# 2013 County and City Extra
## Annual Metro, City, and County Data Book
### *21st Edition*

# 2013 County and City Extra

## Annual Metro, City, and County Data Book

### *21st Edition*

Edited by Deirdre A. Gaquin
and Mary Meghan Ryan

Lanham, MD

Published in the United States of America
by Bernan Press, a wholly owned subsidiary of
The Rowman & Littlefield Publishing Group, Inc.
4501 Forbes Boulevard, Suite 200
Lanham, Maryland 20706

Bernan Press
800-865-3457
www.bernan.com

ISBN: 978-1-59888-633-7

E-ISBN: 978-1-59888-634-4

ISSN: 1059-9096

# Contents

# INTRODUCTION

*County and City Extra* is an annual publication that provides the most up-to-date statistical information available for every state, county, metropolitan area, and congressional district, as well as all cities in the United States with a 2010 census population of 25,000 or more. Data for places, including towns and cities with populations of fewer than 25,000 people are published by Bernan Press in a separate companion volume, *Places, Towns and Townships*. These two volumes are designed to meet the needs of libraries, businesses, and other organizations or individuals who desire convenient and timely sources of the most frequently sought information about geographic entities within the United States. The annual updating of *County and City Extra* for more than 20 years ensures its stature as a reliable and authoritative source for statistical information.

Bernan Press has recently published a new companion volume, the *State and Metropolitan Area Data Book,* previously published by the Census Bureau. This new edition provides an expanded collection of data about states and metropolitan areas, including micropolitan areas and their component counties.

*County and City Extra, Places, Towns and Townships, and State and Metropolitan Area Data Book* are large volumes, but are not big enough to accommodate the wealth of information from the decennial census and the American Community Survey. Two additional volumes in the *County and City Extra* series include this information. *County and City Extra: Special Decennial Census Edition* provides detailed population and housing data from the 2010 census and was published by Bernan Press in December 2011. *The Who, What, and Where of America: Understanding the American Community Survey* includes social and economic details from the American Community Survey and was published by Bernan Press in 2012.

The American Community Survey (ACS) is a national survey that has replaced the census long form as the key source of detailed social and economic data. *County and City Extra* includes data from both the 2010 census and the ACS.

## New and Updated Information for the 2013 Edition

*County and City Extra* includes updated data including 2012 population estimates for states, counties, metropolitan areas, and cities. Also included are the latest available data for education, vital statistics, income and poverty, employment and unemployment, residential construction, production by industry, health resources, crime, land use, the distribution of federal funds, city government finances, weather statistics, and many other topics.

Table E (Congressional Districts) includes a wide selection of 2011 American Community Survey data for the newly established congressional districts of the 113th Congress, along with the 113th congressional representatives.

In February 2013, the Office of Management and Budget released a completely new list of Core Based Statistical Areas (metropolitan and micropolitan areas) based on the 2010 census and some changes in the way these areas are defined. Although they are not yet used in the data in this book, these newly delineated areas are presented in a new Appendix C, together with their component counties and their 2010 census and 2012 estimated populations.

This edition includes data from the 2010 census, 2011 and 2012 population estimates, and the ACS. Annual ACS data are now available for all states and almost all metropolitan areas (all geographic areas with populations of 65,000 or more), but three years are needed to build a sample large enough for reliable estimates for areas of 20,000 to 64,999, and smaller areas need five years of data collection.

With the now annual release of 1-year, 3-year, and 5-year estimates, *County and City Extra* uses ACS data to replace all of the detailed data from the 2000 census. ACS data for 2011 are included in Table A (States) and Table E (Congressional Districts)—all areas with populations of 65,000 or more. Table B (Counties), Table C (Metropolitan areas), and Table D (Cities) include 5-year data (2007–2011). The release of 5-year data for even the smallest geographic areas means that annual social and economic characteristics are now available for all counties and cities.

Although some of the state data are also included in Table B (States and Counties), the separate state data table offers several important features:

- Additional data not available at the county level are provided. Examples include population projections, health insurance coverage, number of immigrants, personal tax payments, information about health service firms not subject to federal tax, and exports by state of origin.

- Additional data that exceeds the space limitations for counties can be found for states. Examples are age of householder, more detailed information about employment in retail trade and services, and the expanded presentation of federal grants and payments to individuals by type.

- State totals can be found more quickly and compared more readily.

Appendix F, **Source Notes and Explanations**, includes Internet references for all data sources. Some of the data can be directly found in data tables on the web sites; some can be assembled through on-line access tools; others can be obtained by downloading files and processing them with statistical software; and some need to be ordered from the agencies.

## Rankings

The rankings present the geography types by various subjects, including population, land area, population density, population change, age, immigration, birth rate, housing characteristics, race, Hispanic origin, educational attainment, income, unemployment rate, per capita local taxes, poverty rate, defense contracts, value of agricultural products, and violent crime rate.

## Subjects Covered and Volume Organization

A summary of the **subjects covered** in each of the five tables appears on **page ix**. The **colored map** portfolio begins on **page xiii**.

The main body of this volume contains five basic parts. Each part includes a table that is preceded by highlights and rankings, as well as the complete column headings for the table. **Part A**, which begins on **page 1**, contains data for states. **Part B**, beginning on **page 51**, contains information for states and counties. The county geography codes include county typology codes from the Economic Research Service of the Department of Agriculture. These codes characterize counties by size of the largest place as well as by other criteria for nonmetropolitan counties. (See Appendix A for the definition of each code.) **Part C**, beginning on **page 773**, contains information for metropolitan areas. Statistics for cities with a 2010 census population of 25,000 or more can be found in **Part D**, which begins on **page 895**. **Part E**, beginning on **page 1175**, contains data for the congressional districts of the 113th Congress.

A contents page preceding tables B through E lists the page number on which the data for a given geographic area begin. Counties and cities are listed alphabetically by state. Metropolitan areas are listed alphabetically, except that metropolitan divisions are listed alphabetically within the metropolitan statistical area of which they are components. Congressional districts are listed in numeric order within states.

The appendixes include definitions of geographic concepts (**Appendix A**), sources and definitions of each data item included in this volume (**Appendix F**), an alphabetical listing of metropolitan areas with their component counties delineated as of December 2009, with 2010 census populations (**Appendix B**), a listing of metropolitan and micropolitan areas and their component counties as of February 2013, with 2010 census populations and 2012 estimated populations (**Appendix C**), a list of cities by county (**Appendix E**), and maps showing congressional districts, counties, and selected places within each state (**Appendix D**).

## Symbols

**D**    Indicates that the number has been withheld to avoid disclosure of information pertaining to a specific orga-
nization or individual, or because the number does not meet statistical standards for publication.

**NA**    Indicates that data are not available.

**X**    Indicates that data are not applicable or are not meaningful for this geographic unit.

In this volume, a figure that is less than half the unit of measure shown will appear as zero.

## Sources

The great majority of the data in this volume have been obtained from federal government sources. A few items are obtained from private sources that are widely recognized as reliable basic sources of those particular data items. For a complete list of these sources, see **Appendix F**.

Data included in this volume meet the publication standards established by the U.S. Census Bureau and the other federal statistical agencies from which they were obtained. Every effort has been made to select data that are accurate, meaningful, and useful. All data from censuses, surveys, and administrative records are subject to errors arising from factors such as sampling variability, reporting errors, incomplete coverage, nonresponse, imputations, and processing error. Responsibility of the editors and publishers of this volume is limited to reasonable care in the reproduction and presentation of data obtained from sources believed to be reliable.

*County and City Extra: Annual Metro, City, and County Data Book* is part of Bernan Press's *County and City Extra* series. The editors of *County and City Extra* acknowledge the contributions of Courtenay Slater and the late George Hall, the originators of this publication. Their initial contributions continue to enrich the *County and City Extra* series. As always, we are especially grateful to the many federal agency personnel who assisted us in obtaining the data, provided excellent resources on their Web sites, and patiently answered questions.

**Deirdre A. Gaquin** has been a data use consultant to private organizations, government agencies, and universities for over 30 years. Prior to that, she was Director of Data Access Services at Data Use & Access Laboratories, a pioneer in private sector distribution of federal statistical data. A former president of the Association of Public Data Users, Ms. Gaquin has served on numerous boards, panels, and task forces concerned with federal statistical data and has worked on five decennial censuses. She holds a Master of Urban Planning (MUP) degree from Hunter College. Ms. Gaquin is also an editor of Bernan Press's *The Who, What, and Where of America: Understanding the American Community Survey*; *Places, Towns and Townships*; *The Congressional District Atlas*, *The Almanac of American Education*, and the *State and Metropolitan Area Data Book*.

**Mary Meghan Ryan** is the senior research editor for Bernan Press. She is also the editor for the *Handbook of U.S. Labor Statistics*, *State Profiles*, and the associate editor for *Business Statistics of the United States*.

# SUBJECTS COVERED, BY GEOGRAPHY TYPE

State data begin on page 1
County data begin on page 51
Metropolitan area data begin on page 773
City data begin on page 895
Congressional district data begin on page 1175

| Subject | Column Number | | | | |
|---|---|---|---|---|---|
| | Table A. States | Table B. States and Counties | Table C. Metropolitan Areas | Table D. Cities | Table E. Congressional Districts |
| Land area | 1 | 1 | 1 | 1 | 1 |
| **Population** | | | | | |
| Total persons, 1990 | 31 | | | | |
| Total persons, 2000 | 32 | 20 | 20 | 23 | |
| Total persons, 2010 | 33 | 21 | 21 | 24 | |
| Total persons, 2012 | 2 | 2 | 2 | 2 | |
| Rank, 2012 | 3 | 3 | 3 | 3 | |
| Persons per square kilometer | 4 | 4 | 4 | 4 | 3 |
| Race and Hispanic or Latino origin, 2010 | 45–50 | | | | |
| Race and Hispanic or Latino origin, 2011 | 5–9 | 5–9 | 5–9 | 5–10 | 4–11 |
| Immigrants | 24 | | | | |
| Foreign-born population | 22 | | | 11 | 13 |
| Percent born in state of residence | 23 | | | | 14 |
| Age distribution, 2010 | 52–61 | | | 12–20 | |
| Age distribution, 2011 | 10–19 | 10–18 | 10–18 | | 15–23 |
| Median age | 20, 62 | | | 21 | 24 |
| Percent female | 21 | 19 | 19 | 22 | 12 |
| Percent population change, 1990–2000 | 34 | | | | |
| Percent population change, 2000–2010 | 35 | 22 | 22 | 25 | |
| Percent population change, 2010–2012 | 36 | 23 | 23 | 26 | |
| Components of population change | 37–41 | 24–26 | 24–26 | | |
| Daytime population | | 33–34 | 33–34 | | |
| Population projections | 42–44 | | | | |
| **Households** | | | | | |
| Total households, 2010 | 64 | 27 | 27 | 27 | |
| Total households, 2011 | 25 | | | | 28 |
| Percent change in number of households | 26, 65 | 28 | 28 | | |
| Household type | 28–30, 67–68 | 30–31 | 30–31 | 29–30 | 30–33 |
| Persons per household | 27, 66 | 29 | 29 | 28 | 29 |
| Persons in group quarters | | 32 | 32 | 31–34 | 34–39 |
| **Housing** | | | | | |
| Housing units in 2010 | 69–78 | 87–88 | 87–88 | 47–49 | |
| Housing units in 2011 | 79–92 | | | | 40–45 |
| Housing units in 2007–2011 | | 89–96 | 89–96 | 50–57 | |
| Percent change in number of housing units | 70, 80 | 88 | 88 | 48 | |
| Housing costs | 73–77, 83–90 | 91–95 | 91–95 | 52–57 | 43–45 |
| Substandard housing units | 78, 91 | 96 | 96 | | |
| Percent with no vehicle available | | | | 58 | |
| Percent who lived in same house one year ago | 92 | | | 59 | |
| Percent who lived outside city one year ago | | | | 60 | |
| New residential construction | 93–95 | 178–179 | 178–179 | 69–71 | |
| Manufactured housing | 96 | | | | |
| **Vital statistics** | | | | | |
| Births | 97–98 | 35–36 | 35–36 | | |
| Deaths | 99–103 | 37–38 | 37–38 | | |

# SUBJECTS COVERED, BY GEOGRAPHY TYPE — Continued

State data begin on page 1
County data begin on page 51
Metropolitan area data begin on page 773
City data begin on page 895
Congressional district data begin on page 1175

| Subject | Column Number | | | | |
| --- | --- | --- | --- | --- | --- |
| | Table A. States | Table B. States and Counties | Table C. Metropolitan Areas | Table D. Cities | Table E. Congressional Districts |
| **Health** | | | | | |
| Persons in nursing facilities | | | | 33 | 37 |
| Medicare enrollees | 106 | 41–43 | 41–43 | | |
| Persons lacking health insurance | 104–105 | 39–40 | 39–40 | | 59 |
| **Crime** | 107–110 | 44–47 | 44–47 | 35–38 | |
| **Education** | | | | | |
| School enrollment | 111–112 | 48–49 | 48–49 | | 25 |
| Educational attainment | 113–116 | 50–51 | 50–51 | 39–41 | 26–27 |
| Expenditures for education | 117–118 | 52–53 | 52–53 | | |
| **Income** | | | | | |
| Personal income | 134–149 | 62–74 | 62–74 | | |
| Per capita income | 122, 136, 149 | 54, 64 | 54, 64 | 42 | 46 |
| Household income | 123–126 | 55–58 | 55–58 | 43–45 | 47–48 |
| Poverty | 127–133 | 59–61 | 59–61 | 46 | 49–50 |
| Food stamps | | | | | 51 |
| Personal income by type | 138–140 | 66–68 | 66–68 | | |
| Earnings by industry | 150–158 | 75–83 | 75–83 | | |
| Transfer payments | 141–146 | 69–74 | 69–74 | | |
| Gross state product | 159 | | | | |
| Personal tax payments | 147 | | | | |
| Disposable personal income | 148–149 | | | | |
| Social Security | 160–162 | 84–86 | 84–86 | | 60–62 |
| **Labor Force and Employment** | | | | | |
| Labor force and unemployment | 167–171 | 97–100 | 97–100 | 61–68 | 52–54 |
| Employment in selected occupations | 163–166 | 101–103 | 101–103 | | 55–58 |
| Employment by industry | 172–183, 207–216 | 104–112 | 104–112 | | |
| **Exports of goods produced** | 119–121 | | | | |
| **Establishments, employment, sales, and payroll** | | | | | |
| Manufacturing | 207–216 | 151–154 | 151–154 | 88–91 | |
| Construction | 217–221 | | | | |
| Wholesale trade | 222–226 | 135–138 | 135–138 | 72–75 | |
| Retail trade | 227–235 | 139–142 | 139–142 | 76–79 | |
| Information | 236–246 | | | | |
| Utilities | 247–251 | | | | |
| Transportation and warehousing | 252–256 | | | | |
| Finance and insurance | 257–261 | | | | |
| Real estate and rental and leasing | 262–266 | 143–146 | 143–146 | 80–83 | |
| Professional, scientific, and technical services | 267–275 | 147–150 | 147–150 | 84–87 | |
| Health care and social assistance | 276–289 | 159–162 | 159–162 | 100–103 | |
| Arts, entertainment and recreation | 290–294 | | | 96–99 | |
| Accommodation and food services | 295–300 | 155–158 | 155–158 | 92–95 | |
| Other services, except public administration | 301–308 | 163–166 | 163–166 | 104–107 | |

# SUBJECTS COVERED, BY GEOGRAPHY TYPE — Continued

State data begin on page 1
County data begin on page 51
Metropolitan area data begin on page 773
City data begin on page 895
Congressional district data begin on page 1175

| Subject | Column Number | | | | |
| --- | --- | --- | --- | --- | --- |
| | Table A. States | Table B. States and Counties | Table C. Metropolitan Areas | Table D. Cities | Table E. Congressional Districts |
| Government employment | 309–311 | 194–196 | 194–196 | 140 | |
| Agriculture | 184–202 | 113–132 | 113–132 | | |
| Land and water | 203–206 | 133–134 | 133–134 | | |
| Government finances | 331–350 | 180–193 | 180–193 | 117–139 | |
| Federal funds and grants | 312–330 | 167–177 | 167–177 | 108–116 | |
| Voting and elections | 351–355 | 197–199 | 197–199 | | |
| Climate | | | | 141–147 | |

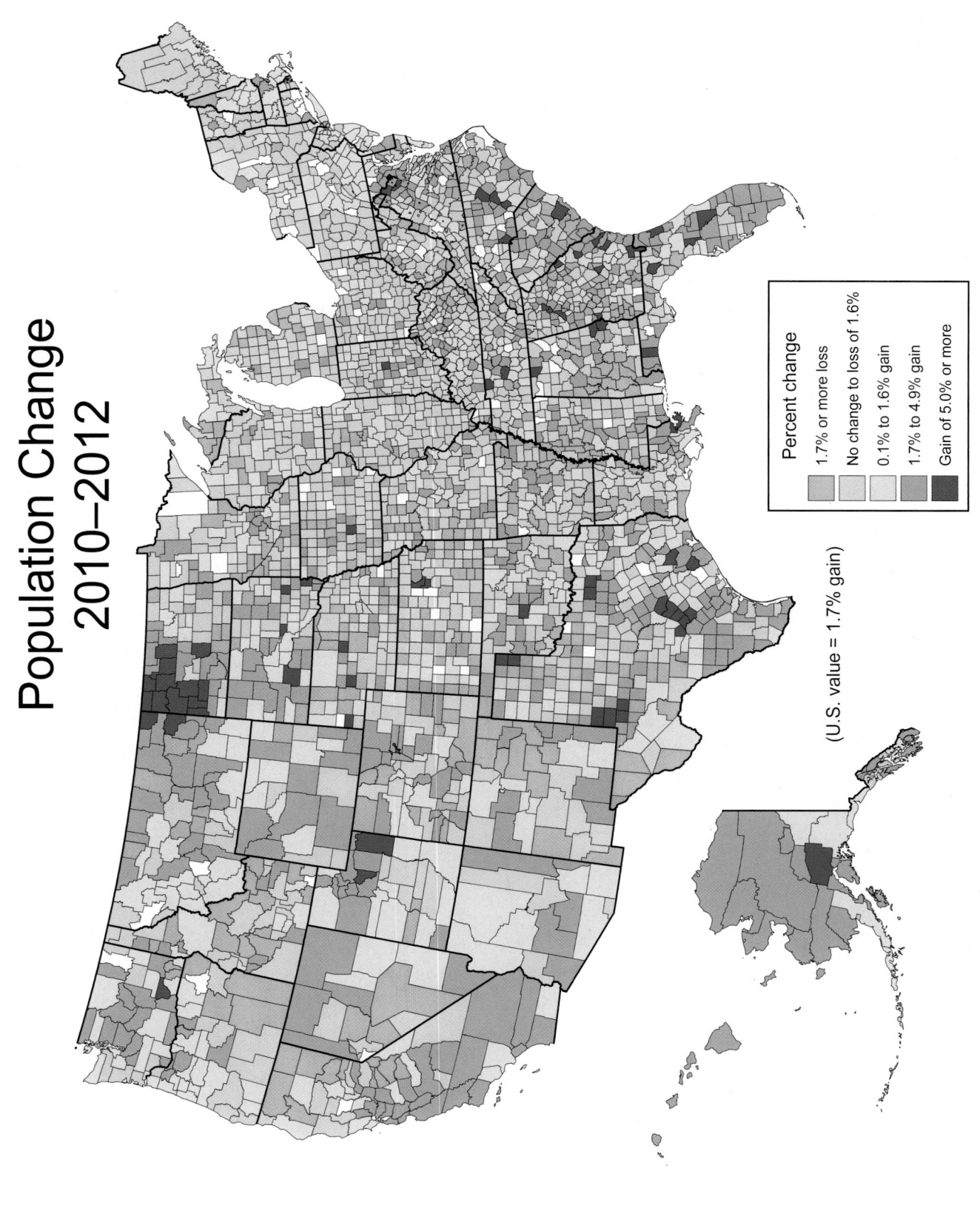

## Population Change 2010–2012

**Percent change**

- 1.7% or more loss
- No change to loss of 1.6%
- 0.1% to 1.6% gain
- 1.7% to 4.9% gain
- Gain of 5.0% or more

(U.S. value = 1.7% gain)

# Black, Not Hispanic or Latino, Population 2011

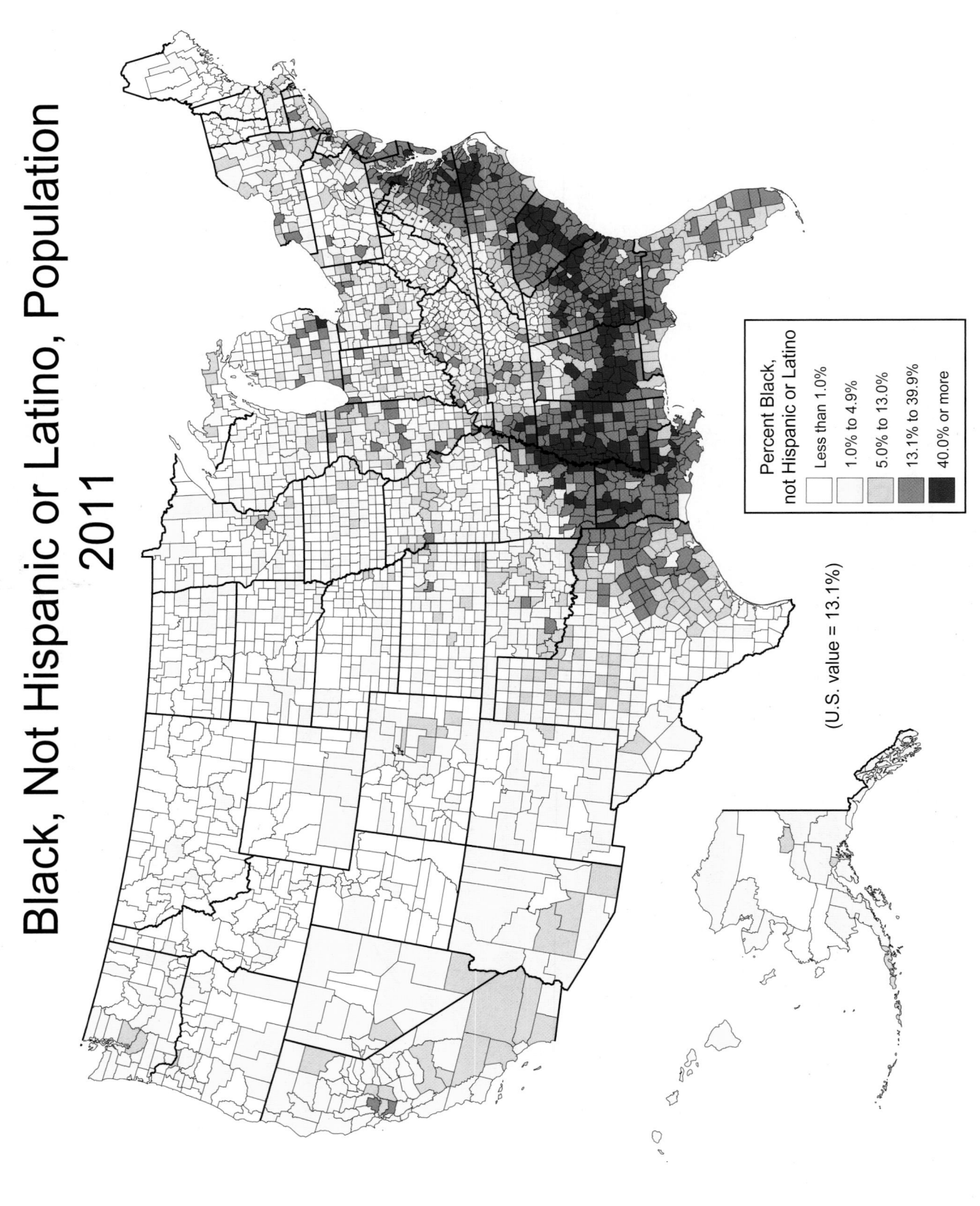

Black, Not Hispanic or Latino, Population
2011

Percent Black,
not Hispanic or Latino

Less than 1.0%
1.0% to 4.9%
5.0% to 13.0%
13.1% to 39.9%
40.0% or more

(U.S. value = 13.1%)

# Hispanic or Latino Population 2011

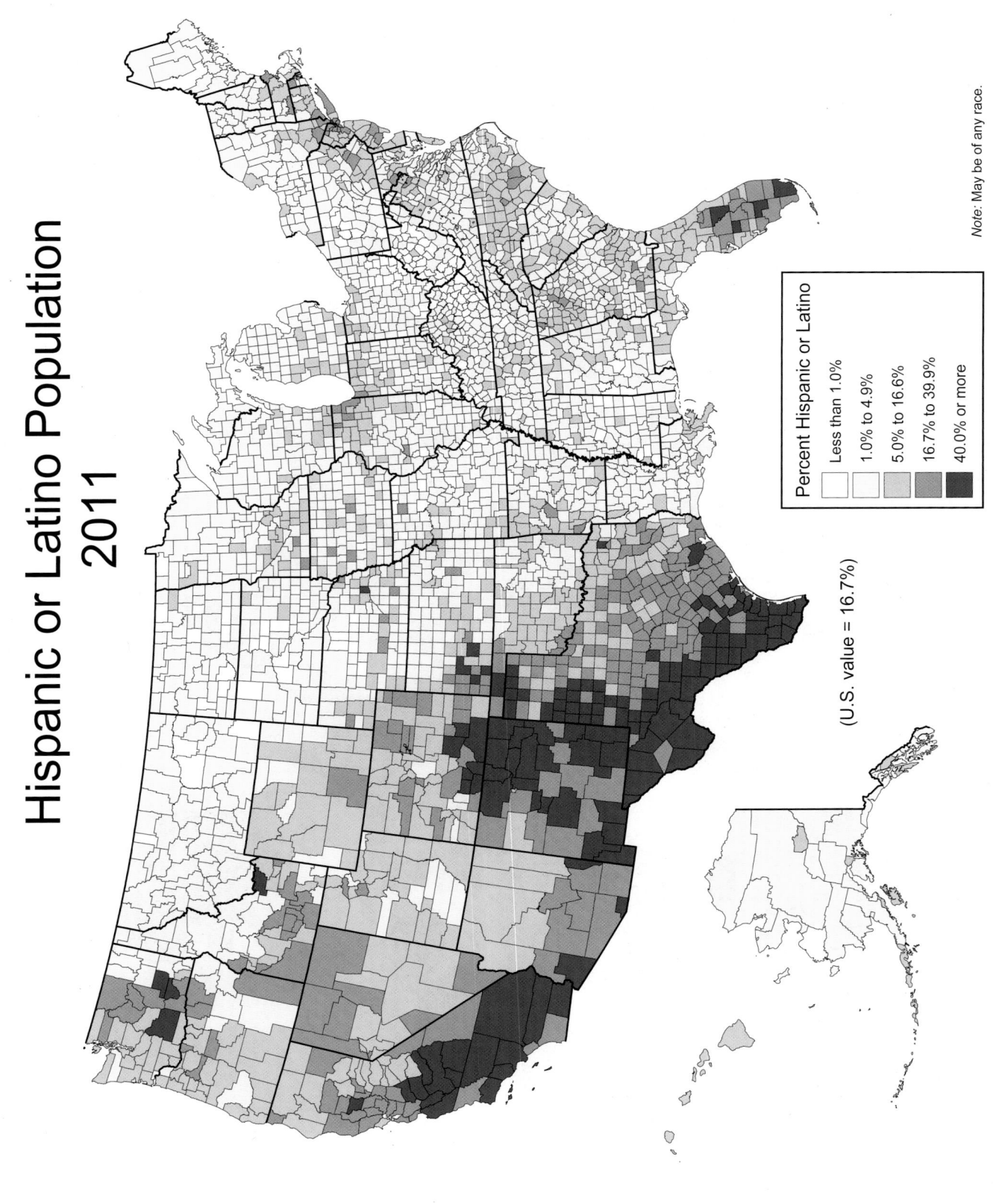

Note: May be of any race.

Percent Hispanic or Latino

- Less than 1.0%
- 1.0% to 4.9%
- 5.0% to 16.6%
- 16.7% to 39.9%
- 40.0% or more

(U.S. value = 16.7%)

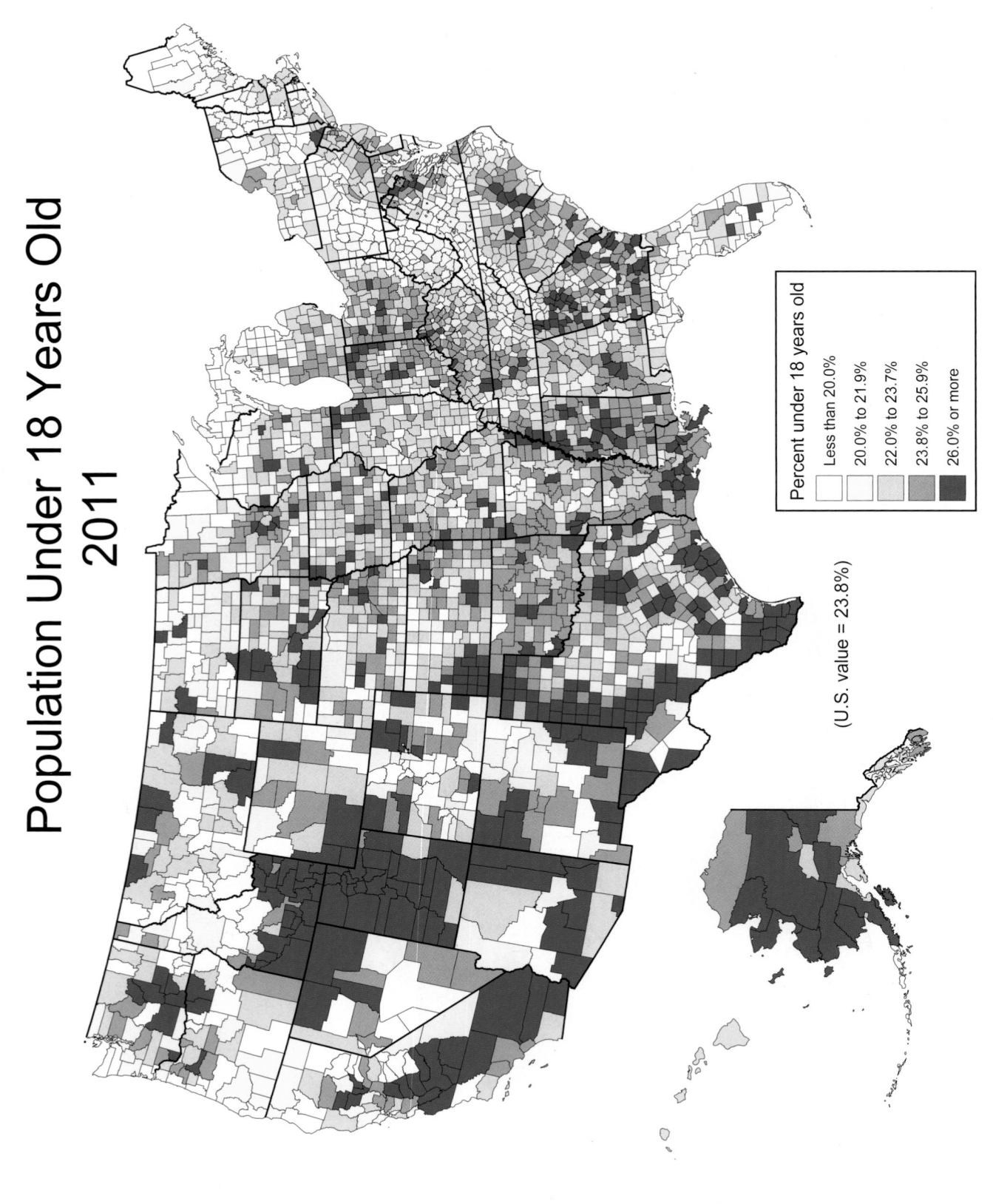

# Population Under 18 Years Old
## 2011

**Percent under 18 years old**

- Less than 20.0%
- 20.0% to 21.9%
- 22.0% to 23.7%
- 23.8% to 25.9%
- 26.0% or more

(U.S. value = 23.8%)

# Population 65 Years Old and Over
## 2011

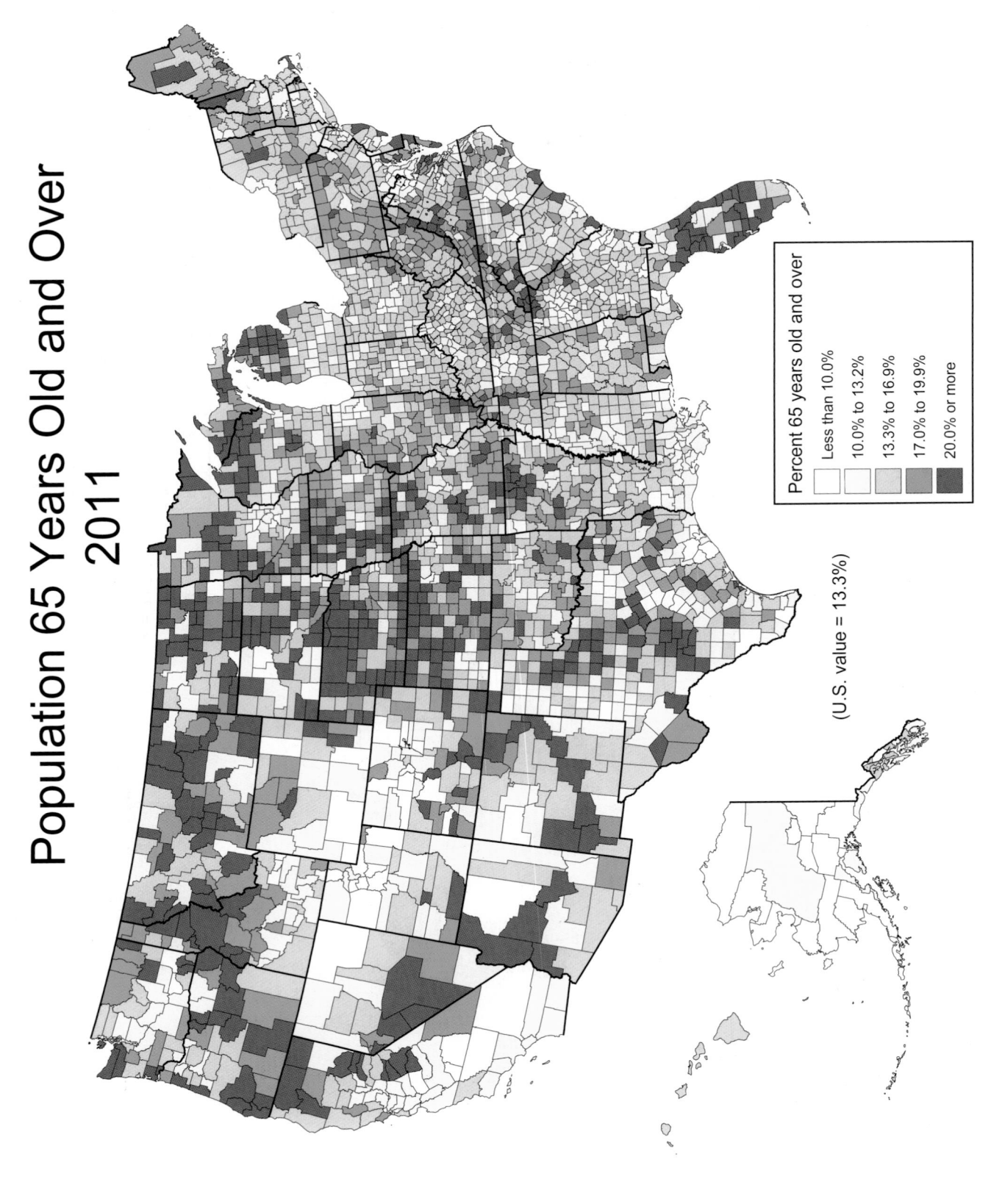

Percent 65 years old and over

| | |
|---|---|
| | Less than 10.0% |
| | 10.0% to 13.2% |
| | 13.3% to 16.9% |
| | 17.0% to 19.9% |
| | 20.0% or more |

(U.S. value = 13.3%)

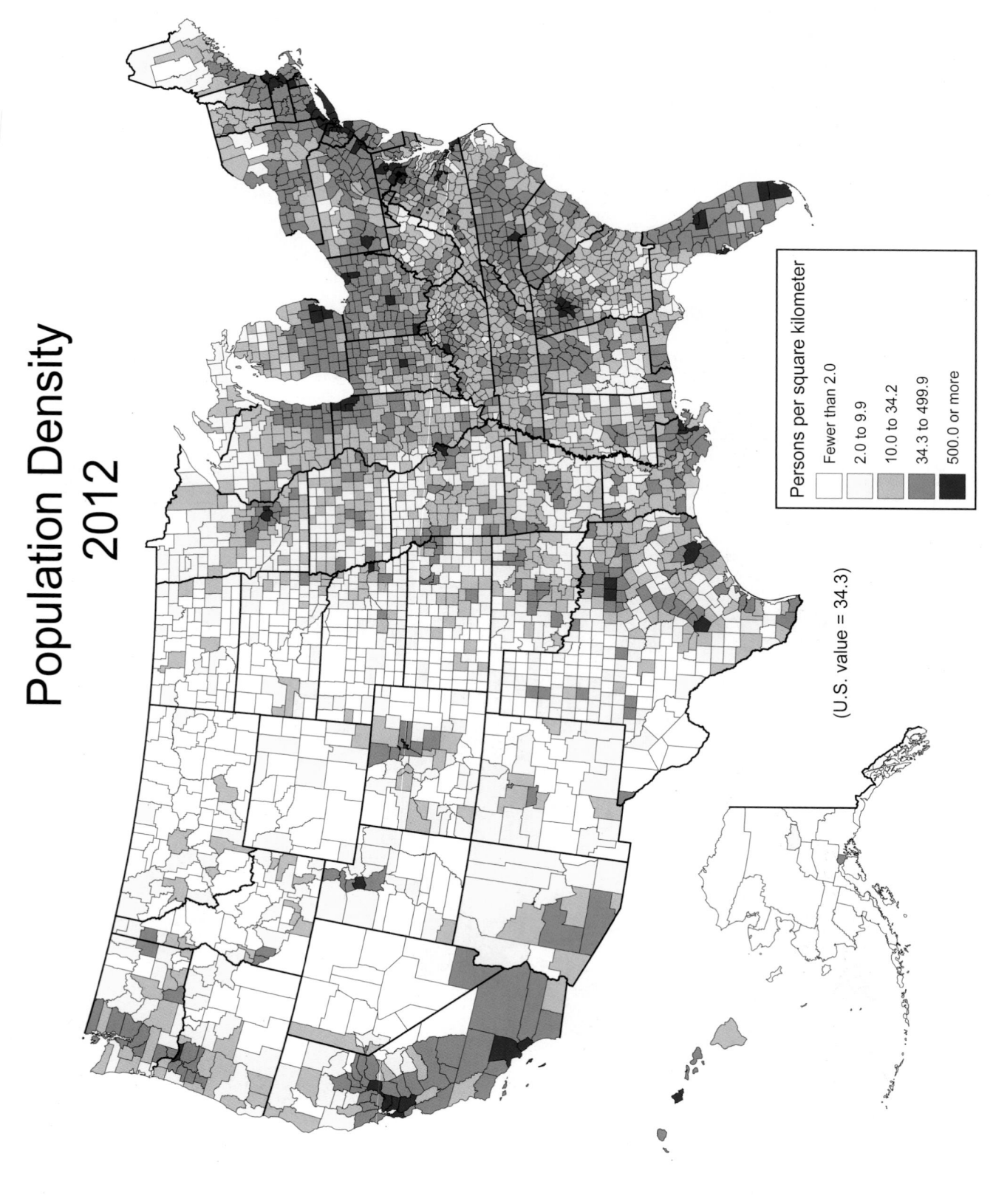

## Population Density
## 2012

Persons per square kilometer

Fewer than 2.0
2.0 to 9.9
10.0 to 34.2
34.3 to 499.9
500.0 or more

(U.S. value = 34.3)

# Unemployment Rate
# 2012

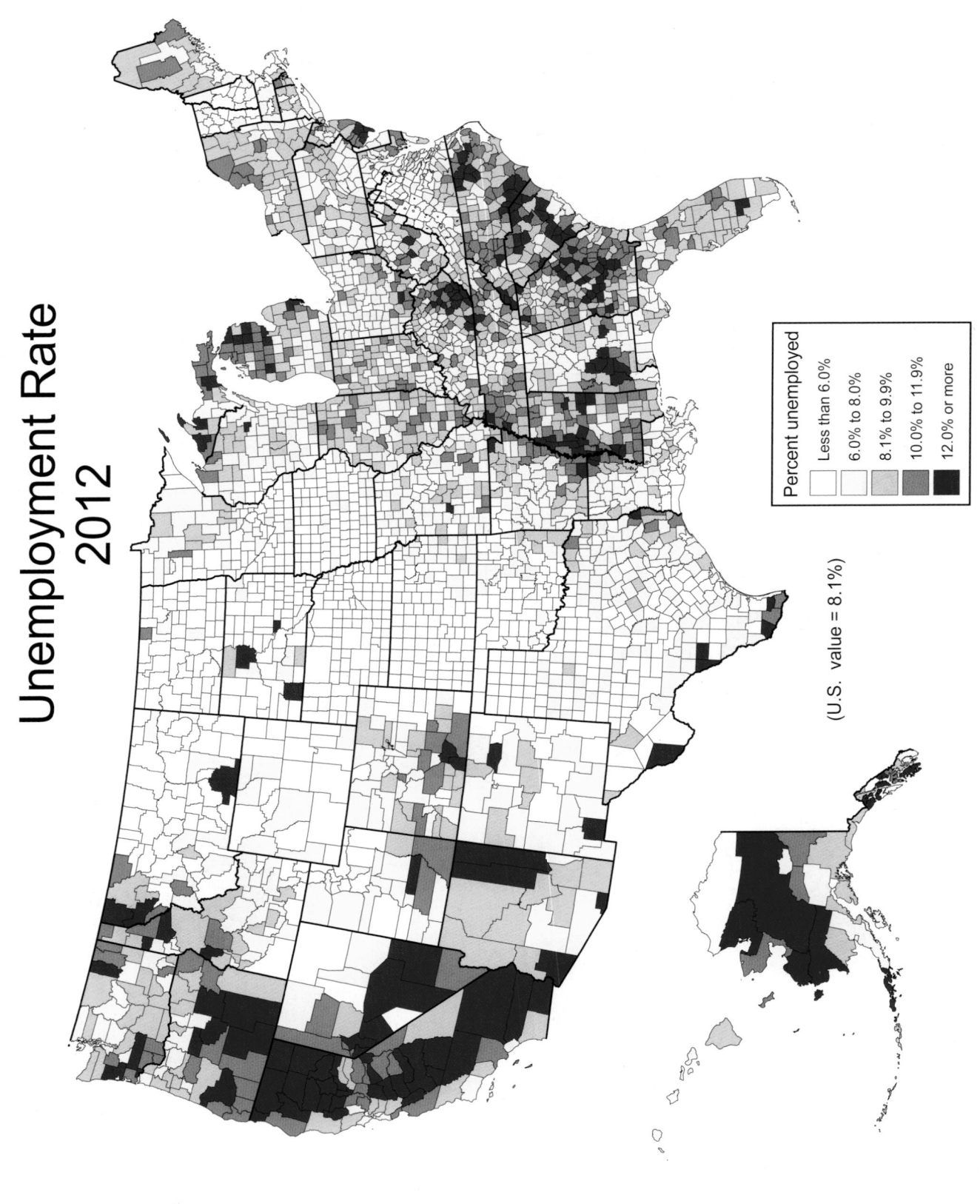

Percent unemployed

Less than 6.0%
6.0% to 8.0%
8.1% to 9.9%
10.0% to 11.9%
12.0% or more

(U.S. value = 8.1%)

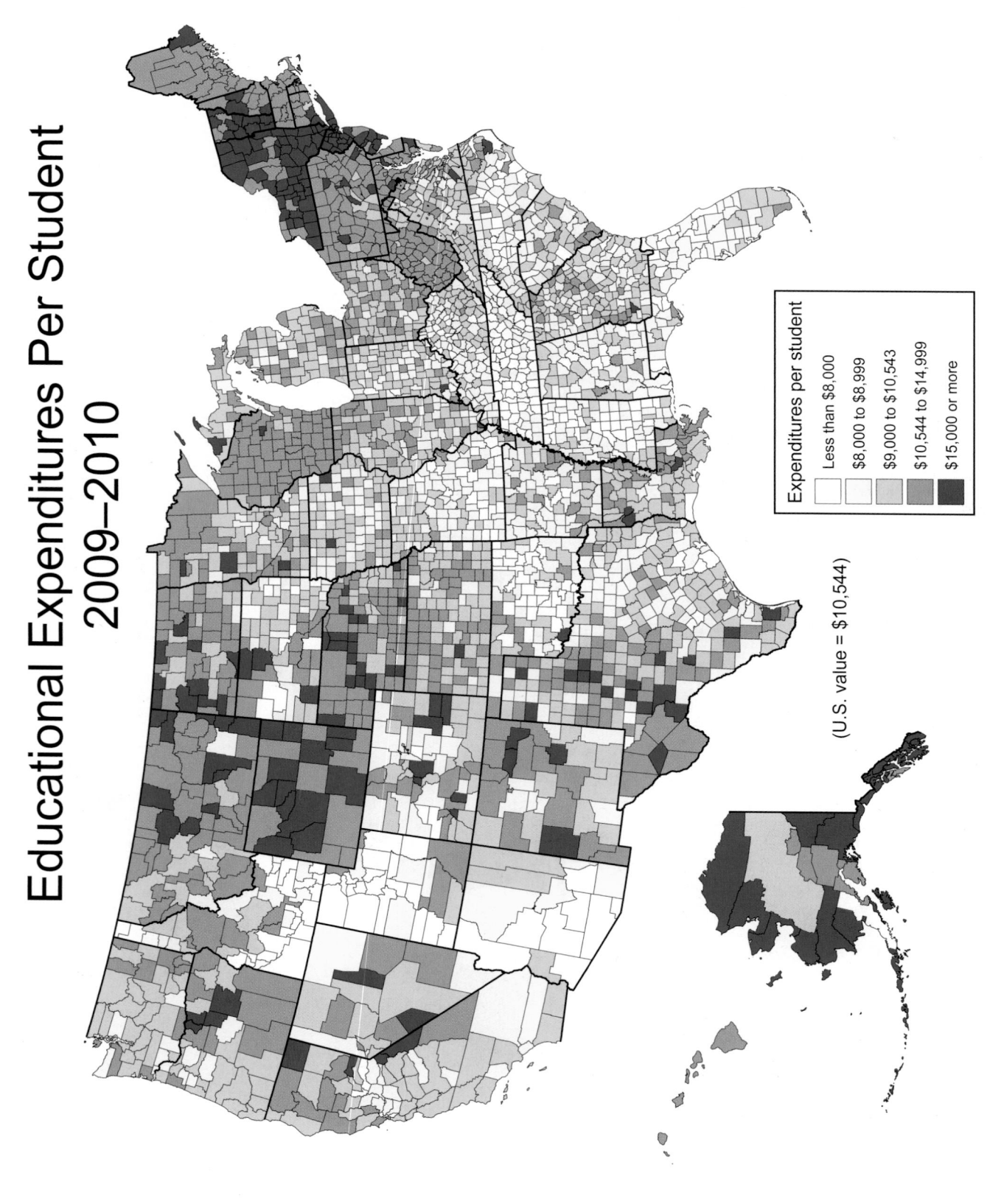

Educational Expenditures Per Student
2009–2010

Expenditures per student

Less than $8,000
$8,000 to $8,999
$9,000 to $10,543
$10,544 to $14,999
$15,000 or more

(U.S. value = $10,544)

# Population with High School Diploma or Less
## 2007–2011

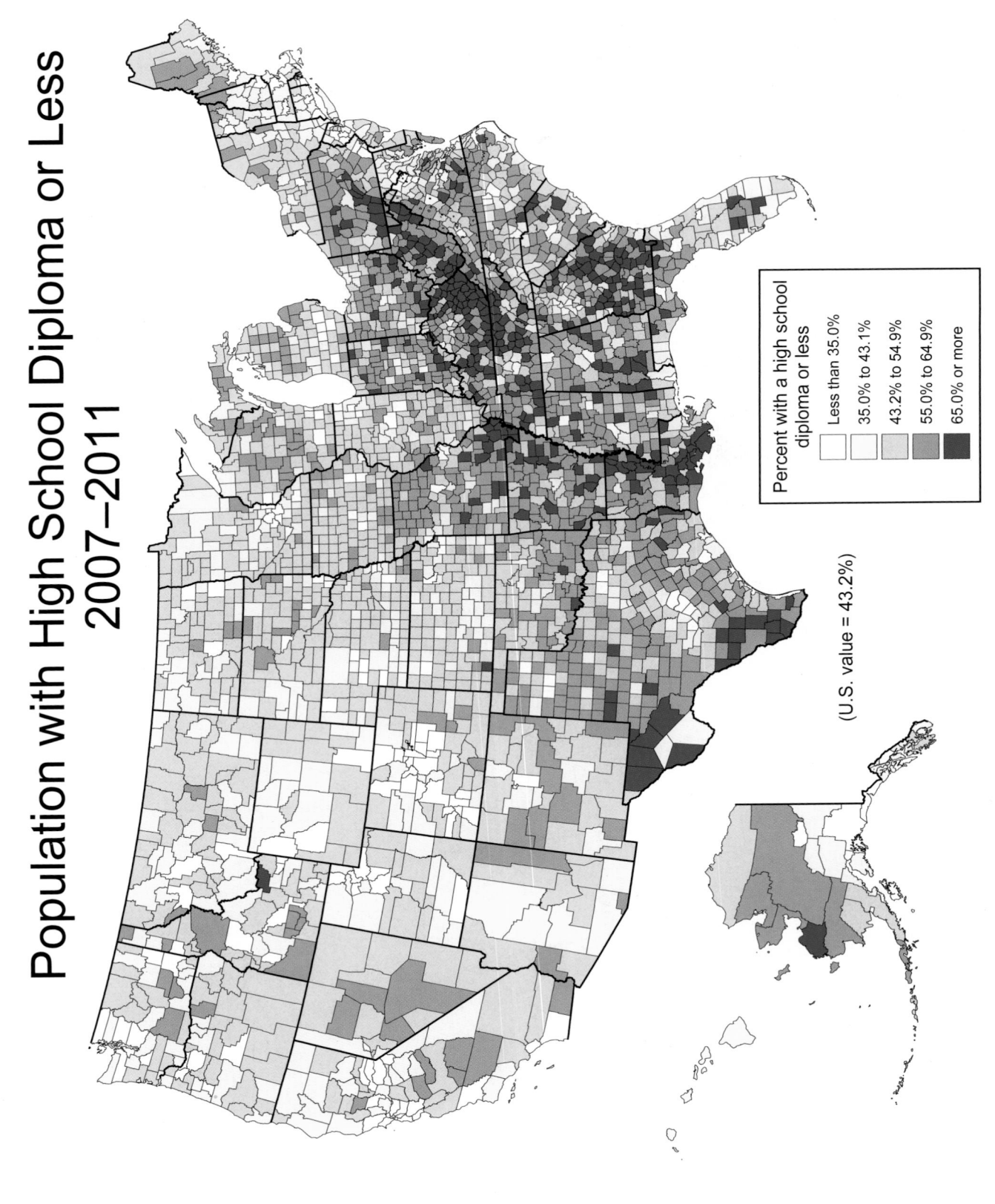

Percent with a high school diploma or less

- Less than 35.0%
- 35.0% to 43.1%
- 43.2% to 54.9%
- 55.0% to 64.9%
- 65.0% or more

(U.S. value = 43.2%)

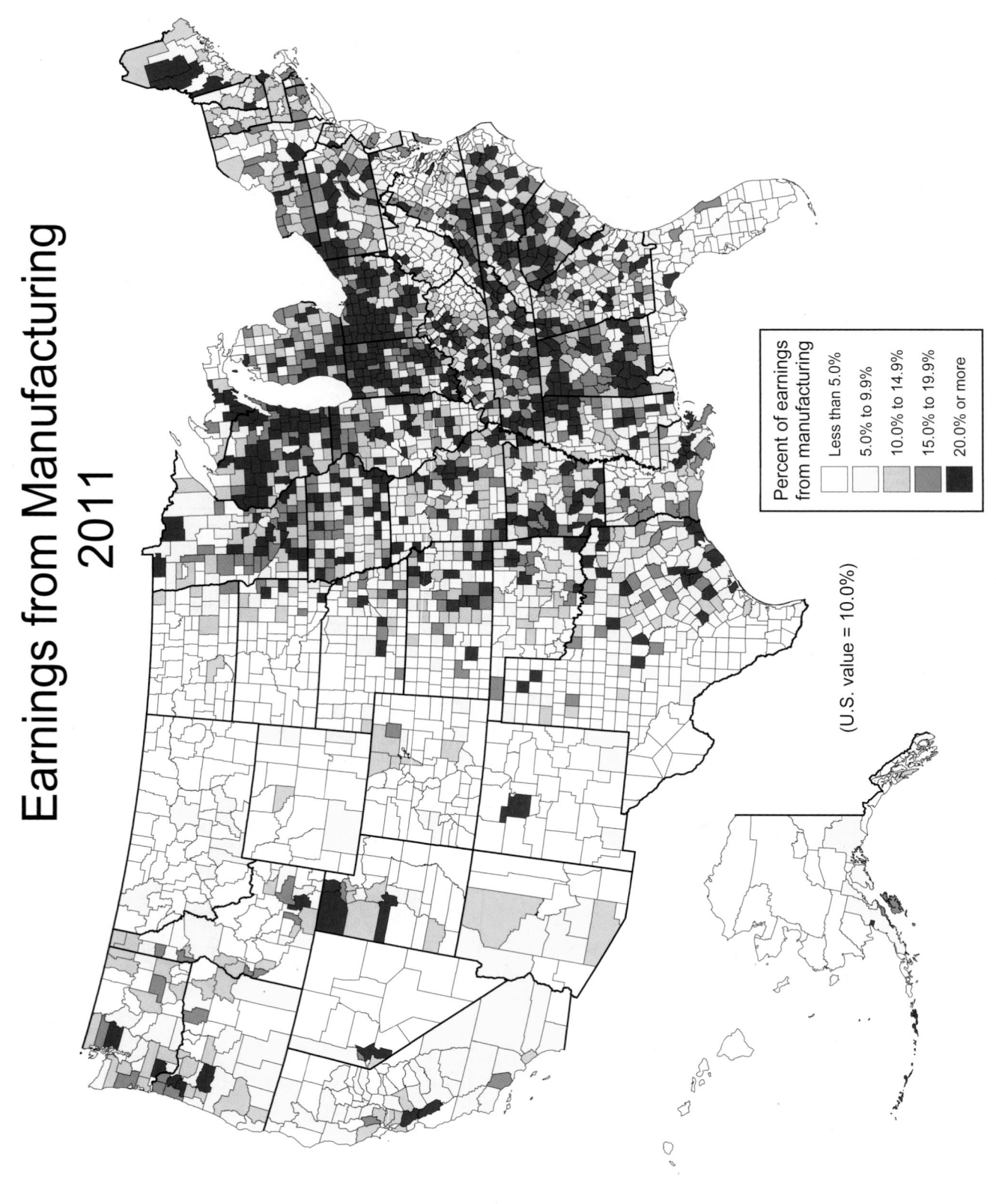

Earnings from Manufacturing
2011

Percent of earnings
from manufacturing

Less than 5.0%
5.0% to 9.9%
10.0% to 14.9%
15.0% to 19.9%
20.0% or more

(U.S. value = 10.0%)

# Employment in Management, Business, Science, and Arts Occupations: 2007–2011

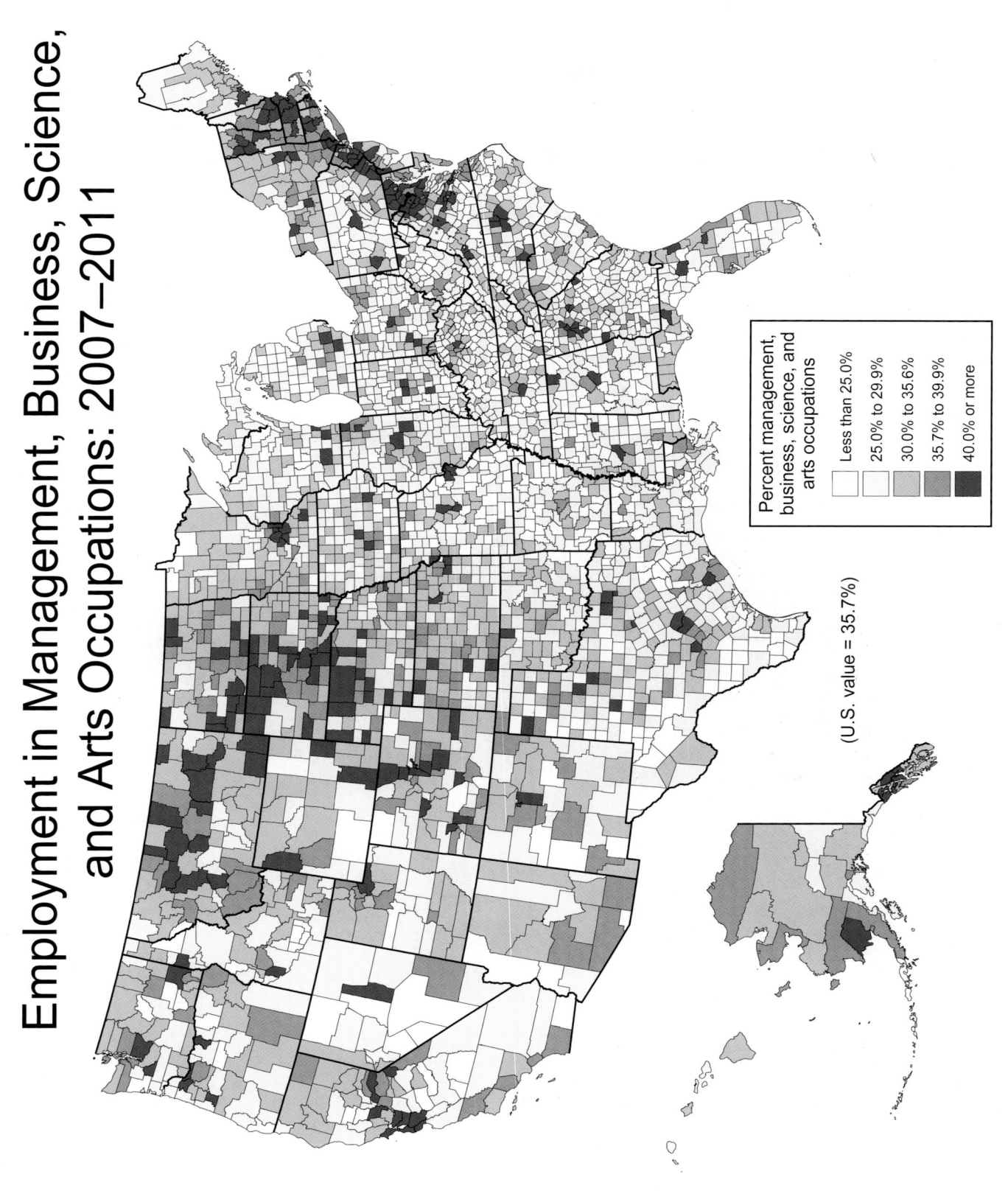

Percent management, business, science, and arts occupations

Less than 25.0%
25.0% to 29.9%
30.0% to 35.6%
35.7% to 39.9%
40.0% or more

(U.S. value = 35.7%)

# Land in Farms 2007

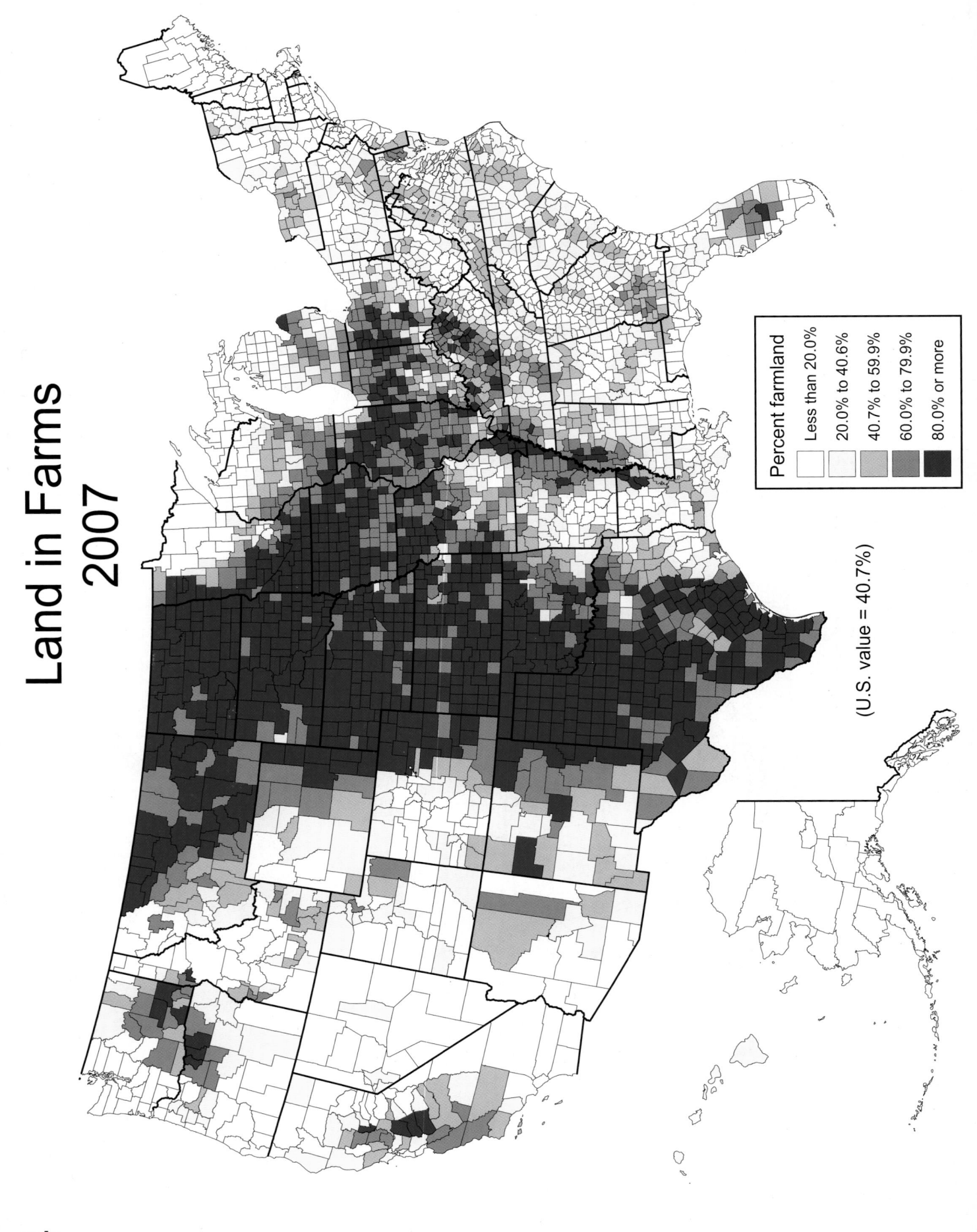

Percent farmland

- Less than 20.0%
- 20.0% to 40.6%
- 40.7% to 59.9%
- 60.0% to 79.9%
- 80.0% or more

(U.S. value = 40.7%)

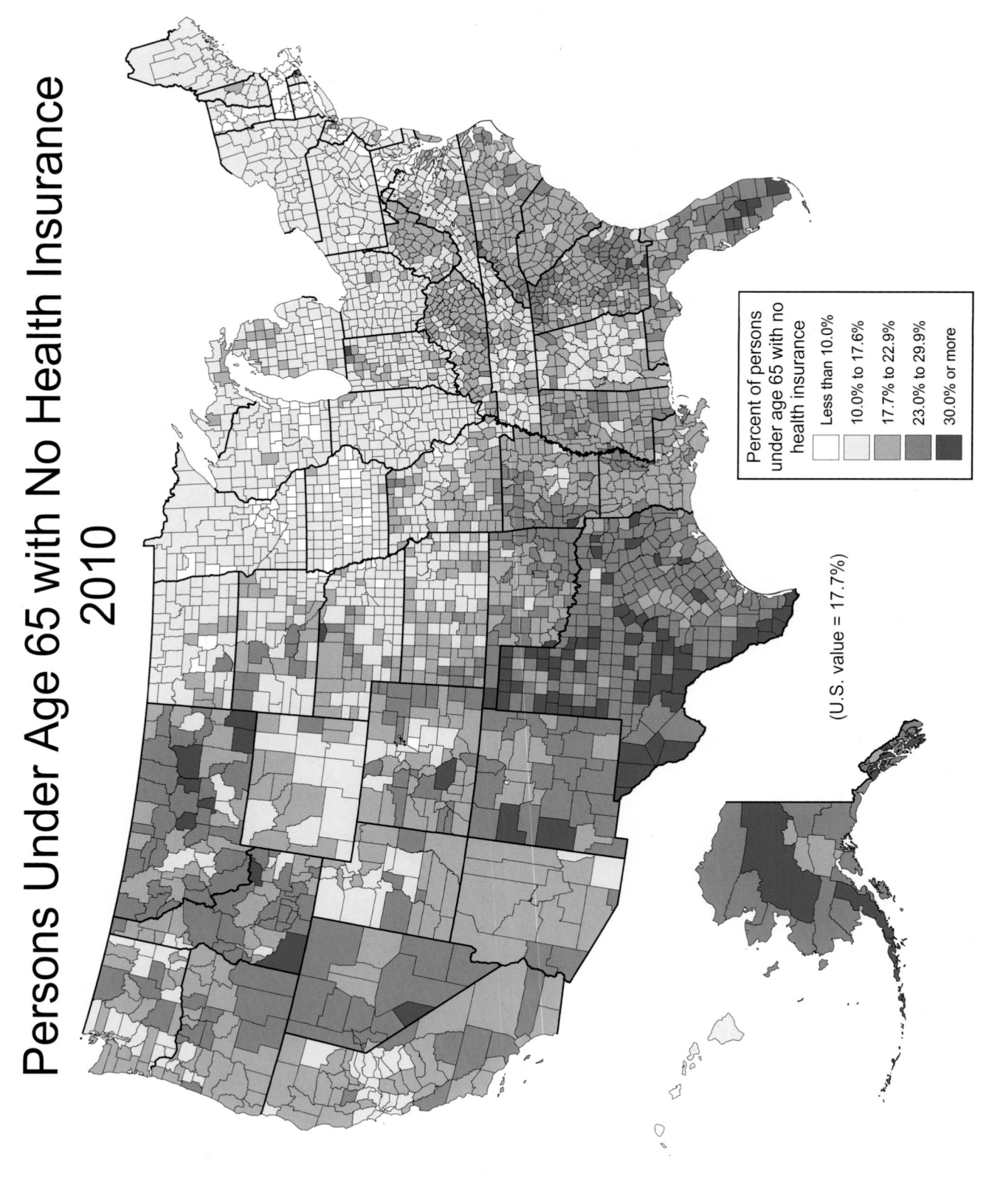

# Persons Under Age 65 with No Health Insurance
## 2010

Percent of persons under age 65 with no health insurance

- Less than 10.0%
- 10.0% to 17.6%
- 17.7% to 22.9%
- 23.0% to 29.9%
- 30.0% or more

(U.S. value = 17.7%)

# Median Household Income
## 2011

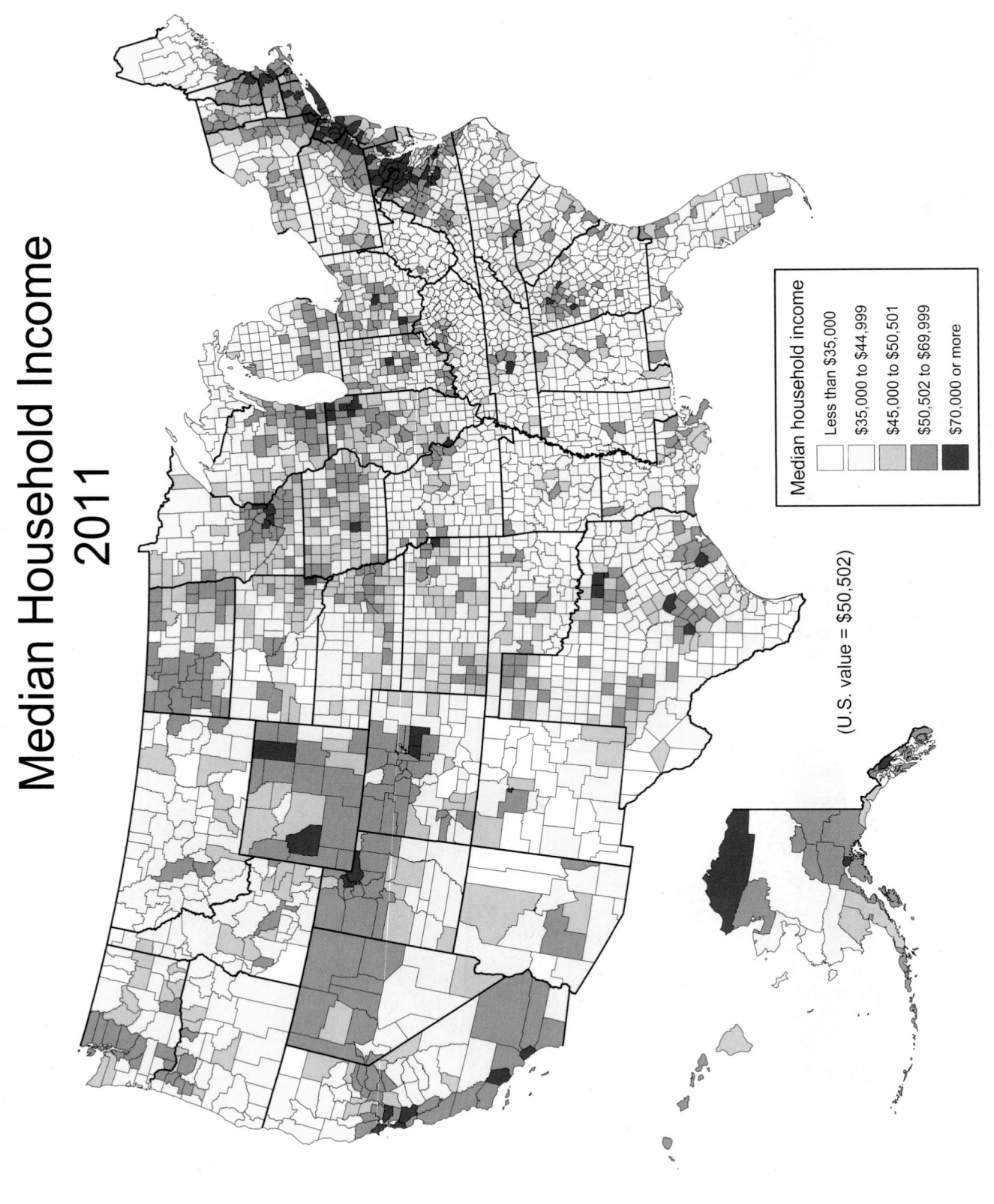

Median household income

- Less than $35,000
- $35,000 to $44,999
- $45,000 to $50,501
- $50,502 to $69,999
- $70,000 or more

(U.S. value = $50,502)

# Percent in Poverty
## 2011

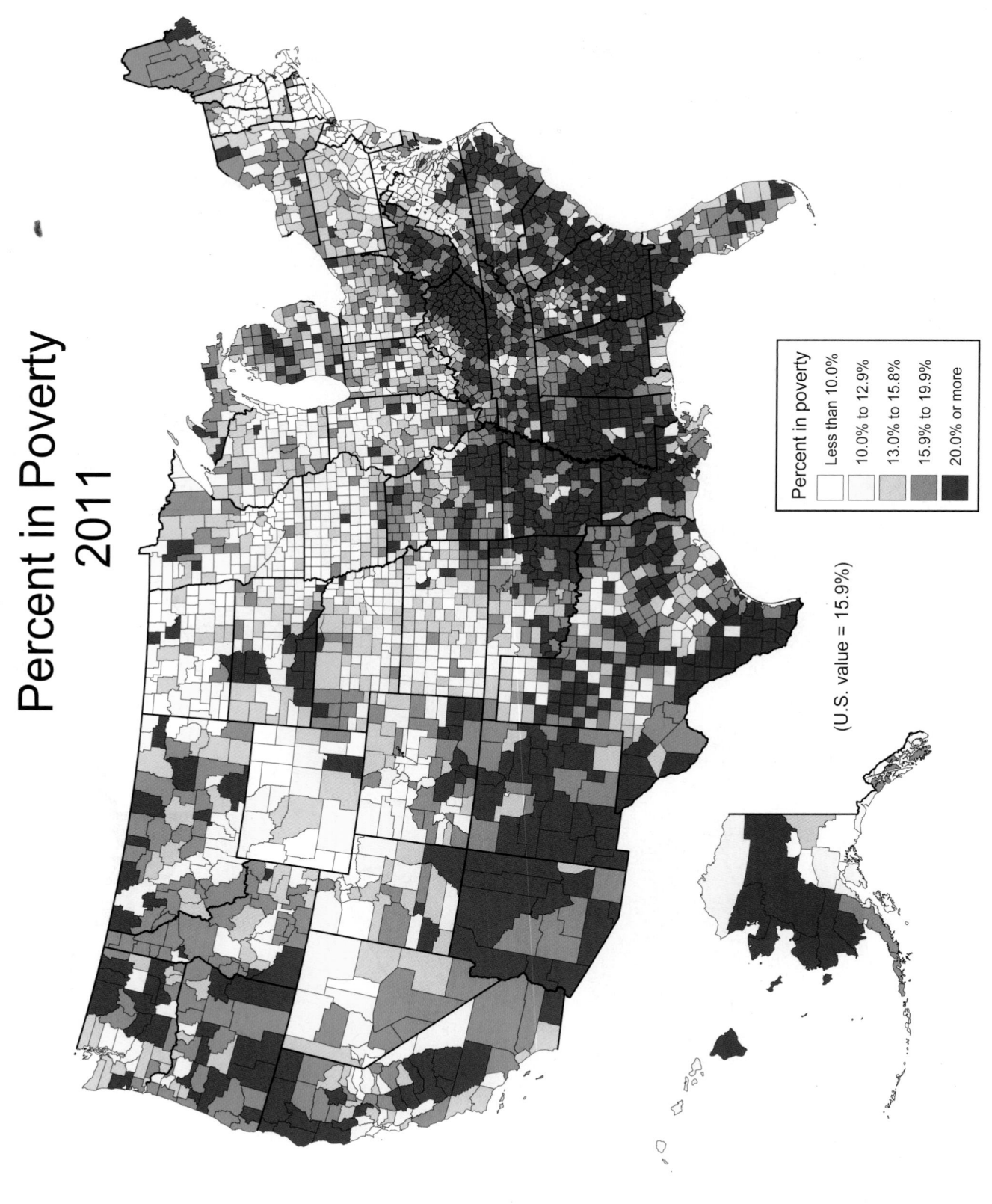

Percent in poverty
- Less than 10.0%
- 10.0% to 12.9%
- 13.0% to 15.8%
- 15.9% to 19.9%
- 20.0% or more

(U.S. value = 15.9%)

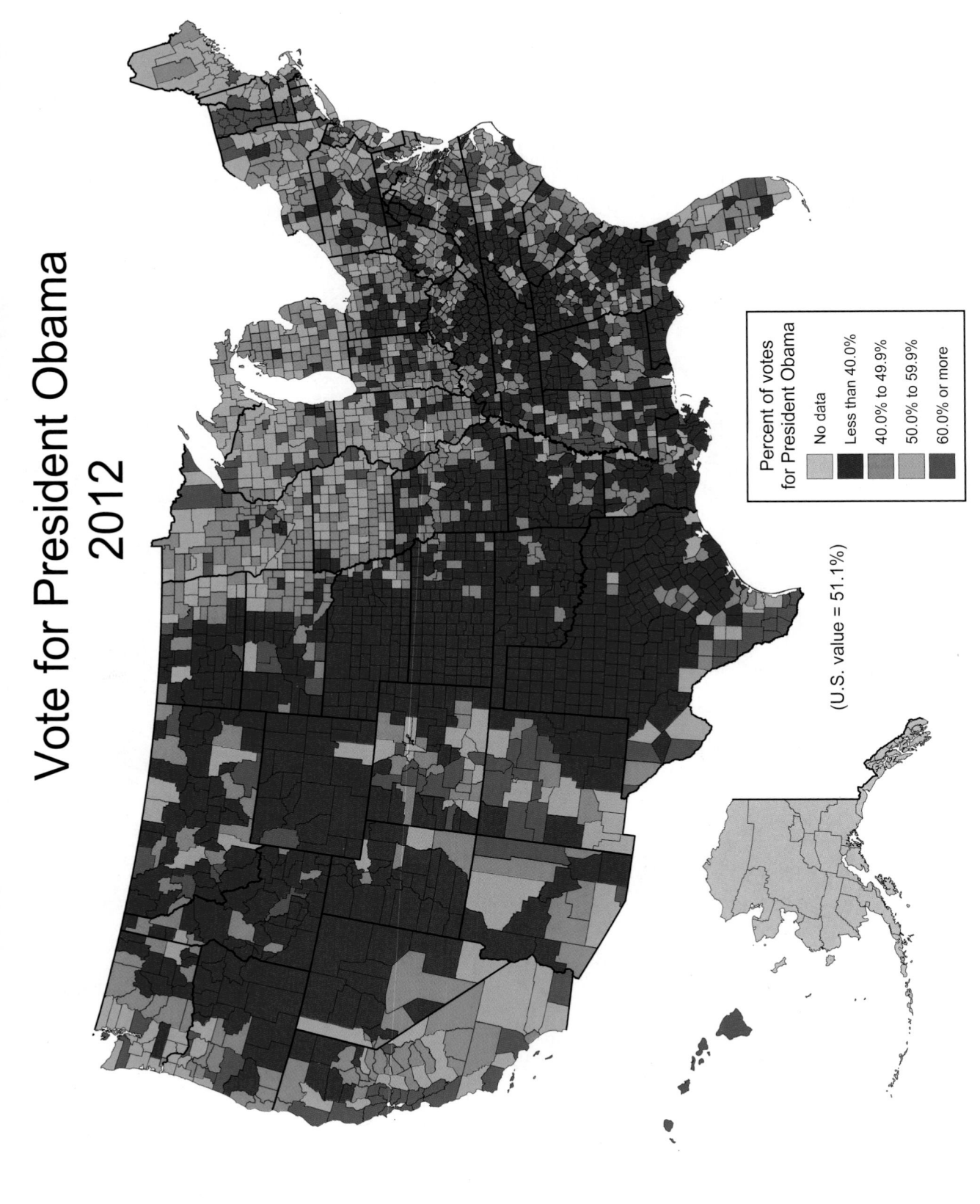

Vote for President Obama
2012

Percent of votes
for President Obama

No data
Less than 40.0%
40.0% to 49.9%
50.0% to 59.9%
60.0% or more

(U.S. value = 51.1%)

# PART A.

# States

(For explanation of symbols, see page viii)

# State Highlights and Rankings

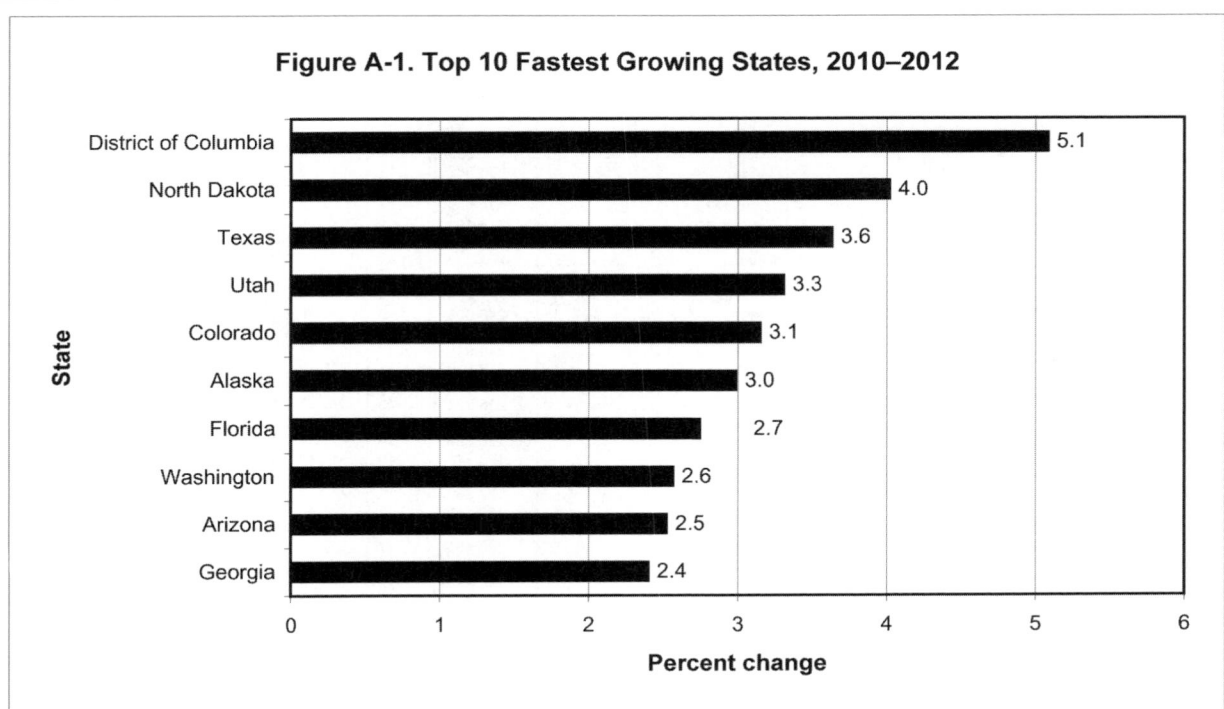

**Figure A-1. Top 10 Fastest Growing States, 2010–2012**

District of Columbia: 5.1
North Dakota: 4.0
Texas: 3.6
Utah: 3.3
Colorado: 3.1
Alaska: 3.0
Florida: 2.7
Washington: 2.6
Arizona: 2.5
Georgia: 2.4

State (y-axis)
Percent change (x-axis): 0, 1, 2, 3, 4, 5, 6

There is no simple relationship between population size and land area for most of the geographic entities included in this publication. According to the Census Bureau's 2012 estimates, state populations ranged from a high of over 38.0 million in California to a low of 576,412 in Wyoming. (The median population for states—with half having a larger population and half having a smaller population—was nearly 4.4 million people.) California was also one of the largest states in land area (ranking third). Alaska was by far the largest state in area; it was more than twice the size of Texas, the second-largest state, even though its population rank was close to the bottom (ranked 47th). Texas was also the second-largest state in terms of total population with over 26.0 million residents. At the other end of the geographic size spectrum were many of the New England states (with Rhode Island ranking as the smallest), plus Delaware, Hawaii, and New Jersey. As a consequence of differing area size and population rank, New Jersey was the most densely settled state, with 465 persons per square kilometer, while Alaska was the least densely settled, with about 0.5 persons per square kilometer. California, which had the largest population and third-largest land area, ranked 12th in terms of population density (94 persons per square kilometer). From 2010 through 2012, the District of Columbia experienced the fastest growth at 5.1 percent followed by North Dakota at 4.0 percent even though they ranked 49th and 48th respectively in population among all the states. The 15 most populous states remained almost unchanged between 2010 and 2012, but there were changes within their ranks. Georgia became the 8th most populous state, pushing ahead of Michigan, and Indiana dropped to 16th with Arizona moving up to 15th in population in 2012, continuing a steady increase up from 16th in 2010 and 20th in 2000.

Not surprisingly, states with higher population density also had higher proportions of developed land. According to the Department of Agriculture's most recent National Resources Inventory, 35.5 percent of New Jersey's land was developed. Connecticut had the second highest proportion with 32.5 percent, followed by Massachusetts at 32.1 percent. Among the reporting states, Nevada had the lowest proportion of developed land, at just 0.8 percent, followed by Wyoming and Montana, each with 1.1 percent of its land developed. Nearly 85 percent of Nevada's land was owned by the federal government. This was by far the highest percentage in the nation. Federal land accounted for about 20 percent of the United States' total land area. (Estimates are not available for Alaska, Hawaii, and the District of Columbia. See Appendix F for definitions and additional information.)

The total population of the United States increased 1.7 percent between 2010 and 2012, with 24 states matching or exceeding this rate of growth and the remainder growing more slowly. The District of Columbia outpaced all the states with a population increase of 5.1 percent in two years. This reflects a national trend of population growth in inner cities. North Dakota ranked first among the states with a population increase of 4.0 percent from 2010 to 2012, primarily caused by an oil boom. Despite its growth, North Dakota ranked 48th for both total population and density. It was among 5 states with population densities of fewer than 5 persons per square kilometer. Texas, Florida, and Georgia ranked among the top 10 states for total population and for population growth from 2010 to 2012. New Hampshire, Rhode Island and Vermont all ranked among the 10 least populous states, as well as among the 10 states with the lowest population growth between 2010 and 2012. While most states have increased their populations in the two years, Rhode Island's population dropped by 0.2 percent. Sixteen other states experienced increases below one percent. Louisiana's population has rebounded from a loss of about 250,000 residents after Hurricane Katrina hit the state in August 2005. Its 2012 population of 4.6 million is slightly higher than its 2005 estimated population on July 1 of that year.

# States and the District of Columbia
## Selected Rankings

| Population, 2012 | | | Land Area, 2010 | | | | Population density, 2012 | | | |
|---|---|---|---|---|---|---|---|---|---|---|
| Popu-lation rank | State | Popu-lation [col 2] | Popu-lation rank | Land area rank | State | Land area (square kilometers) [col 1] | Popu-lation rank | Density rank | State | Density (per square kilometer) [col 4] |
| | United States | 313 914 040 | | | United States | 9 147 593 | | | United States | 34.3 |
| 1 | California | 38 041 430 | 47 | 1 | Alaska | 1 477 953 | 49 | 1 | District of Columbia | 4 002.0 |
| 2 | Texas | 26 059 203 | 2 | 2 | Texas | 676 587 | 11 | 2 | New Jersey | 465.4 |
| 3 | New York | 19 570 261 | 1 | 3 | California | 403 466 | 43 | 3 | Rhode Island | 392.2 |
| 4 | Florida | 19 317 568 | 44 | 4 | Montana | 376 962 | 14 | 4 | Massachusetts | 329.0 |
| 5 | Illinois | 12 875 255 | 36 | 5 | New Mexico | 314 161 | 29 | 5 | Connecticut | 286.3 |
| 6 | Pennsylvania | 12 763 536 | 15 | 6 | Arizona | 294 207 | 19 | 6 | Maryland | 234.1 |
| 7 | Ohio | 11 544 225 | 35 | 7 | Nevada | 284 332 | 45 | 7 | Delaware | 181.7 |
| 8 | Georgia | 9 919 945 | 22 | 8 | Colorado | 268 431 | 3 | 8 | New York | 160.3 |
| 9 | Michigan | 9 883 360 | 51 | 9 | Wyoming | 251 470 | 4 | 9 | Florida | 139.1 |
| 10 | North Carolina | 9 752 073 | 27 | 10 | Oregon | 248 608 | 6 | 10 | Pennsylvania | 110.1 |
| 11 | New Jersey | 8 864 590 | 39 | 11 | Idaho | 214 045 | 7 | 11 | Ohio | 109.1 |
| 12 | Virginia | 8 185 867 | 34 | 12 | Utah | 212 818 | 1 | 12 | California | 94.3 |
| 13 | Washington | 6 897 012 | 33 | 13 | Kansas | 211 754 | 5 | 13 | Illinois | 89.5 |
| 14 | Massachusetts | 6 646 144 | 21 | 14 | Minnesota | 206 232 | 40 | 14 | Hawaii | 83.7 |
| 15 | Arizona | 6 553 255 | 37 | 15 | Nebraska | 198 974 | 12 | 15 | Virginia | 80.0 |
| 16 | Indiana | 6 537 334 | 46 | 16 | South Dakota | 196 350 | 10 | 16 | North Carolina | 77.4 |
| 17 | Tennessee | 6 456 243 | 48 | 17 | North Dakota | 178 711 | 16 | 17 | Indiana | 70.5 |
| 18 | Missouri | 6 021 988 | 18 | 18 | Missouri | 178 040 | 9 | 18 | Michigan | 67.5 |
| 19 | Maryland | 5 884 563 | 28 | 19 | Oklahoma | 177 660 | 8 | 19 | Georgia | 66.6 |
| 20 | Wisconsin | 5 726 398 | 13 | 20 | Washington | 172 119 | 24 | 20 | South Carolina | 60.7 |
| 21 | Minnesota | 5 379 139 | 8 | 21 | Georgia | 148 959 | 17 | 21 | Tennessee | 60.5 |
| 22 | Colorado | 5 187 582 | 9 | 22 | Michigan | 146 435 | 42 | 22 | New Hampshire | 57.0 |
| 23 | Alabama | 4 822 023 | 30 | 23 | Iowa | 144 669 | 26 | 23 | Kentucky | 42.8 |
| 24 | South Carolina | 4 723 723 | 5 | 24 | Illinois | 143 793 | 25 | 24 | Louisiana | 41.1 |
| 25 | Louisiana | 4 601 893 | 20 | 25 | Wisconsin | 140 268 | 20 | 25 | Wisconsin | 40.8 |
| 26 | Kentucky | 4 380 415 | 4 | 26 | Florida | 138 887 | 13 | 26 | Washington | 40.1 |
| 27 | Oregon | 3 899 353 | 32 | 27 | Arkansas | 134 771 | 2 | 27 | Texas | 38.5 |
| 28 | Oklahoma | 3 814 820 | 23 | 28 | Alabama | 131 171 | 23 | 28 | Alabama | 36.8 |
| 29 | Connecticut | 3 590 347 | 10 | 29 | North Carolina | 125 920 | 18 | 29 | Missouri | 33.8 |
| 30 | Iowa | 3 074 186 | 3 | 30 | New York | 122 057 | 38 | 30 | West Virginia | 29.8 |
| 31 | Mississippi | 2 984 926 | 31 | 31 | Mississippi | 121 531 | 50 | 31 | Vermont | 26.2 |
| 32 | Arkansas | 2 949 131 | 6 | 32 | Pennsylvania | 115 883 | 21 | 32 | Minnesota | 26.1 |
| 33 | Kansas | 2 885 905 | 25 | 33 | Louisiana | 111 898 | 31 | 33 | Mississippi | 24.6 |
| 34 | Utah | 2 855 287 | 17 | 34 | Tennessee | 106 798 | 15 | 34 | Arizona | 22.3 |
| 35 | Nevada | 2 758 931 | 7 | 35 | Ohio | 105 829 | 32 | 35 | Arkansas | 21.9 |
| 36 | New Mexico | 2 085 538 | 12 | 36 | Virginia | 102 279 | 28 | 36 | Oklahoma | 21.5 |
| 37 | Nebraska | 1 855 525 | 26 | 37 | Kentucky | 102 269 | 30 | 37 | Iowa | 21.2 |
| 38 | West Virginia | 1 855 413 | 16 | 38 | Indiana | 92 789 | 22 | 38 | Colorado | 19.3 |
| 39 | Idaho | 1 595 728 | 41 | 39 | Maine | 79 883 | 41 | 39 | Maine | 16.6 |
| 40 | Hawaii | 1 392 313 | 24 | 40 | South Carolina | 77 857 | 27 | 40 | Oregon | 15.7 |
| 41 | Maine | 1 329 192 | 38 | 41 | West Virginia | 62 259 | 33 | 41 | Kansas | 13.6 |
| 42 | New Hampshire | 1 320 718 | 19 | 42 | Maryland | 25 142 | 34 | 42 | Utah | 13.4 |
| 43 | Rhode Island | 1 050 292 | 50 | 43 | Vermont | 23 871 | 35 | 43 | Nevada | 9.7 |
| 44 | Montana | 1 005 141 | 42 | 44 | New Hampshire | 23 187 | 37 | 44 | Nebraska | 9.3 |
| 45 | Delaware | 917 092 | 14 | 45 | Massachusetts | 20 202 | 39 | 45 | Idaho | 7.5 |
| 46 | South Dakota | 833 354 | 11 | 46 | New Jersey | 19 047 | 36 | 46 | New Mexico | 6.6 |
| 47 | Alaska | 731 449 | 40 | 47 | Hawaii | 16 635 | 46 | 47 | South Dakota | 4.2 |
| 48 | North Dakota | 699 628 | 29 | 48 | Connecticut | 12 542 | 48 | 48 | North Dakota | 3.9 |
| 49 | District of Columbia | 632 323 | 45 | 49 | Delaware | 5 047 | 44 | 49 | Montana | 2.7 |
| 50 | Vermont | 626 011 | 43 | 50 | Rhode Island | 2 678 | 51 | 50 | Wyoming | 2.3 |
| 51 | Wyoming | 576 412 | 49 | 51 | District of Columbia | 158 | 47 | 51 | Alaska | 0.5 |

# States and the District of Columbia
## Selected Rankings

### Percent population change, 2010-2012

| Population rank | Percent change rank | State | Percent change [col 36] |
|---|---|---|---|
|  |  | United States | 1.7 |
| 49 | 1 | District of Columbia | 5.1 |
| 48 | 2 | North Dakota | 4.0 |
| 2 | 3 | Texas | 3.6 |
| 34 | 4 | Utah | 3.3 |
| 22 | 5 | Colorado | 3.1 |
| 47 | 6 | Alaska | 3.0 |
| 4 | 7 | Florida | 2.7 |
| 13 | 8 | Washington | 2.6 |
| 15 | 9 | Arizona | 2.5 |
| 8 | 10 | Georgia | 2.4 |
| 40 | 10 | Hawaii | 2.4 |
| 46 | 10 | South Dakota | 2.4 |
| 10 | 13 | North Carolina | 2.3 |
| 12 | 13 | Virginia | 2.3 |
| 51 | 13 | Wyoming | 2.3 |
| 35 | 16 | Nevada | 2.2 |
| 1 | 17 | California | 2.1 |
| 45 | 17 | Delaware | 2.1 |
| 24 | 17 | South Carolina | 2.1 |
| 19 | 20 | Maryland | 1.9 |
| 39 | 21 | Idaho | 1.8 |
| 27 | 21 | Oregon | 1.8 |
| 28 | 23 | Oklahoma | 1.7 |
| 17 | 23 | Tennessee | 1.7 |
| 44 | 25 | Montana | 1.6 |
| 37 | 25 | Nebraska | 1.6 |
| 25 | 27 | Louisiana | 1.5 |
| 14 | 27 | Massachusetts | 1.5 |
| 21 | 29 | Minnesota | 1.4 |
| 36 | 30 | New Mexico | 1.3 |
| 32 | 31 | Arkansas | 1.1 |
| 33 | 31 | Kansas | 1.1 |
| 3 | 33 | New York | 1.0 |
| 23 | 34 | Alabama | 0.9 |
| 30 | 34 | Iowa | 0.9 |
| 26 | 34 | Kentucky | 0.9 |
| 16 | 37 | Indiana | 0.8 |
| 11 | 37 | New Jersey | 0.8 |
| 20 | 39 | Wisconsin | 0.7 |
| 31 | 40 | Mississippi | 0.6 |
| 18 | 40 | Missouri | 0.6 |
| 29 | 42 | Connecticut | 0.5 |
| 6 | 42 | Pennsylvania | 0.5 |
| 5 | 44 | Illinois | 0.3 |
| 42 | 44 | New Hampshire | 0.3 |
| 41 | 46 | Maine | 0.1 |
| 7 | 46 | Ohio | 0.1 |
| 38 | 46 | West Virginia | 0.1 |
| 9 | 49 | Michigan | 0.0 |
| 50 | 49 | Vermont | 0.0 |
| 43 | 51 | Rhode Island | -0.2 |

### Percent under 18 years old, 2011

| Population rank | Under 18 years old rank | State | Percent under 18 years old [cols 10 + 11] |
|---|---|---|---|
|  |  | United States | 23.7 |
| 34 | 1 | Utah | 31.2 |
| 2 | 2 | Texas | 27.1 |
| 39 | 3 | Idaho | 27.0 |
| 47 | 4 | Alaska | 26.1 |
| 8 | 5 | Georgia | 25.4 |
| 33 | 6 | Kansas | 25.2 |
| 31 | 6 | Mississippi | 25.2 |
| 15 | 8 | Arizona | 25.1 |
| 37 | 9 | Nebraska | 25.0 |
| 36 | 10 | New Mexico | 24.9 |
| 28 | 11 | Oklahoma | 24.7 |
| 46 | 11 | South Dakota | 24.7 |
| 1 | 13 | California | 24.6 |
| 16 | 14 | Indiana | 24.5 |
| 25 | 15 | Louisiana | 24.4 |
| 35 | 15 | Nevada | 24.4 |
| 32 | 17 | Arkansas | 24.2 |
| 5 | 18 | Illinois | 24.1 |
| 22 | 19 | Colorado | 24.0 |
| 21 | 20 | Minnesota | 23.9 |
| 30 | 21 | Iowa | 23.7 |
| 10 | 21 | North Carolina | 23.7 |
| 51 | 21 | Wyoming | 23.7 |
| 23 | 24 | Alabama | 23.5 |
| 18 | 24 | Missouri | 23.5 |
| 26 | 26 | Kentucky | 23.4 |
| 7 | 27 | Ohio | 23.3 |
| 17 | 27 | Tennessee | 23.3 |
| 9 | 29 | Michigan | 23.2 |
| 11 | 29 | New Jersey | 23.2 |
| 13 | 29 | Washington | 23.2 |
| 20 | 29 | Wisconsin | 23.2 |
| 19 | 33 | Maryland | 23.1 |
| 24 | 33 | South Carolina | 23.1 |
| 12 | 35 | Virginia | 22.9 |
| 45 | 36 | Delaware | 22.6 |
| 29 | 37 | Connecticut | 22.4 |
| 44 | 38 | Montana | 22.3 |
| 27 | 38 | Oregon | 22.3 |
| 40 | 40 | Hawaii | 22.2 |
| 48 | 41 | North Dakota | 22.1 |
| 3 | 42 | New York | 22.0 |
| 6 | 43 | Pennsylvania | 21.7 |
| 14 | 44 | Massachusetts | 21.3 |
| 42 | 45 | New Hampshire | 21.2 |
| 4 | 46 | Florida | 21.0 |
| 43 | 47 | Rhode Island | 20.9 |
| 38 | 48 | West Virginia | 20.7 |
| 41 | 49 | Maine | 20.3 |
| 50 | 50 | Vermont | 20.1 |
| 49 | 51 | District Of Columbia | 17.0 |

### Percent 65 years old and over, 2011

| Population rank | 65 years old and over rank | State | Percent 65 years old and over [cols 17 + 18 + 19] |
|---|---|---|---|
|  |  | United States | 13.3 |
| 4 | 1 | Florida | 17.6 |
| 41 | 2 | Maine | 16.3 |
| 38 | 3 | West Virginia | 16.2 |
| 6 | 4 | Pennsylvania | 15.6 |
| 44 | 5 | Montana | 15.2 |
| 50 | 6 | Vermont | 15.0 |
| 30 | 7 | Iowa | 14.9 |
| 45 | 8 | Delaware | 14.7 |
| 40 | 8 | Hawaii | 14.7 |
| 43 | 8 | Rhode Island | 14.7 |
| 32 | 11 | Arkansas | 14.6 |
| 29 | 12 | Connecticut | 14.4 |
| 48 | 12 | North Dakota | 14.4 |
| 46 | 12 | South Dakota | 14.4 |
| 7 | 15 | Ohio | 14.3 |
| 27 | 15 | Oregon | 14.3 |
| 15 | 17 | Arizona | 14.2 |
| 18 | 17 | Missouri | 14.2 |
| 9 | 19 | Michigan | 14.1 |
| 24 | 19 | South Carolina | 14.1 |
| 23 | 21 | Alabama | 14.0 |
| 14 | 21 | Massachusetts | 14.0 |
| 42 | 21 | New Hampshire | 14.0 |
| 20 | 24 | Wisconsin | 13.9 |
| 11 | 25 | New Jersey | 13.7 |
| 3 | 25 | New York | 13.7 |
| 28 | 25 | Oklahoma | 13.7 |
| 17 | 25 | Tennessee | 13.7 |
| 37 | 29 | Nebraska | 13.6 |
| 36 | 29 | New Mexico | 13.6 |
| 26 | 31 | Kentucky | 13.5 |
| 33 | 32 | Kansas | 13.3 |
| 16 | 33 | Indiana | 13.2 |
| 10 | 33 | North Carolina | 13.2 |
| 21 | 35 | Minnesota | 13.1 |
| 31 | 36 | Mississippi | 13.0 |
| 39 | 37 | Idaho | 12.8 |
| 5 | 38 | Illinois | 12.7 |
| 13 | 38 | Washington | 12.7 |
| 51 | 38 | Wyoming | 12.7 |
| 25 | 41 | Louisiana | 12.5 |
| 19 | 41 | Maryland | 12.5 |
| 35 | 41 | Nevada | 12.5 |
| 12 | 41 | Virginia | 12.5 |
| 1 | 45 | California | 11.7 |
| 49 | 46 | District Of Columbia | 11.4 |
| 22 | 47 | Colorado | 11.3 |
| 8 | 48 | Georgia | 11.0 |
| 2 | 49 | Texas | 10.5 |
| 34 | 50 | Utah | 9.2 |
| 47 | 51 | Alaska | 8.1 |

# States and the District of Columbia
## Selected Rankings

### Percent born in state of residence, 2011

| Population rank | Born in state of residence rank | State | Percent born in state of residence [col 23] |
|---|---|---|---|
| | | United States | 58.9 |
| 25 | 1 | Louisiana | 78.0 |
| 9 | 2 | Michigan | 76.6 |
| 7 | 3 | Ohio | 75.1 |
| 6 | 4 | Pennsylvania | 74.0 |
| 30 | 5 | Iowa | 72.5 |
| 20 | 6 | Wisconsin | 71.8 |
| 31 | 7 | Mississippi | 71.5 |
| 38 | 8 | West Virginia | 71.0 |
| 23 | 9 | Alabama | 70.2 |
| 26 | 10 | Kentucky | 70.1 |
| 16 | 11 | Indiana | 68.9 |
| 21 | 12 | Minnesota | 68.6 |
| 48 | 13 | North Dakota | 67.7 |
| 5 | 14 | Illinois | 67.0 |
| 18 | 15 | Missouri | 66.2 |
| 37 | 16 | Nebraska | 65.8 |
| 46 | 17 | South Dakota | 64.7 |
| 41 | 18 | Maine | 64.3 |
| 3 | 19 | New York | 63.6 |
| 14 | 20 | Massachusetts | 62.9 |
| 34 | 21 | Utah | 61.7 |
| 17 | 22 | Tennessee | 61.4 |
| 32 | 23 | Arkansas | 61.2 |
| 28 | 24 | Oklahoma | 61.1 |
| 2 | 25 | Texas | 60.6 |
| 24 | 26 | South Carolina | 59.4 |
| 33 | 27 | Kansas | 59.0 |
| 43 | 28 | Rhode Island | 58.5 |
| 10 | 29 | North Carolina | 58.0 |
| 8 | 30 | Georgia | 55.8 |
| 29 | 31 | Connecticut | 55.5 |
| 44 | 31 | Montana | 55.5 |
| 40 | 33 | Hawaii | 54.6 |
| 1 | 34 | California | 54.3 |
| 36 | 35 | New Mexico | 52.2 |
| 11 | 36 | New Jersey | 52.1 |
| 50 | 37 | Vermont | 50.7 |
| 12 | 38 | Virginia | 50.3 |
| 19 | 39 | Maryland | 48.0 |
| 13 | 40 | Washington | 47.3 |
| 39 | 41 | Idaho | 46.5 |
| 27 | 42 | Oregon | 46.2 |
| 45 | 43 | Delaware | 45.4 |
| 42 | 44 | New Hampshire | 42.5 |
| 22 | 45 | Colorado | 42.4 |
| 51 | 46 | Wyoming | 40.7 |
| 47 | 47 | Alaska | 39.8 |
| 15 | 48 | Arizona | 38.4 |
| 49 | 49 | District of Columbia | 38.2 |
| 4 | 50 | Florida | 35.5 |
| 35 | 51 | Nevada | 25.3 |

### Number of immigrants, 2011

| Population rank | Immigrant rank | State | Number of immigrants [col 24] |
|---|---|---|---|
| | | United States | 1 062 040 |
| 1 | 1 | California | 210 591 |
| 3 | 2 | New York | 148 426 |
| 4 | 3 | Florida | 109 229 |
| 2 | 4 | Texas | 94 481 |
| 11 | 5 | New Jersey | 55 547 |
| 5 | 6 | Illinois | 38 325 |
| 14 | 7 | Massachusetts | 32 236 |
| 12 | 8 | Virginia | 27 767 |
| 8 | 9 | Georgia | 27 015 |
| 19 | 10 | Maryland | 25 778 |
| 6 | 11 | Pennsylvania | 25 397 |
| 13 | 12 | Washington | 23 789 |
| 15 | 13 | Arizona | 20 333 |
| 9 | 14 | Michigan | 18 347 |
| 10 | 15 | North Carolina | 17 571 |
| 7 | 16 | Ohio | 13 857 |
| 22 | 17 | Colorado | 13 547 |
| 29 | 18 | Connecticut | 12 577 |
| 21 | 19 | Minnesota | 12 389 |
| 35 | 20 | Nevada | 10 449 |
| 17 | 21 | Tennessee | 8 279 |
| 16 | 22 | Indiana | 8 262 |
| 27 | 23 | Oregon | 7694 |
| 40 | 24 | Hawaii | 7 296 |
| 18 | 25 | Missouri | 7 048 |
| 34 | 26 | Utah | 6 426 |
| 20 | 27 | Wisconsin | 6 245 |
| 26 | 28 | Kentucky | 5 403 |
| 33 | 29 | Kansas | 5 086 |
| 30 | 30 | Iowa | 4 624 |
| 37 | 31 | Nebraska | 4 535 |
| 28 | 32 | Oklahoma | 4 503 |
| 25 | 33 | Louisiana | 4 226 |
| 24 | 34 | South Carolina | 4 216 |
| 23 | 35 | Alabama | 4 063 |
| 36 | 36 | New Mexico | 3 767 |
| 43 | 37 | Rhode Island | 3 681 |
| 32 | 38 | Arkansas | 2 874 |
| 49 | 39 | District of Columbia | 2 724 |
| 39 | 40 | Idaho | 2 602 |
| 42 | 41 | New Hampshire | 2478 |
| 45 | 42 | Delaware | 2 355 |
| 47 | 43 | Alaska | 1 799 |
| 31 | 44 | Mississippi | 1 666 |
| 41 | 45 | Maine | 1 467 |
| 46 | 46 | South Dakota | 1 337 |
| 48 | 47 | North Dakota | 948 |
| 50 | 48 | Vermont | 943 |
| 38 | 49 | West Virginia | 830 |
| 44 | 50 | Montana | 511 |
| 51 | 51 | Wyoming | 420 |

### Birth rate, 2010

| Population rank | Birth rate rank | State | Birth rate (per 1,000 population) [col 98] |
|---|---|---|---|
| | | United States | 13.0 |
| 34 | 1 | Utah | 18.9 |
| 47 | 2 | Alaska | 16.2 |
| 2 | 3 | Texas | 15.4 |
| 49 | 4 | District of Columbia | 15.2 |
| 39 | 5 | Idaho | 14.8 |
| 46 | 6 | South Dakota | 14.5 |
| 33 | 7 | Kansas | 14.2 |
| 37 | 7 | Nebraska | 14.2 |
| 28 | 7 | Oklahoma | 14.2 |
| 40 | 10 | Hawaii | 14.0 |
| 8 | 11 | Georgia | 13.8 |
| 25 | 11 | Louisiana | 13.8 |
| 15 | 13 | Arizona | 13.7 |
| 1 | 13 | California | 13.7 |
| 31 | 15 | Mississippi | 13.5 |
| 36 | 15 | New Mexico | 13.5 |
| 48 | 15 | North Dakota | 13.5 |
| 51 | 18 | Wyoming | 13.4 |
| 35 | 19 | Nevada | 13.3 |
| 32 | 20 | Arkansas | 13.2 |
| 22 | 20 | Colorado | 13.2 |
| 5 | 22 | Illinois | 12.9 |
| 16 | 22 | Indiana | 12.9 |
| 26 | 22 | Kentucky | 12.9 |
| 21 | 22 | Minnesota | 12.9 |
| 12 | 22 | Virginia | 12.9 |
| 13 | 22 | Washington | 12.9 |
| 19 | 28 | Maryland | 12.8 |
| 18 | 28 | Missouri | 12.8 |
| 10 | 28 | North Carolina | 12.8 |
| 45 | 31 | Delaware | 12.7 |
| 30 | 31 | Iowa | 12.7 |
| 3 | 33 | New York | 12.6 |
| 24 | 33 | South Carolina | 12.6 |
| 17 | 36 | Tennessee | 12.5 |
| 44 | 37 | Montana | 12.2 |
| 11 | 37 | New Jersey | 12.2 |
| 7 | 39 | Ohio | 12.1 |
| 20 | 40 | Wisconsin | 12.0 |
| 27 | 41 | Oregon | 11.9 |
| 9 | 42 | Michigan | 11.6 |
| 23 | 43 | Alabama | 11.4 |
| 6 | 44 | Pennsylvania | 11.3 |
| 14 | 45 | Massachusetts | 11.1 |
| 38 | 46 | West Virginia | 11.0 |
| 29 | 47 | Connecticut | 10.6 |
| 43 | 47 | Rhode Island | 10.6 |
| 50 | 49 | Vermont | 9.9 |
| 41 | 50 | Maine | 9.8 |
| 42 | 50 | New Hampshire | 9.8 |

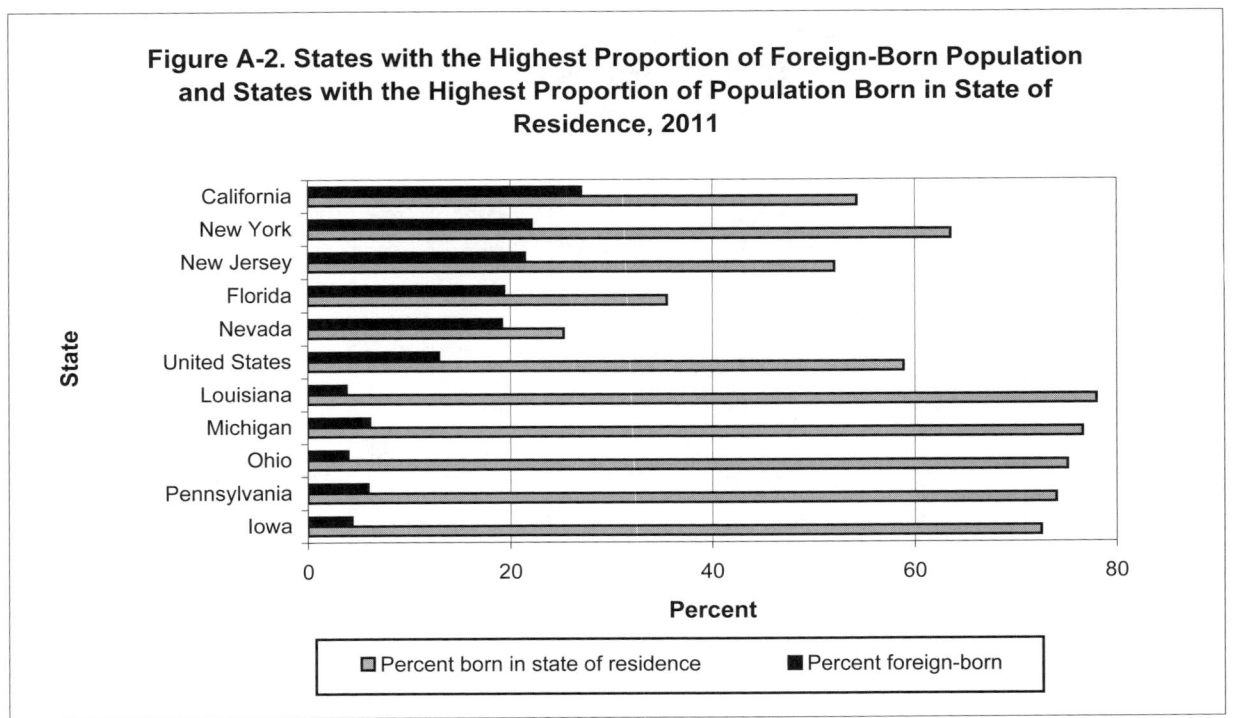

**Figure A-2. States with the Highest Proportion of Foreign-Born Population and States with the Highest Proportion of Population Born in State of Residence, 2011**

The U.S. median age increased slightly from 37.2 years in 2010 to 37.3 years in 2011, primarily caused by the aging Baby Boomer population. This increase was much less than the jump from 32.1 years to 35.3 years between 1990 and 2000. The population between 55 and 64 years showed the largest proportional increase, while the proportion between 35 and 44 showed the largest decrease. The population under age 18 also decreased, but there were increases in the young adult age groups, ages 18 to 34, sometimes referred to as the Echo Boom. The median age by state ranged from 29.6 years in Utah to 43.2 years in Maine. Utah had the highest proportion of young residents; in 2011, 31.3 percent of the state's population was younger than 18 years old. The population age 65 years and over ranged from 8.1 percent in Alaska to 17.6 percent in Florida. Alaska, Wyoming, Nevada, and North Dakota had the lowest proportions of female residents, and were among just nine states in which males outnumbered females. The District of Columbia had the highest proportion of female residents with 52.7 percent, followed by Rhode Island with 51.6 percent.

Natural growth is the difference between the number of births and the number of deaths. Vermont had the fewest births between 2010 and 2012. West Virginia was the only state to have more deaths than births, but a net migration of more than 5,665 people prevented the state from having a population loss from 2010 to 2012. California, the largest state in the nation, had 622,096 more births than deaths and 172,716 new residents through net migration. From 2010 to 2012, California gained 276,809 residents from foreign countries and lost 104,093 residents to other states. Texas and Florida each had a net gain of over 400,000 new residents during this period. In Texas, about 67 percent of these new residents were from other states; in Florida, half were from other states. Fifteen states had a net loss of residents due to internal migration. New York lost over 224,000 residents to other states, only slightly offset by about 14,500 new residents from foreign countries. No state had a net loss of residents because of international migration.

In ten states, more than 70 percent of the residents were born in that same state. Louisiana ranked highest with 78.0 percent. The ten highest rates were mainly in the Midwest and the South. Twelve states and the District of Columbia had proportions less than 50 percent. Nevada had the lowest proportion by far, with just 25.3 percent of its residents having been born in the state. Nationally, 58.9 percent of Americans lived in the state of their birth.

The U.S. birth rate in 2010 was 13.0, the lowest rate ever recorded. Utah had the highest birth rate in the nation, with 18.9 births per 1,000 population. Alaska had the second highest birth rate at 16.2 followed by Texas with a birth rate of 15.4. Maine and New Hampshire had the lowest birth rates in the nation, at 9.8 births per 1,000 population Utah had the lowest crude death rate with 5.1 deaths per 1,000 population followed by Alaska at 5.2 deaths. However, both states had a relatively young population (In Utah, 42.9 percent of the population was under 25 years old while 36.7 percent of the population was under 25 in Alaska). Once adjusted for age, Alaska's death rate increased to 7.6, just above the U.S. rate of 7.4 surpassing 27 states and equaling four others. However, the age-adjusted death rate for Utah remained much lower at 6.6. West Virginia, Alabama, and Arkansas had the highest crude death rates in the nation. With a very high proportion of persons age 65 and over, West Virginia had the highest age-adjusted death rate along with Mississippi, which had a greater mix of younger and older residents. Florida had, by far, the highest proportion of senior citizens. However, Florida also had a high proportion of younger people, which helped give the state a crude death rate outside the top ten, at 9.2 per 1,000 population. When Florida's death rate was age-adjusted, it dropped to 6.7, which was well below the national age-adjusted rate of 7.4. Mississippi, The District of Columbia, and Louisiana had the highest infant mortality rates, while Iowa, Minnesota, and Oregon had the lowest infant death rates.

# States and the District of Columbia
## Selected Rankings

| Percent of owners with a mortgage paying 30 percent or more of income for housing expenses, 2011 | | | | Median value of owner-occupied housing units, 2011 | | | | Median gross rent of renter-occupied housing units, 2011 | | | |
|---|---|---|---|---|---|---|---|---|---|---|---|
| Population rank | Percent of income for housing rank | State | Percent owner-occupied [col 83] | Population rank | Median value rank | State | Median value (dollars) [col 88] | Population rank | Median rent rank | State | Median rent (dollars) [col 90] |
| | | United States...... | 36.6 | | | United States...... | 173 600 | | | United States...... | 871 |
| 40 | 1 | Hawaii | 49.1 | 40 | 1 | Hawaii | 487 400 | 40 | 1 | Hawaii | 1 308 |
| 1 | 2 | California | 48.7 | 49 | 2 | District of Columbia | 422 400 | 49 | 2 | District of Columbia | 1 216 |
| 11 | 3 | New Jersey | 47.1 | 1 | 3 | California | 355 600 | 1 | 3 | California | 1 174 |
| 4 | 4 | Florida | 45.9 | 14 | 4 | Massachusetts | 326 300 | 19 | 4 | Maryland | 1 153 |
| 35 | 5 | Nevada | 42.4 | 11 | 5 | New Jersey | 324 900 | 11 | 5 | New Jersey | 1 135 |
| 3 | 6 | New York | 41.1 | 19 | 6 | Maryland | 287 100 | 12 | 6 | Virginia | 1 062 |
| 43 | 6 | Rhode Island | 41.1 | 3 | 7 | New York | 285 300 | 3 | 7 | New York | 1 058 |
| 27 | 8 | Oregon | 41.0 | 29 | 8 | Connecticut | 278 700 | 47 | 8 | Alaska | 1 049 |
| 29 | 9 | Connecticut | 40.4 | 13 | 9 | Washington | 256 300 | 14 | 9 | Massachusetts | 1 034 |
| 42 | 10 | New Hampshire | 39.8 | 43 | 10 | Rhode Island | 245 500 | 29 | 10 | Connecticut | 1 021 |
| 13 | 11 | Washington | 39.2 | 12 | 11 | Virginia | 243 100 | 45 | 11 | Delaware | 960 |
| 15 | 12 | Arizona | 38.9 | 47 | 12 | Alaska | 238 300 | 4 | 12 | Florida | 949 |
| 5 | 13 | Illinois | 38.6 | 42 | 13 | New Hampshire | 237 500 | 42 | 13 | New Hampshire | 939 |
| 14 | 13 | Massachusetts | 38.6 | 45 | 14 | Delaware | 236 900 | 35 | 14 | Nevada | 936 |
| 44 | 15 | Montana | 37.1 | 22 | 15 | Colorado | 233 700 | 13 | 15 | Washington | 930 |
| 19 | 16 | Maryland | 36.9 | 27 | 16 | Oregon | 232 900 | 22 | 16 | Colorado | 900 |
| 50 | 16 | Vermont | 36.9 | 50 | 17 | Vermont | 213 700 | 43 | 17 | Rhode Island | 875 |
| 39 | 18 | Idaho | 36.7 | 34 | 18 | Utah | 207 500 | 5 | 18 | Illinois | 859 |
| 8 | 19 | Georgia | 36.5 | 44 | 19 | Montana | 184 100 | 15 | 19 | Arizona | 850 |
| 49 | 20 | District of Columbia | 35.5 | 21 | 20 | Minnesota | 183 500 | 50 | 20 | Vermont | 849 |
| 41 | 20 | Maine | 35.5 | 51 | 21 | Wyoming | 179 900 | 27 | 21 | Oregon | 840 |
| 22 | 22 | Colorado | 34.7 | 5 | 22 | Illinois | 178 500 | 8 | 22 | Georgia | 833 |
| 45 | 22 | Delaware | 34.7 | 41 | 23 | Maine | 171 600 | 34 | 23 | Utah | 822 |
| 34 | 24 | Utah | 34.2 | 20 | 24 | Wisconsin | 166 700 | 2 | 24 | Texas | 813 |
| 31 | 25 | Mississippi | 34.1 | 6 | 25 | Pennsylvania | 164 800 | 21 | 25 | Minnesota | 787 |
| 24 | 25 | South Carolina | 34.1 | 36 | 26 | New Mexico | 159 000 | 6 | 26 | Pennsylvania | 786 |
| 36 | 27 | New Mexico | 34.0 | 39 | 27 | Idaho | 158 800 | 51 | 27 | Wyoming | 759 |
| 9 | 28 | Michigan | 33.7 | 35 | 28 | Nevada | 158 000 | 25 | 28 | Louisiana | 747 |
| 10 | 28 | North Carolina | 33.7 | 15 | 29 | Arizona | 153 800 | 41 | 28 | Maine | 747 |
| 12 | 30 | Virginia | 33.3 | 10 | 30 | North Carolina | 153 700 | 10 | 30 | North Carolina | 745 |
| 20 | 30 | Wisconsin | 33.3 | 4 | 31 | Florida | 151 000 | 24 | 31 | South Carolina | 741 |
| 6 | 32 | Pennsylvania | 33.2 | 8 | 32 | Georgia | 147 100 | 9 | 32 | Michigan | 739 |
| 17 | 33 | Tennessee | 32.5 | 25 | 33 | Louisiana | 139 400 | 20 | 32 | Wisconsin | 739 |
| 21 | 34 | Minnesota | 32.1 | 17 | 34 | Tennessee | 138 300 | 36 | 34 | New Mexico | 729 |
| 47 | 35 | Alaska | 32.0 | 18 | 35 | Missouri | 136 900 | 17 | 35 | Tennessee | 715 |
| 23 | 36 | Alabama | 31.5 | 24 | 36 | South Carolina | 136 000 | 33 | 36 | Kansas | 709 |
| 2 | 37 | Texas | 31.4 | 46 | 37 | South Dakota | 131 400 | 18 | 37 | Missouri | 708 |
| 7 | 38 | Ohio | 30.7 | 7 | 38 | Ohio | 129 600 | 16 | 38 | Indiana | 707 |
| 25 | 39 | Louisiana | 29.6 | 48 | 39 | North Dakota | 128 600 | 7 | 39 | Ohio | 692 |
| 18 | 40 | Missouri | 29.3 | 33 | 40 | Kansas | 128 300 | 39 | 40 | Idaho | 689 |
| 28 | 41 | Oklahoma | 28.2 | 2 | 41 | Texas | 127 700 | 31 | 40 | Mississippi | 689 |
| 26 | 42 | Kentucky | 28.0 | 37 | 42 | Nebraska | 127 400 | 23 | 42 | Alabama | 687 |
| 32 | 43 | Arkansas | 27.5 | 30 | 43 | Iowa | 123 400 | 28 | 43 | Oklahoma | 675 |
| 33 | 44 | Kansas | 26.8 | 23 | 44 | Alabama | 122 700 | 37 | 44 | Nebraska | 673 |
| 51 | 44 | Wyoming | 26.8 | 16 | 45 | Indiana | 122 400 | 44 | 45 | Montana | 650 |
| 16 | 46 | Indiana | 26.5 | 26 | 46 | Kentucky | 120 600 | 30 | 46 | Iowa | 643 |
| 38 | 46 | West Virginia | 26.5 | 9 | 47 | Michigan | 118 100 | 32 | 47 | Arkansas | 639 |
| 46 | 48 | South Dakota | 24.9 | 28 | 48 | Oklahoma | 112 600 | 26 | 48 | Kentucky | 626 |
| 37 | 49 | Nebraska | 24.8 | 32 | 49 | Arkansas | 106 300 | 48 | 48 | North Dakota | 626 |
| 30 | 50 | Iowa | 23.6 | 31 | 50 | Mississippi | 99 900 | 46 | 50 | South Dakota | 612 |
| 48 | 51 | North Dakota | 19.1 | 38 | 51 | West Virginia | 99 300 | 38 | 51 | West Virginia | 599 |

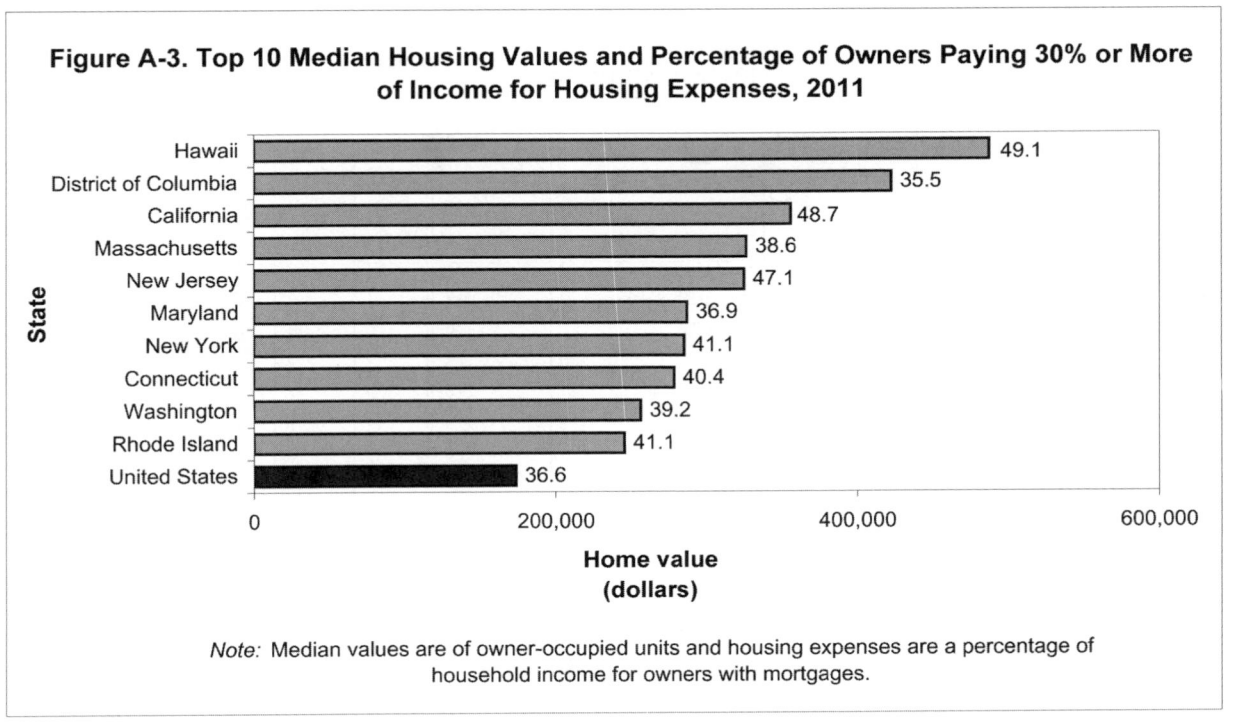

**Figure A-3. Top 10 Median Housing Values and Percentage of Owners Paying 30% or More of Income for Housing Expenses, 2011**

| State | Percentage |
|---|---|
| Hawaii | 49.1 |
| District of Columbia | 35.5 |
| California | 48.7 |
| Massachusetts | 38.6 |
| New Jersey | 47.1 |
| Maryland | 36.9 |
| New York | 41.1 |
| Connecticut | 40.4 |
| Washington | 39.2 |
| Rhode Island | 41.1 |
| United States | 36.6 |

*Note:* Median values are of owner-occupied units and housing expenses are a percentage of household income for owners with mortgages.

In 2011, homeowners paid a median of 24.7 percent of their incomes for monthly owner costs (mortgage, insurance, taxes, utilities, fuel, etc.). This ranged from a high of 29.7 percent in Hawaii to 19.2 percent in North Dakota. Nationally, 36.6 percent of owners with a mortgage paid 30 percent or more of income for housing expenses in 2011. Hawaii had the highest proportion, with 49.1 percent followed by California and New Jersey which both had more than 47 percent of homeowners with a mortgage paying 30 percent or more of their income. In 13 states, less than 30 percent of all mortgaged owners paid this high level of owner costs. North Dakota had the lowest proportion in the nation with 19.1 percent. Four states and the District of Columbia had median home values exceeding $300,000 in 2011, led by Hawaii with a median home value of $487,400. Nationally, the median value of owner-occupied housing units was $173,600. Hawaii also had the highest median gross rent, at $1,308. The District of Columbia, California, Maryland, New Jersey, New York, Virginia, Massachusetts, Connecticut, and Alaska all had median gross monthly rents exceeding $1,000.

Many minority groups had above average growth rates since 2000. Currently, in four states and the District of Columbia, the minority population outnumbers non-Hispanic Whites. Nationally, 65.0 percent of the U.S. population was non-Hispanic White alone or in combination, but the racial and ethnic compositions of the states varied widely. In Hawaii, the state with the highest proportion of minorities, Asian and Pacific Islander alone or in combination was the largest race group, representing over 75 percent of the state's population. Hispanics made up over 46 percent of New Mexico's residents and about 38 percent of residents in both California and Texas. The District of Columbia had the highest proportion of Black residents at just over half the population, down from 60.5 percent in 2000. Among the states, Mississippi and Louisiana ranked first and second, with Black populations of 37.6 and 32.7 percent, respectively. Alaska had the highest proportion of American Indians and Alaska Natives, who made up 18.7 percent of the population. Oklahoma, New Mexico, and South Dakota all had high proportions of American Indian populations. As might be expected, the states

with the largest number of minorities were among the states with the highest total populations. New York was home to nearly 3 million Blacks, and California had the largest number of Hispanics, Asian and Pacific Islanders, and American Indians and Alaska Natives. California had over 380,000 non-Hispanic American Indian and Alaska Native residents, though they made up just 1.0 percent of the state's population. Oklahoma ranked second for both the total number of Native Americans as well as for their representative proportion of the state's population. Despite having only about 80,000 Native American residents, South Dakota had the third highest proportion in the nation.

# States and the District of Columbia
## Selected Rankings

| Popu-lation rank | Percent White rank | State | Percent White [col 5] | Popu-lation rank | Percent Black rank | State | Percent Black [col 6] | Popu-lation rank | Hispanic or Latino rank | State | Percent Hispanic or Latino [col 9] |
|---|---|---|---|---|---|---|---|---|---|---|---|
| | | **Percent White, not Hispanic or Latino, alone or in combination, 2011** | | | | **Percent Black, not Hispanic or Latino, alone or in combination, 2011** | | | | **Percent Hispanic or Latino,[1] 2011** | |
| | | United States .................... | 65.0 | | | United States .................... | 13.1 | | | United States .................... | 16.7 |
| 41 | 1 | Maine ........................... | 95.7 | 49 | 1 | District of Columbia .......... | 50.5 | 36 | 1 | New Mexico .................... | 46.7 |
| 50 | 1 | Vermont ........................ | 95.7 | 31 | 2 | Mississippi ..................... | 37.6 | 2 | 2 | Texas ........................... | 38.1 |
| 38 | 3 | West Virginia ................. | 94.3 | 25 | 3 | Louisiana ...................... | 32.7 | 1 | 2 | California ....................... | 38.1 |
| 42 | 4 | New Hampshire ............. | 93.4 | 8 | 4 | Georgia ......................... | 31.1 | 15 | 4 | Arizona ......................... | 30.1 |
| 48 | 5 | North Dakota ................. | 90.0 | 19 | 5 | Maryland ....................... | 30.3 | 35 | 5 | Nevada ......................... | 27.1 |
| 30 | 6 | Iowa ............................. | 89.7 | 24 | 6 | South Carolina ............... | 28.5 | 4 | 6 | Florida .......................... | 22.9 |
| 44 | 7 | Montana ........................ | 89.6 | 23 | 7 | Alabama ........................ | 26.8 | 22 | 7 | Colorado ....................... | 20.9 |
| 26 | 8 | Kentucky ....................... | 87.5 | 45 | 8 | Delaware ....................... | 22.2 | 11 | 8 | New Jersey .................... | 18.1 |
| 51 | 9 | Wyoming ....................... | 86.9 | 10 | 8 | North Carolina ............... | 22.2 | 3 | 9 | New York ....................... | 18.0 |
| 46 | 10 | South Dakota ................. | 86.1 | 12 | 10 | Virginia ......................... | 20.2 | 5 | 10 | Illinois .......................... | 16.2 |
| 39 | 11 | Idaho ............................ | 85.3 | 17 | 11 | Tennessee ..................... | 17.4 | 29 | 11 | Connecticut .................... | 13.8 |
| 21 | 12 | Minnesota ...................... | 84.6 | 4 | 12 | Florida .......................... | 16.1 | 34 | 12 | Utah ............................. | 13.2 |
| 20 | 13 | Wisconsin ...................... | 84.4 | 32 | 13 | Arkansas ....................... | 16.0 | 43 | 13 | Rhode Island .................. | 12.8 |
| 37 | 14 | Nebraska ....................... | 83.2 | 3 | 14 | New York ....................... | 15.4 | 27 | 14 | Oregon ......................... | 12.0 |
| 16 | 15 | Indiana ......................... | 82.7 | 5 | 15 | Illinois .......................... | 15.0 | 13 | 15 | Washington .................... | 11.6 |
| 7 | 16 | Ohio ............................. | 82.6 | 9 | 15 | Michigan ........................ | 15.0 | 39 | 16 | Idaho ............................ | 11.5 |
| 18 | 17 | Missouri ........................ | 82.5 | 11 | 17 | New Jersey .................... | 13.6 | 33 | 17 | Kansas .......................... | 10.8 |
| 34 | 18 | Utah ............................. | 81.7 | 7 | 18 | Ohio ............................. | 13.2 | 14 | 18 | Massachusetts ................ | 9.9 |
| 27 | 19 | Oregon ......................... | 80.8 | 18 | 19 | Missouri ........................ | 12.4 | 49 | 19 | District of Columbia .......... | 9.5 |
| 6 | 20 | Pennsylvania .................. | 80.4 | 2 | 20 | Texas ........................... | 12.1 | 37 | 19 | Nebraska ....................... | 9.5 |
| 33 | 21 | Kansas .......................... | 79.9 | 6 | 21 | Pennsylvania .................. | 11.4 | 40 | 21 | Hawaii ........................... | 9.2 |
| 9 | 22 | Michigan ........................ | 78.2 | 29 | 22 | Connecticut .................... | 10.4 | 28 | 21 | Oklahoma ...................... | 9.2 |
| 43 | 23 | Rhode Island .................. | 78.0 | 16 | 23 | Indiana ......................... | 10.0 | 51 | 23 | Wyoming ....................... | 9.1 |
| 14 | 24 | Massachusetts ................ | 77.8 | 35 | 24 | Nevada ......................... | 8.8 | 8 | 23 | Georgia ......................... | 9.1 |
| 17 | 25 | Tennessee ..................... | 76.7 | 26 | 25 | Kentucky ....................... | 8.7 | 10 | 25 | North Carolina ................ | 8.6 |
| 32 | 26 | Arkansas ....................... | 75.7 | 28 | 26 | Oklahoma ...................... | 8.6 | 19 | 26 | Maryland ....................... | 8.4 |
| 13 | 27 | Washington .................... | 75.4 | 14 | 27 | Massachusetts ................ | 7.2 | 45 | 26 | Delaware ....................... | 8.4 |
| 28 | 28 | Oklahoma ...................... | 73.0 | 33 | 28 | Kansas .......................... | 6.9 | 12 | 28 | Virginia ......................... | 8.2 |
| 29 | 29 | Connecticut .................... | 72.3 | 20 | 28 | Wisconsin ...................... | 6.9 | 32 | 29 | Arkansas ....................... | 6.6 |
| 22 | 30 | Colorado ....................... | 71.6 | 1 | 30 | California ....................... | 6.6 | 16 | 30 | Indiana ......................... | 6.2 |
| 47 | 31 | Alaska .......................... | 69.4 | 43 | 31 | Rhode Island .................. | 6.5 | 20 | 31 | Wisconsin ...................... | 6.1 |
| 23 | 32 | Alabama ........................ | 67.9 | 21 | 32 | Minnesota ...................... | 6.1 | 6 | 32 | Pennsylvania .................. | 5.9 |
| 45 | 33 | Delaware ....................... | 66.7 | 37 | 33 | Nebraska ....................... | 5.3 | 47 | 33 | Alaska .......................... | 5.8 |
| 12 | 34 | Virginia ......................... | 66.5 | 15 | 34 | Arizona ......................... | 4.6 | 24 | 34 | South Carolina ................ | 5.3 |
| 10 | 35 | North Carolina ............... | 66.4 | 22 | 34 | Colorado ....................... | 4.6 | 30 | 35 | Iowa ............................. | 5.2 |
| 24 | 36 | South Carolina ............... | 65.2 | 13 | 34 | Washington .................... | 4.6 | 21 | 36 | Minnesota ...................... | 4.9 |
| 5 | 37 | Illinois .......................... | 64.5 | 47 | 37 | Alaska .......................... | 4.5 | 17 | 37 | Tennessee ..................... | 4.7 |
| 25 | 38 | Louisiana ...................... | 61.1 | 38 | 38 | West Virginia ................. | 4.2 | 9 | 38 | Michigan ........................ | 4.5 |
| 11 | 39 | New Jersey .................... | 60.0 | 30 | 39 | Iowa ............................. | 3.7 | 25 | 39 | Louisiana ...................... | 4.4 |
| 3 | 40 | New York ....................... | 59.2 | 40 | 40 | Hawaii ........................... | 2.8 | 23 | 40 | Alabama ........................ | 4.0 |
| 15 | 41 | Arizona ......................... | 59.0 | 27 | 41 | Oregon ......................... | 2.4 | 18 | 41 | Missouri ........................ | 3.7 |
| 4 | 42 | Florida .......................... | 58.7 | 36 | 42 | New Mexico .................... | 2.3 | 7 | 42 | Ohio ............................. | 3.2 |
| 31 | 43 | Mississippi ..................... | 58.5 | 46 | 43 | South Dakota ................. | 1.9 | 26 | 42 | Kentucky ....................... | 3.2 |
| 8 | 44 | Georgia ......................... | 56.8 | 48 | 44 | North Dakota ................. | 1.7 | 44 | 44 | Montana ........................ | 3.1 |
| 19 | 45 | Maryland ....................... | 56.1 | 41 | 45 | Maine ........................... | 1.6 | 42 | 45 | New Hampshire ............. | 2.9 |
| 35 | 46 | Nevada ......................... | 56.0 | 42 | 45 | New Hampshire ............. | 1.6 | 46 | 45 | South Dakota ................. | 2.9 |
| 2 | 47 | Texas ........................... | 45.9 | 50 | 47 | Vermont ........................ | 1.5 | 31 | 45 | Mississippi ..................... | 2.9 |
| 1 | 48 | California ....................... | 41.9 | 34 | 48 | Utah ............................. | 1.4 | 48 | 48 | North Dakota ................. | 2.2 |
| 36 | 49 | New Mexico .................... | 41.4 | 51 | 49 | Wyoming ....................... | 1.3 | 50 | 49 | Vermont ........................ | 1.6 |
| 49 | 50 | District of Columbia .......... | 36.9 | 39 | 50 | Idaho ............................ | 1.0 | 41 | 50 | Maine ........................... | 1.4 |
| 40 | 51 | Hawaii ........................... | 36.8 | 44 | 51 | Montana ........................ | 0.9 | 38 | 51 | West Virginia ................. | 1.3 |

1. May be of any race

# States and the District of Columbia
## Selected Rankings

| Percent high school graduates,[1] 2011 | | | | Percent college graduates (bachelor's degree or more),[1] 2011 | | | | Median household income, 2011 | | | |
|---|---|---|---|---|---|---|---|---|---|---|---|
| Population rank | Percent high school graduates rank | State | Percent high school graduates [col 115] | Population rank | Percent college graduates rank | State | Percent college graduates [col 116] | Population rank | Median income rank | State | Median income (dollars) [col 123] |
| | | United States | 85.9 | | | United States | 28.5 | | | United States | 50 502 |
| 44 | 1 | Montana | 92.3 | 49 | 1 | District of Columbia | 52.5 | 19 | 1 | Maryland | 70 004 |
| 21 | 2 | Minnesota | 92.0 | 14 | 2 | Massachusetts | 39.1 | 47 | 2 | Alaska | 67 825 |
| 51 | 2 | Wyoming | 92.0 | 19 | 3 | Maryland | 36.9 | 11 | 3 | New Jersey | 67 458 |
| 47 | 4 | Alaska | 91.8 | 22 | 4 | Colorado | 36.7 | 29 | 4 | Connecticut | 65 753 |
| 50 | 4 | Vermont | 91.8 | 29 | 5 | Connecticut | 36.2 | 49 | 5 | District of Columbia | 63 124 |
| 42 | 6 | New Hampshire | 91.4 | 50 | 6 | Vermont | 35.4 | 14 | 6 | Massachusetts | 62 859 |
| 37 | 7 | Nebraska | 91.0 | 11 | 7 | New Jersey | 35.3 | 42 | 7 | New Hampshire | 62 647 |
| 41 | 8 | Maine | 90.9 | 12 | 8 | Virginia | 35.1 | 12 | 8 | Virginia | 61 882 |
| 48 | 9 | North Dakota | 90.7 | 42 | 9 | New Hampshire | 33.4 | 40 | 9 | Hawaii | 61 821 |
| 40 | 10 | Hawaii | 90.6 | 3 | 10 | New York | 32.9 | 45 | 10 | Delaware | 58 814 |
| 30 | 10 | Iowa | 90.6 | 21 | 11 | Minnesota | 32.4 | 1 | 11 | California | 57 287 |
| 46 | 10 | South Dakota | 90.6 | 13 | 12 | Washington | 31.9 | 21 | 12 | Minnesota | 56 954 |
| 20 | 13 | Wisconsin | 90.4 | 43 | 13 | Rhode Island | 31.1 | 13 | 13 | Washington | 56 835 |
| 34 | 14 | Utah | 90.3 | 5 | 14 | Illinois | 31.0 | 51 | 14 | Wyoming | 56 322 |
| 22 | 15 | Colorado | 90.2 | 1 | 15 | California | 30.3 | 34 | 15 | Utah | 55 869 |
| 13 | 16 | Washington | 90.1 | 33 | 16 | Kansas | 30.1 | 22 | 16 | Colorado | 55 387 |
| 33 | 17 | Kansas | 90.0 | 34 | 17 | Utah | 29.7 | 3 | 17 | New York | 55 246 |
| 27 | 18 | Oregon | 89.4 | 27 | 18 | Oregon | 29.3 | 43 | 18 | Rhode Island | 53 636 |
| 14 | 19 | Massachusetts | 89.2 | 40 | 19 | Hawaii | 29.1 | 5 | 19 | Illinois | 53 234 |
| 29 | 20 | Connecticut | 89.1 | 45 | 20 | Delaware | 28.8 | 50 | 20 | Vermont | 52 776 |
| 19 | 21 | Maryland | 88.9 | 41 | 21 | Maine | 28.4 | 48 | 21 | North Dakota | 51 704 |
| 9 | 22 | Michigan | 88.8 | 44 | 22 | Montana | 28.2 | 20 | 22 | Wisconsin | 50 395 |
| 39 | 23 | Idaho | 88.6 | 37 | 23 | Nebraska | 27.9 | 37 | 23 | Nebraska | 50 296 |
| 6 | 23 | Pennsylvania | 88.6 | 8 | 24 | Georgia | 27.6 | 6 | 24 | Pennsylvania | 50 228 |
| 7 | 25 | Ohio | 88.3 | 6 | 25 | Pennsylvania | 27.0 | 30 | 25 | Iowa | 49 427 |
| 11 | 26 | New Jersey | 88.1 | 10 | 26 | North Carolina | 26.9 | 2 | 26 | Texas | 49 392 |
| 12 | 27 | Virginia | 87.8 | 15 | 27 | Arizona | 26.6 | 33 | 27 | Kansas | 48 964 |
| 18 | 28 | Missouri | 87.6 | 20 | 28 | Wisconsin | 26.5 | 35 | 28 | Nevada | 48 927 |
| 16 | 29 | Indiana | 87.3 | 47 | 29 | Alaska | 26.4 | 46 | 29 | South Dakota | 48 321 |
| 49 | 30 | District of Columbia | 87.2 | 2 | 29 | Texas | 26.4 | 27 | 30 | Oregon | 46 816 |
| 5 | 30 | Illinois | 87.2 | 48 | 31 | North Dakota | 26.3 | 15 | 31 | Arizona | 46 709 |
| 45 | 32 | Delaware | 87.0 | 46 | 31 | South Dakota | 26.3 | 16 | 32 | Indiana | 46 438 |
| 28 | 33 | Oklahoma | 86.3 | 18 | 33 | Missouri | 26.1 | 41 | 33 | Maine | 46 033 |
| 4 | 34 | Florida | 85.9 | 4 | 34 | Florida | 25.8 | 8 | 34 | Georgia | 46 007 |
| 15 | 35 | Arizona | 85.7 | 30 | 34 | Iowa | 25.8 | 9 | 35 | Michigan | 45 981 |
| 3 | 36 | New York | 85.0 | 9 | 36 | Michigan | 25.6 | 7 | 36 | Ohio | 45 749 |
| 43 | 37 | Rhode Island | 84.8 | 36 | 36 | New Mexico | 25.6 | 18 | 37 | Missouri | 45 247 |
| 10 | 38 | North Carolina | 84.7 | 39 | 38 | Idaho | 25.2 | 4 | 38 | Florida | 44 299 |
| 8 | 39 | Georgia | 84.3 | 7 | 39 | Ohio | 24.7 | 44 | 39 | Montana | 44 222 |
| 24 | 40 | South Carolina | 84.2 | 51 | 39 | Wyoming | 24.7 | 10 | 40 | North Carolina | 43 916 |
| 17 | 40 | Tennessee | 84.2 | 24 | 41 | South Carolina | 24.1 | 39 | 41 | Idaho | 43 341 |
| 38 | 40 | West Virginia | 84.2 | 28 | 42 | Oklahoma | 23.8 | 28 | 42 | Oklahoma | 43 225 |
| 35 | 43 | Nevada | 84.0 | 17 | 43 | Tennessee | 23.6 | 24 | 43 | South Carolina | 42 367 |
| 32 | 44 | Arkansas | 83.8 | 16 | 44 | Indiana | 23.0 | 36 | 44 | New Mexico | 41 963 |
| 36 | 45 | New Mexico | 83.2 | 35 | 45 | Nevada | 22.5 | 25 | 45 | Louisiana | 41 734 |
| 26 | 46 | Kentucky | 83.1 | 23 | 46 | Alabama | 22.3 | 17 | 46 | Tennessee | 41 693 |
| 23 | 47 | Alabama | 82.7 | 26 | 47 | Kentucky | 21.1 | 23 | 47 | Alabama | 41 415 |
| 25 | 48 | Louisiana | 82.5 | 25 | 47 | Louisiana | 21.1 | 26 | 48 | Kentucky | 41 141 |
| 1 | 49 | California | 81.1 | 32 | 49 | Arkansas | 20.3 | 32 | 49 | Arkansas | 38 758 |
| 31 | 49 | Mississippi | 81.1 | 31 | 50 | Mississippi | 19.8 | 38 | 50 | West Virginia | 38 482 |
| 2 | 49 | Texas | 81.1 | 38 | 51 | West Virginia | 18.5 | 31 | 51 | Mississippi | 36 919 |

1. Persons 25 years old and over

# States and the District of Columbia
## Selected Rankings

| Unemployment rate, 2012 | | | | Per capita state taxes, 2011 | | | | Exports of goods by state of origin, 2012 | | | |
|---|---|---|---|---|---|---|---|---|---|---|---|
| Popu-lation rank | Unem-ployment rate rank | State | Unem-ployment rate [col 171] | Popu-lation rank | State taxes rank | State | State taxes per capita (dollars) [col 337] | Popu-lation rank | Exports rank | State | Exports (milions of dollars) [col 119] |
| | | United States | 8.1 | | | United States | X | | | United States | 1 547 138 |
| 35 | 1 | Nevada | 11.1 | 47 | 1 | Alaska | 7 662 | 2 | 1 | Texas | 265 352 |
| 1 | 2 | California | 10.5 | 48 | 2 | North Dakota | 5 589 | 1 | 2 | California | 161 700 |
| 43 | 3 | Rhode Island | 10.4 | 51 | 3 | Wyoming | 4 333 | 3 | 3 | New York | 79 189 |
| 11 | 4 | New Jersey | 9.5 | 50 | 4 | Vermont | 4 291 | 13 | 4 | Washington | 75 525 |
| 10 | 4 | North Carolina | 9.5 | 29 | 5 | Connecticut | 3 751 | 5 | 5 | Illinois | 68 026 |
| 31 | 6 | Mississippi | 9.2 | 21 | 6 | Minnesota | 3 546 | 4 | 6 | Florida | 66 398 |
| 9 | 7 | Michigan | 9.1 | 40 | 7 | Hawaii | 3 533 | 25 | 7 | Louisiana | 63 156 |
| 24 | 7 | South Carolina | 9.1 | 3 | 8 | New York | 3 491 | 9 | 8 | Michigan | 56 902 |
| 8 | 9 | Georgia | 9.0 | 14 | 9 | Massachusetts | 3 353 | 7 | 9 | Ohio | 48 535 |
| 49 | 10 | District of Columbia | 8.9 | 45 | 10 | Delaware | 3 327 | 6 | 10 | Pennsylvania | 38 869 |
| 5 | 10 | Illinois | 8.9 | 1 | 11 | California | 3 096 | 11 | 11 | New Jersey | 37 035 |
| 27 | 12 | Oregon | 8.7 | 11 | 12 | New Jersey | 3 082 | 8 | 12 | Georgia | 35 892 |
| 4 | 13 | Florida | 8.6 | 38 | 13 | West Virginia | 2 772 | 16 | 13 | Indiana | 34 385 |
| 3 | 14 | New York | 8.5 | 41 | 14 | Maine | 2 768 | 17 | 14 | Tennessee | 31 126 |
| 29 | 15 | Connecticut | 8.4 | 19 | 15 | Maryland | 2 746 | 10 | 15 | North Carolina | 28 747 |
| 16 | 15 | Indiana | 8.4 | 32 | 16 | Arkansas | 2 715 | 14 | 16 | Massachusetts | 25 549 |
| 15 | 17 | Arizona | 8.3 | 20 | 17 | Wisconsin | 2 687 | 24 | 17 | South Carolina | 25 247 |
| 26 | 18 | Kentucky | 8.2 | 43 | 18 | Rhode Island | 2 604 | 20 | 18 | Wisconsin | 23 097 |
| 13 | 18 | Washington | 8.2 | 13 | 19 | Washington | 2 549 | 26 | 19 | Kentucky | 22 092 |
| 22 | 20 | Colorado | 8.0 | 6 | 20 | Pennsylvania | 2 539 | 21 | 20 | Minnesota | 20 565 |
| 17 | 20 | Tennessee | 8.0 | 36 | 21 | New Mexico | 2 392 | 23 | 21 | Alabama | 19 526 |
| 6 | 22 | Pennsylvania | 7.9 | 9 | 22 | Michigan | 2 384 | 34 | 22 | Utah | 18 939 |
| 23 | 23 | Alabama | 7.3 | 33 | 23 | Kansas | 2 378 | 15 | 23 | Arizona | 18 357 |
| 32 | 23 | Arkansas | 7.3 | 30 | 24 | Iowa | 2 363 | 27 | 24 | Oregon | 18 300 |
| 41 | 23 | Maine | 7.3 | 26 | 25 | Kentucky | 2 335 | 12 | 25 | Virginia | 18 239 |
| 38 | 23 | West Virginia | 7.3 | 35 | 26 | Nevada | 2 325 | 29 | 26 | Connecticut | 15 866 |
| 7 | 27 | Ohio | 7.2 | 10 | 27 | North Carolina | 2 320 | 30 | 27 | Iowa | 14 604 |
| 45 | 28 | Delaware | 7.1 | 44 | 28 | Montana | 2 308 | 18 | 28 | Missouri | 13 910 |
| 39 | 28 | Idaho | 7.1 | 16 | 29 | Indiana | 2 288 | 19 | 29 | Maryland | 11 781 |
| 47 | 30 | Alaska | 7.0 | 5 | 30 | Illinois | 2 287 | 31 | 30 | Mississippi | 11 779 |
| 18 | 31 | Missouri | 6.9 | 31 | 31 | Mississippi | 2 254 | 33 | 31 | Kansas | 11 660 |
| 36 | 31 | New Mexico | 6.9 | 37 | 32 | Nebraska | 2 254 | 38 | 32 | West Virginia | 11 362 |
| 20 | 31 | Wisconsin | 6.9 | 7 | 33 | Ohio | 2 181 | 35 | 33 | Nevada | 10 190 |
| 19 | 34 | Maryland | 6.8 | 12 | 34 | Virginia | 2 150 | 22 | 34 | Colorado | 8 164 |
| 2 | 34 | Texas | 6.8 | 27 | 35 | Oregon | 2 095 | 32 | 35 | Arkansas | 7 621 |
| 14 | 36 | Massachusetts | 6.7 | 39 | 36 | Idaho | 2 058 | 37 | 36 | Nebraska | 7 449 |
| 25 | 37 | Louisiana | 6.4 | 28 | 37 | Oklahoma | 2 048 | 28 | 37 | Oklahoma | 6 576 |
| 44 | 38 | Montana | 6.0 | 34 | 38 | Utah | 1 944 | 39 | 38 | Idaho | 6 113 |
| 12 | 39 | Virginia | 5.9 | 25 | 39 | Louisiana | 1 938 | 45 | 39 | Delaware | 5 157 |
| 40 | 40 | Hawaii | 5.8 | 22 | 40 | Colorado | 1 850 | 47 | 40 | Alaska | 4 596 |
| 33 | 41 | Kansas | 5.7 | 23 | 41 | Alabama | 1 798 | 50 | 41 | Vermont | 4 306 |
| 34 | 41 | Utah | 5.7 | 42 | 42 | New Hampshire | 1 760 | 48 | 42 | North Dakota | 4 288 |
| 21 | 43 | Minnesota | 5.6 | 17 | 43 | Tennessee | 1 755 | 42 | 43 | New Hampshire | 3 485 |
| 42 | 44 | New Hampshire | 5.5 | 4 | 44 | Florida | 1 708 | 41 | 44 | Maine | 3 058 |
| 51 | 45 | Wyoming | 5.4 | 2 | 45 | Texas | 1 682 | 36 | 45 | New Mexico | 2 980 |
| 30 | 46 | Iowa | 5.2 | 18 | 46 | Missouri | 1 682 | 43 | 46 | Rhode Island | 2 376 |
| 28 | 46 | Oklahoma | 5.2 | 46 | 47 | South Dakota | 1 674 | 49 | 47 | District of Columbia | 2 015 |
| 50 | 48 | Vermont | 5.0 | 15 | 48 | Arizona | 1 673 | 44 | 48 | Montana | 1 573 |
| 46 | 49 | South Dakota | 4.4 | 24 | 49 | South Carolina | 1 643 | 46 | 49 | South Dakota | 1 550 |
| 37 | 50 | Nebraska | 3.9 | 8 | 50 | Georgia | 1 630 | 51 | 50 | Wyoming | 1 421 |
| 48 | 51 | North Dakota | 3.1 | 49 | X | District of Columbia | X | 40 | 51 | Hawaii | 726 |

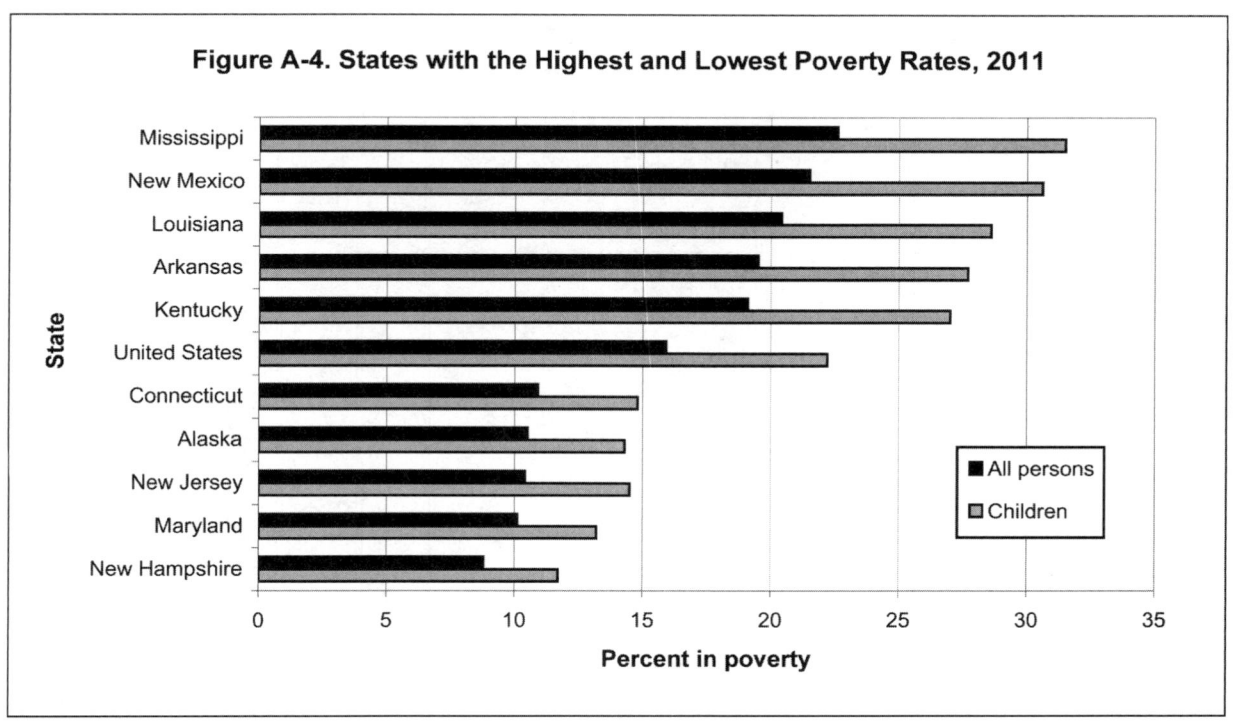

**Figure A-4. States with the Highest and Lowest Poverty Rates, 2011**

Nationally, 85.9 percent of the population 25 years old and over has graduated from high school. Seventeen states had high school attainment levels of 90 percent or more, led by Montana with 92.3 percent. States in the Midwest and the West tended to have above average high school attainment rates although California, Texas, and Mississippi all had the lowest rate in the nation at 81.1 percent. States with above average high school attainment levels do not necessarily have high proportions of college graduates. Nationally, 28.5 percent of the population held bachelor's degrees. In the District of Columbia, 52.5 percent of the population had graduated from college. Even when compared with other large cities, the District of Columbia had among the 10 highest proportions of college graduates in the nation. Of the 50 states, Massachusetts, Colorado, Connecticut, New Jersey, Maryland, Vermont, and Virginia each had more than 35 percent of their populations holding bachelor's degrees or more. States in the Northeast tended to have above average college attainment levels, while states in the South had below average rates.

Median household income ranged from $36,919 in Mississippi to $70,004 in Maryland. Nationally, the median household income was $50,502. In nine states—Mississippi, West Virginia, Kentucky, Arkansas, Alabama, Louisiana, South Carolina, Tennessee, and New Mexico—more than 30 percent of households had incomes below $25,000. Maryland and the District of Columbia had the highest proportions of households earning $100,000 or more, at 33.4 percent and 33.0 percent respectively, followed by New Jersey at 32.9 percent and Connecticut at 31.1 percent.

The poverty threshold for an individual was $11,484 in 2011. Mississippi had the highest poverty rate in the nation, with 22.6 percent of its population living in poverty. New Mexico, Louisiana, Kentucky, and Arkansas, Arizona, and Georgia all had poverty rates of 19 percent or higher. The threshold for a four-person family was $23,021. Among children under 18 years old living in families, 22.2 percent were living in poverty. Over 30 percent of children in Mississippi, the District of Columbia, and New Mexico lived in poverty. New Hampshire had the lowest proportion of children in poverty, at 11.7 percent. Mississippi had the highest proportion of residents 65 years and over living in poverty at 13.5 percent.

The United States labor force increased by 0.9 percent between 2011 and 2012. From 2000 to 2008, it grew about an average of 1 percent a year but then declined from 2009 to 2011. Twenty-one states experienced a decline in their labor force between 2011 and 2012. Arizona experienced the largest decline, dropping 1.3 percent. Meanwhile, the labor force in the District of Columbia grew by 3.9 percent in the same period. In 2012, the unemployment rate was 8.1 percent, down from 8.9 percent in 2011, but three states still had unemployment rates at 10 percent or higher. At 11.1 percent, Nevada had the highest unemployment rate in the nation, followed by California at 10.5 percent. Michigan ranked 7th again in 2012, tied with South Carolina with an unemployment rate of 9.1 percent, after ranking first or second from 2006 through 2010. North Dakota, Nebraska, and South Dakota had the lowest unemployment rates in 2012—all below 5 percent.

# States and the District of Columbia
## Selected Rankings

| Percent of persons below the poverty level, 2011 | | | | Percent of children under 18 years old below the poverty level, 2011 | | | | Percent of persons lacking health insurance, 2011 | | | |
|---|---|---|---|---|---|---|---|---|---|---|---|
| Population rank | Poverty rate rank | State | Poverty rate [col 127] | Population rank | Poverty rate rank | State | Poverty rate [col 128] | Population rank | Percent lacking health insurance rank | State | Percent lacking health insurance [col 104] |
| | | United States | 15.9 | | | United States | 22.2 | | | United States | 15.7 |
| 31 | 1 | Mississippi | 22.6 | 31 | 1 | Mississippi | 31.5 | 2 | 1 | Texas | 23.8 |
| 36 | 2 | New Mexico | 21.5 | 36 | 2 | New Mexico | 30.6 | 35 | 2 | Nevada | 22.6 |
| 25 | 3 | Louisiana | 20.4 | 49 | 3 | District of Columbia | 30.2 | 25 | 3 | Louisiana | 20.8 |
| 32 | 4 | Arkansas | 19.5 | 25 | 4 | Louisiana | 28.6 | 4 | 4 | Florida | 19.8 |
| 8 | 5 | Georgia | 19.1 | 32 | 5 | Arkansas | 27.7 | 1 | 5 | California | 19.7 |
| 26 | 5 | Kentucky | 19.1 | 24 | 6 | South Carolina | 27.6 | 36 | 6 | New Mexico | 19.6 |
| 23 | 7 | Alabama | 19.0 | 23 | 7 | Alabama | 27.4 | 8 | 7 | Georgia | 19.2 |
| 15 | 7 | Arizona | 19.0 | 26 | 8 | Kentucky | 27.0 | 24 | 8 | South Carolina | 19.0 |
| 24 | 9 | South Carolina | 18.9 | 15 | 9 | Arizona | 26.9 | 44 | 9 | Montana | 18.3 |
| 49 | 10 | District of Columbia | 18.7 | 2 | 10 | Texas | 26.4 | 47 | 10 | Alaska | 18.2 |
| 38 | 11 | West Virginia | 18.6 | 8 | 11 | Georgia | 26.1 | 51 | 11 | Wyoming | 17.8 |
| 2 | 12 | Texas | 18.5 | 17 | 12 | Tennessee | 26.0 | 32 | 12 | Arkansas | 17.5 |
| 17 | 13 | Tennessee | 18.3 | 10 | 13 | North Carolina | 25.3 | 15 | 13 | Arizona | 17.3 |
| 10 | 14 | North Carolina | 17.9 | 38 | 13 | West Virginia | 25.3 | 39 | 14 | Idaho | 16.9 |
| 9 | 15 | Michigan | 17.5 | 4 | 15 | Florida | 24.6 | 28 | 14 | Oklahoma | 16.9 |
| 27 | 15 | Oregon | 17.5 | 9 | 16 | Michigan | 24.4 | 10 | 16 | North Carolina | 16.3 |
| 28 | 17 | Oklahoma | 17.2 | 7 | 17 | Ohio | 23.8 | 31 | 17 | Mississippi | 16.2 |
| 4 | 18 | Florida | 17.0 | 27 | 18 | Oregon | 23.2 | 22 | 18 | Colorado | 15.7 |
| 1 | 19 | California | 16.6 | 28 | 19 | Oklahoma | 23.0 | 11 | 19 | New Jersey | 15.4 |
| 39 | 20 | Idaho | 16.5 | 1 | 20 | California | 22.5 | 18 | 20 | Missouri | 14.9 |
| 7 | 21 | Ohio | 16.4 | 16 | 20 | Indiana | 22.5 | 38 | 20 | West Virginia | 14.9 |
| 16 | 22 | Indiana | 16.0 | 3 | 22 | New York | 22.3 | 5 | 22 | Illinois | 14.7 |
| 3 | 22 | New York | 16.0 | 18 | 23 | Missouri | 21.7 | 34 | 23 | Utah | 14.6 |
| 35 | 24 | Nevada | 15.9 | 35 | 24 | Nevada | 21.6 | 13 | 24 | Washington | 14.5 |
| 18 | 25 | Missouri | 15.8 | 43 | 24 | Rhode Island | 21.6 | 26 | 25 | Kentucky | 14.4 |
| 5 | 26 | Illinois | 15.0 | 5 | 26 | Illinois | 21.3 | 19 | 26 | Maryland | 13.8 |
| 44 | 27 | Montana | 14.8 | 39 | 27 | Idaho | 19.9 | 27 | 26 | Oregon | 13.8 |
| 43 | 28 | Rhode Island | 14.7 | 6 | 28 | Pennsylvania | 19.2 | 7 | 28 | Ohio | 13.7 |
| 41 | 29 | Maine | 14.1 | 44 | 29 | Montana | 19.1 | 33 | 29 | Kansas | 13.5 |
| 46 | 30 | South Dakota | 13.9 | 33 | 30 | Kansas | 18.4 | 12 | 30 | Virginia | 13.4 |
| 13 | 30 | Washington | 13.9 | 41 | 31 | Maine | 18.2 | 17 | 31 | Tennessee | 13.3 |
| 33 | 32 | Kansas | 13.8 | 20 | 32 | Wisconsin | 17.9 | 23 | 32 | Alabama | 13.0 |
| 6 | 32 | Pennsylvania | 13.8 | 46 | 33 | South Dakota | 17.8 | 46 | 32 | South Dakota | 13.0 |
| 22 | 34 | Colorado | 13.5 | 13 | 33 | Washington | 17.8 | 9 | 34 | Michigan | 12.5 |
| 34 | 34 | Utah | 13.5 | 37 | 35 | Nebraska | 17.6 | 42 | 34 | New Hampshire | 12.5 |
| 37 | 36 | Nebraska | 13.1 | 22 | 36 | Colorado | 17.5 | 37 | 36 | Nebraska | 12.3 |
| 20 | 36 | Wisconsin | 13.1 | 30 | 37 | Iowa | 17.0 | 3 | 37 | New York | 12.2 |
| 30 | 38 | Iowa | 12.8 | 45 | 38 | Delaware | 16.8 | 16 | 38 | Indiana | 12.0 |
| 48 | 39 | North Dakota | 12.2 | 40 | 39 | Hawaii | 16.7 | 43 | 38 | Rhode Island | 12.0 |
| 40 | 40 | Hawaii | 12.0 | 34 | 40 | Utah | 15.6 | 6 | 40 | Pennsylvania | 10.8 |
| 45 | 41 | Delaware | 11.9 | 51 | 41 | Wyoming | 15.2 | 20 | 41 | Wisconsin | 10.4 |
| 21 | 41 | Minnesota | 11.9 | 21 | 42 | Minnesota | 15.0 | 45 | 42 | Delaware | 10.0 |
| 14 | 43 | Massachusetts | 11.6 | 12 | 42 | Virginia | 15.0 | 30 | 42 | Iowa | 10.0 |
| 50 | 44 | Vermont | 11.5 | 14 | 44 | Massachusetts | 14.9 | 41 | 42 | Maine | 10.0 |
| 12 | 44 | Virginia | 11.5 | 29 | 45 | Connecticut | 14.8 | 21 | 45 | Minnesota | 9.2 |
| 51 | 46 | Wyoming | 11.3 | 11 | 46 | New Jersey | 14.5 | 48 | 46 | North Dakota | 9.1 |
| 29 | 47 | Connecticut | 10.9 | 47 | 47 | Alaska | 14.3 | 29 | 47 | Connecticut | 8.6 |
| 47 | 48 | Alaska | 10.5 | 50 | 48 | Vermont | 14.2 | 50 | 47 | Vermont | 8.6 |
| 11 | 49 | New Jersey | 10.4 | 48 | 49 | North Dakota | 14.1 | 49 | 49 | District of Columbia | 8.4 |
| 19 | 50 | Maryland | 10.1 | 19 | 50 | Maryland | 13.2 | 40 | 50 | Hawaii | 7.8 |
| 42 | 51 | New Hampshire | 8.8 | 42 | 51 | New Hampshire | 11.7 | 14 | 51 | Massachusetts | 3.4 |

# States and the District of Columbia
## Selected Rankings

| | Defense contracts, 2009–2010 | | | | Value of agricultural products sold, 2007 | | | | Violent crime rate, 2011 (violent crimes known to police) | | |
|---|---|---|---|---|---|---|---|---|---|---|---|
| Popu-rank | Defense contract rank | State | Defense contracts (millions of dollars) [col 314] | Popu-lation rank | Agri-cultural sales rank | State | Value of sales (millions of dollars) [col 197] | Popu-lation rank | Violent crime rate rank | State | Violent crime rate (per 100,000 population) [col 108] |
| | | United States ............... | 329 873 | | | United States ................... | 297 220 | | | United States ................... | 15.7 |
| 1 | 1 | California ............... | 41 323 | 1 | 1 | California .......................... | 33 885 | 49 | 1 | District Of Columbia ......... | 1 202.1 |
| 12 | 2 | Virginia ............... | 40 378 | 2 | 2 | Texas ............................ | 21 001 | 17 | 2 | Tennessee ...................... | 608.2 |
| 2 | 3 | Texas ................ | 30 331 | 30 | 3 | Iowa ............................... | 20 418 | 47 | 3 | Alaska ............................ | 606.5 |
| 4 | 4 | Florida ................ | 12 814 | 37 | 4 | Nebraska ......................... | 15 506 | 24 | 4 | South Carolina ................. | 571.9 |
| 14 | 5 | Massachusetts ............... | 12 674 | 33 | 5 | Kansas ............................ | 14 413 | 36 | 5 | New Mexico ..................... | 567.5 |
| 19 | 6 | Maryland ............... | 12 018 | 5 | 6 | Illinois ............................. | 13 329 | 35 | 6 | Nevada ........................... | 562.1 |
| 6 | 7 | Pennsylvania ............... | 11 901 | 21 | 7 | Minnesota ......................... | 13 180 | 45 | 7 | Delaware ......................... | 559.5 |
| 29 | 8 | Connecticut ............... | 11 114 | 10 | 8 | North Carolina .................. | 10 314 | 25 | 8 | Louisiana ........................ | 555.3 |
| 15 | 9 | Arizona ............... | 10 831 | 20 | 9 | Wisconsin ......................... | 8 967 | 4 | 9 | Florida ............................ | 515.3 |
| 18 | 10 | Missouri ............... | 10 335 | 16 | 10 | Indiana ............................ | 8 271 | 19 | 10 | Maryland ......................... | 494.1 |
| 3 | 11 | New York ............... | 8 810 | 4 | 11 | Florida ............................. | 7 785 | 32 | 11 | Arkansas ......................... | 480.9 |
| 20 | 12 | Wisconsin ............... | 8 469 | 18 | 12 | Missouri ........................... | 7 513 | 28 | 12 | Oklahoma ........................ | 454.8 |
| 8 | 13 | Georgia ............... | 8 378 | 32 | 13 | Arkansas .......................... | 7 509 | 18 | 13 | Missouri .......................... | 447.4 |
| 23 | 14 | Alabama ............... | 8 140 | 8 | 14 | Georgia ............................ | 7 113 | 9 | 14 | Michigan .......................... | 445.3 |
| 11 | 15 | New Jersey ............... | 7 858 | 7 | 15 | Ohio ............................... | 7 070 | 5 | 15 | Illinois ............................ | 429.3 |
| 5 | 16 | Illinois ............... | 7 119 | 13 | 16 | Washington ....................... | 6 793 | 14 | 16 | Massachusetts ................. | 428.4 |
| 25 | 18 | Louisiana ............... | 5 842 | 46 | 17 | South Dakota ..................... | 6 570 | 23 | 17 | Alabama .......................... | 420.1 |
| 22 | 19 | Colorado ............... | 5 632 | 48 | 18 | North Dakota .................... | 6 084 | 1 | 18 | California ......................... | 411.1 |
| 26 | 20 | Kentucky ............... | 5 181 | 22 | 19 | Colorado .......................... | 6 061 | 2 | 19 | Texas ............................. | 408.5 |
| 13 | 21 | Washington ............... | 5 151 | 6 | 20 | Pennsylvania ..................... | 5 809 | 15 | 20 | Arizona ........................... | 405.9 |
| 49 | 22 | District of Columbia ........... | 4 651 | 28 | 21 | Oklahoma ......................... | 5 806 | 3 | 21 | New York ......................... | 398.1 |
| 24 | 23 | South Carolina ............... | 4 497 | 9 | 22 | Michigan ........................... | 5 753 | 8 | 22 | Georgia ........................... | 373.2 |
| 16 | 24 | Indiana ............... | 4 370 | 39 | 23 | Idaho .............................. | 5 689 | 18 | 23 | Pennsylvania .................... | 355.0 |
| 9 | 25 | Michigan ............... | 4 080 | 31 | 24 | Mississippi ........................ | 4 877 | 33 | 24 | Kansas ........................... | 353.9 |
| 10 | 26 | North Carolina ............... | 3 627 | 26 | 25 | Kentucky .......................... | 4 825 | 10 | 25 | North Carolina ................. | 349.8 |
| 17 | 27 | Tennessee ............... | 3 101 | 3 | 26 | New York .......................... | 4 419 | 16 | 26 | Indiana ........................... | 331.8 |
| 34 | 28 | Utah ............... | 2 522 | 23 | 27 | Alabama ........................... | 4 416 | 22 | 27 | Colorado ......................... | 320.2 |
| 28 | 29 | Oklahoma ............... | 2 410 | 27 | 28 | Oregon ............................ | 4 386 | 38 | 28 | West Virginia .................... | 315.9 |
| 40 | 30 | Hawaii ............... | 2 351 | 15 | 29 | Arizona ............................ | 3 235 | 11 | 29 | New Jersey ...................... | 308.4 |
| 33 | 31 | Kansas ............... | 1 941 | 12 | 30 | Virginia ............................ | 2 906 | 7 | 30 | Ohio ............................... | 307.4 |
| 47 | 32 | Alaska ............... | 1 776 | 44 | 31 | Montana ........................... | 2 803 | 13 | 31 | Washington ...................... | 294.6 |
| 31 | 33 | Mississippi ............... | 1 634 | 25 | 32 | Louisiana .......................... | 2 618 | 40 | 32 | Hawaii ............................ | 287.2 |
| 30 | 34 | Iowa ............... | 1 557 | 17 | 33 | Tennessee ........................ | 2 617 | 29 | 33 | Connecticut ..................... | 272.8 |
| 21 | 35 | Minnesota ............... | 1 520 | 24 | 34 | South Carolina .................. | 2 353 | 31 | 34 | Mississippi ...................... | 269.8 |
| 36 | 35 | New Mexico ............... | 1 520 | 36 | 35 | New Mexico ...................... | 2 175 | 44 | 35 | Montana .......................... | 267.5 |
| 7 | 35 | Ohio ............... | 6 064 | 19 | 36 | Maryland .......................... | 1 835 | 30 | 36 | Iowa ............................... | 255.6 |
| 41 | 37 | Maine ............... | 1 336 | 34 | 37 | Utah ............................... | 1 416 | 46 | 37 | South Dakota ................... | 254.1 |
| 35 | 38 | Nevada ............... | 1 315 | 51 | 38 | Wyoming ........................... | 1 158 | 37 | 38 | Nebraska ........................ | 253.2 |
| 32 | 39 | Arkansas ............... | 1 138 | 45 | 39 | Delaware .......................... | 1 083 | 27 | 39 | Oregon ........................... | 247.6 |
| 42 | 40 | New Hampshire ............... | 1 092 | 11 | 40 | New Jersey ....................... | 987 | 43 | 40 | Rhode Island .................... | 247.5 |
| 27 | 41 | Oregon ............... | 891 | 50 | 41 | Vermont ........................... | 674 | 48 | 41 | North Dakota .................... | 247.0 |
| 37 | 42 | Nebraska ............... | 793 | 41 | 42 | Maine .............................. | 617 | 26 | 42 | Kentucky ......................... | 238.2 |
| 43 | 43 | Rhode Island ............... | 777 | 38 | 43 | West Virginia ..................... | 592 | 20 | 43 | Wisconsin ........................ | 236.9 |
| 50 | 44 | Vermont ............... | 711 | 29 | 44 | Connecticut ....................... | 552 | 21 | 44 | Minnesota ........................ | 221.2 |
| 46 | 45 | South Dakota ............... | 561 | 40 | 45 | Hawaii ............................. | 514 | 51 | 45 | Wyoming .......................... | 219.3 |
| 38 | 46 | West Virginia ............... | 345 | 35 | 46 | Nevada ............................ | 513 | 39 | 46 | Idaho .............................. | 200.9 |
| 44 | 47 | Montana ............... | 313 | 14 | 47 | Massachusetts ................... | 490 | 12 | 47 | Virginia ........................... | 196.7 |
| 48 | 48 | North Dakota ............... | 288 | 42 | 48 | New Hampshire ................. | 199 | 34 | 48 | Utah ............................... | 195.0 |
| 39 | 49 | Idaho ............... | 265 | 43 | 49 | Rhode Island .................... | 66 | 42 | 49 | New Hampshire ............... | 188.0 |
| 45 | 50 | Delaware ............... | 218 | 47 | 50 | Alaska ............................. | 57 | 50 | 50 | Vermont .......................... | 135.2 |
| 51 | 51 | Wyoming ............... | 155 | 49 | X | District of Columbia .......... | X | 41 | 51 | Maine ............................. | 123.2 |

## Table A. States — **Land Area and Population Characteristics**

| State code | STATE | Land area,[1] 2010 (sq km) | Total persons, 2012 | Rank | Per square kilometer | White | Black | American Indian, Alaska Native | Asian and Pacific Islander | Hispanic or Latino[2] (percent) | Under 5 years | 5 to 17 years | 18 to 24 years | 25 to 34 years | 35 to 44 years | 45 to 54 years |
|---|---|---|---|---|---|---|---|---|---|---|---|---|---|---|---|---|
| | | | Population, 2012 | | | Race alone or in combination, not Hispanic or Latino (percent) | | | | | Age (percent) | | | | | |
| | | 1 | 2 | 3 | 4 | 5 | 6 | 7 | 8 | 9 | 10 | 11 | 12 | 13 | 14 | 15 |

1. Dry land or land partially or temporarily covered by water.   2. May be of any race.

## Table A. States — **Population Characteristics, Immigration, and Households**

| STATE | 55 to 64 years | 65 to 74 years | 75 to 84 years | 85 years and over | Median age | Percent female | Percent foreign born | Percent born in state of residence | Immigrants admitted to legal status, 2011 | Number | Percent change, 2010–2011 | Persons per house-hold | Married couple | Female house-holder[1] | House-holder living alone |
|---|---|---|---|---|---|---|---|---|---|---|---|---|---|---|---|
| | Age (percent) (cont.) | | | | | | | | | Households, 2011 | | | | Household type | |
| | 16 | 17 | 18 | 19 | 20 | 21 | 22 | 23 | 24 | 25 | 26 | 27 | 28 | 29 | 30 |

1. No spouse present.

## Table A. States — **Population Change**

| STATE | 1990 | 2000 | 2010 | 1990–2000 | 2000–2010 | 2010–2012 | Births | Deaths | Net migration | Inter-national | Net internal | 2020 | 2025 | 2030 |
|---|---|---|---|---|---|---|---|---|---|---|---|---|---|---|
| | Census counts | | | Percent change | | | Components of change, 2010–2012 | | Migration | | | Projections | | |
| | 31 | 32 | 33 | 34 | 35 | 36 | 37 | 38 | 39 | 40 | 41 | 42 | 43 | 44 |

## Table A. States — **Population Characteristics**

| STATE | White alone | Black alone | American Indian, Alaska Native alone | Asian and Pacific Islander alone | Some other race or two or more races | Percent Hispanic or Latino[1] | Percent foreign born | Under 5 years | 5 to 17 years | 18 to 24 years | 25 to 34 years | 35 to 44 years | 45 to 54 years | 55 to 64 years | 65 to 74 years | 75 to 84 years | 85 years and over | Median age | Percent female |
|---|---|---|---|---|---|---|---|---|---|---|---|---|---|---|---|---|---|---|---|
| | Race (percent) | | | | | | | Age (percent) | | | | | | | | | | | |
| | 45 | 46 | 47 | 48 | 49 | 50 | 51 | 52 | 53 | 54 | 55 | 56 | 57 | 58 | 59 | 60 | 61 | 62 | 63 |

1. May be of any race.

## Table A. States — **Households and Housing Units**

| | Households, 2010 | | | | | Housing units, 2010 | | | | | | | | | |
| STATE | | | | Percent | | | | Occupied units | | | | | | | |
| | | | | | | | | | | Owner-occupied | | | | Renter-occupied | | |
| | | | | | | | | | | | Median owner cost | | | | | |
| | Number | Percent change, 2000–2010 | Persons per house-hold | Female family house-holder[1] | One person | Total | Percent change, 2000–2010 | Total | Percent | Median value[2] (dollars) | With a mort-gage | Without a mort-gage[3] | Median rent[4] (dollars) | Median rent as a percent of income | Sub-standard units[5] (percent) |
| | 64 | 65 | 66 | 67 | 68 | 69 | 70 | 71 | 72 | 73 | 74 | 75 | 76 | 77 | 78 |

1. No spouse present.    2. Specified owner-occupied units.    3. Median monthly costs is often in the minimum category—10.0 percent or less, which is indicated as 10.0 percent.
4. Specified renter-occupied units.    5. Overcrowded or lacking complete plumbing facilities.

## Table A. States — **Housing Units**

| | Housing units, 2011 | | | | | | | | | | | | | |
| STATE | | | Occupied units | | | | | | | | | | | |
| | | | | | Percent who pay 30 percent or more of income for housing expenses | | Median owner cost as a percent of income | | | | | | | |
| | Total | Percent change, 2010–2011 | Total | Percent owner-occupied | Owners with a mort-gage | Renter | With a mort-gage | Without a mort-gage[1] | Median monthly housing costs (dollars) | Median value of units[2] (dollars) | Percent valued over $500,000 | Median gross rent[3] (dollars) | Sub-standard units[4] (percent) | Percent living in a different house than 1 year ago |
| | 79 | 80 | 81 | 82 | 83 | 84 | 85 | 86 | 87 | 88 | 89 | 90 | 91 | 92 |

1. Median monthly costs is often in the minimum category—10.0 percent or less, which is indicated as 10.0 percent.    2. Specified owner-occupied units.    3. Specified renter-occupied units.
4. Overcrowded or lacking complete plumbing facilities.

## Table A. States — **Residential Construction, Vital Statistics, and Health**

| | Value of residential construction authorized by building permits, 2011 | | | | Births, 2010 | | Deaths, 2009 | | | | | Percent lacking health insurance, 2011 | | |
| STATE | | | | | | | | Number | | Rate | | | | |
| | | | | | | | | | | | Total | | | |
| | New con-struction ($1,000) | Number of housing units | Percent single family | Manu-factured housing units put in place, 2011 (1,000) | Total | Rate[1] | Total | Infant[2] | Crude[1] | Age-adjusted | Infant[3] | All persons | Children under 18 years | Medicare enrollees, 2012 |
| | 93 | 94 | 95 | 96 | 97 | 98 | 99 | 100 | 101 | 102 | 103 | 104 | 105 | 106 |

1. Per 1,000 resident population.    2. Deaths of infants under 1 year old.    3. Deaths of infants under 1 year old per 1,000 live births.

## Table A. States — **Crime and Education**

| | Serious crime known to police,[1] 2011 | | | | Public elementary and secondary school enrollment, 2010–2011 | | Educational attainment[3] (percent) | | | | Local government expenditures for education, 2009–2010 | |
| STATE | Violent Crime | | Property Crime | | | | 2010 | | 2011 | | | |
| | | | | | | | High school graduate or more | Bachelor's degree or more | High school graduate or more | Bachelor's degree or more | | |
| | Number | Rate[2] | Number | Rate[2] | Total | Student/ teacher ratio | | | | | Total current expenditures (mil dol) | Current expenditures per student (dollars) |
| | 107 | 108 | 109 | 110 | 111 | 112 | 113 | 114 | 115 | 116 | 117 | 118 |

1. Data for serious crimes have not been adjusted for underreporting; this may affect comparability between geographic areas and over time.    2. Per 100,000 population estimated by the FBI.    3. Persons 25 years old and over.

## Table A. States — **Exports, Income, and Poverty**

| STATE | Exports of goods by state of origin, 2012 (mil dol) | | | Income, 2011 | | | | | Percent below poverty level, 2011 | | | | | | |
|---|---|---|---|---|---|---|---|---|---|---|---|---|---|---|---|
| | | | | Per capita income (dollars) | Households | | | | | | | | Families with children under 18 | | |
| | Total | Manu-factured | Non-manu-factured | | Median income (dollars) | Percent with income of $25,000 or less | Percent with income of $100,000 or more | Median income of family of four | All persons | Children under 18 years | Persons 65 years and over | All families | Married-couple families | Male house-holder[1] families | Female house-holder[1] families |
| | 119 | 120 | 121 | 122 | 123 | 124 | 125 | 126 | 127 | 128 | 129 | 130 | 131 | 132 | 133 |

1. No spouse present.

## Table A. States — **Personal Income**

| STATE | Personal income, 2011 | | | | | | | | | | | | |
|---|---|---|---|---|---|---|---|---|---|---|---|---|---|
| | Total (mil dol) | Per capita[1] | | Sources of personal income (mil dol) | | | | | | | | | |
| | | | | | | | | | Transfer payments | | | | |
| | | | | | | | | | | Government payments to individuals | | | |
| | | Percent change, 2010–2011 | Dollars | Rank | Wages and salaries[2] | Proprietors' income | Dividends, interest, and rent | Total | Total | Social Security | Medical payments | Income main-tenance | Unemploy-ment insurance |
| | 134 | 135 | 136 | 137 | 138 | 139 | 140 | 141 | 142 | 143 | 144 | 145 | 146 |

1. Based on the resident population estimated as of July 1 of the year shown.    2. Includes supplements to wages and salaries.

## Table A. States — **Personal Income and Earnings**

| STATE | Personal tax payments, 2011 (mil dol) | Disposable personal income, 2011 | | Earnings, 2011 | | | | | | | | | Gross state product, 2011 (mil dol) |
|---|---|---|---|---|---|---|---|---|---|---|---|---|---|
| | | | | Percent by selected industries | | | | | | | | | |
| | | | | | Goods-related[2] | | Service-related and other[3] | | | | | | |
| | | Total (mil dol) | Per capita[1] (dollars) | Total (mil dol) | Farm | Total | Manu-facturing | Total | Retail trade | Finance, insurance, real estate, rental and leasing | Health care and social assist-ance | Government | |
| | 147 | 148 | 149 | 150 | 151 | 152 | 153 | 154 | 155 | 156 | 157 | 158 | 159 |

1. Based on the resident population estimated as of July 1 of the year shown.    2. Total includes mining, construction, and manufacturing.    3. Includes private sector earnings in forestry, fishing, related activities, and other; utilities; wholesale trade; transportation and warehousing; and information.

## Table A. States — **Social Security, Employment, and Labor Force**

| STATE | Social Security beneficiaries, December 2011 | | Supple-mental Security Income recipients[1], December 2011 | Civilian employment and selected occupations,[2] 2011 | | | | Civilian labor force (annual average), 2012 | | | | |
|---|---|---|---|---|---|---|---|---|---|---|---|---|
| | | | | | Percent | | | | | | Unemployed | |
| | Number | Rate[1] | | Total | Management, business, science and art occupations | Services, sales, and office occupations | Construction and production occupations | Total (1,000) | Percent change, 2011–2012 | Employed (1,000) | Total (1,000) | Rate[3] |
| | 160 | 161 | 162 | 163 | 164 | 165 | 166 | 167 | 168 | 169 | 170 | 171 |

1. Per 1,000 resident population estimated as of July 1 of the year shown.    2. Persons 16 years old and over.    3. Percent of civilian labor force.

## Table A. States — Nonfarm Employment and Earnings

| STATE | Private nonfarm employment and earnings, 2012 | | | | | | | | | | | |
| | Employed | | Manufacturing | | | Employment (1,000) | | | | | | |
| | | | | Average earnings of production workers | | | | | | | | |
| | Total (1,000) | Percent change, 2011–2012 | Employment (1,000) | Hourly | Weekly | Construction | Transportation and public utilities | Wholesale trade | Retail trade | Information | Financial activities | Services[1] |
|---|---|---|---|---|---|---|---|---|---|---|---|---|
| | 172 | 173 | 174 | 175 | 176 | 177 | 178 | 179 | 180 | 181 | 182 | 183 |

1. Includes professional and business services, educational and health services, leisure and hospitality, and other services.

## Table A. States — Agriculture

| STATE | Agriculture, 2007 | | | | | | | | | | | |
| | Farms | | | | | Land in farms | | | | | Value of land and buildings (dollars) | |
| | | Percent with: | | | | | | Acres | | | | |
| | Number | Fewer than 50 acres | 500 acres or more | Farm operators whose principal occupation is farming (percent) | Government payments, average per farm (dollars) | Acreage (1,000) | Percent change, 2002–2007 | Average size of farm | Total irrigated (1,000) | Total cropland (1,000) | Average per farm | Average per acre |
|---|---|---|---|---|---|---|---|---|---|---|---|---|
| | 184 | 185 | 186 | 187 | 188 | 189 | 190 | 191 | 192 | 193 | 194 | 195 |

## Table A. States — Agriculture, Land, and Water

| STATE | Agriculture, 2007 (cont.) | | | | | | | Land, 2007 | | | |
| | Value of machinery and equipment, average per farm (dollars) | Value of products sold | | | | Percent of farms with sales of: | | | | | Water consumption, 2005 (mil gal per day) |
| | | | | Percent from: | | | | | | | |
| | | Total (mil dol) | Average per farm (dollars) | Crops | Livestock and poultry products | $10,000 or more | $100,000 or more | Cropland (percent) | Owned by the federal government (percent) | Developed (percent) | |
|---|---|---|---|---|---|---|---|---|---|---|---|
| | 196 | 197 | 198 | 199 | 200 | 201 | 202 | 203 | 204 | 205 | 206 |

## Table A. States — Manufactures and Construction

| STATE | Manufactures, 2011 | | | | | | | | | | Construction, 2007 | | | |
| | All employees | | | Production workers | | | | | | | | Employees | | |
| | | | | | | | Wages | | | | | | | |
| | Number (1,000) | Percent change, 2010–2011 | Annual payroll (mil dol) | Number (1,000) | Work hours (millions) | Total (mil dol) | Average per worker (dollars) | Value added by manufacture (mil dol) | Value of shipments (mil dol) | Total capital expenditures (mil dol) | Number of establishments | Number | Percent change, 2002–2007 | Value (mil dol) | Annual payroll (mil dol) |
|---|---|---|---|---|---|---|---|---|---|---|---|---|---|---|
| | 207 | 208 | 209 | 210 | 211 | 212 | 213 | 214 | 215 | 216 | 217 | 218 | 219 | 220 | 221 |

## Table A. States — **Wholesale Trade and Retail Trade**

| STATE | Wholesale trade, 2007 | | | | | Retail trade,[1] 2007 | | | | | | | | |
|---|---|---|---|---|---|---|---|---|---|---|---|---|---|---|
| | | Employees | | | | | Employees | | | | | | | |
| | Number of establishments | Number | Percent change, 2002–2007 | Sales (mil dol) | Annual payroll (mil dol) | Number of establishments | Total | Percent change, 2002–2007 | Motor vehicle and parts dealers | Food and beverage stores | Clothing and clothing accessory stores | General merchandise stores | Sales (mil dol) | Annual payroll (mil dol) |
| | 222 | 223 | 224 | 225 | 226 | 227 | 228 | 229 | 230 | 231 | 232 | 233 | 234 | 235 |

1. Establishments with payroll.

## Table A. States — **Information**

| STATE | Information, 2007 | | | | | | | | | | |
|---|---|---|---|---|---|---|---|---|---|---|---|
| | | Employees | | | | | | | | | |
| | Number of establishments | Number | Percent change, 2002–2007 | Publishing, except Internet | Motion picture and sound recording | Broadcasting, except Internet | Internet publishing and broadcasting and web search portals | Telecom-munications | Data processing, hosting, and related services | Receipts (mil dol) | Annual payroll (mil dol) |
| | 236 | 237 | 238 | 239 | 240 | 241 | 242 | 243 | 244 | 245 | 246 |

## Table A. States — **Utilities, Transportation and Warehousing, and Finance and Insurance**

| STATE | Utilities, 2007 | | | | | Transportation and warehousing, 2007 | | | | | Finance and insurance, 2007 | | | | |
|---|---|---|---|---|---|---|---|---|---|---|---|---|---|---|---|
| | | Employees | | | | | Employees | | | | | Employees | | | |
| | Number of establishments | Number | Percent change, 2002–2007 | Receipts (mil dol) | Annual payroll (mil dol) | Number of establishments | Number | Percent change, 2002–2007 | Receipts (mil dol) | Annual payroll (mil dol) | Number of establishments | Number | Percent change, 2002–2007 | Receipts (mil dol) | Annual payroll (mil dol) |
| | 247 | 248 | 249 | 250 | 251 | 252 | 253 | 254 | 255 | 256 | 257 | 258 | 259 | 260 | 261 |

## Table A. States — **Real Estate and Rental and Leasing and Professional, Scientific, and Technical Services**

| STATE | Real estate and rental and leasing, 2007 | | | | | Professional, scientific, and technical services, 2007 | | | | | | | | |
|---|---|---|---|---|---|---|---|---|---|---|---|---|---|---|
| | | Employees | | | | | Employees | | | | | | | |
| | Number of establishments | Number | Percent change, 2002–2007 | Receipts (mil dol) | Annual payroll (mil dol) | Number of establishments | Total | Percent change, 2002–2007 | Legal services | Accounting and related services | Architectural, engineering, and related services | Computer systems design and related services | Receipts (mil dol) | Annual payroll (mil dol) |
| | 262 | 263 | 264 | 265 | 266 | 267 | 268 | 269 | 270 | 271 | 272 | 273 | 274 | 275 |

## Table A. States — **Health Care and Social Assistance**

| STATE | Health care and social assistance, 2007 | | | | | | | | | | | | |
|---|---|---|---|---|---|---|---|---|---|---|---|---|---|
| | Subject to federal tax | | | | | | Tax-exempt | | | | | | |
| | | Employees | | | | | | | Employees | | | | | |
| | Number of establishments | Total | Percent change, 2002–2007 | Ambulatory health care services | Hospitals | Receipts (mil dol) | Annual payroll (mil dol) | Number of establishments | Total | Percent change, 2002–2007 | Ambulatory health care services | Hospitals | Receipts (mil dol) | Annual payroll (mil dol) |
| | 276 | 277 | 278 | 279 | 280 | 281 | 282 | 283 | 284 | 285 | 286 | 287 | 288 | 289 |

## Table A. States — **Arts, Entertainment, and Recreation and Accommodation and Food Services**

| STATE | Arts, entertainment, and recreation, 2007 | | | | | Accommodation and food services, 2007 | | | | |
|---|---|---|---|---|---|---|---|---|---|---|
| | | Employees | | | | | Employees | | | |
| | Number of establishments | Number | Percent change, 2002–2007 | Receipts (mil dol) | Annual payroll (mil dol) | Number of establishments | Total | Percent change, 2002–2007 | Food services and drinking places | Receipts (mil dol) | Annual payroll (mil dol) |
| | 290 | 291 | 292 | 293 | 294 | 295 | 296 | 297 | 298 | 299 | 300 |

## Table A. States — **Other Services, Except Public Administration, and Government Employment**

| STATE | Other services, except public administration, 2007 | | | | | | | | Government employment, 2011 | | |
|---|---|---|---|---|---|---|---|---|---|---|---|
| | | Employees | | | | | | | | | |
| | Number of establishments | Total | Percent change, 2002–2007 | Repair and maintenance | Personal and laundry services | Religious, civic, and similar services | Receipts (mil dol) | Annual payroll (mil dol) | Federal civilian | Federal military | State and local |
| | 301 | 302 | 303 | 304 | 305 | 306 | 307 | 308 | 309 | 310 | 311 |

## Table A. States — **Federal Funds**

| STATE | Federal funds and grants, 2009–2010 (mil dol) | | | | | | | | | | | |
|---|---|---|---|---|---|---|---|---|---|---|---|---|
| | | | Procurement contract awards | | Direct payments to individuals | | | | | | | |
| | Total | Salaries and wages | Defense | Other | Total | Social Security and government retirement | Medicare | Unemployment compensation | Food Stamps | Supplemental Security Income | Agricultural assistance | Housing assistance |
| | 312 | 313 | 314 | 315 | 316 | 317 | 318 | 319 | 320 | 321 | 322 | 323 |

## Table A. States — **Federal Funds and State Government Finances**

| STATE | Federal funds and grants, 2009–2010 (mil dol) (cont.) | | | | | | | State government finances, 2011 | | | | | | | |
|---|---|---|---|---|---|---|---|---|---|---|---|---|---|---|---|
| | Grants | | | | | | | | From federal government | | From own sources | | | | |
| | | | | | | | | | | | | | Taxes | | Taxes per capita[2] (dollars) |
| | Total[1] | Medicaid and other health-related | Nutrition and family welfare | Disasters and emergency prepared-ness | Housing and community develop-ment | Employ-ment and training | Energy and environ-ment | Total | Total | Per capita[2] (dollars) | Total | Total | Sales and gross receipts | Total | Sales and gross receipts |
| | 324 | 325 | 326 | 327 | 328 | 329 | 330 | 331 | 332 | 333 | 334 | 335 | 336 | 337 | 338 |

1. Includes program categories not shown separately.    2. Based on resident population estimated as of July 1 of the year shown.

## Table A. States — **State Government Finances and Voting**

| STATE | State government finances, 2011 (cont.) | | | | | | | | | | Debt outstanding | | Voting and registration, November 2012 | | Presidential election,[2] 2012 (percent of vote cast) | | |
|---|---|---|---|---|---|---|---|---|---|---|---|---|---|---|---|---|---|
| | General expenditures (mil dol) | | | | | | | | | | | | | | | | |
| | | | Direct general expenditures | | By selected function | | | | | | | | | | | | |
| | Total | To local govern-ments | Total | Per capita[1] (dollars) | Educa-tion | Health and hospitals | High-ways | Public safety | Public welfare | Natural resources, parks, and recreation | Total (mil dol) | Per capita[1] | Percent registered | Percent voted | Demo-cratic | Repub-lican | All other |
| | 339 | 340 | 341 | 342 | 343 | 344 | 345 | 346 | 347 | 348 | 349 | 350 | 351 | 352 | 353 | 354 | 355 |

1. Based on resident population estimated as of July 1 of the year shown.    2. © 2013 Election Data Services, Inc. All rights reserved.

# Table A. States — Land Area and Population Characteristics

| State code | STATE | Land area,[1] 2010 (sq km) | Population, 2012 | | | Population characteristics, 2011 | | | | | | | | | | |
|---|---|---|---|---|---|---|---|---|---|---|---|---|---|---|---|---|
| | | | Total persons, 2012 | Rank | Per square kilometer | Race alone or in combination, not Hispanic or Latino (percent) | | | | Hispanic or Latino[2] (percent) | Age (percent) | | | | | |
| | | | | | | White | Black | American Indian, Alaska Native | Asian and Pacific Islander | | Under 5 years | 5 to 17 years | 18 to 24 years | 25 to 34 years | 35 to 44 years | 45 to 54 years |
| | | 1 | 2 | 3 | 4 | 5 | 6 | 7 | 8 | 9 | 10 | 11 | 12 | 13 | 14 | 15 |
| 00 | UNITED STATES | 9 147 593 | 313 914 040 | X | 34.3 | 65.0 | 13.1 | 1.3 | 5.9 | 16.7 | 6.5 | 17.3 | 10.0 | 13.4 | 13.0 | 14.4 |
| 01 | Alabama | 131 171 | 4 822 023 | 23 | 36.8 | 67.9 | 26.8 | 1.1 | 1.5 | 4.0 | 6.3 | 17.1 | 10.1 | 12.8 | 12.7 | 14.3 |
| 02 | Alaska | 1 477 953 | 731 449 | 47 | 0.5 | 69.4 | 4.5 | 18.7 | 8.5 | 5.8 | 7.5 | 18.5 | 10.6 | 14.8 | 12.7 | 15.2 |
| 04 | Arizona | 294 207 | 6 553 255 | 15 | 22.3 | 59.0 | 4.6 | 4.6 | 3.7 | 30.1 | 6.9 | 18.1 | 9.9 | 13.4 | 12.7 | 13.0 |
| 05 | Arkansas | 134 771 | 2 949 131 | 32 | 21.9 | 75.7 | 16.0 | 1.5 | 1.8 | 6.6 | 6.7 | 17.5 | 9.7 | 13.0 | 12.4 | 13.7 |
| 06 | California | 403 466 | 38 041 430 | 1 | 94.3 | 41.9 | 6.6 | 1.0 | 15.1 | 38.1 | 6.7 | 17.9 | 10.5 | 14.4 | 13.7 | 13.9 |
| 08 | Colorado | 268 431 | 5 187 582 | 22 | 19.3 | 71.6 | 4.6 | 1.3 | 3.8 | 20.9 | 6.7 | 17.4 | 9.8 | 14.6 | 13.7 | 16.0 |
| 09 | Connecticut | 12 542 | 3 590 347 | 29 | 286.3 | 72.3 | 10.4 | 0.6 | 4.5 | 13.8 | 5.5 | 16.9 | 9.2 | 12.0 | 13.1 | 16.0 |
| 10 | Delaware | 5 047 | 917 092 | 45 | 181.7 | 66.7 | 22.2 | 0.9 | 3.9 | 8.4 | 6.1 | 16.4 | 10.1 | 12.6 | 12.5 | 14.7 |
| 11 | District of Columbia | 158 | 632 323 | 49 | 4 002.0 | 36.9 | 50.5 | 0.8 | 4.7 | 9.5 | 5.9 | 11.2 | 13.6 | 21.6 | 13.3 | 12.3 |
| 12 | Florida | 138 887 | 19 317 568 | 4 | 139.1 | 58.7 | 16.1 | 0.6 | 3.2 | 22.9 | 5.6 | 15.3 | 9.3 | 12.3 | 12.6 | 14.4 |
| 13 | Georgia | 148 959 | 9 919 945 | 8 | 66.6 | 56.8 | 31.1 | 0.7 | 3.9 | 9.1 | 7.0 | 18.4 | 10.1 | 13.8 | 14.1 | 14.2 |
| 15 | Hawaii | 16 635 | 1 392 313 | 40 | 83.7 | 36.8 | 2.8 | 1.7 | 75.4 | 9.2 | 6.4 | 15.7 | 9.6 | 14.0 | 12.7 | 13.8 |
| 16 | Idaho | 214 045 | 1 595 728 | 39 | 7.5 | 85.3 | 1.0 | 1.9 | 2.2 | 11.5 | 7.5 | 19.5 | 9.9 | 13.3 | 12.1 | 13.0 |
| 17 | Illinois | 143 793 | 12 875 255 | 5 | 89.5 | 64.5 | 15.0 | 0.5 | 5.3 | 16.2 | 6.4 | 17.6 | 9.7 | 13.9 | 13.2 | 14.4 |
| 18 | Indiana | 92 789 | 6 537 334 | 16 | 70.5 | 82.7 | 10.0 | 0.6 | 2.1 | 6.2 | 6.6 | 17.9 | 10.1 | 12.8 | 12.7 | 14.4 |
| 19 | Iowa | 144 669 | 3 074 186 | 30 | 21.2 | 89.7 | 3.7 | 0.7 | 2.3 | 5.2 | 6.5 | 17.1 | 10.1 | 12.7 | 11.8 | 14.1 |
| 20 | Kansas | 211 754 | 2 885 905 | 33 | 13.6 | 79.9 | 6.9 | 1.8 | 3.1 | 10.8 | 7.1 | 18.1 | 10.2 | 13.3 | 12.0 | 13.9 |
| 21 | Kentucky | 102 269 | 4 380 415 | 26 | 42.8 | 87.5 | 8.7 | 0.7 | 1.5 | 3.2 | 6.4 | 16.9 | 9.6 | 13.0 | 13.0 | 14.6 |
| 22 | Louisiana | 111 898 | 4 601 893 | 25 | 41.1 | 61.1 | 32.7 | 1.1 | 2.0 | 4.4 | 6.9 | 17.5 | 10.4 | 14.0 | 12.2 | 14.1 |
| 23 | Maine | 79 883 | 1 329 192 | 41 | 16.6 | 95.7 | 1.6 | 1.3 | 1.5 | 1.4 | 5.1 | 15.2 | 8.7 | 11.0 | 12.5 | 16.2 |
| 24 | Maryland | 25 142 | 5 884 563 | 19 | 234.1 | 56.1 | 30.3 | 0.8 | 6.6 | 8.4 | 6.3 | 16.8 | 9.6 | 13.4 | 13.4 | 15.5 |
| 25 | Massachusetts | 20 202 | 6 646 144 | 14 | 329.0 | 77.8 | 7.2 | 0.6 | 6.3 | 9.9 | 5.6 | 15.8 | 10.3 | 13.2 | 13.1 | 15.3 |
| 26 | Michigan | 146 435 | 9 883 360 | 9 | 67.5 | 78.2 | 15.0 | 1.3 | 3.1 | 4.5 | 5.9 | 17.3 | 10.1 | 11.8 | 12.6 | 15.0 |
| 27 | Minnesota | 206 232 | 5 379 139 | 21 | 26.1 | 84.6 | 6.1 | 1.7 | 4.8 | 4.9 | 6.6 | 17.3 | 9.4 | 13.7 | 12.5 | 15.0 |
| 28 | Mississippi | 121 531 | 2 984 926 | 31 | 24.6 | 58.5 | 37.6 | 0.8 | 1.2 | 2.9 | 7.0 | 18.2 | 10.4 | 13.1 | 12.4 | 13.8 |
| 29 | Missouri | 178 040 | 6 021 988 | 18 | 33.8 | 82.5 | 12.4 | 1.1 | 2.3 | 3.7 | 6.4 | 17.1 | 9.8 | 13.1 | 12.2 | 14.6 |
| 30 | Montana | 376 962 | 1 005 141 | 44 | 2.7 | 89.6 | 0.9 | 7.6 | 1.2 | 3.1 | 6.2 | 16.1 | 9.8 | 12.5 | 11.2 | 14.5 |
| 31 | Nebraska | 198 974 | 1 855 525 | 37 | 9.3 | 83.2 | 5.3 | 1.3 | 2.4 | 9.5 | 7.1 | 17.8 | 10.0 | 13.5 | 11.9 | 13.8 |
| 32 | Nevada | 284 332 | 2 758 931 | 35 | 9.7 | 56.0 | 8.8 | 1.5 | 9.8 | 27.1 | 6.8 | 17.5 | 9.2 | 14.3 | 13.9 | 13.8 |
| 33 | New Hampshire | 23 187 | 1 320 718 | 42 | 57.0 | 93.4 | 1.6 | 0.7 | 2.7 | 2.9 | 5.1 | 16.1 | 9.5 | 11.2 | 13.1 | 16.9 |
| 34 | New Jersey | 19 047 | 8 864 590 | 11 | 465.4 | 60.0 | 13.6 | 0.5 | 9.2 | 18.1 | 6.1 | 17.1 | 8.8 | 12.7 | 13.7 | 15.6 |
| 35 | New Mexico | 314 161 | 2 085 538 | 36 | 6.6 | 41.4 | 2.3 | 9.2 | 1.9 | 46.7 | 7.0 | 17.9 | 9.9 | 13.2 | 11.9 | 13.8 |
| 36 | New York | 122 057 | 19 570 261 | 3 | 160.3 | 59.2 | 15.4 | 0.7 | 8.4 | 18.0 | 6.0 | 16.0 | 10.2 | 13.9 | 13.2 | 14.7 |
| 37 | North Carolina | 125 920 | 9 752 073 | 10 | 77.4 | 66.4 | 22.2 | 1.7 | 2.8 | 8.6 | 6.5 | 17.2 | 9.9 | 13.1 | 13.6 | 14.2 |
| 38 | North Dakota | 178 711 | 699 628 | 48 | 3.9 | 90.0 | 1.7 | 6.2 | 1.5 | 2.2 | 6.6 | 15.5 | 12.3 | 13.8 | 11.0 | 13.8 |
| 39 | Ohio | 105 829 | 11 544 225 | 7 | 109.1 | 82.6 | 13.2 | 0.7 | 2.2 | 3.2 | 6.2 | 17.2 | 9.6 | 12.4 | 12.5 | 14.8 |
| 40 | Oklahoma | 177 660 | 3 814 820 | 28 | 21.5 | 73.0 | 8.6 | 12.2 | 2.5 | 9.2 | 7.0 | 17.7 | 10.2 | 13.6 | 12.1 | 13.6 |
| 41 | Oregon | 248 608 | 3 899 353 | 27 | 15.7 | 80.8 | 2.4 | 2.4 | 5.5 | 12.0 | 6.1 | 16.2 | 9.4 | 13.7 | 12.9 | 13.7 |
| 42 | Pennsylvania | 115 883 | 12 763 536 | 6 | 110.1 | 80.4 | 11.4 | 0.5 | 3.3 | 5.9 | 5.7 | 16.0 | 9.9 | 12.1 | 12.4 | 15.0 |
| 44 | Rhode Island | 2 678 | 1 050 292 | 43 | 392.2 | 78.0 | 6.5 | 1.0 | 3.6 | 12.8 | 5.3 | 15.6 | 11.5 | 12.3 | 12.6 | 15.2 |
| 45 | South Carolina | 77 857 | 4 723 723 | 24 | 60.7 | 65.2 | 28.5 | 0.8 | 1.8 | 5.3 | 6.5 | 16.6 | 10.3 | 12.9 | 12.7 | 14.1 |
| 46 | South Dakota | 196 350 | 833 354 | 46 | 4.2 | 86.1 | 1.9 | 9.6 | 1.4 | 2.9 | 7.2 | 17.4 | 10.1 | 13.1 | 11.3 | 13.9 |
| 47 | Tennessee | 106 798 | 6 456 243 | 17 | 60.5 | 76.7 | 17.4 | 0.8 | 1.9 | 4.7 | 6.3 | 17.0 | 9.6 | 13.0 | 13.2 | 14.4 |
| 48 | Texas | 676 587 | 26 059 203 | 2 | 38.5 | 45.9 | 12.1 | 0.7 | 4.5 | 38.1 | 7.6 | 19.5 | 10.2 | 14.4 | 13.6 | 13.5 |
| 49 | Utah | 212 818 | 2 855 287 | 34 | 13.4 | 81.7 | 1.4 | 1.5 | 4.1 | 13.2 | 9.3 | 21.9 | 11.6 | 15.9 | 12.2 | 10.9 |
| 50 | Vermont | 23 871 | 626 011 | 50 | 26.2 | 95.7 | 1.5 | 1.1 | 1.8 | 1.6 | 5.0 | 15.1 | 10.6 | 11.3 | 12.1 | 16.0 |
| 51 | Virginia | 102 279 | 8 185 867 | 12 | 80.0 | 66.5 | 20.2 | 0.8 | 6.8 | 8.2 | 6.3 | 16.6 | 10.1 | 13.8 | 13.5 | 14.9 |
| 53 | Washington | 172 119 | 6 897 012 | 13 | 40.1 | 75.4 | 4.6 | 2.5 | 9.9 | 11.6 | 6.5 | 16.7 | 9.7 | 14.1 | 13.3 | 14.3 |
| 54 | West Virginia | 62 259 | 1 855 413 | 38 | 29.8 | 94.3 | 4.2 | 0.7 | 1.0 | 1.3 | 5.6 | 15.2 | 9.2 | 11.9 | 12.6 | 14.6 |
| 55 | Wisconsin | 140 268 | 5 726 398 | 20 | 40.8 | 84.4 | 6.9 | 1.3 | 2.8 | 6.1 | 6.2 | 17.0 | 9.7 | 12.8 | 12.4 | 15.1 |
| 56 | Wyoming | 251 470 | 576 412 | 51 | 2.3 | 86.9 | 1.3 | 2.9 | 1.4 | 9.1 | 7.0 | 16.8 | 10.1 | 13.9 | 11.7 | 14.2 |

1. Dry land or land partially or temporarily covered by water.    2. May be of any race.

**24**

# Table A. States — **Population Characteristics, Immigration, and Households**

| STATE | Population characteristics, 2011 (cont.) Age (percent) (cont.) | | | | | | | | Immigrants admitted to legal status, 2011 | Households, 2011 | | | Household type | | |
|---|---|---|---|---|---|---|---|---|---|---|---|---|---|---|---|
| | 55 to 64 years | 65 to 74 years | 75 to 84 years | 85 years and over | Median age | Percent female | Percent foreign born | Percent born in state of residence | | Number | Percent change, 2010–2011 | Persons per house-hold | Married couple | Female house-holder[1] | House-holder living alone |
| | 16 | 17 | 18 | 19 | 20 | 21 | 22 | 23 | 24 | 25 | 26 | 27 | 28 | 29 | 30 |
| UNITED STATES | 12.2 | 7.2 | 4.2 | 1.8 | 37.3 | 50.8 | 13.0 | 58.9 | 1 062 040 | 114 991 725 | 0.4 | 2.64 | 48.3 | 13.1 | 27.7 |
| Alabama | 12.7 | 7.9 | 4.5 | 1.6 | 38.0 | 51.5 | 3.4 | 70.2 | 4 063 | 1 844 546 | 1.6 | 2.54 | 48.2 | 15.3 | 28.2 |
| Alaska | 12.6 | 5.2 | 2.1 | 0.7 | 33.8 | 48.1 | 7.1 | 39.8 | 1 799 | 257 330 | 1.1 | 2.71 | 49.5 | 11.8 | 25.2 |
| Arizona | 11.7 | 8.0 | 4.5 | 1.7 | 36.3 | 50.3 | 13.4 | 38.4 | 20 333 | 2 356 055 | 0.9 | 2.69 | 47.1 | 13.0 | 27.6 |
| Arkansas | 12.4 | 8.2 | 4.6 | 1.8 | 37.6 | 50.9 | 4.4 | 61.2 | 2 874 | 1 127 621 | 1.1 | 2.54 | 49.3 | 13.6 | 28.1 |
| California | 11.2 | 6.3 | 3.7 | 1.7 | 35.4 | 50.3 | 27.0 | 54.3 | 210 591 | 12 468 743 | 0.5 | 2.96 | 48.6 | 13.7 | 24.5 |
| Colorado | 12.3 | 6.4 | 3.4 | 1.4 | 36.2 | 49.8 | 9.7 | 42.4 | 13 547 | 1 975 388 | 0.8 | 2.53 | 49.1 | 10.0 | 28.8 |
| Connecticut | 12.9 | 7.4 | 4.6 | 2.4 | 40.3 | 51.3 | 13.4 | 55.5 | 12 577 | 1 351 643 | -0.5 | 2.56 | 48.9 | 13.3 | 28.4 |
| Delaware | 12.8 | 8.3 | 4.6 | 1.8 | 39.1 | 51.5 | 8.4 | 45.4 | 2 355 | 333 192 | 1.3 | 2.65 | 48.5 | 14.0 | 25.3 |
| District of Columbia | 10.8 | 6.2 | 3.5 | 1.7 | 33.7 | 52.7 | 13.5 | 38.2 | 2 724 | 268 670 | 6.5 | 2.15 | 21.3 | 17.0 | 45.2 |
| Florida | 12.8 | 9.3 | 5.8 | 2.5 | 41.1 | 51.1 | 19.4 | 35.5 | 109 229 | 7 106 283 | 1.0 | 2.62 | 46.3 | 13.3 | 29.2 |
| Georgia | 11.4 | 6.5 | 3.3 | 1.2 | 35.5 | 51.1 | 9.6 | 55.8 | 27 015 | 3 494 542 | 0.3 | 2.74 | 47.7 | 15.5 | 26.6 |
| Hawaii | 13.1 | 7.7 | 4.7 | 2.4 | 38.5 | 49.8 | 17.9 | 54.6 | 7 296 | 448 563 | 0.6 | 2.97 | 51.2 | 12.6 | 24.1 |
| Idaho | 11.9 | 7.3 | 3.9 | 1.7 | 34.9 | 49.9 | 6.0 | 46.5 | 2 602 | 580 193 | 0.6 | 2.68 | 55.0 | 9.3 | 24.8 |
| Illinois | 11.9 | 6.8 | 4.1 | 1.9 | 36.8 | 50.9 | 14.0 | 67.0 | 38 325 | 4 737 208 | -0.3 | 2.65 | 47.9 | 13.0 | 29.0 |
| Indiana | 12.3 | 7.1 | 4.2 | 1.8 | 37.1 | 50.8 | 4.7 | 68.9 | 8 262 | 2 467 111 | -0.2 | 2.57 | 49.3 | 12.7 | 27.9 |
| Iowa | 12.7 | 7.5 | 5.0 | 2.5 | 38.1 | 50.4 | 4.4 | 72.5 | 4 624 | 1 216 765 | -0.5 | 2.44 | 51.4 | 9.2 | 29.5 |
| Kansas | 12.1 | 6.8 | 4.4 | 2.1 | 36.0 | 50.3 | 6.9 | 59.0 | 5 086 | 1 101 701 | 0.0 | 2.53 | 50.6 | 10.7 | 28.4 |
| Kentucky | 12.8 | 7.7 | 4.3 | 1.6 | 38.2 | 50.8 | 3.2 | 70.1 | 5 403 | 1 672 134 | -0.7 | 2.54 | 49.5 | 13.0 | 28.2 |
| Louisiana | 12.2 | 7.0 | 4.0 | 1.5 | 35.9 | 51.1 | 3.8 | 78.0 | 4 226 | 1 702 030 | 0.7 | 2.61 | 43.7 | 17.1 | 28.9 |
| Maine | 15.1 | 8.8 | 5.2 | 2.2 | 43.2 | 51.1 | 3.2 | 64.3 | 1 467 | 552 051 | 1.2 | 2.34 | 49.1 | 9.8 | 28.4 |
| Maryland | 12.5 | 6.9 | 3.9 | 1.8 | 38.1 | 51.6 | 13.9 | 48.0 | 25 778 | 2 134 517 | 0.3 | 2.67 | 46.6 | 14.9 | 27.8 |
| Massachusetts | 12.7 | 7.2 | 4.5 | 2.3 | 39.3 | 51.6 | 14.9 | 62.9 | 32 236 | 2 532 067 | 0.5 | 2.51 | 46.4 | 12.8 | 29.3 |
| Michigan | 13.2 | 7.5 | 4.5 | 2.0 | 39.2 | 50.9 | 6.1 | 76.6 | 18 347 | 3 772 433 | -0.9 | 2.56 | 48.2 | 12.8 | 29.0 |
| Minnesota | 12.4 | 6.9 | 4.2 | 2.1 | 37.5 | 50.3 | 7.3 | 68.6 | 12 389 | 2 096 477 | 0.2 | 2.48 | 50.9 | 9.5 | 28.6 |
| Mississippi | 12.1 | 7.4 | 4.1 | 1.5 | 36.1 | 51.4 | 2.2 | 71.5 | 1 666 | 1 080 991 | 0.1 | 2.67 | 45.1 | 18.8 | 27.6 |
| Missouri | 12.5 | 7.7 | 4.6 | 2.0 | 38.1 | 51.0 | 4.0 | 66.2 | 7 048 | 2 341 074 | -0.4 | 2.49 | 48.9 | 12.4 | 28.6 |
| Montana | 14.5 | 8.4 | 4.7 | 2.1 | 40.0 | 49.8 | 2.0 | 55.5 | 511 | 404 250 | 0.4 | 2.40 | 49.4 | 9.3 | 30.6 |
| Nebraska | 12.1 | 6.8 | 4.5 | 2.2 | 36.2 | 50.3 | 6.3 | 65.8 | 4 535 | 723 800 | 0.6 | 2.48 | 51.1 | 9.7 | 28.8 |
| Nevada | 12.0 | 7.6 | 3.7 | 1.2 | 36.6 | 49.5 | 19.2 | 25.3 | 10 449 | 982 352 | -0.8 | 2.74 | 45.8 | 12.8 | 27.7 |
| New Hampshire | 14.1 | 7.7 | 4.4 | 1.9 | 41.6 | 50.6 | 5.6 | 42.5 | 2 478 | 516 454 | 0.2 | 2.47 | 53.6 | 9.9 | 25.3 |
| New Jersey | 12.3 | 7.2 | 4.4 | 2.1 | 39.2 | 51.3 | 21.5 | 52.1 | 55 547 | 3 167 629 | -0.2 | 2.73 | 50.7 | 13.6 | 26.2 |
| New Mexico | 12.8 | 7.7 | 4.2 | 1.6 | 36.7 | 50.5 | 10.1 | 52.2 | 3 767 | 767 285 | 0.3 | 2.66 | 45.6 | 14.2 | 28.7 |
| New York | 12.3 | 7.2 | 4.4 | 2.1 | 38.1 | 51.5 | 22.2 | 63.6 | 148 426 | 7 187 938 | -0.1 | 2.63 | 44.1 | 15.1 | 29.5 |
| North Carolina | 12.3 | 7.5 | 4.1 | 1.6 | 37.6 | 51.3 | 7.3 | 58.0 | 17 571 | 3 683 364 | 0.3 | 2.55 | 48.5 | 13.9 | 28.0 |
| North Dakota | 12.6 | 7.0 | 4.9 | 2.5 | 36.7 | 49.4 | 2.4 | 67.7 | 948 | 283 440 | 1.1 | 2.32 | 50.2 | 7.9 | 31.1 |
| Ohio | 13.1 | 7.5 | 4.7 | 2.1 | 39.1 | 51.2 | 4.0 | 75.1 | 13 857 | 4 538 555 | 0.3 | 2.48 | 47.1 | 12.9 | 30.1 |
| Oklahoma | 12.1 | 7.6 | 4.4 | 1.7 | 36.2 | 50.5 | 5.5 | 61.1 | 4 503 | 1 442 731 | 0.7 | 2.55 | 49.6 | 12.2 | 28.3 |
| Oregon | 13.7 | 7.9 | 4.3 | 2.1 | 38.6 | 50.5 | 9.8 | 46.2 | 7 694 | 1 516 979 | 0.7 | 2.50 | 48.4 | 10.0 | 28.4 |
| Pennsylvania | 13.3 | 7.8 | 5.2 | 2.5 | 40.4 | 51.2 | 5.9 | 74.0 | 25 397 | 4 937 333 | 0.0 | 2.49 | 48.1 | 12.1 | 29.7 |
| Rhode Island | 12.9 | 7.3 | 4.8 | 2.6 | 39.7 | 51.7 | 13.5 | 58.5 | 3 681 | 412 259 | 2.5 | 2.45 | 44.0 | 13.4 | 30.6 |
| South Carolina | 13.0 | 8.3 | 4.2 | 1.6 | 38.2 | 51.3 | 4.7 | 59.4 | 4 216 | 1 768 834 | 0.4 | 2.57 | 48.3 | 15.1 | 27.3 |
| South Dakota | 12.5 | 7.2 | 4.8 | 2.4 | 36.9 | 49.9 | 2.7 | 64.7 | 1 337 | 323 215 | 1.3 | 2.44 | 50.5 | 9.7 | 28.8 |
| Tennessee | 12.8 | 7.9 | 4.3 | 1.6 | 38.3 | 51.3 | 4.4 | 61.4 | 8 279 | 2 467 428 | 1.1 | 2.53 | 48.2 | 13.3 | 29.0 |
| Texas | 10.7 | 6.0 | 3.3 | 1.3 | 33.7 | 50.4 | 16.4 | 60.6 | 94 481 | 8 850 370 | 1.3 | 2.84 | 50.1 | 14.5 | 25.0 |
| Utah | 9.0 | 5.1 | 2.9 | 1.2 | 29.5 | 49.8 | 8.4 | 61.7 | 6 426 | 884 253 | 0.5 | 3.13 | 60.4 | 10.2 | 19.8 |
| Vermont | 14.9 | 8.3 | 4.6 | 2.1 | 41.9 | 50.7 | 3.9 | 50.7 | 943 | 257 358 | 0.2 | 2.34 | 49.8 | 8.6 | 27.6 |
| Virginia | 12.3 | 7.1 | 3.8 | 1.6 | 37.5 | 50.9 | 11.1 | 50.3 | 27 767 | 2 990 650 | -0.1 | 2.63 | 50.8 | 12.2 | 26.3 |
| Washington | 12.8 | 7.1 | 3.8 | 1.8 | 37.3 | 50.1 | 13.3 | 47.3 | 23 789 | 2 632 621 | 1.0 | 2.54 | 49.5 | 10.6 | 27.5 |
| West Virginia | 14.7 | 9.0 | 5.3 | 2.0 | 41.5 | 50.7 | 1.3 | 71.0 | 830 | 735 408 | -0.9 | 2.46 | 48.5 | 11.7 | 30.1 |
| Wisconsin | 12.8 | 7.2 | 4.5 | 2.1 | 38.7 | 50.3 | 4.7 | 71.8 | 6 245 | 2 275 352 | -0.2 | 2.44 | 49.8 | 10.1 | 28.8 |
| Wyoming | 13.6 | 7.2 | 3.9 | 1.6 | 36.9 | 49.0 | 3.2 | 40.7 | 420 | 222 539 | -0.1 | 2.49 | 51.4 | 8.7 | 27.0 |

# Table A. States — Population Change

| STATE | Population, 1990–2010 Census counts | | | Percent change | | | Components of change, 2010–2012 | | | | | Population, 2020–2030 Projections | | |
|---|---|---|---|---|---|---|---|---|---|---|---|---|---|---|
| | 1990 | 2000 | 2010 | 1990–2000 | 2000–2010 | 2010–2012 | Births | Deaths | Net migration | International | Net internal | 2020 | 2025 | 2030 |
| | 31 | 32 | 33 | 34 | 35 | 36 | 37 | 38 | 39 | 40 | 41 | 42 | 43 | 44 |
| UNITED STATES | 248 709 873 | 281 421 906 | 308 745 538 | 13.2 | 9.7 | 1.7 | 8 918 468 | 5 602 865 | 1 850 929 | 1 850 929 | X | 335 804 546 | 349 439 199 | 363 584 435 |
| Alabama | 4 040 587 | 4 447 100 | 4 779 736 | 10.1 | 7.5 | 0.9 | 137 514 | 109 105 | 13 545 | 12 288 | 1 257 | 4 728 915 | 4 800 092 | 4 874 243 |
| Alaska | 550 043 | 626 932 | 710 231 | 14.0 | 13.3 | 3.0 | 25 889 | 7 589 | 2 638 | 4 471 | -1 833 | 774 421 | 820 881 | 867 674 |
| Arizona | 3 665 228 | 5 130 632 | 6 392 017 | 40.0 | 24.6 | 2.5 | 193 899 | 106 658 | 73 049 | 24 790 | 48 259 | 8 456 448 | 9 531 537 | 10 712 397 |
| Arkansas | 2 350 725 | 2 673 400 | 2 915 918 | 13.7 | 9.1 | 1.1 | 85 342 | 64 590 | 12 111 | 6 627 | 5 484 | 3 060 219 | 3 151 005 | 3 240 208 |
| California | 29 760 021 | 33 871 648 | 37 253 956 | 13.8 | 10.0 | 2.1 | 1 159 112 | 537 016 | 172 716 | 276 809 | -104 093 | 42 206 743 | 44 305 177 | 46 444 861 |
| Colorado | 3 294 394 | 4 301 261 | 5 029 196 | 30.6 | 16.9 | 3.1 | 147 515 | 71 725 | 80 587 | 18 291 | 62 296 | 5 278 867 | 5 522 803 | 5 792 357 |
| Connecticut | 3 287 116 | 3 405 565 | 3 574 097 | 3.6 | 4.9 | 0.5 | 83 174 | 65 102 | -811 | 33 660 | -34 471 | 3 675 650 | 3 691 016 | 3 688 630 |
| Delaware | 666 168 | 783 600 | 897 934 | 17.6 | 14.6 | 2.1 | 25 491 | 17 482 | 11 278 | 5 097 | 6 181 | 963 209 | 990 694 | 1 012 658 |
| District of Columbia | 606 900 | 572 059 | 601 723 | -5.7 | 5.2 | 5.1 | 20 537 | 10 593 | 20 369 | 6 199 | 14 170 | 480 540 | 455 108 | 433 414 |
| Florida | 12 937 926 | 15 982 378 | 18 801 310 | 23.5 | 17.6 | 2.7 | 476 020 | 392 110 | 431 042 | 212 039 | 219 003 | 23 406 525 | 25 912 458 | 28 685 769 |
| Georgia | 6 478 216 | 8 186 453 | 9 687 653 | 26.4 | 18.3 | 2.4 | 297 798 | 160 842 | 90 782 | 54 699 | 36 083 | 10 843 753 | 11 438 622 | 12 017 838 |
| Hawaii | 1 108 229 | 1 211 537 | 1 360 301 | 9.3 | 12.3 | 2.4 | 41 798 | 22 275 | 13 124 | 17 361 | -4 237 | 1 412 373 | 1 438 720 | 1 466 046 |
| Idaho | 1 006 749 | 1 293 953 | 1 567 582 | 28.5 | 21.1 | 1.8 | 50 637 | 26 175 | 3 100 | 3 914 | -814 | 1 741 333 | 1 852 627 | 1 969 624 |
| Illinois | 11 430 602 | 12 419 293 | 12 830 632 | 8.6 | 3.3 | 0.3 | 369 642 | 228 958 | -95 069 | 61 128 | -156 197 | 13 236 720 | 13 340 507 | 13 432 892 |
| Indiana | 5 544 159 | 6 080 485 | 6 483 802 | 9.7 | 6.6 | 0.8 | 189 041 | 129 580 | -5 532 | 18 806 | -24 338 | 6 627 008 | 6 721 322 | 6 810 108 |
| Iowa | 2 776 755 | 2 926 324 | 3 046 355 | 5.4 | 4.1 | 0.9 | 85 272 | 63 778 | 5 995 | 9 269 | -3 274 | 3 020 496 | 2 993 222 | 2 955 172 |
| Kansas | 2 477 574 | 2 688 418 | 2 853 118 | 8.5 | 6.1 | 1.1 | 91 020 | 54 764 | -3 599 | 10 693 | -14 292 | 2 890 566 | 2 919 002 | 2 940 084 |
| Kentucky | 3 685 296 | 4 041 769 | 4 339 367 | 9.7 | 7.4 | 0.9 | 125 523 | 96 274 | 12 051 | 13 127 | -1 076 | 4 424 431 | 4 489 662 | 4 554 998 |
| Louisiana | 4 219 973 | 4 468 976 | 4 533 372 | 5.9 | 1.4 | 1.5 | 142 118 | 93 427 | 19 435 | 13 470 | 5 965 | 4 719 160 | 4 762 398 | 4 802 633 |
| Maine | 1 227 928 | 1 274 923 | 1 328 361 | 3.8 | 4.2 | 0.1 | 29 066 | 28 931 | 1 014 | 2 348 | -1 334 | 1 408 665 | 1 414 402 | 1 411 097 |
| Maryland | 4 781 468 | 5 296 486 | 5 773 552 | 10.8 | 9.0 | 1.9 | 162 714 | 98 598 | 47 519 | 55 059 | -7 540 | 6 497 626 | 6 762 732 | 7 022 251 |
| Massachusetts | 6 016 425 | 6 349 097 | 6 547 629 | 5.5 | 3.1 | 1.5 | 163 810 | 119 214 | 56 572 | 66 293 | -9 721 | 6 855 546 | 6 938 636 | 7 012 009 |
| Michigan | 9 295 297 | 9 938 444 | 9 883 640 | 6.9 | -0.6 | 0.0 | 254 152 | 198 341 | -56 325 | 37 043 | -93 368 | 10 695 993 | 10 713 730 | 10 694 172 |
| Minnesota | 4 375 099 | 4 919 479 | 5 303 925 | 12.4 | 7.8 | 1.4 | 151 960 | 88 548 | 12 156 | 27 231 | -15 075 | 5 900 769 | 6 108 787 | 6 306 130 |
| Mississippi | 2 573 216 | 2 844 658 | 2 967 297 | 10.5 | 4.3 | 0.6 | 89 282 | 66 148 | -6 610 | 5 782 | -12 392 | 3 044 812 | 3 069 420 | 3 092 410 |
| Missouri | 5 117 073 | 5 595 211 | 5 988 927 | 9.3 | 7.0 | 0.6 | 169 040 | 123 646 | -12 326 | 16 273 | -28 599 | 6 199 882 | 6 315 366 | 6 430 173 |
| Montana | 799 065 | 902 195 | 989 415 | 12.9 | 9.7 | 1.6 | 26 740 | 19 636 | 8 447 | 1 136 | 7 311 | 1 022 735 | 1 037 387 | 1 044 898 |
| Nebraska | 1 578 385 | 1 711 263 | 1 826 341 | 8.4 | 6.7 | 1.6 | 59 344 | 34 073 | 3 977 | 6 485 | -2 508 | 1 802 678 | 1 812 787 | 1 820 247 |
| Nevada | 1 201 833 | 1 998 257 | 2 700 551 | 66.3 | 35.1 | 2.2 | 81 640 | 43 829 | 20 711 | 17 973 | 2 738 | 3 452 283 | 3 863 298 | 4 282 102 |
| New Hampshire | 1 109 252 | 1 235 786 | 1 316 470 | 11.4 | 6.5 | 0.3 | 28 428 | 23 334 | -389 | 3 951 | -4 340 | 1 524 751 | 1 586 348 | 1 646 471 |
| New Jersey | 7 730 188 | 8 414 350 | 8 791 894 | 8.9 | 4.5 | 0.8 | 230 222 | 154 982 | -1 594 | 101 658 | -103 252 | 9 461 635 | 9 636 644 | 9 802 440 |
| New Mexico | 1 515 069 | 1 819 046 | 2 059 179 | 20.1 | 13.2 | 1.3 | 63 673 | 36 198 | -1 069 | 4 229 | -5 298 | 2 084 341 | 2 106 584 | 2 099 708 |
| New York | 17 990 455 | 18 976 457 | 19 378 102 | 5.5 | 2.1 | 1.0 | 543 408 | 333 712 | -14 551 | 209 917 | -224 468 | 19 576 920 | 19 540 179 | 19 477 429 |
| North Carolina | 6 628 637 | 8 049 313 | 9 535 483 | 21.4 | 18.5 | 2.3 | 270 488 | 178 941 | 122 575 | 50 439 | 72 136 | 10 709 289 | 11 449 153 | 12 227 739 |
| North Dakota | 638 800 | 642 200 | 672 591 | 0.5 | 4.7 | 4.0 | 20 393 | 13 299 | 19 506 | 2 117 | 17 389 | 630 112 | 620 777 | 606 566 |
| Ohio | 10 847 115 | 11 353 140 | 11 536 504 | 4.7 | 1.6 | 0.1 | 305 848 | 245 688 | -51 037 | 33 491 | -84 528 | 11 605 738 | 11 550 528 | 11 550 528 |
| Oklahoma | 3 145 585 | 3 450 654 | 3 751 351 | 9.7 | 8.7 | 1.7 | 114 749 | 79 477 | 27 256 | 10 896 | 16 360 | 3 735 690 | 3 820 994 | 3 913 251 |
| Oregon | 2 842 321 | 3 421 399 | 3 831 074 | 20.4 | 12.0 | 1.8 | 101 333 | 71 781 | 38 753 | 14 374 | 24 379 | 4 260 393 | 4 536 418 | 4 833 918 |
| Pennsylvania | 11 881 643 | 12 281 054 | 12 702 379 | 3.4 | 3.4 | 0.5 | 320 606 | 283 295 | 26 819 | 54 466 | -27 647 | 12 787 354 | 12 801 945 | 12 768 184 |
| Rhode Island | 1 003 464 | 1 048 319 | 1 052 567 | 4.5 | 0.4 | -0.2 | 24 409 | 20 912 | -5 712 | 7 547 | -13 259 | 1 154 230 | 1 157 855 | 1 152 941 |
| South Carolina | 3 486 703 | 4 012 012 | 4 625 364 | 15.1 | 15.3 | 2.1 | 128 897 | 95 175 | 63 360 | 16 276 | 47 084 | 4 822 577 | 4 989 550 | 5 148 569 |
| South Dakota | 696 004 | 754 844 | 814 180 | 8.5 | 7.9 | 2.4 | 26 110 | 15 876 | 8 822 | 1 875 | 6 947 | 801 939 | 801 845 | 800 462 |
| Tennessee | 4 877 185 | 5 689 283 | 6 346 105 | 16.7 | 11.5 | 1.7 | 179 801 | 135 379 | 65 779 | 19 160 | 46 619 | 6 780 670 | 7 073 125 | 7 380 634 |
| Texas | 16 986 510 | 20 851 820 | 25 145 561 | 22.8 | 20.6 | 3.6 | 856 583 | 381 060 | 432 773 | 142 419 | 290 354 | 28 634 896 | 30 865 134 | 33 317 744 |
| Utah | 1 722 850 | 2 233 169 | 2 763 885 | 29.6 | 23.8 | 3.3 | 115 478 | 33 363 | 9 173 | 10 049 | -876 | 2 990 094 | 3 225 680 | 3 485 367 |
| Vermont | 562 758 | 608 827 | 625 741 | 8.2 | 2.8 | 0.0 | 13 415 | 11 827 | -1 134 | 1 269 | -2 403 | 690 686 | 703 288 | 711 867 |
| Virginia | 6 187 358 | 7 078 515 | 8 001 024 | 14.4 | 13.0 | 2.3 | 228 798 | 134 908 | 88 259 | 65 960 | 22 299 | 8 917 395 | 9 364 304 | 9 825 019 |
| Washington | 4 866 692 | 5 894 121 | 6 724 540 | 21.1 | 14.1 | 2.6 | 194 307 | 109 513 | 88 104 | 47 019 | 41 085 | 7 432 136 | 7 996 400 | 8 624 801 |
| West Virginia | 1 793 477 | 1 808 344 | 1 852 994 | 0.8 | 2.5 | 0.1 | 45 849 | 49 008 | 5 665 | 1 925 | 3 740 | 1 801 112 | 1 766 435 | 1 719 959 |
| Wisconsin | 4 891 769 | 5 363 675 | 5 686 986 | 9.6 | 6.0 | 0.7 | 153 926 | 106 193 | -8 256 | 12 797 | -21 053 | 6 004 954 | 6 088 374 | 6 150 764 |
| Wyoming | 453 588 | 493 782 | 563 626 | 8.9 | 14.1 | 2.3 | 16 657 | 9 937 | 5 881 | 734 | 5 147 | 530 948 | 529 031 | 522 979 |

# Table A. States — **Population Characteristics**

| STATE | Race (percent) | | | | | | | Age (percent) | | | | | | | | | | | |
|---|---|---|---|---|---|---|---|---|---|---|---|---|---|---|---|---|---|---|---|
| | White alone | Black alone | American Indian, Alaska Native alone | Asian and Pacific Islander alone | Some other race or two or more races | Percent Hispanic or Latino[1] | Percent foreign born | Under 5 years | 5 to 17 years | 18 to 24 years | 25 to 34 years | 35 to 44 years | 45 to 54 years | 55 to 64 years | 65 to 74 years | 75 to 84 years | 85 years and over | Median age | Percent female |
| | 45 | 46 | 47 | 48 | 49 | 50 | 51 | 52 | 53 | 54 | 55 | 56 | 57 | 58 | 59 | 60 | 61 | 62 | 63 |
| UNITED STATES ........ | 72.4 | 12.6 | 0.9 | 5.0 | 9.1 | 16.3 | 12.9 | 6.5 | 17.5 | 9.9 | 13.3 | 13.3 | 14.6 | 11.8 | 7.0 | 4.2 | 1.8 | 37.2 | 50.8 |
| Alabama.................. | 68.5 | 26.2 | 0.6 | 1.2 | 3.5 | 3.9 | 3.5 | 6.4 | 17.3 | 10.0 | 12.6 | 13.0 | 14.5 | 12.3 | 7.8 | 4.4 | 1.6 | 37.9 | 51.5 |
| Alaska.................... | 66.7 | 3.3 | 14.8 | 6.4 | 8.9 | 5.5 | 6.9 | 7.6 | 18.8 | 10.5 | 14.5 | 13.1 | 15.6 | 12.1 | 5.0 | 2.1 | 0.6 | 33.8 | 48.0 |
| Arizona.................. | 73.0 | 4.1 | 4.6 | 3.0 | 15.3 | 29.6 | 13.4 | 7.1 | 18.4 | 9.9 | 13.4 | 12.9 | 13.2 | 11.4 | 7.8 | 4.4 | 1.6 | 35.9 | 50.3 |
| Arkansas................ | 77.0 | 15.4 | 0.8 | 1.4 | 5.4 | 6.4 | 4.5 | 6.8 | 17.6 | 9.7 | 12.6 | 12.6 | 14.0 | 12.0 | 8.0 | 4.6 | 1.8 | 37.4 | 50.9 |
| California............... | 57.6 | 6.2 | 1.0 | 13.4 | 21.9 | 37.6 | 27.2 | 6.8 | 18.2 | 10.5 | 14.2 | 13.9 | 14.1 | 10.8 | 6.1 | 3.7 | 1.6 | 35.2 | 50.3 |
| Colorado ............... | 81.3 | 4.0 | 1.1 | 2.9 | 10.6 | 20.7 | 9.8 | 6.8 | 17.5 | 9.7 | 14.4 | 13.9 | 14.8 | 11.9 | 6.2 | 3.4 | 1.4 | 36.1 | 49.9 |
| Connecticut............ | 77.6 | 10.1 | 0.3 | 3.8 | 8.2 | 13.4 | 13.6 | 5.7 | 17.2 | 9.1 | 11.8 | 13.6 | 16.1 | 12.4 | 7.1 | 4.6 | 2.4 | 40.0 | 51.3 |
| Delaware................ | 68.9 | 21.4 | 0.5 | 3.2 | 6.1 | 8.2 | 8.0 | 6.2 | 16.7 | 10.1 | 12.3 | 12.9 | 14.9 | 12.4 | 8.1 | 4.5 | 1.8 | 38.8 | 51.6 |
| District of Columbia .......... | 38.5 | 50.7 | 0.3 | 3.6 | 7.0 | 9.1 | 13.5 | 5.4 | 11.3 | 14.5 | 20.9 | 13.4 | 12.6 | 10.6 | 6.1 | 3.5 | 1.8 | 33.8 | 52.8 |
| Florida.................. | 75.0 | 16.0 | 0.4 | 2.5 | 6.1 | 22.5 | 19.4 | 5.7 | 15.6 | 9.3 | 12.1 | 12.9 | 14.6 | 12.4 | 9.2 | 5.7 | 2.4 | 40.7 | 51.1 |
| Georgia................. | 59.7 | 30.5 | 0.3 | 3.3 | 6.1 | 8.8 | 9.7 | 7.1 | 18.6 | 10.0 | 13.6 | 14.4 | 14.4 | 11.0 | 6.3 | 3.1 | 1.2 | 35.3 | 51.2 |
| Hawaii.................. | 24.7 | 1.6 | 0.3 | 48.6 | 24.8 | 8.9 | 18.2 | 6.4 | 15.9 | 9.6 | 13.3 | 13.0 | 14.2 | 12.9 | 7.4 | 4.7 | 2.3 | 38.6 | 49.9 |
| Idaho................... | 89.1 | 0.6 | 1.4 | 1.3 | 7.6 | 11.2 | 5.5 | 7.8 | 19.6 | 9.9 | 13.3 | 12.2 | 13.3 | 11.5 | 7.0 | 3.8 | 1.7 | 34.6 | 49.9 |
| Illinois.................. | 71.5 | 14.5 | 0.3 | 4.6 | 9.0 | 15.8 | 13.7 | 6.5 | 17.9 | 9.7 | 13.9 | 13.5 | 14.6 | 11.5 | 6.6 | 4.0 | 1.9 | 36.6 | 51.0 |
| Indiana................. | 84.3 | 9.1 | 0.3 | 1.6 | 4.7 | 6.0 | 4.6 | 6.7 | 18.1 | 10.0 | 12.7 | 13.0 | 14.6 | 11.9 | 7.0 | 4.3 | 1.7 | 37.0 | 50.8 |
| Iowa.................... | 91.3 | 2.9 | 0.4 | 1.8 | 3.6 | 5.0 | 4.6 | 6.6 | 17.3 | 10.6 | 12.6 | 12.0 | 14.4 | 12.2 | 7.4 | 5.0 | 2.5 | 38.1 | 50.5 |
| Kansas.................. | 83.8 | 5.9 | 1.0 | 2.5 | 6.9 | 10.5 | 6.5 | 7.2 | 18.3 | 10.1 | 13.0 | 12.2 | 14.2 | 11.6 | 6.7 | 4.3 | 2.1 | 36.0 | 50.4 |
| Kentucky............... | 87.8 | 7.8 | 0.2 | 1.2 | 3.0 | 3.1 | 3.2 | 6.5 | 17.1 | 9.5 | 13.0 | 13.3 | 14.8 | 12.4 | 7.5 | 4.2 | 1.6 | 38.1 | 50.8 |
| Louisiana............... | 62.6 | 32.0 | 0.7 | 1.5 | 3.1 | 4.2 | 3.8 | 6.9 | 17.7 | 10.5 | 13.7 | 12.5 | 14.4 | 11.8 | 6.9 | 3.9 | 1.5 | 35.8 | 51.0 |
| Maine................... | 95.2 | 1.2 | 0.6 | 1.0 | 1.9 | 1.3 | 3.4 | 5.2 | 15.4 | 8.7 | 10.9 | 12.9 | 16.5 | 14.5 | 8.5 | 5.3 | 2.1 | 42.7 | 51.1 |
| Maryland............... | 58.2 | 29.4 | 0.4 | 5.6 | 6.5 | 8.2 | 13.9 | 6.3 | 17.1 | 9.7 | 13.2 | 13.8 | 15.6 | 12.1 | 6.7 | 3.9 | 1.7 | 38.0 | 51.6 |
| Massachusetts.......... | 80.4 | 6.6 | 0.3 | 5.3 | 7.3 | 9.6 | 15.0 | 5.6 | 16.1 | 10.4 | 12.9 | 13.5 | 15.5 | 12.3 | 7.0 | 4.6 | 2.2 | 39.1 | 51.6 |
| Michigan............... | 78.9 | 14.2 | 0.6 | 2.4 | 3.8 | 4.4 | 6.0 | 6.0 | 17.7 | 9.9 | 11.7 | 12.9 | 15.3 | 12.7 | 7.3 | 4.5 | 1.9 | 38.9 | 50.9 |
| Minnesota.............. | 85.3 | 5.2 | 1.1 | 4.0 | 4.3 | 4.7 | 7.1 | 6.7 | 17.5 | 9.5 | 13.5 | 12.8 | 15.2 | 11.9 | 6.7 | 4.2 | 2.0 | 37.4 | 50.4 |
| Mississippi............. | 59.1 | 37.0 | 0.5 | 0.9 | 2.4 | 2.7 | 2.1 | 7.1 | 18.4 | 10.3 | 12.6 | 12.6 | 14.1 | 11.7 | 7.2 | 4.1 | 1.5 | 36.0 | 51.4 |
| Missouri................ | 82.8 | 11.6 | 0.5 | 1.7 | 3.4 | 3.5 | 3.9 | 6.5 | 17.3 | 9.8 | 12.9 | 12.5 | 14.8 | 12.1 | 7.5 | 4.5 | 2.0 | 37.9 | 51.0 |
| Montana................ | 89.4 | 0.4 | 6.3 | 0.7 | 3.1 | 2.9 | 2.0 | 6.3 | 16.3 | 9.6 | 12.3 | 11.4 | 15.1 | 14.0 | 8.2 | 4.7 | 2.0 | 39.8 | 49.8 |
| Nebraska............... | 86.1 | 4.5 | 1.0 | 1.9 | 6.5 | 9.2 | 6.1 | 7.2 | 17.9 | 10.0 | 13.2 | 12.1 | 14.2 | 11.7 | 6.7 | 4.7 | 2.2 | 36.2 | 50.4 |
| Nevada.................. | 66.2 | 8.1 | 1.2 | 7.8 | 16.7 | 26.5 | 18.8 | 6.9 | 17.7 | 9.2 | 14.3 | 14.2 | 13.9 | 11.7 | 7.3 | 3.6 | 1.1 | 36.3 | 49.5 |
| New Hampshire........ | 93.9 | 1.1 | 0.2 | 2.2 | 2.5 | 2.8 | 5.3 | 5.3 | 16.5 | 9.4 | 11.0 | 13.6 | 17.2 | 13.5 | 7.4 | 4.4 | 1.8 | 41.1 | 50.7 |
| New Jersey............. | 68.6 | 13.7 | 0.3 | 8.3 | 9.1 | 17.7 | 21.0 | 6.2 | 17.3 | 8.7 | 12.6 | 14.1 | 15.7 | 11.9 | 7.0 | 4.5 | 2.0 | 39.0 | 51.3 |
| New Mexico ........... | 68.4 | 2.1 | 9.4 | 1.5 | 18.7 | 46.3 | 9.9 | 7.0 | 18.1 | 9.9 | 12.8 | 12.1 | 14.2 | 12.5 | 7.5 | 4.3 | 1.5 | 36.7 | 50.6 |
| New York............... | 65.7 | 15.9 | 0.6 | 7.3 | 10.4 | 17.6 | 22.2 | 6.0 | 16.4 | 10.2 | 13.7 | 13.5 | 14.9 | 11.9 | 7.0 | 4.5 | 2.0 | 38.0 | 51.6 |
| North Carolina.......... | 68.5 | 21.5 | 1.3 | 2.3 | 6.5 | 8.4 | 7.5 | 6.6 | 17.3 | 9.8 | 13.0 | 13.9 | 14.4 | 11.9 | 7.3 | 4.1 | 1.6 | 37.4 | 51.3 |
| North Dakota........... | 90.0 | 1.2 | 5.4 | 1.0 | 2.3 | 2.0 | 2.5 | 6.6 | 15.7 | 12.0 | 13.1 | 11.2 | 14.4 | 12.2 | 7.0 | 5.1 | 2.5 | 37.0 | 49.5 |
| Ohio.................... | 82.7 | 12.2 | 0.2 | 1.7 | 3.2 | 3.1 | 4.1 | 6.2 | 17.4 | 9.5 | 12.4 | 12.8 | 15.1 | 12.6 | 7.4 | 4.7 | 2.0 | 38.8 | 51.2 |
| Oklahoma.............. | 72.2 | 7.4 | 8.6 | 1.8 | 10.0 | 8.9 | 5.5 | 7.0 | 17.7 | 10.2 | 13.5 | 12.3 | 14.0 | 11.7 | 7.5 | 4.4 | 1.6 | 36.2 | 50.5 |
| Oregon................. | 83.6 | 1.8 | 1.4 | 4.0 | 9.1 | 11.7 | 9.8 | 6.2 | 16.4 | 9.4 | 13.7 | 13.0 | 14.1 | 13.3 | 7.6 | 4.3 | 2.0 | 38.4 | 50.5 |
| Pennsylvania........... | 81.9 | 10.8 | 0.2 | 2.7 | 4.3 | 5.7 | 5.8 | 5.7 | 16.2 | 9.9 | 11.9 | 12.7 | 15.3 | 12.8 | 7.7 | 5.3 | 2.5 | 40.1 | 51.3 |
| Rhode Island........... | 81.4 | 5.7 | 0.6 | 3.0 | 9.3 | 12.4 | 12.8 | 5.5 | 15.8 | 11.4 | 12.0 | 13.0 | 15.4 | 12.4 | 7.0 | 4.9 | 2.5 | 39.4 | 51.7 |
| South Carolina ........ | 66.2 | 27.9 | 0.4 | 1.4 | 4.2 | 5.1 | 4.7 | 6.5 | 16.8 | 10.3 | 12.7 | 13.0 | 14.3 | 12.6 | 8.0 | 4.1 | 1.6 | 37.9 | 51.4 |
| South Dakota........... | 85.9 | 1.3 | 8.8 | 0.9 | 3.0 | 2.7 | 2.7 | 7.3 | 17.6 | 10.0 | 12.8 | 11.3 | 14.6 | 12.0 | 7.1 | 4.8 | 2.4 | 36.9 | 50.0 |
| Tennessee.............. | 77.6 | 16.7 | 0.3 | 1.5 | 3.9 | 4.6 | 4.5 | 6.4 | 17.1 | 9.6 | 12.8 | 13.5 | 14.6 | 12.4 | 7.7 | 4.2 | 1.6 | 38.0 | 51.3 |
| Texas................... | 70.4 | 11.8 | 0.7 | 3.9 | 13.2 | 37.6 | 16.4 | 7.7 | 19.6 | 10.2 | 14.3 | 13.8 | 13.7 | 10.3 | 5.9 | 3.3 | 1.2 | 33.6 | 50.4 |
| Utah.................... | 86.1 | 1.1 | 1.2 | 2.9 | 8.7 | 13.0 | 8.0 | 9.5 | 22.0 | 11.5 | 16.2 | 12.0 | 11.1 | 8.7 | 5.0 | 2.9 | 1.1 | 29.2 | 49.8 |
| Vermont................ | 95.3 | 1.0 | 0.4 | 1.3 | 2.0 | 1.5 | 4.4 | 5.1 | 15.5 | 10.4 | 11.2 | 12.5 | 16.4 | 14.4 | 7.9 | 4.5 | 2.1 | 41.5 | 50.7 |
| Virginia................. | 68.6 | 19.4 | 0.4 | 5.6 | 6.1 | 7.9 | 11.4 | 6.4 | 16.8 | 10.0 | 13.6 | 13.9 | 15.2 | 11.9 | 6.9 | 3.8 | 1.5 | 37.5 | 50.9 |
| Washington............. | 77.3 | 3.6 | 1.5 | 7.8 | 9.9 | 11.2 | 13.1 | 6.5 | 17.0 | 9.7 | 13.9 | 13.5 | 14.7 | 12.4 | 6.8 | 3.7 | 1.8 | 37.3 | 50.2 |
| West Virginia.......... | 93.9 | 3.4 | 0.2 | 0.7 | 1.8 | 1.2 | 1.2 | 5.6 | 15.3 | 9.1 | 11.7 | 12.8 | 14.9 | 14.3 | 8.8 | 5.2 | 2.0 | 41.3 | 50.7 |
| Wisconsin.............. | 86.2 | 6.3 | 1.0 | 2.3 | 4.2 | 5.9 | 4.5 | 6.3 | 17.3 | 9.7 | 12.6 | 12.8 | 15.4 | 12.3 | 7.0 | 4.6 | 2.1 | 38.5 | 50.4 |
| Wyoming............... | 90.7 | 0.8 | 2.4 | 0.9 | 5.2 | 8.9 | 2.8 | 7.1 | 16.9 | 10.0 | 13.6 | 11.9 | 14.8 | 13.0 | 7.0 | 3.8 | 1.6 | 36.8 | 49.0 |

1. May be of any race.

## Table A. States — **Households and Housing Units**

| STATE | Households, 2010 Number | Percent change, 2000–2010 | Persons per house-hold | Percent Female family house-holder[1] | Percent One person | Housing units, 2010 Total | Percent change, 2000–2010 | Occupied units Total | Owner-occupied Percent | Median owner cost Median value[2] (dollars) | Median owner cost With a mort-gage | Median owner cost Without a mort-gage[3] | Renter-occupied Median rent[4] (dollars) | Median rent as a percent of income | Sub-standard units[5] (percent) |
|---|---|---|---|---|---|---|---|---|---|---|---|---|---|---|---|
| | 64 | 65 | 66 | 67 | 68 | 69 | 70 | 71 | 72 | 73 | 74 | 75 | 76 | 77 | 78 |
| UNITED STATES | 116 716 292 | 10.7 | 2.58 | 13.1 | 26.7 | 131 791 065 | 13.7 | 114 567 419 | 65.4 | 179 900 | 25.1 | 12.8 | 855 | 31.6 | 3.9 |
| Alabama | 1 883 791 | 8.4 | 2.48 | 15.3 | 27.4 | 2 174 428 | 10.7 | 1 815 152 | 70.1 | 123 900 | 23.0 | 12.3 | 667 | 32.2 | 2.4 |
| Alaska | 258 058 | 16.5 | 2.65 | 10.7 | 25.6 | 307 065 | 17.7 | 254 610 | 63.9 | 241 400 | 23.3 | 10.8 | 981 | 29.0 | 10.2 |
| Arizona | 2 380 990 | 25.2 | 2.63 | 12.4 | 26.1 | 2 846 738 | 30.0 | 2 334 050 | 65.2 | 168 800 | 26.5 | 11.3 | 844 | 31.6 | 5.1 |
| Arkansas | 1 147 084 | 10.0 | 2.47 | 13.4 | 27.1 | 1 317 818 | 12.3 | 1 114 902 | 67.4 | 106 300 | 21.5 | 10.9 | 638 | 29.9 | 3.2 |
| California | 12 577 498 | 9.3 | 2.90 | 13.3 | 23.3 | 13 682 976 | 12.0 | 12 406 475 | 55.6 | 370 900 | 30.6 | 11.4 | 1 163 | 33.8 | 9.1 |
| Colorado | 1 972 868 | 19.0 | 2.49 | 10.1 | 27.9 | 2 214 262 | 22.5 | 1 960 585 | 65.9 | 236 600 | 25.2 | 10.7 | 863 | 31.2 | 3.2 |
| Connecticut | 1 371 087 | 5.3 | 2.52 | 12.9 | 27.3 | 1 488 215 | 7.4 | 1 358 809 | 68.0 | 288 800 | 26.8 | 17.6 | 992 | 32.1 | 2.4 |
| Delaware | 342 297 | 14.6 | 2.55 | 14.2 | 25.6 | 406 489 | 18.5 | 328 765 | 73.0 | 243 600 | 24.8 | 11.8 | 952 | 32.3 | 2.9 |
| District of Columbia | 266 707 | 7.4 | 2.11 | 16.4 | 44.0 | 296 836 | 8.0 | 252 388 | 42.5 | 426 900 | 24.8 | 11.0 | 1 198 | 30.4 | 3.5 |
| Florida | 7 420 802 | 17.1 | 2.48 | 13.5 | 27.2 | 8 994 091 | 23.2 | 7 035 068 | 68.1 | 164 200 | 29.5 | 14.4 | 947 | 35.5 | 3.1 |
| Georgia | 3 585 584 | 19.3 | 2.63 | 15.8 | 25.4 | 4 091 482 | 24.7 | 3 482 420 | 66.2 | 156 200 | 25.2 | 12.3 | 819 | 32.4 | 3.2 |
| Hawaii | 455 338 | 12.9 | 2.89 | 12.6 | 23.3 | 519 992 | 12.9 | 445 812 | 58.0 | 525 400 | 30.1 | 10.1 | 1 291 | 33.5 | 9.1 |
| Idaho | 579 408 | 23.4 | 2.66 | 9.6 | 23.8 | 668 634 | 26.7 | 576 709 | 69.6 | 165 100 | 24.7 | 10.6 | 683 | 30.5 | 3.6 |
| Illinois | 4 836 972 | 5.3 | 2.59 | 12.9 | 27.8 | 5 297 077 | 8.4 | 4 752 857 | 67.7 | 191 800 | 25.9 | 13.8 | 848 | 31.5 | 3.1 |
| Indiana | 2 502 154 | 7.1 | 2.52 | 12.4 | 26.9 | 2 797 172 | 10.5 | 2 470 905 | 70.3 | 123 300 | 21.6 | 11.0 | 683 | 30.8 | 2.2 |
| Iowa | 1 221 576 | 6.3 | 2.41 | 9.3 | 28.4 | 1 337 563 | 8.5 | 1 223 439 | 72.4 | 123 400 | 21.3 | 11.5 | 629 | 28.1 | 1.7 |
| Kansas | 1 112 096 | 7.1 | 2.49 | 10.4 | 27.8 | 1 234 037 | 9.1 | 1 101 658 | 68.1 | 127 300 | 21.8 | 11.8 | 682 | 28.1 | 2.2 |
| Kentucky | 1 719 965 | 8.1 | 2.45 | 12.7 | 27.5 | 1 928 617 | 10.1 | 1 684 348 | 68.6 | 121 600 | 22.2 | 11.3 | 613 | 29.8 | 2.5 |
| Louisiana | 1 728 360 | 4.4 | 2.55 | 17.2 | 26.9 | 1 967 947 | 6.5 | 1 689 822 | 67.6 | 137 500 | 21.6 | 10.5 | 736 | 31.7 | 3.7 |
| Maine | 557 219 | 7.5 | 2.32 | 10.0 | 28.6 | 722 217 | 10.8 | 545 417 | 72.7 | 179 100 | 24.1 | 13.9 | 707 | 29.8 | 2.5 |
| Maryland | 2 156 411 | 8.9 | 2.61 | 14.6 | 26.1 | 2 380 605 | 11.0 | 2 127 439 | 67.0 | 301 400 | 25.4 | 12.9 | 1 131 | 30.8 | 2.4 |
| Massachusetts | 2 547 075 | 4.2 | 2.48 | 12.5 | 28.7 | 2 808 727 | 7.1 | 2 520 419 | 62.2 | 334 100 | 26.1 | 15.3 | 1 009 | 30.4 | 2.0 |
| Michigan | 3 872 508 | 2.3 | 2.49 | 13.2 | 27.9 | 4 531 231 | 7.0 | 3 806 621 | 72.8 | 123 300 | 24.6 | 13.9 | 730 | 33.3 | 2.1 |
| Minnesota | 2 087 227 | 10.1 | 2.48 | 9.5 | 28.0 | 2 348 242 | 13.7 | 2 091 548 | 73.0 | 194 300 | 24.1 | 11.9 | 764 | 30.2 | 2.3 |
| Mississippi | 1 115 768 | 6.6 | 2.58 | 18.5 | 26.3 | 1 276 441 | 9.9 | 1 079 999 | 69.8 | 100 100 | 23.5 | 12.0 | 672 | 33.2 | 4.0 |
| Missouri | 2 375 611 | 8.2 | 2.45 | 12.3 | 28.3 | 2 714 017 | 11.1 | 2 350 628 | 69.0 | 139 000 | 22.6 | 11.7 | 682 | 30.1 | 2.2 |
| Montana | 409 607 | 14.2 | 2.35 | 9.0 | 29.7 | 483 006 | 17.1 | 402 747 | 69.7 | 181 200 | 24.1 | 11.3 | 642 | 28.3 | 2.8 |
| Nebraska | 721 130 | 8.2 | 2.46 | 9.8 | 28.7 | 797 677 | 10.4 | 719 304 | 67.4 | 127 600 | 21.4 | 12.6 | 669 | 27.7 | 2.2 |
| Nevada | 1 006 250 | 34.0 | 2.65 | 12.7 | 25.7 | 1 175 070 | 42.0 | 989 811 | 57.2 | 174 800 | 28.1 | 12.2 | 952 | 31.6 | 5.0 |
| New Hampshire | 518 973 | 9.3 | 2.46 | 9.7 | 25.6 | 614 996 | 12.4 | 515 431 | 71.7 | 243 000 | 26.5 | 16.5 | 951 | 30.3 | 1.9 |
| New Jersey | 3 214 360 | 4.9 | 2.68 | 13.3 | 25.2 | 3 554 909 | 7.4 | 3 172 421 | 66.4 | 339 200 | 28.7 | 18.9 | 1 114 | 32.4 | 4.1 |
| New Mexico | 791 395 | 16.7 | 2.55 | 14.0 | 28.0 | 902 242 | 15.6 | 765 183 | 67.9 | 161 200 | 24.3 | 10.0 | 699 | 29.3 | 4.7 |
| New York | 7 317 755 | 3.7 | 2.57 | 14.9 | 29.1 | 8 108 211 | 5.6 | 7 196 427 | 54.3 | 296 500 | 26.3 | 15.5 | 1 020 | 31.7 | 5.5 |
| North Carolina | 3 745 155 | 19.6 | 2.48 | 13.7 | 27.0 | 4 333 479 | 23.0 | 3 670 859 | 67.2 | 154 200 | 24.0 | 12.5 | 731 | 31.3 | 2.8 |
| North Dakota | 281 192 | 9.3 | 2.30 | 8.2 | 31.5 | 318 099 | 9.8 | 280 412 | 66.9 | 123 000 | 19.6 | 10.0 | 583 | 25.8 | 1.3 |
| Ohio | 4 603 435 | 3.5 | 2.44 | 13.1 | 28.9 | 5 128 113 | 7.2 | 4 525 066 | 68.4 | 134 400 | 23.0 | 13.1 | 685 | 31.1 | 1.8 |
| Oklahoma | 1 460 450 | 8.8 | 2.49 | 12.3 | 27.5 | 1 666 205 | 10.0 | 1 432 959 | 67.8 | 111 400 | 21.9 | 11.2 | 659 | 28.9 | 3.0 |
| Oregon | 1 518 938 | 13.9 | 2.47 | 10.5 | 27.4 | 1 676 476 | 15.4 | 1 507 137 | 62.5 | 244 500 | 27.3 | 12.9 | 816 | 32.7 | 3.4 |
| Pennsylvania | 5 018 904 | 5.1 | 2.45 | 12.2 | 28.6 | 5 568 820 | 6.1 | 4 936 030 | 70.1 | 165 500 | 23.8 | 13.7 | 763 | 30.4 | 1.6 |
| Rhode Island | 413 600 | 1.3 | 2.44 | 13.5 | 29.6 | 463 416 | 5.4 | 402 295 | 60.8 | 254 500 | 27.7 | 15.4 | 868 | 30.9 | 2.6 |
| South Carolina | 1 801 181 | 17.4 | 2.49 | 15.6 | 26.5 | 2 140 337 | 22.0 | 1 761 393 | 68.7 | 138 100 | 23.5 | 12.0 | 728 | 32.2 | 2.7 |
| South Dakota | 322 282 | 11.0 | 2.42 | 9.7 | 29.4 | 364 031 | 12.6 | 318 955 | 68.0 | 129 700 | 21.9 | 10.9 | 591 | 26.9 | 2.7 |
| Tennessee | 2 493 552 | 11.7 | 2.48 | 13.9 | 26.9 | 2 815 087 | 15.4 | 2 440 663 | 68.1 | 139 000 | 23.7 | 11.4 | 697 | 31.4 | 2.5 |
| Texas | 8 922 933 | 20.7 | 2.75 | 14.1 | 24.2 | 9 996 209 | 22.5 | 8 738 664 | 63.6 | 128 100 | 23.4 | 12.5 | 801 | 30.2 | 5.8 |
| Utah | 877 692 | 25.2 | 3.10 | 9.7 | 18.7 | 981 821 | 27.7 | 880 025 | 69.9 | 217 200 | 24.8 | 10.0 | 796 | 29.5 | 4.6 |
| Vermont | 256 442 | 6.6 | 2.34 | 9.6 | 28.2 | 322 698 | 9.6 | 256 922 | 70.4 | 216 800 | 26.0 | 16.3 | 823 | 31.8 | 2.2 |
| Virginia | 3 056 058 | 13.2 | 2.54 | 12.4 | 26.0 | 3 368 674 | 16.0 | 2 992 732 | 67.7 | 249 100 | 24.7 | 11.4 | 1 019 | 30.2 | 2.6 |
| Washington | 2 620 076 | 15.4 | 2.51 | 10.5 | 27.2 | 2 888 594 | 17.9 | 2 606 863 | 63.1 | 271 800 | 26.7 | 12.1 | 908 | 30.6 | 3.4 |
| West Virginia | 763 831 | 3.7 | 2.36 | 11.2 | 28.4 | 882 213 | 4.5 | 741 940 | 74.6 | 95 100 | 20.1 | 10.0 | 571 | 29.7 | 1.8 |
| Wisconsin | 2 279 768 | 9.4 | 2.43 | 10.3 | 28.2 | 2 625 477 | 13.1 | 2 279 532 | 68.7 | 169 400 | 24.5 | 14.0 | 715 | 29.8 | 2.2 |
| Wyoming | 226 879 | 17.2 | 2.42 | 8.9 | 28.0 | 262 286 | 17.2 | 222 803 | 69.7 | 180 100 | 22.0 | 10.0 | 693 | 25.3 | 2.8 |

1. No spouse present.   2. Specified owner-occupied units.   3. Median monthly costs is often in the minimum category—10.0 percent or less, which is indicated as 10.0 percent.
4. Specified renter-occupied units.   5. Overcrowded or lacking complete plumbing facilities.

# Table A. States — **Housing Units**

| STATE | Housing units, 2011 | | | | | | | | | | | | | |
|---|---|---|---|---|---|---|---|---|---|---|---|---|---|---|
| | | | Occupied units | | | | | | | | | | | |
| | | | | | Percent who pay 30 percent or more of income for housing expenses | | Median owner cost as a percent of income | | | | | | | |
| | Total | Percent change, 2010–2011 | Total | Percent owner-occupied | Owners with a mort-gage | Renter | With a mort-gage | Without a mort-gage[1] | Median monthly housing costs (dollars) | Median value of units[2] (dollars) | Percent valued over $500,000 | Median gross rent[3] (dollars) | Sub-standard units[4] (percent) | Percent living in a different house than 1 year ago |
| | 79 | 80 | 81 | 82 | 83 | 84 | 85 | 86 | 87 | 88 | 89 | 90 | 91 | 92 |
| UNITED STATES................. | 132 316 248 | 0.4 | 114 991 725 | 64.6 | 36.6 | 53.4 | 24.7 | 12.9 | 979 | 173 600 | 9.9 | 871 | 3.9 | 15.2 |
| Alabama.............................. | 2 182 199 | 0.4 | 1 844 546 | 69.9 | 31.5 | 53.8 | 22.5 | 12.2 | 729 | 122 700 | 3.3 | 687 | 2.5 | 15.2 |
| Alaska................................ | 311 182 | 1.3 | 257 330 | 63.1 | 32.0 | 44.3 | 23.5 | 11.7 | 1 186 | 238 300 | 6.7 | 1 049 | 10.5 | 19.7 |
| Arizona.............................. | 2 864 360 | 0.6 | 2 356 055 | 63.7 | 38.9 | 51.9 | 25.3 | 11.5 | 947 | 153 800 | 5.9 | 850 | 5.4 | 20.2 |
| Arkansas............................ | 1 324 471 | 0.5 | 1 127 621 | 66.6 | 27.5 | 52.6 | 21.1 | 11.0 | 657 | 106 300 | 2.1 | 639 | 3.0 | 16.7 |
| California............................ | 13 721 187 | 0.3 | 12 468 743 | 54.9 | 48.7 | 57.7 | 29.6 | 11.8 | 1 374 | 355 600 | 31.7 | 1 174 | 8.8 | 16.1 |
| Colorado............................ | 2 224 661 | 0.5 | 1 975 388 | 64.4 | 34.7 | 51.6 | 24.3 | 10.8 | 1 111 | 233 700 | 11.2 | 900 | 3.1 | 19.8 |
| Connecticut......................... | 1 494 042 | 0.4 | 1 351 643 | 67.4 | 40.4 | 55.2 | 26.4 | 17.1 | 1 361 | 278 700 | 16.8 | 1 021 | 2.4 | 11.5 |
| Delaware............................ | 409 779 | 0.8 | 333 192 | 71.6 | 34.7 | 52.7 | 24.1 | 11.2 | 1 113 | 236 900 | 6.3 | 960 | 2.0 | 13.5 |
| District of Columbia.............. | 298 908 | 0.7 | 268 670 | 41.2 | 35.5 | 49.3 | 24.2 | 10.0 | 1 401 | 422 400 | 41.1 | 1 216 | 3.6 | 19.9 |
| Florida............................... | 9 027 271 | 0.4 | 7 106 283 | 66.7 | 45.9 | 60.9 | 28.5 | 14.1 | 993 | 151 000 | 6.3 | 949 | 3.0 | 16.6 |
| Georgia ............................. | 4 103 118 | 0.3 | 3 494 542 | 64.6 | 36.5 | 54.9 | 24.5 | 12.4 | 940 | 147 100 | 4.6 | 833 | 3.1 | 16.6 |
| Hawaii................................ | 522 314 | 0.4 | 448 563 | 56.8 | 49.1 | 58.9 | 29.7 | 10.0 | 1 424 | 487 400 | 48.3 | 1 308 | 10.2 | 14.5 |
| Idaho................................. | 674 394 | 0.9 | 580 193 | 68.7 | 36.7 | 51.5 | 24.7 | 10.3 | 801 | 158 800 | 4.0 | 689 | 3.9 | 17.6 |
| Illinois............................... | 5 296 209 | 0.0 | 4 737 208 | 67.3 | 38.6 | 53.1 | 25.6 | 14.0 | 1 037 | 178 500 | 7.0 | 859 | 3.1 | 12.9 |
| Indiana .............................. | 2 800 799 | 0.1 | 2 467 111 | 69.7 | 26.5 | 51.9 | 21.2 | 11.3 | 788 | 122 400 | 2.0 | 707 | 2.3 | 14.9 |
| Iowa.................................. | 1 340 588 | 0.2 | 1 216 765 | 72.4 | 23.6 | 47.7 | 20.9 | 12.0 | 740 | 123 400 | 2.0 | 643 | 1.9 | 15.0 |
| Kansas.............................. | 1 237 738 | 0.3 | 1 101 701 | 67.8 | 26.8 | 46.6 | 21.9 | 12.6 | 798 | 128 300 | 2.9 | 709 | 2.7 | 16.3 |
| Kentucky............................ | 1 932 731 | 0.2 | 1 672 134 | 68.9 | 28.0 | 51.1 | 21.7 | 11.5 | 681 | 120 600 | 2.7 | 626 | 2.4 | 14.6 |
| Louisiana............................ | 1 978 974 | 0.6 | 1 702 030 | 66.4 | 29.6 | 55.6 | 21.7 | 10.3 | 725 | 139 400 | 3.0 | 747 | 3.3 | 14.4 |
| Maine................................ | 725 650 | 0.5 | 552 051 | 71.0 | 35.5 | 53.9 | 24.4 | 14.6 | 853 | 171 600 | 5.2 | 747 | 2.0 | 14.8 |
| Maryland............................ | 2 391 508 | 0.5 | 2 134 517 | 67.3 | 36.9 | 53.6 | 24.9 | 12.9 | 1 410 | 287 100 | 17.3 | 1 153 | 2.7 | 13.0 |
| Massachusetts .................... | 2 819 028 | 0.4 | 2 532 067 | 62.1 | 38.6 | 51.7 | 25.8 | 15.7 | 1 328 | 326 300 | 19.5 | 1 034 | 2.2 | 13.1 |
| Michigan............................ | 4 525 654 | -0.1 | 3 772 433 | 71.7 | 33.7 | 55.5 | 23.7 | 14.0 | 853 | 118 100 | 2.6 | 739 | 2.1 | 14.6 |
| Minnesota........................... | 2 354 075 | 0.2 | 2 096 477 | 72.8 | 32.1 | 50.4 | 23.5 | 12.1 | 1 006 | 183 500 | 5.4 | 787 | 2.5 | 14.7 |
| Mississippi.......................... | 1 281 760 | 0.4 | 1 080 991 | 69.8 | 34.1 | 55.6 | 23.4 | 12.1 | 665 | 99 900 | 1.9 | 689 | 3.1 | 13.9 |
| Missouri............................. | 2 723 449 | 0.3 | 2 341 074 | 68.0 | 29.3 | 49.8 | 22.3 | 12.4 | 799 | 136 900 | 3.3 | 708 | 2.2 | 16.4 |
| Montana............................. | 489 168 | 1.3 | 404 250 | 67.9 | 37.1 | 46.6 | 25.0 | 11.9 | 726 | 184 100 | 7.6 | 650 | 2.5 | 16.1 |
| Nebraska............................ | 801 182 | 0.4 | 723 800 | 66.9 | 24.8 | 43.6 | 20.9 | 12.5 | 780 | 127 400 | 2.0 | 673 | 2.3 | 17.2 |
| Nevada.............................. | 1 183 917 | 0.8 | 982 352 | 56.3 | 42.4 | 52.3 | 27.1 | 12.1 | 1 060 | 158 000 | 4.6 | 936 | 5.0 | 22.5 |
| New Hampshire ................... | 617 702 | 0.4 | 516 454 | 71.5 | 39.8 | 50.3 | 26.5 | 17.4 | 1 223 | 237 500 | 5.8 | 939 | 1.7 | 12.6 |
| New Jersey ......................... | 3 562 720 | 0.2 | 3 167 629 | 65.0 | 47.1 | 54.6 | 29.0 | 19.2 | 1 491 | 324 900 | 20.1 | 1 135 | 4.3 | 10.3 |
| New Mexico......................... | 908 168 | 0.7 | 767 285 | 68.2 | 34.0 | 53.3 | 23.5 | 10.3 | 752 | 159 000 | 5.7 | 729 | 5.2 | 14.7 |
| New York............................ | 8 119 804 | 0.1 | 7 187 938 | 53.6 | 41.1 | 54.4 | 26.3 | 15.3 | 1 177 | 285 300 | 23.0 | 1 058 | 5.6 | 11.4 |
| North Carolina..................... | 4 362 956 | 0.7 | 3 683 364 | 66.5 | 33.7 | 53.1 | 23.5 | 12.3 | 840 | 153 700 | 5.3 | 745 | 3.0 | 15.4 |
| North Dakota....................... | 320 888 | 0.9 | 283 440 | 65.7 | 19.1 | 42.6 | 19.2 | 10.0 | 671 | 128 600 | 1.9 | 626 | 1.7 | 17.0 |
| Ohio.................................. | 5 133 528 | 0.1 | 4 538 555 | 67.0 | 30.7 | 51.7 | 22.8 | 13.1 | 819 | 129 600 | 2.4 | 692 | 1.8 | 14.5 |
| Oklahoma........................... | 1 674 724 | 0.5 | 1 442 731 | 67.0 | 28.2 | 48.3 | 21.8 | 11.5 | 712 | 112 600 | 2.4 | 675 | 3.2 | 17.4 |
| Oregon.............................. | 1 684 244 | 0.5 | 1 516 979 | 60.8 | 41.0 | 55.5 | 26.7 | 13.1 | 968 | 232 900 | 9.7 | 840 | 3.3 | 18.3 |
| Pennsylvania....................... | 5 579 394 | 0.2 | 4 937 333 | 69.5 | 33.2 | 51.4 | 23.7 | 14.1 | 885 | 164 800 | 5.1 | 786 | 1.8 | 12.0 |
| Rhode Island....................... | 464 741 | 0.3 | 412 259 | 60.6 | 41.1 | 50.7 | 26.9 | 17.0 | 1 140 | 245 500 | 10.1 | 875 | 2.5 | 13.1 |
| South Carolina .................... | 2 157 063 | 0.8 | 1 768 834 | 69.2 | 34.1 | 54.2 | 23.5 | 11.9 | 784 | 136 000 | 5.6 | 741 | 2.4 | 15.6 |
| South Dakota....................... | 366 521 | 0.7 | 323 215 | 68.5 | 24.9 | 39.7 | 21.7 | 11.5 | 693 | 131 400 | 2.5 | 612 | 2.8 | 15.4 |
| Tennessee ......................... | 2 829 125 | 0.5 | 2 467 428 | 67.3 | 32.5 | 52.9 | 23.5 | 11.8 | 770 | 138 300 | 4.1 | 715 | 2.3 | 15.6 |
| Texas ................................ | 10 099 242 | 1.0 | 8 850 370 | 62.9 | 31.4 | 49.9 | 23.0 | 12.5 | 891 | 127 700 | 3.9 | 813 | 5.7 | 17.1 |
| Utah.................................. | 993 125 | 1.2 | 884 253 | 69.4 | 34.2 | 51.2 | 24.5 | 10.0 | 1 019 | 207 500 | 6.2 | 822 | 3.9 | 17.1 |
| Vermont.............................. | 324 385 | 0.5 | 257 358 | 71.3 | 36.9 | 53.4 | 25.5 | 16.6 | 1 042 | 213 700 | 6.8 | 849 | 1.9 | 13.6 |
| Virginia.............................. | 3 387 801 | 0.6 | 2 990 650 | 67.3 | 33.3 | 50.3 | 24.0 | 11.2 | 1 193 | 243 100 | 15.3 | 1 062 | 2.4 | 15.1 |
| Washington ......................... | 2 907 605 | 0.7 | 2 632 621 | 62.8 | 39.2 | 50.7 | 26.1 | 12.6 | 1 136 | 256 300 | 13.3 | 930 | 3.5 | 17.5 |
| West Virginia....................... | 881 821 | 0.0 | 735 408 | 72.3 | 26.5 | 48.9 | 19.9 | 10.0 | 550 | 99 300 | 1.9 | 599 | 1.9 | 12.4 |
| Wisconsin........................... | 2 634 806 | 0.4 | 2 275 352 | 67.9 | 33.3 | 48.9 | 24.1 | 14.1 | 898 | 166 700 | 3.6 | 739 | 2.2 | 14.2 |
| Wyoming............................ | 265 554 | 1.2 | 222 539 | 70.6 | 26.8 | 36.6 | 21.5 | 10.0 | 826 | 179 900 | 4.8 | 759 | 2.4 | 17.5 |

1. Excludes units where gross rent as a percentage of household income cannot be calculated.   2. Median monthly costs is often in the minimum category—10.0 percent or less, which is indicated as 10.0 percent.   3. Specified owner-occupied units.   4. Specified renter-occupied units.   5. Overcrowded or lacking complete plumbing facilities.

# Table A. States — Residential Construction, Vital Statistics, and Health

| STATE | Value of residential construction authorized by building permits, 2011 | | | Manu-factured housing units put in place, 2011 (1,000) | Births, 2010 | | Deaths, 2009 | | | | | Percent lacking health insurance, 2011 | | Medicare enrollees, 2012 |
|---|---|---|---|---|---|---|---|---|---|---|---|---|---|---|
| | New con-struction ($1,000) | Number of housing units | Percent single family | | Total | Rate[1] | Number | | Rate | | | All persons | Children under 18 years | |
| | | | | | | | Total | Infant[2] | Crude[1] | Total Age-adjusted | Infant[3] | | | |
| | 93 | 94 | 95 | 96 | 97 | 98 | 99 | 100 | 101 | 102 | 103 | 104 | 105 | 106 |
| UNITED STATES.............. | 105 268 541 | 624 061 | 67.1 | 47 | 3 999 386 | 13.0 | 2 437 163 | 26 412 | 7.9 | 7.4 | 6.39 | 15.7 | 9.4 | 49 682 146 |
| Alabama............................ | 1 704 064 | 11 667 | 75.9 | 2.4 | 60 050 | 12.6 | 47 470 | 517 | 10.1 | 9.2 | 8.28 | 13.0 | 7.3 | 896 274 |
| Alaska.............................. | 203 975 | 877 | 81.3 | (D) | 11 471 | 16.2 | 3 618 | 77 | 5.2 | 7.6 | 6.80 | 18.2 | 10.7 | 72 898 |
| Arizona............................ | 2 580 351 | 13 007 | 79.2 | 0.8 | 87 477 | 13.7 | 45 816 | 556 | 6.9 | 6.5 | 5.99 | 17.3 | 13.5 | 1 009 292 |
| Arkansas.......................... | 861 479 | 6 800 | 60.9 | 1.0 | 38 540 | 13.2 | 28 673 | 307 | 9.9 | 8.7 | 7.71 | 17.5 | 8.1 | 558 620 |
| California......................... | 9 638 517 | 45 471 | 47.7 | 1.3 | 510 198 | 13.7 | 232 736 | 2 602 | 6.3 | 6.5 | 4.94 | 19.7 | 10.8 | 5 111 208 |
| Colorado.......................... | 2 859 669 | 13 502 | 64.6 | 0.8 | 66 355 | 13.2 | 31 173 | 429 | 6.2 | 6.9 | 6.25 | 15.7 | 4.3 | 688 283 |
| Connecticut...................... | 679 237 | 3 173 | 68.1 | 0.2 | 37 708 | 10.6 | 28 585 | 214 | 8.1 | 6.8 | 5.50 | 8.6 | 13.0 | 595 294 |
| Delaware.......................... | 370 169 | 2 954 | 82.6 | 0.2 | 11 364 | 12.7 | 7 534 | 91 | 8.5 | 7.5 | 7.87 | 10.0 | 10.9 | 161 422 |
| District of Columbia........... | 609 369 | 4 612 | 4.9 | (D) | 9 165 | 15.2 | 4 834 | 89 | 8.1 | 8.1 | 9.85 | 8.4 | 4.1 | 82 493 |
| Florida............................. | 8 814 610 | 42 360 | 75.2 | 2.0 | 214 590 | 11.4 | 169 924 | 1 522 | 9.2 | 6.7 | 6.87 | 19.8 | 11.3 | 3 621 057 |
| Georgia............................ | 2 760 775 | 18 493 | 74.7 | 1.3 | 133 947 | 13.8 | 69 712 | 1 049 | 7.1 | 8.2 | 7.42 | 19.2 | 6.2 | 1 350 944 |
| Hawaii.............................. | 653 884 | 2 743 | 59.5 | (D) | 18 988 | 14.0 | 9 914 | 116 | 7.7 | 6.2 | 6.14 | 7.8 | 5.6 | 221 514 |
| Idaho............................... | 732 769 | 3 815 | 82.9 | 0.4 | 23 198 | 14.8 | 11 098 | 129 | 7.2 | 7.2 | 5.43 | 16.9 | 4.9 | 249 626 |
| Illinois............................. | 2 118 058 | 11 809 | 57.9 | 0.9 | 165 200 | 12.9 | 100 056 | 1 177 | 7.8 | 7.4 | 6.88 | 14.7 | 9.4 | 1 934 703 |
| Indiana............................ | 1 975 556 | 12 618 | 73.9 | 0.4 | 83 940 | 12.9 | 55 973 | 678 | 8.7 | 8.2 | 7.82 | 12.0 | 5.6 | 1 064 511 |
| Iowa................................ | 1 245 724 | 7 526 | 78.1 | 0.2 | 38 719 | 12.7 | 27 544 | 182 | 9.2 | 7.2 | 4.58 | 10.0 | 4.9 | 537 430 |
| Kansas............................ | 860 729 | 5 386 | 64.4 | 0.3 | 40 649 | 14.2 | 24 024 | 289 | 8.5 | 7.6 | 6.98 | 13.5 | 9.4 | 453 927 |
| Kentucky.......................... | 915 114 | 7 782 | 61.6 | 2.1 | 55 784 | 12.9 | 41 380 | 397 | 9.6 | 9.0 | 6.90 | 14.4 | 4.6 | 804 245 |
| Louisiana.......................... | 1 918 793 | 12 173 | 81.8 | 4.0 | 62 379 | 13.8 | 40 282 | 568 | 9.0 | 8.9 | 8.74 | 20.8 | 11.6 | 729 271 |
| Maine............................... | 435 668 | 2 744 | 83.1 | 0.3 | 12 970 | 9.8 | 12 594 | 76 | 9.6 | 7.6 | 5.64 | 10.0 | 6.3 | 281 968 |
| Maryland .......................... | 2 204 630 | 13 481 | 62.0 | 0.2 | 73 801 | 12.8 | 43 843 | 546 | 7.7 | 7.6 | 7.27 | 13.8 | 10.0 | 844 862 |
| Massachusetts................... | 1 761 071 | 7 725 | 63.4 | 0.1 | 72 865 | 11.1 | 52 308 | 379 | 7.9 | 6.8 | 5.05 | 3.4 | 2.5 | 1 125 661 |
| Michigan.......................... | 1 688 198 | 9 341 | 85.0 | 1.0 | 114 531 | 11.6 | 86 455 | 881 | 8.7 | 7.9 | 7.51 | 12.5 | 5.4 | 1 754 367 |
| Minnesota........................ | 1 763 836 | 8 890 | 75.7 | 0.3 | 68 610 | 12.9 | 37 851 | 326 | 7.2 | 6.5 | 4.61 | 9.2 | 6.4 | 836 205 |
| Mississippi....................... | 724 061 | 5 273 | 81.0 | 1.9 | 40 036 | 13.5 | 28 275 | 431 | 9.6 | 9.3 | 10.05 | 16.2 | 9.0 | 523 625 |
| Missouri........................... | 1 425 673 | 9 242 | 65.6 | 0.7 | 76 759 | 12.8 | 54 263 | 565 | 9.1 | 8.0 | 7.16 | 14.9 | 11.5 | 1 058 418 |
| Montana........................... | 285 875 | 1 914 | 63.1 | 0.3 | 12 060 | 12.2 | 8 730 | 72 | 9.0 | 7.6 | 5.87 | 18.3 | 12.3 | 181 710 |
| Nebraska.......................... | 726 319 | 5 203 | 69.1 | 0.1 | 25 918 | 14.2 | 14 810 | 146 | 8.2 | 7.2 | 5.42 | 12.3 | 8.2 | 291 333 |
| Nevada............................ | 789 438 | 6 163 | 76.0 | 0.1 | 35 934 | 13.3 | 19 224 | 220 | 7.3 | 7.8 | 5.85 | 22.6 | 21.0 | 394 066 |
| New Hampshire ................. | 432 254 | 2 346 | 68.5 | 0.1 | 12 874 | 9.8 | 10 100 | 65 | 7.6 | 6.8 | 4.86 | 12.5 | 7.4 | 240 551 |
| New Jersey....................... | 2 043 104 | 12 952 | 50.0 | 0.1 | 106 922 | 12.2 | 68 277 | 566 | 7.8 | 6.9 | 5.13 | 15.4 | 9.4 | 1 397 532 |
| New Mexico...................... | 677 704 | 4 067 | 83.6 | 0.9 | 27 850 | 13.5 | 15 643 | 153 | 7.8 | 7.4 | 5.28 | 19.6 | 9.9 | 336 413 |
| New York.......................... | 3 355 501 | 22 575 | 37.2 | 1.1 | 244 375 | 12.6 | 146 475 | 1 323 | 7.5 | 6.7 | 5.33 | 12.2 | 6.6 | 3 138 042 |
| North Carolina................... | 5 053 273 | 32 804 | 75.8 | 2.6 | 122 350 | 12.8 | 77 117 | 1 004 | 8.2 | 8.0 | 7.92 | 16.3 | 9.3 | 1 604 085 |
| North Dakota..................... | 783 616 | 6 201 | 47.0 | 0.6 | 9 104 | 13.5 | 5 914 | 55 | 9.1 | 7.2 | 6.11 | 9.1 | 4.7 | 112 330 |
| Ohio................................ | 2 259 867 | 13 762 | 67.7 | 0.6 | 139 128 | 12.1 | 107 156 | 1 112 | 9.3 | 8.1 | 7.68 | 13.7 | 8.7 | 2 003 455 |
| Oklahoma......................... | 1 285 644 | 8 782 | 73.4 | 2.0 | 53 238 | 14.2 | 35 601 | 428 | 9.7 | 8.9 | 7.85 | 16.9 | 6.4 | 635 525 |
| Oregon............................ | 1 407 354 | 7 663 | 63.3 | 0.6 | 45 540 | 11.9 | 31 636 | 227 | 8.3 | 7.3 | 4.82 | 13.8 | 7.4 | 671 822 |
| Pennsylvania..................... | 2 545 786 | 14 967 | 78.8 | 1.3 | 143 321 | 11.3 | 124 780 | 1 052 | 9.9 | 7.7 | 7.18 | 10.8 | 7.6 | 2 385 084 |
| Rhode Island..................... | 129 276 | 700 | 81.6 | (D) | 11 177 | 10.6 | 9 395 | 71 | 8.9 | 7.2 | 6.21 | 12.0 | 5.8 | 191 420 |
| South Carolina .................. | 2 760 219 | 15 542 | 82.7 | 1.4 | 58 342 | 12.6 | 40 449 | 430 | 8.9 | 8.2 | 7.09 | 19.0 | 13.3 | 839 989 |
| South Dakota .................... | 391 886 | 2 813 | 69.7 | 0.8 | 11 811 | 14.5 | 6 923 | 80 | 8.5 | 6.9 | 6.70 | 13.0 | 7.5 | 143 014 |
| Tennessee ........................ | 2 353 489 | 14 977 | 76.9 | 1.5 | 79 495 | 12.5 | 58 288 | 658 | 9.3 | 8.7 | 8.00 | 13.3 | 5.9 | 1 132 942 |
| Texas............................... | 14 736 206 | 97 450 | 67.2 | 6.6 | 386 118 | 15.4 | 163 249 | 2 402 | 6.6 | 7.5 | 5.98 | 23.8 | 15.4 | 3 256 477 |
| Utah................................ | 1 759 629 | 9 983 | 68.7 | 0.3 | 52 258 | 18.9 | 14 138 | 285 | 5.1 | 6.6 | 5.29 | 14.6 | 10.7 | 307 361 |
| Vermont............................ | 221 336 | 1 299 | 62.0 | 0.1 | 6 223 | 9.9 | 5 034 | 38 | 8.1 | 6.8 | 6.22 | 8.6 | 4.0 | 119 759 |
| Virginia............................ | 3 390 840 | 23 297 | 67.1 | 0.8 | 103 002 | 12.9 | 58 653 | 751 | 7.4 | 7.5 | 7.15 | 13.4 | 5.9 | 1 226 577 |
| Washington....................... | 4 036 365 | 20 864 | 63.1 | 0.6 | 86 539 | 12.9 | 48 270 | 438 | 7.2 | 7.1 | 4.90 | 14.5 | 8.8 | 1 055 977 |
| West Virginia..................... | 306 401 | 2 220 | 71.5 | 0.9 | 20 470 | 11.0 | 21 386 | 165 | 11.8 | 9.5 | 7.76 | 14.9 | 9.7 | 396 705 |
| Wisconsin......................... | 1 605 963 | 9 939 | 65.4 | 0.3 | 68 487 | 12.0 | 45 697 | 431 | 8.1 | 7.1 | 6.08 | 10.4 | 5.8 | 966 151 |
| Wyoming.......................... | 425 156 | 2 114 | 68.7 | 0.2 | 7 556 | 13.4 | 4 283 | 47 | 7.9 | 7.8 | 5.96 | 17.8 | 10.0 | 85 708 |

1.  Per 1,000 resident population.    2.  Deaths of infants under 1 year old.    3.  Deaths of infants under 1 year old per 1,000 live births.

# Table A. States — **Crime and Education**

| STATE | Serious crime known to police,[1] 2011 | | | | Public elementary and secondary school enrollment, 2010–2011 | | Educational attainment[3] (percent) | | | | Local government expenditures for education, 2009–2010 | |
|---|---|---|---|---|---|---|---|---|---|---|---|---|
| | Violent Crime | | Property Crime | | | | 2010 | | 2011 | | | |
| | Number | Rate[2] | Number | Rate[2] | Total | Student/ teacher ratio | High school graduate or more | Bachelor's degree or more | High school graduate or more | Bachelor's degree or more | Total current expenditures (mil dol) | Current expenditures per student (dollars) |
| | 107 | 108 | 109 | 110 | 111 | 112 | 113 | 114 | 115 | 116 | 117 | 118 |
| UNITED STATES................ | 1 203 564 | 386.3 | 9 063 173 | 2 908.7 | 49 484 181 | 16.0 | 85.6 | 28.2 | 85.9 | 28.5 | 525 498 | 10 652 |
| Alabama.............................. | 20 174 | 420.1 | 173 190 | 3 606.1 | 755 552 | 15.3 | 82.1 | 21.9 | 82.7 | 22.3 | 6 671 | 8 907 |
| Alaska................................ | 4 383 | 606.5 | 19 028 | 2 632.8 | 132 104 | 16.2 | 91.0 | 27.9 | 91.8 | 26.4 | 2 084 | 15 829 |
| Arizona.............................. | 26 311 | 405.9 | 230 422 | 3 554.5 | 1 071 751 | 21.4 | 85.6 | 25.9 | 85.7 | 26.6 | 8 588 | 7 968 |
| Arkansas............................ | 14 129 | 480.9 | 110 295 | 3 754.1 | 482 114 | 14.1 | 82.9 | 19.5 | 83.8 | 20.3 | 4 460 | 9 281 |
| California............................ | 154 944 | 411.1 | 973 901 | 2 583.8 | 6 289 578 | 24.1 | 80.7 | 30.1 | 81.1 | 30.3 | 58 249 | 9 300 |
| Colorado............................ | 16 383 | 320.2 | 133 361 | 2 606.3 | 843 316 | 17.4 | 89.7 | 36.4 | 90.2 | 36.7 | 7 429 | 8 926 |
| Connecticut........................ | 9 767 | 272.8 | 77 609 | 2 167.4 | 560 546 | 13.1 | 88.6 | 35.5 | 89.1 | 36.2 | 8 853 | 15 698 |
| Delaware............................ | 5 075 | 559.5 | 30 939 | 3 410.6 | 129 403 | 14.5 | 87.7 | 27.8 | 87.0 | 28.8 | 1 550 | 12 222 |
| District of Columbia............. | 7 429 | 1 202.1 | 29 636 | 4 795.5 | 71 284 | 12.0 | 87.4 | 50.1 | 87.2 | 52.5 | 1 452 | 20 910 |
| Florida............................... | 98 199 | 515.3 | 671 200 | 3 522.0 | 2 643 347 | 15.1 | 85.5 | 25.8 | 85.9 | 25.8 | 23 349 | 8 863 |
| Georgia.............................. | 36 634 | 373.2 | 355 952 | 3 626.5 | 1 677 067 | 14.9 | 84.3 | 27.3 | 84.3 | 27.6 | 15 730 | 9 432 |
| Hawaii............................... | 3 949 | 287.2 | 45 889 | 3 337.8 | 179 601 | 15.8 | 89.9 | 29.5 | 90.6 | 29.1 | 2 111 | 11 714 |
| Idaho................................. | 3 184 | 200.9 | 32 787 | 2 068.6 | 275 859 | 17.6 | 88.3 | 24.4 | 88.6 | 25.2 | 1 962 | 7 100 |
| Illinois............................... | 429 | 429.3 | 346 025 | 2 688.8 | 2 091 654 | 15.7 | 86.9 | 30.8 | 87.2 | 31.0 | 24 696 | 11 739 |
| Indiana............................... | 21 626 | 331.8 | 206 055 | 3 161.8 | 1 047 232 | 18.0 | 87.0 | 22.7 | 87.3 | 23.0 | 9 921 | 9 479 |
| Iowa.................................. | 7 826 | 255.6 | 71 361 | 2 330.3 | 495 775 | 14.3 | 90.6 | 24.9 | 90.6 | 25.8 | 4 794 | 9 748 |
| Kansas............................... | 10 162 | 353.9 | 88 438 | 3 080.1 | 483 701 | 14.0 | 89.2 | 29.8 | 90.0 | 30.1 | 4 732 | 9 972 |
| Kentucky............................ | 10 406 | 238.2 | 118 358 | 2 708.6 | 673 128 | 16.0 | 81.9 | 20.5 | 83.1 | 21.1 | 6 092 | 8 957 |
| Louisiana........................... | 25 406 | 555.3 | 168 744 | 3 688.5 | 696 558 | 14.3 | 81.9 | 21.4 | 82.5 | 21.1 | 7 393 | 10 701 |
| Maine................................ | 1 636 | 123.2 | 33 809 | 2 545.5 | 189 077 | 12.3 | 90.3 | 26.8 | 90.9 | 28.4 | 2 356 | 12 452 |
| Maryland............................ | 28 797 | 494.1 | 166 699 | 2 860.2 | 852 211 | 14.6 | 88.1 | 36.1 | 88.9 | 36.9 | 11 884 | 14 007 |
| Massachusetts..................... | 28 219 | 428.4 | 148 790 | 2 258.7 | 955 563 | 13.9 | 89.1 | 39.0 | 89.2 | 39.1 | 14 067 | 14 699 |
| Michigan............................ | 43 983 | 445.3 | 257 979 | 2 612.1 | 1 587 067 | 17.9 | 88.7 | 25.2 | 88.8 | 25.6 | 17 228 | 10 447 |
| Minnesota.......................... | 11 825 | 221.2 | 136 264 | 2 549.4 | 838 037 | 15.9 | 91.8 | 31.8 | 92.0 | 32.4 | 8 927 | 10 665 |
| Mississippi......................... | 8 036 | 269.8 | 90 115 | 3 025.5 | 490 526 | 15.2 | 81.0 | 19.5 | 81.1 | 19.8 | 3 991 | 8 104 |
| Missouri............................. | 26 889 | 447.4 | 198 882 | 3 308.8 | 918 710 | 13.8 | 86.9 | 25.6 | 87.6 | 26.1 | 8 923 | 9 721 |
| Montana............................. | 2 670 | 267.5 | 23 155 | 2 319.7 | 141 693 | 13.7 | 91.7 | 28.8 | 92.3 | 28.2 | 1 498 | 10 565 |
| Nebraska............................ | 4 665 | 253.2 | 50 726 | 2 752.9 | 298 500 | 13.4 | 90.4 | 28.6 | 91.0 | 27.9 | 3 248 | 11 460 |
| Nevada.............................. | 15 309 | 562.1 | 69 731 | 2 560.5 | 437 149 | 20.0 | 84.7 | 21.7 | 84.0 | 22.5 | 3 593 | 8 376 |
| New Hampshire ................... | 2 478 | 188.0 | 30 106 | 2 283.9 | 194 711 | 12.7 | 91.5 | 32.8 | 91.4 | 33.4 | 2 577 | 13 072 |
| New Jersey......................... | 27 203 | 308.4 | 189 719 | 2 150.7 | 1 402 548 | 12.7 | 88.0 | 35.4 | 88.1 | 35.3 | 24 261 | 17 379 |
| New Mexico........................ | 11 817 | 567.5 | 73 534 | 3 531.5 | 338 122 | 15.1 | 83.3 | 25.0 | 83.2 | 25.6 | 3 217 | 9 621 |
| New York ........................... | 77 490 | 398.1 | 372 255 | 1 912.4 | 2 734 955 | 12.9 | 84.9 | 32.5 | 85.0 | 32.9 | 50 251 | 18 167 |
| North Carolina..................... | 33 774 | 349.8 | 340 562 | 3 526.8 | 1 490 605 | 15.2 | 84.7 | 26.5 | 84.7 | 26.9 | 12 200 | 8 225 |
| North Dakota....................... | 1 689 | 247.0 | 13 246 | 1 936.7 | 96 323 | 11.4 | 90.3 | 27.6 | 90.7 | 26.3 | 1 000 | 10 519 |
| Ohio.................................. | 35 484 | 307.4 | 387 297 | 3 354.7 | 1 754 191 | 16.1 | 88.1 | 24.6 | 88.3 | 24.7 | 19 802 | 11 224 |
| Oklahoma........................... | 17 243 | 454.8 | 127 252 | 3 356.2 | 659 911 | 16.0 | 86.2 | 22.9 | 86.3 | 23.8 | 5 192 | 7 929 |
| Oregon.............................. | 9 586 | 247.6 | 120 594 | 3 114.6 | 570 720 | 20.3 | 88.8 | 28.8 | 89.4 | 29.3 | 5 402 | 9 268 |
| Pennsylvania....................... | 45 240 | 355.0 | 283 179 | 2 222.3 | 1 793 284 | 13.8 | 88.4 | 27.1 | 88.6 | 27.0 | 22 734 | 12 729 |
| Rhode Island....................... | 2 602 | 247.5 | 28 141 | 2 676.8 | 143 793 | 12.8 | 83.5 | 30.2 | 84.8 | 31.1 | 2 137 | 14 723 |
| South Carolina .................... | 26 760 | 571.9 | 182 685 | 3 904.2 | 725 838 | 16.1 | 84.1 | 24.5 | 84.2 | 24.1 | 6 566 | 9 080 |
| South Dakota ...................... | 2 094 | 254.1 | 14 979 | 1 817.7 | 126 128 | 13.3 | 89.6 | 26.3 | 90.6 | 26.3 | 1 116 | 9 020 |
| Tennessee ......................... | 38 944 | 608.2 | 230 261 | 3 595.9 | 987 422 | 14.8 | 83.6 | 23.1 | 84.2 | 23.6 | 7 895 | 8 117 |
| Texas................................ | 104 873 | 408.5 | 891 499 | 3 472.3 | 4 935 715 | 14.7 | 80.7 | 25.9 | 81.1 | 26.4 | 42 622 | 8 788 |
| Utah.................................. | 5 494 | 195.0 | 83 758 | 2 973.1 | 585 552 | 22.8 | 90.6 | 29.3 | 90.3 | 29.7 | 3 635 | 6 452 |
| Vermont............................. | 847 | 135.2 | 14 464 | 2 309.0 | 96 858 | 11.6 | 91.0 | 33.6 | 91.8 | 35.4 | 1 464 | 16 006 |
| Virginia.............................. | 15 923 | 196.7 | 182 141 | 2 249.6 | 1 251 440 | 17.6 | 86.5 | 34.2 | 87.8 | 35.1 | 13 194 | 10 594 |
| Washington........................ | 20 121 | 294.6 | 244 146 | 3 574.6 | 1 043 788 | 19.4 | 89.8 | 31.1 | 90.1 | 31.9 | 9 833 | 9 497 |
| West Virginia....................... | 5 861 | 315.9 | 42 189 | 2 273.9 | 282 879 | 13.9 | 83.2 | 17.5 | 84.2 | 18.5 | 3 316 | 11 730 |
| Wisconsin........................... | 13 532 | 236.9 | 138 949 | 2 432.7 | 872 286 | 15.1 | 90.1 | 26.3 | 90.4 | 26.5 | 9 919 | 11 453 |
| Wyoming............................ | 1 246 | 219.3 | 12 877 | 2 266.4 | 89 009 | 12.5 | 92.3 | 24.1 | 92.0 | 24.7 | 1 335 | 15 232 |

1. Data for serious crimes have not been adjusted for underreporting; this may affect comparability between geographic areas and over time.     2. Per 100,000 population estimated by the FBI.     3. Persons 25 years old and over.

# Table A. States — **Exports, Income, and Poverty**

| STATE | Exports of goods by state of origin, 2012 (mil dol) — Total | Manu- factured | Non- manu- factured | Income, 2011 — Per capita income (dollars) | Households — Median income (dollars) | Percent with income of $25,000 or less | Percent with income of $100,000 or more | Median income of family of four | Percent below poverty level, 2011 — All persons | Children under 18 years | Persons 65 years and over | All families | Families with children under 18 — Married- couple families | Male house- holder[1] families | Female house- holder[1] families |
|---|---|---|---|---|---|---|---|---|---|---|---|---|---|---|---|
| | 119 | 120 | 121 | 122 | 123 | 124 | 125 | 126 | 127 | 128 | 129 | 130 | 131 | 132 | 133 |
| UNITED STATES ............. | 1 547 138 | 1 162 991 | 162 597 | 26 708 | 50 502 | 25.0 | 20.8 | 74 563 | 15.9 | 22.2 | 9.3 | 11.7 | 8.8 | 23.6 | 40.8 |
| Alabama.......................... | 19 526 | 16 680 | 2 289 | 22 711 | 41 415 | 31.6 | 14.7 | 63 388 | 19.0 | 27.4 | 10.3 | 14.9 | 10.2 | 26.8 | 49.8 |
| Alaska............................. | 4 596 | 458 | 4 094 | 31 405 | 67 825 | 15.1 | 28.8 | 86 581 | 10.5 | 14.3 | 6.3 | 6.9 | 4.7 | 20.6 | 23.7 |
| Arizona........................... | 18 357 | 11 526 | 2 993 | 23 793 | 46 709 | 26.5 | 17.6 | 59 786 | 19.0 | 26.9 | 8.5 | 14.1 | 13.0 | 29.1 | 42.1 |
| Arkansas......................... | 7 621 | 5 347 | 633 | 21 203 | 38 758 | 33.4 | 12.4 | 55 444 | 19.5 | 27.7 | 10.5 | 14.9 | 11.3 | 27.4 | 48.2 |
| California......................... | 161 700 | 104 433 | 20 183 | 27 859 | 57 287 | 22.1 | 26.9 | 74 122 | 16.6 | 22.5 | 10.0 | 12.4 | 11.0 | 23.6 | 37.4 |
| Colorado......................... | 8 164 | 6 731 | 577 | 29 804 | 55 387 | 21.5 | 23.8 | 85 027 | 13.5 | 17.5 | 7.8 | 9.1 | 7.2 | 18.8 | 36.5 |
| Connecticut..................... | 15 866 | 14 132 | 916 | 35 932 | 65 753 | 19.3 | 31.3 | 100 451 | 10.9 | 14.8 | 6.8 | 7.9 | 4.0 | 19.7 | 33.0 |
| Delaware......................... | 5 157 | 4 226 | 57 | 29 123 | 58 814 | 19.2 | 24.7 | 83 424 | 11.9 | 16.8 | 5.7 | 8.0 | 4.1 | 18.6 | 31.4 |
| District of Columbia ........ | 2 015 | 1 953 | 32 | 44 578 | 63 124 | 23.1 | 33.0 | 76 230 | 18.7 | 30.2 | 12.5 | 15.4 | 5.5 | 25.7 | 38.1 |
| Florida............................ | 66 398 | 52 084 | 4 040 | 24 905 | 44 299 | 27.8 | 16.3 | 63 937 | 17.0 | 24.6 | 10.0 | 12.4 | 10.8 | 26.6 | 37.9 |
| Georgia........................... | 35 892 | 30 085 | 3 051 | 23 604 | 46 007 | 27.9 | 17.7 | 65 851 | 19.1 | 26.1 | 10.9 | 14.7 | 10.7 | 26.6 | 43.1 |
| Hawaii............................. | 726 | 512 | 162 | 27 353 | 61 821 | 17.8 | 27.3 | 82 973 | 12.0 | 16.7 | 8.2 | 8.6 | 7.0 | 15.7 | 31.5 |
| Idaho.............................. | 6 113 | 3 348 | 423 | 21 152 | 43 341 | 26.9 | 13.5 | 61 058 | 16.5 | 19.9 | 6.8 | 11.6 | 9.4 | 21.9 | 48.0 |
| Illinois............................ | 68 026 | 54 764 | 4 630 | 27 880 | 53 234 | 23.7 | 22.5 | 79 138 | 15.0 | 21.3 | 8.2 | 11.0 | 8.0 | 20.0 | 41.2 |
| Indiana............................ | 34 385 | 31 725 | 486 | 23 524 | 46 438 | 26.3 | 15.1 | 69 328 | 16.0 | 22.5 | 7.2 | 11.7 | 7.5 | 26.6 | 44.9 |
| Iowa................................ | 14 604 | 12 309 | 1 882 | 25 667 | 49 427 | 23.7 | 16.6 | 76 777 | 12.8 | 17.0 | 6.9 | 8.1 | 5.9 | 17.5 | 38.4 |
| Kansas............................ | 11 660 | 8 730 | 2 219 | 25 438 | 48 964 | 23.8 | 17.5 | 74 853 | 13.8 | 18.4 | 7.2 | 9.2 | 7.0 | 16.6 | 40.9 |
| Kentucky......................... | 22 092 | 18 429 | 591 | 22 300 | 41 141 | 31.8 | 13.8 | 66 409 | 19.1 | 27.0 | 11.8 | 14.7 | 10.5 | 30.9 | 51.3 |
| Louisiana ........................ | 63 156 | 41 510 | 21 211 | 22 882 | 41 734 | 32.1 | 16.3 | 68 921 | 20.4 | 28.6 | 12.7 | 16.1 | 7.5 | 26.1 | 50.3 |
| Maine.............................. | 3 058 | 2 285 | 661 | 25 802 | 46 033 | 27.7 | 15.5 | 78 310 | 14.1 | 18.2 | 8.0 | 9.3 | 6.8 | 23.9 | 39.2 |
| Maryland ......................... | 11 781 | 8 115 | 1 023 | 34 500 | 70 004 | 16.8 | 33.4 | 106 707 | 10.1 | 13.2 | 7.5 | 7.1 | 3.5 | 14.0 | 26.3 |
| Massachusetts................. | 25 549 | 20 737 | 1 570 | 34 041 | 62 859 | 21.5 | 30.2 | 101 523 | 11.6 | 14.9 | 9.3 | 8.3 | 4.3 | 16.2 | 35.0 |
| Michigan.......................... | 56 902 | 48 736 | 3 246 | 24 409 | 45 981 | 27.5 | 16.9 | 72 366 | 17.5 | 24.4 | 8.2 | 12.5 | 9.2 | 29.0 | 45.7 |
| Minnesota........................ | 20 565 | 17 208 | 2 008 | 29 404 | 56 954 | 20.7 | 22.7 | 87 319 | 11.9 | 15.0 | 8.0 | 7.6 | 4.9 | 18.6 | 35.4 |
| Mississippi ...................... | 11 779 | 9 571 | 820 | 19 583 | 36 919 | 35.0 | 11.5 | 58 047 | 22.6 | 31.5 | 13.5 | 17.4 | 9.1 | 25.5 | 51.8 |
| Missouri........................... | 13 910 | 11 198 | 2 052 | 24 634 | 45 247 | 27.1 | 15.9 | 70 687 | 15.8 | 21.7 | 8.2 | 11.5 | 7.6 | 23.6 | 42.5 |
| Montana........................... | 1 573 | 1 096 | 431 | 23 893 | 44 222 | 27.6 | 13.2 | 65 695 | 14.8 | 19.1 | 8.1 | 9.7 | 7.9 | 20.2 | 42.5 |
| Nebraska......................... | 7 449 | 5 504 | 1 666 | 26 243 | 50 296 | 23.9 | 17.6 | 75 495 | 13.1 | 17.6 | 7.8 | 9.1 | 6.9 | 17.5 | 40.6 |
| Nevada............................ | 10 190 | 7 884 | 1 076 | 24 968 | 48 927 | 23.6 | 18.3 | 65 212 | 15.9 | 21.6 | 9.4 | 11.9 | 11.6 | 18.8 | 32.1 |
| New Hampshire................ | 3 485 | 2 709 | 259 | 31 871 | 62 647 | 18.1 | 27.2 | 97 441 | 8.8 | 11.7 | 6.2 | 5.6 | 3.5 | 11.3 | 31.6 |
| New Jersey...................... | 37 035 | 28 781 | 3 040 | 34 090 | 67 458 | 18.5 | 32.9 | 101 682 | 10.4 | 14.5 | 7.8 | 7.8 | 4.7 | 17.4 | 30.8 |
| New Mexico...................... | 2 980 | 2 449 | 122 | 22 829 | 41 963 | 31.1 | 15.8 | 60 368 | 21.5 | 30.6 | 11.8 | 16.6 | 13.7 | 30.5 | 45.7 |
| New York.......................... | 79 189 | 46 215 | 10 831 | 30 679 | 55 246 | 24.5 | 25.5 | 81 522 | 16.0 | 22.3 | 11.7 | 12.3 | 8.8 | 24.4 | 38.7 |
| North Carolina.................. | 28 747 | 24 189 | 1 937 | 24 107 | 43 916 | 28.4 | 16.2 | 63 665 | 17.9 | 25.3 | 9.7 | 13.2 | 9.4 | 27.2 | 44.2 |
| North Dakota.................... | 4 288 | 2 459 | 1 730 | 28 055 | 51 704 | 24.2 | 18.7 | 84 896 | 12.2 | 14.1 | 10.5 | 7.9 | 4.0 | 18.0 | 43.9 |
| Ohio................................ | 45 535 | 42 011 | 2 319 | 24 750 | 45 749 | 27.4 | 16.3 | 72 764 | 16.4 | 23.8 | 7.7 | 12.0 | 7.9 | 27.4 | 45.6 |
| Oklahoma........................ | 6 576 | 5 530 | 416 | 23 016 | 43 225 | 28.8 | 14.5 | 63 069 | 17.2 | 23.0 | 9.5 | 12.8 | 9.5 | 21.3 | 43.9 |
| Oregon............................ | 18 300 | 13 100 | 3 355 | 25 228 | 46 816 | 26.4 | 16.5 | 65 950 | 17.5 | 23.2 | 7.4 | 11.9 | 10.7 | 25.9 | 44.7 |
| Pennsylvania ................... | 38 869 | 30 724 | 3 093 | 26 933 | 50 228 | 25.0 | 19.4 | 80 414 | 13.8 | 19.2 | 8.0 | 9.6 | 5.5 | 21.9 | 41.2 |
| Rhode Island.................... | 2 376 | 1 520 | 682 | 29 277 | 53 636 | 24.8 | 23.5 | 82 086 | 14.7 | 21.6 | 10.2 | 10.6 | 6.6 | 16.7 | 41.9 |
| South Carolina................. | 24 247 | 23 039 | 680 | 22 598 | 42 367 | 30.0 | 14.8 | 60 143 | 18.9 | 27.6 | 10.1 | 14.3 | 9.7 | 28.5 | 47.4 |
| South Dakota................... | 1 550 | 1 454 | 71 | 15.0 | 72 460 | 13.9 | 17.8 | 11.1 | 9.6 | 5.1 | 29.9 | 38.9 | | | |
| Tennessee....................... | 31 126 | 22 922 | 1 742 | 23 320 | 41 693 | 30.2 | 14.4 | 63 719 | 18.3 | 26.0 | 10.7 | 13.7 | 10.8 | 31.3 | 46.1 |
| Texas.............................. | 265 352 | 210 597 | 13 673 | 24 682 | 49 392 | 25.5 | 20.4 | 65 932 | 18.5 | 26.4 | 11.4 | 14.4 | 12.5 | 24.7 | 42.3 |
| Utah................................ | 18 939 | 17 622 | 678 | 22 497 | 55 869 | 19.9 | 19.7 | 65 240 | 13.5 | 15.6 | 5.3 | 10.4 | 8.6 | 21.2 | 40.1 |
| Vermont .......................... | 4 306 | 2 808 | 88 | 28 089 | 52 776 | 22.1 | 18.7 | 84 011 | 11.5 | 14.2 | 7.0 | 6.9 | 5.1 | 16.7 | 33.9 |
| Virginia............................ | 18 239 | 14 058 | 2 472 | 32 123 | 61 882 | 19.3 | 28.5 | 89 803 | 11.5 | 15.0 | 7.5 | 8.2 | 5.0 | 15.4 | 34.9 |
| Washington...................... | 75 525 | 56 814 | 15 863 | 29 278 | 56 835 | 20.6 | 23.3 | 81 582 | 13.9 | 17.8 | 8.5 | 9.4 | 7.2 | 19.5 | 37.1 |
| West Virginia ................... | 11 362 | 3 611 | 7 498 | 22 060 | 38 482 | 33.8 | 12.4 | 65 403 | 18.6 | 25.3 | 9.4 | 13.7 | 11.6 | 25.7 | 51.6 |
| Wisconsin ........................ | 23 097 | 20 427 | 1 109 | 26 212 | 50 395 | 23.7 | 17.3 | 79 648 | 13.1 | 17.9 | 7.5 | 8.8 | 5.7 | 21.9 | 39.3 |
| Wyoming.......................... | 1 421 | 1 255 | 130 | 27 973 | 56 322 | 19.4 | 20.7 | 77 137 | 11.3 | 15.2 | 6.2 | 7.9 | 6.8 | 18.8 | 37.5 |

1. No spouse present.

# Table A. States — **Personal Income**

| | Personal income, 2011 | | | | | | | | | | | | |
| STATE | | | Per capita[1] | | Sources of personal income (mil dol) | | | | | | | | |
| | | | | | | | | | Transfer payments | | | | |
| | | | | | | | | | | Government payments to individuals | | | |
| | Total (mil dol) | Percent change, 2010–2011 | Dollars | Rank | Wages and salaries[2] | Proprietors' income | Dividends, interest, and rent | Total | Total | Social Security | Medical payments | Income main-tenance | Unemploy-ment insurance |
|---|---|---|---|---|---|---|---|---|---|---|---|---|---|
| | 134 | 135 | 136 | 137 | 138 | 139 | 140 | 141 | 142 | 143 | 144 | 145 | 146 |
| UNITED STATES............... | 12 949 905 | 5.2 | 41 560 | X | 8 273 601 | 1 180 598 | 2 093 469 | 2 319 212 | 2 249 960 | 713 276 | 974 728 | 278 037 | 108 555 |
| Alabama............................. | 167 517 | 3.8 | 34 880 | 43 | 100 742 | 12 848 | 25 631 | 38 248 | 37 103 | 13 163 | 14 534 | 5 376 | 935 |
| Alaska................................ | 33 003 | 5.6 | 45 665 | 11 | 24 029 | 3 133 | 4 876 | 5 166 | 5 011 | 1 010 | 2 041 | 613 | 268 |
| Arizona.............................. | 227 287 | 4.9 | 35 062 | 42 | 140 994 | 17 947 | 35 899 | 47 519 | 46 089 | 14 751 | 19 578 | 5 095 | 1 335 |
| Arkansas........................... | 99 127 | 4.8 | 33 740 | 46 | 58 694 | 7 810 | 16 158 | 23 871 | 23 222 | 7 968 | 9 794 | 2 785 | 709 |
| California........................... | 1 645 138 | 5.2 | 43 647 | 18 | 1 053 192 | 155 507 | 288 922 | 261 743 | 253 437 | 66 693 | 112 081 | 34 586 | 17 694 |
| Colorado............................ | 225 410 | 6.1 | 44 053 | 14 | 147 569 | 25 801 | 37 699 | 29 542 | 28 419 | 9 386 | 11 236 | 2 878 | 1 831 |
| Connecticut ...................... | 207 329 | 4.6 | 57 902 | 2 | 125 819 | 21 222 | 40 015 | 28 961 | 28 170 | 9 115 | 13 280 | 2 540 | 1 966 |
| Delaware ........................... | 37 600 | 6.0 | 41 449 | 23 | 26 453 | 2 980 | 5 810 | 7 370 | 7 170 | 2 483 | 3 294 | 665 | 264 |
| District of Columbia............ | 45 598 | 5.8 | 73 783 | 1 | 78 568 | 5 950 | 5 542 | 5 744 | 5 608 | 904 | 3 168 | 902 | 304 |
| Florida .............................. | 755 358 | 4.6 | 39 636 | 27 | 411 815 | 47 242 | 187 304 | 153 284 | 148 828 | 51 009 | 64 484 | 17 695 | 4 467 |
| Georgia ............................. | 353 142 | 5.3 | 35 979 | 40 | 235 756 | 29 006 | 51 490 | 62 981 | 60 823 | 19 588 | 23 157 | 9 871 | 2 557 |
| Hawaii ............................... | 59 014 | 5.7 | 42 925 | 19 | 39 472 | 3 778 | 10 653 | 9 417 | 9 124 | 3 057 | 3 643 | 1 304 | 489 |
| Idaho ................................. | 52 116 | 5.1 | 32 881 | 50 | 30 066 | 6 355 | 8 650 | 10 093 | 9 743 | 3 551 | 3 625 | 1 157 | 443 |
| Illinois ............................... | 562 662 | 4.3 | 43 721 | 17 | 377 568 | 48 260 | 91 355 | 87 461 | 84 617 | 28 203 | 34 361 | 11 030 | 5 490 |
| Indiana .............................. | 232 586 | 5.3 | 35 689 | 41 | 150 322 | 18 214 | 30 987 | 46 177 | 44 735 | 16 717 | 17 705 | 4 889 | 2 030 |
| Iowa................................... | 126 032 | 9.1 | 41 156 | 24 | 74 924 | 18 158 | 18 783 | 22 176 | 21 498 | 7 844 | 8 710 | 2 082 | 852 |
| Kansas.............................. | 117 386 | 6.5 | 40 883 | 25 | 74 110 | 13 024 | 18 415 | 19 310 | 18 680 | 6 708 | 7 663 | 2 105 | 839 |
| Kentucky ........................... | 148 510 | 5.1 | 33 989 | 45 | 96 276 | 10 585 | 19 955 | 35 720 | 34 760 | 11 385 | 14 335 | 4 488 | 1 377 |
| Louisiana........................... | 176 356 | 4.5 | 38 549 | 29 | 108 485 | 17 175 | 26 806 | 34 843 | 33 697 | 9 947 | 15 681 | 5 145 | 658 |
| Maine................................. | 50 869 | 4.6 | 38 299 | 30 | 30 155 | 4 021 | 7 646 | 11 701 | 11 408 | 3 742 | 5 262 | 1 224 | 363 |
| Maryland ........................... | 295 236 | 5.0 | 50 656 | 6 | 182 430 | 20 090 | 46 603 | 39 464 | 38 182 | 11 885 | 17 572 | 4 253 | 1 702 |
| Massachusetts ................... | 352 243 | 5.1 | 53 471 | 3 | 239 035 | 29 870 | 58 208 | 55 951 | 54 494 | 15 446 | 26 592 | 6 425 | 3 733 |
| Michigan ............................ | 358 152 | 5.6 | 36 264 | 37 | 227 396 | 25 069 | 49 359 | 81 711 | 79 526 | 28 284 | 32 247 | 10 459 | 3 875 |
| Minnesota .......................... | 238 166 | 5.5 | 44 560 | 12 | 160 186 | 20 444 | 38 934 | 38 651 | 37 469 | 12 129 | 16 755 | 3 768 | 1 846 |
| Mississippi ........................ | 95 313 | 4.1 | 32 000 | 51 | 54 169 | 8 081 | 11 882 | 24 768 | 24 047 | 7 419 | 10 886 | 3 673 | 508 |
| Missouri............................. | 228 218 | 4.6 | 37 969 | 31 | 146 657 | 21 078 | 35 245 | 46 044 | 44 717 | 15 423 | 19 929 | 4 719 | 1 500 |
| Montana ............................ | 35 952 | 5.4 | 36 016 | 39 | 20 935 | 3 521 | 7 352 | 6 917 | 6 697 | 2 486 | 2 492 | 651 | 248 |
| Nebraska........................... | 78 220 | 8.4 | 42 450 | 20 | 48 628 | 11 725 | 12 847 | 11 897 | 11 490 | 4 095 | 4 760 | 1 152 | 307 |
| Nevada.............................. | 100 665 | 4.0 | 36 964 | 35 | 64 090 | 7 898 | 19 413 | 16 552 | 15 952 | 5 609 | 5 815 | 1 885 | 1 475 |
| New Hampshire .................. | 60 480 | 4.5 | 45 881 | 10 | 36 546 | 5 586 | 8 852 | 8 934 | 8 642 | 3 556 | 3 450 | 861 | 223 |
| New Jersey ........................ | 462 494 | 4.2 | 52 430 | 4 | 273 352 | 40 181 | 71 603 | 69 895 | 67 945 | 21 875 | 29 244 | 6 476 | 6 316 |
| New Mexico ....................... | 71 073 | 4.4 | 34 133 | 44 | 43 700 | 5 318 | 10 591 | 15 990 | 15 532 | 4 526 | 6 671 | 2 224 | 640 |
| New York ........................... | 995 185 | 4.5 | 51 126 | 5 | 662 290 | 107 108 | 161 174 | 182 843 | 178 541 | 45 840 | 93 403 | 22 178 | 7 544 |
| North Carolina.................... | 347 905 | 5.2 | 36 028 | 38 | 227 690 | 24 656 | 51 690 | 71 211 | 69 101 | 23 515 | 27 985 | 8 636 | 4 113 |
| North Dakota...................... | 32 306 | 12.8 | 47 236 | 8 | 21 286 | 5 084 | 4 906 | 4 510 | 4 360 | 1 520 | 1 827 | 414 | 95 |
| Ohio................................... | 436 818 | 5.4 | 37 836 | 32 | 283 910 | 34 430 | 58 789 | 93 528 | 90 974 | 28 633 | 38 965 | 11 120 | 3 350 |
| Oklahoma........................... | 142 862 | 6.9 | 37 679 | 33 | 85 026 | 17 201 | 21 512 | 27 882 | 27 048 | 9 141 | 11 225 | 3 274 | 619 |
| Oregon.............................. | 145 300 | 5.4 | 37 527 | 34 | 93 001 | 11 371 | 26 016 | 29 487 | 28 630 | 9 747 | 10 782 | 3 324 | 2 011 |
| Pennsylvania...................... | 538 909 | 4.8 | 42 291 | 21 | 336 565 | 44 925 | 80 802 | 110 439 | 107 620 | 35 674 | 48 884 | 10 190 | 6 567 |
| Rhode Island...................... | 46 125 | 4.3 | 43 875 | 16 | 27 864 | 3 232 | 7 505 | 9 515 | 9 283 | 2 740 | 4 205 | 1 065 | 609 |
| South Carolina ................... | 156 231 | 4.7 | 33 388 | 49 | 96 784 | 9 965 | 22 107 | 36 270 | 35 242 | 12 459 | 13 592 | 4 572 | 1 232 |
| South Dakota...................... | 36 439 | 12.8 | 44 217 | 13 | 19 011 | 7 301 | 7 209 | 5 369 | 5 187 | 1 935 | 2 129 | 563 | 61 |
| Tennessee ......................... | 234 154 | 4.9 | 36 567 | 36 | 144 048 | 27 717 | 28 652 | 50 835 | 49 421 | 16 520 | 21 027 | 6 805 | 1 633 |
| Texas................................. | 1 030 750 | 6.8 | 40 147 | 26 | 659 450 | 138 170 | 142 470 | 160 440 | 154 756 | 44 990 | 69 084 | 22 904 | 5 671 |
| Utah................................... | 94 401 | 5.9 | 33 509 | 47 | 65 634 | 8 073 | 14 739 | 13 437 | 12 815 | 4 387 | 4 711 | 1 762 | 522 |
| Vermont.............................. | 26 042 | 4.7 | 41 572 | 22 | 15 598 | 2 176 | 4 416 | 5 371 | 5 233 | 1 711 | 2 412 | 602 | 165 |
| Virginia.............................. | 373 312 | 5.4 | 46 107 | 9 | 257 102 | 23 144 | 57 609 | 50 329 | 48 566 | 17 408 | 19 272 | 5 601 | 1 259 |
| Washington ........................ | 299 685 | 5.8 | 43 878 | 15 | 195 845 | 24 281 | 51 035 | 49 152 | 47 655 | 15 324 | 17 420 | 5 853 | 3 225 |
| West Virginia ...................... | 61 976 | 5.1 | 33 403 | 48 | 36 879 | 4 068 | 7 278 | 17 034 | 16 624 | 5 870 | 6 918 | 1 850 | 411 |
| Wisconsin .......................... | 226 042 | 4.5 | 39 575 | 28 | 147 053 | 17 137 | 35 513 | 39 852 | 38 588 | 14 664 | 15 507 | 4 079 | 2 079 |
| Wyoming ............................ | 27 214 | 6.3 | 47 898 | 7 | 16 433 | 2 680 | 6 563 | 3 606 | 3 481 | 1 241 | 1 335 | 270 | 144 |

1. Based on the resident population estimated as of July 1 of the year shown.    2. Includes supplements to wages and salaries.

# Table A. States — Personal Income and Earnings

| STATE | Personal tax payments, 2011 (mil dol) | Disposable personal income, 2011 Total (mil dol) | Per capita[1] (dollars) | Earnings, 2011 Total (mil dol) | Farm | Goods-related[2] Total | Manu-facturing | Service-related and other[3] Total | Retail trade | Finance, insurance, real estate, rental and leasing | Health care and social assist-ance | Government | Gross state product, 2011 (mil dol) |
|---|---|---|---|---|---|---|---|---|---|---|---|---|---|
| | 147 | 148 | 149 | 150 | 151 | 152 | 153 | 154 | 155 | 156 | 157 | 158 | 159 |
| UNITED STATES | 1 396 553 | 11 553 352 | 37 078 | 9 454 199 | 1.1 | 16.5 | 10.0 | 64.8 | 6.1 | 9.3 | 11.0 | 17.6 | 14 981 020 |
| Alabama | 14 530 | 152 988 | 31 854 | 113 590 | 0.4 | 20.2 | 13.4 | 56.4 | 6.9 | 6.3 | 10.6 | 22.9 | 173 122 |
| Alaska | 3 068 | 29 935 | 41 420 | 27 162 | 0.0 | 18.1 | 2.7 | 49.4 | 5.5 | 5.0 | 10.3 | 32.5 | 51 376 |
| Arizona | 19 749 | 207 538 | 32 015 | 158 942 | 0.7 | 14.6 | 8.4 | 66.6 | 7.9 | 9.4 | 12.5 | 18.1 | 258 447 |
| Arkansas | 8 582 | 90 545 | 30 819 | 66 505 | 2.1 | 19.8 | 13.0 | 58.4 | 7.0 | 5.7 | 11.7 | 19.8 | 105 846 |
| California | 201 246 | 1 443 892 | 38 308 | 1 208 698 | 1.3 | 15.4 | 10.3 | 66.3 | 6.0 | 8.0 | 9.6 | 17.1 | 1 958 904 |
| Colorado | 24 723 | 200 688 | 39 221 | 173 370 | 0.7 | 15.0 | 6.2 | 66.6 | 5.5 | 9.7 | 8.8 | 17.7 | 264 308 |
| Connecticut | 32 329 | 175 000 | 48 873 | 147 040 | 0.1 | 16.5 | 11.7 | 70.1 | 5.4 | 18.7 | 11.5 | 13.3 | 230 090 |
| Delaware | 4 289 | 33 311 | 36 721 | 29 433 | 0.5 | 12.2 | 6.7 | 71.1 | 6.0 | 15.8 | 12.6 | 16.1 | 65 755 |
| District of Columbia | 5 284 | 40 314 | 65 233 | 84 518 | 0.0 | 1.4 | 0.2 | 55.7 | 0.9 | 4.7 | 5.3 | 42.8 | 107 593 |
| Florida | 65 997 | 689 361 | 36 173 | 459 056 | 0.5 | 9.9 | 4.9 | 72.2 | 7.9 | 9.8 | 13.0 | 17.5 | 754 255 |
| Georgia | 34 833 | 318 309 | 32 430 | 264 761 | 0.7 | 14.2 | 9.4 | 65.9 | 6.1 | 8.2 | 9.5 | 19.1 | 418 943 |
| Hawaii | 5 297 | 53 717 | 39 073 | 43 250 | 0.7 | 8.8 | 1.8 | 55.0 | 6.0 | 5.4 | 9.4 | 35.6 | 66 991 |
| Idaho | 4 391 | 47 725 | 30 111 | 36 421 | 5.9 | 17.0 | 10.1 | 58.8 | 7.6 | 5.8 | 11.5 | 18.3 | 57 927 |
| Illinois | 63 371 | 499 291 | 38 797 | 425 828 | 1.4 | 16.4 | 11.5 | 67.5 | 5.2 | 10.8 | 10.2 | 14.7 | 670 727 |
| Indiana | 22 746 | 209 840 | 32 199 | 168 537 | 1.8 | 27.7 | 21.2 | 55.8 | 6.1 | 5.7 | 12.4 | 14.7 | 278 128 |
| Iowa | 11 485 | 114 547 | 37 406 | 93 082 | 10.1 | 21.1 | 15.3 | 53.1 | 6.2 | 9.5 | 9.8 | 15.7 | 148 986 |
| Kansas | 11 704 | 105 682 | 36 807 | 87 133 | 4.2 | 20.5 | 14.1 | 55.4 | 5.8 | 6.7 | 10.6 | 19.9 | 130 923 |
| Kentucky | 14 117 | 134 393 | 30 758 | 106 861 | 1.0 | 20.6 | 13.6 | 55.6 | 6.4 | 6.1 | 12.1 | 22.8 | 164 799 |
| Louisiana | 14 826 | 161 530 | 35 308 | 125 660 | 0.8 | 23.0 | 10.1 | 57.1 | 6.4 | 5.9 | 10.9 | 19.1 | 247 720 |
| Maine | 4 764 | 46 105 | 34 713 | 34 176 | 0.6 | 16.8 | 10.4 | 63.7 | 8.3 | 7.4 | 16.3 | 18.9 | 51 585 |
| Maryland | 36 434 | 258 802 | 44 404 | 202 520 | 0.2 | 12.0 | 5.0 | 61.8 | 5.5 | 7.3 | 11.0 | 26.0 | 301 100 |
| Massachusetts | 49 477 | 302 765 | 45 960 | 268 905 | 0.1 | 14.1 | 9.4 | 73.9 | 4.8 | 12.7 | 13.5 | 11.9 | 391 771 |
| Michigan | 35 685 | 322 467 | 32 651 | 252 466 | 1.1 | 21.2 | 16.5 | 61.8 | 6.2 | 6.2 | 12.8 | 15.9 | 385 248 |
| Minnesota | 28 344 | 209 822 | 39 257 | 180 631 | 2.9 | 18.0 | 13.0 | 65.3 | 5.3 | 10.0 | 12.4 | 13.8 | 281 712 |
| Mississippi | 7 406 | 87 906 | 29 514 | 62 249 | 1.8 | 20.6 | 12.6 | 52.6 | 7.4 | 4.9 | 11.1 | 25.0 | 97 810 |
| Missouri | 21 555 | 206 664 | 34 383 | 167 736 | 1.4 | 16.3 | 10.5 | 65.4 | 6.5 | 7.6 | 12.0 | 16.8 | 249 525 |
| Montana | 3 392 | 32 559 | 32 618 | 24 455 | 2.5 | 15.1 | 4.3 | 59.8 | 8.2 | 6.0 | 13.5 | 22.6 | 37 990 |
| Nebraska | 7 358 | 70 862 | 38 457 | 60 353 | 9.8 | 15.2 | 9.2 | 57.9 | 5.7 | 8.1 | 10.4 | 17.0 | 94 160 |
| Nevada | 9 337 | 91 328 | 33 536 | 71 989 | 0.3 | 12.3 | 3.7 | 70.3 | 7.1 | 7.0 | 9.0 | 17.1 | 130 366 |
| New Hampshire | 5 812 | 54 669 | 41 472 | 42 133 | 0.1 | 19.2 | 12.9 | 67.4 | 8.9 | 8.9 | 13.1 | 13.3 | 63 556 |
| New Jersey | 58 047 | 404 447 | 45 850 | 313 533 | 0.1 | 13.4 | 8.5 | 71.0 | 6.4 | 10.6 | 11.2 | 15.4 | 486 989 |
| New Mexico | 5 708 | 65 365 | 31 392 | 49 018 | 2.5 | 14.8 | 4.5 | 54.7 | 6.7 | 4.6 | 11.2 | 28.0 | 79 414 |
| New York | 147 987 | 847 190 | 43 524 | 769 398 | 0.2 | 9.0 | 4.8 | 75.8 | 5.0 | 20.5 | 10.9 | 15.0 | 1 157 969 |
| North Carolina | 34 028 | 313 877 | 32 505 | 252 346 | 0.9 | 17.6 | 12.3 | 59.6 | 6.3 | 8.2 | 10.3 | 21.9 | 439 862 |
| North Dakota | 3 245 | 29 062 | 42 492 | 26 370 | 12.0 | 19.4 | 5.3 | 50.8 | 5.9 | 5.9 | 10.7 | 17.8 | 40 328 |
| Ohio | 44 942 | 391 876 | 33 943 | 318 341 | 1.1 | 20.7 | 15.3 | 62.6 | 6.2 | 7.6 | 13.0 | 15.7 | 483 962 |
| Oklahoma | 12 751 | 130 151 | 34 327 | 102 227 | 0.9 | 23.9 | 9.4 | 53.4 | 6.6 | 5.8 | 10.2 | 21.8 | 154 966 |
| Oregon | 16 129 | 129 171 | 33 361 | 104 372 | 1.3 | 18.6 | 12.9 | 62.7 | 6.7 | 6.4 | 12.7 | 17.4 | 194 742 |
| Pennsylvania | 59 174 | 479 735 | 37 647 | 381 490 | 0.4 | 17.6 | 11.0 | 68.6 | 5.9 | 8.2 | 14.4 | 13.3 | 578 839 |
| Rhode Island | 4 722 | 41 404 | 39 383 | 31 097 | 0.0 | 14.1 | 9.1 | 67.1 | 5.7 | 9.9 | 14.8 | 18.5 | 50 091 |
| South Carolina | 13 384 | 142 847 | 30 528 | 106 749 | 0.3 | 19.4 | 13.9 | 57.5 | 7.4 | 6.9 | 9.4 | 22.8 | 165 785 |
| South Dakota | 2 542 | 33 897 | 41 133 | 26 312 | 18.4 | 14.1 | 8.4 | 50.8 | 6.4 | 7.0 | 12.7 | 16.8 | 40 117 |
| Tennessee | 16 733 | 217 420 | 33 954 | 171 765 | 0.2 | 18.5 | 12.4 | 66.4 | 7.3 | 7.4 | 14.8 | 14.9 | 266 527 |
| Texas | 90 255 | 940 495 | 36 631 | 797 621 | 0.5 | 22.9 | 9.6 | 61.0 | 5.9 | 8.3 | 9.4 | 15.7 | 1 308 132 |
| Utah | 8 743 | 85 658 | 30 405 | 73 707 | 0.4 | 18.9 | 10.6 | 61.7 | 7.4 | 8.3 | 8.8 | 19.0 | 124 483 |
| Vermont | 2 417 | 23 625 | 37 714 | 17 775 | 1.3 | 19.2 | 12.0 | 60.6 | 8.0 | 5.9 | 14.3 | 18.8 | 25 905 |
| Virginia | 44 521 | 328 790 | 40 608 | 280 246 | 0.2 | 11.3 | 5.8 | 63.0 | 5.0 | 6.5 | 8.5 | 25.5 | 428 909 |
| Washington | 26 758 | 272 928 | 39 960 | 220 126 | 1.4 | 16.7 | 10.9 | 61.5 | 6.4 | 6.0 | 10.2 | 20.4 | 355 083 |
| West Virginia | 5 630 | 56 346 | 30 369 | 40 946 | -0.1 | 23.3 | 8.7 | 54.1 | 7.0 | 4.3 | 14.2 | 22.7 | 66 821 |
| Wisconsin | 24 077 | 201 965 | 35 359 | 164 189 | 1.8 | 24.6 | 19.3 | 58.8 | 6.1 | 7.6 | 12.7 | 14.8 | 254 818 |
| Wyoming | 2 673 | 24 541 | 43 194 | 19 112 | 1.3 | 29.5 | 3.9 | 45.4 | 6.0 | 5.2 | 7.4 | 23.9 | 37 617 |

1. Based on the resident population estimated as of July 1 of the year shown.    2. Includes mining, construction, and manufacturing.    3. Includes private sector earnings in forestry, fishing, related activities, and other; utilities; wholesale trade; transportation and warehousing; and information.

# Table A. States — Social Security, Employment, and Labor Force

| STATE | Social Security beneficiaries, December 2011 | | Supplemental Security Income recipients, December 2011 | Civilian employment and selected occupations,[2] 2011 | | | | Civilian labor force (annual average), 2012 | | | | |
|---|---|---|---|---|---|---|---|---|---|---|---|---|
| | | | | | Percent | | | | | | Unemployed | |
| | Number | Rate[1] | | Total | Management, business, science and art occupations | Services, sales, and office occupations | Construction and production occupations | Total (1,000) | Percent change, 2011–2012 | Employed (1,000) | Total (1,000) | Rate[3] |
| | 160 | 161 | 162 | 163 | 164 | 165 | 166 | 167 | 168 | 169 | 170 | 171 |
| UNITED STATES | 53 972 162 | 173.2 | 8 111 751 | 140 399 548 | 36.0 | 42.8 | 21.2 | 154 975 | 0.9 | 142 469 | 12 506 | 8.1 |
| Alabama | 1 037 438 | 216.0 | 174 853 | 1 981 095 | 32.9 | 41.8 | 25.3 | 2 156 | -1.2 | 1 999 | 157 | 7.3 |
| Alaska | 82 109 | 113.6 | 12 719 | 344 343 | 36.0 | 40.5 | 23.5 | 366 | 0.2 | 341 | 26 | 7.0 |
| Arizona | 1 104 545 | 170.4 | 112 939 | 2 687 991 | 34.3 | 47.0 | 18.7 | 3 030 | -0.6 | 2 779 | 252 | 8.3 |
| Arkansas | 647 077 | 220.2 | 109 660 | 1 235 755 | 31.1 | 42.1 | 26.9 | 1 356 | -0.3 | 1 257 | 99 | 7.3 |
| California | 5 129 529 | 136.1 | 1 284 629 | 16 426 694 | 36.7 | 43.2 | 20.2 | 18 495 | 0.5 | 16 560 | 1 935 | 10.5 |
| Colorado | 721 274 | 141.0 | 68 815 | 2 492 419 | 40.1 | 41.4 | 18.5 | 2 743 | 0.7 | 2 524 | 220 | 8.0 |
| Connecticut | 630 447 | 176.1 | 59 784 | 1 742 494 | 40.9 | 42.0 | 17.1 | 1 879 | -1.2 | 1 722 | 157 | 8.4 |
| Delaware | 176 885 | 195.0 | 16 240 | 420 365 | 37.6 | 41.9 | 20.5 | 444 | 0.8 | 412 | 32 | 7.1 |
| District of Columbia | 75 755 | 122.6 | 25 633 | 310 607 | 60.8 | 31.8 | 7.4 | 362 | 3.9 | 329 | 32 | 8.9 |
| Florida | 3 894 179 | 204.3 | 506 458 | 8 101 898 | 33.1 | 49.0 | 18.0 | 9 369 | 1.0 | 8 562 | 807 | 8.6 |
| Georgia | 1 524 263 | 155.3 | 238 903 | 4 193 776 | 35.2 | 42.2 | 22.6 | 4 806 | 0.8 | 4 372 | 434 | 9.0 |
| Hawaii | 234 314 | 170.4 | 25 356 | 629 523 | 34.0 | 47.5 | 18.5 | 652 | -0.9 | 614 | 38 | 5.8 |
| Idaho | 278 563 | 175.8 | 28 213 | 684 916 | 33.8 | 42.0 | 24.2 | 773 | 0.9 | 719 | 55 | 7.1 |
| Illinois | 2 065 432 | 160.5 | 276 258 | 5 926 849 | 36.0 | 42.5 | 21.4 | 6 593 | 0.2 | 6 008 | 585 | 8.9 |
| Indiana | 1 219 879 | 187.2 | 122 130 | 2 934 500 | 31.9 | 41.2 | 26.9 | 3 150 | -0.3 | 2 886 | 264 | 8.4 |
| Iowa | 592 000 | 193.3 | 48 927 | 1 538 756 | 33.8 | 41.2 | 25.0 | 1 639 | -1.3 | 1 553 | 86 | 5.2 |
| Kansas | 498 707 | 173.7 | 47 336 | 1 389 038 | 36.3 | 40.4 | 23.3 | 1 489 | -0.6 | 1 404 | 85 | 5.7 |
| Kentucky | 913 548 | 209.1 | 192 721 | 1 838 401 | 32.9 | 41.1 | 26.0 | 2 075 | 0.2 | 1 904 | 171 | 8.2 |
| Louisiana | 809 450 | 176.9 | 178 806 | 1 973 939 | 31.1 | 44.3 | 24.6 | 2 084 | 0.7 | 1 949 | 134 | 6.4 |
| Maine | 306 600 | 230.8 | 36 259 | 643 104 | 35.1 | 42.8 | 22.0 | 706 | 0.4 | 655 | 52 | 7.3 |
| Maryland | 872 919 | 149.8 | 111 494 | 2 894 566 | 43.7 | 40.5 | 15.8 | 3 123 | 1.0 | 2 910 | 213 | 6.8 |
| Massachusetts | 1 161 122 | 176.3 | 197 327 | 3 284 720 | 43.3 | 40.7 | 16.0 | 3 475 | 0.2 | 3 242 | 234 | 6.7 |
| Michigan | 2 016 684 | 204.2 | 264 706 | 4 191 878 | 34.6 | 42.6 | 22.9 | 4 657 | -0.4 | 4 232 | 426 | 9.1 |
| Minnesota | 904 803 | 169.3 | 88 768 | 2 728 881 | 38.7 | 40.4 | 20.8 | 2 969 | 0.0 | 2 802 | 168 | 5.6 |
| Mississippi | 609 651 | 204.7 | 126 223 | 1 181 295 | 31.1 | 40.8 | 28.1 | 1 333 | -0.4 | 1 211 | 122 | 9.2 |
| Missouri | 1 188 437 | 197.7 | 137 167 | 2 742 057 | 34.5 | 43.3 | 22.3 | 2 993 | -1.0 | 2 785 | 207 | 6.9 |
| Montana | 198 230 | 198.6 | 18 196 | 479 988 | 34.3 | 43.7 | 21.9 | 508 | 1.7 | 477 | 31 | 6.0 |
| Nebraska | 313 087 | 169.9 | 26 501 | 943 643 | 34.0 | 41.1 | 24.8 | 1 021 | 1.4 | 981 | 40 | 3.9 |
| Nevada | 424 836 | 156.0 | 44 064 | 1 204 882 | 27.2 | 54.4 | 18.4 | 1 379 | -0.9 | 1 226 | 152 | 11.1 |
| New Hampshire | 262 952 | 199.5 | 18 695 | 684 806 | 39.8 | 39.8 | 20.5 | 742 | 0.6 | 701 | 41 | 5.5 |
| New Jersey | 1 500 403 | 170.1 | 173 000 | 4 152 513 | 40.4 | 42.2 | 17.5 | 4 595 | 1.1 | 4 159 | 436 | 9.5 |
| New Mexico | 370 911 | 178.1 | 61 806 | 869 773 | 35.5 | 43.8 | 20.7 | 936 | 0.5 | 871 | 65 | 6.9 |
| New York | 3 337 276 | 171.4 | 689 019 | 8 959 015 | 38.1 | 45.0 | 16.9 | 9 587 | 0.6 | 8 773 | 815 | 8.5 |
| North Carolina | 1 808 331 | 187.3 | 224 962 | 4 195 808 | 35.6 | 41.2 | 23.1 | 4 723 | 1.4 | 4 275 | 448 | 9.5 |
| North Dakota | 121 335 | 177.4 | 8 349 | 370 830 | 34.6 | 40.4 | 25.0 | 392 | 2.6 | 380 | 12 | 3.1 |
| Ohio | 2 166 271 | 187.6 | 295 042 | 5 213 453 | 34.2 | 42.4 | 23.4 | 5 748 | -1.0 | 5 335 | 413 | 7.2 |
| Oklahoma | 717 398 | 189.2 | 95 644 | 1 681 759 | 32.9 | 42.1 | 25.0 | 1 803 | 1.0 | 1 709 | 94 | 5.2 |
| Oregon | 734 841 | 189.8 | 78 143 | 1 710 336 | 36.0 | 42.6 | 21.4 | 1 963 | -0.6 | 1 792 | 171 | 8.7 |
| Pennsylvania | 2 617 879 | 205.4 | 367 586 | 5 853 320 | 35.7 | 42.2 | 22.1 | 6 487 | 1.4 | 5 973 | 513 | 7.9 |
| Rhode Island | 207 122 | 197.0 | 32 218 | 511 235 | 37.2 | 45.6 | 17.3 | 560 | -0.4 | 502 | 58 | 10.4 |
| South Carolina | 956 097 | 204.3 | 114 974 | 1 968 925 | 31.6 | 43.8 | 24.6 | 2 167 | 0.0 | 1 970 | 197 | 9.1 |
| South Dakota | 156 102 | 189.4 | 14 151 | 415 623 | 34.8 | 42.3 | 22.9 | 446 | 0.4 | 426 | 20 | 4.4 |
| Tennessee | 1 287 683 | 201.1 | 179 325 | 2 784 462 | 33.1 | 42.3 | 24.5 | 3 114 | -0.1 | 2 864 | 249 | 8.0 |
| Texas | 3 551 961 | 138.3 | 640 422 | 11 455 069 | 34.7 | 42.5 | 22.7 | 12 597 | 0.9 | 11 743 | 855 | 6.8 |
| Utah | 335 444 | 119.1 | 29 447 | 1 260 806 | 36.0 | 42.5 | 21.5 | 1 354 | 0.5 | 1 276 | 77 | 5.7 |
| Vermont | 132 268 | 211.1 | 15 652 | 327 302 | 40.5 | 38.5 | 21.0 | 356 | -0.6 | 339 | 18 | 5.0 |
| Virginia | 1 318 580 | 162.9 | 151 013 | 3 860 131 | 42.3 | 39.8 | 17.9 | 4 210 | 0.3 | 3 962 | 247 | 5.9 |
| Washington | 1 127 126 | 165.0 | 142 932 | 3 117 998 | 38.5 | 41.1 | 20.5 | 3 481 | 0.0 | 3 197 | 284 | 8.2 |
| West Virginia | 451 039 | 243.1 | 80 796 | 748 558 | 32.0 | 42.6 | 25.3 | 805 | 0.2 | 746 | 59 | 7.3 |
| Wisconsin | 1 085 632 | 190.1 | 110 959 | 2 819 477 | 33.5 | 40.8 | 25.8 | 3 052 | -0.4 | 2 840 | 211 | 6.9 |
| Wyoming | 93 748 | 165.0 | 6 531 | 289 976 | 31.3 | 39.7 | 29.0 | 306 | 0.9 | 290 | 16 | 5.4 |
| | | | | | | | | 155 049 | | | | |

1. Per 1,000 resident population estimated as of July 1 of the year shown.　　2. Persons 16 years old and over.　　3. Percent of civilian labor force.

## Table A. States — Nonfarm Employment and Earnings

Private nonfarm employment and earnings, 2012

| STATE | Employed Total (1,000) | Employed Percent change, 2011–2012 | Manufacturing Employment (1,000) | Mfg. Avg. earnings prod. workers Hourly | Mfg. Avg. earnings prod. workers Weekly | Construction | Transportation and public utilities | Wholesale trade | Retail trade | Information | Financial activities | Services[1] |
|---|---|---|---|---|---|---|---|---|---|---|---|---|
| | 172 | 173 | 174 | 175 | 176 | 177 | 178 | 179 | 180 | 181 | 182 | 183 |
| UNITED STATES | 133 739 | 1.7 | 11 919 | 19.08 | 794.81 | 5 641.0 | 25 516 | 5 672.7 | 14 874.9 | 2 678 | 7 786 | 57 432.0 |
| Alabama | 1 882.6 | 0.7 | 243 | 18.31 | 780.01 | 79.1 | 69.2 | 72.7 | 223.4 | 22.5 | 92.5 | 691.1 |
| Alaska | 334.1 | 1.4 | 14 | 17.89 | 763.90 | 16.6 | 21.8 | 6.2 | 35.8 | 6.2 | 13.3 | 119.6 |
| Arizona | 2 460.3 | 2.0 | 155 | 18.17 | 746.79 | 115.7 | 84.1 | 97.3 | 297.1 | 38.2 | 176.5 | 1 072.9 |
| Arkansas | 1 177.4 | 0.6 | 156 | 15.20 | 632.32 | 47.4 | 61.8 | 47.5 | 133.5 | 14.5 | 49.1 | 441.1 |
| California | 14 394.5 | 2.1 | 1 253 | 20.20 | 830.22 | 587.5 | 486.5 | 676.8 | 1 561.8 | 430.4 | 774.6 | 6 219.1 |
| Colorado | 2 310 | 2.3 | 132 | 25.13 | 947.40 | 115.1 | 71.4 | 94.1 | 243.5 | 69.7 | 146.1 | 1 013.2 |
| Connecticut | 1 639 | 0.8 | 165 | 23.94 | 967.18 | 51.1 | 50.3 | 63.3 | 181.8 | 31.1 | 132.3 | 724.9 |
| Delaware | 418.5 | 0.3 | 26 | 15.74 | 577.66 | 18.4 | 12.6 | 12.4 | 50.6 | 5.5 | 42.3 | 187.4 |
| District of Columbia | 731.8 | 0.8 | 1 | NA | NA | 13.5 | 4.1 | 5.0 | 18.7 | 17.3 | 28.1 | 401.6 |
| Florida | 7 400.1 | 1.8 | 317 | 19.64 | 803.28 | 341.5 | 240.4 | 317.7 | 979.0 | 133.4 | 497.5 | 3 489.5 |
| Georgia | 3 952.8 | 1.3 | 355 | 17.89 | 719.18 | 141.0 | 187.3 | 201.7 | 444.3 | 100.5 | 227.2 | 1 606.1 |
| Hawaii | 605.3 | 1.9 | 13 | 19.15 | 723.87 | 29.5 | 28.3 | 17.7 | 68.6 | 8.3 | 27.0 | 286.5 |
| Idaho | 622 | 1.9 | 57 | 20.92 | 847.26 | 31.3 | 21.6 | 27.3 | 77.3 | 9.3 | 30.3 | 247.5 |
| Illinois | 5 744.4 | 1.2 | 583 | 19.17 | 791.72 | 187.9 | 264.5 | 294.3 | 596.9 | 100.1 | 366.1 | 2 509.6 |
| Indiana | 2 902.1 | 2.1 | 482 | 18.50 | 771.45 | 124.4 | 132.3 | 116.5 | 312.8 | 35.5 | 130.3 | 1 132.8 |
| Iowa | 1 508.4 | 1.5 | 211 | 17.41 | 708.59 | 64.4 | 62.5 | 68.6 | 175.7 | 27.1 | 101.6 | 541.7 |
| Kansas | 1 357.8 | 1.4 | 163 | 18.46 | 779.01 | 55.1 | 55.8 | 59.0 | 142.3 | 28.3 | 74.6 | 510.6 |
| Kentucky | 1 824.4 | 1.6 | 223 | 18.43 | 748.26 | 67.3 | 95 | 73.0 | 202.7 | 26.3 | 86.7 | 692.5 |
| Louisiana | 1 925.6 | 1.3 | 142 | 20.43 | 870.32 | 126.5 | 83.1 | 72.5 | 222.5 | 24.9 | 94.0 | 755.3 |
| Maine | 597.6 | 0.5 | 51 | 20.50 | 846.65 | 25.6 | 16.8 | 19.4 | 81.1 | 7.9 | 31.4 | 260.8 |
| Maryland | 2 574.5 | 1.3 | 109 | 16.64 | 693.89 | 145.2 | 79.3 | 86.4 | 285.0 | 39.9 | 143.0 | 1 182.1 |
| Massachusetts | 3 273.6 | 1.4 | 252 | 20.90 | 831.82 | 114.6 | 84.8 | 121.1 | 344.8 | 86.8 | 206.2 | 1 625.3 |
| Michigan | 4 024.2 | 1.8 | 537 | 24.64 | 900.89 | 127.3 | 121.2 | 158.9 | 448.4 | 53.1 | 196.2 | 1 764.1 |
| Minnesota | 2 727.6 | 1.5 | 305 | 24.97 | 782.95 | 94.8 | 91.7 | 128.9 | 282.7 | 53.7 | 177.1 | 1 174.8 |
| Mississippi | 1 103.4 | 1.0 | 137 | 19.31 | 663.03 | 48.3 | 47.9 | 34.4 | 133.5 | 12.5 | 44.2 | 390.0 |
| Missouri | 2 669.4 | 0.5 | 248 | 21.46 | 740.05 | 104.0 | 93.7 | 117.8 | 302.3 | 58.2 | 164.1 | 1 139.5 |
| Montana | 440.5 | 2.2 | 18 | 17.88 | 656.20 | 22.9 | 16.7 | 16.3 | 55.3 | 6.9 | 21.4 | 184.3 |
| Nebraska | 2 669.4 | 0.5 | 95 | 19.50 | 670.59 | 42.9 | 52.7 | 41.3 | 105.2 | 17.2 | 70.9 | 366.6 |
| Nevada | 1 142.7 | 1.6 | 39 | 16.00 | 619.20 | 51.8 | 53.1 | 32.9 | 132.3 | 12.5 | 54.2 | 602.3 |
| New Hampshire | 633.2 | 1.0 | 66 | 26.06 | 748.77 | 22.2 | 14.7 | 26.7 | 94.3 | 12 | 34.9 | 270.1 |
| New Jersey | 3 895.5 | 1.2 | 246 | 19.33 | 802.20 | 130.4 | 165 | 213.3 | 444.0 | 77.7 | 249.0 | 1 748.9 |
| New Mexico | 804.1 | 0.1 | 30 | 15.70 | 648.41 | 40.7 | 23.2 | 21.2 | 90.6 | 13.6 | 33.0 | 334.0 |
| New York | 8 799.9 | 1.3 | 458 | 18.54 | 743.45 | 311.9 | 262.2 | 334.3 | 912.7 | 260.6 | 682.7 | 4 111.7 |
| North Carolina | 3 988.1 | 1.8 | 440 | 16.55 | 678.55 | 171.9 | 120.9 | 171.8 | 451.6 | 69.3 | 203.1 | 1 640.5 |
| North Dakota | 429.8 | 8.3 | 25 | 18.06 | 722.40 | 29.6 | 24.5 | 25.3 | 47.1 | 6.9 | 21.9 | 145.1 |
| Ohio | 5 171 | 1.5 | 656 | 19.35 | 801.09 | 933.5 | 188.5 | 224.2 | 558.7 | 74.4 | 279.3 | 2 240.7 |
| Oklahoma | 1 607.6 | 1.9 | 482 | 16.89 | 685.73 | 685.7 | 289.4 | 60.7 | 172.6 | 22.5 | 79.9 | 607.4 |
| Oregon | 1 638.2 | 1.1 | 211 | 18.67 | 752.40 | 752.4 | 316.4 | 75.2 | 187.0 | 32.5 | 90.2 | 659.6 |
| Pennsylvania | 5 729.7 | 0.7 | 567 | 18.26 | 734.05 | 734.1 | 241.3 | 227.5 | 633.1 | 90.2 | 310.2 | 2 675.6 |
| Rhode Island | 465 | 0.8 | 40 | 18.26 | 730.40 | 730.4 | 10.8 | 16.8 | 46.7 | 9.6 | 31.5 | 233.8 |
| South Carolina | 1 858.2 | 1.4 | 220 | 17.01 | 716.12 | 1 858.2 | 62.2 | 66.1 | 226.0 | 25.7 | 98.8 | 731.5 |
| South Dakota | 414 | 1.6 | 41 | 16.95 | 686.48 | 686.5 | 12.5 | 19.5 | 51.0 | 6.2 | 28.7 | 156.3 |
| Tennessee | 2 714.3 | 2.0 | 314 | 16.64 | 695.55 | 695.6 | 141.1 | 120.7 | 313.3 | 43 | 137.6 | 1 112.1 |
| Texas | 10 879.8 | 2.9 | 863 | 18.55 | 814.35 | 814.4 | 449.2 | 541.0 | 1 184.0 | 197 | 659.5 | 4 335.8 |
| Utah | 1 249.2 | 3.4 | 117 | 17.99 | 732.19 | 69.0 | 354.3 | 47.7 | 143.9 | 31.4 | 69.4 | 484.4 |
| Vermont | 303.2 | 1.2 | 32 | 18.22 | 685.07 | 14.2 | 55.6 | 9.3 | 37.7 | 4.7 | 12.0 | 130.2 |
| Virginia | 3 727 | 1.1 | 232 | 18.54 | 741.60 | 175.9 | 115.6 | 111.4 | 404.8 | 71.8 | 188.2 | 1 703.9 |
| Washington | 2 871.3 | 1.6 | 280 | 24.14 | 1 013.88 | 138.5 | 92.9 | 123.9 | 319.3 | 104.7 | 142.9 | 1 121.7 |
| West Virginia | 765.2 | 1.2 | 49 | 18.61 | 738.82 | 35.6 | 135.4 | 23.4 | 87.6 | 9.5 | 28.0 | 319.8 |
| Wisconsin | 2 784.6 | 0.9 | 455 | 18.05 | 734.64 | 93.0 | 511.1 | 116.7 | 294.4 | 46.2 | 162.6 | 1 102.6 |
| Wyoming | 289.7 | 0.9 | 9 | 22.69 | 923.48 | 21.7 | 14.7 | 9.2 | 29.4 | 3.9 | 10.8 | 88.8 |

1. Includes professional and business services, educational and health services, leisure and hospitality, and other services.

# Table A. States — **Agriculture**

| STATE | Agriculture, 2007 | | | | | | | | | | | |
|---|---|---|---|---|---|---|---|---|---|---|---|---|
| | Farms | | | | | Land in farms | | | | | Value of land and buildings (dollars) | |
| | | Percent with: | | | | | | | Acres | | | |
| | Number | Fewer than 50 acres | 500 acres or more | Farm operators whose principal occupation is farming (percent) | Government payments, average per farm (dollars) | Acreage (1,000) | Percent change, 2002–2007 | Average size of farm | Total irrigated (1,000) | Total cropland (1,000) | Average per farm | Average per acre |
| | 184 | 185 | 186 | 187 | 188 | 189 | 190 | 191 | 192 | 193 | 194 | 195 |
| UNITED STATES | 2 204 792 | 38.7 | 14.6 | 45.1 | 9 523 | 922 096 | -1.7 | 418 | 56 599 | 406 425 | 791 138 | 1 892 |
| Alabama | 48 753 | 40.2 | 7.7 | 39.8 | 8 642 | 9 034 | 1.5 | 185 | 113 | 3 143 | 424 674 | 2 292 |
| Alaska | 686 | 48.0 | 13.1 | 53.2 | 21 086 | 882 | -2.1 | 1 285 | 3 730 | 86 238 | 502 342 | 391 |
| Arizona | 15 637 | 80.1 | 8.1 | 61.1 | 49 077 | 26 118 | -1.8 | 1 670 | 876 | 1 205 | 1 249 929 | 748 |
| Arkansas | 49 346 | 35.9 | 12.4 | 44.5 | 23 510 | 13 873 | -4.3 | 281 | 4 461 | 8 432 | 658 732 | 2 343 |
| California | 81 033 | 65.8 | 9.5 | 50.5 | 32 273 | 25 365 | -8.1 | 313 | 8 016 | 9 465 | 2 005 768 | 6 408 |
| Colorado | 37 054 | 36.8 | 25.5 | 40.4 | 13 479 | 31 605 | 1.6 | 853 | 2 868 | 11 484 | 892 170 | 1 046 |
| Connecticut | 4 916 | 63.6 | 2.1 | 46.2 | 11 710 | 406 | 13.6 | 83 | 10 | 164 | 1 045 133 | 12 667 |
| Delaware | 2 546 | 57.1 | 9.6 | 59.1 | 9 364 | 510 | -5.5 | 200 | 105 | 433 | 2 073 605 | 10 347 |
| District of Columbia | X | X | X | X | X | X | X | X | X | X | X | X |
| Florida | 47 463 | 69.2 | 5.5 | 44.0 | 9 722 | 9 232 | -11.4 | 195 | 1 552 | 2 953 | 1 096 718 | 5 639 |
| Georgia | 47 846 | 41.3 | 9.2 | 42.0 | 15 435 | 10 151 | -5.5 | 212 | 1 018 | 4 478 | 661 201 | 3 117 |
| Hawaii | 7 521 | 90.2 | 2.1 | 51.3 | 10 908 | 1 121 | -13.8 | 149 | 58 635 | 177 626 | 1 146 213 | 7 688 |
| Idaho | 25 349 | 48.9 | 16.9 | 45.7 | 10 798 | 11 497 | -2.3 | 454 | 3 300 | 5 919 | 894 497 | 1 972 |
| Illinois | 76 860 | 38.0 | 21.0 | 48.4 | 8 577 | 26 775 | -2.0 | 348 | 474 | 23 708 | 1 321 080 | 3 792 |
| Indiana | 60 938 | 48.0 | 12.6 | 41.9 | 7 272 | 14 773 | -1.9 | 242 | 397 | 12 716 | 868 699 | 3 583 |
| Iowa | 92 856 | 28.6 | 20.8 | 52.4 | 9 425 | 30 748 | -3.1 | 331 | 190 | 26 316 | 1 122 023 | 3 388 |
| Kansas | 65 531 | 18.6 | 30.9 | 47.1 | 9 613 | 46 346 | -1.9 | 707 | 2 763 | 28 216 | 644 039 | 911 |
| Kentucky | 85 260 | 35.0 | 5.8 | 39.8 | 3 494 | 13 993 | 1.1 | 164 | 59 | 7 278 | 440 213 | 2 682 |
| Louisiana | 30 106 | 45.4 | 11.4 | 41.8 | 15 943 | 8 110 | 3.6 | 269 | 954 | 4 691 | 554 270 | 2 058 |
| Maine | 8 136 | 42.1 | 6.3 | 43.5 | 6 042 | 1 348 | -1.6 | 166 | 21 | 529 | 364 807 | 2 203 |
| Maryland | 12 834 | 47.9 | 7.1 | 48.8 | 7 277 | 2 052 | -1.2 | 160 | 93 | 1 405 | 1 124 529 | 7 034 |
| Massachusetts | 7 691 | 66.1 | 1.5 | 48.0 | 7 763 | 518 | -0.1 | 67 | 23 | 187 | 829 090 | 12 313 |
| Michigan | 56 014 | 44.5 | 8.2 | 44.3 | 5 115 | 10 032 | -1.1 | 179 | 500 | 7 804 | 610 556 | 3 409 |
| Minnesota | 80 992 | 25.5 | 17.9 | 48.9 | 7 869 | 26 918 | -2.2 | 332 | 506 | 21 949 | 853 968 | 2 569 |
| Mississippi | 41 959 | 29.3 | 10.8 | 38.0 | 13 463 | 11 456 | 3.2 | 273 | 1 369 | 5 531 | 510 454 | 1 870 |
| Missouri | 107 825 | 26.9 | 13.0 | 41.8 | 7 084 | 29 027 | -3.1 | 269 | 1 200 | 16 406 | 586 478 | 2 179 |
| Montana | 29 524 | 25.0 | 43.0 | 50.7 | 16 971 | 61 388 | 3.0 | 2 079 | 2 013 | 18 242 | 1 611 155 | 775 |
| Nebraska | 47 712 | 18.6 | 39.7 | 60.5 | 11 091 | 45 480 | -0.9 | 953 | 8 559 | 21 486 | 1 104 392 | 1 159 |
| Nevada | 3 131 | 48.8 | 21.2 | 52.7 | 12 105 | 5 865 | -7.3 | 1 873 | 691 | 754 | 1 148 693 | 613 |
| New Hampshire | 4 166 | 51.8 | 3.8 | 46.3 | 5 848 | 472 | 6.1 | 113 | 2 | 129 | 558 385 | 4 929 |
| New Jersey | 10 327 | 75.2 | 2.9 | 44.8 | 8 154 | 733 | -9.0 | 71 | 95 | 489 | 1 089 883 | 15 346 |
| New Mexico | 20 930 | 52.0 | 23.1 | 48.0 | 13 030 | 43 238 | -3.5 | 2 066 | 830 | 2 334 | 696 081 | 337 |
| New York | 36 352 | 32.2 | 8.4 | 54.0 | 5 913 | 7 175 | -6.3 | 197 | 68 | 4 315 | 449 010 | 2 275 |
| North Carolina | 52 913 | 48.7 | 6.7 | 45.8 | 10 633 | 8 475 | -6.7 | 160 | 232 | 4 895 | 656 080 | 4 096 |
| North Dakota | 31 970 | 8.3 | 51.7 | 57.9 | 13 462 | 39 675 | 1.0 | 1 241 | 236 | 27 527 | 957 053 | 771 |
| Ohio | 75 861 | 42.4 | 8.9 | 43.1 | 6 099 | 13 957 | -4.3 | 184 | 38 | 10 833 | 649 130 | 3 528 |
| Oklahoma | 86 565 | 26.0 | 17.6 | 41.6 | 7 754 | 35 087 | 4.2 | 405 | 535 | 13 008 | 468 809 | 1 157 |
| Oregon | 38 553 | 61.4 | 10.6 | 46.2 | 14 954 | 16 400 | -4.0 | 425 | 1 845 | 5 010 | 804 145 | 1 890 |
| Pennsylvania | 63 163 | 41.0 | 3.9 | 45.5 | 4 356 | 7 809 | 0.8 | 124 | 38 | 4 870 | 590 376 | 4 775 |
| Rhode Island | 1 219 | 68.7 | 0.6 | 50.9 | 7 353 | 68 | 10.8 | 56 | 4 | 24 | 936 229 | 16 828 |
| South Carolina | 25 867 | 42.3 | 7.4 | 37.7 | 8 717 | 4 889 | 0.9 | 189 | 132 | 2 151 | 540 200 | 2 858 |
| South Dakota | 31 169 | 15.5 | 46.7 | 60.2 | 11 817 | 43 666 | -0.3 | 1 401 | 374 | 19 094 | 1 255 332 | 896 |
| Tennessee | 79 280 | 44.4 | 4.6 | 38.9 | 5 528 | 10 970 | -6.1 | 138 | 81 | 6 047 | 467 420 | 3 378 |
| Texas | 247 437 | 37.9 | 16.2 | 39.9 | 15 010 | 130 399 | 0.4 | 527 | 5 010 | 33 667 | 669 154 | 1 270 |
| Utah | 16 700 | 55.8 | 13.2 | 38.0 | 7 689 | 11 095 | -5.4 | 664 | 1 134 | 1 838 | 829 816 | 1 249 |
| Vermont | 6 984 | 35.8 | 7.6 | 49.6 | 5 014 | 1 233 | -0.9 | 177 | 2 | 517 | 512 684 | 2 903 |
| Virginia | 47 383 | 39.5 | 7.0 | 42.8 | 5 577 | 8 104 | -6.0 | 171 | 82 | 3 274 | 720 538 | 4 213 |
| Washington | 39 284 | 61.1 | 11.4 | 45.9 | 20 042 | 14 973 | -2.3 | 381 | 1 736 | 7 609 | 759 146 | 1 992 |
| West Virginia | 23 618 | 29.5 | 5.3 | 41.5 | 1 348 | 3 698 | 3.2 | 157 | 2 | 942 | 373 435 | 2 385 |
| Wisconsin | 78 463 | 31.6 | 7.8 | 47.2 | 4 124 | 15 191 | -3.5 | 194 | 377 | 10 116 | 624 428 | 3 225 |
| Wyoming | 11 069 | 24.0 | 38.3 | 49.2 | 10 092 | 30 170 | -12.3 | 2 726 | 1 551 | 2 576 | 1 397 691 | 513 |

| STATE | Value of machinery and equipment, average per farm (dollars) | Value of products sold — Total (mil dol) | Value of products sold — Average per farm (dollars) | Percent from: Crops | Percent from: Livestock and poultry products | Percent of farms with sales of: $10,000 or more | Percent of farms with sales of: $100,000 or more | Cropland (percent) | Owned by the federal government (percent) | Developed (percent) | Water consumption, 2005 (mil gal per day) |
|---|---|---|---|---|---|---|---|---|---|---|---|
| | 196 | 197 | 198 | 199 | 200 | 201 | 202 | 203 | 204 | 205 | 206 |
| UNITED STATES.................. | 88 357 | 297 220 | 134 807 | 48.3 | 51.7 | 40.2 | 16.2 | 18.4 | 20.7 | 5.7 | 460 000 |
| Alabama................................ | 60 810 | 4 416 | 90 570 | 15.3 | 84.7 | 30.8 | 9.7 | 6.6 | 3.0 | 8.8 | 11 200 |
| Alaska.................................. | 78 837 | 57 | 83 119 | 43.4 | 56.6 | 41.3 | 11.2 | NA | NA | NA | 1 180 |
| Arizona................................ | 66 291 | 3 235 | 206 852 | 59.1 | 40.9 | 18.6 | 6.7 | 1.0 | 41.7 | 2.7 | 7 000 |
| Arkansas.............................. | 90 823 | 7 509 | 152 166 | 38.6 | 61.4 | 40.4 | 16.4 | 21.7 | 9.1 | 5.3 | 12 800 |
| California............................. | 108 145 | 33 885 | 418 164 | 67.6 | 32.4 | 53.4 | 23.5 | 9.3 | 45.9 | 6.1 | 51 300 |
| Colorado.............................. | 99 344 | 6 061 | 163 576 | 32.7 | 67.3 | 36.1 | 13.8 | 11.4 | 35.7 | 2.9 | 15 300 |
| Connecticut.......................... | 64 090 | 552 | 112 195 | 72.8 | 27.2 | 34.6 | 10.0 | 5.4 | 0.5 | 32.9 | 4 210 |
| Delaware.............................. | 119 718 | 1 083 | 425 387 | 19.4 | 80.6 | 59.0 | 38.8 | 27.4 | 2.0 | 18.3 | 1 140 |
| District of Columbia.............. | X | X | X | X | X | X | X | NA | NA | NA | 11 |
| Florida................................. | 54 604 | 7 785 | 164 027 | 80 | 20 | 35 | 11 | 8 | 10.0 | 8.3 | 20 500 |
| Georgia................................ | 76 948 | 7 113 | 148 662 | 30.1 | 69.9 | 32.3 | 14.2 | 10.6 | 5.6 | 12.3 | 6 100 |
| Hawaii.................................. | 40 666 | 514 | 68 292 | 83.7 | 16.3 | 34.3 | 7.0 | NA | NA | NA | 2 120 |
| Idaho................................... | 114 383 | 5 689 | 224 418 | 40.9 | 59.1 | 39.9 | 17.0 | 9.8 | 62.7 | 1.7 | 21 900 |
| Illinois................................. | 136 609 | 13 329 | 173 421 | 81.6 | 18.4 | 53.1 | 30.3 | 66.3 | 1.4 | 9.4 | 17 000 |
| Indiana................................. | 103 427 | 8 271 | 135 733 | 64.3 | 35.7 | 45.6 | 20.8 | 57.1 | 2.0 | 10.6 | 10 500 |
| Iowa.................................... | 136 771 | 20 418 | 219 890 | 50.7 | 49.3 | 61.4 | 35.6 | 70.7 | 0.5 | 5.3 | 3 770 |
| Kansas................................. | 114 261 | 14 413 | 219 944 | 33.9 | 66.1 | 51.5 | 21.7 | 48.7 | 1.0 | 4.0 | 4 240 |
| Kentucky.............................. | 57 591 | 4 825 | 56 586 | 29.1 | 70.9 | 33.5 | 6.9 | 20.0 | 5.0 | 8.1 | 4 850 |
| Louisiana............................. | 78 998 | 2 618 | 86 959 | 61.3 | 38.7 | 30.7 | 10.7 | NA | 4.2 | 5.9 | 13 000 |
| Maine.................................. | 65 961 | 617 | 75 859 | 52.9 | 47.1 | 31.1 | 9.5 | 1.8 | 1.0 | 4.1 | 678 |
| Maryland.............................. | 98 823 | 1 835 | 142 987 | 34.3 | 65.7 | 41.5 | 17.6 | 18.0 | 2.2 | 19.0 | 8 400 |
| Massachusetts....................... | 56 373 | 490 | 63 687 | 74.4 | 25.6 | 35.8 | 10.4 | 4.5 | 1.8 | 32.1 | 4 030 |
| Michigan.............................. | 90 742 | 5 753 | 102 710 | 57.9 | 42.1 | 38.1 | 14.2 | 21.0 | 8.8 | 11.3 | 13 100 |
| Minnesota............................ | 131 698 | 13 180 | 162 738 | 53.5 | 46.5 | 50.7 | 27.4 | 38.3 | 6.2 | 4.4 | 4 530 |
| Mississippi........................... | 73 558 | 4 877 | 116 227 | 34.2 | 65.8 | 28.8 | 10.8 | 15.4 | 5.9 | 5.9 | 3 280 |
| Missouri............................... | 68 171 | 7 513 | 69 677 | 46.5 | 53.5 | 42.0 | 11.0 | 29.8 | 4.3 | 6.6 | 9 860 |
| Montana............................... | 103 494 | 2 803 | 94 942 | 45.4 | 54.6 | 46.8 | 21.6 | 14.8 | 28.8 | 1.1 | 11 300 |
| Nebraska.............................. | 157 427 | 15 506 | 324 992 | 44.1 | 55.9 | 68.5 | 41.0 | 39.4 | 1.3 | 2.3 | 14 100 |
| Nevada................................ | 111 799 | 513 | 163 931 | 42.7 | 57.3 | 43.0 | 19.6 | 0.7 | 84.6 | 0.8 | 2 670 |
| New Hampshire ..................... | 58 413 | 199 | 47 780 | 53.5 | 46.5 | 27.9 | 6.9 | 1.8 | 12.8 | 11.7 | 1 480 |
| New Jersey ........................... | 68 374 | 987 | 95 564 | 86.3 | 13.7 | 32.7 | 11.1 | 9.4 | 2.8 | 35.5 | 8 280 |
| New Mexico .......................... | 55 457 | 2 175 | 103 922 | 25.4 | 74.6 | 27.1 | 8.1 | 1.9 | 33.9 | 1.6 | 3 740 |
| New York .............................. | 97 550 | 4 419 | 121 551 | 35.3 | 64.7 | 45.4 | 18.8 | 15.9 | 0.7 | 12.1 | 17 000 |
| North Carolina....................... | 76 793 | 10 314 | 194 917 | 25.3 | 74.7 | 35.2 | 15.7 | 15.5 | 7.4 | 14.2 | 14 400 |
| North Dakota......................... | 174 683 | 6 084 | 190 310 | 82.8 | 17.2 | 57.9 | 35.9 | 52.9 | 3.9 | 2.2 | 1 500 |
| Ohio.................................... | 88 352 | 7 070 | 93 200 | 58.1 | 41.9 | 43.7 | 15.9 | 41.8 | 1.4 | 15.7 | 12 900 |
| Oklahoma............................. | 63 642 | 5 806 | 67 072 | 20.5 | 79.5 | 37.1 | 8.3 | 19.6 | 2.6 | 4.6 | 1 940 |
| Oregon................................. | 79 175 | 4 386 | 113 769 | 67.9 | 32.1 | 32.5 | 12.1 | 5.8 | 50.3 | 2.2 | 8 090 |
| Pennsylvania......................... | 72 988 | 5 809 | 91 965 | 32.2 | 67.8 | 38.5 | 16.9 | 17.0 | 2.5 | 15.0 | 10 600 |
| Rhode Island......................... | 65 343 | 66 | 54 067 | 84.4 | 15.6 | 36.5 | 9.6 | 2.2 | 0.4 | 28.6 | 454 |
| South Carolina ...................... | 64 977 | 2 353 | 90 953 | 33.9 | 66.1 | 23.4 | 7.0 | 11.2 | 5.2 | 13.4 | 8 790 |
| South Dakota......................... | 155 652 | 6 570 | 210 801 | 51.5 | 48.5 | 65.4 | 38.3 | 34.0 | 6.3 | 2.0 | 561 |
| Tennessee............................ | 58 882 | 2 617 | 33 015 | 43.9 | 56.1 | 25.2 | 4.8 | 15.4 | 4.8 | 11.3 | 12 100 |
| Texas.................................. | 64 350 | 21 001 | 84 874 | 31.3 | 68.7 | 29.0 | 7.1 | 14.0 | 1.7 | 5.0 | 30 000 |
| Utah.................................... | 75 365 | 1 416 | 84 771 | 26.3 | 73.7 | 34.9 | 9.7 | 2.6 | 63.1 | 1.4 | 5 730 |
| Vermont............................... | 74 500 | 674 | 96 465 | 14.7 | 85.3 | 41.1 | 15.4 | 8.8 | 6.9 | 6.4 | 586 |
| Virginia................................ | 65 870 | 2 906 | 61 334 | 29.5 | 70.5 | 32.9 | 7.9 | 10.2 | 9.8 | 11.4 | 11 900 |
| Washington........................... | 83 468 | 6 793 | 172 917 | 70.0 | 30.0 | 33.9 | 15.2 | 14.7 | 27.1 | 5.6 | 6 320 |
| West Virginia......................... | 38 871 | 592 | 25 051 | 13.2 | 86.8 | 20.1 | 3.2 | 4.9 | 7.8 | 7.4 | 5 390 |
| Wisconsin............................. | 96 278 | 8 967 | 114 288 | 29.8 | 70.2 | 45.2 | 21.2 | 27.9 | 5.1 | 7.6 | 9 640 |
| Wyoming.............................. | 97 356 | 1 158 | 104 575 | 18.5 | 81.5 | 47.7 | 19.2 | 3.4 | 45.9 | 1.1 | 5 150 |

# Table A. States — **Manufactures and Construction**

| STATE | Manufactures, 2011 | | | | | | | | | | Construction, 2007 | | | | |
|---|---|---|---|---|---|---|---|---|---|---|---|---|---|---|---|
| | All employees | | | Production workers | | | | Value added by manufacture (mil dol) | Value of shipments (mil dol) | Total capital expenditures (mil dol) | Number of establishments | Employees | | Value (mil dol) | Annual payroll (mil dol) |
| | | | | | | Wages | | | | | | | | | |
| | Number (1,000) | Percent change, 2010–2011 | Annual payroll (mil dol) | Number (1,000) | Work hours (millions) | Total (mil dol) | Average per worker (dollars) | | | | | Number | Percent change, 2002–2007 | | |
| | 207 | 208 | 209 | 210 | 211 | 212 | 213 | 214 | 215 | 216 | 217 | 218 | 219 | 220 | 221 |
| UNITED STATES | 10 649 | 1.4 | 559 518 | 7 440 | 14 867 | 313 710 | 42 165 | 2 295 220 | 5 498 599 | 146 652 | 729 345 | 7 316 240 | 1.7 | 1 731 842 | 331 003 |
| Alabama | 213 | -0.4 | 10 001 | 161 | 327 | 6 469 | 40 096 | 43 374 | 113 195 | 3 496 | 9 239 | 107 166 | 8.7 | 24 714 | 4 188 |
| Alaska | 11 | 4.2 | 469 | 9 | 19 | 329 | 36 547 | 1 740 | 8 323 | 145 | 2 404 | 22 082 | 3.4 | 6 263 | 1 352 |
| Arizona | 127 | -1.4 | 7 829 | 72 | 145 | 3 185 | 44 525 | 27 192 | 50 048 | 1 368 | 15 470 | 221 585 | 26.7 | 56 159 | 9 182 |
| Arkansas | 146 | 0.0 | 5 977 | 117 | 231 | 4 224 | 36 238 | 23 737 | 59 897 | 1 455 | 5 764 | 50 407 | 8.1 | 10 341 | 1 814 |
| California | 1 114 | 0.1 | 66 869 | 694 | 1 374 | 29 834 | 43 014 | 231 029 | 497 755 | 13 474 | 72 173 | 873 789 | 0.4 | 217 933 | 43 134 |
| Colorado | 110 | 2.3 | 6 068 | 74 | 149 | 3 191 | 43 258 | 23 270 | 49 230 | 1 441 | 17 787 | 173 559 | -1.0 | 42 990 | 7 711 |
| Connecticut | 155 | -0.4 | 9 488 | 95 | 185 | 4 510 | 47 619 | 29 885 | 51 946 | 1 274 | 9 004 | 71 649 | -6.5 | 18 056 | 3 830 |
| Delaware | 27 | -4.9 | 1 452 | 19 | 38 | 776 | 41 455 | 7 421 | 20 626 | 733 | 2 724 | 25 646 | 2.0 | 5 609 | 1 150 |
| District of Columbia | 1 | -27.5 | 41 | 1 | 1 | 22 | 34 012 | 104 | 182 | 6 | 375 | 7 833 | 30.7 | 2 473 | 422 |
| Florida | 255 | -0.7 | 12 893 | 170 | 333 | 6 489 | 38 248 | 46 016 | 92 182 | 2 872 | 51 143 | 473 703 | 11.5 | 117 804 | 19 587 |
| Georgia | 313 | 1.1 | 14 318 | 240 | 487 | 9 075 | 37 754 | 65 055 | 144 395 | 4 814 | 20 568 | 223 557 | 1.0 | 59 375 | 9 651 |
| Hawaii | 11 | -0.5 | 431 | 7 | 13 | 232 | 34 716 | 1 457 | 7 695 | 101 | 2 771 | 35 523 | 30.2 | 10 420 | 1 907 |
| Idaho | 48 | -4.0 | 2 375 | 36 | 72 | 1 475 | 40 535 | 11 428 | 22 895 | 858 | 7 919 | 50 382 | 39.6 | 10 052 | 1 730 |
| Illinois | 535 | 0.5 | 29 008 | 366 | 744 | 15 654 | 42 715 | 115 314 | 275 279 | 7 878 | 30 236 | 272 682 | -11.9 | 72 778 | 14 623 |
| Indiana | 429 | 3.5 | 21 509 | 321 | 645 | 14 017 | 43 633 | 100 287 | 232 142 | 4 876 | 15 640 | 147 467 | -0.5 | 30 164 | 6 456 |
| Iowa | 192 | 4.8 | 9 502 | 140 | 283 | 5 701 | 40 706 | 39 521 | 102 091 | 2 257 | 8 019 | 70 357 | 4.7 | 14 961 | 2 900 |
| Kansas | 151 | 1.4 | 7 645 | 108 | 216 | 4 628 | 42 944 | 31 534 | 84 277 | 2 500 | 7 159 | 67 769 | -1.3 | 13 829 | 2 793 |
| Kentucky | 202 | 2.5 | 9 293 | 156 | 309 | 6 354 | 40 748 | 38 181 | 118 970 | 3 286 | 8 615 | 83 154 | -0.9 | 16 493 | 3 131 |
| Louisiana | 125 | 2.1 | 7 594 | 91 | 186 | 4 765 | 52 646 | 61 561 | 270 123 | 3 791 | 8 564 | 135 781 | 9.7 | 25 569 | 5 806 |
| Maine | 48 | 0.4 | 2 325 | 34 | 66 | 1 452 | 43 126 | 7 866 | 15 853 | 644 | 4 942 | 29 908 | -1.6 | 5 441 | 1 128 |
| Maryland | 104 | 0.0 | 5 998 | 66 | 128 | 2 774 | 42 234 | 23 203 | 41 836 | 1 525 | 15 618 | 191 293 | 5.5 | 44 327 | 8 953 |
| Massachusetts | 224 | -0.6 | 13 638 | 139 | 278 | 6 270 | 45 234 | 45 417 | 80 477 | 3 218 | 17 194 | 135 485 | -18.2 | 36 835 | 7 470 |
| Michigan | 461 | 6.2 | 25 129 | 336 | 680 | 15 665 | 46 588 | 84 244 | 221 204 | 6 836 | 21 790 | 160 110 | -26.9 | 35 373 | 7 244 |
| Minnesota | 290 | 1.2 | 15 214 | 192 | 381 | 7 811 | 40 761 | 53 376 | 121 021 | 2 925 | 15 863 | 134 584 | -9.3 | 37 052 | 6 821 |
| Mississippi | 128 | -0.5 | 5 461 | 100 | 194 | 3 593 | 36 079 | 20 323 | 60 471 | 1 414 | 4 737 | 55 936 | 13.7 | 11 765 | 2 093 |
| Missouri | 231 | 1.8 | 11 388 | 170 | 331 | 7 192 | 42 221 | 45 121 | 107 703 | 2 316 | 15 230 | 164 362 | 6.8 | 35 463 | 7 141 |
| Montana | 13 | 3.0 | 638 | 10 | 19 | 403 | 41 968 | 3 354 | 11 706 | 278 | 5 316 | 30 353 | 34.9 | 6 158 | 1 105 |
| Nebraska | 90 | 2.0 | 3 817 | 69 | 143 | 2 630 | 38 036 | 19 174 | 52 946 | 894 | 5 447 | 44 605 | -3.0 | 8 490 | 1 667 |
| Nevada | 39 | -1.7 | 2 080 | 26 | 52 | 1 062 | 41 172 | 8 172 | 14 923 | 524 | 5 280 | 122 900 | 29.0 | 29 314 | 5 743 |
| New Hampshire | 70 | 1.4 | 3 947 | 43 | 86 | 1 781 | 41 163 | 10 637 | 19 653 | 581 | 4 357 | 30 054 | -10.4 | 5 960 | 1 366 |
| New Jersey | 235 | -2.2 | 14 357 | 150 | 302 | 6 552 | 43 567 | 47 285 | 107 436 | 2 673 | 23 142 | 180 251 | -14.4 | 46 383 | 9 643 |
| New Mexico | 25 | 0.7 | 1 294 | 17 | 34 | 731 | 42 760 | 18 400 | 28 594 | 1 188 | 5 306 | 55 006 | 21.5 | 10 324 | 2 003 |
| New York | 419 | 0.4 | 22 260 | 278 | 543 | 11 376 | 40 909 | 77 618 | 151 374 | 5 291 | 43 409 | 349 415 | -5.6 | 90 318 | 18 393 |
| North Carolina | 388 | 0.7 | 17 342 | 293 | 581 | 10 832 | 37 025 | 102 559 | 200 420 | 4 133 | 25 457 | 242 488 | 7.6 | 55 786 | 9 364 |
| North Dakota | 22 | 6.4 | 968 | 16 | 32 | 629 | 38 700 | 4 238 | 13 403 | 288 | 2 082 | 19 378 | 14.9 | 3 674 | 768 |
| Ohio | 599 | 2.7 | 30 907 | 433 | 871 | 18 968 | 43 843 | 118 817 | 292 737 | 7 397 | 22 937 | 224 342 | -12.8 | 48 315 | 10 016 |
| Oklahoma | 125 | 6.7 | 5 951 | 94 | 192 | 3 807 | 40 650 | 23 715 | 69 833 | 1 715 | 7 611 | 69 842 | 11.4 | 14 132 | 2 608 |
| Oregon | 129 | 3.3 | 6 543 | 92 | 181 | 3 692 | 40 291 | 37 150 | 59 665 | 1 344 | 13 434 | 102 974 | 17.0 | 23 265 | 4 443 |
| Pennsylvania | 530 | 0.8 | 27 231 | 372 | 738 | 15 800 | 42 491 | 100 737 | 237 600 | 6 411 | 28 505 | 265 925 | -4.1 | 59 187 | 12 480 |
| Rhode Island | 36 | -2.2 | 1 997 | 24 | 48 | 1 000 | 42 255 | 5 652 | 11 175 | 393 | 3 587 | 21 658 | -20.6 | 5 777 | 1 082 |
| South Carolina | 194 | 2.3 | 9 408 | 147 | 293 | 6 069 | 41 396 | 37 582 | 90 737 | 2 930 | 12 118 | 108 199 | -2.4 | 22 820 | 3 910 |
| South Dakota | 39 | 3.8 | 1 633 | 29 | 58 | 1 023 | 35 489 | 6 164 | 16 152 | 332 | 3 128 | 20 601 | 8.2 | 3 944 | 723 |
| Tennessee | 277 | 0.3 | 13 121 | 203 | 408 | 8 039 | 39 565 | 54 420 | 132 135 | 4 509 | 10 907 | 124 488 | 0.4 | 27 964 | 5 210 |
| Texas | 701 | 1.8 | 38 534 | 489 | 994 | 21 946 | 44 894 | 216 794 | 671 372 | 17 619 | 37 200 | 596 499 | 7.5 | 146 638 | 26 534 |
| Utah | 100 | 1.7 | 5 290 | 65 | 130 | 2 732 | 41 735 | 26 720 | 50 788 | 1 799 | 10 055 | 88 880 | 31.5 | 20 012 | 3 375 |
| Vermont | 28 | 0.7 | 1 537 | 18 | 37 | 748 | 41 321 | 5 017 | 10 550 | 377 | 2 838 | 17 475 | 10.0 | 3 171 | 678 |
| Virginia | 222 | -0.8 | 11 189 | 158 | 312 | 6 476 | 41 089 | 54 557 | 94 688 | 2 603 | 22 431 | 235 312 | 11.1 | 51 968 | 10 004 |
| Washington | 230 | 3.3 | 13 306 | 153 | 303 | 7 370 | 48 202 | 52 683 | 115 059 | 2 442 | 22 382 | 199 064 | 18.6 | 48 104 | 9 568 |
| West Virginia | 50 | 1.0 | 2 527 | 38 | 74 | 1 678 | 44 651 | 10 140 | 23 977 | 712 | 3 992 | 31 965 | 9.3 | 5 033 | 1 200 |
| Wisconsin | 428 | 3.6 | 21 168 | 309 | 611 | 12 331 | 39 856 | 72 804 | 163 107 | 4 423 | 14 673 | 126 261 | -11.2 | 28 611 | 5 941 |
| Wyoming | 8 | 10.1 | 557 | 6 | 11 | 349 | 59 102 | 3 180 | 8 757 | 291 | 2 803 | 22 534 | 30.1 | 4 250 | 956 |

# Table A. States — Wholesale Trade and Retail Trade

| STATE | Wholesale trade, 2007 | | | | | Retail trade,[1] 2007 | | | | | | | | |
|---|---|---|---|---|---|---|---|---|---|---|---|---|---|---|
| | Number of establishments | Employees Number | Percent change, 2002–2007 | Sales (mil dol) | Annual payroll (mil dol) | Number of establishments | Employees Total | Percent change, 2002–2007 | Motor vehicle and parts dealers | Food and beverage stores | Clothing and clothing accessory stores | General merchandise stores | Sales (mil dol) | Annual payroll (mil dol) |
| | 222 | 223 | 224 | 225 | 226 | 227 | 228 | 229 | 230 | 231 | 232 | 233 | 234 | 235 |
| UNITED STATES | 434 983 | 6 227 389 | 5.9 | 6 515 709 | 336 207 | 1 128 112 | 15 515 396 | 5.9 | 1 914 466 | 2 827 162 | 1 644 025 | 2 763 474 | 3 917 663 | 362 819 |
| Alabama | 5 663 | 81 076 | 8.2 | 68 625 | 3 600 | 19 722 | 238 922 | 7.4 | 31 887 | 35 110 | 23 832 | 54 410 | 57 345 | 5 112 |
| Alaska | 753 | 9 063 | 22.1 | 7 355 | 443 | 2 641 | 34 977 | 6.0 | 4 517 | 7 519 | 2 333 | 8 105 | 9 303 | 937 |
| Arizona | 7 045 | 102 200 | 15.4 | 85 607 | 5 224 | 19 384 | 337 529 | 25.7 | 47 174 | 67 301 | 28 497 | 64 405 | 86 759 | 8 011 |
| Arkansas | 3 501 | 47 949 | 11.8 | 63 511 | 2 019 | 11 906 | 140 018 | 4.3 | D | 18 949 | 10 948 | D | 32 974 | 2 889 |
| California | 61 451 | 888 079 | 9.5 | 925 328 | 53 724 | 114 438 | 1 683 023 | 10.4 | 212 872 | 323 171 | 212 039 | 262 169 | 455 032 | 44 329 |
| Colorado | 7 290 | 105 366 | 4.2 | 101 410 | 6 147 | 19 428 | 261 962 | 5.9 | 31 207 | 46 934 | 24 488 | 46 357 | 65 897 | 6 538 |
| Connecticut | 4 620 | 75 993 | -3.9 | 143 640 | 4 923 | 13 807 | 196 133 | 2.3 | 23 359 | 41 163 | 24 850 | 23 395 | 52 165 | 5 160 |
| Delaware | 983 | 19 452 | -8.1 | 28 365 | 1 467 | 3 907 | 55 432 | 6.8 | 7 360 | 8 859 | 5 468 | 8 764 | 14 202 | 1 323 |
| District of Columbia | 416 | 5 184 | -10.3 | 3 247 | 333 | 1 827 | 19 117 | 3.3 | D | 5 287 | 4 003 | D | 3 844 | 486 |
| Florida | 32 361 | 326 878 | 9.2 | 323 340 | 15 150 | 73 794 | 1 016 290 | 12.6 | 132 389 | 199 431 | 118 091 | 174 854 | 262 341 | 24 050 |
| Georgia | 14 165 | 213 227 | 6.1 | 254 298 | 11 604 | 36 218 | 475 344 | 6.2 | 62 488 | 83 542 | 51 939 | 89 896 | 117 517 | 10 760 |
| Hawaii | 1 844 | 20 252 | 4.3 | 12 672 | 836 | 5 012 | 70 661 | 10.8 | 7 390 | 12 966 | 12 215 | 12 724 | 17 612 | 1 766 |
| Idaho | 2 103 | 26 519 | 15.6 | 20 210 | 1 136 | 6 300 | 80 447 | 15.5 | 12 293 | 10 928 | 4 892 | 16 553 | 20 527 | 1 834 |
| Illinois | 20 062 | 320 942 | -3.2 | 405 962 | 18 813 | 43 055 | 639 147 | 6.3 | 72 057 | 111 756 | 68 703 | 117 382 | 165 451 | 14 895 |
| Indiana | 8 147 | 115 868 | 5.7 | 101 259 | 5 324 | 23 692 | 333 172 | -3.0 | 42 332 | 50 449 | 28 083 | 70 472 | 78 746 | 7 123 |
| Iowa | 5 017 | 64 891 | 4.6 | 55 108 | 2 724 | 13 203 | 177 156 | 0.5 | 21 717 | 34 508 | 13 035 | 33 571 | 39 235 | 3 561 |
| Kansas | 4 544 | 57 551 | -0.6 | 69 668 | 2 789 | 11 463 | 149 672 | 3.3 | 18 661 | 26 074 | 12 203 | 30 111 | 34 538 | 3 134 |
| Kentucky | 4 485 | 70 882 | 2.4 | 94 546 | 3 409 | 16 404 | 214 782 | 0.3 | 26 128 | 33 299 | 17 512 | 47 875 | 50 406 | 4 502 |
| Louisiana | 5 614 | 75 568 | 2.7 | 67 152 | 3 460 | 17 135 | 231 365 | 1.3 | 30 846 | 35 276 | 22 636 | 47 780 | 56 543 | 5 096 |
| Maine | 1 629 | 18 734 | -3.6 | 12 458 | 790 | 6 911 | 83 279 | 3.8 | 10 679 | 17 274 | 6 140 | 11 617 | 20 444 | 1 894 |
| Maryland | 5 997 | 99 648 | 6.6 | 83 494 | 5 590 | 19 601 | 294 806 | 3.2 | 39 773 | 57 680 | 35 385 | 45 187 | 75 664 | 7 291 |
| Massachusetts | 8 765 | 152 513 | -1.6 | 145 729 | 10 030 | 25 469 | 360 218 | 0.3 | 36 748 | 90 032 | 45 200 | 38 996 | 88 083 | 8 916 |
| Michigan | 12 047 | 172 356 | -3.2 | 226 532 | 9 367 | 37 619 | 470 794 | -9.6 | 48 960 | 76 602 | 45 331 | 105 937 | 109 103 | 10 001 |
| Minnesota | 8 623 | 138 822 | 9.5 | 140 335 | 8 537 | 20 777 | 307 034 | 0.2 | 32 763 | 53 089 | 26 289 | 57 166 | 71 384 | 6 686 |
| Mississippi | 2 922 | 37 214 | 5.4 | 27 995 | 1 466 | 12 452 | 141 426 | 4.1 | 17 947 | 18 625 | 12 686 | 34 157 | 33 751 | 2 911 |
| Missouri | 8 338 | 129 138 | 1.4 | 117 329 | 5 802 | 23 360 | 317 318 | 1.8 | 40 043 | 45 890 | 26 639 | 65 680 | 76 575 | 7 155 |
| Montana | 1 461 | 14 184 | 3.3 | 10 741 | 559 | 5 258 | 58 883 | 11.3 | 8 311 | 8 692 | 3 659 | 9 791 | 14 687 | 1 318 |
| Nebraska | 3 093 | 38 752 | 5.3 | 34 283 | 1 721 | 7 888 | 108 209 | 2.4 | 12 325 | 18 326 | 7 804 | 20 056 | 26 487 | 2 231 |
| Nevada | 3 046 | 41 664 | 31.1 | 27 115 | 2 031 | 8 492 | 139 829 | 24.5 | 18 723 | 22 123 | 19 203 | 24 415 | 37 434 | 3 692 |
| New Hampshire | 1 886 | 24 960 | 6.0 | 19 023 | 1 490 | 6 603 | 98 333 | 4.8 | 12 997 | 20 704 | 8 378 | 14 523 | 25 354 | 2 380 |
| New Jersey | 16 174 | 283 501 | 3.5 | 366 292 | 18 714 | 34 482 | 460 843 | 6.0 | 48 275 | 107 638 | 63 287 | 57 782 | 124 814 | 12 050 |
| New Mexico | 2 036 | 22 943 | 15.5 | 14 702 | 966 | 7 208 | 97 385 | 8.9 | 13 659 | 13 897 | 7 455 | 20 724 | 24 470 | 2 251 |
| New York | 34 672 | 412 962 | -0.1 | 438 854 | 23 018 | 76 637 | 892 863 | 6.6 | 78 920 | 194 012 | 138 550 | 114 888 | 230 718 | 22 337 |
| North Carolina | 12 256 | 180 664 | 11.4 | 148 758 | 9 342 | 36 592 | 466 577 | 7.2 | 62 076 | 75 817 | 47 335 | 87 515 | 114 578 | 10 343 |
| North Dakota | 1 525 | 17 596 | 10.3 | 15 408 | 741 | 3 361 | 44 054 | 6.6 | 5 853 | 7 242 | 2 947 | 8 011 | 10 527 | 891 |
| Ohio | 15 332 | 243 652 | 3.8 | 241 334 | 12 100 | 40 075 | 591 237 | -3.4 | 72 230 | 99 666 | 50 924 | 114 955 | 138 816 | 12 729 |
| Oklahoma | 4 584 | 61 265 | 12.0 | 66 516 | 2 802 | 13 554 | 170 984 | 1.8 | D | 21 975 | 14 278 | D | 43 095 | 3 610 |
| Oregon | 5 789 | 77 547 | 4.0 | 72 660 | 3 943 | 14 991 | 204 793 | 11.5 | 27 048 | 38 697 | 17 632 | 40 184 | 50 371 | 4 916 |
| Pennsylvania | 15 769 | 246 422 | 5.3 | 229 254 | 13 164 | 46 532 | 672 042 | 1.5 | 80 992 | 143 626 | 65 190 | 108 007 | 166 843 | 14 862 |
| Rhode Island | 1 479 | 21 502 | 21.6 | 12 557 | 1 062 | 4 080 | 50 865 | 0.4 | 5 484 | 11 571 | 5 639 | 5 973 | 12 286 | 1 215 |
| South Carolina | 5 034 | 68 229 | 13.0 | 55 125 | 3 111 | 18 886 | 231 685 | 8.8 | 28 786 | 41 184 | 26 215 | 42 730 | 54 298 | 4 878 |
| South Dakota | 1 425 | 15 655 | 4.6 | 14 765 | 623 | 4 172 | 50 842 | 3.4 | 6 713 | 9 025 | 2 880 | 9 028 | 12 266 | 1 045 |
| Tennessee | 7 413 | 123 575 | 1.3 | 126 919 | 6 065 | 24 234 | 320 739 | 5.3 | 42 090 | 48 065 | 31 283 | 65 120 | 77 547 | 7 245 |
| Texas | 31 898 | 495 225 | 12.6 | 663 680 | 27 146 | 78 795 | 1 138 440 | 10.9 | 156 304 | 192 056 | 125 866 | 224 986 | 311 335 | 26 395 |
| Utah | 3 659 | 52 935 | 20.1 | 38 764 | 2 503 | 8 984 | 142 266 | 16.9 | 18 008 | 22 968 | 12 114 | 26 087 | 36 574 | 3 241 |
| Vermont | 852 | 10 628 | -1.5 | 5 893 | 472 | 3 852 | 40 416 | 0.8 | 5 116 | 9 473 | 3 301 | 2 499 | 9 310 | 939 |
| Virginia | 7 740 | 120 111 | 13.7 | 94 659 | 6 059 | 29 633 | 431 634 | 7.4 | 57 291 | 70 445 | 47 329 | 75 598 | 105 663 | 9 992 |
| Washington | 9 743 | 132 047 | 9.0 | 116 016 | 6 919 | 23 075 | 328 053 | 10.6 | 44 839 | 59 754 | 29 651 | 59 721 | 92 969 | 8 585 |
| West Virginia | 1 580 | 20 653 | 2.4 | 15 506 | 868 | 7 047 | 92 227 | 3.2 | 11 609 | 16 316 | 6 260 | 20 406 | 20 539 | 1 776 |
| Wisconsin | 7 326 | 117 706 | 4.4 | 94 009 | 5 707 | 21 205 | 320 140 | 2.7 | 37 848 | 56 874 | 21 749 | 60 781 | 72 283 | 6 778 |
| Wyoming | 826 | 7 646 | 22.2 | 7 699 | 372 | 2 951 | 32 033 | 11.2 | 4 644 | 5 302 | 1 659 | 5 766 | 8 958 | 758 |

1. Establishments with payroll.

# Table A. States — **Information**

| STATE | Number of establishments | Information, 2007 — Employees — Number | Percent change, 2002–2007 | Publishing, except Internet | Motion picture and sound recording | Broadcasting, except Internet | Internet publishing and broadcasting and web search portals | Telecommunications | Data processing, hosting, and related services | Receipts (mil dol) | Annual payroll (mil dol) |
|---|---|---|---|---|---|---|---|---|---|---|---|
| | 236 | 237 | 238 | 239 | 240 | 241 | 242 | 243 | 244 | 245 | 246 |
| UNITED STATES | 141 566 | 3 496 773 | -6.4 | 1 093 047 | 335 807 | 294 876 | 75 506 | 1 250 993 | 393 741 | 1 072 343 | 228 837 |
| Alabama | 1 700 | 40 054 | 0.1 | 13 226 | 2 109 | 3 991 | 110 | 16 907 | 3 562 | NA | 1 875 |
| Alaska | 407 | 6 754 | -5.4 | 983 | 590 | 926 | D | 4 121 | 103 | NA | 374 |
| Arizona | 2 275 | 52 573 | -7.4 | 15 967 | 3 690 | 4 143 | 524 | 17 966 | 9 635 | NA | 3 006 |
| Arkansas | 1 034 | 26 074 | -17.1 | D | D | D | D | 9 273 | D | NA | 1 343 |
| California | 21 068 | 556 535 | -1.3 | 166 140 | 142 848 | 35 660 | 30 580 | 129 756 | 47 851 | NA | 48 147 |
| Colorado | 3 183 | 84 564 | -17.2 | 24 635 | 4 730 | 5 621 | D | 35 283 | 13 369 | NA | 5 663 |
| Connecticut | 1 834 | 40 345 | -16.3 | 12 288 | D | 4 073 | D | 13 380 | 4 805 | NA | 2 556 |
| Delaware | 383 | 8 565 | 4.9 | D | D | D | D | 3 537 | D | NA | 457 |
| District of Columbia | 749 | 24 499 | -14.1 | 10 544 | D | D | 934 | 4 689 | D | NA | 2 129 |
| Florida | 8 296 | 175 382 | -5.0 | 50 552 | 13 190 | 17 527 | 1 783 | 73 873 | 17 265 | NA | 9 663 |
| Georgia | 4 328 | 122 496 | -15.7 | 29 487 | 6 548 | 12 544 | 2 971 | 54 327 | 14 641 | NA | 8 156 |
| Hawaii | 622 | 10 083 | -13.6 | 2 409 | 1 080 | 1 012 | 52 | 4 672 | 797 | NA | 510 |
| Idaho | 717 | 15 163 | 37.9 | 3 267 | 866 | 1 352 | D | 7 681 | 1 828 | NA | 528 |
| Illinois | 5 696 | 136 589 | -8.9 | 45 443 | 9 545 | 9 391 | 3 221 | 46 662 | 20 343 | NA | 8 630 |
| Indiana | 2 282 | 45 786 | -7.7 | 14 847 | 3 746 | 4 461 | 112 | 17 838 | 4 375 | NA | 2 089 |
| Iowa | 1 590 | 34 397 | -22.2 | 11 130 | 1 758 | 2 716 | 45 | 10 635 | 8 066 | NA | 1 426 |
| Kansas | 1 502 | 52 737 | 6.0 | 9 902 | 1 653 | 2 622 | 182 | 33 823 | 3 597 | NA | 3 064 |
| Kentucky | 1 594 | 33 996 | 15.4 | 7 694 | 1 837 | 3 219 | 572 | 12 130 | 7 836 | NA | 1 252 |
| Louisiana | 1 455 | 30 537 | -2.8 | 5 866 | 2 191 | 3 468 | 68 | 17 171 | 1 609 | NA | 1 361 |
| Maine | 777 | 13 520 | 14.7 | 4 235 | 546 | 1 225 | 102 | 5 353 | 852 | NA | 523 |
| Maryland | 2 571 | 63 081 | -13.2 | 15 239 | D | 6 334 | D | 26 069 | 9 536 | NA | 3 764 |
| Massachusetts | 3 772 | 110 038 | -11.7 | 51 791 | 4 212 | 5 552 | D | 30 501 | 13 623 | NA | 8 623 |
| Michigan | 3 791 | 77 639 | -20.0 | 26 606 | 6 017 | 6 296 | 347 | 28 682 | 9 182 | NA | 4 314 |
| Minnesota | 2 772 | 70 314 | 0.2 | 32 666 | 4 123 | 4 831 | 637 | 18 110 | 9 547 | NA | 4 232 |
| Mississippi | 1 017 | 15 902 | -19.9 | 3 290 | 970 | 1 930 | D | 8 728 | 761 | NA | 646 |
| Missouri | 2 627 | 73 040 | -11.1 | 20 630 | 3 802 | 5 463 | 510 | 28 911 | 13 041 | NA | 3 880 |
| Montana | 638 | 9 500 | 1.5 | 2 648 | D | 1 135 | D | 3 949 | 1 023 | NA | 343 |
| Nebraska | 957 | 20 217 | -10.3 | 7 748 | 1 316 | 1 809 | D | 5 361 | 3 338 | NA | 984 |
| Nevada | 1 109 | 17 914 | 0.4 | 4 621 | 1 775 | 2 787 | 389 | 6 907 | 1 368 | NA | 973 |
| New Hampshire | 790 | 15 482 | 5.9 | 8 604 | 824 | 666 | D | 4 387 | 710 | NA | 1 149 |
| New Jersey | 4 092 | 134 356 | 5.0 | 46 384 | D | D | D | 61 510 | 13 802 | NA | 8 950 |
| New Mexico | 828 | 13 987 | -7.6 | 3 017 | 1 186 | 1 503 | D | 7 737 | 412 | NA | 495 |
| New York | 11 326 | 301 340 | -2.1 | 94 777 | 34 555 | 48 850 | D | 77 655 | 21 289 | NA | 22 558 |
| North Carolina | 3 481 | 76 413 | -1.5 | 23 062 | 4 656 | 6 291 | 609 | 33 854 | 6 856 | NA | 4 263 |
| North Dakota | 367 | 7 124 | -7.5 | 2 910 | 345 | 1 261 | D | 1 790 | 611 | NA | 332 |
| Ohio | 4 199 | 97 360 | -13.8 | 32 911 | 5 711 | 7 982 | 5 160 | 34 879 | 10 095 | NA | 5 178 |
| Oklahoma | 1 585 | 32 481 | -10.8 | D | D | D | D | 17 759 | D | NA | 1 463 |
| Oregon | 1 992 | 39 258 | -1.7 | 13 074 | 3 121 | 3 330 | 325 | 12 853 | 6 211 | NA | 2 055 |
| Pennsylvania | 5 302 | 137 115 | -4.7 | 45 951 | 7 704 | 9 256 | 756 | 54 148 | 13 664 | NA | 7 774 |
| Rhode Island | 394 | 8 059 | -8.4 | 2 778 | 374 | 927 | D | 3 097 | 386 | NA | 416 |
| South Carolina | 1 410 | 33 052 | 11.3 | 8 239 | 1 825 | 3 324 | 152 | 16 878 | 2 213 | NA | 1 581 |
| South Dakota | 437 | 7 296 | -8.8 | 1 968 | 475 | 1 177 | D | 3 170 | 462 | NA | 313 |
| Tennessee | 2 491 | 50 778 | -6.3 | 13 093 | 5 330 | 6 313 | D | 21 126 | 4 465 | NA | 2 370 |
| Texas | 9 541 | 250 410 | -11.4 | 62 632 | 14 855 | 18 854 | 1 548 | 111 021 | 39 565 | NA | 15 460 |
| Utah | 1 412 | 33 310 | -4.8 | 11 345 | 3 278 | 1 726 | 918 | 9 619 | 6 121 | NA | 1 762 |
| Vermont | 514 | 6 048 | -17.6 | 1 993 | 404 | 720 | D | 1 778 | 637 | NA | 255 |
| Virginia | 4 064 | 104 147 | -20.5 | 27 600 | 5 140 | 7 133 | D | 48 597 | 13 230 | NA | 7 533 |
| Washington | 3 301 | 111 840 | 10.0 | 59 057 | 5 065 | 4 532 | 2 532 | 29 709 | 9 182 | NA | 11 277 |
| West Virginia | 679 | 10 285 | -18.8 | 2 633 | 553 | 1 541 | 6 | 4 726 | 764 | NA | 387 |
| Wisconsin | 2 286 | 54 179 | -2.0 | 19 751 | 3 497 | 5 327 | 307 | 16 856 | 8 376 | NA | 2 625 |
| Wyoming | 329 | 4 159 | -1.4 | 1 293 | 499 | 515 | D | 1 549 | 234 | NA | 151 |

# Table A. States — Utilities, Transportation and Warehousing, and Finance and Insurance

| STATE | Utilities, 2007 Number of establishments | Employees Number | Employees Percent change, 2002–2007 | Receipts (mil dol) | Annual payroll (mil dol) | Transportation and warehousing, 2007 Number of establishments | Employees Number | Employees Percent change, 2002–2007 | Receipts (mil dol) | Annual payroll (mil dol) | Finance and insurance, 2007 Number of establishments | Employees Number | Employees Percent change, 2002–2007 | Receipts (mil dol) | Annual payroll (mil dol) |
|---|---|---|---|---|---|---|---|---|---|---|---|---|---|---|---|
| | 247 | 248 | 249 | 250 | 251 | 252 | 253 | 254 | 255 | 256 | 257 | 258 | 259 | 260 | 261 |
| UNITED STATES | 16 578 | 637 247 | -3.9 | 584 193 | 51 654 | 219 706 | 4 454 383 | 22.0 | 639 916 | 173 183 | 501 713 | 6 607 511 | 0.4 | 3 669 303 | 502 417 |
| Alabama | 373 | 14 396 | -10.1 | NA | 1 171 | 3 266 | 61 799 | 19.0 | 8 167 | 2 210 | 7 059 | 72 010 | -3.0 | NA | 3 912 |
| Alaska | 90 | 1 731 | 0.6 | NA | 125 | 1 125 | 20 143 | 30.3 | 5 495 | 1 114 | 810 | 7 778 | 9.5 | NA | 437 |
| Arizona | 227 | 11 957 | NA | NA | 952 | 3 405 | 83 777 | 10.1 | 9 626 | 3 271 | 10 496 | 147 894 | NA | NA | 7 997 |
| Arkansas | 346 | 7 127 | -3.1 | NA | 514 | 2 613 | 60 118 | 1.9 | 7 420 | 2 199 | 4 579 | 37 798 | 11.3 | NA | 1 685 |
| California | 1 145 | 63 954 | 11.3 | NA | 5 437 | 21 616 | 452 017 | 13.8 | 70 603 | 18 055 | 54 395 | 720 191 | 5.7 | NA | 57 431 |
| Colorado | 371 | 8 468 | -0.4 | NA | 614 | 3 463 | 64 731 | 36.9 | 10 471 | 2 450 | 10 905 | 107 119 | 5.2 | NA | 6 920 |
| Connecticut | 151 | 10 210 | -3.5 | NA | 997 | 1 714 | 44 117 | 9.7 | 5 273 | 1 739 | 6 431 | 137 353 | -5.9 | NA | 16 598 |
| Delaware | 49 | 2 615 | -2.1 | NA | 224 | 725 | 11 638 | 33.7 | 1 050 | 402 | 2 117 | 42 443 | -11.8 | NA | 3 031 |
| District of Columbia | 37 | 2 029 | NA | NA | 201 | 197 | 8 810 | 52.5 | 3 765 | 607 | 1 036 | 19 474 | NA | NA | 2 486 |
| Florida | 588 | 30 920 | 8.6 | NA | 2 218 | 13 417 | 218 128 | 23.7 | 40 830 | 8 204 | 34 389 | 371 543 | 8.8 | NA | 21 520 |
| Georgia | 561 | 24 495 | -3.8 | NA | 1 821 | 6 430 | 169 568 | 44.7 | 22 064 | 7 499 | 15 707 | 179 053 | 0.1 | NA | 11 189 |
| Hawaii | 54 | 2 953 | 20.8 | NA | 214 | 883 | 32 361 | 100.0 | 4 275 | 1 108 | 1 672 | 20 747 | 13.6 | NA | 1 095 |
| Idaho | 186 | 3 330 | -10.1 | NA | 233 | 1 772 | 16 991 | 31.7 | 2 198 | 544 | 2 997 | 22 586 | 27.0 | NA | 980 |
| Illinois | 455 | 27 635 | -21.0 | NA | 2 551 | 11 753 | 237 877 | 30.8 | 36 208 | 9 947 | 24 106 | 348 163 | -0.2 | NA | 28 584 |
| Indiana | 605 | 14 982 | -2.2 | NA | 1 016 | 5 282 | 118 144 | 21.7 | 16 577 | 4 108 | 10 453 | 110 143 | 1.6 | NA | 5 739 |
| Iowa | 260 | 7 718 | -5.0 | NA | 507 | 3 778 | 54 447 | 24.4 | 6 825 | 1 909 | 6 261 | 91 157 | -4.1 | NA | 4 756 |
| Kansas | 230 | 9 158 | 38.7 | NA | 474 | 2 656 | 46 861 | 15.5 | 5 881 | 1 647 | 6 065 | 61 657 | 11.6 | NA | 3 224 |
| Kentucky | 329 | 8 282 | -9.1 | NA | 578 | 3 176 | 78 936 | 17.5 | 11 791 | 3 517 | 6 594 | 66 825 | -2.8 | NA | 3 076 |
| Louisiana | 532 | 10 857 | -8.8 | NA | 928 | 3 805 | 72 064 | 11.9 | 12 491 | 3 284 | 7 825 | 64 290 | -1.2 | NA | 3 096 |
| Maine | 84 | 2 513 | -12.0 | NA | 165 | 1 251 | 15 211 | 14.9 | 1 658 | 523 | 2 031 | 26 977 | -0.1 | NA | 1 380 |
| Maryland | 115 | 10 058 | -17.8 | NA | 1 162 | 3 704 | 67 301 | 20.1 | 7 266 | 2 548 | 8 553 | 125 201 | 2.4 | NA | 8 944 |
| Massachusetts | 243 | 13 230 | -6.9 | NA | 1 139 | 3 741 | 79 518 | 11.4 | 10 036 | 2 998 | 9 941 | 222 383 | 3.0 | NA | 22 299 |
| Michigan | 397 | 22 221 | NA | NA | 1 734 | 5 876 | 106 859 | 16.8 | 17 723 | 4 454 | 15 165 | 175 299 | -1.2 | NA | 9 308 |
| Minnesota | 269 | 11 780 | -5.6 | NA | 876 | 4 739 | 80 323 | 39.9 | 15 056 | 3 185 | 10 114 | 156 603 | 2.5 | NA | 10 928 |
| Mississippi | 586 | 8 677 | 0.7 | NA | 587 | 2 340 | 36 419 | 23.3 | 4 041 | 1 251 | 4 906 | 35 919 | 6.6 | NA | 1 514 |
| Missouri | 375 | 16 032 | -18.0 | NA | 1 199 | 5 091 | 89 027 | 13.0 | 14 974 | 3 277 | 11 219 | 137 221 | 0.3 | NA | 7 277 |
| Montana | 194 | 2 761 | -9.7 | NA | 184 | 1 350 | 11 658 | 28.2 | 1 640 | 375 | 2 110 | 17 011 | 25.1 | NA | 715 |
| Nebraska | 130 | 1 296 | 8.1 | NA | 147 | 2 334 | 47 793 | 63.4 | 6 323 | 1 629 | 4 169 | 64 519 | 12.5 | NA | 3 280 |
| Nevada | 108 | 5 327 | -7.0 | NA | 442 | 1 543 | 48 376 | 68.6 | 5 319 | 1 548 | 4 841 | 42 034 | 16.7 | NA | 2 098 |
| New Hampshire | 97 | 3 178 | -3.8 | NA | 240 | 847 | 12 703 | -17.5 | 1 384 | 439 | 2 095 | 28 111 | 10.2 | NA | 1 763 |
| New Jersey | 337 | 18 334 | -13.7 | NA | 1 728 | 7 440 | 181 595 | 12.4 | 25 333 | 7 536 | 12 886 | 213 509 | -4.0 | NA | 18 545 |
| New Mexico | 220 | 5 012 | -0.6 | NA | 331 | 1 374 | 17 192 | 27.7 | 2 181 | 577 | 2 973 | 25 485 | -37.4 | NA | 1 216 |
| New York | 547 | 38 328 | -17.0 | NA | 3 490 | 12 067 | 242 097 | 21.2 | 35 690 | 9 358 | 28 241 | 590 838 | -24.4 | NA | 104 090 |
| North Carolina | 392 | 20 490 | -0.1 | NA | 1 648 | 5 971 | 116 932 | 21.8 | 13 265 | 4 252 | 13 722 | 192 422 | 8.7 | NA | 12 575 |
| North Dakota | 114 | 3 331 | 0.5 | NA | 265 | 1 051 | 10 258 | 26.6 | 1 579 | 347 | 1 666 | 16 220 | 24.0 | NA | 662 |
| Ohio | 610 | 26 511 | 5.8 | NA | 2 159 | 7 612 | 177 614 | 10.4 | 22 380 | 6 906 | 19 047 | 266 355 | 2.4 | NA | 15 422 |
| Oklahoma | 334 | 9 822 | 1.5 | NA | 632 | 2 704 | 48 079 | 35.5 | 6 441 | 1 912 | 6 727 | 60 399 | 8.3 | NA | 2 702 |
| Oregon | 268 | 7 984 | -4.7 | NA | 657 | 3 254 | 57 290 | 17.1 | 7 203 | 2 209 | 6 729 | 66 714 | 3.6 | NA | 3 570 |
| Pennsylvania | 611 | 29 183 | -13.8 | NA | 2 790 | 8 158 | 206 663 | 20.0 | 21 206 | 7 109 | 18 954 | 279 472 | -10.0 | NA | 18 603 |
| Rhode Island | 28 | 1 283 | -17.3 | NA | 99 | 703 | 10 686 | 14.2 | 1 275 | 345 | 1 594 | 31 415 | 19.7 | NA | 1 882 |
| South Carolina | 323 | 12 139 | 21.3 | NA | 769 | 2 759 | 56 053 | 19.8 | 6 300 | 2 042 | 7 549 | 66 489 | 1.7 | NA | 3 036 |
| South Dakota | 151 | 2 122 | 2.8 | NA | 127 | 1 102 | 9 168 | 21.8 | 1 253 | 286 | 1 916 | 29 806 | 27.3 | NA | 1 187 |
| Tennessee | 150 | 3 249 | -7.0 | NA | 169 | 4 218 | 132 044 | 11.6 | 15 208 | 4 701 | 10 242 | 116 358 | 1.4 | NA | 6 629 |
| Texas | 1 860 | 46 175 | -11.2 | NA | 3 958 | 16 274 | 373 340 | 37.3 | 62 952 | 15 768 | 37 761 | 465 405 | 11.6 | NA | 28 764 |
| Utah | 203 | 4 639 | 9.9 | NA | 346 | 2 194 | 49 364 | 30.1 | 7 522 | 1 942 | 5 351 | 58 648 | 38.9 | NA | 2 769 |
| Vermont | 47 | 1 902 | 7.6 | NA | 167 | 539 | 6 243 | 14.0 | 717 | 202 | 1 039 | 9 422 | -17.7 | NA | 532 |
| Virginia | 312 | 16 629 | 10.1 | NA | 1 395 | 5 358 | 95 040 | 14.1 | 10 993 | 3 316 | 12 396 | 168 511 | 5.8 | NA | 10 456 |
| Washington | 297 | 5 819 | 3.6 | NA | 396 | 5 111 | 87 038 | 33.3 | 14 983 | 3 626 | 11 061 | 119 201 | 7.4 | NA | 7 280 |
| West Virginia | 211 | 6 448 | 4.2 | NA | 463 | 1 403 | 16 588 | 8.3 | 2 764 | 613 | 2 174 | 19 975 | -10.6 | NA | 752 |
| Wisconsin | 265 | 15 721 | 11.1 | NA | 1 244 | 5 606 | 104 717 | 19.5 | 12 814 | 3 723 | 9 663 | 144 531 | 7.6 | NA | 8 191 |
| Wyoming | 111 | 2 236 | 0.8 | NA | 170 | 916 | 8 667 | 47.8 | 1 425 | 372 | 981 | 6 854 | 6.0 | NA | 291 |

| STATE | Real estate and rental and leasing, 2007 | | | | | Professional, scientific, and technical services, 2007 | | | | | | | | |
|---|---|---|---|---|---|---|---|---|---|---|---|---|---|---|
| | Number of establishments | Employees Number | Employees Percent change, 2002–2007 | Receipts (mil dol) | Annual payroll (mil dol) | Number of establishments | Total | Employees Percent change, 2002–2007 | Legal services | Accounting and related services | Architectural, engineering, and related services | Computer systems design and related services | Receipts (mil dol) | Annual payroll (mil dol) |
| | 262 | 263 | 264 | 265 | 266 | 267 | 268 | 269 | 270 | 271 | 272 | 273 | 274 | 275 |
| UNITED STATES | 384 297 | 2 188 479 | 12.3 | 485 059 | 84 765 | 847 492 | 7 870 414 | 8.7 | 1 203 763 | 1 375 685 | 1 432 209 | 1 252 197 | 1 251 004 | 502 074 |
| Alabama | 4 554 | 27 100 | 27.2 | 4 073 | 823 | 9 489 | 94 051 | 15.7 | D | 15 126 | 25 354 | 14 691 | 13 863 | 5 072 |
| Alaska | 852 | 4 370 | 2.8 | 841 | 160 | 1 828 | 12 843 | 11.3 | 2 010 | 1 521 | 5 419 | 831 | 2 042 | 759 |
| Arizona | 9 441 | 52 627 | NA | 10 078 | 1 994 | 16 640 | 129 368 | 20.7 | 17 688 | 21 946 | 27 186 | 23 092 | 17 802 | 7 311 |
| Arkansas | 3 162 | 14 115 | 15.1 | 1 968 | 375 | 5 609 | 32 361 | 6.2 | D | 7 407 | 6 711 | 2 134 | 3 443 | 1 325 |
| California | 51 597 | 312 488 | 14.1 | 76 805 | 13 447 | 112 709 | 1 260 896 | 8.3 | 145 772 | 364 118 | 185 972 | 169 890 | 200 037 | 82 881 |
| Colorado | 10 011 | 47 568 | 1.1 | 8 461 | 1 793 | 22 629 | 160 601 | 3.0 | 17 955 | 17 283 | 39 320 | 37 318 | 29 572 | 10 800 |
| Connecticut | 3 609 | 22 455 | -3.0 | 5 687 | 994 | 9 881 | 102 071 | -4.7 | D | 11 868 | 16 515 | 13 484 | 15 895 | 8 029 |
| Delaware | 1 248 | 5 807 | 1.7 | 11 057 | 222 | 2 390 | 23 389 | 1.9 | D | 2 610 | 3 568 | 3 902 | 4 269 | 1 722 |
| District of Columbia | 1 140 | 9 663 | NA | 2 748 | 625 | 4 595 | 89 006 | 6.6 | 35 547 | 4 379 | 6 494 | 12 379 | 25 809 | 9 137 |
| Florida | 33 653 | 170 859 | 25.3 | 32 235 | 6 094 | 69 263 | 430 211 | 13.6 | 91 579 | 62 515 | 89 807 | 55 962 | 61 990 | 24 395 |
| Georgia | 12 620 | 65 875 | 10.1 | 14 022 | 2 903 | 27 752 | 215 705 | 12.0 | 32 613 | 35 950 | 44 517 | 36 072 | 35 259 | 12 809 |
| Hawaii | 2 084 | 16 759 | 13.6 | 3 974 | 654 | 3 291 | 22 460 | 5.9 | D | 3 424 | 5 908 | 2 452 | 3 172 | 1 229 |
| Idaho | 2 530 | 8 371 | 49.7 | 1 242 | 234 | 4 209 | 31 650 | -0.6 | 4 631 | 3 580 | 9 229 | 1 901 | 3 822 | 1 491 |
| Illinois | 13 899 | 87 468 | 0.7 | 21 725 | 3 985 | 38 934 | 369 279 | 5.8 | 60 900 | 70 693 | 47 136 | 52 381 | 62 953 | 24 624 |
| Indiana | 6 389 | 34 272 | 1.2 | 5 448 | 1 062 | 13 017 | 96 189 | -1.7 | D | 19 014 | 21 049 | 8 902 | 12 184 | 4 809 |
| Iowa | 2 969 | 14 667 | 7.4 | 2 556 | 473 | 6 214 | 42 376 | 12.0 | 7 996 | 9 570 | 5 363 | 4 530 | 5 043 | 1 896 |
| Kansas | 3 314 | 15 160 | 3.5 | 2 429 | 440 | 7 078 | 56 302 | 5.7 | D | 12 215 | 12 266 | 8 234 | 7 889 | 2 753 |
| Kentucky | 3 898 | 20 146 | 11.8 | 3 894 | 593 | 8 114 | 61 944 | 11.5 | D | 11 253 | 11 185 | 9 205 | 7 917 | 2 852 |
| Louisiana | 4 625 | 30 922 | 5.3 | 6 015 | 1 195 | 11 190 | 85 415 | 6.8 | 20 106 | 16 657 | 27 672 | 4 887 | 11 967 | 4 265 |
| Maine | 1 771 | 6 942 | 15.0 | 1 054 | 209 | 3 484 | 22 242 | 1.5 | 4 348 | 3 085 | 5 191 | 2 374 | 2 916 | 1 087 |
| Maryland | 6 768 | 49 766 | 9.7 | 12 392 | 2 263 | 19 516 | 251 806 | 26.9 | D | 21 041 | 38 889 | 72 913 | 40 162 | 16 882 |
| Massachusetts | 7 053 | 48 576 | 11.6 | 14 030 | 2 288 | 21 974 | 252 905 | 5.5 | 32 489 | 25 994 | 46 532 | 46 723 | 51 285 | 21 358 |
| Michigan | 8 862 | 54 874 | NA | 12 859 | 1 686 | 22 691 | 251 684 | -7.5 | 27 771 | 51 164 | 57 694 | 28 751 | 29 800 | 15 402 |
| Minnesota | 6 889 | 39 430 | 6.5 | 9 208 | 1 317 | 16 678 | 141 819 | 13.3 | 21 404 | 20 035 | 20 294 | 22 362 | 20 575 | 8 473 |
| Mississippi | 2 517 | 10 169 | 5.2 | 1 735 | 284 | 4 770 | 30 999 | 6.8 | D | 6 352 | 6 128 | 3 251 | 3 986 | 1 357 |
| Missouri | 7 003 | 39 625 | 3.0 | 7 186 | 1 249 | 13 582 | 132 339 | 10.3 | D | 22 088 | 21 693 | 25 803 | 19 916 | 7 540 |
| Montana | 1 892 | 6 410 | 34.6 | 848 | 153 | 3 455 | 16 889 | 8.1 | 3 210 | 2 924 | 4 424 | 1 415 | 1 802 | 685 |
| Nebraska | 2 032 | 9 974 | 6.0 | 1 646 | 292 | 4 220 | 40 829 | 31.6 | 5 560 | 10 983 | 5 718 | 6 226 | 4 851 | 2 018 |
| Nevada | 4 613 | 31 603 | 62.2 | 6 187 | 1 106 | 7 925 | 58 085 | 25.4 | 9 593 | 8 275 | 17 170 | 5 486 | 8 991 | 3 272 |
| New Hampshire | 1 534 | 7 266 | -3.1 | 1 372 | 248 | 3 993 | 29 453 | 1.7 | D | 6 964 | 4 848 | 5 577 | 3 758 | 1 584 |
| New Jersey | 9 618 | 64 021 | 11.0 | 16 348 | 2 939 | 31 141 | 331 838 | 15.5 | D | 45 727 | 43 790 | 76 963 | 52 696 | 23 765 |
| New Mexico | 2 525 | 11 678 | 26.1 | 1 955 | 356 | 4 832 | 44 310 | 43.2 | 5 732 | 5 561 | 8 713 | 3 977 | 6 186 | 2 589 |
| New York | 32 588 | 171 601 | 7.2 | 49 867 | 7 942 | 58 526 | 565 273 | 0.4 | 129 554 | 91 780 | 66 137 | 63 579 | 115 484 | 42 815 |
| North Carolina | 11 258 | 53 563 | 15.9 | 11 175 | 1 881 | 22 488 | 184 998 | 17.3 | 24 385 | 28 145 | 31 819 | 28 769 | 26 574 | 10 883 |
| North Dakota | 770 | 3 748 | 10.4 | 669 | 96 | 1 445 | 9 794 | -10.7 | 1 678 | 1 666 | 2 069 | 1 250 | 1 122 | 420 |
| Ohio | 10 973 | 67 048 | 5.6 | 15 011 | 2 339 | 25 083 | 228 670 | -4.7 | 39 115 | 37 230 | 44 190 | 33 677 | 33 028 | 12 619 |
| Oklahoma | 4 003 | 24 887 | 30.3 | 3 852 | 806 | 9 174 | 65 879 | 12.4 | 12 586 | 15 304 | 12 412 | 9 186 | 8 084 | 3 062 |
| Oregon | 6 391 | 30 978 | 16.1 | 5 077 | 950 | 11 465 | 85 253 | 10.0 | 12 504 | 14 448 | 16 090 | 10 583 | 9 964 | 4 967 |
| Pennsylvania | 9 904 | 68 954 | 7.2 | 13 603 | 2 612 | 29 726 | 298 754 | -2.4 | 54 156 | 48 633 | 58 726 | 38 256 | 46 680 | 18 523 |
| Rhode Island | 1 233 | 6 493 | 13.4 | 1 463 | 227 | 3 110 | 22 892 | 16.9 | D | 3 561 | 3 543 | 6 163 | 2 796 | 1 182 |
| South Carolina | 5 473 | 30 417 | 23.8 | 5 194 | 990 | 9 518 | 74 923 | 17.2 | 15 302 | 15 902 | 18 083 | 5 925 | 9 484 | 3 658 |
| South Dakota | 888 | 3 844 | 8.2 | 524 | 90 | 1 750 | 10 197 | -2.2 | 1 869 | 2 052 | 1 666 | 919 | 1 108 | 391 |
| Tennessee | 6 087 | 37 737 | 14.8 | 6 950 | 1 243 | 11 339 | 100 859 | 4.7 | 15 457 | 21 889 | 19 552 | 10 974 | 12 836 | 5 100 |
| Texas | 26 593 | 173 745 | 13.0 | 36 399 | 7 067 | 57 586 | 540 528 | 9.1 | 81 046 | 76 120 | 144 800 | 79 341 | 91 869 | 35 742 |
| Utah | 4 886 | 20 413 | 41.4 | 3 391 | 617 | 8 255 | 68 452 | 31.5 | 8 319 | 18 562 | 11 171 | 8 730 | 8 373 | 3 212 |
| Vermont | 797 | 3 395 | 20.2 | 497 | 96 | 2 122 | 16 534 | 30.1 | 2 203 | 5 776 | 2 152 | 1 989 | 1 637 | 658 |
| Virginia | 9 475 | 60 502 | 21.3 | 12 637 | 2 409 | 27 254 | 387 272 | 25.0 | 28 391 | 29 108 | 65 996 | 148 375 | 68 693 | 27 939 |
| Washington | 10 480 | 51 196 | 7.3 | 10 467 | 1 819 | 19 394 | 159 711 | 12.2 | 22 408 | 21 957 | 37 630 | 24 995 | 24 809 | 10 391 |
| West Virginia | 1 586 | 7 055 | 6.6 | 1 171 | 175 | 2 960 | 22 233 | 4.3 | 5 998 | 3 247 | 4 715 | 2 145 | 2 650 | 921 |
| Wisconsin | 5 119 | 27 226 | 5.4 | 4 043 | 789 | 11 305 | 98 050 | 9.0 | D | 17 712 | 17 133 | 12 681 | 12 871 | 5 028 |
| Wyoming | 1 121 | 4 651 | 49.7 | 992 | 160 | 1 899 | 8 827 | 21.2 | 1 559 | 1 271 | 2 570 | 592 | 1 093 | 393 |

# Table A. States — Health Care and Social Assistance

| STATE | Health care and social assistance, 2007 | | | | | | | | | | | | |
|---|---|---|---|---|---|---|---|---|---|---|---|---|---|
| | Subject to federal tax | | | | | | Tax-exempt | | | | | | |
| | | Employees | | | | | | | Employees | | | | |
| | Number of establishments | Total | Percent change, 2002–2007 | Ambulatory health care services | Hospitals | Receipts (mil dol) | Annual payroll (mil dol) | Number of establishments | Total | Percent change, 2002–2007 | Ambulatory health care services | Hospitals | Receipts (mil dol) | Annual payroll (mil dol) |
| | 276 | 277 | 278 | 279 | 280 | 281 | 282 | 283 | 284 | 285 | 286 | 287 | 288 | 289 |
| UNITED STATES | 647 120 | 8 322 326 | 18.5 | 4 984 940 | 601 899 | 818 395 | 330 888 | 137 506 | 8 469 748 | 5.5 | 718 501 | 4 926 944 | 849 882 | 331 832 |
| Alabama | 8 502 | 134 925 | 19.3 | 71 265 | 18 878 | 12 637 | 5 167 | 1 890 | 103 145 | 3.2 | 9 310 | 69 965 | 9 968 | 3 723 |
| Alaska | 1 603 | 15 416 | 59.8 | 10 193 | 1 740 | 1 821 | 714 | 528 | 25 202 | -3.0 | 4 401 | 12 925 | 2 842 | 1 077 |
| Arizona | 13 643 | 154 061 | 35.1 | 91 394 | D | 16 656 | 6 572 | 1 803 | 124 772 | 26.1 | 11 535 | D | 13 751 | 5 081 |
| Arkansas | 5 718 | 77 215 | 19.8 | 39 750 | 9 239 | 7 151 | 2 895 | 1 498 | 75 649 | 8.1 | 6 435 | D | 6 289 | 2 387 |
| California | 84 335 | 883 552 | 15.2 | 563 016 | 63 134 | 102 703 | 38 944 | 12 953 | 708 878 | 6.2 | 55 838 | 433 199 | 88 903 | 33 587 |
| Colorado | 11 557 | 127 029 | 21.3 | 75 024 | 9 821 | 12 599 | 5 234 | 2 087 | 111 913 | 14.6 | 16 882 | 64 076 | 11 729 | 4 491 |
| Connecticut | 7 687 | 122 425 | 11.8 | 68 206 | D | 11 535 | 5 062 | 2 362 | 130 935 | 9.0 | 14 051 | D | 13 278 | 5 378 |
| Delaware | 1 877 | 25 319 | 26.8 | 15 335 | D | 2 621 | 1 156 | 502 | 29 421 | 7.1 | 2 200 | 17 353 | 2 810 | 1 215 |
| District of Columbia | 1 419 | 19 710 | 9.3 | 10 263 | 3 431 | 2 099 | 944 | 711 | 41 365 | -6.7 | 1 484 | 23 722 | 5 151 | 1 998 |
| Florida | 46 687 | 538 050 | 13.8 | 318 090 | 70 644 | 61 637 | 22 586 | 4 992 | 365 954 | 9.4 | 33 165 | 219 986 | 40 393 | 14 648 |
| Georgia | 18 379 | 229 101 | 14.5 | 135 432 | 19 522 | 23 274 | 9 145 | 2 461 | 190 195 | 8.8 | 11 570 | 132 958 | 20 669 | 7 336 |
| Hawaii | 2 778 | 29 023 | 45.3 | 20 431 | D | 2 979 | 1 244 | 706 | 34 617 | -4.4 | 4 955 | D | 3 586 | 1 477 |
| Idaho | 3 974 | 44 499 | 31.1 | 24 110 | 2 799 | 3 510 | 1 423 | 571 | 29 433 | 8.2 | 1 609 | 20 808 | 2 701 | 1 088 |
| Illinois | 25 651 | 325 085 | 15.9 | 205 032 | 11 797 | 32 056 | 13 445 | 5 411 | 381 584 | 0.2 | 20 692 | 228 320 | 37 987 | 14 564 |
| Indiana | 11 919 | 181 493 | 21.8 | 102 701 | 13 359 | 17 015 | 6 813 | 3 053 | 188 600 | 1.4 | 13 317 | 115 514 | 17 754 | 6 640 |
| Iowa | 5 399 | 70 263 | 14.1 | 40 123 | D | 5 854 | 2 732 | 2 458 | 128 022 | 6.9 | 6 804 | D | 9 518 | 3 872 |
| Kansas | 5 778 | 83 531 | 16.6 | 48 409 | 7 241 | 7 948 | 3 176 | 1 917 | 94 997 | 3.3 | 6 005 | 49 462 | 7 181 | 2 968 |
| Kentucky | 8 686 | 115 673 | 13.0 | 62 383 | 7 842 | 10 090 | 4 218 | 1 914 | 119 609 | 2.8 | 10 428 | 78 156 | 12 062 | 4 177 |
| Louisiana | 9 725 | 145 174 | 11.6 | 77 250 | 21 393 | 13 179 | 4 935 | 1 820 | 110 905 | -3.4 | 3 396 | 71 075 | 10 507 | 3 926 |
| Maine | 3 203 | 39 757 | 10.4 | 21 408 | D | 3 016 | 1 397 | 1 672 | 64 394 | 11.2 | 7 955 | D | 5 577 | 2 294 |
| Maryland | 12 542 | 143 677 | 15.8 | 91 164 | D | 15 364 | 6 218 | 2 762 | 172 104 | 10.2 | 8 902 | 162 079 | 18 463 | 6 871 |
| Massachusetts | 12 828 | 202 678 | 8.1 | 113 995 | 11 095 | 21 342 | 9 280 | 5 027 | 308 334 | 6.7 | 30 689 | 207 748 | 30 605 | 12 896 |
| Michigan | 21 150 | 228 681 | 10.0 | 156 808 | 2 591 | 21 055 | 9 169 | 4 883 | 320 801 | 5.4 | 24 972 | 207 748 | 31 703 | 12 420 |
| Minnesota | 10 263 | 157 035 | 25.2 | 93 957 | D | 13 230 | 6 021 | 3 733 | 229 109 | 1.9 | 22 776 | D | 20 768 | 8 851 |
| Mississippi | 4 858 | 72 601 | 18.0 | 37 002 | 11 694 | 7 229 | 2 753 | 1 018 | 74 257 | 5.4 | 3 996 | 54 573 | 6 885 | 2 619 |
| Missouri | 12 881 | 159 529 | 14.2 | 84 426 | 13 808 | 14 102 | 5 912 | 3 103 | 202 811 | 3.3 | 15 615 | 124 941 | 18 785 | 7 007 |
| Montana | 2 438 | 21 763 | 18.1 | 13 791 | D | 1 945 | 802 | 863 | 36 097 | 8.3 | 2 481 | D | 3 026 | 1 182 |
| Nebraska | 3 830 | 49 338 | 19.7 | 27 155 | 2 050 | 4 447 | 1 889 | 1 090 | 65 590 | 2.6 | 2 796 | 39 933 | 5 634 | 2 219 |
| Nevada | 5 269 | 72 716 | 37.5 | 39 241 | 17 329 | 9 226 | 3 345 | 503 | 23 917 | 1.0 | 1 516 | 15 577 | 2 965 | 1 053 |
| New Hampshire | 2 655 | 32 711 | 11.4 | 18 356 | D | 3 096 | 1 386 | 837 | 51 006 | 14.5 | 2 822 | 8 546 | 4 990 | 1 992 |
| New Jersey | 22 056 | 253 078 | 18.0 | 169 075 | 3 984 | 26 416 | 10 530 | 3 721 | 250 292 | 6.5 | 20 063 | 149 193 | 25 498 | 10 784 |
| New Mexico | 3 713 | 57 423 | 42.1 | 28 655 | 7 403 | 4 855 | 1 958 | 1 019 | 48 073 | 14.0 | 5 072 | 25 291 | 3 980 | 1 823 |
| New York | 41 201 | 459 964 | 15.3 | 341 364 | 4 431 | 46 578 | 18 428 | 12 747 | 866 075 | 3.7 | 98 596 | 411 842 | 82 017 | 35 995 |
| North Carolina | 17 964 | 286 998 | 36.1 | 160 857 | 6 844 | 22 795 | 10 133 | 3 748 | 236 399 | 12.4 | 15 003 | 155 137 | 23 894 | 8 915 |
| North Dakota | 1 176 | 14 135 | 16.4 | 9 015 | 1 404 | 1 427 | 571 | 572 | 38 062 | 6.3 | 1 465 | 18 719 | 2 480 | 1 145 |
| Ohio | 22 693 | 346 386 | 13.0 | 204 606 | 6 227 | 28 637 | 12 631 | 5 272 | 394 808 | 4.7 | 30 467 | 247 224 | 37 246 | 14 990 |
| Oklahoma | 8 577 | 121 175 | 26.5 | 58 561 | 21 197 | 10 860 | 4 172 | 1 755 | 79 602 | -2.2 | 6 397 | D | 7 503 | 2 653 |
| Oregon | 9 011 | 91 816 | 18.6 | 58 522 | D | 9 445 | 3 751 | 2 250 | 100 417 | 13.6 | 10 889 | D | 10 715 | 4 144 |
| Pennsylvania | 27 138 | 368 531 | 20.3 | 228 474 | 21 985 | 35 089 | 15 093 | 8 018 | 506 212 | 5.7 | 43 780 | 252 464 | 46 889 | 18 339 |
| Rhode Island | 2 502 | 34 762 | 20.5 | 19 520 | D | 3 015 | 1 310 | 772 | 47 185 | 6.2 | 4 505 | D | 4 146 | 1 782 |
| South Carolina | 7 883 | 115 669 | 23.3 | 64 005 | 13 933 | 11 213 | 4 523 | 1 408 | 84 547 | -1.5 | 4 245 | 57 911 | 9 195 | 3 238 |
| South Dakota | 1 535 | 17 404 | -0.1 | 10 080 | 1 187 | 1 697 | 667 | 706 | 39 076 | 7.2 | 3 632 | 22 299 | 3 070 | 1 372 |
| Tennessee | 11 720 | 185 582 | 23.8 | 104 883 | 23 380 | 19 249 | 7 600 | 2 547 | 152 159 | 4.6 | 11 097 | 97 202 | 14 550 | 5 494 |
| Texas | 48 875 | 780 459 | 26.2 | 450 190 | 105 928 | 71 221 | 27 772 | 6 116 | 386 154 | 2.0 | 28 558 | 257 127 | 42 609 | 15 346 |
| Utah | 5 731 | 67 064 | 19.3 | 38 665 | D | 6 411 | 2 365 | 661 | 45 582 | 10.8 | 3 873 | D | 4 449 | 1 791 |
| Vermont | 1 469 | 15 381 | 14.9 | 8 992 | D | 1 147 | 532 | 707 | 26 536 | 11.1 | 6 426 | D | 2 390 | 963 |
| Virginia | 14 942 | 203 981 | 19.5 | 121 014 | 18 113 | 19 705 | 8 418 | 2 598 | 167 086 | 5.9 | 11 227 | 101 016 | 17 817 | 6 544 |
| Washington | 15 513 | 172 010 | 19.4 | 103 216 | D | 16 739 | 6 871 | 2 961 | 173 151 | 10.1 | 21 900 | D | 19 148 | 7 479 |
| West Virginia | 3 741 | 51 790 | 5.0 | 25 186 | 6 094 | 4 339 | 1 708 | 1 119 | 62 873 | -2.1 | 6 739 | 38 307 | 5 536 | 2 121 |
| Wisconsin | 11 149 | 165 008 | 14.9 | 96 982 | D | 15 006 | 6 808 | 3 268 | 204 281 | 5.9 | 19 528 | D | 18 835 | 7 274 |
| Wyoming | 1 297 | 11 680 | 20.6 | 7 368 | 644 | 1 139 | 470 | 413 | 17 562 | 13.3 | 718 | 9 886 | 1 437 | 603 |

# Table A. States — Arts, Entertainment, and Recreation and Accommodation and Food Services

| STATE | Arts, entertainment, and recreation, 2007 | | | | | Accommodation and food services, 2007 | | | | | |
|---|---|---|---|---|---|---|---|---|---|---|---|
| | | Employees | | | | | Employees | | | | |
| | Number of establishments | Number | Percent change, 2002–2007 | Receipts (mil dol) | Annual payroll (mil dol) | Number of establishments | Total | Percent change, 2002–2007 | Food services and drinking places | Receipts (mil dol) | Annual payroll (mil dol) |
| | 290 | 291 | 292 | 293 | 294 | 295 | 296 | 297 | 298 | 299 | 300 |
| UNITED STATES | 124 620 | 2 061 348 | 11.5 | 189 417 | 58 359 | 634 361 | 11 600 751 | 14.6 | 9 630 090 | 613 796 | 170 827 |
| Alabama | 1 129 | 17 981 | 24.2 | 1 256 | 300 | 8 093 | 150 791 | 17.5 | 136 439 | 6 426 | 1 751 |
| Alaska | 495 | 4 456 | 20.1 | 350 | 72 | 1 996 | 25 638 | 8.3 | 19 114 | 1 851 | 530 |
| Arizona | 1 819 | 46 524 | 18.2 | 4 275 | 1 322 | 11 610 | 250 716 | 21.5 | 199 909 | 13 269 | 3 766 |
| Arkansas | 812 | 9 212 | 15.4 | 484 | 141 | 5 112 | 89 933 | 15.5 | 79 512 | 3 560 | 994 |
| California | 20 090 | 302 015 | 5.2 | 36 444 | 11 869 | 75 989 | 1 366 926 | 19.3 | 1 128 817 | 80 853 | 22 375 |
| Colorado | 2 414 | 49 688 | 9.8 | 3 911 | 1 256 | 12 075 | 231 721 | 12.2 | 186 986 | 11 440 | 3 408 |
| Connecticut | 1 652 | 25 179 | 8.4 | 2 546 | 730 | 7 941 | 132 001 | 11.5 | 100 129 | 9 138 | 2 483 |
| Delaware | 389 | 6 855 | -8.9 | 545 | 139 | 1 850 | 32 194 | 19.4 | 28 359 | 1 911 | 469 |
| District of Columbia | 290 | 7 318 | 3.2 | 876 | 319 | 2 148 | 52 998 | 22.4 | 37 156 | 4 278 | 1 238 |
| Florida | 7 537 | 166 847 | 13.7 | 15 381 | 4 218 | 35 012 | 746 214 | 20.1 | 598 276 | 41 922 | 11 470 |
| Georgia | 2 797 | 45 047 | 27.7 | 3 422 | 1 137 | 18 640 | 355 423 | 21.3 | 312 688 | 16 976 | 4 704 |
| Hawaii | 502 | 11 988 | 12.1 | 824 | 246 | 3 528 | 98 353 | 14.8 | 60 304 | 8 042 | 2 210 |
| Idaho | 718 | 9 020 | 30.0 | 397 | 126 | 3 482 | 56 662 | 24.7 | 45 340 | 2 416 | 663 |
| Illinois | 4 608 | 79 603 | 9.2 | 7 329 | 2 242 | 26 774 | 468 827 | 11.4 | 409 186 | 25 469 | 6 894 |
| Indiana | 2 175 | 35 876 | 14.0 | 3 025 | 953 | 12 932 | 254 293 | 10.0 | 221 408 | 11 670 | 3 175 |
| Iowa | 1 453 | 21 677 | 6.1 | 1 534 | 363 | 7 014 | 116 838 | 11.7 | 96 927 | 4 738 | 1 276 |
| Kansas | 1 114 | 15 643 | 16.6 | 807 | 232 | 5 866 | 104 795 | 13.8 | 92 897 | 4 192 | 1 174 |
| Kentucky | 1 341 | 18 556 | 15.6 | 1 205 | 368 | 7 309 | 151 551 | 11.1 | 136 285 | 6 301 | 1 787 |
| Louisiana | 1 356 | 24 761 | -16.6 | 2 801 | 674 | 8 169 | 180 289 | 6.0 | 142 855 | 9 730 | 2 579 |
| Maine | 894 | 7 792 | 22.1 | 505 | 134 | 3 938 | 49 363 | 9.8 | 39 919 | 2 516 | 748 |
| Maryland | 2 149 | 37 507 | 17.5 | 2 776 | 976 | 10 802 | 192 619 | 9.1 | 170 707 | 10 758 | 2 916 |
| Massachusetts | 3 078 | 52 731 | 12.7 | 4 691 | 1 612 | 16 039 | 257 302 | 6.6 | 225 602 | 14 917 | 4 340 |
| Michigan | 3 654 | 55 118 | -7.2 | 4 792 | 1 482 | 19 678 | 339 181 | 2.9 | 302 866 | 14 537 | 4 207 |
| Minnesota | 2 747 | 42 057 | 13.4 | 2 924 | 1 057 | 11 340 | 221 081 | 8.9 | 181 622 | 10 424 | 2 978 |
| Mississippi | 673 | 8 179 | -12.0 | 525 | 146 | 4 817 | 119 626 | 9.3 | 79 146 | 7 045 | 1 812 |
| Missouri | 2 161 | 37 529 | 12.3 | 3 411 | 1 254 | 12 261 | 241 438 | 11.9 | 207 557 | 11 071 | 3 109 |
| Montana | 1 083 | 10 294 | 11.3 | 674 | 140 | 3 360 | 46 137 | 12.8 | 36 177 | 2 079 | 554 |
| Nebraska | 841 | 11 364 | 10.6 | 622 | 168 | 4 241 | 69 142 | 10.3 | 61 544 | 2 686 | 749 |
| Nevada | 1 261 | 30 274 | 13.3 | 3 367 | 783 | 5 570 | 325 544 | 21.0 | 97 104 | 28 816 | 8 595 |
| New Hampshire | 739 | 11 595 | 10.6 | 776 | 245 | 3 508 | 55 268 | 15.5 | 45 825 | 2 631 | 800 |
| New Jersey | 3 543 | 51 054 | 16.4 | 3 867 | 1 273 | 19 526 | 291 327 | 8.3 | 221 700 | 19 994 | 5 232 |
| New Mexico | 664 | 14 341 | 5.4 | 1 488 | 304 | 4 090 | 80 415 | 14.9 | 64 319 | 3 734 | 1 055 |
| New York | 11 230 | 158 275 | 15.6 | 21 135 | 6 424 | 43 791 | 591 653 | 12.1 | 504 817 | 39 813 | 10 956 |
| North Carolina | 3 422 | 55 306 | 19.0 | 4 462 | 1 458 | 18 268 | 343 235 | 21.8 | 302 669 | 16 127 | 4 395 |
| North Dakota | 407 | 4 581 | 29.4 | 198 | 56 | 1 840 | 30 307 | 15.8 | 23 926 | 1 214 | 338 |
| Ohio | 4 077 | 65 326 | 3.5 | 5 526 | 1 849 | 23 959 | 436 598 | 4.2 | 401 245 | 17 780 | 5 079 |
| Oklahoma | 1 099 | 26 237 | 77.3 | 2 569 | 487 | 6 900 | 129 159 | 16.2 | 117 572 | 5 107 | 1 401 |
| Oregon | 1 597 | 24 334 | 8.4 | 1 476 | 546 | 10 241 | 150 538 | 15.8 | 127 821 | 7 556 | 2 153 |
| Pennsylvania | 4 648 | 83 594 | 13.7 | 6 702 | 2 299 | 26 910 | 420 209 | 10.0 | 369 097 | 19 625 | 5 454 |
| Rhode Island | 524 | 8 829 | 32.9 | 679 | 192 | 2 926 | 44 426 | 15.2 | 40 319 | 2 149 | 622 |
| South Carolina | 1 547 | 25 300 | 18.8 | 1 426 | 426 | 9 291 | 182 899 | 19.7 | 156 272 | 8 383 | 2 311 |
| South Dakota | 661 | 6 436 | 17.2 | 469 | 101 | 2 426 | 36 710 | 13.9 | 27 654 | 1 623 | 436 |
| Tennessee | 2 377 | 32 436 | 18.2 | 3 421 | 1 079 | 11 592 | 239 379 | 18.1 | 210 513 | 10 627 | 3 009 |
| Texas | 6 260 | 109 689 | 12.6 | 8 824 | 2 855 | 43 509 | 866 189 | 21.0 | 768 821 | 42 055 | 11 502 |
| Utah | 842 | 18 487 | -1.1 | 961 | 336 | 4 541 | 91 808 | 13.7 | 74 282 | 3 981 | 1 149 |
| Vermont | 474 | 8 009 | 0.8 | 379 | 112 | 1 942 | 31 176 | 4.4 | 19 700 | 1 368 | 428 |
| Virginia | 2 730 | 51 160 | 11.2 | 3 803 | 1 097 | 15 765 | 302 446 | 18.0 | 256 469 | 15 340 | 4 273 |
| Washington | 2 675 | 57 631 | 14.4 | 4 907 | 1 538 | 15 893 | 233 235 | 16.8 | 199 322 | 12 389 | 3 618 |
| West Virginia | 699 | 10 801 | 12.6 | 1 354 | 180 | 3 650 | 61 711 | 18.7 | 51 734 | 2 553 | 713 |
| Wisconsin | 2 738 | 42 791 | 22.1 | 3 028 | 969 | 14 439 | 227 475 | 13.3 | 192 650 | 9 247 | 2 535 |
| Wyoming | 435 | 4 045 | -0.6 | 269 | 75 | 1 768 | 26 992 | 11.7 | 18 532 | 1 469 | 412 |

| | Other services, except public administration, 2007 | | | | | | | | Government employment, 2011 | | |
| | Employees | | | | | | | | | | |
| STATE | Number of establishments | Total | Percent change, 2002–2007 | Repair and maintenance | Personal and laundry services | Religious, civic, and similar services | Receipts (mil dol) | Annual payroll (mil dol) | Federal civilian | Federal military | State and local |
| | 301 | 302 | 303 | 304 | 305 | 306 | 307 | 308 | 309 | 310 | 311 |
|---|---|---|---|---|---|---|---|---|---|---|---|
| UNITED STATES | 540 148 | 3 479 011 | 0.1 | 1 261 083 | 1 337 539 | 880 389 | 405 284 | 99 123 | 2 921 000 | 2 095 000 | 19 285 000 |
| Alabama | 6 718 | 40 488 | -2.8 | 18 034 | 15 757 | 6 697 | 4 154 | 1 050 | 57 594 | 32 806 | 317 687 |
| Alaska | 1 328 | 7 566 | -0.9 | 2 487 | 2 387 | 2 692 | 811 | 223 | 17 071 | 28 134 | 63 831 |
| Arizona | 8 906 | 68 368 | 19.6 | 27 251 | 24 794 | 16 323 | 6 220 | 1 726 | 57 269 | 34 280 | 348 709 |
| Arkansas | 4 153 | 23 188 | -3.8 | 9 961 | 8 460 | 4 767 | 2 188 | 558 | 21 101 | 17 994 | 195 115 |
| California | 57 626 | 399 336 | -1.4 | 158 848 | 149 940 | 90 548 | 52 326 | 11 914 | 255 703 | 220 651 | 2 144 996 |
| Colorado | 10 151 | 62 767 | -2.1 | 23 065 | 22 293 | 17 409 | 7 789 | 1 823 | 55 007 | 55 993 | 343 702 |
| Connecticut | 7 392 | 47 992 | 3.7 | 14 885 | 21 839 | 11 268 | 5 061 | 1 395 | 18 060 | 14 569 | 228 858 |
| Delaware | 1 587 | 10 012 | -14.9 | 3 300 | 4 593 | 2 119 | 898 | 265 | 5 842 | 8 803 | 58 178 |
| District of Columbia | 3 284 | 49 853 | 5.4 | 703 | 6 308 | 42 842 | 15 500 | 3 154 | 210 239 | 18 467 | 39 217 |
| Florida | 35 597 | 201 687 | 5.1 | 66 378 | 82 991 | 52 318 | 20 757 | 5 174 | 134 267 | 98 362 | 948 214 |
| Georgia | 14 588 | 98 047 | 15.3 | 42 248 | 38 992 | 16 807 | 10 386 | 2 837 | 104 540 | 102 282 | 575 590 |
| Hawaii | 2 916 | 20 119 | 4.3 | 3 805 | 7 864 | 8 450 | 1 918 | 513 | 34 935 | 57 632 | 90 555 |
| Idaho | 2 640 | 13 681 | 4.6 | 6 567 | 4 464 | 2 650 | 1 094 | 316 | 12 732 | 9 592 | 103 830 |
| Illinois | 23 510 | 167 675 | -5.3 | 62 578 | 60 360 | 44 737 | 20 639 | 5 203 | 85 985 | 44 784 | 758 500 |
| Indiana | 11 458 | 75 292 | -5.0 | 29 915 | 26 816 | 18 561 | 8 451 | 1 893 | 38 373 | 22 329 | 389 202 |
| Iowa | 6 088 | 31 869 | -5.5 | 12 559 | 11 772 | 7 538 | 3 063 | 779 | 18 045 | 13 013 | 236 638 |
| Kansas | 5 498 | 31 665 | -1.7 | 12 126 | 12 139 | 7 400 | 3 326 | 804 | 27 356 | 37 988 | 234 601 |
| Kentucky | 6 150 | 40 956 | -1.2 | 17 582 | 16 359 | 7 015 | 3 751 | 1 009 | 40 949 | 60 002 | 284 812 |
| Louisiana | 6 637 | 42 223 | -8.7 | 20 353 | 14 686 | 7 184 | 4 664 | 1 170 | 31 621 | 40 854 | 324 867 |
| Maine | 2 840 | 13 297 | -4.3 | 4 697 | 4 439 | 4 161 | 1 280 | 328 | 14 684 | 7 406 | 86 686 |
| Maryland | 10 365 | 77 368 | 3.9 | 25 182 | 32 326 | 19 860 | 9 689 | 2 487 | 176 373 | 48 769 | 345 293 |
| Massachusetts | 13 516 | 90 268 | -0.9 | 27 823 | 38 899 | 23 546 | 9 841 | 2 690 | 48 402 | 20 906 | 380 613 |
| Michigan | 17 040 | 101 568 | -10.3 | 38 528 | 40 665 | 22 375 | 10 844 | 2 648 | 53 386 | 20 496 | 558 187 |
| Minnesota | 11 137 | 81 829 | 4.7 | 23 556 | 28 659 | 29 614 | 8 301 | 2 355 | 32 404 | 20 786 | 360 360 |
| Mississippi | 3 853 | 20 421 | -7.9 | 8 894 | 7 307 | 4 220 | 1 950 | 490 | 26 085 | 30 795 | 222 437 |
| Missouri | 11 111 | 67 476 | -6.8 | 27 126 | 26 623 | 13 727 | 6 771 | 1 800 | 60 721 | 37 867 | 384 050 |
| Montana | 2 287 | 10 323 | 0.3 | 4 533 | 2 727 | 3 063 | 995 | 246 | 13 878 | 8 224 | 74 137 |
| Nebraska | 4 073 | 22 543 | -1.7 | 9 368 | 7 918 | 5 257 | 2 391 | 543 | 16 691 | 13 346 | 145 006 |
| Nevada | 3 571 | 27 234 | 15.0 | 10 557 | 12 199 | 4 478 | 2 584 | 702 | 17 750 | 17 967 | 130 347 |
| New Hampshire | 2 886 | 16 153 | -3.5 | 5 849 | 6 420 | 3 884 | 1 574 | 458 | 7 427 | 4 658 | 83 856 |
| New Jersey | 19 047 | 105 659 | -0.4 | 35 166 | 50 036 | 20 457 | 11 204 | 3 003 | 53 901 | 25 798 | 545 933 |
| New Mexico | 2 953 | 18 061 | 0.4 | 8 051 | 5 410 | 4 600 | 1 690 | 450 | 32 610 | 18 196 | 163 024 |
| New York | 42 575 | 249 391 | -0.5 | 56 440 | 98 809 | 94 142 | 39 147 | 8 073 | 121 187 | 61 472 | 1 295 149 |
| North Carolina | 14 105 | 85 304 | 3.4 | 34 948 | 32 550 | 17 806 | 9 362 | 2 217 | 69 699 | 144 936 | 646 446 |
| North Dakota | 1 708 | 9 261 | -5.4 | 2 869 | 3 190 | 3 202 | 746 | 199 | 9 691 | 11 668 | 62 969 |
| Ohio | 20 349 | 135 272 | -8.6 | 48 306 | 57 766 | 29 200 | 13 048 | 3 464 | 80 543 | 36 158 | 700 757 |
| Oklahoma | 5 541 | 31 654 | -2.5 | 12 605 | 12 458 | 6 591 | 3 318 | 759 | 49 211 | 38 193 | 284 491 |
| Oregon | 6 888 | 39 129 | 4.0 | 16 415 | 13 094 | 9 620 | 4 462 | 1 091 | 28 837 | 12 391 | 253 494 |
| Pennsylvania | 25 316 | 154 379 | 0.2 | 51 384 | 62 406 | 40 589 | 17 622 | 3 933 | 103 076 | 35 532 | 664 346 |
| Rhode Island | 2 382 | 14 379 | -0.9 | 4 226 | 5 847 | 4 306 | 1 449 | 373 | 10 261 | 7 376 | 54 474 |
| South Carolina | 7 088 | 45 520 | 7.7 | 18 456 | 16 777 | 10 287 | 3 902 | 1 127 | 32 828 | 54 069 | 306 039 |
| South Dakota | 1 815 | 8 518 | -2.7 | 3 471 | 2 725 | 2 322 | 750 | 182 | 11 560 | 8 801 | 64 761 |
| Tennessee | 8 811 | 62 425 | 6.7 | 23 758 | 26 667 | 12 000 | 6 339 | 1 681 | 51 033 | 23 350 | 380 193 |
| Texas | 34 462 | 253 503 | 2.5 | 116 002 | 93 700 | 43 801 | 25 779 | 6 994 | 202 169 | 185 308 | 1 597 210 |
| Utah | 4 141 | 26 236 | 9.5 | 12 620 | 9 314 | 4 302 | 2 356 | 653 | 36 676 | 16 943 | 183 962 |
| Vermont | 1 629 | 7 269 | -1.7 | 2 306 | 2 133 | 2 830 | 799 | 183 | 6 472 | 4 330 | 46 131 |
| Virginia | 15 072 | 111 129 | 1.3 | 34 685 | 41 436 | 35 008 | 16 498 | 3 915 | 191 928 | 146 801 | 533 049 |
| Washington | 12 324 | 71 213 | 3.7 | 27 026 | 27 518 | 16 669 | 8 921 | 2 030 | 74 077 | 81 182 | 470 095 |
| West Virginia | 2 927 | 16 527 | -4.0 | 6 735 | 5 647 | 4 145 | 1 550 | 388 | 23 548 | 9 662 | 128 169 |
| Wisconsin | 10 724 | 66 392 | -2.8 | 23 560 | 27 506 | 15 326 | 6 360 | 1 679 | 29 496 | 16 750 | 385 310 |
| Wyoming | 1 385 | 6 526 | 4.0 | 3 296 | 1 554 | 1 676 | 766 | 179 | 7 707 | 6 329 | 60 924 |

# Table A. States — **Federal Funds**

| STATE | Federal funds and grants, 2009–2010 (mil dol) | | | | | | | | | | | |
|---|---|---|---|---|---|---|---|---|---|---|---|---|
| | | | Procurement contract awards | | Direct payments to individuals | | | | | | | |
| | Total | Salaries and wages | Defense | Other | Total | Social Security and government retirement | Medicare | Unemploy-ment compen-sation | Food Stamps | Supple-mental Security Income | Agricultural assistance | Housing assistance |
| | 312 | 313 | 314 | 315 | 316 | 317 | 318 | 319 | 320 | 321 | 322 | 323 |
| UNITED STATES................. | 3 251 309 | 341 628 | 329 873 | 184 951 | 1 719 574 | 858 956 | 508 446 | 67 420 | 64 593 | 47 304 | 17 287 | 13 795 |
| Alabama............................... | 56 496 | 5 613 | 8 140 | 2 342 | 31 128 | 16 937 | 8 286 | 533 | 1 226 | 1 040 | 241 | 331 |
| Alaska.................................. | 12 615 | 4 055 | 1 776 | 688 | 2 631 | 1 531 | 349 | 228 | 159 | 59 | 19 | 21 |
| Arizona................................ | 64 427 | 4 980 | 10 831 | 1 982 | 32 273 | 17 842 | 7 041 | 860 | 1 588 | 693 | 133 | 82 |
| Arkansas............................. | 28 904 | 2 418 | 1 138 | 613 | 17 893 | 9 722 | 4 417 | 451 | 686 | 641 | 526 | 91 |
| California............................. | 333 809 | 24 585 | 41 323 | 16 214 | 172 819 | 78 068 | 56 261 | 10 191 | 5 694 | 6 775 | 795 | 1 114 |
| Colorado.............................. | 49 687 | 8 519 | 5 632 | 4 735 | 22 008 | 12 450 | 4 655 | 1 084 | 688 | 389 | 291 | 155 |
| Connecticut......................... | 55 978 | 1 903 | 11 114 | 843 | 33 820 | 9 783 | 20 602 | 1 335 | 570 | 365 | 33 | 230 |
| Delaware.............................. | 8 076 | 708 | 218 | 145 | 4 951 | 2 957 | 1 150 | 168 | 171 | 98 | 67 | 50 |
| District of Columbia.............. | 61 920 | 23 030 | 4 651 | 16 599 | 6 769 | 2 624 | 1 280 | 197 | 196 | 163 | 54 | 115 |
| Florida................................. | 186 704 | 12 964 | 12 814 | 5 167 | 127 692 | 61 448 | 46 594 | 2 687 | 4 417 | 2 927 | 335 | 483 |
| Georgia............................... | 92 387 | 17 372 | 8 378 | 4 083 | 45 804 | 24 719 | 10 240 | 1 365 | 2 565 | 1 341 | 395 | 417 |
| Hawaii................................. | 20 855 | 7 898 | 2 351 | 394 | 7 187 | 4 218 | 1 489 | 328 | 358 | 150 | 15 | 45 |
| Idaho................................... | 14 252 | 1 245 | 265 | 2 368 | 7 393 | 4 391 | 1 320 | 306 | 300 | 167 | 267 | 28 |
| Illinois................................. | 109 967 | 7 949 | 7 119 | 4 482 | 66 357 | 32 013 | 19 805 | 3 605 | 2 784 | 1 831 | 855 | 740 |
| Indiana................................ | 58 603 | 4 360 | 4 370 | 1 128 | 36 780 | 18 937 | 8 988 | 1 217 | 1 291 | 745 | 458 | 288 |
| Iowa.................................... | 28 379 | 1 902 | 1 557 | 816 | 17 710 | 9 175 | 4 609 | 587 | 526 | 289 | 879 | 56 |
| Kansas................................ | 29 046 | 5 818 | 1 941 | 1 119 | 15 431 | 8 306 | 4 125 | 568 | 403 | 280 | 742 | 86 |
| Kentucky............................. | 57 271 | 9 205 | 5 181 | 2 306 | 31 077 | 13 649 | 11 693 | 784 | 1 186 | 1 187 | 460 | 196 |
| Louisiana............................. | 53 214 | 4 703 | 5 842 | 1 449 | 26 134 | 11 960 | 8 703 | 464 | 1 286 | 1 073 | 350 | 152 |
| Maine.................................. | 14 644 | 1 134 | 1 336 | 400 | 7 987 | 4 679 | 1 837 | 233 | 356 | 213 | 102 | 74 |
| Maryland.............................. | 96 261 | 15 041 | 12 018 | 14 505 | 40 256 | 18 444 | 14 531 | 901 | 878 | 674 | 93 | 342 |
| Massachusetts..................... | 82 454 | 4 506 | 12 674 | 3 314 | 39 608 | 17 313 | 13 691 | 2 309 | 1 172 | 1 099 | 40 | 852 |
| Michigan.............................. | 90 921 | 4 798 | 4 080 | 2 386 | 59 079 | 30 769 | 17 108 | 2 571 | 2 809 | 1 635 | 302 | 333 |
| Minnesota............................ | 44 376 | 3 368 | 1 520 | 1 430 | 27 529 | 13 727 | 7 575 | 1 435 | 632 | 546 | 693 | 193 |
| Mississippi.......................... | 31 419 | 3 017 | 1 634 | 1 032 | 17 865 | 9 042 | 4 606 | 259 | 847 | 742 | 517 | 106 |
| Missouri.............................. | 70 348 | 7 321 | 10 335 | 2 668 | 36 022 | 18 408 | 9 846 | 912 | 1 361 | 813 | 547 | 200 |
| Montana.............................. | 10 758 | 1 195 | 313 | 507 | 5 805 | 3 301 | 1 153 | 178 | 177 | 103 | 378 | 27 |
| Nebraska............................. | 16 532 | 1 783 | 793 | 514 | 9 935 | 5 308 | 2 142 | 198 | 238 | 150 | 685 | 43 |
| Nevada................................ | 19 771 | 1 942 | 1 315 | 1 092 | 11 720 | 6 993 | 2 281 | 901 | 415 | 252 | 25 | 43 |
| New Hampshire ................... | 11 335 | 880 | 1 092 | 343 | 6 709 | 4 199 | 1 478 | 196 | 152 | 105 | 45 | 73 |
| New Jersey.......................... | 80 990 | 5 578 | 7 858 | 2 379 | 49 719 | 23 841 | 16 834 | 3 639 | 1 030 | 983 | 60 | 654 |
| New Mexico......................... | 27 959 | 2 768 | 1 520 | 5 979 | 10 972 | 6 261 | 2 011 | 457 | 542 | 368 | 74 | 36 |
| New York............................. | 202 266 | 13 936 | 8 810 | 5 073 | 111 343 | 49 785 | 37 803 | 4 730 | 4 985 | 4 025 | 157 | 2 335 |
| North Carolina...................... | 90 737 | 15 349 | 3 627 | 2 464 | 49 198 | 28 314 | 10 371 | 2 289 | 2 072 | 1 297 | 754 | 304 |
| North Dakota........................ | 8 696 | 1 083 | 288 | 397 | 4 690 | 2 159 | 921 | 74 | 95 | 46 | 1 052 | 20 |
| Ohio.................................... | 106 449 | 6 975 | 6 064 | 2 765 | 66 245 | 33 289 | 20 460 | 2 517 | 2 737 | 1 850 | 357 | 736 |
| Oklahoma............................ | 38 455 | 5 575 | 2 410 | 965 | 21 669 | 11 994 | 5 584 | 400 | 900 | 578 | 282 | 88 |
| Oregon................................ | 33 974 | 2 569 | 891 | 1 156 | 20 664 | 11 620 | 4 615 | 1 240 | 1 073 | 458 | 211 | 85 |
| Pennsylvania....................... | 145 934 | 8 803 | 11 901 | 7 451 | 88 367 | 41 144 | 31 745 | 4 169 | 2 333 | 2 315 | 139 | 649 |
| Rhode Island........................ | 11 759 | 997 | 777 | 224 | 6 609 | 3 140 | 1 989 | 381 | 238 | 193 | 10 | 191 |
| South Carolina ..................... | 46 578 | 4 618 | 4 497 | 3 675 | 25 579 | 15 285 | 5 204 | 666 | 1 256 | 640 | 236 | 206 |
| South Dakota ....................... | 9 507 | 1 031 | 561 | 352 | 5 313 | 2 545 | 995 | 47 | 153 | 80 | 706 | 20 |
| Tennessee .......................... | 68 866 | 3 837 | 3 101 | 7 040 | 40 793 | 20 062 | 13 284 | 853 | 1 966 | 1 054 | 261 | 321 |
| Texas.................................. | 225 725 | 29 926 | 30 331 | 10 263 | 110 580 | 56 814 | 27 712 | 3 555 | 5 447 | 3 609 | 1 368 | 503 |
| Utah.................................... | 23 545 | 3 195 | 2 522 | 1 237 | 11 606 | 5 855 | 3 539 | 378 | 368 | 171 | 41 | 19 |
| Vermont............................... | 7 405 | 724 | 711 | 220 | 3 369 | 1 929 | 757 | 151 | 128 | 78 | 40 | 30 |
| Virginia................................ | 136 083 | 21 112 | 40 378 | 17 960 | 44 405 | 27 413 | 8 408 | 815 | 1 213 | 891 | 216 | 264 |
| Washington ......................... | 70 437 | 11 539 | 5 151 | 4 890 | 34 133 | 19 564 | 6 976 | 2 086 | 1 387 | 919 | 539 | 166 |
| West Virginia........................ | 21 511 | 1 936 | 345 | 1 438 | 12 822 | 7 228 | 3 417 | 266 | 487 | 513 | 22 | 69 |
| Wisconsin............................ | 54 866 | 2 926 | 8 469 | 1 336 | 30 143 | 16 180 | 7 536 | 1 530 | 1 000 | 653 | 348 | 118 |
| Wyoming.............................. | 6 211 | 709 | 155 | 414 | 2 678 | 1 608 | 567 | 128 | 52 | 36 | 72 | 14 |

# Table A. States — Federal Funds and State Government Finances

| | Federal funds and grants, 2009–2010 (mil dol) (cont.) | | | | | | | State government finances, 2011 | | | | | | | |
| | Grants | | | | | | | General revenue (mil dol) | | | | | | | |
| | | | | | | | | | From federal government | | From own sources | | | | |
| | | | | | | | | | | | | Taxes | | Taxes per capita² (dollars) | |
| STATE | Total¹ | Medicaid and other health-related | Nutrition and family welfare | Disasters and emergency preparedness | Housing and community development | Employment and training | Energy and environment | Total | Total | Per capita² (dollars) | Total | Total | Sales and gross receipts | Total | Sales and gross receipts |
| | 324 | 325 | 326 | 327 | 328 | 329 | 330 | 331 | 332 | 333 | 334 | 335 | 336 | 337 | 338 |
|---|---|---|---|---|---|---|---|---|---|---|---|---|---|---|---|
| UNITED STATES | 675 282 | 357 482 | 74 796 | 6 668 | 35 874 | 9 978 | 26 085 | X | X | X | X | X | X | X | |
| Alabama | 9 273 | 4 947 | 949 | 47 | 382 | 138 | 370 | 23 277 | 8 882 | 1 849 | 14 395 | 8 636 | 4 575 | 1 798 | 953 |
| Alaska | 3 465 | 1 066 | 283 | 16 | 174 | 56 | 260 | 12 666 | 3 041 | 4 207 | 9 625 | 5 538 | 256 | 7 662 | 354 |
| Arizona | 14 361 | 8 501 | 1 461 | 13 | 711 | 146 | 449 | 27 049 | 12 360 | 1 907 | 14 688 | 10 848 | 6 206 | 1 673 | 957 |
| Arkansas | 6 843 | 3 731 | 681 | 77 | 265 | 101 | 109 | 17 454 | 6 313 | 2 149 | 11 141 | 7 976 | 3 877 | 2 715 | 1 320 |
| California | 78 869 | 41 931 | 11 744 | 149 | 4 891 | 1 300 | 2 723 | 211 358 | 68 431 | 1 816 | 142 927 | 116 695 | 45 148 | 3 096 | 1 198 |
| Colorado | 8 793 | 3 665 | 968 | 8 | 400 | 130 | 569 | 21 864 | 7 008 | 1 370 | 14 856 | 9 468 | 3 797 | 1 850 | 742 |
| Connecticut | 8 299 | 4 769 | 848 | 20 | 522 | 141 | 189 | 23 508 | 6 561 | 1 832 | 16 947 | 13 432 | 5 523 | 3 751 | 1 542 |
| Delaware | 2 055 | 983 | 207 | 8 | 78 | 28 | 105 | 7 310 | 1 891 | 2 085 | 5 419 | 3 018 | 493 | 3 327 | 544 |
| District of Columbia | 10 872 | 2 283 | 378 | 17 | 343 | 226 | 866 | X | X | X | X | X | X | X | X |
| Florida | 28 066 | 14 386 | 3 377 | 110 | 1 636 | 394 | 808 | 75 290 | 27 804 | 1 459 | 47 486 | 32 558 | 27 156 | 1 708 | 1 425 |
| Georgia | 16 751 | 8 037 | 2 202 | 100 | 937 | 217 | 368 | 37 168 | 15 266 | 1 555 | 21 901 | 16 003 | 7 109 | 1 630 | 724 |
| Hawaii | 3 026 | 1 233 | 331 | 6 | 170 | 50 | 141 | 10 204 | 2 918 | 2 123 | 7 285 | 4 858 | 3 336 | 3 533 | 2 426 |
| Idaho | 2 980 | 1 473 | 283 | 9 | 71 | 68 | 199 | 7 344 | 2 805 | 1 770 | 4 539 | 3 262 | 1 613 | 2 058 | 1 018 |
| Illinois | 24 060 | 12 148 | 2 914 | 260 | 1 735 | 405 | 770 | 58 202 | 19 587 | 1 522 | 38 615 | 29 433 | 13 614 | 2 287 | 1 058 |
| Indiana | 11 965 | 6 229 | 1 305 | 25 | 634 | 226 | 611 | 31 450 | 10 858 | 1 666 | 20 592 | 14 909 | 8 832 | 2 288 | 1 355 |
| Iowa | 6 394 | 2 962 | 662 | 245 | 698 | 92 | 100 | 18 097 | 7 044 | 2 300 | 11 053 | 7 236 | 3 326 | 2 363 | 1 086 |
| Kansas | 4 736 | 2 242 | 600 | 123 | 134 | 63 | 157 | 15 019 | 4 941 | 1 721 | 10 078 | 6 828 | 3 333 | 2 378 | 1 161 |
| Kentucky | 9 502 | 5 483 | 1 065 | 78 | 358 | 137 | 161 | 23 573 | 9 025 | 2 066 | 14 548 | 10 203 | 4 894 | 2 335 | 1 120 |
| Louisiana | 15 088 | 6 251 | 1 239 | 2 910 | 1 732 | 117 | 213 | 26 939 | 12 533 | 2 740 | 14 406 | 8 865 | 5 131 | 1 938 | 1 122 |
| Maine | 3 787 | 2 187 | 340 | 6 | 152 | 58 | 251 | 8 249 | 3 241 | 2 440 | 5 008 | 3 676 | 1 683 | 2 768 | 1 267 |
| Maryland | 14 441 | 7 702 | 1 138 | 53 | 710 | 256 | 631 | 32 999 | 11 336 | 1 945 | 21 663 | 16 003 | 6 654 | 2 746 | 1 142 |
| Massachusetts | 22 352 | 14 088 | 1 527 | 87 | 1 329 | 215 | 867 | 44 898 | 14 137 | 2 146 | 30 761 | 22 090 | 7 109 | 3 353 | 1 079 |
| Michigan | 20 577 | 11 166 | 2 753 | 7 | 938 | 542 | 1 032 | 54 727 | 19 914 | 2 016 | 34 813 | 23 540 | 12 920 | 2 384 | 1 308 |
| Minnesota | 10 528 | 6 007 | 1 249 | 26 | 437 | 187 | 224 | 33 452 | 9 819 | 1 837 | 23 632 | 18 953 | 8 236 | 3 546 | 1 541 |
| Mississippi | 7 871 | 4 460 | 857 | 186 | 233 | 96 | 259 | 17 807 | 8 727 | 2 930 | 9 081 | 6 714 | 4 320 | 2 254 | 1 450 |
| Missouri | 14 003 | 7 869 | 1 213 | 87 | 520 | 199 | 969 | 27 083 | 12 015 | 1 999 | 15 068 | 10 110 | 4 627 | 1 682 | 770 |
| Montana | 2 939 | 1 080 | 272 | 7 | 96 | 54 | 254 | 5 769 | 2 415 | 2 419 | 3 354 | 2 304 | 533 | 2 308 | 534 |
| Nebraska | 3 507 | 1 703 | 412 | 38 | 120 | 51 | 132 | 9 389 | 3 402 | 1 846 | 5 988 | 4 153 | 2 033 | 2 254 | 1 103 |
| Nevada | 3 702 | 1 312 | 424 | 4 | 225 | 92 | 446 | 10 444 | 2 827 | 1 038 | 7 617 | 6 332 | 4 689 | 2 325 | 1 722 |
| New Hampshire | 2 311 | 1 133 | 210 | 14 | 121 | 43 | 102 | 6 252 | 2 159 | 1 637 | 4 094 | 2 320 | 904 | 1 760 | 686 |
| New Jersey | 15 457 | 8 132 | 1 858 | 131 | 1 042 | 273 | 572 | 51 676 | 14 793 | 1 677 | 36 884 | 27 183 | 11 922 | 3 082 | 1 352 |
| New Mexico | 6 720 | 3 713 | 586 | 4 | 160 | 60 | 251 | 14 949 | 6 364 | 3 056 | 8 585 | 4 980 | 2 574 | 2 392 | 1 236 |
| New York | 63 104 | 39 959 | 6 704 | 144 | 3 570 | 553 | 1 202 | 148 841 | 60 200 | 3 093 | 88 641 | 67 945 | 22 368 | 3 491 | 1 149 |
| North Carolina | 20 099 | 11 595 | 2 009 | 25 | 645 | 303 | 976 | 45 858 | 16 049 | 1 662 | 29 809 | 22 406 | 9 935 | 2 320 | 1 029 |
| North Dakota | 2 237 | 630 | 203 | 141 | 75 | 24 | 280 | 6 683 | 1 737 | 2 540 | 4 946 | 3 822 | 1 169 | 5 589 | 1 710 |
| Ohio | 24 399 | 13 660 | 3 021 | 16 | 1 216 | 405 | 848 | 61 984 | 24 133 | 2 090 | 37 851 | 25 177 | 12 591 | 2 181 | 1 091 |
| Oklahoma | 7 855 | 3 961 | 1 024 | 118 | 353 | 91 | 302 | 20 190 | 7 874 | 2 077 | 12 316 | 7 766 | 3 236 | 2 048 | 854 |
| Oregon | 8 694 | 4 360 | 926 | 49 | 346 | 207 | 457 | 20 817 | 7 609 | 1 965 | 13 208 | 8 112 | 1 097 | 2 095 | 283 |
| Pennsylvania | 29 411 | 16 147 | 2 977 | 32 | 1 242 | 427 | 1 337 | 69 499 | 23 843 | 1 871 | 45 657 | 32 352 | 16 784 | 2 539 | 1 317 |
| Rhode Island | 3 152 | 1 753 | 292 | 53 | 144 | 55 | 58 | 7 141 | 2 732 | 2 598 | 4 409 | 2 738 | 1 448 | 2 604 | 1 377 |
| South Carolina | 8 210 | 4 833 | 854 | 8 | 250 | 144 | 157 | 22 792 | 8 690 | 1 857 | 14 102 | 7 687 | 4 066 | 1 643 | 869 |
| South Dakota | 2 250 | 762 | 216 | 56 | 89 | 34 | 233 | 4 124 | 1 879 | 2 280 | 2 245 | 1 380 | 1 153 | 1 674 | 1 400 |
| Tennessee | 14 094 | 8 036 | 1 361 | 200 | 545 | 150 | 286 | 27 520 | 12 117 | 1 892 | 15 403 | 11 235 | 8 604 | 1 755 | 1 344 |
| Texas | 44 624 | 23 604 | 5 505 | 534 | 3 383 | 492 | 1 098 | 107 190 | 42 859 | 1 669 | 64 331 | 43 188 | 33 798 | 1 682 | 1 316 |
| Utah | 4 987 | 2 084 | 491 | 11 | 123 | 76 | 654 | 13 835 | 4 365 | 1 549 | 9 470 | 5 476 | 2 543 | 1 944 | 903 |
| Vermont | 2 380 | 1 088 | 192 | 0 | 72 | 35 | 161 | 5 628 | 2 035 | 3 249 | 3 593 | 2 688 | 904 | 4 291 | 1 443 |
| Virginia | 12 228 | 5 484 | 1 143 | 277 | 593 | 274 | 427 | 39 194 | 10 513 | 1 298 | 28 682 | 17 409 | 5 851 | 2 150 | 723 |
| Washington | 14 725 | 7 161 | 1 608 | 46 | 656 | 259 | 1 130 | 34 993 | 10 944 | 1 602 | 24 049 | 17 411 | 14 104 | 2 549 | 2 065 |
| West Virginia | 4 970 | 2 463 | 511 | 32 | 132 | 53 | 422 | 12 646 | 4 749 | 2 559 | 7 898 | 5 143 | 2 419 | 2 772 | 1 304 |
| Wisconsin | 11 992 | 6 592 | 1 312 | 56 | 461 | 210 | 655 | 32 133 | 10 536 | 1 845 | 21 597 | 15 347 | 6 809 | 2 687 | 1 192 |
| Wyoming | 2 254 | 442 | 115 | 1 | 28 | 25 | 242 | 6 056 | 2 401 | 4 225 | 3 656 | 2 462 | 987 | 4 333 | 1 738 |

1. Includes program categories not shown separately.    2. Based on resident population estimated as of July 1 of the year shown.

# Table A. States — State Government Finances and Voting

| STATE | Total | To local govern-ments | Total | Per capita[1] (dollars) | Education | Health and hospitals | High-ways | Public safety | Public welfare | Natural resources, parks, and recreation | Total (mil dol) | Per capita[1] | Percent registered | Percent voted | Demo-cratic | Repub-lican | All other |
|---|---|---|---|---|---|---|---|---|---|---|---|---|---|---|---|---|---|
| | 339 | 340 | 341 | 342 | 343 | 344 | 345 | 346 | 347 | 348 | 349 | 350 | 351 | 352 | 353 | 354 | 355 |
| UNITED STATES.............. | X | X | X | X | X | X | X | X | X | X | X | X | 65.1 | 56.5 | 51.1 | 47.2 | 3.6 |
| Alabama..................... | 28 061 | 6 801 | 17 490 | 3 642 | 5 961 891 | 2 558 | 1 616 | 747 | 5 962 | 307 | 9 067 | 1 888 | 71.1 | 59.9 | 38.4 | 60.5 | 1.1 |
| Alaska........................ | 11 320 | 1 723 | 8 233 | 11 392 | 1 917 737 | 429 | 1 412 | 402 | 19 177 | 412 | 6 418 | 8 880 | 69.9 | 56.0 | 40.8 | 54.8 | 4.4 |
| Arizona....................... | 32 875 | 8 668 | 19 455 | 3 001 | 9 511 299 | 1 875 | 2 038 | 1 146 | 95 113 | 354 | 14 163 | 2 185 | 57.8 | 49.6 | 44.6 | 53.7 | 1.8 |
| Arkansas.................... | 18 862 | 5 152 | 11 708 | 3 985 | 4 493 896 | 1 135 | 1 081 | 509 | 44 939 | 399 | 3 749 | 1 276 | 62.6 | 51.1 | 36.9 | 60.6 | 2.6 |
| California.................... | 280 213 | 91 502 | 133 491 | 3 542 | 77 464 948 | 18 650 | 10 624 | 8 236 | 774 649 | 4 382 | 149 671 | 3 971 | 54.2 | 47.5 | 60.2 | 37.1 | 2.6 |
| Colorado.................... | 29 169 | 7 091 | 15 939 | 3 115 | 5 663 074 | 1 892 | 1 436 | 1 162 | 56 631 | 464 | 16 335 | 3 192 | 69.0 | 51.5 | 51.5 | 46.1 | 2.4 |
| Connecticut................ | 28 094 | 4 486 | 17 763 | 4 961 | 6 362 163 | 2 409 | 1 013 | 900 | 63 622 | 179 | 30 524 | 8 524 | 64.6 | 57.5 | 58.1 | 40.7 | 1.2 |
| Delaware.................... | 7 936 | 1 293 | 5 765 | 6 355 | 1 762 406 | 447 | 461 | 381 | 17 624 | 138 | 5 808 | 6 403 | 67.8 | 62.2 | 58.6 | 40.0 | 1.4 |
| District of Columbia............. | | | | | | | | | | | | | 74.4 | 67.7 | 90.9 | 7.3 | 1.8 |
| Florida........................ | 84 633 | 19 725 | 52 260 | 2 742 | 22 303 | 4 698 | 5 449 | 2 904 | 223 026 | 1 251 | 43 472 | 2 281 | 60.5 | 53.9 | 50.0 | 49.1 | 0.9 |
| Georgia...................... | 44 750 | 10 600 | 26 810 | 2 732 | 10 367 | 1 998 | 1 641 | 1 760 | 103 669 | 755 | 13 403 | 1 365 | 66.4 | 58.1 | 45.5 | 53.3 | 1.2 |
| Hawaii........................ | 11 476 | 208 | 9 755 | 7 096 | 2 087 | 1 287 | 357 | 223 | 20 868 | 207 | 7 913 | 5 756 | 54.1 | 47.4 | 70.5 | 27.8 | 1.6 |
| Idaho......................... | 8 733 | 2 036 | 5 368 | 3 387 | 2 175 | 203 | 836 | 271 | 21 749 | 230 | 3 928 | 2 478 | 65.9 | 60.2 | 32.6 | 64.5 | 2.8 |
| Illinois....................... | 74 655 | 15 711 | 43 793 | 3 403 | 19 508 | 3 418 | 1 954 | 1 954 | 195 082 | 433 | 64 801 | 5 035 | 66.6 | 56.2 | 57.6 | 40.7 | 1.7 |
| Indiana...................... | 35 262 | 9 265 | 21 637 | 3 320 | 8 397 | 743 | 2 680 | 888 | 83 970 | 377 | 22 144 | 3 398 | 67.4 | 57.7 | 43.9 | 54.1 | 1.9 |
| Iowa.......................... | 19 937 | 5 152 | 12 067 | 3 941 | 4 901 | 1 342 | 1 591 | 429 | 49 008 | 339 | 7 574 | 2 473 | 75.2 | 66.7 | 52.0 | 46.2 | 1.8 |
| Kansas...................... | 16 687 | 4 209 | 10 318 | 3 594 | 3 531 | 1 551 | 1 239 | 441 | 35 307 | 251 | 6 893 | 2 401 | 69.2 | 58.9 | 38.0 | 59.7 | 2.3 |
| Kentucky.................... | 29 370 | 5 069 | 19 607 | 4 487 | 7 334 | 1 906 | 1 936 | 714 | 73 342 | 467 | 14 522 | 3 324 | 70.0 | 57.6 | 37.8 | 60.5 | 1.7 |
| Louisiana................... | 33 396 | 6 580 | 22 555 | 4 930 | 6 426 | 2 803 | 2 185 | 1 160 | 64 258 | 1 220 | 18 447 | 4 032 | 75.2 | 64.7 | 40.6 | 57.8 | 1.6 |
| Maine........................ | 9 099 | 1 302 | 6 703 | 5 047 | 2 905 | 500 | 647 | 214 | 29 052 | 194 | 5 904 | 4 445 | 75.5 | 67.2 | 56.3 | 41.0 | 2.7 |
| Maryland.................... | 37 673 | 8 124 | 24 181 | 4 149 | 9 274 | 2 345 | 2 196 | 1 905 | 92 743 | 596 | 25 250 | 4 332 | 64.9 | 58.7 | 62.0 | 35.9 | 2.1 |
| Massachusetts.................. | 52 551 | 8 826 | 34 355 | 5 215 | 14 716 | 1 627 | 1 908 | 1 810 | 147 155 | 587 | 74 316 | 11 281 | 72.7 | 65.4 | 60.7 | 37.5 | 1.8 |
| Michigan.................... | 63 109 | 19 878 | 32 323 | 3 273 | 14 927 | 3 678 | 2 464 | 1 963 | 149 267 | 370 | 30 975 | 3 136 | 75.0 | 65.4 | 54.2 | 44.7 | 1.1 |
| Minnesota.................. | 38 488 | 11 102 | 21 568 | 4 035 | 10 872 | 922 | 2 565 | 905 | 108 723 | 971 | 12 897 | 2 413 | 76.1 | 70.5 | 52.7 | 45.0 | 2.4 |
| Mississippi................. | 20 157 | 5 253 | 12 293 | 4 127 | 5 437 | 1 507 | 1 378 | 459 | 54 369 | 390 | 6 768 | 2 272 | 82.8 | 73.3 | 43.8 | 55.3 | 0.9 |
| Missouri..................... | 30 647 | 5 948 | 19 824 | 3 298 | 7 587 | 2 895 | 2 033 | 939 | 75 867 | 345 | 20 682 | 3 441 | 74.8 | 62.3 | 44.4 | 53.8 | 1.9 |
| Montana..................... | 7 105 | 1 353 | 4 729 | 4 738 | 1 390 | 218 | 709 | 237 | 13 901 | 291 | 4 267 | 4 274 | 72.0 | 64.5 | 41.7 | 55.4 | 2.9 |
| Nebraska.................... | 9 356 | 2 307 | 6 310 | 3 425 | 2 091 | 716 | 602 | 338 | 20 909 | 289 | 2 346 | 1 273 | 65.7 | 58.2 | 38.0 | 59.8 | 2.2 |
| Nevada...................... | 13 203 | 3 905 | 6 086 | 2 235 | 2 128 | 469 | 773 | 378 | 21 276 | 150 | 4 201 | 1 543 | 57.7 | 51.4 | 52.4 | 45.7 | 2.0 |
| New Hampshire ................. | 7 638 | 1 191 | 5 184 | 3 933 | 1 945 | 138 | 553 | 169 | 19 450 | 102 | 8 450 | 6 410 | 73.1 | 66.9 | 52.0 | 46.4 | 1.6 |
| New Jersey................ | 67 114 | 11 167 | 37 565 | 4 259 | 14 214 | 3 358 | 3 179 | 2 074 | 142 140 | 909 | 64 005 | 7 256 | 64.3 | 54.5 | 58.3 | 40.6 | 1.0 |
| New Mexico................ | 17 865 | 4 326 | 11 269 | 5 412 | 4 329 | 1 415 | 806 | 550 | 43 291 | 289 | 8 119 | 3 899 | 63.0 | 56.5 | 53.0 | 42.8 | 4.2 |
| New York.................... | 184 009 | 59 698 | 86 380 | 4 438 | 51 132 | 14 942 | 4 880 | 3 949 | 511 317 | 1 029 | 134 929 | 6 932 | 59.0 | 50.9 | 63.4 | 35.2 | 1.3 |
| North Carolina............. | 53 089 | 13 633 | 30 702 | 3 179 | 11 619 | 3 189 | 3 433 | 1 958 | 116 195 | 834 | 18 593 | 1 922 | 72.9 | 62.3 | 48.4 | 50.4 | 1.3 |
| North Dakota.............. | 5 516 | 1 301 | 3 731 | 5 456 | 913 | 176 | 717 | 119 | 9 134 | 285 | 2 061 | 3 013 | 72.5 | 62.2 | 38.7 | 58.3 | 3.0 |
| Ohio.......................... | 79 153 | 18 412 | 42 079 | 3 645 | 18 422 | 5 142 | 3 494 | 1 918 | 184 220 | 515 | 30 926 | 2 679 | 69.4 | 61.7 | 50.7 | 47.7 | 1.6 |
| Oklahoma................... | 22 378 | 4 478 | 14 534 | 3 833 | 5 457 | 1 087 | 2 049 | 748 | 54 567 | 318 | 10 255 | 2 705 | 64.3 | 51.0 | 33.2 | 66.8 | 0.0 |
| Oregon...................... | 27 335 | 5 775 | 15 335 | 3 961 | 6 027 | 2 125 | 1 672 | 872 | 60 266 | 546 | 14 069 | 3 634 | 69.6 | 63.3 | 54.2 | 42.1 | 3.6 |
| Pennsylvania............... | 90 792 | 19 945 | 53 513 | 4 199 | 23 707 | 6 290 | 7 790 | 2 794 | 237 075 | 969 | 45 267 | 3 552 | 69.0 | 59.1 | 52.1 | 46.7 | 1.2 |
| Rhode Island.............. | 8 271 | 1 074 | 5 334 | 5 074 | 2 403 | 230 | 255 | 253 | 24 033 | 49 | 9 174 | 8 726 | 67.5 | 57.4 | 62.7 | 35.3 | 2.1 |
| South Carolina............ | 29 352 | 5 586 | 18 074 | 3 863 | 6 831 | 2 431 | 1 171 | 638 | 68 313 | 281 | 15 341 | 3 279 | 70.5 | 56.4 | 44.1 | 54.6 | 1.4 |
| South Dakota.............. | 4 498 | 775 | 3 288 | 3 990 | 966 | 209 | 607 | 145 | 9 656 | 208 | 3 545 | 4 301 | 73.7 | 60.1 | 39.9 | 57.9 | 2.2 |
| Tennessee.................. | 30 841 | 7 105 | 20 461 | 3 195 | 10 747 | 1 534 | 1 705 | 1 018 | 107 466 | 403 | 5 899 | 921 | 66.2 | 53.7 | 39.1 | 59.5 | 1.4 |
| Texas........................ | 125 940 | 29 666 | 78 934 | 3 074 | 31 269 | 6 929 | 6 558 | 4 647 | 312 693 | 1 124 | 38 530 | 1 501 | 57.7 | 46.4 | 41.4 | 57.2 | 1.4 |
| Utah.......................... | 16 683 | 3 106 | 11 602 | 4 118 | 2 812 | 1 305 | 1 514 | 441 | 28 125 | 222 | 7 206 | 2 558 | 59.4 | 53.3 | 24.7 | 72.8 | 2.5 |
| Vermont...................... | 5 854 | 1 553 | 3 838 | 6 126 | 1 463 | 211 | 419 | 219 | 14 629 | 97 | 3 485 | 5 564 | 72.0 | 62.1 | 66.6 | 31.0 | 2.5 |
| Virginia...................... | 45 549 | 11 489 | 28 861 | 3 565 | 9 348 | 4 273 | 3 328 | 2 211 | 93 479 | 802 | 26 479 | 3 270 | 69.1 | 62.0 | 51.2 | 47.3 | 1.6 |
| Washington................ | 46 000 | 9 347 | 27 542 | 4 032 | 8 669 | 3 849 | 3 030 | 1 325 | 86 689 | 1 020 | 28 154 | 4 122 | 67.6 | 60.7 | 56.2 | 41.3 | 2.5 |
| West Virginia.............. | 13 000 | 2 534 | 8 912 | 4 803 | 3 288 | 439 | 1 224 | 352 | 32 877 | 288 | 7 406 | 3 992 | 67.6 | 47.5 | 35.5 | 62.3 | 2.2 |
| Wisconsin.................. | 39 350 | 10 429 | 22 612 | 3 959 | 8 969 | 1 933 | 2 432 | 1 295 | 89 692 | 746 | 22 879 | 4 006 | 76.3 | 71.9 | 52.8 | 45.9 | 1.3 |
| Wyoming.................... | 5 674 | 1 653 | 3 252 | 5 723 | 740 | 286 | 537 | 187 | 7 399 | 383 | 1 364 | 2 401 | 62.8 | 57.8 | 27.8 | 68.6 | 3.5 |

1. Based on resident population estimated as of July 1 of the year shown.   2. © 2013 Election Data Services, Inc. All rights reserved.

# States and Counties

(For explanation of symbols, see page viii)

Page

# County Highlights and Rankings

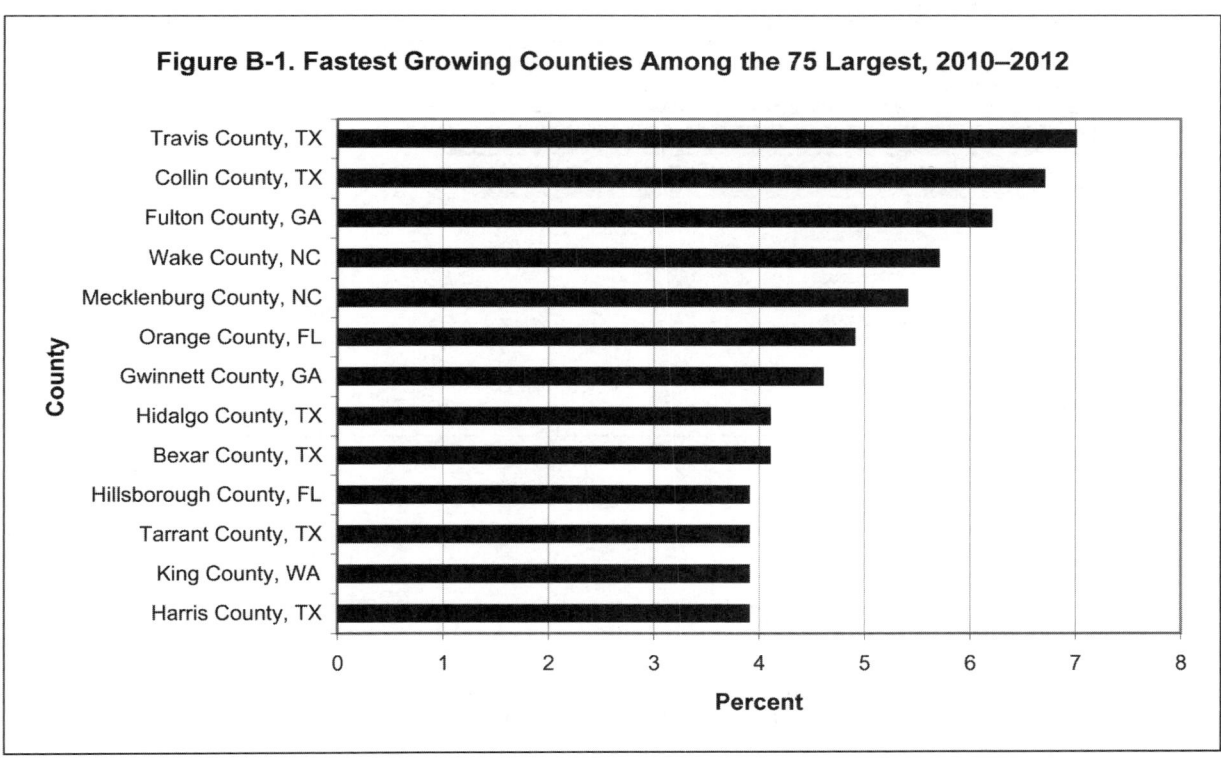

**Figure B-1. Fastest Growing Counties Among the 75 Largest, 2010–2012**

Two years after the 2010 census, the 2012 population estimates show that Los Angeles County, CA, remains, by far, the most populous county, with 9.9 million residents. Next is Cook County, IL, which includes Chicago, with over 5.2 million people. Its population declined 3.4 percent from 2000 to 2010 but increased 0.7 percent from 2010 to 2012. Among the 75 most populous counties, the highest growth rates from 2010 to 2012 were found in the West and the South. Since 2010, the fastest-growing of these large counties was Travis, TX, in the Austin metropolitan area. During the past two years, Travis County's population increased by 7.0 percent. In 2012, it ranked 37th among the most populous counties. Collin, County, TX (Dallas) and Fulton County, GA (Atlanta) each had population growth rates exceeding 6 percent while Wake County, NC (Raleigh) and Mecklenburg County, NC (Charlotte) both had population growth rates over 5 percent. Nearly 1600 counties lost population during this period. The largest proportional losses were in counties with very small populations. Among the largest counties, only Cuyahoga County, OH (Cleveland) and Wayne County, MI (Detroit), declined in population between 2010 and 2012. Sixteen counties had population growth rates at or above 10 percent from 2010 to 2012. None of these fast-growing counties had more than 42,000 residents, St. Bernard Parish was the largest with 41,635, still well below its pre-Katrina population of about 65,000.

Within states, the number and physical size of counties varied considerably: Delaware had 3 counties while Texas had 254 counties. For the 3,143 counties (and county equivalents—see Appendix A) in the United States, population in 2012 ranged from 9.9 million in Los Angeles, CA, to 71 in Loving County, TX. Other particularly large counties in terms of population are Cook County, IL (over 5.2 million people), encompassing Chicago and its suburbs, Harris County, TX (containing Houston) with 4.25 million people, and Maricopa County, AZ (containing Phoenix), with over 3.9 million people. There were 41 counties with a population of 1,000,000 or more; these counties combined contain more than one-fourth of the U.S. population. Over half of the U.S. population lived in the 147 largest counties, those with a population of 450,000 or more. At the other extreme, there were 35 counties with fewer than 1,000 people in 2012. The median county population size was 25,827.

In terms of land area, counties range from the nearly 377,000 square kilometers of Yukon-Koyukuk Census Area, AK; to Kalawao County, HI, with 31 square kilometers; New York County, NY (Manhattan), with 59 square kilometers; Bristol County, RI, with 63 square kilometers; and Arlington County, VA, with 67 square kilometers.[1] Counties tend to be larger in the western United States (most of the largest 50 in size are in that region). The median land area for all U.S. counties was about 1,600 square kilometers in 2010.

---

[1]Several independent cities in Virginia, which are treated as counties for tabulation purposes, were excluded here.

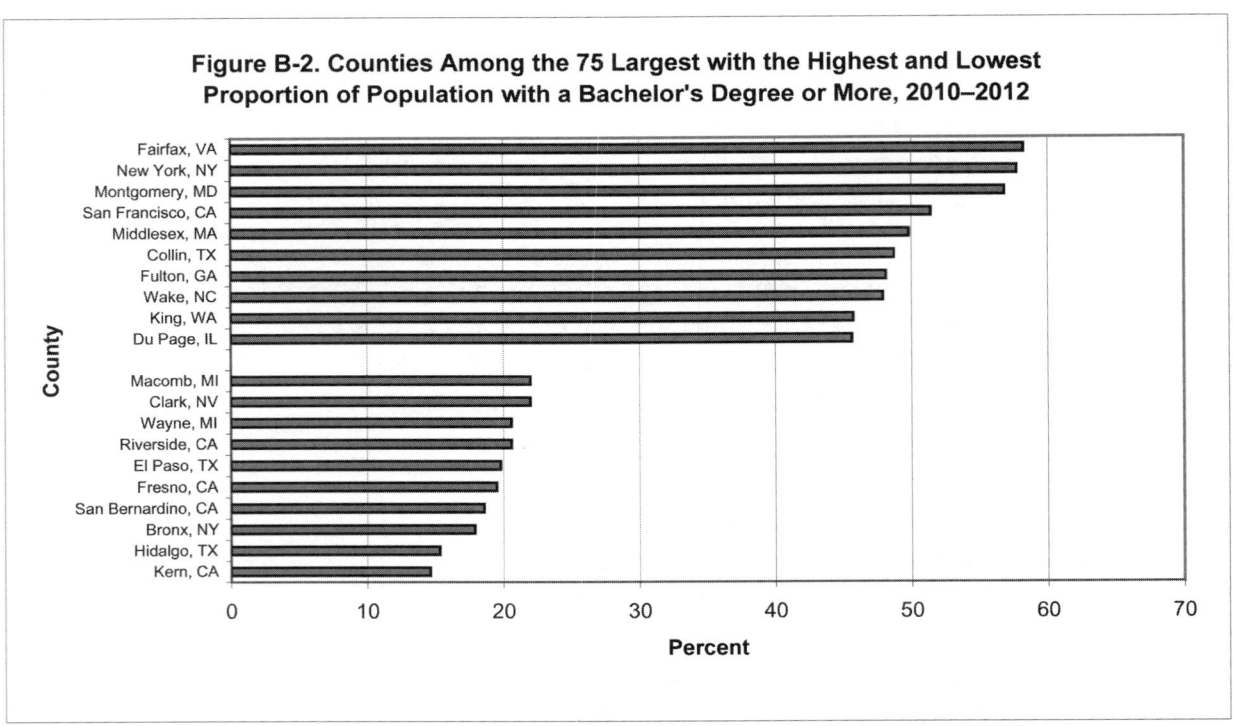

**Figure B-2. Counties Among the 75 Largest with the Highest and Lowest Proportion of Population with a Bachelor's Degree or More, 2010–2012**

While New York County, NY, had one of the smallest land areas, it had by far the highest population density among U.S. counties in 2012, with over 27,000 persons per square kilometer. No other county approached that density (although three other New York City boroughs were among the top five counties in population density). San Francisco had the highest population density outside of New York City, with Suffolk County, MA (Boston); Philadelphia County, PA; and Washington, DC, also among the top 10 counties. The median county only had about 17 persons per square kilometer, with only 113 counties having more than 500 persons per square kilometer. The nation's largest county in terms of population (Los Angeles) had a population density of 947.9 persons per square kilometer. This density ranked 21st among the 75 most populous U.S. counties.

Proportionally large year-to-year labor force changes are not unusual for counties with small populations. The 2012 annual averages reflect a national labor force that increased by 0.9 percent. Among the 75 most populous counties, five counties' labor forces grew by 2.0 percent or more between 2011 and 2012. Kern County, CA was the only county among the top 75 most populous that experienced an increase in its labor force of over 3 percent. Eleven counties experienced increases of between 1.5 and 1.9 percent. Nearly 1,800 counties experienced declines in their labor forces from 2011 to 2012, with 91 counties losing 5 percent or more. Among the most populous 75 counties, 20 counties had decreases in their labor forces, led by St. Louis, MO at 1.5 percent.

The national annual average unemployment rate was 8.1 percent in 2012 down from 8.9 in 2011 and 9.6 in 2010 but still much higher than the unemployment rate of 5.8 percent in 2008. Over 1,200 counties had unemployment rates above

the national average of 8.1 percent in 2012 and over 568 counties had unemployment rates greater than 10 percent, down from 1,100 counties in 2010 but still much higher than the 125 counties in 2008. Of the 10 counties with the highest unemployment rates, only Imperial County, CA, and Yuma County, AZ, had populations over 100,000. Among the 75 most populous counties, 39 exceeded the national unemployment rate of 8.1 percent. Unemployment exceeded 15 percent in Fresno County, CA. Fairfax County, VA, had the lowest unemployment rate at 4.2 percent followed by Montgomery County, MD at 5.1 percent and Honolulu County, HI, at 5.2 percent. In 2012, seven counties had an unemployment rate below 6 percent.

Among the 75 largest counties, the two with the highest unemployment rates, Fresno and Kern counties in CA, ranked among the top counties for agricultural sales. Meanwhile, Wayne County, MI which ranked second highest in manufacturing employment had the sixth highest unemployment rate among the 75 most populous counties. Two of the lowest unemployment rates were in the two counties that topped the rankings for employment in professional, scientific, and technical occupations (Fairfax County, VA and Montgomery County, MD.) These two counties were also at the top of the rankings for median household income and educational attainment, with more than 56 percent of residents holding bachelor's, master's, doctoral or professional degrees. Six large counties had college-educated proportions of less than 20 percent, and five out of the six were among the ten counties with the highest unemployment rates. Nationally, 28.5 percent of the population held bachelor's degrees or higher in 2011.

# 75 Largest Counties by 2012 Population
## Selected Rankings

| Population, 2012 | | | Land area, 2010 | | | | Population density, 2012 | | | |
|---|---|---|---|---|---|---|---|---|---|---|
| Population rank | County | Population [col 2] | Population rank | Land area rank | County | Land area (Square kilometers) [col 1] | Population rank | Density rank | County | Density (per square kilometer) [col 4] |
| 1 | Los Angeles, CA | 9 962 789 | 12 | 1 | San Bernardino, CA | 51 947 | 20 | 1 | New York, NY | 27 442.2 |
| 2 | Cook, IL | 5 231 351 | 4 | 2 | Maricopa, AZ | 23 828 | 8 | 2 | Kings, NY | 14 019.9 |
| 3 | Harris, TX | 4 253 700 | 42 | 3 | Pima, AZ | 23 794 | 26 | 3 | Bronx, NY | 12 921.8 |
| 4 | Maricopa, AZ | 3 942 169 | 61 | 4 | Kern, CA | 21 062 | 10 | 4 | Queens, NY | 8 088.2 |
| 5 | San Diego, CA | 3 177 063 | 14 | 5 | Clark, NV | 20 439 | 67 | 5 | San Francisco, CA | 6 825.3 |
| 6 | Orange, CA | 3 090 132 | 11 | 6 | Riverside, CA | 18 665 | 22 | 6 | Philadelphia, PA | 4 460.0 |
| 7 | Miami-Dade | 2 591 035 | 49 | 7 | Fresno, CA | 15 431 | 75 | 7 | Essex, NJ | 2 409.0 |
| 8 | Kings, NY | 2 565 635 | 5 | 8 | San Diego, CA | 10 895 | 2 | 8 | Cook, IL | 2 137.0 |
| 9 | Dallas, TX | 2 453 843 | 1 | 9 | Los Angeles, CA | 10 510 | 28 | 9 | Nassau, NY | 1 830.7 |
| 10 | Queens, NY | 2 272 771 | 13 | 10 | King, WA | 5 479 | 47 | 10 | Milwaukee, WI | 1 528.3 |
| 11 | Riverside, CA | 2 268 783 | 27 | 11 | Palm Beach, FL | 5 102 | 56 | 11 | Bergen, NJ | 1 523.9 |
| 12 | San Bernardino, CA | 2 081 313 | 7 | 12 | Miami-Dade, FL | 4 915 | 6 | 12 | Orange, CA | 1 508.9 |
| 13 | King, WA | 2 007 440 | 64 | 13 | Ventura, CA | 4 774 | 53 | 13 | Pinellas, FL | 1 299.5 |
| 14 | Clark, NV | 2 000 759 | 3 | 14 | Harris, TX | 4 412 | 18 | 14 | Wayne, MI | 1 130.8 |
| 15 | Tarrant, TX | 1 880 153 | 70 | 15 | Pierce, WA | 4 324 | 36 | 15 | Fairfax, VA | 1 104.2 |
| 16 | Santa Clara, CA | 1 837 504 | 72 | 16 | Hidalgo, TX | 4 069 | 52 | 16 | DuPage, IL | 1 094.3 |
| 17 | Broward, FL | 1 815 137 | 73 | 17 | Worcester, MA | 3 913 | 9 | 17 | Dallas, TX | 1 087.2 |
| 18 | Wayne, MI | 1 792 365 | 16 | 18 | Santa Clara, CA | 3 341 | 30 | 18 | Cuyahoga, OH | 1 068.5 |
| 19 | Bexar, TX | 1 785 704 | 19 | 19 | Bexar, TX | 3211 | 68 | 19 | Middlesex, NJ | 1 028.8 |
| 20 | New York, NY | 1 619 090 | 17 | 20 | Broward, Fl | 3 133 | 3 | 20 | Harris, TX | 964.1 |
| 21 | Alameda, CA | 1 554 720 | 54 | 21 | Erie, NY | 2 701 | 1 | 21 | Los Angeles, CA | 947.9 |
| 22 | Philadelphia, PA | 1 547 607 | 29 | 22 | Hillsborough, FL | 2 642 | 55 | 22 | Marion, IN | 895.7 |
| 23 | Middlesex, MA | 1 537 215 | 66 | 23 | El Paso, TX | 2 623 | 34 | 23 | Franklin, OH | 867.6 |
| 24 | Suffolk, NY | 1 499 273 | 37 | 24 | Travis, TX | 2 565 | 46 | 24 | Westchester, NY | 862.5 |
| 25 | Sacramento, CA | 1 450 121 | 25 | 25 | Sacramento, CA | 2 498 | 15 | 25 | Tarrant, TX | 840.5 |
| 26 | Bronx, NY | 1 408 473 | 2 | 26 | Cook, IL | 2 448 | 35 | 26 | Hennepin, MN | 826.1 |
| 27 | Palm Beach, FL | 1 356 545 | 24 | 27 | Suffolk, NY | 2 362 | 21 | 27 | Alameda, CA | 812.3 |
| 28 | Nassau, NY | 1 349 233 | 33 | 28 | Orange, FL | 2 340 | 40 | 28 | Montgomery, MD | 789.9 |
| 29 | Hillsborough, FL | 1 277 746 | 9 | 29 | Dallas, TX | 2 257 | 74 | 29 | Hamilton, OH | 763.1 |
| 30 | Cuyahoga, OH | 1 265 111 | 32 | 30 | Oakland, MI | 2 247 | 41 | 30 | St. Louis, MO | 760.8 |
| 31 | Allegheny, PA | 1 229 338 | 15 | 31 | Tarrant, TX | 2 237 | 63 | 31 | Gwinnett, GA | 755.2 |
| 32 | Oakland, MI | 1 220 657 | 65 | 32 | Collin, TX | 2 179 | 23 | 32 | Middlesex, MA | 725.8 |
| 33 | Orange, FL | 1 202 234 | 48 | 33 | Wake, NC | 2 163 | 43 | 33 | Fulton, GA | 716.8 |
| 34 | Franklin, OH | 1 195 537 | 23 | 34 | Middlesex, MA | 2 118 | 45 | 34 | Mecklenburg, NC | 714.1 |
| 35 | Hennepin, MN | 1 184 576 | 6 | 35 | Orange, CA | 2 048 | 58 | 35 | Prince George's, MD | 704.9 |
| 36 | Fairfax, VA | 1 118 602 | 50 | 36 | Shelby, TN | 1 977 | 62 | 36 | Macomb, MI | 682.8 |
| 37 | Travis, TX | 1 095 584 | 59 | 37 | Duval, FL | 1 974 | 31 | 37 | Allegheny, PA | 650.1 |
| 38 | Contra Costa, CA | 1 079 597 | 39 | 38 | Salt Lake, UT | 1 923 | 71 | 38 | Montgomery, PA | 646.3 |
| 39 | Salt Lake, UT | 1 063 842 | 21 | 39 | Alameda, CA | 1 914 | 24 | 39 | Suffolk, NY | 634.7 |
| 40 | Montgomery, MD | 1 004 709 | 57 | 40 | Hartford, CT | 1 904 | 44 | 40 | Honolulu, HI | 627.5 |
| 41 | St. Louis, MO | 1 000 438 | 31 | 41 | Allegheny, PA | 1 891 | 38 | 41 | Contra Costa, CA | 582.3 |
| 42 | Pima, AZ | 992 394 | 38 | 42 | Contra Costa, CA | 1 854 | 25 | 42 | Sacramento, CA | 580.5 |
| 43 | Fulton, GA | 977 773 | 51 | 43 | Fairfield, CT | 1 618 | 17 | 43 | Broward, Fl | 579.4 |
| 44 | Honolulu, HI | 976 372 | 18 | 44 | Wayne, MI | 1 585 | 51 | 44 | Fairfield, CT | 577.2 |
| 45 | Mecklenburg, NC | 969 031 | 60 | 45 | New Haven, CT | 1 566 | 19 | 45 | Bexar, TX | 556.1 |
| 46 | Westchester, NY | 961 670 | 44 | 46 | Honolulu, HI | 1 556 | 39 | 46 | Salt Lake, UT | 553.2 |
| 47 | Milwaukee, WI | 955 205 | 69 | 47 | Baltimore, MD | 1 550 | 60 | 47 | New Haven, CT | 551.0 |
| 48 | Wake, NC | 952 151 | 35 | 48 | Hennepin, MN | 1 434 | 16 | 48 | Santa Clara, CA | 550.0 |
| 49 | Fresno, CA | 947 895 | 34 | 49 | Franklin, OH | 1 378 | 32 | 49 | Oakland, MI | 543.2 |
| 50 | Shelby, TN | 940 764 | 43 | 50 | Fulton, GA | 1 364 | 69 | 50 | Baltimore, MD | 527.4 |
| 51 | Fairfield, CT | 933 835 | 45 | 51 | Mecklenburg, NC | 1 357 | 7 | 51 | Miami-Dade, FL | 527.2 |
| 52 | DuPage, IL | 927 987 | 41 | 52 | St. Louis, MO | 1 315 | 33 | 52 | Orange, FL | 513.8 |
| 53 | Pinellas, FL | 921 319 | 40 | 53 | Montgomery, MD | 1 272 | 29 | 53 | Hillsborough, FL | 483.6 |
| 54 | Erie, NY | 919 086 | 71 | 54 | Montgomery, PA | 1 251 | 50 | 54 | Shelby, TN | 475.9 |
| 55 | Marion, IN | 918 977 | 58 | 55 | Prince George's, MD | 1 250 | 57 | 55 | Hartford, CT | 471.2 |
| 56 | Bergen, NJ | 918 888 | 62 | 56 | Macomb, MI | 1 241 | 59 | 56 | Duval, FL | 445.6 |
| 57 | Hartford, CT | 897 259 | 30 | 57 | Cuyahoga, OH | 1 184 | 48 | 57 | Wake, NC | 440.2 |
| 58 | Prince George's, MD | 881 138 | 46 | 58 | Westchester, NY | 1 115 | 37 | 58 | Travis, TX | 427.1 |
| 59 | Duval, FL | 879 602 | 63 | 59 | Gwinnett, GA | 1 115 | 65 | 59 | Collin, TX | 383.0 |
| 60 | New Haven, CT | 862 813 | 74 | 60 | Hamilton, OH | 1 051 | 13 | 60 | King, WA | 366.4 |
| 61 | Kern, CA | 856 158 | 55 | 61 | Marion, IN | 1 026 | 54 | 61 | Erie, NY | 340.3 |
| 62 | Macomb, MI | 847 383 | 36 | 62 | Fairfax, VA | 1 013 | 66 | 62 | El Paso, TX | 315.4 |
| 63 | Gwinnett, GA | 842 046 | 52 | 63 | DuPage, IL | 848 | 5 | 63 | San Diego, CA | 291.6 |
| 64 | Ventura, CA | 835 981 | 68 | 64 | Middlesex, NJ | 800 | 27 | 64 | Palm Beach, FL | 265.9 |
| 65 | Collin, TX | 834 642 | 28 | 65 | Nassau, NY | 737 | 73 | 65 | Worcester, MA | 206.0 |
| 66 | El Paso, TX | 827 398 | 53 | 66 | Pinellas, FL | 709 | 72 | 66 | Hidalgo, TX | 198.2 |
| 67 | San Francisco, CA | 825 863 | 47 | 67 | Milwaukee, WI | 625 | 70 | 67 | Pierce, WA | 187.7 |
| 68 | Middlesex, MA | 823 041 | 56 | 68 | Bergen, NJ | 603 | 64 | 68 | Ventura, CA | 175.1 |
| 69 | Baltimore, MD | 817 455 | 22 | 69 | Philadelphia, PA | 347 | 4 | 69 | Maricopa, AZ | 165.4 |
| 70 | Pierce, WA | 811 681 | 75 | 70 | Essex, NJ | 327 | 11 | 70 | Riverside, CA | 121.6 |
| 71 | Montgomery, PA | 808 460 | 10 | 71 | Queens, NY | 281 | 14 | 71 | Clark, NV | 97.9 |
| 72 | Hidalgo, TX | 806 552 | 8 | 72 | Kings, NY | 183 | 49 | 72 | Fresno, CA | 61.4 |
| 73 | Worcester, MA | 806 163 | 67 | 73 | San Francisco, CA | 121 | 42 | 73 | Pima, AZ | 41.7 |
| 74 | Hamilton, OH | 802 038 | 26 | 74 | Bronx, NY | 109 | 61 | 74 | Kern, CA | 40.6 |
| 75 | Essex, NJ | 787 744 | 20 | 75 | New York, NY | 59 | 12 | 75 | San Bernardino, CA | 40.1 |

# 75 Largest Counties by 2012 Population
## Selected Rankings

| Percent population change, 2010-2012 | | | | Employment/residence ratio, 2007-2011 | | | | Percent White, not Hispanic or Latino, alone or in combination, 2011 | | | |
|---|---|---|---|---|---|---|---|---|---|---|---|
| Population rank | Percent change rank | County | Percent change [col 23] | Population rank | Number of employees per resident rank | County | Number of employees per resident [col 34] | Population rank | White rank | County | Percent white [col 5] |
| 37 | 1 | Travis, TX | 7.0 | 20 | 1 | New York, NY | 2.82 | 62 | 1 | Macomb, MI | 85.0 |
| 65 | 2 | Collin, TX | 6.7 | 43 | 2 | Fulton, GA | 1.84 | 73 | 2 | Worcester, MA | 82.2 |
| 43 | 3 | Fulton, GA | 6.2 | 67 | 3 | San Francisco, CA | 1.38 | 31 | 3 | Allegheny, PA | 82.0 |
| 48 | 4 | Wake, NC | 5.7 | 35 | 4 | Hennepin, MN | 1.37 | 71 | 4 | Montgomery, PA | 80.1 |
| 45 | 5 | Mecklenburg, NC | 5.4 | 55 | 5 | Marion, IN | 1.33 | 54 | 5 | Erie, NY | 78.7 |
| 33 | 6 | Orange, FL | 4.9 | 74 | 6 | Hamilton, OH | 1.32 | 23 | 6 | Middlesex, MA | 78.6 |
| 63 | 7 | Gwinnett, GA | 4.6 | 9 | 7 | Dallas, TX | 1.31 | 53 | 7 | Pinellas, FL | 77.9 |
| 19 | 8 | Bexar, TX | 4.1 | 45 | 8 | Mecklenburg, NC | 1.29 | 32 | 8 | Oakland,MI | 76.3 |
| 72 | 8 | Hidalgo, TX | 4.1 | 33 | 9 | Orange, FL | 1.26 | 39 | 9 | Salt Lake, UT | 75.5 |
| 3 | 10 | Harris, TX | 3.9 | 30 | 10 | Cuyahoga, OH | 1.24 | 70 | 10 | Pierce, WA | 75.0 |
| 13 | 10 | King, WA | 3.9 | 34 | 11 | Franklin, OH | 1.20 | 35 | 11 | Hennepin, MN | 74.0 |
| 15 | 10 | Tarrant, TX | 3.9 | 37 | 11 | Travis, TX | 1.20 | 24 | 12 | Suffolk, NY | 72.0 |
| 29 | 10 | Hillsborough, FL | 3.9 | 41 | 11 | St. Louis, MO | 1.20 | 52 | 13 | DuPage, IL | 71.1 |
| 7 | 14 | Miami-Dade, FL | 3.8 | 22 | 14 | Philadelphia, PA | 1.19 | 41 | 14 | St. Louis, MO | 70.2 |
| 17 | 14 | Broward, Fl | 3.8 | 52 | 14 | DuPage, IL | 1.19 | 34 | 15 | Franklin, OH | 69.6 |
| 9 | 16 | Dallas, TX | 3.6 | 50 | 16 | Shelby, TN | 1.18 | 74 | 16 | Hamilton, OH | 69.3 |
| 11 | 16 | Riverside, CA | 3.6 | 57 | 16 | Hartford, CT | 1.18 | 60 | 17 | New Haven, CT | 68.6 |
| 36 | 18 | Fairfax, VA | 3.4 | 59 | 16 | Duval, FL | 1.18 | 13 | 18 | King, WA | 68.0 |
| 40 | 18 | Montgomery, MD | 3.4 | 13 | 19 | King, WA | 1.16 | 51 | 19 | Fairfield, CT | 67.1 |
| 4 | 20 | Maricopa, AZ | 3.3 | 31 | 19 | Allegheny, PA | 1.16 | 57 | 20 | Hartford, CT | 67.0 |
| 39 | 20 | Salt Lake, UT | 3.3 | 71 | 19 | Montgomery, PA | 1.16 | 28 | 21 | Nassau, NY | 65.7 |
| 66 | 20 | El Paso, TX | 3.3 | 3 | 22 | Harris, TX | 1.15 | 65 | 22 | Collin, TX | 64.1 |
| 16 | 23 | Santa Clara, CA | 3.1 | 32 | 22 | Oakland,MI | 1.15 | 69 | 23 | Baltimore, MD | 63.7 |
| 21 | 24 | Alameda, CA | 2.9 | 39 | 24 | Salt Lake, UT | 1.14 | 48 | 24 | Wake, NC | 63.6 |
| 38 | 24 | Contra Costa, CA | 2.9 | 16 | 25 | Santa Clara, CA | 1.12 | 30 | 25 | Cuyahoga, OH | 62.7 |
| 27 | 26 | Palm Beach, FL | 2.8 | 29 | 26 | Hillsborough, FL | 1.11 | 56 | 25 | Bergen, NJ | 62.7 |
| 34 | 26 | Franklin, OH | 2.8 | 47 | 27 | Milwaukee, WI | 1.10 | 55 | 27 | Marion, IN | 61.5 |
| 35 | 26 | Hennepin, MN | 2.8 | 2 | 28 | Cook, IL | 1.09 | 27 | 28 | Palm Beach, FL | 60.5 |
| 6 | 29 | Orange, CA | 2.7 | 23 | 28 | Middlesex, MA | 1.09 | 4 | 29 | Maricopa, AZ | 59.9 |
| 5 | 30 | San Diego, CA | 2.6 | 75 | 30 | Essex, NJ | 1.08 | 59 | 30 | Duval, FL | 58.3 |
| 67 | 30 | San Francisco, CA | 2.6 | 18 | 31 | Wayne, MI | 1.07 | 46 | 31 | Westchester, NY | 58.0 |
| 14 | 32 | Clark, NV | 2.5 | 54 | 31 | Erie, NY | 1.07 | 36 | 32 | Fairfax, VA | 56.6 |
| 8 | 33 | Kings, NY | 2.4 | 6 | 33 | Orange, CA | 1.06 | 42 | 33 | Pima, AZ | 56.4 |
| 44 | 33 | Honolulu, HI | 2.4 | 7 | 33 | Miami-Dade, FL | 1.06 | 47 | 34 | Milwaukee, WI | 56.0 |
| 12 | 35 | San Bernardino, CA | 2.3 | 19 | 33 | Bexar, TX | 1.06 | 29 | 35 | Hillsborough, FL | 54.9 |
| 23 | 35 | Middlesex, MA | 2.3 | 51 | 33 | Fairfield, CT | 1.06 | 15 | 36 | Tarrant, TX | 52.7 |
| 25 | 37 | Sacramento, CA | 2.2 | 48 | 37 | Wake, NC | 1.05 | 45 | 37 | Mecklenburg, NC | 51.9 |
| 20 | 38 | New York, NY | 2.1 | 1 | 38 | Los Angeles, CA | 1.03 | 37 | 38 | Travis, TX | 51.8 |
| 58 | 38 | Prince George's, MD | 2.1 | 25 | 38 | Sacramento, CA | 1.03 | 25 | 39 | Sacramento, CA | 51.6 |
| 70 | 38 | Pierce, WA | 2.1 | 27 | 38 | Palm Beach, FL | 1.03 | 18 | 40 | Wayne, MI | 51.4 |
| 61 | 41 | Kern, CA | 2.0 | 38 | 38 | Pinellas, FL | 1.03 | 40 | 41 | Montgomery, MD | 50.8 |
| 10 | 42 | Queens, NY | 1.9 | 4 | 42 | Maricopa, AZ | 1.02 | 5 | 42 | San Diego, CA | 50.6 |
| 49 | 42 | Fresno, CA | 1.9 | 5 | 42 | San Diego, CA | 1.02 | 38 | 43 | Contra Costa, CA | 50.5 |
| 51 | 42 | Fairfield, CT | 1.9 | 14 | 44 | Clark, NV | 1.01 | 64 | 44 | Ventura, CA | 50.1 |
| 59 | 45 | Duval, FL | 1.8 | 21 | 44 | Alameda, CA | 1.01 | 14 | 45 | Clark, NV | 50.0 |
| 26 | 46 | Bronx, NY | 1.7 | 49 | 44 | Fresno, CA | 1.01 | 68 | 46 | Middlesex, NJ | 49.6 |
| 55 | 46 | Marion, IN | 1.7 | 36 | 47 | Fairfax, VA | 1.00 | 20 | 47 | New York, NY | 49.4 |
| 68 | 48 | Middlesex, NJ | 1.6 | 42 | 47 | Pima, AZ | 1.00 | 33 | 48 | Orange, FL | 47.2 |
| 1 | 49 | Los Angeles, CA | 1.5 | 44 | 47 | Honolulu, HI | 1.00 | 6 | 49 | Orange, CA | 45.6 |
| 32 | 49 | Oakland,MI | 1.5 | 61 | 47 | Kern, CA | 1.00 | 63 | 50 | Gwinnett, GA | 44.9 |
| 56 | 49 | Bergen, NJ | 1.5 | 66 | 47 | El Paso, TX | 1.00 | 2 | 51 | Cook, IL | 44.8 |
| 64 | 49 | Ventura, CA | 1.5 | 15 | 52 | Tarrant, TX | 0.98 | 67 | 52 | San Francisco, CA | 44.4 |
| 69 | 49 | Baltimore, MD | 1.5 | 46 | 53 | Westchester, NY | 0.97 | 17 | 53 | Broward, Fl | 44.2 |
| 22 | 54 | Philadelphia, PA | 1.4 | 56 | 53 | Bergen, NJ | 0.97 | 43 | 54 | Fulton, GA | 42.1 |
| 50 | 54 | Shelby, TN | 1.4 | 68 | 55 | Middlesex, NJ | 0.96 | 11 | 55 | Riverside, CA | 41.0 |
| 46 | 56 | Westchester, NY | 1.3 | 72 | 55 | Hidalgo, TX | 0.96 | 50 | 56 | Shelby, TN | 39.6 |
| 42 | 57 | Pima, AZ | 1.2 | 40 | 57 | Montgomery, MD | 0.93 | 61 | 56 | Kern, CA | 39.6 |
| 52 | 57 | DuPage, IL | 1.2 | 17 | 58 | Broward, Fl | 0.92 | 22 | 58 | Philadelphia, PA | 38.3 |
| 71 | 59 | Montgomery, PA | 1.1 | 60 | 58 | New Haven, CT | 0.92 | 16 | 59 | Santa Clara, CA | 37.3 |
| 73 | 60 | Worcester, MA | 1.0 | 12 | 60 | San Bernardino, CA | 0.91 | 21 | 60 | Alameda, CA | 37.1 |
| 47 | 61 | Milwaukee, WI | 0.8 | 63 | 61 | Gwinnett, GA | 0.90 | 8 | 61 | Kings, NY | 36.7 |
| 62 | 61 | Macomb, MI | 0.8 | 28 | 62 | Nassau, NY | 0.89 | 75 | 62 | Essex, NJ | 34.5 |
| 2 | 63 | Cook, IL | 0.7 | 64 | 62 | Ventura, CA | 0.89 | 12 | 63 | San Bernardino, CA | 34.4 |
| 28 | 63 | Nassau, NY | 0.7 | 65 | 64 | Collin, TX | 0.88 | 49 | 64 | Fresno, CA | 33.9 |
| 31 | 65 | Allegheny, PA | 0.5 | 69 | 64 | Baltimore, MD | 0.88 | 9 | 65 | Dallas, TX | 33.8 |
| 53 | 65 | Pinellas, FL | 0.5 | 70 | 64 | Pierce, WA | 0.88 | 3 | 66 | Harris, TX | 33.6 |
| 75 | 65 | Essex, NJ | 0.5 | 24 | 67 | Suffolk, NY | 0.87 | 44 | 67 | Honolulu, HI | 32.6 |
| 24 | 68 | Suffolk, NY | 0.4 | 73 | 67 | Worcester, MA | 0.87 | 19 | 68 | Bexar, TX | 31.3 |
| 57 | 68 | Hartford, CT | 0.4 | 62 | 69 | Macomb, MI | 0.84 | 1 | 69 | Los Angeles, CA | 29.2 |
| 41 | 70 | St. Louis, MO | 0.1 | 11 | 70 | Riverside, CA | 0.81 | 10 | 70 | Queens, NY | 28.7 |
| 54 | 71 | Erie, NY | 0.0 | 38 | 71 | Contra Costa, CA | 0.78 | 58 | 71 | Prince George's, MD | 16.6 |
| 60 | 71 | New Haven, CT | 0.0 | 58 | 72 | Prince George's, MD | 0.74 | 7 | 72 | Miami-Dade, FL | 16.5 |
| 74 | 71 | Hamilton, OH | 0.0 | 8 | 73 | Kings, NY | 0.73 | 66 | 73 | El Paso, TX | 14.3 |
| 30 | 74 | Cuyahoga, OH | -1.2 | 26 | 74 | Bronx, NY | 0.70 | 26 | 74 | Bronx, NY | 11.9 |
| 18 | 75 | Wayne, MI | -1.5 | 10 | 75 | Queens, NY | 0.66 | 72 | 75 | Hidalgo, TX | 7.9 |

# 75 Largest Counties by 2012 Population
## Selected Rankings

| Percent Black, not Hispanic or Latino, alone or in combination, 2011 | | | | Percent American Indian, Alaska Native, alone or in combination, 2011 | | | | Percent Asian or Pacific Islander, alone or in combination, 2011 | | | |
|---|---|---|---|---|---|---|---|---|---|---|---|
| Population rank | Black rank | County | Percent black [col 6] | Population rank | American Indian Alaska native rank | County | Percent American Indian, Alaska native [col 7] | Population rank | Asian or Pacific Islander rank | County | Percent Asian or Pacific Islander [col 8] |
| 58 | 1 | Prince George's, MD | 64.6 | 42 | 1 | Pima, AZ | 3.0 | 44 | 1 | Honolulu, HI | 78.5 |
| 50 | 2 | Shelby, TN | 52.5 | 70 | 2 | Pierce, WA | 2.6 | 67 | 2 | San Francisco, CA | 36.1 |
| 43 | 3 | Fulton, GA | 44.6 | 4 | 3 | Maricopa, AZ | 2.1 | 16 | 3 | Santa Clara, CA | 34.9 |
| 22 | 4 | Philadelphia, PA | 43.2 | 13 | 4 | King, WA | 1.7 | 21 | 4 | Alameda, CA | 30.1 |
| 18 | 5 | Wayne, MI | 41.1 | 25 | 5 | Sacramento, CA | 1.6 | 10 | 5 | Queens, NY | 25.4 |
| 75 | 6 | Essex, NJ | 40.2 | 44 | 5 | Honolulu, HI | 1.6 | 68 | 6 | Middlesex, NJ | 22.8 |
| 8 | 7 | Kings, NY | 32.7 | 35 | 7 | Hennepin, MN | 1.5 | 6 | 7 | Orange, CA | 20.1 |
| 45 | 8 | Mecklenburg, NC | 31.4 | 61 | 8 | Kern, CA | 1.4 | 36 | 8 | Fairfax, VA | 19.8 |
| 26 | 9 | Bronx, NY | 30.8 | 47 | 9 | Milwaukee, WI | 1.2 | 13 | 9 | King, WA | 18.2 |
| 30 | 10 | Cuyahoga, OH | 30.4 | 49 | 9 | Fresno, CA | 1.2 | 25 | 10 | Sacramento, CA | 18.0 |
| 59 | 11 | Duval, FL | 30.0 | 11 | 11 | Riverside, CA | 1.1 | 38 | 11 | Contra Costa, CA | 17.7 |
| 55 | 12 | Marion, IN | 27.9 | 39 | 11 | Salt Lake, UT | 1.1 | 56 | 12 | Bergen, NJ | 15.7 |
| 47 | 13 | Milwaukee, WI | 27.5 | 5 | 13 | San Diego, CA | 1.0 | 40 | 13 | Montgomery, MD | 15.6 |
| 69 | 14 | Baltimore, MD | 27.3 | 12 | 13 | San Bernardino, CA | 1.0 | 1 | 14 | Los Angeles, CA | 15.2 |
| 17 | 15 | Broward, Fl | 26.9 | 14 | 13 | Clark, NV | 1.0 | 5 | 15 | San Diego, CA | 13.4 |
| 74 | 16 | Hamilton, OH | 26.8 | 18 | 13 | Wayne, MI | 1.0 | 65 | 16 | Collin, TX | 12.5 |
| 2 | 17 | Cook, IL | 24.8 | 21 | 13 | Alameda, CA | 1.0 | 20 | 17 | New York, NY | 12.4 |
| 63 | 18 | Gwinnett, GA | 24.4 | 38 | 13 | Contra Costa, CA | 1.0 | 8 | 18 | Kings, NY | 11.6 |
| 41 | 19 | St. Louis, MO | 24.1 | 15 | 19 | Tarrant, TX | 0.9 | 14 | 19 | Clark, NV | 11.5 |
| 34 | 20 | Franklin, OH | 22.7 | 34 | 19 | Franklin, OH | 0.9 | 63 | 19 | Gwinnett, GA | 11.5 |
| 9 | 21 | Dallas, TX | 22.3 | 45 | 19 | Mecklenburg, NC | 0.9 | 52 | 21 | DuPage, IL | 11.2 |
| 48 | 22 | Wake, NC | 21.4 | 48 | 19 | Wake, NC | 0.9 | 23 | 22 | Middlesex, MA | 10.7 |
| 33 | 23 | Orange, FL | 20.7 | 54 | 19 | Erie, NY | 0.9 | 49 | 23 | Fresno, CA | 10.6 |
| 10 | 24 | Queens, NY | 19.2 | 58 | 19 | Prince George's, MD | 0.9 | 70 | 24 | Pierce, WA | 10.4 |
| 3 | 25 | Harris, TX | 18.8 | 62 | 19 | Macomb, MI | 0.9 | 28 | 25 | Nassau, NY | 8.7 |
| 40 | 26 | Montgomery, MD | 18.2 | 65 | 19 | Collin, TX | 0.9 | 64 | 26 | Ventura, CA | 8.4 |
| 27 | 27 | Palm Beach, FL | 17.7 | 10 | 27 | Queens, NY | 0.8 | 12 | 27 | San Bernardino, CA | 7.7 |
| 7 | 28 | Miami-Dade, FL | 17.5 | 22 | 27 | Philadelphia, PA | 0.8 | 11 | 28 | Riverside, CA | 7.4 |
| 29 | 29 | Hillsborough, FL | 16.9 | 32 | 27 | Oakland,MI | 0.8 | 35 | 29 | Hennepin, MN | 7.3 |
| 15 | 30 | Tarrant, TX | 15.3 | 59 | 27 | Duval, FL | 0.8 | 71 | 30 | Montgomery, PA | 7.2 |
| 32 | 31 | Oakland,MI | 14.7 | 64 | 27 | Ventura, CA | 0.8 | 22 | 31 | Philadelphia, PA | 7.1 |
| 46 | 32 | Westchester, NY | 14.3 | 67 | 27 | San Francisco, CA | 0.8 | 2 | 32 | Cook, IL | 7.0 |
| 31 | 33 | Allegheny, PA | 14.2 | 69 | 27 | Baltimore, MD | 0.8 | 3 | 33 | Harris, TX | 6.8 |
| 20 | 34 | New York, NY | 14.1 | 9 | 34 | Dallas, TX | 0.7 | 32 | 34 | Oakland,MI | 6.6 |
| 54 | 35 | Erie, NY | 14.0 | 16 | 34 | Santa Clara, CA | 0.7 | 37 | 34 | Travis, TX | 6.6 |
| 57 | 36 | Hartford, CT | 13.4 | 29 | 34 | Hillsborough, FL | 0.7 | 43 | 36 | Fulton, GA | 6.4 |
| 21 | 37 | Alameda, CA | 13.3 | 37 | 34 | Travis, TX | 0.7 | 46 | 36 | Westchester, NY | 6.4 |
| 35 | 37 | Hennepin, MN | 13.3 | 40 | 34 | Montgomery, MD | 0.7 | 48 | 38 | Wake, NC | 6.2 |
| 60 | 39 | New Haven, CT | 12.9 | 43 | 34 | Fulton, GA | 0.7 | 39 | 39 | Salt Lake, UT | 6.1 |
| 25 | 40 | Sacramento, CA | 11.5 | 53 | 34 | Pinellas, FL | 0.7 | 69 | 40 | Baltimore, MD | 6.0 |
| 28 | 41 | Nassau, NY | 11.4 | 55 | 34 | Marion, IN | 0.7 | 33 | 41 | Orange, FL | 5.9 |
| 14 | 42 | Clark, NV | 11.2 | 74 | 34 | Hamilton, OH | 0.7 | 9 | 42 | Dallas, TX | 5.6 |
| 51 | 43 | Fairfield, CT | 11.0 | 1 | 43 | Los Angeles, CA | 0.6 | 15 | 43 | Tarrant, TX | 5.5 |
| 53 | 43 | Pinellas, FL | 11.0 | 6 | 43 | Orange, CA | 0.6 | 51 | 43 | Fairfield, CT | 5.5 |
| 36 | 45 | Fairfax, VA | 10.1 | 19 | 43 | Bexar, TX | 0.6 | 45 | 45 | Mecklenburg, NC | 5.4 |
| 38 | 46 | Contra Costa, CA | 10.0 | 30 | 43 | Cuyahoga, OH | 0.6 | 59 | 45 | Duval, FL | 5.4 |
| 62 | 47 | Macomb, MI | 9.9 | 33 | 43 | Orange, FL | 0.6 | 75 | 45 | Essex, NJ | 5.4 |
| 68 | 48 | Middlesex, NJ | 9.7 | 36 | 43 | Fairfax, VA | 0.6 | 61 | 48 | Kern, CA | 5.1 |
| 71 | 49 | Montgomery, PA | 9.5 | 41 | 43 | St. Louis, MO | 0.6 | 57 | 49 | Hartford, CT | 4.9 |
| 65 | 50 | Collin, TX | 9.3 | 50 | 43 | Shelby, TN | 0.6 | 58 | 49 | Prince George's, MD | 4.9 |
| 12 | 51 | San Bernardino, CA | 9.2 | 57 | 43 | Hartford, CT | 0.6 | 73 | 51 | Worcester, MA | 4.8 |
| 1 | 52 | Los Angeles, CA | 8.9 | 60 | 43 | New Haven, CT | 0.6 | 34 | 52 | Franklin, OH | 4.7 |
| 37 | 53 | Travis, TX | 8.8 | 63 | 43 | Gwinnett, GA | 0.6 | 4 | 53 | Maricopa, AZ | 4.5 |
| 70 | 53 | Pierce, WA | 8.8 | 73 | 43 | Worcester, MA | 0.6 | 29 | 54 | Hillsborough, FL | 4.3 |
| 24 | 55 | Suffolk, NY | 7.6 | 75 | 43 | Essex, NJ | 0.6 | 17 | 55 | Broward, Fl | 4.2 |
| 19 | 56 | Bexar, TX | 7.5 | 3 | 56 | Harris, TX | 0.5 | 41 | 55 | St. Louis, MO | 4.2 |
| 13 | 57 | King, WA | 7.4 | 8 | 56 | Kings, NY | 0.5 | 24 | 57 | Suffolk, NY | 4.1 |
| 11 | 58 | Riverside, CA | 6.8 | 17 | 56 | Broward, Fl | 0.5 | 26 | 57 | Bronx, NY | 4.1 |
| 67 | 59 | San Francisco, CA | 6.7 | 20 | 56 | New York, NY | 0.5 | 60 | 57 | New Haven, CT | 4.1 |
| 61 | 60 | Kern, CA | 6.0 | 24 | 56 | Suffolk, NY | 0.5 | 47 | 60 | Milwaukee, WI | 4.0 |
| 56 | 61 | Bergen, NJ | 5.9 | 26 | 56 | Bronx, NY | 0.5 | 62 | 61 | Macomb, MI | 3.8 |
| 5 | 62 | San Diego, CA | 5.7 | 31 | 56 | Allegheny, PA | 0.5 | 53 | 62 | Pinellas, FL | 3.7 |
| 4 | 63 | Maricopa, AZ | 5.5 | 66 | 56 | El Paso, TX | 0.5 | 42 | 63 | Pima, AZ | 3.5 |
| 23 | 64 | Middlesex, MA | 5.3 | 68 | 56 | Middlesex, NJ | 0.5 | 31 | 64 | Allegheny, PA | 3.4 |
| 49 | 64 | Fresno, CA | 5.3 | 2 | 65 | Cook, IL | 0.4 | 18 | 65 | Wayne, MI | 3.3 |
| 52 | 66 | DuPage, IL | 5.2 | 23 | 65 | Middlesex, MA | 0.4 | 54 | 66 | Erie, NY | 3.2 |
| 73 | 67 | Worcester, MA | 4.5 | 27 | 65 | Palm Beach, FL | 0.4 | 19 | 67 | Bexar, TX | 3.1 |
| 42 | 68 | Pima, AZ | 4.0 | 28 | 65 | Nassau, NY | 0.4 | 27 | 67 | Palm Beach, FL | 3.1 |
| 44 | 69 | Honolulu, HI | 3.5 | 46 | 65 | Westchester, NY | 0.4 | 30 | 67 | Cuyahoga, OH | 3.1 |
| 66 | 70 | El Paso, TX | 3.2 | 51 | 65 | Fairfield, CT | 0.4 | 50 | 70 | Shelby, TN | 2.8 |
| 16 | 71 | Santa Clara, CA | 3.0 | 52 | 65 | DuPage, IL | 0.4 | 55 | 71 | Marion, IN | 2.6 |
| 64 | 72 | Ventura, CA | 2.1 | 71 | 65 | Montgomery, PA | 0.4 | 74 | 71 | Hamilton, OH | 2.6 |
| 6 | 73 | Orange, CA | 2.0 | 56 | 73 | Bergen, NJ | 0.3 | 7 | 73 | Miami-Dade, FL | 1.9 |
| 39 | 74 | Salt Lake, UT | 1.9 | 7 | 74 | Miami-Dade, FL | 0.2 | 66 | 74 | El Paso, TX | 1.5 |
| 72 | 75 | Hidalgo, TX | 0.5 | 72 | 75 | Hidalgo, TX | 0.1 | 72 | 75 | Hidalgo, TX | 1.0 |

# 75 Largest Counties by 2012 Population
## Selected Rankings

| | Percent Hispanic or Latino,[1] 2011 | | | | Percent under 18 years old, 2011 | | | | Percent 65 years old and over, 2011 | | |
|---|---|---|---|---|---|---|---|---|---|---|---|
| Population rank | Hispanic or Latino rank | County | Percent Hispanic or Latino [col 9] | Population rank | Under 18 years old rank | County | Percent under 18 years old [cols 10 and 11] | Population rank | 65 years old and over rank | County | Percent 65 years old and over [cols 17 and 18] |
| 72 | 1 | Hidalgo, TX | 90.7 | 72 | 1 | Hidalgo, TX | 34.4 | 27 | 27 | Palm Beach, FL | 21.8 |
| 66 | 2 | El Paso, TX | 81.4 | 61 | 2 | Kern, CA | 29.9 | 53 | 53 | Pinellas, FL | 21.4 |
| 7 | 3 | Miami-Dade, FL | 64.5 | 66 | 3 | El Paso, TX | 29.7 | 31 | 31 | Allegheny, PA | 16.6 |
| 19 | 4 | Bexar, TX | 58.9 | 49 | 4 | Fresno, CA | 29.6 | 42 | 42 | Pima, AZ | 15.9 |
| 26 | 5 | Bronx, NY | 53.8 | 39 | 5 | Salt Lake, UT | 28.9 | 54 | 54 | Erie, NY | 15.7 |
| 49 | 6 | Fresno, CA | 50.9 | 12 | 6 | San Bernardino, CA | 28.7 | 30 | 30 | Cuyahoga, OH | 15.6 |
| 61 | 7 | Kern, CA | 50.0 | 63 | 6 | Gwinnett, GA | 28.7 | 28 | 28 | Nassau, NY | 15.4 |
| 12 | 8 | San Bernardino, CA | 49.9 | 65 | 8 | Collin, TX | 28.3 | 71 | 71 | Montgomery, PA | 15.3 |
| 1 | 9 | Los Angeles, CA | 48.1 | 3 | 9 | Harris, TX | 27.8 | 41 | 41 | St. Louis, MO | 15.2 |
| 11 | 10 | Riverside, CA | 46.1 | 11 | 9 | Riverside, CA | 27.8 | 56 | 56 | Bergen, NJ | 15.2 |
| 3 | 11 | Harris, TX | 41.4 | 15 | 9 | Tarrant, TX | 27.8 | 44 | 44 | Honolulu, HI | 14.8 |
| 64 | 12 | Ventura, CA | 40.9 | 9 | 12 | Dallas, TX | 27.6 | 46 | 46 | Westchester, NY | 14.8 |
| 9 | 13 | Dallas, TX | 38.9 | 19 | 13 | Bexar, TX | 26.9 | 57 | 57 | Hartford, CT | 14.7 |
| 42 | 14 | Pima, AZ | 35.1 | 26 | 14 | Bronx, NY | 26.4 | 69 | 69 | Baltimore, MD | 14.7 |
| 6 | 15 | Orange, CA | 34.1 | 4 | 15 | Maricopa, AZ | 26.0 | 60 | 60 | New Haven, CT | 14.6 |
| 37 | 16 | Travis, TX | 33.9 | 50 | 15 | Shelby, TN | 26.0 | 62 | 62 | Macomb, MI | 14.6 |
| 5 | 17 | San Diego, CA | 32.5 | 48 | 17 | Wake, NC | 25.8 | 17 | 17 | Broward, Fl | 14.3 |
| 4 | 18 | Maricopa, AZ | 30.0 | 64 | 18 | Ventura, CA | 25.3 | 7 | 7 | Miami-Dade, FL | 14.2 |
| 14 | 19 | Clark, NV | 29.7 | 45 | 19 | Mecklenburg, NC | 25.2 | 24 | 24 | Suffolk, NY | 13.9 |
| 10 | 20 | Queens, NY | 27.8 | 25 | 20 | Sacramento, CA | 25.2 | 20 | 20 | New York, NY | 13.7 |
| 33 | 21 | Orange, FL | 27.5 | 55 | 20 | Marion, IN | 25.2 | 51 | 51 | Fairfield, CT | 13.7 |
| 15 | 22 | Tarrant, TX | 27.3 | 18 | 22 | Wayne, MI | 24.9 | 67 | 67 | San Francisco, CA | 13.7 |
| 16 | 23 | Santa Clara, CA | 27.2 | 47 | 22 | Milwaukee, WI | 24.9 | 32 | 32 | Oakland, MI | 13.6 |
| 17 | 24 | Broward, Fl | 25.8 | 14 | 24 | Clark, NV | 24.8 | 23 | 23 | Middlesex, MA | 13.3 |
| 20 | 25 | New York, NY | 25.6 | 75 | 25 | Essex, NJ | 24.7 | 74 | 74 | Hamilton, OH | 13.3 |
| 29 | 26 | Hillsborough, FL | 25.1 | 38 | 26 | Contra Costa, CA | 24.5 | 10 | 10 | Queens, NY | 13.0 |
| 38 | 27 | Contra Costa, CA | 24.8 | 52 | 27 | DuPage, IL | 24.4 | 73 | 73 | Worcester, MA | 12.9 |
| 2 | 28 | Cook, IL | 24.4 | 51 | 28 | Fairfield, CT | 24.3 | 18 | 18 | Wayne, MI | 12.8 |
| 21 | 29 | Alameda, CA | 22.8 | 70 | 29 | Pierce, WA | 24.3 | 38 | 38 | Contra Costa, CA | 12.8 |
| 46 | 30 | Westchester, NY | 22.4 | 1 | 30 | Los Angeles, CA | 24.1 | 40 | 40 | Montgomery, MD | 12.5 |
| 25 | 31 | Sacramento, CA | 22.0 | 6 | 30 | Orange, CA | 24.1 | 68 | 68 | Middlesex, NJ | 12.5 |
| 75 | 32 | Essex, NJ | 20.8 | 36 | 32 | Fairfax, VA | 24.1 | 4 | 4 | Maricopa, AZ | 12.4 |
| 63 | 33 | Gwinnett, GA | 20.5 | 16 | 33 | Santa Clara, CA | 23.9 | 2 | 2 | Cook, IL | 12.1 |
| 8 | 34 | Kings, NY | 20.0 | 37 | 33 | Travis, TX | 23.9 | 22 | 22 | Philadelphia, PA | 12.1 |
| 27 | 35 | Palm Beach, FL | 19.6 | 34 | 35 | Franklin, OH | 23.8 | 64 | 64 | Ventura, CA | 12.1 |
| 68 | 36 | Middlesex, NJ | 18.9 | 40 | 36 | Montgomery, MD | 23.7 | 11 | 11 | Riverside, CA | 12.0 |
| 40 | 37 | Montgomery, MD | 17.5 | 43 | 36 | Fulton, GA | 23.7 | 52 | 52 | DuPage, IL | 12.0 |
| 39 | 38 | Salt Lake, UT | 17.4 | 46 | 38 | Westchester, NY | 23.6 | 6 | 6 | Orange, CA | 11.9 |
| 51 | 38 | Fairfield, CT | 17.4 | 8 | 39 | Kings, NY | 23.6 | 29 | 29 | Hillsborough, FL | 11.9 |
| 24 | 40 | Suffolk, NY | 17.0 | 2 | 40 | Cook, IL | 23.5 | 14 | 14 | Clark, NV | 11.8 |
| 56 | 41 | Bergen, NJ | 16.8 | 58 | 40 | Prince George's, MD | 23.5 | 75 | 75 | Essex, NJ | 11.7 |
| 36 | 42 | Fairfax, VA | 15.8 | 74 | 40 | Hamilton, OH | 23.5 | 8 | 8 | Kings, NY | 11.6 |
| 57 | 43 | Hartford, CT | 15.7 | 24 | 43 | Suffolk, NY | 23.4 | 35 | 35 | Hennepin, MN | 11.6 |
| 60 | 44 | New Haven, CT | 15.4 | 33 | 43 | Orange, FL | 23.4 | 5 | 5 | San Diego, CA | 11.5 |
| 67 | 44 | San Francisco, CA | 15.4 | 29 | 45 | Hillsborough, FL | 23.3 | 25 | 25 | Sacramento, CA | 11.5 |
| 58 | 46 | Prince George's, MD | 15.2 | 59 | 45 | Duval, FL | 23.3 | 59 | 59 | Duval, FL | 11.5 |
| 65 | 46 | Collin, TX | 15.2 | 5 | 47 | San Diego, CA | 23.2 | 21 | 21 | Alameda, CA | 11.4 |
| 28 | 48 | Nassau, NY | 15.0 | 32 | 48 | Oakland, MI | 23.0 | 47 | 47 | Milwaukee, WI | 11.4 |
| 47 | 49 | Milwaukee, WI | 13.6 | 41 | 48 | St. Louis, MO | 23.0 | 16 | 16 | Santa Clara, CA | 11.3 |
| 52 | 49 | DuPage, IL | 13.6 | 73 | 48 | Worcester, MA | 23.0 | 1 | 1 | Los Angeles, CA | 11.2 |
| 22 | 51 | Philadelphia, PA | 12.6 | 28 | 51 | Nassau, NY | 22.9 | 13 | 13 | King, WA | 11.2 |
| 45 | 52 | Mecklenburg, NC | 12.4 | 68 | 52 | Middlesex, NJ | 22.7 | 70 | 70 | Pierce, WA | 11.2 |
| 48 | 53 | Wake, NC | 10.0 | 42 | 53 | Pima, AZ | 22.7 | 26 | 26 | Bronx, NY | 10.7 |
| 55 | 54 | Marion, IN | 9.6 | 62 | 54 | Macomb, MI | 22.6 | 55 | 55 | Marion, IN | 10.7 |
| 73 | 54 | Worcester, MA | 9.6 | 71 | 54 | Montgomery, PA | 22.6 | 50 | 50 | Shelby, TN | 10.5 |
| 70 | 56 | Pierce, WA | 9.4 | 22 | 56 | Philadelphia, PA | 22.5 | 19 | 19 | Bexar, TX | 10.4 |
| 13 | 57 | King, WA | 9.2 | 35 | 56 | Hennepin, MN | 22.5 | 49 | 49 | Fresno, CA | 10.3 |
| 44 | 58 | Honolulu, HI | 8.5 | 57 | 56 | Hartford, CT | 22.5 | 66 | 66 | El Paso, TX | 10.3 |
| 53 | 59 | Pinellas, FL | 8.3 | 21 | 59 | Alameda, CA | 22.3 | 36 | 36 | Fairfax, VA | 10.2 |
| 43 | 60 | Fulton, GA | 8.1 | 30 | 59 | Cuyahoga, OH | 22.3 | 34 | 34 | Franklin, OH | 10.1 |
| 59 | 61 | Duval, FL | 7.9 | 56 | 61 | Bergen, NJ | 22.2 | 33 | 33 | Orange, FL | 10.0 |
| 35 | 62 | Hennepin, MN | 6.9 | 17 | 62 | Broward, Fl | 22.0 | 58 | 58 | Prince George's, MD | 9.8 |
| 23 | 63 | Middlesex, MA | 6.8 | 44 | 62 | Honolulu, HI | 22.0 | 72 | 72 | Hidalgo, TX | 9.5 |
| 50 | 64 | Shelby, TN | 5.8 | 60 | 64 | New Haven, CT | 21.9 | 12 | 12 | San Bernardino, CA | 9.2 |
| 18 | 65 | Wayne, MI | 5.4 | 69 | 65 | Baltimore, MD | 21.8 | 43 | 43 | Fulton, GA | 9.2 |
| 30 | 66 | Cuyahoga, OH | 4.9 | 7 | 66 | Miami-Dade, FL | 21.4 | 15 | 15 | Tarrant, TX | 9.1 |
| 34 | 66 | Franklin, OH | 4.9 | 54 | 67 | Erie, NY | 21.2 | 61 | 61 | Kern, CA | 9.1 |
| 54 | 68 | Erie, NY | 4.7 | 13 | 68 | King, WA | 21.1 | 45 | 45 | Mecklenburg, NC | 9.0 |
| 69 | 69 | Baltimore, MD | 4.4 | 23 | 68 | Middlesex, MA | 21.1 | 9 | 9 | Dallas, TX | 8.9 |
| 71 | 69 | Montgomery, PA | 4.4 | 10 | 70 | Queens, NY | 20.6 | 39 | 39 | Salt Lake, UT | 8.9 |
| 32 | 71 | Oakland, MI | 3.6 | 27 | 71 | Palm Beach, FL | 20.2 | 48 | 48 | Wake, NC | 8.9 |
| 74 | 72 | Hamilton, OH | 2.7 | 31 | 72 | Allegheny, PA | 19.5 | 3 | 3 | Harris, TX | 8.3 |
| 41 | 73 | St. Louis, MO | 2.6 | 53 | 73 | Pinellas, FL | 17.5 | 65 | 65 | Collin, TX | 8.1 |
| 62 | 74 | Macomb, MI | 2.4 | 20 | 74 | New York, NY | 14.8 | 37 | 37 | Travis, TX | 7.5 |
| 31 | 75 | Allegheny, PA | 1.7 | 67 | 75 | San Francisco, CA | 13.5 | 63 | 63 | Gwinnett, GA | 7.2 |

1. May be of any race.

# 75 Largest Counties by 2012 Population
## Selected Rankings

| Percent female-headed family households, 2010 | | | | Birth rate, 2011 | | | | Percent under 65 who have no health insurance, 2010 | | | |
| --- | --- | --- | --- | --- | --- | --- | --- | --- | --- | --- | --- |
| Population rank | Female households rank | County | Percent female households [col 30] | Population rank | Live birth rate rank | County | Birth rate [col 36] | Population rank | No health insurance rank | County | Percent with no health insurance [col 40] |
| 26 | 1 | Bronx, NY | 31.1 | 72 | 1 | Hidalgo, TX | 21.2 | 72 | 1 | Hidalgo, TX | 38.1 |
| 22 | 2 | Philadelphia, PA | 22.5 | 39 | 2 | Salt Lake, UT | 17.3 | 7 | 2 | Miami-Dade, FL | 35.8 |
| 50 | 3 | Shelby, TN | 21.7 | 9 | 3 | Dallas, TX | 17.2 | 66 | 3 | El Paso, TX | 32.8 |
| 18 | 4 | Wayne, MI | 20.7 | 3 | 4 | Harris, TX | 17.1 | 9 | 4 | Dallas, TX | 31.0 |
| 75 | 5 | Essex, NJ | 20.6 | 49 | 5 | Fresno, CA | 16.9 | 3 | 5 | Harris, TX | 29.9 |
| 8 | 6 | Kings, NY | 20.5 | 61 | 5 | Kern, CA | 16.9 | 17 | 6 | Broward, Fl | 27.1 |
| 58 | 7 | Prince George's, MD | 20.4 | 66 | 5 | El Paso, TX | 16.9 | 27 | 7 | Palm Beach, FL | 26.3 |
| 66 | 8 | El Paso, TX | 20.3 | 55 | 8 | Marion, IN | 16.6 | 1 | 8 | Los Angeles, CA | 25.9 |
| 7 | 9 | Miami-Dade, FL | 18.8 | 8 | 9 | Kings, NY | 16.4 | 14 | 9 | Clark, NV | 25.4 |
| 72 | 9 | Hidalgo, TX | 18.8 | 26 | 10 | Bronx, NY | 16.3 | 33 | 10 | Orange, FL | 24.7 |
| 47 | 11 | Milwaukee, WI | 17.4 | 47 | 11 | Milwaukee, WI | 15.8 | 63 | 11 | Gwinnett, GA | 24.5 |
| 55 | 12 | Marion, IN | 17.1 | 15 | 12 | Tarrant, TX | 15.5 | 15 | 12 | Tarrant, TX | 23.6 |
| 49 | 13 | Fresno, CA | 16.9 | 37 | 13 | Travis, TX | 15.3 | 11 | 13 | Riverside, CA | 23.4 |
| 30 | 14 | Cuyahoga, OH | 16.7 | 19 | 14 | Bexar, TX | 15.2 | 61 | 13 | Kern, CA | 23.4 |
| 59 | 14 | Duval, FL | 16.7 | 22 | 14 | Philadelphia, PA | 15.2 | 19 | 15 | Bexar, TX | 23.1 |
| 19 | 16 | Bexar, TX | 16.6 | 34 | 14 | Franklin, OH | 15.2 | 43 | 16 | Fulton, GA | 22.9 |
| 10 | 17 | Queens, NY | 16.4 | 50 | 14 | Shelby, TN | 15.2 | 37 | 17 | Travis, TX | 22.7 |
| 12 | 18 | San Bernardino, CA | 16.2 | 12 | 18 | San Bernardino, CA | 15.1 | 29 | 18 | Hillsborough, FL | 22.6 |
| 9 | 19 | Dallas, TX | 16.0 | 45 | 19 | Mecklenburg, NC | 14.8 | 12 | 19 | San Bernardino, CA | 22.5 |
| 33 | 20 | Orange, FL | 15.7 | 59 | 20 | Duval, FL | 14.5 | 53 | 20 | Pinellas, FL | 22.3 |
| 43 | 20 | Fulton, GA | 15.7 | 63 | 21 | Gwinnett, GA | 14.3 | 49 | 21 | Fresno, CA | 21.9 |
| 61 | 20 | Kern, CA | 15.7 | 2 | 22 | Cook, IL | 14.2 | 10 | 22 | Queens, NY | 20.7 |
| 2 | 23 | Cook, IL | 15.6 | 43 | 23 | Fulton, GA | 14.1 | 6 | 23 | Orange, CA | 19.9 |
| 74 | 24 | Hamilton, OH | 15.4 | 4 | 24 | Maricopa, AZ | 14.0 | 55 | 23 | Marion, IN | 19.9 |
| 1 | 25 | Los Angeles, CA | 15.3 | 5 | 24 | San Diego, CA | 14.0 | 2 | 25 | Cook, IL | 19.7 |
| 3 | 25 | Harris, TX | 15.3 | 14 | 24 | Clark, NV | 14.0 | 59 | 26 | Duval, FL | 19.3 |
| 17 | 25 | Broward, Fl | 15.3 | 25 | 27 | Sacramento, CA | 13.8 | 4 | 27 | Maricopa, AZ | 19.2 |
| 25 | 28 | Sacramento, CA | 14.8 | 74 | 27 | Hamilton, OH | 13.8 | 5 | 28 | San Diego, CA | 19.1 |
| 29 | 28 | Hillsborough, FL | 14.8 | 11 | 29 | Riverside, CA | 13.7 | 75 | 28 | Essex, NJ | 19.1 |
| 45 | 30 | Mecklenburg, NC | 14.6 | 44 | 29 | Honolulu, HI | 13.7 | 45 | 30 | Mecklenburg, NC | 18.4 |
| 57 | 31 | Hartford, CT | 14.5 | 58 | 29 | Prince George's, MD | 13.7 | 42 | 31 | Pima, AZ | 18.2 |
| 60 | 31 | New Haven, CT | 14.5 | 36 | 32 | Fairfax, VA | 13.6 | 64 | 31 | Ventura, CA | 18.2 |
| 69 | 31 | Baltimore, MD | 14.5 | 48 | 32 | Wake, NC | 13.6 | 39 | 33 | Salt Lake, UT | 17.9 |
| 34 | 34 | Franklin, OH | 14.4 | 70 | 32 | Pierce, WA | 13.6 | 50 | 34 | Shelby, TN | 17.7 |
| 41 | 35 | St. Louis, MO | 14.2 | 1 | 35 | Los Angeles, CA | 13.5 | 18 | 35 | Wayne, MI | 17.5 |
| 63 | 35 | Gwinnett, GA | 14.2 | 35 | 35 | Hennepin, MN | 13.5 | 26 | 36 | Bronx, NY | 17.0 |
| 15 | 37 | Tarrant, TX | 13.8 | 10 | 37 | Queens, NY | 13.4 | 58 | 36 | Prince George's, MD | 17.0 |
| 54 | 38 | Erie, NY | 13.7 | 40 | 37 | Montgomery, MD | 13.4 | 65 | 38 | Collin, TX | 16.7 |
| 14 | 39 | Clark, NV | 13.5 | 75 | 37 | Essex, NJ | 13.4 | 22 | 39 | Philadelphia, PA | 16.5 |
| 11 | 40 | Riverside, CA | 13.3 | 16 | 40 | Santa Clara, CA | 13.3 | 8 | 40 | Kings, NY | 16.2 |
| 70 | 41 | Pierce, WA | 13.0 | 64 | 40 | Ventura, CA | 13.3 | 25 | 41 | Sacramento, CA | 16.0 |
| 21 | 42 | Alameda, CA | 12.9 | 18 | 42 | Wayne, MI | 13.2 | 48 | 42 | Wake, NC | 15.5 |
| 42 | 43 | Pima, AZ | 12.8 | 29 | 43 | Hillsborough, FL | 12.8 | 70 | 43 | Pierce, WA | 15.3 |
| 46 | 43 | Westchester, NY | 12.8 | 33 | 43 | Orange, FL | 12.8 | 30 | 44 | Cuyahoga, OH | 15.2 |
| 44 | 45 | Honolulu, HI | 12.7 | 65 | 43 | Collin, TX | 12.8 | 21 | 45 | Alameda, CA | 15.1 |
| 62 | 45 | Macomb, MI | 12.7 | 21 | 46 | Alameda, CA | 12.7 | 34 | 45 | Franklin, OH | 15.1 |
| 4 | 47 | Maricopa, AZ | 12.4 | 6 | 47 | Orange, CA | 12.6 | 68 | 45 | Middlesex, NJ | 15.1 |
| 38 | 47 | Contra Costa, CA | 12.4 | 13 | 48 | King, WA | 12.4 | 56 | 48 | Bergen, NJ | 14.6 |
| 51 | 49 | Fairfield, CT | 12.3 | 20 | 48 | New York, NY | 12.4 | 67 | 49 | San Francisco, CA | 14.5 |
| 31 | 50 | Allegheny, PA | 12.2 | 42 | 48 | Pima, AZ | 12.4 | 38 | 50 | Contra Costa, CA | 14.3 |
| 73 | 50 | Worcester, MA | 12.2 | 7 | 51 | Miami-Dade, FL | 12.3 | 47 | 50 | Milwaukee, WI | 14.3 |
| 5 | 52 | San Diego, CA | 12.1 | 68 | 52 | Middlesex, NJ | 12.1 | 13 | 52 | King, WA | 14.2 |
| 20 | 53 | New York, NY | 11.9 | 69 | 53 | Baltimore, MD | 12.0 | 74 | 52 | Hamilton, OH | 14.2 |
| 53 | 53 | Pinellas, FL | 11.9 | 30 | 54 | Cuyahoga, OH | 11.9 | 62 | 54 | Macomb, MI | 14.0 |
| 64 | 55 | Ventura, CA | 11.8 | 17 | 55 | Broward, Fl | 11.8 | 16 | 55 | Santa Clara, CA | 13.8 |
| 68 | 55 | Middlesex, NJ | 11.8 | 23 | 56 | Middlesex, MA | 11.6 | 40 | 56 | Montgomery, MD | 13.2 |
| 24 | 57 | Suffolk, NY | 11.7 | 38 | 57 | Contra Costa, CA | 11.5 | 36 | 57 | Fairfax, VA | 12.9 |
| 27 | 57 | Palm Beach, FL | 11.7 | 52 | 57 | DuPage, IL | 11.5 | 46 | 58 | Westchester, NY | 12.7 |
| 28 | 57 | Nassau, NY | 11.7 | 41 | 59 | St. Louis, MO | 11.4 | 20 | 59 | New York, NY | 12.4 |
| 6 | 60 | Orange, CA | 11.6 | 46 | 59 | Westchester, NY | 11.4 | 32 | 60 | Oakland, MI | 12.2 |
| 48 | 61 | Wake, NC | 11.5 | 71 | 59 | Montgomery, PA | 11.4 | 69 | 61 | Baltimore, MD | 12.1 |
| 40 | 62 | Montgomery, MD | 11.3 | 73 | 62 | Worcester, MA | 11.3 | 51 | 62 | Fairfield, CT | 12.0 |
| 32 | 63 | Oakland, MI | 11.1 | 24 | 63 | Suffolk, NY | 11.2 | 24 | 63 | Suffolk, NY | 11.8 |
| 37 | 64 | Travis, TX | 11.0 | 51 | 63 | Fairfield, CT | 11.2 | 41 | 64 | St. Louis, MO | 11.7 |
| 39 | 65 | Salt Lake, UT | 10.9 | 32 | 65 | Oakland, MI | 10.8 | 28 | 65 | Nassau, NY | 11.6 |
| 56 | 65 | Bergen, NJ | 10.9 | 57 | 65 | Hartford, CT | 10.8 | 35 | 66 | Hennepin, MN | 11.4 |
| 16 | 67 | Santa Clara, CA | 10.7 | 28 | 67 | Nassau, NY | 10.7 | 52 | 67 | DuPage, IL | 11.0 |
| 35 | 68 | Hennepin, MN | 10.3 | 60 | 67 | New Haven, CT | 10.7 | 60 | 68 | New Haven, CT | 10.5 |
| 23 | 69 | Middlesex, MA | 10.1 | 62 | 67 | Macomb, MI | 10.7 | 31 | 69 | Allegheny, PA | 10.4 |
| 65 | 70 | Collin, TX | 9.6 | 67 | 70 | San Francisco, CA | 10.6 | 54 | 70 | Erie, NY | 10.0 |
| 52 | 71 | DuPage, IL | 9.5 | 31 | 71 | Allegheny, PA | 10.5 | 57 | 70 | Hartford, CT | 10.0 |
| 71 | 71 | Montgomery, PA | 9.5 | 54 | 71 | Erie, NY | 10.5 | 71 | 72 | Montgomery, PA | 8.1 |
| 36 | 73 | Fairfax, VA | 9.2 | 27 | 73 | Palm Beach, FL | 10.3 | 44 | 73 | Honolulu, HI | 7.9 |
| 13 | 74 | King, WA | 9.1 | 56 | 74 | Bergen, NJ | 9.8 | 73 | 74 | Worcester, MA | 4.8 |
| 67 | 75 | San Francisco, CA | 8.3 | 53 | 75 | Pinellas, FL | 9.2 | 23 | 75 | Middlesex, MA | 4.5 |

# 75 Largest Counties by 2012 Population
## Selected Rankings

| Percent college graduates (bachelor's degree or more), 2007–2011 | | | | Expenditures per student, 2009–2010 | | | | Per capita personal income, 2011 | | | |
|---|---|---|---|---|---|---|---|---|---|---|---|
| Population rank | College graduates rank | County | Percent college graduates [col 51] | Population rank | Expenditures rank | County | Expenditures per student (dollars) [col 53] | Population rank | Per capita income rank | County | Per capita income (dollars) [col 64] |
| 36 | 1 | Fairfax, VA | 58.2 | 46 | 1 | Westchester, NY | 22 351 | 20 | 1 | New York, NY | 121 301 |
| 20 | 2 | New York, NY | 57.7 | 28 | 2 | Nassau, NY | 21 964 | 51 | 2 | Fairfield, CT | 78 504 |
| 40 | 3 | Montgomery, MD | 56.8 | 24 | 3 | Suffolk, NY | 19 813 | 46 | 3 | Westchester, NY | 75 855 |
| 67 | 4 | San Francisco, CA | 51.4 | 75 | 4 | Essex, NJ | 19 074 | 67 | 4 | San Francisco, CA | 74 349 |
| 23 | 5 | Middlesex, MA | 49.8 | 20 | 5 | Kings, NY | 19 015 | 40 | 5 | Montgomery, MD | 69 762 |
| 65 | 6 | Collin, TX | 48.7 | 8 | 5 | Queens, NY | 19 015 | 36 | 6 | Fairfax, VA | 69 008 |
| 43 | 7 | Fulton, GA | 48.1 | 10 | 5 | New York, NY | 19 015 | 28 | 7 | Nassau, NY | 67 776 |
| 48 | 8 | Wake, NC | 47.9 | 26 | 5 | Bronx, NY | 19 015 | 56 | 8 | Bergen, NJ | 66 096 |
| 13 | 9 | King, WA | 45.7 | 56 | 9 | Bergen, NJ | 17 178 | 71 | 9 | Montgomery, PA | 64 718 |
| 52 | 10 | DuPage, IL | 45.6 | 51 | 10 | Fairfield, CT | 15 732 | 23 | 10 | Middlesex, MA | 62 324 |
| 16 | 11 | Santa Clara, CA | 45.5 | 68 | 11 | Middlesex, MA | 15 653 | 16 | 11 | Santa Clara, CA | 61 833 |
| 56 | 12 | Bergen, NJ | 45.1 | 40 | 12 | Montgomery, MD | 15 582 | 13 | 12 | King, WA | 57 837 |
| 35 | 13 | Hennepin, MN | 44.7 | 71 | 13 | Montgomery, PA | 15 459 | 35 | 13 | Hennepin, MN | 57 476 |
| 46 | 14 | Westchester, NY | 44.5 | 60 | 14 | New Haven, CT | 15 047 | 43 | 14 | Fulton, GA | 57 451 |
| 71 | 15 | Montgomery, PA | 44.4 | 57 | 15 | Hartford, CT | 14 848 | 38 | 15 | Contra Costa, CA | 57 011 |
| 37 | 16 | Travis, TX | 44.0 | 31 | 16 | Allegheny, PA | 14 174 | 52 | 16 | DuPage, IL | 54 509 |
| 51 | 16 | Fairfield, CT | 44.0 | 54 | 17 | Erie, NY | 14 146 | 57 | 17 | Hartford, CT | 53 974 |
| 32 | 18 | Oakland, MI | 42.4 | 58 | 18 | Prince George's, MD | 14 020 | 27 | 18 | Palm Beach, FL | 53 500 |
| 28 | 19 | Nassau, NY | 41.2 | 23 | 19 | Middlesex, MA | 13 782 | 32 | 19 | Oakland, MI | 5 3297 |
| 21 | 20 | Alameda, CA | 40.8 | 22 | 20 | Philadelphia, PA | 13 436 | 75 | 20 | Essex, NJ | 52 956 |
| 45 | 21 | Mecklenburg, NC | 40.4 | 69 | 21 | Baltimore, MD | 13 260 | 41 | 21 | St. Louis, MO | 52 783 |
| 41 | 22 | St. Louis, MO | 39.3 | 30 | 22 | Cuyahoga, OH | 12 829 | 65 | 22 | Collin, TX | 52 419 |
| 68 | 23 | Middlesex, NJ | 38.9 | 52 | 23 | DuPage, IL | 12 775 | 24 | 23 | Suffolk, NY | 52 350 |
| 38 | 24 | Contra Costa, CA | 38.4 | 2 | 24 | Cook, IL | 12 727 | 69 | 24 | Baltimore, MD | 50 926 |
| 6 | 25 | Orange, CA | 36.2 | 36 | 25 | Fairfax, VA | 12 554 | 6 | 25 | Orange, CA | 50 440 |
| 34 | 26 | Franklin, OH | 35.5 | 41 | 26 | St. Louis, MO | 12 535 | 21 | 26 | Alameda, CA | 49 617 |
| 69 | 27 | Baltimore, MD | 35.2 | 67 | 27 | San Francisco, CA | 12 471 | 60 | 27 | New Haven, CT | 49 478 |
| 63 | 28 | Gwinnett, GA | 34.7 | 47 | 28 | Milwaukee, WI | 12 317 | 68 | 28 | Middlesex, NJ | 49 203 |
| 31 | 29 | Allegheny, PA | 34.5 | 74 | 29 | Hamilton, OH | 12 192 | 3 | 29 | Harris, TX | 48 935 |
| 5 | 30 | San Diego, CA | 34.2 | 73 | 30 | Worcester, MA | 12 050 | 31 | 30 | Allegheny, PA | 48 812 |
| 57 | 31 | Hartford, CT | 33.9 | 34 | 31 | Franklin, OH | 11 895 | 2 | 31 | Cook, IL | 46 937 |
| 2 | 32 | Cook, IL | 33.7 | 44 | 32 | Honolulu, HI | 11 754 | 74 | 32 | Hamilton, OH | 46 881 |
| 73 | 33 | Worcester, MA | 33.3 | 43 | 33 | Fulton, GA | 11 656 | 5 | 33 | San Diego, CA | 46 800 |
| 74 | 34 | Hamilton, OH | 32.9 | 35 | 34 | Hennepin, MN | 11 642 | 44 | 34 | Honolulu, HI | 46 624 |
| 24 | 35 | Suffolk, NY | 32.4 | 32 | 35 | Oakland, MI | 11 342 | 64 | 35 | Ventura, CA | 45 855 |
| 60 | 36 | New Haven, CT | 32.3 | 18 | 36 | Wayne, MI | 10 877 | 45 | 36 | Mecklenburg, NC | 45 610 |
| 27 | 37 | Palm Beach, FL | 32.2 | 55 | 37 | Marion, IN | 10 795 | 73 | 37 | Worcester, MA | 45 548 |
| 75 | 38 | Essex, NJ | 31.7 | 62 | 38 | Macomb, MI | 10 386 | 9 | 38 | Dallas, TX | 45 402 |
| 44 | 39 | Honolulu, HI | 31.2 | 1 | 39 | Los Angeles, CA | 10 026 | 53 | 39 | Pinellas, FL | 44 622 |
| 64 | 40 | Ventura, CA | 31.0 | 13 | 40 | King, WA | 9 699 | 30 | 40 | Cuyahoga, OH | 43 735 |
| 39 | 41 | Salt Lake, UT | 30.2 | 16 | 41 | Santa Clara, CA | 9 581 | 37 | 41 | Travis, TX | 43 198 |
| 33 | 42 | Orange, FL | 30.0 | 49 | 42 | Fresno, CA | 9 436 | 17 | 42 | Broward, Fl | 42 768 |
| 17 | 43 | Broward, Fl | 29.9 | 37 | 43 | Travis, TX | 9 380 | 1 | 43 | Los Angeles, CA | 42 564 |
| 10 | 44 | Queens, NY | 29.8 | 70 | 44 | Pierce, WA | 9 362 | 48 | 44 | Wake, NC | 42 555 |
| 54 | 44 | Erie, NY | 29.8 | 63 | 45 | Gwinnett, GA | 9 296 | 10 | 45 | Queens, NY | 42 017 |
| 58 | 46 | Prince George's, MD | 29.7 | 17 | 46 | Broward, FL | 9 290 | 54 | 46 | Erie, NY | 41 245 |
| 42 | 47 | Pima, AZ | 29.5 | 61 | 47 | Kern, CA | 9 190 | 70 | 47 | Pierce, WA | 40 992 |
| 1 | 48 | Los Angeles, CA | 29.2 | 72 | 48 | Hidalgo, TX | 9 180 | 15 | 48 | Tarrant, TX | 40 965 |
| 8 | 48 | Kings, NY | 29.2 | 5 | 49 | San Diego, CA | 9 134 | 50 | 49 | Shelby, TN | 40 763 |
| 4 | 50 | Maricopa, AZ | 29.1 | 27 | 50 | Palm Beach, FL | 9 113 | 58 | 50 | Prince George's, MD | 40 215 |
| 29 | 51 | Hillsborough, FL | 29.0 | 7 | 51 | Miami-Dade | 9 017 | 59 | 51 | Duval, FL | 39 858 |
| 15 | 52 | Tarrant, TX | 28.9 | 50 | 52 | Shelby, TN | 8 922 | 34 | 52 | Franklin, OH | 39 646 |
| 30 | 53 | Cuyahoga, OH | 28.6 | 59 | 53 | Duval, FL | 8 907 | 8 | 53 | Kings, NY | 39 351 |
| 50 | 54 | Shelby, TN | 28.3 | 25 | 54 | Sacramento, CA | 8 900 | 29 | 54 | Hillsborough, FL | 39 180 |
| 9 | 55 | Dallas, TX | 28.1 | 21 | 55 | Alameda, CA | 8 891 | 39 | 55 | Salt Lake, UT | 39 081 |
| 3 | 56 | Harris, TX | 27.9 | 66 | 56 | El Paso, TX | 8 890 | 22 | 56 | Philadelphia, PA | 39 041 |
| 25 | 57 | Sacramento, CA | 27.7 | 53 | 57 | Pinellas, FL | 8 783 | 47 | 57 | Milwaukee, WI | 38 881 |
| 47 | 58 | Milwaukee, WI | 27.1 | 38 | 58 | Contra Costa, CA | 8 778 | 55 | 58 | Marion, IN | 38 309 |
| 55 | 58 | Marion, IN | 27.1 | 3 | 59 | Harris, TX | 8 711 | 25 | 59 | Sacramento, CA | 38 202 |
| 53 | 60 | Pinellas, FL | 27.0 | 19 | 60 | Bexar, TX | 8 695 | 4 | 60 | Maricopa, AZ | 38 071 |
| 7 | 61 | Miami-Dade, FL | 26.2 | 6 | 61 | Orange, CA | 8 589 | 7 | 61 | Miami-Dade, FL | 37 834 |
| 19 | 62 | Bexar, TX | 25.6 | 9 | 61 | Dallas, TX | 8 589 | 19 | 62 | Bexar, TX | 36 177 |
| 59 | 63 | Duval, FL | 25.2 | 64 | 63 | Ventura, CA | 8 523 | 33 | 63 | Orange, FL | 35 990 |
| 70 | 64 | Pierce, WA | 23.6 | 29 | 64 | Hillsborough, FL | 8 487 | 62 | 64 | Macomb, MI | 35 717 |
| 22 | 65 | Philadelphia, PA | 22.6 | 12 | 65 | San Bernardino, CA | 8 367 | 14 | 65 | Clark, NV | 35 680 |
| 14 | 66 | Clark, NV | 22.0 | 11 | 66 | Riverside, CA | 8 331 | 42 | 66 | Pima, AZ | 34 961 |
| 62 | 66 | Macomb, MI | 22.0 | 14 | 67 | Clark, NV | 8 262 | 18 | 67 | Wayne, MI | 34 012 |
| 11 | 68 | Riverside, CA | 20.6 | 65 | 68 | Collin, TX | 8 232 | 63 | 68 | Gwinnett, GA | 32 861 |
| 18 | 68 | Wayne, MI | 20.6 | 45 | 69 | Mecklenburg, NC | 8 228 | 26 | 69 | Bronx, NY | 31 788 |
| 66 | 70 | El Paso, TX | 19.8 | 33 | 70 | Orange, FL | 8 206 | 49 | 70 | Fresno, CA | 31 542 |
| 49 | 71 | Fresno, CA | 19.5 | 15 | 71 | Tarrant, TX | 8 018 | 61 | 71 | Kern, CA | 31 400 |
| 12 | 72 | San Bernardino, CA | 18.6 | 42 | 72 | Pima, AZ | 7 953 | 66 | 72 | El Paso, TX | 30 088 |
| 26 | 73 | Bronx, NY | 17.9 | 4 | 73 | Maricopa, AZ | 7 784 | 12 | 73 | San Bernardino, CA | 29 998 |
| 72 | 74 | Hidalgo, TX | 15.3 | 48 | 74 | Wake, NC | 7 686 | 11 | 74 | Riverside, CA | 29 927 |
| 61 | 75 | Kern, CA | 14.6 | 39 | 75 | Salt Lake, UT | 6 110 | 72 | 75 | Hidalgo, TX | 21 620 |

# 75 Largest Counties by 2012 Population
## Selected Rankings

| Median household income, 2011 | | | | Median value of owner-occupied housing units, 2007–2011 | | | | Median gross rent of renter-occupied housing units, 2007–2011 | | | |
|---|---|---|---|---|---|---|---|---|---|---|---|
| Popu-lation rank | Median income rank | County | Median income (dollars) [col 58] | Popu-lation rank | Median value rank | County | Median value (dollars) [col 91] | Popu-lation rank | Median rent rank | County | Median rent (dollars) [col 94] |
| 36 | 1 | Fairfax, VA | 105 409 | 20 | 1 | New York, NY | 842 300 | 36 | 1 | Fairfax, VA | 1 572 |
| 40 | 2 | Montgomery, MD | 92 288 | 67 | 2 | San Francisco, CA | 767 300 | 40 | 2 | Montgomery, MD | 1 473 |
| 28 | 3 | Nassau, NY | 91 162 | 16 | 3 | Santa Clara, CA | 681 100 | 6 | 3 | Orange, CA | 1 463 |
| 16 | 4 | Santa Clara, CA | 84 741 | 6 | 4 | Orange, CA | 575 100 | 24 | 4 | Suffolk, NY | 1 461 |
| 24 | 5 | Suffolk, NY | 83 360 | 8 | 5 | Kings, NY | 570 800 | 16 | 5 | Santa Clara, CA | 1 459 |
| 65 | 6 | Collin, TX | 82 765 | 44 | 6 | Honolulu, HI | 560 300 | 28 | 6 | Nassau, NY | 1 447 |
| 56 | 7 | Bergen, NJ | 79 037 | 21 | 7 | Alameda, CA | 558 300 | 64 | 7 | Ventura, CA | 1 428 |
| 51 | 8 | Fairfield, CT | 77 065 | 46 | 8 | Westchester, NY | 547 000 | 67 | 8 | San Francisco, CA | 1 388 |
| 23 | 9 | Middlesex, MA | 76 803 | 64 | 9 | Ventura, CA | 515 900 | 44 | 9 | Honolulu, HI | 1 381 |
| 46 | 10 | Westchester, NY | 76 728 | 36 | 10 | Fairfax, VA | 493 100 | 20 | 10 | New York, NY | 1 316 |
| 71 | 11 | Montgomery, PA | 76 172 | 38 | 11 | Contra Costa, CA | 490 200 | 38 | 11 | Contra Costa, CA | 1 309 |
| 38 | 12 | Contra Costa, CA | 74 241 | 28 | 12 | Nassau, NY | 478 600 | 56 | 12 | Bergen, NJ | 1 289 |
| 52 | 13 | DuPage, IL | 74 122 | 1 | 13 | Los Angeles, CA | 478 300 | 5 | 13 | San Diego, CA | 1 261 |
| 64 | 14 | Ventura, CA | 74 019 | 56 | 14 | Bergen, NJ | 474 200 | 46 | 14 | Westchester, NY | 1 252 |
| 68 | 15 | Middlesex, NJ | 73 914 | 10 | 15 | Queens, NY | 474 000 | 51 | 15 | Fairfield, CT | 1 249 |
| 6 | 16 | Orange, CA | 72 046 | 40 | 16 | Montgomery, MD | 469 900 | 23 | 16 | Middlesex, MA | 1 243 |
| 58 | 17 | Prince George's, MD | 70 114 | 51 | 17 | Fairfield, CT | 466 700 | 10 | 17 | Queens, NY | 1 235 |
| 67 | 18 | San Francisco, CA | 69 354 | 5 | 18 | San Diego, CA | 455 000 | 21 | 18 | Alameda, CA | 1 228 |
| 13 | 19 | King, WA | 68 596 | 24 | 19 | Suffolk, NY | 411 000 | 68 | 19 | Middlesex, NJ | 1 216 |
| 21 | 20 | Alameda, CA | 67 295 | 23 | 20 | Middlesex, MA | 410 100 | 58 | 20 | Prince George's, MD | 1 180 |
| 20 | 21 | New York, NY | 65 833 | 13 | 21 | King, WA | 402 300 | 17 | 21 | Broward, Fl | 1 162 |
| 44 | 22 | Honolulu, HI | 65 489 | 26 | 22 | Bronx, NY | 391 300 | 1 | 22 | Los Angeles, CA | 1 161 |
| 48 | 23 | Wake, NC | 62 436 | 75 | 23 | Essex, NJ | 389 800 | 27 | 23 | Palm Beach, FL | 1 148 |
| 69 | 24 | Baltimore, MD | 62 309 | 68 | 24 | Middlesex, NJ | 349 000 | 11 | 24 | Riverside, CA | 1 141 |
| 32 | 25 | Oakland,MI | 61 961 | 58 | 25 | Prince George's, MD | 312 800 | 12 | 25 | San Bernardino, CA | 1 092 |
| 57 | 26 | Hartford, CT | 60 947 | 52 | 26 | DuPage, IL | 309 800 | 69 | 26 | Baltimore, MD | 1 082 |
| 35 | 27 | Hennepin, MN | 60 811 | 71 | 27 | Montgomery, PA | 297 900 | 71 | 27 | Montgomery, PA | 1 078 |
| 73 | 28 | Worcester, MA | 60 396 | 25 | 28 | Sacramento, CA | 285 000 | 8 | 28 | Kings, NY | 1 076 |
| 5 | 29 | San Diego, CA | 59 290 | 11 | 29 | Riverside, CA | 284 100 | 13 | 29 | King, WA | 1 060 |
| 60 | 30 | New Haven, CT | 58 985 | 12 | 30 | San Bernardino, CA | 278 400 | 7 | 30 | Miami-Dade, FL | 1 053 |
| 63 | 31 | Gwinnett, GA | 56 944 | 73 | 31 | Worcester, MA | 274 900 | 14 | 31 | Clark, NV | 1 049 |
| 39 | 32 | Salt Lake, UT | 56 166 | 60 | 32 | New Haven, CT | 270 900 | 52 | 32 | DuPage, IL | 1 047 |
| 70 | 33 | Pierce, WA | 55 215 | 69 | 33 | Baltimore, MD | 269 400 | 60 | 33 | New Haven, CT | 1 030 |
| 41 | 34 | St. Louis, MO | 55 131 | 70 | 34 | Pierce, WA | 265 200 | 75 | 34 | Essex, NJ | 1 024 |
| 43 | 35 | Fulton, GA | 54 893 | 2 | 35 | Cook, IL | 256 900 | 33 | 35 | Orange, FL | 1 016 |
| 37 | 36 | Travis, TX | 53 303 | 43 | 36 | Fulton, GA | 250 300 | 25 | 36 | Sacramento, CA | 1 003 |
| 10 | 37 | Queens, NY | 53 124 | 57 | 37 | Hartford, CT | 248 000 | 65 | 37 | Collin, TX | 996 |
| 15 | 38 | Tarrant, TX | 52 882 | 7 | 38 | Miami-Dade, FL | 246 800 | 63 | 38 | Gwinnett, GA | 980 |
| 11 | 39 | Riverside, CA | 52 491 | 35 | 39 | Hennepin, MN | 244 100 | 26 | 39 | Bronx, NY | 966 |
| 1 | 40 | Los Angeles, CA | 52 239 | 39 | 40 | Salt Lake, UT | 240 900 | 70 | 40 | Pierce, WA | 948 |
| 25 | 41 | Sacramento, CA | 52 236 | 27 | 41 | Palm Beach, FL | 236 600 | 43 | 41 | Fulton, GA | 946 |
| 45 | 42 | Mecklenburg, NC | 52 111 | 49 | 42 | Fresno, CA | 236 400 | 57 | 42 | Hartford, CT | 944 |
| 75 | 43 | Essex, NJ | 51 021 | 48 | 43 | Wake, NC | 227 600 | 29 | 43 | Hillsborough, FL | 936 |
| 12 | 44 | San Bernardino, CA | 51 017 | 14 | 44 | Clark, NV | 226 200 | 4 | 44 | Maricopa, AZ | 934 |
| 62 | 45 | Macomb, MI | 50 958 | 17 | 45 | Broward, FL | 225 300 | 2 | 45 | Cook, IL | 932 |
| 3 | 46 | Harris, TX | 50 924 | 4 | 46 | Maricopa, AZ | 219 300 | 53 | 46 | Pinellas, FL | 931 |
| 2 | 47 | Cook, IL | 50 806 | 33 | 47 | Orange, FL | 211 100 | 37 | 47 | Travis, TX | 930 |
| 4 | 48 | Maricopa, AZ | 50 785 | 37 | 48 | Travis, TX | 210 500 | 59 | 48 | Duval, FL | 920 |
| 31 | 49 | Allegheny, PA | 49 682 | 65 | 49 | Collin, TX | 202 000 | 32 | 49 | Oakland,MI | 894 |
| 27 | 50 | Palm Beach, FL | 48 973 | 61 | 50 | Kern, CA | 196 000 | 73 | 50 | Worcester, MA | 883 |
| 17 | 51 | Broward, Fl | 48 478 | 32 | 51 | Oakland,MI | 190 500 | 35 | 51 | Hennepin, MN | 877 |
| 14 | 52 | Clark, NV | 48 343 | 42 | 51 | Pima, AZ | 190 500 | 48 | 52 | Wake, NC | 869 |
| 54 | 53 | Erie, NY | 47 505 | 63 | 53 | Gwinnett, GA | 190 100 | 45 | 53 | Mecklenburg, NC | 857 |
| 9 | 54 | Dallas, TX | 47 335 | 45 | 54 | Mecklenburg, NC | 187 300 | 9 | 54 | Dallas, TX | 855 |
| 34 | 55 | Franklin, OH | 47 174 | 29 | 55 | Hillsborough, FL | 185 900 | 15 | 54 | Tarrant, TX | 855 |
| 29 | 56 | Hillsborough, FL | 46 592 | 41 | 56 | St. Louis, MO | 178 800 | 39 | 56 | Salt Lake, UT | 851 |
| 19 | 57 | Bexar, TX | 46 589 | 53 | 57 | Pinellas, FL | 172 900 | 22 | 57 | Philadelphia, PA | 850 |
| 74 | 58 | Hamilton, OH | 46 125 | 59 | 58 | Duval, FL | 170 300 | 49 | 57 | Fresno, CA | 850 |
| 59 | 59 | Duval, FL | 45 995 | 47 | 59 | Milwaukee, WI | 165 300 | 3 | 59 | Harris, TX | 849 |
| 61 | 60 | Kern, CA | 44 903 | 34 | 60 | Franklin, OH | 155 200 | 61 | 60 | Kern, CA | 840 |
| 33 | 61 | Orange, FL | 44 635 | 62 | 61 | Macomb, MI | 148 600 | 41 | 61 | St. Louis, MO | 821 |
| 42 | 62 | Pima, AZ | 44 102 | 74 | 62 | Hamilton, OH | 147 800 | 50 | 62 | Shelby, TN | 812 |
| 50 | 63 | Shelby, TN | 44 051 | 22 | 63 | Philadelphia, PA | 140 700 | 19 | 63 | Bexar, TX | 791 |
| 53 | 64 | Pinellas, FL | 42 761 | 50 | 64 | Shelby, TN | 136 200 | 34 | 64 | Franklin, OH | 787 |
| 49 | 65 | Fresno, CA | 42 572 | 15 | 65 | Tarrant, TX | 136 100 | 62 | 65 | Macomb, MI | 779 |
| 8 | 66 | Kings, NY | 42 437 | 30 | 66 | Cuyahoga, OH | 134 900 | 18 | 66 | Wayne, MI | 775 |
| 30 | 67 | Cuyahoga, OH | 41 609 | 3 | 67 | Harris, TX | 132 300 | 47 | 67 | Milwaukee, WI | 771 |
| 47 | 68 | Milwaukee, WI | 40 780 | 9 | 68 | Dallas, TX | 129 300 | 42 | 68 | Pima, AZ | 769 |
| 7 | 69 | Miami-Dade, FL | 40 476 | 19 | 69 | Bexar, TX | 121 200 | 55 | 69 | Marion, IN | 735 |
| 55 | 70 | Marion, IN | 39 957 | 55 | 70 | Marion, IN | 120 700 | 30 | 70 | Cuyahoga, OH | 716 |
| 66 | 71 | El Paso, TX | 39 116 | 54 | 71 | Erie, NY | 120 600 | 31 | 71 | Allegheny, PA | 713 |
| 18 | 72 | Wayne, MI | 38 479 | 31 | 72 | Allegheny, PA | 118 700 | 54 | 72 | Erie, NY | 704 |
| 22 | 73 | Philadelphia, PA | 34 433 | 18 | 73 | Wayne, MI | 110 000 | 74 | 73 | Hamilton, OH | 673 |
| 26 | 74 | Bronx, NY | 32 137 | 66 | 74 | El Paso, TX | 108 000 | 66 | 74 | El Paso, TX | 660 |
| 72 | 75 | Hidalgo, TX | 31 021 | 72 | 75 | Hidalgo, TX | 75 500 | 72 | 75 | Hidalgo, TX | 620 |

# 75 Largest Counties by 2012 Population
## Selected Rankings

| Percent of population below the poverty level, 2011 | | | | Percent under 18 years old below the poverty level, 2011 | | | | Unemployment rate, 2012 | | | |
|---|---|---|---|---|---|---|---|---|---|---|---|
| Population rank | Poverty rate rank | County | Poverty rate [col 59] | Population rank | Poverty rate for children rank | County | Poverty rate for children under 18 years [col 60] | Population rank | Unemployment rate rank | County | Unemployment rate [col 100] |
| 72 | 1 | Hidalgo, TX | 37.3 | 72 | 1 | Hidalgo, TX | 47.9 | 49 | 1 | Fresno, CA | 15.2 |
| 26 | 2 | Bronx, NY | 30.3 | 26 | 2 | Bronx, NY | 40.9 | 61 | 2 | Kern, CA | 13.3 |
| 22 | 3 | Philadelphia, PA | 27.9 | 22 | 3 | Philadelphia, PA | 38.7 | 26 | 3 | Bronx, NY | 12.7 |
| 18 | 4 | Wayne, MI | 26.1 | 18 | 4 | Wayne, MI | 37.9 | 11 | 4 | Riverside, CA | 12.2 |
| 49 | 5 | Fresno, CA | 25.8 | 49 | 5 | Fresno, CA | 35.4 | 12 | 5 | San Bernardino, CA | 12.0 |
| 61 | 6 | Kern, CA | 24.6 | 61 | 6 | Kern, CA | 34.6 | 18 | 6 | Wayne, MI | 11.7 |
| 66 | 6 | El Paso, TX | 24.6 | 66 | 7 | El Paso, TX | 34.1 | 14 | 7 | Clark, NV | 11.2 |
| 8 | 8 | Kings, NY | 23.6 | 8 | 8 | Kings, NY | 33.8 | 72 | 8 | Hidalgo, TX | 11.0 |
| 47 | 9 | Milwaukee, WI | 21.8 | 47 | 9 | Milwaukee, WI | 31.9 | 1 | 9 | Los Angeles, CA | 10.9 |
| 50 | 10 | Shelby, TN | 21.5 | 55 | 9 | Marion, IN | 31.9 | 22 | 10 | Philadelphia, PA | 10.8 |
| 55 | 11 | Marion, IN | 21.3 | 50 | 11 | Shelby, TN | 31.0 | 75 | 10 | Essex, NJ | 10.8 |
| 7 | 12 | Miami-Dade, FL | 20.9 | 9 | 12 | Dallas, TX | 30.0 | 25 | 12 | Sacramento, CA | 10.6 |
| 42 | 13 | Pima, AZ | 20.4 | 42 | 13 | Pima, AZ | 29.4 | 62 | 13 | Macomb, MI | 10.4 |
| 9 | 14 | Dallas, TX | 20.0 | 3 | 14 | Harris, TX | 29.1 | 8 | 14 | Kings, NY | 9.9 |
| 43 | 14 | Fulton, GA | 20.0 | 30 | 15 | Cuyahoga, OH | 29.0 | 43 | 15 | Fulton, GA | 9.6 |
| 3 | 16 | Harris, TX | 19.4 | 7 | 16 | Miami-Dade, FL | 28.9 | 45 | 16 | Mecklenburg, NC | 9.4 |
| 12 | 16 | San Bernardino, CA | 19.4 | 74 | 17 | Hamilton, OH | 27.7 | 2 | 17 | Cook, IL | 9.3 |
| 30 | 18 | Cuyahoga, OH | 18.8 | 43 | 18 | Fulton, GA | 27.0 | 7 | 17 | Miami-Dade, FL | 9.3 |
| 34 | 18 | Franklin, OH | 18.8 | 20 | 19 | New York, NY | 26.7 | 66 | 17 | El Paso, TX | 9.3 |
| 33 | 20 | Orange, FL | 18.5 | 2 | 20 | Cook, IL | 26.6 | 60 | 20 | New Haven, CT | 9.2 |
| 74 | 20 | Hamilton, OH | 18.5 | 34 | 21 | Franklin, OH | 26.5 | 32 | 21 | Oakland,MI | 9.1 |
| 1 | 22 | Los Angeles, CA | 18.4 | 12 | 22 | San Bernardino, CA | 26.2 | 50 | 21 | Shelby, TN | 9.1 |
| 20 | 22 | New York, NY | 18.4 | 1 | 23 | Los Angeles, CA | 25.9 | 21 | 23 | Alameda, CA | 9.0 |
| 37 | 24 | Travis, TX | 18.1 | 33 | 24 | Orange, FL | 25.8 | 38 | 23 | Contra Costa, CA | 9.0 |
| 19 | 25 | Bexar, TX | 17.9 | 19 | 25 | Bexar, TX | 25.6 | 64 | 23 | Ventura, CA | 9.0 |
| 2 | 26 | Cook, IL | 17.8 | 59 | 26 | Duval, FL | 25.5 | 5 | 26 | San Diego, CA | 8.9 |
| 25 | 27 | Sacramento, CA | 17.7 | 4 | 27 | Maricopa, AZ | 25.1 | 70 | 26 | Pierce, WA | 8.9 |
| 59 | 27 | Duval, FL | 17.7 | 25 | 28 | Sacramento, CA | 24.9 | 27 | 28 | Palm Beach, FL | 8.8 |
| 29 | 29 | Hillsborough, FL | 17.6 | 27 | 29 | Palm Beach, FL | 24.1 | 59 | 28 | Duval, FL | 8.8 |
| 4 | 30 | Maricopa, AZ | 17.4 | 37 | 29 | Travis, TX | 24.1 | 55 | 30 | Marion, IN | 8.7 |
| 75 | 31 | Essex, NJ | 17.2 | 15 | 31 | Tarrant, TX | 23.8 | 57 | 30 | Hartford, CT | 8.7 |
| 45 | 32 | Mecklenburg, NC | 17.1 | 45 | 31 | Mecklenburg, NC | 23.8 | 29 | 32 | Hillsborough, FL | 8.5 |
| 11 | 33 | Riverside, CA | 16.9 | 29 | 33 | Hillsborough, FL | 23.7 | 53 | 32 | Pinellas, FL | 8.5 |
| 14 | 34 | Clark, NV | 16.8 | 53 | 34 | Pinellas, FL | 23.6 | 68 | 32 | Middlesex, NJ | 8.5 |
| 15 | 34 | Tarrant, TX | 16.8 | 14 | 35 | Clark, NV | 23.4 | 16 | 35 | Santa Clara, CA | 8.4 |
| 10 | 36 | Queens, NY | 16.0 | 75 | 35 | Essex, NJ | 23.4 | 47 | 35 | Milwaukee, WI | 8.4 |
| 27 | 37 | Palm Beach, FL | 15.8 | 11 | 37 | Riverside, CA | 23.0 | 10 | 37 | Queens, NY | 8.3 |
| 63 | 38 | Gwinnett, GA | 15.7 | 54 | 38 | Erie, NY | 22.6 | 33 | 37 | Orange, FL | 8.3 |
| 54 | 39 | Erie, NY | 15.3 | 10 | 39 | Queens, NY | 21.8 | 54 | 37 | Erie, NY | 8.3 |
| 5 | 40 | San Diego, CA | 15.2 | 63 | 40 | Gwinnett, GA | 21.5 | 56 | 40 | Bergen, NJ | 8.1 |
| 53 | 41 | Pinellas, FL | 15.0 | 62 | 41 | Macomb, MI | 20.6 | 63 | 41 | Gwinnett, GA | 7.8 |
| 17 | 42 | Broward, Fl | 14.9 | 17 | 42 | Broward, Fl | 20.5 | 20 | 42 | New York, NY | 7.7 |
| 39 | 43 | Salt Lake, UT | 14.5 | 5 | 43 | San Diego, CA | 19.2 | 6 | 43 | Orange, CA | 7.6 |
| 62 | 44 | Macomb, MI | 14.1 | 31 | 44 | Allegheny, PA | 19.1 | 24 | 43 | Suffolk, NY | 7.6 |
| 67 | 45 | San Francisco, CA | 13.8 | 60 | 44 | New Haven, CT | 19.1 | 51 | 43 | Fairfield, CT | 7.6 |
| 35 | 46 | Hennepin, MN | 13.6 | 39 | 46 | Salt Lake, UT | 18.8 | 48 | 46 | Wake, NC | 7.5 |
| 31 | 47 | Allegheny, PA | 13.4 | 6 | 47 | Orange, CA | 17.9 | 73 | 46 | Worcester, MA | 7.5 |
| 21 | 48 | Alameda, CA | 13.2 | 35 | 48 | Hennepin, MN | 17.7 | 17 | 48 | Broward, Fl | 7.4 |
| 6 | 49 | Orange, CA | 13.0 | 21 | 49 | Alameda, CA | 16.8 | 30 | 49 | Cuyahoga, OH | 7.3 |
| 60 | 50 | New Haven, CT | 12.9 | 57 | 49 | Hartford, CT | 16.8 | 42 | 49 | Pima, AZ | 7.3 |
| 70 | 51 | Pierce, WA | 12.7 | 41 | 51 | St. Louis, MO | 16.6 | 52 | 49 | DuPage, IL | 7.3 |
| 57 | 52 | Hartford, CT | 12.4 | 70 | 51 | Pierce, WA | 16.6 | 67 | 49 | San Francisco, CA | 7.3 |
| 13 | 53 | King, WA | 12.1 | 48 | 53 | Wake, NC | 16.4 | 69 | 49 | Baltimore, MD | 7.3 |
| 38 | 54 | Contra Costa, CA | 11.9 | 64 | 53 | Ventura, CA | 16.4 | 9 | 54 | Dallas, TX | 7.2 |
| 41 | 54 | St. Louis, MO | 11.9 | 73 | 55 | Worcester, MA | 16.2 | 46 | 54 | Westchester, NY | 7.2 |
| 48 | 56 | Wake, NC | 11.6 | 67 | 56 | San Francisco, CA | 16.0 | 4 | 56 | Maricopa, AZ | 7.1 |
| 73 | 56 | Worcester, MA | 11.6 | 32 | 57 | Oakland,MI | 14.9 | 28 | 56 | Nassau, NY | 7.1 |
| 64 | 58 | Ventura, CA | 11.5 | 38 | 58 | Contra Costa, CA | 14.6 | 74 | 58 | Hamilton, OH | 7.0 |
| 32 | 59 | Oakland,MI | 11.2 | 13 | 59 | King, WA | 14.5 | 31 | 59 | Allegheny, PA | 6.9 |
| 16 | 60 | Santa Clara, CA | 10.7 | 44 | 60 | Honolulu, HI | 13.9 | 13 | 60 | King, WA | 6.8 |
| 44 | 61 | Honolulu, HI | 10.3 | 46 | 61 | Westchester, NY | 13.6 | 58 | 60 | Prince George's, MD | 6.8 |
| 46 | 62 | Westchester, NY | 10.0 | 16 | 62 | Santa Clara, CA | 12.6 | 71 | 60 | Montgomery, PA | 6.8 |
| 69 | 63 | Baltimore, MD | 9.6 | 69 | 63 | Baltimore, MD | 12.5 | 41 | 64 | St. Louis, MO | 6.7 |
| 51 | 64 | Fairfield, CT | 9.4 | 51 | 64 | Fairfield, CT | 12.4 | 15 | 65 | Tarrant, TX | 6.6 |
| 58 | 64 | Prince George's, MD | 9.4 | 58 | 64 | Prince George's, MD | 12.4 | 19 | 65 | Bexar, TX | 6.6 |
| 68 | 66 | Middlesex, NJ | 8.5 | 52 | 66 | DuPage, IL | 11.0 | 34 | 67 | Franklin, OH | 6.1 |
| 23 | 67 | Middlesex, MA | 8.3 | 68 | 67 | Middlesex, NJ | 10.8 | 65 | 67 | Collin, TX | 6.1 |
| 65 | 68 | Collin, TX | 8.2 | 65 | 68 | Collin, TX | 9.9 | 37 | 69 | Travis, TX | 5.7 |
| 52 | 69 | DuPage, IL | 7.8 | 23 | 69 | Middlesex, MA | 9.3 | 39 | 70 | Salt Lake, UT | 5.5 |
| 28 | 70 | Nassau, NY | 7.0 | 28 | 69 | Nassau, NY | 9.3 | 23 | 71 | Middlesex, MA | 5.3 |
| 24 | 71 | Suffolk, NY | 6.9 | 24 | 71 | Suffolk, NY | 9.0 | 35 | 71 | Hennepin, MN | 5.3 |
| 36 | 72 | Fairfax, VA | 6.8 | 36 | 71 | Fairfax, VA | 9.0 | 44 | 73 | Honolulu, HI | 5.2 |
| 40 | 73 | Montgomery, MD | 6.7 | 40 | 73 | Montgomery, MD | 8.8 | 40 | 74 | Montgomery, MD | 5.1 |
| 56 | 74 | Bergen, NJ | 6.6 | 56 | 74 | Bergen, NJ | 8.2 | 36 | 75 | Fairfax, VA | 4.2 |
| 71 | 75 | Montgomery, PA | 6.5 | 71 | 75 | Montgomery, PA | 7.2 | | | | |

# 75 Largest Counties by 2012 Population
## Selected Rankings

| Manufacturing employment as a percent of total nonfarm employment, 2011 | | | | Professional, scientific and technical employment as a percent of total nonfarm employment, 2011 | | | | Per capita local government taxes, 2007 | | | |
|---|---|---|---|---|---|---|---|---|---|---|---|
| Population rank | Manufacturing rank | County | Percent employed in manufacturing [col 107/col 105] | Population rank | Professional services rank | County | Percent employed in professional services [col 110/col 105] | Population rank | Local taxes rank | County | Per capita local taxes (dollars) [col 183] |
| 62 | 1 | Macomb, MI | 20.4 | 36 | 1 | Fairfax, VA | 33.2 | 28 | 1 | Nassau, NY | 4 802 |
| 18 | 2 | Wayne, MI | 12.0 | 40 | 2 | Montgomery, MD | 18.3 | 20 | 2 | New York, NY | 4 612 |
| 73 | 3 | Worcester, MA | 11.6 | 67 | 3 | San Francisco, CA | 16.5 | 8 | 2 | Kings, NY | 4 612 |
| 6 | 4 | Orange, CA | 11.4 | 23 | 4 | Middlesex, MA | 14.6 | 10 | 2 | Queens, NY | 4 612 |
| 47 | 5 | Milwaukee, WI | 11.1 | 16 | 5 | Santa Clara, CA | 14.1 | 26 | 2 | Bronx, NY | 4 612 |
| 57 | 6 | Hartford, CT | 10.6 | 20 | 6 | New York, NY | 13.8 | 46 | 6 | Westchester, NY | 4 398 |
| 21 | 6 | Alameda, CA | 10.6 | 32 | 7 | Oakland,MI | 12.8 | 24 | 7 | Suffolk, NY | 3 925 |
| 74 | 6 | Hamilton, OH | 10.6 | 68 | 8 | Middlesex, NJ | 12.7 | 67 | 8 | San Francisco, CA | 3 651 |
| 30 | 6 | Cuyahoga, OH | 10.6 | 43 | 9 | Fulton, GA | 12.1 | 40 | 9 | Montgomery, MD | 3 306 |
| 15 | 10 | Tarrant, TX | 10.5 | 37 | 10 | Travis, TX | 11.9 | 56 | 10 | Bergen, NJ | 3 227 |
| 49 | 10 | Fresno, CA | 10.5 | 1 | 11 | Los Angeles, CA | 11.8 | 51 | 11 | Fairfield, CT | 3 019 |
| 54 | 12 | Erie, NY | 10.4 | 62 | 12 | Macomb, MI | 10.8 | 27 | 12 | Palm Beach, FL | 2 908 |
| 16 | 12 | Santa Clara, CA | 10.4 | 5 | 12 | San Diego, CA | 10.8 | 36 | 13 | Fairfax, VA | 2 820 |
| 24 | 14 | Suffolk, NY | 9.9 | 21 | 14 | Alameda, CA | 10.5 | 30 | 14 | Cuyahoga, OH | 2 658 |
| 12 | 14 | San Bernardino, CA | 9.9 | 58 | 15 | Prince George's, MD | 10.4 | 43 | 15 | Fulton, GA | 2 622 |
| 60 | 16 | New Haven, CT | 9.8 | 71 | 16 | Montgomery, PA | 9.6 | 52 | 16 | DuPage, IL | 2 513 |
| 1 | 16 | Los Angeles, CA | 9.8 | 48 | 16 | Wake, NC | 9.6 | 34 | 17 | Franklin, OH | 2 490 |
| 64 | 18 | Ventura, CA | 9.3 | 35 | 18 | Hennepin, MN | 9.5 | 16 | 18 | Santa Clara, CA | 2 486 |
| 39 | 19 | Salt Lake, UT | 9.2 | 29 | 19 | Hillsborough, FL | 9.4 | 22 | 19 | Philadelphia, PA | 2 484 |
| 52 | 19 | DuPage, IL | 9.2 | 9 | 20 | Dallas, TX | 9.3 | 68 | 20 | Middlesex, NJ | 2 407 |
| 55 | 21 | Marion, IN | 8.8 | 13 | 21 | King, WA | 9.2 | 65 | 21 | Collin, TX | 2 376 |
| 35 | 22 | Hennepin, MN | 8.7 | 41 | 22 | St. Louis, MO | 9.1 | 71 | 22 | Montgomery, PA | 2 350 |
| 11 | 22 | Riverside, CA | 8.7 | 38 | 22 | Contra Costa, CA | 9.1 | 21 | 23 | Alameda, CA | 2 329 |
| 42 | 24 | Pima, AZ | 8.5 | 74 | 24 | Hamilton, OH | 9.0 | 75 | 24 | Essex, NJ | 2 328 |
| 3 | 24 | Harris, TX | 8.5 | 75 | 24 | Essex, NJ | 9.0 | 2 | 25 | Cook, IL | 2 315 |
| 5 | 26 | San Diego, CA | 8.4 | 2 | 26 | Cook, IL | 8.9 | 9 | 26 | Dallas, TX | 2 300 |
| 51 | 27 | Fairfield, CT | 8.3 | 64 | 27 | Ventura, CA | 8.8 | 57 | 27 | Hartford, CT | 2 289 |
| 2 | 28 | Cook, IL | 8.2 | 6 | 28 | Orange, CA | 8.7 | 37 | 28 | Travis, TX | 2 252 |
| 56 | 29 | Bergen, NJ | 8.1 | 51 | 28 | Fairfield, CT | 8.7 | 13 | 29 | King, WA | 2 220 |
| 71 | 29 | Montgomery, PA | 8.1 | 3 | 30 | Harris, TX | 8.6 | 7 | 30 | Miami-Dade, FL | 2 211 |
| 68 | 31 | Middlesex, NJ | 8.0 | 31 | 30 | Allegheny, PA | 8.6 | 74 | 31 | Hamilton, OH | 2 210 |
| 53 | 32 | Pinellas, FL | 7.7 | 17 | 32 | Broward, Fl | 8.2 | 17 | 32 | Broward, Fl | 2 115 |
| 9 | 33 | Dallas, TX | 7.5 | 65 | 33 | Collin, TX | 8.1 | 23 | 33 | Middlesex, MA | 2 093 |
| 23 | 34 | Middlesex, MA | 7.1 | 18 | 34 | Wayne, NY | 8.0 | 31 | 34 | Allegheny, PA | 2 086 |
| 32 | 35 | Oakland,MI | 7.0 | 28 | 34 | Nassau, NY | 8.0 | 60 | 34 | New Haven, CT | 2 086 |
| 13 | 36 | King, WA | 6.9 | 69 | 34 | Baltimore, MD | 8.0 | 3 | 36 | Harris, TX | 2 028 |
| 70 | 36 | Pierce, WA | 6.9 | 56 | 34 | Bergen, NJ | 8.0 | 38 | 37 | Contra Costa, CA | 2 003 |
| 66 | 38 | El Paso, TX | 6.7 | 52 | 34 | DuPage, IL | 8.0 | 15 | 38 | Tarrant, TX | 1 990 |
| 61 | 39 | Kern, CA | 6.6 | 63 | 39 | Gwinnett, GA | 7.7 | 54 | 39 | Erie, NY | 1 985 |
| 4 | 40 | Maricopa, AZ | 6.5 | 24 | 39 | Suffolk, NY | 7.7 | 33 | 40 | Orange, FL | 1 984 |
| 63 | 40 | Gwinnett, GA | 6.5 | 27 | 39 | Palm Beach, FL | 7.7 | 58 | 41 | Prince George's, MD | 1 958 |
| 75 | 42 | Essex, NJ | 6.4 | 53 | 39 | Pinellas, FL | 7.7 | 53 | 42 | Pinellas, FL | 1 906 |
| 41 | 42 | St. Louis, MO | 6.4 | 25 | 39 | Sacramento, CA | 7.7 | 50 | 43 | Shelby, TN | 1 888 |
| 50 | 44 | Shelby, TN | 6.1 | 45 | 44 | Mecklenburg, NC | 7.6 | 41 | 44 | St. Louis, MO | 1 882 |
| 65 | 45 | Collin, TX | 5.9 | 22 | 45 | Philadelphia, PA | 7.5 | 32 | 45 | Oakland,MI | 1 833 |
| 69 | 46 | Baltimore, MD | 5.7 | 34 | 46 | Franklin, OH | 7.3 | 5 | 46 | San Diego, CA | 1 831 |
| 38 | 47 | Contra Costa, CA | 5.6 | 7 | 47 | Miami-Dade, FL | 7.2 | 69 | 47 | Baltimore, MD | 1 825 |
| 31 | 47 | Allegheny, PA | 5.6 | 46 | 47 | Westchester, NY | 7.2 | 6 | 48 | Orange, CA | 1 804 |
| 59 | 49 | Duval, FL | 5.4 | 57 | 49 | Hartford, CT | 7.0 | 45 | 49 | Mecklenburg, NC | 1 742 |
| 37 | 50 | Travis, TX | 5.2 | 55 | 50 | Marion, IN | 6.9 | 1 | 50 | Los Angeles, CA | 1 740 |
| 34 | 51 | Franklin, OH | 5.1 | 39 | 50 | Salt Lake, UT | 6.9 | 14 | 51 | Clark, NV | 1 720 |
| 19 | 52 | Bexar, TX | 4.9 | 47 | 52 | Milwaukee, WI | 6.7 | 63 | 52 | Gwinnett, GA | 1 698 |
| 25 | 53 | Sacramento, CA | 4.8 | 33 | 52 | Orange, CA | 6.7 | 29 | 53 | Hillsborough, FL | 1 665 |
| 45 | 54 | Mecklenburg, NC | 4.6 | 30 | 52 | Cuyahoga, OH | 6.7 | 64 | 54 | Ventura, CA | 1 642 |
| 10 | 54 | Queens, NY | 4.6 | 4 | 55 | Maricopa, AZ | 6.5 | 55 | 55 | Marion, IN | 1 641 |
| 33 | 56 | Orange, FL | 4.4 | 61 | 55 | Kern, CA | 6.5 | 11 | 56 | Riverside, CA | 1 601 |
| 22 | 57 | Philadelphia, PA | 3.9 | 54 | 57 | Erie, NY | 6.3 | 47 | 57 | Milwaukee, WI | 1 600 |
| 8 | 57 | Kings, NY | 3.9 | 44 | 58 | Honolulu, HI | 6.2 | 25 | 58 | Sacramento, CA | 1 564 |
| 7 | 59 | Miami-Dade, FL | 3.8 | 19 | 59 | Bexar, TX | 6.0 | 18 | 59 | Wayne, MI | 1 561 |
| 48 | 59 | Wake, NC | 3.8 | 59 | 60 | Duval, FL | 5.8 | 35 | 60 | Hennepin, MN | 1 558 |
| 29 | 59 | Hillsborough, FL | 3.8 | 73 | 61 | Worcester, MA | 5.6 | 4 | 61 | Maricopa, AZ | 1 505 |
| 58 | 62 | Prince George's, MD | 3.4 | 15 | 62 | Tarrant, TX | 5.4 | 19 | 62 | Bexar, TX | 1 461 |
| 28 | 62 | Nassau, NY | 3.4 | 14 | 63 | Clark, NV | 5.3 | 70 | 63 | Pierce, WA | 1 415 |
| 17 | 62 | Broward, Fl | 3.4 | 42 | 63 | Pima, AZ | 5.3 | 59 | 64 | Duval, FL | 1 385 |
| 46 | 65 | Westchester, NY | 3.3 | 60 | 65 | New Haven, CT | 5.2 | 73 | 65 | Worcester, MA | 1 374 |
| 72 | 66 | Hidalgo, TX | 3.0 | 49 | 66 | Fresno, CA | 4.9 | 12 | 66 | San Bernardino, CA | 1 368 |
| 44 | 67 | Honolulu, HI | 2.8 | 66 | 67 | El Paso, TX | 4.6 | 42 | 67 | Pima, AZ | 1 333 |
| 26 | 67 | Bronx, NY | 2.8 | 50 | 68 | Shelby, TN | 3.8 | 62 | 68 | Macomb, MI | 1 296 |
| 27 | 69 | Palm Beach, FL | 2.7 | 70 | 69 | Pierce, WA | 3.7 | 61 | 69 | Kern, CA | 1 292 |
| 14 | 70 | Clark, NV | 2.6 | 72 | 69 | Hidalgo, TX | 3.7 | 39 | 70 | Salt Lake, UT | 1 279 |
| 43 | 71 | Fulton, GA | 2.5 | 11 | 71 | Riverside, CA | 3.4 | 48 | 71 | Wake, NC | 1 270 |
| 40 | 72 | Montgomery, MD | 2.0 | 12 | 71 | San Bernardino, CA | 3.4 | 66 | 72 | El Paso, TX | 1 219 |
| 67 | 73 | San Francisco, CA | 1.6 | 8 | 73 | Kings, NY | 3.3 | 49 | 73 | Fresno, CA | 1 189 |
| 36 | 74 | Fairfax, VA | 1.4 | 10 | 74 | Queens, NY | 2.6 | 44 | 74 | Honolulu, HI | 1 000 |
| 20 | 75 | New York, NY | 1.0 | 26 | 75 | Bronx, NY | 1.7 | 72 | 75 | Hidalgo, TX | 968 |

# 75 Largest Counties by 2012 Population
## Selected Rankings

| | Violent crime rate, 2011 | | | | Military as a percent of all federal employment, 2011 | | | | Percent of votes for Barack Obama, 2012 | | |
|---|---|---|---|---|---|---|---|---|---|---|---|
| Population rank | Violent crime rate rank | County | Violent crime rate per 100,000 population [col 46] | Population rank | Military employment rank | County | military federal employment [col 195/col 194+195] | Population rank | Vote for Obama rank | County | Percent of votes for Obama [col 197] |
| 22 | 1 | Philadelphia, PA | 1 194 | 70 | 1 | Pierce, WA | 74.0 | 58 | 1 | Prince George's, MD | 88.9 |
| 50 | 2 | Shelby, TN | 1 188 | 5 | 2 | San Diego, CA | 69.6 | 26 | 2 | Bronx, NY | 88.7 |
| 55 | 3 | Marion, IN | 1 078 | 66 | 3 | El Paso, TX | 68.1 | 20 | 3 | New York, NY | 85.7 |
| 18 | 4 | Wayne, MI | 1 048 | 44 | 4 | Honolulu, HI | 62.9 | 67 | 4 | San Francisco, CA | 84.2 |
| 43 | 5 | Fulton, GA | 873 | 12 | 5 | San Bernardino, CA | 60.0 | 22 | 5 | Philadelphia, PA | 83.1 |
| 47 | 6 | Milwaukee, WI | 757 | 65 | 6 | Collin, TX | 59.7 | 8 | 6 | Kings, NY | 79.4 |
| 33 | 7 | Orange, FL | 745 | 14 | 7 | Clark, NV | 56.1 | 21 | 7 | Alameda, CA | 78.8 |
| 7 | 8 | Miami-Dade, FL | 724 | 59 | 8 | Duval, FL | 52.2 | 2 | 8 | Cook, IL | 76.2 |
| 21 | 9 | Alameda, CA | 706 | 19 | 9 | Bexar, TX | 50.0 | 75 | 9 | Essex, NJ | 76.0 |
| 3 | 10 | Harris, TX | 690 | 63 | 10 | Gwinnett, GA | 49.7 | 10 | 10 | Queens, NY | 75.1 |
| 75 | 11 | Essex, NJ | 689 | 73 | 11 | Worcester, MA | 44.8 | 18 | 11 | Wayne, MI | 74.1 |
| 67 | 12 | San Francisco, CA | 671 | 71 | 11 | Montgomery, PA | 44.8 | 40 | 12 | Montgomery, MD | 71.6 |
| 59 | 13 | Duval, FL | 638 | 64 | 13 | Ventura, CA | 44.6 | 13 | 13 | King, WA | 70.3 |
| 20 | 14 | New York, NY | 625 | 56 | 14 | Bergen, NJ | 40.9 | 44 | 14 | Honolulu, HI | 69.8 |
| 8 | 14 | Kings, NY | 625 | 42 | 15 | Pima, AZ | 40.7 | 16 | 15 | Santa Clara, CA | 69.4 |
| 10 | 14 | Queens, NY | 625 | 68 | 16 | Middlesex, NJ | 39.2 | 1 | 16 | Los Angeles, CA | 69.2 |
| 26 | 14 | Bronx, NY | 625 | 8 | 16 | Kings, NY | 39.2 | 72 | 17 | Hidalgo, TX | 69.0 |
| 14 | 18 | Clark, NV | 624 | 4 | 18 | Maricopa, AZ | 38.6 | 30 | 18 | Cuyahoga, OH | 68.9 |
| 2 | 19 | Cook, IL | 620 | 51 | 19 | Fairfield, CT | 37.9 | 38 | 19 | Contra Costa, CA | 68.0 |
| 53 | 20 | Pinellas, FL | 607 | 29 | 20 | Hillsborough, FL | 37.0 | 47 | 20 | Milwaukee, WI | 67.3 |
| 58 | 21 | Prince George's, MD | 593 | 41 | 21 | St. Louis, MO | 36.6 | 43 | 21 | Fulton, GA | 67.2 |
| 49 | 22 | Fresno, CA | 553 | 48 | 22 | Wake, NC | 36.5 | 17 | 22 | Broward, FL | 67.1 |
| 30 | 23 | Cuyahoga, OH | 540 | 11 | 23 | Riverside, CA | 35.0 | 66 | 23 | El Paso, TX | 65.9 |
| 45 | 23 | Mecklenburg, NC | 540 | 72 | 24 | Hidalgo, TX | 34.3 | 57 | 24 | Hartford, CT | 65.2 |
| 69 | 25 | Baltimore, MD | 528 | 32 | 25 | Oakland, MI | 34.2 | 23 | 25 | Middlesex, MA | 64.2 |
| 61 | 26 | Kern, CA | 523 | 17 | 26 | Broward, Fl | 32.7 | 37 | 26 | Travis, TX | 63.9 |
| 25 | 27 | Sacramento, CA | 521 | 28 | 27 | Nassau, NY | 31.9 | 55 | 27 | Marion, IN | 63.8 |
| 27 | 28 | Palm Beach, FL | 492 | 39 | 28 | Salt Lake, UT | 31.8 | 46 | 28 | Westchester, NY | 63.4 |
| 17 | 29 | Broward, FL | 490 | 45 | 29 | Mecklenburg, NC | 31.6 | 35 | 28 | Hennepin, MN | 63.4 |
| 34 | 30 | Franklin, OH | 486 | 6 | 30 | Orange, CA | 31.2 | 50 | 28 | Shelby, TN | 63.4 |
| 74 | 31 | Hamilton, OH | 474 | 27 | 31 | Palm Beach, FL | 29.8 | 45 | 31 | Mecklenburg, NC | 61.8 |
| 1 | 32 | Los Angeles, CA | 464 | 53 | 32 | Pinellas, FL | 29.7 | 27 | 32 | Palm Beach, FL | 61.2 |
| 54 | 33 | Erie, NY | 455 | 3 | 33 | Harris, TX | 29.5 | 60 | 33 | New Haven, CT | 61.0 |
| 9 | 34 | Dallas, TX | 453 | 21 | 34 | Alameda, CA | 28.2 | 68 | 34 | Middlesex, NJ | 60.4 |
| 19 | 35 | Bexar, TX | 450 | 23 | 35 | Middlesex, MA | 27.8 | 36 | 35 | Fairfax, VA | 60.1 |
| 15 | 36 | Tarrant, TX | 442 | 52 | 36 | DuPage, IL | 27.7 | 71 | 36 | Montgomery, PA | 60.0 |
| 73 | 37 | Worcester, MA | 439 | 61 | 37 | Kern, CA | 27.1 | 34 | 37 | Franklin, OH | 59.7 |
| 42 | 38 | Pima, AZ | 432 | 7 | 37 | Miami-Dade, FL | 27.1 | 41 | 38 | St. Louis, MO | 59.5 |
| 70 | 39 | Pierce, WA | 420 | 1 | 39 | Los Angeles, CA | 26.9 | 33 | 39 | Orange, CA | 59.0 |
| 35 | 40 | Hennepin, MN | 418 | 35 | 40 | Hennepin, MN | 26.8 | 51 | 40 | Fairfield, CT | 58.6 |
| 12 | 41 | San Bernardino, CA | 415 | 38 | 41 | Contra Costa, CA | 26.1 | 14 | 41 | Clark, NV | 58.5 |
| 31 | 42 | Allegheny, PA | 412 | 15 | 42 | Tarrant, TX | 25.9 | 25 | 41 | Sacramento, CA | 58.5 |
| 66 | 43 | El Paso, TX | 396 | 46 | 43 | Westchester, NY | 25.8 | 54 | 43 | Erie, NY | 58.0 |
| 4 | 44 | Maricopa, AZ | 388 | 60 | 44 | New Haven, CT | 25.3 | 7 | 44 | Miami-Dade, FL | 57.9 |
| 60 | 45 | New Haven, CT | 384 | 13 | 44 | King, WA | 25.3 | 31 | 45 | Allegheny, PA | 57.3 |
| 29 | 46 | Hillsborough, FL | 371 | 25 | 46 | Sacramento, CA | 24.8 | 9 | 45 | Dallas, TX | 57.3 |
| 38 | 47 | Contra Costa, CA | 370 | 47 | 47 | Milwaukee, WI | 24.4 | 48 | 47 | Wake, NC | 56.7 |
| 37 | 48 | Travis, TX | 367 | 16 | 48 | Santa Clara, CA | 24.2 | 32 | 48 | Oakland, MI | 56.5 |
| 5 | 49 | San Diego, CA | 352 | 26 | 49 | Bronx, NY | 24.1 | 69 | 49 | Baltimore, MD | 56.2 |
| 13 | 50 | King, WA | 343 | 57 | 50 | Hartford, CT | 24.0 | 73 | 50 | Worcester, MA | 55.8 |
| 39 | 51 | Salt Lake, UT | 324 | 50 | 51 | Shelby, TN | 23.2 | 64 | 51 | Ventura, CA | 55.2 |
| 57 | 51 | Hartford, CT | 324 | 58 | 52 | Prince George's, MD | 22.3 | 70 | 51 | Pierce, WA | 55.2 |
| 41 | 53 | St. Louis, MO | 306 | 37 | 53 | Travis, TX | 21.3 | 52 | 53 | Du Page, IL | 54.7 |
| 11 | 54 | Riverside, CA | 299 | 2 | 54 | Cook, IL | 21.2 | 56 | 54 | Bergen, NJ | 54.3 |
| 72 | 55 | Hidalgo, TX | 295 | 33 | 55 | Orange, FL | 20.9 | 5 | 55 | San Diego, CA | 54.1 |
| 51 | 56 | Fairfield, CT | 294 | 18 | 56 | Wayne, MI | 20.6 | 28 | 56 | Nassau, NY | 53.8 |
| 62 | 57 | Macomb, MI | 291 | 31 | 56 | Allegheny, PA | 20.6 | 53 | 57 | Pinellas, FL | 53.6 |
| 48 | 58 | Wake, NC | 258 | 34 | 58 | Franklin, OH | 20.5 | 62 | 58 | Macomb, MI | 53.4 |
| 46 | 59 | Westchester, NY | 256 | 10 | 58 | Queens, NY | 20.5 | 29 | 59 | Hillsborough, FL | 53.2 |
| 16 | 60 | Santa Clara, CA | 253 | 9 | 60 | Dallas, TX | 18.9 | 74 | 60 | Hamilton, OH | 53.0 |
| 23 | 61 | Middlesex, MA | 250 | 74 | 61 | Hamilton, OH | 18.8 | 24 | 61 | Suffolk, NY | 52.6 |
| 44 | 62 | Honolulu, HI | 246 | 62 | 61 | Macomb, MI | 18.8 | 42 | 62 | Pima, AZ | 52.4 |
| 63 | 63 | Gwinnett, GA | 225 | 55 | 63 | Marion, IN | 18.5 | 19 | 62 | Bexar, TX | 52.4 |
| 6 | 64 | Orange, CA | 214 | 24 | 63 | Suffolk, NY | 18.5 | 12 | 64 | San Bernardino, CA | 52.1 |
| 64 | 65 | Ventura, CA | 205 | 30 | 65 | Cuyahoga, OH | 18.0 | 3 | 65 | Harris, TX | 50.4 |
| 32 | 66 | Oakland, MI | 193 | 54 | 66 | Erie, NY | 16.6 | 49 | 66 | Fresno, CA | 50.2 |
| 68 | 67 | Middlesex, NJ | 184 | 43 | 67 | Fulton, GA | 16.0 | 11 | 66 | Riverside, CA | 50.2 |
| 71 | 68 | Montgomery, PA | 178 | 36 | 68 | Fairfax, VA | 15.5 | 59 | 68 | Duval, FL | 48.7 |
| 65 | 69 | Collin, TX | 174 | 75 | 69 | Essex, NJ | 15.2 | 39 | 68 | Salt Lake, UT | 48.7 |
| 40 | 70 | Montgomery, MD | 172 | 49 | 70 | Fresno, CA | 13.7 | 6 | 70 | Orange, CA | 47.6 |
| 28 | 71 | Nassau, NY | 164 | 69 | 71 | Baltimore, MD | 13.6 | 63 | 71 | Gwinnett, GA | 44.5 |
| 24 | 72 | Suffolk, NY | 146 | 22 | 72 | Philadelphia, PA | 13.0 | 4 | 72 | Maricopa, AZ | 44.1 |
| 56 | 73 | Bergen, NJ | 95 | 40 | 73 | Montgomery, MD | 12.5 | 15 | 73 | Tarrant, TX | 43.7 |
| 52 | 74 | DuPage, IL | 94 | 20 | 74 | New York, NY | 11.4 | 61 | 74 | Kern, CA | 40.1 |
| 36 | 75 | Fairfax, VA | 90 | 67 | 75 | San Francisco, CA | 10.3 | 65 | 75 | Collin, TX | 36.8 |

# All Counties
## Selected Rankings

| | Defense contracts, 2009–2010 | | | | Non-defense contracts, 2009–2010 | | | | Federal grants, 2009–2010 | | |
|---|---|---|---|---|---|---|---|---|---|---|---|
| Population rank | Defense contracts rank | County | contracts (millions of dollars) [col 172] | Population rank | Non-defense contracts rank | County | contracts (millions of dollars) [col 173] | Population rank | Grants rank | County | (millions of dollars) [col 174 + 175 + 176 + 177] |
| 36 | 1 | Fairfax, VA | 16 146 | 99 | 1 | District of Columbia | 16 599 | 20 | 1 | New York, NY | 34 534.3 |
| 5 | 2 | San Diego, CA | 11 593 | 36 | 2 | Fairfax, VA | 8 126 | 1 | 2 | Los Angeles, CA | 21 340.9 |
| 1 | 3 | Los Angeles, CA | 10 637 | 40 | 3 | Montgomery, MD | 6 596 | 25 | 3 | Sacramento, CA | 15 259.3 |
| 15 | 4 | Tarrant, TX | 9 370 | 1 | 4 | Los Angeles, CA | 5 805 | 2 | 4 | Cook, IL | 12 589.1 |
| 369 | 5 | Winnebago, WI | 7 100 | 287 | 5 | Arlington, VA | 4 850 | 37 | 5 | Travis, TX | 11 329.2 |
| 23 | 6 | Middlesex, MA | 5 847 | 3 | 6 | Harris, TX | 4 427 | 99 | 6 | District of Columbia | 10 872.0 |
| 42 | 7 | Pima, AZ | 5 269 | 58 | 7 | Prince George's, MD | 4 171 | 80 | 7 | Suffolk, MA | 9 637.6 |
| 192 | 8 | Madison, AL | 5 247 | 727 | 8 | Anderson, TN | 3 682 | 4 | 8 | Maricopa, AZ | 7 815.8 |
| 287 | 9 | Arlington, VA | 4 902 | 346 | 9 | Benton, WA | 3 128 | 22 | 9 | Philadelphia, PA | 7 464.9 |
| 16 | 10 | Santa Clara, CA | 4 709 | 21 | 10 | Alameda, CA | 2 904 | 7 | 10 | Miami-Dade, FL | 7 415.2 |
| 99 | 11 | District of Columbia | 4 651 | 92 | 11 | Bernalillo, NM | 2 895 | 104 | 11 | Baltimore city, MD | 7 211.8 |
| 41 | 12 | St. Louis, MO | 4 569 | 117 | 12 | Jefferson, CO | 2 422 | 212 | 12 | Albany, NY | 6 947.8 |
| 4 | 13 | Maricopa, AZ | 4 436 | 384 | 13 | Aiken, SC | 2 326 | 150 | 13 | East Baton Rouge, LA | 6 872.9 |
| 51 | 14 | Fairfield, CT | 4 046 | 20 | 14 | New York, NY | 2 225 | 43 | 14 | Fulton, GA | 6 868.0 |
| 77 | 15 | Essex, MA | 3 844 | 1 912 | 15 | Los Alamos, NM | 2 216 | 34 | 15 | Franklin, OH | 6 841.1 |
| 19 | 16 | Bexar, TX | 3 694 | 43 | 16 | Fulton, GA | 2 021 | 233 | 16 | Leon, FL | 6 780.4 |
| 84 | 17 | Cobb, GA | 3 624 | 2 | 17 | Cook, IL | 1 997 | 245 | 17 | Dauphin, PA | 6 580.6 |
| 243 | 18 | New London, CT | 3 521 | 91 | 18 | Jackson, MO | 1 453 | 5 | 18 | San Diego, CA | 5 774.5 |
| 25 | 19 | Sacramento, CA | 3 512 | 31 | 19 | Allegheny, PA | 1 430 | 13 | 19 | King, WA | 5 218.8 |
| 33 | 20 | Orange, FL | 3 417 | 23 | 20 | Middlesex, MA | 1 415 | 3 | 20 | Harris, TX | 4 941.0 |
| 205 | 21 | St. Louis city, MO | 3 415 | 559 | 21 | Bonneville, ID | 1 359 | 18 | 21 | Wayne, MI | 4 934.9 |
| 57 | 22 | Hartford, CT | 3 292 | 71 | 22 | Montgomery, PA | 1 326 | 67 | 22 | San Francisco, CA | 4 870.0 |
| 9 | 23 | Dallas, TX | 3 142 | 5 | 23 | San Diego, CA | 1 289 | 95 | 23 | Davidson, TN | 4 661.1 |
| 78 | 24 | Jefferson, KY | 3 080 | 115 | 24 | Brevard, FL | 1 237 | 55 | 24 | Marion, IN | 4 574.9 |
| 350 | 25 | Newport News City, VA | 3 014 | 128 | 25 | Chester, PA | 1 223 | 23 | 25 | Middlesex, MA | 4 530.6 |
| 193 | 26 | Loudoun, VA | 2 972 | 9 | 26 | Dallas, TX | 1 166 | 48 | 26 | Wake, NC | 4 489.3 |
| 97 | 27 | El Paso, CO | 2 888 | 22 | 27 | Philadelphia, PA | 1 142 | 235 | 27 | Ingham, MI | 4 228.1 |
| 100 | 28 | Monmouth, NJ | 2 858 | 434 | 28 | Alexandria City, VA | 1 128 | 318 | 28 | Sangamon, IL | 4 169.2 |
| 13 | 29 | King, WA | 2 724 | 192 | 29 | Madison, AL | 1 127 | 21 | 29 | Alameda, CA | 4 003.6 |
| 3 | 30 | Harris, TX | 2 658 | 806 | 30 | McCracken, KY | 1 079 | 130 | 30 | Dane, WI | 3 888.9 |
| 40 | 31 | Montgomery, MD | 2 556 | 16 | 31 | Santa Clara, CA | 1 071 | 181 | 31 | Mercer, NJ | 3 794.3 |
| 179 | 32 | Orleans, LA | 2 495 | 24 | 32 | Suffolk, NY | 1 039 | 30 | 32 | Cuyahoga, OH | 3 602.4 |
| 500 | 33 | Potter, TX | 2 428 | 52 | 33 | Du Page, IL | 948 | 98 | 33 | Denver, CO | 3 576.2 |
| 62 | 34 | Macomb, MI | 2 324 | 104 | 34 | Baltimore city, MD | 944 | 31 | 34 | Allegheny, PA | 3 499.7 |
| 12 | 35 | San Bernardino, CA | 2 318 | 69 | 35 | Baltimore, MD | 915 | 57 | 35 | Hartford, CT | 3 474.4 |
| 44 | 36 | Honolulu, HI | 2 218 | 14 | 36 | Clark, NV | 893 | 298 | 36 | Richmond City, VA | 3 338.0 |
| 159 | 37 | Prince William, VA | 2 205 | 368 | 37 | Monroe, PA | 865 | 16 | 37 | Santa Clara, CA | 3 243.1 |
| 2 | 38 | Cook, IL | 2 149 | 4 | 38 | Maricopa, AZ | 848 | 205 | 38 | St. Louis city, MO | 3 201.5 |
| 267 | 39 | Norfolk City, VA | 2 127 | 35 | 39 | Hennepin, MN | 831 | 6 | 39 | Orange, CA | 3 060.1 |
| 544 | 40 | St. Mary's, MD | 2 124 | 13 | 40 | King, WA | 829 | 126 | 40 | Ramsey, MN | 2 997.3 |
| 115 | 41 | Brevard, FL | 2 092 | 238 | 41 | Durham, NC | 819 | 9 | 41 | Dallas, TX | 2 983.2 |
| 149 | 42 | Virginia Beach City, VA | 2 086 | 30 | 42 | Cuyahoga, OH | 811 | 39 | 42 | Salt Lake, UT | 2 896.9 |
| 6 | 43 | Orange, CA | 2 026 | 67 | 43 | San Francisco, CA | 799 | 35 | 43 | Hennepin, MN | 2 860.4 |
| 52 | 44 | Du Page, IL | 1 993 | 80 | 44 | Suffolk, MA | 795 | 718 | 44 | Cole, MO | 2 797.9 |
| 31 | 45 | Allegheny, PA | 1 885 | 18 | 45 | Wayne, MI | 780 | 19 | 45 | Bexar, TX | 2 793.9 |
| 113 | 46 | Anne Arundel, MD | 1 879 | 270 | 46 | Frederick, MD | 719 | 76 | 46 | Multnomah, OR | 2 791.1 |
| 79 | 47 | Monroe, NY | 1 844 | 182 | 47 | Charleston, SC | 714 | 47 | 47 | Milwaukee, WI | 2 780.4 |
| 74 | 48 | Hamilton, OH | 1 792 | 82 | 48 | San Mateo, CA | 698 | 75 | 48 | Essex, NJ | 2 775.4 |
| 148 | 49 | Burlington, NJ | 1 770 | 37 | 49 | Travis, TX | 698 | 256 | 49 | Thurston, WA | 2 738.6 |
| 108 | 50 | Arapahoe, CO | 1 715 | 29 | 50 | Hillsborough, FL | 688 | 81 | 50 | Oklahoma, OK | 2 673.0 |
| 28 | 51 | Nassau, NY | 1 714 | 98 | 51 | Denver, CO | 654 | 101 | 51 | Providence, RI | 2 502.8 |
| 50 | 52 | Shelby, TN | 1 628 | 500 | 52 | Potter, TX | 638 | 172 | 52 | Pulaski, AR | 2 460.9 |
| 112 | 53 | Bristol, MA | 1 585 | 443 | 53 | Kootenai, ID | 618 | 44 | 53 | Honolulu, HI | 2 409.4 |
| 182 | 54 | Charleston, SC | 1 579 | 218 | 54 | Howard, MD | 594 | 42 | 54 | Pima, AZ | 2 291.8 |
| 218 | 55 | Howard, MD | 1 577 | 50 | 55 | Shelby, TN | 594 | 60 | 55 | New Haven, CT | 2 265.9 |
| 128 | 56 | Chester, PA | 1 541 | 86 | 56 | De Kalb, GA | 589 | 279 | 56 | Montgomery, AL | 2 228.5 |
| 333 | 57 | Okaloosa, FL | 1 398 | 19 | 57 | Bexar, TX | 583 | 54 | 57 | Erie, NY | 2 162.0 |
| 652 | 58 | Hunt, TX | 1 391 | 975 | 58 | Box Elder, UT | 573 | 264 | 58 | Hinds, MS | 2 131.5 |
| 155 | 59 | York, PA | 1 324 | 33 | 59 | Orange, FL | 568 | 74 | 59 | Hamilton, OH | 2 120.9 |
| 55 | 60 | Marion, IN | 1 290 | 95 | 60 | Davidson, TN | 560 | 204 | 60 | Marion, OR | 2 105.4 |
| 110 | 61 | Delaware, PA | 1 289 | 213 | 61 | Boulder, CO | 533 | 24 | 61 | Suffolk, NY | 2 087.6 |
| 202 | 62 | Bell, TX | 1 281 | 15 | 62 | Tarrant, TX | 532 | 12 | 62 | San Bernardino, CA | 2 071.2 |
| 200 | 63 | Cumberland, NC | 1 227 | 179 | 63 | Orleans, LA | 527 | 238 | 63 | Durham, NC | 2 066.5 |
| 444 | 64 | Cambria, PA | 1 181 | 191 | 64 | Hamilton, TN | 508 | 50 | 64 | Shelby, TN | 2 021.8 |
| 307 | 65 | Yolo, CA | 1 145 | 455 | 65 | Hampton City, VA | 498 | 984 | 65 | Franklin, KY | 2 016.9 |
| 29 | 66 | Hillsborough, FL | 1 144 | 193 | 66 | Loudoun, VA | 491 | 170 | 66 | Richland, SC | 1 949.8 |
| 34 | 67 | Franklin, OH | 1 130 | 703 | 67 | Leavenworth, KS | 490 | 151 | 67 | Polk, IA | 1 943.3 |
| 291 | 68 | Linn, IA | 1 129 | 76 | 68 | Multnomah, OR | 481 | 394 | 68 | Rensselaer, NY | 1 879.5 |
| 156 | 69 | Jefferson, LA | 1 123 | 7 | 69 | Miami-Dade, FL | 473 | 79 | 69 | Monroe, NY | 1 829.4 |
| 250 | 70 | St. Joseph, IN | 1 122 | 124 | 70 | Kane, IL | 470 | 331 | 70 | Kanawha, WV | 1 797.8 |
| 129 | 71 | Sedgwick, KS | 1 075 | 32 | 71 | Oakland, MI | 459 | 179 | 71 | Orleans, LA | 1 786.0 |
| 382 | 72 | Greene, OH | 1 074 | 1 062 | 72 | Hancock, MS | 444 | 40 | 72 | Montgomery, MD | 1 749.1 |
| 143 | 73 | Onondaga, NY | 1 051 | 242 | 73 | Rutherford, TN | 443 | 73 | 73 | Worcester, MA | 1 731.9 |
| 65 | 74 | Collin, TX | 1 047 | 6 | 74 | Orange, CA | 431 | 11 | 74 | Riverside, CA | 1 686.2 |
| 53 | 75 | Pinellas, FL | 978 | 55 | 75 | Marion, IN | 429 | 189 | 75 | Washtenaw, MI | 1 661.7 |

# 75 Counties with Highest Agricultural Sales
## Selected Rankings

| Value of agricultural sales, 2007 | | | Average agricultural sales per farm, 2007 | | | | Number of farms, 2007 | | | |
|---|---|---|---|---|---|---|---|---|---|---|
| Value of sales rank | County | Value of sales (millions of dollars) [col 125] | Value of sales rank | Average sales rank | County | Average sales per farm (dollars) [col 126] | Value of sales rank | Number of farms rank | County | Number of farms [col 113] |
| 1 | Fresno County, CA | 3 731 | 35 | 1 | Haskell County, KS | 2 896 342 | 19 | 1 | San Diego County, CA | 6 687 |
| 2 | Tulare County, CA | 3 335 | 11 | 2 | Imperial County, CA | 2 854 543 | 1 | 2 | Fresno County, CA | 6 081 |
| 3 | Kern County, CA | 3 204 | 32 | 3 | Scott County, KS | 2 753 403 | 18 | 3 | Lancaster County, PA | 5 462 |
| 4 | Merced County, CA | 2 330 | 34 | 4 | Hartley County, TX | 2 569 176 | 2 | 4 | Tulare County, CA | 5 240 |
| 5 | Monterey County, CA | 2 179 | 43 | 5 | Hansford County, TX | 2 437 187 | 6 | 5 | Stanislaus County, CA | 4 114 |
| 6 | Stanislaus County, CA | 1 821 | 23 | 6 | Yuma County, AZ | 2 123 822 | 8 | 6 | Weld County, CO | 3 921 |
| 7 | San Joaquin County, CA | 1 564 | 22 | 7 | Castro County, TX | 2 006 911 | 7 | 7 | San Joaquin County, CA | 3 624 |
| 8 | Weld County, CO | 1 539 | 5 | 8 | Monterey County, CA | 1 816 906 | 12 | 8 | Yakima County, WA | 3 540 |
| 9 | Kings County, CA | 1 358 | 16 | 9 | Deaf Smith County, TX | 1 802 762 | 20 | 9 | Riverside County, CA | 3 463 |
| 10 | Ventura County, CA | 1 316 | 46 | 10 | Grant County, KS | 1 769 655 | 40 | 10 | Sonoma County, CA | 3 429 |
| 11 | Imperial County, CA | 1 290 | 25 | 11 | Parmer County, TX | 1 689 485 | 54 | 11 | Stearns County, MN | 3 368 |
| 12 | Yakima County, WA | 1 204 | 68 | 12 | Moore County, TX | 1 636 750 | 63 | 12 | Dane County, WI | 3 331 |
| 13 | Sampson County, NC | 1 196 | 3 | 13 | Kern County, CA | 1 513 532 | 59 | 13 | Hillsborough County, FL | 2 843 |
| 14 | Grant County, WA | 1 190 | 38 | 14 | Gray County, KS | 1 461 694 | 48 | 14 | San Luis Obispo County, CA | 2 784 |
| 15 | Duplin County, NC | 1 176 | 73 | 15 | Wichita County, KS | 1 389 261 | 45 | 15 | Marion County, OR | 2 670 |
| 16 | Deaf Smith County, TX | 1 148 | 37 | 16 | Finney County, KS | 1 344 046 | 4 | 16 | Merced County, CA | 2 607 |
| 17 | Sioux County, IA | 1 121 | 47 | 17 | Hendry County, FL | 1 319 602 | 39 | 17 | Miami-Dade County, FL | 2 498 |
| 18 | Lancaster County, PA | 1 072 | 72 | 18 | Sherman County, TX | 1 239 944 | 10 | 18 | Ventura County, CA | 2 437 |
| 19 | San Diego County, CA | 1 054 | 50 | 19 | Dallam County, TX | 1 223 139 | 3 | 19 | Kern County, CA | 2 117 |
| 20 | Riverside County, CA | 1 012 | 9 | 20 | Kings County, CA | 1 203 198 | 52 | 20 | Rockingham County, VA | 1 970 |
| 21 | Madera County, CA | 990 | 64 | 21 | Phelps County, NE | 1 119 572 | 14 | 21 | Grant County, WA | 1 858 |
| 22 | Castro County, TX | 973 | 30 | 22 | Pinal County, AZ | 1 018 867 | 29 | 22 | Maricopa County, AZ | 1 793 |
| 23 | Yuma County, AZ | 960 | 15 | 23 | Duplin County, NC | 1 014 902 | 60 | 23 | Darke County, OH | 1 772 |
| 24 | Santa Barbara County, CA | 951 | 13 | 24 | Sampson County, NC | 994 457 | 49 | 24 | Chester County, PA | 1 733 |
| 25 | Parmer County, TX | 938 | 27 | 25 | Cuming County, NE | 992 599 | 21 | 25 | Madera County, CA | 1 708 |
| 26 | Palm Beach County, FL | 932 | 41 | 26 | Cassia County, ID | 973 170 | 17 | 26 | Sioux County, IA | 1 664 |
| 27 | Cuming County, NE | 857 | 42 | 27 | Gooding County, ID | 938 978 | 53 | 27 | Benton County, WA | 1 630 |
| 28 | Sussex County, DE | 849 | 4 | 28 | Merced County, CA | 893 904 | 24 | 28 | Santa Barbara County, CA | 1 597 |
| 29 | Maricopa County, AZ | 814 | 70 | 29 | Swisher County, TX | 860 821 | 67 | 29 | Plymouth County, IA | 1 442 |
| 30 | Pinal County, AZ | 800 | 44 | 30 | Dawson County, NE | 808 444 | 33 | 30 | San Bernardino County, CA | 1 405 |
| 31 | Texas County, OK | 780 | 69 | 31 | Jerome County, ID | 764 237 | 65 | 31 | Kossuth County, IA | 1 395 |
| 32 | Scott County, KS | 763 | 31 | 32 | Texas County, OK | 751 318 | 28 | 32 | Sussex County, DE | 1 374 |
| 33 | San Bernardino County, CA | 744 | 26 | 33 | Palm Beach County, FL | 737 712 | 51 | 33 | Mercer County, OH | 1 302 |
| 34 | Hartley County, TX | 725 | 36 | 34 | Yuma County, CO | 733 393 | 62 | 34 | Twin Falls County, ID | 1 296 |
| 35 | Haskell County, KS | 718 | 61 | 35 | Ford County, KS | 713 970 | 26 | 35 | Palm Beach County, FL | 1 263 |
| 36 | Yuma County, CO | 711 | 57 | 36 | Wayne County, NC | 693 190 | 13 | 36 | Sampson County, NC | 1 203 |
| 37 | Finney County, KS | 694 | 17 | 37 | Sioux County, IA | 673 764 | 5 | 37 | Monterey County, CA | 1 199 |
| 38 | Gray County, KS | 691 | 74 | 38 | Santa Cruz County, CA | 656 037 | 55 | 38 | Custer County, NE | 1 187 |
| 39 | Miami-Dade County, FL | 661 | 14 | 39 | Grant County, WA | 640 576 | 15 | 39 | Duplin County, NC | 1 159 |
| 40 | Sonoma County, CA | 648 | 2 | 40 | Tulare County, CA | 636 453 | 9 | 40 | Kings County, CA | 1 129 |
| 41 | Cassia County, ID | 627 | 56 | 41 | Fayette County, KY | 622 377 | 71 | 41 | Lyon County, IA | 1 087 |
| 42 | Gooding County, ID | 624 | 28 | 42 | Sussex County, DE | 617 862 | 31 | 42 | Texas County, OK | 1 038 |
| 43 | Hansford County, TX | 590 | 1 | 43 | Fresno County, CA | 613 476 | 75 | 43 | Carroll County, IA | 978 |
| 44 | Dawson County, NE | 589 | 24 | 44 | Santa Barbara County, CA | 595 696 | 36 | 44 | Yuma County, CO | 970 |
| 45 | Marion County, OR | 587 | 21 | 45 | Madera County, CA | 579 696 | 58 | 45 | Morgan County, CO | 894 |
| 46 | Grant County, KS | 577 | 58 | 46 | Morgan County, CO | 552 420 | 66 | 46 | Franklin County, WA | 891 |
| 47 | Hendry County, FL | 567 | 10 | 47 | Ventura County, CA | 540 137 | 27 | 47 | Cuming County, NE | 863 |
| 48 | San Luis Obispo County, CA | 561 | 33 | 48 | San Bernardino County, CA | 529 296 | 56 | 48 | Fayette County, KY | 810 |
| 49 | Chester County, PA | 553 | 66 | 49 | Franklin County, WA | 524 145 | 30 | 49 | Pinal County, AZ | 785 |
| 50 | Dallam County, TX | 553 | 29 | 50 | Maricopa County, AZ | 453 704 | 44 | 50 | Dawson County, NE | 728 |
| 51 | Mercer County, OH | 535 | 75 | 51 | Carroll County, IA | 452 612 | 57 | 51 | Wayne County, NC | 723 |
| 52 | Rockingham County, VA | 534 | 6 | 52 | Stanislaus County, CA | 442 529 | 74 | 52 | Santa Cruz County, CA | 682 |
| 53 | Benton County, WA | 526 | 55 | 53 | Custer County, NE | 432 831 | 42 | 53 | Gooding County, ID | 665 |
| 54 | Stearns County, MN | 519 | 7 | 54 | San Joaquin County, CA | 431 665 | 61 | 54 | Ford County, KS | 664 |
| 55 | Custer County, NE | 514 | 71 | 55 | Lyon County, IA | 416 847 | 41 | 55 | Cassia County, ID | 644 |
| 56 | Fayette County, KY | 504 | 51 | 56 | Mercer County, OH | 411 051 | 16 | 56 | Deaf Smith County, TX | 637 |
| 57 | Wayne County, NC | 501 | 8 | 57 | Weld County, CO | 392 520 | 69 | 57 | Jerome County, ID | 604 |
| 58 | Morgan County, CO | 494 | 62 | 58 | Twin Falls County, ID | 364 090 | 25 | 58 | Parmer County, TX | 555 |
| 59 | Hillsborough County, FL | 488 | 12 | 59 | Yakima County, WA | 340 058 | 70 | 59 | Swisher County, TX | 527 |
| 60 | Darke County, OH | 480 | 65 | 60 | Kossuth County, IA | 335 347 | 37 | 60 | Finney County, KS | 516 |
| 61 | Ford County, KS | 474 | 67 | 61 | Plymouth County, IA | 324 065 | 22 | 61 | Castro County, TX | 485 |
| 62 | Twin Falls County, ID | 472 | 53 | 62 | Benton County, WA | 322 649 | 38 | 62 | Gray County, KS | 473 |
| 63 | Dane County, WI | 471 | 49 | 63 | Chester County, PA | 319 267 | 50 | 63 | Dallam County, TX | 452 |
| 64 | Phelps County, NE | 470 | 20 | 64 | Riverside County, CA | 292 244 | 11 | 63 | Imperial County, CA | 452 |
| 65 | Kossuth County, IA | 468 | 52 | 65 | Rockingham County, VA | 271 138 | 23 | 63 | Yuma County, AZ | 452 |
| 66 | Franklin County, WA | 467 | 60 | 66 | Darke County, OH | 270 741 | 47 | 66 | Hendry County, FL | 430 |
| 67 | Plymouth County, IA | 467 | 39 | 67 | Miami-Dade County, FL | 264 652 | 64 | 67 | Phelps County, NE | 420 |
| 68 | Moore County, TX | 463 | 45 | 68 | Marion County, OR | 219 754 | 72 | 68 | Sherman County, TX | 362 |
| 69 | Jerome County, ID | 462 | 48 | 69 | San Luis Obispo County, CA | 201 368 | 46 | 69 | Grant County, KS | 326 |
| 70 | Swisher County, TX | 454 | 18 | 70 | Lancaster County, PA | 196 293 | 73 | 70 | Wichita County, KS | 323 |
| 71 | Lyon County, IA | 453 | 40 | 71 | Sonoma County, CA | 188 854 | 68 | 71 | Moore County, TX | 283 |
| 72 | Sherman County, TX | 449 | 59 | 72 | Hillsborough County, FL | 171 727 | 34 | 72 | Hartley County, TX | 282 |
| 73 | Wichita County, KS | 449 | 19 | 73 | San Diego County, CA | 157 646 | 32 | 73 | Scott County, KS | 277 |
| 74 | Santa Cruz County, CA | 447 | 54 | 74 | Stearns County, MN | 154 226 | 35 | 74 | Haskell County, KS | 248 |
| 75 | Carroll County, IA | 443 | 63 | 75 | Dane County, WI | 141 277 | 43 | 75 | Hansford County, TX | 242 |

# 75 Counties with Highest Agricultural Sales
## Selected Rankings

| Average size of farm, 2007 | | | | Average value of land and buildings per farm, 2007 | | | | Average value of land and buildings per acre, 2007 | | | |
|---|---|---|---|---|---|---|---|---|---|---|---|
| Value of sales rank | Size of farm rank | County | Average size of farm (acres) [col 119] | Value of sales rank | Land and buildings per farm rank | County | Average value per farm (dollars) [col 122] | Value of sales rank | Value of land and buildings per acre rank | County | Average value per acre (dollars) [col 123] |
| 34 | 1 | Hartley County, TX | 3 230 | 3 | 1 | Kern County, CA | 5 160 784 | 39 | 1 | Miami-Dade County, FL | 27 648 |
| 43 | 2 | Hansford County, TX | 2 419 | 5 | 2 | Monterey County, CA | 5 144 255 | 10 | 2 | Ventura County, CA | 22 782 |
| 50 | 3 | Dallam County, TX | 2 073 | 11 | 3 | Imperial County, CA | 5 001 024 | 74 | 3 | Santa Cruz County, CA | 22 423 |
| 68 | 4 | Moore County, TX | 1 955 | 30 | 4 | Pinal County, AZ | 4 853 351 | 19 | 4 | San Diego County, CA | 19 247 |
| 32 | 5 | Scott County, KS | 1 636 | 23 | 5 | Yuma County, AZ | 3 893 483 | 40 | 5 | Sonoma County, CA | 15 887 |
| 72 | 6 | Sherman County, TX | 1 614 | 47 | 6 | Hendry County, FL | 3 673 204 | 20 | 6 | Riverside County, CA | 15 765 |
| 73 | 7 | Wichita County, KS | 1 609 | 9 | 7 | Kings County, CA | 3 295 061 | 49 | 7 | Chester County, PA | 10 740 |
| 35 | 8 | Haskell County, KS | 1 608 | 24 | 8 | Santa Barbara County, CA | 3 223 533 | 28 | 8 | Sussex County, DE | 10 234 |
| 16 | 9 | Deaf Smith County, TX | 1 485 | 4 | 9 | Merced County, CA | 2 879 524 | 59 | 9 | Hillsborough County, FL | 10 190 |
| 37 | 10 | Finney County, KS | 1 473 | 21 | 10 | Madera County, CA | 2 699 315 | 7 | 10 | San Joaquin County, CA | 10 168 |
| 36 | 11 | Yuma County, CO | 1 376 | 40 | 11 | Sonoma County, CA | 2 459 725 | 6 | 11 | Stanislaus County, CA | 9 476 |
| 55 | 12 | Custer County, NE | 1 360 | 10 | 12 | Ventura County, CA | 2 421 700 | 18 | 12 | Lancaster County, PA | 9 324 |
| 30 | 13 | Pinal County, AZ | 1 334 | 29 | 13 | Maricopa County, AZ | 2 300 844 | 29 | 13 | Maricopa County, AZ | 8 498 |
| 22 | 14 | Castro County, TX | 1 170 | 48 | 14 | San Luis Obispo County, CA | 2 236 326 | 23 | 14 | Yuma County, AZ | 8 361 |
| 31 | 15 | Texas County, OK | 1 162 | 34 | 15 | Hartley County, TX | 2 184 140 | 2 | 15 | Tulare County, CA | 8 266 |
| 38 | 16 | Gray County, KS | 1 155 | 1 | 16 | Fresno County, CA | 2 132 914 | 1 | 16 | Fresno County, CA | 7 927 |
| 3 | 17 | Kern County, CA | 1 116 | 7 | 17 | San Joaquin County, CA | 2 069 142 | 4 | 17 | Merced County, CA | 7 210 |
| 5 | 18 | Monterey County, CA | 1 108 | 28 | 18 | Sussex County, DE | 2 006 959 | 24 | 18 | Santa Barbara County, CA | 7 081 |
| 47 | 19 | Hendry County, FL | 1 082 | 43 | 19 | Hansford County, TX | 1 949 295 | 45 | 19 | Marion County, OR | 6 908 |
| 70 | 20 | Swisher County, TX | 1 068 | 2 | 20 | Tulare County, CA | 1 843 502 | 21 | 20 | Madera County, CA | 6 783 |
| 46 | 21 | Grant County, KS | 1 035 | 6 | 21 | Stanislaus County, CA | 1 817 304 | 56 | 21 | Fayette County, KY | 6 594 |
| 25 | 22 | Parmer County, TX | 1 010 | 50 | 22 | Dallam County, TX | 1 751 802 | 52 | 22 | Rockingham County, VA | 6 150 |
| 41 | 23 | Cassia County, ID | 1 001 | 26 | 23 | Palm Beach County, FL | 1 712 306 | 9 | 23 | Kings County, CA | 5 465 |
| 61 | 24 | Ford County, KS | 955 | 35 | 24 | Haskell County, KS | 1 708 092 | 11 | 24 | Imperial County, CA | 5 290 |
| 11 | 25 | Imperial County, CA | 945 | 68 | 25 | Moore County, TX | 1 677 878 | 51 | 25 | Mercer County, OH | 4 882 |
| 44 | 26 | Dawson County, NE | 880 | 41 | 26 | Cassia County, ID | 1 665 431 | 5 | 26 | Monterey County, CA | 4 645 |
| 58 | 27 | Morgan County, CO | 814 | 64 | 27 | Phelps County, NE | 1 663 392 | 3 | 27 | Kern County, CA | 4 626 |
| 64 | 28 | Phelps County, NE | 810 | 20 | 28 | Riverside County, CA | 1 614 969 | 48 | 28 | San Luis Obispo County, CA | 4 546 |
| 66 | 29 | Franklin County, WA | 684 | 74 | 29 | Santa Cruz County, CA | 1 561 362 | 17 | 29 | Sioux County, IA | 4 534 |
| 9 | 30 | Kings County, CA | 603 | 65 | 30 | Kossuth County, IA | 1 553 530 | 63 | 30 | Dane County, WI | 4 330 |
| 14 | 31 | Grant County, WA | 586 | 66 | 31 | Franklin County, WA | 1 477 309 | 71 | 31 | Lyon County, IA | 4 202 |
| 8 | 32 | Weld County, CO | 533 | 14 | 32 | Grant County, WA | 1 460 726 | 60 | 32 | Darke County, OH | 4 195 |
| 48 | 33 | San Luis Obispo County, CA | 492 | 55 | 33 | Yuma County, CO | 1 438 070 | 57 | 33 | Wayne County, NC | 4 160 |
| 12 | 34 | Yakima County, WA | 466 | 16 | 34 | Custer County, NE | 1 386 763 | 26 | 34 | Palm Beach County, FL | 4 114 |
| 23 | 34 | Yuma County, AZ | 466 | 75 | 35 | Deaf Smith County, TX | 1 356 340 | 15 | 35 | Duplin County, NC | 4 082 |
| 24 | 36 | Santa Barbara County, CA | 455 | 36 | 36 | Carroll County, IA | 1 347 857 | 42 | 36 | Gooding County, ID | 3 980 |
| 65 | 37 | Kossuth County, IA | 431 | 42 | 37 | Gooding County, ID | 1 335 076 | 13 | 37 | Sampson County, NC | 3 738 |
| 27 | 38 | Cuming County, NE | 417 | 72 | 38 | Sherman County, TX | 1 313 201 | 75 | 38 | Carroll County, IA | 3 681 |
| 26 | 39 | Palm Beach County, FL | 416 | 17 | 39 | Sioux County, IA | 1 304 456 | 30 | 39 | Pinal County, AZ | 3 638 |
| 4 | 40 | Merced County, CA | 399 | 67 | 40 | Plymouth County, IA | 1 301 406 | 67 | 40 | Plymouth County, IA | 3 628 |
| 21 | 41 | Madera County, CA | 398 | 71 | 41 | Lyon County, IA | 1 248 886 | 65 | 41 | Kossuth County, IA | 3 603 |
| 53 | 42 | Benton County, WA | 388 | 32 | 42 | Scott County, KS | 1 218 245 | 69 | 42 | Jerome County, ID | 3 439 |
| 75 | 43 | Carroll County, IA | 366 | 22 | 43 | Castro County, TX | 1 209 915 | 47 | 43 | Hendry County, FL | 3 396 |
| 33 | 43 | San Bernardino County, CA | 366 | 44 | 44 | Dawson County, NE | 1 176 513 | 33 | 44 | San Bernardino County, CA | 3 167 |
| 67 | 45 | Plymouth County, IA | 359 | 33 | 45 | San Bernardino County, CA | 1 159 028 | 54 | 45 | Stearns County, MN | 2 830 |
| 62 | 46 | Twin Falls County, ID | 339 | 37 | 46 | Finney County, KS | 1 153 579 | 14 | 46 | Grant County, WA | 2 495 |
| 42 | 47 | Gooding County, ID | 335 | 56 | 47 | Fayette County, KY | 1 106 925 | 27 | 47 | Cuming County, NE | 2 493 |
| 69 | 48 | Jerome County, ID | 313 | 51 | 48 | Mercer County, OH | 1 098 799 | 62 | 48 | Twin Falls County, ID | 2 479 |
| 71 | 49 | Lyon County, IA | 297 | 73 | 49 | Wichita County, KS | 1 077 030 | 53 | 49 | Benton County, WA | 2 323 |
| 17 | 50 | Sioux County, IA | 288 | 69 | 50 | Jerome County, ID | 1 074 850 | 66 | 50 | Franklin County, WA | 2 161 |
| 29 | 51 | Maricopa County, AZ | 271 | 27 | 51 | Cuming County, NE | 1 040 286 | 64 | 51 | Phelps County, NE | 2 053 |
| 1 | 52 | Fresno County, CA | 269 | 49 | 52 | Chester County, PA | 1 034 252 | 41 | 52 | Cassia County, ID | 1 664 |
| 13 | 53 | Sampson County, NC | 267 | 25 | 53 | Parmer County, TX | 1 029 842 | 8 | 53 | Weld County, CO | 1 550 |
| 57 | 54 | Wayne County, NC | 242 | 57 | 54 | Wayne County, NC | 1 008 378 | 12 | 54 | Yakima County, WA | 1 530 |
| 51 | 55 | Mercer County, OH | 225 | 13 | 55 | Sampson County, NC | 998 921 | 44 | 55 | Dawson County, NE | 1 337 |
| 2 | 56 | Tulare County, CA | 223 | 38 | 56 | Gray County, KS | 983 325 | 58 | 56 | Morgan County, CO | 1 093 |
| 15 | 57 | Duplin County, NC | 214 | 53 | 57 | Benton County, WA | 901 747 | 35 | 57 | Haskell County, KS | 1 062 |
| 54 | 58 | Stearns County, MN | 210 | 58 | 58 | Morgan County, CO | 890 238 | 36 | 58 | Yuma County, CO | 1 045 |
| 7 | 59 | San Joaquin County, CA | 204 | 19 | 59 | San Diego County, CA | 874 683 | 22 | 59 | Castro County, TX | 1 034 |
| 60 | 60 | Darke County, OH | 198 | 15 | 60 | Duplin County, NC | 873 575 | 55 | 60 | Custer County, NE | 1 020 |
| 28 | 61 | Sussex County, DE | 196 | 62 | 61 | Twin Falls County, ID | 840 836 | 25 | 61 | Parmer County, TX | 1 019 |
| 6 | 62 | Stanislaus County, CA | 192 | 60 | 62 | Darke County, OH | 829 604 | 16 | 62 | Deaf Smith County, TX | 913 |
| 56 | 63 | Fayette County, KY | 168 | 46 | 63 | Grant County, KS | 827 976 | 68 | 63 | Moore County, TX | 858 |
| 63 | 64 | Dane County, WI | 161 | 8 | 64 | Weld County, CO | 825 561 | 38 | 64 | Gray County, KS | 852 |
| 40 | 65 | Sonoma County, CA | 155 | 45 | 65 | Marion County, OR | 795 988 | 50 | 65 | Dallam County, TX | 845 |
| 52 | 66 | Rockingham County, VA | 118 | 31 | 66 | Texas County, OK | 791 501 | 72 | 66 | Sherman County, TX | 814 |
| 45 | 67 | Marion County, OR | 115 | 59 | 67 | Hillsborough County, FL | 787 847 | 43 | 67 | Hansford County, TX | 806 |
| 10 | 68 | Ventura County, CA | 106 | 70 | 68 | Swisher County, TX | 775 406 | 46 | 68 | Grant County, KS | 800 |
| 20 | 69 | Riverside County, CA | 102 | 39 | 69 | Miami-Dade County, FL | 742 119 | 37 | 69 | Finney County, KS | 783 |
| 49 | 70 | Chester County, PA | 96 | 52 | 70 | Rockingham County, VA | 727 644 | 32 | 70 | Scott County, KS | 744 |
| 18 | 71 | Lancaster County, PA | 78 | 18 | 71 | Lancaster County, PA | 726 059 | 70 | 71 | Swisher County, TX | 726 |
| 59 | 72 | Hillsborough County, FL | 77 | 12 | 72 | Yakima County, WA | 712 970 | 61 | 72 | Ford County, KS | 712 |
| 74 | 73 | Santa Cruz County, CA | 70 | 63 | 73 | Dane County, WI | 696 424 | 31 | 73 | Texas County, OK | 681 |
| 19 | 74 | San Diego County, CA | 45 | 61 | 74 | Ford County, KS | 680 092 | 34 | 74 | Hartley County, TX | 676 |
| 39 | 75 | Miami-Dade County, FL | 27 | 54 | 75 | Stearns County, MN | 595 214 | 73 | 75 | Wichita County, KS | 669 |

## Table B. States and Counties — **Land Area and Population**

| STATE/ County code | CBSA code[1] | County type[2] | STATE County | Land area,[3] (sq km) 2010 | Population 2012 — Total persons | Population 2012 — Rank | Population 2012 — Per square kilometer | Race alone or in combination, not Hispanic or Latino (percent) — White | Race — Black | Race — American Indian, Alaska Native | Race — Asian and Pacific Islander | Percent Hispanic or Latino[4] | Age (percent) — Under 5 years | Age — 5 to 17 years | Age — 18 to 24 years | Age — 25 to 34 years | Age — 35 to 44 years | Age — 45 to 54 years |
|---|---|---|---|---|---|---|---|---|---|---|---|---|---|---|---|---|---|---|
| | | | | 1 | 2 | 3 | 4 | 5 | 6 | 7 | 8 | 9 | 10 | 11 | 12 | 13 | 14 | 15 |

1. CBSA = Core Based Statistical Area. See Appendix A for explanation. See Appendix B for list of metropolitan areas with component counties.   2. County type code from the Economic Research Service of USDA Rural-Urban Continuum Codes. See Appendix A for definition.   3. Dry land or land partially or temporarily covered by water.   4. May be of any race.

## Table B. States and Counties — **Population and Households**

| STATE County | Population, 2011 (cont.) Age (percent) (cont.) — 55 to 64 years | 65 to 74 years | 75 years and over | Percent female | Population change and components of change, 2000–2012 — Total persons 2000 | Total persons 2010 | Percent change 2000–2010 | Percent change 2010–2012 | Components of change, 2010–2012 — Births | Deaths | Net migration | Households, 2010 — Number | Percent change, 2000–2010 | Persons per household | Female family householder[1] Percent | One person |
|---|---|---|---|---|---|---|---|---|---|---|---|---|---|---|---|---|
| | 16 | 17 | 18 | 19 | 20 | 21 | 22 | 23 | 24 | 25 | 26 | 27 | 28 | 29 | 30 | 31 |

1. No spouse present.

## Table B. States and Counties — **Population, Vital Statistics, Medicare, and Crime**

| STATE County | Daytime population, 2007–2011 — Persons in group quarters, 2010 | Number | Employment/ residence ratio | Births, 2011 — Total | Rate[1] | Deaths, 2011 — Number | Rate[1] | Persons under 65 with no health insurance, 2010 — Number | Percent | Medicare, 2012 — Eligible for Medicare | Enrolled in Medicare Advantage | Enrolled in a Medicare prescription drug plan | Serious crimes known to police,[2] 2011 Total — Number | Rate[3] |
|---|---|---|---|---|---|---|---|---|---|---|---|---|---|---|
| | 32 | 33 | 34 | 35 | 36 | 37 | 38 | 39 | 40 | 41 | 42 | 43 | 44 | 45 |

1. Per 1,000 estimated resident population.   2. Data for serious crimes have not been adjusted for underreporting; this may affect comparability between geographic areas and over time.   3. Per 100,000 population estimated by the FBI.

## Table B. States and Counties — **Crime, Education, Money Income, and Poverty**

| STATE County | Serious crimes known to police, 2011 (cont.)[1] Rate[2] — Violent | Property | Education — School enrollment and attainment, 2007–2011 Enrollment[3] — Total | Percent private | Attainment[4] (percent) — High school graduate or less | Bachelor's degree or more | Local government expenditures,[5] 2009–2010 — Total current expenditures (mil dol) | Current expenditures per student (dollars) | Money income, 2007–2011 — Per capita income[6] (dollars) | Households Median income — Dollars | Percent change, 2000 to 2007–2011 (constant 2011 dollars) | Percent with income of $200,000 or more | Income and poverty, 2011 — Median household income (dollars) | Percent below poverty level — All persons | Children under 18 years | Children 5 to 17 years in families |
|---|---|---|---|---|---|---|---|---|---|---|---|---|---|---|---|---|
| | 46 | 47 | 48 | 49 | 50 | 51 | 52 | 53 | 54 | 55 | 56 | 57 | 58 | 59 | 60 | 61 |

1. Data for serious crimes have not been adjusted for underreporting; this may affect comparability between geographic areas and over time.   2. Per 100,000 population estimated by the FBI.   3. All persons 3 years old and over enrolled in nursery school through college.   4. Persons 25 years old and over.   5. Elementary and secondary education expenditures.   6. Based on population estimated by the American Community Survey, 2007–2011.

## Table B.  States and Counties  —  **Personal Income**

| | Personal income, 2011 | | | | | | | | | | | | |
| STATE County | | | Per capita[1] | | | | | | Transfer payments (mil dol) | | | | | |
| | | | | | | | | | | | Government payments to individuals | | | |
| | Total (mil dol) | Percent change, 2010– 2011 | Dollars | Rank | Wages and salaries[2] (mil dol) | Proprietors' income (mil dol) | Dividends, interest, and rent (mil dol) | Total | Total | Social Security | Medical payments | Income mainte- nance | Unemploy- ment insurance |
| | 62 | 63 | 64 | 65 | 66 | 67 | 68 | 69 | 70 | 71 | 72 | 73 | 74 |

1. Based on the resident population estimated as of July 1 of the year shown.     2. Includes supplements to wages and salaries.

## Table B.  States and Counties  —  **Earnings, Social Security, and Housing**

| | Earnings, 2011 | | | | | | | | | Social Security beneficiaries, December 2011 | | | Housing units, 2010 | |
| STATE County | | | Percent by selected industries | | | | | | | | | | | |
| | | | Goods-related[1] | | Service-related and health | | | | | | | Supple- mental Security Income recipients, December 2011 | | |
| | Total (mil dol) | Farm | Total | Manu- facturing | Infor- mation and profes- sional and technical services | Retail trade | Finance, insur- ance, and real estate | Health care and social services | Govern- ment | Number | Rate[2] | | Total | Percent change, 2000– 2010 |
| | 75 | 76 | 77 | 78 | 79 | 80 | 81 | 82 | 83 | 84 | 85 | 86 | 87 | 88 |

1. Includes mining, construction, and manufacturing.     2. Per 1,000 resident population enumerated in the 2010 census.

## Table B.  States and Counties  —  **Housing, Labor Force, and Employment**

| | Housing units, 2007–2011 | | | | | | | | Civilian labor force, 2012 | | | | Civilian employment,[6] 2007–2011 | | |
| STATE County | | | Occupied units | | | | | | | | Unemployment | | | Percent | |
| | | | Owner-occupied | | | Renter-occupied | | | | | | | | | |
| | | | | | Median owner cost as a percent of income | | | | | | | | | | Con- struction, produc- tion, and mainte- nance occu- pations |
| | Total | Percent | Median value[1] | With a mort- gage | Without a mort- gage[2] | Median rent[3] | Median rent as a per- cent of income | Sub- stand- ard units[4] (percent) | Total | Percent change, 2011– 2012 | Total | Rate[5] | Total | Manage- ment, business, science and arts | |
| | 89 | 90 | 91 | 92 | 93 | 94 | 95 | 96 | 97 | 98 | 99 | 100 | 101 | 102 | 103 |

1. Specified owner-occupied units.     2. A value of 9.9 represents 9.9 percent or less.     3. Specified renter-occupied units. A value of 10.0 represents 10 percent or less.     4. Overcrowded or lacking complete plumbing facilities.     5. Percent of civilian labor force.     6. Persons 16 years old and over.

## Table B.  States and Counties  —  **Nonfarm Employment and Agriculture**

| | Private nonfarm establishments, employment and payroll, 2011 | | | | | | | | | Agriculture, 2007 | | | |
| STATE County | | | Employment | | | | | | Annual payroll | | Farms | | | |
| | | | | | | | | | | | | Percent with: | | |
| | Number of establish- ments | Total | Health care and social assistance | Manufac- turing | Retail trade | Finance and insurance | Professional, scientific, and technical services | | Total (mil dol) | Average per employee (dollars) | Number | Fewer than 50 acres | 500 acres or more | Farm operators whose principal occu- pation is farming (percent) |
| | 104 | 105 | 106 | 107 | 108 | 109 | 110 | | 111 | 112 | 113 | 114 | 115 | 116 |

## Table B. States and Counties — Agriculture

| STATE County | Agriculture, 2007 (cont.) | | | | | | | | | | | | | | | |
| | Land in farms | | | | | Value of land and buildings (dollars) | | | Value of products sold | | | | Percent of farms with sales of: | | Government payments | |
| | | | Acres | | | | | Value of machinery and equipment, average per farm (dollars) | | | Percent from: | | | | | |
| | Acreage (1,000) | Percent change, 2002–2007 | Average size of farm | Total irrigated (1,000) | Total cropland (1,000) | Average per farm | Average per acre | | Total (mil dol) | Average per farm (dollars) | Crops | Live-stock and poultry products | $10,000 or more | $100,000 or more | Total ($1,000) | Percent of farms |
| --- | --- | --- | --- | --- | --- | --- | --- | --- | --- | --- | --- | --- | --- | --- | --- | --- |
| | 117 | 118 | 119 | 120 | 121 | 122 | 123 | 124 | 125 | 126 | 127 | 128 | 129 | 130 | 131 | 132 |

## Table B. States and Counties — Water Use, Wholesale Trade, Retail Trade, and Real Estate

| STATE County | Water use, 2005 | | Wholesale trade,[1] 2007 | | | | Retail trade,[2] 2007 | | | | Real estate and rental and leasing,[2] 2007 | | | |
| | Total water withdrawn (mil gal/day) | Gallons withdrawn per person | Number of establish-ments | Number of employees | Sales (mil dol) | Annual payroll (mil dol) | Number of establish-ments | Number of employees | Sales (mil dol) | Annual payroll (mil dol) | Number of establish-ments | Number of employees | Receipts (mil dol) | Annual payroll (mil dol) |
| --- | --- | --- | --- | --- | --- | --- | --- | --- | --- | --- | --- | --- | --- | --- |
| | 133 | 134 | 135 | 136 | 137 | 138 | 139 | 140 | 141 | 142 | 143 | 144 | 145 | 146 |

1. Merchant wholesalers, except manufacturers' sales branches and offices.    2. Employer establishments.

## Table B. States and Counties — Professional Services, Manufacturing, and Accommodation and Food Services

| STATE County | Professional, scientific, and technical services,[1] 2007 | | | | Manufacturing, 2007 | | | | Accommodation and food services, 2007 | | | |
| | Number of establish-ments | Number of employees | Receipts (mil dol) | Annual payroll (mil dol) | Number of establish-ments | Number of employees | Receipts (mil dol) | Annual payroll (mil dol) | Number of establish-ments | Number of employees | Sales (mil dol) | Annual payroll (mil dol) |
| --- | --- | --- | --- | --- | --- | --- | --- | --- | --- | --- | --- | --- |
| | 147 | 148 | 149 | 150 | 151 | 152 | 153 | 154 | 155 | 156 | 157 | 158 |

1. Establishment subject to federal tax.

## Table B. States and Counties — Health Care and Social Assistance, Other Services, and Federal Funds

| STATE County | Health care and social assistance, 2007 | | | | Other services, 2007 | | | | Federal funds and grants, 2009–2010 | | | |
| | | | | | | | | | Expenditures (mil dol) | | | |
| | | | | | | | | | | Direct payments for individuals[1] | | |
| | Number of establish-ments | Number of employees | Receipts (mil dol) | Annual payroll (mil dol) | Number of establish-ments | Number of employees | Receipts (mil dol) | Annual payroll (mil dol) | Total | Social Security and government retirement | Medicare | Food Stamps and Supplemental Security Income |
| --- | --- | --- | --- | --- | --- | --- | --- | --- | --- | --- | --- | --- |
| | 159 | 160 | 161 | 162 | 163 | 164 | 165 | 166 | 167 | 168 | 169 | 170 |

1. State totals may include programs not allocated by county.

**Table B. States and Counties** — **Federal Funds, Residential Construction, and Local Government Finances**

| | Federal funds and grants, 2009–2010 (cont.) | | | | | | | Value of residential construction authorized by building permits, 2011 | | Local government finances, 2007 | | | | | |
| --- | --- | --- | --- | --- | --- | --- | --- | --- | --- | --- | --- | --- | --- | --- | --- |
| | Expenditures (mil dol) (cont.) | | | | | | | | | General revenue | | | | | |
| | Procurement contract awards | | | Grants[1] | | | | | | | | | Taxes | | |
| STATE County | | | | | | | | | | | | | | Per capita[2] (dollars) | |
| | Salaries and wages | Defense | Other | Medicaid and other health-related | Nutrition and family welfare | Education | Other | New construction ($1,000) | Number of housing units | Total (mil dol) | Inter-govern-mental (mil dol) | Total (mil dol) | Total | Property |
| | 171 | 172 | 173 | 174 | 175 | 176 | 177 | 178 | 179 | 180 | 181 | 182 | 183 | 184 |

1. State totals may include programs not allocated by county.    2. Based on the resident population estimated as of July 1 of the year shown.

**Table B. States and Counties** — **Local Government Finances, Government Employment, and Voting**

| | Local government finances, 2007 (cont.) | | | | | | | | | Government employment, 2011 | | | Presidential election,[2] 2012 | | |
| --- | --- | --- | --- | --- | --- | --- | --- | --- | --- | --- | --- | --- | --- | --- | --- |
| | Direct general expenditure | | | | | | | Debt outstanding | | | | | Percent of vote cast: | | |
| | | | Percent of total for: | | | | | | | | | | | | |
| STATE County | Total (mil dol) | Per capita[1] (dollars) | Educa-tion | Health and hospitals | Police protec-tion | Public welfare | High-ways | Total (mil dol) | Per capita[1] (dollars) | Federal civilian | Federal military | State and local | Demo-cratic | Republi-can | All other |
| | 185 | 186 | 187 | 188 | 189 | 190 | 191 | 192 | 193 | 194 | 195 | 196 | 197 | 198 | 199 |

1. Based on the resident population estimated as of July 1 of the year shown.    2. © 2013 Election Data Services, Inc. All rights reserved.

# Table B. States and Counties — **Land Area and Population**

| STATE/ County code | CBSA code[1] | County type[2] | STATE County | Land area,[3] (sq km) 2010 | Total persons | Rank | Per square kilometer | White | Black | American Indian, Alaska Native | Asian and Pacific Islander | Percent Hispanic or Latino[4] | Under 5 years | 5 to 17 years | 18 to 24 years | 25 to 34 years | 35 to 44 years | 45 to 54 years |
|---|---|---|---|---|---|---|---|---|---|---|---|---|---|---|---|---|---|---|
| | | | | 1 | 2 | 3 | 4 | 5 | 6 | 7 | 8 | 9 | 10 | 11 | 12 | 13 | 14 | 15 |
| 00 000 | ... | X | UNITED STATES ............ | 9 147 593 | 313 914 040 | X | 34.3 | 65.0 | 13.1 | 1.3 | 5.9 | 16.7 | 6.5 | 17.3 | 10.0 | 13.4 | 13.0 | 14.4 |
| 01 000 | ... | X | ALABAMA ......................... | 131 171 | 4 822 023 | X | 36.8 | 67.9 | 26.8 | 1.1 | 1.5 | 4.0 | 6.3 | 17.1 | 10.1 | 12.8 | 12.7 | 14.3 |
| 01 001 | 33860 | 2 | Autauga ........................ | 1 540 | 55 514 | 907 | 36.0 | 77.6 | 18.8 | 0.9 | 1.4 | 2.6 | 6.5 | 19.5 | 8.9 | 12.1 | 14.7 | 14.9 |
| 01 003 | 19300 | 4 | Baldwin ......................... | 4 118 | 190 790 | 332 | 46.3 | 84.4 | 10.0 | 1.3 | 1.1 | 4.5 | 6.0 | 16.8 | 7.5 | 11.6 | 12.6 | 14.5 |
| 01 005 | 21640 | 6 | Barbour ......................... | 2 292 | 27 201 | 1 523 | 11.9 | 47.3 | 46.9 | 0.6 | 0.7 | 5.3 | 6.2 | 15.6 | 8.7 | 14.1 | 13.0 | 14.5 |
| 01 007 | 13820 | 1 | Bibb ............................... | 1 612 | 22 597 | 1 707 | 14.0 | 75.3 | 22.6 | 0.7 | 0.3 | 2.0 | 5.6 | 16.4 | 9.0 | 14.3 | 14.3 | 14.8 |
| 01 009 | 13820 | 1 | Blount ............................ | 1 670 | 57 826 | 882 | 34.6 | 89.0 | 2.0 | 1.1 | 0.4 | 8.6 | 6.2 | 18.2 | 8.0 | 12.2 | 13.5 | 13.9 |
| 01 011 | ... | 6 | Bullock .......................... | 1 613 | 10 474 | 2 397 | 6.5 | 23.4 | 68.6 | 0.4 | 0.5 | 7.7 | 7.0 | 14.9 | 8.4 | 14.7 | 12.6 | 15.2 |
| 01 013 | ... | 6 | Butler ............................ | 2 012 | 20 307 | 1 825 | 10.1 | 54.4 | 43.6 | 0.6 | 1.1 | 1.1 | 6.5 | 17.1 | 7.9 | 12.2 | 11.4 | 14.0 |
| 01 015 | 11500 | 3 | Calhoun ......................... | 1 569 | 117 296 | 518 | 74.8 | 74.6 | 21.3 | 1.0 | 1.2 | 3.4 | 6.1 | 16.7 | 10.6 | 12.5 | 12.2 | 14.1 |
| 01 017 | 46740 | 6 | Chambers ...................... | 1 545 | 34 064 | 1 327 | 22.0 | 59.0 | 39.0 | 0.6 | 0.8 | 1.7 | 5.7 | 16.6 | 8.3 | 11.1 | 12.6 | 14.6 |
| 01 019 | ... | 8 | Cherokee ....................... | 1 434 | 26 021 | 1 562 | 18.1 | 92.8 | 5.5 | 1.1 | 0.5 | 1.4 | 5.1 | 16.0 | 7.3 | 9.9 | 12.7 | 15.0 |
| 01 021 | 13820 | 1 | Chilton .......................... | 1 794 | 43 819 | 1 090 | 24.4 | 81.6 | 10.3 | 0.7 | 0.5 | 7.8 | 6.8 | 18.0 | 8.3 | 12.9 | 13.3 | 14.1 |
| 01 023 | ... | 9 | Choctaw ........................ | 2 366 | 13 633 | 2 206 | 5.8 | 55.8 | 43.5 | 0.3 | 0.2 | 0.6 | 5.1 | 16.9 | 7.3 | 10.0 | 11.7 | 15.4 |
| 01 025 | ... | 7 | Clarke ........................... | 3 208 | 25 161 | 1 601 | 7.8 | 54.1 | 44.2 | 0.7 | 0.5 | 1.2 | 5.6 | 18.6 | 8.0 | 10.9 | 12.4 | 14.8 |
| 01 027 | ... | 9 | Clay .............................. | 1 564 | 13 435 | 2 217 | 8.6 | 81.5 | 15.7 | 1.1 | 0.4 | 2.9 | 5.6 | 16.7 | 7.7 | 10.5 | 12.5 | 14.9 |
| 01 029 | ... | 8 | Cleburne ........................ | 1 451 | 14 832 | 2 122 | 10.2 | 93.0 | 4.4 | 0.7 | 0.4 | 2.4 | 6.0 | 17.4 | 7.9 | 10.9 | 13.3 | 14.4 |
| 01 031 | 21460 | 6 | Coffee ........................... | 1 759 | 51 252 | 965 | 29.1 | 73.8 | 17.9 | 2.0 | 2.0 | 6.4 | 6.7 | 17.5 | 8.7 | 13.5 | 13.0 | 13.7 |
| 01 033 | 22520 | 3 | Colbert .......................... | 1 535 | 54 446 | 918 | 35.5 | 80.5 | 16.9 | 1.1 | 0.7 | 2.2 | 5.6 | 16.3 | 8.2 | 11.4 | 12.4 | 14.8 |
| 01 035 | ... | 9 | Conecuh ......................... | 2 202 | 12 981 | 2 241 | 5.9 | 51.6 | 46.7 | 0.8 | 0.3 | 1.5 | 5.8 | 16.6 | 8.0 | 10.0 | 11.2 | 14.8 |
| 01 037 | 10760 | 8 | Coosa ............................ | 1 686 | 10 966 | 2 362 | 6.5 | 66.4 | 31.0 | 0.9 | 0.3 | 2.2 | 4.9 | 16.1 | 7.5 | 10.4 | 13.3 | 16.7 |
| 01 039 | ... | 7 | Covington ....................... | 2 669 | 37 955 | 1 225 | 14.2 | 84.8 | 13.3 | 1.2 | 0.7 | 1.4 | 5.9 | 16.6 | 7.8 | 11.0 | 11.8 | 14.5 |
| 01 041 | ... | 8 | Crenshaw ....................... | 1 577 | 14 083 | 2 169 | 8.9 | 72.0 | 24.8 | 1.0 | 1.9 | 1.7 | 6.2 | 17.3 | 8.0 | 11.1 | 12.6 | 15.0 |
| 01 043 | 18980 | 6 | Cullman ......................... | 1 903 | 80 440 | 686 | 42.3 | 93.2 | 1.6 | 1.1 | 0.6 | 4.5 | 6.1 | 16.8 | 8.6 | 11.9 | 12.6 | 14.6 |
| 01 045 | 21460 | 4 | Dale .............................. | 1 453 | 50 444 | 972 | 34.7 | 72.9 | 20.3 | 1.5 | 2.0 | 5.6 | 7.1 | 17.4 | 9.1 | 14.5 | 12.1 | 13.8 |
| 01 047 | 42820 | 4 | Dallas ........................... | 2 535 | 42 864 | 1 115 | 16.9 | 29.5 | 69.4 | 0.4 | 0.5 | 0.8 | 7.3 | 19.0 | 9.2 | 11.5 | 10.9 | 14.4 |
| 01 049 | 22840 | 6 | DeKalb .......................... | 2 013 | 71 080 | 752 | 35.3 | 82.7 | 2.1 | 2.6 | 0.5 | 14.0 | 7.0 | 18.6 | 8.3 | 12.6 | 13.4 | 13.5 |
| 01 051 | 33860 | 2 | Elmore ........................... | 1 602 | 80 629 | 685 | 50.3 | 75.1 | 21.5 | 0.9 | 1.0 | 2.8 | 6.0 | 17.1 | 9.6 | 13.2 | 14.4 | 15.2 |
| 01 053 | ... | 6 | Escambia ....................... | 2 448 | 37 994 | 1 223 | 15.5 | 62.3 | 32.5 | 4.1 | 0.5 | 2.0 | 6.2 | 16.5 | 8.4 | 13.2 | 13.5 | 14.4 |
| 01 055 | 23460 | 3 | Etowah .......................... | 1 386 | 104 392 | 564 | 75.3 | 80.0 | 15.9 | 0.9 | 0.9 | 3.5 | 6.0 | 16.9 | 8.6 | 11.6 | 13.1 | 14.1 |
| 01 057 | ... | 6 | Fayette .......................... | 1 626 | 16 983 | 1 984 | 10.4 | 86.3 | 12.1 | 0.6 | 0.5 | 1.4 | 5.7 | 16.1 | 8.2 | 10.4 | 11.9 | 14.7 |
| 01 059 | ... | 6 | Franklin ......................... | 1 642 | 31 761 | 1 393 | 19.3 | 80.0 | 4.6 | 0.9 | 0.4 | 15.1 | 7.1 | 17.6 | 8.8 | 12.8 | 13.0 | 13.5 |
| 01 061 | 20020 | 3 | Geneva .......................... | 1 488 | 26 931 | 1 532 | 18.1 | 85.5 | 10.5 | 1.5 | 0.6 | 3.4 | 5.8 | 16.2 | 8.0 | 10.8 | 12.4 | 14.6 |
| 01 063 | 46220 | 3 | Greene .......................... | 1 676 | 8 876 | 2 529 | 5.3 | 18.6 | 80.4 | 0.3 | 0.3 | 0.9 | 6.2 | 17.8 | 8.9 | 10.0 | 10.1 | 14.6 |
| 01 065 | 46220 | 3 | Hale .............................. | 1 668 | 15 388 | 2 081 | 9.2 | 40.3 | 58.3 | 0.3 | 0.4 | 1.1 | 6.0 | 18.1 | 8.8 | 11.3 | 10.7 | 15.4 |
| 01 067 | 20020 | 3 | Henry ............................ | 1 455 | 17 287 | 1 964 | 11.9 | 68.6 | 28.6 | 0.7 | 0.5 | 2.5 | 5.7 | 16.9 | 7.2 | 10.7 | 12.3 | 13.9 |
| 01 069 | 20020 | 3 | Houston ......................... | 1 502 | 103 402 | 566 | 68.8 | 69.6 | 26.6 | 0.9 | 1.2 | 3.1 | 6.5 | 17.8 | 8.2 | 12.8 | 12.8 | 14.3 |
| 01 071 | 42460 | 6 | Jackson .......................... | 2 792 | 53 019 | 938 | 19.0 | 92.1 | 4.0 | 3.0 | 0.5 | 2.6 | 5.5 | 16.6 | 7.7 | 10.9 | 13.2 | 14.7 |
| 01 073 | 13820 | 1 | Jefferson ........................ | 2 878 | 660 009 | 93 | 229.3 | 52.2 | 42.4 | 0.6 | 1.7 | 4.0 | 6.8 | 16.7 | 9.6 | 14.4 | 12.5 | 14.1 |
| 01 075 | ... | 9 | Lamar ............................ | 1 567 | 14 259 | 2 156 | 9.1 | 86.8 | 12.2 | 0.6 | 0.2 | 1.3 | 5.5 | 16.6 | 7.3 | 9.8 | 12.4 | 14.8 |
| 01 077 | 22520 | 3 | Lauderdale ...................... | 1 729 | 92 542 | 625 | 53.5 | 86.2 | 10.7 | 0.9 | 1.0 | 2.4 | 5.6 | 15.7 | 10.8 | 11.3 | 11.9 | 14.1 |
| 01 079 | 19460 | 3 | Lawrence ........................ | 1 789 | 33 838 | 1 330 | 18.9 | 80.6 | 12.4 | 8.8 | 0.4 | 1.9 | 5.9 | 16.8 | 8.3 | 11.1 | 13.4 | 16.0 |
| 01 081 | 12220 | 3 | Lee ............................... | 1 574 | 147 257 | 428 | 93.6 | 70.8 | 23.3 | 0.7 | 3.1 | 3.4 | 5.9 | 15.9 | 21.8 | 13.6 | 11.9 | 11.9 |
| 01 083 | 26620 | 2 | Limestone ....................... | 1 450 | 87 654 | 648 | 60.5 | 79.5 | 13.7 | 1.2 | 1.4 | 5.7 | 6.4 | 17.3 | 8.0 | 13.5 | 14.4 | 15.8 |
| 01 085 | 33860 | 2 | Lowndes ......................... | 1 854 | 10 857 | 2 370 | 5.9 | 26.1 | 72.7 | 0.5 | 0.3 | 1.1 | 6.7 | 17.5 | 10.4 | 10.8 | 10.7 | 15.6 |
| 01 087 | 46260 | 6 | Macon ........................... | 1 577 | 20 535 | 1 812 | 13.0 | 16.7 | 81.5 | 0.6 | 0.6 | 1.8 | 5.1 | 14.4 | 20.8 | 9.8 | 9.7 | 12.5 |
| 01 089 | 26620 | 2 | Madison ......................... | 2 076 | 343 080 | 192 | 165.3 | 67.9 | 25.0 | 1.6 | 3.1 | 4.7 | 6.1 | 17.2 | 10.2 | 13.4 | 12.8 | 16.1 |
| 01 091 | ... | 7 | Marengo ......................... | 2 530 | 20 401 | 1 821 | 8.1 | 46.3 | 51.8 | 0.4 | 0.5 | 1.7 | 6.0 | 18.0 | 8.7 | 10.4 | 12.1 | 14.2 |
| 01 093 | ... | 8 | Marion ........................... | 1 923 | 30 327 | 1 422 | 15.8 | 92.9 | 4.6 | 0.8 | 0.4 | 2.2 | 5.4 | 16.1 | 7.7 | 10.6 | 12.9 | 14.8 |
| 01 095 | 10700 | 4 | Marshall ......................... | 1 466 | 94 776 | 612 | 64.6 | 84.2 | 2.5 | 1.2 | 0.8 | 12.5 | 7.0 | 18.0 | 8.8 | 12.3 | 12.8 | 13.8 |
| 01 097 | 33660 | 2 | Mobile ........................... | 3 184 | 413 936 | 165 | 130.0 | 59.3 | 35.3 | 1.4 | 2.3 | 2.5 | 6.8 | 18.0 | 10.0 | 13.0 | 12.2 | 14.2 |
| 01 099 | ... | 7 | Monroe .......................... | 2 656 | 22 602 | 1 706 | 8.5 | 55.9 | 42.2 | 1.7 | 0.6 | 1.1 | 5.9 | 19.0 | 8.2 | 10.4 | 12.2 | 14.5 |
| 01 101 | 33860 | 2 | Montgomery ..................... | 2 031 | 230 149 | 279 | 113.3 | 39.3 | 55.2 | 0.6 | 2.6 | 3.6 | 6.8 | 18.0 | 11.9 | 14.2 | 12.4 | 13.1 |
| 01 103 | 19460 | 3 | Morgan .......................... | 1 500 | 120 395 | 506 | 80.3 | 78.6 | 12.8 | 1.6 | 0.9 | 7.8 | 6.3 | 17.5 | 8.4 | 12.6 | 13.1 | 14.9 |
| 01 105 | ... | 8 | Perry ............................. | 1 864 | 10 181 | 2 426 | 5.5 | 30.4 | 67.9 | 0.3 | 0.5 | 1.3 | 6.5 | 17.8 | 13.5 | 10.5 | 10.2 | 12.9 |
| 01 107 | ... | 8 | Pickens .......................... | 2 283 | 19 405 | 1 860 | 8.5 | 56.6 | 41.7 | 0.5 | 0.3 | 1.7 | 6.0 | 17.0 | 8.4 | 10.8 | 11.1 | 15.4 |
| 01 109 | 45980 | 6 | Pike .............................. | 1 741 | 33 182 | 1 349 | 19.1 | 58.4 | 37.3 | 1.2 | 2.2 | 2.4 | 5.8 | 14.2 | 21.5 | 11.9 | 10.6 | 11.6 |
| 01 111 | ... | 6 | Randolph ........................ | 1 504 | 22 675 | 1 701 | 15.1 | 76.1 | 20.8 | 0.8 | 0.4 | 2.9 | 5.8 | 17.7 | 8.5 | 10.4 | 12.0 | 14.3 |
| 01 113 | 17980 | 2 | Russell .......................... | 1 661 | 57 820 | 883 | 34.8 | 53.3 | 42.1 | 1.0 | 1.3 | 4.1 | 7.0 | 17.8 | 9.8 | 14.6 | 12.4 | 14.0 |
| 01 115 | 13820 | 1 | St. Clair ......................... | 1 637 | 85 237 | 661 | 52.1 | 87.8 | 9.4 | 1.0 | 0.9 | 2.2 | 6.5 | 17.0 | 7.7 | 13.4 | 14.0 | 14.9 |
| 01 117 | 13820 | 1 | Shelby ........................... | 2 033 | 200 941 | 313 | 98.8 | 80.5 | 11.6 | 0.6 | 2.4 | 6.0 | 6.5 | 18.7 | 7.7 | 13.7 | 15.0 | 14.9 |
| 01 119 | ... | 8 | Sumter ........................... | 2 341 | 13 427 | 2 218 | 5.7 | 25.4 | 73.4 | 0.3 | 0.4 | 0.9 | 5.3 | 16.0 | 17.1 | 9.3 | 10.2 | 13.6 |
| 01 121 | 45180 | 4 | Talladega ........................ | 1 908 | 81 762 | 678 | 42.9 | 65.3 | 32.4 | 0.7 | 0.6 | 2.1 | 5.9 | 17.2 | 8.8 | 12.0 | 13.4 | 14.6 |
| 01 123 | 10760 | 6 | Tallapoosa ...................... | 1 856 | 41 168 | 1 148 | 22.2 | 69.9 | 27.0 | 0.7 | 0.7 | 2.7 | 5.9 | 16.0 | 8.1 | 10.5 | 12.2 | 14.6 |
| 01 125 | 46220 | 3 | Tuscaloosa ...................... | 3 423 | 198 596 | 321 | 58.0 | 65.4 | 30.2 | 0.6 | 1.6 | 3.1 | 6.0 | 15.2 | 20.3 | 13.2 | 11.4 | 11.9 |
| 01 127 | 13820 | 1 | Walker ........................... | 2 049 | 66 221 | 795 | 32.3 | 91.1 | 6.5 | 0.9 | 0.5 | 2.1 | 5.8 | 16.6 | 8.1 | 11.4 | 12.7 | 14.6 |

1. CBSA = Core Based Statistical Area. See Appendix A for explanation. See Appendix B for list of metropolitan areas with component counties. 2. County type code from the Economic Research Service of USDA Rural-Urban Continuum Codes. See Appendix A for definition. 3. Dry land or land partially or temporarily covered by water. 4. May be of any race.

# Table B. States and Counties — Population and Households

| STATE County | Population, 2011 (cont.) Age (percent) (cont.) 55 to 64 years | 65 to 74 years | 75 years and over | Percent female | Population change and components of change, 2000–2012 Total persons 2000 | 2010 | Percent change 2000–2010 | 2010–2012 | Components of change, 2010–2012 Births | Deaths | Net migration | Households, 2010 Number | Percent change, 2000–2010 | Persons per household | Percent Female family householder[1] | One person |
|---|---|---|---|---|---|---|---|---|---|---|---|---|---|---|---|---|
| | 16 | 17 | 18 | 19 | 20 | 21 | 22 | 23 | 24 | 25 | 26 | 27 | 28 | 29 | 30 | 31 |
| UNITED STATES | 12.2 | 7.2 | 6.1 | 50.8 | 281 421 906 | 308 745 538 | 9.7 | 1.7 | 8 918 468 | 5 602 865 | 1 850 929 | 116 716 292 | 10.7 | 2.58 | 13.1 | 26.7 |
| ALABAMA | 12.7 | 7.9 | 6.1 | 51.5 | 4 447 100 | 4 779 736 | 7.5 | 0.9 | 137 514 | 109 105 | 13 545 | 1 883 791 | 8.4 | 2.48 | 15.3 | 27.4 |
| Autauga | 11.1 | 7.5 | 4.8 | 51.2 | 43 671 | 54 571 | 25.0 | 1.7 | 1 506 | 989 | 381 | 20 221 | 26.4 | 2.68 | 13.7 | 22.0 |
| Baldwin | 13.9 | 10.0 | 7.1 | 51.2 | 140 415 | 182 265 | 29.8 | 4.7 | 4 846 | 4 012 | 7 519 | 73 180 | 32.2 | 2.46 | 11.1 | 25.1 |
| Barbour | 13.3 | 8.4 | 6.2 | 46.5 | 29 038 | 27 457 | -5.4 | -0.9 | 607 | 686 | -188 | 9 820 | -5.7 | 2.47 | 19.8 | 28.5 |
| Bibb | 12.3 | 7.9 | 5.4 | 46.1 | 20 826 | 22 915 | 10.0 | -1.4 | 499 | 505 | -309 | 7 953 | 7.2 | 2.60 | 14.4 | 24.5 |
| Blount | 13.1 | 9.0 | 6.0 | 50.6 | 51 024 | 57 322 | 12.3 | 0.9 | 1 573 | 1 257 | 143 | 21 578 | 12.0 | 2.63 | 9.7 | 22.2 |
| Bullock | 13.6 | 7.7 | 5.9 | 45.7 | 11 714 | 10 914 | -6.8 | -4.0 | 355 | 254 | -557 | 3 745 | -6.0 | 2.46 | 26.8 | 32.8 |
| Butler | 13.9 | 8.8 | 8.3 | 53.1 | 21 399 | 20 947 | -2.1 | -3.1 | 532 | 579 | -618 | 8 491 | 1.1 | 2.43 | 19.8 | 29.7 |
| Calhoun | 13.3 | 8.2 | 6.4 | 51.9 | 112 249 | 118 572 | 5.6 | -1.1 | 3 169 | 3 059 | -1 333 | 47 331 | 4.5 | 2.44 | 15.2 | 27.7 |
| Chambers | 14.2 | 9.4 | 7.6 | 52.2 | 36 583 | 34 215 | -6.5 | -0.4 | 853 | 1 046 | 37 | 13 933 | -4.1 | 2.42 | 19.1 | 29.1 |
| Cherokee | 15.6 | 11.4 | 7.0 | 50.4 | 23 988 | 25 989 | 8.3 | 0.1 | 451 | 693 | 253 | 10 626 | 9.3 | 2.42 | 10.4 | 26.0 |
| Chilton | 12.5 | 8.2 | 5.9 | 50.7 | 39 593 | 43 643 | 10.2 | 0.4 | 1 280 | 1 023 | -80 | 16 558 | 8.3 | 2.61 | 12.0 | 23.5 |
| Choctaw | 14.5 | 11.1 | 8.0 | 52.3 | 15 922 | 13 859 | -13.0 | -1.6 | 306 | 380 | -156 | 5 866 | -7.8 | 2.34 | 15.8 | 31.7 |
| Clarke | 13.1 | 9.4 | 7.2 | 52.9 | 27 867 | 25 833 | -7.3 | -2.6 | 614 | 722 | -563 | 10 337 | -2.3 | 2.47 | 17.5 | 28.1 |
| Clay | 13.4 | 10.6 | 8.1 | 51.1 | 14 254 | 13 932 | -2.3 | -3.6 | 312 | 458 | -348 | 5 670 | -1.6 | 2.41 | 12.8 | 27.2 |
| Cleburne | 14.0 | 9.6 | 6.6 | 50.4 | 14 123 | 14 972 | 6.0 | -0.9 | 355 | 423 | -107 | 5 891 | 5.4 | 2.51 | 10.3 | 25.1 |
| Coffee | 12.2 | 8.2 | 6.5 | 50.7 | 43 615 | 49 948 | 14.5 | 2.6 | 1 607 | 1 150 | 846 | 19 849 | 13.9 | 2.49 | 12.9 | 25.4 |
| Colbert | 13.8 | 9.6 | 7.9 | 51.9 | 54 984 | 54 428 | -1.0 | 0.0 | 1 386 | 1 508 | 162 | 22 773 | 1.4 | 2.37 | 13.7 | 28.8 |
| Conecuh | 15.1 | 10.8 | 7.8 | 51.5 | 14 089 | 13 228 | -6.1 | -1.9 | 333 | 428 | -160 | 5 625 | -2.9 | 2.34 | 19.1 | 30.9 |
| Coosa | 17.3 | 8.2 | 5.7 | 50.1 | 12 202 | 11 539 | -5.4 | -5.0 | 184 | 252 | -563 | 4 794 | 2.4 | 2.38 | 14.1 | 27.9 |
| Covington | 13.9 | 10.0 | 8.6 | 51.6 | 37 631 | 37 765 | 0.4 | 0.5 | 1 067 | 1 113 | 210 | 15 531 | -0.7 | 2.39 | 13.1 | 28.1 |
| Crenshaw | 13.8 | 8.7 | 7.2 | 51.7 | 13 665 | 13 906 | 1.8 | 1.3 | 390 | 392 | 174 | 5 652 | 1.3 | 2.44 | 15.6 | 28.1 |
| Cullman | 13.2 | 9.4 | 6.8 | 50.5 | 77 483 | 80 406 | 3.8 | 0.0 | 2 157 | 2 103 | -23 | 31 864 | 3.8 | 2.49 | 10.4 | 25.7 |
| Dale | 12.2 | 8.0 | 5.8 | 50.8 | 49 129 | 50 251 | 2.3 | 0.4 | 1 663 | 1 101 | -368 | 20 065 | 6.3 | 2.46 | 14.6 | 27.3 |
| Dallas | 13.2 | 8.3 | 6.2 | 53.7 | 46 365 | 43 820 | -5.5 | -2.2 | 1 461 | 1 219 | -1 216 | 17 064 | -4.4 | 2.52 | 27.1 | 30.0 |
| DeKalb | 12.5 | 8.2 | 5.9 | 50.7 | 64 452 | 71 109 | 10.3 | 0.0 | 2 109 | 1 635 | -524 | 26 842 | 6.9 | 2.62 | 11.0 | 24.6 |
| Elmore | 12.2 | 7.5 | 4.8 | 51.2 | 65 874 | 79 303 | 20.4 | 1.7 | 2 348 | 1 595 | 583 | 28 301 | 24.5 | 2.61 | 13.1 | 22.0 |
| Escambia | 12.5 | 9.0 | 6.3 | 48.4 | 38 440 | 38 319 | -0.3 | -0.8 | 1 054 | 982 | -392 | 14 157 | -1.0 | 2.48 | 17.3 | 27.7 |
| Etowah | 14.0 | 8.8 | 7.1 | 51.6 | 103 459 | 104 430 | 0.9 | 0.0 | 2 810 | 3 229 | 447 | 42 036 | 1.0 | 2.43 | 14.3 | 28.1 |
| Fayette | 14.6 | 10.6 | 7.8 | 50.6 | 18 495 | 17 241 | -6.8 | -1.5 | 422 | 551 | -125 | 7 100 | -5.2 | 2.39 | 12.3 | 27.5 |
| Franklin | 12.1 | 8.7 | 6.5 | 50.2 | 31 223 | 31 704 | 1.5 | 0.2 | 1 061 | 861 | -140 | 12 286 | 0.2 | 2.56 | 12.3 | 26.1 |
| Geneva | 14.3 | 10.2 | 7.6 | 51.2 | 25 764 | 26 790 | 4.0 | 0.5 | 622 | 762 | 265 | 10 920 | 4.2 | 2.43 | 13.3 | 26.7 |
| Greene | 16.0 | 8.5 | 7.9 | 53.1 | 9 974 | 9 045 | -9.3 | -1.9 | 267 | 214 | -219 | 3 764 | -4.2 | 2.39 | 24.9 | 34.4 |
| Hale | 13.9 | 8.6 | 7.3 | 52.7 | 17 185 | 15 760 | -8.3 | -2.4 | 416 | 428 | -366 | 6 273 | -2.2 | 2.46 | 21.5 | 29.5 |
| Henry | 15.2 | 10.5 | 7.6 | 52.1 | 16 310 | 17 302 | 6.1 | -0.1 | 418 | 463 | 24 | 6 994 | 7.2 | 2.45 | 14.6 | 25.9 |
| Houston | 12.7 | 8.3 | 6.5 | 52.2 | 88 787 | 101 547 | 14.4 | 1.8 | 3 103 | 2 270 | 1 040 | 40 969 | 14.3 | 2.44 | 16.2 | 27.2 |
| Jackson | 14.2 | 10.3 | 6.8 | 50.8 | 53 926 | 53 227 | -1.3 | -0.4 | 1 281 | 1 412 | -79 | 21 513 | -0.5 | 2.45 | 11.3 | 26.2 |
| Jefferson | 12.8 | 6.9 | 6.4 | 52.7 | 662 047 | 658 466 | -0.5 | 0.2 | 21 809 | 15 401 | -4 656 | 263 568 | 0.1 | 2.44 | 18.4 | 30.1 |
| Lamar | 14.6 | 10.7 | 8.4 | 51.4 | 15 904 | 14 564 | -8.4 | -2.1 | 303 | 448 | -154 | 6 103 | -5.6 | 2.35 | 11.6 | 28.8 |
| Lauderdale | 13.6 | 9.3 | 7.8 | 52.2 | 87 966 | 92 709 | 5.4 | -0.2 | 2 155 | 2 405 | 130 | 38 680 | 7.2 | 2.35 | 12.2 | 28.9 |
| Lawrence | 13.3 | 9.3 | 5.9 | 51.1 | 34 803 | 34 339 | -1.3 | -1.5 | 836 | 844 | -481 | 13 654 | 0.9 | 2.50 | 12.6 | 24.2 |
| Lee | 9.8 | 5.5 | 3.7 | 50.6 | 115 092 | 140 247 | 21.9 | 5.0 | 3 324 | 1 928 | 5 512 | 55 682 | 21.8 | 2.44 | 13.0 | 27.9 |
| Limestone | 12.3 | 7.5 | 5.0 | 49.4 | 65 676 | 82 782 | 26.0 | 5.9 | 2 346 | 1 515 | 3 954 | 31 446 | 27.4 | 2.54 | 11.4 | 23.7 |
| Lowndes | 13.1 | 9.1 | 6.1 | 53.2 | 13 473 | 11 299 | -16.1 | -3.9 | 380 | 350 | -485 | 4 352 | -11.3 | 2.57 | 25.4 | 26.9 |
| Macon | 13.3 | 7.9 | 6.5 | 54.0 | 24 105 | 21 452 | -11.0 | -4.3 | 527 | 588 | -880 | 8 499 | -5.0 | 2.32 | 25.6 | 35.0 |
| Madison | 11.8 | 7.0 | 5.4 | 51.0 | 276 700 | 334 811 | 21.0 | 2.5 | 9 497 | 5 953 | 4 730 | 134 700 | 22.5 | 2.43 | 12.8 | 28.7 |
| Marengo | 13.9 | 8.9 | 7.9 | 52.8 | 22 539 | 21 027 | -6.7 | -3.0 | 530 | 585 | -601 | 8 535 | -2.6 | 2.43 | 19.5 | 29.6 |
| Marion | 14.0 | 10.8 | 7.7 | 50.3 | 31 214 | 30 776 | -1.4 | -1.5 | 670 | 913 | -211 | 12 651 | -0.4 | 2.36 | 12.1 | 28.4 |
| Marshall | 12.4 | 8.6 | 6.4 | 50.7 | 82 231 | 93 019 | 13.1 | 1.9 | 3 242 | 2 371 | 894 | 35 810 | 10.0 | 2.57 | 12.1 | 25.4 |
| Mobile | 12.5 | 7.5 | 5.7 | 52.0 | 399 843 | 412 992 | 3.3 | 0.2 | 12 955 | 9 222 | -2 660 | 158 435 | 5.5 | 2.56 | 18.8 | 26.5 |
| Monroe | 13.7 | 8.9 | 7.2 | 52.0 | 24 324 | 23 068 | -5.2 | -2.0 | 570 | 587 | -450 | 9 214 | -1.8 | 2.48 | 18.1 | 27.4 |
| Montgomery | 11.5 | 6.5 | 5.5 | 52.5 | 223 510 | 229 363 | 2.6 | 0.3 | 7 430 | 4 525 | -2 097 | 89 981 | 4.5 | 2.45 | 20.9 | 30.4 |
| Morgan | 12.8 | 8.2 | 6.1 | 50.8 | 111 064 | 119 490 | 7.6 | 0.8 | 3 318 | 2 665 | 313 | 47 030 | 7.9 | 2.50 | 12.9 | 25.9 |
| Perry | 12.5 | 8.8 | 7.4 | 53.0 | 11 861 | 10 591 | -10.7 | -3.9 | 312 | 315 | -417 | 3 947 | -8.9 | 2.50 | 27.1 | 29.3 |
| Pickens | 14.0 | 9.4 | 7.8 | 52.4 | 20 949 | 19 746 | -5.7 | -1.7 | 551 | 569 | -325 | 8 012 | -0.9 | 2.42 | 18.4 | 30.1 |
| Pike | 11.3 | 7.6 | 5.5 | 52.3 | 29 605 | 32 899 | 11.1 | 0.9 | 930 | 740 | 81 | 13 210 | 10.7 | 2.34 | 16.2 | 30.3 |
| Randolph | 14.1 | 9.8 | 7.4 | 51.4 | 22 380 | 22 913 | 2.4 | -1.0 | 507 | 625 | -150 | 9 164 | 6.0 | 2.46 | 13.9 | 27.9 |
| Russell | 11.8 | 7.2 | 5.4 | 51.9 | 49 756 | 52 947 | 6.4 | 9.2 | 2 066 | 1 318 | 4 046 | 21 229 | 7.5 | 2.47 | 21.3 | 29.1 |
| St. Clair | 12.9 | 8.3 | 5.3 | 50.0 | 64 742 | 83 593 | 29.1 | 2.0 | 2 426 | 1 771 | 945 | 31 624 | 31.0 | 2.58 | 11.2 | 22.5 |
| Shelby | 12.3 | 6.7 | 4.4 | 51.1 | 143 293 | 195 085 | 36.1 | 3.0 | 5 434 | 2 779 | 3 086 | 74 072 | 35.6 | 2.60 | 9.4 | 23.2 |
| Sumter | 13.2 | 7.9 | 7.4 | 54.7 | 14 798 | 13 763 | -7.0 | -2.4 | 347 | 344 | -343 | 5 629 | -1.4 | 2.32 | 24.2 | 34.8 |
| Talladega | 13.7 | 8.4 | 6.0 | 51.4 | 80 321 | 82 291 | 2.5 | -0.6 | 2 049 | 2 148 | -397 | 31 890 | 4.0 | 2.48 | 17.5 | 26.7 |
| Tallapoosa | 14.7 | 10.4 | 7.5 | 51.6 | 41 475 | 41 616 | 0.3 | -1.1 | 1 070 | 1 188 | -334 | 16 985 | 2.0 | 2.42 | 15.9 | 27.2 |
| Tuscaloosa | 11.1 | 5.9 | 5.0 | 51.5 | 164 875 | 194 656 | 18.1 | 2.0 | 5 548 | 3 736 | 2 188 | 76 141 | 18.0 | 2.42 | 14.9 | 29.2 |
| Walker | 14.3 | 9.7 | 7.0 | 51.3 | 70 713 | 67 023 | -5.2 | -1.2 | 1 780 | 2 060 | -525 | 26 571 | -6.3 | 2.49 | 13.3 | 25.8 |

1. No spouse present.

# Table B. States and Counties — Population, Vital Statistics, Medicare, and Crime

| STATE County | Daytime population, 2007–2011 | | | Births, 2011 | | Deaths, 2011 | | Persons under 65 with no health insurance, 2010 | | Medicare, 2012 | | | Serious crimes known to police,[2] 2011 Total | |
|---|---|---|---|---|---|---|---|---|---|---|---|---|---|---|
| | Persons in group quarters, 2010 | Number | Employ-ment/resi-dence ratio | Total | Rate[1] | Number | Rate[1] | Number | Percent | Eligible for Medicare | Enrolled in Medicare Advantage | Enrolled in a Medicare prescription drug plan | Number | Rate[3] |
| | 32 | 33 | 34 | 35 | 36 | 37 | 38 | 39 | 40 | 41 | 42 | 43 | 44 | 45 |
| UNITED STATES | 7 987 323 | 306 603 772 | 1.00 | 4 008 000 | 12.9 | 2 450 126 | 7.9 | 46 556 803 | 17.7 | 50 090 694 | 12 260 498 | 19 145 925 | 10 266 737 | 3 295 |
| ALABAMA | 115 816 | 4 710 983 | 0.98 | 59 866 | 12.5 | 47 768 | 9.9 | 681 437 | 16.9 | 903 548 | 195 561 | 337 794 | 193 364 | 4 026 |
| Autauga | 455 | 42 649 | 0.54 | 660 | 11.9 | 423 | 7.7 | 6 467 | 13.6 | 9 099 | 2 706 | 2 210 | 1 831 | 3 339 |
| Baldwin | 2 307 | 166 289 | 0.83 | 2 109 | 11.3 | 1 723 | 9.2 | 28 586 | 19.1 | 39 586 | 11 381 | 11 438 | 5 192 | 2 835 |
| Barbour | 3 193 | 27 729 | 1.02 | 292 | 10.8 | 316 | 11.7 | 3 782 | 18.5 | 5 829 | 765 | 2 873 | 742 | 2 689 |
| Bibb | 2 224 | 18 907 | 0.57 | 225 | 9.9 | 215 | 9.4 | 3 166 | 17.7 | 4 454 | 1 494 | 1 450 | NA | NA |
| Blount | 489 | 44 535 | 0.47 | 690 | 12.0 | 556 | 9.6 | 9 351 | 19.3 | 10 853 | 4 288 | 3 058 | 1 411 | 2 450 |
| Bullock | 1 690 | 10 374 | 0.87 | 165 | 15.7 | 112 | 10.6 | 1 285 | 16.2 | 1 781 | 371 | 885 | 178 | 1 623 |
| Butler | 333 | 19 884 | 0.88 | 258 | 12.5 | 248 | 12.0 | 2 971 | 17.1 | 4 530 | 389 | 2 580 | 849 | 4 034 |
| Calhoun | 2 919 | 123 392 | 1.12 | 1 385 | 11.8 | 1 344 | 11.4 | 15 920 | 16.1 | 24 795 | 2 726 | 9 891 | 5 693 | 4 778 |
| Chambers | 458 | 30 456 | 0.70 | 373 | 11.0 | 461 | 13.6 | 5 324 | 18.8 | 8 236 | 1 093 | 4 320 | 1 633 | 4 750 |
| Cherokee | 290 | 21 972 | 0.62 | 202 | 7.8 | 295 | 11.3 | 3 980 | 18.8 | 6 228 | 1 300 | 2 738 | 1 149 | 4 400 |
| Chilton | 393 | 35 816 | 0.57 | 569 | 13.0 | 437 | 10.0 | 7 481 | 20.0 | 8 135 | 3 450 | 2 094 | 1 738 | 3 963 |
| Choctaw | 129 | 13 753 | 0.95 | 132 | 9.7 | 170 | 12.5 | 2 013 | 17.9 | 3 591 | 205 | 2 150 | 90 | 646 |
| Clarke | 280 | 26 809 | 1.09 | 264 | 10.3 | 309 | 12.0 | 3 559 | 16.6 | 5 783 | 867 | 2 938 | 529 | 2 038 |
| Clay | 255 | 12 951 | 0.80 | 137 | 9.9 | 196 | 14.1 | 2 129 | 18.8 | 3 273 | 368 | 1 619 | 178 | 1 272 |
| Cleburne | 178 | 12 110 | 0.52 | 162 | 10.9 | 198 | 13.3 | 2 202 | 17.6 | 3 283 | 358 | 1 639 | NA | NA |
| Coffee | 600 | 46 558 | 0.87 | 702 | 13.9 | 499 | 9.9 | 7 680 | 18.1 | 9 357 | 716 | 3 808 | 1 687 | 3 361 |
| Colbert | 474 | 55 263 | 1.04 | 611 | 11.2 | 647 | 11.9 | 6 536 | 14.7 | 12 823 | 1 073 | 6 211 | 1 916 | 3 503 |
| Conecuh | 45 | 12 706 | 0.85 | 151 | 11.5 | 187 | 14.3 | 2 011 | 18.6 | 3 338 | 325 | 1 853 | 489 | 3 849 |
| Coosa | 124 | 8 975 | 0.45 | 85 | 7.9 | 124 | 11.6 | 1 592 | 16.8 | 2 415 | 250 | 1 183 | 278 | 2 886 |
| Covington | 575 | 37 182 | 0.96 | 446 | 11.7 | 491 | 12.9 | 5 360 | 17.5 | 9 084 | 594 | 4 917 | 938 | 2 472 |
| Crenshaw | 132 | 12 600 | 0.77 | 173 | 12.4 | 168 | 12.1 | 2 193 | 18.9 | 3 233 | 628 | 1 452 | 294 | 2 133 |
| Cullman | 1 056 | 74 900 | 0.83 | 961 | 11.9 | 937 | 11.6 | 12 640 | 18.9 | 17 295 | 3 306 | 7 924 | 2 289 | 2 833 |
| Dale | 917 | 51 229 | 1.06 | 723 | 14.4 | 504 | 10.1 | 6 359 | 14.9 | 9 197 | 757 | 3 583 | 1 684 | 3 335 |
| Dallas | 786 | 44 464 | 1.04 | 644 | 14.9 | 535 | 12.3 | 6 008 | 16.1 | 9 329 | 1 574 | 4 923 | 3 484 | 7 913 |
| DeKalb | 782 | 66 180 | 0.84 | 926 | 13.0 | 728 | 10.2 | 14 290 | 23.5 | 13 919 | 2 121 | 6 866 | 2 006 | 2 808 |
| Elmore | 5 483 | 62 954 | 0.53 | 996 | 12.4 | 687 | 8.6 | 9 236 | 14.3 | 14 169 | 3 692 | 3 419 | 2 047 | 2 569 |
| Escambia | 3 199 | 38 827 | 1.06 | 479 | 12.6 | 443 | 11.6 | 5 738 | 19.5 | 8 029 | 725 | 4 261 | 1 436 | 3 730 |
| Etowah | 2 085 | 98 896 | 0.87 | 1 232 | 11.8 | 1 443 | 13.8 | 15 817 | 18.3 | 23 394 | 3 938 | 8 759 | 5 111 | 4 871 |
| Fayette | 291 | 15 716 | 0.75 | 186 | 10.8 | 234 | 13.6 | 2 369 | 16.9 | 4 601 | 514 | 2 253 | 267 | 1 541 |
| Franklin | 272 | 29 449 | 0.84 | 470 | 14.7 | 365 | 11.4 | 6 198 | 23.2 | 6 396 | 445 | 3 532 | 877 | 2 778 |
| Geneva | 229 | 22 076 | 0.58 | 281 | 10.5 | 331 | 12.4 | 4 339 | 19.7 | 6 315 | 557 | 3 110 | 713 | 2 649 |
| Greene | 45 | 8 921 | 0.91 | 121 | 13.6 | 85 | 9.5 | 1 368 | 18.1 | 2 061 | 127 | 1 218 | 341 | 4 042 |
| Hale | 334 | 13 852 | 0.62 | 189 | 12.3 | 183 | 11.9 | 2 184 | 16.6 | 3 677 | 209 | 2 022 | NA | NA |
| Henry | 199 | 14 882 | 0.63 | 173 | 9.9 | 203 | 11.7 | 2 585 | 18.3 | 4 107 | 765 | 1 715 | 302 | 1 737 |
| Houston | 1 416 | 107 674 | 1.17 | 1 361 | 13.3 | 995 | 9.7 | 14 356 | 16.7 | 20 441 | 2 424 | 9 467 | 3 875 | 3 798 |
| Jackson | 597 | 49 758 | 0.83 | 564 | 10.6 | 610 | 11.4 | 8 206 | 18.6 | 11 809 | 1 125 | 6 485 | 1 399 | 2 653 |
| Jefferson | 15 774 | 723 885 | 1.23 | 9 452 | 14.3 | 6 799 | 10.3 | 90 222 | 16.1 | 117 300 | 46 168 | 30 279 | 39 317 | 5 968 |
| Lamar | 217 | 13 414 | 0.78 | 137 | 9.6 | 195 | 13.6 | 2 023 | 17.3 | 3 715 | 270 | 2 177 | 106 | 724 |
| Lauderdale | 1 891 | 87 667 | 0.88 | 937 | 10.1 | 1 058 | 11.4 | 11 498 | 15.2 | 19 657 | 1 725 | 9 339 | 2 075 | 2 227 |
| Lawrence | 229 | 27 838 | 0.53 | 359 | 10.5 | 376 | 11.0 | 5 562 | 19.0 | 7 156 | 525 | 3 645 | 717 | 2 078 |
| Lee | 4 410 | 129 116 | 0.86 | 1 536 | 10.7 | 840 | 5.9 | 19 495 | 15.8 | 18 103 | 1 888 | 7 157 | 4 883 | 3 465 |
| Limestone | 2 907 | 70 514 | 0.69 | 1 000 | 11.7 | 659 | 7.7 | 11 663 | 16.7 | 14 216 | 2 048 | 5 646 | 1 240 | 1 491 |
| Lowndes | 96 | 10 560 | 0.74 | 165 | 14.8 | 154 | 13.8 | 1 627 | 17.0 | 2 535 | 927 | 849 | 372 | 3 277 |
| Macon | 1 772 | 20 371 | 0.86 | 235 | 11.1 | 283 | 13.4 | 2 757 | 16.4 | 4 227 | 860 | 1 366 | 759 | 3 521 |
| Madison | 8 042 | 363 725 | 1.22 | 4 152 | 12.2 | 2 542 | 7.5 | 40 438 | 14.1 | 52 684 | 6 211 | 16 692 | 14 030 | 4 170 |
| Marengo | 254 | 20 982 | 0.98 | 235 | 11.4 | 243 | 11.7 | 2 930 | 16.8 | 5 058 | 397 | 2 894 | 705 | 3 358 |
| Marion | 868 | 30 752 | 1.00 | 299 | 9.8 | 390 | 12.7 | 4 248 | 17.3 | 6 764 | 704 | 3 568 | 733 | 2 370 |
| Marshall | 1 047 | 92 496 | 1.01 | 1 395 | 14.8 | 1 045 | 11.1 | 16 893 | 21.5 | 18 542 | 1 714 | 9 033 | 3 972 | 4 250 |
| Mobile | 6 808 | 419 942 | 1.06 | 5 734 | 13.9 | 4 069 | 9.9 | 66 095 | 18.6 | 72 730 | 28 422 | 19 094 | 22 472 | 5 415 |
| Monroe | 230 | 22 939 | 0.97 | 258 | 11.3 | 254 | 11.2 | 3 548 | 18.4 | 4 886 | 639 | 2 679 | 738 | 3 375 |
| Montgomery | 9 082 | 265 969 | 1.37 | 3 161 | 13.6 | 2 012 | 8.7 | 30 580 | 15.8 | 37 154 | 9 401 | 9 720 | 12 166 | 5 279 |
| Morgan | 2 133 | 117 911 | 0.99 | 1 472 | 12.3 | 1 136 | 9.5 | 19 086 | 18.9 | 22 736 | 1 818 | 10 620 | 3 563 | 2 968 |
| Perry | 721 | 9 466 | 0.64 | 136 | 13.1 | 142 | 13.7 | 1 397 | 17.0 | 2 354 | 128 | 1 436 | NA | NA |
| Pickens | 334 | 16 907 | 0.58 | 239 | 12.4 | 253 | 13.1 | 2 812 | 17.4 | 4 733 | 263 | 2 540 | 201 | 1 045 |
| Pike | 1 963 | 33 843 | 1.10 | 405 | 12.3 | 336 | 10.2 | 4 750 | 17.6 | 5 732 | 1 092 | 2 351 | 1 232 | 3 727 |
| Randolph | 407 | 19 768 | 0.65 | 225 | 9.9 | 261 | 11.5 | 3 403 | 18.2 | 5 125 | 562 | 2 596 | 647 | 2 810 |
| Russell | 574 | 44 871 | 0.64 | 411 | 7.5 | 575 | 10.5 | 8 025 | 17.4 | 10 000 | 1 928 | 3 928 | 2 654 | 5 041 |
| St. Clair | 1 967 | 66 382 | 0.54 | 1 096 | 13.0 | 766 | 9.1 | 10 777 | 15.2 | 14 930 | 6 006 | 3 715 | 2 172 | 2 586 |
| Shelby | 2 574 | 173 936 | 0.81 | 2 441 | 12.3 | 1 183 | 6.0 | 20 999 | 12.3 | 28 287 | 9 845 | 7 117 | 4 148 | 2 124 |
| Sumter | 718 | 12 979 | 0.83 | 142 | 10.5 | 152 | 11.3 | 2 094 | 18.8 | 2 811 | 147 | 1 769 | 311 | 2 281 |
| Talladega | 3 143 | 81 228 | 0.97 | 892 | 10.9 | 967 | 11.8 | 10 988 | 16.2 | 17 816 | 3 980 | 7 526 | 3 828 | 4 630 |
| Tallapoosa | 576 | 39 235 | 0.86 | 471 | 11.3 | 533 | 12.8 | 5 879 | 17.3 | 10 085 | 927 | 5 275 | 1 342 | 3 292 |
| Tuscaloosa | 10 423 | 196 731 | 1.06 | 2 434 | 12.3 | 1 626 | 8.2 | 28 690 | 17.5 | 30 907 | 2 695 | 12 316 | 8 062 | 4 122 |
| Walker | 866 | 63 127 | 0.83 | 810 | 12.2 | 906 | 13.6 | 9 249 | 16.7 | 16 577 | 5 357 | 4 793 | NA | NA |

1. Per 1,000 estimated resident population.   2. Data for serious crimes have not been adjusted for underreporting; this may affect comparability between geographic areas and over time.   3. Per 100,000 population estimated by the FBI.

# Table B. States and Counties — Crime, Education, Money Income, and Poverty

| STATE County | Serious crimes known to police, 2011 (cont.)[1] Rate[2] Violent | Property | Education — School enrollment and attainment, 2007–2011 Enrollment[3] Total | Percent private | Attainment[4] (percent) High school graduate or less | Bachelor's degree or more | Local government expenditures,[5] 2009–2010 Total current expenditures (mil dol) | Current expenditures per student (dollars) | Money income, 2007–2011 Per capita income[6] (dollars) | Households Median income Dollars | Percent change, 2000 to 2007–2011 (constant 2011 dollars) | Percent with income of $200,000 or more | Income and poverty, 2011 Median household income (dollars) | Percent below poverty level All persons | Children under 18 years | Children 5 to 17 years in families |
|---|---|---|---|---|---|---|---|---|---|---|---|---|---|---|---|---|
| | 46 | 47 | 48 | 49 | 50 | 51 | 52 | 53 | 54 | 55 | 56 | 57 | 58 | 59 | 60 | 61 |
| UNITED STATES | 386 | 2 909 | 81 677 036 | 16.7 | 43.2 | 28.2 | 518 885.9 | 10 544 | 27 915 | 52 762 | -6.9 | 4.5 | 50 502 | 15.9 | 22.5 | 20.8 |
| ALABAMA | 420 | 3 606 | 1 217 101 | 14.6 | 49.5 | 22.0 | 6 650.7 | 8 881 | 23 483 | 42 934 | -6.8 | 2.5 | 41 427 | 19.1 | 27.6 | 25.8 |
| Autauga | 244 | 3 095 | 15 268 | 21.1 | 48.6 | 21.6 | 74.4 | 7 385 | 25 035 | 53 899 | -5.0 | 1.8 | 48 863 | 14.9 | 21.0 | 19.4 |
| Baldwin | 211 | 2 624 | 40 236 | 15.3 | 41.3 | 27.2 | 230.5 | 8 268 | 27 217 | 51 321 | -5.6 | 3.6 | 50 144 | 13.4 | 20.5 | 18.9 |
| Barbour | 156 | 2 534 | 6 064 | 12.7 | 60.6 | 13.9 | 35.1 | 8 998 | 15 899 | 34 041 | 0.4 | 0.4 | 30 117 | 29.5 | 39.8 | 37.2 |
| Bibb | NA | NA | 5 145 | 6.7 | 66.1 | 9.8 | 30.2 | 8 406 | 18 462 | 40 506 | -4.5 | 0.5 | 37 347 | 22.2 | 30.5 | 28.2 |
| Blount | 227 | 2 222 | 13 003 | 10.0 | 62.8 | 11.3 | 74.1 | 7 482 | 21 185 | 45 404 | -4.6 | 1.4 | 41 940 | 14.9 | 22.2 | 21.3 |
| Bullock | 301 | 1 322 | 2 262 | 10.1 | 62.7 | 14.4 | 15.3 | 9 318 | 20 678 | 31 955 | 14.9 | 3.9 | 26 038 | 32.8 | 41.1 | 40.7 |
| Butler | 608 | 3 426 | 5 225 | 9.0 | 62.7 | 12.4 | 29.1 | 8 598 | 17 091 | 31 273 | -6.6 | 0.6 | 30 489 | 24.1 | 35.7 | 33.2 |
| Calhoun | 509 | 4 269 | 29 245 | 11.3 | 55.8 | 15.8 | 159.2 | 8 574 | 20 903 | 39 467 | -8.0 | 1.6 | 39 060 | 20.9 | 31.8 | 31.1 |
| Chambers | 538 | 4 212 | 7 838 | 10.8 | 62.1 | 10.5 | 41.2 | 8 311 | 17 705 | 32 186 | -19.6 | 0.8 | 33 500 | 23.7 | 39.1 | 37.8 |
| Cherokee | 383 | 4 017 | 5 170 | 8.2 | 61.0 | 11.3 | 36.5 | 8 885 | 21 673 | 37 833 | -9.2 | 1.7 | 34 738 | 23.8 | 36.6 | 32.9 |
| Chilton | 379 | 3 585 | 9 529 | 12.4 | 63.4 | 12.4 | 59.5 | 7 669 | 20 826 | 40 418 | -8.1 | 1.6 | 38 833 | 18.3 | 28.4 | 27.7 |
| Choctaw | 86 | 560 | 3 302 | 17.7 | 65.7 | 10.5 | 17.5 | 9 471 | 18 201 | 32 188 | -3.7 | 1.8 | 32 940 | 27.3 | 35.9 | 34.0 |
| Clarke | 239 | 1 799 | 6 901 | 9.8 | 62.3 | 13.2 | 43.1 | 8 657 | 18 471 | 29 668 | -19.8 | 1.9 | 32 642 | 26.3 | 35.2 | 30.6 |
| Clay | 321 | 950 | 3 164 | 10.7 | 65.6 | 9.1 | 17.4 | 8 243 | 18 284 | 35 410 | -5.9 | 0.2 | 32 454 | 18.7 | 28.5 | 26.2 |
| Cleburne | NA | NA | 3 368 | 8.7 | 66.3 | 9.4 | 22.6 | 8 507 | 18 881 | 38 785 | -6.8 | 1.1 | 39 153 | 17.2 | 25.9 | 24.4 |
| Coffee | 387 | 2 975 | 12 014 | 7.9 | 48.5 | 21.3 | 79.4 | 8 632 | 22 953 | 42 065 | -7.5 | 1.7 | 42 173 | 16.9 | 24.0 | 23.8 |
| Colbert | 404 | 3 099 | 12 275 | 5.2 | 53.0 | 17.4 | 80.0 | 9 545 | 21 693 | 40 247 | -6.7 | 1.8 | 37 269 | 18.7 | 28.4 | 26.0 |
| Conecuh | 669 | 3 180 | 3 142 | 13.8 | 65.7 | 11.6 | 18.1 | 10 708 | 16 673 | 27 977 | -6.3 | 1.2 | 26 914 | 27.9 | 40.3 | 38.1 |
| Coosa | 343 | 2 543 | 2 446 | 9.0 | 68.6 | 9.5 | 12.8 | 9 636 | 19 966 | 37 191 | -7.8 | 0.5 | 34 391 | 25.5 | 35.6 | 31.2 |
| Covington | 190 | 2 282 | 8 268 | 9.4 | 59.1 | 12.9 | 53.0 | 8 602 | 20 246 | 33 544 | -5.7 | 1.8 | 32 138 | 24.2 | 34.2 | 34.6 |
| Crenshaw | 450 | 1 683 | 3 106 | 10.5 | 60.8 | 11.6 | 19.6 | 8 103 | 21 993 | 38 041 | 8.1 | 2.1 | 34 534 | 18.2 | 27.9 | 26.4 |
| Cullman | 204 | 2 629 | 18 915 | 12.7 | 56.1 | 14.2 | 107.9 | 8 344 | 20 621 | 38 703 | -11.1 | 1.3 | 39 395 | 18.2 | 27.9 | 27.6 |
| Dale | 465 | 2 870 | 12 397 | 13.3 | 47.0 | 17.6 | 58.4 | 8 812 | 22 326 | 45 491 | 5.3 | 1.2 | 41 568 | 18.8 | 27.5 | 25.9 |
| Dallas | 922 | 6 991 | 12 236 | 11.9 | 59.6 | 13.6 | 72.0 | 8 822 | 17 259 | 26 909 | -14.7 | 1.0 | 25 859 | 35.7 | 49.9 | 44.2 |
| DeKalb | 319 | 2 488 | 16 584 | 5.6 | 64.3 | 10.7 | 100.4 | 8 460 | 18 788 | 36 853 | -9.4 | 1.5 | 35 487 | 20.3 | 29.5 | 29.2 |
| Elmore | 182 | 2 387 | 19 368 | 18.5 | 48.9 | 21.2 | 103.4 | 7 977 | 23 828 | 54 831 | -1.5 | 2.2 | 54 866 | 13.8 | 20.7 | 19.3 |
| Escambia | 597 | 3 132 | 8 269 | 11.3 | 61.5 | 11.8 | 53.0 | 8 995 | 16 509 | 31 638 | -17.3 | 0.5 | 32 838 | 25.5 | 31.5 | 29.4 |
| Etowah | 488 | 4 383 | 23 450 | 11.5 | 50.5 | 15.3 | 133.7 | 8 137 | 20 818 | 37 772 | -10.2 | 1.3 | 34 927 | 21.0 | 30.4 | 29.8 |
| Fayette | 156 | 1 385 | 3 709 | 7.5 | 63.7 | 10.9 | 22.1 | 8 604 | 18 336 | 33 378 | -13.4 | 0.5 | 32 648 | 22.5 | 32.9 | 30.2 |
| Franklin | 317 | 2 461 | 6 914 | 4.3 | 62.9 | 11.4 | 50.8 | 8 775 | 18 715 | 35 831 | -2.4 | 1.6 | 33 705 | 19.9 | 32.5 | 30.7 |
| Geneva | 349 | 2 299 | 5 559 | 5.2 | 62.4 | 10.3 | 32.1 | 8 060 | 20 120 | 35 237 | -1.3 | 0.9 | 33 835 | 24.4 | 42.3 | 38.1 |
| Greene | 1 197 | 2 845 | 2 446 | 6.3 | 64.6 | 10.6 | 14.7 | 10 565 | 15 210 | 23 004 | -14.0 | 1.5 | 24 738 | 35.1 | 47.3 | 43.2 |
| Hale | NA | NA | 4 436 | 10.6 | 64.1 | 10.0 | 26.0 | 8 850 | 16 480 | 29 236 | -16.1 | 0.5 | 31 044 | 28.5 | 41.0 | 37.4 |
| Henry | 276 | 1 461 | 3 972 | 16.3 | 60.1 | 14.8 | 22.4 | 7 878 | 20 079 | 39 948 | -2.5 | 0.4 | 39 788 | 18.7 | 29.2 | 26.5 |
| Houston | 430 | 3 367 | 23 558 | 17.2 | 51.3 | 18.8 | 133.7 | 8 563 | 23 152 | 41 766 | -10.2 | 2.3 | 40 428 | 17.5 | 29.2 | 28.1 |
| Jackson | 247 | 2 406 | 11 992 | 8.4 | 61.2 | 13.5 | 81.8 | 9 521 | 19 770 | 36 383 | -15.8 | 0.7 | 36 746 | 17.9 | 25.1 | 23.5 |
| Jefferson | 737 | 5 231 | 170 023 | 17.8 | 41.0 | 29.0 | 1 033.1 | 9 873 | 26 962 | 45 750 | -8.1 | 3.7 | 42 053 | 18.7 | 27.2 | 26.6 |
| Lamar | 41 | 683 | 3 139 | 6.8 | 66.2 | 9.4 | 19.3 | 8 200 | 20 865 | 34 711 | -8.4 | 1.8 | 34 731 | 22.1 | 31.4 | 28.6 |
| Lauderdale | 125 | 2 103 | 22 668 | 13.6 | 51.5 | 21.6 | 118.7 | 8 986 | 22 692 | 39 702 | -11.8 | 2.0 | 40 195 | 16.4 | 24.0 | 21.6 |
| Lawrence | 226 | 1 852 | 8 135 | 9.9 | 62.6 | 12.3 | 47.3 | 9 024 | 19 676 | 40 009 | -6.1 | 0.4 | 38 132 | 18.0 | 27.1 | 25.1 |
| Lee | 210 | 3 255 | 52 053 | 9.9 | 41.5 | 31.2 | 180.2 | 8 881 | 23 015 | 42 320 | 1.3 | 2.1 | 42 539 | 21.4 | 20.7 | 19.3 |
| Limestone | 105 | 1 386 | 18 969 | 13.4 | 51.1 | 21.1 | 106.4 | 8 973 | 24 157 | 47 199 | -6.5 | 2.2 | 46 760 | 13.9 | 21.1 | 19.3 |
| Lowndes | 458 | 2 819 | 2 793 | 19.5 | 64.0 | 13.7 | 23.9 | 12 519 | 17 671 | 27 905 | -10.3 | 2.3 | 28 043 | 27.1 | 39.9 | 38.0 |
| Macon | 422 | 3 099 | 7 408 | 39.4 | 50.1 | 21.1 | 26.8 | 9 812 | 16 763 | 29 355 | 2.7 | 1.2 | 27 591 | 30.9 | 43.0 | 39.2 |
| Madison | 542 | 3 629 | 92 091 | 16.6 | 33.6 | 37.4 | 475.2 | 9 125 | 30 708 | 57 453 | -4.8 | 4.8 | 55 298 | 13.8 | 19.8 | 18.3 |
| Marengo | 362 | 2 996 | 5 185 | 12.5 | 56.0 | 17.8 | 39.7 | 8 872 | 19 075 | 35 165 | -3.6 | 1.1 | 31 995 | 24.6 | 33.9 | 30.8 |
| Marion | 239 | 2 131 | 6 343 | 7.3 | 64.9 | 8.5 | 42.3 | 8 404 | 18 358 | 31 799 | -14.3 | 1.4 | 30 926 | 25.6 | 33.2 | 29.9 |
| Marshall | 250 | 3 999 | 20 514 | 7.6 | 58.3 | 15.2 | 147.8 | 8 942 | 20 590 | 38 563 | -11.2 | 2.2 | 38 876 | 19.1 | 27.9 | 27.2 |
| Mobile | 608 | 4 807 | 110 388 | 20.5 | 50.7 | 20.1 | 562.1 | 8 712 | 22 306 | 42 187 | -7.3 | 2.3 | 41 867 | 19.7 | 29.9 | 27.7 |
| Monroe | 590 | 2 785 | 5 458 | 11.6 | 65.3 | 10.4 | 35.2 | 8 566 | 17 408 | 29 849 | -24.0 | 0.6 | 31 072 | 28.7 | 41.6 | 38.3 |
| Montgomery | 342 | 4 937 | 64 277 | 22.2 | 41.9 | 31.2 | 282.5 | 8 895 | 24 991 | 44 587 | -8.2 | 3.2 | 42 962 | 23.2 | 33.9 | 30.3 |
| Morgan | 220 | 2 748 | 28 364 | 11.4 | 50.6 | 19.0 | 186.3 | 9 394 | 23 552 | 45 564 | -10.7 | 1.7 | 43 615 | 16.8 | 27.3 | 26.5 |
| Perry | NA | NA | 2 973 | 14.8 | 65.3 | 12.6 | 18.2 | 9 463 | 14 283 | 27 222 | -0.2 | 0.9 | 22 175 | 33.0 | 47.3 | 45.0 |
| Pickens | 203 | 842 | 4 828 | 11.2 | 64.8 | 10.3 | 27.0 | 9 138 | 16 310 | 29 096 | -17.9 | 0.0 | 31 079 | 26.5 | 35.3 | 30.7 |
| Pike | 457 | 3 270 | 11 796 | 8.0 | 55.0 | 23.4 | 42.1 | 9 405 | 19 335 | 31 179 | -9.6 | 1.4 | 32 345 | 25.6 | 33.5 | 32.8 |
| Randolph | 330 | 2 480 | 5 153 | 11.7 | 62.4 | 12.2 | 32.3 | 8 382 | 20 147 | 35 823 | -7.5 | 1.1 | 34 517 | 22.1 | 31.2 | 29.0 |
| Russell | 408 | 4 633 | 13 664 | 13.2 | 56.1 | 12.6 | 83.3 | 8 674 | 18 233 | 33 754 | -9.1 | 0.3 | 32 632 | 20.1 | 30.2 | 29.4 |
| St. Clair | 211 | 2 375 | 18 100 | 14.4 | 54.9 | 14.6 | 98.6 | 7 848 | 22 974 | 49 200 | -2.3 | 2.0 | 48 040 | 17.3 | 25.2 | 23.8 |
| Shelby | 152 | 1 971 | 50 986 | 21.2 | 30.9 | 40.0 | 238.9 | 8 619 | 34 226 | 68 883 | -8.0 | 6.2 | 66 362 | 8.1 | 11.5 | 9.8 |
| Sumter | 315 | 1 965 | 4 384 | 6.0 | 60.3 | 13.6 | 22.4 | 10 230 | 14 122 | 21 964 | -14.0 | 0.5 | 23 531 | 39.1 | 45.5 | 41.9 |
| Talladega | 313 | 4 316 | 19 278 | 10.1 | 60.2 | 12.3 | 112.9 | 8 977 | 18 882 | 36 609 | -14.3 | 0.5 | 33 856 | 26.2 | 35.2 | 29.6 |
| Tallapoosa | 466 | 2 826 | 9 266 | 9.4 | 55.6 | 17.1 | 56.5 | 8 862 | 22 792 | 39 423 | -5.0 | 1.9 | 37 686 | 18.8 | 29.8 | 27.0 |
| Tuscaloosa | 427 | 3 694 | 61 006 | 9.3 | 46.2 | 26.0 | 237.9 | 8 512 | 22 449 | 43 538 | -6.4 | 2.3 | 42 086 | 20.2 | 26.6 | 25.7 |
| Walker | NA | NA | 14 466 | 8.1 | 59.6 | 10.0 | 102.6 | 9 267 | 20 881 | 37 161 | -5.3 | 1.2 | 35 423 | 22.1 | 29.7 | 25.9 |

1. Data for serious crimes have not been adjusted for underreporting; this may affect comparability between geographic areas and over time.  2. Per 100,000 population estimated by the FBI.  3. All persons 3 years old and over enrolled in nursery school through college.  4. Persons 25 years old and over.  5. Elementary and secondary education expenditures.  6. Based on population estimated by the American Community Survey, 2007–2011.

# Table B. States and Counties — **Personal Income**

| | Personal income, 2011 | | | | | | | Transfer payments (mil dol) | | | | | |
| STATE County | Total (mil dol) | Percent change, 2010–2011 | Per capita¹ Dollars | Rank | Wages and salaries² (mil dol) | Proprietors' income (mil dol) | Dividends, interest, and rent (mil dol) | Total | Government payments to individuals Total | Social Security | Medical payments | Income mainte- nance | Unemploy- ment insurance |
|---|---|---|---|---|---|---|---|---|---|---|---|---|---|
| | 62 | 63 | 64 | 65 | 66 | 67 | 68 | 69 | 70 | 71 | 72 | 73 | 74 |
| UNITED STATES | 12 949 905 | 5.2 | 41 560 | X | 8 273 601 | 1 180 598 | 2 093 469 | 2 319 212 | 2 249 960 | 713 276 | 974 728 | 278 037 | 108 555 |
| ALABAMA | 167 517 | 3.8 | 34 880 | X | 100 742 | 12 848 | 25 631 | 38 248 | 37 103 | 13 163 | 14 534 | 5 376 | 935 |
| Autauga | 1 805 | 5.3 | 32 657 | 1 767 | 497 | 113 | 206 | 370 | 358 | 132 | 132 | 49 | 10 |
| Baldwin | 7 100 | 6.7 | 38 024 | 969 | 2 579 | 443 | 1 399 | 1 448 | 1 364 | 596 | 501 | 127 | 32 |
| Barbour | 727 | 0.9 | 26 807 | 2 786 | 394 | 48 | 113 | 242 | 236 | 78 | 97 | 42 | 5 |
| Bibb | 550 | 2.9 | 24 180 | 3 022 | 200 | 36 | 58 | 188 | 183 | 64 | 81 | 25 | 4 |
| Blount | 1 570 | 3.0 | 27 220 | 2 732 | 359 | 88 | 202 | 416 | 403 | 161 | 160 | 48 | 10 |
| Bullock | 244 | 0.7 | 23 188 | 3 051 | 117 | 9 | 30 | 93 | 90 | 22 | 41 | 19 | 3 |
| Butler | 590 | 1.0 | 28 562 | 2 530 | 270 | 40 | 72 | 199 | 195 | 61 | 82 | 36 | 5 |
| Calhoun | 3 741 | 2.6 | 31 758 | 1 940 | 2 447 | 194 | 564 | 1 000 | 974 | 335 | 387 | 135 | 23 |
| Chambers | 984 | 5.4 | 28 994 | 2 450 | 345 | 50 | 123 | 337 | 329 | 123 | 128 | 54 | 8 |
| Cherokee | 700 | 2.2 | 26 869 | 2 781 | 207 | 45 | 105 | 229 | 223 | 91 | 87 | 28 | 5 |
| Chilton | 1 266 | 4.7 | 28 844 | 2 479 | 369 | 60 | 149 | 345 | 335 | 120 | 137 | 49 | 8 |
| Choctaw | 409 | 0.4 | 30 050 | 2 281 | 217 | 34 | 50 | 143 | 140 | 54 | 56 | 20 | 3 |
| Clarke | 792 | 1.9 | 30 810 | 2 141 | 388 | 76 | 109 | 251 | 245 | 84 | 99 | 44 | 7 |
| Clay | 364 | -0.8 | 26 288 | 2 852 | 146 | 27 | 49 | 126 | 123 | 45 | 52 | 16 | 3 |
| Cleburne | 429 | 1.2 | 28 916 | 2 465 | 122 | 30 | 44 | 116 | 113 | 45 | 45 | 15 | 3 |
| Coffee | 1 852 | 3.3 | 36 653 | 1 117 | 605 | 132 | 302 | 398 | 387 | 129 | 155 | 42 | 7 |
| Colbert | 1 730 | 2.5 | 31 743 | 1 944 | 1 219 | 102 | 252 | 505 | 493 | 194 | 183 | 58 | 13 |
| Conecuh | 370 | 1.2 | 28 222 | 2 580 | 145 | 32 | 47 | 142 | 139 | 46 | 55 | 25 | 3 |
| Coosa | 254 | -1.9 | 23 678 | 3 039 | 64 | 9 | 33 | 91 | 88 | 35 | 33 | 14 | 2 |
| Covington | 1 119 | 2.1 | 29 399 | 2 395 | 546 | 67 | 169 | 357 | 348 | 123 | 145 | 46 | 7 |
| Crenshaw | 420 | -1.4 | 30 217 | 2 251 | 159 | 42 | 50 | 126 | 123 | 42 | 52 | 19 | 3 |
| Cullman | 2 466 | 0.7 | 30 616 | 2 172 | 1 147 | 153 | 362 | 680 | 662 | 252 | 269 | 70 | 15 |
| Dale | 1 521 | 2.2 | 30 393 | 2 222 | 1 846 | 68 | 195 | 416 | 405 | 124 | 170 | 57 | 8 |
| Dallas | 1 240 | 2.6 | 28 615 | 2 521 | 621 | 96 | 156 | 476 | 466 | 121 | 188 | 109 | 12 |
| DeKalb | 1 826 | -2.5 | 25 586 | 2 922 | 857 | 138 | 261 | 555 | 539 | 193 | 213 | 78 | 15 |
| Elmore | 2 723 | 4.1 | 33 975 | 1 515 | 800 | 134 | 320 | 581 | 563 | 206 | 213 | 76 | 14 |
| Escambia | 1 075 | 4.5 | 28 227 | 2 579 | 594 | 83 | 151 | 336 | 327 | 116 | 129 | 51 | 7 |
| Etowah | 3 321 | 2.8 | 31 844 | 1 918 | 1 555 | 220 | 462 | 967 | 944 | 347 | 386 | 116 | 20 |
| Fayette | 462 | 1.9 | 26 884 | 2 779 | 160 | 25 | 65 | 163 | 159 | 63 | 62 | 21 | 3 |
| Franklin | 844 | 1.3 | 26 457 | 2 828 | 430 | 40 | 109 | 267 | 260 | 91 | 115 | 36 | 7 |
| Geneva | 805 | 1.5 | 30 047 | 2 283 | 209 | 49 | 107 | 248 | 242 | 85 | 102 | 32 | 4 |
| Greene | 283 | 4.0 | 31 678 | 1 960 | 91 | 29 | 49 | 94 | 92 | 26 | 37 | 22 | 2 |
| Hale | 470 | 1.9 | 30 458 | 2 209 | 132 | 52 | 61 | 166 | 162 | 48 | 71 | 31 | 3 |
| Henry | 555 | 5.1 | 31 888 | 1 910 | 162 | 39 | 83 | 170 | 166 | 58 | 61 | 20 | 3 |
| Houston | 3 719 | 3.9 | 36 330 | 1 162 | 2 262 | 254 | 629 | 801 | 778 | 289 | 293 | 121 | 18 |
| Jackson | 1 630 | 2.5 | 30 591 | 2 181 | 724 | 123 | 240 | 445 | 433 | 173 | 179 | 51 | 11 |
| Jefferson | 29 042 | 4.4 | 44 074 | 435 | 21 621 | 4 225 | 5 139 | 5 490 | 5 341 | 1 789 | 2 170 | 773 | 128 |
| Lamar | 393 | 3.9 | 27 430 | 2 695 | 149 | 28 | 53 | 142 | 138 | 52 | 59 | 17 | 3 |
| Lauderdale | 2 989 | 3.5 | 32 211 | 1 841 | 1 239 | 238 | 506 | 735 | 714 | 296 | 268 | 79 | 19 |
| Lawrence | 994 | 2.4 | 29 144 | 2 430 | 340 | 72 | 103 | 266 | 259 | 108 | 94 | 36 | 8 |
| Lee | 4 190 | 5.6 | 29 208 | 2 424 | 2 280 | 287 | 684 | 781 | 749 | 274 | 245 | 122 | 24 |
| Limestone | 2 924 | 6.8 | 34 250 | 1 479 | 1 198 | 314 | 336 | 559 | 540 | 208 | 187 | 65 | 15 |
| Lowndes | 359 | 1.0 | 32 176 | 1 848 | 149 | 43 | 34 | 115 | 113 | 32 | 42 | 30 | 3 |
| Macon | 586 | 2.4 | 27 644 | 2 663 | 284 | 18 | 63 | 193 | 188 | 52 | 64 | 44 | 5 |
| Madison | 14 149 | 4.5 | 41 601 | 608 | 13 077 | 629 | 2 376 | 2 029 | 1 953 | 736 | 713 | 231 | 64 |
| Marengo | 692 | 2.5 | 33 467 | 1 612 | 322 | 78 | 93 | 215 | 211 | 71 | 84 | 38 | 4 |
| Marion | 804 | 1.1 | 26 237 | 2 859 | 400 | 63 | 124 | 263 | 256 | 97 | 108 | 33 | 6 |
| Marshall | 2 876 | 1.8 | 30 543 | 2 189 | 1 416 | 93 | 414 | 727 | 706 | 258 | 294 | 93 | 17 |
| Mobile | 13 524 | 3.9 | 32 779 | 1 744 | 9 608 | 961 | 1 896 | 3 467 | 3 347 | 1 075 | 1 334 | 582 | 91 |
| Monroe | 643 | 0.7 | 28 245 | 2 576 | 340 | 61 | 86 | 215 | 210 | 71 | 81 | 37 | 6 |
| Montgomery | 8 913 | 3.5 | 38 414 | 923 | 7 777 | 829 | 1 417 | 1 834 | 1 783 | 528 | 646 | 371 | 45 |
| Morgan | 3 947 | 2.9 | 32 904 | 1 724 | 2 417 | 216 | 602 | 897 | 870 | 348 | 347 | 103 | 24 |
| Perry | 300 | 2.7 | 28 941 | 2 459 | 101 | 20 | 37 | 121 | 118 | 30 | 48 | 30 | 3 |
| Pickens | 559 | 2.2 | 28 910 | 2 467 | 155 | 32 | 75 | 198 | 193 | 64 | 83 | 30 | 4 |
| Pike | 1 128 | 1.9 | 34 269 | 1 476 | 658 | 93 | 152 | 307 | 300 | 77 | 108 | 45 | 6 |
| Randolph | 598 | -0.3 | 26 263 | 2 856 | 185 | 37 | 92 | 209 | 204 | 72 | 74 | 31 | 5 |
| Russell | 1 742 | 7.1 | 31 920 | 1 900 | 591 | 57 | 168 | 453 | 441 | 139 | 154 | 87 | 11 |
| St. Clair | 2 721 | 5.8 | 32 240 | 1 838 | 751 | 85 | 287 | 590 | 571 | 224 | 229 | 68 | 15 |
| Shelby | 8 855 | 6.2 | 44 734 | 402 | 4 380 | 293 | 1 455 | 1 051 | 1 007 | 463 | 356 | 87 | 30 |
| Sumter | 346 | 1.1 | 25 680 | 2 911 | 151 | 26 | 43 | 132 | 129 | 36 | 46 | 31 | 3 |
| Talladega | 2 517 | 3.0 | 30 820 | 2 140 | 1 396 | 99 | 283 | 742 | 724 | 254 | 301 | 113 | 18 |
| Tallapoosa | 1 286 | 3.1 | 30 899 | 2 124 | 530 | 59 | 204 | 401 | 392 | 149 | 148 | 54 | 9 |
| Tuscaloosa | 6 848 | 4.5 | 34 724 | 1 417 | 4 721 | 483 | 1 059 | 1 388 | 1 343 | 462 | 531 | 188 | 35 |
| Walker | 2 211 | 2.5 | 33 167 | 1 681 | 835 | 169 | 269 | 720 | 705 | 253 | 305 | 74 | 12 |

1. Based on the resident population estimated as of July 1 of the year shown.   2. Includes supplements to wages and salaries.

# Table B. States and Counties — Earnings, Social Security, and Housing

| | Earnings, 2011 | | | | | | | | | Social Security beneficiaries, December 2011 | | | Housing units, 2010 | |
| | | | | Percent by selected industries | | | | | | | | | | |
| | | | Goods-related[1] | | Service-related and health | | | | | | | | | |
| STATE County | Total (mil dol) | Farm | Total | Manu-facturing | Infor-mation and profes-sional and technical services | Retail trade | Finance, insur-ance, and real estate | Health care and social services | Govern-ment | Number | Rate[2] | Supple-mental Security Income recipients, December 2011 | Total | Percent change, 2000–2010 |
|---|---|---|---|---|---|---|---|---|---|---|---|---|---|---|
| | 75 | 76 | 77 | 78 | 79 | 80 | 81 | 82 | 83 | 84 | 85 | 86 | 87 | 88 |
| UNITED STATES | 9 454 199 | 1.1 | 16.5 | 10.0 | 13.1 | 6.1 | 9.3 | 11.0 | 17.6 | 53 972 162 | 173 | 8 111 751 | 131 704 730 | 13.6 |
| ALABAMA | 113 590 | 0.4 | 20.2 | 13.4 | 9.5 | 6.9 | 6.3 | 10.6 | 22.9 | 1 037 438 | 216 | 174 853 | 2 171 853 | 10.6 |
| Autauga | 609 | 3.7 | 21.6 | 14.1 | 3.5 | 11.1 | 5.5 | D | 20.4 | 10 455 | 189 | 1 445 | 22 135 | 25.3 |
| Baldwin | 3 022 | 0.4 | 15.3 | 7.4 | 5.6 | 13.8 | 7.8 | 12.1 | 16.4 | 43 915 | 235 | 3 319 | 104 061 | 40.1 |
| Barbour | 442 | 1.9 | 33.5 | 28.4 | D | 6.9 | 2.8 | 7.1 | 21.6 | 6 720 | 248 | 1 625 | 11 829 | -5.1 |
| Bibb | 236 | 2.4 | D | 7.4 | 1.7 | 6.8 | 2.0 | D | 29.9 | 5 350 | 235 | 1 071 | 8 981 | 7.6 |
| Blount | 447 | -3.5 | 21.3 | 12.8 | D | 9.6 | 3.2 | D | 24.7 | 12 715 | 220 | 1 471 | 23 887 | 12.9 |
| Bullock | 126 | 2.7 | D | D | D | D | 2.5 | 11.7 | 30.4 | 2 025 | 192 | 708 | 4 493 | -4.1 |
| Butler | 310 | 1.9 | 21.5 | 17.0 | D | 9.5 | 2.6 | D | 16.1 | 5 260 | 255 | 1 276 | 9 964 | 0.1 |
| Calhoun | 2 641 | 0.1 | D | 13.1 | 5.5 | 7.2 | 2.6 | 9.2 | 36.4 | 28 520 | 242 | 4 689 | 53 289 | 3.8 |
| Chambers | 395 | 0.3 | 22.4 | 18.3 | D | 9.9 | 2.4 | D | 18.7 | 9 650 | 284 | 1 642 | 17 004 | 4.5 |
| Cherokee | 253 | 2.4 | 21.0 | 16.8 | D | 12.5 | 4.2 | 7.5 | 25.3 | 7 355 | 282 | 1 009 | 16 267 | 16.0 |
| Chilton | 429 | 2.8 | D | 15.5 | 2.7 | 11.1 | 3.1 | D | 22.9 | 9 650 | 220 | 1 559 | 19 278 | 9.2 |
| Choctaw | 250 | -0.2 | 51.9 | 44.7 | D | 8.9 | 1.7 | D | 10.7 | 4 350 | 320 | 929 | 7 269 | -7.3 |
| Clarke | 464 | 2.3 | D | 22.8 | D | 10.8 | 4.5 | D | 21.6 | 6 855 | 267 | 1 534 | 12 638 | 0.0 |
| Clay | 173 | 0.8 | 35.3 | 31.2 | 2.5 | 5.8 | 3.3 | D | 27.1 | 3 825 | 276 | 615 | 6 776 | 2.5 |
| Cleburne | 152 | 5.1 | D | 12.6 | 1.3 | 9.4 | 2.1 | 2.9 | 27.6 | 3 835 | 259 | 538 | 6 718 | 8.5 |
| Coffee | 737 | 1.1 | 19.3 | 14.9 | 10.2 | 11.0 | 4.3 | 12.3 | 19.5 | 10 525 | 208 | 1 439 | 22 330 | 12.6 |
| Colbert | 1 321 | 1.1 | 30.3 | 20.3 | 2.0 | 7.9 | 3.1 | 9.7 | 26.9 | 14 885 | 273 | 2 237 | 25 758 | 3.1 |
| Conecuh | 177 | 3.6 | D | 12.4 | 1.9 | 5.8 | 1.3 | D | 23.9 | 3 945 | 301 | 871 | 7 093 | -2.4 |
| Coosa | 73 | 3.9 | 40.4 | 38.1 | D | D | D | 3.9 | 26.4 | 2 865 | 267 | 508 | 6 478 | 5.6 |
| Covington | 614 | 0.8 | 21.8 | 16.2 | 3.0 | 9.8 | 3.5 | D | 18.3 | 10 370 | 272 | 1 558 | 18 829 | 1.3 |
| Crenshaw | 201 | 3.4 | 26.6 | 22.1 | D | 5.3 | 3.0 | D | 15.8 | 3 700 | 266 | 725 | 6 735 | 1.4 |
| Cullman | 1 300 | -2.5 | D | 17.8 | 4.8 | 9.9 | 4.3 | 14.1 | 16.7 | 20 075 | 249 | 2 655 | 37 054 | 5.2 |
| Dale | 1 914 | 0.3 | D | 23.1 | 3.3 | 2.0 | 0.9 | 1.6 | 54.1 | 10 585 | 212 | 1 860 | 22 677 | 4.1 |
| Dallas | 717 | 3.7 | D | 24.8 | D | 8.0 | 2.6 | 13.4 | 20.9 | 10 930 | 252 | 4 371 | 20 208 | -1.2 |
| DeKalb | 995 | -1.0 | D | 28.5 | 3.4 | 8.6 | 3.2 | 10.1 | 17.5 | 16 225 | 227 | 2 414 | 31 109 | 10.9 |
| Elmore | 934 | 0.4 | 24.9 | 16.5 | 4.8 | 11.5 | 3.9 | 9.4 | 23.7 | 16 085 | 201 | 2 236 | 32 657 | 26.9 |
| Escambia | 678 | 2.9 | 28.3 | 21.6 | 2.0 | 7.6 | 3.9 | 7.1 | 29.7 | 9 535 | 250 | 1 520 | 16 486 | -0.4 |
| Etowah | 1 776 | -0.7 | 21.5 | 16.4 | 4.1 | 8.4 | 4.8 | D | 16.8 | 27 415 | 263 | 4 729 | 47 454 | 3.3 |
| Fayette | 185 | -0.8 | 22.5 | 16.4 | D | 10.5 | 3.0 | D | 32.5 | 5 260 | 306 | 912 | 8 437 | -0.4 |
| Franklin | 470 | 0.0 | 40.3 | 36.8 | 1.9 | 6.8 | 3.6 | D | 21.7 | 7 535 | 236 | 1 150 | 14 022 | 2.0 |
| Geneva | 258 | 4.2 | D | 10.5 | D | 8.2 | 4.1 | D | 27.8 | 7 270 | 271 | 1 258 | 12 687 | 4.7 |
| Greene | 121 | 17.8 | 20.6 | 17.5 | D | 4.0 | 1.5 | D | 25.2 | 2 480 | 278 | 924 | 5 007 | -2.1 |
| Hale | 184 | 17.7 | 22.7 | 15.6 | 1.9 | 6.1 | 2.3 | D | 25.1 | 4 420 | 287 | 1 194 | 7 655 | -1.3 |
| Henry | 202 | 7.1 | D | 15.0 | D | 5.6 | 2.5 | D | 18.6 | 4 720 | 271 | 667 | 8 891 | 10.6 |
| Houston | 2 516 | 0.7 | 14.6 | 7.6 | 5.0 | 10.4 | 4.2 | 17.6 | 18.6 | 23 260 | 227 | 3 976 | 45 319 | 14.5 |
| Jackson | 847 | 3.6 | D | 27.7 | 3.2 | 8.7 | 2.7 | 5.4 | 25.8 | 13 835 | 260 | 1 735 | 24 786 | 2.6 |
| Jefferson | 25 847 | 0.0 | 15.6 | 6.8 | 11.8 | 5.5 | 10.1 | 14.3 | 15.8 | 134 120 | 204 | 25 065 | 300 552 | 4.3 |
| Lamar | 178 | 2.6 | D | 27.3 | D | 7.0 | 3.8 | 7.1 | 18.1 | 4 375 | 306 | 632 | 7 354 | -2.2 |
| Lauderdale | 1 477 | 3.7 | 17.0 | 10.9 | 5.3 | 11.9 | 4.8 | 15.4 | 19.7 | 22 610 | 244 | 2 823 | 43 791 | 8.3 |
| Lawrence | 412 | 7.0 | D | 31.4 | 1.8 | 7.3 | 2.1 | D | 19.0 | 8 475 | 248 | 1 393 | 15 229 | 1.5 |
| Lee | 2 567 | 0.1 | 17.2 | 11.7 | 5.1 | 7.5 | 4.5 | 7.2 | 37.1 | 20 920 | 146 | 3 298 | 62 391 | 24.0 |
| Limestone | 1 511 | 3.5 | D | 9.8 | 7.4 | 10.1 | 2.7 | 4.9 | 32.9 | 16 295 | 191 | 2 049 | 34 977 | 30.0 |
| Lowndes | 192 | 12.2 | D | 38.1 | D | 3.5 | 1.7 | 2.3 | 16.3 | 2 965 | 266 | 1 029 | 5 140 | -11.3 |
| Macon | 301 | 1.5 | D | D | 2.3 | 3.4 | 1.1 | D | 66.4 | 4 610 | 218 | 1 285 | 10 259 | -3.5 |
| Madison | 13 705 | 0.3 | 14.0 | 11.5 | 25.5 | 4.7 | 2.8 | 6.5 | 32.4 | 55 675 | 164 | 6 666 | 146 447 | 21.6 |
| Marengo | 399 | 2.4 | 27.6 | 21.9 | 2.4 | 7.0 | 3.9 | D | 21.8 | 5 915 | 286 | 1 676 | 10 237 | 1.1 |
| Marion | 463 | 0.4 | D | 30.9 | 2.1 | 7.7 | 3.9 | D | 18.0 | 7 995 | 261 | 1 156 | 14 737 | 2.2 |
| Marshall | 1 509 | -2.2 | D | 28.5 | 4.9 | 9.8 | 4.4 | 6.6 | 21.4 | 21 140 | 224 | 2 902 | 40 342 | 11.0 |
| Mobile | 10 569 | 0.2 | 20.2 | 12.3 | 8.3 | 6.6 | 9.0 | 11.2 | 17.3 | 84 270 | 204 | 14 844 | 178 196 | 7.9 |
| Monroe | 401 | 1.8 | 27.5 | 25.2 | D | 7.5 | 2.6 | D | 19.2 | 5 835 | 256 | 1 118 | 11 333 | -0.1 |
| Montgomery | 8 607 | 0.2 | 15.7 | 9.7 | 9.3 | 5.4 | 6.9 | 10.6 | 32.6 | 42 050 | 181 | 10 032 | 101 641 | 6.5 |
| Morgan | 2 633 | -0.1 | 40.7 | 32.7 | 4.0 | 7.0 | 3.9 | 8.0 | 15.2 | 26 235 | 219 | 3 349 | 51 193 | 8.0 |
| Perry | 121 | 7.3 | 22.2 | 19.7 | 1.2 | 4.9 | D | 8.2 | 27.3 | 2 900 | 280 | 1 266 | 4 737 | -12.4 |
| Pickens | 188 | 5.0 | D | 16.4 | D | 7.5 | 2.4 | D | 24.8 | 5 530 | 286 | 1 320 | 9 483 | -0.4 |
| Pike | 751 | -0.4 | 25.5 | 21.1 | 2.2 | 6.5 | 3.6 | D | 23.1 | 6 540 | 199 | 1 703 | 15 267 | 8.9 |
| Randolph | 222 | -1.0 | D | 17.0 | 3.1 | 10.9 | 3.8 | D | 28.0 | 5 950 | 261 | 941 | 11 982 | 16.5 |
| Russell | 648 | 1.2 | 34.1 | 26.8 | 2.6 | 10.0 | 4.8 | 8.8 | 22.2 | 11 520 | 211 | 2 104 | 24 595 | 7.7 |
| St. Clair | 835 | -1.2 | D | 15.9 | 4.4 | 9.5 | 4.0 | 7.9 | 19.9 | 17 335 | 205 | 2 114 | 35 541 | 30.2 |
| Shelby | 4 673 | 0.1 | 14.8 | 7.0 | 10.8 | 7.4 | 15.7 | 7.1 | 10.3 | 31 485 | 159 | 2 467 | 80 970 | 36.6 |
| Sumter | 177 | 6.3 | 13.8 | 10.4 | D | 5.7 | 2.0 | D | 39.1 | 3 280 | 243 | 1 239 | 6 786 | -2.4 |
| Talladega | 1 494 | 0.8 | D | 38.2 | 2.1 | 5.7 | 2.0 | 8.5 | 19.4 | 20 610 | 252 | 4 370 | 37 088 | 7.6 |
| Tallapoosa | 589 | 0.3 | D | 16.9 | 4.0 | 8.8 | 4.2 | D | 19.6 | 11 790 | 283 | 1 877 | 22 111 | 7.8 |
| Tuscaloosa | 5 204 | 0.0 | 29.1 | 18.0 | 6.1 | 6.3 | 3.8 | 9.3 | 28.1 | 35 875 | 182 | 6 869 | 84 872 | 18.8 |
| Walker | 1 004 | -0.8 | 18.0 | 9.0 | 4.9 | 11.9 | 4.3 | 16.2 | 17.8 | 19 965 | 300 | 3 434 | 30 816 | -4.9 |

1. Includes mining, construction, and manufacturing.    2. Per 1,000 resident population enumerated in the 2010 census.

# Table B. States and Counties — Housing, Labor Force, and Employment

| STATE County | Housing units, 2007–2011 Occupied units Total | Percent | Owner-occupied Median value[1] | Median owner cost as a percent of income With a mortgage | Without a mortgage[2] | Renter-occupied Median rent[3] | Median rent as a percent of income | Sub-standard units[4] (percent) | Civilian labor force, 2012 Total | Percent change, 2011–2012 | Unemployment Total | Rate[5] | Civilian employment,[6] 2007–2011 Total | Percent Management, business, science and arts | Construction, production, and maintenance occupations |
|---|---|---|---|---|---|---|---|---|---|---|---|---|---|---|---|
| | 89 | 90 | 91 | 92 | 93 | 94 | 95 | 96 | 97 | 98 | 99 | 100 | 101 | 102 | 103 |
| UNITED STATES............ | 114 761 359 | 66.1 | 186 200 | 25.0 | 12.6 | 871 | 30.9 | 3.7 | 155 049 194 | 0.3 | 12 512 946 | 8.1 | 141 832 499 | 35.7 | 21.8 |
| ALABAMA ...................... | 1 831 269 | 70.7 | 120 800 | 22.2 | 11.7 | 674 | 30.7 | 2.4 | 2 156 301 | -1.2 | 157 119 | 7.3 | 2 027 919 | 31.6 | 26.9 |
| Autauga........................... | 19 998 | 77.7 | 137 500 | 21.4 | 10.8 | 832 | 27.6 | 2.6 | 25 480 | -0.9 | 1 644 | 6.5 | 24 139 | 31.2 | 25.1 |
| Baldwin........................... | 70 757 | 76.2 | 175 700 | 24.2 | 11.3 | 863 | 30.4 | 2.5 | 83 743 | -0.5 | 5 666 | 6.8 | 79 963 | 32.3 | 22.2 |
| Barbour........................... | 9 589 | 66.4 | 91 600 | 22.2 | 14.3 | 547 | 33.6 | 3.3 | 9 088 | -4.8 | 1 016 | 11.2 | 9 637 | 27.0 | 33.7 |
| Bibb................................ | 7 225 | 83.0 | 87 500 | 21.7 | 11.1 | 558 | 26.4 | 1.0 | 9 083 | -0.8 | 694 | 7.6 | 9 353 | 21.5 | 39.5 |
| Blount............................. | 20 954 | 79.9 | 111 500 | 21.7 | 11.0 | 561 | 24.5 | 3.0 | 26 358 | -0.6 | 1 639 | 6.2 | 24 174 | 25.2 | 34.0 |
| Bullock........................... | 3 760 | 79.6 | 68 000 | 23.9 | 14.3 | 402 | 39.6 | 2.7 | 3 533 | -3.9 | 473 | 13.4 | 4 007 | 21.8 | 43.0 |
| Butler............................. | 8 090 | 71.1 | 74 300 | 24.1 | 14.4 | 522 | 33.0 | 3.3 | 8 903 | -1.8 | 966 | 10.9 | 8 076 | 24.1 | 31.5 |
| Calhoun.......................... | 45 923 | 70.1 | 99 600 | 21.7 | 11.8 | 593 | 30.5 | 1.6 | 52 372 | -2.6 | 3 966 | 7.6 | 47 597 | 26.8 | 31.9 |
| Chambers........................ | 13 562 | 71.4 | 82 400 | 23.0 | 12.8 | 605 | 32.8 | 2.8 | 14 659 | -1.1 | 1 360 | 9.3 | 13 570 | 23.5 | 34.4 |
| Cherokee......................... | 11 508 | 75.8 | 96 200 | 22.1 | 13.5 | 524 | 31.0 | 1.7 | 11 455 | -1.6 | 814 | 7.1 | 10 369 | 25.0 | 39.8 |
| Chilton............................ | 16 277 | 75.3 | 104 300 | 22.8 | 12.0 | 607 | 30.5 | 3.6 | 19 920 | -0.6 | 1 298 | 6.5 | 18 051 | 24.9 | 35.9 |
| Choctaw.......................... | 5 165 | 84.8 | 61 400 | 22.2 | 13.1 | 613 | 29.6 | 3.1 | 4 992 | -0.4 | 447 | 9.0 | 4 439 | 28.3 | 39.6 |
| Clarke............................. | 9 114 | 77.1 | 79 900 | 21.4 | 14.5 | 488 | 30.6 | 3.2 | 9 566 | -4.8 | 1 160 | 12.1 | 8 488 | 27.2 | 35.1 |
| Clay................................ | 5 837 | 76.4 | 83 400 | 24.1 | 10.8 | 424 | 23.4 | 3.9 | 5 044 | -3.8 | 470 | 9.3 | 5 608 | 25.4 | 43.5 |
| Cleburne......................... | 5 521 | 78.5 | 88 200 | 20.8 | 11.1 | 549 | 29.2 | 4.9 | 6 272 | -1.8 | 434 | 6.9 | 5 996 | 25.5 | 38.7 |
| Coffee............................. | 18 799 | 70.6 | 121 800 | 21.5 | 9.9 | 606 | 28.5 | 2.0 | 21 256 | -1.7 | 1 316 | 6.2 | 19 379 | 32.5 | 28.3 |
| Colbert............................ | 22 322 | 72.7 | 97 300 | 21.1 | 12.2 | 592 | 28.8 | 1.6 | 24 971 | -1.1 | 1 889 | 7.6 | 22 318 | 27.3 | 32.5 |
| Conecuh.......................... | 4 712 | 79.4 | 76 700 | 20.1 | 12.8 | 516 | 37.3 | 5.3 | 4 312 | -4.0 | 502 | 11.6 | 4 029 | 27.1 | 32.4 |
| Coosa............................. | 4 667 | 84.6 | 79 200 | 25.2 | 13.6 | 513 | 35.1 | 3.2 | 4 243 | -0.4 | 347 | 8.2 | 4 424 | 20.9 | 41.7 |
| Covington........................ | 14 742 | 74.0 | 86 100 | 21.8 | 13.7 | 535 | 31.5 | 3.4 | 16 548 | -0.3 | 1 245 | 7.5 | 15 322 | 24.3 | 36.8 |
| Crenshaw........................ | 5 650 | 69.1 | 75 400 | 23.1 | 12.9 | 505 | 21.7 | 1.7 | 6 462 | -3.3 | 466 | 7.2 | 5 886 | 28.6 | 31.8 |
| Cullman.......................... | 31 364 | 75.3 | 102 300 | 22.1 | 11.7 | 592 | 29.9 | 2.1 | 38 205 | 0.0 | 2 447 | 6.4 | 33 204 | 26.1 | 34.9 |
| Dale................................ | 19 454 | 61.3 | 96 800 | 18.5 | 9.9 | 619 | 25.8 | 1.9 | 19 859 | -1.9 | 1 446 | 7.3 | 19 746 | 25.7 | 31.5 |
| Dallas............................. | 16 913 | 61.5 | 70 200 | 22.2 | 15.2 | 553 | 37.8 | 7.2 | 14 464 | -4.1 | 1 986 | 13.7 | 14 867 | 25.4 | 36.1 |
| DeKalb............................ | 26 196 | 78.0 | 87 400 | 23.2 | 12.1 | 522 | 26.1 | 5.2 | 27 998 | -3.4 | 2 373 | 8.5 | 28 745 | 23.0 | 41.9 |
| Elmore............................ | 28 085 | 76.9 | 143 200 | 22.0 | 10.9 | 709 | 28.1 | 3.2 | 35 119 | -0.8 | 2 402 | 6.8 | 33 540 | 34.8 | 24.3 |
| Escambia......................... | 13 860 | 72.0 | 84 500 | 20.4 | 13.4 | 549 | 36.3 | 2.6 | 14 404 | -2.1 | 1 285 | 8.9 | 13 097 | 26.7 | 29.9 |
| Etowah............................ | 41 160 | 73.3 | 102 000 | 22.3 | 13.1 | 600 | 28.5 | 2.2 | 45 402 | -0.9 | 3 275 | 7.2 | 40 621 | 29.5 | 31.0 |
| Fayette............................ | 7 240 | 73.7 | 72 200 | 22.4 | 11.8 | 495 | 33.9 | 1.0 | 6 443 | -2.5 | 513 | 8.0 | 6 723 | 24.2 | 39.7 |
| Franklin........................... | 12 376 | 68.9 | 81 400 | 20.8 | 12.6 | 506 | 26.8 | 3.7 | 13 126 | -2.3 | 1 071 | 8.2 | 13 280 | 20.6 | 44.4 |
| Geneva............................ | 10 892 | 71.2 | 82 000 | 21.8 | 9.9 | 538 | 27.4 | 2.8 | 10 913 | -2.2 | 757 | 6.9 | 11 233 | 22.5 | 35.3 |
| Greene............................ | 3 357 | 71.4 | 77 100 | 29.1 | 14.9 | 494 | 35.8 | 3.9 | 3 054 | -1.5 | 347 | 11.4 | 2 925 | 22.4 | 34.6 |
| Hale................................ | 5 858 | 75.8 | 73 500 | 23.9 | 18.0 | 469 | 28.9 | 3.5 | 5 663 | -0.9 | 560 | 9.9 | 5 734 | 23.2 | 39.7 |
| Henry.............................. | 6 783 | 80.7 | 95 100 | 22.2 | 12.1 | 528 | 28.4 | 1.2 | 7 057 | -2.0 | 515 | 7.3 | 6 681 | 26.7 | 30.4 |
| Houston........................... | 38 500 | 66.8 | 120 500 | 20.1 | 10.0 | 626 | 28.5 | 1.8 | 45 224 | -1.9 | 3 168 | 7.0 | 44 251 | 29.8 | 26.0 |
| Jackson........................... | 21 629 | 76.2 | 88 900 | 21.8 | 11.1 | 498 | 29.9 | 2.0 | 25 697 | -2.1 | 1 817 | 7.1 | 21 999 | 24.8 | 39.8 |
| Jefferson......................... | 259 394 | 66.0 | 141 700 | 23.7 | 12.5 | 779 | 32.5 | 1.6 | 305 558 | -0.5 | 20 692 | 6.8 | 297 766 | 36.4 | 19.3 |
| Lamar.............................. | 6 016 | 73.4 | 70 000 | 19.3 | 11.2 | 401 | 27.7 | 1.3 | 5 296 | -1.1 | 401 | 7.6 | 5 783 | 24.7 | 38.7 |
| Lauderdale....................... | 38 315 | 71.3 | 108 100 | 21.8 | 10.6 | 570 | 31.6 | 1.3 | 44 351 | -1.3 | 2 962 | 6.7 | 39 302 | 28.1 | 27.2 |
| Lawrence......................... | 13 531 | 78.7 | 95 000 | 22.5 | 12.8 | 493 | 26.8 | 1.1 | 15 246 | -2.0 | 1 232 | 8.1 | 14 002 | 23.6 | 38.5 |
| Lee.................................. | 55 176 | 63.2 | 144 100 | 23.3 | 12.6 | 707 | 33.6 | 2.0 | 68 739 | 1.2 | 4 316 | 6.3 | 62 255 | 36.8 | 23.8 |
| Limestone....................... | 30 821 | 77.2 | 128 700 | 21.4 | 9.9 | 579 | 27.9 | 3.3 | 40 004 | -1.0 | 2 491 | 6.2 | 34 539 | 32.8 | 29.7 |
| Lowndes.......................... | 4 215 | 74.2 | 64 900 | 26.6 | 18.8 | 563 | 30.2 | 6.3 | 4 114 | -2.1 | 580 | 14.1 | 3 906 | 18.5 | 40.1 |
| Macon............................. | 8 031 | 67.9 | 77 900 | 26.5 | 14.0 | 573 | 36.5 | 2.8 | 8 547 | -2.2 | 837 | 9.8 | 8 109 | 23.0 | 24.1 |
| Madison........................... | 128 869 | 70.1 | 160 400 | 19.3 | 9.9 | 701 | 27.8 | 1.7 | 171 797 | -1.0 | 10 704 | 6.2 | 157 335 | 43.3 | 18.4 |
| Marengo.......................... | 8 359 | 73.4 | 88 500 | 21.5 | 11.7 | 482 | 31.8 | 3.6 | 7 622 | -2.5 | 713 | 9.4 | 7 660 | 26.6 | 35.1 |
| Marion............................. | 12 806 | 75.3 | 75 900 | 23.3 | 12.0 | 431 | 28.4 | 2.1 | 11 266 | -2.1 | 1 027 | 9.1 | 11 880 | 25.4 | 38.6 |
| Marshall.......................... | 34 587 | 72.2 | 107 000 | 21.5 | 11.5 | 587 | 29.2 | 3.8 | 40 310 | -0.9 | 2 837 | 7.0 | 38 481 | 26.1 | 36.7 |
| Mobile............................. | 155 638 | 67.9 | 124 100 | 23.2 | 12.5 | 723 | 34.0 | 2.8 | 186 408 | -2.6 | 15 617 | 8.4 | 173 345 | 29.8 | 25.7 |
| Monroe............................ | 8 943 | 74.5 | 77 900 | 21.8 | 12.9 | 536 | 32.6 | 2.3 | 7 432 | -5.2 | 912 | 12.3 | 8 243 | 24.1 | 38.3 |
| Montgomery ..................... | 88 091 | 63.1 | 124 000 | 22.8 | 10.5 | 780 | 33.4 | 2.6 | 103 607 | -1.0 | 8 000 | 7.7 | 101 275 | 35.3 | 19.8 |
| Morgan............................ | 46 129 | 72.1 | 117 300 | 20.4 | 10.0 | 588 | 25.4 | 2.3 | 56 840 | -1.5 | 3 994 | 7.0 | 53 277 | 29.3 | 31.1 |
| Perry............................... | 3 690 | 63.6 | 62 200 | 21.7 | 16.3 | 448 | 38.1 | 7.7 | 3 457 | -4.3 | 446 | 12.9 | 3 225 | 26.2 | 28.5 |
| Pickens........................... | 7 852 | 72.3 | 81 200 | 20.7 | 12.6 | 456 | 31.0 | 1.8 | 7 706 | -2.3 | 692 | 9.0 | 7 050 | 19.9 | 37.3 |
| Pike................................. | 12 967 | 56.4 | 102 800 | 21.4 | 11.6 | 553 | 35.3 | 2.2 | 15 484 | -2.3 | 1 079 | 7.0 | 14 136 | 27.7 | 28.2 |
| Randolph......................... | 8 949 | 74.1 | 91 200 | 23.2 | 12.0 | 531 | 29.0 | 5.7 | 8 596 | -4.3 | 762 | 8.9 | 9 121 | 24.9 | 39.8 |
| Russell............................ | 20 453 | 63.2 | 96 200 | 24.5 | 12.7 | 668 | 31.8 | 3.0 | 23 132 | -0.4 | 2 113 | 9.1 | 21 055 | 22.8 | 27.4 |
| St. Clair.......................... | 30 588 | 81.3 | 129 700 | 22.8 | 11.0 | 720 | 26.5 | 2.5 | 37 834 | -0.4 | 2 405 | 6.4 | 35 417 | 27.8 | 31.3 |
| Shelby............................. | 72 694 | 79.8 | 198 900 | 21.8 | 10.1 | 869 | 26.8 | 1.6 | 104 461 | 0.1 | 5 192 | 5.0 | 96 110 | 42.2 | 16.5 |
| Sumter............................ | 5 036 | 67.6 | 75 300 | 22.9 | 17.6 | 479 | 47.0 | 5.2 | 4 476 | -2.4 | 521 | 11.6 | 4 923 | 25.2 | 28.9 |
| Talladega......................... | 31 597 | 70.7 | 89 100 | 22.6 | 13.3 | 571 | 30.7 | 2.7 | 36 856 | -0.9 | 2 997 | 8.1 | 31 603 | 24.7 | 35.3 |
| Tallapoosa....................... | 16 404 | 73.5 | 96 600 | 22.6 | 10.9 | 557 | 29.1 | 4.3 | 17 333 | -0.5 | 1 479 | 8.5 | 17 690 | 28.4 | 34.6 |
| Tuscaloosa....................... | 68 711 | 63.8 | 150 600 | 22.4 | 10.2 | 749 | 35.0 | 1.9 | 92 770 | -0.1 | 6 140 | 6.6 | 85 727 | 32.3 | 26.7 |
| Walker............................. | 25 779 | 77.1 | 83 600 | 20.9 | 12.4 | 577 | 29.1 | 1.7 | 27 395 | -0.5 | 2 049 | 7.5 | 24 776 | 24.4 | 34.5 |

1. Specified owner-occupied units.    2. A value of 9.9 represents 9.9 percent or less.    3. Specified renter-occupied units. A value of 10.0 represents 10 percent or less.    4. Overcrowded or lacking complete plumbing facilities.    5. Percent of civilian labor force.    6. Persons 16 years old and over.

| STATE County | Number of establish-ments | Total | Health care and social assistance | Manufac-turing | Retail trade | Finance and insurance | Professional, scientific, and technical services | Total (mil dol) | Average per employee (dollars) | Number | Fewer than 50 acres | 500 acres or more | Farm operators whose principal occu-pation is farming (percent) |
|---|---|---|---|---|---|---|---|---|---|---|---|---|---|
| | Private nonfarm establishments, employment and payroll, 2011 | | | | | | | | | Agriculture, 2007 | | | |
| | | Employment | | | | | | Annual payroll | | Farms | | Percent with: | |
| | 104 | 105 | 106 | 107 | 108 | 109 | 110 | 111 | 112 | 113 | 114 | 115 | 116 |
| UNITED STATES | 7 354 043 | 113 425 965 | 18 059 112 | 10 984 361 | 14 698 563 | 5 886 602 | 7 929 910 | 5 164 898 | 45 535 | 2 204 792 | 38.7 | 14.6 | 45.1 |
| ALABAMA | 97 743 | 1 573 138 | 235 237 | 227 628 | 225 793 | 69 040 | 93 488 | 59 241 | 37 658 | 48 753 | 40.2 | 7.7 | 39.8 |
| Autauga | 835 | 10 290 | 1 381 | D | 2 726 | 417 | 280 | 277 | 26 888 | 415 | 29.4 | 11.6 | 36.1 |
| Baldwin | 4 624 | 51 386 | 6 560 | 3 575 | 12 468 | 1 574 | 1 742 | 1 516 | 29 505 | 1 139 | 52.4 | 8.8 | 42.0 |
| Barbour | 501 | 7 572 | 725 | 3 436 | 975 | 230 | 110 | 220 | 29 053 | 623 | 19.7 | 16.1 | 36.4 |
| Bibb | 285 | 2 980 | 590 | 359 | 540 | 76 | 40 | 96 | 32 152 | 211 | 37.4 | 9.0 | 37.9 |
| Blount | 690 | 6 345 | 890 | 1 264 | 1 221 | 264 | 189 | 178 | 28 054 | 1 414 | 45.2 | 2.6 | 42.9 |
| Bullock | 113 | D | D | D | 257 | D | 18 | D | D | 277 | 20.6 | 31.4 | 48.7 |
| Butler | 411 | 5 354 | D | 1 091 | 942 | 151 | D | 143 | 26 792 | 490 | 28.8 | 6.7 | 44.7 |
| Calhoun | 2 333 | 36 093 | 6 095 | 5 900 | 6 207 | 915 | 1 557 | 1 166 | 32 318 | 735 | 51.6 | 2.0 | 40.7 |
| Chambers | 557 | 6 419 | 1 310 | 1 394 | 1 156 | D | 122 | 195 | 30 325 | 336 | 27.1 | 18.5 | 37.5 |
| Cherokee | 351 | 3 590 | 430 | 1 055 | 847 | D | 49 | 100 | 27 783 | 654 | 36.4 | 9.3 | 33.0 |
| Chilton | 709 | 6 644 | 777 | 1 305 | 1 425 | 242 | 106 | 186 | 28 015 | 645 | 38.8 | 6.4 | 46.0 |
| Choctaw | 264 | 2 754 | 309 | D | 353 | 96 | 49 | 133 | 48 164 | 264 | 39.4 | 10.6 | 42.4 |
| Clarke | 601 | 6 430 | 961 | 1 450 | 1 493 | D | 82 | 202 | 31 423 | 321 | 37.4 | 10.0 | 31.5 |
| Clay | 184 | 3 001 | 627 | 1 262 | 295 | 93 | D | 81 | 27 086 | 432 | 28.2 | 6.9 | 39.1 |
| Cleburne | 157 | 1 567 | 63 | D | 303 | 61 | D | 57 | 36 592 | 380 | 38.4 | 2.1 | 49.5 |
| Coffee | 953 | 12 407 | 2 011 | 3 217 | 2 275 | 543 | 536 | 340 | 27 394 | 971 | 29.4 | 8.5 | 36.6 |
| Colbert | 1 257 | 18 980 | 2 830 | 4 355 | 2 846 | D | 967 | 667 | 35 159 | 736 | 47.8 | 7.2 | 33.6 |
| Conecuh | 212 | 2 316 | D | 349 | 321 | 46 | 16 | 67 | 28 852 | 401 | 29.7 | 9.7 | 45.4 |
| Coosa | 90 | 921 | 29 | 587 | 96 | 10 | 11 | 29 | 31 417 | 207 | 19.3 | 13.0 | 36.7 |
| Covington | 864 | 10 827 | 1 790 | 2 469 | 1 956 | 331 | 293 | 314 | 29 040 | 1 096 | 31.2 | 6.4 | 40.1 |
| Crenshaw | 237 | 3 280 | 529 | 1 127 | 292 | 93 | 41 | 102 | 31 210 | 638 | 22.4 | 9.2 | 35.1 |
| Cullman | 1 693 | 21 195 | 3 426 | 4 056 | 3 289 | 730 | 460 | 671 | 31 647 | 2 465 | 49.9 | 1.9 | 45.2 |
| Dale | 815 | 13 631 | 1 396 | 331 | 1 198 | 394 | 932 | 596 | 43 759 | 528 | 24.8 | 12.9 | 35.4 |
| Dallas | 785 | 10 789 | 2 110 | 3 240 | 1 804 | 330 | 205 | 330 | 30 595 | 555 | 28.1 | 23.8 | 36.4 |
| DeKalb | 1 095 | 16 549 | 2 264 | 6 334 | 2 385 | 480 | 418 | 486 | 29 388 | 2 426 | 49.5 | 2.4 | 43.0 |
| Elmore | 1 096 | 14 103 | 2 070 | 3 352 | 2 742 | 412 | 415 | 413 | 29 301 | 626 | 47.4 | 6.5 | 39.5 |
| Escambia | 747 | 9 454 | 1 231 | 1 443 | 1 690 | 443 | 169 | 292 | 30 840 | 502 | 41.6 | 13.3 | 44.4 |
| Etowah | 1 979 | 28 470 | 7 041 | 4 709 | 4 410 | 1 004 | 630 | 892 | 31 344 | 1 004 | 52.7 | 2.1 | 33.5 |
| Fayette | 334 | 3 656 | 851 | 633 | 631 | 91 | D | 116 | 31 699 | 401 | 21.9 | 9.0 | 31.9 |
| Franklin | 549 | 9 765 | 1 197 | D | 1 020 | 356 | D | 280 | 28 704 | 958 | 29.9 | 5.2 | 41.6 |
| Geneva | 417 | 3 884 | 645 | D | 778 | 191 | D | 115 | 29 653 | 1 108 | 30.3 | 8.1 | 40.5 |
| Greene | 97 | 1 102 | D | 369 | 172 | 28 | 8 | 35 | 31 583 | 316 | 20.3 | 20.6 | 49.7 |
| Hale | 189 | 2 151 | 430 | D | 339 | 69 | D | 63 | 29 126 | 479 | 24.8 | 19.8 | 45.1 |
| Henry | 300 | 2 739 | D | 264 | 393 | 130 | 38 | 83 | 30 325 | 478 | 19.2 | 17.2 | 44.6 |
| Houston | 2 746 | 43 457 | 9 031 | 4 180 | 7 923 | 1 086 | 1 205 | 1 485 | 34 183 | 841 | 37.2 | 10.2 | 40.5 |
| Jackson | 845 | 11 683 | 1 535 | 4 840 | 1 900 | 356 | 313 | 344 | 29 403 | 1 523 | 44.4 | 6.4 | 32.1 |
| Jefferson | 16 278 | 313 651 | 53 236 | 23 472 | 38 756 | 22 032 | 16 340 | 13 991 | 44 605 | 470 | 58.9 | 2.8 | 38.5 |
| Lamar | 246 | 2 758 | D | D | 335 | 135 | 59 | 90 | 32 661 | 422 | 32.5 | 6.2 | 30.3 |
| Lauderdale | 1 968 | 24 479 | 4 246 | 2 991 | 5 325 | 944 | 837 | 664 | 27 145 | 1 697 | 46.8 | 4.5 | 34.1 |
| Lawrence | 407 | 4 734 | 701 | D | 810 | 115 | D | 225 | 47 494 | 1 601 | 43.8 | 3.9 | 40.0 |
| Lee | 2 343 | 35 565 | 5 462 | 5 402 | 6 352 | 854 | 1 149 | 1 014 | 28 498 | 356 | 40.4 | 7.3 | 46.3 |
| Limestone | 1 228 | 13 590 | 1 788 | 2 565 | 2 651 | D | 453 | 437 | 32 157 | 1 352 | 47.6 | 6.1 | 35.1 |
| Lowndes | 114 | 2 145 | D | 1 208 | 219 | 45 | D | 109 | 50 730 | 405 | 24.7 | 24.2 | 45.9 |
| Macon | 201 | 5 269 | D | D | 411 | D | 38 | 191 | 36 245 | 385 | 26.8 | 15.3 | 32.7 |
| Madison | 7 997 | 149 519 | 20 567 | 16 452 | 18 820 | 3 336 | 34 666 | 6 924 | 46 308 | 1 187 | 52.9 | 6.8 | 43.9 |
| Marengo | 475 | 5 583 | 913 | 1 332 | 988 | 200 | 78 | 186 | 33 237 | 555 | 25.0 | 17.1 | 40.2 |
| Marion | 521 | 6 622 | 1 238 | 2 112 | 1 011 | 314 | 82 | 208 | 31 347 | 787 | 30.1 | 2.9 | 35.6 |
| Marshall | 1 834 | 31 089 | 3 681 | 9 932 | 4 660 | 821 | 730 | 891 | 28 667 | 1 731 | 55.6 | 1.8 | 39.5 |
| Mobile | 8 659 | 149 033 | 22 199 | 16 198 | 20 241 | 5 537 | 9 726 | 5 845 | 39 218 | 876 | 60.8 | 4.8 | 39.7 |
| Monroe | 393 | 5 190 | 740 | 993 | 890 | 185 | D | 194 | 37 321 | 505 | 43.8 | 11.1 | 41.6 |
| Montgomery | 5 541 | 98 984 | 15 787 | 11 903 | 12 960 | 4 234 | 6 065 | 3 837 | 38 769 | 620 | 32.6 | 22.4 | 42.1 |
| Morgan | 2 654 | 42 646 | 5 904 | 11 319 | 5 837 | 1 419 | 1 743 | 1 562 | 36 624 | 1 457 | 50.2 | 3.8 | 37.8 |
| Perry | 131 | 1 434 | 165 | 356 | 177 | 75 | D | 39 | 27 397 | 390 | 25.6 | 20.3 | 43.8 |
| Pickens | 280 | 2 716 | 732 | 526 | 424 | 188 | 32 | 75 | 27 787 | 503 | 29.8 | 8.7 | 47.7 |
| Pike | 643 | 10 431 | 1 198 | 1 555 | 1 496 | 342 | D | 347 | 33 295 | 709 | 26.8 | 12.8 | 37.7 |
| Randolph | 339 | 3 493 | 687 | 875 | 758 | 158 | 43 | 89 | 25 614 | 610 | 26.7 | 7.0 | 41.1 |
| Russell | 834 | 10 598 | 1 374 | D | 1 877 | 438 | 222 | 335 | 31 610 | 303 | 35.3 | 14.5 | 39.3 |
| St. Clair | 1 203 | 12 870 | 1 451 | 2 469 | 2 257 | 438 | 395 | 390 | 30 283 | 621 | 46.2 | 2.7 | 39.6 |
| Shelby | 4 802 | 74 851 | 5 877 | 5 102 | 9 500 | 9 551 | 4 099 | 3 351 | 44 767 | 474 | 51.3 | 4.2 | 39.5 |
| Sumter | 205 | 2 655 | 586 | D | 314 | 58 | D | 78 | 29 432 | 431 | 24.6 | 21.8 | 40.6 |
| Talladega | 1 283 | 21 592 | 2 765 | 7 917 | 2 806 | 574 | D | 807 | 37 392 | 625 | 40.2 | 7.2 | 40.5 |
| Tallapoosa | 739 | 9 674 | 2 160 | 1 719 | 1 647 | 345 | 202 | 286 | 29 614 | 377 | 31.0 | 4.5 | 32.4 |
| Tuscaloosa | 3 968 | 70 099 | 11 508 | 11 770 | 9 886 | 1 680 | 2 180 | 2 727 | 38 903 | 613 | 40.3 | 8.2 | 41.3 |
| Walker | 1 279 | 14 861 | 3 283 | 1 875 | 3 223 | 595 | 510 | 492 | 33 095 | 629 | 51.4 | 3.7 | 42.0 |

# Table B. States and Counties — Agriculture

| STATE County | Land in farms | | | | | Value of land and buildings (dollars) | | Value of machinery and equipment, average per farm (dollars) | Value of products sold | | | | Percent of farms with sales of: | | Government payments | |
|---|---|---|---|---|---|---|---|---|---|---|---|---|---|---|---|---|
| | Acreage (1,000) | Percent change, 2002–2007 | Acres | | | Average per farm | Average per acre | | Total (mil dol) | Average per farm (dollars) | Percent from: | | $10,000 or more | $100,000 or more | Total ($1,000) | Percent of farms |
| | | | Average size of farm | Total irrigated (1,000) | Total cropland (1,000) | | | | | | Crops | Live-stock and poultry products | | | | |
| | 117 | 118 | 119 | 120 | 121 | 122 | 123 | 124 | 125 | 126 | 127 | 128 | 129 | 130 | 131 | 132 |
| UNITED STATES............ | 922 096 | -1.7 | 418 | 56 599.3 | 406 424.9 | 791 138 | 1 892 | 88 357 | 297 220.5 | 134 807 | 48.3 | 51.7 | 40.2 | 16.2 | 7 983 922 | 38.0 |
| ALABAMA ...................... | 9 034 | 1.5 | 185 | 112.8 | 3 143.0 | 424 674 | 2 292 | 60 810 | 4 415.6 | 90 570 | 15.3 | 84.7 | 30.8 | 9.7 | 124 692 | 29.6 |
| Autauga.......................... | 110 | -6.8 | 266 | 1.2 | 42.3 | 518 368 | 1 947 | 61 478 | 16.8 | 40 405 | D | D | 30.8 | 5.3 | 1 357 | 28.4 |
| Baldwin........................... | 190 | 5.0 | 167 | 10.2 | 103.0 | 544 907 | 3 270 | 76 160 | 100.3 | 88 087 | 80.4 | 19.6 | 31.9 | 9.6 | 5 144 | 27.0 |
| Barbour........................... | 199 | 4.2 | 320 | 2.8 | 56.9 | 562 887 | 1 761 | 57 809 | 71.4 | 114 628 | 8.4 | 91.6 | 27.6 | 9.1 | 2 647 | 60.7 |
| Bibb................................ | 38 | -15.6 | 181 | 0.2 | 8.6 | 405 116 | 2 244 | 42 852 | D | D | D | D | 24.6 | 2.8 | 61 | 10.4 |
| Blount............................ | 151 | 5.6 | 107 | 0.6 | 46.7 | 342 438 | 3 201 | 56 286 | 160.2 | 113 327 | 4.2 | 95.8 | 35.9 | 12.7 | 583 | 15.3 |
| Bullock........................... | 134 | -8.2 | 484 | D | 32.9 | 977 472 | 2 021 | 80 117 | 40.8 | 147 278 | 67.4 | 32.6 | 36.5 | 9.7 | 1 074 | 30.7 |
| Butler............................. | 93 | 12.0 | 189 | 0.1 | 25.2 | 402 861 | 2 132 | 60 671 | 95.2 | 194 360 | 2.3 | 97.7 | 27.6 | 9.6 | 633 | 30.2 |
| Calhoun.......................... | 76 | 1.3 | 104 | 1.7 | 26.0 | 329 225 | 3 176 | 56 359 | 69.1 | 93 960 | 14.8 | 85.2 | 25.3 | 7.8 | 391 | 13.3 |
| Chambers....................... | 105 | 12.9 | 312 | 0.3 | 14.3 | 565 077 | 1 809 | 49 848 | 6.5 | 19 386 | D | D | 26.8 | 6.0 | 320 | 22.0 |
| Cherokee........................ | 133 | 9.9 | 203 | 1.2 | 58.3 | 442 197 | 2 176 | 75 888 | 60.0 | 91 744 | 28.3 | 71.7 | 29.5 | 6.9 | 2 838 | 44.6 |
| Chilton........................... | 100 | 2.0 | 155 | 0.7 | 28.8 | 431 332 | 2 776 | 52 825 | 15.2 | 23 635 | 56.4 | 43.6 | 31.8 | 3.9 | 322 | 11.0 |
| Choctaw.......................... | 55 | 0.0 | 208 | D | 9.3 | 358 189 | 1 719 | 50 383 | 11.2 | 42 423 | 4.1 | 95.9 | 20.1 | 3.8 | 95 | 12.9 |
| Clarke............................ | 74 | 29.8 | 230 | 0.1 | 10.6 | 376 945 | 1 641 | 39 578 | D | D | D | D | 19.0 | 0.6 | 223 | 19.9 |
| Clay............................... | 74 | -11.9 | 172 | 0.0 | 14.2 | 403 829 | 2 344 | 61 856 | 34.3 | 79 351 | 1.8 | 98.2 | 35.4 | 7.2 | 99 | 13.2 |
| Cleburne........................ | 49 | 11.4 | 130 | 0.5 | 12.2 | 400 588 | 3 076 | 60 095 | 66.6 | 175 330 | 2.4 | 97.6 | 37.6 | 17.1 | 58 | 11.8 |
| Coffee............................ | 211 | 7.1 | 217 | 4.2 | 80.7 | 472 149 | 2 171 | 65 967 | 196.6 | 202 436 | 6.6 | 93.4 | 31.3 | 14.5 | 5 695 | 64.1 |
| Colbert........................... | 129 | -2.3 | 175 | 2.4 | 60.0 | 377 879 | 2 158 | 59 190 | 42.4 | 57 648 | 22.7 | 77.3 | 26.0 | 6.1 | 2 843 | 36.3 |
| Conecuh......................... | 86 | 4.9 | 215 | 0.1 | 22.7 | 394 747 | 1 834 | 50 249 | 7.9 | 19 756 | 24.2 | 75.8 | 27.4 | 2.7 | 903 | 42.9 |
| Coosa............................. | 45 | 15.4 | 219 | 0.0 | 8.5 | 457 731 | 2 087 | 42 972 | D | D | D | 0.0 | 30.9 | 1.0 | 19 | 9.2 |
| Covington....................... | 200 | -1.0 | 183 | 1.2 | 64.1 | 409 242 | 2 241 | 59 559 | 85.6 | 78 110 | 12.6 | 87.4 | 29.8 | 10.4 | 3 980 | 48.2 |
| Crenshaw....................... | 132 | 1.5 | 208 | 0.7 | 33.5 | 442 221 | 2 131 | 56 913 | 112.0 | 175 513 | 1.1 | 98.9 | 32.3 | 14.4 | 1 516 | 51.1 |
| Cullman.......................... | 230 | -0.4 | 93 | 0.8 | 87.8 | 346 699 | 3 719 | 68 459 | 405.9 | 164 654 | 2.1 | 97.9 | 43.1 | 21.4 | 916 | 13.6 |
| Dale............................... | 138 | -0.7 | 262 | 2.6 | 54.2 | 552 202 | 2 110 | 66 705 | 76.3 | 144 444 | 10.4 | 89.6 | 31.8 | 13.6 | 2 307 | 52.7 |
| Dallas............................ | 257 | 8.9 | 463 | 2.9 | 83.1 | 763 677 | 1 649 | 80 264 | 43.9 | 79 187 | 27.1 | 72.9 | 30.3 | 8.3 | 5 069 | 46.1 |
| DeKalb........................... | 235 | -0.8 | 97 | 1.0 | 91.7 | 335 689 | 3 462 | 58 895 | 414.3 | 170 775 | 2.9 | 97.1 | 37.0 | 17.0 | 1 383 | 23.4 |
| Elmore............................ | 103 | -1.0 | 164 | 2.0 | 43.4 | 427 939 | 2 606 | 59 112 | 15.0 | 23 901 | 62.9 | 37.1 | 24.1 | 5.1 | 1 526 | 19.5 |
| Escambia........................ | 113 | 20.2 | 225 | 1.9 | 58.3 | 473 576 | 2 107 | 82 735 | 23.5 | 46 754 | 83.8 | 16.2 | 31.3 | 12.5 | 5 344 | 44.0 |
| Etowah........................... | 94 | 4.4 | 94 | 0.6 | 29.6 | 282 306 | 3 009 | 44 457 | 66.2 | 65 894 | 5.3 | 94.7 | 23.2 | 7.0 | 518 | 11.2 |
| Fayette........................... | 79 | 5.3 | 197 | 0.4 | 24.1 | 334 144 | 1 700 | 62 850 | 13.0 | 32 314 | 15.7 | 84.3 | 25.2 | 2.7 | 724 | 40.9 |
| Franklin.......................... | 141 | -3.4 | 147 | 0.2 | 36.1 | 310 585 | 2 112 | 45 661 | 133.5 | 139 302 | 1.2 | 98.8 | 36.5 | 14.4 | 491 | 21.6 |
| Geneva........................... | 221 | -2.6 | 199 | 3.0 | 90.0 | 411 435 | 2 066 | 57 252 | 130.6 | 117 859 | 14.3 | 85.7 | 32.9 | 13.3 | 6 583 | 61.6 |
| Greene............................ | 136 | 6.3 | 429 | 0.3 | 36.3 | 663 679 | 1 546 | 66 754 | 23.0 | 72 831 | 4.3 | 95.7 | 30.7 | 8.9 | 842 | 37.7 |
| Hale................................ | 169 | 5.0 | 353 | 0.1 | 35.6 | 646 418 | 1 829 | 86 369 | 57.8 | 120 732 | D | D | 37.2 | 12.3 | 1 200 | 38.6 |
| Henry.............................. | 166 | 9.9 | 347 | 5.0 | 79.7 | 629 450 | 1 816 | 79 994 | 39.6 | 82 863 | 35.7 | 64.3 | 37.2 | 10.0 | 4 820 | 59.6 |
| Houston.......................... | 205 | 9.0 | 243 | 13.4 | 114.9 | 517 102 | 2 125 | 72 552 | 55.7 | 66 196 | 54.3 | 45.7 | 33.8 | 9.5 | 8 206 | 57.6 |
| Jackson.......................... | 243 | 6.1 | 159 | 0.7 | 112.5 | 336 077 | 2 108 | 55 577 | 99.7 | 65 443 | 14.2 | 85.8 | 27.9 | 7.6 | 2 037 | 32.0 |
| Jefferson......................... | 40 | -4.8 | 86 | 0.2 | 12.2 | 295 663 | 3 435 | 45 990 | D | D | 0.0 | D | 17.2 | 0.9 | 74 | 7.2 |
| Lamar............................. | 85 | -2.3 | 201 | 0.1 | 18.6 | 285 879 | 1 425 | 43 373 | D | D | D | 0.0 | 14.7 | 0.9 | 416 | 34.1 |
| Lauderdale...................... | 228 | 9.6 | 134 | 1.1 | 108.2 | 312 507 | 2 329 | 49 841 | 45.0 | 26 497 | 35.1 | 64.9 | 26.9 | 4.7 | 4 399 | 33.9 |
| Lawrence........................ | 222 | -5.1 | 139 | 4.1 | 116.1 | 361 656 | 2 603 | 62 009 | 145.0 | 90 589 | 12.2 | 87.8 | 28.7 | 9.1 | 6 311 | 43.4 |
| Lee................................. | 63 | -14.9 | 177 | 0.8 | 13.9 | 534 602 | 3 012 | 57 383 | D | D | D | D | 28.7 | 2.8 | 497 | 16.3 |
| Limestone....................... | 237 | 4.9 | 175 | 7.4 | 150.0 | 466 517 | 2 659 | 64 855 | 70.8 | 52 359 | 47.1 | 52.9 | 29.3 | 7.8 | 7 749 | 38.3 |
| Lowndes......................... | 187 | -5.1 | 461 | 3.1 | 42.2 | 752 337 | 1 631 | 82 834 | 57.8 | 142 652 | D | D | 39.8 | 11.9 | 1 575 | 32.8 |
| Macon............................ | 117 | -9.3 | 303 | 2.6 | 34.8 | 570 812 | 1 882 | 68 543 | 13.4 | 34 909 | 69.4 | 30.6 | 26.0 | 4.7 | 1 466 | 32.2 |
| Madison.......................... | 199 | 0.5 | 168 | 6.5 | 122.8 | 449 482 | 2 677 | 64 015 | 37.5 | 31 582 | 73.1 | 26.9 | 27.4 | 5.2 | 5 477 | 29.8 |
| Marengo.......................... | 178 | -5.8 | 321 | 0.0 | 36.6 | 537 958 | 1 676 | 55 070 | 16.5 | 29 747 | 13.2 | 86.8 | 32.6 | 3.8 | 1 392 | 30.1 |
| Marion............................ | 117 | -1.7 | 149 | 0.3 | 30.3 | 299 773 | 2 013 | 54 228 | 70.2 | 89 246 | 4.8 | 95.2 | 26.3 | 9.1 | 694 | 31.9 |
| Marshall.......................... | 155 | -3.7 | 89 | 1.2 | 61.5 | 330 979 | 3 707 | 61 866 | 238.2 | 137 603 | 2.8 | 97.2 | 32.5 | 11.8 | 1 181 | 20.6 |
| Mobile............................ | 114 | 12.9 | 130 | 3.5 | 44.2 | 414 764 | 3 197 | 69 495 | 83.2 | 94 946 | 90.1 | 9.9 | 29.3 | 10.0 | 2 538 | 12.9 |
| Monroe........................... | 119 | -0.8 | 235 | 0.8 | 45.9 | 421 544 | 1 792 | 75 376 | 19.2 | 38 114 | 48.4 | 51.6 | 30.1 | 6.5 | 2 822 | 44.0 |
| Montgomery .................... | 223 | 4.7 | 360 | 0.6 | 59.8 | 700 766 | 1 948 | 66 319 | 41.7 | 67 185 | 24.8 | 75.2 | 36.5 | 8.9 | 1 251 | 24.5 |
| Morgan........................... | 162 | 8.7 | 111 | 0.4 | 72.8 | 317 198 | 2 861 | 52 686 | 96.9 | 66 473 | 6.3 | 93.7 | 30.1 | 7.2 | 1 432 | 18.9 |
| Perry.............................. | 166 | 0.6 | 425 | 0.1 | 39.7 | 679 727 | 1 599 | 68 219 | 17.5 | 44 995 | 11.1 | 88.9 | 32.8 | 9.2 | 1 390 | 38.5 |
| Pickens.......................... | 131 | -8.4 | 260 | 0.6 | 28.6 | 487 719 | 1 876 | 58 308 | 109.8 | 218 332 | 2.4 | 97.6 | 38.4 | 19.7 | 650 | 22.9 |
| Pike................................ | 179 | -4.3 | 253 | 2.4 | 53.0 | 547 958 | 2 168 | 70 915 | 110.9 | 156 401 | 5.7 | 94.3 | 34.4 | 13.3 | 2 852 | 47.5 |
| Randolph........................ | 115 | 4.5 | 188 | 0.2 | 19.9 | 455 760 | 2 423 | 57 114 | 74.9 | 122 861 | 1.2 | 98.8 | 37.0 | 14.1 | 153 | 19.2 |
| Russell........................... | 94 | -10.5 | 311 | 2.6 | 24.3 | 679 298 | 2 186 | 68 426 | 11.9 | 39 204 | 59.0 | 41.0 | 21.5 | 2.6 | 1 551 | 29.4 |
| St. Clair.......................... | 72 | -13.3 | 115 | 1.8 | 21.0 | 406 441 | 3 526 | 64 661 | 58.9 | 94 770 | 12.8 | 87.2 | 28.8 | 7.9 | 150 | 6.0 |
| Shelby............................ | 55 | -14.1 | 116 | 2.2 | 21.1 | 428 945 | 3 710 | 57 847 | 9.8 | 20 599 | 67.3 | 32.7 | 23.4 | 2.7 | 543 | 13.5 |
| Sumter............................ | 181 | 2.3 | 420 | 0.5 | 35.7 | 605 468 | 1 442 | 49 646 | 17.9 | 41 434 | 6.3 | 93.7 | 32.3 | 6.7 | 887 | 37.1 |
| Talladega........................ | 119 | 9.2 | 190 | 3.2 | 48.6 | 442 771 | 2 325 | 64 540 | 28.4 | 45 414 | 23.7 | 76.3 | 30.2 | 5.3 | 1 058 | 24.5 |
| Tallapoosa...................... | 64 | -17.9 | 170 | D | 13.1 | 420 894 | 2 476 | 52 311 | 6.6 | 17 548 | 21.1 | 78.9 | 23.9 | 2.1 | 324 | 16.4 |
| Tuscaloosa..................... | 111 | 7.8 | 180 | 1.2 | 38.2 | 445 608 | 2 470 | 65 369 | 25.4 | 41 417 | 28.4 | 71.6 | 23.3 | 6.5 | 1 387 | 18.8 |
| Walker............................ | 70 | -6.7 | 112 | 0.5 | 20.9 | 281 205 | 2 513 | 55 815 | 52.6 | 83 564 | 5.3 | 94.7 | 24.3 | 7.9 | 95 | 9.4 |

| STATE County | Water use, 2005 | | Wholesale trade,[1] 2007 | | | | Retail trade,[2] 2007 | | | | Real estate and rental and leasing,[2] 2007 | | | |
|---|---|---|---|---|---|---|---|---|---|---|---|---|---|---|
| | Total water withdrawn (mil gal/day) | Gallons withdrawn per person | Number of establish-ments | Number of employees | Sales (mil dol) | Annual payroll (mil dol) | Number of establish-ments | Number of employees | Sales (mil dol) | Annual payroll (mil dol) | Number of establish-ments | Number of employees | Receipts (mil dol) | Annual payroll (mil dol) |
| | 133 | 134 | 135 | 136 | 137 | 138 | 139 | 140 | 141 | 142 | 143 | 144 | 145 | 146 |
| UNITED STATES............ | 407 313.9 | 1 373 | 369 387 | 5 098 545 | 4 174 286.5 | 260 532.1 | 1 128 112 | 15 515 396 | 3 917 663.5 | 362 818.7 | 384 297 | 2 188 479 | 485 058.6 | 84 764.9 |
| ALABAMA ........................ | 9 957.6 | 2 185 | 4 824 | 70 469 | 52 252.8 | 3 032.2 | 19 722 | 238 922 | 57 344.9 | 5 112.0 | 4 554 | 27 100 | 4 073.2 | 823.4 |
| Autauga................................ | 43.7 | 898 | 26 | D | D | D | 182 | 2 373 | 598.2 | 56.4 | 31 | D | D | D |
| Baldwin................................ | 69.0 | 424 | 183 | D | D | D | 1 019 | 12 920 | 2 966.5 | 282.6 | 358 | 1 987 | 266.7 | 59.5 |
| Barbour................................ | 16.5 | 580 | 19 | D | D | D | 104 | 994 | 188.3 | 17.4 | 20 | D | D | D |
| Bibb.................................... | 5.0 | 231 | 13 | D | D | D | 64 | 515 | 124.7 | 10.6 | 11 | 27 | 3.5 | 0.9 |
| Blount................................. | 19.0 | 340 | 32 | D | D | D | 155 | 1 263 | 319.7 | 25.4 | 16 | 49 | 3.6 | 0.7 |
| Bullock................................ | 5.4 | 492 | 6 | D | D | D | 22 | 251 | 43.8 | 4.8 | 4 | 10 | 0.7 | 0.1 |
| Butler................................. | 4.4 | 211 | 10 | 74 | 56.7 | 2.9 | 106 | 1 084 | 229.3 | 19.6 | 21 | 88 | 3.8 | 0.7 |
| Calhoun................................ | 29.0 | 258 | 104 | D | D | D | 552 | 6 854 | 1 543.0 | 139.1 | 93 | 459 | 66.3 | 10.2 |
| Chambers............................. | 8.4 | 237 | 16 | D | D | D | 130 | 1 205 | 264.7 | 23.9 | 17 | 79 | 7.5 | 1.3 |
| Cherokee............................. | 7.2 | 294 | 17 | 74 | 62.3 | 2.5 | 86 | 884 | 186.3 | 17.5 | 18 | 58 | 8.3 | 1.1 |
| Chilton................................ | 6.3 | 150 | 23 | 292 | 155.1 | 10.5 | 170 | 1 503 | 359.9 | 31.1 | 27 | 87 | 6.4 | 1.2 |
| Choctaw............................... | 49.6 | 3 348 | 13 | 57 | 52.9 | 2.1 | 66 | 360 | 84.6 | 6.1 | 4 | 9 | 0.5 | 0.1 |
| Clarke.................................. | 4.9 | 180 | 14 | 206 | 85.8 | 6.1 | 153 | 1 477 | 344.3 | 28.7 | 22 | 74 | 6.2 | 1.5 |
| Clay.................................... | 2.7 | 193 | 5 | D | D | D | 50 | 358 | 70.6 | 5.3 | 7 | 17 | 1.3 | 0.5 |
| Cleburne.............................. | 2.4 | 164 | 4 | 10 | 5.9 | 0.3 | 49 | 362 | 133.4 | 10.3 | 3 | D | D | D |
| Coffee.................................. | 13.0 | 284 | 25 | 275 | 131.6 | 9.7 | 224 | 2 514 | 639.6 | 54.9 | 62 | 261 | 29.7 | 6.7 |
| Colbert................................. | 1 363.2 | 24 939 | 84 | 848 | 351.4 | 30.2 | 238 | 2 912 | 821.3 | 66.4 | 38 | 211 | 23.1 | 4.0 |
| Conecuh............................... | 2.4 | 179 | 7 | 174 | 76.7 | 4.9 | 45 | 303 | 71.2 | 4.5 | 8 | 12 | 1.0 | 0.2 |
| Coosa.................................. | 1.0 | 90 | 7 | 37 | 31.6 | 1.8 | 18 | 89 | 20.5 | 1.4 | 7 | 10 | 1.1 | 0.1 |
| Covington............................. | 13.5 | 366 | 39 | 610 | 338.7 | 17.7 | 191 | 1 902 | 424.9 | 39.2 | 33 | 128 | 12.1 | 2.4 |
| Crenshaw............................. | 3.2 | 235 | 13 | 346 | 131.9 | 14.4 | 50 | 343 | 75.5 | 6.5 | 7 | 17 | 0.9 | 0.3 |
| Cullman............................... | 32.7 | 409 | 91 | D | D | D | 341 | 3 346 | 867.1 | 69.6 | 56 | 231 | 26.1 | 5.9 |
| Dale.................................... | 12.2 | 251 | 22 | 257 | 69.3 | 7.5 | 149 | 1 431 | 332.5 | 27.0 | 31 | 169 | 21.1 | 3.6 |
| Dallas................................. | 17.8 | 401 | 31 | D | D | D | 200 | 2 085 | 437.4 | 41.8 | 39 | 119 | 14.0 | 2.5 |
| DeKalb................................ | 16.4 | 244 | 43 | D | D | D | 269 | 2 532 | 635.2 | 55.3 | 36 | 153 | 11.8 | 3.4 |
| Elmore................................. | 14.8 | 200 | 32 | 291 | 104.9 | 8.8 | 225 | 2 479 | 618.3 | 50.6 | 48 | 125 | 17.4 | 3.1 |
| Escambia............................. | 42.8 | 1 125 | 27 | 221 | 93.1 | 6.5 | 190 | 1 639 | 379.6 | 33.5 | 25 | 119 | 10.3 | 2.1 |
| Etowah................................ | 173.9 | 1 685 | 96 | 1 064 | 518.4 | 36.1 | 453 | 4 786 | 1 114.8 | 92.7 | 79 | 428 | 68.7 | 12.1 |
| Fayette................................ | 3.9 | 216 | 7 | 34 | 22.5 | 1.1 | 62 | 633 | 130.4 | 11.5 | 6 | 15 | 0.9 | 0.2 |
| Franklin............................... | 7.1 | 231 | 20 | 111 | 67.4 | 3.5 | 119 | 1 060 | 269.1 | 19.3 | 15 | 45 | 4.6 | 0.6 |
| Geneva................................ | 7.6 | 296 | 21 | 423 | 231.7 | 23.0 | 102 | 872 | 170.0 | 15.0 | 8 | 27 | 1.7 | 0.4 |
| Greene................................. | 398.6 | 41 257 | 3 | D | D | D | 28 | 185 | 33.6 | 3.0 | 1 | D | D | D |
| Hale.................................... | 28.4 | 1 550 | 6 | D | D | D | 49 | 361 | 86.7 | 7.0 | 5 | D | D | D |
| Henry................................... | 5.8 | 350 | 14 | D | D | D | 60 | 425 | 92.6 | 8.2 | 13 | 21 | 1.9 | 0.3 |
| Houston............................... | 131.8 | 1 398 | 159 | D | D | D | 618 | 7 934 | 1 909.6 | 179.1 | 122 | 553 | 81.5 | 17.2 |
| Jackson............................... | 1 498.2 | 27 926 | 38 | D | D | D | 187 | 1 923 | 411.0 | 37.0 | 28 | 106 | 11.4 | 2.6 |
| Jefferson.............................. | 81.0 | 123 | 1 052 | 18 937 | 13 756.8 | 930.6 | 3 026 | 42 765 | 11 066.3 | 971.5 | 810 | 7 976 | 1 193.0 | 289.1 |
| Lamar.................................. | 2.3 | 150 | 6 | D | D | D | 51 | 349 | 70.8 | 6.0 | 5 | 22 | 1.1 | 0.3 |
| Lauderdale ........................... | 17.2 | 196 | 78 | 1 286 | 514.6 | 34.0 | 445 | 5 190 | 1 131.6 | 100.7 | 86 | 345 | 45.1 | 8.5 |
| Lawrence.............................. | 67.4 | 1 949 | 11 | 34 | 23.8 | 1.0 | 86 | 825 | 167.0 | 15.6 | 7 | 30 | 2.8 | 1.0 |
| Lee...................................... | 21.5 | 175 | 68 | D | D | D | 472 | 6 391 | 1 451.6 | 125.3 | 122 | 636 | 79.4 | 15.0 |
| Limestone ............................ | 2 013.9 | 28 578 | 51 | 407 | 248.3 | 17.8 | 246 | 2 611 | 723.2 | 58.8 | 55 | 156 | 24.0 | 3.9 |
| Lowndes.............................. | 6.0 | 457 | 2 | D | D | D | 32 | 395 | 103.6 | 7.1 | 7 | D | D | D |
| Macon.................................. | 9.9 | 436 | 9 | D | D | D | 50 | 455 | 87.5 | 7.1 | 11 | D | D | D |
| Madison............................... | 70.5 | 236 | 342 | 4 519 | 2 970.4 | 212.4 | 1 348 | 18 840 | 4 438.7 | 421.1 | 432 | 2 091 | 345.3 | 65.4 |
| Marengo............................... | 26.8 | 1 224 | 25 | 133 | 64.6 | 4.2 | 109 | 1 039 | 197.2 | 18.8 | 17 | 85 | 24.8 | 3.5 |
| Marion................................. | 7.8 | 260 | 23 | 195 | 162.5 | 6.2 | 110 | 976 | 209.9 | 18.1 | 14 | 33 | 3.9 | 0.6 |
| Marshall............................... | 27.1 | 316 | 86 | 1 486 | 1 138.7 | 55.3 | 465 | 4 990 | 1 357.7 | 102.8 | 80 | 603 | 39.4 | 8.6 |
| Mobile................................. | 1 130.9 | 2 817 | 546 | 6 904 | 3 268.7 | 296.1 | 1 644 | 22 271 | 5 225.5 | 483.4 | 448 | 2 460 | 417.2 | 77.8 |
| Monroe................................ | 60.0 | 2 529 | 15 | 148 | 92.8 | 7.2 | 93 | 872 | 212.6 | 16.1 | 13 | 50 | 5.5 | 1.1 |
| Montgomery.......................... | 69.7 | 315 | 290 | 5 684 | 3 275.6 | 235.8 | 1 009 | 14 325 | 3 238.2 | 314.6 | 303 | 2 358 | 292.8 | 72.5 |
| Morgan................................ | 124.8 | 1 097 | 163 | 2 046 | 1 213.9 | 86.5 | 545 | 5 851 | 1 637.6 | 128.4 | 102 | 418 | 60.2 | 10.4 |
| Perry................................... | 12.4 | 1 090 | 4 | 69 | 10.4 | 1.8 | 37 | 178 | 34.1 | 3.4 | 3 | D | D | D |
| Pickens................................ | 5.7 | 281 | 12 | 72 | 36.6 | 1.8 | 66 | 524 | 113.2 | 9.2 | 6 | 31 | 1.0 | 0.6 |
| Pike..................................... | 7.0 | 236 | 22 | D | D | D | 147 | 1 578 | 367.9 | 31.5 | 28 | 89 | 21.5 | 1.7 |
| Randolph.............................. | 2.8 | 122 | 8 | 61 | 26.8 | 0.9 | 95 | 714 | 161.4 | 15.1 | 20 | 49 | 5.8 | 1.0 |
| Russell................................ | 43.7 | 886 | 16 | D | D | D | 165 | 2 010 | 428.2 | 38.5 | 46 | 157 | 23.2 | 3.5 |
| St. Clair............................... | 21.0 | 290 | 68 | 726 | 317.5 | 30.1 | 232 | 2 502 | 581.3 | 51.6 | 45 | 157 | 28.4 | 3.8 |
| Shelby................................. | 833.3 | 4 860 | 328 | 4 622 | 4 385.6 | 255.4 | 707 | 10 135 | 2 520.5 | 237.8 | 217 | 1 474 | 454.8 | 57.9 |
| Sumter................................. | 10.3 | 743 | 13 | 173 | 76.5 | 4.8 | 47 | 334 | 59.6 | 4.4 | 9 | 25 | 3.1 | 0.9 |
| Talladega.............................. | 78.3 | 973 | 59 | D | D | D | 310 | 3 233 | 730.7 | 63.6 | 52 | 400 | 28.6 | 4.9 |
| Tallapoosa............................ | 14.6 | 360 | 22 | D | D | D | 155 | 1 534 | 362.3 | 33.3 | 38 | 139 | 26.6 | 4.2 |
| Tuscaloosa........................... | 36.0 | 213 | 142 | 1 655 | 760.6 | 72.6 | 781 | 10 551 | 2 445.9 | 223.5 | 198 | 1 170 | 173.8 | 32.0 |
| Walker................................. | 969.5 | 13 826 | 52 | 300 | 256.4 | 13.2 | 322 | 3 789 | 903.6 | 74.7 | 41 | 159 | 24.7 | 4.2 |

1. Merchant wholesalers, except manufacturers' sales branches and offices.   2. Employer establishments.

Items 133—146

| STATE County | Professional, scientific, and technical services,[1] 2007 | | | | Manufacturing, 2007 | | | | Accommodation and food services, 2007 | | | |
|---|---|---|---|---|---|---|---|---|---|---|---|---|
| | Number of establish-ments | Number of employees | Receipts (mil dol) | Annual payroll (mil dol) | Number of establish-ments | Number of employees | Receipts (mil dol) | Annual payroll (mil dol) | Number of establish-ments | Number of employees | Sales (mil dol) | Annual payroll (mil dol) |
| | 147 | 148 | 149 | 150 | 151 | 152 | 153 | 154 | 155 | 156 | 157 | 158 |
| UNITED STATES | 842 607 | 7 678 304 | 1 220 434.1 | 489 965.4 | 332 536 | 13 395 670 | 5 319 456.3 | 613 768.6 | 634 361 | 11 600 751 | 613 795.7 | 170 826.8 |
| ALABAMA | 9 437 | 92 759 | 13 623.2 | 4 996.4 | 4 928 | 271 986 | 112 858.8 | 11 351.6 | 8 093 | 150 791 | 6 426.3 | 1 751.4 |
| Autauga | 61 | 386 | 42.3 | 15.5 | 33 | 1 506 | D | D | 92 | 2 182 | 88.2 | 25.5 |
| Baldwin | 458 | D | D | D | 162 | 4 795 | 1 410.3 | 169.3 | 414 | 8 368 | 437.0 | 122.4 |
| Barbour | 48 | D | D | D | 38 | D | D | D | 45 | D | D | D |
| Bibb | 14 | D | D | D | NA | NA | NA | NA | 19 | 255 | 10.8 | 2.6 |
| Blount | 47 | 229 | 16.7 | 8.2 | 53 | 1 517 | 341.5 | 44.3 | 46 | 490 | 20.9 | 5.1 |
| Bullock | 7 | 20 | 2.6 | 0.9 | 3 | D | D | D | 8 | 110 | 3.7 | 1.1 |
| Butler | 25 | 85 | 6.9 | 2.2 | 23 | 1 170 | 399.1 | 38.5 | 40 | 673 | 28.4 | 7.5 |
| Calhoun | 171 | D | D | D | 141 | 6 961 | 2 680.0 | 279.3 | 224 | 5 129 | 186.5 | 51.5 |
| Chambers | 29 | D | D | D | 27 | D | 667.3 | 73.6 | 47 | 611 | 23.2 | 5.9 |
| Cherokee | 17 | 60 | 6.3 | 1.5 | 24 | 1 171 | 307.4 | 34.7 | 39 | 354 | 13.9 | 3.7 |
| Chilton | 39 | D | D | D | 52 | 1 444 | D | 41.8 | 60 | 868 | 34.1 | 8.5 |
| Choctaw | 18 | 51 | 3.3 | 1.1 | 7 | D | D | D | 21 | 170 | 11.3 | 1.5 |
| Clarke | 30 | 94 | 13.2 | 2.1 | 31 | 1 592 | 571.5 | 70.2 | 53 | 611 | 23.6 | 5.4 |
| Clay | 10 | 56 | 5.2 | 0.8 | 12 | 2 526 | 330.9 | 72.9 | 12 | 139 | 4.4 | 1.1 |
| Cleburne | 8 | 36 | 1.7 | 0.6 | NA | NA | NA | NA | 13 | 164 | 4.1 | 1.0 |
| Coffee | 71 | 373 | 45.2 | 11.2 | 36 | 3 128 | 613.8 | 80.6 | 89 | 1 474 | 50.1 | 13.2 |
| Colbert | 94 | D | D | D | 112 | 4 162 | 2 083.2 | 185.2 | 99 | 1 560 | 61.9 | 16.2 |
| Conecuh | 11 | 19 | 2.2 | 0.4 | 12 | 672 | 183.5 | 21.5 | 16 | 202 | 8.7 | 1.9 |
| Coosa | 6 | 15 | 1.7 | 0.7 | 9 | 782 | 89.6 | D | 3 | 5 | 0.6 | 0.1 |
| Covington | 63 | 301 | 28.4 | 9.7 | 34 | 2 476 | 561.2 | 76.7 | 67 | 745 | 30.3 | 7.2 |
| Crenshaw | 11 | 31 | 2.8 | 0.8 | 10 | 986 | 270.8 | 29.1 | 11 | 173 | 5.6 | 1.4 |
| Cullman | 118 | 566 | 38.5 | 14.0 | 124 | 5 306 | 1 393.4 | 188.9 | 126 | 2 457 | 102.3 | 25.6 |
| Dale | 81 | 974 | 129.4 | 45.3 | 35 | 652 | 115.0 | 19.8 | 85 | 1 219 | 37.2 | 10.1 |
| Dallas | 45 | D | D | D | 46 | 3 594 | 1 174.8 | 137.7 | 63 | 855 | 33.7 | 7.9 |
| DeKalb | 79 | 399 | 30.1 | 13.1 | 134 | 9 028 | 1 831.6 | 304.3 | 108 | 1 426 | 67.9 | 18.3 |
| Elmore | 86 | 449 | 79.2 | 17.0 | 73 | 3 312 | 766.3 | 130.3 | 82 | 1 209 | 47.9 | 11.8 |
| Escambia | 41 | 176 | 16.2 | 5.4 | 39 | 1 660 | 665.3 | 80.5 | 54 | 728 | 31.9 | 7.6 |
| Etowah | 156 | 876 | 76.6 | 26.8 | 118 | 5 430 | 1 253.0 | 203.7 | 177 | 3 381 | 138.0 | 38.1 |
| Fayette | 15 | 47 | 3.4 | 1.1 | 25 | 974 | 186.2 | 28.5 | 22 | 258 | 10.9 | 2.6 |
| Franklin | 28 | 123 | 9.7 | 2.8 | 49 | 4 071 | 672.0 | 135.0 | 51 | 691 | 25.4 | 6.1 |
| Geneva | 34 | D | D | D | 27 | 960 | 153.3 | 27.2 | 31 | 313 | 10.4 | 2.7 |
| Greene | 6 | D | D | D | NA | NA | NA | NA | 6 | 58 | 1.2 | 0.4 |
| Hale | 8 | D | D | D | 11 | 820 | D | D | 12 | 148 | 3.1 | 0.8 |
| Henry | 22 | D | D | D | 17 | 826 | 425.8 | 25.3 | 25 | 252 | 7.4 | 1.8 |
| Houston | 236 | D | D | D | 126 | 5 562 | 1 310.7 | 201.1 | 226 | 4 442 | 177.2 | 48.6 |
| Jackson | 55 | D | D | D | 70 | 5 707 | 1 525.4 | 206.5 | 77 | 1 068 | 39.3 | 10.6 |
| Jefferson | 1 946 | D | D | D | 674 | 28 833 | 10 261.0 | 1 331.4 | 1 271 | 26 530 | 1 268.2 | 354.2 |
| Lamar | 18 | 51 | 4.3 | 1.5 | 17 | 1 113 | 234.9 | 49.9 | 19 | 153 | 6.0 | 1.4 |
| Lauderdale | 176 | D | D | D | 91 | 3 150 | 1 083.7 | 116.1 | 150 | 3 568 | 136.6 | 40.1 |
| Lawrence | 35 | 112 | 7.7 | 2.4 | 24 | 1 411 | D | D | 42 | 543 | 22.7 | 6.0 |
| Lee | 189 | D | D | D | 123 | D | D | D | 271 | 5 515 | 201.2 | 55.8 |
| Limestone | 98 | 666 | 92.9 | 34.5 | 72 | 4 272 | 947.3 | 173.9 | 96 | 1 548 | 68.1 | 17.2 |
| Lowndes | 8 | 58 | 9.4 | 3.3 | 13 | 1 103 | 1 156.9 | 63.8 | 6 | 14 | 0.6 | 0.1 |
| Macon | 15 | D | D | D | NA | NA | NA | NA | 22 | 436 | 19.4 | 5.5 |
| Madison | 1 276 | 31 697 | 5 668.6 | 2 209.6 | 319 | 23 499 | 8 650.7 | 1 129.7 | 643 | 13 989 | 596.3 | 167.6 |
| Marengo | 25 | 88 | 11.0 | 2.2 | 25 | 1 886 | 542.1 | 74.7 | 41 | 422 | 16.7 | 3.9 |
| Marion | 23 | 75 | 5.0 | 1.5 | 48 | 3 474 | 794.5 | 114.3 | 46 | 491 | 19.1 | 5.3 |
| Marshall | 133 | 623 | 54.6 | 17.9 | 125 | 10 842 | 3 029.5 | 334.0 | 169 | 2 473 | 103.5 | 27.5 |
| Mobile | 901 | D | D | D | 385 | 16 776 | 12 407.2 | 840.9 | 652 | 13 252 | 562.4 | 155.0 |
| Monroe | 25 | 62 | 4.4 | 1.3 | 28 | 2 329 | 1 251.9 | 119.7 | 32 | 349 | 14.8 | 3.3 |
| Montgomery | 662 | 6 385 | 890.0 | 341.8 | 199 | 12 828 | 7 956.6 | 567.2 | 473 | 9 754 | 402.9 | 112.8 |
| Morgan | 227 | 1 451 | 116.6 | 48.1 | 199 | 12 152 | D | D | 207 | 3 756 | 154.7 | 41.4 |
| Perry | 6 | D | D | D | NA | NA | NA | NA | 11 | 58 | 2.6 | 0.5 |
| Pickens | 18 | 42 | 2.5 | 0.7 | 22 | 630 | 107.6 | 18.7 | 16 | 138 | 6.3 | 1.7 |
| Pike | 34 | 173 | 14.6 | 4.0 | 32 | D | D | D | 63 | 1 197 | 45.7 | 11.8 |
| Randolph | 20 | 78 | 4.2 | 1.6 | 21 | 1 537 | 401.7 | 49.3 | 30 | 219 | 9.2 | 2.4 |
| Russell | 48 | D | D | D | 37 | D | D | D | 84 | 1 428 | 56.4 | 14.7 |
| St. Clair | 93 | 475 | 40.8 | 16.1 | 76 | 2 830 | 985.4 | 102.2 | 109 | 1 641 | 70.3 | 18.8 |
| Shelby | 570 | D | D | D | 191 | 6 672 | 1 723.0 | 272.3 | 334 | 6 596 | 301.9 | 83.6 |
| Sumter | 12 | 32 | 2.0 | 0.5 | NA | NA | NA | NA | 20 | 262 | 8.2 | 2.1 |
| Talladega | 72 | 310 | 21.8 | 8.1 | 88 | 9 749 | 9 054.2 | 514.4 | 111 | 1 775 | 67.1 | 17.7 |
| Tallapoosa | 57 | 209 | 24.5 | 9.2 | 39 | 1 473 | D | 39.7 | 65 | 843 | 28.2 | 7.9 |
| Tuscaloosa | 356 | 2 555 | 223.1 | 83.7 | 154 | 13 216 | 10 852.5 | 715.5 | 377 | 8 183 | 327.4 | 87.4 |
| Walker | 98 | 558 | 46.1 | 21.7 | 59 | 1 679 | 314.8 | 52.3 | 102 | 1 565 | 73.9 | 17.9 |

1. Establishment subject to federal tax.

# Table B. States and Counties — Health Care and Social Assistance, Other Services, and Federal Funds

| STATE County | Health care and social assistance, 2007 | | | | Other services, 2007 | | | | Federal funds and grants, 2009–2010 Expenditures (mil dol) | | | |
|---|---|---|---|---|---|---|---|---|---|---|---|---|
| | | | | | | | | | Total | Direct payments for individuals[1] | | |
| | Number of establishments | Number of employees | Receipts (mil dol) | Annual payroll (mil dol) | Number of establishments | Number of employees | Receipts (mil dol) | Annual payroll (mil dol) | | Social Security and government retirement | Medicare | Food Stamps and Supplemental Security Income |
| | 159 | 160 | 161 | 162 | 163 | 164 | 165 | 166 | 167 | 168 | 169 | 170 |
| UNITED STATES............ | 784 626 | 16 792 074 | 1 668 276.8 | 662 719.9 | 540 148 | 3 479 011 | 405 284.0 | 99 123.3 | 3 251 308.5 | 858 961.1 | 508 581.6 | 111 896.6 |
| ALABAMA ......................... | 10 392 | 238 070 | 22 604.9 | 8 890.1 | 6 718 | 40 488 | 4 154.1 | 1 050.0 | 56 495.7 | 16 936.5 | 8 286.0 | 2 266.2 |
| Autauga................................. | 82 | 1 059 | 82.1 | 29.5 | 65 | D | D | D | 349.3 | 196.7 | 54.1 | 16.7 |
| Baldwin.................................. | 388 | 6 647 | 624.0 | 230.6 | 274 | 1 202 | 169.0 | 32.1 | 1 178.4 | 733.3 | 226.1 | 34.4 |
| Barbour................................. | 59 | D | D | D | 32 | D | D | D | 251.5 | 85.8 | 64.9 | 19.1 |
| Bibb....................................... | 30 | 602 | 33.2 | 14.3 | 22 | D | D | D | 172.2 | 74.9 | 42.6 | 9.7 |
| Blount.................................... | 47 | 805 | 57.0 | 24.2 | 59 | 241 | 17.5 | 4.6 | 304.4 | 154.1 | 75.0 | 17.4 |
| Bullock.................................. | 17 | 365 | 25.3 | 8.9 | 9 | 19 | 1.4 | 0.3 | 114.6 | 26.4 | 27.0 | 10.7 |
| Butler.................................... | 42 | 798 | 63.4 | 25.1 | 25 | 152 | 6.0 | 3.6 | 202.5 | 71.6 | 56.1 | 16.2 |
| Calhoun................................ | 283 | 6 307 | 545.7 | 206.7 | 186 | 944 | 81.3 | 22.1 | 1 726.3 | 565.6 | 229.3 | 61.1 |
| Chambers.............................. | 66 | 1 070 | 95.8 | 34.1 | 41 | D | D | D | 306.3 | 141.6 | 82.4 | 21.0 |
| Cherokee............................... | 30 | 389 | 28.4 | 12.3 | 19 | 70 | 5.4 | 1.3 | 184.8 | 90.1 | 42.5 | 9.1 |
| Chilton.................................. | 65 | 808 | 53.3 | 23.4 | 35 | D | D | D | 288.6 | 131.3 | 78.3 | 18.4 |
| Choctaw................................ | 27 | 283 | 18.8 | 8.4 | 20 | 51 | 5.8 | 1.2 | 147.4 | 56.0 | 36.3 | 10.1 |
| Clarke................................... | 58 | 1 007 | 72.7 | 29.6 | 40 | 190 | 17.0 | 3.5 | 263.3 | 102.8 | 58.3 | 23.2 |
| Clay...................................... | 23 | 665 | 34.4 | 15.6 | 13 | D | D | D | 134.8 | 55.4 | 31.5 | 4.2 |
| Cleburne............................... | 13 | D | D | D | 10 | 60 | 6.3 | 1.6 | 105.8 | 51.4 | 22.5 | 5.5 |
| Coffee................................... | 104 | D | D | D | 62 | D | D | D | 2 081.3 | 234.3 | 82.6 | 15.4 |
| Colbert.................................. | 140 | 2 680 | 261.2 | 103.9 | 83 | 572 | 69.8 | 16.2 | 526.1 | 244.4 | 114.4 | 22.5 |
| Conecuh................................ | 23 | 371 | 30.4 | 11.2 | 15 | 30 | 4.0 | 0.8 | 148.7 | 51.0 | 38.7 | 13.9 |
| Coosa.................................... | 8 | D | D | D | 6 | 14 | 1.6 | 0.3 | 93.1 | 43.8 | 19.7 | 6.1 |
| Covington.............................. | 98 | 1 692 | 136.6 | 49.2 | 49 | 224 | 20.1 | 5.4 | 377.9 | 154.8 | 97.1 | 19.4 |
| Crenshaw.............................. | 15 | D | D | D | 15 | D | D | D | 139.8 | 50.0 | 34.5 | 6.8 |
| Cullman................................ | 184 | 3 542 | 317.2 | 123.9 | 110 | 515 | 45.3 | 12.2 | 626.1 | 298.1 | 154.5 | 27.4 |
| Dale...................................... | 72 | D | D | D | 57 | D | D | D | 644.3 | 218.7 | 92.3 | 27.5 |
| Dallas................................... | 119 | 2 172 | 185.6 | 73.4 | 64 | 419 | 35.7 | 8.0 | 614.7 | 165.9 | 114.8 | 62.1 |
| DeKalb.................................. | 109 | 2 260 | 160.7 | 62.4 | 59 | 206 | 16.1 | 4.0 | 471.6 | 209.5 | 110.1 | 23.4 |
| Elmore.................................. | 122 | 1 880 | 122.5 | 48.8 | 77 | D | D | D | 525.1 | 308.5 | 90.7 | 22.1 |
| Escambia.............................. | 79 | 1 323 | 98.7 | 38.8 | 59 | 225 | 17.1 | 4.0 | 316.2 | 132.2 | 77.5 | 19.6 |
| Etowah.................................. | 302 | 6 515 | 626.7 | 229.8 | 121 | 691 | 54.0 | 15.8 | 966.6 | 420.9 | 248.2 | 51.1 |
| Fayette.................................. | 58 | 896 | 48.2 | 21.4 | 23 | D | D | D | 153.9 | 62.2 | 36.2 | 9.4 |
| Franklin................................ | 78 | 1 317 | 97.3 | 37.1 | 37 | 135 | 11.5 | 3.0 | 275.4 | 110.2 | 74.8 | 13.6 |
| Geneva.................................. | 42 | D | D | D | 22 | D | D | D | 255.5 | 111.5 | 60.7 | 11.3 |
| Greene.................................. | 9 | D | D | D | 8 | 30 | 1.7 | 0.5 | 111.5 | 28.9 | 23.6 | 12.9 |
| Hale...................................... | 17 | D | D | D | 7 | 17 | 1.2 | 0.3 | 182.5 | 66.4 | 40.0 | 15.5 |
| Henry.................................... | 28 | D | D | D | 18 | D | D | D | 173.4 | 70.1 | 35.4 | 8.7 |
| Houston................................ | 320 | 9 099 | 920.9 | 365.4 | 198 | 1 104 | 104.3 | 24.4 | 744.4 | 372.7 | 136.6 | 47.1 |
| Jackson................................ | 112 | D | D | D | 43 | 161 | 14.7 | 3.7 | 669.1 | 216.0 | 99.8 | 20.9 |
| Jefferson............................... | 1 730 | 54 356 | 6 502.2 | 2 422.6 | 1 192 | 9 162 | 1 145.4 | 295.9 | 7 448.9 | 2 361.7 | 1 540.5 | 352.9 |
| Lamar................................... | 21 | 346 | 17.8 | 8.1 | 15 | 46 | 3.6 | 0.9 | 144.2 | 60.4 | 35.2 | 7.5 |
| Lauderdale ........................... | 265 | 4 604 | 399.7 | 147.1 | 136 | 821 | 51.1 | 15.7 | 750.5 | 403.1 | 154.8 | 30.9 |
| Lawrence.............................. | 40 | 732 | 46.9 | 19.7 | 32 | 101 | 8.3 | 2.1 | 239.9 | 100.5 | 51.4 | 13.4 |
| Lee....................................... | 221 | 6 157 | 469.5 | 191.8 | 152 | 748 | 49.7 | 14.2 | 762.5 | 321.6 | 107.1 | 38.7 |
| Limestone............................. | 130 | 1 927 | 136.8 | 58.8 | 75 | 358 | 26.2 | 6.9 | 519.2 | 259.7 | 84.1 | 24.0 |
| Lowndes................................ | 9 | 288 | 25.9 | 4.6 | 4 | D | D | D | 139.5 | 34.8 | 22.7 | 13.7 |
| Macon................................... | 27 | 1 920 | 130.1 | 93.4 | 17 | D | D | D | 320.6 | 90.0 | 43.6 | 25.3 |
| Madison................................ | 871 | 18 475 | 1 883.4 | 769.3 | 494 | 3 661 | 593.3 | 96.2 | 9 801.8 | 1 302.8 | 303.7 | 96.4 |
| Marengo................................ | 61 | 973 | 71.1 | 28.3 | 37 | 137 | 9.1 | 2.0 | 221.5 | 71.0 | 51.4 | 22.7 |
| Marion .................................. | 72 | 1 139 | 95.0 | 36.9 | 32 | 96 | 7.9 | 2.2 | 264.1 | 105.3 | 67.1 | 10.7 |
| Marshall................................ | 201 | 3 356 | 290.8 | 108.0 | 107 | 378 | 27.1 | 6.8 | 781.0 | 352.5 | 164.4 | 29.6 |
| Mobile.................................. | 741 | 23 845 | 2 160.0 | 894.7 | 666 | 4 681 | 412.6 | 116.5 | 3 934.1 | 1 327.4 | 768.5 | 269.2 |
| Monroe................................. | 31 | 725 | 49.6 | 21.0 | 22 | 76 | 6.9 | 1.4 | 211.7 | 76.7 | 49.9 | 14.5 |
| Montgomery.......................... | 704 | 16 381 | 1 747.0 | 658.7 | 508 | 3 504 | 329.9 | 96.2 | 4 910.7 | 796.3 | 363.5 | 149.4 |
| Morgan.................................. | 344 | 6 131 | 501.0 | 200.4 | 180 | 1 058 | 91.4 | 26.4 | 869.8 | 455.1 | 179.6 | 35.3 |
| Perry..................................... | 18 | 306 | 15.5 | 7.6 | 4 | D | D | D | 134.1 | 33.4 | 31.6 | 16.5 |
| Pickens................................. | 26 | 646 | 40.6 | 17.4 | 17 | D | D | D | 238.0 | 74.9 | 54.5 | 16.7 |
| Pike...................................... | 65 | 1 086 | 92.5 | 34.2 | 38 | D | D | D | 360.9 | 95.7 | 66.4 | 21.3 |
| Randolph.............................. | 41 | 720 | 44.4 | 19.9 | 24 | 70 | 5.1 | 1.5 | 193.1 | 82.3 | 45.8 | 11.1 |
| Russell.................................. | 75 | 1 653 | 105.4 | 40.5 | 68 | 342 | 22.5 | 7.6 | 459.3 | 222.9 | 87.1 | 33.3 |
| St. Clair................................ | 94 | 1 669 | 120.3 | 45.2 | 91 | 398 | 35.5 | 8.3 | 425.1 | 241.2 | 95.7 | 23.3 |
| Shelby.................................. | 392 | 5 709 | 522.6 | 203.0 | 324 | 2 137 | 191.2 | 61.4 | 918.4 | 372.0 | 135.4 | 23.1 |
| Sumter.................................. | 24 | 447 | 27.5 | 10.7 | 7 | 24 | 1.5 | 0.4 | 169.2 | 42.9 | 30.2 | 18.4 |
| Talladega.............................. | 170 | 3 016 | 230.4 | 90.0 | 79 | 365 | 29.2 | 8.5 | 743.4 | 305.0 | 173.8 | 52.0 |
| Tallapoosa............................ | 97 | D | D | D | 46 | 204 | 16.7 | 4.3 | 375.7 | 170.6 | 85.9 | 24.8 |
| Tuscaloosa............................ | 396 | D | D | D | 242 | 1 742 | 134.7 | 38.3 | 1 626.5 | 543.5 | 268.3 | 83.6 |
| Walker.................................. | 174 | 3 208 | 273.4 | 108.2 | 85 | 441 | 37.0 | 10.5 | 694.7 | 326.2 | 185.7 | 31.1 |

1. State totals may include programs not allocated by county.

**Federal Funds, Residential Construction, and Local Government Finances**

| STATE County | Salaries and wages | Defense | Other | Medicaid and other health-related | Nutrition and family welfare | Education | Other | New construction ($1,000) | Number of housing units | Total (mil dol) | Inter-governmental (mil dol) | Total (mil dol) | Total | Property |
|---|---|---|---|---|---|---|---|---|---|---|---|---|---|---|
| | 171 | 172 | 173 | 174 | 175 | 176 | 177 | 178 | 179 | 180 | 181 | 182 | 183 | 184 |
| UNITED STATES............. | 341 627.5 | 329 872.9 | 184 951.4 | 357 482.0 | 74 796.2 | 57 254.8 | 185 749.4 | 105 268 541 | 624 061 | X | X | X | X | X |
| ALABAMA ...................... | 5 613.2 | 8 140.1 | 2 341.6 | 4 946.9 | 949.1 | 816.7 | 2 560.7 | 1 704 064 | 11 667 | X | X | X | X | X |
| Autauga.......................... | 26.7 | 0.0 | 1.6 | 35.8 | 5.4 | 2.9 | 2.7 | 24 365 | 106 | 112.8 | 64.4 | 31.9 | 639 | 206 |
| Baldwin.......................... | 35.5 | 3.9 | 14.1 | 54.3 | 16.2 | 6.7 | 16.3 | 134 054 | 756 | 616.5 | 180.5 | 213.4 | 1 243 | 523 |
| Barbour.......................... | 12.9 | 0.8 | 0.9 | 48.2 | 5.9 | 2.7 | 2.4 | 7 366 | 55 | 73.5 | 43.3 | 17.4 | 623 | 269 |
| Bibb ............................... | 15.1 | 0.0 | 1.6 | 21.4 | 3.4 | 2.2 | 0.4 | 1 890 | 11 | 56.0 | 31.1 | 7.7 | 357 | 143 |
| Blount ............................ | 9.7 | 0.0 | 1.5 | 35.9 | 5.2 | 3.0 | 0.7 | 764 | 2 | 101.6 | 68.9 | 18.9 | 334 | 165 |
| Bullock........................... | 3.9 | 2.8 | 0.5 | 34.6 | 3.4 | 0.9 | 2.8 | 0 | 0 | 31.9 | 23.0 | 5.4 | 504 | 349 |
| Butler............................. | 5.3 | 0.0 | 0.9 | 39.3 | 5.2 | 2.7 | 1.2 | 1 502 | 11 | 58.6 | 37.7 | 15.1 | 750 | 266 |
| Calhoun.......................... | 233.1 | 415.3 | 58.5 | 104.4 | 16.3 | 9.1 | 7.4 | 10 862 | 83 | 507.7 | 186.6 | 103.4 | 915 | 334 |
| Chambers........................ | 7.5 | 0.0 | 1.1 | 40.6 | 5.8 | 2.5 | 1.1 | 425 | 2 | 80.8 | 40.0 | 24.1 | 694 | 288 |
| Cherokee........................ | 13.1 | 0.0 | 1.4 | 19.6 | 3.0 | 2.2 | 0.9 | 4 231 | 49 | 50.7 | 32.0 | 13.6 | 553 | 278 |
| Chilton........................... | 8.0 | 0.0 | 1.5 | 35.8 | 4.9 | 3.1 | 3.9 | 2 344 | 17 | 120.0 | 55.4 | 23.3 | 551 | 280 |
| Choctaw ......................... | 3.2 | 0.2 | 0.6 | 33.8 | 3.9 | 1.1 | 0.1 | 0 | 0 | 31.8 | 18.5 | 6.4 | 450 | 390 |
| Clarke............................ | 10.0 | 6.8 | 1.0 | 45.7 | 6.0 | 2.6 | 5.1 | 400 | 4 | 68.5 | 39.5 | 21.4 | 808 | 226 |
| Clay ............................... | 14.8 | 0.6 | 3.6 | 18.4 | 2.1 | 0.9 | 1.8 | 0 | 0 | 50.6 | 25.5 | 4.9 | 357 | 199 |
| Cleburne......................... | 4.8 | 0.1 | 1.4 | 15.9 | 1.8 | 1.0 | 1.0 | 250 | 1 | 39.0 | 27.6 | 6.7 | 455 | 244 |
| Coffee............................ | 878.6 | 776.0 | 16.5 | 42.7 | 6.2 | 5.7 | 3.8 | 23 026 | 216 | 166.3 | 98.8 | 30.4 | 650 | 241 |
| Colbert........................... | 16.7 | 3.3 | 26.5 | 51.2 | 7.6 | 6.8 | 13.3 | 11 089 | 127 | 236.0 | 85.6 | 44.0 | 806 | 364 |
| Conecuh.......................... | 2.5 | 0.0 | 0.6 | 31.9 | 3.4 | 1.2 | 0.8 | 0 | 0 | 31.2 | 21.9 | 5.2 | 398 | 222 |
| Coosa............................. | 4.2 | 3.2 | 0.5 | 12.0 | 2.1 | 0.8 | 0.2 | 0 | 0 | 24.0 | 15.1 | 5.1 | 473 | 267 |
| Covington........................ | 19.5 | 5.5 | 1.9 | 52.5 | 5.7 | 4.7 | 3.5 | 1 898 | 17 | 96.6 | 55.8 | 19.0 | 512 | 211 |
| Crenshaw........................ | 6.7 | 0.5 | 0.8 | 33.3 | 2.4 | 1.1 | 1.0 | 861 | 8 | 31.4 | 21.1 | 5.6 | 408 | 238 |
| Cullman.......................... | 30.2 | 0.1 | 3.4 | 73.8 | 9.3 | 5.8 | 3.0 | 5 609 | 69 | 249.2 | 107.1 | 34.5 | 428 | 206 |
| Dale............................... | 130.4 | 102.3 | 4.4 | 41.4 | 6.7 | 4.7 | 3.3 | 2 238 | 26 | 118.1 | 58.0 | 21.2 | 439 | 192 |
| Dallas............................ | 18.9 | 85.3 | 4.3 | 108.6 | 17.2 | 8.4 | 7.5 | 13 057 | 76 | 124.6 | 77.3 | 33.4 | 775 | 344 |
| DeKalb........................... | 14.8 | 0.1 | 5.4 | 77.0 | 6.8 | 4.8 | 3.4 | 3 392 | 26 | 158.5 | 90.6 | 37.5 | 552 | 219 |
| Elmore ........................... | 34.2 | 1.2 | 2.5 | 41.8 | 11.4 | 5.0 | 1.0 | 10 539 | 142 | 164.4 | 85.7 | 29.5 | 381 | 158 |
| Escambia........................ | 9.0 | 4.6 | 1.2 | 40.2 | 6.6 | 3.5 | 5.4 | 1 617 | 11 | 109.0 | 45.9 | 25.2 | 671 | 278 |
| Etowah .......................... | 42.2 | 4.3 | 15.2 | 119.3 | 15.8 | 11.8 | 10.7 | 11 975 | 99 | 268.4 | 133.0 | 101.5 | 983 | 266 |
| Fayette........................... | 15.1 | 0.0 | 0.8 | 24.0 | 2.3 | 1.3 | 0.4 | 220 | 3 | 53.5 | 36.0 | 10.0 | 567 | 211 |
| Franklin.......................... | 7.6 | 8.7 | 1.4 | 47.0 | 4.2 | 3.4 | 1.8 | 1 860 | 35 | 76.4 | 44.0 | 14.5 | 477 | 236 |
| Geneva........................... | 12.5 | 1.6 | 2.2 | 38.4 | 4.0 | 1.7 | 1.2 | 1 614 | 11 | 94.1 | 36.3 | 10.4 | 406 | 178 |
| Greene............................ | 2.2 | 0.2 | 0.5 | 35.0 | 3.8 | 1.1 | 1.5 | 313 | 3 | 27.4 | 16.7 | 5.3 | 579 | 395 |
| Hale............................... | 8.9 | 0.2 | 0.9 | 36.9 | 5.3 | 1.7 | 1.6 | 840 | 6 | 41.5 | 27.9 | 5.2 | 288 | 134 |
| Henry ............................ | 3.7 | 0.9 | 0.8 | 26.0 | 3.3 | 2.7 | 0.8 | 5 530 | 41 | 44.9 | 20.6 | 9.2 | 554 | 236 |
| Houston.......................... | 29.1 | 10.4 | 7.0 | 87.1 | 19.4 | 8.3 | 10.5 | 47 371 | 236 | 462.3 | 111.2 | 87.2 | 897 | 262 |
| Jackson.......................... | 11.1 | 2.5 | 212.1 | 69.7 | 7.5 | 3.4 | 21.3 | 4 511 | 37 | 167.5 | 71.5 | 29.4 | 554 | 170 |
| Jefferson......................... | 860.4 | 76.4 | 344.0 | 995.0 | 107.4 | 58.8 | 404.8 | 285 121 | 1 718 | 2 986.9 | 888.6 | 1 357.7 | 2 061 | 781 |
| Lamar............................. | 3.9 | 5.4 | 0.7 | 25.1 | 2.2 | 1.4 | 0.5 | 98 | 1 | 35.4 | 24.2 | 5.8 | 398 | 171 |
| Lauderdale...................... | 33.0 | 4.7 | 4.4 | 73.7 | 11.4 | 5.7 | 6.2 | 9 632 | 113 | 578.4 | 108.7 | 71.9 | 812 | 332 |
| Lawrence........................ | 6.3 | 0.6 | 1.0 | 44.5 | 5.0 | 2.7 | 0.4 | 0 | 0 | 89.6 | 47.4 | 9.2 | 270 | 135 |
| Lee ................................ | 70.4 | 22.7 | 10.2 | 66.3 | 18.2 | 7.9 | 59.1 | 191 657 | 957 | 728.3 | 134.9 | 132.6 | 1 016 | 470 |
| Limestone....................... | 18.8 | 7.4 | 2.8 | 51.5 | 6.3 | 5.2 | 17.6 | 17 644 | 95 | 197.6 | 82.2 | 30.9 | 418 | 209 |
| Lowndes......................... | 4.2 | 13.3 | 0.3 | 29.7 | 6.9 | 6.0 | 2.2 | 357 | 3 | 34.6 | 20.2 | 11.3 | 889 | 499 |
| Macon............................ | 41.4 | 1.0 | 19.8 | 52.9 | 8.6 | 8.3 | 16.1 | 1 019 | 5 | 52.3 | 30.2 | 12.8 | 571 | 280 |
| Madison.......................... | 1 342.0 | 5 246.7 | 1 127.0 | 156.3 | 28.7 | 30.3 | 88.6 | 263 440 | 1 924 | 1 644.2 | 673.0 | 333.0 | 1 065 | 459 |
| Marengo......................... | 8.1 | 4.8 | 1.0 | 49.5 | 6.1 | 1.7 | 0.4 | 469 | 4 | 64.2 | 43.1 | 14.4 | 675 | 254 |
| Marion............................ | 29.8 | 0.0 | 1.2 | 37.2 | 3.8 | 2.0 | 2.7 | 855 | 8 | 71.8 | 42.0 | 17.7 | 597 | 206 |
| Marshall.......................... | 26.6 | 8.2 | 64.6 | 85.9 | 9.3 | 6.6 | 10.5 | 7 464 | 46 | 344.2 | 134.0 | 64.1 | 731 | 314 |
| Mobile............................ | 317.4 | 507.9 | 65.7 | 333.9 | 74.8 | 37.7 | 104.8 | 143 429 | 1 541 | 1 348.0 | 605.0 | 535.3 | 1 324 | 417 |
| Monroe........................... | 6.4 | 0.1 | 1.0 | 42.4 | 5.1 | 3.7 | 1.2 | 0 | 0 | 85.2 | 44.2 | 10.6 | 465 | 262 |
| Montgomery .................... | 767.6 | 408.1 | 93.1 | 331.9 | 189.6 | 378.8 | 1 328.2 | 104 296 | 721 | 607.0 | 283.3 | 258.4 | 1 144 | 284 |
| Morgan........................... | 44.1 | 15.9 | 6.6 | 83.3 | 23.8 | 7.9 | 9.0 | 16 734 | 103 | 419.4 | 144.4 | 95.3 | 828 | 400 |
| Perry.............................. | 7.8 | 0.0 | 0.4 | 32.7 | 5.8 | 1.7 | 0.7 | 0 | 0 | 38.2 | 27.7 | 6.6 | 626 | 219 |
| Pickens........................... | 8.9 | 16.6 | 5.3 | 47.9 | 6.0 | 1.8 | 2.7 | 414 | 4 | 45.8 | 32.6 | 6.4 | 325 | 227 |
| Pike ............................... | 17.1 | 0.4 | 1.2 | 54.8 | 11.3 | 4.3 | 36.3 | 6 070 | 77 | 70.3 | 42.1 | 16.9 | 565 | 214 |
| Randolph......................... | 4.1 | 0.6 | 1.0 | 32.3 | 3.3 | 1.5 | 0.5 | 0 | 0 | 55.7 | 34.4 | 14.0 | 622 | 398 |
| Russell............................ | 13.3 | 0.6 | 2.1 | 62.3 | 11.2 | 4.1 | 6.1 | 109 835 | 588 | 141.5 | 77.6 | 38.8 | 772 | 385 |
| St. Clair .......................... | 15.8 | 6.4 | -7.1 | 32.8 | 8.9 | 4.6 | 1.2 | 19 850 | 169 | 154.5 | 85.6 | 46.5 | 596 | 249 |
| Shelby ............................ | 38.4 | 203.2 | 28.3 | 33.0 | 11.6 | 6.1 | 54.1 | 77 093 | 434 | 467.0 | 175.9 | 176.0 | 966 | 522 |
| Sumter............................ | 16.4 | 0.2 | 0.7 | 38.6 | 7.8 | 2.7 | 2.2 | 375 | 2 | 36.9 | 23.7 | 8.5 | 639 | 278 |
| Talladega......................... | 42.3 | 17.1 | 5.7 | 97.0 | 19.6 | 8.8 | 11.3 | 8 929 | 108 | 189.6 | 104.6 | 55.7 | 694 | 324 |
| Tallapoosa....................... | 15.0 | 1.7 | 1.7 | 43.9 | 9.1 | 4.4 | 7.2 | 3 138 | 13 | 114.2 | 66.5 | 25.8 | 634 | 302 |
| Tuscaloosa...................... | 102.3 | 122.5 | 150.6 | 156.8 | 27.8 | 18.7 | 79.9 | 98 185 | 734 | 871.6 | 242.3 | 163.0 | 916 | 347 |
| Walker............................ | 23.0 | 5.3 | 3.6 | 75.2 | 12.7 | 6.9 | 5.6 | 1 720 | 11 | 139.8 | 84.2 | 34.6 | 502 | 153 |

1. State totals may include programs not allocated by county.    2. Based on the resident population estimated as of July 1 of the year shown.

# Table B. States and Counties — Local Government Finances, Government Employment, and Voting

| STATE County | Local government finances, 2007 (cont.) — Direct general expenditure — Total (mil dol) | Per capita[1] (dollars) | Percent of total for: Education | Health and hospitals | Police protection | Public welfare | High-ways | Debt outstanding — Total (mil dol) | Per capita[1] (dollars) | Government employment, 2011 — Federal civilian | Federal military | State and local | Presidential election,[2] 2012 — Percent of vote cast: Democratic | Republican | All other |
|---|---|---|---|---|---|---|---|---|---|---|---|---|---|---|---|
| | 185 | 186 | 187 | 188 | 189 | 190 | 191 | 192 | 193 | 194 | 195 | 196 | 197 | 198 | 199 |
| UNITED STATES............ | X | X | X | X | X | X | X | X | X | 2 921 000 | 2 095 000 | 19 285 000 | 51.1 | 47.2 | 1.7 |
| ALABAMA ........................ | X | X | X | X | X | X | X | X | X | 57 594 | 32 806 | 317 687 | 38.7 | 60.3 | 0.9 |
| Autauga.......................... | 116.2 | 2 325 | 62.2 | 0.2 | 6.5 | 0.4 | 5.6 | 172.4 | 3 451 | 83 | 268 | 2 222 | 25.8 | 73.6 | 0.6 |
| Baldwin.......................... | 726.3 | 4 228 | 45.6 | 16.8 | 4.1 | 0.1 | 6.8 | 1 059.3 | 6 167 | 315 | 904 | 8 323 | 23.8 | 75.3 | 0.9 |
| Barbour.......................... | 72.1 | 2 581 | 49.7 | 15.4 | 8.1 | 0.0 | 3.7 | 38.4 | 1 374 | 62 | 143 | 1 790 | 49.0 | 50.4 | 0.6 |
| Bibb............................... | 55.9 | 2 594 | 54.3 | 23.1 | 3.5 | 0.0 | 4.6 | 60.1 | 2 790 | 98 | 110 | 1 281 | 26.6 | 72.4 | 1.0 |
| Blount............................ | 111.7 | 1 972 | 71.8 | 1.6 | 5.0 | 0.1 | 7.0 | 49.8 | 880 | 93 | 279 | 1 989 | 14.5 | 84.0 | 1.5 |
| Bullock.......................... | 32.3 | 2 992 | 51.2 | 18.4 | 5.7 | 0.7 | 10.3 | 9.8 | 909 | 36 | 51 | 699 | 74.1 | 25.7 | 0.2 |
| Butler............................ | 63.0 | 3 126 | 48.6 | 8.0 | 5.4 | 0.5 | 8.9 | 99.7 | 4 944 | 38 | 100 | 899 | 43.1 | 56.5 | 0.4 |
| Calhoun......................... | 494.3 | 4 370 | 38.2 | 35.3 | 3.6 | 0.2 | 4.0 | 141.5 | 1 251 | 5 206 | 670 | 8 059 | 33.2 | 65.7 | 1.1 |
| Chambers....................... | 80.9 | 2 328 | 54.1 | 0.2 | 8.2 | 0.0 | 6.3 | 67.3 | 1 936 | 53 | 164 | 1 359 | 45.5 | 53.9 | 0.6 |
| Cherokee........................ | 51.3 | 2 088 | 72.5 | 0.1 | 4.1 | 0.2 | 8.8 | 48.9 | 1 991 | 50 | 126 | 1 221 | 23.7 | 74.9 | 1.4 |
| Chilton.......................... | 115.8 | 2 739 | 49.8 | 21.7 | 5.0 | 0.0 | 5.1 | 28.2 | 666 | 66 | 212 | 1 764 | 20.7 | 78.5 | 0.8 |
| Choctaw......................... | 31.8 | 2 246 | 61.3 | 0.0 | 5.0 | 0.0 | 10.7 | 42.8 | 3 017 | 27 | 66 | 516 | 46.1 | 53.5 | 0.4 |
| Clarke............................ | 72.7 | 2 744 | 64.3 | 0.2 | 5.8 | 0.2 | 9.3 | 104.0 | 3 925 | 84 | 124 | 1 863 | 44.0 | 55.6 | 0.4 |
| Clay............................... | 50.7 | 3 681 | 33.5 | 42.2 | 4.3 | 0.1 | 7.2 | 3.5 | 256 | 54 | 67 | 957 | 25.8 | 73.1 | 1.1 |
| Cleburne........................ | 38.6 | 2 623 | 56.6 | 0.0 | 4.6 | 14.2 | 9.4 | 33.5 | 2 281 | 49 | 72 | 790 | 18.0 | 80.3 | 1.7 |
| Coffee........................... | 131.6 | 2 812 | 67.9 | 0.5 | 4.8 | 0.5 | 5.3 | 48.2 | 1 030 | 211 | 244 | 2 473 | 25.2 | 74.1 | 0.6 |
| Colbert.......................... | 246.5 | 4 516 | 39.4 | 32.8 | 3.2 | 0.2 | 4.4 | 140.4 | 2 572 | 1 066 | 264 | 4 155 | 39.1 | 59.3 | 1.6 |
| Conecuh......................... | 36.2 | 2 747 | 51.0 | 0.1 | 5.3 | 4.8 | 13.7 | 13.7 | 1 039 | 27 | 63 | 762 | 49.4 | 50.0 | 0.6 |
| Coosa............................ | 23.4 | 2 154 | 55.7 | 0.5 | 6.9 | 0.9 | 18.1 | 11.6 | 1 066 | 23 | 52 | 366 | 40.9 | 58.4 | 0.8 |
| Covington....................... | 105.6 | 2 855 | 52.2 | 0.1 | 7.1 | 0.5 | 16.1 | 209.3 | 5 655 | 123 | 184 | 2 035 | 20.5 | 78.8 | 0.7 |
| Crenshaw....................... | 33.7 | 2 441 | 59.3 | 1.1 | 3.9 | 0.4 | 12.4 | 21.1 | 1 525 | 39 | 67 | 581 | 30.8 | 68.7 | 0.5 |
| Cullman.......................... | 246.5 | 3 060 | 44.6 | 35.1 | 2.9 | 0.6 | 3.4 | 142.7 | 1 772 | 228 | 390 | 4 042 | 16.6 | 81.8 | 1.5 |
| Dale.............................. | 123.2 | 2 558 | 47.5 | 22.5 | 4.5 | 0.2 | 4.7 | 60.2 | 1 250 | 3 213 | 4 060 | 2 234 | 27.3 | 71.9 | 0.8 |
| Dallas............................ | 121.3 | 2 815 | 58.8 | 0.1 | 10.5 | 0.2 | 5.9 | 48.4 | 1 124 | 178 | 210 | 2 787 | 67.1 | 32.6 | 0.3 |
| DeKalb........................... | 156.3 | 2 297 | 62.1 | 2.9 | 3.9 | 0.5 | 7.1 | 99.8 | 1 467 | 168 | 345 | 3 264 | 23.6 | 74.8 | 1.7 |
| Elmore........................... | 149.6 | 1 930 | 72.0 | 0.6 | 4.6 | 0.0 | 6.2 | 121.0 | 1 561 | 146 | 388 | 3 944 | 24.2 | 75.1 | 0.7 |
| Escambia........................ | 107.5 | 2 859 | 49.5 | 25.7 | 6.0 | 0.0 | 5.7 | 41.8 | 1 111 | 61 | 184 | 3 940 | 35.4 | 63.9 | 0.8 |
| Etowah.......................... | 274.7 | 2 661 | 50.8 | 1.8 | 7.6 | 0.2 | 3.9 | 247.2 | 2 395 | 343 | 506 | 5 120 | 30.2 | 68.4 | 1.4 |
| Fayette.......................... | 40.1 | 2 273 | 58.3 | 0.8 | 3.6 | 0.0 | 8.4 | 24.7 | 1 402 | 38 | 83 | 1 215 | 25.1 | 73.9 | 1.0 |
| Franklin.......................... | 94.4 | 3 100 | 59.6 | 0.1 | 3.3 | 0.5 | 4.6 | 71.2 | 2 339 | 98 | 154 | 1 859 | 29.7 | 68.8 | 1.5 |
| Geneva.......................... | 75.2 | 2 925 | 45.5 | 26.8 | 3.9 | 0.7 | 10.1 | 28.4 | 1 104 | 61 | 130 | 1 501 | 18.3 | 80.8 | 0.9 |
| Greene........................... | 30.1 | 3 274 | 57.1 | 18.1 | 3.6 | 0.0 | 5.1 | 8.0 | 874 | 25 | 43 | 622 | 83.1 | 16.5 | 0.4 |
| Hale.............................. | 45.0 | 2 482 | 60.4 | 13.6 | 4.5 | 0.1 | 7.5 | 18.2 | 1 006 | 50 | 75 | 868 | 60.7 | 39.0 | 0.4 |
| Henry............................ | 43.6 | 2 623 | 57.4 | 0.1 | 4.9 | 20.1 | 0.5 | 33.0 | 1 984 | 42 | 84 | 710 | 34.9 | 64.6 | 0.5 |
| Houston......................... | 483.7 | 4 978 | 27.3 | 46.3 | 4.4 | 0.0 | 3.7 | 380.4 | 3 915 | 332 | 507 | 7 898 | 29.3 | 70.1 | 0.6 |
| Jackson.......................... | 175.8 | 3 315 | 47.4 | 23.6 | 3.7 | 0.5 | 5.0 | 142.9 | 2 694 | 496 | 258 | 3 177 | 30.5 | 67.5 | 2.0 |
| Jefferson........................ | 2 974.3 | 4 515 | 40.7 | 4.1 | 6.1 | 0.1 | 5.4 | 8 267.4 | 12 550 | 8 212 | 3 513 | 51 544 | 52.2 | 47.1 | 0.8 |
| Lamar............................ | 35.5 | 2 455 | 55.8 | 3.3 | 4.0 | 0.1 | 11.2 | 20.2 | 1 396 | 37 | 69 | 615 | 22.8 | 76.6 | 0.6 |
| Lauderdale ..................... | 304.3 | 3 436 | 44.2 | 29.0 | 3.7 | 0.1 | 4.3 | 319.4 | 3 606 | 304 | 453 | 4 801 | 35.0 | 63.2 | 1.9 |
| Lawrence........................ | 87.9 | 2 568 | 55.7 | 10.0 | 9.9 | 0.6 | 9.2 | 188.0 | 5 491 | 86 | 165 | 1 408 | 35.2 | 63.2 | 1.6 |
| Lee............................... | 542.0 | 4 153 | 36.5 | 35.4 | 3.4 | 0.1 | 4.0 | 632.6 | 4 847 | 306 | 746 | 15 572 | 39.6 | 59.3 | 1.1 |
| Limestone....................... | 208.6 | 2 822 | 50.2 | 24.6 | 3.7 | 0.3 | 4.4 | 180.3 | 2 440 | 1 520 | 413 | 5 239 | 28.4 | 70.3 | 1.2 |
| Lowndes......................... | 33.8 | 2 662 | 67.5 | 0.4 | 5.0 | 0.2 | 12.8 | 33.8 | 2 668 | 33 | 54 | 586 | 74.9 | 24.9 | 0.3 |
| Macon............................ | 51.6 | 2 311 | 57.2 | 7.4 | 3.1 | 0.0 | 1.2 | 103.9 | 4 653 | 910 | 113 | 2 153 | 86.9 | 12.8 | 0.3 |
| Madison.......................... | 1 447.7 | 4 629 | 31.2 | 39.9 | 4.2 | 0.0 | 2.9 | 1 962.4 | 6 275 | 19 343 | 2 981 | 23 847 | 41.9 | 56.9 | 1.2 |
| Marengo......................... | 64.1 | 3 013 | 66.4 | 3.1 | 3.9 | 0.4 | 4.3 | 27.9 | 1 309 | 62 | 115 | 1 637 | 51.7 | 48.1 | 0.3 |
| Marion........................... | 69.1 | 2 336 | 64.6 | 2.6 | 2.4 | 0.1 | 4.4 | 85.1 | 2 878 | 78 | 148 | 1 540 | 21.0 | 77.2 | 1.8 |
| Marshall......................... | 348.5 | 3 977 | 41.9 | 34.8 | 3.9 | 0.5 | 2.6 | 297.6 | 3 396 | 252 | 455 | 5 873 | 21.2 | 77.6 | 1.2 |
| Mobile........................... | 1 241.0 | 3 069 | 48.4 | 3.3 | 6.9 | 0.5 | 4.8 | 1 144.8 | 2 831 | 2 693 | 2 988 | 24 641 | 45.3 | 54.0 | 0.7 |
| Monroe.......................... | 88.1 | 3 872 | 42.9 | 31.8 | 4.4 | 0.2 | 7.4 | 19.2 | 844 | 56 | 110 | 1 485 | 44.7 | 54.9 | 0.5 |
| Montgomery ................... | 701.0 | 3 105 | 40.8 | 1.6 | 7.6 | 0.4 | 5.5 | 369.4 | 1 636 | 6 739 | 3 960 | 26 873 | 59.4 | 40.1 | 0.5 |
| Morgan........................... | 445.2 | 3 870 | 41.6 | 21.0 | 4.3 | 0.3 | 2.0 | 449.0 | 3 903 | 315 | 583 | 6 749 | 27.5 | 71.3 | 1.3 |
| Perry............................. | 39.9 | 3 763 | 45.9 | 21.7 | 3.2 | 0.2 | 7.2 | 21.4 | 2 023 | 25 | 88 | 585 | 72.4 | 27.3 | 0.4 |
| Pickens.......................... | 45.4 | 2 313 | 63.5 | 1.2 | 5.5 | 0.1 | 8.5 | 30.5 | 1 554 | 54 | 94 | 857 | 45.6 | 54.0 | 0.4 |
| Pike.............................. | 77.2 | 2 578 | 52.9 | 0.3 | 7.9 | 0.2 | 10.7 | 56.4 | 1 885 | 88 | 162 | 3 258 | 42.1 | 57.4 | 0.5 |
| Randolph........................ | 48.0 | 2 139 | 68.6 | 2.7 | 5.2 | 0.4 | 7.6 | 31.0 | 1 384 | 50 | 110 | 1 163 | 29.5 | 69.1 | 1.4 |
| Russell........................... | 150.1 | 2 990 | 61.1 | 0.1 | 6.8 | 0.0 | 5.2 | 285.6 | 5 692 | 88 | 264 | 2 711 | 53.3 | 46.0 | 0.7 |
| St. Clair......................... | 163.4 | 2 094 | 62.7 | 0.4 | 6.5 | 0.1 | 5.0 | 254.7 | 3 263 | 111 | 408 | 2 858 | 17.9 | 81.1 | 1.0 |
| Shelby........................... | 462.1 | 2 538 | 58.6 | 1.4 | 6.3 | 0.2 | 4.4 | 500.4 | 2 748 | 326 | 957 | 8 073 | 22.8 | 76.2 | 1.1 |
| Sumter........................... | 39.2 | 2 948 | 58.2 | 1.1 | 4.2 | 0.1 | 13.7 | 16.2 | 1 217 | 39 | 65 | 1 327 | 75.0 | 24.7 | 0.4 |
| Talladega........................ | 313.0 | 3 900 | 38.1 | 3.0 | 2.8 | 0.1 | 3.3 | 147.4 | 1 837 | 484 | 395 | 4 806 | 40.3 | 58.8 | 0.9 |
| Tallapoosa...................... | 122.3 | 3 001 | 51.0 | 15.5 | 6.2 | 0.1 | 4.1 | 98.7 | 2 422 | 91 | 201 | 2 043 | 31.4 | 67.9 | 0.7 |
| Tuscaloosa...................... | 904.2 | 5 082 | 30.3 | 43.1 | 4.0 | 0.0 | 5.0 | 590.5 | 3 319 | 1 656 | 968 | 22 065 | 41.6 | 57.5 | 0.9 |
| Walker........................... | 157.6 | 2 290 | 69.4 | 0.1 | 5.5 | 0.1 | 5.3 | 105.2 | 1 529 | 180 | 323 | 3 251 | 25.9 | 72.3 | 1.8 |

1. Based on the resident population estimated as of July 1 of the year shown.   2. © 2013 Election Data Services, Inc. All rights reserved.

# Table B. States and Counties — Land Area and Population

| STATE/ County code | CBSA code[1] | County type[2] | STATE County | Land area,[3] (sq km) 2010 | Population 2012 | | | Population characteristics[6], 2011 | | | | | | | | | | |
|---|---|---|---|---|---|---|---|---|---|---|---|---|---|---|---|---|---|---|
| | | | | | | | | Race alone or in combination, not Hispanic or Latino (percent) | | | | | Age (percent) | | | | | |
| | | | | | Total persons | Rank | Per square kilometer | White | Black | American Indian, Alaska Native | Asian and Pacific Islander | Percent Hispanic or Latino[4] | Under 5 years | 5 to 17 years | 18 to 24 years | 25 to 34 years | 35 to 44 years | 45 to 54 years |
| | | | | 1 | 2 | 3 | 4 | 5 | 6 | 7 | 8 | 9 | 10 | 11 | 12 | 13 | 14 | 15 |
| | | | ALABAMA—Cont'd | | | | | | | | | | | | | | | |
| 01 129 | ... | 8 | Washington | 2 798 | 17 109 | 1 970 | 6.1 | 66.3 | 25.4 | 8.0 | 0.4 | 1.0 | 5.7 | 19.1 | 8.4 | 10.7 | 12.2 | 15.1 |
| 01 131 | ... | 8 | Wilcox | 2 301 | 11 431 | 2 333 | 5.0 | 27.2 | 72.0 | 0.3 | 0.2 | 0.7 | 5.8 | 20.5 | 8.4 | 10.5 | 11.3 | 14.0 |
| 01 133 | ... | 6 | Winston | 1 588 | 24 108 | 1 637 | 15.2 | 95.3 | 1.3 | 1.4 | 0.4 | 2.8 | 5.4 | 16.1 | 7.4 | 10.5 | 12.6 | 15.2 |
| 02 000 | ... | X | ALASKA | 1 477 953 | 731 449 | X | 0.5 | 69.4 | 4.5 | 18.7 | 8.5 | 5.8 | 7.5 | 18.5 | 10.6 | 14.8 | 12.7 | 15.2 |
| 02 013 | ... | 9 | Aleutians East | 18 083 | 3 161 | 2 965 | 0.2 | 17.1 | 7.7 | 26.8 | 39.2 | 12.8 | 3.3 | 8.2 | 9.2 | 16.0 | 18.8 | 24.2 |
| 02 016 | ... | 7 | Aleutians West | 11 371 | 5 547 | 2 800 | 0.5 | 33.7 | 6.8 | 16.7 | 33.1 | 14.0 | 3.8 | 10.1 | 8.1 | 17.6 | 19.9 | 22.5 |
| 02 020 | 11260 | 2 | Anchorage | 4 415 | 298 610 | 220 | 67.6 | 68.1 | 7.2 | 11.6 | 12.8 | 7.9 | 7.5 | 18.2 | 11.3 | 15.9 | 13.0 | 14.8 |
| 02 050 | ... | 7 | Bethel | 105 076 | 17 746 | 1 931 | 0.2 | 15.4 | 0.9 | 85.0 | 1.7 | 1.4 | 10.8 | 25.5 | 11.7 | 13.6 | 10.7 | 12.7 |
| 02 060 | ... | 9 | Bristol Bay | 1 305 | 991 | 3 109 | 0.8 | 62.6 | 1.8 | 45.5 | 3.2 | 2.8 | 4.5 | 18.4 | 7.3 | 11.5 | 12.6 | 21.7 |
| 02 068 | ... | 8 | Denali | 33 026 | 1 875 | 3 067 | 0.1 | 91.5 | 1.5 | 6.7 | 1.8 | 2.6 | 5.7 | 16.3 | 4.6 | 12.6 | 15.4 | 19.2 |
| 02 070 | ... | 9 | Dillingham | 48 093 | 5 034 | 2 835 | 0.1 | 26.5 | 1.0 | 77.0 | 1.6 | 2.3 | 9.6 | 23.1 | 11.4 | 13.0 | 9.5 | 14.9 |
| 02 090 | 21820 | 3 | Fairbanks North Star | 19 006 | 100 272 | 588 | 5.3 | 78.7 | 6.0 | 10.5 | 4.9 | 6.3 | 8.0 | 17.3 | 13.5 | 17.1 | 12.4 | 13.4 |
| 02 100 | ... | 9 | Haines | 6 005 | 2 552 | 3 006 | 0.4 | 86.8 | 1.3 | 13.4 | 1.7 | 2.3 | 4.9 | 15.1 | 4.6 | 10.1 | 11.9 | 18.1 |
| 02 105 | ... | | Hoonah-Angoon | 19 489 | 2 129 | 3 041 | 0.1 | 56.6 | 1.4 | 45.9 | 2.2 | 3.8 | 5.9 | 14.2 | 6.9 | 10.8 | 10.3 | 17.4 |
| 02 110 | 27940 | 5 | Juneau | 6 998 | 32 556 | 1 370 | 4.7 | 74.4 | 1.9 | 17.9 | 9.8 | 5.4 | 6.2 | 17.0 | 8.9 | 14.1 | 13.6 | 17.0 |
| 02 122 | ... | 7 | Kenai Peninsula | 41 635 | 56 900 | 892 | 1.4 | 87.3 | 1.0 | 11.3 | 2.8 | 3.2 | 6.3 | 17.1 | 8.3 | 11.5 | 12.0 | 16.5 |
| 02 130 | 28540 | 7 | Ketchikan Gateway | 12 583 | 13 779 | 2 189 | 1.1 | 73.4 | 1.4 | 20.4 | 9.5 | 4.3 | 6.7 | 17.1 | 8.6 | 13.5 | 12.5 | 16.2 |
| 02 150 | 28980 | 7 | Kodiak Island | 16 963 | 14 239 | 2 159 | 0.8 | 57.5 | 1.5 | 17.3 | 22.7 | 7.9 | 8.3 | 20.0 | 10.1 | 15.0 | 12.7 | 15.4 |
| 02 164 | ... | 9 | Lake and Peninsula | 61 258 | 1 654 | 3 077 | 0.0 | 32.7 | 2.6 | 70.1 | 2.1 | 3.3 | 8.4 | 20.8 | 11.4 | 14.5 | 9.7 | 16.5 |
| 02 170 | 11260 | 2 | Matanuska-Susitna | 63 734 | 93 925 | 616 | 1.5 | 87.6 | 1.8 | 10.0 | 3.0 | 3.9 | 7.4 | 21.0 | 8.7 | 13.0 | 13.2 | 15.7 |
| 02 180 | ... | 7 | Nome | 59 471 | 9 915 | 2 449 | 0.2 | 22.3 | 1.0 | 79.5 | 2.0 | 1.6 | 10.7 | 23.5 | 11.6 | 14.4 | 10.9 | 12.7 |
| 02 185 | ... | 7 | North Slope | 229 720 | 9 643 | 2 460 | 0.0 | 37.1 | 1.8 | 56.4 | 7.4 | 3.0 | 7.8 | 16.4 | 10.6 | 15.3 | 12.5 | 19.3 |
| 02 188 | ... | 7 | Northwest Arctic | 92 133 | 7 810 | 2 614 | 0.1 | 17.2 | 1.3 | 85.0 | 2.0 | 1.1 | 11.9 | 23.2 | 13.4 | 13.5 | 10.5 | 12.5 |
| 02 195 | ... | | Petersburg | 8 500 | 3 844 | 2 918 | 0.5 | 75.0 | 2.1 | 22.5 | 5.7 | 3.9 | 6.1 | 16.8 | 7.9 | 11.6 | 12.4 | 16.5 |
| 02 198 | ... | | Prince of Wales-Hyder | 10 160 | 5 751 | 2 789 | 0.6 | 56.5 | 1.2 | 45.8 | 2.2 | 2.8 | 7.2 | 18.1 | 7.7 | 11.0 | 12.5 | 16.8 |
| 02 220 | ... | 7 | Sitka | 7 434 | 9 046 | 2 515 | 1.2 | 71.2 | 1.6 | 22.9 | 8.3 | 5.0 | 7.0 | 16.0 | 7.7 | 14.4 | 13.0 | 15.4 |
| 02 230 | ... | | Skagway | 1 172 | 959 | 3 110 | 0.8 | 92.1 | 1.1 | 6.5 | 1.7 | 2.8 | 5.5 | 9.4 | 6.1 | 19.0 | 16.7 | 16.1 |
| 02 240 | ... | 8 | Southeast Fairbanks | 64 151 | 7 144 | 2 669 | 0.1 | 82.3 | 1.9 | 14.8 | 2.1 | 3.7 | 7.2 | 18.9 | 8.2 | 13.1 | 12.5 | 16.2 |
| 02 261 | ... | 9 | Valdez-Cordova | 88 681 | 9 717 | 2 458 | 0.1 | 77.3 | 1.3 | 18.1 | 6.2 | 3.9 | 6.8 | 17.5 | 8.1 | 12.6 | 12.0 | 18.2 |
| 02 270 | ... | 9 | Wade Hampton | 44 241 | 7 809 | 2 615 | 0.2 | 6.0 | 0.5 | 95.0 | 0.7 | 0.2 | 12.4 | 28.5 | 14.0 | 12.2 | 10.0 | 10.6 |
| 02 275 | ... | | Wrangell | 6 582 | 2 403 | 3 014 | 0.4 | 80.2 | 1.2 | 23.2 | 3.5 | 1.7 | 5.3 | 16.4 | 7.0 | 9.2 | 9.7 | 17.3 |
| 02 282 | ... | 9 | Yakutat | 19 812 | 668 | 3 132 | 0.0 | 52.0 | 2.9 | 44.6 | 13.8 | 2.8 | 6.3 | 17.2 | 7.9 | 11.3 | 15.3 | 15.3 |
| 02 290 | ... | 8 | Yukon-Koyukuk | 376 856 | 5 770 | 2 785 | 0.0 | 27.9 | 0.8 | 74.9 | 1.2 | 1.4 | 8.0 | 19.7 | 10.4 | 11.6 | 9.8 | 15.7 |
| 04 000 | ... | X | ARIZONA | 294 207 | 6 553 255 | X | 22.3 | 59.0 | 4.6 | 4.6 | 3.7 | 30.1 | 6.9 | 18.1 | 9.9 | 13.4 | 12.7 | 13.0 |
| 04 001 | ... | 6 | Apache | 29 001 | 73 195 | 743 | 2.5 | 21.6 | 1.3 | 71.2 | 0.8 | 6.8 | 8.5 | 23.0 | 10.4 | 11.1 | 10.9 | 13.0 |
| 04 003 | 43420 | 4 | Cochise | 15 969 | 132 088 | 473 | 8.3 | 60.0 | 5.0 | 1.5 | 3.4 | 32.6 | 6.5 | 16.3 | 9.7 | 12.8 | 10.8 | 12.9 |
| 04 005 | 22380 | 3 | Coconino | 48 223 | 136 011 | 457 | 2.8 | 57.0 | 2.0 | 27.1 | 2.5 | 13.9 | 6.6 | 16.5 | 18.8 | 13.2 | 11.1 | 12.7 |
| 04 007 | 37740 | 6 | Gila | 12 323 | 53 144 | 936 | 4.3 | 65.9 | 0.8 | 15.2 | 0.9 | 18.4 | 6.0 | 15.5 | 7.3 | 8.7 | 9.2 | 13.5 |
| 04 009 | 40940 | 6 | Graham | 11 972 | 37 416 | 1 236 | 3.1 | 52.9 | 2.3 | 14.1 | 1.2 | 30.8 | 8.3 | 19.7 | 11.9 | 14.4 | 12.2 | 11.7 |
| 04 011 | 40940 | 7 | Greenlee | 4 774 | 8 802 | 2 534 | 1.8 | 48.8 | 1.6 | 2.7 | 0.8 | 47.3 | 7.5 | 21.3 | 8.6 | 13.2 | 12.1 | 13.2 |
| 04 012 | ... | 6 | La Paz | 11 654 | 20 281 | 1 826 | 1.7 | 63.1 | 1.2 | 12.2 | 0.9 | 24.5 | 5.1 | 13.1 | 6.0 | 8.0 | 7.8 | 11.2 |
| 04 013 | 38060 | 1 | Maricopa | 23 828 | 3 942 169 | 4 | 165.4 | 59.9 | 5.5 | 2.1 | 4.5 | 30.0 | 7.2 | 18.8 | 9.9 | 14.2 | 13.6 | 13.1 |
| 04 015 | 29420 | 4 | Mohave | 34 476 | 203 334 | 309 | 5.9 | 80.5 | 1.4 | 2.8 | 1.9 | 15.2 | 5.3 | 14.9 | 6.9 | 9.3 | 9.7 | 13.8 |
| 04 017 | 43320 | 4 | Navajo | 25 771 | 107 094 | 555 | 4.2 | 44.9 | 1.6 | 43.0 | 1.0 | 11.1 | 8.0 | 21.3 | 9.7 | 11.0 | 10.8 | 13.0 |
| 04 019 | 46060 | 2 | Pima | 23 794 | 992 394 | 42 | 41.7 | 56.4 | 4.0 | 3.0 | 3.5 | 35.1 | 6.3 | 16.4 | 11.0 | 13.0 | 11.6 | 13.1 |
| 04 021 | 38060 | 1 | Pinal | 13 897 | 387 365 | 173 | 27.9 | 60.1 | 5.0 | 5.5 | 2.6 | 28.7 | 7.6 | 18.5 | 7.8 | 14.5 | 13.3 | 11.7 |
| 04 023 | 35700 | 4 | Santa Cruz | 3 204 | 47 303 | 1 022 | 14.8 | 16.2 | 0.4 | 0.4 | 0.6 | 82.7 | 7.7 | 22.4 | 9.1 | 10.1 | 11.8 | 13.2 |
| 04 025 | 39140 | 3 | Yavapai | 21 040 | 212 637 | 296 | 10.1 | 83.0 | 1.0 | 2.2 | 1.6 | 13.9 | 4.7 | 13.8 | 7.0 | 8.8 | 9.4 | 13.6 |
| 04 027 | 49740 | 3 | Yuma | 14 281 | 200 022 | 316 | 14.0 | 35.6 | 2.3 | 1.5 | 1.7 | 60.1 | 7.6 | 20.0 | 11.4 | 12.7 | 11.4 | 11.4 |
| 05 000 | ... | X | ARKANSAS | 134 771 | 2 949 131 | X | 21.9 | 75.7 | 16.0 | 1.5 | 1.8 | 6.6 | 6.7 | 17.5 | 9.7 | 13.0 | 12.4 | 13.7 |
| 05 001 | ... | 6 | Arkansas | 2 561 | 18 892 | 1 880 | 7.4 | 71.7 | 24.9 | 0.8 | 0.9 | 3.0 | 6.2 | 17.1 | 7.6 | 12.0 | 11.9 | 14.1 |
| 05 003 | ... | 7 | Ashley | 2 397 | 21 524 | 1 752 | 9.0 | 68.5 | 26.3 | 0.7 | 0.4 | 5.0 | 6.5 | 17.8 | 8.1 | 10.7 | 12.7 | 14.2 |
| 05 005 | 34260 | 7 | Baxter | 1 436 | 41 048 | 1 153 | 28.6 | 96.8 | 0.5 | 1.5 | 0.7 | 1.8 | 4.6 | 13.3 | 6.0 | 8.7 | 9.7 | 13.2 |
| 05 007 | 22220 | 2 | Benton | 2 195 | 232 268 | 278 | 105.8 | 77.9 | 2.1 | 2.6 | 3.6 | 15.7 | 7.8 | 19.8 | 8.2 | 14.7 | 14.0 | 13.0 |
| 05 009 | 25460 | 7 | Boone | 1 529 | 37 327 | 1 238 | 24.4 | 96.1 | 0.8 | 1.9 | 0.8 | 2.0 | 5.8 | 16.9 | 8.2 | 11.3 | 12.1 | 14.1 |
| 05 011 | ... | 6 | Bradley | 1 682 | 11 397 | 2 336 | 6.8 | 58.6 | 27.6 | 0.6 | 0.3 | 13.9 | 7.1 | 16.5 | 8.6 | 11.8 | 11.8 | 13.4 |
| 05 013 | 15780 | 9 | Calhoun | 1 628 | 5 307 | 2 818 | 3.3 | 74.2 | 22.6 | 0.9 | 0.6 | 3.1 | 5.0 | 14.6 | 9.8 | 10.3 | 12.4 | 16.8 |
| 05 015 | ... | 6 | Carroll | 1 632 | 27 610 | 1 508 | 16.9 | 84.6 | 0.7 | 2.1 | 0.9 | 13.3 | 5.8 | 16.5 | 7.1 | 10.2 | 10.9 | 14.0 |
| 05 017 | ... | 7 | Chicot | 1 669 | 11 433 | 2 332 | 6.9 | 41.2 | 53.3 | 0.6 | 0.7 | 5.0 | 7.0 | 15.9 | 8.4 | 11.2 | 10.7 | 14.5 |
| 05 019 | 11660 | 7 | Clark | 2 243 | 22 936 | 1 692 | 10.2 | 70.9 | 24.1 | 1.1 | 0.9 | 4.3 | 5.3 | 13.8 | 22.9 | 10.0 | 9.7 | 12.0 |
| 05 021 | ... | 7 | Clay | 1 656 | 15 684 | 2 066 | 9.5 | 97.4 | 0.8 | 1.1 | 0.3 | 1.5 | 5.3 | 16.6 | 7.7 | 10.0 | 12.3 | 14.1 |
| 05 023 | ... | 6 | Cleburne | 1 434 | 25 808 | 1 575 | 18.0 | 96.5 | 0.7 | 1.5 | 0.4 | 2.2 | 5.2 | 14.7 | 6.8 | 9.8 | 10.7 | 14.6 |

1. CBSA = Core Based Statistical Area. See Appendix A for explanation. See Appendix B for list of metropolitan areas with component counties.  2. County type code from the Economic Research Service of USDA Rural-Urban Continuum Codes. See Appendix A for definition.  3. Dry land or land partially or temporarily covered by water.  4. May be of any race.

| STATE County | Population, 2011 (cont.) Age (percent) (cont.) 55 to 64 years | 65 to 74 years | 75 years and over | Percent female | Population change and components of change, 2000–2012 Total persons 2000 | 2010 | Percent change 2000– 2010 | 2010– 2012 | Components of change, 2010–2012 Births | Deaths | Net migration | Households, 2010 Number | Percent change, 2000– 2010 | Persons per house-hold | Percent Female family house-holder[1] | One per-son |
|---|---|---|---|---|---|---|---|---|---|---|---|---|---|---|---|---|
| | 16 | 17 | 18 | 19 | 20 | 21 | 22 | 23 | 24 | 25 | 26 | 27 | 28 | 29 | 30 | 31 |
| ALABAMA—Cont'd | | | | | | | | | | | | | | | | |
| Washington | 13.7 | 9.0 | 6.1 | 50.7 | 18 097 | 17 581 | -2.9 | -2.7 | 366 | 450 | -404 | 6 758 | 0.8 | 2.58 | 13.3 | 24.5 |
| Wilcox | 14.1 | 8.5 | 6.9 | 52.7 | 13 183 | 11 670 | -11.5 | -2.0 | 318 | 298 | -262 | 4 484 | -6.1 | 2.58 | 27.3 | 28.4 |
| Winston | 14.5 | 10.9 | 7.2 | 51.0 | 24 843 | 24 484 | -1.4 | -1.5 | 501 | 710 | -152 | 10 163 | 0.6 | 2.38 | 10.9 | 27.1 |
| ALASKA | 12.6 | 5.2 | 2.8 | 48.1 | 626 932 | 710 231 | 13.3 | 3.0 | 25 889 | 7 589 | 2 638 | 258 058 | 16.5 | 2.65 | 10.7 | 25.6 |
| Aleutians East | 14.4 | 4.1 | 1.7 | 32.8 | 2 697 | 3 141 | 16.5 | 0.6 | 41 | 11 | -14 | 553 | 5.1 | 2.56 | 13.4 | 26.6 |
| Aleutians West | 14.3 | 3.1 | 0.7 | 32.4 | 5 465 | 5 561 | 1.8 | -0.3 | 64 | 10 | -78 | 1 212 | -4.6 | 2.49 | 9.6 | 32.4 |
| Anchorage | 11.8 | 4.8 | 2.8 | 49.3 | 260 283 | 291 826 | 12.1 | 2.3 | 10 658 | 3 037 | -850 | 107 332 | 13.2 | 2.64 | 11.7 | 24.9 |
| Bethel | 8.7 | 4.0 | 2.3 | 48.0 | 16 006 | 17 013 | 6.3 | 4.3 | 1 015 | 198 | -86 | 4 651 | 10.1 | 3.59 | 17.2 | 20.2 |
| Bristol Bay | 15.7 | 5.4 | 2.9 | 46.5 | 1 258 | 997 | -20.7 | -0.6 | 31 | 15 | -25 | 423 | -13.7 | 2.32 | 6.9 | 32.4 |
| Denali | 17.8 | 6.8 | 1.6 | 45.3 | 1 893 | 1 826 | -3.5 | 2.7 | 49 | 5 | -1 | 806 | 2.7 | 2.22 | 3.0 | 35.1 |
| Dillingham | 11.2 | 4.9 | 2.5 | 48.5 | 4 922 | 4 847 | -1.5 | 3.9 | 272 | 50 | -36 | 1 563 | 2.2 | 3.07 | 17.2 | 25.6 |
| Fairbanks North Star | 11.5 | 4.5 | 2.3 | 47.3 | 82 840 | 97 581 | 17.8 | 2.8 | 3 716 | 857 | -215 | 36 441 | 22.4 | 2.56 | 8.8 | 26.7 |
| Haines | 20.9 | 9.2 | 5.3 | 49.1 | 2 392 | 2 508 | 4.8 | 1.8 | 55 | 25 | 12 | 1 149 | 15.9 | 2.18 | 7.8 | 31.7 |
| Hoonah-Angoon | 20.5 | 9.8 | 4.1 | 46.5 | NA | 2 150 | NA | -1.0 | 52 | 28 | -49 | 913 | NA | 2.35 | 8.5 | 31.0 |
| Juneau | 14.5 | 5.6 | 3.1 | 49.3 | 30 711 | 31 275 | 1.8 | 4.1 | 939 | 285 | 620 | 12 187 | 5.6 | 2.49 | 10.4 | 26.9 |
| Kenai Peninsula | 16.5 | 7.7 | 4.1 | 47.8 | 49 691 | 55 400 | 11.5 | 2.7 | 1 575 | 851 | 764 | 22 161 | 20.2 | 2.42 | 8.1 | 28.6 |
| Ketchikan Gateway | 14.9 | 6.5 | 4.0 | 48.6 | 14 070 | 13 477 | -4.2 | 2.2 | 414 | 182 | 68 | 5 305 | -1.7 | 2.49 | 11.6 | 27.9 |
| Kodiak Island | 11.5 | 4.9 | 2.1 | 47.0 | 13 913 | 13 592 | -2.3 | 4.8 | 518 | 92 | 220 | 4 630 | 4.7 | 2.86 | 10.9 | 22.1 |
| Lake and Peninsula | 10.4 | 5.9 | 2.4 | 46.8 | 1 823 | 1 631 | -10.5 | 1.4 | 73 | 16 | -35 | 553 | -6.0 | 2.88 | 14.6 | 23.0 |
| Matanuska-Susitna | 12.7 | 5.5 | 2.8 | 48.4 | 59 322 | 88 995 | 50.0 | 5.5 | 3 022 | 964 | 2 811 | 31 824 | 54.8 | 2.75 | 8.7 | 22.3 |
| Nome | 9.9 | 4.0 | 2.4 | 46.9 | 9 196 | 9 492 | 3.2 | 4.5 | 565 | 157 | -8 | 2 815 | 4.5 | 3.29 | 17.5 | 23.5 |
| North Slope | 14.0 | 3.0 | 1.2 | 37.4 | 7 385 | 9 430 | 27.7 | 2.3 | 388 | 68 | -106 | 2 029 | -3.8 | 3.34 | 19.9 | 23.6 |
| Northwest Arctic | 8.6 | 3.8 | 2.5 | 46.4 | 7 208 | 7 523 | 4.4 | 3.8 | 513 | 75 | -162 | 1 919 | 7.8 | 3.72 | 21.0 | 21.0 |
| Petersburg | 16.8 | 7.9 | 4.0 | 48.5 | 0 | 3 815 | NA | 0.8 | 108 | 44 | -44 | 1 599 | NA | 2.36 | 9.4 | 29.2 |
| Prince of Wales-Hyder | 16.6 | 7.1 | 3.0 | 45.2 | 0 | 5 559 | NA | 3.5 | 174 | 32 | 46 | 2 194 | NA | 2.51 | 10.5 | 29.9 |
| Sitka | 14.6 | 6.7 | 5.2 | 49.3 | 8 835 | 8 881 | 0.5 | 1.9 | 247 | 111 | 26 | 3 545 | 8.1 | 2.43 | 10.7 | 29.0 |
| Skagway | 17.5 | 7.0 | 2.7 | 47.8 | 0 | 968 | NA | -0.9 | 17 | 44 | 16 | 436 | NA | 2.15 | 4.6 | 33.5 |
| Southeast Fairbanks | 14.2 | 6.6 | 3.0 | 45.1 | 6 174 | 7 029 | 13.8 | 1.6 | 263 | 88 | -62 | 2 567 | 22.4 | 2.59 | 6.7 | 27.4 |
| Valdez-Cordova | 16.2 | 5.9 | 2.7 | 46.6 | 10 195 | 9 636 | -5.5 | 0.8 | 275 | 96 | -112 | 3 966 | 2.1 | 2.38 | 8.2 | 32.0 |
| Wade Hampton | 6.8 | 3.4 | 2.1 | 47.6 | 7 028 | 7 459 | 6.1 | 4.7 | 551 | 124 | -76 | 1 745 | 8.9 | 4.27 | 23.3 | 15.1 |
| Wrangell | 18.8 | 10.5 | 5.9 | 47.9 | 0 | 2 369 | NA | 1.4 | 62 | 54 | 31 | 1 053 | NA | 2.23 | 9.0 | 32.6 |
| Yakutat | 15.8 | 7.7 | 3.1 | 45.5 | 808 | 662 | -18.1 | 0.9 | 20 | 2 | -15 | 270 | 1.9 | 2.39 | 10.7 | 34.1 |
| Yukon-Koyukuk | 14.3 | 6.4 | 4.2 | 45.5 | 6 551 | 5 588 | -14.7 | 3.3 | 212 | 68 | -2 | 2 217 | -4.0 | 2.51 | 17.1 | 35.1 |
| ARIZONA | 11.7 | 8.0 | 6.2 | 50.3 | 5 130 632 | 6 392 017 | 24.6 | 2.5 | 193 899 | 106 658 | 73 049 | 2 380 990 | 25.2 | 2.63 | 12.4 | 26.1 |
| Apache | 11.1 | 7.4 | 4.6 | 50.2 | 69 423 | 71 518 | 3.0 | 2.3 | 2 595 | 1 310 | 407 | 22 771 | 14.0 | 3.10 | 21.2 | 24.8 |
| Cochise | 13.5 | 10.3 | 7.3 | 49.0 | 117 755 | 131 346 | 11.5 | 0.6 | 3 916 | 2 635 | -531 | 50 865 | 15.9 | 2.46 | 11.5 | 28.2 |
| Coconino | 11.6 | 5.9 | 3.4 | 50.6 | 116 320 | 134 421 | 15.6 | 1.2 | 3 998 | 1 606 | -831 | 46 711 | 15.5 | 2.69 | 12.7 | 24.5 |
| Gila | 16.6 | 13.6 | 9.7 | 50.4 | 51 335 | 53 597 | 4.4 | -0.8 | 1 459 | 1 460 | -409 | 22 000 | 9.2 | 2.39 | 11.1 | 29.3 |
| Graham | 10.1 | 6.5 | 5.1 | 46.3 | 33 489 | 37 220 | 11.1 | 0.5 | 1 304 | 608 | -497 | 11 120 | 9.9 | 3.01 | 15.5 | 21.7 |
| Greenlee | 12.0 | 6.1 | 5.8 | 48.0 | 8 547 | 8 437 | -1.3 | 4.3 | 268 | 100 | 191 | 3 188 | 2.3 | 2.64 | 9.6 | 27.8 |
| La Paz | 15.4 | 20.6 | 12.8 | 48.9 | 19 715 | 20 489 | 3.9 | -1.0 | 386 | 519 | -64 | 9 198 | 10.0 | 2.19 | 9.4 | 32.1 |
| Maricopa | 10.8 | 6.9 | 5.5 | 50.5 | 3 072 149 | 3 817 117 | 24.2 | 3.3 | 120 826 | 57 453 | 61 214 | 1 411 583 | 24.6 | 2.67 | 12.4 | 25.9 |
| Mohave | 16.1 | 14.4 | 9.6 | 49.9 | 155 032 | 200 186 | 29.1 | 1.6 | 4 681 | 5 863 | 4 268 | 82 539 | 31.4 | 2.39 | 10.4 | 26.7 |
| Navajo | 12.4 | 8.6 | 5.2 | 49.8 | 97 470 | 107 449 | 10.2 | -0.3 | 3 815 | 1 892 | -2 287 | 35 658 | 18.7 | 2.95 | 17.1 | 23.0 |
| Pima | 12.8 | 8.6 | 7.3 | 50.8 | 843 746 | 980 263 | 16.2 | 1.2 | 26 942 | 18 947 | 4 363 | 388 660 | 16.9 | 2.46 | 12.8 | 29.2 |
| Pinal | 11.8 | 9.4 | 5.4 | 47.6 | 179 727 | 375 770 | 109.1 | 3.1 | 10 880 | 5 048 | 5 129 | 125 590 | 104.7 | 2.78 | 11.7 | 20.5 |
| Santa Cruz | 12.0 | 8.1 | 5.7 | 52.3 | 38 381 | 47 420 | 23.6 | -0.2 | 1 577 | 699 | -1 000 | 15 437 | 30.7 | 3.05 | 17.1 | 19.0 |
| Yavapai | 17.6 | 14.4 | 10.8 | 51.0 | 167 517 | 211 033 | 26.0 | 0.8 | 4 120 | 5 439 | 2 896 | 90 903 | 29.5 | 2.28 | 9.0 | 29.1 |
| Yuma | 9.6 | 8.8 | 7.0 | 49.4 | 160 026 | 195 751 | 22.3 | 2.2 | 7 132 | 3 079 | 200 | 64 767 | 20.3 | 2.93 | 13.8 | 19.6 |
| ARKANSAS | 12.4 | 8.2 | 6.4 | 50.9 | 2 673 400 | 2 915 918 | 9.1 | 1.1 | 85 342 | 64 590 | 12 111 | 1 147 084 | 10.0 | 2.47 | 13.4 | 27.1 |
| Arkansas | 14.5 | 8.6 | 7.9 | 51.4 | 20 749 | 19 019 | -8.3 | -0.7 | 540 | 550 | -105 | 8 005 | -5.3 | 2.35 | 15.3 | 29.4 |
| Ashley | 13.5 | 9.7 | 6.9 | 51.6 | 24 209 | 21 853 | -9.7 | -1.5 | 620 | 548 | -405 | 8 765 | -6.6 | 2.47 | 14.9 | 26.1 |
| Baxter | 15.7 | 15.8 | 13.0 | 51.9 | 38 386 | 41 513 | 8.1 | -1.1 | 783 | 1 477 | 224 | 18 748 | 9.9 | 2.18 | 8.6 | 29.5 |
| Benton | 10.2 | 6.8 | 5.5 | 50.6 | 153 406 | 221 339 | 44.3 | 4.9 | 7 264 | 3 370 | 6 887 | 82 087 | 41.0 | 2.67 | 9.9 | 22.5 |
| Boone | 13.3 | 10.1 | 8.2 | 50.9 | 33 948 | 36 903 | 8.7 | 1.1 | 937 | 933 | 444 | 15 120 | 9.2 | 2.41 | 9.6 | 26.6 |
| Bradley | 13.2 | 9.1 | 8.4 | 51.5 | 12 600 | 11 508 | -8.7 | -1.0 | 325 | 348 | -83 | 4 673 | -3.3 | 2.42 | 15.1 | 30.3 |
| Calhoun | 15.1 | 8.9 | 7.3 | 49.1 | 5 744 | 5 368 | -6.5 | -1.1 | 84 | 102 | -71 | 2 262 | -2.4 | 2.30 | 12.8 | 30.3 |
| Carroll | 16.0 | 11.5 | 8.0 | 50.7 | 25 357 | 27 446 | 8.2 | 0.6 | 700 | 621 | 97 | 11 393 | 11.8 | 2.39 | 9.6 | 28.2 |
| Chicot | 13.8 | 9.7 | 8.8 | 50.7 | 14 117 | 11 800 | -16.4 | -3.1 | 365 | 389 | -347 | 4 579 | -12.0 | 2.42 | 21.1 | 31.6 |
| Clark | 11.1 | 8.0 | 7.1 | 52.3 | 23 546 | 22 995 | -2.3 | -0.3 | 543 | 551 | -50 | 8 783 | -1.4 | 2.32 | 13.7 | 29.3 |
| Clay | 13.9 | 10.9 | 9.1 | 51.0 | 17 609 | 16 083 | -8.7 | -2.5 | 274 | 486 | -174 | 6 845 | -7.7 | 2.33 | 10.3 | 29.6 |
| Cleburne | 14.5 | 13.3 | 10.5 | 50.6 | 24 046 | 25 970 | 8.0 | -0.6 | 574 | 787 | 79 | 11 078 | 8.7 | 2.31 | 8.6 | 26.9 |

1. No spouse present.

# Table B. States and Counties — Population, Vital Statistics, Medicare, and Crime

| STATE County | Persons in group quarters, 2010 | Daytime population, 2007–2011 Number | Daytime population, 2007–2011 Employment/ residence ratio | Births, 2011 Total | Births, 2011 Rate[1] | Deaths, 2011 Number | Deaths, 2011 Rate[1] | Persons under 65 with no health insurance, 2010 Number | Persons under 65 with no health insurance, 2010 Percent | Medicare, 2012 Eligible for Medicare | Medicare, 2012 Enrolled in Medicare Advantage | Medicare, 2012 Enrolled in a Medicare prescription drug plan | Serious crimes known to police,[2] 2011 Total Number | Serious crimes known to police,[2] 2011 Total Rate[3] |
|---|---|---|---|---|---|---|---|---|---|---|---|---|---|---|
| | 32 | 33 | 34 | 35 | 36 | 37 | 38 | 39 | 40 | 41 | 42 | 43 | 44 | 45 |
| ALABAMA—Cont'd | | | | | | | | | | | | | | |
| Washington | 147 | 16 911 | 0.91 | 168 | 9.7 | 193 | 11.1 | 2 839 | 19.0 | 3 698 | 382 | 1 927 | 277 | 1 568 |
| Wilcox | 108 | 12 014 | 1.06 | 137 | 11.9 | 118 | 10.3 | 1 727 | 17.6 | 2 942 | 230 | 1 872 | 96 | 819 |
| Winston | 301 | 24 816 | 1.02 | 235 | 9.7 | 300 | 12.3 | 3 860 | 19.3 | 5 643 | 676 | 3 031 | 501 | 2 036 |
| ALASKA | 26 352 | 707 641 | 1.02 | 11 193 | 15.5 | 3 338 | 4.6 | 138 777 | 21.4 | 72 196 | 0 | 27 603 | 23 411 | 3 239 |
| Aleutians East | 1 726 | 3 250 | 1.07 | 20 | 6.3 | 0 | 0.0 | 1 247 | 41.2 | 156 | D | 41 | NA | NA |
| Aleutians West | 2 543 | 6 109 | 1.15 | 28 | 5.1 | 2 | 0.4 | 1 624 | 31.3 | 181 | D | 54 | NA | NA |
| Anchorage | 8 450 | 297 679 | 1.07 | 4 574 | 15.5 | 1 355 | 4.6 | 49 058 | 18.4 | 29 478 | 140 | 11 278 | NA | NA |
| Bethel | 338 | 17 282 | 1.05 | 441 | 25.3 | 79 | 4.5 | 4 495 | 27.8 | 1 185 | D | 643 | NA | NA |
| Bristol Bay | 16 | 1 289 | 1.51 | 11 | 10.7 | 5 | 4.9 | 200 | 22.1 | 115 | D | 28 | NA | NA |
| Denali | 36 | 2 216 | 1.43 | 22 | 11.9 | 0 | 0.0 | 328 | 19.5 | 191 | D | 49 | NA | NA |
| Dillingham | 52 | 4 935 | 1.05 | 113 | 22.7 | 16 | 3.2 | 1 373 | 29.9 | 427 | D | 219 | NA | NA |
| Fairbanks North Star | 4 313 | 95 302 | 0.98 | 1 639 | 16.5 | 383 | 3.9 | 17 920 | 20.3 | 8 430 | 34 | 2 762 | NA | NA |
| Haines | 0 | 2 475 | 0.96 | 24 | 9.4 | 10 | 3.9 | 631 | 28.9 | 461 | D | 191 | NA | NA |
| Hoonah-Angoon | 0 | 1 939 | 0.91 | 22 | 10.4 | 12 | 5.7 | 660 | 34.7 | NA | NA | NA | NA | NA |
| Juneau | 887 | 31 583 | 1.02 | 391 | 12.2 | 121 | 3.8 | 5 455 | 19.3 | 3 737 | 11 | 1 177 | NA | NA |
| Kenai Peninsula | 1 722 | 53 149 | 0.93 | 686 | 12.2 | 392 | 7.0 | 11 385 | 23.6 | 8 565 | 43 | 3 536 | NA | NA |
| Ketchikan Gateway | 246 | 13 828 | 1.06 | 185 | 13.6 | 75 | 5.5 | 2 815 | 23.3 | 1 885 | D | 751 | NA | NA |
| Kodiak Island | 336 | 13 633 | 1.02 | 227 | 16.4 | 43 | 3.1 | 3 524 | 28.1 | 1 221 | D | 449 | NA | NA |
| Lake and Peninsula | 37 | 1 601 | 1.09 | 33 | 19.8 | 9 | 5.4 | 511 | 33.9 | 165 | D | 69 | NA | NA |
| Matanuska-Susitna | 1 370 | 74 026 | 0.65 | 1 301 | 14.1 | 397 | 4.3 | 17 312 | 21.2 | 9 757 | 56 | 3 807 | NA | NA |
| Nome | 219 | 9 535 | 1.03 | 248 | 25.2 | 56 | 5.7 | 2 615 | 29.3 | 721 | D | 297 | NA | NA |
| North Slope | 2 652 | 16 553 | 2.94 | 177 | 18.6 | 29 | 3.1 | 2 288 | 25.2 | 451 | D | 113 | NA | NA |
| Northwest Arctic | 382 | 7 785 | 1.10 | 222 | 28.7 | 31 | 4.0 | 2 063 | 28.9 | 502 | D | 255 | NA | NA |
| Petersburg | 43 | 4 133 | 1.16 | 48 | 12.5 | 34 | 8.9 | 839 | 24.7 | NA | NA | NA | NA | NA |
| Prince of Wales-Hyder | 50 | 5 557 | 1.01 | 72 | 12.6 | 23 | 4.0 | 1 721 | 34.0 | NA | NA | NA | NA | NA |
| Sitka | 255 | 8 948 | 1.01 | 109 | 12.2 | 38 | 4.2 | 2 057 | 26.3 | 1 157 | D | 358 | NA | NA |
| Skagway | 32 | 1 035 | 0.89 | 11 | 11.8 | 25 | 26.7 | 214 | 24.3 | NA | NA | NA | NA | NA |
| Southeast Fairbanks | 369 | 7 504 | 1.16 | 114 | 16.0 | 34 | 4.8 | 1 748 | 27.5 | 978 | D | 403 | NA | NA |
| Valdez-Cordova | 201 | 10 060 | 1.11 | 119 | 12.2 | 45 | 4.6 | 2 205 | 25.0 | 1 143 | D | 462 | NA | NA |
| Wade Hampton | 9 | 7 505 | 1.02 | 234 | 30.5 | 52 | 6.8 | 2 020 | 27.9 | 487 | D | 314 | NA | NA |
| Wrangell | 19 | 2 323 | 0.97 | 24 | 10.1 | 44 | 18.5 | 527 | 25.9 | NA | NA | NA | NA | NA |
| Yakutat | 18 | 794 | 1.13 | 8 | 12.4 | 0 | 0.0 | 179 | 29.7 | 89 | D | 36 | NA | NA |
| Yukon-Koyukuk | 31 | 5 613 | 1.00 | 90 | 15.9 | 28 | 5.0 | 1 763 | 34.2 | 714 | D | 311 | NA | NA |
| ARIZONA | 139 384 | 6 313 214 | 0.99 | 87 887 | 13.6 | 45 899 | 7.1 | 1 042 809 | 19.3 | 1 009 603 | 376 511 | 288 975 | 256 733 | 3 960 |
| Apache | 941 | 70 073 | 0.96 | 1 158 | 16.0 | 551 | 7.6 | 13 555 | 21.4 | 10 247 | 949 | 5 428 | 446 | 646 |
| Cochise | 6 271 | 130 894 | 1.01 | 1 783 | 13.4 | 1 108 | 8.3 | 17 605 | 17.1 | 26 338 | 7 408 | 6 792 | 4 047 | 3 161 |
| Coconino | 8 834 | 133 248 | 1.00 | 1 802 | 13.4 | 703 | 5.2 | 24 623 | 21.4 | 15 235 | 1 810 | 7 223 | 5 150 | 3 778 |
| Gila | 917 | 53 393 | 1.00 | 670 | 12.6 | 659 | 12.4 | 7 952 | 19.5 | 14 012 | 1 559 | 6 495 | 1 302 | 2 442 |
| Graham | 3 751 | 35 861 | 0.93 | 568 | 15.3 | 247 | 6.6 | 5 424 | 18.6 | 4 957 | 1 455 | 2 015 | 679 | 2 421 |
| Greenlee | 35 | 9 939 | 1.47 | 116 | 13.5 | 36 | 4.2 | 1 100 | 15.1 | 1 159 | 262 | 417 | NA | NA |
| La Paz | 388 | 20 910 | 1.06 | 181 | 8.9 | 217 | 10.6 | 3 450 | 25.5 | 4 874 | 740 | 1 765 | 466 | 2 640 |
| Maricopa | 53 177 | 3 839 064 | 1.02 | 54 493 | 14.0 | 24 817 | 6.4 | 634 846 | 19.2 | 534 519 | 224 925 | 141 449 | 159 169 | 4 112 |
| Mohave | 2 629 | 187 900 | 0.82 | 2 099 | 10.4 | 2 485 | 12.3 | 30 734 | 20.4 | 52 571 | 11 869 | 19 362 | 6 872 | 3 385 |
| Navajo | 2 227 | 108 479 | 1.03 | 1 772 | 16.5 | 812 | 7.6 | 17 828 | 19.4 | 18 171 | 3 331 | 8 630 | 2 718 | 2 494 |
| Pima | 24 139 | 973 775 | 1.00 | 12 223 | 12.4 | 8 255 | 8.3 | 147 455 | 18.2 | 173 473 | 77 507 | 40 065 | 28 227 | 2 839 |
| Pinal | 26 245 | 302 272 | 0.60 | 5 245 | 13.7 | 2 074 | 5.4 | 58 673 | 19.3 | 56 938 | 21 135 | 15 289 | 10 878 | 2 876 |
| Santa Cruz | 384 | 47 352 | 1.04 | 713 | 15.0 | 309 | 6.5 | 9 782 | 23.9 | 7 554 | 3 498 | 1 831 | 955 | 2 025 |
| Yavapai | 3 525 | 207 260 | 0.96 | 1 885 | 8.9 | 2 309 | 10.9 | 31 553 | 20.0 | 61 531 | 14 132 | 22 010 | 5 283 | 2 468 |
| Yuma | 5 921 | 192 794 | 0.98 | 3 179 | 15.8 | 1 317 | 6.6 | 38 228 | 23.9 | 28 024 | 5 931 | 10 204 | 4 437 | 2 570 |
| ARKANSAS | 78 931 | 2 898 634 | 1.00 | 38 156 | 13.0 | 28 478 | 9.7 | 500 134 | 20.6 | 563 896 | 94 396 | 269 838 | 124 424 | 4 235 |
| Arkansas | 247 | 20 503 | 1.16 | 250 | 13.2 | 222 | 11.8 | 2 972 | 19.0 | 4 034 | 375 | 2 474 | 756 | 3 945 |
| Ashley | 191 | 21 999 | 1.00 | 284 | 13.1 | 245 | 11.3 | 3 586 | 19.9 | 4 863 | 461 | 3 197 | 596 | 2 707 |
| Baxter | 595 | 42 326 | 1.05 | 356 | 8.6 | 660 | 15.9 | 6 554 | 22.2 | 14 178 | 3 151 | 5 573 | 1 257 | 3 005 |
| Benton | 2 061 | 222 198 | 1.06 | 3 192 | 14.0 | 1 457 | 6.4 | 37 746 | 19.4 | 34 469 | 9 738 | 12 862 | 5 384 | 2 420 |
| Boone | 465 | 38 646 | 1.11 | 388 | 10.5 | 431 | 11.6 | 6 386 | 21.3 | 9 127 | 1 730 | 4 063 | 1 079 | 2 965 |
| Bradley | 220 | 11 809 | 1.05 | 154 | 13.4 | 150 | 13.1 | 2 524 | 27.2 | 2 523 | 226 | 1 629 | 239 | 2 221 |
| Calhoun | 175 | 4 906 | 0.78 | 41 | 8.0 | 48 | 9.3 | 927 | 21.9 | 1 192 | 95 | 705 | 43 | 795 |
| Carroll | 230 | 27 001 | 0.99 | 316 | 11.5 | 277 | 10.1 | 6 412 | 29.1 | 6 394 | 1 538 | 2 575 | 747 | 2 701 |
| Chicot | 722 | 11 885 | 0.98 | 163 | 13.9 | 174 | 14.8 | 1 903 | 21.3 | 2 673 | 141 | 1 844 | 183 | 1 539 |
| Clark | 2 612 | 23 512 | 1.05 | 240 | 10.5 | 254 | 11.1 | 3 543 | 20.8 | 4 277 | 701 | 1 951 | 764 | 3 298 |
| Clay | 125 | 14 459 | 0.73 | 135 | 8.5 | 223 | 14.0 | 2 817 | 22.2 | 4 114 | 473 | 2 284 | 230 | 1 419 |
| Cleburne | 339 | 24 747 | 0.89 | 258 | 10.0 | 355 | 13.7 | 4 577 | 23.3 | 7 298 | 732 | 3 698 | 942 | 3 600 |

1. Per 1,000 estimated resident population.  2. Data for serious crimes have not been adjusted for underreporting; this may affect comparability between geographic areas and over time.  3. Per 100,000 population estimated by the FBI.

# Table B. States and Counties — Crime, Education, Money Income, and Poverty

| STATE County | Serious crimes known to police, 2011 (cont.)[1] Rate[2] | | Education School enrollment and attainment, 2007–2011 Enrollment[3] | | Attainment[4] (percent) | | Local government expenditures,[5] 2009–2010 | | Money income, 2007–2011 | Households | | | Income and poverty, 2011 Percent below poverty level | | |
|---|---|---|---|---|---|---|---|---|---|---|---|---|---|---|---|
| | Violent | Property | Total | Per-cent private | High school grad-uate or less | Bach-elor's degree or more | Total current expendi-tures (mil dol) | Current expendi-tures per student (dollars) | Per capita income[6] (dollars) | Median income Dollars | Percent change, 2000 to 2007–2011 (constant 2011 dollars) | Percent with income of $200,000 or more | Median house-hold income (dollars) | All per-sons | Children under 18 years | Children 5 to 17 years in families |
| | 46 | 47 | 48 | 49 | 50 | 51 | 52 | 53 | 54 | 55 | 56 | 57 | 58 | 59 | 60 | 61 |
| ALABAMA—Cont'd | | | | | | | | | | | | | | | | |
| Washington | 243 | 1 325 | 4 303 | 7.8 | 66.6 | 10.1 | 30.1 | 8 568 | 19 836 | 40 286 | -3.2 | 0.8 | 39 203 | 18.9 | 27.4 | 22.3 |
| Wilcox | 239 | 580 | 3 020 | 12.7 | 66.3 | 12.0 | 20.5 | 9 915 | 12 683 | 23 750 | 5.7 | 0.8 | 20 990 | 39.9 | 51.2 | 44.8 |
| Winston | 134 | 1 902 | 5 294 | 3.5 | 61.4 | 11.5 | 40.2 | 9 083 | 18 568 | 32 557 | -15.2 | 2.0 | 31 018 | 19.8 | 30.3 | 28.6 |
| ALASKA | 606 | 2 633 | 191 754 | 11.9 | 35.9 | 27.2 | 2 069.0 | 15 714 | 31 944 | 69 014 | -0.9 | 4.9 | 65 699 | 10.8 | 14.7 | 13.6 |
| Aleutians East | NA | NA | 282 | 11.7 | 56.0 | 17.8 | 8.5 | 32 630 | 24 387 | 57 083 | -11.7 | 2.4 | 51 289 | 17.8 | 17.5 | 16.0 |
| Aleutians West | NA | NA | 849 | 7.5 | 52.1 | 11.1 | 10.9 | 21 650 | 31 188 | 75 179 | -9.3 | 2.3 | 59 362 | 10.1 | 9.2 | 7.9 |
| Anchorage | NA | NA | 80 317 | 13.0 | 31.1 | 32.3 | 673.3 | 13 489 | 35 580 | 75 485 | 0.7 | 6.8 | 71 237 | 8.5 | 12.2 | 11.7 |
| Bethel | NA | NA | 5 544 | 1.6 | 60.9 | 12.5 | 124.9 | 25 453 | 18 392 | 52 063 | 8.0 | 3.7 | 43 314 | 23.5 | 30.3 | 27.5 |
| Bristol Bay | NA | NA | 323 | 8.0 | 31.9 | 19.6 | 20.7 | 37 989 | 35 981 | 80 000 | 13.6 | 4.7 | 61 905 | 9.1 | 11.2 | 9.2 |
| Denali | NA | NA | 355 | 23.1 | 37.4 | 24.2 | 6.7 | 14 360 | 38 804 | 82 898 | 14.4 | 2.4 | 68 899 | 5.8 | 7.9 | 6.6 |
| Dillingham | NA | NA | 1 591 | 4.1 | 49.0 | 19.2 | 28.0 | 24 819 | 22 603 | 57 681 | -0.8 | 5.5 | 46 427 | 21.3 | 27.4 | 24.6 |
| Fairbanks North Star | NA | NA | 27 292 | 11.7 | 33.3 | 27.7 | 238.8 | 14 887 | 31 532 | 68 922 | 4.0 | 3.6 | 64 396 | 9.5 | 11.0 | 10.3 |
| Haines | NA | NA | 502 | 4.6 | 37.4 | 31.6 | 5.7 | 18 423 | 30 090 | 51 667 | -6.1 | 3.7 | 51 350 | 11.2 | 17.2 | 14.9 |
| Hoonah-Angoon | NA | NA | 368 | 6.3 | 40.5 | 27.9 | 8.3 | 29 381 | 28 398 | 49 545 | 0.0 | 1.7 | 40 896 | 18.5 | 24.6 | 23.2 |
| Juneau | NA | NA | 7 954 | 12.3 | 27.0 | 36.4 | 77.9 | 15 384 | 37 294 | 77 465 | -7.5 | 4.9 | 74 219 | 7.5 | 10.4 | 8.9 |
| Kenai Peninsula | NA | NA | 13 192 | 11.1 | 39.5 | 23.1 | 138.9 | 14 830 | 30 256 | 59 256 | -5.4 | 2.9 | 60 360 | 10.6 | 13.9 | 12.6 |
| Ketchikan Gateway | NA | NA | 2 852 | 17.0 | 38.4 | 24.6 | 34.7 | 15 384 | 29 998 | 57 243 | -17.4 | 2.8 | 59 092 | 11.6 | 15.1 | 13.8 |
| Kodiak Island | NA | NA | 3 846 | 15.5 | 32.9 | 24.5 | 46.9 | 18 076 | 26 720 | 66 326 | -10.1 | 3.7 | 66 935 | 9.6 | 10.8 | 9.5 |
| Lake and Peninsula | NA | NA | 450 | 10.9 | 44.5 | 19.8 | NA | NA | 21 210 | 51 429 | 4.5 | 1.6 | 47 612 | 16.4 | 22.0 | 20.2 |
| Matanuska-Susitna | NA | NA | 24 126 | 16.1 | 39.0 | 20.9 | 220.4 | 13 140 | 29 292 | 70 343 | 1.7 | 4.1 | 68 999 | 11.6 | 14.7 | 13.3 |
| Nome | NA | NA | 2 999 | 1.4 | 58.5 | 15.7 | 66.0 | 28 471 | 20 325 | 52 435 | -5.9 | 2.7 | 44 766 | 26.4 | 32.2 | 30.5 |
| North Slope | NA | NA | 2 779 | 2.1 | 53.4 | 17.6 | 62.8 | 34 584 | 35 423 | 76 667 | -10.1 | 4.0 | 73 744 | 11.5 | 14.1 | 13.2 |
| Northwest Arctic | NA | NA | 2 243 | 3.1 | 62.5 | 12.2 | 54.4 | 27 409 | 21 751 | 59 893 | -3.5 | 1.0 | 54 680 | 23.9 | 27.8 | 26.6 |
| Petersburg | NA | NA | 845 | 7.5 | 37.1 | 24.2 | 11.6 | 19 388 | 31 279 | 64 216 | 0.0 | 1.9 | 54 434 | 10.6 | 14.4 | 12.8 |
| Prince of Wales-Hyder | NA | NA | 1 230 | 5.4 | 50.9 | 16.1 | 27.2 | 20 827 | 24 902 | 45 513 | 0.0 | 2.0 | 42 649 | 17.1 | 23.1 | 21.2 |
| Sitka | NA | NA | 2 210 | 5.4 | 29.1 | 34.7 | 21.3 | 12 031 | 32 451 | 69 798 | -0.4 | 3.9 | 61 956 | 8.4 | 10.7 | 10.0 |
| Skagway | NA | NA | 208 | 1.9 | 35.8 | 28.8 | 2.9 | 27 381 | 36 108 | 73 000 | 0.0 | 10.2 | 61 025 | 4.6 | 9.4 | 10.2 |
| Southeast Fairbanks | NA | NA | 2 001 | 14.2 | 37.1 | 20.8 | 23.7 | 16 714 | 29 014 | 59 917 | 14.4 | 1.5 | 55 617 | 13.9 | 19.6 | 17.4 |
| Valdez-Cordova | NA | NA | 2 434 | 13.0 | 31.3 | 24.5 | 29.7 | 19 277 | 31 029 | 62 238 | -5.4 | 3.0 | 63 887 | 9.3 | 11.3 | 9.7 |
| Wade Hampton | NA | NA | 2 732 | 1.7 | 68.7 | 6.9 | 62.7 | 26 062 | 11 476 | 39 583 | -2.9 | 0.5 | 33 206 | 33.6 | 41.5 | 40.5 |
| Wrangell | NA | NA | 586 | 12.1 | 47.2 | 19.3 | 6.0 | 18 987 | 29 643 | 50 000 | 0.0 | 5.2 | 43 120 | 12.3 | 18.8 | 16.5 |
| Yakutat | NA | NA | 152 | 2.0 | 33.2 | 25.8 | 3.0 | 27 261 | 37 556 | 74 844 | 18.5 | 3.5 | 47 575 | 12.8 | 17.1 | 15.6 |
| Yukon-Koyukuk | NA | NA | 1 492 | 8.0 | 56.6 | 10.1 | 53.2 | 9 557 | 19 923 | 35 335 | -8.7 | 0.6 | 33 578 | 22.1 | 28.7 | 26.4 |
| ARIZONA | 406 | 3 555 | 1 688 671 | 10.9 | 39.5 | 26.4 | 8 390.6 | 7 804 | 25 784 | 50 752 | -7.3 | 3.5 | 46 710 | 19.0 | 27.2 | 25.7 |
| Apache | 90 | 557 | 21 670 | 5.7 | 58.9 | 10.1 | 136.1 | 10 294 | 12 626 | 31 011 | -1.6 | 0.9 | 30 837 | 36.5 | 43.9 | 40.0 |
| Cochise | 641 | 2 520 | 32 077 | 9.8 | 40.0 | 21.9 | 166.3 | 8 213 | 23 296 | 45 906 | 5.9 | 2.0 | 41 237 | 19.6 | 30.8 | 29.3 |
| Coconino | 414 | 3 363 | 44 837 | 4.6 | 35.6 | 31.5 | 178.0 | 8 848 | 22 607 | 49 615 | -3.9 | 2.5 | 45 051 | 21.6 | 26.8 | 26.5 |
| Gila | 285 | 2 157 | 10 478 | 10.4 | 49.0 | 15.5 | 67.1 | 8 145 | 20 098 | 37 905 | -9.2 | 1.1 | 35 898 | 25.7 | 37.7 | 37.6 |
| Graham | 934 | 1 487 | 10 535 | 6.9 | 49.2 | 14.4 | 48.0 | 7 449 | 16 116 | 43 083 | 7.6 | 0.7 | 40 548 | 26.0 | 31.1 | 29.9 |
| Greenlee | NA | NA | 2 365 | 9.4 | 49.7 | 11.9 | 14.2 | 8 851 | 20 366 | 49 390 | -7.1 | 0.0 | 51 145 | 13.9 | 17.7 | 16.2 |
| La Paz | 278 | 2 362 | 3 145 | 3.7 | 55.9 | 9.3 | 25.6 | 10 140 | 21 358 | 32 220 | -7.6 | 0.9 | 30 679 | 24.2 | 37.7 | 35.4 |
| Maricopa | 388 | 3 724 | 1 033 720 | 11.6 | 37.7 | 29.1 | 5 328.3 | 7 784 | 27 841 | 55 099 | -10.0 | 4.4 | 50 785 | 17.4 | 25.1 | 23.4 |
| Mohave | 201 | 3 183 | 41 353 | 10.6 | 50.0 | 12.2 | 176.9 | 6 735 | 21 457 | 40 573 | -4.7 | 1.5 | 35 998 | 21.7 | 37.4 | 35.4 |
| Navajo | 358 | 2 136 | 31 065 | 7.1 | 48.2 | 14.3 | 182.9 | 9 406 | 17 004 | 38 975 | 1.0 | 0.8 | 32 425 | 32.4 | 44.5 | 42.2 |
| Pima | 432 | 2 407 | 264 429 | 11.5 | 36.4 | 29.5 | 1 170.4 | 7 953 | 25 477 | 46 341 | -6.6 | 3.0 | 44 102 | 20.4 | 29.4 | 28.5 |
| Pinal | 218 | 2 658 | 83 899 | 10.5 | 45.1 | 18.1 | 390.3 | 7 590 | 21 419 | 51 212 | 5.8 | 1.6 | 45 170 | 17.4 | 22.9 | 23.5 |
| Santa Cruz | 144 | 1 881 | 13 983 | 5.2 | 58.0 | 18.0 | 76.1 | 7 208 | 17 577 | 38 092 | -5.0 | 2.1 | 35 500 | 26.2 | 35.1 | 33.0 |
| Yavapai | 349 | 2 119 | 42 907 | 13.5 | 36.8 | 24.2 | 187.3 | 7 306 | 26 028 | 44 084 | -6.4 | 2.3 | 41 437 | 18.4 | 28.9 | 25.7 |
| Yuma | 329 | 2 241 | 52 208 | 6.7 | 54.1 | 13.9 | 243.1 | 6 437 | 18 778 | 41 441 | -4.6 | 1.4 | 37 894 | 22.3 | 32.1 | 30.7 |
| ARKANSAS | 481 | 3 754 | 737 547 | 11.1 | 52.5 | 19.6 | 4 381.3 | 9 117 | 21 833 | 40 149 | -7.6 | 2.0 | 38 889 | 19.3 | 27.8 | 25.5 |
| Arkansas | 277 | 3 669 | 4 299 | 8.2 | 59.4 | 13.0 | 28.2 | 8 620 | 22 220 | 38 986 | -4.8 | 1.2 | 37 922 | 18.5 | 28.3 | 24.8 |
| Ashley | 195 | 2 512 | 5 411 | 3.1 | 62.7 | 12.5 | 36.4 | 8 914 | 19 264 | 35 657 | -16.8 | 1.1 | 37 170 | 19.8 | 30.6 | 29.1 |
| Baxter | 96 | 2 910 | 7 957 | 6.2 | 51.9 | 14.9 | 42.7 | 8 226 | 21 968 | 35 589 | -9.4 | 1.5 | 33 312 | 16.8 | 28.1 | 26.2 |
| Benton | 271 | 2 149 | 54 910 | 13.4 | 45.1 | 27.6 | 309.1 | 8 304 | 25 934 | 52 159 | -4.1 | 3.5 | 52 644 | 12.1 | 18.3 | 16.1 |
| Boone | 223 | 2 742 | 8 318 | 7.7 | 55.5 | 14.2 | 59.9 | 9 432 | 21 803 | 37 703 | -6.9 | 1.6 | 38 411 | 16.9 | 27.1 | 24.7 |
| Bradley | 232 | 1 989 | 2 582 | 5.5 | 68.4 | 11.4 | 20.8 | 10 350 | 19 283 | 32 337 | -3.5 | 2.2 | 31 118 | 24.4 | 36.1 | 34.7 |
| Calhoun | 111 | 684 | 1 210 | 1.0 | 67.8 | 6.7 | 5.9 | 9 482 | 15 998 | 30 625 | -20.2 | 0.1 | 35 464 | 16.5 | 22.4 | 20.1 |
| Carroll | 231 | 2 470 | 5 220 | 10.8 | 56.2 | 17.1 | 33.6 | 8 727 | 20 320 | 36 031 | -4.4 | 1.5 | 33 579 | 18.7 | 29.8 | 27.2 |
| Chicot | 404 | 1 136 | 2 690 | 10.8 | 70.0 | 13.2 | 19.2 | 11 037 | 15 593 | 23 954 | -19.4 | 1.1 | 27 966 | 33.4 | 48.2 | 48.0 |
| Clark | 384 | 2 913 | 8 026 | 19.5 | 53.5 | 22.3 | 48.8 | 12 547 | 18 090 | 32 998 | -15.3 | 1.8 | 34 478 | 23.1 | 30.3 | 27.8 |
| Clay | 86 | 1 333 | 3 459 | 6.9 | 66.6 | 9.3 | 22.9 | 8 240 | 18 494 | 31 135 | -9.0 | 0.7 | 32 564 | 20.1 | 28.9 | 26.4 |
| Cleburne | 210 | 3 390 | 4 803 | 5.7 | 55.4 | 16.3 | 29.5 | 8 819 | 21 614 | 38 510 | -9.5 | 1.3 | 42 265 | 16.2 | 26.2 | 24.3 |

1. Data for serious crimes have not been adjusted for underreporting; this may affect comparability between geographic areas and over time.   2. Per 100,000 population estimated by the FBI.   3. All persons 3 years old and over enrolled in nursery school through college.   4. Persons 25 years old and over.   5. Elementary and secondary education expenditures.   6. Based on population estimated by the American Community Survey, 2007–2011.

# Table B. States and Counties — **Personal Income**

| STATE County | Total (mil dol) | Percent change, 2010–2011 | Per capita[1] Dollars | Per capita[1] Rank | Wages and salaries[2] (mil dol) | Proprietors' income (mil dol) | Dividends, interest, and rent (mil dol) | Transfer payments (mil dol) Total | Government payments to individuals Total | Social Security | Medical payments | Income mainte-nance | Unemploy-ment insurance |
|---|---|---|---|---|---|---|---|---|---|---|---|---|---|
| | 62 | 63 | 64 | 65 | 66 | 67 | 68 | 69 | 70 | 71 | 72 | 73 | 74 |
| ALABAMA—Cont'd | | | | | | | | | | | | | |
| Washington | 494 | 2.1 | 28 477 | 2 544 | 261 | 28 | 57 | 153 | 149 | 55 | 59 | 22 | 4 |
| Wilcox | 298 | 2.2 | 25 996 | 2 879 | 142 | 21 | 46 | 135 | 132 | 38 | 50 | 36 | 3 |
| Winston | 632 | 1.2 | 25 982 | 2 882 | 281 | 13 | 106 | 237 | 232 | 80 | 107 | 26 | 6 |
| ALASKA | 33 003 | 5.6 | 45 665 | X | 24 029 | 3 133 | 4 876 | 5 166 | 5 011 | 1 010 | 2 041 | 613 | 268 |
| Aleutians East | 89 | 7.4 | 27 980 | 2 617 | 90 | 3 | 9 | 11 | 10 | 2 | 3 | 1 | 1 |
| Aleutians West | 175 | 9.3 | 31 845 | 1 917 | 216 | 17 | 20 | 20 | 19 | 2 | 6 | 2 | 2 |
| Anchorage | 15 062 | 5.2 | 50 958 | 187 | 11 877 | 1 795 | 2 374 | 2 105 | 2 042 | 398 | 831 | 244 | 93 |
| Bethel | 559 | 5.2 | 32 108 | 1 860 | 365 | 18 | 40 | 167 | 163 | 13 | 89 | 31 | 10 |
| Bristol Bay | 51 | 4.4 | 49 727 | 212 | 79 | 5 | 7 | 10 | 10 | 2 | 5 | 1 | 0 |
| Denali | 112 | 6.7 | 60 191 | 66 | 118 | 1 | 14 | 27 | 26 | 3 | 17 | 2 | 1 |
| Dillingham | 199 | 6.4 | 40 046 | 742 | 138 | 17 | 26 | 39 | 38 | 5 | 17 | 8 | 2 |
| Fairbanks North Star | 4 228 | 7.8 | 42 626 | 527 | 3 450 | 242 | 625 | 646 | 626 | 116 | 258 | 68 | 31 |
| Haines | 175 | 5.2 | 68 517 | 27 | 47 | 81 | 20 | 23 | 22 | 6 | 10 | 2 | 1 |
| Hoonah-Angoon | 83 | 7.1 | 39 307 | 822 | 33 | 8 | 14 | 22 | 22 | 4 | 10 | 2 | 2 |
| Juneau | 1 552 | 4.9 | 48 242 | 262 | 1 157 | 49 | 269 | 203 | 196 | 46 | 74 | 22 | 9 |
| Kenai Peninsula | 2 351 | 5.9 | 41 772 | 595 | 1 137 | 226 | 408 | 458 | 446 | 123 | 176 | 43 | 25 |
| Ketchikan Gateway | 702 | 3.6 | 51 631 | 172 | 434 | 87 | 116 | 115 | 113 | 27 | 48 | 14 | 6 |
| Kodiak Island | 610 | 6.5 | 43 951 | 442 | 468 | 65 | 98 | 79 | 77 | 17 | 29 | 10 | 5 |
| Lake and Peninsula | 62 | 7.2 | 37 023 | 1 073 | 42 | 1 | 11 | 14 | 13 | 2 | 6 | 2 | 1 |
| Matanuska-Susitna | 3 853 | 6.6 | 41 905 | 581 | 1 063 | 299 | 405 | 543 | 523 | 137 | 146 | 63 | 36 |
| Nome | 347 | 4.7 | 35 160 | 1 347 | 223 | 13 | 32 | 100 | 98 | 10 | 55 | 17 | 5 |
| North Slope | 460 | -2.0 | 48 447 | 257 | 1 569 | 4 | 47 | 49 | 46 | 9 | 18 | 6 | 3 |
| Northwest Arctic | 268 | 4.9 | 34 720 | 1 419 | 214 | 10 | 20 | 81 | 79 | 7 | 49 | 11 | 4 |
| Petersburg | 185 | 4.8 | 48 203 | 263 | 87 | 37 | 38 | 34 | 33 | 8 | 15 | 3 | 2 |
| Prince of Wales-Hyder | 178 | 4.3 | 30 954 | 2 110 | 102 | 14 | 24 | 45 | 44 | 10 | 16 | 6 | 4 |
| Sitka | 394 | 5.3 | 44 044 | 437 | 257 | 55 | 76 | 60 | 58 | 15 | 23 | 6 | 3 |
| Skagway | 57 | 4.5 | 60 683 | 63 | 37 | 9 | 9 | 6 | 6 | 1 | 1 | 1 | 1 |
| Southeast Fairbanks | 319 | 5.0 | 44 716 | 403 | 227 | 17 | 34 | 61 | 60 | 12 | 25 | 8 | 4 |
| Valdez-Cordova | 442 | 3.9 | 45 289 | 381 | 321 | 42 | 77 | 64 | 62 | 16 | 23 | 6 | 5 |
| Wade Hampton | 169 | 5.7 | 21 992 | 3 085 | 89 | 2 | 11 | 80 | 78 | 6 | 39 | 19 | 5 |
| Wrangell | 84 | 5.5 | 35 250 | 1 330 | 43 | 7 | 17 | 22 | 21 | 6 | 9 | 2 | 1 |
| Yakutat | 27 | 5.4 | 41 766 | 596 | 16 | 1 | 3 | 6 | 6 | 1 | 3 | 1 | 0 |
| Yukon-Koyukuk | 211 | 9.3 | 37 259 | 1 052 | 132 | 8 | 31 | 76 | 74 | 8 | 42 | 12 | 5 |
| ARIZONA | 227 287 | 4.9 | 35 062 | X | 140 994 | 17 947 | 35 899 | 47 519 | 46 089 | 14 751 | 19 578 | 5 095 | 1 335 |
| Apache | 1 869 | 2.3 | 25 813 | 2 900 | 1 063 | 62 | 180 | 817 | 801 | 114 | 443 | 155 | 20 |
| Cochise | 4 763 | 5.0 | 35 738 | 1 258 | 2 864 | 209 | 684 | 1 296 | 1 268 | 346 | 615 | 133 | 26 |
| Coconino | 4 621 | 3.9 | 34 353 | 1 464 | 2 901 | 352 | 750 | 947 | 917 | 207 | 434 | 125 | 32 |
| Gila | 1 692 | 3.9 | 31 846 | 1 916 | 738 | 79 | 289 | 670 | 658 | 208 | 342 | 67 | 11 |
| Graham | 937 | 3.7 | 25 215 | 2 946 | 412 | 31 | 109 | 343 | 335 | 71 | 192 | 40 | 7 |
| Greenlee | 270 | 8.2 | 31 333 | 2 034 | 276 | 8 | 21 | 76 | 74 | 18 | 44 | 6 | 2 |
| La Paz | 593 | 9.7 | 29 053 | 2 443 | 231 | 93 | 84 | 200 | 196 | 65 | 94 | 21 | 4 |
| Maricopa | 147 724 | 5.3 | 38 071 | 961 | 100 094 | 13 317 | 22 347 | 25 949 | 25 091 | 8 063 | 10 062 | 2 659 | 739 |
| Mohave | 5 291 | 4.3 | 26 145 | 2 865 | 2 013 | 342 | 831 | 1 782 | 1 737 | 766 | 619 | 181 | 44 |
| Navajo | 2 744 | 3.2 | 25 554 | 2 925 | 1 340 | 128 | 346 | 1 113 | 1 090 | 236 | 542 | 189 | 30 |
| Pima | 34 596 | 4.0 | 34 961 | 1 379 | 19 827 | 1 948 | 6 608 | 8 192 | 7 974 | 2 491 | 3 761 | 838 | 183 |
| Pinal | 9 302 | 6.4 | 24 287 | 3 015 | 2 835 | 425 | 1 129 | 2 548 | 2 463 | 832 | 1 159 | 245 | 67 |
| Santa Cruz | 1 194 | 3.6 | 25 037 | 2 961 | 727 | 90 | 222 | 349 | 338 | 91 | 151 | 67 | 15 |
| Yavapai | 6 248 | 3.9 | 29 490 | 2 379 | 2 438 | 316 | 1 684 | 1 832 | 1 785 | 890 | 586 | 129 | 42 |
| Yuma | 5 442 | 4.9 | 27 091 | 2 753 | 3 236 | 547 | 616 | 1 405 | 1 362 | 353 | 533 | 242 | 112 |
| ARKANSAS | 99 127 | 4.8 | 33 740 | X | 58 694 | 7 810 | 16 158 | 23 871 | 23 222 | 7 968 | 9 794 | 2 785 | 709 |
| Arkansas | 759 | 4.3 | 40 173 | 727 | 460 | 121 | 110 | 176 | 171 | 57 | 76 | 21 | 9 |
| Ashley | 755 | 5.7 | 34 789 | 1 406 | 428 | 88 | 97 | 222 | 217 | 74 | 97 | 27 | 7 |
| Baxter | 1 343 | 4.1 | 32 335 | 1 815 | 610 | 77 | 334 | 462 | 452 | 207 | 177 | 29 | 9 |
| Benton | 8 361 | 6.8 | 36 744 | 1 106 | 5 999 | 516 | 1 393 | 1 242 | 1 192 | 505 | 425 | 120 | 43 |
| Boone | 1 131 | 4.2 | 30 524 | 2 193 | 648 | 97 | 205 | 327 | 319 | 125 | 127 | 30 | 8 |
| Bradley | 350 | 5.6 | 30 467 | 2 206 | 148 | 39 | 46 | 127 | 124 | 35 | 65 | 15 | 4 |
| Calhoun | 146 | 0.3 | 28 356 | 2 563 | 171 | 6 | 17 | 41 | 40 | 17 | 15 | 4 | 2 |
| Carroll | 746 | 4.4 | 27 121 | 2 750 | 367 | 44 | 175 | 216 | 210 | 89 | 82 | 20 | 6 |
| Chicot | 379 | 6.2 | 32 320 | 1 819 | 143 | 76 | 46 | 129 | 127 | 34 | 61 | 22 | 4 |
| Clark | 695 | 3.4 | 30 386 | 2 224 | 401 | 42 | 116 | 210 | 205 | 61 | 96 | 21 | 7 |
| Clay | 487 | 3.5 | 30 639 | 2 166 | 153 | 80 | 73 | 158 | 154 | 55 | 69 | 15 | 6 |
| Cleburne | 905 | 5.5 | 34 924 | 1 384 | 300 | 97 | 185 | 248 | 243 | 103 | 96 | 18 | 6 |

1. Based on the resident population estimated as of July 1 of the year shown.  2. Includes supplements to wages and salaries.

| STATE County | Total (mil dol) | Farm | Total | Manu- facturing | Infor- mation and profes- sional and technical services | Retail trade | Finance, insur- ance, and real estate | Health care and social services | Govern- ment | Number | Rate[2] | Supple- mental Security Income recipients, December 2011 | Total | Percent change, 2000– 2010 |
|---|---|---|---|---|---|---|---|---|---|---|---|---|---|---|
| | 75 | 76 | 77 | 78 | 79 | 80 | 81 | 82 | 83 | 84 | 85 | 86 | 87 | 88 |
| ALABAMA—Cont'd | | | | | | | | | | | | | | |
| Washington | 289 | 1.7 | D | 40.4 | D | 3.4 | D | D | 16.3 | 4 515 | 260 | 801 | 8 407 | 3.5 |
| Wilcox | 163 | 4.3 | 33.2 | 30.1 | D | 5.6 | D | D | 24.8 | 3 625 | 316 | 1 641 | 5 649 | -8.6 |
| Winston | 294 | -4.7 | D | 34.8 | 2.0 | 7.6 | 3.5 | 9.1 | 20.8 | 6 635 | 273 | 1 021 | 13 469 | 7.7 |
| ALASKA | 27 162 | 0.0 | 18.1 | 2.7 | 8.2 | 5.5 | 5.0 | 10.3 | 32.5 | 82 109 | 114 | 12 719 | 306 967 | 17.6 |
| Aleutians East | 93 | 0.0 | D | D | D | 1.3 | D | D | 17.2 | 160 | 50 | 0 | 747 | 3.2 |
| Aleutians West | 233 | -0.2 | 49.4 | 47.1 | D | 4.4 | 2.5 | 3.2 | 15.1 | 195 | 35 | 21 | 1 929 | -13.7 |
| Anchorage | 13 672 | 0.0 | 13.0 | 0.9 | 12.4 | 5.4 | 6.4 | 11.2 | 29.1 | 31 275 | 106 | 5 774 | 113 032 | 12.6 |
| Bethel | 382 | 0.0 | 4.1 | 0.9 | 2.9 | 4.9 | D | D | 43.7 | 1 555 | 89 | 470 | 5 919 | 14.1 |
| Bristol Bay | 84 | 0.0 | D | 43.6 | D | 1.6 | D | D | 21.8 | 130 | 126 | 0 | 969 | -1.0 |
| Denali | 119 | 0.0 | D | 0.0 | D | D | D | 0.5 | 27.5 | 215 | 116 | 0 | 1 771 | 31.1 |
| Dillingham | 155 | 0.0 | D | D | D | 4.3 | D | 25.2 | 26.1 | 540 | 109 | 128 | 2 427 | 4.1 |
| Fairbanks North Star | 3 692 | 0.2 | 13.3 | 1.4 | 4.2 | 5.4 | 2.8 | 8.0 | 51.6 | 9 220 | 93 | 1 127 | 41 783 | 25.5 |
| Haines | 127 | 0.0 | D | 5.7 | D | 10.8 | D | D | 9.6 | 500 | 196 | 58 | 1 631 | 14.9 |
| Hoonah-Angoon | 41 | 0.0 | D | D | D | 5.2 | D | 4.6 | 51.8 | 390 | 185 | 51 | 1 771 | 10.3 |
| Juneau | 1 207 | -0.3 | D | 1.3 | D | 5.9 | 3.5 | 7.7 | 50.4 | 3 935 | 122 | 657 | 13 055 | 6.3 |
| Kenai Peninsula | 1 363 | 0.0 | 23.2 | 5.6 | 3.8 | 7.5 | 4.1 | 12.4 | 26.4 | 9 620 | 171 | 1 036 | 30 578 | 22.9 |
| Ketchikan Gateway | 521 | 0.0 | 12.0 | 5.5 | 3.3 | 8.8 | 4.8 | 10.5 | 33.9 | 2 070 | 152 | 271 | 6 166 | -1.8 |
| Kodiak Island | 533 | 0.0 | 21.6 | 18.1 | D | 3.6 | 4.0 | D | 39.6 | 1 405 | 101 | 147 | 5 303 | 2.8 |
| Lake and Peninsula | 43 | 0.0 | D | 7.2 | D | D | D | 0.0 | 45.0 | 185 | 111 | 21 | 1 502 | -3.5 |
| Matanuska-Susitna | 1 362 | 0.4 | 16.1 | 0.8 | 8.6 | 10.7 | 4.5 | 16.6 | 23.9 | 11 175 | 122 | 1 509 | 41 329 | 51.2 |
| Nome | 236 | 0.0 | D | D | D | 4.9 | 4.5 | 21.7 | 45.0 | 975 | 99 | 230 | 4 008 | 9.8 |
| North Slope | 1 573 | 0.0 | D | D | D | 0.7 | D | D | 9.8 | 625 | 66 | 27 | 2 500 | -1.5 |
| Northwest Arctic | 223 | 0.0 | D | D | D | D | D | D | 27.6 | 700 | 91 | 120 | 2 707 | 6.6 |
| Petersburg | 124 | 0.0 | D | D | 2.3 | 5.7 | D | D | 34.2 | 645 | 168 | 48 | 1 994 | 0.2 |
| Prince of Wales-Hyder | 116 | 0.0 | 8.4 | 4.2 | D | 7.6 | 4.5 | 4.5 | 47.0 | 830 | 145 | 120 | 2 992 | 1.7 |
| Sitka | 312 | 0.0 | 17.4 | 10.1 | D | 5.7 | 2.7 | 15.2 | 33.6 | 1 210 | 135 | 101 | 4 102 | 12.4 |
| Skagway | 46 | 0.0 | D | D | D | 19.8 | D | 0.5 | 27.1 | 90 | 96 | 0 | 636 | 26.7 |
| Southeast Fairbanks | 244 | 0.0 | D | D | 7.5 | 4.4 | 0.9 | D | 33.9 | 1 070 | 150 | 167 | 3 915 | 21.4 |
| Valdez-Cordova | 362 | 0.0 | 12.3 | 6.0 | 4.7 | 4.9 | 4.2 | 5.4 | 30.3 | 1 260 | 129 | 122 | 6 102 | 18.5 |
| Wade Hampton | 91 | 0.0 | D | D | D | 7.8 | D | D | 68.1 | 750 | 98 | 221 | 2 183 | 5.8 |
| Wrangell | 50 | 0.0 | 12.5 | 8.3 | D | 7.2 | D | D | 44.5 | 485 | 204 | 48 | 1 428 | 5.9 |
| Yakutat | 17 | 0.0 | D | D | D | 5.9 | D | D | 48.3 | 100 | 155 | 0 | 450 | -9.8 |
| Yukon-Koyukuk | 140 | 0.0 | D | D | D | 4.9 | D | 10.1 | 52.7 | 800 | 141 | 209 | 4 038 | 3.5 |
| ARIZONA | 158 942 | 0.7 | 14.6 | 8.4 | 9.9 | 7.9 | 9.4 | 12.5 | 18.1 | 1 104 545 | 170 | 112 939 | 2 844 526 | 29.9 |
| Apache | 1 125 | -1.1 | 4.7 | 0.5 | 1.3 | 4.0 | D | 9.5 | 64.5 | 11 245 | 155 | 4 506 | 32 514 | 2.8 |
| Cochise | 3 073 | 2.4 | D | D | 11.8 | 5.4 | D | 6.5 | 54.9 | 29 090 | 218 | 2 955 | 59 041 | 15.5 |
| Coconino | 3 253 | 0.3 | 14.6 | 10.2 | 3.6 | 7.2 | 4.6 | 16.2 | 32.3 | 16 695 | 124 | 2 832 | 63 321 | 18.5 |
| Gila | 817 | -0.2 | D | D | D | 7.5 | 3.4 | 12.4 | 31.8 | 15 690 | 295 | 1 483 | 32 698 | 16.0 |
| Graham | 443 | 2.7 | D | 2.3 | 14.6 | 9.9 | 2.2 | 12.4 | 37.5 | 5 790 | 156 | 793 | 12 980 | 13.6 |
| Greenlee | 284 | 0.7 | D | 0.0 | D | 2.0 | D | 2.9 | 9.1 | 1 425 | 166 | 139 | 4 372 | 16.8 |
| La Paz | 324 | 22.7 | 4.0 | 1.8 | 1.8 | 9.4 | 2.3 | 4.4 | 37.7 | 5 385 | 264 | 491 | 16 049 | 6.1 |
| Maricopa | 113 411 | 0.3 | 15.1 | 8.7 | 10.9 | 8.1 | 11.2 | 12.1 | 12.8 | 584 315 | 151 | 56 702 | 1 639 279 | 31.1 |
| Mohave | 2 355 | 0.8 | 12.8 | 6.3 | 4.1 | 13.1 | 5.4 | 21.9 | 19.6 | 58 670 | 290 | 4 208 | 110 911 | 38.5 |
| Navajo | 1 467 | 0.8 | 11.0 | 2.6 | 6.9 | 8.2 | 2.7 | 11.3 | 37.9 | 20 060 | 187 | 5 009 | 56 938 | 20.1 |
| Pima | 21 775 | 0.1 | 16.0 | 10.5 | 9.7 | 6.6 | 6.4 | 15.1 | 25.7 | 187 530 | 190 | 19 295 | 440 909 | 20.2 |
| Pinal | 3 260 | 6.9 | 12.8 | 5.8 | 2.9 | 7.3 | 2.9 | 7.8 | 38.6 | 62 775 | 164 | 5 682 | 159 222 | 96.2 |
| Santa Cruz | 818 | -0.1 | D | 2.4 | 3.9 | 11.0 | 3.6 | 2.9 | 42.9 | 8 245 | 173 | 1 286 | 18 010 | 38.2 |
| Yavapai | 2 754 | 0.3 | 14.9 | 5.4 | 5.0 | 10.6 | 5.9 | 15.7 | 23.1 | 66 330 | 313 | 3 456 | 110 432 | 35.1 |
| Yuma | 3 783 | 9.0 | 6.6 | 2.7 | 5.8 | 6.6 | 3.3 | 10.5 | 36.0 | 31 300 | 156 | 4 102 | 87 850 | 18.5 |
| ARKANSAS | 66 505 | 2.1 | 19.8 | 13.0 | 6.7 | 7.0 | 5.7 | 11.7 | 19.8 | 647 077 | 220 | 109 660 | 1 316 299 | 12.2 |
| Arkansas | 581 | 8.4 | 33.1 | 29.8 | 2.3 | 6.7 | 3.5 | 6.9 | 11.4 | 4 620 | 245 | 731 | 9 436 | -2.4 |
| Ashley | 517 | 9.4 | 46.1 | 38.5 | D | 5.3 | 2.6 | 6.7 | 11.7 | 5 725 | 264 | 1 026 | 10 137 | -4.5 |
| Baxter | 687 | 0.6 | D | 16.8 | 5.3 | 9.7 | 7.0 | 25.4 | 13.7 | 15 920 | 383 | 1 112 | 22 580 | 13.5 |
| Benton | 6 516 | 0.2 | 13.0 | 8.8 | 9.9 | 5.3 | 6.2 | 6.3 | 8.3 | 38 455 | 169 | 3 337 | 93 084 | 44.9 |
| Boone | 745 | 1.0 | D | 12.1 | 4.4 | 8.6 | 5.8 | 8.7 | 22.7 | 10 460 | 282 | 1 098 | 16 827 | 9.1 |
| Bradley | 187 | 4.7 | D | 14.6 | D | 5.9 | 3.9 | 12.4 | 22.7 | 2 905 | 253 | 558 | 5 860 | -1.2 |
| Calhoun | 177 | -0.2 | 74.3 | 69.9 | D | D | D | 1.3 | 7.9 | 1 380 | 268 | 172 | 2 897 | -3.8 |
| Carroll | 411 | 2.0 | D | 30.2 | 2.7 | 8.0 | 6.2 | D | 15.7 | 7 385 | 268 | 621 | 13 559 | 14.6 |
| Chicot | 218 | 26.2 | 9.9 | 4.2 | 1.5 | 5.9 | 6.0 | D | 22.8 | 3 105 | 265 | 989 | 5 421 | -9.3 |
| Clark | 443 | 1.8 | 21.8 | 20.2 | 3.5 | 9.2 | 4.0 | D | 26.7 | 4 945 | 216 | 698 | 10 385 | 2.2 |
| Clay | 233 | 24.4 | 13.7 | 10.0 | D | 6.3 | 2.9 | 8.1 | 19.0 | 4 785 | 301 | 730 | 8 031 | -5.5 |
| Cleburne | 397 | 0.9 | 28.6 | 14.2 | 2.5 | 9.6 | 5.5 | D | 13.2 | 8 240 | 318 | 712 | 15 826 | 15.2 |

1. Includes mining, construction, and manufacturing.    2. Per 1,000 resident population enumerated in the 2010 census.

# Table B. States and Counties — Housing, Labor Force, and Employment

| | Housing units, 2007–2011 | | | | | | | | | Civilian labor force, 2012 | | | | Civilian employment,[6] 2007–2011 | | |
| | Occupied units | | | | | | | | | | Unemployment | | Percent | | |
| | | | Owner-occupied | | | | Renter-occupied | | | | | | | | | |
| STATE County | Total | Percent | Median value[1] | Median owner cost as a percent of income | | Median rent[3] | Median rent as a percent of income | Sub-standard units[4] (percent) | Total | Percent change, 2011–2012 | Total | Rate[5] | Total | Manage-ment, business, science and arts | Con-struction, produc-tion, and mainte-nance occu-pations |
| | | | | With a mort-gage | Without a mort-gage[2] | | | | | | | | | | | |
| | 89 | 90 | 91 | 92 | 93 | 94 | 95 | 96 | 97 | 98 | 99 | 100 | 101 | 102 | 103 |
| **ALABAMA—Cont'd** | | | | | | | | | | | | | | | |
| Washington | 6 489 | 85.0 | 85 600 | 21.1 | 13.1 | 583 | 27.5 | 3.5 | 6 567 | -3.7 | 751 | 11.4 | 6 338 | 23.9 | 46.4 |
| Wilcox | 3 732 | 78.7 | 54 500 | 27.5 | 16.2 | 400 | 34.2 | 3.7 | 3 206 | -2.8 | 525 | 16.4 | 2 636 | 19.8 | 39.6 |
| Winston | 9 568 | 75.0 | 83 500 | 24.7 | 12.6 | 445 | 31.1 | 1.3 | 9 006 | -2.9 | 879 | 9.8 | 9 483 | 22.1 | 43.8 |
| **ALASKA** | 252 920 | 64.3 | 235 100 | 23.8 | 11.1 | 1 017 | 27.5 | 9.8 | 366 297 | 0.2 | 25 586 | 7.0 | 336 026 | 35.3 | 23.9 |
| Aleutians East | 336 | 51.5 | 121 700 | 18.8 | 11.4 | 790 | 22.3 | 7.4 | 1 167 | -0.8 | 147 | 12.6 | 2 562 | 8.9 | 80.2 |
| Aleutians West | 1 255 | 38.3 | 193 800 | 20.1 | 14.8 | 1 197 | 22.1 | 13.1 | 3 215 | 1.4 | 292 | 9.1 | 4 021 | 15.5 | 61.6 |
| Anchorage | 105 123 | 61.4 | 276 200 | 24.0 | 11.4 | 1 058 | 28.1 | 4.9 | 157 001 | 0.3 | 8 551 | 5.4 | 144 394 | 38.5 | 18.5 |
| Bethel | 4 295 | 64.4 | 171 100 | 19.1 | 12.7 | 941 | 19.8 | 56.5 | 7 142 | 0.2 | 1 086 | 15.2 | 6 100 | 38.1 | 20.3 |
| Bristol Bay | 424 | 55.0 | 172 300 | 16.0 | 9.9 | 1 057 | 23.2 | 6.4 | 1 002 | -7.1 | 44 | 4.4 | 530 | 38.3 | 24.7 |
| Denali | 699 | 67.1 | 179 500 | 17.3 | 9.9 | 572 | 11.5 | 17.6 | 1 360 | 0.0 | 139 | 10.2 | 1 006 | 27.8 | 35.7 |
| Dillingham | 1 369 | 56.8 | 182 500 | 16.0 | 13.6 | 931 | 21.7 | 26.4 | 2 148 | 1.9 | 206 | 9.6 | 1 853 | 40.1 | 19.5 |
| Fairbanks North Star | 35 583 | 59.2 | 212 800 | 25.1 | 10.2 | 1 105 | 29.1 | 9.4 | 46 697 | 0.1 | 2 915 | 6.2 | 45 413 | 33.0 | 26.0 |
| Haines | 1 176 | 68.4 | 173 800 | 24.1 | 9.9 | 792 | 28.1 | 9.7 | 1 315 | -4.2 | 107 | 8.1 | 1 294 | 34.8 | 26.7 |
| Hoonah-Angoon | 966 | 62.5 | 208 200 | 25.1 | 10.0 | 698 | 22.5 | 15.1 | 1 141 | 5.1 | 175 | 15.3 | 978 | 40.5 | 23.9 |
| Juneau | 12 379 | 64.5 | 299 100 | 25.0 | 12.1 | 1 135 | 26.1 | 5.4 | 18 427 | 0.3 | 895 | 4.9 | 17 352 | 42.3 | 16.5 |
| Kenai Peninsula | 22 390 | 73.5 | 200 000 | 22.9 | 9.9 | 812 | 28.2 | 9.8 | 27 543 | 0.7 | 2 311 | 8.4 | 25 057 | 29.9 | 28.8 |
| Ketchikan Gateway | 5 479 | 57.3 | 254 900 | 23.8 | 11.0 | 990 | 29.6 | 3.5 | 8 164 | -0.6 | 552 | 6.8 | 6 503 | 30.9 | 28.7 |
| Kodiak Island | 4 445 | 53.7 | 214 000 | 23.5 | 14.1 | 963 | 26.0 | 10.2 | 6 923 | -0.6 | 431 | 6.2 | 6 218 | 25.6 | 31.8 |
| Lake and Peninsula | 562 | 62.1 | 157 600 | 25.0 | 12.1 | 732 | 16.5 | 24.9 | 1 166 | 2.0 | 87 | 7.5 | 710 | 37.5 | 34.9 |
| Matanuska-Susitna | 30 609 | 78.7 | 216 500 | 24.4 | 11.4 | 969 | 29.4 | 9.4 | 43 764 | 0.1 | 3 509 | 8.0 | 38 301 | 32.6 | 28.3 |
| Nome | 2 756 | 52.9 | 144 200 | 20.2 | 14.7 | 1 003 | 22.9 | 34.7 | 4 159 | 1.3 | 484 | 11.6 | 3 611 | 37.8 | 24.9 |
| North Slope | 1 966 | 44.5 | 137 500 | 14.6 | 9.9 | 936 | 16.3 | 32.0 | 5 501 | 1.7 | 294 | 5.3 | 4 033 | 37.1 | 29.8 |
| Northwest Arctic | 1 797 | 54.4 | 131 100 | 21.3 | 15.3 | 1 074 | 19.7 | 48.4 | 3 100 | 1.3 | 467 | 15.1 | 2 578 | 30.9 | 33.7 |
| Petersburg | 1 564 | 76.3 | 182 500 | 18.6 | 17.3 | 760 | 23.3 | 4.9 | 1 663 | -0.2 | 174 | 10.5 | 2 083 | 33.4 | 32.4 |
| Prince of Wales-Hyder | 2 351 | 68.0 | 145 000 | 24.9 | 10.8 | 638 | 20.8 | 12.4 | 2 467 | -1.3 | 348 | 14.1 | 2 480 | 34.9 | 32.7 |
| Sitka | 3 632 | 53.6 | 315 200 | 23.3 | 9.9 | 1 047 | 33.0 | 7.5 | 4 611 | 0.3 | 257 | 5.6 | 4 836 | 38.2 | 23.2 |
| Skagway | 430 | 61.4 | 310 300 | 33.1 | 10.7 | 1 059 | 18.5 | 4.0 | 691 | 3.4 | 82 | 11.9 | 735 | 28.6 | 29.4 |
| Southeast Fairbanks | 2 523 | 65.2 | 158 900 | 23.5 | 11.0 | 991 | 19.9 | 18.9 | 3 398 | -4.3 | 380 | 11.2 | 3 103 | 29.6 | 31.5 |
| Valdez-Cordova | 3 793 | 76.4 | 167 700 | 18.2 | 9.9 | 809 | 27.7 | 13.5 | 5 202 | 0.0 | 464 | 8.9 | 4 564 | 31.0 | 29.8 |
| Wade Hampton | 1 714 | 67.0 | 85 100 | 14.3 | 11.6 | 532 | 14.3 | 66.9 | 2 781 | 0.1 | 599 | 21.5 | 2 030 | 35.0 | 25.3 |
| Wrangell | 1 004 | 76.0 | 168 500 | 23.8 | 9.9 | 789 | 27.7 | 5.9 | 1 055 | 0.3 | 93 | 8.8 | 1 166 | 30.9 | 25.9 |
| Yakutat | 259 | 51.4 | 155 500 | 15.5 | 9.9 | 1 000 | 21.3 | 18.1 | 289 | -3.7 | 27 | 9.3 | 490 | 28.2 | 41.6 |
| Yukon-Koyukuk | 2 041 | 70.1 | 102 500 | 20.3 | 13.0 | 654 | 21.9 | 46.9 | 3 208 | 2.4 | 471 | 14.7 | 2 025 | 34.4 | 30.2 |
| **ARIZONA** | 2 344 215 | 66.6 | 197 400 | 26.2 | 11.1 | 881 | 30.9 | 4.9 | 3 030 238 | -0.6 | 251 659 | 8.3 | 2 739 077 | 34.7 | 19.6 |
| Apache | 18 953 | 76.2 | 83 200 | 22.7 | 9.9 | 526 | 19.1 | 27.6 | 21 954 | -1.8 | 4 298 | 19.6 | 19 203 | 30.5 | 25.8 |
| Cochise | 48 917 | 69.2 | 155 700 | 22.9 | 10.6 | 762 | 28.0 | 3.4 | 58 923 | -4.3 | 4 844 | 8.2 | 48 437 | 35.9 | 18.7 |
| Coconino | 45 266 | 61.3 | 246 600 | 25.6 | 9.9 | 927 | 32.2 | 9.4 | 72 988 | -1.0 | 5 936 | 8.1 | 65 122 | 32.2 | 20.3 |
| Gila | 19 924 | 76.8 | 154 200 | 28.1 | 11.5 | 697 | 33.2 | 4.8 | 22 498 | -1.1 | 2 116 | 9.4 | 18 357 | 26.9 | 24.9 |
| Graham | 11 100 | 74.2 | 121 100 | 23.3 | 11.6 | 624 | 24.1 | 6.5 | 14 701 | 2.0 | 1 315 | 8.9 | 12 327 | 30.0 | 30.6 |
| Greenlee | 3 292 | 47.9 | 73 200 | 21.9 | 11.1 | 390 | 10.0 | 5.3 | 4 182 | 1.2 | 250 | 6.0 | 3 329 | 27.6 | 43.8 |
| La Paz | 10 374 | 74.6 | 95 700 | 26.0 | 9.9 | 567 | 26.4 | 10.4 | 7 687 | 2.2 | 705 | 9.2 | 6 911 | 23.6 | 26.3 |
| Maricopa | 1 394 016 | 65.2 | 219 300 | 26.2 | 11.1 | 934 | 30.9 | 4.4 | 1 896 987 | -0.4 | 135 413 | 7.1 | 1 736 116 | 36.0 | 18.9 |
| Mohave | 80 389 | 71.2 | 158 200 | 27.9 | 11.5 | 831 | 31.4 | 3.8 | 85 127 | -2.4 | 8 394 | 9.9 | 73 759 | 24.7 | 23.1 |
| Navajo | 34 921 | 72.8 | 130 400 | 24.8 | 9.9 | 644 | 24.1 | 15.9 | 39 928 | -1.3 | 6 077 | 15.2 | 35 757 | 29.4 | 25.7 |
| Pima | 382 366 | 64.0 | 190 500 | 25.5 | 11.7 | 769 | 31.8 | 4.1 | 462 748 | -1.2 | 33 581 | 7.3 | 420 203 | 36.3 | 17.6 |
| Pinal | 121 281 | 76.5 | 144 500 | 27.4 | 11.7 | 924 | 31.6 | 4.3 | 140 041 | -0.6 | 12 413 | 8.9 | 128 157 | 31.2 | 24.1 |
| Santa Cruz | 13 114 | 68.9 | 152 700 | 24.8 | 10.7 | 664 | 33.9 | 4.6 | 17 915 | -2.7 | 3 090 | 17.2 | 16 984 | 23.5 | 21.9 |
| Yavapai | 90 309 | 71.8 | 216 900 | 28.7 | 12.0 | 831 | 31.6 | 3.4 | 92 545 | -0.7 | 7 951 | 8.6 | 86 200 | 30.4 | 20.6 |
| Yuma | 69 993 | 70.4 | 138 600 | 27.1 | 10.5 | 775 | 31.2 | 8.3 | 92 015 | 2.0 | 25 277 | 27.5 | 68 215 | 25.5 | 28.0 |
| **ARKANSAS** | 1 121 386 | 67.5 | 105 100 | 21.0 | 11.0 | 637 | 29.6 | 3.1 | 1 355 851 | -0.3 | 98 834 | 7.3 | 1 252 276 | 30.6 | 28.1 |
| Arkansas | 8 089 | 66.6 | 79 000 | 19.8 | 11.1 | 603 | 29.8 | 1.6 | 10 959 | -4.4 | 840 | 7.7 | 8 964 | 26.8 | 33.5 |
| Ashley | 8 828 | 74.0 | 61 800 | 19.9 | 12.0 | 511 | 29.7 | 2.8 | 8 941 | -5.0 | 1 115 | 12.5 | 8 712 | 25.7 | 38.1 |
| Baxter | 18 581 | 77.4 | 121 900 | 23.2 | 11.1 | 610 | 32.5 | 2.1 | 17 281 | -0.1 | 1 333 | 7.7 | 15 442 | 29.3 | 25.2 |
| Benton | 80 140 | 69.5 | 155 700 | 21.6 | 10.3 | 746 | 25.9 | 3.1 | 111 186 | 2.2 | 6 338 | 5.7 | 99 466 | 34.8 | 25.6 |
| Boone | 14 596 | 72.8 | 108 400 | 21.8 | 11.3 | 545 | 28.2 | 3.1 | 17 070 | -1.2 | 1 220 | 7.1 | 15 809 | 28.2 | 25.8 |
| Bradley | 4 906 | 70.4 | 63 900 | 23.0 | 10.3 | 533 | 29.4 | 5.0 | 4 718 | -2.4 | 475 | 10.1 | 4 743 | 23.6 | 38.7 |
| Calhoun | 2 037 | 82.1 | 51 300 | 21.7 | 14.8 | 475 | 25.6 | 0.2 | 2 320 | -5.8 | 208 | 9.0 | 2 345 | 17.9 | 49.1 |
| Carroll | 11 418 | 71.8 | 118 200 | 26.1 | 10.0 | 585 | 29.4 | 3.2 | 13 903 | -1.9 | 761 | 5.5 | 12 043 | 25.2 | 35.7 |
| Chicot | 4 674 | 68.8 | 54 700 | 27.3 | 16.2 | 481 | 32.2 | 3.1 | 4 416 | -3.8 | 460 | 10.4 | 3 950 | 30.5 | 31.9 |
| Clark | 8 072 | 66.9 | 78 700 | 21.6 | 11.2 | 564 | 35.1 | 2.0 | 10 676 | -0.9 | 994 | 9.3 | 10 020 | 30.6 | 26.5 |
| Clay | 6 850 | 74.3 | 59 100 | 20.2 | 12.7 | 453 | 28.2 | 1.9 | 5 939 | -5.7 | 738 | 12.4 | 6 461 | 28.5 | 34.8 |
| Cleburne | 10 678 | 78.1 | 116 800 | 22.2 | 11.9 | 617 | 28.3 | 2.2 | 11 900 | -1.3 | 853 | 7.2 | 9 843 | 28.0 | 34.8 |

1. Specified owner-occupied units. 2. A value of 9.9 represents 9.9 percent or less. 3. Specified renter-occupied units. A value of 10.0 represents 10 percent or less. 4. Overcrowded or lacking complete plumbing facilities. 5. Percent of civilian labor force. 6. Persons 16 years old and over.

# Table B. States and Counties — Nonfarm Employment and Agriculture

| | Private nonfarm establishments, employment and payroll, 2011 | | | | | | | | | Agriculture, 2007 | | | |
| | | Employment | | | | | | Annual payroll | | Farms | | | |
| | | | | | | | | | | | Percent with: | | |
| STATE County | Number of establish-ments | Total | Health care and social assistance | Manufac-turing | Retail trade | Finance and insurance | Professional, scientific, and technical services | Total (mil dol) | Average per employee (dollars) | Number | Fewer than 50 acres | 500 acres or more | Farm operators whose principal occu-pation is farming (percent) |
|---|---|---|---|---|---|---|---|---|---|---|---|---|---|
| | 104 | 105 | 106 | 107 | 108 | 109 | 110 | 111 | 112 | 113 | 114 | 115 | 116 |
| ALABAMA—Cont'd | | | | | | | | | | | | | |
| Washington | 225 | 3 356 | 297 | 1 687 | 297 | 84 | D | 198 | 59 137 | 473 | 36.6 | 7.0 | 39.5 |
| Wilcox | 201 | 1 835 | D | D | 242 | 95 | D | 67 | 36 264 | 368 | 32.9 | 25.3 | 53.3 |
| Winston | 464 | 6 572 | 700 | 2 769 | 869 | 746 | 77 | 178 | 27 123 | 626 | 38.5 | 2.2 | 41.1 |
| ALASKA | 20 119 | 254 996 | 44 084 | 13 125 | 32 548 | 7 350 | 17 417 | 13 394 | 52 526 | 686 | 48.0 | 13.1 | 53.2 |
| Aleutians East | 58 | D | D | D | 62 | D | D | D | D | NA | NA | NA | NA |
| Aleutians West | 123 | 4 609 | 110 | 3 260 | 140 | D | D | 140 | 30 471 | NA | NA | NA | NA |
| Anchorage | 8 428 | 144 136 | 22 136 | 2 787 | 14 761 | 4 876 | 12 724 | 8 306 | 57 627 | 278 | 50.4 | 6.1 | 52.5 |
| Bethel | 238 | 3 188 | D | D | 770 | D | D | 134 | 42 077 | NA | NA | NA | NA |
| Bristol Bay | 63 | 534 | D | D | D | D | D | 37 | 68 436 | NA | NA | NA | NA |
| Denali | 102 | D | D | NA | 22 | D | 0 | 51 | D | NA | NA | NA | NA |
| Dillingham | 103 | 1 273 | 590 | D | 231 | D | D | 56 | 43 615 | NA | NA | NA | NA |
| Fairbanks North Star | 2 455 | 26 951 | 5 443 | 553 | 4 746 | 730 | 1 812 | 1 241 | 46 062 | 212 | 34.0 | 22.2 | 56.1 |
| Haines | 133 | 604 | 126 | D | 126 | D | D | 27 | 44 475 | NA | NA | NA | NA |
| Hoonah-Angoon | NA | NA | NA | NA | NA | NA | NA | NA | NA | | | | |
| Juneau | 1 112 | 10 848 | 2 295 | 225 | 1 769 | D | 505 | 486 | 44 767 | 37 | 91.9 | 0.0 | 51.4 |
| Kenai Peninsula | 1 993 | 13 712 | 3 569 | 605 | 2 446 | 290 | 529 | 618 | 45 056 | 124 | 56.5 | 5.6 | 50.0 |
| Ketchikan Gateway | 580 | 4 805 | D | 414 | 825 | 239 | D | 225 | 46 928 | NA | NA | NA | NA |
| Kodiak Island | 482 | 4 722 | D | 1 739 | 454 | 67 | D | 177 | 37 454 | NA | NA | NA | NA |
| Lake and Peninsula | 53 | 167 | NA | 17 | 19 | D | D | 15 | 92 593 | NA | NA | NA | NA |
| Matanuska-Susitna | 1 938 | 15 571 | 3 435 | 180 | 3 121 | 433 | 784 | 682 | 43 813 | NA | NA | NA | NA |
| Nome | 163 | 1 935 | 776 | D | 339 | D | D | 92 | 47 444 | NA | NA | NA | NA |
| North Slope | 137 | 2 833 | D | D | D | D | D | 185 | 65 237 | NA | NA | NA | NA |
| Northwest Arctic | 73 | 1 713 | D | NA | D | D | D | 118 | 69 108 | NA | NA | NA | NA |
| Petersburg | NA | NA | NA | NA | NA | NA | NA | NA | NA | | | | |
| Prince of Wales-Hyder | NA | NA | NA | NA | NA | NA | NA | NA | NA | | | | |
| Sitka | 388 | 2 978 | 910 | 333 | 429 | 69 | 39 | 128 | 42 868 | NA | NA | NA | NA |
| Skagway | NA | NA | NA | NA | NA | NA | NA | NA | NA | | | | |
| Southeast Fairbanks | 196 | 949 | 101 | D | 216 | 21 | D | 34 | 35 960 | NA | NA | NA | NA |
| Valdez-Cordova | 429 | 2 843 | 369 | 139 | 326 | D | 96 | 168 | 59 115 | NA | NA | NA | NA |
| Wade Hampton | 73 | 695 | D | D | 331 | D | D | 15 | 21 029 | NA | NA | NA | NA |
| Wrangell | NA | NA | NA | NA | NA | NA | NA | NA | NA | | | | |
| Yakutat | 28 | 128 | D | D | 40 | NA | NA | 6 | 48 750 | NA | NA | NA | NA |
| Yukon-Koyukuk | 115 | 432 | D | D | 174 | NA | D | 27 | 61 414 | NA | NA | NA | NA |
| ARIZONA | 130 305 | 2 108 561 | 314 612 | 137 532 | 306 972 | 129 576 | 128 576 | 86 533 | 41 039 | 15 637 | 80.1 | 8.1 | 61.1 |
| Apache | 467 | 7 219 | 3 145 | D | 1 104 | 79 | 216 | 244 | 33 864 | 4 243 | 95.3 | 1.5 | 70.4 |
| Cochise | 2 315 | 28 909 | 4 702 | 437 | 5 700 | 545 | 5 870 | 917 | 31 730 | 1 065 | 35.1 | 24.1 | 48.5 |
| Coconino | 3 529 | 44 547 | 7 756 | D | 7 698 | 916 | 1 576 | 1 494 | 33 527 | 1 597 | 94.3 | 2.8 | 67.3 |
| Gila | 1 017 | 11 413 | 2 421 | D | 2 055 | 206 | 359 | 419 | 36 753 | 279 | 78.5 | 4.7 | 60.2 |
| Graham | 512 | 8 633 | 1 373 | D | 1 539 | 115 | D | 358 | 41 488 | 343 | 60.1 | 16.0 | 43.4 |
| Greenlee | 75 | 2 170 | D | NA | 132 | D | D | 49 | 22 710 | 127 | 40.2 | 16.5 | 57.5 |
| La Paz | 342 | 3 983 | 595 | 245 | 1 048 | 71 | D | 110 | 27 592 | 99 | 28.3 | 43.4 | 70.7 |
| Maricopa | 83 468 | 1 449 079 | 199 158 | 94 036 | 197 939 | 108 161 | 93 754 | 63 370 | 43 731 | 1 793 | 79.6 | 7.8 | 50.7 |
| Mohave | 3 600 | 39 743 | 8 726 | 2 552 | 9 782 | 1 039 | 1 081 | 1 202 | 30 233 | 334 | 57.8 | 21.6 | 48.8 |
| Navajo | 1 742 | 16 982 | 3 549 | D | 3 875 | 403 | 430 | 539 | 31 753 | 2 949 | 94.1 | 2.3 | 70.8 |
| Pima | 20 059 | 300 956 | 57 630 | 25 633 | 46 397 | 11 901 | 16 042 | 11 231 | 37 317 | 622 | 74.0 | 12.1 | 41.2 |
| Pinal | 3 199 | 44 197 | 6 996 | 2 718 | 8 979 | 878 | 1 063 | 1 397 | 31 605 | 785 | 52.1 | 23.2 | 52.5 |
| Santa Cruz | 1 128 | 10 588 | 1 061 | 367 | 2 408 | 265 | 197 | 295 | 27 838 | 193 | 45.1 | 17.6 | 39.9 |
| Yavapai | 5 495 | 50 662 | 10 876 | 2 621 | 10 369 | 1 308 | 1 521 | 1 546 | 30 518 | 756 | 63.0 | 13.8 | 46.2 |
| Yuma | 2 897 | 39 826 | 6 409 | 2 629 | 7 786 | 1 160 | 1 207 | 1 169 | 29 364 | 452 | 60.6 | 19.5 | 57.5 |
| ARKANSAS | 64 471 | 980 644 | 171 336 | 156 024 | 136 814 | 36 729 | 33 583 | 35 312 | 36 009 | 49 346 | 35.9 | 12.4 | 44.5 |
| Arkansas | 542 | 8 452 | 1 049 | 3 446 | 1 172 | 250 | 93 | 283 | 33 542 | 539 | 17.3 | 42.3 | 61.0 |
| Ashley | 440 | 7 332 | 905 | D | 854 | 188 | D | 286 | 38 950 | 436 | 47.9 | 15.1 | 43.8 |
| Baxter | 1 072 | 12 561 | 3 421 | 2 198 | 2 249 | 496 | 402 | 380 | 30 271 | 668 | 45.5 | 5.4 | 37.3 |
| Benton | 5 289 | 101 258 | 7 776 | 9 763 | 10 027 | 2 538 | 5 707 | 5 032 | 49 694 | 2 151 | 49.2 | 3.7 | 46.3 |
| Boone | 852 | 12 387 | 2 343 | 1 928 | 1 904 | 813 | 266 | 437 | 35 287 | 1 266 | 34.7 | 9.3 | 41.8 |
| Bradley | 262 | 2 556 | 520 | 489 | 386 | 113 | 32 | 70 | 27 302 | 219 | 37.9 | 1.8 | 45.7 |
| Calhoun | 76 | 544 | D | D | 110 | D | NA | 18 | 32 237 | 101 | 31.7 | 6.9 | 30.7 |
| Carroll | 678 | 7 667 | 694 | 3 043 | 1 141 | 260 | 141 | 201 | 26 234 | 1 139 | 32.0 | 9.9 | 47.4 |
| Chicot | 227 | 2 367 | 846 | 95 | 399 | 112 | 40 | 62 | 26 284 | 382 | 20.2 | 37.7 | 59.2 |
| Clark | 497 | 6 964 | 955 | D | 1 195 | 245 | 191 | 189 | 27 141 | 430 | 38.6 | 8.6 | 32.1 |
| Clay | 290 | 3 025 | 740 | 576 | 458 | 98 | 45 | 81 | 26 791 | 731 | 27.1 | 25.0 | 49.9 |
| Cleburne | 602 | 6 051 | 817 | 1 352 | 1 094 | D | 176 | 166 | 27 390 | 905 | 37.7 | 5.1 | 34.7 |

# Table B. States and Counties — **Agriculture**

| STATE County | Agriculture, 2007 (cont.) | | | | | | | | | | | | | | | |
| | Land in farms | | | | | Value of land and buildings (dollars) | | | Value of products sold | | | | Percent of farms with sales of: | | Government payments | |
| | | | Acres | | | | | Value of machinery and equipment, average per farm (dollars) | | | Percent from: | | | | | |
| | Acreage (1,000) | Percent change, 2002–2007 | Average size of farm | Total irrigated (1,000) | Total cropland (1,000) | Average per farm | Average per acre | | Total (mil dol) | Average per farm (dollars) | Crops | Live-stock and poultry products | $10,000 or more | $100,000 or more | Total ($1,000) | Percent of farms |
| | 117 | 118 | 119 | 120 | 121 | 122 | 123 | 124 | 125 | 126 | 127 | 128 | 129 | 130 | 131 | 132 |
| **ALABAMA—Cont'd** | | | | | | | | | | | | | | | | |
| Washington | 84 | 13.5 | 177 | 0.1 | 19.0 | 373 658 | 2 114 | 57 902 | 30.8 | 65 074 | 8.4 | 91.6 | 32.3 | 10.1 | 342 | 20.5 |
| Wilcox | 169 | 5.6 | 459 | 0.2 | 33.4 | 634 093 | 1 382 | 46 064 | 7.6 | 20 682 | 21.7 | 78.3 | 22.3 | 4.3 | 1 126 | 46.5 |
| Winston | 65 | -1.5 | 103 | 0.0 | 20.5 | 266 819 | 2 588 | 50 374 | 65.5 | 104 601 | 1.8 | 98.2 | 37.9 | 17.4 | 144 | 12.5 |
| **ALASKA** | 882 | -2.1 | 1 285 | 3.7 | 86.2 | 502 342 | 391 | 78 837 | 57.0 | 83 119 | 43.4 | 56.6 | 41.3 | 11.2 | 1 645 | 11.4 |
| Aleutians East | NA | NA | NA | NA | NA | NA | NA | NA | NA | NA | NA | NA | NA | NA | NA | NA |
| Aleutians West | NA | NA | NA | NA | NA | NA | NA | NA | NA | NA | NA | NA | NA | NA | NA | NA |
| Anchorage | 38 | -19.1 | 138 | 1.7 | 17.0 | 488 278 | 3 536 | 72 515 | 31.8 | 114 216 | 49.6 | 50.4 | 41.0 | 14.4 | 110 | 6.1 |
| Bethel | NA | NA | NA | NA | NA | NA | NA | NA | NA | NA | NA | NA | NA | NA | NA | NA |
| Bristol Bay | NA | NA | NA | NA | NA | NA | NA | NA | NA | NA | NA | NA | NA | NA | NA | NA |
| Denali | NA | NA | NA | NA | NA | NA | NA | NA | NA | NA | NA | NA | NA | NA | NA | NA |
| Dillingham | NA | NA | NA | NA | NA | NA | NA | NA | NA | NA | NA | NA | NA | NA | NA | NA |
| Fairbanks North Star | 111 | 0.9 | 523 | 2.0 | 63.6 | 406 163 | 777 | 74 337 | 7.1 | 33 375 | 83.2 | 16.8 | 42.5 | 7.5 | 1 356 | 23.6 |
| Haines | NA | NA | NA | NA | NA | NA | NA | NA | NA | NA | NA | NA | NA | NA | NA | NA |
| Hoonah-Angoon | | | | | | | | | | | | | | | | |
| Juneau | 1 | NA | 14 | 0.0 | 0.0 | 757 354 | 54 518 | 216 319 | 11.8 | 318 120 | 7.7 | 92.3 | 70.3 | 35.1 | 0 | 0.0 |
| Kenai Peninsula | 38 | 5.6 | 309 | 0.0 | 5.3 | 409 882 | 1 327 | 50 729 | D | D | D | D | 33.9 | 4.0 | 38 | 6.5 |
| Ketchikan Gateway | NA | NA | NA | NA | NA | NA | NA | NA | NA | NA | NA | NA | NA | NA | NA | NA |
| Kodiak Island | NA | NA | NA | NA | NA | NA | NA | NA | NA | NA | NA | NA | NA | NA | NA | NA |
| Lake and Peninsula | NA | NA | NA | NA | NA | NA | NA | NA | NA | NA | NA | NA | NA | NA | NA | NA |
| Matanuska-Susitna | NA | NA | NA | NA | NA | NA | NA | NA | NA | NA | NA | NA | NA | NA | NA | NA |
| Nome | NA | NA | NA | NA | NA | NA | NA | NA | NA | NA | NA | NA | NA | NA | NA | NA |
| North Slope | NA | NA | NA | NA | NA | NA | NA | NA | NA | NA | NA | NA | NA | NA | NA | NA |
| Northwest Arctic | NA | NA | NA | NA | NA | NA | NA | NA | NA | NA | NA | NA | NA | NA | NA | NA |
| Petersburg | | | | | | | | | | | | | | | | |
| Prince of Wales-Hyder | | | | | | | | | | | | | | | | |
| Sitka | NA | NA | NA | NA | NA | NA | NA | NA | NA | NA | NA | NA | NA | NA | NA | NA |
| Skagway | | | | | | | | | | | | | | | | |
| Southeast Fairbanks | NA | NA | NA | NA | NA | NA | NA | NA | NA | NA | NA | NA | NA | NA | NA | NA |
| Valdez-Cordova | NA | NA | NA | NA | NA | NA | NA | NA | NA | NA | NA | NA | NA | NA | NA | NA |
| Wade Hampton | NA | NA | NA | NA | NA | NA | NA | NA | NA | NA | NA | NA | NA | NA | NA | NA |
| Wrangell | NA | NA | NA | NA | NA | NA | NA | NA | NA | NA | NA | NA | NA | NA | NA | NA |
| Yakutat | NA | NA | NA | NA | NA | NA | NA | NA | NA | NA | NA | NA | NA | NA | NA | NA |
| Yukon-Koyukuk | NA | NA | NA | NA | NA | NA | NA | NA | NA | NA | NA | NA | NA | NA | NA | NA |
| **ARIZONA** | 26 118 | -1.8 | 1 670 | 876.2 | 1 205.4 | 1 249 929 | 748 | 66 291 | 3 234.6 | 206 852 | 59.1 | 40.9 | 18.6 | 6.7 | 55 947 | 7.3 |
| Apache | D | D | D | 9.3 | 27.5 | 263 783 | 194 | 15 511 | 12.6 | 2 975 | 38.2 | 61.8 | 5.3 | 0.2 | 28 | 1.6 |
| Cochise | 824 | -15.0 | 774 | 67.6 | 141.2 | 1 475 858 | 1 907 | 77 792 | 117.1 | 109 981 | 63.5 | 36.5 | 34.3 | 10.1 | 3 698 | 13.8 |
| Coconino | 6 102 | NA | 3 821 | 2.2 | 20.5 | 752 116 | 197 | 22 738 | D | D | 0.0 | D | 7.4 | 1.9 | 372 | 3.0 |
| Gila | 1 166 | NA | 4 181 | 3.2 | 3.7 | 1 589 706 | 380 | 44 594 | 4.4 | 15 748 | 39.2 | 60.7 | 20.1 | 2.2 | 153 | 4.3 |
| Graham | 1 346 | NA | 3 923 | 28.3 | 35.3 | 2 161 265 | 551 | 157 473 | D | D | D | 0.0 | 33.8 | 12.2 | 2 974 | 30.3 |
| Greenlee | 35 | 29.6 | 278 | 5.3 | 6.7 | 650 667 | 2 343 | 71 100 | 6.2 | 48 895 | 23.8 | 76.2 | 38.6 | 7.9 | 315 | 28.3 |
| La Paz | D | D | D | 100.5 | 123.3 | 3 175 260 | 1 085 | 363 805 | 136.6 | 1 379 731 | 98.1 | 1.9 | 69.7 | 40.4 | 4 192 | 34.3 |
| Maricopa | 485 | -22.6 | 271 | 199.4 | 267.3 | 2 300 844 | 8 498 | 116 343 | 813.5 | 453 704 | 48.7 | 51.3 | 32.8 | 15.5 | 17 150 | 10.3 |
| Mohave | 858 | 8.2 | 2 570 | 17.1 | 31.2 | 1 450 681 | 564 | 57 373 | 18.6 | 55 783 | 65.2 | 34.8 | 28.1 | 5.1 | 761 | 4.5 |
| Navajo | 4 503 | -2.0 | 1 527 | 8.6 | 16.9 | 421 707 | 276 | 19 304 | 46.5 | 19 344 | 9.7 | 90.3 | 6.1 | 0.7 | 77 | 2.6 |
| Pima | D | D | D | 35.7 | 49.6 | 1 951 879 | 446 | 80 179 | 67.5 | 108 521 | 73.2 | 26.8 | 27.2 | 9.8 | 3 771 | 6.6 |
| Pinal | 1 047 | -9.9 | 1 334 | 215.1 | 256.0 | 4 853 351 | 3 638 | 240 548 | 799.8 | 1 018 867 | 29.3 | 70.7 | 44.5 | 27.4 | 17 624 | 30.8 |
| Santa Cruz | 130 | -2.3 | 671 | 1.7 | 8.0 | 1 537 974 | 2 291 | 46 385 | 4.3 | 22 133 | 10.7 | 89.3 | 31.1 | 4.1 | 156 | 4.1 |
| Yavapai | 639 | -11.3 | 845 | 7.9 | 25.3 | 1 503 944 | 1 779 | 52 064 | D | D | D | D | 26.2 | 5.0 | 282 | 3.6 |
| Yuma | 210 | -9.1 | 466 | 184.2 | 193.1 | 3 893 483 | 8 361 | 373 336 | 960.0 | 2 123 822 | D | D | 60.0 | 37.4 | 4 395 | 20.8 |
| **ARKANSAS** | 13 873 | -4.3 | 281 | 4 460.7 | 8 432.2 | 658 732 | 2 343 | 90 823 | 7 508.8 | 152 166 | 38.6 | 61.4 | 40.4 | 16.4 | 269 448 | 23.2 |
| Arkansas | 405 | 3.8 | 752 | 310.7 | 359.0 | 1 568 961 | 2 088 | 244 440 | 180.1 | 334 046 | 99.7 | 0.3 | 60.1 | 46.0 | 14 310 | 85.2 |
| Ashley | 154 | -7.8 | 354 | 90.8 | 120.1 | 811 284 | 2 294 | 103 494 | 64.7 | 148 425 | 85.3 | 14.7 | 33.9 | 17.7 | 5 578 | 31.7 |
| Baxter | 97 | -5.8 | 145 | D | 18.8 | 398 818 | 2 742 | 42 098 | 17.5 | 26 231 | 4.2 | 95.8 | 24.7 | 2.8 | 135 | 10.0 |
| Benton | 255 | -18.5 | 118 | 0.4 | 101.1 | 579 942 | 4 900 | 68 428 | 434.0 | 201 747 | 1.6 | 98.4 | 43.4 | 17.0 | 495 | 6.6 |
| Boone | 242 | -14.8 | 191 | 0.2 | 57.6 | 518 871 | 2 714 | 56 403 | 119.8 | 94 634 | 1.7 | 98.3 | 45.8 | 11.4 | 1 476 | 39.3 |
| Bradley | 25 | -13.8 | 115 | 0.9 | 9.6 | 332 369 | 2 884 | 54 957 | 29.9 | 136 326 | 11.8 | 88.2 | 42.5 | 18.3 | 53 | 8.7 |
| Calhoun | 16 | -15.8 | 162 | D | 6.2 | 353 653 | 2 177 | 55 110 | 2.9 | 28 958 | D | D | 25.7 | 4.0 | 65 | 23.8 |
| Carroll | 243 | -9.7 | 213 | 0.5 | 64.8 | 541 070 | 2 541 | 62 119 | 261.1 | 229 244 | 0.9 | 99.1 | 52.6 | 20.8 | 413 | 14.9 |
| Chicot | 286 | 6.3 | 747 | 141.8 | 221.3 | 1 320 053 | 1 766 | 199 901 | 129.1 | 337 977 | 65.8 | 34.2 | 59.7 | 42.4 | 9 232 | 75.7 |
| Clark | 82 | -16.3 | 190 | 0.4 | 29.9 | 397 138 | 2 087 | 51 666 | 16.9 | 39 250 | 13.4 | 86.6 | 29.5 | 6.5 | 315 | 19.5 |
| Clay | 330 | -3.8 | 452 | 227.0 | 293.4 | 1 008 541 | 2 231 | 166 226 | 142.1 | 194 350 | 98.1 | 1.9 | 44.3 | 28.6 | 12 282 | 71.3 |
| Cleburne | 130 | 4.0 | 143 | 0.2 | 38.5 | 405 826 | 2 829 | 57 358 | 56.1 | 62 014 | 2.9 | 97.1 | 29.3 | 8.0 | 646 | 18.3 |

| STATE County | Water use, 2005 | | Wholesale trade,[1] 2007 | | | | Retail trade,[2] 2007 | | | | Real estate and rental and leasing,[2] 2007 | | | |
|---|---|---|---|---|---|---|---|---|---|---|---|---|---|---|
| | Total water withdrawn (mil gal/day) | Gallons withdrawn per person | Number of establish-ments | Number of employees | Sales (mil dol) | Annual payroll (mil dol) | Number of establish-ments | Number of employees | Sales (mil dol) | Annual payroll (mil dol) | Number of establish-ments | Number of employees | Receipts (mil dol) | Annual payroll (mil dol) |
| | 133 | 134 | 135 | 136 | 137 | 138 | 139 | 140 | 141 | 142 | 143 | 144 | 145 | 146 |
| ALABAMA—Cont'd | | | | | | | | | | | | | | |
| Washington | 99.2 | 5 580 | 5 | 78 | 32.9 | 2.8 | 47 | 325 | 76.3 | 5.9 | 2 | D | D | D |
| Wilcox | 23.7 | 1 828 | 7 | 43 | 21.3 | 1.4 | 46 | 298 | 75.7 | 5.5 | 7 | 14 | 0.5 | 0.1 |
| Winston | 1.9 | 78 | 29 | 310 | 165.6 | 10.5 | 108 | 915 | 166.7 | 16.6 | 11 | 32 | 2.4 | 0.4 |
| ALASKA | 1 055.1 | 1 590 | 658 | 8 262 | 4 563.6 | 391.6 | 2 641 | 34 977 | 9 303.4 | 936.8 | 852 | 4 370 | 840.6 | 160.2 |
| Aleutians East | 3.4 | 1 275 | 1 | D | D | D | 9 | 52 | 9.3 | 1.2 | 2 | D | D | D |
| Aleutians West | 4.8 | 905 | 10 | 82 | 62.1 | 4.0 | 14 | 155 | 46.8 | 5.1 | 6 | 39 | 10.0 | 2.0 |
| Anchorage | 107.7 | 387 | 339 | 5 498 | 2 914.0 | 261.0 | 923 | 15 842 | 4 482.7 | 441.8 | 378 | 2 416 | 453.5 | 94.0 |
| Bethel | 0.5 | 26 | 4 | 26 | 3.5 | 0.3 | 54 | 831 | 96.8 | 13.5 | 6 | 45 | 7.9 | 1.0 |
| Bristol Bay | 0.2 | 158 | 3 | D | D | D | 9 | 50 | 12.8 | 1.5 | 2 | D | D | D |
| Denali | 16.2 | 8 897 | NA | NA | NA | NA | 10 | 33 | 11.0 | 0.9 | NA | NA | NA | NA |
| Dillingham | 0.8 | 173 | 2 | D | D | D | 19 | 209 | 42.7 | 4.8 | 6 | 25 | 3.6 | 0.6 |
| Fairbanks North Star | 38.3 | 437 | 72 | D | D | D | 339 | 5 236 | 1 574.3 | 146.7 | 136 | 745 | 152.5 | 29.9 |
| Haines | 3.5 | 1 604 | 2 | D | D | D | 18 | 115 | 16.2 | 2.9 | 4 | 8 | 0.7 | 0.1 |
| Hoonah-Angoon | | | NA | NA | NA | NA | NA | NA | NA | NA | NA | NA | NA | NA |
| Juneau | 603.7 | 19 352 | 33 | D | D | D | 172 | 1 933 | 465.3 | 52.0 | 58 | 241 | 41.1 | 5.9 |
| Kenai Peninsula | 27.4 | 534 | 46 | 353 | 193.7 | 16.1 | 265 | 2 537 | 666.9 | 62.5 | 66 | 169 | 38.2 | 5.3 |
| Ketchikan Gateway | 14.3 | 1 086 | 10 | D | D | D | 109 | 961 | 268.9 | 31.2 | 22 | 82 | 16.1 | 2.5 |
| Kodiak Island | 9.4 | 692 | 37 | D | D | D | 45 | 481 | 108.2 | 11.6 | 15 | 75 | 7.8 | 2.2 |
| Lake and Peninsula | 0.4 | 265 | 1 | D | D | D | 4 | D | D | D | 3 | 9 | 0.5 | 0.1 |
| Matanuska-Susitna | 6.7 | 90 | 36 | 368 | 137.0 | 14.9 | 233 | 3 200 | 853.9 | 86.9 | 72 | 272 | 37.4 | 6.8 |
| Nome | 0.6 | 67 | 4 | D | D | D | 33 | 399 | 63.2 | 7.8 | 7 | 24 | 5.2 | 0.5 |
| North Slope | 175.7 | 25 489 | 8 | 202 | 135.2 | 14.6 | 18 | 233 | 70.1 | 6.7 | 5 | D | D | D |
| Northwest Arctic | 8.0 | 1 098 | 1 | D | D | D | 15 | 201 | 41.6 | 4.9 | 3 | 2 | 0.4 | 0.0 |
| Petersburg | | | NA | NA | NA | NA | NA | NA | NA | NA | NA | NA | NA | NA |
| Prince of Wales-Hyder | | | NA | NA | NA | NA | NA | NA | NA | NA | NA | NA | NA | NA |
| Sitka | 9.1 | 1 013 | 15 | D | D | D | 62 | 465 | 94.9 | 12.6 | 15 | 49 | 7.8 | 1.9 |
| Skagway | | | NA | NA | NA | NA | NA | NA | NA | NA | NA | NA | NA | NA |
| Southeast Fairbanks | 0.7 | 104 | 2 | D | D | D | 38 | 208 | 47.3 | 4.0 | 8 | 10 | 1.0 | 0.1 |
| Valdez-Cordova | 13.1 | 1 303 | 14 | 86 | 81.2 | 4.7 | 56 | 370 | 79.7 | 7.7 | 17 | 45 | 17.1 | 2.4 |
| Wade Hampton | 0.5 | 61 | 1 | D | D | D | 25 | 283 | 39.5 | 4.0 | 2 | D | D | D |
| Wrangell | | | NA | NA | NA | NA | NA | NA | NA | NA | NA | NA | NA | NA |
| Yakutat | 0.6 | 953 | 3 | 20 | 10.0 | 1.8 | 6 | D | D | D | 1 | D | D | D |
| Yukon-Koyukuk | 0.7 | 109 | 2 | D | D | D | 34 | 299 | 41.6 | 6.5 | 3 | 5 | 0.3 | 0.1 |
| ARIZONA | 6 244.7 | 1 051 | 5 874 | 84 029 | 57 573.5 | 4 116.4 | 19 384 | 337 529 | 86 758.8 | 8 010.8 | 9 441 | 52 627 | 10 077.6 | 1 994.3 |
| Apache | 35.2 | 508 | 12 | 32 | 18.1 | 0.8 | 104 | 1 189 | 276.9 | 24.1 | 20 | 56 | 5.9 | 0.9 |
| Cochise | 254.4 | 2 018 | 54 | 359 | 102.3 | 10.4 | 455 | 6 305 | 1 313.7 | 129.1 | 139 | 504 | 65.1 | 12.4 |
| Coconino | 48.0 | 387 | 98 | 1 149 | 475.6 | 40.2 | 674 | 7 861 | 1 691.7 | 169.3 | 237 | 754 | 187.5 | 24.2 |
| Gila | 28.0 | 543 | 29 | D | D | D | 186 | 2 450 | 550.8 | 55.6 | 82 | 269 | 35.9 | 7.5 |
| Graham | 172.9 | 5 228 | 19 | 193 | 68.0 | 7.5 | 97 | 1 602 | 389.4 | 36.2 | 29 | D | D | D |
| Greenlee | 31.6 | 4 195 | 2 | D | D | D | 19 | 159 | 35.6 | 2.8 | 1 | D | D | D |
| La Paz | 628.5 | 31 055 | 10 | 107 | 65.9 | 3.7 | 88 | 1 006 | 394.4 | 19.1 | 17 | 57 | 6.0 | 1.3 |
| Maricopa | 1 967.0 | 541 | 4 176 | 66 783 | 49 760.3 | 3 457.2 | 11 468 | 217 746 | 58 688.3 | 5 332.6 | 6 123 | 37 987 | 7 796.5 | 1 564.0 |
| Mohave | 138.6 | 741 | 117 | 976 | 423.8 | 33.0 | 730 | 10 672 | 2 837.7 | 248.0 | 280 | 876 | 133.3 | 22.7 |
| Navajo | 67.5 | 622 | 38 | 289 | 209.5 | 12.0 | 340 | 4 399 | 1 237.5 | 102.4 | 142 | 350 | 56.9 | 10.1 |
| Pima | 306.8 | 332 | 744 | 8 132 | 3 056.8 | 324.6 | 2 982 | 51 830 | 11 928.5 | 1 208.9 | 1 449 | 8 133 | 1 211.7 | 251.8 |
| Pinal | 1 289.2 | 5 616 | 110 | 930 | 450.4 | 35.9 | 524 | 8 552 | 2 033.1 | 175.2 | 202 | 689 | 107.5 | 18.1 |
| Santa Cruz | 19.4 | 461 | 157 | D | D | D | 257 | 3 058 | 681.3 | 60.7 | 61 | 265 | 42.6 | 5.5 |
| Yavapai | 91.5 | 460 | 175 | 1 652 | 831.4 | 61.1 | 920 | 11 795 | 2 695.4 | 266.6 | 469 | 1 776 | 293.9 | 55.4 |
| Yuma | 1 166.1 | 6 433 | 133 | D | D | D | 540 | 8 905 | 2 004.6 | 180.2 | 190 | 734 | 119.2 | 17.5 |
| ARKANSAS | 11 428.3 | 4 112 | 2 977 | 38 988 | 29 659.8 | 1 536.3 | 11 906 | 140 018 | 32 974.3 | 2 889.2 | 3 162 | 14 115 | 1 968.1 | 374.9 |
| Arkansas | 966.4 | 48 144 | 30 | 303 | 134.6 | 12.2 | 111 | 1 231 | 286.3 | 25.4 | 19 | 58 | 6.1 | 1.3 |
| Ashley | 232.3 | 10 021 | 18 | 114 | 107.3 | 4.7 | 95 | 881 | 170.8 | 16.6 | 13 | 46 | 4.8 | 0.8 |
| Baxter | 5.8 | 145 | 19 | D | D | D | 242 | 2 460 | 486.8 | 48.7 | 50 | 202 | 22.7 | 4.5 |
| Benton | 440.9 | 2 359 | 216 | D | D | D | 751 | 9 896 | 2 390.6 | 223.0 | 308 | 1 204 | 165.9 | 34.3 |
| Boone | 3.1 | 87 | 32 | D | D | D | 166 | 2 038 | 466.9 | 42.2 | 38 | 104 | 13.6 | 2.4 |
| Bradley | 1.9 | 153 | 10 | 137 | 42.8 | 4.2 | 50 | 346 | 71.5 | 6.0 | 9 | 20 | 1.6 | 0.4 |
| Calhoun | 0.6 | 102 | 2 | D | D | D | 20 | 65 | 17.9 | 1.0 | 2 | D | D | D |
| Carroll | 11.5 | 426 | 14 | 78 | 24.1 | 2.9 | 167 | 1 339 | 265.4 | 25.8 | 36 | 70 | 6.4 | 1.3 |
| Chicot | 319.9 | 24 558 | 13 | 113 | 120.6 | 4.0 | 50 | 426 | 67.0 | 7.0 | 11 | 30 | 3.5 | 0.6 |
| Clark | 6.6 | 287 | 13 | D | D | D | 102 | 1 184 | 247.8 | 25.8 | 36 | 112 | 11.1 | 2.2 |
| Clay | 478.7 | 28 876 | 12 | 265 | 116.9 | 7.9 | 67 | 531 | 132.6 | 9.8 | 10 | 22 | 1.5 | 0.4 |
| Cleburne | 8.6 | 338 | 18 | 123 | 54.4 | 3.0 | 123 | 1 131 | 282.4 | 23.2 | 34 | 83 | 8.3 | 2.0 |

1. Merchant wholesalers, except manufacturers' sales branches and offices.  2. Employer establishments.

| STATE County | Professional, scientific, and technical services,[1] 2007 | | | | Manufacturing, 2007 | | | | Accommodation and food services, 2007 | | | |
|---|---|---|---|---|---|---|---|---|---|---|---|---|
| | Number of establishments | Number of employees | Receipts (mil dol) | Annual payroll (mil dol) | Number of establishments | Number of employees | Receipts (mil dol) | Annual payroll (mil dol) | Number of establishments | Number of employees | Sales (mil dol) | Annual payroll (mil dol) |
| | 147 | 148 | 149 | 150 | 151 | 152 | 153 | 154 | 155 | 156 | 157 | 158 |
| ALABAMA—Cont'd | | | | | | | | | | | | |
| Washington | 14 | 178 | 25.9 | 9.1 | 15 | 1 397 | 1 153.4 | 85.3 | 9 | D | D | D |
| Wilcox | 11 | D | D | D | 13 | 876 | D | D | 19 | 112 | 12.9 | 1.2 |
| Winston | 23 | 70 | 5.7 | 1.9 | 68 | 4 439 | 797.8 | 112.0 | 40 | 511 | 16.6 | 4.4 |
| ALASKA | 1 799 | 12 509 | 2 006.8 | 745.4 | 544 | 13 298 | 8 204.0 | 489.5 | 1 996 | 25 638 | 1 851.3 | 529.8 |
| Aleutians East | NA | NA | NA | NA | 5 | D | D | D | 12 | D | D | D |
| Aleutians West | 2 | D | D | D | 14 | 2 314 | 634.8 | 77.1 | 12 | 103 | 14.7 | 2.9 |
| Anchorage | 1 092 | D | D | D | 194 | 2 305 | D | D | 720 | 14 031 | 933.3 | 283.9 |
| Bethel | 5 | D | D | D | NA | NA | NA | NA | 18 | 39 | 4.1 | 0.8 |
| Bristol Bay | 1 | D | D | D | NA | NA | NA | NA | 19 | 74 | 13.3 | 3.9 |
| Denali | 2 | D | D | D | NA | NA | NA | NA | 30 | 110 | 37.1 | 10.5 |
| Dillingham | 4 | D | D | D | NA | NA | NA | NA | 18 | 51 | 7.2 | 1.9 |
| Fairbanks North Star | 228 | 1 329 | 174.9 | 64.7 | 78 | 745 | D | 37.3 | 220 | 3 430 | 221.6 | 60.9 |
| Haines | 4 | 6 | 0.3 | 0.1 | NA | NA | NA | NA | 19 | 64 | 6.4 | 1.5 |
| Hoonah-Angoon | NA | NA | NA | NA | NA | NA | NA | NA | NA | NA | NA | NA |
| Juneau | 95 | D | D | D | NA | NA | NA | NA | 97 | 1 228 | 86.9 | 21.6 |
| Kenai Peninsula | 111 | D | D | D | 64 | 982 | D | 57.4 | 260 | 1 677 | 131.2 | 33.5 |
| Ketchikan Gateway | 26 | D | D | D | 14 | 500 | D | 16.7 | 57 | 546 | 45.6 | 12.1 |
| Kodiak Island | 25 | 65 | 12.4 | 2.5 | 22 | 1 644 | D | 51.5 | 42 | 404 | 26.3 | 6.9 |
| Lake and Peninsula | 3 | 9 | 1.0 | 0.5 | NA | NA | NA | NA | 14 | D | D | D |
| Matanuska-Susitna | 132 | D | D | D | NA | NA | NA | NA | 185 | 1 774 | 113.7 | 30.2 |
| Nome | 5 | D | D | D | NA | NA | NA | NA | 15 | 166 | 10.2 | 2.9 |
| North Slope | 4 | 14 | 2.8 | 1.3 | NA | NA | NA | NA | 20 | 414 | 56.3 | 20.0 |
| Northwest Arctic | 1 | D | D | D | NA | NA | NA | NA | 4 | D | D | D |
| Petersburg | NA | NA | NA | NA | NA | NA | NA | NA | NA | NA | NA | NA |
| Prince of Wales-Hyder | NA | NA | NA | NA | NA | NA | NA | NA | NA | NA | NA | NA |
| Sitka | 15 | 48 | 4.0 | 1.1 | NA | NA | NA | NA | 41 | 500 | 27.1 | 8.2 |
| Skagway | NA | NA | NA | NA | NA | NA | NA | NA | NA | NA | NA | NA |
| Southeast Fairbanks | 11 | 23 | 5.5 | 1.2 | NA | NA | NA | NA | 30 | 165 | 22.2 | 4.1 |
| Valdez-Cordova | 21 | D | D | D | 14 | 569 | 543.4 | 19.2 | 56 | 264 | 23.1 | 6.2 |
| Wade Hampton | 1 | D | D | D | NA | NA | NA | NA | NA | NA | NA | NA |
| Wrangell | NA | NA | NA | NA | NA | NA | NA | NA | NA | NA | NA | NA |
| Yakutat | NA | NA | NA | NA | NA | NA | NA | NA | 7 | 21 | 3.8 | 1.1 |
| Yukon-Koyukuk | 1 | D | D | D | NA | NA | NA | NA | 12 | 77 | 5.4 | 1.6 |
| ARIZONA | 16 563 | 128 188 | 17 617.1 | 7 239.5 | 5 074 | 172 438 | 57 977.8 | 8 774.3 | 11 610 | 250 716 | 13 268.5 | 3 766.3 |
| Apache | 27 | D | D | D | NA | NA | NA | NA | 68 | 1 033 | 47.8 | 13.3 |
| Cochise | 208 | D | D | D | 56 | 576 | 181.3 | 20.6 | 277 | 4 100 | 171.4 | 47.8 |
| Coconino | 322 | D | D | D | 109 | 4 219 | 1 526.8 | 240.5 | 531 | 11 181 | 717.7 | 181.9 |
| Gila | 91 | 370 | 34.4 | 12.2 | NA | NA | NA | NA | 137 | 2 021 | 106.7 | 29.5 |
| Graham | 27 | 373 | 10.5 | 11.2 | NA | NA | NA | NA | 53 | 955 | 34.7 | 8.3 |
| Greenlee | 4 | 28 | 0.9 | 0.4 | NA | NA | NA | NA | 16 | 116 | 4.9 | 1.2 |
| La Paz | 15 | D | D | D | NA | NA | NA | NA | 73 | 719 | 38.0 | 9.3 |
| Maricopa | 11 727 | D | D | D | 3 398 | 121 062 | 40 182.1 | 6 043.4 | 6 750 | 156 678 | 8 408.9 | 2 446.3 |
| Mohave | 251 | D | D | D | 164 | 3 814 | 1 350.0 | 139.6 | 381 | 6 380 | 274.3 | 77.3 |
| Navajo | 117 | D | D | D | 57 | D | D | D | 244 | 3 308 | 191.5 | 45.7 |
| Pima | 2 692 | 16 250 | 1 886.4 | 777.8 | 760 | 30 567 | 10 365.2 | 1 877.0 | 1 758 | 42 002 | 2 135.2 | 601.8 |
| Pinal | 227 | D | D | D | 122 | 3 896 | 2 149.9 | 151.8 | 328 | 6 063 | 341.9 | 88.3 |
| Santa Cruz | 63 | D | D | D | NA | NA | NA | NA | 100 | 1 481 | 67.2 | 19.8 |
| Yavapai | 584 | D | D | D | 233 | 3 618 | 764.0 | 143.6 | 578 | 8 737 | 456.5 | 126.2 |
| Yuma | 208 | D | D | D | 82 | 2 856 | 891.6 | 88.0 | 316 | 5 942 | 271.9 | 69.6 |
| ARKANSAS | 5 588 | D | D | D | 3 088 | 184 568 | 60 735.6 | 6 518.4 | 5 112 | 89 933 | 3 559.8 | 994.1 |
| Arkansas | 28 | 85 | 7.6 | 2.7 | 33 | 3 964 | 1 702.2 | 127.5 | 43 | 448 | 15.5 | 4.2 |
| Ashley | 27 | 95 | 9.1 | 3.0 | 26 | 2 733 | D | 125.4 | 25 | 442 | 15.3 | 4.1 |
| Baxter | 75 | 413 | 29.1 | 11.0 | 57 | 2 496 | 550.1 | 90.6 | 108 | 1 555 | 60.3 | 16.1 |
| Benton | 535 | 4 702 | 472.6 | 240.4 | 199 | 12 403 | D | 432.3 | 362 | 7 511 | 295.7 | 85.8 |
| Boone | 66 | D | D | D | 69 | D | D | D | 63 | 1 023 | 41.9 | 11.7 |
| Bradley | 14 | 36 | 2.4 | 0.8 | 5 | 916 | 177.0 | 27.3 | 15 | 176 | 6.2 | 1.5 |
| Calhoun | NA | NA | NA | NA | NA | NA | NA | NA | 4 | 30 | 0.8 | 0.2 |
| Carroll | 51 | 139 | 10.0 | 3.4 | 41 | 2 866 | D | 74.2 | 143 | 1 424 | 54.0 | 15.8 |
| Chicot | 16 | 53 | 2.6 | 1.2 | 8 | 503 | D | 8.5 | 18 | 169 | 6.1 | 1.6 |
| Clark | 28 | 198 | 14.7 | 6.8 | 28 | 2 196 | 433.9 | 53.9 | 50 | 908 | 32.7 | 9.5 |
| Clay | 16 | 36 | 2.7 | 0.7 | 17 | 651 | 111.8 | 18.7 | 16 | 205 | 6.3 | 1.7 |
| Cleburne | 31 | 104 | 7.0 | 2.1 | 40 | 1 360 | 205.6 | 43.3 | 58 | 784 | 29.2 | 9.0 |

1. Establishment subject to federal tax.

Table B. States and Counties — **Health Care and Social Assistance, Other Services, and Federal Funds**

| | Health care and social assistance, 2007 | | | | Other services, 2007 | | | | Federal funds and grants, 2009–2010 | | | |
| --- | --- | --- | --- | --- | --- | --- | --- | --- | --- | --- | --- | --- |
| | | | | | | | | | Expenditures (mil dol) | | | |
| | | | | | | | | | | Direct payments for individuals[1] | | |
| STATE County | Number of establishments | Number of employees | Receipts (mil dol) | Annual payroll (mil dol) | Number of establishments | Number of employees | Receipts (mil dol) | Annual payroll (mil dol) | Total | Social Security and government retirement | Medicare | Food Stamps and Supplemental Security Income |
| | 159 | 160 | 161 | 162 | 163 | 164 | 165 | 166 | 167 | 168 | 169 | 170 |
| **ALABAMA—Cont'd** | | | | | | | | | | | | |
| Washington | 21 | 295 | 16.4 | 8.4 | 8 | 16 | 1.3 | 0.2 | 145.1 | 60.9 | 33.2 | 10.4 |
| Wilcox | 20 | 247 | 12.7 | 6.2 | 10 | D | D | D | 174.6 | 43.7 | 30.4 | 22.1 |
| Winston | 42 | 915 | 59.1 | 23.9 | 23 | D | D | D | 218.8 | 94.0 | 65.2 | 10.5 |
| **ALASKA** | 2 131 | 40 618 | 4 662.6 | 1 791.5 | 1 328 | 7 566 | 811.3 | 222.9 | 12 615.3 | 1 531.3 | 348.7 | 218.8 |
| Aleutians East | 9 | D | D | D | 2 | D | D | D | 45.4 | 3.8 | 0.3 | 0.5 |
| Aleutians West | 17 | 146 | 9.7 | 4.9 | 6 | 29 | 13.9 | 1.4 | 35.4 | 2.3 | 1.0 | 0.3 |
| Anchorage | 1 033 | 20 722 | 2 678.4 | 964.1 | 580 | 4 060 | 441.0 | 125.5 | 4 812.4 | 674.3 | 136.4 | 72.3 |
| Bethel | 11 | D | D | D | 13 | 78 | 8.7 | 1.9 | 391.9 | 13.1 | 6.7 | 20.2 |
| Bristol Bay | 3 | 5 | 1.0 | 0.4 | 1 | D | D | D | 81.0 | 7.4 | 1.6 | 0.1 |
| Denali | 2 | D | D | D | 1 | D | D | D | 134.2 | 2.0 | 2.1 | 0.0 |
| Dillingham | 5 | D | D | D | 6 | 15 | 0.8 | 0.3 | 52.3 | 6.8 | 0.0 | 3.7 |
| Fairbanks North Star | 267 | 4 867 | 570.5 | 223.9 | 195 | 1 081 | 106.8 | 31.3 | 1 546.6 | 196.7 | 45.0 | 19.0 |
| Haines | 8 | 113 | 6.8 | 3.0 | 7 | 18 | 1.2 | 0.3 | 19.5 | 7.3 | 2.6 | 0.8 |
| Hoonah-Angoon | NA | NA | NA | NA | NA | NA | NA | NA | NA | NA | NA | NA |
| Juneau | 138 | 2 215 | 200.8 | 85.5 | 85 | 433 | 40.0 | 12.0 | 779.7 | 72.9 | 21.7 | 7.4 |
| Kenai Peninsula | 191 | 2 671 | 226.4 | 97.5 | 135 | 602 | 67.2 | 18.4 | 356.7 | 150.4 | 40.4 | 12.7 |
| Ketchikan Gateway | 31 | D | D | D | 35 | 133 | 12.7 | 3.3 | 147.6 | 35.6 | 13.7 | 5.3 |
| Kodiak Island | 42 | 534 | 56.7 | 22.0 | 26 | 130 | 13.7 | 3.0 | 182.6 | 18.0 | 3.5 | 3.5 |
| Lake and Peninsula | NA | NA | NA | NA | 1 | D | D | D | 13.5 | 0.5 | 2.5 | 1.7 |
| Matanuska-Susitna | 232 | 2 692 | 253.8 | 102.7 | 113 | 498 | 57.1 | 13.6 | 361.8 | 197.4 | 31.7 | 21.0 |
| Nome | 23 | D | D | D | 14 | 74 | 6.4 | 1.2 | 156.1 | 11.8 | 3.6 | 9.1 |
| North Slope | 3 | D | D | D | 8 | 67 | 8.3 | 3.3 | 64.2 | 7.9 | 2.3 | 1.0 |
| Northwest Arctic | 4 | D | D | D | 6 | D | D | D | 68.5 | 8.0 | 2.5 | 6.8 |
| Petersburg | NA | NA | NA | NA | NA | NA | NA | NA | NA | NA | NA | NA |
| Prince of Wales-Hyder | NA | NA | NA | NA | NA | NA | NA | NA | NA | NA | NA | NA |
| Sitka | 28 | 855 | 86.1 | 38.9 | 21 | 93 | 8.2 | 1.8 | 98.3 | 22.8 | 7.8 | 2.0 |
| Skagway | NA | NA | NA | NA | NA | NA | NA | NA | NA | NA | NA | NA |
| Southeast Fairbanks | 9 | 115 | 7.1 | 2.8 | 9 | 17 | 1.3 | 0.4 | 119.2 | 15.2 | 3.4 | 2.8 |
| Valdez-Cordova | 24 | 470 | 35.3 | 13.2 | 25 | 96 | 9.5 | 2.5 | 1 253.8 | 22.8 | 5.0 | 2.2 |
| Wade Hampton | 3 | D | D | D | 1 | D | D | D | 127.3 | 6.5 | 2.7 | 14.4 |
| Wrangell | NA | NA | NA | NA | NA | NA | NA | NA | NA | NA | NA | NA |
| Yakutat | 2 | D | D | D | NA | NA | NA | NA | 8.9 | 1.9 | 0.0 | 0.1 |
| Yukon-Koyukuk | 4 | D | D | D | 5 | D | D | D | 121.0 | 14.3 | 1.2 | 7.7 |
| **ARIZONA** | 15 446 | 278 833 | 30 406.8 | 11 653.5 | 8 906 | 68 368 | 6 219.6 | 1 725.6 | 64 426.8 | 17 842.1 | 7 040.6 | 2 280.3 |
| Apache | 57 | 2 616 | 184.3 | 96.8 | 35 | D | D | D | 1 676.0 | 170.2 | 60.8 | 104.4 |
| Cochise | 273 | 4 773 | 380.3 | 152.0 | 162 | 718 | 44.2 | 12.3 | 3 090.8 | 624.0 | 155.9 | 69.3 |
| Coconino | 389 | 6 628 | 878.6 | 305.9 | 247 | 1 493 | 100.8 | 32.2 | 1 357.4 | 341.8 | 109.5 | 63.7 |
| Gila | 141 | 2 366 | 197.5 | 78.0 | 64 | 262 | 22.1 | 5.3 | 635.9 | 260.0 | 114.5 | 34.7 |
| Graham | 70 | 1 242 | 104.3 | 41.1 | 43 | 287 | 30.5 | 10.0 | 319.6 | 90.5 | 39.1 | 20.2 |
| Greenlee | 8 | 121 | 6.8 | 4.2 | NA | NA | NA | NA | 56.0 | 21.1 | 10.1 | 3.6 |
| La Paz | 20 | 516 | 59.3 | 23.4 | 25 | D | D | D | 157.7 | 79.1 | 0.0 | 12.9 |
| Maricopa | 9 683 | 175 051 | 19 740.9 | 7 610.8 | 5 509 | 45 671 | 4 392.2 | 1 195.4 | 31 522.5 | 9 346.5 | 4 078.3 | 1 138.8 |
| Mohave | 456 | 7 612 | 911.1 | 284.4 | 315 | 1 895 | 129.4 | 38.0 | 1 474.8 | 868.4 | 294.3 | 80.2 |
| Navajo | 216 | 3 152 | 333.4 | 133.9 | 125 | 1 120 | 135.7 | 39.9 | 1 281.0 | 318.3 | 95.0 | 95.8 |
| Pima | 2 672 | 51 151 | 5 459.8 | 2 073.5 | 1 494 | 12 045 | 1 020.6 | 289.4 | 14 248.6 | 3 301.3 | 1 318.0 | 381.9 |
| Pinal | 325 | 5 819 | 476.3 | 211.5 | 241 | 1 445 | 89.3 | 28.5 | 2 009.8 | 775.8 | 269.8 | 103.5 |
| Santa Cruz | 70 | 1 055 | 89.8 | 31.8 | 52 | 155 | 11.8 | 3.5 | 603.0 | 112.8 | 38.1 | 24.0 |
| Yavapai | 737 | 10 268 | 930.0 | 370.7 | 386 | 1 822 | 141.9 | 41.0 | 1 624.2 | 996.3 | 244.7 | 51.4 |
| Yuma | 329 | 6 463 | 654.6 | 235.7 | 208 | 1 217 | 85.2 | 26.0 | 1 761.7 | 495.9 | 212.6 | 96.0 |
| **ARKANSAS** | 7 216 | 152 864 | 13 439.6 | 5 282.0 | 4 153 | 23 188 | 2 187.8 | 558.0 | 28 904.0 | 9 722.2 | 4 416.7 | 1 327.7 |
| Arkansas | 49 | 1 087 | 64.4 | 26.9 | 35 | 137 | 8.9 | 2.7 | 242.2 | 67.7 | 46.1 | 11.9 |
| Ashley | 46 | 567 | 44.8 | 19.0 | 25 | 131 | 10.8 | 2.8 | 231.7 | 82.4 | 50.8 | 14.7 |
| Baxter | 158 | 3 168 | 311.6 | 116.2 | 99 | 409 | 25.9 | 7.6 | 413.0 | 242.7 | 92.8 | 12.7 |
| Benton | 409 | 6 176 | 563.0 | 220.0 | 274 | D | D | D | 957.0 | 534.3 | 170.1 | 26.3 |
| Boone | 109 | 2 109 | 151.5 | 59.9 | 63 | D | D | D | 344.4 | 160.0 | 56.1 | 12.9 |
| Bradley | 31 | 574 | 40.8 | 16.0 | 22 | 71 | 6.8 | 1.5 | 134.7 | 42.1 | 31.0 | 8.7 |
| Calhoun | 5 | D | D | D | 2 | D | D | D | 178.7 | 16.1 | 8.5 | 2.6 |
| Carroll | 54 | 743 | 59.7 | 26.3 | 40 | 132 | 8.8 | 2.4 | 191.3 | 98.9 | 37.0 | 6.3 |
| Chicot | 42 | 773 | 49.1 | 21.0 | 17 | 57 | 4.3 | 1.0 | 197.9 | 42.1 | 33.7 | 15.0 |
| Clark | 57 | D | D | D | 38 | 115 | 12.9 | 2.9 | 202.2 | 75.2 | 44.0 | 9.5 |
| Clay | 27 | 643 | 31.4 | 16.3 | 24 | 60 | 5.1 | 1.3 | 196.5 | 64.0 | 43.7 | 7.6 |
| Cleburne | 43 | 718 | 54.9 | 20.7 | 42 | 153 | 12.2 | 2.8 | 224.6 | 126.9 | 46.8 | 8.3 |

1. State totals may include programs not allocated by county.

Items 159—170

Table B. States and Counties — **Federal Funds, Residential Construction, and Local Government Finances**

| STATE County | Salaries and wages | Defense | Other | Medicaid and other health-related | Nutrition and family welfare | Education | Other | New construction ($1,000) | Number of housing units | Total (mil dol) | Inter-governmental (mil dol) | Total (mil dol) | Total | Property |
|---|---|---|---|---|---|---|---|---|---|---|---|---|---|---|
| | 171 | 172 | 173 | 174 | 175 | 176 | 177 | 178 | 179 | 180 | 181 | 182 | 183 | 184 |
| ALABAMA—Cont'd | | | | | | | | | | | | | | |
| Washington | 3.7 | 0.0 | 0.9 | 28.9 | 3.5 | 1.3 | 0.9 | 0 | 0 | 42.5 | 26.9 | 11.3 | 656 | 499 |
| Wilcox | 13.4 | 1.0 | 1.1 | 50.7 | 5.0 | 1.5 | 1.0 | 0 | 0 | 39.8 | 21.8 | 5.7 | 450 | 308 |
| Winston | 9.7 | 0.0 | 3.6 | 27.3 | 3.3 | 1.7 | 2.4 | 230 | 2 | 73.9 | 48.4 | 13.6 | 563 | 202 |
| ALASKA | 4 055.1 | 1 776.3 | 687.9 | 1 065.9 | 283.0 | 354.9 | 1 761.4 | 0 | 56 | X | X | X | X | X |
| Aleutians East | 2.2 | 31.9 | 0.6 | 0.0 | 0.6 | 1.5 | 1.3 | 0 | 0 | 24.3 | 12.2 | 6.6 | 2 484 | 0 |
| Aleutians West | 3.0 | 20.0 | 3.1 | 0.7 | 1.3 | 1.0 | 2.2 | 98 | 1 | 53.7 | 16.6 | 19.2 | 3 985 | 869 |
| Anchorage | 1 131.2 | 964.4 | 298.3 | 325.6 | 76.6 | 45.8 | 1 024.4 | 117 246 | 447 | 1 185.7 | 493.7 | 469.1 | 1 677 | 1 461 |
| Bethel | 14.6 | 46.2 | 3.6 | 176.2 | 12.2 | 36.2 | 45.8 | 1 500 | 7 | 41.1 | 18.3 | 7.5 | 438 | 2 |
| Bristol Bay | 3.4 | 8.1 | 6.1 | 29.2 | 0.3 | 3.8 | 20.6 | 0 | 0 | 10.7 | 5.5 | 2.9 | 2 929 | 1 992 |
| Denali | 17.1 | 86.3 | 26.0 | 0.0 | 0.4 | 0.0 | 0.0 | NA | NA | 8.6 | 5.8 | 2.2 | 1 210 | 130 |
| Dillingham | 4.1 | 0.7 | 1.5 | 2.3 | 3.9 | 9.3 | 10.6 | NA | NA | 30.3 | 20.6 | 4.8 | 962 | 329 |
| Fairbanks North Star | 343.6 | 493.1 | 116.7 | 114.0 | 33.8 | 18.3 | 135.5 | 7 484 | 39 | 327.0 | 164.7 | 114.5 | 1 174 | 1 041 |
| Haines | 1.1 | 0.2 | 0.4 | 4.5 | 0.5 | 0.4 | 1.6 | 227 | 1 | 11.4 | 5.2 | 4.5 | 1 989 | 907 |
| Hoonah-Angoon | NA | NA | NA | NA | NA | NA | NA | NA | NA | NA | NA | NA | NA | NA |
| Juneau | 97.8 | 2.0 | 52.7 | 56.5 | 51.2 | 126.1 | 274.9 | 9 288 | 40 | 256.9 | 62.8 | 80.7 | 2 631 | 1 223 |
| Kenai Peninsula | 33.5 | 8.1 | 12.7 | 53.1 | 15.4 | 7.2 | 18.2 | 14 923 | 71 | 338.5 | 112.0 | 101.2 | 1 906 | 1 105 |
| Ketchikan Gateway | 34.8 | 0.0 | 20.0 | 27.3 | 3.4 | 2.3 | 4.8 | 5 710 | 41 | 103.6 | 29.2 | 30.6 | 2 311 | 960 |
| Kodiak Island | 81.8 | 1.5 | 36.7 | 12.3 | 5.9 | 3.2 | 13.0 | 2 919 | 13 | 87.1 | 43.1 | 20.7 | 1 593 | 801 |
| Lake and Peninsula | 2.3 | 0.0 | 0.5 | 0.0 | 1.0 | 0.1 | 4.0 | NA | NA | 17.0 | 12.4 | 2.1 | 1 388 | 0 |
| Matanuska-Susitna | 21.2 | 0.4 | 19.4 | 22.2 | 19.4 | 6.3 | 12.1 | 14 379 | 77 | 318.7 | 179.9 | 108.4 | 1 311 | 992 |
| Nome | 10.4 | 9.3 | 6.9 | 49.8 | 9.9 | 20.8 | 13.1 | 380 | 2 | 47.0 | 24.3 | 7.2 | 773 | 291 |
| North Slope | 2.7 | 0.4 | 10.3 | 12.1 | 2.5 | 10.8 | 10.4 | 6 218 | 28 | 357.0 | 67.9 | 203.3 | 30 983 | 30 944 |
| Northwest Arctic | 4.3 | 3.4 | 2.3 | 2.6 | 5.2 | 12.7 | 15.3 | 900 | 3 | 91.0 | 66.2 | 3.3 | 445 | 0 |
| Petersburg | NA | NA | NA | NA | NA | NA | NA | NA | NA | NA | NA | NA | NA | NA |
| Prince of Wales-Hyder | NA | NA | NA | NA | NA | NA | NA | NA | NA | NA | NA | NA | NA | NA |
| Sitka | 24.2 | 0.0 | 7.4 | 14.8 | 2.9 | 1.6 | 2.8 | 2 363 | 12 | 73.7 | 25.6 | 15.5 | 1 746 | 560 |
| Skagway | NA | NA | NA | NA | NA | NA | NA | NA | NA | NA | NA | NA | NA | NA |
| Southeast Fairbanks | 15.5 | 46.9 | 4.2 | 22.6 | 2.0 | 1.3 | 2.9 | NA | NA | 2.1 | 1.2 | 0.0 | 0 | 0 |
| Valdez-Cordova | 1 125.6 | 44.5 | 12.2 | 14.4 | 3.7 | 2.1 | 18.6 | 2 480 | 13 | 73.8 | 17.8 | 35.0 | 3 688 | 3 307 |
| Wade Hampton | 2.8 | 0.0 | 1.2 | 48.1 | 1.4 | 19.3 | 26.4 | NA | NA | 13.0 | 6.0 | 1.1 | 140 | 13 |
| Wrangell | NA | NA | NA | NA | NA | NA | NA | NA | NA | NA | NA | NA | NA | NA |
| Yakutat | 1.5 | 0.0 | 1.0 | 0.5 | 0.3 | 0.2 | 2.6 | 290 | 2 | 6.6 | 3.5 | 2.0 | 2 946 | 1 496 |
| Yukon-Koyukuk | 9.5 | 8.8 | 4.2 | 49.0 | 4.0 | 3.8 | 15.6 | 0 | 0 | 40.5 | 34.2 | 0.7 | 124 | 47 |
| ARIZONA | 4 980.4 | 10 831.4 | 1 981.7 | 8 500.6 | 1 460.7 | 1 186.1 | 3 213.5 | 2 580 351 | 13 007 | X | X | X | X | X |
| Apache | 138.6 | 5.3 | 138.3 | 611.5 | 57.9 | 83.4 | 184.0 | 8 024 | 40 | 248.0 | 187.9 | 26.6 | 381 | 301 |
| Cochise | 1 063.7 | 765.6 | 46.6 | 254.7 | 26.6 | 17.3 | 40.4 | 62 243 | 319 | 442.4 | 211.0 | 125.8 | 984 | 710 |
| Coconino | 171.0 | 6.3 | 128.3 | 330.2 | 40.9 | 50.2 | 48.2 | 18 820 | 100 | 557.6 | 231.7 | 219.0 | 1 718 | 965 |
| Gila | 29.0 | 0.2 | 12.5 | 129.7 | 12.5 | 14.3 | 17.3 | 13 747 | 72 | 194.1 | 97.0 | 68.4 | 1 316 | 752 |
| Graham | 23.0 | 0.2 | 6.6 | 95.2 | 7.4 | 17.0 | 3.3 | 12 916 | 135 | 133.9 | 82.0 | 24.7 | 711 | 339 |
| Greenlee | 2.4 | 0.0 | 0.5 | 15.2 | 1.8 | 0.8 | 0.2 | 887 | 4 | 34.9 | 18.3 | 11.1 | 1 426 | 1 208 |
| La Paz | 19.0 | 0.4 | 11.1 | 0.7 | 5.4 | 8.2 | 9.7 | 900 | 5 | 81.0 | 49.3 | 19.6 | 972 | 667 |
| Maricopa | 1 801.8 | 4 436.4 | 848.2 | 3 913.4 | 820.8 | 751.3 | 2 330.3 | 1 694 542 | 8 103 | 15 566.3 | 5 955.4 | 5 840.3 | 1 505 | 864 |
| Mohave | 36.4 | 6.0 | 15.3 | 84.6 | 25.0 | 12.8 | 29.3 | 39 177 | 196 | 613.2 | 254.1 | 253.3 | 1 299 | 749 |
| Navajo | 91.5 | 0.9 | 50.5 | 433.4 | 31.4 | 60.4 | 29.9 | 16 153 | 100 | 579.2 | 236.6 | 122.4 | 1 100 | 653 |
| Pima | 1 074.4 | 5 268.8 | 388.9 | 1 668.4 | 174.1 | 107.4 | 341.9 | 458 236 | 2 242 | 3 481.7 | 1 650.1 | 1 289.2 | 1 333 | 911 |
| Pinal | 118.4 | 7.8 | 85.4 | 436.0 | 48.7 | 25.8 | 78.7 | 126 271 | 978 | 1 134.1 | 500.3 | 385.4 | 1 288 | 694 |
| Santa Cruz | 105.5 | 7.6 | 158.1 | 133.5 | 12.0 | 5.4 | 2.6 | 11 724 | 51 | 189.6 | 106.2 | 56.6 | 1 321 | 702 |
| Yavapai | 70.5 | 1.1 | 46.3 | 147.1 | 24.0 | 12.9 | 5.6 | 67 532 | 302 | 692.9 | 249.7 | 293.3 | 1 380 | 903 |
| Yuma | 235.1 | 324.8 | 45.2 | 209.7 | 51.8 | 19.1 | 30.8 | 49 179 | 360 | 669.9 | 368.7 | 193.9 | 1 017 | 548 |
| ARKANSAS | 2 417.8 | 1 137.5 | 613.5 | 3 731.0 | 680.6 | 539.7 | 1 891.7 | 861 479 | 6 800 | X | X | X | X | X |
| Arkansas | 20.6 | 1.2 | 20.6 | 41.1 | 4.5 | 1.3 | 2.8 | 1 745 | 13 | 69.8 | 34.1 | 14.4 | 742 | 300 |
| Ashley | 6.4 | 0.0 | 1.8 | 52.4 | 5.2 | 1.6 | 1.2 | 0 | 0 | 67.5 | 37.1 | 15.6 | 700 | 268 |
| Baxter | 15.8 | 11.4 | 4.1 | 22.4 | 4.5 | 2.5 | -0.1 | 608 | 4 | 70.6 | 36.0 | 21.0 | 501 | 192 |
| Benton | 61.1 | 5.7 | 52.4 | 53.4 | 17.2 | 8.4 | 6.5 | 160 080 | 753 | 524.9 | 265.0 | 143.6 | 707 | 286 |
| Boone | 13.3 | 0.5 | 4.1 | 33.5 | 7.4 | 4.0 | 43.0 | 2 621 | 17 | 84.0 | 57.3 | 16.7 | 455 | 188 |
| Bradley | 17.4 | 0.0 | 0.6 | 24.5 | 5.0 | 0.8 | 1.6 | 391 | 5 | 33.0 | 22.4 | 6.0 | 502 | 198 |
| Calhoun | 1.2 | 129.6 | 0.2 | 14.4 | 1.1 | 0.3 | 4.4 | 180 | 1 | 15.7 | 5.9 | 2.5 | 451 | 259 |
| Carroll | 24.2 | 0.5 | 2.0 | 16.8 | 2.7 | 1.5 | 0.3 | 1 089 | 11 | 57.7 | 29.5 | 14.1 | 515 | 234 |
| Chicot | 3.9 | 1.1 | 0.6 | 70.0 | 5.3 | 1.8 | 2.5 | 312 | 10 | 50.3 | 23.5 | 8.9 | 726 | 289 |
| Clark | 13.3 | 0.2 | 1.4 | 33.8 | 4.0 | 4.9 | 1.4 | 1 465 | 14 | 53.7 | 34.4 | 10.3 | 435 | 170 |
| Clay | 6.3 | 0.8 | 1.0 | 49.4 | 3.0 | 1.4 | 6.3 | 687 | 10 | 46.9 | 24.5 | 7.0 | 434 | 240 |
| Cleburne | 6.4 | 2.1 | 1.4 | 24.6 | 3.3 | 2.2 | 0.5 | 1 742 | 16 | 45.0 | 25.9 | 12.1 | 477 | 213 |

1. State totals may include programs not allocated by county.   2. Based on the resident population estimated as of July 1 of the year shown.

# Table B. States and Counties — Local Government Finances, Government Employment, and Voting

| STATE County | Direct general expenditure Total (mil dol) | Per capita[1] (dollars) | Percent of total for: Educa-tion | Health and hospitals | Police protec-tion | Public welfare | High-ways | Debt outstanding Total (mil dol) | Per capita[1] (dollars) | Government employment, 2011 Federal civilian | Federal military | State and local | Presidential election,[2] 2012 Percent of vote cast: Demo-cratic | Republi-can | All other |
|---|---|---|---|---|---|---|---|---|---|---|---|---|---|---|---|
| | 185 | 186 | 187 | 188 | 189 | 190 | 191 | 192 | 193 | 194 | 195 | 196 | 197 | 198 | 199 |
| **ALABAMA—Cont'd** | | | | | | | | | | | | | | | |
| Washington | 44.3 | 2 570 | 70.0 | 2.9 | 2.8 | 0.1 | 10.2 | 27.0 | 1 568 | 35 | 84 | 958 | 35.0 | 64.4 | 0.6 |
| Wilcox | 40.6 | 3 173 | 55.2 | 10.2 | 2.5 | 0.5 | 9.6 | 42.9 | 3 357 | 64 | 56 | 742 | 71.0 | 28.8 | 0.2 |
| Winston | 76.7 | 3 162 | 55.8 | 22.6 | 2.7 | 0.5 | 5.3 | 50.6 | 2 088 | 75 | 118 | 1 142 | 17.5 | 80.8 | 1.7 |
| **ALASKA** | X | X | X | X | X | X | X | X | X | 17 071 | 28 134 | 63 831 | 37.9 | 59.4 | 2.7 |
| Aleutians East | 29.0 | 10 877 | 25.2 | 30.6 | 3.1 | 0.0 | 2.1 | 54.2 | 20 332 | 22 | 23 | 257 | NA | 0.0 | 0.0 |
| Aleutians West | 44.1 | 9 139 | 16.5 | 0.2 | 8.3 | 0.0 | 10.8 | 12.6 | 2 608 | 15 | 47 | 463 | NA | 0.0 | 0.0 |
| Anchorage | 1 137.1 | 4 066 | 49.8 | 2.1 | 7.4 | 0.0 | 8.5 | 1 799.6 | 6 435 | 9 543 | 14 104 | 20 498 | NA | 0.0 | 0.0 |
| Bethel | 37.9 | 2 203 | 0.0 | 0.4 | 7.2 | 0.0 | 3.2 | 9.0 | 525 | 88 | 127 | 2 961 | NA | 0.0 | 0.0 |
| Bristol Bay | 9.8 | 9 831 | 38.2 | 11.0 | 7.1 | 0.0 | 7.2 | 1.8 | 1 846 | 55 | 0 | 175 | NA | 0.0 | 0.0 |
| Denali | 8.4 | 4 596 | 80.0 | 1.6 | 0.0 | 0.0 | 1.0 | 1.6 | 894 | 233 | 18 | 155 | NA | 0.0 | 0.0 |
| Dillingham | 29.9 | 5 989 | 33.5 | 2.1 | 3.9 | 0.0 | 3.6 | 25.1 | 5 022 | 53 | 36 | 672 | NA | 0.0 | 0.0 |
| Fairbanks North Star | 291.2 | 2 987 | 60.0 | 1.2 | 2.8 | 0.0 | 3.6 | 185.0 | 1 898 | 3 444 | 9 784 | 8 050 | NA | 0.0 | 0.0 |
| Haines | 9.0 | 3 959 | 47.0 | 2.4 | 5.1 | 0.2 | 5.3 | 20.0 | 8 769 | 12 | 19 | 191 | NA | 0.0 | 0.0 |
| Hoonah-Angoon | NA | NA | NA | NA | NA | NA | NA | NA | NA | 104 | 15 | 253 | | | |
| Juneau | 245.8 | 8 008 | 33.2 | 26.7 | 5.4 | 0.0 | 3.7 | 234.1 | 7 629 | 840 | 495 | 6 377 | NA | 0.0 | 0.0 |
| Kenai Peninsula | 319.3 | 6 014 | 34.2 | 28.8 | 2.2 | 0.0 | 3.6 | 121.6 | 2 290 | 407 | 503 | 4 299 | NA | 0.0 | 0.0 |
| Ketchikan Gateway | 118.6 | 8 966 | 24.2 | 3.1 | 3.5 | 0.0 | 3.8 | 202.2 | 15 284 | 267 | 270 | 1 760 | NA | 0.0 | 0.0 |
| Kodiak Island | 85.2 | 6 553 | 44.4 | 0.6 | 4.5 | 0.1 | 2.8 | 32.1 | 2 471 | 349 | 1 054 | 1 156 | NA | 0.0 | 0.0 |
| Lake and Peninsula | 20.0 | 12 979 | 80.4 | 0.1 | 0.0 | 0.0 | 0.4 | 9.6 | 6 212 | 43 | 12 | 357 | NA | 0.0 | 0.0 |
| Matanuska-Susitna | 318.4 | 3 852 | 65.3 | 2.8 | 2.7 | 0.0 | 6.2 | 294.2 | 3 558 | 217 | 670 | 4 253 | NA | 0.0 | 0.0 |
| Nome | 50.9 | 5 461 | 23.0 | 0.5 | 3.5 | 0.0 | 3.5 | 9.5 | 1 024 | 66 | 72 | 1 660 | NA | 0.0 | 0.0 |
| North Slope | 271.9 | 41 440 | 21.5 | 3.7 | 3.3 | 1.2 | 7.1 | 541.4 | 82 524 | 24 | 69 | 1 898 | NA | 0.0 | 0.0 |
| Northwest Arctic | 92.0 | 12 346 | 70.8 | 0.1 | 1.1 | 0.0 | 0.4 | 73.0 | 9 793 | 48 | 56 | 1 045 | NA | 0.0 | 0.0 |
| Petersburg | NA | NA | NA | NA | NA | NA | NA | NA | NA | 108 | 57 | 486 | | | |
| Prince of Wales-Hyder | NA | NA | NA | NA | NA | NA | NA | NA | NA | 99 | 42 | 780 | | | |
| Sitka | 70.5 | 7 941 | 31.0 | 21.2 | 6.7 | 0.0 | 2.7 | 87.2 | 9 826 | 151 | 246 | 1 044 | NA | 0.0 | 0.0 |
| Skagway | NA | NA | NA | NA | NA | NA | NA | NA | NA | 56 | 0 | 103 | | | |
| Southeast Fairbanks | 1.8 | 260 | 0.1 | 3.4 | 0.0 | 0.0 | 11.0 | 1.1 | 161 | 466 | 58 | 463 | NA | 0.0 | 0.0 |
| Valdez-Cordova | 63.8 | 6 715 | 19.0 | 3.4 | 3.4 | 0.0 | 5.4 | 27.5 | 2 900 | 159 | 223 | 1 189 | NA | 0.0 | 0.0 |
| Wade Hampton | 11.8 | 1 547 | 31.4 | 1.6 | 10.1 | 0.0 | 1.7 | 2.0 | 256 | 24 | 56 | 1 563 | NA | 0.0 | 0.0 |
| Wrangell | NA | NA | NA | NA | NA | NA | NA | NA | NA | 53 | 17 | 269 | | | |
| Yakutat | 5.0 | 7 194 | 58.3 | 3.4 | 9.1 | 0.0 | 7.5 | 1.3 | 1 836 | 25 | 0 | 114 | NA | 0.0 | 0.0 |
| Yukon-Koyukuk | 42.0 | 7 201 | 75.5 | 4.0 | 1.3 | 0.0 | 0.8 | 6.9 | 1 186 | 100 | 41 | 1 340 | NA | 0.0 | 0.0 |
| **ARIZONA** | X | X | X | X | X | X | X | X | X | 57 269 | 34 280 | 348 709 | 45.1 | 53.6 | 1.2 |
| Apache | 239.0 | 3 416 | 69.7 | 2.1 | 1.1 | 0.5 | 6.0 | 387.5 | 5 537 | 3 036 | 156 | 8 631 | 63.4 | 35.2 | 1.3 |
| Cochise | 425.8 | 3 330 | 43.8 | 3.2 | 8.8 | 7.0 | 6.6 | 151.9 | 1 188 | 5 898 | 5 671 | 6 761 | 38.8 | 59.5 | 1.7 |
| Coconino | 485.8 | 3 812 | 39.5 | 2.6 | 9.4 | 1.2 | 10.3 | 462.9 | 3 632 | 3 014 | 304 | 13 358 | 57.8 | 40.8 | 1.3 |
| Gila | 186.8 | 3 592 | 39.4 | 3.5 | 8.8 | 2.8 | 8.1 | 88.0 | 1 692 | 488 | 114 | 4 442 | 35.3 | 63.1 | 1.6 |
| Graham | 132.1 | 3 799 | 60.0 | 1.8 | 3.7 | 1.3 | 9.1 | 244.4 | 7 028 | 431 | 80 | 2 306 | 29.0 | 69.8 | 1.2 |
| Greenlee | 30.8 | 3 978 | 42.5 | 6.3 | 2.5 | 0.0 | 8.1 | 43.1 | 5 555 | 31 | 19 | 528 | 40.0 | 58.8 | 1.2 |
| La Paz | 75.5 | 3 744 | 34.6 | 3.6 | 10.4 | 0.0 | 10.5 | 32.3 | 1 603 | 318 | 44 | 1 936 | 34.7 | 63.2 | 2.1 |
| Maricopa | 15 068.8 | 3 884 | 40.5 | 4.5 | 7.6 | 1.7 | 5.4 | 26 279.2 | 6 773 | 20 444 | 12 827 | 192 828 | 44.1 | 54.7 | 1.2 |
| Mohave | 607.7 | 3 117 | 33.3 | 2.7 | 8.5 | 0.8 | 7.5 | 509.9 | 2 616 | 510 | 437 | 7 505 | 32.7 | 65.6 | 1.7 |
| Navajo | 482.1 | 4 332 | 51.1 | 16.2 | 3.9 | 0.3 | 4.0 | 291.8 | 2 622 | 1 725 | 231 | 8 124 | 43.5 | 55.2 | 1.3 |
| Pima | 3 541.9 | 3 662 | 35.0 | 8.9 | 8.4 | 2.7 | 6.5 | 4 775.0 | 4 937 | 12 629 | 8 681 | 61 835 | 52.4 | 46.4 | 1.2 |
| Pinal | 1 035.0 | 3 459 | 44.2 | 2.9 | 6.1 | 4.3 | 9.2 | 861.5 | 2 879 | 1 770 | 825 | 18 117 | 42.2 | 56.7 | 1.2 |
| Santa Cruz | 170.1 | 3 971 | 46.8 | 1.1 | 9.5 | 2.5 | 7.3 | 99.7 | 2 328 | 1 731 | 103 | 2 189 | 65.3 | 34.0 | 0.8 |
| Yavapai | 676.3 | 3 181 | 35.2 | 1.6 | 7.3 | 4.9 | 10.7 | 475.8 | 2 237 | 1 447 | 467 | 9 170 | 37.0 | 61.4 | 1.6 |
| Yuma | 749.5 | 3 933 | 47.7 | 1.1 | 6.0 | 0.3 | 6.6 | 534.1 | 2 803 | 3 797 | 4 321 | 10 979 | 42.6 | 56.3 | 1.1 |
| **ARKANSAS** | X | X | X | X | X | X | X | X | X | 21 101 | 17 994 | 195 115 | 38.9 | 58.7 | 2.4 |
| Arkansas | 70.1 | 3 615 | 41.4 | 11.9 | 4.3 | 0.0 | 7.0 | 67.8 | 3 499 | 199 | 81 | 1 039 | 37.5 | 60.0 | 2.5 |
| Ashley | 60.0 | 2 689 | 62.2 | 0.0 | 3.5 | 0.0 | 5.0 | 142.8 | 6 397 | 75 | 93 | 1 182 | 34.4 | 62.6 | 3.0 |
| Baxter | 69.5 | 1 657 | 56.8 | 0.2 | 7.2 | 0.1 | 9.7 | 122.7 | 2 925 | 153 | 178 | 1 606 | 32.7 | 64.3 | 3.0 |
| Benton | 559.1 | 2 753 | 59.9 | 3.9 | 4.1 | 0.0 | 6.6 | 725.9 | 3 574 | 471 | 977 | 8 679 | 30.7 | 67.2 | 2.1 |
| Boone | 81.0 | 2 209 | 69.7 | 0.1 | 4.6 | 0.0 | 4.2 | 47.2 | 1 287 | 176 | 159 | 3 099 | 28.7 | 68.3 | 3.0 |
| Bradley | 32.9 | 2 744 | 67.0 | 0.1 | 4.1 | 0.0 | 4.8 | 15.4 | 1 288 | 35 | 49 | 876 | 41.6 | 56.0 | 2.4 |
| Calhoun | 15.0 | 2 709 | 42.7 | 0.2 | 5.5 | 1.9 | 6.2 | 91.4 | 16 509 | 11 | 22 | 274 | 31.2 | 65.9 | 2.9 |
| Carroll | 54.1 | 1 973 | 55.4 | 0.0 | 6.7 | 0.0 | 6.5 | 50.7 | 1 850 | 83 | 118 | 1 149 | 39.4 | 57.5 | 3.1 |
| Chicot | 44.8 | 3 638 | 43.4 | 31.9 | 4.8 | 0.0 | 4.8 | 21.6 | 1 754 | 41 | 50 | 997 | 58.4 | 40.7 | 0.9 |
| Clark | 51.9 | 2 199 | 65.3 | 0.1 | 5.7 | 0.0 | 6.0 | 45.7 | 1 937 | 102 | 98 | 2 574 | 46.9 | 50.7 | 2.4 |
| Clay | 48.5 | 3 006 | 54.0 | 23.4 | 3.2 | 0.0 | 6.4 | 17.7 | 1 096 | 51 | 68 | 904 | 40.7 | 55.0 | 4.3 |
| Cleburne | 43.4 | 1 707 | 68.5 | 0.1 | 4.7 | 0.4 | 8.7 | 60.4 | 2 377 | 92 | 111 | 899 | 26.0 | 70.2 | 3.7 |

1. Based on the resident population estimated as of July 1 of the year shown.   2. © 2013 Election Data Services, Inc. All rights reserved.

Items 185—199

# Table B. States and Counties — Land Area and Population

| STATE/County code | CBSA code[1] | County type[2] | STATE County | Land area,[3] (sq km) 2010 | Population 2012 Total persons | Rank | Per square kilometer | Race alone or in combination, not Hispanic or Latino (percent) White | Black | American Indian, Alaska Native | Asian and Pacific Islander | Percent Hispanic or Latino[4] | Age (percent) Under 5 years | 5 to 17 years | 18 to 24 years | 25 to 34 years | 35 to 44 years | 45 to 54 years |
|---|---|---|---|---|---|---|---|---|---|---|---|---|---|---|---|---|---|---|
| | | | | 1 | 2 | 3 | 4 | 5 | 6 | 7 | 8 | 9 | 10 | 11 | 12 | 13 | 14 | 15 |
| | | | ARKANSAS—Cont'd | | | | | | | | | | | | | | | |
| 05 025 | 38220 | 3 | Cleveland | 1 548 | 8 627 | 2 554 | 5.6 | 85.6 | 12.3 | 0.7 | 0.3 | 1.8 | 6.4 | 18.2 | 7.4 | 11.3 | 12.4 | 14.2 |
| 05 027 | 31620 | 7 | Columbia | 1 984 | 24 473 | 1 625 | 12.3 | 60.3 | 36.5 | 0.7 | 1.0 | 2.4 | 6.2 | 16.4 | 13.7 | 11.5 | 11.2 | 12.9 |
| 05 029 | ... | 6 | Conway | 1 430 | 21 287 | 1 768 | 14.9 | 84.1 | 11.9 | 1.5 | 0.7 | 3.7 | 6.4 | 17.3 | 8.3 | 11.1 | 11.6 | 14.8 |
| 05 031 | 27860 | 3 | Craighead | 1 832 | 99 735 | 590 | 54.4 | 80.5 | 14.0 | 0.9 | 1.5 | 4.6 | 7.2 | 17.7 | 12.7 | 14.6 | 12.4 | 12.5 |
| 05 033 | 22900 | 2 | Crawford | 1 536 | 61 946 | 840 | 40.3 | 88.7 | 2.0 | 3.6 | 1.8 | 6.3 | 6.5 | 19.3 | 8.5 | 12.0 | 12.8 | 14.7 |
| 05 035 | 32820 | 1 | Crittenden | 1 579 | 50 021 | 977 | 31.7 | 46.2 | 51.2 | 0.7 | 0.9 | 2.1 | 8.0 | 20.5 | 9.2 | 13.1 | 12.5 | 14.2 |
| 05 037 | ... | 6 | Cross | 1 596 | 17 683 | 1 935 | 11.1 | 75.0 | 23.0 | 0.8 | 0.8 | 1.5 | 6.3 | 18.3 | 7.8 | 11.2 | 12.5 | 14.9 |
| 05 039 | ... | 6 | Dallas | 1 729 | 7 987 | 2 600 | 4.6 | 54.7 | 42.5 | 1.2 | 0.3 | 2.6 | 5.9 | 17.5 | 7.5 | 10.3 | 11.1 | 14.2 |
| 05 041 | ... | 6 | Desha | 1 990 | 12 545 | 2 271 | 6.3 | 47.5 | 47.3 | 0.8 | 0.6 | 4.7 | 7.4 | 18.5 | 8.2 | 11.7 | 10.7 | 14.3 |
| 05 043 | ... | 7 | Drew | 2 145 | 18 743 | 1 886 | 8.7 | 68.4 | 28.6 | 0.7 | 0.8 | 2.7 | 6.5 | 16.9 | 12.7 | 11.9 | 11.2 | 13.9 |
| 05 045 | 30780 | 2 | Faulkner | 1 678 | 118 704 | 512 | 70.7 | 83.6 | 11.2 | 1.3 | 1.8 | 4.0 | 6.9 | 17.2 | 15.9 | 14.5 | 12.5 | 12.8 |
| 05 047 | 22900 | 2 | Franklin | 1 577 | 18 045 | 1 919 | 11.4 | 94.5 | 1.2 | 2.2 | 1.4 | 2.2 | 6.4 | 17.7 | 8.5 | 11.0 | 12.3 | 13.8 |
| 05 049 | ... | 9 | Fulton | 1 601 | 12 318 | 2 287 | 7.7 | 97.5 | 1.0 | 1.8 | 0.5 | 0.9 | 5.5 | 15.3 | 6.7 | 8.8 | 10.5 | 14.3 |
| 05 051 | 26300 | 3 | Garland | 1 755 | 96 903 | 604 | 55.2 | 85.4 | 9.0 | 1.5 | 1.1 | 5.0 | 5.6 | 15.3 | 7.8 | 10.9 | 11.2 | 13.7 |
| 05 053 | 30780 | 2 | Grant | 1 636 | 17 986 | 1 921 | 11.0 | 94.3 | 2.9 | 1.0 | 0.5 | 2.3 | 6.0 | 18.0 | 7.9 | 11.9 | 13.2 | 15.3 |
| 05 055 | 37500 | 6 | Greene | 1 496 | 43 163 | 1 104 | 28.9 | 95.9 | 1.1 | 1.3 | 0.5 | 2.4 | 6.7 | 18.5 | 8.8 | 12.6 | 13.2 | 13.9 |
| 05 057 | 26260 | 6 | Hempstead | 1 884 | 22 373 | 1 716 | 11.9 | 57.7 | 29.9 | 1.1 | 0.7 | 12.1 | 7.7 | 18.4 | 8.5 | 12.0 | 11.7 | 14.2 |
| 05 059 | ... | 6 | Hot Spring | 1 593 | 33 394 | 1 343 | 21.0 | 85.3 | 11.5 | 1.4 | 0.6 | 2.9 | 6.0 | 17.1 | 8.3 | 12.0 | 12.1 | 14.5 |
| 05 061 | ... | 7 | Howard | 1 524 | 13 735 | 2 195 | 9.0 | 67.9 | 20.8 | 1.3 | 1.0 | 10.2 | 7.6 | 18.8 | 8.2 | 11.8 | 11.7 | 14.3 |
| 05 063 | 12900 | 7 | Independence | 1 979 | 37 025 | 1 245 | 18.7 | 90.5 | 2.6 | 1.1 | 1.1 | 5.9 | 6.7 | 17.3 | 8.7 | 12.0 | 12.5 | 14.1 |
| 05 065 | ... | 9 | Izard | 1 504 | 13 474 | 2 214 | 9.0 | 95.5 | 2.0 | 1.6 | 0.4 | 1.8 | 4.6 | 14.2 | 6.6 | 9.8 | 11.2 | 14.8 |
| 05 067 | ... | 3 | Jackson | 1 642 | 17 600 | 1 943 | 10.7 | 79.4 | 17.4 | 1.2 | 0.7 | 2.7 | 5.5 | 15.2 | 8.4 | 13.5 | 13.3 | 14.9 |
| 05 069 | 38220 | 3 | Jefferson | 2 255 | 74 723 | 732 | 33.1 | 42.4 | 55.2 | 0.8 | 1.2 | 1.7 | 6.3 | 17.2 | 11.1 | 12.5 | 11.6 | 14.4 |
| 05 071 | ... | 6 | Johnson | 1 709 | 25 901 | 1 568 | 15.2 | 83.9 | 2.0 | 1.7 | 1.1 | 12.8 | 7.0 | 17.9 | 10.2 | 12.6 | 11.9 | 13.9 |
| 05 073 | ... | 8 | Lafayette | 1 368 | 7 447 | 2 647 | 5.4 | 60.9 | 36.9 | 0.6 | 0.6 | 1.9 | 5.9 | 16.7 | 8.6 | 9.8 | 10.7 | 14.6 |
| 05 075 | ... | 6 | Lawrence | 1 522 | 17 012 | 1 979 | 11.2 | 97.4 | 1.3 | 1.1 | 0.4 | 1.0 | 5.6 | 17.0 | 9.4 | 10.8 | 11.8 | 14.0 |
| 05 077 | ... | 6 | Lee | 1 561 | 10 216 | 2 424 | 6.5 | 43.1 | 54.8 | 1.0 | 0.7 | 1.9 | 5.5 | 14.8 | 9.0 | 14.5 | 13.2 | 13.8 |
| 05 079 | 38220 | 3 | Lincoln | 1 454 | 14 101 | 2 168 | 9.7 | 66.3 | 30.3 | 0.6 | 0.3 | 3.4 | 4.8 | 14.2 | 10.8 | 16.1 | 14.8 | 15.3 |
| 05 081 | ... | 6 | Little River | 1 379 | 12 919 | 2 248 | 9.4 | 75.8 | 19.9 | 2.4 | 0.6 | 3.1 | 6.0 | 17.5 | 7.4 | 11.0 | 12.5 | 13.8 |
| 05 083 | ... | 6 | Logan | 1 834 | 21 983 | 1 732 | 12.0 | 93.1 | 2.0 | 2.0 | 2.1 | 2.4 | 6.0 | 18.2 | 7.7 | 10.5 | 11.7 | 15.2 |
| 05 085 | 30780 | 2 | Lonoke | 1 996 | 69 839 | 761 | 35.0 | 88.7 | 6.8 | 1.1 | 1.4 | 3.5 | 6.8 | 20.3 | 8.3 | 14.0 | 14.2 | 14.1 |
| 05 087 | 22220 | 2 | Madison | 2 161 | 15 645 | 2 070 | 7.2 | 92.9 | 0.9 | 2.0 | 0.8 | 5.0 | 5.9 | 17.9 | 7.7 | 10.8 | 12.0 | 15.1 |
| 05 089 | ... | 9 | Marion | 1 546 | 16 568 | 2 006 | 10.7 | 96.6 | 0.7 | 1.8 | 0.5 | 1.9 | 4.5 | 13.0 | 6.5 | 8.1 | 9.9 | 15.5 |
| 05 091 | 45500 | 3 | Miller | 1 620 | 43 634 | 1 095 | 26.9 | 71.8 | 24.5 | 1.4 | 0.8 | 3.0 | 7.2 | 17.1 | 9.1 | 13.7 | 12.6 | 13.8 |
| 05 093 | 14180 | 4 | Mississippi | 2 332 | 45 562 | 1 057 | 19.5 | 61.4 | 34.6 | 0.7 | 0.9 | 3.7 | 7.5 | 20.4 | 9.3 | 12.8 | 12.0 | 14.0 |
| 05 095 | ... | 7 | Monroe | 1 572 | 7 828 | 2 612 | 5.0 | 56.5 | 40.9 | 1.0 | 0.8 | 2.0 | 6.2 | 16.2 | 8.1 | 9.6 | 11.0 | 14.5 |
| 05 097 | ... | 8 | Montgomery | 2 020 | 9 340 | 2 487 | 4.6 | 94.1 | 0.8 | 2.2 | 0.8 | 4.0 | 5.0 | 15.2 | 6.9 | 8.3 | 10.5 | 15.6 |
| 05 099 | 26260 | 7 | Nevada | 1 600 | 8 925 | 2 526 | 5.6 | 66.0 | 31.2 | 0.9 | 0.5 | 2.8 | 6.8 | 16.8 | 8.2 | 10.7 | 11.4 | 14.3 |
| 05 101 | 25460 | 9 | Newton | 2 126 | 8 086 | 2 595 | 3.8 | 96.5 | 0.7 | 2.8 | 0.6 | 1.8 | 4.9 | 15.5 | 7.0 | 10.0 | 10.4 | 14.6 |
| 05 103 | 15780 | 7 | Ouachita | 1 898 | 25 396 | 1 593 | 13.4 | 57.5 | 40.7 | 0.9 | 0.7 | 1.7 | 6.7 | 16.5 | 8.0 | 10.9 | 10.8 | 14.9 |
| 05 105 | 30780 | 2 | Perry | 1 428 | 10 339 | 2 410 | 7.2 | 94.2 | 2.5 | 1.5 | 0.4 | 2.5 | 5.9 | 16.7 | 8.0 | 10.3 | 12.7 | 15.2 |
| 05 107 | 25760 | 7 | Phillips | 1 802 | 20 784 | 1 790 | 11.5 | 35.6 | 62.6 | 0.7 | 0.6 | 1.5 | 7.8 | 20.1 | 9.4 | 11.1 | 10.0 | 13.7 |
| 05 109 | ... | 9 | Pike | 1 556 | 11 247 | 2 340 | 7.2 | 89.0 | 3.6 | 1.3 | 0.7 | 6.8 | 6.1 | 18.3 | 7.8 | 10.4 | 13.0 | 14.2 |
| 05 111 | 27860 | 3 | Poinsett | 1 964 | 24 307 | 1 633 | 12.4 | 89.7 | 8.0 | 0.8 | 0.4 | 2.3 | 6.6 | 17.7 | 8.4 | 11.6 | 12.3 | 14.1 |
| 05 113 | ... | 7 | Polk | 2 221 | 20 471 | 1 817 | 9.2 | 91.3 | 0.7 | 3.2 | 0.7 | 6.2 | 5.9 | 17.3 | 7.2 | 10.1 | 11.2 | 13.8 |
| 05 115 | 40780 | 5 | Pope | 2 104 | 62 765 | 832 | 29.8 | 88.0 | 3.6 | 1.8 | 1.4 | 7.1 | 6.6 | 16.4 | 14.5 | 12.3 | 11.7 | 13.5 |
| 05 117 | ... | 8 | Prairie | 1 678 | 8 458 | 2 568 | 5.0 | 86.3 | 12.5 | 0.9 | 0.3 | 1.0 | 5.1 | 15.9 | 7.0 | 9.7 | 11.9 | 15.1 |
| 05 119 | 30780 | 2 | Pulaski | 1 968 | 388 953 | 172 | 197.6 | 56.6 | 35.7 | 1.0 | 2.5 | 6.0 | 7.0 | 16.9 | 9.2 | 15.3 | 12.9 | 13.8 |
| 05 121 | ... | 7 | Randolph | 1 689 | 17 930 | 1 924 | 10.6 | 96.5 | 1.3 | 1.3 | 0.4 | 1.7 | 6.1 | 16.9 | 8.4 | 10.9 | 11.7 | 14.0 |
| 05 123 | 22620 | 6 | St. Francis | 1 644 | 27 858 | 1 500 | 16.9 | 43.0 | 52.2 | 1.0 | 0.8 | 4.3 | 6.6 | 16.9 | 8.5 | 14.7 | 11.3 | 14.5 |
| 05 125 | 30780 | 2 | Saline | 1 874 | 111 845 | 539 | 59.7 | 89.4 | 5.6 | 1.2 | 1.2 | 3.9 | 6.4 | 17.8 | 7.3 | 13.3 | 13.6 | 14.0 |
| 05 127 | ... | 6 | Scott | 2 311 | 11 010 | 2 357 | 4.8 | 86.8 | 1.5 | 3.1 | 3.7 | 7.0 | 6.5 | 18.7 | 8.7 | 10.5 | 11.5 | 14.5 |
| 05 129 | ... | 9 | Searcy | 1 725 | 8 007 | 2 599 | 4.6 | 96.6 | 0.7 | 2.9 | 0.4 | 1.7 | 4.8 | 15.3 | 6.4 | 9.9 | 10.7 | 14.7 |
| 05 131 | 22900 | 2 | Sebastian | 1 378 | 127 304 | 484 | 92.4 | 75.0 | 7.5 | 3.0 | 4.6 | 12.6 | 7.1 | 18.0 | 9.6 | 13.1 | 12.6 | 14.1 |
| 05 133 | ... | 7 | Sevier | 1 464 | 17 177 | 1 966 | 11.7 | 62.0 | 4.8 | 2.9 | 0.6 | 31.5 | 8.7 | 20.6 | 9.0 | 12.8 | 12.8 | 12.4 |
| 05 135 | ... | 7 | Sharp | 1 565 | 17 054 | 1 975 | 10.9 | 96.0 | 1.1 | 2.2 | 0.4 | 1.8 | 5.3 | 16.0 | 6.5 | 8.8 | 10.4 | 13.4 |
| 05 137 | ... | 9 | Stone | 1 571 | 12 663 | 2 263 | 8.1 | 96.0 | 0.6 | 1.9 | 0.6 | 1.5 | 5.0 | 15.6 | 6.3 | 9.3 | 9.9 | 14.5 |
| 05 139 | 20980 | 5 | Union | 2 692 | 40 867 | 1 157 | 15.2 | 62.4 | 33.4 | 0.8 | 0.8 | 3.8 | 6.6 | 17.2 | 8.2 | 11.9 | 12.1 | 14.6 |
| 05 141 | ... | 8 | Van Buren | 1 834 | 17 030 | 1 978 | 9.3 | 95.4 | 1.0 | 1.9 | 0.5 | 2.8 | 4.7 | 15.4 | 6.5 | 8.9 | 10.9 | 14.8 |
| 05 143 | 22220 | 2 | Washington | 2 440 | 211 411 | 297 | 86.6 | 75.7 | 3.8 | 2.1 | 4.8 | 15.8 | 7.4 | 17.9 | 14.3 | 16.1 | 12.7 | 11.9 |
| 05 145 | 42620 | 4 | White | 2 681 | 78 493 | 700 | 29.3 | 90.6 | 4.9 | 1.3 | 0.8 | 4.0 | 6.6 | 17.3 | 12.6 | 12.3 | 12.0 | 13.6 |
| 05 147 | ... | 9 | Woodruff | 1 520 | 7 100 | 2 674 | 4.7 | 70.9 | 27.9 | 1.0 | 0.6 | 1.3 | 6.1 | 16.4 | 7.2 | 10.0 | 11.9 | 14.6 |
| 05 149 | 40780 | 6 | Yell | 2 409 | 21 932 | 1 733 | 9.1 | 77.3 | 1.8 | 1.2 | 1.6 | 19.2 | 7.0 | 18.9 | 8.3 | 11.6 | 12.4 | 13.9 |

1. CBSA = Core Based Statistical Area. See Appendix A for explanation. See Appendix B for list of metropolitan areas with component counties.   2. County type code from the Economic Research Service of USDA Rural-Urban Continuum Codes. See Appendix A for definition.   3. Dry land or land partially or temporarily covered by water.   4. May be of any race.

# Table B. States and Counties — **Population and Households**

| | Population, 2011 (cont.) — Age (percent) (cont.) | | | | Population change and components of change, 2000–2012 | | | | | | | Households, 2010 | | | | |
| | 55 to 64 years | 65 to 74 years | 75 years and over | Percent female | Total persons 2000 | Total persons 2010 | Percent change 2000–2010 | Percent change 2010–2012 | Births | Deaths | Net migration | Number | Percent change, 2000–2010 | Persons per house-hold | Female family house-holder[1] | One per-son |
| STATE County | 16 | 17 | 18 | 19 | 20 | 21 | 22 | 23 | 24 | 25 | 26 | 27 | 28 | 29 | 30 | 31 |
|---|---|---|---|---|---|---|---|---|---|---|---|---|---|---|---|---|
| **ARKANSAS—Cont'd** | | | | | | | | | | | | | | | | |
| Cleveland | 13.8 | 9.3 | 7.1 | 51.0 | 8 571 | 8 689 | 1.4 | -0.7 | 202 | 210 | -52 | 3 416 | 4.4 | 2.53 | 11.7 | 23.7 |
| Columbia | 11.8 | 8.3 | 7.8 | 52.2 | 25 603 | 24 552 | -4.1 | -0.3 | 666 | 644 | -111 | 9 759 | -2.2 | 2.38 | 16.3 | 30.2 |
| Conway | 13.2 | 9.4 | 7.9 | 50.7 | 20 336 | 21 273 | 4.6 | 0.1 | 604 | 497 | -81 | 8 463 | 6.2 | 2.48 | 11.8 | 26.4 |
| Craighead | 10.8 | 6.8 | 5.4 | 51.1 | 82 148 | 96 443 | 17.4 | 3.4 | 3 069 | 1 915 | 2 101 | 37 291 | 15.4 | 2.49 | 13.9 | 26.5 |
| Crawford | 12.5 | 8.2 | 5.5 | 50.7 | 53 247 | 61 948 | 16.3 | 0.0 | 1 657 | 1 278 | -360 | 23 447 | 19.0 | 2.62 | 11.8 | 23.0 |
| Crittenden | 11.4 | 6.5 | 4.6 | 52.5 | 50 866 | 50 902 | 0.1 | -1.7 | 1 817 | 1 074 | -1 646 | 19 026 | 3.0 | 2.64 | 23.6 | 25.9 |
| Cross | 13.0 | 9.0 | 6.9 | 51.7 | 19 526 | 17 870 | -8.5 | -1.0 | 506 | 434 | -256 | 7 002 | -5.3 | 2.52 | 15.1 | 26.2 |
| Dallas | 15.2 | 9.6 | 8.8 | 51.2 | 9 210 | 8 116 | -11.9 | -1.6 | 197 | 190 | -145 | 3 280 | -6.8 | 2.35 | 15.7 | 30.0 |
| Desha | 13.5 | 9.3 | 6.5 | 52.9 | 15 341 | 13 008 | -15.2 | -3.6 | 395 | 408 | -458 | 5 321 | -10.1 | 2.43 | 21.5 | 29.6 |
| Drew | 12.1 | 7.9 | 6.9 | 51.2 | 18 723 | 18 509 | -1.1 | 1.3 | 492 | 400 | 145 | 7 360 | 0.3 | 2.41 | 15.6 | 27.8 |
| Faulkner | 10.1 | 5.9 | 4.3 | 51.1 | 86 014 | 113 237 | 31.6 | 4.8 | 3 491 | 1 752 | 3 644 | 42 614 | 33.7 | 2.56 | 11.6 | 23.4 |
| Franklin | 13.3 | 9.2 | 7.8 | 50.4 | 17 771 | 18 125 | 2.0 | -0.4 | 449 | 441 | -76 | 7 037 | 2.3 | 2.51 | 10.8 | 24.9 |
| Fulton | 16.2 | 13.2 | 9.4 | 51.1 | 11 642 | 12 245 | 5.2 | 0.6 | 252 | 395 | 209 | 5 196 | 8.0 | 2.32 | 9.3 | 28.1 |
| Garland | 14.6 | 11.4 | 9.7 | 51.5 | 88 068 | 96 024 | 9.0 | 0.9 | 2 451 | 2 850 | 1 192 | 40 994 | 8.4 | 2.29 | 11.9 | 29.6 |
| Grant | 12.9 | 8.9 | 5.9 | 50.2 | 16 464 | 17 853 | 8.4 | 0.7 | 414 | 389 | 121 | 6 933 | 11.1 | 2.55 | 10.2 | 22.4 |
| Greene | 12.1 | 8.2 | 6.1 | 51.0 | 37 331 | 42 090 | 12.7 | 2.5 | 1 267 | 997 | 801 | 16 425 | 11.4 | 2.53 | 12.4 | 24.2 |
| Hempstead | 12.5 | 8.5 | 6.6 | 51.7 | 23 587 | 22 609 | -4.1 | -1.0 | 719 | 542 | -411 | 8 839 | -1.3 | 2.52 | 16.9 | 27.2 |
| Hot Spring | 14.2 | 9.0 | 6.8 | 48.9 | 30 353 | 32 923 | 8.5 | 1.4 | 794 | 749 | 439 | 12 664 | 5.5 | 2.48 | 12.3 | 25.2 |
| Howard | 12.2 | 8.4 | 7.0 | 51.5 | 14 300 | 13 789 | -3.6 | -0.4 | 428 | 330 | -152 | 5 365 | -1.9 | 2.54 | 15.0 | 26.3 |
| Independence | 12.9 | 8.6 | 7.3 | 51.1 | 34 233 | 36 647 | 7.1 | 1.0 | 1 056 | 919 | 260 | 14 391 | 6.9 | 2.48 | 10.8 | 25.9 |
| Izard | 15.6 | 12.9 | 10.4 | 48.4 | 13 249 | 13 696 | 3.4 | -1.6 | 252 | 398 | -66 | 5 731 | 5.3 | 2.26 | 8.4 | 29.7 |
| Jackson | 13.2 | 9.1 | 7.0 | 50.4 | 18 418 | 17 997 | -2.3 | -2.2 | 415 | 500 | -325 | 6 724 | -3.5 | 2.38 | 14.4 | 30.1 |
| Jefferson | 13.2 | 7.6 | 6.0 | 50.8 | 84 278 | 77 435 | -8.1 | -3.5 | 2 146 | 1 855 | -3 033 | 28 873 | -5.5 | 2.49 | 21.5 | 28.4 |
| Johnson | 11.8 | 8.3 | 6.4 | 50.5 | 22 781 | 25 540 | 12.1 | 1.4 | 782 | 549 | 147 | 9 812 | 12.3 | 2.55 | 11.3 | 25.3 |
| Lafayette | 13.9 | 11.6 | 8.1 | 51.5 | 8 559 | 7 645 | -10.7 | -2.6 | 160 | 208 | -155 | 3 150 | -8.3 | 2.39 | 17.0 | 29.2 |
| Lawrence | 12.8 | 10.3 | 8.3 | 51.2 | 17 774 | 17 415 | -2.0 | -2.3 | 393 | 573 | -234 | 6 938 | -2.4 | 2.42 | 11.0 | 27.7 |
| Lee | 13.5 | 8.6 | 7.3 | 44.5 | 12 580 | 10 424 | -17.1 | -2.0 | 222 | 239 | -192 | 3 624 | -13.3 | 2.39 | 22.0 | 31.2 |
| Lincoln | 11.7 | 6.6 | 5.7 | 39.7 | 14 492 | 14 134 | -2.5 | -0.2 | 273 | 323 | 9 | 4 207 | -1.4 | 2.54 | 15.3 | 25.2 |
| Little River | 14.1 | 10.5 | 7.1 | 51.3 | 13 628 | 13 171 | -3.4 | -1.9 | 297 | 397 | -145 | 5 411 | -1.0 | 2.41 | 14.3 | 27.9 |
| Logan | 13.1 | 10.0 | 7.5 | 50.0 | 22 486 | 22 353 | -0.6 | -1.7 | 579 | 649 | -313 | 8 704 | 0.1 | 2.50 | 11.5 | 25.9 |
| Lonoke | 10.9 | 6.8 | 4.6 | 50.7 | 52 828 | 68 356 | 29.4 | 2.2 | 2 084 | 1 302 | 726 | 25 295 | 31.3 | 2.68 | 12.3 | 20.5 |
| Madison | 14.4 | 9.2 | 6.9 | 49.9 | 14 243 | 15 717 | 10.3 | -0.5 | 422 | 323 | -163 | 6 174 | 13.0 | 2.53 | 8.2 | 24.2 |
| Marion | 18.2 | 15.2 | 9.2 | 50.2 | 16 140 | 16 653 | 3.2 | -0.5 | 321 | 541 | 152 | 7 411 | 9.4 | 2.23 | 8.2 | 28.3 |
| Miller | 12.6 | 8.1 | 5.9 | 50.7 | 40 443 | 43 462 | 7.5 | 0.4 | 1 378 | 925 | -258 | 17 219 | 10.1 | 2.44 | 17.0 | 27.4 |
| Mississippi | 11.7 | 6.9 | 5.4 | 51.4 | 51 979 | 46 480 | -10.6 | -2.0 | 1 452 | 1 126 | -1 246 | 17 741 | -8.3 | 2.58 | 19.6 | 27.1 |
| Monroe | 15.1 | 10.3 | 8.9 | 52.1 | 10 254 | 8 149 | -20.5 | -3.9 | 217 | 290 | -252 | 3 481 | -15.2 | 2.32 | 16.8 | 32.8 |
| Montgomery | 15.4 | 13.0 | 10.1 | 50.1 | 9 245 | 9 487 | 2.6 | -1.5 | 192 | 300 | -29 | 4 000 | 5.7 | 2.34 | 7.7 | 27.4 |
| Nevada | 13.9 | 10.0 | 8.0 | 51.5 | 9 955 | 8 997 | -9.6 | -0.8 | 253 | 255 | -72 | 3 697 | -5.0 | 2.39 | 16.0 | 28.5 |
| Newton | 16.3 | 13.0 | 8.4 | 49.7 | 8 608 | 8 330 | -3.2 | -2.9 | 163 | 229 | -180 | 3 571 | 2.0 | 2.32 | 7.9 | 29.1 |
| Ouachita | 14.7 | 9.2 | 8.3 | 52.8 | 28 790 | 26 120 | -9.3 | -2.8 | 720 | 793 | -669 | 11 003 | -5.3 | 2.34 | 18.0 | 30.5 |
| Perry | 13.7 | 9.9 | 7.6 | 50.6 | 10 209 | 10 445 | 2.3 | -1.0 | 256 | 285 | -84 | 4 170 | 4.5 | 2.47 | 10.7 | 25.8 |
| Phillips | 12.7 | 8.6 | 6.7 | 53.1 | 26 445 | 21 757 | -17.7 | -4.5 | 704 | 601 | -1 095 | 8 491 | -12.6 | 2.53 | 25.8 | 30.1 |
| Pike | 12.6 | 10.0 | 7.4 | 50.2 | 11 303 | 11 291 | -0.1 | -0.4 | 265 | 316 | 15 | 4 457 | -1.0 | 2.49 | 10.5 | 26.1 |
| Poinsett | 13.2 | 9.5 | 6.7 | 51.5 | 25 614 | 24 583 | -4.0 | -1.1 | 704 | 740 | -234 | 9 754 | -2.7 | 2.49 | 15.1 | 26.6 |
| Polk | 14.5 | 11.5 | 8.4 | 50.9 | 20 229 | 20 662 | 2.1 | -0.9 | 545 | 611 | -116 | 8 450 | 5.0 | 2.43 | 9.6 | 26.7 |
| Pope | 11.6 | 7.5 | 5.9 | 50.5 | 54 469 | 61 754 | 13.4 | 1.6 | 1 766 | 1 202 | 452 | 23 353 | 12.8 | 2.50 | 11.5 | 24.9 |
| Prairie | 14.9 | 11.4 | 8.8 | 50.6 | 9 539 | 8 715 | -8.6 | -2.9 | 186 | 257 | -188 | 3 685 | -5.4 | 2.33 | 11.0 | 27.7 |
| Pulaski | 12.7 | 6.6 | 5.5 | 51.9 | 361 474 | 382 748 | 5.9 | 1.6 | 12 673 | 7 545 | 1 248 | 158 772 | 7.3 | 2.36 | 16.6 | 31.8 |
| Randolph | 13.4 | 9.9 | 8.7 | 51.0 | 18 195 | 17 969 | -1.2 | -0.2 | 445 | 533 | 56 | 7 299 | 0.5 | 2.41 | 10.7 | 27.7 |
| St. Francis | 12.5 | 7.3 | 5.2 | 45.5 | 29 329 | 28 258 | -3.7 | -1.4 | 790 | 614 | -580 | 9 616 | -4.3 | 2.51 | 23.4 | 28.7 |
| Saline | 12.6 | 9.0 | 6.0 | 50.7 | 83 529 | 107 118 | 28.2 | 4.4 | 2 825 | 2 026 | 3 695 | 41 441 | 30.4 | 2.55 | 10.8 | 21.9 |
| Scott | 12.4 | 10.4 | 6.8 | 49.5 | 10 996 | 11 233 | 2.2 | -2.0 | 314 | 282 | -263 | 4 368 | 1.0 | 2.55 | 10.0 | 26.7 |
| Searcy | 16.5 | 11.9 | 9.9 | 50.2 | 8 261 | 8 195 | -0.8 | -2.3 | 164 | 231 | -114 | 3 574 | 1.4 | 2.27 | 7.4 | 30.3 |
| Sebastian | 12.1 | 7.4 | 5.9 | 50.9 | 115 071 | 125 744 | 9.3 | 1.2 | 3 958 | 2 573 | 227 | 49 599 | 9.5 | 2.49 | 13.0 | 28.4 |
| Sevier | 10.7 | 7.1 | 5.8 | 50.2 | 15 757 | 17 058 | 8.3 | 0.7 | 611 | 368 | -119 | 5 975 | 4.7 | 2.83 | 12.2 | 23.2 |
| Sharp | 15.2 | 13.4 | 10.9 | 50.5 | 17 119 | 17 264 | 0.8 | -1.2 | 385 | 538 | -71 | 7 360 | 2.1 | 2.32 | 9.8 | 28.2 |
| Stone | 16.2 | 13.5 | 9.6 | 50.7 | 11 499 | 12 394 | 7.8 | 2.2 | 281 | 341 | 323 | 5 325 | 11.7 | 2.30 | 7.2 | 28.9 |
| Union | 13.7 | 8.2 | 7.5 | 51.3 | 45 629 | 41 639 | -8.7 | -1.9 | 1 154 | 1 224 | -701 | 16 951 | -5.8 | 2.43 | 15.9 | 28.5 |
| Van Buren | 15.0 | 12.4 | 10.7 | 50.3 | 16 192 | 17 295 | 6.8 | -1.5 | 380 | 523 | -113 | 7 433 | 8.9 | 2.30 | 8.5 | 29.6 |
| Washington | 9.8 | 5.6 | 4.3 | 50.0 | 157 715 | 203 065 | 28.8 | 4.1 | 7 214 | 2 948 | 4 005 | 76 389 | 27.0 | 2.56 | 10.6 | 27.5 |
| White | 11.4 | 8.0 | 6.3 | 51.1 | 67 165 | 77 076 | 14.8 | 1.8 | 2 183 | 1 726 | 956 | 29 342 | 16.7 | 2.52 | 11.2 | 24.7 |
| Woodruff | 15.4 | 10.2 | 8.2 | 51.9 | 8 741 | 7 260 | -16.9 | -2.2 | 199 | 234 | -135 | 3 134 | -11.2 | 2.28 | 15.7 | 32.7 |
| Yell | 12.3 | 8.6 | 7.0 | 50.2 | 21 139 | 22 185 | 4.9 | -1.1 | 684 | 521 | -415 | 8 219 | 3.7 | 2.66 | 11.4 | 24.3 |

1. No spouse present.

# Table B. States and Counties — Population, Vital Statistics, Medicare, and Crime

| STATE County | Persons in group quarters, 2010 | Daytime population, 2007–2011 | | Births, 2011 | | Deaths, 2011 | | Persons under 65 with no health insurance, 2010 | | Medicare, 2012 | | | Serious crimes known to police,[2] 2011 Total | |
|---|---|---|---|---|---|---|---|---|---|---|---|---|---|---|
| | | Number | Employment/residence ratio | Total | Rate[1] | Number | Rate[1] | Number | Percent | Eligible for Medicare | Enrolled in Medicare Advantage | Enrolled in a Medicare prescription drug plan | Number | Rate[3] |
| | 32 | 33 | 34 | 35 | 36 | 37 | 38 | 39 | 40 | 41 | 42 | 43 | 44 | 45 |
| ARKANSAS—Cont'd | | | | | | | | | | | | | | |
| Cleveland | 52 | 6 872 | 0.44 | 87 | 10.0 | 85 | 9.8 | 1 505 | 20.8 | 1 841 | 151 | 1 077 | 135 | 1 542 |
| Columbia | 1 315 | 24 926 | 1.03 | 304 | 12.5 | 312 | 12.8 | 3 675 | 18.9 | 5 104 | 470 | 3 216 | 764 | 3 088 |
| Conway | 286 | 20 565 | 0.92 | 274 | 12.9 | 192 | 9.0 | 3 525 | 20.2 | 4 833 | 866 | 2 349 | 857 | 3 998 |
| Craighead | 3 579 | 100 492 | 1.13 | 1 380 | 14.0 | 826 | 8.4 | 16 966 | 20.7 | 16 211 | 1 912 | 9 126 | 4 260 | 4 545 |
| Crawford | 540 | 55 166 | 0.77 | 744 | 12.0 | 548 | 8.8 | 12 289 | 23.1 | 11 953 | 4 238 | 4 250 | 1 540 | 2 467 |
| Crittenden | 701 | 46 129 | 0.78 | 826 | 16.3 | 495 | 9.8 | 8 325 | 18.6 | 8 094 | 1 107 | 4 507 | 4 580 | 8 930 |
| Cross | 225 | 16 490 | 0.80 | 224 | 12.6 | 208 | 11.7 | 3 019 | 20.2 | 3 728 | 543 | 2 043 | 437 | 2 427 |
| Dallas | 405 | 9 000 | 1.30 | 88 | 10.9 | 82 | 10.2 | 1 242 | 19.8 | 1 863 | 303 | 1 024 | 202 | 2 470 |
| Desha | 56 | 13 417 | 1.05 | 187 | 14.7 | 186 | 14.6 | 2 391 | 22.0 | 2 739 | 240 | 1 688 | NA | NA |
| Drew | 785 | 17 840 | 0.91 | 215 | 11.6 | 168 | 9.1 | 2 928 | 19.4 | 3 415 | 232 | 2 084 | 711 | 3 813 |
| Faulkner | 4 055 | 101 562 | 0.82 | 1 545 | 13.3 | 732 | 6.3 | 17 647 | 17.9 | 16 006 | 1 173 | 8 455 | 4 279 | 3 750 |
| Franklin | 447 | 16 964 | 0.83 | 211 | 11.7 | 186 | 10.3 | 3 084 | 20.6 | 3 919 | 972 | 1 650 | 408 | 2 234 |
| Fulton | 165 | 11 019 | 0.70 | 115 | 9.4 | 192 | 15.6 | 2 282 | 24.3 | 3 294 | 576 | 1 601 | 244 | 1 978 |
| Garland | 2 166 | 96 154 | 1.01 | 1 100 | 11.3 | 1 241 | 12.8 | 17 327 | 23.2 | 25 698 | 4 274 | 11 396 | 5 477 | 5 661 |
| Grant | 143 | 14 000 | 0.52 | 188 | 10.5 | 155 | 8.6 | 2 667 | 17.6 | 3 386 | 421 | 1 589 | 348 | 1 935 |
| Greene | 602 | 41 179 | 0.97 | 535 | 12.5 | 456 | 10.7 | 7 010 | 19.6 | 8 624 | 1 432 | 4 432 | 2 316 | 5 461 |
| Hempstead | 301 | 22 556 | 0.99 | 326 | 14.5 | 232 | 10.3 | 4 568 | 24.1 | 4 214 | 642 | 2 318 | 981 | 4 306 |
| Hot Spring | 1 571 | 28 249 | 0.65 | 363 | 11.0 | 328 | 10.0 | 5 163 | 19.7 | 6 958 | 899 | 3 241 | NA | NA |
| Howard | 181 | 15 322 | 1.25 | 209 | 15.1 | 153 | 11.0 | 3 017 | 26.1 | 2 894 | 366 | 1 660 | 325 | 2 339 |
| Independence | 900 | 37 781 | 1.10 | 474 | 12.9 | 400 | 10.9 | 6 109 | 20.2 | 7 910 | 708 | 4 611 | 1 719 | 4 656 |
| Izard | 769 | 12 407 | 0.74 | 117 | 8.7 | 191 | 14.2 | 2 272 | 23.2 | 3 697 | 522 | 1 886 | 218 | 1 580 |
| Jackson | 2 000 | 18 410 | 1.07 | 182 | 10.2 | 215 | 12.0 | 2 973 | 22.6 | 3 897 | 322 | 2 429 | 769 | 4 241 |
| Jefferson | 5 530 | 80 488 | 1.09 | 1 005 | 13.2 | 832 | 10.9 | 10 842 | 17.5 | 14 315 | 2 774 | 6 837 | 5 502 | 7 143 |
| Johnson | 558 | 25 127 | 0.97 | 342 | 13.3 | 242 | 9.4 | 5 176 | 24.4 | 5 116 | 1 094 | 2 381 | 709 | 2 755 |
| Lafayette | 111 | 6 826 | 0.67 | 80 | 10.6 | 106 | 14.1 | 1 400 | 23.2 | 1 737 | 149 | 1 085 | 137 | 1 779 |
| Lawrence | 595 | 16 272 | 0.83 | 180 | 10.5 | 271 | 15.8 | 2 925 | 21.2 | 4 219 | 530 | 2 385 | 260 | 1 482 |
| Lee | 1 756 | 10 397 | 0.94 | 95 | 9.2 | 125 | 12.1 | 1 446 | 20.5 | 2 002 | 470 | 1 097 | 219 | 2 085 |
| Lincoln | 3 445 | 13 064 | 0.75 | 121 | 8.6 | 154 | 11.0 | 1 848 | 20.6 | 2 262 | 264 | 1 277 | 126 | 940 |
| Little River | 123 | 12 136 | 0.82 | 154 | 11.8 | 168 | 12.9 | 2 146 | 19.8 | 2 915 | 285 | 1 628 | 304 | 2 291 |
| Logan | 580 | 20 540 | 0.78 | 260 | 11.7 | 288 | 12.9 | 3 608 | 19.9 | 5 280 | 1 138 | 2 430 | 683 | 3 033 |
| Lonoke | 572 | 51 507 | 0.50 | 891 | 12.8 | 577 | 8.3 | 10 685 | 17.6 | 10 740 | 1 439 | 4 847 | 2 409 | 3 649 |
| Madison | 79 | 13 237 | 0.62 | 179 | 11.3 | 133 | 8.4 | 3 425 | 26.1 | 3 343 | 806 | 1 384 | 144 | 1 069 |
| Marion | 141 | 15 349 | 0.78 | 141 | 8.5 | 252 | 15.2 | 2 990 | 23.8 | 4 973 | 1 108 | 2 033 | 367 | 2 187 |
| Miller | 1 480 | 39 274 | 0.77 | 625 | 14.3 | 419 | 9.6 | 7 111 | 19.6 | 7 737 | 1 163 | 3 930 | 2 811 | 6 419 |
| Mississippi | 767 | 49 592 | 1.17 | 652 | 14.2 | 511 | 11.1 | 7 137 | 17.9 | 8 353 | 1 343 | 4 570 | 2 849 | 6 083 |
| Monroe | 84 | 7 914 | 0.86 | 106 | 13.1 | 126 | 15.6 | 1 336 | 20.6 | 2 013 | 291 | 1 218 | 106 | 1 291 |
| Montgomery | 121 | 8 628 | 0.75 | 89 | 9.4 | 138 | 14.6 | 1 872 | 25.8 | 2 445 | 278 | 1 188 | 23 | 241 |
| Nevada | 157 | 8 049 | 0.71 | 111 | 12.3 | 115 | 12.8 | 1 469 | 20.2 | 2 101 | 380 | 1 114 | 261 | 2 879 |
| Newton | 51 | 6 735 | 0.55 | 74 | 9.0 | 116 | 14.0 | 1 712 | 26.0 | 2 252 | 434 | 1 044 | 89 | 1 060 |
| Ouachita | 352 | 24 858 | 0.87 | 325 | 12.6 | 352 | 13.6 | 4 028 | 18.8 | 5 915 | 1 212 | 2 895 | 747 | 2 838 |
| Perry | 152 | 7 953 | 0.42 | 120 | 11.5 | 129 | 12.4 | 1 715 | 19.9 | 2 598 | 397 | 1 210 | 222 | 2 109 |
| Phillips | 246 | 21 269 | 0.89 | 341 | 15.9 | 289 | 13.5 | 3 079 | 17.0 | 4 305 | 799 | 2 483 | NA | NA |
| Pike | 196 | 10 668 | 0.86 | 120 | 10.7 | 143 | 12.7 | 2 303 | 25.3 | 2 509 | 304 | 1 363 | 100 | 879 |
| Poinsett | 341 | 21 751 | 0.70 | 310 | 12.6 | 330 | 13.5 | 4 106 | 20.2 | 5 546 | 764 | 3 465 | 875 | 3 533 |
| Polk | 155 | 20 332 | 0.98 | 240 | 11.6 | 274 | 13.3 | 4 240 | 25.7 | 5 190 | 466 | 2 560 | 543 | 2 608 |
| Pope | 3 330 | 62 445 | 1.05 | 787 | 12.6 | 503 | 8.1 | 10 137 | 20.1 | 11 291 | 1 963 | 5 258 | 1 965 | 3 158 |
| Prairie | 131 | 7 488 | 0.64 | 88 | 10.2 | 116 | 13.5 | 1 559 | 22.6 | 2 017 | 203 | 1 249 | 72 | 883 |
| Pulaski | 7 938 | 449 075 | 1.38 | 5 648 | 14.6 | 3 270 | 8.5 | 60 673 | 18.3 | 65 284 | 9 696 | 28 151 | 31 006 | 8 040 |
| Randolph | 349 | 16 445 | 0.75 | 205 | 11.4 | 249 | 13.8 | 3 178 | 22.1 | 4 457 | 916 | 2 227 | 54 | 298 |
| St. Francis | 4 085 | 28 557 | 1.04 | 354 | 12.2 | 291 | 10.4 | 3 849 | 18.7 | 4 729 | 891 | 2 534 | 1 702 | 5 978 |
| Saline | 1 425 | 81 175 | 0.51 | 1 218 | 11.1 | 856 | 7.8 | 14 956 | 16.4 | 20 743 | 2 712 | 8 810 | 3 602 | 3 337 |
| Scott | 79 | 10 645 | 0.86 | 141 | 12.5 | 117 | 10.4 | 2 381 | 25.8 | 2 560 | 616 | 1 187 | 307 | 2 817 |
| Searcy | 71 | 7 294 | 0.72 | 69 | 8.6 | 107 | 13.3 | 1 800 | 28.3 | 2 360 | 414 | 1 182 | 37 | 448 |
| Sebastian | 2 235 | 142 131 | 1.32 | 1 748 | 13.8 | 1 121 | 8.8 | 25 565 | 23.8 | 22 775 | 6 151 | 9 356 | 5 992 | 4 757 |
| Sevier | 173 | 16 749 | 0.99 | 282 | 16.3 | 155 | 9.0 | 4 650 | 31.6 | 2 733 | 211 | 1 588 | 325 | 1 891 |
| Sharp | 189 | 16 449 | 0.83 | 172 | 9.9 | 227 | 13.1 | 2 895 | 22.3 | 5 698 | 952 | 2 803 | NA | NA |
| Stone | 151 | 12 222 | 0.96 | 120 | 9.5 | 152 | 12.1 | 2 406 | 25.4 | 3 730 | 511 | 1 796 | 225 | 1 802 |
| Union | 524 | 43 968 | 1.13 | 536 | 12.9 | 559 | 13.5 | 6 330 | 18.3 | 9 401 | 1 004 | 5 397 | 1 839 | 4 589 |
| Van Buren | 189 | 16 857 | 0.93 | 151 | 8.8 | 241 | 14.1 | 2 907 | 22.0 | 4 940 | 818 | 2 356 | 360 | 2 066 |
| Washington | 7 563 | 204 580 | 1.04 | 3 205 | 15.4 | 1 260 | 6.1 | 41 210 | 23.3 | 27 111 | 5 003 | 11 363 | 7 452 | 3 690 |
| White | 3 252 | 73 284 | 0.91 | 989 | 12.7 | 756 | 9.7 | 12 615 | 19.9 | 14 726 | 1 943 | 7 410 | 2 818 | 3 657 |
| Woodruff | 106 | 6 851 | 0.82 | 87 | 12.0 | 95 | 13.1 | 1 300 | 22.2 | 1 758 | 172 | 1 081 | NA | NA |
| Yell | 323 | 19 962 | 0.77 | 324 | 14.7 | 234 | 10.6 | 5 196 | 28.0 | 4 297 | 602 | 2 179 | 517 | 2 313 |

1. Per 1,000 estimated resident population.   2. Data for serious crimes have not been adjusted for underreporting; this may affect comparability between geographic areas and over time.   3. Per 100,000 population estimated by the FBI.

# Table B. States and Counties — Crime, Education, Money Income, and Poverty

| STATE County | Serious crimes known to police, 2011 (cont.)[1] Rate[2] Violent | Property | Education School enrollment and attainment, 2007–2011 Enrollment[3] Total | Per cent private | High school graduate or less | Bach-elor's degree or more | Local government expenditures,[5] 2009–2010 Total current expendi-tures (mil dol) | Current expendi-tures per student (dollars) | Money income, 2007–2011 Per capita income[6] (dollars) | Households Median income Dollars | Percent change, 2000 to 2007–2011 (constant 2011 dollars) | Percent with income of $200,000 or more | Income and poverty, 2011 Median house-hold income (dollars) | Percent below poverty level All per-sons | Children under 18 years | Children 5 to 17 years in families |
|---|---|---|---|---|---|---|---|---|---|---|---|---|---|---|---|---|
| | 46 | 47 | 48 | 49 | 50 | 51 | 52 | 53 | 54 | 55 | 56 | 57 | 58 | 59 | 60 | 61 |
| ARKANSAS—Cont'd | | | | | | | | | | | | | | | | |
| Cleveland | 57 | 1 485 | 2 278 | 3.2 | 61.1 | 14.0 | 12.0 | 8 241 | 19 269 | 34 292 | -21.6 | 0.7 | 41 864 | 16.7 | 24.6 | 22.4 |
| Columbia | 384 | 2 704 | 7 544 | 7.4 | 52.6 | 20.5 | 31.3 | 8 677 | 20 146 | 36 163 | -3.1 | 1.4 | 33 533 | 26.4 | 37.3 | 36.1 |
| Conway | 215 | 3 784 | 4 919 | 11.0 | 61.3 | 14.0 | 37.5 | 11 169 | 20 202 | 31 890 | -24.3 | 1.5 | 37 830 | 23.0 | 30.8 | 29.5 |
| Craighead | 388 | 4 156 | 26 591 | 7.4 | 50.3 | 23.7 | 133.4 | 8 041 | 22 505 | 40 221 | -8.1 | 2.7 | 39 410 | 20.6 | 28.3 | 25.1 |
| Crawford | 375 | 2 092 | 15 349 | 9.0 | 56.4 | 13.2 | 95.7 | 8 390 | 18 732 | 40 409 | -9.0 | 0.7 | 37 552 | 18.0 | 27.3 | 24.8 |
| Crittenden | 1 728 | 7 203 | 15 162 | 5.9 | 58.0 | 13.5 | 98.6 | 8 871 | 19 007 | 35 264 | -13.3 | 1.3 | 34 905 | 26.6 | 39.9 | 38.7 |
| Cross | 261 | 2 166 | 4 512 | 4.7 | 67.8 | 12.0 | 31.5 | 8 756 | 18 179 | 38 432 | -3.1 | 0.4 | 35 268 | 19.2 | 28.3 | 26.0 |
| Dallas | 257 | 2 214 | 1 916 | 6.1 | 67.2 | 12.7 | 8.3 | 8 233 | 16 704 | 30 011 | -16.5 | 1.4 | 30 728 | 21.5 | 34.3 | 32.4 |
| Desha | NA | NA | 3 270 | 8.0 | 64.9 | 13.4 | 26.4 | 9 484 | 19 320 | 30 786 | -5.5 | 0.6 | 30 186 | 27.6 | 39.9 | 36.6 |
| Drew | 434 | 3 378 | 5 353 | 12.4 | 54.9 | 19.8 | 39.6 | 12 482 | 18 220 | 32 038 | -17.1 | 0.4 | 35 627 | 22.6 | 31.3 | 27.9 |
| Faulkner | 277 | 3 473 | 34 188 | 16.2 | 44.0 | 25.9 | 145.3 | 8 291 | 23 344 | 47 649 | -7.6 | 2.2 | 49 314 | 14.7 | 17.7 | 16.2 |
| Franklin | 378 | 1 856 | 4 476 | 4.4 | 57.1 | 12.4 | 32.6 | 9 977 | 18 810 | 34 819 | -16.4 | 1.7 | 38 245 | 20.9 | 28.4 | 26.6 |
| Fulton | 146 | 1 832 | 2 548 | 10.0 | 63.4 | 11.5 | 13.8 | 8 679 | 18 149 | 33 281 | -3.4 | 0.5 | 33 696 | 21.4 | 33.5 | 30.0 |
| Garland | 492 | 5 169 | 20 676 | 10.0 | 47.3 | 20.6 | 128.7 | 9 000 | 22 955 | 38 210 | -10.8 | 2.4 | 35 651 | 20.9 | 32.4 | 28.4 |
| Grant | 161 | 1 773 | 4 097 | 8.6 | 58.8 | 15.1 | 36.0 | 7 555 | 22 590 | 50 927 | 1.4 | 1.9 | 46 538 | 11.5 | 18.3 | 16.6 |
| Greene | 377 | 5 084 | 10 171 | 6.9 | 61.6 | 12.1 | 59.5 | 8 245 | 19 262 | 39 090 | -6.1 | 0.8 | 37 893 | 17.4 | 25.6 | 23.5 |
| Hempstead | 628 | 3 679 | 5 754 | 7.0 | 57.7 | 14.5 | 40.2 | 10 575 | 17 822 | 34 885 | -9.7 | 0.9 | 30 922 | 24.7 | 38.0 | 35.2 |
| Hot Spring | NA | NA | 7 457 | 5.7 | 58.4 | 12.3 | 46.9 | 8 597 | 18 378 | 38 188 | -10.3 | 0.6 | 38 082 | 20.3 | 30.0 | 28.1 |
| Howard | 216 | 2 123 | 3 506 | 2.8 | 64.7 | 12.7 | 26.9 | 8 574 | 18 415 | 37 146 | -4.1 | 1.0 | 33 079 | 20.9 | 30.5 | 29.7 |
| Independence | 371 | 4 284 | 8 518 | 7.4 | 58.8 | 13.2 | 54.6 | 8 910 | 19 927 | 34 878 | -19.1 | 1.4 | 34 690 | 21.4 | 27.9 | 25.7 |
| Izard | 43 | 1 536 | 2 487 | 9.4 | 59.1 | 12.7 | 20.3 | 10 872 | 18 081 | 31 865 | -8.1 | 0.5 | 31 245 | 20.5 | 31.7 | 28.4 |
| Jackson | 259 | 3 982 | 3 913 | 5.8 | 70.4 | 8.0 | 27.9 | 9 026 | 15 833 | 31 352 | -7.4 | 0.6 | 32 750 | 23.9 | 34.8 | 32.7 |
| Jefferson | 981 | 6 161 | 21 799 | 7.2 | 55.4 | 16.9 | 125.8 | 9 700 | 19 080 | 37 682 | -10.9 | 0.9 | 37 704 | 24.3 | 35.7 | 32.6 |
| Johnson | 171 | 2 584 | 5 514 | 14.9 | 63.1 | 16.0 | 36.4 | 8 561 | 18 541 | 31 400 | -16.7 | 1.8 | 34 182 | 20.8 | 29.8 | 26.9 |
| Lafayette | 117 | 1 662 | 1 856 | 5.8 | 66.9 | 12.8 | 12.3 | 9 896 | 17 464 | 30 152 | -10.1 | 2.0 | 30 057 | 24.2 | 35.4 | 32.9 |
| Lawrence | 165 | 1 316 | 4 431 | 16.3 | 66.5 | 9.4 | 33.2 | 10 206 | 15 506 | 32 337 | -11.7 | 0.2 | 32 678 | 23.0 | 34.4 | 30.1 |
| Lee | 105 | 1 980 | 2 428 | 14.5 | 72.8 | 6.5 | 14.9 | 12 249 | 12 615 | 25 270 | -8.7 | 0.0 | 27 894 | 35.2 | 46.4 | 42.9 |
| Lincoln | 52 | 888 | 2 978 | 4.0 | 70.2 | 9.0 | 14.2 | 8 128 | 15 183 | 31 480 | -21.2 | 1.3 | 35 854 | 25.4 | 28.8 | 26.1 |
| Little River | 173 | 2 117 | 2 892 | 6.4 | 59.1 | 12.5 | 20.0 | 9 501 | 20 258 | 38 564 | -2.9 | 0.4 | 38 937 | 17.6 | 27.8 | 25.4 |
| Logan | 258 | 2 775 | 5 469 | 8.8 | 64.5 | 11.2 | 31.0 | 8 562 | 19 464 | 38 447 | 0.5 | 1.5 | 34 000 | 20.0 | 31.2 | 28.5 |
| Lonoke | 323 | 3 326 | 18 213 | 8.0 | 49.6 | 17.3 | 106.4 | 7 836 | 22 725 | 51 096 | -6.1 | 1.0 | 49 579 | 13.7 | 18.8 | 17.0 |
| Madison | 156 | 913 | 3 629 | 8.5 | 66.1 | 12.2 | 20.6 | 8 825 | 18 199 | 35 579 | -5.5 | 1.1 | 34 292 | 22.6 | 31.2 | 28.1 |
| Marion | 304 | 1 883 | 3 090 | 8.9 | 54.2 | 14.5 | 16.6 | 9 370 | 19 508 | 34 063 | -5.6 | 2.2 | 32 685 | 20.5 | 34.5 | 32.2 |
| Miller | 591 | 5 828 | 10 087 | 8.5 | 56.8 | 12.9 | 63.7 | 9 605 | 20 013 | 40 200 | -3.8 | 1.0 | 37 728 | 21.5 | 32.4 | 29.7 |
| Mississippi | 779 | 5 304 | 12 538 | 2.7 | 61.9 | 12.6 | 86.3 | 9 587 | 18 125 | 34 267 | -7.6 | 1.3 | 33 426 | 25.4 | 36.3 | 35.0 |
| Monroe | 37 | 1 254 | 2 182 | 4.6 | 62.7 | 13.7 | 14.3 | 11 032 | 17 074 | 28 306 | -7.4 | 1.1 | 27 758 | 31.6 | 47.5 | 43.4 |
| Montgomery | 42 | 199 | 1 929 | 6.8 | 60.8 | 11.3 | 10.1 | 8 889 | 20 417 | 34 934 | -9.0 | 2.4 | 31 603 | 21.9 | 35.0 | 32.0 |
| Nevada | 232 | 2 648 | 2 119 | 9.2 | 61.1 | 10.3 | 13.0 | 9 307 | 20 523 | 38 006 | 4.4 | 1.4 | 31 590 | 23.5 | 35.0 | 33.3 |
| Newton | 119 | 941 | 1 609 | 10.9 | 61.5 | 12.6 | 14.1 | 10 483 | 16 768 | 29 702 | -11.1 | 0.3 | 31 224 | 21.3 | 36.4 | 32.0 |
| Ouachita | 315 | 2 523 | 6 353 | 5.9 | 57.6 | 13.2 | 47.8 | 10 452 | 19 079 | 33 008 | -16.7 | 0.4 | 35 095 | 24.1 | 37.6 | 35.3 |
| Perry | 200 | 1 910 | 2 253 | 5.6 | 61.7 | 11.5 | 13.4 | 7 858 | 20 257 | 42 514 | 1.3 | 0.2 | 38 868 | 16.4 | 27.2 | 25.6 |
| Phillips | NA | NA | 6 111 | 11.1 | 58.0 | 12.2 | 56.6 | 13 131 | 15 948 | 28 225 | -6.0 | 1.1 | 26 892 | 34.0 | 51.0 | 47.5 |
| Pike | 220 | 659 | 2 719 | 4.9 | 60.7 | 11.3 | 11.7 | 8 963 | 17 596 | 32 457 | -13.2 | 0.4 | 30 054 | 20.5 | 32.4 | 30.0 |
| Poinsett | 359 | 3 173 | 5 391 | 6.2 | 69.3 | 9.4 | 45.6 | 10 043 | 17 014 | 31 939 | -10.9 | 0.5 | 30 761 | 25.0 | 37.1 | 35.5 |
| Polk | 298 | 2 311 | 4 582 | 6.4 | 56.9 | 10.6 | 34.4 | 8 920 | 18 327 | 32 395 | -4.7 | 0.8 | 31 030 | 22.1 | 35.3 | 31.9 |
| Pope | 294 | 2 864 | 16 541 | 6.4 | 52.4 | 20.4 | 88.8 | 8 876 | 20 118 | 40 325 | -6.9 | 1.3 | 38 095 | 22.1 | 30.1 | 28.4 |
| Prairie | 98 | 785 | 1 874 | 3.3 | 69.1 | 9.9 | 11.1 | 8 493 | 18 704 | 36 194 | -10.6 | 0.2 | 36 088 | 21.7 | 31.3 | 27.9 |
| Pulaski | 1 135 | 6 905 | 101 098 | 19.4 | 38.6 | 31.3 | 598.8 | 10 481 | 27 666 | 45 897 | -10.8 | 3.7 | 43 898 | 16.6 | 23.3 | 21.8 |
| Randolph | 44 | 254 | 4 371 | 10.0 | 60.5 | 11.5 | 23.9 | 8 757 | 18 995 | 33 072 | -11.2 | 2.0 | 33 210 | 23.4 | 35.4 | 32.5 |
| St. Francis | 527 | 5 451 | 6 353 | 9.8 | 64.0 | 10.2 | 48.7 | 10 524 | 13 834 | 26 360 | -25.3 | 1.0 | 28 467 | 32.9 | 43.8 | 39.4 |
| Saline | 246 | 3 092 | 25 631 | 12.9 | 47.5 | 22.9 | 112.9 | 7 552 | 25 417 | 52 982 | -7.8 | 1.6 | 54 372 | 10.0 | 15.2 | 14.4 |
| Scott | 174 | 2 642 | 2 850 | 4.2 | 64.7 | 11.1 | 23.4 | 8 579 | 17 697 | 38 910 | 9.1 | 0.9 | 31 163 | 22.3 | 37.0 | 33.4 |
| Searcy | 121 | 327 | 1 712 | 15.1 | 66.4 | 8.5 | 17.5 | 10 685 | 15 053 | 29 384 | 1.7 | 0.1 | 26 990 | 28.6 | 46.6 | 41.5 |
| Sebastian | 576 | 4 180 | 31 003 | 10.0 | 49.8 | 19.0 | 173.0 | 8 854 | 23 175 | 40 680 | -11.1 | 2.9 | 38 404 | 21.2 | 31.2 | 27.3 |
| Sevier | 180 | 1 711 | 3 965 | 5.9 | 65.7 | 9.2 | 37.6 | 11 137 | 15 698 | 35 289 | -13.3 | 0.6 | 30 899 | 21.7 | 31.6 | 29.8 |
| Sharp | NA | NA | 3 793 | 6.3 | 60.4 | 12.8 | 24.2 | 8 152 | 16 146 | 29 590 | -12.9 | 0.5 | 28 760 | 24.5 | 37.8 | 35.1 |
| Stone | 216 | 1 586 | 2 418 | 13.3 | 58.6 | 11.8 | 14.6 | 8 391 | 17 190 | 31 364 | 4.6 | 0.4 | 29 182 | 22.9 | 38.5 | 34.9 |
| Union | 661 | 3 928 | 10 121 | 8.4 | 54.3 | 16.5 | 69.3 | 8 822 | 21 393 | 37 794 | -6.1 | 1.7 | 37 193 | 21.5 | 31.8 | 27.3 |
| Van Buren | 321 | 1 745 | 3 346 | 7.3 | 58.1 | 12.7 | 21.8 | 9 097 | 18 341 | 32 906 | -9.7 | 1.1 | 34 513 | 22.1 | 39.1 | 33.9 |
| Washington | 403 | 3 288 | 60 497 | 9.1 | 46.5 | 27.6 | 312.8 | 8 685 | 23 109 | 41 474 | -11.5 | 2.7 | 39 230 | 20.1 | 27.0 | 24.8 |
| White | 250 | 3 407 | 21 302 | 27.5 | 55.0 | 18.4 | 110.6 | 8 628 | 21 327 | 41 618 | -4.3 | 1.6 | 42 958 | 18.0 | 23.6 | 22.0 |
| Woodruff | NA | NA | 1 636 | 2.2 | 71.1 | 9.6 | 6.8 | 12 445 | 19 167 | 27 047 | -9.4 | 1.0 | 27 357 | 27.3 | 38.5 | 35.2 |
| Yell | 255 | 2 058 | 5 294 | 3.8 | 69.8 | 10.5 | 39.1 | 8 878 | 17 367 | 37 477 | -4.0 | 0.5 | 33 747 | 19.5 | 28.1 | 25.5 |

1. Data for serious crimes have not been adjusted for underreporting; this may affect comparability between geographic areas and over time. 2. Per 100,000 population estimated by the FBI. 3. All persons 3 years old and over enrolled in nursery school through college. 4. Persons 25 years old and over. 5. Elementary and secondary education expenditures. 6. Based on population estimated by the American Community Survey, 2007–2011.

# Table B. States and Counties — **Personal Income**

| STATE County | Personal income, 2011 Total (mil dol) | Percent change, 2010–2011 | Per capita[1] Dollars | Per capita[1] Rank | Wages and salaries[2] (mil dol) | Proprietors' income (mil dol) | Dividends, interest, and rent (mil dol) | Transfer payments (mil dol) Total | Government payments to individuals Total | Social Security | Medical payments | Income mainte-nance | Unemploy-ment insurance |
|---|---|---|---|---|---|---|---|---|---|---|---|---|---|
| | 62 | 63 | 64 | 65 | 66 | 67 | 68 | 69 | 70 | 71 | 72 | 73 | 74 |
| **ARKANSAS—Cont'd** | | | | | | | | | | | | | |
| Cleveland | 278 | 0.6 | 32 051 | 1 872 | 42 | 5 | 29 | 74 | 72 | 25 | 30 | 8 | 2 |
| Columbia | 811 | 5.0 | 33 253 | 1 666 | 425 | 60 | 158 | 229 | 223 | 73 | 94 | 31 | 6 |
| Conway | 702 | 5.0 | 33 021 | 1 704 | 323 | 54 | 85 | 206 | 201 | 67 | 88 | 22 | 5 |
| Craighead | 3 204 | 5.6 | 32 588 | 1 782 | 2 071 | 351 | 434 | 751 | 730 | 229 | 314 | 91 | 22 |
| Crawford | 1 716 | 3.3 | 27 699 | 2 653 | 863 | 124 | 207 | 488 | 474 | 168 | 202 | 54 | 15 |
| Crittenden | 1 609 | 3.3 | 31 850 | 1 915 | 716 | 163 | 155 | 448 | 437 | 114 | 187 | 93 | 17 |
| Cross | 550 | 3.9 | 30 939 | 2 114 | 224 | 70 | 73 | 161 | 157 | 52 | 70 | 22 | 5 |
| Dallas | 242 | 0.1 | 30 035 | 2 284 | 115 | 13 | 30 | 95 | 93 | 27 | 49 | 10 | 3 |
| Desha | 422 | 5.1 | 33 101 | 1 690 | 206 | 70 | 56 | 132 | 130 | 36 | 61 | 21 | 4 |
| Drew | 574 | 3.9 | 31 086 | 2 080 | 273 | 63 | 75 | 171 | 167 | 48 | 71 | 21 | 6 |
| Faulkner | 3 869 | 7.2 | 33 255 | 1 665 | 2 073 | 175 | 481 | 768 | 742 | 232 | 329 | 72 | 26 |
| Franklin | 552 | 2.3 | 30 593 | 2 180 | 218 | 19 | 88 | 151 | 147 | 55 | 62 | 16 | 4 |
| Fulton | 329 | 4.8 | 26 723 | 2 799 | 76 | 39 | 49 | 121 | 119 | 44 | 53 | 11 | 2 |
| Garland | 3 434 | 4.8 | 35 355 | 1 316 | 1 531 | 213 | 874 | 1 007 | 985 | 375 | 429 | 88 | 22 |
| Grant | 586 | 4.1 | 32 601 | 1 780 | 157 | 36 | 74 | 128 | 124 | 48 | 47 | 12 | 4 |
| Greene | 1 226 | 4.5 | 28 709 | 2 501 | 654 | 93 | 201 | 347 | 338 | 120 | 143 | 40 | 12 |
| Hempstead | 655 | 7.0 | 29 075 | 2 441 | 425 | 24 | 77 | 203 | 198 | 58 | 90 | 30 | 6 |
| Hot Spring | 912 | 5.5 | 27 724 | 2 652 | 379 | 37 | 117 | 287 | 280 | 100 | 124 | 29 | 8 |
| Howard | 386 | 5.5 | 27 810 | 2 639 | 280 | 41 | 50 | 126 | 123 | 41 | 58 | 15 | 3 |
| Independence | 1 146 | 3.6 | 31 088 | 2 078 | 680 | 113 | 178 | 322 | 314 | 109 | 138 | 31 | 10 |
| Izard | 355 | 4.1 | 26 469 | 2 826 | 123 | 27 | 55 | 139 | 136 | 52 | 55 | 11 | 3 |
| Jackson | 555 | 3.1 | 31 055 | 2 086 | 245 | 64 | 79 | 182 | 178 | 52 | 92 | 20 | 5 |
| Jefferson | 2 411 | 2.5 | 31 627 | 1 972 | 1 708 | 133 | 313 | 697 | 680 | 189 | 254 | 116 | 24 |
| Johnson | 632 | 3.0 | 24 551 | 3 003 | 348 | 28 | 81 | 196 | 190 | 69 | 78 | 24 | 5 |
| Lafayette | 204 | 2.8 | 27 125 | 2 749 | 58 | 20 | 32 | 75 | 73 | 23 | 33 | 11 | 2 |
| Lawrence | 469 | 2.3 | 27 323 | 2 715 | 169 | 47 | 73 | 173 | 169 | 55 | 82 | 18 | 5 |
| Lee | 316 | 9.6 | 30 642 | 2 165 | 94 | 92 | 36 | 93 | 91 | 25 | 41 | 18 | 3 |
| Lincoln | 364 | 2.4 | 25 991 | 2 880 | 137 | 21 | 31 | 98 | 94 | 30 | 40 | 15 | 3 |
| Little River | 392 | 3.5 | 30 182 | 2 255 | 238 | 23 | 43 | 114 | 111 | 42 | 46 | 12 | 3 |
| Logan | 597 | 3.3 | 26 773 | 2 793 | 234 | 33 | 81 | 218 | 213 | 70 | 102 | 22 | 5 |
| Lonoke | 2 286 | 5.9 | 32 972 | 1 712 | 544 | 144 | 280 | 497 | 482 | 155 | 206 | 50 | 14 |
| Madison | 346 | -1.6 | 21 921 | 3 087 | 130 | 29 | 58 | 109 | 106 | 44 | 40 | 12 | 3 |
| Marion | 442 | 4.5 | 26 684 | 2 804 | 139 | 25 | 84 | 166 | 162 | 70 | 61 | 15 | 4 |
| Miller | 1 468 | 6.0 | 33 539 | 1 596 | 646 | 167 | 181 | 364 | 354 | 108 | 165 | 50 | 9 |
| Mississippi | 1 505 | 7.3 | 32 741 | 1 751 | 1 034 | 148 | 164 | 419 | 409 | 116 | 175 | 75 | 16 |
| Monroe | 256 | 5.9 | 31 733 | 1 948 | 89 | 31 | 34 | 89 | 88 | 26 | 42 | 13 | 3 |
| Montgomery | 228 | 2.4 | 24 211 | 3 018 | 64 | 18 | 39 | 88 | 86 | 32 | 36 | 8 | 3 |
| Nevada | 270 | 5.6 | 29 912 | 2 307 | 101 | 11 | 37 | 100 | 98 | 28 | 51 | 12 | 2 |
| Newton | 216 | 5.6 | 26 127 | 2 867 | 42 | 14 | 33 | 74 | 73 | 29 | 29 | 9 | 2 |
| Ouachita | 802 | 2.9 | 31 006 | 2 100 | 329 | 27 | 116 | 257 | 251 | 86 | 106 | 34 | 7 |
| Perry | 333 | 3.4 | 32 041 | 1 875 | 61 | 22 | 40 | 96 | 94 | 36 | 39 | 10 | 3 |
| Phillips | 671 | 3.8 | 31 314 | 2 038 | 266 | 91 | 78 | 247 | 242 | 56 | 113 | 51 | 8 |
| Pike | 323 | 2.7 | 28 651 | 2 514 | 97 | 40 | 55 | 99 | 96 | 34 | 45 | 9 | 3 |
| Poinsett | 744 | 4.9 | 30 350 | 2 228 | 225 | 99 | 72 | 243 | 238 | 75 | 112 | 34 | 6 |
| Polk | 500 | 1.5 | 24 263 | 3 016 | 227 | 35 | 83 | 190 | 186 | 70 | 73 | 20 | 4 |
| Pope | 1 808 | 4.0 | 29 007 | 2 449 | 1 258 | 69 | 252 | 468 | 454 | 160 | 180 | 49 | 15 |
| Prairie | 274 | 3.6 | 31 744 | 1 943 | 63 | 44 | 32 | 83 | 81 | 27 | 38 | 8 | 3 |
| Pulaski | 16 973 | 4.3 | 43 938 | 443 | 15 267 | 1 525 | 3 298 | 3 131 | 3 046 | 942 | 1 271 | 396 | 90 |
| Randolph | 493 | 3.0 | 27 362 | 2 706 | 181 | 46 | 68 | 185 | 181 | 60 | 77 | 18 | 6 |
| St. Francis | 738 | 4.3 | 26 373 | 2 843 | 378 | 87 | 73 | 246 | 240 | 64 | 104 | 49 | 8 |
| Saline | 4 276 | 7.4 | 39 040 | 853 | 934 | 153 | 563 | 777 | 753 | 315 | 303 | 63 | 22 |
| Scott | 261 | 2.8 | 23 116 | 3 055 | 113 | 16 | 34 | 96 | 93 | 34 | 40 | 12 | 2 |
| Searcy | 208 | 3.5 | 25 926 | 2 889 | 59 | 23 | 29 | 85 | 84 | 30 | 38 | 9 | 2 |
| Sebastian | 4 710 | 4.8 | 37 052 | 1 072 | 3 398 | 444 | 942 | 979 | 951 | 328 | 397 | 111 | 32 |
| Sevier | 396 | -0.2 | 22 926 | 3 061 | 205 | 18 | 48 | 125 | 121 | 37 | 52 | 16 | 4 |
| Sharp | 438 | 3.3 | 25 214 | 2 947 | 136 | 10 | 82 | 201 | 198 | 79 | 83 | 18 | 4 |
| Stone | 320 | 4.6 | 25 411 | 2 936 | 99 | 26 | 68 | 131 | 128 | 49 | 55 | 12 | 3 |
| Union | 1 754 | 4.3 | 42 335 | 556 | 1 004 | 196 | 387 | 400 | 390 | 141 | 162 | 52 | 11 |
| Van Buren | 503 | 8.8 | 29 457 | 2 384 | 189 | 25 | 89 | 172 | 169 | 69 | 68 | 15 | 5 |
| Washington | 6 894 | 4.7 | 33 220 | 1 669 | 4 950 | 461 | 1 258 | 1 129 | 1 083 | 387 | 420 | 140 | 40 |
| White | 2 316 | 4.5 | 29 624 | 2 357 | 1 230 | 171 | 355 | 605 | 588 | 209 | 241 | 60 | 20 |
| Woodruff | 227 | 8.7 | 31 375 | 2 023 | 83 | 25 | 34 | 85 | 83 | 23 | 43 | 11 | 2 |
| Yell | 591 | 3.1 | 26 772 | 2 794 | 241 | 35 | 81 | 177 | 172 | 59 | 80 | 20 | 4 |

1. Based on the resident population estimated as of July 1 of the year shown.    2. Includes supplements to wages and salaries.

# Table B. States and Counties — Earnings, Social Security, and Housing

| STATE County | Earnings, 2011 | | | | | | | | | Social Security beneficiaries, December 2011 | | Supple-mental Security Income recipients, December 2011 | Housing units, 2010 | |
| | Total (mil dol) | Farm | Goods-related[1] | | Service-related and health | | | | Govern-ment | Number | Rate[2] | | Total | Percent change, 2000–2010 |
| | | | Total | Manu-facturing | Infor-mation and profes-sional and technical services | Retail trade | Finance, insur-ance, and real estate | Health care and social services | | | | | | |
| | 75 | 76 | 77 | 78 | 79 | 80 | 81 | 82 | 83 | 84 | 85 | 86 | 87 | 88 |

ARKANSAS—Cont'd

| STATE County | 75 | 76 | 77 | 78 | 79 | 80 | 81 | 82 | 83 | 84 | 85 | 86 | 87 | 88 |
|---|---|---|---|---|---|---|---|---|---|---|---|---|---|---|
| Cleveland | 47 | -7.3 | 11.4 | 7.7 | D | D | D | 7.9 | 37.9 | 2 030 | 234 | 263 | 4 064 | 6.0 |
| Columbia | 485 | 0.5 | 41.2 | 26.8 | 3.2 | 6.0 | 4.7 | D | 19.4 | 5 910 | 242 | 1 304 | 11 596 | 0.3 |
| Conway | 377 | 2.8 | 32.1 | 16.4 | 1.7 | 8.4 | 3.0 | 8.8 | 18.1 | 5 545 | 261 | 981 | 9 720 | 7.7 |
| Craighead | 2 422 | 3.0 | 19.6 | 14.2 | 4.2 | 7.8 | 5.7 | 21.1 | 17.3 | 18 760 | 191 | 3 847 | 40 515 | 15.3 |
| Crawford | 987 | 0.5 | 31.0 | 20.2 | D | 6.3 | 4.9 | 7.1 | 13.3 | 14 255 | 230 | 2 070 | 26 115 | 22.5 |
| Crittenden | 879 | 6.1 | D | 11.3 | 2.3 | 7.1 | 5.1 | 10.9 | 18.1 | 9 615 | 190 | 3 655 | 21 489 | 4.8 |
| Cross | 294 | 13.5 | 12.8 | 10.1 | D | 9.4 | 7.3 | 10.4 | 20.9 | 4 360 | 245 | 938 | 7 853 | -2.2 |
| Dallas | 128 | 1.0 | 24.7 | 21.0 | D | 8.5 | 3.1 | D | 14.3 | 2 200 | 273 | 444 | 4 305 | -2.2 |
| Desha | 276 | 20.2 | 22.2 | 19.3 | 1.9 | 6.0 | 4.7 | D | 17.6 | 3 160 | 248 | 815 | 6 261 | -6.0 |
| Drew | 336 | 6.2 | 14.0 | 10.3 | 2.3 | 8.6 | 4.2 | D | 31.0 | 3 975 | 215 | 774 | 8 408 | 1.5 |
| Faulkner | 2 248 | 0.1 | 23.4 | 9.3 | 12.7 | 7.6 | 4.7 | 11.1 | 18.2 | 18 350 | 158 | 2 609 | 46 612 | 34.9 |
| Franklin | 237 | -1.6 | 32.9 | 19.6 | 2.1 | 8.0 | 4.6 | D | 24.9 | 4 600 | 255 | 583 | 8 021 | 4.5 |
| Fulton | 115 | 10.2 | D | 3.4 | D | 7.2 | 5.8 | D | 27.9 | 3 770 | 307 | 494 | 6 778 | 13.5 |
| Garland | 1 744 | 0.3 | 13.5 | 6.3 | 5.9 | 11.7 | 6.2 | 22.7 | 16.9 | 28 795 | 296 | 3 636 | 50 548 | 12.4 |
| Grant | 194 | 1.4 | D | 18.8 | 3.3 | 7.8 | 4.7 | D | 23.7 | 3 790 | 211 | 416 | 7 758 | 11.5 |
| Greene | 747 | 5.7 | D | 34.1 | D | 7.2 | 3.9 | 10.2 | 15.9 | 10 180 | 238 | 1 810 | 17 892 | 10.7 |
| Hempstead | 449 | -0.5 | D | 17.2 | 1.1 | 6.2 | 2.9 | D | 21.2 | 4 880 | 216 | 1 039 | 10 419 | 2.5 |
| Hot Spring | 416 | 1.1 | D | 19.0 | D | 6.8 | 3.8 | 10.5 | 22.9 | 8 185 | 249 | 1 195 | 14 332 | 7.1 |
| Howard | 321 | 5.4 | D | 43.5 | D | 6.6 | 2.1 | D | 13.5 | 3 385 | 244 | 515 | 6 238 | -0.9 |
| Independence | 793 | 2.6 | 27.4 | 22.5 | D | 7.8 | 4.1 | 18.9 | 14.8 | 9 215 | 250 | 1 347 | 16 187 | 9.1 |
| Izard | 149 | 3.6 | D | 6.6 | D | 8.7 | 7.1 | 13.7 | 33.8 | 4 335 | 323 | 514 | 7 232 | 9.7 |
| Jackson | 309 | 10.1 | D | 18.5 | 2.1 | 7.9 | 3.6 | D | 23.0 | 4 450 | 249 | 914 | 7 601 | -4.5 |
| Jefferson | 1 841 | 2.8 | D | 16.8 | D | 6.3 | 3.8 | 12.7 | 30.6 | 15 985 | 210 | 4 473 | 33 006 | -3.9 |
| Johnson | 375 | -1.0 | D | 29.9 | 1.7 | 7.2 | 3.6 | D | 17.5 | 6 000 | 233 | 983 | 11 311 | 14.0 |
| Lafayette | 77 | 17.7 | 16.8 | 2.1 | D | 5.0 | 3.0 | D | 23.4 | 2 005 | 267 | 511 | 4 353 | -4.5 |
| Lawrence | 216 | 8.5 | 14.7 | 8.7 | D | 9.2 | 4.1 | D | 28.9 | 4 905 | 286 | 897 | 8 000 | -1.1 |
| Lee | 186 | 37.7 | D | D | D | 4.6 | 2.2 | D | 23.0 | 2 355 | 228 | 895 | 4 356 | -8.6 |
| Lincoln | 158 | 11.3 | D | 9.0 | D | 3.4 | 2.3 | D | 43.2 | 2 585 | 185 | 546 | 4 860 | -1.9 |
| Little River | 260 | 2.2 | D | 50.0 | D | 5.4 | 2.1 | 2.7 | 17.9 | 3 335 | 257 | 435 | 6 460 | 0.4 |
| Logan | 266 | 3.9 | 28.1 | 19.2 | 2.4 | 8.4 | 4.9 | 10.5 | 26.9 | 6 150 | 276 | 909 | 10 108 | 1.7 |
| Lonoke | 688 | 7.2 | 20.3 | 10.8 | 3.6 | 9.5 | 7.2 | 9.0 | 22.1 | 12 555 | 181 | 1 809 | 27 239 | 31.3 |
| Madison | 159 | 3.8 | D | 25.9 | 3.4 | 8.6 | 3.6 | 5.3 | 21.6 | 3 935 | 249 | 431 | 7 481 | 14.4 |
| Marion | 164 | 0.8 | 37.3 | 33.2 | 4.2 | 9.6 | 7.5 | 6.8 | 19.3 | 5 720 | 345 | 580 | 9 354 | 13.6 |
| Miller | 813 | 2.7 | 31.1 | 22.2 | D | 6.8 | 4.5 | 4.9 | 14.9 | 8 825 | 202 | 1 981 | 19 281 | 8.8 |
| Mississippi | 1 182 | 6.7 | 44.0 | 39.6 | 5.0 | 4.9 | 2.3 | D | 12.9 | 10 160 | 221 | 3 537 | 20 459 | -8.3 |
| Monroe | 120 | 15.3 | 7.4 | 3.8 | 2.0 | 9.0 | 6.2 | D | 20.0 | 2 310 | 286 | 630 | 4 455 | -12.1 |
| Montgomery | 82 | 2.2 | D | 4.7 | D | 7.8 | 6.2 | D | 34.1 | 2 760 | 293 | 342 | 5 763 | 14.2 |
| Nevada | 112 | 1.9 | D | D | D | 6.8 | 2.6 | 12.5 | 19.8 | 2 440 | 271 | 557 | 4 563 | -4.0 |
| Newton | 56 | 4.6 | D | 3.3 | D | 6.4 | D | D | 41.7 | 2 655 | 321 | 437 | 4 664 | 8.1 |
| Ouachita | 356 | 0.3 | 19.0 | 12.8 | D | 9.1 | 4.3 | D | 28.4 | 6 965 | 269 | 1 507 | 13 121 | -2.4 |
| Perry | 83 | 10.4 | D | D | D | 5.9 | D | D | 25.8 | 3 000 | 288 | 420 | 4 907 | 4.4 |
| Phillips | 357 | 20.1 | 6.6 | 4.6 | D | 7.1 | 4.0 | 13.1 | 22.4 | 5 115 | 239 | 2 148 | 10 126 | -6.7 |
| Pike | 137 | 18.1 | D | 5.2 | 1.5 | 8.3 | D | D | 24.2 | 2 975 | 264 | 370 | 5 580 | 0.8 |
| Poinsett | 324 | 18.8 | D | 9.1 | D | 6.6 | 5.6 | 6.5 | 20.2 | 6 585 | 269 | 1 657 | 10 923 | -1.2 |
| Polk | 263 | -1.4 | D | 17.9 | 3.0 | 9.7 | 5.6 | D | 21.7 | 6 010 | 292 | 706 | 10 002 | 8.3 |
| Pope | 1 327 | -0.2 | 25.5 | 16.6 | 3.2 | 7.1 | 3.5 | 10.0 | 17.6 | 13 225 | 212 | 1 986 | 25 551 | 11.8 |
| Prairie | 107 | 35.1 | D | D | D | 5.1 | 3.3 | 6.0 | 18.9 | 2 295 | 266 | 357 | 4 503 | -6.0 |
| Pulaski | 16 792 | 0.1 | 10.6 | 5.1 | 11.6 | 6.2 | 8.2 | 12.2 | 26.3 | 72 520 | 188 | 16 114 | 175 555 | 8.9 |
| Randolph | 226 | 10.6 | D | 11.9 | D | 8.0 | 3.1 | 18.1 | 23.0 | 5 170 | 287 | 753 | 8 513 | 3.0 |
| St. Francis | 464 | 10.1 | 9.1 | 6.4 | D | 7.7 | 3.9 | 13.8 | 32.7 | 5 610 | 201 | 2 067 | 10 903 | -3.0 |
| Saline | 1 087 | 0.0 | D | 7.0 | 3.6 | 15.8 | 4.5 | 13.1 | 24.3 | 23 240 | 212 | 2 309 | 44 811 | 32.5 |
| Scott | 128 | 1.8 | D | 30.9 | D | 6.5 | 3.5 | D | 22.4 | 3 070 | 272 | 446 | 5 193 | 5.5 |
| Searcy | 82 | 1.9 | D | 6.4 | D | 8.0 | 5.6 | 13.3 | 28.2 | 2 775 | 345 | 477 | 4 900 | 14.2 |
| Sebastian | 3 843 | 0.0 | 29.5 | 20.7 | 7.8 | 6.5 | 4.2 | 15.8 | 12.8 | 26 335 | 207 | 4 165 | 54 651 | 10.8 |
| Sevier | 223 | 1.9 | D | D | 1.0 | 7.9 | 3.8 | D | 26.0 | 3 145 | 182 | 439 | 6 887 | 7.0 |
| Sharp | 146 | 2.3 | D | 3.6 | 4.2 | 10.2 | 9.1 | D | 27.3 | 6 720 | 387 | 859 | 9 822 | 5.1 |
| Stone | 125 | 1.2 | 11.5 | 5.1 | D | 15.6 | 5.3 | 16.4 | 27.0 | 4 295 | 341 | 638 | 6 712 | 17.4 |
| Union | 1 200 | -0.3 | 35.4 | 18.7 | 2.2 | 6.2 | 4.6 | 9.7 | 11.6 | 11 030 | 266 | 2 054 | 19 653 | -4.9 |
| Van Buren | 214 | 1.9 | 17.5 | 1.6 | 2.6 | 8.6 | 4.7 | 11.4 | 18.4 | 5 705 | 334 | 638 | 10 345 | 12.9 |
| Washington | 5 412 | 0.3 | 16.9 | 11.6 | 5.2 | 6.7 | 5.5 | 12.9 | 20.1 | 30 620 | 148 | 3 997 | 87 808 | 36.4 |
| White | 1 401 | 1.3 | 24.6 | 9.5 | 3.1 | 8.2 | 4.6 | 13.2 | 13.9 | 17 175 | 220 | 2 407 | 32 488 | 17.7 |
| Woodruff | 109 | 22.8 | D | 10.6 | D | 4.7 | 2.9 | 9.3 | 24.7 | 2 065 | 286 | 476 | 3 893 | -4.7 |
| Yell | 276 | 2.0 | D | 29.2 | D | 5.3 | 5.1 | D | 26.9 | 5 080 | 230 | 770 | 9 752 | 6.5 |

1. Includes mining, construction, and manufacturing.    2. Per 1,000 resident population enumerated in the 2010 census.

| STATE County | Housing units, 2007–2011 | | | | | | | | Civilian labor force, 2012 | | Unemployment | | Civilian employment,[6] 2007–2011 | | |
|---|---|---|---|---|---|---|---|---|---|---|---|---|---|---|---|
| | Occupied units | | | | | | | | | | | | | Percent | |
| | | | Owner-occupied | | | Renter-occupied | | | | | | | | | |
| | | | | Median owner cost as a percent of income | | | | | | | | | | | Con-struction, produc-tion, and mainte-nance occu-pations |
| | | | | With a mort-gage | Without a mort-gage[2] | Median rent[3] | Median rent as a per-cent of income | Sub-stand-ard units[4] (percent) | | Percent change, 2011–2012 | | | | Manage-ment, business, science and arts | |
| | Total | Percent | Median value[1] | | | | | | Total | | Total | Rate[5] | Total | | |
| | 89 | 90 | 91 | 92 | 93 | 94 | 95 | 96 | 97 | 98 | 99 | 100 | 101 | 102 | 103 |
| ARKANSAS—Cont'd | | | | | | | | | | | | | | | |
| Cleveland | 3 292 | 77.6 | 74 900 | 19.9 | 11.6 | 579 | 30.7 | 2.4 | 4 056 | -1.7 | 283 | 7.0 | 3 381 | 32.8 | 31.7 |
| Columbia | 9 799 | 71.1 | 79 500 | 18.5 | 11.2 | 544 | 36.0 | 3.0 | 10 182 | -3.6 | 866 | 8.5 | 9 896 | 30.7 | 27.2 |
| Conway | 8 137 | 73.6 | 82 900 | 20.2 | 12.5 | 551 | 32.0 | 3.0 | 9 878 | -3.8 | 753 | 7.6 | 8 084 | 26.7 | 37.7 |
| Craighead | 36 815 | 60.2 | 111 900 | 19.3 | 10.5 | 621 | 30.6 | 2.5 | 49 181 | 1.0 | 3 298 | 6.7 | 43 232 | 34.3 | 24.7 |
| Crawford | 23 174 | 71.7 | 99 400 | 20.8 | 10.6 | 581 | 27.7 | 3.2 | 27 762 | -0.4 | 2 064 | 7.4 | 26 723 | 27.0 | 33.0 |
| Crittenden | 18 757 | 56.9 | 99 200 | 23.1 | 12.7 | 650 | 33.6 | 4.8 | 20 872 | -0.3 | 2 328 | 11.2 | 20 864 | 25.9 | 29.3 |
| Cross | 6 823 | 68.0 | 73 600 | 22.1 | 13.2 | 622 | 25.7 | 1.4 | 8 102 | -3.1 | 662 | 8.2 | 7 757 | 22.5 | 34.4 |
| Dallas | 3 065 | 69.5 | 58 400 | 21.2 | 11.6 | 435 | 34.1 | 4.8 | 3 499 | -2.9 | 361 | 10.3 | 2 781 | 23.3 | 41.3 |
| Desha | 5 313 | 58.8 | 58 100 | 19.0 | 11.3 | 525 | 32.8 | 2.0 | 5 494 | -2.9 | 576 | 10.5 | 5 363 | 32.7 | 35.2 |
| Drew | 7 378 | 66.5 | 73 500 | 19.6 | 12.3 | 576 | 35.2 | 3.2 | 7 906 | -2.7 | 857 | 10.8 | 7 798 | 33.7 | 28.0 |
| Faulkner | 41 540 | 65.9 | 130 900 | 19.6 | 9.9 | 688 | 29.5 | 2.0 | 58 554 | 0.8 | 3 850 | 6.6 | 53 485 | 34.6 | 24.3 |
| Franklin | 6 763 | 75.4 | 85 800 | 20.0 | 9.9 | 554 | 27.1 | 2.1 | 7 891 | 0.0 | 531 | 6.7 | 7 145 | 23.1 | 34.4 |
| Fulton | 4 819 | 78.4 | 87 300 | 22.6 | 10.0 | 492 | 28.8 | 1.2 | 5 216 | 0.0 | 356 | 6.8 | 4 528 | 28.5 | 31.9 |
| Garland | 40 002 | 70.1 | 128 400 | 23.9 | 10.8 | 693 | 30.5 | 2.6 | 42 431 | 0.6 | 3 183 | 7.5 | 39 255 | 30.3 | 23.5 |
| Grant | 6 629 | 80.9 | 102 500 | 19.7 | 9.9 | 672 | 24.5 | 2.8 | 8 396 | 0.4 | 542 | 6.5 | 8 075 | 27.3 | 35.8 |
| Greene | 16 378 | 66.3 | 92 800 | 20.3 | 10.8 | 603 | 28.6 | 2.5 | 19 047 | 0.7 | 1 682 | 8.8 | 17 747 | 24.9 | 37.2 |
| Hempstead | 8 719 | 69.8 | 69 000 | 19.5 | 11.1 | 549 | 29.7 | 3.3 | 10 975 | 0.7 | 785 | 7.2 | 9 936 | 23.3 | 39.4 |
| Hot Spring | 11 998 | 74.6 | 81 600 | 21.6 | 11.4 | 578 | 23.6 | 2.4 | 15 883 | 0.3 | 1 035 | 6.5 | 13 164 | 26.4 | 32.5 |
| Howard | 5 015 | 67.4 | 71 900 | 20.9 | 11.1 | 543 | 27.3 | 5.1 | 5 962 | -3.5 | 425 | 7.1 | 6 228 | 23.8 | 42.5 |
| Independence | 14 776 | 72.0 | 86 700 | 19.9 | 10.7 | 565 | 31.7 | 3.5 | 16 440 | -3.3 | 1 427 | 8.7 | 15 437 | 25.9 | 33.9 |
| Izard | 5 891 | 76.2 | 79 200 | 22.2 | 12.9 | 492 | 33.3 | 2.8 | 5 429 | -0.7 | 445 | 8.2 | 4 774 | 27.5 | 28.7 |
| Jackson | 6 383 | 70.7 | 58 100 | 20.4 | 13.1 | 528 | 30.9 | 2.4 | 7 321 | -1.3 | 704 | 9.6 | 6 071 | 24.7 | 33.8 |
| Jefferson | 28 062 | 64.5 | 78 400 | 20.0 | 12.1 | 641 | 32.7 | 2.7 | 33 952 | -1.9 | 3 203 | 9.4 | 30 252 | 27.9 | 25.9 |
| Johnson | 9 626 | 70.2 | 86 200 | 18.9 | 9.9 | 565 | 32.0 | 3.7 | 11 334 | -2.8 | 767 | 6.8 | 10 341 | 19.1 | 44.5 |
| Lafayette | 2 746 | 74.4 | 50 600 | 20.6 | 12.1 | 531 | 28.1 | 0.7 | 2 741 | -3.4 | 272 | 9.9 | 2 706 | 25.6 | 31.5 |
| Lawrence | 6 693 | 69.8 | 58 700 | 20.3 | 11.5 | 495 | 28.7 | 2.4 | 7 161 | -2.4 | 645 | 9.0 | 6 517 | 24.0 | 36.1 |
| Lee | 3 484 | 64.0 | 51 600 | 25.0 | 15.0 | 498 | 32.9 | 1.7 | 3 184 | -3.5 | 360 | 11.3 | 3 030 | 19.7 | 26.7 |
| Lincoln | 4 073 | 68.3 | 61 900 | 19.0 | 10.6 | 522 | 30.8 | 3.5 | 5 049 | -1.0 | 460 | 9.1 | 4 414 | 22.3 | 43.0 |
| Little River | 5 369 | 77.9 | 78 200 | 18.3 | 10.6 | 521 | 26.9 | 2.0 | 6 078 | 0.8 | 422 | 6.9 | 5 724 | 20.3 | 42.2 |
| Logan | 8 285 | 78.2 | 80 200 | 18.6 | 9.9 | 478 | 32.2 | 3.2 | 9 861 | 0.3 | 752 | 7.6 | 8 920 | 27.0 | 37.2 |
| Lonoke | 24 667 | 74.2 | 117 200 | 20.5 | 9.9 | 670 | 27.2 | 3.0 | 32 908 | 0.5 | 2 007 | 6.1 | 30 882 | 30.9 | 26.1 |
| Madison | 5 887 | 77.6 | 99 400 | 21.8 | 9.9 | 532 | 27.3 | 3.8 | 7 460 | 1.7 | 394 | 5.3 | 6 495 | 22.9 | 40.3 |
| Marion | 7 055 | 81.6 | 92 100 | 22.7 | 11.4 | 557 | 28.5 | 3.5 | 6 545 | -1.1 | 531 | 8.1 | 6 393 | 25.7 | 29.7 |
| Miller | 16 552 | 65.6 | 89 400 | 21.0 | 10.5 | 660 | 29.1 | 2.2 | 20 474 | -0.6 | 1 363 | 6.7 | 18 164 | 24.1 | 32.1 |
| Mississippi | 17 136 | 59.2 | 72 400 | 18.5 | 12.6 | 577 | 28.7 | 4.5 | 21 537 | -2.1 | 2 158 | 10.0 | 17 946 | 25.5 | 39.0 |
| Monroe | 3 462 | 62.9 | 58 900 | 19.8 | 14.2 | 507 | 33.2 | 2.5 | 3 463 | -1.3 | 290 | 8.4 | 2 989 | 27.1 | 33.1 |
| Montgomery | 3 725 | 84.6 | 75 500 | 20.9 | 11.6 | 477 | 34.8 | 3.2 | 3 845 | -3.5 | 296 | 7.7 | 3 522 | 30.6 | 37.5 |
| Nevada | 3 707 | 73.4 | 57 800 | 22.6 | 11.3 | 591 | 23.0 | 3.9 | 4 318 | -0.2 | 298 | 6.9 | 3 601 | 24.3 | 40.4 |
| Newton | 3 506 | 82.2 | 76 400 | 23.0 | 9.9 | 367 | 25.8 | 5.5 | 3 484 | -1.2 | 263 | 7.5 | 3 658 | 24.7 | 39.5 |
| Ouachita | 10 782 | 70.1 | 63 400 | 19.6 | 11.6 | 499 | 28.4 | 1.9 | 11 338 | -5.1 | 1 072 | 9.5 | 10 157 | 27.0 | 34.0 |
| Perry | 4 013 | 82.8 | 82 400 | 18.9 | 9.9 | 666 | 25.6 | 3.9 | 4 678 | 0.5 | 375 | 8.0 | 4 450 | 25.9 | 41.6 |
| Phillips | 8 102 | 55.6 | 60 400 | 23.0 | 12.2 | 573 | 35.1 | 5.2 | 8 284 | -3.7 | 901 | 10.9 | 7 561 | 32.5 | 23.3 |
| Pike | 4 123 | 75.0 | 74 900 | 17.6 | 11.6 | 478 | 28.6 | 2.4 | 4 383 | -6.2 | 380 | 8.7 | 4 420 | 23.8 | 43.3 |
| Poinsett | 9 427 | 66.1 | 66 000 | 21.3 | 12.5 | 467 | 30.0 | 3.0 | 10 601 | 0.3 | 826 | 7.8 | 9 601 | 22.2 | 36.8 |
| Polk | 7 979 | 77.5 | 82 500 | 24.5 | 9.9 | 534 | 28.8 | 1.7 | 8 194 | -2.3 | 634 | 7.7 | 8 254 | 23.6 | 36.6 |
| Pope | 22 599 | 69.5 | 103 300 | 20.6 | 9.9 | 607 | 29.2 | 2.5 | 29 987 | -1.2 | 2 127 | 7.1 | 28 136 | 27.1 | 28.8 |
| Prairie | 3 685 | 73.6 | 73 800 | 20.4 | 11.7 | 501 | 27.9 | 2.3 | 3 877 | -2.5 | 283 | 7.3 | 3 624 | 28.4 | 31.1 |
| Pulaski | 154 346 | 60.6 | 139 800 | 21.4 | 11.3 | 752 | 30.7 | 2.4 | 188 199 | 0.7 | 12 469 | 6.6 | 181 056 | 38.8 | 17.5 |
| Randolph | 7 271 | 75.6 | 69 800 | 20.2 | 11.7 | 495 | 31.7 | 2.6 | 7 297 | -3.7 | 721 | 9.9 | 6 627 | 30.4 | 34.5 |
| St. Francis | 9 060 | 55.3 | 66 400 | 22.3 | 14.8 | 548 | 34.3 | 2.8 | 9 635 | -1.1 | 1 056 | 11.0 | 8 743 | 24.7 | 30.9 |
| Saline | 40 132 | 76.9 | 135 300 | 20.1 | 10.1 | 754 | 29.1 | 2.5 | 53 195 | 0.7 | 3 203 | 6.0 | 49 543 | 33.2 | 24.4 |
| Scott | 4 156 | 74.5 | 76 700 | 20.1 | 9.9 | 527 | 26.4 | 4.9 | 4 678 | -1.0 | 307 | 6.6 | 4 283 | 25.5 | 43.8 |
| Searcy | 3 421 | 75.2 | 79 000 | 24.9 | 10.3 | 431 | 33.2 | 3.5 | 3 308 | -3.2 | 256 | 7.7 | 3 231 | 20.9 | 32.1 |
| Sebastian | 48 441 | 63.3 | 113 100 | 19.9 | 10.8 | 591 | 28.7 | 3.4 | 60 062 | -0.3 | 4 355 | 7.3 | 54 923 | 29.6 | 29.8 |
| Sevier | 5 825 | 72.8 | 73 900 | 24.1 | 9.9 | 485 | 27.8 | 6.0 | 6 651 | -3.5 | 519 | 7.8 | 6 618 | 20.6 | 48.2 |
| Sharp | 7 106 | 81.5 | 77 300 | 23.4 | 11.8 | 566 | 40.4 | 3.8 | 6 085 | -4.2 | 604 | 9.9 | 5 610 | 28.0 | 33.5 |
| Stone | 5 141 | 80.1 | 93 200 | 26.9 | 10.9 | 484 | 27.9 | 6.0 | 4 265 | -5.8 | 414 | 9.7 | 4 717 | 29.2 | 30.1 |
| Union | 16 757 | 69.8 | 72 300 | 18.1 | 11.6 | 572 | 30.2 | 3.4 | 17 445 | -2.4 | 1 497 | 8.6 | 16 842 | 28.4 | 31.3 |
| Van Buren | 7 097 | 77.1 | 81 600 | 22.6 | 11.1 | 537 | 28.4 | 3.8 | 7 224 | -2.4 | 642 | 8.9 | 5 844 | 19.3 | 38.4 |
| Washington | 76 841 | 56.3 | 153 700 | 22.4 | 10.5 | 671 | 29.9 | 5.4 | 105 303 | 2.2 | 5 653 | 5.4 | 98 383 | 33.7 | 24.1 |
| White | 29 529 | 68.2 | 94 400 | 19.8 | 10.3 | 590 | 28.3 | 3.9 | 34 825 | -0.3 | 2 775 | 8.0 | 32 539 | 27.9 | 28.6 |
| Woodruff | 3 256 | 58.9 | 57 300 | 20.5 | 11.2 | 411 | 28.3 | 2.7 | 3 154 | -3.0 | 338 | 10.7 | 2 982 | 25.5 | 34.2 |
| Yell | 7 927 | 70.8 | 79 900 | 19.6 | 10.5 | 555 | 27.3 | 8.7 | 10 030 | -1.3 | 601 | 6.0 | 9 056 | 18.7 | 42.0 |

1. Specified owner-occupied units.    2. A value of 9.9 represents 9.9 percent or less.    3. Specified renter-occupied units. A value of 10.0 represents 10 percent or less.    4. Overcrowded or lacking complete plumbing facilities.    5. Percent of civilian labor force.    6. Persons 16 years old and over.

| STATE County | Private nonfarm establishments, employment and payroll, 2011 | | | | | | | | | Agriculture, 2007 | | | |
|---|---|---|---|---|---|---|---|---|---|---|---|---|---|
| | | Employment | | | | | | Annual payroll | | Farms | | | |
| | | | | | | | | | | | Percent with: | | |
| | Number of establishments | Total | Health care and social assistance | Manufacturing | Retail trade | Finance and insurance | Professional, scientific, and technical services | Total (mil dol) | Average per employee (dollars) | Number | Fewer than 50 acres | 500 acres or more | Farm operators whose principal occupation is farming (percent) |
| | 104 | 105 | 106 | 107 | 108 | 109 | 110 | 111 | 112 | 113 | 114 | 115 | 116 |
| **ARKANSAS—Cont'd** | | | | | | | | | | | | | |
| Cleveland | 77 | 505 | D | 68 | D | 18 | D | 13 | 26 384 | 241 | 44.4 | 6.2 | 61.4 |
| Columbia | 592 | 7 612 | 1 281 | 2 354 | 1 079 | 281 | 168 | 251 | 33 000 | 306 | 32.7 | 7.2 | 42.8 |
| Conway | 411 | 5 202 | D | D | 905 | 138 | 108 | 162 | 31 155 | 994 | 33.3 | 7.5 | 49.5 |
| Craighead | 2 404 | 36 274 | 8 214 | 5 489 | 6 269 | 1 156 | 941 | 1 216 | 33 522 | 736 | 42.9 | 25.0 | 47.7 |
| Crawford | 1 080 | 21 031 | 1 940 | 4 150 | 1 937 | 419 | 277 | 601 | 28 594 | 1 026 | 51.4 | 3.7 | 37.3 |
| Crittenden | 842 | 13 361 | 2 042 | 1 547 | 2 097 | 275 | 239 | 400 | 29 971 | 266 | 13.9 | 51.9 | 69.2 |
| Cross | 363 | 4 191 | 773 | 620 | 759 | 267 | 76 | 119 | 28 463 | 364 | 23.9 | 38.7 | 61.0 |
| Dallas | 207 | 2 463 | 750 | D | 376 | 61 | 19 | 63 | 25 456 | 106 | 28.3 | 8.5 | 32.1 |
| Desha | 323 | 3 531 | 582 | D | 601 | 152 | 67 | 109 | 30 886 | 273 | 22.0 | 49.1 | 69.2 |
| Drew | 413 | 4 842 | 996 | 811 | 915 | 176 | 114 | 126 | 25 930 | 368 | 29.3 | 15.5 | 40.5 |
| Faulkner | 2 372 | 35 818 | 4 964 | 3 903 | 5 302 | 1 055 | 922 | 1 307 | 36 494 | 1 341 | 43.0 | 4.8 | 35.3 |
| Franklin | 268 | 3 180 | 514 | 914 | 445 | 153 | 82 | 100 | 31 292 | 759 | 29.6 | 10.1 | 48.1 |
| Fulton | 175 | 1 441 | 492 | 128 | 225 | D | 45 | 34 | 23 555 | 702 | 24.6 | 13.0 | 40.7 |
| Garland | 2 663 | 31 328 | 7 135 | 2 319 | 5 748 | 930 | 1 528 | 891 | 28 452 | 439 | 56.9 | 2.1 | 38.3 |
| Grant | 266 | 2 904 | D | 1 152 | 447 | 90 | 53 | 87 | 29 875 | 282 | 50.4 | 3.9 | 43.6 |
| Greene | 785 | 14 012 | 1 713 | 4 550 | 1 800 | 574 | D | 385 | 27 506 | 770 | 37.8 | 17.1 | 45.1 |
| Hempstead | 394 | 6 716 | 961 | 1 884 | 879 | 181 | 87 | 244 | 36 320 | 894 | 30.4 | 11.3 | 43.6 |
| Hot Spring | 485 | 5 974 | 1 177 | 1 363 | 904 | 224 | 102 | 190 | 31 848 | 644 | 49.5 | 3.4 | 38.5 |
| Howard | 290 | 5 838 | 788 | 3 248 | 639 | 107 | 50 | 150 | 25 648 | 592 | 28.5 | 6.6 | 53.4 |
| Independence | 784 | 14 820 | 3 247 | 4 094 | 1 757 | D | 213 | 474 | 32 013 | 1 121 | 32.0 | 9.7 | 42.9 |
| Izard | 209 | 1 981 | 722 | D | 418 | D | D | 51 | 25 604 | 639 | 21.0 | 13.1 | 43.5 |
| Jackson | 314 | 3 692 | 862 | 947 | 717 | D | 94 | 118 | 32 080 | 445 | 24.7 | 33.7 | 58.0 |
| Jefferson | 1 408 | 22 971 | 4 736 | 4 857 | 3 458 | 834 | 1 193 | 781 | 34 007 | 489 | 36.6 | 26.0 | 50.3 |
| Johnson | 387 | 7 455 | 1 101 | 2 652 | 901 | 145 | 85 | 192 | 25 786 | 607 | 33.1 | 6.4 | 48.1 |
| Lafayette | 112 | 826 | 175 | D | 141 | 57 | 23 | 32 | 39 068 | 313 | 31.6 | 15.7 | 52.1 |
| Lawrence | 284 | 2 789 | 599 | 348 | 587 | D | D | 73 | 26 289 | 592 | 20.4 | 25.0 | 54.2 |
| Lee | 130 | 992 | 302 | D | D | D | 37 | 29 | 29 580 | 251 | 19.5 | 45.4 | 68.9 |
| Lincoln | 157 | 1 663 | D | D | 197 | D | D | 50 | 30 162 | 384 | 28.9 | 20.1 | 53.9 |
| Little River | 166 | 2 837 | 334 | D | 361 | D | D | 132 | 46 464 | 482 | 31.7 | 10.2 | 36.7 |
| Logan | 389 | 3 919 | 765 | D | 684 | 267 | 63 | 107 | 27 364 | 942 | 31.4 | 5.9 | 46.9 |
| Lonoke | 987 | 10 709 | 2 102 | 1 478 | 2 275 | 413 | 314 | 264 | 24 669 | 832 | 34.3 | 21.6 | 48.4 |
| Madison | 184 | 2 368 | 262 | 1 021 | 446 | 75 | D | 62 | 26 133 | 1 339 | 30.2 | 8.7 | 38.0 |
| Marion | 225 | 3 030 | 305 | 1 485 | 573 | 115 | 47 | 77 | 25 302 | 463 | 28.1 | 13.6 | 44.7 |
| Miller | 713 | 11 385 | 956 | D | 1 447 | 234 | 258 | 374 | 32 806 | 601 | 41.8 | 10.8 | 37.4 |
| Mississippi | 856 | 15 660 | 1 828 | 5 123 | 1 856 | 326 | 132 | 616 | 39 311 | 369 | 16.3 | 52.8 | 70.5 |
| Monroe | 187 | 1 621 | 344 | 102 | 276 | 64 | D | 40 | 24 951 | 229 | 18.8 | 48.5 | 65.1 |
| Montgomery | 141 | 942 | D | D | 156 | 57 | 16 | 25 | 26 306 | 456 | 29.8 | 6.6 | 42.1 |
| Nevada | 126 | 1 810 | D | D | D | 41 | D | 56 | 30 681 | 395 | 33.9 | 6.1 | 34.9 |
| Newton | 90 | 647 | 224 | D | 85 | D | 16 | 14 | 21 419 | 636 | 28.9 | 6.3 | 34.3 |
| Ouachita | 539 | 7 869 | 1 223 | 2 435 | 1 059 | 229 | D | 266 | 33 855 | 222 | 36.0 | 5.0 | 36.0 |
| Perry | 109 | 848 | 205 | D | 190 | D | D | 27 | 31 810 | 453 | 38.4 | 5.5 | 39.1 |
| Phillips | 445 | 4 461 | 1 137 | 341 | 1 076 | D | 86 | 121 | 27 229 | 307 | 20.8 | 54.1 | 70.0 |
| Pike | 179 | 1 593 | D | 230 | 236 | 92 | D | 38 | 23 677 | 425 | 32.5 | 11.5 | 48.5 |
| Poinsett | 356 | 3 713 | 591 | 722 | 959 | 167 | 40 | 99 | 26 638 | 418 | 20.8 | 50.7 | 68.9 |
| Polk | 473 | 5 193 | 1 052 | 1 245 | 944 | 156 | 94 | 127 | 24 531 | 1 007 | 43.2 | 4.4 | 42.7 |
| Pope | 1 505 | 22 622 | 3 002 | 4 591 | 3 420 | 859 | 491 | 712 | 31 479 | 1 080 | 41.9 | 5.9 | 40.4 |
| Prairie | 154 | 913 | 220 | D | 174 | D | 30 | 22 | 23 926 | 539 | 19.9 | 32.5 | 54.4 |
| Pulaski | 12 007 | 208 571 | 48 368 | 13 054 | 25 020 | 12 702 | 10 854 | 8 531 | 40 904 | 484 | 59.3 | 8.7 | 39.7 |
| Randolph | 328 | 3 591 | D | 831 | 615 | 113 | D | 87 | 24 204 | 766 | 28.5 | 14.8 | 38.0 |
| St. Francis | 479 | 5 644 | 1 325 | D | 1 153 | 205 | D | 147 | 26 042 | 310 | 26.1 | 32.6 | 58.1 |
| Saline | 1 745 | 18 502 | 4 116 | 1 191 | 3 966 | 528 | 543 | 523 | 28 275 | 371 | 53.9 | 4.9 | 38.0 |
| Scott | 151 | 2 075 | 252 | D | 301 | 41 | D | 57 | 27 270 | 593 | 30.4 | 5.7 | 58.3 |
| Searcy | 117 | 1 028 | 360 | 133 | 260 | 45 | 31 | 21 | 20 358 | 617 | 19.9 | 16.0 | 39.2 |
| Sebastian | 3 504 | 61 739 | 10 922 | 14 522 | 8 219 | 1 694 | 1 619 | 2 228 | 36 081 | 931 | 51.2 | 3.2 | 35.3 |
| Sevier | 264 | 4 961 | 511 | D | 707 | 145 | D | 120 | 24 132 | 598 | 39.3 | 6.5 | 43.5 |
| Sharp | 317 | 2 658 | 551 | D | 658 | 226 | D | 65 | 24 448 | 723 | 24.8 | 13.3 | 38.5 |
| Stone | 231 | 2 110 | 589 | 113 | 549 | 101 | 45 | 46 | 22 009 | 556 | 24.1 | 12.1 | 45.1 |
| Union | 1 166 | 16 873 | 2 232 | 2 867 | 2 353 | 516 | 251 | 699 | 41 400 | 356 | 45.8 | 2.2 | 44.1 |
| Van Buren | 333 | 3 175 | 673 | D | 600 | D | 72 | 103 | 32 437 | 566 | 27.0 | 7.8 | 41.3 |
| Washington | 4 769 | 76 535 | 12 793 | 11 844 | 10 866 | 2 387 | 2 885 | 2 813 | 36 749 | 2 915 | 50.4 | 3.7 | 39.0 |
| White | 1 515 | 22 911 | 3 669 | 2 539 | 3 573 | 634 | 482 | 708 | 30 887 | 2 199 | 41.7 | 7.4 | 35.8 |
| Woodruff | 139 | 1 289 | D | D | 232 | 41 | 8 | 37 | 28 744 | 262 | 18.7 | 43.5 | 66.8 |
| Yell | 316 | 4 794 | 889 | D | 523 | 116 | 67 | 118 | 24 691 | 993 | 37.3 | 7.3 | 49.1 |

# Table B. States and Counties — **Agriculture**

| | Agriculture, 2007 (cont.) | | | | | | | | | | | | | | | |
| STATE County | Land in farms | | | | | Value of land and buildings (dollars) | | Value of machinery and equipment, average per farm (dollars) | Value of products sold | | | | Percent of farms with sales of: | | Government payments | |
| | | | Acres | | | | | | | | Percent from: | | | | | |
| | Acreage (1,000) | Percent change, 2002–2007 | Average size of farm | Total irrigated (1,000) | Total cropland (1,000) | Average per farm | Average per acre | | Total (mil dol) | Average per farm (dollars) | Crops | Live-stock and poultry products | $10,000 or more | $100,000 or more | Total ($1,000) | Percent of farms |
| | 117 | 118 | 119 | 120 | 121 | 122 | 123 | 124 | 125 | 126 | 127 | 128 | 129 | 130 | 131 | 132 |
| ARKANSAS—Cont'd | | | | | | | | | | | | | | | | |
| Cleveland | 31 | -13.9 | 129 | D | 9.3 | 456 860 | 3 542 | 103 715 | 148.1 | 614 358 | 0.2 | 99.8 | 46.9 | 36.1 | 114 | 10.8 |
| Columbia | 47 | -14.5 | 154 | 0.1 | 15.1 | 378 703 | 2 463 | 59 218 | 45.1 | 147 521 | 21.6 | 78.4 | 40.2 | 13.1 | 14 | 2.6 |
| Conway | 187 | 8.1 | 188 | 11.4 | 88.5 | 477 573 | 2 537 | 68 347 | 133.6 | 134 387 | 8.2 | 91.8 | 42.0 | 16.7 | 950 | 15.3 |
| Craighead | 337 | -3.7 | 458 | 244.4 | 301.7 | 1 119 008 | 2 444 | 183 029 | 158.9 | 215 945 | 96.5 | 3.5 | 45.4 | 28.9 | 16 297 | 49.3 |
| Crawford | 119 | -21.2 | 116 | 2.1 | 51.7 | 377 401 | 3 248 | 64 864 | 58.5 | 57 040 | 18.5 | 81.5 | 28.2 | 5.9 | 171 | 4.1 |
| Crittenden | 314 | 2.6 | 1 179 | 138.1 | 278.8 | 2 534 662 | 2 149 | 311 200 | 99.6 | 374 542 | 99.7 | 0.3 | 71.1 | 47.0 | 9 794 | 79.7 |
| Cross | 283 | -13.2 | 777 | 191.6 | 254.4 | 1 554 190 | 1 999 | 258 712 | 111.6 | 306 713 | 99.2 | 0.8 | 55.5 | 39.8 | 11 044 | 76.4 |
| Dallas | 20 | -23.1 | 188 | D | 4.9 | 319 298 | 1 699 | 41 597 | 1.4 | 13 069 | D | D | 13.2 | 0.9 | 28 | 6.6 |
| Desha | 306 | 7.4 | 1 123 | 229.7 | 280.5 | 2 142 086 | 1 908 | 319 493 | 140.7 | 515 542 | 97.5 | 2.5 | 67.8 | 52.0 | 11 044 | 80.2 |
| Drew | 124 | 6.9 | 338 | 59.3 | 80.7 | 663 259 | 1 963 | 102 233 | 57.3 | 155 809 | 62.7 | 37.3 | 39.1 | 17.1 | 3 292 | 36.1 |
| Faulkner | 190 | -15.6 | 142 | 4.3 | 71.5 | 431 415 | 3 043 | 52 710 | 19.9 | 14 807 | 29.4 | 70.6 | 25.9 | 2.2 | 1 080 | 11.6 |
| Franklin | 153 | -13.1 | 201 | 0.8 | 52.8 | 488 050 | 2 424 | 57 037 | 112.2 | 147 812 | 2.9 | 97.1 | 49.0 | 17.1 | 186 | 7.6 |
| Fulton | 177 | -29.2 | 252 | 0.0 | 28.9 | 449 098 | 1 779 | 42 612 | 25.8 | 36 709 | 2.5 | 97.5 | 37.6 | 6.3 | 245 | 15.4 |
| Garland | 39 | -15.2 | 90 | 0.1 | 11.4 | 329 321 | 3 662 | 37 905 | 12.2 | 27 887 | 19.4 | 80.6 | 19.1 | 3.4 | 41 | 3.2 |
| Grant | 35 | -5.4 | 123 | 0.1 | 11.8 | 352 330 | 2 871 | 59 597 | 19.2 | 68 097 | 5.0 | 95.0 | 29.1 | 6.7 | 17 | 2.5 |
| Greene | 267 | 1.9 | 347 | 164.6 | 229.3 | 866 235 | 2 496 | 132 788 | 115.8 | 150 355 | 91.4 | 8.6 | 39.0 | 18.3 | 9 479 | 53.9 |
| Hempstead | 211 | 3.4 | 236 | 1.7 | 66.6 | 494 672 | 2 100 | 79 349 | 167.1 | 186 933 | 3.0 | 97.0 | 47.3 | 18.8 | 943 | 18.7 |
| Hot Spring | 72 | -2.7 | 112 | 0.4 | 25.4 | 300 367 | 2 682 | 47 624 | 16.2 | 25 111 | 9.3 | 90.7 | 22.8 | 3.0 | 147 | 6.4 |
| Howard | 111 | 0.9 | 187 | 0.9 | 34.7 | 489 781 | 2 619 | 75 078 | 184.1 | 310 915 | 1.0 | 99.0 | 63.5 | 36.5 | 98 | 13.3 |
| Independence | 250 | -13.2 | 223 | 30.3 | 99.6 | 480 607 | 2 158 | 75 429 | 123.6 | 110 286 | 17.6 | 82.4 | 34.9 | 9.4 | 1 801 | 11.9 |
| Izard | 170 | -20.9 | 267 | 0.2 | 38.0 | 485 383 | 1 820 | 51 103 | 40.3 | 63 071 | 2.9 | 97.1 | 39.4 | 5.5 | 396 | 20.3 |
| Jackson | 302 | -9.0 | 679 | 178.1 | 266.4 | 1 372 634 | 2 022 | 191 313 | 106.9 | 240 120 | 95.7 | 4.3 | 55.3 | 36.6 | 9 169 | 63.4 |
| Jefferson | 303 | 9.8 | 620 | 200.2 | 259.2 | 1 309 975 | 2 114 | 177 731 | 135.9 | 277 980 | 86.5 | 13.5 | 44.8 | 24.9 | 9 774 | 60.1 |
| Johnson | 106 | -10.2 | 174 | 0.9 | 40.7 | 444 923 | 2 552 | 62 939 | 134.7 | 221 858 | 2.7 | 97.3 | 41.4 | 15.3 | 176 | 4.9 |
| Lafayette | 98 | -5.8 | 312 | 16.8 | 55.2 | 599 365 | 1 922 | 105 487 | 91.3 | 291 576 | 17.7 | 82.3 | 54.6 | 33.5 | 1 545 | 27.2 |
| Lawrence | 264 | -10.8 | 445 | 131.0 | 200.8 | 962 044 | 2 160 | 148 669 | 108.0 | 182 476 | 77.5 | 22.5 | 57.8 | 25.7 | 6 375 | 43.6 |
| Lee | 302 | 8.6 | 1 205 | 174.5 | 288.4 | 2 420 253 | 2 008 | 409 243 | 128.0 | 509 932 | 98.6 | 1.4 | 69.7 | 43.4 | 9 276 | 72.1 |
| Lincoln | 186 | -6.5 | 484 | 99.9 | 131.6 | 1 053 345 | 2 174 | 177 183 | 171.3 | 446 044 | 33.3 | 66.7 | 51.3 | 32.6 | 5 969 | 44.8 |
| Little River | 139 | -5.4 | 289 | 2.7 | 50.9 | 514 254 | 1 780 | 61 524 | 66.5 | 137 996 | 13.1 | 86.9 | 41.1 | 13.5 | 529 | 16.2 |
| Logan | 160 | -20.0 | 170 | 1.9 | 64.1 | 436 497 | 2 564 | 59 457 | 139.9 | 148 513 | 3.9 | 96.1 | 45.2 | 14.3 | 271 | 7.9 |
| Lonoke | 371 | 2.8 | 446 | 211.4 | 293.2 | 961 455 | 2 154 | 144 964 | 152.3 | 183 071 | 78.1 | 21.9 | 40.9 | 20.9 | 11 364 | 45.8 |
| Madison | 260 | -11.9 | 194 | 0.6 | 73.1 | 578 016 | 2 982 | 57 534 | 160.1 | 119 587 | 1.7 | 98.3 | 42.2 | 14.4 | 338 | 12.2 |
| Marion | 130 | -9.1 | 282 | 0.0 | 28.7 | 555 231 | 1 971 | 61 396 | 34.8 | 75 167 | 2.2 | 97.8 | 41.7 | 6.9 | 393 | 25.7 |
| Miller | 175 | 10.8 | 291 | 1.6 | 101.2 | 544 285 | 1 870 | 62 406 | 48.7 | 81 094 | 41.9 | 58.1 | 33.3 | 11.0 | 1 309 | 12.3 |
| Mississippi | 461 | -1.7 | 1 250 | 269.6 | 451.9 | 2 804 745 | 2 243 | 443 313 | 195.6 | 530 072 | 99.7 | 0.3 | 77.5 | 55.0 | 22 535 | 79.7 |
| Monroe | 242 | 4.3 | 1 058 | 163.2 | 211.0 | 2 121 750 | 2 006 | 280 942 | 93.9 | 410 189 | 96.4 | 3.6 | 63.3 | 43.2 | 7 348 | 83.0 |
| Montgomery | 74 | -5.1 | 162 | 0.9 | 27.1 | 464 258 | 2 872 | 60 654 | 48.2 | 105 809 | 2.3 | 97.7 | 41.0 | 17.5 | 62 | 4.8 |
| Nevada | 65 | -20.7 | 165 | 0.0 | 23.8 | 341 772 | 2 070 | 56 264 | 48.5 | 122 759 | 2.6 | 97.4 | 43.3 | 12.7 | 178 | 15.7 |
| Newton | 113 | -13.7 | 178 | 0.1 | 24.5 | 417 453 | 2 350 | 40 388 | 19.0 | 29 907 | 4.9 | 95.1 | 32.2 | 2.5 | 332 | 29.7 |
| Ouachita | 33 | 0.0 | 146 | 0.0 | 10.6 | 336 515 | 2 298 | 39 698 | 16.7 | 75 083 | 9.1 | 90.9 | 28.4 | 8.6 | 49 | 7.7 |
| Perry | 73 | 7.4 | 160 | 5.4 | 33.0 | 394 537 | 2 459 | 60 564 | 33.0 | 72 767 | 19.0 | 81.0 | 42.2 | 10.6 | 366 | 14.3 |
| Phillips | 437 | 32.8 | 1 424 | 245.4 | 424.2 | 2 575 578 | 1 808 | 404 817 | 185.1 | 602 891 | 99.7 | 0.3 | 74.3 | 54.1 | 15 803 | 78.5 |
| Pike | 84 | 23.5 | 197 | 0.6 | 23.7 | 452 519 | 2 301 | 77 947 | 92.9 | 218 585 | 0.8 | 99.2 | 51.1 | 25.2 | 115 | 13.2 |
| Poinsett | 341 | -10.7 | 815 | 262.2 | 323.0 | 1 826 209 | 2 241 | 290 355 | 154.2 | 368 805 | 99.5 | 0.5 | 68.2 | 51.4 | 14 351 | 78.5 |
| Polk | 133 | -8.9 | 132 | 0.6 | 45.0 | 387 972 | 2 930 | 52 564 | 135.5 | 134 587 | 1.2 | 98.8 | 37.4 | 15.3 | 77 | 3.8 |
| Pope | 154 | -8.9 | 142 | 4.0 | 65.8 | 412 029 | 2 895 | 64 043 | 148.9 | 137 836 | 4.1 | 95.9 | 38.2 | 13.4 | 334 | 6.9 |
| Prairie | 332 | 7.8 | 616 | 176.3 | 234.7 | 1 142 050 | 1 855 | 189 385 | 102.1 | 189 402 | 93.8 | 6.2 | 45.6 | 28.6 | 10 866 | 71.2 |
| Pulaski | 95 | -19.5 | 196 | 26.9 | 61.9 | 482 049 | 2 458 | 59 774 | 27.4 | 56 643 | 67.9 | 32.1 | 25.6 | 8.5 | 1 371 | 15.3 |
| Randolph | 252 | 2.4 | 329 | 67.3 | 135.0 | 641 603 | 1 948 | 74 749 | 64.2 | 83 876 | 67.3 | 32.7 | 36.2 | 10.6 | 3 220 | 20.8 |
| St. Francis | 255 | -8.6 | 823 | 144.8 | 225.9 | 1 668 825 | 2 028 | 232 547 | 91.7 | 295 816 | 97.5 | 2.5 | 51.6 | 33.9 | 8 326 | 70.0 |
| Saline | 45 | -19.6 | 121 | 0.8 | 15.6 | 375 996 | 3 115 | 58 900 | 5.6 | 15 078 | 50.4 | 49.6 | 21.0 | 2.4 | 31 | 5.4 |
| Scott | 96 | -22.6 | 163 | D | 31.8 | 405 451 | 2 492 | 63 344 | 112.5 | 189 790 | 1.3 | 98.7 | 46.2 | 19.1 | 111 | 5.7 |
| Searcy | 195 | 6.6 | 316 | 0.0 | 38.4 | 565 789 | 1 791 | 45 799 | 12.3 | 19 881 | 5.9 | 94.1 | 35.0 | 4.1 | 392 | 18.6 |
| Sebastian | 104 | -14.8 | 112 | 0.7 | 36.8 | 341 550 | 3 044 | 47 115 | 67.4 | 72 362 | 2.7 | 97.3 | 29.3 | 7.5 | 80 | 2.5 |
| Sevier | 117 | -5.6 | 195 | 0.3 | 30.6 | 472 133 | 2 422 | 63 753 | 149.0 | 249 103 | 0.6 | 99.4 | 48.7 | 23.1 | 154 | 14.2 |
| Sharp | 184 | 3.4 | 255 | 0.3 | 36.7 | 473 599 | 1 860 | 48 669 | 56.7 | 78 375 | 1.4 | 98.6 | 33.3 | 10.1 | 146 | 6.5 |
| Stone | 142 | -13.4 | 256 | 0.2 | 38.5 | 519 845 | 2 030 | 56 209 | 43.7 | 78 570 | 2.3 | 97.7 | 39.0 | 10.3 | 566 | 27.3 |
| Union | 38 | -5.0 | 107 | 0.1 | 11.6 | 364 004 | 3 418 | 61 407 | 74.1 | 208 262 | 1.2 | 98.8 | 33.4 | 16.3 | 57 | 2.5 |
| Van Buren | 114 | -13.6 | 202 | 0.5 | 33.9 | 495 478 | 2 454 | 54 719 | 15.5 | 27 388 | 8.2 | 91.8 | 35.3 | 5.1 | 299 | 15.0 |
| Washington | 327 | -11.1 | 112 | 0.8 | 112.0 | 463 747 | 4 131 | 52 447 | 418.0 | 143 384 | 1.9 | 98.1 | 33.8 | 11.0 | 264 | 3.5 |
| White | 411 | 4.3 | 187 | 43.2 | 202.2 | 464 706 | 2 484 | 50 213 | 119.2 | 54 225 | 28.7 | 71.3 | 23.0 | 5.1 | 5 848 | 24.6 |
| Woodruff | 274 | -0.4 | 1 047 | 169.5 | 246.6 | 2 110 227 | 2 015 | 271 357 | 91.7 | 349 856 | 97.5 | 2.5 | 61.8 | 42.7 | 6 997 | 83.6 |
| Yell | 175 | -3.3 | 176 | 4.2 | 67.0 | 439 230 | 2 491 | 61 287 | 162.5 | 163 612 | 3.4 | 96.6 | 40.4 | 16.7 | 501 | 10.3 |

# Table B. States and Counties — Water Use, Wholesale Trade, Retail Trade, and Real Estate

| STATE County | Water use, 2005 | | Wholesale trade,[1] 2007 | | | | Retail trade,[2] 2007 | | | | Real estate and rental and leasing,[2] 2007 | | | |
|---|---|---|---|---|---|---|---|---|---|---|---|---|---|---|
| | Total water withdrawn (mil gal/day) | Gallons withdrawn per person | Number of establishments | Number of employees | Sales (mil dol) | Annual payroll (mil dol) | Number of establishments | Number of employees | Sales (mil dol) | Annual payroll (mil dol) | Number of establishments | Number of employees | Receipts (mil dol) | Annual payroll (mil dol) |
| | 133 | 134 | 135 | 136 | 137 | 138 | 139 | 140 | 141 | 142 | 143 | 144 | 145 | 146 |
| **ARKANSAS—Cont'd** | | | | | | | | | | | | | | |
| Cleveland | 0.9 | 104 | 3 | 12 | 1.2 | 0.2 | 11 | 81 | 12.3 | 0.8 | 1 | D | D | D |
| Columbia | 5.9 | 238 | 22 | D | D | D | 116 | 1 100 | 197.9 | 19.3 | 27 | 139 | 16.9 | 4.2 |
| Conway | 19.4 | 936 | 20 | 236 | 124.9 | 5.9 | 90 | 960 | 270.4 | 20.1 | 9 | 38 | 11.3 | 1.1 |
| Craighead | 409.7 | 4 724 | 129 | 1 418 | 605.9 | 56.8 | 499 | 6 536 | 1 440.9 | 125.1 | 103 | 473 | 73.6 | 11.8 |
| Crawford | 8.6 | 148 | 49 | D | D | D | 158 | 1 937 | 452.5 | 39.4 | 60 | 169 | 24.3 | 5.6 |
| Crittenden | 160.5 | 3 093 | 53 | 663 | 795.8 | 28.3 | 175 | 2 313 | 750.5 | 44.9 | 37 | 153 | 20.4 | 4.7 |
| Cross | 644.3 | 33 493 | 17 | 265 | 174.7 | 9.2 | 73 | 693 | 185.7 | 15.2 | 22 | 149 | 13.0 | 3.0 |
| Dallas | 1.5 | 176 | 6 | 22 | 10.9 | 0.5 | 52 | 399 | 79.7 | 7.7 | 7 | 17 | 2.1 | 0.4 |
| Desha | 413.6 | 28 807 | 22 | 195 | 230.9 | 8.2 | 85 | 598 | 119.2 | 10.9 | 18 | 56 | 3.9 | 0.8 |
| Drew | 89.6 | 4 791 | 12 | 106 | 87.6 | 3.7 | 96 | 932 | 199.0 | 17.6 | 21 | 66 | 6.5 | 1.4 |
| Faulkner | 17.2 | 177 | 71 | 601 | 266.1 | 23.0 | 381 | 5 250 | 1 227.7 | 102.7 | 120 | 384 | 52.8 | 9.7 |
| Franklin | 3.9 | 215 | 7 | 25 | 3.1 | 0.4 | 55 | 483 | 140.2 | 9.1 | 7 | 19 | 1.1 | 0.3 |
| Fulton | 2.4 | 204 | 7 | 25 | 8.2 | 1.1 | 46 | 236 | 42.4 | 3.4 | 3 | 5 | 0.3 | 0.1 |
| Garland | 19.9 | 212 | 91 | D | D | D | 523 | 5 898 | 1 443.4 | 126.9 | 158 | 614 | 88.0 | 14.6 |
| Grant | 2.7 | 156 | 13 | 130 | 48.5 | 4.1 | 49 | 460 | 107.6 | 9.0 | 7 | 41 | 2.7 | 0.8 |
| Greene | 227.4 | 5 771 | 47 | D | D | D | 180 | 1 655 | 373.1 | 33.6 | 29 | 85 | 12.1 | 1.7 |
| Hempstead | 7.5 | 322 | 15 | 157 | 32.8 | 3.8 | 87 | 973 | 204.4 | 19.2 | 20 | 77 | 9.7 | 1.7 |
| Hot Spring | 323.2 | 10 337 | 17 | 154 | 77.0 | 5.7 | 101 | 941 | 207.4 | 19.2 | 19 | 122 | 8.2 | 2.9 |
| Howard | 5.6 | 388 | 12 | 73 | 45.1 | 3.0 | 63 | 591 | 160.8 | 12.2 | 12 | 32 | 3.3 | 0.5 |
| Independence | 104.6 | 3 011 | 29 | 464 | 175.0 | 14.1 | 167 | 1 664 | 384.2 | 34.4 | 28 | 98 | 10.9 | 2.3 |
| Izard | 5.0 | 373 | 4 | D | D | D | 51 | 417 | 104.7 | 7.7 | 8 | 53 | 3.3 | 0.8 |
| Jackson | 405.7 | 23 050 | 27 | 217 | 95.4 | 6.2 | 72 | 669 | 190.9 | 13.4 | 18 | 48 | 4.6 | 0.8 |
| Jefferson | 349.3 | 4 276 | 66 | D | D | D | 321 | 4 024 | 867.4 | 79.8 | 76 | D | D | D |
| Johnson | 5.3 | 221 | 9 | 83 | 44.2 | 2.8 | 81 | 938 | 196.8 | 16.5 | 19 | 57 | 8.8 | 1.6 |
| Lafayette | 41.2 | 5 134 | 3 | D | D | D | 24 | 194 | 32.9 | 3.1 | 7 | 11 | 0.8 | 0.1 |
| Lawrence | 248.2 | 14 467 | 15 | 114 | 58.0 | 3.3 | 75 | 644 | 163.7 | 14.7 | 10 | 30 | 2.2 | 0.4 |
| Lee | 272.2 | 23 577 | 11 | 136 | 84.7 | 4.0 | 20 | 205 | 35.8 | 3.0 | 8 | 18 | 2.2 | 0.5 |
| Lincoln | 206.4 | 14 472 | 8 | D | D | D | 31 | 248 | 57.5 | 4.1 | 6 | D | D | D |
| Little River | 14.4 | 1 089 | 8 | 32 | 13.5 | 1.0 | 45 | 335 | 88.2 | 7.1 | 5 | 12 | 0.8 | 0.1 |
| Logan | 5.9 | 257 | 6 | D | D | D | 78 | 700 | 178.1 | 13.4 | 13 | 31 | 2.6 | 0.5 |
| Lonoke | 534.3 | 8 808 | 42 | 320 | 161.6 | 10.8 | 185 | 2 041 | 497.2 | 40.9 | 49 | 144 | 13.4 | 2.8 |
| Madison | 2.1 | 142 | 3 | D | D | D | 40 | 446 | 114.7 | 8.2 | 5 | 6 | 0.3 | 0.1 |
| Marion | 2.0 | 122 | 4 | D | D | D | 41 | 501 | 87.9 | 9.5 | 14 | 19 | 2.3 | 0.3 |
| Miller | 125.8 | 2 914 | 42 | D | D | D | 142 | 1 474 | 407.7 | 30.7 | 21 | 66 | 10.5 | 1.5 |
| Mississippi | 279.9 | 5 842 | 51 | D | D | D | 191 | 1 911 | 421.9 | 37.1 | 45 | 180 | 24.3 | 4.1 |
| Monroe | 316.5 | 34 020 | 13 | 100 | 64.7 | 3.7 | 44 | 364 | 82.2 | 6.2 | 4 | 9 | 1.1 | 0.1 |
| Montgomery | 1.5 | 160 | 3 | D | D | D | 25 | 152 | 32.4 | 2.8 | 10 | 41 | 1.4 | 0.4 |
| Nevada | 2.1 | 219 | 5 | D | D | D | 28 | 295 | 136.8 | 5.1 | 6 | 14 | 0.9 | 0.2 |
| Newton | 1.4 | 166 | 2 | D | D | D | 16 | 67 | 13.3 | 1.2 | 3 | 9 | 0.7 | 0.1 |
| Ouachita | 59.5 | 2 197 | 22 | D | D | D | 113 | 1 086 | 185.7 | 18.9 | 22 | D | D | D |
| Perry | 14.6 | 1 393 | 3 | 12 | 1.5 | 0.2 | 22 | 194 | 32.8 | 3.5 | 6 | 9 | 0.9 | 0.4 |
| Phillips | 210.3 | 8 723 | 33 | D | D | D | 99 | 1 120 | 229.4 | 22.1 | 22 | 53 | 5.1 | 1.2 |
| Pike | 1.7 | 150 | 17 | 163 | 92.1 | 3.6 | 35 | 276 | 52.8 | 5.0 | 8 | 26 | 1.5 | 0.3 |
| Poinsett | 772.6 | 30 479 | 21 | D | D | D | 88 | 883 | 193.1 | 14.7 | 12 | 72 | 6.1 | 1.4 |
| Polk | 3.6 | 176 | 22 | 126 | 47.8 | 2.5 | 98 | 861 | 176.9 | 16.8 | 18 | 128 | 10.4 | 2.6 |
| Pope | 1 164.8 | 20 586 | 71 | 426 | 234.5 | 16.1 | 303 | 3 633 | 919.3 | 73.8 | 78 | 241 | 45.3 | 6.0 |
| Prairie | 355.8 | 39 039 | 8 | 59 | 28.4 | 2.0 | 38 | 201 | 39.5 | 3.0 | 5 | 9 | 0.9 | 0.4 |
| Pulaski | 84.0 | 229 | 704 | 13 507 | 13 419.0 | 594.4 | 1 771 | 25 621 | 6 163.1 | 566.9 | 644 | 3 614 | 671.4 | 113.1 |
| Randolph | 141.4 | 7 657 | 10 | 89 | 39.3 | 2.1 | 67 | 708 | 137.4 | 12.4 | 15 | 41 | 3.6 | 0.6 |
| St. Francis | 313.4 | 11 232 | 20 | D | D | D | 136 | 1 248 | 353.8 | 26.3 | 17 | 54 | 4.8 | 0.8 |
| Saline | 9.3 | 102 | 68 | 751 | 265.2 | 31.5 | 301 | 3 996 | 1 157.7 | 90.7 | 78 | 225 | 27.2 | 4.7 |
| Scott | 2.8 | 251 | 8 | 39 | 9.2 | 1.2 | 28 | 299 | 48.7 | 5.3 | 5 | 11 | 0.8 | 0.2 |
| Searcy | 1.0 | 124 | 3 | D | D | D | 33 | 299 | 59.1 | 5.1 | 6 | 31 | 0.9 | 0.2 |
| Sebastian | 39.4 | 332 | 198 | 2 474 | 1 313.8 | 95.9 | 604 | 8 058 | 1 825.5 | 167.8 | 170 | 919 | 158.6 | 26.8 |
| Sevier | 2.6 | 156 | 4 | D | D | D | 73 | 657 | 160.6 | 12.6 | 8 | 32 | 3.0 | 0.6 |
| Sharp | 5.3 | 304 | 7 | D | D | D | 73 | 648 | 156.0 | 12.1 | 17 | 35 | 4.4 | 0.7 |
| Stone | 2.4 | 207 | 8 | 75 | 32.6 | 1.6 | 62 | 583 | 108.4 | 13.4 | 10 | 13 | 1.8 | 0.2 |
| Union | 20.7 | 469 | 55 | D | D | D | 237 | 2 457 | 526.4 | 47.3 | 37 | 184 | 35.1 | 5.2 |
| Van Buren | 3.0 | 182 | 14 | 81 | 50.7 | 2.2 | 66 | 603 | 152.1 | 12.4 | 6 | 34 | 4.9 | 0.7 |
| Washington | 3.8 | 21 | 236 | 2 578 | 1 328.1 | 110.5 | 798 | 11 512 | 2 723.3 | 247.4 | 289 | 2 262 | 196.0 | 59.1 |
| White | 91.5 | 1 283 | 63 | D | D | D | 311 | 3 384 | 803.5 | 69.1 | 70 | 267 | 34.4 | 6.8 |
| Woodruff | 351.5 | 43 402 | 12 | 183 | 90.9 | 7.2 | 32 | 263 | 64.7 | 3.8 | 7 | 11 | 1.0 | 0.1 |
| Yell | 9.8 | 458 | 9 | 24 | 5.8 | 0.6 | 57 | 575 | 109.3 | 9.4 | 11 | 20 | 1.8 | 0.3 |

1. Merchant wholesalers, except manufacturers' sales branches and offices.　2. Employer establishments.

| STATE County | Professional, scientific, and technical services,[1] 2007 | | | | Manufacturing, 2007 | | | | Accommodation and food services, 2007 | | | |
|---|---|---|---|---|---|---|---|---|---|---|---|---|
| | Number of establish-ments | Number of employees | Receipts (mil dol) | Annual payroll (mil dol) | Number of establish-ments | Number of employees | Receipts (mil dol) | Annual payroll (mil dol) | Number of establish-ments | Number of employees | Sales (mil dol) | Annual payroll (mil dol) |
| | 147 | 148 | 149 | 150 | 151 | 152 | 153 | 154 | 155 | 156 | 157 | 158 |
| ARKANSAS—Cont'd | | | | | | | | | | | | |
| Cleveland | 1 | D | D | D | NA | NA | NA | NA | 2 | D | D | D |
| Columbia | 33 | 149 | 10.4 | 3.9 | 35 | 2 688 | 1 164.3 | 93.4 | 38 | 590 | 21.8 | 5.5 |
| Conway | 31 | 94 | 7.4 | 2.5 | 27 | 1 137 | 432.6 | 43.4 | 36 | 424 | 16.2 | 3.9 |
| Craighead | 173 | D | D | D | 120 | 6 455 | 1 830.3 | 229.9 | 178 | 3 963 | 146.7 | 41.4 |
| Crawford | 90 | D | D | D | 62 | 3 576 | 848.0 | 97.1 | 84 | 1 364 | 53.2 | 15.2 |
| Crittenden | 53 | D | D | D | 44 | 1 396 | 701.3 | 55.1 | 82 | 1 626 | 65.1 | 17.6 |
| Cross | 28 | 74 | 5.2 | 1.8 | 11 | 664 | D | 17.9 | 24 | 369 | 12.5 | 3.3 |
| Dallas | 10 | 23 | 1.6 | 0.4 | 13 | 749 | 184.5 | 27.2 | 13 | 115 | 4.6 | 1.3 |
| Desha | 23 | 59 | 4.5 | 1.4 | 14 | 982 | 400.8 | 43.4 | 28 | 279 | 9.8 | 2.5 |
| Drew | 28 | 105 | 7.6 | 2.7 | 24 | 891 | 156.1 | 30.2 | 31 | 657 | 19.7 | 5.1 |
| Faulkner | 214 | 759 | 76.5 | 22.7 | 100 | 5 342 | 1 587.6 | 216.5 | 165 | 3 781 | 137.9 | 37.1 |
| Franklin | 15 | D | D | D | 19 | 954 | 327.7 | 28.9 | 21 | 262 | 10.4 | 2.7 |
| Fulton | 15 | 57 | 3.6 | 1.5 | NA | NA | NA | NA | 16 | 163 | 5.3 | 1.6 |
| Garland | 218 | D | D | D | 119 | 2 786 | 661.7 | 99.9 | 265 | 5 080 | 203.3 | 62.2 |
| Grant | 14 | D | D | D | 18 | 1 294 | 489.9 | D | 18 | 249 | 10.2 | 2.4 |
| Greene | 55 | 360 | 20.1 | 8.0 | 53 | 4 942 | 1 434.1 | 160.7 | 61 | 984 | 37.6 | 10.4 |
| Hempstead | 15 | 45 | 4.1 | 1.5 | 30 | D | D | D | 38 | 586 | 21.2 | 6.0 |
| Hot Spring | 22 | 105 | 7.0 | 2.4 | 33 | 1 749 | 858.5 | 62.4 | 32 | 456 | 16.8 | 4.4 |
| Howard | 18 | 62 | 4.1 | 1.2 | 23 | 3 645 | 1 081.1 | 100.3 | 16 | 307 | 9.2 | 2.5 |
| Independence | 57 | 343 | 17.6 | 5.6 | 44 | 4 491 | 920.0 | 147.5 | 59 | 990 | 34.7 | 9.7 |
| Izard | 5 | D | D | D | NA | NA | NA | NA | 13 | 111 | 3.3 | 1.0 |
| Jackson | 24 | D | D | D | 17 | 982 | D | 33.4 | 26 | 237 | 9.7 | 2.7 |
| Jefferson | 89 | D | D | D | 60 | 4 684 | D | D | 140 | 2 147 | 87.1 | 22.4 |
| Johnson | 26 | 99 | 7.6 | 2.5 | 37 | 2 798 | 546.8 | 71.9 | 35 | 480 | 20.5 | 5.0 |
| Lafayette | 7 | 32 | 1.4 | 0.3 | NA | NA | NA | NA | 5 | 50 | 1.5 | 0.4 |
| Lawrence | 13 | 42 | 2.4 | 0.8 | NA | NA | NA | NA | 19 | 292 | 9.3 | 2.4 |
| Lee | 11 | 47 | 4.4 | 1.2 | NA | NA | NA | NA | 7 | 84 | 2.8 | 0.7 |
| Lincoln | 9 | D | D | D | 5 | D | D | D | 14 | D | D | D |
| Little River | 13 | 70 | 5.4 | 1.6 | 16 | 1 339 | D | 83.8 | 14 | 166 | 6.1 | 1.5 |
| Logan | 28 | 66 | 7.5 | 1.9 | 23 | 1 824 | 692.1 | 51.9 | 27 | 312 | 10.0 | 2.9 |
| Lonoke | 92 | D | D | D | 38 | 1 502 | D | 56.4 | 75 | 1 222 | 46.4 | 12.7 |
| Madison | 13 | D | D | D | 21 | 1 082 | D | 31.4 | 13 | 126 | 3.2 | 1.0 |
| Marion | 13 | 40 | 2.3 | 0.9 | 20 | 1 756 | 350.1 | 49.7 | 32 | 237 | 8.6 | 2.1 |
| Miller | 39 | 187 | 25.6 | 6.7 | 29 | 2 246 | 712.9 | 129.1 | 66 | 1 188 | 43.7 | 12.7 |
| Mississippi | 49 | 195 | 17.2 | 5.6 | 51 | 5 962 | 5 010.2 | 319.6 | 81 | 1 091 | 45.8 | 11.8 |
| Monroe | 11 | 33 | 1.8 | 0.6 | NA | NA | NA | NA | 16 | 212 | 8.2 | 2.2 |
| Montgomery | 9 | 22 | 1.2 | 0.5 | NA | NA | NA | NA | 17 | 232 | 18.2 | 5.1 |
| Nevada | 4 | 19 | 1.6 | 0.5 | 8 | D | D | D | 9 | 95 | 3.2 | 0.9 |
| Newton | 6 | D | D | D | NA | NA | NA | NA | 12 | 46 | 3.3 | 0.7 |
| Ouachita | 27 | 154 | 17.1 | 5.0 | 32 | D | D | D | 26 | 421 | 14.6 | 3.7 |
| Perry | 8 | D | D | D | NA | NA | NA | NA | 5 | 58 | 1.7 | 0.5 |
| Phillips | 39 | D | D | D | NA | NA | NA | NA | 29 | 382 | 13.5 | 3.7 |
| Pike | 3 | D | D | D | NA | NA | NA | NA | 14 | 162 | 6.8 | 1.7 |
| Poinsett | 21 | D | D | D | 19 | 834 | 172.0 | 29.1 | 37 | 361 | 11.6 | 2.8 |
| Polk | 34 | 107 | 8.8 | 2.6 | 38 | 1 218 | 303.5 | 34.5 | 35 | 418 | 14.4 | 3.8 |
| Pope | 138 | D | D | D | 75 | 4 620 | 1 436.7 | 159.3 | 113 | 2 349 | 79.4 | 21.3 |
| Prairie | 7 | 21 | 2.2 | 0.5 | NA | NA | NA | NA | 14 | 90 | 4.3 | 0.8 |
| Pulaski | 1 549 | D | D | D | 382 | 15 031 | 5 969.5 | 665.4 | 858 | 17 807 | 810.0 | 231.0 |
| Randolph | 21 | 81 | 6.0 | 2.0 | 35 | 822 | 148.1 | 28.1 | 22 | 413 | 13.9 | 3.6 |
| St. Francis | 35 | D | D | D | 12 | 1 011 | D | 30.7 | 45 | 739 | 28.5 | 7.5 |
| Saline | 136 | 438 | 40.4 | 14.1 | 74 | 1 579 | 366.9 | 63.9 | 117 | 1 919 | 81.2 | 23.3 |
| Scott | 9 | 14 | 1.4 | 0.3 | 19 | 1 070 | 203.0 | 27.2 | 16 | 100 | 3.1 | 0.8 |
| Searcy | 8 | 31 | 1.5 | 0.4 | NA | NA | NA | NA | 11 | 73 | 2.9 | 0.9 |
| Sebastian | 297 | D | D | D | 198 | 19 654 | 5 676.5 | 648.5 | 262 | 5 124 | 207.8 | 56.8 |
| Sevier | 12 | 47 | 2.4 | 0.7 | 9 | D | D | D | 14 | 191 | 6.9 | 1.6 |
| Sharp | 19 | 41 | 2.5 | 0.7 | NA | NA | NA | NA | 41 | 387 | 13.0 | 3.3 |
| Stone | 8 | D | D | D | NA | NA | NA | NA | 29 | 316 | 12.1 | 2.9 |
| Union | 66 | D | D | D | 60 | 4 711 | 3 901.9 | 198.3 | 70 | 975 | 40.0 | 9.8 |
| Van Buren | 18 | 60 | 4.4 | 1.5 | NA | NA | NA | NA | 22 | 319 | 12.5 | 3.1 |
| Washington | 570 | D | D | D | 213 | 14 703 | 3 497.6 | 482.9 | 454 | 9 536 | 355.7 | 102.3 |
| White | 77 | 343 | 30.6 | 11.0 | 79 | 3 831 | 1 168.2 | 128.4 | 116 | 2 005 | 79.8 | 20.4 |
| Woodruff | 6 | D | D | D | NA | NA | NA | NA | 7 | 45 | 1.3 | 0.3 |
| Yell | 19 | D | D | D | 17 | 2 683 | 449.6 | 65.3 | 22 | 318 | 9.2 | 2.5 |

1. Establishment subject to federal tax.

| STATE County | Health care and social assistance, 2007 | | | | Other services, 2007 | | | | Federal funds and grants, 2009–2010 Expenditures (mil dol) | | | |
|---|---|---|---|---|---|---|---|---|---|---|---|---|
| | | | | | | | | | | Direct payments for individuals[1] | | |
| | Number of establish- ments | Number of employees | Receipts (mil dol) | Annual payroll (mil dol) | Number of establish- ments | Number of employees | Receipts (mil dol) | Annual payroll (mil dol) | Total | Social Security and government retirement | Medicare | Food Stamps and Supplemental Security Income |
| | 159 | 160 | 161 | 162 | 163 | 164 | 165 | 166 | 167 | 168 | 169 | 170 |
| ARKANSAS—Cont'd | | | | | | | | | | | | |
| Cleveland | 8 | D | D | D | 7 | D | D | D | 66.7 | 30.8 | 13.6 | 4.0 |
| Columbia | 63 | 1 190 | 69.7 | 27.3 | 39 | 169 | 11.7 | 3.3 | 249.8 | 84.8 | 50.5 | 21.0 |
| Conway | 45 | 556 | 32.1 | 12.5 | 16 | 98 | 22.6 | 5.1 | 203.4 | 82.3 | 40.2 | 10.5 |
| Craighead | 307 | 7 706 | 769.0 | 283.2 | 141 | 835 | 67.6 | 16.9 | 670.1 | 274.5 | 104.2 | 36.6 |
| Crawford | 92 | 1 542 | 100.4 | 46.9 | 67 | 420 | 33.1 | 9.9 | 383.4 | 197.8 | 71.8 | 23.1 |
| Crittenden | 117 | 1 897 | 166.2 | 65.5 | 71 | 476 | 34.7 | 9.7 | 487.2 | 132.5 | 80.9 | 46.5 |
| Cross | 47 | 657 | 43.2 | 16.2 | 22 | 49 | 4.1 | 1.0 | 189.6 | 58.4 | 32.7 | 11.1 |
| Dallas | 22 | 877 | 45.3 | 17.9 | 14 | 42 | 2.9 | 0.8 | 88.7 | 30.0 | 24.8 | 6.2 |
| Desha | 34 | 600 | 42.0 | 15.6 | 17 | 40 | 2.2 | 0.6 | 182.0 | 41.9 | 34.9 | 12.8 |
| Drew | 41 | 1 011 | 46.4 | 21.7 | 21 | 143 | 9.9 | 3.7 | 169.2 | 53.9 | 30.5 | 7.6 |
| Faulkner | 273 | 4 581 | 366.0 | 136.1 | 121 | 571 | 44.6 | 12.3 | 607.0 | 294.5 | 84.1 | 30.3 |
| Franklin | 28 | 574 | 26.5 | 12.1 | 15 | 59 | 5.7 | 1.1 | 147.4 | 65.9 | 30.5 | 6.6 |
| Fulton | 27 | 418 | 17.8 | 9.1 | 10 | 27 | 1.4 | 0.4 | 108.1 | 53.4 | 22.4 | 8.8 |
| Garland | 276 | 6 590 | 613.4 | 244.4 | 179 | 1 309 | 80.6 | 26.6 | 1 017.6 | 513.5 | 231.6 | 44.9 |
| Grant | 20 | 237 | 13.0 | 5.7 | 18 | D | D | D | 108.6 | 60.7 | 20.6 | 4.5 |
| Greene | 86 | 1 572 | 117.8 | 42.4 | 45 | 145 | 12.1 | 3.4 | 304.9 | 136.1 | 56.1 | 16.6 |
| Hempstead | 54 | 1 160 | 72.6 | 26.7 | 36 | D | D | D | 192.2 | 62.5 | 47.9 | 13.9 |
| Hot Spring | 44 | 1 070 | 62.1 | 27.3 | 28 | 135 | 9.1 | 2.4 | 240.9 | 109.2 | 58.7 | 13.4 |
| Howard | 30 | 589 | 32.7 | 12.6 | 21 | 88 | 6.8 | 2.0 | 126.0 | 48.9 | 32.2 | 5.5 |
| Independence | 106 | 2 730 | 243.6 | 90.6 | 54 | 249 | 16.7 | 5.0 | 322.1 | 129.5 | 59.8 | 17.0 |
| Izard | 22 | 589 | 41.6 | 12.9 | 16 | 78 | 3.0 | 1.0 | 139.7 | 61.8 | 29.0 | 6.1 |
| Jackson | 56 | 1 002 | 67.9 | 26.0 | 22 | 161 | 7.9 | 2.3 | 234.9 | 53.2 | 70.6 | 11.7 |
| Jefferson | 267 | 4 422 | 387.1 | 142.7 | 94 | 665 | 44.7 | 17.2 | 1 151.3 | 286.0 | 138.0 | 71.5 |
| Johnson | 44 | 977 | 63.5 | 26.3 | 27 | 161 | 6.2 | 2.9 | 173.2 | 79.2 | 34.6 | 9.5 |
| Lafayette | 9 | 217 | 7.5 | 4.0 | 5 | D | D | D | 91.4 | 25.0 | 22.9 | 7.0 |
| Lawrence | 29 | 608 | 34.6 | 16.2 | 19 | 58 | 4.6 | 1.0 | 204.4 | 70.0 | 41.6 | 10.9 |
| Lee | 20 | 243 | 17.6 | 6.9 | 11 | 18 | 1.5 | 0.4 | 161.7 | 27.4 | 23.6 | 17.0 |
| Lincoln | 14 | D | D | D | 15 | D | D | D | 111.7 | 33.9 | 19.7 | 8.3 |
| Little River | 17 | 362 | 19.4 | 9.9 | 13 | D | D | D | 114.0 | 51.0 | 24.4 | 6.0 |
| Logan | 44 | 695 | 40.6 | 15.7 | 27 | 88 | 7.0 | 1.9 | 198.0 | 85.8 | 37.6 | 11.3 |
| Lonoke | 96 | 1 085 | 74.7 | 29.8 | 59 | 215 | 16.1 | 4.9 | 424.9 | 232.8 | 68.4 | 16.5 |
| Madison | 16 | D | D | D | 11 | D | D | D | 113.1 | 63.6 | 17.2 | 4.6 |
| Marion | 18 | 379 | 12.1 | 5.8 | 14 | 36 | 2.8 | 0.6 | 146.6 | 77.5 | 25.5 | 6.5 |
| Miller | 69 | 1 367 | 81.7 | 29.5 | 40 | 274 | 20.9 | 5.8 | 359.2 | 133.8 | 86.5 | 31.0 |
| Mississippi | 124 | 1 699 | 115.5 | 45.6 | 44 | 208 | 13.8 | 3.9 | 492.0 | 140.3 | 86.4 | 45.3 |
| Monroe | 21 | 337 | 12.4 | 6.4 | 13 | 58 | 5.0 | 0.9 | 141.2 | 29.5 | 24.9 | 11.0 |
| Montgomery | 11 | D | D | D | 7 | D | D | D | 80.5 | 37.2 | 18.2 | 3.6 |
| Nevada | 14 | 441 | 17.8 | 8.4 | 13 | D | D | D | 106.9 | 32.4 | 25.8 | 6.1 |
| Newton | 9 | 218 | 7.0 | 3.1 | 4 | D | D | D | 77.6 | 31.1 | 11.3 | 4.5 |
| Ouachita | 61 | D | D | D | 34 | D | D | D | 306.0 | 105.4 | 64.0 | 20.4 |
| Perry | 16 | 162 | 9.4 | 3.8 | 6 | D | D | D | 84.7 | 42.0 | 17.5 | 3.6 |
| Phillips | 80 | 1 168 | 78.4 | 28.1 | 30 | D | D | D | 368.8 | 65.2 | 58.6 | 38.3 |
| Pike | 13 | 300 | 10.9 | 5.0 | 8 | 52 | 4.0 | 1.1 | 85.7 | 38.6 | 21.4 | 3.9 |
| Poinsett | 39 | 506 | 23.6 | 11.3 | 20 | 52 | 4.0 | 1.1 | 283.7 | 83.7 | 51.8 | 21.5 |
| Polk | 52 | 947 | 53.0 | 22.8 | 26 | 84 | 5.4 | 1.4 | 186.7 | 84.9 | 40.0 | 9.6 |
| Pope | 146 | 2 593 | 180.7 | 78.6 | 99 | 515 | 33.5 | 10.3 | 443.6 | 191.8 | 65.6 | 20.8 |
| Prairie | 18 | 180 | 10.2 | 4.5 | 11 | 34 | 1.9 | 0.5 | 107.3 | 31.4 | 21.5 | 3.7 |
| Pulaski | 1 462 | 39 444 | 4 389.9 | 1 688.5 | 856 | 5 641 | 690.3 | 155.4 | 6 517.7 | 1 391.0 | 574.8 | 186.6 |
| Randolph | 37 | 769 | 53.7 | 21.7 | 18 | 43 | 3.7 | 0.9 | 160.9 | 65.9 | 30.8 | 9.0 |
| St. Francis | 59 | 1 290 | 76.2 | 31.5 | 26 | D | D | D | 367.4 | 84.2 | 50.4 | 33.1 |
| Saline | 174 | 3 387 | 248.2 | 100.2 | 128 | 668 | 53.1 | 16.7 | 383.8 | 207.2 | 78.2 | 15.4 |
| Scott | 16 | 269 | 15.5 | 6.5 | 8 | 38 | 1.7 | 1.5 | 90.3 | 41.9 | 17.9 | 5.1 |
| Searcy | 13 | 292 | 11.4 | 5.0 | 2 | D | D | D | 97.1 | 37.0 | 16.5 | 5.0 |
| Sebastian | 403 | 11 362 | 1 021.0 | 423.8 | 201 | 981 | 81.7 | 22.2 | 920.3 | 398.3 | 173.5 | 45.8 |
| Sevier | 33 | 593 | 28.4 | 12.8 | 23 | 90 | 4.9 | 1.4 | 108.0 | 45.8 | 26.8 | 5.9 |
| Sharp | 40 | 501 | 19.8 | 8.7 | 26 | 112 | 7.8 | 1.9 | 179.6 | 92.6 | 42.8 | 7.9 |
| Stone | 20 | 458 | 25.7 | 11.5 | 13 | 41 | 3.8 | 1.3 | 119.6 | 55.7 | 23.3 | 5.8 |
| Union | 135 | 2 440 | 192.8 | 79.3 | 81 | 446 | 42.6 | 10.8 | 426.9 | 164.7 | 94.6 | 25.3 |
| Van Buren | 34 | 682 | 39.2 | 17.1 | 24 | 159 | 13.5 | 2.6 | 154.1 | 79.7 | 34.4 | 9.2 |
| Washington | 494 | 11 569 | 1 179.7 | 472.0 | 314 | D | D | D | 1 252.7 | 477.0 | 151.7 | 43.6 |
| White | 154 | 3 259 | 282.5 | 110.2 | 100 | 573 | 46.7 | 16.1 | 554.5 | 268.0 | 102.4 | 26.1 |
| Woodruff | 22 | 161 | 10.0 | 3.8 | 9 | 18 | 1.4 | 0.3 | 126.5 | 27.1 | 27.3 | 7.7 |
| Yell | 45 | 791 | 46.1 | 18.4 | 13 | 55 | 4.1 | 1.0 | 179.6 | 75.8 | 36.3 | 8.4 |

1. State totals may include programs not allocated by county.

# Table B. States and Counties — Federal Funds, Residential Construction, and Local Government Finances

| | Federal funds and grants, 2009–2010 (cont.) | | | | | | | Value of residential construction authorized by building permits, 2011 | | Local government finances, 2007 | | | | |
| STATE County | Expenditures (mil dol) (cont.) | | | | | | | | | General revenue | | | | |
| | Procurement contract awards | | | Grants[1] | | | | | | | | Taxes | | |
| | | | | | | | | | | | | | Per capita[2] (dollars) | |
| | Salaries and wages | Defense | Other | Medicaid and other health-related | Nutrition and family welfare | Education | Other | New construction ($1,000) | Number of housing units | Total (mil dol) | Inter-govern-mental (mil dol) | Total (mil dol) | Total | Property |
| | 171 | 172 | 173 | 174 | 175 | 176 | 177 | 178 | 179 | 180 | 181 | 182 | 183 | 184 |
| ARKANSAS—Cont'd | | | | | | | | | | | | | | |
| Cleveland | 1.4 | 0.0 | 0.3 | 13.2 | 2.1 | 0.8 | 0.2 | 0 | 0 | 18.3 | 14.5 | 2.0 | 223 | 142 |
| Columbia | 13.3 | 5.9 | 1.1 | 53.7 | 4.9 | 3.2 | 2.4 | 480 | 3 | 71.5 | 34.9 | 12.6 | 519 | 199 |
| Conway | 12.8 | 0.8 | 1.2 | 38.7 | 4.3 | 1.6 | 1.6 | 869 | 10 | 56.9 | 35.8 | 10.3 | 499 | 193 |
| Craighead | 53.7 | 11.3 | 9.6 | 82.0 | 11.1 | 8.5 | 14.8 | 61 396 | 751 | 237.3 | 130.7 | 63.4 | 693 | 328 |
| Crawford | 13.3 | 8.6 | 7.0 | 40.8 | 10.7 | 4.0 | 3.5 | 12 467 | 113 | 143.7 | 99.5 | 27.0 | 458 | 171 |
| Crittenden | 31.2 | 2.1 | 3.0 | 133.2 | 12.7 | 6.1 | 8.0 | 7 531 | 43 | 165.4 | 98.5 | 35.3 | 678 | 186 |
| Cross | 6.7 | 2.4 | 1.1 | 37.4 | 4.8 | 1.5 | 8.2 | 5 686 | 42 | 47.5 | 33.1 | 9.3 | 497 | 248 |
| Dallas | 3.9 | 0.0 | 0.5 | 19.6 | 2.0 | 0.8 | 0.3 | 135 | 1 | 17.9 | 11.5 | 4.1 | 496 | 160 |
| Desha | 6.9 | 0.4 | 0.7 | 46.6 | 5.2 | 1.6 | 3.2 | 0 | 0 | 52.7 | 28.3 | 12.0 | 873 | 410 |
| Drew | 15.4 | 2.8 | 1.9 | 29.9 | 3.6 | 3.7 | 1.8 | 1 635 | 22 | 72.3 | 38.0 | 10.6 | 568 | 198 |
| Faulkner | 45.1 | 1.3 | 4.6 | 42.5 | 16.3 | 5.3 | 56.8 | 42 724 | 245 | 241.3 | 128.2 | 56.4 | 538 | 199 |
| Franklin | 17.8 | 0.9 | 2.4 | 17.2 | 2.7 | 2.0 | 0.6 | 658 | 8 | 43.2 | 31.0 | 7.9 | 438 | 221 |
| Fulton | 2.6 | 0.0 | -1.0 | 17.2 | 1.9 | 0.6 | 0.5 | 0 | 0 | 21.1 | 13.8 | 2.9 | 249 | 118 |
| Garland | 42.3 | 22.1 | 39.0 | 77.7 | 12.8 | 8.8 | 7.4 | 7 174 | 37 | 219.2 | 115.5 | 56.9 | 591 | 174 |
| Grant | 5.7 | 0.0 | 0.8 | 12.0 | 2.2 | 1.4 | 0.2 | 1 682 | 51 | 46.6 | 34.9 | 7.2 | 410 | 204 |
| Greene | 15.7 | 0.9 | 1.5 | 50.7 | 5.4 | 2.8 | 2.7 | 12 792 | 144 | 104.5 | 57.6 | 21.4 | 530 | 218 |
| Hempstead | 9.2 | 6.3 | 1.3 | 34.7 | 5.5 | 3.0 | 1.6 | 3 090 | 49 | 61.9 | 41.9 | 10.6 | 458 | 174 |
| Hot Spring | 18.1 | 0.0 | 1.3 | 29.2 | 5.1 | 2.0 | 0.5 | 531 | 3 | 66.8 | 44.6 | 13.8 | 435 | 200 |
| Howard | 12.6 | 0.3 | 0.8 | 19.9 | 2.9 | 1.1 | 0.9 | 255 | 3 | 38.7 | 24.9 | 7.9 | 562 | 195 |
| Independence | 21.7 | 0.1 | 2.7 | 54.5 | 6.8 | 3.9 | 13.0 | 2 950 | 18 | 90.4 | 59.2 | 16.4 | 475 | 256 |
| Izard | 2.9 | 0.1 | 0.7 | 20.6 | 2.1 | 1.2 | 7.7 | 123 | 1 | 29.8 | 21.7 | 4.9 | 381 | 192 |
| Jackson | 11.1 | 0.0 | 0.8 | 56.1 | 3.8 | 1.6 | 3.7 | 605 | 3 | 43.1 | 24.8 | 10.7 | 623 | 284 |
| Jefferson | 93.8 | 256.5 | 42.6 | 169.1 | 19.3 | 14.9 | 18.1 | 6 441 | 67 | 213.4 | 134.7 | 49.3 | 624 | 263 |
| Johnson | 7.6 | 0.1 | 4.6 | 28.2 | 3.6 | 1.8 | 1.7 | 1 633 | 16 | 50.8 | 33.4 | 10.9 | 440 | 193 |
| Lafayette | 2.1 | 0.1 | 0.5 | 27.3 | 2.3 | 0.8 | -0.1 | 0 | 0 | 19.5 | 11.7 | 3.7 | 477 | 206 |
| Lawrence | 15.1 | 0.0 | 1.2 | 42.0 | 3.6 | 1.8 | 3.1 | 0 | 0 | 59.5 | 33.4 | 8.2 | 486 | 244 |
| Lee | 3.7 | 4.6 | 1.0 | 60.4 | 5.4 | 1.3 | 1.4 | 51 | 1 | 23.4 | 17.0 | 3.4 | 317 | 143 |
| Lincoln | 2.0 | 0.0 | 0.5 | 35.0 | 2.9 | 0.7 | 1.3 | 325 | 2 | 20.8 | 15.3 | 3.2 | 237 | 122 |
| Little River | 3.1 | 2.8 | 0.6 | 19.9 | 2.5 | 0.8 | 0.7 | 440 | 9 | 40.9 | 17.5 | 7.6 | 595 | 269 |
| Logan | 19.8 | 0.0 | 2.5 | 33.5 | 3.8 | 1.4 | 1.0 | 1 218 | 21 | 46.0 | 31.0 | 8.4 | 371 | 190 |
| Lonoke | 23.6 | 0.0 | 2.4 | 38.4 | 7.1 | 7.9 | 3.6 | 23 395 | 254 | 160.4 | 101.3 | 27.0 | 424 | 178 |
| Madison | 3.6 | 0.1 | 0.7 | 18.2 | 2.1 | 0.9 | 0.9 | 0 | 0 | 27.4 | 18.9 | 4.8 | 310 | 168 |
| Marion | 2.8 | 5.8 | 2.5 | 14.4 | 2.3 | 1.0 | 6.6 | 1 140 | 10 | 24.7 | 16.2 | 5.7 | 341 | 180 |
| Miller | 10.5 | 1.9 | 3.1 | 58.9 | 10.8 | 3.2 | 4.6 | 8 099 | 45 | 104.7 | 63.6 | 23.2 | 545 | 226 |
| Mississippi | 11.0 | 7.0 | 5.2 | 124.2 | 20.1 | 6.1 | 6.2 | 3 622 | 29 | 158.2 | 79.6 | 29.3 | 628 | 182 |
| Monroe | 4.8 | 0.0 | 0.7 | 46.4 | 3.2 | 0.9 | 1.9 | 120 | 1 | 24.6 | 16.7 | 4.8 | 547 | 315 |
| Montgomery | 3.8 | 0.8 | 1.2 | 11.7 | 1.3 | 0.3 | 0.4 | NA | NA | 17.2 | 12.9 | 2.7 | 299 | 138 |
| Nevada | 17.0 | 0.0 | 0.7 | 19.0 | 2.3 | 0.7 | 2.3 | 312 | 2 | 23.6 | 12.9 | 3.7 | 395 | 166 |
| Newton | 3.5 | 0.0 | 1.1 | 22.1 | 2.5 | 0.5 | 0.8 | 150 | 1 | 25.9 | 22.2 | 1.8 | 219 | 170 |
| Ouachita | 17.8 | 7.4 | 2.0 | 63.5 | 6.1 | 1.7 | 11.4 | 1 123 | 7 | 70.5 | 51.7 | 10.7 | 412 | 180 |
| Perry | 3.7 | 0.0 | 0.8 | 14.1 | 1.5 | 0.6 | 0.1 | 0 | 0 | 18.6 | 14.1 | 2.8 | 267 | 141 |
| Phillips | 12.8 | 3.7 | 1.7 | 131.1 | 13.8 | 4.2 | 3.2 | 2 369 | 29 | 74.9 | 54.6 | 10.3 | 468 | 207 |
| Pike | 4.2 | 0.0 | 0.7 | 13.2 | 1.6 | 1.0 | 0.4 | NA | NA | 29.5 | 20.2 | 4.8 | 441 | 182 |
| Poinsett | 11.1 | 0.2 | 1.7 | 70.9 | 5.5 | 2.1 | 2.6 | 1 332 | 14 | 61.2 | 44.1 | 9.9 | 399 | 189 |
| Polk | 17.7 | 0.2 | 2.2 | 20.9 | 3.6 | 3.1 | 0.9 | 1 700 | 22 | 62.8 | 32.0 | 6.9 | 340 | 127 |
| Pope | 45.6 | 1.6 | 9.2 | 54.9 | 16.0 | 4.7 | 8.7 | 6 051 | 81 | 138.6 | 82.6 | 34.9 | 592 | 209 |
| Prairie | 10.3 | 9.7 | 0.5 | 17.5 | 1.8 | 0.8 | 0.5 | 845 | 5 | 20.5 | 12.8 | 4.2 | 480 | 276 |
| Pulaski | 1 083.4 | 440.8 | 237.5 | 523.9 | 194.3 | 287.6 | 1 455.1 | 232 916 | 2 341 | 1 290.8 | 584.0 | 373.8 | 1 000 | 446 |
| Randolph | 2.9 | 0.0 | 0.7 | 29.5 | 5.6 | 1.2 | 1.1 | 1 546 | 11 | 38.5 | 25.2 | 9.5 | 525 | 328 |
| St. Francis | 42.4 | 0.4 | 2.2 | 109.2 | 11.0 | 3.2 | 8.9 | 3 612 | 43 | 79.2 | 50.4 | 14.2 | 529 | 194 |
| Saline | 21.9 | 8.1 | 2.2 | 28.3 | 11.0 | 3.3 | 3.5 | 54 812 | 339 | 171.2 | 102.4 | 40.5 | 421 | 202 |
| Scott | 4.9 | 0.0 | 1.5 | 14.1 | 1.8 | 0.7 | 1.7 | 250 | 3 | 22.6 | 17.2 | 2.8 | 252 | 124 |
| Searcy | 5.4 | 0.0 | 0.5 | 27.9 | 1.7 | 0.6 | 1.1 | 450 | 5 | 15.8 | 10.7 | 3.3 | 413 | 304 |
| Sebastian | 123.5 | 12.0 | 20.7 | 73.7 | 14.6 | 8.3 | 13.6 | 52 734 | 363 | 358.6 | 181.3 | 115.4 | 947 | 305 |
| Sevier | 6.3 | 0.3 | 1.6 | 12.6 | 2.3 | 1.4 | 1.3 | 270 | 5 | 48.4 | 34.0 | 7.1 | 435 | 135 |
| Sharp | 4.1 | 0.0 | 1.0 | 24.6 | 3.1 | 1.1 | 1.0 | 110 | 3 | 41.9 | 27.1 | 6.0 | 338 | 131 |
| Stone | 3.4 | 0.0 | 1.4 | 26.4 | 1.9 | 0.6 | 0.1 | 380 | 5 | 19.6 | 13.8 | 3.9 | 322 | 139 |
| Union | 20.4 | 1.0 | 4.6 | 83.9 | 13.1 | 4.3 | 7.7 | 532 | 6 | 111.0 | 63.2 | 32.5 | 753 | 245 |
| Van Buren | 3.0 | 0.0 | 0.4 | 22.5 | 2.6 | 0.8 | 0.8 | 399 | 3 | 34.1 | 20.7 | 8.4 | 509 | 217 |
| Washington | 133.6 | 151.4 | 71.4 | 77.0 | 20.4 | 15.4 | 75.5 | 96 046 | 449 | 558.8 | 286.5 | 168.7 | 868 | 263 |
| White | 35.8 | 0.1 | 3.7 | 76.7 | 9.6 | 6.2 | 1.4 | 22 912 | 200 | 165.5 | 108.0 | 33.1 | 450 | 135 |
| Woodruff | 5.2 | 0.1 | 0.7 | 38.2 | 2.7 | 3.2 | 0.8 | 210 | 4 | 24.9 | 16.8 | 2.8 | 368 | 196 |
| Yell | 17.2 | 1.2 | 2.0 | 30.7 | 3.1 | 1.4 | 0.7 | 234 | 3 | 54.6 | 41.7 | 7.2 | 329 | 165 |

1. State totals may include programs not allocated by county.   2. Based on the resident population estimated as of July 1 of the year shown.

# Table B. States and Counties — Local Government Finances, Government Employment, and Voting

| STATE County | Local government finances, 2007 (cont.) | | | | | | | | | Government employment, 2011 | | | Presidential election,[2] 2012 | | |
| | Direct general expenditure | | | | | | | Debt outstanding | | | | | Percent of vote cast: | | |
| | | | Percent of total for: | | | | | | | | | | | | |
| | Total (mil dol) | Per capita[1] (dollars) | Education | Health and hospitals | Police protection | Public welfare | Highways | Total (mil dol) | Per capita[1] (dollars) | Federal civilian | Federal military | State and local | Democratic | Republican | All other |
| | 185 | 186 | 187 | 188 | 189 | 190 | 191 | 192 | 193 | 194 | 195 | 196 | 197 | 198 | 199 |
| ARKANSAS—Cont'd | | | | | | | | | | | | | | | |
| Cleveland | 20.1 | 2 293 | 64.7 | 0.1 | 2.4 | 0.0 | 6.8 | 6.6 | 751 | 13 | 37 | 379 | 26.0 | 69.9 | 4.1 |
| Columbia | 67.8 | 2 784 | 45.2 | 24.3 | 3.6 | 0.0 | 4.6 | 54.7 | 2 246 | 44 | 105 | 1 893 | 37.2 | 61.3 | 1.5 |
| Conway | 58.0 | 2 797 | 69.4 | 0.1 | 5.1 | 0.0 | 5.1 | 41.1 | 1 984 | 60 | 91 | 1 417 | 38.7 | 57.6 | 3.7 |
| Craighead | 235.4 | 2 572 | 56.3 | 0.8 | 5.4 | 0.1 | 6.5 | 446.0 | 4 871 | 366 | 429 | 7 430 | 36.5 | 61.0 | 2.6 |
| Crawford | 161.6 | 2 738 | 77.2 | 0.1 | 4.1 | 0.0 | 3.8 | 143.9 | 2 437 | 98 | 266 | 2 233 | 25.5 | 71.5 | 3.0 |
| Crittenden | 167.9 | 3 222 | 60.1 | 0.2 | 6.8 | 0.0 | 3.9 | 290.4 | 5 573 | 101 | 217 | 2 783 | 56.6 | 41.9 | 1.5 |
| Cross | 43.5 | 2 328 | 67.2 | 0.4 | 4.9 | 0.3 | 5.8 | 20.2 | 1 080 | 59 | 76 | 1 073 | 36.2 | 61.6 | 2.2 |
| Dallas | 17.8 | 2 162 | 57.2 | 2.5 | 6.4 | 0.0 | 5.9 | 12.2 | 1 480 | 21 | 35 | 395 | 44.3 | 53.0 | 2.7 |
| Desha | 50.7 | 3 674 | 55.9 | 15.7 | 5.4 | 0.0 | 4.7 | 45.3 | 3 280 | 65 | 55 | 931 | 54.9 | 42.7 | 2.4 |
| Drew | 70.5 | 3 763 | 54.5 | 21.5 | 4.5 | 0.0 | 6.8 | 24.4 | 1 302 | 62 | 79 | 2 101 | 39.3 | 58.4 | 2.3 |
| Faulkner | 257.6 | 2 456 | 63.3 | 0.0 | 5.5 | 0.0 | 3.8 | 380.3 | 3 626 | 212 | 515 | 7 381 | 36.3 | 61.6 | 2.1 |
| Franklin | 40.7 | 2 241 | 74.5 | 2.8 | 3.5 | 0.1 | 5.9 | 37.2 | 2 048 | 154 | 77 | 872 | 28.9 | 68.1 | 3.0 |
| Fulton | 20.9 | 1 778 | 62.3 | 13.2 | 3.0 | 0.2 | 8.0 | 6.3 | 539 | 31 | 53 | 658 | 38.9 | 57.8 | 3.3 |
| Garland | 214.2 | 2 223 | 58.7 | 0.3 | 6.5 | 0.0 | 3.5 | 179.2 | 1 860 | 534 | 418 | 4 400 | 36.4 | 61.4 | 2.3 |
| Grant | 44.6 | 2 552 | 75.0 | 0.0 | 3.7 | 0.1 | 4.3 | 27.1 | 1 552 | 31 | 77 | 891 | 23.0 | 73.9 | 3.1 |
| Greene | 94.0 | 2 327 | 61.9 | 0.2 | 4.1 | 0.1 | 4.3 | 103.3 | 2 557 | 88 | 183 | 2 006 | 33.4 | 63.0 | 3.6 |
| Hempstead | 60.9 | 2 621 | 67.5 | 0.2 | 4.4 | 0.1 | 5.5 | 26.0 | 1 119 | 114 | 97 | 1 716 | 39.0 | 58.1 | 2.8 |
| Hot Spring | 68.8 | 2 159 | 68.6 | 0.1 | 3.8 | 0.0 | 5.6 | 78.3 | 2 459 | 73 | 141 | 1 900 | 35.9 | 60.3 | 3.8 |
| Howard | 36.7 | 2 622 | 66.3 | 0.1 | 4.1 | 0.0 | 5.6 | 18.5 | 1 320 | 63 | 60 | 794 | 36.0 | 61.0 | 3.0 |
| Independence | 92.4 | 2 672 | 60.6 | 0.1 | 3.7 | 0.9 | 4.6 | 129.9 | 3 759 | 146 | 158 | 2 312 | 30.0 | 67.1 | 2.9 |
| Izard | 32.7 | 2 522 | 78.3 | 0.1 | 2.7 | 0.0 | 4.5 | 27.0 | 2 078 | 34 | 58 | 1 117 | 34.3 | 61.2 | 4.5 |
| Jackson | 41.5 | 2 409 | 53.4 | 1.0 | 6.3 | 0.5 | 6.0 | 36.8 | 2 138 | 44 | 77 | 1 486 | 39.5 | 55.9 | 4.6 |
| Jefferson | 232.7 | 2 946 | 64.8 | 0.2 | 6.3 | 0.0 | 3.3 | 126.0 | 1 596 | 1 886 | 360 | 7 262 | 62.2 | 35.9 | 1.9 |
| Johnson | 47.6 | 1 922 | 70.8 | 0.0 | 3.3 | 0.0 | 7.4 | 43.7 | 1 765 | 94 | 110 | 1 075 | 37.1 | 60.2 | 2.7 |
| Lafayette | 15.6 | 2 008 | 73.9 | 0.1 | 5.5 | 0.3 | 4.2 | 4.2 | 546 | 25 | 32 | 354 | 39.0 | 58.1 | 2.9 |
| Lawrence | 61.3 | 3 637 | 53.6 | 18.8 | 2.8 | 3.7 | 3.9 | 20.2 | 1 198 | 61 | 74 | 1 278 | 36.7 | 57.6 | 5.7 |
| Lee | 22.6 | 2 083 | 62.6 | 0.5 | 6.1 | 0.0 | 4.7 | 2.7 | 245 | 40 | 44 | 819 | 60.1 | 38.6 | 1.2 |
| Lincoln | 19.6 | 1 429 | 68.1 | 0.0 | 3.7 | 0.0 | 8.1 | 16.7 | 1 214 | 26 | 60 | 1 333 | 38.8 | 57.0 | 4.2 |
| Little River | 43.4 | 3 388 | 48.2 | 15.2 | 3.2 | 4.8 | 5.1 | 90.7 | 7 077 | 49 | 56 | 896 | 34.0 | 63.0 | 3.0 |
| Logan | 45.2 | 2 000 | 70.6 | 1.6 | 4.3 | 0.1 | 4.4 | 43.8 | 1 940 | 125 | 96 | 1 391 | 28.9 | 67.7 | 3.4 |
| Lonoke | 162.4 | 2 554 | 72.3 | 0.1 | 3.7 | 0.0 | 4.0 | 114.6 | 1 803 | 109 | 298 | 2 865 | 25.1 | 72.6 | 2.2 |
| Madison | 27.2 | 1 764 | 76.6 | 0.0 | 6.4 | 0.0 | 8.3 | 18.4 | 1 194 | 46 | 68 | 613 | 33.9 | 62.8 | 3.4 |
| Marion | 24.9 | 1 498 | 61.0 | 0.1 | 7.3 | 0.1 | 14.2 | 21.1 | 1 270 | 40 | 71 | 619 | 33.3 | 63.2 | 3.5 |
| Miller | 109.4 | 2 565 | 61.2 | 0.1 | 8.9 | 0.0 | 3.8 | 120.5 | 2 825 | 60 | 188 | 2 202 | 32.3 | 65.8 | 1.9 |
| Mississippi | 155.1 | 3 325 | 50.1 | 0.2 | 5.1 | 0.4 | 3.2 | 777.7 | 16 667 | 108 | 197 | 3 029 | 47.6 | 49.8 | 2.6 |
| Monroe | 23.8 | 2 736 | 63.5 | 0.5 | 5.2 | 0.5 | 7.0 | 8.0 | 917 | 27 | 35 | 503 | 46.8 | 50.9 | 2.3 |
| Montgomery | 16.1 | 1 781 | 69.4 | 0.1 | 2.3 | 0.0 | 8.7 | 22.6 | 2 501 | 58 | 40 | 529 | 30.1 | 65.3 | 4.6 |
| Nevada | 25.0 | 2 662 | 48.8 | 19.0 | 4.2 | 0.0 | 8.0 | 22.6 | 2 406 | 26 | 39 | 479 | 40.6 | 56.7 | 2.7 |
| Newton | 25.1 | 3 006 | 83.3 | 0.0 | 2.3 | 0.0 | 7.6 | 12.2 | 1 467 | 60 | 35 | 459 | 29.8 | 65.4 | 4.8 |
| Ouachita | 70.8 | 2 715 | 71.5 | 0.0 | 3.8 | 0.0 | 5.0 | 37.0 | 1 421 | 103 | 111 | 1 997 | 43.6 | 54.5 | 1.9 |
| Perry | 17.9 | 1 721 | 71.3 | 0.5 | 4.3 | 0.1 | 7.5 | 10.8 | 1 039 | 27 | 45 | 450 | 31.6 | 64.1 | 4.3 |
| Phillips | 77.1 | 3 500 | 65.0 | 0.1 | 2.9 | 0.0 | 2.5 | 39.5 | 1 793 | 69 | 92 | 1 626 | 63.5 | 34.5 | 2.0 |
| Pike | 30.0 | 2 776 | 71.3 | 6.2 | 2.9 | 0.0 | 4.6 | 18.1 | 1 680 | 66 | 48 | 615 | 27.5 | 68.8 | 3.8 |
| Poinsett | 62.6 | 2 520 | 73.2 | 0.1 | 5.0 | 0.0 | 4.8 | 33.7 | 1 355 | 68 | 105 | 1 216 | 34.6 | 61.8 | 3.6 |
| Polk | 63.5 | 3 144 | 52.5 | 31.0 | 2.3 | 0.0 | 2.6 | 34.1 | 1 690 | 96 | 88 | 1 156 | 25.5 | 71.3 | 3.3 |
| Pope | 130.6 | 2 215 | 65.8 | 1.2 | 7.2 | 0.3 | 6.0 | 149.7 | 2 539 | 299 | 267 | 4 180 | 27.2 | 70.5 | 2.3 |
| Prairie | 18.5 | 2 121 | 58.9 | 2.2 | 6.0 | 0.0 | 10.8 | 10.6 | 1 207 | 43 | 37 | 359 | 31.0 | 65.7 | 3.3 |
| Pulaski | 1 320.8 | 3 532 | 43.2 | 4.6 | 6.6 | 0.0 | 4.5 | 1 288.0 | 3 445 | 9 096 | 6 951 | 46 147 | 55.1 | 43.5 | 1.4 |
| Randolph | 36.5 | 2 020 | 64.8 | 0.1 | 6.0 | 0.0 | 8.5 | 7.2 | 399 | 35 | 77 | 1 105 | 39.1 | 57.2 | 3.7 |
| St. Francis | 66.2 | 2 462 | 68.1 | 0.3 | 6.5 | 0.2 | 4.1 | 14.7 | 545 | 665 | 120 | 1 626 | 57.7 | 41.2 | 1.1 |
| Saline | 191.5 | 1 991 | 61.4 | 0.2 | 6.2 | 0.0 | 5.1 | 238.4 | 2 478 | 86 | 470 | 4 635 | 28.4 | 69.4 | 2.2 |
| Scott | 20.1 | 1 782 | 65.1 | 0.0 | 5.9 | 0.0 | 8.0 | 14.1 | 1 246 | 77 | 48 | 489 | 26.4 | 69.9 | 3.8 |
| Searcy | 15.5 | 1 917 | 68.5 | 0.0 | 5.1 | 0.0 | 6.5 | 4.4 | 540 | 47 | 34 | 468 | 25.0 | 70.9 | 4.2 |
| Sebastian | 336.5 | 2 764 | 50.6 | 0.1 | 4.6 | 0.1 | 9.6 | 515.8 | 4 236 | 1 073 | 561 | 6 987 | 31.6 | 66.3 | 2.1 |
| Sevier | 44.8 | 2 744 | 74.3 | 0.1 | 4.1 | 0.0 | 4.3 | 13.0 | 798 | 72 | 74 | 1 191 | 28.2 | 68.2 | 3.6 |
| Sharp | 41.4 | 2 321 | 64.3 | 0.0 | 4.2 | 0.0 | 7.3 | 31.5 | 1 763 | 47 | 75 | 842 | 33.6 | 62.5 | 3.9 |
| Stone | 19.2 | 1 601 | 70.6 | 0.0 | 5.6 | 0.1 | 10.8 | 2.6 | 219 | 65 | 54 | 572 | 30.0 | 66.4 | 3.6 |
| Union | 102.1 | 2 362 | 63.3 | 0.1 | 4.8 | 0.0 | 6.8 | 56.8 | 1 315 | 149 | 179 | 2 578 | 36.0 | 62.2 | 1.8 |
| Van Buren | 31.6 | 1 917 | 66.4 | 0.2 | 7.9 | 0.4 | 7.0 | 27.7 | 1 677 | 36 | 73 | 747 | 32.1 | 63.8 | 4.1 |
| Washington | 608.4 | 3 131 | 52.0 | 0.2 | 5.5 | 0.0 | 7.9 | 880.2 | 4 530 | 1 778 | 912 | 15 440 | 42.4 | 55.5 | 2.0 |
| White | 165.7 | 2 257 | 67.3 | 0.1 | 8.9 | 0.2 | 5.1 | 131.7 | 1 794 | 179 | 336 | 3 724 | 25.0 | 72.2 | 2.8 |
| Woodruff | 25.6 | 3 345 | 51.9 | 0.3 | 4.8 | 21.1 | 6.2 | 12.1 | 1 586 | 45 | 31 | 543 | 51.1 | 43.7 | 5.2 |
| Yell | 49.6 | 2 278 | 72.8 | 0.1 | 5.6 | 0.0 | 5.7 | 24.3 | 1 114 | 138 | 95 | 1 270 | 33.2 | 63.1 | 3.7 |

1. Based on the resident population estimated as of July 1 of the year shown.    2. © 2013 Election Data Services, Inc. All rights reserved.

# Table B. States and Counties — Land Area and Population

| STATE/ County code | CBSA code[1] | County type[2] | STATE County | Land area,[3] (sq km) 2010 | Total persons | Rank | Per square kilometer | White | Black | American Indian, Alaska Native | Asian and Pacific Islander | Percent Hispanic or Latino[4] | Under 5 years | 5 to 17 years | 18 to 24 years | 25 to 34 years | 35 to 44 years | 45 to 54 years |
|---|---|---|---|---|---|---|---|---|---|---|---|---|---|---|---|---|---|---|
| | | | | 1 | 2 | 3 | 4 | 5 | 6 | 7 | 8 | 9 | 10 | 11 | 12 | 13 | 14 | 15 |
| 06 000 | ... | X | CALIFORNIA | 403 466 | 38 041 430 | X | 94.3 | 41.9 | 6.6 | 1.0 | 15.1 | 38.1 | 6.7 | 17.9 | 10.5 | 14.4 | 13.7 | 13.9 |
| 06 001 | 41860 | 1 | Alameda | 1 914 | 1 554 720 | 21 | 812.3 | 37.1 | 13.3 | 1.0 | 30.1 | 22.8 | 6.4 | 15.9 | 9.8 | 15.1 | 14.9 | 14.6 |
| 06 003 | ... | 8 | Alpine | 1 912 | 1 129 | 3 104 | 0.6 | 72.5 | 1.5 | 19.2 | 1.2 | 7.7 | 4.7 | 14.5 | 6.1 | 8.6 | 11.7 | 17.4 |
| 06 005 | ... | 6 | Amador | 1 540 | 37 035 | 1 244 | 24.0 | 81.6 | 3.1 | 2.6 | 2.2 | 12.9 | 3.7 | 12.7 | 6.7 | 9.7 | 11.6 | 16.1 |
| 06 007 | 17020 | 3 | Butte | 4 238 | 221 539 | 285 | 52.3 | 77.6 | 2.4 | 3.0 | 5.9 | 14.7 | 5.5 | 15.0 | 15.8 | 11.9 | 10.3 | 12.5 |
| 06 009 | ... | 6 | Calaveras | 2 642 | 44 742 | 1 074 | 16.9 | 85.4 | 1.4 | 2.8 | 2.4 | 10.8 | 4.3 | 14.8 | 6.3 | 8.3 | 9.6 | 15.8 |
| 06 011 | ... | 6 | Colusa | 2 980 | 21 411 | 1 761 | 7.2 | 40.1 | 1.2 | 1.8 | 2.0 | 56.1 | 8.4 | 21.2 | 9.1 | 12.8 | 12.5 | 12.7 |
| 06 013 | 41860 | 1 | Contra Costa | 1 854 | 1 079 597 | 38 | 582.3 | 50.5 | 10.0 | 1.0 | 17.7 | 24.8 | 6.3 | 18.2 | 8.4 | 12.4 | 13.9 | 15.4 |
| 06 015 | 18860 | 7 | Del Norte | 2 606 | 28 290 | 1 479 | 10.9 | 67.3 | 4.5 | 8.7 | 4.4 | 18.4 | 5.9 | 15.2 | 8.7 | 14.6 | 13.1 | 15.1 |
| 06 017 | 40900 | 1 | El Dorado | 4 423 | 180 561 | 351 | 40.8 | 82.1 | 1.3 | 1.9 | 5.3 | 12.3 | 5.0 | 17.2 | 7.6 | 9.6 | 11.7 | 17.4 |
| 06 019 | 23420 | 2 | Fresno | 15 431 | 947 895 | 49 | 61.4 | 33.9 | 5.3 | 1.2 | 10.6 | 50.9 | 8.5 | 21.1 | 11.6 | 14.4 | 12.2 | 12.2 |
| 06 021 | ... | 6 | Glenn | 3 403 | 27 992 | 1 495 | 8.2 | 56.5 | 1.3 | 2.5 | 3.1 | 38.4 | 7.7 | 20.0 | 9.3 | 12.5 | 11.6 | 13.4 |
| 06 023 | 21700 | 5 | Humboldt | 9 241 | 134 827 | 465 | 14.6 | 80.7 | 2.0 | 7.4 | 4.2 | 10.2 | 5.6 | 14.0 | 13.3 | 14.4 | 11.2 | 13.2 |
| 06 025 | 20940 | 3 | Imperial | 10 817 | 176 948 | 356 | 16.4 | 14.1 | 3.1 | 1.1 | 1.8 | 80.6 | 7.9 | 20.9 | 11.2 | 14.0 | 12.9 | 12.6 |
| 06 027 | 13860 | 7 | Inyo | 26 368 | 18 495 | 1 896 | 0.7 | 67.7 | 1.2 | 11.4 | 1.8 | 20.1 | 5.9 | 15.2 | 6.8 | 10.9 | 10.4 | 15.2 |
| 06 029 | 12540 | 2 | Kern | 21 062 | 856 158 | 61 | 40.6 | 39.6 | 6.0 | 1.4 | 5.1 | 50.0 | 8.6 | 21.3 | 11.3 | 14.7 | 12.8 | 12.7 |
| 06 031 | 25260 | 3 | Kings | 3 599 | 151 364 | 417 | 42.1 | 36.8 | 7.5 | 1.3 | 5.2 | 51.4 | 8.4 | 19.2 | 11.6 | 16.8 | 14.2 | 13.2 |
| 06 033 | 17340 | 4 | Lake | 3 254 | 63 983 | 820 | 19.7 | 76.5 | 2.6 | 4.0 | 2.5 | 17.7 | 5.5 | 15.2 | 7.7 | 10.3 | 10.5 | 15.4 |
| 06 035 | 45000 | 6 | Lassen | 11 762 | 33 658 | 1 335 | 2.9 | 68.4 | 9.4 | 4.2 | 2.4 | 18.0 | 4.6 | 12.9 | 10.6 | 18.4 | 15.7 | 15.4 |
| 06 037 | 31100 | 1 | Los Angeles | 10 510 | 9 962 789 | 1 | 947.9 | 29.2 | 8.9 | 0.6 | 15.2 | 48.1 | 6.6 | 17.5 | 10.8 | 15.1 | 14.4 | 13.9 |
| 06 039 | 31460 | 3 | Madera | 5 535 | 152 218 | 413 | 27.5 | 38.8 | 3.9 | 1.9 | 2.5 | 54.5 | 7.8 | 20.4 | 10.5 | 13.8 | 12.5 | 12.6 |
| 06 041 | 41860 | 1 | Marin | 1 348 | 256 069 | 258 | 190.0 | 75.3 | 3.4 | 0.8 | 7.8 | 15.7 | 5.4 | 15.2 | 5.8 | 9.7 | 14.0 | 16.5 |
| 06 043 | ... | 8 | Mariposa | 3 752 | 17 905 | 1 925 | 4.8 | 85.1 | 1.3 | 4.4 | 2.2 | 9.9 | 4.2 | 13.4 | 6.6 | 9.6 | 9.5 | 16.7 |
| 06 045 | 46380 | 4 | Mendocino | 9 081 | 87 428 | 651 | 9.6 | 70.4 | 1.3 | 5.4 | 2.8 | 22.9 | 6.1 | 16.1 | 7.9 | 12.1 | 11.6 | 13.6 |
| 06 047 | 32900 | 3 | Merced | 5 012 | 262 305 | 254 | 52.3 | 32.8 | 3.9 | 0.9 | 8.6 | 55.7 | 8.5 | 22.6 | 11.9 | 13.8 | 12.3 | 12.1 |
| 06 049 | ... | 6 | Modoc | 10 147 | 9 327 | 2 490 | 0.9 | 80.3 | 1.6 | 4.4 | 1.8 | 14.3 | 5.2 | 16.3 | 6.2 | 9.4 | 10.8 | 14.4 |
| 06 051 | ... | 7 | Mono | 7 897 | 14 348 | 2 145 | 1.8 | 68.9 | 1.0 | 2.3 | 2.6 | 27.0 | 6.1 | 15.1 | 9.3 | 16.3 | 13.3 | 16.1 |
| 06 053 | 41500 | 2 | Monterey | 8 497 | 426 762 | 161 | 50.2 | 32.4 | 3.4 | 0.8 | 8.0 | 56.1 | 8.0 | 18.8 | 11.0 | 15.1 | 13.0 | 12.6 |
| 06 055 | 34900 | 3 | Napa | 1 938 | 139 045 | 450 | 71.7 | 57.5 | 2.3 | 1.1 | 8.4 | 32.9 | 5.9 | 17.0 | 8.9 | 12.4 | 12.8 | 14.4 |
| 06 057 | 46020 | 4 | Nevada | 2 481 | 98 292 | 597 | 39.6 | 88.4 | 0.9 | 2.0 | 2.4 | 8.9 | 4.3 | 14.4 | 6.8 | 9.8 | 10.5 | 15.3 |
| 06 059 | 31100 | 1 | Orange | 2 048 | 3 090 132 | 6 | 1 508.9 | 45.6 | 2.0 | 0.6 | 20.1 | 34.1 | 6.3 | 17.8 | 10.1 | 13.8 | 14.3 | 14.7 |
| 06 061 | 40900 | 1 | Placer | 3 644 | 361 682 | 184 | 99.3 | 78.2 | 1.9 | 1.5 | 8.2 | 13.3 | 5.8 | 18.2 | 7.8 | 11.3 | 13.1 | 15.1 |
| 06 063 | ... | 7 | Plumas | 6 612 | 19 399 | 1 861 | 2.9 | 87.3 | 1.5 | 3.9 | 1.8 | 8.5 | 4.6 | 13.2 | 7.4 | 8.9 | 9.0 | 15.5 |
| 06 065 | 40140 | 1 | Riverside | 18 665 | 2 268 783 | 11 | 121.6 | 41.0 | 6.8 | 1.1 | 7.4 | 46.1 | 7.3 | 20.5 | 10.5 | 13.0 | 13.2 | 13.3 |
| 06 067 | 40900 | 1 | Sacramento | 2 498 | 1 450 121 | 25 | 580.5 | 51.6 | 11.5 | 1.6 | 18.0 | 22.0 | 7.0 | 18.2 | 10.1 | 14.7 | 13.3 | 13.9 |
| 06 069 | 41940 | 1 | San Benito | 3 597 | 56 884 | 894 | 15.8 | 39.2 | 1.1 | 0.9 | 3.5 | 56.9 | 7.2 | 21.3 | 9.5 | 12.6 | 13.4 | 14.8 |
| 06 071 | 40140 | 1 | San Bernardino | 51 947 | 2 081 313 | 12 | 40.1 | 34.4 | 9.2 | 1.0 | 7.7 | 49.9 | 7.7 | 21.0 | 11.4 | 14.0 | 13.2 | 13.5 |
| 06 073 | 41740 | 1 | San Diego | 10 895 | 3 177 063 | 5 | 291.6 | 50.6 | 5.7 | 1.0 | 13.4 | 32.5 | 6.6 | 16.6 | 11.7 | 15.4 | 13.4 | 13.7 |
| 06 075 | 41860 | 1 | San Francisco | 121 | 825 863 | 67 | 6 825.3 | 44.4 | 6.7 | 0.8 | 36.1 | 15.4 | 4.5 | 9.0 | 8.9 | 21.4 | 16.4 | 13.7 |
| 06 077 | 44700 | 2 | San Joaquin | 3 604 | 702 612 | 87 | 195.0 | 38.0 | 7.9 | 1.2 | 16.8 | 39.4 | 7.8 | 21.1 | 10.4 | 13.3 | 13.1 | 13.3 |
| 06 079 | 42020 | 3 | San Luis Obispo | 8 543 | 274 804 | 241 | 32.2 | 72.4 | 2.6 | 1.3 | 4.9 | 21.3 | 4.9 | 13.5 | 15.9 | 11.5 | 10.7 | 13.7 |
| 06 081 | 41860 | 1 | San Mateo | 1 161 | 739 311 | 82 | 636.8 | 44.6 | 3.3 | 0.6 | 29.3 | 25.6 | 6.4 | 15.7 | 7.6 | 13.9 | 14.9 | 15.2 |
| 06 083 | 42060 | 2 | Santa Barbara | 7 084 | 431 249 | 157 | 60.9 | 49.1 | 2.3 | 1.0 | 6.4 | 43.4 | 6.4 | 16.2 | 16.2 | 13.2 | 11.6 | 12.6 |
| 06 085 | 41940 | 1 | Santa Clara | 3 341 | 1 837 504 | 16 | 550.0 | 37.3 | 3.0 | 0.7 | 34.9 | 27.2 | 6.9 | 17.0 | 8.8 | 15.1 | 15.5 | 14.7 |
| 06 087 | 42100 | 2 | Santa Cruz | 1 153 | 266 776 | 249 | 231.4 | 61.5 | 1.6 | 1.2 | 6.1 | 32.7 | 5.7 | 15.0 | 14.8 | 12.4 | 12.3 | 14.2 |
| 06 089 | 39820 | 3 | Shasta | 9 778 | 178 586 | 354 | 18.3 | 85.2 | 1.6 | 4.2 | 3.9 | 8.8 | 5.7 | 16.3 | 9.0 | 11.5 | 10.8 | 14.5 |
| 06 091 | ... | 8 | Sierra | 2 469 | 3 086 | 2 970 | 1.2 | 88.7 | 1.0 | 2.0 | 1.2 | 8.9 | 3.8 | 12.6 | 5.1 | 7.9 | 9.8 | 17.1 |
| 06 093 | ... | 7 | Siskiyou | 16 260 | 44 154 | 1 083 | 2.7 | 82.8 | 2.2 | 6.1 | 2.5 | 10.7 | 5.4 | 15.1 | 7.2 | 9.6 | 9.8 | 14.6 |
| 06 095 | 46700 | 2 | Solano | 2 128 | 420 757 | 162 | 197.7 | 44.6 | 16.0 | 1.4 | 18.9 | 24.6 | 6.4 | 17.6 | 9.9 | 13.5 | 12.8 | 15.1 |
| 06 097 | 42220 | 2 | Sonoma | 4 081 | 491 829 | 137 | 120.5 | 68.2 | 2.1 | 1.6 | 5.6 | 25.4 | 5.8 | 16.0 | 9.4 | 12.8 | 12.3 | 14.8 |
| 06 099 | 33700 | 2 | Stanislaus | 3 872 | 521 726 | 125 | 134.7 | 48.3 | 3.2 | 1.4 | 7.3 | 42.6 | 7.7 | 20.6 | 10.5 | 13.7 | 12.8 | 13.3 |
| 06 101 | 49700 | 3 | Sutter | 1 560 | 95 022 | 611 | 60.9 | 52.3 | 2.6 | 2.1 | 17.0 | 29.4 | 7.4 | 19.7 | 9.8 | 13.4 | 12.3 | 13.4 |
| 06 103 | 39780 | 4 | Tehama | 7 640 | 63 406 | 825 | 8.3 | 73.5 | 1.2 | 3.4 | 1.9 | 22.6 | 6.8 | 18.2 | 8.5 | 11.3 | 11.2 | 14.3 |
| 06 105 | ... | 8 | Trinity | 8 234 | 13 526 | 2 212 | 1.6 | 87.0 | 1.0 | 7.2 | 1.6 | 7.4 | 4.3 | 13.7 | 5.9 | 9.2 | 10.0 | 16.2 |
| 06 107 | 47300 | 2 | Tulare | 12 495 | 451 977 | 147 | 36.2 | 33.2 | 1.6 | 1.3 | 4.1 | 61.3 | 9.2 | 23.1 | 10.8 | 14.0 | 12.3 | 11.7 |
| 06 109 | 38020 | 4 | Tuolumne | 5 752 | 54 008 | 924 | 9.4 | 83.6 | 2.6 | 3.0 | 2.0 | 11.3 | 4.1 | 12.9 | 7.7 | 11.3 | 10.6 | 14.7 |
| 06 111 | 37100 | 2 | Ventura | 4 774 | 835 981 | 64 | 175.1 | 50.1 | 2.1 | 0.8 | 8.4 | 40.9 | 6.6 | 18.7 | 10.0 | 12.9 | 13.2 | 14.8 |
| 06 113 | 40900 | 1 | Yolo | 2 628 | 204 118 | 307 | 77.7 | 52.0 | 3.2 | 1.3 | 16.6 | 30.5 | 6.0 | 15.9 | 21.1 | 13.3 | 11.5 | 12.0 |
| 06 115 | 49700 | 3 | Yuba | 1 636 | 72 926 | 745 | 44.6 | 61.9 | 4.3 | 3.7 | 9.0 | 25.9 | 8.4 | 20.4 | 10.3 | 14.7 | 12.0 | 12.9 |
| 08 000 | ... | X | COLORADO | 268 431 | 5 187 582 | X | 19.3 | 71.6 | 4.6 | 1.3 | 3.8 | 20.9 | 6.7 | 17.4 | 9.8 | 14.6 | 13.7 | 14.4 |
| 08 001 | 19740 | 1 | Adams | 3 024 | 459 598 | 145 | 152.0 | 54.6 | 3.5 | 1.2 | 4.4 | 38.2 | 8.3 | 20.1 | 9.2 | 16.2 | 14.7 | 13.1 |
| 08 003 | ... | 7 | Alamosa | 1 872 | 16 148 | 2 034 | 8.6 | 50.3 | 1.5 | 1.8 | 1.5 | 46.5 | 7.9 | 16.3 | 16.5 | 12.7 | 10.3 | 12.8 |
| 08 005 | 19740 | 1 | Arapahoe | 2 067 | 595 546 | 108 | 288.1 | 65.7 | 11.0 | 1.1 | 6.5 | 18.7 | 6.9 | 18.4 | 8.5 | 14.9 | 14.3 | 14.5 |
| 08 007 | ... | 7 | Archuleta | 3 497 | 12 070 | 2 295 | 3.5 | 79.2 | 0.7 | 2.3 | 1.1 | 18.3 | 5.0 | 14.5 | 5.4 | 9.6 | 9.9 | 16.1 |
| 08 009 | ... | 9 | Baca | 6 617 | 3 751 | 2 926 | 0.6 | 89.0 | 0.9 | 1.8 | 0.4 | 9.2 | 5.7 | 15.5 | 5.8 | 9.9 | 9.8 | 13.9 |
| 08 011 | ... | 7 | Bent | 3 918 | 5 773 | 2 782 | 1.5 | 59.8 | 7.4 | 1.9 | 1.0 | 30.5 | 4.2 | 12.2 | 8.7 | 16.2 | 15.6 | 15.5 |

1. CBSA = Core Based Statistical Area. See Appendix A for explanation. See Appendix B for list of metropolitan areas with component counties.   2. County type code from the Economic Research Service of USDA Rural-Urban Continuum Codes. See Appendix A for definition.   3. Dry land or land partially or temporarily covered by water.   4. May be of any race.

# Table B. States and Counties — **Population and Households**

| STATE County | Population, 2011 (cont.) Age (percent) (cont.) 55 to 64 years | 65 to 74 years | 75 years and over | Percent female | Population change and components of change, 2000–2012 Total persons 2000 | Total persons 2010 | Percent change 2000–2010 | Percent change 2010–2012 | Components of change, 2010–2012 Births | Deaths | Net migration | Households, 2010 Number | Percent change, 2000–2010 | Persons per household | Percent Female family householder[1] | One person |
|---|---|---|---|---|---|---|---|---|---|---|---|---|---|---|---|---|
| | 16 | 17 | 18 | 19 | 20 | 21 | 22 | 23 | 24 | 25 | 26 | 27 | 28 | 29 | 30 | 31 |
| CALIFORNIA | 11.2 | 6.3 | 5.4 | 50.3 | 33 871 648 | 37 253 956 | 10.0 | 2.1 | 1 159 112 | 537 016 | 172 716 | 12 577 498 | 9.3 | 2.90 | 13.3 | 23.3 |
| Alameda | 11.8 | 6.2 | 5.2 | 50.9 | 1 443 741 | 1 510 271 | 4.6 | 2.9 | 44 111 | 20 674 | 21 665 | 545 138 | 4.2 | 2.70 | 12.9 | 26.0 |
| Alpine | 21.2 | 9.6 | 6.1 | 47.7 | 1 208 | 1 175 | -2.7 | -3.9 | 9 | 12 | -50 | 497 | 2.9 | 2.32 | 8.0 | 29.4 |
| Amador | 18.0 | 12.3 | 9.2 | 45.6 | 35 100 | 38 091 | 8.5 | -2.8 | 632 | 926 | -757 | 14 569 | 14.2 | 2.30 | 8.6 | 26.8 |
| Butte | 13.4 | 8.1 | 7.5 | 50.5 | 203 171 | 220 000 | 8.3 | 0.7 | 5 493 | 4 863 | 1 024 | 87 618 | 10.1 | 2.45 | 11.6 | 27.9 |
| Calaveras | 19.0 | 13.4 | 8.4 | 50.0 | 40 554 | 45 578 | 12.4 | -1.8 | 748 | 1 027 | -534 | 18 886 | 14.7 | 2.39 | 8.6 | 24.7 |
| Colusa | 11.3 | 6.6 | 5.3 | 48.6 | 18 804 | 21 419 | 13.9 | 0.0 | 784 | 299 | -494 | 7 056 | 15.7 | 3.00 | 11.2 | 20.9 |
| Contra Costa | 12.6 | 7.0 | 5.8 | 51.2 | 948 816 | 1 049 025 | 10.6 | 2.9 | 28 112 | 16 129 | 18 689 | 375 364 | 9.1 | 2.77 | 12.4 | 22.7 |
| Del Norte | 13.5 | 7.7 | 6.0 | 44.4 | 27 507 | 28 610 | 4.0 | -1.1 | 754 | 555 | -523 | 9 907 | 8.0 | 2.50 | 13.3 | 28.1 |
| El Dorado | 16.2 | 9.0 | 6.3 | 50.0 | 156 299 | 181 058 | 15.8 | -0.3 | 3 743 | 3 033 | -1 105 | 70 223 | 19.1 | 2.55 | 8.8 | 22.1 |
| Fresno | 9.8 | 5.5 | 4.8 | 50.0 | 799 407 | 930 450 | 16.4 | 1.9 | 36 236 | 13 970 | -4 730 | 289 391 | 14.4 | 3.15 | 16.9 | 19.8 |
| Glenn | 12.1 | 7.3 | 6.1 | 49.5 | 26 453 | 28 122 | 6.3 | -0.5 | 951 | 473 | -610 | 9 800 | 6.8 | 2.84 | 11.7 | 22.2 |
| Humboldt | 14.8 | 7.5 | 6.0 | 49.9 | 126 518 | 134 623 | 6.4 | 0.2 | 3 423 | 2 659 | -501 | 56 031 | 9.4 | 2.31 | 10.9 | 31.8 |
| Imperial | 9.9 | 5.6 | 4.9 | 48.5 | 142 361 | 174 528 | 22.6 | 1.4 | 6 990 | 2 029 | -2 539 | 49 126 | 24.7 | 3.34 | 19.6 | 17.0 |
| Inyo | 16.2 | 10.1 | 9.4 | 49.7 | 17 945 | 18 546 | 3.3 | -0.3 | 512 | 445 | -115 | 8 049 | 4.5 | 2.25 | 10.0 | 33.9 |
| Kern | 9.5 | 5.3 | 3.8 | 48.4 | 661 645 | 839 631 | 26.9 | 2.0 | 33 060 | 12 046 | -4 358 | 254 610 | 22.0 | 3.15 | 15.7 | 17.5 |
| Kings | 8.7 | 4.6 | 3.5 | 43.6 | 129 461 | 152 982 | 18.2 | -1.1 | 5 792 | 1 758 | -5 743 | 41 233 | 19.8 | 3.19 | 15.9 | 17.5 |
| Lake | 17.0 | 10.6 | 7.7 | 49.8 | 58 309 | 64 665 | 10.9 | -1.1 | 1 580 | 1 683 | -538 | 26 548 | 10.7 | 2.39 | 12.2 | 29.7 |
| Lassen | 12.1 | 5.8 | 4.5 | 35.6 | 33 828 | 34 895 | 3.2 | -3.5 | 712 | 497 | -1 462 | 10 058 | 4.5 | 2.50 | 10.3 | 25.6 |
| Los Angeles | 10.7 | 6.0 | 5.2 | 50.7 | 9 519 338 | 9 818 605 | 3.1 | 1.5 | 302 441 | 133 505 | -22 066 | 3 241 204 | 3.4 | 2.98 | 15.3 | 24.2 |
| Madera | 10.8 | 6.7 | 4.9 | 51.8 | 123 109 | 150 865 | 22.5 | 0.9 | 5 411 | 2 102 | -1 931 | 43 317 | 19.8 | 3.28 | 13.3 | 16.7 |
| Marin | 16.1 | 9.7 | 7.6 | 50.8 | 247 289 | 252 409 | 2.1 | 1.5 | 5 251 | 3 948 | 2 489 | 103 210 | 2.5 | 2.36 | 8.8 | 30.8 |
| Mariposa | 18.4 | 12.6 | 9.0 | 49.2 | 17 130 | 18 251 | 6.5 | -1.9 | 352 | 371 | -326 | 7 693 | 16.3 | 2.28 | 7.6 | 28.4 |
| Mendocino | 14.8 | 9.0 | 6.9 | 50.0 | 86 265 | 87 841 | 1.8 | -0.5 | 2 366 | 1 750 | -1 000 | 34 945 | 5.0 | 2.46 | 11.5 | 29.7 |
| Merced | 9.1 | 5.3 | 4.3 | 49.6 | 210 554 | 255 793 | 21.5 | 2.5 | 9 841 | 3 454 | 127 | 75 642 | 18.5 | 3.32 | 15.8 | 17.4 |
| Modoc | 17.0 | 12.0 | 8.5 | 49.7 | 9 449 | 9 686 | 2.5 | -3.7 | 216 | 271 | -304 | 4 064 | 7.4 | 2.30 | 10.0 | 29.4 |
| Mono | 13.8 | 6.7 | 3.3 | 47.0 | 12 853 | 14 202 | 10.5 | 1.0 | 327 | 103 | -103 | 5 768 | 12.3 | 2.42 | 5.6 | 27.6 |
| Monterey | 10.6 | 5.7 | 5.2 | 48.6 | 401 762 | 415 057 | 3.3 | 2.8 | 15 665 | 5 200 | 1 500 | 125 946 | 3.9 | 3.15 | 12.7 | 21.7 |
| Napa | 13.3 | 8.0 | 7.3 | 50.1 | 124 279 | 136 484 | 9.8 | 1.9 | 3 636 | 2 683 | 1 621 | 48 876 | 7.7 | 2.69 | 10.3 | 25.3 |
| Nevada | 18.7 | 11.3 | 8.8 | 50.6 | 92 033 | 98 764 | 7.3 | -0.5 | 1 703 | 1 939 | -171 | 41 527 | 12.6 | 2.35 | 8.7 | 26.3 |
| Orange | 11.1 | 6.4 | 5.5 | 50.5 | 2 846 289 | 3 010 232 | 5.8 | 2.7 | 88 284 | 39 829 | 32 074 | 992 781 | 6.1 | 2.99 | 11.6 | 20.9 |
| Placer | 13.0 | 8.6 | 7.2 | 51.2 | 248 399 | 348 432 | 40.3 | 3.8 | 8 646 | 6 050 | 10 338 | 132 627 | 42.0 | 2.60 | 9.2 | 23.0 |
| Plumas | 19.8 | 13.3 | 8.3 | 49.9 | 20 824 | 20 007 | -3.9 | -3.0 | 371 | 512 | -482 | 8 977 | -0.3 | 2.20 | 8.0 | 29.8 |
| Riverside | 10.1 | 6.6 | 5.4 | 50.2 | 1 545 387 | 2 189 641 | 41.7 | 3.6 | 71 555 | 32 410 | 39 391 | 686 260 | 35.6 | 3.14 | 13.3 | 19.3 |
| Sacramento | 11.4 | 6.1 | 5.4 | 51.0 | 1 223 499 | 1 418 788 | 16.0 | 2.2 | 45 179 | 22 806 | 9 064 | 513 945 | 13.3 | 2.71 | 14.8 | 26.0 |
| San Benito | 11.2 | 5.7 | 4.3 | 50.1 | 53 234 | 55 269 | 3.8 | 2.9 | 1 668 | 622 | 580 | 16 805 | 5.8 | 3.27 | 12.6 | 15.4 |
| San Bernardino | 10.1 | 5.3 | 3.9 | 50.3 | 1 709 434 | 2 035 210 | 19.1 | 2.3 | 71 488 | 27 617 | 2 428 | 611 618 | 15.7 | 3.26 | 16.2 | 17.7 |
| San Diego | 11.0 | 6.0 | 5.5 | 49.8 | 2 813 833 | 3 095 313 | 10.0 | 2.6 | 100 498 | 44 443 | 26 655 | 1 086 865 | 9.3 | 2.75 | 12.1 | 24.0 |
| San Francisco | 12.3 | 6.8 | 6.9 | 49.2 | 776 733 | 805 235 | 3.7 | 2.6 | 19 444 | 12 788 | 14 030 | 345 811 | 4.9 | 2.26 | 8.3 | 38.6 |
| San Joaquin | 10.4 | 5.8 | 4.8 | 50.1 | 563 598 | 685 306 | 21.6 | 2.5 | 24 244 | 10 484 | 3 590 | 215 007 | 18.4 | 3.12 | 15.4 | 19.7 |
| San Luis Obispo | 14.1 | 8.2 | 7.4 | 48.8 | 246 681 | 269 637 | 9.3 | 1.9 | 5 889 | 4 832 | 4 171 | 102 016 | 10.0 | 2.48 | 9.3 | 26.2 |
| San Mateo | 12.8 | 7.1 | 6.5 | 50.8 | 707 161 | 718 451 | 1.6 | 2.9 | 20 560 | 10 404 | 11 043 | 257 837 | 1.5 | 2.75 | 10.8 | 24.5 |
| Santa Barbara | 10.8 | 6.5 | 6.6 | 49.8 | 399 347 | 423 895 | 6.1 | 1.7 | 13 255 | 6 452 | 725 | 142 104 | 4.0 | 2.86 | 10.9 | 24.8 |
| Santa Clara | 10.8 | 6.1 | 5.2 | 49.8 | 1 682 585 | 1 781 642 | 5.9 | 3.1 | 54 502 | 20 999 | 23 286 | 604 204 | 6.8 | 2.90 | 10.7 | 21.8 |
| Santa Cruz | 14.0 | 6.4 | 5.2 | 50.2 | 255 602 | 262 382 | 2.7 | 1.7 | 7 241 | 3 803 | 1 030 | 94 355 | 3.5 | 2.66 | 10.5 | 26.4 |
| Shasta | 14.9 | 9.7 | 7.6 | 50.9 | 163 256 | 177 223 | 8.6 | 0.8 | 4 659 | 4 356 | 993 | 70 346 | 10.9 | 2.48 | 12.2 | 25.9 |
| Sierra | 21.8 | 13.4 | 8.6 | 49.7 | 3 555 | 3 240 | -8.9 | -4.8 | 44 | 85 | -119 | 1 482 | -2.5 | 2.16 | 7.2 | 31.2 |
| Siskiyou | 18.2 | 11.4 | 8.7 | 50.3 | 44 301 | 44 900 | 1.4 | -1.7 | 1 010 | 1 197 | -532 | 19 505 | 5.1 | 2.28 | 9.9 | 31.1 |
| Solano | 12.9 | 6.6 | 5.1 | 50.0 | 394 542 | 413 344 | 4.8 | 1.8 | 11 802 | 6 487 | 2 142 | 141 758 | 8.7 | 2.83 | 14.7 | 21.9 |
| Sonoma | 14.6 | 7.8 | 6.6 | 50.8 | 458 614 | 483 878 | 5.5 | 1.6 | 12 465 | 8 672 | 4 199 | 185 825 | 7.8 | 2.55 | 10.6 | 27.3 |
| Stanislaus | 10.5 | 5.9 | 5.0 | 50.5 | 446 997 | 514 453 | 15.1 | 1.4 | 17 531 | 7 997 | -2 174 | 165 180 | 13.8 | 3.08 | 14.6 | 19.3 |
| Sutter | 11.0 | 7.0 | 6.0 | 50.4 | 78 930 | 94 737 | 20.0 | 0.3 | 3 108 | 1 593 | -1 239 | 31 437 | 16.3 | 2.98 | 12.8 | 21.0 |
| Tehama | 13.4 | 9.2 | 7.1 | 50.2 | 56 039 | 63 463 | 13.2 | -0.1 | 1 770 | 1 288 | -562 | 23 767 | 13.1 | 2.63 | 12.8 | 24.0 |
| Trinity | 20.0 | 12.5 | 8.2 | 48.2 | 13 022 | 13 786 | 5.9 | -1.9 | 242 | 348 | -141 | 6 083 | 8.9 | 2.20 | 8.8 | 32.0 |
| Tulare | 9.3 | 5.3 | 4.3 | 49.8 | 368 021 | 442 179 | 20.2 | 2.2 | 18 591 | 6 062 | -2 643 | 130 352 | 18.1 | 3.36 | 16.1 | 16.6 |
| Tuolumne | 17.5 | 11.8 | 9.3 | 47.2 | 54 501 | 55 365 | 1.6 | -2.5 | 968 | 1 253 | -1 103 | 22 156 | 5.5 | 2.30 | 9.2 | 28.3 |
| Ventura | 11.8 | 6.5 | 5.6 | 50.3 | 753 197 | 823 318 | 9.3 | 1.5 | 25 125 | 11 582 | -733 | 266 920 | 9.7 | 3.04 | 11.8 | 19.9 |
| Yolo | 10.1 | 5.5 | 4.7 | 51.3 | 168 660 | 200 849 | 19.1 | 1.6 | 5 400 | 2 566 | 411 | 70 872 | 19.4 | 2.74 | 11.3 | 22.9 |
| Yuba | 11.0 | 5.9 | 4.3 | 49.6 | 60 219 | 72 155 | 19.8 | 1.1 | 2 722 | 1 075 | -861 | 24 307 | 18.4 | 2.92 | 14.3 | 21.2 |
| COLORADO | 12.3 | 6.4 | 4.8 | 49.8 | 4 301 261 | 5 029 196 | 16.9 | 3.1 | 147 515 | 71 725 | 80 587 | 1 972 868 | 19.0 | 2.49 | 10.1 | 27.9 |
| Adams | 9.9 | 4.9 | 3.6 | 49.6 | 348 618 | 441 603 | NA | 4.1 | 15 506 | 5 450 | 7 637 | 153 764 | 20.0 | 2.85 | 13.0 | 22.3 |
| Alamosa | 12.0 | 6.7 | 4.8 | 50.0 | 14 966 | 15 445 | 3.2 | 4.6 | 530 | 249 | 411 | 5 995 | 9.7 | 2.45 | 13.1 | 30.2 |
| Arapahoe | 12.1 | 5.9 | 4.5 | 50.9 | 487 967 | 572 003 | 17.2 | 4.1 | 17 011 | 7 581 | 13 481 | 224 011 | 17.3 | 2.53 | 11.8 | 28.0 |
| Archuleta | 20.7 | 12.0 | 6.9 | 49.4 | 9 898 | 12 084 | 22.1 | -0.1 | 256 | 185 | -94 | 5 267 | 32.3 | 2.27 | 7.8 | 26.7 |
| Baca | 14.8 | 11.5 | 13.1 | 50.6 | 4 517 | 3 788 | -16.1 | -1.0 | 90 | 131 | -6 | 1 685 | -11.5 | 2.20 | 7.4 | 35.0 |
| Bent | 13.1 | 7.6 | 6.9 | 35.0 | 5 998 | 6 499 | 8.4 | -11.2 | 105 | 121 | -727 | 1 832 | -8.5 | 2.34 | 12.8 | 32.0 |

1. No spouse present.

Table B. States and Counties — **Population, Vital Statistics, Medicare, and Crime**

| STATE County | Persons in group quarters, 2010 | Daytime population, 2007–2011 Number | Employment/residence ratio | Births, 2011 Total | Rate[1] | Deaths, 2011 Number | Rate[1] | Persons under 65 with no health insurance, 2010 Number | Percent | Medicare, 2012 Eligible for Medicare | Enrolled in Medicare Advantage | Enrolled in a Medicare prescription drug plan | Serious crimes known to police,[2] 2011 Total Number | Rate[3] |
|---|---|---|---|---|---|---|---|---|---|---|---|---|---|---|
| | 32 | 33 | 34 | 35 | 36 | 37 | 38 | 39 | 40 | 41 | 42 | 43 | 44 | 45 |
| CALIFORNIA | 819 816 | 36 967 527 | 1.00 | 508 069 | 13.5 | 234 045 | 6.2 | 6 720 279 | 20.7 | 5 171 312 | 1 892 465 | 1 817 325 | 1 128 845 | 2 995 |
| Alameda | 37 442 | 1 500 231 | 1.01 | 19 372 | 12.7 | 8 950 | 5.9 | 199 327 | 15.1 | 202 631 | 84 892 | 65 126 | 63 444 | 4 152 |
| Alpine | 24 | 1 639 | 1.91 | 4 | 3.6 | 3 | 2.7 | 161 | 15.7 | 201 | 11 | 106 | 112 | 9 420 |
| Amador | 4 551 | 38 991 | 1.06 | 277 | 7.3 | 396 | 10.4 | 4 097 | 15.8 | 9 356 | 1 738 | 3 855 | 1 070 | 2 776 |
| Butte | 4 942 | 218 043 | 0.99 | 2 403 | 10.9 | 2 182 | 9.9 | 34 814 | 19.0 | 44 093 | 766 | 24 965 | 5 951 | 2 674 |
| Calaveras | 493 | 39 489 | 0.65 | 330 | 7.3 | 478 | 10.6 | 5 868 | 16.5 | 11 290 | 1 457 | 4 994 | 1 276 | 2 767 |
| Colusa | 225 | 21 468 | 1.02 | 345 | 16.0 | 114 | 5.3 | 4 560 | 24.2 | 3 094 | 207 | 1 814 | 541 | 2 496 |
| Contra Costa | 10 314 | 933 883 | 0.78 | 12 289 | 11.5 | 7 039 | 6.6 | 129 974 | 14.3 | 160 627 | 70 717 | 45 126 | 33 901 | 3 194 |
| Del Norte | 3 818 | 29 043 | 1.05 | 347 | 12.1 | 248 | 8.7 | 3 437 | 16.2 | 5 339 | 408 | 2 840 | 921 | 3 182 |
| El Dorado | 1 643 | 155 675 | 0.70 | 1 634 | 9.0 | 1 348 | 7.5 | 20 841 | 13.6 | 33 828 | 9 985 | 11 256 | 3 483 | 1 901 |
| Fresno | 17 523 | 924 213 | 1.01 | 15 958 | 16.9 | 6 161 | 6.5 | 181 235 | 21.9 | 116 513 | 29 070 | 56 155 | 45 521 | 4 912 |
| Glenn | 316 | 27 209 | 0.92 | 418 | 14.9 | 211 | 7.5 | 5 457 | 22.6 | 4 987 | 52 | 2 940 | 707 | 2 485 |
| Humboldt | 5 014 | 133 974 | 1.01 | 1 521 | 11.3 | 1 193 | 8.9 | 23 158 | 20.2 | 24 421 | 734 | 13 494 | 4 651 | 3 415 |
| Imperial | 10 684 | 170 192 | 0.98 | 3 062 | 17.3 | 844 | 4.8 | 33 176 | 22.6 | 25 128 | 1 915 | 15 836 | 6 156 | 3 647 |
| Inyo | 433 | 19 427 | 1.11 | 215 | 11.6 | 186 | 10.1 | 2 952 | 19.9 | 4 058 | 58 | 2 162 | 335 | 1 785 |
| Kern | 36 757 | 830 119 | 1.00 | 14 378 | 16.9 | 5 318 | 6.2 | 171 643 | 23.4 | 98 895 | 33 370 | 38 502 | 34 518 | 4 063 |
| Kings | 21 580 | 151 680 | 0.99 | 2 528 | 16.4 | 770 | 5.0 | 23 607 | 19.6 | 14 582 | 1 635 | 7 702 | 3 978 | 2 570 |
| Lake | 1 085 | 59 875 | 0.81 | 707 | 11.0 | 761 | 11.8 | 10 726 | 20.2 | 15 283 | 700 | 8 367 | 2 066 | 3 158 |
| Lassen | 9 779 | 35 970 | 1.10 | 319 | 9.3 | 223 | 6.5 | 3 104 | 14.3 | 4 422 | 56 | 2 049 | 598 | 1 694 |
| Los Angeles | 171 681 | 9 934 403 | 1.03 | 133 239 | 13.5 | 58 426 | 5.9 | 2 248 384 | 25.9 | 1 254 353 | 508 040 | 457 962 | 274 252 | 2 761 |
| Madera | 8 624 | 147 407 | 0.95 | 2 376 | 15.5 | 880 | 5.8 | 28 784 | 22.8 | 20 908 | 6 371 | 8 419 | 4 604 | 3 016 |
| Marin | 9 044 | 254 347 | 1.03 | 2 374 | 9.3 | 1 692 | 6.6 | 23 851 | 11.8 | 49 286 | 16 975 | 17 267 | 5 218 | 2 043 |
| Mariposa | 725 | 17 334 | 0.87 | 148 | 8.1 | 160 | 8.8 | 2 412 | 16.9 | 4 397 | 186 | 2 043 | 420 | 2 274 |
| Mendocino | 2 044 | 88 953 | 1.04 | 1 057 | 12.1 | 759 | 8.7 | 15 858 | 21.5 | 18 941 | 1 174 | 10 417 | 1 998 | 2 248 |
| Merced | 4 896 | 241 565 | 0.87 | 4 260 | 16.4 | 1 510 | 5.8 | 49 697 | 21.7 | 30 697 | 2 251 | 17 116 | 10 541 | 4 073 |
| Modoc | 357 | 9 392 | 0.94 | 106 | 11.1 | 121 | 12.7 | 1 720 | 22.5 | 2 390 | 165 | 1 219 | 191 | 1 949 |
| Mono | 222 | 14 533 | 1.07 | 146 | 10.2 | 49 | 3.4 | 3 011 | 23.6 | 1 274 | 38 | 608 | 360 | 2 505 |
| Monterey | 18 702 | 410 839 | 1.00 | 6 808 | 16.1 | 2 259 | 5.4 | 86 376 | 24.3 | 53 521 | 510 | 28 688 | 11 844 | 2 820 |
| Napa | 4 918 | 141 419 | 1.10 | 1 565 | 11.3 | 1 209 | 8.8 | 21 105 | 18.7 | 25 080 | 9 183 | 7 274 | 3 251 | 2 354 |
| Nevada | 1 175 | 93 122 | 0.88 | 761 | 7.7 | 835 | 8.5 | 13 832 | 17.5 | 23 596 | 3 645 | 10 353 | 1 706 | 1 707 |
| Orange | 39 236 | 3 071 161 | 1.06 | 38 498 | 12.6 | 17 161 | 5.6 | 527 030 | 19.9 | 409 719 | 183 643 | 122 933 | 68 167 | 2 238 |
| Placer | 3 807 | 335 408 | 0.95 | 3 746 | 10.5 | 2 565 | 7.2 | 36 419 | 12.4 | 65 436 | 28 691 | 16 060 | 8 317 | 2 359 |
| Plumas | 277 | 20 212 | 1.00 | 166 | 8.4 | 223 | 11.3 | 2 945 | 18.9 | 5 416 | 332 | 2 720 | 490 | 2 421 |
| Riverside | 35 829 | 1 997 190 | 0.81 | 30 783 | 13.7 | 14 065 | 6.3 | 448 271 | 23.4 | 295 334 | 148 382 | 74 344 | 69 863 | 3 154 |
| Sacramento | 23 787 | 1 426 322 | 1.03 | 19 811 | 13.8 | 9 898 | 6.9 | 199 328 | 16.0 | 207 508 | 87 441 | 59 401 | 52 911 | 3 686 |
| San Benito | 289 | 47 774 | 0.71 | 728 | 13.0 | 278 | 5.0 | 10 225 | 20.5 | 6 719 | 268 | 3 605 | 1 111 | 1 987 |
| San Bernardino | 40 054 | 1 953 848 | 0.91 | 31 140 | 15.1 | 12 032 | 5.8 | 411 749 | 22.5 | 235 695 | 119 420 | 60 682 | 65 785 | 3 195 |
| San Diego | 101 966 | 3 086 589 | 1.02 | 44 076 | 14.0 | 19 373 | 6.2 | 511 168 | 19.1 | 426 740 | 175 340 | 118 221 | 76 111 | 2 430 |
| San Francisco | 24 264 | 964 917 | 1.38 | 8 593 | 10.6 | 5 572 | 6.9 | 99 476 | 14.5 | 130 021 | 48 376 | 52 916 | 39 244 | 4 817 |
| San Joaquin | 14 354 | 652 426 | 0.89 | 10 557 | 15.2 | 4 525 | 6.5 | 117 928 | 19.4 | 91 198 | 27 878 | 38 034 | 34 836 | 5 024 |
| San Luis Obispo | 17 006 | 265 139 | 0.98 | 2 632 | 9.7 | 2 078 | 7.6 | 38 754 | 18.2 | 49 939 | 4 578 | 23 671 | 6 876 | 2 520 |
| San Mateo | 8 853 | 711 210 | 1.00 | 9 092 | 12.5 | 4 528 | 6.2 | 83 186 | 13.4 | 109 577 | 46 641 | 27 770 | 15 509 | 2 134 |
| Santa Barbara | 17 782 | 432 395 | 1.07 | 5 842 | 13.7 | 2 845 | 6.7 | 75 530 | 21.3 | 65 093 | 8 905 | 32 993 | 10 740 | 2 504 |
| Santa Clara | 30 350 | 1 864 624 | 1.12 | 23 999 | 13.3 | 9 073 | 5.0 | 216 019 | 13.8 | 229 849 | 82 048 | 85 557 | 43 533 | 2 415 |
| Santa Cruz | 10 969 | 247 440 | 0.90 | 3 191 | 12.1 | 1 693 | 6.4 | 41 184 | 18.3 | 37 946 | 2 657 | 20 889 | 9 913 | 3 734 |
| Shasta | 2 654 | 178 424 | 1.02 | 2 052 | 11.5 | 1 884 | 10.6 | 25 788 | 17.7 | 42 098 | 2 415 | 22 619 | 6 256 | 3 489 |
| Sierra | 33 | 3 026 | 0.80 | 22 | 7.1 | 46 | 14.8 | 468 | 18.2 | 777 | 25 | 395 | 61 | 1 861 |
| Siskiyou | 474 | 45 377 | 1.04 | 446 | 10.0 | 537 | 12.1 | 7 022 | 19.5 | 11 467 | 885 | 5 787 | 1 018 | 2 241 |
| Solano | 12 452 | 369 815 | 0.77 | 5 121 | 12.3 | 2 852 | 6.8 | 51 013 | 14.3 | 60 671 | 26 820 | 11 498 | 13 889 | 3 321 |
| Sonoma | 10 043 | 459 121 | 0.91 | 5 444 | 11.2 | 3 769 | 7.7 | 72 057 | 17.5 | 84 235 | 31 997 | 26 994 | 10 009 | 2 044 |
| Stanislaus | 6 305 | 494 508 | 0.91 | 7 713 | 14.9 | 3 467 | 6.7 | 89 607 | 19.6 | 72 342 | 27 902 | 27 190 | 21 671 | 4 163 |
| Sutter | 1 060 | 86 025 | 0.78 | 1 363 | 14.4 | 693 | 7.3 | 17 798 | 21.6 | 14 710 | 328 | 8 357 | 3 046 | 3 178 |
| Tehama | 842 | 59 769 | 0.86 | 779 | 12.2 | 559 | 8.8 | 11 421 | 21.5 | 13 492 | 165 | 7 772 | 1 801 | 2 805 |
| Trinity | 385 | 13 415 | 0.94 | 107 | 7.8 | 158 | 11.5 | 2 210 | 20.2 | 3 484 | 189 | 1 738 | 172 | 1 233 |
| Tulare | 4 772 | 428 077 | 0.95 | 8 115 | 18.1 | 2 640 | 5.9 | 92 846 | 23.3 | 53 227 | 5 706 | 30 514 | 17 153 | 3 834 |
| Tuolumne | 4 482 | 55 965 | 1.01 | 441 | 8.0 | 544 | 9.9 | 6 502 | 16.3 | 13 673 | 497 | 6 970 | 1 364 | 2 435 |
| Ventura | 10 600 | 773 434 | 0.89 | 11 060 | 13.3 | 5 083 | 6.1 | 130 774 | 18.2 | 119 422 | 32 899 | 44 034 | 15 874 | 1 906 |
| Yolo | 6 709 | 211 826 | 1.15 | 2 402 | 11.9 | 1 123 | 5.6 | 28 425 | 16.2 | 24 761 | 11 379 | 6 317 | 5 857 | 2 882 |
| Yuba | 1 171 | 67 655 | 0.84 | 1 203 | 16.6 | 456 | 6.3 | 11 971 | 18.6 | 10 591 | 558 | 5 785 | 2 354 | 3 225 |
| COLORADO | 115 878 | 4 953 970 | 1.00 | 66 213 | 12.9 | 31 123 | 6.1 | 777 411 | 17.7 | 695 295 | 9 621 | 204 905 | 149 744 | 2 927 |
| Adams | 4 027 | 388 824 | 0.78 | 7 016 | 15.5 | 2 348 | 5.2 | 92 360 | 23.0 | 48 451 | 24 390 | 10 525 | 14 533 | 3 235 |
| Alamosa | 740 | 17 495 | 1.33 | 252 | 16.0 | 103 | 6.6 | 2 664 | 20.4 | 2 370 | 599 | 1 069 | 721 | 4 588 |
| Arapahoe | 4 920 | 549 928 | 0.95 | 7 681 | 13.1 | 3 313 | 5.7 | 93 629 | 18.3 | 71 979 | 30 237 | 16 946 | 17 454 | 2 999 |
| Archuleta | 129 | 11 831 | 0.94 | 114 | 9.5 | 91 | 7.6 | 2 138 | 21.6 | 2 615 | 288 | 1 169 | 209 | 1 700 |
| Baca | 82 | 3 809 | 1.00 | 37 | 9.7 | 66 | 17.4 | 738 | 25.8 | 988 | D | 617 | 17 | 441 |
| Bent | 2 208 | 5 818 | 0.82 | 51 | 8.2 | 51 | 8.2 | 695 | 19.5 | 962 | 51 | 457 | 46 | 696 |

1. Per 1,000 estimated resident population.   2. Data for serious crimes have not been adjusted for underreporting; this may affect comparability between geographic areas and over time.   3. Per 100,000 population estimated by the FBI.

# Table B. States and Counties — Crime, Education, Money Income, and Poverty

| STATE County | Serious crimes known to police, 2011 (cont.)[1] Rate[2] Violent | Property | Education School enrollment and attainment, 2007–2011 Enrollment[3] Total | Percent private | Attainment[4] (percent) High school graduate or less | Bachelor's degree or more | Local government expenditures,[5] 2009–2010 Total current expenditures (mil dol) | Current expenditures per student (dollars) | Money income, 2007–2011 Per capita income[6] (dollars) | Households Median income Dollars | Percent change, 2000 to 2007–2011 (constant 2011 dollars) | Percent with income of $200,000 or more | Income and poverty, 2011 Median household income (dollars) | Percent below poverty level All persons | Children under 18 years | Children 5 to 17 years in families |
|---|---|---|---|---|---|---|---|---|---|---|---|---|---|---|---|---|
| | 46 | 47 | 48 | 49 | 50 | 51 | 52 | 53 | 54 | 55 | 56 | 57 | 58 | 59 | 60 | 61 |
| CALIFORNIA | 411 | 2 584 | 10 516 923 | 14.1 | 40.3 | 30.2 | 57 581.9 | 9 281 | 29 634 | 61 632 | -3.9 | 6.9 | 57 275 | 16.6 | 22.8 | 21.7 |
| Alameda | 706 | 3 446 | 409 744 | 15.5 | 33.9 | 40.8 | 1 908.2 | 8 891 | 34 937 | 70 821 | -6.2 | 9.2 | 67 295 | 13.2 | 16.8 | 15.6 |
| Alpine | 589 | 8 831 | 404 | 13.6 | 33.9 | 32.0 | 4.0 | 35 839 | 29 576 | 59 018 | 4.4 | 5.0 | 46 706 | 17.4 | 29.3 | 25.3 |
| Amador | 254 | 2 522 | 7 642 | 12.5 | 42.1 | 18.8 | 39.0 | 8 731 | 28 030 | 56 180 | -1.6 | 2.6 | 51 553 | 14.0 | 19.3 | 16.5 |
| Butte | 259 | 2 415 | 67 176 | 8.0 | 36.8 | 24.0 | 304.9 | 9 840 | 23 431 | 42 971 | -0.3 | 1.9 | 39 208 | 22.6 | 28.0 | 25.6 |
| Calaveras | 260 | 2 507 | 9 242 | 12.2 | 37.8 | 20.7 | 63.9 | 10 115 | 28 667 | 55 256 | -0.2 | 2.6 | 50 599 | 12.5 | 20.4 | 17.7 |
| Colusa | 212 | 2 284 | 6 001 | 7.0 | 55.1 | 13.0 | 49.0 | 10 378 | 21 271 | 49 558 | 4.7 | 2.6 | 47 469 | 13.2 | 19.5 | 18.5 |
| Contra Costa | 370 | 2 824 | 283 527 | 16.4 | 31.2 | 38.4 | 1 461.8 | 8 778 | 38 141 | 79 135 | -8.0 | 11.1 | 74 244 | 11.9 | 14.6 | 14.0 |
| Del Norte | 553 | 2 629 | 6 814 | 14.8 | 52.0 | 14.3 | 43.5 | 9 955 | 19 247 | 37 588 | -6.1 | 2.0 | 35 598 | 25.4 | 33.7 | 31.6 |
| El Dorado | 213 | 1 688 | 47 124 | 11.5 | 30.2 | 30.8 | 253.6 | 8 941 | 34 385 | 68 815 | -1.0 | 7.0 | 61 970 | 10.3 | 13.4 | 12.1 |
| Fresno | 553 | 4 359 | 286 887 | 7.5 | 50.4 | 19.5 | 1 808.3 | 9 436 | 20 638 | 46 903 | 0.0 | 3.0 | 42 572 | 25.8 | 35.4 | 33.0 |
| Glenn | 228 | 2 256 | 7 848 | 11.8 | 51.6 | 15.5 | 58.5 | 10 743 | 21 254 | 43 239 | -0.3 | 3.2 | 40 221 | 19.2 | 26.6 | 24.9 |
| Humboldt | 323 | 3 092 | 36 451 | 7.9 | 36.2 | 26.3 | 174.7 | 10 117 | 24 209 | 40 376 | -4.2 | 2.2 | 39 526 | 21.1 | 26.3 | 24.1 |
| Imperial | 268 | 3 379 | 53 712 | 4.9 | 58.6 | 12.8 | 355.7 | 9 788 | 16 593 | 39 402 | -8.4 | 1.9 | 36 898 | 26.0 | 33.2 | 30.0 |
| Inyo | 362 | 1 423 | 3 895 | 9.6 | 39.6 | 22.5 | 41.6 | 11 976 | 27 532 | 49 571 | 4.9 | 1.2 | 44 928 | 12.7 | 20.4 | 19.5 |
| Kern | 523 | 3 540 | 244 546 | 8.7 | 55.3 | 14.6 | 1 600.0 | 9 190 | 20 167 | 48 021 | 0.3 | 2.7 | 44 903 | 24.6 | 34.6 | 33.5 |
| Kings | 350 | 2 220 | 42 092 | 10.8 | 55.4 | 12.5 | 253.4 | 8 847 | 18 296 | 48 838 | 1.2 | 1.8 | 48 319 | 21.2 | 29.5 | 27.5 |
| Lake | 506 | 2 652 | 14 497 | 6.8 | 44.2 | 16.2 | 92.1 | 10 474 | 22 238 | 39 525 | -1.2 | 1.8 | 35 882 | 23.0 | 33.8 | 31.2 |
| Lassen | 340 | 1 354 | 6 891 | 16.6 | 46.6 | 12.4 | 45.3 | 9 527 | 19 339 | 52 484 | 7.1 | 2.3 | 47 938 | 19.3 | 19.3 | 17.4 |
| Los Angeles | 464 | 2 297 | 2 807 907 | 15.4 | 44.8 | 29.2 | 15 936.9 | 10 026 | 27 954 | 56 266 | -1.2 | 6.3 | 52 239 | 18.4 | 25.9 | 25.1 |
| Madera | 523 | 2 493 | 41 313 | 6.6 | 55.8 | 14.0 | 264.2 | 8 913 | 18 817 | 47 724 | -2.6 | 2.6 | 44 795 | 23.6 | 33.5 | 30.5 |
| Marin | 212 | 1 831 | 57 470 | 27.2 | 20.7 | 54.0 | 346.8 | 11 505 | 54 605 | 89 605 | -6.9 | 17.4 | 78 470 | 9.4 | 10.8 | 10.1 |
| Mariposa | 298 | 1 977 | 3 416 | 7.6 | 40.7 | 20.5 | 22.7 | 10 440 | 27 209 | 49 174 | 5.2 | 2.2 | 42 175 | 15.7 | 24.3 | 22.3 |
| Mendocino | 543 | 1 705 | 20 106 | 11.1 | 41.6 | 22.1 | 146.5 | 11 460 | 23 585 | 44 527 | -8.4 | 2.0 | 41 236 | 20.2 | 31.4 | 29.0 |
| Merced | 544 | 3 529 | 81 303 | 6.0 | 58.5 | 12.3 | 522.4 | 9 286 | 18 304 | 43 945 | -8.4 | 2.7 | 40 016 | 26.8 | 35.8 | 35.7 |
| Modoc | 429 | 1 520 | 2 227 | 10.6 | 43.0 | 16.2 | 17.2 | 16 341 | 20 769 | 35 402 | -4.7 | 1.6 | 34 654 | 21.5 | 32.3 | 28.8 |
| Mono | 341 | 2 164 | 2 742 | 6.8 | 35.8 | 30.3 | 26.5 | 15 770 | 28 789 | 60 469 | -0.5 | 2.0 | 48 758 | 10.8 | 16.2 | 15.6 |
| Monterey | 465 | 2 356 | 116 010 | 10.2 | 50.0 | 23.2 | 692.4 | 9 755 | 25 508 | 59 737 | -8.4 | 5.4 | 52 746 | 17.1 | 24.5 | 23.0 |
| Napa | 327 | 2 027 | 33 403 | 16.6 | 37.7 | 30.7 | 214.7 | 10 564 | 35 309 | 68 641 | -1.7 | 8.8 | 61 179 | 12.0 | 16.6 | 14.8 |
| Nevada | 268 | 1 439 | 21 476 | 13.2 | 27.5 | 32.4 | 163.4 | 9 455 | 31 607 | 58 077 | -6.2 | 4.4 | 53 833 | 12.1 | 17.4 | 15.3 |
| Orange | 214 | 2 024 | 859 058 | 14.9 | 34.9 | 36.2 | 4 314.2 | 8 589 | 34 416 | 75 762 | -4.6 | 9.9 | 72 046 | 13.0 | 17.9 | 16.5 |
| Placer | 197 | 2 162 | 92 584 | 15.0 | 26.7 | 34.6 | 506.7 | 7 801 | 35 583 | 74 645 | -3.9 | 7.1 | 69 581 | 8.5 | 9.9 | 8.7 |
| Plumas | 514 | 1 907 | 4 244 | 13.9 | 36.2 | 21.1 | 27.6 | 11 645 | 28 104 | 44 151 | -10.0 | 2.5 | 44 923 | 14.8 | 21.9 | 19.8 |
| Riverside | 299 | 2 855 | 636 900 | 11.7 | 46.4 | 20.6 | 3 528.7 | 8 331 | 24 516 | 58 365 | 0.8 | 4.3 | 52 491 | 16.9 | 23.0 | 22.1 |
| Sacramento | 521 | 3 165 | 409 710 | 13.0 | 36.9 | 27.7 | 2 098.3 | 8 900 | 27 180 | 56 553 | -4.4 | 3.9 | 52 236 | 17.7 | 24.9 | 23.1 |
| San Benito | 351 | 1 636 | 16 223 | 13.1 | 48.1 | 18.3 | 101.7 | 9 020 | 26 300 | 65 570 | -15.5 | 5.0 | 62 618 | 12.4 | 17.6 | 15.9 |
| San Bernardino | 415 | 2 780 | 627 639 | 11.1 | 48.7 | 18.6 | 3 494.0 | 8 367 | 21 932 | 55 853 | -1.7 | 3.3 | 51 017 | 19.4 | 26.2 | 24.6 |
| San Diego | 352 | 2 079 | 861 453 | 14.2 | 34.1 | 34.2 | 4 543.7 | 9 134 | 30 955 | 63 857 | 0.5 | 6.5 | 59 290 | 15.2 | 19.2 | 18.4 |
| San Francisco | 671 | 4 146 | 169 209 | 29.6 | 28.7 | 51.4 | 693.5 | 12 471 | 46 777 | 72 947 | -2.2 | 12.6 | 69 354 | 13.8 | 16.0 | 17.5 |
| San Joaquin | 821 | 4 203 | 204 621 | 12.3 | 50.0 | 17.6 | 1 160.3 | 8 545 | 22 857 | 53 764 | -3.5 | 3.5 | 50 376 | 18.2 | 25.0 | 22.8 |
| San Luis Obispo | 249 | 2 271 | 75 632 | 9.9 | 33.0 | 30.8 | 314.7 | 9 089 | 30 204 | 58 630 | 2.3 | 4.9 | 53 877 | 15.1 | 17.5 | 16.7 |
| San Mateo | 216 | 1 917 | 181 212 | 23.0 | 29.2 | 43.9 | 915.4 | 10 081 | 45 346 | 87 633 | -8.4 | 15.0 | 81 378 | 7.9 | 10.0 | 9.4 |
| Santa Barbara | 386 | 2 118 | 130 843 | 10.8 | 37.6 | 31.3 | 604.3 | 9 161 | 30 330 | 61 896 | -1.8 | 6.7 | 59 494 | 15.4 | 21.1 | 20.9 |
| Santa Clara | 253 | 2 162 | 488 570 | 20.2 | 29.8 | 45.5 | 2 540.2 | 9 581 | 40 698 | 89 064 | -11.3 | 14.7 | 84 741 | 10.7 | 12.6 | 12.1 |
| Santa Cruz | 440 | 3 294 | 77 725 | 11.3 | 31.9 | 38.1 | 369.1 | 9 485 | 32 975 | 66 030 | -9.4 | 8.0 | 61 228 | 14.9 | 18.5 | 17.2 |
| Shasta | 726 | 2 763 | 44 667 | 16.0 | 38.8 | 19.7 | 274.2 | 9 882 | 23 691 | 44 058 | -5.0 | 2.7 | 41 796 | 19.4 | 25.3 | 22.9 |
| Sierra | 153 | 1 708 | 555 | 10.8 | 47.3 | 18.6 | 7.4 | 16 280 | 26 137 | 50 308 | 4.0 | 1.1 | 45 060 | 13.6 | 19.8 | 17.7 |
| Siskiyou | 341 | 1 900 | 10 241 | 12.5 | 38.3 | 22.6 | 80.2 | 12 185 | 22 335 | 37 865 | -5.0 | 1.2 | 35 175 | 24.4 | 31.6 | 28.4 |
| Solano | 431 | 2 890 | 113 107 | 12.7 | 37.8 | 24.2 | 566.6 | 8 397 | 29 367 | 69 914 | -4.3 | 5.3 | 63 090 | 13.6 | 18.4 | 15.9 |
| Sonoma | 348 | 1 697 | 122 769 | 12.5 | 34.6 | 31.8 | 667.0 | 9 393 | 33 119 | 64 343 | -10.2 | 6.2 | 60 792 | 12.2 | 15.9 | 14.0 |
| Stanislaus | 477 | 3 686 | 150 625 | 9.2 | 52.2 | 16.4 | 992.0 | 9 450 | 21 820 | 50 671 | -6.4 | 2.7 | 44 287 | 23.3 | 31.6 | 29.0 |
| Sutter | 358 | 2 820 | 26 200 | 9.5 | 46.2 | 18.9 | 158.8 | 7 761 | 22 464 | 50 010 | -3.5 | 2.5 | 48 749 | 15.8 | 24.5 | 21.9 |
| Tehama | 542 | 2 263 | 15 852 | 10.0 | 49.3 | 12.6 | 108.7 | 10 552 | 20 689 | 38 753 | -8.0 | 1.6 | 37 297 | 19.5 | 27.6 | 25.4 |
| Trinity | 244 | 989 | 2 595 | 10.1 | 37.9 | 19.3 | 25.5 | 14 894 | 22 551 | 37 672 | 0.7 | 1.4 | 33 163 | 21.4 | 33.3 | 30.4 |
| Tulare | 426 | 3 408 | 135 054 | 6.7 | 56.4 | 12.9 | 908.6 | 9 372 | 17 986 | 43 550 | -5.1 | 2.3 | 40 599 | 25.6 | 33.7 | 32.9 |
| Tuolumne | 189 | 2 246 | 11 685 | 12.5 | 41.2 | 17.9 | 65.7 | 10 058 | 26 084 | 47 359 | -9.4 | 3.4 | 43 530 | 16.6 | 24.3 | 22.2 |
| Ventura | 205 | 1 701 | 231 620 | 15.1 | 36.9 | 31.0 | 1 205.4 | 8 523 | 32 740 | 76 728 | -4.8 | 8.8 | 74 019 | 11.5 | 16.4 | 15.2 |
| Yolo | 280 | 2 602 | 73 701 | 7.9 | 34.6 | 38.4 | 263.0 | 8 932 | 28 631 | 57 920 | 5.2 | 5.5 | 50 174 | 21.3 | 20.5 | 19.6 |
| Yuba | 467 | 2 757 | 20 763 | 7.8 | 47.9 | 12.7 | 135.4 | 9 649 | 20 046 | 46 617 | 13.4 | 1.8 | 43 299 | 19.6 | 27.0 | 27.5 |
| COLORADO | 320 | 2 606 | 1 321 417 | 13.9 | 33.3 | 36.3 | 7 359.2 | 8 847 | 30 816 | 57 685 | -9.5 | 4.8 | 55 530 | 13.4 | 17.7 | 15.9 |
| Adams | 404 | 2 830 | 113 466 | 12.0 | 49.0 | 20.7 | 696.2 | 8 525 | 24 384 | 56 089 | 0.0 | 2.2 | 52 429 | 16.1 | 22.7 | 20.8 |
| Alamosa | 293 | 4 296 | 5 199 | 5.7 | 43.4 | 24.7 | 26.9 | 11 375 | 20 429 | 38 299 | -3.7 | 3.4 | 36 870 | 22.7 | 29.9 | 30.7 |
| Arapahoe | 324 | 2 675 | 150 074 | 14.6 | 30.8 | 38.3 | 992.1 | 9 030 | 32 482 | 59 937 | -17.1 | 5.6 | 57 042 | 12.0 | 16.4 | 14.5 |
| Archuleta | 236 | 1 464 | 2 535 | 10.9 | 36.4 | 33.5 | 12.8 | 8 411 | 29 361 | 60 170 | 17.6 | 4.9 | 48 043 | 14.9 | 26.6 | 24.4 |
| Baca | 52 | 389 | 765 | 3.4 | 44.7 | 17.5 | 10.4 | 10 372 | 21 322 | 37 111 | -2.2 | 2.1 | 34 168 | 20.5 | 31.1 | 28.4 |
| Bent | 106 | 590 | 1 090 | 3.6 | 62.0 | 11.3 | 8.0 | 9 368 | 15 390 | 35 667 | -6.1 | 0.7 | 35 522 | 32.4 | 34.7 | 31.7 |

1. Data for serious crimes have not been adjusted for underreporting; this may affect comparability between geographic areas and over time. 2. Per 100,000 population estimated by the FBI. 3. All persons 3 years old and over enrolled in nursery school through college. 4. Persons 25 years old and over. 5. Elementary and secondary education expenditures. 6. Based on population estimated by the American Community Survey, 2007–2011.

# Table B. States and Counties — **Personal Income**

| | Personal income, 2011 | | | | | | | | | | | | |
| STATE County | Total (mil dol) | Percent change, 2010–2011 | Per capita[1] Dollars | Rank | Wages and salaries[2] (mil dol) | Proprietors' income (mil dol) | Dividends, interest, and rent (mil dol) | Transfer payments (mil dol) Total | Government payments to individuals Total | Social Security | Medical payments | Income mainte-nance | Unemploy-ment insurance |
|---|---|---|---|---|---|---|---|---|---|---|---|---|---|
| | 62 | 63 | 64 | 65 | 66 | 67 | 68 | 69 | 70 | 71 | 72 | 73 | 74 |
| CALIFORNIA | 1 645 138 | 5.2 | 43 647 | X | 1 053 192 | 155 507 | 288 922 | 261 743 | 253 437 | 66 693 | 112 081 | 34 586 | 17 694 |
| Alameda | 75 908 | 5.4 | 49 617 | 216 | 52 415 | 4 986 | 12 212 | 10 684 | 10 346 | 2 580 | 4 884 | 1 221 | 777 |
| Alpine | 54 | 13.3 | 49 274 | 226 | 49 | 3 | 13 | 12 | 12 | 2 | 7 | 1 | 0 |
| Amador | 1 355 | 3.4 | 35 689 | 1 265 | 616 | 96 | 304 | 325 | 316 | 136 | 120 | 20 | 19 |
| Butte | 7 347 | 4.3 | 33 356 | 1 641 | 3 429 | 760 | 1 427 | 1 974 | 1 926 | 593 | 784 | 250 | 100 |
| Calaveras | 1 614 | 4.2 | 35 828 | 1 245 | 366 | 151 | 373 | 424 | 414 | 167 | 162 | 33 | 25 |
| Colusa | 1 007 | 8.8 | 46 741 | 311 | 403 | 393 | 128 | 152 | 148 | 41 | 65 | 16 | 17 |
| Contra Costa | 60 779 | 5.3 | 57 011 | 96 | 26 083 | 4 517 | 10 979 | 7 163 | 6 927 | 2 304 | 2 918 | 625 | 516 |
| Del Norte | 780 | 3.3 | 27 220 | 2 732 | 390 | 52 | 128 | 270 | 264 | 68 | 120 | 43 | 10 |
| El Dorado | 9 041 | 3.5 | 49 967 | 207 | 2 624 | 858 | 1 555 | 1 289 | 1 249 | 494 | 472 | 86 | 92 |
| Fresno | 29 741 | 4.2 | 31 542 | 1 991 | 17 073 | 3 419 | 4 265 | 7 111 | 6 902 | 1 446 | 2 939 | 1 390 | 518 |
| Glenn | 1 035 | 8.8 | 36 796 | 1 102 | 377 | 300 | 167 | 222 | 215 | 64 | 94 | 29 | 14 |
| Humboldt | 4 489 | 3.9 | 33 308 | 1 654 | 2 205 | 426 | 980 | 1 173 | 1 143 | 326 | 497 | 144 | 49 |
| Imperial | 5 020 | 4.2 | 28 351 | 2 565 | 2 782 | 624 | 511 | 1 380 | 1 341 | 265 | 518 | 283 | 168 |
| Inyo | 700 | 4.8 | 37 905 | 985 | 392 | 70 | 140 | 155 | 151 | 53 | 68 | 13 | 8 |
| Kern | 26 744 | 6.6 | 31 400 | 2 015 | 16 546 | 3 699 | 3 259 | 5 437 | 5 249 | 1 301 | 2 042 | 1 039 | 379 |
| Kings | 4 522 | 9.7 | 29 407 | 2 394 | 2 678 | 702 | 544 | 887 | 854 | 182 | 362 | 155 | 64 |
| Lake | 2 147 | 3.9 | 33 375 | 1 634 | 656 | 145 | 358 | 685 | 671 | 212 | 295 | 83 | 36 |
| Lassen | 987 | 3.9 | 28 855 | 2 477 | 618 | 81 | 139 | 226 | 218 | 56 | 99 | 27 | 12 |
| Los Angeles | 420 913 | 4.4 | 42 564 | 533 | 281 652 | 47 450 | 72 720 | 74 863 | 72 675 | 14 962 | 36 600 | 11 530 | 4 275 |
| Madera | 4 378 | 7.6 | 28 631 | 2 518 | 2 137 | 767 | 627 | 1 014 | 980 | 283 | 391 | 165 | 70 |
| Marin | 21 872 | 4.9 | 85 761 | 4 | 7 904 | 2 345 | 6 224 | 1 711 | 1 655 | 724 | 620 | 87 | 91 |
| Mariposa | 620 | 3.6 | 34 103 | 1 494 | 245 | 50 | 129 | 168 | 164 | 62 | 69 | 13 | 9 |
| Mendocino | 3 170 | 3.9 | 36 211 | 1 187 | 1 373 | 314 | 795 | 842 | 823 | 242 | 384 | 99 | 36 |
| Merced | 7 406 | 6.5 | 28 497 | 2 538 | 3 250 | 1 204 | 929 | 1 936 | 1 878 | 385 | 848 | 346 | 141 |
| Modoc | 344 | 6.8 | 36 148 | 1 193 | 122 | 66 | 63 | 100 | 98 | 30 | 45 | 11 | 4 |
| Mono | 592 | 7.2 | 41 370 | 627 | 345 | 68 | 151 | 55 | 51 | 17 | 16 | 5 | 7 |
| Monterey | 17 356 | 4.1 | 41 138 | 648 | 9 941 | 1 963 | 3 688 | 2 601 | 2 509 | 696 | 1 011 | 316 | 215 |
| Napa | 7 077 | 6.1 | 51 253 | 180 | 4 098 | 583 | 1 533 | 985 | 955 | 333 | 416 | 62 | 62 |
| Nevada | 4 370 | 4.3 | 44 313 | 428 | 1 521 | 485 | 1 162 | 820 | 798 | 340 | 298 | 53 | 46 |
| Orange | 154 132 | 4.8 | 50 440 | 197 | 99 325 | 16 057 | 28 482 | 17 949 | 17 273 | 5 493 | 7 044 | 1 822 | 1 291 |
| Placer | 17 313 | 6.0 | 48 476 | 256 | 8 039 | 1 347 | 3 173 | 2 425 | 2 346 | 941 | 826 | 149 | 178 |
| Plumas | 778 | 3.4 | 39 339 | 820 | 322 | 70 | 201 | 210 | 206 | 72 | 86 | 15 | 12 |
| Riverside | 67 025 | 4.8 | 29 927 | 2 303 | 30 074 | 4 737 | 10 731 | 13 950 | 13 454 | 4 117 | 5 084 | 1 890 | 1 111 |
| Sacramento | 54 862 | 3.9 | 38 202 | 942 | 41 053 | 3 957 | 8 183 | 11 375 | 11 057 | 2 650 | 5 009 | 1 584 | 762 |
| San Benito | 1 964 | 4.3 | 35 029 | 1 365 | 730 | 135 | 310 | 320 | 307 | 94 | 114 | 38 | 35 |
| San Bernardino | 61 958 | 3.9 | 29 998 | 2 291 | 35 418 | 3 895 | 7 458 | 13 446 | 12 993 | 3 082 | 5 318 | 2 382 | 977 |
| San Diego | 146 956 | 5.3 | 46 800 | 309 | 98 688 | 11 353 | 26 732 | 20 650 | 19 978 | 5 529 | 8 394 | 2 198 | 1 481 |
| San Francisco | 60 433 | 8.2 | 74 349 | 15 | 58 089 | 8 929 | 10 538 | 6 143 | 5 963 | 1 453 | 2 896 | 714 | 379 |
| San Joaquin | 21 592 | 3.8 | 31 013 | 2 096 | 11 201 | 1 905 | 3 091 | 5 398 | 5 244 | 1 201 | 2 431 | 786 | 432 |
| San Luis Obispo | 10 966 | 5.1 | 40 322 | 714 | 5 544 | 1 067 | 2 866 | 1 759 | 1 699 | 690 | 604 | 142 | 100 |
| San Mateo | 50 597 | 5.5 | 69 577 | 25 | 32 711 | 4 220 | 11 557 | 4 042 | 3 882 | 1 551 | 1 429 | 264 | 282 |
| Santa Barbara | 19 303 | 5.4 | 45 219 | 385 | 11 211 | 1 854 | 5 384 | 2 574 | 2 480 | 882 | 925 | 259 | 144 |
| Santa Clara | 111 880 | 9.1 | 61 833 | 54 | 104 096 | 6 727 | 19 134 | 10 539 | 10 139 | 3 013 | 4 340 | 1 004 | 826 |
| Santa Cruz | 12 920 | 5.5 | 48 883 | 239 | 5 289 | 1 207 | 2 696 | 1 686 | 1 627 | 511 | 642 | 160 | 142 |
| Shasta | 6 305 | 3.3 | 35 466 | 1 300 | 3 042 | 532 | 1 169 | 1 890 | 1 851 | 572 | 808 | 206 | 107 |
| Sierra | 113 | 5.6 | 36 307 | 1 168 | 37 | 6 | 25 | 28 | 27 | 11 | 9 | 3 | 2 |
| Siskiyou | 1 510 | 3.2 | 33 928 | 1 526 | 614 | 149 | 339 | 486 | 476 | 148 | 207 | 55 | 25 |
| Solano | 15 859 | 3.7 | 38 078 | 959 | 8 538 | 688 | 2 279 | 2 808 | 2 717 | 810 | 1 021 | 316 | 239 |
| Sonoma | 22 127 | 5.5 | 45 331 | 380 | 10 879 | 1 961 | 5 067 | 3 330 | 3 222 | 1 181 | 1 299 | 244 | 232 |
| Stanislaus | 16 652 | 4.2 | 32 115 | 1 858 | 8 661 | 1 689 | 2 344 | 3 845 | 3 731 | 964 | 1 572 | 577 | 312 |
| Sutter | 3 219 | 4.1 | 33 908 | 1 529 | 1 258 | 564 | 498 | 706 | 685 | 184 | 289 | 92 | 60 |
| Tehama | 1 755 | 4.8 | 27 592 | 2 671 | 753 | 165 | 317 | 559 | 545 | 182 | 218 | 76 | 27 |
| Trinity | 417 | 4.2 | 30 389 | 2 223 | 125 | 31 | 93 | 148 | 145 | 46 | 68 | 15 | 6 |
| Tulare | 13 316 | 7.3 | 29 640 | 2 353 | 6 564 | 2 160 | 1 764 | 3 322 | 3 222 | 660 | 1 389 | 672 | 230 |
| Tuolumne | 2 016 | 4.3 | 36 680 | 1 113 | 851 | 128 | 501 | 510 | 498 | 198 | 193 | 41 | 27 |
| Ventura | 38 141 | 4.5 | 45 855 | 343 | 20 450 | 2 641 | 6 824 | 5 055 | 4 872 | 1 639 | 1 910 | 486 | 386 |
| Yolo | 7 455 | 3.4 | 36 896 | 1 085 | 6 020 | 587 | 1 388 | 1 232 | 1 188 | 318 | 486 | 143 | 88 |
| Yuba | 2 209 | 4.8 | 30 437 | 2 215 | 1 319 | 167 | 277 | 693 | 678 | 136 | 327 | 105 | 41 |
| COLORADO | 225 410 | 6.1 | 44 053 | X | 147 569 | 25 801 | 37 699 | 29 542 | 28 419 | 9 386 | 11 236 | 2 878 | 1 831 |
| Adams | 14 925 | 5.6 | 33 061 | 1 698 | 9 135 | 1 139 | 1 427 | 2 408 | 2 308 | 674 | 950 | 299 | 182 |
| Alamosa | 525 | 5.4 | 33 402 | 1 628 | 355 | 61 | 74 | 123 | 120 | 26 | 50 | 21 | 6 |
| Arapahoe | 28 656 | 4.7 | 48 989 | 232 | 20 826 | 5 902 | 4 725 | 3 154 | 3 025 | 1 022 | 1 206 | 315 | 210 |
| Archuleta | 379 | 5.5 | 31 536 | 1 994 | 139 | 53 | 111 | 82 | 79 | 37 | 24 | 8 | 5 |
| Baca | 170 | 8.5 | 44 860 | 397 | 50 | 62 | 29 | 35 | 34 | 12 | 17 | 3 | 1 |
| Bent | 149 | 2.5 | 23 827 | 3 034 | 61 | 21 | 26 | 41 | 40 | 10 | 17 | 7 | 2 |

1. Based on the resident population estimated as of July 1 of the year shown.  2. Includes supplements to wages and salaries.

# Table B. States and Counties — Earnings, Social Security, and Housing

| STATE County | Earnings, 2011 | | | | | | | | | Social Security beneficiaries, December 2011 | | | Housing units, 2010 | |
|---|---|---|---|---|---|---|---|---|---|---|---|---|---|---|
| | | | | Percent by selected industries | | | | | | | | | | |
| | | | Goods-related[1] | | Service-related and health | | | | | | | Supplemental Security Income recipients, December 2011 | | |
| | Total (mil dol) | Farm | Total | Manu-facturing | Information and professional and technical services | Retail trade | Finance, insurance, and real estate | Health care and social services | Govern-ment | Number | Rate[2] | Total | Total | Percent change, 2000–2010 |
| | 75 | 76 | 77 | 78 | 79 | 80 | 81 | 82 | 83 | 84 | 85 | 86 | 87 | 88 |
| CALIFORNIA | 1 208 698 | 1.3 | 15.4 | 10.3 | 17.6 | 6.0 | 8.0 | 9.6 | 17.1 | 5 129 529 | 136 | 1 284 629 | 13 680 081 | 12.0 |
| Alameda | 57 402 | 0.0 | 17.1 | 11.2 | 18.1 | 5.5 | 4.1 | 11.6 | 16.2 | 191 820 | 125 | 53 658 | 582 549 | 7.8 |
| Alpine | 53 | 0.0 | 4.9 | 0.0 | D | D | D | 1.0 | 29.2 | 205 | 186 | 42 | 1 760 | 16.2 |
| Amador | 712 | 0.3 | 12.5 | 6.0 | 7.1 | 8.2 | 3.0 | 11.5 | 42.3 | 10 040 | 265 | 695 | 18 032 | 19.9 |
| Butte | 4 189 | 6.3 | 10.6 | 4.9 | 6.9 | 9.1 | 4.8 | 19.2 | 21.3 | 47 585 | 216 | 11 581 | 95 835 | 12.1 |
| Calaveras | 518 | 1.2 | D | 3.0 | 6.5 | 8.8 | 3.5 | D | 29.0 | 12 260 | 272 | 1 112 | 27 925 | 21.7 |
| Colusa | 795 | 48.2 | D | 6.0 | 1.1 | 3.4 | 1.7 | D | 15.0 | 3 435 | 159 | 567 | 7 883 | 16.4 |
| Contra Costa | 30 601 | 0.2 | 19.9 | 11.7 | 14.8 | 6.2 | 10.6 | 13.8 | 11.9 | 159 930 | 150 | 25 805 | 400 263 | 12.9 |
| Del Norte | 442 | 2.1 | D | 1.5 | D | 8.3 | 2.0 | 15.0 | 50.0 | 5 810 | 203 | 2 061 | 11 186 | 7.2 |
| El Dorado | 3 481 | 0.0 | 13.0 | 3.1 | 12.7 | 7.5 | 12.0 | 12.6 | 19.9 | 36 065 | 199 | 3 131 | 88 159 | 23.7 |
| Fresno | 20 492 | 7.9 | 12.0 | 7.1 | 6.3 | 6.8 | 5.5 | 12.8 | 21.9 | 121 670 | 129 | 42 186 | 315 531 | 16.6 |
| Glenn | 677 | 40.9 | D | 5.1 | D | 3.9 | 1.9 | D | 18.7 | 5 435 | 193 | 1 169 | 10 778 | 8.0 |
| Humboldt | 2 630 | 1.5 | D | 4.5 | 6.5 | 10.2 | 5.0 | 13.5 | 28.9 | 26 410 | 196 | 6 979 | 61 559 | 10.1 |
| Imperial | 3 406 | 14.4 | D | 3.9 | 2.3 | 7.1 | 2.4 | 4.4 | 39.3 | 27 175 | 153 | 10 547 | 56 067 | 27.7 |
| Inyo | 462 | 2.0 | 12.7 | 7.3 | D | 8.2 | 1.8 | 4.8 | 44.7 | 4 215 | 228 | 455 | 9 478 | 4.8 |
| Kern | 20 245 | 9.5 | 19.2 | 5.1 | 5.8 | 5.7 | 3.2 | 8.0 | 23.3 | 109 465 | 129 | 33 616 | 284 367 | 22.8 |
| Kings | 3 380 | 18.1 | 10.7 | 8.3 | 2.0 | 4.4 | 1.8 | 8.2 | 42.3 | 16 130 | 105 | 4 711 | 43 867 | 20.0 |
| Lake | 802 | 1.1 | D | 2.3 | 5.1 | 10.1 | 2.9 | 16.8 | 26.1 | 17 055 | 265 | 3 844 | 35 492 | 9.1 |
| Lassen | 699 | 5.6 | D | 0.2 | D | 4.8 | 1.6 | 7.5 | 66.3 | 4 880 | 143 | 999 | 12 710 | 5.9 |
| Los Angeles | 329 102 | 0.0 | 12.9 | 9.1 | 21.3 | 5.7 | 8.5 | 9.8 | 14.1 | 1 181 910 | 120 | 418 384 | 3 445 076 | 5.3 |
| Madera | 2 904 | 21.7 | D | 7.1 | 3.5 | 5.7 | 1.7 | 14.5 | 22.4 | 22 985 | 150 | 4 751 | 49 140 | 21.7 |
| Marin | 10 249 | 0.2 | 7.8 | 1.5 | 21.9 | 7.4 | 14.1 | 11.7 | 12.4 | 47 120 | 185 | 3 801 | 111 214 | 5.9 |
| Mariposa | 295 | 0.8 | 8.3 | 1.8 | D | 6.0 | D | 3.1 | 43.5 | 4 805 | 264 | 519 | 10 188 | 15.4 |
| Mendocino | 1 686 | 1.2 | 15.8 | 8.7 | 6.5 | 11.6 | 3.6 | 13.2 | 23.5 | 19 610 | 224 | 3 830 | 40 323 | 9.2 |
| Merced | 4 453 | 20.1 | D | 9.1 | 3.5 | 6.6 | 2.4 | 9.5 | 23.7 | 33 570 | 129 | 11 172 | 83 698 | 22.1 |
| Modoc | 189 | 28.2 | D | D | D | 5.4 | 1.6 | D | 37.9 | 2 565 | 270 | 451 | 5 192 | 8.0 |
| Mono | 413 | 2.2 | D | 0.7 | 4.2 | 5.8 | 4.2 | 1.9 | 34.2 | 1 325 | 93 | 110 | 13 912 | 18.3 |
| Monterey | 11 904 | 8.6 | 7.0 | 3.4 | 6.3 | 6.0 | 3.6 | 7.7 | 27.4 | 55 480 | 132 | 9 314 | 139 048 | 5.6 |
| Napa | 4 681 | 2.4 | 25.2 | 19.5 | 6.9 | 5.6 | 5.3 | 11.6 | 15.9 | 25 100 | 182 | 2 654 | 54 759 | 12.8 |
| Nevada | 2 006 | -0.1 | 19.6 | 6.9 | 10.8 | 8.6 | 6.7 | 13.9 | 19.5 | 25 055 | 254 | 2 018 | 52 590 | 18.8 |
| Orange | 115 382 | 0.0 | 18.5 | 12.0 | 14.8 | 6.3 | 12.8 | 8.9 | 10.0 | 390 615 | 128 | 72 713 | 1 048 907 | 8.2 |
| Placer | 9 386 | 0.2 | 17.1 | 7.4 | 9.7 | 11.1 | 11.0 | 16.0 | 12.8 | 66 935 | 187 | 5 605 | 152 648 | 42.3 |
| Plumas | 392 | 1.7 | D | 8.6 | 4.2 | 6.1 | 3.0 | 6.9 | 36.1 | 5 670 | 287 | 717 | 15 566 | 16.3 |
| Riverside | 34 811 | 0.9 | 16.6 | 7.9 | 6.6 | 9.9 | 4.7 | 10.6 | 23.9 | 315 990 | 141 | 58 813 | 800 707 | 37.0 |
| Sacramento | 45 009 | 0.3 | 9.1 | 4.3 | 13.2 | 5.5 | 7.0 | 11.1 | 35.3 | 209 055 | 146 | 64 312 | 555 932 | 17.1 |
| San Benito | 865 | 4.9 | D | 20.6 | D | 13.0 | 3.3 | 4.9 | 22.3 | 7 300 | 130 | 937 | 17 870 | 8.3 |
| San Bernardino | 39 313 | 0.4 | 13.6 | 7.8 | 5.6 | 8.3 | 4.2 | 12.1 | 25.8 | 252 180 | 122 | 70 202 | 699 637 | 16.3 |
| San Diego | 110 042 | 0.4 | 13.5 | 8.5 | 17.2 | 5.4 | 6.9 | 8.4 | 26.4 | 427 485 | 136 | 83 160 | 1 164 786 | 12.0 |
| San Francisco | 67 018 | 0.0 | 4.0 | 1.3 | 29.8 | 3.9 | 18.8 | 5.3 | 15.0 | 113 580 | 140 | 45 469 | 376 942 | 8.8 |
| San Joaquin | 13 106 | 5.3 | 14.6 | 9.0 | 4.3 | 7.6 | 4.7 | 13.1 | 20.0 | 96 410 | 138 | 29 095 | 233 755 | 23.6 |
| San Luis Obispo | 6 611 | 1.9 | 14.9 | 6.3 | 8.9 | 8.7 | 5.0 | 11.7 | 21.5 | 51 645 | 190 | 5 230 | 117 315 | 14.7 |
| San Mateo | 36 931 | 0.1 | 15.7 | 10.8 | 28.5 | 5.2 | 11.8 | 7.6 | 7.2 | 105 565 | 145 | 12 881 | 271 031 | 4.0 |
| Santa Barbara | 13 065 | 3.5 | 15.0 | 8.4 | 13.9 | 6.4 | 5.4 | 10.7 | 21.2 | 66 610 | 156 | 9 642 | 152 834 | 6.9 |
| Santa Clara | 110 823 | 0.1 | 29.5 | 26.5 | 30.1 | 4.2 | 4.3 | 6.8 | 7.0 | 211 340 | 117 | 48 367 | 631 920 | 9.1 |
| Santa Cruz | 6 496 | 5.0 | D | 7.2 | 9.2 | 7.5 | 4.4 | 13.8 | 18.8 | 38 925 | 147 | 5 854 | 104 476 | 5.7 |
| Shasta | 3 574 | 0.6 | D | 3.9 | 6.4 | 10.2 | 4.6 | 19.3 | 22.6 | 45 995 | 259 | 9 959 | 77 313 | 12.4 |
| Sierra | 43 | 3.9 | D | D | D | D | D | 11.0 | 48.3 | 850 | 273 | 101 | 2 328 | 5.7 |
| Siskiyou | 763 | 6.4 | D | 5.2 | 5.3 | 7.8 | 2.8 | 12.9 | 31.4 | 12 370 | 278 | 2 570 | 23 910 | 8.9 |
| Solano | 9 226 | 1.0 | 20.1 | 11.0 | 4.2 | 7.2 | 4.7 | 15.7 | 27.8 | 63 110 | 152 | 12 361 | 152 698 | 13.5 |
| Sonoma | 12 840 | 1.2 | 22.1 | 14.3 | 11.7 | 7.6 | 6.0 | 13.8 | 14.5 | 85 465 | 175 | 9 784 | 204 572 | 11.7 |
| Stanislaus | 10 350 | 8.5 | 18.9 | 14.2 | 4.2 | 7.7 | 4.1 | 16.5 | 16.8 | 77 895 | 150 | 21 600 | 179 503 | 19.0 |
| Sutter | 1 822 | 15.8 | 11.4 | 5.5 | 4.2 | 9.8 | 4.1 | 13.0 | 15.1 | 15 610 | 164 | 3 902 | 33 858 | 19.6 |
| Tehama | 918 | 10.1 | D | 9.7 | 2.6 | 8.1 | 2.3 | 11.3 | 23.7 | 14 860 | 234 | 3 505 | 26 987 | 14.6 |
| Trinity | 156 | 2.7 | D | 5.1 | 4.4 | 8.2 | 1.9 | D | 50.3 | 3 800 | 277 | 755 | 8 681 | 8.8 |
| Tulare | 8 724 | 17.3 | 11.5 | 7.6 | 3.6 | 7.1 | 3.0 | 7.0 | 22.2 | 58 550 | 130 | 18 887 | 141 696 | 18.4 |
| Tuolumne | 979 | 0.0 | 11.7 | 4.9 | 6.6 | 8.2 | 3.2 | 19.6 | 32.9 | 14 915 | 271 | 1 721 | 31 244 | 10.3 |
| Ventura | 23 091 | 3.3 | 21.6 | 15.7 | 9.9 | 6.7 | 9.7 | 8.9 | 17.3 | 120 935 | 145 | 16 571 | 281 695 | 11.9 |
| Yolo | 6 607 | 3.4 | 10.2 | 5.4 | 7.5 | 5.0 | 3.2 | 6.7 | 41.5 | 24 925 | 123 | 5 629 | 75 054 | 21.9 |
| Yuba | 1 486 | 6.3 | 6.7 | 2.4 | 3.3 | 3.6 | 1.3 | 9.9 | 56.5 | 11 840 | 163 | 4 125 | 27 635 | 22.1 |
| COLORADO | 173 370 | 0.7 | 15.0 | 6.2 | 17.9 | 5.5 | 9.7 | 8.8 | 17.7 | 721 274 | 141 | 68 815 | 2 212 898 | 22.4 |
| Adams | 10 274 | 0.4 | 19.5 | 8.9 | 7.7 | 7.2 | 4.4 | 9.5 | 16.9 | 52 145 | 116 | 6 401 | 163 136 | 28.4 |
| Alamosa | 416 | 6.9 | D | 1.3 | 6.6 | 9.3 | 4.8 | D | 26.7 | 2 535 | 161 | 539 | 6 554 | 7.7 |
| Arapahoe | 26 729 | 0.1 | 9.8 | 2.1 | 28.3 | 5.3 | 14.8 | 9.0 | 9.1 | 74 000 | 127 | 6 927 | 238 301 | 20.8 |
| Archuleta | 192 | -1.1 | 13.6 | 1.2 | D | 12.5 | 10.5 | D | 19.8 | 2 895 | 241 | 124 | 8 762 | 41.1 |
| Baca | 112 | 49.1 | D | D | D | 5.6 | D | 0.8 | 25.3 | 1 060 | 279 | 86 | 2 248 | -4.9 |
| Bent | 83 | 25.5 | D | D | D | 4.1 | 3.2 | 1.8 | 38.5 | 980 | 157 | 196 | 2 242 | -5.2 |

1. Includes mining, construction, and manufacturing.  2. Per 1,000 resident population enumerated in the 2010 census.

| STATE County | Total | Percent | Median value[1] | With a mortgage | Without a mortgage[2] | Median rent[3] | Median rent as a percent of income | Substandard units[4] (percent) | Total | Percent change, 2011–2012 | Total | Rate[5] | Total | Management, business, science and arts | Construction, production, and maintenance occupations |
|---|---|---|---|---|---|---|---|---|---|---|---|---|---|---|---|
| | 89 | 90 | 91 | 92 | 93 | 94 | 95 | 96 | 97 | 98 | 99 | 100 | 101 | 102 | 103 |
| CALIFORNIA | 12 433 172 | 56.7 | 421 600 | 30.9 | 11.3 | 1 185 | 33.0 | 8.5 | 18 494 881 | 0.5 | 1 934 533 | 10.5 | 16 603 417 | 36.5 | 20.6 |
| Alameda | 536 160 | 54.5 | 558 300 | 30.3 | 10.2 | 1 228 | 30.9 | 5.9 | 775 855 | 1.4 | 69 963 | 9.0 | 718 035 | 44.6 | 16.9 |
| Alpine | 357 | 80.4 | 395 600 | 30.8 | 11.7 | 796 | 29.3 | 0.6 | 459 | -9.6 | 61 | 13.3 | 529 | 48.8 | 19.1 |
| Amador | 14 283 | 78.5 | 318 400 | 31.3 | 12.7 | 1 011 | 30.8 | 1.1 | 16 673 | -2.2 | 1 960 | 11.8 | 13 260 | 33.3 | 21.5 |
| Butte | 85 219 | 60.3 | 254 900 | 29.0 | 12.8 | 878 | 35.7 | 4.0 | 102 063 | 0.1 | 12 493 | 12.2 | 87 965 | 34.2 | 19.6 |
| Calaveras | 18 865 | 78.7 | 312 000 | 30.5 | 14.4 | 1 031 | 29.2 | 2.1 | 19 430 | -2.0 | 2 531 | 13.0 | 18 391 | 33.6 | 24.6 |
| Colusa | 6 989 | 63.5 | 244 200 | 29.1 | 12.2 | 885 | 29.0 | 8.8 | 11 860 | 0.1 | 2 369 | 20.0 | 8 853 | 24.7 | 36.2 |
| Contra Costa | 370 925 | 68.3 | 490 200 | 30.8 | 11.4 | 1 309 | 32.8 | 4.4 | 535 782 | 1.3 | 48 167 | 9.0 | 483 584 | 41.8 | 15.9 |
| Del Norte | 9 818 | 61.5 | 239 800 | 27.9 | 13.2 | 869 | 35.8 | 4.3 | 11 381 | -2.4 | 1 521 | 13.4 | 9 316 | 29.3 | 16.5 |
| El Dorado | 68 812 | 75.3 | 409 400 | 30.7 | 12.9 | 1 098 | 31.9 | 3.2 | 90 525 | 0.2 | 9 371 | 10.4 | 83 412 | 38.2 | 16.6 |
| Fresno | 285 338 | 55.0 | 236 400 | 27.9 | 10.9 | 850 | 33.7 | 10.7 | 442 453 | -0.3 | 67 426 | 15.2 | 367 858 | 28.5 | 28.5 |
| Glenn | 9 483 | 66.2 | 233 800 | 28.7 | 10.5 | 742 | 31.5 | 4.8 | 12 841 | -0.2 | 1 884 | 14.7 | 11 107 | 24.4 | 33.5 |
| Humboldt | 53 724 | 57.3 | 314 400 | 28.9 | 12.4 | 859 | 36.9 | 3.6 | 60 144 | -0.6 | 6 287 | 10.5 | 59 407 | 32.9 | 20.3 |
| Imperial | 48 117 | 55.7 | 169 600 | 29.1 | 12.4 | 699 | 32.8 | 10.6 | 78 282 | 0.2 | 22 132 | 28.3 | 58 017 | 24.4 | 27.2 |
| Inyo | 7 910 | 62.7 | 271 100 | 26.7 | 13.0 | 882 | 35.2 | 4.2 | 9 375 | -1.2 | 878 | 9.4 | 8 737 | 29.7 | 19.7 |
| Kern | 250 999 | 60.1 | 196 000 | 27.9 | 11.3 | 840 | 32.8 | 9.3 | 396 657 | 3.1 | 52 681 | 13.3 | 312 748 | 26.0 | 32.4 |
| Kings | 40 716 | 54.6 | 208 100 | 27.1 | 10.2 | 864 | 29.7 | 8.9 | 60 886 | -0.1 | 9 321 | 15.3 | 52 895 | 24.2 | 35.0 |
| Lake | 25 654 | 65.2 | 235 900 | 31.6 | 15.0 | 891 | 36.6 | 4.9 | 25 519 | -0.2 | 3 834 | 15.0 | 24 493 | 28.2 | 25.2 |
| Lassen | 10 097 | 65.2 | 199 200 | 26.0 | 12.6 | 855 | 31.4 | 4.6 | 13 083 | -2.6 | 1 650 | 12.6 | 10 453 | 31.0 | 17.9 |
| Los Angeles | 3 218 518 | 47.8 | 478 300 | 32.6 | 11.0 | 1 161 | 34.2 | 12.5 | 4 879 674 | -1.0 | 533 951 | 10.9 | 4 501 382 | 35.0 | 21.2 |
| Madera | 42 032 | 62.2 | 245 500 | 31.5 | 11.7 | 861 | 31.5 | 11.1 | 68 167 | 0.7 | 9 295 | 13.6 | 52 804 | 23.3 | 35.6 |
| Marin | 102 832 | 63.0 | 840 900 | 30.1 | 11.1 | 1 571 | 32.6 | 2.9 | 140 287 | 2.9 | 8 861 | 6.3 | 124 781 | 51.4 | 11.1 |
| Mariposa | 7 607 | 70.9 | 248 900 | 28.3 | 10.1 | 748 | 28.4 | 2.2 | 9 446 | -1.4 | 1 038 | 11.0 | 7 602 | 31.4 | 21.5 |
| Mendocino | 34 102 | 61.6 | 380 800 | 34.0 | 13.7 | 940 | 34.2 | 5.8 | 42 776 | 0.0 | 4 153 | 9.7 | 38 812 | 29.5 | 25.4 |
| Merced | 74 079 | 55.2 | 197 700 | 29.7 | 10.7 | 806 | 34.1 | 9.6 | 111 322 | 0.8 | 18 953 | 17.0 | 94 066 | 22.5 | 35.9 |
| Modoc | 3 947 | 68.5 | 162 500 | 24.6 | 12.5 | 613 | 33.6 | 4.3 | 3 932 | 1.3 | 529 | 13.5 | 3 573 | 37.7 | 20.9 |
| Mono | 5 416 | 57.2 | 428 600 | 30.9 | 15.7 | 1 096 | 36.0 | 5.6 | 8 301 | -5.3 | 871 | 10.5 | 8 001 | 36.3 | 13.4 |
| Monterey | 125 217 | 51.4 | 497 400 | 32.8 | 10.6 | 1 160 | 31.6 | 12.0 | 226 510 | 2.1 | 25 743 | 11.4 | 175 425 | 27.6 | 30.3 |
| Napa | 49 640 | 63.3 | 521 700 | 30.0 | 11.7 | 1 279 | 32.4 | 6.6 | 77 843 | 1.9 | 6 080 | 7.8 | 64 899 | 35.6 | 23.4 |
| Nevada | 41 561 | 73.3 | 412 600 | 33.1 | 14.2 | 1 138 | 35.8 | 3.3 | 50 742 | -0.8 | 4 753 | 9.4 | 44 232 | 37.9 | 17.3 |
| Orange | 987 164 | 60.3 | 575 100 | 30.5 | 10.1 | 1 463 | 32.9 | 9.6 | 1 618 677 | 1.2 | 122 716 | 7.6 | 1 441 313 | 39.6 | 17.3 |
| Placer | 130 736 | 72.3 | 387 400 | 29.7 | 12.7 | 1 190 | 32.1 | 2.2 | 178 818 | 0.5 | 16 824 | 9.4 | 157 609 | 41.6 | 14.6 |
| Plumas | 9 434 | 69.9 | 266 100 | 28.9 | 15.2 | 779 | 28.6 | 3.6 | 9 478 | -3.0 | 1 396 | 14.7 | 7 948 | 34.6 | 23.8 |
| Riverside | 672 896 | 69.2 | 284 100 | 32.6 | 13.5 | 1 141 | 35.3 | 7.5 | 944 458 | 0.5 | 115 639 | 12.2 | 868 898 | 29.3 | 24.4 |
| Sacramento | 510 976 | 58.6 | 285 000 | 29.4 | 10.8 | 1 003 | 33.1 | 5.0 | 680 349 | 0.3 | 71 834 | 10.6 | 621 437 | 37.1 | 17.0 |
| San Benito | 16 785 | 63.8 | 432 900 | 33.8 | 13.2 | 1 202 | 32.7 | 8.2 | 26 611 | 1.1 | 3 695 | 13.9 | 24 917 | 27.8 | 28.9 |
| San Bernardino | 598 822 | 64.2 | 278 400 | 30.6 | 11.8 | 1 092 | 34.8 | 9.2 | 860 895 | 0.6 | 102 953 | 12.0 | 815 102 | 28.2 | 26.8 |
| San Diego | 1 064 048 | 55.2 | 455 000 | 31.2 | 10.7 | 1 261 | 33.6 | 6.1 | 1 599 133 | 1.1 | 142 810 | 8.9 | 1 382 856 | 39.8 | 16.5 |
| San Francisco | 338 366 | 37.1 | 767 300 | 30.2 | 10.0 | 1 388 | 27.9 | 7.6 | 477 632 | 2.7 | 34 859 | 7.3 | 447 467 | 50.5 | 10.1 |
| San Joaquin | 212 902 | 60.7 | 264 600 | 31.4 | 11.3 | 993 | 34.5 | 8.2 | 298 468 | -0.5 | 45 264 | 15.2 | 269 072 | 28.2 | 29.0 |
| San Luis Obispo | 101 993 | 60.1 | 480 200 | 31.1 | 11.5 | 1 165 | 36.4 | 3.2 | 143 069 | 2.6 | 11 531 | 8.1 | 121 788 | 36.0 | 17.6 |
| San Mateo | 256 423 | 60.1 | 763 100 | 30.3 | 10.1 | 1 508 | 29.3 | 7.6 | 394 322 | 2.8 | 26 525 | 6.7 | 362 719 | 43.5 | 14.6 |
| Santa Barbara | 141 635 | 53.6 | 523 800 | 30.7 | 10.7 | 1 303 | 34.4 | 8.7 | 229 464 | 1.6 | 18 289 | 8.0 | 195 736 | 35.5 | 21.9 |
| Santa Clara | 599 652 | 58.7 | 681 100 | 29.6 | 9.9 | 1 459 | 28.3 | 7.5 | 910 983 | 1.9 | 76 633 | 8.4 | 850 552 | 49.5 | 15.2 |
| Santa Cruz | 93 834 | 59.4 | 613 500 | 32.8 | 11.9 | 1 325 | 33.8 | 7.3 | 151 139 | 1.0 | 16 848 | 11.1 | 127 947 | 40.7 | 19.9 |
| Shasta | 69 147 | 65.3 | 246 800 | 30.2 | 13.0 | 882 | 35.8 | 3.5 | 81 245 | -1.5 | 10 896 | 13.4 | 69 420 | 33.3 | 20.0 |
| Sierra | 1 328 | 76.8 | 304 700 | 22.9 | 12.1 | 913 | 31.3 | 1.0 | 1 497 | -7.2 | 214 | 14.3 | 1 300 | 32.4 | 32.2 |
| Siskiyou | 19 782 | 64.8 | 232 200 | 31.5 | 13.3 | 758 | 35.5 | 5.0 | 19 489 | -2.1 | 2 979 | 15.3 | 16 929 | 32.6 | 22.9 |
| Solano | 139 312 | 64.9 | 340 100 | 30.0 | 10.1 | 1 222 | 32.8 | 4.4 | 217 024 | 0.8 | 21 995 | 10.1 | 181 725 | 33.6 | 21.4 |
| Sonoma | 184 170 | 61.5 | 477 300 | 31.6 | 12.5 | 1 223 | 33.0 | 5.2 | 256 878 | 0.2 | 22 005 | 8.6 | 232 866 | 35.2 | 20.3 |
| Stanislaus | 164 933 | 60.8 | 232 000 | 30.7 | 12.3 | 962 | 34.6 | 7.2 | 239 461 | 0.3 | 36 324 | 15.2 | 205 958 | 26.6 | 30.9 |
| Sutter | 31 668 | 60.9 | 233 000 | 28.2 | 11.8 | 867 | 31.3 | 6.8 | 42 810 | -0.2 | 7 544 | 17.6 | 37 995 | 28.6 | 29.7 |
| Tehama | 23 810 | 64.4 | 208 000 | 30.4 | 11.8 | 813 | 32.1 | 6.8 | 25 251 | -0.9 | 3 517 | 13.9 | 22 885 | 25.5 | 28.9 |
| Trinity | 5 731 | 72.4 | 264 200 | 25.9 | 11.8 | 744 | 31.3 | 4.9 | 5 019 | -0.5 | 792 | 15.8 | 4 841 | 33.9 | 20.8 |
| Tulare | 128 324 | 58.9 | 191 500 | 28.5 | 11.5 | 781 | 31.7 | 11.8 | 207 634 | -0.5 | 32 860 | 15.8 | 167 498 | 23.7 | 36.6 |
| Tuolumne | 22 157 | 70.8 | 304 700 | 31.8 | 13.6 | 905 | 34.3 | 3.3 | 25 918 | -0.2 | 3 015 | 11.6 | 20 559 | 29.4 | 22.8 |
| Ventura | 264 982 | 65.8 | 515 900 | 30.3 | 11.1 | 1 428 | 33.1 | 6.7 | 440 649 | 1.0 | 39 865 | 9.0 | 384 192 | 37.3 | 20.8 |
| Yolo | 69 860 | 54.0 | 365 500 | 27.6 | 9.9 | 1 086 | 34.9 | 5.4 | 98 475 | 0.8 | 11 276 | 11.5 | 91 834 | 44.3 | 18.2 |
| Yuba | 23 885 | 59.3 | 194 200 | 29.9 | 11.2 | 829 | 31.9 | 8.7 | 27 772 | -0.2 | 4 701 | 16.9 | 25 417 | 27.1 | 27.5 |
| COLORADO | 1 941 193 | 66.8 | 236 700 | 25.0 | 10.2 | 883 | 30.7 | 2.9 | 2 743 264 | 0.7 | 219 729 | 8.0 | 2 476 167 | 39.3 | 19.3 |
| Adams | 149 508 | 67.5 | 192 300 | 26.5 | 11.9 | 911 | 30.9 | 4.6 | 234 436 | 1.0 | 21 674 | 9.2 | 210 688 | 28.0 | 27.8 |
| Alamosa | 5 743 | 65.3 | 130 400 | 22.0 | 10.2 | 547 | 30.2 | 3.3 | 8 766 | 0.0 | 800 | 9.1 | 6 559 | 29.1 | 24.6 |
| Arapahoe | 221 136 | 65.1 | 231 200 | 24.9 | 9.9 | 914 | 31.8 | 3.1 | 323 283 | 1.1 | 25 079 | 7.8 | 289 548 | 39.3 | 17.5 |
| Archuleta | 3 951 | 78.2 | 303 800 | 24.7 | 9.9 | 866 | 28.1 | 3.1 | 6 125 | -0.7 | 574 | 9.4 | 5 380 | 33.1 | 22.8 |
| Baca | 1 675 | 75.5 | 71 500 | 20.8 | 12.5 | 460 | 23.3 | 1.5 | 2 357 | -5.0 | 94 | 4.0 | 1 875 | 33.0 | 28.5 |
| Bent | 1 975 | 65.7 | 74 300 | 24.4 | 11.4 | 612 | 27.2 | 4.0 | 2 262 | -10.6 | 192 | 8.5 | 1 937 | 32.5 | 30.7 |

1. Specified owner-occupied units.    2. A value of 9.9 represents 9.9 percent or less.    3. Specified renter-occupied units. A value of 10.0 represents 10 percent or less.    4. Overcrowded or lacking complete plumbing facilities.    5. Percent of civilian labor force.    6. Persons 16 years old and over.

| STATE County | Private nonfarm establishments, employment and payroll, 2011 | | | | | | | | Agriculture, 2007 | | | |
|---|---|---|---|---|---|---|---|---|---|---|---|---|
| | | Employment | | | | | Annual payroll | | Farms | | | |
| | | | | | | | | | | Percent with: | | Farm operators whose principal occupation is farming (percent) |
| | Number of establishments | Total | Health care and social assistance | Manufacturing | Retail trade | Finance and insurance | Professional, scientific, and technical services | Total (mil dol) | Average per employee (dollars) | Number | Fewer than 50 acres | 500 acres or more | |
| | 104 | 105 | 106 | 107 | 108 | 109 | 110 | 111 | 112 | 113 | 114 | 115 | 116 |
| CALIFORNIA | 849 316 | 12 698 427 | 1 714 414 | 1 134 193 | 1 517 573 | 571 421 | 1 212 869 | 663 571 | 52 256 | 81 033 | 65.8 | 9.5 | 50.5 |
| Alameda | 35 921 | 567 151 | 79 260 | 60 292 | 61 615 | 14 931 | 59 782 | 33 282 | 58 682 | 525 | 60.4 | 12.0 | 37.5 |
| Alpine | 46 | 711 | D | NA | D | D | 10 | 12 | 16 328 | 7 | 14.3 | 14.3 | 28.6 |
| Amador | 750 | 7 646 | 1 282 | D | 1 527 | 201 | 249 | 258 | 33 798 | 479 | 54.9 | 9.4 | 49.3 |
| Butte | 4 606 | 53 193 | 12 880 | 3 836 | 9 326 | 2 307 | 2 527 | 1 776 | 33 380 | 2 048 | 64.5 | 7.9 | 51.6 |
| Calaveras | 907 | 5 579 | 996 | 334 | 1 010 | 148 | 279 | 174 | 31 265 | 631 | 59.4 | 12.4 | 45.6 |
| Colusa | 357 | 3 879 | 457 | 584 | 542 | 115 | 49 | 141 | 36 415 | 814 | 31.2 | 26.9 | 57.0 |
| Contra Costa | 21 868 | 290 961 | 50 765 | 16 303 | 40 812 | 22 690 | 26 570 | 16 537 | 56 835 | 634 | 73.8 | 9.0 | 41.8 |
| Del Norte | 449 | 4 059 | 1 170 | D | 880 | 110 | 123 | 116 | 28 550 | 85 | 52.9 | 8.2 | 43.5 |
| El Dorado | 4 182 | 39 870 | 6 667 | 2 414 | 5 666 | 2 927 | 2 335 | 1 493 | 37 458 | 1 268 | 79.1 | 1.6 | 42.8 |
| Fresno | 15 700 | 227 628 | 40 047 | 23 958 | 32 546 | 9 704 | 11 174 | 8 465 | 37 190 | 6 081 | 61.3 | 10.8 | 57.1 |
| Glenn | 473 | 4 327 | 515 | 618 | 632 | 132 | 161 | 189 | 43 648 | 1 242 | 49.4 | 15.3 | 58.8 |
| Humboldt | 3 304 | 33 551 | 7 326 | 2 285 | 7 021 | 1 108 | 1 720 | 1 041 | 31 031 | 852 | 52.3 | 16.5 | 54.7 |
| Imperial | 2 350 | 29 516 | 4 502 | 3 276 | 7 269 | D | 822 | 904 | 30 618 | 452 | 28.1 | 39.4 | 71.0 |
| Inyo | 531 | 5 149 | 1 115 | D | 930 | 97 | 116 | 163 | 31 629 | 94 | 43.6 | 28.7 | 50.0 |
| Kern | 11 982 | 179 232 | 27 475 | 11 773 | 28 115 | 6 180 | 11 567 | 7 421 | 41 405 | 2 117 | 43.0 | 24.7 | 57.4 |
| Kings | 1 599 | 22 896 | 4 757 | 3 771 | 4 049 | 543 | 451 | 783 | 34 201 | 1 129 | 53.3 | 17.7 | 57.8 |
| Lake | 1 047 | 8 671 | 2 381 | 273 | 2 041 | 220 | 239 | 272 | 31 339 | 845 | 66.4 | 4.9 | 41.7 |
| Lassen | 415 | 3 466 | 821 | D | 831 | 100 | 156 | 107 | 30 846 | 459 | 35.9 | 22.9 | 52.7 |
| Los Angeles | 245 261 | 3 648 846 | 487 608 | 357 728 | 378 434 | 159 799 | 428 881 | 180 344 | 49 425 | 1 734 | 86.9 | 2.8 | 35.8 |
| Madera | 1 882 | 25 329 | 5 759 | 3 171 | 3 344 | 462 | 489 | 885 | 34 932 | 1 708 | 46.4 | 13.1 | 54.4 |
| Marin | 9 483 | 94 284 | 14 772 | 1 810 | 13 388 | 7 731 | 8 943 | 5 138 | 54 498 | 255 | 43.5 | 31.8 | 59.2 |
| Mariposa | 351 | 3 272 | 462 | 93 | 429 | 33 | 36 | 86 | 26 369 | 302 | 45.0 | 21.5 | 44.7 |
| Mendocino | 2 464 | 21 148 | 4 290 | 2 235 | 4 365 | 567 | 810 | 684 | 32 351 | 1 136 | 50.1 | 13.4 | 51.3 |
| Merced | 2 830 | 39 914 | 6 604 | 8 468 | 7 652 | 1 049 | 828 | 1 356 | 33 969 | 2 607 | 55.7 | 12.6 | 59.5 |
| Modoc | 154 | 1 310 | 477 | NA | 223 | 32 | 34 | 40 | 30 305 | 448 | 21.4 | 36.2 | 60.0 |
| Mono | 561 | 6 451 | D | D | 679 | D | 131 | 168 | 26 119 | 84 | 33.3 | 23.8 | 45.2 |
| Monterey | 8 216 | 96 528 | 14 125 | 5 653 | 16 108 | 3 152 | 7 822 | 3 907 | 40 473 | 1 199 | 45.0 | 24.9 | 64.1 |
| Napa | 3 880 | 56 022 | 10 768 | 10 262 | 6 593 | 1 281 | 1 603 | 2 563 | 45 741 | 1 638 | 73.0 | 5.3 | 41.4 |
| Nevada | 2 978 | 26 399 | 4 455 | 1 959 | 3 972 | 736 | 1 395 | 955 | 36 184 | 690 | 78.4 | 3.8 | 42.8 |
| Orange | 86 473 | 1 300 673 | 142 783 | 148 190 | 139 719 | 76 910 | 113 308 | 67 332 | 51 767 | 325 | 82.8 | 2.8 | 40.9 |
| Placer | 9 282 | 121 639 | 17 006 | 3 845 | 20 077 | 6 775 | 10 646 | 5 493 | 45 155 | 1 488 | 81.7 | 2.6 | 45.0 |
| Plumas | 621 | 3 576 | 904 | D | 598 | 150 | 104 | 133 | 37 151 | 142 | 52.1 | 15.5 | 49.3 |
| Riverside | 33 421 | 469 182 | 66 298 | 40 650 | 81 672 | 11 359 | 16 054 | 16 250 | 34 634 | 3 463 | 87.1 | 2.9 | 48.0 |
| Sacramento | 27 029 | 406 048 | 72 053 | 19 664 | 56 365 | 25 875 | 31 278 | 17 841 | 43 938 | 1 393 | 70.9 | 9.0 | 47.9 |
| San Benito | 894 | 9 426 | 1 242 | 1 965 | 1 355 | 245 | 198 | 349 | 36 992 | 625 | 57.0 | 21.3 | 55.5 |
| San Bernardino | 31 204 | 511 293 | 78 244 | 50 391 | 78 283 | 15 395 | 17 355 | 18 620 | 36 418 | 1 405 | 82.6 | 2.3 | 48.3 |
| San Diego | 75 837 | 1 128 909 | 145 431 | 94 413 | 138 742 | 51 882 | 121 359 | 55 585 | 49 237 | 6 687 | 91.1 | 1.3 | 37.8 |
| San Francisco | 30 924 | 493 972 | 60 820 | 8 139 | 40 411 | 48 025 | 81 631 | 39 600 | 80 166 | 6 | 100.0 | 0.0 | 33.3 |
| San Joaquin | 10 697 | 159 882 | 26 540 | 18 011 | 23 929 | 5 301 | 4 347 | 6 016 | 37 627 | 3 624 | 64.1 | 8.6 | 55.9 |
| San Luis Obispo | 7 720 | 81 045 | 14 881 | 5 318 | 13 530 | 2 572 | 4 645 | 2 954 | 36 443 | 2 784 | 56.7 | 12.5 | 49.6 |
| San Mateo | 19 724 | 311 675 | 31 964 | D | 33 723 | 14 160 | 31 186 | 24 099 | 77 320 | 329 | 64.4 | 7.6 | 48.6 |
| Santa Barbara | 11 064 | 133 803 | 19 329 | 12 222 | 18 824 | 4 332 | 12 312 | 6 178 | 46 175 | 1 597 | 64.9 | 11.1 | 50.9 |
| Santa Clara | 44 568 | 865 069 | 91 720 | 89 606 | 78 586 | 24 968 | 121 968 | 78 231 | 90 433 | 1 068 | 75.2 | 6.1 | 46.9 |
| Santa Cruz | 6 673 | 68 341 | 11 831 | 4 509 | 11 100 | 2 021 | 4 546 | 2 863 | 41 899 | 682 | 77.7 | 2.2 | 61.9 |
| Shasta | 4 205 | 46 057 | 10 416 | 1 934 | 8 859 | 1 856 | 2 035 | 1 593 | 34 584 | 1 473 | 69.5 | 8.5 | 46.8 |
| Sierra | 68 | 255 | D | D | D | D | D | 10 | 37 698 | 50 | 8.0 | 16.0 | 72.0 |
| Siskiyou | 1 104 | 8 236 | 1 663 | 730 | 1 474 | 292 | 332 | 246 | 29 872 | 846 | 36.5 | 21.2 | 53.2 |
| Solano | 6 629 | 97 762 | 19 352 | 8 897 | 17 381 | 3 490 | 3 697 | 4 149 | 42 438 | 890 | 62.0 | 12.1 | 52.8 |
| Sonoma | 13 080 | 144 934 | 22 539 | 17 447 | 22 520 | 7 322 | 8 273 | 6 500 | 44 845 | 3 429 | 72.4 | 5.3 | 47.3 |
| Stanislaus | 8 289 | 122 473 | 22 718 | 18 407 | 21 417 | 3 639 | 4 803 | 4 806 | 39 237 | 4 114 | 69.4 | 6.1 | 54.1 |
| Sutter | 1 678 | 18 936 | 3 341 | 1 472 | 4 210 | 688 | 613 | 689 | 36 370 | 1 263 | 50.9 | 13.5 | 59.2 |
| Tehama | 987 | 11 009 | 1 892 | 1 671 | 1 801 | 266 | 213 | 385 | 34 928 | 1 752 | 62.9 | 9.1 | 50.1 |
| Trinity | 258 | 1 461 | 340 | D | 322 | 49 | 68 | 45 | 30 563 | 181 | 50.3 | 13.8 | 33.7 |
| Tulare | 6 109 | 83 911 | 14 497 | 12 035 | 14 400 | 3 037 | 2 498 | 2 916 | 34 746 | 5 240 | 64.3 | 8.0 | 53.2 |
| Tuolumne | 1 343 | 12 007 | 2 940 | 753 | 2 086 | 322 | 471 | 418 | 34 807 | 366 | 50.5 | 15.6 | 47.3 |
| Ventura | 19 576 | 238 849 | 31 190 | 22 133 | 37 550 | 15 911 | 21 092 | 11 285 | 47 246 | 2 437 | 77.8 | 4.1 | 47.7 |
| Yolo | 3 807 | 57 978 | 6 386 | 5 691 | 7 222 | 1 726 | 3 417 | 2 451 | 42 272 | 983 | 46.5 | 17.8 | 53.9 |
| Yuba | 797 | 8 745 | 2 068 | 469 | 1 257 | 265 | 429 | 303 | 34 689 | 828 | 62.9 | 8.5 | 50.4 |
| COLORADO | 150 889 | 1 972 271 | 257 481 | 117 810 | 242 477 | 92 251 | 170 484 | 92 655 | 46 979 | 37 054 | 36.8 | 25.5 | 40.4 |
| Adams | 8 146 | 131 739 | 18 796 | 9 090 | 16 665 | 2 163 | 5 145 | 5 511 | 41 835 | 895 | 52.1 | 20.0 | 35.6 |
| Alamosa | 495 | 5 390 | 1 739 | D | 1 103 | 338 | 155 | 166 | 30 740 | 316 | 20.9 | 30.4 | 51.9 |
| Arapahoe | 16 789 | 239 377 | 29 296 | 8 241 | 29 610 | 20 192 | 21 261 | 12 988 | 54 257 | 627 | 59.0 | 12.6 | 27.1 |
| Archuleta | 459 | 2 594 | 233 | 68 | 486 | 98 | 95 | 65 | 25 088 | 306 | 35.3 | 20.3 | 35.9 |
| Baca | 87 | 602 | D | D | D | D | 10 | 17 | 27 410 | 777 | 3.2 | 58.8 | 39.6 |
| Bent | 61 | 582 | 44 | D | 82 | D | D | 16 | 28 096 | 311 | 17.4 | 49.2 | 56.3 |

| STATE County | Land in farms | | | | | Value of land and buildings (dollars) | | Value of machinery and equipment, average per farm (dollars) | Value of products sold | | | | Percent of farms with sales of: | | Government payments | |
|---|---|---|---|---|---|---|---|---|---|---|---|---|---|---|---|---|
| | Acres | | | | | | | | | | Percent from: | | | | | |
| | Acreage (1,000) | Percent change, 2002–2007 | Average size of farm | Total irrigated (1,000) | Total cropland (1,000) | Average per farm | Average per acre | | Total (mil dol) | Average per farm (dollars) | Crops | Live-stock and poultry products | $10,000 or more | $100,000 or more | Total ($1,000) | Percent of farms |
| | 117 | 118 | 119 | 120 | 121 | 122 | 123 | 124 | 125 | 126 | 127 | 128 | 129 | 130 | 131 | 132 |
| CALIFORNIA | 25 365 | -8.1 | 313 | 8 016.2 | 9 464.6 | 2 005 768 | 6 408 | 108 145 | 33 885.1 | 418 164 | 67.6 | 32.4 | 53.4 | 23.5 | 240 242 | 9.2 |
| Alameda | 205 | -6.0 | 390 | 9.7 | 30.5 | 1 511 370 | 3 878 | 53 082 | 50.4 | 95 919 | 67.9 | 32.1 | 40.4 | 9.3 | 365 | 5.7 |
| Alpine | 2 | NA | 259 | D | 0.5 | 1 771 429 | 6 851 | 71 453 | D | D | D | D | 42.9 | 14.3 | 0 | 0.0 |
| Amador | 163 | -16.0 | 341 | 10.1 | 15.6 | 1 626 088 | 4 764 | 46 973 | 20.7 | 43 217 | 63.3 | 36.7 | 37.8 | 9.6 | 91 | 2.3 |
| Butte | 374 | -2.1 | 183 | 202.2 | 222.7 | 1 371 244 | 7 513 | 108 816 | 342.8 | 167 366 | 96.5 | 3.5 | 53.6 | 25.5 | 14 780 | 14.3 |
| Calaveras | 201 | -23.0 | 319 | 4.9 | 12.1 | 1 167 695 | 3 665 | 50 209 | 16.5 | 26 146 | 26.6 | 73.4 | 30.0 | 4.8 | 49 | 2.4 |
| Colusa | 474 | -2.3 | 582 | 277.3 | 299.0 | 2 317 659 | 3 979 | 227 223 | 386.3 | 474 570 | 97.9 | 2.1 | 74.8 | 51.1 | 21 222 | 54.8 |
| Contra Costa | 147 | 16.7 | 232 | 27.4 | 35.9 | 1 531 291 | 6 605 | 72 166 | 70.8 | 111 687 | 84.2 | 15.8 | 33.6 | 12.8 | 192 | 3.0 |
| Del Norte | 18 | 38.5 | 214 | 7.7 | 8.0 | 1 453 524 | 6 800 | 106 770 | 32.5 | 382 445 | 40.5 | 59.5 | 37.6 | 16.5 | D | 7.1 |
| El Dorado | 107 | -8.5 | 84 | 9.9 | 15.3 | 858 053 | 10 161 | 35 905 | 19.9 | 15 732 | 83.9 | 16.1 | 26.3 | 3.0 | 149 | 1.8 |
| Fresno | 1 636 | -15.2 | 269 | 984.5 | 1 102.2 | 2 132 914 | 7 927 | 147 707 | 3 730.5 | 613 476 | 67.0 | 33.0 | 71.6 | 33.6 | 24 737 | 9.2 |
| Glenn | 489 | -3.4 | 394 | 236.1 | 250.3 | 1 899 672 | 4 823 | 147 291 | 405.4 | 326 441 | 76.0 | 24.0 | 69.0 | 39.5 | 15 457 | 33.5 |
| Humboldt | 597 | -5.8 | 701 | 17.5 | 33.9 | 1 723 851 | 2 458 | 84 426 | 149.8 | 175 873 | D | D | 43.5 | 15.0 | 515 | 9.5 |
| Imperial | 427 | -16.9 | 945 | 376.5 | 396.7 | 5 001 024 | 5 290 | 413 760 | 1 290.3 | 2 854 543 | 54.5 | 45.5 | 83.2 | 61.9 | 4 885 | 29.2 |
| Inyo | 293 | 29.1 | 3 112 | 32.5 | 8.3 | 2 959 058 | 951 | 71 730 | 14.5 | 153 740 | 38.7 | 61.3 | 52.1 | 23.4 | D | 3.2 |
| Kern | 2 362 | -13.5 | 1 116 | 786.3 | 942.8 | 5 160 784 | 4 626 | 253 255 | 3 204.1 | 1 513 532 | 79.6 | 20.4 | 59.6 | 40.3 | 27 346 | 17.1 |
| Kings | 681 | 5.4 | 603 | 421.6 | 512.9 | 3 295 061 | 5 465 | 245 730 | 1 358.4 | 1 203 198 | 48.0 | 52.0 | 63.7 | 41.9 | 23 258 | 35.5 |
| Lake | 124 | -13.9 | 147 | 13.6 | 29.0 | 1 349 648 | 9 182 | 45 940 | 61.1 | 72 310 | 97.7 | 2.3 | 33.6 | 8.3 | 154 | 2.4 |
| Lassen | 459 | -4.8 | 1 000 | 69.9 | 82.6 | 1 383 204 | 1 383 | 108 010 | 55.5 | 120 923 | 65.8 | 34.2 | 38.6 | 12.9 | 160 | 4.4 |
| Los Angeles | 108 | -2.7 | 63 | 29.7 | 49.2 | 877 388 | 14 027 | 67 008 | 325.9 | 187 935 | 92.7 | 7.3 | 27.8 | 11.2 | 138 | 1.6 |
| Madera | 680 | -0.3 | 398 | 281.7 | 290.7 | 2 699 315 | 6 783 | 139 667 | 990.1 | 579 696 | 63.2 | 36.8 | 64.8 | 38.8 | 4 608 | 11.3 |
| Marin | 133 | -11.9 | 523 | 1.6 | 12.0 | 2 641 781 | 5 055 | 83 556 | 57.9 | 226 944 | 10.5 | 89.5 | 55.3 | 25.1 | 603 | 13.3 |
| Mariposa | 213 | -2.7 | 704 | D | 4.4 | 1 160 104 | 1 649 | 52 874 | 11.5 | 37 960 | 4.2 | 95.8 | 31.8 | 6.0 | 131 | 1.7 |
| Mendocino | 609 | -13.9 | 536 | 27.1 | 53.8 | 2 846 283 | 5 312 | 57 225 | 122.4 | 107 754 | 87.1 | 12.9 | 47.6 | 15.2 | 719 | 7.5 |
| Merced | 1 041 | 3.5 | 399 | 514.2 | 537.7 | 2 879 524 | 7 210 | 198 153 | 2 330.4 | 893 904 | 37.7 | 62.3 | 72.7 | 39.6 | 11 968 | 19.8 |
| Modoc | 598 | -1.8 | 1 334 | 132.7 | 145.8 | 1 946 852 | 1 459 | 122 736 | 70.8 | 158 059 | 61.6 | 38.4 | 55.8 | 26.8 | 825 | 20.8 |
| Mono | 45 | -16.7 | 531 | 22.2 | 10.5 | 1 639 748 | 3 088 | 86 028 | 9.8 | 116 313 | 40.7 | 59.3 | 45.2 | 28.6 | 0 | 0.0 |
| Monterey | 1 328 | 5.3 | 1 108 | 233.0 | 311.1 | 5 144 255 | 4 645 | 305 191 | 2 178.5 | 1 816 906 | 98.2 | 1.8 | 59.8 | 37.9 | 1 316 | 7.8 |
| Napa | 223 | -6.3 | 136 | 51.6 | 66.2 | 3 696 510 | 27 122 | 76 502 | 376.9 | 230 078 | 98.7 | 1.3 | 72.6 | 31.2 | 233 | 1.6 |
| Nevada | 70 | -14.6 | 102 | 7.2 | 7.3 | 745 506 | 7 331 | 40 004 | 9.5 | 13 722 | 55.1 | 44.9 | 23.3 | 3.3 | 227 | 3.8 |
| Orange | 87 | 27.9 | 269 | 9.0 | 14.6 | 3 253 936 | 12 095 | 166 005 | 336.4 | 1 035 046 | 99.2 | 0.8 | 49.5 | 26.8 | 38 | 3.4 |
| Placer | 132 | 0.8 | 89 | 30.2 | 50.3 | 905 331 | 10 188 | 39 564 | 45.0 | 30 220 | 68.1 | 31.9 | 24.1 | 4.3 | 2 838 | 4.0 |
| Plumas | 120 | -29.8 | 847 | 20.2 | 18.5 | 1 550 857 | 1 831 | 68 115 | D | D | D | D | 32.4 | 9.9 | D | 1.4 |
| Riverside | 355 | -37.9 | 102 | 168.1 | 219.9 | 1 614 969 | 15 765 | 66 421 | 1 012.0 | 292 244 | 71.3 | 28.7 | 47.7 | 13.7 | 5 740 | 2.4 |
| Sacramento | 329 | 4.8 | 236 | 113.4 | 133.6 | 1 585 376 | 6 721 | 94 739 | 346.1 | 248 485 | 59.8 | 40.2 | 38.3 | 18.3 | 3 631 | 11.1 |
| San Benito | 580 | 0.3 | 928 | 30.4 | 55.2 | 2 585 410 | 2 787 | 107 836 | 222.9 | 356 577 | 83.3 | 16.7 | 49.1 | 17.6 | 396 | 7.4 |
| San Bernardino | 514 | 0.0 | 366 | 29.0 | 35.9 | 1 159 028 | 3 167 | 86 262 | 743.7 | 529 296 | 19.9 | 80.1 | 41.9 | 19.3 | 1 240 | 4.2 |
| San Diego | 304 | -25.5 | 45 | 62.2 | 102.5 | 874 683 | 19 247 | 40 032 | 1 054.2 | 157 646 | 91.2 | 8.8 | 42.0 | 10.8 | 342 | 0.5 |
| San Francisco | 0 | NA | 1 | 0.0 | 0.0 | 533 333 | 457 143 | 53 354 | 0.6 | 107 333 | 100.0 | 0.0 | 66.7 | 16.7 | 0 | 0.0 |
| San Joaquin | 738 | -9.2 | 204 | 454.0 | 492.0 | 2 069 142 | 10 168 | 127 313 | 1 564.4 | 431 665 | 63.4 | 36.6 | 65.5 | 33.9 | 4 444 | 8.5 |
| San Luis Obispo | 1 370 | 3.9 | 492 | 98.9 | 299.6 | 2 236 326 | 4 546 | 69 792 | 560.6 | 201 368 | 93.2 | 6.8 | 46.3 | 15.9 | 4 492 | 8.2 |
| San Mateo | 57 | 35.7 | 174 | 3.6 | 10.4 | 1 620 751 | 9 340 | 85 246 | 135.6 | 412 008 | 97.6 | 2.4 | 45.0 | 18.8 | 25 | 2.7 |
| Santa Barbara | 727 | -4.0 | 455 | 95.1 | 125.0 | 3 223 533 | 7 081 | 104 111 | 951.3 | 595 696 | 96.0 | 4.0 | 57.2 | 25.9 | 132 | 1.0 |
| Santa Clara | 300 | -6.5 | 281 | 22.2 | 33.3 | 1 605 690 | 5 719 | 77 811 | 235.9 | 220 906 | 94.6 | 5.4 | 36.5 | 11.5 | 132 | 2.9 |
| Santa Cruz | 47 | -29.9 | 70 | 19.6 | 23.6 | 1 561 362 | 22 423 | 101 383 | 447.4 | 656 037 | 96.9 | 3.1 | 59.4 | 30.4 | 40 | 0.7 |
| Shasta | 391 | 17.1 | 265 | 48.7 | 40.2 | 837 861 | 3 158 | 43 514 | 44.7 | 30 329 | D | D | 22.6 | 4.1 | 252 | 3.8 |
| Sierra | 29 | -50.8 | 576 | 7.0 | 6.2 | 1 502 130 | 2 609 | 67 892 | 2.0 | 40 062 | 29.3 | 70.8 | 56.0 | 14.0 | 47 | 6.0 |
| Siskiyou | 598 | -2.0 | 706 | 144.1 | 164.4 | 1 766 360 | 2 501 | 111 641 | 136.4 | 161 220 | 78.9 | 21.1 | 39.7 | 16.2 | 2 395 | 22.2 |
| Solano | 358 | 2.0 | 403 | 146.0 | 154.9 | 1 985 813 | 4 934 | 99 718 | 244.3 | 274 489 | 83.1 | 16.9 | 41.0 | 19.3 | 2 289 | 17.4 |
| Sonoma | 531 | -15.3 | 155 | 78.3 | 134.4 | 2 459 725 | 15 887 | 68 139 | 647.6 | 188 854 | 65.2 | 34.8 | 56.9 | 20.6 | 711 | 2.6 |
| Stanislaus | 789 | -0.1 | 192 | 375.0 | 351.2 | 1 817 304 | 9 476 | 119 526 | 1 820.6 | 442 529 | 40.4 | 59.6 | 61.4 | 28.7 | 4 379 | 10.0 |
| Sutter | 360 | -3.2 | 285 | 231.7 | 274.4 | 1 868 657 | 6 559 | 141 018 | 317.6 | 251 471 | 98.0 | 2.0 | 67.5 | 32.2 | 16 822 | 26.4 |
| Tehama | 532 | -38.3 | 304 | 76.1 | 94.2 | 967 204 | 3 184 | 63 403 | 143.0 | 81 597 | 73.0 | 27.0 | 43.9 | 11.7 | 1 065 | 7.0 |
| Trinity | 125 | 19.0 | 690 | 1.4 | 3.0 | 858 580 | 1 244 | 43 511 | 3.2 | 17 496 | 32.8 | 67.2 | 26.5 | 3.3 | 75 | 8.3 |
| Tulare | 1 169 | -16.1 | 223 | 550.3 | 638.8 | 1 843 502 | 8 266 | 125 007 | 3 335.0 | 636 453 | 36.2 | 63.8 | 69.9 | 32.8 | 20 335 | 11.3 |
| Tuolumne | 117 | -22.0 | 320 | 2.1 | 5.6 | 1 086 881 | 3 398 | 45 256 | 18.7 | 50 965 | 8.3 | 91.7 | 26.5 | 4.6 | 37 | 2.5 |
| Ventura | 259 | -22.0 | 106 | 91.3 | 113.9 | 2 421 700 | 22 782 | 95 150 | 1 316.3 | 540 137 | 99.0 | 1.0 | 62.2 | 25.2 | 554 | 1.9 |
| Yolo | 480 | -12.7 | 488 | 246.3 | 311.3 | 2 665 291 | 5 460 | 172 234 | 384.2 | 390 864 | 92.9 | 7.1 | 57.3 | 27.9 | 8 306 | 30.0 |
| Yuba | 161 | -31.2 | 194 | 71.0 | 71.0 | 1 152 483 | 5 931 | 96 461 | 112.9 | 136 363 | 84.4 | 15.6 | 42.4 | 20.4 | 5 161 | 17.5 |
| COLORADO | 31 605 | 1.6 | 853 | 2 868.0 | 11 483.9 | 892 170 | 1 046 | 99 344 | 6 061.1 | 163 576 | 32.7 | 67.3 | 36.1 | 13.8 | 155 980 | 31.2 |
| Adams | 702 | 0.1 | 784 | 17.0 | 546.9 | 931 948 | 1 189 | 102 027 | 153.4 | 171 439 | 88.2 | 11.8 | 29.5 | 13.7 | 6 242 | 38.1 |
| Alamosa | 177 | -13.7 | 559 | 94.0 | 91.1 | 885 117 | 1 584 | 176 244 | 91.4 | 289 281 | 94.1 | 5.9 | 51.3 | 25.9 | 684 | 26.6 |
| Arapahoe | 252 | -24.3 | 402 | 1.7 | 151.3 | 615 585 | 1 533 | 63 458 | 28.8 | 45 989 | 83.4 | 16.6 | 17.9 | 6.1 | 1 847 | 27.6 |
| Archuleta | 150 | 45.6 | 489 | 14.5 | 18.9 | 811 945 | 1 661 | 59 412 | 7.4 | 24 146 | 9.8 | 90.2 | 24.8 | 5.9 | 173 | 8.8 |
| Baca | 1 301 | 20.5 | 1 674 | 55.7 | 718.7 | 1 090 687 | 651 | 133 172 | 111.2 | 143 117 | 54.6 | 45.4 | 42.3 | 24.3 | 11 448 | 80.1 |
| Bent | 877 | 19.2 | 2 820 | 50.5 | 185.7 | 1 461 869 | 518 | 144 804 | 82.2 | 264 373 | 23.1 | 76.9 | 55.3 | 27.3 | 1 816 | 56.3 |

# Table B. States and Counties — Water Use, Wholesale Trade, Retail Trade, and Real Estate

| STATE County | Water use, 2005 | | Wholesale trade,[1] 2007 | | | | Retail trade,[2] 2007 | | | | Real estate and rental and leasing,[2] 2007 | | | |
|---|---|---|---|---|---|---|---|---|---|---|---|---|---|---|
| | Total water withdrawn (mil gal/day) | Gallons withdrawn per person | Number of establishments | Number of employees | Sales (mil dol) | Annual payroll (mil dol) | Number of establishments | Number of employees | Sales (mil dol) | Annual payroll (mil dol) | Number of establishments | Number of employees | Receipts (mil dol) | Annual payroll (mil dol) |
| | 133 | 134 | 135 | 136 | 137 | 138 | 139 | 140 | 141 | 142 | 143 | 144 | 145 | 146 |
| CALIFORNIA | 45 719.7 | 1 265 | 53 963 | 745 785 | 598 456.5 | 42 334.5 | 114 438 | 1 683 023 | 455 032.3 | 44 328.9 | 51 597 | 312 488 | 76 805.0 | 13 446.7 |
| Alameda | 171.8 | 119 | 2 553 | 45 364 | 35 674.0 | 2 786.6 | 4 503 | 67 335 | 17 909.1 | 1 882.1 | 2 032 | 12 754 | 3 081.7 | 508.7 |
| Alpine | 15.1 | 13 037 | NA | NA | NA | NA | 4 | D | D | D | 1 | D | D | D |
| Amador | 24.1 | 625 | 24 | D | D | D | 163 | 1 960 | 1 800.8 | 49.7 | 44 | 98 | 16.4 | 2.6 |
| Butte | 789.9 | 3 688 | 165 | 1 824 | 796.4 | 71.6 | 798 | 11 316 | 2 400.7 | 256.8 | 264 | 1 462 | 158.8 | 32.6 |
| Calaveras | 17.3 | 369 | 20 | 77 | 24.2 | 3.3 | 151 | 1 388 | 292.8 | 32.6 | 61 | 173 | 29.5 | 3.9 |
| Colusa | 916.3 | 43 436 | 18 | 224 | 183.2 | 11.6 | 60 | 506 | 208.5 | 12.1 | 17 | 42 | 5.8 | 1.2 |
| Contra Costa | 1 679.1 | 1 650 | 779 | 7 116 | 6 644.0 | 409.6 | 2 822 | 46 065 | 11 763.8 | 1 242.9 | 1 452 | 7 236 | 1 607.0 | 311.8 |
| Del Norte | 9.0 | 314 | 9 | D | D | D | 74 | 1 029 | 206.3 | 22.6 | 35 | 122 | 16.6 | 3.0 |
| El Dorado | 46.0 | 260 | 118 | 718 | 363.6 | 32.8 | 591 | 6 384 | 1 619.7 | 175.6 | 265 | 1 545 | 190.8 | 40.7 |
| Fresno | 3 260.2 | 3 715 | 814 | 12 843 | 7 846.8 | 582.0 | 2 579 | 38 046 | 9 808.3 | 905.0 | 755 | 4 478 | 695.2 | 132.1 |
| Glenn | 741.2 | 26 701 | 29 | 415 | 148.4 | 14.4 | 85 | 766 | 204.0 | 18.0 | 25 | 97 | 9.0 | 2.3 |
| Humboldt | 137.2 | 1 069 | 99 | D | D | D | 659 | 7 782 | 1 726.4 | 172.4 | 186 | 622 | 102.8 | 15.7 |
| Imperial | 2 144.9 | 13 765 | 212 | D | D | D | 534 | 8 052 | 1 727.3 | 170.2 | 134 | 555 | 73.4 | 12.5 |
| Inyo | 80.4 | 4 430 | 15 | D | D | D | 116 | 975 | 242.0 | 21.8 | 28 | 94 | 10.6 | 2.5 |
| Kern | 2 663.6 | 3 519 | 559 | 7 850 | 5 730.5 | 377.0 | 1 993 | 30 123 | 7 876.0 | 725.6 | 627 | 3 414 | 565.5 | 112.8 |
| Kings | 1 380.4 | 9 625 | 60 | D | D | D | 326 | 4 267 | 1 035.9 | 93.9 | 95 | 343 | 55.4 | 7.2 |
| Lake | 45.2 | 694 | 21 | D | D | D | 196 | 2 267 | 557.9 | 50.6 | 67 | 223 | 28.2 | 5.0 |
| Lassen | 246.9 | 7 104 | 7 | D | D | D | 95 | 993 | 260.4 | 24.5 | 25 | 65 | 6.1 | 1.3 |
| Los Angeles | 3 811.1 | 384 | 21 677 | 259 831 | 198 435.8 | 12 262.9 | 30 179 | 418 153 | 119 111.8 | 10 849.2 | 14 085 | 90 847 | 26 790.4 | 4 129.2 |
| Madera | 834.8 | 5 846 | 79 | 678 | 353.1 | 28.8 | 368 | 3 883 | 1 010.2 | 89.3 | 100 | 409 | 36.7 | 9.4 |
| Marin | 36.8 | 149 | 381 | 3 631 | 2 373.1 | 218.5 | 1 161 | 15 432 | 4 589.3 | 472.8 | 633 | 3 122 | 1 148.2 | 137.8 |
| Mariposa | 9.2 | 511 | 7 | D | D | D | 72 | 427 | 84.5 | 8.6 | 21 | 85 | 9.3 | 2.4 |
| Mendocino | 58.1 | 659 | 84 | D | D | D | 492 | 5 097 | 1 259.1 | 120.7 | 141 | 597 | 91.3 | 12.6 |
| Merced | 1 624.9 | 6 723 | 97 | D | D | D | 578 | 8 005 | 2 001.3 | 179.9 | 153 | 641 | 85.6 | 15.1 |
| Modoc | 313.8 | 32 950 | 8 | D | D | D | 33 | 271 | 53.0 | 5.4 | 11 | D | D | D |
| Mono | 211.1 | 16 879 | 9 | D | D | D | 90 | 812 | 154.3 | 16.9 | 65 | 346 | 39.5 | 9.9 |
| Monterey | 1 129.2 | 2 740 | 392 | D | D | D | 1 497 | 18 392 | 4 541.1 | 487.8 | 487 | 2 423 | 500.6 | 86.6 |
| Napa | 51.8 | 390 | 143 | D | D | D | 537 | 6 463 | 1 665.0 | 180.7 | 206 | 893 | 153.0 | 31.1 |
| Nevada | 88.9 | 903 | 88 | D | D | D | 443 | 4 713 | 1 077.2 | 124.6 | 185 | 820 | 142.5 | 26.1 |
| Orange | 717.6 | 240 | 6 559 | 94 938 | 97 963.6 | 5 642.5 | 9 991 | 159 810 | 45 022.5 | 4 304.3 | 5 566 | 43 366 | 10 688.2 | 2 161.6 |
| Placer | 209.2 | 660 | 334 | 5 272 | 3 898.6 | 275.6 | 1 254 | 22 112 | 6 180.1 | 604.9 | 602 | 4 113 | 674.9 | 146.7 |
| Plumas | 79.3 | 3 691 | 5 | D | D | D | 118 | 769 | 175.3 | 17.6 | 42 | 77 | 13.7 | 2.8 |
| Riverside | 1 257.5 | 646 | 1 601 | 22 180 | 16 912.3 | 979.6 | 5 320 | 89 543 | 24 146.4 | 2 257.3 | 2 189 | 11 787 | 2 056.8 | 376.9 |
| Sacramento | 774.3 | 568 | 1 144 | 16 959 | 15 728.1 | 773.4 | 3 821 | 63 609 | 15 600.0 | 1 613.6 | 1 673 | 9 979 | 1 677.6 | 360.4 |
| San Benito | 69.4 | 1 241 | 36 | 1 645 | 319.6 | 60.7 | 124 | 1 522 | 352.9 | 40.7 | 56 | 115 | 16.5 | 3.4 |
| San Bernardino | 586.1 | 298 | 2 284 | 33 335 | 27 579.9 | 1 434.7 | 5 018 | 84 312 | 21 717.4 | 2 018.8 | 1 771 | 9 935 | 2 310.1 | 354.5 |
| San Diego | 4 085.1 | 1 393 | 4 002 | 55 934 | 33 704.9 | 4 120.7 | 9 948 | 151 425 | 38 710.6 | 3 889.2 | 5 810 | 33 067 | 7 190.2 | 1 345.2 |
| San Francisco | 1 668.3 | 2 256 | 1 195 | 11 786 | 10 562.2 | 668.1 | 3 710 | 45 079 | 12 400.0 | 1 395.9 | 1 843 | 14 332 | 4 309.7 | 984.3 |
| San Joaquin | 1 483.5 | 2 234 | 558 | 9 517 | 9 001.3 | 437.3 | 1 756 | 27 329 | 7 109.7 | 653.0 | 634 | 3 363 | 577.5 | 104.4 |
| San Luis Obispo | 2 774.1 | 10 858 | 277 | 2 329 | 955.0 | 104.1 | 1 262 | 14 652 | 3 548.4 | 353.6 | 475 | 2 050 | 293.4 | 56.7 |
| San Mateo | 151.1 | 216 | 1 076 | 15 170 | 12 607.8 | 1 094.9 | 2 216 | 36 139 | 10 198.8 | 1 084.2 | 1 246 | 8 041 | 2 077.1 | 365.1 |
| Santa Barbara | 239.6 | 598 | 438 | 5 713 | 4 023.6 | 350.4 | 1 605 | 20 281 | 4 983.4 | 524.4 | 681 | 3 452 | 620.7 | 119.5 |
| Santa Clara | 296.1 | 174 | 2 487 | 61 835 | 60 644.1 | 6 157.9 | 5 297 | 86 410 | 26 491.5 | 2 906.4 | 2 608 | 14 831 | 5 172.6 | 748.6 |
| Santa Cruz | 73.7 | 295 | 273 | D | D | D | 981 | 12 454 | 3 725.4 | 316.0 | 380 | 1 793 | 311.1 | 58.6 |
| Shasta | 236.2 | 1 313 | 179 | 1 748 | 829.0 | 69.4 | 722 | 10 287 | 2 526.4 | 260.1 | 225 | 1 201 | 128.2 | 26.1 |
| Sierra | 63.4 | 18 465 | 2 | D | D | D | 14 | D | D | D | NA | NA | NA | NA |
| Siskiyou | 384.8 | 8 502 | 37 | 358 | 169.1 | 11.2 | 209 | 1 859 | 403.3 | 37.2 | 67 | 203 | 22.1 | 4.1 |
| Solano | 467.9 | 1 137 | 249 | D | D | D | 1 167 | 19 117 | 4 828.0 | 482.7 | 404 | 1 913 | 347.9 | 58.5 |
| Sonoma | 114.3 | 245 | 585 | 7 631 | 3 953.6 | 454.3 | 1 925 | 26 177 | 6 427.2 | 718.5 | 718 | 3 237 | 604.1 | 114.2 |
| Stanislaus | 1 457.9 | 2 884 | 397 | 5 460 | 3 759.1 | 248.8 | 1 500 | 23 394 | 5 661.9 | 561.1 | 500 | 2 988 | 472.6 | 90.3 |
| Sutter | 833.7 | 9 381 | 66 | 1 421 | 879.0 | 71.7 | 304 | 4 614 | 1 065.4 | 112.0 | 99 | 602 | 60.4 | 12.9 |
| Tehama | 538.8 | 8 804 | 32 | D | D | D | 180 | 2 244 | 735.4 | 54.7 | 60 | 216 | 23.8 | 4.7 |
| Trinity | 21.6 | 1 588 | 4 | D | D | D | 52 | 383 | 69.2 | 6.7 | 8 | D | D | D |
| Tulare | 2 275.0 | 5 537 | 337 | D | D | D | 1 140 | 16 005 | 3 900.9 | 367.4 | 294 | 1 260 | 189.1 | 32.3 |
| Tuolumne | 33.8 | 570 | 37 | D | D | D | 213 | 2 419 | 582.4 | 56.1 | 90 | 271 | 39.9 | 6.6 |
| Ventura | 1 198.6 | 1 506 | 1 024 | D | D | D | 2 766 | 40 773 | 11 083.6 | 1 074.8 | 1 051 | 5 064 | 1 006.1 | 196.0 |
| Yolo | 738.8 | 3 995 | 251 | 6 048 | 6 483.6 | 271.2 | 500 | 7 812 | 1 765.7 | 189.2 | 268 | 1 560 | 247.0 | 53.4 |
| Yuba | 351.7 | 5 238 | 27 | D | D | D | 126 | 1 522 | 423.6 | 35.0 | 37 | 121 | 20.5 | 2.6 |
| COLORADO | 13 627.7 | 2 921 | 5 850 | 81 144 | 53 599.0 | 4 191.0 | 19 428 | 261 962 | 65 896.8 | 6 537.5 | 10 011 | 47 568 | 8 460.9 | 1 793.0 |
| Adams | 185.3 | 464 | 654 | 15 465 | 11 193.4 | 747.5 | 997 | 17 192 | 4 848.9 | 466.9 | 455 | 3 029 | 458.8 | 98.1 |
| Alamosa | 272.1 | 17 807 | 17 | 136 | 85.3 | 4.7 | 90 | 1 115 | 263.0 | 27.6 | 26 | 122 | 14.2 | 2.8 |
| Arapahoe | 84.9 | 161 | 684 | 9 551 | 5 774.1 | 550.7 | 1 890 | 32 052 | 9 932.0 | 848.7 | 1 109 | 6 048 | 1 207.1 | 241.7 |
| Archuleta | 71.5 | 6 014 | 8 | 29 | 8.8 | 0.8 | 104 | 647 | 142.7 | 14.9 | 51 | 178 | 37.2 | 4.7 |
| Baca | 127.8 | 31 403 | 16 | 43 | 52.7 | 1.2 | 17 | 124 | 32.9 | 2.5 | 3 | 3 | 0.1 | 0.0 |
| Bent | 211.3 | 38 024 | 1 | D | D | D | 16 | 85 | 16.4 | 1.4 | 2 | D | D | D |

1. Merchant wholesalers, except manufacturers' sales branches and offices.    2. Employer establishments.

# Table B. States and Counties — Professional Services, Manufacturing, and Accommodation and Food Services

| STATE County | Professional, scientific, and technical services,[1] 2007 | | | | Manufacturing, 2007 | | | | Accommodation and food services, 2007 | | | |
|---|---|---|---|---|---|---|---|---|---|---|---|---|
| | Number of establish-ments | Number of employees | Receipts (mil dol) | Annual payroll (mil dol) | Number of establish-ments | Number of employees | Receipts (mil dol) | Annual payroll (mil dol) | Number of establish-ments | Number of employees | Sales (mil dol) | Annual payroll (mil dol) |
| | 147 | 148 | 149 | 150 | 151 | 152 | 153 | 154 | 155 | 156 | 157 | 158 |
| CALIFORNIA | 111 954 | 1 231 372 | 194 406.3 | 80 738.1 | 44 296 | 1 448 485 | 491 372.1 | 71 247.3 | 75 989 | 1 366 926 | 80 852.8 | 22 374.8 |
| Alameda | 5 143 | D | D | D | 2 081 | 81 002 | 25 236.9 | 4 645.4 | 3 385 | 47 408 | 2 807.8 | 770.0 |
| Alpine | 5 | D | D | D | NA | NA | NA | NA | 12 | D | D | D |
| Amador | 77 | 279 | 26.1 | 8.9 | 51 | 760 | 143.0 | 29.4 | 109 | 1 249 | 61.2 | 17.1 |
| Butte | 426 | D | D | D | 224 | 4 404 | 987.4 | 150.6 | 429 | 7 708 | 355.8 | 96.7 |
| Calaveras | 80 | 347 | 36.7 | 12.9 | NA | NA | NA | NA | 114 | 976 | 42.4 | 11.1 |
| Colusa | 22 | 50 | 3.9 | 1.1 | 24 | 745 | 288.4 | 27.5 | 39 | 1 124 | 91.6 | 21.0 |
| Contra Costa | 3 273 | D | D | D | 622 | 18 551 | 32 021.4 | 1 146.1 | 1 777 | 28 524 | 1 562.3 | 433.1 |
| Del Norte | 38 | 135 | 13.1 | 4.2 | NA | NA | NA | NA | 74 | 748 | 32.2 | 7.9 |
| El Dorado | 538 | 2 808 | 515.1 | 151.4 | 204 | 3 534 | 662.2 | 142.5 | 447 | 5 885 | 301.7 | 83.5 |
| Fresno | 1 564 | D | D | D | 646 | 26 898 | 7 827.3 | 1 018.0 | 1 460 | 25 553 | 1 147.2 | 320.9 |
| Glenn | 36 | 149 | 11.0 | 3.4 | 31 | 721 | 278.3 | 27.7 | 58 | 608 | 31.0 | 8.3 |
| Humboldt | 259 | D | D | D | 158 | 3 105 | 877.0 | 117.7 | 352 | 4 649 | 209.0 | 58.4 |
| Imperial | 153 | D | D | D | 58 | 2 846 | 1 207.9 | 96.9 | 261 | 3 719 | 167.8 | 46.2 |
| Inyo | 34 | D | D | D | NA | NA | NA | NA | 98 | 1 570 | 91.7 | 25.3 |
| Kern | 1 123 | D | D | D | 390 | 12 789 | 9 456.2 | 583.7 | 1 203 | 19 344 | 940.3 | 252.2 |
| Kings | 101 | 535 | 52.9 | 16.9 | 73 | 4 291 | 2 107.7 | 148.7 | 171 | 4 209 | 360.1 | 77.5 |
| Lake | 79 | D | D | D | NA | NA | NA | NA | 133 | 1 325 | 68.1 | 17.3 |
| Lassen | 33 | 120 | 11.9 | 4.0 | NA | NA | NA | NA | 61 | 651 | 29.7 | 7.6 |
| Los Angeles | 30 754 | D | D | D | 15 158 | 451 656 | 153 343.7 | 20 520.1 | 19 476 | 339 815 | 20 238.1 | 5 570.1 |
| Madera | 124 | D | D | D | 116 | 4 143 | 1 452.9 | 170.3 | 192 | 2 265 | 125.1 | 33.1 |
| Marin | 1 797 | D | D | D | 229 | 2 205 | 397.2 | 88.0 | 694 | 10 913 | 626.6 | 185.9 |
| Mariposa | 21 | 76 | 5.8 | 1.9 | NA | NA | NA | NA | 51 | 1 430 | 133.0 | 27.5 |
| Mendocino | 206 | D | D | D | 146 | 3 057 | 773.4 | 113.6 | 347 | 3 796 | 194.2 | 53.6 |
| Merced | 170 | D | D | D | 122 | 9 208 | 3 954.2 | 348.6 | 302 | 5 130 | 219.4 | 55.2 |
| Modoc | 11 | 35 | 3.7 | 0.8 | NA | NA | NA | NA | 26 | 156 | 8.8 | 2.0 |
| Mono | 36 | 217 | 24.3 | 9.6 | NA | NA | NA | NA | 138 | 3 848 | 217.4 | 68.9 |
| Monterey | 818 | D | D | D | 301 | 7 333 | 2 227.6 | 268.4 | 983 | 18 026 | 1 197.1 | 345.4 |
| Napa | 419 | D | D | D | 436 | 13 165 | 4 529.3 | 632.4 | 363 | 8 904 | 620.4 | 195.4 |
| Nevada | 389 | D | D | D | 164 | 2 488 | 664.6 | 156.1 | 235 | 5 604 | 199.4 | 64.4 |
| Orange | 14 013 | D | D | D | 5 351 | 177 115 | 49 131.9 | 8 641.4 | 6 854 | 141 702 | 8 247.8 | 2 366.7 |
| Placer | 1 188 | D | D | D | 292 | 9 197 | 3 023.4 | 354.3 | 824 | 16 575 | 773.6 | 228.8 |
| Plumas | 57 | D | D | D | 21 | 593 | 130.6 | 26.5 | 112 | 560 | 30.1 | 8.5 |
| Riverside | 3 174 | D | D | D | 1 611 | 56 388 | 13 623.5 | 2 314.9 | 3 292 | 73 824 | 4 835.3 | 1 275.0 |
| Sacramento | 3 735 | D | D | D | 925 | 26 030 | 7 282.8 | 1 126.9 | 2 634 | 45 903 | 2 252.9 | 628.3 |
| San Benito | 70 | 206 | 25.8 | 7.8 | 63 | 2 867 | 630.3 | 102.0 | 93 | 1 109 | 50.2 | 14.6 |
| San Bernardino | 2 488 | D | D | D | 2 057 | 65 702 | 18 907.3 | 2 540.2 | 3 112 | 54 839 | 2 754.7 | 746.0 |
| San Diego | 11 972 | 117 497 | 18 834.7 | 7 694.0 | 3 182 | 102 168 | 27 541.1 | 5 244.6 | 6 599 | 144 287 | 9 551.5 | 2 567.2 |
| San Francisco | 5 600 | D | D | D | 788 | 11 339 | 2 077.5 | 422.5 | 3 525 | 66 365 | 5 039.2 | 1 496.8 |
| San Joaquin | 801 | D | D | D | 585 | 23 442 | 8 272.5 | 938.6 | 1 079 | 15 195 | 745.8 | 199.3 |
| San Luis Obispo | 930 | 5 709 | 593.8 | 222.6 | 377 | 6 517 | 2 548.2 | 260.4 | 850 | 14 903 | 767.9 | 219.7 |
| San Mateo | 2 916 | D | D | D | 742 | 30 221 | 17 918.2 | 1 975.0 | 1 785 | 30 836 | 2 107.2 | 613.5 |
| Santa Barbara | 1 359 | D | D | D | 505 | 13 149 | 3 174.1 | 676.8 | 1 029 | 21 380 | 1 361.5 | 360.1 |
| Santa Clara | 7 815 | 123 627 | 21 567.5 | 13 553.6 | 2 620 | 142 713 | 45 088.8 | 10 295.9 | 4 097 | 68 514 | 4 147.6 | 1 159.3 |
| Santa Cruz | 914 | D | D | D | 329 | 6 689 | 1 502.4 | 301.6 | 657 | 9 774 | 513.8 | 148.8 |
| Shasta | 400 | D | D | D | 167 | 2 794 | 662.9 | 117.1 | 403 | 5 862 | 281.0 | 74.9 |
| Sierra | 4 | D | D | D | NA | NA | NA | NA | 16 | D | D | D |
| Siskiyou | 98 | D | D | D | 38 | 911 | 257.8 | 36.0 | 149 | 1 684 | 78.5 | 22.0 |
| Solano | 598 | D | D | D | 296 | 10 357 | 8 377.3 | 578.9 | 731 | 12 523 | 573.3 | 153.4 |
| Sonoma | 1 538 | D | D | D | 885 | 24 077 | 5 841.9 | 1 201.2 | 1 173 | 17 739 | 1 005.4 | 283.8 |
| Stanislaus | 701 | D | D | D | 443 | 24 127 | 9 476.0 | 1 032.9 | 842 | 13 881 | 615.1 | 171.7 |
| Sutter | 129 | D | D | D | 71 | 1 549 | 494.9 | 61.3 | 153 | 2 498 | 100.7 | 28.1 |
| Tehama | 75 | 280 | 29.1 | 10.2 | 47 | 2 356 | 556.7 | 97.0 | 124 | 1 215 | 56.1 | 14.8 |
| Trinity | 22 | 82 | 8.1 | 2.6 | NA | NA | NA | NA | 53 | 291 | 14.6 | 3.7 |
| Tulare | 446 | D | D | D | 278 | 12 443 | 5 016.0 | 458.3 | 558 | 8 282 | 379.4 | 102.8 |
| Tuolumne | 120 | D | D | D | 66 | 1 030 | 222.5 | 40.4 | 169 | 1 817 | 86.5 | 23.6 |
| Ventura | 2 597 | 16 457 | 6 370.8 | 1 032.7 | 954 | 33 602 | 8 769.0 | 1 643.4 | 1 602 | 29 832 | 1 478.2 | 422.9 |
| Yolo | 395 | D | D | D | 177 | 5 743 | 1 853.3 | 235.7 | 399 | 8 693 | 840.3 | 159.7 |
| Yuba | 70 | D | D | D | 45 | 921 | 170.0 | 33.3 | 85 | 1 055 | 52.4 | 14.0 |
| COLORADO | 22 522 | 156 859 | 28 932.6 | 10 515.7 | 5 288 | 137 880 | 46 332.0 | 6 789.7 | 12 075 | 231 721 | 11 440.4 | 3 408.2 |
| Adams | 658 | D | D | D | 417 | 11 757 | 6 161.5 | 515.1 | 635 | 11 997 | 578.0 | 164.1 |
| Alamosa | 51 | D | D | D | NA | NA | NA | NA | 48 | 766 | 30.3 | 9.2 |
| Arapahoe | 2 727 | D | D | D | 436 | 8 358 | 2 043.0 | 395.2 | 1 136 | 20 947 | 1 008.5 | 301.4 |
| Archuleta | 43 | 119 | 10.1 | 3.5 | NA | NA | NA | NA | 64 | 649 | 33.2 | 9.0 |
| Baca | 3 | 5 | 0.5 | 0.1 | NA | NA | NA | NA | 8 | D | D | D |
| Bent | 2 | D | D | D | NA | NA | NA | NA | 10 | 98 | 3.0 | 0.8 |

1. Establishment subject to federal tax.

# Table B. States and Counties — Health Care and Social Assistance, Other Services, and Federal Funds

| STATE County | Health care and social assistance, 2007 | | | | Other services, 2007 | | | | Federal funds and grants, 2009–2010 Expenditures (mil dol) | | | |
| | | | | | | | | | | Direct payments for individuals[1] | | |
| | Number of establishments | Number of employees | Receipts (mil dol) | Annual payroll (mil dol) | Number of establishments | Number of employees | Receipts (mil dol) | Annual payroll (mil dol) | Total | Social Security and government retirement | Medicare | Food Stamps and Supplemental Security Income |
| | 159 | 160 | 161 | 162 | 163 | 164 | 165 | 166 | 167 | 168 | 169 | 170 |
| CALIFORNIA | 97 288 | 1 592 430 | 191 605.7 | 72 531.1 | 57 626 | 399 336 | 52 326.5 | 11 913.7 | 333 809.3 | 78 067.9 | 56 261.1 | 12 469.4 |
| Alameda | 4 238 | 74 258 | 9 681.4 | 3 987.0 | 2 742 | 19 921 | 2 359.3 | 670.7 | 14 633.9 | 3 043.5 | 2 487.2 | 529.6 |
| Alpine | 4 | D | D | D | 1 | D | D | D | 7.9 | 2.6 | 1.6 | 0.3 |
| Amador | 89 | 1 281 | 127.6 | 48.1 | 50 | 158 | 17.4 | 4.4 | 280.5 | 152.4 | 78.0 | 6.1 |
| Butte | 737 | 12 120 | 1 179.3 | 427.5 | 321 | 2 168 | 173.6 | 49.9 | 1 788.2 | 699.6 | 453.6 | 104.9 |
| Calaveras | 99 | 1 134 | 106.8 | 40.4 | 63 | 226 | 18.2 | 4.9 | 353.5 | 181.6 | 88.9 | 11.3 |
| Colusa | 25 | D | D | D | 22 | 94 | 10.4 | 2.6 | 156.4 | 50.7 | 36.7 | 6.5 |
| Contra Costa | 2 737 | 44 257 | 5 652.4 | 2 302.8 | 1 528 | 8 902 | 1 054.4 | 276.2 | 6 802.1 | 2 508.5 | 1 559.0 | 238.8 |
| Del Norte | 75 | 1 352 | 117.0 | 51.3 | 26 | 98 | 10.5 | 2.1 | 241.7 | 89.7 | 49.9 | 19.1 |
| El Dorado | 452 | 5 802 | 624.8 | 240.9 | 285 | 1 513 | 137.8 | 38.8 | 1 057.1 | 532.1 | 266.8 | 29.0 |
| Fresno | 2 099 | 36 707 | 4 150.8 | 1 713.0 | 1 069 | 7 309 | 704.7 | 191.7 | 5 953.8 | 1 736.7 | 991.7 | 468.5 |
| Glenn | 37 | 479 | 33.7 | 14.5 | 21 | 51 | 6.9 | 1.1 | 221.0 | 72.1 | 51.5 | 11.3 |
| Humboldt | 462 | 6 762 | 589.0 | 217.0 | 259 | 1 304 | 157.0 | 32.8 | 1 130.5 | 385.3 | 233.2 | 65.6 |
| Imperial | 265 | 4 257 | 394.1 | 142.6 | 163 | 1 046 | 83.2 | 25.1 | 1 240.1 | 314.4 | 226.8 | 84.2 |
| Inyo | 63 | 1 047 | 92.8 | 38.2 | 44 | 164 | 16.2 | 4.2 | 211.4 | 53.0 | 44.5 | 5.1 |
| Kern | 1 456 | 25 119 | 2 746.4 | 1 042.9 | 857 | 5 637 | 569.1 | 145.0 | 5 744.5 | 1 632.6 | 1 074.6 | 328.6 |
| Kings | 204 | 4 106 | 433.8 | 153.1 | 105 | 582 | 47.0 | 13.4 | 994.5 | 260.9 | 141.1 | 49.3 |
| Lake | 154 | 2 242 | 237.7 | 86.7 | 79 | 258 | 24.4 | 7.0 | 621.3 | 245.0 | 200.2 | 37.3 |
| Lassen | 61 | 722 | 75.5 | 23.7 | 29 | 92 | 7.4 | 1.9 | 315.4 | 87.7 | 42.7 | 10.5 |
| Los Angeles | 27 728 | 444 806 | 53 200.9 | 19 568.8 | 16 089 | 117 748 | 15 230.4 | 3 369.6 | 82 544.3 | 16 317.2 | 17 792.2 | 4 259.6 |
| Madera | 221 | 5 836 | 554.7 | 255.8 | 119 | 609 | 48.9 | 12.9 | 847.3 | 327.4 | 188.3 | 45.6 |
| Marin | 1 066 | 13 958 | 1 595.2 | 649.1 | 617 | 4 249 | 630.4 | 167.2 | 1 694.9 | 772.6 | 429.9 | 32.9 |
| Mariposa | 31 | 456 | 29.9 | 13.3 | 18 | 62 | 5.6 | 1.4 | 211.5 | 68.4 | 34.9 | 4.4 |
| Mendocino | 294 | 4 185 | 369.1 | 147.2 | 165 | 674 | 74.3 | 16.3 | 773.3 | 277.9 | 177.1 | 36.3 |
| Merced | 443 | 6 048 | 592.2 | 235.3 | 209 | 899 | 73.9 | 19.3 | 1 519.8 | 461.0 | 273.2 | 126.0 |
| Modoc | 18 | D | D | D | 7 | 54 | 4.5 | 1.2 | 263.9 | 38.4 | 18.8 | 4.6 |
| Mono | 28 | D | D | D | 53 | 199 | 20.1 | 5.0 | 87.7 | 29.4 | 7.6 | 1.1 |
| Monterey | 970 | 13 789 | 1 876.6 | 723.7 | 556 | 3 651 | 425.9 | 104.6 | 3 298.5 | 932.2 | 553.5 | 91.2 |
| Napa | 425 | 10 004 | 1 150.0 | 502.2 | 219 | 1 172 | 142.5 | 38.4 | 1 011.6 | 412.9 | 312.3 | 21.3 |
| Nevada | 365 | 4 469 | 451.4 | 171.9 | 176 | 878 | 94.0 | 25.8 | 808.5 | 362.2 | 171.8 | 16.1 |
| Orange | 9 967 | 133 174 | 16 300.4 | 5 915.0 | 5 111 | 34 627 | 3 636.0 | 967.4 | 18 041.8 | 5 889.5 | 4 181.8 | 633.2 |
| Placer | 979 | 13 655 | 1 934.7 | 676.1 | 547 | 7 590 | 1 955.4 | 444.6 | 1 942.3 | 1 169.9 | 310.5 | 43.2 |
| Plumas | 53 | 912 | 75.2 | 30.3 | 41 | 128 | 10.6 | 3.0 | 249.2 | 92.2 | 48.1 | 5.9 |
| Riverside | 3 779 | 57 969 | 6 621.0 | 2 365.0 | 2 474 | 15 480 | 1 335.4 | 383.7 | 11 146.5 | 4 760.9 | 2 742.7 | 488.0 |
| Sacramento | 3 232 | 70 675 | 9 072.3 | 3 587.6 | 2 200 | 17 591 | 1 974.9 | 573.8 | 26 522.5 | 3 517.6 | 1 883.2 | 659.1 |
| San Benito | 100 | D | D | D | 69 | 251 | 22.4 | 5.7 | 241.6 | 99.6 | 51.0 | 8.2 |
| San Bernardino | 3 446 | 71 731 | 8 350.6 | 3 149.6 | 2 336 | 16 862 | 1 592.3 | 467.0 | 13 406.5 | 3 684.2 | 2 370.5 | 751.9 |
| San Diego | 7 924 | 133 893 | 15 954.7 | 5 872.9 | 5 176 | 37 084 | 3 732.5 | 1 015.3 | 37 302.9 | 7 771.6 | 4 652.8 | 790.1 |
| San Francisco | 2 967 | 57 946 | 7 752.0 | 3 039.4 | 2 239 | 17 261 | 5 992.0 | 626.7 | 11 738.0 | 1 638.2 | 1 876.8 | 363.5 |
| San Joaquin | 1 351 | 26 658 | 3 045.8 | 1 141.3 | 879 | 5 576 | 462.8 | 144.6 | 4 164.3 | 1 413.7 | 851.2 | 287.4 |
| San Luis Obispo | 864 | 14 341 | 1 341.2 | 546.4 | 464 | 2 808 | 222.0 | 60.3 | 1 783.4 | 769.8 | 416.5 | 44.5 |
| San Mateo | 2 095 | 30 901 | 4 046.3 | 1 591.8 | 1 411 | 9 356 | 2 520.3 | 331.9 | 5 434.4 | 1 785.3 | 1 106.7 | 94.8 |
| Santa Barbara | 1 322 | 19 124 | 2 076.4 | 784.0 | 767 | 5 005 | 816.9 | 141.4 | 3 677.4 | 1 037.4 | 621.1 | 91.6 |
| Santa Clara | 5 061 | D | D | D | 2 901 | 19 386 | 2 816.0 | 658.4 | 16 008.4 | 3 253.3 | 2 064.5 | 466.3 |
| Santa Cruz | 863 | 11 416 | 1 441.4 | 505.0 | 452 | 2 702 | 258.2 | 72.1 | 1 598.2 | 550.8 | 387.8 | 56.7 |
| Shasta | 661 | 10 015 | 1 124.5 | 420.3 | 320 | 1 697 | 168.2 | 43.3 | 1 678.2 | 724.9 | 355.0 | 93.5 |
| Sierra | 11 | D | D | D | NA | NA | NA | NA | 36.2 | 12.7 | 9.3 | 0.8 |
| Siskiyou | 117 | 1 721 | 151.9 | 59.3 | 71 | 212 | 20.9 | 5.1 | 488.5 | 193.6 | 101.0 | 22.3 |
| Solano | 861 | 18 135 | 2 136.5 | 895.9 | 541 | 3 240 | 324.0 | 92.5 | 3 454.6 | 1 261.9 | 407.1 | 118.6 |
| Sonoma | 1 516 | 23 219 | 2 623.9 | 1 065.9 | 873 | 4 877 | 508.1 | 138.8 | 3 142.9 | 1 300.7 | 800.3 | 86.8 |
| Stanislaus | 1 108 | 21 628 | 2 662.6 | 967.7 | 650 | 4 205 | 380.9 | 119.5 | 3 048.2 | 1 091.0 | 705.9 | 198.7 |
| Sutter | 251 | 3 085 | 409.2 | 116.9 | 132 | 741 | 61.9 | 16.6 | 575.9 | 243.5 | 128.1 | 28.8 |
| Tehama | 129 | 1 917 | 171.5 | 62.1 | 71 | 614 | 31.8 | 23.9 | 520.3 | 183.0 | 107.2 | 23.1 |
| Trinity | 29 | 198 | 12.9 | 4.7 | 17 | D | D | D | 139.3 | 59.4 | 29.5 | 6.6 |
| Tulare | 806 | 13 734 | 1 295.3 | 493.8 | 384 | 2 298 | 208.1 | 62.9 | 2 559.9 | 749.5 | 525.0 | 196.5 |
| Tuolumne | 173 | 2 662 | 307.7 | 112.2 | 76 | 435 | 41.0 | 11.2 | 460.8 | 229.4 | 111.9 | 16.5 |
| Ventura | 2 317 | 29 522 | 3 140.0 | 1 200.9 | 1 196 | 7 303 | 839.6 | 195.9 | 5 559.1 | 1 945.1 | 1 102.6 | 147.1 |
| Yolo | 364 | 5 936 | 660.5 | 234.6 | 282 | 2 000 | 208.0 | 63.8 | 2 866.1 | 377.2 | 208.0 | 55.2 |
| Yuba | 96 | 2 708 | 313.1 | 111.6 | 54 | 250 | 33.9 | 9.9 | 789.0 | 195.8 | 117.2 | 45.2 |
| COLORADO | 13 644 | 238 942 | 24 328.4 | 9 724.8 | 10 151 | 62 767 | 7 789.2 | 1 823.2 | 49 686.9 | 12 450.4 | 4 655.3 | 1 076.3 |
| Adams | 582 | 18 364 | 2 227.9 | 770.6 | 620 | 4 315 | 458.5 | 122.1 | 2 110.8 | 726.5 | 399.6 | 92.7 |
| Alamosa | 69 | 1 507 | 114.3 | 48.0 | 44 | 222 | 11.6 | 3.6 | 136.0 | 37.5 | 15.6 | 8.8 |
| Arapahoe | 1 714 | 28 246 | 3 010.4 | 1 196.9 | 1 110 | 7 321 | 943.9 | 242.5 | 5 218.0 | 1 576.6 | 394.3 | 86.1 |
| Archuleta | 37 | 186 | 13.3 | 4.7 | 29 | 139 | 10.0 | 3.2 | 66.7 | 43.7 | 5.7 | 1.6 |
| Baca | 7 | D | D | D | 6 | D | D | D | 62.5 | 21.6 | 9.6 | 1.3 |
| Bent | 7 | D | D | D | 3 | D | D | D | 57.5 | 22.9 | 8.2 | 3.6 |

1. State totals may include programs not allocated by county.

# Federal Funds, Residential Construction, and Local Government Finances

| STATE County | Federal funds and grants, 2009–2010 (cont.) | | | | | | | Value of residential construction authorized by building permits, 2011 | | Local government finances, 2007 | | | | |
|---|---|---|---|---|---|---|---|---|---|---|---|---|---|---|
| | Expenditures (mil dol) (cont.) | | | | | | | | | General revenue | | | | |
| | Procurement contract awards | | | Grants[1] | | | | | | | | Taxes | | |
| | | | | | | | | | | | | | Per capita[2] (dollars) | |
| | Salaries and wages | Defense | Other | Medicaid and other health-related | Nutrition and family welfare | Education | Other | New construction ($1,000) | Number of housing units | Total (mil dol) | Inter-govern-mental (mil dol) | Total (mil dol) | Total | Property |
| | 171 | 172 | 173 | 174 | 175 | 176 | 177 | 178 | 179 | 180 | 181 | 182 | 183 | 184 |
| CALIFORNIA | 24 584.6 | 41 323.3 | 16 213.6 | 41 931.1 | 11 743.7 | 6 113.7 | 19 080.4 | 9 638 517 | 45 471 | X | X | X | X | X |
| Alameda | 998.9 | 358.9 | 2 903.6 | 2 556.4 | 318.6 | 159.9 | 968.7 | 516 026 | 2 172 | 11 177.5 | 4 672.4 | 3 410.6 | 2 329 | 1 552 |
| Alpine | 0.4 | 0.4 | 0.4 | 1.0 | 0.3 | 0.4 | 0.4 | 1 625 | 3 | 22.6 | 9.4 | 8.4 | 7 298 | 6 225 |
| Amador | 6.9 | 0.5 | 2.1 | 16.6 | 9.1 | 0.4 | 6.2 | 11 316 | 80 | 143.0 | 64.1 | 52.4 | 1 355 | 1 126 |
| Butte | 47.0 | 0.5 | 36.4 | 263.4 | 44.7 | 22.7 | 34.9 | 42 692 | 240 | 1 116.2 | 653.8 | 247.0 | 1 129 | 888 |
| Calaveras | 8.3 | 4.4 | 4.3 | 26.1 | 11.2 | 8.1 | 7.8 | 8 640 | 29 | 196.0 | 76.1 | 77.9 | 1 662 | 1 464 |
| Colusa | 4.3 | 0.0 | 0.8 | 18.6 | 8.2 | 1.4 | 7.6 | 2 849 | 14 | 134.9 | 76.4 | 29.4 | 1 379 | 1 125 |
| Contra Costa | 582.9 | 245.6 | 403.6 | 749.7 | 189.3 | 56.4 | 171.9 | 191 488 | 861 | 5 949.8 | 2 045.3 | 2 042.3 | 2 003 | 1 567 |
| Del Norte | 10.1 | 0.1 | 8.3 | 28.8 | 10.1 | 2.1 | 21.3 | 10 257 | 89 | 126.5 | 81.5 | 22.5 | 776 | 618 |
| El Dorado | 54.6 | 18.6 | 25.1 | 62.5 | 32.4 | 9.3 | 18.3 | 54 457 | 141 | 905.5 | 353.8 | 309.9 | 1 764 | 1 477 |
| Fresno | 601.7 | 72.9 | 167.6 | 992.0 | 274.8 | 96.6 | 252.1 | 278 260 | 1 622 | 4 901.8 | 2 877.0 | 1 069.3 | 1 189 | 832 |
| Glenn | 15.7 | 1.6 | 7.7 | 25.3 | 10.6 | 2.7 | 7.4 | 4 662 | 26 | 175.5 | 105.8 | 28.4 | 1 012 | 815 |
| Humboldt | 74.5 | 3.7 | 25.3 | 167.8 | 36.0 | 20.9 | 58.1 | 29 410 | 263 | 682.1 | 405.0 | 137.6 | 1 068 | 833 |
| Imperial | 178.5 | 47.7 | 59.2 | 199.4 | 50.0 | 23.2 | 20.8 | 37 648 | 257 | 1 139.1 | 670.3 | 166.9 | 1 031 | 684 |
| Inyo | 19.8 | 12.6 | 35.0 | 19.8 | 6.6 | 4.4 | 8.9 | 2 901 | 6 | 178.6 | 65.8 | 46.9 | 2 689 | 1 941 |
| Kern | 772.0 | 484.6 | 233.1 | 712.0 | 203.4 | 69.5 | 80.2 | 150 696 | 969 | 5 502.3 | 2 722.3 | 1 021.3 | 1 292 | 1 083 |
| Kings | 195.1 | 28.9 | 66.6 | 129.2 | 37.8 | 20.1 | 11.0 | 28 528 | 222 | 632.3 | 386.7 | 115.8 | 778 | 616 |
| Lake | 11.6 | 1.7 | 2.7 | 90.4 | 15.3 | 4.5 | 8.1 | 7 104 | 43 | 274.3 | 152.0 | 75.3 | 1 164 | 974 |
| Lassen | 66.0 | 37.8 | 18.4 | 32.5 | 7.8 | 3.9 | 2.8 | 3 886 | 21 | 147.1 | 102.0 | 25.7 | 733 | 617 |
| Los Angeles | 4 489.4 | 10 637.0 | 5 805.2 | 13 950.6 | 2 840.6 | 852.6 | 3 697.1 | 2 177 034 | 9 895 | 61 779.9 | 29 562.5 | 17 192.0 | 1 740 | 1 120 |
| Madera | 44.6 | 0.9 | 7.9 | 144.3 | 33.6 | 9.9 | 14.9 | 31 281 | 291 | 598.1 | 351.0 | 131.1 | 895 | 715 |
| Marin | 87.4 | 31.3 | 32.2 | 168.7 | 43.9 | 10.8 | 50.5 | 57 542 | 181 | 1 337.5 | 345.9 | 672.0 | 2 709 | 2 236 |
| Mariposa | 33.4 | 0.0 | 46.6 | 10.3 | 5.2 | 0.9 | 6.7 | 6 571 | 28 | 94.9 | 40.1 | 29.8 | 1 655 | 1 024 |
| Mendocino | 22.8 | 23.3 | 7.5 | 126.7 | 44.5 | 16.6 | 25.8 | 13 054 | 106 | 854.4 | 264.3 | 130.6 | 1 513 | 1 213 |
| Merced | 54.0 | 54.7 | 64.5 | 260.0 | 73.7 | 26.1 | 48.7 | 29 805 | 157 | 1 419.6 | 825.1 | 251.4 | 1 024 | 823 |
| Modoc | 163.4 | 0.0 | 9.1 | 11.1 | 4.9 | 1.9 | 4.1 | 1 809 | 11 | 72.2 | 42.5 | 11.7 | 1 272 | 1 143 |
| Mono | 14.1 | 16.6 | 8.6 | 2.7 | 3.6 | 1.2 | 1.8 | 5 916 | 15 | 181.4 | 41.4 | 73.4 | 5 735 | 4 264 |
| Monterey | 588.4 | 385.9 | 170.6 | 285.9 | 114.4 | 35.1 | 93.0 | 38 140 | 156 | 2 775.3 | 1 150.3 | 709.4 | 1 740 | 1 280 |
| Napa | 22.6 | 24.8 | 9.1 | 102.5 | 32.0 | 10.9 | 35.0 | 55 850 | 154 | 773.9 | 256.2 | 327.3 | 2 469 | 1 962 |
| Nevada | 28.0 | 137.7 | 8.3 | 53.8 | 15.4 | 5.7 | 5.9 | 22 201 | 91 | 498.3 | 164.9 | 163.7 | 1 687 | 1 415 |
| Orange | 1 410.9 | 2 026.2 | 430.5 | 1 678.3 | 610.6 | 166.1 | 605.1 | 820 241 | 4 352 | 14 874.7 | 5 845.1 | 5 406.3 | 1 804 | 1 344 |
| Placer | 99.9 | 18.5 | 20.5 | 139.2 | 44.8 | 11.6 | 17.0 | 236 223 | 812 | 2 164.9 | 613.3 | 790.5 | 2 374 | 1 911 |
| Plumas | 22.0 | 0.5 | 25.9 | 19.3 | 7.9 | 2.7 | 20.5 | 6 524 | 42 | 183.1 | 66.1 | 45.2 | 2 192 | 1 924 |
| Riverside | 688.7 | 396.1 | 149.5 | 966.4 | 347.2 | 121.1 | 251.5 | 650 619 | 3 264 | 12 026.7 | 5 366.7 | 3 319.0 | 1 601 | 1 198 |
| Sacramento | 895.1 | 3 511.6 | 382.0 | 2 115.5 | 2 695.9 | 3 035.5 | 7 412.4 | 250 737 | 1 286 | 8 376.8 | 3 982.9 | 2 168.3 | 1 564 | 1 088 |
| San Benito | 11.9 | 18.6 | 5.6 | 27.1 | 12.5 | 4.0 | 0.4 | 9 030 | 32 | 325.2 | 148.3 | 76.0 | 1 390 | 1 254 |
| San Bernardino | 1 673.8 | 2 317.9 | 299.3 | 1 236.2 | 390.1 | 144.8 | 300.1 | 264 133 | 1 472 | 11 930.8 | 6 580.8 | 2 747.7 | 1 368 | 985 |
| San Diego | 4 765.8 | 11 593.0 | 1 288.7 | 3 866.8 | 677.8 | 239.4 | 990.5 | 1 089 286 | 5 370 | 16 065.9 | 6 632.0 | 5 448.0 | 1 831 | 1 394 |
| San Francisco | 1 362.1 | 509.8 | 798.8 | 3 305.9 | 182.3 | 149.8 | 1 232.0 | 481 144 | 1 818 | 7 150.7 | 2 481.0 | 2 793.0 | 3 651 | 1 970 |
| San Joaquin | 285.9 | 93.9 | 65.0 | 739.1 | 153.5 | 47.5 | 89.5 | 182 054 | 933 | 3 836.6 | 1 957.0 | 986.4 | 1 470 | 1 065 |
| San Luis Obispo | 126.0 | 56.0 | 25.0 | 176.0 | 70.7 | 13.3 | 44.4 | 92 274 | 306 | 1 183.8 | 434.3 | 521.1 | 1 986 | 1 598 |
| San Mateo | 299.5 | 441.4 | 697.8 | 589.1 | 124.2 | 35.3 | 210.6 | 288 782 | 751 | 3 894.9 | 1 068.6 | 1 716.6 | 2 428 | 1 815 |
| Santa Barbara | 416.1 | 701.1 | 65.0 | 332.1 | 93.3 | 38.4 | 201.3 | 80 063 | 231 | 2 499.6 | 956.2 | 791.8 | 1 959 | 1 459 |
| Santa Clara | 953.4 | 4 708.7 | 1 070.8 | 2 000.2 | 334.3 | 115.6 | 793.0 | 700 940 | 3 065 | 11 364.0 | 3 646.1 | 4 347.8 | 2 486 | 1 854 |
| Santa Cruz | 53.2 | 9.7 | 19.4 | 275.4 | 54.0 | 21.4 | 116.7 | 35 096 | 208 | 1 409.1 | 614.7 | 454.6 | 1 806 | 1 403 |
| Shasta | 96.8 | 3.9 | 75.2 | 199.0 | 50.8 | 18.4 | 30.1 | 23 168 | 138 | 953.9 | 513.4 | 222.1 | 1 238 | 962 |
| Sierra | 3.1 | 0.0 | 1.5 | 6.0 | 0.7 | 0.3 | 1.6 | 1 211 | 6 | 28.7 | 17.8 | 7.6 | 2 292 | 2 079 |
| Siskiyou | 42.6 | -0.1 | 21.0 | 59.6 | 13.3 | 5.3 | 14.2 | 10 726 | 52 | 258.1 | 160.7 | 51.1 | 1 153 | 950 |
| Solano | 689.1 | 363.8 | 49.4 | 264.2 | 71.7 | 24.2 | 163.2 | 81 456 | 387 | 2 176.4 | 1 047.1 | 670.5 | 1 641 | 1 187 |
| Sonoma | 203.3 | 47.1 | 78.1 | 359.9 | 84.6 | 26.4 | 103.0 | 131 369 | 632 | 2 520.7 | 903.4 | 933.6 | 2 010 | 1 589 |
| Stanislaus | 93.7 | 18.4 | 33.7 | 535.9 | 145.3 | 36.1 | 78.6 | 28 290 | 164 | 2 994.5 | 1 529.2 | 678.5 | 1 327 | 984 |
| Sutter | 19.7 | 0.5 | 17.0 | 76.4 | 20.1 | 6.1 | 7.6 | 12 258 | 77 | 479.7 | 254.2 | 117.8 | 1 280 | 912 |
| Tehama | 16.4 | 0.1 | 94.8 | 61.6 | 17.5 | 10.1 | 1.5 | 8 673 | 48 | 262.5 | 169.4 | 60.9 | 997 | 809 |
| Trinity | 15.8 | 0.0 | 4.6 | 12.5 | 4.9 | 1.7 | 3.3 | 3 355 | 25 | 114.5 | 61.3 | 11.6 | 819 | 718 |
| Tulare | 77.9 | 12.8 | 73.0 | 569.1 | 116.0 | 40.5 | 68.2 | 135 666 | 922 | 2 844.1 | 1 469.6 | 387.4 | 919 | 613 |
| Tuolumne | 30.2 | 2.3 | 12.7 | 36.9 | 11.4 | 2.1 | 1.9 | 9 114 | 46 | 258.0 | 95.4 | 69.2 | 1 241 | 1 059 |
| Ventura | 602.1 | 681.1 | 175.4 | 445.3 | 153.9 | 52.6 | 159.5 | 116 433 | 568 | 4 288.6 | 1 876.2 | 1 310.9 | 1 642 | 1 348 |
| Yolo | 208.4 | 1 145.3 | 61.1 | 504.8 | 39.7 | 17.7 | 180.3 | 58 393 | 252 | 917.9 | 389.3 | 324.8 | 1 658 | 1 064 |
| Yuba | 224.5 | 12.4 | 2.4 | 125.0 | 21.8 | 13.2 | 6.3 | 9 612 | 69 | 407.1 | 227.4 | 84.9 | 1 178 | 1 038 |
| COLORADO | 8 518.5 | 5 631.6 | 4 735.5 | 3 665.3 | 967.6 | 778.9 | 3 381.1 | 2 859 669 | 13 502 | X | X | X | X | X |
| Adams | 430.4 | 33.4 | 58.6 | 209.2 | 47.8 | 26.2 | 33.4 | 124 403 | 565 | 1 681.3 | 572.8 | 694.2 | 1 643 | 1 031 |
| Alamosa | 11.4 | 0.0 | 5.5 | 35.3 | 4.5 | 2.9 | 1.2 | 4 747 | 53 | 51.7 | 30.0 | 14.1 | 918 | 649 |
| Arapahoe | 414.5 | 1 714.8 | 276.0 | 463.3 | 52.7 | 34.8 | 141.5 | 201 827 | 806 | 2 344.3 | 696.2 | 1 054.5 | 1 935 | 1 290 |
| Archuleta | 3.2 | 0.2 | 2.6 | 5.5 | 1.5 | 0.5 | 1.2 | 8 620 | 36 | 47.5 | 13.6 | 23.9 | 1 898 | 1 256 |
| Baca | 2.1 | 0.0 | 0.4 | 7.3 | 1.3 | 0.5 | 0.1 | 150 | 2 | 60.8 | 32.3 | 9.0 | 2 335 | 1 473 |
| Bent | 2.3 | 1.3 | 0.8 | 11.0 | 1.8 | 0.5 | 0.8 | 5 | 1 | 41.8 | 12.5 | 5.5 | 941 | 726 |

1. State totals may include programs not allocated by county.   2. Based on the resident population estimated as of July 1 of the year shown.

# Table B. States and Counties — Local Government Finances, Government Employment, and Voting

| STATE County | Local government finances, 2007 (cont.) Direct general expenditure Total (mil dol) | Per capita¹ (dollars) | Education | Health and hospitals | Police protection | Public welfare | Highways | Debt outstanding Total (mil dol) | Per capita¹ (dollars) | Government employment, 2011 Federal civilian | Federal military | State and local | Presidential election,² 2012 Democratic | Republican | All other |
|---|---|---|---|---|---|---|---|---|---|---|---|---|---|---|---|
| | | | Percent of total for: | | | | | | | | | | Percent of vote cast: | | |
| | 185 | 186 | 187 | 188 | 189 | 190 | 191 | 192 | 193 | 194 | 195 | 196 | 197 | 198 | 199 |
| CALIFORNIA | X | X | X | X | X | X | X | X | X | 255 703 | 220 651 | 2 144 996 | 61.0 | 37.0 | 2.0 |
| Alameda | 11 620.2 | 7 936 | 23.2 | 10.8 | 5.2 | 5.0 | 2.3 | 21 002.9 | 14 344 | 9 850 | 3 872 | 95 084 | 78.8 | 19.3 | 2.0 |
| Alpine | 24.4 | 21 295 | 21.9 | 6.8 | 8.6 | 5.6 | 8.7 | 2.2 | 1 927 | 10 | 0 | 258 | 61.0 | 36.4 | 2.6 |
| Amador | 154.7 | 3 998 | 30.8 | 5.3 | 7.9 | 4.8 | 7.2 | 119.7 | 3 094 | 87 | 60 | 4 594 | 41.5 | 56.1 | 2.3 |
| Butte | 1 112.9 | 5 087 | 41.0 | 5.4 | 4.3 | 12.0 | 2.7 | 441.7 | 2 019 | 577 | 352 | 14 393 | 49.8 | 47.5 | 2.7 |
| Calaveras | 181.4 | 3 872 | 42.8 | 5.4 | 5.3 | 7.3 | 5.9 | 119.0 | 2 540 | 131 | 71 | 2 123 | 42.1 | 55.1 | 2.8 |
| Colusa | 134.7 | 6 322 | 39.8 | 5.1 | 5.2 | 5.4 | 6.2 | 28.6 | 1 344 | 79 | 34 | 2 043 | 40.0 | 58.1 | 2.0 |
| Contra Costa | 6 279.4 | 6 158 | 37.0 | 12.8 | 5.4 | 6.2 | 6.1 | 6 116.2 | 5 998 | 4 871 | 1 719 | 41 205 | 68.0 | 30.2 | 1.8 |
| Del Norte | 128.1 | 4 413 | 36.0 | 9.7 | 3.7 | 14.6 | 2.9 | 28.8 | 994 | 163 | 57 | 3 582 | 45.4 | 52.1 | 2.5 |
| El Dorado | 935.8 | 5 327 | 34.2 | 4.1 | 4.5 | 4.3 | 6.3 | 644.1 | 3 666 | 803 | 288 | 9 792 | 43.6 | 54.1 | 2.2 |
| Fresno | 4 984.7 | 5 543 | 47.6 | 6.2 | 5.4 | 9.9 | 3.3 | 3 891.0 | 4 326 | 10 253 | 1 633 | 54 961 | 50.2 | 48.1 | 1.7 |
| Glenn | 173.1 | 6 157 | 41.2 | 7.6 | 5.2 | 12.0 | 3.6 | 29.9 | 1 062 | 279 | 45 | 1 764 | 37.8 | 59.8 | 2.4 |
| Humboldt | 669.9 | 5 199 | 39.8 | 9.2 | 4.2 | 9.7 | 3.0 | 255.4 | 1 982 | 756 | 403 | 12 222 | 62.3 | 34.1 | 3.6 |
| Imperial | 1 068.8 | 6 603 | 47.6 | 16.7 | 3.8 | 7.4 | 2.8 | 843.5 | 5 211 | 2 527 | 539 | 15 219 | 62.2 | 36.1 | 1.7 |
| Inyo | 179.4 | 10 284 | 27.1 | 37.5 | 4.3 | 3.4 | 3.5 | 35.2 | 2 014 | 404 | 29 | 2 719 | 43.9 | 53.0 | 3.1 |
| Kern | 5 086.6 | 6 433 | 43.2 | 8.2 | 3.5 | 7.3 | 1.6 | 2 907.0 | 3 676 | 10 739 | 3 999 | 46 849 | 40.1 | 57.9 | 2.0 |
| Kings | 609.8 | 4 096 | 45.4 | 5.7 | 5.8 | 8.7 | 3.3 | 264.9 | 1 780 | 1 218 | 5 679 | 11 546 | 42.0 | 56.1 | 1.9 |
| Lake | 286.6 | 4 432 | 42.0 | 7.1 | 5.3 | 11.2 | 3.4 | 93.7 | 1 448 | 144 | 102 | 3 618 | 58.2 | 38.9 | 2.9 |
| Lassen | 148.1 | 4 228 | 51.3 | 5.5 | 3.8 | 9.7 | 5.7 | 63.0 | 1 799 | 1 870 | 56 | 4 742 | 31.5 | 65.7 | 2.8 |
| Los Angeles | 56 883.7 | 5 758 | 38.2 | 9.7 | 7.3 | 8.0 | 2.9 | 73 718.0 | 7 462 | 49 343 | 18 152 | 518 252 | 69.2 | 28.8 | 2.0 |
| Madera | 691.1 | 4 717 | 49.3 | 3.3 | 3.4 | 8.0 | 4.8 | 386.0 | 2 635 | 315 | 242 | 10 184 | 42.4 | 55.7 | 1.9 |
| Marin | 1 467.3 | 5 914 | 32.4 | 6.4 | 6.2 | 3.8 | 4.0 | 3 555.3 | 14 330 | 825 | 632 | 14 643 | 78.0 | 20.2 | 1.8 |
| Mariposa | 90.2 | 5 001 | 29.2 | 21.9 | 6.4 | 9.6 | 5.4 | 29.9 | 1 655 | 832 | 29 | 1 168 | 42.5 | 54.9 | 2.6 |
| Mendocino | 813.6 | 9 431 | 27.1 | 7.8 | 2.6 | 6.6 | 2.5 | 443.6 | 5 142 | 287 | 169 | 6 460 | 69.6 | 26.8 | 3.6 |
| Merced | 1 437.0 | 5 853 | 49.3 | 3.6 | 3.8 | 9.6 | 3.0 | 688.0 | 2 802 | 762 | 413 | 16 040 | 53.3 | 45.0 | 1.7 |
| Modoc | 75.0 | 8 156 | 37.7 | 25.9 | 3.7 | 6.9 | 8.2 | 3.9 | 421 | 261 | 15 | 954 | 29.7 | 67.4 | 2.9 |
| Mono | 178.7 | 13 957 | 21.9 | 28.8 | 5.1 | 3.3 | 8.6 | 98.5 | 7 692 | 218 | 269 | 1 277 | 55.5 | 42.3 | 2.2 |
| Monterey | 2 680.5 | 6 576 | 35.2 | 21.3 | 4.5 | 4.9 | 4.8 | 1 456.7 | 3 574 | 5 938 | 6 491 | 25 118 | 68.2 | 29.9 | 2.0 |
| Napa | 789.2 | 5 954 | 41.2 | 5.1 | 6.7 | 3.7 | 4.4 | 766.1 | 5 779 | 358 | 219 | 9 515 | 65.1 | 32.7 | 2.2 |
| Nevada | 491.3 | 5 063 | 29.8 | 21.7 | 4.8 | 5.5 | 5.6 | 270.6 | 2 789 | 384 | 156 | 5 438 | 51.4 | 46.1 | 2.5 |
| Orange | 14 291.5 | 4 769 | 43.2 | 3.0 | 7.4 | 5.6 | 4.0 | 21 438.8 | 7 153 | 11 617 | 5 267 | 135 252 | 47.6 | 50.2 | 2.2 |
| Placer | 2 195.6 | 6 595 | 38.8 | 2.4 | 4.8 | 4.3 | 8.1 | 2 949.2 | 8 859 | 720 | 584 | 16 596 | 43.4 | 54.7 | 1.9 |
| Plumas | 182.4 | 8 846 | 29.2 | 34.4 | 3.6 | 4.9 | 4.8 | 74.2 | 3 597 | 435 | 31 | 1 899 | 42.8 | 54.7 | 2.5 |
| Riverside | 12 014.0 | 5 794 | 40.8 | 7.9 | 5.5 | 6.1 | 4.5 | 13 422.4 | 6 473 | 7 081 | 3 810 | 112 314 | 50.2 | 47.9 | 1.9 |
| Sacramento | 8 735.5 | 6 300 | 33.6 | 6.0 | 5.1 | 8.8 | 6.5 | 15 639.4 | 11 278 | 9 033 | 2 978 | 172 295 | 58.5 | 39.5 | 2.0 |
| San Benito | 313.4 | 5 732 | 35.7 | 24.5 | 3.4 | 4.7 | 8.9 | 109.4 | 2 001 | 151 | 89 | 2 449 | 60.5 | 37.7 | 1.8 |
| San Bernardino | 11 125.3 | 5 541 | 42.3 | 10.4 | 5.8 | 7.2 | 3.7 | 10 184.1 | 5 072 | 14 312 | 21 471 | 98 928 | 52.1 | 45.8 | 2.2 |
| San Diego | 16 037.1 | 5 391 | 40.2 | 9.0 | 6.0 | 6.5 | 2.9 | 17 352.6 | 5 833 | 47 046 | 107 893 | 178 469 | 54.1 | 43.9 | 1.9 |
| San Francisco | 6 597.0 | 8 624 | 16.0 | 22.5 | 5.2 | 8.9 | 3.0 | 10 649.8 | 13 922 | 14 581 | 1 669 | 87 394 | 84.2 | 13.7 | 2.2 |
| San Joaquin | 3 766.6 | 5 613 | 43.4 | 8.4 | 5.5 | 8.1 | 2.8 | 3 448.9 | 5 140 | 4 042 | 1 182 | 31 404 | 54.4 | 43.8 | 1.8 |
| San Luis Obispo | 1 122.2 | 4 276 | 38.3 | 5.7 | 6.4 | 8.8 | 5.0 | 704.1 | 2 683 | 612 | 490 | 19 818 | 51.4 | 46.0 | 2.6 |
| San Mateo | 3 829.0 | 5 416 | 31.8 | 10.9 | 7.4 | 5.0 | 3.5 | 4 385.4 | 6 203 | 3 786 | 1 318 | 26 729 | 73.5 | 24.7 | 1.8 |
| Santa Barbara | 2 477.1 | 6 129 | 37.4 | 14.0 | 5.5 | 5.4 | 4.7 | 1 475.7 | 3 651 | 3 997 | 3 410 | 30 458 | 60.4 | 37.5 | 2.1 |
| Santa Clara | 11 104.3 | 6 349 | 32.9 | 16.1 | 5.0 | 5.5 | 2.9 | 14 916.6 | 8 529 | 10 044 | 3 211 | 76 155 | 69.4 | 28.6 | 2.0 |
| Santa Cruz | 1 495.0 | 5 939 | 37.8 | 6.0 | 4.3 | 8.0 | 3.1 | 1 194.1 | 4 743 | 514 | 421 | 17 440 | 77.5 | 19.8 | 2.7 |
| Shasta | 983.2 | 5 480 | 41.0 | 6.6 | 5.0 | 9.3 | 2.5 | 684.3 | 3 814 | 1 396 | 295 | 11 443 | 35.9 | 61.7 | 2.4 |
| Sierra | 30.1 | 9 032 | 32.9 | 8.7 | 11.1 | 8.5 | 11.8 | 3.3 | 985 | 56 | 0 | 335 | 37.3 | 58.2 | 4.5 |
| Siskiyou | 255.7 | 5 772 | 45.4 | 7.4 | 5.4 | 6.9 | 6.9 | 32.9 | 742 | 799 | 70 | 3 298 | 43.3 | 53.7 | 3.1 |
| Solano | 2 178.6 | 5 332 | 37.7 | 4.8 | 8.0 | 6.8 | 5.1 | 2 079.0 | 5 088 | 4 068 | 7 280 | 20 059 | 63.4 | 34.8 | 1.8 |
| Sonoma | 2 662.5 | 5 733 | 35.4 | 8.3 | 6.4 | 4.9 | 4.3 | 2 522.0 | 5 430 | 1 568 | 1 411 | 24 775 | 73.6 | 24.0 | 2.3 |
| Stanislaus | 2 929.4 | 5 730 | 52.0 | 7.3 | 4.7 | 8.4 | 2.9 | 3 299.0 | 6 453 | 876 | 825 | 25 147 | 49.9 | 48.1 | 2.0 |
| Sutter | 485.2 | 5 271 | 44.3 | 7.4 | 5.6 | 5.7 | 2.0 | 241.0 | 2 618 | 156 | 152 | 4 153 | 40.7 | 57.4 | 1.9 |
| Tehama | 268.9 | 4 401 | 52.5 | 5.3 | 5.2 | 12.7 | 4.1 | 27.0 | 441 | 262 | 101 | 3 508 | 36.6 | 60.7 | 2.7 |
| Trinity | 110.6 | 7 800 | 29.9 | 5.4 | 2.2 | 5.7 | 7.6 | 30.1 | 2 124 | 269 | 22 | 992 | 50.7 | 46.1 | 3.2 |
| Tulare | 2 828.2 | 6 709 | 40.6 | 21.2 | 3.1 | 8.7 | 2.8 | 1 178.2 | 2 795 | 1 250 | 713 | 30 018 | 41.5 | 56.8 | 1.7 |
| Tuolumne | 277.1 | 4 966 | 35.1 | 18.1 | 4.7 | 6.4 | 3.6 | 112.5 | 2 017 | 391 | 87 | 4 885 | 42.4 | 55.1 | 2.4 |
| Ventura | 4 176.2 | 5 231 | 39.4 | 8.7 | 7.5 | 4.3 | 4.1 | 2 696.6 | 3 378 | 7 412 | 5 963 | 35 211 | 55.2 | 42.9 | 1.9 |
| Yolo | 1 018.3 | 5 200 | 34.4 | 4.1 | 5.4 | 7.9 | 6.9 | 1 052.2 | 5 372 | 3 533 | 330 | 32 237 | 67.1 | 30.8 | 2.1 |
| Yuba | 411.9 | 5 714 | 60.2 | 1.8 | 3.7 | 11.6 | 3.6 | 202.3 | 2 806 | 1 412 | 3 846 | 5 572 | 41.4 | 56.1 | 2.5 |
| COLORADO | X | X | X | X | X | X | X | X | X | 55 007 | 55 993 | 343 747 | 53.7 | 44.7 | 1.6 |
| Adams | 1 807.7 | 4 279 | 40.3 | 0.3 | 5.0 | 6.2 | 5.4 | 3 374.9 | 7 988 | 1 534 | 1 631 | 25 169 | 58.2 | 39.9 | 1.9 |
| Alamosa | 56.4 | 3 681 | 50.0 | 5.3 | 6.8 | 4.1 | 3.5 | 61.5 | 4 017 | 174 | 42 | 2 163 | 56.0 | 41.9 | 2.1 |
| Arapahoe | 2 432.7 | 4 463 | 39.8 | 1.7 | 7.1 | 2.7 | 5.7 | 5 251.0 | 9 633 | 3 174 | 3 039 | 32 712 | 55.7 | 42.8 | 1.5 |
| Archuleta | 46.5 | 3 699 | 30.0 | 6.4 | 5.8 | 3.5 | 13.5 | 70.1 | 5 572 | 55 | 32 | 633 | 42.8 | 54.9 | 2.3 |
| Baca | 57.5 | 14 857 | 58.2 | 16.2 | 0.9 | 5.1 | 7.1 | 9.0 | 2 327 | 39 | 10 | 722 | 24.6 | 72.3 | 3.1 |
| Bent | 41.6 | 7 116 | 21.8 | 0.4 | 3.6 | 12.8 | 4.8 | 13.7 | 2 336 | 47 | 22 | 629 | 41.6 | 56.1 | 2.3 |

1. Based on the resident population estimated as of July 1 of the year shown.  2. © 2013 Election Data Services, Inc. All rights reserved.

Items 185—199

# Table B. States and Counties — Land Area and Population

| STATE/ County code | CBSA code[1] | County type[2] | STATE County | Land area,[3] (sq km) 2010 | Population 2012 | | | Population characteristics[6], 2011 | | | | | | | | | | |
|---|---|---|---|---|---|---|---|---|---|---|---|---|---|---|---|---|---|---|
| | | | | | | | | Race alone or in combination, not Hispanic or Latino (percent) | | | | | Age (percent) | | | | | |
| | | | | | Total persons | Rank | Per square kilometer | White | Black | Amer- ican Indian, Alaska Native | Asian and Pacific Islander | Percent Hispanic or Latino[4] | Under 5 years | 5 to 17 years | 18 to 24 years | 25 to 34 years | 35 to 44 years | 45 to 54 years |
| | | | | 1 | 2 | 3 | 4 | 5 | 6 | 7 | 8 | 9 | 10 | 11 | 12 | 13 | 14 | 15 |
| | | | COLORADO—Cont'd | | | | | | | | | | | | | | | |
| 08 013 | 14500 | 2 | Boulder | 1 881 | 305 318 | 213 | 162.3 | 80.7 | 1.4 | 0.9 | 5.4 | 13.7 | 5.4 | 15.4 | 15.2 | 13.0 | 13.5 | 14.5 |
| 08 014 | 19740 | 1 | Broomfield | 86 | 58 298 | 879 | 677.9 | 80.4 | 1.7 | 1.2 | 7.1 | 11.6 | 6.6 | 18.3 | 8.3 | 15.2 | 15.8 | 14.5 |
| 08 015 | ... | 7 | Chaffee | 2 625 | 18 150 | 1 913 | 6.9 | 87.1 | 1.9 | 1.5 | 0.9 | 9.7 | 4.2 | 12.1 | 6.7 | 11.8 | 11.5 | 15.2 |
| 08 017 | ... | 9 | Cheyenne | 4 606 | 1 874 | 3 068 | 0.4 | 87.7 | 0.8 | 1.1 | 0.7 | 10.3 | 6.6 | 17.9 | 6.4 | 11.5 | 10.6 | 14.1 |
| 08 019 | 19740 | 1 | Clear Creek | 1 024 | 9 026 | 2 519 | 8.8 | 92.6 | 1.0 | 1.3 | 1.0 | 5.4 | 4.5 | 12.1 | 5.0 | 10.2 | 14.5 | 20.0 |
| 08 021 | ... | 9 | Conejos | 3 334 | 8 275 | 2 588 | 2.5 | 43.5 | 0.5 | 1.2 | 0.6 | 55.2 | 7.2 | 20.7 | 8.4 | 9.9 | 10.5 | 13.8 |
| 08 023 | ... | 9 | Costilla | 3 178 | 3 594 | 2 937 | 1.1 | 33.6 | 0.7 | 1.4 | 1.3 | 64.2 | 4.2 | 15.7 | 7.5 | 8.1 | 9.5 | 15.0 |
| 08 025 | ... | 8 | Crowley | 2 039 | 5 365 | 2 814 | 2.6 | 58.9 | 9.5 | 2.5 | 1.2 | 28.9 | 3.6 | 9.8 | 10.1 | 19.7 | 16.9 | 16.9 |
| 08 027 | ... | 8 | Custer | 1 913 | 4 249 | 2 888 | 2.2 | 92.8 | 1.4 | 1.4 | 0.8 | 5.0 | 3.0 | 12.8 | 4.0 | 6.5 | 9.1 | 15.6 |
| 08 029 | ... | 6 | Delta | 2 958 | 30 432 | 1 421 | 10.3 | 83.9 | 0.8 | 1.5 | 0.8 | 14.3 | 5.3 | 16.3 | 6.8 | 9.7 | 10.3 | 14.3 |
| 08 031 | 19740 | 1 | Denver | 396 | 634 265 | 98 | 1 601.7 | 54.4 | 10.4 | 1.3 | 4.3 | 31.8 | 7.4 | 14.3 | 9.8 | 21.0 | 15.0 | 11.8 |
| 08 033 | ... | 9 | Dolores | 2 764 | 1 994 | 3 054 | 0.7 | 91.8 | 1.7 | 3.7 | 0.8 | 4.7 | 6.1 | 15.8 | 5.4 | 10.2 | 11.9 | 14.8 |
| 08 035 | 19740 | 1 | Douglas | 2 176 | 298 215 | 221 | 137.0 | 86.7 | 1.8 | 0.7 | 5.1 | 7.8 | 7.1 | 22.6 | 5.9 | 11.2 | 17.6 | 16.6 |
| 08 037 | 20780 | 5 | Eagle | 4 363 | 51 874 | 955 | 11.9 | 67.6 | 0.7 | 0.6 | 1.4 | 30.4 | 7.3 | 17.2 | 8.0 | 18.2 | 17.3 | 14.5 |
| 08 039 | 19740 | 1 | Elbert | 4 794 | 23 383 | 1 669 | 4.9 | 92.0 | 1.2 | 1.4 | 1.5 | 5.7 | 4.6 | 19.7 | 6.4 | 7.1 | 13.2 | 21.6 |
| 08 041 | 17820 | 2 | El Paso | 5 508 | 644 964 | 97 | 117.1 | 74.7 | 7.5 | 1.5 | 4.7 | 15.4 | 7.1 | 18.6 | 11.1 | 14.5 | 12.8 | 14.5 |
| 08 043 | 15860 | 4 | Fremont | 3 971 | 46 788 | 1 030 | 11.8 | 81.2 | 4.3 | 2.4 | 0.9 | 12.6 | 4.3 | 12.8 | 7.3 | 14.0 | 13.5 | 15.5 |
| 08 045 | ... | 5 | Garfield | 7 634 | 56 953 | 891 | 7.5 | 69.6 | 0.8 | 1.1 | 1.1 | 28.6 | 7.9 | 19.0 | 8.3 | 15.0 | 14.4 | 14.4 |
| 08 047 | 19740 | 1 | Gilpin | 388 | 5 491 | 2 806 | 14.2 | 91.5 | 1.1 | 1.6 | 1.8 | 5.6 | 4.8 | 12.6 | 4.7 | 10.1 | 16.2 | 20.7 |
| 08 049 | ... | 8 | Grand | 4 782 | 14 195 | 2 163 | 3.0 | 90.4 | 0.7 | 0.9 | 1.3 | 7.9 | 5.3 | 14.6 | 6.8 | 13.5 | 14.0 | 17.5 |
| 08 051 | ... | 7 | Gunnison | 8 389 | 15 475 | 2 077 | 1.8 | 89.3 | 0.9 | 1.1 | 1.3 | 8.8 | 4.8 | 13.0 | 18.5 | 15.1 | 13.4 | 12.8 |
| 08 053 | ... | 9 | Hinsdale | 2 894 | 810 | 3 118 | 0.3 | 94.7 | 1.3 | 1.2 | 1.1 | 3.4 | 6.5 | 13.5 | 6.9 | 9.4 | 10.7 | 16.0 |
| 08 055 | ... | 6 | Huerfano | 4 121 | 6 596 | 2 715 | 1.6 | 62.4 | 0.7 | 1.6 | 0.8 | 35.6 | 4.3 | 12.6 | 6.0 | 7.4 | 8.5 | 15.0 |
| 08 057 | ... | 9 | Jackson | 4 180 | 1 348 | 3 092 | 0.3 | 88.2 | 0.6 | 1.4 | 0.1 | 10.5 | 3.9 | 13.7 | 6.7 | 10.0 | 11.6 | 17.8 |
| 08 059 | 19740 | 1 | Jefferson | 1 979 | 545 358 | 117 | 275.6 | 81.1 | 1.5 | 1.1 | 3.5 | 14.6 | 5.5 | 16.3 | 8.4 | 12.5 | 13.1 | 16.6 |
| 08 061 | ... | 9 | Kiowa | 4 578 | 1 444 | 3 085 | 0.3 | 93.3 | 0.6 | 0.9 | 0.2 | 6.1 | 5.8 | 16.8 | 5.6 | 10.3 | 9.2 | 15.4 |
| 08 063 | ... | 7 | Kit Carson | 5 597 | 8 094 | 2 594 | 1.4 | 77.6 | 2.4 | 1.1 | 0.9 | 19.0 | 6.8 | 16.3 | 7.4 | 13.9 | 12.3 | 15.1 |
| 08 065 | 20780 | 7 | Lake | 976 | 7 338 | 2 651 | 7.5 | 58.4 | 0.8 | 1.3 | 0.8 | 39.9 | 8.0 | 17.5 | 9.7 | 14.9 | 14.2 | 13.2 |
| 08 067 | 20420 | 6 | La Plata | 4 382 | 52 401 | 949 | 12.0 | 81.5 | 0.9 | 5.9 | 1.4 | 12.2 | 5.6 | 14.4 | 12.6 | 13.1 | 12.4 | 14.7 |
| 08 069 | 22660 | 2 | Larimer | 6 724 | 310 487 | 209 | 46.2 | 85.8 | 1.4 | 1.1 | 2.9 | 10.8 | 5.6 | 15.2 | 14.7 | 13.9 | 12.0 | 13.5 |
| 08 071 | ... | 7 | Las Animas | 12 361 | 14 945 | 2 111 | 1.2 | 54.3 | 1.7 | 1.8 | 1.0 | 42.2 | 5.3 | 15.0 | 9.0 | 10.7 | 10.8 | 14.7 |
| 08 073 | ... | 8 | Lincoln | 6 676 | 5 453 | 2 809 | 0.8 | 79.9 | 5.9 | 1.6 | 1.3 | 12.7 | 5.8 | 13.9 | 8.4 | 15.3 | 12.1 | 16.3 |
| 08 075 | 44540 | 7 | Logan | 4 762 | 22 631 | 1 703 | 4.8 | 78.8 | 4.3 | 1.2 | 1.0 | 15.7 | 5.0 | 14.5 | 11.4 | 14.5 | 12.6 | 14.9 |
| 08 077 | 24300 | 3 | Mesa | 8 622 | 147 848 | 424 | 17.1 | 84.1 | 1.0 | 1.4 | 1.5 | 13.6 | 6.8 | 16.6 | 9.8 | 13.3 | 11.2 | 13.7 |
| 08 079 | ... | 9 | Mineral | 2 268 | 709 | 3 128 | 0.3 | 95.5 | 1.1 | 1.3 | 0.7 | 2.5 | 3.1 | 10.9 | 4.5 | 9.2 | 8.5 | 17.4 |
| 08 081 | ... | 7 | Moffat | 12 285 | 13 200 | 2 231 | 1.1 | 83.5 | 0.8 | 1.5 | 1.0 | 14.8 | 7.5 | 19.0 | 8.2 | 13.3 | 11.7 | 15.4 |
| 08 083 | ... | 6 | Montezuma | 5 256 | 25 431 | 1 591 | 4.8 | 76.4 | 0.8 | 12.1 | 0.9 | 11.6 | 6.4 | 16.6 | 7.2 | 10.7 | 11.1 | 14.7 |
| 08 085 | 33940 | 7 | Montrose | 5 803 | 40 725 | 1 161 | 7.0 | 78.1 | 0.7 | 1.3 | 1.0 | 20.3 | 6.3 | 18.0 | 6.5 | 10.8 | 11.3 | 14.3 |
| 08 087 | 22820 | 6 | Morgan | 3 316 | 28 472 | 1 470 | 8.6 | 62.0 | 2.8 | 0.8 | 0.9 | 34.4 | 7.9 | 20.2 | 8.6 | 12.3 | 11.7 | 13.7 |
| 08 089 | ... | 6 | Otero | 3 268 | 18 698 | 1 888 | 5.7 | 57.3 | 1.0 | 1.2 | 1.2 | 40.5 | 6.4 | 18.2 | 8.6 | 10.8 | 10.5 | 13.4 |
| 08 091 | ... | 9 | Ouray | 1 403 | 4 530 | 2 867 | 3.2 | 93.5 | 0.6 | 1.0 | 1.0 | 5.1 | 3.6 | 14.3 | 4.0 | 7.0 | 11.6 | 17.8 |
| 08 093 | 19740 | 1 | Park | 5 682 | 16 029 | 2 045 | 2.8 | 92.9 | 1.0 | 1.8 | 1.3 | 4.9 | 4.4 | 13.7 | 5.2 | 8.4 | 13.0 | 21.3 |
| 08 095 | ... | 9 | Phillips | 1 782 | 4 367 | 2 877 | 2.5 | 79.2 | 0.9 | 0.5 | 1.0 | 19.1 | 6.0 | 18.2 | 7.0 | 10.3 | 10.9 | 14.1 |
| 08 097 | ... | 7 | Pitkin | 2 514 | 17 263 | 1 965 | 6.9 | 88.8 | 0.8 | 0.5 | 1.9 | 9.1 | 4.2 | 12.9 | 5.9 | 15.4 | 15.3 | 17.1 |
| 08 099 | ... | 7 | Prowers | 4 243 | 12 389 | 2 280 | 2.9 | 62.6 | 0.8 | 0.9 | 0.6 | 35.7 | 7.6 | 19.7 | 9.4 | 11.5 | 10.8 | 13.3 |
| 08 101 | 39380 | 3 | Pueblo | 6 180 | 160 852 | 390 | 26.0 | 55.1 | 2.2 | 1.3 | 1.2 | 41.6 | 6.5 | 17.7 | 9.5 | 12.1 | 11.7 | 13.6 |
| 08 103 | ... | 9 | Rio Blanco | 8 342 | 6 857 | 2 694 | 0.8 | 86.8 | 1.5 | 1.6 | 1.2 | 10.8 | 7.6 | 17.3 | 9.8 | 13.4 | 11.3 | 15.2 |
| 08 105 | ... | 7 | Rio Grande | 2 362 | 11 943 | 2 302 | 5.1 | 54.9 | 0.6 | 1.5 | 0.7 | 43.3 | 6.5 | 18.3 | 7.9 | 10.8 | 11.0 | 14.1 |
| 08 107 | ... | 7 | Routt | 6 118 | 23 334 | 1 674 | 3.8 | 91.3 | 0.7 | 0.9 | 1.3 | 6.9 | 5.3 | 14.9 | 7.7 | 15.3 | 15.2 | 16.5 |
| 08 109 | ... | 9 | Saguache | 8 206 | 6 304 | 2 739 | 0.8 | 57.8 | 0.6 | 1.9 | 1.3 | 39.8 | 6.4 | 15.4 | 7.6 | 10.1 | 10.4 | 15.6 |
| 08 111 | ... | 9 | San Juan | 1 004 | 690 | 3 130 | 0.7 | 86.0 | 0.4 | 1.2 | 1.2 | 12.9 | 4.5 | 12.9 | 5.6 | 14.9 | 12.7 | 16.3 |
| 08 113 | ... | 9 | San Miguel | 3 332 | 7 580 | 2 635 | 2.3 | 88.9 | 0.8 | 1.0 | 1.4 | 9.4 | 6.0 | 13.2 | 5.9 | 17.0 | 17.3 | 17.1 |
| 08 115 | ... | 9 | Sedgwick | 1 419 | 2 383 | 3 017 | 1.7 | 86.0 | 1.0 | 1.0 | 1.0 | 12.3 | 4.8 | 14.1 | 6.5 | 9.3 | 10.0 | 14.4 |
| 08 117 | 43540 | 7 | Summit | 1 576 | 28 044 | 1 492 | 17.8 | 83.6 | 1.0 | 0.7 | 1.5 | 14.3 | 5.4 | 11.8 | 8.9 | 20.4 | 16.2 | 15.3 |
| 08 119 | 17820 | 2 | Teller | 1 443 | 23 389 | 1 668 | 16.2 | 92.0 | 1.0 | 1.8 | 1.4 | 5.6 | 4.3 | 15.6 | 5.7 | 8.0 | 11.8 | 19.6 |
| 08 121 | ... | 9 | Washington | 6 522 | 4 766 | 2 855 | 0.7 | 90.0 | 1.1 | 0.7 | 0.6 | 8.8 | 5.6 | 16.7 | 7.3 | 9.8 | 11.2 | 15.6 |
| 08 123 | 24540 | 3 | Weld | 10 327 | 263 691 | 253 | 25.5 | 68.5 | 1.3 | 1.1 | 1.9 | 28.5 | 7.7 | 19.8 | 10.9 | 13.8 | 13.7 | 13.3 |
| 08 125 | ... | 7 | Yuma | 6 124 | 10 119 | 2 434 | 1.7 | 77.1 | 0.5 | 0.6 | 0.4 | 22.0 | 7.6 | 18.8 | 7.6 | 12.4 | 11.7 | 13.5 |
| 09 000 | ... | X | CONNECTICUT | 12 542 | 3 590 347 | X | 286.3 | 72.3 | 10.4 | 0.6 | 4.5 | 13.8 | 5.5 | 16.9 | 9.2 | 12.0 | 13.1 | 16.0 |
| 09 001 | 14860 | 2 | Fairfield | 1 618 | 933 835 | 51 | 577.2 | 67.1 | 11.0 | 0.4 | 5.5 | 17.4 | 6.0 | 18.3 | 8.0 | 11.7 | 13.9 | 16.2 |
| 09 003 | 25540 | 1 | Hartford | 1 904 | 897 259 | 57 | 471.2 | 67.0 | 13.4 | 0.6 | 4.9 | 15.7 | 5.6 | 16.9 | 8.9 | 12.5 | 13.2 | 15.7 |
| 09 005 | 45860 | 4 | Litchfield | 2 384 | 187 530 | 338 | 78.7 | 92.1 | 1.7 | 0.5 | 2.1 | 4.8 | 4.6 | 16.4 | 6.9 | 9.4 | 12.7 | 18.0 |
| 09 007 | 25540 | 1 | Middlesex | 956 | 165 602 | 380 | 173.2 | 87.5 | 5.3 | 0.5 | 3.3 | 5.0 | 4.8 | 15.9 | 7.9 | 10.6 | 13.2 | 17.0 |
| 09 009 | 35300 | 2 | New Haven | 1 566 | 862 813 | 60 | 551.0 | 68.6 | 12.9 | 0.6 | 4.1 | 15.4 | 5.5 | 16.4 | 9.9 | 12.7 | 12.8 | 15.3 |
| 09 011 | 35980 | 2 | New London | 1 722 | 274 170 | 243 | 159.2 | 80.4 | 6.8 | 1.7 | 5.2 | 8.8 | 5.3 | 16.0 | 9.9 | 12.1 | 12.6 | 16.2 |

1. CBSA = Core Based Statistical Area. See Appendix A for explanation. See Appendix B for list of metropolitan areas with component counties. 2. County type code from the Economic Research Service of USDA Rural-Urban Continuum Codes. See Appendix A for definition. 3. Dry land or land partially or temporarily covered by water. 4. May be of any race.

# Table B. States and Counties — **Population and Households**

| | Population, 2011 (cont.) | | | | Population change and components of change, 2000-2012 | | | | | | | Households, 2010 | | | | |
| | Age (percent) (cont.) | | | | Total persons | | Percent change | | Components of change, 2010-2012 | | | | | | Percent | |
| STATE County | 55 to 64 years | 65 to 74 years | 75 years and over | Percent female | 2000 | 2010 | 2000-2010 | 2010-2012 | Births | Deaths | Net migration | Number | Percent change, 2000-2010 | Persons per house-hold | Female family house-holder[1] | One per-son |
|---|---|---|---|---|---|---|---|---|---|---|---|---|---|---|---|---|
| | 16 | 17 | 18 | 19 | 20 | 21 | 22 | 23 | 24 | 25 | 26 | 27 | 28 | 29 | 30 | 31 |
| COLORADO—Cont'd | | | | | | | | | | | | | | | | |
| Boulder | 12.5 | 6.0 | 4.5 | 49.8 | 269 814 | 294 567 | NA | 3.6 | 6 708 | 3 502 | 7 430 | 119 300 | 4.0 | 2.39 | 7.7 | 29.0 |
| Broomfield | 10.9 | 5.8 | 4.7 | 50.4 | 38 272 | 55 889 | NA | 4.3 | 1 611 | 679 | 1 480 | 21 414 | NA | 2.60 | 8.0 | 23.9 |
| Chaffee | 18.1 | 11.7 | 8.8 | 46.8 | 16 242 | 17 809 | 9.6 | 1.9 | 341 | 337 | 345 | 7 601 | 15.4 | 2.15 | 6.7 | 30.1 |
| Cheyenne | 15.1 | 7.9 | 9.9 | 50.3 | 2 231 | 1 836 | -17.7 | 2.1 | 49 | 48 | 33 | 786 | -10.7 | 2.28 | 5.9 | 33.8 |
| Clear Creek | 20.4 | 9.2 | 4.1 | 47.9 | 9 322 | 9 088 | -2.5 | -0.7 | 121 | 134 | -61 | 4 208 | 4.7 | 2.14 | 6.1 | 31.9 |
| Conejos | 13.8 | 8.3 | 7.2 | 50.4 | 8 400 | 8 256 | -1.7 | 0.2 | 256 | 176 | -75 | 3 118 | 4.6 | 2.64 | 11.1 | 27.5 |
| Costilla | 17.0 | 14.3 | 8.7 | 48.3 | 3 663 | 3 524 | -3.8 | 2.0 | 65 | 52 | 52 | 1 550 | 3.1 | 2.27 | 11.6 | 33.5 |
| Crowley | 11.8 | 6.5 | 4.7 | 28.7 | 5 518 | 5 823 | 5.5 | -7.9 | 76 | 73 | -470 | 1 306 | -3.8 | 2.41 | 10.6 | 30.2 |
| Custer | 25.4 | 15.7 | 7.8 | 48.8 | 3 503 | 4 255 | 21.5 | -0.1 | 49 | 78 | 26 | 1 925 | 30.1 | 2.13 | 3.9 | 30.1 |
| Delta | 16.2 | 11.8 | 9.3 | 49.8 | 27 834 | 30 952 | 11.2 | -1.7 | 757 | 766 | -519 | 12 703 | 14.9 | 2.38 | 7.9 | 27.4 |
| Denver | 10.5 | 5.4 | 4.8 | 49.9 | 554 636 | 600 158 | 8.2 | 5.7 | 23 048 | 9 735 | 20 764 | 263 107 | 10.0 | 2.22 | 10.6 | 40.6 |
| Dolores | 15.6 | 12.2 | 8.0 | 48.5 | 1 844 | 2 064 | 11.9 | -3.4 | 41 | 26 | -93 | 899 | 14.5 | 2.30 | 5.9 | 29.7 |
| Douglas | 11.2 | 5.1 | 2.7 | 50.5 | 175 766 | 285 465 | 62.4 | 4.5 | 7 785 | 2 094 | 6 768 | 102 018 | 67.5 | 2.79 | 7.1 | 18.0 |
| Eagle | 11.3 | 4.6 | 1.6 | 47.9 | 41 659 | 52 197 | 25.3 | -0.6 | 1 508 | 201 | -1 695 | 19 236 | 27.0 | 2.71 | 6.4 | 22.2 |
| Elbert | 17.1 | 7.2 | 3.2 | 49.9 | 19 872 | 23 086 | 16.2 | 1.3 | 389 | 255 | 125 | 8 380 | 23.8 | 2.75 | 5.8 | 15.5 |
| El Paso | 11.3 | 5.8 | 4.4 | 50.0 | 516 929 | 622 263 | 20.4 | 3.6 | 20 253 | 8 272 | 10 690 | 235 959 | 22.6 | 2.56 | 11.3 | 26.0 |
| Fremont | 14.7 | 9.9 | 8.0 | 42.0 | 46 145 | 46 824 | 1.5 | -0.1 | 837 | 1 138 | 239 | 16 582 | 8.9 | 2.30 | 9.6 | 29.0 |
| Garfield | 12.2 | 5.2 | 3.7 | 48.6 | 43 791 | 56 389 | 28.8 | 1.0 | 1 896 | 661 | -691 | 20 359 | 25.4 | 2.73 | 8.5 | 22.3 |
| Gilpin | 20.8 | 7.4 | 2.8 | 47.0 | 4 757 | 5 441 | 14.4 | 0.9 | 99 | 47 | 1 | 2 460 | 20.4 | 2.19 | 5.1 | 29.0 |
| Grand | 17.3 | 7.5 | 3.5 | 46.6 | 12 442 | 14 843 | 19.3 | -4.4 | 262 | 116 | -796 | 6 469 | 27.5 | 2.26 | 5.4 | 29.4 |
| Gunnison | 13.1 | 6.2 | 3.0 | 45.9 | 13 956 | 15 324 | 9.8 | 1.0 | 350 | 130 | -68 | 6 516 | 15.3 | 2.22 | 5.2 | 30.5 |
| Hinsdale | 18.8 | 12.4 | 5.8 | 47.3 | 790 | 843 | 6.7 | -3.9 | 19 | 3 | -48 | 362 | 0.8 | 2.17 | 3.0 | 27.9 |
| Huerfano | 19.8 | 15.2 | 11.3 | 50.2 | 7 862 | 6 711 | -14.6 | -1.7 | 120 | 214 | -25 | 3 137 | 1.8 | 2.09 | 9.3 | 36.9 |
| Jackson | 16.6 | 11.7 | 8.0 | 47.5 | 1 577 | 1 394 | -11.6 | -3.3 | 22 | 16 | -59 | 649 | -1.8 | 2.14 | 4.6 | 33.3 |
| Jefferson | 14.5 | 7.4 | 5.7 | 50.3 | 525 507 | 534 543 | NA | 2.0 | 12 387 | 8 550 | 7 023 | 218 160 | 5.9 | 2.42 | 9.9 | 27.4 |
| Kiowa | 15.7 | 10.1 | 11.1 | 50.8 | 1 622 | 1 398 | -13.8 | 3.3 | 31 | 35 | 37 | 619 | -6.9 | 2.24 | 5.8 | 32.3 |
| Kit Carson | 12.2 | 8.6 | 7.3 | 44.9 | 8 011 | 8 270 | 3.2 | -2.1 | 232 | 178 | -248 | 3 038 | 1.6 | 2.37 | 7.7 | 31.6 |
| Lake | 13.5 | 5.9 | 3.1 | 46.8 | 7 812 | 7 310 | -6.4 | 0.4 | 226 | 60 | -147 | 2 953 | -0.8 | 2.43 | 8.0 | 29.6 |
| La Plata | 15.0 | 7.5 | 4.8 | 49.1 | 43 941 | 51 334 | 16.8 | 2.1 | 1 234 | 673 | 522 | 21 100 | 21.7 | 2.35 | 8.1 | 27.0 |
| Larimer | 12.8 | 6.9 | 5.4 | 50.4 | 251 494 | 299 630 | 19.1 | 3.6 | 7 555 | 4 130 | 7 247 | 120 295 | 23.8 | 2.42 | 8.2 | 25.9 |
| Las Animas | 16.0 | 10.5 | 8.0 | 48.6 | 15 207 | 15 507 | 2.0 | -3.6 | 328 | 393 | -497 | 6 384 | 3.4 | 2.29 | 11.6 | 32.4 |
| Lincoln | 11.3 | 8.2 | 8.7 | 41.7 | 6 087 | 5 467 | -10.2 | -0.3 | 126 | 111 | -29 | 1 948 | -5.3 | 2.28 | 8.5 | 33.6 |
| Logan | 12.3 | 7.3 | 7.5 | 43.1 | 20 504 | 22 709 | 10.8 | -0.3 | 483 | 434 | -127 | 8 047 | 6.6 | 2.34 | 9.5 | 31.4 |
| Mesa | 13.4 | 8.1 | 7.2 | 50.3 | 116 255 | 146 723 | 26.2 | 0.8 | 4 277 | 2 889 | -218 | 58 095 | 26.8 | 2.46 | 10.0 | 26.5 |
| Mineral | 23.6 | 14.8 | 8.1 | 48.9 | 831 | 712 | -14.3 | -0.4 | 12 | 12 | -7 | 355 | -5.8 | 2.01 | 4.8 | 32.4 |
| Moffat | 13.8 | 6.5 | 4.6 | 48.8 | 13 184 | 13 795 | 4.6 | -4.3 | 427 | 198 | -841 | 5 465 | 9.7 | 2.51 | 9.0 | 26.6 |
| Montezuma | 16.2 | 9.6 | 7.4 | 50.5 | 23 830 | 25 535 | 7.2 | -0.4 | 676 | 610 | -158 | 10 541 | 14.6 | 2.40 | 11.5 | 27.4 |
| Montrose | 14.4 | 10.2 | 8.3 | 50.8 | 33 432 | 41 276 | 23.5 | -1.3 | 1 020 | 896 | -667 | 16 484 | 26.4 | 2.47 | 9.1 | 25.8 |
| Morgan | 11.2 | 7.2 | 7.2 | 50.5 | 27 171 | 28 159 | 3.6 | 1.1 | 981 | 560 | -181 | 10 294 | 7.9 | 2.68 | 10.6 | 25.5 |
| Otero | 13.7 | 9.6 | 8.9 | 51.2 | 20 311 | 18 831 | -7.3 | -0.7 | 533 | 492 | -160 | 7 729 | -2.4 | 2.38 | 13.8 | 30.6 |
| Ouray | 23.1 | 13.6 | 5.1 | 50.6 | 3 742 | 4 436 | 18.5 | 2.1 | 60 | 47 | 74 | 2 022 | 28.3 | 2.19 | 4.9 | 26.5 |
| Park | 21.2 | 9.6 | 3.3 | 47.3 | 14 523 | 16 206 | 11.6 | -1.1 | 239 | 192 | -222 | 7 174 | 21.7 | 2.25 | 5.1 | 27.0 |
| Phillips | 13.1 | 8.9 | 11.6 | 50.5 | 4 480 | 4 442 | -0.8 | -1.7 | 119 | 122 | -71 | 1 819 | 2.1 | 2.41 | 6.3 | 31.1 |
| Pitkin | 16.5 | 8.9 | 3.7 | 47.3 | 14 872 | 17 148 | 15.3 | 0.7 | 333 | 85 | -139 | 8 152 | 19.8 | 2.09 | 5.3 | 38.0 |
| Prowers | 13.0 | 7.6 | 7.0 | 50.4 | 14 483 | 12 551 | -13.3 | -1.3 | 370 | 303 | -237 | 4 935 | -7.0 | 2.48 | 12.6 | 28.3 |
| Pueblo | 13.3 | 8.1 | 7.4 | 50.8 | 141 472 | 159 063 | 12.4 | 1.1 | 4 282 | 3 567 | 1 146 | 62 972 | 15.4 | 2.46 | 14.1 | 28.9 |
| Rio Blanco | 12.9 | 7.3 | 5.2 | 48.1 | 5 986 | 6 666 | 11.4 | 2.9 | 223 | 94 | 63 | 2 647 | 14.8 | 2.43 | 6.5 | 26.7 |
| Rio Grande | 14.9 | 9.2 | 7.3 | 50.1 | 12 413 | 11 982 | -3.5 | -0.3 | 346 | 278 | -108 | 4 779 | 1.7 | 2.47 | 11.8 | 26.6 |
| Routt | 16.1 | 6.2 | 2.7 | 47.0 | 19 690 | 23 509 | 19.4 | -0.7 | 532 | 209 | -510 | 9 892 | 24.4 | 2.34 | 5.7 | 26.1 |
| Saguache | 19.1 | 9.9 | 5.0 | 48.8 | 5 917 | 6 108 | 3.2 | 3.2 | 148 | 92 | 139 | 2 640 | 14.8 | 2.31 | 10.6 | 33.0 |
| San Juan | 21.2 | 8.1 | 3.8 | 42.3 | 558 | 699 | 25.3 | -1.3 | 8 | 9 | -12 | 344 | 27.9 | 2.03 | 6.7 | 40.7 |
| San Miguel | 15.5 | 5.9 | 2.0 | 45.9 | 6 594 | 7 359 | 11.6 | 3.0 | 156 | 33 | 97 | 3 454 | 14.6 | 2.13 | 5.6 | 37.5 |
| Sedgwick | 17.1 | 11.5 | 12.2 | 49.8 | 2 747 | 2 379 | -13.4 | 0.2 | 58 | 76 | 23 | 1 093 | -6.2 | 2.14 | 7.1 | 35.1 |
| Summit | 13.4 | 6.7 | 1.9 | 45.2 | 23 548 | 27 994 | 18.9 | 0.2 | 669 | 125 | -512 | 11 754 | 28.9 | 2.36 | 4.7 | 25.7 |
| Teller | 20.9 | 10.2 | 3.8 | 49.1 | 20 555 | 23 350 | 13.6 | 0.2 | 425 | 329 | -67 | 9 805 | 22.7 | 2.37 | 6.4 | 23.6 |
| Washington | 14.4 | 9.8 | 9.5 | 48.8 | 4 926 | 4 814 | -2.3 | -1.0 | 95 | 102 | -62 | 1 980 | -0.5 | 2.34 | 6.1 | 31.4 |
| Weld | 11.0 | 5.8 | 4.1 | 49.8 | 180 926 | 252 825 | NA | 4.3 | 8 437 | 3 165 | 5 448 | 89 349 | 41.3 | 2.76 | 9.9 | 21.5 |
| Yuma | 12.4 | 8.1 | 7.9 | 50.2 | 9 841 | 10 043 | 2.1 | 0.8 | 327 | 206 | -67 | 3 952 | 4.0 | 2.49 | 6.9 | 28.3 |
| CONNECTICUT | 12.9 | 7.4 | 7.0 | 51.3 | 3 405 565 | 3 574 097 | 4.9 | 0.5 | 83 174 | 65 102 | -811 | 1 371 087 | 5.3 | 2.52 | 12.9 | 27.3 |
| Fairfield | 12.1 | 7.0 | 6.7 | 51.3 | 882 567 | 916 829 | 3.9 | 1.9 | 23 078 | 14 370 | 8 674 | 335 545 | 3.5 | 2.68 | 12.3 | 24.9 |
| Hartford | 12.8 | 7.3 | 7.4 | 51.6 | 857 183 | 894 014 | 4.3 | 0.4 | 21 552 | 17 452 | -709 | 350 854 | 4.7 | 2.47 | 14.5 | 28.7 |
| Litchfield | 15.6 | 8.8 | 7.7 | 50.8 | 182 193 | 189 927 | 4.2 | -1.3 | 3 375 | 3 826 | -1 852 | 76 640 | 7.1 | 2.44 | 9.4 | 26.6 |
| Middlesex | 14.7 | 8.4 | 7.4 | 51.1 | 155 071 | 165 676 | 6.8 | 0.0 | 3 298 | 3 086 | -225 | 67 202 | 9.6 | 2.39 | 9.4 | 28.2 |
| New Haven | 12.7 | 7.3 | 7.3 | 51.8 | 824 008 | 862 477 | 4.7 | 0.0 | 20 519 | 16 825 | -3 171 | 334 502 | 4.8 | 2.49 | 14.5 | 28.9 |
| New London | 13.3 | 7.7 | 6.8 | 50.1 | 259 088 | 274 055 | 5.8 | 0.0 | 6 180 | 5 172 | -800 | 107 057 | 7.2 | 2.44 | 11.8 | 27.6 |

1. No spouse present.

# Table B. States and Counties — Population, Vital Statistics, Medicare, and Crime

| STATE County | Daytime population, 2007–2011 Persons in group quarters, 2010 | Daytime population Number | Daytime population Employment/residence ratio | Births, 2011 Total | Births Rate[1] | Deaths, 2011 Number | Deaths Rate[1] | Persons under 65 with no health insurance, 2010 Number | Persons under 65 Percent | Medicare, 2012 Eligible for Medicare | Medicare Enrolled in Medicare Advantage | Medicare Enrolled in a Medicare prescription drug plan | Serious crimes known to police,[2] 2011 Total Number | Serious crimes Total Rate[3] |
|---|---|---|---|---|---|---|---|---|---|---|---|---|---|---|
| | 32 | 33 | 34 | 35 | 36 | 37 | 38 | 39 | 40 | 41 | 42 | 43 | 44 | 45 |
| **COLORADO—Cont'd** | | | | | | | | | | | | | | |
| Boulder | 8 949 | 320 108 | 1.18 | 3 066 | 10.2 | 1 510 | 5.0 | 37 869 | 14.7 | 37 898 | 13 066 | 11 007 | 6 584 | 2 197 |
| Broomfield | 282 | 58 203 | 1.13 | 686 | 12.0 | 268 | 4.7 | 5 870 | 11.6 | 7 135 | 3 468 | 1 482 | 1 136 | 1 998 |
| Chaffee | 1 436 | 17 924 | 1.03 | 144 | 8.0 | 135 | 7.5 | 2 633 | 20.3 | 4 286 | 707 | 1 738 | 290 | 1 601 |
| Cheyenne | 42 | 2 414 | 1.15 | 22 | 11.7 | 20 | 10.7 | 382 | 25.8 | 320 | 15 | 167 | 3 | 161 |
| Clear Creek | 84 | 7 414 | 0.68 | 63 | 7.0 | 56 | 6.2 | 942 | 12.0 | 1 367 | 428 | 389 | 171 | 2 087 |
| Conejos | 36 | 6 949 | 0.60 | 118 | 14.2 | 71 | 8.6 | 1 542 | 22.1 | 1 622 | 482 | 774 | 4 | 48 |
| Costilla | 0 | 3 294 | 0.81 | 27 | 7.4 | 27 | 7.4 | 800 | 29.2 | 982 | 261 | 448 | NA | NA |
| Crowley | 2 682 | 5 831 | 0.98 | 35 | 6.1 | 35 | 6.1 | 527 | 20.2 | 750 | 84 | 383 | 3 | 51 |
| Custer | 150 | 3 587 | 0.82 | 21 | 5.0 | 34 | 8.1 | 725 | 22.9 | 1 179 | 177 | 428 | 41 | 947 |
| Delta | 713 | 29 134 | 0.88 | 335 | 11.0 | 346 | 11.4 | 5 514 | 22.9 | 7 406 | 1 842 | 2 736 | 541 | 1 802 |
| Denver | 15 981 | 743 493 | 1.50 | 10 167 | 16.4 | 4 271 | 6.9 | 109 574 | 20.7 | 77 799 | 36 567 | 20 278 | 26 503 | 4 340 |
| Dolores | 0 | 1 780 | 0.72 | 20 | 9.7 | 9 | 4.4 | 472 | 28.2 | 460 | 40 | 195 | 26 | 1 238 |
| Douglas | 651 | 238 109 | 0.70 | 3 506 | 12.0 | 864 | 3.0 | 19 361 | 7.3 | 27 990 | 10 714 | 7 087 | 3 798 | 1 308 |
| Eagle | 55 | 51 204 | 0.99 | 729 | 14.1 | 86 | 1.7 | 11 516 | 23.6 | 3 679 | 264 | 1 824 | 1 077 | 2 028 |
| Elbert | 73 | 15 568 | 0.37 | 176 | 7.6 | 104 | 4.5 | 2 729 | 13.1 | 3 036 | 805 | 917 | NA | NA |
| El Paso | 19 141 | 611 228 | 1.00 | 8 868 | 13.9 | 3 604 | 5.7 | 88 912 | 16.3 | 81 204 | 21 137 | 19 720 | 21 330 | 3 373 |
| Fremont | 8 704 | 46 279 | 0.95 | 363 | 7.7 | 500 | 10.6 | 4 962 | 16.3 | 10 169 | 2 557 | 3 455 | 852 | 1 788 |
| Garfield | 884 | 54 971 | 0.97 | 892 | 15.9 | 304 | 5.4 | 12 445 | 24.6 | 5 976 | 651 | 2 789 | 738 | 1 536 |
| Gilpin | 49 | 7 322 | 1.68 | 49 | 9.0 | 18 | 3.3 | 580 | 11.8 | 667 | 228 | 167 | 198 | 3 577 |
| Grand | 222 | 14 416 | 0.97 | 127 | 8.7 | 44 | 3.0 | 2 764 | 21.0 | 1 759 | 198 | 733 | 249 | 1 649 |
| Gunnison | 850 | 16 047 | 1.09 | 155 | 10.1 | 58 | 3.8 | 3 172 | 24.0 | 1 750 | 71 | 806 | 414 | 2 655 |
| Hinsdale | 56 | 727 | 0.99 | 9 | 10.8 | 0 | 0.0 | 147 | 21.0 | 191 | 14 | 77 | 13 | 1 515 |
| Huerfano | 165 | 6 831 | 1.00 | 56 | 8.6 | 88 | 13.5 | 1 031 | 20.7 | 1 993 | 278 | 967 | 122 | 2 029 |
| Jackson | 2 | 1 546 | 1.06 | 9 | 6.6 | 6 | 4.4 | 285 | 25.0 | 300 | D | 161 | 6 | 423 |
| Jefferson | 7 427 | 483 062 | 0.82 | 5 564 | 10.3 | 3 705 | 6.9 | 66 744 | 14.5 | 83 862 | 43 237 | 14 918 | 15 442 | 2 839 |
| Kiowa | 14 | 1 757 | 1.03 | 11 | 7.7 | 17 | 11.9 | 214 | 19.5 | 310 | D | 206 | 0 | 0 |
| Kit Carson | 1 075 | 8 326 | 1.04 | 107 | 13.1 | 83 | 10.2 | 1 565 | 26.5 | 1 426 | 50 | 879 | 120 | 1 426 |
| Lake | 133 | 5 767 | 0.64 | 112 | 15.1 | 26 | 3.5 | 1 722 | 26.4 | 781 | 46 | 347 | 101 | 1 358 |
| La Plata | 1 715 | 52 147 | 1.05 | 573 | 11.0 | 305 | 5.9 | 8 554 | 19.5 | 7 530 | 690 | 3 274 | NA | NA |
| Larimer | 8 530 | 288 186 | 0.95 | 3 380 | 11.1 | 1 739 | 5.7 | 40 267 | 15.6 | 45 017 | 10 985 | 16 058 | 8 273 | 2 714 |
| Las Animas | 858 | 15 810 | 1.04 | 153 | 10.2 | 175 | 11.6 | 2 361 | 19.7 | 3 412 | 530 | 1 461 | NA | NA |
| Lincoln | 1 030 | 5 860 | 1.21 | 61 | 11.2 | 50 | 9.2 | 749 | 21.0 | 934 | 35 | 520 | 22 | 396 |
| Logan | 3 904 | 22 107 | 0.97 | 216 | 9.5 | 203 | 9.0 | 3 041 | 19.4 | 3 748 | 388 | 2 073 | 487 | 2 108 |
| Mesa | 3 631 | 142 401 | 0.97 | 1 943 | 13.2 | 1 280 | 8.7 | 24 352 | 20.0 | 26 618 | 9 850 | 8 269 | 4 482 | 3 017 |
| Mineral | 0 | 771 | 1.13 | 4 | 5.6 | 4 | 5.6 | 128 | 22.9 | 214 | 25 | 124 | 3 | 414 |
| Moffat | 102 | 12 784 | 0.88 | 211 | 15.7 | 94 | 7.0 | 2 216 | 18.1 | 1 821 | 90 | 870 | 315 | 2 244 |
| Montezuma | 237 | 24 544 | 0.93 | 319 | 12.5 | 267 | 10.5 | 4 648 | 21.9 | 5 135 | 509 | 2 466 | 577 | 2 221 |
| Montrose | 542 | 39 224 | 0.91 | 479 | 11.7 | 399 | 9.7 | 7 526 | 22.4 | 8 708 | 1 915 | 3 426 | 914 | 2 176 |
| Morgan | 564 | 27 844 | 0.99 | 438 | 15.5 | 219 | 7.8 | 5 621 | 23.7 | 4 400 | 314 | 2 428 | 414 | 1 492 |
| Otero | 433 | 18 803 | 1.00 | 222 | 11.8 | 213 | 11.3 | 2 966 | 19.6 | 4 254 | 591 | 2 210 | 347 | 1 854 |
| Ouray | 0 | 4 267 | 0.95 | 25 | 5.7 | 18 | 4.1 | 810 | 22.1 | 981 | 152 | 436 | 46 | 1 287 |
| Park | 92 | 11 383 | 0.43 | 120 | 7.5 | 84 | 5.2 | 2 692 | 18.9 | 2 450 | 607 | 724 | 139 | 843 |
| Phillips | 60 | 4 445 | 1.03 | 58 | 13.2 | 61 | 13.9 | 871 | 24.6 | 883 | 20 | 587 | 28 | 620 |
| Pitkin | 72 | 24 259 | 1.75 | 151 | 8.8 | 31 | 1.8 | 3 040 | 20.1 | 2 172 | 80 | 1 239 | 404 | 2 316 |
| Prowers | 315 | 12 475 | 0.98 | 170 | 13.5 | 134 | 10.7 | 2 535 | 24.3 | 2 184 | 50 | 1 338 | 291 | 2 279 |
| Pueblo | 4 321 | 156 303 | 0.97 | 1 961 | 12.2 | 1 561 | 9.7 | 22 972 | 17.4 | 31 674 | 9 408 | 11 331 | 8 014 | 4 952 |
| Rio Blanco | 235 | 7 189 | 1.18 | 99 | 14.6 | 45 | 6.6 | 1 042 | 18.7 | 987 | 182 | 429 | 69 | 1 017 |
| Rio Grande | 198 | 11 444 | 0.90 | 163 | 13.6 | 124 | 10.4 | 1 978 | 19.8 | 2 643 | 565 | 1 405 | 221 | 1 813 |
| Routt | 335 | 24 287 | 1.08 | 239 | 10.3 | 92 | 4.0 | 3 628 | 17.1 | 2 520 | 171 | 1 241 | 457 | 1 985 |
| Saguache | 18 | 5 852 | 0.89 | 66 | 10.6 | 47 | 7.5 | 1 765 | 34.0 | 938 | 156 | 383 | 118 | 1 899 |
| San Juan | 0 | 905 | 1.24 | 4 | 5.8 | 2 | 2.9 | 145 | 23.4 | 107 | D | 44 | 27 | 3 797 |
| San Miguel | 9 | 8 564 | 1.25 | 68 | 9.1 | 19 | 2.5 | 1 795 | 26.4 | 667 | 73 | 282 | 190 | 2 538 |
| Sedgwick | 35 | 2 309 | 0.92 | 23 | 9.7 | 35 | 14.8 | 454 | 25.1 | 611 | 26 | 367 | 24 | 992 |
| Summit | 273 | 29 479 | 1.12 | 306 | 10.9 | 56 | 2.0 | 5 490 | 21.3 | 2 397 | 197 | 1 018 | 836 | 2 935 |
| Teller | 132 | 20 387 | 0.76 | 202 | 8.6 | 145 | 6.2 | 2 972 | 14.7 | 4 259 | 1 148 | 1 176 | 305 | 1 284 |
| Washington | 184 | 4 203 | 0.79 | 43 | 9.0 | 47 | 9.9 | 971 | 26.2 | 902 | 14 | 548 | 90 | 1 837 |
| Weld | 5 895 | 224 405 | 0.79 | 3 788 | 14.6 | 1 326 | 5.1 | 42 498 | 19.0 | 31 698 | 8 121 | 12 095 | 6 018 | 2 384 |
| Yuma | 196 | 10 337 | 1.08 | 140 | 13.9 | 87 | 8.6 | 2 102 | 25.4 | 1 769 | 42 | 1 222 | 69 | 675 |
| **CONNECTICUT** | 118 152 | 3 547 530 | 0.99 | 37 319 | 10.4 | 28 244 | 7.9 | 309 864 | 10.4 | 599 182 | 133 584 | 259 087 | 87 376 | 2 440 |
| Fairfield | 19 168 | 938 416 | 1.06 | 10 396 | 11.2 | 6 191 | 6.7 | 93 423 | 12.0 | 140 054 | 29 898 | 61 036 | 20 089 | 2 230 |
| Hartford | 28 227 | 965 938 | 1.18 | 9 668 | 10.8 | 7 640 | 8.5 | 74 640 | 10.0 | 155 172 | 38 151 | 66 881 | 24 966 | 2 861 |
| Litchfield | 2 804 | 161 561 | 0.71 | 1 524 | 8.1 | 1 675 | 8.9 | 14 291 | 9.0 | 36 302 | 5 777 | 16 793 | NA | NA |
| Middlesex | 5 085 | 152 502 | 0.85 | 1 472 | 8.9 | 1 298 | 7.8 | 11 484 | 8.4 | 30 581 | 6 323 | 13 305 | NA | NA |
| New Haven | 29 198 | 826 521 | 0.92 | 9 190 | 10.7 | 7 322 | 8.5 | 75 254 | 10.5 | 147 093 | 37 341 | 59 155 | 27 127 | 3 347 |
| New London | 12 782 | 276 925 | 1.03 | 2 735 | 10.0 | 2 286 | 8.4 | 21 416 | 9.6 | 47 859 | 7 226 | 21 829 | NA | NA |

1. Per 1,000 estimated resident population.  2. Data for serious crimes have not been adjusted for underreporting; this may affect comparability between geographic areas and over time.  3. Per 100,000 population estimated by the FBI.

# Table B. States and Counties — Crime, Education, Money Income, and Poverty

| STATE County | Serious crimes known to police, 2011 (cont.)[1] Rate[2] Violent | Property | Education — School enrollment and attainment, 2007–2011 Enrollment[3] Total | Percent private | Attainment[4] (percent) High school graduate or less | Bachelor's degree or more | Local government expenditures,[5] 2009–2010 Total current expenditures (mil dol) | Current expenditures per student (dollars) | Money income, 2007–2011 Per capita income[6] (dollars) | Households Median income Dollars | Percent change, 2000 to 2007–2011 (constant 2011 dollars) | Percent with income of $200,000 or more | Income and poverty, 2011 Median household income (dollars) | Percent below poverty level All persons | Children under 18 years | Children 5 to 17 years in families |
|---|---|---|---|---|---|---|---|---|---|---|---|---|---|---|---|---|
| | 46 | 47 | 48 | 49 | 50 | 51 | 52 | 53 | 54 | 55 | 56 | 57 | 58 | 59 | 60 | 61 |
| COLORADO—Cont'd | | | | | | | | | | | | | | | | |
| Boulder | 201 | 1 996 | 91 246 | 12.7 | 19.3 | 57.7 | [7]497.6 | [7]8 929 | 37 720 | 66 479 | 0.0 | 8.4 | 68 101 | 13.8 | 13.0 | 11.7 |
| Broomfield | 58 | 1 940 | 15 611 | 19.4 | 22.7 | 45.6 | [7] | [7] | 36 783 | 76 531 | -11.3 | 6.9 | 79 051 | 6.5 | 7.8 | 6.8 |
| Chaffee | 55 | 1 545 | 2 971 | 13.6 | 38.6 | 32.2 | 20.3 | 9 859 | 26 795 | 43 684 | -5.9 | 2.4 | 44 156 | 12.9 | 19.8 | 17.9 |
| Cheyenne | 0 | 161 | 543 | 13.1 | 48.1 | 15.6 | 4.6 | 16 081 | 22 877 | 47 188 | -5.7 | 0.5 | 46 965 | 12.9 | 23.7 | 22.2 |
| Clear Creek | 256 | 1 831 | 1 783 | 11.3 | 27.8 | 39.9 | 9.9 | 10 122 | 35 345 | 62 756 | -8.9 | 4.5 | 65 420 | 8.9 | 14.3 | 12.7 |
| Conejos | 12 | 36 | 2 208 | 3.9 | 51.7 | 20.6 | 15.7 | 9 395 | 18 094 | 34 435 | 3.1 | 0.7 | 32 588 | 19.8 | 28.4 | 26.1 |
| Costilla | NA | NA | 845 | 1.3 | 58.0 | 15.3 | 5.4 | 11 534 | 18 622 | 25 949 | -1.6 | 0.9 | 26 125 | 26.0 | 38.3 | 33.5 |
| Crowley | 51 | 0 | 1 066 | 10.1 | 64.7 | 10.7 | 4.3 | 8 632 | 17 746 | 40 636 | 12.3 | 4.0 | 30 279 | 48.1 | 40.6 | 37.4 |
| Custer | 185 | 762 | 651 | 4.5 | 38.1 | 30.8 | 4.5 | 9 231 | 28 008 | 43 358 | -7.5 | 4.1 | 45 791 | 15.6 | 28.7 | 24.3 |
| Delta | 147 | 1 656 | 6 236 | 8.1 | 49.8 | 17.7 | 41.9 | 7 852 | 23 495 | 41 856 | -5.4 | 2.4 | 41 442 | 16.6 | 24.8 | 21.7 |
| Denver | 609 | 3 732 | 142 808 | 22.5 | 35.1 | 41.3 | 818.9 | 9 767 | 32 051 | 47 499 | -10.9 | 5.1 | 47 584 | 18.7 | 26.2 | 25.0 |
| Dolores | 143 | 1 095 | 448 | 4.0 | 49.9 | 15.5 | 3.0 | 10 430 | 22 729 | 44 077 | 1.4 | 0.6 | 39 650 | 13.3 | 16.4 | 15.6 |
| Douglas | 134 | 1 173 | 84 546 | 17.4 | 16.2 | 54.6 | 468.3 | 7 813 | 43 461 | 101 193 | -9.6 | 12.1 | 95 973 | 4.3 | 4.9 | 4.0 |
| Eagle | 115 | 1 913 | 11 355 | 17.2 | 30.7 | 46.9 | 66.2 | 10 606 | 38 174 | 70 914 | -16.2 | 8.7 | 67 190 | 9.8 | 14.5 | 13.4 |
| Elbert | NA | NA | 6 095 | 11.5 | 32.6 | 30.2 | 30.6 | 8 209 | 34 527 | 79 367 | -5.9 | 6.0 | 78 029 | 7.9 | 11.4 | 9.4 |
| El Paso | 381 | 2 993 | 176 382 | 19.9 | 29.7 | 35.1 | 922.1 | 8 439 | 28 624 | 57 079 | -9.8 | 3.9 | 54 857 | 13.2 | 18.0 | 15.9 |
| Fremont | 195 | 1 593 | 7 920 | 15.7 | 53.3 | 16.5 | 44.7 | 8 052 | 19 657 | 38 979 | -15.5 | 1.4 | 41 493 | 18.0 | 24.8 | 22.7 |
| Garfield | 102 | 1 434 | 14 264 | 11.8 | 41.6 | 24.8 | 97.5 | 8 471 | 27 901 | 63 929 | 0.7 | 3.0 | 57 617 | 10.7 | 14.9 | 14.6 |
| Gilpin | 199 | 3 378 | 1 033 | 7.6 | 31.7 | 27.4 | 4.4 | 12 166 | 33 439 | 59 394 | -15.3 | 4.1 | 60 537 | 7.8 | 11.5 | 9.0 |
| Grand | 252 | 1 397 | 3 034 | 9.2 | 36.4 | 29.6 | 18.1 | 9 571 | 30 519 | 64 281 | -0.3 | 3.1 | 56 980 | 10.4 | 15.9 | 14.0 |
| Gunnison | 205 | 2 450 | 4 662 | 13.0 | 23.6 | 47.0 | 15.6 | 8 586 | 28 862 | 50 073 | 0.5 | 4.7 | 43 069 | 17.9 | 18.2 | 15.3 |
| Hinsdale | 117 | 1 399 | 56 | 37.5 | 23.2 | 41.5 | 1.4 | 14 602 | 38 528 | 77 321 | 53.6 | 4.3 | 49 024 | 10.7 | 27.7 | 26.7 |
| Huerfano | 183 | 1 846 | 1 293 | 10.4 | 45.0 | 25.0 | 8.7 | 9 913 | 22 167 | 29 737 | -14.6 | 2.1 | 30 655 | 22.0 | 37.7 | 34.1 |
| Jackson | 0 | 423 | 311 | 4.2 | 45.1 | 21.8 | 2.7 | 11 526 | 24 466 | 48 571 | 13.1 | 0.0 | 43 206 | 16.1 | 28.5 | 24.5 |
| Jefferson | 220 | 2 619 | 132 693 | 14.6 | 28.9 | 39.7 | 764.2 | 8 857 | 35 587 | 67 827 | 0.0 | 5.8 | 64 412 | 9.0 | 12.2 | 11.1 |
| Kiowa | 0 | 0 | 461 | 0.0 | 39.9 | 23.0 | 4.2 | 15 279 | 24 098 | 41 542 | 0.9 | 2.8 | 41 427 | 12.6 | 18.4 | 16.0 |
| Kit Carson | 107 | 1 319 | 1 953 | 12.4 | 48.9 | 15.4 | 13.6 | 9 452 | 21 674 | 43 194 | -3.5 | 0.5 | 43 078 | 16.2 | 22.1 | 20.4 |
| Lake | 282 | 1 076 | 1 850 | 7.8 | 39.9 | 21.7 | 20.1 | 16 612 | 21 063 | 40 543 | -20.3 | 1.0 | 42 768 | 16.4 | 26.9 | 26.0 |
| La Plata | NA | NA | 13 169 | 11.0 | 26.9 | 41.0 | 65.5 | 9 488 | 30 592 | 56 910 | 5.0 | 4.2 | 52 276 | 11.1 | 15.0 | 14.1 |
| Larimer | 198 | 2 516 | 90 582 | 9.9 | 25.6 | 43.1 | 363.7 | 8 467 | 30 276 | 57 215 | -12.9 | 3.9 | 55 501 | 13.8 | 14.0 | 12.4 |
| Las Animas | NA | NA | 3 663 | 4.7 | 45.0 | 18.2 | 25.3 | 9 547 | 22 357 | 40 617 | 6.4 | 0.6 | 40 191 | 19.5 | 27.1 | 24.9 |
| Lincoln | 180 | 216 | 909 | 10.9 | 60.9 | 12.3 | 13.9 | 15 232 | 20 579 | 43 375 | 0.7 | 2.4 | 42 734 | 17.7 | 23.6 | 22.6 |
| Logan | 100 | 2 008 | 5 429 | 6.9 | 45.0 | 16.4 | 28.1 | 8 890 | 23 601 | 42 324 | -4.2 | 2.1 | 43 823 | 18.0 | 21.4 | 18.8 |
| Mesa | 304 | 2 713 | 36 430 | 12.0 | 40.6 | 26.1 | 186.3 | 8 206 | 27 680 | 52 986 | 9.4 | 3.1 | 47 778 | 12.2 | 16.3 | 15.4 |
| Mineral | 0 | 414 | 59 | 22.0 | 30.0 | 39.7 | 1.8 | 18 119 | 50 502 | 54 375 | 15.6 | 4.6 | 46 956 | 11.2 | 20.6 | 17.6 |
| Moffat | 214 | 2 031 | 3 884 | 7.3 | 48.0 | 14.1 | 21.2 | 8 354 | 23 810 | 50 758 | -9.5 | 0.5 | 52 257 | 11.9 | 17.5 | 14.9 |
| Montezuma | 208 | 2 013 | 5 096 | 8.7 | 40.2 | 26.1 | 38.0 | 9 438 | 25 612 | 45 623 | 5.3 | 2.9 | 41 817 | 16.4 | 26.0 | 24.5 |
| Montrose | 167 | 2 010 | 9 340 | 16.9 | 48.8 | 22.9 | 53.7 | 7 820 | 23 498 | 47 479 | -0.2 | 2.0 | 43 035 | 16.6 | 25.3 | 21.3 |
| Morgan | 76 | 1 417 | 7 259 | 4.4 | 54.0 | 14.6 | 56.8 | 10 342 | 19 753 | 42 792 | -8.3 | 1.2 | 41 246 | 15.3 | 20.3 | 18.9 |
| Otero | 230 | 1 624 | 5 078 | 5.2 | 51.5 | 13.6 | 33.8 | 10 040 | 17 396 | 31 246 | -22.2 | 0.7 | 30 420 | 23.9 | 35.1 | 30.5 |
| Ouray | 84 | 1 203 | 970 | 9.4 | 24.9 | 42.1 | 8.7 | 14 315 | 31 329 | 61 935 | 9.2 | 6.1 | 57 922 | 9.8 | 17.4 | 14.9 |
| Park | 61 | 782 | 3 148 | 7.2 | 30.4 | 33.8 | 32.1 | 17 346 | 30 908 | 61 284 | -12.5 | 1.6 | 58 565 | 9.9 | 15.8 | 14.0 |
| Phillips | 0 | 620 | 1 088 | 6.0 | 45.2 | 19.3 | 11.8 | 12 415 | 20 995 | 44 717 | 2.9 | 1.5 | 43 826 | 12.4 | 17.1 | 15.2 |
| Pitkin | 132 | 2 184 | 3 381 | 22.4 | 15.2 | 56.5 | 21.8 | 12 864 | 57 179 | 68 242 | -14.9 | 13.8 | 69 229 | 7.5 | 9.3 | 8.1 |
| Prowers | 149 | 2 130 | 3 456 | 2.5 | 47.4 | 18.9 | 23.3 | 9 355 | 19 337 | 34 513 | -14.6 | 1.0 | 36 563 | 21.0 | 30.2 | 26.3 |
| Pueblo | 517 | 4 435 | 41 911 | 10.5 | 43.2 | 21.5 | 225.7 | 8 281 | 22 056 | 41 273 | -6.7 | 1.8 | 40 764 | 19.0 | 27.3 | 24.3 |
| Rio Blanco | 103 | 914 | 1 540 | 11.9 | 42.3 | 23.0 | 12.2 | 10 049 | 27 771 | 63 125 | 24.0 | 1.6 | 60 022 | 10.1 | 11.8 | 10.6 |
| Rio Grande | 98 | 1 714 | 3 049 | 8.3 | 47.9 | 19.2 | 18.4 | 8 112 | 18 762 | 37 885 | -11.9 | 1.2 | 37 472 | 18.5 | 30.6 | 28.3 |
| Routt | 195 | 1 790 | 4 629 | 17.8 | 21.4 | 47.9 | 38.6 | 12 750 | 34 435 | 64 230 | -11.3 | 4.2 | 64 998 | 8.7 | 11.9 | 10.9 |
| Saguache | 209 | 1 690 | 1 290 | 1.8 | 54.0 | 20.1 | 11.2 | 11 683 | 20 194 | 33 672 | -2.2 | 1.9 | 30 746 | 29.7 | 42.2 | 40.3 |
| San Juan | 281 | 3 516 | 91 | 24.2 | 28.0 | 26.5 | 1.1 | 16 848 | 25 839 | 36 378 | -12.4 | 0.0 | 36 547 | 18.0 | 24.1 | 23.2 |
| San Miguel | 107 | 2 431 | 1 302 | 23.4 | 21.7 | 50.4 | 11.9 | 12 207 | 44 490 | 66 789 | 2.0 | 7.6 | 57 578 | 11.1 | 16.4 | 16.1 |
| Sedgwick | 207 | 785 | 474 | 5.7 | 49.4 | 15.0 | 10.1 | 7 493 | 23 515 | 36 797 | -3.6 | 2.2 | 37 511 | 13.8 | 22.0 | 19.4 |
| Summit | 126 | 2 809 | 4 923 | 12.5 | 24.0 | 49.2 | 31.6 | 10 238 | 35 218 | 67 915 | -11.1 | 4.4 | 60 397 | 10.5 | 13.8 | 12.5 |
| Teller | 156 | 1 128 | 5 086 | 12.2 | 32.9 | 29.9 | 28.9 | 8 846 | 28 569 | 57 931 | -14.5 | 1.7 | 60 313 | 9.3 | 15.1 | 12.9 |
| Washington | 163 | 1 674 | 1 054 | 10.4 | 45.1 | 18.6 | 10.7 | 11 664 | 24 814 | 43 945 | 0.4 | 2.5 | 43 433 | 12.6 | 19.7 | 17.4 |
| Weld | 293 | 2 091 | 73 290 | 9.0 | 41.6 | 25.6 | 301.1 | 8 184 | 25 233 | 55 825 | -2.3 | 3.0 | 51 773 | 14.4 | 18.3 | 16.0 |
| Yuma | 69 | 607 | 2 384 | 4.0 | 48.8 | 16.4 | 17.4 | 9 782 | 21 825 | 44 991 | 0.5 | 1.1 | 46 246 | 13.6 | 19.7 | 18.6 |
| CONNECTICUT | 273 | 2 167 | 947 323 | 21.1 | 39.6 | 35.7 | 8 181.4 | 14 724 | 37 627 | 69 243 | -4.9 | 8.7 | 65 822 | 10.8 | 14.6 | 13.3 |
| Fairfield | 294 | 1 935 | 246 238 | 24.8 | 34.9 | 44.0 | 2 291.2 | 15 732 | 48 922 | 82 558 | -6.3 | 16.7 | 77 065 | 9.4 | 12.4 | 11.6 |
| Hartford | 324 | 2 537 | 237 020 | 18.8 | 40.9 | 33.9 | 2 092.3 | 14 848 | 33 991 | 64 007 | -6.6 | 6.5 | 60 947 | 12.4 | 16.8 | 15.8 |
| Litchfield | NA | NA | 45 714 | 19.7 | 39.1 | 32.7 | 388.3 | 14 519 | 37 249 | 71 497 | -5.9 | 6.6 | 68 658 | 7.8 | 8.9 | 7.6 |
| Middlesex | NA | NA | 41 488 | 22.5 | 34.8 | 38.3 | 344.5 | 10 150 | 39 347 | 77 095 | -3.5 | 7.8 | 75 714 | 6.7 | 7.9 | 6.9 |
| New Haven | 384 | 2 964 | 229 599 | 24.5 | 42.7 | 32.3 | 1 926.2 | 15 047 | 32 509 | 62 497 | -5.2 | 5.9 | 58 985 | 12.9 | 19.1 | 17.3 |
| New London | NA | NA | 67 666 | 17.5 | 41.2 | 30.9 | 580.4 | 14 411 | 33 478 | 67 010 | -2.0 | 5.2 | 63 561 | 9.0 | 12.2 | 11.1 |

1. Data for serious crimes have not been adjusted for underreporting; this may affect comparability between geographic areas and over time.   2. Per 100,000 population estimated by the FBI.   3. All persons 3 years old and over enrolled in nursery school through college.   4. Persons 25 years old and over.   5. Elementary and secondary education expenditures.   6. Based on population estimated by the American Community Survey, 2007–2011.   7. Broomfield county is included with Boulder county.

| STATE County | Total (mil dol) | Percent change, 2010–2011 | Per capita[1] Dollars | Per capita[1] Rank | Wages and salaries[2] (mil dol) | Proprietors' income (mil dol) | Dividends, interest, and rent (mil dol) | Transfer payments (mil dol) Total | Government payments to individuals Total | Social Security | Medical payments | Income maintenance | Unemployment insurance |
|---|---|---|---|---|---|---|---|---|---|---|---|---|---|
| | 62 | 63 | 64 | 65 | 66 | 67 | 68 | 69 | 70 | 71 | 72 | 73 | 74 |
| COLORADO—Cont'd | | | | | | | | | | | | | |
| Boulder | 15 536 | 5.2 | 51 893 | 164 | 11 351 | 1 556 | 3 481 | 1 408 | 1 341 | 521 | 510 | 100 | 89 |
| Broomfield | 2 345 | 7.4 | 40 892 | 668 | 2 601 | 235 | 364 | 267 | 254 | 101 | 97 | 14 | 18 |
| Chaffee | 578 | 5.9 | 32 246 | 1 837 | 268 | 40 | 173 | 128 | 124 | 56 | 46 | 9 | 5 |
| Cheyenne | 108 | 2.7 | 57 591 | 88 | 40 | 43 | 18 | 13 | 13 | 4 | 7 | 1 | 0 |
| Clear Creek | 499 | 2.1 | 55 335 | 111 | 195 | 104 | 89 | 47 | 45 | 20 | 15 | 3 | 3 |
| Conejos | 213 | 9.1 | 25 638 | 2 918 | 55 | 30 | 30 | 67 | 65 | 17 | 29 | 11 | 3 |
| Costilla | 99 | 9.2 | 27 127 | 2 748 | 29 | 9 | 14 | 35 | 35 | 11 | 14 | 6 | 1 |
| Crowley | 96 | 2.8 | 16 752 | 3 113 | 55 | 5 | 13 | 34 | 32 | 9 | 14 | 5 | 1 |
| Custer | 146 | 7.5 | 34 793 | 1 404 | 36 | 19 | 43 | 34 | 33 | 16 | 10 | 2 | 1 |
| Delta | 953 | 5.9 | 31 307 | 2 041 | 379 | 78 | 183 | 242 | 235 | 94 | 91 | 22 | 12 |
| Denver | 33 811 | 7.0 | 54 537 | 119 | 33 165 | 7 400 | 5 216 | 4 008 | 3 871 | 1 005 | 1 693 | 499 | 242 |
| Dolores | 60 | 9.9 | 29 250 | 2 417 | 9 | 9 | 12 | 14 | 14 | 6 | 5 | 1 | 1 |
| Douglas | 20 879 | 10.4 | 71 463 | 21 | 6 339 | 485 | 2 595 | 1 008 | 943 | 427 | 257 | 44 | 81 |
| Eagle | 2 521 | 4.5 | 48 618 | 249 | 1 452 | 425 | 626 | 148 | 136 | 55 | 38 | 11 | 20 |
| Elbert | 1 034 | 6.3 | 44 606 | 413 | 146 | 50 | 137 | 115 | 109 | 45 | 39 | 7 | 7 |
| El Paso | 25 421 | 6.9 | 39 909 | 758 | 18 151 | 1 447 | 3 769 | 3 971 | 3 839 | 1 086 | 1 412 | 387 | 225 |
| Fremont | 1 299 | 4.7 | 27 440 | 2 693 | 662 | 66 | 222 | 363 | 353 | 129 | 143 | 34 | 16 |
| Garfield | 2 130 | 5.4 | 37 858 | 990 | 1 407 | 203 | 388 | 256 | 244 | 81 | 96 | 22 | 23 |
| Gilpin | 238 | 5.9 | 43 444 | 475 | 267 | 16 | 35 | 24 | 23 | 9 | 7 | 2 | 2 |
| Grand | 560 | 4.6 | 38 504 | 908 | 264 | 80 | 134 | 66 | 62 | 26 | 22 | 5 | 6 |
| Gunnison | 528 | 4.5 | 34 293 | 1 470 | 366 | 44 | 153 | 62 | 59 | 22 | 19 | 5 | 5 |
| Hinsdale | 34 | 5.1 | 41 284 | 635 | 10 | 3 | 15 | 5 | 5 | 2 | 2 | 0 | 0 |
| Huerfano | 205 | 3.5 | 31 380 | 2 022 | 70 | 11 | 45 | 84 | 83 | 24 | 38 | 10 | 3 |
| Jackson | 61 | 9.2 | 44 604 | 414 | 25 | 15 | 14 | 9 | 9 | 4 | 3 | 1 | 0 |
| Jefferson | 24 391 | 3.5 | 45 179 | 389 | 13 444 | 1 532 | 4 599 | 3 182 | 3 063 | 1 171 | 1 229 | 218 | 196 |
| Kiowa | 62 | -4.8 | 43 447 | 472 | 29 | 15 | 10 | 12 | 11 | 4 | 6 | 1 | 0 |
| Kit Carson | 321 | 5.5 | 39 383 | 816 | 123 | 110 | 52 | 50 | 48 | 18 | 22 | 4 | 2 |
| Lake | 217 | 5.2 | 29 274 | 2 413 | 84 | 10 | 38 | 38 | 36 | 11 | 15 | 4 | 3 |
| La Plata | 2 256 | 3.6 | 43 453 | 471 | 1 270 | 326 | 527 | 277 | 266 | 101 | 101 | 21 | 16 |
| Larimer | 12 150 | 6.1 | 39 767 | 771 | 7 329 | 898 | 2 320 | 1 684 | 1 617 | 610 | 623 | 126 | 97 |
| Las Animas | 481 | 3.8 | 31 961 | 1 896 | 248 | 29 | 81 | 149 | 146 | 39 | 64 | 16 | 6 |
| Lincoln | 170 | 6.3 | 31 153 | 2 073 | 101 | 21 | 33 | 34 | 33 | 10 | 16 | 3 | 1 |
| Logan | 785 | 5.4 | 34 725 | 1 416 | 385 | 160 | 141 | 144 | 139 | 46 | 60 | 15 | 6 |
| Mesa | 5 173 | 5.1 | 35 169 | 1 345 | 3 056 | 372 | 970 | 1 026 | 993 | 349 | 382 | 96 | 61 |
| Mineral | 32 | 9.2 | 45 243 | 384 | 18 | 2 | 11 | 6 | 5 | 3 | 2 | 0 | 0 |
| Moffat | 551 | 7.3 | 40 945 | 663 | 302 | 79 | 65 | 79 | 76 | 27 | 31 | 8 | 6 |
| Montezuma | 865 | 4.9 | 34 015 | 1 506 | 389 | 60 | 169 | 193 | 187 | 67 | 80 | 20 | 9 |
| Montrose | 1 269 | 3.3 | 30 933 | 2 118 | 629 | 172 | 258 | 305 | 296 | 113 | 116 | 31 | 18 |
| Morgan | 944 | 9.7 | 33 489 | 1 603 | 582 | 109 | 128 | 186 | 179 | 56 | 82 | 21 | 8 |
| Otero | 592 | 4.6 | 31 370 | 2 025 | 266 | 56 | 88 | 195 | 191 | 47 | 82 | 25 | 8 |
| Ouray | 183 | 2.4 | 41 898 | 582 | 56 | 18 | 62 | 29 | 28 | 14 | 9 | 2 | 2 |
| Park | 546 | 2.4 | 33 936 | 1 525 | 98 | 34 | 105 | 84 | 80 | 37 | 22 | 7 | 6 |
| Phillips | 176 | 13.3 | 40 055 | 740 | 67 | 52 | 31 | 33 | 32 | 11 | 16 | 2 | 1 |
| Pitkin | 1 353 | 5.9 | 79 086 | 8 | 856 | 215 | 534 | 66 | 62 | 31 | 18 | 2 | 7 |
| Prowers | 426 | 4.7 | 33 985 | 1 511 | 201 | 73 | 81 | 98 | 96 | 26 | 42 | 16 | 3 |
| Pueblo | 5 099 | 5.5 | 31 760 | 1 939 | 2 872 | 305 | 753 | 1 414 | 1 378 | 376 | 597 | 182 | 64 |
| Rio Blanco | 277 | 6.5 | 40 792 | 677 | 217 | 38 | 35 | 37 | 35 | 13 | 14 | 2 | 2 |
| Rio Grande | 407 | 5.9 | 34 051 | 1 504 | 174 | 65 | 76 | 104 | 102 | 33 | 39 | 17 | 5 |
| Routt | 1 200 | 5.1 | 51 628 | 173 | 693 | 161 | 369 | 96 | 91 | 36 | 33 | 6 | 9 |
| Saguache | 155 | 8.9 | 24 820 | 2 981 | 72 | 11 | 28 | 39 | 38 | 11 | 16 | 6 | 3 |
| San Juan | 21 | 5.3 | 29 854 | 2 315 | 9 | 2 | 5 | 3 | 3 | 1 | 1 | 0 | 0 |
| San Miguel | 358 | 4.4 | 47 742 | 272 | 210 | 55 | 117 | 23 | 22 | 9 | 6 | 2 | 3 |
| Sedgwick | 120 | 11.9 | 50 745 | 194 | 34 | 40 | 18 | 23 | 23 | 8 | 11 | 2 | 1 |
| Summit | 1 304 | 5.5 | 46 627 | 313 | 778 | 144 | 439 | 88 | 81 | 36 | 23 | 6 | 10 |
| Teller | 988 | 4.7 | 42 297 | 557 | 307 | 43 | 165 | 150 | 145 | 63 | 45 | 12 | 9 |
| Washington | 196 | 14.8 | 41 158 | 647 | 55 | 61 | 32 | 31 | 30 | 11 | 13 | 3 | 1 |
| Weld | 7 756 | 7.2 | 29 986 | 2 294 | 4 513 | 786 | 1 119 | 1 349 | 1 292 | 425 | 526 | 141 | 92 |
| Yuma | 430 | 14.3 | 42 572 | 531 | 185 | 135 | 77 | 62 | 60 | 21 | 28 | 6 | 2 |
| CONNECTICUT | 207 329 | 4.6 | 57 902 | X | 125 819 | 21 222 | 40 015 | 28 961 | 28 170 | 9 115 | 13 280 | 2 540 | 1 966 |
| Fairfield | 72 687 | 4.3 | 78 504 | 9 | 42 770 | 9 641 | 16 294 | 6 961 | 6 756 | 2 193 | 3 283 | 590 | 447 |
| Hartford | 48 291 | 5.4 | 53 974 | 131 | 38 810 | 4 923 | 8 292 | 7 805 | 7 607 | 2 320 | 3 691 | 765 | 506 |
| Litchfield | 10 032 | 4.9 | 53 139 | 139 | 3 303 | 926 | 2 170 | 1 372 | 1 330 | 568 | 536 | 74 | 102 |
| Middlesex | 8 999 | 4.2 | 54 198 | 127 | 4 192 | 763 | 1 797 | 1 147 | 1 110 | 473 | 435 | 66 | 84 |
| New Haven | 42 606 | 4.8 | 49 478 | 221 | 23 506 | 3 469 | 7 064 | 7 650 | 7 459 | 2 204 | 3 628 | 743 | 522 |
| New London | 12 978 | 3.6 | 47 452 | 284 | 8 816 | 782 | 2 588 | 2 150 | 2 091 | 713 | 935 | 169 | 155 |

1. Based on the resident population estimated as of July 1 of the year shown.  2. Includes supplements to wages and salaries.

| STATE County | Earnings, 2011 | | | | | | | | | Social Security beneficiaries, December 2011 | | Supple-mental Security Income recipients, December 2011 | Housing units, 2010 | |
|---|---|---|---|---|---|---|---|---|---|---|---|---|---|---|
| | | | | Percent by selected industries | | | | | | | | | | |
| | | | Goods-related[1] | | Service-related and health | | | | | | | | | |
| | Total (mil dol) | Farm | Total | Manu-facturing | Infor-mation and profes-sional and technical services | Retail trade | Finance, insur-ance, and real estate | Health care and social services | Govern-ment | Number | Rate[2] | | Total | Percent change, 2000–2010 |
| | 75 | 76 | 77 | 78 | 79 | 80 | 81 | 82 | 83 | 84 | 85 | 86 | 87 | 88 |
| COLORADO—Cont'd | | | | | | | | | | | | | | |
| Boulder | 12 907 | 0.1 | 16.3 | 12.5 | 30.3 | 4.8 | 6.4 | 9.4 | 15.2 | 37 330 | 125 | 2 445 | 127 071 | 14.0 |
| Broomfield | 2 836 | 0.0 | 23.6 | 19.4 | 34.0 | 6.5 | 5.5 | 3.0 | 2.8 | 7 140 | 124 | 326 | 22 646 | 54.5 |
| Chaffee | 308 | 0.5 | 12.6 | 2.0 | 5.9 | 11.7 | 8.2 | 6.9 | 29.7 | 4 490 | 250 | 222 | 10 020 | 19.4 |
| Cheyenne | 82 | 46.9 | D | D | D | 2.7 | D | 0.0 | 17.5 | 320 | 171 | 11 | 975 | -11.8 |
| Clear Creek | 298 | 0.0 | 36.5 | 0.3 | 11.6 | 3.2 | 8.2 | D | 12.8 | 1 455 | 161 | 83 | 5 685 | 10.9 |
| Conejos | 85 | 20.5 | D | 0.4 | D | 8.8 | D | 9.6 | 28.8 | 1 745 | 210 | 365 | 4 286 | 10.3 |
| Costilla | 37 | 24.3 | D | D | D | 4.2 | D | D | 33.9 | 1 055 | 288 | 226 | 2 613 | 18.7 |
| Crowley | 60 | 6.4 | D | 0.0 | 0.7 | 4.8 | D | D | 46.9 | 825 | 144 | 156 | 1 559 | 1.1 |
| Custer | 55 | 6.2 | 30.2 | 3.1 | D | 8.2 | 7.1 | D | 19.7 | 1 250 | 297 | 43 | 3 956 | 32.4 |
| Delta | 458 | 3.3 | 26.2 | 5.8 | 4.3 | 8.7 | 4.2 | 8.4 | 27.2 | 7 930 | 260 | 466 | 14 572 | 17.8 |
| Denver | 40 565 | 0.0 | 13.1 | 3.4 | 19.8 | 3.0 | 14.3 | 7.1 | 14.6 | 78 340 | 126 | 14 624 | 285 797 | 13.8 |
| Dolores | 25 | 27.6 | D | D | D | 6.9 | D | 2.8 | 30.8 | 525 | 255 | 27 | 1 468 | 23.1 |
| Douglas | 6 823 | 0.0 | 9.7 | 2.5 | 23.4 | 7.5 | 12.2 | 7.2 | 9.6 | 28 675 | 98 | 931 | 106 859 | 68.7 |
| Eagle | 1 877 | 0.3 | D | 0.8 | 7.5 | 8.0 | 15.7 | 9.5 | 10.0 | 3 690 | 71 | 85 | 31 312 | 41.6 |
| Elbert | 196 | 2.6 | D | 3.6 | 11.0 | 7.9 | 6.3 | 2.2 | 22.5 | 3 295 | 142 | 92 | 8 939 | 25.7 |
| El Paso | 19 598 | 0.0 | 9.3 | 4.9 | 14.7 | 5.8 | 6.3 | 8.0 | 39.1 | 86 985 | 137 | 7 763 | 252 852 | 24.9 |
| Fremont | 728 | -0.2 | 10.7 | 4.3 | D | 7.5 | 3.0 | 12.2 | 48.9 | 11 000 | 232 | 1 014 | 19 242 | 12.2 |
| Garfield | 1 610 | 0.2 | 29.8 | 1.6 | 6.4 | 7.5 | 6.5 | 9.4 | 17.3 | 6 230 | 111 | 318 | 23 309 | 34.5 |
| Gilpin | 283 | 0.0 | D | D | 1.7 | 0.3 | 0.6 | D | 9.7 | 695 | 127 | 25 | 3 560 | 21.1 |
| Grand | 344 | 2.6 | 13.3 | 1.3 | 9.4 | 7.1 | 8.4 | 3.3 | 20.1 | 1 855 | 128 | 56 | 16 061 | 47.4 |
| Gunnison | 410 | 0.4 | D | 0.8 | 6.4 | 7.3 | 5.3 | 3.7 | 24.8 | 1 805 | 117 | 73 | 11 412 | 24.9 |
| Hinsdale | 12 | 7.6 | D | 0.0 | D | D | D | D | 29.3 | 190 | 229 | 0 | 1 388 | 6.4 |
| Huerfano | 82 | -0.2 | D | 5.3 | 4.4 | 10.6 | 3.5 | D | 26.4 | 2 080 | 319 | 284 | 5 075 | 10.4 |
| Jackson | 40 | 30.7 | D | D | D | 7.7 | D | 1.6 | 22.1 | 305 | 223 | 13 | 1 286 | 12.3 |
| Jefferson | 14 977 | 0.0 | 18.5 | 12.9 | 16.0 | 6.7 | 7.5 | 10.3 | 17.8 | 84 665 | 157 | 5 072 | 229 967 | 8.6 |
| Kiowa | 45 | 38.0 | D | D | D | 1.9 | D | 0.0 | 26.2 | 325 | 227 | 11 | 805 | -1.5 |
| Kit Carson | 233 | 39.2 | D | 2.2 | 1.9 | 4.1 | 3.5 | 2.6 | 14.6 | 1 530 | 188 | 79 | 3 527 | 2.8 |
| Lake | 94 | 0.0 | D | D | 4.3 | 6.3 | 2.4 | D | 40.0 | 835 | 112 | 65 | 4 271 | 9.1 |
| La Plata | 1 596 | 0.3 | 18.9 | 1.6 | 10.0 | 7.0 | 10.4 | 12.0 | 21.2 | 7 900 | 152 | 406 | 25 860 | 24.5 |
| Larimer | 8 227 | 0.4 | 21.6 | 13.6 | 13.5 | 6.8 | 5.7 | 13.0 | 20.0 | 46 310 | 152 | 2 536 | 132 722 | 25.9 |
| Las Animas | 277 | 0.6 | 19.8 | 1.6 | D | 7.6 | 5.4 | 10.7 | 29.5 | 3 475 | 231 | 539 | 8 217 | 7.7 |
| Lincoln | 122 | 10.8 | D | D | D | 7.8 | 3.8 | 5.2 | 42.6 | 915 | 168 | 68 | 2 420 | 0.6 |
| Logan | 545 | 14.1 | 11.0 | 3.4 | 3.0 | 11.2 | 3.6 | D | 22.6 | 3 905 | 173 | 382 | 8 981 | 6.2 |
| Mesa | 3 428 | 0.2 | 21.0 | 4.1 | 6.8 | 8.0 | 6.7 | 15.1 | 17.4 | 28 070 | 191 | 2 288 | 62 644 | 28.6 |
| Mineral | 20 | -2.4 | D | D | D | 7.2 | D | D | 18.0 | 230 | 325 | 0 | 1 201 | 7.3 |
| Moffat | 381 | 5.8 | 30.9 | 1.0 | D | 7.7 | 2.8 | D | 17.0 | 2 070 | 154 | 159 | 6 196 | 10.0 |
| Montezuma | 449 | 2.2 | 15.4 | 3.3 | 4.1 | 10.5 | 4.1 | D | 31.0 | 5 555 | 218 | 444 | 12 094 | 15.2 |
| Montrose | 801 | 0.9 | 21.7 | 7.3 | 5.4 | 9.7 | 5.7 | 11.9 | 22.4 | 9 410 | 229 | 653 | 18 250 | 28.5 |
| Morgan | 691 | 7.9 | 37.5 | 19.7 | D | 4.7 | 4.0 | D | 15.4 | 4 685 | 166 | 434 | 11 490 | 10.4 |
| Otero | 322 | 8.4 | D | 6.7 | 3.1 | 7.9 | 4.8 | D | 25.2 | 4 300 | 228 | 781 | 8 969 | 1.8 |
| Ouray | 74 | 1.2 | 18.5 | 1.7 | 11.1 | 9.7 | 6.5 | D | 24.1 | 1 025 | 235 | 31 | 3 083 | 43.7 |
| Park | 131 | 0.1 | D | 2.0 | 13.1 | 6.4 | 4.5 | 3.2 | 30.9 | 2 670 | 166 | 100 | 13 947 | 30.4 |
| Phillips | 119 | 36.6 | D | 0.4 | D | 4.2 | 3.4 | D | 21.8 | 915 | 208 | 57 | 2 087 | 3.6 |
| Pitkin | 1 071 | 0.1 | D | 0.5 | 10.6 | 6.3 | 15.5 | 3.2 | 13.0 | 2 085 | 122 | 20 | 12 953 | 28.3 |
| Prowers | 275 | 15.8 | 14.0 | 5.4 | D | 9.1 | 5.0 | 5.5 | 25.4 | 2 285 | 182 | 354 | 5 942 | -0.6 |
| Pueblo | 3 178 | 0.3 | D | 10.8 | 4.2 | 7.9 | 3.7 | 19.2 | 22.8 | 32 820 | 204 | 6 001 | 69 526 | 18.0 |
| Rio Blanco | 255 | 2.7 | 46.2 | 0.8 | D | 5.2 | 1.3 | 0.8 | 22.5 | 1 010 | 149 | 37 | 3 309 | 15.9 |
| Rio Grande | 239 | 7.3 | D | 2.3 | 2.4 | 5.1 | 3.7 | D | 19.9 | 2 975 | 249 | 433 | 6 630 | 10.4 |
| Routt | 854 | 1.3 | 21.1 | 0.9 | 8.4 | 8.1 | 9.6 | 9.5 | 11.4 | 2 570 | 111 | 88 | 16 303 | 45.4 |
| Saguache | 82 | 19.7 | D | 1.5 | D | 6.3 | 1.5 | 2.9 | 27.9 | 970 | 156 | 91 | 3 843 | 24.5 |
| San Juan | 11 | 0.0 | D | D | D | D | D | D | 33.6 | 105 | 152 | 0 | 756 | 19.6 |
| San Miguel | 265 | 0.4 | D | 2.3 | 7.7 | 6.7 | 10.2 | 3.6 | 16.7 | 675 | 90 | 24 | 6 638 | 27.7 |
| Sedgwick | 74 | 54.6 | D | 1.2 | D | 3.3 | D | D | 19.5 | 650 | 275 | 42 | 1 415 | 2.0 |
| Summit | 922 | 0.0 | D | 0.5 | 9.9 | 9.4 | 11.8 | 7.2 | 14.1 | 2 395 | 86 | 37 | 29 842 | 23.3 |
| Teller | 350 | -0.6 | 16.3 | 0.9 | 10.8 | 8.0 | 4.5 | 5.2 | 18.5 | 4 740 | 203 | 199 | 12 643 | 22.0 |
| Washington | 116 | 46.4 | D | D | D | 5.2 | D | 0.8 | 18.2 | 925 | 194 | 43 | 2 434 | 5.5 |
| Weld | 5 299 | 4.0 | 30.1 | 11.7 | 4.4 | 6.0 | 6.0 | 8.6 | 14.5 | 33 650 | 130 | 3 292 | 96 281 | 45.5 |
| Yuma | 320 | 41.9 | 12.4 | 2.3 | 1.8 | 4.6 | 3.9 | 3.3 | 15.0 | 1 805 | 179 | 116 | 4 466 | 4.0 |
| CONNECTICUT | 147 040 | 0.1 | 16.5 | 11.7 | 11.7 | 5.4 | 18.7 | 11.5 | 13.3 | 630 447 | 176 | 59 784 | 1 487 891 | 7.4 |
| Fairfield | 52 411 | 0.0 | D | 9.7 | 14.4 | 5.2 | 28.0 | 8.4 | 7.1 | 143 870 | 155 | 11 577 | 361 221 | 6.4 |
| Hartford | 43 734 | 0.1 | 16.5 | 12.5 | 11.1 | 4.7 | 22.6 | 11.6 | 13.5 | 164 020 | 183 | 19 935 | 374 249 | 6.0 |
| Litchfield | 4 229 | 0.5 | 27.4 | 15.2 | 7.4 | 8.6 | 4.9 | 13.2 | 13.6 | 38 740 | 205 | 1 683 | 87 550 | 10.4 |
| Middlesex | 4 955 | 0.1 | D | 17.2 | 8.4 | 6.6 | 5.4 | 15.5 | 17.6 | 31 740 | 191 | 1 479 | 74 837 | 11.2 |
| New Haven | 26 975 | 0.1 | D | 11.0 | 10.6 | 6.1 | 7.5 | 16.2 | 14.8 | 155 530 | 181 | 18 536 | 362 004 | 6.2 |
| New London | 9 597 | 0.4 | 21.6 | 17.0 | 8.9 | 5.5 | 3.2 | 11.0 | 31.1 | 50 970 | 186 | 3 686 | 120 994 | 9.3 |

1. Includes mining, construction, and manufacturing.    2. Per 1,000 resident population enumerated in the 2010 census.

# Table B. States and Counties — Housing, Labor Force, and Employment

| | Housing units, 2007–2011 | | | | | | | | Civilian labor force, 2012 | | Unemployment | | Civilian employment,[6] 2007–2011 | | |
|---|---|---|---|---|---|---|---|---|---|---|---|---|---|---|---|
| | Occupied units | | | | | | | | | | | | | Percent | |
| | | Owner-occupied | | | | Renter-occupied | | | | | | | | | |
| STATE County | Total | Percent | Median value[1] | With a mortgage | Without a mortgage[2] | Median rent[3] | Median rent as a percent of income | Substandard units[4] (percent) | Total | Percent change, 2011–2012 | Total | Rate[5] | Total | Management, business, science and arts | Construction, production, and maintenance occupations |
| | 89 | 90 | 91 | 92 | 93 | 94 | 95 | 96 | 97 | 98 | 99 | 100 | 101 | 102 | 103 |
| COLORADO—Cont'd | | | | | | | | | | | | | | | |
| Boulder | 118 545 | 64.2 | 353 000 | 24.0 | 9.9 | 1 026 | 35.2 | 2.8 | 179 816 | 1.8 | 10 899 | 6.1 | 155 375 | 51.7 | 12.0 |
| Broomfield | 20 841 | 72.1 | 270 500 | 23.2 | 12.0 | 1 037 | 28.2 | 2.3 | 31 506 | 1.4 | 2 249 | 7.1 | 28 829 | 49.2 | 14.3 |
| Chaffee | 7 715 | 74.5 | 244 600 | 27.5 | 9.9 | 770 | 30.3 | 1.9 | 8 554 | 1.2 | 605 | 7.1 | 8 182 | 34.0 | 22.0 |
| Cheyenne | 869 | 79.6 | 83 200 | 20.1 | 9.9 | 462 | 18.2 | 2.2 | 1 276 | -5.5 | 50 | 3.9 | 1 105 | 37.8 | 27.3 |
| Clear Creek | 4 031 | 80.5 | 279 600 | 26.9 | 11.7 | 826 | 24.7 | 1.1 | 5 600 | 1.6 | 416 | 7.4 | 5 329 | 35.9 | 23.3 |
| Conejos | 3 062 | 77.2 | 110 200 | 23.6 | 11.1 | 502 | 28.6 | 6.4 | 3 793 | -0.7 | 376 | 9.9 | 3 244 | 36.1 | 22.9 |
| Costilla | 1 325 | 76.8 | 102 600 | 29.6 | 12.5 | 489 | 48.0 | 4.2 | 1 469 | 2.4 | 187 | 12.7 | 1 385 | 24.3 | 42.5 |
| Crowley | 1 180 | 77.7 | 83 600 | 21.3 | 11.8 | 548 | 25.7 | 4.2 | 1 692 | -2.4 | 173 | 10.2 | 1 456 | 25.5 | 30.6 |
| Custer | 1 827 | 84.1 | 225 600 | 30.7 | 11.1 | 704 | 26.1 | 3.2 | 1 904 | -1.8 | 131 | 6.9 | 1 534 | 40.5 | 19.9 |
| Delta | 12 660 | 74.6 | 198 400 | 24.9 | 12.3 | 721 | 29.6 | 2.5 | 16 257 | 0.0 | 1 387 | 8.5 | 12 613 | 30.2 | 32.0 |
| Denver | 258 132 | 51.7 | 243 400 | 25.2 | 10.6 | 832 | 30.2 | 3.7 | 328 933 | 1.0 | 27 880 | 8.5 | 308 945 | 41.5 | 16.9 |
| Dolores | 871 | 80.9 | 130 800 | 27.8 | 9.9 | 618 | 21.8 | 2.5 | 1 018 | 0.8 | 97 | 9.5 | 945 | 27.7 | 38.1 |
| Douglas | 100 795 | 81.5 | 337 900 | 23.9 | 9.9 | 1 227 | 26.0 | 0.8 | 162 971 | 1.5 | 10 357 | 6.4 | 146 604 | 53.1 | 9.4 |
| Eagle | 18 362 | 62.8 | 530 200 | 28.7 | 13.2 | 1 169 | 29.1 | 4.7 | 29 793 | 1.7 | 2 405 | 8.1 | 31 542 | 32.4 | 21.2 |
| Elbert | 8 175 | 90.6 | 344 200 | 28.1 | 10.8 | 956 | 32.3 | 1.6 | 12 824 | 1.3 | 919 | 7.2 | 11 889 | 39.0 | 20.7 |
| El Paso | 230 620 | 65.6 | 217 000 | 24.5 | 9.9 | 854 | 29.6 | 2.4 | 300 909 | -0.1 | 27 948 | 9.3 | 275 699 | 40.3 | 17.3 |
| Fremont | 17 294 | 71.9 | 158 200 | 26.4 | 11.7 | 695 | 32.3 | 2.1 | 19 831 | -1.1 | 2 000 | 10.1 | 14 830 | 28.6 | 23.0 |
| Garfield | 20 186 | 65.4 | 343 700 | 27.5 | 9.9 | 1 127 | 30.5 | 5.1 | 33 230 | 0.8 | 2 662 | 8.0 | 29 292 | 29.2 | 29.9 |
| Gilpin | 2 442 | 70.5 | 320 700 | 26.4 | 9.9 | 1 042 | 38.9 | 0.5 | 3 581 | 1.4 | 232 | 6.5 | 3 128 | 35.0 | 17.4 |
| Grand | 5 186 | 75.5 | 283 200 | 24.8 | 9.9 | 877 | 26.7 | 2.3 | 8 616 | -0.2 | 652 | 7.6 | 8 137 | 32.1 | 24.4 |
| Gunnison | 6 351 | 58.2 | 338 100 | 27.7 | 9.9 | 858 | 30.4 | 3.2 | 8 983 | -0.9 | 596 | 6.6 | 8 871 | 32.7 | 22.7 |
| Hinsdale | 322 | 78.6 | 284 800 | 23.8 | 9.9 | 837 | 20.2 | 0.0 | 555 | -8.4 | 21 | 3.8 | 363 | 42.4 | 16.8 |
| Huerfano | 3 096 | 69.0 | 149 100 | 29.0 | 11.8 | 647 | 32.8 | 6.0 | 3 137 | -2.5 | 382 | 12.2 | 2 198 | 38.7 | 22.3 |
| Jackson | 736 | 72.3 | 122 600 | 18.5 | 9.9 | 676 | 22.5 | 2.0 | 1 118 | -8.9 | 43 | 3.8 | 829 | 27.6 | 39.8 |
| Jefferson | 217 763 | 71.4 | 259 400 | 24.4 | 10.0 | 924 | 29.7 | 1.9 | 305 325 | 1.2 | 23 080 | 7.6 | 280 618 | 42.9 | 17.2 |
| Kiowa | 719 | 71.2 | 75 100 | 20.0 | 10.2 | 599 | 26.9 | 0.4 | 959 | -4.8 | 39 | 4.1 | 866 | 40.1 | 21.0 |
| Kit Carson | 3 003 | 70.4 | 115 900 | 23.4 | 12.7 | 629 | 22.0 | 1.8 | 4 522 | -2.0 | 212 | 4.7 | 3 907 | 32.2 | 27.0 |
| Lake | 2 648 | 67.4 | 171 600 | 26.1 | 11.7 | 862 | 37.8 | 6.9 | 3 656 | 0.6 | 365 | 10.0 | 3 533 | 29.1 | 35.0 |
| La Plata | 20 769 | 69.2 | 342 600 | 26.0 | 9.9 | 964 | 29.5 | 3.1 | 30 260 | 0.7 | 2 010 | 6.6 | 27 365 | 37.8 | 20.2 |
| Larimer | 118 791 | 67.0 | 244 600 | 25.1 | 9.9 | 887 | 33.8 | 1.6 | 180 713 | 1.2 | 11 637 | 6.4 | 154 002 | 42.9 | 17.2 |
| Las Animas | 6 356 | 69.0 | 147 600 | 25.6 | 12.6 | 744 | 31.7 | 3.4 | 7 956 | 0.3 | 851 | 10.7 | 6 545 | 25.6 | 34.0 |
| Lincoln | 1 930 | 70.8 | 104 600 | 23.3 | 9.9 | 624 | 26.5 | 2.7 | 3 069 | -1.6 | 164 | 5.3 | 1 926 | 31.6 | 19.7 |
| Logan | 8 126 | 70.3 | 121 400 | 21.0 | 12.1 | 573 | 24.1 | 2.8 | 11 196 | -0.6 | 742 | 6.6 | 11 308 | 22.7 | 28.4 |
| Mesa | 58 288 | 71.9 | 222 800 | 24.4 | 9.9 | 837 | 29.9 | 3.2 | 78 619 | -0.1 | 7 235 | 9.2 | 69 053 | 33.0 | 25.4 |
| Mineral | 368 | 85.9 | 284 700 | 22.9 | 10.1 | 694 | 26.9 | 0.0 | 504 | 7.2 | 24 | 4.8 | 383 | 39.4 | 30.8 |
| Moffat | 5 347 | 74.4 | 178 400 | 23.8 | 12.5 | 741 | 29.2 | 1.9 | 8 261 | -1.6 | 639 | 7.7 | 6 870 | 22.1 | 35.9 |
| Montezuma | 10 950 | 71.1 | 191 500 | 24.6 | 10.9 | 734 | 29.7 | 4.5 | 13 121 | 0.0 | 1 121 | 8.5 | 11 606 | 34.8 | 22.4 |
| Montrose | 16 591 | 72.8 | 202 200 | 24.6 | 11.6 | 813 | 29.5 | 3.3 | 19 734 | -1.2 | 2 076 | 10.5 | 18 273 | 26.9 | 30.8 |
| Morgan | 10 513 | 63.4 | 136 700 | 24.6 | 13.7 | 677 | 27.3 | 6.6 | 15 570 | -0.7 | 1 032 | 6.6 | 12 672 | 25.9 | 38.7 |
| Otero | 7 453 | 64.3 | 93 300 | 23.1 | 12.8 | 588 | 32.7 | 2.9 | 9 037 | -2.8 | 860 | 9.5 | 7 333 | 33.7 | 21.7 |
| Ouray | 1 688 | 75.5 | 442 600 | 37.0 | 11.4 | 1 202 | 28.4 | 1.3 | 2 650 | 2.8 | 187 | 7.1 | 2 042 | 42.5 | 20.6 |
| Park | 7 000 | 88.7 | 246 100 | 27.6 | 9.9 | 1 216 | 37.1 | 1.2 | 8 968 | 1.2 | 676 | 7.5 | 8 777 | 32.3 | 26.3 |
| Phillips | 1 792 | 73.0 | 121 200 | 23.2 | 11.1 | 595 | 26.8 | 6.1 | 2 409 | -3.1 | 117 | 4.9 | 2 015 | 32.0 | 31.7 |
| Pitkin | 7 401 | 66.6 | 664 300 | 29.1 | 10.8 | 1 334 | 26.7 | 3.0 | 10 772 | 0.1 | 795 | 7.4 | 10 173 | 44.9 | 11.6 |
| Prowers | 4 996 | 66.4 | 83 100 | 19.3 | 13.5 | 547 | 26.8 | 2.2 | 6 645 | -3.7 | 434 | 6.5 | 5 902 | 32.3 | 29.3 |
| Pueblo | 61 858 | 68.5 | 140 700 | 25.4 | 12.0 | 679 | 34.3 | 2.0 | 75 795 | -0.7 | 8 089 | 10.7 | 65 675 | 30.5 | 21.3 |
| Rio Blanco | 2 499 | 72.9 | 201 600 | 20.8 | 9.9 | 713 | 23.7 | 3.0 | 4 265 | -2.4 | 256 | 6.0 | 3 300 | 28.7 | 37.6 |
| Rio Grande | 3 960 | 73.0 | 141 600 | 27.2 | 10.7 | 559 | 29.0 | 2.2 | 6 456 | -1.9 | 610 | 9.4 | 4 714 | 29.3 | 30.2 |
| Routt | 9 929 | 72.5 | 434 700 | 28.5 | 10.5 | 1 198 | 28.8 | 1.9 | 14 340 | 0.8 | 1 045 | 7.3 | 14 091 | 38.9 | 22.2 |
| Saguache | 2 695 | 70.7 | 131 400 | 28.8 | 10.3 | 604 | 28.8 | 5.5 | 3 283 | -1.0 | 340 | 10.4 | 2 774 | 24.4 | 38.2 |
| San Juan | 404 | 47.5 | 259 500 | 23.9 | 9.9 | 789 | 35.3 | 5.9 | 602 | 3.8 | 51 | 8.5 | 461 | 34.9 | 19.3 |
| San Miguel | 3 453 | 61.1 | 487 100 | 32.4 | 12.3 | 1 095 | 29.4 | 3.9 | 5 053 | -0.4 | 379 | 7.5 | 4 894 | 38.1 | 16.5 |
| Sedgwick | 1 070 | 74.4 | 83 500 | 19.3 | 11.9 | 506 | 20.6 | 1.2 | 1 624 | -0.2 | 79 | 4.9 | 1 095 | 29.5 | 29.6 |
| Summit | 11 001 | 68.6 | 465 200 | 28.3 | 11.6 | 1 163 | 27.3 | 3.1 | 16 678 | 0.4 | 1 201 | 7.2 | 17 713 | 35.4 | 20.5 |
| Teller | 9 051 | 84.5 | 229 600 | 26.0 | 9.9 | 881 | 32.8 | 2.0 | 12 279 | -0.9 | 994 | 8.1 | 11 263 | 38.6 | 17.4 |
| Washington | 2 089 | 70.7 | 117 000 | 23.0 | 11.4 | 564 | 23.9 | 1.9 | 2 876 | -0.6 | 136 | 4.7 | 2 433 | 36.6 | 26.4 |
| Weld | 88 242 | 71.1 | 193 300 | 25.4 | 11.2 | 801 | 31.9 | 4.4 | 124 972 | 1.2 | 10 915 | 8.7 | 119 511 | 32.8 | 26.4 |
| Yuma | 3 839 | 68.5 | 117 700 | 23.1 | 10.5 | 581 | 22.6 | 3.0 | 6 497 | -3.5 | 258 | 4.0 | 4 763 | 27.2 | 40.0 |
| CONNECTICUT | 1 360 115 | 68.9 | 293 100 | 26.5 | 17.0 | 1 020 | 31.4 | 2.3 | 1 879 452 | -1.2 | 157 058 | 8.4 | 1 764 755 | 40.5 | 17.8 |
| Fairfield | 332 139 | 70.4 | 466 700 | 28.2 | 18.1 | 1 249 | 32.3 | 3.0 | 476 031 | -0.9 | 36 266 | 7.6 | 442 427 | 43.4 | 15.5 |
| Hartford | 348 438 | 66.3 | 248 000 | 25.1 | 16.5 | 944 | 31.0 | 2.3 | 460 959 | -1.4 | 40 246 | 8.7 | 437 182 | 40.4 | 17.0 |
| Litchfield | 76 477 | 78.9 | 279 600 | 26.4 | 16.9 | 898 | 30.4 | 1.2 | 104 165 | -1.0 | 8 055 | 7.7 | 99 778 | 39.1 | 20.6 |
| Middlesex | 66 798 | 76.1 | 306 900 | 26.2 | 14.7 | 991 | 28.2 | 1.4 | 93 191 | -1.2 | 6 601 | 7.1 | 86 647 | 44.3 | 17.1 |
| New Haven | 330 396 | 64.8 | 270 900 | 27.2 | 18.5 | 1 030 | 33.2 | 2.4 | 448 745 | -0.9 | 41 181 | 9.2 | 424 782 | 39.0 | 19.0 |
| New London | 107 115 | 69.4 | 265 700 | 25.8 | 15.0 | 987 | 28.8 | 1.7 | 147 124 | -2.3 | 12 468 | 8.5 | 133 983 | 37.5 | 18.2 |

1. Specified owner-occupied units.   2. A value of 9.9 represents 9.9 percent or less.   3. Specified renter-occupied units. A value of 10.0 represents 10 percent or less.   4. Overcrowded or lacking complete plumbing facilities.   5. Percent of civilian labor force.   6. Persons 16 years old and over.

# Table B. States and Counties — Nonfarm Employment and Agriculture

| STATE County | Number of establish-ments | Total | Health care and social assistance | Manufac-turing | Retail trade | Finance and insurance | Professional, scientific, and technical services | Total (mil dol) | Average per employee (dollars) | Number | Fewer than 50 acres | 500 acres or more | Farm operators whose principal occu-pation is farming (percent) |
|---|---|---|---|---|---|---|---|---|---|---|---|---|---|
| | 104 | 105 | 106 | 107 | 108 | 109 | 110 | 111 | 112 | 113 | 114 | 115 | 116 |
| COLORADO—Cont'd | | | | | | | | | | | | | |
| Boulder | 11 419 | 131 872 | 18 598 | 13 934 | 16 536 | 4 125 | 24 315 | 6 982 | 52 946 | 746 | 67.2 | 6.4 | 38.6 |
| Broomfield | 1 718 | 30 797 | 1 566 | 2 744 | 4 983 | 832 | 4 576 | 1 784 | 57 925 | 24 | 66.7 | 12.5 | 29.2 |
| Chaffee | 822 | 5 036 | 666 | 145 | 999 | 244 | 226 | 138 | 27 380 | 223 | 43.0 | 17.5 | 48.4 |
| Cheyenne | 64 | 929 | D | NA | D | D | 5 | 48 | 51 807 | 380 | 3.4 | 65.8 | 46.1 |
| Clear Creek | 341 | 2 533 | 35 | 44 | 211 | D | 81 | 91 | 36 109 | 27 | 51.9 | 18.5 | 25.9 |
| Conejos | 95 | 659 | 213 | D | 187 | D | D | 19 | 28 956 | 535 | 24.3 | 22.1 | 44.1 |
| Costilla | 48 | 213 | D | D | D | D | D | 5 | 25 418 | 241 | 34.9 | 19.1 | 34.9 |
| Crowley | 42 | 605 | D | NA | 89 | 29 | D | 17 | 28 048 | 268 | 17.2 | 43.7 | 49.6 |
| Custer | 141 | 574 | D | 32 | 111 | D | 31 | 16 | 27 653 | 226 | 14.2 | 27.9 | 41.6 |
| Delta | 853 | 6 288 | 1 545 | 555 | 1 180 | 280 | 214 | 212 | 33 643 | 1 294 | 57.1 | 7.1 | 43.0 |
| Denver | 21 961 | 373 970 | 47 643 | 16 284 | 25 985 | 23 263 | 35 674 | 20 873 | 55 815 | 24 | 95.8 | 0.0 | 25.0 |
| Dolores | 45 | 191 | 30 | D | D | D | D | 6 | 30 016 | 279 | 18.3 | 28.0 | 33.7 |
| Douglas | 7 414 | 78 310 | 8 007 | 1 501 | 14 766 | 5 489 | 5 293 | 4 010 | 51 207 | 1 080 | 61.8 | 7.0 | 32.6 |
| Eagle | 3 126 | 29 625 | 1 820 | 212 | 3 660 | 733 | 1 131 | 929 | 31 346 | 152 | 40.1 | 23.0 | 33.6 |
| Elbert | 517 | 1 933 | 121 | 145 | 399 | D | 201 | 63 | 32 772 | 1 402 | 32.4 | 23.2 | 35.3 |
| El Paso | 15 743 | 212 287 | 30 904 | 11 059 | 28 567 | 9 204 | 17 716 | 8 589 | 40 459 | 1 529 | 46.8 | 17.1 | 34.5 |
| Fremont | 832 | 7 610 | 2 082 | 441 | 1 577 | 267 | 154 | 205 | 26 940 | 924 | 66.6 | 12.0 | 36.1 |
| Garfield | 2 428 | 18 169 | 2 630 | 218 | 3 004 | 635 | 951 | 810 | 44 601 | 623 | 48.6 | 16.9 | 40.1 |
| Gilpin | 110 | 4 794 | 35 | D | 23 | D | 32 | 155 | 32 286 | 27 | 37.0 | 18.5 | 33.3 |
| Grand | 818 | 6 824 | 292 | 91 | 651 | D | 713 | 186 | 27 200 | 229 | 27.1 | 29.3 | 38.0 |
| Gunnison | 1 064 | 6 383 | 498 | 82 | 916 | 135 | 345 | 187 | 29 237 | 217 | 30.0 | 29.5 | 40.6 |
| Hinsdale | 74 | 201 | D | NA | D | D | D | 5 | 24 736 | 21 | 14.3 | 14.3 | 61.9 |
| Huerfano | 163 | 1 283 | 456 | D | 264 | 27 | 67 | 34 | 26 426 | 309 | 10.0 | 46.6 | 41.7 |
| Jackson | 62 | 369 | D | D | 67 | D | D | 11 | 28 759 | 120 | 15.8 | 61.7 | 55.0 |
| Jefferson | 15 986 | 184 960 | 23 915 | 17 470 | 27 222 | 8 043 | 25 917 | 8 370 | 45 255 | 540 | 68.9 | 6.9 | 29.1 |
| Kiowa | 41 | D | D | NA | D | D | D | 7 | D | 425 | 4.7 | 58.1 | 40.2 |
| Kit Carson | 245 | 1 860 | 290 | 126 | 300 | 117 | D | 57 | 30 787 | 786 | 5.6 | 59.0 | 50.5 |
| Lake | 183 | 1 209 | D | D | 175 | D | D | 29 | 23 841 | 29 | 37.9 | 24.1 | 24.1 |
| La Plata | 2 258 | 18 368 | 2 743 | 628 | 3 182 | 909 | 1 046 | 696 | 37 906 | 1 076 | 45.4 | 10.8 | 36.5 |
| Larimer | 9 356 | 104 622 | 17 593 | 10 073 | 16 860 | 3 356 | 9 334 | 4 110 | 39 289 | 1 757 | 60.8 | 9.2 | 34.1 |
| Las Animas | 387 | 3 352 | 783 | 73 | 685 | D | 111 | 95 | 28 344 | 585 | 16.4 | 52.1 | 45.5 |
| Lincoln | 126 | 1 229 | 274 | D | D | 64 | 31 | 39 | 31 751 | 542 | 6.6 | 65.3 | 49.3 |
| Logan | 582 | 5 286 | 1 149 | 330 | 1 214 | 194 | 101 | 157 | 29 728 | 1 035 | 10.7 | 44.5 | 45.7 |
| Mesa | 4 529 | 49 509 | 9 330 | 2 305 | 8 363 | 1 843 | 2 842 | 1 840 | 37 159 | 1 767 | 71.0 | 6.6 | 36.6 |
| Mineral | 65 | D | D | D | D | D | D | D | D | 6 | 6.7 | 26.7 | 0.0 |
| Moffat | 424 | 3 785 | 483 | 65 | 737 | D | 91 | 164 | 43 342 | 503 | 25.6 | 32.4 | 29.8 |
| Montezuma | 747 | 6 456 | 1 304 | 254 | 1 239 | 190 | 240 | 204 | 31 564 | 1 123 | 47.5 | 11.8 | 37.8 |
| Montrose | 1 236 | 10 514 | 2 286 | 1 034 | 2 125 | 355 | 463 | 348 | 33 140 | 1 045 | 51.4 | 12.0 | 40.6 |
| Morgan | 659 | 8 815 | 1 214 | 2 844 | 951 | 247 | 117 | 304 | 34 445 | 894 | 20.8 | 30.1 | 45.2 |
| Otero | 450 | 4 705 | D | 456 | 773 | 176 | 106 | 123 | 26 089 | 569 | 33.4 | 25.1 | 47.1 |
| Ouray | 255 | 910 | 48 | 28 | D | D | 66 | 27 | 30 091 | 105 | 38.1 | 25.7 | 47.6 |
| Park | 437 | 1 151 | D | 54 | 188 | 31 | 96 | 34 | 29 228 | 282 | 25.2 | 28.0 | 39.0 |
| Phillips | 133 | 966 | D | 26 | 153 | 41 | D | 32 | 33 260 | 334 | 13.2 | 54.5 | 54.8 |
| Pitkin | 1 549 | 15 916 | 747 | 107 | 1 464 | 269 | 748 | 525 | 32 962 | 82 | 32.9 | 17.1 | 48.8 |
| Prowers | 330 | 2 775 | 610 | 167 | 721 | 218 | 94 | 76 | 27 255 | 636 | 11.9 | 47.5 | 47.0 |
| Pueblo | 3 093 | 45 865 | 12 205 | 4 201 | 7 887 | 1 190 | 1 595 | 1 493 | 32 552 | 881 | 41.2 | 23.7 | 38.7 |
| Rio Blanco | 236 | 1 760 | D | D | 204 | 73 | 52 | 97 | 55 327 | 285 | 31.6 | 33.0 | 41.4 |
| Rio Grande | 364 | 2 846 | 434 | 95 | 417 | 120 | 62 | 77 | 26 923 | 390 | 23.6 | 26.2 | 60.8 |
| Routt | 1 541 | 15 479 | 1 152 | 127 | 1 562 | 282 | 570 | 574 | 37 084 | 610 | 36.7 | 25.2 | 28.4 |
| Saguache | 123 | 739 | 71 | D | 77 | D | 14 | 22 | 30 000 | 242 | 8.3 | 45.9 | 62.4 |
| San Juan | 70 | 177 | D | 6 | 25 | NA | 6 | 4 | 23 712 | 0 | 0.0 | 0.0 | 0.0 |
| San Miguel | 630 | 4 565 | 141 | D | 488 | D | 215 | 120 | 26 306 | 123 | 31.7 | 29.3 | 39.8 |
| Sedgwick | 68 | 371 | D | 30 | 88 | D | D | 9 | 25 094 | 193 | 8.8 | 53.9 | 62.7 |
| Summit | 2 075 | 18 873 | 835 | 136 | 3 101 | 250 | 681 | 457 | 24 229 | 41 | 12.2 | 39.0 | 43.9 |
| Teller | 684 | 5 071 | 455 | 51 | 750 | 141 | 256 | 160 | 31 458 | 126 | 46.8 | 23.8 | 32.5 |
| Washington | 104 | 488 | 40 | D | 67 | D | 22 | 17 | 35 537 | 1 010 | 9.5 | 47.3 | 43.9 |
| Weld | 5 125 | 66 594 | 8 121 | 11 464 | 8 040 | 3 597 | 2 184 | 2 883 | 43 293 | 3 921 | 34.4 | 18.1 | 40.9 |
| Yuma | 361 | 2 556 | 587 | 76 | 431 | D | 60 | 86 | 33 833 | 970 | 11.2 | 55.2 | 51.4 |
| CONNECTICUT | 88 040 | 1 442 620 | 265 810 | 150 646 | 180 535 | 115 490 | 101 163 | 82 131 | 56 932 | 4 916 | 63.6 | 2.1 | 46.2 |
| Fairfield | 26 725 | 398 342 | 62 118 | 33 141 | 48 321 | 38 774 | 34 556 | 31 040 | 77 922 | 310 | 71.0 | 2.6 | 47.4 |
| Hartford | 22 470 | 432 172 | 78 750 | 45 972 | 50 176 | 55 108 | 30 058 | 23 410 | 54 168 | 790 | 65.3 | 1.8 | 47.8 |
| Litchfield | 4 909 | 51 070 | 9 970 | 8 407 | 8 530 | 1 502 | 1 722 | 2 050 | 40 147 | 979 | 61.1 | 3.2 | 45.5 |
| Middlesex | 4 139 | 58 100 | 13 478 | 10 371 | 8 396 | 1 865 | 2 527 | 2 539 | 43 700 | 393 | 79.6 | 0.8 | 41.5 |
| New Haven | 19 261 | 325 467 | 71 493 | 32 012 | 41 737 | 11 717 | 16 868 | 15 243 | 46 834 | 573 | 70.5 | 1.4 | 50.6 |
| New London | 5 675 | 105 276 | 16 975 | D | 13 882 | 2 104 | 9 185 | 4 777 | 45 377 | 793 | 58.9 | 1.5 | 44.6 |

# Table B. States and Counties — **Agriculture**

| STATE County | Land in farms | | | | | Value of land and buildings (dollars) | | Value of machinery and equipment, average per farm (dollars) | Value of products sold | | | | Percent of farms with sales of: | | Government payments | |
|---|---|---|---|---|---|---|---|---|---|---|---|---|---|---|---|---|
| | | | Acres | | | | | | | | Percent from: | | | | | |
| | Acreage (1,000) | Percent change, 2002–2007 | Average size of farm | Total irrigated (1,000) | Total cropland (1,000) | Average per farm | Average per acre | | Total (mil dol) | Average per farm (dollars) | Crops | Live-stock and poultry products | $10,000 or more | $100,000 or more | Total ($1,000) | Percent of farms |
| | 117 | 118 | 119 | 120 | 121 | 122 | 123 | 124 | 125 | 126 | 127 | 128 | 129 | 130 | 131 | 132 |
| COLORADO—Cont'd | | | | | | | | | | | | | | | | |
| Boulder | 138 | 27.8 | 185 | 33.9 | 54.4 | 588 686 | 3 190 | 66 628 | 34.0 | 45 625 | 76.4 | 23.6 | 31.2 | 6.8 | 376 | 11.1 |
| Broomfield | 6 | NA | 260 | 1.0 | 4.9 | 431 533 | 1 657 | 50 167 | 1.0 | 39 928 | 51.9 | 48.1 | 12.5 | 8.3 | 20 | 25.0 |
| Chaffee | 79 | 11.3 | 356 | 15.1 | 21.9 | 752 697 | 2 114 | 64 166 | 8.1 | 36 284 | 37.9 | 62.1 | 35.9 | 9.9 | 33 | 5.8 |
| Cheyenne | 900 | 21.6 | 2 367 | 33.0 | 512.0 | 1 528 587 | 646 | 155 582 | 71.1 | 187 099 | 76.3 | 23.7 | 51.6 | 33.2 | 6 890 | 80.3 |
| Clear Creek | 12 | NA | 461 | 0.1 | 1.4 | 579 421 | 1 256 | 50 000 | 0.1 | 4 690 | D | D | 7.4 | 0.0 | D | 7.4 |
| Conejos | 229 | -14.6 | 427 | 119.1 | 123.0 | 534 397 | 1 250 | 97 926 | 31.6 | 59 007 | 59.6 | 40.4 | 46.5 | 14.2 | 671 | 27.1 |
| Costilla | 401 | 13.3 | 1 665 | 63.5 | 59.0 | 1 356 077 | 815 | 143 398 | 26.7 | 110 623 | 85.7 | 14.3 | 34.4 | 13.3 | 393 | 29.5 |
| Crowley | 451 | 20.3 | 1 684 | 9.8 | 62.4 | 850 123 | 505 | 75 316 | 110.9 | 413 888 | 1.4 | 98.6 | 34.7 | 13.4 | 1 345 | 49.3 |
| Custer | 138 | 13.1 | 610 | 18.2 | 26.0 | 1 000 638 | 1 641 | 80 386 | 8.4 | 37 274 | 26.7 | 73.3 | 33.2 | 8.4 | 94 | 9.7 |
| Delta | 253 | -3.4 | 195 | 66.2 | 67.3 | 565 016 | 2 895 | 61 140 | 46.8 | 36 167 | 43.1 | 56.9 | 34.3 | 6.6 | 725 | 9.1 |
| Denver | 1 | NA | 25 | D | 0.2 | 369 472 | 14 560 | 46 939 | 0.6 | 23 356 | D | D | 29.2 | 12.5 | 1 | 12.5 |
| Dolores | 174 | 9.4 | 623 | 9.4 | 82.1 | 657 975 | 1 056 | 65 143 | 8.8 | 31 719 | 70.0 | 30.0 | 28.7 | 9.3 | 1 114 | 62.7 |
| Douglas | 189 | -5.0 | 175 | 3.5 | 35.1 | 563 587 | 3 217 | 50 075 | 15.9 | 14 760 | 47.7 | 52.3 | 17.4 | 2.0 | 163 | 4.0 |
| Eagle | 124 | 6.9 | 816 | 11.1 | 12.3 | 932 684 | 1 143 | 83 714 | 4.8 | 31 816 | 29.8 | 70.2 | 30.9 | 5.9 | 210 | 6.6 |
| Elbert | 1 134 | 6.2 | 809 | 12.4 | 224.0 | 820 923 | 1 015 | 64 340 | 40.7 | 29 047 | 32.5 | 67.5 | 26.1 | 5.8 | 2 488 | 18.5 |
| El Paso | 616 | -24.1 | 403 | 15.9 | 88.7 | 538 722 | 1 336 | 54 664 | 39.4 | 25 783 | 50.5 | 49.5 | 21.1 | 3.2 | 806 | 8.8 |
| Fremont | 296 | 11.7 | 320 | 11.8 | 25.6 | 498 287 | 1 556 | 46 486 | 19.3 | 20 894 | 24.8 | 75.2 | 18.4 | 2.2 | 140 | 7.6 |
| Garfield | 335 | -17.1 | 538 | 43.7 | 50.4 | 974 591 | 1 811 | 79 960 | 22.2 | 35 639 | 30.8 | 69.2 | 34.3 | 10.0 | 358 | 7.1 |
| Gilpin | 13 | 116.7 | 492 | D | 0.3 | 629 973 | 1 280 | 32 368 | 0.3 | 12 157 | 0.6 | 99.4 | 18.5 | 7.4 | D | 7.4 |
| Grand | 208 | -5.5 | 910 | 43.1 | 38.8 | 1 376 888 | 1 513 | 110 654 | 9.4 | 40 897 | 15.7 | 84.3 | 31.9 | 10.9 | 108 | 5.2 |
| Gunnison | 174 | 5.5 | 800 | 40.7 | 33.8 | 1 432 979 | 1 790 | 80 419 | 10.7 | 49 450 | 16.8 | 83.2 | 40.1 | 12.4 | 16 | 2.3 |
| Hinsdale | 6 | -33.3 | 281 | 1.9 | 0.8 | 772 668 | 2 752 | 40 109 | 0.8 | 39 310 | 0.0 | 100.0 | 42.9 | 28.6 | D | 9.5 |
| Huerfano | 519 | -14.6 | 1 678 | 13.9 | 35.8 | 1 121 356 | 668 | 65 511 | 12.3 | 39 691 | 28.2 | 71.8 | 35.6 | 7.1 | 211 | 11.3 |
| Jackson | 387 | -11.6 | 3 226 | 89.6 | 80.3 | 3 148 162 | 976 | 153 620 | 21.2 | 176 660 | 18.3 | 81.7 | 51.7 | 29.2 | 95 | 6.7 |
| Jefferson | 93 | 3.3 | 173 | 4.2 | 15.2 | 588 271 | 3 405 | 44 815 | 11.1 | 20 568 | 81.4 | 18.6 | 15.4 | 3.7 | 42 | 3.7 |
| Kiowa | 958 | 6.8 | 2 254 | 3.3 | 616.8 | 1 223 630 | 543 | 137 062 | 68.4 | 160 918 | 75.9 | 24.1 | 44.5 | 24.2 | 7 870 | 79.1 |
| Kit Carson | 1 352 | 8.4 | 1 721 | 118.0 | 885.8 | 1 338 431 | 778 | 243 340 | 337.0 | 428 735 | 34.1 | 65.9 | 53.8 | 33.8 | 13 422 | 79.4 |
| Lake | 15 | -11.8 | 512 | 2.7 | 6.1 | 873 671 | 1 707 | 44 603 | 0.6 | 21 114 | D | D | 20.7 | 6.9 | D | 6.9 |
| La Plata | 570 | 1.2 | 530 | 66.0 | 76.8 | 734 070 | 1 385 | 73 039 | 19.8 | 18 393 | 39.7 | 60.3 | 27.7 | 4.2 | 1 045 | 14.6 |
| Larimer | 490 | -6.1 | 279 | 63.4 | 120.0 | 695 145 | 2 494 | 63 923 | 128.1 | 72 921 | 38.9 | 61.1 | 26.0 | 6.8 | 803 | 9.0 |
| Las Animas | 2 179 | -5.5 | 3 725 | 35.1 | 109.5 | 1 708 606 | 459 | 71 216 | 25.4 | 43 414 | 13.4 | 86.6 | 40.3 | 12.0 | 1 431 | 26.3 |
| Lincoln | 1 400 | -2.0 | 2 583 | 9.7 | 576.0 | 1 488 765 | 576 | 132 201 | 71.0 | 130 939 | 60.1 | 39.9 | 50.0 | 29.9 | 8 037 | 69.6 |
| Logan | 1 132 | 1.9 | 1 094 | 100.3 | 603.0 | 951 244 | 870 | 136 747 | 442.1 | 427 157 | 18.0 | 82.0 | 55.9 | 25.6 | 9 604 | 74.1 |
| Mesa | 373 | -3.1 | 211 | 64.3 | 131.2 | 703 108 | 3 335 | 57 102 | 61.2 | 34 652 | 49.4 | 50.6 | 28.1 | 5.7 | 476 | 7.9 |
| Mineral | 9 | 125.0 | 591 | 0.8 | 1.8 | 1 042 017 | 1 763 | 27 487 | 0.1 | 8 427 | D | D | 20.0 | 0.0 | 0 | 0.0 |
| Moffat | 837 | -17.8 | 1 663 | 28.5 | 135.1 | 1 200 473 | 722 | 74 555 | 28.3 | 56 269 | 13.2 | 86.8 | 29.4 | 11.7 | 1 749 | 31.4 |
| Montezuma | 704 | -14.0 | 627 | 57.1 | 103.9 | 577 679 | 921 | 66 298 | 26.7 | 23 752 | 64.8 | 35.2 | 30.9 | 5.5 | 1 273 | 14.5 |
| Montrose | 321 | -4.2 | 307 | 85.7 | 93.3 | 732 730 | 2 385 | 82 249 | 67.2 | 64 268 | 34.6 | 65.4 | 39.5 | 10.1 | 1 059 | 18.1 |
| Morgan | 728 | -4.0 | 814 | 94.6 | 323.0 | 890 238 | 1 093 | 148 005 | 493.9 | 552 420 | 12.9 | 87.1 | 51.0 | 22.9 | 6 459 | 58.1 |
| Otero | 624 | 14.3 | 1 097 | 55.2 | 92.9 | 657 569 | 599 | 121 810 | 111.2 | 195 408 | 24.0 | 76.0 | 50.8 | 21.6 | 1 654 | 46.0 |
| Ouray | 94 | -13.0 | 894 | 10.7 | 10.2 | 1 289 511 | 1 443 | 83 245 | 3.6 | 34 328 | 17.0 | 83.0 | 41.9 | 8.6 | 8 | 3.8 |
| Park | 324 | 8.7 | 1 148 | 9.9 | 55.9 | 979 334 | 853 | 48 960 | 5.3 | 18 659 | 3.6 | 96.4 | 20.2 | 2.8 | 42 | 3.5 |
| Phillips | 431 | -8.5 | 1 291 | 63.7 | 355.6 | 1 441 720 | 1 117 | 237 350 | 143.0 | 428 092 | 51.9 | 48.1 | 63.2 | 45.2 | 5 613 | 78.7 |
| Pitkin | 29 | 20.8 | 348 | 10.0 | 4.8 | 883 951 | 2 540 | 80 543 | 2.0 | 24 714 | 22.1 | 77.9 | 29.3 | 7.3 | D | 4.9 |
| Prowers | 1 037 | 20.3 | 1 631 | 103.2 | 552.5 | 1 125 165 | 690 | 164 018 | 263.3 | 414 027 | 31.2 | 68.8 | 48.7 | 25.2 | 7 499 | 68.2 |
| Pueblo | 911 | 17.7 | 1 034 | 24.6 | 73.5 | 692 240 | 670 | 68 533 | 49.3 | 55 904 | 32.2 | 67.8 | 29.3 | 8.3 | 1 667 | 18.8 |
| Rio Blanco | 387 | 2.7 | 1 356 | 23.0 | 55.2 | 1 302 220 | 960 | 86 839 | 15.6 | 54 607 | 10.7 | 89.3 | 36.8 | 14.0 | 573 | 24.9 |
| Rio Grande | 179 | 4.7 | 459 | 102.8 | 114.4 | 1 017 332 | 2 218 | 170 004 | 85.4 | 218 871 | 91.4 | 8.6 | 56.9 | 26.9 | 835 | 29.0 |
| Routt | 533 | 18.4 | 874 | 43.5 | 129.9 | 1 192 414 | 1 365 | 85 124 | 34.1 | 55 926 | 13.6 | 86.4 | 30.5 | 9.5 | 1 072 | 21.1 |
| Saguache | 287 | -39.8 | 1 187 | 103.3 | 118.2 | 1 550 459 | 1 306 | 252 425 | 91.5 | 377 916 | 85.9 | 14.1 | 57.0 | 36.4 | 541 | 33.5 |
| San Juan | 0 | NA | 0 | 0.0 | 0.0 | 0 | 0 | 0 | 0.0 | 0 | 0.0 | 0.0 | 0.0 | 0.0 | 0 | 0.0 |
| San Miguel | 151 | 0.0 | 1 227 | 12.7 | 17.8 | 1 764 631 | 1 438 | 69 276 | 3.4 | 27 235 | 19.5 | 80.5 | 29.3 | 5.7 | 157 | 13.8 |
| Sedgwick | 297 | 8.4 | 1 537 | 40.0 | 196.4 | 1 475 381 | 960 | 205 608 | 70.3 | 364 131 | 53.1 | 46.9 | 68.4 | 45.6 | 2 665 | 78.2 |
| Summit | 48 | 71.4 | 1 166 | 10.5 | 7.1 | 1 801 830 | 1 545 | 87 226 | 1.1 | 26 753 | 42.0 | 58.0 | 29.3 | 9.8 | D | 2.4 |
| Teller | 73 | -1.4 | 581 | 1.4 | 8.8 | 740 055 | 1 274 | 42 770 | 1.1 | 8 485 | 4.7 | 95.3 | 16.7 | 1.6 | D | 0.8 |
| Washington | 1 376 | -2.3 | 1 362 | 37.6 | 854.4 | 991 634 | 728 | 119 086 | 130.2 | 128 884 | 55.3 | 44.7 | 49.1 | 22.8 | 12 742 | 75.3 |
| Weld | 2 089 | 15.3 | 533 | 327.8 | 987.9 | 825 561 | 1 550 | 123 541 | 1 539.1 | 392 520 | 17.7 | 82.3 | 39.8 | 16.4 | 15 403 | 39.4 |
| Yuma | 1 334 | -1.5 | 1 376 | 263.8 | 697.8 | 1 438 070 | 1 045 | 207 395 | 711.4 | 733 393 | 26.9 | 73.1 | 56.1 | 35.3 | 13 685 | 69.2 |
| CONNECTICUT | 406 | 13.7 | 83 | 9.9 | 163.7 | 1 045 133 | 12 667 | 64 090 | 551.6 | 112 195 | 72.8 | 27.2 | 34.6 | 10.0 | 4 122 | 7.2 |
| Fairfield | 40 | 207.7 | 128 | 0.2 | 6.6 | 1 850 189 | 14 505 | 64 999 | 37.3 | 120 273 | 77.7 | 22.3 | 39.4 | 11.3 | 19 | 2.6 |
| Hartford | 54 | 8.0 | 68 | 5.7 | 29.6 | 992 236 | 14 651 | 89 534 | 133.6 | 169 091 | 94.7 | 5.3 | 44.6 | 15.7 | 422 | 4.6 |
| Litchfield | 87 | -7.4 | 89 | 0.3 | 39.2 | 1 127 534 | 12 628 | 54 661 | 47.4 | 48 435 | 57.8 | 42.2 | 34.2 | 7.2 | 1 533 | 9.9 |
| Middlesex | 17 | -5.6 | 42 | 0.7 | 7.4 | 729 070 | 17 237 | 54 704 | 55.8 | 141 866 | 96.9 | 3.1 | 22.9 | 6.6 | 96 | 3.3 |
| New Haven | 46 | 76.9 | 80 | 1.5 | 13.8 | 1 061 198 | 13 310 | 64 600 | 90.2 | 157 370 | 90.3 | 9.7 | 36.8 | 12.7 | 344 | 6.1 |
| New London | 63 | 6.8 | 80 | 0.6 | 25.1 | 953 549 | 11 931 | 52 855 | 110.1 | 138 800 | 46.5 | 53.5 | 29.8 | 8.1 | 479 | 9.6 |

# Table B. States and Counties — Water Use, Wholesale Trade, Retail Trade, and Real Estate

| STATE County | Water use, 2005 | | Wholesale trade,[1] 2007 | | | | Retail trade,[2] 2007 | | | | Real estate and rental and leasing,[2] 2007 | | | |
|---|---|---|---|---|---|---|---|---|---|---|---|---|---|---|
| | Total water withdrawn (mil gal/day) | Gallons withdrawn per person | Number of establishments | Number of employees | Sales (mil dol) | Annual payroll (mil dol) | Number of establishments | Number of employees | Sales (mil dol) | Annual payroll (mil dol) | Number of establishments | Number of employees | Receipts (mil dol) | Annual payroll (mil dol) |
| | 133 | 134 | 135 | 136 | 137 | 138 | 139 | 140 | 141 | 142 | 143 | 144 | 145 | 146 |
| COLORADO—Cont'd | | | | | | | | | | | | | | |
| Boulder | 203.7 | 726 | 397 | 5 129 | 2 782.1 | 427.1 | 1 244 | 17 620 | 4 039.3 | 444.5 | 669 | 2 365 | 441.7 | 83.2 |
| Broomfield | 5.2 | 120 | 68 | D | D | D | 279 | 5 355 | 1 139.8 | 111.3 | 91 | 525 | 105.3 | 15.3 |
| Chaffee | 122.9 | 7 244 | 16 | 71 | 23.6 | 1.7 | 135 | 989 | 252.6 | 24.4 | 74 | 210 | 25.9 | 4.7 |
| Cheyenne | 39.3 | 20 097 | 5 | 46 | 51.2 | 1.9 | 11 | 67 | 13.0 | 1.1 | 1 | D | D | D |
| Clear Creek | 1.7 | 186 | 13 | 33 | 7.0 | 0.8 | 48 | 238 | 73.1 | 6.2 | 23 | 180 | 6.5 | 1.5 |
| Conejos | 359.3 | 42 205 | 5 | 8 | 3.6 | 0.2 | 20 | 179 | 33.1 | 3.6 | 2 | D | D | D |
| Costilla | 173.0 | 50 529 | 2 | D | D | D | 8 | 24 | 5.7 | 0.4 | NA | NA | NA | NA |
| Crowley | 34.3 | 6 343 | NA | NA | NA | NA | 9 | 84 | 15.7 | 1.8 | 1 | D | D | D |
| Custer | 45.3 | 11 741 | 3 | D | D | D | 21 | 145 | 58.7 | 3.0 | 15 | 38 | 3.0 | 0.6 |
| Delta | 466.0 | 15 562 | 25 | 231 | 60.9 | 8.4 | 141 | 1 319 | 312.9 | 29.1 | 42 | 90 | 14.1 | 2.6 |
| Denver | 236.4 | 424 | 1 174 | 21 245 | 14 920.9 | 1 064.5 | 2 271 | 27 979 | 6 835.4 | 752.6 | 1 451 | 11 600 | 2 536.4 | 623.7 |
| Dolores | 34.7 | 19 015 | 5 | 33 | 19.2 | 0.9 | 8 | 58 | 15.0 | 0.9 | NA | NA | NA | NA |
| Douglas | 43.4 | 174 | 236 | D | D | D | 845 | 15 346 | 3 765.5 | 361.9 | 498 | 1 368 | 239.1 | 45.7 |
| Eagle | 156.8 | 3 300 | 70 | D | D | D | 449 | 4 343 | 928.8 | 120.2 | 414 | 1 728 | 268.8 | 66.5 |
| Elbert | 36.6 | 1 607 | 17 | 51 | 13.8 | 1.5 | 38 | 251 | 80.7 | 6.4 | 18 | 22 | 5.5 | 0.5 |
| El Paso | 157.1 | 278 | 457 | 5 400 | 2 810.6 | 264.3 | 2 079 | 31 302 | 7 950.2 | 773.3 | 1 132 | 3 870 | 588.1 | 114.0 |
| Fremont | 150.9 | 3 158 | 21 | D | D | D | 143 | 1 531 | 352.4 | 34.1 | 46 | 217 | 26.5 | 3.8 |
| Garfield | 352.1 | 7 069 | 63 | 625 | 442.4 | 32.2 | 325 | 3 798 | 1 184.7 | 116.0 | 182 | 676 | 114.7 | 22.6 |
| Gilpin | 0.6 | 126 | NA | NA | NA | NA | 7 | 13 | 3.2 | 0.1 | 7 | 10 | 0.8 | 0.2 |
| Grand | 230.7 | 17 460 | 6 | 17 | 5.1 | 0.5 | 124 | 918 | 193.1 | 21.3 | 99 | 720 | 75.7 | 17.4 |
| Gunnison | 559.7 | 39 346 | 10 | D | D | D | 142 | 1 024 | 211.6 | 21.9 | 92 | 233 | 27.6 | 6.0 |
| Hinsdale | 70.4 | 91 961 | NA | NA | NA | NA | 15 | 33 | 7.8 | 0.8 | 11 | D | D | D |
| Huerfano | 36.5 | 4 697 | 1 | D | D | D | 32 | 222 | 55.3 | 4.4 | 12 | 19 | 3.5 | 0.4 |
| Jackson | 428.5 | 295 939 | 1 | D | D | D | 13 | 88 | 19.4 | 1.9 | 2 | D | D | D |
| Jefferson | 86.9 | 165 | 529 | 4 492 | 2 514.1 | 238.5 | 2 054 | 31 020 | 7 282.2 | 750.6 | 925 | 3 134 | 538.0 | 104.9 |
| Kiowa | 8.6 | 6 055 | 8 | 18 | 27.0 | 0.5 | 6 | 50 | 8.0 | 0.7 | NA | NA | NA | NA |
| Kit Carson | 284.8 | 37 261 | 17 | 184 | 166.3 | 6.1 | 46 | 348 | 84.4 | 6.5 | 7 | 19 | 2.4 | 0.7 |
| Lake | 14.7 | 1 896 | 1 | D | D | D | 30 | 235 | 51.4 | 4.6 | 17 | 71 | 6.8 | 1.4 |
| La Plata | 383.5 | 8 082 | 59 | D | D | D | 345 | 3 345 | 790.4 | 83.2 | 169 | 552 | 109.5 | 17.3 |
| Larimer | 504.4 | 1 855 | 290 | 3 156 | 1 265.2 | 146.8 | 1 306 | 17 510 | 3 922.9 | 402.7 | 562 | 2 181 | 327.1 | 63.6 |
| Las Animas | 67.7 | 4 381 | 14 | 119 | 51.6 | 3.4 | 62 | 733 | 164.4 | 16.0 | 23 | 84 | 10.2 | 1.8 |
| Lincoln | 6.4 | 1 141 | 2 | D | D | D | 36 | 336 | 134.7 | 7.3 | 3 | 6 | 0.3 | 0.0 |
| Logan | 290.4 | 14 017 | 25 | D | D | D | 106 | 1 135 | 281.3 | 24.9 | 22 | 67 | 7.2 | 1.4 |
| Mesa | 926.3 | 7 132 | 219 | 2 463 | 1 179.3 | 103.2 | 693 | 8 856 | 2 389.5 | 223.8 | 323 | 1 101 | 246.9 | 40.1 |
| Mineral | 21.8 | 23 380 | 1 | D | D | D | 11 | 45 | 6.0 | 0.7 | 3 | 4 | 0.8 | 0.0 |
| Moffat | 165.4 | 12 325 | 27 | 159 | 73.2 | 6.9 | 77 | 707 | 213.0 | 18.7 | 20 | 41 | 6.5 | 0.8 |
| Montezuma | 249.7 | 10 075 | 24 | 160 | 52.1 | 5.6 | 117 | 1 335 | 301.4 | 31.2 | 34 | 111 | 18.7 | 2.8 |
| Montrose | 705.8 | 18 831 | 48 | D | D | D | 208 | 2 195 | 610.9 | 58.3 | 67 | 200 | 33.8 | 6.8 |
| Morgan | 293.5 | 10 484 | 30 | D | D | D | 105 | 1 071 | 232.8 | 22.1 | 35 | 84 | 7.9 | 1.6 |
| Otero | 393.5 | 20 183 | 24 | 188 | 59.8 | 4.9 | 87 | 837 | 171.5 | 17.4 | 21 | 119 | 14.7 | 2.4 |
| Ouray | 103.9 | 24 383 | 3 | 11 | 1.0 | 0.3 | 46 | 207 | 27.0 | 4.1 | 9 | 12 | 3.1 | 0.3 |
| Park | 22.0 | 1 296 | 8 | 17 | 3.4 | 0.5 | 47 | 209 | 55.4 | 5.1 | 31 | 39 | 4.9 | 1.0 |
| Phillips | 104.5 | 22 785 | 11 | 121 | 150.9 | 4.4 | 23 | 165 | 45.6 | 3.4 | 4 | 6 | 0.4 | 0.4 |
| Pitkin | 130.9 | 8 776 | 18 | 85 | 64.7 | 7.1 | 250 | 1 864 | 399.5 | 57.1 | 204 | 1 213 | 210.3 | 49.3 |
| Prowers | 488.0 | 35 129 | 21 | 174 | 82.0 | 4.3 | 69 | 709 | 147.0 | 14.6 | 17 | 49 | 4.6 | 0.9 |
| Pueblo | 301.3 | 1 991 | 85 | 850 | 431.0 | 37.8 | 548 | 8 064 | 1 864.6 | 192.4 | 165 | 667 | 94.9 | 18.3 |
| Rio Blanco | 241.3 | 40 405 | 2 | D | D | D | 43 | 247 | 54.7 | 5.0 | 8 | 11 | 1.8 | 0.4 |
| Rio Grande | 729.9 | 59 692 | 29 | 435 | 218.2 | 13.2 | 62 | 465 | 110.2 | 10.6 | 15 | 55 | 5.2 | 0.8 |
| Routt | 203.9 | 9 565 | 40 | 246 | 187.8 | 12.1 | 223 | 1 982 | 421.5 | 45.9 | 148 | 1 082 | 165.7 | 30.9 |
| Saguache | 509.2 | 72 415 | 12 | 156 | 57.1 | 5.4 | 18 | 86 | 20.9 | 1.6 | 1 | D | D | D |
| San Juan | 0.3 | 468 | 1 | D | D | D | 14 | 44 | 6.6 | 0.7 | 1 | D | D | D |
| San Miguel | 28.4 | 3 933 | 1 | D | D | D | 75 | 572 | 97.8 | 12.8 | 89 | 362 | 61.5 | 9.4 |
| Sedgwick | 99.7 | 39 427 | 5 | D | D | D | 12 | 106 | 33.3 | 1.9 | 1 | D | D | D |
| Summit | 66.0 | 2 651 | 26 | D | D | D | 371 | 3 391 | 641.0 | 73.9 | 271 | 1 980 | 236.7 | 51.6 |
| Teller | 6.4 | 293 | 14 | 78 | 26.3 | 2.0 | 79 | 668 | 169.0 | 14.4 | 51 | 158 | 15.2 | 3.2 |
| Washington | 120.7 | 26 041 | 7 | 44 | 42.6 | 1.9 | 20 | 87 | 23.1 | 1.3 | 2 | D | D | D |
| Weld | 773.0 | 3 377 | 248 | D | D | D | 650 | 8 735 | 2 246.1 | 212.9 | 227 | 838 | 115.6 | 23.7 |
| Yuma | 397.3 | 40 590 | 26 | 178 | 193.6 | 6.2 | 68 | 462 | 106.1 | 7.8 | 8 | 31 | 5.8 | 0.9 |
| CONNECTICUT | 3 758.4 | 1 071 | 3 848 | 58 291 | 107 917.0 | 3 587.9 | 13 807 | 196 133 | 52 165.5 | 5 160.4 | 3 609 | 22 455 | 5 686.6 | 994.0 |
| Fairfield | 652.0 | 722 | 1 220 | 17 035 | 78 881.6 | 1 391.9 | 3 770 | 53 738 | 15 702.2 | 1 648.8 | 1 174 | 7 465 | 2 283.4 | 450.7 |
| Hartford | 145.4 | 166 | 1 014 | 19 472 | 15 631.4 | 1 021.7 | 3 423 | 53 241 | 13 820.7 | 1 310.7 | 932 | 6 289 | 1 204.5 | 248.3 |
| Litchfield | 99.4 | 523 | 176 | D | D | D | 788 | 9 059 | 2 458.2 | 239.8 | 162 | 680 | 89.9 | 18.1 |
| Middlesex | 224.4 | 1 375 | 171 | 2 189 | 953.9 | 111.5 | 749 | 8 300 | 2 129.2 | 209.8 | 146 | 915 | 233.2 | 38.1 |
| New Haven | 342.7 | 405 | 980 | 14 619 | 9 890.7 | 814.1 | 3 172 | 46 058 | 11 785.3 | 1 112.5 | 780 | 5 470 | 1 611.1 | 192.9 |
| New London | 2 259.1 | 8 473 | 147 | D | D | D | 1 123 | 15 660 | 3 883.0 | 390.4 | 232 | D | D | D |

1. Merchant wholesalers, except manufacturers' sales branches and offices.　　2. Employer establishments.

# Table B. States and Counties — Professional Services, Manufacturing, and Accommodation and Food Services

| STATE County | Professional, scientific, and technical services,[1] 2007 | | | | Manufacturing, 2007 | | | | Accommodation and food services, 2007 | | | |
|---|---|---|---|---|---|---|---|---|---|---|---|---|
| | Number of establishments | Number of employees | Receipts (mil dol) | Annual payroll (mil dol) | Number of establishments | Number of employees | Receipts (mil dol) | Annual payroll (mil dol) | Number of establishments | Number of employees | Sales (mil dol) | Annual payroll (mil dol) |
| | 147 | 148 | 149 | 150 | 151 | 152 | 153 | 154 | 155 | 156 | 157 | 158 |
| COLORADO—Cont'd | | | | | | | | | | | | |
| Boulder | 2 447 | 23 459 | 5 054.5 | 1 781.8 | 534 | 16 791 | 3 855.9 | 896.9 | 815 | 14 563 | 668.9 | 208.4 |
| Broomfield | 271 | D | D | D | 85 | 3 939 | 2 255.5 | 192.9 | 137 | 3 370 | 163.4 | 53.3 |
| Chaffee | 87 | D | D | D | NA | NA | NA | NA | 107 | 1 197 | 49.2 | 14.6 |
| Cheyenne | 5 | 5 | 0.4 | 0.1 | NA | NA | NA | NA | 3 | 10 | 0.4 | 0.1 |
| Clear Creek | 59 | 77 | 9.4 | 3.9 | NA | NA | NA | NA | 49 | 481 | 25.0 | 7.6 |
| Conejos | 4 | 5 | 0.3 | 0.1 | NA | NA | NA | NA | 12 | 49 | 4.5 | 0.9 |
| Costilla | 1 | D | D | D | NA | NA | NA | NA | 5 | D | D | D |
| Crowley | 1 | D | D | D | NA | NA | NA | NA | 3 | D | D | D |
| Custer | 16 | 28 | 1.9 | 0.8 | NA | NA | NA | NA | 19 | 125 | 5.5 | 1.5 |
| Delta | 80 | D | D | D | 48 | 570 | 141.4 | 19.1 | 80 | 708 | 26.9 | 7.6 |
| Denver | 3 856 | D | D | D | 840 | 19 480 | 5 189.9 | 826.0 | 1 778 | 38 701 | 2 279.0 | 656.3 |
| Dolores | 4 | 4 | 0.4 | 0.1 | NA | NA | NA | NA | 5 | 22 | 1.7 | 0.7 |
| Douglas | 1 360 | D | D | D | 130 | 6 965 | 1 950.8 | 442.7 | 467 | 9 878 | 435.1 | 136.6 |
| Eagle | 422 | D | D | D | NA | NA | NA | NA | 254 | 7 882 | 469.7 | 152.7 |
| Elbert | 80 | 198 | 20.3 | 7.8 | NA | NA | NA | NA | 16 | 177 | 6.9 | 1.8 |
| El Paso | 2 328 | D | D | D | 499 | D | D | D | 1 240 | 24 124 | 1 153.8 | 350.5 |
| Fremont | 63 | 184 | 13.7 | 4.2 | 51 | 663 | 168.8 | 29.6 | 97 | 1 120 | 40.8 | 12.0 |
| Garfield | 317 | 1 270 | 163.3 | 63.5 | NA | NA | NA | NA | 187 | 2 900 | 161.2 | 46.3 |
| Gilpin | 16 | D | D | D | NA | NA | NA | NA | 9 | 1 610 | 291.5 | 49.5 |
| Grand | 97 | D | D | D | NA | NA | NA | NA | 133 | 1 581 | 73.9 | 24.8 |
| Gunnison | 121 | D | D | D | NA | NA | NA | NA | 123 | 2 501 | 89.7 | 29.8 |
| Hinsdale | 5 | D | D | D | NA | NA | NA | NA | 18 | 58 | 3.6 | 0.9 |
| Huerfano | 11 | 26 | 1.8 | 0.6 | NA | NA | NA | NA | 31 | 221 | 9.7 | 2.8 |
| Jackson | 3 | 6 | 0.8 | 0.1 | NA | NA | NA | NA | 11 | 49 | 2.4 | 0.7 |
| Jefferson | 2 934 | D | D | D | 489 | 16 816 | 6 566.6 | 1 063.6 | 1 109 | 21 096 | 960.5 | 293.0 |
| Kiowa | 2 | D | D | D | NA | NA | NA | NA | 2 | D | D | D |
| Kit Carson | 15 | 41 | 2.4 | 1.0 | NA | NA | NA | NA | 22 | 194 | 10.3 | 2.2 |
| Lake | 13 | D | D | D | NA | NA | NA | NA | 36 | 412 | 12.6 | 4.3 |
| La Plata | 342 | D | D | D | 65 | 748 | D | 22.5 | 204 | 4 188 | 206.2 | 63.3 |
| Larimer | 1 327 | 7 876 | 867.5 | 387.3 | 420 | 11 764 | 3 226.8 | 664.5 | 807 | 14 244 | 604.4 | 181.9 |
| Las Animas | 28 | 112 | 15.3 | 5.6 | NA | NA | NA | NA | 43 | 547 | 22.4 | 6.0 |
| Lincoln | 13 | 66 | 6.3 | 1.8 | NA | NA | NA | NA | 17 | 194 | 8.4 | 2.4 |
| Logan | 39 | 175 | 11.5 | 5.9 | NA | NA | NA | NA | 43 | 553 | 23.3 | 6.3 |
| Mesa | 547 | D | D | D | 177 | 2 691 | 539.6 | 104.9 | 301 | 6 307 | 268.8 | 77.6 |
| Mineral | 4 | 4 | 0.4 | 0.1 | NA | NA | NA | NA | 18 | 62 | 9.5 | 2.8 |
| Moffat | 41 | 152 | 12.2 | 5.3 | NA | NA | NA | NA | 37 | 556 | 35.3 | 6.8 |
| Montezuma | 79 | D | D | D | NA | NA | NA | NA | 86 | 1 424 | 84.9 | 22.0 |
| Montrose | 138 | D | D | D | 66 | 1 436 | 218.2 | 38.8 | 85 | 1 363 | 51.1 | 16.9 |
| Morgan | 37 | D | D | D | 31 | 2 463 | D | 85.3 | 55 | 741 | 27.7 | 8.1 |
| Otero | 33 | D | D | D | NA | NA | NA | NA | 57 | 558 | 20.3 | 5.3 |
| Ouray | 36 | 65 | 8.5 | 3.3 | NA | NA | NA | NA | 56 | 397 | 21.2 | 6.4 |
| Park | 58 | 102 | 10.3 | 4.1 | NA | NA | NA | NA | 44 | 224 | 11.1 | 3.6 |
| Phillips | 6 | 15 | 1.6 | 0.4 | NA | NA | NA | NA | 9 | 63 | 1.9 | 0.5 |
| Pitkin | 274 | D | D | D | NA | NA | NA | NA | 146 | 4 550 | 270.8 | 91.9 |
| Prowers | 31 | 87 | 12.0 | 2.7 | NA | NA | NA | NA | 37 | 393 | 16.3 | 3.9 |
| Pueblo | 251 | D | D | D | 106 | 3 838 | 1 705.8 | 180.3 | 344 | 5 602 | 220.9 | 61.8 |
| Rio Blanco | 20 | 46 | 4.0 | 1.2 | NA | NA | NA | NA | 31 | 278 | 11.3 | 3.2 |
| Rio Grande | 20 | 58 | 5.1 | 2.2 | NA | NA | NA | NA | 40 | 328 | 14.2 | 3.9 |
| Routt | 186 | D | D | D | NA | NA | NA | NA | 130 | 4 813 | 184.4 | 61.6 |
| Saguache | 11 | 16 | 1.3 | 0.6 | NA | NA | NA | NA | 10 | D | D | D |
| San Juan | 4 | D | D | D | NA | NA | NA | NA | 22 | 67 | 5.1 | 1.6 |
| San Miguel | 83 | 214 | 27.7 | 9.1 | NA | NA | NA | NA | 74 | 1 422 | 77.1 | 22.8 |
| Sedgwick | 5 | 10 | 0.8 | 0.2 | NA | NA | NA | NA | 8 | 59 | 1.7 | 0.5 |
| Summit | 220 | D | D | D | NA | NA | NA | NA | 208 | 6 952 | 281.6 | 97.8 |
| Teller | 95 | D | D | D | NA | NA | NA | NA | 76 | 1 790 | 128.0 | 38.1 |
| Washington | 7 | 17 | 1.2 | 0.4 | NA | NA | NA | NA | 8 | 46 | 1.5 | 0.4 |
| Weld | 462 | D | D | D | 284 | 10 186 | 4 193.7 | 451.8 | 379 | 6 099 | 217.2 | 63.8 |
| Yuma | 23 | D | D | D | NA | NA | NA | NA | 31 | 284 | 8.8 | 2.3 |
| CONNECTICUT | 9 828 | 101 384 | 15 771.7 | 7 988.8 | 4 924 | 190 790 | 58 404.9 | 10 345.1 | 7 941 | 132 001 | 9 138.4 | 2 483.1 |
| Fairfield | 3 778 | 38 942 | 7 103.5 | 3 058.3 | 1 029 | 42 123 | 20 028.4 | 2 455.4 | 2 094 | 27 883 | 1 861.9 | 523.1 |
| Hartford | 2 304 | 29 103 | 5 011.1 | 2 180.3 | 1 392 | 63 880 | 15 016.2 | 3 584.0 | 1 956 | 32 809 | 1 638.0 | 483.8 |
| Litchfield | 457 | D | D | D | 405 | D | D | 509.9 | 424 | 4 558 | 245.2 | 70.5 |
| Middlesex | 396 | D | D | D | 280 | 10 104 | 3 336.0 | 530.4 | 410 | 5 266 | 293.4 | 89.8 |
| New Haven | 2 015 | D | D | D | 1 289 | 40 188 | 10 493.0 | 1 976.9 | 1 920 | 24 768 | 1 345.9 | 371.7 |
| New London | 555 | D | D | D | 201 | D | D | 848.8 | 690 | 30 404 | 3 444.7 | 856.8 |

1. Establishment subject to federal tax.

# Table B. States and Counties — Health Care and Social Assistance, Other Services, and Federal Funds

| STATE County | Health care and social assistance, 2007 | | | | Other services, 2007 | | | | Federal funds and grants, 2009–2010 | | | |
| | | | | | | | | | Expenditures (mil dol) | | | |
| | | | | | | | | | | Direct payments for individuals[1] | | |
| | Number of establishments | Number of employees | Receipts (mil dol) | Annual payroll (mil dol) | Number of establishments | Number of employees | Receipts (mil dol) | Annual payroll (mil dol) | Total | Social Security and government retirement | Medicare | Food Stamps and Supplemental Security Income |
| | 159 | 160 | 161 | 162 | 163 | 164 | 165 | 166 | 167 | 168 | 169 | 170 |
|---|---|---|---|---|---|---|---|---|---|---|---|---|
| COLORADO—Cont'd | | | | | | | | | | | | |
| Boulder | 1 158 | 17 109 | 1 712.5 | 716.4 | 711 | 4 509 | 794.5 | 161.0 | 3 118.2 | 722.8 | 256.8 | 37.7 |
| Broomfield | 110 | 1 007 | 89.0 | 35.0 | 92 | 760 | 127.7 | 45.5 | 63.5 | 7.9 | 0.0 | 3.5 |
| Chaffee | 60 | 661 | 58.9 | 22.2 | 43 | 153 | 10.4 | 3.2 | 123.5 | 66.4 | 21.3 | 3.5 |
| Cheyenne | 1 | D | D | D | 6 | 11 | 0.8 | 0.2 | 46.2 | 7.0 | 6.3 | 0.2 |
| Clear Creek | 15 | D | D | D | 15 | 33 | 3.5 | 1.0 | 38.3 | 23.1 | 6.6 | 1.1 |
| Conejos | 10 | D | D | D | 4 | D | D | D | 86.7 | 21.4 | 12.9 | 5.6 |
| Costilla | 7 | 27 | 0.9 | 0.4 | 2 | D | D | D | 53.0 | 14.9 | 6.7 | 3.6 |
| Crowley | 4 | 80 | 3.2 | 1.5 | 1 | D | D | D | 33.7 | 12.5 | 6.3 | 3.0 |
| Custer | 3 | D | D | D | 6 | D | D | D | 31.1 | 21.7 | 3.3 | 0.7 |
| Delta | 82 | 1 316 | 91.7 | 38.5 | 56 | 204 | 20.6 | 5.1 | 250.6 | 118.0 | 52.3 | 8.5 |
| Denver | 1 981 | 45 826 | 5 232.8 | 2 172.8 | 1 627 | 12 532 | 1 821.5 | 381.8 | 8 557.6 | 1 446.4 | 1 016.3 | 279.4 |
| Dolores | 5 | D | D | D | NA | NA | NA | NA | 16.1 | 7.1 | 2.4 | 0.3 |
| Douglas | 598 | 7 186 | 765.6 | 283.9 | 468 | 2 646 | 224.2 | 66.6 | 575.5 | 353.9 | 30.9 | 4.3 |
| Eagle | 144 | D | D | D | 174 | 1 998 | 140.3 | 36.4 | 117.6 | 51.4 | 8.8 | 1.1 |
| Elbert | 19 | 138 | 8.9 | 3.3 | 34 | 83 | 7.9 | 2.3 | 84.7 | 57.6 | 10.6 | 2.3 |
| El Paso | 1 733 | 27 411 | 2 913.8 | 1 102.7 | 1 078 | 8 039 | 1 315.5 | 256.3 | 11 076.8 | 2 061.6 | 467.8 | 136.8 |
| Fremont | 104 | 2 028 | 126.5 | 52.7 | 48 | 169 | 12.8 | 3.6 | 392.3 | 175.2 | 62.0 | 13.6 |
| Garfield | 143 | 2 266 | 286.8 | 106.0 | 147 | 719 | 64.6 | 20.0 | 208.0 | 99.0 | 36.0 | 6.1 |
| Gilpin | 5 | D | D | D | 7 | D | D | D | 17.2 | 12.7 | 1.6 | 0.3 |
| Grand | 32 | 230 | 19.0 | 8.1 | 42 | 99 | 15.3 | 3.1 | 55.7 | 28.9 | 11.2 | 0.6 |
| Gunnison | 54 | 513 | 37.8 | 14.4 | 63 | 183 | 25.9 | 4.2 | 102.4 | 23.3 | 6.8 | 1.5 |
| Hinsdale | 1 | D | D | D | 5 | D | D | D | 5.0 | 2.8 | 0.6 | 0.1 |
| Huerfano | 17 | 417 | 18.1 | 8.9 | 9 | 28 | 3.2 | 0.5 | 89.5 | 31.9 | 22.4 | 3.7 |
| Jackson | 3 | D | D | D | 2 | D | D | D | 11.6 | 4.7 | 1.6 | 0.2 |
| Jefferson | 1 441 | 21 470 | 1 946.8 | 821.0 | 1 124 | 5 971 | 579.9 | 150.6 | 5 795.9 | 1 269.9 | 475.3 | 59.3 |
| Kiowa | 2 | D | D | D | 3 | D | D | D | 25.8 | 9.0 | 4.3 | 0.2 |
| Kit Carson | 22 | 328 | 18.6 | 8.3 | 15 | 46 | 4.9 | 0.9 | 85.4 | 32.3 | 13.9 | 1.3 |
| Lake | 13 | D | D | D | 12 | 31 | 2.1 | 0.5 | 30.8 | 12.4 | 7.0 | 0.9 |
| La Plata | 223 | 2 766 | 275.7 | 106.7 | 126 | 582 | 47.7 | 15.2 | 282.2 | 123.0 | 45.0 | 6.3 |
| Larimer | 908 | 15 177 | 1 400.5 | 610.6 | 612 | 3 123 | 286.8 | 77.2 | 1 879.7 | 719.3 | 236.7 | 38.7 |
| Las Animas | 41 | 543 | 43.0 | 15.1 | 43 | 580 | 34.6 | 11.5 | 169.0 | 58.4 | 30.4 | 8.7 |
| Lincoln | 6 | 212 | 15.7 | 7.9 | 14 | D | D | D | 48.2 | 15.9 | 11.1 | 1.0 |
| Logan | 72 | 1 203 | 81.0 | 32.7 | 55 | 261 | 26.9 | 7.3 | 154.8 | 56.9 | 32.9 | 5.4 |
| Mesa | 425 | 8 480 | 847.4 | 336.2 | 317 | 1 599 | 160.1 | 42.3 | 1 064.5 | 462.6 | 163.9 | 33.6 |
| Mineral | 2 | D | D | D | 4 | D | D | D | 4.6 | 3.0 | 0.5 | 0.0 |
| Moffat | 43 | 485 | 44.5 | 15.3 | 29 | 217 | 17.2 | 4.7 | 83.3 | 31.5 | 15.5 | 2.9 |
| Montezuma | 94 | 1 118 | 83.6 | 31.4 | 55 | 183 | 15.4 | 3.5 | 235.2 | 83.8 | 31.3 | 7.6 |
| Montrose | 157 | 2 065 | 164.6 | 68.3 | 85 | 397 | 33.0 | 9.2 | 287.2 | 143.6 | 48.0 | 7.5 |
| Morgan | 69 | 1 093 | 94.8 | 36.5 | 45 | 146 | 12.1 | 3.3 | 218.2 | 64.7 | 39.7 | 7.9 |
| Otero | 62 | 1 398 | 79.2 | 35.4 | 37 | 108 | 8.9 | 1.9 | 240.0 | 75.8 | 44.1 | 14.0 |
| Ouray | 18 | 60 | 4.6 | 1.7 | 9 | 16 | 2.0 | 0.3 | 18.6 | 12.7 | 3.1 | 0.3 |
| Park | 16 | 64 | 3.5 | 1.2 | 29 | D | D | D | 60.7 | 44.9 | 5.4 | 1.6 |
| Phillips | 9 | 261 | 15.8 | 7.3 | 13 | 43 | 5.2 | 1.1 | 48.5 | 14.5 | 11.9 | 0.6 |
| Pitkin | 80 | 709 | 110.5 | 37.2 | 105 | 777 | 101.4 | 24.2 | 42.5 | 23.5 | 5.8 | 0.3 |
| Prowers | 32 | 637 | 46.1 | 18.0 | 24 | 100 | 8.1 | 1.9 | 107.6 | 33.3 | 20.6 | 6.2 |
| Pueblo | 410 | 11 085 | 872.7 | 388.5 | 237 | 1 160 | 92.3 | 25.4 | 1 440.6 | 554.1 | 256.1 | 92.2 |
| Rio Blanco | 11 | 258 | 22.3 | 9.2 | 12 | 50 | 3.8 | 0.9 | 37.2 | 15.0 | 8.6 | 0.7 |
| Rio Grande | 34 | 417 | 24.3 | 9.5 | 31 | 93 | 11.1 | 2.4 | 108.7 | 38.3 | 14.8 | 9.9 |
| Routt | 100 | 1 147 | 124.5 | 50.9 | 76 | 362 | 30.4 | 8.3 | 77.9 | 37.6 | 10.8 | 1.4 |
| Saguache | 7 | 49 | 2.7 | 1.2 | 9 | D | D | D | 50.7 | 15.2 | 6.3 | 4.6 |
| San Juan | 2 | D | D | D | 2 | D | D | D | 3.5 | 1.7 | 0.4 | 0.1 |
| San Miguel | 26 | 128 | 8.7 | 3.4 | 38 | 245 | 37.5 | 5.7 | 43.9 | 9.2 | 1.9 | 0.4 |
| Sedgwick | 4 | D | D | D | 4 | D | D | D | 32.8 | 9.8 | 8.5 | 0.9 |
| Summit | 84 | 942 | 87.7 | 34.3 | 112 | 478 | 47.6 | 12.2 | 62.0 | 40.9 | 4.0 | 0.4 |
| Teller | 63 | 313 | 20.6 | 8.0 | 49 | 183 | 12.7 | 3.0 | 117.8 | 89.1 | 10.5 | 3.6 |
| Washington | 7 | 31 | 1.5 | 0.5 | 9 | D | D | D | 50.4 | 16.8 | 9.2 | 0.7 |
| Weld | 429 | 8 538 | 763.1 | 292.3 | 340 | 1 513 | 161.2 | 40.0 | 1 076.8 | 454.9 | 177.6 | 43.9 |
| Yuma | 27 | 574 | 43.7 | 17.8 | 24 | 53 | 5.5 | 1.0 | 134.2 | 70.9 | 15.4 | 1.6 |
| CONNECTICUT | 10 049 | 253 360 | 24 813.2 | 10 440.0 | 7 392 | 47 992 | 5 061.3 | 1 395.4 | 55 978.3 | 9 783.0 | 20 601.7 | 935.0 |
| Fairfield | 2 739 | 60 497 | 6 923.5 | 2 604.2 | 2 056 | 13 357 | 1 722.7 | 431.1 | 13 539.9 | 2 248.1 | 4 982.5 | 184.7 |
| Hartford | 2 686 | 72 837 | 7 022.9 | 3 107.3 | 1 989 | 15 781 | 1 599.2 | 458.6 | 16 782.1 | 2 484.7 | 6 135.1 | 317.9 |
| Litchfield | 503 | 9 629 | 820.4 | 349.7 | 391 | 1 900 | 158.3 | 57.7 | 1 636.2 | 585.1 | 776.3 | 20.7 |
| Middlesex | 476 | 12 803 | 1 175.5 | 543.0 | 325 | 1 527 | 158.7 | 43.3 | 1 618.6 | 490.4 | 733.6 | 20.3 |
| New Haven | 2 371 | 68 663 | 6 467.8 | 2 792.6 | 1 772 | 10 629 | 948.2 | 288.9 | 11 538.3 | 2 403.0 | 5 657.1 | 291.9 |
| New London | 703 | 16 048 | 1 467.8 | 617.5 | 479 | 2 549 | 234.3 | 59.3 | 6 569.1 | 887.6 | 1 336.7 | 55.3 |

1. State totals may include programs not allocated by county.

# Table B. States and Counties — Federal Funds, Residential Construction, and Local Government Finances

| | Federal funds and grants, 2009–2010 (cont.) | | | | | | | Value of residential construction authorized by building permits, 2011 | | Local government finances, 2007 | | | | |
| | Expenditures (mil dol) (cont.) | | | | | | | | | General revenue | | | | |
| | | Procurement contract awards | | Grants[1] | | | | | | | | Taxes | | |
| STATE County | | | | | | | | | | | | | Per capita[2] (dollars) | |
| | Salaries and wages | Defense | Other | Medicaid and other health-related | Nutrition and family welfare | Education | Other | New construction ($1,000) | Number of housing units | Total (mil dol) | Inter-governmental (mil dol) | Total (mil dol) | Total | Property |
|---|---|---|---|---|---|---|---|---|---|---|---|---|---|---|
| | 171 | 172 | 173 | 174 | 175 | 176 | 177 | 178 | 179 | 180 | 181 | 182 | 183 | 184 |
| COLORADO—Cont'd | | | | | | | | | | | | | | |
| Boulder | 317.0 | 183.9 | 532.6 | 216.3 | 30.3 | 21.4 | 757.2 | 132 006 | 661 | 1 187.5 | 282.9 | 670.7 | 2 311 | 1 403 |
| Broomfield | 1.1 | 25.6 | 7.1 | 0.3 | 0.0 | 0.6 | 15.0 | 65 583 | 229 | 185.2 | 11.5 | 96.0 | 1 787 | 626 |
| Chaffee | 6.3 | 0.1 | 3.1 | 15.3 | 2.9 | 0.6 | 3.2 | 16 368 | 69 | 74.1 | 17.4 | 21.9 | 1 304 | 843 |
| Cheyenne | 19.6 | 0.0 | 0.2 | 2.6 | 0.4 | 0.1 | 1.0 | 0 | 0 | 15.0 | 4.9 | 5.2 | 2 969 | 2 454 |
| Clear Creek | 2.7 | 0.0 | 0.8 | 2.1 | 0.9 | 0.7 | 0.0 | 3 697 | 16 | 47.0 | 12.3 | 20.9 | 2 331 | 1 956 |
| Conejos | 3.1 | 0.0 | 1.1 | 37.2 | 2.8 | 0.7 | 0.2 | 2 241 | 13 | 33.3 | 20.8 | 5.5 | 687 | 498 |
| Costilla | 1.0 | 0.0 | 0.2 | 22.1 | 1.9 | 0.3 | 0.8 | 4 995 | 22 | 19.4 | 12.2 | 4.9 | 1 488 | 1 392 |
| Crowley | 1.3 | 0.0 | 0.3 | 7.3 | 1.3 | 0.2 | 0.1 | 179 | 2 | 10.4 | 6.6 | 2.8 | 415 | 309 |
| Custer | 1.3 | 0.0 | 0.3 | 2.6 | 0.6 | 0.2 | 0.1 | 14 398 | 66 | 12.9 | 4.2 | 6.1 | 1 514 | 1 248 |
| Delta | 13.8 | 0.0 | 3.0 | 34.0 | 4.9 | 2.1 | 7.3 | 5 764 | 50 | 142.5 | 44.4 | 33.0 | 1 087 | 669 |
| Denver | 1 009.2 | 169.1 | 654.0 | 1 122.9 | 402.5 | 449.0 | 1 601.8 | 316 561 | 2 685 | 4 170.1 | 842.5 | 1 713.4 | 2 912 | 1 079 |
| Dolores | 0.9 | 0.0 | 0.2 | 2.5 | 0.5 | 0.2 | 0.3 | 0 | 0 | 6.5 | 3.5 | 2.3 | 1 181 | 979 |
| Douglas | 19.1 | 67.2 | 53.1 | 4.9 | 9.9 | 3.3 | 7.4 | 293 373 | 1 295 | 1 076.3 | 237.9 | 561.6 | 2 064 | 1 496 |
| Eagle | 15.6 | 7.9 | 8.1 | 3.9 | 3.7 | 2.1 | 14.0 | 43 010 | 53 | 378.4 | 42.2 | 205.6 | 4 002 | 2 534 |
| Elbert | 3.9 | 0.0 | 0.7 | 3.7 | 1.5 | 0.7 | 0.1 | 7 245 | 30 | 78.2 | 28.4 | 24.9 | 1 094 | 976 |
| El Paso | 4 744.1 | 2 888.3 | 107.2 | 233.5 | 67.7 | 61.3 | 67.5 | 601 921 | 2 220 | 2 391.6 | 721.9 | 756.8 | 1 289 | 707 |
| Fremont | 74.4 | 0.0 | 9.6 | 42.6 | 8.5 | 2.3 | 2.2 | 8 848 | 46 | 107.9 | 48.2 | 39.7 | 837 | 554 |
| Garfield | 22.2 | 0.7 | 8.9 | 12.8 | 4.1 | 2.7 | 10.2 | 8 388 | 33 | 310.3 | 76.5 | 163.2 | 3 044 | 2 152 |
| Gilpin | 0.9 | 0.0 | 0.2 | 0.6 | 0.5 | 0.2 | 0.1 | 5 554 | 16 | 71.5 | 15.5 | 45.5 | 8 946 | 4 271 |
| Grand | 7.0 | 0.0 | 4.0 | 1.6 | 1.3 | 0.9 | -0.1 | 35 201 | 155 | 117.2 | 12.7 | 54.9 | 4 035 | 2 635 |
| Gunnison | 8.8 | 0.4 | 49.8 | 3.3 | 1.5 | 0.7 | 3.3 | 16 416 | 50 | 95.4 | 15.8 | 40.1 | 2 680 | 1 662 |
| Hinsdale | 0.1 | 0.0 | 0.7 | 0.5 | 0.1 | 0.1 | 0.1 | 1 757 | 9 | 5.2 | 1.9 | 2.4 | 2 822 | 1 911 |
| Huerfano | 1.3 | 0.0 | 1.0 | 23.0 | 2.5 | 0.6 | 2.2 | 4 360 | 30 | 66.5 | 24.1 | 18.4 | 2 351 | 1 806 |
| Jackson | 2.2 | 0.0 | 1.8 | 0.5 | 0.2 | 0.2 | 0.2 | 434 | 2 | 8.1 | 4.0 | 2.3 | 1 690 | 1 242 |
| Jefferson | 757.3 | 400.4 | 2 422.3 | 138.2 | 48.2 | 39.2 | 128.8 | 163 702 | 958 | 1 765.0 | 511.7 | 886.8 | 1 675 | 1 268 |
| Kiowa | 1.4 | 0.0 | 0.2 | 1.6 | 0.3 | 0.2 | 0.0 | 80 | 1 | 14.3 | 5.1 | 4.0 | 2 996 | 2 595 |
| Kit Carson | 3.0 | 0.4 | 0.6 | 7.8 | 1.5 | 0.6 | 0.6 | 0 | 0 | 41.1 | 15.2 | 11.2 | 1 412 | 1 202 |
| Lake | 3.6 | 0.0 | 1.1 | 2.8 | 1.7 | 0.5 | 0.5 | 3 214 | 17 | 102.2 | 20.9 | 47.2 | 5 960 | 5 555 |
| La Plata | 26.6 | 0.4 | 16.6 | 27.2 | 9.0 | 4.7 | 12.9 | 32 111 | 154 | 188.4 | 41.6 | 117.0 | 2 361 | 1 673 |
| Larimer | 212.8 | 26.2 | 223.3 | 157.5 | 30.1 | 13.6 | 166.3 | 211 693 | 1 192 | 1 133.2 | 287.5 | 531.6 | 1 848 | 1 167 |
| Las Animas | 4.7 | 0.8 | 0.9 | 49.4 | 4.8 | 3.2 | 1.5 | 2 458 | 22 | 87.0 | 35.8 | 39.7 | 2 483 | 1 605 |
| Lincoln | 2.0 | 0.0 | 0.4 | 6.6 | 1.6 | 0.3 | 0.1 | 490 | 4 | 39.3 | 19.5 | 8.1 | 1 513 | 986 |
| Logan | 6.7 | 0.2 | 4.3 | 19.4 | 4.3 | 1.6 | 8.1 | 2 335 | 13 | 75.9 | 31.1 | 29.9 | 1 421 | 847 |
| Mesa | 89.3 | 38.4 | 99.1 | 98.5 | 13.1 | 8.5 | 20.1 | 67 323 | 359 | 480.7 | 186.9 | 192.8 | 1 387 | 752 |
| Mineral | 0.3 | 0.0 | 0.2 | 0.0 | 0.1 | 0.1 | 0.4 | 1 999 | 9 | 6.3 | 2.9 | 2.1 | 2 205 | 1 599 |
| Moffat | 8.9 | 0.0 | 12.3 | 6.0 | 2.1 | 0.9 | 0.4 | 2 372 | 10 | 71.8 | 19.0 | 28.6 | 2 092 | 1 617 |
| Montezuma | 18.9 | 0.0 | 31.7 | 24.6 | 5.0 | 4.1 | 9.8 | 1 043 | 9 | 108.1 | 41.5 | 31.9 | 1 265 | 787 |
| Montrose | 23.5 | 0.3 | 15.5 | 29.5 | 5.4 | 2.4 | 6.2 | 8 385 | 51 | 186.6 | 53.0 | 54.4 | 1 377 | 722 |
| Morgan | 9.9 | 0.0 | 42.2 | 24.8 | 7.0 | 2.4 | 5.2 | 2 961 | 10 | 99.3 | 34.9 | 39.5 | 1 412 | 1 186 |
| Otero | 8.3 | 0.2 | 1.5 | 53.9 | 12.7 | 3.6 | 17.4 | 422 | 3 | 78.6 | 43.2 | 23.2 | 1 229 | 525 |
| Ouray | 1.1 | 0.0 | 0.3 | 0.6 | 0.4 | 0.2 | 0.0 | 9 590 | 19 | 25.3 | 5.4 | 13.6 | 3 102 | 2 435 |
| Park | 3.8 | 0.1 | 1.0 | 1.1 | 1.6 | 0.5 | 0.2 | 12 894 | 73 | 49.3 | 20.1 | 22.8 | 1 339 | 1 233 |
| Phillips | 1.3 | 0.0 | 0.4 | 4.7 | 0.9 | 0.4 | 3.0 | 865 | 2 | 32.2 | 10.7 | 7.0 | 1 558 | 1 175 |
| Pitkin | 6.6 | 0.1 | 1.7 | 1.1 | 0.8 | 0.2 | 2.0 | 59 045 | 33 | 274.9 | 24.5 | 125.5 | 8 306 | 3 549 |
| Prowers | 3.1 | 0.0 | 0.6 | 20.9 | 3.7 | 2.0 | 1.6 | 199 | 2 | 87.7 | 30.5 | 17.1 | 1 296 | 854 |
| Pueblo | 85.8 | 42.0 | 20.4 | 258.3 | 33.6 | 16.6 | 39.7 | 20 893 | 118 | 490.8 | 226.0 | 183.4 | 1 187 | 747 |
| Rio Blanco | 4.7 | 0.0 | 1.6 | 2.7 | 0.7 | 0.7 | 0.6 | 5 098 | 16 | 55.3 | 16.8 | 24.2 | 3 883 | 2 552 |
| Rio Grande | 6.7 | 0.0 | 2.0 | 23.7 | 4.1 | 1.2 | 2.3 | 2 929 | 14 | 46.3 | 22.5 | 15.0 | 1 291 | 951 |
| Routt | 6.9 | 0.0 | 8.1 | 4.2 | 1.8 | 1.0 | 5.2 | 25 374 | 42 | 151.5 | 30.3 | 78.8 | 3 519 | 1 880 |
| Saguache | 3.0 | 0.0 | 0.9 | 12.1 | 3.5 | 0.7 | 0.3 | 4 049 | 25 | 21.6 | 11.6 | 7.3 | 1 055 | 1 017 |
| San Juan | 0.4 | 0.0 | 0.4 | 0.0 | 0.1 | 0.1 | 0.3 | 100 | 1 | 4.4 | 1.5 | 2.2 | 3 900 | 2 628 |
| San Miguel | 3.4 | 0.0 | 1.1 | 2.1 | 0.7 | 0.8 | 24.0 | 25 989 | 28 | 98.0 | 12.4 | 53.6 | 7 114 | 4 544 |
| Sedgwick | 1.5 | 0.0 | 0.3 | 4.7 | 0.5 | 0.3 | 0.1 | 0 | 0 | 18.9 | 4.8 | 3.7 | 1 568 | 1 286 |
| Summit | 3.7 | 0.6 | 5.0 | 2.7 | 1.8 | 0.6 | 1.0 | 69 969 | 154 | 188.1 | 14.0 | 106.3 | 4 004 | 2 863 |
| Teller | 3.8 | 0.6 | 2.1 | 2.3 | 2.8 | 0.8 | 0.7 | 13 505 | 55 | 84.0 | 33.1 | 33.3 | 1 528 | 1 076 |
| Washington | 3.6 | 0.0 | 1.2 | 5.2 | 1.4 | 0.4 | 0.0 | 276 | 1 | 29.2 | 13.1 | 7.9 | 1 713 | 1 601 |
| Weld | 57.0 | 27.5 | 23.5 | 135.0 | 20.5 | 17.0 | 66.4 | 179 964 | 889 | 851.6 | 256.5 | 359.0 | 1 473 | 1 074 |
| Yuma | 4.1 | 0.0 | 0.8 | 8.4 | 2.2 | 0.9 | 2.3 | 294 | 3 | 80.5 | 19.4 | 19.4 | 2 007 | 1 652 |
| CONNECTICUT | 1 902.7 | 11 113.6 | 843.0 | 4 768.8 | 847.6 | 497.3 | 2 185.2 | 679 237 | 3 173 | X | X | X | X | X |
| Fairfield | 303.9 | 4 045.9 | 346.9 | 869.6 | 127.7 | 52.2 | 278.3 | 322 224 | 937 | 4 018.8 | 884.0 | 2 701.7 | 3 019 | 2 940 |
| Hartford | 632.7 | 3 292.2 | 226.2 | 1 367.9 | 311.9 | 291.7 | 1 502.9 | 100 503 | 600 | 3 596.0 | 1 271.1 | 2 007.4 | 2 289 | 2 247 |
| Litchfield | 39.7 | 37.2 | 9.4 | 113.3 | 22.9 | 13.3 | 8.2 | 39 816 | 111 | 671.9 | 175.9 | 440.0 | 2 337 | 2 298 |
| Middlesex | 38.5 | 117.2 | 12.4 | 140.5 | 19.0 | 8.5 | 21.2 | 33 397 | 190 | 579.7 | 163.5 | 372.1 | 2 267 | 2 246 |
| New Haven | 480.1 | 79.2 | 179.4 | 1 810.1 | 129.2 | 70.3 | 256.3 | 85 098 | 689 | 3 404.4 | 1 294.9 | 1 764.1 | 2 086 | 2 046 |
| New London | 342.9 | 3 520.5 | 55.9 | 234.1 | 35.3 | 19.9 | 33.0 | 41 551 | 209 | 1 033.0 | 375.8 | 540.4 | 2 021 | 1 959 |

1. State totals may include programs not allocated by county.  2. Based on the resident population estimated as of July 1 of the year shown.

# Table B. States and Counties — Local Government Finances, Government Employment, and Voting

| | Local government finances, 2007 (cont.) | | | | | | | | | Government employment, 2011 | | | Presidential election,[2] 2012 | | |
| | Direct general expenditure | | | | | | | Debt outstanding | | | | | Percent of vote cast: | | |
| | | | | Percent of total for: | | | | | | | | | | | |
| STATE County | Total (mil dol) | Per capita[1] (dollars) | Education | Health and hospitals | Police protection | Public welfare | Highways | Total (mil dol) | Per capita[1] (dollars) | Federal civilian | Federal military | State and local | Democratic | Republican | All other |
| | 185 | 186 | 187 | 188 | 189 | 190 | 191 | 192 | 193 | 194 | 195 | 196 | 197 | 198 | 199 |
| COLORADO—Cont'd | | | | | | | | | | | | | | | |
| Boulder | 1 157.4 | 3 987 | 40.7 | 0.9 | 7.7 | 2.8 | 6.3 | 2 072.2 | 7 139 | 2 142 | 911 | 28 805 | 72.3 | 26.1 | 1.6 |
| Broomfield | 237.8 | 4 429 | 0.0 | 1.7 | 5.2 | 3.9 | 4.5 | 1 531.1 | 28 518 | 139 | 155 | 1 102 | 54.9 | 43.3 | 1.8 |
| Chaffee | 72.5 | 4 318 | 28.6 | 34.2 | 3.9 | 2.1 | 5.5 | 97.0 | 5 779 | 87 | 48 | 1 647 | 49.0 | 49.1 | 1.9 |
| Cheyenne | 13.3 | 7 520 | 37.7 | 0.8 | 2.4 | 17.9 | 11.2 | 9.7 | 5 503 | 13 | 0 | 307 | 17.8 | 80.1 | 2.1 |
| Clear Creek | 41.3 | 4 617 | 27.2 | 5.5 | 6.6 | 7.1 | 7.9 | 31.8 | 3 550 | 43 | 24 | 649 | 57.8 | 39.9 | 2.3 |
| Conejos | 28.5 | 3 524 | 56.2 | 5.2 | 2.8 | 2.7 | 9.1 | 4.4 | 542 | 52 | 22 | 516 | 55.6 | 42.7 | 1.7 |
| Costilla | 18.1 | 5 467 | 37.6 | 5.9 | 2.8 | 4.6 | 17.7 | 4.9 | 1 495 | 11 | 10 | 322 | 73.4 | 24.5 | 2.2 |
| Crowley | 11.1 | 1 667 | 47.7 | 0.5 | 4.3 | 9.9 | 8.3 | 3.2 | 485 | 12 | 16 | 506 | 35.4 | 62.6 | 1.9 |
| Custer | 12.1 | 3 000 | 37.3 | 13.1 | 6.5 | 2.4 | 10.2 | 5.6 | 1 391 | 15 | 11 | 229 | 34.7 | 63.6 | 1.7 |
| Delta | 138.7 | 4 574 | 31.8 | 31.2 | 3.4 | 4.0 | 6.0 | 88.1 | 2 905 | 173 | 82 | 2 174 | 32.9 | 65.2 | 1.8 |
| Denver | 3 934.0 | 6 687 | 19.1 | 18.2 | 4.2 | 2.8 | 1.5 | 9 470.6 | 16 097 | 14 170 | 2 493 | 57 660 | 75.5 | 23.0 | 1.5 |
| Dolores | 9.0 | 4 689 | 37.3 | 2.1 | 9.3 | 1.5 | 27.7 | 4.6 | 2 421 | 11 | 0 | 196 | 30.3 | 67.2 | 2.5 |
| Douglas | 1 103.2 | 4 054 | 44.0 | 0.5 | 5.1 | 1.0 | 10.3 | 2 170.4 | 7 976 | 378 | 790 | 10 530 | 40.8 | 58.0 | 1.2 |
| Eagle | 353.5 | 6 882 | 18.2 | 2.8 | 5.3 | 0.8 | 8.0 | 889.1 | 17 311 | 141 | 141 | 3 006 | 60.9 | 37.8 | 1.3 |
| Elbert | 63.8 | 2 806 | 57.0 | 0.8 | 3.9 | 5.0 | 8.5 | 200.8 | 8 839 | 36 | 63 | 945 | 28.9 | 69.0 | 2.1 |
| El Paso | 2 427.4 | 4 133 | 43.5 | 16.9 | 5.3 | 1.7 | 4.3 | 3 848.7 | 6 554 | 13 368 | 41 023 | 35 068 | 39.9 | 58.7 | 1.4 |
| Fremont | 103.4 | 2 183 | 50.2 | 0.4 | 8.4 | 6.2 | 5.0 | 100.2 | 2 114 | 1 128 | 128 | 4 233 | 34.4 | 63.6 | 2.0 |
| Garfield | 336.0 | 6 265 | 46.7 | 7.8 | 3.9 | 3.9 | 5.1 | 586.6 | 10 937 | 297 | 152 | 4 898 | 49.2 | 49.2 | 1.6 |
| Gilpin | 57.9 | 11 364 | 7.4 | 0.6 | 8.6 | 2.0 | 7.9 | 99.5 | 19 553 | 10 | 15 | 424 | 59.2 | 38.0 | 2.8 |
| Grand | 109.5 | 8 044 | 21.4 | 11.1 | 4.4 | 0.8 | 8.9 | 182.9 | 13 435 | 142 | 39 | 1 133 | 48.6 | 49.7 | 1.7 |
| Gunnison | 85.9 | 5 735 | 16.8 | 23.7 | 5.5 | 3.3 | 13.8 | 76.9 | 5 136 | 184 | 42 | 1 815 | 62.6 | 35.3 | 2.1 |
| Hinsdale | 5.2 | 6 208 | 23.6 | 14.6 | 7.6 | 1.1 | 12.2 | 1.0 | 1 223 | 0 | 0 | 86 | 40.1 | 57.4 | 2.5 |
| Huerfano | 59.9 | 7 643 | 18.9 | 34.3 | 8.5 | 2.4 | 11.0 | 16.8 | 2 146 | 15 | 18 | 475 | 54.6 | 43.4 | 2.0 |
| Jackson | 7.9 | 5 748 | 38.5 | 3.2 | 5.2 | 1.8 | 20.7 | 5.7 | 4 129 | 47 | 0 | 147 | 30.3 | 68.3 | 1.3 |
| Jefferson | 1 778.7 | 3 360 | 47.7 | 1.1 | 8.2 | 1.9 | 4.7 | 1 876.5 | 3 545 | 8 967 | 1 480 | 27 002 | 53.6 | 44.6 | 1.8 |
| Kiowa | 14.2 | 10 633 | 24.6 | 36.5 | 3.2 | 3.7 | 11.7 | 0.4 | 274 | 24 | 0 | 262 | 20.9 | 76.3 | 2.8 |
| Kit Carson | 44.1 | 5 560 | 32.8 | 23.5 | 2.7 | 3.1 | 17.2 | 7.6 | 956 | 47 | 22 | 767 | 26.5 | 71.3 | 2.2 |
| Lake | 100.3 | 12 671 | 69.7 | 15.2 | 1.2 | 1.2 | 1.8 | 37.4 | 4 731 | 63 | 20 | 758 | 61.9 | 35.9 | 2.2 |
| La Plata | 158.1 | 3 190 | 42.3 | 0.2 | 9.7 | 3.1 | 10.1 | 235.7 | 4 756 | 388 | 140 | 5 243 | 57.4 | 41.1 | 1.5 |
| Larimer | 1 068.3 | 3 715 | 36.2 | 4.8 | 7.0 | 2.5 | 11.5 | 1 529.2 | 5 317 | 2 594 | 848 | 25 232 | 54.0 | 44.3 | 1.7 |
| Las Animas | 105.5 | 6 592 | 25.2 | 2.1 | 6.1 | 1.3 | 20.1 | 25.3 | 1 580 | 69 | 41 | 1 785 | 52.7 | 45.6 | 1.7 |
| Lincoln | 38.3 | 7 188 | 44.6 | 18.6 | 2.1 | 6.1 | 10.7 | 10.7 | 2 015 | 26 | 15 | 951 | 23.7 | 74.5 | 1.8 |
| Logan | 89.8 | 4 266 | 50.8 | 0.5 | 4.2 | 3.4 | 6.8 | 57.6 | 2 737 | 68 | 61 | 2 417 | 31.7 | 66.9 | 1.4 |
| Mesa | 515.5 | 3 707 | 37.5 | 1.5 | 9.2 | 4.5 | 14.9 | 409.8 | 2 946 | 1 510 | 401 | 8 049 | 34.5 | 64.0 | 1.5 |
| Mineral | 6.6 | 6 842 | 30.9 | 27.6 | 5.0 | 0.6 | 10.2 | 0.0 | 0 | 0 | 0 | 80 | 43.3 | 53.6 | 3.0 |
| Moffat | 70.4 | 5 161 | 28.7 | 26.3 | 5.4 | 5.6 | 9.2 | 37.3 | 2 736 | 162 | 36 | 1 050 | 26.9 | 70.4 | 2.6 |
| Montezuma | 102.8 | 4 076 | 40.5 | 3.5 | 6.6 | 6.9 | 5.4 | 44.2 | 1 751 | 378 | 69 | 2 503 | 39.4 | 58.9 | 1.7 |
| Montrose | 184.1 | 4 658 | 32.4 | 29.6 | 4.5 | 2.4 | 4.2 | 137.0 | 3 467 | 321 | 111 | 2 719 | 33.9 | 63.7 | 2.4 |
| Morgan | 97.7 | 3 494 | 48.5 | 1.5 | 4.8 | 4.4 | 10.4 | 91.8 | 3 284 | 135 | 76 | 2 235 | 37.3 | 61.3 | 1.5 |
| Otero | 72.4 | 3 841 | 50.7 | 1.7 | 5.3 | 13.8 | 3.5 | 22.7 | 1 206 | 123 | 51 | 1 690 | 44.0 | 54.5 | 1.6 |
| Ouray | 22.1 | 5 045 | 34.8 | 2.8 | 4.1 | 3.4 | 8.6 | 31.1 | 7 100 | 11 | 12 | 361 | 53.5 | 44.7 | 1.9 |
| Park | 45.6 | 2 684 | 37.7 | 4.3 | 6.1 | 5.7 | 8.3 | 27.7 | 1 627 | 58 | 43 | 780 | 45.3 | 52.2 | 2.5 |
| Phillips | 35.0 | 7 788 | 36.0 | 40.8 | 2.6 | 1.8 | 4.4 | 10.6 | 2 355 | 21 | 12 | 563 | 27.5 | 71.3 | 1.2 |
| Pitkin | 274.4 | 18 164 | 17.6 | 27.8 | 2.9 | 1.0 | 2.4 | 338.2 | 22 389 | 101 | 46 | 1 985 | 73.7 | 24.9 | 1.3 |
| Prowers | 79.0 | 5 996 | 33.2 | 34.3 | 4.8 | 5.0 | 4.1 | 362.0 | 27 467 | 42 | 34 | 1 431 | 32.2 | 65.9 | 1.8 |
| Pueblo | 498.3 | 3 224 | 43.3 | 0.9 | 6.1 | 4.6 | 4.6 | 446.2 | 2 887 | 1 008 | 450 | 11 850 | 56.7 | 41.8 | 1.5 |
| Rio Blanco | 48.7 | 7 828 | 25.4 | 16.2 | 5.4 | 1.6 | 19.1 | 13.1 | 2 101 | 78 | 18 | 1 060 | 20.8 | 77.4 | 1.7 |
| Rio Grande | 39.7 | 3 412 | 51.1 | 5.2 | 6.4 | 0.7 | 11.5 | 12.5 | 1 078 | 113 | 32 | 815 | 45.0 | 53.8 | 1.2 |
| Routt | 135.7 | 6 064 | 29.1 | 1.3 | 4.2 | 2.3 | 15.5 | 174.5 | 7 796 | 125 | 63 | 1 739 | 62.7 | 35.8 | 1.5 |
| Saguache | 21.4 | 3 088 | 56.6 | 3.0 | 3.4 | 0.0 | 16.6 | 11.3 | 1 630 | 46 | 17 | 508 | 63.0 | 34.7 | 2.3 |
| San Juan | 4.4 | 7 830 | 26.5 | 4.0 | 10.9 | 2.4 | 12.4 | 1.4 | 2 460 | 0 | 0 | 70 | 53.2 | 44.0 | 2.8 |
| San Miguel | 82.9 | 11 010 | 16.2 | 5.0 | 5.6 | 0.8 | 14.8 | 142.0 | 18 854 | 51 | 20 | 750 | 77.0 | 21.4 | 1.6 |
| Sedgwick | 21.4 | 9 162 | 22.5 | 52.1 | 2.5 | 0.6 | 4.1 | 9.8 | 4 208 | 22 | 0 | 324 | 34.6 | 63.4 | 1.9 |
| Summit | 198.3 | 7 469 | 27.9 | 3.0 | 4.5 | 1.5 | 5.5 | 156.9 | 5 909 | 51 | 76 | 2 362 | 65.8 | 32.8 | 1.4 |
| Teller | 80.8 | 3 705 | 38.0 | 4.8 | 8.0 | 4.2 | 6.3 | 46.2 | 2 116 | 58 | 63 | 1 252 | 35.0 | 63.1 | 1.9 |
| Washington | 28.8 | 6 223 | 41.1 | 0.3 | 4.6 | 4.2 | 18.9 | 11.6 | 2 498 | 55 | 13 | 461 | 21.1 | 77.6 | 1.4 |
| Weld | 813.1 | 3 336 | 41.4 | 2.0 | 5.9 | 2.3 | 7.6 | 908.7 | 3 728 | 587 | 702 | 14 811 | 44.7 | 53.4 | 1.9 |
| Yuma | 84.4 | 8 737 | 26.9 | 42.3 | 2.8 | 3.6 | 7.7 | 69.0 | 7 141 | 55 | 27 | 936 | 24.9 | 73.3 | 1.8 |
| CONNECTICUT | X | X | X | X | X | X | X | X | X | 18 060 | 14 569 | 228 858 | 60.7 | 38.1 | 1.1 |
| Fairfield | 3 883.2 | 4 339 | 56.0 | 0.9 | 5.8 | 0.7 | 2.3 | 3 327.6 | 3 718 | 2 982 | 1 822 | 43 482 | 58.6 | 40.6 | 0.7 |
| Hartford | 3 604.9 | 4 111 | 56.9 | 0.7 | 5.5 | 0.9 | 3.2 | 1 922.2 | 2 192 | 5 604 | 1 772 | 66 718 | 65.2 | 33.7 | 1.1 |
| Litchfield | 726.3 | 3 858 | 67.3 | 0.8 | 3.7 | 0.3 | 5.0 | 344.2 | 1 828 | 442 | 367 | 7 823 | 51.6 | 46.7 | 1.7 |
| Middlesex | 625.8 | 3 813 | 65.0 | 0.7 | 3.6 | 0.2 | 5.3 | 287.5 | 1 751 | 342 | 323 | 10 633 | 60.8 | 37.8 | 1.5 |
| New Haven | 3 336.5 | 3 946 | 57.5 | 0.9 | 4.8 | 0.5 | 3.5 | 2 951.8 | 3 491 | 5 572 | 1 890 | 44 780 | 61.0 | 37.8 | 1.2 |
| New London | 1 092.9 | 4 087 | 63.7 | 0.4 | 4.8 | 0.6 | 5.1 | 682.5 | 2 553 | 2 570 | 7 841 | 33 032 | 59.9 | 38.8 | 1.3 |

1. Based on the resident population estimated as of July 1 of the year shown.    2. © 2013 Election Data Services, Inc. All rights reserved.

| STATE/ County code | CBSA code[1] | County type[2] | STATE County | Population 2012 | | | | Population characteristics[6], 2011 | | | | | | | | | | | |
| | | | | | | | | Race alone or in combination, not Hispanic or Latino (percent) | | | | | Age (percent) | | | | | |
| | | | | Land area,[3] (sq km) 2010 | Total persons | Rank | Per square kilometer | White | Black | American Indian, Alaska Native | Asian and Pacific Islander | Percent Hispanic or Latino[4] | Under 5 years | 5 to 17 years | 18 to 24 years | 25 to 34 years | 35 to 44 years | 45 to 54 years |
| | | | | 1 | 2 | 3 | 4 | 5 | 6 | 7 | 8 | 9 | 10 | 11 | 12 | 13 | 14 | 15 |
| | | | CONNECTICUT—Cont'd | | | | | | | | | | | | | | | |
| 09 013 | 25540 | 1 | Tolland | 1 062 | 151 539 | 416 | 142.7 | 88.3 | 3.9 | 0.5 | 4.2 | 4.6 | 4.4 | 15.3 | 16.6 | 10.3 | 12.3 | 16.2 |
| 09 015 | 48740 | 4 | Windham | 1 328 | 117 599 | 516 | 88.6 | 86.6 | 2.6 | 1.0 | 1.7 | 9.9 | 5.3 | 16.5 | 10.6 | 11.9 | 13.2 | 16.2 |
| 10 000 | ... | X | DELAWARE | 5 047 | 917 092 | X | 181.7 | 66.7 | 22.2 | 0.9 | 3.9 | 8.4 | 6.1 | 16.4 | 10.1 | 12.6 | 12.5 | 14.7 |
| 10 001 | 20100 | 3 | Kent | 1 518 | 167 626 | 373 | 110.4 | 67.2 | 25.4 | 1.3 | 3.1 | 6.0 | 6.7 | 17.8 | 11.0 | 12.5 | 12.3 | 14.2 |
| 10 003 | 37980 | 1 | New Castle | 1 104 | 546 076 | 116 | 494.6 | 62.9 | 24.4 | 0.7 | 5.0 | 9.0 | 6.1 | 16.7 | 10.9 | 13.4 | 13.2 | 15.0 |
| 10 005 | 42580 | 4 | Sussex | 2 424 | 203 390 | 308 | 83.9 | 76.9 | 13.6 | 0.9 | 1.5 | 8.9 | 5.8 | 14.5 | 7.2 | 10.6 | 10.8 | 14.2 |
| 11 000 | ... | X | DISTRICT OF COLUMBIA | 158 | 632 323 | X | 4 002.0 | 36.9 | 50.5 | 0.8 | 4.7 | 9.5 | 5.9 | 11.2 | 13.6 | 21.6 | 13.3 | 12.3 |
| 11 001 | 47900 | 1 | District of Columbia | 158 | 632 323 | 99 | 4 002.0 | 36.9 | 50.5 | 0.8 | 4.7 | 9.5 | 5.9 | 11.2 | 13.6 | 21.6 | 13.3 | 12.3 |
| 12 000 | ... | X | FLORIDA | 138 887 | 19 317 568 | X | 139.1 | 58.7 | 16.1 | 0.6 | 3.2 | 22.9 | 5.6 | 15.3 | 9.3 | 12.3 | 12.6 | 14.4 |
| 12 001 | 23540 | 3 | Alachua | 2 266 | 251 417 | 263 | 111.0 | 65.3 | 20.9 | 0.8 | 6.4 | 8.9 | 5.3 | 12.1 | 25.0 | 14.2 | 10.1 | 11.3 |
| 12 003 | 27260 | 1 | Baker | 1 516 | 27 086 | 1 528 | 17.9 | 83.1 | 14.4 | 0.8 | 0.9 | 2.2 | 6.9 | 18.8 | 9.2 | 13.5 | 13.7 | 14.5 |
| 12 005 | 37460 | 3 | Bay | 1 964 | 171 903 | 363 | 87.5 | 81.1 | 12.0 | 1.4 | 3.2 | 5.1 | 6.2 | 15.5 | 9.4 | 13.3 | 12.4 | 15.4 |
| 12 007 | ... | 6 | Bradford | 761 | 27 049 | 1 529 | 35.5 | 74.4 | 21.2 | 0.8 | 1.1 | 3.9 | 5.8 | 13.8 | 8.8 | 15.3 | 13.3 | 15.5 |
| 12 009 | 37340 | 2 | Brevard | 2 631 | 547 307 | 115 | 208.0 | 79.1 | 10.8 | 0.8 | 3.1 | 8.4 | 4.8 | 14.6 | 7.9 | 10.2 | 10.9 | 16.4 |
| 12 011 | 33100 | 1 | Broward | 3 133 | 1 815 137 | 17 | 579.4 | 44.2 | 26.9 | 0.5 | 4.2 | 25.8 | 5.9 | 16.1 | 8.6 | 13.1 | 14.0 | 15.8 |
| 12 013 | ... | 6 | Calhoun | 1 469 | 14 723 | 2 127 | 10.0 | 78.9 | 14.9 | 1.9 | 1.1 | 5.4 | 6.0 | 15.5 | 8.5 | 13.5 | 13.6 | 14.5 |
| 12 015 | 39460 | 3 | Charlotte | 1 762 | 162 449 | 386 | 92.2 | 86.9 | 6.1 | 0.6 | 1.8 | 5.9 | 3.3 | 10.5 | 5.5 | 7.0 | 8.4 | 12.9 |
| 12 017 | 26140 | 4 | Citrus | 1 507 | 139 360 | 449 | 92.5 | 90.4 | 3.3 | 0.8 | 1.8 | 4.9 | 3.8 | 11.6 | 5.7 | 7.1 | 8.8 | 13.3 |
| 12 019 | 27260 | 1 | Clay | 1 565 | 194 345 | 327 | 124.2 | 78.5 | 10.8 | 1.0 | 4.2 | 8.0 | 6.0 | 19.6 | 8.7 | 11.4 | 13.9 | 15.6 |
| 12 021 | 34940 | 2 | Collier | 5 176 | 332 427 | 197 | 64.2 | 65.9 | 6.7 | 0.4 | 1.5 | 26.3 | 5.2 | 14.0 | 6.9 | 10.1 | 10.7 | 12.5 |
| 12 023 | 29380 | 6 | Columbia | 2 066 | 67 966 | 781 | 32.9 | 75.4 | 18.5 | 1.1 | 1.6 | 5.1 | 6.2 | 16.0 | 9.8 | 12.3 | 11.7 | 14.7 |
| 12 027 | 11580 | 6 | DeSoto | 1 650 | 34 712 | 1 308 | 21.0 | 56.2 | 13.0 | 0.4 | 0.8 | 30.4 | 6.4 | 16.0 | 10.4 | 13.4 | 11.6 | 12.3 |
| 12 029 | ... | 6 | Dixie | 1 826 | 16 126 | 2 036 | 8.8 | 87.2 | 9.0 | 1.0 | 0.7 | 3.4 | 5.5 | 13.7 | 7.2 | 11.3 | 11.2 | 15.3 |
| 12 031 | 27260 | 1 | Duval | 1 974 | 879 602 | 59 | 445.6 | 58.3 | 30.0 | 0.8 | 5.4 | 7.9 | 6.9 | 16.4 | 10.3 | 15.2 | 13.2 | 14.6 |
| 12 033 | 37860 | 2 | Escambia | 1 700 | 302 715 | 215 | 178.1 | 68.4 | 23.8 | 1.6 | 4.1 | 4.9 | 6.3 | 15.1 | 12.8 | 13.0 | 11.1 | 14.2 |
| 12 035 | 37380 | 4 | Flagler | 1 257 | 98 359 | 596 | 78.2 | 77.2 | 11.8 | 0.7 | 2.9 | 9.0 | 4.8 | 14.6 | 6.3 | 9.2 | 11.0 | 13.1 |
| 12 037 | ... | 6 | Franklin | 1 385 | 11 686 | 2 318 | 8.4 | 80.3 | 14.6 | 1.1 | 0.8 | 4.8 | 4.9 | 11.7 | 7.7 | 15.6 | 12.4 | 14.8 |
| 12 039 | 45220 | 2 | Gadsden | 1 337 | 46 528 | 1 039 | 34.8 | 34.0 | 55.4 | 0.5 | 0.9 | 10.1 | 7.0 | 16.9 | 8.7 | 12.4 | 12.4 | 14.5 |
| 12 041 | 23540 | 3 | Gilchrist | 906 | 16 815 | 1 993 | 18.6 | 88.3 | 6.1 | 0.8 | 0.7 | 5.2 | 5.3 | 15.9 | 12.6 | 9.8 | 10.9 | 13.8 |
| 12 043 | ... | 6 | Glades | 2 088 | 13 107 | 2 235 | 6.3 | 61.3 | 12.7 | 4.4 | 0.8 | 21.8 | 5.3 | 13.6 | 8.0 | 13.1 | 12.9 | 12.8 |
| 12 045 | ... | 6 | Gulf | 1 461 | 15 718 | 2 061 | 10.8 | 75.9 | 19.4 | 1.1 | 0.8 | 4.5 | 4.2 | 11.8 | 7.8 | 14.9 | 14.7 | 15.9 |
| 12 047 | ... | 6 | Hamilton | 1 331 | 14 708 | 2 128 | 11.1 | 55.6 | 34.4 | 0.9 | 1.0 | 9.3 | 5.3 | 14.2 | 13.2 | 13.3 | 12.6 | 14.4 |
| 12 049 | 48100 | 6 | Hardee | 1 652 | 27 514 | 1 513 | 16.7 | 48.3 | 7.4 | 0.6 | 1.4 | 43.1 | 8.1 | 19.5 | 11.2 | 13.6 | 12.1 | 12.0 |
| 12 051 | 17500 | 4 | Hendry | 2 986 | 37 447 | 1 234 | 12.5 | 35.2 | 13.5 | 1.6 | 1.0 | 49.4 | 7.9 | 19.7 | 10.9 | 14.2 | 13.1 | 12.7 |
| 12 053 | 45300 | 1 | Hernando | 1 224 | 173 422 | 360 | 141.7 | 82.7 | 5.6 | 0.7 | 1.7 | 10.6 | 4.8 | 14.8 | 6.7 | 8.9 | 10.7 | 13.5 |
| 12 055 | 42700 | 4 | Highlands | 2 633 | 98 128 | 598 | 37.3 | 71.0 | 9.7 | 0.8 | 1.8 | 17.8 | 5.1 | 13.1 | 6.6 | 8.7 | 8.9 | 11.5 |
| 12 057 | 45300 | 1 | Hillsborough | 2 642 | 1 277 746 | 29 | 483.6 | 54.9 | 16.9 | 0.7 | 4.3 | 25.1 | 6.4 | 16.9 | 10.3 | 14.4 | 13.9 | 14.5 |
| 12 059 | ... | 6 | Holmes | 1 240 | 19 804 | 1 845 | 16.0 | 89.6 | 6.8 | 1.9 | 0.9 | 2.6 | 5.7 | 15.7 | 9.0 | 12.0 | 12.4 | 14.5 |
| 12 061 | 42680 | 3 | Indian River | 1 302 | 140 567 | 446 | 108.0 | 77.8 | 9.4 | 0.5 | 1.7 | 11.6 | 4.6 | 14.0 | 6.7 | 9.0 | 9.9 | 13.4 |
| 12 063 | ... | 6 | Jackson | 2 377 | 48 968 | 1 000 | 20.6 | 67.5 | 27.3 | 1.2 | 1.0 | 4.6 | 5.2 | 14.4 | 9.3 | 12.8 | 14.1 | 14.7 |
| 12 065 | 45220 | 2 | Jefferson | 1 549 | 14 256 | 2 157 | 9.2 | 59.9 | 35.8 | 0.7 | 0.8 | 3.9 | 5.3 | 13.2 | 7.5 | 11.6 | 12.7 | 16.1 |
| 12 067 | ... | 8 | Lafayette | 1 407 | 8 804 | 2 532 | 6.3 | 71.0 | 16.6 | 0.5 | 0.5 | 12.4 | 5.2 | 14.7 | 11.8 | 16.2 | 15.2 | 13.6 |
| 12 069 | 36740 | 1 | Lake | 2 430 | 303 186 | 214 | 124.8 | 75.3 | 10.3 | 0.9 | 2.4 | 12.6 | 5.4 | 15.2 | 6.8 | 9.8 | 11.6 | 13.2 |
| 12 071 | 15980 | 2 | Lee | 2 032 | 645 293 | 96 | 317.6 | 71.6 | 8.5 | 0.5 | 1.9 | 18.6 | 5.2 | 14.2 | 7.6 | 10.5 | 11.1 | 13.0 |
| 12 073 | 45220 | 2 | Leon | 1 727 | 283 769 | 233 | 164.3 | 60.3 | 31.2 | 0.8 | 3.7 | 5.9 | 5.3 | 13.5 | 24.3 | 13.9 | 10.6 | 11.7 |
| 12 075 | ... | 8 | Levy | 2 896 | 40 025 | 1 172 | 13.8 | 81.5 | 10.3 | 1.0 | 0.9 | 7.7 | 5.6 | 15.1 | 7.5 | 10.0 | 10.9 | 14.9 |
| 12 077 | ... | 8 | Liberty | 2 164 | 8 276 | 2 587 | 3.8 | 73.9 | 18.9 | 1.4 | 0.6 | 6.6 | 5.3 | 15.9 | 8.5 | 16.6 | 15.6 | 15.9 |
| 12 079 | ... | 6 | Madison | 1 802 | 18 907 | 1 878 | 10.5 | 55.9 | 39.0 | 0.8 | 0.5 | 4.9 | 6.2 | 15.3 | 9.7 | 12.6 | 11.9 | 14.1 |
| 12 081 | 35840 | 2 | Manatee | 1 924 | 333 895 | 196 | 173.5 | 74.1 | 9.4 | 0.5 | 2.2 | 15.1 | 5.6 | 14.8 | 7.1 | 10.2 | 11.1 | 13.4 |
| 12 083 | 36100 | 2 | Marion | 4 104 | 335 125 | 195 | 81.7 | 74.7 | 12.8 | 0.8 | 1.8 | 11.2 | 5.1 | 14.0 | 7.2 | 9.8 | 10.5 | 13.1 |
| 12 085 | 38940 | 2 | Martin | 1 408 | 148 817 | 423 | 105.7 | 80.8 | 5.8 | 0.5 | 1.5 | 12.4 | 4.2 | 13.2 | 6.4 | 8.7 | 10.1 | 14.8 |
| 12 086 | 33100 | 1 | Miami-Dade | 4 915 | 2 591 035 | 7 | 527.2 | 16.5 | 17.5 | 0.2 | 1.9 | 64.5 | 5.9 | 15.5 | 10.0 | 13.7 | 14.7 | 14.9 |
| 12 087 | 28580 | 4 | Monroe | 2 547 | 74 809 | 730 | 29.4 | 71.6 | 6.1 | 0.9 | 1.7 | 21.0 | 4.4 | 10.6 | 6.9 | 12.3 | 13.0 | 17.1 |
| 12 089 | 27260 | 1 | Nassau | 1 680 | 74 629 | 733 | 44.4 | 88.4 | 7.1 | 0.9 | 1.4 | 3.5 | 5.3 | 16.0 | 7.7 | 10.4 | 12.6 | 15.5 |
| 12 091 | 18880 | 3 | Okaloosa | 2 409 | 190 083 | 333 | 78.9 | 79.5 | 10.7 | 1.2 | 4.9 | 7.2 | 6.5 | 15.6 | 10.2 | 14.3 | 11.6 | 15.4 |
| 12 093 | 36380 | 4 | Okeechobee | 1 991 | 39 467 | 1 183 | 19.8 | 65.5 | 8.7 | 1.0 | 1.2 | 24.5 | 6.6 | 17.4 | 9.1 | 12.8 | 12.2 | 13.0 |
| 12 095 | 36740 | 1 | Orange | 2 340 | 1 202 234 | 33 | 513.8 | 47.2 | 20.7 | 0.6 | 5.9 | 27.5 | 6.4 | 17.0 | 12.5 | 15.7 | 14.2 | 14.0 |
| 12 097 | 36740 | 1 | Osceola | 3 438 | 287 416 | 229 | 83.6 | 40.9 | 10.4 | 0.6 | 3.4 | 46.3 | 6.6 | 19.3 | 9.9 | 13.3 | 14.4 | 14.3 |
| 12 099 | 33100 | 1 | Palm Beach | 5 102 | 1 356 545 | 27 | 265.9 | 60.5 | 17.7 | 0.4 | 3.1 | 19.6 | 5.3 | 14.9 | 8.0 | 11.2 | 12.2 | 14.1 |
| 12 101 | 45300 | 1 | Pasco | 1 934 | 470 391 | 141 | 243.2 | 80.8 | 5.1 | 0.8 | 2.8 | 12.1 | 5.4 | 15.5 | 7.1 | 10.6 | 12.8 | 14.3 |
| 12 103 | 45300 | 1 | Pinellas | 709 | 921 319 | 53 | 1 299.5 | 77.9 | 11.0 | 0.7 | 3.7 | 8.3 | 4.6 | 12.9 | 7.3 | 11.0 | 11.7 | 15.8 |
| 12 105 | 29460 | 2 | Polk | 4 656 | 616 158 | 105 | 132.3 | 65.3 | 15.1 | 0.7 | 2.2 | 18.1 | 6.3 | 16.9 | 8.9 | 11.9 | 12.0 | 13.1 |

1. CBSA = Core Based Statistical Area. See Appendix A for explanation. See Appendix B for list of metropolitan areas with component counties.   2. County type code from the Economic Research Service of USDA Rural-Urban Continuum Codes. See Appendix A for definition.   3. Dry land or land partially or temporarily covered by water.   4. May be of any race.

# Table B. States and Counties — **Population and Households**

| | Population, 2011 (cont.) | | | | Population change and components of change, 2000–2012 | | | | | | | Households, 2010 | | | | |
|---|---|---|---|---|---|---|---|---|---|---|---|---|---|---|---|---|
| | Age (percent) (cont.) | | | | Total persons | | Percent change | | Components of change, 2010–2012 | | | | | | Percent | |
| STATE County | 55 to 64 years | 65 to 74 years | 75 years and over | Percent female | 2000 | 2010 | 2000–2010 | 2010–2012 | Births | Deaths | Net migration | Number | Percent change, 2000–2010 | Persons per house-hold | Female family house-holder[1] | One per-son |
| | 16 | 17 | 18 | 19 | 20 | 21 | 22 | 23 | 24 | 25 | 26 | 27 | 28 | 29 | 30 | 31 |
| CONNECTICUT—Cont'd | | | | | | | | | | | | | | | | |
| Tolland | 12.7 | 7.0 | 5.3 | 49.5 | 136 364 | 152 691 | 12.0 | -0.8 | 2 606 | 2 160 | -1 549 | 54 477 | 10.2 | 2.51 | 8.6 | 24.2 |
| Windham | 13.1 | 7.1 | 6.0 | 50.4 | 109 091 | 118 428 | 8.6 | -0.7 | 2 566 | 2 211 | -1 179 | 44 810 | 8.9 | 2.54 | 12.3 | 24.6 |
| DELAWARE | 12.8 | 8.3 | 6.4 | 51.5 | 783 600 | 897 934 | 14.6 | 2.1 | 25 491 | 17 482 | 11 278 | 342 297 | 14.6 | 2.55 | 14.2 | 25.6 |
| Kent | 11.7 | 8.1 | 5.8 | 51.8 | 126 697 | 162 310 | 28.1 | 3.3 | 5 098 | 3 170 | 3 304 | 60 278 | 27.6 | 2.62 | 14.9 | 23.6 |
| New Castle | 12.1 | 6.8 | 5.8 | 51.5 | 500 265 | 538 479 | 7.6 | 1.4 | 15 317 | 9 460 | 2 041 | 202 651 | 7.3 | 2.57 | 14.9 | 26.1 |
| Sussex | 15.7 | 12.6 | 8.7 | 51.2 | 156 638 | 197 145 | 25.9 | 3.2 | 5 076 | 4 852 | 5 933 | 79 368 | 26.8 | 2.45 | 11.7 | 25.6 |
| DISTRICT OF COLUMBIA | 10.8 | 6.2 | 5.2 | 52.7 | 572 059 | 601 723 | 5.2 | 5.1 | 20 537 | 10 593 | 20 369 | 266 707 | 7.4 | 2.11 | 16.4 | 44.0 |
| District of Columbia | 10.8 | 6.2 | 5.2 | 52.7 | 572 059 | 601 723 | 5.2 | 5.1 | 20 537 | 10 593 | 20 369 | 266 707 | 7.4 | 2.11 | 16.4 | 44.0 |
| FLORIDA | 12.8 | 9.3 | 8.3 | 51.1 | 15 982 378 | 18 801 310 | 17.6 | 2.7 | 476 020 | 392 110 | 431 042 | 7 420 802 | 17.1 | 2.48 | 13.5 | 27.2 |
| Alachua | 10.9 | 6.1 | 5.0 | 51.6 | 217 955 | 247 336 | 13.5 | 1.6 | 6 387 | 3 819 | 1 602 | 100 516 | 14.9 | 2.32 | 12.8 | 30.2 |
| Baker | 11.9 | 7.1 | 4.4 | 47.9 | 22 259 | 27 115 | 21.8 | -0.1 | 774 | 509 | -286 | 8 772 | 24.5 | 2.82 | 14.2 | 19.3 |
| Bay | 12.9 | 8.2 | 6.6 | 50.5 | 148 217 | 168 852 | 13.9 | 1.8 | 4 881 | 3 652 | 1 824 | 68 438 | 14.8 | 2.41 | 13.0 | 27.5 |
| Bradford | 12.7 | 8.3 | 6.5 | 43.8 | 26 088 | 28 520 | 9.3 | -5.2 | 706 | 664 | -1 565 | 9 479 | 11.6 | 2.53 | 15.0 | 25.1 |
| Brevard | 14.4 | 10.8 | 10.0 | 51.1 | 476 230 | 543 376 | 14.1 | 0.7 | 11 209 | 13 404 | 6 286 | 229 692 | 15.9 | 2.33 | 11.8 | 28.4 |
| Broward | 12.2 | 7.3 | 7.0 | 51.5 | 1 623 018 | 1 748 066 | 7.7 | 3.8 | 46 965 | 32 473 | 53 032 | 686 047 | 4.8 | 2.52 | 15.3 | 28.8 |
| Calhoun | 12.3 | 9.2 | 7.0 | 45.8 | 13 017 | 14 625 | 12.4 | 0.7 | 341 | 334 | 60 | 5 061 | 13.3 | 2.52 | 13.7 | 27.1 |
| Charlotte | 17.3 | 18.5 | 16.6 | 51.4 | 141 627 | 159 978 | 13.0 | 1.5 | 2 167 | 5 096 | 5 571 | 73 370 | 14.9 | 2.14 | 8.5 | 28.5 |
| Citrus | 16.8 | 17.9 | 14.9 | 51.6 | 118 085 | 141 236 | 19.6 | -1.3 | 2 342 | 5 168 | 1 075 | 63 304 | 20.3 | 2.20 | 9.1 | 28.3 |
| Clay | 12.5 | 7.4 | 4.9 | 51.1 | 140 814 | 190 865 | 35.5 | 1.8 | 4 705 | 3 169 | 1 973 | 68 792 | 36.9 | 2.76 | 12.9 | 18.8 |
| Collier | 13.3 | 14.6 | 12.6 | 50.6 | 251 377 | 321 520 | 27.9 | 3.4 | 7 357 | 6 565 | 9 897 | 133 179 | 29.3 | 2.38 | 8.6 | 26.7 |
| Columbia | 13.5 | 9.2 | 6.7 | 48.5 | 56 513 | 67 531 | 19.5 | 0.6 | 1 769 | 1 620 | 304 | 24 941 | 19.2 | 2.52 | 14.7 | 25.7 |
| DeSoto | 11.5 | 10.5 | 7.9 | 43.3 | 32 209 | 34 862 | 8.2 | -0.4 | 922 | 632 | -473 | 11 445 | 6.5 | 2.71 | 12.8 | 22.8 |
| Dixie | 15.4 | 12.8 | 7.7 | 46.3 | 13 827 | 16 422 | 18.8 | -1.8 | 358 | 444 | -216 | 6 316 | 21.3 | 2.37 | 11.7 | 28.1 |
| Duval | 12.0 | 6.4 | 5.1 | 51.5 | 778 879 | 864 263 | 11.0 | 1.8 | 27 883 | 16 239 | 3 991 | 342 450 | 12.7 | 2.47 | 16.7 | 28.4 |
| Escambia | 12.8 | 8.0 | 6.6 | 50.6 | 294 410 | 297 619 | 1.1 | 1.7 | 8 701 | 6 788 | 3 288 | 116 238 | 4.7 | 2.41 | 16.3 | 28.9 |
| Flagler | 15.7 | 14.6 | 10.7 | 51.9 | 49 832 | 95 696 | 92.0 | 2.8 | 1 823 | 2 256 | 3 082 | 39 186 | 84.0 | 2.42 | 11.0 | 23.1 |
| Franklin | 14.7 | 11.4 | 6.7 | 42.4 | 11 057 | 11 549 | 4.4 | 1.2 | 240 | 241 | 139 | 4 254 | 3.9 | 2.29 | 10.9 | 29.3 |
| Gadsden | 14.0 | 8.1 | 6.0 | 51.2 | 45 087 | 46 389 | 2.9 | 0.3 | 1 397 | 1 048 | -1 602 | 16 952 | 6.3 | 2.61 | 22.6 | 25.5 |
| Gilchrist | 14.0 | 10.0 | 7.7 | 47.7 | 14 437 | 16 939 | 17.3 | -0.7 | 406 | 382 | -146 | 6 121 | 21.9 | 2.58 | 11.5 | 23.4 |
| Glades | 13.0 | 13.0 | 8.3 | 42.2 | 10 576 | 12 884 | 21.8 | 1.7 | 165 | 242 | 209 | 4 533 | 17.7 | 2.52 | 9.0 | 25.8 |
| Gulf | 14.0 | 9.7 | 7.1 | 40.2 | 13 332 | 15 863 | 19.0 | -0.9 | 284 | 365 | -83 | 5 335 | 8.2 | 2.33 | 10.8 | 28.6 |
| Hamilton | 13.4 | 8.2 | 5.4 | 41.1 | 13 327 | 14 799 | 11.0 | -0.6 | 370 | 255 | -213 | 4 617 | 11.0 | 2.54 | 16.9 | 26.5 |
| Hardee | 10.1 | 7.7 | 5.6 | 46.5 | 26 938 | 27 731 | 2.9 | -0.8 | 964 | 423 | -797 | 8 245 | 1.0 | 3.12 | 14.2 | 19.2 |
| Hendry | 9.6 | 6.9 | 5.0 | 45.9 | 36 210 | 39 140 | 8.1 | -4.3 | 1 371 | 662 | -2 499 | 12 025 | 10.8 | 3.09 | 15.2 | 19.4 |
| Hernando | 14.4 | 13.7 | 12.4 | 52.3 | 130 802 | 172 778 | 32.1 | 0.4 | 3 384 | 5 574 | 2 894 | 71 745 | 29.4 | 2.38 | 11.4 | 25.4 |
| Highlands | 13.6 | 16.5 | 16.0 | 51.2 | 87 366 | 98 786 | 13.1 | -0.7 | 2 082 | 3 170 | 515 | 42 604 | 13.7 | 2.28 | 9.9 | 28.5 |
| Hillsborough | 11.7 | 6.4 | 5.5 | 51.1 | 998 948 | 1 229 226 | 23.1 | 3.9 | 36 686 | 21 416 | 32 976 | 474 030 | 21.1 | 2.55 | 14.8 | 27.1 |
| Holmes | 13.1 | 10.2 | 7.4 | 47.0 | 18 564 | 19 927 | 7.3 | -0.6 | 450 | 523 | -50 | 7 354 | 6.3 | 2.47 | 12.0 | 26.3 |
| Indian River | 14.7 | 13.4 | 14.2 | 51.7 | 112 947 | 138 028 | 22.2 | 1.8 | 2 830 | 3 932 | 3 578 | 60 176 | 22.5 | 2.26 | 9.8 | 29.8 |
| Jackson | 13.4 | 9.0 | 7.1 | 45.2 | 46 755 | 49 746 | 6.4 | -1.6 | 1 090 | 1 228 | -617 | 17 417 | 4.8 | 2.40 | 15.6 | 28.9 |
| Jefferson | 16.0 | 10.2 | 7.3 | 47.6 | 12 902 | 14 761 | 14.4 | -3.4 | 284 | 322 | -484 | 5 646 | 20.3 | 2.38 | 15.1 | 28.1 |
| Lafayette | 10.5 | 7.5 | 5.2 | 38.3 | 7 022 | 8 870 | 26.3 | -0.7 | 183 | 186 | -77 | 2 580 | 20.4 | 2.63 | 10.9 | 24.2 |
| Lake | 13.4 | 13.4 | 11.3 | 51.6 | 210 528 | 297 052 | 41.1 | 2.1 | 6 725 | 7 868 | 7 538 | 121 289 | 37.2 | 2.42 | 10.6 | 25.2 |
| Lee | 14.3 | 13.4 | 10.7 | 50.9 | 440 888 | 618 754 | 40.3 | 4.3 | 14 027 | 13 633 | 25 704 | 259 818 | 37.8 | 2.35 | 10.3 | 26.7 |
| Leon | 10.9 | 5.6 | 4.3 | 52.5 | 239 452 | 275 487 | 15.0 | 3.0 | 6 754 | 3 666 | 5 196 | 110 945 | 14.9 | 2.35 | 14.0 | 30.1 |
| Levy | 15.9 | 12.1 | 7.9 | 50.8 | 34 450 | 40 801 | 18.4 | -1.9 | 879 | 1 078 | -594 | 16 404 | 18.3 | 2.45 | 13.0 | 26.0 |
| Liberty | 11.1 | 6.8 | 4.3 | 38.8 | 7 021 | 8 365 | 19.1 | -1.1 | 185 | 170 | -109 | 2 525 | 13.6 | 2.57 | 13.6 | 25.1 |
| Madison | 13.9 | 9.2 | 7.2 | 47.7 | 18 733 | 19 224 | 2.6 | -1.6 | 479 | 453 | -358 | 6 985 | 5.4 | 2.48 | 18.3 | 27.6 |
| Manatee | 14.2 | 12.3 | 11.4 | 51.7 | 264 002 | 322 833 | 22.3 | 3.4 | 7 613 | 7 518 | 10 879 | 135 729 | 20.7 | 2.34 | 10.8 | 28.5 |
| Marion | 14.1 | 14.4 | 11.8 | 52.1 | 258 916 | 331 298 | 28.0 | 1.2 | 7 551 | 9 483 | 5 875 | 137 726 | 29.0 | 2.35 | 12.0 | 26.7 |
| Martin | 14.8 | 13.4 | 14.3 | 50.5 | 126 731 | 146 318 | 15.5 | 1.7 | 2 639 | 3 891 | 3 847 | 63 899 | 15.6 | 2.23 | 8.6 | 31.0 |
| Miami-Dade | 11.2 | 7.5 | 6.7 | 51.4 | 2 253 362 | 2 496 435 | 10.8 | 3.8 | 70 089 | 41 938 | 66 334 | 867 352 | 11.7 | 2.83 | 18.8 | 23.5 |
| Monroe | 17.9 | 10.9 | 6.8 | 46.8 | 79 589 | 73 090 | -8.2 | 2.4 | 1 569 | 1 475 | 1 662 | 32 629 | -7.0 | 2.18 | 8.0 | 30.8 |
| Nassau | 15.4 | 10.6 | 6.5 | 50.7 | 57 663 | 73 314 | 27.1 | 1.8 | 1 698 | 1 588 | 1 202 | 28 794 | 31.0 | 2.53 | 10.5 | 21.9 |
| Okaloosa | 12.2 | 7.9 | 6.3 | 49.7 | 170 498 | 180 822 | 6.1 | 5.1 | 5 800 | 3 408 | 6 820 | 72 379 | 9.2 | 2.43 | 11.8 | 26.1 |
| Okeechobee | 11.6 | 9.7 | 7.5 | 46.4 | 35 910 | 39 996 | 11.4 | -1.3 | 1 207 | 885 | -1 036 | 14 013 | 11.3 | 2.68 | 12.5 | 23.9 |
| Orange | 10.3 | 5.6 | 4.4 | 50.7 | 896 344 | 1 145 956 | 27.8 | 4.9 | 33 841 | 15 251 | 37 622 | 421 847 | 25.4 | 2.64 | 15.7 | 24.9 |
| Osceola | 10.9 | 6.8 | 4.6 | 50.8 | 172 493 | 268 685 | 55.8 | 7.0 | 8 423 | 3 695 | 13 762 | 90 603 | 48.6 | 2.93 | 16.6 | 17.9 |
| Palm Beach | 12.4 | 10.0 | 11.8 | 51.6 | 1 131 184 | 1 320 134 | 16.7 | 2.8 | 30 626 | 29 863 | 36 096 | 544 227 | 14.8 | 2.39 | 11.7 | 30.1 |
| Pasco | 13.4 | 11.1 | 9.9 | 51.4 | 344 765 | 464 697 | 34.8 | 1.2 | 10 501 | 12 044 | 7 414 | 189 612 | 28.5 | 2.42 | 11.2 | 26.2 |
| Pinellas | 15.1 | 10.5 | 10.9 | 52.0 | 921 482 | 916 542 | -0.5 | 0.5 | 18 589 | 25 750 | 12 653 | 415 876 | 0.2 | 2.16 | 11.9 | 35.4 |
| Polk | 12.5 | 10.2 | 8.1 | 51.0 | 483 924 | 602 095 | 24.4 | 2.3 | 16 386 | 13 083 | 11 078 | 227 485 | 21.5 | 2.59 | 13.7 | 23.8 |

1. No spouse present.

# Table B. States and Counties — Population, Vital Statistics, Medicare, and Crime

| STATE County | Persons in group quarters, 2010 | Daytime population, 2007–2011 Number | Employment/residence ratio | Births, 2011 Total | Rate[1] | Deaths, 2011 Number | Rate[1] | Persons under 65 with no health insurance, 2010 Number | Percent | Medicare, 2012 Eligible for Medicare | Enrolled in Medicare Advantage | Enrolled in a Medicare prescription drug plan | Serious crimes known to police,[2] 2011 Total Number | Rate[3] |
|---|---|---|---|---|---|---|---|---|---|---|---|---|---|---|
| | 32 | 33 | 34 | 35 | 36 | 37 | 38 | 39 | 40 | 41 | 42 | 43 | 44 | 45 |
| CONNECTICUT—Cont'd | | | | | | | | | | | | | | |
| Tolland | 16 117 | 122 800 | 0.63 | 1 189 | 7.8 | 898 | 5.9 | 9 002 | 7.6 | 22 336 | 5 005 | 9 892 | NA | NA |
| Windham | 4 771 | 102 867 | 0.74 | 1 145 | 9.7 | 934 | 7.9 | 10 354 | 10.4 | 19 785 | 3 863 | 10 196 | NA | NA |
| DELAWARE | 24 413 | 895 009 | 1.01 | 11 172 | 12.3 | 7 633 | 8.4 | 86 894 | 11.6 | 162 810 | 8 599 | 78 750 | 36 014 | 3 970 |
| Kent | 4 322 | 152 575 | 0.90 | 2 214 | 13.4 | 1 406 | 8.5 | 14 714 | 10.7 | 28 676 | 1 398 | 12 052 | 7 038 | 4 292 |
| New Castle | 17 154 | 555 123 | 1.07 | 6 712 | 12.4 | 4 124 | 7.6 | 49 361 | 10.8 | 83 516 | 5 202 | 41 628 | 20 952 | 3 851 |
| Sussex | 2 937 | 187 311 | 0.91 | 2 246 | 11.2 | 2 103 | 10.5 | 22 818 | 14.7 | 50 618 | 1 999 | 25 070 | 8 317 | 4 176 |
| DISTRICT OF COLUMBIA | 40 021 | 1 069 960 | 2.60 | 9 003 | 14.6 | 4 773 | 7.7 | 45 483 | 9.0 | 82 991 | 8 583 | 34 746 | 37 065 | 5 998 |
| District of Columbia | 40 021 | 1 069 960 | 2.60 | 9 003 | 14.6 | 4 773 | 7.7 | 45 483 | 9.0 | 82 991 | 8 583 | 34 746 | 37 065 | 5 998 |
| FLORIDA | 421 709 | 18 642 360 | 0.99 | 213 292 | 11.2 | 171 257 | 9.0 | 3 853 392 | 25.3 | 3 624 805 | 1 258 680 | 1 182 462 | 769 399 | 4 037 |
| Alachua | 13 920 | 261 765 | 1.14 | 2 831 | 11.4 | 1 690 | 6.8 | 42 323 | 20.3 | 34 339 | 4 131 | 13 955 | 10 511 | 4 193 |
| Baker | 2 344 | 22 848 | 0.61 | 353 | 13.0 | 212 | 7.8 | 4 038 | 18.4 | 4 063 | 739 | 1 759 | 359 | 1 306 |
| Bay | 3 817 | 170 160 | 1.03 | 2 209 | 13.0 | 1 610 | 9.5 | 31 413 | 22.2 | 31 841 | 3 674 | 12 870 | 8 339 | 4 872 |
| Bradford | 4 492 | 27 014 | 0.83 | 324 | 11.5 | 304 | 10.8 | 4 096 | 20.3 | 4 912 | 597 | 2 310 | 768 | 2 726 |
| Brevard | 7 735 | 534 591 | 0.97 | 4 943 | 9.1 | 5 854 | 10.8 | 87 870 | 20.7 | 126 864 | 40 824 | 33 306 | 21 417 | 3 888 |
| Broward | 16 892 | 1 677 174 | 0.92 | 20 927 | 11.8 | 14 331 | 8.1 | 401 954 | 27.1 | 265 352 | 132 273 | 69 763 | 78 781 | 4 446 |
| Calhoun | 1 891 | 13 416 | 0.74 | 158 | 10.7 | 140 | 9.5 | 2 497 | 23.4 | 2 570 | 536 | 1 171 | 123 | 830 |
| Charlotte | 3 012 | 155 871 | 0.92 | 974 | 6.1 | 2 208 | 13.8 | 23 632 | 22.9 | 52 998 | 13 670 | 19 170 | 4 433 | 2 734 |
| Citrus | 2 251 | 135 726 | 0.88 | 1 035 | 7.4 | 2 315 | 16.5 | 21 036 | 22.1 | 49 147 | 12 097 | 17 197 | 3 580 | 2 501 |
| Clay | 1 251 | 152 273 | 0.57 | 2 127 | 11.1 | 1 365 | 7.1 | 29 125 | 17.4 | 30 956 | 5 160 | 10 097 | 5 536 | 2 861 |
| Collier | 4 546 | 327 765 | 1.06 | 3 371 | 10.3 | 2 742 | 8.4 | 68 849 | 29.5 | 75 607 | 11 864 | 35 265 | 7 105 | 2 180 |
| Columbia | 4 606 | 66 101 | 0.95 | 817 | 12.1 | 708 | 10.5 | 11 605 | 21.8 | 13 193 | 1 669 | 5 679 | 2 796 | 4 085 |
| DeSoto | 3 798 | 33 856 | 0.94 | 436 | 12.5 | 261 | 7.5 | 8 875 | 34.4 | 6 026 | 1 115 | 2 665 | 999 | 2 827 |
| Dixie | 1 430 | 14 997 | 0.74 | 167 | 10.1 | 194 | 11.8 | 2 577 | 21.7 | 3 717 | 541 | 1 728 | 508 | 3 052 |
| Duval | 19 985 | 935 797 | 1.18 | 12 585 | 14.5 | 7 232 | 8.3 | 145 240 | 19.3 | 127 930 | 30 607 | 47 820 | 44 522 | 5 082 |
| Escambia | 17 959 | 310 957 | 1.10 | 3 962 | 13.2 | 3 034 | 10.1 | 48 336 | 20.3 | 58 370 | 12 350 | 18 633 | 16 048 | 5 320 |
| Flagler | 684 | 84 343 | 0.71 | 854 | 8.8 | 953 | 9.8 | 16 774 | 23.3 | 27 612 | 9 159 | 8 073 | 2 375 | 2 448 |
| Franklin | 1 828 | 11 350 | 0.96 | 115 | 9.9 | 96 | 8.3 | 2 080 | 26.8 | 2 362 | 439 | 1 024 | 351 | 2 998 |
| Gadsden | 2 161 | 42 562 | 0.77 | 662 | 14.3 | 448 | 9.7 | 9 266 | 23.9 | 8 656 | 3 476 | 2 627 | 1 108 | 2 387 |
| Gilchrist | 1 128 | 14 589 | 0.63 | 182 | 10.7 | 174 | 10.2 | 3 039 | 23.1 | 3 298 | 491 | 1 429 | 296 | 1 724 |
| Glades | 1 483 | 11 463 | 0.73 | 79 | 6.3 | 105 | 8.3 | 2 819 | 32.8 | 2 000 | 471 | 766 | 311 | 2 381 |
| Gulf | 3 450 | 14 931 | 0.83 | 119 | 7.5 | 169 | 10.7 | 2 236 | 22.5 | 3 040 | 371 | 1 578 | 257 | 1 598 |
| Hamilton | 3 064 | 14 110 | 0.86 | 176 | 12.0 | 106 | 7.2 | 2 158 | 21.9 | 2 555 | 325 | 1 274 | 393 | 2 620 |
| Hardee | 1 984 | 27 365 | 0.97 | 450 | 16.1 | 168 | 6.0 | 7 327 | 32.4 | 3 823 | 599 | 2 018 | 876 | 3 116 |
| Hendry | 1 942 | 38 754 | 0.98 | 622 | 15.9 | 304 | 7.8 | 11 458 | 34.5 | 4 833 | 832 | 2 430 | 1 568 | 3 952 |
| Hernando | 1 828 | 157 177 | 0.75 | 1 502 | 8.7 | 2 511 | 14.5 | 29 606 | 23.3 | 50 047 | 23 190 | 11 047 | 5 720 | 3 266 |
| Highlands | 1 733 | 97 609 | 0.96 | 952 | 9.7 | 1 378 | 14.0 | 18 923 | 28.5 | 28 920 | 6 005 | 12 060 | 3 183 | 3 179 |
| Hillsborough | 22 065 | 1 281 723 | 1.11 | 16 270 | 12.8 | 9 329 | 7.4 | 241 193 | 22.6 | 184 169 | 77 083 | 50 220 | 37 147 | 2 981 |
| Holmes | 1 732 | 17 950 | 0.68 | 209 | 10.5 | 216 | 10.9 | 3 174 | 21.2 | 4 529 | 492 | 2 117 | 324 | 1 604 |
| Indian River | 1 794 | 138 314 | 1.02 | 1 266 | 9.1 | 1 730 | 12.5 | 25 651 | 25.9 | 39 180 | 6 824 | 16 140 | 4 409 | 3 151 |
| Jackson | 7 994 | 48 739 | 0.95 | 511 | 10.4 | 555 | 11.3 | 6 419 | 18.6 | 10 369 | 1 202 | 4 650 | 1 285 | 2 597 |
| Jefferson | 1 339 | 12 498 | 0.63 | 135 | 9.2 | 132 | 9.0 | 2 484 | 22.4 | 3 028 | 1 103 | 956 | 308 | 2 059 |
| Lafayette | 2 094 | 8 051 | 0.84 | 79 | 8.8 | 83 | 9.3 | 1 633 | 28.3 | 942 | 88 | 482 | 76 | 845 |
| Lake | 3 987 | 270 057 | 0.78 | 3 053 | 10.1 | 3 420 | 11.4 | 49 874 | 22.4 | 79 743 | 18 570 | 29 817 | 8 914 | 2 960 |
| Lee | 8 488 | 604 861 | 0.95 | 6 308 | 10.0 | 5 852 | 9.3 | 127 288 | 27.2 | 144 273 | 39 238 | 54 897 | 19 711 | 3 143 |
| Leon | 14 994 | 290 903 | 1.13 | 3 051 | 11.0 | 1 585 | 5.7 | 40 413 | 17.2 | 33 119 | 12 718 | 7 907 | 13 916 | 4 984 |
| Levy | 635 | 35 537 | 0.66 | 427 | 10.6 | 473 | 11.8 | 7 609 | 23.5 | 9 979 | 1 736 | 4 395 | 1 514 | 3 661 |
| Liberty | 1 882 | 7 903 | 0.85 | 78 | 9.4 | 67 | 8.1 | 1 219 | 21.6 | 1 213 | 335 | 451 | 45 | 531 |
| Madison | 1 933 | 17 723 | 0.78 | 214 | 11.2 | 202 | 10.6 | 3 281 | 22.7 | 3 780 | 748 | 1 873 | 603 | 3 095 |
| Manatee | 4 817 | 303 667 | 0.86 | 3 436 | 10.5 | 3 233 | 9.9 | 59 650 | 24.4 | 76 066 | 21 973 | 26 885 | 14 839 | 4 535 |
| Marion | 8 239 | 322 875 | 0.94 | 3 402 | 10.2 | 4 144 | 12.5 | 59 070 | 24.7 | 95 234 | 31 651 | 29 994 | 10 049 | 2 992 |
| Martin | 3 933 | 148 598 | 1.05 | 1 173 | 8.0 | 1 706 | 11.6 | 23 856 | 23.2 | 38 316 | 7 490 | 15 615 | 4 042 | 2 725 |
| Miami-Dade | 40 057 | 2 539 249 | 1.06 | 31 317 | 12.3 | 18 117 | 7.1 | 758 908 | 35.8 | 394 991 | 220 104 | 121 905 | 138 000 | 5 454 |
| Monroe | 2 020 | 75 855 | 1.07 | 694 | 9.4 | 632 | 8.6 | 17 087 | 28.7 | 14 032 | 1 007 | 6 615 | 3 580 | 4 832 |
| Nassau | 543 | 61 393 | 0.65 | 762 | 10.3 | 690 | 9.3 | 11 589 | 19.1 | 15 179 | 3 051 | 6 309 | 1 635 | 2 200 |
| Okaloosa | 4 883 | 189 352 | 1.08 | 2 521 | 13.7 | 1 529 | 8.3 | 29 019 | 19.3 | 32 094 | 3 005 | 9 282 | 6 033 | 3 392 |
| Okeechobee | 2 503 | 39 436 | 0.96 | 540 | 13.5 | 369 | 9.2 | 8 982 | 28.9 | 7 251 | 2 123 | 2 737 | 1 599 | 3 944 |
| Orange | 33 704 | 1 274 979 | 1.26 | 14 981 | 12.8 | 6 584 | 5.6 | 250 534 | 24.7 | 142 082 | 52 135 | 41 085 | 59 658 | 5 136 |
| Osceola | 3 262 | 233 644 | 0.73 | 3 706 | 13.4 | 1 591 | 5.8 | 64 504 | 27.1 | 40 693 | 19 690 | 9 785 | 11 289 | 4 145 |
| Palm Beach | 19 972 | 1 325 663 | 1.03 | 13 733 | 10.3 | 13 089 | 9.8 | 268 136 | 26.3 | 271 316 | 91 500 | 98 901 | 52 371 | 3 914 |
| Pasco | 5 674 | 398 716 | 0.65 | 4 748 | 10.2 | 5 325 | 11.4 | 80 781 | 22.2 | 105 697 | 50 876 | 24 526 | 16 045 | 3 432 |
| Pinellas | 19 678 | 927 673 | 1.03 | 8 403 | 9.2 | 11 440 | 12.5 | 158 352 | 22.3 | 207 400 | 85 788 | 57 437 | 40 863 | 4 398 |
| Polk | 12 261 | 572 976 | 0.89 | 7 412 | 12.2 | 5 683 | 9.3 | 117 796 | 24.4 | 123 620 | 48 914 | 35 375 | 22 649 | 3 711 |

1. Per 1,000 estimated resident population.   2. Data for serious crimes have not been adjusted for underreporting; this may affect comparability between geographic areas and over time.   3. Per 100,000 population estimated by the FBI.

# Table B. States and Counties — Crime, Education, Money Income, and Poverty

| STATE County | Serious crimes known to police, 2011 (cont.)[1] Rate[2] Violent | Property | Education School enrollment and attainment, 2007–2011 Enrollment[3] Total | Percent private | Attainment[4] (percent) High school graduate or less | Bachelor's degree or more | Local government expenditures,[5] 2009–2010 Total current expenditures (mil dol) | Current expenditures per student (dollars) | Money income, 2007–2011 Per capita income[6] (dollars) | Households Median income Dollars | Percent change, 2000 to 2007–2011 (constant 2011 dollars) | Percent with income of $200,000 or more | Income and poverty, 2011 Median household income (dollars) | Percent below poverty level All persons | Children under 18 years | Children 5 to 17 years in families |
|---|---|---|---|---|---|---|---|---|---|---|---|---|---|---|---|---|
| | 46 | 47 | 48 | 49 | 50 | 51 | 52 | 53 | 54 | 55 | 56 | 57 | 58 | 59 | 60 | 61 |
| CONNECTICUT—Cont'd | | | | | | | | | | | | | | | | |
| Tolland | NA | NA | 49 091 | 10.5 | 35.0 | 36.5 | 310.6 | 13 706 | 33 929 | 80 333 | 0.8 | 5.6 | 77 124 | 8.0 | 7.4 | 6.1 |
| Windham | NA | NA | 30 507 | 10.1 | 51.8 | 22.0 | 247.8 | 14 194 | 27 634 | 60 063 | -1.4 | 2.6 | 54 911 | 10.6 | 15.0 | 12.9 |
| DELAWARE | 559 | 3 411 | 233 082 | 21.1 | 44.3 | 28.0 | 1 545.8 | 12 191 | 29 659 | 59 317 | -7.3 | 4.4 | 58 159 | 12.6 | 18.8 | 17.1 |
| Kent | 626 | 3 666 | 44 495 | 16.2 | 48.9 | 20.0 | 285.9 | 11 346 | 24 374 | 54 783 | -0.9 | 1.8 | 51 045 | 14.9 | 22.7 | 19.9 |
| New Castle | 580 | 3 272 | 150 088 | 24.1 | 40.4 | 32.7 | 918.5 | 12 435 | 31 988 | 64 158 | -9.3 | 5.5 | 63 087 | 12.0 | 16.2 | 14.8 |
| Sussex | 484 | 3 692 | 38 499 | 15.1 | 51.1 | 21.9 | 341.4 | 12 306 | 27 580 | 53 215 | 0.5 | 3.3 | 51 060 | 12.4 | 23.1 | 21.4 |
| DISTRICT OF COLUMBIA | 1 202 | 4 796 | 154 369 | 44.2 | 32.4 | 50.5 | 1 222.8 | 17 611 | 43 993 | 61 835 | 14.1 | 10.5 | 62 087 | 19.1 | 30.9 | 30.5 |
| District of Columbia | 1 202 | 4 796 | 154 369 | 44.2 | 32.4 | 50.5 | 1 222.8 | 17 611 | 43 993 | 61 835 | 14.1 | 10.5 | 62 087 | 19.1 | 30.9 | 30.5 |
| FLORIDA | 515 | 3 522 | 4 524 992 | 17.9 | 44.6 | 26.0 | 22 966.9 | 8 718 | 26 733 | 47 827 | -8.7 | 3.7 | 44 250 | 17.0 | 25.1 | 23.5 |
| Alachua | 625 | 3 567 | 93 630 | 8.5 | 30.7 | 41.1 | 241.9 | 8 364 | 25 172 | 41 373 | -2.5 | 3.9 | 39 825 | 23.5 | 21.8 | 21.3 |
| Baker | 167 | 1 139 | 6 291 | 9.0 | 69.6 | 7.4 | 40.1 | 7 753 | 19 985 | 47 041 | -13.0 | 2.5 | 42 564 | 18.6 | 24.2 | 23.0 |
| Bay | 535 | 4 338 | 38 882 | 11.4 | 44.7 | 21.0 | 208.8 | 8 062 | 25 370 | 48 225 | -1.0 | 2.0 | 44 204 | 14.4 | 23.3 | 21.6 |
| Bradford | 433 | 2 293 | 5 553 | 14.1 | 62.7 | 8.8 | 30.4 | 9 293 | 17 270 | 41 397 | -7.5 | 1.2 | 39 271 | 23.1 | 30.0 | 29.7 |
| Brevard | 592 | 3 296 | 124 912 | 19.6 | 39.5 | 26.4 | 578.8 | 7 993 | 27 927 | 50 068 | -7.5 | 3.2 | 46 494 | 14.2 | 22.6 | 21.3 |
| Broward | 490 | 3 956 | 451 218 | 22.2 | 41.0 | 29.9 | 2 379.6 | 9 290 | 28 720 | 51 782 | -8.0 | 4.5 | 48 478 | 14.9 | 20.5 | 19.0 |
| Calhoun | 88 | 742 | 2 874 | 4.2 | 69.0 | 7.9 | 19.7 | 8 826 | 14 486 | 31 142 | -13.2 | 0.8 | 32 395 | 25.9 | 31.8 | 29.9 |
| Charlotte | 244 | 2 490 | 25 935 | 16.0 | 47.0 | 20.9 | 152.4 | 8 995 | 26 902 | 45 112 | -8.2 | 1.9 | 41 346 | 13.2 | 24.2 | 22.5 |
| Citrus | 309 | 2 192 | 23 424 | 12.7 | 53.6 | 16.5 | 142.0 | 8 831 | 22 939 | 38 189 | -8.8 | 1.3 | 35 041 | 17.3 | 31.2 | 28.2 |
| Clay | 401 | 2 461 | 53 551 | 13.7 | 41.2 | 23.2 | 287.0 | 7 982 | 26 650 | 59 994 | -9.0 | 3.0 | 54 867 | 10.9 | 15.1 | 13.7 |
| Collier | 315 | 1 865 | 62 128 | 15.1 | 42.3 | 31.6 | 431.1 | 10 092 | 37 335 | 56 876 | -12.8 | 8.2 | 51 039 | 16.2 | 30.7 | 28.1 |
| Columbia | 640 | 3 445 | 16 011 | 12.6 | 54.2 | 13.1 | 87.0 | 8 666 | 19 224 | 38 589 | -7.4 | 1.0 | 36 452 | 21.7 | 31.8 | 29.3 |
| DeSoto | 481 | 2 346 | 7 238 | 8.5 | 68.7 | 11.4 | 43.6 | 8 746 | 16 034 | 36 407 | -12.2 | 1.3 | 32 753 | 31.0 | 41.9 | 40.9 |
| Dixie | 421 | 2 631 | 2 909 | 9.2 | 62.7 | 8.9 | 17.8 | 8 409 | 18 374 | 34 243 | -2.8 | 0.7 | 30 801 | 25.2 | 36.3 | 35.6 |
| Duval | 638 | 4 445 | 228 366 | 20.7 | 42.2 | 25.2 | 1 091.8 | 8 907 | 26 394 | 49 964 | -9.1 | 2.9 | 45 995 | 17.7 | 25.5 | 24.0 |
| Escambia | 720 | 4 599 | 75 210 | 22.4 | 42.8 | 23.3 | 347.5 | 8 557 | 23 773 | 43 707 | -8.1 | 2.5 | 41 072 | 18.5 | 28.3 | 26.1 |
| Flagler | 321 | 2 128 | 19 259 | 15.8 | 43.8 | 22.0 | 103.1 | 7 846 | 24 455 | 48 708 | -10.3 | 2.3 | 47 095 | 14.7 | 25.8 | 22.5 |
| Franklin | 888 | 2 110 | 1 672 | 6.9 | 55.8 | 17.6 | 15.2 | 11 725 | 21 009 | 37 017 | 2.5 | 1.4 | 35 288 | 22.3 | 30.7 | 29.7 |
| Gadsden | 511 | 1 877 | 10 942 | 13.0 | 60.2 | 13.2 | 56.7 | 8 947 | 17 657 | 33 453 | -20.7 | 0.6 | 34 154 | 25.2 | 37.5 | 36.6 |
| Gilchrist | 204 | 1 520 | 3 480 | 16.8 | 59.7 | 11.4 | 24.1 | 8 822 | 18 869 | 38 467 | -6.1 | 1.2 | 38 046 | 19.5 | 29.4 | 27.3 |
| Glades | 314 | 2 067 | 2 253 | 6.4 | 60.8 | 10.3 | 13.8 | 9 649 | 18 248 | 39 611 | -4.7 | 0.7 | 38 825 | 22.2 | 33.6 | 31.9 |
| Gulf | 373 | 1 225 | 2 853 | 8.5 | 60.7 | 13.3 | 19.0 | 9 367 | 18 371 | 41 291 | 1.0 | 0.5 | 37 373 | 23.2 | 28.1 | 25.4 |
| Hamilton | 367 | 2 253 | 2 787 | 12.2 | 67.7 | 8.4 | 18.5 | 10 153 | 15 484 | 36 683 | 6.0 | 1.9 | 29 482 | 31.9 | 39.2 | 36.3 |
| Hardee | 285 | 2 832 | 6 432 | 4.5 | 70.9 | 9.3 | 43.3 | 8 616 | 15 760 | 38 046 | -6.6 | 1.4 | 33 058 | 31.8 | 45.4 | 43.0 |
| Hendry | 633 | 3 320 | 9 952 | 7.6 | 71.7 | 9.4 | 60.3 | 8 726 | 14 858 | 37 989 | -16.2 | 1.0 | 35 247 | 29.6 | 39.8 | 36.1 |
| Hernando | 313 | 2 953 | 36 087 | 11.9 | 51.6 | 16.2 | 176.9 | 7 722 | 22 540 | 42 700 | -2.9 | 1.4 | 40 411 | 16.6 | 27.9 | 25.5 |
| Highlands | 294 | 2 885 | 17 357 | 11.8 | 57.3 | 14.5 | 109.0 | 9 010 | 19 860 | 34 913 | -14.3 | 1.1 | 33 692 | 18.8 | 32.8 | 32.0 |
| Hillsborough | 371 | 2 610 | 329 477 | 16.6 | 42.0 | 29.0 | 1 640.3 | 8 487 | 27 282 | 50 195 | -8.6 | 4.0 | 46 592 | 17.6 | 23.7 | 21.7 |
| Holmes | 322 | 1 282 | 4 072 | 8.5 | 67.7 | 10.1 | 28.6 | 8 546 | 15 404 | 33 510 | -11.1 | 0.5 | 33 211 | 26.1 | 36.8 | 34.2 |
| Indian River | 322 | 2 830 | 26 630 | 15.1 | 42.0 | 26.4 | 148.7 | 8 378 | 31 732 | 46 363 | -13.4 | 5.5 | 42 053 | 13.9 | 23.3 | 22.3 |
| Jackson | 376 | 2 221 | 10 579 | 13.1 | 55.4 | 13.6 | 65.9 | 8 977 | 18 368 | 39 869 | -0.7 | 1.5 | 35 193 | 20.5 | 28.6 | 25.9 |
| Jefferson | 668 | 1 390 | 2 692 | 28.7 | 55.8 | 15.5 | 11.3 | 9 454 | 19 788 | 42 096 | -5.5 | 1.3 | 40 252 | 18.7 | 27.9 | 26.4 |
| Lafayette | 133 | 712 | 2 047 | 10.6 | 59.6 | 10.3 | 11.0 | 9 432 | 19 201 | 49 713 | 20.1 | 0.8 | 40 407 | 23.8 | 27.7 | 24.3 |
| Lake | 361 | 2 600 | 60 107 | 17.7 | 47.6 | 20.1 | 319.1 | 7 772 | 25 440 | 47 665 | -4.6 | 2.1 | 44 965 | 13.9 | 21.3 | 21.3 |
| Lee | 353 | 2 790 | 126 928 | 13.7 | 46.0 | 24.6 | 707.5 | 8 790 | 28 946 | 49 444 | -9.2 | 4.1 | 45 515 | 15.3 | 25.9 | 23.9 |
| Leon | 727 | 4 256 | 106 715 | 11.9 | 29.6 | 43.1 | 272.3 | 7 642 | 26 332 | 45 827 | -9.5 | 3.2 | 44 857 | 22.7 | 22.5 | 20.4 |
| Levy | 392 | 3 269 | 8 998 | 14.5 | 58.7 | 12.2 | 51.9 | 8 749 | 19 244 | 35 920 | -1.3 | 1.4 | 33 544 | 22.0 | 32.7 | 28.8 |
| Liberty | 83 | 448 | 1 549 | 6.0 | 64.1 | 13.2 | 13.4 | 8 967 | 16 291 | 40 893 | 5.0 | 1.0 | 37 446 | 23.5 | 28.1 | 25.3 |
| Madison | 688 | 2 407 | 3 966 | 9.9 | 63.9 | 10.9 | 25.6 | 9 395 | 16 398 | 36 557 | 2.0 | 1.4 | 31 578 | 25.9 | 36.5 | 35.3 |
| Manatee | 625 | 3 910 | 65 852 | 15.4 | 44.5 | 26.0 | 384.0 | 8 942 | 27 918 | 48 181 | -7.7 | 3.4 | 43 494 | 15.9 | 26.7 | 23.6 |
| Marion | 497 | 2 496 | 64 937 | 16.8 | 52.6 | 16.8 | 362.4 | 8 627 | 22 328 | 40 103 | -7.0 | 1.9 | 36 425 | 17.6 | 30.0 | 27.9 |
| Martin | 241 | 2 484 | 28 361 | 18.4 | 38.0 | 29.9 | 159.9 | 8 878 | 35 822 | 53 612 | -7.8 | 7.1 | 50 417 | 12.7 | 21.9 | 19.5 |
| Miami-Dade | 724 | 4 730 | 634 419 | 21.1 | 50.1 | 26.2 | 3 118.1 | 9 017 | 23 348 | 43 957 | -9.5 | 4.1 | 40 476 | 20.9 | 28.9 | 28.4 |
| Monroe | 478 | 4 354 | 11 881 | 15.2 | 39.9 | 27.8 | 100.0 | 12 071 | 35 074 | 53 889 | -5.6 | 6.6 | 51 152 | 13.8 | 22.0 | 22.0 |
| Nassau | 175 | 2 025 | 16 973 | 15.2 | 48.1 | 21.8 | 88.3 | 7 947 | 29 368 | 58 933 | -5.2 | 4.2 | 54 706 | 11.4 | 17.6 | 15.2 |
| Okaloosa | 427 | 2 865 | 44 391 | 11.2 | 37.0 | 26.9 | 248.3 | 8 614 | 28 505 | 54 140 | -3.3 | 4.0 | 49 643 | 13.7 | 22.2 | 20.2 |
| Okeechobee | 496 | 3 448 | 8 775 | 7.7 | 66.4 | 10.1 | 58.1 | 8 343 | 19 493 | 36 929 | -10.2 | 1.9 | 33 806 | 26.1 | 36.2 | 34.8 |
| Orange | 745 | 4 391 | 326 820 | 19.8 | 40.3 | 30.0 | 1 421.8 | 8 206 | 25 494 | 49 731 | -10.8 | 3.8 | 44 635 | 18.5 | 25.8 | 24.5 |
| Osceola | 585 | 3 560 | 70 976 | 14.1 | 50.9 | 18.0 | 431.9 | 8 284 | 20 440 | 46 479 | -9.9 | 1.6 | 40 933 | 16.0 | 24.4 | 22.9 |
| Palm Beach | 492 | 3 422 | 294 845 | 20.2 | 39.5 | 32.2 | 1 595.0 | 9 113 | 33 960 | 52 951 | -13.0 | 6.3 | 48 973 | 15.8 | 24.1 | 22.3 |
| Pasco | 311 | 3 096 | 100 691 | 16.5 | 48.0 | 19.7 | 573.2 | 8 536 | 24 116 | 44 103 | -0.9 | 1.8 | 40 859 | 15.7 | 21.2 | 19.0 |
| Pinellas | 607 | 3 792 | 186 739 | 18.1 | 42.1 | 27.0 | 924.3 | 8 783 | 29 232 | 45 891 | -8.4 | 3.4 | 42 761 | 15.0 | 25.3 | 22.4 |
| Polk | 417 | 3 294 | 140 435 | 15.8 | 54.6 | 18.0 | 819.6 | 8 670 | 21 952 | 44 398 | -8.7 | 1.9 | 40 258 | 19.2 | 30.2 | 28.3 |

1. Data for serious crimes have not been adjusted for underreporting; this may affect comparability between geographic areas and over time. 2. Per 100,000 population estimated by the FBI. 3. All persons 3 years old and over enrolled in nursery school through college. 4. Persons 25 years old and over. 5. Elementary and secondary education expenditures. 6. Based on population estimated by the American Community Survey, 2007–2011.

# Table B. States and Counties — Personal Income

| STATE County | Personal income, 2011 | | | | | | | | | | | | |
|---|---|---|---|---|---|---|---|---|---|---|---|---|---|
| | | | Per capita[1] | | | | | Transfer payments (mil dol) | | | | | |
| | | | | | | | | | Government payments to individuals | | | | |
| | Total (mil dol) | Percent change, 2010–2011 | Dollars | Rank | Wages and salaries[2] (mil dol) | Proprietors' income (mil dol) | Dividends, interest, and rent (mil dol) | Total | Total | Social Security | Medical payments | Income maintenance | Unemployment insurance |
| | 62 | 63 | 64 | 65 | 66 | 67 | 68 | 69 | 70 | 71 | 72 | 73 | 74 |
| CONNECTICUT—Cont'd | | | | | | | | | | | | | |
| Tolland | 7 110 | 3.8 | 46 624 | 314 | 2 417 | 469 | 1 119 | 919 | 886 | 351 | 345 | 50 | 75 |
| Windham | 4 625 | 3.7 | 39 141 | 840 | 2 005 | 248 | 691 | 957 | 931 | 294 | 426 | 84 | 74 |
| DELAWARE | 37 600 | 6.0 | 41 449 | X | 26 453 | 2 980 | 5 810 | 7 370 | 7 170 | 2 483 | 3 294 | 665 | 264 |
| Kent | 5 489 | 5.1 | 33 302 | 1 656 | 3 407 | 546 | 689 | 1 295 | 1 260 | 417 | 536 | 145 | 46 |
| New Castle | 25 101 | 6.9 | 46 315 | 326 | 19 922 | 1 970 | 3 708 | 4 055 | 3 935 | 1 312 | 1 836 | 370 | 163 |
| Sussex | 7 009 | 3.5 | 34 988 | 1 375 | 3 123 | 463 | 1 413 | 2 019 | 1 975 | 754 | 922 | 150 | 55 |
| DISTRICT OF COLUMBIA | 45 598 | 5.8 | 73 783 | X | 78 568 | 5 950 | 5 542 | 5 744 | 5 608 | 904 | 3 168 | 902 | 304 |
| District of Columbia | 45 598 | 5.8 | 73 783 | 16 | 78 568 | 5 950 | 5 542 | 5 744 | 5 608 | 904 | 3 168 | 902 | 304 |
| FLORIDA | 755 358 | 4.6 | 39 636 | X | 411 815 | 47 242 | 187 304 | 153 284 | 148 828 | 51 009 | 64 484 | 17 695 | 4 467 |
| Alachua | 8 931 | 3.6 | 35 816 | 1 247 | 6 580 | 347 | 1 764 | 1 634 | 1 579 | 490 | 657 | 196 | 34 |
| Baker | 690 | 3.0 | 25 426 | 2 935 | 295 | 18 | 77 | 192 | 186 | 58 | 82 | 26 | 6 |
| Bay | 6 296 | 3.2 | 37 068 | 1 070 | 3 887 | 299 | 1 202 | 1 441 | 1 371 | 436 | 579 | 160 | 43 |
| Bradford | 821 | 3.0 | 29 059 | 2 442 | 310 | 26 | 90 | 226 | 220 | 102 | 30 | 5 | 5 |
| Brevard | 20 671 | 3.6 | 38 028 | 967 | 11 580 | 944 | 4 287 | 4 801 | 4 681 | 1 866 | 1 889 | 382 | 147 |
| Broward | 76 134 | 4.7 | 42 768 | 523 | 41 961 | 5 063 | 16 493 | 12 604 | 12 208 | 3 730 | 5 547 | 1 527 | 466 |
| Calhoun | 329 | 2.9 | 22 318 | 3 077 | 121 | 19 | 45 | 114 | 111 | 33 | 53 | 15 | 2 |
| Charlotte | 5 644 | 4.7 | 35 161 | 1 346 | 1 866 | 250 | 1 851 | 1 725 | 1 687 | 785 | 683 | 97 | 30 |
| Citrus | 4 575 | 3.4 | 32 675 | 1 762 | 1 553 | 165 | 1 250 | 1 628 | 1 596 | 723 | 645 | 111 | 27 |
| Clay | 6 440 | 4.3 | 33 476 | 1 605 | 1 940 | 181 | 979 | 1 284 | 1 241 | 445 | 473 | 124 | 40 |
| Collier | 19 447 | 5.1 | 59 264 | 75 | 6 457 | 1 182 | 10 308 | 2 550 | 2 464 | 1 153 | 925 | 203 | 60 |
| Columbia | 1 904 | 2.1 | 28 209 | 2 584 | 1 016 | 50 | 352 | 579 | 564 | 182 | 235 | 79 | 14 |
| DeSoto | 857 | 3.5 | 24 574 | 2 999 | 417 | 49 | 181 | 254 | 247 | 82 | 110 | 36 | 6 |
| Dixie | 342 | 3.0 | 20 728 | 3 097 | 102 | 19 | 54 | 147 | 143 | 52 | 57 | 21 | 3 |
| Duval | 34 705 | 3.8 | 39 858 | 761 | 29 744 | 2 709 | 5 733 | 6 374 | 6 182 | 1 781 | 2 564 | 912 | 239 |
| Escambia | 10 782 | 4.7 | 36 047 | 1 204 | 7 709 | 426 | 1 863 | 2 596 | 2 511 | 788 | 1 043 | 324 | 57 |
| Flagler | 3 230 | 6.5 | 33 170 | 1 678 | 802 | 22 | 935 | 871 | 849 | 419 | 288 | 69 | 21 |
| Franklin | 338 | 3.5 | 29 147 | 2 429 | 138 | 24 | 92 | 104 | 98 | 31 | 47 | 11 | 2 |
| Gadsden | 1 282 | 1.7 | 27 778 | 2 644 | 581 | 43 | 209 | 384 | 374 | 113 | 148 | 81 | 11 |
| Gilchrist | 524 | 3.7 | 30 828 | 2 137 | 128 | 38 | 66 | 134 | 130 | 46 | 54 | 17 | 3 |
| Glades | 300 | 4.8 | 23 725 | 3 037 | 92 | 41 | 60 | 68 | 66 | 28 | 22 | 9 | 2 |
| Gulf | 412 | 2.8 | 26 029 | 2 876 | 166 | 17 | 82 | 137 | 132 | 44 | 64 | 13 | 3 |
| Hamilton | 293 | 3.6 | 20 005 | 3 104 | 188 | 6 | 46 | 113 | 110 | 35 | 47 | 19 | 2 |
| Hardee | 694 | 3.8 | 24 898 | 2 972 | 332 | 69 | 105 | 181 | 175 | 50 | 79 | 33 | 4 |
| Hendry | 1 106 | 1.7 | 28 285 | 2 573 | 556 | 115 | 171 | 262 | 254 | 66 | 111 | 53 | 12 |
| Hernando | 5 319 | 3.4 | 30 729 | 2 151 | 1 603 | 209 | 1 225 | 1 838 | 1 799 | 741 | 751 | 146 | 37 |
| Highlands | 2 940 | 3.6 | 29 809 | 2 321 | 1 145 | 114 | 785 | 1 022 | 1 001 | 409 | 423 | 92 | 17 |
| Hillsborough | 49 671 | 4.9 | 39 180 | 835 | 37 219 | 3 907 | 9 788 | 8 782 | 8 489 | 2 584 | 3 452 | 1 283 | 302 |
| Holmes | 523 | 3.7 | 26 324 | 2 846 | 136 | 37 | 68 | 197 | 192 | 58 | 91 | 25 | 2 |
| Indian River | 7 080 | 5.1 | 50 977 | 185 | 2 247 | 299 | 3 434 | 1 358 | 1 327 | 589 | 545 | 98 | 34 |
| Jackson | 1 431 | 3.7 | 29 033 | 2 447 | 655 | 100 | 223 | 476 | 465 | 138 | 231 | 54 | 7 |
| Jefferson | 424 | 2.3 | 28 954 | 2 456 | 106 | 16 | 82 | 117 | 114 | 40 | 45 | 17 | 3 |
| Lafayette | 171 | 2.9 | 19 121 | 3 108 | 69 | 13 | 33 | 44 | 42 | 13 | 19 | 6 | 1 |
| Lake | 10 188 | 5.1 | 33 846 | 1 540 | 3 570 | 384 | 2 262 | 2 964 | 2 897 | 1 158 | 1 271 | 237 | 63 |
| Lee | 27 161 | 5.4 | 43 022 | 508 | 10 447 | 1 580 | 10 783 | 5 282 | 5 129 | 2 158 | 2 048 | 472 | 139 |
| Leon | 10 236 | 3.2 | 36 823 | 1 099 | 7 650 | 624 | 2 012 | 1 530 | 1 467 | 486 | 484 | 218 | 42 |
| Levy | 1 093 | 3.7 | 27 231 | 2 731 | 339 | 57 | 203 | 373 | 363 | 138 | 147 | 45 | 8 |
| Liberty | 201 | 1.7 | 24 211 | 3 018 | 91 | 6 | 24 | 52 | 51 | 16 | 22 | 8 | 1 |
| Madison | 475 | 2.0 | 24 853 | 2 977 | 180 | 31 | 71 | 171 | 167 | 50 | 74 | 27 | 3 |
| Manatee | 13 308 | 4.4 | 40 678 | 689 | 5 236 | 1 020 | 4 082 | 2 675 | 2 599 | 1 129 | 983 | 249 | 62 |
| Marion | 10 877 | 4.3 | 32 709 | 1 755 | 4 185 | 395 | 2 602 | 3 300 | 3 226 | 1 370 | 1 230 | 331 | 71 |
| Martin | 7 787 | 4.7 | 52 798 | 146 | 3 028 | 405 | 3 654 | 1 303 | 1 270 | 592 | 515 | 73 | 28 |
| Miami-Dade | 96 658 | 4.8 | 37 834 | 992 | 62 315 | 9 284 | 15 697 | 21 415 | 20 847 | 4 224 | 11 247 | 3 605 | 700 |
| Monroe | 4 354 | 5.4 | 58 941 | 79 | 2 002 | 246 | 1 747 | 548 | 515 | 205 | 214 | 44 | 13 |
| Nassau | 3 420 | 5.3 | 46 099 | 334 | 953 | 100 | 910 | 569 | 553 | 229 | 217 | 50 | 16 |
| Okaloosa | 7 914 | 6.5 | 43 132 | 499 | 5 861 | 354 | 1 643 | 1 410 | 1 336 | 436 | 548 | 124 | 30 |
| Okeechobee | 1 037 | 2.9 | 25 831 | 2 897 | 455 | 63 | 177 | 350 | 342 | 103 | 170 | 42 | 10 |
| Orange | 42 076 | 4.9 | 35 990 | 1 211 | 38 025 | 3 485 | 6 358 | 7 406 | 7 147 | 1 964 | 2 955 | 1 173 | 300 |
| Osceola | 7 504 | 6.4 | 27 171 | 2 741 | 3 386 | 209 | 985 | 1 983 | 1 921 | 548 | 829 | 355 | 75 |
| Palm Beach | 71 432 | 4.4 | 53 500 | 135 | 31 330 | 4 679 | 27 921 | 10 933 | 10 637 | 4 174 | 4 668 | 939 | 304 |
| Pasco | 14 974 | 5.4 | 32 102 | 1 863 | 4 567 | 282 | 2 917 | 4 124 | 4 017 | 1 553 | 1 676 | 373 | 102 |
| Pinellas | 40 936 | 3.9 | 44 622 | 411 | 22 203 | 2 267 | 10 957 | 8 558 | 8 327 | 2 992 | 3 808 | 703 | 217 |
| Polk | 20 385 | 4.4 | 33 447 | 1 617 | 9 663 | 1 136 | 4 412 | 4 799 | 4 660 | 1 763 | 1 802 | 655 | 137 |

1. Based on the resident population estimated as of July 1 of the year shown.  2. Includes supplements to wages and salaries.

# Table B. States and Counties — **Earnings, Social Security, and Housing**

| STATE County | Earnings, 2011 | | | | | | | | | Social Security beneficiaries, December 2011 | | Supplemental Security Income recipients, December 2011 | Housing units, 2010 | |
|---|---|---|---|---|---|---|---|---|---|---|---|---|---|---|
| | | | Percent by selected industries | | | | | | | | | | | |
| | | | Goods-related[1] | | Service-related and health | | | | | | | | | |
| | Total (mil dol) | Farm | Total | Manu-facturing | Infor-mation and profes-sional and technical services | Retail trade | Finance, insur-ance, and real estate | Health care and social services | Govern-ment | Number | Rate[2] | | Total | Percent change, 2000–2010 |
| | 75 | 76 | 77 | 78 | 79 | 80 | 81 | 82 | 83 | 84 | 85 | 86 | 87 | 88 |
| CONNECTICUT—Cont'd | | | | | | | | | | | | | | |
| Tolland | 2 886 | 0.5 | D | 7.2 | 7.5 | 6.5 | 4.4 | 11.8 | 36.2 | 23 675 | 155 | 958 | 57 963 | 12.4 |
| Windham | 2 253 | 0.5 | D | 18.9 | 5.2 | 7.9 | 3.0 | 16.0 | 20.9 | 21 900 | 185 | 1 930 | 49 073 | 11.6 |
| DELAWARE | 29 433 | 0.5 | D | 6.7 | 13.6 | 6.0 | 15.8 | 12.6 | 16.1 | 176 885 | 195 | 16 240 | 405 885 | 18.3 |
| Kent | 3 954 | 1.4 | D | D | 4.0 | 7.8 | 7.7 | 11.3 | 39.6 | 31 990 | 194 | 3 686 | 65 338 | 29.4 |
| New Castle | 21 893 | 0.0 | D | D | 16.7 | 4.8 | 18.6 | 12.3 | 12.2 | 90 740 | 167 | 9 588 | 217 511 | 9.0 |
| Sussex | 3 587 | 2.1 | 22.0 | 13.2 | 4.9 | 10.9 | 7.3 | 16.3 | 14.0 | 54 155 | 270 | 2 966 | 123 036 | 32.2 |
| DISTRICT OF COLUMBIA | 84 518 | 0.0 | 1.4 | 0.2 | 25.5 | 0.9 | 4.7 | 5.3 | 42.8 | 75 755 | 123 | 25 633 | 296 719 | 8.0 |
| District of Columbia | 84 518 | 0.0 | 1.4 | 0.2 | 25.5 | 0.9 | 4.7 | 5.3 | 42.8 | 75 755 | 123 | 25 633 | 296 719 | 8.0 |
| FLORIDA | 459 056 | 0.5 | 9.9 | 4.9 | 12.0 | 7.9 | 9.8 | 13.0 | 17.5 | 3 894 179 | 204 | 506 458 | 8 989 580 | 23.1 |
| Alachua | 6 927 | 0.3 | D | 4.4 | 7.8 | 6.2 | 5.5 | 17.6 | 39.6 | 37 340 | 150 | 5 422 | 112 766 | 18.6 |
| Baker | 313 | 0.0 | 6.4 | 3.6 | 3.1 | 8.3 | 1.9 | D | 44.7 | 4 750 | 175 | 623 | 9 687 | 27.6 |
| Bay | 4 186 | 0.0 | 11.0 | 4.7 | 9.6 | 8.1 | 5.2 | 11.0 | 31.6 | 35 190 | 207 | 4 463 | 99 650 | 27.0 |
| Bradford | 336 | 0.0 | D | 3.7 | 3.5 | 9.4 | 2.2 | D | 37.3 | 5 605 | 198 | 869 | 11 011 | 14.6 |
| Brevard | 12 524 | 0.1 | 19.3 | 15.3 | 11.1 | 6.7 | 4.5 | 13.4 | 18.4 | 138 755 | 255 | 10 439 | 269 864 | 21.5 |
| Broward | 47 024 | 0.0 | 9.0 | 3.9 | 14.1 | 8.8 | 10.4 | 10.3 | 15.5 | 284 245 | 160 | 39 670 | 810 388 | 9.4 |
| Calhoun | 140 | 4.9 | D | 1.4 | D | 8.1 | D | 15.5 | 37.4 | 2 910 | 197 | 566 | 5 999 | 14.3 |
| Charlotte | 2 116 | 1.0 | 7.2 | 1.3 | 6.5 | 13.0 | 6.0 | 24.8 | 17.9 | 57 175 | 356 | 2 399 | 100 632 | 26.2 |
| Citrus | 1 718 | 0.1 | 9.6 | 1.2 | 6.3 | 11.1 | 4.0 | 23.4 | 15.2 | 54 320 | 388 | 2 821 | 78 026 | 25.4 |
| Clay | 2 121 | -0.1 | 9.8 | 3.3 | 8.0 | 12.0 | 5.5 | 17.7 | 21.1 | 34 165 | 178 | 2 520 | 75 478 | 40.4 |
| Collier | 7 639 | 1.9 | 11.3 | 2.5 | 8.2 | 9.3 | 11.5 | 15.3 | 11.6 | 77 900 | 237 | 3 314 | 197 298 | 36.5 |
| Columbia | 1 066 | 0.1 | D | 8.5 | D | 11.0 | 4.2 | 14.4 | 34.2 | 15 035 | 223 | 2 528 | 28 636 | 21.5 |
| DeSoto | 466 | 10.4 | 9.3 | 5.9 | 1.8 | 13.7 | 2.7 | 11.0 | 24.6 | 6 715 | 192 | 928 | 14 590 | 7.2 |
| Dixie | 121 | 1.4 | D | D | D | 7.0 | D | 3.9 | 39.9 | 4 405 | 267 | 763 | 9 319 | 26.6 |
| Duval | 32 453 | 0.1 | 9.8 | 5.4 | 11.6 | 6.3 | 14.7 | 12.2 | 18.0 | 139 930 | 161 | 22 554 | 388 486 | 17.8 |
| Escambia | 8 135 | 0.3 | 9.7 | 4.6 | 8.0 | 6.6 | 6.1 | 16.0 | 33.7 | 64 560 | 216 | 9 684 | 136 703 | 9.7 |
| Flagler | 824 | 1.0 | D | 4.5 | 10.2 | 11.2 | 4.0 | 15.7 | 25.5 | 30 310 | 311 | 1 567 | 48 595 | 98.7 |
| Franklin | 162 | 0.0 | D | D | 5.6 | 10.7 | 7.9 | D | 33.6 | 2 575 | 222 | 363 | 8 652 | 20.6 |
| Gadsden | 624 | 3.6 | 20.3 | 8.6 | D | 6.0 | 2.1 | 4.0 | 39.8 | 9 810 | 213 | 2 702 | 19 506 | 10.2 |
| Gilchrist | 165 | 8.5 | 9.1 | 1.5 | D | 4.9 | 1.9 | D | 34.4 | 3 845 | 226 | 436 | 7 307 | 23.7 |
| Glades | 133 | 20.2 | 8.4 | 5.3 | D | 2.7 | 1.1 | D | 22.2 | 2 205 | 175 | 194 | 6 979 | 20.5 |
| Gulf | 183 | 0.0 | 8.5 | 2.2 | 5.7 | 7.9 | 6.8 | 11.8 | 37.0 | 3 370 | 213 | 369 | 9 110 | 20.0 |
| Hamilton | 195 | -0.1 | D | D | 1.2 | 3.4 | 1.2 | D | 33.5 | 2 930 | 200 | 602 | 5 778 | 16.4 |
| Hardee | 401 | 17.0 | D | 2.0 | D | 6.4 | 3.4 | D | 23.0 | 4 395 | 158 | 789 | 9 722 | -1.0 |
| Hendry | 671 | 23.5 | D | 3.5 | 5.4 | 5.0 | 2.4 | 4.4 | 19.3 | 5 510 | 141 | 1 293 | 14 564 | 18.5 |
| Hernando | 1 811 | 0.1 | 9.4 | 4.3 | 4.9 | 11.9 | 4.6 | 25.2 | 19.4 | 56 450 | 326 | 3 644 | 84 504 | 34.7 |
| Highlands | 1 259 | 6.1 | D | 2.5 | 3.5 | 10.8 | 3.7 | 24.2 | 18.3 | 31 805 | 322 | 2 479 | 55 386 | 13.4 |
| Hillsborough | 41 126 | 0.5 | 8.7 | 4.2 | 16.5 | 6.9 | 12.4 | 11.8 | 15.4 | 201 760 | 159 | 36 407 | 536 092 | 25.9 |
| Holmes | 173 | 1.7 | D | 5.9 | 2.7 | 7.9 | 2.8 | D | 41.4 | 5 160 | 260 | 882 | 8 641 | 8.0 |
| Indian River | 2 547 | 1.6 | D | 4.3 | 9.4 | 10.9 | 7.4 | 18.6 | 13.6 | 41 905 | 302 | 2 032 | 76 346 | 31.9 |
| Jackson | 755 | 8.5 | 9.2 | 4.2 | D | 7.8 | 2.9 | D | 41.3 | 11 725 | 238 | 1 980 | 21 003 | 7.8 |
| Jefferson | 122 | 3.5 | D | 0.4 | D | 6.9 | 3.2 | D | 33.7 | 3 260 | 222 | 653 | 6 632 | 26.3 |
| Lafayette | 82 | 14.6 | D | 2.2 | D | 5.4 | D | D | 43.4 | 1 120 | 125 | 147 | 3 328 | 25.1 |
| Lake | 3 954 | 1.2 | 12.0 | 4.6 | 6.1 | 11.6 | 5.6 | 19.8 | 18.8 | 86 245 | 287 | 5 965 | 144 996 | 41.0 |
| Lee | 12 027 | 0.2 | 10.5 | 2.8 | 11.6 | 10.1 | 7.2 | 12.2 | 20.6 | 153 955 | 244 | 10 863 | 371 099 | 51.2 |
| Leon | 8 274 | 0.1 | D | 1.5 | 14.4 | 6.0 | 6.9 | 13.0 | 38.8 | 35 525 | 128 | 5 291 | 124 136 | 19.4 |
| Levy | 395 | 8.8 | D | 5.1 | 3.0 | 10.4 | 4.7 | 7.3 | 26.2 | 11 380 | 283 | 1 458 | 20 123 | 21.4 |
| Liberty | 97 | -0.2 | 10.4 | 9.4 | D | 2.6 | D | 23.2 | 44.2 | 1 385 | 167 | 283 | 3 357 | 6.4 |
| Madison | 212 | 7.9 | D | 9.2 | D | 7.1 | 2.7 | 10.5 | 33.6 | 4 340 | 227 | 973 | 8 481 | 8.2 |
| Manatee | 6 256 | 2.9 | 15.4 | 9.0 | 11.1 | 8.9 | 7.0 | 13.4 | 12.9 | 81 425 | 249 | 5 254 | 172 690 | 25.0 |
| Marion | 4 580 | -0.2 | 14.8 | 8.6 | 6.5 | 10.8 | 5.8 | 15.9 | 22.3 | 104 990 | 316 | 8 314 | 164 050 | 33.7 |
| Martin | 3 433 | 1.0 | D | 5.5 | 11.3 | 10.2 | 7.5 | 17.0 | 10.9 | 40 755 | 276 | 1 497 | 78 131 | 19.3 |
| Miami-Dade | 71 598 | 0.3 | 7.4 | 3.2 | 13.2 | 7.3 | 10.6 | 11.7 | 15.8 | 381 305 | 149 | 145 629 | 989 435 | 16.1 |
| Monroe | 2 247 | 0.0 | D | 0.5 | 7.3 | 10.5 | 6.2 | 6.7 | 26.5 | 14 955 | 202 | 1 196 | 52 764 | 2.2 |
| Nassau | 1 053 | 0.0 | 12.5 | 9.2 | 5.6 | 7.8 | 4.8 | 9.5 | 24.6 | 16 475 | 222 | 1 116 | 35 009 | 35.1 |
| Okaloosa | 6 216 | 0.1 | 7.9 | 4.0 | 10.7 | 6.0 | 5.0 | 6.8 | 47.3 | 34 875 | 190 | 2 812 | 92 407 | 17.6 |
| Okeechobee | 517 | 8.9 | D | 6.2 | D | 9.4 | 3.3 | D | 24.9 | 8 200 | 204 | 911 | 18 509 | 19.4 |
| Orange | 41 510 | 0.2 | 9.6 | 5.4 | 13.9 | 6.3 | 10.0 | 10.6 | 11.4 | 157 370 | 135 | 30 248 | 487 839 | 35.0 |
| Osceola | 3 595 | 0.5 | D | 1.7 | 4.1 | 9.9 | 8.0 | 14.7 | 20.2 | 46 545 | 169 | 8 900 | 128 170 | 77.3 |
| Palm Beach | 36 009 | 0.7 | 8.3 | 3.5 | 13.4 | 7.7 | 12.8 | 13.7 | 12.5 | 287 480 | 215 | 20 426 | 664 594 | 19.4 |
| Pasco | 4 849 | 0.2 | 10.2 | 4.0 | 5.7 | 12.1 | 5.2 | 21.6 | 19.9 | 119 340 | 256 | 9 757 | 228 928 | 31.8 |
| Pinellas | 24 470 | 0.0 | 13.9 | 9.4 | 12.2 | 8.1 | 11.3 | 16.2 | 12.8 | 224 145 | 244 | 19 688 | 503 634 | 4.6 |
| Polk | 10 799 | 1.0 | 14.7 | 9.0 | 5.9 | 8.6 | 8.1 | 14.4 | 15.0 | 137 250 | 225 | 18 193 | 281 214 | 24.2 |

1. Includes mining, construction, and manufacturing.    2. Per 1,000 resident population enumerated in the 2010 census.

| STATE County | Housing units, 2007–2011 | | | | | | | | Civilian labor force, 2012 | | | | Civilian employment,[6] 2007–2011 | | |
|---|---|---|---|---|---|---|---|---|---|---|---|---|---|---|---|
| | | | Occupied units | | | | | | | | Unemployment | | | Percent | |
| | | | Owner-occupied | | | | Renter-occupied | | | | | | | | |
| | | | | Median owner cost as a percent of income | | | | | | | | | | | |
| | Total | Percent | Median value[1] | With a mortgage | Without a mortgage[2] | Median rent[3] | Median rent as a percent of income | Sub-stand-ard units[4] (percent) | Total | Percent change, 2011–2012 | Total | Rate[5] | Total | Manage-ment, business, science and arts | Con-struction, produc-tion, and mainte-nance occu-pations |
| | 89 | 90 | 91 | 92 | 93 | 94 | 95 | 96 | 97 | 98 | 99 | 100 | 101 | 102 | 103 |
| CONNECTICUT—Cont'd | | | | | | | | | | | | | | | |
| Tolland | 54 386 | 76.4 | 266 300 | 24.1 | 13.9 | 993 | 29.7 | 0.9 | 85 687 | -1.1 | 6 199 | 7.2 | 81 010 | 43.5 | 18.2 |
| Windham | 44 366 | 70.9 | 227 000 | 27.0 | 16.3 | 852 | 28.3 | 2.1 | 63 559 | -1.7 | 6 050 | 9.5 | 58 946 | 30.4 | 26.4 |
| DELAWARE | 332 837 | 73.0 | 244 100 | 24.7 | 11.3 | 975 | 31.5 | 2.4 | 444 042 | 0.8 | 31 598 | 7.1 | 420 057 | 37.4 | 20.1 |
| Kent | 57 629 | 72.4 | 208 300 | 25.7 | 11.8 | 954 | 32.0 | 2.0 | 75 502 | 0.3 | 5 703 | 7.6 | 70 155 | 32.6 | 24.4 |
| New Castle | 199 922 | 70.5 | 254 400 | 24.0 | 10.5 | 987 | 31.4 | 2.3 | 275 794 | 1.0 | 19 369 | 7.0 | 264 252 | 41.2 | 17.4 |
| Sussex | 75 286 | 79.9 | 246 900 | 26.6 | 12.3 | 939 | 31.5 | 2.9 | 92 746 | 0.5 | 6 526 | 7.0 | 85 650 | 29.8 | 24.8 |
| DISTRICT OF COLUMBIA | 260 136 | 42.8 | 442 600 | 24.7 | 10.7 | 1 135 | 29.7 | 3.5 | 361 610 | 3.9 | 32 340 | 8.9 | 300 913 | 58.6 | 7.6 |
| District of Columbia | 260 136 | 42.8 | 442 600 | 24.7 | 10.7 | 1 135 | 29.7 | 3.5 | 361 610 | 3.9 | 32 340 | 8.9 | 300 913 | 58.6 | 7.6 |
| FLORIDA | 7 140 096 | 69.0 | 188 600 | 29.4 | 14.1 | 981 | 34.8 | 2.9 | 9 368 500 | 1.0 | 806 808 | 8.6 | 8 258 511 | 33.1 | 19.1 |
| Alachua | 97 542 | 54.5 | 185 100 | 24.9 | 11.3 | 880 | 38.1 | 2.2 | 133 909 | 1.3 | 8 888 | 6.6 | 116 156 | 45.1 | 11.6 |
| Baker | 8 333 | 76.1 | 142 600 | 25.8 | 10.5 | 708 | 33.2 | 3.7 | 12 407 | 0.4 | 972 | 7.8 | 10 563 | 26.7 | 26.5 |
| Bay | 68 819 | 65.7 | 168 400 | 25.9 | 12.0 | 924 | 29.9 | 2.3 | 90 582 | -0.3 | 7 484 | 8.3 | 76 890 | 31.4 | 21.6 |
| Bradford | 9 188 | 76.6 | 121 400 | 23.6 | 13.5 | 602 | 30.9 | 3.1 | 12 157 | -2.5 | 871 | 7.2 | 9 893 | 23.8 | 26.2 |
| Brevard | 219 669 | 75.3 | 171 200 | 27.4 | 12.8 | 909 | 32.7 | 1.7 | 268 281 | -0.3 | 24 746 | 9.2 | 233 820 | 36.5 | 19.4 |
| Broward | 665 037 | 68.2 | 225 300 | 32.7 | 18.6 | 1 162 | 36.5 | 3.5 | 1 015 805 | 1.7 | 75 388 | 7.4 | 845 492 | 35.2 | 16.4 |
| Calhoun | 4 796 | 74.0 | 80 200 | 25.7 | 11.6 | 569 | 33.2 | 5.0 | 5 758 | -2.4 | 467 | 8.1 | 4 390 | 24.2 | 24.6 |
| Charlotte | 71 059 | 80.3 | 166 700 | 31.1 | 14.2 | 928 | 32.4 | 1.1 | 70 478 | 0.4 | 6 199 | 8.8 | 56 092 | 30.5 | 19.9 |
| Citrus | 59 915 | 83.3 | 134 800 | 27.4 | 12.3 | 770 | 35.5 | 1.5 | 56 804 | 0.5 | 5 547 | 9.8 | 45 137 | 27.7 | 21.8 |
| Clay | 67 592 | 77.5 | 178 900 | 25.0 | 9.9 | 988 | 29.1 | 1.4 | 97 581 | 0.9 | 7 459 | 7.6 | 85 088 | 33.9 | 20.6 |
| Collier | 119 554 | 76.1 | 317 200 | 32.5 | 14.4 | 1 045 | 34.3 | 3.5 | 150 903 | 2.0 | 12 824 | 8.5 | 130 779 | 29.1 | 20.7 |
| Columbia | 24 127 | 70.1 | 127 100 | 27.1 | 10.6 | 724 | 29.4 | 3.6 | 31 183 | -0.9 | 2 522 | 8.1 | 25 170 | 29.3 | 26.1 |
| DeSoto | 10 462 | 75.6 | 114 900 | 30.9 | 10.3 | 717 | 28.5 | 7.2 | 14 298 | -7.9 | 1 312 | 9.2 | 12 833 | 19.9 | 35.6 |
| Dixie | 5 380 | 80.6 | 104 400 | 25.9 | 12.2 | 579 | 24.3 | 2.7 | 5 606 | -1.6 | 609 | 10.9 | 5 306 | 25.6 | 38.0 |
| Duval | 330 821 | 63.2 | 170 300 | 26.4 | 12.1 | 920 | 32.1 | 2.3 | 447 805 | 0.7 | 39 318 | 8.8 | 406 350 | 33.1 | 19.5 |
| Escambia | 111 928 | 67.3 | 145 000 | 25.8 | 12.1 | 842 | 33.8 | 2.5 | 140 706 | -0.1 | 11 759 | 8.4 | 125 086 | 31.7 | 19.2 |
| Flagler | 36 232 | 81.2 | 201 300 | 31.5 | 13.6 | 1 068 | 34.6 | 1.4 | 35 348 | 0.8 | 4 096 | 11.6 | 35 423 | 34.6 | 18.4 |
| Franklin | 4 618 | 66.0 | 170 100 | 25.2 | 14.0 | 738 | 33.1 | 2.9 | 5 355 | -2.0 | 360 | 6.7 | 4 392 | 23.3 | 27.2 |
| Gadsden | 16 488 | 69.7 | 109 000 | 26.8 | 12.7 | 714 | 40.9 | 5.4 | 19 468 | -1.5 | 1 776 | 9.1 | 16 115 | 26.6 | 22.8 |
| Gilchrist | 6 009 | 81.2 | 119 600 | 23.7 | 13.0 | 761 | 33.6 | 4.2 | 7 643 | 0.6 | 608 | 8.0 | 6 249 | 26.6 | 29.6 |
| Glades | 3 903 | 77.7 | 95 200 | 26.0 | 11.1 | 766 | 27.2 | 4.9 | 4 948 | -5.9 | 450 | 9.1 | 4 529 | 16.5 | 34.4 |
| Gulf | 5 385 | 74.8 | 150 600 | 29.5 | 12.9 | 773 | 27.4 | 2.7 | 6 026 | -3.1 | 510 | 8.5 | 5 728 | 27.6 | 25.3 |
| Hamilton | 4 441 | 73.1 | 75 600 | 26.3 | 9.9 | 616 | 31.6 | 5.4 | 4 643 | -3.5 | 480 | 10.3 | 4 602 | 23.0 | 30.5 |
| Hardee | 7 850 | 73.8 | 104 100 | 26.9 | 11.0 | 746 | 30.2 | 8.6 | 11 684 | -4.3 | 1 074 | 9.2 | 10 545 | 19.3 | 46.3 |
| Hendry | 11 013 | 70.0 | 103 400 | 30.0 | 11.7 | 787 | 28.9 | 6.3 | 16 466 | -5.5 | 2 249 | 13.7 | 14 991 | 16.7 | 39.6 |
| Hernando | 70 809 | 82.4 | 145 000 | 28.7 | 13.1 | 882 | 35.6 | 1.9 | 62 431 | 0.7 | 6 821 | 10.9 | 60 239 | 28.3 | 21.7 |
| Highlands | 39 970 | 79.4 | 115 600 | 28.1 | 13.1 | 717 | 34.0 | 2.6 | 41 160 | -2.1 | 3 830 | 9.3 | 32 737 | 24.7 | 25.4 |
| Hillsborough | 463 425 | 62.4 | 185 900 | 27.5 | 13.4 | 936 | 33.3 | 2.7 | 629 444 | 1.4 | 53 389 | 8.5 | 575 542 | 36.3 | 17.7 |
| Holmes | 6 761 | 79.1 | 86 800 | 24.5 | 11.5 | 595 | 30.5 | 2.0 | 8 793 | -1.3 | 626 | 7.1 | 6 587 | 25.0 | 27.4 |
| Indian River | 57 467 | 76.3 | 179 300 | 28.5 | 14.2 | 889 | 36.4 | 2.1 | 63 435 | 0.3 | 6 747 | 10.6 | 54 526 | 30.6 | 22.1 |
| Jackson | 16 440 | 79.1 | 97 200 | 22.1 | 12.7 | 582 | 30.5 | 2.2 | 22 115 | -1.6 | 1 576 | 7.1 | 17 269 | 31.1 | 21.3 |
| Jefferson | 5 313 | 73.9 | 125 000 | 22.3 | 12.5 | 692 | 32.5 | 0.7 | 6 555 | -1.3 | 515 | 7.9 | 5 846 | 32.2 | 21.6 |
| Lafayette | 2 474 | 80.1 | 153 500 | 23.8 | 9.9 | 613 | 27.9 | 2.5 | 3 020 | -5.0 | 222 | 7.4 | 3 606 | 24.9 | 27.4 |
| Lake | 118 253 | 77.7 | 167 900 | 27.6 | 13.7 | 946 | 33.9 | 2.2 | 129 931 | 1.4 | 11 711 | 9.0 | 120 313 | 31.9 | 20.4 |
| Lee | 243 017 | 73.8 | 181 000 | 30.5 | 14.1 | 957 | 33.7 | 3.0 | 286 397 | 1.3 | 25 493 | 8.9 | 251 857 | 29.0 | 20.6 |
| Leon | 109 508 | 55.0 | 195 300 | 24.5 | 11.3 | 908 | 38.9 | 3.7 | 146 998 | -1.2 | 10 620 | 7.2 | 137 214 | 45.2 | 12.4 |
| Levy | 16 034 | 77.3 | 108 400 | 24.7 | 12.1 | 651 | 32.0 | 2.9 | 16 461 | -3.1 | 1 569 | 9.5 | 15 327 | 24.3 | 29.3 |
| Liberty | 2 142 | 75.3 | 80 600 | 22.9 | 11.6 | 673 | 35.5 | 8.0 | 3 136 | -4.7 | 226 | 7.2 | 2 646 | 31.0 | 32.2 |
| Madison | 6 939 | 74.9 | 94 100 | 24.9 | 13.0 | 680 | 35.4 | 3.9 | 7 219 | -0.6 | 732 | 10.1 | 7 324 | 26.0 | 32.2 |
| Manatee | 131 318 | 73.0 | 195 300 | 29.6 | 14.1 | 931 | 33.7 | 2.6 | 142 219 | 1.2 | 12 279 | 8.6 | 133 336 | 32.7 | 20.3 |
| Marion | 133 977 | 78.4 | 142 000 | 28.3 | 12.9 | 839 | 35.6 | 2.1 | 133 573 | -0.2 | 13 296 | 10.0 | 119 750 | 27.6 | 22.6 |
| Martin | 59 316 | 78.8 | 238 200 | 29.2 | 13.9 | 992 | 32.1 | 1.5 | 64 439 | 0.6 | 5 677 | 8.8 | 59 814 | 37.1 | 16.9 |
| Miami-Dade | 825 337 | 57.6 | 246 800 | 35.2 | 17.0 | 1 053 | 38.7 | 5.7 | 1 299 265 | 1.5 | 120 533 | 9.3 | 1 131 458 | 30.3 | 20.6 |
| Monroe | 28 272 | 64.3 | 463 100 | 38.7 | 14.3 | 1 269 | 36.2 | 5.1 | 48 306 | 2.8 | 2 423 | 5.0 | 37 739 | 27.7 | 21.7 |
| Nassau | 27 664 | 79.9 | 202 300 | 24.8 | 11.2 | 897 | 27.2 | 2.6 | 37 607 | 0.6 | 2 879 | 7.7 | 31 996 | 30.2 | 27.8 |
| Okaloosa | 71 609 | 66.9 | 196 800 | 26.1 | 11.3 | 981 | 31.9 | 2.2 | 98 219 | 0.5 | 6 120 | 6.2 | 82 776 | 35.0 | 18.6 |
| Okeechobee | 13 857 | 74.7 | 124 300 | 31.0 | 12.8 | 762 | 35.3 | 6.9 | 18 559 | -2.1 | 1 891 | 10.2 | 15 397 | 20.3 | 30.5 |
| Orange | 408 605 | 59.6 | 211 100 | 29.5 | 13.0 | 1 016 | 35.7 | 2.8 | 636 186 | 1.7 | 53 011 | 8.3 | 562 866 | 33.9 | 17.4 |
| Osceola | 93 100 | 64.8 | 170 200 | 33.5 | 14.0 | 1 046 | 36.5 | 2.9 | 140 696 | 1.3 | 13 054 | 9.3 | 121 538 | 25.3 | 21.5 |
| Palm Beach | 523 559 | 72.6 | 236 600 | 32.0 | 16.7 | 1 148 | 36.3 | 2.9 | 634 732 | 1.6 | 55 831 | 8.8 | 579 516 | 34.7 | 16.7 |
| Pasco | 184 270 | 78.3 | 145 100 | 28.4 | 13.7 | 896 | 33.7 | 1.7 | 192 137 | 1.2 | 19 026 | 9.9 | 185 077 | 33.7 | 18.9 |
| Pinellas | 401 598 | 69.6 | 172 900 | 29.3 | 15.9 | 931 | 33.0 | 1.8 | 441 416 | 1.4 | 37 628 | 8.5 | 420 024 | 36.7 | 16.8 |
| Polk | 221 975 | 71.7 | 133 200 | 26.7 | 13.0 | 858 | 33.1 | 3.7 | 271 538 | 0.4 | 26 542 | 9.8 | 244 360 | 29.0 | 25.2 |

1. Specified owner-occupied units.   2. A value of 9.9 represents 9.9 percent or less.   3. Specified renter-occupied units. A value of 10.0 represents 10 percent or less.   4. Overcrowded or lacking complete plumbing facilities.   5. Percent of civilian labor force.   6. Persons 16 years old and over.

| | Private nonfarm establishments, employment and payroll, 2011 | | | | | | | | | Agriculture, 2007 | | | |
| | | Employment | | | | | | Annual payroll | | Farms | | | |
| | | | | | | | | | | | | Percent with: | |
| STATE County | Number of establishments | Total | Health care and social assistance | Manufacturing | Retail trade | Finance and insurance | Professional, scientific, and technical services | Total (mil dol) | Average per employee (dollars) | Number | Fewer than 50 acres | 500 acres or more | Farm operators whose principal occupation is farming (percent) |
|---|---|---|---|---|---|---|---|---|---|---|---|---|---|
| | 104 | 105 | 106 | 107 | 108 | 109 | 110 | 111 | 112 | 113 | 114 | 115 | 116 |
| **CONNECTICUT—Cont'd** | | | | | | | | | | | | | |
| Tolland | 2 398 | 29 450 | 5 991 | 3 527 | 4 657 | 558 | 1 122 | 1 059 | 35 969 | 484 | 62.8 | 2.1 | 45.7 |
| Windham | 2 097 | 28 805 | 6 555 | 5 360 | 4 689 | 667 | 605 | 1 085 | 37 676 | 594 | 51.2 | 2.9 | 46.3 |
| **DELAWARE** | 24 132 | 359 602 | 59 793 | 27 715 | 51 664 | 35 450 | 24 315 | 17 553 | 48 813 | 2 546 | 57.1 | 9.6 | 59.1 |
| Kent | 3 177 | 48 100 | 9 061 | 5 000 | 8 831 | 1 139 | 2 026 | 1 667 | 34 648 | 825 | 57.0 | 9.3 | 58.4 |
| New Castle | 15 448 | 251 479 | 40 540 | 13 429 | 30 557 | 31 984 | 19 838 | 13 889 | 55 229 | 347 | 62.8 | 8.9 | 49.9 |
| Sussex | 5 313 | 57 764 | 10 132 | 9 286 | 12 267 | 1 708 | 1 612 | 1 842 | 31 884 | 1 374 | 55.7 | 10.0 | 61.8 |
| **DISTRICT OF COLUMBIA** | 21 545 | 477 623 | 64 928 | 1 001 | 19 752 | 17 528 | 96 916 | 32 872 | 68 824 | NA | NA | NA | NA |
| District of Columbia | 21 545 | 477 623 | 64 928 | 1 001 | 19 752 | 17 528 | 96 916 | 32 872 | 68 824 | NA | NA | NA | NA |
| **FLORIDA** | 490 851 | 6 732 639 | 969 536 | 276 352 | 940 764 | 331 921 | 433 745 | 265 464 | 39 429 | 47 463 | 69.2 | 5.5 | 44.0 |
| Alachua | 5 733 | 80 828 | 20 774 | 3 094 | 13 188 | 4 086 | 4 879 | 2 824 | 34 937 | 1 532 | 71.7 | 4.6 | 40.0 |
| Baker | 369 | 5 199 | 1 852 | 130 | 833 | 126 | D | 158 | 30 435 | 344 | 77.9 | 1.7 | 36.3 |
| Bay | 4 374 | 55 989 | 9 357 | 3 468 | 10 235 | 2 053 | 3 362 | 1 821 | 32 517 | 133 | 69.2 | 2.3 | 38.3 |
| Bradford | 438 | 4 242 | 881 | 132 | 898 | 95 | 120 | 120 | 28 185 | 479 | 72.2 | 1.3 | 34.9 |
| Brevard | 12 746 | 166 490 | 28 831 | 19 054 | 24 999 | 5 932 | 17 352 | 6 814 | 40 930 | 531 | 79.8 | 4.9 | 46.7 |
| Broward | 55 700 | 596 817 | 89 644 | 20 448 | 94 523 | 32 634 | 48 934 | 25 261 | 42 326 | 547 | 92.3 | 0.5 | 50.3 |
| Calhoun | 196 | 1 647 | 569 | D | 331 | 58 | D | 40 | 24 455 | 242 | 52.1 | 5.0 | 35.5 |
| Charlotte | 3 542 | 32 974 | 8 492 | 308 | 7 993 | 1 183 | 1 268 | 970 | 29 415 | 242 | 57.9 | 13.6 | 49.2 |
| Citrus | 2 641 | 25 543 | 7 551 | 254 | 5 362 | 696 | 860 | 830 | 32 508 | 411 | 70.3 | 4.4 | 47.0 |
| Clay | 3 481 | 35 545 | 6 505 | 1 063 | 8 288 | 972 | 2 809 | 1 054 | 29 652 | 374 | 78.6 | 1.9 | 47.7 |
| Collier | 9 888 | 101 687 | 16 716 | 2 287 | 18 565 | 3 601 | 4 494 | 3 869 | 38 044 | 322 | 70.5 | 9.9 | 53.1 |
| Columbia | 1 325 | 16 999 | 4 228 | 893 | 2 947 | 543 | 613 | 532 | 31 309 | 982 | 71.4 | 3.6 | 42.0 |
| DeSoto | 409 | 4 614 | 1 087 | D | 949 | 162 | D | 166 | 36 021 | 1 035 | 71.3 | 6.9 | 39.2 |
| Dixie | 173 | 1 282 | 136 | 441 | 239 | 40 | D | 34 | 26 196 | 217 | 59.4 | 6.9 | 46.1 |
| Duval | 23 144 | 382 633 | 58 383 | 20 832 | 46 248 | 43 900 | 22 219 | 16 969 | 44 347 | 371 | 79.2 | 3.2 | 46.4 |
| Escambia | 6 529 | 96 255 | 18 272 | 3 816 | 15 241 | 5 138 | 5 097 | 3 359 | 34 901 | 725 | 64.0 | 5.4 | 38.2 |
| Flagler | 1 733 | 15 813 | 2 511 | 715 | 3 079 | 507 | 428 | 434 | 27 460 | 82 | 47.6 | 24.4 | 53.7 |
| Franklin | 298 | 2 052 | 181 | D | 435 | D | D | 48 | 23 519 | 15 | 86.7 | 0.0 | 53.3 |
| Gadsden | 638 | 8 854 | 3 053 | 1 149 | 1 173 | 169 | 160 | 272 | 30 760 | 385 | 51.9 | 4.7 | 41.8 |
| Gilchrist | 196 | 1 349 | 452 | 165 | 204 | 48 | 54 | 38 | 27 890 | 569 | 65.2 | 6.5 | 43.2 |
| Glades | 92 | 865 | D | 133 | D | D | D | 28 | 32 723 | 311 | 64.0 | 13.8 | 43.1 |
| Gulf | 305 | 2 029 | 511 | 35 | 336 | D | 128 | 58 | 28 777 | 53 | 64.2 | 3.8 | 47.2 |
| Hamilton | 177 | 2 434 | 217 | D | 318 | D | D | 112 | 46 093 | 322 | 39.8 | 11.2 | 35.7 |
| Hardee | 397 | 4 122 | 1 343 | 135 | 707 | 235 | D | 127 | 30 888 | 1 081 | 56.1 | 8.7 | 39.9 |
| Hendry | 540 | 5 712 | 1 007 | D | 1 141 | 243 | 169 | 178 | 31 177 | 430 | 54.9 | 19.3 | 49.5 |
| Hernando | 2 854 | 29 140 | 7 645 | 1 242 | 6 981 | 754 | 1 086 | 816 | 28 020 | 768 | 79.9 | 2.6 | 44.8 |
| Highlands | 1 903 | 19 530 | 5 286 | 611 | 4 349 | 1 230 | 625 | 540 | 27 657 | 832 | 59.9 | 12.9 | 48.8 |
| Hillsborough | 32 023 | 499 099 | 70 953 | 18 821 | 62 931 | 43 581 | 46 971 | 21 865 | 43 809 | 2 843 | 83.6 | 2.3 | 45.1 |
| Holmes | 276 | 1 907 | 648 | 134 | 328 | D | 82 | 46 | 23 876 | 1 037 | 28.8 | 4.3 | 34.7 |
| Indian River | 3 840 | 37 876 | 7 588 | 1 806 | 7 851 | 1 222 | 1 554 | 1 282 | 33 846 | 415 | 68.7 | 9.6 | 50.1 |
| Jackson | 780 | 8 842 | 1 822 | 484 | 1 839 | 315 | 227 | 251 | 28 350 | 1 321 | 36.3 | 10.9 | 42.9 |
| Jefferson | 247 | 1 606 | 278 | 72 | 355 | 92 | 53 | 38 | 23 851 | 642 | 50.2 | 9.2 | 34.6 |
| Lafayette | 98 | 767 | 156 | D | 150 | D | 22 | 18 | 23 881 | 236 | 37.7 | 9.7 | 55.5 |
| Lake | 6 208 | 66 844 | 15 435 | 2 649 | 13 502 | 1 859 | 2 534 | 2 035 | 30 448 | 1 814 | 79.4 | 2.6 | 40.3 |
| Lee | 15 629 | 171 148 | 28 466 | 4 070 | 33 882 | 5 465 | 9 306 | 5 809 | 33 942 | 944 | 86.4 | 4.1 | 37.7 |
| Leon | 7 253 | 89 580 | 16 766 | 1 610 | 15 563 | 4 515 | 9 454 | 3 235 | 36 108 | 324 | 66.7 | 5.9 | 34.9 |
| Levy | 711 | 5 167 | 561 | 406 | 1 508 | 241 | 149 | 134 | 25 885 | 1 018 | 70.1 | 5.6 | 47.2 |
| Liberty | 81 | 870 | 121 | D | 130 | 20 | D | 26 | 29 546 | 53 | 47.2 | 7.5 | 37.7 |
| Madison | 308 | 2 688 | 643 | D | 541 | 78 | 75 | 68 | 25 191 | 678 | 33.9 | 8.6 | 42.0 |
| Manatee | 7 595 | 83 991 | 13 866 | 7 516 | 15 730 | 2 772 | 3 073 | 2 765 | 32 924 | 794 | 64.1 | 8.8 | 43.8 |
| Marion | 6 638 | 72 006 | 14 822 | 5 087 | 14 947 | 2 400 | 3 764 | 2 267 | 31 489 | 3 496 | 81.9 | 1.9 | 50.6 |
| Martin | 4 921 | 49 363 | 8 875 | 2 407 | 9 474 | 1 801 | 2 766 | 1 708 | 34 608 | 492 | 76.4 | 8.5 | 40.9 |
| Miami-Dade | 74 585 | 823 116 | 127 889 | 31 498 | 120 926 | 42 880 | 59 649 | 35 057 | 42 591 | 2 498 | 93.2 | 0.9 | 50.4 |
| Monroe | 3 487 | 27 579 | 2 238 | 170 | 5 358 | 845 | 1 104 | 864 | 31 317 | 23 | 95.7 | 0.0 | 30.4 |
| Nassau | 1 588 | 14 878 | 2 344 | 1 226 | 2 965 | 366 | 486 | 493 | 33 155 | 449 | 76.2 | 1.1 | 38.3 |
| Okaloosa | 4 961 | 58 506 | 8 381 | 2 552 | 11 500 | 2 540 | 5 634 | 2 027 | 34 642 | 567 | 47.6 | 3.5 | 36.3 |
| Okeechobee | 729 | 6 231 | 1 211 | 205 | 1 626 | D | 197 | 181 | 29 111 | 656 | 56.1 | 17.4 | 47.9 |
| Orange | 31 565 | 613 870 | 62 777 | 27 274 | 72 533 | 21 851 | 41 055 | 24 239 | 39 486 | 825 | 84.6 | 3.3 | 46.5 |
| Osceola | 4 814 | 58 464 | 9 572 | 1 190 | 12 117 | 1 210 | 1 756 | 1 667 | 28 518 | 381 | 65.4 | 15.2 | 50.4 |
| Palm Beach | 41 970 | 436 202 | 71 787 | 11 748 | 67 069 | 21 818 | 33 727 | 19 035 | 43 638 | 1 263 | 87.8 | 5.3 | 54.4 |
| Pasco | 8 378 | 77 738 | 17 182 | 2 599 | 19 500 | 2 524 | 3 725 | 2 350 | 30 234 | 1 210 | 78.5 | 4.0 | 45.1 |
| Pinellas | 26 114 | 341 953 | 64 780 | 26 455 | 47 234 | 23 801 | 26 414 | 13 893 | 40 627 | 134 | 97.0 | 0.0 | 24.6 |
| Polk | 10 718 | 161 846 | 26 544 | 13 582 | 23 278 | 11 011 | 8 813 | 5 855 | 36 176 | 2 768 | 66.2 | 6.4 | 42.5 |

# Table B. States and Counties — Agriculture

| STATE County | Land in farms Acreage (1,000) | Percent change, 2002–2007 | Acres Average size of farm | Total irrigated (1,000) | Total cropland (1,000) | Value of land and buildings (dollars) Average per farm | Average per acre | Value of machinery and equipment, average per farm (dollars) | Value of products sold Total (mil dol) | Average per farm (dollars) | Percent from: Crops | Live-stock and poultry products | Percent of farms with sales of: $10,000 or more | $100,000 or more | Government payments Total ($1,000) | Percent of farms |
|---|---|---|---|---|---|---|---|---|---|---|---|---|---|---|---|---|
| | 117 | 118 | 119 | 120 | 121 | 122 | 123 | 124 | 125 | 126 | 127 | 128 | 129 | 130 | 131 | 132 |
| CONNECTICUT—Cont'd | | | | | | | | | | | | | | | | |
| Tolland | 39 | 5.4 | 81 | 0.6 | 16.8 | 979 030 | 12 047 | 64 011 | 37.6 | 77 630 | 53.4 | 46.6 | 31.2 | 7.2 | 318 | 6.0 |
| Windham | 60 | -1.6 | 101 | 0.2 | 25.1 | 929 269 | 9 179 | 66 079 | 39.7 | 66 837 | 30.0 | 70.0 | 34.7 | 10.8 | 911 | 9.8 |
| DELAWARE | 510 | -5.6 | 200 | 104.6 | 432.8 | 2 073 605 | 10 347 | 119 718 | 1 083.0 | 425 387 | 19.4 | 80.6 | 59.0 | 38.8 | 8 896 | 37.3 |
| Kent | 174 | -5.9 | 211 | 29.1 | 146.5 | 2 091 272 | 9 926 | 122 692 | 188.4 | 228 352 | D | D | 46.7 | 26.1 | 3 285 | 37.3 |
| New Castle | 67 | -5.6 | 193 | 2.7 | 51.9 | 2 295 500 | 11 892 | 102 370 | 45.7 | 131 708 | D | D | 43.8 | 13.0 | 1 045 | 34.0 |
| Sussex | 269 | -5.3 | 196 | 72.8 | 234.3 | 2 006 959 | 10 234 | 122 313 | 848.9 | 617 862 | 15.1 | 84.9 | 70.3 | 53.1 | 4 565 | 38.1 |
| DISTRICT OF COLUMBIA.. | NA | NA | NA | NA | NA | NA | NA | NA | NA | NA | NA | NA | NA | NA | NA | NA |
| District of Columbia | NA | NA | NA | NA | NA | NA | NA | NA | NA | NA | NA | NA | NA | NA | NA | NA |
| FLORIDA | 9 232 | -11.4 | 195 | 1 552.1 | 2 953.3 | 1 096 718 | 5 639 | 54 604 | 7 785.2 | 164 027 | 80.4 | 19.6 | 34.6 | 11.0 | 45 343 | 9.8 |
| Alachua | 173 | -22.4 | 113 | 13.4 | 65.6 | 820 508 | 7 273 | 49 395 | 92.1 | 60 102 | 70.6 | 29.4 | 27.6 | 5.5 | 1 212 | 7.0 |
| Baker | 27 | 50.0 | 78 | 0.7 | 4.7 | 496 345 | 6 389 | 27 699 | D | D | D | 0.0 | 18.0 | 4.1 | 50 | 4.4 |
| Bay | 12 | 9.1 | 94 | D | 2.7 | 718 873 | 7 667 | 33 325 | 5.0 | 37 813 | 92.3 | 7.7 | 19.5 | 2.3 | 5 | 4.5 |
| Bradford | 30 | -33.3 | 62 | 0.2 | 8.5 | 426 399 | 6 895 | 33 893 | 13.9 | 29 054 | 16.9 | 83.1 | 23.8 | 3.3 | D | 0.6 |
| Brevard | 167 | -11.2 | 315 | 20.5 | 22.1 | 1 238 223 | 3 936 | 56 362 | 46.7 | 87 913 | 85.2 | 14.8 | 50.1 | 9.0 | 21 | 1.5 |
| Broward | 9 | -62.5 | 16 | 1.7 | 4.9 | 424 408 | 26 571 | 32 949 | 50.3 | 91 945 | 97.0 | 3.0 | 29.4 | 10.2 | 680 | 5.5 |
| Calhoun | 39 | -20.4 | 162 | 1.5 | 16.6 | 707 352 | 4 378 | 68 275 | 16.2 | 67 048 | 84.4 | 15.6 | 19.4 | 5.0 | 772 | 24.0 |
| Charlotte | 166 | -13.5 | 686 | 20.0 | 28.7 | 2 224 000 | 3 241 | 61 849 | 65.6 | 270 921 | 89.5 | 10.5 | 39.7 | 16.5 | 306 | 2.5 |
| Citrus | 40 | -14.9 | 97 | 1.4 | 9.7 | 746 230 | 7 664 | 43 628 | 14.4 | 35 006 | 66.2 | 33.8 | 20.9 | 4.9 | 157 | 4.1 |
| Clay | 42 | -46.8 | 111 | 0.9 | 5.7 | 585 985 | 5 276 | 36 344 | D | D | 0.0 | D | 13.1 | 3.2 | 9 | 3.2 |
| Collier | 110 | -39.2 | 341 | 31.4 | 69.9 | 2 039 523 | 5 974 | 87 700 | 278.8 | 865 906 | 98.5 | 1.5 | 40.7 | 20.5 | 132 | 4.3 |
| Columbia | 86 | -4.4 | 88 | 2.7 | 30.0 | 618 208 | 7 063 | 36 690 | D | D | D | D | 16.3 | 3.3 | 334 | 9.7 |
| DeSoto | 260 | -33.0 | 251 | 56.2 | 91.3 | 1 397 534 | 5 557 | 59 069 | 219.9 | 212 491 | 84.4 | 15.6 | 49.4 | 13.6 | 123 | 1.1 |
| Dixie | 42 | 35.5 | 194 | 3.0 | 7.6 | 716 085 | 3 698 | 45 628 | 8.4 | 38 512 | 32.9 | 67.1 | 20.7 | 1.8 | D | 5.1 |
| Duval | 27 | -12.9 | 72 | 2.0 | 5.7 | 639 475 | 8 861 | 32 759 | D | D | 0.0 | D | 17.3 | 3.2 | 18 | 2.4 |
| Escambia | 82 | 26.2 | 113 | 2.6 | 52.3 | 536 368 | 4 744 | 56 997 | 31.9 | 44 064 | 87.0 | 13.0 | 24.1 | 7.0 | 4 193 | 36.7 |
| Flagler | 58 | -14.7 | 712 | 6.8 | 8.7 | 2 833 332 | 3 979 | 88 146 | 35.1 | 428 538 | 97.6 | 2.4 | 43.9 | 20.7 | 27 | 4.9 |
| Franklin | 1 | NA | 34 | 0.0 | D | 87 243 | 2 566 | 51 131 | 0.7 | 48 282 | 0.0 | 100.0 | 60.0 | 20.0 | 0 | 0.0 |
| Gadsden | 47 | -30.9 | 122 | 2.2 | 15.2 | 675 924 | 5 526 | 62 515 | 96.0 | 249 427 | 98.2 | 1.8 | 24.9 | 3.9 | 194 | 21.0 |
| Gilchrist | 71 | -12.3 | 125 | 7.8 | 32.8 | 840 009 | 6 723 | 50 514 | 76.7 | 134 745 | 21.1 | 78.9 | 26.5 | 5.1 | 565 | 11.4 |
| Glades | 402 | -1.5 | 1 294 | 46.7 | 50.8 | 6 796 878 | 5 252 | 76 580 | 85.3 | 274 330 | 69.4 | 30.6 | 32.2 | 14.8 | 237 | 3.9 |
| Gulf | 5 | 0.0 | 89 | D | 1.3 | 425 195 | 4 752 | 41 005 | 1.1 | 20 137 | 22.9 | 77.2 | 22.6 | 9.4 | D | 3.8 |
| Hamilton | 65 | 25.0 | 201 | 5.5 | 20.0 | 973 465 | 4 839 | 49 506 | 14.4 | 44 775 | 75.9 | 24.1 | 25.5 | 4.7 | 500 | 39.8 |
| Hardee | 280 | -19.1 | 259 | 44.1 | 66.3 | 1 578 924 | 6 098 | 58 750 | 232.0 | 214 579 | 73.1 | 26.9 | 56.9 | 21.2 | 217 | 2.4 |
| Hendry | 465 | -15.8 | 1 082 | 188.8 | 262.4 | 3 673 204 | 3 396 | 136 706 | 567.4 | 1 319 602 | 95.5 | 4.5 | 60.5 | 32.6 | 626 | 5.1 |
| Hernando | 56 | -13.8 | 73 | 1.5 | 16.5 | 716 829 | 9 789 | 37 988 | 35.7 | 46 456 | 49.3 | 50.7 | 19.4 | 5.2 | 94 | 1.2 |
| Highlands | 476 | -17.5 | 572 | 73.7 | 120.5 | 2 353 234 | 4 111 | 87 582 | 326.0 | 391 829 | 80.8 | 19.2 | 58.4 | 25.2 | 493 | 3.1 |
| Hillsborough | 220 | -22.8 | 77 | 29.9 | 86.4 | 787 847 | 10 190 | 52 850 | 488.2 | 171 727 | 89.3 | 10.7 | 33.0 | 10.8 | 58 | 0.8 |
| Holmes | 152 | 67.0 | 146 | 2.0 | 46.0 | 621 851 | 4 248 | 40 589 | 24.1 | 23 209 | 16.8 | 83.2 | 21.1 | 3.5 | 2 726 | 53.3 |
| Indian River | 157 | -17.8 | 379 | 66.9 | 81.3 | 1 986 694 | 5 245 | 104 511 | 136.1 | 327 910 | D | D | 61.0 | 24.1 | 68 | 3.6 |
| Jackson | 311 | 37.0 | 236 | 20.3 | 144.0 | 875 624 | 3 715 | 55 873 | 69.7 | 52 751 | D | D | 25.8 | 7.6 | 6 638 | 47.7 |
| Jefferson | 147 | 10.5 | 230 | 2.1 | 34.0 | 1 035 244 | 4 508 | 35 153 | 22.1 | 34 427 | 53.7 | 46.3 | 26.9 | 3.4 | 1 201 | 31.3 |
| Lafayette | 81 | -12.0 | 344 | 7.4 | 17.3 | 1 306 640 | 3 794 | 92 611 | 138.7 | 587 594 | 4.2 | 95.8 | 43.6 | 25.8 | 458 | 29.2 |
| Lake | 121 | -32.8 | 67 | 15.0 | 34.7 | 705 893 | 10 546 | 39 374 | 188.5 | 103 925 | 97.1 | 2.9 | 40.1 | 9.4 | 38 | 0.9 |
| Lee | 86 | -31.7 | 91 | 14.6 | 22.0 | 982 569 | 10 818 | 39 788 | 116.1 | 122 945 | 97.1 | 2.9 | 26.2 | 6.1 | 142 | 1.2 |
| Leon | 91 | 23.0 | 280 | 1.5 | 13.0 | 1 070 670 | 3 823 | 50 769 | 4.4 | 13 646 | 79.2 | 20.8 | 20.7 | 2.5 | 165 | 6.2 |
| Levy | 174 | -3.3 | 171 | 14.5 | 73.2 | 891 435 | 5 209 | 50 965 | 75.7 | 74 354 | 59.9 | 40.1 | 30.9 | 9.6 | 2 733 | 5.9 |
| Liberty | 24 | 140.0 | 446 | D | 0.7 | 828 227 | 1 859 | 39 369 | 1.2 | 22 034 | 5.1 | 94.9 | 32.1 | 7.5 | D | 1.9 |
| Madison | 149 | -5.1 | 220 | 3.1 | 40.3 | 1 001 957 | 4 558 | 53 827 | 43.4 | 63 953 | 17.6 | 82.4 | 28.3 | 6.6 | 725 | 27.3 |
| Manatee | 225 | -25.2 | 284 | 50.8 | 77.3 | 1 759 488 | 6 206 | 77 276 | 311.8 | 392 702 | 93.6 | 6.4 | 40.3 | 15.9 | 11 | 0.4 |
| Marion | 267 | -1.5 | 76 | 9.7 | 59.9 | 725 733 | 9 518 | 46 830 | 173.7 | 49 696 | 15.7 | 84.3 | 22.6 | 5.9 | 476 | 1.3 |
| Martin | 129 | -37.4 | 263 | 48.5 | 51.9 | 1 594 655 | 6 064 | 61 270 | 158.5 | 322 171 | 84.9 | 15.1 | 33.7 | 12.0 | 291 | 6.1 |
| Miami-Dade | 67 | -25.6 | 27 | 39.0 | 53.8 | 742 119 | 27 648 | 45 341 | 661.1 | 264 652 | D | D | 51.5 | 18.3 | 5 450 | 8.9 |
| Monroe | 0 | NA | 8 | 0.0 | 0.2 | 214 565 | 26 390 | 61 786 | 1.9 | 83 356 | 44.0 | 56.0 | 47.8 | 21.7 | D | 8.7 |
| Nassau | 31 | NA | 70 | 0.3 | 4.2 | 441 968 | 6 345 | 28 798 | 8.3 | 18 584 | 9.1 | 90.9 | 14.7 | 1.6 | 1 | 0.9 |
| Okaloosa | 66 | 20.0 | 116 | 0.4 | 24.3 | 628 564 | 5 410 | 38 958 | D | D | D | D | 13.1 | 3.4 | 1 641 | 36.2 |
| Okeechobee | 338 | -13.8 | 516 | 20.5 | 40.9 | 2 374 399 | 4 603 | 82 412 | 177.6 | 270 745 | 24.8 | 75.2 | 37.7 | 14.0 | 337 | 6.6 |
| Orange | 136 | -7.5 | 165 | 11.9 | 20.7 | 1 084 345 | 6 574 | 60 921 | 269.9 | 327 176 | 98.0 | 2.0 | 50.2 | 24.5 | D | 0.1 |
| Osceola | 646 | -1.1 | 1 696 | 31.4 | 44.5 | 4 339 729 | 2 558 | 103 685 | 90.9 | 238 571 | 67.6 | 32.4 | 44.9 | 18.4 | 230 | 2.4 |
| Palm Beach | 526 | -1.9 | 416 | 387.8 | 450.7 | 1 712 306 | 4 114 | 127 234 | 931.7 | 737 732 | 99.1 | 0.9 | 41.7 | 18.8 | 2 455 | 6.1 |
| Pasco | 150 | -11.2 | 124 | 10.6 | 37.8 | 953 274 | 7 692 | 37 716 | 111.3 | 91 963 | 43.7 | 56.3 | 31.9 | 8.4 | 231 | 2.1 |
| Pinellas | 1 | -50.0 | 11 | 0.2 | D | 267 805 | 24 664 | 25 608 | 2.4 | 17 850 | 78.6 | 21.4 | 29.1 | 4.5 | D | 1.5 |
| Polk | 549 | -12.4 | 198 | 98.4 | 136.3 | 1 417 168 | 7 144 | 57 381 | 399.0 | 144 132 | 91.1 | 8.9 | 62.7 | 22.8 | 211 | 1.7 |

| STATE County | Water use, 2005 | | Wholesale trade,[1] 2007 | | | | Retail trade,[2] 2007 | | | | Real estate and rental and leasing,[2] 2007 | | | |
|---|---|---|---|---|---|---|---|---|---|---|---|---|---|---|
| | Total water withdrawn (mil gal/day) | Gallons withdrawn per person | Number of establishments | Number of employees | Sales (mil dol) | Annual payroll (mil dol) | Number of establishments | Number of employees | Sales (mil dol) | Annual payroll (mil dol) | Number of establishments | Number of employees | Receipts (mil dol) | Annual payroll (mil dol) |
| | 133 | 134 | 135 | 136 | 137 | 138 | 139 | 140 | 141 | 142 | 143 | 144 | 145 | 146 |
| CONNECTICUT—Cont'd | | | | | | | | | | | | | | |
| Tolland................................. | 17.6 | 119 | 69 | 571 | 214.3 | 25.7 | 406 | 5 207 | 1 206.3 | 126.3 | 110 | 457 | 62.7 | 12.2 |
| Windham.............................. | 17.9 | 154 | 71 | 1 132 | 546.7 | 60.0 | 376 | 4 870 | 1 180.6 | 122.0 | 73 | D | D | D |
| DELAWARE ...................... | 1 017.2 | 1 206 | 819 | 9 065 | 5 727.4 | 416.9 | 3 907 | 55 432 | 14 202.1 | 1 322.8 | 1 248 | 5 807 | 11 057.2 | 222.4 |
| Kent...................................... | 37.6 | 261 | 100 | D | D | D | 632 | 9 614 | 2 589.2 | 224.6 | 127 | 604 | 91.0 | 22.0 |
| New Castle........................... | 498.4 | 953 | 559 | D | D | D | 2 093 | 33 010 | 8 633.4 | 795.0 | 823 | 3 786 | 10 740.6 | 155.1 |
| Sussex.................................. | 481.3 | 2 726 | 160 | D | D | D | 1 182 | 12 808 | 2 979.4 | 303.1 | 298 | 1 417 | 225.5 | 45.3 |
| DISTRICT OF COLUMBIA.. | 9.7 | 17 | 316 | 3 680 | 2 118.0 | 216.4 | 1 827 | 19 117 | 3 843.7 | 485.9 | 1 140 | 9 663 | 2 747.8 | 624.8 |
| District of Columbia.............. | 9.7 | 17 | 316 | 3 680 | 2 118.0 | 216.4 | 1 827 | 19 117 | 3 843.7 | 485.9 | 1 140 | 9 663 | 2 747.8 | 624.8 |
| FLORIDA............................ | 18 307.9 | 1 022 | 27 442 | 279 300 | 221 641.5 | 12 566.1 | 73 794 | 1 016 290 | 262 341.1 | 24 049.7 | 33 653 | 170 859 | 32 235.4 | 6 094.2 |
| Alachua ................................ | 60.1 | 249 | 188 | D | D | D | 969 | 14 610 | 3 152.2 | 300.1 | 397 | 2 048 | 311.6 | 59.0 |
| Baker.................................... | 7.2 | 300 | 8 | D | D | D | 74 | 888 | 180.6 | 16.3 | 11 | D | D | D |
| Bay....................................... | 291.9 | 1 805 | 174 | 1 481 | 645.0 | 62.9 | 816 | 10 186 | 2 472.0 | 227.1 | 314 | 1 172 | 167.7 | 33.6 |
| Bradford................................ | 6.7 | 239 | 14 | D | D | D | 87 | 961 | 215.6 | 20.7 | 22 | 47 | 6.2 | 1.0 |
| Brevard................................ | 957.3 | 1 799 | 493 | 3 683 | 1 852.7 | 155.1 | 2 073 | 28 911 | 6 594.0 | 630.4 | 777 | 2 795 | 401.1 | 74.8 |
| Broward................................ | 1 837.9 | 1 056 | 3 946 | 37 891 | 31 411.6 | 1 819.5 | 7 382 | 104 336 | 30 886.3 | 2 710.6 | 3 624 | 18 044 | 3 555.6 | 648.1 |
| Calhoun................................ | 3.4 | 246 | 12 | D | D | D | 42 | 295 | 64.8 | 6.2 | 5 | 13 | 1.1 | 0.2 |
| Charlotte............................... | 40.1 | 260 | 94 | 592 | 211.7 | 22.0 | 582 | 8 761 | 1 898.1 | 187.9 | 289 | 877 | 120.7 | 22.1 |
| Citrus................................... | 1 707.1 | 12 871 | 84 | D | D | D | 516 | 5 836 | 1 405.6 | 131.1 | 202 | 605 | 59.4 | 12.3 |
| Clay...................................... | 22.6 | 133 | 115 | 803 | 394.3 | 34.8 | 609 | 9 363 | 2 005.7 | 195.5 | 230 | 797 | 143.2 | 21.4 |
| Collier................................... | 193.2 | 608 | 331 | 2 678 | 1 649.0 | 137.9 | 1 500 | 20 122 | 5 186.5 | 535.5 | 958 | 2 874 | 552.3 | 118.0 |
| Columbia............................... | 12.3 | 199 | 75 | 871 | 478.6 | 35.6 | 265 | 3 113 | 862.2 | 74.2 | 66 | 206 | 31.5 | 5.4 |
| DeSoto.................................. | 66.7 | 2 047 | 20 | D | D | D | 75 | 1 023 | 280.8 | 23.1 | 38 | 106 | 13.0 | 2.2 |
| Dixie..................................... | 3.8 | 244 | 4 | D | D | D | 34 | 237 | 49.1 | 4.2 | 7 | 11 | 1.1 | 0.1 |
| Duval.................................... | 771.6 | 896 | 1 154 | 19 865 | 17 205.8 | 969.5 | 3 464 | 51 916 | 13 316.7 | 1 228.5 | 1 427 | 8 481 | 2 040.1 | 368.9 |
| Escambia.............................. | 329.0 | 1 084 | 278 | 3 171 | 1 838.9 | 126.6 | 1 233 | 16 777 | 4 055.7 | 374.3 | 413 | 1 539 | 278.0 | 45.0 |
| Flagler .................................. | 19.3 | 245 | 53 | D | D | D | 208 | 2 899 | 684.1 | 66.3 | 195 | 508 | 66.9 | 13.8 |
| Franklin................................ | 2.6 | 239 | 8 | D | D | D | 71 | 438 | 92.3 | 9.3 | 33 | 194 | 20.5 | 6.1 |
| Gadsden............................... | 17.0 | 355 | 34 | 707 | 384.0 | 23.9 | 137 | 1 462 | 440.3 | 29.4 | 29 | 88 | 13.3 | 2.2 |
| Gilchrist................................ | 14.8 | 911 | 3 | 10 | 2.3 | 0.2 | 41 | 239 | 52.5 | 4.7 | 8 | 38 | 4.6 | 1.0 |
| Glades.................................. | 104.4 | 9 731 | 5 | D | D | D | 15 | 83 | 13.1 | 1.4 | 5 | 14 | 1.1 | 0.2 |
| Gulf....................................... | 2.7 | 161 | 3 | D | D | D | 48 | 371 | 76.3 | 7.3 | 22 | 68 | 8.6 | 1.6 |
| Hamilton............................... | 54.8 | 3 831 | 4 | D | D | D | 54 | 343 | 103.2 | 5.6 | 4 | 22 | 1.8 | 0.3 |
| Hardee.................................. | 32.5 | 1 188 | 21 | D | D | D | 75 | 740 | 400.1 | 16.0 | 25 | 65 | 8.3 | 1.3 |
| Hendry.................................. | 395.9 | 10 317 | 32 | 273 | 212.1 | 8.3 | 131 | 1 373 | 345.7 | 28.2 | 29 | 94 | 10.3 | 1.9 |
| Hernando.............................. | 48.6 | 322 | 114 | 592 | 177.9 | 20.8 | 469 | 7 191 | 1 654.1 | 156.1 | 192 | 467 | 63.0 | 9.8 |
| Highlands ............................. | 118.3 | 1 266 | 83 | D | D | D | 364 | 4 513 | 1 089.6 | 99.0 | 112 | 337 | 52.6 | 8.1 |
| Hillsborough ......................... | 2 014.0 | 1 780 | 1 764 | 28 080 | 17 752.9 | 1 233.9 | 4 369 | 70 015 | 19 110.3 | 1 745.9 | 1 983 | 12 821 | 2 504.2 | 500.3 |
| Holmes................................. | 3.8 | 197 | 14 | D | D | D | 49 | 332 | 73.1 | 5.5 | 8 | 18 | 1.4 | 0.3 |
| Indian River.......................... | 285.7 | 2 197 | 132 | D | D | D | 699 | 9 096 | 1 851.7 | 203.3 | 260 | 945 | 146.5 | 24.1 |
| Jackson................................ | 119.5 | 2 405 | 26 | 185 | 70.6 | 5.2 | 188 | 2 056 | 541.9 | 43.0 | 47 | 131 | 13.1 | 2.5 |
| Jefferson.............................. | 13.2 | 930 | 9 | 39 | 43.7 | 1.5 | 55 | 390 | 88.7 | 6.6 | 10 | 24 | 1.9 | 0.4 |
| Lafayette.............................. | 7.9 | 985 | 4 | D | D | D | 20 | 139 | 66.5 | 3.1 | 2 | D | D | D |
| Lake...................................... | 85.7 | 326 | 224 | 1 745 | 726.3 | 62.3 | 1 003 | 14 137 | 3 441.9 | 310.3 | 477 | 2 116 | 266.9 | 69.5 |
| Lee ....................................... | 709.1 | 1 291 | 589 | 5 590 | 2 271.6 | 225.7 | 2 624 | 38 417 | 9 193.1 | 923.2 | 1 307 | 5 643 | 1 000.1 | 171.3 |
| Leon...................................... | 43.0 | 159 | 228 | 2 254 | 791.2 | 88.4 | 1 043 | 16 881 | 3 533.8 | 343.1 | 451 | 2 412 | 361.5 | 68.3 |
| Levy...................................... | 28.7 | 757 | 32 | 170 | 62.8 | 4.2 | 145 | 1 546 | 346.4 | 32.8 | 44 | 129 | 10.2 | 2.0 |
| Liberty.................................. | 1.0 | 136 | 4 | D | D | D | 16 | 76 | 24.4 | 1.4 | 1 | D | D | D |
| Madison................................ | 14.3 | 725 | 9 | D | D | D | 71 | 585 | 124.8 | 9.4 | 13 | 25 | 2.4 | 0.4 |
| Manatee................................ | 141.4 | 465 | 303 | 3 314 | 1 725.5 | 148.1 | 1 163 | 16 937 | 3 874.8 | 382.0 | 550 | 2 227 | 390.6 | 66.0 |
| Marion................................... | 54.4 | 179 | 318 | 3 812 | 1 639.5 | 149.7 | 1 208 | 16 639 | 4 218.8 | 379.2 | 466 | 1 598 | 217.9 | 39.9 |
| Martin.................................... | 138.7 | 983 | 195 | 1 393 | 741.6 | 65.3 | 809 | 10 666 | 2 470.4 | 243.3 | 326 | 1 595 | 203.0 | 40.7 |
| Miami-Dade .......................... | 602.3 | 249 | 7 819 | 65 657 | 60 760.1 | 2 818.0 | 10 293 | 123 559 | 34 530.5 | 3 055.6 | 4 935 | 25 546 | 5 367.9 | 985.2 |
| Monroe.................................. | 1.7 | 20 | 86 | D | D | D | 657 | 6 267 | 1 387.6 | 146.7 | 308 | 808 | 150.5 | 26.5 |
| Nassau................................. | 54.9 | 834 | 37 | D | D | D | 280 | 2 998 | 630.9 | 63.0 | 97 | D | D | D |
| Okaloosa.............................. | 26.4 | 140 | 110 | 563 | 236.9 | 23.0 | 903 | 12 427 | 3 031.0 | 272.4 | 398 | 1 772 | 260.5 | 57.0 |
| Okeechobee.......................... | 54.5 | 1 443 | 29 | 179 | 85.3 | 6.0 | 156 | 1 680 | 430.6 | 37.5 | 49 | 115 | 16.5 | 3.3 |
| Orange.................................. | 258.0 | 247 | 1 643 | 23 425 | 17 080.7 | 1 148.0 | 4 670 | 71 848 | 19 195.6 | 1 653.3 | 2 383 | 26 517 | 6 177.0 | 1 053.1 |
| Osceola................................ | 146.8 | 624 | 128 | 1 819 | 3 044.2 | 69.6 | 822 | 12 171 | 2 868.7 | 264.6 | 504 | 4 643 | 732.0 | 155.4 |
| Palm Beach........................... | 1 532.5 | 1 211 | 2 007 | 17 634 | 12 017.5 | 900.5 | 5 564 | 76 129 | 19 321.7 | 1 916.5 | 2 691 | 12 359 | 2 083.2 | 503.8 |
| Pasco ................................... | 2 168.2 | 5 329 | 311 | 1 847 | 807.4 | 70.4 | 1 336 | 18 995 | 4 746.2 | 426.6 | 529 | 1 602 | 197.5 | 35.1 |
| Pinellas................................ | 483.8 | 511 | 1 247 | 14 111 | 12 378.4 | 625.8 | 3 850 | 52 539 | 14 826.9 | 1 232.7 | 1 687 | 7 648 | 1 222.6 | 268.2 |
| Polk...................................... | 219.3 | 405 | 580 | 8 024 | 13 241.7 | 337.4 | 1 876 | 25 321 | 6 420.1 | 586.4 | 741 | 3 423 | 517.8 | 95.9 |

1. Merchant wholesalers, except manufacturers' sales branches and offices.     2. Employer establishments.

| STATE County | Professional, scientific, and technical services,[1] 2007 | | | | Manufacturing, 2007 | | | | Accommodation and food services, 2007 | | | |
|---|---|---|---|---|---|---|---|---|---|---|---|---|
| | Number of establish-ments | Number of employees | Receipts (mil dol) | Annual payroll (mil dol) | Number of establish-ments | Number of employees | Receipts (mil dol) | Annual payroll (mil dol) | Number of establish-ments | Number of employees | Sales (mil dol) | Annual payroll (mil dol) |
| | 147 | 148 | 149 | 150 | 151 | 152 | 153 | 154 | 155 | 156 | 157 | 158 |
| CONNECTICUT—Cont'd | | | | | | | | | | | | |
| Tolland | 200 | D | D | D | 141 | 3 962 | 1 021.8 | 185.1 | 211 | 3 472 | 173.1 | 48.7 |
| Windham | 123 | D | D | D | 187 | 6 135 | 1 776.5 | 254.7 | 236 | 2 841 | 136.3 | 38.7 |
| DELAWARE | 2 383 | D | D | D | 673 | 34 866 | 25 679.9 | 1 759.7 | 1 850 | 32 194 | 1 910.8 | 468.8 |
| Kent | 248 | D | D | D | 87 | 5 253 | 2 361.8 | 213.8 | 236 | 5 352 | 447.9 | 76.2 |
| New Castle | 1 804 | D | D | D | 421 | 18 556 | 20 268.8 | 1 167.8 | 1 051 | 19 118 | 999.2 | 267.2 |
| Sussex | 331 | D | D | D | 165 | 11 057 | 3 049.3 | 378.0 | 563 | 7 724 | 463.7 | 125.4 |
| DISTRICT OF COLUMBIA.. | 4 373 | 82 107 | 24 177.7 | 8 660.6 | 137 | 2 015 | 332.8 | 80.8 | 2 148 | 52 998 | 4 278.2 | 1 238.4 |
| District of Columbia | 4 373 | 82 107 | 24 177.7 | 8 660.6 | 137 | 2 015 | 332.8 | 80.8 | 2 148 | 52 998 | 4 278.2 | 1 238.4 |
| FLORIDA | 69 083 | 427 536 | 61 599.8 | 24 264.5 | 14 324 | 355 386 | 104 832.9 | 15 227.2 | 35 012 | 746 214 | 41 922.1 | 11 470.0 |
| Alachua | 792 | 5 262 | 625.4 | 263.6 | 147 | 3 803 | D | D | 524 | 11 170 | 494.0 | 133.7 |
| Baker | 16 | 90 | 7.2 | 2.9 | NA | NA | NA | NA | 34 | 446 | 19.8 | 4.8 |
| Bay | 406 | D | D | D | 116 | 3 702 | 1 254.3 | 153.4 | 442 | 9 154 | 480.4 | 135.8 |
| Bradford | 44 | 163 | 11.9 | 4.2 | NA | NA | NA | NA | 42 | 752 | 37.1 | 9.1 |
| Brevard | 1 683 | 19 711 | 3 364.7 | 1 589.6 | 473 | 22 772 | 6 767.6 | 1 172.5 | 1 019 | 19 057 | 855.5 | 240.1 |
| Broward | 9 509 | 46 243 | 6 635.1 | 2 550.4 | 1 734 | 29 333 | 7 160.8 | 1 185.5 | 3 693 | 70 373 | 4 209.1 | 1 140.1 |
| Calhoun | 9 | 19 | 1.1 | 0.5 | NA | NA | NA | NA | 20 | 285 | 9.3 | 2.8 |
| Charlotte | 366 | D | D | D | NA | NA | NA | NA | 240 | 4 322 | 178.0 | 53.2 |
| Citrus | 274 | D | D | D | NA | NA | NA | NA | 188 | 2 931 | 109.7 | 32.4 |
| Clay | 423 | D | D | D | 81 | 1 464 | D | D | 274 | 5 413 | 213.8 | 61.9 |
| Collier | 1 271 | D | D | D | 228 | 3 035 | 606.7 | 109.5 | 704 | 17 421 | 1 037.2 | 308.3 |
| Columbia | 115 | D | D | D | 38 | 988 | 351.5 | 37.5 | 120 | 2 220 | 103.3 | 25.9 |
| DeSoto | 32 | 189 | 14.9 | 6.1 | NA | NA | NA | NA | 38 | 579 | 24.3 | 6.5 |
| Dixie | 13 | 63 | 3.5 | 2.0 | 11 | 529 | D | D | 23 | 192 | 7.4 | 1.6 |
| Duval | 3 126 | D | D | D | 647 | 26 119 | 11 222.1 | 1 242.1 | 1 811 | 34 979 | 1 719.4 | 488.1 |
| Escambia | 778 | D | D | D | 191 | 5 152 | 2 117.0 | 253.4 | 534 | 11 014 | 493.9 | 137.2 |
| Flagler | 197 | 674 | 105.6 | 46.6 | 52 | 1 031 | 235.7 | 29.9 | 131 | 2 401 | 114.8 | 31.6 |
| Franklin | 21 | 41 | 7.2 | 2.0 | NA | NA | NA | NA | 43 | 623 | 37.6 | 10.4 |
| Gadsden | 48 | D | D | D | 33 | 1 462 | 262.9 | 50.8 | 38 | 466 | 18.9 | 4.7 |
| Gilchrist | 18 | 64 | 4.4 | 1.6 | NA | NA | NA | NA | 19 | 163 | 8.1 | 2.0 |
| Glades | 6 | D | D | D | NA | NA | NA | NA | 11 | 110 | 4.9 | 1.3 |
| Gulf | 31 | 143 | 14.6 | 5.4 | NA | NA | NA | NA | 25 | 298 | 18.8 | 3.4 |
| Hamilton | 11 | 19 | 1.8 | 0.3 | 1 | D | D | D | 18 | 151 | 7.9 | 1.6 |
| Hardee | 23 | 105 | 7.0 | 2.5 | NA | NA | NA | NA | 25 | 413 | 17.9 | 3.4 |
| Hendry | 41 | 193 | 17.3 | 7.0 | 22 | 1 014 | D | D | 71 | 754 | 37.3 | 9.3 |
| Hernando | 281 | D | D | D | 80 | 1 111 | 312.5 | 44.1 | 237 | 4 101 | 166.2 | 44.3 |
| Highlands | 152 | D | D | D | 56 | 927 | 306.1 | 33.1 | 133 | 2 408 | 100.8 | 28.0 |
| Hillsborough | 4 983 | 40 574 | 6 205.8 | 2 518.5 | 911 | 28 213 | 9 444.9 | 1 112.6 | 2 117 | 47 384 | 2 619.8 | 706.8 |
| Holmes | 24 | 160 | 6.1 | 3.4 | NA | NA | NA | NA | 18 | 206 | 8.3 | 2.3 |
| Indian River | 473 | 2 076 | 235.3 | 97.2 | 99 | 2 179 | 413.0 | 87.7 | 232 | 4 557 | 190.5 | 56.2 |
| Jackson | 46 | 253 | 23.5 | 9.1 | 22 | 636 | 180.6 | 21.1 | 72 | 1 014 | 43.2 | 11.1 |
| Jefferson | 20 | 98 | 8.7 | 3.2 | NA | NA | NA | NA | 18 | 79 | 7.0 | 1.2 |
| Lafayette | 8 | 28 | 1.4 | 0.5 | NA | NA | NA | NA | 9 | 47 | 2.7 | 0.6 |
| Lake | 644 | D | D | D | 163 | 3 531 | 825.5 | 132.4 | 428 | 8 283 | 436.0 | 110.6 |
| Lee | 1 848 | 10 115 | 1 305.2 | 511.3 | 403 | 5 988 | 1 181.8 | 222.6 | 1 095 | 23 070 | 1 192.0 | 344.2 |
| Leon | 1 373 | D | D | D | 100 | 2 155 | 593.4 | 90.3 | 594 | 13 745 | 551.6 | 150.8 |
| Levy | 47 | 205 | 15.6 | 6.1 | 27 | 681 | 131.0 | 22.3 | 75 | 862 | 32.4 | 8.2 |
| Liberty | 2 | D | D | D | NA | NA | NA | NA | 4 | 60 | 3.4 | 0.8 |
| Madison | 21 | 111 | 5.6 | 2.5 | NA | NA | NA | NA | 21 | 356 | 12.3 | 3.1 |
| Manatee | 919 | D | D | D | 297 | 10 012 | 2 985.1 | 434.2 | 529 | 9 788 | 443.8 | 129.5 |
| Marion | 698 | 3 459 | 361.6 | 132.0 | 221 | 8 904 | 1 841.5 | 320.9 | 443 | 7 784 | 353.1 | 100.0 |
| Martin | 675 | D | D | D | 154 | 3 242 | 856.1 | 118.6 | 329 | 6 648 | 279.0 | 85.3 |
| Miami-Dade | 11 294 | 60 310 | 9 603.2 | 3 755.1 | 2 312 | 40 446 | 9 347.1 | 1 556.0 | 4 358 | 91 230 | 6 005.9 | 1 659.8 |
| Monroe | 325 | D | D | D | NA | NA | NA | NA | 484 | 9 814 | 748.1 | 202.4 |
| Nassau | 164 | 495 | 62.3 | 23.3 | 33 | D | 696.2 | 68.0 | 152 | 3 971 | 287.0 | 78.0 |
| Okaloosa | 637 | D | D | D | 98 | 3 858 | 656.7 | 166.4 | 431 | 10 619 | 491.9 | 148.9 |
| Okeechobee | 51 | 202 | 14.3 | 5.1 | NA | NA | NA | NA | 59 | 914 | 46.9 | 11.5 |
| Orange | 4 656 | D | D | D | 822 | 30 097 | 10 921.8 | 1 555.9 | 2 426 | 87 369 | 6 645.1 | 1 567.8 |
| Osceola | 423 | D | D | D | 88 | 1 907 | 644.9 | 75.7 | 532 | 14 153 | 890.5 | 239.0 |
| Palm Beach | 6 944 | 35 002 | 6 092.8 | 2 284.2 | 995 | 13 919 | 4 240.7 | 628.6 | 2 618 | 56 542 | 3 088.6 | 919.0 |
| Pasco | 875 | D | D | D | 211 | 3 057 | 745.2 | 122.8 | 581 | 10 306 | 432.4 | 126.7 |
| Pinellas | 4 036 | D | D | D | 1 121 | 33 564 | 8 062.0 | 1 483.6 | 2 060 | 37 374 | 1 925.1 | 545.3 |
| Polk | 1 093 | 6 654 | 781.8 | 310.5 | 438 | 16 160 | 7 178.0 | 697.4 | 765 | 16 084 | 699.6 | 199.4 |

1. Establishment subject to federal tax.

# Table B. States and Counties — Health Care and Social Assistance, Other Services, and Federal Funds

| STATE County | Health care and social assistance, 2007 | | | | Other services, 2007 | | | | Federal funds and grants, 2009–2010 Expenditures (mil dol) | | | |
|---|---|---|---|---|---|---|---|---|---|---|---|---|
| | | | | | | | | | | Direct payments for individuals[1] | | |
| | Number of establishments | Number of employees | Receipts (mil dol) | Annual payroll (mil dol) | Number of establishments | Number of employees | Receipts (mil dol) | Annual payroll (mil dol) | Total | Social Security and government retirement | Medicare | Food Stamps and Supplemental Security Income |
| | 159 | 160 | 161 | 162 | 163 | 164 | 165 | 166 | 167 | 168 | 169 | 170 |
| CONNECTICUT—Cont'd | | | | | | | | | | | | |
| Tolland | 297 | 5 867 | 434.0 | 197.6 | 201 | 1 517 | 177.9 | 39.1 | 948.1 | 351.7 | 324.7 | 12.0 |
| Windham | 274 | 7 016 | 501.3 | 228.1 | 179 | 732 | 62.2 | 17.4 | 1 262.9 | 330.9 | 655.7 | 32.2 |
| DELAWARE | 2 379 | 54 740 | 5 430.9 | 2 370.5 | 1 587 | 10 012 | 898.4 | 264.6 | 8 076.3 | 2 957.4 | 1 149.8 | 269.6 |
| Kent | 354 | 7 773 | 672.8 | 269.3 | 249 | 1 460 | 100.8 | 32.3 | 2 016.4 | 584.1 | 142.1 | 46.2 |
| New Castle | 1 517 | 37 843 | 3 886.5 | 1 750.7 | 982 | 6 854 | 671.1 | 195.4 | 4 010.3 | 1 475.4 | 716.4 | 169.7 |
| Sussex | 508 | 9 124 | 871.6 | 350.6 | 356 | 1 698 | 126.5 | 36.8 | 1 614.8 | 897.7 | 291.3 | 53.7 |
| DISTRICT OF COLUMBIA | 2 130 | 61 075 | 7 250.2 | 2 942.1 | 3 284 | 49 853 | 15 499.7 | 3 154.3 | 61 919.8 | 2 623.8 | 1 280.2 | 358.8 |
| District of Columbia | 2 130 | 61 075 | 7 250.2 | 2 942.1 | 3 284 | 49 853 | 15 499.7 | 3 154.3 | 61 919.8 | 2 623.8 | 1 280.2 | 358.8 |
| FLORIDA | 51 679 | 904 004 | 102 029.3 | 37 234.1 | 35 597 | 201 687 | 20 757.0 | 5 173.7 | 186 703.8 | 61 447.7 | 46 593.9 | 7 344.1 |
| Alachua | 708 | D | D | D | 379 | 2 781 | 655.1 | 87.6 | 2 382.5 | 652.3 | 441.7 | 104.7 |
| Baker | 39 | 1 844 | 109.1 | 65.5 | 30 | D | D | D | 158.1 | 73.8 | 38.8 | 12.4 |
| Bay | 493 | 9 501 | 985.3 | 354.0 | 315 | 1 767 | 122.2 | 38.1 | 2 261.4 | 730.5 | 337.2 | 74.5 |
| Bradford | 38 | 913 | 59.5 | 26.4 | 28 | 139 | 11.0 | 3.1 | 346.7 | 80.4 | 68.1 | 15.5 |
| Brevard | 1 417 | 26 415 | 2 796.8 | 1 085.6 | 1 039 | 4 868 | 395.3 | 121.0 | 8 154.8 | 2 539.4 | 1 110.3 | 165.0 |
| Broward | 5 732 | 88 155 | 10 883.5 | 3 647.7 | 4 174 | 22 705 | 2 171.8 | 586.7 | 12 480.1 | 4 158.7 | 4 960.3 | 545.3 |
| Calhoun | 28 | 525 | 29.7 | 12.6 | 7 | D | D | D | 132.1 | 39.3 | 44.3 | 8.7 |
| Charlotte | 474 | 7 731 | 897.1 | 308.2 | 275 | 1 186 | 90.0 | 24.7 | 1 438.9 | 829.2 | 490.9 | 31.4 |
| Citrus | 340 | 6 762 | 661.8 | 239.8 | 221 | 857 | 52.8 | 16.3 | 1 313.3 | 779.9 | 398.5 | 44.8 |
| Clay | 376 | 6 167 | 611.2 | 227.6 | 288 | 1 423 | 89.0 | 29.3 | 1 111.8 | 747.9 | 169.7 | 31.9 |
| Collier | 914 | 14 861 | 1 796.1 | 703.8 | 828 | 4 364 | 393.3 | 113.0 | 2 069.4 | 1 202.8 | 492.5 | 54.2 |
| Columbia | 155 | 3 542 | 372.3 | 149.5 | 82 | 340 | 29.7 | 6.6 | 648.1 | 253.0 | 145.2 | 41.2 |
| DeSoto | 53 | 1 134 | 96.7 | 39.1 | 23 | 82 | 4.2 | 1.3 | 249.7 | 90.7 | 96.9 | 16.7 |
| Dixie | 12 | D | D | D | 8 | 25 | 1.8 | 0.5 | 127.7 | 60.4 | 34.5 | 11.5 |
| Duval | 2 292 | 52 877 | 5 928.8 | 2 230.4 | 1 745 | 11 890 | 1 242.6 | 358.0 | 9 298.6 | 2 704.4 | 1 759.9 | 371.3 |
| Escambia | 751 | 19 847 | 2 101.2 | 785.1 | 477 | 2 727 | 229.0 | 69.1 | 3 839.2 | 1 364.1 | 699.8 | 161.7 |
| Flagler | 149 | 1 807 | 175.1 | 70.7 | 126 | 484 | 35.2 | 9.4 | 631.4 | 469.7 | 101.0 | 17.6 |
| Franklin | 24 | D | D | D | 22 | 99 | 5.9 | 1.9 | 112.0 | 38.3 | 42.5 | 4.7 |
| Gadsden | 60 | D | D | D | 42 | 147 | 11.2 | 3.2 | 509.9 | 134.4 | 151.2 | 44.6 |
| Gilchrist | 21 | D | D | D | 11 | 25 | 3.0 | 0.7 | 108.2 | 57.6 | 25.5 | 6.5 |
| Glades | 9 | D | D | D | 6 | 25 | 1.5 | 0.4 | 47.4 | 21.9 | 14.0 | 0.3 |
| Gulf | 25 | 387 | 18.1 | 8.5 | 18 | 93 | 4.4 | 1.1 | 150.5 | 58.7 | 52.9 | 7.3 |
| Hamilton | 18 | 275 | 14.3 | 5.8 | 12 | 41 | 2.6 | 0.7 | 128.8 | 43.9 | 38.9 | 8.5 |
| Hardee | 59 | 1 242 | 82.1 | 35.1 | 25 | 71 | 4.9 | 1.3 | 226.8 | 58.0 | 62.1 | 20.2 |
| Hendry | 63 | 843 | 55.0 | 23.6 | 49 | 170 | 12.3 | 3.2 | 283.3 | 76.9 | 61.9 | 25.2 |
| Hernando | 411 | 6 711 | 741.9 | 248.6 | 230 | 1 115 | 65.9 | 21.1 | 1 619.8 | 915.0 | 520.6 | 58.3 |
| Highlands | 300 | 4 876 | 483.4 | 180.7 | 142 | 540 | 40.7 | 10.4 | 966.6 | 478.8 | 327.5 | 33.9 |
| Hillsborough | 3 248 | 63 269 | 7 585.5 | 2 791.8 | 2 065 | 16 278 | 1 576.0 | 415.9 | 11 330.2 | 3 202.8 | 2 213.7 | 521.9 |
| Holmes | 33 | 623 | 31.4 | 14.7 | 16 | 55 | 4.4 | 1.3 | 236.2 | 74.6 | 74.0 | 14.6 |
| Indian River | 446 | 7 230 | 836.4 | 300.9 | 264 | 1 169 | 97.0 | 26.7 | 1 224.1 | 654.7 | 422.4 | 26.9 |
| Jackson | 91 | 1 819 | 135.0 | 54.3 | 56 | 297 | 27.7 | 6.9 | 614.0 | 181.8 | 182.0 | 26.8 |
| Jefferson | 27 | D | D | D | 15 | 62 | 2.4 | 0.8 | 157.1 | 46.4 | 48.1 | 10.4 |
| Lafayette | 10 | D | D | D | 5 | D | D | D | 42.8 | 15.1 | 11.8 | 2.5 |
| Lake | 704 | 13 216 | 1 382.3 | 533.6 | 450 | 1 864 | 145.2 | 43.3 | 2 918.9 | 1 921.0 | 644.8 | 84.4 |
| Lee | 1 389 | 25 867 | 3 068.2 | 1 115.8 | 1 206 | 6 552 | 589.9 | 162.5 | 4 275.2 | 2 289.1 | 1 205.1 | 133.0 |
| Leon | 676 | 15 657 | 1 691.6 | 614.8 | 629 | 4 537 | 704.3 | 161.8 | 8 324.6 | 646.7 | 314.7 | 90.5 |
| Levy | 59 | 583 | 34.1 | 13.8 | 61 | 156 | 13.3 | 2.8 | 327.2 | 152.9 | 87.5 | 19.8 |
| Liberty | 11 | D | D | D | 3 | D | D | D | 60.7 | 19.6 | 18.4 | 4.0 |
| Madison | 39 | 754 | 42.5 | 17.9 | 21 | 63 | 4.5 | 1.4 | 224.5 | 61.5 | 73.8 | 13.4 |
| Manatee | 793 | 12 166 | 1 279.6 | 448.6 | 524 | 2 524 | 167.0 | 48.4 | 2 496.2 | 1 153.1 | 688.4 | 82.8 |
| Marion | 817 | 14 493 | 1 590.4 | 566.1 | 467 | 2 408 | 201.6 | 51.4 | 2 844.7 | 1 621.9 | 717.0 | 121.2 |
| Martin | 506 | 8 500 | 859.2 | 340.2 | 379 | 2 024 | 155.2 | 49.0 | 1 188.6 | 645.1 | 404.3 | 28.3 |
| Miami-Dade | 8 311 | 120 152 | 15 042.3 | 5 194.3 | 5 065 | 27 878 | 3 185.8 | 659.3 | 27 110.5 | 4 568.7 | 9 894.6 | 1 956.9 |
| Monroe | 210 | 2 293 | 264.8 | 91.3 | 257 | 1 118 | 110.4 | 28.1 | 839.0 | 249.5 | 194.7 | 23.8 |
| Nassau | 131 | 1 974 | 161.7 | 63.9 | 106 | D | D | D | 671.8 | 295.9 | 101.0 | 17.0 |
| Okaloosa | 499 | 8 357 | 845.8 | 312.4 | 393 | 2 053 | 166.4 | 46.1 | 3 812.1 | 1 006.3 | 281.1 | 43.9 |
| Okeechobee | 103 | 1 591 | 153.7 | 50.6 | 55 | 235 | 16.9 | 4.8 | 353.5 | 134.2 | 128.7 | 15.3 |
| Orange | 2 611 | 57 144 | 5 905.1 | 2 466.0 | 2 012 | 15 428 | 1 610.4 | 450.9 | 10 500.4 | 2 435.0 | 1 618.2 | 397.2 |
| Osceola | 407 | 7 041 | 965.6 | 297.2 | 329 | 1 411 | 156.7 | 33.0 | 1 243.5 | 712.1 | 283.0 | 107.2 |
| Palm Beach | 4 815 | 67 881 | 8 382.6 | 2 978.3 | 3 180 | 17 714 | 1 812.2 | 460.1 | 10 665.1 | 4 385.8 | 3 739.3 | 307.3 |
| Pasco | 1 016 | 15 549 | 1 718.4 | 624.2 | 638 | 2 901 | 211.0 | 61.0 | 3 440.6 | 1 620.0 | 1 279.7 | 119.9 |
| Pinellas | 3 194 | 61 564 | 6 733.7 | 2 496.3 | 2 104 | 10 928 | 963.9 | 283.2 | 10 365.3 | 3 904.9 | 3 329.4 | 326.1 |
| Polk | 971 | 24 347 | 2 613.7 | 926.8 | 727 | 3 850 | 323.5 | 94.6 | 4 156.6 | 1 954.4 | 1 105.1 | 266.6 |

1. State totals may include programs not allocated by county.

# Table B. States and Counties — Federal Funds, Residential Construction, and Local Government Finances

| | Federal funds and grants, 2009–2010 (cont.) | | | | | | | Value of residential construction authorized by building permits, 2011 | | Local government finances, 2007 | | | | |
| | Expenditures (mil dol) (cont.) | | | | | | | | | General revenue | | | | |
| | Procurement contract awards | | Grants[1] | | | | | | | | | Taxes | | |
| | | | | | | | | | | | | | Per capita[2] (dollars) | |
| STATE County | Salaries and wages | Defense | Other | Medicaid and other health-related | Nutrition and family welfare | Education | Other | New construction ($1,000) | Number of housing units | Total (mil dol) | Inter-govern-mental (mil dol) | Total (mil dol) | Total | Property |
|---|---|---|---|---|---|---|---|---|---|---|---|---|---|---|
| | 171 | 172 | 173 | 174 | 175 | 176 | 177 | 178 | 179 | 180 | 181 | 182 | 183 | 184 |
| CONNECTICUT—Cont'd | | | | | | | | | | | | | | |
| Tolland | 32.0 | 11.4 | 7.1 | 84.0 | 14.8 | 15.5 | 62.0 | 42 658 | 333 | 472.6 | 169.4 | 255.4 | 1 724 | 1 702 |
| Windham | 33.0 | 10.1 | 5.7 | 132.2 | 20.2 | 8.2 | 8.7 | 13 990 | 104 | 403.6 | 205.6 | 164.2 | 1 403 | 1 382 |
| DELAWARE | 707.6 | 218.1 | 144.5 | 983.3 | 207.3 | 285.8 | 578.8 | 370 169 | 2 954 | X | X | X | X | X |
| Kent | 309.0 | 144.0 | 10.1 | 177.8 | 24.9 | 223.7 | 297.7 | 85 575 | 680 | 410.9 | 241.0 | 85.8 | 564 | 439 |
| New Castle | 322.4 | 71.5 | 120.9 | 613.1 | 106.0 | 32.6 | 261.5 | 59 146 | 695 | 1 559.8 | 739.2 | 503.8 | 954 | 744 |
| Sussex | 76.2 | 2.7 | 13.5 | 192.4 | 22.8 | 21.0 | 14.6 | 225 447 | 1 579 | 628.9 | 320.9 | 162.8 | 883 | 592 |
| DISTRICT OF COLUMBIA.. | 23 029.5 | 4 651.0 | 16 598.9 | 2 282.6 | 377.8 | 730.2 | 7 481.4 | 609 369 | 4 612 | X | X | X | X | X |
| District of Columbia | 23 029.5 | 4 651.0 | 16 598.9 | 2 282.6 | 377.8 | 730.2 | 7 481.4 | 609 368 | 4 612 | 9 746.6 | 2 999.0 | 5 192.2 | 8 826 | 2 577 |
| FLORIDA | 12 964.5 | 12 814.2 | 5 166.5 | 14 386.2 | 3 377.4 | 3 471.7 | 6 831.1 | 8 814 610 | 42 360 | X | X | X | X | X |
| Alachua | 222.8 | 16.6 | 158.6 | 444.6 | 39.0 | 24.3 | 173.3 | 63 100 | 444 | 879.0 | 308.3 | 303.4 | 1 264 | 977 |
| Baker | 5.7 | 0.0 | 2.6 | 15.4 | 5.1 | 2.4 | 0.9 | 5 281 | 29 | 78.3 | 41.3 | 19.6 | 762 | 458 |
| Bay | 420.0 | 425.6 | 56.4 | 109.4 | 33.1 | 14.2 | 12.5 | 41 970 | 343 | 877.5 | 228.1 | 282.9 | 1 725 | 1 267 |
| Bradford | 134.1 | 6.0 | 1.1 | 33.0 | 5.4 | 1.7 | 0.3 | 1 059 | 18 | 76.0 | 42.8 | 20.2 | 703 | 465 |
| Brevard | 617.8 | 2 092.1 | 1 237.4 | 154.1 | 63.8 | 28.4 | 65.6 | 235 830 | 882 | 1 940.6 | 575.9 | 770.6 | 1 437 | 1 095 |
| Broward | 672.6 | 202.1 | 285.6 | 601.0 | 203.9 | 104.8 | 326.9 | 279 497 | 2 444 | 10 074.0 | 2 472.5 | 3 722.3 | 2 115 | 1 746 |
| Calhoun | 2.7 | 0.0 | 0.9 | 29.2 | 2.8 | 1.2 | 1.0 | 744 | 6 | 47.7 | 37.4 | 6.3 | 467 | 330 |
| Charlotte | 26.1 | 0.8 | 5.5 | 16.6 | 19.3 | 4.9 | 5.5 | 52 752 | 312 | 668.6 | 125.2 | 347.4 | 2 273 | 1 705 |
| Citrus | 18.8 | 2.0 | 4.4 | 34.3 | 15.4 | 6.7 | 3.8 | 31 509 | 142 | 373.7 | 114.1 | 198.3 | 1 414 | 1 165 |
| Clay | 28.7 | 15.8 | 34.2 | 32.2 | 17.3 | 8.8 | 3.1 | 84 746 | 475 | 614.7 | 277.7 | 180.9 | 994 | 747 |
| Collier | 53.2 | 61.7 | 19.9 | 63.1 | 62.5 | 11.5 | 14.8 | 425 480 | 1 320 | 1 632.7 | 314.3 | 935.7 | 2 963 | 2 487 |
| Columbia | 56.7 | 2.7 | 40.9 | 71.6 | 15.9 | 5.5 | 5.4 | 7 058 | 52 | 196.2 | 108.9 | 56.3 | 828 | 564 |
| DeSoto | 3.5 | 0.1 | 0.8 | 24.6 | 6.6 | 3.0 | 0.9 | 14 330 | 95 | 126.6 | 62.6 | 34.8 | 1 004 | 657 |
| Dixie | 1.3 | 0.0 | 0.3 | 13.4 | 3.9 | 1.4 | 0.4 | 2 147 | 17 | 43.6 | 24.2 | 13.0 | 872 | 719 |
| Duval | 1 367.7 | 899.9 | 287.6 | 768.0 | 148.7 | 91.8 | 255.8 | 231 302 | 1 589 | 3 373.9 | 1 176.6 | 1 176.3 | 1 385 | 982 |
| Escambia | 455.2 | 482.4 | 154.1 | 310.1 | 60.8 | 28.6 | 50.1 | 70 671 | 638 | 1 092.9 | 466.7 | 327.9 | 1 070 | 727 |
| Flagler | 13.8 | 0.4 | 3.2 | 7.1 | 6.8 | 2.9 | 4.1 | 47 584 | 152 | 366.4 | 107.4 | 156.2 | 1 767 | 1 578 |
| Franklin | 2.0 | 0.7 | 0.4 | 18.7 | 2.7 | 1.0 | 0.3 | 1 380 | 5 | 74.6 | 27.2 | 34.0 | 3 385 | 3 140 |
| Gadsden | 11.9 | 13.1 | 1.6 | 107.1 | 16.5 | 7.2 | 17.6 | 13 491 | 81 | 129.1 | 73.7 | 33.6 | 713 | 429 |
| Gilchrist | 2.6 | 0.0 | 0.7 | 9.8 | 3.2 | 0.8 | 0.5 | 1 055 | 20 | 43.3 | 25.2 | 12.0 | 703 | 566 |
| Glades | 1.5 | 0.3 | 0.2 | 2.6 | 1.5 | 1.1 | 0.0 | 199 | 2 | 33.0 | 13.9 | 13.4 | 1 208 | 1 011 |
| Gulf | 1.4 | 0.0 | 0.3 | 21.1 | 5.1 | 1.2 | 0.2 | 10 209 | 45 | 63.0 | 17.7 | 31.1 | 2 215 | 2 035 |
| Hamilton | 2.4 | 0.0 | 0.5 | 27.0 | 3.5 | 2.4 | 0.0 | 1 301 | 15 | 88.0 | 54.0 | 19.2 | 1 345 | 1 124 |
| Hardee | 15.0 | 0.0 | 0.9 | 29.2 | 6.9 | 2.5 | 3.0 | 2 405 | 14 | 83.1 | 42.7 | 30.3 | 1 052 | 859 |
| Hendry | 4.4 | 56.3 | 0.6 | 22.5 | 9.1 | 2.8 | 9.3 | 3 503 | 32 | 173.9 | 58.1 | 62.1 | 1 567 | 1 117 |
| Hernando | 27.4 | 7.1 | 6.6 | 38.4 | 26.5 | 6.8 | 3.4 | 32 097 | 405 | 769.7 | 222.7 | 387.4 | 2 291 | 2 043 |
| Highlands | 21.7 | 6.7 | 4.3 | 47.0 | 13.6 | 6.3 | 4.1 | 13 694 | 77 | 285.9 | 117.4 | 111.1 | 1 118 | 880 |
| Hillsborough | 1 636.3 | 1 144.0 | 688.4 | 991.9 | 182.6 | 110.8 | 271.3 | 1 086 143 | 4 181 | 5 300.4 | 2 140.9 | 1 956.4 | 1 665 | 1 265 |
| Holmes | 12.2 | 0.2 | 0.9 | 45.5 | 6.8 | 1.6 | 3.4 | 3 181 | 19 | 63.2 | 37.6 | 10.9 | 565 | 295 |
| Indian River | 33.2 | 0.1 | 10.4 | 38.1 | 17.6 | 6.6 | 5.8 | 126 231 | 372 | 581.3 | 109.6 | 324.0 | 2 458 | 1 835 |
| Jackson | 43.1 | 0.1 | 5.7 | 129.2 | 12.3 | 4.4 | 7.8 | 5 310 | 43 | 220.3 | 96.3 | 32.6 | 662 | 353 |
| Jefferson | 3.0 | 0.0 | 0.6 | 38.4 | 3.5 | 1.6 | 1.1 | 5 168 | 28 | 35.8 | 19.7 | 13.0 | 898 | 587 |
| Lafayette | 1.2 | 2.9 | 0.3 | 5.6 | 1.4 | 0.5 | 0.2 | 879 | 4 | 18.0 | 11.7 | 4.2 | 521 | 422 |
| Lake | 58.1 | 5.4 | 25.7 | 84.7 | 30.5 | 16.1 | 25.5 | 136 420 | 517 | 1 014.6 | 287.3 | 370.0 | 1 229 | 927 |
| Lee | 190.7 | 4.9 | 41.8 | 138.2 | 62.1 | 27.1 | 94.8 | 313 138 | 1 587 | 3 868.3 | 890.3 | 1 485.2 | 2 515 | 2 088 |
| Leon | 187.2 | 28.9 | 34.9 | 680.4 | 620.2 | 2 155.9 | 3 323.9 | 102 801 | 883 | 1 107.2 | 417.3 | 357.6 | 1 370 | 1 014 |
| Levy | 8.9 | 0.1 | 1.8 | 31.7 | 6.9 | 5.5 | 7.1 | 6 769 | 54 | 115.2 | 52.4 | 42.8 | 1 096 | 902 |
| Liberty | 2.6 | 0.0 | 0.9 | 13.0 | 1.3 | 0.7 | 0.0 | 1 604 | 12 | 26.9 | 19.2 | 4.5 | 574 | 466 |
| Madison | 3.4 | 0.0 | 1.2 | 55.2 | 5.5 | 3.3 | 1.3 | 3 367 | 27 | 85.3 | 45.2 | 15.9 | 840 | 620 |
| Manatee | 99.7 | 212.6 | 18.5 | 96.2 | 41.0 | 18.7 | 34.7 | 258 943 | 1 641 | 1 320.2 | 336.3 | 547.9 | 1 739 | 1 557 |
| Marion | 57.6 | 15.9 | 17.1 | 163.8 | 42.2 | 18.5 | 24.2 | 74 066 | 361 | 968.0 | 357.1 | 320.2 | 986 | 783 |
| Martin | 24.8 | 4.0 | 9.3 | 31.7 | 17.9 | 5.5 | 11.8 | 111 232 | 224 | 600.8 | 145.7 | 335.9 | 2 413 | 2 086 |
| Miami-Dade | 1 812.5 | 396.7 | 472.7 | 5 786.5 | 443.0 | 166.9 | 1 018.8 | 311 632 | 2 618 | 14 420.4 | 4 219.0 | 5 277.1 | 2 211 | 1 651 |
| Monroe | 194.8 | 67.5 | 15.2 | 59.6 | 11.0 | 4.9 | 10.7 | 65 861 | 135 | 555.6 | 152.3 | 250.2 | 3 416 | 2 591 |
| Nassau | 198.6 | 3.6 | 2.5 | 35.1 | 8.6 | 3.2 | 3.1 | 76 174 | 327 | 256.3 | 72.9 | 129.7 | 1 895 | 1 558 |
| Okaloosa | 868.9 | 1 397.5 | 25.3 | 84.9 | 28.9 | 14.3 | 25.7 | 194 035 | 749 | 652.5 | 245.8 | 266.4 | 1 468 | 1 264 |
| Okeechobee | 6.3 | 11.6 | 1.6 | 29.5 | 7.8 | 3.4 | 2.3 | 10 680 | 42 | 141.7 | 74.5 | 37.4 | 927 | 791 |
| Orange | 827.1 | 3 417.4 | 568.4 | 467.5 | 142.8 | 86.8 | 219.7 | 855 727 | 4 083 | 5 766.6 | 1 741.8 | 2 115.7 | 1 984 | 1 352 |
| Osceola | 32.8 | 6.3 | 7.2 | 32.2 | 24.9 | 13.4 | 11.0 | 162 857 | 785 | 1 213.1 | 336.5 | 456.7 | 1 785 | 1 166 |
| Palm Beach | 463.0 | 446.9 | 309.7 | 401.8 | 160.8 | 57.8 | 230.1 | 716 805 | 2 470 | 7 017.5 | 1 555.2 | 3 682.6 | 2 908 | 2 513 |
| Pasco | 118.3 | 17.6 | 15.0 | 114.3 | 53.2 | 20.1 | 17.6 | 217 119 | 1 401 | 1 400.0 | 532.5 | 500.5 | 1 082 | 760 |
| Pinellas | 618.1 | 978.1 | 331.9 | 393.4 | 124.9 | 56.7 | 136.9 | 89 364 | 355 | 3 780.7 | 1 010.6 | 1 748.4 | 1 906 | 1 530 |
| Polk | 153.2 | 49.3 | 24.1 | 306.9 | 97.8 | 47.9 | 49.1 | 211 033 | 1 156 | 2 004.3 | 841.8 | 655.6 | 1 141 | 856 |

1. State totals may include programs not allocated by county.　　2. Based on the resident population estimated as of July 1 of the year shown.

# Table B. States and Counties — Local Government Finances, Government Employment, and Voting

| STATE County | Local government finances, 2007 (cont.) Direct general expenditure Total (mil dol) | Per capita[1] (dollars) | Percent of total for: Education | Health and hospitals | Police protection | Public welfare | Highways | Debt outstanding Total (mil dol) | Per capita[1] (dollars) | Government employment, 2011 Federal civilian | Federal military | State and local | Presidential election,[2] 2012 Percent of vote cast: Democratic | Republican | All other |
|---|---|---|---|---|---|---|---|---|---|---|---|---|---|---|---|
| | 185 | 186 | 187 | 188 | 189 | 190 | 191 | 192 | 193 | 194 | 195 | 196 | 197 | 198 | 199 |
| **CONNECTICUT—Cont'd** | | | | | | | | | | | | | | | |
| Tolland | 463.8 | 3 131 | 65.8 | 0.4 | 2.5 | 0.6 | 4.1 | 305.4 | 2 062 | 278 | 324 | 14 686 | 59.6 | 38.8 | 1.6 |
| Windham | 380.0 | 3 247 | 72.0 | 0.5 | 2.7 | 0.3 | 4.2 | 167.6 | 1 432 | 270 | 230 | 7 704 | 60.7 | 37.7 | 1.6 |
| **DELAWARE** | X | X | X | X | X | X | X | X | X | 5 842 | 8 803 | 58 178 | 61.9 | 36.9 | 1.1 |
| Kent | 421.6 | 2 769 | 68.9 | 0.9 | 5.1 | 0.0 | 1.8 | 243.8 | 1 601 | 1 994 | 4 429 | 17 154 | 54.4 | 44.6 | 1.1 |
| New Castle | 1 767.4 | 3 346 | 58.5 | 0.8 | 8.9 | 0.0 | 0.9 | 1 463.8 | 2 771 | 3 299 | 3 179 | 33 316 | 69.7 | 29.1 | 1.2 |
| Sussex | 577.3 | 3 133 | 62.5 | 3.1 | 4.7 | 0.0 | 2.7 | 433.1 | 2 350 | 549 | 1 195 | 7 708 | 45.2 | 53.8 | 0.9 |
| **DISTRICT OF COLUMBIA** | X | X | X | X | X | X | X | X | X | 210 239 | 18 467 | 39 217 | 92.5 | 6.5 | 1.0 |
| District of Columbia | 8 490.4 | 14 432 | 18.2 | 6.3 | 5.9 | 25.5 | 1.2 | 10 769.8 | 18 307 | 210 239 | 18 467 | 39 217 | 92.5 | 6.5 | 1.0 |
| **FLORIDA** | X | X | X | X | X | X | X | X | X | 134 267 | 98 362 | 948 214 | 51.0 | 48.2 | 0.8 |
| Alachua | 860.4 | 3 584 | 41.4 | 2.6 | 8.6 | 0.7 | 3.1 | 1 728.0 | 7 197 | 4 425 | 578 | 37 327 | 60.2 | 38.6 | 1.1 |
| Baker | 71.8 | 2 789 | 58.9 | 3.7 | 6.5 | 0.8 | 6.2 | 35.5 | 1 378 | 65 | 53 | 2 661 | 21.0 | 78.4 | 0.5 |
| Bay | 846.1 | 5 159 | 36.6 | 29.6 | 5.2 | 0.0 | 3.0 | 797.3 | 4 862 | 3 862 | 3 698 | 10 763 | 29.2 | 69.9 | 1.0 |
| Bradford | 80.3 | 2 790 | 47.4 | 3.4 | 4.6 | 0.0 | 8.8 | 18.7 | 651 | 35 | 68 | 2 445 | 29.4 | 69.7 | 0.9 |
| Brevard | 1 977.4 | 3 688 | 44.4 | 8.3 | 6.0 | 0.3 | 4.8 | 2 145.2 | 4 001 | 6 420 | 2 903 | 22 499 | 44.3 | 54.7 | 0.9 |
| Broward | 10 081.9 | 5 730 | 30.6 | 21.2 | 8.5 | 1.5 | 1.6 | 9 068.5 | 5 154 | 8 017 | 3 888 | 90 936 | 67.1 | 32.4 | 0.5 |
| Calhoun | 48.6 | 3 575 | 43.0 | 1.4 | 3.8 | 0.6 | 27.8 | 2.1 | 153 | 24 | 29 | 1 029 | 29.2 | 69.6 | 1.2 |
| Charlotte | 645.6 | 4 225 | 30.2 | 3.1 | 8.6 | 1.3 | 9.5 | 627.2 | 4 104 | 326 | 315 | 5 679 | 45.8 | 53.1 | 1.1 |
| Citrus | 364.3 | 2 599 | 45.6 | 4.9 | 7.3 | 1.9 | 7.4 | 383.9 | 2 739 | 228 | 277 | 4 647 | 41.3 | 57.4 | 1.3 |
| Clay | 541.8 | 2 977 | 57.3 | 0.9 | 6.8 | 0.5 | 3.3 | 495.4 | 2 721 | 360 | 380 | 7 162 | 28.2 | 71.1 | 0.7 |
| Collier | 1 757.0 | 5 563 | 38.1 | 2.3 | 8.8 | 0.2 | 8.2 | 3 007.6 | 9 523 | 663 | 641 | 12 121 | 38.3 | 60.8 | 0.8 |
| Columbia | 191.4 | 2 815 | 61.7 | 3.7 | 4.9 | 0.2 | 7.0 | 63.2 | 929 | 1 338 | 133 | 4 595 | 32.6 | 66.4 | 1.0 |
| DeSoto | 105.3 | 3 038 | 45.7 | 2.0 | 6.4 | 0.6 | 4.7 | 52.9 | 1 526 | 39 | 68 | 2 120 | 43.3 | 55.6 | 1.1 |
| Dixie | 41.6 | 2 782 | 49.6 | 6.6 | 6.2 | 0.0 | 6.0 | 11.8 | 788 | 12 | 32 | 963 | 26.5 | 71.5 | 2.0 |
| Duval | 3 152.0 | 3 712 | 43.1 | 0.7 | 5.9 | 2.6 | 2.7 | 12 819.4 | 15 097 | 15 821 | 17 301 | 38 511 | 48.7 | 50.6 | 0.6 |
| Escambia | 1 136.7 | 3 710 | 42.8 | 4.8 | 5.6 | 0.4 | 4.2 | 1 783.8 | 5 822 | 6 113 | 12 425 | 15 568 | 39.9 | 59.2 | 0.9 |
| Flagler | 414.3 | 4 686 | 35.3 | 1.3 | 4.2 | 0.2 | 7.2 | 447.0 | 5 057 | 144 | 190 | 3 535 | 50.4 | 48.8 | 0.7 |
| Franklin | 71.6 | 7 138 | 51.9 | 7.3 | 7.9 | 0.1 | 6.4 | 78.9 | 7 869 | 15 | 36 | 1 059 | 35.4 | 63.3 | 1.3 |
| Gadsden | 137.5 | 2 914 | 57.6 | 0.9 | 5.8 | 0.7 | 8.9 | 31.2 | 661 | 110 | 90 | 4 949 | 69.2 | 30.3 | 0.5 |
| Gilchrist | 45.8 | 2 690 | 57.6 | 2.6 | 5.4 | 0.6 | 7.7 | 4.9 | 285 | 30 | 33 | 1 134 | 25.5 | 72.3 | 2.1 |
| Glades | 36.5 | 3 287 | 50.8 | 3.0 | 11.3 | 0.1 | 4.0 | 5.8 | 523 | 23 | 25 | 501 | 41.1 | 57.7 | 1.2 |
| Gulf | 57.3 | 4 074 | 36.8 | 7.1 | 7.8 | 0.3 | 7.6 | 20.8 | 1 482 | 13 | 31 | 1 343 | 29.8 | 69.1 | 1.1 |
| Hamilton | 74.3 | 5 198 | 26.4 | 1.8 | 4.1 | 0.2 | 13.1 | 5.6 | 395 | 28 | 29 | 1 300 | 42.3 | 56.9 | 0.8 |
| Hardee | 89.3 | 3 099 | 54.0 | 3.5 | 10.9 | 0.0 | 7.7 | 14.9 | 518 | 47 | 54 | 1 690 | 34.6 | 64.3 | 1.1 |
| Hendry | 171.9 | 4 340 | 43.4 | 13.1 | 5.1 | 1.8 | 5.0 | 47.4 | 1 197 | 84 | 76 | 2 250 | 45.9 | 53.1 | 0.9 |
| Hernando | 653.7 | 3 866 | 36.0 | 1.3 | 4.4 | 0.1 | 4.7 | 658.1 | 3 893 | 319 | 339 | 5 957 | 47.7 | 51.2 | 1.1 |
| Highlands | 291.4 | 2 933 | 56.7 | 2.2 | 7.1 | 0.3 | 4.5 | 217.9 | 2 193 | 248 | 193 | 3 894 | 40.5 | 58.6 | 1.0 |
| Hillsborough | 4 899.7 | 4 171 | 40.9 | 2.3 | 6.6 | 2.4 | 3.6 | 6 543.0 | 5 570 | 14 292 | 8 385 | 65 218 | 53.2 | 46.0 | 0.8 |
| Holmes | 60.1 | 3 124 | 48.0 | 12.9 | 4.3 | 0.7 | 7.3 | 13.0 | 676 | 62 | 39 | 1 403 | 16.8 | 81.9 | 1.3 |
| Indian River | 528.1 | 4 006 | 35.5 | 3.8 | 7.4 | 0.6 | 7.4 | 540.1 | 4 097 | 383 | 271 | 5 030 | 42.1 | 56.9 | 1.0 |
| Jackson | 202.4 | 4 106 | 43.1 | 31.3 | 3.3 | 0.0 | 6.8 | 59.4 | 1 205 | 497 | 96 | 5 199 | 35.6 | 63.6 | 0.8 |
| Jefferson | 36.7 | 2 536 | 43.4 | 2.3 | 9.1 | 0.0 | 8.2 | 8.4 | 578 | 35 | 34 | 787 | 51.4 | 47.7 | 0.9 |
| Lafayette | 18.3 | 2 285 | 59.7 | 4.6 | 3.5 | 0.6 | 5.5 | 4.3 | 542 | 16 | 17 | 685 | 19.1 | 79.8 | 1.1 |
| Lake | 1 081.5 | 3 592 | 42.9 | 8.4 | 5.7 | 0.4 | 5.3 | 1 563.5 | 5 193 | 565 | 588 | 12 782 | 42.8 | 56.4 | 0.8 |
| Lee | 3 524.7 | 5 968 | 29.1 | 19.2 | 4.5 | 0.4 | 5.9 | 4 370.1 | 7 400 | 2 422 | 1 297 | 34 191 | 44.5 | 54.8 | 0.7 |
| Leon | 1 113.7 | 4 268 | 41.4 | 0.9 | 6.3 | 0.0 | 10.2 | 3 166.0 | 12 133 | 1 704 | 641 | 51 876 | 61.7 | 37.5 | 0.8 |
| Levy | 110.7 | 2 835 | 53.9 | 3.9 | 8.1 | 0.7 | 4.8 | 27.9 | 715 | 77 | 112 | 1 972 | 35.8 | 62.8 | 1.4 |
| Liberty | 26.0 | 3 306 | 60.0 | 1.8 | 4.1 | 1.3 | 12.1 | 6.4 | 819 | 38 | 16 | 786 | 27.3 | 71.4 | 1.3 |
| Madison | 87.8 | 4 633 | 50.2 | 12.8 | 6.7 | 0.4 | 3.5 | 26.1 | 1 375 | 42 | 37 | 1 428 | 47.9 | 51.0 | 1.0 |
| Manatee | 1 493.6 | 4 740 | 42.3 | 1.5 | 6.5 | 1.7 | 3.6 | 1 825.9 | 5 795 | 776 | 671 | 11 307 | 46.1 | 53.1 | 0.8 |
| Marion | 959.0 | 2 952 | 50.3 | 1.7 | 10.2 | 0.7 | 8.4 | 760.8 | 2 342 | 719 | 652 | 16 595 | 43.7 | 55.3 | 1.0 |
| Martin | 568.8 | 4 086 | 35.2 | 5.6 | 8.1 | 1.6 | 3.9 | 377.9 | 2 715 | 271 | 290 | 5 513 | 42.8 | 56.4 | 0.8 |
| Miami-Dade | 14 688.6 | 6 153 | 33.7 | 10.0 | 6.5 | 3.0 | 2.0 | 20 249.0 | 8 482 | 19 938 | 7 405 | 124 157 | 57.9 | 41.8 | 0.4 |
| Monroe | 599.5 | 8 187 | 30.1 | 4.1 | 17.2 | 0.6 | 2.2 | 556.4 | 7 598 | 1 280 | 1 594 | 4 570 | 51.9 | 47.0 | 1.1 |
| Nassau | 234.8 | 3 430 | 40.2 | 3.6 | 6.3 | 1.1 | 6.5 | 241.6 | 3 529 | 612 | 145 | 2 761 | 27.7 | 71.5 | 0.7 |
| Okaloosa | 652.0 | 3 592 | 50.0 | 1.8 | 7.1 | 0.3 | 4.7 | 355.6 | 1 959 | 8 138 | 15 242 | 7 959 | 27.1 | 72.0 | 0.9 |
| Okeechobee | 129.5 | 3 212 | 49.4 | 0.9 | 13.0 | 1.1 | 5.5 | 47.2 | 1 170 | 66 | 78 | 2 198 | 39.9 | 59.1 | 0.9 |
| Orange | 5 375.1 | 5 042 | 38.8 | 3.3 | 6.1 | 0.7 | 4.7 | 10 479.2 | 9 829 | 9 860 | 2 608 | 60 985 | 59.0 | 40.4 | 0.6 |
| Osceola | 1 207.3 | 4 720 | 41.1 | 1.6 | 5.8 | 2.1 | 6.6 | 2 077.6 | 8 121 | 380 | 541 | 11 439 | 59.6 | 39.8 | 0.6 |
| Palm Beach | 6 853.8 | 5 412 | 32.9 | 3.3 | 7.3 | 2.4 | 2.4 | 7 088.2 | 5 597 | 6 361 | 2 695 | 56 186 | 61.2 | 38.3 | 0.5 |
| Pasco | 1 443.0 | 3 119 | 53.3 | 1.5 | 5.0 | 0.3 | 4.2 | 1 492.2 | 3 225 | 751 | 911 | 15 997 | 47.7 | 51.2 | 1.1 |
| Pinellas | 3 564.2 | 3 885 | 35.9 | 2.9 | 9.6 | 3.4 | 3.2 | 3 766.6 | 4 106 | 7 210 | 3 045 | 37 350 | 53.6 | 45.3 | 1.1 |
| Polk | 1 985.5 | 3 455 | 50.8 | 2.7 | 6.7 | 0.9 | 6.0 | 2 648.1 | 4 607 | 1 184 | 1 223 | 27 652 | 46.5 | 52.6 | 0.9 |

1. Based on the resident population estimated as of July 1 of the year shown.  2. © 2013 Election Data Services, Inc. All rights reserved.

# Table B. States and Counties — Land Area and Population

| STATE/ County code | CBSA code[1] | County type[2] | STATE County | Land area,[3] (sq km) 2010 | Population 2012 | | | Race alone or in combination, not Hispanic or Latino (percent) | | | | | Age (percent) | | | | | |
| | | | | | Total persons | Rank | Per square kilometer | White | Black | American Indian, Alaska Native | Asian and Pacific Islander | Percent Hispanic or Latino[4] | Under 5 years | 5 to 17 years | 18 to 24 years | 25 to 34 years | 35 to 44 years | 45 to 54 years |
| | | | | 1 | 2 | 3 | 4 | 5 | 6 | 7 | 8 | 9 | 10 | 11 | 12 | 13 | 14 | 15 |
| | | | FLORIDA—Cont'd | | | | | | | | | | | | | | | |
| 12 107 | 37260 | 4 | Putnam | 1 885 | 73 263 | 741 | 38.9 | 73.3 | 16.8 | 0.9 | 1.0 | 9.4 | 6.2 | 16.3 | 8.2 | 10.4 | 10.3 | 14.4 |
| 12 109 | 27260 | 1 | St. Johns | 1 556 | 202 188 | 312 | 129.9 | 86.1 | 6.3 | 0.7 | 2.9 | 5.5 | 5.1 | 17.6 | 7.7 | 9.9 | 13.2 | 16.0 |
| 12 111 | 38940 | 2 | St. Lucie | 1 481 | 283 866 | 232 | 191.7 | 62.4 | 19.4 | 0.7 | 2.3 | 16.8 | 5.7 | 16.2 | 7.7 | 10.9 | 12.1 | 14.0 |
| 12 113 | 37860 | 2 | Santa Rosa | 2 620 | 158 512 | 397 | 60.5 | 86.7 | 6.5 | 1.7 | 3.2 | 4.6 | 5.9 | 17.6 | 8.5 | 12.5 | 13.4 | 16.2 |
| 12 115 | 35840 | 2 | Sarasota | 1 440 | 386 147 | 174 | 268.2 | 85.4 | 5.2 | 0.5 | 1.8 | 8.2 | 3.8 | 11.7 | 5.9 | 8.2 | 9.7 | 13.4 |
| 12 117 | 36740 | 1 | Seminole | 801 | 430 838 | 158 | 537.9 | 67.3 | 11.6 | 0.7 | 4.6 | 17.7 | 5.4 | 17.0 | 10.0 | 13.3 | 13.6 | 15.8 |
| 12 119 | 45540 | 4 | Sumter | 1 417 | 101 620 | 576 | 71.7 | 83.7 | 9.4 | 0.7 | 1.0 | 6.0 | 2.3 | 6.4 | 3.6 | 6.7 | 7.6 | 8.6 |
| 12 121 | ... | 6 | Suwannee | 1 783 | 43 656 | 1 094 | 24.5 | 78.2 | 12.1 | 1.1 | 0.9 | 9.0 | 6.3 | 16.5 | 7.8 | 11.3 | 11.2 | 13.8 |
| 12 123 | ... | 6 | Taylor | 2 702 | 22 744 | 1 697 | 8.4 | 74.1 | 21.2 | 1.6 | 1.1 | 3.6 | 5.8 | 13.7 | 8.8 | 13.5 | 13.2 | 15.1 |
| 12 125 | ... | 6 | Union | 631 | 15 212 | 2 091 | 24.1 | 71.9 | 22.7 | 0.7 | 0.6 | 5.2 | 5.1 | 14.1 | 9.0 | 15.5 | 14.0 | 16.3 |
| 12 127 | 19660 | 2 | Volusia | 2 852 | 496 950 | 135 | 174.2 | 76.3 | 10.9 | 0.8 | 2.1 | 11.5 | 4.9 | 13.7 | 9.0 | 10.4 | 11.1 | 14.7 |
| 12 129 | 45220 | 2 | Wakulla | 1 571 | 30 818 | 1 414 | 19.6 | 80.5 | 15.4 | 1.3 | 0.9 | 3.6 | 5.5 | 16.4 | 8.0 | 14.0 | 15.2 | 16.6 |
| 12 131 | ... | 6 | Walton | 2 687 | 57 582 | 886 | 21.4 | 86.5 | 6.6 | 1.9 | 1.5 | 5.5 | 5.8 | 14.4 | 7.3 | 12.5 | 12.6 | 15.6 |
| 12 133 | ... | 6 | Washington | 1 509 | 24 892 | 1 613 | 16.5 | 79.5 | 16.0 | 2.1 | 1.1 | 3.2 | 5.4 | 15.5 | 8.7 | 12.7 | 13.7 | 15.3 |
| 13 000 | ... | X | GEORGIA | 148 959 | 9 919 945 | X | 66.6 | 56.8 | 31.1 | 0.7 | 3.9 | 9.1 | 7.0 | 18.4 | 10.1 | 13.8 | 14.1 | 14.2 |
| 13 001 | ... | 7 | Appling | 1 313 | 18 368 | 1 903 | 14.0 | 70.3 | 19.6 | 0.4 | 0.9 | 9.4 | 6.9 | 18.3 | 8.3 | 12.4 | 13.0 | 14.1 |
| 13 003 | 20060 | 9 | Atkinson | 879 | 8 284 | 2 586 | 9.4 | 57.0 | 17.8 | 0.7 | 0.5 | 24.8 | 8.9 | 20.7 | 9.3 | 13.5 | 13.2 | 13.0 |
| 13 005 | ... | 7 | Bacon | 670 | 11 198 | 2 346 | 16.7 | 76.1 | 16.6 | 0.3 | 0.6 | 7.5 | 7.3 | 18.5 | 8.3 | 13.5 | 13.2 | 12.8 |
| 13 007 | 10500 | 3 | Baker | 886 | 3 366 | 2 951 | 3.8 | 48.3 | 45.9 | 0.6 | 1.2 | 4.9 | 6.4 | 18.6 | 9.0 | 10.5 | 12.2 | 16.0 |
| 13 009 | 33300 | 4 | Baldwin | 668 | 46 367 | 1 042 | 69.4 | 54.9 | 41.7 | 0.5 | 1.8 | 2.2 | 5.9 | 14.5 | 18.6 | 12.0 | 10.7 | 13.5 |
| 13 011 | ... | 8 | Banks | 601 | 18 316 | 1 907 | 30.5 | 89.6 | 3.4 | 0.8 | 1.2 | 6.1 | 5.9 | 18.9 | 8.5 | 11.4 | 14.4 | 15.0 |
| 13 013 | 12060 | 1 | Barrow | 415 | 70 169 | 760 | 169.1 | 75.5 | 12.6 | 0.7 | 3.9 | 9.1 | 7.9 | 20.0 | 8.2 | 15.4 | 14.8 | 13.5 |
| 13 015 | 12060 | 1 | Bartow | 1 190 | 100 661 | 583 | 84.6 | 80.4 | 11.2 | 0.8 | 1.2 | 7.9 | 6.8 | 19.4 | 8.7 | 12.8 | 14.7 | 14.8 |
| 13 017 | 22340 | 7 | Ben Hill | 648 | 17 538 | 1 946 | 27.1 | 58.4 | 34.9 | 0.7 | 1.0 | 6.1 | 7.9 | 18.2 | 8.9 | 12.5 | 11.7 | 13.6 |
| 13 019 | ... | 6 | Berrien | 1 170 | 19 041 | 1 871 | 16.3 | 83.0 | 11.6 | 0.6 | 0.7 | 5.0 | 6.5 | 18.4 | 8.7 | 12.1 | 13.0 | 14.4 |
| 13 021 | 31420 | 3 | Bibb | 647 | 156 462 | 402 | 241.8 | 42.8 | 52.8 | 0.6 | 2.1 | 3.1 | 7.4 | 18.2 | 10.6 | 13.2 | 11.9 | 13.6 |
| 13 023 | ... | 6 | Bleckley | 559 | 12 913 | 2 249 | 23.1 | 69.0 | 28.1 | 0.3 | 1.0 | 2.4 | 5.6 | 16.6 | 16.6 | 10.5 | 10.8 | 13.9 |
| 13 025 | 15260 | 3 | Brantley | 1 146 | 18 587 | 1 893 | 16.2 | 93.7 | 4.1 | 1.0 | 0.6 | 2.0 | 6.9 | 19.4 | 8.6 | 11.6 | 13.4 | 15.1 |
| 13 027 | 46660 | 3 | Brooks | 1 277 | 15 403 | 2 079 | 12.1 | 59.0 | 35.3 | 0.7 | 0.8 | 5.2 | 6.6 | 16.9 | 8.0 | 11.6 | 11.7 | 14.9 |
| 13 029 | 42340 | 2 | Bryan | 1 129 | 32 214 | 1 385 | 28.5 | 77.7 | 15.8 | 0.8 | 2.6 | 5.2 | 7.3 | 21.8 | 7.9 | 13.0 | 14.6 | 15.2 |
| 13 031 | 44340 | 4 | Bulloch | 1 743 | 72 694 | 746 | 41.7 | 65.5 | 29.6 | 0.6 | 2.1 | 3.7 | 5.6 | 14.1 | 29.6 | 12.4 | 10.0 | 10.4 |
| 13 033 | 12260 | 2 | Burke | 2 142 | 23 125 | 1 684 | 10.8 | 47.2 | 49.7 | 0.6 | 0.7 | 2.9 | 7.3 | 20.1 | 9.7 | 12.1 | 11.7 | 14.3 |
| 13 035 | 12060 | 1 | Butts | 478 | 23 524 | 1 662 | 49.2 | 69.2 | 27.8 | 0.6 | 0.7 | 2.8 | 6.0 | 16.2 | 9.5 | 14.1 | 13.6 | 15.0 |
| 13 037 | ... | 8 | Calhoun | 726 | 6 504 | 2 723 | 9.0 | 35.0 | 60.7 | 0.4 | 0.4 | 4.1 | 5.4 | 14.1 | 8.6 | 15.6 | 15.0 | 15.2 |
| 13 039 | 41220 | 4 | Camden | 1 588 | 51 402 | 963 | 32.4 | 70.1 | 20.6 | 0.9 | 2.5 | 5.4 | 7.7 | 18.6 | 13.1 | 14.7 | 12.4 | 13.7 |
| 13 043 | ... | 7 | Candler | 629 | 11 117 | 2 352 | 17.7 | 62.7 | 25.8 | 0.4 | 0.8 | 11.1 | 7.1 | 18.5 | 10.1 | 11.9 | 11.9 | 12.6 |
| 13 045 | 12060 | 1 | Carroll | 1 293 | 111 580 | 540 | 86.3 | 74.0 | 19.4 | 0.7 | 1.2 | 6.4 | 7.0 | 18.1 | 12.8 | 13.5 | 13.1 | 13.2 |
| 13 047 | 16860 | 2 | Catoosa | 420 | 65 046 | 810 | 154.9 | 93.1 | 3.3 | 0.9 | 1.7 | 2.5 | 6.1 | 18.4 | 8.2 | 12.3 | 14.4 | 14.3 |
| 13 049 | ... | 6 | Charlton | 2 004 | 13 295 | 2 225 | 6.6 | 63.5 | 32.6 | 0.9 | 0.9 | 3.5 | 5.4 | 13.9 | 16.1 | 14.6 | 15.9 | 15.9 |
| 13 051 | 42340 | 2 | Chatham | 1 104 | 276 434 | 239 | 250.4 | 51.7 | 40.5 | 0.7 | 3.2 | 5.7 | 7.0 | 15.5 | 12.9 | 16.1 | 11.8 | 12.7 |
| 13 053 | 17980 | 2 | Chattahoochee | 644 | 13 037 | 2 239 | 20.2 | 63.7 | 20.2 | 1.5 | 3.7 | 14.0 | 9.3 | 16.7 | 27.2 | 22.9 | 10.3 | 5.9 |
| 13 055 | 44900 | 6 | Chattooga | 812 | 25 725 | 1 578 | 31.7 | 83.6 | 12.3 | 0.6 | 0.6 | 4.2 | 6.0 | 16.3 | 8.6 | 12.9 | 13.5 | 14.8 |
| 13 057 | 12060 | 1 | Cherokee | 1 092 | 221 315 | 286 | 202.7 | 82.0 | 6.6 | 0.8 | 2.3 | 9.9 | 7.0 | 20.0 | 7.8 | 12.9 | 16.2 | 15.2 |
| 13 059 | 12020 | 3 | Clarke | 309 | 120 266 | 507 | 389.2 | 58.9 | 26.7 | 0.4 | 5.0 | 10.5 | 6.0 | 11.3 | 31.6 | 16.1 | 9.9 | 8.5 |
| 13 061 | ... | 9 | Clay | 506 | 3 116 | 2 967 | 6.2 | 38.3 | 60.3 | 0.8 | 0.6 | 0.9 | 6.3 | 16.3 | 8.5 | 9.6 | 8.9 | 13.8 |
| 13 063 | 12060 | 1 | Clayton | 367 | 265 888 | 251 | 724.5 | 16.7 | 65.4 | 0.7 | 5.5 | 13.5 | 8.3 | 20.7 | 10.7 | 15.2 | 14.9 | 13.6 |
| 13 065 | ... | 6 | Clinch | 2 073 | 6 718 | 2 706 | 3.2 | 67.6 | 28.8 | 0.9 | 0.5 | 3.4 | 7.5 | 18.9 | 9.3 | 11.6 | 12.5 | 13.4 |
| 13 067 | 12060 | 1 | Cobb | 879 | 707 442 | 84 | 804.8 | 57.5 | 25.9 | 0.7 | 5.3 | 12.5 | 6.9 | 18.4 | 9.1 | 14.6 | 15.5 | 15.1 |
| 13 069 | 20060 | 7 | Coffee | 1 489 | 43 170 | 1 103 | 29.0 | 61.0 | 28.1 | 0.5 | 1.0 | 10.4 | 7.1 | 18.2 | 10.6 | 14.1 | 13.8 | 13.8 |
| 13 071 | 34220 | 6 | Colquitt | 1 409 | 46 137 | 1 046 | 32.7 | 59.2 | 22.7 | 0.5 | 0.9 | 17.6 | 8.4 | 19.5 | 9.3 | 13.0 | 12.7 | 12.7 |
| 13 073 | 12260 | 2 | Columbia | 751 | 131 627 | 476 | 175.3 | 74.8 | 16.3 | 0.7 | 5.2 | 5.3 | 6.5 | 20.1 | 8.4 | 12.7 | 14.1 | 15.3 |
| 13 075 | ... | 6 | Cook | 588 | 16 923 | 1 988 | 28.8 | 65.6 | 27.9 | 0.6 | 1.0 | 5.9 | 7.4 | 19.3 | 8.6 | 12.4 | 13.0 | 13.5 |
| 13 077 | 12060 | 1 | Coweta | 1 142 | 130 929 | 478 | 114.6 | 73.6 | 18.2 | 0.7 | 2.1 | 7.0 | 6.9 | 19.8 | 7.8 | 12.8 | 15.2 | 15.1 |
| 13 079 | 31420 | 3 | Crawford | 841 | 12 600 | 2 266 | 15.0 | 73.8 | 23.2 | 1.0 | 0.5 | 2.8 | 5.5 | 17.0 | 8.4 | 10.8 | 13.3 | 17.0 |
| 13 081 | 18380 | 6 | Crisp | 706 | 23 606 | 1 658 | 33.4 | 52.0 | 44.0 | 0.4 | 1.0 | 3.4 | 7.0 | 18.4 | 9.3 | 12.0 | 11.8 | 13.7 |
| 13 083 | 16860 | 2 | Dade | 451 | 16 490 | 2 013 | 36.6 | 95.5 | 1.7 | 1.1 | 1.1 | 1.9 | 5.3 | 15.7 | 12.7 | 11.4 | 11.9 | 14.6 |
| 13 085 | 12060 | 1 | Dawson | 546 | 22 422 | 1 713 | 41.1 | 93.4 | 1.3 | 1.0 | 0.8 | 4.1 | 5.3 | 16.6 | 8.2 | 11.5 | 13.2 | 15.3 |
| 13 087 | 12460 | 6 | Decatur | 1 547 | 27 509 | 1 514 | 17.8 | 52.8 | 41.4 | 0.6 | 0.8 | 5.3 | 6.9 | 18.6 | 9.4 | 11.9 | 12.6 | 14.2 |
| 13 089 | 12060 | 1 | DeKalb | 693 | 707 089 | 86 | 1 020.3 | 31.2 | 54.3 | 0.7 | 5.8 | 9.8 | 7.4 | 16.5 | 9.8 | 17.1 | 15.2 | 13.8 |
| 13 091 | ... | 7 | Dodge | 1 284 | 21 329 | 1 766 | 16.6 | 66.1 | 30.2 | 0.5 | 0.7 | 3.4 | 6.2 | 16.6 | 10.1 | 12.0 | 13.4 | 14.3 |
| 13 093 | ... | 6 | Dooly | 1 015 | 14 318 | 2 149 | 14.1 | 44.2 | 49.1 | 0.5 | 0.9 | 6.1 | 5.5 | 15.3 | 8.2 | 13.9 | 13.5 | 15.2 |
| 13 095 | 10500 | 3 | Dougherty | 851 | 94 501 | 613 | 111.0 | 29.6 | 67.2 | 0.6 | 1.2 | 2.5 | 7.6 | 18.1 | 13.0 | 13.3 | 11.3 | 12.5 |
| 13 097 | 12060 | 1 | Douglas | 518 | 133 971 | 468 | 258.6 | 50.4 | 40.0 | 0.7 | 2.1 | 8.6 | 7.2 | 20.6 | 8.6 | 12.9 | 16.2 | 14.8 |
| 13 099 | ... | 6 | Early | 1 328 | 10 594 | 2 391 | 8.0 | 48.3 | 49.3 | 0.6 | 0.6 | 1.8 | 6.9 | 19.1 | 8.4 | 10.3 | 11.6 | 13.9 |
| 13 101 | 46660 | 3 | Echols | 1 075 | 3 988 | 2 907 | 3.7 | 64.1 | 4.9 | 2.3 | 0.6 | 29.4 | 8.5 | 19.8 | 10.0 | 16.5 | 13.2 | 12.5 |

1. CBSA = Core Based Statistical Area. See Appendix A for explanation. See Appendix B for list of metropolitan areas with component counties.　2. County type code from the Economic Research Service of USDA Rural-Urban Continuum Codes. See Appendix A for definition.　3. Dry land or land partially or temporarily covered by water.　4. May be of any race.

# Table B. States and Counties — Population and Households

| | Population, 2011 (cont.) | | | | Population change and components of change, 2000-2012 | | | | | | | Households, 2010 | | | | |
|---|---|---|---|---|---|---|---|---|---|---|---|---|---|---|---|---|
| | Age (percent) (cont.) | | | | Total persons | | Percent change | | Components of change, 2010-2012 | | | | | | Percent | |
| STATE County | 55 to 64 years | 65 to 74 years | 75 years and over | Percent female | 2000 | 2010 | 2000-2010 | 2010-2012 | Births | Deaths | Net migration | Number | Percent change, 2000-2010 | Persons per house-hold | Female family house-holder[1] | One per-son |
| | 16 | 17 | 18 | 19 | 20 | 21 | 22 | 23 | 24 | 25 | 26 | 27 | 28 | 29 | 30 | 31 |
| **FLORIDA—Cont'd** | | | | | | | | | | | | | | | | |
| Putnam | 14.9 | 10.9 | 8.5 | 50.5 | 70 423 | 74 364 | 5.6 | -1.5 | 1 950 | 2 022 | -994 | 29 409 | 5.6 | 2.48 | 14.4 | 26.8 |
| St. Johns | 14.4 | 9.1 | 7.0 | 51.4 | 123 135 | 190 039 | 54.3 | 6.4 | 4 032 | 3 304 | 11 118 | 75 338 | 51.8 | 2.49 | 9.6 | 23.7 |
| St. Lucie | 13.0 | 10.8 | 9.6 | 51.2 | 192 695 | 277 789 | 44.2 | 2.2 | 6 750 | 6 296 | 5 319 | 108 523 | 41.1 | 2.53 | 12.9 | 24.2 |
| Santa Rosa | 12.8 | 8.1 | 5.1 | 49.6 | 117 743 | 151 372 | 28.6 | 4.7 | 4 035 | 2 653 | 5 688 | 56 910 | 30.0 | 2.59 | 11.4 | 21.3 |
| Sarasota | 15.6 | 15.6 | 16.1 | 52.2 | 325 957 | 379 448 | 16.4 | 1.8 | 6 337 | 11 348 | 11 818 | 175 746 | 17.2 | 2.13 | 8.7 | 32.1 |
| Seminole | 12.6 | 6.8 | 5.6 | 51.6 | 365 196 | 422 718 | 15.8 | 1.9 | 9 762 | 6 571 | 4 642 | 164 706 | 18.0 | 2.55 | 13.5 | 24.7 |
| Sumter | 19.3 | 29.6 | 16.0 | 48.2 | 53 345 | 93 420 | 75.1 | 8.8 | 989 | 2 656 | 9 029 | 41 361 | 99.1 | 2.04 | 5.7 | 25.0 |
| Suwannee | 13.8 | 10.7 | 8.5 | 49.6 | 34 844 | 41 551 | 19.2 | 5.1 | 1 070 | 1 117 | 2 122 | 15 953 | 18.5 | 2.52 | 13.0 | 25.6 |
| Taylor | 13.9 | 9.6 | 6.5 | 44.3 | 19 256 | 22 570 | 17.2 | 0.8 | 584 | 476 | 71 | 7 920 | 10.4 | 2.44 | 14.5 | 26.9 |
| Union | 15.4 | 7.0 | 3.6 | 35.4 | 13 442 | 15 535 | 15.6 | -2.1 | 353 | 456 | -246 | 4 048 | 20.2 | 2.66 | 15.1 | 23.8 |
| Volusia | 14.7 | 11.1 | 10.4 | 51.2 | 443 343 | 494 593 | 11.6 | 0.5 | 10 484 | 13 460 | 5 602 | 208 236 | 12.7 | 2.31 | 12.1 | 29.5 |
| Wakulla | 13.0 | 7.2 | 4.1 | 44.9 | 22 863 | 30 776 | 34.6 | 0.1 | 689 | 467 | -179 | 10 490 | 24.1 | 2.61 | 13.3 | 22.3 |
| Walton | 14.8 | 10.4 | 6.6 | 48.7 | 40 601 | 55 043 | 35.6 | 4.6 | 1 396 | 1 124 | 2 224 | 22 301 | 34.8 | 2.38 | 11.1 | 27.6 |
| Washington | 12.8 | 9.6 | 6.3 | 45.4 | 20 973 | 24 896 | 18.7 | 0.0 | 532 | 619 | 55 | 8 864 | 11.8 | 2.50 | 13.0 | 25.6 |
| **GEORGIA** | 11.4 | 6.5 | 4.5 | 51.1 | 8 186 453 | 9 687 653 | 18.3 | 2.4 | 297 798 | 160 842 | 90 782 | 3 585 584 | 19.3 | 2.63 | 15.8 | 25.4 |
| Appling | 13.1 | 8.4 | 5.4 | 49.3 | 17 419 | 18 236 | 4.7 | 0.7 | 590 | 431 | -22 | 6 969 | 5.5 | 2.56 | 12.6 | 26.3 |
| Atkinson | 10.6 | 6.6 | 4.2 | 49.7 | 7 609 | 8 375 | 10.1 | -1.1 | 297 | 126 | -277 | 2 983 | 9.8 | 2.80 | 15.3 | 22.9 |
| Bacon | 13.1 | 7.9 | 5.4 | 50.4 | 10 103 | 11 096 | 9.8 | 0.9 | 334 | 265 | 37 | 4 214 | 9.9 | 2.56 | 14.8 | 25.7 |
| Baker | 16.8 | 6.2 | 4.4 | 51.2 | 4 074 | 3 451 | -15.3 | -2.5 | 74 | 32 | -128 | 1 372 | -9.4 | 2.52 | 15.9 | 30.5 |
| Baldwin | 12.2 | 7.4 | 5.2 | 51.1 | 44 700 | 45 720 | 2.3 | 1.4 | 1 087 | 919 | 442 | 16 788 | 13.8 | 2.45 | 19.2 | 26.9 |
| Banks | 13.0 | 8.4 | 4.6 | 49.4 | 14 422 | 18 395 | 27.5 | -0.4 | 400 | 266 | -247 | 6 700 | 24.9 | 2.75 | 10.2 | 20.2 |
| Barrow | 10.4 | 6.0 | 3.8 | 50.6 | 46 144 | 69 367 | 50.3 | 1.2 | 2 358 | 1 116 | -472 | 23 971 | 46.6 | 2.88 | 13.4 | 18.8 |
| Bartow | 11.6 | 6.8 | 4.3 | 50.6 | 76 019 | 100 157 | 31.8 | 0.5 | 2 892 | 1 837 | -559 | 35 782 | 31.7 | 2.77 | 13.5 | 21.0 |
| Ben Hill | 12.9 | 8.0 | 6.3 | 52.2 | 17 484 | 17 634 | 0.9 | -0.5 | 603 | 452 | -242 | 6 794 | 1.8 | 2.55 | 19.1 | 26.7 |
| Berrien | 12.3 | 8.8 | 5.8 | 50.4 | 16 235 | 19 286 | 18.8 | -1.3 | 493 | 424 | -321 | 7 443 | 18.9 | 2.57 | 13.6 | 25.2 |
| Bibb | 12.2 | 6.9 | 6.0 | 52.7 | 153 887 | 155 547 | 1.1 | 0.6 | 5 261 | 3 675 | -687 | 60 295 | 1.1 | 2.48 | 22.0 | 30.3 |
| Bleckley | 10.5 | 8.4 | 6.9 | 52.5 | 11 666 | 13 063 | 12.0 | -1.1 | 318 | 272 | -208 | 4 660 | 6.6 | 2.49 | 15.5 | 26.5 |
| Brantley | 13.2 | 7.3 | 4.5 | 50.3 | 14 629 | 18 411 | 25.9 | 1.0 | 475 | 392 | 83 | 6 885 | 26.7 | 2.66 | 13.2 | 22.1 |
| Brooks | 13.7 | 9.7 | 6.9 | 51.2 | 16 450 | 16 243 | -1.3 | -5.2 | 421 | 413 | -858 | 6 457 | 4.9 | 2.52 | 16.8 | 27.6 |
| Bryan | 11.1 | 5.6 | 3.6 | 50.6 | 23 417 | 30 233 | 29.1 | 6.6 | 1 059 | 451 | 1 352 | 10 738 | 32.7 | 2.81 | 13.9 | 17.7 |
| Bulloch | 8.9 | 5.4 | 3.7 | 50.0 | 55 983 | 70 217 | 25.4 | 3.5 | 1 879 | 1 116 | 1 676 | 25 575 | 23.3 | 2.56 | 13.2 | 25.0 |
| Burke | 12.8 | 7.2 | 4.9 | 51.8 | 22 243 | 23 316 | 4.8 | -0.8 | 727 | 524 | -404 | 8 553 | 7.5 | 2.70 | 24.1 | 24.3 |
| Butts | 12.4 | 7.9 | 5.3 | 47.3 | 19 522 | 23 655 | 21.2 | -0.6 | 653 | 515 | -274 | 7 881 | 22.1 | 2.70 | 15.6 | 21.8 |
| Calhoun | 12.2 | 7.0 | 6.9 | 41.4 | 6 320 | 6 694 | 5.9 | -2.8 | 154 | 118 | -262 | 2 002 | 2.0 | 2.49 | 22.6 | 32.5 |
| Camden | 10.2 | 6.5 | 3.2 | 49.3 | 43 664 | 50 513 | 15.7 | 1.8 | 1 755 | 590 | -291 | 18 047 | 22.7 | 2.69 | 14.3 | 20.1 |
| Candler | 13.2 | 8.9 | 5.7 | 50.7 | 9 577 | 10 998 | 14.8 | 1.1 | 324 | 270 | 38 | 4 041 | 19.7 | 2.65 | 15.7 | 25.5 |
| Carroll | 10.9 | 6.8 | 4.5 | 51.2 | 87 268 | 110 527 | 26.7 | 1.0 | 3 473 | 2 045 | -453 | 39 187 | 24.1 | 2.73 | 14.1 | 21.7 |
| Catoosa | 12.7 | 8.0 | 5.6 | 51.4 | 53 282 | 63 942 | 20.0 | 1.7 | 1 643 | 1 119 | 494 | 24 475 | 19.8 | 2.59 | 12.6 | 23.1 |
| Charlton | 10.3 | 7.5 | 4.5 | 39.6 | 10 282 | 12 171 | 18.4 | 9.2 | 302 | 171 | 948 | 3 927 | 17.5 | 2.64 | 15.2 | 23.1 |
| Chatham | 11.5 | 6.9 | 5.6 | 51.6 | 232 048 | 265 128 | 14.3 | 4.3 | 8 894 | 5 047 | 7 472 | 103 038 | 14.7 | 2.45 | 17.5 | 28.7 |
| Chattahoochee | 3.9 | 2.4 | 1.3 | 37.0 | 14 882 | 11 267 | -24.3 | 15.7 | 461 | 56 | 1 336 | 2 686 | -8.4 | 2.98 | 16.2 | 19.1 |
| Chattooga | 13.0 | 8.4 | 6.6 | 48.2 | 25 470 | 26 015 | 2.1 | -1.1 | 650 | 603 | -328 | 9 548 | -0.3 | 2.52 | 14.0 | 26.6 |
| Cherokee | 11.4 | 6.4 | 3.5 | 50.6 | 141 903 | 214 346 | 51.1 | 3.3 | 6 395 | 2 511 | 3 065 | 75 936 | 53.4 | 2.80 | 10.1 | 18.8 |
| Clarke | 7.8 | 4.8 | 3.9 | 52.0 | 101 489 | 116 714 | 15.0 | 3.0 | 3 253 | 1 459 | 1 745 | 45 414 | 14.4 | 2.37 | 13.4 | 30.6 |
| Clay | 17.2 | 11.3 | 8.2 | 54.5 | 3 357 | 3 183 | -5.2 | -2.1 | 90 | 75 | -77 | 1 331 | -1.2 | 2.35 | 22.8 | 31.6 |
| Clayton | 9.7 | 4.4 | 2.5 | 52.0 | 236 517 | 259 424 | 9.7 | 2.5 | 9 305 | 3 278 | 322 | 90 633 | 10.2 | 2.82 | 25.3 | 25.4 |
| Clinch | 13.3 | 8.5 | 5.0 | 50.8 | 6 878 | 6 798 | -1.2 | -1.2 | 224 | 135 | -171 | 2 572 | 2.4 | 2.58 | 19.4 | 25.7 |
| Cobb | 11.2 | 5.5 | 3.6 | 51.4 | 607 751 | 688 078 | 13.2 | 2.8 | 21 180 | 8 479 | 6 745 | 260 056 | 14.3 | 2.61 | 13.0 | 25.6 |
| Coffee | 11.2 | 6.8 | 4.5 | 48.5 | 37 413 | 42 356 | 13.2 | 1.9 | 1 342 | 775 | 241 | 14 817 | 11.0 | 2.68 | 17.4 | 24.1 |
| Colquitt | 11.1 | 7.6 | 5.7 | 50.7 | 42 053 | 45 498 | 8.2 | 1.4 | 1 708 | 884 | -180 | 16 317 | 5.3 | 2.73 | 17.3 | 24.0 |
| Columbia | 12.4 | 6.3 | 4.2 | 51.4 | 89 288 | 124 053 | 38.9 | 6.1 | 3 559 | 1 647 | 5 599 | 44 898 | 44.3 | 2.75 | 12.3 | 18.6 |
| Cook | 11.9 | 8.1 | 5.7 | 51.1 | 15 771 | 17 212 | 9.1 | -1.7 | 513 | 403 | -425 | 6 339 | 7.8 | 2.69 | 16.5 | 23.6 |
| Coweta | 11.6 | 6.7 | 4.1 | 51.0 | 89 215 | 127 317 | 42.7 | 2.8 | 3 689 | 1 884 | 1 813 | 45 673 | 45.3 | 2.77 | 13.1 | 19.6 |
| Crawford | 14.3 | 8.8 | 4.8 | 49.4 | 12 495 | 12 630 | 1.1 | -0.2 | 271 | 261 | -48 | 4 822 | 8.1 | 2.59 | 13.3 | 22.2 |
| Crisp | 13.7 | 7.7 | 6.3 | 51.8 | 21 996 | 23 439 | 6.6 | 0.7 | 712 | 584 | 46 | 9 079 | 8.9 | 2.53 | 21.3 | 26.8 |
| Dade | 13.6 | 8.7 | 6.1 | 50.6 | 15 154 | 16 633 | 9.8 | -0.9 | 362 | 358 | -143 | 6 291 | 11.7 | 2.49 | 10.4 | 25.1 |
| Dawson | 14.8 | 10.3 | 4.8 | 49.9 | 15 999 | 22 330 | 39.6 | 0.4 | 550 | 336 | -151 | 8 433 | 39.0 | 2.61 | 9.5 | 19.7 |
| Decatur | 12.2 | 7.8 | 6.4 | 51.0 | 28 240 | 27 842 | -1.4 | -1.2 | 863 | 706 | -496 | 10 390 | 0.1 | 2.58 | 20.0 | 26.4 |
| DeKalb | 10.9 | 5.4 | 4.0 | 51.9 | 665 865 | 691 893 | 3.9 | 2.2 | 24 169 | 9 357 | -53 | 271 809 | 9.0 | 2.50 | 18.3 | 31.4 |
| Dodge | 12.2 | 8.8 | 6.3 | 47.7 | 19 171 | 21 796 | 13.7 | -2.1 | 560 | 558 | -531 | 8 177 | 15.8 | 2.43 | 16.4 | 28.7 |
| Dooly | 14.0 | 8.9 | 5.5 | 45.7 | 11 525 | 14 918 | 29.4 | -4.0 | 281 | 243 | -646 | 5 286 | 35.2 | 2.45 | 19.1 | 28.8 |
| Dougherty | 11.7 | 6.7 | 5.6 | 53.2 | 96 065 | 94 565 | -1.6 | -0.1 | 3 414 | 1 804 | -1 761 | 36 508 | 2.7 | 2.47 | 25.6 | 30.2 |
| Douglas | 10.6 | 5.8 | 3.2 | 51.8 | 92 174 | 132 403 | 43.6 | 1.2 | 3 897 | 1 892 | -359 | 46 624 | 42.1 | 2.81 | 17.3 | 21.5 |
| Early | 12.8 | 9.4 | 7.4 | 52.8 | 12 354 | 11 008 | -10.9 | -3.8 | 335 | 290 | -457 | 4 228 | -9.9 | 2.56 | 21.3 | 27.3 |
| Echols | 10.0 | 4.9 | 4.6 | 49.6 | 3 754 | 4 034 | 7.5 | -1.1 | 120 | 45 | -134 | 1 329 | 5.1 | 3.04 | 14.0 | 16.7 |

1. No spouse present.

# Table B. States and Counties — Population, Vital Statistics, Medicare, and Crime

| STATE County | Persons in group quarters, 2010 | Daytime population, 2007–2011 Number | Employment/ residence ratio | Births, 2011 Total | Rate[1] | Deaths, 2011 Number | Rate[1] | Persons under 65 with no health insurance, 2010 Number | Percent | Medicare, 2012 Eligible for Medicare | Enrolled in Medicare Advantage | Enrolled in a Medicare prescription drug plan | Serious crimes known to police,[2] 2011 Total Number | Rate[3] |
|---|---|---|---|---|---|---|---|---|---|---|---|---|---|---|
| | 32 | 33 | 34 | 35 | 36 | 37 | 38 | 39 | 40 | 41 | 42 | 43 | 44 | 45 |
| **FLORIDA—Cont'd** | | | | | | | | | | | | | | |
| Putnam | 1 407 | 69 025 | 0.78 | 906 | 12.2 | 874 | 11.8 | 13 803 | 23.3 | 17 074 | 3 252 | 7 743 | 3 988 | 5 291 |
| St. Johns | 2 798 | 168 124 | 0.79 | 1 774 | 9.1 | 1 411 | 7.2 | 25 671 | 16.3 | 37 295 | 6 225 | 14 566 | 5 322 | 2 763 |
| St. Lucie | 3 053 | 248 880 | 0.76 | 3 052 | 10.9 | 2 732 | 9.7 | 58 743 | 26.6 | 60 870 | 18 208 | 20 987 | 9 502 | 3 375 |
| Santa Rosa | 4 244 | 123 863 | 0.60 | 1 738 | 11.3 | 1 164 | 7.6 | 25 198 | 19.7 | 26 028 | 5 737 | 7 905 | 2 669 | 1 739 |
| Sarasota | 5 622 | 391 569 | 1.09 | 2 808 | 7.3 | 4 971 | 13.0 | 63 016 | 24.5 | 113 420 | 22 252 | 48 011 | 14 676 | 3 816 |
| Seminole | 3 515 | 393 576 | 0.87 | 4 320 | 10.2 | 2 908 | 6.8 | 74 939 | 20.4 | 62 275 | 20 001 | 18 838 | 12 269 | 2 863 |
| Sumter | 8 952 | 93 052 | 1.13 | 449 | 4.6 | 1 086 | 11.1 | 8 543 | 19.2 | 49 225 | 12 879 | 17 659 | 1 136 | 1 209 |
| Suwannee | 1 393 | 39 367 | 0.88 | 479 | 11.4 | 479 | 11.4 | 7 935 | 24.3 | 9 894 | 1 266 | 4 819 | 1 040 | 2 469 |
| Taylor | 3 254 | 22 434 | 1.01 | 274 | 12.1 | 201 | 8.9 | 3 039 | 19.1 | 4 296 | 596 | 1 962 | 537 | 2 347 |
| Union | 4 778 | 15 993 | 1.10 | 159 | 10.3 | 198 | 12.9 | 1 970 | 20.7 | 1 820 | 212 | 769 | 206 | 1 308 |
| Volusia | 12 809 | 471 830 | 0.88 | 4 785 | 9.7 | 5 885 | 11.9 | 94 014 | 24.7 | 118 912 | 47 535 | 33 270 | 20 728 | 4 150 |
| Wakulla | 3 428 | 24 009 | 0.53 | 311 | 10.0 | 206 | 6.6 | 4 414 | 18.4 | 4 523 | 1 952 | 1 071 | 841 | 2 696 |
| Walton | 2 065 | 55 020 | 1.03 | 628 | 11.3 | 479 | 8.6 | 10 404 | 23.5 | 10 736 | 1 365 | 4 495 | 1 666 | 2 986 |
| Washington | 2 694 | 22 719 | 0.79 | 248 | 9.9 | 275 | 11.0 | 4 043 | 21.9 | 5 111 | 551 | 2 297 | 397 | 1 573 |
| **GEORGIA** | 253 199 | 9 601 041 | 1.00 | 134 442 | 13.7 | 70 688 | 7.2 | 1 848 505 | 21.9 | 1 368 053 | 334 070 | 551 387 | 392 586 | 4 000 |
| Appling | 426 | 18 422 | 1.03 | 257 | 14.0 | 166 | 9.0 | 3 845 | 24.9 | 3 323 | 598 | 1 777 | 801 | 4 335 |
| Atkinson | 20 | 7 727 | 0.79 | 137 | 16.3 | 59 | 7.0 | 2 373 | 32.0 | 1 230 | 209 | 708 | 128 | 1 509 |
| Bacon | 325 | 10 661 | 0.89 | 148 | 13.2 | 98 | 8.7 | 2 460 | 26.4 | 1 949 | 353 | 1 051 | NA | NA |
| Baker | 0 | 3 224 | 0.74 | 33 | 10.7 | 33 | 10.7 | 655 | 22.6 | 676 | 108 | 357 | 16 | 458 |
| Baldwin | 4 569 | 47 600 | 1.07 | 503 | 11.3 | 418 | 9.4 | 7 316 | 20.2 | 7 599 | 2 975 | 2 422 | 1 921 | 4 147 |
| Banks | 0 | 15 553 | 0.68 | 176 | 9.6 | 117 | 6.4 | 4 132 | 25.7 | 3 016 | 653 | 1 495 | 722 | 3 874 |
| Barrow | 289 | 55 148 | 0.57 | 1 055 | 15.1 | 471 | 6.7 | 15 103 | 23.9 | 9 302 | 2 383 | 3 850 | 2 023 | 2 878 |
| Bartow | 990 | 93 395 | 0.87 | 1 334 | 13.3 | 788 | 7.8 | 19 683 | 22.2 | 14 940 | 3 199 | 6 532 | 4 668 | 4 631 |
| Ben Hill | 308 | 17 750 | 1.01 | 283 | 16.0 | 208 | 11.8 | 3 515 | 23.5 | 3 398 | 697 | 1 708 | 321 | 1 797 |
| Berrien | 176 | 17 071 | 0.73 | 233 | 12.0 | 195 | 10.1 | 3 989 | 24.1 | 3 380 | 702 | 1 641 | 620 | 3 173 |
| Bibb | 6 051 | 177 231 | 1.37 | 2 405 | 15.4 | 1 624 | 10.4 | 24 823 | 19.0 | 27 494 | 7 103 | 10 976 | 11 712 | 7 442 |
| Bleckley | 1 439 | 11 940 | 0.75 | 141 | 10.6 | 123 | 9.3 | 1 899 | 19.4 | 2 350 | 313 | 934 | 494 | 3 733 |
| Brantley | 66 | 13 714 | 0.40 | 226 | 12.3 | 189 | 10.3 | 3 836 | 23.8 | 3 005 | 533 | 1 562 | 370 | 1 984 |
| Brooks | 0 | 13 524 | 0.59 | 191 | 12.0 | 178 | 11.2 | 3 435 | 25.2 | 3 225 | 643 | 1 611 | 583 | 3 670 |
| Bryan | 98 | 22 931 | 0.51 | 457 | 14.6 | 190 | 6.1 | 4 878 | 17.7 | 3 930 | 855 | 1 485 | 777 | 2 537 |
| Bulloch | 4 818 | 66 103 | 0.90 | 803 | 11.0 | 478 | 6.6 | 13 638 | 23.0 | 8 360 | 1 503 | 3 738 | 2 360 | 3 317 |
| Burke | 283 | 22 196 | 0.88 | 342 | 14.6 | 229 | 9.7 | 4 176 | 20.4 | 3 988 | 1 173 | 1 698 | 975 | 4 127 |
| Butts | 2 345 | 21 357 | 0.76 | 296 | 12.6 | 251 | 10.7 | 3 701 | 20.0 | 3 979 | 1 095 | 1 569 | 769 | 3 209 |
| Calhoun | 1 701 | 6 426 | 0.94 | 74 | 11.0 | 46 | 6.8 | 1 045 | 24.6 | 1 025 | 265 | 587 | 104 | 1 533 |
| Camden | 1 877 | 47 582 | 0.90 | 791 | 15.7 | 265 | 5.3 | 7 689 | 17.4 | 6 402 | 1 021 | 2 532 | 1 756 | 3 530 |
| Candler | 287 | 9 781 | 0.75 | 138 | 12.2 | 128 | 11.4 | 2 492 | 26.9 | 2 050 | 449 | 1 056 | 194 | 1 741 |
| Carroll | 3 583 | 103 972 | 0.86 | 1 596 | 14.4 | 909 | 8.2 | 21 170 | 22.3 | 17 298 | 4 469 | 7 309 | 3 755 | 3 353 |
| Catoosa | 461 | 50 974 | 0.56 | 739 | 11.5 | 527 | 8.2 | 10 587 | 19.2 | 11 151 | 2 435 | 5 343 | 1 972 | 3 044 |
| Charlton | 1 791 | 11 399 | 0.67 | 142 | 10.6 | 79 | 5.9 | 1 881 | 21.0 | 1 838 | 278 | 984 | 286 | 2 319 |
| Chatham | 12 891 | 289 532 | 1.24 | 3 949 | 14.5 | 2 206 | 8.1 | 47 053 | 21.3 | 40 405 | 11 093 | 14 331 | 12 467 | 4 641 |
| Chattahoochee | 3 267 | 17 259 | 1.88 | 148 | 12.6 | 28 | 2.4 | 1 126 | 15.1 | 562 | 85 | 203 | 73 | 640 |
| Chattooga | 1 941 | 23 855 | 0.77 | 303 | 11.8 | 277 | 10.8 | 4 567 | 22.3 | 5 171 | 1 274 | 2 686 | 458 | 1 774 |
| Cherokee | 1 406 | 168 944 | 0.58 | 2 911 | 13.3 | 1 028 | 4.7 | 34 470 | 17.9 | 27 049 | 7 467 | 9 318 | 3 577 | 1 647 |
| Clarke | 9 183 | 135 705 | 1.39 | 1 514 | 12.9 | 680 | 5.8 | 22 148 | 22.8 | 13 525 | 2 775 | 5 176 | 5 692 | 4 813 |
| Clay | 58 | 2 876 | 0.60 | 35 | 11.3 | 42 | 13.5 | 527 | 20.7 | 705 | 192 | 342 | 16 | 496 |
| Clayton | 4 037 | 245 563 | 0.87 | 4 196 | 16.0 | 1 380 | 5.3 | 65 081 | 27.3 | 26 389 | 8 203 | 9 325 | 14 874 | 5 659 |
| Clinch | 155 | 7 125 | 1.12 | 103 | 15.2 | 63 | 9.3 | 1 288 | 21.9 | 1 321 | 227 | 786 | 229 | 3 325 |
| Cobb | 9 068 | 667 090 | 0.95 | 9 507 | 13.6 | 3 632 | 5.2 | 122 349 | 19.8 | 78 365 | 20 585 | 26 498 | 19 078 | 2 737 |
| Coffee | 2 657 | 42 984 | 1.05 | 594 | 13.9 | 366 | 8.5 | 8 820 | 25.1 | 6 333 | 1 207 | 3 488 | NA | NA |
| Colquitt | 1 005 | 43 283 | 0.90 | 768 | 16.8 | 421 | 9.2 | 10 396 | 26.6 | 7 879 | 1 453 | 4 049 | 1 412 | 3 185 |
| Columbia | 640 | 97 998 | 0.59 | 1 527 | 11.9 | 718 | 5.6 | 17 549 | 15.8 | 16 417 | 3 584 | 4 280 | 2 829 | 2 251 |
| Cook | 143 | 14 912 | 0.69 | 252 | 14.7 | 174 | 10.2 | 3 788 | 25.5 | 3 044 | 529 | 1 616 | 526 | 3 177 |
| Coweta | 588 | 103 154 | 0.63 | 1 651 | 12.7 | 798 | 6.2 | 20 055 | 17.6 | 17 450 | 4 103 | 6 900 | 3 181 | 2 466 |
| Crawford | 133 | 9 331 | 0.36 | 119 | 9.5 | 105 | 8.4 | 2 546 | 23.4 | 2 200 | 597 | 886 | 571 | 4 462 |
| Crisp | 506 | 24 179 | 1.09 | 313 | 13.2 | 264 | 11.1 | 4 154 | 21.0 | 3 915 | 940 | 2 080 | 1 559 | 6 565 |
| Dade | 993 | 13 553 | 0.57 | 152 | 9.2 | 165 | 10.0 | 2 800 | 21.1 | 3 114 | 722 | 1 512 | 371 | 2 202 |
| Dawson | 299 | 20 056 | 0.79 | 245 | 10.9 | 147 | 6.5 | 4 095 | 21.7 | 3 574 | 729 | 1 599 | 566 | 2 502 |
| Decatur | 1 069 | 27 666 | 0.98 | 398 | 14.4 | 324 | 11.7 | 5 261 | 22.8 | 5 077 | 1 082 | 2 579 | 891 | 3 159 |
| DeKalb | 13 049 | 670 890 | 0.94 | 10 977 | 15.7 | 3 966 | 5.7 | 159 225 | 25.8 | 81 508 | 25 235 | 27 522 | 41 257 | 5 950 |
| Dodge | 1 951 | 19 858 | 0.77 | 251 | 11.5 | 230 | 10.5 | 3 694 | 21.7 | 3 730 | 764 | 1 761 | 969 | 4 735 |
| Dooly | 1 978 | 14 183 | 0.94 | 133 | 9.1 | 116 | 8.0 | 2 586 | 23.7 | 2 081 | 476 | 960 | NA | NA |
| Dougherty | 4 331 | 108 492 | 1.38 | 1 554 | 16.4 | 881 | 9.3 | 16 259 | 20.3 | 15 477 | 2 998 | 6 817 | 6 182 | 6 452 |
| Douglas | 1 368 | 112 669 | 0.69 | 1 762 | 13.2 | 837 | 6.3 | 24 352 | 20.3 | 15 633 | 3 982 | 5 721 | 4 671 | 3 482 |
| Early | 172 | 11 194 | 1.02 | 155 | 14.4 | 142 | 13.2 | 1 798 | 19.8 | 2 253 | 557 | 1 117 | 402 | 3 689 |
| Echols | 0 | 2 654 | 0.21 | 49 | 11.9 | 19 | 4.6 | 1 320 | 36.3 | 470 | 68 | 240 | 39 | 954 |

1. Per 1,000 estimated resident population.  2. Data for serious crimes have not been adjusted for underreporting; this may affect comparability between geographic areas and over time.  3. Per 100,000 population estimated by the FBI.

# Table B. States and Counties — Crime, Education, Money Income, and Poverty

| STATE County | Serious crimes known to police, 2011 (cont.)[1] Rate[2] Violent | Property | Education School enrollment and attainment, 2007–2011 Enrollment[3] Total | Percent private | Attainment[4] (percent) High school graduate or less | Bachelor's degree or more | Local government expenditures,[5] 2009–2010 Total current expenditures (mil dol) | Current expenditures per student (dollars) | Money income, 2007–2011 Per capita income[6] (dollars) | Households Median income Dollars | Percent change, 2000 to 2007–2011 (constant 2011 dollars) | Percent with income of $200,000 or more | Income and poverty, 2011 Median household income (dollars) | Percent below poverty level All persons | Children under 18 years | Children 5 to 17 years in families |
|---|---|---|---|---|---|---|---|---|---|---|---|---|---|---|---|---|
| | 46 | 47 | 48 | 49 | 50 | 51 | 52 | 53 | 54 | 55 | 56 | 57 | 58 | 59 | 60 | 61 |
| **FLORIDA—Cont'd** | | | | | | | | | | | | | | | | |
| Putnam | 797 | 4 493 | 15 230 | 10.0 | 62.6 | 12.5 | 101.9 | 8 922 | 18 609 | 34 174 | -10.2 | 0.7 | 31 150 | 27.9 | 42.1 | 38.3 |
| St. Johns | 314 | 2 449 | 47 495 | 21.3 | 30.0 | 39.3 | 243.3 | 7 937 | 36 694 | 64 153 | -5.2 | 7.9 | 63 299 | 9.4 | 12.4 | 10.6 |
| St. Lucie | 399 | 2 976 | 64 306 | 13.0 | 52.2 | 17.9 | 330.5 | 8 472 | 23 172 | 44 947 | -8.5 | 1.8 | 41 384 | 20.3 | 31.7 | 28.9 |
| Santa Rosa | 146 | 1 594 | 39 646 | 12.7 | 39.1 | 25.6 | 191.4 | 7 485 | 26 507 | 55 913 | -1.1 | 3.0 | 53 155 | 11.3 | 16.3 | 14.7 |
| Sarasota | 383 | 3 433 | 66 753 | 16.9 | 40.1 | 29.3 | 433.0 | 10 489 | 33 096 | 49 212 | -13.1 | 4.5 | 47 457 | 11.7 | 19.3 | 17.7 |
| Seminole | 362 | 2 501 | 119 844 | 17.1 | 33.6 | 34.0 | 509.8 | 7 910 | 29 894 | 58 908 | -11.5 | 5.0 | 54 449 | 11.5 | 16.5 | 15.0 |
| Sumter | 188 | 1 020 | 8 857 | 11.5 | 50.9 | 20.0 | 67.4 | 8 921 | 25 070 | 44 817 | 3.5 | 1.3 | 44 595 | 14.5 | 34.9 | 35.3 |
| Suwannee | 435 | 2 035 | 8 553 | 10.8 | 62.1 | 10.1 | 48.5 | 7 921 | 19 094 | 37 775 | -6.6 | 1.3 | 34 947 | 24.7 | 36.4 | 36.0 |
| Taylor | 686 | 1 661 | 4 488 | 21.5 | 60.7 | 10.8 | 28.4 | 8 926 | 18 291 | 38 005 | -6.3 | 1.2 | 33 863 | 22.7 | 30.9 | 28.6 |
| Union | 229 | 1 080 | 2 879 | 5.7 | 63.3 | 10.0 | 20.6 | 8 805 | 14 210 | 45 645 | -2.2 | 0.3 | 40 743 | 25.3 | 26.1 | 23.6 |
| Volusia | 501 | 3 649 | 112 287 | 20.4 | 45.4 | 20.8 | 520.8 | 8 358 | 24 536 | 44 169 | -7.1 | 2.3 | 38 477 | 17.4 | 27.1 | 25.8 |
| Wakulla | 292 | 2 404 | 7 105 | 13.8 | 51.1 | 17.3 | 41.6 | 7 927 | 22 089 | 54 151 | 8.0 | 0.9 | 50 716 | 14.6 | 20.8 | 18.6 |
| Walton | 357 | 2 629 | 11 126 | 11.8 | 45.0 | 24.9 | 72.8 | 10 243 | 27 064 | 46 926 | 7.2 | 3.7 | 44 763 | 14.3 | 24.8 | 23.8 |
| Washington | 273 | 1 300 | 5 362 | 9.3 | 60.8 | 12.3 | 37.3 | 9 763 | 18 382 | 37 036 | -1.8 | 1.0 | 35 004 | 24.3 | 33.9 | 30.7 |
| **GEORGIA** | 373 | 3 627 | 2 670 757 | 15.5 | 45.4 | 27.5 | 15 644.7 | 9 381 | 25 383 | 49 736 | -13.2 | 3.8 | 45 886 | 19.2 | 26.6 | 24.8 |
| Appling | 211 | 4 124 | 4 009 | 4.6 | 68.3 | 9.3 | 33.1 | 9 368 | 18 899 | 34 989 | -14.4 | 0.2 | 35 164 | 21.1 | 34.0 | 31.0 |
| Atkinson | 236 | 1 273 | 2 298 | 2.9 | 75.7 | 8.3 | 15.2 | 8 941 | 15 172 | 32 814 | -8.2 | 1.2 | 28 693 | 31.4 | 44.3 | 43.3 |
| Bacon | NA | NA | 2 546 | 12.5 | 73.7 | 8.0 | 16.2 | 8 683 | 16 561 | 32 065 | -11.7 | 0.6 | 31 301 | 24.5 | 35.3 | 32.3 |
| Baker | 114 | 343 | 966 | 1.1 | 64.4 | 9.7 | 5.7 | 15 092 | 17 838 | 27 255 | -33.5 | 2.4 | 33 347 | 28.4 | 41.9 | 37.2 |
| Baldwin | 237 | 3 910 | 13 652 | 14.9 | 55.3 | 19.0 | 51.7 | 9 483 | 17 953 | 36 429 | -23.3 | 1.2 | 34 304 | 29.2 | 35.9 | 33.5 |
| Banks | 102 | 3 772 | 4 371 | 10.4 | 68.5 | 11.1 | 24.7 | 8 561 | 20 149 | 41 397 | -20.4 | 2.0 | 42 673 | 19.0 | 28.0 | 25.2 |
| Barrow | 474 | 2 405 | 17 400 | 9.1 | 55.7 | 16.1 | 106.4 | 8 491 | 20 740 | 50 604 | -16.7 | 1.1 | 50 996 | 15.6 | 22.6 | 23.0 |
| Bartow | 336 | 4 295 | 24 458 | 11.6 | 58.2 | 16.7 | 167.7 | 8 973 | 22 324 | 49 060 | -16.8 | 1.8 | 45 072 | 19.1 | 28.7 | 25.2 |
| Ben Hill | 129 | 1 668 | 4 639 | 7.2 | 63.6 | 9.3 | 29.2 | 8 799 | 16 234 | 31 943 | -12.7 | 0.8 | 29 425 | 29.1 | 43.2 | 41.8 |
| Berrien | 251 | 2 922 | 4 890 | 8.1 | 63.5 | 11.3 | 26.9 | 8 362 | 16 885 | 32 512 | -19.9 | 0.4 | 33 417 | 24.0 | 34.7 | 31.6 |
| Bibb | 517 | 6 926 | 43 905 | 20.8 | 50.9 | 22.6 | 227.9 | 9 076 | 21 754 | 37 975 | -18.6 | 3.0 | 35 125 | 25.4 | 35.0 | 32.2 |
| Bleckley | 302 | 3 430 | 4 011 | 12.1 | 67.0 | 12.3 | 23.3 | 9 606 | 18 149 | 35 997 | -20.3 | 1.9 | 39 461 | 21.7 | 28.6 | 26.6 |
| Brantley | 252 | 1 732 | 4 691 | 5.8 | 72.0 | 4.6 | 29.2 | 8 131 | 18 464 | 38 374 | -6.4 | 0.4 | 36 300 | 22.3 | 30.9 | 28.8 |
| Brooks | 667 | 3 003 | 3 950 | 7.6 | 58.5 | 13.9 | 23.0 | 9 743 | 22 812 | 40 186 | 10.6 | 1.9 | 29 282 | 29.8 | 41.2 | 41.5 |
| Bryan | 166 | 2 370 | 8 706 | 11.9 | 38.8 | 29.0 | 52.2 | 7 156 | 28 911 | 64 651 | -1.0 | 2.8 | 63 092 | 12.2 | 19.1 | 17.3 |
| Bulloch | 188 | 3 129 | 28 868 | 5.4 | 45.6 | 26.3 | 92.5 | 9 629 | 17 918 | 33 902 | -14.9 | 1.6 | 33 192 | 31.0 | 30.8 | 29.6 |
| Burke | 830 | 3 298 | 6 796 | 12.4 | 64.0 | 9.1 | 49.2 | 10 374 | 15 690 | 32 188 | -14.5 | 0.5 | 31 188 | 31.0 | 43.4 | 40.7 |
| Butts | 296 | 2 912 | 5 139 | 17.6 | 67.7 | 8.1 | 31.7 | 8 917 | 21 130 | 49 339 | -8.4 | 1.1 | 40 330 | 20.2 | 29.4 | 28.0 |
| Calhoun | 251 | 1 283 | 1 500 | 20.2 | 66.9 | 9.3 | 8.2 | 12 291 | 13 428 | 32 986 | -0.6 | 0.4 | 27 860 | 40.5 | 41.6 | 38.5 |
| Camden | 382 | 3 148 | 14 364 | 11.7 | 41.9 | 20.3 | 84.6 | 8 750 | 22 228 | 51 061 | -7.9 | 1.0 | 50 207 | 14.7 | 20.4 | 19.4 |
| Candler | 179 | 1 562 | 2 539 | 6.9 | 64.2 | 15.4 | 18.1 | 8 920 | 16 962 | 37 315 | 10.5 | 1.4 | 28 263 | 27.3 | 40.3 | 36.7 |
| Carroll | 267 | 3 086 | 32 591 | 9.5 | 55.9 | 18.4 | 166.3 | 8 643 | 20 739 | 45 752 | -12.7 | 1.8 | 43 237 | 19.5 | 25.4 | 23.6 |
| Catoosa | 190 | 2 854 | 16 379 | 13.4 | 48.7 | 17.8 | 97.2 | 9 026 | 22 368 | 46 549 | -13.8 | 1.1 | 47 111 | 14.4 | 21.1 | 19.0 |
| Charlton | 122 | 2 198 | 2 427 | 7.5 | 70.5 | 8.7 | 16.5 | 9 342 | 17 623 | 42 307 | 12.4 | 2.8 | 31 582 | 32.6 | 34.9 | 33.0 |
| Chatham | 400 | 4 241 | 72 643 | 24.7 | 41.0 | 29.6 | 332.5 | 9 592 | 25 394 | 45 985 | -9.8 | 3.2 | 42 383 | 22.5 | 34.6 | 34.3 |
| Chattahoochee | 158 | 482 | 4 091 | 10.3 | 31.1 | 28.4 | 9.7 | 10 718 | 21 648 | 49 969 | -0.3 | 1.5 | 41 476 | 20.2 | 19.4 | 19.8 |
| Chattooga | 155 | 1 619 | 5 770 | 6.7 | 69.2 | 7.8 | 38.3 | 9 141 | 14 924 | 32 224 | -22.2 | 0.5 | 33 350 | 22.5 | 28.2 | 26.5 |
| Cherokee | 107 | 1 540 | 57 581 | 19.2 | 35.5 | 33.6 | 330.4 | 8 628 | 29 968 | 66 717 | -18.9 | 4.8 | 65 769 | 9.6 | 12.7 | 11.8 |
| Clarke | 363 | 4 451 | 50 364 | 7.2 | 37.4 | 40.7 | 157.0 | 12 606 | 19 596 | 34 151 | -10.9 | 2.5 | 30 880 | 39.2 | 37.7 | 35.3 |
| Clay | 310 | 186 | 729 | 10.7 | 65.8 | 9.5 | 4.7 | 14 423 | 12 619 | 24 750 | -14.5 | 0.0 | 26 420 | 36.3 | 54.0 | 48.8 |
| Clayton | 523 | 5 136 | 78 517 | 13.8 | 50.6 | 17.8 | 466.6 | 9 271 | 18 835 | 42 936 | -25.5 | 0.9 | 37 706 | 25.2 | 35.4 | 33.2 |
| Clinch | 421 | 2 904 | 1 506 | 6.3 | 66.3 | 13.9 | 13.1 | 9 200 | 15 980 | 33 143 | -8.3 | 0.0 | 30 237 | 26.8 | 38.8 | 35.6 |
| Cobb | 232 | 2 505 | 192 750 | 18.5 | 29.7 | 44.0 | 1 072.2 | 9 316 | 33 514 | 65 423 | -16.9 | 6.9 | 57 995 | 13.2 | 17.6 | 16.9 |
| Coffee | NA | NA | 10 694 | 3.8 | 65.3 | 11.8 | 67.9 | 8 691 | 16 854 | 34 327 | -17.2 | 1.5 | 32 351 | 27.9 | 40.1 | 40.4 |
| Colquitt | 214 | 2 971 | 11 463 | 6.0 | 65.7 | 11.9 | 82.9 | 9 171 | 17 922 | 33 345 | -13.5 | 1.7 | 30 669 | 28.9 | 38.3 | 35.6 |
| Columbia | 91 | 2 159 | 35 186 | 15.1 | 35.4 | 34.3 | 194.4 | 8 334 | 30 109 | 66 556 | -11.5 | 5.5 | 62 717 | 8.2 | 11.1 | 10.0 |
| Cook | 284 | 2 893 | 4 505 | 1.5 | 66.9 | 9.9 | 31.2 | 9 355 | 18 755 | 35 306 | -5.2 | 1.4 | 32 812 | 27.8 | 41.0 | 36.4 |
| Coweta | 219 | 2 247 | 33 775 | 16.0 | 45.3 | 26.2 | 190.9 | 6 899 | 26 117 | 61 015 | -14.3 | 2.6 | 56 878 | 13.9 | 20.4 | 17.3 |
| Crawford | 219 | 4 244 | 2 710 | 7.9 | 59.4 | 11.7 | 17.2 | 9 175 | 20 244 | 37 746 | -26.1 | 1.2 | 41 855 | 19.5 | 29.9 | 25.9 |
| Crisp | 518 | 6 047 | 5 886 | 6.4 | 62.5 | 11.5 | 41.9 | 9 558 | 17 140 | 32 616 | -9.0 | 1.3 | 29 134 | 32.5 | 45.9 | 43.1 |
| Dade | 392 | 1 810 | 4 514 | 28.7 | 54.6 | 17.6 | 20.8 | 8 325 | 21 110 | 41 629 | -12.6 | 1.9 | 41 233 | 17.5 | 24.2 | 21.7 |
| Dawson | 66 | 2 435 | 5 161 | 9.4 | 52.2 | 21.9 | 35.6 | 10 161 | 25 158 | 51 989 | -18.9 | 3.0 | 53 339 | 12.2 | 21.0 | 18.6 |
| Decatur | 408 | 2 751 | 7 887 | 6.4 | 59.1 | 12.2 | 51.8 | 9 102 | 17 968 | 31 391 | -19.3 | 2.0 | 31 054 | 31.9 | 46.4 | 43.0 |
| DeKalb | 568 | 5 382 | 190 563 | 25.0 | 33.7 | 39.3 | 1 033.4 | 10 062 | 28 843 | 51 712 | -22.0 | 5.0 | 48 293 | 19.8 | 28.8 | 28.4 |
| Dodge | 454 | 4 280 | 4 772 | 5.8 | 64.8 | 13.6 | 35.2 | 10 438 | 16 756 | 33 829 | -9.2 | 0.3 | 31 696 | 27.4 | 39.0 | 36.8 |
| Dooly | NA | NA | 3 159 | 11.4 | 70.6 | 10.2 | 14.5 | 10 049 | 15 515 | 30 830 | -18.4 | 1.7 | 29 970 | 32.4 | 40.2 | 36.1 |
| Dougherty | 715 | 5 737 | 29 945 | 8.8 | 49.8 | 18.6 | 153.0 | 9 483 | 19 204 | 32 364 | -22.5 | 2.2 | 30 186 | 31.0 | 40.2 | 38.6 |
| Douglas | 283 | 3 199 | 38 042 | 15.0 | 45.2 | 24.2 | 212.2 | 8 505 | 24 457 | 54 763 | -19.1 | 2.7 | 50 501 | 16.2 | 21.8 | 21.1 |
| Early | 578 | 3 111 | 3 136 | 6.9 | 63.9 | 13.5 | 24.0 | 10 044 | 17 313 | 27 645 | -20.1 | 1.6 | 31 345 | 28.2 | 39.5 | 36.1 |
| Echols | 49 | 905 | 933 | 2.4 | 76.2 | 6.9 | 7.0 | 8 944 | 14 179 | 29 476 | -15.5 | 1.6 | 32 543 | 26.0 | 40.0 | 39.2 |

1. Data for serious crimes have not been adjusted for underreporting; this may affect comparability between geographic areas and over time.  2. Per 100,000 population estimated by the FBI.  3. All persons 3 years old and over enrolled in nursery school through college.  4. Persons 25 years old and over.  5. Elementary and secondary education expenditures.  6. Based on population estimated by the American Community Survey, 2007–2011.

# Table B. States and Counties — Personal Income

| STATE County | Personal income, 2011 Total (mil dol) | Percent change, 2010–2011 | Per capita[1] Dollars | Rank | Wages and salaries[2] (mil dol) | Proprietors' income (mil dol) | Dividends, interest, and rent (mil dol) | Transfer payments (mil dol) Total | Government payments to individuals Total | Social Security | Medical payments | Income maintenance | Unemployment insurance |
|---|---|---|---|---|---|---|---|---|---|---|---|---|---|
| | 62 | 63 | 64 | 65 | 66 | 67 | 68 | 69 | 70 | 71 | 72 | 73 | 74 |
| FLORIDA—Cont'd | | | | | | | | | | | | | |
| Putnam | 2 047 | 2.0 | 27 644 | 2 663 | 846 | 32 | 342 | 736 | 719 | 240 | 300 | 107 | 18 |
| St. Johns | 10 120 | 7.4 | 51 677 | 170 | 2 821 | 266 | 2 792 | 1 321 | 1 277 | 563 | 493 | 91 | 33 |
| St. Lucie | 8 627 | 4.6 | 30 768 | 2 144 | 3 130 | 303 | 2 218 | 2 476 | 2 414 | 890 | 1 028 | 264 | 78 |
| Santa Rosa | 5 569 | 6.6 | 36 141 | 1 194 | 1 685 | 146 | 877 | 1 068 | 1 020 | 370 | 402 | 95 | 24 |
| Sarasota | 20 551 | 4.5 | 53 769 | 134 | 7 201 | 1 119 | 8 668 | 3 879 | 3 789 | 1 690 | 1 636 | 215 | 71 |
| Seminole | 17 391 | 3.8 | 40 914 | 666 | 8 466 | 1 089 | 2 759 | 2 569 | 2 475 | 922 | 933 | 271 | 109 |
| Sumter | 2 720 | 8.0 | 27 824 | 2 636 | 1 117 | 59 | 688 | 1 189 | 1 168 | 729 | 322 | 51 | 10 |
| Suwannee | 1 175 | 3.9 | 27 988 | 2 615 | 445 | 88 | 193 | 404 | 395 | 138 | 177 | 48 | 7 |
| Taylor | 613 | 3.7 | 27 011 | 2 763 | 348 | 19 | 111 | 186 | 181 | 62 | 77 | 27 | 4 |
| Union | 293 | 1.9 | 19 049 | 3 109 | 186 | 10 | 36 | 85 | 81 | 25 | 34 | 14 | 2 |
| Volusia | 16 544 | 3.4 | 33 436 | 1 619 | 7 050 | 525 | 4 513 | 4 561 | 4 451 | 1 729 | 1 804 | 428 | 127 |
| Wakulla | 903 | 3.7 | 29 157 | 2 426 | 235 | 30 | 116 | 198 | 190 | 65 | 77 | 24 | 6 |
| Walton | 1 864 | 5.6 | 33 403 | 1 627 | 835 | 115 | 553 | 401 | 370 | 150 | 132 | 41 | 9 |
| Washington | 615 | 3.2 | 24 660 | 2 992 | 264 | 19 | 88 | 228 | 222 | 68 | 100 | 27 | 4 |
| GEORGIA | 353 142 | 5.3 | 35 979 | X | 235 756 | 29 006 | 51 490 | 62 981 | 60 823 | 19 588 | 23 157 | 9 871 | 2 557 |
| Appling | 493 | 4.5 | 26 781 | 2 791 | 355 | 30 | 59 | 147 | 143 | 44 | 63 | 23 | 6 |
| Atkinson | 186 | 5.4 | 22 165 | 3 082 | 68 | 27 | 22 | 65 | 63 | 15 | 28 | 13 | 2 |
| Bacon | 279 | 5.4 | 24 861 | 2 976 | 134 | 29 | 35 | 91 | 88 | 25 | 41 | 13 | 3 |
| Baker | 122 | 8.2 | 39 650 | 786 | 23 | 37 | 14 | 29 | 29 | 9 | 11 | 7 | 1 |
| Baldwin | 1 267 | 3.3 | 28 533 | 2 536 | 669 | 61 | 220 | 404 | 394 | 109 | 172 | 56 | 13 |
| Banks | 511 | 1.8 | 27 985 | 2 616 | 171 | 41 | 68 | 118 | 114 | 44 | 44 | 16 | 4 |
| Barrow | 2 136 | 5.3 | 30 556 | 2 186 | 684 | 110 | 211 | 400 | 384 | 137 | 155 | 53 | 17 |
| Bartow | 2 788 | 3.0 | 27 762 | 2 648 | 1 620 | 254 | 336 | 633 | 611 | 224 | 228 | 95 | 27 |
| Ben Hill | 470 | 3.3 | 26 606 | 2 810 | 242 | 35 | 83 | 171 | 167 | 43 | 73 | 30 | 5 |
| Berrien | 548 | 4.9 | 28 286 | 2 572 | 165 | 80 | 72 | 162 | 157 | 44 | 71 | 25 | 5 |
| Bibb | 5 581 | 4.0 | 35 676 | 1 269 | 4 159 | 405 | 961 | 1 451 | 1 417 | 368 | 592 | 265 | 43 |
| Bleckley | 396 | 5.0 | 29 787 | 2 325 | 133 | 45 | 62 | 108 | 105 | 28 | 41 | 15 | 4 |
| Brantley | 421 | 3.8 | 22 900 | 3 062 | 87 | 15 | 39 | 134 | 130 | 40 | 54 | 20 | 5 |
| Brooks | 501 | 5.1 | 31 531 | 1 996 | 119 | 52 | 73 | 136 | 132 | 41 | 53 | 24 | 4 |
| Bryan | 1 258 | 7.7 | 40 085 | 736 | 257 | 71 | 142 | 187 | 180 | 59 | 70 | 21 | 7 |
| Bulloch | 1 774 | 4.4 | 24 335 | 3 014 | 974 | 106 | 278 | 424 | 408 | 116 | 137 | 69 | 18 |
| Burke | 671 | 5.7 | 28 549 | 2 533 | 391 | 71 | 77 | 215 | 210 | 55 | 80 | 50 | 6 |
| Butts | 596 | 2.1 | 25 336 | 2 941 | 253 | 30 | 73 | 181 | 176 | 59 | 76 | 25 | 7 |
| Calhoun | 150 | 2.3 | 22 287 | 3 079 | 53 | 24 | 23 | 50 | 48 | 13 | 22 | 10 | 1 |
| Camden | 1 616 | 6.4 | 32 058 | 1 871 | 1 231 | 36 | 199 | 295 | 285 | 94 | 106 | 39 | 11 |
| Candler | 283 | 5.0 | 25 082 | 2 960 | 109 | 34 | 35 | 98 | 95 | 27 | 45 | 17 | 3 |
| Carroll | 3 220 | 4.1 | 28 964 | 2 454 | 1 848 | 149 | 423 | 797 | 772 | 258 | 298 | 119 | 30 |
| Catoosa | 1 916 | 5.4 | 29 685 | 2 344 | 589 | 135 | 187 | 404 | 390 | 167 | 132 | 49 | 14 |
| Charlton | 249 | 6.3 | 18 523 | 3 110 | 101 | 8 | 29 | 87 | 84 | 24 | 38 | 13 | 3 |
| Chatham | 11 264 | 6.4 | 41 480 | 618 | 7 971 | 609 | 2 028 | 2 054 | 1 996 | 590 | 713 | 274 | 69 |
| Chattahoochee | 401 | 6.3 | 34 166 | 1 490 | 2 003 | 3 | 64 | 38 | 37 | 7 | 9 | 12 | 2 |
| Chattooga | 607 | 2.1 | 23 576 | 3 043 | 239 | 32 | 78 | 215 | 209 | 74 | 89 | 30 | 6 |
| Cherokee | 8 054 | 7.6 | 36 898 | 1 083 | 2 235 | 357 | 1 008 | 1 002 | 953 | 424 | 331 | 78 | 49 |
| Clarke | 3 003 | 2.6 | 25 587 | 2 921 | 3 464 | 207 | 671 | 658 | 632 | 191 | 230 | 108 | 27 |
| Clay | 93 | 2.0 | 29 996 | 2 292 | 27 | 7 | 14 | 32 | 31 | 9 | 13 | 7 | 1 |
| Clayton | 6 997 | 4.9 | 26 755 | 2 796 | 5 979 | 360 | 680 | 1 693 | 1 636 | 373 | 642 | 384 | 86 |
| Clinch | 175 | 6.2 | 25 834 | 2 896 | 98 | 11 | 18 | 69 | 68 | 17 | 34 | 12 | 2 |
| Cobb | 32 034 | 4.5 | 45 923 | 339 | 19 613 | 3 456 | 4 513 | 3 459 | 3 305 | 1 213 | 1 192 | 407 | 179 |
| Coffee | 1 076 | 5.1 | 25 011 | 2 956 | 619 | 79 | 170 | 326 | 317 | 85 | 134 | 60 | 12 |
| Colquitt | 1 241 | 4.1 | 27 196 | 2 740 | 591 | 113 | 175 | 363 | 353 | 103 | 146 | 66 | 11 |
| Columbia | 5 473 | 6.8 | 42 717 | 524 | 1 338 | 215 | 747 | 691 | 663 | 250 | 227 | 59 | 25 |
| Cook | 427 | 2.9 | 24 944 | 2 968 | 148 | 57 | 56 | 139 | 136 | 40 | 57 | 25 | 5 |
| Coweta | 4 387 | 6.1 | 33 842 | 1 541 | 1 480 | 176 | 578 | 744 | 715 | 268 | 275 | 94 | 30 |
| Crawford | 394 | 4.5 | 31 327 | 2 035 | 56 | 37 | 44 | 91 | 89 | 30 | 32 | 16 | 3 |
| Crisp | 630 | 4.1 | 26 565 | 2 814 | 299 | 58 | 106 | 205 | 199 | 52 | 86 | 44 | 7 |
| Dade | 446 | 3.6 | 26 906 | 2 775 | 135 | 21 | 57 | 117 | 113 | 44 | 48 | 12 | 4 |
| Dawson | 728 | 3.7 | 32 395 | 1 805 | 273 | 57 | 126 | 138 | 133 | 54 | 53 | 13 | 5 |
| Decatur | 795 | 3.8 | 28 718 | 2 498 | 347 | 106 | 120 | 250 | 244 | 67 | 89 | 52 | 8 |
| DeKalb | 28 179 | 3.7 | 40 262 | 719 | 19 126 | 3 355 | 4 152 | 4 091 | 3 936 | 1 161 | 1 467 | 763 | 202 |
| Dodge | 508 | 3.8 | 23 183 | 3 052 | 221 | 33 | 71 | 167 | 163 | 46 | 71 | 30 | 6 |
| Dooly | 297 | 2.5 | 20 384 | 3 101 | 123 | 33 | 50 | 98 | 95 | 26 | 40 | 20 | 4 |
| Dougherty | 2 719 | 2.9 | 28 689 | 2 507 | 2 560 | 153 | 465 | 893 | 872 | 211 | 326 | 198 | 27 |
| Douglas | 3 969 | 4.7 | 29 761 | 2 328 | 1 648 | 150 | 403 | 762 | 733 | 238 | 278 | 121 | 38 |
| Early | 388 | 6.6 | 35 966 | 1 213 | 222 | 64 | 48 | 103 | 101 | 29 | 40 | 25 | 3 |
| Echols | 96 | 2.5 | 23 181 | 3 053 | 25 | 14 | 9 | 21 | 21 | 6 | 8 | 4 | 1 |

1. Based on the resident population estimated as of July 1 of the year shown.   2. Includes supplements to wages and salaries.

# Table B. States and Counties — Earnings, Social Security, and Housing

| STATE County | Earnings, 2011 | | | | | | | | | Social Security beneficiaries, December 2011 | | | Housing units, 2010 | |
| | Total (mil dol) | Farm | Goods-related[1] | | Service-related and health | | | | Govern-ment | Number | Rate[2] | Supple-mental Security Income recipients, December 2011 | Total | Percent change, 2000–2010 |
| | | | Total | Manu-facturing | Infor-mation and profes-sional and technical services | Retail trade | Finance, insur-ance, and real estate | Health care and social services | | | | | | |
| | 75 | 76 | 77 | 78 | 79 | 80 | 81 | 82 | 83 | 84 | 85 | 86 | 87 | 88 |
| FLORIDA—Cont'd | | | | | | | | | | | | | | |
| Putnam | 879 | 1.5 | 20.7 | 16.6 | D | 8.6 | 4.7 | 11.8 | 28.6 | 19 550 | 264 | 2 962 | 37 337 | 10.2 |
| St. Johns | 3 087 | 1.0 | D | 5.7 | 7.6 | 9.2 | 8.4 | 13.1 | 16.9 | 39 910 | 204 | 2 207 | 89 830 | 54.9 |
| St. Lucie | 3 433 | 0.8 | 8.1 | 3.4 | 6.0 | 10.1 | 5.2 | 16.7 | 24.0 | 66 795 | 238 | 6 033 | 137 029 | 50.1 |
| Santa Rosa | 1 831 | 0.7 | 8.9 | 1.7 | 11.4 | 8.7 | 3.6 | 11.2 | 30.6 | 28 980 | 188 | 2 297 | 64 760 | 31.8 |
| Sarasota | 8 320 | 0.1 | 11.0 | 4.0 | 11.4 | 9.6 | 11.1 | 19.3 | 11.5 | 118 930 | 311 | 4 193 | 228 413 | 25.2 |
| Seminole | 9 555 | 0.1 | 11.3 | 3.9 | 17.0 | 9.6 | 11.4 | 10.3 | 11.2 | 68 260 | 161 | 6 575 | 181 307 | 23.3 |
| Sumter | 1 176 | 0.9 | 19.5 | 5.1 | D | 8.6 | 3.7 | 12.0 | 27.0 | 49 670 | 508 | 1 491 | 53 026 | 110.4 |
| Suwannee | 533 | 8.3 | D | D | 3.3 | 10.0 | 1.8 | 9.4 | 26.8 | 11 410 | 272 | 1 417 | 19 164 | 22.2 |
| Taylor | 366 | 0.1 | D | 30.4 | 2.9 | 8.6 | 1.9 | D | 22.3 | 4 920 | 217 | 764 | 11 004 | 14.1 |
| Union | 197 | 1.0 | D | 3.5 | D | 3.4 | D | D | 63.6 | 2 150 | 140 | 374 | 4 508 | 20.7 |
| Volusia | 7 575 | 0.6 | 11.7 | 6.7 | 7.0 | 10.3 | 5.9 | 19.5 | 17.3 | 131 685 | 266 | 10 623 | 254 226 | 20.0 |
| Wakulla | 265 | 0.2 | 22.8 | 16.5 | 5.8 | 8.2 | 2.6 | D | 37.7 | 5 210 | 168 | 562 | 12 804 | 30.4 |
| Walton | 950 | 1.4 | D | 2.0 | 5.2 | 11.4 | 8.0 | 9.4 | 18.9 | 11 770 | 211 | 1 068 | 45 132 | 55.2 |
| Washington | 283 | 0.8 | D | 5.6 | 3.4 | 7.7 | 2.5 | D | 41.0 | 5 870 | 235 | 1 016 | 10 796 | 13.6 |
| GEORGIA | 264 761 | 0.7 | 14.2 | 9.4 | 13.7 | 6.1 | 8.2 | 9.5 | 19.1 | 1 524 263 | 155 | 238 903 | 4 088 801 | 24.6 |
| Appling | 386 | 3.6 | 14.1 | 9.2 | 1.7 | 5.3 | 1.9 | 3.3 | 18.0 | 3 780 | 205 | 715 | 8 512 | 8.4 |
| Atkinson | 95 | 21.9 | D | 24.2 | D | 5.2 | D | D | 19.8 | 1 460 | 174 | 363 | 3 522 | 11.1 |
| Bacon | 163 | 8.8 | 17.4 | 15.6 | D | 5.7 | D | D | 16.5 | 2 215 | 198 | 432 | 4 801 | 7.5 |
| Baker | 60 | 63.5 | D | D | D | 1.2 | D | 2.1 | 10.1 | 795 | 258 | 228 | 1 652 | -5.1 |
| Baldwin | 730 | 0.0 | 17.3 | 13.5 | D | 8.9 | 3.8 | 14.0 | 38.6 | 8 535 | 192 | 1 453 | 20 159 | 17.3 |
| Banks | 212 | 4.2 | 22.8 | 16.5 | 10.8 | 12.5 | 1.3 | D | 18.5 | 3 595 | 197 | 415 | 7 595 | 30.8 |
| Barrow | 794 | 1.0 | D | 12.9 | D | 10.0 | 3.9 | 7.8 | 20.2 | 10 850 | 155 | 1 545 | 26 400 | 52.6 |
| Bartow | 1 874 | 0.4 | 34.7 | 28.1 | 6.1 | 6.4 | 3.9 | 7.7 | 15.0 | 17 200 | 171 | 2 191 | 39 823 | 38.5 |
| Ben Hill | 276 | 3.9 | 23.4 | 21.2 | D | 7.3 | 3.7 | D | 24.3 | 3 785 | 214 | 830 | 7 942 | 4.2 |
| Berrien | 244 | 25.0 | D | 17.3 | 5.0 | 8.7 | 3.3 | 4.6 | 17.0 | 3 855 | 199 | 743 | 8 709 | 22.7 |
| Bibb | 4 564 | 0.0 | D | 8.1 | 7.4 | 8.3 | 12.2 | 21.9 | 13.4 | 30 370 | 194 | 7 004 | 69 662 | 3.7 |
| Bleckley | 178 | 17.5 | D | D | D | 6.8 | 3.9 | 5.3 | 30.0 | 2 585 | 195 | 389 | 5 304 | 9.0 |
| Brantley | 102 | 0.9 | D | 5.3 | D | 5.3 | 2.0 | 4.4 | 38.3 | 3 430 | 187 | 530 | 8 086 | 24.6 |
| Brooks | 171 | 25.1 | 10.0 | 7.0 | D | 4.9 | 2.9 | 7.6 | 18.8 | 3 630 | 228 | 762 | 7 706 | 8.3 |
| Bryan | 328 | 1.5 | 16.7 | 6.6 | 5.3 | 10.0 | 4.8 | D | 28.6 | 4 550 | 145 | 559 | 11 842 | 36.5 |
| Bulloch | 1 079 | 3.1 | 13.5 | 6.4 | D | 8.2 | 4.6 | 12.2 | 32.7 | 9 430 | 129 | 1 697 | 28 794 | 26.6 |
| Burke | 462 | 8.2 | 7.5 | 5.6 | D | 4.8 | 1.8 | D | 16.7 | 4 775 | 203 | 1 244 | 9 865 | 11.6 |
| Butts | 283 | 1.0 | 16.8 | 12.4 | D | 7.3 | 3.9 | D | 28.4 | 4 630 | 197 | 595 | 9 357 | 26.6 |
| Calhoun | 78 | 25.6 | D | D | D | 3.7 | 6.8 | D | 39.2 | 1 165 | 173 | 313 | 2 409 | 4.5 |
| Camden | 1 267 | 0.0 | 7.3 | 5.2 | 7.2 | 4.2 | 3.8 | 4.0 | 61.8 | 7 300 | 145 | 807 | 21 114 | 24.5 |
| Candler | 144 | 13.7 | 12.3 | 6.5 | 6.3 | 8.8 | 3.7 | 4.7 | 23.5 | 2 365 | 210 | 536 | 4 761 | 22.3 |
| Carroll | 1 997 | 0.5 | D | 19.8 | D | 7.9 | 3.3 | 15.4 | 20.0 | 20 180 | 182 | 2 954 | 44 607 | 30.9 |
| Catoosa | 723 | 0.2 | 16.7 | 9.4 | 2.9 | 12.2 | 4.1 | 15.1 | 19.1 | 12 765 | 198 | 1 279 | 26 606 | 22.2 |
| Charlton | 109 | 1.1 | D | 9.4 | D | 4.5 | D | 3.3 | 27.8 | 2 055 | 153 | 347 | 4 475 | 16.0 |
| Chatham | 8 580 | 0.0 | 18.7 | 14.7 | 5.3 | 6.4 | 4.2 | 13.3 | 23.0 | 44 175 | 163 | 6 342 | 119 323 | 19.6 |
| Chattahoochee | 2 006 | 0.0 | D | D | D | 0.2 | D | D | 93.3 | 685 | 58 | 146 | 3 376 | 1.8 |
| Chattooga | 271 | 1.7 | 41.4 | 37.4 | 4.0 | 8.4 | 2.6 | D | 25.2 | 6 075 | 236 | 917 | 10 977 | 2.8 |
| Cherokee | 2 592 | -0.1 | 19.6 | 8.8 | 8.8 | 9.8 | 6.2 | 9.2 | 18.4 | 29 455 | 135 | 1 639 | 82 360 | 58.5 |
| Clarke | 3 672 | 0.0 | D | 13.3 | 4.1 | 6.3 | 5.3 | 17.1 | 35.3 | 14 820 | 126 | 2 963 | 51 068 | 21.2 |
| Clay | 35 | 19.8 | D | 0.0 | D | 4.9 | D | 7.8 | 37.1 | 820 | 264 | 213 | 2 102 | 9.2 |
| Clayton | 6 339 | 0.0 | D | 5.0 | 2.5 | 5.9 | 2.3 | 7.0 | 13.9 | 30 915 | 118 | 7 533 | 104 705 | 21.1 |
| Clinch | 109 | 4.5 | 36.0 | 34.5 | D | 3.4 | D | 3.3 | 20.7 | 1 530 | 226 | 401 | 3 007 | 6.0 |
| Cobb | 23 069 | 0.0 | 17.9 | 8.8 | 17.1 | 6.5 | 8.6 | 9.3 | 9.1 | 83 515 | 120 | 8 375 | 286 490 | 20.6 |
| Coffee | 698 | 5.6 | 21.0 | 17.1 | 2.9 | 10.0 | 3.2 | 12.0 | 18.7 | 7 410 | 173 | 1 574 | 17 061 | 9.3 |
| Colquitt | 704 | 10.5 | 20.3 | 17.2 | D | 9.1 | 4.3 | D | 25.0 | 8 950 | 196 | 2 023 | 18 311 | 4.3 |
| Columbia | 1 553 | 0.1 | D | 11.4 | 7.7 | 13.4 | 5.8 | 10.1 | 18.4 | 18 290 | 143 | 1 308 | 48 626 | 45.9 |
| Cook | 206 | 24.9 | D | 11.3 | D | 6.0 | 2.9 | D | 20.8 | 3 475 | 203 | 672 | 7 287 | 11.1 |
| Coweta | 1 656 | 0.8 | D | 14.4 | 6.1 | 10.4 | 4.2 | 11.2 | 18.3 | 19 585 | 151 | 1 963 | 50 171 | 51.2 |
| Crawford | 93 | 12.4 | D | 2.0 | D | 7.0 | 4.3 | 5.6 | 22.1 | 2 595 | 206 | 464 | 5 292 | 8.6 |
| Crisp | 356 | 7.8 | 14.2 | 11.4 | D | 9.2 | 4.4 | D | 19.9 | 4 490 | 189 | 1 104 | 10 734 | 12.3 |
| Dade | 156 | -1.0 | D | 18.6 | D | 7.8 | 4.3 | 6.2 | 18.4 | 3 565 | 215 | 411 | 7 305 | 17.4 |
| Dawson | 330 | 1.1 | D | 10.0 | 4.6 | 21.4 | 6.1 | 5.4 | 17.4 | 3 995 | 178 | 332 | 10 425 | 45.5 |
| Decatur | 453 | 15.4 | D | 6.3 | 2.9 | 11.0 | 4.3 | D | 27.4 | 5 800 | 209 | 1 331 | 12 125 | 1.3 |
| DeKalb | 22 481 | 0.0 | D | 4.2 | 15.0 | 5.4 | 7.4 | 10.7 | 18.3 | 87 795 | 125 | 16 595 | 304 968 | 16.7 |
| Dodge | 253 | 5.8 | D | 10.1 | 2.4 | 8.0 | 3.8 | D | 38.0 | 4 155 | 190 | 928 | 9 857 | 20.4 |
| Dooly | 156 | 15.8 | 22.9 | 21.9 | 0.8 | 6.1 | 4.9 | D | 25.5 | 2 360 | 162 | 579 | 6 328 | 40.7 |
| Dougherty | 2 714 | 0.7 | 13.4 | 9.8 | 7.4 | 6.7 | 3.6 | 17.9 | 28.5 | 17 540 | 185 | 4 984 | 40 801 | 2.9 |
| Douglas | 1 798 | 0.0 | D | 9.1 | 4.3 | 12.3 | 4.8 | 11.1 | 18.3 | 17 990 | 135 | 2 453 | 51 672 | 48.3 |
| Early | 286 | 20.4 | 26.7 | 23.5 | 1.5 | 5.0 | D | D | 18.9 | 2 505 | 232 | 691 | 4 975 | -6.8 |
| Echols | 39 | 20.2 | D | D | 0.9 | D | D | D | 21.4 | 535 | 130 | 98 | 1 558 | 5.2 |

1. Includes mining, construction, and manufacturing.  2. Per 1,000 resident population enumerated in the 2010 census.

| STATE County | Housing units, 2007–2011 Total (89) | Percent (90) | Owner-occupied Median value[1] (91) | Median owner cost as a percent of income With a mortgage (92) | Without a mortgage[2] (93) | Renter-occupied Median rent[3] (94) | Median rent as a percent of income (95) | Sub-standard units[4] (percent) (96) | Civilian labor force, 2012 Total (97) | Percent change, 2011–2012 (98) | Unemployment Total (99) | Rate[5] (100) | Civilian employment,[6] 2007–2011 Total (101) | Percent Management, business, science and arts (102) | Construction, production, and mainte-nance occupations (103) |
|---|---|---|---|---|---|---|---|---|---|---|---|---|---|---|---|
| **FLORIDA—Cont'd** | | | | | | | | | | | | | | | |
| Putnam | 29 061 | 77.2 | 105 300 | 26.0 | 11.6 | 610 | 35.6 | 3.1 | 30 988 | -4.2 | 3 465 | 11.2 | 26 004 | 23.8 | 34.4 |
| St. Johns | 71 807 | 76.9 | 279 700 | 27.2 | 13.0 | 1 056 | 31.0 | 1.2 | 100 951 | 1.0 | 6 923 | 6.9 | 87 445 | 41.9 | 13.4 |
| St. Lucie | 103 900 | 75.3 | 157 600 | 33.3 | 14.8 | 1 039 | 36.7 | 2.5 | 125 941 | 0.6 | 13 931 | 11.1 | 110 467 | 26.5 | 23.1 |
| Santa Rosa | 55 956 | 76.3 | 173 400 | 25.9 | 11.3 | 956 | 30.8 | 1.8 | 74 421 | 0.4 | 5 762 | 7.7 | 64 536 | 32.8 | 21.5 |
| Sarasota | 169 256 | 76.2 | 213 400 | 30.9 | 14.4 | 1 013 | 34.3 | 1.4 | 162 993 | 1.3 | 14 048 | 8.6 | 151 327 | 32.6 | 17.7 |
| Seminole | 150 443 | 71.5 | 225 500 | 27.3 | 12.2 | 1 049 | 32.1 | 1.6 | 240 792 | 1.7 | 18 878 | 7.8 | 207 571 | 41.3 | 13.5 |
| Sumter | 40 294 | 89.6 | 186 800 | 26.0 | 12.3 | 751 | 26.6 | 1.9 | 36 272 | 0.4 | 2 667 | 7.4 | 21 304 | 26.7 | 24.1 |
| Suwannee | 15 810 | 73.6 | 108 900 | 24.9 | 12.2 | 700 | 32.2 | 2.9 | 18 953 | -1.7 | 1 467 | 7.7 | 15 698 | 25.2 | 30.7 |
| Taylor | 7 632 | 83.5 | 89 700 | 20.8 | 13.1 | 616 | 34.2 | 2.0 | 9 452 | 1.2 | 880 | 9.3 | 8 060 | 21.7 | 30.5 |
| Union | 3 665 | 66.4 | 113 500 | 23.8 | 9.9 | 598 | 23.6 | 2.0 | 5 146 | -4.2 | 375 | 7.3 | 5 088 | 25.3 | 17.4 |
| Volusia | 197 382 | 75.0 | 172 100 | 28.7 | 14.6 | 890 | 35.9 | 1.5 | 252 690 | 0.2 | 22 340 | 8.8 | 207 221 | 30.6 | 20.3 |
| Wakulla | 10 539 | 84.2 | 136 900 | 23.7 | 10.6 | 908 | 31.4 | 2.5 | 15 020 | -1.5 | 1 065 | 7.1 | 12 988 | 34.1 | 20.4 |
| Walton | 22 454 | 74.0 | 174 000 | 28.9 | 11.9 | 976 | 34.7 | 2.6 | 33 207 | 3.6 | 1 855 | 5.6 | 23 763 | 31.9 | 21.4 |
| Washington | 8 727 | 76.8 | 96 600 | 26.2 | 11.9 | 618 | 33.4 | 3.7 | 9 851 | -2.9 | 922 | 9.4 | 8 734 | 24.4 | 26.9 |
| **GEORGIA** | 3 490 754 | 66.8 | 160 200 | 24.4 | 11.7 | 835 | 31.3 | 2.9 | 4 806 103 | 0.8 | 434 495 | 9.0 | 4 288 924 | 35.1 | 23.1 |
| Appling | 7 062 | 71.0 | 82 300 | 27.4 | 9.9 | 470 | 19.7 | 3.2 | 9 692 | 1.1 | 1 000 | 10.3 | 7 727 | 23.2 | 42.9 |
| Atkinson | 2 745 | 69.1 | 61 100 | 19.9 | 11.3 | 398 | 24.5 | 6.4 | 3 029 | -0.3 | 405 | 13.4 | 3 202 | 17.2 | 49.0 |
| Bacon | 3 909 | 66.0 | 67 300 | 19.8 | 10.2 | 517 | 35.4 | 1.4 | 4 525 | -0.1 | 445 | 9.8 | 3 915 | 25.7 | 37.2 |
| Baker | 1 262 | 67.4 | 71 200 | 33.3 | 11.1 | 473 | 39.3 | 7.5 | 1 380 | 0.1 | 120 | 8.7 | 1 035 | 38.8 | 28.0 |
| Baldwin | 16 317 | 60.3 | 113 700 | 24.7 | 12.3 | 682 | 37.5 | 2.2 | 17 974 | -1.0 | 2 156 | 12.0 | 17 280 | 33.5 | 23.0 |
| Banks | 6 583 | 78.5 | 149 300 | 25.0 | 11.7 | 671 | 29.3 | 7.1 | 10 248 | 0.1 | 680 | 6.6 | 8 041 | 25.1 | 41.1 |
| Barrow | 23 404 | 77.0 | 137 300 | 25.0 | 11.9 | 824 | 33.8 | 3.0 | 34 700 | 1.1 | 2 909 | 8.4 | 30 876 | 27.6 | 26.4 |
| Bartow | 34 477 | 70.1 | 147 000 | 24.2 | 10.5 | 762 | 33.4 | 2.5 | 48 895 | 0.9 | 4 500 | 9.2 | 43 150 | 29.8 | 29.8 |
| Ben Hill | 6 344 | 63.2 | 77 100 | 26.5 | 13.3 | 605 | 30.4 | 4.9 | 6 781 | -0.8 | 877 | 12.9 | 6 437 | 26.4 | 34.6 |
| Berrien | 7 213 | 70.2 | 74 500 | 23.5 | 11.1 | 494 | 32.5 | 1.9 | 8 005 | 0.8 | 813 | 10.2 | 7 051 | 25.8 | 38.3 |
| Bibb | 57 189 | 57.5 | 121 900 | 24.0 | 12.3 | 712 | 35.6 | 2.6 | 75 036 | 0.9 | 7 356 | 9.8 | 61 823 | 33.4 | 19.7 |
| Bleckley | 4 182 | 71.3 | 81 200 | 20.0 | 12.3 | 642 | 36.1 | 1.0 | 5 133 | -2.2 | 695 | 13.5 | 4 729 | 28.0 | 27.2 |
| Brantley | 6 735 | 84.1 | 74 400 | 22.0 | 11.7 | 477 | 24.7 | 2.0 | 7 771 | 1.0 | 863 | 11.1 | 7 179 | 26.0 | 38.2 |
| Brooks | 6 330 | 72.2 | 96 300 | 23.9 | 10.2 | 536 | 36.0 | 4.1 | 7 397 | 1.4 | 633 | 8.6 | 6 783 | 23.8 | 37.6 |
| Bryan | 10 705 | 73.7 | 182 200 | 23.0 | 9.9 | 969 | 31.1 | 1.7 | 16 271 | 2.0 | 1 242 | 7.6 | 13 601 | 35.4 | 22.1 |
| Bulloch | 24 826 | 54.4 | 140 100 | 22.9 | 10.8 | 671 | 41.6 | 2.6 | 32 752 | 1.0 | 3 408 | 10.4 | 30 243 | 32.9 | 24.9 |
| Burke | 7 745 | 71.5 | 78 900 | 24.3 | 12.4 | 555 | 31.6 | 4.2 | 9 892 | 0.4 | 1 145 | 11.6 | 8 598 | 23.4 | 34.4 |
| Butts | 7 931 | 76.8 | 140 400 | 24.9 | 11.0 | 751 | 28.0 | 3.1 | 10 028 | 0.7 | 1 067 | 10.6 | 9 680 | 22.8 | 35.7 |
| Calhoun | 1 782 | 71.9 | 60 100 | 20.7 | 17.2 | 412 | 30.6 | 2.1 | 2 167 | -4.3 | 232 | 10.7 | 2 471 | 16.3 | 34.4 |
| Camden | 18 015 | 69.3 | 163 000 | 24.7 | 11.3 | 833 | 27.5 | 3.0 | 21 073 | 2.8 | 1 899 | 9.0 | 19 928 | 31.1 | 22.1 |
| Candler | 3 711 | 67.0 | 79 400 | 26.6 | 12.7 | 523 | 21.0 | 3.3 | 4 498 | 2.2 | 463 | 10.3 | 4 564 | 19.7 | 39.7 |
| Carroll | 39 473 | 68.2 | 136 100 | 24.1 | 11.9 | 763 | 33.4 | 3.0 | 52 426 | 1.0 | 5 072 | 9.7 | 47 650 | 28.8 | 30.4 |
| Catoosa | 24 143 | 74.6 | 133 100 | 23.1 | 9.9 | 675 | 28.5 | 2.5 | 34 631 | 0.5 | 2 282 | 6.6 | 29 613 | 30.8 | 26.1 |
| Charlton | 3 739 | 78.8 | 84 900 | 22.9 | 9.9 | 679 | 23.3 | 1.1 | 4 480 | -0.7 | 511 | 11.4 | 4 317 | 19.0 | 34.8 |
| Chatham | 100 658 | 58.7 | 176 400 | 25.7 | 12.5 | 904 | 32.2 | 1.8 | 137 965 | 1.9 | 11 809 | 8.6 | 116 133 | 33.7 | 21.2 |
| Chattahoochee | 2 544 | 31.4 | 88 300 | 18.6 | 11.1 | 1 206 | 28.4 | 4.8 | 2 182 | 1.2 | 400 | 18.3 | 1 981 | 25.9 | 24.9 |
| Chattooga | 9 031 | 71.2 | 78 300 | 23.4 | 13.2 | 579 | 27.7 | 7.6 | 10 429 | -0.6 | 1 123 | 10.8 | 9 325 | 22.3 | 45.4 |
| Cherokee | 75 784 | 79.9 | 198 000 | 24.7 | 11.0 | 957 | 30.0 | 2.0 | 114 541 | 1.2 | 8 263 | 7.2 | 104 602 | 39.2 | 17.5 |
| Clarke | 41 349 | 45.6 | 161 100 | 24.4 | 11.5 | 744 | 36.2 | 2.9 | 68 767 | 1.2 | 4 831 | 7.0 | 51 636 | 41.2 | 16.3 |
| Clay | 1 194 | 71.9 | 71 700 | 21.5 | 17.1 | 558 | 44.1 | 6.5 | 1 299 | -7.9 | 122 | 9.4 | 841 | 26.0 | 34.8 |
| Clayton | 85 875 | 59.1 | 121 300 | 27.6 | 12.0 | 870 | 34.1 | 4.5 | 130 580 | 0.8 | 14 471 | 11.1 | 116 502 | 23.5 | 29.3 |
| Clinch | 2 585 | 69.5 | 70 800 | 23.1 | 13.3 | 424 | 21.6 | 6.1 | 2 670 | -1.0 | 290 | 10.9 | 2 437 | 20.6 | 45.3 |
| Cobb | 258 710 | 68.6 | 210 100 | 23.5 | 9.9 | 958 | 30.4 | 2.8 | 377 191 | 1.2 | 30 656 | 8.1 | 351 300 | 43.8 | 15.6 |
| Coffee | 14 714 | 69.6 | 79 400 | 24.0 | 11.2 | 575 | 29.6 | 4.3 | 15 347 | -1.1 | 2 010 | 13.1 | 15 955 | 22.9 | 34.7 |
| Colquitt | 15 978 | 64.1 | 85 600 | 21.9 | 12.4 | 582 | 32.1 | 5.4 | 19 900 | -1.0 | 1 835 | 9.2 | 19 185 | 23.0 | 39.4 |
| Columbia | 43 070 | 80.4 | 169 600 | 22.4 | 9.9 | 923 | 27.9 | 1.3 | 66 807 | 0.0 | 4 550 | 6.8 | 56 114 | 41.6 | 18.7 |
| Cook | 6 521 | 71.9 | 87 500 | 25.3 | 11.3 | 722 | 36.1 | 3.2 | 6 447 | -2.7 | 719 | 11.2 | 7 085 | 26.1 | 38.2 |
| Coweta | 45 227 | 75.2 | 178 500 | 24.3 | 11.8 | 904 | 29.0 | 2.2 | 64 107 | 1.5 | 5 331 | 8.3 | 58 369 | 32.0 | 26.3 |
| Crawford | 4 773 | 81.3 | 88 300 | 23.2 | 12.9 | 636 | 45.9 | 3.6 | 6 205 | 1.1 | 583 | 9.4 | 5 317 | 25.8 | 35.1 |
| Crisp | 8 826 | 59.3 | 92 100 | 23.8 | 11.4 | 577 | 33.0 | 3.6 | 9 304 | 0.0 | 1 146 | 12.3 | 8 652 | 27.1 | 33.2 |
| Dade | 6 290 | 78.7 | 125 500 | 24.4 | 11.8 | 650 | 26.6 | 2.1 | 8 211 | 1.0 | 618 | 7.5 | 7 455 | 27.9 | 26.7 |
| Dawson | 8 049 | 78.6 | 193 800 | 28.8 | 9.9 | 862 | 32.5 | 3.0 | 11 397 | 0.8 | 879 | 7.7 | 10 001 | 29.0 | 26.4 |
| Decatur | 10 371 | 62.9 | 105 400 | 20.6 | 13.1 | 575 | 37.6 | 7.6 | 11 163 | 1.7 | 1 259 | 11.3 | 10 572 | 26.0 | 29.5 |
| DeKalb | 265 137 | 58.2 | 185 100 | 26.1 | 12.4 | 952 | 32.6 | 3.1 | 369 188 | 1.2 | 34 217 | 9.3 | 334 788 | 42.2 | 16.7 |
| Dodge | 8 197 | 70.3 | 70 400 | 20.8 | 14.4 | 525 | 24.8 | 1.5 | 8 777 | -1.8 | 1 010 | 11.5 | 7 632 | 27.7 | 31.8 |
| Dooly | 4 803 | 68.4 | 66 800 | 22.4 | 11.7 | 508 | 32.5 | 2.7 | 4 551 | -0.7 | 596 | 13.1 | 4 553 | 27.2 | 33.0 |
| Dougherty | 36 013 | 48.4 | 102 100 | 24.0 | 13.5 | 652 | 33.3 | 3.2 | 43 111 | 0.0 | 4 562 | 10.6 | 36 755 | 28.8 | 25.7 |
| Douglas | 45 451 | 71.6 | 153 900 | 25.9 | 9.9 | 928 | 29.8 | 2.6 | 68 619 | 0.9 | 6 318 | 9.2 | 59 857 | 32.2 | 25.0 |
| Early | 4 122 | 65.4 | 77 900 | 23.4 | 12.5 | 474 | 37.1 | 2.7 | 5 413 | 0.4 | 454 | 8.4 | 3 619 | 26.1 | 34.2 |
| Echols | 1 292 | 63.2 | 100 200 | 21.3 | 12.4 | 668 | 31.8 | 11.1 | 2 048 | 2.2 | 146 | 7.1 | 1 736 | 18.5 | 43.0 |

1. Specified owner-occupied units.   2. A value of 9.9 represents 9.9 percent or less.   3. Specified renter-occupied units. A value of 10.0 represents 10 percent or less.   4. Overcrowded or lacking complete plumbing facilities.   5. Percent of civilian labor force.   6. Persons 16 years old and over.

| STATE County | Number of establish-ments | Total | Health care and social assistance | Manufac-turing | Retail trade | Finance and insurance | Professional, scientific, and technical services | Total (mil dol) | Average per employee (dollars) | Number | Fewer than 50 acres | 500 acres or more | Farm operators whose principal occu-pation is farming (percent) |
|---|---|---|---|---|---|---|---|---|---|---|---|---|---|
| | 104 | 105 | 106 | 107 | 108 | 109 | 110 | 111 | 112 | 113 | 114 | 115 | 116 |
| **FLORIDA—Cont'd** | | | | | | | | | | | | | |
| Putnam | 1 273 | 12 735 | 2 335 | D | 2 588 | 351 | 346 | 393 | 30 885 | 469 | 71.0 | 8.1 | 44.1 |
| St. Johns | 4 956 | 45 074 | 7 056 | 1 430 | 8 675 | 1 809 | 2 318 | 1 458 | 32 353 | 194 | 60.8 | 13.9 | 61.3 |
| St. Lucie | 4 827 | 53 587 | 10 376 | 1 997 | 13 662 | 1 263 | 1 869 | 1 726 | 32 209 | 365 | 55.3 | 14.8 | 49.0 |
| Santa Rosa | 2 432 | 21 329 | 3 323 | 277 | 4 759 | 637 | 1 555 | 725 | 34 000 | 594 | 51.3 | 3.9 | 33.3 |
| Sarasota | 12 385 | 120 752 | 24 761 | 4 868 | 20 359 | 5 505 | 9 380 | 4 279 | 35 439 | 305 | 77.4 | 6.6 | 43.3 |
| Seminole | 12 335 | 142 151 | 16 135 | 6 359 | 24 308 | 11 981 | 10 291 | 5 401 | 37 997 | 395 | 87.6 | 2.3 | 40.5 |
| Sumter | 1 131 | 15 132 | 2 066 | 713 | 2 936 | 482 | 369 | 465 | 30 712 | 837 | 66.1 | 4.8 | 43.8 |
| Suwannee | 658 | 8 202 | 1 501 | 1 832 | 1 478 | 141 | 248 | 200 | 24 431 | 1 075 | 50.9 | 6.9 | 51.1 |
| Taylor | 402 | 4 682 | 616 | D | 1 010 | 89 | 138 | 164 | 34 985 | 132 | 48.5 | 9.1 | 39.4 |
| Union | 134 | 1 826 | D | D | 147 | D | D | 62 | 33 740 | 275 | 57.5 | 4.4 | 38.2 |
| Volusia | 11 693 | 126 547 | 26 001 | 7 432 | 23 274 | 4 413 | 6 279 | 3 993 | 31 553 | 1 243 | 84.5 | 2.4 | 46.7 |
| Wakulla | 402 | 3 100 | 201 | D | 766 | D | 121 | 87 | 27 988 | 147 | 75.5 | 4.8 | 42.9 |
| Walton | 1 716 | 15 483 | 1 597 | D | 3 487 | 298 | 410 | 475 | 30 683 | 754 | 36.1 | 8.4 | 35.1 |
| Washington | 362 | 3 662 | 866 | D | 786 | D | 158 | 96 | 26 313 | 462 | 33.8 | 5.2 | 38.5 |
| **GEORGIA** | 214 635 | 3 328 033 | 444 294 | 329 372 | 437 549 | 160 454 | 221 572 | 141 481 | 42 512 | 47 846 | 41.3 | 9.2 | 42.0 |
| Appling | 382 | 5 359 | 1 054 | 584 | 673 | 124 | 44 | 217 | 40 508 | 494 | 41.3 | 9.1 | 49.6 |
| Atkinson | 87 | 981 | 32 | 481 | 151 | D | D | 28 | 28 037 | 195 | 20.5 | 20.5 | 48.2 |
| Bacon | 217 | 2 500 | D | 592 | 313 | 139 | 48 | 71 | 28 518 | 326 | 38.7 | 9.5 | 41.4 |
| Baker | 25 | 241 | D | NA | 33 | D | D | 8 | 33 095 | 156 | 28.2 | 29.5 | 66.7 |
| Baldwin | 816 | 12 844 | 4 301 | 1 506 | 2 135 | 381 | D | 362 | 28 168 | 170 | 39.4 | 7.1 | 48.2 |
| Banks | 278 | 3 347 | 145 | D | 985 | 54 | D | 84 | 25 031 | 530 | 49.2 | 1.1 | 51.5 |
| Barrow | 1 047 | 12 865 | 1 363 | D | 2 315 | 372 | 830 | 409 | 31 775 | 466 | 65.9 | 1.5 | 40.1 |
| Bartow | 1 823 | 27 488 | 2 629 | 7 261 | 3 665 | 706 | 804 | 981 | 35 681 | 501 | 56.3 | 5.8 | 36.1 |
| Ben Hill | 335 | 4 978 | 711 | 1 544 | 801 | 156 | 221 | 135 | 27 196 | 227 | 31.3 | 17.6 | 41.4 |
| Berrien | 278 | 2 927 | 336 | 1 209 | 436 | 121 | D | 127 | 43 222 | 417 | 27.8 | 15.6 | 48.0 |
| Bibb | 4 179 | 70 595 | 15 042 | 4 809 | 10 579 | 8 398 | 2 392 | 2 524 | 35 751 | 123 | 39.8 | 4.1 | 48.8 |
| Bleckley | 164 | 2 175 | 290 | 699 | 330 | 74 | 59 | 52 | 23 834 | 308 | 31.2 | 19.2 | 43.8 |
| Brantley | 180 | 1 217 | D | 116 | 301 | D | D | 33 | 27 031 | 225 | 46.7 | 2.7 | 39.6 |
| Brooks | 203 | 1 990 | 528 | D | 310 | 66 | 26 | 54 | 27 159 | 457 | 32.2 | 19.9 | 39.8 |
| Bryan | 576 | 5 282 | 1 114 | 308 | 921 | D | 280 | 145 | 27 517 | 77 | 41.6 | 9.1 | 40.3 |
| Bulloch | 1 360 | 16 855 | 2 567 | 1 572 | 3 397 | 568 | 507 | 427 | 25 357 | 669 | 31.8 | 14.9 | 39.0 |
| Burke | 304 | 5 832 | 516 | 903 | 735 | 137 | 61 | 304 | 52 121 | 468 | 24.1 | 19.9 | 42.1 |
| Butts | 347 | 3 772 | 530 | 551 | 658 | D | D | 106 | 28 097 | 146 | 41.8 | 4.8 | 52.1 |
| Calhoun | 75 | 722 | 247 | NA | D | 38 | D | 21 | 28 785 | 141 | 14.9 | 40.4 | 58.2 |
| Camden | 803 | 8 143 | 918 | 236 | 2 582 | 324 | 375 | 205 | 25 133 | 57 | 40.4 | 14.0 | 28.1 |
| Candler | 223 | 2 159 | 503 | 174 | 421 | D | 52 | 58 | 26 759 | 283 | 30.4 | 12.7 | 38.2 |
| Carroll | 1 932 | 29 544 | 4 427 | 6 706 | 4 562 | 788 | 621 | 1 099 | 37 198 | 1 054 | 47.5 | 1.4 | 41.8 |
| Catoosa | 885 | 12 002 | 1 979 | 1 662 | 2 585 | 429 | 245 | 355 | 29 562 | 261 | 56.7 | 1.1 | 34.9 |
| Charlton | 145 | 1 637 | D | D | 211 | 37 | D | 52 | 31 487 | 113 | 34.5 | 9.7 | 34.5 |
| Chatham | 7 065 | 117 852 | 18 512 | 11 987 | 15 964 | 3 044 | 5 279 | 4 389 | 37 245 | 33 | 60.6 | 9.1 | 42.4 |
| Chattahoochee | 70 | 1 092 | D | D | 97 | D | 104 | 40 | 36 919 | 22 | 50.0 | 4.5 | 22.7 |
| Chattooga | 315 | 4 302 | 357 | D | 652 | 130 | 103 | 117 | 27 096 | 309 | 30.1 | 6.5 | 36.6 |
| Cherokee | 4 552 | 38 776 | 4 890 | 3 517 | 8 098 | 1 387 | 2 446 | 1 195 | 30 815 | 452 | 75.9 | 1.1 | 49.8 |
| Clarke | 2 931 | 43 616 | 9 666 | 5 191 | 7 221 | 1 215 | 1 650 | 1 447 | 33 169 | 116 | 57.8 | 2.6 | 24.1 |
| Clay | 41 | D | 34 | NA | 87 | 9 | D | D | D | 90 | 22.2 | 26.7 | 44.4 |
| Clayton | 3 914 | 69 776 | 7 014 | 3 700 | 11 272 | 2 088 | 971 | 2 392 | 34 287 | 48 | 79.2 | 0.0 | 45.8 |
| Clinch | 121 | 1 652 | D | D | 150 | 22 | 30 | 50 | 30 358 | 109 | 47.7 | 11.0 | 42.2 |
| Cobb | 18 728 | 288 112 | 29 752 | D | 35 003 | 16 407 | 24 975 | 14 047 | 48 755 | 129 | 76.7 | 3.9 | 35.7 |
| Coffee | 835 | 11 632 | 1 779 | 2 455 | 1 934 | 349 | 235 | 348 | 29 907 | 605 | 28.8 | 14.2 | 47.9 |
| Colquitt | 860 | 11 211 | 2 059 | 3 035 | 1 872 | 312 | 183 | 307 | 27 376 | 644 | 33.1 | 14.4 | 51.2 |
| Columbia | 2 136 | 26 653 | 3 062 | 3 070 | 5 904 | 732 | 1 081 | 868 | 32 548 | 186 | 55.4 | 2.2 | 30.6 |
| Cook | 313 | 2 661 | 409 | 515 | 474 | 104 | 73 | 66 | 24 743 | 253 | 38.3 | 11.5 | 51.8 |
| Coweta | 2 024 | 26 122 | 3 287 | 4 106 | 5 184 | 607 | 712 | 820 | 31 378 | 445 | 53.0 | 4.7 | 35.3 |
| Crawford | 102 | 466 | D | 44 | 97 | D | D | 13 | 27 766 | 188 | 35.6 | 8.5 | 49.5 |
| Crisp | 507 | 6 311 | 1 240 | 1 029 | 1 367 | 218 | 68 | 170 | 26 901 | 229 | 27.9 | 17.0 | 43.7 |
| Dade | 215 | 2 344 | 210 | 504 | 456 | 96 | D | 79 | 33 539 | 266 | 47.7 | 1.9 | 34.2 |
| Dawson | 591 | 6 380 | 313 | 1 250 | 2 784 | 141 | 156 | 139 | 21 863 | 208 | 62.5 | 3.8 | 45.2 |
| Decatur | 583 | 6 394 | 932 | 1 282 | 1 506 | 222 | 132 | 191 | 29 904 | 351 | 21.9 | 18.8 | 46.4 |
| DeKalb | 16 003 | 252 081 | 40 238 | 11 064 | 30 946 | 9 279 | 16 334 | 11 421 | 45 307 | 38 | 86.8 | 0.0 | 50.0 |
| Dodge | 336 | 3 662 | 901 | D | 719 | 161 | 90 | 97 | 26 551 | 427 | 25.3 | 12.4 | 38.4 |
| Dooly | 162 | 1 891 | 156 | 722 | 324 | D | 21 | 52 | 27 462 | 329 | 27.7 | 24.6 | 52.0 |
| Dougherty | 2 387 | 37 548 | 8 408 | 3 050 | 6 419 | 1 157 | 2 336 | 1 267 | 33 737 | 129 | 43.4 | 24.8 | 49.6 |
| Douglas | 2 416 | 32 296 | 4 585 | 2 603 | 7 276 | 769 | 1 141 | 1 007 | 31 187 | 136 | 69.9 | 1.5 | 37.5 |
| Early | 215 | 2 639 | D | D | 346 | 104 | D | 126 | 47 597 | 418 | 24.2 | 22.7 | 40.7 |
| Echols | 20 | 74 | D | D | D | D | NA | 2 | 28 811 | 59 | 30.5 | 13.6 | 39.0 |

# Table B. States and Counties — **Agriculture**

| | Agriculture, 2007 (cont.) | | | | | | | | | | | | | | |
| | Land in farms | | | | Value of land and buildings (dollars) | | | Value of products sold | | | | | Percent of farms with sales of: | | Government payments | |
| | | | Acres | | | | | | | | Percent from: | | | | | |
| STATE County | Acreage (1,000) | Percent change, 2002–2007 | Average size of farm | Total irrigated (1,000) | Total cropland (1,000) | Average per farm | Average per acre | Value of machinery and equipment, average per farm (dollars) | Total (mil dol) | Average per farm (dollars) | Crops | Live-stock and poultry products | $10,000 or more | $100,000 or more | Total ($1,000) | Percent of farms |
| | 117 | 118 | 119 | 120 | 121 | 122 | 123 | 124 | 125 | 126 | 127 | 128 | 129 | 130 | 131 | 132 |
| **FLORIDA—Cont'd** | | | | | | | | | | | | | | | | |
| Putnam | 74 | -20.4 | 159 | 4.6 | 12.0 | 845 062 | 5 321 | 48 714 | 37.5 | 80 046 | 86.5 | 13.5 | 31.3 | 7.2 | 52 | 2.1 |
| St. Johns | 34 | -10.5 | 173 | 14.4 | 19.6 | 1 520 754 | 8 795 | 122 298 | 53.5 | 275 647 | 98.0 | 2.0 | 33.0 | 17.0 | 30 | 3.6 |
| St. Lucie | 153 | -31.1 | 421 | 69.3 | 62.6 | 2 585 978 | 6 150 | 93 088 | 144.3 | 395 297 | 92.9 | 7.1 | 57.3 | 28.2 | 182 | 2.7 |
| Santa Rosa | 70 | -16.7 | 118 | 2.6 | 33.3 | 683 136 | 5 782 | 48 021 | 20.8 | 34 966 | 80.8 | 19.2 | 25.1 | 6.4 | 2 806 | 43.9 |
| Sarasota | 61 | -49.6 | 200 | 2.3 | 8.7 | 1 528 612 | 7 639 | 56 547 | 31.0 | 101 741 | D | D | 27.5 | 10.2 | 79 | 2.0 |
| Seminole | 36 | 28.6 | 90 | 1.8 | 4.5 | 764 620 | 8 498 | 24 886 | 20.8 | 52 729 | 91.7 | 8.3 | 31.6 | 5.6 | 0 | 0.0 |
| Sumter | 160 | -14.4 | 191 | 2.0 | 29.4 | 1 103 939 | 5 783 | 46 671 | 29.4 | 35 153 | D | D | 24.1 | 5.4 | 222 | 6.9 |
| Suwannee | 167 | -1.8 | 156 | 20.1 | 68.2 | 962 912 | 6 180 | 62 945 | 197.8 | 183 980 | 25.0 | 75.0 | 34.6 | 12.7 | 1 295 | 13.1 |
| Taylor | 34 | -37.0 | 254 | D | 1.8 | 1 192 797 | 4 695 | 44 450 | 3.7 | 27 852 | D | D | 20.5 | 3.0 | 30 | 6.8 |
| Union | 47 | -21.7 | 169 | 1.0 | 7.2 | 779 433 | 4 604 | 44 787 | D | D | D | 0.0 | 26.5 | 5.1 | 56 | 9.5 |
| Volusia | 83 | -11.7 | 67 | 9.1 | 18.3 | 662 001 | 9 881 | 38 989 | 125.5 | 101 001 | 94.9 | 5.1 | 36.7 | 10.2 | 47 | 1.3 |
| Wakulla | 28 | 154.5 | 193 | 0.3 | 2.0 | 609 659 | 3 162 | 34 966 | 1.6 | 11 212 | 58.6 | 41.4 | 21.1 | 0.7 | 122 | 5.4 |
| Walton | 127 | 58.8 | 168 | 0.7 | 46.7 | 760 624 | 4 521 | 47 674 | 25.5 | 33 884 | 19.1 | 80.9 | 22.0 | 5.6 | 1 972 | 43.0 |
| Washington | 74 | 39.6 | 160 | 0.9 | 22.7 | 713 217 | 4 463 | 45 794 | 5.8 | 12 469 | 46.7 | 53.3 | 18.8 | 2.4 | 1 064 | 52.6 |
| **GEORGIA** | 10 151 | -5.5 | 212 | 1 017.8 | 4 478.2 | 661 201 | 3 117 | 76 948 | 7 112.9 | 148 662 | 30.1 | 69.9 | 32.3 | 14.2 | 224 523 | 30.4 |
| Appling | 102 | -14.3 | 206 | 9.1 | 61.6 | 544 006 | 2 646 | 107 135 | 75.1 | 152 113 | 37.0 | 63.0 | 43.5 | 19.0 | 4 160 | 43.1 |
| Atkinson | 77 | 8.5 | 396 | 5.6 | 28.4 | 1 101 543 | 2 782 | 111 265 | 60.0 | 307 934 | 24.0 | 76.0 | 51.3 | 25.1 | 2 021 | 53.3 |
| Bacon | 63 | -6.0 | 194 | 6.0 | 29.9 | 515 224 | 2 656 | 105 268 | 58.2 | 178 558 | 31.5 | 68.5 | 43.6 | 15.6 | 1 128 | 39.3 |
| Baker | 135 | 7.1 | 867 | 22.0 | 51.6 | 2 173 489 | 2 508 | 249 122 | 42.1 | 269 639 | 61.5 | 38.5 | 42.9 | 32.7 | 2 986 | 68.6 |
| Baldwin | 30 | -16.7 | 176 | 0.1 | 8.7 | 419 267 | 2 380 | 53 128 | 6.0 | 35 090 | 12.1 | 87.9 | 27.1 | 1.8 | 43 | 10.6 |
| Banks | 47 | -19.0 | 88 | 0.7 | 11.9 | 554 298 | 6 293 | 76 605 | 144.2 | 272 128 | 0.3 | 99.7 | 47.5 | 35.7 | 105 | 10.2 |
| Barrow | 34 | -5.6 | 73 | 0.1 | 10.0 | 452 630 | 6 229 | 41 904 | 41.6 | 89 249 | 2.0 | 98.0 | 23.8 | 7.7 | 39 | 6.0 |
| Bartow | 65 | -20.7 | 130 | 3.0 | 24.5 | 590 027 | 4 540 | 63 243 | 94.0 | 187 537 | 13.9 | 86.1 | 29.5 | 15.2 | 565 | 16.2 |
| Ben Hill | 75 | 31.6 | 329 | 8.0 | 36.6 | 727 713 | 2 210 | 101 292 | 20.1 | 88 530 | 75.6 | 24.4 | 37.9 | 19.8 | 2 191 | 62.1 |
| Berrien | 119 | -5.6 | 285 | 14.5 | 59.9 | 786 367 | 2 760 | 109 173 | 61.1 | 146 503 | 67.6 | 32.4 | 45.8 | 24.7 | 3 623 | 45.3 |
| Bibb | 14 | -53.3 | 117 | 0.1 | 5.1 | 440 157 | 3 758 | 40 467 | 6.1 | 49 512 | 13.8 | 86.2 | 30.1 | 4.9 | 82 | 12.2 |
| Bleckley | 88 | 60.0 | 286 | 17.5 | 57.0 | 736 698 | 2 577 | 94 384 | 19.0 | 61 842 | 93.0 | 7.0 | 33.4 | 17.9 | 2 982 | 59.4 |
| Brantley | 25 | -21.9 | 113 | 0.4 | 10.8 | 302 862 | 2 690 | 59 991 | 8.3 | 36 897 | 37.9 | 62.1 | 19.6 | 4.4 | 584 | 23.1 |
| Brooks | 189 | -6.9 | 414 | 19.1 | 91.8 | 1 185 393 | 2 866 | 108 240 | 81.2 | 177 775 | 75.4 | 24.6 | 44.4 | 20.6 | 5 997 | 53.6 |
| Bryan | 20 | 17.6 | 264 | D | 6.5 | 503 395 | 1 910 | 67 460 | 1.9 | 24 258 | 82.5 | 17.5 | 14.3 | 3.9 | 312 | 18.2 |
| Bulloch | 197 | -4.4 | 295 | 7.8 | 118.8 | 772 465 | 2 623 | 91 312 | 55.6 | 83 061 | 69.9 | 30.1 | 37.7 | 14.8 | 7 444 | 54.6 |
| Burke | 192 | -12.3 | 410 | 17.7 | 111.1 | 999 897 | 2 440 | 105 946 | 48.7 | 104 005 | 64.1 | 35.9 | 39.1 | 10.9 | 4 257 | 38.2 |
| Butts | 25 | -32.4 | 174 | 0.1 | 6.4 | 617 679 | 3 546 | 50 042 | 3.5 | 24 112 | 33.1 | 66.9 | 17.8 | 6.2 | 74 | 26.0 |
| Calhoun | 123 | 4.2 | 869 | 30.3 | 67.0 | 1 728 410 | 1 988 | 316 913 | 63.1 | 447 746 | 58.8 | 41.2 | 56.0 | 39.7 | 5 142 | 74.5 |
| Camden | 13 | 8.3 | 235 | 0.2 | 3.3 | 415 652 | 1 768 | 29 533 | 0.4 | 7 476 | 63.6 | 36.4 | 15.8 | 1.8 | 19 | 5.3 |
| Candler | 74 | 17.5 | 261 | 3.7 | 36.8 | 706 614 | 2 705 | 102 498 | 24.4 | 86 367 | 71.0 | 29.0 | 34.3 | 13.1 | 1 776 | 47.0 |
| Carroll | 96 | 2.1 | 91 | 0.7 | 25.5 | 484 930 | 5 313 | 50 961 | 155.2 | 147 228 | 1.9 | 98.1 | 26.5 | 9.6 | 295 | 8.7 |
| Catoosa | 21 | -22.2 | 79 | 0.1 | 8.2 | 440 698 | 5 589 | 49 795 | 29.3 | 112 240 | D | D | 28.0 | 10.7 | 31 | 7.3 |
| Charlton | 20 | 33.3 | 181 | 0.1 | 3.2 | 383 047 | 2 119 | 47 002 | 9.5 | 83 881 | 4.2 | 95.8 | 17.7 | 4.4 | 43 | 3.5 |
| Chatham | 4 | -55.6 | 130 | 0.1 | 1.2 | 595 223 | 4 570 | 72 863 | 5.9 | 179 463 | 94.9 | 5.1 | 30.3 | 15.2 | D | 3.0 |
| Chattahoochee | 4 | 0.0 | 194 | 0.0 | 0.4 | 470 693 | 2 429 | 72 661 | D | D | 0.0 | D | 9.1 | 4.5 | D | |
| Chattooga | 53 | -3.6 | 172 | 0.3 | 16.1 | 563 567 | 3 281 | 60 194 | 11.1 | 35 925 | 11.0 | 89.0 | 25.6 | 5.8 | 410 | 24.3 |
| Cherokee | 23 | -36.1 | 52 | 0.1 | 7.2 | 467 059 | 9 018 | 39 871 | 40.5 | 89 588 | 8.7 | 91.3 | 28.3 | 11.9 | 51 | 7.1 |
| Clarke | 10 | -28.6 | 90 | 0.1 | 3.0 | 440 776 | 4 890 | 40 602 | 40.1 | 345 005 | D | D | 25.0 | 6.0 | 69 | 22.4 |
| Clay | 45 | 7.1 | 495 | 9.4 | 23.8 | 1 237 349 | 2 499 | 108 633 | 11.5 | 127 914 | 94.0 | 6.0 | 31.1 | 17.8 | 1 542 | 56.7 |
| Clayton | 2 | -33.3 | 35 | 0.0 | 0.6 | 207 059 | 5 843 | 32 334 | 0.2 | 3 441 | 72.7 | 27.3 | 12.5 | 0.0 | 0 | 0.0 |
| Clinch | 19 | -38.7 | 173 | 1.8 | 6.0 | 468 678 | 2 702 | 88 055 | 13.5 | 123 751 | 75.6 | 24.4 | 46.8 | 26.6 | 26 | 11.9 |
| Cobb | 9 | -18.2 | 66 | 0.0 | 3.2 | 375 173 | 5 693 | 47 261 | 2.9 | 22 475 | 90.2 | 9.8 | 12.4 | 1.6 | 32 | 14.0 |
| Coffee | 185 | -2.1 | 306 | 18.0 | 98.9 | 763 316 | 2 497 | 122 486 | 147.9 | 244 540 | 30.9 | 69.1 | 41.2 | 20.3 | 5 872 | 53.6 |
| Colquitt | 197 | -13.6 | 305 | 44.1 | 114.6 | 889 153 | 2 913 | 146 905 | 256.5 | 398 301 | 55.5 | 44.5 | 48.1 | 27.0 | 8 831 | 55.1 |
| Columbia | 19 | -17.4 | 101 | 0.1 | 4.7 | 397 851 | 3 929 | 43 121 | 3.7 | 20 057 | 27.6 | 72.4 | 17.2 | 2.7 | 13 | 9.1 |
| Cook | 65 | -4.4 | 257 | 10.8 | 38.4 | 746 721 | 2 900 | 111 437 | 97.9 | 386 837 | 51.9 | 48.1 | 41.1 | 18.6 | 2 908 | 57.3 |
| Coweta | 75 | 23.0 | 168 | 0.5 | 18.6 | 619 703 | 3 694 | 59 614 | 11.3 | 25 365 | 39.1 | 60.9 | 17.5 | 1.8 | 233 | 5.2 |
| Crawford | 38 | 0.0 | 200 | 4.5 | 15.1 | 590 638 | 2 950 | 77 090 | 32.9 | 174 985 | 43.1 | 56.9 | 25.0 | 14.4 | 212 | 14.9 |
| Crisp | 83 | -20.2 | 364 | 17.3 | 49.2 | 816 730 | 2 246 | 118 230 | 29.9 | 130 376 | 83.1 | 16.9 | 41.9 | 20.5 | 3 765 | 57.2 |
| Dade | 35 | 25.0 | 133 | 0.0 | 7.4 | 421 129 | 3 177 | 55 144 | 14.7 | 55 381 | 2.7 | 97.3 | 19.2 | 4.1 | 67 | 7.5 |
| Dawson | 17 | -15.0 | 81 | 0.1 | 4.3 | 561 380 | 6 907 | 91 070 | 68.2 | 328 043 | 1.0 | 99.0 | 33.7 | 23.6 | 22 | 6.7 |
| Decatur | 180 | 12.5 | 513 | 47.9 | 106.5 | 1 363 102 | 2 659 | 156 925 | 114.3 | 325 749 | 86.7 | 13.3 | 41.3 | 21.7 | 7 126 | 69.8 |
| DeKalb | 1 | 0.0 | 25 | 0.0 | 0.6 | 258 686 | 10 208 | 41 456 | 0.5 | 12 184 | 97.8 | 2.2 | 13.2 | 7.9 | 7 | 13.2 |
| Dodge | 127 | -8.6 | 298 | 13.5 | 46.6 | 598 796 | 2 007 | 58 102 | 20.9 | 48 914 | 87.0 | 13.0 | 22.7 | 8.4 | 3 355 | 58.8 |
| Dooly | 156 | -8.8 | 473 | 37.2 | 106.6 | 988 541 | 2 090 | 188 260 | 73.9 | 224 715 | 66.1 | 33.9 | 50.5 | 34.7 | 8 570 | 67.5 |
| Dougherty | 88 | -10.2 | 681 | 15.2 | 33.1 | 1 744 680 | 2 563 | 167 925 | 32.2 | 249 245 | 94.0 | 6.0 | 34.1 | 22.5 | 1 442 | 34.1 |
| Douglas | 7 | -12.5 | 52 | 0.2 | 2.9 | 379 781 | 7 260 | 43 902 | 3.8 | 27 973 | 32.2 | 67.8 | 22.1 | 3.7 | 20 | 7.4 |
| Early | 178 | 11.3 | 425 | 33.1 | 99.5 | 1 018 724 | 2 398 | 138 914 | 50.7 | 121 263 | 87.1 | 12.9 | 45.2 | 26.3 | 7 543 | 67.2 |
| Echols | 14 | -51.7 | 243 | 4.0 | 6.8 | 786 885 | 3 240 | 131 916 | 17.9 | 303 237 | 96.1 | 3.9 | 30.5 | 16.9 | 129 | 23.7 |

| STATE County | Water use, 2005 | | Wholesale trade,[1] 2007 | | | | Retail trade,[2] 2007 | | | | Real estate and rental and leasing,[2] 2007 | | | |
|---|---|---|---|---|---|---|---|---|---|---|---|---|---|---|
| | Total water withdrawn (mil gal/day) | Gallons withdrawn per person | Number of establishments | Number of employees | Sales (mil dol) | Annual payroll (mil dol) | Number of establishments | Number of employees | Sales (mil dol) | Annual payroll (mil dol) | Number of establishments | Number of employees | Receipts (mil dol) | Annual payroll (mil dol) |
| | 133 | 134 | 135 | 136 | 137 | 138 | 139 | 140 | 141 | 142 | 143 | 144 | 145 | 146 |
| FLORIDA—Cont'd | | | | | | | | | | | | | | |
| Putnam | 73.9 | 1 001 | 24 | D | D | D | 261 | 2 918 | 671.6 | 60.2 | 72 | 182 | 22.0 | 3.9 |
| St. Johns | 34.9 | 222 | 165 | 1 817 | 871.1 | 83.5 | 763 | 8 967 | 2 039.7 | 189.1 | 376 | 1 383 | 207.0 | 41.8 |
| St. Lucie | 1 352.3 | 5 634 | 244 | 1 899 | 693.6 | 72.5 | 705 | 13 381 | 3 697.7 | 335.1 | 327 | 1 014 | 174.2 | 31.8 |
| Santa Rosa | 29.0 | 212 | 72 | 266 | 148.9 | 8.9 | 363 | 4 472 | 1 108.0 | 96.6 | 178 | 469 | 55.3 | 10.7 |
| Sarasota | 41.0 | 111 | 477 | 3 442 | 1 560.3 | 147.8 | 1 764 | 22 887 | 5 599.5 | 561.1 | 929 | 3 175 | 539.4 | 103.3 |
| Seminole | 68.8 | 167 | 661 | 6 783 | 2 852.7 | 314.2 | 1 800 | 28 169 | 6 872.1 | 642.2 | 877 | 3 376 | 682.0 | 120.3 |
| Sumter | 24.7 | 333 | 42 | D | D | D | 178 | 2 696 | 672.1 | 52.1 | 90 | 153 | 19.7 | 3.7 |
| Suwannee | 103.1 | 2 700 | 31 | 271 | 108.7 | 6.3 | 152 | 1 606 | 353.8 | 33.3 | 29 | 66 | 7.7 | 1.1 |
| Taylor | 49.2 | 2 311 | 14 | D | D | D | 93 | 980 | 207.1 | 18.6 | 21 | 76 | 6.8 | 1.2 |
| Union | 3.3 | 219 | 2 | D | D | D | 28 | 146 | 42.0 | 3.6 | 2 | D | D | D |
| Volusia | 171.2 | 346 | 443 | 4 426 | 2 002.9 | 168.8 | 1 970 | 26 205 | 6 099.9 | 575.9 | 842 | 3 978 | 531.8 | 101.5 |
| Wakulla | 10.9 | 404 | 13 | 63 | 7.0 | 1.5 | 63 | 908 | 167.7 | 17.2 | 15 | 41 | 4.6 | 0.7 |
| Walton | 11.7 | 218 | 47 | 722 | 205.1 | 21.7 | 381 | 3 317 | 705.0 | 72.2 | 176 | 950 | 145.3 | 33.0 |
| Washington | 3.6 | 156 | 9 | D | D | D | 70 | 805 | 177.3 | 16.0 | 18 | 42 | 3.0 | 0.9 |
| GEORGIA | 5 442.4 | 600 | 11 545 | 166 619 | 141 962.4 | 8 246.5 | 36 218 | 475 344 | 117 516.9 | 10 760.2 | 12 620 | 65 875 | 14 021.9 | 2 903.2 |
| Appling | 63.0 | 3 510 | 20 | 112 | 58.1 | 3.1 | 83 | 705 | 179.4 | 14.1 | 8 | 38 | 4.3 | 0.6 |
| Atkinson | 7.9 | 980 | 6 | D | D | D | 26 | 162 | 35.7 | 2.6 | 1 | D | D | D |
| Bacon | 6.4 | 619 | 15 | 171 | 120.7 | 5.0 | 45 | 313 | 68.6 | 5.3 | 3 | 9 | 0.4 | 0.1 |
| Baker | 34.4 | 8 279 | 2 | D | D | D | 5 | 43 | 5.3 | 0.4 | 2 | D | D | D |
| Baldwin | 7.6 | 169 | 25 | D | D | D | 199 | 2 326 | 524.2 | 46.9 | 34 | D | D | D |
| Banks | 3.5 | 220 | 12 | 108 | 23.3 | 3.0 | 68 | 994 | 233.9 | 19.9 | 4 | D | D | D |
| Barrow | 8.6 | 144 | 64 | 1 476 | 466.3 | 50.4 | 159 | 2 308 | 660.9 | 59.8 | 59 | 165 | 22.7 | 3.4 |
| Bartow | 107.8 | 1 208 | 120 | 1 378 | 649.0 | 51.3 | 342 | 4 069 | 1 177.4 | 96.3 | 137 | 466 | 51.6 | 11.9 |
| Ben Hill | 10.7 | 617 | 9 | D | D | D | 96 | 987 | 225.0 | 17.5 | 11 | 44 | 4.5 | 0.9 |
| Berrien | 6.9 | 411 | 20 | 132 | 68.4 | 3.3 | 77 | 478 | 129.2 | 10.4 | 7 | 16 | 1.5 | 0.2 |
| Bibb | 18.7 | 121 | 209 | 2 975 | 1 613.7 | 132.6 | 860 | 11 834 | 2 536.2 | 250.1 | 223 | 1 223 | 221.8 | 34.9 |
| Bleckley | 13.6 | 1 116 | 6 | 42 | 16.9 | 2.2 | 50 | 385 | 76.3 | 6.5 | 6 | 36 | 1.1 | 1.0 |
| Brantley | 2.8 | 183 | 3 | D | D | D | 37 | 249 | 62.4 | 3.9 | 3 | 10 | 0.7 | 0.1 |
| Brooks | 4.5 | 273 | 12 | 66 | 65.9 | 2.6 | 43 | 302 | 88.2 | 6.5 | 8 | D | D | D |
| Bryan | 3.1 | 109 | 20 | 249 | 154.4 | 13.0 | 96 | 705 | 225.0 | 15.6 | 39 | 105 | 21.5 | 3.2 |
| Bulloch | 16.9 | 275 | 48 | D | D | D | 292 | 3 603 | 733.4 | 71.6 | 88 | 319 | 45.9 | 6.6 |
| Burke | 83.8 | 3 598 | 22 | D | D | D | 64 | 686 | 177.5 | 15.4 | 12 | 31 | 3.4 | 0.6 |
| Butts | 3.5 | 166 | 17 | 364 | 465.4 | 12.1 | 69 | 760 | 295.5 | 15.2 | 28 | 60 | 7.6 | 1.2 |
| Calhoun | 27.0 | 4 526 | 7 | 42 | 16.5 | 1.4 | 21 | 133 | 19.6 | 2.0 | NA | NA | NA | NA |
| Camden | 6.7 | 146 | 10 | D | D | D | 188 | 2 512 | 648.3 | 55.9 | 59 | 201 | 26.4 | 3.6 |
| Candler | 11.1 | 1 078 | 6 | 43 | 24.3 | 0.9 | 63 | 463 | 114.5 | 8.9 | 6 | 20 | 1.6 | 0.3 |
| Carroll | 14.4 | 137 | 78 | 1 560 | 985.9 | 58.9 | 390 | 4 606 | 1 252.5 | 98.0 | 98 | 364 | 49.7 | 9.0 |
| Catoosa | 6.7 | 110 | 40 | 444 | 151.2 | 15.6 | 203 | 3 053 | 795.1 | 70.5 | 44 | 144 | 24.3 | 4.1 |
| Charlton | 1.2 | 115 | 5 | 34 | 46.0 | 1.7 | 46 | 258 | 68.4 | 4.8 | 5 | 33 | 1.3 | 0.4 |
| Chatham | 241.3 | 1 012 | 327 | 4 287 | 3 780.1 | 216.0 | 1 287 | 17 094 | 4 004.2 | 381.0 | 409 | 2 007 | 351.2 | 63.6 |
| Chattahoochee | 1.2 | 82 | 1 | D | D | D | 11 | 69 | 13.0 | 1.0 | 1 | D | D | D |
| Chattooga | 12.3 | 462 | 13 | 47 | 66.4 | 1.8 | 77 | 798 | 147.2 | 13.8 | 5 | D | D | D |
| Cherokee | 29.3 | 159 | 233 | 1 702 | 849.0 | 71.4 | 545 | 8 242 | 2 114.9 | 193.8 | 255 | 721 | 125.4 | 20.3 |
| Clarke | 7.6 | 72 | 106 | 1 994 | 1 782.5 | 84.1 | 553 | 7 752 | 1 669.1 | 161.5 | 224 | 839 | 128.3 | 24.3 |
| Clay | 0.7 | 204 | 5 | 12 | 1.5 | 0.3 | 9 | 64 | 11.0 | 0.9 | 2 | D | D | D |
| Clayton | 15.6 | 58 | 276 | 6 131 | 3 582.3 | 253.8 | 808 | 12 447 | 3 207.0 | 297.7 | 231 | 1 247 | 302.1 | 44.0 |
| Clinch | 1.9 | 269 | 2 | D | D | D | 26 | 135 | 39.8 | 2.7 | 4 | 19 | 0.6 | 0.1 |
| Cobb | 414.7 | 625 | 1 189 | 20 206 | 15 524.8 | 1 094.7 | 2 413 | 39 613 | 10 480.7 | 961.7 | 1 235 | 7 548 | 2 171.2 | 383.1 |
| Coffee | 16.1 | 407 | 47 | 433 | 323.9 | 17.3 | 208 | 1 981 | 458.7 | 39.9 | 35 | D | D | D |
| Colquitt | 36.8 | 837 | 44 | 370 | 184.9 | 10.9 | 195 | 1 997 | 432.4 | 43.1 | 42 | 142 | 18.6 | 3.1 |
| Columbia | 15.6 | 150 | 71 | 791 | 357.5 | 32.5 | 308 | 5 023 | 1 406.3 | 126.7 | 93 | 380 | 71.4 | 10.9 |
| Cook | 11.1 | 680 | 16 | 125 | 51.5 | 5.2 | 78 | 530 | 118.1 | 9.7 | 11 | 34 | 4.1 | 0.8 |
| Coweta | 42.4 | 386 | 68 | 815 | 524.6 | 33.6 | 343 | 4 895 | 1 291.0 | 111.5 | 141 | 390 | 65.7 | 12.3 |
| Crawford | 4.9 | 378 | 5 | D | D | D | 20 | 98 | 18.2 | 1.5 | NA | NA | NA | NA |
| Crisp | 18.8 | 854 | 34 | D | D | D | 131 | 1 538 | 326.5 | 28.8 | 30 | 220 | 16.8 | 4.3 |
| Dade | 2.9 | 181 | 4 | D | D | D | 65 | 516 | 189.3 | 8.3 | 5 | D | D | D |
| Dawson | 2.7 | 137 | 16 | 144 | 103.9 | 6.0 | 185 | 2 524 | 466.6 | 44.2 | 27 | 84 | 27.0 | 2.3 |
| Decatur | 42.0 | 1 466 | 28 | D | D | D | 158 | 1 945 | 395.4 | 33.4 | 20 | 55 | 10.8 | 1.0 |
| DeKalb | 88.8 | 131 | 905 | 11 028 | 9 361.1 | 559.4 | 2 456 | 35 506 | 7 973.4 | 810.1 | 1 086 | 5 761 | 1 542.4 | 311.4 |
| Dodge | 19.9 | 1 018 | 13 | 82 | 9.8 | 1.3 | 91 | 851 | 167.1 | 16.2 | 15 | 86 | 7.5 | 1.9 |
| Dooly | 26.3 | 2 238 | 13 | 115 | 61.9 | 3.8 | 42 | 303 | 151.4 | 7.3 | 2 | D | D | D |
| Dougherty | 158.8 | 1 673 | 148 | 2 086 | 1 175.7 | 81.2 | 538 | 6 934 | 1 543.7 | 136.4 | 146 | 654 | 87.9 | 17.3 |
| Douglas | 27.4 | 243 | 114 | 1 552 | 929.2 | 69.7 | 447 | 8 396 | 2 055.8 | 192.2 | 135 | 553 | 78.5 | 16.0 |
| Early | 123.9 | 10 277 | 16 | 68 | 131.9 | 2.1 | 59 | 401 | 75.8 | 6.3 | 8 | 22 | 1.8 | 0.4 |
| Echols | 6.3 | 1 477 | 1 | D | D | D | 2 | D | D | D | 1 | D | D | D |

1. Merchant wholesalers, except manufacturers' sales branches and offices.  2. Employer establishments.

# Table B. States and Counties — Professional Services, Manufacturing, and Accommodation and Food Services

| STATE County | Professional, scientific, and technical services,[1] 2007 | | | | Manufacturing, 2007 | | | | Accommodation and food services, 2007 | | | |
|---|---|---|---|---|---|---|---|---|---|---|---|---|
| | Number of establishments | Number of employees | Receipts (mil dol) | Annual payroll (mil dol) | Number of establishments | Number of employees | Receipts (mil dol) | Annual payroll (mil dol) | Number of establishments | Number of employees | Sales (mil dol) | Annual payroll (mil dol) |
| | 147 | 148 | 149 | 150 | 151 | 152 | 153 | 154 | 155 | 156 | 157 | 158 |
| FLORIDA—Cont'd | | | | | | | | | | | | |
| Putnam | 100 | D | D | D | 40 | 2 163 | 982.6 | 91.3 | 96 | 1 103 | 48.9 | 11.5 |
| St. Johns | 724 | D | D | D | 104 | 2 074 | 533.3 | 81.9 | 442 | 9 172 | 507.6 | 153.6 |
| St. Lucie | 503 | D | D | D | 141 | 2 864 | 916.5 | 113.2 | 336 | 6 503 | 268.3 | 76.3 |
| Santa Rosa | 264 | D | D | D | 55 | 558 | 74.9 | 17.6 | 184 | 3 385 | 135.1 | 36.4 |
| Sarasota | 1 768 | D | D | D | 333 | 7 786 | 1 366.7 | 328.9 | 806 | 16 412 | 844.4 | 251.9 |
| Seminole | 1 944 | D | D | D | 400 | 7 482 | 1 634.7 | 296.1 | 804 | 16 975 | 764.1 | 226.1 |
| Sumter | 99 | D | D | D | 29 | 889 | 367.9 | 33.5 | 95 | 2 367 | 79.9 | 22.5 |
| Suwannee | 53 | 241 | 18.6 | 5.8 | 23 | D | D | D | 40 | 633 | 31.9 | 7.5 |
| Taylor | 32 | 138 | 9.7 | 3.6 | 23 | 1 428 | 595.5 | 69.1 | 41 | 306 | 20.0 | 4.0 |
| Union | 10 | 30 | 2.0 | 0.8 | NA | NA | NA | NA | 20 | 148 | 10.5 | 1.9 |
| Volusia | 1 353 | D | D | D | 369 | 9 491 | 1 948.6 | 366.2 | 1 006 | 19 359 | 899.2 | 245.8 |
| Wakulla | 47 | D | D | D | 8 | D | D | D | 34 | 489 | 20.1 | 5.1 |
| Walton | 191 | D | D | D | NA | NA | NA | NA | 165 | 4 382 | 312.7 | 93.2 |
| Washington | 30 | 200 | 16.3 | 6.5 | 13 | 676 | D | 16.0 | 36 | 525 | 18.1 | 4.4 |
| GEORGIA | 27 668 | 213 419 | 34 966.0 | 12 689.5 | 8 699 | 411 158 | 144 280.8 | 16 128.1 | 18 640 | 355 423 | 16 976.2 | 4 704.4 |
| Appling | 20 | 63 | 4.8 | 1.4 | 23 | 948 | 347.1 | 39.1 | 31 | 444 | 15.8 | 4.2 |
| Atkinson | 5 | 8 | 0.4 | 0.1 | 12 | 663 | D | D | 6 | 40 | 0.9 | 0.2 |
| Bacon | 12 | 57 | 3.4 | 1.4 | 15 | 817 | 165.4 | 20.7 | 15 | 141 | 5.9 | 1.5 |
| Baker | 2 | D | D | D | NA | NA | NA | NA | 2 | D | D | D |
| Baldwin | 57 | D | D | D | 30 | D | D | D | 85 | 1 781 | 57.9 | 15.8 |
| Banks | 12 | 37 | 3.7 | 1.4 | NA | NA | NA | NA | 46 | 950 | 44.3 | 12.4 |
| Barrow | 89 | 687 | 60.2 | 28.3 | 65 | 2 159 | 768.4 | 77.4 | 73 | 1 711 | 125.1 | 25.0 |
| Bartow | 142 | 858 | 84.3 | 31.1 | 143 | 8 447 | 3 723.6 | 359.4 | 184 | 3 306 | 140.7 | 41.9 |
| Ben Hill | 15 | 178 | 14.6 | 6.9 | 34 | 2 445 | D | D | 38 | 632 | 20.0 | 4.9 |
| Berrien | 13 | 29 | 2.0 | 0.7 | 12 | 1 872 | 415.9 | 57.5 | 21 | 285 | 9.3 | 2.6 |
| Bibb | 405 | D | D | D | 147 | 5 429 | 1 693.9 | 236.8 | 395 | 7 493 | 306.3 | 81.2 |
| Bleckley | 10 | 45 | 2.9 | 1.4 | 6 | D | D | D | 10 | 221 | 6.6 | 1.4 |
| Brantley | 4 | D | D | D | NA | NA | NA | NA | 10 | 94 | 4.3 | 1.1 |
| Brooks | 13 | D | D | D | NA | NA | NA | NA | 10 | D | D | D |
| Bryan | 66 | D | D | D | NA | NA | NA | NA | 65 | 841 | 34.8 | 8.3 |
| Bulloch | 115 | 641 | 64.0 | 20.8 | 48 | 1 904 | 523.8 | 63.9 | 133 | 2 611 | 95.3 | 25.9 |
| Burke | 15 | D | D | D | 15 | 788 | D | 29.4 | 22 | 306 | 11.1 | 2.8 |
| Butts | 28 | 124 | 10.3 | 3.1 | 17 | 726 | 287.0 | 19.9 | 28 | 393 | 18.0 | 4.2 |
| Calhoun | 3 | 5 | 0.5 | 0.1 | NA | NA | NA | NA | 5 | 18 | 0.9 | 0.2 |
| Camden | 76 | 367 | 32.8 | 11.7 | NA | NA | NA | NA | 101 | 1 825 | 71.8 | 19.8 |
| Candler | 16 | 63 | 4.9 | 1.5 | NA | NA | NA | NA | 20 | 394 | 14.7 | 3.2 |
| Carroll | 149 | 846 | 63.8 | 23.3 | 134 | 8 222 | 3 175.6 | 317.4 | 201 | 3 552 | 142.4 | 38.6 |
| Catoosa | 60 | 274 | 25.3 | 10.1 | 56 | 2 563 | 562.1 | 90.2 | 93 | 1 862 | 76.5 | 20.7 |
| Charlton | 6 | 20 | 1.4 | 0.5 | NA | NA | NA | NA | 19 | 222 | 9.8 | 2.6 |
| Chatham | 694 | D | D | D | 185 | 13 508 | D | 786.4 | 807 | 16 946 | 872.9 | 237.9 |
| Chattahoochee | 19 | D | D | D | NA | NA | NA | NA | 4 | 24 | 0.8 | 0.2 |
| Chattooga | 18 | D | D | D | 22 | 3 502 | 629.6 | 84.8 | 34 | D | D | D |
| Cherokee | 711 | 2 756 | 381.9 | 120.5 | 188 | 4 008 | 823.7 | 146.0 | 308 | 6 116 | 246.9 | 71.8 |
| Clarke | 283 | D | D | D | 91 | 6 632 | 1 971.2 | 255.2 | 331 | 7 062 | 293.4 | 80.3 |
| Clay | 1 | D | D | D | NA | NA | NA | NA | 1 | D | D | D |
| Clayton | 256 | 4 947 | 1 113.8 | 358.3 | 127 | 4 254 | 1 604.6 | 179.7 | 414 | 8 175 | 398.9 | 121.1 |
| Clinch | 9 | 28 | 3.2 | 1.1 | 9 | 851 | D | 33.4 | 11 | 89 | 3.3 | 0.7 |
| Cobb | 3 360 | 23 747 | 4 225.6 | 1 464.5 | 540 | 20 106 | 5 651.6 | 1 033.3 | 1 460 | 28 640 | 1 393.5 | 395.8 |
| Coffee | 58 | 269 | 22.7 | 8.3 | 48 | 3 503 | D | D | 67 | 1 313 | 47.1 | 12.7 |
| Colquitt | 63 | 203 | 19.6 | 5.4 | 59 | 3 472 | 599.5 | 90.0 | 59 | 904 | 35.0 | 9.5 |
| Columbia | 208 | D | D | D | 52 | 3 637 | 2 411.2 | 183.2 | 164 | 3 198 | 119.1 | 31.8 |
| Cook | 25 | 102 | 10.3 | 3.4 | 33 | 976 | 360.7 | 32.8 | 38 | 410 | 18.1 | 4.5 |
| Coweta | 202 | 742 | 83.0 | 29.5 | 87 | 5 466 | 2 270.1 | 227.6 | 159 | 3 633 | 146.6 | 42.7 |
| Crawford | 3 | D | D | D | NA | NA | NA | NA | 6 | 59 | 1.4 | 0.3 |
| Crisp | 25 | D | D | D | 29 | 1 405 | 410.8 | 54.4 | 51 | 1 062 | 39.0 | 11.2 |
| Dade | 12 | D | D | D | 15 | 889 | 187.8 | 31.7 | 22 | 412 | 15.8 | 4.2 |
| Dawson | 55 | 221 | 24.4 | 7.8 | NA | NA | NA | NA | 51 | 1 049 | 49.9 | 14.0 |
| Decatur | 38 | 165 | 11.5 | 4.5 | 34 | 2 301 | 1 021.4 | 74.8 | 50 | 600 | 24.1 | 5.7 |
| DeKalb | 2 872 | D | D | D | 511 | 19 626 | 7 489.0 | 821.2 | 1 425 | 22 495 | 1 207.7 | 320.2 |
| Dodge | 24 | 98 | 8.1 | 2.9 | 15 | 762 | 199.1 | 24.5 | 28 | 366 | 12.5 | 3.5 |
| Dooly | 5 | 11 | 1.0 | 0.3 | 12 | 1 118 | 303.8 | 34.4 | 16 | 180 | 6.6 | 1.8 |
| Dougherty | 214 | D | D | D | 78 | 5 380 | D | 260.0 | 216 | 4 151 | 171.0 | 42.7 |
| Douglas | 251 | 1 122 | 115.6 | 38.2 | 116 | 3 656 | 989.9 | 149.6 | 214 | 5 146 | 212.3 | 59.0 |
| Early | 14 | D | D | D | 16 | 912 | 832.3 | 72.6 | 21 | 164 | 6.3 | 1.5 |
| Echols | NA | NA | NA | NA | NA | NA | NA | NA | NA | NA | NA | NA |

1. Establishment subject to federal tax.

# Table B. States and Counties — Health Care and Social Assistance, Other Services, and Federal Funds

| STATE County | Health care and social assistance, 2007 | | | | Other services, 2007 | | | | Federal funds and grants, 2009–2010 Expenditures (mil dol) | | | |
|---|---|---|---|---|---|---|---|---|---|---|---|---|
| | | | | | | | | | | Direct payments for individuals[1] | | |
| | Number of establish-ments | Number of employees | Receipts (mil dol) | Annual payroll (mil dol) | Number of establish-ments | Number of employees | Receipts (mil dol) | Annual payroll (mil dol) | Total | Social Security and government retirement | Medicare | Food Stamps and Supplemental Security Income |
| | 159 | 160 | 161 | 162 | 163 | 164 | 165 | 166 | 167 | 168 | 169 | 170 |
| FLORIDA—Cont'd | | | | | | | | | | | | |
| Putnam | 146 | 2 213 | 203.5 | 70.2 | 99 | 444 | 34.2 | 9.1 | 726.8 | 290.7 | 221.9 | 55.2 |
| St. Johns | 432 | 6 152 | 554.8 | 213.0 | 316 | D | D | D | 1 318.0 | 669.2 | 256.9 | 32.1 |
| St. Lucie | 581 | 8 754 | 998.2 | 331.1 | 355 | 1 685 | 132.8 | 36.8 | 2 010.2 | 1 076.9 | 574.1 | 88.1 |
| Santa Rosa | 232 | 3 352 | 311.7 | 109.1 | 172 | 741 | 54.3 | 17.1 | 1 088.8 | 642.8 | 177.6 | 36.4 |
| Sarasota | 1 451 | 23 670 | 2 493.2 | 935.9 | 907 | 4 837 | 410.7 | 111.7 | 3 891.0 | 2 130.6 | 1 274.0 | 72.0 |
| Seminole | 1 141 | 15 588 | 1 600.4 | 612.0 | 820 | 5 329 | 433.5 | 137.6 | 2 168.5 | 1 041.1 | 531.5 | 98.9 |
| Sumter | 83 | 1 335 | 136.0 | 51.0 | 59 | 245 | 17.9 | 4.5 | 608.2 | 277.5 | 123.1 | 24.3 |
| Suwannee | 64 | 1 372 | 106.0 | 37.5 | 43 | 178 | 15.2 | 4.1 | 368.1 | 163.9 | 106.5 | 19.7 |
| Taylor | 45 | 757 | 60.6 | 27.8 | 29 | 106 | 8.8 | 2.4 | 218.6 | 69.3 | 65.4 | 13.8 |
| Union | 18 | D | D | D | 6 | 22 | 1.3 | 0.4 | 93.2 | 32.1 | 24.1 | 15.2 |
| Volusia | 1 246 | 24 171 | 2 513.9 | 949.0 | 1 028 | 5 409 | 499.6 | 119.4 | 4 310.1 | 2 079.7 | 1 282.7 | 171.3 |
| Wakulla | 20 | D | D | D | 35 | 79 | 9.4 | 2.2 | 149.6 | 72.8 | 34.5 | 8.3 |
| Walton | 100 | 1 534 | 133.4 | 51.6 | 77 | 401 | 42.0 | 10.4 | 689.9 | 178.7 | 85.4 | 15.6 |
| Washington | 42 | 1 042 | 53.0 | 22.9 | 22 | 70 | 5.6 | 1.2 | 269.2 | 87.1 | 88.3 | 13.6 |
| GEORGIA | 20 840 | 419 296 | 43 943.0 | 16 481.2 | 14 588 | 98 047 | 10 386.0 | 2 836.9 | 92 387.1 | 24 719.0 | 10 240.4 | 3 905.7 |
| Appling | 29 | 811 | 43.7 | 19.7 | 29 | 118 | 9.8 | 2.5 | 143.0 | 47.7 | 32.5 | 9.7 |
| Atkinson | 5 | D | D | D | 1 | D | D | D | 69.4 | 19.7 | 16.3 | 4.6 |
| Bacon | 17 | 436 | 35.8 | 11.1 | 18 | D | D | D | 94.2 | 28.6 | 22.6 | 8.3 |
| Baker | 5 | D | D | D | 2 | D | D | D | 31.6 | 4.0 | 5.8 | 2.2 |
| Baldwin | 107 | D | D | D | 58 | 353 | 21.3 | 6.6 | 333.8 | 127.8 | 65.3 | 23.1 |
| Banks | 15 | 130 | 8.9 | 2.7 | 11 | 47 | 5.1 | 1.0 | 72.2 | 36.6 | 14.3 | 4.0 |
| Barrow | 67 | 1 176 | 98.4 | 51.1 | 77 | 294 | 23.0 | 6.6 | 369.8 | 174.5 | 58.1 | 19.1 |
| Bartow | 158 | 2 538 | 286.3 | 94.7 | 115 | 547 | 53.6 | 15.1 | 468.6 | 246.8 | 76.3 | 26.7 |
| Ben Hill | 31 | 601 | 40.9 | 17.8 | 29 | D | D | D | 159.6 | 59.8 | 35.7 | 12.4 |
| Berrien | 25 | D | D | D | 14 | 45 | 3.2 | 0.7 | 143.3 | 61.1 | 33.0 | 9.4 |
| Bibb | 557 | 15 350 | 1 686.3 | 611.8 | 302 | 1 835 | 190.0 | 51.3 | 1 711.4 | 581.9 | 343.7 | 137.1 |
| Bleckley | 21 | 330 | 20.1 | 7.4 | 15 | 40 | 4.7 | 0.9 | 102.7 | 34.4 | 24.7 | 6.0 |
| Brantley | 10 | D | D | D | 14 | 39 | 3.9 | 0.6 | 104.7 | 49.5 | 21.6 | 9.5 |
| Brooks | 20 | D | D | D | 23 | D | D | D | 135.4 | 45.5 | 29.2 | 13.0 |
| Bryan | 39 | D | D | D | 35 | 163 | 9.3 | 2.6 | 3 496.3 | 98.1 | 25.5 | 10.3 |
| Bulloch | 163 | 2 345 | 259.9 | 79.3 | 99 | 479 | 37.6 | 9.8 | 370.0 | 134.6 | 56.6 | 24.7 |
| Burke | 33 | 484 | 32.0 | 13.1 | 20 | 57 | 3.3 | 0.8 | 212.0 | 68.0 | 34.7 | 20.9 |
| Butts | 27 | 700 | 37.8 | 16.3 | 27 | 178 | 30.7 | 3.4 | 157.3 | 80.0 | 30.5 | 7.7 |
| Calhoun | 8 | 262 | 13.4 | 6.9 | 5 | D | D | D | 68.2 | 21.0 | 14.7 | 5.8 |
| Camden | 99 | 889 | 90.2 | 32.3 | 53 | 261 | 17.7 | 5.5 | 587.7 | 161.8 | 28.8 | 14.7 |
| Candler | 15 | 409 | 25.1 | 12.2 | 4 | 22 | 1.9 | 0.4 | 87.6 | 29.1 | 20.2 | 7.1 |
| Carroll | 188 | 4 028 | 431.0 | 169.3 | 124 | 596 | 51.5 | 12.5 | 663.9 | 324.4 | 132.5 | 36.6 |
| Catoosa | 96 | 2 366 | 207.9 | 82.0 | 61 | 359 | 20.9 | 6.5 | 262.7 | 146.1 | 52.0 | 16.4 |
| Charlton | 10 | 218 | 15.5 | 5.9 | 8 | 15 | 1.5 | 0.3 | 287.1 | 32.7 | 18.3 | 6.1 |
| Chatham | 682 | 18 344 | 1 941.2 | 793.5 | 460 | 3 091 | 275.9 | 83.1 | 3 475.4 | 782.4 | 424.3 | 148.9 |
| Chattahoochee | 5 | D | D | D | 7 | 105 | 8.2 | 2.7 | 847.8 | 12.3 | 3.1 | 2.8 |
| Chattooga | 24 | D | D | D | 18 | D | D | D | 193.0 | 84.0 | 46.8 | 11.3 |
| Cherokee | 362 | 3 977 | 378.5 | 141.6 | 327 | 1 341 | 106.2 | 33.0 | 580.8 | 351.4 | 94.2 | 18.5 |
| Clarke | 394 | 8 593 | 871.8 | 372.4 | 209 | 1 635 | 186.6 | 31.3 | 908.7 | 251.3 | 103.2 | 45.2 |
| Clay | 7 | 99 | 3.6 | 1.6 | 2 | D | D | D | 49.5 | 9.1 | 5.3 | 4.0 |
| Clayton | 405 | 7 206 | 763.0 | 298.9 | 293 | 1 549 | 133.4 | 38.7 | 1 277.7 | 598.0 | 213.7 | 114.4 |
| Clinch | 11 | 158 | 13.2 | 4.3 | 7 | 20 | 1.4 | 0.4 | 66.2 | 19.7 | 17.6 | 5.9 |
| Cobb | 1 567 | 29 429 | 3 293.2 | 1 282.3 | 1 259 | 13 391 | 902.7 | 459.0 | 6 730.9 | 1 587.2 | 486.3 | 113.6 |
| Coffee | 95 | D | D | D | 57 | D | D | D | 282.9 | 97.9 | 57.7 | 23.9 |
| Colquitt | 97 | 2 018 | 153.0 | 59.9 | 60 | 326 | 23.7 | 7.7 | 378.0 | 129.5 | 71.9 | 33.9 |
| Columbia | 187 | 2 303 | 172.5 | 75.1 | 148 | 920 | 62.3 | 19.0 | 1 854.8 | 308.6 | 56.7 | 16.8 |
| Cook | 31 | 437 | 30.1 | 10.8 | 13 | 50 | 3.1 | 0.9 | 120.9 | 47.0 | 26.7 | 9.6 |
| Coweta | 160 | 2 909 | 277.0 | 113.6 | 143 | 553 | 51.2 | 14.5 | 576.1 | 330.8 | 102.5 | 28.5 |
| Crawford | 9 | D | D | D | 11 | 28 | 1.8 | 0.6 | 56.5 | 25.9 | 12.3 | 5.5 |
| Crisp | 58 | 1 212 | 96.1 | 34.8 | 29 | D | D | D | 213.5 | 65.1 | 44.7 | 21.7 |
| Dade | 14 | D | D | D | 13 | D | D | D | 106.6 | 54.2 | 23.5 | 5.8 |
| Dawson | 32 | 252 | 21.6 | 9.4 | 40 | 159 | 15.8 | 3.9 | 107.5 | 65.3 | 17.1 | 4.4 |
| Decatur | 60 | 1 010 | 71.2 | 31.8 | 41 | 227 | 11.1 | 3.5 | 267.6 | 74.6 | 40.2 | 23.3 |
| DeKalb | 1 747 | 38 838 | 4 338.3 | 1 602.9 | 1 072 | 7 368 | 837.2 | 238.7 | 5 146.4 | 1 107.9 | 741.8 | 273.7 |
| Dodge | 55 | 1 150 | 69.9 | 28.1 | 20 | 109 | 6.9 | 1.9 | 195.1 | 76.0 | 39.2 | 12.1 |
| Dooly | 12 | 144 | 7.5 | 3.1 | 9 | 30 | 3.2 | 0.6 | 115.6 | 31.8 | 22.4 | 8.2 |
| Dougherty | 307 | 8 298 | 838.5 | 311.6 | 188 | 1 106 | 85.5 | 25.7 | 1 183.2 | 313.9 | 154.4 | 101.8 |
| Douglas | 235 | 4 268 | 392.5 | 151.3 | 212 | 1 027 | 121.2 | 32.5 | 505.5 | 285.8 | 97.2 | 30.7 |
| Early | 23 | 254 | 26.1 | 10.4 | 14 | 34 | 3.2 | 0.8 | 127.0 | 33.0 | 21.9 | 13.1 |
| Echols | 3 | D | D | D | 1 | D | D | D | 15.1 | 3.9 | 2.6 | 1.2 |

1. State totals may include programs not allocated by county.

# Table B. States and Counties — Federal Funds, Residential Construction, and Local Government Finances

| STATE County | Federal funds and grants, 2009–2010 (cont.) | | | | | | | Value of residential construction authorized by building permits, 2011 | | Local government finances, 2007 | | | | |
|---|---|---|---|---|---|---|---|---|---|---|---|---|---|---|
| | Expenditures (mil dol) (cont.) | | | | | | | | | General revenue | | | | |
| | Procurement contract awards | | | Grants[1] | | | | | | | | Taxes | | |
| | | | | | | | | | | | | | Per capita[2] (dollars) | |
| | Salaries and wages | Defense | Other | Medicaid and other health-related | Nutrition and family welfare | Education | Other | New construction ($1,000) | Number of housing units | Total (mil dol) | Inter-govern-mental (mil dol) | Total (mil dol) | Total | Property |
| | 171 | 172 | 173 | 174 | 175 | 176 | 177 | 178 | 179 | 180 | 181 | 182 | 183 | 184 |
| FLORIDA—Cont'd | | | | | | | | | | | | | | |
| Putnam | 10.2 | 2.7 | 3.3 | 84.6 | 17.3 | 12.5 | 8.2 | 5 213 | 36 | 424.7 | 166.8 | 197.8 | 2 680 | 2 486 |
| St. Johns | 147.0 | 51.4 | 49.6 | 61.7 | 15.6 | 6.6 | 13.9 | 361 202 | 1 491 | 706.5 | 182.6 | 334.3 | 1 906 | 1 729 |
| St. Lucie | 58.8 | 1.7 | 12.4 | 87.1 | 30.2 | 15.3 | 21.0 | 49 941 | 315 | 1 305.2 | 387.7 | 525.8 | 2 015 | 1 652 |
| Santa Rosa | 58.9 | 49.8 | 9.5 | 59.3 | 21.6 | 7.4 | 5.3 | 102 900 | 567 | 416.8 | 206.5 | 129.6 | 881 | 763 |
| Sarasota | 128.7 | 11.6 | 20.4 | 89.7 | 35.7 | 16.3 | 91.3 | 216 935 | 744 | 2 157.0 | 280.9 | 912.6 | 2 453 | 1 888 |
| Seminole | 126.0 | 56.4 | 29.3 | 124.2 | 42.4 | 19.5 | 31.0 | 185 400 | 1 120 | 1 430.6 | 535.1 | 602.5 | 1 471 | 1 075 |
| Sumter | 93.1 | 0.9 | 36.8 | 35.5 | 7.9 | 3.3 | 2.9 | 669 081 | 2 655 | 230.4 | 41.0 | 80.2 | 1 110 | 843 |
| Suwannee | 13.8 | 0.0 | 1.7 | 45.6 | 7.0 | 3.5 | 0.5 | 5 332 | 28 | 160.3 | 94.3 | 45.2 | 1 144 | 887 |
| Taylor | 3.1 | 18.3 | 1.3 | 33.2 | 6.4 | 2.4 | 2.8 | 2 067 | 21 | 70.3 | 33.0 | 25.3 | 1 281 | 1 006 |
| Union | 1.7 | 0.0 | 0.4 | 14.9 | 2.3 | 0.7 | 0.7 | 844 | 9 | 37.5 | 27.3 | 5.2 | 345 | 231 |
| Volusia | 119.4 | 115.2 | 49.7 | 230.3 | 58.2 | 31.4 | 57.5 | 186 655 | 1 024 | 2 373.1 | 574.3 | 864.5 | 1 728 | 1 379 |
| Wakulla | 6.4 | 0.3 | 3.8 | 14.5 | 4.1 | 1.9 | 0.9 | 6 200 | 47 | 83.5 | 44.5 | 25.8 | 866 | 693 |
| Walton | 343.7 | 1.8 | 1.5 | 44.4 | 7.7 | 2.9 | 4.2 | 199 050 | 552 | 262.8 | 60.4 | 161.9 | 3 061 | 2 492 |
| Washington | 6.3 | 0.0 | 6.1 | 53.8 | 4.6 | 3.3 | 0.7 | 2 855 | 23 | 81.0 | 52.3 | 17.2 | 752 | 619 |
| GEORGIA | 17 372.0 | 8 377.5 | 4 083.2 | 8 036.6 | 2 202.4 | 1 977.0 | 4 534.7 | 2 760 775 | 18 493 | X | X | X | X | X |
| Appling | 3.9 | 0.2 | 1.7 | 34.8 | 5.0 | 1.7 | 0.7 | 222 | 2 | 85.1 | 24.2 | 27.6 | 1 539 | 926 |
| Atkinson | 1.9 | 0.0 | 0.4 | 19.1 | 3.0 | 0.8 | 0.0 | 900 | 4 | 25.0 | 13.7 | 6.4 | 780 | 437 |
| Bacon | 1.6 | 2.8 | 0.3 | 17.8 | 3.6 | 1.1 | 1.0 | 0 | 0 | 30.2 | 15.8 | 10.7 | 1 018 | 559 |
| Baker | 0.5 | 0.3 | 0.1 | 9.5 | 1.2 | 0.5 | 0.0 | 0 | 0 | 9.8 | 4.7 | 4.3 | 1 139 | 873 |
| Baldwin | 21.9 | 0.0 | 1.2 | 47.5 | 11.1 | 4.3 | 8.1 | 6 290 | 82 | 187.4 | 55.2 | 45.1 | 980 | 559 |
| Banks | 1.5 | 0.0 | 0.3 | 12.4 | 2.2 | 0.8 | 0.0 | 125 | 1 | 43.6 | 15.0 | 22.2 | 1 342 | 658 |
| Barrow | 57.2 | 10.8 | 2.1 | 33.8 | 6.9 | 3.2 | 0.8 | 8 948 | 119 | 176.7 | 65.2 | 80.9 | 1 205 | 690 |
| Bartow | 17.9 | 16.6 | 16.1 | 37.9 | 18.5 | 6.1 | 0.9 | 13 820 | 77 | 340.1 | 116.5 | 158.8 | 1 710 | 868 |
| Ben Hill | 2.6 | 0.2 | 1.2 | 34.8 | 5.0 | 1.6 | 0.7 | 1 392 | 16 | 81.0 | 26.1 | 20.7 | 1 174 | 631 |
| Berrien | 2.9 | 0.0 | 0.6 | 22.4 | 4.0 | 1.0 | 0.7 | 5 580 | 31 | 45.6 | 22.8 | 17.7 | 1 058 | 632 |
| Bibb | 167.9 | 11.9 | 44.5 | 234.9 | 40.8 | 22.2 | 38.8 | 24 118 | 308 | 554.3 | 201.2 | 244.8 | 1 582 | 867 |
| Bleckley | 1.9 | 0.0 | 0.5 | 18.1 | 2.3 | 2.3 | 0.2 | 1 253 | 10 | 34.1 | 19.5 | 9.8 | 797 | 485 |
| Brantley | 2.6 | 0.0 | 0.8 | 13.4 | 3.3 | 1.9 | 0.2 | 1 630 | 17 | 41.5 | 24.3 | 13.8 | 893 | 491 |
| Brooks | 2.1 | 0.0 | 0.6 | 30.7 | 5.6 | 2.0 | 0.8 | 3 532 | 24 | 49.2 | 19.1 | 15.0 | 920 | 637 |
| Bryan | 2 922.3 | 411.6 | 2.1 | 15.6 | 4.7 | 1.5 | 0.1 | 64 099 | 434 | 91.2 | 36.4 | 41.9 | 1 391 | 802 |
| Bulloch | 25.0 | 1.4 | 2.3 | 51.3 | 11.5 | 5.6 | 3.4 | 43 436 | 526 | 190.9 | 74.7 | 70.8 | 1 069 | 477 |
| Burke | 13.8 | 1.9 | 1.3 | 51.1 | 7.5 | 2.9 | 0.8 | 2 764 | 23 | 108.9 | 26.4 | 43.6 | 1 915 | 1 518 |
| Butts | 6.5 | 0.4 | 0.9 | 20.9 | 8.1 | 1.4 | 0.2 | 464 | 5 | 75.3 | 25.4 | 36.6 | 1 541 | 901 |
| Calhoun | 1.4 | 0.0 | 0.3 | 19.3 | 2.0 | 0.7 | -1.0 | 80 | 1 | 26.3 | 10.2 | 5.7 | 935 | 606 |
| Camden | 213.6 | 125.0 | 4.7 | 15.7 | 8.7 | 8.0 | 0.5 | 13 571 | 90 | 163.6 | 70.0 | 63.9 | 1 313 | 802 |
| Candler | 4.2 | 0.0 | 0.4 | 18.6 | 3.2 | 1.0 | 0.2 | 147 | 3 | 44.6 | 15.3 | 11.8 | 1 114 | 604 |
| Carroll | 21.6 | 14.1 | 4.2 | 70.3 | 14.4 | 7.9 | 8.1 | 15 261 | 204 | 297.7 | 123.7 | 118.1 | 1 055 | 521 |
| Catoosa | 6.9 | 0.6 | 2.4 | 23.1 | 8.8 | 3.5 | 0.2 | 14 168 | 84 | 156.2 | 70.3 | 62.1 | 997 | 479 |
| Charlton | 2.9 | 0.0 | 209.8 | 12.1 | 3.2 | 1.7 | 0.0 | 1 614 | 9 | 44.4 | 16.3 | 16.3 | 1 536 | 1 121 |
| Chatham | 1 181.0 | 324.2 | 29.8 | 256.6 | 65.2 | 29.6 | 48.2 | 109 337 | 1 057 | 1 573.2 | 251.8 | 552.1 | 2 222 | 1 376 |
| Chattahoochee | 0.8 | 812.5 | 8.0 | 4.6 | 1.1 | 1.1 | 0.2 | 466 | 3 | 10.6 | 6.7 | 2.6 | 272 | 117 |
| Chattooga | 3.2 | 0.0 | 0.9 | 32.8 | 6.1 | 2.1 | 3.2 | 168 | 2 | 63.7 | 33.1 | 19.9 | 742 | 393 |
| Cherokee | 29.9 | 7.4 | 10.7 | 34.1 | 15.1 | 5.7 | 1.4 | 97 832 | 439 | 567.9 | 184.3 | 270.2 | 1 322 | 991 |
| Clarke | 116.6 | 5.4 | 31.3 | 154.2 | 26.8 | 15.6 | 109.1 | 20 420 | 171 | 739.6 | 115.6 | 143.5 | 1 258 | 890 |
| Clay | 2.0 | 13.9 | 0.2 | 11.1 | 1.3 | 0.3 | 0.1 | 1 210 | 9 | 10.7 | 5.0 | 4.2 | 1 303 | 835 |
| Clayton | 111.7 | 47.9 | 12.8 | 63.3 | 32.5 | 24.2 | 24.0 | 15 905 | 106 | 952.9 | 336.7 | 458.1 | 1 683 | 937 |
| Clinch | 1.7 | 1.5 | 0.4 | 13.7 | 2.6 | 0.8 | 0.1 | 0 | 0 | 35.0 | 11.5 | 9.1 | 1 303 | 888 |
| Cobb | 249.9 | 3 623.6 | 259.2 | 108.9 | 72.1 | 34.5 | 62.9 | 331 300 | 1 758 | 2 215.9 | 678.0 | 1 146.8 | 1 657 | 1 141 |
| Coffee | 17.3 | 0.0 | 1.5 | 50.0 | 10.1 | 3.9 | 0.8 | 4 845 | 40 | 129.0 | 71.3 | 41.9 | 1 046 | 505 |
| Colquitt | 9.9 | 1.7 | 1.8 | 67.6 | 28.6 | 4.2 | 6.3 | 10 953 | 66 | 207.1 | 69.7 | 43.1 | 962 | 504 |
| Columbia | 1 402.0 | 1.4 | 3.9 | 26.3 | 10.4 | 3.4 | 13.0 | 190 027 | 1 265 | 307.9 | 115.7 | 141.7 | 1 299 | 745 |
| Cook | 2.4 | 0.0 | 0.6 | 23.3 | 4.5 | 2.8 | 0.1 | 3 623 | 21 | 50.0 | 24.0 | 17.3 | 1 052 | 567 |
| Coweta | 33.1 | 1.7 | 6.1 | 49.3 | 12.0 | 4.8 | 1.6 | 98 054 | 329 | 292.1 | 120.2 | 136.4 | 1 147 | 604 |
| Crawford | 0.8 | 0.0 | 0.2 | 9.3 | 1.6 | 1.0 | -1.1 | 2 582 | 14 | 27.6 | 14.2 | 9.6 | 770 | 600 |
| Crisp | 15.7 | 0.0 | 0.9 | 47.2 | 7.0 | 3.6 | 0.7 | 1 845 | 15 | 150.1 | 38.7 | 34.0 | 1 537 | 736 |
| Dade | 2.2 | 0.0 | 0.7 | 16.0 | 2.9 | 0.9 | 0.0 | 85 | 1 | 35.8 | 16.2 | 15.8 | 983 | 445 |
| Dawson | 4.8 | 0.9 | 1.1 | 10.6 | 2.4 | 0.4 | 0.0 | 9 609 | 37 | 72.7 | 17.2 | 46.9 | 2 183 | 1 220 |
| Decatur | 19.2 | 1.9 | 4.4 | 46.9 | 8.4 | 3.9 | 0.6 | 3 521 | 27 | 169.4 | 53.7 | 31.9 | 1 118 | 573 |
| DeKalb | 1 394.9 | 55.3 | 589.1 | 291.0 | 107.3 | 55.5 | 303.5 | 69 871 | 580 | 2 685.0 | 740.3 | 1 070.6 | 1 452 | 1 050 |
| Dodge | 8.8 | 0.5 | 0.7 | 42.0 | 5.9 | 2.3 | 2.9 | 878 | 13 | 100.2 | 31.1 | 15.8 | 789 | 386 |
| Dooly | 3.4 | 0.0 | 0.5 | 29.1 | 5.0 | 1.2 | 2.9 | 0 | 0 | 37.2 | 13.4 | 14.0 | 1 210 | 724 |
| Dougherty | 162.7 | 111.4 | 62.3 | 149.9 | 35.3 | 17.3 | 17.1 | 4 899 | 54 | 372.4 | 164.5 | 136.4 | 1 425 | 856 |
| Douglas | 24.2 | 0.7 | 4.6 | 30.4 | 12.5 | 5.7 | 2.4 | 7 040 | 54 | 431.8 | 149.4 | 203.8 | 1 637 | 887 |
| Early | 3.0 | 0.0 | 0.6 | 33.7 | 4.1 | 1.4 | 7.2 | 1 147 | 7 | 54.6 | 19.2 | 16.1 | 1 358 | 775 |
| Echols | 0.1 | 0.0 | 0.0 | 3.9 | 0.8 | 0.4 | 1.8 | 243 | 3 | 10.1 | 5.3 | 4.0 | 978 | 804 |

1. State totals may include programs not allocated by county.　　2. Based on the resident population estimated as of July 1 of the year shown.

# Table B. States and Counties — **Local Government Finances, Government Employment, and Voting**

| STATE County | Direct general expenditure Total (mil dol) | Per capita[1] (dollars) | Education | Health and hospitals | Police protection | Public welfare | Highways | Debt outstanding Total (mil dol) | Per capita[1] (dollars) | Federal civilian | Federal military | State and local | Demo-cratic | Republi-can | All other |
|---|---|---|---|---|---|---|---|---|---|---|---|---|---|---|---|
| | 185 | 186 | 187 | 188 | 189 | 190 | 191 | 192 | 193 | 194 | 195 | 196 | 197 | 198 | 199 |
| **FLORIDA—Cont'd** | | | | | | | | | | | | | | | |
| Putnam | 388.8 | 5 266 | 39.8 | 1.5 | 3.8 | 0.3 | 5.0 | 171.3 | 2 321 | 127 | 144 | 4 187 | 39.9 | 59.2 | 0.9 |
| St. Johns | 871.6 | 4 968 | 40.3 | 1.6 | 4.4 | 0.8 | 6.0 | 1 605.0 | 9 148 | 577 | 394 | 8 055 | 33.8 | 65.4 | 0.8 |
| St. Lucie | 1 335.9 | 5 119 | 44.1 | 0.7 | 6.3 | 0.7 | 10.7 | 2 238.9 | 8 580 | 752 | 625 | 12 287 | 55.7 | 43.5 | 0.8 |
| Santa Rosa | 403.6 | 2 745 | 57.9 | 1.0 | 7.8 | 0.0 | 4.7 | 98.5 | 670 | 800 | 1 429 | 5 522 | 25.6 | 73.5 | 1.0 |
| Sarasota | 1 904.4 | 5 118 | 29.5 | 25.6 | 5.3 | 0.0 | 6.6 | 1 715.3 | 4 610 | 1 045 | 759 | 12 952 | 49.5 | 49.6 | 0.9 |
| Seminole | 1 396.5 | 3 410 | 52.0 | 0.7 | 7.6 | 0.1 | 8.9 | 762.8 | 1 863 | 1 210 | 831 | 16 096 | 48.2 | 51.0 | 0.7 |
| Sumter | 215.1 | 2 977 | 34.2 | 1.0 | 8.4 | 0.8 | 4.3 | 598.0 | 8 278 | 1 541 | 191 | 2 955 | 36.1 | 63.2 | 0.7 |
| Suwannee | 141.7 | 3 584 | 68.4 | 1.2 | 3.3 | 0.0 | 7.0 | 54.4 | 1 377 | 109 | 82 | 2 531 | 27.8 | 71.0 | 1.2 |
| Taylor | 71.4 | 3 613 | 51.2 | 5.6 | 6.9 | 0.4 | 5.0 | 47.7 | 2 411 | 33 | 44 | 1 654 | 29.9 | 68.9 | 1.1 |
| Union | 36.8 | 2 454 | 54.8 | 2.9 | 3.8 | 0.7 | 11.3 | 2.8 | 184 | 19 | 30 | 2 453 | 24.6 | 74.4 | 1.0 |
| Volusia | 2 294.2 | 4 585 | 36.0 | 21.7 | 6.6 | 0.5 | 3.7 | 3 233.2 | 6 461 | 1 282 | 1 065 | 19 931 | 52.4 | 46.7 | 0.9 |
| Wakulla | 78.4 | 2 637 | 57.7 | 3.5 | 12.4 | 0.1 | 7.7 | 19.8 | 667 | 88 | 60 | 1 846 | 36.9 | 61.7 | 1.3 |
| Walton | 257.0 | 4 860 | 30.3 | 3.7 | 11.6 | 0.6 | 13.2 | 131.2 | 2 482 | 158 | 141 | 2 936 | 26.5 | 72.3 | 1.1 |
| Washington | 77.9 | 3 405 | 66.7 | 0.7 | 6.3 | 0.0 | 7.8 | 15.6 | 680 | 38 | 49 | 2 145 | 25.7 | 73.5 | 0.8 |
| **GEORGIA** | X | X | X | X | X | X | X | X | X | 104 540 | 102 282 | 575 590 | 47.0 | 52.2 | 0.8 |
| Appling | 91.2 | 5 081 | 37.6 | 33.7 | 2.8 | 1.5 | 4.9 | 36.4 | 2 027 | 47 | 55 | 1 471 | 26.4 | 72.7 | 0.9 |
| Atkinson | 26.0 | 3 159 | 58.4 | 1.1 | 3.8 | 1.3 | 4.1 | 6.1 | 742 | 23 | 25 | 386 | 32.3 | 66.8 | 0.9 |
| Bacon | 30.2 | 2 872 | 57.7 | 1.1 | 4.0 | 0.9 | 7.9 | 4.3 | 411 | 21 | 34 | 572 | 20.7 | 78.4 | 0.8 |
| Baker | 9.5 | 2 517 | 66.0 | 3.5 | 4.5 | 0.7 | 10.4 | 0.7 | 196 | 0 | 0 | 126 | 50.1 | 49.1 | 0.8 |
| Baldwin | 176.6 | 3 835 | 30.6 | 41.7 | 3.7 | 0.1 | 3.1 | 113.8 | 2 470 | 68 | 150 | 6 068 | 51.9 | 47.3 | 0.8 |
| Banks | 47.3 | 2 859 | 70.4 | 2.2 | 3.6 | 0.1 | 4.2 | 51.1 | 3 084 | 15 | 55 | 849 | 16.5 | 82.1 | 1.5 |
| Barrow | 201.1 | 2 995 | 64.2 | 2.2 | 6.2 | 0.4 | 2.9 | 260.8 | 3 885 | 137 | 211 | 2 810 | 27.1 | 71.7 | 1.2 |
| Bartow | 329.8 | 3 553 | 57.3 | 1.3 | 7.0 | 0.3 | 5.1 | 385.6 | 4 153 | 189 | 303 | 4 866 | 26.8 | 72.0 | 1.3 |
| Ben Hill | 81.7 | 4 631 | 38.9 | 28.4 | 4.1 | 0.4 | 3.8 | 17.3 | 980 | 27 | 53 | 1 459 | 42.9 | 56.6 | 0.5 |
| Berrien | 44.7 | 2 674 | 62.9 | 2.4 | 4.5 | 0.2 | 8.2 | 26.0 | 1 557 | 33 | 58 | 907 | 22.8 | 76.0 | 1.2 |
| Bibb | 563.4 | 3 641 | 45.8 | 5.5 | 7.9 | 0.5 | 3.4 | 551.4 | 3 564 | 1 094 | 569 | 9 788 | 58.7 | 40.7 | 0.5 |
| Bleckley | 33.2 | 2 696 | 62.7 | 1.2 | 8.4 | 0.9 | 5.6 | 3.7 | 300 | 28 | 40 | 1 190 | 27.2 | 72.1 | 0.7 |
| Brantley | 38.9 | 2 522 | 74.2 | 1.8 | 3.0 | 0.4 | 6.2 | 11.9 | 768 | 26 | 85 | 794 | 17.8 | 80.9 | 1.2 |
| Brooks | 49.9 | 3 051 | 46.6 | 18.4 | 4.7 | 0.2 | 7.5 | 12.3 | 752 | 29 | 48 | 683 | 43.0 | 56.6 | 0.4 |
| Bryan | 89.6 | 2 975 | 60.1 | 2.0 | 7.8 | 0.7 | 6.1 | 27.1 | 898 | 193 | 95 | 1 443 | 28.3 | 70.9 | 0.8 |
| Bulloch | 207.3 | 3 132 | 53.8 | 9.7 | 6.2 | 0.0 | 5.2 | 41.0 | 620 | 132 | 227 | 7 010 | 40.1 | 59.3 | 0.7 |
| Burke | 111.7 | 4 908 | 43.4 | 0.7 | 3.3 | 0.4 | 5.2 | 721.7 | 31 720 | 47 | 71 | 1 479 | 54.4 | 45.1 | 0.5 |
| Butts | 71.7 | 3 019 | 52.4 | 1.1 | 6.2 | 0.2 | 5.3 | 78.8 | 3 315 | 48 | 71 | 1 603 | 33.7 | 65.4 | 0.9 |
| Calhoun | 25.1 | 4 114 | 43.6 | 32.6 | 3.6 | 0.8 | 4.4 | 2.5 | 405 | 21 | 20 | 767 | 60.7 | 39.0 | 0.3 |
| Camden | 167.2 | 3 435 | 53.8 | 2.8 | 6.2 | 0.2 | 6.7 | 30.5 | 625 | 2 290 | 4 290 | 2 370 | 37.9 | 61.5 | 0.6 |
| Candler | 43.5 | 4 121 | 40.2 | 30.3 | 3.6 | 0.1 | 3.8 | 12.1 | 1 149 | 22 | 34 | 700 | 34.4 | 65.0 | 0.7 |
| Carroll | 305.8 | 2 731 | 61.0 | 0.6 | 6.1 | 0.1 | 2.7 | 425.9 | 3 804 | 203 | 336 | 7 732 | 33.0 | 65.9 | 1.2 |
| Catoosa | 157.4 | 2 529 | 77.9 | 0.7 | 4.0 | 0.6 | 1.7 | 136.2 | 2 188 | 92 | 194 | 2 565 | 24.6 | 74.4 | 1.0 |
| Charlton | 40.2 | 3 794 | 44.7 | 22.9 | 5.2 | 0.1 | 9.0 | 5.9 | 556 | 46 | 40 | 557 | 32.5 | 66.9 | 0.6 |
| Chatham | 1 581.2 | 6 364 | 20.5 | 34.5 | 5.8 | 0.2 | 4.0 | 1 231.6 | 4 957 | 2 947 | 7 169 | 15 703 | 56.9 | 42.5 | 0.6 |
| Chattahoochee | 11.8 | 1 253 | 71.6 | 1.5 | 4.1 | 5.2 | 3.3 | 5.7 | 604 | 102 | 16 783 | 292 | 50.2 | 49.1 | 0.7 |
| Chattooga | 66.5 | 2 480 | 62.1 | 1.3 | 5.1 | 0.2 | 4.3 | 24.2 | 904 | 34 | 78 | 1 451 | 31.3 | 67.1 | 1.7 |
| Cherokee | 573.7 | 2 807 | 66.7 | 1.4 | 4.1 | 0.4 | 5.5 | 827.3 | 4 048 | 282 | 658 | 7 534 | 23.8 | 74.9 | 1.2 |
| Clarke | 724.0 | 6 347 | 21.2 | 54.4 | 3.1 | 0.1 | 1.7 | 345.0 | 3 025 | 1 229 | 459 | 22 768 | 65.0 | 33.7 | 1.3 |
| Clay | 10.6 | 3 320 | 48.3 | 4.1 | 4.7 | 1.6 | 10.5 | 2.5 | 792 | 45 | 0 | 222 | 61.0 | 38.8 | 0.2 |
| Clayton | 881.9 | 3 240 | 57.6 | 3.2 | 6.7 | 0.6 | 4.5 | 452.4 | 1 662 | 1 141 | 811 | 13 940 | 83.0 | 16.6 | 0.4 |
| Clinch | 37.9 | 5 414 | 37.0 | 43.9 | 2.8 | 0.2 | 2.9 | 29.3 | 4 193 | 17 | 20 | 493 | 36.7 | 62.2 | 1.1 |
| Cobb | 2 127.6 | 3 075 | 55.3 | 2.1 | 6.6 | 0.7 | 4.5 | 1 230.8 | 1 779 | 2 388 | 2 687 | 32 067 | 44.8 | 54.2 | 1.0 |
| Coffee | 125.3 | 3 127 | 66.4 | 0.4 | 4.7 | 0.1 | 6.4 | 28.6 | 713 | 100 | 129 | 2 766 | 35.0 | 64.5 | 0.5 |
| Colquitt | 209.0 | 4 665 | 40.8 | 32.6 | 3.0 | 0.1 | 4.1 | 60.4 | 1 348 | 133 | 138 | 3 526 | 30.8 | 68.4 | 0.8 |
| Columbia | 290.5 | 2 662 | 68.4 | 0.5 | 5.4 | 0.3 | 3.9 | 281.4 | 2 580 | 230 | 386 | 4 811 | 28.4 | 71.0 | 0.6 |
| Cook | 49.7 | 3 024 | 57.2 | 1.3 | 6.6 | 0.4 | 7.2 | 39.4 | 2 399 | 31 | 52 | 964 | 35.2 | 64.1 | 0.8 |
| Coweta | 296.4 | 2 492 | 70.3 | 0.5 | 4.8 | 0.1 | 4.0 | 221.7 | 1 864 | 233 | 391 | 5 003 | 29.0 | 70.2 | 0.9 |
| Crawford | 25.3 | 2 025 | 72.4 | 2.0 | 5.8 | 0.2 | 4.0 | 4.2 | 340 | 10 | 38 | 438 | 35.0 | 64.1 | 1.0 |
| Crisp | 142.4 | 6 435 | 31.0 | 44.7 | 4.0 | 0.2 | 2.8 | 26.3 | 1 188 | 55 | 71 | 1 367 | 40.9 | 58.6 | 0.5 |
| Dade | 34.0 | 2 114 | 66.5 | 0.8 | 6.0 | 0.5 | 2.5 | 16.4 | 1 017 | 22 | 50 | 598 | 25.2 | 73.4 | 1.5 |
| Dawson | 77.1 | 3 589 | 55.4 | 2.9 | 4.4 | 1.1 | 3.5 | 68.6 | 3 192 | 49 | 68 | 1 173 | 16.4 | 82.6 | 1.0 |
| Decatur | 139.3 | 4 881 | 41.5 | 28.2 | 4.3 | 0.1 | 4.9 | 36.2 | 1 267 | 59 | 83 | 2 725 | 42.6 | 56.8 | 0.6 |
| DeKalb | 2 893.2 | 3 925 | 39.7 | 25.9 | 4.8 | 0.4 | 2.0 | 2 647.4 | 3 592 | 16 760 | 2 393 | 32 766 | 79.0 | 20.3 | 0.7 |
| Dodge | 82.1 | 4 096 | 43.8 | 36.6 | 2.9 | 0.2 | 3.8 | 30.1 | 1 504 | 44 | 66 | 2 050 | 31.6 | 67.5 | 0.9 |
| Dooly | 39.0 | 3 362 | 62.2 | 1.8 | 6.1 | 0.6 | 6.8 | 14.6 | 1 255 | 51 | 44 | 778 | 51.4 | 47.9 | 0.7 |
| Dougherty | 361.3 | 3 775 | 49.2 | 6.9 | 5.7 | 0.1 | 3.1 | 252.8 | 2 642 | 3 240 | 700 | 7 371 | 67.3 | 32.3 | 0.4 |
| Douglas | 422.5 | 3 394 | 59.0 | 1.4 | 4.6 | 0.5 | 5.9 | 532.3 | 4 276 | 168 | 403 | 5 580 | 50.5 | 48.7 | 0.8 |
| Early | 53.4 | 4 509 | 46.3 | 24.6 | 7.5 | 0.2 | 4.9 | 5.5 | 460 | 45 | 32 | 1 125 | 48.8 | 50.8 | 0.4 |
| Echols | 9.0 | 2 192 | 74.5 | 0.3 | 4.8 | 0.4 | 4.0 | 0.1 | 27 | 0 | 12 | 212 | 16.9 | 82.6 | 0.4 |

1. Based on the resident population estimated as of July 1 of the year shown.    2. © 2013 Election Data Services, Inc. All rights reserved.

| STATE/ County code | CBSA code[1] | County type[2] | STATE County | Land area,[3] (sq km) 2010 | Population 2012 | | | Race alone or in combination, not Hispanic or Latino (percent) | | | | Percent Hispanic or Latino[4] | Age (percent) | | | | | |
|---|---|---|---|---|---|---|---|---|---|---|---|---|---|---|---|---|---|---|
| | | | | | Total persons | Rank | Per square kilometer | White | Black | American Indian, Alaska Native | Asian and Pacific Islander | | Under 5 years | 5 to 17 years | 18 to 24 years | 25 to 34 years | 35 to 44 years | 45 to 54 years |
| | | | | 1 | 2 | 3 | 4 | 5 | 6 | 7 | 8 | 9 | 10 | 11 | 12 | 13 | 14 | 15 |
| | | | GEORGIA—Cont'd | | | | | | | | | | | | | | | |
| 13 103 | 42340 | 2 | Effingham | 1 237 | 53 293 | 933 | 43.1 | 81.7 | 14.7 | 0.9 | 1.3 | 3.1 | 6.7 | 21.1 | 8.5 | 13.1 | 14.6 | 15.4 |
| 13 105 | ... | 6 | Elbert | 909 | 19 684 | 1 850 | 21.7 | 64.7 | 29.7 | 0.5 | 0.9 | 4.7 | 6.5 | 16.3 | 8.9 | 11.2 | 11.7 | 14.6 |
| 13 107 | ... | 7 | Emanuel | 1 763 | 22 898 | 1 694 | 13.0 | 60.9 | 33.9 | 0.5 | 0.9 | 4.7 | 7.3 | 18.3 | 9.2 | 13.2 | 11.9 | 13.6 |
| 13 109 | ... | 6 | Evans | 474 | 10 689 | 2 381 | 22.6 | 57.0 | 29.9 | 0.5 | 0.8 | 12.7 | 7.4 | 18.1 | 9.7 | 13.4 | 12.4 | 13.8 |
| 13 111 | ... | 8 | Fannin | 1 002 | 23 492 | 1 663 | 23.4 | 96.7 | 0.9 | 1.0 | 0.5 | 2.0 | 4.7 | 13.8 | 6.3 | 8.9 | 10.5 | 15.0 |
| 13 113 | 12060 | 1 | Fayette | 503 | 107 524 | 552 | 213.8 | 68.6 | 21.1 | 0.7 | 4.8 | 6.5 | 4.4 | 20.7 | 7.6 | 7.5 | 12.7 | 18.3 |
| 13 115 | 40660 | 3 | Floyd | 1 321 | 96 177 | 607 | 72.8 | 74.2 | 15.2 | 0.6 | 1.7 | 9.7 | 6.6 | 17.3 | 10.5 | 12.2 | 12.8 | 13.9 |
| 13 117 | 12060 | 1 | Forsyth | 580 | 187 928 | 337 | 324.0 | 80.4 | 3.4 | 0.7 | 7.2 | 9.6 | 7.2 | 22.7 | 6.0 | 10.7 | 18.1 | 16.0 |
| 13 119 | ... | 8 | Franklin | 677 | 21 894 | 1 737 | 32.3 | 86.0 | 9.6 | 0.6 | 0.9 | 4.2 | 6.1 | 16.4 | 9.7 | 10.9 | 12.2 | 14.1 |
| 13 121 | 12060 | 1 | Fulton | 1 364 | 977 773 | 43 | 716.8 | 42.1 | 44.6 | 0.7 | 6.4 | 8.1 | 6.8 | 16.9 | 10.7 | 16.8 | 15.2 | 13.9 |
| 13 123 | ... | 6 | Gilmer | 1 105 | 28 190 | 1 484 | 25.5 | 88.4 | 0.9 | 0.9 | 0.5 | 10.2 | 5.8 | 15.9 | 7.1 | 10.7 | 12.2 | 14.4 |
| 13 125 | ... | 9 | Glascock | 372 | 3 142 | 2 966 | 8.4 | 88.9 | 9.6 | 0.8 | 0.5 | 1.5 | 5.7 | 20.0 | 7.1 | 10.6 | 14.1 | 15.2 |
| 13 127 | 15260 | 3 | Glynn | 1 087 | 81 022 | 682 | 74.5 | 65.7 | 26.9 | 0.6 | 1.8 | 6.5 | 6.7 | 17.2 | 8.6 | 12.1 | 12.1 | 14.3 |
| 13 129 | 15660 | 6 | Gordon | 922 | 55 766 | 905 | 60.5 | 80.2 | 4.8 | 0.7 | 1.4 | 14.2 | 7.3 | 19.4 | 8.8 | 12.9 | 14.2 | 14.0 |
| 13 131 | ... | 6 | Grady | 1 177 | 25 440 | 1 590 | 21.6 | 60.2 | 28.8 | 1.0 | 0.7 | 10.4 | 7.1 | 18.3 | 8.4 | 12.6 | 12.3 | 14.1 |
| 13 133 | ... | 6 | Greene | 1 003 | 16 092 | 2 039 | 16.0 | 56.2 | 37.7 | 0.6 | 0.6 | 5.8 | 5.3 | 15.0 | 6.5 | 10.6 | 9.9 | 12.8 |
| 13 135 | 12060 | 1 | Gwinnett | 1 115 | 842 046 | 63 | 755.2 | 44.9 | 24.4 | 0.6 | 11.5 | 20.5 | 7.5 | 21.2 | 8.7 | 14.2 | 16.2 | 15.1 |
| 13 137 | 18460 | 6 | Habersham | 717 | 43 520 | 1 099 | 60.7 | 80.6 | 4.5 | 0.7 | 2.6 | 12.9 | 6.5 | 17.2 | 8.8 | 12.5 | 12.9 | 13.5 |
| 13 139 | 23580 | 3 | Hall | 1 017 | 185 416 | 340 | 182.3 | 63.6 | 8.0 | 0.6 | 2.2 | 26.8 | 7.7 | 20.0 | 9.4 | 13.4 | 14.0 | 13.3 |
| 13 141 | 33300 | 7 | Hancock | 1 222 | 8 996 | 2 522 | 7.4 | 24.8 | 73.1 | 0.5 | 0.5 | 1.7 | 4.4 | 13.1 | 9.4 | 13.8 | 11.9 | 15.7 |
| 13 143 | 12060 | 1 | Haralson | 731 | 28 400 | 1 473 | 38.9 | 92.4 | 6.0 | 0.9 | 0.8 | 1.4 | 6.3 | 18.4 | 8.6 | 11.6 | 13.7 | 14.4 |
| 13 145 | 17980 | 2 | Harris | 1 201 | 32 550 | 1 373 | 27.1 | 77.9 | 18.1 | 0.9 | 1.4 | 2.9 | 5.2 | 17.7 | 7.7 | 9.3 | 13.8 | 16.9 |
| 13 147 | ... | 6 | Hart | 602 | 25 518 | 1 585 | 42.4 | 76.8 | 19.6 | 0.4 | 1.0 | 3.3 | 5.9 | 16.3 | 7.9 | 10.6 | 12.1 | 14.6 |
| 13 149 | 12060 | 1 | Heard | 767 | 11 633 | 2 321 | 15.2 | 86.4 | 11.4 | 0.8 | 0.8 | 2.1 | 6.0 | 18.9 | 8.7 | 10.4 | 13.7 | 15.5 |
| 13 151 | 12060 | 1 | Henry | 834 | 209 053 | 300 | 250.7 | 53.6 | 37.8 | 0.8 | 3.8 | 6.0 | 6.5 | 21.9 | 8.8 | 11.9 | 16.4 | 15.3 |
| 13 153 | 47580 | 3 | Houston | 973 | 146 136 | 435 | 150.2 | 61.9 | 29.8 | 0.8 | 3.7 | 6.2 | 7.1 | 19.2 | 9.6 | 14.6 | 13.2 | 15.0 |
| 13 155 | 22340 | 7 | Irwin | 918 | 9 600 | 2 463 | 10.5 | 69.1 | 27.6 | 0.3 | 0.9 | 2.8 | 6.4 | 17.0 | 9.0 | 13.0 | 13.4 | 13.6 |
| 13 157 | ... | 6 | Jackson | 880 | 60 571 | 854 | 68.8 | 84.1 | 8.0 | 0.7 | 2.1 | 6.5 | 7.0 | 19.0 | 7.8 | 12.6 | 15.0 | 14.4 |
| 13 159 | 12060 | 1 | Jasper | 954 | 13 630 | 2 207 | 14.3 | 73.0 | 22.8 | 0.7 | 0.7 | 4.1 | 6.4 | 18.2 | 8.0 | 11.7 | 13.3 | 14.7 |
| 13 161 | ... | 7 | Jeff Davis | 857 | 15 156 | 2 096 | 17.7 | 73.2 | 15.4 | 0.5 | 0.7 | 11.1 | 7.9 | 20.1 | 8.5 | 12.5 | 12.7 | 13.3 |
| 13 163 | ... | 6 | Jefferson | 1 364 | 16 432 | 2 016 | 12.0 | 42.3 | 54.3 | 0.4 | 0.6 | 3.3 | 6.7 | 18.3 | 8.9 | 11.6 | 11.9 | 13.7 |
| 13 165 | ... | 6 | Jenkins | 899 | 9 213 | 2 501 | 10.2 | 54.8 | 40.5 | 0.7 | 0.6 | 4.5 | 7.4 | 19.2 | 8.5 | 9.0 | 11.1 | 13.7 |
| 13 167 | 20140 | 9 | Johnson | 785 | 9 897 | 2 451 | 12.6 | 62.7 | 34.9 | 0.5 | 0.6 | 2.1 | 5.3 | 15.4 | 7.8 | 13.5 | 14.1 | 16.3 |
| 13 169 | 31420 | 3 | Jones | 1 020 | 28 577 | 1 465 | 28.0 | 72.8 | 25.4 | 0.6 | 0.9 | 1.3 | 6.0 | 19.4 | 8.1 | 11.4 | 13.7 | 15.3 |
| 13 171 | 12060 | 1 | Lamar | 475 | 18 057 | 1 918 | 38.0 | 66.2 | 31.8 | 0.7 | 0.7 | 2.2 | 5.8 | 15.5 | 14.2 | 10.8 | 11.9 | 14.1 |
| 13 173 | 46660 | 3 | Lanier | 480 | 10 400 | 2 404 | 21.7 | 69.6 | 24.8 | 1.1 | 1.7 | 4.9 | 8.7 | 17.7 | 10.2 | 16.3 | 12.7 | 13.5 |
| 13 175 | 20140 | 6 | Laurens | 2 091 | 48 041 | 1 012 | 23.0 | 60.4 | 36.4 | 0.5 | 1.4 | 2.4 | 6.9 | 18.5 | 8.7 | 12.0 | 12.7 | 13.9 |
| 13 177 | 10500 | 3 | Lee | 921 | 28 746 | 1 456 | 31.2 | 75.2 | 20.5 | 0.6 | 2.7 | 2.2 | 6.4 | 20.8 | 8.4 | 12.8 | 15.7 | 15.2 |
| 13 179 | 25980 | 3 | Liberty | 1 269 | 65 471 | 808 | 51.6 | 46.4 | 42.1 | 1.1 | 3.8 | 10.4 | 10.8 | 19.4 | 14.6 | 17.6 | 11.6 | 11.5 |
| 13 181 | ... | 8 | Lincoln | 545 | 7 737 | 2 624 | 14.2 | 65.3 | 32.8 | 0.8 | 0.7 | 1.4 | 5.0 | 14.8 | 8.3 | 9.1 | 11.5 | 16.4 |
| 13 183 | 25980 | 3 | Long | 1 037 | 16 048 | 2 043 | 15.5 | 61.1 | 26.6 | 1.0 | 2.0 | 12.0 | 8.8 | 21.4 | 10.4 | 16.2 | 13.5 | 13.1 |
| 13 185 | 46660 | 3 | Lowndes | 1 285 | 114 552 | 527 | 89.1 | 56.7 | 36.9 | 0.7 | 2.3 | 5.2 | 7.5 | 16.7 | 18.5 | 14.3 | 11.6 | 11.9 |
| 13 187 | ... | 6 | Lumpkin | 733 | 30 611 | 1 419 | 41.8 | 92.5 | 2.1 | 1.5 | 0.9 | 4.7 | 5.4 | 14.8 | 15.5 | 12.1 | 11.6 | 13.9 |
| 13 189 | 12260 | 2 | McDuffie | 667 | 21 663 | 1 746 | 32.5 | 56.7 | 40.8 | 0.6 | 0.8 | 2.4 | 7.1 | 18.8 | 8.6 | 11.6 | 12.1 | 14.6 |
| 13 191 | 15260 | 3 | McIntosh | 1 099 | 13 839 | 2 183 | 12.6 | 65.8 | 36.4 | 0.7 | 0.6 | 1.6 | 5.3 | 15.1 | 7.9 | 9.3 | 12.5 | 15.5 |
| 13 193 | ... | 6 | Macon | 1 038 | 14 263 | 2 154 | 13.7 | 34.3 | 60.6 | 0.4 | 1.7 | 3.9 | 5.7 | 15.9 | 10.2 | 14.1 | 12.5 | 15.3 |
| 13 195 | 12020 | 3 | Madison | 731 | 27 922 | 1 497 | 38.2 | 85.7 | 9.4 | 0.7 | 1.0 | 4.4 | 6.0 | 18.0 | 8.4 | 11.7 | 13.0 | 15.5 |
| 13 197 | 17980 | 2 | Marion | 948 | 8 711 | 2 545 | 9.2 | 58.9 | 33.4 | 1.0 | 1.2 | 6.7 | 6.5 | 17.1 | 8.8 | 10.5 | 11.3 | 16.9 |
| 13 199 | 12060 | 1 | Meriwether | 1 298 | 21 273 | 1 770 | 16.4 | 58.0 | 39.8 | 0.7 | 0.9 | 1.7 | 6.2 | 17.0 | 8.6 | 11.3 | 11.3 | 14.7 |
| 13 201 | ... | 8 | Miller | 731 | 5 969 | 2 761 | 8.2 | 69.8 | 28.1 | 0.7 | 0.8 | 1.8 | 6.7 | 16.4 | 8.1 | 11.1 | 11.1 | 13.7 |
| 13 205 | ... | 6 | Mitchell | 1 326 | 23 144 | 1 683 | 17.5 | 47.0 | 48.0 | 0.5 | 0.8 | 4.6 | 7.0 | 17.4 | 9.6 | 13.3 | 13.0 | 14.2 |
| 13 207 | 31420 | 3 | Monroe | 1 025 | 26 637 | 1 542 | 26.0 | 72.6 | 24.3 | 0.6 | 1.2 | 2.2 | 5.4 | 16.7 | 8.5 | 11.4 | 12.7 | 16.3 |
| 13 209 | 47080 | 9 | Montgomery | 620 | 8 913 | 2 527 | 14.4 | 67.3 | 27.0 | 0.4 | 0.7 | 5.7 | 6.0 | 16.3 | 12.5 | 12.2 | 12.7 | 14.2 |
| 13 211 | ... | 6 | Morgan | 900 | 17 881 | 1 926 | 19.9 | 72.6 | 24.2 | 0.7 | 1.0 | 2.8 | 5.7 | 18.6 | 7.5 | 9.9 | 12.8 | 15.2 |
| 13 213 | 19140 | 3 | Murray | 892 | 39 392 | 1 186 | 44.2 | 84.5 | 1.6 | 0.6 | 0.6 | 13.6 | 6.8 | 19.6 | 9.0 | 12.4 | 14.5 | 14.6 |
| 13 215 | 17980 | 2 | Muscogee | 560 | 198 413 | 322 | 354.3 | 45.3 | 46.5 | 0.8 | 3.2 | 6.7 | 7.6 | 17.7 | 11.6 | 15.4 | 12.2 | 13.1 |
| 13 217 | 12060 | 1 | Newton | 705 | 101 505 | 577 | 144.0 | 53.4 | 41.5 | 0.6 | 1.4 | 4.8 | 7.2 | 21.0 | 9.1 | 12.4 | 15.3 | 14.0 |
| 13 219 | 12020 | 3 | Oconee | 477 | 33 619 | 1 337 | 70.5 | 86.4 | 6.1 | 0.4 | 3.7 | 4.5 | 5.7 | 21.6 | 7.6 | 9.4 | 14.4 | 16.5 |
| 13 221 | 12020 | 3 | Oglethorpe | 1 137 | 14 618 | 2 131 | 12.9 | 77.3 | 18.8 | 0.8 | 1.0 | 4.0 | 5.6 | 17.7 | 7.9 | 11.4 | 13.6 | 15.9 |
| 13 223 | 12060 | 1 | Paulding | 809 | 144 800 | 438 | 179.0 | 76.1 | 18.1 | 0.9 | 1.5 | 5.3 | 7.4 | 22.0 | 8.2 | 13.3 | 17.4 | 14.7 |
| 13 225 | 22980 | 6 | Peach | 389 | 27 622 | 1 507 | 71.0 | 46.1 | 46.3 | 0.7 | 1.2 | 7.1 | 6.5 | 16.3 | 16.8 | 11.7 | 11.0 | 13.9 |
| 13 227 | 12060 | 1 | Pickens | 601 | 29 268 | 1 441 | 48.7 | 94.8 | 1.8 | 0.9 | 0.7 | 2.9 | 5.7 | 16.1 | 7.3 | 10.5 | 13.2 | 14.5 |
| 13 229 | 48180 | 6 | Pierce | 820 | 18 844 | 1 882 | 23.0 | 84.7 | 10.0 | 0.8 | 0.7 | 5.0 | 6.8 | 19.0 | 7.7 | 12.0 | 13.0 | 14.0 |
| 13 231 | 12060 | 1 | Pike | 560 | 17 810 | 1 929 | 31.8 | 87.0 | 11.6 | 0.8 | 0.8 | 1.2 | 5.6 | 20.8 | 7.8 | 10.4 | 14.8 | 15.6 |
| 13 233 | 16340 | 6 | Polk | 804 | 41 188 | 1 147 | 51.2 | 73.9 | 13.6 | 0.5 | 1.0 | 12.3 | 7.7 | 18.8 | 9.0 | 12.8 | 12.4 | 13.7 |
| 13 235 | ... | 6 | Pulaski | 645 | 11 720 | 2 315 | 18.2 | 62.9 | 32.3 | 0.6 | 1.2 | 3.8 | 5.7 | 15.4 | 8.2 | 12.8 | 13.3 | 15.4 |

1. CBSA = Core Based Statistical Area. See Appendix A for explanation. See Appendix B for list of metropolitan areas with component counties.   2. County type code from the Economic Research Service of USDA Rural-Urban Continuum Codes. See Appendix A for definition.   3. Dry land or land partially or temporarily covered by water.   4. May be of any race.

# Table B. States and Counties — **Population and Households**

| STATE County | Age (percent) (cont.) 55 to 64 years | 65 to 74 years | 75 years and over | Percent female | Total persons 2000 | 2010 | Percent change 2000–2010 | 2010–2012 | Components of change, 2010–2012 Births | Deaths | Net migration | Households, 2010 Number | Percent change, 2000–2010 | Persons per house-hold | Female family house-holder[1] | One per-son |
|---|---|---|---|---|---|---|---|---|---|---|---|---|---|---|---|---|
| | 16 | 17 | 18 | 19 | 20 | 21 | 22 | 23 | 24 | 25 | 26 | 27 | 28 | 29 | 30 | 31 |
| GEORGIA—Cont'd | | | | | | | | | | | | | | | | |
| Effingham | 11.0 | 6.2 | 3.4 | 50.2 | 37 535 | 52 250 | 39.2 | 2.0 | 1 478 | 792 | 355 | 18 092 | 37.6 | 2.85 | 12.7 | 17.3 |
| Elbert | 13.5 | 9.5 | 7.8 | 52.2 | 20 511 | 20 166 | -1.7 | -2.4 | 542 | 522 | -499 | 8 063 | 0.7 | 2.47 | 16.5 | 26.9 |
| Emanuel | 12.4 | 8.2 | 5.9 | 50.9 | 21 837 | 22 598 | 3.5 | 1.3 | 751 | 629 | 140 | 8 430 | 4.8 | 2.57 | 19.1 | 26.5 |
| Evans | 11.1 | 8.1 | 5.9 | 50.5 | 10 495 | 11 000 | 4.8 | -2.8 | 359 | 265 | -411 | 4 033 | 6.7 | 2.63 | 17.4 | 25.9 |
| Fannin | 17.8 | 13.4 | 9.6 | 51.1 | 19 798 | 23 682 | 19.6 | -0.8 | 444 | 617 | -48 | 10 187 | 21.7 | 2.31 | 9.5 | 27.1 |
| Fayette | 14.9 | 8.3 | 5.6 | 51.7 | 91 263 | 106 567 | 16.8 | 0.9 | 1 785 | 1 600 | 810 | 38 167 | 21.1 | 2.78 | 10.3 | 18.1 |
| Floyd | 12.3 | 7.8 | 6.6 | 51.5 | 90 565 | 96 317 | 6.4 | -0.1 | 2 772 | 2 259 | -604 | 35 930 | 5.6 | 2.58 | 14.8 | 26.0 |
| Forsyth | 10.1 | 5.9 | 3.3 | 50.3 | 98 407 | 175 511 | 78.4 | 7.1 | 4 960 | 1 963 | 9 013 | 59 433 | 71.9 | 2.94 | 8.0 | 15.9 |
| Franklin | 13.3 | 9.9 | 7.4 | 50.6 | 20 285 | 22 084 | 8.9 | -0.9 | 615 | 557 | -239 | 8 540 | 8.3 | 2.51 | 11.2 | 26.2 |
| Fulton | 10.6 | 5.3 | 3.9 | 51.1 | 816 006 | 920 581 | 12.8 | 6.2 | 29 745 | 13 879 | 40 490 | 376 377 | 17.2 | 2.36 | 15.7 | 35.4 |
| Gilmer | 15.6 | 11.7 | 6.7 | 49.9 | 23 456 | 28 292 | 20.6 | -0.4 | 699 | 561 | -233 | 11 314 | 24.7 | 2.48 | 8.9 | 24.5 |
| Glascock | 11.9 | 8.0 | 7.2 | 51.5 | 2 556 | 3 082 | 20.6 | 1.9 | 66 | 76 | 54 | 1 162 | 15.7 | 2.58 | 13.4 | 26.6 |
| Glynn | 13.5 | 9.1 | 6.5 | 52.5 | 67 568 | 79 626 | 17.8 | 1.8 | 2 286 | 1 686 | 810 | 31 774 | 16.8 | 2.46 | 16.2 | 27.5 |
| Gordon | 11.5 | 7.3 | 4.6 | 50.2 | 44 104 | 55 186 | 25.1 | 1.1 | 1 663 | 1 033 | -32 | 19 715 | 21.9 | 2.77 | 12.9 | 21.6 |
| Grady | 12.5 | 8.6 | 6.1 | 51.2 | 23 659 | 25 011 | 5.7 | 1.7 | 836 | 527 | 107 | 9 418 | 7.1 | 2.63 | 16.7 | 24.3 |
| Greene | 17.5 | 15.1 | 7.3 | 51.1 | 14 406 | 15 994 | 11.0 | 0.6 | 365 | 426 | 156 | 6 519 | 19.0 | 2.43 | 15.8 | 25.0 |
| Gwinnett | 9.9 | 4.5 | 2.7 | 50.7 | 588 448 | 805 321 | 36.9 | 4.6 | 26 191 | 7 939 | 18 163 | 268 519 | 32.7 | 2.98 | 14.2 | 19.1 |
| Habersham | 12.6 | 9.0 | 6.9 | 52.8 | 35 902 | 43 041 | 19.9 | 1.1 | 1 174 | 895 | 208 | 15 472 | 16.7 | 2.63 | 10.5 | 23.2 |
| Hall | 10.7 | 6.7 | 4.8 | 49.9 | 139 277 | 179 684 | 29.0 | 3.2 | 5 900 | 2 809 | 2 388 | 60 691 | 28.1 | 2.91 | 12.4 | 20.3 |
| Hancock | 15.3 | 9.7 | 6.6 | 44.6 | 10 076 | 9 429 | -6.4 | -4.6 | 202 | 236 | -374 | 3 341 | 3.2 | 2.38 | 23.7 | 31.3 |
| Haralson | 12.3 | 8.7 | 5.9 | 51.2 | 25 690 | 28 780 | 12.0 | -1.3 | 804 | 766 | -422 | 10 757 | 9.5 | 2.64 | 13.3 | 23.2 |
| Harris | 15.7 | 8.8 | 5.0 | 50.1 | 23 695 | 32 024 | 35.2 | 1.6 | 669 | 612 | 439 | 11 823 | 34.0 | 2.67 | 10.3 | 18.5 |
| Hart | 14.4 | 10.4 | 7.8 | 50.6 | 22 997 | 25 213 | 9.6 | 1.2 | 600 | 652 | 320 | 10 121 | 11.1 | 2.43 | 13.6 | 27.4 |
| Heard | 13.0 | 8.5 | 5.3 | 50.2 | 11 012 | 11 834 | 7.5 | -1.7 | 267 | 270 | -207 | 4 400 | 8.8 | 2.66 | 13.6 | 23.8 |
| Henry | 10.4 | 5.5 | 3.2 | 52.0 | 119 341 | 203 922 | 70.9 | 2.5 | 5 720 | 2 724 | 2 085 | 70 255 | 69.8 | 2.89 | 16.4 | 18.5 |
| Houston | 10.8 | 6.0 | 4.4 | 51.3 | 110 765 | 139 900 | 26.3 | 4.5 | 4 584 | 2 357 | 3 878 | 53 051 | 29.7 | 2.61 | 16.2 | 24.0 |
| Irwin | 11.9 | 9.0 | 6.6 | 48.6 | 9 931 | 9 538 | -4.0 | 0.7 | 235 | 254 | 71 | 3 495 | -4.1 | 2.54 | 17.0 | 25.8 |
| Jackson | 11.5 | 8.0 | 4.7 | 50.4 | 41 589 | 60 485 | 45.4 | 1.0 | 1 815 | 1 097 | -776 | 21 343 | 41.7 | 2.80 | 11.3 | 18.7 |
| Jasper | 14.2 | 8.0 | 5.4 | 50.6 | 11 426 | 13 900 | 21.7 | -1.9 | 402 | 285 | -397 | 5 044 | 20.8 | 2.74 | 13.8 | 20.8 |
| Jeff Davis | 11.9 | 8.2 | 4.8 | 50.3 | 12 684 | 15 068 | 18.8 | 0.6 | 503 | 319 | -88 | 5 689 | 17.8 | 2.63 | 15.6 | 24.2 |
| Jefferson | 13.8 | 8.3 | 6.7 | 51.4 | 17 266 | 16 930 | -1.9 | -2.9 | 505 | 483 | -543 | 6 241 | -1.5 | 2.63 | 23.4 | 26.0 |
| Jenkins | 13.8 | 8.5 | 7.0 | 52.4 | 8 575 | 8 340 | -2.7 | 10.5 | 230 | 216 | 830 | 3 192 | -0.7 | 2.59 | 20.3 | 28.7 |
| Johnson | 13.0 | 8.4 | 6.1 | 44.1 | 8 560 | 9 980 | 16.6 | -0.8 | 201 | 217 | -77 | 3 347 | 6.9 | 2.46 | 18.3 | 29.1 |
| Jones | 13.1 | 7.9 | 5.1 | 51.4 | 23 639 | 28 669 | 21.3 | -0.3 | 700 | 569 | -302 | 10 586 | 22.3 | 2.68 | 14.5 | 21.4 |
| Lamar | 13.1 | 8.6 | 5.8 | 52.2 | 15 912 | 18 317 | 15.1 | -1.4 | 475 | 482 | -256 | 6 618 | 15.9 | 2.55 | 15.7 | 25.6 |
| Lanier | 10.6 | 5.9 | 4.4 | 49.3 | 7 241 | 10 078 | 39.2 | 3.2 | 291 | 212 | 237 | 3 608 | 39.1 | 2.72 | 15.6 | 22.3 |
| Laurens | 12.7 | 8.2 | 6.5 | 52.2 | 44 874 | 48 434 | 7.9 | -0.8 | 1 475 | 1 186 | -740 | 18 641 | 9.1 | 2.54 | 18.4 | 26.2 |
| Lee | 12.0 | 5.5 | 3.2 | 49.8 | 24 757 | 28 298 | 14.3 | 1.6 | 823 | 414 | 28 | 9 706 | 17.9 | 2.83 | 13.6 | 16.4 |
| Liberty | 8.2 | 4.3 | 2.1 | 50.5 | 61 610 | 63 453 | 3.0 | 3.2 | 3 248 | 667 | -698 | 22 155 | 14.3 | 2.75 | 21.5 | 20.7 |
| Lincoln | 16.7 | 11.5 | 6.7 | 50.7 | 8 348 | 7 996 | -4.2 | -3.2 | 135 | 188 | -211 | 3 281 | 0.9 | 2.42 | 14.2 | 27.6 |
| Long | 9.6 | 4.1 | 2.9 | 50.2 | 10 304 | 14 464 | 40.4 | 11.0 | 417 | 141 | 1 290 | 5 023 | 40.5 | 2.81 | 18.1 | 22.4 |
| Lowndes | 9.6 | 5.7 | 4.1 | 51.0 | 92 115 | 109 233 | 18.6 | 4.9 | 4 047 | 1 872 | 3 120 | 39 747 | 21.7 | 2.59 | 16.9 | 24.5 |
| Lumpkin | 13.3 | 8.5 | 4.8 | 50.3 | 21 016 | 29 966 | 42.6 | 2.2 | 687 | 539 | 478 | 10 989 | 45.8 | 2.56 | 9.6 | 22.2 |
| McDuffie | 13.2 | 8.5 | 5.6 | 53.0 | 21 231 | 21 875 | 3.0 | -1.0 | 703 | 561 | -347 | 8 289 | 4.0 | 2.60 | 21.4 | 24.2 |
| McIntosh | 16.5 | 11.9 | 6.7 | 51.2 | 10 847 | 14 333 | 32.1 | -3.4 | 258 | 243 | -522 | 5 971 | 42.1 | 2.39 | 14.7 | 28.4 |
| Macon | 13.5 | 8.0 | 4.9 | 45.7 | 14 074 | 14 740 | 4.7 | -3.2 | 327 | 354 | -457 | 4 999 | 3.4 | 2.56 | 24.0 | 29.2 |
| Madison | 13.5 | 8.6 | 5.2 | 50.4 | 25 730 | 28 120 | 9.3 | -0.7 | 731 | 554 | -383 | 10 508 | 7.2 | 2.66 | 12.1 | 21.5 |
| Marion | 14.0 | 10.1 | 4.9 | 50.6 | 7 144 | 8 742 | 22.4 | -0.4 | 234 | 186 | -83 | 3 420 | 28.2 | 2.53 | 16.5 | 26.9 |
| Meriwether | 14.5 | 9.9 | 6.5 | 52.1 | 22 534 | 21 992 | -2.4 | -3.3 | 552 | 567 | -701 | 8 522 | 3.3 | 2.55 | 18.7 | 26.8 |
| Miller | 13.5 | 10.3 | 9.1 | 52.0 | 6 383 | 6 125 | -4.0 | -2.5 | 173 | 205 | -122 | 2 426 | -2.5 | 2.46 | 15.6 | 27.3 |
| Mitchell | 11.8 | 7.8 | 5.8 | 48.1 | 23 932 | 23 498 | -1.8 | -1.5 | 682 | 534 | -514 | 8 055 | -0.1 | 2.65 | 23.2 | 25.0 |
| Monroe | 14.7 | 8.5 | 5.8 | 49.8 | 21 757 | 26 424 | 21.5 | 0.8 | 601 | 614 | 199 | 9 662 | 25.2 | 2.61 | 13.1 | 21.9 |
| Montgomery | 12.8 | 8.5 | 4.8 | 48.4 | 8 270 | 9 123 | 10.3 | -2.3 | 228 | 190 | -272 | 3 287 | 12.6 | 2.55 | 15.5 | 24.9 |
| Morgan | 14.1 | 9.5 | 6.7 | 51.5 | 15 457 | 17 868 | 15.6 | 0.1 | 446 | 310 | -111 | 6 660 | 19.8 | 2.66 | 14.7 | 20.7 |
| Murray | 11.5 | 7.4 | 4.0 | 50.4 | 36 506 | 39 628 | 8.6 | -0.6 | 1 122 | 780 | -589 | 14 080 | 6.0 | 2.80 | 12.8 | 19.8 |
| Muscogee | 10.9 | 6.0 | 5.5 | 51.7 | 186 291 | 189 885 | 1.9 | 4.5 | 7 376 | 3 939 | 5 088 | 74 081 | 6.1 | 2.47 | 21.3 | 29.9 |
| Newton | 10.7 | 6.3 | 4.0 | 52.4 | 62 001 | 99 958 | 61.2 | 1.5 | 3 036 | 1 567 | 84 | 34 390 | 56.3 | 2.85 | 19.0 | 19.6 |
| Oconee | 13.3 | 7.0 | 4.6 | 51.3 | 26 225 | 32 808 | 25.1 | 2.5 | 714 | 407 | 485 | 11 622 | 28.4 | 2.81 | 9.5 | 16.3 |
| Oglethorpe | 13.3 | 9.0 | 5.7 | 50.2 | 12 635 | 14 899 | 17.9 | -1.9 | 320 | 296 | -327 | 5 647 | 16.5 | 2.61 | 12.5 | 23.3 |
| Paulding | 9.2 | 4.9 | 2.7 | 51.0 | 81 678 | 142 324 | 74.3 | 1.7 | 4 027 | 1 723 | 18 | 48 105 | 71.3 | 2.94 | 12.8 | 16.6 |
| Peach | 11.8 | 7.2 | 4.8 | 51.5 | 23 668 | 27 695 | 17.0 | -0.3 | 799 | 522 | -386 | 9 958 | 18.0 | 2.58 | 19.2 | 24.8 |
| Pickens | 15.3 | 11.1 | 6.3 | 51.0 | 22 983 | 29 431 | 28.1 | -0.6 | 674 | 715 | -147 | 11 291 | 26.0 | 2.57 | 9.9 | 21.2 |
| Pierce | 12.7 | 9.0 | 5.7 | 50.8 | 15 636 | 18 758 | 20.0 | 0.5 | 529 | 417 | -28 | 7 083 | 18.9 | 2.63 | 13.6 | 21.8 |
| Pike | 12.3 | 8.0 | 4.8 | 51.0 | 13 688 | 17 869 | 30.5 | -0.3 | 378 | 342 | -114 | 6 187 | 30.1 | 2.84 | 11.0 | 17.6 |
| Polk | 11.8 | 8.0 | 5.8 | 50.7 | 38 127 | 41 475 | 8.8 | -0.7 | 1 346 | 1 027 | -608 | 15 092 | 7.7 | 2.72 | 14.8 | 23.6 |
| Pulaski | 14.1 | 9.2 | 5.8 | 56.8 | 9 588 | 12 010 | 25.3 | -2.4 | 228 | 234 | -285 | 4 475 | 31.3 | 2.40 | 17.6 | 29.3 |

1. No spouse present.

# Table B. States and Counties — Population, Vital Statistics, Medicare, and Crime

| STATE County | Persons in group quarters, 2010 | Daytime population, 2007–2011 Number | Employment/ residence ratio | Births, 2011 Total | Rate[1] | Deaths, 2011 Number | Rate[1] | Persons under 65 with no health insurance, 2010 Number | Percent | Medicare, 2012 Eligible for Medicare | Enrolled in Medicare Advantage | Enrolled in a Medicare prescription drug plan | Serious crimes known to police,[2] 2011 Total Number | Rate[3] |
|---|---|---|---|---|---|---|---|---|---|---|---|---|---|---|
| | 32 | 33 | 34 | 35 | 36 | 37 | 38 | 39 | 40 | 41 | 42 | 43 | 44 | 45 |
| **GEORGIA—Cont'd** | | | | | | | | | | | | | | |
| Effingham | 607 | 39 056 | 0.47 | 638 | 12.1 | 319 | 6.1 | 8 147 | 17.3 | 6 635 | 1 405 | 2 544 | 696 | 1 315 |
| Elbert | 220 | 19 500 | 0.90 | 258 | 13.0 | 257 | 12.9 | 4 013 | 24.1 | 4 642 | 1 171 | 2 121 | 1 010 | 4 943 |
| Emanuel | 916 | 21 792 | 0.92 | 352 | 15.6 | 272 | 12.1 | 4 974 | 26.5 | 4 386 | 989 | 2 398 | 413 | 2 000 |
| Evans | 404 | 11 754 | 1.18 | 170 | 15.4 | 115 | 10.4 | 2 337 | 25.7 | 1 927 | 510 | 894 | 229 | 2 055 |
| Fannin | 161 | 21 779 | 0.80 | 199 | 8.4 | 263 | 11.1 | 4 857 | 26.4 | 6 268 | 1 086 | 2 795 | 579 | 2 552 |
| Fayette | 557 | 100 715 | 0.89 | 803 | 7.5 | 682 | 6.3 | 11 770 | 12.8 | 17 278 | 3 426 | 6 638 | 1 733 | 1 605 |
| Floyd | 3 733 | 100 097 | 1.10 | 1 280 | 13.3 | 1 008 | 10.5 | 17 347 | 21.9 | 18 019 | 3 176 | 9 277 | 4 210 | 4 314 |
| Forsyth | 642 | 156 262 | 0.82 | 2 237 | 12.3 | 812 | 4.5 | 23 099 | 14.5 | 19 220 | 5 379 | 6 663 | 2 554 | 1 436 |
| Franklin | 610 | 22 511 | 1.05 | 294 | 13.4 | 264 | 12.1 | 4 343 | 24.2 | 4 805 | 949 | 2 435 | 648 | 2 896 |
| Fulton | 31 392 | 1 273 283 | 1.84 | 13 387 | 14.1 | 6 201 | 6.5 | 186 396 | 22.9 | 107 822 | 31 376 | 41 259 | 59 803 | 6 412 |
| Gilmer | 282 | 26 999 | 0.89 | 330 | 11.7 | 273 | 9.6 | 6 416 | 27.7 | 6 215 | 1 177 | 2 893 | 470 | 1 640 |
| Glascock | 89 | 2 343 | 0.43 | 30 | 9.7 | 41 | 13.3 | 517 | 19.8 | 549 | 97 | 273 | NA | NA |
| Glynn | 1 453 | 86 310 | 1.22 | 1 055 | 13.1 | 742 | 9.2 | 15 361 | 23.0 | 14 971 | 2 545 | 6 633 | 4 965 | 6 154 |
| Gordon | 670 | 53 628 | 0.95 | 760 | 13.7 | 470 | 8.5 | 12 150 | 25.2 | 8 746 | 1 339 | 4 615 | 1 757 | 3 174 |
| Grady | 200 | 21 483 | 0.62 | 373 | 14.8 | 229 | 9.1 | 5 736 | 26.9 | 4 621 | 992 | 2 238 | 551 | 2 174 |
| Greene | 168 | 16 564 | 1.11 | 159 | 9.9 | 181 | 11.3 | 2 811 | 22.4 | 4 417 | 999 | 2 081 | 513 | 3 166 |
| Gwinnett | 5 682 | 755 715 | 0.90 | 11 828 | 14.3 | 3 302 | 4.0 | 182 933 | 24.5 | 74 262 | 19 870 | 26 643 | 22 118 | 2 711 |
| Habersham | 2 384 | 41 638 | 0.93 | 543 | 12.5 | 405 | 9.4 | 9 055 | 26.5 | 8 195 | 1 949 | 3 636 | 866 | 1 986 |
| Hall | 3 141 | 177 119 | 0.99 | 2 672 | 14.6 | 1 238 | 6.8 | 40 656 | 25.8 | 27 125 | 6 504 | 11 250 | 4 789 | 2 631 |
| Hancock | 1 471 | 8 822 | 0.70 | 86 | 9.1 | 118 | 12.6 | 1 448 | 22.0 | 1 993 | 777 | 805 | 142 | 1 486 |
| Haralson | 354 | 26 840 | 0.83 | 364 | 12.7 | 326 | 11.4 | 5 049 | 20.6 | 5 474 | 1 447 | 2 519 | 1 212 | 4 157 |
| Harris | 442 | 22 162 | 0.36 | 297 | 9.2 | 268 | 8.3 | 4 294 | 15.7 | 5 223 | 1 177 | 1 806 | 410 | 1 305 |
| Hart | 663 | 23 312 | 0.81 | 254 | 10.0 | 276 | 10.9 | 4 749 | 23.5 | 5 594 | 1 093 | 2 662 | 1 013 | 3 966 |
| Heard | 132 | 10 149 | 0.63 | 108 | 9.2 | 111 | 9.5 | 2 124 | 20.8 | 2 063 | 534 | 966 | 222 | 1 852 |
| Henry | 933 | 163 808 | 0.61 | 2 607 | 12.6 | 1 187 | 5.7 | 33 922 | 18.2 | 24 156 | 6 694 | 8 246 | 6 216 | 3 009 |
| Houston | 1 599 | 140 118 | 1.04 | 1 992 | 13.8 | 1 012 | 7.0 | 22 375 | 18.0 | 19 719 | 2 431 | 5 573 | 6 417 | 4 527 |
| Irwin | 663 | 8 519 | 0.68 | 111 | 11.5 | 106 | 11.0 | 1 915 | 25.6 | 1 866 | 394 | 989 | 343 | 3 549 |
| Jackson | 757 | 54 047 | 0.78 | 833 | 13.6 | 474 | 7.7 | 11 343 | 21.4 | 9 877 | 2 385 | 3 966 | 1 563 | 2 610 |
| Jasper | 94 | 10 672 | 0.45 | 177 | 12.7 | 120 | 8.6 | 2 743 | 22.7 | 2 424 | 637 | 1 057 | 367 | 2 606 |
| Jeff Davis | 111 | 14 200 | 0.90 | 232 | 15.3 | 164 | 10.8 | 3 308 | 25.2 | 2 613 | 398 | 1 508 | 596 | 3 904 |
| Jefferson | 527 | 16 626 | 0.96 | 226 | 13.6 | 238 | 14.3 | 3 126 | 22.2 | 3 439 | 701 | 1 758 | 350 | 2 132 |
| Jenkins | 84 | 7 390 | 0.67 | 114 | 14.0 | 102 | 12.5 | 1 823 | 25.8 | 1 571 | 420 | 798 | NA | NA |
| Johnson | 1 737 | 8 668 | 0.60 | 104 | 10.4 | 107 | 10.7 | 1 597 | 22.8 | 1 772 | 349 | 957 | 162 | 1 668 |
| Jones | 321 | 20 521 | 0.34 | 314 | 11.0 | 242 | 8.5 | 4 713 | 19.0 | 4 843 | 1 570 | 1 775 | 638 | 2 197 |
| Lamar | 1 455 | 15 662 | 0.66 | 213 | 11.7 | 202 | 11.1 | 3 197 | 22.0 | 3 378 | 1 070 | 1 337 | 599 | 3 339 |
| Lanier | 260 | 7 806 | 0.45 | 126 | 12.1 | 92 | 8.8 | 2 232 | 25.4 | 1 331 | 202 | 703 | 245 | 2 399 |
| Laurens | 1 058 | 49 070 | 1.05 | 663 | 13.8 | 504 | 10.5 | 7 446 | 18.2 | 9 339 | 2 212 | 3 989 | 2 298 | 4 683 |
| Lee | 828 | 20 492 | 0.40 | 353 | 12.4 | 185 | 6.5 | 4 207 | 16.7 | 3 506 | 620 | 1 284 | 745 | 2 652 |
| Liberty | 2 579 | 67 340 | 1.10 | 1 449 | 22.1 | 307 | 4.7 | 9 766 | 17.5 | 5 104 | 911 | 1 588 | 2 351 | 3 657 |
| Lincoln | 67 | 6 613 | 0.57 | 64 | 8.1 | 87 | 11.1 | 1 636 | 25.1 | 1 772 | 404 | 756 | NA | NA |
| Long | 328 | 9 561 | 0.26 | 170 | 11.2 | 71 | 4.7 | 3 498 | 26.3 | 1 201 | 187 | 490 | NA | NA |
| Lowndes | 6 410 | 115 770 | 1.18 | 1 794 | 16.0 | 843 | 7.5 | 20 802 | 22.4 | 14 538 | 2 382 | 6 560 | 3 976 | 3 617 |
| Lumpkin | 1 782 | 25 155 | 0.67 | 285 | 9.5 | 223 | 7.4 | 5 782 | 23.6 | 4 977 | 1 027 | 2 151 | 669 | 2 203 |
| McDuffie | 318 | 21 267 | 0.94 | 320 | 14.8 | 245 | 11.3 | 3 754 | 20.0 | 4 073 | 1 269 | 1 512 | NA | NA |
| McIntosh | 71 | 12 355 | 0.70 | 124 | 8.8 | 98 | 6.9 | 2 728 | 23.3 | 2 515 | 543 | 1 092 | 422 | 3 370 |
| Macon | 1 960 | 13 692 | 0.82 | 145 | 10.1 | 159 | 11.0 | 2 588 | 23.5 | 2 138 | 642 | 1 028 | 255 | 2 195 |
| Madison | 204 | 21 796 | 0.48 | 336 | 12.0 | 239 | 8.6 | 5 875 | 24.2 | 5 257 | 1 262 | 1 975 | 956 | 3 496 |
| Marion | 79 | 7 224 | 0.59 | 109 | 12.5 | 82 | 9.4 | 1 908 | 25.5 | 1 363 | 340 | 560 | NA | NA |
| Meriwether | 253 | 19 623 | 0.71 | 253 | 11.7 | 241 | 11.1 | 3 962 | 21.7 | 4 529 | 1 610 | 1 961 | 826 | 3 861 |
| Miller | 168 | 5 688 | 0.81 | 82 | 13.4 | 74 | 12.1 | 1 059 | 21.5 | 1 158 | 252 | 619 | 70 | 1 128 |
| Mitchell | 2 135 | 23 968 | 1.04 | 310 | 13.2 | 228 | 9.7 | 3 875 | 21.0 | 4 125 | 893 | 2 086 | 778 | 3 322 |
| Monroe | 1 208 | 22 359 | 0.66 | 268 | 10.1 | 269 | 10.1 | 4 019 | 18.5 | 4 778 | 1 018 | 1 975 | 744 | 2 779 |
| Montgomery | 732 | 7 960 | 0.68 | 105 | 11.6 | 80 | 8.8 | 1 769 | 24.6 | 1 477 | 332 | 774 | NA | NA |
| Morgan | 154 | 18 436 | 1.07 | 202 | 11.2 | 128 | 7.1 | 3 197 | 21.4 | 3 619 | 996 | 1 420 | 405 | 2 339 |
| Murray | 254 | 35 623 | 0.73 | 508 | 12.8 | 355 | 9.0 | 8 776 | 25.0 | 6 388 | 751 | 3 835 | 1 053 | 2 623 |
| Muscogee | 7 017 | 213 665 | 1.31 | 3 320 | 17.1 | 1 745 | 9.0 | 31 655 | 19.5 | 29 584 | 7 059 | 9 829 | 13 475 | 7 004 |
| Newton | 1 792 | 84 030 | 0.65 | 1 364 | 13.5 | 697 | 6.9 | 18 720 | 21.1 | 14 146 | 3 610 | 5 397 | 3 625 | 3 579 |
| Oconee | 117 | 28 097 | 0.73 | 327 | 9.8 | 172 | 5.2 | 4 711 | 16.2 | 4 788 | 957 | 1 592 | 595 | 1 790 |
| Oglethorpe | 177 | 10 856 | 0.37 | 151 | 10.3 | 133 | 9.1 | 3 042 | 23.9 | 2 636 | 517 | 1 103 | 712 | 4 717 |
| Paulding | 662 | 100 435 | 0.40 | 1 809 | 12.6 | 740 | 5.2 | 23 214 | 17.6 | 14 573 | 3 513 | 5 321 | 3 396 | 2 359 |
| Peach | 2 028 | 26 280 | 0.90 | 402 | 14.4 | 237 | 8.5 | 5 055 | 22.3 | 4 574 | 952 | 1 586 | 1 841 | 6 561 |
| Pickens | 360 | 26 663 | 0.78 | 311 | 10.6 | 288 | 9.8 | 5 010 | 20.5 | 7 067 | 1 359 | 3 129 | 702 | 2 354 |
| Pierce | 142 | 15 558 | 0.60 | 233 | 12.4 | 200 | 10.7 | 3 719 | 23.1 | 3 664 | 597 | 1 973 | 207 | 1 089 |
| Pike | 268 | 13 030 | 0.38 | 188 | 10.6 | 160 | 9.0 | 3 210 | 20.8 | 2 936 | 733 | 1 191 | 124 | 699 |
| Polk | 373 | 37 721 | 0.78 | 610 | 14.8 | 469 | 11.4 | 8 646 | 24.2 | 7 771 | 1 540 | 3 563 | 1 874 | 4 475 |
| Pulaski | 1 248 | 10 697 | 0.76 | 112 | 9.5 | 116 | 9.9 | 1 917 | 21.4 | 1 942 | 288 | 905 | NA | NA |

1. Per 1,000 estimated resident population.   2. Data for serious crimes have not been adjusted for underreporting; this may affect comparability between geographic areas and over time.   3. Per 100,000 population estimated by the FBI.

# Table B. States and Counties — Crime, Education, Money Income, and Poverty

| | Serious crimes known to police, 2011 (cont.)[1] | | Education | | | | | | Money income, 2007–2011 | | | | Income and poverty, 2011 | | | |
| | Rate[2] | | School enrollment and attainment, 2007–2011 | | | | Local government expenditures,[5] 2009–2010 | | | Households | | | Percent below poverty level | | | |
| | | | Enrollment[3] | | Attainment[4] (percent) | | | | | | Median income | | | | | |
| STATE County | Violent | Property | Total | Per-cent private | High school grad-uate or less | Bach-elor's degree or more | Total current expendi-tures (mil dol) | Current expendi-tures per student (dollars) | Per capita income[6] (dollars) | Dollars | Percent change, 2000 to 2007–2011 (constant 2011 dollars) | Percent with income of $200,000 or more | Median house-hold income (dollars) | All per-sons | Children under 18 years | Children 5 to 17 years in families |
| | 46 | 47 | 48 | 49 | 50 | 51 | 52 | 53 | 54 | 55 | 56 | 57 | 58 | 59 | 60 | 61 |

GEORGIA—Cont'd

| | 46 | 47 | 48 | 49 | 50 | 51 | 52 | 53 | 54 | 55 | 56 | 57 | 58 | 59 | 60 | 61 |
|---|---|---|---|---|---|---|---|---|---|---|---|---|---|---|---|---|
| Effingham | 136 | 1 179 | 14 902 | 9.9 | 55.2 | 15.8 | 95.3 | 8 312 | 24 136 | 58 935 | -6.1 | 1.7 | 59 502 | 12.3 | 18.2 | 16.5 |
| Elbert | 338 | 4 606 | 4 817 | 9.6 | 68.9 | 11.4 | 36.3 | 10 591 | 17 978 | 32 634 | -15.9 | 0.7 | 33 068 | 23.3 | 34.0 | 31.9 |
| Emanuel | 165 | 1 835 | 5 450 | 9.7 | 66.2 | 10.0 | 39.4 | 8 728 | 16 318 | 30 427 | -7.6 | 1.3 | 30 459 | 28.8 | 41.5 | 39.6 |
| Evans | 179 | 1 875 | 2 842 | 11.8 | 61.6 | 12.7 | 16.1 | 8 802 | 18 547 | 38 000 | 10.6 | 0.5 | 30 858 | 28.4 | 41.3 | 38.9 |
| Fannin | 419 | 2 133 | 4 337 | 14.9 | 61.8 | 14.8 | 31.0 | 9 995 | 20 085 | 34 554 | -16.4 | 0.5 | 34 775 | 21.5 | 37.8 | 34.2 |
| Fayette | 79 | 1 526 | 31 564 | 15.7 | 27.4 | 41.7 | 188.0 | 8 654 | 35 405 | 81 498 | -15.3 | 8.2 | 74 476 | 8.7 | 11.5 | 9.7 |
| Floyd | 498 | 3 816 | 25 556 | 22.1 | 54.9 | 18.1 | 169.5 | 10 511 | 21 213 | 43 129 | -10.3 | 2.4 | 40 159 | 20.6 | 29.8 | 27.8 |
| Forsyth | 209 | 1 227 | 49 329 | 18.8 | 30.5 | 42.8 | 290.5 | 8 492 | 35 277 | 88 262 | -5.1 | 9.4 | 85 137 | 8.0 | 9.8 | 8.7 |
| Franklin | 121 | 2 775 | 5 170 | 14.2 | 63.5 | 14.0 | 33.4 | 8 891 | 19 524 | 33 086 | -23.7 | 0.5 | 31 042 | 22.5 | 33.9 | 31.4 |
| Fulton | 873 | 5 539 | 256 548 | 22.8 | 29.4 | 48.1 | 1 623.8 | 11 656 | 37 711 | 57 582 | -9.9 | 9.9 | 54 893 | 20.0 | 27.0 | 25.6 |
| Gilmer | 87 | 1 552 | 5 866 | 9.0 | 59.7 | 14.3 | 48.5 | 11 580 | 20 624 | 37 091 | -21.8 | 2.3 | 36 359 | 26.3 | 43.0 | 40.0 |
| Glascock | NA | NA | 722 | 10.0 | 68.0 | 9.9 | 6.1 | 9 415 | 17 265 | 36 275 | -9.7 | 0.1 | 35 247 | 18.8 | 23.5 | 20.4 |
| Glynn | 620 | 5 535 | 18 817 | 9.4 | 43.9 | 25.9 | 131.4 | 10 262 | 27 767 | 49 828 | -4.8 | 3.9 | 44 238 | 19.6 | 31.1 | 29.5 |
| Gordon | 329 | 2 845 | 13 933 | 9.5 | 63.1 | 13.6 | 90.8 | 8 798 | 18 781 | 41 336 | -21.2 | 1.1 | 42 253 | 18.6 | 28.3 | 27.2 |
| Grady | 249 | 1 926 | 6 317 | 7.3 | 66.4 | 10.5 | 37.3 | 8 357 | 17 683 | 32 091 | -17.1 | 1.1 | 33 368 | 28.4 | 37.6 | 34.6 |
| Greene | 247 | 2 919 | 3 434 | 15.5 | 63.9 | 18.7 | 25.2 | 12 124 | 24 479 | 38 209 | -15.5 | 4.1 | 39 209 | 25.0 | 43.1 | 42.1 |
| Gwinnett | 225 | 2 486 | 235 704 | 15.2 | 36.0 | 34.7 | 1 512.0 | 9 296 | 26 712 | 63 076 | -22.8 | 4.2 | 56 944 | 15.7 | 21.5 | 20.4 |
| Habersham | 151 | 1 835 | 10 255 | 14.1 | 57.2 | 18.1 | 64.4 | 9 294 | 19 710 | 41 222 | -15.9 | 1.6 | 39 879 | 18.8 | 27.6 | 26.1 |
| Hall | 156 | 2 475 | 45 355 | 12.3 | 52.8 | 22.1 | 276.1 | 8 555 | 24 572 | 52 050 | -14.2 | 3.7 | 49 324 | 17.8 | 25.5 | 23.4 |
| Hancock | 147 | 1 340 | 1 794 | 3.1 | 68.9 | 13.8 | 14.2 | 11 540 | 11 714 | 24 483 | -17.6 | 0.2 | 26 107 | 34.4 | 42.9 | 37.8 |
| Haralson | 617 | 3 539 | 6 924 | 8.0 | 66.2 | 12.0 | 52.5 | 8 944 | 19 472 | 38 664 | -9.5 | 1.0 | 37 495 | 20.4 | 28.8 | 27.0 |
| Harris | 76 | 1 229 | 8 408 | 12.6 | 39.4 | 27.7 | 45.6 | 9 321 | 31 363 | 67 299 | 4.4 | 6.3 | 64 048 | 10.6 | 15.7 | 13.9 |
| Hart | 325 | 3 641 | 5 565 | 13.0 | 61.0 | 14.9 | 32.5 | 9 426 | 19 252 | 35 685 | -19.5 | 1.4 | 36 327 | 21.3 | 29.5 | 28.1 |
| Heard | 267 | 1 585 | 2 941 | 5.7 | 68.1 | 7.0 | 19.8 | 9 122 | 17 381 | 39 167 | -12.2 | 0.8 | 35 765 | 28.0 | 39.3 | 33.9 |
| Henry | 167 | 2 841 | 63 083 | 18.3 | 42.5 | 25.2 | 344.6 | 8 415 | 25 949 | 64 251 | -17.0 | 2.3 | 58 130 | 13.0 | 20.5 | 18.4 |
| Houston | 332 | 4 196 | 41 780 | 9.7 | 41.4 | 24.5 | 237.7 | 8 874 | 25 329 | 55 738 | -5.4 | 2.3 | 51 851 | 14.3 | 21.4 | 19.6 |
| Irwin | 259 | 3 291 | 2 317 | 6.9 | 64.9 | 7.5 | 16.9 | 9 673 | 17 062 | 40 379 | -1.2 | 0.3 | 33 602 | 24.6 | 34.5 | 32.6 |
| Jackson | 124 | 2 486 | 15 245 | 11.2 | 57.9 | 17.6 | 104.0 | 9 031 | 22 465 | 52 883 | -2.9 | 1.6 | 49 400 | 15.6 | 21.3 | 20.3 |
| Jasper | 107 | 2 499 | 3 284 | 19.6 | 56.1 | 16.7 | 18.8 | 8 486 | 20 440 | 44 404 | -17.6 | 2.7 | 43 618 | 20.4 | 30.9 | 29.2 |
| Jeff Davis | 413 | 3 491 | 3 646 | 4.4 | 68.6 | 11.6 | 23.7 | 7 909 | 17 127 | 35 336 | -4.2 | 0.2 | 32 248 | 25.0 | 35.9 | 35.3 |
| Jefferson | 219 | 1 912 | 4 310 | 11.8 | 71.4 | 8.5 | 26.8 | 8 688 | 14 974 | 29 129 | -17.3 | 0.5 | 27 703 | 30.7 | 42.3 | 38.0 |
| Jenkins | NA | NA | 2 405 | 7.3 | 67.9 | 13.5 | 14.3 | 9 420 | 15 243 | 25 467 | -21.5 | 1.3 | 25 807 | 35.8 | 53.7 | 51.1 |
| Johnson | 237 | 1 431 | 2 096 | 6.9 | 67.4 | 11.5 | 12.3 | 10 180 | 16 178 | 31 301 | -2.8 | 2.7 | 28 585 | 31.4 | 37.3 | 34.0 |
| Jones | 62 | 2 135 | 7 622 | 15.2 | 51.2 | 17.3 | 46.3 | 8 268 | 23 185 | 51 265 | -12.3 | 2.0 | 48 792 | 16.2 | 21.8 | 19.7 |
| Lamar | 446 | 2 893 | 4 992 | 10.3 | 60.5 | 10.9 | 22.8 | 9 148 | 18 058 | 39 684 | -20.7 | 0.9 | 40 769 | 19.6 | 28.7 | 27.3 |
| Lanier | 245 | 2 155 | 2 134 | 3.8 | 57.9 | 13.5 | 14.7 | 8 174 | 17 472 | 40 878 | 3.8 | 1.9 | 33 929 | 24.8 | 36.3 | 35.7 |
| Laurens | 330 | 4 353 | 11 932 | 6.9 | 62.7 | 16.0 | 80.4 | 8 470 | 19 358 | 37 640 | -12.9 | 1.7 | 34 865 | 24.9 | 35.8 | 33.1 |
| Lee | 306 | 2 346 | 8 844 | 8.8 | 48.3 | 18.5 | 47.0 | 7 492 | 24 121 | 58 252 | -11.2 | 3.0 | 60 652 | 12.7 | 18.0 | 15.5 |
| Liberty | 358 | 3 299 | 20 212 | 10.8 | 44.2 | 17.3 | 96.7 | 9 312 | 20 034 | 44 146 | -2.3 | 1.3 | 40 659 | 16.8 | 22.1 | 21.2 |
| Lincoln | NA | NA | 1 634 | 2.6 | 65.5 | 10.2 | 14.1 | 11 149 | 20 242 | 36 741 | -14.8 | 0.7 | 35 183 | 24.1 | 33.1 | 29.1 |
| Long | NA | NA | 3 732 | 6.2 | 62.4 | 8.9 | 19.6 | 7 429 | 15 661 | 38 785 | -6.2 | 0.0 | 35 244 | 24.7 | 34.1 | 31.7 |
| Lowndes | 316 | 3 301 | 33 589 | 7.8 | 48.3 | 22.4 | 165.8 | 9 403 | 20 040 | 38 535 | -11.2 | 1.7 | 34 252 | 27.1 | 33.4 | 30.8 |
| Lumpkin | 336 | 1 868 | 9 111 | 10.5 | 51.9 | 20.0 | 34.6 | 9 028 | 20 949 | 43 704 | -17.4 | 1.6 | 44 422 | 18.0 | 26.6 | 25.5 |
| McDuffie | NA | NA | 5 630 | 6.8 | 64.8 | 12.8 | 43.1 | 10 280 | 17 760 | 36 841 | -14.5 | 1.4 | 36 907 | 23.1 | 36.3 | 33.4 |
| McIntosh | 176 | 3 195 | 3 094 | 13.6 | 60.6 | 15.2 | 16.9 | 9 378 | 20 395 | 37 194 | -8.5 | 0.5 | 34 787 | 21.7 | 35.5 | 33.6 |
| Macon | 336 | 1 860 | 3 727 | 11.5 | 68.1 | 11.8 | 18.6 | 10 012 | 14 398 | 28 726 | -12.2 | 0.5 | 27 934 | 28.5 | 36.6 | 33.1 |
| Madison | 713 | 2 783 | 6 893 | 14.3 | 65.6 | 12.5 | 45.3 | 9 412 | 18 992 | 41 407 | -15.6 | 0.8 | 40 123 | 20.0 | 28.9 | 26.5 |
| Marion | NA | NA | 2 090 | 4.8 | 70.7 | 6.3 | 13.1 | 9 322 | 17 532 | 32 610 | -17.1 | 0.3 | 34 189 | 24.1 | 37.3 | 35.1 |
| Meriwether | 220 | 3 641 | 4 815 | 16.2 | 71.5 | 9.2 | 32.8 | 9 848 | 18 145 | 37 028 | -13.9 | 0.5 | 34 589 | 21.6 | 35.5 | 33.2 |
| Miller | 209 | 918 | 1 466 | 10.7 | 61.8 | 11.3 | 9.7 | 8 830 | 19 558 | 33 248 | -9.9 | 1.0 | 33 063 | 25.2 | 37.4 | 35.1 |
| Mitchell | 380 | 2 942 | 5 864 | 13.3 | 68.8 | 10.7 | 39.4 | 9 770 | 16 489 | 37 597 | 4.8 | 1.1 | 31 088 | 30.6 | 39.4 | 36.0 |
| Monroe | 153 | 2 626 | 6 460 | 18.9 | 57.6 | 18.3 | 39.1 | 9 767 | 23 671 | 48 632 | -18.5 | 1.5 | 51 747 | 14.7 | 22.2 | 19.8 |
| Montgomery | NA | NA | 2 445 | 24.1 | 62.2 | 15.4 | 10.9 | 9 896 | 16 884 | 34 933 | -14.4 | 1.1 | 34 379 | 25.7 | 35.3 | 33.4 |
| Morgan | 139 | 2 201 | 4 465 | 15.5 | 53.3 | 24.5 | 30.8 | 9 141 | 27 459 | 46 918 | -13.7 | 5.9 | 46 176 | 16.5 | 25.4 | 22.8 |
| Murray | 142 | 2 481 | 9 907 | 4.3 | 71.9 | 7.4 | 62.2 | 8 053 | 16 748 | 37 004 | -25.9 | 0.6 | 36 230 | 24.8 | 29.3 | 26.3 |
| Muscogee | 485 | 6 519 | 54 556 | 10.6 | 44.7 | 21.7 | 310.1 | 9 553 | 22 726 | 41 088 | -12.5 | 2.4 | 37 564 | 19.8 | 30.1 | 29.0 |
| Newton | 393 | 3 186 | 28 837 | 16.9 | 49.8 | 19.4 | 170.5 | 8 682 | 21 246 | 51 691 | -14.7 | 1.5 | 44 089 | 18.5 | 26.3 | 23.3 |
| Oconee | 135 | 1 655 | 9 887 | 19.5 | 28.2 | 45.2 | 59.4 | 9 187 | 33 863 | 75 136 | 0.8 | 7.5 | 71 707 | 8.8 | 11.6 | 9.5 |
| Oglethorpe | 411 | 4 306 | 3 859 | 11.7 | 56.5 | 14.8 | 21.5 | 8 843 | 19 052 | 43 255 | -10.0 | 1.5 | 44 066 | 17.4 | 24.6 | 22.4 |
| Paulding | 128 | 2 231 | 41 731 | 12.7 | 49.0 | 22.3 | 233.7 | 8 216 | 23 700 | 63 023 | -10.5 | 1.5 | 59 185 | 11.8 | 16.4 | 15.8 |
| Peach | 649 | 5 912 | 9 337 | 10.1 | 54.1 | 17.8 | 38.9 | 9 777 | 18 735 | 41 333 | -11.1 | 1.0 | 39 838 | 25.8 | 33.0 | 31.6 |
| Pickens | 117 | 2 237 | 6 244 | 11.3 | 53.8 | 21.9 | 45.0 | 10 057 | 26 206 | 50 582 | -9.5 | 3.7 | 50 282 | 14.6 | 26.5 | 24.1 |
| Pierce | 89 | 1 000 | 4 598 | 4.5 | 63.3 | 11.4 | 30.9 | 8 677 | 18 287 | 37 489 | -7.1 | 0.7 | 38 290 | 21.2 | 32.4 | 28.4 |
| Pike | 39 | 660 | 5 018 | 13.3 | 54.6 | 15.6 | 26.1 | 7 340 | 21 922 | 56 433 | -5.8 | 1.1 | 54 457 | 14.0 | 19.6 | 17.2 |
| Polk | 413 | 4 062 | 10 104 | 10.8 | 65.5 | 11.2 | 64.5 | 8 568 | 18 274 | 38 514 | -11.8 | 0.8 | 36 326 | 23.9 | 32.7 | 31.3 |
| Pulaski | NA | NA | 2 346 | 3.8 | 69.1 | 7.3 | 14.5 | 9 238 | 16 679 | 32 424 | -24.7 | 0.3 | 34 820 | 22.8 | 31.0 | 28.6 |

1. Data for serious crimes have not been adjusted for underreporting; this may affect comparability between geographic areas and over time.   2. Per 100,000 population estimated by the FBI.   3. All persons 3 years old and over enrolled in nursery school through college.   4. Persons 25 years old and over.   5. Elementary and secondary education expenditures.   6. Based on population estimated by the American Community Survey, 2007–2011.

# Table B. States and Counties — **Personal Income**

| | Personal income, 2011 | | | | | | | | | | | | |
|---|---|---|---|---|---|---|---|---|---|---|---|---|---|
| | | Per capita[1] | | | | | | Transfer payments (mil dol) | | | | | |
| | | | | | | | | | Government payments to individuals | | | | |
| STATE<br>County | Total<br>(mil dol) | Percent<br>change,<br>2010–<br>2011 | Dollars | Rank | Wages and<br>salaries[2]<br>(mil dol) | Proprietors'<br>income<br>(mil dol) | Dividends,<br>interest,<br>and rent<br>(mil dol) | Total | Total | Social<br>Security | Medical<br>payments | Income<br>mainte-<br>nance | Unemploy-<br>ment<br>insurance |
| | 62 | 63 | 64 | 65 | 66 | 67 | 68 | 69 | 70 | 71 | 72 | 73 | 74 |
| GEORGIA—Cont'd | | | | | | | | | | | | | |
| Effingham | 1 816 | 5.9 | 34 485 | 1 437 | 473 | 45 | 156 | 287 | 275 | 102 | 98 | 37 | 12 |
| Elbert | 571 | 2.3 | 28 713 | 2 499 | 245 | 37 | 105 | 190 | 186 | 63 | 79 | 28 | 8 |
| Emanuel | 597 | 4.1 | 26 434 | 2 831 | 269 | 43 | 74 | 221 | 216 | 58 | 91 | 40 | 6 |
| Evans | 306 | 2.5 | 27 657 | 2 661 | 165 | 22 | 47 | 86 | 84 | 25 | 35 | 17 | 2 |
| Fannin | 682 | 5.1 | 28 759 | 2 492 | 212 | 55 | 123 | 226 | 220 | 91 | 91 | 20 | 6 |
| Fayette | 4 792 | 4.3 | 44 460 | 426 | 2 012 | 302 | 872 | 611 | 587 | 268 | 201 | 42 | 23 |
| Floyd | 3 183 | 3.6 | 33 159 | 1 682 | 1 897 | 201 | 497 | 806 | 785 | 266 | 303 | 109 | 28 |
| Forsyth | 7 520 | 9.8 | 41 354 | 630 | 3 307 | 21 | 1 060 | 674 | 634 | 298 | 215 | 41 | 35 |
| Franklin | 633 | 3.2 | 28 956 | 2 455 | 280 | 70 | 108 | 191 | 186 | 67 | 78 | 24 | 6 |
| Fulton | 54 556 | 6.9 | 57 451 | 90 | 62 923 | 9 511 | 9 058 | 5 486 | 5 276 | 1 515 | 1 898 | 1 018 | 258 |
| Gilmer | 782 | 1.7 | 27 624 | 2 668 | 285 | 62 | 134 | 246 | 239 | 91 | 105 | 23 | 8 |
| Glascock | 70 | 4.5 | 22 659 | 3 068 | 15 | 3 | 9 | 26 | 25 | 8 | 12 | 3 | 1 |
| Glynn | 2 944 | 4.1 | 36 619 | 1 122 | 1 808 | 143 | 689 | 629 | 612 | 223 | 244 | 76 | 21 |
| Gordon | 1 467 | 3.9 | 26 382 | 2 840 | 937 | 97 | 175 | 367 | 354 | 125 | 141 | 54 | 16 |
| Grady | 702 | 5.0 | 27 801 | 2 642 | 248 | 73 | 111 | 179 | 174 | 59 | 64 | 37 | 5 |
| Greene | 616 | 4.8 | 38 429 | 921 | 228 | 43 | 168 | 166 | 162 | 65 | 64 | 22 | 4 |
| Gwinnett | 27 108 | 5.4 | 32 861 | 1 730 | 19 313 | 1 324 | 3 250 | 3 336 | 3 154 | 1 099 | 1 101 | 492 | 196 |
| Habersham | 1 172 | 3.7 | 27 075 | 2 755 | 570 | 56 | 208 | 310 | 301 | 116 | 116 | 30 | 10 |
| Hall | 5 858 | 6.6 | 32 001 | 1 891 | 3 833 | 402 | 1 010 | 1 108 | 1 067 | 410 | 402 | 135 | 40 |
| Hancock | 198 | 4.2 | 21 059 | 3 092 | 53 | 12 | 27 | 96 | 94 | 26 | 43 | 18 | 3 |
| Haralson | 812 | 2.3 | 28 347 | 2 566 | 329 | 31 | 110 | 245 | 238 | 79 | 93 | 31 | 7 |
| Harris | 1 585 | 8.9 | 49 114 | 229 | 155 | 119 | 208 | 190 | 183 | 78 | 57 | 20 | 7 |
| Hart | 672 | 3.2 | 26 552 | 2 816 | 291 | 36 | 130 | 206 | 201 | 79 | 78 | 27 | 7 |
| Heard | 309 | 0.6 | 26 289 | 2 851 | 145 | 9 | 27 | 87 | 84 | 29 | 33 | 14 | 3 |
| Henry | 6 250 | 5.7 | 30 143 | 2 261 | 2 348 | 272 | 670 | 1 069 | 1 024 | 370 | 349 | 153 | 55 |
| Houston | 4 990 | 5.3 | 34 674 | 1 423 | 4 075 | 218 | 674 | 895 | 864 | 243 | 344 | 133 | 31 |
| Irwin | 275 | 5.7 | 28 454 | 2 548 | 82 | 49 | 46 | 81 | 79 | 24 | 33 | 13 | 3 |
| Jackson | 1 841 | 3.3 | 30 048 | 2 282 | 862 | 89 | 239 | 400 | 386 | 145 | 156 | 47 | 14 |
| Jasper | 414 | 4.6 | 29 818 | 2 320 | 82 | 21 | 55 | 99 | 96 | 35 | 34 | 17 | 4 |
| Jeff Davis | 379 | 4.6 | 24 979 | 2 966 | 171 | 52 | 48 | 120 | 116 | 36 | 49 | 21 | 4 |
| Jefferson | 442 | 4.2 | 26 509 | 2 821 | 215 | 37 | 59 | 166 | 162 | 45 | 70 | 34 | 5 |
| Jenkins | 204 | 5.0 | 25 016 | 2 963 | 53 | 17 | 28 | 81 | 79 | 20 | 35 | 17 | 2 |
| Johnson | 208 | 4.3 | 20 901 | 3 095 | 71 | 8 | 27 | 85 | 83 | 22 | 39 | 15 | 3 |
| Jones | 974 | 4.5 | 34 168 | 1 489 | 154 | 34 | 107 | 191 | 185 | 73 | 64 | 30 | 7 |
| Lamar | 485 | 2.7 | 26 630 | 2 806 | 151 | 29 | 57 | 154 | 149 | 49 | 51 | 20 | 6 |
| Lanier | 265 | 5.8 | 25 434 | 2 934 | 56 | 17 | 30 | 71 | 68 | 17 | 31 | 13 | 2 |
| Laurens | 1 420 | 2.1 | 29 622 | 2 358 | 832 | 83 | 201 | 417 | 406 | 124 | 156 | 79 | 15 |
| Lee | 1 177 | 6.2 | 41 198 | 643 | 232 | 43 | 123 | 156 | 150 | 53 | 53 | 23 | 7 |
| Liberty | 1 829 | 6.9 | 27 940 | 2 625 | 3 140 | 40 | 238 | 354 | 343 | 69 | 120 | 74 | 18 |
| Lincoln | 229 | 2.1 | 29 093 | 2 440 | 54 | 13 | 39 | 71 | 69 | 25 | 28 | 10 | 2 |
| Long | 325 | 8.2 | 21 473 | 3 089 | 42 | 6 | 31 | 78 | 75 | 15 | 28 | 16 | 3 |
| Lowndes | 3 462 | 4.5 | 30 938 | 2 115 | 2 510 | 205 | 558 | 774 | 751 | 198 | 300 | 127 | 27 |
| Lumpkin | 828 | 5.8 | 27 573 | 2 673 | 314 | 40 | 147 | 192 | 186 | 72 | 67 | 20 | 7 |
| McDuffie | 676 | 4.1 | 31 174 | 2 068 | 292 | 36 | 88 | 193 | 188 | 54 | 79 | 36 | 6 |
| McIntosh | 329 | 3.6 | 23 235 | 3 050 | 77 | 16 | 52 | 110 | 107 | 35 | 45 | 15 | 3 |
| Macon | 325 | 3.5 | 22 530 | 3 072 | 142 | 34 | 41 | 118 | 114 | 27 | 57 | 21 | 4 |
| Madison | 819 | 2.3 | 29 317 | 2 407 | 141 | 36 | 110 | 211 | 205 | 75 | 83 | 28 | 7 |
| Marion | 235 | 5.5 | 26 821 | 2 785 | 57 | 12 | 22 | 60 | 58 | 17 | 22 | 13 | 2 |
| Meriwether | 604 | 4.8 | 27 952 | 2 623 | 207 | 28 | 89 | 198 | 193 | 60 | 74 | 38 | 7 |
| Miller | 207 | 8.5 | 33 685 | 1 566 | 64 | 39 | 37 | 52 | 51 | 16 | 23 | 9 | 1 |
| Mitchell | 622 | 4.0 | 26 493 | 2 823 | 305 | 63 | 85 | 192 | 187 | 52 | 77 | 42 | 5 |
| Monroe | 1 049 | 5.8 | 39 397 | 814 | 323 | 24 | 126 | 184 | 178 | 69 | 67 | 24 | 7 |
| Montgomery | 238 | 3.9 | 26 251 | 2 858 | 65 | 21 | 31 | 68 | 66 | 20 | 26 | 11 | 3 |
| Morgan | 646 | 4.0 | 35 966 | 1 213 | 259 | 56 | 131 | 140 | 136 | 53 | 52 | 19 | 4 |
| Murray | 996 | 2.0 | 25 177 | 2 952 | 436 | 19 | 93 | 271 | 262 | 88 | 107 | 41 | 12 |
| Muscogee | 7 689 | 7.6 | 39 611 | 793 | 5 605 | 288 | 1 323 | 1 576 | 1 536 | 406 | 542 | 311 | 49 |
| Newton | 2 604 | 5.3 | 25 830 | 2 898 | 1 045 | 53 | 311 | 657 | 635 | 210 | 245 | 114 | 30 |
| Oconee | 1 780 | 7.1 | 53 361 | 136 | 390 | 41 | 296 | 170 | 163 | 73 | 57 | 15 | 6 |
| Oglethorpe | 450 | 1.9 | 30 618 | 2 171 | 69 | 35 | 59 | 95 | 92 | 36 | 32 | 14 | 3 |
| Paulding | 5 237 | 8.0 | 36 485 | 1 138 | 858 | 178 | 365 | 621 | 589 | 228 | 189 | 80 | 37 |
| Peach | 829 | 5.1 | 29 801 | 2 322 | 375 | 55 | 97 | 224 | 218 | 57 | 84 | 39 | 8 |
| Pickens | 1 071 | 4.9 | 36 407 | 1 147 | 323 | 36 | 229 | 249 | 242 | 109 | 93 | 21 | 8 |
| Pierce | 528 | 3.7 | 28 147 | 2 594 | 155 | 36 | 68 | 161 | 156 | 47 | 64 | 22 | 5 |
| Pike | 543 | 4.7 | 30 608 | 2 174 | 101 | 24 | 65 | 117 | 113 | 45 | 42 | 14 | 4 |
| Polk | 1 090 | 3.7 | 26 456 | 2 829 | 491 | 43 | 135 | 339 | 329 | 109 | 144 | 47 | 12 |
| Pulaski | 308 | 3.4 | 26 252 | 2 857 | 124 | 13 | 49 | 82 | 79 | 24 | 35 | 13 | 2 |

1. Based on the resident population estimated as of July 1 of the year shown.    2. Includes supplements to wages and salaries.

# Table B. States and Counties — Earnings, Social Security, and Housing

| STATE County | Earnings, 2011 | | | | | | | | | Social Security beneficiaries, December 2011 | | Housing units, 2010 | |
|---|---|---|---|---|---|---|---|---|---|---|---|---|---|
| | | | Percent by selected industries | | | | | | | | | | |
| | | | Goods-related[1] | | Service-related and health | | | | | | | Supplemental Security Income recipients, December 2011 | | |
| | Total (mil dol) | Farm | Total | Manufacturing | Information and professional and technical services | Retail trade | Finance, insurance, and real estate | Health care and social services | Government | Number | Rate[2] | | Total | Percent change, 2000–2010 |
| | 75 | 76 | 77 | 78 | 79 | 80 | 81 | 82 | 83 | 84 | 85 | 86 | 87 | 88 |
| GEORGIA—Cont'd | | | | | | | | | | | | | | |
| Effingham | 518 | 0.2 | D | 26.8 | 4.6 | 7.2 | 2.8 | 3.8 | 28.2 | 7 705 | 146 | 880 | 19 884 | 40.3 |
| Elbert | 282 | 0.9 | 35.3 | 29.0 | D | 6.1 | 3.7 | D | 26.2 | 5 285 | 266 | 841 | 9 583 | 4.9 |
| Emanuel | 311 | 4.1 | 24.3 | 21.4 | 3.0 | 8.0 | 3.7 | D | 29.0 | 5 190 | 230 | 1 300 | 9 968 | 5.8 |
| Evans | 187 | 6.2 | 38.3 | 31.7 | 1.7 | 7.0 | D | D | 16.8 | 2 185 | 197 | 451 | 4 664 | 6.5 |
| Fannin | 267 | -0.3 | D | D | D | 11.5 | 6.4 | D | 18.1 | 7 195 | 303 | 687 | 16 207 | 45.6 |
| Fayette | 2 314 | 0.0 | D | 8.2 | 8.7 | 8.5 | 5.3 | 13.1 | 15.3 | 18 260 | 169 | 856 | 40 793 | 24.7 |
| Floyd | 2 098 | 0.1 | D | 16.8 | 6.1 | 5.8 | 4.2 | 25.9 | 16.0 | 20 530 | 214 | 3 078 | 40 551 | 10.7 |
| Forsyth | 3 328 | 0.1 | 23.5 | 14.1 | 12.3 | 6.1 | 3.4 | 8.9 | 11.7 | 20 170 | 111 | 925 | 64 052 | 75.5 |
| Franklin | 350 | 7.9 | D | 19.0 | 2.0 | 7.6 | 3.0 | D | 15.6 | 5 555 | 254 | 789 | 10 553 | 13.4 |
| Fulton | 72 434 | 0.0 | 7.2 | 4.5 | 26.5 | 3.5 | 14.4 | 7.7 | 10.5 | 112 555 | 119 | 23 917 | 437 105 | 25.4 |
| Gilmer | 347 | 3.9 | D | 17.9 | D | 9.9 | 5.8 | 6.9 | 18.8 | 7 075 | 250 | 629 | 16 564 | 38.9 |
| Glascock | 17 | 1.2 | D | 0.0 | D | 3.6 | D | D | 45.1 | 660 | 214 | 86 | 1 519 | 27.4 |
| Glynn | 1 952 | 0.0 | D | 8.8 | 5.2 | 7.9 | 4.7 | 9.2 | 33.4 | 16 635 | 207 | 1 882 | 40 716 | 24.8 |
| Gordon | 1 034 | 0.6 | 46.1 | 42.4 | D | 6.8 | 2.9 | 8.5 | 14.1 | 10 045 | 181 | 1 349 | 22 278 | 29.9 |
| Grady | 321 | 9.6 | D | 10.3 | 2.8 | 8.1 | D | 6.8 | 19.5 | 5 180 | 205 | 1 077 | 10 760 | 7.7 |
| Greene | 272 | 4.3 | D | 8.7 | D | 8.2 | 7.0 | D | 14.9 | 4 795 | 299 | 603 | 8 688 | 30.6 |
| Gwinnett | 20 637 | 0.0 | D | 10.4 | 15.2 | 9.1 | 8.8 | 6.5 | 10.3 | 80 740 | 98 | 10 295 | 291 547 | 39.0 |
| Habersham | 625 | 0.2 | D | 27.4 | 4.1 | 8.3 | 4.0 | 5.3 | 24.5 | 9 195 | 212 | 855 | 18 146 | 24.0 |
| Hall | 4 234 | 0.1 | 24.6 | 19.3 | 4.1 | 6.9 | 8.0 | 15.1 | 12.9 | 30 295 | 165 | 2 812 | 68 825 | 34.8 |
| Hancock | 65 | 1.3 | D | D | D | 6.9 | D | D | 51.8 | 2 260 | 240 | 474 | 5 360 | 25.2 |
| Haralson | 360 | -1.8 | D | 26.5 | D | 9.7 | 3.2 | D | 22.4 | 6 390 | 223 | 976 | 12 287 | 14.6 |
| Harris | 274 | -0.3 | 18.4 | 4.8 | D | 4.2 | 8.6 | D | 20.9 | 5 820 | 180 | 459 | 13 397 | 30.2 |
| Hart | 326 | 4.7 | 31.1 | 26.4 | 5.0 | 7.7 | 2.7 | 7.8 | 17.7 | 6 305 | 249 | 715 | 13 007 | 17.0 |
| Heard | 154 | -1.7 | D | 15.7 | D | 1.6 | D | 1.8 | 19.3 | 2 415 | 206 | 397 | 5 148 | 14.1 |
| Henry | 2 620 | 0.1 | 12.7 | 7.2 | 4.0 | 10.7 | 6.1 | 11.8 | 23.4 | 27 860 | 134 | 3 039 | 76 533 | 77.3 |
| Houston | 4 293 | 0.1 | D | 6.5 | 7.3 | 5.0 | 2.1 | 5.1 | 61.0 | 21 090 | 147 | 3 172 | 58 325 | 31.0 |
| Irwin | 131 | 30.5 | 11.2 | 8.0 | D | 4.8 | D | D | 31.2 | 2 125 | 220 | 413 | 4 033 | -2.8 |
| Jackson | 951 | 2.1 | D | 27.5 | D | 9.4 | 3.5 | 4.1 | 15.7 | 11 235 | 183 | 1 303 | 23 752 | 46.4 |
| Jasper | 103 | 2.1 | D | 20.3 | 2.7 | 5.8 | 3.8 | D | 27.6 | 2 755 | 198 | 336 | 6 153 | 28.0 |
| Jeff Davis | 224 | 7.1 | 19.3 | 18.2 | 1.5 | 8.9 | 2.2 | 3.2 | 17.6 | 3 090 | 204 | 538 | 6 488 | 16.2 |
| Jefferson | 252 | 6.3 | D | 18.6 | 1.8 | 6.8 | 3.9 | D | 20.8 | 3 900 | 234 | 1 020 | 7 298 | 1.1 |
| Jenkins | 71 | 14.1 | 5.6 | 0.9 | D | 6.0 | D | 6.0 | 37.1 | 1 790 | 220 | 470 | 4 221 | 8.0 |
| Johnson | 78 | -0.2 | 14.9 | 7.7 | 0.9 | 4.5 | D | 12.8 | 35.9 | 1 940 | 194 | 504 | 4 120 | 13.4 |
| Jones | 188 | 1.4 | 15.2 | 1.4 | D | 6.1 | D | D | 30.1 | 5 580 | 196 | 727 | 11 688 | 26.1 |
| Lamar | 181 | 4.2 | D | 16.8 | D | 7.9 | D | 4.3 | 32.5 | 3 865 | 212 | 454 | 7 474 | 21.6 |
| Lanier | 73 | 15.6 | 9.8 | 5.9 | D | 6.2 | D | 9.6 | 28.1 | 1 575 | 151 | 367 | 4 249 | 41.1 |
| Laurens | 915 | 0.8 | 18.5 | 12.5 | D | 8.3 | 3.5 | D | 28.9 | 10 685 | 223 | 2 083 | 21 368 | 8.5 |
| Lee | 275 | 6.1 | D | 2.9 | D | 9.9 | 3.0 | D | 25.6 | 4 025 | 141 | 457 | 10 276 | 16.6 |
| Liberty | 3 180 | 0.0 | 5.1 | 3.9 | 1.3 | 1.9 | 1.1 | 1.2 | 83.3 | 6 055 | 93 | 1 104 | 26 731 | 21.6 |
| Lincoln | 67 | -1.4 | D | D | 1.7 | 8.9 | 4.4 | 2.3 | 28.4 | 2 040 | 259 | 252 | 4 786 | 6.0 |
| Long | 47 | 3.7 | D | D | D | 2.6 | D | 2.0 | 58.6 | 1 405 | 93 | 276 | 6 039 | 42.7 |
| Lowndes | 2 715 | 0.2 | D | 7.0 | 4.9 | 8.3 | 4.4 | 11.6 | 39.0 | 16 795 | 150 | 3 314 | 43 921 | 20.1 |
| Lumpkin | 354 | 1.1 | D | 8.9 | D | 7.2 | 3.0 | 9.4 | 40.7 | 5 565 | 185 | 537 | 12 925 | 56.6 |
| McDuffie | 328 | 4.9 | D | 23.8 | 4.2 | 8.7 | 2.9 | 7.7 | 23.8 | 4 675 | 216 | 984 | 9 319 | 4.5 |
| McIntosh | 93 | 1.1 | D | 1.1 | D | 8.8 | 2.3 | 1.2 | 36.2 | 2 875 | 203 | 452 | 9 220 | 60.8 |
| Macon | 177 | 13.1 | D | 28.1 | D | 4.2 | 1.8 | D | 23.2 | 2 400 | 167 | 696 | 6 136 | 11.7 |
| Madison | 177 | 3.2 | D | 7.0 | D | 6.4 | 4.1 | D | 34.0 | 6 160 | 221 | 882 | 11 784 | 12.0 |
| Marion | 69 | -1.4 | D | 27.9 | 1.7 | 6.5 | D | 5.0 | 26.4 | 1 495 | 171 | 302 | 4 156 | 32.8 |
| Meriwether | 236 | 2.3 | 22.4 | 14.8 | 1.5 | 7.2 | 3.9 | D | 33.6 | 5 050 | 234 | 962 | 9 957 | 8.1 |
| Miller | 102 | 33.9 | 3.1 | 0.7 | D | 6.9 | 5.5 | D | 28.5 | 1 335 | 217 | 254 | 2 791 | 0.8 |
| Mitchell | 367 | 16.6 | 28.9 | 27.6 | D | 6.1 | 3.0 | D | 21.4 | 4 650 | 198 | 1 136 | 8 996 | 1.3 |
| Monroe | 347 | 0.6 | D | 2.7 | D | 5.5 | 2.0 | 5.4 | 32.3 | 5 295 | 199 | 592 | 10 710 | 27.0 |
| Montgomery | 86 | 17.6 | 9.9 | 6.0 | 0.6 | 9.4 | 9.5 | D | 22.9 | 1 740 | 192 | 312 | 3 921 | 12.3 |
| Morgan | 315 | 3.6 | 23.7 | 16.8 | 7.7 | 8.1 | 6.1 | 4.1 | 17.8 | 4 065 | 226 | 417 | 7 472 | 21.9 |
| Murray | 456 | -1.9 | D | 44.2 | D | 7.0 | 2.8 | D | 17.4 | 7 420 | 188 | 1 105 | 15 979 | 11.6 |
| Muscogee | 5 892 | 0.0 | 11.0 | 7.2 | 7.7 | 5.7 | 14.4 | 12.9 | 30.7 | 33 650 | 173 | 6 890 | 82 690 | 8.5 |
| Newton | 1 098 | 0.3 | D | 30.0 | 3.9 | 7.1 | 2.9 | 9.4 | 22.4 | 16 360 | 162 | 2 506 | 38 342 | 66.5 |
| Oconee | 430 | 2.2 | D | 5.1 | 7.2 | 7.9 | 9.7 | 10.4 | 19.9 | 5 260 | 158 | 347 | 12 383 | 30.0 |
| Oglethorpe | 103 | 29.9 | 13.6 | 3.2 | D | 4.8 | 2.8 | D | 25.8 | 3 000 | 204 | 445 | 6 484 | 20.8 |
| Paulding | 1 036 | 0.0 | D | 5.6 | 6.4 | 11.5 | 4.4 | 8.2 | 26.4 | 16 875 | 118 | 1 648 | 52 130 | 78.2 |
| Peach | 431 | 10.6 | 30.1 | 25.4 | 1.2 | 9.2 | 2.2 | D | 29.6 | 4 915 | 177 | 958 | 11 050 | 21.5 |
| Pickens | 359 | -3.2 | 22.3 | 12.1 | 5.4 | 9.6 | 7.7 | 15.6 | 20.1 | 7 770 | 264 | 584 | 13 692 | 28.1 |
| Pierce | 191 | 7.6 | 17.1 | 7.7 | D | 7.7 | 3.2 | 6.2 | 22.8 | 4 000 | 213 | 711 | 7 986 | 19.0 |
| Pike | 126 | -1.0 | D | 13.5 | D | 4.6 | 3.5 | D | 26.9 | 3 470 | 195 | 327 | 6 820 | 34.6 |
| Polk | 534 | 1.2 | D | 31.1 | D | 9.5 | 2.1 | 5.2 | 17.8 | 8 905 | 216 | 1 352 | 16 908 | 12.3 |
| Pulaski | 137 | 8.9 | D | D | 5.9 | 6.4 | D | D | 24.3 | 2 130 | 182 | 374 | 5 151 | 30.6 |

1. Includes mining, construction, and manufacturing.  2. Per 1,000 resident population enumerated in the 2010 census.

# Table B. States and Counties — Housing, Labor Force, and Employment

| | Housing units, 2007–2011 | | | | | | | | Civilian labor force, 2012 | | | | Civilian employment,[6] 2007–2011 | | |
| STATE County | Occupied units | | | | | | | | | | Unemployment | | | Percent | |
| | | | Owner-occupied | | | Renter-occupied | | | | | | | | | | |
| | | | | Median owner cost as a percent of income | | | | | | | | | | | | Con-struction, produc-tion, and mainte-nance occu-pations |
| | Total | Percent | Median value[1] | With a mort-gage | Without a mort-gage[2] | Median rent[3] | Median rent as a per-cent of income | Sub-stand-ard units[4] (percent) | Total | Percent change, 2011–2012 | Total | Rate[5] | Total | Manage-ment, business, science and arts | |
| | 89 | 90 | 91 | 92 | 93 | 94 | 95 | 96 | 97 | 98 | 99 | 100 | 101 | 102 | 103 |
| **GEORGIA—Cont'd** | | | | | | | | | | | | | | | |
| Effingham | 17 856 | 75.1 | 154 600 | 23.2 | 10.6 | 852 | 28.5 | 3.7 | 27 860 | 1.8 | 2 140 | 7.7 | 23 582 | 29.6 | 32.5 |
| Elbert | 7 697 | 72.3 | 82 200 | 23.7 | 11.3 | 551 | 30.1 | 3.6 | 9 162 | -3.1 | 1 078 | 11.8 | 8 085 | 22.0 | 39.9 |
| Emanuel | 8 108 | 65.7 | 80 200 | 27.8 | 13.4 | 523 | 26.8 | 3.4 | 9 994 | -2.5 | 1 127 | 11.3 | 8 432 | 25.7 | 36.7 |
| Evans | 4 114 | 67.4 | 89 800 | 21.9 | 12.0 | 536 | 22.1 | 3.4 | 4 877 | -1.0 | 431 | 8.8 | 4 321 | 25.2 | 36.6 |
| Fannin | 10 287 | 80.4 | 168 900 | 31.1 | 12.0 | 567 | 32.0 | 2.7 | 10 549 | -2.3 | 1 012 | 9.6 | 9 127 | 24.9 | 32.3 |
| Fayette | 37 930 | 84.6 | 247 500 | 24.3 | 10.5 | 1 065 | 30.5 | 1.0 | 53 452 | 1.9 | 4 242 | 7.9 | 49 740 | 42.9 | 18.0 |
| Floyd | 34 823 | 66.8 | 120 000 | 23.4 | 12.1 | 687 | 32.1 | 3.4 | 48 706 | 0.8 | 4 857 | 10.0 | 40 675 | 30.6 | 27.6 |
| Forsyth | 55 465 | 86.7 | 274 200 | 23.6 | 9.9 | 1 095 | 30.6 | 1.6 | 94 156 | 1.6 | 6 388 | 6.8 | 79 923 | 45.6 | 14.8 |
| Franklin | 8 774 | 71.8 | 129 100 | 24.8 | 11.4 | 566 | 31.2 | 2.2 | 10 016 | -2.5 | 1 064 | 10.6 | 9 036 | 29.2 | 32.3 |
| Fulton | 362 603 | 55.3 | 250 300 | 24.9 | 13.0 | 946 | 30.5 | 3.0 | 463 788 | 1.2 | 44 661 | 9.6 | 442 363 | 47.6 | 12.4 |
| Gilmer | 11 533 | 71.6 | 152 100 | 26.2 | 11.2 | 682 | 29.7 | 4.4 | 12 462 | -2.6 | 1 275 | 10.2 | 11 967 | 23.1 | 36.4 |
| Glascock | 1 220 | 68.6 | 68 700 | 19.7 | 15.0 | 523 | 29.9 | 1.9 | 1 138 | -2.4 | 130 | 11.4 | 1 264 | 20.1 | 43.4 |
| Glynn | 30 980 | 63.9 | 180 400 | 23.7 | 10.9 | 792 | 28.6 | 3.7 | 37 526 | 0.6 | 3 636 | 9.7 | 36 014 | 31.4 | 19.8 |
| Gordon | 19 085 | 68.2 | 124 500 | 24.1 | 11.8 | 647 | 31.5 | 2.2 | 25 986 | 1.4 | 2 609 | 10.0 | 24 333 | 24.0 | 38.0 |
| Grady | 9 308 | 64.9 | 98 000 | 23.8 | 13.4 | 631 | 33.8 | 3.4 | 11 850 | -0.6 | 905 | 7.6 | 9 192 | 28.9 | 29.7 |
| Greene | 6 205 | 73.3 | 125 000 | 28.2 | 13.6 | 668 | 38.9 | 2.5 | 7 277 | 0.4 | 701 | 9.6 | 5 593 | 19.3 | 35.0 |
| Gwinnett | 262 169 | 70.9 | 190 100 | 25.4 | 10.7 | 980 | 31.7 | 3.5 | 438 826 | 1.4 | 34 422 | 7.8 | 387 109 | 37.6 | 20.5 |
| Habersham | 15 055 | 76.4 | 146 900 | 24.3 | 11.7 | 636 | 29.2 | 4.1 | 19 559 | -0.3 | 1 737 | 8.9 | 16 927 | 26.9 | 32.8 |
| Hall | 60 939 | 69.6 | 174 400 | 25.0 | 11.1 | 838 | 30.5 | 5.3 | 90 910 | 1.7 | 6 814 | 7.5 | 80 531 | 28.9 | 34.2 |
| Hancock | 2 970 | 77.8 | 72 000 | 37.7 | 18.9 | 683 | 32.4 | 4.0 | 3 000 | -2.5 | 510 | 17.0 | 2 678 | 25.1 | 30.4 |
| Haralson | 10 626 | 73.3 | 112 900 | 23.6 | 13.9 | 674 | 29.7 | 5.8 | 12 725 | 1.0 | 1 213 | 9.5 | 11 069 | 27.2 | 34.4 |
| Harris | 11 321 | 88.5 | 209 400 | 22.7 | 11.8 | 957 | 27.5 | 1.4 | 17 102 | 0.6 | 1 169 | 6.8 | 14 683 | 43.3 | 19.7 |
| Hart | 9 617 | 77.8 | 114 600 | 25.5 | 11.0 | 571 | 38.9 | 2.6 | 10 161 | -2.5 | 1 113 | 11.0 | 9 693 | 28.6 | 30.3 |
| Heard | 4 364 | 74.0 | 86 800 | 23.5 | 13.2 | 659 | 27.3 | 2.7 | 5 033 | 1.2 | 514 | 10.2 | 4 540 | 21.0 | 37.2 |
| Henry | 68 128 | 78.3 | 167 600 | 25.3 | 10.9 | 1 045 | 29.8 | 2.1 | 106 795 | 1.2 | 9 570 | 9.0 | 92 540 | 33.1 | 22.6 |
| Houston | 50 871 | 68.1 | 134 200 | 20.9 | 9.9 | 783 | 27.8 | 2.5 | 71 633 | 0.3 | 5 450 | 7.6 | 61 407 | 38.3 | 22.2 |
| Irwin | 3 162 | 78.3 | 78 900 | 21.8 | 11.6 | 592 | 31.5 | 2.2 | 3 593 | -1.0 | 428 | 11.9 | 3 600 | 23.5 | 37.1 |
| Jackson | 21 266 | 76.9 | 163 700 | 25.4 | 11.4 | 749 | 29.5 | 2.0 | 27 935 | 1.5 | 2 434 | 8.7 | 26 665 | 30.9 | 29.5 |
| Jasper | 5 052 | 75.5 | 121 600 | 24.5 | 13.8 | 737 | 42.2 | 2.7 | 6 486 | 0.9 | 624 | 9.6 | 5 931 | 25.4 | 32.8 |
| Jeff Davis | 5 695 | 71.0 | 83 800 | 20.9 | 9.9 | 428 | 26.2 | 3.3 | 5 294 | -3.6 | 735 | 13.9 | 5 893 | 21.6 | 42.0 |
| Jefferson | 6 227 | 70.4 | 69 800 | 24.2 | 16.2 | 495 | 31.0 | 4.3 | 6 814 | -0.9 | 944 | 13.9 | 5 914 | 22.7 | 31.3 |
| Jenkins | 2 954 | 71.0 | 67 300 | 29.5 | 14.0 | 497 | 32.5 | 4.3 | 2 529 | 0.6 | 434 | 17.2 | 2 977 | 20.2 | 34.3 |
| Johnson | 3 366 | 71.8 | 66 000 | 19.8 | 15.1 | 481 | 27.2 | 3.0 | 3 569 | -1.2 | 463 | 13.0 | 3 519 | 22.4 | 37.7 |
| Jones | 10 466 | 80.9 | 137 300 | 24.0 | 11.2 | 767 | 28.7 | 1.2 | 14 753 | 1.3 | 1 265 | 8.6 | 12 430 | 31.1 | 26.2 |
| Lamar | 6 307 | 66.8 | 120 800 | 26.7 | 14.5 | 680 | 29.5 | 2.5 | 8 497 | 0.6 | 900 | 10.6 | 7 032 | 25.0 | 31.6 |
| Lanier | 3 350 | 64.5 | 130 600 | 28.0 | 9.9 | 629 | 35.2 | 5.8 | 4 780 | 1.5 | 366 | 7.7 | 3 425 | 25.4 | 28.8 |
| Laurens | 17 636 | 68.3 | 89 600 | 22.5 | 11.6 | 580 | 26.6 | 2.6 | 20 584 | -2.7 | 2 414 | 11.7 | 18 880 | 27.6 | 28.7 |
| Lee | 9 522 | 75.6 | 149 700 | 21.5 | 11.8 | 830 | 26.1 | 0.9 | 15 620 | 0.2 | 1 162 | 7.4 | 12 986 | 36.3 | 21.9 |
| Liberty | 22 907 | 50.9 | 125 700 | 23.1 | 11.2 | 834 | 28.4 | 2.8 | 25 745 | -0.9 | 2 498 | 9.7 | 22 466 | 28.2 | 25.9 |
| Lincoln | 3 346 | 82.6 | 103 600 | 24.7 | 19.4 | 536 | 24.9 | 2.4 | 3 701 | -1.4 | 381 | 10.3 | 3 301 | 19.1 | 31.2 |
| Long | 4 748 | 63.3 | 85 100 | 25.5 | 9.9 | 651 | 28.1 | 2.9 | 7 690 | -1.0 | 547 | 7.1 | 5 409 | 21.8 | 36.1 |
| Lowndes | 38 605 | 58.3 | 132 200 | 24.1 | 10.9 | 740 | 31.9 | 2.4 | 53 740 | 1.7 | 4 687 | 8.7 | 45 657 | 29.0 | 22.4 |
| Lumpkin | 10 841 | 71.7 | 169 800 | 27.6 | 13.4 | 837 | 32.6 | 2.3 | 13 058 | 1.6 | 1 214 | 9.3 | 12 910 | 30.2 | 23.1 |
| McDuffie | 8 292 | 65.1 | 99 600 | 26.3 | 11.6 | 612 | 29.8 | 1.4 | 10 220 | -0.9 | 1 039 | 10.2 | 8 812 | 22.4 | 33.9 |
| McIntosh | 5 583 | 78.6 | 99 000 | 23.7 | 12.6 | 514 | 31.3 | 4.9 | 5 782 | 1.4 | 615 | 10.6 | 6 031 | 27.0 | 31.6 |
| Macon | 4 716 | 65.0 | 68 900 | 25.9 | 14.4 | 444 | 29.2 | 3.6 | 4 958 | -2.1 | 731 | 14.7 | 5 126 | 27.7 | 41.2 |
| Madison | 9 379 | 75.7 | 128 000 | 24.1 | 10.2 | 671 | 33.4 | 2.8 | 16 365 | 0.7 | 1 110 | 6.8 | 12 134 | 26.1 | 31.0 |
| Marion | 3 223 | 73.4 | 78 200 | 24.0 | 13.9 | 444 | 28.5 | 2.5 | 3 974 | 0.1 | 320 | 8.1 | 3 318 | 15.5 | 43.8 |
| Meriwether | 8 183 | 69.9 | 94 200 | 25.9 | 12.2 | 664 | 31.3 | 2.9 | 9 082 | 0.0 | 1 024 | 11.3 | 8 922 | 19.0 | 42.8 |
| Miller | 2 552 | 72.4 | 81 000 | 21.6 | 15.6 | 513 | 21.6 | 5.3 | 3 483 | -1.1 | 221 | 6.3 | 2 404 | 24.3 | 31.7 |
| Mitchell | 8 021 | 65.8 | 81 100 | 21.8 | 12.0 | 586 | 31.8 | 5.6 | 10 055 | 1.6 | 906 | 9.0 | 8 409 | 24.6 | 36.4 |
| Monroe | 9 291 | 79.7 | 143 000 | 22.2 | 12.4 | 688 | 35.8 | 1.4 | 14 336 | 1.0 | 1 171 | 8.2 | 11 658 | 31.8 | 30.6 |
| Montgomery | 3 291 | 70.8 | 76 600 | 24.6 | 11.6 | 547 | 27.5 | 2.7 | 4 623 | -0.5 | 468 | 10.1 | 3 621 | 28.1 | 36.9 |
| Morgan | 6 478 | 75.1 | 184 700 | 27.0 | 10.9 | 793 | 30.4 | 0.5 | 9 383 | 1.9 | 751 | 8.0 | 7 839 | 37.6 | 24.7 |
| Murray | 14 300 | 70.3 | 99 200 | 23.0 | 12.3 | 618 | 28.8 | 7.8 | 17 105 | -3.3 | 2 096 | 12.3 | 15 549 | 20.8 | 47.2 |
| Muscogee | 72 087 | 54.9 | 134 900 | 23.7 | 11.2 | 758 | 31.4 | 1.9 | 85 897 | 0.6 | 7 843 | 9.1 | 74 411 | 34.2 | 18.7 |
| Newton | 33 634 | 75.3 | 144 500 | 26.8 | 11.5 | 942 | 39.4 | 2.5 | 48 450 | 0.6 | 4 992 | 10.3 | 43 236 | 29.7 | 27.3 |
| Oconee | 11 155 | 82.0 | 234 400 | 21.8 | 9.9 | 838 | 29.6 | 1.6 | 19 773 | 1.2 | 1 090 | 5.5 | 15 469 | 47.4 | 15.9 |
| Oglethorpe | 4 793 | 82.3 | 134 500 | 24.1 | 12.4 | 616 | 21.9 | 3.0 | 8 411 | 0.7 | 563 | 6.7 | 6 212 | 30.9 | 28.1 |
| Paulding | 47 691 | 81.5 | 147 700 | 23.8 | 10.3 | 932 | 30.0 | 2.0 | 72 990 | 1.0 | 6 133 | 8.4 | 66 097 | 32.5 | 24.8 |
| Peach | 9 188 | 69.2 | 118 900 | 22.5 | 11.6 | 649 | 36.1 | 3.0 | 12 716 | 2.2 | 1 387 | 10.9 | 11 246 | 26.8 | 32.8 |
| Pickens | 11 116 | 79.4 | 169 900 | 26.2 | 11.5 | 771 | 33.4 | 2.0 | 14 434 | 0.5 | 1 197 | 8.3 | 12 788 | 25.4 | 27.3 |
| Pierce | 6 914 | 74.7 | 79 900 | 21.3 | 11.5 | 454 | 27.7 | 3.9 | 8 516 | 1.3 | 780 | 9.2 | 7 492 | 25.3 | 33.0 |
| Pike | 6 012 | 83.3 | 156 500 | 24.4 | 13.3 | 875 | 30.3 | 1.8 | 8 264 | 1.3 | 755 | 9.1 | 7 581 | 31.4 | 31.1 |
| Polk | 14 675 | 70.3 | 109 200 | 24.0 | 13.6 | 638 | 32.0 | 3.4 | 20 749 | 1.2 | 1 838 | 8.9 | 16 640 | 22.1 | 38.8 |
| Pulaski | 4 245 | 72.0 | 81 200 | 25.0 | 10.6 | 492 | 26.5 | 2.9 | 4 403 | -0.8 | 422 | 9.6 | 4 454 | 24.0 | 30.6 |

1. Specified owner-occupied units.   2. A value of 9.9 represents 9.9 percent or less.   3. Specified renter-occupied units. A value of 10.0 represents 10 percent or less.   4. Overcrowded or lacking complete plumbing facilities.   5. Percent of civilian labor force.   6. Persons 16 years old and over.

| STATE County | Private nonfarm establishments, employment and payroll, 2011 | | | | | | | | | Agriculture, 2007 | | | |
|---|---|---|---|---|---|---|---|---|---|---|---|---|---|
| | | Employment | | | | | | Annual payroll | | Farms | | | |
| | | | | | | | | | | | | Percent with: | |
| | Number of establishments | Total | Health care and social assistance | Manufacturing | Retail trade | Finance and insurance | Professional, scientific, and technical services | Total (mil dol) | Average per employee (dollars) | Number | Fewer than 50 acres | 500 acres or more | Farm operators whose principal occupation is farming (percent) |
| | 104 | 105 | 106 | 107 | 108 | 109 | 110 | 111 | 112 | 113 | 114 | 115 | 116 |

GEORGIA—Cont'd

| | | | | | | | | | | | | | |
|---|---|---|---|---|---|---|---|---|---|---|---|---|---|
| Effingham | 680 | 7 083 | 949 | D | 1 275 | 197 | 252 | 255 | 35 938 | 203 | 46.3 | 9.4 | 36.9 |
| Elbert | 457 | 4 854 | 602 | 1 811 | 642 | 143 | D | 131 | 26 969 | 507 | 38.1 | 4.5 | 43.4 |
| Emanuel | 393 | 4 889 | 844 | 1 685 | 825 | 158 | 218 | 132 | 26 941 | 511 | 24.1 | 14.3 | 35.4 |
| Evans | 220 | 3 771 | 495 | D | 461 | D | 67 | 98 | 26 070 | 212 | 30.7 | 16.5 | 38.7 |
| Fannin | 541 | 4 344 | 1 083 | 291 | 994 | 196 | 175 | 114 | 26 302 | 243 | 56.0 | 1.2 | 42.0 |
| Fayette | 3 113 | 36 287 | 5 019 | 2 260 | 6 427 | 1 044 | 2 658 | 1 341 | 36 952 | 154 | 50.0 | 0.6 | 50.6 |
| Floyd | 1 927 | 32 780 | 7 971 | 6 095 | 4 129 | D | 746 | 1 127 | 34 393 | 553 | 42.0 | 6.5 | 40.0 |
| Forsyth | 5 055 | 58 013 | 6 223 | 6 692 | 7 834 | 1 628 | 4 817 | 2 501 | 43 118 | 306 | 67.0 | 1.6 | 45.8 |
| Franklin | 422 | 5 508 | 684 | 1 362 | 857 | 154 | 78 | 153 | 27 828 | 851 | 47.6 | 1.9 | 51.1 |
| Fulton | 32 776 | 685 868 | 71 062 | 16 834 | 48 925 | 51 539 | 83 008 | 42 790 | 62 388 | 204 | 71.6 | 2.0 | 45.1 |
| Gilmer | 537 | 5 628 | D | D | 1 102 | 228 | D | 152 | 26 979 | 397 | 49.9 | 2.3 | 52.9 |
| Glascock | 25 | 209 | D | D | 17 | D | D | 5 | 23 278 | 93 | 14.0 | 8.6 | 36.6 |
| Glynn | 2 393 | 29 135 | 4 853 | 2 274 | 4 690 | 757 | 908 | 926 | 31 782 | 50 | 74.0 | 4.0 | 34.0 |
| Gordon | 1 006 | 18 012 | 1 586 | 6 404 | 2 335 | 328 | 228 | 570 | 31 661 | 839 | 54.1 | 2.5 | 42.8 |
| Grady | 407 | 3 795 | 381 | D | 839 | 167 | 91 | 108 | 28 464 | 445 | 35.5 | 12.4 | 47.0 |
| Greene | 381 | 4 358 | 417 | 417 | 565 | 181 | 104 | 132 | 30 228 | 247 | 30.8 | 13.4 | 42.9 |
| Gwinnett | 20 920 | 285 475 | 24 589 | 18 508 | 42 007 | 13 817 | 22 106 | 12 720 | 44 557 | 181 | 75.1 | 0.6 | 47.5 |
| Habersham | 798 | 11 288 | 1 286 | D | 1 667 | 653 | 253 | 319 | 28 218 | 372 | 57.0 | 1.1 | 48.4 |
| Hall | 3 860 | 59 760 | 11 062 | 15 344 | 7 860 | 1 761 | 1 691 | 2 292 | 38 359 | 799 | 60.6 | 1.6 | 40.3 |
| Hancock | 75 | 680 | D | D | 109 | D | D | 15 | 22 535 | 172 | 20.9 | 8.1 | 48.8 |
| Haralson | 416 | 4 798 | 742 | 1 474 | 842 | 175 | 95 | 172 | 35 930 | 367 | 46.3 | 2.2 | 34.1 |
| Harris | 377 | 3 590 | 212 | 1 286 | 296 | 42 | 79 | 80 | 22 282 | 371 | 48.2 | 5.1 | 30.5 |
| Hart | 387 | 5 047 | 591 | 1 781 | 897 | 98 | 96 | 171 | 33 951 | 657 | 47.8 | 2.9 | 49.2 |
| Heard | 117 | 1 161 | D | D | 97 | 25 | D | 36 | 31 234 | 187 | 36.9 | 2.7 | 42.8 |
| Henry | 3 266 | 41 605 | 5 888 | 2 663 | 8 371 | 1 697 | 1 514 | 1 287 | 30 943 | 298 | 58.4 | 1.3 | 49.3 |
| Houston | 2 280 | 34 278 | 6 020 | 3 840 | 6 495 | 1 087 | 3 749 | 1 032 | 30 093 | 298 | 54.0 | 5.7 | 51.0 |
| Irwin | 140 | 1 630 | D | 127 | 159 | D | D | 47 | 28 584 | 387 | 20.9 | 22.7 | 47.8 |
| Jackson | 1 136 | 15 519 | 968 | 4 465 | 2 508 | 340 | 576 | 531 | 34 222 | 892 | 55.3 | 3.3 | 39.8 |
| Jasper | 162 | 1 318 | D | 389 | D | 63 | D | 35 | 26 736 | 333 | 40.5 | 6.0 | 35.7 |
| Jeff Davis | 247 | 3 369 | 280 | 1 081 | 759 | 96 | D | 94 | 27 773 | 224 | 39.7 | 17.0 | 50.9 |
| Jefferson | 314 | 3 921 | D | 918 | 617 | 177 | 50 | 127 | 32 315 | 315 | 25.1 | 17.1 | 38.7 |
| Jenkins | 98 | 708 | 168 | D | 167 | 35 | D | 18 | 25 730 | 247 | 19.0 | 16.6 | 36.4 |
| Johnson | 125 | 1 144 | 257 | 158 | 144 | D | D | 31 | 26 715 | 281 | 22.8 | 11.0 | 32.7 |
| Jones | 332 | 2 493 | 363 | D | 413 | 102 | D | 72 | 28 759 | 206 | 35.9 | 4.9 | 47.6 |
| Lamar | 227 | 2 341 | 243 | 515 | 437 | D | D | 64 | 27 418 | 271 | 44.3 | 5.2 | 37.6 |
| Lanier | 103 | 901 | D | 84 | 148 | D | 17 | 22 | 24 555 | 107 | 40.2 | 15.9 | 43.9 |
| Laurens | 1 048 | 14 846 | 2 915 | 2 627 | 2 509 | 520 | 359 | 482 | 32 451 | 664 | 30.4 | 9.3 | 36.9 |
| Lee | 371 | 3 231 | 419 | D | 608 | 147 | 78 | 91 | 28 084 | 198 | 34.8 | 25.3 | 44.9 |
| Liberty | 812 | 11 917 | 1 844 | 1 428 | 2 037 | 272 | 945 | 396 | 33 263 | 62 | 50.0 | 11.3 | 35.5 |
| Lincoln | 135 | 827 | D | D | 150 | D | 22 | 23 | 27 318 | 199 | 44.2 | 5.0 | 34.7 |
| Long | 70 | 345 | 23 | D | 63 | D | D | 7 | 20 983 | 73 | 42.5 | 9.6 | 45.2 |
| Lowndes | 2 725 | 37 162 | 6 760 | 2 942 | 6 424 | 934 | 1 225 | 1 051 | 28 276 | 470 | 46.8 | 6.6 | 33.2 |
| Lumpkin | 481 | 4 346 | 817 | 588 | 725 | 113 | D | 124 | 28 537 | 292 | 65.4 | 2.1 | 43.8 |
| McDuffie | 450 | 6 240 | 953 | 2 034 | 1 134 | 158 | 96 | 177 | 28 352 | 213 | 43.7 | 9.4 | 38.5 |
| McIntosh | 191 | 1 236 | 48 | 26 | 478 | D | D | 27 | 21 929 | 58 | 58.6 | 8.6 | 51.7 |
| Macon | 184 | 2 008 | 418 | 738 | 261 | 52 | D | 66 | 33 108 | 336 | 25.6 | 18.2 | 47.6 |
| Madison | 359 | 2 104 | 312 | D | 452 | D | 82 | 52 | 24 817 | 771 | 49.5 | 1.9 | 38.7 |
| Marion | 71 | 1 166 | D | D | 269 | D | D | 30 | 25 985 | 185 | 30.3 | 16.2 | 44.3 |
| Meriwether | 304 | 2 962 | 599 | 673 | 562 | 140 | D | 91 | 30 867 | 437 | 41.6 | 5.9 | 35.5 |
| Miller | 131 | 1 097 | 375 | D | D | 43 | 30 | 31 | 28 354 | 213 | 23.0 | 24.4 | 57.3 |
| Mitchell | 374 | 6 291 | 483 | D | 611 | 171 | D | 164 | 26 104 | 441 | 29.0 | 23.6 | 52.6 |
| Monroe | 491 | 6 656 | 803 | 590 | D | 173 | 156 | 202 | 30 289 | 204 | 39.7 | 8.8 | 48.0 |
| Montgomery | 108 | 1 022 | 33 | 188 | 122 | 82 | D | 27 | 26 008 | 228 | 30.3 | 10.1 | 26.3 |
| Morgan | 450 | 5 610 | 627 | 1 083 | 928 | 174 | D | 176 | 31 436 | 657 | 39.7 | 4.9 | 39.3 |
| Murray | 404 | 7 741 | 465 | 4 331 | 817 | D | 64 | 218 | 28 223 | 308 | 51.9 | 2.6 | 35.4 |
| Muscogee | 4 314 | 76 940 | 13 185 | 6 469 | 11 351 | D | 4 364 | 2 811 | 36 541 | 43 | 32.6 | 9.3 | 62.8 |
| Newton | 1 312 | 16 391 | 2 234 | 3 761 | 2 503 | 521 | 556 | 593 | 36 161 | 306 | 58.5 | 5.6 | 38.2 |
| Oconee | 942 | 7 808 | 1 161 | 563 | 1 629 | 394 | 574 | 253 | 32 359 | 420 | 47.1 | 4.3 | 32.1 |
| Oglethorpe | 170 | 1 088 | 125 | 65 | D | 43 | D | 27 | 24 876 | 477 | 40.7 | 9.0 | 49.1 |
| Paulding | 1 586 | 14 363 | 1 925 | 852 | 4 011 | 330 | 508 | 384 | 26 702 | 181 | 56.4 | 0.6 | 50.3 |
| Peach | 467 | 5 944 | 743 | D | 783 | 146 | 126 | 182 | 30 692 | 213 | 55.4 | 8.9 | 41.8 |
| Pickens | 644 | 5 694 | 1 125 | 720 | 1 226 | 261 | 163 | 174 | 30 637 | 333 | 60.1 | 1.2 | 37.5 |
| Pierce | 313 | 2 943 | 262 | D | 376 | 114 | 90 | 79 | 26 978 | 431 | 45.5 | 5.1 | 40.6 |
| Pike | 220 | 1 412 | D | D | 165 | D | 71 | 38 | 27 030 | 392 | 49.5 | 3.6 | 37.5 |
| Polk | 595 | 9 667 | 845 | 3 224 | 1 454 | 203 | 108 | 292 | 30 173 | 363 | 43.5 | 2.2 | 41.3 |
| Pulaski | 189 | 1 947 | 608 | D | 361 | 74 | 72 | 58 | 29 947 | 190 | 31.6 | 19.5 | 41.6 |

# Table B. States and Counties — Agriculture

| STATE County | Agriculture, 2007 (cont.) | | | | | | | | | | | | | | | |
|---|---|---|---|---|---|---|---|---|---|---|---|---|---|---|---|---|
| | Land in farms | | | | | Value of land and buildings (dollars) | | Value of machinery and equipment, average per farm (dollars) | Value of products sold | | | | Percent of farms with sales of: | | Government payments | |
| | | | Acres | | | | | | | | Percent from: | | | | | |
| | Acreage (1,000) | Percent change, 2002–2007 | Average size of farm | Total irrigated (1,000) | Total cropland (1,000) | Average per farm | Average per acre | | Total (mil dol) | Average per farm (dollars) | Crops | Live-stock and poultry products | $10,000 or more | $100,000 or more | Total ($1,000) | Percent of farms |
| | 117 | 118 | 119 | 120 | 121 | 122 | 123 | 124 | 125 | 126 | 127 | 128 | 129 | 130 | 131 | 132 |
| GEORGIA—Cont'd | | | | | | | | | | | | | | | | |
| Effingham | 40 | -24.5 | 199 | 0.0 | 14.7 | 636 927 | 3 198 | 70 116 | 5.0 | 24 788 | 77.9 | 22.1 | 27.6 | 5.4 | 546 | 28.6 |
| Elbert | 63 | 0.0 | 124 | 0.1 | 19.2 | 429 051 | 3 458 | 53 690 | 50.4 | 99 468 | 3.4 | 96.6 | 23.9 | 10.5 | 599 | 26.4 |
| Emanuel | 139 | -13.1 | 271 | 7.6 | 54.9 | 589 051 | 2 173 | 77 017 | 20.4 | 39 889 | 79.5 | 20.5 | 24.3 | 10.6 | 3 814 | 52.1 |
| Evans | 53 | 10.4 | 249 | 2.8 | 23.4 | 602 807 | 2 422 | 68 410 | 30.8 | 145 066 | 35.8 | 64.2 | 35.4 | 16.5 | 1 031 | 41.0 |
| Fannin | 19 | 26.7 | 77 | D | 4.5 | 420 832 | 5 436 | 45 444 | 18.1 | 74 598 | 9.1 | 90.9 | 19.3 | 8.6 | 6 | 7.8 |
| Fayette | 12 | -33.3 | 80 | 0.1 | 2.7 | 535 895 | 6 689 | 41 882 | 2.8 | 18 473 | 75.9 | 24.1 | 20.8 | 1.3 | 6 | 8.4 |
| Floyd | 85 | -6.6 | 153 | 1.1 | 28.0 | 565 269 | 3 695 | 63 954 | 49.4 | 89 350 | 5.9 | 94.1 | 26.6 | 8.0 | 769 | 16.8 |
| Forsyth | 20 | -41.2 | 65 | 0.2 | 5.7 | 539 890 | 8 344 | 67 074 | 40.0 | 130 628 | 16.3 | 83.7 | 30.7 | 16.3 | 44 | 6.2 |
| Franklin | 81 | -5.8 | 96 | 0.5 | 25.9 | 616 510 | 6 448 | 70 653 | 326.2 | 383 284 | 0.9 | 99.1 | 42.4 | 27.0 | 222 | 13.3 |
| Fulton | 16 | -42.9 | 76 | 0.3 | 3.6 | 423 093 | 5 548 | 31 360 | 4.0 | 19 768 | 85.5 | 14.5 | 21.1 | 2.9 | 22 | 4.4 |
| Gilmer | 37 | 48.0 | 92 | 0.1 | 9.6 | 694 848 | 7 550 | 66 506 | 194.2 | 489 115 | 1.2 | 98.8 | 44.3 | 35.3 | 166 | 10.3 |
| Glascock | 21 | 0.0 | 228 | 0.1 | 6.6 | 491 038 | 2 151 | 48 329 | 1.5 | 15 659 | 41.1 | 58.9 | 23.7 | 3.2 | 386 | 32.3 |
| Glynn | 6 | -25.0 | 117 | 0.1 | 0.4 | 415 516 | 3 559 | 77 507 | 0.3 | 5 993 | 37.3 | 62.3 | 24.0 | 0.0 | 0 | 0.0 |
| Gordon | 79 | 3.9 | 94 | 0.9 | 31.1 | 507 095 | 5 377 | 57 810 | 182.0 | 216 983 | 1.9 | 98.1 | 30.5 | 15.4 | 380 | 15.3 |
| Grady | 119 | -6.3 | 267 | 8.0 | 56.4 | 799 170 | 2 989 | 89 873 | 79.5 | 178 547 | 65.7 | 34.3 | 40.9 | 15.5 | 3 857 | 53.0 |
| Greene | 55 | 5.8 | 224 | 0.5 | 13.7 | 888 978 | 3 968 | 77 363 | 64.0 | 259 013 | D | D | 38.1 | 13.0 | 77 | 14.2 |
| Gwinnett | 8 | -55.6 | 46 | 0.3 | 3.3 | 443 536 | 9 614 | 61 858 | 15.9 | 87 639 | 81.1 | 18.9 | 28.2 | 11.0 | 23 | 3.9 |
| Habersham | 29 | -25.6 | 79 | 0.3 | 8.4 | 550 333 | 6 989 | 69 204 | 101.3 | 272 329 | 0.8 | 99.2 | 46.8 | 27.4 | 90 | 7.0 |
| Hall | 57 | -8.1 | 72 | 0.2 | 15.4 | 532 486 | 7 426 | 53 349 | 185.1 | 227 192 | 0.6 | 99.4 | 31.0 | 19.3 | 213 | 11.3 |
| Hancock | 38 | -9.5 | 221 | 0.1 | 8.6 | 556 330 | 2 517 | 47 801 | 3.4 | 19 970 | 26.3 | 73.7 | 20.3 | 4.7 | 52 | 9.9 |
| Haralson | 34 | -15.0 | 94 | 0.1 | 11.3 | 385 787 | 4 116 | 48 977 | 43.3 | 118 114 | 1.4 | 98.6 | 16.1 | 4.9 | 76 | 11.2 |
| Harris | 61 | -9.0 | 164 | 0.1 | 11.9 | 546 578 | 3 333 | 37 994 | 2.7 | 7 248 | 66.2 | 33.8 | 15.1 | 0.8 | 41 | 4.9 |
| Hart | 70 | 7.7 | 107 | 1.5 | 28.8 | 613 357 | 5 724 | 69 738 | 204.6 | 311 413 | 1.7 | 98.3 | 37.3 | 20.2 | 420 | 23.3 |
| Heard | 24 | -42.9 | 126 | D | 5.9 | 523 055 | 4 145 | 67 915 | 28.3 | 151 501 | 3.1 | 96.9 | 26.7 | 7.5 | 50 | 10.7 |
| Henry | 24 | -58.6 | 79 | 0.2 | 8.3 | 473 022 | 5 990 | 43 401 | 5.3 | 17 873 | 70.6 | 29.4 | 21.5 | 3.0 | 145 | 11.4 |
| Houston | 47 | -37.3 | 157 | 4.5 | 20.3 | 577 908 | 3 692 | 64 949 | 15.6 | 52 338 | 44.8 | 55.2 | 28.9 | 6.4 | 1 095 | 24.2 |
| Irwin | 145 | 5.1 | 376 | 30.6 | 88.3 | 845 066 | 2 249 | 146 151 | 46.0 | 118 822 | 84.2 | 15.8 | 53.0 | 24.3 | 7 205 | 75.7 |
| Jackson | 85 | -15.0 | 95 | 0.6 | 24.5 | 588 108 | 6 181 | 51 686 | 166.9 | 187 137 | 1.7 | 98.3 | 34.2 | 18.5 | 165 | 6.7 |
| Jasper | 56 | 9.8 | 169 | 0.3 | 12.4 | 649 775 | 3 835 | 42 173 | 20.8 | 62 329 | 3.1 | 96.9 | 18.9 | 3.0 | 75 | 12.6 |
| Jeff Davis | 58 | 3.6 | 259 | 9.3 | 38.1 | 578 015 | 2 228 | 119 805 | 23.0 | 102 856 | 69.8 | 30.2 | 32.6 | 17.9 | 2 350 | 45.5 |
| Jefferson | 109 | -20.4 | 346 | 14.6 | 61.7 | 742 772 | 2 148 | 86 810 | 29.3 | 93 092 | 69.7 | 30.3 | 39.0 | 15.9 | 2 569 | 61.0 |
| Jenkins | 85 | -10.5 | 343 | 10.0 | 42.0 | 656 814 | 1 915 | 66 491 | 14.8 | 59 769 | 75.7 | 24.3 | 25.5 | 10.9 | 1 669 | 51.0 |
| Johnson | 67 | -11.8 | 237 | 1.6 | 21.2 | 465 570 | 1 967 | 41 804 | 4.8 | 16 966 | 74.5 | 25.4 | 19.6 | 3.2 | 686 | 42.0 |
| Jones | 32 | -8.6 | 157 | 0.3 | 8.6 | 559 361 | 3 559 | 54 788 | 7.5 | 36 387 | 13.5 | 86.5 | 30.6 | 4.9 | 50 | 5.4 |
| Lamar | 36 | -14.3 | 132 | 1.3 | 13.1 | 548 341 | 4 165 | 64 304 | 43.9 | 162 151 | 9.3 | 90.7 | 28.8 | 10.0 | 88 | 18.5 |
| Lanier | 53 | 1.9 | 497 | 8.4 | 21.8 | 1 178 519 | 2 372 | 135 457 | 17.5 | 163 780 | 92.3 | 7.7 | 29.9 | 15.9 | 1 247 | 41.1 |
| Laurens | 165 | -14.9 | 248 | 6.4 | 55.3 | 526 545 | 2 119 | 57 077 | 14.5 | 21 882 | 65.7 | 34.3 | 20.6 | 6.0 | 2 914 | 53.9 |
| Lee | 126 | -14.3 | 638 | 15.8 | 50.2 | 1 595 988 | 2 502 | 150 389 | 30.9 | 156 095 | 67.5 | 32.5 | 38.9 | 19.7 | 2 417 | 45.5 |
| Liberty | 9 | -43.8 | 151 | 0.0 | 1.2 | 307 199 | 2 032 | 46 021 | 0.2 | 3 080 | 39.8 | 60.2 | 8.1 | 0.0 | 34 | 11.3 |
| Lincoln | 28 | -9.7 | 139 | 0.0 | 6.9 | 407 572 | 2 937 | 31 999 | 1.5 | 7 354 | 12.4 | 87.6 | 18.1 | 0.5 | 60 | 17.1 |
| Long | 13 | -45.8 | 180 | 0.5 | 4.8 | 395 719 | 2 198 | 92 928 | 5.3 | 73 158 | 14.5 | 85.5 | 27.4 | 6.8 | 120 | 19.2 |
| Lowndes | 68 | -8.1 | 145 | 4.2 | 27.8 | 534 956 | 3 702 | 58 969 | 22.1 | 46 931 | 89.2 | 10.8 | 27.2 | 8.1 | 1 372 | 33.2 |
| Lumpkin | 22 | 4.8 | 75 | 0.1 | 5.0 | 493 787 | 6 549 | 45 546 | 48.8 | 167 180 | 1.1 | 98.9 | 28.4 | 15.1 | 99 | 14.0 |
| McDuffie | 36 | -23.4 | 170 | 0.5 | 9.6 | 483 053 | 2 849 | 49 554 | 24.9 | 117 022 | D | D | 29.6 | 4.2 | 90 | 17.4 |
| McIntosh | 9 | -18.2 | 157 | 0.0 | 2.6 | 368 010 | 2 343 | 43 432 | 0.6 | 10 483 | 6.1 | 93.9 | 15.5 | 1.7 | D | 3.4 |
| Macon | 122 | 7.0 | 364 | 16.9 | 54.0 | 1 028 759 | 2 824 | 124 100 | 157.4 | 468 500 | 12.6 | 87.4 | 47.3 | 31.3 | 3 198 | 50.9 |
| Madison | 76 | 0.0 | 99 | 0.3 | 25.3 | 500 466 | 5 044 | 67 020 | 140.9 | 182 719 | 1.1 | 98.9 | 33.1 | 17.1 | 289 | 16.5 |
| Marion | 47 | -9.6 | 252 | 3.4 | 14.6 | 632 544 | 2 510 | 64 239 | 32.1 | 173 291 | 12.3 | 87.7 | 36.8 | 16.8 | 372 | 31.4 |
| Meriwether | 81 | -3.6 | 186 | 0.8 | 22.2 | 678 251 | 3 637 | 41 468 | 8.6 | 19 585 | 51.0 | 49.0 | 20.8 | 3.7 | 267 | 14.9 |
| Miller | 102 | 7.4 | 478 | 37.7 | 65.8 | 1 273 797 | 2 667 | 165 163 | 42.5 | 199 486 | 78.3 | 21.7 | 54.0 | 30.5 | 4 255 | 61.0 |
| Mitchell | 204 | 10.3 | 464 | 47.7 | 126.6 | 1 212 128 | 2 615 | 155 875 | 250.2 | 567 384 | 34.2 | 65.8 | 53.3 | 39.0 | 7 338 | 56.5 |
| Monroe | 39 | -37.1 | 193 | 0.2 | 9.1 | 624 973 | 3 244 | 69 841 | 36.2 | 177 513 | 1.0 | 99.0 | 33.8 | 9.8 | 214 | 15.2 |
| Montgomery | 52 | -29.7 | 226 | 2.6 | 17.4 | 560 558 | 2 477 | 49 832 | 10.2 | 44 817 | 79.7 | 20.3 | 21.1 | 7.5 | 898 | 46.1 |
| Morgan | 92 | 3.4 | 141 | 1.8 | 31.0 | 725 864 | 5 159 | 64 941 | 71.9 | 109 383 | 6.7 | 93.3 | 29.4 | 10.4 | 626 | 28.5 |
| Murray | 40 | -4.8 | 130 | 0.4 | 15.3 | 521 263 | 4 021 | 54 610 | 51.5 | 167 144 | 3.3 | 96.7 | 34.7 | 14.3 | 74 | 10.4 |
| Muscogee | 8 | -46.7 | 179 | D | 2.8 | 581 738 | 3 251 | 37 532 | 0.1 | 3 069 | 41.7 | 58.3 | 7.0 | 0.0 | D | 4.7 |
| Newton | 39 | -13.3 | 126 | 0.2 | 9.9 | 540 261 | 4 290 | 44 566 | 4.7 | 15 238 | 19.2 | 80.8 | 22.2 | 4.6 | 54 | 12.1 |
| Oconee | 49 | -9.3 | 116 | 1.0 | 13.6 | 635 315 | 5 470 | 51 107 | 79.8 | 190 070 | 22.2 | 77.8 | 31.0 | 10.2 | 330 | 24.5 |
| Oglethorpe | 87 | 55.4 | 182 | 0.8 | 23.7 | 664 911 | 3 661 | 74 478 | 166.1 | 348 288 | 2.7 | 97.3 | 35.6 | 20.8 | 476 | 15.9 |
| Paulding | 11 | -35.3 | 63 | 0.0 | 3.5 | 416 839 | 6 609 | 40 108 | 17.0 | 94 050 | 11.8 | 88.2 | 25.4 | 6.6 | 2 | 2.2 |
| Peach | 40 | 2.6 | 188 | 5.6 | 23.5 | 702 024 | 3 738 | 73 240 | 20.8 | 97 707 | 80.5 | 19.5 | 24.9 | 9.4 | 454 | 12.7 |
| Pickens | 24 | 41.2 | 71 | 0.3 | 8.0 | 470 848 | 6 603 | 64 071 | 72.5 | 217 567 | 1.1 | 98.9 | 28.8 | 13.2 | 30 | 5.7 |
| Pierce | 72 | -27.3 | 166 | 8.3 | 34.9 | 475 208 | 2 855 | 73 206 | 24.0 | 55 743 | 75.1 | 24.9 | 36.7 | 8.1 | 2 281 | 47.8 |
| Pike | 46 | 4.5 | 118 | 0.8 | 14.5 | 490 571 | 4 172 | 54 754 | 13.9 | 35 456 | 23.9 | 76.1 | 18.9 | 3.3 | 184 | 18.4 |
| Polk | 44 | -15.4 | 121 | 0.1 | 15.5 | 512 580 | 4 241 | 61 487 | 36.3 | 99 892 | 3.6 | 96.4 | 26.4 | 8.0 | 305 | 18.5 |
| Pulaski | 57 | -14.9 | 300 | 12.7 | 34.0 | 794 591 | 2 651 | 93 682 | 18.9 | 99 467 | 87.0 | 13.0 | 31.6 | 18.4 | 2 532 | 58.4 |

| STATE County | Water use, 2005 | | Wholesale trade,[1] 2007 | | | | Retail trade,[2] 2007 | | | | Real estate and rental and leasing,[2] 2007 | | | |
|---|---|---|---|---|---|---|---|---|---|---|---|---|---|---|
| | Total water withdrawn (mil gal/day) | Gallons withdrawn per person | Number of establishments | Number of employees | Sales (mil dol) | Annual payroll (mil dol) | Number of establishments | Number of employees | Sales (mil dol) | Annual payroll (mil dol) | Number of establishments | Number of employees | Receipts (mil dol) | Annual payroll (mil dol) |
| | 133 | 134 | 135 | 136 | 137 | 138 | 139 | 140 | 141 | 142 | 143 | 144 | 145 | 146 |
| GEORGIA—Cont'd | | | | | | | | | | | | | | |
| Effingham | 150.8 | 3 214 | 12 | 95 | 63.0 | 4.8 | 108 | 1 190 | 322.6 | 26.1 | 39 | 111 | 14.9 | 1.9 |
| Elbert | 3.4 | 163 | 44 | 377 | 106.3 | 11.2 | 88 | 650 | 137.0 | 13.0 | 10 | 23 | 1.7 | 0.4 |
| Emanuel | 6.7 | 301 | 27 | 172 | 93.4 | 4.3 | 104 | 896 | 184.0 | 17.8 | 19 | 54 | 6.2 | 1.0 |
| Evans | 4.2 | 371 | 5 | D | D | D | 54 | 451 | 153.9 | 11.5 | 5 | 21 | 2.4 | 0.3 |
| Fannin | 2.8 | 127 | 22 | 139 | 41.8 | 4.1 | 122 | 1 173 | 293.1 | 24.1 | 51 | 97 | 18.4 | 1.9 |
| Fayette | 14.8 | 142 | 190 | 1 798 | 877.2 | 81.8 | 464 | 7 315 | 1 390.0 | 147.0 | 216 | 535 | 80.7 | 15.7 |
| Floyd | 588.9 | 6 252 | 94 | 1 274 | 636.2 | 46.9 | 431 | 4 718 | 1 039.8 | 94.0 | 82 | 353 | 58.0 | 10.1 |
| Forsyth | 28.5 | 203 | 386 | 4 565 | 2 503.5 | 249.0 | 541 | 7 952 | 1 960.9 | 194.3 | 314 | 829 | 147.9 | 30.9 |
| Franklin | 4.2 | 193 | 20 | 334 | 107.8 | 7.5 | 115 | 985 | 315.1 | 22.2 | 17 | 31 | 2.1 | 0.5 |
| Fulton | 152.0 | 166 | 1 596 | 28 186 | 40 824.1 | 1 744.0 | 3 625 | 54 054 | 13 239.7 | 1 361.0 | 2 312 | 20 719 | 4 881.9 | 1 234.2 |
| Gilmer | 10.9 | 400 | 20 | 160 | 45.8 | 5.2 | 117 | 1 298 | 370.5 | 32.8 | 32 | 84 | 13.0 | 1.9 |
| Glascock | 0.3 | 122 | NA | NA | NA | NA | 3 | 14 | 4.8 | 0.2 | NA | NA | NA | NA |
| Glynn | 112.1 | 1 559 | 93 | 598 | 270.9 | 20.8 | 507 | 4 954 | 1 351.8 | 117.0 | 195 | 721 | 93.4 | 20.4 |
| Gordon | 15.1 | 301 | 70 | D | D | D | 249 | 2 641 | 659.4 | 53.3 | 55 | 170 | 32.2 | 4.4 |
| Grady | 10.4 | 423 | 23 | 356 | 201.3 | 10.3 | 87 | 762 | 168.1 | 15.8 | 21 | 75 | 6.5 | 1.4 |
| Greene | 3.9 | 249 | 18 | 90 | 31.9 | 4.1 | 77 | 638 | 137.1 | 12.9 | 30 | 54 | 8.0 | 1.7 |
| Gwinnett | 9.2 | 13 | 1 774 | 33 042 | 28 829.1 | 1 851.4 | 2 959 | 47 523 | 13 857.0 | 1 178.7 | 1 212 | 5 730 | 1 396.1 | 258.1 |
| Habersham | 13.2 | 333 | 35 | D | D | D | 175 | 1 983 | 492.1 | 40.0 | 33 | 240 | 23.3 | 5.0 |
| Hall | 108.6 | 655 | 252 | 3 732 | 4 914.5 | 170.8 | 630 | 8 134 | 2 220.7 | 206.5 | 229 | 558 | 125.5 | 18.4 |
| Hancock | 1.5 | 153 | NA | NA | NA | NA | 18 | 98 | 21.0 | 2.4 | 2 | D | D | D |
| Haralson | 3.4 | 119 | 19 | 174 | 53.2 | 6.6 | 96 | 969 | 313.1 | 21.1 | 14 | 40 | 3.5 | 0.6 |
| Harris | 12.6 | 453 | 10 | D | D | D | 51 | 335 | 66.1 | 5.6 | 15 | D | D | D |
| Hart | 3.8 | 157 | 19 | 227 | 59.0 | 7.3 | 94 | 879 | 170.7 | 15.6 | 19 | 72 | 8.9 | 2.3 |
| Heard | 65.9 | 5 807 | 2 | D | D | D | 21 | 113 | 24.8 | 2.1 | 1 | D | D | D |
| Henry | 35.0 | 208 | 101 | 1 508 | 3 076.6 | 71.4 | 556 | 8 291 | 1 907.4 | 183.5 | 210 | 636 | 116.4 | 19.8 |
| Houston | 29.4 | 233 | 49 | D | D | D | 452 | 6 600 | 1 524.3 | 143.9 | 133 | 510 | 72.6 | 12.5 |
| Irwin | 17.6 | 1 741 | 14 | 160 | 94.1 | 4.4 | 34 | 137 | 27.3 | 2.6 | 4 | 8 | 1.1 | 0.4 |
| Jackson | 21.2 | 405 | 63 | 1 050 | 568.8 | 32.8 | 232 | 2 175 | 559.4 | 47.1 | 62 | 144 | 19.4 | 2.7 |
| Jasper | 2.7 | 202 | 3 | D | D | D | 30 | 228 | 33.4 | 3.6 | 6 | D | D | D |
| Jeff Davis | 5.6 | 427 | 12 | 138 | 35.9 | 4.2 | 74 | 751 | 204.4 | 15.4 | 8 | 32 | 4.5 | 0.7 |
| Jefferson | 20.5 | 1 212 | 14 | 141 | 127.2 | 3.6 | 74 | 694 | 129.4 | 12.6 | 13 | D | D | D |
| Jenkins | 4.9 | 560 | 2 | D | D | D | 33 | 212 | 53.9 | 3.8 | 2 | D | D | D |
| Johnson | 3.0 | 319 | 11 | D | D | D | 21 | 145 | 25.2 | 2.2 | 2 | D | D | D |
| Jones | 29.6 | 1 104 | 12 | 86 | 42.4 | 4.2 | 42 | 364 | 70.6 | 6.8 | 18 | D | D | D |
| Lamar | 2.9 | 177 | 4 | D | D | D | 48 | 480 | 114.0 | 10.9 | 5 | D | D | D |
| Lanier | 2.2 | 287 | 2 | D | D | D | 18 | D | D | D | 4 | D | D | D |
| Laurens | 30.1 | 642 | 47 | 663 | 252.1 | 18.7 | 262 | 2 779 | 613.1 | 51.4 | 46 | D | D | D |
| Lee | 7.6 | 243 | 10 | 216 | 118.3 | 8.8 | 48 | 584 | 124.0 | 15.5 | 25 | 75 | 11.3 | 1.9 |
| Liberty | 14.0 | 243 | 7 | D | D | D | 191 | 1 946 | 539.3 | 41.0 | 51 | 233 | 28.9 | 5.8 |
| Lincoln | 0.9 | 111 | 6 | 27 | 9.4 | 0.8 | 31 | 218 | 39.6 | 3.7 | 4 | 9 | 0.7 | 0.2 |
| Long | 3.0 | 269 | 2 | D | D | D | 13 | 58 | 17.4 | 1.0 | 4 | 5 | 0.5 | 0.1 |
| Lowndes | 30.3 | 314 | 130 | 1 731 | 756.5 | 55.9 | 569 | 7 019 | 1 804.8 | 142.9 | 131 | 764 | 80.8 | 18.7 |
| Lumpkin | 3.2 | 133 | 12 | 171 | 37.4 | 5.1 | 86 | 806 | 206.6 | 18.7 | 28 | 116 | 15.5 | 2.8 |
| McDuffie | 5.9 | 269 | 10 | D | D | D | 109 | 1 196 | 350.4 | 26.9 | 21 | 90 | 11.3 | 2.2 |
| McIntosh | 1.1 | 98 | 3 | D | D | D | 69 | 574 | 114.0 | 10.2 | 12 | 15 | 4.1 | 0.3 |
| Macon | 31.5 | 2 290 | 12 | 80 | 39.5 | 3.1 | 38 | 282 | 47.9 | 5.1 | 7 | 28 | 2.6 | 0.6 |
| Madison | 3.6 | 130 | 16 | 186 | 57.8 | 5.5 | 60 | 501 | 119.2 | 8.5 | 13 | D | D | D |
| Marion | 3.1 | 431 | 4 | D | D | D | 25 | 337 | 71.7 | 7.2 | NA | NA | NA | NA |
| Meriwether | 2.4 | 105 | 8 | D | D | D | 88 | 682 | 100.8 | 12.0 | 9 | 28 | 1.8 | 0.5 |
| Miller | 22.1 | 3 547 | 3 | 37 | 15.0 | 1.2 | 42 | 257 | 53.5 | 4.3 | 6 | 8 | 0.6 | 0.1 |
| Mitchell | 39.4 | 1 656 | 27 | 302 | 169.2 | 8.2 | 102 | 816 | 151.0 | 14.6 | 15 | 70 | 5.4 | 1.4 |
| Monroe | 62.8 | 2 640 | 19 | D | D | D | 71 | 526 | 114.4 | 10.7 | 17 | D | D | D |
| Montgomery | 2.5 | 276 | 8 | D | D | D | 22 | 100 | 24.7 | 2.1 | 4 | 6 | 0.6 | 0.0 |
| Morgan | 2.9 | 167 | 16 | 200 | 54.9 | 5.7 | 91 | 1 014 | 276.4 | 21.1 | 27 | 63 | 7.8 | 1.5 |
| Murray | 6.3 | 154 | 29 | 338 | 89.4 | 12.4 | 101 | 818 | 218.9 | 18.1 | 11 | 40 | 4.8 | 1.0 |
| Muscogee | 33.9 | 183 | 173 | 1 906 | 1 173.6 | 81.2 | 845 | 12 642 | 2 889.2 | 260.7 | 259 | 1 549 | 292.8 | 54.0 |
| Newton | 14.6 | 169 | 52 | 512 | 226.6 | 19.6 | 223 | 2 699 | 679.4 | 57.2 | 70 | 256 | 33.2 | 5.8 |
| Oconee | 2.0 | 68 | 28 | 254 | 72.9 | 10.7 | 101 | 1 557 | 326.4 | 33.3 | 60 | 114 | 14.4 | 3.5 |
| Oglethorpe | 2.0 | 146 | 8 | 27 | 8.5 | 0.9 | 36 | 256 | 69.6 | 4.7 | 2 | D | D | D |
| Paulding | 4.8 | 42 | 62 | 366 | 176.5 | 15.2 | 233 | 3 920 | 973.0 | 83.7 | 78 | 243 | 44.9 | 9.5 |
| Peach | 10.6 | 429 | 19 | D | D | D | 118 | 945 | 317.4 | 22.1 | 25 | 61 | 11.7 | 2.1 |
| Pickens | 4.9 | 171 | 21 | 108 | 112.0 | 4.4 | 110 | 1 335 | 320.5 | 27.0 | 49 | 105 | 15.3 | 3.0 |
| Pierce | 3.5 | 204 | 18 | D | D | D | 67 | 460 | 99.7 | 8.7 | 6 | 22 | 1.6 | 0.3 |
| Pike | 1.6 | 98 | 9 | 97 | 16.7 | 2.9 | 35 | 183 | 33.9 | 3.1 | 9 | 33 | 2.8 | 0.4 |
| Polk | 8.9 | 219 | 17 | D | D | D | 145 | 1 500 | 314.7 | 29.7 | 23 | 68 | 6.9 | 1.4 |
| Pulaski | 16.7 | 1 719 | 8 | 80 | 21.4 | 1.8 | 47 | 391 | 84.5 | 7.5 | 12 | 22 | 2.2 | 0.3 |

1. Merchant wholesalers, except manufacturers' sales branches and offices.   2. Employer establishments.

# Table B. States and Counties — **Professional Services, Manufacturing, and Accommodation and Food Services**

| STATE County | Professional, scientific, and technical services,[1] 2007 | | | | Manufacturing, 2007 | | | | Accommodation and food services, 2007 | | | |
|---|---|---|---|---|---|---|---|---|---|---|---|---|
| | Number of establishments | Number of employees | Receipts (mil dol) | Annual payroll (mil dol) | Number of establishments | Number of employees | Receipts (mil dol) | Annual payroll (mil dol) | Number of establishments | Number of employees | Sales (mil dol) | Annual payroll (mil dol) |
| | 147 | 148 | 149 | 150 | 151 | 152 | 153 | 154 | 155 | 156 | 157 | 158 |
| GEORGIA—Cont'd | | | | | | | | | | | | |
| Effingham | 56 | D | D | D | 25 | D | D | D | 49 | 637 | 26.1 | 6.6 |
| Elbert | 26 | 84 | 5.8 | 1.5 | 108 | 2 522 | 515.2 | 82.4 | 29 | 437 | 14.6 | 4.3 |
| Emanuel | 27 | 189 | 26.3 | 9.6 | 30 | 1 936 | 448.4 | 51.9 | 33 | 406 | 14.8 | 3.5 |
| Evans | 12 | 60 | 5.1 | 1.6 | 14 | 1 895 | 354.8 | 47.9 | 17 | 161 | 6.4 | 1.7 |
| Fannin | 41 | 183 | 12.8 | 5.2 | NA | NA | NA | NA | 59 | 651 | 29.7 | 8.4 |
| Fayette | 431 | D | D | D | 113 | 3 690 | 1 744.7 | 170.2 | 204 | 4 586 | 171.2 | 49.2 |
| Floyd | 174 | 703 | 80.1 | 24.8 | 109 | 7 726 | 3 346.1 | 312.7 | 198 | 3 423 | 144.3 | 38.1 |
| Forsyth | 855 | 4 197 | 650.9 | 207.2 | 223 | 8 127 | 2 318.6 | 329.8 | 240 | 3 904 | 183.1 | 48.4 |
| Franklin | 31 | D | D | D | 41 | 2 180 | 430.4 | 69.3 | 45 | 664 | 22.8 | 6.3 |
| Fulton | 6 560 | 77 813 | 16 269.2 | 5 882.0 | 677 | 24 993 | 10 428.5 | 1 051.8 | 2 782 | 66 711 | 4 133.8 | 1 154.9 |
| Gilmer | 52 | 207 | 14.8 | 5.4 | 34 | 2 099 | 354.6 | 64.1 | 57 | 872 | 36.6 | 10.8 |
| Glascock | 1 | D | D | D | NA | NA | NA | NA | 2 | D | D | D |
| Glynn | 268 | D | D | D | 73 | 2 554 | D | 123.6 | 251 | 7 394 | 398.3 | 162.5 |
| Gordon | 73 | 232 | 23.8 | 8.3 | 104 | 6 291 | 2 528.1 | 214.2 | 89 | 1 358 | 62.5 | 16.2 |
| Grady | 14 | 58 | 5.6 | 1.5 | 22 | 771 | 183.2 | 28.0 | 26 | 364 | 13.1 | 2.7 |
| Greene | 39 | 120 | 15.6 | 5.5 | 14 | 533 | 673.2 | 20.7 | 27 | 897 | 60.6 | 15.9 |
| Gwinnett | 3 256 | D | D | D | 772 | 22 797 | 6 480.3 | 1 030.7 | 1 629 | 27 397 | 1 264.7 | 353.6 |
| Habersham | 59 | 250 | 23.8 | 7.1 | 58 | 4 357 | 968.5 | 140.7 | 81 | 995 | 41.8 | 10.5 |
| Hall | 419 | D | D | D | 265 | 17 296 | 6 069.0 | 602.5 | 272 | 4 930 | 224.1 | 62.5 |
| Hancock | 3 | D | D | D | NA | NA | NA | NA | 9 | 28 | 1.0 | 0.3 |
| Haralson | 36 | 141 | 13.6 | 4.2 | 37 | 2 239 | 952.1 | 87.8 | 34 | 409 | 14.6 | 3.7 |
| Harris | 32 | D | D | D | 20 | 693 | D | D | 38 | 731 | 43.5 | 14.2 |
| Hart | 34 | 118 | 10.9 | 3.5 | 31 | 1 246 | 244.8 | 48.7 | 36 | 480 | 16.8 | 4.4 |
| Heard | 7 | D | D | D | NA | NA | NA | NA | 6 | 50 | 1.9 | 0.5 |
| Henry | 305 | D | D | D | 82 | 3 092 | 1 695.8 | 122.6 | 348 | 6 217 | 243.2 | 63.1 |
| Houston | 281 | D | D | D | 64 | 2 511 | 1 422.9 | 97.2 | 248 | 5 246 | 206.1 | 54.8 |
| Irwin | 5 | 30 | 2.9 | 0.9 | NA | NA | NA | NA | 6 | 97 | 2.6 | 0.7 |
| Jackson | 98 | 417 | 50.4 | 17.0 | 77 | 5 675 | 1 801.5 | 202.3 | 58 | 811 | 33.3 | 9.3 |
| Jasper | 8 | D | D | D | 19 | 839 | 187.5 | 27.7 | 11 | 104 | 3.4 | 0.9 |
| Jeff Davis | 17 | 87 | 3.9 | 1.8 | 24 | 1 229 | 242.9 | 34.3 | 21 | 364 | 9.9 | 2.6 |
| Jefferson | 13 | 44 | 3.0 | 0.9 | 30 | 1 343 | 303.6 | 47.6 | 26 | 327 | 11.2 | 2.6 |
| Jenkins | 4 | 13 | 0.9 | 0.4 | 10 | 665 | 116.9 | 20.6 | 13 | 140 | 3.8 | 1.0 |
| Johnson | 3 | 8 | 0.4 | 0.2 | NA | NA | NA | NA | 6 | 39 | 1.4 | 0.4 |
| Jones | 32 | 95 | 7.3 | 2.9 | NA | NA | NA | NA | 20 | 369 | 13.4 | 3.5 |
| Lamar | 20 | 83 | 4.2 | 1.2 | NA | NA | NA | NA | 28 | 379 | 12.0 | 3.3 |
| Lanier | 6 | D | D | D | NA | NA | NA | NA | 10 | D | D | D |
| Laurens | 73 | 322 | 29.7 | 11.1 | 47 | 3 870 | D | D | 97 | 1 608 | 66.8 | 17.8 |
| Lee | 23 | 79 | 9.0 | 2.3 | NA | NA | NA | NA | 16 | 205 | 6.9 | 2.0 |
| Liberty | 54 | D | D | D | 17 | D | D | D | 95 | 1 665 | 62.9 | 15.9 |
| Lincoln | 9 | 30 | 2.5 | 1.0 | NA | NA | NA | NA | 11 | 106 | 5.2 | 1.0 |
| Long | 3 | D | D | D | NA | NA | NA | NA | 6 | 102 | 1.8 | 0.6 |
| Lowndes | 211 | D | D | D | 106 | 4 324 | 2 237.8 | 162.9 | 252 | 5 498 | 209.5 | 55.3 |
| Lumpkin | 37 | 121 | 9.3 | 4.5 | 28 | 1 063 | 207.8 | 30.8 | 53 | 757 | 33.4 | 9.1 |
| McDuffie | 28 | D | D | D | 36 | 1 983 | D | 67.7 | 41 | 637 | 23.6 | 5.6 |
| McIntosh | 16 | D | D | D | NA | NA | NA | NA | 40 | 531 | 19.8 | 5.4 |
| Macon | 9 | 16 | 1.5 | 0.6 | 17 | 733 | 397.4 | 32.9 | 19 | 191 | 5.6 | 1.5 |
| Madison | 30 | D | D | D | 30 | 505 | D | 17.2 | 23 | 182 | 7.2 | 1.7 |
| Marion | 6 | D | D | D | NA | NA | NA | NA | 7 | 18 | 1.0 | 0.2 |
| Meriwether | 13 | 41 | 3.7 | 1.2 | 15 | 812 | 233.4 | 33.8 | 31 | 434 | 14.8 | 4.5 |
| Miller | 9 | 37 | 1.4 | 0.5 | NA | NA | NA | NA | 10 | 96 | 2.9 | 0.9 |
| Mitchell | 26 | 183 | 8.8 | 4.1 | 19 | D | D | 69.8 | 29 | 333 | 15.4 | 4.4 |
| Monroe | 42 | 99 | 9.0 | 2.8 | 19 | 855 | 118.1 | 25.9 | 42 | 668 | 23.8 | 7.2 |
| Montgomery | 7 | 12 | 0.8 | 0.2 | NA | NA | NA | NA | 7 | 61 | 2.9 | 0.7 |
| Morgan | 46 | 222 | 23.2 | 8.9 | 27 | 1 105 | 239.5 | 40.0 | 56 | 1 004 | 40.3 | 10.8 |
| Murray | 20 | D | D | D | 82 | 5 446 | 1 605.7 | 153.3 | 43 | 573 | 24.6 | 6.6 |
| Muscogee | 348 | D | D | D | 141 | 7 055 | 2 111.4 | 266.7 | 418 | 9 898 | 428.2 | 120.7 |
| Newton | 127 | 565 | 48.1 | 16.7 | 90 | 4 175 | 2 205.1 | 187.4 | 103 | 1 714 | 93.5 | 20.3 |
| Oconee | 145 | 709 | 58.9 | 25.7 | 31 | 747 | D | 25.4 | 58 | 946 | 38.9 | 9.6 |
| Oglethorpe | 18 | D | D | D | NA | NA | NA | NA | 9 | 45 | 1.8 | 0.5 |
| Paulding | 141 | 582 | 59.3 | 24.0 | 61 | 1 114 | 255.4 | 38.9 | 123 | 2 863 | 109.0 | 31.0 |
| Peach | 32 | 117 | 8.2 | 2.7 | 30 | 4 378 | 1 057.8 | 124.1 | 49 | 761 | 28.7 | 6.8 |
| Pickens | 83 | 177 | 18.3 | 6.4 | 44 | 694 | 104.8 | 23.0 | 49 | 719 | 27.8 | 7.8 |
| Pierce | 23 | D | D | D | NA | NA | NA | NA | 19 | 343 | 8.7 | 2.4 |
| Pike | 24 | 59 | 6.1 | 1.7 | NA | NA | NA | NA | 12 | 53 | 2.4 | 0.6 |
| Polk | 34 | D | D | D | 35 | 3 271 | 698.6 | 117.8 | 63 | 843 | 35.2 | 8.7 |
| Pulaski | 12 | 80 | 5.0 | 2.2 | NA | NA | NA | NA | 21 | 432 | 13.7 | 3.5 |

1. Establishment subject to federal tax.

# Table B. States and Counties — Health Care and Social Assistance, Other Services, and Federal Funds

| | Health care and social assistance, 2007 | | | | Other services, 2007 | | | | Federal funds and grants, 2009–2010 | | | |
| | | | | | | | | | Expenditures (mil dol) | | | |
| | | | | | | | | | | Direct payments for individuals[1] | | |
| STATE County | Number of establishments | Number of employees | Receipts (mil dol) | Annual payroll (mil dol) | Number of establishments | Number of employees | Receipts (mil dol) | Annual payroll (mil dol) | Total | Social Security and government retirement | Medicare | Food Stamps and Supplemental Security Income |
| | 159 | 160 | 161 | 162 | 163 | 164 | 165 | 166 | 167 | 168 | 169 | 170 |
| GEORGIA—Cont'd | | | | | | | | | | | | |
| Effingham | 46 | D | D | D | 43 | 213 | 21.2 | 5.4 | 213.9 | 121.8 | 31.2 | 13.5 |
| Elbert | 39 | 615 | 41.6 | 16.2 | 27 | 84 | 7.5 | 2.1 | 193.3 | 72.6 | 42.5 | 13.5 |
| Emanuel | 52 | 897 | 54.7 | 24.8 | 30 | 127 | 12.0 | 2.5 | 260.2 | 72.2 | 43.3 | 17.2 |
| Evans | 20 | 448 | 32.8 | 14.4 | 16 | 114 | 8.4 | 2.2 | 86.9 | 32.6 | 17.9 | 6.9 |
| Fannin | 67 | 865 | 78.7 | 33.2 | 26 | 161 | 11.2 | 2.9 | 200.2 | 102.5 | 45.5 | 7.7 |
| Fayette | 301 | 4 309 | 437.3 | 158.9 | 211 | 1 273 | 101.7 | 31.7 | 635.1 | 373.8 | 66.5 | 8.6 |
| Floyd | 259 | 7 910 | 785.1 | 310.9 | 108 | D | D | D | 705.5 | 304.8 | 152.1 | 42.4 |
| Forsyth | 368 | 4 193 | 403.4 | 152.7 | 274 | 1 618 | 308.6 | 83.9 | 436.6 | 267.5 | 55.8 | 10.4 |
| Franklin | 38 | 768 | 56.6 | 21.8 | 28 | 171 | 15.6 | 3.5 | 177.2 | 79.5 | 41.2 | 8.3 |
| Fulton | 3 204 | 67 143 | 8 483.0 | 3 072.6 | 2 139 | 20 887 | 3 560.9 | 707.4 | 16 634.2 | 2 239.6 | 1 134.7 | 608.8 |
| Gilmer | 45 | 625 | 43.7 | 16.5 | 49 | 424 | 21.9 | 6.0 | 176.9 | 97.0 | 38.2 | 7.2 |
| Glascock | 5 | D | D | D | 3 | D | D | D | 27.4 | 10.6 | 6.8 | 0.9 |
| Glynn | 265 | 4 708 | 897.7 | 183.8 | 151 | 912 | 72.1 | 21.1 | 905.8 | 287.7 | 141.3 | 33.7 |
| Gordon | 74 | 1 314 | 133.1 | 51.2 | 50 | 355 | 32.4 | 10.3 | 286.3 | 135.4 | 57.4 | 15.8 |
| Grady | 36 | 452 | 41.7 | 13.6 | 29 | 153 | 14.2 | 3.7 | 162.6 | 62.1 | 31.2 | 17.4 |
| Greene | 35 | 393 | 33.9 | 13.4 | 24 | 98 | 11.7 | 3.9 | 143.2 | 67.2 | 25.2 | 10.5 |
| Gwinnett | 1 583 | 21 698 | 2 302.0 | 879.7 | 1 431 | 8 527 | 813.1 | 257.3 | 2 250.5 | 1 097.8 | 266.8 | 79.8 |
| Habersham | 87 | 1 406 | 93.6 | 41.9 | 46 | 170 | 15.2 | 4.7 | 292.2 | 131.7 | 54.1 | 8.5 |
| Hall | 398 | 8 599 | 1 046.7 | 384.6 | 272 | 1 384 | 136.1 | 36.5 | 1 157.9 | 440.8 | 154.3 | 39.2 |
| Hancock | 8 | D | D | D | 7 | 20 | 1.5 | 0.3 | 99.8 | 29.1 | 23.8 | 8.6 |
| Haralson | 41 | 608 | 53.4 | 22.9 | 39 | 171 | 11.0 | 3.1 | 199.7 | 87.4 | 43.5 | 14.4 |
| Harris | 23 | 212 | 11.1 | 4.6 | 19 | D | D | D | 165.2 | 98.6 | 21.1 | 6.2 |
| Hart | 36 | 697 | 50.1 | 20.7 | 23 | 80 | 5.8 | 1.3 | 168.0 | 72.3 | 35.9 | 9.5 |
| Heard | 6 | D | D | D | 7 | D | D | D | 64.4 | 27.5 | 14.0 | 5.7 |
| Henry | 351 | 5 004 | 459.2 | 183.6 | 242 | 1 172 | 91.9 | 27.6 | 777.4 | 463.2 | 96.1 | 28.5 |
| Houston | 256 | 4 784 | 461.8 | 176.5 | 166 | 932 | 67.1 | 17.0 | 2 499.9 | 601.1 | 113.9 | 48.8 |
| Irwin | 18 | 529 | 39.7 | 13.8 | 9 | D | D | D | 80.7 | 24.2 | 15.3 | 5.5 |
| Jackson | 63 | 975 | 58.9 | 30.1 | 67 | 230 | 23.7 | 7.1 | 335.6 | 192.3 | 55.5 | 17.4 |
| Jasper | 13 | 169 | 12.5 | 5.4 | 13 | D | D | D | 76.2 | 36.2 | 13.7 | 5.2 |
| Jeff Davis | 18 | 264 | 19.8 | 7.6 | 13 | 39 | 1.8 | 0.6 | 102.4 | 39.5 | 22.4 | 7.2 |
| Jefferson | 25 | 501 | 41.1 | 13.6 | 19 | 57 | 3.3 | 0.9 | 188.3 | 54.5 | 39.0 | 15.2 |
| Jenkins | 8 | 258 | 12.8 | 6.3 | 10 | 23 | 3.1 | 0.6 | 84.1 | 22.7 | 19.0 | 6.4 |
| Johnson | 11 | D | D | D | 9 | 29 | 2.3 | 0.7 | 84.4 | 26.1 | 20.0 | 7.4 |
| Jones | 24 | D | D | D | 22 | 57 | 3.6 | 1.0 | 117.3 | 57.4 | 23.4 | 7.5 |
| Lamar | 21 | 204 | 18.2 | 5.5 | 13 | 147 | 10.7 | 4.0 | 125.6 | 55.0 | 24.0 | 6.5 |
| Lanier | 15 | D | D | D | 4 | D | D | D | 58.4 | 20.1 | 13.9 | 5.1 |
| Laurens | 133 | D | D | D | 66 | 335 | 24.6 | 6.6 | 495.6 | 174.4 | 73.4 | 29.5 |
| Lee | 25 | 322 | 19.4 | 7.1 | 27 | 141 | 11.6 | 3.5 | 112.9 | 64.9 | 14.1 | 6.6 |
| Liberty | 66 | D | D | D | 68 | D | D | D | 470.3 | 174.8 | 32.3 | 27.5 |
| Lincoln | 6 | 33 | 2.1 | 1.1 | 13 | 71 | 5.1 | 1.1 | 71.5 | 30.8 | 17.9 | 3.7 |
| Long | 4 | D | D | D | 4 | D | D | D | 55.7 | 28.5 | 6.3 | 5.1 |
| Lowndes | 321 | 7 074 | 593.7 | 243.1 | 162 | 794 | 64.4 | 21.3 | 1 032.9 | 294.2 | 119.7 | 58.6 |
| Lumpkin | 53 | 609 | 52.9 | 19.8 | 33 | 108 | 9.5 | 2.3 | 181.7 | 71.1 | 19.5 | 5.7 |
| McDuffie | 48 | 1 011 | 55.9 | 26.0 | 35 | 120 | 39.1 | 3.3 | 174.6 | 69.4 | 38.4 | 14.8 |
| McIntosh | 13 | D | D | D | 15 | 33 | 3.4 | 0.8 | 102.7 | 43.1 | 20.6 | 8.2 |
| Macon | 21 | 460 | 37.2 | 13.5 | 9 | D | D | D | 158.4 | 34.3 | 30.3 | 7.7 |
| Madison | 17 | D | D | D | 21 | D | D | D | 181.4 | 87.7 | 34.8 | 14.2 |
| Marion | 7 | D | D | D | 5 | D | D | D | 54.8 | 17.2 | 7.8 | 6.6 |
| Meriwether | 36 | 717 | 52.9 | 25.7 | 18 | 48 | 4.0 | 1.0 | 177.7 | 69.0 | 35.5 | 13.8 |
| Miller | 14 | 388 | 24.0 | 11.9 | 10 | 36 | 2.7 | 0.7 | 62.5 | 18.7 | 12.1 | 4.3 |
| Mitchell | 25 | 500 | 35.8 | 14.2 | 33 | 191 | 13.8 | 3.8 | 200.7 | 60.1 | 35.7 | 19.9 |
| Monroe | 39 | D | D | D | 30 | 130 | 16.3 | 4.0 | 139.1 | 65.9 | 25.0 | 8.3 |
| Montgomery | 5 | 15 | 1.0 | 0.4 | 4 | 10 | 0.8 | 0.3 | 69.4 | 22.5 | 14.4 | 4.4 |
| Morgan | 28 | 500 | 29.7 | 15.4 | 35 | 135 | 11.8 | 2.8 | 117.9 | 57.5 | 24.6 | 6.5 |
| Murray | 33 | 505 | 39.2 | 14.5 | 28 | 113 | 9.1 | 2.8 | 180.9 | 88.4 | 35.0 | 10.9 |
| Muscogee | 555 | 13 088 | 1 332.5 | 521.1 | 353 | 2 323 | 178.4 | 54.7 | 4 790.6 | 737.8 | 259.8 | 142.3 |
| Newton | 133 | 2 037 | 203.9 | 75.8 | 90 | 414 | 33.3 | 9.6 | 477.4 | 265.1 | 83.3 | 33.9 |
| Oconee | 81 | D | D | D | 47 | 474 | 42.8 | 13.1 | 133.3 | 81.7 | 22.5 | 4.1 |
| Oglethorpe | 10 | D | D | D | 11 | D | D | D | 67.8 | 27.4 | 13.4 | 4.6 |
| Paulding | 109 | 1 492 | 105.5 | 40.6 | 108 | 455 | 30.3 | 9.8 | 328.7 | 205.0 | 44.1 | 17.4 |
| Peach | 40 | D | D | D | 31 | D | D | D | 269.2 | 114.7 | 35.9 | 20.8 |
| Pickens | 50 | 1 003 | 72.6 | 28.5 | 42 | 188 | 15.7 | 5.0 | 179.1 | 112.4 | 29.6 | 6.1 |
| Pierce | 27 | 298 | 11.5 | 6.2 | 26 | 68 | 4.5 | 1.0 | 138.9 | 67.7 | 24.9 | 9.7 |
| Pike | 15 | D | D | D | 15 | 57 | 3.4 | 1.0 | 371.9 | 52.1 | 17.4 | 4.6 |
| Polk | 42 | 891 | 53.3 | 23.2 | 45 | 495 | 46.0 | 11.2 | 356.4 | 131.7 | 74.1 | 21.1 |
| Pulaski | 24 | 786 | 61.5 | 28.0 | 10 | 14 | 1.0 | 0.3 | 95.6 | 38.3 | 19.5 | 5.8 |

1. State totals may include programs not allocated by county.

# Table B. States and Counties — Federal Funds, Residential Construction, and Local Government Finances

| STATE County | Federal funds and grants, 2009–2010 (cont.) | | | | | | | Value of residential construction authorized by building permits, 2011 | | Local government finances, 2007 | | | | |
|---|---|---|---|---|---|---|---|---|---|---|---|---|---|---|
| | Expenditures (mil dol) (cont.) | | | | | | | | | General revenue | | | | |
| | | Procurement contract awards | | Grants[1] | | | | | | | | Taxes | | |
| | | | | | | | | | | | | | Per capita[2] (dollars) | |
| | Salaries and wages | Defense | Other | Medicaid and other health-related | Nutrition and family welfare | Education | Other | New construction ($1,000) | Number of housing units | Total (mil dol) | Inter-govern-mental (mil dol) | Total (mil dol) | Total | Property |
| | 171 | 172 | 173 | 174 | 175 | 176 | 177 | 178 | 179 | 180 | 181 | 182 | 183 | 184 |
| GEORGIA—Cont'd | | | | | | | | | | | | | | |
| Effingham | 16.7 | 0.0 | 1.4 | 18.6 | 5.3 | 1.6 | 0.0 | 19 583 | 134 | 173.0 | 67.8 | 71.3 | 1 406 | 759 |
| Elbert | 13.2 | 1.9 | 2.5 | 38.2 | 5.2 | 1.7 | 0.5 | 3 234 | 37 | 74.3 | 26.2 | 20.5 | 1 000 | 599 |
| Emanuel | 20.8 | 0.0 | 10.2 | 61.5 | 10.7 | 2.0 | 7.9 | 478 | 7 | 148.3 | 41.1 | 22.4 | 996 | 527 |
| Evans | 2.7 | 0.3 | 0.5 | 18.7 | 2.8 | 1.1 | 0.6 | 890 | 8 | 57.6 | 16.9 | 9.9 | 861 | 416 |
| Fannin | 4.5 | 0.5 | 1.4 | 29.5 | 4.3 | 1.5 | 1.7 | 19 098 | 107 | 60.4 | 22.1 | 32.1 | 1 422 | 810 |
| Fayette | 134.7 | 13.9 | 7.9 | 9.7 | 8.7 | 2.7 | 0.1 | 20 582 | 70 | 379.6 | 108.5 | 207.1 | 1 951 | 1 445 |
| Floyd | 35.5 | 0.0 | 8.9 | 86.1 | 19.0 | 7.5 | 5.0 | 9 546 | 109 | 530.9 | 181.6 | 115.9 | 1 212 | 720 |
| Forsyth | 15.5 | 35.9 | 7.1 | 24.2 | 8.7 | 8.1 | 0.4 | 158 485 | 1 174 | 499.7 | 139.8 | 274.8 | 1 729 | 1 050 |
| Franklin | 4.3 | 1.1 | 1.1 | 31.2 | 3.3 | 1.8 | 1.8 | 430 | 3 | 63.8 | 25.0 | 28.8 | 1 322 | 709 |
| Fulton | 2 486.2 | 825.0 | 2 021.2 | 1 802.2 | 584.2 | 1 240.0 | 3 241.6 | 286 889 | 1 954 | 5 576.3 | 1 414.3 | 2 601.7 | 2 622 | 1 793 |
| Gilmer | 6.2 | 0.0 | 1.3 | 20.1 | 3.9 | 1.6 | 0.2 | 6 412 | 47 | 84.9 | 31.0 | 42.2 | 1 486 | 913 |
| Glascock | 0.9 | 0.0 | 0.2 | 6.7 | 0.5 | 0.3 | 0.0 | NA | NA | 10.3 | 4.7 | 4.6 | 1 669 | 1 247 |
| Glynn | 197.3 | 11.7 | 122.0 | 51.3 | 20.2 | 6.5 | 18.4 | 78 178 | 304 | 509.4 | 71.8 | 164.3 | 2 193 | 1 434 |
| Gordon | 29.3 | 4.2 | 5.9 | 24.7 | 8.0 | 3.2 | 0.5 | 4 369 | 29 | 166.9 | 68.6 | 64.9 | 1 247 | 579 |
| Grady | 3.4 | 0.0 | 0.8 | 32.8 | 5.9 | 3.0 | 0.4 | 4 274 | 34 | 68.1 | 33.5 | 24.3 | 971 | 521 |
| Greene | 7.3 | 0.0 | 1.0 | 24.4 | 4.8 | 1.3 | 0.3 | 24 664 | 63 | 56.7 | 14.9 | 33.3 | 2 124 | 1 277 |
| Gwinnett | 224.1 | 223.7 | 118.2 | 63.3 | 56.4 | 26.0 | 37.0 | 129 727 | 873 | 2 583.5 | 793.0 | 1 318.2 | 1 698 | 1 182 |
| Habersham | 8.3 | 0.5 | 7.5 | 29.9 | 5.7 | 1.0 | 34.0 | 13 901 | 112 | 162.0 | 65.0 | 54.3 | 1 286 | 706 |
| Hall | 62.2 | 264.1 | 41.1 | 74.7 | 41.3 | 9.3 | 3.2 | 36 666 | 228 | 1 091.0 | 200.0 | 285.5 | 1 585 | 843 |
| Hancock | 1.4 | 0.0 | 0.3 | 29.4 | 6.0 | 1.0 | 0.0 | 1 596 | 12 | 29.3 | 11.8 | 12.9 | 1 349 | 1 106 |
| Haralson | 4.7 | -0.4 | 1.3 | 25.3 | 5.5 | 2.7 | 0.6 | 3 713 | 42 | 90.4 | 40.3 | 33.3 | 1 159 | 602 |
| Harris | 6.0 | 0.2 | 2.8 | 22.2 | 4.5 | 1.3 | 0.1 | 23 596 | 93 | 73.2 | 27.0 | 36.5 | 1 254 | 885 |
| Hart | 7.5 | 2.0 | 0.7 | 32.8 | 4.0 | 1.8 | 0.3 | 4 902 | 33 | 61.3 | 21.8 | 30.1 | 1 241 | 741 |
| Heard | 1.3 | 0.0 | 0.3 | 11.1 | 2.9 | 0.9 | 0.1 | 1 478 | 11 | 45.6 | 13.3 | 28.1 | 2 470 | 1 010 |
| Henry | 119.8 | 0.8 | 8.6 | 29.7 | 11.5 | 4.6 | 1.7 | 46 914 | 250 | 629.9 | 190.0 | 337.9 | 1 816 | 1 157 |
| Houston | 982.5 | 572.7 | 67.4 | 55.7 | 25.1 | 7.4 | 2.1 | 107 962 | 653 | 597.5 | 168.8 | 172.5 | 1 316 | 721 |
| Irwin | 5.5 | 3.6 | -3.6 | 19.0 | 2.8 | 1.0 | 0.4 | 1 491 | 11 | 41.2 | 15.8 | 9.3 | 932 | 649 |
| Jackson | 11.9 | 0.1 | 2.5 | 41.3 | 7.5 | 3.1 | 0.7 | 16 702 | 116 | 249.3 | 66.3 | 99.6 | 1 681 | 1 010 |
| Jasper | 1.9 | 0.0 | 1.2 | 12.7 | 3.7 | 0.8 | 0.2 | 4 554 | 34 | 38.4 | 13.8 | 17.2 | 1 258 | 953 |
| Jeff Davis | 2.1 | 0.0 | 0.5 | 20.1 | 4.0 | 0.9 | 0.2 | 280 | 4 | 62.6 | 22.2 | 14.5 | 1 090 | 523 |
| Jefferson | 3.3 | 0.0 | 3.8 | 56.9 | 6.7 | 1.8 | 1.2 | 1 976 | 17 | 66.1 | 27.1 | 20.5 | 1 245 | 736 |
| Jenkins | 1.5 | 0.0 | 0.7 | 25.5 | 3.6 | 1.9 | 0.3 | 930 | 9 | 28.2 | 13.5 | 7.4 | 857 | 519 |
| Johnson | 1.7 | 0.0 | 0.3 | 23.6 | 2.9 | 1.0 | 0.2 | 0 | 0 | 19.6 | 10.7 | 6.7 | 703 | 420 |
| Jones | 3.0 | 0.0 | 2.5 | 15.7 | 3.9 | 3.1 | 0.0 | 1 866 | 17 | 66.3 | 35.2 | 25.7 | 943 | 605 |
| Lamar | 3.1 | 0.1 | 0.7 | 16.5 | 3.6 | 1.0 | 0.7 | 3 510 | 28 | 44.6 | 15.7 | 17.7 | 1 044 | 641 |
| Lanier | 1.1 | 0.0 | 0.2 | 13.0 | 2.1 | 0.7 | 0.0 | 1 600 | 21 | 21.0 | 13.5 | 6.5 | 812 | 529 |
| Laurens | 52.8 | 15.5 | 45.0 | 77.2 | 11.7 | 4.9 | 1.0 | 1 649 | 25 | 156.4 | 72.7 | 45.6 | 959 | 425 |
| Lee | 3.1 | 0.1 | 0.8 | 11.9 | 3.5 | 1.3 | 0.0 | 12 457 | 109 | 82.4 | 35.4 | 35.1 | 1 061 | 673 |
| Liberty | 120.0 | 34.7 | 1.8 | 26.6 | 15.0 | 14.0 | 11.1 | 41 449 | 201 | 203.9 | 94.3 | 63.2 | 1 045 | 547 |
| Lincoln | 1.4 | 0.0 | 0.3 | 12.4 | 2.0 | 0.8 | 0.1 | 5 113 | 30 | 25.9 | 12.5 | 9.8 | 1 207 | 805 |
| Long | 1.4 | 0.3 | 0.2 | 7.5 | 1.8 | 1.0 | 0.0 | NA | NA | 26.3 | 16.6 | 7.4 | 658 | 463 |
| Lowndes | 283.1 | 89.1 | 4.2 | 87.7 | 25.6 | 9.8 | 10.0 | 46 588 | 612 | 321.0 | 135.1 | 141.2 | 1 387 | 660 |
| Lumpkin | 51.8 | 2.5 | 1.0 | 17.6 | 3.2 | 0.7 | 2.0 | 7 479 | 48 | 66.2 | 22.6 | 31.3 | 1 178 | 815 |
| McDuffie | 6.6 | 0.0 | 0.8 | 35.3 | 5.2 | 2.0 | 0.4 | 1 898 | 12 | 88.5 | 39.9 | 25.1 | 1 165 | 559 |
| McIntosh | 10.0 | 0.3 | 0.4 | 15.0 | 3.6 | 1.0 | 0.2 | 9 759 | 75 | 31.8 | 11.3 | 16.0 | 1 405 | 815 |
| Macon | 2.2 | 34.2 | 0.5 | 35.3 | 6.2 | 1.6 | 1.1 | 520 | 7 | 35.1 | 16.0 | 14.5 | 1 075 | 746 |
| Madison | 4.6 | 0.0 | 1.1 | 30.8 | 4.8 | 1.9 | 0.4 | 4 906 | 28 | 73.2 | 41.6 | 24.4 | 872 | 577 |
| Marion | 2.3 | 0.2 | 0.2 | 16.3 | 2.2 | 0.9 | 0.2 | 627 | 7 | 20.6 | 11.2 | 7.4 | 1 055 | 765 |
| Meriwether | 4.6 | 0.0 | 1.3 | 42.0 | 7.2 | 2.4 | 0.3 | 3 271 | 21 | 90.0 | 33.4 | 31.6 | 1 388 | 1 056 |
| Miller | 1.6 | 0.1 | 0.3 | 12.6 | 2.1 | 0.7 | 0.2 | 0 | 0 | 41.3 | 10.1 | 7.7 | 1 249 | 831 |
| Mitchell | 5.3 | 1.4 | 0.8 | 51.9 | 8.7 | 2.5 | 1.8 | 2 329 | 21 | 94.2 | 34.4 | 25.6 | 1 061 | 667 |
| Monroe | 17.2 | 0.0 | 0.8 | 16.0 | 2.2 | 1.4 | 0.5 | 7 106 | 47 | 91.4 | 20.4 | 39.0 | 1 550 | 1 131 |
| Montgomery | 1.7 | 0.0 | 0.4 | 19.3 | 2.4 | 0.8 | 0.1 | 1 132 | 8 | 23.2 | 13.3 | 6.8 | 750 | 453 |
| Morgan | 3.8 | 0.0 | 0.9 | 18.6 | 3.4 | 1.1 | 0.2 | 8 497 | 34 | 65.6 | 20.1 | 35.1 | 1 934 | 1 161 |
| Murray | 6.7 | 11.0 | 2.1 | 16.3 | 6.3 | 2.8 | 0.2 | 2 243 | 23 | 100.0 | 50.3 | 38.6 | 950 | 531 |
| Muscogee | 3 032.0 | 266.2 | 11.5 | 189.5 | 51.8 | 21.4 | 32.2 | 33 828 | 369 | 707.6 | 323.8 | 242.6 | 1 297 | 913 |
| Newton | 19.5 | 1.0 | 4.0 | 40.0 | 11.7 | 5.5 | 5.8 | 7 545 | 54 | 373.2 | 109.9 | 127.0 | 1 322 | 893 |
| Oconee | 7.4 | 0.2 | 1.9 | 9.3 | 3.3 | 1.1 | 0.4 | 23 901 | 91 | 101.8 | 32.5 | 55.7 | 1 777 | 1 159 |
| Oglethorpe | 1.9 | 0.0 | 0.5 | 15.5 | 2.8 | 1.1 | 0.0 | 2 504 | 37 | 32.7 | 15.3 | 13.7 | 981 | 739 |
| Paulding | 11.8 | 1.4 | 3.0 | 23.5 | 9.2 | 4.0 | 1.9 | 27 411 | 187 | 350.4 | 161.9 | 149.0 | 1 165 | 719 |
| Peach | 13.6 | 1.9 | 12.4 | 29.5 | 8.5 | 7.0 | 8.8 | 8 808 | 69 | 113.0 | 32.9 | 33.3 | 1 297 | 695 |
| Pickens | 5.6 | 0.2 | 1.7 | 16.0 | 4.5 | 1.4 | 0.6 | 7 809 | 41 | 78.1 | 22.5 | 43.7 | 1 435 | 895 |
| Pierce | 3.3 | 0.1 | 1.5 | 19.6 | 4.1 | 1.3 | 0.1 | 2 618 | 23 | 46.1 | 25.0 | 16.9 | 948 | 561 |
| Pike | 280.7 | 0.0 | 0.7 | 12.6 | 2.0 | 0.8 | 0.0 | 1 851 | 9 | 44.7 | 22.3 | 17.6 | 1 025 | 787 |
| Polk | 26.6 | 27.8 | 10.4 | 49.5 | 9.6 | 3.1 | 0.6 | 3 211 | 22 | 116.4 | 56.4 | 43.1 | 1 039 | 652 |
| Pulaski | 1.5 | 0.1 | 0.4 | 20.6 | 2.7 | 0.7 | 1.1 | 1 018 | 13 | 35.3 | 21.4 | 10.5 | 1 068 | 629 |

1. State totals may include programs not allocated by county.    2. Based on the resident population estimated as of July 1 of the year shown.

# Table B. States and Counties — Local Government Finances, Government Employment, and Voting

| STATE County | Total (mil dol) | Per capita¹ (dollars) | Education | Health and hospitals | Police protection | Public welfare | Highways | Total (mil dol) | Per capita¹ (dollars) | Federal civilian | Federal military | State and local | Democratic | Republican | All other |
|---|---|---|---|---|---|---|---|---|---|---|---|---|---|---|---|
| | 185 | 186 | 187 | 188 | 189 | 190 | 191 | 192 | 193 | 194 | 195 | 196 | 197 | 198 | 199 |
| GEORGIA—Cont'd | | | | | | | | | | | | | | | |
| Effingham | 170.9 | 3 368 | 58.7 | 13.7 | 3.8 | 0.3 | 4.2 | 92.3 | 1 820 | 66 | 159 | 2 762 | 24.3 | 75.0 | 0.7 |
| Elbert | 75.5 | 3 676 | 45.3 | 21.2 | 6.0 | 1.7 | 1.7 | 17.2 | 838 | 133 | 60 | 1 276 | 40.5 | 58.5 | 1.0 |
| Emanuel | 150.0 | 6 678 | 27.2 | 55.4 | 1.7 | 0.1 | 2.6 | 64.8 | 2 884 | 89 | 68 | 1 880 | 37.2 | 62.0 | 0.8 |
| Evans | 60.4 | 5 247 | 30.6 | 48.2 | 2.6 | 0.0 | 4.0 | 2.4 | 205 | 33 | 33 | 655 | 35.6 | 63.9 | 0.5 |
| Fannin | 62.5 | 2 766 | 62.6 | 2.8 | 4.7 | 0.7 | 11.8 | 24.9 | 1 103 | 41 | 71 | 928 | 24.7 | 73.8 | 1.6 |
| Fayette | 375.6 | 3 538 | 60.1 | 2.2 | 5.8 | 1.0 | 4.8 | 354.6 | 3 341 | 525 | 334 | 4 800 | 34.2 | 64.9 | 0.9 |
| Floyd | 541.5 | 5 663 | 32.4 | 42.5 | 2.6 | 0.1 | 2.8 | 233.9 | 2 446 | 230 | 292 | 6 257 | 31.2 | 67.6 | 1.1 |
| Forsyth | 558.6 | 3 515 | 60.9 | 0.2 | 4.4 | 0.3 | 9.4 | 684.3 | 4 306 | 176 | 548 | 6 273 | 20.4 | 78.5 | 1.1 |
| Franklin | 76.7 | 3 520 | 58.1 | 1.9 | 8.7 | 0.4 | 5.3 | 47.8 | 2 193 | 48 | 66 | 1 108 | 23.7 | 75.2 | 1.1 |
| Fulton | 4 992.6 | 5 032 | 34.2 | 0.7 | 7.2 | 1.6 | 2.8 | 15 916.7 | 16 043 | 20 122 | 3 827 | 75 936 | 67.2 | 32.1 | 0.7 |
| Gilmer | 95.7 | 3 371 | 66.4 | 2.8 | 3.0 | 0.1 | 4.0 | 44.2 | 1 556 | 84 | 85 | 1 216 | 23.4 | 75.4 | 1.1 |
| Glascock | 10.0 | 3 605 | 58.0 | 1.1 | 3.2 | 1.3 | 5.7 | 1.4 | 494 | 0 | 0 | 197 | 14.7 | 84.2 | 1.1 |
| Glynn | 478.7 | 6 389 | 27.5 | 42.6 | 3.9 | 0.1 | 1.4 | 447.1 | 5 967 | 1 814 | 282 | 6 843 | 38.0 | 61.4 | 0.6 |
| Gordon | 168.9 | 3 246 | 55.5 | 1.5 | 4.5 | 0.3 | 5.9 | 64.4 | 1 238 | 87 | 168 | 2 677 | 24.2 | 74.5 | 1.3 |
| Grady | 74.7 | 2 983 | 60.3 | 1.6 | 4.0 | 0.3 | 5.4 | 64.5 | 2 576 | 74 | 76 | 1 153 | 37.8 | 61.7 | 0.5 |
| Greene | 51.6 | 3 297 | 47.2 | 0.3 | 8.0 | 0.8 | 6.1 | 26.3 | 1 680 | 41 | 48 | 757 | 42.2 | 57.2 | 0.6 |
| Gwinnett | 2 724.9 | 3 510 | 58.7 | 1.3 | 5.4 | 0.2 | 5.5 | 3 370.3 | 4 341 | 2 517 | 2 488 | 32 377 | 44.5 | 54.7 | 0.8 |
| Habersham | 174.1 | 4 119 | 39.0 | 39.2 | 3.2 | 0.1 | 2.7 | 166.6 | 3 942 | 112 | 130 | 2 915 | 19.6 | 79.5 | 1.0 |
| Hall | 1 105.6 | 6 136 | 27.0 | 44.1 | 2.1 | 0.6 | 1.6 | 1 620.4 | 8 994 | 487 | 552 | 9 706 | 24.1 | 75.0 | 0.8 |
| Hancock | 24.8 | 2 595 | 62.6 | 2.0 | 4.6 | 1.3 | 3.8 | 16.5 | 1 728 | 14 | 28 | 786 | 81.4 | 18.3 | 0.3 |
| Haralson | 93.8 | 3 265 | 63.5 | 1.6 | 5.2 | 0.1 | 5.5 | 34.3 | 1 194 | 48 | 86 | 1 594 | 20.3 | 78.0 | 1.7 |
| Harris | 66.4 | 2 282 | 67.9 | 2.1 | 4.8 | 0.1 | 3.6 | 39.5 | 1 359 | 60 | 97 | 1 125 | 28.1 | 71.4 | 0.5 |
| Hart | 64.2 | 2 649 | 59.9 | 2.1 | 4.7 | 0.5 | 6.9 | 26.6 | 1 096 | 92 | 76 | 1 079 | 33.6 | 65.4 | 1.0 |
| Heard | 41.2 | 3 615 | 50.7 | 2.1 | 5.1 | 1.3 | 6.8 | 39.3 | 3 448 | 14 | 35 | 643 | 24.7 | 74.2 | 1.2 |
| Henry | 663.7 | 3 567 | 59.0 | 0.2 | 5.3 | 0.7 | 8.5 | 1 056.7 | 5 680 | 1 019 | 627 | 8 247 | 45.9 | 53.4 | 0.7 |
| Houston | 604.1 | 4 611 | 46.0 | 28.7 | 3.8 | 0.2 | 4.5 | 126.5 | 966 | 16 881 | 4 236 | 9 261 | 39.5 | 59.7 | 0.8 |
| Irwin | 42.5 | 4 279 | 44.8 | 30.4 | 3.8 | 0.2 | 7.3 | 14.3 | 1 443 | 26 | 29 | 899 | 31.3 | 68.1 | 0.7 |
| Jackson | 285.2 | 4 813 | 54.9 | 14.8 | 4.3 | 0.2 | 5.5 | 406.4 | 6 858 | 136 | 185 | 2 948 | 21.6 | 77.4 | 1.0 |
| Jasper | 42.3 | 3 095 | 60.4 | 11.0 | 4.7 | 0.1 | 2.9 | 18.1 | 1 323 | 21 | 42 | 629 | 32.8 | 66.3 | 0.9 |
| Jeff Davis | 60.7 | 4 564 | 41.7 | 32.6 | 3.2 | 0.1 | 8.4 | 17.4 | 1 305 | 26 | 46 | 833 | 25.7 | 73.3 | 1.0 |
| Jefferson | 66.2 | 4 023 | 45.1 | 20.0 | 3.9 | 1.4 | 3.2 | 20.2 | 1 226 | 44 | 50 | 1 123 | 57.4 | 42.3 | 0.3 |
| Jenkins | 32.6 | 3 796 | 57.7 | 16.8 | 2.7 | 0.1 | 3.3 | 6.8 | 797 | 20 | 25 | 563 | 43.1 | 56.3 | 0.6 |
| Johnson | 22.6 | 2 373 | 54.3 | 2.4 | 4.7 | 0.3 | 4.7 | 5.3 | 552 | 16 | 30 | 647 | 32.8 | 66.5 | 0.6 |
| Jones | 65.8 | 2 418 | 67.3 | 0.6 | 5.0 | 0.5 | 5.8 | 17.1 | 628 | 35 | 86 | 1 110 | 36.8 | 62.6 | 0.7 |
| Lamar | 40.4 | 2 382 | 53.6 | 1.3 | 5.7 | 0.1 | 3.1 | 46.1 | 2 717 | 39 | 55 | 1 091 | 35.8 | 63.4 | 0.8 |
| Lanier | 20.6 | 2 596 | 76.0 | 0.4 | 6.9 | 0.2 | 4.8 | 3.6 | 448 | 14 | 31 | 434 | 37.0 | 62.2 | 0.8 |
| Laurens | 172.7 | 3 634 | 51.4 | 11.4 | 5.1 | 0.3 | 6.6 | 61.9 | 1 303 | 1 217 | 145 | 3 111 | 39.0 | 60.5 | 0.6 |
| Lee | 78.8 | 2 383 | 70.6 | 2.4 | 3.5 | 0.1 | 3.4 | 55.0 | 1 664 | 37 | 86 | 1 487 | 23.7 | 75.8 | 0.5 |
| Liberty | 209.4 | 3 462 | 52.0 | 15.6 | 4.5 | 0.1 | 3.1 | 41.2 | 682 | 4 416 | 19 222 | 3 074 | 64.0 | 35.6 | 0.5 |
| Lincoln | 24.9 | 3 074 | 54.6 | 3.0 | 3.7 | 5.5 | 4.5 | 12.5 | 1 541 | 15 | 24 | 446 | 37.4 | 61.8 | 0.8 |
| Long | 24.9 | 2 204 | 71.6 | 0.7 | 5.7 | 1.4 | 8.8 | 5.1 | 448 | 10 | 46 | 622 | 37.3 | 61.4 | 1.2 |
| Lowndes | 348.4 | 3 423 | 52.0 | 7.4 | 6.1 | 0.6 | 9.4 | 52.6 | 517 | 1 151 | 4 840 | 10 440 | 45.0 | 54.3 | 0.7 |
| Lumpkin | 64.8 | 2 439 | 54.5 | 2.4 | 5.0 | 0.5 | 3.3 | 81.7 | 3 075 | 74 | 308 | 2 169 | 23.3 | 75.2 | 1.5 |
| McDuffie | 88.6 | 4 112 | 53.9 | 20.9 | 3.7 | 1.4 | 2.7 | 2.0 | 91 | 36 | 122 | 1 468 | 42.3 | 57.2 | 0.5 |
| McIntosh | 31.6 | 2 763 | 55.7 | 5.3 | 6.8 | 0.1 | 5.6 | 8.0 | 704 | 25 | 43 | 655 | 46.6 | 52.7 | 0.7 |
| Macon | 34.8 | 2 573 | 56.1 | 1.7 | 6.4 | 0.4 | 5.8 | 8.2 | 605 | 24 | 43 | 891 | 65.3 | 34.4 | 0.4 |
| Madison | 72.7 | 2 594 | 73.5 | 3.2 | 2.8 | 0.3 | 3.6 | 23.5 | 839 | 48 | 84 | 1 223 | 26.2 | 72.6 | 1.3 |
| Marion | 19.6 | 2 786 | 71.4 | 0.2 | 2.3 | 2.2 | 2.7 | 8.6 | 1 218 | 38 | 26 | 341 | 43.4 | 55.7 | 0.9 |
| Meriwether | 88.8 | 3 904 | 45.7 | 17.5 | 4.2 | 0.5 | 3.0 | 49.8 | 2 188 | 44 | 65 | 1 743 | 47.0 | 52.4 | 0.6 |
| Miller | 43.4 | 7 039 | 28.1 | 51.5 | 3.5 | 0.0 | 4.3 | 25.0 | 4 059 | 19 | 18 | 609 | 29.9 | 69.4 | 0.8 |
| Mitchell | 97.1 | 4 021 | 41.9 | 23.9 | 4.8 | 0.0 | 4.5 | 42.3 | 1 751 | 79 | 71 | 1 596 | 47.7 | 51.7 | 0.6 |
| Monroe | 86.7 | 3 449 | 43.1 | 12.9 | 5.7 | 0.1 | 3.9 | 164.3 | 6 534 | 35 | 80 | 2 229 | 33.8 | 65.4 | 0.8 |
| Montgomery | 22.3 | 2 466 | 63.2 | 2.6 | 2.5 | 0.8 | 8.1 | 4.2 | 461 | 23 | 27 | 410 | 29.1 | 70.2 | 0.7 |
| Morgan | 66.0 | 3 634 | 50.5 | 6.1 | 4.3 | 0.9 | 9.9 | 17.5 | 964 | 44 | 54 | 1 196 | 33.8 | 65.4 | 0.8 |
| Murray | 94.8 | 2 331 | 72.0 | 3.0 | 3.6 | 0.8 | 5.6 | 71.5 | 1 758 | 106 | 119 | 1 413 | 26.6 | 71.9 | 1.5 |
| Muscogee | 680.7 | 3 639 | 48.6 | 7.9 | 4.9 | 2.1 | 3.4 | 540.0 | 2 887 | 6 517 | 5 925 | 13 206 | 59.6 | 39.9 | 0.5 |
| Newton | 396.1 | 4 125 | 41.9 | 16.8 | 3.5 | 0.2 | 5.0 | 309.6 | 3 224 | 198 | 304 | 4 263 | 50.3 | 49.1 | 0.7 |
| Oconee | 108.3 | 3 454 | 55.6 | 1.4 | 3.7 | 0.8 | 6.0 | 105.0 | 3 349 | 169 | 101 | 1 410 | 28.2 | 70.7 | 1.1 |
| Oglethorpe | 33.0 | 2 365 | 64.5 | 2.4 | 2.1 | 1.0 | 2.1 | 2.9 | 204 | 16 | 44 | 613 | 34.6 | 64.3 | 1.1 |
| Paulding | 376.2 | 2 941 | 69.0 | 0.8 | 4.1 | 0.1 | 4.2 | 423.1 | 3 308 | 122 | 432 | 4 795 | 30.2 | 68.8 | 1.0 |
| Peach | 100.0 | 3 894 | 40.7 | 13.9 | 5.0 | 0.1 | 2.1 | 49.5 | 1 929 | 112 | 88 | 2 371 | 53.1 | 46.3 | 0.6 |
| Pickens | 75.5 | 2 475 | 59.5 | 2.6 | 5.0 | 0.2 | 5.6 | 32.0 | 1 048 | 53 | 89 | 1 351 | 20.3 | 78.2 | 1.5 |
| Pierce | 45.6 | 2 548 | 71.6 | 3.6 | 3.0 | 0.6 | 4.1 | 7.8 | 438 | 46 | 57 | 890 | 18.5 | 81.0 | 0.6 |
| Pike | 43.7 | 2 539 | 72.4 | 1.8 | 5.8 | 0.2 | 3.0 | 21.8 | 1 265 | 30 | 53 | 715 | 19.2 | 79.8 | 1.0 |
| Polk | 126.5 | 3 052 | 59.5 | 2.8 | 5.1 | 0.5 | 4.4 | 42.0 | 1 014 | 58 | 124 | 1 659 | 28.7 | 69.8 | 1.5 |
| Pulaski | 38.6 | 3 921 | 40.1 | 1.6 | 3.7 | 0.3 | 4.0 | 8.1 | 825 | 19 | 35 | 736 | 34.8 | 64.6 | 0.6 |

1. Based on the resident population estimated as of July 1 of the year shown.   2. © 2013 Election Data Services, Inc. All rights reserved.

# Table B. States and Counties — **Land Area and Population**

| STATE/ County code | CBSA code[1] | County type[2] | STATE County | Land area,[3] (sq km) 2010 | Total persons | Rank | Per square kilometer | White | Black | American Indian, Alaska Native | Asian and Pacific Islander | Percent Hispanic or Latino[4] | Under 5 years | 5 to 17 years | 18 to 24 years | 25 to 34 years | 35 to 44 years | 45 to 54 years |
|---|---|---|---|---|---|---|---|---|---|---|---|---|---|---|---|---|---|---|
| | | | | | | | | | | | | | | | | | | |
| | | | | 1 | 2 | 3 | 4 | 5 | 6 | 7 | 8 | 9 | 10 | 11 | 12 | 13 | 14 | 15 |
| | | | GEORGIA—Cont'd | | | | | | | | | | | | | | | |
| 13 237 | ... | 6 | Putnam | 893 | 21 198 | 1 774 | 23.7 | 66.4 | 26.6 | 0.5 | 0.8 | 6.6 | 6.1 | 15.4 | 7.4 | 11.2 | 11.2 | 13.9 |
| 13 239 | 21640 | 9 | Quitman | 392 | 2 404 | 3 013 | 6.1 | 49.5 | 48.7 | 0.2 | 0.4 | 1.6 | 4.7 | 15.1 | 8.5 | 8.5 | 10.3 | 12.3 |
| 13 241 | ... | 9 | Rabun | 958 | 16 297 | 2 026 | 17.0 | 89.0 | 1.7 | 0.9 | 1.1 | 8.4 | 4.9 | 15.8 | 7.3 | 9.5 | 11.3 | 13.8 |
| 13 243 | ... | 6 | Randolph | 1 109 | 7 327 | 2 653 | 6.6 | 37.4 | 60.8 | 0.2 | 0.4 | 1.7 | 6.5 | 15.5 | 9.4 | 11.1 | 9.5 | 14.9 |
| 13 245 | 12260 | 2 | Richmond | 840 | 202 587 | 311 | 241.2 | 39.6 | 54.9 | 0.8 | 2.7 | 4.3 | 7.5 | 17.2 | 12.3 | 15.3 | 11.3 | 13.2 |
| 13 247 | 12060 | 1 | Rockdale | 336 | 85 820 | 658 | 255.4 | 42.1 | 46.6 | 0.7 | 2.4 | 9.9 | 6.6 | 19.6 | 9.2 | 11.6 | 13.9 | 15.4 |
| 13 249 | 11140 | 8 | Schley | 432 | 4 990 | 2 839 | 11.6 | 72.5 | 23.0 | 0.4 | 1.0 | 3.8 | 5.8 | 22.7 | 8.0 | 9.7 | 14.6 | 14.1 |
| 13 251 | ... | 6 | Screven | 1 671 | 14 202 | 2 161 | 8.5 | 55.0 | 43.2 | 0.7 | 0.7 | 1.4 | 6.9 | 18.0 | 8.9 | 11.2 | 11.4 | 14.0 |
| | | | | | | | | | | | | | | | | | | |
| 13 253 | ... | 6 | Seminole | 609 | 8 947 | 2 525 | 14.7 | 63.5 | 33.4 | 0.5 | 0.6 | 2.9 | 5.7 | 17.3 | 7.7 | 9.7 | 11.1 | 14.7 |
| 13 255 | 12060 | 1 | Spalding | 509 | 63 865 | 823 | 125.5 | 61.8 | 33.7 | 0.7 | 1.3 | 4.0 | 7.1 | 17.8 | 9.0 | 13.0 | 12.8 | 13.7 |
| 13 257 | 45740 | 7 | Stephens | 464 | 25 891 | 1 569 | 55.8 | 84.8 | 12.4 | 0.7 | 1.2 | 2.6 | 6.1 | 16.1 | 9.9 | 11.1 | 11.7 | 13.9 |
| 13 259 | ... | 8 | Stewart | 1 188 | 6 042 | 2 757 | 5.1 | 28.8 | 45.7 | 0.6 | 1.1 | 24.8 | 4.7 | 10.6 | 11.5 | 19.5 | 14.5 | 13.0 |
| 13 261 | 11140 | 6 | Sumter | 1 250 | 31 554 | 1 400 | 25.2 | 41.3 | 51.7 | 0.6 | 1.6 | 5.7 | 7.0 | 18.0 | 13.2 | 12.7 | 11.4 | 12.8 |
| 13 263 | ... | 8 | Talbot | 1 014 | 6 517 | 2 722 | 6.4 | 39.5 | 58.8 | 0.7 | 0.6 | 1.6 | 5.4 | 14.4 | 8.8 | 8.7 | 11.2 | 17.3 |
| 13 265 | ... | 8 | Taliaferro | 504 | 1 680 | 3 076 | 3.3 | 37.0 | 60.8 | 0.6 | 0.7 | 2.5 | 5.8 | 13.6 | 9.0 | 9.3 | 10.6 | 15.4 |
| 13 267 | ... | 6 | Tattnall | 1 242 | 25 384 | 1 595 | 20.4 | 59.7 | 29.7 | 0.4 | 0.7 | 10.3 | 6.1 | 15.1 | 10.3 | 16.2 | 14.8 | 14.7 |
| 13 269 | ... | 8 | Taylor | 976 | 8 420 | 2 570 | 8.6 | 59.3 | 38.4 | 0.3 | 0.8 | 2.0 | 6.0 | 18.2 | 8.9 | 9.5 | 12.3 | 15.3 |
| | | | | | | | | | | | | | | | | | | |
| 13 271 | ... | 7 | Telfair | 1 133 | 16 349 | 2 022 | 14.4 | 51.5 | 35.4 | 0.3 | 0.8 | 12.7 | 5.3 | 14.3 | 8.1 | 15.7 | 15.4 | 15.1 |
| 13 273 | 10500 | 3 | Terrell | 869 | 9 045 | 2 516 | 10.4 | 36.9 | 60.9 | 0.4 | 0.6 | 2.1 | 7.2 | 17.0 | 9.6 | 11.8 | 10.4 | 14.9 |
| 13 275 | 45620 | 4 | Thomas | 1 410 | 44 724 | 1 075 | 31.7 | 58.8 | 37.3 | 0.8 | 1.1 | 3.1 | 6.8 | 18.0 | 8.3 | 11.6 | 12.2 | 14.7 |
| 13 277 | 45700 | 4 | Tift | 671 | 41 064 | 1 152 | 61.2 | 57.7 | 31.0 | 0.5 | 1.6 | 10.3 | 6.9 | 18.2 | 13.0 | 13.1 | 12.0 | 13.0 |
| 13 279 | 47080 | 7 | Toombs | 943 | 27 315 | 1 519 | 29.0 | 62.4 | 25.9 | 0.4 | 1.0 | 11.3 | 8.1 | 19.6 | 8.6 | 12.7 | 12.1 | 13.0 |
| 13 281 | ... | 9 | Towns | 431 | 10 495 | 2 395 | 24.4 | 96.3 | 1.1 | 0.5 | 0.6 | 2.1 | 3.5 | 11.6 | 10.1 | 7.3 | 9.3 | 11.7 |
| 13 283 | ... | 7 | Treutlen | 517 | 6 769 | 2 701 | 13.1 | 64.9 | 33.1 | 0.4 | 0.4 | 2.0 | 6.9 | 17.8 | 9.4 | 13.6 | 11.7 | 13.6 |
| 13 285 | 29300 | 4 | Troup | 1 072 | 68 468 | 773 | 63.9 | 60.8 | 34.5 | 0.5 | 2.0 | 3.5 | 7.0 | 19.1 | 10.0 | 12.5 | 12.8 | 14.0 |
| 13 287 | ... | 6 | Turner | 739 | 8 410 | 2 572 | 11.4 | 54.5 | 41.0 | 0.5 | 0.8 | 3.9 | 6.4 | 17.3 | 9.4 | 12.5 | 12.0 | 13.4 |
| | | | | | | | | | | | | | | | | | | |
| 13 289 | 31420 | 3 | Twiggs | 928 | 8 447 | 2 569 | 9.1 | 56.7 | 41.8 | 0.7 | 0.5 | 1.5 | 5.7 | 15.0 | 8.4 | 9.9 | 10.7 | 17.2 |
| 13 291 | ... | 9 | Union | 834 | 21 451 | 1 757 | 25.7 | 95.8 | 1.2 | 1.0 | 0.7 | 2.6 | 4.2 | 13.3 | 6.1 | 8.1 | 10.1 | 13.8 |
| 13 293 | 45580 | 6 | Upson | 838 | 26 630 | 1 544 | 31.8 | 68.9 | 28.4 | 0.6 | 0.9 | 2.4 | 6.1 | 17.1 | 9.0 | 11.2 | 12.5 | 14.8 |
| 13 295 | 16860 | 2 | Walker | 1 156 | 68 094 | 780 | 58.9 | 92.9 | 5.3 | 0.7 | 0.7 | 1.7 | 5.8 | 17.1 | 7.9 | 12.2 | 13.3 | 14.6 |
| 13 297 | 12060 | 1 | Walton | 844 | 84 575 | 665 | 100.2 | 78.8 | 16.5 | 0.7 | 1.6 | 3.7 | 6.6 | 19.7 | 8.1 | 11.7 | 14.4 | 14.8 |
| 13 299 | 48180 | 4 | Ware | 2 311 | 35 821 | 1 280 | 15.5 | 65.9 | 30.1 | 0.6 | 1.2 | 3.5 | 6.8 | 16.4 | 9.6 | 12.8 | 12.3 | 13.6 |
| 13 301 | ... | 8 | Warren | 736 | 5 578 | 2 799 | 7.6 | 38.1 | 60.6 | 0.3 | 0.5 | 1.0 | 6.3 | 16.3 | 8.2 | 10.1 | 10.5 | 15.2 |
| 13 303 | ... | 7 | Washington | 1 757 | 20 879 | 1 784 | 11.9 | 44.6 | 53.1 | 0.3 | 0.7 | 2.1 | 6.6 | 16.6 | 9.2 | 12.9 | 12.1 | 15.9 |
| 13 305 | 27700 | 6 | Wayne | 1 662 | 30 305 | 1 423 | 18.2 | 72.9 | 20.9 | 0.7 | 1.0 | 6.0 | 7.2 | 17.5 | 8.4 | 13.4 | 14.2 | 14.2 |
| | | | | | | | | | | | | | | | | | | |
| 13 307 | ... | 8 | Webster | 542 | 2 793 | 2 989 | 5.2 | 54.0 | 41.8 | 0.5 | 0.7 | 3.9 | 4.6 | 19.9 | 7.8 | 9.4 | 12.9 | 14.9 |
| 13 309 | ... | 9 | Wheeler | 765 | 7 888 | 2 607 | 10.3 | 56.9 | 38.2 | 0.4 | 0.4 | 4.9 | 5.0 | 12.4 | 10.5 | 18.6 | 15.6 | 15.9 |
| 13 311 | ... | 8 | White | 623 | 27 556 | 1 512 | 44.2 | 94.3 | 2.7 | 1.0 | 0.8 | 2.4 | 5.5 | 16.7 | 8.4 | 10.0 | 11.9 | 14.7 |
| 13 313 | 19140 | 3 | Whitfield | 752 | 103 359 | 567 | 137.4 | 62.2 | 4.4 | 0.5 | 1.5 | 32.3 | 7.8 | 20.4 | 9.7 | 13.3 | 13.7 | 13.2 |
| 13 315 | ... | 9 | Wilcox | 978 | 9 068 | 2 513 | 9.3 | 59.8 | 36.0 | 0.6 | 0.6 | 3.8 | 5.1 | 14.0 | 8.9 | 15.4 | 14.3 | 14.7 |
| 13 317 | ... | 6 | Wilkes | 1 216 | 10 076 | 2 437 | 8.3 | 53.8 | 43.0 | 0.4 | 0.7 | 3.6 | 6.1 | 16.0 | 7.1 | 10.3 | 11.5 | 14.7 |
| 13 319 | ... | 8 | Wilkinson | 1 159 | 9 577 | 2 465 | 8.3 | 58.7 | 38.8 | 0.6 | 0.6 | 2.3 | 6.8 | 17.4 | 8.0 | 10.9 | 11.3 | 15.5 |
| 13 321 | 10500 | 3 | Worth | 1 478 | 21 741 | 1 741 | 14.7 | 68.5 | 29.3 | 0.6 | 0.7 | 1.9 | 6.2 | 17.5 | 9.7 | 11.2 | 11.9 | 14.8 |
| | | | | | | | | | | | | | | | | | | |
| 15 000 | ... | X | HAWAII | 16 635 | 1 392 313 | X | 83.7 | 36.8 | 2.8 | 1.7 | 75.4 | 9.2 | 6.4 | 15.7 | 9.6 | 14.0 | 12.7 | 13.8 |
| 15 001 | 25900 | 5 | Hawaii | 10 434 | 189 191 | 336 | 18.1 | 48.2 | 1.4 | 2.5 | 68.5 | 11.8 | 6.4 | 16.2 | 8.4 | 12.1 | 11.3 | 14.2 |
| 15 003 | 26180 | 2 | Honolulu | 1 556 | 976 372 | 44 | 627.5 | 32.6 | 3.5 | 1.6 | 78.5 | 8.5 | 6.5 | 15.5 | 10.3 | 14.6 | 12.8 | 13.4 |
| 15 005 | ... | 9 | Kalawao | 31 | 90 | 3 142 | 2.9 | 41.1 | 2.2 | 4.4 | 67.8 | 1.1 | 0.0 | 0.0 | 3.3 | 8.9 | 13.3 | 17.8 |
| 15 007 | 28180 | 5 | Kauai | 1 606 | 68 434 | 774 | 42.6 | 45.0 | 1.4 | 1.8 | 68.8 | 9.7 | 6.4 | 16.0 | 7.4 | 12.4 | 12.1 | 14.7 |
| 15 009 | 27980 | 5 | Maui | 3 008 | 158 226 | 399 | 52.6 | 45.0 | 1.4 | 1.6 | 67.1 | 10.4 | 6.4 | 16.4 | 7.5 | 13.4 | 13.4 | 15.2 |
| | | | | | | | | | | | | | | | | | | |
| 16 000 | ... | X | IDAHO | 214 045 | 1 595 728 | X | 7.5 | 85.3 | 1.0 | 1.9 | 2.2 | 11.5 | 7.5 | 19.5 | 9.9 | 13.3 | 12.1 | 13.0 |
| 16 001 | 14260 | 2 | Ada | 2 726 | 409 061 | 167 | 150.1 | 88.3 | 1.6 | 1.3 | 3.7 | 7.3 | 6.9 | 19.1 | 8.9 | 14.7 | 14.1 | 13.9 |
| 16 003 | ... | 8 | Adams | 3 530 | 3 915 | 2 914 | 1.1 | 95.4 | 0.5 | 1.9 | 0.8 | 2.8 | 4.9 | 13.9 | 5.9 | 8.3 | 9.2 | 15.9 |
| 16 005 | 38540 | 3 | Bannock | 2 880 | 83 800 | 668 | 29.1 | 87.8 | 1.2 | 3.4 | 2.5 | 7.0 | 8.0 | 19.0 | 12.9 | 14.9 | 11.0 | 11.5 |
| 16 007 | ... | 7 | Bear Lake | 2 525 | 5 907 | 2 772 | 2.3 | 95.0 | 0.3 | 0.7 | 0.7 | 4.1 | 7.0 | 20.7 | 6.4 | 10.3 | 10.1 | 12.7 |
| 16 009 | ... | 6 | Benewah | 2 011 | 9 117 | 2 509 | 4.5 | 87.7 | 0.8 | 10.9 | 1.1 | 3.0 | 6.2 | 17.1 | 6.7 | 9.0 | 10.5 | 15.2 |
| 16 011 | 13940 | 6 | Bingham | 5 423 | 45 474 | 1 058 | 8.4 | 76.1 | 0.5 | 5.9 | 1.3 | 17.6 | 9.3 | 23.3 | 8.5 | 12.9 | 11.2 | 12.4 |
| 16 013 | ... | 7 | Blaine | 6 847 | 21 146 | 1 776 | 3.1 | 78.0 | 0.3 | 0.6 | 1.2 | 20.7 | 6.2 | 17.7 | 6.0 | 12.0 | 13.8 | 16.2 |
| 16 015 | 14260 | 2 | Boise | 4 919 | 6 835 | 2 696 | 1.4 | 94.7 | 0.6 | 2.0 | 1.2 | 3.6 | 4.1 | 16.8 | 4.8 | 6.7 | 11.5 | 17.3 |
| | | | | | | | | | | | | | | | | | | |
| 16 017 | ... | 6 | Bonner | 4 493 | 40 476 | 1 166 | 9.0 | 96.1 | 0.4 | 2.0 | 1.0 | 2.4 | 5.0 | 16.1 | 6.1 | 9.8 | 11.1 | 15.4 |
| 16 019 | 26820 | 3 | Bonneville | 4 833 | 106 684 | 559 | 22.1 | 86.1 | 0.9 | 1.0 | 1.5 | 11.8 | 9.4 | 21.8 | 8.4 | 14.7 | 11.4 | 12.4 |
| 16 021 | ... | 7 | Boundary | 3 286 | 10 808 | 2 375 | 3.3 | 93.6 | 0.6 | 2.7 | 1.2 | 3.8 | 5.8 | 18.7 | 6.1 | 9.7 | 11.1 | 14.1 |
| 16 023 | ... | 8 | Butte | 5 780 | 2 740 | 2 996 | 0.5 | 94.2 | 0.9 | 1.2 | 0.8 | 4.2 | 6.4 | 20.8 | 6.5 | 9.1 | 9.2 | 14.7 |
| 16 025 | ... | 9 | Camas | 2 783 | 1 077 | 3 106 | 0.4 | 90.6 | 1.6 | 2.1 | 0.4 | 7.8 | 5.6 | 17.0 | 3.6 | 13.3 | 12.5 | 15.8 |
| 16 027 | 14260 | 2 | Canyon | 1 521 | 193 888 | 329 | 127.5 | 73.6 | 0.8 | 1.5 | 1.8 | 24.1 | 8.8 | 22.4 | 9.4 | 13.6 | 11.3 | 11.8 |

1. CBSA = Core Based Statistical Area. See Appendix A for explanation. See Appendix B for list of metropolitan areas with component counties.    2. County type code from the Economic Research Service of USDA Rural-Urban Continuum Codes. See Appendix A for definition.    3. Dry land or land partially or temporarily covered by water.    4. May be of any race.

# Table B. States and Counties — **Population and Households**

| STATE County | 55 to 64 years | 65 to 74 years | 75 years and over | Percent female | 2000 | 2010 | 2000– 2010 | 2010– 2012 | Births | Deaths | Net migration | Number | Percent change, 2000– 2010 | Persons per house-hold | Female family house-holder[1] | One per-son |
|---|---|---|---|---|---|---|---|---|---|---|---|---|---|---|---|---|
| | 16 | 17 | 18 | 19 | 20 | 21 | 22 | 23 | 24 | 25 | 26 | 27 | 28 | 29 | 30 | 31 |
| **GEORGIA—Cont'd** | | | | | | | | | | | | | | | | |
| Putnam | 15.9 | 12.1 | 6.7 | 51.6 | 18 812 | 21 218 | 12.8 | -0.1 | 566 | 519 | -49 | 8 601 | 16.2 | 2.45 | 14.2 | 24.7 |
| Quitman | 16.5 | 14.9 | 9.1 | 52.4 | 2 598 | 2 513 | -3.3 | -4.3 | 60 | 52 | -115 | 1 053 | 0.6 | 2.39 | 15.8 | 30.6 |
| Rabun | 15.7 | 13.0 | 8.9 | 50.6 | 15 050 | 16 276 | 8.1 | 0.1 | 346 | 427 | 95 | 6 780 | 8.0 | 2.34 | 9.6 | 28.5 |
| Randolph | 14.9 | 9.4 | 8.8 | 53.7 | 7 791 | 7 719 | -0.9 | -5.1 | 195 | 149 | -445 | 3 187 | 9.6 | 2.33 | 22.7 | 33.5 |
| Richmond | 11.6 | 6.5 | 5.1 | 51.6 | 199 775 | 200 549 | 0.4 | 1.0 | 6 845 | 4 187 | -549 | 76 924 | 4.1 | 2.47 | 22.6 | 30.4 |
| Rockdale | 12.5 | 6.7 | 4.5 | 52.4 | 70 111 | 85 215 | 21.5 | 0.7 | 2 339 | 1 358 | -379 | 30 027 | 24.8 | 2.81 | 18.9 | 21.0 |
| Schley | 10.9 | 10.2 | 3.9 | 52.0 | 3 766 | 5 010 | 33.0 | -0.4 | 114 | 60 | -71 | 1 872 | 30.5 | 2.68 | 13.8 | 25.6 |
| Screven | 14.1 | 8.7 | 6.7 | 51.2 | 15 374 | 14 593 | -5.1 | -2.7 | 450 | 395 | -455 | 5 596 | -3.5 | 2.53 | 18.6 | 27.3 |
| Seminole | 14.4 | 11.3 | 8.2 | 52.2 | 9 369 | 8 729 | -6.8 | 2.5 | 237 | 213 | 197 | 3 509 | -1.8 | 2.46 | 17.9 | 26.4 |
| Spalding | 12.6 | 8.2 | 5.7 | 51.5 | 58 417 | 64 073 | 9.7 | -0.3 | 1 948 | 1 543 | -692 | 23 565 | 9.5 | 2.67 | 19.4 | 23.5 |
| Stephens | 14.0 | 10.0 | 7.2 | 52.0 | 25 435 | 26 175 | 2.9 | -1.1 | 675 | 708 | -269 | 10 289 | 3.4 | 2.49 | 13.2 | 25.7 |
| Stewart | 11.7 | 7.7 | 6.7 | 39.0 | 5 252 | 6 058 | 15.3 | -0.3 | 123 | 169 | -201 | 1 862 | -7.2 | 2.35 | 21.8 | 32.2 |
| Sumter | 11.8 | 7.3 | 5.8 | 52.3 | 33 200 | 32 819 | -1.1 | -3.9 | 871 | 710 | -1 443 | 12 123 | 0.8 | 2.55 | 23.0 | 27.6 |
| Talbot | 17.3 | 10.8 | 6.1 | 52.4 | 6 498 | 6 865 | 5.6 | -5.1 | 140 | 151 | -344 | 2 832 | 11.6 | 2.42 | 19.2 | 28.9 |
| Taliaferro | 15.9 | 11.2 | 9.2 | 51.3 | 2 077 | 1 717 | -17.3 | -2.2 | 32 | 56 | -12 | 759 | -12.8 | 2.25 | 22.0 | 33.2 |
| Tattnall | 10.8 | 7.2 | 4.7 | 41.7 | 22 305 | 25 520 | 14.4 | -0.5 | 785 | 537 | -435 | 8 210 | 16.3 | 2.52 | 14.1 | 27.7 |
| Taylor | 13.8 | 9.6 | 6.4 | 52.7 | 8 815 | 8 906 | 1.0 | -5.5 | 200 | 169 | -533 | 3 522 | 7.3 | 2.44 | 19.6 | 30.1 |
| Telfair | 12.6 | 7.4 | 6.1 | 42.4 | 11 794 | 16 500 | 39.9 | -0.9 | 335 | 312 | -189 | 5 543 | 33.9 | 2.41 | 17.2 | 30.8 |
| Terrell | 13.9 | 8.8 | 6.4 | 51.3 | 10 970 | 9 315 | -15.1 | -2.9 | 292 | 220 | -346 | 3 519 | -12.1 | 2.57 | 24.4 | 26.7 |
| Thomas | 13.0 | 8.7 | 6.8 | 52.6 | 42 737 | 44 720 | 4.6 | 0.0 | 1 335 | 1 073 | -248 | 17 573 | 7.8 | 2.50 | 18.3 | 27.2 |
| Tift | 11.3 | 6.9 | 5.6 | 51.8 | 38 407 | 40 118 | 4.5 | 2.4 | 1 389 | 881 | 418 | 14 836 | 6.6 | 2.60 | 17.6 | 25.6 |
| Toombs | 11.7 | 8.2 | 6.0 | 52.7 | 26 067 | 27 223 | 4.4 | 0.3 | 968 | 639 | -224 | 10 375 | 5.0 | 2.59 | 18.3 | 27.2 |
| Towns | 15.6 | 17.3 | 13.6 | 52.3 | 9 319 | 10 471 | 12.4 | 0.2 | 170 | 352 | 194 | 4 510 | 12.8 | 2.17 | 7.6 | 30.1 |
| Treutlen | 12.6 | 7.8 | 6.4 | 50.0 | 6 854 | 6 885 | 0.5 | -1.7 | 178 | 161 | -130 | 2 543 | 0.5 | 2.53 | 18.1 | 27.1 |
| Troup | 12.1 | 6.8 | 5.7 | 51.9 | 58 779 | 67 044 | 14.1 | 2.1 | 2 067 | 1 456 | 804 | 24 828 | 13.3 | 2.62 | 20.3 | 25.1 |
| Turner | 12.7 | 9.2 | 7.1 | 50.1 | 9 504 | 8 930 | -6.0 | -5.8 | 258 | 208 | -593 | 3 339 | -2.8 | 2.56 | 19.4 | 27.1 |
| Twiggs | 16.1 | 10.7 | 6.3 | 51.1 | 10 590 | 9 023 | -14.8 | -6.4 | 201 | 291 | -493 | 3 634 | -5.2 | 2.46 | 16.5 | 27.6 |
| Union | 17.6 | 15.9 | 11.0 | 51.2 | 17 289 | 21 356 | 23.5 | 0.4 | 365 | 546 | 219 | 9 116 | 27.3 | 2.30 | 8.0 | 26.2 |
| Upson | 13.5 | 9.3 | 6.7 | 52.0 | 27 597 | 27 153 | -1.6 | -1.9 | 729 | 838 | -425 | 10 716 | -0.1 | 2.49 | 17.6 | 27.4 |
| Walker | 13.4 | 8.9 | 6.6 | 50.9 | 61 053 | 68 756 | 12.6 | -1.0 | 1 613 | 1 547 | -746 | 26 497 | 12.3 | 2.54 | 13.1 | 24.7 |
| Walton | 11.9 | 7.6 | 5.1 | 51.2 | 60 687 | 83 768 | 38.0 | 1.0 | 2 320 | 1 663 | 192 | 29 583 | 38.8 | 2.81 | 13.9 | 18.7 |
| Ware | 12.5 | 8.4 | 7.6 | 50.4 | 35 483 | 36 312 | 2.3 | -1.4 | 1 115 | 930 | -743 | 13 654 | 1.3 | 2.48 | 17.7 | 28.4 |
| Warren | 14.6 | 10.4 | 8.4 | 53.6 | 6 336 | 5 834 | -7.9 | -4.4 | 150 | 174 | -240 | 2 315 | -4.9 | 2.48 | 23.4 | 28.3 |
| Washington | 12.7 | 7.8 | 6.2 | 49.0 | 21 176 | 21 187 | 0.1 | -1.5 | 562 | 519 | -365 | 7 547 | 1.5 | 2.56 | 22.4 | 27.2 |
| Wayne | 12.1 | 7.7 | 5.4 | 47.7 | 26 565 | 30 099 | 13.3 | 0.7 | 914 | 711 | 18 | 10 562 | 13.3 | 2.63 | 14.9 | 23.6 |
| Webster | 14.4 | 8.9 | 7.3 | 50.6 | 2 390 | 2 799 | 17.1 | -0.2 | 37 | 24 | -31 | 1 119 | 22.8 | 2.50 | 16.4 | 26.6 |
| Wheeler | 11.7 | 6.0 | 4.4 | 34.8 | 6 179 | 7 421 | 20.1 | 6.3 | 139 | 124 | 434 | 2 152 | 7.0 | 2.54 | 15.5 | 26.0 |
| White | 14.4 | 11.2 | 7.2 | 51.3 | 19 944 | 27 144 | 36.1 | 1.5 | 550 | 594 | 432 | 10 646 | 35.7 | 2.52 | 10.7 | 22.8 |
| Whitfield | 10.5 | 6.6 | 4.8 | 50.0 | 83 525 | 102 599 | 22.8 | 0.7 | 3 347 | 1 607 | -955 | 35 180 | 19.7 | 2.89 | 13.4 | 21.4 |
| Wilcox | 12.4 | 8.1 | 7.1 | 41.2 | 8 577 | 9 255 | 7.9 | -2.0 | 229 | 234 | -203 | 2 891 | 3.8 | 2.50 | 15.7 | 25.9 |
| Wilkes | 14.8 | 11.2 | 8.3 | 52.1 | 10 687 | 10 593 | -0.9 | -4.9 | 266 | 305 | -478 | 4 263 | -1.2 | 2.40 | 18.8 | 29.6 |
| Wilkinson | 13.8 | 9.5 | 6.7 | 52.0 | 10 220 | 9 563 | -6.4 | 0.1 | 304 | 269 | -37 | 3 666 | -4.2 | 2.58 | 18.3 | 24.8 |
| Worth | 13.6 | 9.0 | 6.1 | 51.8 | 21 967 | 21 679 | -1.3 | 0.3 | 520 | 472 | 11 | 8 214 | 1.3 | 2.62 | 17.1 | 23.4 |
| **HAWAII** | 13.1 | 7.7 | 7.1 | 49.8 | 1 211 537 | 1 360 301 | 12.3 | 2.4 | 41 798 | 22 275 | 13 124 | 455 338 | 12.9 | 2.89 | 12.6 | 23.3 |
| Hawaii | 16.2 | 8.5 | 6.6 | 49.8 | 148 677 | 185 079 | 24.5 | 2.2 | 5 405 | 3 112 | 1 876 | 67 096 | 26.6 | 2.70 | 12.3 | 25.1 |
| Honolulu | 12.1 | 7.4 | 7.4 | 49.8 | 876 156 | 953 207 | 8.8 | 2.4 | 29 935 | 15 810 | 9 490 | 311 047 | 8.6 | 2.95 | 12.7 | 22.8 |
| Kalawao | 26.7 | 8.9 | 21.1 | 53.3 | 147 | 90 | -38.8 | 0.0 | 0 | 0 | 0 | 69 | -40.0 | 1.26 | 1.4 | 73.9 |
| Kauai | 15.5 | 8.5 | 7.1 | 49.8 | 58 463 | 67 091 | 14.8 | 2.0 | 1 938 | 1 121 | 567 | 23 240 | 15.1 | 2.84 | 12.6 | 22.6 |
| Maui | 14.3 | 7.7 | 5.7 | 49.9 | 128 094 | 154 834 | 20.9 | 2.2 | 4 520 | 2 232 | 1 191 | 53 886 | 23.9 | 2.82 | 12.3 | 24.3 |
| **IDAHO** | 11.9 | 7.3 | 5.5 | 49.9 | 1 293 953 | 1 567 582 | 21.1 | 1.8 | 50 637 | 26 175 | 3 100 | 579 408 | 23.4 | 2.66 | 9.6 | 23.8 |
| Ada | 11.5 | 6.1 | 4.7 | 49.9 | 300 904 | 392 365 | 30.4 | 4.3 | 11 386 | 5 405 | 10 477 | 148 445 | 30.9 | 2.58 | 10.0 | 25.0 |
| Adams | 20.5 | 14.0 | 7.4 | 48.8 | 3 476 | 3 976 | 14.4 | -1.5 | 63 | 60 | -63 | 1 748 | 23.0 | 2.26 | 5.8 | 26.8 |
| Bannock | 11.3 | 6.2 | 5.2 | 50.3 | 75 565 | 82 839 | 9.6 | 1.2 | 3 099 | 1 410 | -706 | 30 682 | 12.8 | 2.64 | 10.7 | 24.9 |
| Bear Lake | 14.0 | 10.3 | 8.4 | 50.1 | 6 411 | 5 986 | -6.6 | -1.3 | 169 | 159 | -89 | 2 281 | 1.0 | 2.61 | 6.3 | 24.0 |
| Benewah | 16.1 | 11.8 | 7.4 | 49.1 | 9 171 | 9 285 | 1.2 | -1.8 | 240 | 253 | -153 | 3 837 | 7.2 | 2.40 | 9.3 | 27.3 |
| Bingham | 10.9 | 6.5 | 5.1 | 49.7 | 41 735 | 45 607 | 9.3 | -0.3 | 1 711 | 723 | -1 126 | 14 999 | 12.6 | 3.02 | 10.5 | 18.5 |
| Blaine | 15.4 | 8.5 | 4.2 | 49.0 | 18 991 | 21 376 | 12.6 | -1.1 | 519 | 217 | -549 | 8 823 | 13.4 | 2.39 | 7.3 | 28.7 |
| Boise | 21.7 | 12.3 | 4.7 | 48.2 | 6 670 | 7 028 | 5.4 | -2.7 | 97 | 118 | -176 | 2 974 | 13.7 | 2.35 | 5.6 | 25.3 |
| Bonner | 18.4 | 11.2 | 6.9 | 49.7 | 36 835 | 40 877 | 11.0 | -1.0 | 845 | 836 | -440 | 17 100 | 16.4 | 2.37 | 7.9 | 26.0 |
| Bonneville | 10.7 | 6.1 | 5.0 | 50.1 | 82 522 | 104 234 | 26.3 | 2.4 | 4 230 | 1 674 | -163 | 36 629 | 27.4 | 2.81 | 10.1 | 22.4 |
| Boundary | 16.5 | 10.8 | 7.1 | 49.5 | 9 871 | 10 972 | 11.2 | -1.5 | 263 | 264 | -162 | 4 421 | 19.3 | 2.47 | 7.6 | 27.5 |
| Butte | 15.6 | 10.1 | 7.5 | 48.7 | 2 899 | 2 891 | -0.3 | -5.2 | 64 | 45 | -182 | 1 129 | 3.7 | 2.54 | 7.8 | 26.4 |
| Camas | 15.0 | 11.4 | 5.7 | 47.3 | 991 | 1 117 | 12.7 | -3.6 | 26 | 9 | -67 | 487 | 23.0 | 2.29 | 5.1 | 28.3 |
| Canyon | 10.1 | 6.5 | 4.8 | 50.5 | 131 441 | 188 923 | 43.7 | 2.6 | 6 857 | 2 812 | 843 | 63 604 | 41.3 | 2.92 | 12.3 | 20.1 |

1. No spouse present.

# Table B. States and Counties — **Population, Vital Statistics, Medicare, and Crime**

| STATE County | Persons in group quarters, 2010 | Daytime population, 2007–2011 Number | Employ-ment/resi-dence ratio | Births, 2011 Total | Rate[1] | Deaths, 2011 Number | Rate[1] | Persons under 65 with no health insurance, 2010 Number | Percent | Medicare, 2012 Eligible for Medicare | Enrolled in Medicare Advantage | Enrolled in a Medicare prescription drug plan | Serious crimes known to police,[2] 2011 Total Number | Rate[3] |
|---|---|---|---|---|---|---|---|---|---|---|---|---|---|---|
| | 32 | 33 | 34 | 35 | 36 | 37 | 38 | 39 | 40 | 41 | 42 | 43 | 44 | 45 |
| GEORGIA—Cont'd | | | | | | | | | | | | | | |
| Putnam | 172 | 18 962 | 0.75 | 241 | 11.3 | 235 | 11.0 | 4 087 | 23.8 | 4 685 | 980 | 1 902 | 705 | 3 280 |
| Quitman | 0 | 2 060 | 0.49 | 31 | 12.6 | 21 | 8.5 | 478 | 24.2 | 649 | 167 | 277 | 43 | 1 689 |
| Rabun | 390 | 16 849 | 1.09 | 168 | 10.3 | 209 | 12.8 | 3 506 | 27.7 | 4 189 | 610 | 2 142 | 238 | 1 443 |
| Randolph | 308 | 7 254 | 0.83 | 95 | 12.6 | 62 | 8.2 | 1 357 | 22.1 | 1 520 | 336 | 821 | 149 | 1 905 |
| Richmond | 10 508 | 232 643 | 1.40 | 3 117 | 15.5 | 1 840 | 9.1 | 33 236 | 19.6 | 31 696 | 9 419 | 9 324 | 14 658 | 7 214 |
| Rockdale | 864 | 82 907 | 0.96 | 1 082 | 12.6 | 592 | 6.9 | 16 920 | 22.4 | 12 109 | 3 435 | 4 240 | 3 928 | 4 550 |
| Schley | 0 | 4 242 | 0.67 | 51 | 10.2 | 34 | 6.8 | 955 | 22.0 | 711 | 178 | 350 | 75 | 1 478 |
| Screven | 420 | 13 694 | 0.81 | 206 | 14.3 | 177 | 12.3 | 2 695 | 22.4 | 2 849 | 579 | 1 363 | 349 | 2 458 |
| Seminole | 100 | 8 320 | 0.85 | 102 | 11.6 | 103 | 11.7 | 1 506 | 21.4 | 2 152 | 457 | 1 049 | 161 | 1 820 |
| Spalding | 1 226 | 62 112 | 0.94 | 890 | 13.9 | 669 | 10.4 | 11 874 | 21.7 | 12 065 | 3 195 | 5 102 | 3 498 | 5 388 |
| Stephens | 548 | 26 146 | 1.02 | 312 | 12.0 | 337 | 13.0 | 5 104 | 23.9 | 5 845 | 1 106 | 2 854 | 1 048 | 3 952 |
| Stewart | 1 675 | 5 545 | 0.84 | 61 | 10.3 | 69 | 11.7 | 769 | 21.4 | 962 | 221 | 500 | 29 | 472 |
| Sumter | 1 907 | 33 558 | 1.06 | 393 | 12.1 | 318 | 9.8 | 5 940 | 22.0 | 5 480 | 1 428 | 2 646 | 1 905 | 5 729 |
| Talbot | 17 | 5 382 | 0.37 | 67 | 9.9 | 77 | 11.4 | 1 160 | 20.3 | 1 433 | 373 | 608 | 51 | 917 |
| Taliaferro | 7 | 1 526 | 0.55 | 13 | 7.6 | 20 | 11.7 | 363 | 26.3 | 419 | 141 | 181 | NA | NA |
| Tattnall | 4 859 | 23 269 | 0.82 | 349 | 13.6 | 230 | 9.0 | 4 958 | 27.7 | 3 647 | 954 | 1 627 | 467 | 2 306 |
| Taylor | 322 | 7 977 | 0.70 | 100 | 11.8 | 80 | 9.4 | 1 571 | 21.5 | 1 613 | 470 | 770 | 111 | 1 230 |
| Telfair | 3 127 | 16 377 | 1.04 | 161 | 10.0 | 156 | 9.7 | 2 637 | 23.4 | 2 272 | 470 | 1 221 | 218 | 1 304 |
| Terrell | 270 | 8 926 | 0.82 | 140 | 15.0 | 96 | 10.3 | 1 608 | 20.8 | 1 991 | 553 | 908 | 198 | 2 098 |
| Thomas | 848 | 47 301 | 1.17 | 613 | 13.7 | 479 | 10.7 | 7 732 | 20.6 | 9 270 | 2 131 | 4 329 | 1 895 | 4 463 |
| Tift | 1 568 | 44 323 | 1.25 | 600 | 14.5 | 390 | 9.4 | 8 342 | 24.7 | 6 807 | 1 496 | 3 159 | 2 460 | 6 052 |
| Toombs | 387 | 28 630 | 1.13 | 444 | 16.2 | 305 | 11.1 | 5 584 | 23.9 | 5 176 | 943 | 2 878 | 1 066 | 4 604 |
| Towns | 698 | 10 961 | 1.12 | 82 | 7.7 | 152 | 14.3 | 1 625 | 23.8 | 3 725 | 828 | 1 489 | 195 | 1 838 |
| Treutlen | 452 | 5 835 | 0.55 | 84 | 12.3 | 80 | 11.7 | 1 276 | 22.7 | 1 269 | 334 | 664 | NA | NA |
| Troup | 2 073 | 72 272 | 1.21 | 912 | 13.5 | 670 | 9.9 | 11 840 | 20.7 | 11 072 | 2 553 | 5 406 | 2 852 | 4 199 |
| Turner | 371 | 7 858 | 0.64 | 121 | 13.6 | 100 | 11.3 | 1 809 | 24.9 | 1 833 | 474 | 935 | 320 | 3 537 |
| Twiggs | 89 | 7 826 | 0.51 | 86 | 9.8 | 137 | 15.6 | 1 693 | 22.6 | 2 109 | 602 | 899 | 183 | 2 261 |
| Union | 379 | 20 527 | 0.91 | 171 | 8.1 | 223 | 10.6 | 4 007 | 26.0 | 6 572 | 1 357 | 2 673 | 153 | 707 |
| Upson | 474 | 25 359 | 0.81 | 341 | 12.6 | 373 | 13.8 | 4 804 | 21.3 | 5 957 | 1 751 | 2 744 | 910 | 3 308 |
| Walker | 1 323 | 56 785 | 0.58 | 712 | 10.3 | 716 | 10.4 | 12 533 | 21.8 | 13 466 | 3 037 | 6 673 | 1 890 | 2 713 |
| Walton | 682 | 67 462 | 0.58 | 1 023 | 12.1 | 729 | 8.6 | 15 231 | 20.8 | 12 906 | 3 141 | 5 262 | 2 584 | 3 045 |
| Ware | 2 409 | 39 676 | 1.27 | 501 | 13.7 | 425 | 11.7 | 6 456 | 22.4 | 7 465 | 1 194 | 4 251 | 2 043 | 5 553 |
| Warren | 89 | 5 193 | 0.68 | 61 | 10.7 | 68 | 11.9 | 987 | 20.7 | 1 285 | 352 | 598 | NA | NA |
| Washington | 1 896 | 21 683 | 1.07 | 260 | 12.3 | 228 | 10.8 | 3 610 | 21.8 | 3 921 | 1 321 | 1 638 | 699 | 3 295 |
| Wayne | 2 316 | 28 878 | 0.90 | 419 | 13.8 | 305 | 10.1 | 5 634 | 23.4 | 5 286 | 1 081 | 2 623 | 1 965 | 6 444 |
| Webster | 0 | 2 102 | 0.47 | 15 | 5.4 | 9 | 3.2 | 645 | 27.1 | 488 | 122 | 226 | 32 | 1 128 |
| Wheeler | 1 959 | 7 455 | 1.06 | 69 | 8.7 | 70 | 8.8 | 1 074 | 23.2 | 1 019 | 194 | 520 | 67 | 891 |
| White | 365 | 24 271 | 0.78 | 254 | 9.3 | 254 | 9.3 | 5 551 | 25.2 | 5 764 | 1 276 | 2 653 | 709 | 2 578 |
| Whitfield | 1 002 | 114 120 | 1.30 | 1 542 | 14.9 | 706 | 6.8 | 24 288 | 26.8 | 14 989 | 1 781 | 8 752 | 3 450 | 3 399 |
| Wilcox | 2 019 | 8 736 | 0.84 | 101 | 10.9 | 110 | 11.8 | 1 428 | 23.6 | 1 596 | 366 | 687 | 122 | 1 593 |
| Wilkes | 344 | 9 879 | 0.83 | 114 | 11.2 | 147 | 14.4 | 1 884 | 22.6 | 2 438 | 538 | 1 230 | 274 | 2 553 |
| Wilkinson | 110 | 9 219 | 0.88 | 149 | 15.8 | 121 | 12.8 | 1 601 | 20.1 | 2 142 | 577 | 814 | 210 | 2 415 |
| Worth | 149 | 17 361 | 0.47 | 230 | 10.5 | 194 | 8.8 | 4 094 | 22.2 | 3 679 | 616 | 1 727 | 556 | 2 582 |
| HAWAII | 42 880 | 1 347 513 | 1.00 | 18 501 | 13.5 | 9 730 | 7.1 | 102 658 | 8.9 | 223 765 | 15 465 | 9 456 | 49 838 | 3 625 |
| Hawaii | 3 644 | 182 936 | 1.00 | 2 376 | 12.7 | 1 397 | 7.5 | 18 684 | 11.7 | 32 984 | 13 704 | 10 188 | 5 200 | 2 780 |
| Honolulu | 35 300 | 944 728 | 1.00 | 13 246 | 13.7 | 6 870 | 7.1 | 63 196 | 7.9 | 156 177 | 71 793 | 37 658 | 32 982 | 3 423 |
| Kalawao | 3 | 108 | 2.11 | 0 | 0.0 | 0 | 0.0 | 0 | 0.0 | 20 | D | 0 | NA | NA |
| Kauai | 1 161 | 66 390 | 1.00 | 842 | 12.4 | 474 | 7.0 | 5 647 | 9.8 | 11 745 | 4 580 | 3 765 | 2 861 | 4 219 |
| Maui | 2 772 | 153 351 | 1.01 | 2 037 | 13.0 | 989 | 6.3 | 15 131 | 11.1 | 22 839 | 10 885 | 5 691 | 6 296 | 4 023 |
| IDAHO | 28 951 | 1 533 165 | 0.98 | 22 954 | 14.5 | 11 275 | 7.1 | 273 440 | 20.3 | 251 496 | 76 496 | 89 797 | 35 971 | 2 269 |
| Ada | 9 714 | 406 712 | 1.10 | 5 024 | 12.5 | 2 303 | 5.7 | 56 856 | 16.5 | 55 506 | 23 362 | 13 104 | 8 548 | 2 155 |
| Adams | 21 | 3 774 | 0.88 | 29 | 7.3 | 25 | 6.3 | 829 | 26.7 | 1 008 | 161 | 399 | 30 | 746 |
| Bannock | 1 792 | 80 817 | 0.98 | 1 414 | 16.9 | 604 | 7.2 | 13 024 | 18.1 | 12 165 | 3 792 | 5 237 | 2 670 | 3 188 |
| Bear Lake | 31 | 5 721 | 0.88 | 88 | 14.7 | 74 | 12.3 | 985 | 20.3 | 1 286 | 128 | 690 | 113 | 1 867 |
| Benewah | 70 | 9 825 | 1.14 | 108 | 11.7 | 119 | 12.9 | 1 688 | 22.4 | 2 260 | 500 | 1 033 | 65 | 692 |
| Bingham | 323 | 42 081 | 0.84 | 785 | 17.1 | 315 | 6.9 | 9 571 | 23.9 | 6 685 | 1 457 | 2 993 | 874 | 1 895 |
| Blaine | 258 | 22 374 | 1.09 | 252 | 11.9 | 89 | 4.2 | 4 486 | 23.8 | 3 243 | 527 | 1 463 | 261 | 1 208 |
| Boise | 34 | 6 776 | 0.89 | 49 | 7.0 | 53 | 7.5 | 1 256 | 21.4 | 1 457 | 588 | 347 | 132 | 1 995 |
| Bonner | 353 | 40 183 | 0.96 | 385 | 9.4 | 358 | 8.8 | 7 136 | 21.3 | 9 007 | 2 418 | 3 178 | 899 | 2 175 |
| Bonneville | 1 172 | 107 582 | 1.11 | 1 907 | 18.0 | 720 | 6.8 | 16 063 | 17.4 | 14 550 | 2 930 | 6 502 | 2 717 | 2 576 |
| Boundary | 73 | 10 569 | 0.93 | 119 | 11.0 | 132 | 12.2 | 2 218 | 24.4 | 2 463 | 690 | 835 | 129 | 1 163 |
| Butte | 18 | 4 785 | 2.66 | 32 | 11.3 | 15 | 5.3 | 500 | 21.0 | 568 | 37 | 302 | 7 | 239 |
| Camas | 0 | 1 017 | 0.63 | 15 | 13.3 | 2 | 1.8 | 270 | 28.8 | 169 | 20 | 69 | 14 | 1 240 |
| Canyon | 3 335 | 170 725 | 0.79 | 3 104 | 16.2 | 1 218 | 6.4 | 37 369 | 22.7 | 27 577 | 13 122 | 7 323 | 5 071 | 2 655 |

1. Per 1,000 estimated resident population.    2. Data for serious crimes have not been adjusted for underreporting; this may affect comparability between geographic areas and over time.    3. Per 100,000 population estimated by the FBI.

# Table B. States and Counties — Crime, Education, Money Income, and Poverty

| STATE County | Serious crimes known to police, 2011 (cont.)[1] — Rate[2] | | Education — School enrollment and attainment, 2007–2011 | | | | Local government expenditures,[5] 2009–2010 | | Money income, 2007–2011 | | | | Income and poverty, 2011 | | | |
|---|---|---|---|---|---|---|---|---|---|---|---|---|---|---|---|---|
| | | | Enrollment[3] | | Attainment[4] (percent) | | | | | Households — Median income | | | | Percent below poverty level | | |
| | Violent | Property | Total | Per-cent private | High school graduate or less | Bach-elor's degree or more | Total current expendi-tures (mil dol) | Current expendi-tures per student (dollars) | Per capita income[6] (dollars) | Dollars | Percent change, 2000 to 2007–2011 (constant 2011 dollars) | Percent with income of $200,000 or more | Median house-hold income (dollars) | All per-sons | Children under 18 years | Children 5 to 17 years in families |
| | 46 | 47 | 48 | 49 | 50 | 51 | 52 | 53 | 54 | 55 | 56 | 57 | 58 | 59 | 60 | 61 |
| **GEORGIA—Cont'd** | | | | | | | | | | | | | | | | |
| Putnam | 581 | 2 698 | 4 513 | 20.5 | 56.4 | 18.9 | 32.4 | 11 762 | 27 000 | 41 756 | -16.3 | 4.1 | 40 168 | 18.7 | 33.4 | 31.7 |
| Quitman | 471 | 1 218 | 491 | 2.6 | 68.7 | 7.6 | 4.8 | 12 386 | 14 894 | 32 656 | -6.5 | 0.8 | 28 621 | 27.5 | 44.0 | 39.4 |
| Rabun | 24 | 1 419 | 3 171 | 13.2 | 50.4 | 24.2 | 25.5 | 10 879 | 22 423 | 33 533 | -26.7 | 2.7 | 34 394 | 20.5 | 33.0 | 30.2 |
| Randolph | 141 | 1 764 | 1 983 | 29.7 | 61.7 | 14.8 | 15.0 | 11 306 | 19 523 | 29 071 | -2.1 | 2.8 | 27 950 | 30.8 | 43.4 | 41.8 |
| Richmond | 504 | 6 710 | 54 444 | 13.7 | 49.9 | 19.7 | 303.7 | 9 361 | 20 393 | 39 090 | -12.5 | 1.5 | 37 352 | 25.2 | 35.8 | 34.7 |
| Rockdale | 408 | 4 142 | 24 448 | 19.5 | 44.6 | 23.7 | 154.4 | 9 784 | 24 606 | 55 819 | -22.9 | 2.7 | 51 106 | 15.5 | 24.5 | 23.1 |
| Schley | 158 | 1 320 | 1 306 | 4.3 | 65.5 | 11.3 | 13.9 | 9 808 | 16 815 | 34 691 | -19.8 | 0.0 | 37 669 | 19.7 | 26.4 | 22.6 |
| Screven | 148 | 2 311 | 3 841 | 7.8 | 67.2 | 11.9 | 22.5 | 8 628 | 16 647 | 31 963 | -19.2 | 0.7 | 32 990 | 27.1 | 39.0 | 36.2 |
| Seminole | 192 | 1 628 | 2 216 | 10.3 | 57.3 | 10.9 | 15.6 | 9 567 | 18 692 | 29 639 | -19.0 | 2.5 | 30 489 | 28.6 | 44.6 | 39.6 |
| Spalding | 434 | 4 954 | 16 134 | 12.6 | 62.0 | 14.0 | 103.0 | 9 483 | 19 547 | 41 163 | -15.8 | 1.8 | 38 914 | 23.4 | 34.6 | 31.3 |
| Stephens | 249 | 3 703 | 6 768 | 20.1 | 63.6 | 14.2 | 41.9 | 10 161 | 18 592 | 37 502 | -5.7 | 2.6 | 37 536 | 22.7 | 33.5 | 31.1 |
| Stewart | 49 | 424 | 1 331 | 12.7 | 67.1 | 12.0 | 7.1 | 13 128 | 15 944 | 30 417 | -9.1 | 0.2 | 26 010 | 39.1 | 44.9 | 44.2 |
| Sumter | 740 | 4 989 | 9 642 | 13.3 | 58.3 | 18.2 | 48.8 | 9 546 | 18 368 | 34 416 | -17.5 | 1.0 | 31 937 | 28.9 | 41.3 | 39.1 |
| Talbot | 180 | 738 | 1 544 | 21.0 | 66.0 | 11.2 | 8.7 | 13 520 | 18 051 | 33 404 | -7.0 | 0.9 | 31 290 | 24.3 | 36.8 | 34.4 |
| Taliaferro | NA | NA | 394 | 7.4 | 75.0 | 8.5 | 3.2 | 14 342 | 13 347 | 24 125 | -24.8 | 0.8 | 25 807 | 29.8 | 50.3 | 49.6 |
| Tattnall | 94 | 2 212 | 5 223 | 11.6 | 70.8 | 11.3 | 30.7 | 8 544 | 15 741 | 33 863 | -12.5 | 1.5 | 31 531 | 35.3 | 43.5 | 35.4 |
| Taylor | 144 | 1 086 | 2 139 | 9.4 | 67.2 | 6.8 | 15.9 | 10 362 | 15 594 | 27 479 | -19.1 | 1.0 | 30 308 | 26.9 | 36.2 | 32.1 |
| Telfair | 138 | 1 166 | 3 031 | 4.6 | 74.2 | 10.2 | 16.7 | 9 407 | 12 959 | 23 777 | -32.5 | 0.4 | 27 831 | 36.4 | 44.3 | 40.3 |
| Terrell | 371 | 1 727 | 2 403 | 16.7 | 68.4 | 10.2 | 15.9 | 10 499 | 15 896 | 30 552 | -15.0 | 0.3 | 30 552 | 36.3 | 47.8 | 44.1 |
| Thomas | 289 | 3 893 | 11 053 | 12.2 | 54.6 | 19.1 | 74.8 | 8 857 | 20 716 | 34 419 | -18.1 | 2.5 | 34 611 | 26.3 | 33.8 | 31.0 |
| Tift | 603 | 5 449 | 11 626 | 8.6 | 54.2 | 17.0 | 67.4 | 8 845 | 18 704 | 37 414 | -15.0 | 1.5 | 33 669 | 26.4 | 38.3 | 34.3 |
| Toombs | 363 | 4 241 | 7 081 | 9.9 | 59.3 | 14.0 | 46.0 | 8 286 | 18 466 | 32 462 | -10.3 | 2.4 | 32 915 | 26.1 | 39.4 | 38.0 |
| Towns | 94 | 1 744 | 2 265 | 35.7 | 53.4 | 21.0 | 13.4 | 11 863 | 21 642 | 39 309 | -8.9 | 1.5 | 36 858 | 19.4 | 32.7 | 29.6 |
| Treutlen | NA | NA | 1 555 | 6.6 | 71.4 | 9.2 | 10.4 | 8 729 | 18 030 | 31 848 | -4.3 | 1.9 | 30 131 | 28.0 | 40.7 | 37.1 |
| Troup | 287 | 3 912 | 18 111 | 11.5 | 54.8 | 19.6 | 117.6 | 9 319 | 20 351 | 41 961 | -12.4 | 1.8 | 39 370 | 22.4 | 32.1 | 30.4 |
| Turner | 542 | 2 995 | 2 230 | 11.4 | 65.8 | 11.4 | 17.6 | 10 546 | 17 265 | 29 851 | -13.9 | 0.6 | 25 480 | 28.2 | 43.0 | 40.4 |
| Twiggs | 99 | 2 162 | 2 213 | 16.8 | 75.9 | 8.7 | 11.8 | 11 878 | 16 022 | 27 715 | -35.1 | 0.7 | 34 528 | 23.1 | 33.9 | 31.8 |
| Union | 69 | 638 | 4 113 | 25.2 | 45.1 | 21.1 | 32.3 | 9 094 | 24 124 | 43 146 | 0.2 | 2.4 | 39 206 | 18.4 | 31.1 | 28.2 |
| Upson | 156 | 3 151 | 6 741 | 8.5 | 61.7 | 11.0 | 40.5 | 8 676 | 17 482 | 34 068 | -19.1 | 0.2 | 33 483 | 22.0 | 31.6 | 29.3 |
| Walker | 369 | 2 344 | 15 291 | 13.1 | 58.0 | 13.6 | 96.9 | 9 089 | 20 459 | 39 578 | -9.5 | 1.2 | 37 813 | 18.6 | 27.0 | 24.7 |
| Walton | 266 | 2 778 | 21 459 | 15.8 | 53.1 | 17.7 | 128.7 | 8 673 | 22 993 | 51 347 | -18.2 | 2.0 | 52 747 | 15.3 | 23.1 | 21.5 |
| Ware | 383 | 5 170 | 8 540 | 4.7 | 60.8 | 13.4 | 61.8 | 10 160 | 18 513 | 35 431 | -7.5 | 1.4 | 31 529 | 27.2 | 36.1 | 35.3 |
| Warren | NA | NA | 1 459 | 10.7 | 74.5 | 5.9 | 8.2 | 10 352 | 17 423 | 33 330 | -9.8 | 1.1 | 30 946 | 27.0 | 39.6 | 36.6 |
| Washington | 264 | 3 031 | 4 618 | 8.2 | 67.9 | 10.9 | 34.1 | 10 490 | 15 840 | 31 784 | -21.3 | 0.7 | 34 117 | 26.1 | 33.6 | 31.5 |
| Wayne | 712 | 5 732 | 7 301 | 7.9 | 61.6 | 10.7 | 47.5 | 8 845 | 18 441 | 39 470 | -10.8 | 0.9 | 37 082 | 23.9 | 33.9 | 32.1 |
| Webster | 35 | 1 093 | 457 | 24.1 | 66.5 | 11.8 | 4.8 | 9 283 | 20 524 | 29 583 | -21.7 | 1.3 | 32 842 | 23.1 | 34.3 | 28.6 |
| Wheeler | 40 | 851 | 1 329 | 2.3 | 78.5 | 8.1 | 9.6 | 9 596 | 9 412 | 31 456 | -3.1 | 0.0 | 29 780 | 42.2 | 40.5 | 39.3 |
| White | 236 | 2 342 | 5 591 | 22.3 | 49.3 | 19.6 | 45.9 | 11 855 | 23 849 | 39 666 | -18.6 | 1.9 | 39 753 | 15.8 | 27.5 | 25.3 |
| Whitfield | 253 | 3 145 | 27 655 | 7.3 | 61.5 | 14.8 | 183.8 | 9 086 | 20 139 | 42 379 | -20.3 | 2.5 | 38 452 | 17.8 | 25.1 | 23.9 |
| Wilcox | 183 | 1 410 | 1 797 | 5.1 | 67.9 | 9.2 | 11.3 | 8 314 | 12 561 | 31 712 | -14.5 | 0.4 | 30 500 | 32.8 | 40.1 | 36.5 |
| Wilkes | 391 | 2 162 | 2 465 | 6.6 | 62.7 | 15.5 | 16.2 | 9 613 | 17 397 | 28 989 | -22.3 | 0.9 | 30 720 | 23.3 | 35.8 | 34.0 |
| Wilkinson | 138 | 2 277 | 2 239 | 7.5 | 66.5 | 12.4 | 20.0 | 12 439 | 18 488 | 37 500 | -15.1 | 1.0 | 38 570 | 18.3 | 30.5 | 29.0 |
| Worth | 79 | 2 503 | 5 591 | 13.9 | 66.8 | 8.3 | 31.0 | 8 593 | 18 810 | 38 336 | -12.3 | 1.0 | 35 308 | 26.7 | 37.0 | 33.6 |
| **HAWAII** | 287 | 3 338 | 331 875 | 24.0 | 38.5 | 29.5 | 2 118.0 | 11 754 | 29 203 | 67 116 | -0.2 | 5.5 | 62 071 | 12.1 | 16.8 | 15.9 |
| Hawaii | 262 | 2 518 | 43 057 | 19.8 | 40.9 | 25.9 | (7) | (7) | 25 573 | 53 591 | -0.3 | 3.0 | 46 186 | 20.4 | 29.9 | 28.7 |
| Honolulu | 246 | 3 177 | 239 307 | 26.0 | 37.4 | 31.2 | (7)2 118.0 | (7)11 754 | 30 016 | 71 263 | 1.7 | 6.1 | 65 489 | 10.3 | 13.9 | 13.3 |
| Kalawao | NA | NA | 4 | 0.0 | 33.3 | 36.8 | (7) | (7) | 49 995 | 56 875 | 351.3 | 0.0 | 0 | 0.0 | 0.0 | 0.0 |
| Kauai | 348 | 3 871 | 14 714 | 14.2 | 40.1 | 24.3 | (7) | (7) | 26 591 | 64 422 | 6.0 | 3.7 | 56 937 | 12.9 | 18.3 | 17.1 |
| Maui | 236 | 3 788 | 34 793 | 20.1 | 42.1 | 25.7 | (7) | (7) | 29 654 | 64 583 | -3.3 | 5.9 | 57 789 | 12.8 | 17.7 | 15.8 |
| **IDAHO** | 201 | 2 069 | 428 368 | 14.2 | 39.9 | 24.6 | 1 947.0 | 7 049 | 22 788 | 46 890 | -7.6 | 2.2 | 43 345 | 16.5 | 21.3 | 19.2 |
| Ada | 201 | 1 953 | 110 574 | 12.5 | 29.5 | 35.2 | 495.3 | 7 095 | 27 956 | 55 304 | -11.2 | 3.7 | 50 701 | 13.4 | 15.7 | 13.8 |
| Adams | 25 | 721 | 735 | 10.1 | 49.8 | 19.5 | 4.3 | 10 357 | 24 015 | 36 845 | -4.0 | 2.2 | 32 752 | 17.1 | 27.4 | 25.7 |
| Bannock | 215 | 2 973 | 24 970 | 8.5 | 35.5 | 27.0 | 93.0 | 6 642 | 21 457 | 45 347 | -8.4 | 1.4 | 41 749 | 18.7 | 23.8 | 21.3 |
| Bear Lake | 116 | 1 751 | 1 433 | 9.7 | 47.9 | 16.6 | 7.8 | 6 930 | 19 484 | 43 897 | 1.1 | 0.2 | 42 327 | 14.0 | 20.4 | 17.8 |
| Benewah | 234 | 458 | 2 069 | 4.3 | 56.1 | 12.1 | 13.5 | 8 987 | 18 831 | 37 508 | -11.9 | 0.5 | 39 327 | 16.3 | 24.4 | 22.2 |
| Bingham | 95 | 1 800 | 13 088 | 8.2 | 47.2 | 16.2 | 67.9 | 6 751 | 18 918 | 46 169 | -6.1 | 1.2 | 45 354 | 15.5 | 21.6 | 19.9 |
| Blaine | 204 | 1 004 | 4 689 | 21.1 | 27.0 | 45.1 | 48.3 | 14 672 | 33 408 | 62 906 | -7.7 | 4.6 | 60 448 | 10.4 | 16.3 | 14.4 |
| Boise | 166 | 1 829 | 1 604 | 10.7 | 41.0 | 19.9 | 9.2 | 9 678 | 23 894 | 47 128 | -9.7 | 0.6 | 48 657 | 15.7 | 22.1 | 18.2 |
| Bonner | 111 | 2 064 | 8 049 | 15.5 | 41.0 | 22.3 | 40.4 | 7 763 | 24 494 | 42 989 | -2.9 | 2.4 | 41 255 | 17.2 | 24.4 | 21.4 |
| Bonneville | 218 | 2 358 | 28 785 | 13.8 | 36.0 | 26.7 | 127.9 | 6 066 | 23 521 | 51 311 | -9.1 | 2.7 | 49 748 | 13.9 | 19.0 | 17.1 |
| Boundary | 99 | 1 064 | 2 208 | 7.9 | 58.1 | 11.9 | 11.9 | 7 478 | 18 509 | 35 324 | -16.3 | 0.4 | 33 655 | 18.5 | 27.7 | 23.9 |
| Butte | 103 | 137 | 653 | 12.1 | 43.3 | 18.7 | 3.9 | 8 196 | 19 395 | 37 821 | -8.1 | 0.3 | 41 026 | 16.2 | 21.5 | 17.9 |
| Camas | 89 | 1 151 | 305 | 8.2 | 48.1 | 23.7 | 1.9 | 12 106 | 19 726 | 41 184 | -10.7 | 0.0 | 45 439 | 12.4 | 18.7 | 15.9 |
| Canyon | 239 | 2 416 | 52 895 | 16.3 | 49.8 | 16.5 | 232.7 | 6 490 | 18 171 | 42 943 | -11.4 | 1.3 | 39 132 | 20.1 | 26.7 | 23.8 |

1. Data for serious crimes have not been adjusted for underreporting; this may affect comparability between geographic areas and over time. 2. Per 100,000 population estimated by the FBI. 3. All persons 3 years old and over enrolled in nursery school through college. 4. Persons 25 years old and over. 5. Elementary and secondary education expenditures. 6. Based on population estimated by the American Community Survey, 2007–2011. 7. Hawaii, Kalawao, Kauai, and Maui counties are included with Honolulu county.

# Table B. States and Counties — Personal Income

| STATE County | Personal income, 2011 Total (mil dol) | Percent change, 2010–2011 | Per capita[1] Dollars | Per capita[1] Rank | Wages and salaries[2] (mil dol) | Proprietors' income (mil dol) | Dividends, interest, and rent (mil dol) | Transfer payments (mil dol) Total | Government payments to individuals Total | Social Security | Medical payments | Income mainte-nance | Unemploy-ment insurance |
|---|---|---|---|---|---|---|---|---|---|---|---|---|---|
| | 62 | 63 | 64 | 65 | 66 | 67 | 68 | 69 | 70 | 71 | 72 | 73 | 74 |
| **GEORGIA—Cont'd** | | | | | | | | | | | | | |
| Putnam | 683 | 2.6 | 32 005 | 1 889 | 250 | 45 | 143 | 184 | 179 | 70 | 69 | 25 | 6 |
| Quitman | 63 | 0.9 | 25 757 | 2 905 | 17 | 2 | 8 | 24 | 24 | 9 | 9 | 4 | 1 |
| Rabun | 493 | 3.5 | 30 324 | 2 233 | 177 | 34 | 130 | 147 | 144 | 59 | 60 | 12 | 5 |
| Randolph | 215 | 4.7 | 28 495 | 2 539 | 80 | 48 | 28 | 70 | 68 | 19 | 29 | 15 | 2 |
| Richmond | 6 101 | 3.3 | 30 320 | 2 234 | 6 813 | 254 | 971 | 1 741 | 1 698 | 438 | 655 | 336 | 65 |
| Rockdale | 2 731 | 3.7 | 31 840 | 1 920 | 1 634 | 118 | 349 | 545 | 526 | 183 | 186 | 86 | 24 |
| Schley | 103 | 1.5 | 20 566 | 3 099 | 52 | 6 | 13 | 32 | 30 | 10 | 12 | 5 | 1 |
| Screven | 423 | 5.8 | 29 475 | 2 381 | 145 | 37 | 66 | 130 | 127 | 38 | 54 | 24 | 5 |
| Seminole | 315 | 8.5 | 35 865 | 1 234 | 97 | 68 | 42 | 89 | 87 | 29 | 36 | 17 | 2 |
| Spalding | 1 812 | 3.4 | 28 305 | 2 570 | 974 | 96 | 273 | 549 | 535 | 172 | 203 | 102 | 20 |
| Stephens | 793 | 2.6 | 30 553 | 2 187 | 412 | 52 | 124 | 235 | 229 | 82 | 96 | 31 | 7 |
| Stewart | 141 | 2.3 | 23 862 | 3 033 | 58 | 8 | 18 | 50 | 49 | 12 | 23 | 11 | 1 |
| Sumter | 933 | 4.3 | 28 685 | 2 508 | 455 | 77 | 176 | 293 | 286 | 75 | 107 | 64 | 9 |
| Talbot | 177 | 5.7 | 26 273 | 2 854 | 38 | 4 | 22 | 62 | 60 | 19 | 22 | 12 | 2 |
| Taliaferro | 48 | 2.4 | 28 126 | 2 602 | 8 | 3 | 7 | 18 | 18 | 5 | 8 | 3 | 1 |
| Tattnall | 621 | 3.7 | 24 181 | 3 021 | 239 | 65 | 75 | 169 | 163 | 46 | 72 | 28 | 5 |
| Taylor | 221 | 3.4 | 25 979 | 2 883 | 79 | 19 | 27 | 78 | 77 | 21 | 33 | 17 | 2 |
| Telfair | 279 | 5.5 | 17 385 | 3 111 | 135 | 15 | 37 | 117 | 114 | 29 | 56 | 19 | 4 |
| Terrell | 299 | 5.3 | 32 048 | 1 873 | 98 | 40 | 56 | 94 | 92 | 25 | 38 | 23 | 3 |
| Thomas | 1 595 | 5.2 | 35 687 | 1 266 | 1 011 | 104 | 307 | 402 | 392 | 125 | 167 | 63 | 10 |
| Tift | 1 227 | 4.2 | 29 585 | 2 364 | 816 | 114 | 185 | 322 | 313 | 92 | 124 | 59 | 12 |
| Toombs | 849 | 3.6 | 30 934 | 2 117 | 474 | 62 | 110 | 246 | 240 | 68 | 100 | 46 | 9 |
| Towns | 375 | 4.1 | 35 378 | 1 311 | 125 | 21 | 100 | 118 | 116 | 54 | 45 | 6 | 3 |
| Treutlen | 168 | 1.9 | 24 686 | 2 989 | 45 | 15 | 21 | 58 | 57 | 17 | 23 | 11 | 2 |
| Troup | 2 196 | 8.4 | 32 410 | 1 801 | 1 775 | 91 | 335 | 509 | 494 | 162 | 186 | 96 | 20 |
| Turner | 260 | 4.2 | 29 305 | 2 409 | 88 | 33 | 32 | 89 | 87 | 22 | 38 | 19 | 3 |
| Twiggs | 283 | 3.3 | 32 267 | 1 829 | 49 | 4 | 25 | 89 | 87 | 28 | 34 | 17 | 3 |
| Union | 661 | 3.5 | 31 281 | 2 052 | 257 | 33 | 147 | 212 | 207 | 93 | 81 | 14 | 5 |
| Upson | 738 | 5.1 | 27 346 | 2 710 | 306 | 26 | 107 | 239 | 233 | 82 | 91 | 40 | 7 |
| Walker | 1 876 | 4.2 | 27 250 | 2 729 | 556 | 65 | 233 | 573 | 558 | 193 | 249 | 67 | 16 |
| Walton | 2 896 | 6.1 | 34 236 | 1 480 | 904 | 54 | 344 | 555 | 536 | 190 | 221 | 72 | 22 |
| Ware | 980 | 2.8 | 26 878 | 2 780 | 696 | 64 | 149 | 361 | 353 | 88 | 146 | 52 | 10 |
| Warren | 157 | 3.2 | 27 425 | 2 697 | 47 | 7 | 23 | 61 | 59 | 17 | 25 | 12 | 2 |
| Washington | 611 | 5.1 | 28 950 | 2 457 | 316 | 37 | 113 | 185 | 181 | 53 | 78 | 32 | 6 |
| Wayne | 883 | 5.1 | 29 118 | 2 434 | 434 | 45 | 102 | 255 | 248 | 75 | 106 | 39 | 8 |
| Webster | 69 | 5.2 | 24 574 | 2 999 | 24 | 2 | 10 | 20 | 20 | 6 | 8 | 4 | 1 |
| Wheeler | 138 | 5.4 | 17 340 | 3 112 | 63 | 1 | 15 | 46 | 44 | 13 | 19 | 8 | 2 |
| White | 702 | 5.1 | 25 757 | 2 905 | 240 | 38 | 132 | 201 | 195 | 82 | 74 | 20 | 7 |
| Whitfield | 2 894 | 3.7 | 28 044 | 2 610 | 2 643 | 236 | 426 | 664 | 641 | 219 | 252 | 93 | 29 |
| Wilcox | 235 | 9.9 | 25 300 | 2 943 | 61 | 41 | 28 | 75 | 73 | 19 | 36 | 12 | 2 |
| Wilkes | 295 | 2.9 | 28 866 | 2 473 | 121 | 17 | 65 | 104 | 102 | 34 | 44 | 16 | 3 |
| Wilkinson | 270 | 2.0 | 28 592 | 2 525 | 176 | 10 | 32 | 92 | 90 | 32 | 35 | 16 | 3 |
| Worth | 700 | 5.2 | 31 944 | 1 899 | 150 | 71 | 80 | 160 | 155 | 49 | 59 | 32 | 6 |
| **HAWAII** | 59 014 | 5.7 | 42 925 | X | 39 472 | 3 778 | 10 653 | 9 417 | 9 124 | 3 057 | 3 643 | 1 304 | 489 |
| Hawaii | 5 929 | 4.3 | 31 749 | 1 942 | 3 078 | 449 | 1 250 | 1 492 | 1 451 | 463 | 534 | 272 | 93 |
| Honolulu | 44 927 | 6.0 | 46 624 | 314 | 31 532 | 2 664 | 7 782 | 6 328 | 6 125 | 2 101 | 2 401 | 859 | 297 |
| Kalawao | [3]5 686 | [3]5.4 | [3]36 272 | [3]1 177 | [3]3 411 | [3]486 | [3]1 125 | [3]1 090 | [3]1 055 | [3]327 | [3]490 | [3]118 | [3]66 |
| Kauai | 2 472 | 4.9 | 36 520 | 1 134 | 1 450 | 180 | 495 | 508 | 493 | 166 | 218 | 56 | 32 |
| Maui | (3) | | (3) | (3) | (3) | (3) | (3) | (3) | (3) | (3) | (3) | (3) | (3) |
| **IDAHO** | 52 116 | 5.1 | 32 881 | X | 30 066 | 6 355 | 8 650 | 10 093 | 9 743 | 3 551 | 3 625 | 1 157 | 443 |
| Ada | 15 927 | 4.8 | 39 734 | 775 | 10 972 | 2 201 | 2 529 | 2 255 | 2 166 | 809 | 789 | 218 | 114 |
| Adams | 112 | 4.7 | 28 140 | 2 598 | 44 | 8 | 31 | 31 | 30 | 14 | 9 | 3 | 2 |
| Bannock | 2 412 | 3.5 | 28 818 | 2 484 | 1 475 | 155 | 329 | 586 | 567 | 165 | 202 | 76 | 22 |
| Bear Lake | 181 | 4.8 | 30 138 | 2 263 | 69 | 17 | 27 | 44 | 42 | 18 | 16 | 4 | 1 |
| Benewah | 294 | 3.2 | 31 906 | 1 905 | 161 | 25 | 45 | 85 | 83 | 32 | 33 | 8 | 4 |
| Bingham | 1 264 | 6.2 | 27 500 | 2 687 | 651 | 139 | 195 | 270 | 260 | 94 | 97 | 42 | 11 |
| Blaine | 1 261 | 5.9 | 59 465 | 71 | 582 | 140 | 523 | 107 | 103 | 48 | 34 | 6 | 9 |
| Boise | 257 | 4.9 | 36 633 | 1 120 | 56 | 7 | 41 | 49 | 48 | 21 | 15 | 4 | 2 |
| Bonner | 1 283 | 4.0 | 31 433 | 2 011 | 567 | 105 | 325 | 310 | 301 | 128 | 103 | 30 | 17 |
| Bonneville | 3 701 | 4.4 | 34 989 | 1 374 | 1 925 | 495 | 564 | 644 | 621 | 213 | 260 | 83 | 24 |
| Boundary | 289 | 5.8 | 26 714 | 2 801 | 158 | 25 | 54 | 82 | 80 | 32 | 27 | 9 | 4 |
| Butte | 100 | 6.7 | 35 305 | 1 324 | 820 | 20 | 13 | 20 | 20 | 8 | 8 | 2 | 1 |
| Camas | 43 | 15.0 | 38 661 | 887 | 18 | 10 | 5 | 6 | 5 | 2 | 2 | 0 | 1 |
| Canyon | 4 519 | 4.2 | 23 575 | 3 044 | 2 214 | 379 | 608 | 1 224 | 1 182 | 375 | 470 | 187 | 66 |

1. Based on the resident population estimated as of July 1 of the year shown.    2. Includes supplements to wages and salaries.    3. Kalawao county is included with Maui county.

# Table B. States and Counties — Earnings, Social Security, and Housing

| STATE County | Earnings, 2011 | | | | | | | | | Social Security beneficiaries, December 2011 | | | Housing units, 2010 | |
|---|---|---|---|---|---|---|---|---|---|---|---|---|---|---|
| | | | | | Percent by selected industries | | | | | | | | | |
| | | | Goods-related[1] | | Service-related and health | | | | | | | | | |
| | Total (mil dol) | Farm | Total | Manu-facturing | Infor-mation and profes-sional and technical services | Retail trade | Finance, insur-ance, and real estate | Health care and social services | Govern-ment | Number | Rate[2] | Supple-mental Security Income recipients, December 2011 | Total | Percent change, 2000–2010 |
| | 75 | 76 | 77 | 78 | 79 | 80 | 81 | 82 | 83 | 84 | 85 | 86 | 87 | 88 |
| GEORGIA—Cont'd | | | | | | | | | | | | | | |
| Putnam | 295 | 0.9 | 18.3 | 7.9 | D | 11.6 | 4.0 | D | 26.5 | 5 280 | 247 | 491 | 12 804 | 24.1 |
| Quitman | 19 | 9.0 | D | D | D | D | D | D | 35.9 | 730 | 296 | 145 | 2 047 | 15.5 |
| Rabun | 211 | 1.7 | D | 8.6 | 3.7 | 14.7 | 5.7 | D | 20.6 | 4 660 | 286 | 423 | 12 313 | 20.6 |
| Randolph | 128 | 9.6 | D | D | D | 9.1 | 3.5 | D | 23.9 | 1 690 | 224 | 435 | 4 153 | 22.1 |
| Richmond | 7 068 | 0.0 | D | 8.0 | 6.7 | 4.2 | 3.1 | 13.1 | 45.3 | 36 360 | 181 | 7 931 | 86 331 | 4.9 |
| Rockdale | 1 752 | 0.1 | D | 14.3 | 10.5 | 8.7 | 4.2 | 11.5 | 13.8 | 13 700 | 160 | 1 644 | 33 272 | 32.7 |
| Schley | 58 | 1.8 | D | 33.7 | D | 3.5 | D | D | 27.0 | 835 | 166 | 145 | 2 208 | 37.0 |
| Screven | 183 | 15.1 | 27.8 | 24.3 | D | 6.4 | 2.9 | D | 24.8 | 3 265 | 227 | 747 | 6 739 | -1.7 |
| Seminole | 165 | 33.1 | D | D | D | 5.3 | 2.7 | 13.3 | 14.0 | 2 400 | 273 | 493 | 4 797 | 1.2 |
| Spalding | 1 070 | -0.2 | D | 19.0 | 4.0 | 8.3 | 3.6 | 14.3 | 21.7 | 13 755 | 215 | 2 423 | 26 777 | 16.4 |
| Stephens | 464 | -1.1 | D | 19.4 | 3.4 | 7.7 | 4.6 | D | 21.4 | 6 735 | 259 | 1 048 | 12 662 | 8.7 |
| Stewart | 66 | 3.4 | D | 0.0 | D | 2.6 | D | 16.7 | 33.3 | 1 090 | 184 | 278 | 2 383 | 1.2 |
| Sumter | 532 | 8.2 | D | 11.2 | D | 7.2 | 2.7 | 13.3 | 26.1 | 6 270 | 193 | 1 422 | 13 909 | 1.5 |
| Talbot | 42 | 2.3 | 30.9 | 0.0 | D | 2.6 | D | D | 29.5 | 1 580 | 234 | 342 | 3 399 | 18.4 |
| Taliaferro | 10 | 20.8 | D | D | D | 1.9 | D | 0.0 | 48.4 | 460 | 270 | 112 | 1 015 | -6.5 |
| Tattnall | 304 | 19.4 | D | 1.0 | 1.8 | 5.5 | 2.9 | D | 31.9 | 4 110 | 160 | 896 | 9 966 | 16.2 |
| Taylor | 98 | 11.7 | D | 2.9 | D | 6.7 | 2.1 | 5.9 | 23.7 | 1 940 | 228 | 478 | 4 563 | 14.7 |
| Telfair | 150 | 4.2 | D | D | 1.6 | 5.3 | D | D | 24.9 | 2 650 | 165 | 607 | 7 297 | 43.6 |
| Terrell | 137 | 20.7 | 13.6 | 11.9 | 3.0 | 6.4 | 4.6 | D | 21.7 | 2 220 | 238 | 584 | 4 080 | -8.5 |
| Thomas | 1 115 | 3.3 | D | 15.1 | 3.2 | 6.7 | 5.1 | D | 17.3 | 10 390 | 232 | 2 235 | 20 177 | 10.4 |
| Tift | 930 | 5.3 | 10.1 | 6.6 | 5.3 | 9.0 | 3.6 | 8.0 | 31.2 | 7 840 | 189 | 1 541 | 16 434 | 6.7 |
| Toombs | 536 | 6.0 | 14.0 | 8.7 | D | 9.5 | 2.5 | D | 14.8 | 5 830 | 213 | 1 323 | 12 144 | 6.8 |
| Towns | 146 | 2.3 | D | 1.4 | 3.0 | 8.2 | 7.1 | D | 16.9 | 4 105 | 387 | 217 | 7 731 | 23.1 |
| Treutlen | 59 | 13.6 | D | D | 0.7 | 9.9 | D | D | 28.1 | 1 550 | 227 | 367 | 2 992 | 4.4 |
| Troup | 1 866 | 0.0 | D | 32.5 | 7.3 | 9.2 | 4.4 | 9.5 | 11.5 | 12 815 | 189 | 2 106 | 28 046 | 17.8 |
| Turner | 121 | 23.0 | 10.6 | 9.0 | D | 5.7 | D | 3.8 | 23.4 | 2 060 | 232 | 453 | 3 841 | -1.9 |
| Twiggs | 53 | 0.1 | D | D | D | 3.1 | D | D | 27.4 | 2 395 | 273 | 493 | 4 235 | -1.3 |
| Union | 290 | 0.4 | D | 4.0 | 3.5 | 13.4 | 5.2 | D | 26.0 | 7 220 | 342 | 467 | 14 052 | 40.5 |
| Upson | 332 | -0.5 | 28.0 | 21.2 | D | 8.2 | 4.4 | 19.3 | 20.9 | 6 705 | 249 | 1 179 | 12 161 | 4.7 |
| Walker | 621 | 0.7 | D | 31.0 | D | 7.0 | 4.4 | 6.3 | 25.9 | 15 375 | 223 | 1 871 | 30 100 | 17.7 |
| Walton | 958 | 1.3 | D | 13.2 | 3.8 | 13.9 | 2.6 | 7.5 | 21.6 | 14 425 | 171 | 1 800 | 32 435 | 44.1 |
| Ware | 761 | 1.4 | 12.9 | 8.8 | D | 10.0 | 3.5 | D | 20.9 | 7 700 | 211 | 1 756 | 16 326 | 3.1 |
| Warren | 53 | 4.0 | D | 22.8 | D | 6.4 | D | D | 22.3 | 1 475 | 258 | 319 | 2 985 | 7.9 |
| Washington | 353 | 3.1 | 15.9 | 7.6 | 4.5 | 6.4 | 4.4 | D | 29.7 | 4 455 | 211 | 942 | 9 047 | 8.6 |
| Wayne | 479 | 2.4 | 29.4 | 21.3 | D | 7.5 | 2.7 | D | 32.6 | 6 080 | 200 | 1 105 | 12 199 | 12.7 |
| Webster | 26 | 3.9 | D | D | D | 6.2 | D | 0.0 | 25.7 | 515 | 185 | 87 | 1 523 | 36.7 |
| Wheeler | 65 | 1.8 | 1.7 | 0.0 | D | 2.3 | D | 13.2 | 22.7 | 1 165 | 147 | 252 | 2 625 | 7.3 |
| White | 278 | 0.3 | 27.4 | 13.3 | D | 12.3 | 3.9 | D | 22.2 | 6 435 | 236 | 538 | 16 062 | 69.9 |
| Whitfield | 2 878 | 0.0 | 37.7 | 35.7 | 9.2 | 7.4 | 2.1 | 8.5 | 10.1 | 17 070 | 165 | 2 283 | 39 899 | 29.8 |
| Wilcox | 102 | 35.5 | D | D | D | 3.2 | D | 5.0 | 26.3 | 1 780 | 191 | 391 | 3 510 | 5.7 |
| Wilkes | 138 | 3.7 | 21.1 | 17.5 | D | 8.4 | 4.5 | 6.0 | 29.8 | 2 835 | 278 | 477 | 5 158 | 2.7 |
| Wilkinson | 186 | -0.3 | 63.5 | 12.3 | D | 2.4 | D | 2.4 | 12.8 | 2 485 | 263 | 350 | 4 487 | 0.9 |
| Worth | 222 | 26.4 | 12.6 | 7.6 | 1.9 | 7.1 | 2.7 | D | 20.6 | 4 195 | 191 | 802 | 9 251 | 1.7 |
| HAWAII | 43 250 | 0.7 | 8.8 | 1.8 | 7.3 | 6.0 | 5.4 | 9.4 | 35.6 | 234 314 | 170 | 25 356 | 519 508 | 12.8 |
| Hawaii | 3 527 | 2.1 | D | D | D | 8.9 | 5.0 | 10.6 | 25.6 | 36 710 | 197 | 5 192 | 82 324 | 31.4 |
| Honolulu | 34 196 | 0.2 | 8.5 | 1.9 | 7.9 | 5.2 | 5.6 | 9.5 | 39.2 | 159 550 | 166 | 17 144 | 336 899 | 6.6 |
| Kalawao | (3)3 897 | (3)3.0 | (3)D | (3)1.4 | (3)4.7 | (3)8.7 | (3)4.5 | (3)D | (3)18.8 | 0 | 0 | 0 | 113 | -34.3 |
| Kauai | 1 630 | 1.8 | D | D | D | 8.7 | 5.5 | D | 21.5 | 12 945 | 191 | 986 | 29 793 | 17.6 |
| Maui | (3) | (3) | (3) | (3) | (3) | (3) | (3) | (3) | (3) | 25 110 | 160 | 2 034 | 70 379 | 24.8 |
| IDAHO | 36 421 | 5.9 | 17.0 | 10.1 | 10.2 | 7.6 | 5.8 | 11.5 | 18.3 | 278 563 | 176 | 28 213 | 667 796 | 26.5 |
| Ada | 13 173 | 0.4 | 18.0 | 11.2 | 11.4 | 7.3 | 8.6 | 13.7 | 15.2 | 60 190 | 150 | 5 839 | 159 471 | 34.6 |
| Adams | 51 | -1.1 | D | 10.2 | 7.3 | 7.6 | 4.4 | D | 32.8 | 1 090 | 274 | 47 | 2 636 | 33.0 |
| Bannock | 1 630 | 0.9 | D | 8.9 | D | 7.8 | 6.0 | 15.7 | 25.4 | 12 885 | 154 | 1 752 | 33 191 | 14.1 |
| Bear Lake | 86 | 9.6 | D | 1.9 | D | 9.4 | 2.4 | D | 35.1 | 1 395 | 232 | 98 | 3 914 | 19.8 |
| Benewah | 186 | 4.9 | D | 16.5 | 2.2 | 6.3 | 1.1 | D | 35.6 | 2 570 | 279 | 239 | 4 629 | 9.2 |
| Bingham | 790 | 8.1 | D | 15.3 | D | 4.9 | 3.0 | 9.8 | 22.5 | 7 500 | 163 | 852 | 16 141 | 12.9 |
| Blaine | 722 | 2.1 | 16.5 | 4.1 | 16.4 | 8.5 | 9.1 | 8.0 | 12.1 | 3 335 | 157 | 106 | 15 050 | 23.5 |
| Boise | 63 | 0.8 | D | 1.2 | D | 4.4 | D | 3.1 | 41.5 | 1 625 | 231 | 120 | 5 292 | 21.7 |
| Bonner | 672 | 0.6 | 23.2 | 13.7 | 7.9 | 15.0 | 5.2 | 8.1 | 18.2 | 10 190 | 250 | 830 | 24 669 | 25.6 |
| Bonneville | 2 420 | 2.3 | D | 5.0 | 11.8 | 10.0 | 5.1 | 17.1 | 13.5 | 16 395 | 155 | 1 894 | 39 731 | 30.3 |
| Boundary | 183 | 10.1 | D | 11.1 | 3.6 | 7.3 | 2.0 | 8.3 | 30.6 | 2 750 | 255 | 250 | 5 175 | 26.4 |
| Butte | 841 | 2.1 | 0.5 | 0.2 | D | 0.3 | 0.1 | D | 2.5 | 615 | 218 | 55 | 1 354 | 5.0 |
| Camas | 28 | 38.9 | D | D | D | 1.3 | D | D | 21.3 | 180 | 160 | 0 | 831 | 38.3 |
| Canyon | 2 593 | 7.1 | 22.3 | 15.5 | 5.0 | 9.2 | 3.5 | 11.0 | 16.9 | 30 705 | 160 | 4 260 | 69 409 | 44.7 |

1. Includes mining, construction, and manufacturing.  2. Per 1,000 resident population enumerated in the 2010 census.  3. Kalawao county is included with Maui county.

| STATE County | Housing units, 2007–2011 | | | | | | | | Civilian labor force, 2012 | | Unemployment | | Civilian employment,[6] 2007–2011 | | |
|---|---|---|---|---|---|---|---|---|---|---|---|---|---|---|---|
| | Occupied units | | | | | | | | | | | | | Percent | |
| | | | Owner-occupied | | | Renter-occupied | | | | | | | | | |
| | | | | Median owner cost as a percent of income | | | | | | | | | | | Construction, production, and maintenance occupations |
| | | | | With a mortgage | Without a mortgage[2] | Median rent[3] | Median rent as a percent of income | Sub-standard units[4] (percent) | | Percent change, 2011–2012 | | | | Management, business, science and arts | |
| | Total | Percent | Median value[1] | | | | | | Total | | Total | Rate[5] | Total | | |
| | 89 | 90 | 91 | 92 | 93 | 94 | 95 | 96 | 97 | 98 | 99 | 100 | 101 | 102 | 103 |
| GEORGIA—Cont'd | | | | | | | | | | | | | | | |
| Putnam | 8 782 | 77.1 | 150 200 | 23.5 | 12.2 | 740 | 33.9 | 1.6 | 8 902 | -4.8 | 950 | 10.7 | 9 099 | 26.8 | 30.0 |
| Quitman | 946 | 68.2 | 68 600 | 24.4 | 13.5 | 640 | 28.1 | 2.3 | 874 | -5.9 | 97 | 11.1 | 860 | 13.5 | 38.1 |
| Rabun | 6 908 | 75.4 | 183 600 | 27.6 | 14.4 | 703 | 37.5 | 3.5 | 6 392 | -3.3 | 787 | 12.3 | 6 627 | 28.2 | 25.3 |
| Randolph | 3 018 | 73.8 | 61 100 | 24.9 | 13.1 | 487 | 40.8 | 3.7 | 2 642 | -7.2 | 362 | 13.7 | 2 444 | 29.1 | 31.9 |
| Richmond | 73 214 | 57.0 | 101 700 | 24.1 | 12.5 | 724 | 31.0 | 2.4 | 89 272 | 0.0 | 9 242 | 10.4 | 78 899 | 29.8 | 22.6 |
| Rockdale | 29 002 | 70.4 | 164 700 | 25.3 | 10.1 | 946 | 31.8 | 2.7 | 41 962 | 1.2 | 4 246 | 10.1 | 38 836 | 32.7 | 25.2 |
| Schley | 1 743 | 72.2 | 98 200 | 22.9 | 16.4 | 482 | 28.6 | 9.0 | 1 974 | 1.0 | 235 | 11.9 | 2 017 | 31.1 | 41.4 |
| Screven | 4 682 | 77.0 | 79 700 | 23.9 | 13.9 | 474 | 34.5 | 1.5 | 6 930 | -2.3 | 803 | 11.6 | 5 289 | 24.1 | 37.1 |
| Seminole | 3 059 | 80.0 | 74 800 | 24.5 | 13.0 | 597 | 29.5 | 4.1 | 3 771 | -1.2 | 351 | 9.3 | 3 221 | 22.8 | 32.5 |
| Spalding | 22 920 | 63.8 | 121 000 | 25.5 | 13.7 | 757 | 32.0 | 3.5 | 28 831 | 0.6 | 3 253 | 11.3 | 25 500 | 24.1 | 31.1 |
| Stephens | 9 175 | 75.0 | 111 700 | 25.3 | 14.0 | 636 | 32.3 | 4.1 | 13 190 | -0.4 | 1 211 | 9.2 | 10 484 | 27.2 | 28.2 |
| Stewart | 2 183 | 66.9 | 48 800 | 26.3 | 11.5 | 452 | 30.4 | 3.0 | 2 201 | -2.0 | 250 | 11.4 | 2 103 | 28.8 | 30.9 |
| Sumter | 11 473 | 62.0 | 87 500 | 23.1 | 13.9 | 584 | 28.4 | 3.5 | 13 131 | 0.0 | 1 683 | 12.8 | 13 261 | 29.7 | 29.8 |
| Talbot | 2 701 | 79.0 | 83 300 | 26.8 | 17.1 | 534 | 29.7 | 2.4 | 3 161 | -0.1 | 293 | 9.3 | 2 454 | 23.0 | 39.8 |
| Taliaferro | 638 | 70.8 | 67 400 | 21.0 | 17.6 | 460 | 30.6 | 4.4 | 721 | -1.0 | 78 | 10.8 | 567 | 11.1 | 46.6 |
| Tattnall | 7 844 | 68.7 | 78 900 | 22.5 | 12.2 | 482 | 26.9 | 2.8 | 9 446 | -1.7 | 950 | 10.1 | 8 363 | 28.3 | 36.0 |
| Taylor | 3 460 | 71.4 | 64 100 | 21.7 | 14.9 | 524 | 25.5 | 2.0 | 3 375 | -2.8 | 425 | 12.6 | 2 966 | 25.1 | 35.4 |
| Telfair | 5 780 | 60.7 | 56 700 | 22.4 | 14.6 | 481 | 31.9 | 2.5 | 4 438 | -1.4 | 686 | 15.5 | 4 961 | 26.2 | 32.7 |
| Terrell | 3 427 | 62.0 | 75 400 | 24.0 | 12.8 | 516 | 31.3 | 4.9 | 4 114 | -0.7 | 402 | 9.8 | 3 353 | 25.2 | 33.8 |
| Thomas | 17 356 | 59.8 | 128 100 | 23.3 | 12.8 | 677 | 33.8 | 1.6 | 21 967 | 0.4 | 1 761 | 8.0 | 16 485 | 34.1 | 24.7 |
| Tift | 14 164 | 63.4 | 109 700 | 22.3 | 12.0 | 612 | 28.9 | 4.2 | 19 047 | 1.4 | 1 949 | 10.2 | 16 934 | 28.4 | 29.9 |
| Toombs | 10 133 | 61.5 | 92 200 | 21.0 | 11.0 | 566 | 30.4 | 1.7 | 13 792 | -0.3 | 1 460 | 10.6 | 10 943 | 26.3 | 30.1 |
| Towns | 4 499 | 86.3 | 187 600 | 31.5 | 11.8 | 689 | 27.6 | 1.7 | 5 686 | -1.3 | 472 | 8.3 | 4 045 | 23.3 | 34.0 |
| Treutlen | 2 500 | 61.6 | 66 000 | 18.2 | 9.9 | 479 | 26.5 | 1.0 | 2 852 | -2.4 | 398 | 14.0 | 2 305 | 29.6 | 35.5 |
| Troup | 24 233 | 63.8 | 129 100 | 23.5 | 12.4 | 683 | 33.0 | 3.5 | 34 490 | 2.9 | 3 488 | 10.1 | 28 112 | 27.3 | 29.7 |
| Turner | 3 065 | 65.7 | 84 300 | 20.7 | 18.6 | 521 | 28.4 | 4.7 | 4 388 | -3.5 | 420 | 9.6 | 3 347 | 27.8 | 31.5 |
| Twiggs | 3 088 | 78.3 | 68 900 | 23.8 | 13.8 | 594 | 30.9 | 1.3 | 4 114 | 1.5 | 513 | 12.5 | 2 906 | 29.8 | 30.7 |
| Union | 9 118 | 77.6 | 199 600 | 27.1 | 11.5 | 623 | 29.0 | 1.8 | 11 100 | 2.2 | 819 | 7.4 | 8 056 | 34.5 | 21.6 |
| Upson | 10 416 | 68.5 | 92 500 | 24.1 | 12.5 | 590 | 33.2 | 2.8 | 11 613 | -0.8 | 1 292 | 11.1 | 10 546 | 20.9 | 35.9 |
| Walker | 26 256 | 73.8 | 109 300 | 22.9 | 11.9 | 621 | 32.5 | 2.8 | 33 336 | 0.5 | 2 551 | 7.7 | 28 255 | 26.3 | 34.0 |
| Walton | 29 488 | 76.4 | 163 100 | 25.0 | 11.9 | 806 | 34.0 | 2.1 | 41 032 | 0.5 | 3 505 | 8.5 | 38 074 | 29.2 | 26.3 |
| Ware | 13 091 | 66.5 | 83 900 | 20.8 | 12.3 | 591 | 30.8 | 2.9 | 14 769 | 1.3 | 1 640 | 11.1 | 13 564 | 28.7 | 27.2 |
| Warren | 2 269 | 70.8 | 60 100 | 24.2 | 13.7 | 502 | 28.6 | 1.5 | 2 538 | -0.5 | 400 | 15.8 | 2 131 | 14.2 | 48.7 |
| Washington | 7 082 | 72.0 | 81 800 | 25.2 | 10.9 | 562 | 34.7 | 2.1 | 7 749 | -1.0 | 876 | 11.3 | 7 207 | 22.9 | 30.7 |
| Wayne | 10 214 | 70.8 | 86 400 | 20.3 | 10.6 | 553 | 27.3 | 2.7 | 12 038 | -0.3 | 1 388 | 11.5 | 11 660 | 24.6 | 36.2 |
| Webster | 1 270 | 80.8 | 59 800 | 24.3 | 11.8 | 375 | 17.9 | 2.4 | 1 212 | -3.5 | 100 | 8.3 | 1 263 | 36.3 | 34.4 |
| Wheeler | 1 687 | 72.0 | 62 300 | 19.8 | 11.9 | 488 | 23.4 | 2.3 | 2 942 | -1.1 | 300 | 10.2 | 1 641 | 25.4 | 42.0 |
| White | 12 459 | 75.9 | 176 000 | 27.0 | 11.4 | 698 | 33.6 | 1.2 | 12 878 | 2.2 | 1 144 | 8.9 | 12 075 | 30.6 | 28.5 |
| Whitfield | 34 514 | 67.7 | 129 100 | 23.7 | 9.9 | 664 | 29.0 | 6.2 | 42 885 | -3.3 | 4 827 | 11.3 | 44 408 | 22.4 | 40.3 |
| Wilcox | 2 661 | 78.2 | 65 800 | 24.0 | 12.9 | 469 | 34.1 | 3.8 | 3 058 | -1.7 | 375 | 12.3 | 2 485 | 29.7 | 30.7 |
| Wilkes | 4 138 | 70.3 | 96 500 | 29.6 | 17.8 | 569 | 35.3 | 2.3 | 4 341 | -2.3 | 472 | 10.9 | 3 675 | 30.7 | 36.3 |
| Wilkinson | 3 356 | 82.6 | 71 500 | 21.6 | 12.0 | 516 | 24.8 | 3.5 | 4 386 | -2.0 | 422 | 9.6 | 3 460 | 25.6 | 35.5 |
| Worth | 8 039 | 74.0 | 83 500 | 22.3 | 12.2 | 509 | 31.6 | 1.6 | 10 682 | -0.4 | 941 | 8.8 | 8 480 | 23.9 | 33.3 |
| HAWAII | 445 513 | 58.7 | 529 500 | 29.5 | 9.9 | 1 313 | 33.1 | 9.6 | 651 586 | -0.9 | 37 918 | 5.8 | 635 956 | 33.6 | 18.5 |
| Hawaii | 64 270 | 65.9 | 342 100 | 30.3 | 9.9 | 1 043 | 32.5 | 10.1 | 83 381 | -3.5 | 6 950 | 8.3 | 83 640 | 30.0 | 20.9 |
| Honolulu | 307 248 | 56.9 | 560 300 | 28.9 | 9.9 | 1 381 | 33.5 | 9.1 | 457 990 | -0.4 | 23 651 | 5.2 | 441 581 | 35.3 | 17.8 |
| Kalawao | 46 | 0.0 | 0 | 0.0 | 0.0 | 313 | NA | 0.0 | NA | NA | NA | NA | 43 | 62.8 | 18.6 |
| Kauai | 21 884 | 63.6 | 561 600 | 31.7 | 10.5 | 1 228 | 29.2 | 10.1 | 32 694 | -2.1 | 2 410 | 7.4 | 32 372 | 29.9 | 19.8 |
| Maui | 52 065 | 58.3 | 594 400 | 32.0 | 9.9 | 1 299 | 32.5 | 11.8 | 77 520 | -1.0 | 4 907 | 6.3 | 78 320 | 29.5 | 19.1 |
| IDAHO | 575 497 | 70.6 | 171 300 | 24.5 | 10.5 | 709 | 29.1 | 3.2 | 773 300 | 0.9 | 54 621 | 7.1 | 699 895 | 33.2 | 25.2 |
| Ada | 147 753 | 69.0 | 206 200 | 24.1 | 9.9 | 805 | 29.4 | 2.0 | 204 182 | 2.2 | 12 803 | 6.3 | 188 248 | 41.4 | 16.6 |
| Adams | 1 783 | 80.6 | 174 300 | 25.0 | 10.9 | 523 | 23.9 | 3.8 | 1 804 | -0.7 | 251 | 13.9 | 1 759 | 24.2 | 34.3 |
| Bannock | 30 045 | 70.9 | 140 100 | 23.2 | 10.5 | 593 | 29.5 | 2.3 | 40 171 | -0.3 | 2 812 | 7.0 | 37 917 | 32.8 | 23.2 |
| Bear Lake | 2 427 | 82.7 | 135 600 | 18.3 | 11.7 | 568 | 23.5 | 2.2 | 3 273 | -1.0 | 153 | 4.7 | 2 418 | 26.5 | 35.2 |
| Benewah | 3 867 | 74.0 | 119 400 | 23.9 | 12.5 | 554 | 27.0 | 7.3 | 4 115 | -1.4 | 492 | 12.0 | 3 815 | 28.6 | 36.5 |
| Bingham | 14 432 | 78.2 | 133 300 | 22.2 | 9.9 | 556 | 25.9 | 4.5 | 23 388 | 0.6 | 1 433 | 6.1 | 19 034 | 27.4 | 31.3 |
| Blaine | 9 028 | 68.7 | 415 500 | 30.4 | 13.3 | 931 | 22.4 | 3.8 | 12 328 | -1.4 | 820 | 6.7 | 11 775 | 34.6 | 23.9 |
| Boise | 2 990 | 76.5 | 195 800 | 25.6 | 9.9 | 628 | 26.0 | 5.1 | 3 262 | 2.9 | 279 | 8.6 | 2 947 | 39.8 | 27.8 |
| Bonner | 18 399 | 73.2 | 236 200 | 28.4 | 10.5 | 743 | 30.0 | 4.4 | 19 384 | -2.0 | 1 913 | 9.9 | 18 013 | 30.1 | 28.5 |
| Bonneville | 35 849 | 73.6 | 157 400 | 22.7 | 9.9 | 700 | 30.3 | 2.5 | 51 678 | 1.1 | 3 113 | 6.0 | 47 107 | 35.7 | 22.1 |
| Boundary | 4 200 | 80.9 | 177 500 | 27.7 | 11.6 | 612 | 28.3 | 3.4 | 4 931 | 0.8 | 493 | 10.0 | 4 023 | 27.0 | 29.2 |
| Butte | 1 080 | 82.5 | 111 500 | 26.3 | 12.6 | 457 | 22.7 | 2.8 | 1 405 | -5.1 | 101 | 7.2 | 1 196 | 33.8 | 27.9 |
| Camas | 454 | 70.9 | 184 300 | 27.9 | 9.9 | 750 | 29.0 | 2.9 | 591 | -1.3 | 53 | 9.0 | 614 | 29.6 | 40.6 |
| Canyon | 62 824 | 71.2 | 145 400 | 27.0 | 11.1 | 720 | 30.0 | 5.0 | 86 960 | 1.3 | 7 191 | 8.3 | 76 454 | 26.9 | 30.1 |

1. Specified owner-occupied units, lacking complete plumbing facilities.    2. A value of 9.9 represents 9.9 percent or less.    3. Specified renter-occupied units. A value of 10.0 represents 10 percent or less.    4. Overcrowded or lacking complete plumbing facilities.    5. Percent of civilian labor force.    6. Persons 16 years old and over.

# Table B. States and Counties — Nonfarm Employment and Agriculture

| | Private nonfarm establishments, employment and payroll, 2011 | | | | | | | | | Agriculture, 2007 | | | |
| | Employment | | | | | | Annual payroll | | Farms | | | |
| | | | | | | | | | | | Percent with: | | |
| STATE County | Number of establishments | Total | Health care and social assistance | Manufacturing | Retail trade | Finance and insurance | Professional, scientific, and technical services | Total (mil dol) | Average per employee (dollars) | Number | Fewer than 50 acres | 500 acres or more | Farm operators whose principal occupation is farming (percent) |
|---|---|---|---|---|---|---|---|---|---|---|---|---|---|
| | 104 | 105 | 106 | 107 | 108 | 109 | 110 | 111 | 112 | 113 | 114 | 115 | 116 |
| GEORGIA—Cont'd | | | | | | | | | | | | | |
| Putnam | 373 | 4 517 | 410 | 638 | 1 138 | D | 71 | 138 | 30 456 | 215 | 35.8 | 8.4 | 34.4 |
| Quitman | 34 | 209 | D | D | D | D | NA | 6 | 28 502 | 25 | 24.0 | 28.0 | 40.0 |
| Rabun | 449 | 3 784 | 537 | 353 | 994 | 187 | 103 | 107 | 28 209 | 121 | 66.9 | 0.8 | 41.3 |
| Randolph | 130 | 1 289 | D | D | 206 | D | 23 | 38 | 29 597 | 177 | 13.0 | 21.5 | 37.9 |
| Richmond | 4 307 | 82 835 | 22 132 | 7 617 | 9 934 | 2 599 | 3 816 | 3 084 | 37 230 | 154 | 50.0 | 1.9 | 33.1 |
| Rockdale | 1 962 | 27 104 | 3 755 | 3 668 | 4 453 | 683 | 886 | 991 | 36 571 | 108 | 79.6 | 1.9 | 50.0 |
| Schley | 63 | 741 | D | D | 90 | D | D | 27 | 36 729 | 122 | 22.1 | 12.3 | 32.8 |
| Screven | 221 | 2 766 | 473 | 1 074 | 410 | 100 | 35 | 75 | 26 935 | 419 | 24.1 | 21.0 | 39.6 |
| Seminole | 183 | 1 489 | 461 | D | 362 | 95 | 28 | 42 | 28 019 | 182 | 25.3 | 24.2 | 48.4 |
| Spalding | 1 134 | 16 945 | 4 139 | 3 037 | 2 690 | 486 | 384 | 504 | 29 759 | 347 | 64.8 | 2.0 | 35.7 |
| Stephens | 546 | 7 569 | 1 560 | 1 432 | 1 113 | 219 | 145 | 257 | 33 950 | 199 | 51.8 | 1.5 | 43.7 |
| Stewart | 70 | D | 174 | NA | D | 31 | D | 21 | D | 94 | 16.0 | 31.9 | 33.0 |
| Sumter | 656 | 9 543 | 2 586 | 1 255 | 1 420 | 249 | 209 | 276 | 28 973 | 429 | 24.9 | 18.4 | 44.1 |
| Talbot | 57 | 521 | D | D | D | D | D | 18 | 35 253 | 149 | 29.5 | 14.1 | 32.2 |
| Taliaferro | 21 | 71 | D | D | D | D | NA | 2 | 22 690 | 71 | 23.9 | 9.9 | 40.8 |
| Tattnall | 294 | 2 978 | D | D | 494 | 132 | 75 | 91 | 30 397 | 589 | 38.0 | 9.8 | 46.9 |
| Taylor | 118 | 949 | 247 | D | 170 | 47 | D | 29 | 31 044 | 262 | 21.4 | 19.8 | 45.0 |
| Telfair | 199 | 3 017 | 433 | D | 348 | 95 | 44 | 66 | 21 996 | 301 | 21.6 | 11.6 | 36.5 |
| Terrell | 176 | 1 532 | 175 | D | 283 | D | 24 | 41 | 26 853 | 274 | 20.1 | 28.5 | 44.9 |
| Thomas | 1 068 | 15 549 | D | 2 711 | 2 296 | 641 | 424 | 556 | 35 736 | 485 | 33.4 | 19.8 | 42.1 |
| Tift | 1 041 | 15 178 | 3 280 | 1 340 | 2 551 | 421 | 551 | 492 | 32 401 | 404 | 31.4 | 15.6 | 52.5 |
| Toombs | 682 | 8 644 | 1 826 | 1 352 | 1 588 | 289 | 205 | 253 | 29 266 | 341 | 31.1 | 8.5 | 40.2 |
| Towns | 293 | 2 837 | 461 | 41 | 421 | D | 83 | 67 | 23 776 | 116 | 62.1 | 0.0 | 38.8 |
| Treutlen | 85 | 699 | 151 | D | 161 | 25 | D | 14 | 20 464 | 151 | 39.1 | 7.9 | 29.8 |
| Troup | 1 393 | 30 771 | 3 310 | 9 203 | 3 165 | 1 056 | 543 | 1 181 | 38 369 | 241 | 46.1 | 5.8 | 39.8 |
| Turner | 141 | 1 253 | 158 | 236 | 158 | 66 | 38 | 31 | 25 125 | 278 | 32.7 | 24.5 | 42.4 |
| Twiggs | 68 | 731 | D | NA | 72 | D | D | 30 | 41 107 | 121 | 34.7 | 14.0 | 42.1 |
| Union | 516 | 5 023 | 996 | 253 | 1 030 | D | 164 | 138 | 27 500 | 281 | 61.6 | 2.1 | 30.2 |
| Upson | 454 | 5 973 | 1 414 | 1 242 | 986 | 262 | 112 | 179 | 30 020 | 348 | 44.5 | 3.7 | 29.3 |
| Walker | 700 | 10 572 | 1 111 | D | 1 443 | 331 | 199 | 300 | 28 352 | 538 | 43.7 | 4.8 | 42.9 |
| Walton | 1 459 | 15 057 | 1 790 | 1 777 | 2 465 | 436 | 517 | 472 | 31 366 | 490 | 52.2 | 3.7 | 39.6 |
| Ware | 876 | 11 299 | 2 832 | 1 239 | 2 485 | 386 | 240 | 339 | 30 002 | 280 | 43.6 | 7.5 | 39.6 |
| Warren | 67 | 622 | 141 | D | 101 | D | D | 18 | 28 994 | 188 | 31.9 | 8.0 | 34.0 |
| Washington | 346 | 5 532 | 998 | 401 | 824 | D | D | 196 | 35 481 | 425 | 27.1 | 13.9 | 30.8 |
| Wayne | 548 | 5 850 | D | D | 1 304 | 205 | D | 197 | 33 716 | 313 | 43.8 | 7.3 | 44.7 |
| Webster | 25 | D | D | D | D | D | NA | D | D | 114 | 11.4 | 16.7 | 36.8 |
| Wheeler | 74 | 1 055 | D | NA | 69 | D | D | 32 | 30 179 | 143 | 21.0 | 17.5 | 32.9 |
| White | 573 | 4 770 | 468 | 580 | 1 134 | 144 | 82 | 128 | 26 821 | 291 | 59.5 | 1.0 | 48.5 |
| Whitfield | 2 247 | 47 083 | 4 259 | 16 663 | 4 892 | 810 | 1 142 | 1 633 | 34 692 | 480 | 45.6 | 0.8 | 34.2 |
| Wilcox | 86 | 521 | 195 | D | 97 | 53 | D | 13 | 24 202 | 349 | 24.6 | 18.9 | 44.1 |
| Wilkes | 208 | 2 679 | 580 | D | 373 | 96 | D | 72 | 26 938 | 356 | 25.0 | 10.1 | 43.8 |
| Wilkinson | 146 | 1 999 | 162 | D | 151 | 41 | D | 86 | 43 170 | 158 | 29.7 | 9.5 | 43.0 |
| Worth | 283 | 2 411 | 431 | 273 | 482 | 103 | D | 66 | 27 377 | 496 | 30.0 | 23.4 | 46.2 |
| HAWAII | 31 472 | 485 548 | 65 145 | 12 118 | 66 913 | 18 783 | 25 450 | 18 362 | 37 817 | 7 521 | 90.2 | 2.1 | 51.3 |
| Hawaii | 3 966 | 49 068 | 7 957 | 1 263 | 9 175 | 1 225 | 1 746 | 1 586 | 32 317 | 4 650 | 89.9 | 1.9 | 48.6 |
| Honolulu | 21 139 | 337 092 | 48 373 | 9 595 | 44 633 | 16 351 | 20 755 | 13 376 | 39 681 | 967 | 90.6 | 1.6 | 71.5 |
| Kalawao | NA | NA | NA | NA | NA | NA | NA | NA | NA | NA | NA | NA | NA |
| Kauai | 1 905 | 23 784 | 2 693 | 232 | 4 016 | 363 | 635 | 789 | 33 184 | 748 | 90.2 | 3.3 | 52.7 |
| Maui | 4 314 | 60 913 | 6 111 | 1 028 | 9 089 | 745 | 1 416 | 2 138 | 35 095 | 1 156 | 91.3 | 2.8 | 44.6 |
| IDAHO | 42 399 | 482 722 | 80 010 | 53 345 | 72 264 | 20 601 | 30 997 | 16 889 | 34 988 | 25 349 | 48.9 | 16.9 | 45.7 |
| Ada | 11 898 | 164 701 | 27 864 | 15 667 | 20 170 | 9 297 | 10 256 | 6 806 | 41 324 | 1 323 | 81.9 | 3.4 | 31.7 |
| Adams | 125 | 435 | D | D | 73 | D | D | 11 | 24 513 | 258 | 40.7 | 22.5 | 51.2 |
| Bannock | 1 945 | 23 563 | 4 697 | 2 124 | 4 526 | 1 236 | 1 391 | 724 | 30 723 | 937 | 52.6 | 14.7 | 35.6 |
| Bear Lake | 123 | 988 | D | D | 249 | D | D | 24 | 24 158 | 445 | 27.9 | 21.8 | 38.4 |
| Benewah | 232 | 2 182 | 357 | 582 | 309 | 54 | 22 | 73 | 33 531 | 292 | 34.2 | 15.1 | 39.4 |
| Bingham | 796 | 9 602 | D | 2 294 | 1 150 | 301 | 174 | 307 | 31 995 | 1 328 | 56.3 | 18.1 | 47.6 |
| Blaine | 1 344 | 9 932 | 660 | 289 | 1 277 | 259 | 723 | 340 | 34 257 | 193 | 42.0 | 32.6 | 45.1 |
| Boise | 141 | 490 | D | 15 | 88 | D | D | 10 | 21 078 | 105 | 49.5 | 12.4 | 40.0 |
| Bonner | 1 429 | 10 968 | 1 526 | 1 713 | 1 883 | 330 | 461 | 349 | 31 799 | 687 | 52.7 | 4.7 | 47.6 |
| Bonneville | 3 189 | 42 828 | 6 958 | 2 264 | 6 840 | 1 213 | D | 1 671 | 39 011 | 926 | 51.6 | 18.4 | 37.4 |
| Boundary | 350 | 2 234 | 554 | 281 | 352 | D | 81 | 59 | 26 583 | 373 | 47.2 | 10.2 | 47.2 |
| Butte | 66 | 638 | D | D | 71 | 23 | D | 17 | 26 575 | 222 | 24.8 | 26.6 | 51.8 |
| Camas | 25 | 171 | D | D | D | D | NA | 4 | 21 053 | 104 | 26.9 | 34.6 | 44.2 |
| Canyon | 3 437 | 41 541 | 6 202 | 7 976 | 6 799 | 1 036 | 1 140 | 1 198 | 28 841 | 2 368 | 73.8 | 4.7 | 40.5 |

| STATE County | Acreage (1,000) | Percent change, 2002–2007 | Average size of farm | Total irrigated (1,000) | Total cropland (1,000) | Average per farm | Average per acre | Value of machinery and equipment, average per farm (dollars) | Total (mil dol) | Average per farm (dollars) | Crops | Live-stock and poultry products | $10,000 or more | $100,000 or more | Total ($1,000) | Percent of farms |
|---|---|---|---|---|---|---|---|---|---|---|---|---|---|---|---|---|
| | 117 | 118 | 119 | 120 | 121 | 122 | 123 | 124 | 125 | 126 | 127 | 128 | 129 | 130 | 131 | 132 |
| GEORGIA—Cont'd | | | | | | | | | | | | | | | | |
| Putnam | 38 | -7.3 | 176 | 0.5 | 12.4 | 728 384 | 4 149 | 82 524 | 40.7 | 189 287 | 2.1 | 97.9 | 30.7 | 13.0 | 137 | 17.2 |
| Quitman | 11 | -21.4 | 455 | D | 5.5 | 1 164 034 | 2 556 | 55 540 | D | D | D | 0.0 | 20.0 | 8.0 | 248 | 44.0 |
| Rabun | 8 | -20.0 | 66 | 0.6 | 2.4 | 355 197 | 5 420 | 47 368 | 9.1 | 75 302 | 38.4 | 61.6 | 28.9 | 9.1 | 75 | 5.0 |
| Randolph | 90 | 13.9 | 509 | 15.8 | 55.5 | 1 091 378 | 2 146 | 105 986 | 19.9 | 112 191 | 88.9 | 11.1 | 33.3 | 14.7 | 2 525 | 74.6 |
| Richmond | 13 | 8.3 | 81 | 0.0 | 6.3 | 331 942 | 4 083 | 37 369 | 1.3 | 8 343 | 34.6 | 65.4 | 21.4 | 0.0 | 22 | 8.4 |
| Rockdale | 6 | -33.3 | 59 | 0.0 | 1.7 | 321 986 | 5 494 | 49 400 | D | 0.0 | D | D | 17.6 | 0.0 | D | 1.9 |
| Schley | 36 | 2.9 | 297 | 1.3 | 9.6 | 896 270 | 3 015 | 51 961 | 33.2 | 272 317 | 4.5 | 95.5 | 27.0 | 10.7 | 552 | 41.0 |
| Screven | 179 | -2.7 | 426 | 13.6 | 92.0 | 1 004 920 | 2 356 | 88 440 | 29.2 | 69 697 | 85.7 | 14.3 | 33.2 | 13.1 | 2 700 | 65.9 |
| Seminole | 104 | 11.8 | 569 | 45.8 | 71.0 | 1 295 067 | 2 276 | 219 806 | 48.1 | 264 180 | 88.9 | 11.1 | 54.9 | 32.4 | 4 311 | 68.1 |
| Spalding | 26 | 0.0 | 76 | 0.2 | 7.1 | 411 223 | 5 398 | 48 106 | 5.1 | 14 558 | 6.9 | 93.1 | 12.7 | 1.2 | 98 | 12.7 |
| Stephens | 15 | -25.0 | 77 | 0.0 | 4.2 | 394 935 | 5 109 | 47 188 | 43.4 | 218 314 | 0.5 | 99.5 | 33.7 | 15.6 | 50 | 10.6 |
| Stewart | 46 | 35.3 | 490 | 0.4 | 11.7 | 1 203 874 | 2 457 | 78 741 | 5.3 | 56 337 | 48.0 | 52.0 | 35.1 | 11.7 | 676 | 55.3 |
| Sumter | 153 | -8.4 | 357 | 31.9 | 84.7 | 834 664 | 2 341 | 98 626 | 78.3 | 182 423 | 57.7 | 42.3 | 37.5 | 17.2 | 4 040 | 55.9 |
| Talbot | 42 | -6.7 | 280 | 0.1 | 6.7 | 590 495 | 2 112 | 54 855 | 1.0 | 6 555 | 32.7 | 67.3 | 18.8 | 0.7 | 83 | 10.1 |
| Taliaferro | 14 | -26.3 | 199 | D | 5.3 | 519 870 | 2 619 | 56 221 | 6.0 | 84 406 | 2.8 | 97.2 | 23.9 | 8.5 | 17 | 11.3 |
| Tattnall | 136 | -4.9 | 230 | 12.5 | 73.5 | 641 217 | 2 786 | 91 471 | 210.9 | 357 986 | 33.5 | 66.5 | 46.7 | 24.3 | 1 642 | 27.2 |
| Taylor | 87 | 16.0 | 331 | 4.4 | 32.6 | 709 832 | 2 146 | 60 830 | 24.0 | 91 459 | 49.0 | 51.0 | 31.7 | 9.2 | 1 242 | 48.1 |
| Telfair | 62 | -15.1 | 205 | 7.3 | 24.2 | 463 548 | 2 260 | 59 316 | 7.6 | 25 325 | 79.8 | 20.2 | 32.2 | 6.6 | 789 | 57.1 |
| Terrell | 137 | 11.4 | 498 | 29.1 | 80.1 | 1 184 295 | 2 377 | 138 498 | 31.0 | 113 248 | 97.2 | 2.8 | 36.1 | 24.8 | 5 735 | 70.8 |
| Thomas | 204 | 3.0 | 421 | 12.5 | 94.0 | 1 147 428 | 2 725 | 95 260 | 59.6 | 122 977 | 51.3 | 48.7 | 45.8 | 20.8 | 5 539 | 48.7 |
| Tift | 133 | 35.7 | 329 | 28.8 | 77.3 | 848 743 | 2 582 | 105 870 | 68.1 | 168 561 | 94.4 | 5.6 | 51.2 | 25.7 | 5 800 | 57.7 |
| Toombs | 90 | -3.2 | 264 | 10.7 | 30.6 | 564 309 | 2 141 | 69 962 | 46.8 | 137 239 | 79.8 | 20.2 | 29.9 | 13.2 | 1 278 | 43.1 |
| Towns | 7 | -36.4 | 65 | D | 2.3 | 408 219 | 6 319 | 55 925 | 5.1 | 44 192 | 17.5 | 82.5 | 32.8 | 5.2 | 80 | 11.2 |
| Treutlen | 30 | -14.3 | 199 | 5.0 | 10.5 | 442 565 | 2 220 | 73 182 | D | D | D | 0.0 | 13.2 | 3.3 | 561 | 58.3 |
| Troup | 38 | -37.7 | 157 | D | 7.6 | 600 868 | 3 824 | 49 654 | 3.5 | 14 669 | 20.6 | 79.4 | 23.2 | 2.5 | 106 | 6.2 |
| Turner | 116 | 18.4 | 417 | 22.2 | 65.8 | 1 033 969 | 2 479 | 132 939 | 46.0 | 165 347 | 74.5 | 25.5 | 51.1 | 27.7 | 5 335 | 65.1 |
| Twiggs | 45 | 12.5 | 371 | 2.1 | 13.5 | 950 523 | 2 559 | 86 902 | 3.3 | 27 297 | 79.5 | 20.5 | 18.2 | 5.8 | 561 | 28.9 |
| Union | 21 | -16.0 | 75 | 0.0 | 6.1 | 443 060 | 5 941 | 60 385 | 18.7 | 66 402 | D | D | 25.6 | 4.6 | 76 | 11.0 |
| Upson | 48 | 2.1 | 137 | 0.6 | 12.8 | 434 761 | 3 173 | 43 069 | 28.1 | 80 877 | 4.7 | 95.3 | 17.8 | 5.5 | 137 | 10.1 |
| Walker | 71 | -13.4 | 132 | 0.3 | 22.9 | 568 791 | 4 301 | 67 106 | 90.3 | 167 856 | 1.5 | 98.5 | 30.5 | 9.9 | 209 | 15.4 |
| Walton | 54 | -18.2 | 110 | 0.8 | 19.3 | 639 545 | 5 836 | 42 917 | 37.3 | 76 040 | 28.8 | 71.2 | 25.3 | 8.2 | 241 | 25.9 |
| Ware | 50 | -23.1 | 180 | 2.5 | 18.9 | 548 590 | 3 055 | 47 402 | 21.4 | 76 561 | 44.1 | 55.9 | 31.4 | 7.1 | 496 | 26.8 |
| Warren | 37 | -22.9 | 198 | D | 10.7 | 494 741 | 2 501 | 47 957 | 4.9 | 26 255 | 12.3 | 87.7 | 20.7 | 4.3 | 253 | 25.0 |
| Washington | 110 | -11.3 | 259 | 2.3 | 39.8 | 574 658 | 2 217 | 48 376 | 11.7 | 27 528 | 63.8 | 36.2 | 27.8 | 5.6 | 1 639 | 48.5 |
| Wayne | 57 | -10.9 | 181 | 4.6 | 24.1 | 525 441 | 2 896 | 80 308 | 28.7 | 91 710 | 55.6 | 44.4 | 29.4 | 9.3 | 896 | 36.4 |
| Webster | 55 | -16.7 | 480 | 3.3 | 26.4 | 1 086 376 | 2 266 | 75 613 | 8.9 | 78 166 | 56.9 | 43.1 | 28.1 | 10.5 | 1 156 | 77.2 |
| Wheeler | 57 | -5.0 | 400 | 4.1 | 17.5 | 855 491 | 2 140 | 52 972 | 5.9 | 41 120 | 90.2 | 9.8 | 34.3 | 9.8 | 604 | 62.9 |
| White | 21 | -30.0 | 72 | 0.1 | 7.0 | 519 479 | 7 200 | 57 419 | 70.2 | 241 148 | 1.1 | 98.9 | 41.2 | 26.8 | 29 | 7.9 |
| Whitfield | 43 | 0.0 | 89 | 0.1 | 13.8 | 416 808 | 4 680 | 56 827 | 108.4 | 225 793 | 0.6 | 99.4 | 30.6 | 12.3 | 133 | 6.0 |
| Wilcox | 101 | -1.0 | 289 | 21.4 | 58.1 | 645 775 | 2 235 | 107 317 | 68.0 | 194 772 | 50.3 | 49.7 | 42.4 | 24.1 | 4 088 | 69.9 |
| Wilkes | 90 | -9.1 | 252 | 0.4 | 19.3 | 662 337 | 2 626 | 56 773 | 32.5 | 91 363 | 5.1 | 94.9 | 30.3 | 6.7 | 336 | 26.7 |
| Wilkinson | 30 | -3.2 | 189 | 0.0 | 9.5 | 422 091 | 2 230 | 56 663 | 3.4 | 21 533 | 21.4 | 78.6 | 17.1 | 1.3 | 142 | 20.3 |
| Worth | 193 | 7.8 | 388 | 30.2 | 111.1 | 940 534 | 2 423 | 131 943 | 72.0 | 145 192 | 74.1 | 25.9 | 42.3 | 22.2 | 10 212 | 65.1 |
| HAWAII | 1 121 | -13.8 | 149 | 58.6 | 177.6 | 1 146 213 | 7 688 | 40 666 | 513.6 | 68 292 | 83.7 | 16.3 | 34.3 | 7.0 | 2 378 | 2.9 |
| Hawaii | 684 | -16.7 | 147 | 8.1 | 81.8 | 1 022 976 | 6 956 | 31 981 | 202.6 | 43 564 | 74.2 | 25.8 | 32.5 | 5.6 | 1 232 | 2.9 |
| Honolulu | 60 | -15.5 | 62 | 8.4 | 18.9 | 1 106 333 | 17 710 | 61 269 | 126.6 | 130 897 | 84.4 | 15.6 | 48.2 | 15.1 | 294 | 1.8 |
| Kalawao | NA | NA | NA | NA | NA | NA | NA | NA | NA | NA | NA | NA | NA | NA | NA | NA |
| Kauai | 152 | 0.0 | 203 | 14.1 | 22.3 | 1 259 559 | 6 217 | 49 828 | 45.2 | 60 362 | 90.3 | 9.7 | 31.1 | 4.9 | 164 | 2.9 |
| Maui | 226 | -12.1 | 195 | 28.0 | 54.6 | 1 601 950 | 8 210 | 52 480 | 139.3 | 120 524 | 94.8 | 5.2 | 32.2 | 7.4 | 688 | 3.8 |
| IDAHO | 11 497 | -2.3 | 454 | 3 299.9 | 5 918.9 | 894 497 | 1 972 | 114 383 | 5 688.8 | 224 418 | 40.9 | 59.1 | 39.9 | 17.0 | 99 494 | 36.3 |
| Ada | 191 | -14.3 | 145 | 57.0 | 66.1 | 607 769 | 4 199 | 62 480 | 153.0 | 115 670 | 29.4 | 70.6 | 23.3 | 6.6 | 667 | 11.3 |
| Adams | 149 | -24.0 | 578 | 24.9 | 27.8 | 777 096 | 1 346 | 48 639 | 9.1 | 35 379 | 10.8 | 89.2 | 31.0 | 9.3 | 268 | 15.9 |
| Bannock | 322 | -9.8 | 344 | 39.3 | 185.0 | 516 233 | 1 503 | 58 955 | 34.3 | 36 555 | 60.0 | 40.0 | 22.5 | 6.2 | 3 878 | 31.6 |
| Bear Lake | 233 | 9.9 | 524 | 38.7 | 101.5 | 682 885 | 1 304 | 70 615 | 17.3 | 38 886 | 16.0 | 84.0 | 40.9 | 9.7 | 1 604 | 49.4 |
| Benewah | 154 | 11.6 | 526 | 0.3 | 83.4 | 854 158 | 1 624 | 71 787 | 20.4 | 70 023 | 95.9 | 4.0 | 20.5 | 8.9 | 1 415 | 41.4 |
| Bingham | 913 | 11.2 | 687 | 316.9 | 362.1 | 1 194 297 | 1 738 | 160 921 | 355.1 | 267 420 | 73.5 | 26.5 | 43.4 | 20.6 | 7 108 | 29.4 |
| Blaine | 192 | -15.0 | 995 | 44.0 | 54.2 | 1 602 365 | 1 611 | 154 365 | 26.4 | 136 979 | 52.4 | 47.6 | 46.6 | 24.4 | 478 | 37.3 |
| Boise | 44 | -12.0 | 416 | 2.0 | 4.1 | 623 161 | 1 498 | 34 895 | 3.5 | 33 183 | 75.3 | 24.7 | 21.0 | 5.7 | 63 | 6.7 |
| Bonner | 94 | 3.3 | 137 | 2.1 | 28.8 | 583 313 | 4 246 | 48 929 | 10.7 | 15 559 | 62.4 | 37.6 | 19.7 | 2.5 | 70 | 3.8 |
| Bonneville | 453 | -5.2 | 489 | 156.0 | 298.6 | 991 113 | 2 026 | 109 781 | 189.3 | 204 402 | 58.6 | 41.4 | 36.9 | 13.2 | 5 520 | 47.0 |
| Boundary | 74 | -3.9 | 197 | 2.8 | 43.2 | 751 326 | 3 813 | 74 008 | 30.2 | 81 033 | 91.5 | 8.5 | 38.3 | 12.6 | 942 | 17.7 |
| Butte | 121 | 0.0 | 546 | 54.5 | 61.9 | 817 106 | 1 497 | 102 308 | 25.0 | 112 507 | 64.6 | 35.4 | 57.7 | 22.1 | 1 460 | 57.2 |
| Camas | 138 | 3.0 | 1 331 | 16.5 | 81.4 | 1 630 469 | 1 225 | 145 206 | 10.1 | 97 488 | 82.3 | 17.7 | 42.3 | 15.4 | 413 | 58.7 |
| Canyon | 260 | -4.4 | 110 | 197.3 | 191.7 | 672 852 | 6 122 | 82 719 | 420.9 | 177 757 | 41.4 | 58.6 | 35.3 | 12.1 | 1 668 | 19.6 |

# Table B. States and Counties — Water Use, Wholesale Trade, Retail Trade, and Real Estate

| STATE County | Water use, 2005 | | Wholesale trade,[1] 2007 | | | | Retail trade,[2] 2007 | | | | Real estate and rental and leasing,[2] 2007 | | | |
|---|---|---|---|---|---|---|---|---|---|---|---|---|---|---|
| | Total water withdrawn (mil gal/day) | Gallons withdrawn per person | Number of establish-ments | Number of employees | Sales (mil dol) | Annual payroll (mil dol) | Number of establish-ments | Number of employees | Sales (mil dol) | Annual payroll (mil dol) | Number of establish-ments | Number of employees | Receipts (mil dol) | Annual payroll (mil dol) |
| | 133 | 134 | 135 | 136 | 137 | 138 | 139 | 140 | 141 | 142 | 143 | 144 | 145 | 146 |
| GEORGIA—Cont'd | | | | | | | | | | | | | | |
| Putnam | 1 097.2 | 55 331 | 16 | 96 | 75.5 | 3.6 | 95 | 899 | 204.1 | 21.4 | 34 | 203 | 16.3 | 3.0 |
| Quitman | 0.2 | 85 | 3 | D | D | D | 5 | 26 | 2.8 | 0.3 | 1 | D | D | D |
| Rabun | 4.7 | 292 | 5 | D | D | D | 92 | 949 | 234.4 | 23.4 | 27 | 54 | 10.4 | 1.3 |
| Randolph | 10.4 | 1 425 | 9 | 53 | 41.7 | 1.5 | 31 | 211 | 44.3 | 3.6 | 4 | 12 | 0.8 | 0.2 |
| Richmond | 115.7 | 591 | 196 | 2 249 | 916.4 | 94.3 | 895 | 11 084 | 2 505.1 | 233.6 | 233 | 1 449 | 220.1 | 38.5 |
| Rockdale | 14.5 | 184 | 101 | 726 | 515.6 | 33.7 | 329 | 5 488 | 1 450.1 | 138.0 | 98 | 389 | 85.3 | 14.0 |
| Schley | 1.0 | 252 | 3 | D | D | D | 13 | 110 | 18.6 | 1.9 | NA | NA | NA | NA |
| Screven | 14.3 | 929 | 7 | 31 | 17.5 | 0.6 | 51 | 427 | 93.6 | 7.7 | 12 | 36 | 1.9 | 0.5 |
| Seminole | 39.4 | 4 275 | 11 | 58 | 48.8 | 2.1 | 53 | 382 | 76.5 | 6.6 | 5 | 14 | 0.8 | 0.2 |
| Spalding | 14.4 | 234 | 54 | 565 | 604.3 | 20.9 | 252 | 2 948 | 661.6 | 63.1 | 62 | 243 | 28.1 | 5.8 |
| Stephens | 4.6 | 182 | 30 | D | D | D | 101 | 1 164 | 274.7 | 24.5 | 12 | 30 | 3.2 | 0.8 |
| Stewart | 1.1 | 225 | 3 | 16 | 2.6 | 0.4 | 22 | 89 | 23.9 | 1.6 | 1 | D | D | D |
| Sumter | 14.0 | 424 | 31 | 462 | 239.0 | 12.6 | 150 | 1 575 | 326.1 | 29.3 | 24 | 86 | 11.3 | 1.7 |
| Talbot | 2.5 | 367 | 3 | D | D | D | 7 | 23 | 4.7 | 0.3 | NA | NA | NA | NA |
| Taliaferro | 0.2 | 104 | NA | NA | NA | NA | 4 | 14 | 1.7 | 0.2 | 2 | D | D | D |
| Tattnall | 8.2 | 355 | 21 | 446 | 152.0 | 11.9 | 70 | 518 | 102.4 | 9.9 | 11 | 31 | 2.3 | 0.4 |
| Taylor | 5.3 | 592 | 5 | 93 | 21.4 | 3.0 | 28 | 190 | 46.4 | 3.6 | 4 | 10 | 0.7 | 0.1 |
| Telfair | 4.8 | 360 | 12 | 66 | 30.5 | 1.7 | 51 | 396 | 77.3 | 6.5 | 3 | D | D | D |
| Terrell | 16.2 | 1 512 | 10 | D | D | D | 52 | 343 | 68.3 | 5.7 | 5 | D | D | D |
| Thomas | 20.1 | 451 | 63 | 752 | 575.3 | 35.4 | 239 | 2 567 | 627.5 | 55.4 | 44 | 167 | 23.7 | 4.0 |
| Tift | 25.9 | 634 | 70 | 1 205 | 612.2 | 41.2 | 242 | 2 515 | 721.6 | 52.1 | 51 | 217 | 32.4 | 5.0 |
| Toombs | 11.1 | 406 | 35 | 611 | 665.0 | 20.7 | 158 | 1 702 | 386.3 | 33.9 | 25 | 86 | 12.0 | 1.7 |
| Towns | 6.6 | 638 | 11 | 28 | 6.2 | 0.7 | 72 | 446 | 102.3 | 8.6 | 28 | 71 | 16.6 | 1.8 |
| Treutlen | 1.5 | 228 | 5 | D | D | D | 25 | 199 | 30.4 | 3.0 | 1 | D | D | D |
| Troup | 12.6 | 204 | 57 | D | D | D | 295 | 3 357 | 798.8 | 71.3 | 66 | 445 | 41.7 | 9.0 |
| Turner | 15.9 | 1 675 | 15 | 148 | 103.2 | 4.8 | 34 | 193 | 64.5 | 3.4 | 4 | D | D | D |
| Twiggs | 22.2 | 2 156 | 2 | D | D | D | 18 | 99 | 30.3 | 2.1 | 1 | D | D | D |
| Union | 8.1 | 408 | 12 | 99 | 38.1 | 3.3 | 117 | 981 | 246.7 | 20.1 | 60 | 153 | 17.5 | 3.3 |
| Upson | 5.0 | 182 | 3 | D | D | D | 97 | 1 152 | 208.7 | 21.5 | 18 | 37 | 5.5 | 0.9 |
| Walker | 9.9 | 155 | 33 | D | D | D | 170 | 1 472 | 344.2 | 28.5 | 20 | D | D | D |
| Walton | 10.8 | 142 | 63 | 598 | 260.4 | 25.3 | 207 | 2 660 | 797.2 | 64.4 | 91 | 193 | 27.1 | 4.6 |
| Ware | 6.0 | 173 | 45 | 450 | 762.7 | 13.5 | 244 | 2 811 | 621.1 | 55.7 | 34 | 139 | 12.4 | 2.3 |
| Warren | 4.6 | 754 | 4 | D | D | D | 22 | 154 | 23.2 | 3.1 | 2 | D | D | D |
| Washington | 35.7 | 1 776 | 17 | 122 | 70.0 | 4.2 | 94 | 920 | 213.7 | 18.7 | 17 | 84 | 9.9 | 1.3 |
| Wayne | 65.2 | 2 297 | 14 | D | D | D | 134 | 1 367 | 310.3 | 29.3 | 20 | 102 | 7.6 | 1.5 |
| Webster | 2.9 | 1 284 | 4 | 22 | 3.5 | 0.3 | 4 | 29 | 4.7 | 0.5 | NA | NA | NA | NA |
| Wheeler | 4.9 | 723 | 3 | 47 | 8.2 | 0.8 | 19 | 92 | 18.1 | 1.2 | 1 | D | D | D |
| White | 3.7 | 152 | 18 | 154 | 40.4 | 4.5 | 137 | 960 | 280.7 | 23.8 | 28 | 48 | 8.1 | 1.5 |
| Whitfield | 36.9 | 406 | 235 | 3 548 | 1 351.9 | 136.0 | 504 | 5 707 | 1 440.2 | 128.8 | 89 | 372 | 56.7 | 11.0 |
| Wilcox | 12.6 | 1 442 | 3 | D | D | D | 24 | 128 | 27.4 | 2.1 | NA | NA | NA | NA |
| Wilkes | 1.9 | 186 | 6 | 38 | 19.0 | 1.1 | 60 | 401 | 73.4 | 7.0 | 7 | 22 | 2.5 | 0.5 |
| Wilkinson | 18.5 | 1 827 | 7 | 28 | 13.3 | 1.2 | 26 | 153 | 24.3 | 2.6 | NA | NA | NA | NA |
| Worth | 13.8 | 627 | 27 | 188 | 116.4 | 5.8 | 70 | 497 | 132.2 | 11.0 | 13 | 34 | 2.1 | 0.4 |
| HAWAII | 1 893.4 | 1 485 | 1 629 | 17 707 | 8 894.7 | 699.1 | 5 012 | 70 661 | 17 611.9 | 1 766.4 | 2 084 | 16 759 | 3 974.0 | 653.8 |
| Hawaii | 124.8 | 746 | 185 | 1 847 | 732.2 | 62.1 | 722 | 9 730 | 2 566.0 | 250.0 | 303 | 2 729 | 474.1 | 106.3 |
| Honolulu | 1 593.3 | 1 760 | 1 244 | 14 049 | 7 377.1 | 565.1 | 3 058 | 46 613 | 11 518.3 | 1 144.1 | 1 294 | 9 867 | 2 660.2 | 399.9 |
| Kalawao | 0.0 | 180 | NA | NA | NA | NA | NA | NA | NA | NA | NA | NA | NA | NA |
| Kauai | 49.4 | 788 | 61 | 525 | 209.4 | 16.4 | 379 | 4 457 | 1 052.7 | 110.3 | 168 | 1 387 | 245.6 | 50.7 |
| Maui | 126.0 | 900 | 139 | 1 286 | 575.9 | 55.5 | 853 | 9 861 | 2 474.8 | 262.0 | 319 | 2 776 | 594.1 | 96.8 |
| IDAHO | 19 510.2 | 13 652 | 1 846 | 21 844 | 14 286.7 | 900.0 | 6 300 | 80 447 | 20 526.6 | 1 833.6 | 2 530 | 8 371 | 1 241.7 | 233.5 |
| Ada | 1 117.3 | 3 241 | 561 | 7 490 | 6 006.9 | 371.8 | 1 483 | 23 080 | 5 855.1 | 545.1 | 916 | 3 614 | 551.8 | 121.0 |
| Adams | 115.9 | 32 264 | 1 | D | D | D | 17 | 120 | 20.0 | 1.8 | 12 | 17 | 1.7 | 0.2 |
| Bannock | 398.0 | 5 092 | 78 | 636 | 386.6 | 24.1 | 350 | 4 972 | 1 099.2 | 97.7 | 96 | 323 | 52.2 | 6.9 |
| Bear Lake | 107.4 | 17 383 | 4 | 63 | 23.4 | 1.7 | 32 | 288 | 58.7 | 4.0 | 7 | 16 | 1.2 | 0.3 |
| Benewah | 4.4 | 477 | 5 | 37 | 6.1 | 1.0 | 39 | 366 | 93.9 | 7.5 | 5 | 9 | 0.6 | 0.2 |
| Bingham | 1 195.7 | 27 337 | 50 | D | D | D | 124 | 1 357 | 339.9 | 27.6 | 24 | 75 | 8.4 | 1.7 |
| Blaine | 349.5 | 16 510 | 35 | 678 | 285.9 | 29.8 | 201 | 1 579 | 356.0 | 44.6 | 111 | 363 | 59.4 | 10.5 |
| Boise | 11.7 | 1 553 | NA | NA | NA | NA | 21 | 100 | 18.7 | 1.5 | 8 | 13 | 2.0 | 0.2 |
| Bonner | 72.8 | 1 780 | 37 | 275 | 149.7 | 10.8 | 206 | 2 126 | 485.3 | 48.0 | 95 | 257 | 34.8 | 7.1 |
| Bonneville | 882.0 | 9 601 | 158 | 2 081 | 1 881.6 | 89.0 | 512 | 7 375 | 1 871.5 | 159.4 | 142 | 501 | 86.8 | 11.5 |
| Boundary | 7.0 | 662 | 10 | 39 | 19.7 | 1.7 | 45 | 369 | 86.3 | 8.3 | 9 | 9 | 0.9 | 0.2 |
| Butte | 237.4 | 84 558 | 4 | 31 | 5.2 | 0.5 | 15 | 98 | 18.1 | 1.5 | 7 | 26 | 0.8 | 0.2 |
| Camas | 59.2 | 56 333 | NA | NA | NA | NA | 2 | D | D | D | NA | NA | NA | NA |
| Canyon | 658.3 | 3 999 | 182 | 1 766 | 992.9 | 79.2 | 510 | 7 916 | 2 176.0 | 196.0 | 212 | 643 | 67.7 | 12.5 |

1. Merchant wholesalers, except manufacturers' sales branches and offices.   2. Employer establishments.

# Table B. States and Counties — Professional Services, Manufacturing, and Accommodation and Food Services

| STATE County | Professional, scientific, and technical services,[1] 2007 | | | | Manufacturing, 2007 | | | | Accommodation and food services, 2007 | | | |
|---|---|---|---|---|---|---|---|---|---|---|---|---|
| | Number of establishments | Number of employees | Receipts (mil dol) | Annual payroll (mil dol) | Number of establishments | Number of employees | Receipts (mil dol) | Annual payroll (mil dol) | Number of establishments | Number of employees | Sales (mil dol) | Annual payroll (mil dol) |
| | 147 | 148 | 149 | 150 | 151 | 152 | 153 | 154 | 155 | 156 | 157 | 158 |
| GEORGIA—Cont'd | | | | | | | | | | | | |
| Putnam | 37 | 81 | 9.5 | 2.2 | 27 | 1 352 | 316.1 | 42.7 | 39 | 545 | 19.8 | 5.2 |
| Quitman | 1 | D | D | D | NA | NA | NA | NA | 3 | D | D | D |
| Rabun | 31 | 119 | 10.3 | 4.0 | 25 | 591 | 138.7 | 19.4 | 66 | 676 | 41.1 | 10.4 |
| Randolph | 9 | 42 | 2.4 | 1.5 | NA | NA | NA | NA | 14 | 81 | 3.9 | 0.9 |
| Richmond | 437 | 3 181 | 397.2 | 144.3 | 129 | 9 055 | 5 256.3 | 452.0 | 431 | 9 726 | 395.4 | 108.6 |
| Rockdale | 229 | 1 139 | 131.5 | 50.5 | 87 | 4 437 | 1 778.8 | 192.6 | 193 | 4 190 | 196.6 | 49.7 |
| Schley | 2 | D | D | D | 12 | 919 | 215.9 | 32.0 | 6 | 29 | 0.9 | 0.2 |
| Screven | 13 | 39 | 2.4 | 0.8 | 17 | 1 063 | 183.8 | 32.9 | 20 | 206 | 8.3 | 1.9 |
| Seminole | 11 | 40 | 3.7 | 0.9 | NA | NA | NA | NA | 19 | 140 | 5.4 | 1.3 |
| Spalding | 81 | 481 | 51.1 | 19.6 | 57 | 4 266 | 2 285.2 | 170.1 | 111 | 2 023 | 77.4 | 20.8 |
| Stephens | 42 | 160 | 17.9 | 6.2 | 52 | 1 981 | 535.7 | 69.0 | 50 | 771 | 26.2 | 6.8 |
| Stewart | 2 | D | D | D | NA | NA | NA | NA | 7 | 69 | 2.7 | 0.6 |
| Sumter | 34 | D | D | D | 35 | 1 940 | 412.0 | 64.7 | 56 | 1 069 | 33.7 | 9.8 |
| Talbot | 3 | 5 | 0.3 | 0.2 | NA | NA | NA | NA | NA | NA | NA | NA |
| Taliaferro | NA | NA | NA | NA | NA | NA | NA | NA | 1 | D | D | D |
| Tattnall | 17 | 78 | 7.3 | 2.0 | NA | NA | NA | NA | 21 | 269 | 9.5 | 2.2 |
| Taylor | 9 | 11 | 0.8 | 0.1 | NA | NA | NA | NA | 8 | 57 | 1.6 | 0.5 |
| Telfair | 11 | 48 | 3.2 | 1.2 | 13 | D | D | D | 19 | 216 | 11.1 | 2.6 |
| Terrell | 8 | 36 | 3.3 | 1.1 | 14 | 535 | D | 17.8 | 10 | D | D | D |
| Thomas | 78 | 426 | 44.9 | 16.2 | 51 | 3 166 | 657.6 | 112.5 | 82 | 1 313 | 49.9 | 13.5 |
| Tift | 79 | 559 | 47.4 | 20.4 | 54 | 2 370 | 547.5 | 75.6 | 102 | 2 195 | 92.0 | 26.1 |
| Toombs | 46 | 225 | 20.1 | 6.6 | 36 | D | D | D | 65 | 1 042 | 42.3 | 11.2 |
| Towns | 21 | 88 | 6.7 | 2.7 | NA | NA | NA | NA | 42 | 539 | 31.0 | 9.2 |
| Treutlen | 3 | D | D | D | NA | NA | NA | NA | 4 | 50 | 1.8 | 0.5 |
| Troup | 88 | 429 | 42.3 | 18.6 | 92 | 6 857 | 2 470.8 | 288.4 | 131 | 2 359 | 88.7 | 23.8 |
| Turner | 13 | 33 | 2.9 | 0.8 | NA | NA | NA | NA | 17 | 172 | 6.5 | 1.7 |
| Twiggs | 4 | D | D | D | NA | NA | NA | NA | 7 | 29 | 1.3 | 0.4 |
| Union | 49 | 197 | 13.8 | 5.6 | NA | NA | NA | NA | 43 | 452 | 21.6 | 5.7 |
| Upson | 36 | D | D | D | 24 | D | 526.5 | 56.5 | 50 | 569 | 22.9 | 5.3 |
| Walker | 53 | 197 | 21.3 | 9.4 | 65 | 5 417 | 2 060.6 | 181.2 | 56 | 745 | 25.4 | 6.4 |
| Walton | 151 | 574 | 53.1 | 20.3 | 55 | 1 698 | 591.8 | 69.5 | 90 | 1 397 | 58.4 | 15.0 |
| Ware | 61 | D | D | D | 33 | 1 552 | D | 43.2 | 75 | 1 645 | 55.5 | 14.7 |
| Warren | 3 | D | D | D | NA | NA | NA | NA | 7 | 17 | 0.7 | 0.2 |
| Washington | 22 | 193 | 12.6 | 8.9 | NA | NA | NA | NA | 32 | 516 | 16.5 | 4.4 |
| Wayne | 28 | 106 | 6.9 | 5.5 | 28 | 1 505 | 663.4 | 74.0 | 57 | 875 | 32.9 | 8.7 |
| Webster | 1 | D | D | D | NA | NA | NA | NA | 1 | D | D | D |
| Wheeler | 3 | 8 | 0.3 | 0.1 | NA | NA | NA | NA | 3 | D | D | D |
| White | 50 | 122 | 10.1 | 3.1 | 34 | 584 | 103.9 | 20.3 | 88 | 831 | 51.1 | 11.6 |
| Whitfield | 167 | D | D | D | 317 | 22 283 | 7 524.9 | 710.4 | 189 | 3 428 | 144.8 | 38.8 |
| Wilcox | 2 | D | D | D | NA | NA | NA | NA | 3 | 17 | 0.6 | 0.1 |
| Wilkes | 16 | 87 | 7.3 | 3.6 | 17 | 622 | 174.3 | 18.3 | 18 | 176 | 7.1 | 1.7 |
| Wilkinson | 7 | 69 | 5.6 | 1.9 | 15 | 973 | 521.5 | 52.4 | 7 | 39 | 1.4 | 0.4 |
| Worth | 10 | D | D | D | NA | NA | NA | NA | 17 | 178 | 6.5 | 1.7 |
| HAWAII | 3 254 | 21 772 | 3 068.3 | 1 193.5 | 984 | 14 127 | 8 799.3 | 511.5 | 3 528 | 98 353 | 8 042.2 | 2 209.8 |
| Hawaii | 321 | D | D | D | 138 | 1 516 | 290.1 | 53.6 | 421 | 12 280 | 874.7 | 284.5 |
| Honolulu | 2 433 | 18 508 | 2 686.9 | 1 056.8 | 684 | 10 996 | 8 201.9 | 398.9 | 2 347 | 57 064 | 4 123.8 | 1 126.5 |
| Kalawao | NA | NA | NA | NA | NA | NA | NA | NA | NA | NA | NA | NA |
| Kauai | 132 | D | D | D | NA | NA | NA | NA | 234 | 7 082 | 591.5 | 168.8 |
| Maui | 368 | D | D | D | 114 | 1 319 | 262.7 | 50.7 | 526 | 21 927 | 2 452.2 | 630.1 |
| IDAHO | 4 189 | D | D | D | 1 942 | 64 778 | 18 011.0 | 2 829.4 | 3 482 | 56 662 | 2 416.0 | 662.7 |
| Ada | 1 602 | D | D | D | 419 | 21 075 | 4 942.4 | 1 248.3 | 900 | 17 928 | 796.0 | 219.9 |
| Adams | 8 | D | D | D | NA | NA | NA | NA | 16 | D | D | D |
| Bannock | 164 | D | D | D | 58 | D | D | D | 180 | 3 056 | 117.8 | 31.9 |
| Bear Lake | 3 | D | D | D | NA | NA | NA | NA | 15 | D | D | D |
| Benewah | 12 | D | D | D | 10 | 576 | D | 25.0 | 21 | D | D | D |
| Bingham | 49 | 209 | 23.0 | 7.9 | 45 | 2 334 | 624.5 | 79.9 | 55 | 1 046 | 24.3 | 6.2 |
| Blaine | 163 | 727 | 114.2 | 47.3 | NA | NA | NA | NA | 114 | 3 186 | 153.3 | 52.2 |
| Boise | 12 | D | D | D | NA | NA | NA | NA | 23 | 165 | 5.7 | 1.7 |
| Bonner | 145 | 576 | 43.8 | 26.7 | 87 | 2 091 | 498.6 | 79.6 | 124 | 2 018 | 63.3 | 20.8 |
| Bonneville | 382 | D | D | D | 144 | 2 580 | D | 92.8 | 200 | 3 824 | 153.5 | 41.3 |
| Boundary | 27 | 108 | 6.0 | 2.6 | NA | NA | NA | NA | 23 | D | D | D |
| Butte | 2 | D | D | D | NA | NA | NA | NA | 8 | D | D | D |
| Camas | NA | NA | NA | NA | NA | NA | NA | NA | 6 | 89 | 1.5 | 0.4 |
| Canyon | 252 | D | D | D | 233 | 9 848 | D | 335.1 | 242 | 3 905 | 140.9 | 38.1 |

1. Establishment subject to federal tax.

| STATE County | Health care and social assistance, 2007 | | | | Other services, 2007 | | | | Federal funds and grants, 2009–2010 | | | |
|---|---|---|---|---|---|---|---|---|---|---|---|---|
| | | | | | | | | | Expenditures (mil dol) | | | |
| | | | | | | | | | | Direct payments for individuals[1] | | |
| | Number of establishments | Number of employees | Receipts (mil dol) | Annual payroll (mil dol) | Number of establishments | Number of employees | Receipts (mil dol) | Annual payroll (mil dol) | Total | Social Security and government retirement | Medicare | Food Stamps and Supplemental Security Income |
| | 159 | 160 | 161 | 162 | 163 | 164 | 165 | 166 | 167 | 168 | 169 | 170 |
| GEORGIA—Cont'd | | | | | | | | | | | | |
| Putnam | 25 | 380 | 27.0 | 11.2 | 31 | 73 | 5.4 | 1.2 | 145.4 | 77.6 | 28.1 | 8.0 |
| Quitman | 2 | D | D | D | 1 | D | D | D | 23.0 | 4.3 | 6.0 | 2.2 |
| Rabun | 32 | 455 | 36.0 | 13.7 | 34 | 96 | 10.0 | 2.3 | 138.1 | 65.0 | 33.2 | 4.4 |
| Randolph | 8 | 246 | 16.2 | 6.3 | 8 | 22 | 2.2 | 0.4 | 88.7 | 22.8 | 15.4 | 8.8 |
| Richmond | 617 | 20 772 | 2 482.3 | 911.5 | 290 | 1 956 | 193.4 | 49.9 | 2 506.5 | 829.7 | 291.1 | 168.1 |
| Rockdale | 228 | 3 606 | 335.9 | 127.4 | 175 | 838 | 65.4 | 19.0 | 372.8 | 215.9 | 67.4 | 17.9 |
| Schley | 5 | D | D | D | 5 | D | D | D | 30.0 | 11.3 | 6.2 | 2.1 |
| Screven | 20 | 468 | 24.6 | 11.8 | 20 | 65 | 6.7 | 1.5 | 131.5 | 44.1 | 29.7 | 8.9 |
| Seminole | 22 | 464 | 41.2 | 14.3 | 14 | 48 | 2.9 | 0.9 | 91.6 | 32.6 | 18.5 | 8.9 |
| Spalding | 128 | 3 753 | 277.7 | 96.8 | 88 | 502 | 38.6 | 11.8 | 475.6 | 201.9 | 95.6 | 40.5 |
| Stephens | 49 | 1 335 | 108.0 | 45.9 | 36 | 190 | 20.0 | 4.3 | 235.4 | 108.6 | 53.5 | 14.4 |
| Stewart | 12 | 196 | 12.8 | 4.3 | 7 | 18 | 1.8 | 0.4 | 67.6 | 16.2 | 14.2 | 5.8 |
| Sumter | 88 | D | D | D | 49 | D | D | D | 438.3 | 87.7 | 50.9 | 26.4 |
| Talbot | 2 | D | D | D | 6 | 5 | 0.4 | 0.1 | 65.2 | 30.4 | 9.6 | 5.8 |
| Taliaferro | 2 | D | D | D | 3 | D | D | D | 23.6 | 6.4 | 6.0 | 1.5 |
| Tattnall | 26 | 615 | 30.8 | 13.7 | 14 | 42 | 2.9 | 0.6 | 180.8 | 68.0 | 35.4 | 14.0 |
| Taylor | 19 | 267 | 13.4 | 4.6 | 8 | D | D | D | 92.3 | 31.1 | 16.5 | 7.8 |
| Telfair | 18 | 647 | 32.7 | 15.6 | 17 | 69 | 7.8 | 1.6 | 176.4 | 50.3 | 32.2 | 8.9 |
| Terrell | 17 | D | D | D | 16 | D | D | D | 112.4 | 28.3 | 21.3 | 11.0 |
| Thomas | 134 | 3 303 | 369.8 | 130.7 | 74 | 470 | 41.2 | 10.2 | 404.0 | 160.7 | 77.9 | 31.8 |
| Tift | 110 | 2 811 | 267.4 | 121.2 | 65 | 543 | 65.3 | 17.1 | 315.1 | 116.7 | 57.0 | 24.5 |
| Toombs | 117 | 1 787 | 151.4 | 58.2 | 43 | 241 | 19.6 | 5.4 | 230.5 | 87.9 | 46.0 | 19.1 |
| Towns | 25 | 416 | 32.1 | 12.8 | 15 | 35 | 2.2 | 0.6 | 106.1 | 60.6 | 19.1 | 2.1 |
| Treutlen | 9 | 150 | 5.9 | 2.8 | 7 | 29 | 1.7 | 0.5 | 59.6 | 18.2 | 10.7 | 5.4 |
| Troup | 132 | 3 341 | 281.4 | 114.9 | 96 | 456 | 40.6 | 9.8 | 461.6 | 197.3 | 96.5 | 33.3 |
| Turner | 9 | D | D | D | 9 | 31 | 1.4 | 0.4 | 87.7 | 27.6 | 20.4 | 7.8 |
| Twiggs | 8 | D | D | D | 6 | 16 | 1.9 | 0.4 | 81.4 | 31.0 | 15.3 | 7.1 |
| Union | 56 | 941 | 74.6 | 28.9 | 32 | 202 | 19.8 | 4.4 | 175.5 | 104.4 | 32.7 | 4.9 |
| Upson | 61 | 1 360 | 121.7 | 45.9 | 38 | D | D | D | 228.0 | 84.4 | 48.3 | 16.4 |
| Walker | 52 | D | D | D | 48 | D | D | D | 484.5 | 239.9 | 127.5 | 25.4 |
| Walton | 107 | 1 661 | 223.7 | 51.1 | 113 | 349 | 29.1 | 8.1 | 448.8 | 251.8 | 77.3 | 24.8 |
| Ware | 114 | 2 824 | 260.2 | 94.7 | 70 | 349 | 22.5 | 6.3 | 397.3 | 154.4 | 82.8 | 30.3 |
| Warren | 5 | 110 | 6.4 | 3.0 | 7 | D | D | D | 67.8 | 19.3 | 16.2 | 5.4 |
| Washington | 36 | 949 | 48.6 | 23.3 | 34 | 88 | 7.1 | 1.6 | 181.7 | 58.9 | 43.1 | 14.4 |
| Wayne | 56 | 1 634 | 94.1 | 36.4 | 29 | D | D | D | 244.6 | 89.4 | 50.3 | 16.9 |
| Webster | 1 | D | D | D | 2 | D | D | D | 19.8 | 5.9 | 4.0 | 1.5 |
| Wheeler | 9 | 98 | 11.5 | 5.1 | 5 | 12 | 1.3 | 0.3 | 56.5 | 14.8 | 11.9 | 3.7 |
| White | 33 | 427 | 20.9 | 9.8 | 46 | 204 | 15.6 | 4.2 | 147.2 | 87.6 | 25.2 | 4.6 |
| Whitfield | 195 | 3 776 | 441.3 | 168.8 | 138 | 726 | 68.5 | 21.2 | 515.5 | 237.9 | 110.8 | 29.4 |
| Wilcox | 14 | 213 | 9.2 | 3.9 | 6 | 17 | 0.9 | 0.2 | 82.4 | 28.4 | 18.2 | 5.6 |
| Wilkes | 30 | 514 | 28.6 | 13.1 | 14 | 46 | 4.0 | 0.8 | 143.2 | 41.8 | 27.9 | 6.7 |
| Wilkinson | 14 | 141 | 10.9 | 3.9 | 11 | 40 | 2.3 | 0.7 | 90.2 | 38.9 | 20.4 | 7.2 |
| Worth | 27 | D | D | D | 28 | 75 | 7.0 | 1.4 | 153.5 | 55.1 | 27.5 | 15.7 |
| HAWAII | 3 484 | 63 640 | 6 565.0 | 2 721.4 | 2 916 | 20 119 | 1 917.8 | 512.6 | 20 855.2 | 4 218.0 | 1 488.9 | 508.6 |
| Hawaii | 452 | 7 285 | 623.3 | 271.8 | 310 | 1 673 | 162.5 | 42.6 | 1 258.9 | 549.4 | 178.0 | 111.0 |
| Honolulu | 2 473 | 47 727 | 5 055.4 | 2 047.9 | 2 083 | 15 228 | 1 462.7 | 388.7 | 17 392.9 | 3 117.6 | 1 100.2 | 333.7 |
| Kalawao | NA | NA | NA | NA | NA | NA | NA | NA | 1.3 | 0.0 | 1.2 | 0.0 |
| Kauai | 172 | 2 729 | 266.5 | 119.7 | 134 | 866 | 65.6 | 20.6 | 523.7 | 188.4 | 77.5 | 22.8 |
| Maui | 387 | 5 899 | 619.8 | 282.0 | 389 | 2 352 | 227.1 | 60.6 | 771.1 | 362.5 | 131.9 | 41.1 |
| IDAHO | 4 545 | 73 932 | 6 211.0 | 2 510.8 | 2 640 | 13 681 | 1 094.0 | 315.6 | 14 251.7 | 4 390.8 | 1 320.1 | 467.0 |
| Ada | 1 298 | 25 055 | 2 433.7 | 1 020.4 | 790 | 4 663 | 395.2 | 122.6 | 3 296.9 | 1 010.1 | 241.3 | 78.7 |
| Adams | 9 | 44 | 2.1 | 1.0 | 3 | D | D | D | 34.1 | 17.5 | 4.4 | 1.3 |
| Bannock | 291 | D | D | D | 132 | 669 | 59.4 | 14.2 | 597.4 | 240.9 | 71.8 | 36.5 |
| Bear Lake | 14 | 295 | 18.1 | 7.6 | 8 | 23 | 2.2 | 0.4 | 46.4 | 22.2 | 7.9 | 1.6 |
| Benewah | 19 | 362 | 23.0 | 9.7 | 16 | 79 | 6.4 | 2.0 | 114.0 | 40.5 | 15.4 | 4.8 |
| Bingham | 84 | 1 417 | 105.3 | 51.0 | 56 | 310 | 27.0 | 8.5 | 307.3 | 106.8 | 35.6 | 18.4 |
| Blaine | 79 | 595 | 69.3 | 27.7 | 82 | 331 | 45.8 | 10.9 | 87.2 | 44.9 | 11.3 | 2.4 |
| Boise | 5 | 22 | 1.3 | 0.5 | 8 | D | D | D | 46.7 | 22.9 | 4.8 | 1.3 |
| Bonner | 132 | 1 448 | 112.6 | 44.2 | 84 | 376 | 22.5 | 7.1 | 276.4 | 147.6 | 41.2 | 15.6 |
| Bonneville | 464 | D | D | D | 166 | 954 | 83.6 | 22.4 | 1 989.3 | 259.3 | 83.4 | 33.2 |
| Boundary | 34 | 507 | 25.7 | 13.6 | 23 | 36 | 3.3 | 0.8 | 106.0 | 40.2 | 9.1 | 4.4 |
| Butte | 8 | 191 | 8.5 | 5.4 | 3 | 18 | 1.2 | 0.2 | 40.2 | 10.2 | 5.0 | 0.9 |
| Camas | 3 | D | D | D | NA | NA | NA | NA | 7.3 | 2.7 | 0.7 | 0.2 |
| Canyon | 340 | 5 703 | 422.5 | 175.9 | 207 | 1 172 | 83.0 | 24.4 | 969.1 | 448.9 | 132.1 | 61.4 |

1. State totals may include programs not allocated by county.

| STATE County | Salaries and wages | Defense | Other | Medicaid and other health-related | Nutrition and family welfare | Education | Other | New construction ($1,000) | Number of housing units | Total (mil dol) | Inter-governmental (mil dol) | Total (mil dol) | Total | Property |
|---|---|---|---|---|---|---|---|---|---|---|---|---|---|---|
| | 171 | 172 | 173 | 174 | 175 | 176 | 177 | 178 | 179 | 180 | 181 | 182 | 183 | 184 |
| **GEORGIA—Cont'd** | | | | | | | | | | | | | | |
| Putnam | 5.3 | 0.0 | 2.5 | 15.5 | 5.9 | 1.1 | 0.1 | 10 678 | 50 | 85.6 | 17.4 | 40.9 | 2 020 | 1 152 |
| Quitman | 0.7 | 0.0 | 0.2 | 8.0 | 1.0 | 0.3 | 0.0 | 165 | 3 | 9.1 | 5.3 | 3.0 | 1 124 | 730 |
| Rabun | 4.4 | 1.5 | 1.1 | 23.2 | 2.6 | 0.5 | 1.7 | 23 832 | 80 | 58.9 | 13.9 | 37.2 | 2 251 | 1 534 |
| Randolph | 1.8 | 0.0 | 0.4 | 25.3 | 4.6 | 2.8 | 0.4 | 0 | 0 | 38.0 | 13.5 | 8.4 | 1 157 | 668 |
| Richmond | 300.8 | 298.1 | 87.5 | 330.6 | 59.0 | 25.8 | 61.3 | 46 287 | 267 | 667.8 | 316.3 | 198.7 | 1 007 | 612 |
| Rockdale | 13.6 | 0.2 | 2.7 | 19.8 | 9.5 | 6.7 | 9.6 | 8 953 | 30 | 259.3 | 81.2 | 129.2 | 1 574 | 994 |
| Schley | 0.6 | 0.0 | 0.2 | 7.2 | 0.9 | 0.5 | 0.1 | 0 | 0 | 13.9 | 8.1 | 3.6 | 863 | 633 |
| Screven | 2.7 | 0.0 | 0.6 | 34.3 | 4.2 | 1.4 | 0.2 | 1 229 | 7 | 46.3 | 21.9 | 13.7 | 908 | 552 |
| Seminole | 1.7 | 0.0 | 0.4 | 19.3 | 2.7 | 1.0 | 0.1 | 2 132 | 12 | 27.3 | 13.4 | 10.9 | 1 200 | 743 |
| Spalding | 28.6 | 2.3 | 2.5 | 70.9 | 13.4 | 6.7 | 0.6 | 14 547 | 110 | 231.3 | 98.8 | 88.1 | 1 403 | 849 |
| Stephens | 9.3 | 0.8 | 1.7 | 33.5 | 5.0 | 2.1 | 1.5 | 352 | 4 | 110.0 | 43.4 | 33.5 | 1 325 | 810 |
| Stewart | 7.1 | 0.0 | 0.3 | 19.7 | 2.4 | 0.6 | 0.2 | 0 | 0 | 14.5 | 7.3 | 5.7 | 1 237 | 855 |
| Sumter | 13.3 | 0.9 | 2.0 | 57.1 | 10.3 | 3.4 | 161.0 | 4 028 | 25 | 176.4 | 65.4 | 29.6 | 910 | 524 |
| Talbot | 1.6 | 0.0 | 0.4 | 13.2 | 2.5 | 0.6 | 0.2 | 930 | 6 | 18.8 | 7.5 | 9.6 | 1 451 | 1 065 |
| Taliaferro | 0.6 | 0.0 | 0.2 | 7.7 | 0.7 | 0.1 | 0.0 | 260 | 2 | 9.0 | 4.2 | 2.7 | 1 421 | 1 142 |
| Tattnall | 3.7 | 0.0 | 0.8 | 40.5 | 5.6 | 1.4 | 0.5 | 3 373 | 23 | 53.1 | 26.0 | 16.5 | 713 | 412 |
| Taylor | 1.8 | 0.0 | 0.4 | 21.4 | 2.3 | 1.6 | 8.4 | 1 266 | 9 | 25.8 | 14.2 | 8.5 | 969 | 567 |
| Telfair | 2.9 | 0.0 | 41.9 | 32.0 | 4.3 | 1.2 | 0.3 | 208 | 1 | 30.0 | 14.9 | 10.4 | 778 | 387 |
| Terrell | 5.4 | 0.0 | 0.6 | 31.2 | 4.8 | 1.2 | 0.2 | 1 900 | 20 | 32.3 | 15.2 | 10.7 | 1 045 | 669 |
| Thomas | 16.9 | 2.5 | 4.9 | 77.1 | 12.4 | 6.5 | 0.9 | 22 363 | 134 | 172.5 | 75.7 | 42.9 | 948 | 468 |
| Tift | 31.5 | -0.7 | 1.9 | 51.3 | 9.6 | 5.5 | 1.1 | 4 690 | 50 | 318.7 | 52.5 | 61.8 | 1 486 | 678 |
| Toombs | 5.8 | 0.1 | 1.5 | 47.7 | 7.7 | 2.4 | 0.5 | 5 749 | 75 | 156.8 | 46.6 | 23.3 | 839 | 296 |
| Towns | 7.8 | 0.0 | 1.6 | 11.4 | 1.5 | 0.4 | 0.1 | 11 458 | 64 | 37.9 | 15.1 | 17.0 | 1 561 | 728 |
| Treutlen | 1.0 | 0.0 | 0.2 | 18.6 | 2.2 | 0.5 | 0.5 | 2 332 | 13 | 18.6 | 10.5 | 5.0 | 714 | 440 |
| Troup | 16.8 | 7.7 | 2.3 | 78.9 | 13.5 | 6.0 | 3.5 | 16 009 | 95 | 237.9 | 103.1 | 92.1 | 1 449 | 851 |
| Turner | 2.4 | 0.0 | 0.7 | 18.6 | 3.7 | 1.4 | 0.3 | 1 154 | 8 | 34.0 | 17.5 | 10.3 | 1 109 | 708 |
| Twiggs | 4.2 | 0.7 | 0.3 | 16.5 | 3.1 | 1.0 | 1.1 | 650 | 10 | 23.6 | 11.7 | 9.4 | 910 | 629 |
| Union | 6.0 | 0.0 | 2.5 | 20.4 | 3.1 | 0.5 | 0.2 | 10 662 | 59 | 56.8 | 20.4 | 30.0 | 1 430 | 774 |
| Upson | 12.7 | 0.0 | 1.0 | 37.4 | 7.4 | 2.2 | 15.8 | 1 733 | 18 | 76.0 | 34.3 | 30.2 | 1 097 | 658 |
| Walker | 10.3 | -0.1 | 2.3 | 53.6 | 11.1 | 5.5 | 0.8 | 8 591 | 86 | 165.1 | 91.6 | 51.6 | 799 | 438 |
| Walton | 31.6 | 0.3 | 5.0 | 39.0 | 9.7 | 3.9 | 0.9 | 4 842 | 38 | 299.8 | 82.2 | 126.1 | 1 516 | 1 019 |
| Ware | 14.4 | 0.1 | 3.6 | 71.2 | 19.2 | 4.9 | 5.9 | 9 245 | 75 | 138.3 | 62.8 | 47.3 | 1 321 | 621 |
| Warren | 1.5 | 0.0 | 0.4 | 20.9 | 2.6 | 0.7 | 0.2 | 0 | 0 | 17.9 | 7.7 | 7.3 | 1 237 | 883 |
| Washington | 3.8 | 0.0 | 0.8 | 45.4 | 9.1 | 2.1 | 0.6 | 746 | 13 | 95.4 | 27.1 | 33.1 | 1 580 | 962 |
| Wayne | 27.5 | 0.1 | 4.5 | 39.5 | 6.6 | 2.3 | 0.4 | 345 | 3 | 118.2 | 38.8 | 33.2 | 1 142 | 742 |
| Webster | 0.6 | 0.0 | 0.1 | 4.9 | 0.8 | 0.1 | 0.0 | NA | NA | 7.9 | 4.2 | 2.8 | 1 267 | 971 |
| Wheeler | 1.0 | 0.0 | 0.2 | 16.0 | 2.5 | 0.5 | 4.2 | 0 | 0 | 15.9 | 9.7 | 4.5 | 658 | 435 |
| White | 4.3 | 0.0 | 1.1 | 13.9 | 3.0 | 5.3 | 0.8 | 3 916 | 22 | 72.2 | 28.2 | 34.1 | 1 362 | 836 |
| Whitfield | 25.2 | 2.1 | 7.9 | 58.9 | 16.3 | 9.0 | 0.8 | 4 622 | 40 | 358.4 | 147.4 | 112.0 | 1 200 | 604 |
| Wilcox | 1.9 | 0.1 | 0.5 | 20.6 | 2.5 | 0.7 | 0.3 | NA | NA | 20.4 | 12.0 | 6.7 | 778 | 531 |
| Wilkes | 2.9 | 0.0 | 0.5 | 24.0 | 3.3 | 1.0 | 34.0 | 1 396 | 9 | 43.1 | 13.9 | 12.6 | 1 226 | 798 |
| Wilkinson | 2.0 | 0.0 | 0.5 | 16.0 | 3.1 | 1.5 | 0.2 | 158 | 1 | 32.4 | 11.3 | 18.6 | 1 849 | 1 106 |
| Worth | 5.2 | 0.6 | 0.7 | 28.9 | 6.7 | 2.7 | 0.8 | 2 700 | 23 | 53.3 | 28.0 | 18.3 | 861 | 567 |
| HAWAII | 7 897.6 | 2 350.8 | 394.0 | 1 232.7 | 331.2 | 350.8 | 1 110.8 | 653 884 | 2 743 | X | X | X | X | X |
| Hawaii | 104.8 | 26.2 | 21.4 | 113.4 | 27.1 | 9.2 | 92.7 | 181 341 | 689 | 321.3 | 68.5 | 214.5 | 1 240 | 1 048 |
| Honolulu | 7 676.7 | 2 218.2 | 350.0 | 983.8 | 208.1 | 288.2 | 929.3 | 369 974 | 1 724 | 1 503.1 | 212.0 | 905.8 | 1 000 | 754 |
| Kalawao | 0.0 | 0.0 | 0.0 | 0.0 | 0.0 | 0.0 | 0.0 | NA | NA | NA | NA | NA | NA | NA |
| Kauai | 47.1 | 98.5 | 7.6 | 53.2 | 8.0 | 2.7 | 14.1 | 55 955 | 120 | 179.9 | 61.5 | 94.0 | 1 496 | 1 232 |
| Maui | 66.8 | 7.9 | 15.1 | 74.7 | 21.2 | 3.2 | 30.1 | 46 613 | 210 | 378.9 | 65.9 | 240.0 | 1 693 | 1 373 |
| IDAHO | 1 245.3 | 264.9 | 2 368.4 | 1 473.1 | 282.9 | 244.4 | 979.2 | 732 769 | 3 815 | X | X | X | X | X |
| Ada | 461.4 | 33.6 | 146.1 | 258.3 | 77.9 | 128.5 | 768.2 | 339 913 | 1 453 | 1 088.3 | 442.2 | 367.7 | 985 | 914 |
| Adams | 4.3 | 0.2 | 1.8 | 3.6 | 0.5 | 0.1 | 0.1 | 1 504 | 7 | 12.8 | 7.3 | 4.3 | 1 200 | 961 |
| Bannock | 58.7 | 0.4 | 11.7 | 102.0 | 13.6 | 2.9 | 16.2 | 9 704 | 75 | 329.8 | 100.9 | 58.9 | 737 | 692 |
| Bear Lake | 3.0 | 0.0 | 0.6 | 8.6 | 1.3 | 0.1 | 0.1 | 6 130 | 27 | 26.3 | 10.2 | 3.0 | 507 | 481 |
| Benewah | 3.5 | 0.9 | 2.5 | 13.0 | 3.1 | 2.1 | 12.3 | 1 316 | 9 | 42.5 | 14.7 | 4.7 | 508 | 480 |
| Bingham | 20.9 | 12.0 | 3.0 | 59.0 | 10.5 | 2.5 | 5.6 | 7 175 | 65 | 148.4 | 70.1 | 22.4 | 516 | 487 |
| Blaine | 6.9 | 1.7 | 2.6 | 4.4 | 1.6 | 0.2 | 8.3 | 43 596 | 53 | 116.6 | 33.9 | 63.1 | 2 927 | 2 547 |
| Boise | 5.5 | 1.5 | 3.2 | 3.1 | 0.8 | 0.2 | 2.9 | 4 314 | 28 | 17.6 | 10.7 | 4.1 | 543 | 507 |
| Bonner | 12.1 | 2.5 | 5.1 | 39.6 | 5.1 | 0.9 | 5.2 | 3 250 | 51 | 94.4 | 48.0 | 29.9 | 729 | 704 |
| Bonneville | 64.4 | 66.5 | 1 359.4 | 84.9 | 15.0 | 1.5 | 4.0 | 30 016 | 221 | 254.6 | 131.1 | 64.8 | 671 | 642 |
| Boundary | 11.7 | 11.2 | 1.8 | 14.1 | 1.4 | 0.3 | 8.3 | 5 298 | 26 | 35.9 | 16.7 | 6.8 | 621 | 610 |
| Butte | 8.2 | 0.0 | 1.3 | 10.4 | 0.6 | 0.1 | 0.2 | 420 | 4 | 16.5 | 5.0 | 2.9 | 1 058 | 1 031 |
| Camas | 1.4 | 0.0 | 0.8 | 1.0 | 0.1 | 0.0 | 0.1 | 1 255 | 6 | 4.6 | 3.0 | 1.2 | 1 093 | 1 055 |
| Canyon | 44.7 | 0.2 | 13.1 | 206.3 | 27.4 | 4.7 | 13.9 | 42 168 | 331 | 457.9 | 229.1 | 125.4 | 699 | 610 |

1. State totals may include programs not allocated by county.    2. Based on the resident population estimated as of July 1 of the year shown.

**Local Government Finances, Government Employment, and Voting**

| STATE County | \multicolumn{7}{c}{Local government finances, 2007 (cont.)} | | | \multicolumn{2}{c}{Government employment, 2011} | | \multicolumn{3}{c}{Presidential election,[2] 2012} |
|---|---|---|---|---|---|---|---|---|---|---|---|---|---|---|
| | \multicolumn{7}{c}{Direct general expenditure} | \multicolumn{2}{c}{Debt outstanding} | | | | \multicolumn{3}{c}{Percent of vote cast:} |
| | | | \multicolumn{5}{c}{Percent of total for:} | | | | | | | | |
| | Total (mil dol) | Per capita[1] (dollars) | Educa-tion | Health and hospitals | Police protec-tion | Public welfare | High-ways | Total (mil dol) | Per capita[1] (dollars) | Federal civilian | Federal military | State and local | Demo-cratic | Republi-can | All other |
| | 185 | 186 | 187 | 188 | 189 | 190 | 191 | 192 | 193 | 194 | 195 | 196 | 197 | 198 | 199 |
| GEORGIA—Cont'd | | | | | | | | | | | | | | | |
| Putnam | 73.7 | 3 638 | 46.9 | 22.4 | 4.4 | 0.8 | 5.1 | 66.9 | 3 305 | 67 | 64 | 1 601 | 34.0 | 65.3 | 0.7 |
| Quitman | 8.2 | 3 073 | 54.2 | 2.0 | 6.3 | 1.8 | 6.0 | 5.5 | 2 059 | 0 | 0 | 151 | 53.6 | 45.7 | 0.7 |
| Rabun | 58.9 | 3 565 | 56.1 | 4.6 | 4.8 | 0.8 | 7.1 | 22.5 | 1 364 | 54 | 49 | 800 | 26.3 | 72.2 | 1.5 |
| Randolph | 38.6 | 5 288 | 40.9 | 33.1 | 2.9 | 0.0 | 3.8 | 6.7 | 912 | 24 | 23 | 688 | 57.0 | 42.6 | 0.4 |
| Richmond | 773.3 | 3 918 | 42.9 | 17.8 | 4.2 | 0.1 | 2.3 | 1 281.5 | 6 493 | 7 425 | 10 542 | 22 545 | 65.7 | 33.8 | 0.5 |
| Rockdale | 253.2 | 3 086 | 56.2 | 1.6 | 4.7 | 0.3 | 6.0 | 300.3 | 3 660 | 106 | 259 | 4 264 | 54.4 | 44.9 | 0.7 |
| Schley | 14.6 | 3 533 | 71.9 | 1.7 | 3.4 | 0.3 | 5.3 | 6.3 | 1 531 | 0 | 15 | 301 | 27.6 | 72.0 | 0.4 |
| Screven | 49.0 | 3 260 | 53.3 | 14.0 | 5.0 | 0.3 | 6.1 | 6.2 | 409 | 38 | 43 | 924 | 46.7 | 52.8 | 0.5 |
| Seminole | 26.9 | 2 962 | 64.1 | 4.0 | 5.9 | 0.0 | 7.5 | 5.0 | 110 | 18 | 26 | 482 | 41.5 | 57.9 | 0.5 |
| Spalding | 234.2 | 3 728 | 48.8 | 8.8 | 5.7 | 0.1 | 3.4 | 146.2 | 2 328 | 130 | 193 | 4 666 | 40.2 | 58.9 | 0.9 |
| Stephens | 114.5 | 4 533 | 38.6 | 36.7 | 3.5 | 0.4 | 1.9 | 78.9 | 3 123 | 68 | 78 | 1 887 | 25.7 | 73.1 | 1.2 |
| Stewart | 15.0 | 3 230 | 54.0 | 1.0 | 6.0 | 0.0 | 4.5 | 2.1 | 453 | 88 | 18 | 276 | 62.0 | 37.2 | 0.8 |
| Sumter | 178.8 | 5 497 | 31.5 | 45.1 | 2.9 | 0.1 | 1.3 | 52.2 | 1 605 | 138 | 98 | 2 728 | 52.8 | 46.7 | 0.5 |
| Talbot | 17.6 | 2 662 | 56.9 | 4.2 | 5.6 | 1.1 | 6.1 | 8.1 | 1 222 | 16 | 20 | 270 | 64.0 | 35.2 | 0.8 |
| Taliaferro | 7.1 | 3 794 | 53.9 | 2.3 | 9.3 | 2.7 | 3.7 | 1.5 | 819 | 0 | 0 | 122 | 64.9 | 34.2 | 0.8 |
| Tattnall | 49.0 | 2 116 | 62.4 | 2.8 | 4.3 | 0.1 | 5.9 | 21.2 | 914 | 32 | 77 | 2 205 | 28.8 | 70.4 | 0.8 |
| Taylor | 25.3 | 2 893 | 64.1 | 3.0 | 7.3 | 0.3 | 8.6 | 6.1 | 701 | 19 | 26 | 506 | 42.9 | 56.4 | 0.7 |
| Telfair | 32.9 | 2 464 | 59.5 | 2.4 | 5.7 | 0.3 | 5.2 | 17.7 | 1 325 | 34 | 48 | 835 | 42.6 | 56.8 | 0.6 |
| Terrell | 28.2 | 2 749 | 54.6 | 5.0 | 6.5 | 0.1 | 2.5 | 170.3 | 16 600 | 75 | 28 | 532 | 56.6 | 42.8 | 0.6 |
| Thomas | 179.0 | 3 957 | 46.7 | 9.3 | 4.7 | 0.0 | 3.7 | 115.8 | 2 559 | 189 | 137 | 3 621 | 41.8 | 57.7 | 0.5 |
| Tift | 293.6 | 7 056 | 23.0 | 52.6 | 3.0 | 0.0 | 3.0 | 231.6 | 5 565 | 220 | 126 | 5 098 | 33.3 | 66.1 | 0.5 |
| Toombs | 153.2 | 5 506 | 38.6 | 44.1 | 2.0 | 0.1 | 3.6 | 14.1 | 506 | 64 | 83 | 1 644 | 30.6 | 68.7 | 0.7 |
| Towns | 33.9 | 3 112 | 62.2 | 5.9 | 3.9 | 2.2 | 3.4 | 12.5 | 1 149 | 27 | 32 | 516 | 24.2 | 74.8 | 1.0 |
| Treutlen | 18.6 | 2 687 | 61.3 | 3.3 | 7.9 | 1.3 | 3.8 | 7.0 | 1 003 | 11 | 21 | 379 | 37.6 | 61.8 | 0.5 |
| Troup | 242.3 | 3 814 | 51.1 | 10.6 | 5.8 | 0.3 | 3.0 | 190.4 | 2 997 | 127 | 204 | 4 086 | 40.2 | 59.1 | 0.7 |
| Turner | 33.6 | 3 627 | 56.8 | 3.8 | 7.1 | 0.2 | 7.1 | 9.2 | 991 | 30 | 27 | 604 | 40.2 | 59.0 | 0.8 |
| Twiggs | 20.7 | 2 015 | 55.7 | 2.2 | 8.6 | 1.1 | 5.7 | 5.5 | 538 | 10 | 26 | 310 | 53.2 | 46.2 | 0.7 |
| Union | 55.4 | 2 640 | 52.7 | 3.7 | 4.0 | 1.6 | 5.8 | 51.5 | 2 457 | 54 | 64 | 1 570 | 23.4 | 75.4 | 1.3 |
| Upson | 74.3 | 2 694 | 59.9 | 2.6 | 4.3 | 0.1 | 3.5 | 47.0 | 1 706 | 44 | 81 | 1 394 | 35.6 | 63.8 | 0.6 |
| Walker | 159.4 | 2 469 | 62.7 | 12.7 | 4.5 | 1.1 | 2.9 | 75.8 | 1 175 | 105 | 208 | 3 389 | 25.9 | 72.7 | 1.4 |
| Walton | 295.5 | 3 554 | 55.5 | 12.0 | 5.0 | 0.4 | 4.3 | 360.8 | 4 340 | 145 | 255 | 3 583 | 23.5 | 75.6 | 0.8 |
| Ware | 147.2 | 4 108 | 44.6 | 14.2 | 4.4 | 0.3 | 4.4 | 80.7 | 2 252 | 129 | 111 | 3 095 | 32.5 | 66.9 | 0.6 |
| Warren | 16.0 | 2 713 | 61.6 | 3.2 | 3.2 | 0.1 | 10.6 | 2.1 | 352 | 16 | 17 | 281 | 58.4 | 40.9 | 0.7 |
| Washington | 90.8 | 4 337 | 42.1 | 30.4 | 3.9 | 0.1 | 6.9 | 19.2 | 918 | 46 | 64 | 2 384 | 52.0 | 47.6 | 0.5 |
| Wayne | 142.6 | 4 911 | 31.2 | 48.8 | 3.0 | 0.3 | 5.5 | 32.8 | 1 129 | 408 | 91 | 2 416 | 27.1 | 72.0 | 1.0 |
| Webster | 7.9 | 3 501 | 57.9 | 5.5 | 4.8 | 0.9 | 4.2 | 2.9 | 1 276 | 0 | 0 | 142 | 46.4 | 52.9 | 0.7 |
| Wheeler | 15.9 | 2 331 | 73.4 | 2.9 | 4.7 | 0.0 | 4.2 | 1.2 | 180 | 11 | 24 | 333 | 35.9 | 63.7 | 0.4 |
| White | 80.0 | 3 196 | 64.4 | 1.9 | 4.7 | 0.4 | 3.9 | 32.2 | 1 285 | 43 | 82 | 1 166 | 20.2 | 78.7 | 1.1 |
| Whitfield | 376.7 | 4 035 | 48.8 | 11.2 | 3.7 | 0.1 | 4.3 | 244.5 | 2 619 | 153 | 311 | 5 196 | 29.5 | 69.5 | 1.0 |
| Wilcox | 19.2 | 2 228 | 64.7 | 4.7 | 6.5 | 0.7 | 9.0 | 1.2 | 134 | 25 | 28 | 605 | 30.9 | 68.3 | 0.8 |
| Wilkes | 42.6 | 4 149 | 38.9 | 28.7 | 4.6 | 0.9 | 3.6 | 18.4 | 1 795 | 37 | 31 | 819 | 45.8 | 53.5 | 0.6 |
| Wilkinson | 30.6 | 3 044 | 56.6 | 3.0 | 6.4 | 1.1 | 7.2 | 9.1 | 906 | 19 | 28 | 533 | 49.2 | 50.3 | 0.6 |
| Worth | 55.6 | 2 614 | 60.7 | 1.8 | 9.4 | 0.1 | 7.6 | 5.8 | 271 | 39 | 66 | 865 | 30.4 | 69.1 | 0.6 |
| HAWAII | X | X | X | X | X | X | X | X | X | 34 935 | 57 632 | 90 555 | 71.8 | 26.6 | 1.6 |
| Hawaii | 292.2 | 1 689 | 0.0 | 6.3 | 15.5 | 2.1 | 6.7 | 465.1 | 2 688 | 1 431 | 1 402 | 11 049 | 75.9 | 22.2 | 1.8 |
| Honolulu | 1 403.3 | 1 550 | 0.0 | 2.0 | 13.7 | 0.0 | 9.7 | 4 105.7 | 4 534 | 32 059 | 54 454 | 66 778 | 69.8 | 28.7 | 1.4 |
| Kalawao | NA | NA | NA | NA | NA | NA | NA | NA | NA | [3]885 | [3]1 193 | [3]8 786 | NA | NA | NA |
| Kauai | 154.6 | 2 461 | 0.0 | 0.0 | 12.5 | 7.6 | 8.1 | 125.3 | 1 994 | 560 | 583 | 3 942 | 75.0 | 22.9 | 2.1 |
| Maui | 313.2 | 2 209 | 0.0 | 0.3 | 11.2 | 4.6 | 9.1 | 330.0 | 2 327 | [3] | [3] | [3] | 76.7 | 21.5 | 1.8 |
| IDAHO | X | X | X | X | X | X | X | X | X | 12 732 | 9 592 | 103 830 | 36.1 | 61.5 | 2.4 |
| Ada | 1 000.9 | 2 680 | 44.1 | 2.2 | 8.2 | 0.5 | 7.6 | 865.1 | 2 317 | 5 265 | 1 587 | 26 279 | 45.8 | 52.0 | 2.1 |
| Adams | 11.1 | 3 119 | 42.0 | 1.6 | 9.9 | 0.0 | 10.9 | 5.6 | 1 571 | 95 | 15 | 216 | 31.4 | 65.4 | 3.2 |
| Bannock | 348.5 | 4 360 | 25.3 | 42.7 | 4.4 | 0.4 | 5.8 | 139.7 | 1 748 | 567 | 318 | 7 502 | 42.1 | 55.1 | 2.7 |
| Bear Lake | 24.7 | 4 219 | 34.0 | 40.0 | 2.9 | 0.7 | 6.3 | 3.5 | 595 | 53 | 23 | 607 | 17.1 | 80.8 | 2.2 |
| Benewah | 43.4 | 4 699 | 34.2 | 46.0 | 1.7 | 0.4 | 4.8 | 2.3 | 244 | 62 | 35 | 1 312 | 33.8 | 63.5 | 2.7 |
| Bingham | 144.4 | 3 321 | 45.2 | 28.4 | 4.0 | 0.3 | 5.1 | 58.3 | 1 342 | 230 | 174 | 3 657 | 25.8 | 71.3 | 2.9 |
| Blaine | 93.3 | 4 327 | 48.3 | 4.9 | 4.3 | 0.3 | 5.1 | 47.4 | 2 199 | 104 | 80 | 1 388 | 65.7 | 32.5 | 1.8 |
| Boise | 18.3 | 2 423 | 48.6 | 1.9 | 8.4 | 1.0 | 12.7 | 4.1 | 547 | 150 | 27 | 342 | 32.9 | 64.5 | 2.7 |
| Bonner | 91.4 | 2 226 | 45.3 | 3.1 | 6.9 | 0.4 | 6.8 | 23.1 | 562 | 188 | 154 | 2 138 | 40.1 | 57.0 | 2.9 |
| Bonneville | 244.0 | 2 527 | 53.4 | 1.2 | 5.1 | 0.3 | 6.7 | 164.8 | 1 707 | 765 | 401 | 4 963 | 27.4 | 70.3 | 2.3 |
| Boundary | 33.6 | 3 086 | 35.6 | 26.2 | 4.8 | 2.6 | 7.3 | 14.8 | 1 361 | 165 | 41 | 927 | 31.4 | 65.0 | 3.6 |
| Butte | 15.1 | 5 460 | 25.1 | 52.2 | 3.3 | 0.5 | 1.2 | 6.6 | 2 372 | 103 | 23 | 164 | 22.6 | 74.9 | 2.6 |
| Camas | 4.3 | 3 860 | 42.1 | 0.3 | 12.0 | 0.2 | 19.0 | 4.0 | 3 622 | 28 | 0 | 93 | 30.3 | 68.3 | 1.5 |
| Canyon | 450.8 | 2 513 | 51.5 | 0.2 | 6.1 | 0.6 | 4.7 | 390.9 | 2 179 | 361 | 726 | 8 449 | 31.4 | 66.5 | 2.1 |

1. Based on the resident population estimated as of July 1 of the year shown. 2. © 2013 Election Data Services, Inc. All rights reserved. 3. Kalawao county is included with Maui county.

# Table B. States and Counties — Land Area and Population

| STATE/ County code | CBSA code[1] | County type[2] | STATE County | Land area[3] (sq km) 2010 | Total persons | Rank | Per square kilometer | White | Black | American Indian Alaska Native | Asian and Pacific Islander | Percent Hispanic or Latino[4] | Under 5 years | 5 to 17 years | 18 to 24 years | 25 to 34 years | 35 to 44 years | 45 to 54 years |
|---|---|---|---|---|---|---|---|---|---|---|---|---|---|---|---|---|---|---|
| | | | | 1 | 2 | 3 | 4 | 5 | 6 | 7 | 8 | 9 | 10 | 11 | 12 | 13 | 14 | 15 |
| | | | **IDAHO—Cont'd** | | | | | | | | | | | | | | | |
| 16 029 | ... | 6 | Caribou | 4 569 | 6 787 | 2 699 | 1.5 | 94.1 | 0.4 | 1.0 | 1.2 | 4.9 | 7.8 | 20.9 | 6.4 | 11.8 | 10.7 | 13.0 |
| 16 031 | 15420 | 7 | Cassia | 6 644 | 23 249 | 1 678 | 3.5 | 73.3 | 0.3 | 1.0 | 1.2 | 25.2 | 9.0 | 23.7 | 8.7 | 11.8 | 11.2 | 12.0 |
| 16 033 | ... | 8 | Clark | 4 569 | 869 | 3 114 | 0.2 | 57.4 | 0.9 | 0.9 | 0.8 | 41.2 | 7.3 | 23.1 | 8.6 | 12.4 | 12.6 | 11.6 |
| 16 035 | ... | 6 | Clearwater | 6 364 | 8 590 | 2 558 | 1.3 | 93.4 | 0.6 | 3.3 | 1.4 | 3.3 | 4.0 | 13.2 | 5.9 | 9.4 | 10.5 | 15.9 |
| 16 037 | ... | 9 | Custer | 12 745 | 4 331 | 2 882 | 0.3 | 94.4 | 0.4 | 1.3 | 0.6 | 4.3 | 4.8 | 14.0 | 5.1 | 10.2 | 10.5 | 16.6 |
| 16 039 | 34300 | 4 | Elmore | 7 964 | 26 223 | 1 553 | 3.3 | 77.4 | 3.4 | 1.8 | 4.8 | 15.7 | 9.1 | 18.9 | 12.9 | 15.1 | 11.5 | 12.5 |
| 16 041 | 30860 | 3 | Franklin | 1 719 | 12 786 | 2 253 | 7.4 | 92.3 | 0.5 | 0.9 | 0.5 | 6.9 | 9.1 | 25.7 | 7.5 | 12.1 | 11.2 | 11.5 |
| 16 043 | 39940 | 6 | Fremont | 4 827 | 12 957 | 2 243 | 2.7 | 86.0 | 0.5 | 1.2 | 0.8 | 12.6 | 8.2 | 22.6 | 7.4 | 12.9 | 10.7 | 12.4 |
| 16 045 | 14260 | 2 | Gem | 1 453 | 16 673 | 2 000 | 11.5 | 90.4 | 0.6 | 1.4 | 1.2 | 8.2 | 6.1 | 17.9 | 7.3 | 9.7 | 10.8 | 15.0 |
| 16 047 | ... | 7 | Gooding | 1 888 | 15 291 | 2 088 | 8.1 | 70.6 | 0.5 | 1.1 | 0.9 | 28.1 | 8.0 | 21.2 | 8.6 | 12.2 | 11.5 | 12.2 |
| 16 049 | ... | 6 | Idaho | 21 956 | 16 308 | 2 024 | 0.7 | 93.8 | 0.5 | 3.7 | 0.9 | 2.7 | 5.3 | 15.2 | 6.3 | 8.8 | 9.8 | 14.7 |
| 16 051 | 26820 | 3 | Jefferson | 2 832 | 26 684 | 1 540 | 9.4 | 88.2 | 0.5 | 1.1 | 1.0 | 10.4 | 10.2 | 24.9 | 7.8 | 13.6 | 11.7 | 12.1 |
| 16 053 | 46300 | 7 | Jerome | 1 547 | 22 499 | 1 710 | 14.5 | 66.6 | 0.4 | 1.3 | 0.7 | 32.0 | 9.7 | 21.5 | 9.3 | 13.7 | 11.4 | 12.5 |
| 16 055 | 17660 | 3 | Kootenai | 3 222 | 142 357 | 443 | 44.2 | 93.6 | 0.7 | 2.2 | 1.6 | 4.0 | 6.4 | 18.0 | 8.6 | 12.3 | 12.2 | 14.1 |
| 16 057 | 34140 | 4 | Latah | 2 787 | 38 184 | 1 213 | 13.7 | 92.5 | 1.3 | 1.5 | 3.3 | 3.8 | 5.6 | 12.8 | 26.7 | 13.5 | 9.6 | 10.6 |
| 16 059 | ... | 7 | Lemhi | 11 819 | 7 758 | 2 622 | 0.7 | 95.9 | 0.6 | 1.6 | 0.9 | 2.5 | 5.0 | 14.4 | 5.5 | 9.1 | 9.0 | 15.4 |
| 16 061 | ... | 8 | Lewis | 1 240 | 3 889 | 2 917 | 3.1 | 90.8 | 0.8 | 6.3 | 1.0 | 3.5 | 5.7 | 16.0 | 5.9 | 9.4 | 9.2 | 15.2 |
| 16 063 | ... | 9 | Lincoln | 3 112 | 5 277 | 2 821 | 1.7 | 69.6 | 0.7 | 1.2 | 0.8 | 28.7 | 8.5 | 23.2 | 8.2 | 13.5 | 11.7 | 11.6 |
| 16 065 | 39940 | 6 | Madison | 1 215 | 37 456 | 1 233 | 30.8 | 91.5 | 0.8 | 0.7 | 2.1 | 6.1 | 9.2 | 15.5 | 38.1 | 14.4 | 6.2 | 6.0 |
| 16 067 | 15420 | 7 | Minidoka | 1 962 | 20 037 | 1 839 | 10.2 | 66.0 | 0.5 | 1.4 | 0.7 | 32.5 | 8.3 | 20.6 | 8.9 | 11.6 | 10.6 | 13.1 |
| 16 069 | 30300 | 3 | Nez Perce | 2 197 | 39 531 | 1 181 | 18.0 | 90.4 | 0.7 | 6.4 | 1.6 | 3.1 | 5.6 | 16.1 | 9.7 | 12.0 | 11.3 | 13.9 |
| 16 071 | ... | 8 | Oneida | 3 108 | 4 215 | 2 890 | 1.4 | 95.3 | 0.5 | 0.8 | 1.0 | 3.3 | 7.4 | 21.5 | 6.1 | 10.7 | 9.9 | 13.5 |
| 16 073 | 14260 | 2 | Owyhee | 19 854 | 11 439 | 2 330 | 0.6 | 69.7 | 0.5 | 4.3 | 1.0 | 25.9 | 7.6 | 21.3 | 8.4 | 11.4 | 11.6 | 13.1 |
| 16 075 | 36620 | 6 | Payette | 1 054 | 22 639 | 1 702 | 21.5 | 82.7 | 0.5 | 1.9 | 1.7 | 15.2 | 7.6 | 20.4 | 7.8 | 11.2 | 11.7 | 13.7 |
| 16 077 | 38540 | 3 | Power | 3 637 | 7 778 | 2 620 | 2.1 | 66.5 | 0.5 | 2.8 | 1.1 | 30.6 | 9.5 | 21.4 | 9.3 | 11.5 | 11.2 | 12.9 |
| 16 079 | ... | 6 | Shoshone | 6 811 | 12 702 | 2 260 | 1.9 | 94.3 | 0.5 | 2.7 | 0.7 | 3.4 | 4.9 | 15.8 | 6.4 | 9.5 | 11.5 | 15.1 |
| 16 081 | 27220 | 9 | Teton | 1 164 | 10 052 | 2 439 | 8.6 | 81.7 | 0.4 | 0.7 | 0.8 | 17.2 | 9.6 | 19.7 | 6.4 | 16.3 | 17.5 | 13.2 |
| 16 083 | 46300 | 5 | Twin Falls | 4 976 | 78 595 | 699 | 15.8 | 83.5 | 0.7 | 1.3 | 1.7 | 14.1 | 8.2 | 19.2 | 9.4 | 13.8 | 11.4 | 12.6 |
| 16 085 | ... | 8 | Valley | 9 491 | 9 545 | 2 470 | 1.0 | 94.4 | 0.5 | 1.2 | 0.7 | 4.4 | 5.1 | 13.9 | 5.5 | 10.2 | 11.9 | 15.2 |
| 16 087 | ... | 6 | Washington | 3 763 | 10 099 | 2 435 | 2.7 | 81.1 | 0.4 | 1.6 | 1.3 | 16.9 | 5.4 | 18.7 | 6.6 | 8.9 | 11.1 | 13.4 |
| 17 000 | ... | X | **ILLINOIS** | 143 793 | 12 875 255 | X | 89.5 | 64.5 | 15.0 | 0.5 | 5.3 | 16.2 | 6.4 | 17.6 | 9.7 | 13.9 | 13.2 | 14.4 |
| 17 001 | 39500 | 5 | Adams | 2 215 | 67 197 | 787 | 30.3 | 94.2 | 4.6 | 0.5 | 1.0 | 1.3 | 6.4 | 16.6 | 8.9 | 11.8 | 11.4 | 14.4 |
| 17 003 | 16020 | 7 | Alexander | 610 | 7 748 | 2 623 | 12.7 | 61.9 | 36.3 | 0.8 | 0.8 | 2.0 | 6.7 | 15.9 | 9.2 | 10.9 | 11.1 | 14.6 |
| 17 005 | 41180 | 1 | Bond | 985 | 17 644 | 1 938 | 17.9 | 89.5 | 6.8 | 0.9 | 0.8 | 3.2 | 5.3 | 15.0 | 10.3 | 13.3 | 13.0 | 15.0 |
| 17 007 | 40420 | 2 | Boone | 727 | 53 940 | 926 | 74.2 | 76.2 | 2.5 | 0.5 | 1.8 | 20.3 | 6.4 | 21.8 | 8.2 | 10.8 | 14.6 | 14.6 |
| 17 009 | ... | 7 | Brown | 792 | 6 914 | 2 692 | 8.7 | 74.8 | 18.9 | 0.4 | 0.5 | 5.9 | 4.3 | 11.3 | 11.5 | 19.0 | 16.1 | 15.1 |
| 17 011 | 36860 | 6 | Bureau | 2 251 | 34 323 | 1 319 | 15.2 | 89.4 | 1.1 | 0.6 | 1.0 | 7.9 | 5.5 | 17.3 | 7.1 | 10.8 | 11.9 | 14.9 |
| 17 013 | 41180 | 1 | Calhoun | 657 | 5 014 | 2 838 | 7.6 | 98.3 | 0.3 | 0.3 | 0.4 | 1.1 | 5.4 | 16.0 | 7.0 | 9.5 | 11.8 | 15.4 |
| 17 015 | ... | 7 | Carroll | 1 152 | 15 011 | 2 105 | 13.0 | 95.3 | 1.3 | 0.6 | 0.7 | 3.1 | 4.7 | 15.4 | 7.0 | 9.7 | 10.6 | 14.9 |
| 17 017 | ... | 6 | Cass | 973 | 13 338 | 2 220 | 13.7 | 78.9 | 3.3 | 0.4 | 0.7 | 17.3 | 6.5 | 18.3 | 8.0 | 12.2 | 12.7 | 14.1 |
| 17 019 | 16580 | 3 | Champaign | 2 580 | 203 276 | 310 | 78.8 | 72.4 | 13.5 | 0.6 | 10.5 | 5.5 | 5.6 | 13.4 | 25.0 | 14.5 | 10.3 | 11.0 |
| 17 021 | 45380 | 6 | Christian | 1 837 | 34 638 | 1 309 | 18.9 | 96.2 | 2.0 | 0.4 | 0.7 | 1.5 | 6.0 | 16.2 | 8.1 | 11.8 | 12.1 | 15.0 |
| 17 023 | ... | 6 | Clark | 1 299 | 16 209 | 2 031 | 12.5 | 97.6 | 0.9 | 0.5 | 0.5 | 1.3 | 5.4 | 17.2 | 7.4 | 11.3 | 11.9 | 15.5 |
| 17 025 | ... | 7 | Clay | 1 213 | 13 766 | 2 191 | 11.3 | 97.4 | 0.8 | 0.5 | 0.7 | 1.3 | 6.3 | 16.6 | 8.0 | 11.1 | 11.6 | 14.8 |
| 17 027 | 41180 | 1 | Clinton | 1 228 | 38 061 | 1 220 | 31.0 | 92.7 | 4.0 | 0.5 | 0.8 | 2.9 | 5.7 | 16.8 | 8.6 | 13.4 | 13.0 | 15.9 |
| 17 029 | 16660 | 5 | Coles | 1 316 | 53 655 | 929 | 40.8 | 92.4 | 4.8 | 0.5 | 1.4 | 2.3 | 5.1 | 12.9 | 24.4 | 11.1 | 9.5 | 11.8 |
| 17 031 | 16980 | 1 | Cook | 2 448 | 5 231 351 | 2 | 2 137.0 | 44.4 | 24.8 | 0.4 | 7.0 | 24.4 | 6.6 | 16.9 | 9.7 | 16.2 | 13.5 | 13.6 |
| 17 033 | ... | 6 | Crawford | 1 149 | 19 600 | 1 853 | 17.1 | 92.3 | 5.2 | 0.5 | 0.7 | 2.1 | 5.2 | 15.1 | 8.7 | 12.5 | 12.6 | 15.5 |
| 17 035 | 16660 | 9 | Cumberland | 896 | 10 968 | 2 361 | 12.2 | 98.0 | 0.8 | 0.5 | 0.5 | 0.9 | 6.5 | 17.0 | 7.8 | 11.7 | 11.7 | 14.8 |
| 17 037 | 16980 | 1 | DeKalb | 1 635 | 104 704 | 563 | 64.0 | 80.2 | 7.2 | 0.5 | 3.1 | 10.5 | 6.0 | 15.8 | 21.6 | 13.6 | 11.1 | 12.0 |
| 17 039 | ... | 6 | De Witt | 1 030 | 16 434 | 2 015 | 16.0 | 96.4 | 1.1 | 0.5 | 0.8 | 2.2 | 5.7 | 16.7 | 7.2 | 11.3 | 12.7 | 15.5 |
| 17 041 | ... | 6 | Douglas | 1 079 | 19 853 | 1 844 | 18.4 | 95.3 | 0.8 | 0.5 | 0.7 | 6.4 | 7.0 | 18.6 | 7.9 | 12.1 | 11.6 | 14.2 |
| 17 043 | 16980 | 1 | DuPage | 848 | 927 987 | 52 | 1 094.3 | 71.1 | 5.2 | 0.4 | 11.2 | 13.6 | 6.1 | 18.3 | 8.4 | 12.9 | 13.5 | 16.0 |
| 17 045 | ... | 6 | Edgar | 1 615 | 18 191 | 1 911 | 11.3 | 97.9 | 0.8 | 0.5 | 0.4 | 1.2 | 5.5 | 16.5 | 7.0 | 11.4 | 11.6 | 14.8 |
| 17 047 | ... | 9 | Edwards | 576 | 6 684 | 2 709 | 11.6 | 97.9 | 0.9 | 0.5 | 0.5 | 1.0 | 5.5 | 17.1 | 7.4 | 10.1 | 12.5 | 14.9 |
| 17 049 | 20820 | 7 | Effingham | 1 240 | 34 353 | 1 318 | 27.7 | 97.2 | 0.6 | 0.3 | 0.6 | 1.9 | 6.5 | 17.8 | 8.6 | 12.4 | 11.5 | 15.3 |
| 17 051 | ... | 6 | Fayette | 1 856 | 22 014 | 1 731 | 11.9 | 93.5 | 4.8 | 0.5 | 0.6 | 1.5 | 5.6 | 16.4 | 9.2 | 12.7 | 12.6 | 14.7 |
| 17 053 | 16580 | 3 | Ford | 1 258 | 14 008 | 2 176 | 11.1 | 96.2 | 1.1 | 0.6 | 0.5 | 2.4 | 5.7 | 17.6 | 7.0 | 10.7 | 12.0 | 15.3 |
| 17 055 | ... | 5 | Franklin | 1 059 | 39 407 | 1 185 | 37.2 | 97.4 | 0.7 | 0.8 | 0.7 | 1.4 | 6.0 | 16.8 | 7.7 | 11.3 | 12.2 | 14.0 |
| 17 057 | 15900 | 6 | Fulton | 2 242 | 36 651 | 1 257 | 16.3 | 93.3 | 3.9 | 0.6 | 0.6 | 2.5 | 5.2 | 15.4 | 7.9 | 12.4 | 12.9 | 14.3 |
| 17 059 | ... | 8 | Gallatin | 837 | 5 430 | 2 811 | 6.5 | 97.9 | 0.9 | 0.7 | 0.3 | 1.3 | 5.5 | 15.0 | 7.4 | 10.4 | 11.8 | 14.2 |
| 17 061 | ... | 6 | Greene | 1 406 | 13 576 | 2 210 | 9.7 | 97.6 | 1.4 | 0.5 | 0.3 | 0.9 | 5.5 | 17.1 | 7.8 | 11.4 | 12.1 | 15.5 |
| 17 063 | 16980 | 1 | Grundy | 1 083 | 50 281 | 974 | 46.4 | 89.3 | 1.7 | 0.5 | 1.1 | 8.4 | 7.0 | 19.8 | 7.7 | 13.4 | 14.6 | 14.7 |
| 17 065 | 34500 | 7 | Hamilton | 1 126 | 8 370 | 2 573 | 7.4 | 97.6 | 0.8 | 0.5 | 0.4 | 1.4 | 5.9 | 16.7 | 6.8 | 11.5 | 11.0 | 14.3 |
| 17 067 | ... | 7 | Hancock | 2 056 | 18 891 | 1 881 | 9.2 | 97.9 | 0.8 | 0.6 | 0.6 | 1.1 | 5.6 | 16.0 | 6.8 | 10.6 | 10.8 | 14.8 |

1. CBSA = Core Based Statistical Area. See Appendix A for explanation. See Appendix B for list of metropolitan areas with component counties.    2. County type code from the Economic Research Service of USDA Rural-Urban Continuum Codes. See Appendix A for definition.    3. Dry land or land partially or temporarily covered by water.    4. May be of any race.

# Table B. States and Counties — **Population and Households**

| STATE County | \(55\) to 64 years (16) | \(65\) to 74 years (17) | \(75\) years and over (18) | Percent female (19) | Total persons 2000 (20) | Total persons 2010 (21) | Percent change 2000–2010 (22) | Percent change 2010–2012 (23) | Births (24) | Deaths (25) | Net migration (26) | Households 2010 Number (27) | Percent change 2000–2010 (28) | Persons per household (29) | Percent Female family householder[1] (30) | Percent One person (31) |
|---|---|---|---|---|---|---|---|---|---|---|---|---|---|---|---|---|
| **IDAHO—Cont'd** | | | | | | | | | | | | | | | | |
| Caribou | 13.1 | 9.0 | 7.3 | 50.0 | 7 304 | 6 963 | -4.7 | -2.5 | 209 | 169 | -221 | 2 606 | 1.8 | 2.64 | 6.1 | 22.9 |
| Cassia | 10.7 | 6.8 | 6.2 | 49.3 | 21 416 | 22 952 | 7.2 | 1.3 | 916 | 423 | -199 | 7 666 | 8.6 | 2.96 | 9.1 | 21.5 |
| Clark | 10.9 | 8.0 | 5.5 | 44.6 | 1 022 | 982 | -3.9 | -11.5 | 27 | 7 | -135 | 345 | 1.5 | 2.84 | 7.0 | 24.3 |
| Clearwater | 17.8 | 13.8 | 9.4 | 45.7 | 8 930 | 8 761 | -1.9 | -2.0 | 132 | 243 | -61 | 3 660 | 5.9 | 2.23 | 6.4 | 29.3 |
| Custer | 18.8 | 12.3 | 7.6 | 47.1 | 4 342 | 4 368 | 0.6 | -0.8 | 80 | 80 | -40 | 1 936 | 9.4 | 2.25 | 4.8 | 30.2 |
| Elmore | 9.4 | 6.4 | 4.4 | 48.5 | 29 130 | 27 038 | -7.2 | -3.0 | 1 094 | 394 | -1 542 | 10 140 | 11.5 | 2.60 | 9.4 | 23.8 |
| Franklin | 9.8 | 7.0 | 6.0 | 49.4 | 11 329 | 12 786 | 12.9 | 0.0 | 445 | 214 | -228 | 4 079 | 17.3 | 3.11 | 6.3 | 17.9 |
| Fremont | 11.3 | 8.2 | 6.2 | 47.5 | 11 819 | 13 242 | 12.0 | -2.2 | 454 | 232 | -508 | 4 436 | 14.2 | 2.88 | 7.2 | 19.7 |
| Gem | 14.2 | 10.6 | 8.4 | 50.5 | 15 181 | 16 719 | 10.1 | -0.3 | 402 | 437 | -26 | 6 495 | 17.3 | 2.55 | 9.3 | 24.3 |
| Gooding | 10.9 | 8.2 | 7.2 | 48.4 | 14 155 | 15 464 | 9.2 | -1.1 | 506 | 296 | -384 | 5 531 | 9.6 | 2.79 | 8.8 | 24.2 |
| Idaho | 18.1 | 12.9 | 8.8 | 47.6 | 15 511 | 16 267 | 4.9 | 0.3 | 354 | 372 | 51 | 6 834 | 12.3 | 2.30 | 6.6 | 28.6 |
| Jefferson | 9.9 | 5.8 | 3.9 | 49.7 | 19 155 | 26 140 | 36.5 | 2.1 | 1 132 | 306 | -278 | 8 146 | 38.0 | 3.20 | 7.4 | 15.0 |
| Jerome | 10.5 | 6.4 | 5.1 | 48.7 | 18 342 | 22 374 | 22.0 | 0.6 | 915 | 374 | -424 | 7 540 | 19.7 | 2.95 | 9.6 | 20.3 |
| Kootenai | 13.6 | 8.6 | 6.3 | 50.6 | 108 685 | 138 494 | 27.4 | 2.8 | 3 825 | 2 676 | 2 649 | 54 200 | 31.2 | 2.53 | 10.0 | 24.3 |
| Latah | 10.7 | 5.8 | 4.7 | 48.7 | 34 935 | 37 244 | 6.6 | 2.5 | 1 039 | 467 | 376 | 14 708 | 12.6 | 2.32 | 6.1 | 28.2 |
| Lemhi | 18.7 | 13.5 | 9.4 | 48.8 | 7 806 | 7 936 | 1.7 | -2.2 | 160 | 203 | -139 | 3 576 | 9.2 | 2.20 | 6.9 | 31.7 |
| Lewis | 15.6 | 13.4 | 9.5 | 50.0 | 3 747 | 3 821 | 2.0 | 1.8 | 86 | 91 | 72 | 1 657 | 6.6 | 2.26 | 7.6 | 32.6 |
| Lincoln | 11.8 | 6.0 | 5.4 | 48.1 | 4 044 | 5 208 | 28.8 | 1.3 | 173 | 69 | -36 | 1 705 | 17.8 | 3.03 | 7.1 | 20.5 |
| Madison | 5.0 | 3.1 | 2.5 | 52.1 | 27 467 | 37 536 | 36.7 | -0.2 | 2 254 | 293 | -2 082 | 10 611 | 48.8 | 3.44 | 4.8 | 10.1 |
| Minidoka | 11.8 | 8.0 | 6.9 | 49.5 | 20 174 | 20 069 | -0.5 | -0.2 | 696 | 395 | -338 | 7 170 | 2.8 | 2.79 | 9.1 | 22.0 |
| Nez Perce | 13.3 | 9.1 | 9.0 | 50.5 | 37 410 | 39 265 | 5.0 | 0.7 | 996 | 1 054 | 337 | 16 241 | 6.2 | 2.36 | 10.3 | 28.6 |
| Oneida | 14.0 | 8.6 | 8.1 | 49.0 | 4 125 | 4 286 | 3.9 | -1.7 | 115 | 91 | -98 | 1 545 | 8.0 | 2.74 | 6.1 | 22.5 |
| Owyhee | 12.5 | 8.3 | 5.9 | 48.9 | 10 644 | 11 526 | 8.3 | -0.8 | 316 | 202 | -203 | 4 076 | 9.9 | 2.79 | 9.6 | 23.0 |
| Payette | 11.6 | 9.3 | 6.7 | 50.6 | 20 578 | 22 623 | 9.9 | 0.1 | 692 | 457 | -213 | 8 262 | 12.1 | 2.73 | 10.4 | 22.1 |
| Power | 12.0 | 7.4 | 5.0 | 48.4 | 7 538 | 7 817 | 3.7 | -0.5 | 288 | 142 | -192 | 2 641 | 3.2 | 2.94 | 10.1 | 19.8 |
| Shoshone | 16.6 | 11.6 | 8.5 | 49.8 | 13 771 | 12 765 | -7.3 | -0.5 | 271 | 405 | 81 | 5 605 | -5.1 | 2.25 | 8.7 | 31.3 |
| Teton | 10.3 | 4.3 | 2.7 | 47.4 | 5 999 | 10 170 | 69.5 | -1.2 | 378 | 87 | -420 | 3 651 | 75.7 | 2.78 | 5.9 | 21.9 |
| Twin Falls | 11.5 | 7.5 | 6.4 | 50.7 | 64 284 | 77 230 | 20.1 | 1.8 | 2 682 | 1 635 | 343 | 28 760 | 20.6 | 2.65 | 10.5 | 24.3 |
| Valley | 20.3 | 12.1 | 5.7 | 48.5 | 7 651 | 9 862 | 28.9 | -3.2 | 205 | 161 | -377 | 4 393 | 36.9 | 2.23 | 6.0 | 27.9 |
| Washington | 14.7 | 11.7 | 9.5 | 50.8 | 9 977 | 10 198 | 2.2 | -1.0 | 226 | 215 | -109 | 4 034 | 7.2 | 2.50 | 9.7 | 25.8 |
| **ILLINOIS** | 11.9 | 6.8 | 6.0 | 50.9 | 12 419 293 | 12 830 632 | 3.3 | 0.3 | 369 642 | 228 958 | -95 069 | 4 836 972 | 5.3 | 2.59 | 12.9 | 27.8 |
| Adams | 13.1 | 8.4 | 9.1 | 51.4 | 68 277 | 67 103 | -1.7 | 0.1 | 1 777 | 1 734 | 63 | 27 375 | 1.9 | 2.37 | 10.7 | 30.1 |
| Alexander | 14.2 | 9.3 | 8.1 | 49.2 | 9 590 | 8 238 | -14.1 | -5.9 | 222 | 223 | -498 | 3 329 | -12.6 | 2.31 | 18.5 | 33.6 |
| Bond | 13.1 | 7.6 | 7.3 | 47.7 | 17 633 | 17 768 | 0.8 | -0.7 | 438 | 398 | -162 | 6 427 | 4.4 | 2.44 | 9.1 | 26.8 |
| Boone | 11.4 | 7.2 | 5.0 | 50.1 | 41 786 | 54 165 | 29.6 | -0.4 | 1 366 | 734 | -856 | 18 505 | 26.8 | 2.91 | 10.2 | 18.9 |
| Brown | 10.5 | 6.3 | 5.9 | 35.9 | 6 950 | 6 937 | -0.2 | -0.3 | 120 | 146 | 7 | 2 099 | -0.4 | 2.30 | 8.6 | 32.2 |
| Bureau | 14.1 | 9.2 | 9.2 | 51.1 | 35 503 | 34 978 | -1.5 | -1.9 | 793 | 856 | -601 | 14 262 | 0.6 | 2.42 | 9.2 | 28.0 |
| Calhoun | 14.3 | 11.4 | 9.2 | 50.3 | 5 084 | 5 089 | 0.1 | -1.5 | 118 | 130 | -72 | 2 085 | 1.9 | 2.40 | 7.0 | 27.3 |
| Carroll | 16.1 | 11.5 | 10.2 | 50.0 | 16 674 | 15 387 | -7.7 | -2.4 | 289 | 436 | -222 | 6 622 | -2.5 | 2.29 | 8.2 | 29.8 |
| Cass | 12.5 | 7.9 | 7.6 | 49.7 | 13 695 | 13 642 | -0.4 | -2.2 | 363 | 333 | -333 | 5 270 | -1.4 | 2.55 | 10.9 | 26.5 |
| Champaign | 9.9 | 5.3 | 4.9 | 50.1 | 179 669 | 201 081 | 11.9 | 1.1 | 5 242 | 2 666 | -343 | 80 665 | 14.3 | 2.29 | 9.9 | 33.2 |
| Christian | 13.1 | 8.9 | 8.8 | 49.3 | 35 372 | 34 800 | -1.6 | -0.5 | 856 | 902 | -105 | 14 055 | 1.0 | 2.36 | 10.3 | 29.9 |
| Clark | 13.4 | 9.5 | 8.4 | 51.3 | 17 008 | 16 335 | -4.0 | -0.8 | 371 | 491 | 2 | 6 782 | -2.7 | 2.38 | 9.7 | 27.7 |
| Clay | 14.2 | 8.8 | 8.7 | 50.8 | 14 560 | 13 815 | -5.1 | -0.4 | 390 | 425 | -8 | 5 697 | -2.4 | 2.37 | 9.4 | 28.9 |
| Clinton | 12.1 | 7.3 | 7.2 | 48.5 | 35 535 | 37 762 | 6.3 | 0.8 | 901 | 772 | 114 | 14 005 | 9.8 | 2.55 | 8.7 | 25.1 |
| Coles | 11.1 | 7.0 | 7.1 | 51.9 | 53 196 | 53 873 | 1.3 | -0.4 | 1 156 | 1 105 | -257 | 21 463 | 2.0 | 2.30 | 9.9 | 31.4 |
| Cook | 11.4 | 6.4 | 5.7 | 51.5 | 5 376 741 | 5 194 675 | -3.4 | 0.7 | 163 994 | 89 127 | -37 510 | 1 966 356 | -0.4 | 2.60 | 15.6 | 31.0 |
| Crawford | 13.4 | 8.6 | 8.3 | 48.2 | 20 452 | 19 817 | -3.1 | -1.1 | 460 | 551 | -113 | 7 763 | -1.0 | 2.36 | 9.4 | 29.1 |
| Cumberland | 13.6 | 8.8 | 8.1 | 50.1 | 11 253 | 11 048 | -1.8 | -0.7 | 281 | 259 | -102 | 4 377 | 0.2 | 2.50 | 8.6 | 24.3 |
| DeKalb | 9.7 | 5.3 | 4.8 | 50.2 | 88 969 | 105 160 | 18.2 | -0.4 | 2 846 | 1 533 | -1 781 | 38 484 | 21.5 | 2.56 | 10.2 | 25.8 |
| De Witt | 13.7 | 9.3 | 7.8 | 50.4 | 16 798 | 16 561 | -1.4 | -0.8 | 402 | 482 | -48 | 6 811 | 0.6 | 2.39 | 10.0 | 27.5 |
| Douglas | 12.7 | 8.0 | 8.0 | 50.8 | 19 922 | 19 980 | 0.3 | -0.6 | 575 | 416 | -276 | 7 720 | 1.9 | 2.57 | 8.5 | 26.1 |
| DuPage | 12.9 | 6.6 | 5.4 | 51.0 | 904 161 | 916 924 | 1.4 | 1.2 | 23 781 | 12 982 | 675 | 337 132 | 3.5 | 2.68 | 9.5 | 24.3 |
| Edgar | 14.4 | 9.8 | 8.9 | 51.5 | 19 704 | 18 576 | -5.7 | -2.1 | 438 | 538 | -283 | 7 839 | -0.4 | 2.33 | 10.7 | 29.5 |
| Edwards | 14.8 | 9.1 | 8.7 | 50.7 | 6 971 | 6 721 | -3.6 | -0.6 | 148 | 171 | -15 | 2 840 | -2.2 | 2.35 | 8.3 | 28.5 |
| Effingham | 12.7 | 7.8 | 7.4 | 50.2 | 34 264 | 34 242 | -0.1 | 0.3 | 1 030 | 752 | -158 | 13 515 | 4.0 | 2.50 | 9.5 | 26.9 |
| Fayette | 12.5 | 8.4 | 7.9 | 47.4 | 21 802 | 22 140 | 1.6 | -0.6 | 520 | 482 | -147 | 8 311 | 2.0 | 2.45 | 9.7 | 27.2 |
| Ford | 12.8 | 8.7 | 10.2 | 51.0 | 14 241 | 14 081 | -1.1 | -0.5 | 334 | 460 | 41 | 5 676 | 0.7 | 2.41 | 9.8 | 29.2 |
| Franklin | 13.7 | 9.9 | 8.4 | 51.1 | 39 018 | 39 561 | 1.4 | -0.4 | 1 025 | 1 188 | 27 | 16 617 | 1.3 | 2.35 | 11.2 | 30.0 |
| Fulton | 13.7 | 9.3 | 8.9 | 48.2 | 38 250 | 37 069 | -3.1 | -1.1 | 817 | 1 046 | -170 | 14 536 | -2.3 | 2.37 | 10.2 | 28.1 |
| Gallatin | 14.8 | 11.9 | 8.9 | 51.1 | 6 445 | 5 589 | -13.3 | -2.8 | 129 | 207 | -79 | 2 403 | -11.8 | 2.32 | 10.0 | 31.1 |
| Greene | 13.2 | 9.0 | 8.3 | 49.5 | 14 761 | 13 886 | -5.9 | -2.2 | 310 | 381 | -241 | 5 570 | -3.2 | 2.44 | 9.4 | 27.8 |
| Grundy | 11.5 | 6.4 | 4.9 | 50.2 | 37 535 | 50 063 | 33.4 | 0.4 | 1 497 | 858 | -422 | 18 546 | 29.8 | 2.69 | 9.7 | 22.5 |
| Hamilton | 13.8 | 10.3 | 9.7 | 51.2 | 8 621 | 8 457 | -1.9 | -1.0 | 207 | 274 | -13 | 3 489 | 0.8 | 2.39 | 9.2 | 28.1 |
| Hancock | 15.1 | 10.5 | 9.7 | 50.8 | 20 121 | 19 104 | -5.1 | -1.1 | 433 | 456 | -192 | 8 040 | -0.4 | 2.35 | 8.3 | 28.2 |

1. No spouse present.

| STATE County | Persons in group quarters, 2010 | Daytime population, 2007–2011 Number | Employment/ residence ratio | Births, 2011 Total | Rate[1] | Deaths, 2011 Number | Rate[1] | Persons under 65 with no health insurance, 2010 Number | Percent | Medicare, 2012 Eligible for Medicare | Enrolled in Medicare Advantage | Enrolled in a Medicare prescription drug plan | Serious crimes known to police,[2] 2011 Total Number | Rate[3] |
|---|---|---|---|---|---|---|---|---|---|---|---|---|---|---|
| | 32 | 33 | 34 | 35 | 36 | 37 | 38 | 39 | 40 | 41 | 42 | 43 | 44 | 45 |
| **IDAHO—Cont'd** | | | | | | | | | | | | | | |
| Caribou | 79 | 7 403 | 1.17 | 96 | 14.0 | 73 | 10.7 | 1 119 | 19.3 | 1 218 | 200 | 510 | 51 | 724 |
| Cassia | 286 | 23 525 | 1.12 | 416 | 17.9 | 192 | 8.3 | 4 860 | 24.7 | 3 588 | 572 | 1 724 | 350 | 1 508 |
| Clark | 2 | 923 | 1.18 | 11 | 11.6 | 1 | 1.1 | 271 | 32.1 | 127 | 23 | 55 | 12 | 1 208 |
| Clearwater | 607 | 8 871 | 1.04 | 63 | 7.2 | 101 | 11.6 | 1 317 | 21.2 | 2 511 | 335 | 1 287 | 187 | 2 111 |
| Custer | 21 | 4 394 | 1.04 | 32 | 7.4 | 32 | 7.4 | 701 | 19.8 | 962 | 111 | 414 | 29 | 657 |
| Elmore | 632 | 26 087 | 0.95 | 517 | 19.6 | 176 | 6.7 | 5 119 | 21.7 | 3 394 | 454 | 1 140 | 374 | 1 368 |
| Franklin | 102 | 11 211 | 0.72 | 211 | 16.4 | 89 | 6.9 | 2 552 | 23.1 | 1 882 | 44 | 1 129 | 139 | 1 075 |
| Fremont | 460 | 11 206 | 0.66 | 205 | 15.6 | 97 | 7.4 | 3 005 | 27.7 | 2 153 | 444 | 941 | 113 | 844 |
| Gem | 151 | 13 791 | 0.56 | 177 | 10.6 | 185 | 11.1 | 3 061 | 22.9 | 3 836 | 1 485 | 1 120 | 183 | 1 083 |
| Gooding | 52 | 14 821 | 0.93 | 252 | 16.3 | 111 | 7.2 | 3 752 | 29.0 | 2 600 | 416 | 1 181 | 187 | 1 196 |
| Idaho | 524 | 15 414 | 0.89 | 163 | 9.9 | 163 | 9.9 | 2 982 | 24.2 | 3 543 | 457 | 2 015 | 190 | 1 155 |
| Jefferson | 111 | 21 408 | 0.64 | 521 | 19.8 | 134 | 5.1 | 5 064 | 21.5 | 3 200 | 686 | 1 378 | 258 | 976 |
| Jerome | 106 | 21 126 | 0.93 | 430 | 19.0 | 153 | 6.7 | 5 577 | 28.4 | 3 090 | 869 | 1 274 | 485 | 2 144 |
| Kootenai | 1 488 | 131 718 | 0.91 | 1 715 | 12.2 | 1 148 | 8.1 | 23 704 | 20.1 | 27 313 | 8 153 | 9 612 | 4 354 | 3 109 |
| Latah | 3 086 | 34 012 | 0.83 | 454 | 12.0 | 192 | 5.1 | 5 105 | 16.7 | 4 937 | 677 | 1 957 | 952 | 2 528 |
| Lemhi | 80 | 7 855 | 0.99 | 73 | 9.2 | 90 | 11.3 | 1 410 | 23.0 | 2 173 | 311 | 841 | 100 | 1 246 |
| Lewis | 74 | 3 938 | 1.11 | 37 | 9.7 | 44 | 11.5 | 652 | 22.0 | 1 730 | 240 | 926 | 57 | 1 476 |
| Lincoln | 37 | 4 504 | 0.73 | 80 | 15.4 | 23 | 4.4 | 1 331 | 29.0 | 977 | 134 | 438 | 17 | 323 |
| Madison | 1 036 | 37 392 | 1.03 | 1 029 | 27.2 | 127 | 3.4 | 5 538 | 16.2 | 2 455 | 908 | 853 | 314 | 827 |
| Minidoka | 82 | 18 526 | 0.86 | 312 | 15.5 | 179 | 8.9 | 4 268 | 25.2 | 3 094 | 700 | 1 395 | 348 | 1 715 |
| Nez Perce | 966 | 41 919 | 1.16 | 445 | 11.3 | 448 | 11.3 | 5 210 | 16.4 | 8 718 | 1 911 | 3 706 | 1 554 | 3 914 |
| Oneida | 50 | 3 891 | 0.80 | 59 | 14.0 | 38 | 9.0 | 725 | 20.4 | 848 | 126 | 415 | 29 | 669 |
| Owyhee | 160 | 10 221 | 0.72 | 146 | 12.8 | 93 | 8.1 | 3 174 | 32.7 | 1 887 | 649 | 604 | 213 | 1 828 |
| Payette | 94 | 19 933 | 0.71 | 318 | 14.1 | 195 | 8.6 | 4 434 | 23.4 | 4 437 | 1 544 | 1 501 | 549 | 2 400 |
| Power | 47 | 7 727 | 1.02 | 136 | 17.5 | 63 | 8.1 | 1 787 | 26.1 | 1 187 | 265 | 570 | 155 | 1 961 |
| Shoshone | 160 | 12 772 | 0.98 | 130 | 10.3 | 178 | 14.0 | 2 003 | 19.9 | 3 241 | 763 | 1 447 | 272 | 2 108 |
| Teton | 7 | 8 567 | 0.76 | 184 | 18.1 | 35 | 3.4 | 2 802 | 29.6 | 917 | 71 | 490 | 52 | 506 |
| Twin Falls | 1 072 | 77 029 | 1.03 | 1 226 | 15.7 | 739 | 9.5 | 15 610 | 23.8 | 13 203 | 3 098 | 5 770 | 2 124 | 2 720 |
| Valley | 66 | 10 406 | 1.11 | 94 | 9.8 | 63 | 6.5 | 1 950 | 24.2 | 1 913 | 387 | 709 | 259 | 2 598 |
| Washington | 119 | 9 634 | 0.87 | 111 | 10.8 | 86 | 8.4 | 2 106 | 26.3 | 2 418 | 731 | 920 | 77 | 747 |
| **ILLINOIS** | 301 773 | 12 785 110 | 1.00 | 167 000 | 13.0 | 100 651 | 7.8 | 1 717 178 | 15.6 | 1 952 653 | 202 992 | 969 398 | 401 272 | 3 118 |
| Adams | 2 287 | 70 462 | 1.11 | 783 | 11.7 | 784 | 11.7 | 6 583 | 12.1 | 13 732 | 525 | 7 979 | 1 767 | 2 670 |
| Alexander | 543 | 7 877 | 0.84 | 110 | 13.7 | 108 | 13.4 | 887 | 13.8 | 1 724 | 96 | 1 018 | 405 | 4 901 |
| Bond | 2 060 | 16 084 | 0.78 | 189 | 10.7 | 174 | 9.8 | 1 642 | 12.5 | 3 239 | 89 | 2 044 | 215 | 1 207 |
| Boone | 310 | 45 577 | 0.64 | 599 | 11.0 | 307 | 5.6 | 6 847 | 14.4 | 8 235 | 1 506 | 3 371 | 881 | 1 622 |
| Brown | 2 110 | 7 910 | 1.40 | 60 | 8.7 | 66 | 9.6 | 483 | 12.1 | 985 | 44 | 553 | 44 | 632 |
| Bureau | 456 | 31 523 | 0.79 | 365 | 10.5 | 380 | 11.0 | 3 962 | 13.9 | 7 165 | 619 | 3 936 | 521 | 1 553 |
| Calhoun | 90 | 3 933 | 0.47 | 54 | 10.7 | 61 | 12.1 | 589 | 14.5 | 1 214 | 33 | 749 | 69 | 1 669 |
| Carroll | 223 | 13 800 | 0.77 | 119 | 7.8 | 191 | 12.6 | 1 690 | 14.1 | 3 917 | 552 | 1 918 | 213 | 1 574 |
| Cass | 184 | 13 219 | 0.93 | 160 | 11.8 | 152 | 11.2 | 1 784 | 15.6 | 2 414 | 112 | 1 363 | 127 | 928 |
| Champaign | 16 129 | 210 070 | 1.11 | 2 373 | 11.8 | 1 182 | 5.9 | 24 988 | 15.0 | 24 395 | 4 662 | 7 430 | 6 411 | 3 247 |
| Christian | 1 610 | 31 117 | 0.75 | 395 | 11.3 | 397 | 11.4 | 3 502 | 12.8 | 7 279 | 313 | 4 212 | 417 | 1 280 |
| Clark | 221 | 14 385 | 0.74 | 155 | 9.6 | 226 | 14.0 | 1 770 | 13.3 | 3 452 | 366 | 1 987 | 144 | 1 158 |
| Clay | 305 | 13 557 | 0.95 | 175 | 12.7 | 205 | 14.9 | 1 559 | 13.8 | 3 036 | 60 | 1 985 | 200 | 1 443 |
| Clinton | 2 072 | 31 256 | 0.65 | 407 | 10.7 | 348 | 9.2 | 3 595 | 11.8 | 6 612 | 162 | 3 766 | 436 | 1 432 |
| Coles | 4 489 | 55 751 | 1.09 | 531 | 9.8 | 463 | 8.6 | 5 896 | 13.8 | 8 778 | 642 | 4 490 | 872 | 1 614 |
| Cook | 90 282 | 5 385 260 | 1.09 | 73 996 | 14.2 | 39 408 | 7.6 | 891 420 | 19.7 | 738 673 | 82 320 | 379 400 | 208 713 | 4 060 |
| Crawford | 1 495 | 20 260 | 1.05 | 198 | 10.0 | 253 | 12.7 | 1 907 | 12.6 | 4 032 | 112 | 2 009 | 320 | 1 610 |
| Cumberland | 117 | 8 555 | 0.51 | 126 | 11.4 | 109 | 9.8 | 1 254 | 13.7 | 2 150 | 140 | 1 199 | 96 | 1 017 |
| DeKalb | 6 673 | 95 006 | 0.81 | 1 303 | 12.4 | 670 | 6.4 | 12 093 | 13.7 | 12 819 | 565 | 6 292 | 2 773 | 2 757 |
| De Witt | 249 | 14 192 | 0.69 | 182 | 11.0 | 228 | 13.8 | 1 561 | 11.4 | 3 260 | 428 | 1 544 | NA | NA |
| Douglas | 168 | 18 774 | 0.87 | 264 | 13.3 | 182 | 9.2 | 2 865 | 17.1 | 3 671 | 855 | 1 484 | 195 | 1 173 |
| DuPage | 12 140 | 1 002 045 | 1.19 | 10 583 | 11.5 | 5 670 | 6.1 | 88 206 | 11.0 | 128 613 | 7 774 | 65 574 | 15 738 | 1 711 |
| Edgar | 283 | 17 601 | 0.87 | 193 | 10.5 | 239 | 13.0 | 2 004 | 13.4 | 4 019 | 243 | 2 379 | 274 | 1 471 |
| Edwards | 52 | 6 647 | 0.98 | 65 | 9.8 | 76 | 11.5 | 720 | 13.0 | 1 445 | 30 | 931 | 55 | 1 078 |
| Effingham | 440 | 38 422 | 1.25 | 464 | 13.5 | 326 | 9.5 | 3 467 | 12.0 | 6 323 | 138 | 3 733 | 689 | 2 006 |
| Fayette | 1 784 | 20 223 | 0.81 | 225 | 10.2 | 212 | 9.6 | 2 413 | 14.2 | 4 348 | 75 | 2 567 | 267 | 1 285 |
| Ford | 410 | 12 615 | 0.78 | 149 | 10.7 | 201 | 14.4 | 1 412 | 12.5 | 2 818 | 286 | 1 484 | 297 | 2 234 |
| Franklin | 517 | 34 924 | 0.70 | 462 | 11.7 | 527 | 13.3 | 4 643 | 14.5 | 9 198 | 874 | 4 844 | 1 090 | 3 249 |
| Fulton | 2 683 | 32 248 | 0.68 | 370 | 10.0 | 471 | 12.7 | 3 818 | 13.6 | 7 747 | 1 480 | 3 888 | 610 | 1 944 |
| Gallatin | 25 | 5 338 | 0.85 | 57 | 10.3 | 86 | 15.6 | 679 | 15.3 | 1 419 | 56 | 910 | NA | NA |
| Greene | 284 | 11 351 | 0.58 | 138 | 10.0 | 173 | 12.5 | 1 558 | 13.8 | 2 922 | 66 | 1 856 | 185 | 1 528 |
| Grundy | 254 | 43 648 | 0.75 | 690 | 13.8 | 375 | 7.5 | 4 914 | 11.1 | 7 083 | 193 | 3 358 | 1 020 | 2 031 |
| Hamilton | 117 | 7 191 | 0.64 | 88 | 10.4 | 128 | 15.2 | 956 | 14.1 | 1 889 | 96 | 1 133 | NA | NA |
| Hancock | 223 | 15 599 | 0.61 | 189 | 9.9 | 212 | 11.1 | 2 141 | 14.1 | 4 221 | 238 | 2 496 | NA | NA |

1. Per 1,000 estimated resident population.  2. Data for serious crimes have not been adjusted for underreporting; this may affect comparability between geographic areas and over time.  3. Per 100,000 population estimated by the FBI.

# Table B. States and Counties — Crime, Education, Money Income, and Poverty

| STATE County | Serious crimes known to police, 2011 (cont.)[1] Rate[2] Violent | Property | School enrollment and attainment, 2007–2011 Enrollment[3] Total | Per-cent private | Attainment[4] (percent) High school grad-uate or less | Bach-elor's degree or more | Local government expenditures,[5] 2009–2010 Total current expendi-tures (mil dol) | Current expendi-tures per student (dollars) | Per capita income[6] (dollars) | Households Median income Dollars | Percent change, 2000 to 2007–2011 (constant 2011 dollars) | Percent with income of $200,000 or more | Median house-hold income (dollars) | All per-sons | Children under 18 years | Children 5 to 17 years in families |
|---|---|---|---|---|---|---|---|---|---|---|---|---|---|---|---|---|
| | 46 | 47 | 48 | 49 | 50 | 51 | 52 | 53 | 54 | 55 | 56 | 57 | 58 | 59 | 60 | 61 |
| **IDAHO—Cont'd** | | | | | | | | | | | | | | | | |
| Caribou | 99 | 625 | 1 643 | 10.6 | 46.0 | 18.3 | 12.4 | 8 576 | 22 014 | 49 740 | -2.0 | 0.8 | 49 665 | 12.2 | 16.9 | 15.3 |
| Cassia | 142 | 1 366 | 6 518 | 7.8 | 48.2 | 15.8 | 34.0 | 6 737 | 17 651 | 39 551 | -12.1 | 1.7 | 41 393 | 16.7 | 24.1 | 21.7 |
| Clark | 0 | 1 208 | 148 | 0.0 | 65.2 | 7.1 | 2.4 | 11 955 | 19 165 | 39 792 | -6.7 | 0.0 | 40 581 | 18.1 | 27.9 | 24.1 |
| Clearwater | 147 | 1 964 | 1 534 | 10.9 | 54.2 | 14.2 | 11.1 | 9 736 | 20 238 | 42 043 | -2.9 | 1.3 | 38 086 | 17.0 | 28.2 | 24.4 |
| Custer | 68 | 589 | 803 | 5.9 | 51.7 | 22.0 | 6.2 | 9 907 | 23 579 | 43 445 | 0.0 | 0.7 | 44 234 | 13.8 | 20.4 | 17.9 |
| Elmore | 209 | 1 160 | 7 340 | 10.1 | 43.1 | 16.2 | 33.2 | 6 813 | 20 435 | 43 691 | -8.2 | 1.2 | 43 120 | 12.9 | 21.6 | 20.9 |
| Franklin | 31 | 1 044 | 3 595 | 8.0 | 50.3 | 18.0 | 16.7 | 5 481 | 18 722 | 46 344 | -4.8 | 1.7 | 46 348 | 11.1 | 17.1 | 14.9 |
| Fremont | 67 | 777 | 3 324 | 9.8 | 43.5 | 18.6 | 15.7 | 6 723 | 18 709 | 42 178 | -6.5 | 1.6 | 41 411 | 16.8 | 26.2 | 23.8 |
| | | | | | | | | | | | | | | | | |
| Gem | 160 | 923 | 4 150 | 10.8 | 49.4 | 12.9 | 17.2 | 6 521 | 20 660 | 44 442 | -4.5 | 0.7 | 40 541 | 17.7 | 27.4 | 24.2 |
| Gooding | 154 | 1 043 | 3 774 | 8.8 | 57.3 | 12.1 | 22.3 | 7 328 | 18 339 | 40 854 | -5.1 | 1.7 | 39 670 | 18.5 | 27.4 | 25.3 |
| Idaho | 103 | 1 052 | 3 166 | 13.0 | 55.5 | 13.9 | 18.4 | 10 846 | 19 299 | 36 706 | -7.9 | 0.9 | 39 184 | 16.9 | 26.3 | 23.6 |
| Jefferson | 98 | 878 | 7 491 | 12.1 | 41.9 | 19.8 | 36.6 | 6 105 | 19 648 | 52 799 | 3.6 | 1.2 | 47 827 | 14.3 | 19.4 | 17.7 |
| Jerome | 186 | 1 958 | 5 681 | 6.5 | 58.0 | 12.4 | 26.8 | 6 290 | 17 415 | 39 232 | -16.3 | 0.8 | 39 454 | 18.0 | 27.2 | 26.6 |
| Kootenai | 301 | 2 809 | 33 981 | 14.1 | 37.4 | 23.1 | 133.0 | 6 295 | 24 766 | 48 075 | -5.7 | 2.3 | 47 026 | 16.1 | 19.8 | 17.3 |
| Latah | 96 | 2 433 | 15 101 | 8.7 | 28.3 | 43.7 | 42.5 | 8 451 | 21 818 | 39 578 | -9.9 | 1.4 | 42 350 | 18.7 | 17.0 | 15.7 |
| Lemhi | 212 | 1 034 | 1 415 | 16.3 | 39.7 | 21.2 | 8.3 | 8 155 | 24 019 | 40 270 | -1.2 | 2.1 | 36 319 | 18.9 | 29.4 | 26.6 |
| Lewis | 181 | 1 294 | 812 | 9.9 | 44.8 | 15.2 | 9.3 | 10 900 | 18 865 | 35 344 | -16.7 | 0.4 | 40 149 | 20.2 | 28.4 | 25.4 |
| | | | | | | | | | | | | | | | | |
| Lincoln | 114 | 209 | 1 347 | 5.6 | 58.9 | 10.8 | 8.6 | 8 012 | 18 147 | 45 077 | 2.8 | 0.7 | 40 460 | 16.1 | 24.8 | 22.4 |
| Madison | 71 | 756 | 19 856 | 59.2 | 22.3 | 30.9 | 37.2 | 5 966 | 14 314 | 33 791 | -23.2 | 1.5 | 33 343 | 38.5 | 25.9 | 25.8 |
| Minidoka | 138 | 1 577 | 5 174 | 7.7 | 59.6 | 10.0 | 28.4 | 6 905 | 19 537 | 43 194 | -0.1 | 2.5 | 40 779 | 17.4 | 25.1 | 22.6 |
| Nez Perce | 136 | 3 778 | 9 144 | 8.5 | 45.2 | 19.7 | 50.9 | 9 152 | 24 580 | 44 540 | -9.1 | 1.5 | 43 662 | 12.9 | 19.0 | 16.4 |
| Oneida | 0 | 669 | 1 118 | 4.1 | 42.4 | 14.1 | 6.1 | 6 642 | 18 902 | 44 435 | -4.1 | 0.4 | 43 519 | 14.7 | 19.7 | 17.2 |
| Owyhee | 154 | 1 673 | 2 880 | 6.9 | 61.4 | 8.9 | 19.0 | 7 704 | 16 665 | 32 169 | -15.9 | 2.3 | 33 518 | 25.1 | 36.3 | 34.6 |
| Payette | 254 | 2 147 | 6 079 | 10.4 | 52.2 | 14.6 | 27.1 | 6 221 | 19 590 | 44 943 | 0.7 | 0.8 | 39 031 | 19.2 | 26.9 | 24.7 |
| Power | 164 | 1 797 | 2 030 | 4.8 | 52.8 | 15.9 | 14.6 | 8 871 | 18 293 | 41 797 | -3.9 | 0.4 | 39 288 | 17.2 | 26.3 | 24.8 |
| Shoshone | 263 | 1 844 | 2 381 | 6.4 | 52.8 | 12.9 | 19.9 | 10 256 | 19 717 | 37 934 | -1.5 | 0.2 | 36 811 | 19.7 | 28.6 | 24.6 |
| | | | | | | | | | | | | | | | | |
| Teton | 68 | 438 | 2 158 | 9.9 | 33.9 | 33.2 | 11.8 | 7 530 | 23 576 | 52 444 | -7.4 | 2.5 | 51 561 | 12.5 | 21.3 | 20.9 |
| Twin Falls | 224 | 2 496 | 19 289 | 10.3 | 45.3 | 17.3 | 90.8 | 6 823 | 20 619 | 43 146 | -7.4 | 1.6 | 41 942 | 17.7 | 22.9 | 21.7 |
| Valley | 311 | 2 287 | 1 917 | 22.7 | 34.1 | 36.8 | 14.5 | 11 812 | 27 678 | 52 675 | 5.7 | 2.8 | 46 210 | 12.0 | 21.2 | 19.8 |
| Washington | 145 | 601 | 2 462 | 9.9 | 48.7 | 17.8 | 13.9 | 7 393 | 20 896 | 37 878 | -8.4 | 3.0 | 35 232 | 18.8 | 28.0 | 22.9 |
| | | | | | | | | | | | | | | | | |
| **ILLINOIS** | 429 | 2 689 | 3 510 236 | 19.1 | 41.0 | 30.7 | 24 409.2 | 11 597 | 29 376 | 56 576 | -10.1 | 5.0 | 53 271 | 14.9 | 21.3 | 19.9 |
| | | | | | | | | | | | | | | | | |
| Adams | 329 | 2 341 | 16 452 | 21.8 | 48.5 | 21.2 | 98.7 | 9 852 | 24 798 | 45 792 | -2.5 | 2.2 | 43 293 | 15.9 | 23.3 | 20.5 |
| Alexander | 1 440 | 3 461 | 2 122 | 10.9 | 61.3 | 7.9 | 17.0 | 14 199 | 14 617 | 27 727 | -21.1 | 0.4 | 28 499 | 31.3 | 48.2 | 47.8 |
| Bond | 34 | 1 173 | 5 219 | 26.1 | 45.8 | 22.8 | 21.2 | 8 418 | 24 166 | 50 672 | -0.4 | 1.7 | 44 945 | 14.3 | 19.0 | 17.4 |
| Boone | 120 | 1 502 | 14 922 | 16.0 | 52.1 | 19.8 | 107.5 | 9 922 | 26 323 | 61 613 | -12.9 | 5.3 | 57 708 | 10.3 | 14.7 | 13.0 |
| Brown | 101 | 532 | 1 398 | 4.2 | 56.8 | 10.7 | 7.3 | 9 050 | 19 704 | 42 014 | -12.2 | 0.9 | 46 160 | 15.3 | 14.4 | 13.5 |
| Bureau | 116 | 1 436 | 8 081 | 10.4 | 52.3 | 16.3 | 59.1 | 10 317 | 25 344 | 48 046 | -11.6 | 1.7 | 48 474 | 10.7 | 17.1 | 15.1 |
| Calhoun | 314 | 1 355 | 1 085 | 14.3 | 56.3 | 13.9 | 6.9 | 9 673 | 24 643 | 48 958 | 5.5 | 2.2 | 47 218 | 12.5 | 17.8 | 16.3 |
| Carroll | 59 | 1 515 | 3 244 | 7.8 | 53.0 | 16.2 | 27.2 | 10 296 | 26 196 | 45 433 | -9.4 | 1.7 | 42 996 | 15.0 | 24.4 | 20.4 |
| | | | | | | | | | | | | | | | | |
| Cass | 88 | 840 | 3 340 | 6.7 | 61.1 | 13.1 | 21.3 | 8 773 | 19 975 | 41 139 | -13.5 | 0.9 | 40 065 | 14.8 | 24.0 | 21.6 |
| Champaign | 607 | 2 640 | 80 819 | 6.8 | 30.2 | 42.1 | 259.7 | 10 948 | 25 226 | 44 462 | -12.8 | 3.3 | 42 847 | 23.4 | 21.4 | 20.0 |
| Christian | 135 | 1 145 | 7 911 | 9.8 | 56.4 | 12.8 | 65.4 | 10 216 | 23 125 | 43 964 | -10.9 | 1.7 | 46 401 | 13.4 | 20.1 | 18.6 |
| Clark | 330 | 828 | 4 129 | 5.5 | 49.4 | 17.4 | 25.7 | 9 050 | 24 338 | 47 933 | -1.3 | 2.4 | 48 940 | 12.4 | 19.8 | 17.2 |
| Clay | 72 | 1 371 | 2 991 | 2.1 | 57.1 | 13.6 | 21.4 | 8 637 | 21 577 | 38 905 | -5.8 | 1.0 | 38 445 | 14.9 | 22.6 | 21.6 |
| Clinton | 223 | 1 209 | 9 176 | 16.4 | 43.4 | 19.5 | 45.8 | 8 407 | 26 380 | 57 246 | -5.0 | 2.9 | 59 711 | 9.1 | 12.8 | 11.2 |
| Coles | 241 | 1 373 | 19 801 | 5.9 | 43.7 | 24.2 | 77.8 | 11 567 | 21 669 | 38 294 | -12.2 | 2.1 | 40 623 | 21.8 | 21.4 | 19.9 |
| Cook | 620 | 3 440 | 1 398 357 | 23.7 | 40.9 | 33.7 | 10 077.7 | 12 727 | 29 920 | 54 598 | -11.9 | 5.6 | 50 806 | 17.8 | 26.6 | 26.0 |
| Crawford | 277 | 1 333 | 4 433 | 7.8 | 49.6 | 14.8 | 29.9 | 9 681 | 23 387 | 43 923 | 0.0 | 1.9 | 46 307 | 15.1 | 22.3 | 19.3 |
| | | | | | | | | | | | | | | | | |
| Cumberland | 180 | 837 | 2 615 | 9.1 | 53.1 | 12.7 | 15.5 | 8 843 | 21 715 | 43 255 | -11.4 | 1.5 | 47 145 | 12.4 | 19.1 | 17.8 |
| DeKalb | 274 | 2 483 | 39 789 | 7.7 | 38.0 | 28.2 | 207.2 | 11 824 | 24 547 | 54 436 | -12.0 | 2.6 | 52 091 | 15.9 | 16.9 | 15.7 |
| De Witt | NA | NA | 3 768 | 5.3 | 52.5 | 17.0 | 26.9 | 9 136 | 25 914 | 48 750 | -12.5 | 2.0 | 56 147 | 11.6 | 18.1 | 15.1 |
| Douglas | 180 | 992 | 4 534 | 9.1 | 56.2 | 14.7 | 28.3 | 9 516 | 22 339 | 47 921 | -10.0 | 1.0 | 48 671 | 10.0 | 15.6 | 14.5 |
| DuPage | 94 | 1 617 | 257 833 | 23.8 | 28.0 | 45.6 | 2 055.1 | 12 775 | 38 405 | 77 598 | -15.3 | 9.6 | 74 122 | 7.8 | 11.0 | 9.9 |
| Edgar | 306 | 1 165 | 4 002 | 5.4 | 53.1 | 17.2 | 30.6 | 9 509 | 23 897 | 42 947 | -9.6 | 1.6 | 43 596 | 14.4 | 22.1 | 19.4 |
| Edwards | 137 | 941 | 1 581 | 9.7 | 45.7 | 12.5 | 8.7 | 8 788 | 20 907 | 39 071 | -9.0 | 0.9 | 41 239 | 12.0 | 17.2 | 15.1 |
| Effingham | 163 | 1 843 | 8 118 | 14.2 | 46.6 | 19.3 | 48.3 | 9 053 | 25 566 | 50 938 | -4.2 | 2.2 | 48 632 | 10.7 | 16.0 | 14.4 |
| Fayette | 96 | 1 189 | 5 111 | 8.7 | 58.7 | 13.7 | 32.9 | 9 174 | 22 419 | 43 081 | 0.1 | 1.3 | 40 247 | 18.7 | 27.6 | 24.4 |
| | | | | | | | | | | | | | | | | |
| Ford | 354 | 1 880 | 3 277 | 5.7 | 53.6 | 16.3 | 31.9 | 10 168 | 25 302 | 50 332 | -2.1 | 1.4 | 49 206 | 11.1 | 17.2 | 15.5 |
| Franklin | 227 | 3 023 | 9 051 | 5.1 | 48.3 | 12.8 | 66.2 | 9 962 | 19 668 | 36 383 | -5.2 | 0.3 | 36 610 | 18.6 | 28.4 | 26.6 |
| Fulton | 156 | 1 788 | 8 214 | 6.5 | 53.9 | 14.0 | 62.6 | 9 064 | 21 071 | 42 963 | -6.3 | 1.2 | 46 539 | 13.1 | 19.9 | 17.8 |
| Gallatin | NA | NA | 1 096 | 1.1 | 56.8 | 9.8 | 8.0 | 10 768 | 22 674 | 38 577 | 9.4 | 1.7 | 36 722 | 18.3 | 27.7 | 24.8 |
| Greene | 281 | 1 247 | 3 269 | 10.6 | 57.6 | 13.3 | 19.5 | 9 206 | 22 366 | 42 193 | -1.6 | 1.3 | 42 534 | 14.9 | 22.1 | 19.3 |
| Grundy | 110 | 1 922 | 13 462 | 9.0 | 45.0 | 18.1 | 130.1 | 10 273 | 28 159 | 64 592 | -7.5 | 2.5 | 63 685 | 7.1 | 9.5 | 8.6 |
| Hamilton | NA | NA | 1 838 | 3.3 | 53.5 | 13.0 | 12.0 | 9 215 | 22 471 | 39 000 | -5.3 | 1.1 | 41 446 | 15.5 | 25.0 | 22.8 |
| Hancock | NA | NA | 4 255 | 7.2 | 49.5 | 18.9 | 33.1 | 9 654 | 23 027 | 43 567 | -12.0 | 1.1 | 43 850 | 12.1 | 19.0 | 16.7 |

1. Data for serious crimes have not been adjusted for underreporting; this may affect comparability between geographic areas and over time.  2. Per 100,000 population estimated by the FBI.  3. All persons 3 years old and over enrolled in nursery school through college.  4. Persons 25 years old and over.  5. Elementary and secondary education expenditures.  6. Based on population estimated by the American Community Survey, 2007–2011.

| STATE County | Personal income, 2011 | | | | | | | | | | | | |
|---|---|---|---|---|---|---|---|---|---|---|---|---|---|
| | | | Per capita[1] | | | | | Transfer payments (mil dol) | | | | | |
| | | | | | | | | | Government payments to individuals | | | | |
| | Total (mil dol) | Percent change, 2010–2011 | Dollars | Rank | Wages and salaries[2] (mil dol) | Proprietors' income (mil dol) | Dividends, interest, and rent (mil dol) | Total | Total | Social Security | Medical payments | Income mainte-nance | Unemploy-ment insurance |
| | 62 | 63 | 64 | 65 | 66 | 67 | 68 | 69 | 70 | 71 | 72 | 73 | 74 |
| IDAHO—Cont'd | | | | | | | | | | | | | |
| Caribou | 232 | 10.4 | 33 809 | 1 547 | 199 | 28 | 36 | 43 | 42 | 18 | 15 | 4 | 2 |
| Cassia | 800 | 8.1 | 34 515 | 1 435 | 414 | 208 | 115 | 144 | 139 | 49 | 58 | 20 | 4 |
| Clark | 52 | 22.3 | 54 591 | 118 | 27 | 21 | 3 | 5 | 5 | 1 | 2 | 1 | 0 |
| Clearwater | 265 | 3.3 | 30 493 | 2 201 | 133 | 23 | 48 | 83 | 82 | 36 | 29 | 7 | 3 |
| Custer | 148 | 6.2 | 34 186 | 1 487 | 88 | 25 | 34 | 29 | 28 | 13 | 10 | 2 | 1 |
| Elmore | 927 | 1.9 | 35 173 | 1 343 | 628 | 65 | 118 | 155 | 150 | 44 | 52 | 22 | 6 |
| Franklin | 350 | 3.1 | 27 265 | 2 723 | 109 | 47 | 41 | 64 | 61 | 26 | 23 | 8 | 1 |
| Fremont | 322 | 4.9 | 24 545 | 3 004 | 121 | 14 | 62 | 77 | 74 | 29 | 27 | 10 | 3 |
| Gem | 448 | 1.1 | 26 895 | 2 778 | 121 | 29 | 73 | 133 | 130 | 52 | 47 | 14 | 6 |
| Gooding | 637 | 15.0 | 41 179 | 645 | 250 | 219 | 79 | 94 | 91 | 34 | 36 | 11 | 3 |
| Idaho | 458 | 3.0 | 27 827 | 2 635 | 200 | 51 | 104 | 116 | 112 | 47 | 40 | 11 | 6 |
| Jefferson | 726 | 8.5 | 27 612 | 2 669 | 218 | 130 | 76 | 129 | 123 | 46 | 48 | 15 | 6 |
| Jerome | 715 | 7.1 | 31 543 | 1 990 | 354 | 184 | 88 | 126 | 121 | 41 | 49 | 18 | 5 |
| Kootenai | 4 647 | 5.3 | 32 923 | 1 721 | 2 351 | 354 | 844 | 1 014 | 983 | 396 | 352 | 96 | 49 |
| Latah | 1 199 | 4.3 | 31 809 | 1 929 | 619 | 90 | 231 | 202 | 194 | 72 | 61 | 19 | 5 |
| Lemhi | 245 | 3.1 | 30 733 | 2 150 | 102 | 21 | 61 | 74 | 73 | 28 | 30 | 6 | 3 |
| Lewis | 167 | 3.8 | 43 570 | 463 | 59 | 33 | 26 | 57 | 56 | 24 | 24 | 5 | 0 |
| Lincoln | 158 | 9.4 | 30 533 | 2 191 | 66 | 51 | 16 | 31 | 30 | 12 | 10 | 3 | 2 |
| Madison | 726 | 5.9 | 19 184 | 3 107 | 491 | 65 | 107 | 176 | 168 | 35 | 43 | 20 | 3 |
| Minidoka | 635 | 12.8 | 31 486 | 2 005 | 289 | 135 | 89 | 125 | 120 | 41 | 51 | 18 | 4 |
| Nez Perce | 1 428 | 3.9 | 36 109 | 1 198 | 990 | 137 | 236 | 339 | 330 | 125 | 133 | 33 | 7 |
| Oneida | 118 | 4.6 | 28 032 | 2 613 | 38 | 24 | 16 | 28 | 27 | 11 | 12 | 3 | 0 |
| Owyhee | 361 | 7.8 | 31 541 | 1 992 | 102 | 97 | 51 | 67 | 65 | 26 | 25 | 9 | 0 |
| Payette | 653 | 5.6 | 28 869 | 2 472 | 276 | 55 | 100 | 159 | 154 | 61 | 53 | 25 | 5 |
| Power | 240 | 14.3 | 30 936 | 2 116 | 166 | 24 | 35 | 47 | 45 | 16 | 17 | 8 | 2 |
| Shoshone | 419 | 4.9 | 33 097 | 1 691 | 231 | 19 | 60 | 129 | 127 | 48 | 50 | 15 | 8 |
| Teton | 261 | 5.0 | 25 705 | 2 909 | 108 | 28 | 55 | 38 | 36 | 13 | 15 | 4 | 2 |
| Twin Falls | 2 507 | 6.2 | 32 134 | 1 853 | 1 342 | 397 | 403 | 545 | 528 | 183 | 199 | 63 | 21 |
| Valley | 346 | 3.8 | 35 942 | 1 219 | 155 | 36 | 102 | 66 | 64 | 28 | 21 | 5 | 5 |
| Washington | 283 | 4.5 | 27 605 | 2 670 | 109 | 20 | 52 | 82 | 80 | 32 | 28 | 12 | 2 |
| ILLINOIS | 562 662 | 4.3 | 43 721 | X | 377 568 | 48 260 | 91 355 | 87 461 | 84 617 | 28 203 | 34 361 | 11 030 | 5 490 |
| Adams | 2 575 | 4.5 | 38 345 | 929 | 1 644 | 179 | 521 | 505 | 490 | 190 | 179 | 54 | 21 |
| Alexander | 217 | 1.1 | 26 943 | 2 769 | 89 | 9 | 26 | 91 | 89 | 22 | 37 | 22 | 3 |
| Bond | 614 | 4.8 | 34 642 | 1 427 | 220 | 58 | 94 | 126 | 122 | 45 | 47 | 14 | 7 |
| Boone | 1 808 | 5.5 | 33 252 | 1 667 | 813 | 77 | 276 | 306 | 294 | 130 | 92 | 29 | 30 |
| Brown | 197 | 5.9 | 28 616 | 2 520 | 174 | 26 | 34 | 35 | 34 | 13 | 14 | 3 | 1 |
| Bureau | 1 303 | 5.5 | 37 663 | 1 008 | 587 | 141 | 230 | 255 | 248 | 105 | 92 | 22 | 17 |
| Calhoun | 170 | 5.2 | 33 613 | 1 584 | 31 | 15 | 29 | 42 | 41 | 17 | 16 | 3 | 2 |
| Carroll | 544 | 6.0 | 35 880 | 1 229 | 193 | 48 | 115 | 133 | 130 | 52 | 50 | 11 | 7 |
| Cass | 462 | 4.0 | 33 988 | 1 510 | 270 | 53 | 66 | 99 | 96 | 33 | 39 | 10 | 5 |
| Champaign | 7 223 | 2.8 | 35 815 | 1 248 | 5 297 | 486 | 1 481 | 968 | 923 | 303 | 300 | 140 | 73 |
| Christian | 1 345 | 9.9 | 38 569 | 902 | 593 | 187 | 195 | 288 | 281 | 107 | 119 | 27 | 14 |
| Clark | 573 | 5.3 | 35 428 | 1 308 | 195 | 75 | 97 | 127 | 124 | 48 | 49 | 12 | 8 |
| Clay | 454 | 3.3 | 33 079 | 1 695 | 229 | 60 | 72 | 126 | 123 | 41 | 58 | 12 | 6 |
| Clinton | 1 489 | 5.8 | 39 241 | 828 | 501 | 128 | 232 | 257 | 248 | 90 | 107 | 18 | 13 |
| Coles | 1 773 | 5.0 | 32 876 | 1 729 | 1 143 | 132 | 355 | 367 | 355 | 116 | 132 | 40 | 21 |
| Cook | 244 872 | 3.5 | 46 937 | 301 | 183 169 | 26 704 | 38 315 | 39 098 | 37 943 | 10 245 | 17 076 | 5 916 | 2 299 |
| Crawford | 754 | 5.6 | 37 989 | 974 | 525 | 77 | 122 | 145 | 140 | 58 | 52 | 14 | 7 |
| Cumberland | 398 | 7.2 | 35 900 | 1 225 | 104 | 54 | 56 | 79 | 76 | 30 | 29 | 8 | 5 |
| DeKalb | 3 311 | 5.8 | 31 612 | 1 973 | 1 931 | 224 | 547 | 557 | 534 | 188 | 174 | 54 | 46 |
| De Witt | 648 | 8.6 | 39 064 | 849 | 345 | 83 | 95 | 124 | 120 | 47 | 47 | 11 | 6 |
| Douglas | 786 | 8.9 | 39 610 | 794 | 410 | 151 | 133 | 127 | 123 | 52 | 44 | 11 | 7 |
| DuPage | 50 324 | 3.8 | 54 509 | 120 | 41 987 | 4 227 | 8 789 | 4 899 | 4 695 | 2 007 | 1 720 | 344 | 350 |
| Edgar | 646 | 6.3 | 35 098 | 1 358 | 295 | 102 | 97 | 152 | 147 | 56 | 58 | 17 | 9 |
| Edwards | 209 | 6.2 | 31 552 | 1 988 | 117 | 29 | 41 | 47 | 45 | 20 | 17 | 4 | 2 |
| Effingham | 1 299 | 4.8 | 37 882 | 988 | 912 | 116 | 291 | 229 | 221 | 88 | 89 | 21 | 11 |
| Fayette | 630 | 5.3 | 28 478 | 2 543 | 269 | 70 | 112 | 168 | 163 | 59 | 68 | 20 | 9 |
| Ford | 622 | 5.6 | 44 484 | 422 | 221 | 151 | 94 | 101 | 98 | 40 | 38 | 9 | 5 |
| Franklin | 1 175 | 3.2 | 29 656 | 2 350 | 420 | 61 | 175 | 377 | 368 | 130 | 145 | 50 | 18 |
| Fulton | 1 246 | 4.2 | 33 723 | 1 560 | 368 | 105 | 193 | 315 | 307 | 112 | 135 | 28 | 16 |
| Gallatin | 205 | 8.1 | 37 066 | 1 071 | 55 | 36 | 35 | 56 | 55 | 19 | 24 | 7 | 2 |
| Greene | 436 | 5.1 | 31 573 | 1 982 | 112 | 78 | 64 | 111 | 107 | 40 | 43 | 13 | 5 |
| Grundy | 1 746 | 5.1 | 34 829 | 1 398 | 1 144 | 136 | 269 | 283 | 272 | 113 | 97 | 20 | 28 |
| Hamilton | 292 | 7.1 | 34 674 | 1 423 | 72 | 49 | 49 | 75 | 73 | 25 | 33 | 7 | 3 |
| Hancock | 669 | 6.6 | 35 155 | 1 349 | 175 | 116 | 116 | 143 | 139 | 59 | 52 | 12 | 8 |

1. Based on the resident population estimated as of July 1 of the year shown.   2. Includes supplements to wages and salaries.

| STATE County | Earnings, 2011 Total (mil dol) | Farm | Goods-related[1] Total | Manu-facturing | Service-related and health Infor-mation and profes-sional and technical services | Retail trade | Finance, insur-ance, and real estate | Health care and social services | Govern-ment | Social Security beneficiaries, December 2011 Number | Rate[2] | Supple-mental Security Income recipients, December 2011 | Housing units, 2010 Total | Percent change, 2000–2010 |
|---|---|---|---|---|---|---|---|---|---|---|---|---|---|---|
| | 75 | 76 | 77 | 78 | 79 | 80 | 81 | 82 | 83 | 84 | 85 | 86 | 87 | 88 |
| **IDAHO—Cont'd** | | | | | | | | | | | | | | |
| Caribou | 227 | 9.6 | D | D | 2.5 | 3.5 | 2.3 | D | 13.5 | 1 365 | 199 | 66 | 3 226 | 1.2 |
| Cassia | 622 | 32.3 | 14.7 | 10.4 | D | 7.2 | 2.0 | D | 12.0 | 4 035 | 174 | 422 | 8 372 | 6.5 |
| Clark | 48 | 50.8 | D | D | D | D | 2.8 | D | 14.8 | 130 | 137 | 0 | 531 | 1.9 |
| Clearwater | 155 | 3.2 | D | 4.9 | 2.1 | 6.1 | 2.0 | D | 35.9 | 2 830 | 325 | 248 | 4 453 | 7.5 |
| Custer | 113 | 13.8 | D | 0.4 | 4.2 | 4.3 | 1.4 | 2.0 | 21.5 | 1 065 | 246 | 62 | 3 103 | 4.0 |
| Elmore | 692 | 8.3 | D | 2.7 | 1.8 | 4.2 | 1.4 | 2.8 | 67.3 | 3 815 | 145 | 439 | 12 162 | 15.5 |
| Franklin | 156 | 23.3 | D | 3.9 | 3.6 | 8.7 | 2.9 | D | 23.2 | 2 135 | 166 | 162 | 4 528 | 16.9 |
| Fremont | 135 | 1.6 | D | 1.8 | D | 6.5 | 3.3 | 5.1 | 39.8 | 2 355 | 179 | 178 | 8 531 | 23.8 |
| Gem | 150 | 8.6 | D | 5.0 | 2.9 | 7.3 | 3.1 | D | 26.3 | 4 245 | 255 | 419 | 7 099 | 20.6 |
| Gooding | 469 | 56.4 | D | 9.7 | D | 2.4 | 1.3 | D | 9.8 | 2 910 | 188 | 290 | 6 093 | 10.7 |
| Idaho | 251 | 6.3 | 19.2 | 8.7 | 3.3 | 8.3 | 4.0 | 8.9 | 28.3 | 4 005 | 244 | 353 | 8 744 | 16.0 |
| Jefferson | 348 | 28.5 | 20.0 | 11.3 | D | 4.7 | 2.6 | D | 15.3 | 3 715 | 141 | 282 | 8 722 | 38.7 |
| Jerome | 538 | 33.0 | 15.5 | 12.1 | D | 6.6 | 1.7 | 3.9 | 8.2 | 3 490 | 154 | 371 | 8 101 | 20.7 |
| Kootenai | 2 704 | 0.3 | 16.9 | 8.5 | 8.5 | 10.6 | 6.7 | 12.1 | 20.9 | 30 420 | 216 | 2 410 | 63 177 | 35.6 |
| Latah | 709 | 3.4 | D | 3.4 | 7.0 | 6.8 | 2.8 | 9.8 | 46.7 | 5 440 | 144 | 455 | 15 988 | 15.5 |
| Lemhi | 123 | 3.3 | D | 2.7 | 6.3 | 8.3 | 2.8 | 7.5 | 38.6 | 2 395 | 301 | 191 | 4 729 | 13.8 |
| Lewis | 91 | 31.0 | D | 11.9 | D | 6.5 | 1.9 | 4.7 | 21.2 | 1 995 | 522 | 245 | 1 880 | 4.7 |
| Lincoln | 117 | 49.8 | D | D | 1.0 | 2.1 | D | D | 20.7 | 1 075 | 207 | 67 | 1 976 | 19.7 |
| Madison | 557 | 0.1 | D | 5.4 | 7.7 | 8.2 | 3.7 | D | 16.9 | 2 745 | 72 | 212 | 11 280 | 47.8 |
| Minidoka | 424 | 32.8 | 20.4 | 16.0 | 2.9 | 3.5 | 1.5 | D | 14.5 | 3 460 | 172 | 369 | 7 665 | 2.2 |
| Nez Perce | 1 126 | 2.6 | 21.2 | 16.3 | 4.9 | 7.4 | 7.7 | 16.8 | 18.8 | 9 715 | 246 | 1 045 | 17 438 | 7.6 |
| Oneida | 62 | 36.4 | D | 1.0 | 1.6 | 4.9 | D | 2.7 | 26.8 | 945 | 224 | 66 | 1 906 | 8.6 |
| Owyhee | 199 | 54.0 | 8.8 | 3.9 | D | 3.2 | D | D | 15.2 | 2 205 | 193 | 285 | 4 781 | 7.4 |
| Payette | 331 | 9.6 | D | 15.2 | D | 4.1 | D | D | 14.1 | 5 080 | 225 | 588 | 8 945 | 12.5 |
| Power | 189 | 14.1 | 41.3 | 37.4 | D | D | D | 1.1 | 15.0 | 1 330 | 171 | 116 | 2 944 | 3.5 |
| Shoshone | 250 | -0.1 | 34.3 | 3.5 | 4.8 | 15.4 | 2.2 | 5.2 | 19.1 | 3 705 | 292 | 446 | 7 061 | 0.1 |
| Teton | 137 | 4.4 | 19.2 | 3.6 | D | 6.8 | 7.9 | 2.9 | 22.9 | 1 035 | 102 | 62 | 5 478 | 108.2 |
| Twin Falls | 1 739 | 14.5 | 13.3 | 9.2 | 6.4 | 8.9 | 4.5 | 15.4 | 13.1 | 14 665 | 188 | 1 644 | 31 072 | 21.4 |
| Valley | 191 | 0.7 | 11.0 | 0.9 | 5.9 | 10.3 | 9.4 | D | 30.1 | 2 135 | 222 | 106 | 11 789 | 45.8 |
| Washington | 128 | 10.8 | 17.4 | 13.5 | 6.5 | 6.8 | 3.4 | 7.5 | 26.4 | 2 700 | 263 | 258 | 4 529 | 9.4 |
| **ILLINOIS** | 425 828 | 1.4 | 16.4 | 11.5 | 13.3 | 5.2 | 10.8 | 10.2 | 14.7 | 2 065 432 | 160 | 276 258 | 5 296 715 | 8.4 |
| Adams | 1 823 | 4.0 | D | 17.9 | 4.4 | 8.0 | 6.5 | 17.3 | 13.5 | 14 825 | 221 | 1 354 | 29 842 | 1.6 |
| Alexander | 97 | 4.0 | D | 7.0 | 1.6 | 3.3 | 1.6 | D | 35.7 | 1 950 | 243 | 510 | 4 006 | -12.7 |
| Bond | 278 | 12.9 | 19.7 | 15.4 | 2.8 | 3.0 | 2.1 | D | 25.0 | 3 540 | 200 | 333 | 7 089 | 6.0 |
| Boone | 890 | 2.6 | D | 41.6 | 2.6 | 5.2 | 3.9 | 4.2 | 14.9 | 9 140 | 168 | 478 | 19 970 | 29.6 |
| Brown | 199 | 10.2 | D | 0.3 | D | D | D | D | 16.8 | 1 060 | 154 | 94 | 2 462 | 0.2 |
| Bureau | 728 | 11.7 | D | 13.4 | D | 4.9 | 4.3 | D | 16.2 | 7 745 | 224 | 360 | 15 720 | 2.5 |
| Calhoun | 46 | 21.6 | D | D | D | 7.9 | D | D | 25.7 | 1 305 | 259 | 88 | 2 835 | 5.7 |
| Carroll | 241 | 14.8 | D | 18.4 | D | 6.1 | 5.1 | D | 17.9 | 4 120 | 272 | 253 | 8 437 | 6.2 |
| Cass | 323 | 12.3 | 36.2 | 33.5 | D | 5.0 | 3.5 | D | 13.9 | 2 605 | 192 | 260 | 5 836 | 0.9 |
| Champaign | 5 783 | 3.4 | D | 7.3 | 8.4 | 5.0 | 4.9 | 12.8 | 38.4 | 24 920 | 124 | 2 907 | 87 569 | 16.3 |
| Christian | 780 | 18.0 | 29.2 | 23.3 | D | 5.8 | 3.0 | 9.7 | 12.1 | 8 140 | 233 | 700 | 15 563 | 3.8 |
| Clark | 271 | 16.4 | 33.5 | 23.1 | 2.8 | 6.5 | 3.0 | 5.6 | 15.5 | 3 795 | 235 | 300 | 7 772 | -0.6 |
| Clay | 290 | 10.8 | 35.6 | 30.6 | D | 4.9 | 3.5 | D | 17.5 | 3 400 | 248 | 359 | 6 404 | 0.2 |
| Clinton | 629 | 10.5 | D | 7.0 | D | 8.0 | 4.9 | 10.3 | 23.0 | 7 055 | 186 | 431 | 15 311 | 11.0 |
| Coles | 1 275 | 6.3 | 17.2 | 12.4 | D | 6.0 | 3.3 | 15.0 | 29.1 | 9 410 | 175 | 1 037 | 23 425 | 2.9 |
| Cook | 209 873 | 0.0 | 11.9 | 7.9 | 18.0 | 4.1 | 15.0 | 9.7 | 12.8 | 759 125 | 146 | 159 231 | 2 180 359 | 4.0 |
| Crawford | 602 | 5.2 | 50.6 | 39.6 | D | 4.2 | 2.7 | D | 17.2 | 4 460 | 225 | 313 | 8 661 | -1.4 |
| Cumberland | 158 | 20.7 | D | 13.7 | D | 10.3 | D | 8.9 | 15.4 | 2 430 | 219 | 198 | 4 874 | 0.0 |
| DeKalb | 2 155 | 3.8 | D | 11.8 | 3.7 | 7.1 | 3.8 | 12.1 | 33.5 | 13 650 | 130 | 769 | 41 079 | 24.5 |
| De Witt | 428 | 13.0 | 16.3 | 8.5 | D | 6.3 | 2.2 | D | 13.3 | 3 490 | 211 | 251 | 7 521 | 3.3 |
| Douglas | 562 | 17.3 | D | 40.5 | 1.3 | 5.4 | 2.5 | D | 8.7 | 3 980 | 201 | 231 | 8 390 | 4.8 |
| DuPage | 46 214 | 0.0 | 14.5 | 9.7 | 15.6 | 5.6 | 9.3 | 8.5 | 7.9 | 130 955 | 142 | 7 922 | 356 179 | 6.1 |
| Edgar | 397 | 19.4 | D | 21.4 | 2.7 | 4.9 | 6.7 | D | 16.8 | 4 425 | 241 | 445 | 8 803 | 2.2 |
| Edwards | 146 | 12.0 | D | D | D | 3.9 | D | 2.3 | 10.2 | 1 615 | 244 | 99 | 3 187 | -0.4 |
| Effingham | 1 028 | 3.9 | 24.8 | 18.2 | 3.5 | 9.3 | 3.5 | 18.3 | 11.1 | 6 945 | 203 | 472 | 14 570 | 4.4 |
| Fayette | 338 | 11.7 | 19.4 | 11.7 | 2.6 | 7.6 | 3.6 | D | 26.0 | 4 870 | 220 | 499 | 9 302 | 2.8 |
| Ford | 373 | 25.8 | D | 8.3 | 2.2 | 8.2 | 2.2 | D | 11.8 | 3 075 | 220 | 201 | 6 282 | 3.7 |
| Franklin | 481 | 2.7 | 20.1 | 12.5 | D | 9.8 | 3.3 | 10.6 | 25.8 | 10 320 | 260 | 1 399 | 18 525 | 2.3 |
| Fulton | 474 | 12.6 | D | 2.8 | 2.7 | 8.0 | 3.8 | D | 28.6 | 8 600 | 233 | 675 | 16 195 | -0.3 |
| Gallatin | 91 | 32.3 | D | D | D | 5.7 | D | D | 13.8 | 1 570 | 284 | 231 | 2 746 | -10.6 |
| Greene | 190 | 34.5 | D | 4.7 | 2.0 | 5.9 | D | D | 18.6 | 3 190 | 231 | 346 | 6 389 | 0.9 |
| Grundy | 1 280 | 4.6 | 24.0 | 10.8 | D | 5.5 | 2.6 | 8.7 | 11.4 | 7 940 | 158 | 372 | 19 996 | 33.0 |
| Hamilton | 121 | 30.0 | 15.1 | 2.9 | D | 4.3 | 3.6 | 4.4 | 24.0 | 2 095 | 249 | 195 | 4 104 | 3.1 |
| Hancock | 291 | 29.1 | D | 6.4 | 5.7 | 4.9 | 3.5 | D | 18.1 | 4 585 | 241 | 294 | 9 274 | 4.1 |

1. Includes mining, construction, and manufacturing.     2. Per 1,000 resident population enumerated in the 2010 census.

| STATE County | Housing units, 2007–2011 | | | | | | | | Civilian labor force, 2012 | | | | Civilian employment,[6] 2007–2011 | | |
|---|---|---|---|---|---|---|---|---|---|---|---|---|---|---|---|
| | Occupied units | | | | | | | | | | Unemployment | | | Percent | |
| | | | Owner-occupied | | | Renter-occupied | | | | | | | | | |
| | | | | Median owner cost as a percent of income | | | | | | | | | | | Con-struction, produc-tion, and mainte-nance occu-pations |
| | Total | Percent | Median value[1] | With a mort-gage | Without a mort-gage[2] | Median rent[3] | Median rent as a per-cent of income | Sub-stand-ard units[4] (percent) | Total | Percent change, 2011–2012 | Total | Rate[5] | Total | Manage-ment, business, science and arts | |
| | 89 | 90 | 91 | 92 | 93 | 94 | 95 | 96 | 97 | 98 | 99 | 100 | 101 | 102 | 103 |
| **IDAHO—Cont'd** | | | | | | | | | | | | | | | |
| Caribou | 2 637 | 82.3 | 115 700 | 20.1 | 9.9 | 488 | 20.4 | 2.5 | 4 018 | 1.6 | 233 | 5.8 | 3 014 | 30.8 | 36.2 |
| Cassia | 7 569 | 67.8 | 120 000 | 22.8 | 10.5 | 527 | 27.0 | 4.6 | 11 438 | 0.1 | 633 | 5.5 | 9 072 | 26.8 | 38.2 |
| Clark | 323 | 75.9 | 79 700 | 26.9 | 9.9 | 472 | 14.7 | 8.4 | 485 | -11.8 | 32 | 6.6 | 434 | 34.6 | 55.5 |
| Clearwater | 3 612 | 80.5 | 127 600 | 23.7 | 11.5 | 590 | 24.3 | 2.4 | 3 223 | -1.6 | 420 | 13.0 | 3 295 | 28.1 | 30.4 |
| Custer | 1 887 | 79.9 | 144 900 | 21.0 | 9.9 | 445 | 23.3 | 1.2 | 2 551 | 1.5 | 180 | 7.1 | 2 159 | 26.3 | 36.8 |
| Elmore | 9 532 | 67.6 | 144 400 | 23.9 | 9.9 | 691 | 24.8 | 3.3 | 10 848 | -2.8 | 814 | 7.5 | 10 200 | 26.0 | 32.2 |
| Franklin | 4 129 | 79.5 | 167 000 | 25.3 | 9.9 | 579 | 27.6 | 2.8 | 6 110 | 0.6 | 273 | 4.5 | 5 178 | 26.3 | 39.8 |
| Fremont | 4 514 | 82.5 | 139 800 | 22.8 | 11.5 | 614 | 24.0 | 4.6 | 6 162 | 2.5 | 403 | 6.5 | 5 733 | 27.5 | 33.5 |
| Gem | 6 491 | 75.9 | 160 400 | 23.5 | 10.4 | 673 | 32.6 | 2.5 | 7 064 | 1.5 | 645 | 9.1 | 6 958 | 30.1 | 25.6 |
| Gooding | 5 357 | 73.3 | 124 700 | 25.2 | 10.9 | 564 | 26.9 | 5.7 | 8 938 | 0.1 | 456 | 5.1 | 6 401 | 24.7 | 43.9 |
| Idaho | 6 710 | 77.0 | 142 300 | 28.1 | 9.9 | 547 | 25.0 | 3.7 | 7 394 | 0.5 | 691 | 9.3 | 6 222 | 27.0 | 31.6 |
| Jefferson | 8 155 | 81.5 | 158 200 | 24.2 | 9.9 | 640 | 22.6 | 3.9 | 11 976 | 0.9 | 719 | 6.0 | 10 904 | 31.2 | 30.9 |
| Jerome | 7 481 | 64.0 | 135 900 | 23.8 | 9.9 | 685 | 27.6 | 6.6 | 10 793 | 1.0 | 690 | 6.4 | 9 754 | 23.9 | 40.5 |
| Kootenai | 55 301 | 70.7 | 212 300 | 26.8 | 11.7 | 783 | 29.9 | 2.5 | 71 444 | -0.4 | 6 023 | 8.4 | 63 339 | 31.9 | 24.1 |
| Latah | 14 801 | 54.2 | 187 300 | 22.8 | 11.0 | 657 | 33.8 | 2.8 | 17 577 | 1.3 | 1 132 | 6.4 | 18 155 | 41.4 | 17.5 |
| Lemhi | 3 650 | 74.3 | 173 300 | 21.4 | 9.9 | 562 | 30.5 | 3.6 | 3 574 | -1.2 | 354 | 9.9 | 3 657 | 33.0 | 29.6 |
| Lewis | 1 639 | 71.5 | 117 400 | 21.9 | 11.6 | 570 | 30.0 | 1.8 | 1 748 | 1.9 | 101 | 5.8 | 1 459 | 29.9 | 26.7 |
| Lincoln | 1 746 | 76.1 | 121 600 | 20.5 | 9.9 | 569 | 25.7 | 4.6 | 2 603 | -1.5 | 238 | 9.1 | 2 287 | 18.8 | 41.6 |
| Madison | 9 943 | 50.5 | 174 900 | 24.0 | 9.9 | 629 | 41.1 | 7.9 | 17 284 | 3.0 | 948 | 5.5 | 16 664 | 32.9 | 19.7 |
| Minidoka | 6 728 | 75.1 | 106 400 | 20.9 | 9.9 | 545 | 23.4 | 6.4 | 10 434 | 0.2 | 634 | 6.1 | 8 656 | 22.7 | 43.7 |
| Nez Perce | 16 166 | 67.2 | 164 700 | 22.2 | 11.9 | 610 | 27.6 | 1.6 | 18 810 | -0.5 | 1 119 | 5.9 | 18 678 | 28.4 | 26.8 |
| Oneida | 1 560 | 82.5 | 122 500 | 24.4 | 12.4 | 559 | 30.6 | 1.2 | 2 356 | 2.3 | 97 | 4.1 | 1 727 | 37.5 | 32.7 |
| Owyhee | 3 873 | 68.1 | 135 100 | 26.1 | 11.7 | 543 | 25.0 | 6.7 | 4 538 | 3.4 | 213 | 4.7 | 4 408 | 28.4 | 40.2 |
| Payette | 8 361 | 76.0 | 135 500 | 25.4 | 11.3 | 641 | 30.4 | 2.2 | 10 642 | -1.9 | 849 | 8.0 | 9 346 | 26.7 | 31.3 |
| Power | 2 597 | 74.2 | 135 600 | 24.3 | 9.9 | 553 | 21.0 | 6.3 | 3 526 | -0.5 | 284 | 8.1 | 3 416 | 28.4 | 42.4 |
| Shoshone | 5 792 | 70.0 | 140 100 | 23.4 | 12.2 | 570 | 27.1 | 2.7 | 6 258 | -2.7 | 728 | 11.6 | 4 966 | 24.1 | 31.9 |
| Teton | 3 812 | 65.3 | 263 100 | 33.2 | 11.4 | 818 | 23.7 | 4.3 | 5 403 | 1.6 | 310 | 5.7 | 5 228 | 30.3 | 29.1 |
| Twin Falls | 27 940 | 67.8 | 150 900 | 23.9 | 9.9 | 664 | 26.8 | 3.7 | 39 260 | 1.0 | 2 574 | 6.6 | 34 317 | 29.3 | 28.9 |
| Valley | 4 019 | 77.2 | 278 500 | 26.1 | 9.9 | 688 | 26.4 | 4.2 | 4 597 | 0.9 | 526 | 11.4 | 4 825 | 30.6 | 30.4 |
| Washington | 4 041 | 75.8 | 145 900 | 27.1 | 9.9 | 553 | 30.9 | 2.9 | 4 784 | -0.2 | 401 | 8.4 | 4 123 | 29.0 | 34.2 |
| **ILLINOIS** | 4 773 002 | 68.7 | 198 500 | 25.6 | 13.7 | 860 | 30.7 | 3.0 | 6 592 992 | 0.2 | 585 039 | 8.9 | 6 043 771 | 35.9 | 21.8 |
| Adams | 26 722 | 74.9 | 99 900 | 20.5 | 11.2 | 572 | 28.3 | 1.3 | 36 751 | -1.6 | 2 282 | 6.2 | 33 051 | 29.4 | 25.9 |
| Alexander | 3 168 | 67.4 | 56 300 | 20.3 | 14.5 | 333 | 26.3 | 2.5 | 2 858 | -2.7 | 325 | 11.4 | 2 847 | 22.4 | 27.1 |
| Bond | 6 434 | 80.2 | 107 300 | 22.2 | 12.1 | 673 | 25.1 | 0.6 | 8 260 | -1.6 | 719 | 8.7 | 8 119 | 30.2 | 25.9 |
| Boone | 17 960 | 83.2 | 171 300 | 26.2 | 14.0 | 704 | 30.3 | 3.3 | 25 844 | -1.2 | 3 002 | 11.6 | 23 756 | 28.4 | 33.6 |
| Brown | 2 128 | 73.3 | 80 000 | 21.8 | 12.8 | 493 | 26.4 | 2.1 | 3 622 | 0.6 | 160 | 4.4 | 2 581 | 25.8 | 36.9 |
| Bureau | 14 404 | 75.7 | 103 800 | 21.0 | 13.1 | 616 | 26.1 | 1.7 | 18 586 | -2.3 | 1 767 | 9.5 | 16 783 | 24.1 | 33.7 |
| Calhoun | 2 084 | 79.8 | 109 400 | 22.2 | 12.5 | 548 | 23.2 | 2.0 | 2 485 | -1.5 | 248 | 10.0 | 2 248 | 27.5 | 29.3 |
| Carroll | 6 893 | 76.1 | 102 500 | 22.1 | 13.2 | 530 | 25.6 | 1.0 | 7 905 | -2.7 | 704 | 8.9 | 7 308 | 27.9 | 32.1 |
| Cass | 5 082 | 70.8 | 76 900 | 19.7 | 11.7 | 631 | 26.1 | 2.4 | 7 267 | -4.6 | 578 | 8.0 | 6 304 | 21.5 | 41.3 |
| Champaign | 78 900 | 54.6 | 147 900 | 21.8 | 11.2 | 766 | 36.3 | 1.5 | 99 683 | -1.6 | 8 006 | 8.0 | 99 203 | 43.8 | 15.2 |
| Christian | 14 063 | 74.5 | 82 000 | 20.4 | 12.8 | 602 | 28.2 | 2.2 | 17 346 | -2.1 | 1 602 | 9.2 | 15 350 | 26.1 | 28.7 |
| Clark | 6 676 | 77.2 | 84 700 | 19.4 | 12.8 | 590 | 25.1 | 1.2 | 7 873 | -1.2 | 804 | 10.2 | 8 018 | 29.9 | 32.6 |
| Clay | 5 535 | 75.8 | 71 500 | 20.0 | 12.5 | 499 | 26.0 | 1.7 | 6 346 | -1.4 | 672 | 10.6 | 5 890 | 26.8 | 38.7 |
| Clinton | 14 022 | 80.6 | 125 200 | 21.4 | 12.4 | 660 | 23.0 | 1.8 | 19 197 | -1.4 | 1 457 | 7.6 | 18 530 | 30.1 | 28.4 |
| Coles | 21 035 | 62.4 | 93 100 | 21.2 | 12.0 | 617 | 36.1 | 1.7 | 26 227 | -0.5 | 2 332 | 8.9 | 24 468 | 29.9 | 26.3 |
| Cook | 1 934 771 | 59.8 | 256 900 | 28.8 | 15.2 | 932 | 31.6 | 4.4 | 2 608 543 | 1.0 | 241 400 | 9.3 | 2 429 269 | 37.1 | 20.0 |
| Crawford | 7 815 | 79.8 | 70 000 | 18.5 | 11.4 | 578 | 23.7 | 2.0 | 9 466 | -3.4 | 860 | 9.1 | 8 850 | 25.4 | 35.1 |
| Cumberland | 4 163 | 81.2 | 82 100 | 19.8 | 11.7 | 513 | 23.9 | 2.9 | 5 258 | -1.1 | 490 | 9.3 | 5 213 | 24.8 | 33.7 |
| DeKalb | 38 011 | 62.8 | 188 100 | 26.1 | 14.7 | 809 | 33.8 | 2.9 | 59 359 | 1.1 | 4 901 | 8.3 | 52 986 | 31.6 | 23.7 |
| De Witt | 6 728 | 77.5 | 104 400 | 20.0 | 12.9 | 588 | 21.2 | 1.0 | 8 882 | -2.5 | 712 | 8.0 | 7 996 | 28.4 | 30.0 |
| Douglas | 7 589 | 78.2 | 95 000 | 21.6 | 11.7 | 657 | 32.0 | 3.1 | 9 781 | -2.6 | 754 | 7.7 | 9 526 | 25.0 | 35.0 |
| DuPage | 335 651 | 75.9 | 309 800 | 26.6 | 14.0 | 1 047 | 29.1 | 2.2 | 528 233 | 1.4 | 38 348 | 7.3 | 470 591 | 43.9 | 16.1 |
| Edgar | 7 881 | 76.0 | 72 400 | 19.1 | 13.3 | 582 | 24.4 | 0.8 | 9 956 | -1.7 | 923 | 9.3 | 8 541 | 25.0 | 34.9 |
| Edwards | 2 799 | 78.8 | 61 500 | 19.7 | 11.3 | 471 | 23.5 | 0.9 | 3 015 | -3.0 | 248 | 8.2 | 3 071 | 24.5 | 42.2 |
| Effingham | 13 496 | 79.5 | 108 100 | 20.9 | 11.2 | 518 | 25.2 | 1.6 | 18 071 | -1.1 | 1 268 | 7.0 | 17 371 | 28.7 | 29.5 |
| Fayette | 8 296 | 79.2 | 78 400 | 20.0 | 11.1 | 538 | 26.3 | 1.7 | 9 876 | -4.4 | 1 035 | 10.5 | 9 826 | 28.3 | 31.2 |
| Ford | 5 709 | 78.8 | 89 900 | 20.8 | 12.1 | 610 | 23.7 | 0.9 | 6 469 | -2.1 | 552 | 8.5 | 6 791 | 28.6 | 30.0 |
| Franklin | 16 100 | 78.4 | 63 200 | 21.2 | 12.5 | 519 | 27.3 | 1.7 | 17 307 | -1.5 | 1 939 | 11.2 | 15 696 | 25.2 | 29.9 |
| Fulton | 14 717 | 76.6 | 80 800 | 21.9 | 13.6 | 598 | 31.7 | 1.9 | 17 899 | -2.7 | 1 737 | 9.7 | 15 331 | 28.1 | 29.6 |
| Gallatin | 2 382 | 77.2 | 58 700 | 19.1 | 10.9 | 363 | 26.0 | 2.8 | 2 564 | -2.4 | 221 | 8.6 | 2 372 | 28.2 | 33.6 |
| Greene | 5 809 | 76.5 | 71 800 | 20.4 | 11.2 | 498 | 25.6 | 3.1 | 6 588 | -3.5 | 579 | 8.8 | 6 273 | 26.0 | 35.4 |
| Grundy | 18 297 | 75.6 | 191 500 | 24.8 | 13.3 | 910 | 28.4 | 2.5 | 27 823 | 0.4 | 2 839 | 10.2 | 23 504 | 28.9 | 28.0 |
| Hamilton | 3 470 | 82.7 | 74 100 | 19.4 | 12.4 | 417 | 29.7 | 3.1 | 4 178 | -2.2 | 326 | 7.8 | 3 543 | 28.8 | 35.6 |
| Hancock | 7 977 | 80.2 | 81 700 | 20.2 | 12.3 | 500 | 21.2 | 1.9 | 8 862 | -3.9 | 817 | 9.2 | 9 257 | 28.8 | 31.7 |

1. Specified owner-occupied units.   2. A value of 9.9 represents 9.9 percent or less.   3. Specified renter-occupied units. A value of 10.0 represents 10 percent or less.   4. Overcrowded or lacking complete plumbing facilities.   5. Percent of civilian labor force.   6. Persons 16 years old and over.

# Table B. States and Counties — Nonfarm Employment and Agriculture

| STATE County | Number of establish-ments | Total | Health care and social assistance | Manufac-turing | Retail trade | Finance and insurance | Professional, scientific, and technical services | Total (mil dol) | Average per employee (dollars) | Number | Fewer than 50 acres | 500 acres or more | Farm operators whose principal occu-pation is farming (percent) |
|---|---|---|---|---|---|---|---|---|---|---|---|---|---|
| | 104 | 105 | 106 | 107 | 108 | 109 | 110 | 111 | 112 | 113 | 114 | 115 | 116 |
| **IDAHO—Cont'd** | | | | | | | | | | | | | |
| Caribou | 185 | 2 500 | 245 | D | 279 | D | 72 | 140 | 55 912 | 454 | 17.0 | 40.5 | 50.2 |
| Cassia | 639 | 6 645 | 1 290 | 1 154 | 1 334 | 227 | 144 | 190 | 28 643 | 644 | 36.8 | 33.9 | 53.9 |
| Clark | 14 | 77 | D | D | 35 | D | D | 2 | 23 364 | 81 | 19.8 | 51.9 | 54.3 |
| Clearwater | 237 | 1 883 | 570 | 189 | 248 | 39 | 47 | 62 | 32 816 | 241 | 34.0 | 15.8 | 44.0 |
| Custer | 155 | 932 | 43 | D | 132 | 20 | D | 38 | 40 677 | 261 | 36.8 | 21.8 | 51.3 |
| Elmore | 426 | 3 720 | 675 | D | 922 | 197 | D | 97 | 25 975 | 381 | 54.6 | 20.5 | 44.1 |
| Franklin | 289 | 1 956 | D | 216 | 520 | 79 | 63 | 50 | 25 407 | 739 | 37.6 | 17.7 | 41.9 |
| Fremont | 279 | 1 330 | 181 | D | 222 | D | D | 38 | 28 374 | 536 | 30.8 | 23.9 | 48.9 |
| Gem | 331 | 2 109 | 646 | 129 | 354 | 64 | 51 | 52 | 24 841 | 822 | 68.7 | 6.3 | 47.9 |
| Gooding | 332 | 2 521 | 488 | 447 | 372 | 74 | 65 | 76 | 30 302 | 665 | 53.4 | 11.7 | 57.1 |
| Idaho | 465 | 2 974 | 583 | D | 425 | 143 | 115 | 97 | 32 460 | 760 | 26.8 | 31.2 | 51.4 |
| Jefferson | 424 | 3 221 | 324 | 770 | 498 | 77 | 56 | 90 | 27 854 | 826 | 55.8 | 16.3 | 44.9 |
| Jerome | 526 | 5 347 | 469 | 1 365 | 877 | 99 | D | 171 | 31 945 | 604 | 51.0 | 15.1 | 54.0 |
| Kootenai | 4 293 | 42 855 | 8 376 | 3 819 | 7 670 | 1 985 | 2 635 | 1 426 | 33 277 | 826 | 57.9 | 8.0 | 40.0 |
| Latah | 877 | 7 943 | 1 238 | 323 | 1 570 | 244 | 470 | 204 | 25 730 | 1 104 | 30.0 | 14.5 | 36.7 |
| Lemhi | 294 | 1 573 | 442 | D | 358 | 70 | D | 40 | 25 183 | 342 | 48.8 | 22.5 | 57.3 |
| Lewis | 130 | 789 | 67 | 175 | 159 | 27 | D | 20 | 25 828 | 225 | 15.6 | 48.4 | 61.3 |
| Lincoln | 83 | 643 | 134 | D | 78 | D | D | 19 | 29 785 | 258 | 21.3 | 28.3 | 61.2 |
| Madison | 735 | 13 047 | 1 455 | 999 | 1 744 | 264 | 647 | 294 | 22 510 | 450 | 42.9 | 20.9 | 50.2 |
| Minidoka | 410 | 4 380 | 628 | 857 | 482 | D | 127 | 141 | 32 104 | 626 | 51.9 | 13.7 | 53.4 |
| Nez Perce | 1 119 | 16 119 | 3 188 | 2 705 | 2 339 | 1 204 | 460 | 545 | 33 831 | 473 | 35.1 | 27.7 | 51.0 |
| Oneida | 82 | 592 | D | D | D | D | D | 15 | 24 914 | 463 | 21.8 | 30.5 | 39.3 |
| Owyhee | 184 | 1 687 | 151 | 167 | 259 | 27 | 31 | 40 | 23 531 | 620 | 43.1 | 23.9 | 56.9 |
| Payette | 472 | 4 356 | 582 | 981 | 512 | 156 | 99 | 129 | 29 566 | 678 | 65.6 | 6.0 | 43.1 |
| Power | 157 | 2 144 | D | D | D | 71 | D | 76 | 35 585 | 336 | 17.6 | 52.7 | 50.6 |
| Shoshone | 356 | 3 974 | 462 | D | 917 | 87 | 239 | 159 | 40 007 | 39 | 59.0 | 0.0 | 43.6 |
| Teton | 402 | 1 696 | D | 106 | 270 | 63 | 101 | 56 | 32 768 | 299 | 32.4 | 21.4 | 43.1 |
| Twin Falls | 2 439 | 25 427 | 4 857 | 2 621 | 4 850 | 950 | 1 008 | 731 | 28 757 | 1 296 | 48.5 | 12.6 | 54.0 |
| Valley | 549 | 2 834 | 506 | 56 | 450 | 76 | D | 75 | 26 380 | 145 | 44.8 | 22.1 | 46.9 |
| Washington | 206 | 1 566 | D | D | D | 54 | D | 39 | 24 828 | 594 | 44.9 | 19.4 | 46.8 |
| **ILLINOIS** | 312 437 | 5 038 462 | 757 799 | 538 985 | 596 569 | 295 028 | 347 083 | 245 056 | 48 637 | 76 860 | 38.0 | 21.0 | 48.4 |
| Adams | 1 815 | 29 913 | 5 383 | 4 520 | 5 021 | 1 519 | 963 | 1 054 | 35 245 | 1 295 | 32.0 | 19.1 | 45.9 |
| Alexander | 114 | 1 209 | 239 | D | 156 | 38 | D | 40 | 33 341 | 143 | 37.8 | 12.6 | 52.4 |
| Bond | 313 | 3 695 | 611 | 839 | 374 | 113 | 96 | 110 | 29 675 | 673 | 36.1 | 22.3 | 41.6 |
| Boone | 850 | 12 250 | 844 | 5 815 | 1 330 | 223 | D | 512 | 41 808 | 540 | 57.2 | 15.7 | 56.3 |
| Brown | 121 | D | 173 | D | 147 | D | D | D | D | 422 | 26.3 | 19.2 | 39.1 |
| Bureau | 772 | 9 818 | 2 297 | 1 461 | 1 125 | 482 | 355 | 351 | 35 784 | 1 189 | 33.4 | 26.4 | 55.5 |
| Calhoun | 93 | 628 | 106 | D | 111 | 67 | 14 | 13 | 20 982 | 464 | 31.0 | 9.7 | 38.6 |
| Carroll | 411 | 3 474 | 496 | 882 | 474 | 206 | 53 | 105 | 30 137 | 676 | 31.4 | 21.7 | 53.8 |
| Cass | 260 | 4 327 | 371 | D | 480 | 151 | D | 134 | 30 878 | 433 | 33.3 | 23.8 | 46.0 |
| Champaign | 4 107 | 67 327 | D | 6 806 | 10 628 | 2 397 | 3 098 | 2 362 | 35 076 | 1 389 | 32.1 | 27.3 | 55.2 |
| Christian | 736 | 8 675 | 1 870 | 1 004 | 1 371 | 363 | 285 | 292 | 33 660 | 910 | 34.2 | 29.3 | 53.7 |
| Clark | 326 | 3 531 | 365 | D | 363 | 163 | D | 109 | 30 986 | 588 | 38.8 | 23.3 | 54.4 |
| Clay | 354 | 4 468 | 651 | 1 731 | 450 | 155 | 66 | 146 | 32 771 | 707 | 42.4 | 18.4 | 42.7 |
| Clinton | 856 | 8 803 | 1 621 | 937 | 1 557 | 304 | 239 | 249 | 28 304 | 1 031 | 38.0 | 17.7 | 45.0 |
| Coles | 1 230 | 17 685 | 3 877 | 2 644 | 2 624 | 650 | 424 | 576 | 32 574 | 729 | 41.0 | 20.2 | 52.5 |
| Cook | 127 846 | 2 193 827 | 351 134 | 179 615 | 221 585 | 152 441 | 195 825 | 120 287 | 54 830 | 184 | 84.2 | 2.2 | 45.7 |
| Crawford | 440 | 6 899 | 993 | 1 971 | 832 | 231 | D | 259 | 37 496 | 615 | 45.2 | 18.7 | 41.8 |
| Cumberland | 171 | 1 602 | 247 | D | 168 | D | D | 45 | 28 046 | 654 | 46.3 | 13.9 | 37.8 |
| DeKalb | 1 952 | 25 295 | 4 682 | 3 512 | 4 189 | 940 | 851 | 865 | 34 183 | 930 | 36.8 | 26.2 | 57.4 |
| De Witt | 381 | 4 631 | 602 | 385 | 692 | 148 | 92 | 222 | 47 914 | 508 | 40.4 | 26.4 | 56.5 |
| Douglas | 595 | 6 037 | 316 | 2 109 | 1 205 | 234 | 83 | 208 | 34 410 | 657 | 41.4 | 22.2 | 54.9 |
| DuPage | 32 918 | 567 052 | 62 533 | 52 025 | 59 827 | 32 631 | 45 150 | 30 021 | 52 942 | 73 | 82.2 | 5.5 | 34.2 |
| Edgar | 370 | 5 285 | 733 | 1 657 | 762 | 300 | 94 | 172 | 32 558 | 670 | 28.8 | 31.2 | 56.0 |
| Edwards | 154 | D | 113 | D | 163 | D | D | D | D | 365 | 43.6 | 19.5 | 40.5 |
| Effingham | 1 172 | 17 716 | 2 805 | 3 106 | 2 978 | 447 | 300 | 587 | 33 135 | 1 150 | 41.0 | 11.3 | 37.8 |
| Fayette | 481 | 4 741 | 935 | 588 | 953 | 214 | 126 | 121 | 25 506 | 1 132 | 40.5 | 11.4 | 41.4 |
| Ford | 377 | 3 962 | 1 066 | 519 | 504 | 147 | 113 | 135 | 34 133 | 524 | 26.3 | 34.0 | 55.2 |
| Franklin | 776 | 7 068 | 1 468 | 791 | 1 550 | 296 | 279 | 203 | 28 667 | 785 | 50.6 | 14.0 | 37.5 |
| Fulton | 677 | 6 846 | 2 037 | 237 | 1 373 | 327 | 140 | 182 | 26 621 | 1 005 | 30.0 | 21.6 | 46.3 |
| Gallatin | 97 | 650 | 97 | 7 | D | 20 | 24 | 22 | 33 188 | 210 | 36.7 | 32.9 | 56.2 |
| Greene | 266 | 1 827 | 379 | 162 | 385 | 112 | 86 | 49 | 26 601 | 600 | 27.2 | 24.0 | 50.2 |
| Grundy | 1 074 | 14 721 | 1 950 | 1 219 | 1 903 | 392 | 779 | 786 | 53 369 | 450 | 30.0 | 27.1 | 48.0 |
| Hamilton | 196 | 1 294 | 458 | 79 | 172 | D | D | 38 | 29 384 | 685 | 38.2 | 15.8 | 35.6 |
| Hancock | 406 | 2 783 | 570 | D | 437 | 189 | 140 | 87 | 31 317 | 1 063 | 29.1 | 22.1 | 51.8 |

# Table B.  States and Counties  —  **Agriculture**

| STATE County | Agriculture, 2007 (cont.) | | | | | | | | | | | | | | | |
| | Land in farms | | | | | Value of land and buildings (dollars) | | Value of machinery and equipment, average per farm (dollars) | Value of products sold | | | | Percent of farms with sales of: | | Government payments | |
| | | | Acres | | | | | | | | Percent from: | | | | | |
| | Acreage (1,000) | Percent change, 2002–2007 | Average size of farm | Total irrigated (1,000) | Total cropland (1,000) | Average per farm | Average per acre | | Total (mil dol) | Average per farm (dollars) | Crops | Live-stock and poultry products | $10,000 or more | $100,000 or more | Total ($1,000) | Percent of farms |
| | 117 | 118 | 119 | 120 | 121 | 122 | 123 | 124 | 125 | 126 | 127 | 128 | 129 | 130 | 131 | 132 |
| **IDAHO—Cont'd** | | | | | | | | | | | | | | | | |
| Caribou | 421 | -1.4 | 928 | 68.3 | 229.0 | 1 000 425 | 1 078 | 151 325 | 55.0 | 121 172 | 62.6 | 37.4 | 43.0 | 22.9 | 4 178 | 65.6 |
| Cassia | 645 | -13.3 | 1 001 | 249.8 | 372.8 | 1 665 431 | 1 664 | 255 684 | 626.7 | 973 170 | 28.0 | 72.0 | 58.9 | 34.8 | 5 062 | 39.1 |
| Clark | 158 | -11.2 | 1 949 | 32.0 | 45.5 | 1 709 390 | 877 | 196 453 | 30.3 | 374 545 | 75.6 | 24.4 | 54.3 | 34.6 | 727 | 46.9 |
| Clearwater | 70 | -1.4 | 289 | D | 32.4 | 597 891 | 2 071 | 53 036 | 8.0 | 32 988 | 71.3 | 28.7 | 23.2 | 7.9 | 978 | 46.5 |
| Custer | 124 | -6.1 | 476 | 56.0 | 46.9 | 1 122 682 | 2 359 | 89 236 | 17.8 | 68 385 | 25.3 | 74.7 | 44.8 | 16.1 | 685 | 17.6 |
| Elmore | 347 | 0.3 | 910 | 97.9 | 120.8 | 1 253 456 | 1 378 | 148 119 | 284.6 | 747 055 | 25.3 | 74.7 | 34.9 | 18.6 | 886 | 17.6 |
| Franklin | 225 | -7.8 | 304 | 49.4 | 131.8 | 631 735 | 2 076 | 96 436 | 78.8 | 106 576 | 20.2 | 79.8 | 43.4 | 15.6 | 2 456 | 49.0 |
| Fremont | 288 | 0.3 | 538 | 101.8 | 175.7 | 1 012 170 | 1 883 | 164 650 | 86.2 | 160 776 | 87.9 | 12.1 | 42.5 | 18.8 | 3 524 | 55.8 |
| Gem | 191 | -13.6 | 232 | 35.1 | 34.9 | 523 969 | 2 258 | 54 029 | 30.8 | 37 487 | 39.9 | 60.1 | 32.4 | 8.2 | 571 | 23.6 |
| Gooding | 223 | 14.4 | 335 | 132.6 | 133.8 | 1 335 076 | 3 980 | 233 583 | 624.4 | 938 978 | 8.2 | 91.8 | 57.9 | 27.4 | 1 567 | 23.8 |
| Idaho | 591 | -7.5 | 778 | 1.2 | 218.8 | 1 095 170 | 1 409 | 78 506 | 51.4 | 67 582 | 71.5 | 28.5 | 42.9 | 16.7 | 6 634 | 52.4 |
| Jefferson | 325 | 6.6 | 394 | 210.3 | 225.1 | 818 005 | 2 077 | 143 918 | 233.1 | 282 146 | 53.4 | 46.6 | 50.0 | 24.2 | 2 632 | 39.5 |
| Jerome | 189 | 1.6 | 313 | 150.8 | 157.6 | 1 074 850 | 3 439 | 209 468 | 461.6 | 764 237 | 20.4 | 79.6 | 57.9 | 33.9 | 1 710 | 40.6 |
| Kootenai | 131 | -14.9 | 158 | 11.0 | 71.2 | 642 680 | 4 057 | 52 170 | 16.4 | 19 834 | 75.1 | 24.9 | 18.8 | 3.6 | 869 | 17.4 |
| Latah | 344 | 1.2 | 312 | 0.3 | 242.9 | 647 950 | 2 077 | 66 496 | 60.9 | 55 192 | 94.3 | 5.7 | 21.7 | 10.4 | 6 396 | 72.3 |
| Lemhi | 190 | 9.2 | 555 | 77.0 | 53.6 | 879 721 | 1 586 | 78 591 | 21.3 | 62 274 | 6.6 | 93.4 | 42.1 | 16.7 | 828 | 12.9 |
| Lewis | 246 | 13.4 | 1 093 | 0.3 | 184.1 | 1 649 738 | 1 509 | 176 488 | 43.7 | 194 418 | 92.7 | 7.3 | 58.2 | 37.8 | 3 920 | 76.9 |
| Lincoln | 117 | -8.6 | 455 | 68.0 | 68.4 | 976 143 | 2 146 | 178 150 | 131.0 | 507 650 | 16.2 | 83.8 | 60.9 | 30.2 | 1 034 | 50.0 |
| Madison | 211 | 11.1 | 468 | 128.2 | 176.1 | 1 279 118 | 2 733 | 211 179 | 107.8 | 239 494 | 94.4 | 5.6 | 52.9 | 25.6 | 2 824 | 51.8 |
| Minidoka | 226 | -0.9 | 361 | 191.6 | 202.7 | 875 005 | 2 422 | 185 923 | 257.0 | 410 606 | 70.0 | 30.0 | 55.4 | 34.0 | 3 011 | 51.3 |
| Nez Perce | 353 | 2.9 | 747 | 0.6 | 203.6 | 1 095 708 | 1 467 | 118 452 | 58.7 | 124 086 | 93.0 | 7.0 | 37.0 | 20.5 | 5 013 | 53.7 |
| Oneida | 314 | -13.5 | 678 | 38.3 | 204.3 | 794 950 | 1 173 | 82 291 | 27.6 | 59 533 | 64.3 | 35.7 | 39.3 | 13.6 | 4 149 | 70.0 |
| Owyhee | 569 | -0.4 | 918 | 115.2 | 136.6 | 1 256 088 | 1 368 | 138 716 | 206.6 | 333 148 | 25.3 | 74.7 | 55.6 | 28.9 | 1 258 | 32.4 |
| Payette | 166 | 7.1 | 245 | 54.6 | 56.1 | 688 178 | 2 808 | 98 039 | 146.5 | 216 009 | 19.5 | 80.5 | 39.2 | 13.0 | 462 | 23.2 |
| Power | 451 | 6.1 | 1 343 | 114.0 | 351.1 | 1 400 971 | 1 043 | 224 989 | 164.1 | 488 493 | 80.9 | 19.1 | 45.5 | 28.6 | 8 045 | 71.7 |
| Shoshone | 3 | -25.0 | 81 | D | 1.3 | 471 129 | 5 839 | 37 528 | 0.1 | 3 400 | 13.5 | 86.5 | 5.1 | 0.0 | 0 | 0.0 |
| Teton | 122 | -2.4 | 410 | 52.6 | 85.1 | 1 497 180 | 3 655 | 141 413 | 33.0 | 110 230 | 87.1 | 12.9 | 44.1 | 14.7 | 1 016 | 44.5 |
| Twin Falls | 440 | -0.2 | 339 | 244.5 | 267.1 | 840 836 | 2 479 | 144 828 | 471.9 | 364 090 | 29.8 | 70.2 | 59.6 | 28.5 | 2 585 | 43.1 |
| Valley | 62 | -6.1 | 428 | 22.1 | 11.4 | 1 409 537 | 3 294 | 57 304 | 5.1 | 35 505 | 10.3 | 89.7 | 36.6 | 11.0 | 43 | 9.7 |
| Washington | 417 | -11.7 | 702 | 43.9 | 88.4 | 686 593 | 978 | 74 774 | 43.0 | 72 380 | 42.6 | 57.4 | 42.1 | 14.1 | 878 | 36.5 |
| **ILLINOIS** | 26 775 | -2.0 | 348 | 474.5 | 23 707.7 | 1 321 080 | 3 792 | 136 609 | 13 329.1 | 173 421 | 81.6 | 18.4 | 53.1 | 30.3 | 487 293 | 73.9 |
| Adams | 374 | -15.8 | 289 | 1.6 | 284.7 | 1 013 322 | 3 507 | 113 632 | 156.3 | 120 673 | 66.7 | 33.3 | 52.3 | 25.6 | 5 141 | 70.6 |
| Alexander | 48 | -38.5 | 333 | D | 36.7 | 1 030 129 | 3 093 | 83 157 | 13.1 | 91 674 | 97.1 | 2.9 | 42.0 | 14.0 | 715 | 62.9 |
| Bond | 225 | 16.6 | 334 | 0.0 | 203.3 | 1 137 540 | 3 406 | 134 298 | 74.3 | 110 419 | 83.0 | 17.0 | 48.1 | 26.3 | 3 327 | 77.7 |
| Boone | 137 | -6.8 | 254 | 1.8 | 128.8 | 1 255 409 | 4 942 | 112 280 | 81.4 | 150 765 | 86.1 | 13.9 | 48.3 | 28.3 | 3 711 | 54.1 |
| Brown | 151 | 4.9 | 358 | D | 92.1 | 1 091 712 | 3 050 | 87 114 | 42.0 | 99 448 | 72.9 | 27.1 | 48.2 | 22.0 | 2 583 | 83.2 |
| Bureau | 478 | -2.6 | 402 | 10.2 | 439.9 | 1 628 471 | 4 047 | 156 932 | 303.4 | 255 137 | 86.2 | 13.8 | 63.8 | 42.9 | 10 029 | 81.6 |
| Calhoun | 88 | -2.2 | 190 | D | 49.6 | 588 974 | 3 108 | 66 781 | 18.7 | 40 223 | 83.9 | 16.1 | 30.0 | 9.3 | 1 697 | 72.8 |
| Carroll | 265 | 6.9 | 392 | 10.5 | 228.1 | 1 442 019 | 3 676 | 170 529 | 207.0 | 306 250 | 54.0 | 46.0 | 59.0 | 37.1 | 6 184 | 80.6 |
| Cass | 174 | -12.6 | 401 | 21.2 | 143.6 | 1 426 235 | 3 559 | 136 955 | 92.0 | 212 370 | 71.3 | 28.8 | 51.3 | 31.6 | 3 375 | 82.4 |
| Champaign | 550 | -4.7 | 396 | 7.1 | 536.1 | 1 724 299 | 4 351 | 176 444 | 311.5 | 224 235 | 96.0 | 4.0 | 72.8 | 43.3 | 10 743 | 88.0 |
| Christian | 450 | 9.5 | 494 | 0.0 | 430.4 | 2 064 186 | 4 179 | 171 450 | 229.2 | 251 882 | 94.4 | 5.6 | 63.5 | 40.8 | 7 078 | 80.7 |
| Clark | 239 | -13.1 | 406 | 6.4 | 206.0 | 1 312 708 | 3 234 | 158 135 | 103.5 | 175 937 | 84.1 | 15.9 | 48.5 | 27.7 | 4 128 | 78.4 |
| Clay | 210 | -13.6 | 297 | D | 178.3 | 871 635 | 2 937 | 102 294 | 72.8 | 102 946 | 69.6 | 30.4 | 38.9 | 20.1 | 3 698 | 83.7 |
| Clinton | 268 | 5.1 | 260 | 1.2 | 246.4 | 991 561 | 3 808 | 143 602 | 175.9 | 170 627 | 45.4 | 54.6 | 58.5 | 30.6 | 5 123 | 85.4 |
| Coles | 255 | -2.3 | 350 | 0.0 | 235.1 | 1 354 381 | 3 874 | 143 393 | 123.9 | 169 906 | 95.8 | 4.2 | 55.0 | 31.4 | 4 726 | 74.1 |
| Cook | 8 | -66.7 | 45 | 0.2 | 6.5 | 464 325 | 10 422 | 71 712 | 15.3 | 82 988 | 95.0 | 5.0 | 34.8 | 16.8 | 94 | 13.0 |
| Crawford | 205 | -4.2 | 334 | 6.8 | 176.6 | 1 094 677 | 3 278 | 116 138 | 74.7 | 121 406 | 89.9 | 10.1 | 36.6 | 22.3 | 4 548 | 85.9 |
| Cumberland | 145 | -16.2 | 222 | 0.0 | 124.5 | 781 010 | 3 523 | 97 966 | 71.8 | 109 811 | 70.3 | 29.7 | 43.9 | 22.6 | 3 343 | 82.7 |
| DeKalb | 371 | 3.3 | 399 | 0.1 | 356.2 | 1 847 105 | 4 633 | 185 559 | 302.2 | 324 915 | 62.8 | 37.2 | 66.5 | 46.6 | 10 012 | 73.5 |
| De Witt | 199 | -2.0 | 391 | D | 185.6 | 1 630 935 | 4 170 | 149 395 | 96.1 | 189 154 | 92.6 | 7.4 | 59.1 | 37.6 | 3 671 | 75.0 |
| Douglas | 262 | 12.4 | 398 | D | 252.8 | 1 674 156 | 4 206 | 148 029 | 133.9 | 203 880 | 94.6 | 5.4 | 59.4 | 34.1 | 4 785 | 70.2 |
| DuPage | 8 | 0.0 | 109 | D | 6.4 | 817 586 | 7 509 | 57 909 | 14.1 | 192 813 | 99.7 | 0.4 | 37.0 | 19.2 | 113 | 13.7 |
| Edgar | 353 | -0.6 | 526 | 0.2 | 328.3 | 2 011 584 | 3 823 | 182 109 | 189.9 | 283 501 | 88.3 | 11.7 | 67.3 | 40.1 | 6 337 | 77.8 |
| Edwards | 117 | -4.9 | 320 | 0.1 | 100.5 | 890 959 | 2 787 | 101 514 | 32.8 | 89 967 | 87.2 | 12.8 | 41.1 | 21.1 | 2 237 | 83.6 |
| Effingham | 242 | -12.9 | 210 | 0.3 | 204.5 | 759 757 | 3 610 | 101 108 | 127.3 | 110 709 | 55.6 | 44.4 | 50.5 | 22.2 | 4 565 | 75.1 |
| Fayette | 303 | -17.2 | 268 | 0.1 | 254.5 | 789 210 | 2 946 | 103 978 | 104.3 | 92 158 | 86.6 | 13.4 | 42.6 | 20.7 | 4 381 | 73.0 |
| Ford | 271 | -5.2 | 517 | 0.1 | 258.7 | 2 053 439 | 3 975 | 178 916 | 145.9 | 278 379 | 88.4 | 11.6 | 74.0 | 49.2 | 4 552 | 87.6 |
| Franklin | 208 | 15.6 | 265 | D | 183.7 | 671 184 | 2 535 | 80 319 | 56.6 | 72 135 | 80.3 | 19.7 | 28.5 | 15.4 | 3 772 | 68.0 |
| Fulton | 385 | -6.8 | 383 | 0.9 | 280.1 | 1 350 626 | 3 523 | 121 274 | 145.6 | 144 860 | 84.9 | 15.1 | 53.4 | 26.1 | 5 104 | 68.2 |
| Gallatin | 186 | 20.8 | 885 | 20.6 | 171.6 | 2 628 760 | 2 972 | 315 220 | 72.6 | 345 538 | 95.7 | 4.3 | 51.9 | 35.7 | 3 017 | 82.9 |
| Greene | 273 | -13.3 | 455 | 3.8 | 214.8 | 1 651 273 | 3 628 | 150 950 | 135.5 | 225 906 | 63.2 | 36.8 | 56.7 | 30.0 | 4 644 | 79.2 |
| Grundy | 215 | 0.9 | 479 | D | 206.1 | 1 988 655 | 4 153 | 189 410 | 105.2 | 233 714 | 97.1 | 2.9 | 73.6 | 42.0 | 3 404 | 79.3 |
| Hamilton | 220 | -6.0 | 321 | D | 191.9 | 963 280 | 3 001 | 99 151 | 65.4 | 95 405 | 81.0 | 19.0 | 34.0 | 16.5 | 4 309 | 83.1 |
| Hancock | 393 | -9.0 | 370 | 1.3 | 322.2 | 1 228 769 | 3 324 | 119 803 | 188.5 | 177 364 | 71.1 | 28.9 | 58.0 | 32.7 | 6 781 | 77.9 |

# Table B. States and Counties — Water Use, Wholesale Trade, Retail Trade, and Real Estate

| STATE County | Water use, 2005 | | Wholesale trade,[1] 2007 | | | | Retail trade,[2] 2007 | | | | Real estate and rental and leasing,[2] 2007 | | | |
|---|---|---|---|---|---|---|---|---|---|---|---|---|---|---|
| | Total water withdrawn (mil gal/day) | Gallons withdrawn per person | Number of establish-ments | Number of employees | Sales (mil dol) | Annual payroll (mil dol) | Number of establish-ments | Number of employees | Sales (mil dol) | Annual payroll (mil dol) | Number of establish-ments | Number of employees | Receipts (mil dol) | Annual payroll (mil dol) |
| | 133 | 134 | 135 | 136 | 137 | 138 | 139 | 140 | 141 | 142 | 143 | 144 | 145 | 146 |
| **IDAHO—Cont'd** | | | | | | | | | | | | | | |
| Caribou | 379.4 | 53 207 | 14 | 63 | 94.6 | 2.3 | 34 | 340 | 68.4 | 6.0 | 5 | 6 | 0.6 | 0.1 |
| Cassia | 880.9 | 41 309 | 30 | 267 | 335.9 | 8.5 | 128 | 1 436 | 318.9 | 30.2 | 26 | D | D | D |
| Clark | 95.6 | 101 326 | 1 | D | D | D | 3 | D | D | D | NA | NA | NA | NA |
| Clearwater | 15.2 | 1 809 | 5 | 32 | 13.7 | 1.1 | 42 | 265 | 69.8 | 5.8 | 5 | D | D | D |
| Custer | 842.7 | 206 699 | NA | NA | NA | NA | 30 | 150 | 35.1 | 2.7 | 7 | 20 | 0.6 | 0.1 |
| Elmore | 424.7 | 14 830 | 14 | 101 | 53.4 | 4.0 | 75 | 970 | 241.2 | 20.1 | 16 | 50 | 5.6 | 1.0 |
| Franklin | 203.8 | 16 477 | 19 | 146 | 49.5 | 4.5 | 42 | 508 | 113.5 | 9.3 | 11 | D | D | D |
| Fremont | 295.0 | 24 095 | 14 | 184 | 76.7 | 4.9 | 41 | 250 | 68.2 | 4.9 | 6 | 11 | 2.5 | 0.3 |
| Gem | 725.8 | 44 604 | 11 | 75 | 13.6 | 2.7 | 47 | 392 | 113.9 | 8.8 | 20 | 37 | 3.8 | 0.5 |
| Gooding | 1 155.5 | 79 905 | 19 | 174 | 118.9 | 5.0 | 44 | 419 | 88.2 | 6.5 | 9 | D | D | D |
| Idaho | 19.2 | 1 221 | 17 | 115 | 64.8 | 3.7 | 68 | 519 | 97.6 | 11.2 | 14 | 28 | 2.8 | 0.5 |
| Jefferson | 2 108.0 | 97 684 | 23 | D | D | D | 56 | 474 | 92.4 | 8.0 | 13 | 47 | 5.0 | 0.8 |
| Jerome | 1 472.9 | 75 002 | 36 | 226 | 103.7 | 8.4 | 73 | 982 | 300.4 | 21.5 | 26 | 51 | 8.2 | 0.9 |
| Kootenai | 73.2 | 573 | 142 | 1 550 | 843.3 | 64.0 | 609 | 7 398 | 2 175.2 | 187.5 | 249 | 876 | 155.3 | 27.4 |
| Latah | 9.7 | 281 | 24 | D | D | D | 156 | 1 960 | 361.7 | 37.1 | 49 | 120 | 17.6 | 2.9 |
| Lemhi | 240.8 | 30 446 | 5 | D | D | D | 53 | 444 | 123.0 | 8.9 | 19 | 33 | 2.7 | 0.6 |
| Lewis | 2.7 | 720 | 9 | D | D | D | 20 | 138 | 29.7 | 2.3 | 5 | 15 | 1.3 | 0.2 |
| Lincoln | 321.9 | 70 814 | NA | NA | NA | NA | 13 | 77 | 16.9 | 1.1 | 4 | D | D | D |
| Madison | 625.5 | 20 194 | 38 | 475 | 162.0 | 11.6 | 124 | 1 718 | 407.7 | 37.6 | 59 | 174 | 23.4 | 3.1 |
| Minidoka | 649.7 | 34 167 | 40 | 745 | 347.0 | 24.9 | 66 | 543 | 162.9 | 10.4 | 10 | D | D | D |
| Nez Perce | 28.9 | 761 | 45 | D | D | D | 216 | 2 822 | 703.0 | 70.0 | 40 | 160 | 23.0 | 4.7 |
| Oneida | 152.6 | 36 263 | 1 | D | D | D | 15 | 145 | 24.1 | 2.0 | 4 | D | D | D |
| Owyhee | 816.9 | 73 778 | 10 | 71 | 34.6 | 2.8 | 25 | 219 | 50.9 | 4.4 | 10 | 23 | 0.7 | 0.1 |
| Payette | 285.0 | 12 841 | 26 | 187 | 133.1 | 6.3 | 70 | 596 | 145.6 | 14.2 | 29 | 46 | 6.4 | 0.8 |
| Power | 349.2 | 45 034 | 11 | D | D | D | 23 | 213 | 50.4 | 3.9 | 7 | 27 | 1.8 | 0.3 |
| Shoshone | 5.4 | 411 | 9 | 71 | 25.0 | 2.8 | 80 | 1 019 | 623.1 | 32.1 | 11 | 44 | 3.1 | 0.7 |
| Teton | 166.5 | 22 291 | 12 | D | D | D | 46 | 329 | 84.1 | 6.9 | 46 | 56 | 22.5 | 2.4 |
| Twin Falls | 1 691.8 | 24 370 | 123 | 1 301 | 497.6 | 44.6 | 423 | 5 363 | 1 259.1 | 117.5 | 113 | 359 | 49.1 | 8.4 |
| Valley | 68.2 | 8 184 | 11 | 62 | 20.5 | 2.4 | 83 | 643 | 135.6 | 13.5 | 60 | 111 | 16.5 | 2.6 |
| Washington | 187.4 | 18 558 | 12 | 439 | 63.4 | 7.2 | 38 | 335 | 76.3 | 6.1 | 13 | 43 | 3.3 | 0.5 |
| **ILLINOIS** | 15 183.7 | 1 190 | 16 704 | 259 758 | 231 082.8 | 14 319.6 | 43 055 | 639 147 | 165 450.5 | 14 895.5 | 13 899 | 87 468 | 21 725.0 | 3 985.2 |
| Adams | 26.1 | 389 | 114 | D | D | D | 330 | 4 813 | 928.3 | 89.9 | 65 | 294 | 34.9 | 7.0 |
| Alexander | 4.9 | 544 | 7 | D | D | D | 24 | 165 | 22.9 | 2.5 | 2 | D | D | D |
| Bond | 2.9 | 158 | 18 | 414 | 217.6 | 17.0 | 60 | 490 | 104.5 | 8.7 | 13 | D | D | D |
| Boone | 8.1 | 160 | 35 | 223 | 146.2 | 11.0 | 103 | 1 555 | 454.9 | 36.6 | 25 | 68 | 7.9 | 1.3 |
| Brown | 0.5 | 66 | 7 | D | D | D | 25 | 166 | 30.0 | 2.7 | 2 | D | D | D |
| Bureau | 13.5 | 381 | 42 | 823 | 977.6 | 30.0 | 120 | 1 269 | 332.0 | 27.2 | 17 | D | D | D |
| Calhoun | 0.6 | 122 | 2 | D | D | D | 15 | 104 | 22.3 | 2.1 | 2 | D | D | D |
| Carroll | 17.3 | 1 075 | 23 | 250 | 301.8 | 10.5 | 59 | 428 | 88.7 | 7.6 | 10 | 34 | 2.8 | 0.4 |
| Cass | 20.5 | 1 478 | 17 | 355 | 331.3 | 13.2 | 50 | 478 | 115.4 | 9.1 | 6 | D | D | D |
| Champaign | 38.6 | 209 | 170 | 3 166 | 2 576.0 | 118.7 | 667 | 10 960 | 2 347.1 | 213.1 | 233 | 1 655 | 349.4 | 51.0 |
| Christian | 835.6 | 23 753 | 46 | D | D | D | 122 | 1 385 | 369.9 | 30.7 | 20 | 83 | 10.4 | 1.8 |
| Clark | 8.7 | 511 | 17 | 154 | 176.1 | 4.8 | 60 | 390 | 109.6 | 8.2 | 5 | 18 | 2.4 | 0.5 |
| Clay | 2.3 | 161 | 28 | 315 | 168.8 | 9.7 | 55 | 531 | 114.8 | 10.2 | 11 | 30 | 3.6 | 0.7 |
| Clinton | 8.1 | 225 | 48 | 544 | 282.0 | 19.7 | 151 | 1 538 | 383.2 | 35.5 | 22 | 161 | 16.5 | 4.0 |
| Coles | 5.5 | 108 | 59 | 496 | 382.9 | 19.9 | 193 | 2 894 | 635.1 | 60.6 | 47 | 162 | 21.8 | 4.1 |
| Cook | 1 758.0 | 331 | 6 657 | 98 030 | 83 964.6 | 5 379.0 | 16 288 | 241 745 | 60 585.6 | 5 793.8 | 6 626 | 47 857 | 13 137.3 | 2 511.3 |
| Crawford | 102.0 | 5 128 | 15 | 157 | 90.9 | 4.3 | 63 | 709 | 164.2 | 14.0 | 17 | 39 | 4.2 | 0.5 |
| Cumberland | 1.8 | 168 | 18 | D | D | D | 27 | 160 | 22.9 | 2.1 | NA | NA | NA | NA |
| DeKalb | 15.4 | 157 | 72 | 579 | 249.7 | 21.7 | 320 | 4 713 | 1 090.2 | 94.6 | 66 | 524 | 57.2 | 11.2 |
| De Witt | 938.9 | 56 500 | 25 | 262 | 248.9 | 12.4 | 64 | 740 | 188.2 | 14.5 | 9 | 45 | 6.4 | 0.6 |
| Douglas | 4.0 | 198 | 30 | 318 | 290.1 | 13.1 | 136 | 1 081 | 218.4 | 18.9 | 11 | 38 | 5.2 | 1.0 |
| DuPage | 16.0 | 17 | 2 423 | 46 343 | 49 574.9 | 2 924.4 | 3 512 | 65 944 | 18 043.4 | 1 646.3 | 1 485 | 11 690 | 3 917.2 | 614.7 |
| Edgar | 3.2 | 167 | 23 | 197 | 126.7 | 8.0 | 66 | 743 | 197.1 | 16.3 | 9 | 39 | 3.4 | 1.1 |
| Edwards | 0.9 | 137 | 17 | 213 | 147.1 | 7.5 | 27 | 191 | 40.6 | 3.3 | 3 | D | D | D |
| Effingham | 5.0 | 145 | 60 | D | D | D | 205 | 3 141 | 857.8 | 68.7 | 44 | 222 | 36.8 | 6.7 |
| Fayette | 4.4 | 201 | 25 | 396 | 322.6 | 13.3 | 88 | 970 | 227.3 | 19.1 | 12 | 34 | 3.4 | 0.7 |
| Ford | 5.9 | 419 | 30 | 312 | 323.1 | 10.8 | 62 | 599 | 112.3 | 9.1 | 6 | 12 | 1.1 | 0.2 |
| Franklin | 14.7 | 370 | 31 | 191 | 72.7 | 6.6 | 152 | 1 545 | 362.2 | 33.5 | 21 | 75 | 8.2 | 1.3 |
| Fulton | 158.7 | 4 208 | 23 | D | D | D | 128 | 1 343 | 288.9 | 25.5 | 18 | D | D | D |
| Gallatin | 18.9 | 3 074 | 6 | 44 | 23.2 | 1.2 | 18 | 108 | 21.9 | 2.2 | NA | NA | NA | NA |
| Greene | 11.0 | 756 | 22 | 148 | 151.3 | 5.1 | 56 | 389 | 95.9 | 7.6 | 3 | 11 | 0.3 | 0.1 |
| Grundy | 1 560.1 | 35 587 | 46 | 393 | 438.5 | 16.4 | 161 | 1 928 | 522.6 | 42.5 | 41 | 149 | 23.5 | 3.4 |
| Hamilton | 1.0 | 117 | 10 | D | D | D | 33 | 158 | 41.9 | 2.9 | 6 | 41 | 0.5 | 0.2 |
| Hancock | 4.0 | 210 | 28 | 160 | 200.5 | 5.2 | 82 | 569 | 106.5 | 9.8 | 3 | 8 | 3.4 | 0.1 |

1. Merchant wholesalers, except manufacturers' sales branches and offices.    2. Employer establishments.

# Table B. States and Counties — Professional Services, Manufacturing, and Accommodation and Food Services

| STATE County | Professional, scientific, and technical services,[1] 2007 | | | | Manufacturing, 2007 | | | | Accommodation and food services, 2007 | | | |
|---|---|---|---|---|---|---|---|---|---|---|---|---|
| | Number of establish-ments | Number of employees | Receipts (mil dol) | Annual payroll (mil dol) | Number of establish-ments | Number of employees | Receipts (mil dol) | Annual payroll (mil dol) | Number of establish-ments | Number of employees | Sales (mil dol) | Annual payroll (mil dol) |
| | 147 | 148 | 149 | 150 | 151 | 152 | 153 | 154 | 155 | 156 | 157 | 158 |
| IDAHO—Cont'd | | | | | | | | | | | | |
| Caribou | 9 | D | D | D | 11 | D | 443.2 | D | 11 | D | D | D |
| Cassia | 45 | 173 | 14.6 | 4.3 | 28 | 1 032 | 371.3 | 41.2 | 47 | 656 | 33.5 | 6.5 |
| Clark | 2 | D | D | D | NA | NA | NA | NA | 1 | D | D | D |
| Clearwater | 12 | D | D | D | NA | NA | NA | NA | 34 | D | D | D |
| Custer | 8 | D | D | D | NA | NA | NA | NA | 33 | 205 | 11.3 | 2.7 |
| Elmore | 27 | D | D | D | NA | NA | NA | NA | 55 | 702 | 27.0 | 7.9 |
| Franklin | 12 | D | D | D | NA | NA | NA | NA | 20 | 194 | 5.8 | 1.7 |
| Fremont | 12 | 27 | 6.0 | 0.6 | NA | NA | NA | NA | 33 | 170 | 10.1 | 2.7 |
| Gem | 20 | 61 | 4.5 | 1.3 | NA | NA | NA | NA | 28 | 342 | 9.2 | 2.6 |
| Gooding | 20 | 80 | 8.5 | 2.8 | 25 | 510 | D | 20.4 | 30 | D | D | D |
| Idaho | 22 | 88 | 16.0 | 3.6 | NA | NA | NA | NA | 66 | 353 | 14.7 | 3.5 |
| Jefferson | 44 | D | D | D | 33 | 1 069 | D | 26.3 | 24 | 238 | 7.4 | 1.8 |
| Jerome | 30 | D | D | D | 24 | 1 246 | 764.2 | 36.6 | 33 | 329 | 14.0 | 3.5 |
| Kootenai | 438 | D | D | D | 246 | 4 401 | 992.2 | 163.3 | 363 | 6 773 | 303.7 | 96.0 |
| Latah | 84 | D | D | D | NA | NA | NA | NA | 104 | 1 756 | 55.2 | 15.9 |
| Lemhi | 24 | 68 | 4.0 | 1.4 | NA | NA | NA | NA | 34 | 232 | 7.7 | 2.4 |
| Lewis | 1 | D | D | D | NA | NA | NA | NA | 13 | D | D | D |
| Lincoln | 4 | D | D | D | NA | NA | NA | NA | 10 | 68 | 2.4 | 0.7 |
| Madison | 64 | 910 | 38.1 | 11.4 | 35 | D | D | D | 50 | 1 090 | 32.0 | 9.0 |
| Minidoka | 23 | 98 | 7.0 | 2.8 | 27 | 864 | 381.1 | 32.2 | 28 | 336 | 18.9 | 3.4 |
| Nez Perce | 78 | D | D | D | 37 | 2 874 | D | D | 95 | 1 687 | 64.5 | 20.2 |
| Oneida | 1 | D | D | D | NA | NA | NA | NA | 9 | 85 | 2.1 | 0.5 |
| Owyhee | 10 | 35 | 2.9 | 1.1 | NA | NA | NA | NA | 21 | 144 | 4.2 | 1.2 |
| Payette | 28 | D | D | D | 31 | 1 228 | D | 39.9 | 33 | 329 | 12.8 | 2.4 |
| Power | 6 | D | D | D | 8 | D | D | D | 17 | 70 | 2.6 | 0.6 |
| Shoshone | 27 | 254 | 24.2 | 8.1 | NA | NA | NA | NA | 50 | 310 | 11.1 | 3.4 |
| Teton | 32 | D | D | D | NA | NA | NA | NA | 29 | 201 | 10.7 | 2.9 |
| Twin Falls | 221 | D | D | D | 101 | 3 175 | 970.3 | 104.3 | 177 | 2 825 | 112.0 | 29.5 |
| Valley | 47 | 165 | 31.8 | 6.2 | NA | NA | NA | NA | 82 | 803 | 43.2 | 13.0 |
| Washington | 17 | 70 | 4.2 | 1.3 | NA | NA | NA | NA | 25 | D | D | D |
| ILLINOIS | 38 797 | 363 231 | 61 896.1 | 24 197.9 | 15 704 | 663 586 | 257 760.7 | 31 715.9 | 26 774 | 468 827 | 25 469.0 | 6 894.3 |
| Adams | 136 | D | D | D | 96 | D | D | D | 142 | D | D | D |
| Alexander | 9 | D | D | D | NA | NA | NA | NA | 19 | D | D | D |
| Bond | 23 | D | D | D | 16 | 821 | D | 30.0 | 31 | 333 | 13.1 | 3.4 |
| Boone | 73 | D | D | D | 71 | 6 534 | 5 553.7 | 387.3 | 71 | 883 | 40.2 | 10.4 |
| Brown | 8 | D | D | D | NA | NA | NA | NA | 15 | D | D | D |
| Bureau | 41 | D | D | D | 43 | 2 062 | D | D | 78 | 765 | 27.4 | 7.5 |
| Calhoun | 2 | D | D | D | NA | NA | NA | NA | 20 | 138 | 5.4 | 1.4 |
| Carroll | 19 | 66 | 5.4 | 1.6 | 28 | 926 | 320.8 | 34.1 | 40 | 297 | 13.0 | 2.8 |
| Cass | 16 | 59 | 4.6 | 1.5 | 13 | D | D | D | 33 | 235 | 8.1 | 2.0 |
| Champaign | 453 | 2 913 | 299.3 | 127.9 | 143 | 8 995 | 3 248.9 | 337.2 | 502 | 9 836 | 374.5 | 104.4 |
| Christian | 46 | 5 377 | 69.6 | 32.6 | 25 | 1 339 | 392.4 | 46.6 | 76 | 762 | 29.3 | 7.5 |
| Clark | 20 | 132 | 8.2 | 3.8 | 18 | 1 622 | 664.4 | 59.5 | 38 | 543 | 17.0 | 5.0 |
| Clay | 16 | 57 | 4.1 | 1.1 | 17 | 1 980 | 737.1 | 71.3 | 30 | D | D | D |
| Clinton | 50 | 244 | 20.6 | 8.0 | 35 | 1 005 | D | 30.6 | 76 | 808 | 32.4 | 8.6 |
| Coles | 83 | 494 | 43.4 | 15.2 | 54 | 3 537 | D | D | 127 | 2 465 | 75.6 | 21.7 |
| Cook | 18 818 | D | D | D | 6 018 | 236 509 | 77 932.9 | 11 039.2 | 10 887 | 201 766 | 13 094.4 | 3 525.6 |
| Crawford | 30 | 124 | 12.3 | 4.0 | 19 | 2 007 | D | 120.1 | 37 | 423 | 15.3 | 3.9 |
| Cumberland | 7 | 30 | 2.0 | 0.8 | NA | NA | NA | NA | 11 | 140 | 3.1 | 0.9 |
| DeKalb | 158 | D | D | D | 140 | 4 608 | 1 435.9 | 191.2 | 214 | 3 247 | 128.2 | 32.7 |
| De Witt | 29 | 91 | 7.0 | 2.3 | NA | NA | NA | NA | 38 | 483 | 13.9 | 4.1 |
| Douglas | 30 | 108 | 6.4 | 2.3 | 92 | 2 731 | 699.9 | 102.2 | 54 | 674 | 24.5 | 7.2 |
| DuPage | 5 172 | D | D | D | 1 881 | 62 578 | 16 862.5 | 2 977.7 | 2 071 | 41 256 | 2 226.2 | 638.5 |
| Edgar | 28 | 105 | 8.4 | 2.5 | 23 | 2 061 | 521.8 | 75.8 | 28 | 384 | 12.0 | 3.4 |
| Edwards | 11 | 37 | 2.0 | 0.7 | 7 | D | D | D | 8 | 83 | 2.5 | 0.8 |
| Effingham | 57 | 315 | 31.9 | 9.0 | 63 | 3 440 | 890.3 | 119.2 | 107 | 2 265 | 85.2 | 24.3 |
| Fayette | 26 | 132 | 7.8 | 3.6 | 21 | 833 | 174.6 | 24.8 | 46 | 511 | 18.3 | 5.2 |
| Ford | 26 | 93 | 9.0 | 2.7 | 20 | D | D | D | 36 | 302 | 11.4 | 3.2 |
| Franklin | 56 | 345 | 23.3 | 7.6 | 38 | 782 | 223.2 | 25.7 | 82 | 956 | 34.2 | 10.1 |
| Fulton | 43 | D | D | D | NA | NA | NA | NA | 84 | 844 | 29.4 | 8.4 |
| Gallatin | 7 | 21 | 1.6 | 0.7 | NA | NA | NA | NA | 10 | D | D | D |
| Greene | 16 | 79 | 6.7 | 2.7 | NA | NA | NA | NA | 24 | D | D | D |
| Grundy | 93 | D | D | D | 49 | 1 755 | 2 082.4 | D | 101 | 1 406 | 56.3 | 14.7 |
| Hamilton | 11 | 25 | 2.2 | 0.5 | NA | NA | NA | NA | 8 | 95 | 2.8 | 0.8 |
| Hancock | 25 | 127 | 21.2 | 4.9 | 24 | 726 | 193.2 | 35.2 | 34 | 254 | 10.9 | 3.0 |

1. Establishment subject to federal tax.

# Table B. States and Counties — Health Care and Social Assistance, Other Services, and Federal Funds

| STATE County | Health care and social assistance, 2007 | | | | Other services, 2007 | | | | Federal funds and grants, 2009–2010 Expenditures (mil dol) | | | |
|---|---|---|---|---|---|---|---|---|---|---|---|---|
| | | | | | | | | | | Direct payments for individuals[1] | | |
| | Number of establishments | Number of employees | Receipts (mil dol) | Annual payroll (mil dol) | Number of establishments | Number of employees | Receipts (mil dol) | Annual payroll (mil dol) | Total | Social Security and government retirement | Medicare | Food Stamps and Supplemental Security Income |
| | 159 | 160 | 161 | 162 | 163 | 164 | 165 | 166 | 167 | 168 | 169 | 170 |
| IDAHO—Cont'd | | | | | | | | | | | | |
| Caribou | 20 | 224 | 14.8 | 5.7 | 18 | 39 | 4.0 | 0.8 | 43.9 | 20.8 | 6.9 | 1.4 |
| Cassia | 83 | 1 165 | 74.8 | 27.8 | 45 | 135 | 11.9 | 2.5 | 140.0 | 53.9 | 25.1 | 7.5 |
| Clark | 2 | D | D | D | NA | NA | NA | NA | 6.1 | 2.1 | 0.9 | 0.1 |
| Clearwater | 25 | 551 | 34.5 | 17.8 | 10 | 98 | 4.1 | 1.9 | 130.2 | 41.7 | 13.9 | 3.9 |
| Custer | 9 | 49 | 2.1 | 0.8 | 3 | 7 | 0.3 | 0.1 | 38.3 | 16.2 | 6.2 | 1.0 |
| Elmore | 52 | 711 | 46.7 | 17.4 | 40 | 167 | 8.6 | 2.4 | 469.4 | 102.2 | 17.4 | 6.6 |
| Franklin | 27 | D | D | D | 20 | D | D | D | 60.5 | 30.4 | 10.7 | 3.0 |
| Fremont | 18 | 209 | 10.2 | 4.4 | 19 | 62 | 5.8 | 1.4 | 81.7 | 33.7 | 11.6 | 2.6 |
| Gem | 41 | 574 | 33.9 | 13.1 | 29 | D | D | D | 124.8 | 64.1 | 19.4 | 5.6 |
| Gooding | 32 | 482 | 28.8 | 12.2 | 24 | D | D | D | 106.4 | 39.5 | 18.9 | 4.2 |
| Idaho | 35 | 535 | 38.2 | 17.6 | 19 | 51 | 3.1 | 0.6 | 183.1 | 63.3 | 22.3 | 7.1 |
| Jefferson | 33 | D | D | D | 17 | 24 | 3.4 | 0.7 | 114.0 | 52.8 | 17.0 | 5.6 |
| Jerome | 36 | 471 | 26.3 | 13.8 | 45 | 214 | 19.0 | 4.9 | 163.4 | 47.2 | 20.7 | 6.4 |
| Kootenai | 458 | 7 004 | 573.4 | 238.0 | 240 | 1 242 | 82.8 | 24.6 | 1 486.4 | 487.5 | 118.9 | 38.9 |
| Latah | 71 | 1 210 | 92.7 | 36.9 | 59 | 407 | 25.4 | 8.0 | 289.0 | 88.2 | 27.4 | 8.0 |
| Lemhi | 32 | 431 | 24.3 | 10.4 | 27 | 69 | 5.3 | 1.2 | 96.4 | 38.3 | 15.7 | 2.1 |
| Lewis | 15 | 59 | 3.7 | 1.3 | 1 | D | D | D | 83.4 | 31.2 | 8.0 | 3.1 |
| Lincoln | 7 | D | D | D | 2 | D | D | D | 26.4 | 10.2 | 4.2 | 1.0 |
| Madison | 84 | 1 183 | 99.2 | 35.9 | 31 | 163 | 9.6 | 2.5 | 133.8 | 40.0 | 13.8 | 4.2 |
| Minidoka | 39 | 588 | 34.0 | 13.9 | 26 | 186 | 17.1 | 4.5 | 124.6 | 51.4 | 26.8 | 7.8 |
| Nez Perce | 140 | 2 949 | 271.7 | 95.2 | 89 | 484 | 31.7 | 9.5 | 422.7 | 163.3 | 64.7 | 16.4 |
| Oneida | 8 | 174 | 7.8 | 3.5 | 4 | D | D | D | 29.2 | 14.5 | 5.6 | 1.2 |
| Owyhee | 13 | 128 | 6.2 | 3.0 | 8 | D | D | D | 78.7 | 27.1 | 8.4 | 4.5 |
| Payette | 39 | 512 | 29.6 | 11.9 | 21 | D | D | D | 157.5 | 65.9 | 23.3 | 11.1 |
| Power | 12 | D | D | D | 13 | 43 | 4.0 | 0.9 | 55.5 | 17.1 | 6.1 | 3.8 |
| Shoshone | 32 | 458 | 31.1 | 11.8 | 23 | 84 | 5.9 | 1.6 | 148.9 | 57.0 | 30.2 | 13.7 |
| Teton | 29 | D | D | D | 20 | 75 | 6.2 | 1.9 | 38.3 | 12.3 | 6.0 | 0.5 |
| Twin Falls | 311 | 4 734 | 373.6 | 134.8 | 167 | 976 | 70.1 | 20.6 | 524.9 | 220.9 | 80.2 | 24.7 |
| Valley | 40 | 399 | 32.5 | 12.4 | 31 | 109 | 8.9 | 2.7 | 89.5 | 36.7 | 11.7 | 2.9 |
| Washington | 22 | 413 | 24.3 | 9.6 | 11 | 40 | 5.5 | 1.0 | 88.1 | 38.4 | 14.5 | 7.0 |
| ILLINOIS | 31 062 | 706 669 | 70 042.9 | 28 009.4 | 23 510 | 167 675 | 20 639.2 | 5 203.0 | 109 967.5 | 32 012.8 | 19 805.5 | 4 615.9 |
| Adams | 156 | 5 096 | 509.4 | 185.2 | 158 | D | D | D | 548.0 | 221.0 | 114.8 | 22.1 |
| Alexander | 8 | D | D | D | 6 | D | D | D | 122.9 | 29.7 | 24.3 | 9.3 |
| Bond | 30 | D | D | D | 26 | 88 | 7.0 | 2.0 | 148.7 | 52.7 | 28.0 | 4.5 |
| Boone | 65 | 745 | 39.7 | 15.8 | 66 | 345 | 27.5 | 7.9 | 204.7 | 125.5 | 39.0 | 6.3 |
| Brown | 7 | 152 | 8.7 | 4.0 | 10 | D | D | D | 34.6 | 14.4 | 8.3 | 1.4 |
| Bureau | 77 | 2 024 | 157.6 | 64.9 | 76 | 304 | 22.3 | 6.9 | 257.0 | 115.0 | 66.9 | 5.6 |
| Calhoun | 6 | D | D | D | 6 | 6 | 1.0 | 0.2 | 72.7 | 19.8 | 11.1 | 1.5 |
| Carroll | 28 | 550 | 18.9 | 8.6 | 32 | 164 | 12.0 | 3.4 | 130.5 | 66.4 | 32.0 | 3.7 |
| Cass | 23 | 366 | 14.8 | 7.3 | 23 | 100 | 7.2 | 1.9 | 94.8 | 42.6 | 26.1 | 3.1 |
| Champaign | 363 | 10 977 | 1 251.3 | 490.5 | 290 | 2 154 | 428.6 | 56.4 | 1 499.6 | 374.1 | 153.2 | 43.9 |
| Christian | 71 | 1 664 | 107.0 | 42.0 | 68 | 319 | 19.1 | 4.8 | 258.8 | 117.7 | 78.2 | 10.1 |
| Clark | 20 | 393 | 18.9 | 9.1 | 23 | 71 | 4.6 | 1.0 | 123.6 | 55.7 | 33.3 | 4.2 |
| Clay | 37 | 711 | 44.4 | 17.5 | 31 | 116 | 9.0 | 1.8 | 121.1 | 44.7 | 32.5 | 4.3 |
| Clinton | 76 | D | D | D | 62 | 257 | 17.0 | 4.6 | 226.7 | 114.8 | 55.8 | 5.0 |
| Coles | 156 | 3 631 | 290.3 | 105.3 | 100 | 498 | 35.4 | 10.7 | 344.9 | 132.6 | 80.2 | 14.9 |
| Cook | 13 580 | 325 243 | 34 227.7 | 13 682.6 | 9 784 | 79 024 | 11 900.2 | 2 789.2 | 45 944.7 | 11 361.0 | 10 015.8 | 2 820.5 |
| Crawford | 44 | 894 | 54.7 | 21.0 | 44 | 183 | 14.2 | 3.4 | 141.7 | 65.0 | 36.3 | 4.6 |
| Cumberland | 18 | 229 | 15.1 | 6.9 | 14 | 84 | 5.1 | 1.9 | 72.0 | 31.2 | 17.5 | 2.8 |
| DeKalb | 202 | 4 374 | 368.3 | 143.8 | 148 | 838 | 59.9 | 16.2 | 522.7 | 212.2 | 95.3 | 11.9 |
| De Witt | 26 | 473 | 30.1 | 12.3 | 24 | 128 | 7.8 | 2.2 | 111.6 | 53.8 | 30.3 | 4.7 |
| Douglas | 33 | 331 | 19.6 | 8.6 | 30 | 140 | 13.4 | 2.9 | 103.7 | 51.2 | 26.5 | 3.5 |
| DuPage | 2 894 | 56 847 | 6 379.9 | 2 541.4 | 2 038 | 17 829 | 2 120.8 | 647.6 | 7 121.9 | 2 189.7 | 1 000.9 | 90.4 |
| Edgar | 32 | 744 | 53.7 | 21.5 | 29 | 108 | 7.4 | 1.8 | 144.1 | 63.9 | 37.9 | 5.9 |
| Edwards | 15 | 145 | 5.9 | 2.9 | 15 | 54 | 3.0 | 0.9 | 48.7 | 20.7 | 12.6 | 1.5 |
| Effingham | 120 | 2 550 | 231.6 | 88.4 | 95 | 783 | 48.6 | 19.2 | 226.1 | 107.4 | 51.6 | 6.1 |
| Fayette | 47 | 814 | 50.9 | 20.6 | 37 | 121 | 12.0 | 2.4 | 153.7 | 61.2 | 37.6 | 7.5 |
| Ford | 33 | D | D | D | 25 | 79 | 4.8 | 1.1 | 96.3 | 47.9 | 25.2 | 2.8 |
| Franklin | 70 | 1 329 | 77.8 | 32.8 | 62 | 227 | 20.0 | 6.1 | 379.2 | 167.6 | 91.3 | 22.2 |
| Fulton | 67 | 1 528 | 129.4 | 47.1 | 70 | 375 | 15.7 | 4.9 | 285.7 | 124.2 | 90.4 | 12.9 |
| Gallatin | 6 | D | D | D | 10 | 23 | 1.9 | 0.4 | 79.2 | 22.8 | 15.6 | 4.3 |
| Greene | 26 | 481 | 29.3 | 13.5 | 19 | D | D | D | 119.8 | 48.2 | 31.6 | 4.7 |
| Grundy | 97 | 1 780 | 171.5 | 67.5 | 78 | 400 | 33.7 | 9.1 | 219.8 | 122.4 | 57.6 | 6.3 |
| Hamilton | 17 | 422 | 21.2 | 9.4 | 19 | 40 | 3.2 | 0.6 | 82.7 | 29.7 | 18.2 | 3.0 |
| Hancock | 39 | 554 | 32.8 | 13.5 | 32 | 81 | 5.9 | 1.5 | 148.7 | 71.1 | 35.5 | 5.3 |

1. State totals may include programs not allocated by county.

**Federal Funds, Residential Construction, and Local Government Finances**

| STATE County | Federal funds and grants, 2009–2010 (cont.) Expenditures (mil dol) (cont.) Procurement contract awards — Salaries and wages | Defense | Other | Grants[1] — Medicaid and other health-related | Nutrition and family welfare | Education | Other | Value of residential construction authorized by building permits, 2011 — New construction ($1,000) | Number of housing units | Local government finances, 2007 — General revenue — Total (mil dol) | Inter-govern-mental (mil dol) | Taxes — Total (mil dol) | Per capita[2] (dollars) Total | Property |
|---|---|---|---|---|---|---|---|---|---|---|---|---|---|---|
| | 171 | 172 | 173 | 174 | 175 | 176 | 177 | 178 | 179 | 180 | 181 | 182 | 183 | 184 |
| IDAHO—Cont'd | | | | | | | | | | | | | | |
| Caribou | 2.6 | 0.0 | 0.6 | 3.3 | 1.5 | 0.1 | 0.1 | 1 379 | 8 | 35.1 | 15.3 | 7.3 | 1 062 | 1 020 |
| Cassia | 11.2 | 0.0 | 2.0 | 21.9 | 4.4 | 0.6 | 0.5 | 6 005 | 33 | 79.8 | 47.8 | 11.2 | 536 | 509 |
| Clark | 2.2 | 0.0 | 0.1 | 0.0 | 0.1 | 0.1 | 0.0 | 217 | 2 | 4.7 | 3.4 | 0.8 | 916 | 905 |
| Clearwater | 11.8 | 8.7 | 22.0 | 21.9 | 1.8 | 0.2 | 1.7 | 2 609 | 20 | 29.8 | 15.7 | 8.2 | 1 002 | 962 |
| Custer | 6.9 | 0.1 | 2.4 | 3.5 | 0.8 | 0.1 | 0.5 | 480 | 3 | 15.3 | 8.4 | 4.3 | 1 040 | 981 |
| Elmore | 232.1 | 77.5 | 2.4 | 12.9 | 4.4 | 2.8 | 2.2 | 3 156 | 15 | 85.4 | 33.5 | 12.4 | 429 | 398 |
| Franklin | 4.8 | 0.0 | 0.6 | 7.3 | 1.9 | 0.2 | 0.3 | 5 486 | 34 | 42.0 | 20.9 | 4.2 | 348 | 324 |
| Fremont | 6.8 | 0.0 | 2.1 | 11.5 | 2.5 | 0.3 | 0.1 | 4 670 | 31 | 35.5 | 17.7 | 15.1 | 1 208 | 1 165 |
| Gem | 9.5 | 0.0 | 1.7 | 19.8 | 2.7 | 0.4 | 0.2 | 2 418 | 14 | 48.4 | 24.1 | 11.0 | 669 | 587 |
| Gooding | 8.5 | 0.0 | 2.1 | 23.9 | 2.3 | 0.5 | 3.4 | 1 458 | 9 | 54.4 | 26.0 | 10.7 | 754 | 744 |
| Idaho | 20.0 | 0.4 | 25.0 | 26.1 | 2.7 | 1.6 | 0.8 | 711 | 7 | 47.0 | 25.4 | 7.2 | 467 | 439 |
| Jefferson | 4.9 | 0.0 | 2.7 | 12.6 | 4.7 | 0.4 | 1.4 | 8 608 | 51 | 57.7 | 37.7 | 13.4 | 586 | 571 |
| Jerome | 6.1 | 0.0 | 51.3 | 24.0 | 2.1 | 0.6 | 0.4 | 6 476 | 47 | 69.1 | 36.7 | 10.9 | 545 | 516 |
| Kootenai | 61.7 | 13.4 | 618.3 | 103.5 | 13.6 | 2.4 | 5.8 | 102 611 | 623 | 567.8 | 168.3 | 115.8 | 862 | 708 |
| Latah | 18.3 | 4.2 | 16.4 | 33.8 | 4.8 | 4.3 | 44.3 | 11 453 | 91 | 85.8 | 43.5 | 25.6 | 705 | 641 |
| Lemhi | 11.2 | 0.0 | 15.3 | 10.4 | 1.4 | 0.2 | 0.6 | 3 616 | 21 | 36.1 | 12.7 | 4.3 | 563 | 523 |
| Lewis | 2.6 | 0.0 | 0.3 | 19.8 | 1.2 | 0.1 | 1.2 | 201 | 2 | 18.7 | 10.2 | 4.9 | 1 373 | 1 344 |
| Lincoln | 4.5 | 0.0 | 0.5 | 2.1 | 0.8 | 0.2 | 0.0 | 274 | 2 | 16.8 | 10.7 | 3.3 | 737 | 707 |
| Madison | 8.4 | 0.3 | 1.0 | 10.7 | 4.9 | 0.7 | 0.8 | 8 192 | 58 | 114.1 | 42.5 | 20.1 | 549 | 403 |
| Minidoka | 4.4 | 0.0 | 1.5 | 19.8 | 4.5 | 0.5 | 1.8 | 11 198 | 56 | 69.4 | 34.0 | 9.0 | 485 | 461 |
| Nez Perce | 19.6 | 0.4 | 16.5 | 76.8 | 10.9 | 8.4 | 13.0 | 8 982 | 49 | 121.4 | 55.8 | 35.7 | 916 | 873 |
| Oneida | 0.8 | 0.0 | 0.2 | 3.1 | 0.7 | 0.1 | 0.1 | 776 | 10 | 13.9 | 7.9 | 2.3 | 569 | 552 |
| Owyhee | 3.2 | 9.7 | 1.3 | 14.6 | 2.4 | 0.5 | 0.3 | 1 899 | 14 | 38.0 | 22.3 | 11.4 | 1 048 | 892 |
| Payette | 4.4 | 6.0 | 1.1 | 32.7 | 8.7 | 0.6 | 2.0 | 4 831 | 32 | 59.5 | 34.4 | 13.6 | 598 | 551 |
| Power | 1.7 | 0.0 | 0.5 | 5.2 | 1.4 | 0.3 | 3.4 | 965 | 8 | 35.3 | 16.3 | 10.4 | 1 360 | 1 344 |
| Shoshone | 4.1 | 10.8 | 3.6 | 25.0 | 2.1 | 0.3 | 1.2 | 1 385 | 7 | 55.4 | 22.3 | 11.6 | 906 | 852 |
| Teton | 3.4 | 0.6 | 0.4 | 10.4 | 0.8 | 0.1 | 1.5 | 3 204 | 11 | 31.8 | 11.8 | 6.1 | 733 | 490 |
| Twin Falls | 43.7 | 2.2 | 11.1 | 84.7 | 15.6 | 1.9 | 4.3 | 25 483 | 159 | 363.5 | 131.5 | 47.8 | 654 | 611 |
| Valley | 16.1 | 0.0 | 12.2 | 5.2 | 1.3 | 0.1 | 3.0 | 5 800 | 23 | 67.9 | 19.7 | 20.8 | 2 331 | 1 938 |
| Washington | 3.0 | 0.0 | 0.5 | 17.7 | 2.3 | 0.3 | 3.2 | 2 166 | 19 | 49.6 | 21.6 | 6.5 | 642 | 620 |
| ILLINOIS | 7 949.5 | 7 118.7 | 4 481.8 | 12 147.7 | 2 913.9 | 2 151.5 | 6 847.0 | 2 118 058 | 11 809 | X | X | X | X | X |
| Adams | 44.2 | 6.5 | 5.6 | 75.4 | 12.3 | 3.1 | 7.7 | 7 902 | 50 | 190.5 | 93.7 | 61.6 | 918 | 780 |
| Alexander | 3.3 | 2.4 | 0.7 | 42.6 | 3.6 | 0.8 | 1.0 | 135 | 1 | 31.4 | 18.5 | 4.5 | 535 | 452 |
| Bond | 23.8 | 0.1 | 5.7 | 13.7 | 2.8 | 0.3 | 0.6 | 3 806 | 24 | 38.6 | 18.7 | 11.0 | 610 | 592 |
| Boone | 7.2 | 0.2 | 2.0 | 9.1 | 4.6 | 0.8 | 1.3 | 4 128 | 26 | 142.4 | 58.2 | 52.2 | 976 | 921 |
| Brown | 2.2 | 0.0 | 0.4 | 3.3 | 1.1 | 0.1 | 0.1 | 0 | 0 | 13.5 | 7.2 | 4.5 | 682 | 658 |
| Bureau | 12.3 | 23.3 | 0.8 | 11.6 | 4.7 | 0.8 | 1.1 | 4 050 | 22 | 138.1 | 46.4 | 39.7 | 1 133 | 1 093 |
| Calhoun | 2.1 | 9.7 | 0.8 | 6.2 | 1.1 | 1.6 | 0.1 | 1 880 | 11 | 12.4 | 7.0 | 3.3 | 645 | 639 |
| Carroll | 5.1 | 3.4 | 1.5 | 8.3 | 2.7 | 0.4 | 0.2 | 3 853 | 23 | 45.6 | 18.2 | 21.6 | 1 357 | 1 297 |
| Cass | 5.2 | 0.0 | 0.8 | 10.4 | 2.3 | 0.4 | 0.1 | 400 | 3 | 39.2 | 22.3 | 11.0 | 800 | 742 |
| Champaign | 132.3 | 25.0 | 45.7 | 243.8 | 25.8 | 19.3 | 377.3 | 64 276 | 487 | 608.1 | 226.6 | 268.5 | 1 411 | 1 161 |
| Christian | 7.3 | 0.0 | 2.1 | 24.0 | 5.4 | 0.9 | 2.5 | 4 649 | 34 | 98.0 | 53.6 | 30.2 | 873 | 830 |
| Clark | 4.8 | 0.0 | 1.1 | 11.1 | 2.5 | 0.5 | 0.2 | 388 | 4 | 45.7 | 24.9 | 12.5 | 741 | 699 |
| Clay | 3.8 | 0.0 | 0.8 | 19.8 | 2.8 | 0.4 | 1.8 | 1 071 | 6 | 54.9 | 21.8 | 8.7 | 626 | 595 |
| Clinton | 9.0 | 5.7 | 1.5 | 11.6 | 4.9 | 0.6 | 0.0 | 16 202 | 98 | 83.0 | 36.4 | 30.7 | 843 | 830 |
| Coles | 32.8 | 0.3 | 3.0 | 34.4 | 6.9 | 2.1 | 5.4 | 3 648 | 24 | 186.4 | 86.7 | 60.8 | 1 192 | 1 072 |
| Cook | 3 429.7 | 2 148.9 | 1 997.1 | 8 022.8 | 1 321.0 | 370.1 | 2 875.2 | 604 378 | 3 436 | 27 280.1 | 9 218.1 | 12 233.3 | 2 315 | 1 687 |
| Crawford | 4.8 | 0.0 | 1.1 | 13.6 | 3.2 | 0.5 | 3.1 | 5 700 | 38 | 80.5 | 26.1 | 17.2 | 877 | 856 |
| Cumberland | 2.4 | 0.0 | 0.6 | 7.0 | 5.1 | 0.2 | 0.6 | 110 | 1 | 25.1 | 13.3 | 7.6 | 699 | 689 |
| DeKalb | 22.4 | 2.2 | 4.7 | 22.4 | 8.9 | 4.5 | 71.5 | 6 516 | 40 | 383.8 | 126.7 | 171.8 | 1 656 | 1 396 |
| De Witt | 5.1 | 0.0 | 1.0 | 8.3 | 2.5 | 0.3 | 0.6 | 2 375 | 14 | 63.8 | 15.9 | 25.7 | 1 563 | 1 535 |
| Douglas | 5.1 | 0.0 | 1.2 | 7.0 | 2.5 | 0.4 | 0.0 | 1 864 | 12 | 49.4 | 20.6 | 22.1 | 1 128 | 1 093 |
| DuPage | 411.9 | 1 992.7 | 947.6 | 151.4 | 69.8 | 20.1 | 136.6 | 213 464 | 605 | 3 886.1 | 792.9 | 2 334.9 | 2 513 | 2 226 |
| Edgar | 7.3 | 0.0 | 1.2 | 14.5 | 3.4 | 0.5 | 0.6 | 495 | 3 | 50.2 | 24.8 | 17.9 | 945 | 851 |
| Edwards | 2.0 | 0.0 | 0.5 | 3.8 | 1.4 | 0.1 | 0.1 | NA | NA | 14.5 | 7.8 | 4.3 | 656 | 602 |
| Effingham | 22.0 | 0.3 | 2.9 | 17.4 | 7.5 | 1.0 | 2.0 | 6 824 | 32 | 98.7 | 51.2 | 29.9 | 875 | 822 |
| Fayette | 5.5 | 0.0 | 1.3 | 18.2 | 3.6 | 0.7 | 2.9 | 360 | 3 | 50.4 | 26.1 | 14.9 | 692 | 619 |
| Ford | 4.4 | 0.1 | 1.0 | 5.0 | 2.2 | 0.3 | 0.2 | 1 972 | 18 | 42.9 | 19.9 | 17.1 | 1 208 | 1 113 |
| Franklin | 14.6 | 3.1 | 7.3 | 50.8 | 7.6 | 1.6 | 3.3 | 695 | 10 | 130.1 | 68.3 | 21.2 | 536 | 483 |
| Fulton | 12.6 | 0.4 | 2.0 | 20.4 | 6.2 | 1.3 | 1.6 | 5 820 | 39 | 121.4 | 62.6 | 30.6 | 832 | 778 |
| Gallatin | 2.1 | 0.0 | 8.1 | 12.8 | 1.6 | 0.2 | 2.7 | NA | NA | 15.4 | 10.3 | 3.6 | 591 | 551 |
| Greene | 4.1 | 0.5 | 1.0 | 19.0 | 3.0 | 0.5 | 0.3 | 190 | 1 | 32.8 | 17.8 | 9.8 | 706 | 656 |
| Grundy | 9.2 | 6.1 | 2.1 | 5.2 | 3.9 | 0.6 | 0.2 | 12 637 | 115 | 186.2 | 49.2 | 104.6 | 2 218 | 2 150 |
| Hamilton | 3.2 | 0.1 | 0.7 | 12.2 | 1.7 | 0.2 | 0.3 | 0 | 0 | 35.4 | 15.7 | 4.8 | 577 | 575 |
| Hancock | 6.9 | 0.0 | 1.6 | 12.4 | 3.4 | 0.5 | 0.2 | 425 | 2 | 48.6 | 24.1 | 16.5 | 874 | 840 |

1. State totals may include programs not allocated by county.    2. Based on the resident population estimated as of July 1 of the year shown.

## Table B. States and Counties — Local Government Finances, Government Employment, and Voting

| STATE County | Total (mil dol) | Per capita[1] (dollars) | Education | Health and hospitals | Police protection | Public welfare | Highways | Total (mil dol) | Per capita[1] (dollars) | Federal civilian | Federal military | State and local | Democratic | Republican | All other |
|---|---|---|---|---|---|---|---|---|---|---|---|---|---|---|---|
| | 185 | 186 | 187 | 188 | 189 | 190 | 191 | 192 | 193 | 194 | 195 | 196 | 197 | 198 | 199 |
| **IDAHO—Cont'd** | | | | | | | | | | | | | | | |
| Caribou | 32.2 | 4 689 | 42.3 | 24.3 | 5.0 | 0.2 | 9.5 | 4.4 | 640 | 53 | 26 | 619 | 16.7 | 80.4 | 2.8 |
| Cassia | 76.7 | 3 661 | 44.1 | 0.1 | 5.6 | 0.4 | 7.0 | 49.6 | 2 366 | 171 | 88 | 1 486 | 17.0 | 80.5 | 2.6 |
| Clark | 5.0 | 5 474 | 45.1 | 0.2 | 6.2 | 0.4 | 25.1 | 3.8 | 4 177 | 37 | 0 | 108 | 17.1 | 81.3 | 1.6 |
| Clearwater | 27.3 | 3 313 | 40.9 | 1.9 | 7.7 | 1.0 | 9.3 | 8.0 | 976 | 202 | 33 | 802 | 31.0 | 65.8 | 3.2 |
| Custer | 13.3 | 3 199 | 48.1 | 3.7 | 5.4 | 0.4 | 9.2 | 1.7 | 408 | 154 | 16 | 304 | 26.0 | 72.0 | 2.0 |
| Elmore | 82.7 | 2 867 | 38.3 | 30.7 | 5.1 | 0.2 | 7.2 | 29.8 | 1 033 | 871 | 3 583 | 1 365 | 30.7 | 67.2 | 2.1 |
| Franklin | 37.4 | 3 067 | 50.4 | 25.2 | 3.8 | 0.7 | 5.0 | 6.8 | 559 | 35 | 49 | 910 | 11.8 | 83.7 | 4.5 |
| Fremont | 34.1 | 2 724 | 46.5 | 0.9 | 7.1 | 0.9 | 8.1 | 23.0 | 1 838 | 87 | 50 | 1 017 | 18.1 | 79.9 | 2.0 |
| Gem | 44.1 | 2 675 | 43.0 | 18.4 | 3.1 | 0.8 | 4.5 | 20.9 | 1 266 | 82 | 63 | 775 | 27.3 | 70.3 | 2.5 |
| Gooding | 45.8 | 3 214 | 50.5 | 22.9 | 3.2 | 0.6 | 6.9 | 17.5 | 1 228 | 67 | 58 | 1 024 | 27.6 | 69.8 | 2.5 |
| Idaho | 44.2 | 2 879 | 38.7 | 16.2 | 3.4 | 0.9 | 18.3 | 6.1 | 397 | 352 | 62 | 860 | 24.6 | 71.8 | 3.6 |
| Jefferson | 54.3 | 2 378 | 62.9 | 1.3 | 4.2 | 0.6 | 3.8 | 21.8 | 956 | 51 | 99 | 1 260 | 15.7 | 81.8 | 2.5 |
| Jerome | 79.3 | 3 950 | 50.9 | 0.4 | 2.9 | 0.6 | 7.7 | 50.8 | 2 531 | 48 | 86 | 943 | 26.2 | 71.5 | 2.3 |
| Kootenai | 541.9 | 4 031 | 32.3 | 34.0 | 3.6 | 0.5 | 4.0 | 219.9 | 1 636 | 575 | 534 | 9 378 | 35.7 | 62.0 | 2.3 |
| Latah | 82.4 | 2 270 | 51.8 | 0.3 | 10.8 | 0.6 | 8.0 | 33.1 | 911 | 193 | 169 | 6 436 | 51.9 | 45.1 | 3.0 |
| Lemhi | 31.6 | 4 092 | 28.3 | 43.4 | 4.5 | 0.6 | 5.1 | 17.6 | 2 282 | 212 | 30 | 601 | 25.8 | 71.6 | 2.6 |
| Lewis | 17.6 | 4 907 | 49.1 | 1.4 | 5.9 | 0.7 | 12.0 | 6.6 | 1 836 | 40 | 14 | 417 | 26.6 | 70.7 | 2.8 |
| Lincoln | 16.7 | 3 708 | 48.4 | 1.2 | 3.4 | 0.7 | 36.5 | 4.8 | 1 076 | 87 | 20 | 390 | 29.1 | 65.9 | 5.0 |
| Madison | 112.3 | 3 064 | 31.0 | 38.8 | 5.0 | 0.1 | 5.0 | 148.1 | 4 041 | 57 | 143 | 1 946 | 12.5 | 85.2 | 2.3 |
| Minidoka | 65.6 | 3 534 | 42.9 | 19.5 | 3.7 | 4.3 | 4.3 | 48.6 | 2 617 | 57 | 76 | 1 360 | 23.7 | 73.8 | 2.5 |
| Nez Perce | 122.2 | 3 138 | 43.9 | 4.4 | 7.0 | 0.5 | 6.5 | 12.6 | 324 | 203 | 151 | 3 824 | 40.0 | 58.1 | 1.9 |
| Oneida | 13.7 | 3 337 | 45.2 | 21.2 | 5.9 | 0.2 | 7.5 | 4.0 | 983 | 18 | 16 | 424 | 17.6 | 79.7 | 2.6 |
| Owyhee | 36.7 | 3 389 | 52.5 | 0.2 | 3.9 | 0.7 | 7.2 | 16.4 | 1 518 | 59 | 43 | 649 | 23.3 | 74.5 | 2.2 |
| Payette | 64.0 | 2 815 | 60.3 | 0.2 | 6.3 | 0.7 | 6.4 | 28.5 | 1 251 | 36 | 85 | 1 025 | 28.0 | 69.5 | 2.4 |
| Power | 33.0 | 4 296 | 44.1 | 17.8 | 4.7 | 0.3 | 9.7 | 17.4 | 2 261 | 25 | 29 | 643 | 36.1 | 61.7 | 2.1 |
| Shoshone | 62.7 | 4 883 | 42.4 | 16.6 | 4.3 | 0.8 | 12.5 | 48.6 | 3 789 | 78 | 48 | 913 | 44.5 | 52.1 | 3.4 |
| Teton | 29.5 | 3 531 | 36.8 | 28.3 | 2.3 | 0.3 | 5.2 | 28.9 | 3 462 | 41 | 38 | 550 | 49.4 | 48.6 | 2.0 |
| Twin Falls | 357.1 | 4 887 | 42.0 | 33.1 | 2.8 | 0.9 | 3.5 | 165.6 | 2 266 | 415 | 296 | 4 343 | 30.4 | 67.1 | 2.4 |
| Valley | 55.3 | 6 177 | 30.1 | 23.9 | 2.7 | 0.3 | 12.5 | 87.9 | 9 822 | 238 | 36 | 737 | 45.4 | 52.3 | 2.2 |
| Washington | 41.2 | 4 061 | 39.6 | 16.8 | 3.6 | 0.7 | 7.6 | 10.7 | 1 057 | 52 | 39 | 684 | 27.5 | 70.3 | 2.2 |
| **ILLINOIS** | X | X | X | X | X | X | X | X | X | 85 985 | 44 784 | 758 500 | 61.9 | 36.8 | 1.3 |
| Adams | 181.9 | 2 713 | 56.3 | 2.9 | 5.6 | 0.2 | 7.3 | 65.1 | 970 | 323 | 135 | 4 255 | 38.3 | 60.7 | 1.0 |
| Alexander | 31.7 | 3 751 | 46.7 | 0.0 | 4.9 | 0.7 | 6.6 | 5.6 | 658 | 35 | 16 | 533 | 55.6 | 43.0 | 1.4 |
| Bond | 38.4 | 2 122 | 45.6 | 6.8 | 5.2 | 0.1 | 9.6 | 17.7 | 978 | 342 | 35 | 737 | 48.5 | 49.8 | 1.7 |
| Boone | 183.0 | 3 418 | 65.5 | 0.6 | 3.1 | 2.3 | 4.8 | 148.8 | 2 780 | 79 | 109 | 2 135 | 51.1 | 47.0 | 1.9 |
| Brown | 12.9 | 1 972 | 45.4 | 2.1 | 6.0 | 0.0 | 14.2 | 4.9 | 744 | 40 | 14 | 454 | 38.4 | 60.1 | 1.5 |
| Bureau | 137.5 | 3 924 | 37.6 | 21.2 | 4.0 | 3.2 | 8.1 | 52.9 | 1 511 | 141 | 69 | 2 173 | 51.9 | 46.2 | 1.8 |
| Calhoun | 12.9 | 2 488 | 53.0 | 0.7 | 3.4 | 0.1 | 19.5 | 5.6 | 1 086 | 30 | 10 | 218 | 52.7 | 45.2 | 2.0 |
| Carroll | 44.5 | 2 794 | 58.8 | 1.3 | 6.0 | 0.3 | 8.0 | 25.4 | 1 595 | 74 | 30 | 780 | 51.7 | 46.9 | 1.5 |
| Cass | 37.3 | 2 718 | 49.9 | 7.8 | 4.8 | 0.4 | 6.2 | 10.4 | 756 | 58 | 27 | 876 | 49.7 | 48.4 | 1.9 |
| Champaign | 584.6 | 3 073 | 48.8 | 2.5 | 5.7 | 3.6 | 5.4 | 333.6 | 1 754 | 1 244 | 439 | 34 573 | 57.8 | 40.3 | 2.0 |
| Christian | 104.1 | 3 013 | 62.4 | 1.4 | 5.3 | 0.2 | 7.5 | 32.3 | 934 | 80 | 70 | 1 652 | 45.8 | 52.1 | 2.1 |
| Clark | 44.2 | 2 617 | 49.8 | 1.8 | 5.3 | 0.2 | 14.0 | 20.7 | 1 224 | 59 | 32 | 862 | 45.1 | 53.2 | 1.7 |
| Clay | 56.9 | 4 099 | 35.3 | 30.5 | 3.3 | 0.0 | 5.7 | 39.6 | 2 854 | 48 | 27 | 923 | 37.6 | 60.8 | 1.6 |
| Clinton | 80.1 | 2 196 | 50.0 | 1.8 | 7.4 | 0.0 | 10.9 | 46.2 | 1 267 | 106 | 76 | 2 322 | 44.2 | 54.0 | 1.7 |
| Coles | 199.7 | 3 915 | 59.2 | 1.6 | 4.9 | 0.2 | 6.5 | 73.5 | 1 440 | 131 | 112 | 6 308 | 50.8 | 47.6 | 1.7 |
| Cook | 26 539.5 | 5 022 | 36.7 | 4.6 | 7.7 | 1.1 | 3.7 | 44 769.2 | 8 471 | 40 265 | 10 809 | 285 495 | 76.2 | 22.8 | 1.0 |
| Crawford | 79.5 | 4 053 | 36.8 | 40.1 | 2.6 | 0.0 | 6.4 | 31.0 | 1 582 | 57 | 40 | 1 930 | 42.5 | 55.5 | 1.9 |
| Cumberland | 23.6 | 2 178 | 57.8 | 1.6 | 4.8 | 0.2 | 9.6 | 10.7 | 982 | 34 | 22 | 468 | 38.6 | 59.3 | 2.1 |
| DeKalb | 378.7 | 3 651 | 46.6 | 1.9 | 5.8 | 3.2 | 7.4 | 264.5 | 2 550 | 190 | 215 | 13 114 | 57.5 | 40.8 | 1.7 |
| De Witt | 59.6 | 3 627 | 39.3 | 20.7 | 6.1 | 0.1 | 8.7 | 16.5 | 1 006 | 52 | 33 | 1 065 | 42.4 | 55.7 | 1.9 |
| Douglas | 45.7 | 2 331 | 51.0 | 1.5 | 6.7 | 0.2 | 10.2 | 26.9 | 1 370 | 62 | 40 | 992 | 38.6 | 59.9 | 1.5 |
| DuPage | 3 750.1 | 4 036 | 52.2 | 1.0 | 6.5 | 1.7 | 5.2 | 4 021.9 | 4 328 | 4 875 | 1 865 | 44 944 | 54.7 | 43.9 | 1.4 |
| Edgar | 47.3 | 2 498 | 57.8 | 2.9 | 5.9 | 0.1 | 8.3 | 15.5 | 817 | 61 | 37 | 1 078 | 45.3 | 53.3 | 1.4 |
| Edwards | 16.0 | 2 427 | 52.0 | 0.8 | 3.5 | 0.1 | 10.4 | 26.3 | 4 004 | 24 | 13 | 311 | 34.0 | 63.8 | 2.2 |
| Effingham | 95.4 | 2 788 | 48.4 | 2.5 | 6.2 | 0.0 | 8.2 | 32.3 | 942 | 192 | 69 | 1 659 | 31.3 | 67.3 | 1.5 |
| Fayette | 49.0 | 2 282 | 49.6 | 6.3 | 6.8 | 0.1 | 8.3 | 36.3 | 1 689 | 63 | 44 | 1 409 | 41.0 | 56.8 | 2.2 |
| Ford | 46.2 | 3 259 | 59.6 | 1.0 | 5.5 | 0.0 | 6.2 | 16.1 | 1 135 | 55 | 28 | 831 | 34.9 | 63.9 | 1.3 |
| Franklin | 129.5 | 3 279 | 45.3 | 12.5 | 5.7 | 0.4 | 6.2 | 34.2 | 866 | 218 | 79 | 1 948 | 47.6 | 50.4 | 1.9 |
| Fulton | 121.8 | 3 305 | 55.7 | 3.4 | 4.4 | 2.1 | 6.0 | 82.5 | 2 239 | 103 | 74 | 2 487 | 59.6 | 38.3 | 2.1 |
| Gallatin | 14.8 | 2 452 | 49.1 | 0.7 | 2.5 | 0.6 | 19.3 | 4.0 | 658 | 29 | 11 | 257 | 55.5 | 42.4 | 2.1 |
| Greene | 32.3 | 2 325 | 53.0 | 5.2 | 4.7 | 0.4 | 10.9 | 23.2 | 1 669 | 50 | 28 | 705 | 45.1 | 52.6 | 2.3 |
| Grundy | 210.9 | 4 474 | 62.4 | 0.8 | 3.7 | 0.5 | 4.0 | 233.8 | 4 958 | 112 | 100 | 2 440 | 49.9 | 48.2 | 1.9 |
| Hamilton | 36.6 | 4 433 | 28.4 | 38.5 | 0.9 | 0.1 | 17.2 | 8.9 | 1 083 | 38 | 17 | 542 | 42.1 | 55.2 | 2.7 |
| Hancock | 50.6 | 2 684 | 56.5 | 3.5 | 3.7 | 0.0 | 9.3 | 15.3 | 812 | 76 | 38 | 1 155 | 43.7 | 54.5 | 1.8 |

1. Based on the resident population estimated as of July 1 of the year shown.    2. © 2013 Election Data Services, Inc. All rights reserved.

| STATE/ County code | CBSA code[1] | County type[2] | STATE County | Land area,[3] (sq km) 2010 | Total persons | Rank | Per square kilometer | White | Black | American Indian, Alaska Native | Asian and Pacific Islander | Percent Hispanic or Latino[4] | Under 5 years | 5 to 17 years | 18 to 24 years | 25 to 34 years | 35 to 44 years | 45 to 54 years |
|---|---|---|---|---|---|---|---|---|---|---|---|---|---|---|---|---|---|---|
| | | | | 1 | 2 | 3 | 4 | 5 | 6 | 7 | 8 | 9 | 10 | 11 | 12 | 13 | 14 | 15 |
| | | | ILLINOIS—Cont'd | | | | | | | | | | | | | | | |
| 17 069 | ... | 9 | Hardin | 460 | 4 258 | 2 886 | 9.3 | 96.8 | 0.8 | 0.8 | 0.8 | 1.4 | 5.4 | 15.1 | 6.2 | 9.6 | 11.4 | 14.6 |
| 17 071 | 15460 | 9 | Henderson | 981 | 7 043 | 2 678 | 7.2 | 98.0 | 0.7 | 0.6 | 0.5 | 1.2 | 4.4 | 15.2 | 6.4 | 9.2 | 10.6 | 16.8 |
| 17 073 | 19340 | 2 | Henry | 2 132 | 50 155 | 976 | 23.5 | 92.8 | 2.3 | 0.5 | 0.7 | 4.9 | 5.7 | 17.8 | 7.4 | 10.8 | 11.8 | 15.0 |
| 17 075 | ... | 6 | Iroquois | 2 894 | 29 240 | 1 443 | 10.1 | 92.7 | 1.3 | 0.5 | 0.7 | 5.7 | 5.3 | 18.0 | 7.2 | 9.9 | 11.2 | 15.4 |
| 17 077 | 16060 | 5 | Jackson | 1 513 | 60 071 | 863 | 39.7 | 77.2 | 15.4 | 1.0 | 4.5 | 4.3 | 5.1 | 12.2 | 27.1 | 13.3 | 9.4 | 10.6 |
| 17 079 | ... | 7 | Jasper | 1 281 | 9 614 | 2 461 | 7.5 | 98.3 | 0.5 | 0.4 | 0.5 | 0.9 | 5.6 | 16.9 | 7.6 | 11.5 | 11.0 | 16.0 |
| 17 081 | 34500 | 7 | Jefferson | 1 479 | 38 720 | 1 203 | 26.2 | 88.4 | 9.1 | 0.6 | 1.1 | 2.2 | 6.3 | 15.8 | 8.4 | 12.7 | 12.4 | 14.4 |
| 17 083 | 41180 | 1 | Jersey | 956 | 22 742 | 1 698 | 23.8 | 97.7 | 0.9 | 0.8 | 0.7 | 1.1 | 5.3 | 17.0 | 9.6 | 11.2 | 11.9 | 15.7 |
| 17 085 | ... | 6 | Jo Daviess | 1 557 | 22 549 | 1 709 | 14.5 | 96.0 | 0.9 | 0.5 | 0.7 | 2.8 | 5.1 | 15.3 | 6.3 | 9.2 | 10.8 | 14.8 |
| 17 087 | ... | 7 | Johnson | 891 | 12 760 | 2 255 | 14.3 | 88.2 | 8.5 | 0.7 | 0.4 | 3.1 | 4.4 | 14.3 | 8.8 | 12.7 | 12.8 | 15.1 |
| 17 089 | 16980 | 1 | Kane | 1 347 | 522 487 | 124 | 387.9 | 59.7 | 6.1 | 0.3 | 3.9 | 31.1 | 7.5 | 21.1 | 8.4 | 13.2 | 14.5 | 14.4 |
| 17 091 | 28100 | 3 | Kankakee | 1 752 | 113 040 | 530 | 64.5 | 74.4 | 16.0 | 0.6 | 1.4 | 9.2 | 6.6 | 18.4 | 10.2 | 12.5 | 12.4 | 14.0 |
| 17 093 | 16980 | 1 | Kendall | 830 | 118 105 | 515 | 142.3 | 75.1 | 6.4 | 0.5 | 3.6 | 15.9 | 8.3 | 22.6 | 7.0 | 14.9 | 17.4 | 13.2 |
| 17 095 | 23660 | 4 | Knox | 1 855 | 52 247 | 950 | 28.2 | 86.8 | 8.6 | 0.5 | 1.1 | 4.9 | 5.1 | 15.2 | 9.7 | 11.7 | 11.3 | 13.9 |
| 17 097 | 16980 | 1 | Lake | 1 149 | 702 120 | 88 | 611.1 | 66.1 | 7.5 | 0.5 | 7.2 | 20.3 | 6.5 | 20.3 | 9.2 | 11.4 | 13.8 | 16.1 |
| 17 099 | 36860 | 4 | LaSalle | 2 940 | 112 973 | 531 | 38.4 | 88.7 | 2.5 | 0.5 | 1.0 | 8.3 | 5.7 | 17.1 | 8.1 | 11.9 | 11.9 | 15.5 |
| 17 101 | ... | 7 | Lawrence | 964 | 16 604 | 2 001 | 17.2 | 86.4 | 10.1 | 0.4 | 0.4 | 3.5 | 5.2 | 14.0 | 9.4 | 15.1 | 14.0 | 14.9 |
| 17 103 | 19940 | 4 | Lee | 1 877 | 35 037 | 1 299 | 18.7 | 88.9 | 5.6 | 0.5 | 1.0 | 5.1 | 5.5 | 15.5 | 8.1 | 12.0 | 12.6 | 16.4 |
| 17 105 | 38700 | 4 | Livingston | 2 705 | 38 647 | 1 207 | 14.3 | 90.0 | 5.6 | 0.4 | 0.9 | 4.1 | 5.7 | 16.5 | 8.5 | 12.4 | 12.4 | 15.8 |
| 17 107 | 30660 | 6 | Logan | 1 601 | 30 013 | 1 427 | 18.7 | 88.3 | 8.3 | 0.5 | 1.0 | 3.1 | 5.1 | 14.5 | 10.9 | 13.7 | 12.8 | 14.6 |
| 17 109 | 31380 | 5 | McDonough | 1 527 | 32 537 | 1 375 | 21.3 | 89.5 | 5.9 | 0.6 | 2.8 | 2.8 | 4.5 | 11.3 | 29.8 | 10.6 | 8.3 | 10.4 |
| 17 111 | 16980 | 1 | McHenry | 1 562 | 308 145 | 190 | 197.3 | 84.3 | 1.5 | 0.4 | 3.1 | 11.7 | 6.2 | 20.5 | 7.7 | 11.1 | 14.7 | 17.1 |
| 17 113 | 14060 | 3 | McLean | 3 065 | 172 281 | 362 | 56.2 | 83.3 | 8.5 | 0.5 | 5.0 | 4.6 | 6.2 | 16.1 | 18.1 | 13.4 | 12.1 | 13.1 |
| 17 115 | 19500 | 3 | Macon | 1 504 | 110 122 | 543 | 73.2 | 80.3 | 17.9 | 0.5 | 1.5 | 2.0 | 6.3 | 16.4 | 9.4 | 11.7 | 11.4 | 14.2 |
| 17 117 | 41180 | 1 | Macoupin | 2 235 | 47 231 | 1 024 | 21.1 | 97.4 | 1.3 | 0.6 | 0.5 | 1.0 | 5.7 | 16.6 | 8.3 | 11.4 | 11.8 | 15.1 |
| 17 119 | 41180 | 1 | Madison | 1 853 | 267 883 | 248 | 144.6 | 88.0 | 8.8 | 0.7 | 1.4 | 2.9 | 6.0 | 16.5 | 9.9 | 12.9 | 12.4 | 15.1 |
| 17 121 | 16460 | 4 | Marion | 1 482 | 38 894 | 1 199 | 26.2 | 93.6 | 4.8 | 0.7 | 0.9 | 1.5 | 6.4 | 16.6 | 8.2 | 11.1 | 11.4 | 14.6 |
| 17 123 | 37900 | 2 | Marshall | 1 002 | 12 327 | 2 286 | 12.3 | 96.2 | 0.8 | 0.4 | 0.6 | 2.7 | 5.5 | 16.1 | 7.1 | 9.8 | 11.4 | 15.0 |
| 17 125 | ... | 6 | Mason | 1 397 | 14 327 | 2 146 | 10.3 | 97.9 | 0.9 | 0.7 | 0.6 | 1.0 | 4.9 | 16.9 | 7.0 | 10.2 | 11.7 | 15.3 |
| 17 127 | 37140 | 7 | Massac | 614 | 15 234 | 2 089 | 24.8 | 91.5 | 6.8 | 0.9 | 0.7 | 2.0 | 6.2 | 16.7 | 7.3 | 10.8 | 12.2 | 14.8 |
| 17 129 | 44100 | 3 | Menard | 814 | 12 722 | 2 259 | 15.6 | 97.5 | 1.3 | 0.6 | 0.6 | 1.1 | 5.4 | 17.4 | 7.4 | 10.1 | 12.3 | 16.4 |
| 17 131 | 19340 | 2 | Mercer | 1 454 | 16 219 | 2 028 | 11.2 | 97.2 | 0.6 | 0.4 | 0.6 | 1.9 | 5.6 | 16.8 | 6.9 | 10.1 | 11.8 | 15.6 |
| 17 133 | 41180 | 1 | Monroe | 997 | 33 357 | 1 344 | 33.5 | 97.5 | 0.6 | 0.5 | 0.7 | 1.4 | 5.7 | 18.4 | 7.0 | 11.0 | 13.2 | 17.3 |
| 17 135 | ... | 6 | Montgomery | 1 823 | 29 620 | 1 434 | 16.2 | 94.4 | 3.6 | 0.4 | 0.6 | 1.6 | 5.5 | 15.4 | 8.0 | 12.4 | 12.5 | 15.5 |
| 17 137 | 27300 | 4 | Morgan | 1 473 | 35 272 | 1 296 | 23.9 | 90.8 | 7.1 | 0.5 | 0.8 | 2.2 | 5.4 | 15.6 | 10.2 | 12.0 | 11.4 | 14.9 |
| 17 139 | ... | 6 | Moultrie | 870 | 14 933 | 2 112 | 17.2 | 98.0 | 0.7 | 0.5 | 0.4 | 1.0 | 6.4 | 18.4 | 7.3 | 12.1 | 11.4 | 13.9 |
| 17 141 | 40300 | 4 | Ogle | 1 965 | 52 848 | 942 | 26.9 | 89.1 | 1.5 | 0.5 | 0.9 | 9.1 | 5.7 | 18.5 | 7.7 | 10.5 | 12.8 | 16.1 |
| 17 143 | 37900 | 2 | Peoria | 1 604 | 187 254 | 339 | 116.7 | 74.7 | 19.4 | 0.6 | 3.8 | 4.0 | 6.9 | 17.2 | 10.1 | 13.6 | 12.1 | 13.3 |
| 17 145 | ... | 7 | Perry | 1 144 | 22 058 | 1 728 | 19.3 | 87.8 | 9.3 | 0.6 | 0.7 | 2.8 | 5.1 | 15.4 | 10.1 | 13.1 | 13.4 | 14.2 |
| 17 147 | 16580 | 3 | Piatt | 1 138 | 16 504 | 2 011 | 14.5 | 97.7 | 0.9 | 0.5 | 0.6 | 1.2 | 5.4 | 18.1 | 6.6 | 10.4 | 12.0 | 16.8 |
| 17 149 | ... | 7 | Pike | 2 153 | 16 308 | 2 024 | 7.6 | 96.6 | 2.1 | 0.5 | 0.5 | 1.1 | 6.0 | 16.5 | 7.8 | 10.8 | 11.9 | 14.2 |
| 17 151 | ... | 9 | Pope | 955 | 4 272 | 2 883 | 4.5 | 90.9 | 7.0 | 0.9 | 0.6 | 1.5 | 4.0 | 14.6 | 10.9 | 9.4 | 9.6 | 15.0 |
| 17 153 | ... | 9 | Pulaski | 516 | 5 998 | 2 760 | 11.6 | 65.5 | 32.9 | 1.0 | 0.7 | 1.7 | 5.5 | 17.4 | 8.0 | 10.3 | 10.4 | 15.0 |
| 17 155 | 36860 | 8 | Putnam | 415 | 5 886 | 2 775 | 14.2 | 94.4 | 1.2 | 0.5 | 0.5 | 4.3 | 4.9 | 15.8 | 7.0 | 10.3 | 11.1 | 16.6 |
| 17 157 | ... | 6 | Randolph | 1 491 | 32 956 | 1 355 | 22.1 | 86.9 | 10.3 | 0.4 | 0.6 | 2.7 | 5.1 | 14.5 | 7.9 | 14.2 | 13.0 | 15.7 |
| 17 159 | ... | 7 | Richland | 932 | 16 176 | 2 033 | 17.4 | 96.9 | 1.0 | 0.5 | 1.1 | 1.4 | 5.9 | 16.2 | 7.9 | 11.7 | 11.3 | 14.6 |
| 17 161 | 19340 | 2 | Rock Island | 1 108 | 147 457 | 426 | 133.1 | 77.2 | 10.0 | 0.6 | 2.3 | 11.9 | 6.3 | 16.0 | 9.1 | 12.5 | 11.7 | 14.1 |
| 17 163 | 41180 | 1 | St. Clair | 1 704 | 268 858 | 247 | 157.8 | 64.6 | 31.2 | 0.7 | 2.1 | 3.4 | 6.7 | 18.3 | 9.2 | 13.2 | 12.8 | 15.1 |
| 17 165 | 25380 | 7 | Saline | 984 | 24 946 | 1 610 | 25.4 | 93.4 | 5.0 | 0.9 | 0.8 | 1.6 | 5.9 | 16.9 | 8.5 | 10.9 | 11.6 | 14.1 |
| 17 167 | 44100 | 3 | Sangamon | 2 249 | 199 271 | 318 | 88.6 | 84.2 | 13.2 | 0.6 | 2.2 | 1.9 | 6.2 | 17.2 | 8.3 | 13.0 | 12.4 | 15.1 |
| 17 169 | ... | 7 | Schuyler | 1 133 | 7 457 | 2 644 | 6.6 | 94.8 | 3.4 | 0.4 | 0.4 | 1.6 | 5.5 | 15.3 | 6.7 | 10.8 | 13.4 | 15.3 |
| 17 171 | 27300 | 9 | Scott | 650 | 5 290 | 2 820 | 8.1 | 98.5 | 0.5 | 0.5 | 0.4 | 0.9 | 5.7 | 17.2 | 7.1 | 10.6 | 11.7 | 16.3 |
| 17 173 | ... | 7 | Shelby | 1 965 | 22 196 | 1 723 | 11.3 | 98.0 | 0.6 | 0.4 | 0.4 | 1.0 | 5.6 | 16.6 | 7.3 | 10.6 | 11.6 | 15.0 |
| 17 175 | 37900 | 2 | Stark | 746 | 5 946 | 2 764 | 8.0 | 97.5 | 1.0 | 0.5 | 0.8 | 1.2 | 5.3 | 17.9 | 6.8 | 9.9 | 12.1 | 14.8 |
| 17 177 | 23300 | 4 | Stephenson | 1 462 | 46 959 | 1 027 | 32.1 | 86.9 | 10.6 | 0.5 | 1.2 | 3.1 | 6.0 | 16.4 | 7.7 | 10.3 | 11.2 | 15.0 |
| 17 179 | 37900 | 2 | Tazewell | 1 681 | 135 949 | 458 | 80.9 | 95.7 | 1.6 | 0.6 | 1.1 | 2.0 | 6.2 | 17.0 | 7.5 | 12.9 | 12.9 | 14.4 |
| 17 181 | ... | 7 | Union | 1 071 | 17 647 | 1 937 | 16.5 | 93.0 | 1.5 | 0.9 | 0.8 | 5.1 | 5.6 | 15.7 | 8.4 | 10.6 | 11.9 | 15.0 |
| 17 183 | 19180 | 3 | Vermilion | 2 327 | 80 727 | 683 | 34.7 | 81.6 | 14.1 | 0.6 | 1.1 | 4.4 | 6.7 | 17.6 | 8.2 | 11.9 | 11.6 | 14.2 |
| 17 185 | ... | 6 | Wabash | 578 | 11 727 | 2 314 | 20.3 | 97.0 | 1.2 | 0.5 | 0.9 | 1.4 | 6.0 | 16.1 | 8.3 | 11.3 | 11.0 | 14.8 |
| 17 187 | 23660 | 7 | Warren | 1 405 | 17 731 | 1 933 | 12.6 | 88.2 | 2.5 | 0.5 | 1.1 | 8.9 | 5.9 | 16.1 | 12.1 | 10.9 | 11.2 | 13.4 |
| 17 189 | ... | 6 | Washington | 1 457 | 14 598 | 2 133 | 10.0 | 97.2 | 1.1 | 0.4 | 0.6 | 1.5 | 5.2 | 16.1 | 7.8 | 11.6 | 12.0 | 16.3 |
| 17 191 | ... | 7 | Wayne | 1 849 | 16 574 | 2 005 | 9.0 | 97.7 | 0.7 | 0.5 | 0.7 | 1.1 | 6.2 | 16.4 | 7.3 | 11.2 | 11.4 | 14.3 |
| 17 193 | ... | 6 | White | 1 281 | 14 568 | 2 135 | 11.4 | 97.7 | 0.7 | 0.6 | 0.5 | 1.1 | 6.3 | 14.9 | 7.0 | 10.1 | 11.5 | 15.4 |
| 17 195 | 44580 | 4 | Whiteside | 1 772 | 57 846 | 881 | 32.6 | 86.7 | 2.0 | 0.5 | 0.8 | 11.2 | 5.9 | 17.1 | 7.9 | 10.6 | 11.9 | 14.7 |
| 17 197 | 16980 | 1 | Will | 2 168 | 682 518 | 89 | 314.8 | 68.1 | 11.8 | 0.4 | 5.2 | 15.9 | 6.9 | 21.5 | 8.3 | 12.0 | 15.5 | 15.3 |
| 17 199 | 32060 | 5 | Williamson | 1 088 | 66 674 | 790 | 61.3 | 92.5 | 4.9 | 0.8 | 1.3 | 2.0 | 6.0 | 16.0 | 8.2 | 12.9 | 12.6 | 14.4 |

1. CBSA = Core Based Statistical Area. See Appendix A for explanation. See Appendix B for list of metropolitan areas with component counties. 2. County type code from the Economic Research Service of USDA Rural-Urban Continuum Codes. See Appendix A for definition. 3. Dry land or land partially or temporarily covered by water. 4. May be of any race.

# Table B. States and Counties — **Population and Households**

| STATE County | Age (percent) 55 to 64 years | Age (percent) 65 to 74 years | Age (percent) 75 years and over | Percent female | Total persons 2000 | Total persons 2010 | Percent change 2000–2010 | Percent change 2010–2012 | Components of change 2010–2012 Births | Components of change 2010–2012 Deaths | Components of change 2010–2012 Net migration | Households 2010 Number | Households 2010 Percent change 2000–2010 | Households 2010 Persons per household | Households 2010 Percent Female family householder[1] | Households 2010 Percent One person |
|---|---|---|---|---|---|---|---|---|---|---|---|---|---|---|---|---|
| | 16 | 17 | 18 | 19 | 20 | 21 | 22 | 23 | 24 | 25 | 26 | 27 | 28 | 29 | 30 | 31 |
| **ILLINOIS—Cont'd** | | | | | | | | | | | | | | | | |
| Hardin | 16.5 | 12.8 | 8.3 | 49.9 | 4 800 | 4 320 | -10.0 | -1.4 | 89 | 142 | -5 | 1 915 | -3.6 | 2.25 | 9.2 | 31.7 |
| Henderson | 16.1 | 11.8 | 9.4 | 50.7 | 8 213 | 7 331 | -10.7 | -3.9 | 119 | 190 | -216 | 3 149 | -6.4 | 2.31 | 8.7 | 27.3 |
| Henry | 14.1 | 9.1 | 8.3 | 50.2 | 51 020 | 50 486 | -1.0 | -0.7 | 1 189 | 1 242 | -270 | 20 373 | 1.6 | 2.44 | 9.5 | 26.1 |
| Iroquois | 13.9 | 9.7 | 9.4 | 51.1 | 31 334 | 29 718 | -5.2 | -1.6 | 677 | 810 | -322 | 11 956 | -2.2 | 2.45 | 9.3 | 27.2 |
| Jackson | 10.5 | 6.1 | 5.8 | 49.4 | 59 612 | 60 218 | 1.0 | -0.2 | 1 535 | 977 | -727 | 25 538 | 5.5 | 2.20 | 10.2 | 35.1 |
| Jasper | 13.9 | 8.8 | 8.8 | 50.2 | 10 117 | 9 698 | -4.1 | -0.9 | 242 | 236 | -85 | 3 940 | 0.3 | 2.45 | 7.9 | 24.5 |
| Jefferson | 13.8 | 8.7 | 7.4 | 48.5 | 40 045 | 38 827 | -3.0 | -0.3 | 1 064 | 989 | -177 | 15 365 | -0.1 | 2.38 | 11.4 | 29.1 |
| Jersey | 13.1 | 8.6 | 7.6 | 51.0 | 21 668 | 22 985 | 6.1 | -1.1 | 485 | 485 | -238 | 8 828 | 9.0 | 2.51 | 9.7 | 25.0 |
| Jo Daviess | 17.0 | 12.0 | 9.5 | 49.8 | 22 289 | 22 678 | 1.7 | -0.6 | 449 | 540 | -23 | 9 753 | 5.8 | 2.31 | 7.0 | 28.4 |
| Johnson | 14.2 | 10.6 | 7.0 | 44.2 | 12 878 | 12 582 | -2.3 | 1.4 | 244 | 290 | 231 | 4 584 | 9.6 | 2.41 | 8.3 | 25.3 |
| Kane | 10.9 | 5.7 | 4.3 | 50.1 | 404 119 | 515 269 | 27.5 | 1.4 | 16 532 | 6 446 | -3 330 | 170 479 | 27.3 | 2.98 | 11.0 | 19.8 |
| Kankakee | 12.2 | 7.2 | 6.5 | 50.9 | 103 833 | 113 449 | 9.3 | -0.4 | 3 263 | 2 399 | -1 255 | 41 511 | 8.7 | 2.61 | 14.7 | 25.5 |
| Kendall | 9.0 | 4.7 | 2.9 | 50.6 | 54 544 | 114 736 | 110.4 | 2.9 | 3 845 | 1 048 | 552 | 38 022 | 102.3 | 3.01 | 9.2 | 16.4 |
| Knox | 14.2 | 9.4 | 9.4 | 49.9 | 55 836 | 52 919 | -5.2 | -1.3 | 1 172 | 1 434 | -384 | 21 535 | -2.4 | 2.27 | 11.9 | 32.3 |
| Lake | 11.9 | 6.0 | 4.8 | 50.1 | 644 356 | 703 462 | 9.2 | -0.2 | 19 104 | 9 269 | -11 233 | 241 712 | 11.8 | 2.82 | 10.4 | 21.5 |
| LaSalle | 13.2 | 8.2 | 8.3 | 50.0 | 111 509 | 113 924 | 2.2 | -0.8 | 2 796 | 2 807 | -921 | 45 347 | 4.4 | 2.45 | 10.5 | 28.6 |
| Lawrence | 11.9 | 7.8 | 7.8 | 43.9 | 15 452 | 16 833 | 8.9 | -1.4 | 370 | 496 | -111 | 6 130 | -2.8 | 2.34 | 10.7 | 30.1 |
| Lee | 14.0 | 8.4 | 7.6 | 47.5 | 36 062 | 36 031 | -0.1 | -2.8 | 797 | 839 | -962 | 13 758 | 3.8 | 2.41 | 10.0 | 28.8 |
| Livingston | 12.9 | 7.9 | 7.9 | 49.9 | 39 678 | 38 950 | -1.8 | -0.8 | 1 062 | 867 | -494 | 14 613 | 1.7 | 2.43 | 9.9 | 28.6 |
| Logan | 12.6 | 7.8 | 8.0 | 49.2 | 31 183 | 30 305 | -2.8 | -1.0 | 666 | 721 | -267 | 11 070 | -0.4 | 2.34 | 10.6 | 29.2 |
| McDonough | 10.7 | 7.0 | 7.5 | 50.5 | 32 913 | 32 612 | -0.9 | -0.2 | 643 | 683 | -19 | 13 057 | 5.6 | 2.19 | 8.0 | 33.9 |
| McHenry | 12.0 | 6.3 | 4.3 | 50.2 | 260 077 | 308 760 | 18.7 | -0.2 | 7 785 | 4 057 | -4 623 | 109 199 | 22.1 | 2.81 | 8.9 | 19.8 |
| McLean | 10.7 | 5.4 | 4.9 | 51.4 | 150 433 | 169 572 | 12.7 | 1.6 | 4 660 | 2 439 | 551 | 65 104 | 14.7 | 2.44 | 9.6 | 28.1 |
| Macon | 14.1 | 8.3 | 8.2 | 52.1 | 114 706 | 110 768 | -3.4 | -0.6 | 3 180 | 2 605 | -1 181 | 45 855 | -1.5 | 2.33 | 14.1 | 30.9 |
| Macoupin | 14.0 | 8.5 | 8.5 | 50.8 | 49 019 | 47 765 | -2.6 | -1.1 | 1 093 | 1 247 | -385 | 19 381 | 0.7 | 2.42 | 9.8 | 27.0 |
| Madison | 12.7 | 7.5 | 7.0 | 51.2 | 258 941 | 269 282 | 4.0 | -0.5 | 7 126 | 5 966 | -2 480 | 108 094 | 6.0 | 2.46 | 12.2 | 26.8 |
| Marion | 13.9 | 9.3 | 8.6 | 51.2 | 41 691 | 39 437 | -5.4 | -1.4 | 1 089 | 1 055 | -650 | 16 148 | -2.8 | 2.40 | 12.8 | 28.8 |
| Marshall | 15.3 | 10.1 | 9.9 | 50.7 | 13 180 | 12 640 | -4.1 | -2.5 | 288 | 371 | -223 | 5 161 | -1.2 | 2.40 | 7.7 | 26.8 |
| Mason | 14.4 | 10.0 | 9.7 | 50.9 | 16 038 | 14 666 | -8.6 | -2.3 | 305 | 444 | -192 | 6 079 | -4.9 | 2.38 | 10.3 | 28.4 |
| Massac | 13.2 | 9.6 | 9.2 | 52.2 | 15 161 | 15 429 | 1.8 | -1.3 | 427 | 450 | -171 | 6 362 | 1.6 | 2.38 | 12.0 | 29.2 |
| Menard | 15.0 | 8.9 | 7.0 | 51.3 | 12 486 | 12 705 | 1.8 | 0.1 | 281 | 310 | 39 | 5 140 | 5.5 | 2.44 | 9.6 | 24.3 |
| Mercer | 14.7 | 10.1 | 8.5 | 50.4 | 16 957 | 16 434 | -3.1 | -1.3 | 351 | 401 | -178 | 6 734 | 1.7 | 2.41 | 7.9 | 25.8 |
| Monroe | 13.0 | 7.2 | 7.2 | 50.5 | 27 619 | 32 957 | 19.3 | 1.2 | 785 | 637 | 254 | 12 589 | 22.5 | 2.59 | 7.9 | 21.5 |
| Montgomery | 13.4 | 8.4 | 9.0 | 47.7 | 30 652 | 30 104 | -1.8 | -1.6 | 658 | 861 | -264 | 11 652 | 1.3 | 2.38 | 10.2 | 28.4 |
| Morgan | 13.4 | 8.8 | 8.2 | 49.8 | 36 616 | 35 547 | -2.9 | -0.8 | 818 | 818 | -271 | 14 104 | 0.5 | 2.30 | 11.2 | 31.5 |
| Moultrie | 13.1 | 8.4 | 9.0 | 51.4 | 14 287 | 14 846 | 3.9 | 0.6 | 382 | 394 | 97 | 5 758 | 6.5 | 2.51 | 8.9 | 25.5 |
| Ogle | 13.1 | 8.6 | 7.0 | 50.4 | 51 032 | 53 497 | 4.8 | -1.2 | 1 211 | 1 063 | -817 | 20 856 | 8.2 | 2.54 | 9.7 | 24.5 |
| Peoria | 12.8 | 7.3 | 6.7 | 51.5 | 183 433 | 186 494 | 1.7 | 0.4 | 5 924 | 3 865 | -1 223 | 75 793 | 4.2 | 2.39 | 14.1 | 31.0 |
| Perry | 12.9 | 8.3 | 7.5 | 45.7 | 23 094 | 22 350 | -3.2 | -1.3 | 454 | 532 | -209 | 8 335 | -2.0 | 2.38 | 11.3 | 28.6 |
| Piatt | 14.0 | 9.0 | 7.7 | 50.4 | 16 365 | 16 729 | 2.2 | -1.3 | 349 | 366 | -209 | 6 782 | 4.7 | 2.46 | 8.0 | 24.5 |
| Pike | 13.8 | 9.5 | 9.4 | 50.0 | 17 384 | 16 430 | -5.5 | -0.7 | 425 | 437 | -98 | 6 639 | -3.4 | 2.38 | 9.0 | 27.8 |
| Pope | 15.9 | 11.8 | 8.8 | 47.4 | 4 413 | 4 470 | 1.3 | -4.4 | 69 | 89 | -167 | 1 829 | 3.4 | 2.23 | 7.8 | 29.8 |
| Pulaski | 14.8 | 9.6 | 9.0 | 52.5 | 7 348 | 6 161 | -16.2 | -2.6 | 133 | 166 | -131 | 2 642 | -8.7 | 2.32 | 14.3 | 33.4 |
| Putnam | 16.2 | 10.2 | 7.9 | 49.6 | 6 086 | 6 006 | -1.3 | -2.0 | 115 | 142 | -89 | 2 509 | 3.9 | 2.39 | 7.2 | 26.0 |
| Randolph | 13.3 | 8.4 | 7.9 | 45.1 | 33 893 | 33 476 | -1.2 | -1.6 | 784 | 851 | -440 | 12 314 | 1.9 | 2.37 | 10.1 | 28.9 |
| Richland | 13.2 | 9.3 | 9.1 | 51.1 | 16 149 | 16 233 | 0.5 | -0.4 | 425 | 446 | -30 | 6 726 | 1.0 | 2.36 | 9.6 | 29.3 |
| Rock Island | 13.8 | 8.4 | 8.0 | 50.9 | 149 374 | 147 546 | -1.2 | -0.1 | 4 281 | 3 218 | -1 096 | 61 303 | 1.0 | 2.34 | 12.7 | 31.6 |
| St. Clair | 12.1 | 6.5 | 6.1 | 51.8 | 256 082 | 270 056 | 5.5 | -0.4 | 7 981 | 5 512 | -3 609 | 105 045 | 8.5 | 2.53 | 17.7 | 27.5 |
| Saline | 13.5 | 9.8 | 8.7 | 51.1 | 26 733 | 24 913 | -6.8 | 0.1 | 666 | 789 | 172 | 10 379 | -5.6 | 2.32 | 11.7 | 31.9 |
| Sangamon | 13.7 | 7.4 | 6.6 | 52.0 | 188 951 | 197 465 | 4.5 | 0.9 | 5 416 | 4 310 | 747 | 82 986 | 5.4 | 2.33 | 13.2 | 31.8 |
| Schuyler | 14.5 | 9.3 | 9.2 | 47.5 | 7 189 | 7 544 | 4.9 | -1.2 | 151 | 185 | -52 | 3 040 | 2.2 | 2.33 | 7.6 | 28.6 |
| Scott | 12.9 | 9.8 | 8.7 | 51.2 | 5 537 | 5 355 | -3.3 | -1.2 | 118 | 128 | -63 | 2 214 | -0.4 | 2.40 | 9.1 | 27.3 |
| Shelby | 14.4 | 9.9 | 9.0 | 50.3 | 22 893 | 22 363 | -2.3 | -0.7 | 521 | 546 | -127 | 9 216 | 1.8 | 2.40 | 8.0 | 27.1 |
| Stark | 15.2 | 9.1 | 8.8 | 51.0 | 6 332 | 5 994 | -5.3 | -0.8 | 119 | 165 | 7 | 2 425 | -4.0 | 2.43 | 8.0 | 26.8 |
| Stephenson | 14.1 | 9.5 | 9.7 | 51.5 | 48 979 | 47 711 | -2.6 | -1.6 | 1 156 | 1 220 | -688 | 19 845 | 0.3 | 2.36 | 11.2 | 29.7 |
| Tazewell | 13.4 | 8.0 | 7.7 | 50.8 | 128 485 | 135 394 | 5.4 | 0.4 | 3 490 | 3 070 | 213 | 54 146 | 7.6 | 2.45 | 10.2 | 26.3 |
| Union | 14.2 | 10.5 | 8.0 | 50.1 | 18 293 | 17 808 | -2.7 | -0.9 | 414 | 492 | -77 | 7 167 | -1.7 | 2.41 | 10.6 | 28.4 |
| Vermilion | 13.4 | 8.6 | 7.8 | 50.4 | 83 919 | 81 625 | -2.7 | -1.1 | 2 416 | 2 102 | -1 199 | 32 655 | -2.2 | 2.41 | 14.7 | 29.8 |
| Wabash | 14.5 | 8.6 | 9.4 | 51.1 | 12 937 | 11 947 | -7.7 | -1.8 | 318 | 324 | -225 | 5 012 | -3.5 | 2.37 | 9.3 | 29.4 |
| Warren | 13.4 | 9.0 | 8.0 | 51.0 | 18 735 | 17 707 | -5.5 | 0.1 | 435 | 428 | 27 | 6 918 | -3.5 | 2.40 | 9.7 | 28.2 |
| Washington | 13.7 | 8.8 | 8.5 | 49.6 | 15 148 | 14 716 | -2.9 | -0.8 | 289 | 326 | -83 | 5 926 | 1.3 | 2.44 | 7.3 | 25.9 |
| Wayne | 13.7 | 10.4 | 9.2 | 50.7 | 17 151 | 16 760 | -2.3 | -1.1 | 427 | 487 | -126 | 7 102 | -0.6 | 2.35 | 9.1 | 28.4 |
| White | 14.0 | 10.4 | 10.6 | 51.6 | 15 371 | 14 665 | -4.6 | -0.7 | 374 | 530 | 69 | 6 313 | -3.4 | 2.26 | 9.5 | 30.5 |
| Whiteside | 14.0 | 9.1 | 8.8 | 50.8 | 60 653 | 58 498 | -3.6 | -1.1 | 1 494 | 1 418 | -708 | 23 740 | 0.2 | 2.42 | 11.0 | 27.7 |
| Will | 10.7 | 5.6 | 4.1 | 50.3 | 502 266 | 677 560 | 34.9 | 0.7 | 19 282 | 8 796 | -5 524 | 225 256 | 34.4 | 2.97 | 10.9 | 18.5 |
| Williamson | 13.3 | 9.1 | 7.4 | 50.5 | 61 296 | 66 357 | 8.3 | 0.5 | 1 688 | 1 686 | 327 | 27 421 | 8.1 | 2.35 | 11.5 | 29.1 |

1. No spouse present.

# Table B. States and Counties — Population, Vital Statistics, Medicare, and Crime

| STATE County | Persons in group quarters, 2010 | Daytime population, 2007–2011 Number | Daytime population Employ-ment/resi-dence ratio | Births, 2011 Total | Births Rate[1] | Deaths, 2011 Number | Deaths Rate[1] | Persons under 65 with no health insurance, 2010 Number | Percent | Medicare, 2012 Eligible for Medicare | Enrolled in Medicare Advantage | Enrolled in a Medicare prescription drug plan | Serious crimes known to police,[2] 2011 Total Number | Rate[3] |
|---|---|---|---|---|---|---|---|---|---|---|---|---|---|---|
| | 32 | 33 | 34 | 35 | 36 | 37 | 38 | 39 | 40 | 41 | 42 | 43 | 44 | 45 |
| **ILLINOIS—Cont'd** | | | | | | | | | | | | | | |
| Hardin | 17 | 4 086 | 0.81 | 39 | 9.1 | 68 | 15.9 | 459 | 13.3 | 1 166 | 51 | 659 | NA | NA |
| Henderson | 51 | 5 705 | 0.51 | 51 | 7.1 | 86 | 12.0 | 955 | 16.5 | 1 628 | 102 | 917 | 126 | 2 006 |
| Henry | 724 | 42 705 | 0.67 | 522 | 10.4 | 533 | 10.6 | 4 670 | 11.3 | 10 245 | 1 183 | 4 700 | 915 | 1 981 |
| Iroquois | 468 | 26 222 | 0.74 | 301 | 10.2 | 351 | 11.9 | 3 131 | 13.1 | 6 559 | 381 | 4 019 | 419 | 1 497 |
| Jackson | 4 087 | 63 874 | 1.15 | 684 | 11.3 | 408 | 6.8 | 8 565 | 17.1 | 8 525 | 149 | 4 269 | 2 587 | 4 327 |
| Jasper | 54 | 8 591 | 0.75 | 90 | 9.3 | 103 | 10.6 | 1 115 | 14.0 | 2 044 | 84 | 1 286 | 147 | 1 511 |
| Jefferson | 2 203 | 42 948 | 1.24 | 476 | 12.3 | 440 | 11.4 | 4 108 | 13.4 | 7 649 | 337 | 4 494 | 1 404 | 3 605 |
| Jersey | 848 | 18 771 | 0.61 | 217 | 9.5 | 194 | 8.5 | 2 282 | 12.2 | 4 541 | 254 | 2 578 | 537 | 2 330 |
| Jo Daviess | 167 | 20 319 | 0.79 | 200 | 8.8 | 243 | 10.7 | 2 487 | 14.0 | 5 535 | 1 766 | 2 614 | 269 | 1 262 |
| Johnson | 1 553 | 11 670 | 0.72 | 102 | 8.1 | 126 | 10.0 | 1 166 | 13.1 | 2 823 | 147 | 1 261 | 218 | 1 885 |
| Kane | 6 787 | 478 366 | 0.87 | 7 556 | 14.5 | 2 838 | 5.5 | 69 652 | 15.1 | 60 637 | 5 752 | 28 920 | 9 459 | 1 830 |
| Kankakee | 5 107 | 108 996 | 0.92 | 1 493 | 13.1 | 1 088 | 9.6 | 13 722 | 14.5 | 19 597 | 541 | 11 050 | 3 460 | 3 354 |
| Kendall | 208 | 85 080 | 0.53 | 1 713 | 14.7 | 439 | 3.8 | 11 890 | 11.2 | 11 775 | 1 540 | 4 950 | 1 768 | 1 536 |
| Knox | 3 955 | 52 434 | 0.98 | 533 | 10.1 | 600 | 11.3 | 5 440 | 13.6 | 11 541 | 2 022 | 5 956 | 1 659 | 3 254 |
| Lake | 20 709 | 713 484 | 1.04 | 8 782 | 12.4 | 3 991 | 5.7 | 79 658 | 13.0 | 90 194 | 3 018 | 45 733 | 14 171 | 2 029 |
| LaSalle | 2 950 | 108 795 | 0.90 | 1 251 | 11.0 | 1 208 | 10.6 | 12 448 | 13.4 | 21 823 | 1 363 | 11 018 | 2 314 | 2 079 |
| Lawrence | 2 471 | 16 589 | 0.95 | 171 | 10.2 | 222 | 13.3 | 1 692 | 14.3 | 3 148 | 104 | 1 839 | 97 | 679 |
| Lee | 2 872 | 34 438 | 0.90 | 363 | 10.2 | 385 | 10.9 | 3 517 | 12.6 | 7 104 | 372 | 3 860 | 816 | 2 321 |
| Livingston | 3 390 | 38 684 | 0.98 | 485 | 12.5 | 361 | 9.3 | 3 461 | 11.6 | 7 013 | 715 | 3 585 | 837 | 2 142 |
| Logan | 4 361 | 29 008 | 0.89 | 301 | 10.0 | 314 | 10.4 | 2 449 | 11.4 | 5 557 | 245 | 2 626 | 931 | 3 244 |
| McDonough | 4 036 | 33 372 | 1.05 | 288 | 8.8 | 298 | 9.1 | 4 199 | 17.3 | 5 561 | 247 | 2 837 | 790 | 2 415 |
| McHenry | 1 647 | 263 415 | 0.71 | 3 607 | 11.7 | 1 722 | 5.6 | 32 058 | 11.7 | 40 642 | 1 637 | 20 485 | 4 382 | 1 484 |
| McLean | 10 676 | 174 894 | 1.08 | 2 097 | 12.3 | 1 058 | 6.2 | 15 110 | 10.6 | 21 558 | 3 018 | 9 137 | 4 044 | 2 486 |
| Macon | 4 059 | 116 562 | 1.12 | 1 425 | 12.9 | 1 135 | 10.3 | 10 986 | 12.2 | 22 375 | 1 719 | 12 813 | 3 932 | 3 539 |
| Macoupin | 876 | 38 631 | 0.58 | 481 | 10.1 | 583 | 12.2 | 4 703 | 12.0 | 9 879 | 211 | 5 722 | 790 | 1 688 |
| Madison | 3 754 | 250 533 | 0.85 | 3 196 | 11.9 | 2 616 | 9.7 | 26 569 | 11.6 | 48 657 | 9 503 | 22 048 | 7 124 | 2 720 |
| Marion | 758 | 38 650 | 0.94 | 495 | 12.6 | 426 | 10.8 | 4 364 | 13.6 | 8 762 | 144 | 5 359 | 1 449 | 3 838 |
| Marshall | 255 | 10 926 | 0.69 | 135 | 10.8 | 160 | 12.8 | 1 367 | 13.6 | 2 773 | 371 | 1 270 | 150 | 1 341 |
| Mason | 206 | 13 109 | 0.73 | 131 | 9.0 | 190 | 13.1 | 1 632 | 13.9 | 3 576 | 189 | 1 771 | NA | NA |
| Massac | 292 | 14 315 | 0.82 | 201 | 13.0 | 181 | 11.7 | 1 621 | 12.9 | 3 525 | 174 | 1 805 | 375 | 2 423 |
| Menard | 154 | 9 006 | 0.42 | 121 | 9.5 | 136 | 10.7 | 1 186 | 11.2 | 2 391 | 94 | 1 018 | 64 | 611 |
| Mercer | 185 | 12 644 | 0.52 | 164 | 10.0 | 179 | 10.9 | 1 582 | 11.9 | 3 698 | 604 | 1 621 | 275 | 1 703 |
| Monroe | 343 | 25 322 | 0.54 | 348 | 10.4 | 277 | 8.3 | 2 570 | 9.2 | 5 469 | 1 202 | 2 230 | 254 | 768 |
| Montgomery | 2 419 | 29 676 | 0.96 | 298 | 10.0 | 380 | 12.7 | 2 977 | 13.0 | 6 112 | 140 | 3 678 | 658 | 2 206 |
| Morgan | 3 064 | 36 235 | 1.03 | 359 | 10.1 | 356 | 10.0 | 3 282 | 12.1 | 7 347 | 294 | 3 929 | 580 | 1 676 |
| Moultrie | 395 | 14 160 | 0.91 | 158 | 10.7 | 162 | 10.9 | 1 718 | 14.2 | 2 848 | 206 | 1 539 | NA | NA |
| Ogle | 525 | 47 005 | 0.74 | 546 | 10.3 | 456 | 8.6 | 5 668 | 12.6 | 9 746 | 1 401 | 4 657 | 538 | 1 078 |
| Peoria | 4 979 | 209 113 | 1.28 | 2 722 | 14.6 | 1 696 | 9.1 | 19 481 | 12.4 | 32 171 | 6 234 | 13 488 | 7 944 | 4 247 |
| Perry | 2 500 | 20 482 | 0.78 | 208 | 9.3 | 232 | 10.4 | 2 200 | 13.3 | 4 242 | 150 | 2 645 | 238 | 1 062 |
| Piatt | 72 | 13 460 | 0.60 | 158 | 9.5 | 163 | 9.8 | 1 551 | 11.2 | 3 240 | 673 | 1 123 | 184 | 1 197 |
| Pike | 627 | 14 959 | 0.78 | 194 | 11.8 | 201 | 12.3 | 1 925 | 15.0 | 3 494 | 118 | 2 116 | 45 | 273 |
| Pope | 389 | 3 550 | 0.50 | 31 | 7.1 | 29 | 6.6 | 502 | 15.1 | 845 | 42 | 402 | NA | NA |
| Pulaski | 21 | 6 297 | 1.05 | 60 | 9.9 | 62 | 10.3 | 818 | 16.3 | 1 412 | 131 | 774 | 118 | 2 198 |
| Putnam | 2 | 5 397 | 0.78 | 51 | 8.5 | 77 | 12.9 | 619 | 12.6 | 1 261 | 109 | 594 | 54 | 896 |
| Randolph | 4 298 | 33 307 | 0.99 | 361 | 10.8 | 388 | 11.6 | 2 830 | 11.7 | 6 239 | 230 | 3 629 | 287 | 923 |
| Richland | 364 | 15 740 | 0.94 | 188 | 11.6 | 189 | 11.6 | 1 686 | 12.9 | 3 616 | 184 | 2 307 | 386 | 2 371 |
| Rock Island | 4 313 | 158 886 | 1.17 | 1 931 | 13.1 | 1 408 | 9.5 | 17 102 | 14.2 | 28 160 | 4 656 | 10 317 | 4 999 | 3 393 |
| St. Clair | 4 451 | 254 366 | 0.89 | 3 641 | 13.5 | 2 476 | 9.2 | 28 794 | 12.3 | 42 667 | 9 548 | 16 905 | 11 146 | 4 294 |
| Saline | 878 | 25 799 | 1.08 | 303 | 12.1 | 337 | 13.5 | 2 517 | 12.6 | 5 853 | 288 | 3 401 | 821 | 3 519 |
| Sangamon | 3 966 | 211 267 | 1.15 | 2 399 | 12.1 | 1 931 | 9.7 | 18 797 | 11.2 | 34 758 | 2 222 | 13 807 | 11 188 | 5 955 |
| Schuyler | 463 | 6 487 | 0.70 | 71 | 9.5 | 86 | 11.5 | 938 | 15.3 | 1 560 | 80 | 850 | 59 | 780 |
| Scott | 43 | 4 334 | 0.61 | 60 | 11.4 | 60 | 11.4 | 563 | 12.9 | 985 | 37 | 546 | NA | NA |
| Shelby | 205 | 18 571 | 0.62 | 231 | 10.4 | 253 | 11.4 | 2 245 | 12.5 | 4 795 | 118 | 2 705 | 148 | 866 |
| Stark | 92 | 5 176 | 0.69 | 49 | 8.6 | 82 | 14.5 | 586 | 12.3 | 1 262 | 198 | 541 | NA | NA |
| Stephenson | 835 | 46 888 | 0.96 | 517 | 10.9 | 529 | 11.1 | 4 997 | 13.0 | 10 477 | 2 769 | 4 343 | 1 221 | 2 551 |
| Tazewell | 2 843 | 127 675 | 0.89 | 1 540 | 11.4 | 1 345 | 9.9 | 11 142 | 10.0 | 24 767 | 4 357 | 9 521 | 2 703 | 2 257 |
| Union | 566 | 16 263 | 0.76 | 188 | 10.6 | 225 | 12.7 | 2 001 | 13.8 | 4 229 | 203 | 2 186 | 245 | 1 528 |
| Vermilion | 2 903 | 80 601 | 0.96 | 1 075 | 13.2 | 929 | 11.4 | 8 967 | 13.6 | 16 772 | 4 154 | 6 345 | 3 759 | 4 591 |
| Wabash | 88 | 10 593 | 0.74 | 147 | 12.4 | 134 | 11.3 | 1 342 | 13.8 | 2 473 | 68 | 1 527 | 374 | 3 121 |
| Warren | 1 116 | 16 550 | 0.85 | 194 | 10.9 | 190 | 10.7 | 2 012 | 14.7 | 3 166 | 353 | 1 799 | 704 | 4 079 |
| Washington | 246 | 14 758 | 1.00 | 127 | 8.7 | 138 | 9.5 | 1 407 | 11.7 | 2 899 | 98 | 1 683 | 102 | 897 |
| Wayne | 76 | 15 695 | 0.85 | 198 | 11.9 | 214 | 12.9 | 1 902 | 14.2 | 3 749 | 89 | 2 555 | 344 | 2 181 |
| White | 391 | 13 230 | 0.77 | 172 | 11.7 | 230 | 15.7 | 1 581 | 13.8 | 3 603 | 208 | 2 221 | 400 | 3 035 |
| Whiteside | 1 012 | 55 329 | 0.88 | 657 | 11.3 | 617 | 10.6 | 6 823 | 14.3 | 12 515 | 1 202 | 7 195 | 1 383 | 2 549 |
| Will | 8 547 | 589 222 | 0.73 | 8 859 | 13.0 | 3 799 | 5.6 | 74 625 | 12.3 | 82 185 | 5 654 | 38 473 | 12 600 | 1 873 |
| Williamson | 1 870 | 65 192 | 0.97 | 735 | 11.0 | 754 | 11.3 | 7 434 | 13.7 | 13 490 | 832 | 6 816 | 1 405 | 2 395 |

1. Per 1,000 estimated resident population.   2. Data for serious crimes have not been adjusted for underreporting; this may affect comparability between geographic areas and over time.   3. Per 100,000 population estimated by the FBI.

# Table B. States and Counties — Crime, Education, Money Income, and Poverty

| STATE County | Serious crimes known to police, 2011 (cont.)[1] Rate[2] Violent | Property | Education School enrollment and attainment, 2007–2011 Enrollment[3] Total | Percent private | Attainment[4] (percent) High school graduate or less | Bachelor's degree or more | Local government expenditures,[5] 2009–2010 Total current expenditures (mil dol) | Current expenditures per student (dollars) | Money income, 2007–2011 Per capita income[6] (dollars) | Households Median income Dollars | Percent change, 2000 to 2007–2011 (constant 2011 dollars) | Percent with income of $200,000 or more | Income and poverty, 2011 Median household income (dollars) | Percent below poverty level All persons | Children under 18 years | Children 5 to 17 years in families |
|---|---|---|---|---|---|---|---|---|---|---|---|---|---|---|---|---|
| | 46 | 47 | 48 | 49 | 50 | 51 | 52 | 53 | 54 | 55 | 56 | 57 | 58 | 59 | 60 | 61 |
| **ILLINOIS—Cont'd** | | | | | | | | | | | | | | | | |
| Hardin | NA | NA | 834 | 2.6 | 57.3 | 10.6 | 5.9 | 9 553 | 18 749 | 30 875 | -17.4 | 0.4 | 35 596 | 20.4 | 32.1 | 28.6 |
| Henderson | 430 | 1 576 | 1 530 | 10.1 | 53.2 | 15.3 | 9.5 | 9 249 | 23 237 | 47 944 | -2.5 | 0.5 | 45 217 | 12.0 | 21.3 | 19.0 |
| Henry | 156 | 1 825 | 12 100 | 7.7 | 48.1 | 20.3 | 76.7 | 8 865 | 25 931 | 50 698 | -5.8 | 2.4 | 50 445 | 10.2 | 15.7 | 13.8 |
| Iroquois | 71 | 1 426 | 6 981 | 12.9 | 53.9 | 13.7 | 52.0 | 10 716 | 24 563 | 48 248 | -6.1 | 2.5 | 48 577 | 13.3 | 20.9 | 18.5 |
| Jackson | 612 | 3 715 | 25 329 | 6.5 | 35.5 | 35.6 | 86.8 | 11 818 | 19 619 | 32 896 | -2.3 | 1.6 | 32 868 | 33.7 | 34.0 | 30.7 |
| Jasper | 257 | 1 254 | 2 242 | 16.0 | 48.4 | 15.1 | 20.9 | 14 660 | 22 917 | 47 731 | 1.8 | 1.1 | 46 257 | 10.7 | 16.4 | 14.6 |
| Jefferson | 593 | 3 012 | 8 777 | 8.5 | 48.8 | 15.2 | 58.3 | 9 292 | 22 032 | 42 679 | -5.8 | 2.0 | 42 601 | 17.6 | 27.5 | 25.2 |
| Jersey | 338 | 1 991 | 5 704 | 23.2 | 48.1 | 16.6 | 41.3 | 9 060 | 24 940 | 54 469 | -4.1 | 1.2 | 55 416 | 9.9 | 15.1 | 13.3 |
| Jo Daviess | 113 | 1 149 | 4 569 | 11.6 | 48.4 | 23.3 | 38.2 | 11 578 | 28 659 | 52 487 | -3.8 | 2.6 | 51 293 | 9.7 | 15.8 | 14.5 |
| Johnson | 380 | 1 504 | 2 578 | 4.2 | 53.1 | 13.0 | 17.4 | 8 362 | 17 328 | 42 172 | -6.3 | 1.3 | 42 357 | 15.4 | 20.5 | 17.9 |
| Kane | 187 | 1 644 | 145 845 | 16.4 | 41.0 | 31.8 | 1 252.8 | 10 200 | 29 864 | 69 496 | -13.3 | 6.7 | 66 133 | 12.6 | 18.7 | 16.3 |
| Kankakee | 392 | 2 963 | 30 792 | 19.0 | 49.6 | 17.3 | 199.3 | 10 178 | 23 190 | 49 266 | -12.1 | 1.7 | 46 046 | 16.4 | 24.4 | 23.3 |
| Kendall | 119 | 1 417 | 34 151 | 16.4 | 32.8 | 33.7 | 230.6 | 9 471 | 31 325 | 82 649 | -5.3 | 4.6 | 82 934 | 5.1 | 7.2 | 6.7 |
| Knox | 271 | 2 983 | 12 573 | 16.2 | 52.1 | 16.2 | 78.2 | 10 045 | 21 336 | 40 112 | -16.1 | 1.0 | 39 803 | 20.2 | 29.7 | 26.4 |
| Lake | 165 | 1 863 | 202 099 | 18.0 | 32.6 | 41.5 | 1 800.9 | 12 833 | 38 512 | 79 666 | -11.9 | 11.5 | 74 306 | 11.1 | 16.2 | 14.3 |
| LaSalle | 119 | 1 960 | 27 317 | 12.6 | 51.2 | 15.9 | 194.9 | 11 408 | 25 439 | 52 469 | -3.6 | 1.8 | 48 945 | 11.7 | 17.5 | 14.9 |
| Lawrence | 147 | 532 | 3 629 | 12.8 | 57.9 | 10.5 | 20.1 | 8 270 | 17 050 | 38 326 | -6.5 | 0.7 | 38 934 | 14.4 | 21.4 | 19.8 |
| Lee | 176 | 2 144 | 8 539 | 16.5 | 50.7 | 15.4 | 48.6 | 10 097 | 25 303 | 49 451 | -10.6 | 2.8 | 48 388 | 11.3 | 15.9 | 14.3 |
| Livingston | 218 | 1 925 | 9 139 | 8.3 | 56.0 | 13.7 | 74.6 | 11 350 | 23 530 | 52 835 | -5.3 | 1.7 | 53 249 | 12.0 | 16.8 | 15.2 |
| Logan | 314 | 2 930 | 8 025 | 19.7 | 52.3 | 16.8 | 37.5 | 10 628 | 22 136 | 48 714 | -8.4 | 1.8 | 46 863 | 13.6 | 19.2 | 16.7 |
| McDonough | 199 | 2 217 | 13 765 | 5.9 | 38.5 | 33.5 | 44.8 | 13 117 | 18 854 | 34 186 | -21.2 | 1.0 | 38 916 | 20.3 | 22.7 | 20.7 |
| McHenry | 124 | 1 360 | 89 153 | 16.6 | 35.6 | 31.9 | 574.7 | 10 640 | 32 318 | 76 909 | -12.1 | 5.5 | 70 682 | 8.0 | 10.2 | 9.0 |
| McLean | 323 | 2 162 | 57 352 | 15.1 | 32.9 | 41.1 | 251.5 | 9 851 | 29 425 | 59 410 | -6.4 | 3.7 | 59 291 | 15.1 | 14.2 | 13.7 |
| Macon | 512 | 3 027 | 27 712 | 20.9 | 48.0 | 20.8 | 181.8 | 10 710 | 25 797 | 45 987 | -10.0 | 2.9 | 44 725 | 14.8 | 22.4 | 20.2 |
| Macoupin | 158 | 1 530 | 11 460 | 12.6 | 50.8 | 15.3 | 58.2 | 8 057 | 24 141 | 48 739 | -0.3 | 1.4 | 46 525 | 12.5 | 20.1 | 18.2 |
| Madison | 262 | 2 458 | 72 387 | 16.2 | 43.8 | 23.3 | 413.3 | 9 660 | 26 939 | 53 143 | -5.2 | 2.5 | 50 462 | 14.0 | 19.5 | 18.1 |
| Marion | 347 | 3 491 | 9 627 | 9.6 | 51.5 | 13.6 | 76.2 | 10 761 | 21 418 | 40 097 | -15.7 | 0.9 | 40 056 | 17.1 | 29.0 | 27.6 |
| Marshall | 161 | 1 180 | 2 900 | 10.4 | 51.4 | 16.5 | 14.7 | 9 908 | 25 600 | 51 642 | -8.0 | 1.1 | 50 571 | 10.7 | 17.0 | 15.5 |
| Mason | NA | NA | 3 265 | 6.6 | 53.8 | 15.9 | 29.7 | 9 396 | 23 992 | 42 929 | -11.6 | 1.3 | 43 515 | 13.8 | 21.4 | 18.9 |
| Massac | 336 | 2 087 | 3 505 | 5.8 | 48.9 | 15.6 | 22.4 | 8 613 | 20 044 | 40 885 | -3.9 | 0.4 | 39 308 | 18.8 | 28.4 | 26.9 |
| Menard | 19 | 592 | 3 000 | 12.9 | 50.7 | 21.2 | 21.8 | 8 212 | 26 300 | 56 943 | -9.5 | 1.9 | 58 900 | 9.2 | 15.3 | 13.5 |
| Mercer | 149 | 1 554 | 3 788 | 12.7 | 52.0 | 14.0 | 28.0 | 9 220 | 25 878 | 51 216 | -7.2 | 2.0 | 52 351 | 9.3 | 13.5 | 11.5 |
| Monroe | 51 | 717 | 8 548 | 21.4 | 42.0 | 23.6 | 47.1 | 8 935 | 31 570 | 69 291 | -7.2 | 4.9 | 71 766 | 5.2 | 6.3 | 5.1 |
| Montgomery | 443 | 1 763 | 6 488 | 9.8 | 58.5 | 12.5 | 42.1 | 8 945 | 22 205 | 41 925 | -6.3 | 1.3 | 49 430 | 14.5 | 22.1 | 19.1 |
| Morgan | 266 | 1 410 | 9 263 | 24.0 | 51.6 | 20.5 | 56.5 | 10 913 | 23 598 | 44 731 | -10.3 | 1.7 | 43 210 | 14.3 | 21.6 | 20.0 |
| Moultrie | NA | NA | 3 280 | 11.4 | 57.5 | 15.2 | 17.6 | 8 956 | 24 078 | 48 982 | -9.5 | 3.1 | 49 994 | 11.4 | 18.1 | 16.3 |
| Ogle | 62 | 1 016 | 14 046 | 9.2 | 48.2 | 19.0 | 107.7 | 10 824 | 25 803 | 57 094 | -7.0 | 1.6 | 55 009 | 10.4 | 15.2 | 13.2 |
| Peoria | 572 | 3 675 | 49 554 | 25.8 | 40.6 | 28.3 | 299.3 | 10 883 | 28 743 | 50 689 | -6.1 | 4.0 | 49 022 | 18.3 | 28.6 | 26.2 |
| Perry | 98 | 964 | 5 271 | 6.0 | 52.2 | 13.9 | 25.5 | 8 741 | 18 469 | 41 333 | -8.0 | 0.4 | 40 167 | 18.5 | 24.0 | 21.4 |
| Piatt | 208 | 989 | 4 130 | 9.5 | 43.9 | 22.8 | 30.0 | 8 891 | 27 452 | 58 837 | -4.8 | 2.0 | 61 339 | 7.3 | 10.0 | 8.4 |
| Pike | 49 | 225 | 3 804 | 8.1 | 60.8 | 12.1 | 26.9 | 9 684 | 20 383 | 40 668 | -3.2 | 1.1 | 38 743 | 16.1 | 23.1 | 22.6 |
| Pope | NA | NA | 893 | 9.5 | 50.2 | 10.7 | 4.9 | 8 892 | 20 603 | 38 651 | -4.7 | 0.9 | 37 757 | 19.5 | 28.0 | 25.7 |
| Pulaski | 820 | 1 379 | 1 594 | 4.7 | 58.4 | 11.2 | 19.0 | 16 976 | 17 732 | 31 712 | -7.4 | 1.2 | 31 742 | 22.4 | 35.3 | 31.3 |
| Putnam | 83 | 813 | 1 267 | 6.3 | 48.4 | 15.1 | 9.5 | 10 140 | 25 510 | 52 409 | -14.7 | 1.4 | 51 518 | 8.3 | 13.4 | 11.8 |
| Randolph | 119 | 804 | 7 012 | 14.1 | 60.3 | 11.6 | 43.9 | 10 260 | 21 442 | 46 148 | -7.7 | 1.1 | 44 708 | 17.0 | 22.4 | 18.9 |
| Richland | 166 | 2 205 | 3 654 | 9.2 | 44.7 | 18.9 | 22.4 | 8 915 | 23 922 | 42 305 | 0.5 | 2.1 | 42 369 | 14.7 | 22.4 | 20.8 |
| Rock Island | 474 | 2 920 | 36 464 | 20.6 | 45.6 | 22.0 | 232.2 | 10 774 | 25 609 | 46 726 | -10.4 | 2.4 | 44 487 | 14.1 | 22.2 | 20.4 |
| St. Clair | 911 | 3 382 | 76 538 | 13.5 | 40.5 | 24.3 | 513.5 | 11 564 | 25 475 | 50 109 | -5.2 | 2.4 | 49 634 | 19.1 | 30.5 | 28.2 |
| Saline | 296 | 3 223 | 6 130 | 5.9 | 47.5 | 14.0 | 37.8 | 8 741 | 21 626 | 36 083 | -7.1 | 1.0 | 35 999 | 20.8 | 33.4 | 31.8 |
| Sangamon | 921 | 5 034 | 51 004 | 18.1 | 37.2 | 31.2 | 325.1 | 10 668 | 29 167 | 53 508 | -7.7 | 2.9 | 51 537 | 16.0 | 24.7 | 22.3 |
| Schuyler | 106 | 674 | 1 802 | 6.0 | 51.5 | 17.8 | 12.7 | 10 414 | 22 215 | 43 902 | -7.7 | 1.4 | 43 744 | 12.3 | 17.1 | 16.1 |
| Scott | NA | NA | 1 223 | 9.7 | 55.8 | 18.3 | 8.6 | 8 802 | 27 955 | 50 702 | 2.7 | 3.3 | 48 361 | 11.3 | 16.1 | 14.0 |
| Shelby | 117 | 749 | 5 040 | 4.1 | 54.1 | 14.5 | 23.4 | 9 161 | 22 522 | 44 689 | -11.3 | 1.6 | 45 964 | 10.8 | 17.1 | 15.4 |
| Stark | NA | NA | 1 400 | 10.2 | 52.9 | 14.3 | 17.4 | 14 728 | 24 952 | 49 693 | 2.7 | 4.6 | 46 913 | 10.4 | 15.5 | 13.6 |
| Stephenson | 130 | 2 422 | 11 666 | 14.2 | 48.1 | 17.8 | 79.0 | 11 084 | 23 413 | 43 410 | -20.4 | 1.2 | 42 661 | 14.5 | 24.3 | 20.9 |
| Tazewell | 263 | 1 994 | 33 647 | 13.7 | 41.9 | 23.5 | 193.4 | 9 576 | 27 395 | 54 617 | -10.6 | 2.3 | 50 106 | 11.3 | 15.2 | 13.6 |
| Union | 112 | 1 416 | 4 301 | 5.0 | 49.7 | 18.6 | 29.0 | 10 114 | 20 138 | 40 696 | -2.8 | 1.0 | 40 742 | 19.8 | 28.0 | 25.5 |
| Vermilion | 585 | 4 006 | 18 928 | 8.2 | 53.9 | 14.0 | 142.0 | 10 319 | 21 000 | 40 463 | -12.0 | 1.0 | 40 742 | 19.8 | 31.2 | 27.6 |
| Wabash | 225 | 2 896 | 3 046 | 10.8 | 45.5 | 16.0 | 16.4 | 8 667 | 23 629 | 47 426 | 1.9 | 1.7 | 48 743 | 13.5 | 20.7 | 19.2 |
| Warren | 301 | 3 778 | 5 064 | 29.2 | 50.1 | 18.6 | 24.7 | 9 249 | 20 373 | 42 773 | -12.5 | 0.7 | 44 818 | 14.2 | 20.9 | 19.7 |
| Washington | 281 | 615 | 3 283 | 15.1 | 47.2 | 18.1 | 18.5 | 9 143 | 25 177 | 53 036 | -4.0 | 1.1 | 50 465 | 9.5 | 12.7 | 10.8 |
| Wayne | 222 | 1 959 | 3 810 | 9.1 | 51.2 | 12.5 | 24.0 | 9 139 | 22 319 | 40 654 | -1.2 | 1.1 | 40 178 | 12.6 | 20.9 | 19.5 |
| White | 258 | 2 777 | 3 065 | 6.8 | 50.1 | 12.7 | 33.1 | 13 480 | 23 398 | 43 639 | 9.2 | 1.3 | 41 706 | 16.8 | 23.2 | 22.2 |
| Whiteside | 160 | 2 389 | 13 908 | 13.9 | 52.6 | 15.6 | 101.2 | 10 193 | 24 370 | 46 444 | -14.8 | 1.5 | 45 930 | 13.2 | 20.8 | 18.5 |
| Will | 159 | 1 714 | 202 524 | 17.2 | 37.9 | 31.3 | 1 263.7 | 10 671 | 30 199 | 76 533 | -9.0 | 5.5 | 72 053 | 8.4 | 11.4 | 9.6 |
| Williamson | 557 | 1 838 | 16 112 | 8.0 | 42.1 | 22.0 | 97.3 | 9 842 | 22 903 | 41 319 | -4.3 | 1.5 | 41 079 | 16.0 | 23.4 | 21.3 |

1. Data for serious crimes have not been adjusted for underreporting; this may affect comparability between geographic areas and over time.  2. Per 100,000 population estimated by the FBI.  3. All persons 3 years old and over enrolled in nursery school through college.  4. Persons 25 years old and over.  5. Elementary and secondary education expenditures.  6. Based on population estimated by the American Community Survey, 2007–2011.

# Table B. States and Counties — **Personal Income**

| STATE County | Personal income, 2011 | | | | | | | | | | | | |
| | Total (mil dol) | Percent change, 2010–2011 | Per capita[1] Dollars | Per capita[1] Rank | Wages and salaries[2] (mil dol) | Proprietors' income (mil dol) | Dividends, interest, and rent (mil dol) | Transfer payments (mil dol) Total | Government payments to individuals Total | Social Security | Medical payments | Income maintenance | Unemployment insurance |
|---|---|---|---|---|---|---|---|---|---|---|---|---|---|
| | 62 | 63 | 64 | 65 | 66 | 67 | 68 | 69 | 70 | 71 | 72 | 73 | 74 |
| **ILLINOIS—Cont'd** | | | | | | | | | | | | | |
| Hardin | 124 | 2.5 | 28 982 | 2 451 | 41 | 7 | 19 | 47 | 46 | 16 | 22 | 5 | 2 |
| Henderson | 265 | 9.3 | 36 872 | 1 090 | 50 | 48 | 37 | 54 | 53 | 23 | 19 | 5 | 3 |
| Henry | 1 882 | 6.2 | 37 404 | 1 038 | 577 | 214 | 332 | 347 | 336 | 147 | 123 | 30 | 18 |
| Iroquois | 1 155 | 8.5 | 39 189 | 833 | 360 | 226 | 196 | 240 | 233 | 95 | 93 | 22 | 13 |
| Jackson | 2 005 | 2.2 | 33 213 | 1 671 | 1 464 | 135 | 306 | 402 | 389 | 103 | 132 | 69 | 21 |
| Jasper | 344 | 7.4 | 35 451 | 1 303 | 119 | 58 | 71 | 69 | 66 | 28 | 26 | 6 | 4 |
| Jefferson | 1 299 | 3.9 | 33 546 | 1 593 | 987 | 86 | 198 | 334 | 325 | 106 | 136 | 42 | 15 |
| Jersey | 882 | 5.7 | 38 503 | 909 | 214 | 55 | 125 | 166 | 161 | 67 | 62 | 14 | 10 |
| Jo Daviess | 964 | 7.0 | 42 456 | 545 | 353 | 86 | 252 | 167 | 162 | 79 | 56 | 11 | 9 |
| Johnson | 328 | 3.5 | 25 920 | 2 890 | 99 | 25 | 47 | 93 | 90 | 37 | 33 | 9 | 5 |
| Kane | 19 403 | 5.1 | 37 293 | 1 049 | 11 387 | 977 | 2 844 | 2 627 | 2 512 | 941 | 905 | 293 | 230 |
| Kankakee | 3 771 | 3.2 | 33 171 | 1 677 | 2 057 | 198 | 524 | 888 | 863 | 285 | 356 | 112 | 58 |
| Kendall | 4 450 | 9.2 | 38 151 | 951 | 1 299 | 125 | 434 | 424 | 398 | 188 | 99 | 38 | 48 |
| Knox | 1 771 | 3.6 | 33 471 | 1 609 | 966 | 151 | 283 | 485 | 473 | 155 | 204 | 46 | 20 |
| Lake | 39 306 | 4.0 | 55 656 | 106 | 27 268 | 2 280 | 8 427 | 3 637 | 3 484 | 1 414 | 1 256 | 335 | 290 |
| LaSalle | 4 227 | 4.4 | 37 237 | 1 054 | 2 276 | 303 | 789 | 818 | 793 | 333 | 277 | 78 | 58 |
| Lawrence | 479 | 2.8 | 28 625 | 2 519 | 183 | 50 | 80 | 137 | 133 | 44 | 63 | 14 | 6 |
| Lee | 1 235 | 5.3 | 34 815 | 1 400 | 625 | 133 | 206 | 260 | 253 | 103 | 101 | 18 | 15 |
| Livingston | 1 649 | 8.5 | 42 417 | 551 | 741 | 278 | 228 | 263 | 255 | 107 | 100 | 23 | 14 |
| Logan | 1 058 | 7.8 | 35 094 | 1 359 | 470 | 146 | 155 | 212 | 205 | 81 | 81 | 20 | 10 |
| McDonough | 1 060 | 5.0 | 32 538 | 1 787 | 660 | 103 | 187 | 211 | 204 | 69 | 70 | 22 | 11 |
| McHenry | 12 608 | 5.3 | 40 811 | 675 | 5 164 | 323 | 1 879 | 1 531 | 1 462 | 655 | 493 | 95 | 139 |
| McLean | 7 132 | 4.9 | 41 816 | 593 | 5 630 | 564 | 1 037 | 837 | 799 | 322 | 245 | 97 | 56 |
| Macon | 4 495 | 4.3 | 40 591 | 696 | 3 088 | 383 | 756 | 905 | 880 | 326 | 325 | 115 | 49 |
| Macoupin | 1 741 | 5.6 | 36 510 | 1 135 | 469 | 135 | 279 | 378 | 367 | 142 | 151 | 33 | 21 |
| Madison | 10 237 | 3.4 | 38 133 | 953 | 5 338 | 434 | 1 638 | 2 036 | 1 977 | 711 | 785 | 223 | 109 |
| Marion | 1 312 | 2.1 | 33 356 | 1 641 | 650 | 51 | 214 | 425 | 416 | 114 | 195 | 47 | 17 |
| Marshall | 516 | 7.5 | 41 192 | 644 | 148 | 72 | 86 | 99 | 96 | 42 | 35 | 8 | 5 |
| Mason | 552 | 5.9 | 38 136 | 952 | 154 | 67 | 91 | 136 | 133 | 53 | 55 | 13 | 7 |
| Massac | 492 | 5.6 | 31 843 | 1 919 | 250 | 27 | 78 | 145 | 141 | 49 | 60 | 19 | 6 |
| Menard | 528 | 6.8 | 41 543 | 613 | 96 | 62 | 74 | 85 | 82 | 35 | 31 | 7 | 5 |
| Mercer | 665 | 7.3 | 40 639 | 692 | 142 | 81 | 102 | 121 | 118 | 53 | 43 | 9 | 7 |
| Monroe | 1 489 | 6.3 | 44 712 | 405 | 368 | 88 | 263 | 190 | 183 | 82 | 65 | 9 | 12 |
| Montgomery | 980 | 4.0 | 32 821 | 1 736 | 461 | 105 | 180 | 239 | 233 | 88 | 96 | 22 | 15 |
| Morgan | 1 206 | 2.7 | 33 922 | 1 528 | 657 | 144 | 223 | 278 | 270 | 104 | 107 | 29 | 13 |
| Moultrie | 554 | 8.8 | 37 363 | 1 042 | 181 | 102 | 92 | 107 | 104 | 42 | 43 | 8 | 5 |
| Ogle | 1 898 | 7.0 | 35 741 | 1 257 | 914 | 144 | 323 | 349 | 337 | 147 | 113 | 33 | 28 |
| Peoria | 8 478 | 7.9 | 45 375 | 374 | 6 372 | 482 | 1 534 | 1 362 | 1 320 | 486 | 473 | 196 | 79 |
| Perry | 591 | 4.0 | 26 540 | 2 818 | 233 | 40 | 102 | 170 | 165 | 61 | 64 | 21 | 9 |
| Piatt | 808 | 6.5 | 48 481 | 255 | 151 | 111 | 107 | 109 | 105 | 46 | 42 | 6 | 6 |
| Pike | 540 | 5.1 | 32 959 | 1 714 | 176 | 85 | 92 | 129 | 125 | 46 | 54 | 13 | 6 |
| Pope | 121 | 3.4 | 27 582 | 2 672 | 31 | 5 | 17 | 38 | 37 | 13 | 15 | 5 | 2 |
| Pulaski | 198 | 3.5 | 32 688 | 1 760 | 90 | 21 | 21 | 70 | 69 | 18 | 26 | 11 | 3 |
| Putnam | 235 | 4.3 | 39 408 | 813 | 95 | 12 | 46 | 43 | 41 | 20 | 14 | 3 | 3 |
| Randolph | 990 | 4.2 | 29 682 | 2 345 | 571 | 53 | 193 | 244 | 237 | 91 | 93 | 27 | 11 |
| Richland | 508 | 4.4 | 31 293 | 2 045 | 279 | 52 | 100 | 140 | 137 | 47 | 52 | 15 | 6 |
| Rock Island | 5 774 | 3.8 | 39 132 | 842 | 5 409 | 360 | 995 | 1 063 | 1 030 | 406 | 377 | 127 | 56 |
| St. Clair | 9 913 | 3.7 | 36 680 | 1 113 | 6 441 | 382 | 1 540 | 2 086 | 2 027 | 585 | 823 | 329 | 116 |
| Saline | 830 | 3.7 | 33 214 | 1 670 | 498 | 56 | 124 | 252 | 247 | 79 | 107 | 34 | 10 |
| Sangamon | 8 602 | 4.1 | 43 261 | 489 | 6 427 | 697 | 1 455 | 1 387 | 1 343 | 506 | 495 | 178 | 72 |
| Schuyler | 266 | 8.6 | 35 565 | 1 279 | 103 | 38 | 39 | 51 | 49 | 21 | 17 | 5 | 3 |
| Scott | 188 | 6.5 | 35 634 | 1 275 | 50 | 40 | 25 | 36 | 35 | 14 | 14 | 3 | 2 |
| Shelby | 788 | 9.3 | 35 486 | 1 297 | 214 | 152 | 121 | 173 | 168 | 68 | 68 | 14 | 9 |
| Stark | 237 | 14.1 | 41 870 | 586 | 56 | 53 | 36 | 46 | 45 | 17 | 21 | 3 | 2 |
| Stephenson | 1 759 | 4.6 | 36 980 | 1 080 | 966 | 136 | 345 | 378 | 368 | 152 | 128 | 45 | 21 |
| Tazewell | 5 685 | 10.2 | 41 909 | 580 | 4 490 | 266 | 926 | 923 | 893 | 383 | 337 | 78 | 53 |
| Union | 554 | -0.1 | 31 273 | 2 057 | 212 | 24 | 92 | 170 | 166 | 53 | 75 | 20 | 8 |
| Vermilion | 2 659 | 4.5 | 32 619 | 1 775 | 1 512 | 239 | 402 | 687 | 669 | 236 | 238 | 108 | 35 |
| Wabash | 411 | 5.9 | 34 751 | 1 413 | 150 | 39 | 87 | 95 | 92 | 36 | 36 | 11 | 5 |
| Warren | 626 | 8.1 | 35 144 | 1 350 | 263 | 101 | 96 | 126 | 122 | 45 | 48 | 13 | 6 |
| Washington | 574 | 6.9 | 39 530 | 801 | 253 | 73 | 105 | 106 | 103 | 39 | 43 | 7 | 5 |
| Wayne | 563 | 6.5 | 33 827 | 1 545 | 198 | 83 | 102 | 139 | 136 | 50 | 60 | 13 | 6 |
| White | 557 | 6.8 | 37 977 | 975 | 228 | 84 | 108 | 134 | 131 | 49 | 57 | 13 | 5 |
| Whiteside | 2 178 | 5.4 | 37 306 | 1 047 | 1 023 | 215 | 408 | 481 | 469 | 185 | 193 | 43 | 25 |
| Will | 28 938 | 6.3 | 42 459 | 544 | 11 763 | 841 | 3 358 | 3 390 | 3 239 | 1 279 | 1 091 | 347 | 314 |
| Williamson | 2 243 | 2.5 | 33 674 | 1 570 | 1 306 | 120 | 359 | 530 | 515 | 185 | 189 | 64 | 27 |

1. Based on the resident population estimated as of July 1 of the year shown.   2. Includes supplements to wages and salaries.

# Table B. States and Counties — Earnings, Social Security, and Housing

| STATE County | Total (mil dol) | Farm | Goods-related[1] Total | Manu-facturing | Information and professional and technical services | Retail trade | Finance, insurance, and real estate | Health care and social services | Government | Social Security beneficiaries, December 2011 Number | Rate[2] | Supplemental Security Income recipients, December 2011 | Housing units, 2010 Total | Percent change, 2000–2010 |
|---|---|---|---|---|---|---|---|---|---|---|---|---|---|---|
| | 75 | 76 | 77 | 78 | 79 | 80 | 81 | 82 | 83 | 84 | 85 | 86 | 87 | 88 |
| **ILLINOIS—Cont'd** | | | | | | | | | | | | | | |
| Hardin | 48 | 2.3 | D | D | D | 5.1 | D | 25.1 | 23.2 | 1 285 | 300 | 179 | 2 488 | -0.2 |
| Henderson | 99 | 37.3 | D | D | D | 2.9 | D | 5.3 | 19.4 | 1 745 | 242 | 97 | 3 827 | -7.2 |
| Henry | 790 | 13.6 | D | 11.7 | 3.4 | 7.5 | 5.3 | 6.2 | 20.7 | 11 045 | 219 | 646 | 22 161 | 4.2 |
| Iroquois | 586 | 32.1 | 12.8 | 6.6 | 2.1 | 6.1 | 4.3 | 10.9 | 12.4 | 7 200 | 244 | 487 | 13 452 | 0.7 |
| Jackson | 1 599 | 1.7 | 9.1 | 2.2 | 4.3 | 6.3 | 3.4 | 13.4 | 48.3 | 8 855 | 147 | 1 416 | 28 578 | 6.4 |
| Jasper | 177 | 23.4 | 10.3 | 5.2 | D | 7.3 | 3.2 | 1.8 | 17.5 | 2 235 | 230 | 169 | 4 345 | 1.2 |
| Jefferson | 1 072 | 2.3 | D | 21.7 | 4.3 | 7.0 | 4.5 | D | 14.7 | 8 365 | 216 | 987 | 16 954 | -0.2 |
| Jersey | 269 | 10.8 | 8.7 | 1.3 | 6.8 | 9.8 | 2.9 | D | 24.4 | 5 015 | 219 | 369 | 9 848 | 10.4 |
| Jo Daviess | 439 | 11.2 | D | 15.2 | D | 6.8 | 4.8 | D | 16.1 | 5 890 | 259 | 199 | 13 574 | 13.1 |
| Johnson | 125 | 3.6 | D | 1.0 | D | 5.7 | D | D | 44.7 | 2 990 | 236 | 260 | 5 598 | 10.9 |
| Kane | 12 364 | 0.5 | 25.2 | 18.2 | 9.6 | 6.2 | 5.8 | 11.6 | 17.1 | 64 425 | 124 | 4 661 | 182 047 | 31.0 |
| Kankakee | 2 256 | 4.4 | D | 16.2 | D | 7.6 | 4.7 | 18.1 | 17.5 | 21 340 | 188 | 2 731 | 45 246 | 11.4 |
| Kendall | 1 424 | 3.0 | 29.6 | 23.5 | 4.8 | 9.0 | 3.4 | 5.8 | 20.7 | 12 830 | 110 | 588 | 40 321 | 106.5 |
| Knox | 1 117 | 8.7 | D | 5.1 | 4.0 | 8.7 | 3.2 | D | 17.5 | 11 960 | 226 | 1 242 | 24 077 | 1.5 |
| Lake | 29 548 | 0.0 | 24.0 | 20.6 | 10.1 | 6.9 | 7.9 | 7.3 | 15.0 | 93 970 | 133 | 7 377 | 260 310 | 15.2 |
| LaSalle | 2 579 | 5.7 | 25.1 | 17.5 | 4.5 | 8.3 | 3.8 | 10.0 | 15.6 | 24 260 | 214 | 1 456 | 49 978 | 7.6 |
| Lawrence | 233 | 12.3 | D | 10.4 | 2.1 | 5.7 | 8.9 | D | 17.4 | 3 505 | 209 | 316 | 6 936 | -1.1 |
| Lee | 758 | 8.8 | D | 17.7 | D | 5.8 | 2.8 | 16.3 | 19.8 | 7 755 | 219 | 538 | 15 049 | 5.2 |
| Livingston | 1 020 | 21.2 | D | 15.0 | D | 5.7 | 3.3 | 8.5 | 18.3 | 7 815 | 201 | 514 | 15 895 | 3.9 |
| Logan | 616 | 18.5 | D | 12.3 | 2.3 | 6.6 | 3.9 | 9.2 | 23.0 | 6 030 | 200 | 380 | 12 107 | 2.0 |
| McDonough | 762 | 10.1 | D | 12.1 | 2.4 | 6.1 | 3.0 | D | 45.7 | 5 790 | 178 | 582 | 14 419 | 8.5 |
| McHenry | 5 487 | 1.0 | 29.3 | 20.2 | 5.6 | 7.7 | 3.8 | 11.3 | 16.3 | 43 625 | 141 | 1 708 | 116 040 | 24.9 |
| McLean | 6 195 | 3.5 | D | 4.3 | D | 4.8 | 22.1 | 10.0 | 14.2 | 23 450 | 137 | 1 729 | 69 656 | 16.1 |
| Macon | 3 470 | 2.9 | 35.6 | 28.7 | 5.4 | 5.3 | 3.6 | 12.8 | 10.5 | 24 055 | 217 | 3 206 | 50 475 | 0.5 |
| Macoupin | 603 | 14.2 | D | 8.7 | 3.1 | 6.7 | 4.2 | D | 19.3 | 10 860 | 228 | 903 | 21 584 | 2.3 |
| Madison | 5 772 | 1.0 | 28.1 | 19.5 | 7.3 | 7.2 | 4.7 | 11.1 | 17.3 | 52 845 | 197 | 5 578 | 117 106 | 7.5 |
| Marion | 701 | 2.7 | 23.4 | 17.2 | D | 6.8 | 3.7 | 16.6 | 17.8 | 9 245 | 235 | 1 116 | 18 296 | 1.5 |
| Marshall | 221 | 24.9 | 29.9 | 25.0 | 2.1 | 3.1 | 3.3 | 6.8 | 12.2 | 3 070 | 245 | 142 | 5 914 | 0.3 |
| Mason | 221 | 24.1 | D | 2.5 | D | 4.6 | 3.2 | 4.4 | 28.6 | 4 055 | 280 | 302 | 7 077 | 0.6 |
| Massac | 277 | 2.9 | D | 13.7 | 1.2 | 4.3 | 2.4 | D | 18.3 | 3 890 | 252 | 489 | 7 113 | 2.3 |
| Menard | 157 | 31.2 | D | 0.6 | D | 4.7 | 5.3 | D | 22.1 | 2 645 | 208 | 158 | 5 654 | 7.0 |
| Mercer | 222 | 27.8 | 17.0 | 13.0 | 1.9 | 5.2 | 4.1 | 3.5 | 25.8 | 4 015 | 245 | 165 | 7 358 | 3.5 |
| Monroe | 457 | 5.0 | 13.3 | 4.7 | 14.9 | 9.9 | 6.9 | 6.9 | 17.1 | 5 845 | 175 | 160 | 13 392 | 24.6 |
| Montgomery | 566 | 12.8 | 17.5 | 5.4 | 3.4 | 7.8 | 4.1 | D | 19.7 | 6 895 | 231 | 652 | 13 080 | 4.4 |
| Morgan | 801 | 10.6 | 17.0 | 13.0 | 4.1 | 7.2 | 7.0 | 12.4 | 17.7 | 8 125 | 229 | 946 | 15 515 | 1.5 |
| Moultrie | 283 | 22.2 | D | 23.2 | 3.5 | 5.0 | 3.3 | D | 11.1 | 3 115 | 210 | 165 | 6 260 | 9.0 |
| Ogle | 1 058 | 7.6 | D | 17.9 | D | 5.4 | 3.3 | 5.4 | 15.3 | 10 715 | 202 | 549 | 22 561 | 10.5 |
| Peoria | 6 854 | 1.0 | D | 12.2 | 17.5 | 5.0 | 5.5 | 20.9 | 11.0 | 35 335 | 189 | 4 783 | 83 034 | 6.2 |
| Perry | 273 | 4.9 | D | 12.7 | D | 7.0 | 3.9 | 10.5 | 28.6 | 4 675 | 210 | 458 | 9 426 | -0.3 |
| Piatt | 262 | 34.3 | 7.7 | 3.8 | D | 4.8 | 4.8 | 9.6 | 17.4 | 3 355 | 201 | 112 | 7 269 | 6.9 |
| Pike | 261 | 24.1 | D | 1.2 | 2.8 | 8.7 | 5.4 | D | 20.1 | 3 775 | 230 | 362 | 7 951 | -0.7 |
| Pope | 37 | 6.0 | D | D | D | 2.9 | D | D | 47.3 | 1 090 | 249 | 118 | 2 491 | 6.0 |
| Pulaski | 111 | 14.0 | 11.3 | 4.7 | D | 2.9 | D | D | 36.9 | 1 570 | 260 | 306 | 3 155 | -5.9 |
| Putnam | 106 | 11.3 | D | 27.6 | D | D | D | D | 13.5 | 1 400 | 235 | 38 | 3 074 | 6.4 |
| Randolph | 624 | 5.4 | D | 21.1 | D | 7.5 | 3.0 | 7.5 | 30.7 | 6 775 | 203 | 473 | 13 707 | 2.8 |
| Richland | 330 | 9.6 | 13.7 | 7.6 | 2.4 | 6.7 | 5.1 | D | 16.0 | 3 885 | 239 | 413 | 7 513 | 0.6 |
| Rock Island | 5 770 | 0.6 | 18.0 | 14.0 | 5.7 | 4.6 | 5.2 | 9.1 | 22.7 | 30 225 | 205 | 2 837 | 65 756 | 2.0 |
| St. Clair | 6 824 | 0.6 | D | 5.3 | 8.8 | 5.9 | 3.8 | 11.5 | 32.0 | 45 790 | 169 | 8 537 | 116 249 | 11.3 |
| Saline | ♦ 553 | 1.9 | 35.9 | 3.9 | 3.6 | 7.5 | 3.7 | 13.3 | 19.4 | 6 355 | 254 | 1 170 | 11 697 | -5.4 |
| Sangamon | 7 124 | 2.7 | D | 2.9 | 7.4 | 5.5 | 7.3 | 19.4 | 33.3 | 38 900 | 196 | 4 950 | 89 901 | 5.2 |
| Schuyler | 141 | 22.9 | D | 3.0 | 1.0 | 3.9 | D | 3.5 | 20.0 | 1 675 | 224 | 109 | 3 459 | 4.7 |
| Scott | 90 | 41.4 | D | D | D | 3.3 | D | D | 18.0 | 1 065 | 202 | 84 | 2 459 | -0.2 |
| Shelby | 366 | 35.6 | D | 12.7 | D | 4.8 | 4.2 | 7.4 | 13.2 | 5 240 | 236 | 385 | 10 396 | 3.3 |
| Stark | 108 | 36.2 | 12.8 | 11.1 | 3.0 | 6.1 | D | 3.6 | 13.5 | 1 240 | 219 | 63 | 2 674 | -1.9 |
| Stephenson | 1 101 | 6.5 | 34.6 | 24.5 | 3.3 | 5.0 | 8.9 | 13.6 | 13.9 | 11 495 | 242 | 1 071 | 22 081 | 1.7 |
| Tazewell | 4 756 | 1.8 | 52.9 | 47.9 | 2.5 | 4.4 | 3.3 | 4.5 | 8.5 | 27 310 | 201 | 1 769 | 57 516 | 8.6 |
| Union | 236 | 3.3 | D | 5.8 | 3.0 | 9.8 | 3.4 | D | 34.8 | 4 535 | 256 | 657 | 7 924 | 0.4 |
| Vermilion | 1 751 | 8.2 | D | 20.9 | D | 5.8 | 4.1 | 9.2 | 22.1 | 18 620 | 228 | 2 793 | 36 318 | -0.1 |
| Wabash | 189 | 9.1 | 27.4 | 6.9 | 4.6 | 6.2 | 3.7 | D | 27.7 | 2 755 | 233 | 212 | 5 585 | -3.0 |
| Warren | 363 | 22.6 | D | 24.2 | D | 3.9 | D | D | 11.0 | 3 475 | 195 | 289 | 7 682 | -1.4 |
| Washington | 326 | 13.8 | 29.7 | 22.0 | 2.2 | 9.4 | 3.4 | D | 13.2 | 3 015 | 207 | 156 | 6 534 | 2.3 |
| Wayne | 281 | 18.9 | 22.6 | 13.9 | 2.2 | 6.4 | 2.5 | D | 16.1 | 4 095 | 246 | 299 | 7 975 | 0.3 |
| White | 312 | 14.5 | 31.2 | 5.6 | 2.0 | 7.9 | 3.5 | D | 13.8 | 3 925 | 268 | 389 | 7 181 | -2.9 |
| Whiteside | 1 238 | 7.8 | D | 26.4 | D | 9.3 | 3.1 | 6.2 | 23.4 | 13 940 | 239 | 1 099 | 25 770 | 3.0 |
| Will | 12 604 | 0.5 | 21.6 | 13.5 | 6.1 | 8.4 | 4.8 | 10.5 | 17.2 | 88 940 | 130 | 6 609 | 237 501 | 35.3 |
| Williamson | 1 426 | 0.5 | D | 7.9 | 4.5 | 7.8 | 7.6 | 17.1 | 28.2 | 14 700 | 221 | 1 678 | 30 359 | 9.6 |

1. Includes mining, construction, and manufacturing.   2. Per 1,000 resident population enumerated in the 2010 census.

# Table B. States and Counties — Housing, Labor Force, and Employment

| | Housing units, 2007–2011 | | | | | | | | Civilian labor force, 2012 | | | | Civilian employment,[6] 2007–2011 | | |
|---|---|---|---|---|---|---|---|---|---|---|---|---|---|---|---|
| | Occupied units | | | | | | | | | | Unemployment | | | Percent | |
| | | | Owner-occupied | | | Renter-occupied | | | | | | | | | | |
| | | | | Median owner cost as a percent of income | | | | | | | | | | | Con-struction, produc-tion, and mainte-nance occu-pations |
| STATE County | Total | Percent | Median value[1] | With a mort-gage | Without a mort-gage[2] | Median rent[3] | Median rent as a per-cent of income | Sub-stand-ard units[4] (percent) | Total | Percent change, 2011–2012 | Total | Rate[5] | Total | Manage-ment, business, science and arts | |
| | 89 | 90 | 91 | 92 | 93 | 94 | 95 | 96 | 97 | 98 | 99 | 100 | 101 | 102 | 103 |
| ILLINOIS—Cont'd | | | | | | | | | | | | | | | |
| Hardin | 1 856 | 78.3 | 65 700 | 17.5 | 12.9 | 319 | 27.4 | 3.0 | 1 715 | -1.3 | 183 | 10.7 | 1 494 | 24.1 | 33.3 |
| Henderson | 3 155 | 80.3 | 82 900 | 20.5 | 11.2 | 523 | 26.3 | 1.9 | 3 776 | -0.4 | 307 | 8.1 | 3 522 | 27.1 | 33.1 |
| Henry | 20 467 | 78.3 | 109 900 | 20.1 | 12.9 | 644 | 26.8 | 1.6 | 26 856 | -0.4 | 1 976 | 7.4 | 24 137 | 29.3 | 29.5 |
| Iroquois | 11 884 | 75.8 | 99 400 | 21.6 | 12.2 | 666 | 27.7 | 2.0 | 16 358 | -2.0 | 1 364 | 8.3 | 14 208 | 28.4 | 31.3 |
| Jackson | 23 718 | 54.4 | 95 100 | 21.3 | 12.2 | 620 | 39.6 | 2.1 | 31 310 | -2.5 | 2 394 | 7.6 | 26 527 | 37.2 | 15.9 |
| Jasper | 3 985 | 82.6 | 82 700 | 21.1 | 11.5 | 523 | 22.1 | 0.4 | 4 853 | -1.1 | 404 | 8.3 | 4 763 | 29.6 | 32.9 |
| Jefferson | 15 314 | 74.0 | 87 000 | 20.9 | 13.0 | 576 | 30.1 | 2.0 | 19 832 | -1.7 | 1 679 | 8.5 | 16 797 | 25.6 | 29.9 |
| Jersey | 8 650 | 80.5 | 120 800 | 20.8 | 11.9 | 611 | 28.1 | 1.3 | 11 612 | -1.5 | 1 036 | 8.9 | 10 972 | 28.2 | 28.9 |
| Jo Daviess | 9 862 | 78.4 | 142 200 | 23.0 | 13.7 | 629 | 23.3 | 1.0 | 12 573 | -2.2 | 930 | 7.4 | 11 602 | 28.5 | 29.9 |
| Johnson | 4 298 | 82.0 | 93 400 | 21.2 | 12.4 | 509 | 26.6 | 0.9 | 5 058 | -2.0 | 515 | 10.2 | 3 781 | 32.0 | 21.3 |
| Kane | 169 528 | 76.6 | 241 600 | 27.9 | 15.2 | 952 | 32.1 | 4.1 | 279 151 | 1.1 | 24 671 | 8.8 | 245 198 | 34.4 | 24.4 |
| Kankakee | 41 086 | 69.9 | 147 700 | 24.8 | 14.0 | 755 | 33.2 | 2.2 | 55 825 | -0.4 | 6 176 | 11.1 | 50 002 | 28.9 | 28.0 |
| Kendall | 36 856 | 86.2 | 239 300 | 27.6 | 14.6 | 1 129 | 29.8 | 1.2 | 67 410 | 1.3 | 5 271 | 7.8 | 55 798 | 38.9 | 21.3 |
| Knox | 21 704 | 68.2 | 80 700 | 20.6 | 12.6 | 570 | 30.5 | 1.0 | 25 028 | -2.1 | 2 092 | 8.4 | 22 302 | 28.0 | 26.6 |
| Lake | 239 947 | 77.6 | 280 900 | 27.1 | 15.3 | 988 | 30.3 | 2.9 | 359 646 | -0.3 | 31 342 | 8.7 | 335 978 | 41.5 | 18.1 |
| LaSalle | 45 000 | 76.5 | 127 500 | 23.1 | 13.4 | 646 | 27.2 | 1.5 | 57 826 | -2.0 | 6 283 | 10.9 | 53 512 | 25.7 | 30.7 |
| Lawrence | 5 818 | 70.5 | 68 300 | 19.7 | 11.6 | 504 | 25.6 | 1.2 | 7 822 | -2.7 | 654 | 8.4 | 5 471 | 26.0 | 31.1 |
| Lee | 13 721 | 74.7 | 114 700 | 22.1 | 13.3 | 590 | 24.5 | 1.4 | 17 390 | -3.0 | 1 612 | 9.3 | 16 709 | 28.2 | 32.1 |
| Livingston | 14 484 | 75.8 | 105 600 | 22.5 | 12.6 | 613 | 25.3 | 0.8 | 18 114 | -3.3 | 1 486 | 8.2 | 16 837 | 26.1 | 33.8 |
| Logan | 10 992 | 74.1 | 95 700 | 18.9 | 12.3 | 551 | 27.2 | 1.3 | 13 165 | -1.5 | 1 059 | 8.0 | 12 239 | 30.1 | 23.7 |
| McDonough | 12 834 | 60.6 | 87 000 | 20.6 | 11.8 | 655 | 44.6 | 1.4 | 16 214 | -1.0 | 1 211 | 7.5 | 14 975 | 34.2 | 19.5 |
| McHenry | 108 361 | 83.8 | 243 500 | 27.6 | 14.7 | 1 031 | 31.7 | 1.8 | 176 716 | 1.1 | 14 816 | 8.4 | 153 954 | 37.1 | 21.5 |
| McLean | 63 431 | 67.8 | 154 600 | 21.2 | 12.3 | 711 | 28.3 | 1.6 | 90 653 | -0.7 | 6 280 | 6.9 | 87 317 | 40.7 | 15.0 |
| Macon | 44 568 | 70.1 | 92 300 | 19.7 | 11.4 | 634 | 29.1 | 1.6 | 53 617 | -1.4 | 5 689 | 10.6 | 49 050 | 30.9 | 26.4 |
| Macoupin | 19 407 | 77.8 | 94 900 | 20.8 | 12.3 | 584 | 26.4 | 2.2 | 23 558 | -1.5 | 2 244 | 9.5 | 22 407 | 27.9 | 31.2 |
| Madison | 106 792 | 74.4 | 124 300 | 22.1 | 12.4 | 751 | 33.0 | 1.5 | 135 619 | -1.3 | 11 918 | 8.8 | 125 974 | 33.2 | 23.3 |
| Marion | 16 108 | 74.1 | 71 300 | 20.8 | 14.1 | 591 | 29.3 | 2.3 | 17 724 | -1.9 | 1 936 | 10.9 | 17 406 | 24.2 | 31.8 |
| Marshall | 5 061 | 82.8 | 103 200 | 22.3 | 12.5 | 598 | 28.0 | 1.2 | 6 951 | 0.1 | 545 | 7.8 | 5 820 | 25.7 | 33.5 |
| Mason | 6 426 | 79.6 | 81 500 | 19.5 | 12.5 | 595 | 28.7 | 1.4 | 7 276 | -2.1 | 733 | 10.1 | 6 340 | 28.2 | 35.0 |
| Massac | 6 251 | 77.6 | 80 500 | 22.2 | 12.7 | 575 | 26.6 | 2.9 | 7 464 | -1.2 | 661 | 8.9 | 6 412 | 24.8 | 27.8 |
| Menard | 4 959 | 81.5 | 115 200 | 19.7 | 11.7 | 621 | 24.7 | 2.0 | 6 935 | -1.3 | 512 | 7.4 | 6 485 | 33.3 | 23.4 |
| Mercer | 6 889 | 79.9 | 98 200 | 20.2 | 12.4 | 582 | 23.9 | 0.8 | 8 521 | -0.8 | 702 | 8.2 | 8 172 | 29.0 | 34.3 |
| Monroe | 12 311 | 81.1 | 201 300 | 22.4 | 12.5 | 762 | 25.3 | 1.4 | 18 208 | -1.4 | 1 280 | 7.0 | 16 680 | 33.8 | 24.3 |
| Montgomery | 11 667 | 76.4 | 79 500 | 20.6 | 12.5 | 613 | 28.1 | 1.2 | 12 999 | -3.0 | 1 547 | 11.9 | 11 975 | 29.3 | 26.8 |
| Morgan | 13 993 | 70.0 | 93 000 | 20.6 | 11.0 | 583 | 29.0 | 0.7 | 17 060 | -2.1 | 1 457 | 8.5 | 16 805 | 30.7 | 24.3 |
| Moultrie | 5 611 | 78.6 | 93 300 | 20.9 | 12.7 | 592 | 21.8 | 2.0 | 7 618 | -1.6 | 550 | 7.2 | 6 783 | 28.1 | 34.0 |
| Ogle | 20 663 | 74.6 | 153 400 | 23.4 | 14.3 | 653 | 23.5 | 1.7 | 26 026 | -2.7 | 2 818 | 10.8 | 25 569 | 28.2 | 31.4 |
| Peoria | 75 416 | 67.6 | 121 900 | 20.9 | 12.1 | 681 | 29.0 | 1.9 | 97 296 | 0.0 | 8 212 | 8.4 | 85 672 | 37.3 | 19.6 |
| Perry | 8 252 | 78.5 | 76 600 | 21.3 | 12.3 | 512 | 30.3 | 2.3 | 9 172 | -1.7 | 1 037 | 11.3 | 8 854 | 29.7 | 32.7 |
| Piatt | 6 507 | 83.0 | 122 200 | 19.7 | 12.8 | 713 | 24.5 | 1.2 | 8 230 | -1.4 | 642 | 7.8 | 8 368 | 34.8 | 28.6 |
| Pike | 6 650 | 78.0 | 75 300 | 20.1 | 12.7 | 492 | 24.0 | 1.5 | 8 390 | -1.7 | 622 | 7.4 | 7 310 | 21.3 | 32.9 |
| Pope | 1 880 | 76.0 | 87 400 | 20.6 | 14.5 | 500 | 23.9 | 1.7 | 1 811 | -2.8 | 178 | 9.8 | 1 828 | 19.7 | 36.7 |
| Pulaski | 2 457 | 77.1 | 50 500 | 20.6 | 13.4 | 464 | 31.4 | 4.3 | 2 741 | 0.5 | 283 | 10.3 | 2 133 | 25.9 | 32.0 |
| Putnam | 2 482 | 78.2 | 126 800 | 22.2 | 12.4 | 578 | 22.6 | 3.4 | 3 088 | -2.1 | 311 | 10.1 | 2 803 | 22.7 | 36.9 |
| Randolph | 12 022 | 76.2 | 88 700 | 19.8 | 11.1 | 622 | 27.7 | 1.4 | 15 076 | -1.0 | 1 285 | 8.5 | 14 172 | 24.7 | 34.1 |
| Richland | 6 687 | 76.8 | 76 000 | 20.0 | 11.8 | 568 | 24.2 | 1.8 | 6 933 | -3.3 | 647 | 9.3 | 7 391 | 27.7 | 34.5 |
| Rock Island | 60 527 | 71.2 | 113 100 | 21.8 | 12.2 | 622 | 27.5 | 1.8 | 77 192 | -0.6 | 5 986 | 7.8 | 69 379 | 30.5 | 25.7 |
| St. Clair | 103 498 | 67.4 | 126 300 | 23.4 | 13.4 | 761 | 31.1 | 1.6 | 124 857 | -1.6 | 12 156 | 9.7 | 120 077 | 33.6 | 20.2 |
| Saline | 10 414 | 73.7 | 69 400 | 21.3 | 13.2 | 560 | 27.9 | 1.8 | 12 919 | 0.5 | 1 126 | 8.7 | 9 923 | 29.8 | 26.4 |
| Sangamon | 82 422 | 70.9 | 120 900 | 21.0 | 11.4 | 703 | 29.9 | 1.7 | 108 045 | -1.3 | 8 159 | 7.6 | 98 358 | 39.8 | 14.4 |
| Schuyler | 3 081 | 79.5 | 72 500 | 19.3 | 13.2 | 505 | 22.8 | 4.8 | 4 144 | -2.4 | 292 | 7.0 | 3 500 | 23.0 | 35.2 |
| Scott | 2 145 | 74.4 | 83 100 | 18.7 | 10.2 | 507 | 20.5 | 1.3 | 2 660 | -1.4 | 255 | 9.6 | 2 692 | 29.8 | 29.6 |
| Shelby | 8 968 | 80.4 | 86 500 | 20.6 | 11.8 | 588 | 25.4 | 1.4 | 10 726 | -2.0 | 962 | 9.0 | 10 058 | 28.8 | 32.6 |
| Stark | 2 371 | 80.1 | 86 000 | 19.3 | 11.9 | 536 | 22.2 | 1.6 | 2 680 | 0.0 | 240 | 9.0 | 2 692 | 28.8 | 30.4 |
| Stephenson | 19 515 | 71.8 | 104 500 | 22.6 | 13.7 | 584 | 33.4 | 0.7 | 23 711 | -2.3 | 2 240 | 9.4 | 21 981 | 29.2 | 29.0 |
| Tazewell | 54 144 | 78.0 | 128 900 | 20.6 | 11.9 | 660 | 26.3 | 1.1 | 73 872 | 0.3 | 5 592 | 7.6 | 64 462 | 34.3 | 24.9 |
| Union | 6 787 | 74.1 | 88 200 | 19.7 | 13.2 | 519 | 29.8 | 1.4 | 7 840 | -2.6 | 862 | 11.0 | 7 055 | 32.1 | 26.5 |
| Vermilion | 31 979 | 71.1 | 76 100 | 20.6 | 12.1 | 597 | 29.8 | 1.6 | 36 356 | -0.9 | 3 602 | 9.9 | 34 065 | 25.3 | 32.3 |
| Wabash | 4 752 | 79.6 | 79 500 | 19.3 | 12.8 | 580 | 22.9 | 2.8 | 5 909 | -1.4 | 488 | 8.3 | 5 567 | 25.5 | 35.3 |
| Warren | 6 854 | 72.8 | 84 700 | 21.4 | 13.8 | 605 | 27.4 | 2.2 | 9 023 | -2.0 | 679 | 7.5 | 8 155 | 26.1 | 29.3 |
| Washington | 6 013 | 81.8 | 104 400 | 22.6 | 12.1 | 598 | 23.9 | 1.9 | 8 882 | 4.2 | 610 | 6.9 | 7 751 | 29.7 | 33.2 |
| Wayne | 7 241 | 77.0 | 69 300 | 19.2 | 12.1 | 515 | 24.7 | 2.0 | 7 791 | -2.6 | 653 | 8.4 | 7 646 | 25.4 | 37.0 |
| White | 6 327 | 79.6 | 67 800 | 19.8 | 10.1 | 477 | 24.8 | 1.5 | 7 523 | -1.9 | 581 | 7.7 | 6 759 | 24.8 | 31.8 |
| Whiteside | 23 603 | 75.3 | 99 700 | 21.1 | 13.1 | 614 | 28.3 | 2.1 | 29 108 | -1.8 | 2 714 | 9.3 | 27 168 | 27.0 | 30.9 |
| Will | 221 722 | 84.5 | 236 300 | 27.3 | 14.4 | 931 | 31.1 | 2.1 | 370 385 | 1.0 | 33 466 | 9.0 | 322 593 | 35.5 | 23.0 |
| Williamson | 26 764 | 72.3 | 89 100 | 20.3 | 12.6 | 616 | 30.1 | 1.2 | 34 417 | -1.5 | 2 871 | 8.3 | 28 734 | 31.8 | 21.4 |

1. Specified owner-occupied units.   2. A value of 9.9 represents 9.9 percent or less.   3. Specified renter-occupied units. A value of 10.0 represents 10 percent or less.   4. Overcrowded or lacking complete plumbing facilities.   5. Percent of civilian labor force.   6. Persons 16 years old and over.

# Table B. States and Counties — Nonfarm Employment and Agriculture

| | Private nonfarm establishments, employment and payroll, 2011 | | | | | | | | | Agriculture, 2007 | | | |
| | Employment | | | | | | Annual payroll | | Farms | | | |
| | | | | | | | | | | | Percent with: | | |
| STATE County | Number of establishments | Total | Health care and social assistance | Manufacturing | Retail trade | Finance and insurance | Professional, scientific, and technical services | Total (mil dol) | Average per employee (dollars) | Number | Fewer than 50 acres | 500 acres or more | Farm operators whose principal occupation is farming (percent) |
|---|---|---|---|---|---|---|---|---|---|---|---|---|---|
| | 104 | 105 | 106 | 107 | 108 | 109 | 110 | 111 | 112 | 113 | 114 | 115 | 116 |
| ILLINOIS—Cont'd | | | | | | | | | | | | | |
| Hardin | 69 | 755 | 346 | D | 65 | D | D | 25 | 33 662 | 145 | 22.1 | 8.3 | 34.5 |
| Henderson | 103 | 659 | D | D | 122 | 79 | 35 | 15 | 22 012 | 400 | 21.5 | 30.0 | 63.8 |
| Henry | 1 088 | 13 159 | 1 475 | 3 889 | 2 029 | 545 | 335 | 407 | 30 959 | 1 473 | 35.9 | 23.4 | 50.6 |
| Iroquois | 712 | 6 514 | 1 731 | 937 | 967 | 360 | 101 | 200 | 30 779 | 1 471 | 27.9 | 29.4 | 57.4 |
| Jackson | 1 348 | 17 379 | 3 877 | 787 | 3 804 | 589 | 808 | 485 | 27 925 | 810 | 39.8 | 13.0 | 40.7 |
| Jasper | 207 | 1 784 | 133 | D | 228 | 102 | D | 66 | 37 043 | 882 | 38.8 | 19.3 | 46.7 |
| Jefferson | 968 | 16 811 | 3 348 | 3 139 | 2 404 | 453 | 510 | 601 | 35 752 | 1 156 | 43.7 | 10.7 | 30.8 |
| Jersey | 434 | 4 432 | 774 | 118 | 925 | 191 | 179 | 115 | 26 035 | 519 | 34.9 | 23.7 | 51.4 |
| Jo Daviess | 727 | 7 049 | 624 | 1 066 | 910 | D | 253 | 217 | 30 753 | 1 016 | 34.1 | 12.1 | 43.6 |
| Johnson | 179 | 1 352 | 235 | 46 | 202 | 73 | D | 25 | 18 348 | 568 | 34.2 | 6.9 | 35.7 |
| Kane | 12 117 | 175 282 | 21 616 | 28 448 | 23 121 | 7 926 | 9 125 | 6 880 | 39 252 | 759 | 60.1 | 14.9 | 49.9 |
| Kankakee | 2 361 | 35 778 | 7 376 | 4 890 | 5 557 | 1 372 | 744 | 1 213 | 33 905 | 835 | 34.9 | 26.6 | 51.0 |
| Kendall | 1 922 | 20 335 | 1 649 | 2 246 | 4 901 | 585 | 698 | 635 | 31 212 | 424 | 42.7 | 22.4 | 54.2 |
| Knox | 1 083 | 15 265 | 3 580 | 946 | 3 503 | 419 | 360 | 431 | 28 255 | 904 | 36.7 | 22.8 | 53.5 |
| Lake | 19 347 | 307 559 | 31 285 | 42 846 | 39 410 | 13 122 | 27 688 | 19 079 | 62 033 | 396 | 77.5 | 4.3 | 47.5 |
| LaSalle | 2 732 | 37 297 | 5 816 | 4 690 | 6 021 | 1 367 | 1 130 | 1 327 | 35 570 | 1 622 | 29.3 | 27.1 | 53.7 |
| Lawrence | 290 | 3 337 | 636 | 483 | 403 | 319 | 56 | 105 | 31 391 | 421 | 43.2 | 27.3 | 52.5 |
| Lee | 729 | 10 148 | 1 944 | 2 906 | 1 308 | 289 | 259 | 355 | 34 946 | 898 | 31.3 | 27.1 | 58.1 |
| Livingston | 908 | 11 965 | 2 216 | 3 154 | 1 675 | 467 | 341 | 410 | 34 249 | 1 319 | 27.4 | 32.9 | 58.0 |
| Logan | 625 | 7 681 | 1 464 | 947 | 1 100 | 314 | 174 | 231 | 30 094 | 710 | 31.8 | 31.1 | 60.0 |
| McDonough | 686 | 9 503 | 1 852 | 1 496 | 1 598 | 342 | 186 | 262 | 27 525 | 761 | 33.0 | 24.6 | 55.3 |
| McHenry | 7 717 | 83 244 | 10 353 | 16 201 | 14 496 | 2 512 | 3 068 | 3 278 | 39 374 | 1 035 | 65.0 | 11.1 | 50.6 |
| McLean | 3 694 | 76 610 | 8 662 | 4 093 | 9 367 | 22 699 | 2 882 | 3 553 | 46 383 | 1 513 | 35.1 | 30.5 | 53.7 |
| Macon | 2 478 | 45 784 | 7 430 | 7 510 | 5 529 | 1 366 | 1 221 | 1 835 | 40 078 | 708 | 44.1 | 27.0 | 54.5 |
| Macoupin | 917 | 8 614 | 1 739 | 536 | 1 436 | 513 | D | 258 | 29 976 | 1 187 | 38.6 | 20.5 | 49.5 |
| Madison | 5 877 | 84 870 | 13 994 | 12 767 | 12 633 | 3 032 | 3 415 | 3 257 | 38 372 | 1 229 | 46.5 | 15.7 | 47.3 |
| Marion | 949 | 10 532 | 2 753 | 2 459 | 1 368 | 377 | 237 | 341 | 32 419 | 1 077 | 39.7 | 12.3 | 31.5 |
| Marshall | 277 | 2 792 | 443 | 963 | 304 | 112 | 22 | 83 | 29 843 | 500 | 29.2 | 24.0 | 57.2 |
| Mason | 299 | 2 394 | 520 | 111 | 340 | 145 | 24 | 78 | 32 645 | 447 | 27.7 | 40.3 | 60.0 |
| Massac | 235 | 4 396 | 749 | D | 317 | 105 | 30 | 189 | 43 065 | 400 | 41.3 | 10.0 | 39.3 |
| Menard | 216 | 1 372 | 120 | 31 | 255 | D | 73 | 39 | 28 507 | 411 | 45.7 | 24.1 | 46.7 |
| Mercer | 299 | 2 479 | 375 | 641 | 373 | 152 | D | 71 | 28 608 | 785 | 34.9 | 22.5 | 52.6 |
| Monroe | 777 | 7 473 | 982 | 305 | 1 303 | 341 | 618 | 254 | 33 939 | 678 | 44.7 | 17.6 | 43.7 |
| Montgomery | 712 | 7 163 | 1 222 | 711 | 1 561 | 413 | 216 | 230 | 32 099 | 1 029 | 38.1 | 22.2 | 50.9 |
| Morgan | 881 | 12 670 | 2 692 | 1 945 | 1 993 | 818 | 454 | 397 | 31 332 | 740 | 30.9 | 28.1 | 51.8 |
| Moultrie | 305 | 4 252 | 757 | D | 364 | 113 | 104 | 134 | 31 538 | 520 | 51.5 | 19.6 | 51.5 |
| Ogle | 1 083 | 13 674 | 1 565 | 3 672 | 1 417 | 466 | D | 556 | 40 678 | 1 274 | 44.0 | 18.7 | 47.1 |
| Peoria | 4 613 | 108 798 | 20 465 | 9 564 | 11 243 | 4 190 | 4 662 | 6 080 | 55 882 | 877 | 33.6 | 18.0 | 47.2 |
| Perry | 419 | 4 264 | 844 | D | 670 | 174 | 71 | 136 | 31 819 | 589 | 35.5 | 20.5 | 44.5 |
| Piatt | 341 | 2 357 | 364 | D | 470 | 164 | 119 | 76 | 32 202 | 480 | 31.7 | 34.0 | 58.5 |
| Pike | 372 | 3 176 | 651 | 153 | 580 | 224 | 90 | 88 | 27 690 | 967 | 25.1 | 23.7 | 45.1 |
| Pope | 55 | 312 | 167 | D | D | D | D | 5 | 16 500 | 346 | 33.5 | 7.2 | 36.7 |
| Pulaski | 100 | D | 101 | NA | 92 | 56 | D | D | D | 276 | 31.2 | 22.8 | 44.2 |
| Putnam | 129 | 1 060 | D | 404 | 104 | D | D | 51 | 47 880 | 167 | 26.9 | 23.4 | 52.1 |
| Randolph | 681 | 10 221 | 2 148 | 2 858 | 1 401 | 306 | 193 | 339 | 33 130 | 833 | 34.0 | 17.4 | 44.4 |
| Richland | 466 | 5 320 | 989 | 461 | 736 | 213 | D | 168 | 31 549 | 579 | 39.0 | 21.4 | 48.2 |
| Rock Island | 3 308 | 61 019 | 9 230 | 7 704 | 8 186 | 2 928 | 3 073 | 2 976 | 48 771 | 700 | 44.3 | 15.1 | 45.6 |
| St. Clair | 5 377 | 78 424 | 14 922 | 4 934 | 13 658 | 2 614 | 5 123 | 2 717 | 34 643 | 895 | 42.9 | 20.0 | 45.8 |
| Saline | 585 | 7 779 | 1 783 | 381 | 1 350 | 336 | 177 | 298 | 38 321 | 497 | 42.7 | 12.5 | 32.6 |
| Sangamon | 5 096 | 81 550 | 20 858 | 2 885 | 12 113 | 5 200 | 4 073 | 3 139 | 38 486 | 1 153 | 45.1 | 22.4 | 48.0 |
| Schuyler | 148 | 1 245 | D | 83 | D | 59 | D | 38 | 30 531 | 534 | 30.1 | 21.2 | 39.1 |
| Scott | 76 | 612 | D | 139 | 96 | 56 | D | 22 | 36 337 | 350 | 37.1 | 22.6 | 47.1 |
| Shelby | 439 | 4 121 | 658 | 1 048 | 577 | D | D | 128 | 30 996 | 1 185 | 39.5 | 19.4 | 44.1 |
| Stark | 114 | 899 | D | 205 | 155 | 80 | D | 30 | 33 925 | 372 | 29.3 | 32.8 | 61.3 |
| Stephenson | 1 096 | 15 088 | 2 821 | 3 106 | 2 092 | 1 320 | 442 | 566 | 37 522 | 1 178 | 44.5 | 16.2 | 50.3 |
| Tazewell | 2 783 | 43 034 | 5 254 | 7 006 | 6 579 | 1 777 | 1 359 | 1 605 | 37 303 | 998 | 37.5 | 21.4 | 51.8 |
| Union | 351 | 3 331 | 1 234 | D | 680 | 144 | 75 | 87 | 26 066 | 620 | 35.5 | 8.1 | 38.4 |
| Vermilion | 1 492 | 23 300 | 4 723 | 4 798 | 3 483 | 1 137 | 420 | 835 | 35 835 | 1 014 | 38.7 | 27.3 | 52.4 |
| Wabash | 272 | 2 897 | 928 | 186 | 403 | 95 | D | 88 | 30 473 | 225 | 35.1 | 30.2 | 51.6 |
| Warren | 353 | 5 532 | 687 | 1 862 | 552 | 220 | 79 | 145 | 26 168 | 644 | 27.0 | 31.2 | 56.7 |
| Washington | 379 | 5 602 | D | D | 557 | 192 | D | 190 | 33 832 | 779 | 28.0 | 30.9 | 54.2 |
| Wayne | 351 | 3 351 | 824 | D | 604 | 109 | 58 | 100 | 29 894 | 1 233 | 43.5 | 13.7 | 33.8 |
| White | 364 | 3 322 | 591 | D | 519 | D | 72 | 118 | 35 604 | 481 | 36.4 | 24.5 | 45.3 |
| Whiteside | 1 272 | 17 704 | 3 357 | 3 921 | 2 899 | 586 | 358 | 585 | 33 017 | 1 132 | 34.1 | 22.3 | 56.3 |
| Will | 13 911 | 187 180 | 22 911 | 18 880 | 27 623 | 4 913 | 8 471 | 7 574 | 40 462 | 877 | 55.0 | 14.8 | 52.2 |
| Williamson | 1 578 | 22 412 | 6 082 | 1 890 | 3 742 | 1 331 | 551 | 733 | 32 715 | 616 | 47.1 | 7.3 | 32.3 |

Items 104—116

| STATE County | Acreage (1,000) | Percent change, 2002–2007 | Average size of farm | Total irrigated (1,000) | Total cropland (1,000) | Average per farm | Average per acre | Value of machinery and equipment, average per farm (dollars) | Total (mil dol) | Average per farm (dollars) | Crops | Live-stock and poultry products | $10,000 or more | $100,000 or more | Total ($1,000) | Percent of farms |
|---|---|---|---|---|---|---|---|---|---|---|---|---|---|---|---|---|
| | 117 | 118 | 119 | 120 | 121 | 122 | 123 | 124 | 125 | 126 | 127 | 128 | 129 | 130 | 131 | 132 |
| **ILLINOIS—Cont'd** | | | | | | | | | | | | | | | | |
| Hardin | 35 | -12.5 | 240 | 0.0 | 16.4 | 549 014 | 2 292 | 60 083 | 3.0 | 20 803 | 71.1 | 28.9 | 23.4 | 4.1 | 360 | 49.0 |
| Henderson | 170 | -15.4 | 426 | 16.6 | 143.7 | 1 469 607 | 3 449 | 147 170 | 86.0 | 215 083 | 81.6 | 18.4 | 76.0 | 43.5 | 3 468 | 86.0 |
| Henry | 490 | 1.9 | 333 | 7.2 | 446.1 | 1 313 624 | 3 950 | 128 465 | 296.8 | 201 511 | 71.4 | 28.6 | 60.4 | 37.1 | 10 999 | 78.5 |
| Iroquois | 678 | -0.1 | 461 | 4.1 | 646.9 | 1 857 803 | 4 032 | 180 847 | 418.5 | 284 529 | 79.3 | 20.7 | 70.2 | 45.8 | 12 595 | 85.4 |
| Jackson | 224 | 12.0 | 277 | 0.4 | 177.4 | 775 182 | 2 798 | 107 406 | 60.8 | 75 101 | 88.2 | 11.8 | 34.8 | 15.6 | 3 118 | 59.8 |
| Jasper | 243 | -10.3 | 276 | D | 214.4 | 913 218 | 3 309 | 116 937 | 112.9 | 128 057 | 64.8 | 35.2 | 52.3 | 27.6 | 4 187 | 85.7 |
| Jefferson | 233 | -10.0 | 201 | 0.0 | 186.0 | 570 152 | 2 834 | 72 646 | 51.0 | 44 084 | 79.8 | 20.2 | 28.9 | 11.0 | 3 629 | 69.2 |
| Jersey | 189 | 9.2 | 365 | 0.0 | 158.1 | 1 336 206 | 3 660 | 129 502 | 68.7 | 132 420 | 92.6 | 7.4 | 47.8 | 30.8 | 2 559 | 73.4 |
| Jo Daviess | 281 | 6.4 | 277 | 0.1 | 196.0 | 1 108 860 | 4 003 | 109 864 | 136.7 | 134 499 | 53.3 | 46.7 | 46.6 | 20.6 | 5 672 | 78.1 |
| Johnson | 100 | -17.4 | 177 | D | 53.4 | 414 754 | 2 344 | 63 753 | 12.5 | 22 085 | 59.0 | 41.0 | 22.4 | 5.1 | 1 369 | 48.1 |
| Kane | 192 | -3.0 | 253 | 2.9 | 182.0 | 1 231 861 | 4 860 | 175 643 | 198.1 | 261 011 | 88.6 | 11.4 | 48.9 | 28.5 | 4 614 | 40.1 |
| Kankakee | 386 | 11.2 | 462 | 16.0 | 376.2 | 2 000 617 | 4 330 | 187 468 | 244.1 | 292 276 | 88.8 | 11.2 | 70.2 | 41.8 | 5 988 | 75.0 |
| Kendall | 167 | -0.6 | 394 | 2.1 | 160.5 | 1 703 203 | 4 328 | 171 639 | 103.5 | 244 155 | 92.5 | 7.5 | 63.4 | 40.8 | 3 108 | 61.1 |
| Knox | 363 | -7.9 | 401 | D | 301.5 | 1 614 027 | 4 020 | 146 360 | 198.7 | 219 791 | 73.8 | 26.2 | 52.0 | 30.5 | 7 008 | 74.6 |
| Lake | 35 | -10.3 | 87 | 0.6 | 28.5 | 551 511 | 6 326 | 69 788 | 30.8 | 77 839 | 77.6 | 22.4 | 34.8 | 12.4 | 444 | 13.9 |
| LaSalle | 643 | 11.1 | 397 | 3.8 | 614.4 | 1 665 997 | 4 201 | 174 983 | 329.0 | 202 834 | 93.8 | 6.2 | 72.1 | 43.0 | 11 943 | 80.9 |
| Lawrence | 194 | 1.0 | 461 | 15.7 | 179.1 | 1 510 800 | 3 278 | 144 458 | 90.1 | 213 914 | 75.3 | 24.7 | 49.9 | 33.3 | 3 527 | 79.3 |
| Lee | 396 | 1.8 | 441 | 21.7 | 377.6 | 1 900 065 | 4 313 | 174 859 | 214.4 | 238 717 | 91.4 | 8.6 | 65.3 | 46.5 | 8 009 | 80.4 |
| Livingston | 629 | -1.1 | 476 | 0.2 | 599.1 | 1 973 244 | 4 141 | 186 082 | 350.7 | 265 897 | 84.9 | 15.1 | 77.3 | 52.1 | 11 434 | 83.9 |
| Logan | 320 | -10.9 | 451 | 1.3 | 303.1 | 1 896 399 | 4 203 | 156 048 | 180.2 | 253 818 | 89.2 | 10.8 | 63.9 | 44.4 | 6 627 | 86.5 |
| McDonough | 308 | -5.2 | 404 | 0.1 | 267.2 | 1 570 176 | 3 883 | 143 647 | 148.5 | 195 088 | 90.0 | 10.0 | 58.1 | 32.3 | 5 135 | 76.2 |
| McHenry | 216 | -7.3 | 208 | 8.5 | 198.8 | 1 049 568 | 5 039 | 114 010 | 156.5 | 151 231 | 80.0 | 20.0 | 43.4 | 21.7 | 4 280 | 31.1 |
| McLean | 676 | -1.7 | 447 | 2.9 | 647.4 | 1 868 207 | 4 181 | 175 125 | 366.5 | 242 265 | 89.5 | 10.5 | 65.1 | 44.7 | 12 275 | 77.9 |
| Macon | 291 | -9.3 | 410 | 0.0 | 280.7 | 1 831 072 | 4 461 | 177 853 | 156.8 | 221 463 | 96.8 | 3.2 | 58.9 | 37.3 | 5 131 | 74.2 |
| Macoupin | 394 | -7.7 | 332 | 0.0 | 337.0 | 1 273 380 | 3 834 | 131 387 | 184.3 | 155 263 | 78.7 | 21.3 | 50.3 | 26.8 | 6 846 | 75.4 |
| Madison | 313 | 5.7 | 255 | 1.0 | 284.6 | 1 053 742 | 4 138 | 133 828 | 131.9 | 107 345 | 89.5 | 10.5 | 47.8 | 22.4 | 4 419 | 60.5 |
| Marion | 261 | -0.4 | 242 | 0.1 | 212.1 | 755 440 | 3 121 | 93 949 | 78.3 | 72 666 | 84.2 | 15.8 | 31.7 | 15.4 | 5 471 | 78.8 |
| Marshall | 205 | 7.3 | 409 | 2.3 | 183.5 | 1 654 832 | 4 044 | 146 222 | 100.6 | 201 285 | 94.4 | 5.6 | 65.2 | 39.4 | 3 614 | 81.6 |
| Mason | 273 | -4.2 | 612 | 100.5 | 251.3 | 2 017 955 | 3 300 | 221 325 | 121.6 | 272 053 | 96.9 | 3.1 | 63.1 | 46.5 | 4 605 | 85.5 |
| Massac | 90 | -28.0 | 224 | 8.1 | 65.0 | 567 832 | 2 532 | 77 963 | 22.2 | 55 622 | 84.0 | 16.0 | 36.8 | 12.5 | 1 578 | 69.5 |
| Menard | 169 | 9.0 | 410 | 2.7 | 150.9 | 1 572 483 | 3 833 | 147 681 | 80.7 | 196 457 | 92.1 | 7.9 | 45.5 | 30.4 | 3 017 | 77.4 |
| Mercer | 306 | 4.4 | 390 | 9.2 | 265.2 | 1 438 698 | 3 687 | 133 503 | 145.8 | 185 717 | 84.2 | 15.8 | 56.3 | 33.0 | 6 103 | 78.1 |
| Monroe | 178 | 0.6 | 263 | 3.3 | 148.7 | 934 349 | 3 556 | 127 779 | 62.9 | 92 754 | 75.2 | 24.8 | 44.0 | 23.2 | 2 774 | 63.4 |
| Montgomery | 348 | -3.9 | 338 | 0.4 | 315.0 | 1 288 726 | 3 813 | 127 417 | 150.0 | 145 801 | 83.4 | 16.6 | 54.2 | 31.1 | 5 883 | 78.7 |
| Morgan | 321 | 9.6 | 433 | 3.2 | 281.1 | 1 703 819 | 3 934 | 166 922 | 149.5 | 202 050 | 87.6 | 12.4 | 60.8 | 36.4 | 5 226 | 77.2 |
| Moultrie | 168 | -9.7 | 323 | 0.0 | 159.1 | 1 364 294 | 4 228 | 131 838 | 90.7 | 174 510 | 96.2 | 3.8 | 53.7 | 27.5 | 2 890 | 64.0 |
| Ogle | 366 | -1.6 | 288 | 1.2 | 333.6 | 1 304 554 | 4 535 | 108 105 | 258.7 | 203 098 | 67.1 | 32.9 | 54.3 | 31.6 | 8 579 | 69.9 |
| Peoria | 259 | -2.6 | 296 | 2.8 | 220.2 | 1 148 306 | 3 885 | 116 613 | 126.3 | 143 980 | 85.9 | 14.1 | 58.3 | 28.8 | 4 239 | 67.6 |
| Perry | 200 | 3.1 | 340 | D | 171.8 | 953 734 | 2 804 | 100 470 | 41.5 | 70 377 | 90.9 | 9.1 | 46.2 | 21.4 | 2 957 | 80.5 |
| Piatt | 267 | 3.5 | 557 | 0.5 | 259.5 | 2 432 020 | 4 368 | 206 231 | 146.5 | 305 208 | 92.0 | 8.0 | 69.4 | 47.3 | 4 850 | 80.4 |
| Pike | 390 | -8.5 | 403 | 1.3 | 288.1 | 1 417 177 | 3 516 | 116 504 | 170.9 | 176 708 | 69.7 | 30.3 | 48.7 | 26.2 | 6 532 | 77.0 |
| Pope | 61 | -20.8 | 176 | D | 30.9 | 399 521 | 2 273 | 54 068 | 5.4 | 15 589 | 79.5 | 20.5 | 19.1 | 3.2 | 934 | 61.6 |
| Pulaski | 101 | 17.4 | 367 | D | 83.2 | 1 084 029 | 2 957 | 115 253 | 29.5 | 106 751 | 91.3 | 8.7 | 39.5 | 21.0 | 1 798 | 74.6 |
| Putnam | 63 | -11.3 | 375 | 0.5 | 53.9 | 1 478 127 | 3 937 | 214 337 | 64.9 | 388 638 | 94.9 | 5.1 | 61.1 | 36.5 | 1 456 | 81.4 |
| Randolph | 253 | -0.4 | 304 | 0.4 | 202.3 | 976 442 | 3 216 | 126 178 | 73.5 | 88 206 | 83.1 | 16.9 | 48.1 | 19.8 | 3 450 | 75.4 |
| Richland | 203 | -2.9 | 350 | 0.0 | 185.6 | 1 076 855 | 3 074 | 110 702 | 82.5 | 142 524 | 70.4 | 29.6 | 51.5 | 25.2 | 3 419 | 80.7 |
| Rock Island | 179 | 5.3 | 255 | 3.2 | 148.7 | 1 045 315 | 4 096 | 102 621 | 95.3 | 136 152 | 81.5 | 18.5 | 47.3 | 23.7 | 4 037 | 66.3 |
| St. Clair | 307 | 13.7 | 342 | 1.1 | 284.8 | 1 301 234 | 3 799 | 150 091 | 125.6 | 140 368 | 87.8 | 12.2 | 54.1 | 27.5 | 5 099 | 71.8 |
| Saline | 117 | -10.0 | 236 | D | 96.2 | 681 789 | 2 890 | 77 874 | 42.0 | 84 430 | 66.5 | 33.5 | 34.4 | 13.3 | 1 779 | 65.0 |
| Sangamon | 518 | 10.7 | 449 | 0.8 | 485.2 | 1 748 638 | 3 891 | 174 091 | 294.0 | 255 016 | 94.6 | 5.4 | 51.3 | 33.9 | 9 235 | 67.0 |
| Schuyler | 207 | 0.0 | 388 | D | 138.4 | 1 266 603 | 3 260 | 114 478 | 65.4 | 122 398 | 83.8 | 16.2 | 43.4 | 21.9 | 3 377 | 83.1 |
| Scott | 136 | 17.2 | 388 | 5.5 | 109.0 | 1 397 802 | 3 604 | 136 752 | 54.5 | 155 664 | 87.9 | 12.1 | 51.7 | 26.9 | 2 105 | 68.0 |
| Shelby | 387 | -7.9 | 327 | 0.1 | 347.0 | 1 160 282 | 3 550 | 129 810 | 203.3 | 171 600 | 80.7 | 19.3 | 52.8 | 29.1 | 6 153 | 74.9 |
| Stark | 170 | -2.3 | 456 | 0.0 | 159.8 | 1 881 018 | 4 122 | 175 762 | 87.0 | 233 758 | 95.2 | 4.8 | 69.9 | 45.2 | 3 650 | 82.5 |
| Stephenson | 338 | 4.3 | 287 | 0.1 | 306.9 | 1 109 412 | 3 867 | 142 964 | 246.8 | 209 505 | 53.8 | 46.2 | 50.3 | 30.7 | 7 527 | 69.8 |
| Tazewell | 329 | 0.6 | 330 | 31.4 | 306.4 | 1 331 434 | 4 036 | 126 285 | 184.8 | 185 206 | 85.3 | 14.7 | 60.2 | 34.3 | 6 352 | 74.4 |
| Union | 122 | -19.7 | 197 | 0.1 | 75.0 | 522 955 | 2 650 | 64 280 | 25.7 | 41 498 | 78.2 | 21.8 | 26.1 | 8.2 | 1 883 | 60.2 |
| Vermilion | 457 | 1.6 | 451 | 0.7 | 428.1 | 1 781 695 | 3 950 | 178 307 | 224.0 | 220 875 | 95.5 | 4.5 | 61.3 | 37.7 | 8 500 | 78.9 |
| Wabash | 114 | 2.7 | 508 | 1.1 | 104.9 | 1 647 150 | 3 241 | 178 399 | 40.5 | 180 199 | 95.9 | 4.1 | 61.8 | 36.0 | 1 774 | 78.7 |
| Warren | 295 | -9.8 | 458 | D | 260.6 | 1 873 134 | 4 090 | 161 721 | 168.2 | 261 176 | 77.1 | 22.9 | 74.1 | 46.6 | 5 320 | 82.9 |
| Washington | 354 | 6.6 | 454 | D | 324.9 | 1 532 726 | 3 374 | 187 882 | 142.4 | 182 821 | 65.7 | 34.3 | 62.4 | 37.6 | 5 543 | 87.2 |
| Wayne | 333 | -6.5 | 270 | 2.5 | 284.3 | 728 843 | 2 697 | 87 931 | 119.1 | 96 591 | 68.0 | 32.0 | 32.9 | 15.6 | 7 093 | 84.3 |
| White | 297 | 5.7 | 617 | 24.2 | 265.8 | 1 753 235 | 2 840 | 211 083 | 102.7 | 213 483 | 92.1 | 7.9 | 45.5 | 27.0 | 4 872 | 80.9 |
| Whiteside | 405 | 6.9 | 358 | 57.0 | 376.4 | 1 367 865 | 3 820 | 157 131 | 280.8 | 248 037 | 69.3 | 30.7 | 62.5 | 39.4 | 8 643 | 77.7 |
| Will | 221 | -16.6 | 252 | 1.9 | 208.9 | 1 419 945 | 5 639 | 132 564 | 127.6 | 145 492 | 94.6 | 5.4 | 49.7 | 26.1 | 3 392 | 51.0 |
| Williamson | 94 | -10.5 | 153 | 0.0 | 64.8 | 433 076 | 2 834 | 53 815 | 16.2 | 26 324 | 80.3 | 19.7 | 23.4 | 6.8 | 1 383 | 47.2 |

| STATE County | Water use, 2005 Total water withdrawn (mil gal/day) | Gallons withdrawn per person | Wholesale trade,[1] 2007 Number of establishments | Number of employees | Sales (mil dol) | Annual payroll (mil dol) | Retail trade,[2] 2007 Number of establishments | Number of employees | Sales (mil dol) | Annual payroll (mil dol) | Real estate and rental and leasing,[2] 2007 Number of establishments | Number of employees | Receipts (mil dol) | Annual payroll (mil dol) |
|---|---|---|---|---|---|---|---|---|---|---|---|---|---|---|
| | 133 | 134 | 135 | 136 | 137 | 138 | 139 | 140 | 141 | 142 | 143 | 144 | 145 | 146 |
| ILLINOIS—Cont'd | | | | | | | | | | | | | | |
| Hardin | 1.8 | 384 | NA | NA | NA | NA | 11 | 70 | 14.4 | 1.1 | 2 | D | D | D |
| Henderson | 18.2 | 2 287 | 10 | D | D | D | 18 | 103 | 26.1 | 1.7 | 2 | D | D | D |
| Henry | 12.4 | 246 | 60 | D | D | D | 200 | 2 173 | 477.6 | 45.0 | 32 | 74 | 5.8 | 1.1 |
| Iroquois | 5.8 | 190 | 50 | 463 | 614.9 | 16.1 | 99 | 964 | 265.4 | 20.4 | 18 | 46 | 6.8 | 1.2 |
| Jackson | 89.4 | 1 543 | 26 | D | D | D | 244 | 3 759 | 684.1 | 66.9 | 76 | 381 | 38.6 | 6.6 |
| Jasper | 608.9 | 60 766 | 16 | 142 | 257.2 | 4.9 | 34 | 282 | 82.6 | 5.2 | 4 | D | D | D |
| Jefferson | 2.7 | 68 | 49 | D | D | D | 190 | 2 262 | 567.6 | 50.1 | 28 | 101 | 13.5 | 3.1 |
| Jersey | 2.9 | 128 | 24 | D | D | D | 76 | 978 | 250.3 | 21.2 | 13 | 24 | 2.9 | 0.4 |
| Jo Daviess | 7.1 | 315 | 21 | 107 | 120.5 | 4.7 | 145 | 1 060 | 310.7 | 21.6 | 29 | 63 | 11.5 | 1.6 |
| Johnson | 2.6 | 200 | 7 | 40 | 16.7 | 1.0 | 36 | 272 | 65.5 | 5.3 | 4 | D | D | D |
| Kane | 69.6 | 144 | 775 | 10 899 | 9 589.6 | 620.8 | 1 624 | 25 240 | 5 688.3 | 543.7 | 502 | 2 803 | 430.3 | 89.0 |
| Kankakee | 35.3 | 327 | 116 | D | D | D | 389 | 5 737 | 1 258.5 | 118.1 | 105 | 342 | 63.5 | 9.5 |
| Kendall | 13.3 | 168 | 63 | 1 164 | 1 299.8 | 44.8 | 243 | 4 360 | 1 064.0 | 106.6 | 67 | 195 | 25.4 | 4.3 |
| Knox | 2.4 | 46 | 50 | D | D | D | 206 | 3 653 | 681.4 | 67.7 | 36 | 148 | 19.4 | 2.8 |
| Lake | 855.6 | 1 218 | 1 121 | 26 870 | 26 053.3 | 2 054.7 | 2 530 | 44 334 | 20 336.3 | 1 407.1 | 846 | 3 956 | 1 082.2 | 213.0 |
| LaSalle | 121.9 | 1 082 | 131 | 1 577 | 1 208.2 | 59.7 | 478 | 6 904 | 1 739.9 | 149.9 | 103 | 692 | 76.2 | 22.4 |
| Lawrence | 15.6 | 977 | 12 | 220 | 82.7 | 8.3 | 46 | 432 | 81.7 | 8.7 | 8 | 16 | 1.4 | 0.2 |
| Lee | 26.0 | 728 | 31 | D | D | D | 118 | 1 421 | 366.5 | 31.4 | 32 | 162 | 13.2 | 2.9 |
| Livingston | 9.2 | 235 | 51 | D | D | D | 152 | 1 841 | 396.5 | 34.8 | 21 | 61 | 5.4 | 1.3 |
| Logan | 7.4 | 243 | 43 | D | D | D | 109 | 1 234 | 275.5 | 24.4 | 29 | 105 | 12.2 | 2.3 |
| McDonough | 4.5 | 141 | 22 | D | D | D | 142 | 1 657 | 338.1 | 32.0 | 26 | 85 | 14.5 | 2.3 |
| McHenry | 43.5 | 143 | 438 | 4 815 | 2 391.2 | 251.9 | 979 | 15 034 | 3 578.6 | 331.8 | 295 | 1 358 | 178.3 | 39.0 |
| McLean | 16.0 | 100 | 174 | 2 701 | 5 309.3 | 149.1 | 608 | 9 660 | 2 231.4 | 197.0 | 153 | 934 | 139.2 | 24.9 |
| Macon | 40.4 | 366 | 113 | D | D | D | 432 | 6 231 | 1 450.6 | 132.5 | 91 | 454 | 64.6 | 12.6 |
| Macoupin | 9.3 | 188 | 49 | 610 | 350.4 | 24.5 | 160 | 1 464 | 326.0 | 31.8 | 24 | 96 | 6.1 | 1.8 |
| Madison | 387.5 | 1 466 | 231 | 2 470 | 1 643.6 | 113.7 | 906 | 12 733 | 3 104.2 | 285.8 | 241 | 1 284 | 158.5 | 32.3 |
| Marion | 6.6 | 165 | 39 | D | D | D | 168 | 1 434 | 345.7 | 30.7 | 29 | D | D | D |
| Marshall | 7.0 | 526 | 17 | D | D | D | 42 | 329 | 78.5 | 6.1 | 6 | D | D | D |
| Mason | 276.0 | 17 536 | 19 | 206 | 192.3 | 8.1 | 48 | 453 | 98.8 | 7.3 | 3 | 5 | 1.1 | 0.1 |
| Massac | 630.9 | 41 105 | 9 | D | D | D | 44 | 287 | 75.9 | 6.5 | 5 | D | D | D |
| Menard | 3.9 | 308 | 14 | 113 | 128.7 | 4.3 | 33 | 352 | 68.9 | 5.6 | 8 | 58 | 9.5 | 0.5 |
| Mercer | 8.7 | 517 | 16 | D | D | D | 45 | 405 | 85.3 | 7.8 | 4 | 6 | 0.5 | 0.1 |
| Monroe | 2.9 | 92 | 22 | D | D | D | 105 | 1 395 | 405.7 | 35.1 | 37 | 123 | 13.0 | 2.9 |
| Montgomery | 510.2 | 16 786 | 41 | 312 | 254.3 | 13.0 | 138 | 1 647 | 401.5 | 34.2 | 19 | 58 | 5.2 | 1.1 |
| Morgan | 232.1 | 6 497 | 45 | 697 | 425.5 | 23.5 | 162 | 1 984 | 403.1 | 37.0 | 24 | D | D | D |
| Moultrie | 1.6 | 112 | 15 | 86 | 95.2 | 3.5 | 48 | 480 | 118.7 | 9.3 | 4 | D | D | D |
| Ogle | 64.9 | 1 196 | 44 | D | D | D | 151 | 1 587 | 454.3 | 30.1 | 45 | 120 | 13.0 | 2.4 |
| Peoria | 529.6 | 2 905 | 226 | 3 127 | 1 609.8 | 147.5 | 786 | 11 618 | 2 425.9 | 241.0 | 230 | 1 167 | 194.6 | 31.7 |
| Perry | 2.2 | 96 | 8 | 53 | 42.9 | 1.7 | 58 | 650 | 168.3 | 13.9 | 7 | 26 | 1.6 | 0.3 |
| Piatt | 3.3 | 199 | 27 | 237 | 263.9 | 10.1 | 44 | 496 | 118.8 | 10.7 | 7 | 40 | 1.7 | 0.5 |
| Pike | 33.0 | 1 929 | 21 | 171 | 265.3 | 6.1 | 56 | 551 | 136.5 | 10.5 | 8 | 24 | 2.5 | 0.4 |
| Pope | 0.4 | 102 | NA | NA | NA | NA | 11 | 60 | 9.2 | 0.9 | 1 | D | D | D |
| Pulaski | 2.3 | 343 | 5 | D | D | D | 18 | 96 | 31.8 | 1.9 | 1 | D | D | D |
| Putnam | 210.2 | 34 491 | 8 | D | D | D | 14 | 112 | 21.7 | 1.8 | 1 | D | D | D |
| Randolph | 41.4 | 1 249 | 32 | 422 | 166.4 | 17.3 | 116 | 1 472 | 332.3 | 31.0 | 14 | 34 | 3.0 | 0.7 |
| Richland | 3.1 | 194 | 22 | 382 | 250.3 | 11.6 | 70 | 756 | 161.5 | 15.2 | 8 | D | D | D |
| Rock Island | 1 082.3 | 7 322 | 163 | 3 145 | 1 437.5 | 131.4 | 545 | 8 158 | 1 711.4 | 174.9 | 136 | 615 | 96.1 | 14.1 |
| St. Clair | 32.8 | 126 | 182 | 1 800 | 1 661.6 | 72.9 | 976 | 13 864 | 3 087.2 | 299.7 | 245 | 1 167 | 153.2 | 33.2 |
| Saline | 3.3 | 125 | 16 | D | D | D | 120 | 1 214 | 271.2 | 26.0 | 13 | 70 | 6.0 | 1.4 |
| Sangamon | 411.4 | 2 134 | 192 | 2 763 | 1 841.3 | 109.2 | 809 | 12 446 | 2 862.6 | 250.1 | 227 | 1 011 | 153.5 | 24.6 |
| Schuyler | 1.7 | 233 | 3 | D | D | D | 37 | 285 | 53.1 | 6.1 | 4 | D | D | D |
| Scott | 9.4 | 1 739 | 2 | D | D | D | 12 | 119 | 34.9 | 2.3 | 1 | D | D | D |
| Shelby | 3.3 | 149 | 27 | 184 | 157.3 | 6.0 | 72 | 549 | 140.9 | 9.6 | 11 | 27 | 1.7 | 0.4 |
| Stark | 2.0 | 316 | 10 | D | D | D | 19 | 174 | 57.3 | 5.5 | 1 | D | D | D |
| Stephenson | 8.9 | 186 | 46 | D | D | D | 167 | 2 045 | 480.6 | 42.4 | 37 | 105 | 11.6 | 2.5 |
| Tazewell | 123.8 | 952 | 134 | 1 946 | 1 225.1 | 86.6 | 455 | 6 798 | 1 758.1 | 156.7 | 85 | 321 | 55.1 | 8.9 |
| Union | 3.4 | 187 | 8 | 64 | 20.5 | 2.0 | 70 | 678 | 145.1 | 14.2 | 14 | 42 | 4.4 | 0.9 |
| Vermilion | 17.1 | 208 | 77 | D | D | D | 281 | 3 443 | 757.9 | 68.5 | 59 | 254 | 34.3 | 6.6 |
| Wabash | 4.0 | 316 | 12 | 143 | 89.5 | 4.5 | 43 | 496 | 109.2 | 8.4 | 5 | 20 | 1.8 | 0.4 |
| Warren | 3.6 | 206 | 20 | 281 | 219.8 | 10.1 | 66 | 634 | 133.7 | 11.5 | 8 | 19 | 1.7 | 0.3 |
| Washington | 4.0 | 267 | 31 | 482 | 270.5 | 18.8 | 65 | 610 | 197.3 | 15.4 | 14 | 30 | 1.4 | 0.2 |
| Wayne | 4.9 | 289 | 16 | 128 | 126.6 | 6.2 | 68 | 645 | 146.3 | 12.4 | 8 | 22 | 1.9 | 0.5 |
| White | 14.9 | 974 | 26 | 280 | 400.3 | 8.9 | 59 | 491 | 123.1 | 10.0 | 10 | 49 | 4.9 | 1.4 |
| Whiteside | 54.9 | 918 | 64 | 431 | 926.8 | 16.7 | 222 | 2 823 | 570.6 | 57.2 | 47 | 179 | 16.4 | 3.2 |
| Will | 2 630.5 | 4 092 | 699 | 12 694 | 11 061.8 | 636.9 | 1 654 | 28 627 | 6 841.5 | 624.0 | 530 | 2 767 | 424.1 | 80.9 |
| Williamson | 112.9 | 1 775 | 58 | D | D | D | 308 | 3 900 | 987.5 | 84.7 | 61 | 242 | 43.7 | 9.5 |

1. Merchant wholesalers, except manufacturers' sales branches and offices.  2. Employer establishments.

| STATE County | Professional, scientific, and technical services,[1] 2007 | | | | Manufacturing, 2007 | | | | Accommodation and food services, 2007 | | | |
|---|---|---|---|---|---|---|---|---|---|---|---|---|
| | Number of establish-ments | Number of employees | Receipts (mil dol) | Annual payroll (mil dol) | Number of establish-ments | Number of employees | Receipts (mil dol) | Annual payroll (mil dol) | Number of establish-ments | Number of employees | Sales (mil dol) | Annual payroll (mil dol) |
| | 147 | 148 | 149 | 150 | 151 | 152 | 153 | 154 | 155 | 156 | 157 | 158 |
| ILLINOIS—Cont'd | | | | | | | | | | | | |
| Hardin | 4 | D | D | D | NA | NA | NA | NA | 7 | 32 | 1.0 | 0.3 |
| Henderson | 6 | 24 | 1.5 | 0.4 | NA | NA | NA | NA | 20 | 57 | 1.9 | 0.5 |
| Henry | 67 | D | D | D | 57 | 4 272 | D | D | 97 | 1 119 | 42.0 | 10.4 |
| Iroquois | 29 | 111 | 8.9 | 3.6 | 30 | 880 | 338.7 | 24.3 | 64 | 539 | 20.8 | 5.6 |
| Jackson | 119 | D | D | D | 31 | 716 | 177.4 | D | 155 | 3 138 | 108.3 | 31.2 |
| Jasper | 9 | 22 | 1.7 | 0.6 | NA | NA | NA | NA | 13 | 110 | 3.2 | 0.8 |
| Jefferson | 71 | 471 | 39.8 | 17.1 | 36 | D | D | D | 82 | 1 650 | 67.8 | 19.3 |
| Jersey | 27 | 163 | 13.2 | 6.0 | NA | NA | NA | NA | 59 | 749 | 26.7 | 7.4 |
| Jo Daviess | 54 | 184 | 26.7 | 8.1 | 36 | 1 106 | 419.5 | 42.8 | 101 | 1 730 | 81.3 | 22.7 |
| Johnson | 16 | 361 | 9.9 | 3.6 | NA | NA | NA | NA | 16 | 163 | 6.8 | 1.8 |
| Kane | 1 522 | D | D | D | 885 | 34 075 | 9 879.5 | 1 552.1 | 904 | 15 459 | 680.9 | 201.2 |
| Kankakee | 169 | D | D | D | 115 | 5 633 | 3 418.9 | 280.8 | 229 | D | D | D |
| Kendall | 169 | D | D | D | 84 | 2 766 | 685.7 | D | 152 | 2 153 | 99.9 | 25.7 |
| Knox | 65 | D | D | D | 40 | D | D | D | 132 | 1 800 | 68.3 | 19.1 |
| Lake | 3 021 | D | D | D | 922 | 49 414 | 16 381.5 | 3 717.8 | 1 492 | 24 968 | 1 299.3 | 365.8 |
| LaSalle | 181 | D | D | D | 155 | 5 964 | 2 244.0 | 274.7 | 322 | 4 263 | 158.6 | 44.1 |
| Lawrence | 19 | 77 | 7.8 | 2.6 | 12 | D | D | D | 22 | D | D | D |
| Lee | 46 | 271 | 26.3 | 10.7 | 43 | 4 115 | 1 098.2 | 145.9 | 89 | 884 | 35.0 | 8.8 |
| Livingston | 59 | 302 | 24.5 | 10.9 | 55 | 4 021 | 1 261.5 | 188.0 | 79 | 898 | 38.3 | 9.5 |
| Logan | 42 | 177 | 13.7 | 5.2 | 20 | 1 329 | 631.6 | 51.7 | 73 | 844 | 30.4 | 9.4 |
| McDonough | 42 | D | D | D | 22 | 1 369 | 248.8 | 49.9 | 107 | 1 598 | 52.8 | 13.5 |
| McHenry | 973 | 3 730 | 488.0 | 167.7 | 576 | 21 462 | 5 291.2 | 958.4 | 539 | 8 438 | 365.6 | 104.5 |
| McLean | 338 | D | D | D | 115 | 5 497 | 2 578.8 | 270.5 | 375 | 8 558 | 336.1 | 97.4 |
| Macon | 181 | 1 185 | 125.8 | 51.1 | 112 | 8 762 | 9 590.8 | 409.4 | 219 | 4 733 | 170.9 | 52.0 |
| Macoupin | 55 | 471 | 40.2 | 18.2 | 40 | 704 | 180.4 | 25.2 | 84 | 786 | 26.1 | 6.5 |
| Madison | 528 | D | D | D | 213 | 13 490 | 18 978.2 | 769.9 | 596 | 10 249 | 382.7 | 111.6 |
| Marion | 63 | 232 | 15.0 | 6.6 | 56 | 2 930 | 689.7 | 113.5 | 88 | 1 016 | 36.8 | 9.9 |
| Marshall | 13 | D | D | D | 21 | 1 045 | D | D | 30 | 345 | 9.2 | 2.7 |
| Mason | 12 | 34 | 3.0 | 0.8 | NA | NA | NA | NA | 36 | 279 | 10.4 | 2.5 |
| Massac | 12 | D | D | D | 6 | 514 | D | D | 27 | D | D | D |
| Menard | 14 | 77 | 4.9 | 1.5 | NA | NA | NA | NA | 22 | 185 | 6.9 | 1.5 |
| Mercer | 13 | D | D | D | NA | NA | NA | NA | 20 | 222 | 5.6 | 1.8 |
| Monroe | 75 | 766 | 82.7 | 43.1 | NA | NA | NA | NA | 66 | 971 | 35.9 | 10.7 |
| Montgomery | 37 | 217 | 16.7 | 5.1 | 28 | 1 081 | 305.6 | 40.1 | 74 | 992 | 36.4 | 10.8 |
| Morgan | 50 | D | D | D | 34 | 2 349 | D | D | 88 | 1 248 | 44.4 | 13.0 |
| Moultrie | 19 | 100 | 8.6 | 3.6 | 31 | 1 777 | 541.2 | 70.0 | 19 | D | D | D |
| Ogle | 81 | 729 | 46.1 | 21.1 | 68 | 4 590 | 1 137.6 | 192.5 | 108 | 1 140 | 43.4 | 11.8 |
| Peoria | 426 | D | D | D | 165 | 11 683 | 4 951.3 | 502.0 | 486 | 8 169 | 343.1 | 99.3 |
| Perry | 21 | 93 | 6.2 | 2.6 | 19 | 831 | 369.0 | 30.9 | 34 | 526 | 15.4 | 4.5 |
| Piatt | 34 | 119 | 8.9 | 3.9 | NA | NA | NA | NA | 31 | 299 | 10.0 | 2.7 |
| Pike | 18 | 67 | 8.1 | 2.0 | NA | NA | NA | NA | 40 | 434 | 13.7 | 3.7 |
| Pope | 3 | D | D | D | NA | NA | NA | NA | 10 | 26 | 1.2 | 0.2 |
| Pulaski | NA | NA | NA | NA | NA | NA | NA | NA | 9 | D | D | D |
| Putnam | 6 | D | D | D | 10 | 613 | D | D | 13 | 59 | 2.3 | 0.5 |
| Randolph | 39 | 201 | 22.8 | 5.5 | 34 | 3 104 | 532.2 | 80.7 | 74 | 800 | 26.8 | 7.0 |
| Richland | 27 | 84 | 9.2 | 3.1 | 32 | 543 | 94.6 | 17.4 | 31 | 357 | 14.2 | 3.7 |
| Rock Island | 297 | D | D | D | 166 | 7 961 | 3 714.3 | 395.9 | 364 | 5 853 | 224.2 | 64.9 |
| St. Clair | 514 | D | D | D | 181 | 5 788 | 2 324.5 | 245.6 | 564 | 11 181 | 615.4 | 149.4 |
| Saline | 48 | 223 | 27.0 | 7.3 | 27 | 501 | 92.4 | D | 45 | 833 | 28.3 | 7.5 |
| Sangamon | 580 | 4 649 | 562.7 | 228.8 | 117 | D | D | D | 521 | 9 265 | 366.8 | 110.7 |
| Schuyler | 9 | 19 | 1.2 | 0.4 | NA | NA | NA | NA | 14 | D | D | D |
| Scott | 3 | D | D | D | NA | NA | NA | NA | 9 | 33 | 1.7 | 0.4 |
| Shelby | 24 | 164 | 15.4 | 6.3 | 18 | 1 163 | D | 44.9 | 38 | 364 | 14.1 | 4.1 |
| Stark | 14 | D | D | D | NA | NA | NA | NA | 8 | 40 | 1.4 | 0.3 |
| Stephenson | 76 | 460 | 48.5 | 17.0 | 57 | 3 631 | 905.1 | 168.4 | 95 | 1 192 | 44.8 | 13.6 |
| Tazewell | 183 | 1 197 | 106.3 | 47.0 | 121 | 9 985 | 5 145.7 | 395.7 | 334 | 6 334 | 353.9 | 83.9 |
| Union | 24 | 91 | 9.8 | 4.7 | 11 | 584 | 176.1 | 21.0 | 29 | 314 | 10.0 | 4.0 |
| Vermilion | 93 | 396 | 44.7 | 12.9 | 100 | 5 458 | 2 576.4 | 239.7 | 156 | 2 370 | 85.0 | 24.6 |
| Wabash | 21 | 108 | 11.0 | 3.7 | NA | NA | NA | NA | 21 | 301 | 10.2 | 2.9 |
| Warren | 20 | D | D | D | 21 | D | D | D | 29 | 414 | 14.3 | 4.0 |
| Washington | 21 | 97 | 16.2 | 6.1 | 17 | 1 983 | 409.2 | 73.5 | 37 | 313 | 12.3 | 2.9 |
| Wayne | 23 | 54 | 4.6 | 1.1 | 17 | D | D | D | 26 | D | D | D |
| White | 20 | 80 | 5.3 | 1.4 | NA | NA | NA | NA | 26 | 338 | 11.4 | 3.2 |
| Whiteside | 73 | 583 | 128.8 | 24.9 | 103 | 3 985 | 1 022.5 | 178.9 | 119 | 1 647 | 60.6 | 16.4 |
| Will | 1 516 | D | D | D | 642 | 22 470 | 13 628.2 | 1 098.3 | 1 029 | 20 905 | 1 404.9 | 308.1 |
| Williamson | 128 | D | D | D | 50 | 1 863 | 681.4 | 72.1 | 145 | 2 588 | 118.6 | 31.0 |

1. Establishment subject to federal tax.

# Table B. States and Counties — Health Care and Social Assistance, Other Services, and Federal Funds

| STATE County | Health care and social assistance, 2007 | | | | Other services, 2007 | | | | Federal funds and grants, 2009–2010 Expenditures (mil dol) | | | |
|---|---|---|---|---|---|---|---|---|---|---|---|---|
| | | | | | | | | | Total | Direct payments for individuals[1] | | |
| | Number of establishments | Number of employees | Receipts (mil dol) | Annual payroll (mil dol) | Number of establishments | Number of employees | Receipts (mil dol) | Annual payroll (mil dol) | | Social Security and government retirement | Medicare | Food Stamps and Supplemental Security Income |
| | 159 | 160 | 161 | 162 | 163 | 164 | 165 | 166 | 167 | 168 | 169 | 170 |
| **ILLINOIS—Cont'd** | | | | | | | | | | | | |
| Hardin | 11 | 311 | 17.9 | 8.9 | 3 | D | D | D | 48.2 | 17.2 | 12.6 | 3.0 |
| Henderson | 8 | D | D | D | 5 | D | D | D | 57.2 | 27.1 | 12.1 | 1.7 |
| Henry | 87 | 1 421 | 116.2 | 43.3 | 96 | 640 | 48.8 | 11.7 | 337.3 | 170.5 | 82.4 | 9.2 |
| Iroquois | 78 | 1 648 | 93.3 | 42.0 | 52 | 148 | 15.0 | 3.8 | 225.7 | 107.6 | 57.3 | 7.2 |
| Jackson | 161 | 3 872 | 370.4 | 127.7 | 96 | 436 | 42.6 | 7.3 | 445.8 | 142.0 | 73.5 | 30.2 |
| Jasper | 15 | 130 | 5.9 | 2.3 | 23 | 89 | 5.7 | 1.2 | 67.9 | 27.3 | 16.3 | 2.3 |
| Jefferson | 139 | 3 158 | 316.6 | 118.3 | 88 | 391 | 26.6 | 8.1 | 318.8 | 127.2 | 81.8 | 18.0 |
| Jersey | 37 | D | D | D | 33 | 126 | 5.6 | 1.5 | 132.5 | 65.9 | 32.3 | 5.4 |
| Jo Daviess | 41 | 615 | 32.0 | 15.4 | 58 | 277 | 19.9 | 5.5 | 152.6 | 84.6 | 35.5 | 2.8 |
| Johnson | 20 | 192 | 9.4 | 3.9 | 10 | D | D | D | 95.8 | 46.7 | 19.5 | 4.0 |
| Kane | 1 068 | 20 650 | 2 107.5 | 861.5 | 849 | 5 753 | 583.3 | 165.6 | 2 591.9 | 1 072.5 | 425.8 | 88.7 |
| Kankakee | 290 | 6 260 | 618.8 | 228.6 | 193 | 1 080 | 105.7 | 26.6 | 794.0 | 326.4 | 202.6 | 42.4 |
| Kendall | 128 | 1 021 | 95.7 | 35.6 | 148 | 767 | 55.4 | 16.9 | 427.7 | 140.8 | 34.2 | 3.5 |
| Knox | 143 | 4 266 | 356.7 | 134.4 | 83 | 621 | 204.5 | 15.2 | 427.2 | 200.4 | 113.0 | 17.8 |
| Lake | 1 818 | 30 953 | 3 380.3 | 1 372.6 | 1 246 | 8 449 | 787.7 | 218.6 | 4 231.8 | 1 575.2 | 617.8 | 89.6 |
| LaSalle | 277 | 5 599 | 404.0 | 164.3 | 249 | 1 337 | 87.7 | 25.5 | 761.0 | 360.7 | 190.2 | 25.3 |
| Lawrence | 27 | 713 | 33.8 | 13.4 | 28 | 153 | 16.5 | 3.7 | 130.1 | 50.7 | 36.9 | 5.0 |
| Lee | 87 | 2 082 | 161.8 | 71.7 | 64 | 338 | 25.1 | 7.8 | 237.6 | 117.4 | 55.6 | 6.8 |
| Livingston | 67 | 1 622 | 123.6 | 50.2 | 77 | 321 | 29.4 | 7.2 | 233.9 | 107.3 | 65.8 | 8.0 |
| Logan | 59 | 1 296 | 91.4 | 33.5 | 55 | 222 | 16.6 | 3.3 | 200.7 | 86.2 | 53.8 | 7.0 |
| McDonough | 83 | 1 816 | 120.0 | 52.5 | 72 | 265 | 17.8 | 4.6 | 201.8 | 74.7 | 46.2 | 9.2 |
| McHenry | 667 | 10 348 | 1 013.9 | 409.5 | 561 | 3 226 | 240.5 | 75.1 | 1 189.0 | 760.7 | 232.7 | 18.3 |
| McLean | 333 | 8 693 | 875.8 | 354.5 | 260 | 2 362 | 187.8 | 59.7 | 758.0 | 353.8 | 140.8 | 25.7 |
| Macon | 282 | 7 449 | 750.1 | 281.3 | 197 | 1 526 | 222.4 | 33.5 | 1 043.4 | 382.0 | 189.1 | 51.9 |
| Macoupin | 96 | 1 761 | 96.0 | 39.1 | 80 | 276 | 23.7 | 5.6 | 369.0 | 176.6 | 105.5 | 15.0 |
| Madison | 655 | 12 765 | 1 066.8 | 412.7 | 479 | 3 210 | 273.5 | 80.8 | 2 208.0 | 921.9 | 477.5 | 102.3 |
| Marion | 113 | 2 852 | 210.8 | 80.0 | 77 | 279 | 20.3 | 5.3 | 401.3 | 165.8 | 114.6 | 19.9 |
| Marshall | 22 | D | D | D | 21 | D | D | D | 82.4 | 43.2 | 22.5 | 2.4 |
| Mason | 27 | 460 | 28.2 | 12.8 | 27 | 88 | 7.3 | 1.4 | 137.1 | 59.5 | 39.1 | 5.6 |
| Massac | 31 | 628 | 40.7 | 16.7 | 28 | 150 | 8.3 | 3.0 | 138.4 | 56.8 | 36.3 | 6.4 |
| Menard | 15 | D | D | D | 19 | 61 | 4.8 | 1.2 | 80.7 | 39.1 | 18.2 | 2.7 |
| Mercer | 27 | 369 | 21.7 | 9.4 | 23 | 65 | 7.3 | 1.5 | 116.5 | 57.0 | 26.2 | 3.4 |
| Monroe | 70 | 793 | 45.2 | 19.2 | 68 | 292 | 23.6 | 6.6 | 173.4 | 99.4 | 34.1 | 2.0 |
| Montgomery | 75 | 1 538 | 111.7 | 41.8 | 57 | 220 | 17.2 | 4.6 | 237.2 | 104.5 | 59.5 | 10.0 |
| Morgan | 125 | D | D | D | 66 | 273 | 17.1 | 5.0 | 262.8 | 114.3 | 62.9 | 10.8 |
| Moultrie | 30 | 721 | 33.9 | 15.5 | 23 | 66 | 6.6 | 1.7 | 110.6 | 52.7 | 27.5 | 2.6 |
| Ogle | 92 | 1 424 | 86.4 | 34.5 | 80 | 346 | 28.1 | 7.8 | 272.0 | 148.0 | 60.6 | 7.4 |
| Peoria | 536 | 20 744 | 2 106.8 | 883.9 | 338 | 3 786 | 332.4 | 141.5 | 1 686.2 | 552.5 | 305.3 | 85.3 |
| Perry | 44 | 1 018 | 61.6 | 24.8 | 50 | 162 | 13.3 | 2.6 | 155.7 | 71.9 | 42.3 | 8.7 |
| Piatt | 29 | D | D | D | 19 | 70 | 4.2 | 0.9 | 111.7 | 56.9 | 26.9 | 2.1 |
| Pike | 31 | 585 | 41.0 | 15.6 | 29 | 103 | 7.8 | 1.7 | 136.7 | 56.0 | 36.1 | 5.6 |
| Pope | 13 | 143 | 4.9 | 2.5 | 4 | D | D | D | 41.6 | 16.2 | 8.9 | 1.9 |
| Pulaski | 14 | 184 | 6.6 | 2.8 | 14 | 37 | 5.0 | 0.7 | 475.0 | 21.7 | 17.1 | 6.1 |
| Putnam | 4 | 20 | 1.0 | 0.3 | 6 | 17 | 1.2 | 0.3 | 38.4 | 21.8 | 9.6 | 0.7 |
| Randolph | 73 | 2 120 | 147.9 | 69.0 | 66 | 248 | 17.0 | 5.7 | 239.2 | 109.3 | 63.4 | 9.2 |
| Richland | 48 | 945 | 60.5 | 26.1 | 44 | 187 | 13.3 | 3.7 | 134.7 | 54.3 | 28.6 | 5.2 |
| Rock Island | 397 | 9 031 | 742.0 | 324.9 | 263 | 1 765 | 152.2 | 44.1 | 1 673.8 | 524.0 | 247.2 | 54.0 |
| St. Clair | 620 | 14 718 | 1 246.8 | 517.7 | 439 | 2 502 | 196.7 | 60.3 | 3 539.8 | 952.1 | 472.5 | 164.6 |
| Saline | 62 | 2 059 | 116.0 | 53.1 | 53 | D | D | D | 312.6 | 102.4 | 56.4 | 18.0 |
| Sangamon | 462 | D | D | D | 482 | 3 494 | 382.6 | 108.4 | 5 512.3 | 575.4 | 314.8 | 67.4 |
| Schuyler | 15 | 345 | 20.3 | 8.4 | 13 | 39 | 6.0 | 0.7 | 52.5 | 23.7 | 11.9 | 1.8 |
| Scott | 5 | D | D | D | 5 | 14 | 2.2 | 0.3 | 40.3 | 16.7 | 9.4 | 1.0 |
| Shelby | 37 | 683 | 43.3 | 16.3 | 27 | 96 | 7.8 | 1.8 | 176.3 | 75.4 | 45.7 | 5.0 |
| Stark | 7 | D | D | D | 3 | D | D | D | 51.5 | 21.4 | 15.3 | 1.1 |
| Stephenson | 104 | 2 586 | 208.5 | 88.9 | 98 | 594 | 30.6 | 9.9 | 345.8 | 168.6 | 74.5 | 14.8 |
| Tazewell | 238 | 5 102 | 335.4 | 135.1 | 252 | 1 270 | 109.9 | 32.3 | 785.6 | 409.7 | 199.1 | 24.4 |
| Union | 53 | 1 156 | 47.5 | 22.0 | 20 | 71 | 5.3 | 1.5 | 157.3 | 61.6 | 34.4 | 9.8 |
| Vermilion | 149 | 4 729 | 437.7 | 203.4 | 138 | 780 | 54.8 | 14.5 | 774.1 | 302.8 | 150.8 | 44.4 |
| Wabash | 28 | 733 | 42.2 | 16.6 | 23 | D | D | D | 86.0 | 39.1 | 22.3 | 4.5 |
| Warren | 44 | 732 | 33.5 | 13.4 | 34 | 112 | 11.3 | 1.9 | 131.4 | 53.9 | 32.2 | 5.1 |
| Washington | 26 | 489 | 26.2 | 12.1 | 28 | 101 | 5.8 | 1.4 | 119.7 | 47.9 | 34.7 | 2.6 |
| Wayne | 32 | 727 | 41.8 | 18.5 | 28 | 112 | 8.1 | 2.0 | 141.5 | 53.8 | 36.3 | 4.5 |
| White | 38 | 536 | 25.7 | 10.2 | 34 | 141 | 16.1 | 3.9 | 166.8 | 60.1 | 38.1 | 5.6 |
| Whiteside | 112 | 3 834 | 248.3 | 104.9 | 135 | 695 | 71.1 | 14.2 | 433.3 | 231.4 | 105.0 | 14.6 |
| Will | 1 127 | 18 527 | 1 782.4 | 714.9 | 1 013 | 6 548 | 638.9 | 169.8 | 2 344.2 | 1 309.4 | 444.4 | 83.5 |
| Williamson | 210 | 5 288 | 539.0 | 197.2 | 102 | 472 | 44.1 | 10.8 | 704.3 | 224.4 | 107.5 | 26.9 |

1. State totals may include programs not allocated by county.

# Table B. States and Counties — Federal Funds, Residential Construction, and Local Government Finances

| STATE County | Salaries and wages | Defense | Other | Medicaid and other health-related | Nutrition and family welfare | Education | Other | New construction ($1,000) | Number of housing units | Total (mil dol) | Inter-governmental (mil dol) | Total (mil dol) | Per capita Total | Per capita Property |
|---|---|---|---|---|---|---|---|---|---|---|---|---|---|---|
| | 171 | 172 | 173 | 174 | 175 | 176 | 177 | 178 | 179 | 180 | 181 | 182 | 183 | 184 |
| ILLINOIS—Cont'd | | | | | | | | | | | | | | |
| Hardin | 1.1 | 0.0 | 0.3 | 10.7 | 1.3 | 0.2 | 0.8 | 0 | 0 | 12.3 | 9.5 | 1.4 | 302 | 274 |
| Henderson | 2.6 | 0.6 | 0.5 | 4.7 | 1.5 | 0.2 | 0.1 | 334 | 6 | 19.6 | 10.2 | 6.2 | 812 | 798 |
| Henry | 31.1 | 0.5 | 2.2 | 14.1 | 6.8 | 1.0 | 3.6 | 7 204 | 41 | 168.5 | 62.0 | 50.4 | 1 015 | 960 |
| Iroquois | 9.1 | 0.1 | 11.1 | 9.1 | 4.4 | 0.8 | 1.3 | 3 041 | 25 | 82.7 | 36.0 | 33.6 | 1 108 | 1 031 |
| Jackson | 29.6 | 5.8 | 8.1 | 76.7 | 13.2 | 6.1 | 20.3 | 4 726 | 83 | 157.6 | 72.2 | 53.8 | 914 | 696 |
| Jasper | 3.3 | 0.0 | 0.8 | 7.0 | 1.8 | 0.2 | 0.0 | 0 | 0 | 34.5 | 18.0 | 12.5 | 1 283 | 1 270 |
| Jefferson | 17.0 | 0.1 | 3.1 | 43.5 | 8.3 | 2.4 | 2.1 | 0 | 0 | 133.7 | 78.1 | 34.2 | 851 | 660 |
| Jersey | 3.7 | 0.0 | 0.9 | 14.9 | 3.1 | 0.3 | 0.9 | 5 945 | 76 | 74.2 | 23.6 | 16.3 | 724 | 627 |
| Jo Daviess | 6.2 | 0.0 | 2.6 | 7.8 | 3.1 | 0.4 | 0.4 | 9 481 | 34 | 82.4 | 21.4 | 39.3 | 1 761 | 1 700 |
| Johnson | 5.5 | 0.0 | 1.5 | 13.2 | 2.2 | 0.4 | 0.2 | 317 | 3 | 26.3 | 15.8 | 5.3 | 408 | 404 |
| Kane | 212.5 | 45.0 | 470.0 | 127.0 | 50.8 | 11.7 | 34.2 | 95 584 | 477 | 2 427.2 | 666.1 | 1 310.9 | 2 617 | 2 353 |
| Kankakee | 53.7 | 0.2 | 4.7 | 96.5 | 20.0 | 5.2 | 18.9 | 11 642 | 62 | 374.3 | 178.8 | 129.3 | 1 168 | 1 106 |
| Kendall | 192.5 | 32.8 | 3.9 | 3.7 | 4.4 | 1.2 | 3.9 | 27 770 | 169 | 342.3 | 91.9 | 167.4 | 1 729 | 1 583 |
| Knox | 20.9 | 0.0 | 3.4 | 37.3 | 8.3 | 2.9 | 3.6 | 6 209 | 31 | 172.0 | 77.1 | 54.1 | 1 043 | 934 |
| Lake | 535.9 | 685.9 | 316.9 | 171.6 | 68.4 | 25.9 | 54.7 | 143 626 | 628 | 3 294.3 | 796.2 | 1 949.8 | 2 745 | 2 561 |
| LaSalle | 56.3 | 5.5 | 5.7 | 52.6 | 13.5 | 3.1 | 22.5 | 16 492 | 117 | 376.1 | 140.6 | 162.7 | 1 445 | 1 313 |
| Lawrence | 7.0 | 0.1 | 0.9 | 16.1 | 2.9 | 0.5 | 0.6 | 0 | 0 | 34.3 | 20.5 | 7.8 | 499 | 490 |
| Lee | 15.5 | 0.0 | 2.2 | 16.2 | 4.5 | 0.9 | 1.0 | 6 014 | 69 | 110.3 | 41.1 | 46.8 | 1 321 | 1 217 |
| Livingston | 16.3 | 0.1 | 1.9 | 12.0 | 5.3 | 0.8 | 1.0 | 4 483 | 24 | 141.7 | 52.1 | 54.4 | 1 421 | 1 399 |
| Logan | 10.4 | 0.3 | 1.7 | 15.0 | 6.3 | 2.3 | 1.2 | 2 474 | 16 | 71.2 | 30.2 | 27.3 | 910 | 872 |
| McDonough | 17.8 | 0.1 | 1.7 | 15.7 | 4.7 | 0.9 | 2.7 | 1 365 | 19 | 134.5 | 41.1 | 25.6 | 801 | 771 |
| McHenry | 56.4 | 8.1 | 13.0 | 33.0 | 22.5 | 3.4 | 13.0 | 61 062 | 419 | 1 095.7 | 253.3 | 625.2 | 1 979 | 1 795 |
| McLean | 67.4 | 0.3 | 18.6 | 56.5 | 18.9 | 5.3 | 21.8 | 62 499 | 620 | 542.8 | 157.7 | 275.3 | 1 676 | 1 372 |
| Macon | 63.7 | 2.0 | 18.1 | 111.7 | 20.3 | 4.3 | 179.3 | 11 931 | 84 | 391.1 | 180.1 | 140.6 | 1 293 | 1 103 |
| Macoupin | 11.3 | 0.2 | 2.9 | 26.9 | 9.1 | 1.1 | 1.0 | 5 718 | 30 | 116.8 | 66.6 | 33.0 | 684 | 652 |
| Madison | 82.5 | 164.7 | 91.0 | 222.3 | 55.2 | 10.5 | 30.2 | 89 912 | 527 | 883.4 | 401.0 | 318.5 | 1 191 | 1 084 |
| Marion | 14.2 | 0.1 | 3.2 | 44.6 | 10.8 | 2.3 | 3.3 | 617 | 4 | 181.5 | 90.1 | 38.6 | 976 | 826 |
| Marshall | 3.1 | 0.0 | 0.7 | 3.7 | 1.8 | 0.2 | 0.1 | 2 314 | 11 | 32.4 | 11.6 | 15.8 | 1 226 | 1 180 |
| Mason | 5.0 | 3.2 | 2.5 | 11.1 | 2.9 | 0.4 | 0.7 | 1 012 | 8 | 66.1 | 25.3 | 19.2 | 1 269 | 1 208 |
| Massac | 3.5 | 2.2 | 2.8 | 22.7 | 2.9 | 0.5 | 0.3 | 146 | 2 | 67.7 | 30.6 | 11.2 | 743 | 699 |
| Menard | 3.0 | 0.0 | 0.7 | 9.7 | 1.8 | 0.3 | 1.0 | 4 871 | 22 | 41.6 | 18.0 | 14.8 | 1 184 | 1 150 |
| Mercer | 4.4 | 5.1 | 0.9 | 5.8 | 2.7 | 0.2 | 0.2 | 1 641 | 13 | 56.8 | 23.6 | 16.7 | 1 014 | 1 004 |
| Monroe | 8.8 | 0.4 | 5.1 | 12.9 | 2.8 | 0.3 | 0.0 | 20 602 | 94 | 88.0 | 25.5 | 38.9 | 1 202 | 1 120 |
| Montgomery | 17.2 | 0.0 | 1.8 | 22.0 | 4.9 | 1.0 | 3.0 | 4 349 | 26 | 81.8 | 40.1 | 28.0 | 940 | 901 |
| Morgan | 8.0 | 0.0 | 1.6 | 44.4 | 5.1 | 1.4 | 1.8 | 637 | 5 | 95.3 | 51.1 | 32.3 | 915 | 827 |
| Moultrie | 14.9 | 0.0 | 0.6 | 5.8 | 1.8 | 0.3 | 0.0 | 3 035 | 32 | 44.7 | 15.3 | 23.2 | 1 620 | 1 608 |
| Ogle | 11.2 | 4.0 | 2.6 | 13.2 | 5.7 | 0.9 | 1.7 | 5 513 | 28 | 211.1 | 69.4 | 88.6 | 1 610 | 1 562 |
| Peoria | 170.8 | 250.1 | 40.9 | 134.6 | 33.1 | 8.1 | 50.9 | 53 058 | 219 | 694.9 | 273.2 | 260.0 | 1 421 | 1 144 |
| Perry | 4.2 | 0.0 | 1.0 | 16.2 | 3.4 | 0.6 | 0.9 | 8 532 | 51 | 68.3 | 25.6 | 11.4 | 504 | 471 |
| Piatt | 3.5 | 7.8 | 0.8 | 5.0 | 2.2 | 0.3 | 0.1 | 3 072 | 13 | 65.8 | 32.0 | 21.6 | 1 311 | 1 277 |
| Pike | 5.5 | 0.0 | 1.3 | 17.0 | 3.2 | 0.5 | 0.3 | 2 417 | 16 | 44.2 | 24.2 | 12.4 | 744 | 717 |
| Pope | 4.7 | 0.0 | 1.9 | 5.4 | 1.1 | 0.1 | 0.2 | 0 | 0 | 9.6 | 5.9 | 2.4 | 581 | 576 |
| Pulaski | 3.9 | 380.3 | 1.1 | 27.2 | 6.8 | 1.0 | 0.9 | 350 | 4 | 25.0 | 18.0 | 2.6 | 398 | 351 |
| Putnam | 1.9 | 0.0 | 0.5 | 0.8 | 1.0 | 0.1 | 0.1 | 1 893 | 14 | 19.6 | 11.4 | 6.5 | 1 084 | 1 065 |
| Randolph | 13.9 | 0.3 | 5.8 | 19.4 | 6.9 | 0.8 | 0.7 | 6 754 | 69 | 128.2 | 42.3 | 22.8 | 697 | 642 |
| Richland | 4.8 | -0.1 | 1.2 | 15.9 | 2.9 | 1.5 | 0.8 | 1 156 | 8 | 74.8 | 44.2 | 11.6 | 749 | 702 |
| Rock Island | 343.9 | 301.2 | 18.8 | 86.5 | 26.1 | 5.3 | 35.7 | 17 386 | 107 | 548.0 | 224.6 | 203.5 | 1 381 | 1 203 |
| St. Clair | 698.0 | 585.9 | 59.8 | 438.8 | 52.5 | 25.9 | 37.3 | 107 087 | 673 | 1 012.9 | 517.1 | 308.7 | 1 181 | 966 |
| Saline | 7.8 | 2.9 | 22.9 | 50.0 | 4.9 | 1.8 | 33.2 | 0 | 0 | 82.1 | 45.2 | 18.9 | 723 | 649 |
| Sangamon | 269.9 | 25.2 | 32.2 | 272.7 | 394.3 | 939.9 | 2 562.3 | 66 850 | 369 | 661.9 | 257.4 | 279.3 | 1 439 | 1 255 |
| Schuyler | 2.2 | 0.1 | 0.5 | 6.7 | 1.4 | 0.2 | 0.1 | NA | NA | 36.2 | 10.8 | 6.4 | 921 | 919 |
| Scott | 1.8 | 0.1 | 0.4 | 6.6 | 1.1 | 0.1 | 0.1 | NA | NA | 17.1 | 8.9 | 4.1 | 779 | 752 |
| Shelby | 16.0 | 2.5 | 1.4 | 15.7 | 3.3 | 0.5 | 0.6 | 4 650 | 27 | 45.3 | 20.6 | 16.5 | 761 | 743 |
| Stark | 2.2 | 0.0 | 0.5 | 3.3 | 1.2 | 0.1 | 0.1 | 375 | 2 | 17.8 | 6.5 | 8.1 | 1 312 | 1 298 |
| Stephenson | 25.9 | 0.7 | 2.7 | 29.6 | 7.8 | 1.9 | 2.3 | 1 607 | 10 | 168.4 | 74.4 | 59.4 | 1 276 | 1 162 |
| Tazewell | 48.6 | 3.5 | 9.1 | 55.1 | 17.2 | 2.0 | 4.7 | 36 929 | 155 | 457.4 | 181.1 | 176.4 | 1 345 | 1 167 |
| Union | 4.2 | 0.0 | 0.9 | 35.6 | 3.5 | 0.7 | 1.7 | 1 854 | 14 | 75.2 | 31.9 | 14.1 | 773 | 767 |
| Vermilion | 56.9 | 14.7 | 69.5 | 79.2 | 19.3 | 3.6 | 9.5 | 2 036 | 12 | 277.9 | 144.2 | 79.7 | 981 | 836 |
| Wabash | 2.4 | 0.0 | 0.6 | 9.1 | 2.1 | 1.0 | 0.2 | 64 | 1 | 49.6 | 15.8 | 8.1 | 668 | 632 |
| Warren | 7.5 | 0.0 | 1.1 | 15.0 | 5.3 | 0.4 | 1.5 | 2 323 | 11 | 44.2 | 20.5 | 14.8 | 850 | 833 |
| Washington | 4.2 | 0.0 | 1.0 | 8.7 | 2.1 | 0.3 | 1.1 | 5 015 | 34 | 44.2 | 14.9 | 12.0 | 816 | 808 |
| Wayne | 5.1 | 0.0 | 1.1 | 16.5 | 3.1 | 0.6 | 1.0 | 0 | 0 | 38.7 | 23.3 | 9.4 | 567 | 527 |
| White | 4.5 | 0.3 | 11.8 | 22.0 | 7.1 | 0.4 | 0.3 | 0 | 0 | 44.8 | 28.5 | 9.2 | 626 | 582 |
| Whiteside | 21.0 | 0.7 | 2.7 | 27.1 | 13.2 | 1.4 | 2.7 | 7 336 | 45 | 281.2 | 74.0 | 62.7 | 1 059 | 1 002 |
| Will | 102.1 | 81.6 | 60.8 | 116.1 | 53.8 | 13.9 | 31.8 | 129 069 | 538 | 2 329.8 | 670.9 | 1 202.8 | 1 786 | 1 620 |
| Williamson | 95.1 | 109.1 | 39.0 | 67.0 | 9.2 | 2.5 | 3.2 | 19 038 | 205 | 212.3 | 110.3 | 60.6 | 939 | 794 |

1. State totals may include programs not allocated by county.   2. Based on the resident population estimated as of July 1 of the year shown.

# Table B. States and Counties — Local Government Finances, Government Employment, and Voting

| | Local government finances, 2007 (cont.) | | | | | | | | | Government employment, 2011 | | | Presidential election,[2] 2012 | | |
| | Direct general expenditure | | | | | | | Debt outstanding | | | | | Percent of vote cast: | | |
| | | | Percent of total for: | | | | | | | | | | | | |
| STATE County | Total (mil dol) | Per capita[1] (dollars) | Education | Health and hospitals | Police protection | Public welfare | High-ways | Total (mil dol) | Per capita[1] (dollars) | Federal civilian | Federal military | State and local | Demo-cratic | Republi-can | All other |
| | 185 | 186 | 187 | 188 | 189 | 190 | 191 | 192 | 193 | 194 | 195 | 196 | 197 | 198 | 199 |
| ILLINOIS—Cont'd | | | | | | | | | | | | | | | |
| Hardin | 9.8 | 2 201 | 63.4 | 3.2 | 2.7 | 0.2 | 7.8 | 5.1 | 1 130 | 11 | 0 | 247 | 39.6 | 59.0 | 1.5 |
| Henderson | 18.0 | 2 369 | 51.6 | 7.6 | 3.7 | 0.1 | 10.4 | 4.8 | 627 | 40 | 14 | 392 | 58.1 | 40.4 | 1.5 |
| Henry | 163.6 | 3 294 | 42.4 | 16.9 | 6.8 | 1.9 | 6.5 | 85.4 | 1 721 | 121 | 101 | 3 366 | 53.2 | 45.4 | 1.4 |
| Iroquois | 86.2 | 2 847 | 54.0 | 2.9 | 3.7 | 0.1 | 8.7 | 57.7 | 1 904 | 109 | 59 | 1 391 | 34.1 | 64.0 | 1.9 |
| Jackson | 158.1 | 2 687 | 49.4 | 2.5 | 6.8 | 6.9 | 7.7 | 116.9 | 1 986 | 237 | 131 | 13 340 | 59.7 | 37.9 | 2.3 |
| Jasper | 31.6 | 3 260 | 58.9 | 5.8 | 4.1 | 0.1 | 13.8 | 7.1 | 735 | 42 | 19 | 620 | 40.2 | 57.8 | 2.0 |
| Jefferson | 124.5 | 3 098 | 65.5 | 0.9 | 4.3 | 0.1 | 4.8 | 50.8 | 1 265 | 156 | 78 | 2 649 | 43.5 | 54.3 | 2.2 |
| Jersey | 71.8 | 3 198 | 34.6 | 38.4 | 3.9 | 0.2 | 4.3 | 19.3 | 859 | 41 | 46 | 1 133 | 47.6 | 50.4 | 2.0 |
| Jo Daviess | 79.0 | 3 543 | 42.5 | 14.1 | 6.0 | 0.0 | 9.3 | 48.5 | 2 173 | 76 | 45 | 1 280 | 54.5 | 44.0 | 1.5 |
| Johnson | 27.0 | 2 064 | 58.2 | 1.4 | 3.5 | 0.1 | 9.4 | 11.7 | 893 | 74 | 25 | 756 | 31.7 | 66.3 | 2.0 |
| Kane | 2 458.6 | 4 907 | 53.3 | 0.5 | 6.5 | 0.1 | 5.5 | 3 468.0 | 6 922 | 1 700 | 1 041 | 28 148 | 55.2 | 43.4 | 1.3 |
| Kankakee | 395.4 | 3 571 | 54.9 | 1.0 | 6.0 | 0.1 | 5.7 | 256.7 | 2 319 | 251 | 228 | 6 161 | 51.5 | 46.9 | 1.5 |
| Kendall | 408.2 | 4 216 | 60.2 | 0.9 | 3.3 | 0.7 | 7.5 | 672.0 | 6 941 | 130 | 233 | 5 005 | 53.1 | 45.8 | 1.1 |
| Knox | 176.2 | 3 397 | 53.4 | 1.4 | 5.6 | 4.2 | 5.9 | 74.2 | 1 431 | 186 | 106 | 3 400 | 59.2 | 39.3 | 1.6 |
| Lake | 3 247.6 | 4 573 | 54.7 | 1.8 | 5.9 | 0.9 | 4.5 | 2 963.3 | 4 172 | 5 727 | 14 631 | 36 001 | 59.3 | 39.6 | 1.1 |
| LaSalle | 362.1 | 3 216 | 55.5 | 1.6 | 6.0 | 1.5 | 8.8 | 192.2 | 1 706 | 352 | 228 | 6 271 | 54.7 | 43.6 | 1.7 |
| Lawrence | 33.6 | 2 158 | 55.2 | 0.3 | 4.9 | 0.1 | 12.9 | 17.1 | 1 095 | 48 | 33 | 818 | 46.1 | 52.1 | 1.8 |
| Lee | 107.5 | 3 032 | 59.5 | 1.6 | 5.2 | 0.1 | 6.3 | 65.9 | 1 859 | 86 | 73 | 2 128 | 47.6 | 50.6 | 1.8 |
| Livingston | 129.0 | 3 371 | 54.3 | 3.1 | 4.6 | 3.9 | 6.1 | 57.5 | 1 502 | 103 | 78 | 2 619 | 39.6 | 58.8 | 1.6 |
| Logan | 73.6 | 2 458 | 46.7 | 3.5 | 5.5 | 0.1 | 9.0 | 29.5 | 983 | 107 | 60 | 1 983 | 40.7 | 57.6 | 1.7 |
| McDonough | 128.7 | 4 022 | 30.4 | 38.6 | 3.2 | 3.6 | 6.1 | 17.6 | 550 | 98 | 69 | 5 722 | 52.0 | 46.4 | 1.6 |
| McHenry | 1 135.3 | 3 593 | 49.6 | 1.6 | 5.5 | 1.8 | 5.9 | 1 206.1 | 3 817 | 511 | 617 | 14 321 | 51.9 | 46.6 | 1.5 |
| McLean | 563.9 | 3 434 | 44.5 | 1.2 | 5.4 | 1.4 | 5.2 | 651.5 | 3 968 | 711 | 347 | 14 579 | 49.8 | 48.5 | 1.7 |
| Macon | 379.7 | 3 492 | 50.8 | 2.2 | 6.6 | 0.3 | 7.8 | 200.6 | 1 845 | 344 | 229 | 5 619 | 49.8 | 48.7 | 1.5 |
| Macoupin | 115.6 | 2 397 | 61.0 | 2.4 | 7.1 | 0.2 | 8.5 | 58.5 | 1 213 | 123 | 95 | 2 254 | 54.0 | 44.2 | 1.8 |
| Madison | 865.5 | 3 237 | 50.4 | 0.7 | 6.2 | 1.3 | 7.0 | 897.7 | 3 358 | 572 | 539 | 16 066 | 53.7 | 44.6 | 1.7 |
| Marion | 216.5 | 5 468 | 62.2 | 8.6 | 2.5 | 0.2 | 6.5 | 77.7 | 1 964 | 146 | 79 | 2 187 | 48.1 | 50.1 | 1.9 |
| Marshall | 29.2 | 2 274 | 44.2 | 1.6 | 5.2 | 0.1 | 12.5 | 12.2 | 948 | 37 | 25 | 536 | 48.6 | 49.7 | 1.7 |
| Mason | 64.3 | 4 241 | 44.7 | 25.1 | 2.6 | 0.1 | 7.2 | 29.2 | 1 924 | 60 | 29 | 1 147 | 52.0 | 46.1 | 1.8 |
| Massac | 64.6 | 4 273 | 31.3 | 31.0 | 3.7 | 0.0 | 6.7 | 65.9 | 4 360 | 44 | 31 | 944 | 37.5 | 60.8 | 1.7 |
| Menard | 43.4 | 3 482 | 55.7 | 1.7 | 3.5 | 10.2 | 8.0 | 22.1 | 1 769 | 37 | 25 | 740 | 41.9 | 56.8 | 1.3 |
| Mercer | 55.7 | 3 377 | 44.9 | 22.5 | 3.3 | 0.1 | 7.2 | 61.4 | 3 722 | 63 | 33 | 1 100 | 55.2 | 43.3 | 1.4 |
| Monroe | 93.9 | 2 899 | 47.0 | 1.7 | 4.3 | 15.8 | 9.3 | 153.5 | 4 741 | 75 | 67 | 1 445 | 44.0 | 54.6 | 1.4 |
| Montgomery | 79.0 | 2 651 | 48.7 | 3.2 | 5.6 | 0.1 | 11.6 | 49.3 | 1 652 | 100 | 60 | 1 789 | 50.4 | 47.8 | 1.8 |
| Morgan | 92.5 | 2 622 | 54.1 | 1.6 | 8.5 | 3.1 | 9.6 | 13.2 | 374 | 89 | 71 | 2 235 | 48.6 | 49.4 | 1.9 |
| Moultrie | 41.3 | 2 882 | 35.6 | 1.5 | 6.9 | 0.0 | 7.9 | 5.8 | 406 | 30 | 30 | 588 | 42.6 | 55.4 | 1.9 |
| Ogle | 215.9 | 3 924 | 59.0 | 1.4 | 3.6 | 0.1 | 8.6 | 174.7 | 3 176 | 129 | 106 | 2 875 | 45.3 | 52.9 | 1.8 |
| Peoria | 691.5 | 3 779 | 38.9 | 1.4 | 6.2 | 2.2 | 6.3 | 432.2 | 2 362 | 1 644 | 423 | 9 119 | 56.2 | 42.3 | 1.5 |
| Perry | 65.7 | 2 909 | 34.6 | 33.9 | 4.1 | 0.5 | 7.5 | 23.1 | 1 023 | 49 | 44 | 1 198 | 47.0 | 50.9 | 2.1 |
| Piatt | 58.6 | 3 550 | 46.4 | 2.9 | 4.7 | 10.3 | 11.7 | 25.7 | 1 558 | 44 | 33 | 945 | 42.9 | 55.5 | 1.7 |
| Pike | 45.4 | 2 715 | 53.6 | 5.1 | 4.2 | 0.5 | 12.1 | 19.6 | 1 175 | 64 | 33 | 954 | 39.7 | 58.5 | 1.8 |
| Pope | 9.3 | 2 233 | 47.4 | 0.0 | 2.2 | 0.7 | 11.9 | 6.9 | 1 649 | 90 | 0 | 193 | 37.9 | 60.2 | 1.9 |
| Pulaski | 25.1 | 3 870 | 64.2 | 1.7 | 4.7 | 0.9 | 5.5 | 16.3 | 2 519 | 80 | 12 | 719 | 50.1 | 48.7 | 1.2 |
| Putnam | 19.7 | 3 278 | 45.9 | 1.7 | 3.6 | 0.3 | 10.7 | 1.6 | 266 | 22 | 12 | 313 | 56.9 | 41.3 | 1.8 |
| Randolph | 120.8 | 3 689 | 33.0 | 36.4 | 4.0 | 3.2 | 6.3 | 39.1 | 1 193 | 106 | 67 | 2 812 | 48.6 | 49.6 | 1.8 |
| Richland | 74.5 | 4 795 | 76.0 | 0.4 | 2.1 | 0.1 | 5.4 | 20.0 | 1 286 | 57 | 32 | 990 | 41.6 | 56.6 | 1.8 |
| Rock Island | 518.5 | 3 519 | 47.5 | 1.3 | 6.7 | 2.8 | 5.2 | 281.7 | 1 912 | 6 453 | 682 | 7 683 | 61.7 | 37.1 | 1.2 |
| St. Clair | 954.7 | 3 654 | 55.1 | 1.6 | 4.9 | 0.3 | 5.7 | 686.3 | 2 626 | 6 711 | 5 379 | 13 341 | 60.6 | 38.1 | 1.3 |
| Saline | 81.2 | 3 112 | 63.5 | 0.0 | 6.2 | 0.2 | 5.8 | 46.6 | 1 785 | 99 | 50 | 1 900 | 44.5 | 53.4 | 2.2 |
| Sangamon | 635.5 | 3 274 | 54.3 | 1.1 | 8.6 | 1.2 | 5.9 | 1 061.5 | 5 468 | 1 923 | 459 | 25 673 | 51.4 | 47.0 | 1.6 |
| Schuyler | 34.1 | 4 875 | 33.4 | 43.6 | 2.6 | 0.2 | 7.5 | 8.7 | 1 249 | 29 | 15 | 595 | 49.7 | 47.9 | 2.4 |
| Scott | 15.8 | 3 026 | 48.6 | 1.1 | 4.9 | 15.6 | 7.6 | 1.9 | 360 | 22 | 11 | 341 | 41.9 | 56.0 | 2.1 |
| Shelby | 40.8 | 1 877 | 48.0 | 2.6 | 5.3 | 0.2 | 9.4 | 19.3 | 888 | 98 | 44 | 847 | 39.1 | 58.9 | 2.1 |
| Stark | 18.9 | 3 056 | 63.1 | 0.5 | 1.7 | 0.2 | 8.3 | 10.0 | 1 617 | 26 | 11 | 302 | 46.7 | 52.0 | 1.3 |
| Stephenson | 163.6 | 3 512 | 55.0 | 1.6 | 3.9 | 4.7 | 4.8 | 117.2 | 2 517 | 137 | 95 | 2 881 | 52.5 | 45.9 | 1.6 |
| Tazewell | 434.9 | 3 316 | 57.0 | 1.6 | 5.4 | 0.2 | 7.2 | 263.4 | 2 008 | 520 | 271 | 7 035 | 46.0 | 52.1 | 1.9 |
| Union | 70.9 | 3 885 | 53.8 | 23.8 | 3.0 | 0.0 | 5.0 | 19.6 | 1 072 | 50 | 35 | 1 341 | 43.0 | 54.9 | 2.1 |
| Vermilion | 256.8 | 3 163 | 54.1 | 1.5 | 6.1 | 3.3 | 6.8 | 94.9 | 1 168 | 1 481 | 164 | 4 519 | 49.4 | 48.8 | 1.7 |
| Wabash | 48.6 | 3 998 | 32.0 | 37.4 | 4.7 | 0.6 | 8.5 | 14.4 | 1 183 | 30 | 24 | 1 018 | 42.6 | 56.3 | 1.1 |
| Warren | 42.1 | 2 420 | 52.8 | 0.8 | 5.5 | 0.1 | 9.2 | 47.7 | 2 742 | 65 | 36 | 788 | 53.4 | 45.3 | 1.3 |
| Washington | 44.5 | 3 012 | 38.6 | 29.4 | 3.4 | 0.1 | 7.2 | 20.3 | 1 374 | 54 | 29 | 854 | 42.1 | 56.4 | 1.5 |
| Wayne | 44.2 | 2 666 | 50.2 | 1.8 | 3.5 | 0.1 | 8.5 | 17.1 | 1 033 | 59 | 33 | 960 | 31.6 | 66.8 | 1.7 |
| White | 47.3 | 3 225 | 61.8 | 0.8 | 4.4 | 0.2 | 9.0 | 6.9 | 473 | 54 | 29 | 811 | 44.5 | 53.5 | 2.0 |
| Whiteside | 268.1 | 4 528 | 32.6 | 42.1 | 3.2 | 0.7 | 3.7 | 60.4 | 1 020 | 157 | 117 | 4 588 | 58.0 | 40.4 | 1.5 |
| Will | 2 491.9 | 3 699 | 53.5 | 1.3 | 5.8 | 0.7 | 6.2 | 3 575.2 | 5 308 | 971 | 1 373 | 33 006 | 56.0 | 42.8 | 1.2 |
| Williamson | 201.3 | 3 120 | 61.2 | 1.6 | 4.1 | 0.4 | 8.2 | 143.5 | 2 223 | 1 706 | 134 | 3 956 | 41.9 | 56.4 | 1.7 |

1. Based on the resident population estimated as of July 1 of the year shown.   2. © 2013 Election Data Services, Inc. All rights reserved.

| STATE/ County code | CBSA code[1] | County type[2] | STATE County | Land area,[3] (sq km) 2010 | Total persons | Rank | Per square kilometer | White | Black | American Indian, Alaska Native | Asian and Pacific Islander | Percent Hispanic or Latino[4] | Under 5 years | 5 to 17 years | 18 to 24 years | 25 to 34 years | 35 to 44 years | 45 to 54 years |
|---|---|---|---|---|---|---|---|---|---|---|---|---|---|---|---|---|---|---|
| | | | | | | | | Population 2012 | | | | | Population characteristics[6], 2011 | | | | | |
| | | | | | | | | Race alone or in combination, not Hispanic or Latino (percent) | | | | | Age (percent) | | | | | |
| | | | | 1 | 2 | 3 | 4 | 5 | 6 | 7 | 8 | 9 | 10 | 11 | 12 | 13 | 14 | 15 |
| | | | ILLINOIS—Cont'd | | | | | | | | | | | | | | | |
| 17 201 | 40420 | 2 | Winnebago | 1 330 | 292 069 | 225 | 219.6 | 74.1 | 13.3 | 0.6 | 2.9 | 11.2 | 6.6 | 18.0 | 8.4 | 12.4 | 12.8 | 14.7 |
| 17 203 | 37900 | 2 | Woodford | 1 367 | 38 971 | 1 195 | 28.5 | 96.9 | 1.2 | 0.6 | 0.9 | 1.5 | 6.5 | 19.0 | 8.4 | 10.6 | 12.0 | 15.1 |
| 18 000 | ... | X | INDIANA | 92 789 | 6 537 334 | X | 70.5 | 82.7 | 10.0 | 0.6 | 2.1 | 6.2 | 6.6 | 17.9 | 10.1 | 12.8 | 12.7 | 14.4 |
| 18 001 | 19540 | 6 | Adams | 878 | 34 365 | 1 316 | 39.1 | 95.1 | 0.6 | 0.4 | 0.4 | 4.1 | 9.2 | 21.6 | 8.6 | 11.4 | 11.4 | 12.6 |
| 18 003 | 23060 | 2 | Allen | 1 702 | 360 412 | 185 | 211.8 | 78.5 | 13.3 | 0.7 | 3.3 | 6.7 | 7.4 | 19.3 | 9.4 | 13.3 | 12.8 | 13.8 |
| 18 005 | 18020 | 3 | Bartholomew | 1 054 | 79 129 | 694 | 75.1 | 87.7 | 2.7 | 0.5 | 4.0 | 6.3 | 6.6 | 18.2 | 8.0 | 13.1 | 13.4 | 14.1 |
| 18 007 | 29140 | 3 | Benton | 1 053 | 8 804 | 2 532 | 8.4 | 94.1 | 0.9 | 0.5 | 0.3 | 4.9 | 6.5 | 18.8 | 7.4 | 11.4 | 12.4 | 15.2 |
| 18 009 | ... | 6 | Blackford | 428 | 12 502 | 2 272 | 29.2 | 97.9 | 1.2 | 0.7 | 0.4 | 1.1 | 6.1 | 16.7 | 7.5 | 10.3 | 12.2 | 14.9 |
| 18 011 | 26900 | 1 | Boone | 1 095 | 58 944 | 876 | 53.8 | 94.5 | 1.6 | 0.6 | 2.1 | 2.4 | 6.8 | 20.9 | 6.8 | 11.0 | 14.2 | 16.9 |
| 18 013 | 26900 | 1 | Brown | 808 | 15 083 | 2 102 | 18.7 | 97.5 | 0.9 | 0.9 | 0.6 | 1.3 | 4.6 | 15.6 | 6.0 | 8.7 | 11.5 | 16.4 |
| 18 015 | 29140 | 3 | Carroll | 964 | 20 095 | 1 835 | 20.8 | 95.5 | 0.7 | 0.5 | 0.3 | 3.8 | 5.7 | 18.3 | 7.5 | 10.4 | 12.4 | 15.6 |
| 18 017 | 30900 | 4 | Cass | 1 067 | 38 581 | 1 208 | 36.2 | 84.0 | 2.0 | 0.6 | 1.2 | 13.2 | 6.7 | 19.0 | 8.0 | 11.7 | 12.7 | 14.3 |
| 18 019 | 31140 | 1 | Clark | 966 | 111 951 | 537 | 115.9 | 86.9 | 8.1 | 0.7 | 1.2 | 4.9 | 6.6 | 17.0 | 8.1 | 14.1 | 13.6 | 14.8 |
| 18 021 | 45460 | 3 | Clay | 926 | 26 837 | 1 535 | 29.0 | 97.7 | 0.8 | 0.7 | 0.5 | 1.2 | 5.8 | 17.7 | 8.3 | 11.7 | 12.8 | 14.9 |
| 18 023 | 23140 | 6 | Clinton | 1 049 | 33 022 | 1 353 | 31.5 | 85.2 | 0.8 | 0.5 | 0.3 | 13.9 | 7.5 | 19.1 | 8.2 | 12.1 | 12.1 | 14.2 |
| 18 025 | ... | 8 | Crawford | 792 | 10 665 | 2 382 | 13.5 | 97.5 | 0.7 | 0.9 | 0.6 | 1.4 | 5.7 | 17.2 | 7.7 | 10.1 | 12.6 | 16.1 |
| 18 027 | 47780 | 7 | Daviess | 1 112 | 32 064 | 1 389 | 28.8 | 94.3 | 1.0 | 0.5 | 0.7 | 4.3 | 8.2 | 20.6 | 8.8 | 12.0 | 11.2 | 13.3 |
| 18 029 | 17140 | 1 | Dearborn | 790 | 49 831 | 982 | 63.1 | 97.6 | 1.1 | 0.5 | 0.7 | 1.0 | 5.8 | 18.6 | 7.7 | 10.9 | 13.4 | 16.1 |
| 18 031 | 24700 | 6 | Decatur | 965 | 26 042 | 1 560 | 27.0 | 96.8 | 0.7 | 0.5 | 1.1 | 1.7 | 6.3 | 18.6 | 8.1 | 12.1 | 12.7 | 15.1 |
| 18 033 | 12140 | 4 | DeKalb | 940 | 42 321 | 1 124 | 45.0 | 96.4 | 0.8 | 0.5 | 0.7 | 2.4 | 6.6 | 19.5 | 8.1 | 11.9 | 12.8 | 15.2 |
| 18 035 | 34620 | 3 | Delaware | 1 016 | 117 364 | 517 | 115.5 | 89.7 | 8.0 | 0.7 | 1.7 | 1.9 | 5.4 | 14.3 | 20.1 | 10.7 | 10.6 | 12.4 |
| 18 037 | 27540 | 7 | Dubois | 1 107 | 42 071 | 1 128 | 38.0 | 92.7 | 0.6 | 0.3 | 0.6 | 6.3 | 6.5 | 18.6 | 7.1 | 11.9 | 12.4 | 15.8 |
| 18 039 | 21140 | 3 | Elkhart | 1 200 | 199 619 | 317 | 166.3 | 78.5 | 6.8 | 0.6 | 1.4 | 14.5 | 8.0 | 20.3 | 8.9 | 12.8 | 12.9 | 13.3 |
| 18 041 | 18220 | 7 | Fayette | 557 | 24 029 | 1 642 | 43.1 | 97.1 | 1.8 | 0.5 | 0.5 | 1.0 | 6.1 | 17.4 | 7.4 | 11.1 | 12.6 | 13.8 |
| 18 043 | 31140 | 1 | Floyd | 383 | 75 283 | 728 | 196.6 | 90.8 | 6.3 | 0.6 | 1.3 | 2.8 | 5.9 | 17.6 | 8.9 | 12.0 | 13.1 | 15.8 |
| 18 045 | ... | 6 | Fountain | 1 025 | 17 119 | 1 969 | 16.7 | 96.8 | 0.6 | 0.8 | 0.5 | 2.2 | 5.9 | 17.8 | 7.5 | 10.4 | 12.2 | 15.0 |
| 18 047 | 17140 | 1 | Franklin | 996 | 22 969 | 1 691 | 23.1 | 98.2 | 0.5 | 0.5 | 0.4 | 1.1 | 5.9 | 19.6 | 7.3 | 10.1 | 13.2 | 15.9 |
| 18 049 | ... | 7 | Fulton | 954 | 20 737 | 1 794 | 21.7 | 93.7 | 1.3 | 0.7 | 0.7 | 4.4 | 6.5 | 17.9 | 7.5 | 11.2 | 11.9 | 14.6 |
| 18 051 | 21780 | 2 | Gibson | 1 263 | 33 458 | 1 339 | 26.5 | 96.0 | 2.9 | 0.5 | 0.6 | 1.4 | 6.3 | 17.5 | 8.4 | 11.6 | 12.4 | 15.3 |
| 18 053 | 31980 | 4 | Grant | 1 072 | 69 330 | 766 | 64.7 | 88.4 | 8.1 | 0.8 | 1.0 | 3.7 | 5.7 | 15.7 | 13.4 | 10.2 | 11.3 | 14.0 |
| 18 055 | 14020 | 3 | Greene | 1 405 | 32 940 | 1 357 | 23.4 | 97.9 | 0.6 | 0.7 | 0.5 | 1.1 | 5.9 | 17.6 | 7.5 | 10.9 | 12.8 | 15.2 |
| 18 057 | 26900 | 1 | Hamilton | 1 021 | 289 495 | 227 | 283.5 | 87.5 | 4.3 | 0.5 | 5.7 | 3.6 | 7.5 | 22.2 | 5.9 | 13.1 | 16.4 | 15.5 |
| 18 059 | 26900 | 1 | Hancock | 793 | 70 933 | 753 | 89.4 | 94.9 | 2.6 | 0.6 | 1.2 | 1.8 | 6.0 | 19.6 | 7.2 | 11.2 | 13.9 | 16.0 |
| 18 061 | 31140 | 1 | Harrison | 1 255 | 39 134 | 1 194 | 31.2 | 97.1 | 0.9 | 0.6 | 0.7 | 1.6 | 5.8 | 17.3 | 7.7 | 12.1 | 12.7 | 16.1 |
| 18 063 | 26900 | 1 | Hendricks | 1 054 | 150 434 | 421 | 142.7 | 89.3 | 5.6 | 0.6 | 2.7 | 3.1 | 6.7 | 20.2 | 7.2 | 13.0 | 15.1 | 15.2 |
| 18 065 | 35220 | 4 | Henry | 1 015 | 49 345 | 993 | 48.6 | 95.7 | 2.8 | 0.6 | 0.6 | 1.5 | 5.4 | 16.8 | 7.9 | 11.2 | 13.3 | 15.3 |
| 18 067 | 29020 | 3 | Howard | 759 | 82 849 | 673 | 109.2 | 89.0 | 8.2 | 0.8 | 1.4 | 2.7 | 6.2 | 17.1 | 7.9 | 11.5 | 12.1 | 14.8 |
| 18 069 | 26540 | 6 | Huntington | 991 | 36 987 | 1 246 | 37.3 | 96.7 | 1.0 | 0.7 | 0.7 | 1.8 | 6.0 | 17.3 | 10.1 | 11.6 | 12.0 | 15.2 |
| 18 071 | 42980 | 4 | Jackson | 1 319 | 43 083 | 1 106 | 32.7 | 92.2 | 1.2 | 0.6 | 1.1 | 5.9 | 6.5 | 17.9 | 7.8 | 13.1 | 13.1 | 14.7 |
| 18 073 | 16980 | 1 | Jasper | 1 449 | 33 456 | 1 340 | 23.1 | 93.1 | 1.1 | 0.5 | 0.7 | 5.5 | 6.2 | 19.0 | 9.5 | 11.1 | 12.4 | 14.9 |
| 18 075 | ... | 6 | Jay | 994 | 21 366 | 1 763 | 21.5 | 96.2 | 0.6 | 0.4 | 0.6 | 2.9 | 6.9 | 19.6 | 7.9 | 10.8 | 12.4 | 14.1 |
| 18 077 | 31500 | 6 | Jefferson | 934 | 32 554 | 1 371 | 34.9 | 94.9 | 2.3 | 0.6 | 1.0 | 2.3 | 5.7 | 16.5 | 10.0 | 11.7 | 12.8 | 15.2 |
| 18 079 | 35860 | 6 | Jennings | 975 | 28 161 | 1 486 | 28.9 | 96.5 | 1.3 | 0.5 | 0.5 | 2.2 | 6.4 | 19.0 | 8.4 | 10.8 | 13.9 | 15.2 |
| 18 081 | 26900 | 1 | Johnson | 830 | 143 191 | 440 | 172.5 | 93.0 | 1.9 | 0.5 | 2.6 | 3.2 | 6.7 | 19.3 | 8.3 | 12.8 | 13.9 | 14.5 |
| 18 083 | 47180 | 4 | Knox | 1 337 | 38 122 | 1 215 | 28.5 | 94.7 | 3.3 | 0.6 | 0.9 | 1.7 | 5.8 | 15.3 | 13.7 | 11.6 | 10.5 | 14.2 |
| 18 085 | 47700 | 6 | Kosciusko | 1 376 | 77 609 | 704 | 56.4 | 90.5 | 1.3 | 0.6 | 1.2 | 7.5 | 6.7 | 18.5 | 8.9 | 12.4 | 12.3 | 14.5 |
| 18 087 | ... | 6 | LaGrange | 983 | 37 521 | 1 231 | 38.2 | 95.3 | 0.7 | 0.4 | 0.5 | 3.6 | 9.7 | 24.6 | 9.1 | 11.7 | 11.1 | 11.3 |
| 18 089 | 16980 | 1 | Lake | 1 292 | 493 618 | 136 | 382.1 | 56.4 | 25.7 | 0.6 | 1.6 | 17.0 | 6.6 | 18.7 | 8.7 | 12.7 | 12.5 | 14.6 |
| 18 091 | 33140 | 3 | LaPorte | 1 550 | 111 246 | 541 | 71.8 | 82.9 | 11.8 | 0.7 | 0.8 | 5.6 | 6.0 | 16.5 | 8.5 | 13.0 | 12.8 | 15.0 |
| 18 093 | 13260 | 4 | Lawrence | 1 163 | 46 078 | 1 048 | 39.6 | 97.3 | 0.9 | 0.9 | 0.7 | 1.3 | 5.8 | 17.3 | 7.4 | 10.9 | 12.5 | 15.2 |
| 18 095 | 11300 | 3 | Madison | 1 170 | 130 348 | 479 | 111.4 | 87.6 | 9.2 | 0.7 | 0.7 | 3.4 | 6.1 | 16.7 | 9.0 | 12.5 | 12.9 | 14.2 |
| 18 097 | 26900 | 1 | Marion | 1 026 | 918 977 | 55 | 895.7 | 61.5 | 27.9 | 0.7 | 2.6 | 9.6 | 7.7 | 17.5 | 10.2 | 16.2 | 12.9 | 13.8 |
| 18 099 | 38500 | 6 | Marshall | 1 149 | 47 024 | 1 025 | 40.9 | 89.9 | 1.0 | 0.6 | 0.8 | 8.8 | 6.7 | 19.7 | 8.1 | 11.1 | 12.3 | 14.4 |
| 18 101 | ... | 6 | Martin | 870 | 10 260 | 2 421 | 11.8 | 98.2 | 0.7 | 0.5 | 0.4 | 0.9 | 6.1 | 17.6 | 7.2 | 10.4 | 12.5 | 15.6 |
| 18 103 | 37940 | 6 | Miami | 968 | 36 486 | 1 262 | 37.7 | 91.6 | 5.3 | 1.5 | 0.7 | 2.6 | 5.5 | 16.9 | 8.3 | 12.7 | 14.0 | 15.1 |
| 18 105 | 14020 | 3 | Monroe | 1 022 | 141 019 | 445 | 138.0 | 87.7 | 4.2 | 0.8 | 6.5 | 3.1 | 4.6 | 11.5 | 29.6 | 14.0 | 9.8 | 10.4 |
| 18 107 | 18820 | 6 | Montgomery | 1 307 | 38 254 | 1 211 | 29.3 | 93.5 | 1.4 | 0.6 | 0.9 | 4.6 | 6.4 | 17.3 | 10.0 | 10.9 | 12.4 | 14.9 |
| 18 109 | 26900 | 1 | Morgan | 1 046 | 69 356 | 765 | 66.3 | 97.5 | 0.7 | 0.8 | 0.6 | 1.3 | 6.1 | 18.5 | 7.7 | 11.0 | 13.5 | 16.0 |
| 18 111 | 16980 | 1 | Newton | 1 041 | 14 044 | 2 173 | 13.5 | 93.7 | 0.8 | 0.5 | 0.6 | 5.2 | 5.4 | 16.9 | 7.4 | 10.7 | 12.0 | 16.2 |
| 18 113 | 28340 | 6 | Noble | 1 064 | 47 582 | 1 018 | 44.7 | 89.0 | 0.9 | 0.6 | 0.6 | 9.8 | 7.1 | 19.5 | 8.2 | 12.0 | 12.8 | 14.7 |
| 18 115 | 17140 | 1 | Ohio | 223 | 6 079 | 2 754 | 27.3 | 97.6 | 0.9 | 0.4 | 0.5 | 1.3 | 4.6 | 16.6 | 7.4 | 10.0 | 12.5 | 17.0 |
| 18 117 | ... | 6 | Orange | 1 032 | 19 690 | 1 849 | 19.1 | 97.1 | 1.6 | 0.7 | 0.6 | 1.1 | 5.8 | 18.5 | 7.7 | 10.9 | 12.4 | 15.1 |
| 18 119 | 14020 | 3 | Owen | 998 | 21 380 | 1 762 | 21.4 | 97.7 | 0.8 | 0.7 | 0.6 | 1.1 | 5.3 | 17.5 | 7.7 | 10.2 | 12.4 | 16.6 |
| 18 121 | ... | 6 | Parke | 1 152 | 17 069 | 1 974 | 14.8 | 95.5 | 2.7 | 0.6 | 0.4 | 1.4 | 5.7 | 15.1 | 8.6 | 12.0 | 12.9 | 15.7 |
| 18 123 | ... | 6 | Perry | 989 | 19 462 | 1 859 | 19.7 | 95.7 | 2.9 | 0.5 | 0.6 | 1.1 | 5.8 | 15.3 | 8.2 | 13.3 | 12.5 | 15.4 |

1. CBSA = Core Based Statistical Area. See Appendix A for explanation. See Appendix B for list of metropolitan areas with component counties.  2. County type code from the Economic Research Service of USDA Rural-Urban Continuum Codes. See Appendix A for definition.  3. Dry land or land partially or temporarily covered by water.  4. May be of any race.

# Table B. States and Counties — **Population and Households**

| | Population, 2011 (cont.) Age (percent) (cont.) | | | | Population change and components of change, 2000-2012 | | | | | | | Households, 2010 | | | | |
| STATE County | 55 to 64 years | 65 to 74 years | 75 years and over | Percent female | Total persons 2000 | Total persons 2010 | Percent change 2000-2010 | Percent change 2010-2012 | Births | Deaths | Net migration | Number | Percent change, 2000-2010 | Persons per household | Female family householder[1] | One person |
|---|---|---|---|---|---|---|---|---|---|---|---|---|---|---|---|---|
| | 16 | 17 | 18 | 19 | 20 | 21 | 22 | 23 | 24 | 25 | 26 | 27 | 28 | 29 | 30 | 31 |
| **ILLINOIS—Cont'd** | | | | | | | | | | | | | | | | |
| Winnebago | 12.8 | 7.5 | 6.6 | 51.2 | 278 418 | 295 266 | 6.1 | -1.1 | 8 465 | 5 944 | -5 675 | 115 501 | 7.0 | 2.52 | 14.0 | 27.7 |
| Woodford | 13.5 | 7.5 | 7.4 | 50.6 | 35 469 | 38 664 | 9.0 | 0.8 | 1 052 | 846 | 45 | 14 276 | 11.6 | 2.64 | 7.5 | 21.8 |
| **INDIANA** | 12.3 | 7.1 | 6.0 | 50.8 | 6 080 485 | 6 483 802 | 6.6 | 0.8 | 189 041 | 129 580 | -5 532 | 2 502 154 | 7.1 | 2.52 | 12.4 | 26.9 |
| Adams | 11.2 | 6.8 | 7.2 | 50.6 | 33 625 | 34 387 | 2.3 | -0.1 | 1 440 | 639 | -823 | 12 011 | 1.6 | 2.83 | 8.9 | 24.6 |
| Allen | 12.0 | 6.3 | 5.7 | 51.2 | 331 849 | 355 329 | 7.1 | 1.4 | 12 016 | 6 326 | -479 | 137 851 | 7.1 | 2.53 | 13.1 | 28.1 |
| Bartholomew | 12.4 | 8.0 | 6.3 | 50.5 | 71 435 | 76 794 | 7.5 | 3.0 | 2 283 | 1 538 | 1 603 | 29 860 | 6.9 | 2.53 | 10.7 | 25.3 |
| Benton | 12.7 | 8.4 | 7.2 | 50.4 | 9 421 | 8 854 | -6.0 | -0.6 | 210 | 211 | -46 | 3 479 | -2.2 | 2.52 | 9.4 | 27.0 |
| Blackford | 14.4 | 9.5 | 8.2 | 50.6 | 14 048 | 12 766 | -9.1 | -2.1 | 312 | 374 | -212 | 5 236 | -8.0 | 2.41 | 10.9 | 27.7 |
| Boone | 12.0 | 6.2 | 5.3 | 50.7 | 46 107 | 56 640 | 22.8 | 4.1 | 1 585 | 985 | 1 643 | 21 149 | 23.8 | 2.65 | 8.4 | 22.4 |
| Brown | 19.2 | 11.3 | 6.6 | 50.5 | 14 957 | 15 242 | 1.9 | -1.0 | 266 | 315 | -116 | 6 199 | 5.1 | 2.43 | 7.2 | 23.6 |
| Carroll | 14.0 | 9.0 | 7.2 | 50.1 | 20 165 | 20 155 | 0.0 | -0.3 | 468 | 421 | -103 | 7 900 | 2.4 | 2.54 | 7.3 | 24.0 |
| Cass | 12.4 | 7.9 | 7.2 | 50.0 | 40 930 | 38 966 | -4.8 | -1.0 | 1 119 | 898 | -600 | 14 858 | -5.5 | 2.55 | 11.3 | 27.3 |
| Clark | 12.9 | 7.4 | 5.5 | 51.0 | 96 472 | 110 232 | 14.3 | 1.6 | 3 289 | 2 311 | 748 | 44 248 | 14.2 | 2.46 | 12.9 | 27.6 |
| Clay | 13.5 | 8.3 | 7.1 | 50.9 | 26 556 | 26 890 | 1.3 | -0.2 | 670 | 655 | -74 | 10 447 | 2.3 | 2.54 | 10.7 | 24.0 |
| Clinton | 12.3 | 7.4 | 7.1 | 50.6 | 33 866 | 33 224 | -1.9 | -0.6 | 1 043 | 748 | -499 | 12 105 | -3.5 | 2.68 | 11.1 | 23.1 |
| Crawford | 15.2 | 9.4 | 5.9 | 49.4 | 10 743 | 10 713 | -0.3 | -0.4 | 245 | 245 | -48 | 4 303 | 2.9 | 2.48 | 9.7 | 25.6 |
| Daviess | 11.8 | 7.5 | 6.6 | 50.2 | 29 820 | 31 648 | 6.1 | 1.3 | 1 127 | 751 | 54 | 11 329 | 4.0 | 2.74 | 10.0 | 24.6 |
| Dearborn | 14.0 | 7.8 | 5.7 | 50.3 | 46 109 | 50 047 | 8.5 | -0.4 | 1 217 | 942 | -467 | 18 743 | 11.4 | 2.64 | 10.0 | 22.0 |
| Decatur | 12.5 | 7.8 | 6.9 | 50.6 | 24 555 | 25 740 | 4.8 | 1.2 | 701 | 604 | 219 | 9 977 | 6.3 | 2.54 | 10.6 | 25.0 |
| DeKalb | 12.5 | 7.4 | 6.0 | 50.5 | 40 285 | 42 223 | 4.8 | 0.2 | 1 232 | 850 | -276 | 15 951 | 5.4 | 2.61 | 10.5 | 24.3 |
| Delaware | 11.5 | 8.0 | 7.0 | 52.0 | 118 769 | 117 671 | -0.9 | -0.3 | 2 822 | 2 607 | -453 | 46 516 | -1.3 | 2.34 | 12.2 | 29.6 |
| Dubois | 12.9 | 7.6 | 7.1 | 50.7 | 39 674 | 41 889 | 5.6 | 0.4 | 1 149 | 885 | -101 | 16 133 | 8.9 | 2.54 | 8.6 | 24.7 |
| Elkhart | 11.4 | 6.6 | 5.8 | 50.7 | 182 791 | 197 559 | 8.1 | 1.0 | 6 830 | 3 343 | -1 425 | 70 244 | 6.2 | 2.76 | 12.6 | 22.7 |
| Fayette | 14.5 | 9.1 | 7.9 | 50.9 | 25 588 | 24 277 | -5.1 | -1.0 | 625 | 709 | -149 | 9 719 | -4.7 | 2.46 | 12.4 | 26.6 |
| Floyd | 13.5 | 7.2 | 6.0 | 51.6 | 70 823 | 74 578 | 5.3 | 0.9 | 1 944 | 1 565 | 335 | 29 479 | 7.2 | 2.48 | 13.6 | 25.6 |
| Fountain | 13.1 | 9.8 | 8.3 | 50.3 | 17 954 | 17 240 | -4.0 | -0.7 | 440 | 420 | -141 | 6 935 | -1.5 | 2.46 | 10.0 | 26.7 |
| Franklin | 13.4 | 8.0 | 6.5 | 49.9 | 22 151 | 23 087 | 4.2 | -0.5 | 526 | 460 | -171 | 8 579 | 9.0 | 2.67 | 8.4 | 20.5 |
| Fulton | 13.6 | 9.3 | 7.5 | 50.1 | 20 511 | 20 836 | 1.6 | -0.5 | 599 | 515 | -176 | 8 237 | 1.9 | 2.50 | 10.2 | 25.8 |
| Gibson | 13.1 | 8.0 | 7.5 | 50.3 | 32 500 | 33 503 | 3.1 | -0.1 | 885 | 825 | -100 | 13 255 | 3.2 | 2.47 | 9.7 | 26.5 |
| Grant | 13.2 | 8.8 | 7.6 | 52.0 | 73 403 | 70 061 | -4.6 | -1.0 | 1 788 | 1 798 | -696 | 27 245 | -3.8 | 2.39 | 13.4 | 28.8 |
| Greene | 14.0 | 8.8 | 7.3 | 49.9 | 33 157 | 33 165 | 0.0 | -0.7 | 795 | 872 | -181 | 13 487 | 0.9 | 2.44 | 9.4 | 27.0 |
| Hamilton | 10.5 | 5.2 | 3.7 | 51.2 | 182 740 | 274 569 | 50.3 | 5.4 | 8 649 | 3 000 | 9 014 | 99 835 | 51.4 | 2.73 | 8.3 | 20.5 |
| Hancock | 13.0 | 7.7 | 5.4 | 50.8 | 55 391 | 70 002 | 26.4 | 1.3 | 1 765 | 1 287 | 441 | 26 304 | 27.0 | 2.64 | 9.8 | 20.3 |
| Harrison | 13.9 | 8.2 | 6.1 | 49.9 | 34 325 | 39 364 | 14.7 | -0.6 | 930 | 795 | -353 | 15 192 | 17.6 | 2.56 | 9.5 | 22.8 |
| Hendricks | 11.5 | 6.4 | 4.7 | 50.1 | 104 093 | 145 448 | 39.7 | 3.4 | 3 923 | 2 065 | 3 044 | 52 368 | 40.5 | 2.71 | 9.8 | 19.8 |
| Henry | 13.8 | 8.9 | 7.5 | 49.3 | 48 508 | 49 462 | 2.0 | -0.2 | 1 145 | 1 256 | -34 | 19 077 | -2.1 | 2.43 | 11.6 | 27.3 |
| Howard | 13.7 | 9.2 | 7.5 | 51.8 | 84 964 | 82 752 | -2.6 | 0.1 | 2 157 | 1 998 | -93 | 34 301 | -1.4 | 2.38 | 13.1 | 29.4 |
| Huntington | 12.9 | 7.8 | 7.1 | 50.9 | 38 075 | 37 124 | -2.5 | -0.4 | 927 | 883 | -183 | 14 218 | -0.2 | 2.52 | 9.9 | 24.4 |
| Jackson | 12.4 | 7.9 | 6.5 | 50.3 | 41 335 | 42 376 | 2.5 | 1.7 | 1 250 | 977 | 437 | 16 501 | 2.8 | 2.53 | 10.8 | 24.4 |
| Jasper | 12.4 | 8.3 | 6.2 | 50.4 | 30 043 | 33 478 | 11.4 | -0.1 | 866 | 690 | -200 | 12 232 | 14.5 | 2.66 | 9.3 | 20.9 |
| Jay | 12.7 | 8.6 | 6.9 | 50.7 | 21 806 | 21 253 | -2.5 | 0.5 | 680 | 498 | -63 | 8 133 | -3.2 | 2.58 | 10.4 | 25.6 |
| Jefferson | 13.4 | 8.3 | 6.4 | 51.7 | 31 705 | 32 428 | 2.3 | 0.4 | 839 | 780 | 87 | 12 635 | 4.0 | 2.42 | 11.4 | 27.2 |
| Jennings | 12.8 | 8.2 | 4.9 | 49.9 | 27 554 | 28 525 | 3.5 | -1.3 | 771 | 637 | -497 | 10 680 | 5.4 | 2.64 | 11.5 | 22.3 |
| Johnson | 11.8 | 7.0 | 5.6 | 50.8 | 115 209 | 139 654 | 21.2 | 2.5 | 4 062 | 2 629 | 2 040 | 52 242 | 23.1 | 2.63 | 10.2 | 22.6 |
| Knox | 13.0 | 8.3 | 7.6 | 49.6 | 39 256 | 38 440 | -2.1 | -0.8 | 961 | 951 | -319 | 15 249 | -1.9 | 2.35 | 11.1 | 30.1 |
| Kosciusko | 12.8 | 7.8 | 6.0 | 50.3 | 74 057 | 77 358 | 4.5 | 0.3 | 2 177 | 1 481 | -416 | 29 197 | 7.0 | 2.60 | 9.5 | 23.9 |
| LaGrange | 10.7 | 7.0 | 4.9 | 49.8 | 34 909 | 37 128 | 6.4 | 1.1 | 1 620 | 546 | -678 | 11 598 | 3.3 | 3.17 | 7.1 | 18.4 |
| Lake | 12.7 | 7.1 | 6.3 | 51.7 | 484 564 | 496 005 | 2.4 | -0.5 | 14 527 | 10 334 | -6 513 | 188 157 | 3.6 | 2.60 | 17.4 | 27.4 |
| LaPorte | 13.8 | 8.0 | 6.5 | 48.3 | 110 106 | 111 467 | 1.2 | -0.2 | 2 988 | 2 509 | -681 | 42 331 | 3.1 | 2.48 | 12.8 | 27.3 |
| Lawrence | 14.1 | 9.4 | 7.4 | 50.6 | 45 922 | 46 134 | 0.5 | -0.1 | 1 111 | 1 193 | 45 | 18 811 | 1.5 | 2.42 | 10.1 | 27.3 |
| Madison | 13.0 | 8.4 | 7.3 | 50.0 | 133 358 | 131 636 | -1.3 | -1.0 | 3 540 | 3 227 | -1 562 | 51 927 | -2.1 | 2.41 | 13.6 | 28.3 |
| Marion | 11.0 | 5.7 | 5.0 | 51.8 | 860 454 | 903 393 | 5.0 | 1.7 | 33 410 | 16 674 | -962 | 366 176 | 4.0 | 2.42 | 17.1 | 32.0 |
| Marshall | 12.9 | 7.6 | 7.3 | 50.6 | 45 128 | 47 051 | 4.3 | -0.1 | 1 316 | 1 023 | -347 | 17 406 | 5.4 | 2.66 | 9.9 | 24.1 |
| Martin | 14.7 | 9.2 | 6.7 | 49.4 | 10 369 | 10 334 | -0.3 | -0.7 | 271 | 232 | -99 | 4 216 | 0.8 | 2.43 | 9.2 | 28.7 |
| Miami | 13.2 | 8.1 | 6.3 | 46.4 | 36 082 | 36 903 | 2.3 | -1.1 | 857 | 787 | -494 | 13 456 | -1.9 | 2.49 | 11.3 | 26.2 |
| Monroe | 9.7 | 5.5 | 4.9 | 50.2 | 120 563 | 137 974 | 14.4 | 2.2 | 2 869 | 1 823 | 2 041 | 54 864 | 17.0 | 2.24 | 8.1 | 32.5 |
| Montgomery | 12.3 | 8.6 | 7.1 | 49.7 | 37 629 | 38 124 | 1.3 | 0.3 | 1 089 | 874 | -77 | 14 979 | 2.6 | 2.47 | 10.4 | 25.9 |
| Morgan | 13.7 | 8.1 | 5.4 | 50.5 | 66 689 | 68 894 | 3.3 | 0.7 | 1 784 | 1 396 | 99 | 25 765 | 5.4 | 2.65 | 10.1 | 20.3 |
| Newton | 14.4 | 9.9 | 7.2 | 49.4 | 14 566 | 14 244 | -2.2 | -1.4 | 303 | 333 | -164 | 5 503 | 3.1 | 2.56 | 8.7 | 23.8 |
| Noble | 12.9 | 7.1 | 5.8 | 49.9 | 46 275 | 47 536 | 2.7 | 0.1 | 1 373 | 960 | -411 | 17 355 | 3.9 | 2.69 | 10.0 | 22.9 |
| Ohio | 14.6 | 10.4 | 6.8 | 50.2 | 5 623 | 6 128 | 9.0 | -0.8 | 125 | 167 | -12 | 2 477 | 12.5 | 2.45 | 9.8 | 25.2 |
| Orange | 13.6 | 9.0 | 7.0 | 50.5 | 19 306 | 19 840 | 2.8 | -0.8 | 515 | 493 | -180 | 7 872 | 3.3 | 2.49 | 10.4 | 26.7 |
| Owen | 15.0 | 9.3 | 5.9 | 49.8 | 21 786 | 21 575 | -1.0 | -0.9 | 529 | 530 | -202 | 8 486 | 2.5 | 2.52 | 9.2 | 24.0 |
| Parke | 14.1 | 9.3 | 6.6 | 53.4 | 17 241 | 17 339 | 0.6 | -1.6 | 410 | 394 | -280 | 6 222 | -3.0 | 2.51 | 9.4 | 24.8 |
| Perry | 14.0 | 7.8 | 7.6 | 46.9 | 18 899 | 19 338 | 2.3 | 0.6 | 472 | 434 | 78 | 7 476 | 2.8 | 2.38 | 9.7 | 28.7 |

1. No spouse present.

# Table B. States and Counties — Population, Vital Statistics, Medicare, and Crime

| STATE County | Persons in group quarters, 2010 | Daytime population, 2007–2011 | | Births, 2011 | | Deaths, 2011 | | Persons under 65 with no health insurance, 2010 | | Medicare, 2012 | | | Serious crimes known to police,[2] 2011 Total | |
|---|---|---|---|---|---|---|---|---|---|---|---|---|---|---|
| | | Number | Employ-ment/resi-dence ratio | Total | Rate[1] | Number | Rate[1] | Number | Percent | Eligible for Medicare | Enrolled in Medicare Advantage | Enrolled in a Medicare prescription drug plan | Number | Rate[3] |
| | 32 | 33 | 34 | 35 | 36 | 37 | 38 | 39 | 40 | 41 | 42 | 43 | 44 | 45 |
| ILLINOIS—Cont'd | | | | | | | | | | | | | | |
| Winnebago | 4 685 | 299 752 | 1.04 | 3 842 | 13.1 | 2 587 | 8.8 | 38 498 | 15.3 | 52 333 | 10 105 | 23 609 | 12 727 | 4 518 |
| Woodford | 1 021 | 30 524 | 0.57 | 494 | 12.7 | 387 | 10.0 | 3 027 | 9.4 | 6 575 | 852 | 2 840 | 317 | 931 |
| INDIANA | 186 923 | 6 396 454 | 0.98 | 84 732 | 13.0 | 56 499 | 8.7 | 929 589 | 17.0 | 1 074 296 | 209 868 | 486 136 | 227 681 | 3 494 |
| Adams | 421 | 32 816 | 0.90 | 640 | 18.6 | 271 | 7.9 | 6 087 | 20.6 | 5 351 | 2 015 | 2 525 | NA | NA |
| Allen | 6 107 | 369 046 | 1.09 | 5 354 | 14.9 | 2 777 | 7.7 | 52 787 | 17.1 | 55 085 | 22 472 | 21 653 | 11 277 | 3 158 |
| Bartholomew | 1 147 | 84 026 | 1.21 | 1 010 | 13.0 | 647 | 8.3 | 10 396 | 16.0 | 13 589 | 2 011 | 6 091 | 3 322 | 4 325 |
| Benton | 92 | 7 687 | 0.71 | 92 | 10.4 | 93 | 10.5 | 1 308 | 17.6 | 1 672 | 204 | 940 | NA | NA |
| Blackford | 163 | 11 689 | 0.78 | 141 | 11.2 | 177 | 14.1 | 1 683 | 16.2 | 2 971 | 410 | 1 480 | 276 | 2 176 |
| Boone | 574 | 48 711 | 0.74 | 702 | 12.2 | 416 | 7.2 | 5 540 | 11.3 | 8 208 | 1 598 | 3 687 | NA | NA |
| Brown | 163 | 11 997 | 0.53 | 131 | 8.7 | 146 | 9.7 | 2 169 | 17.4 | 3 410 | 766 | 1 293 | 131 | 855 |
| Carroll | 106 | 16 179 | 0.57 | 211 | 10.5 | 183 | 9.1 | 2 676 | 15.9 | 3 848 | 655 | 1 787 | 301 | 1 486 |
| Cass | 1 066 | 38 570 | 0.98 | 511 | 13.2 | 411 | 10.6 | 6 392 | 19.6 | 7 379 | 954 | 3 644 | 1 163 | 2 969 |
| Clark | 1 515 | 101 300 | 0.85 | 1 495 | 13.4 | 1 008 | 9.0 | 15 483 | 16.3 | 19 921 | 3 553 | 9 559 | 6 047 | 5 458 |
| Clay | 341 | 22 843 | 0.66 | 286 | 10.6 | 274 | 10.2 | 3 810 | 16.8 | 5 164 | 552 | 2 650 | NA | NA |
| Clinton | 830 | 30 396 | 0.81 | 475 | 14.3 | 320 | 9.7 | 5 769 | 20.5 | 5 803 | 775 | 2 775 | 1 259 | 3 770 |
| Crawford | 62 | 8 805 | 0.56 | 115 | 10.8 | 123 | 11.5 | 1 672 | 18.3 | 2 194 | 315 | 1 144 | 146 | 1 356 |
| Daviess | 581 | 29 652 | 0.88 | 502 | 15.7 | 327 | 10.2 | 5 777 | 21.4 | 5 097 | 321 | 2 693 | 607 | 1 908 |
| Dearborn | 530 | 41 105 | 0.64 | 556 | 11.1 | 390 | 7.8 | 6 307 | 14.7 | 8 904 | 1 985 | 3 730 | 665 | 1 322 |
| Decatur | 377 | 26 850 | 1.10 | 307 | 11.8 | 257 | 9.9 | 3 741 | 17.1 | 4 791 | 1 000 | 2 309 | NA | NA |
| DeKalb | 615 | 43 050 | 1.05 | 548 | 12.9 | 365 | 8.6 | 5 908 | 16.2 | 7 399 | 3 221 | 2 853 | NA | NA |
| Delaware | 8 830 | 118 733 | 1.03 | 1 277 | 10.9 | 1 126 | 9.6 | 15 957 | 17.2 | 22 066 | 2 776 | 10 231 | 3 954 | 3 343 |
| Dubois | 893 | 47 777 | 1.27 | 512 | 12.1 | 377 | 8.9 | 5 286 | 15.0 | 7 338 | 576 | 4 449 | 244 | 580 |
| Elkhart | 3 804 | 216 349 | 1.21 | 3 061 | 15.4 | 1 462 | 7.3 | 39 869 | 23.3 | 29 650 | 6 994 | 13 474 | 3 132 | 1 577 |
| Fayette | 367 | 22 694 | 0.82 | 297 | 12.2 | 293 | 12.1 | 3 513 | 17.4 | 5 602 | 678 | 3 532 | NA | NA |
| Floyd | 1 329 | 68 133 | 0.83 | 840 | 11.2 | 680 | 9.1 | 8 564 | 13.4 | 13 008 | 1 971 | 6 515 | 3 155 | 4 378 |
| Fountain | 172 | 15 147 | 0.72 | 205 | 11.9 | 192 | 11.2 | 2 312 | 16.4 | 3 662 | 438 | 1 831 | NA | NA |
| Franklin | 187 | 18 220 | 0.53 | 233 | 10.1 | 192 | 8.3 | 3 139 | 16.0 | 4 901 | 1 377 | 2 198 | 258 | 1 112 |
| Fulton | 224 | 18 866 | 0.78 | 266 | 12.7 | 217 | 10.4 | 3 119 | 18.0 | 4 153 | 1 514 | 1 536 | NA | NA |
| Gibson | 738 | 36 252 | 1.18 | 396 | 11.8 | 378 | 11.3 | 3 771 | 13.6 | 6 190 | 1 485 | 2 662 | 634 | 1 883 |
| Grant | 5 022 | 70 671 | 1.02 | 820 | 11.7 | 788 | 11.3 | 9 157 | 16.9 | 14 924 | 2 356 | 6 424 | 2 075 | 2 947 |
| Greene | 281 | 26 689 | 0.56 | 374 | 11.4 | 392 | 11.9 | 4 553 | 16.5 | 6 630 | 511 | 3 304 | 394 | 1 267 |
| Hamilton | 1 628 | 246 967 | 0.84 | 3 797 | 13.4 | 1 245 | 4.4 | 25 410 | 10.3 | 31 000 | 6 718 | 12 687 | 3 094 | 1 293 |
| Hancock | 649 | 55 348 | 0.58 | 801 | 11.4 | 518 | 7.3 | 8 306 | 13.8 | 11 821 | 2 699 | 4 395 | 831 | 1 181 |
| Harrison | 461 | 32 321 | 0.63 | 426 | 10.8 | 323 | 8.2 | 4 960 | 14.8 | 7 155 | 1 070 | 3 594 | 663 | 1 676 |
| Hendricks | 3 360 | 123 479 | 0.72 | 1 742 | 11.8 | 871 | 5.9 | 14 345 | 11.4 | 19 437 | 4 475 | 6 971 | NA | NA |
| Henry | 3 016 | 43 805 | 0.72 | 530 | 10.8 | 542 | 11.0 | 6 236 | 16.1 | 10 227 | 1 576 | 4 129 | 1 812 | 3 645 |
| Howard | 1 282 | 87 600 | 1.13 | 963 | 11.6 | 866 | 10.5 | 10 618 | 15.5 | 17 682 | 1 730 | 7 350 | 3 318 | 3 989 |
| Huntington | 1 330 | 35 006 | 0.87 | 419 | 11.3 | 385 | 10.3 | 5 074 | 16.6 | 7 203 | 3 012 | 2 678 | 650 | 1 742 |
| Jackson | 595 | 43 246 | 1.06 | 543 | 12.6 | 409 | 9.5 | 6 722 | 18.6 | 8 114 | 2 180 | 2 957 | 1 752 | 4 421 |
| Jasper | 926 | 29 729 | 0.76 | 392 | 11.7 | 311 | 9.3 | 4 322 | 15.5 | 5 963 | 464 | 3 268 | NA | NA |
| Jay | 243 | 19 854 | 0.84 | 300 | 14.1 | 230 | 10.8 | 3 106 | 17.4 | 4 304 | 897 | 2 009 | 355 | 1 855 |
| Jefferson | 1 905 | 31 510 | 0.94 | 391 | 12.1 | 339 | 10.5 | 4 282 | 16.5 | 6 509 | 704 | 3 408 | NA | NA |
| Jennings | 298 | 23 852 | 0.61 | 352 | 12.5 | 279 | 9.9 | 4 310 | 17.4 | 5 213 | 948 | 2 257 | 822 | 2 867 |
| Johnson | 2 332 | 116 501 | 0.68 | 1 805 | 12.7 | 1 125 | 7.9 | 17 074 | 14.2 | 21 717 | 4 565 | 8 868 | 4 050 | 3 092 |
| Knox | 2 645 | 39 765 | 1.08 | 412 | 10.7 | 402 | 10.4 | 4 955 | 16.5 | 7 435 | 494 | 4 139 | 1 196 | 3 350 |
| Kosciusko | 1 568 | 77 193 | 1.00 | 979 | 12.7 | 633 | 8.2 | 13 448 | 20.5 | 13 113 | 4 888 | 4 722 | 1 453 | 1 869 |
| LaGrange | 324 | 36 547 | 0.96 | 685 | 18.3 | 239 | 6.4 | 11 483 | 34.9 | 4 995 | 1 465 | 1 935 | 273 | 732 |
| Lake | 6 349 | 479 702 | 0.93 | 6 553 | 13.2 | 4 619 | 9.3 | 71 011 | 16.8 | 81 511 | 4 639 | 42 346 | 22 151 | 4 461 |
| LaPorte | 6 623 | 107 014 | 0.91 | 1 330 | 11.9 | 1 140 | 10.2 | 13 878 | 15.6 | 19 969 | 1 511 | 10 952 | 4 098 | 3 776 |
| Lawrence | 653 | 41 291 | 0.75 | 505 | 10.9 | 518 | 11.2 | 6 653 | 17.4 | 9 416 | 1 310 | 4 034 | 911 | 2 169 |
| Madison | 6 277 | 120 319 | 0.80 | 1 591 | 12.1 | 1 382 | 10.5 | 17 850 | 16.9 | 26 401 | 4 415 | 9 543 | NA | NA |
| Marion | 16 675 | 1 034 410 | 1.33 | 15 097 | 16.6 | 7 305 | 8.0 | 158 414 | 19.9 | 126 755 | 28 218 | 53 916 | 58 006 | 6 731 |
| Marshall | 670 | 45 712 | 0.94 | 596 | 12.7 | 448 | 9.5 | 7 955 | 20.0 | 8 282 | 2 499 | 3 321 | 1 081 | 2 286 |
| Martin | 93 | 13 738 | 1.73 | 124 | 12.0 | 99 | 9.6 | 1 363 | 15.8 | 2 116 | 172 | 1 001 | NA | NA |
| Miami | 3 416 | 32 589 | 0.70 | 386 | 10.5 | 348 | 9.5 | 4 918 | 17.3 | 6 143 | 840 | 2 795 | NA | NA |
| Monroe | 14 976 | 145 474 | 1.15 | 1 281 | 9.2 | 793 | 5.7 | 18 547 | 16.8 | 17 512 | 2 662 | 8 677 | 4 918 | 3 546 |
| Montgomery | 1 171 | 37 870 | 0.98 | 497 | 12.9 | 371 | 9.7 | 5 325 | 17.1 | 7 130 | 1 429 | 3 176 | 1 203 | 3 139 |
| Morgan | 592 | 54 461 | 0.53 | 796 | 11.5 | 570 | 8.2 | 9 538 | 16.1 | 12 211 | 2 259 | 5 052 | NA | NA |
| Newton | 170 | 12 050 | 0.65 | 133 | 9.4 | 150 | 10.6 | 1 949 | 16.6 | 2 589 | 224 | 1 423 | 247 | 1 725 |
| Noble | 831 | 44 991 | 0.88 | 629 | 13.2 | 408 | 8.6 | 8 339 | 20.3 | 7 724 | 3 050 | 2 973 | 619 | 1 363 |
| Ohio | 52 | 4 903 | 0.61 | 57 | 9.4 | 74 | 12.2 | 806 | 15.9 | 1 117 | 221 | 504 | NA | NA |
| Orange | 258 | 19 047 | 0.90 | 230 | 11.5 | 216 | 10.8 | 2 934 | 17.7 | 4 165 | 745 | 2 018 | 23 | 115 |
| Owen | 197 | 17 866 | 0.59 | 232 | 10.8 | 232 | 10.8 | 3 143 | 17.2 | 4 291 | 706 | 1 932 | NA | NA |
| Parke | 1 741 | 14 704 | 0.60 | 182 | 10.6 | 178 | 10.3 | 2 662 | 20.5 | 3 162 | 353 | 1 513 | 106 | 608 |
| Perry | 1 532 | 18 252 | 0.87 | 215 | 11.1 | 187 | 9.7 | 2 398 | 16.0 | 3 622 | 277 | 2 115 | NA | NA |

1. Per 1,000 estimated resident population.   2. Data for serious crimes have not been adjusted for underreporting; this may affect comparability between geographic areas and over time.   3. Per 100,000 population estimated by the FBI.

# Table B. States and Counties — **Crime, Education, Money Income, and Poverty**

| STATE County | Serious crimes known to police, 2011 (cont.)[1] Rate[2] | | Education | | | | | | Money income, 2007–2011 | | | | Income and poverty, 2011 | | | |
|---|---|---|---|---|---|---|---|---|---|---|---|---|---|---|---|---|
| | | | School enrollment and attainment, 2007–2011 | | | | Local government expenditures,[5] 2009–2010 | | | Households | | | Percent below poverty level | | | |
| | | | Enrollment[3] | | Attainment[4] (percent) | | | | | Median income | | | | | | |
| | Violent | Property | Total | Percent private | High school graduate or less | Bachelor's degree or more | Total current expenditures (mil dol) | Current expenditures per student (dollars) | Per capita income[6] (dollars) | Dollars | Percent change, 2000 to 2007–2011 (constant 2011 dollars) | Percent with income of $200,000 or more | Median household income (dollars) | All persons | Children under 18 years | Children 5 to 17 years in families |
| | 46 | 47 | 48 | 49 | 50 | 51 | 52 | 53 | 54 | 55 | 56 | 57 | 58 | 59 | 60 | 61 |
| **ILLINOIS—Cont'd** | | | | | | | | | | | | | | | | |
| Winnebago | 861 | 3 657 | 76 033 | 20.3 | 49.1 | 21.2 | 536.8 | 11 208 | 24 544 | 47 597 | -19.7 | 2.6 | 44 353 | 19.1 | 27.7 | 24.6 |
| Woodford | 44 | 887 | 10 484 | 15.4 | 40.8 | 24.3 | 78.7 | 9 530 | 29 886 | 66 198 | -4.6 | 3.4 | 65 998 | 7.0 | 8.6 | 7.3 |
| **INDIANA** | 332 | 3 162 | 1 737 555 | 16.5 | 49.2 | 22.7 | 10 009.0 | 9 563 | 24 497 | 48 393 | -13.8 | 2.4 | 46 410 | 15.8 | 22.6 | 20.6 |
| Adams | NA | NA | 8 719 | 27.5 | 58.7 | 13.3 | 40.4 | 8 705 | 19 633 | 46 549 | -15.1 | 1.0 | 47 265 | 15.0 | 28.3 | 27.9 |
| Allen | 247 | 2 910 | 100 781 | 21.3 | 42.1 | 26.3 | 531.7 | 9 417 | 24 902 | 49 767 | -13.6 | 2.5 | 47 411 | 17.2 | 24.9 | 23.5 |
| Bartholomew | 167 | 4 158 | 19 535 | 15.8 | 45.2 | 27.2 | 131.4 | 10 724 | 27 518 | 53 692 | -10.0 | 3.0 | 52 669 | 12.7 | 19.5 | 17.6 |
| Benton | NA | NA | 2 250 | 11.1 | 57.5 | 15.1 | 18.7 | 10 024 | 22 461 | 47 240 | -12.1 | 1.1 | 45 644 | 13.0 | 17.8 | 15.4 |
| Blackford | 166 | 2 010 | 2 713 | 5.2 | 66.1 | 10.5 | 19.9 | 9 767 | 21 255 | 40 214 | -14.3 | 0.7 | 38 346 | 16.1 | 24.5 | 22.3 |
| Boone | NA | NA | 15 628 | 14.3 | 35.3 | 39.4 | 94.2 | 8 622 | 36 155 | 68 284 | 1.9 | 9.7 | 63 717 | 8.1 | 9.3 | 7.9 |
| Brown | 13 | 842 | 3 179 | 9.4 | 49.7 | 22.9 | 20.1 | 9 237 | 25 418 | 50 503 | -14.4 | 2.7 | 53 376 | 13.0 | 21.8 | 19.7 |
| Carroll | 99 | 1 387 | 4 706 | 13.7 | 58.0 | 14.4 | 23.0 | 8 420 | 24 007 | 49 232 | -14.6 | 0.9 | 49 216 | 11.6 | 17.3 | 15.5 |
| Cass | 79 | 2 890 | 9 760 | 10.0 | 60.7 | 14.3 | 69.1 | 10 177 | 20 674 | 42 679 | -19.3 | 1.5 | 41 271 | 14.7 | 22.0 | 20.0 |
| Clark | 619 | 4 839 | 25 514 | 15.7 | 50.1 | 18.5 | 148.9 | 8 965 | 24 136 | 49 130 | -9.3 | 1.6 | 49 778 | 13.0 | 18.5 | 17.5 |
| Clay | NA | NA | 6 560 | 12.3 | 56.3 | 14.3 | 39.9 | 8 808 | 20 921 | 46 916 | -5.7 | 0.3 | 44 574 | 13.7 | 21.4 | 19.1 |
| Clinton | 207 | 3 564 | 7 888 | 10.0 | 62.1 | 13.1 | 57.8 | 9 165 | 21 362 | 48 352 | -12.1 | 1.1 | 45 712 | 16.2 | 24.4 | 23.0 |
| Crawford | 84 | 1 272 | 2 231 | 11.2 | 67.4 | 12.5 | 16.7 | 10 397 | 19 202 | 40 354 | -8.4 | 1.0 | 37 674 | 19.5 | 29.8 | 26.6 |
| Daviess | 47 | 1 861 | 7 274 | 19.0 | 63.2 | 11.8 | 42.4 | 9 800 | 20 123 | 45 231 | -1.7 | 1.3 | 43 800 | 15.0 | 23.0 | 21.9 |
| Dearborn | 72 | 1 250 | 12 856 | 18.4 | 53.8 | 17.7 | 92.0 | 10 284 | 25 687 | 57 146 | -13.4 | 2.2 | 56 344 | 8.9 | 13.8 | 12.4 |
| Decatur | NA | NA | 6 413 | 9.5 | 62.4 | 13.8 | 36.4 | 8 113 | 22 425 | 47 810 | -12.4 | 1.2 | 44 574 | 14.5 | 21.5 | 18.8 |
| DeKalb | NA | NA | 11 285 | 17.5 | 54.1 | 15.4 | 88.5 | 11 452 | 22 732 | 47 099 | -22.3 | 1.2 | 46 262 | 13.1 | 18.3 | 16.0 |
| Delaware | 509 | 2 834 | 38 767 | 5.0 | 51.1 | 22.2 | 151.1 | 9 196 | 21 132 | 38 730 | -17.2 | 1.7 | 37 208 | 23.0 | 26.1 | 23.9 |
| Dubois | 14 | 565 | 10 128 | 13.7 | 56.2 | 19.7 | 71.4 | 9 670 | 25 355 | 53 997 | -9.5 | 2.1 | 51 936 | 8.3 | 10.4 | 9.2 |
| Elkhart | 42 | 1 535 | 51 936 | 15.6 | 56.8 | 17.9 | 344.9 | 9 737 | 21 879 | 47 308 | -21.2 | 2.0 | 44 354 | 18.3 | 27.4 | 25.9 |
| Fayette | NA | NA | 5 982 | 7.5 | 65.9 | 8.7 | 43.2 | 10 373 | 18 288 | 35 802 | -31.7 | 0.8 | 37 292 | 21.5 | 30.7 | 28.3 |
| Floyd | 183 | 4 195 | 19 075 | 18.2 | 47.7 | 21.7 | 115.0 | 9 331 | 26 785 | 52 803 | -11.2 | 2.7 | 51 210 | 12.8 | 18.3 | 16.5 |
| Fountain | NA | NA | 4 003 | 9.6 | 61.7 | 10.9 | 26.0 | 7 985 | 21 918 | 44 802 | -13.0 | 0.4 | 44 508 | 11.4 | 18.2 | 16.1 |
| Franklin | 78 | 1 034 | 5 676 | 19.1 | 59.9 | 16.8 | 40.7 | 8 012 | 23 971 | 52 234 | -11.1 | 2.0 | 51 106 | 11.3 | 16.1 | 13.1 |
| Fulton | NA | NA | 4 978 | 9.8 | 60.5 | 13.4 | 22.2 | 8 157 | 21 951 | 42 157 | -18.1 | 1.6 | 42 877 | 14.6 | 23.2 | 21.7 |
| Gibson | 89 | 1 794 | 8 179 | 15.9 | 54.8 | 14.4 | 44.6 | 8 562 | 23 252 | 48 171 | -4.9 | 1.1 | 46 570 | 11.5 | 15.0 | 13.6 |
| Grant | 122 | 2 825 | 19 154 | 27.3 | 58.6 | 16.3 | 109.1 | 9 162 | 20 346 | 39 377 | -19.4 | 1.3 | 38 745 | 17.4 | 25.5 | 22.9 |
| Greene | 16 | 1 251 | 7 838 | 8.2 | 58.8 | 11.0 | 52.5 | 9 449 | 21 974 | 43 869 | -4.4 | 0.9 | 42 877 | 14.3 | 21.0 | 18.7 |
| Hamilton | 47 | 1 246 | 80 414 | 19.9 | 20.7 | 54.4 | 429.8 | 8 208 | 39 842 | 84 449 | -11.9 | 10.1 | 84 939 | 4.6 | 6.2 | 5.5 |
| Hancock | 41 | 1 140 | 18 089 | 13.7 | 44.5 | 24.8 | 109.5 | 8 454 | 28 605 | 62 184 | -18.4 | 3.2 | 61 540 | 7.5 | 10.1 | 8.9 |
| Harrison | 91 | 1 585 | 9 407 | 12.0 | 54.9 | 14.8 | 53.3 | 8 695 | 23 956 | 52 263 | -10.9 | 1.5 | 49 551 | 12.6 | 16.7 | 14.7 |
| Hendricks | NA | NA | 39 150 | 16.3 | 38.5 | 31.6 | 218.2 | 8 220 | 29 173 | 68 192 | -8.5 | 3.6 | 64 239 | 5.6 | 7.4 | 6.8 |
| Henry | 52 | 3 592 | 12 037 | 7.8 | 59.7 | 13.9 | 80.3 | 9 896 | 19 598 | 40 519 | -21.3 | 0.8 | 36 572 | 18.4 | 24.1 | 21.8 |
| Howard | 278 | 3 711 | 20 770 | 9.2 | 50.1 | 19.7 | 134.4 | 9 958 | 23 631 | 45 022 | -23.3 | 1.5 | 40 997 | 17.3 | 24.8 | 22.1 |
| Huntington | 54 | 1 688 | 9 747 | 19.0 | 55.1 | 15.6 | 53.1 | 8 982 | 21 916 | 47 137 | -16.1 | 1.3 | 47 326 | 11.7 | 17.8 | 16.6 |
| Jackson | 267 | 4 153 | 9 660 | 20.4 | 59.0 | 13.4 | 58.8 | 8 788 | 22 062 | 45 666 | -14.2 | 0.9 | 44 921 | 14.1 | 20.0 | 18.0 |
| Jasper | NA | NA | 8 846 | 19.9 | 57.1 | 14.3 | 42.4 | 7 857 | 23 546 | 55 509 | -5.2 | 1.0 | 52 559 | 10.6 | 14.8 | 13.3 |
| Jay | 42 | 1 814 | 5 423 | 6.5 | 65.0 | 9.5 | 35.2 | 9 726 | 19 375 | 40 144 | -16.7 | 1.1 | 38 512 | 15.9 | 27.7 | 25.3 |
| Jefferson | NA | NA | 8 099 | 25.5 | 55.2 | 18.2 | 55.4 | 11 741 | 22 191 | 43 635 | -15.4 | 1.3 | 40 386 | 14.3 | 22.1 | 19.6 |
| Jennings | 192 | 2 675 | 7 315 | 11.0 | 63.1 | 8.1 | 52.4 | 10 240 | 19 570 | 44 815 | -15.8 | 0.4 | 42 577 | 14.5 | 21.6 | 19.4 |
| Johnson | 233 | 2 859 | 36 550 | 17.0 | 44.0 | 26.4 | 216.5 | 8 637 | 28 694 | 62 754 | -11.8 | 3.6 | 61 477 | 9.3 | 13.1 | 11.7 |
| Knox | 101 | 3 249 | 10 453 | 11.7 | 51.9 | 14.6 | 54.6 | 10 503 | 20 841 | 40 391 | -4.6 | 1.4 | 38 653 | 19.7 | 27.0 | 24.3 |
| Kosciusko | 59 | 1 810 | 18 809 | 16.1 | 53.0 | 20.2 | 126.0 | 8 871 | 24 417 | 51 141 | -13.8 | 2.2 | 50 823 | 11.3 | 16.4 | 15.4 |
| LaGrange | 29 | 702 | 8 590 | 29.6 | 70.1 | 10.4 | 55.9 | 9 261 | 18 469 | 47 057 | -18.7 | 1.2 | 42 119 | 12.9 | 21.1 | 20.1 |
| Lake | 386 | 4 076 | 133 329 | 15.6 | 50.2 | 19.5 | 873.5 | 9 976 | 23 726 | 49 443 | -12.5 | 2.1 | 48 143 | 19.3 | 30.2 | 28.3 |
| LaPorte | 165 | 3 611 | 27 440 | 13.0 | 53.0 | 17.0 | 180.3 | 9 868 | 22 968 | 46 934 | -16.1 | 1.8 | 47 201 | 17.3 | 25.9 | 23.8 |
| Lawrence | 186 | 1 983 | 10 720 | 11.1 | 61.3 | 12.9 | 67.8 | 9 248 | 22 189 | 43 195 | -11.8 | 1.5 | 43 471 | 15.4 | 23.1 | 20.4 |
| Madison | NA | NA | 29 967 | 16.8 | 54.9 | 16.8 | 184.1 | 9 514 | 22 150 | 44 035 | -16.2 | 1.3 | 41 766 | 18.9 | 29.4 | 23.6 |
| Marion | 1 078 | 5 653 | 235 624 | 20.4 | 45.6 | 27.1 | 1 535.8 | 10 795 | 24 575 | 43 197 | -20.8 | 2.4 | 39 957 | 21.3 | 31.9 | 30.2 |
| Marshall | 70 | 2 216 | 11 878 | 17.5 | 56.7 | 16.8 | 78.1 | 10 067 | 22 376 | 48 536 | -15.6 | 1.7 | 46 301 | 13.3 | 17.9 | 16.0 |
| Martin | NA | NA | 2 303 | 12.5 | 59.9 | 9.5 | 15.8 | 9 586 | 22 148 | 43 592 | -11.3 | 0.8 | 44 715 | 14.0 | 20.1 | 17.3 |
| Miami | NA | NA | 9 701 | 8.1 | 59.8 | 9.5 | 52.2 | 9 263 | 19 392 | 39 746 | -24.9 | 0.9 | 43 287 | 14.7 | 22.7 | 19.1 |
| Monroe | 244 | 3 302 | 59 482 | 7.5 | 32.5 | 42.5 | 128.9 | 9 307 | 22 306 | 38 524 | -14.3 | 2.6 | 40 262 | 24.7 | 17.6 | 15.7 |
| Montgomery | 191 | 2 949 | 9 452 | 15.1 | 56.7 | 18.0 | 62.2 | 9 867 | 23 322 | 47 929 | -14.0 | 1.6 | 43 176 | 14.8 | 24.1 | 19.6 |
| Morgan | NA | NA | 16 838 | 13.5 | 55.0 | 15.0 | 100.1 | 8 346 | 25 249 | 56 315 | -12.6 | 2.1 | 53 690 | 11.1 | 17.0 | 14.6 |
| Newton | 203 | 1 523 | 3 500 | 13.3 | 65.0 | 8.1 | 22.8 | 9 664 | 23 416 | 48 108 | -13.0 | 1.7 | 44 418 | 15.0 | 22.5 | 18.5 |
| Noble | 51 | 1 312 | 12 027 | 13.4 | 60.1 | 12.7 | 67.3 | 8 504 | 20 600 | 47 768 | -17.1 | 0.5 | 46 690 | 13.1 | 18.7 | 16.6 |
| Ohio | NA | NA | 1 337 | 8.8 | 63.9 | 12.8 | 8.2 | 9 079 | 26 138 | 50 795 | -9.0 | 1.0 | 48 788 | 11.1 | 17.5 | 14.6 |
| Orange | 60 | 55 | 4 322 | 12.0 | 65.0 | 12.2 | 39.1 | 11 600 | 18 811 | 37 618 | -11.7 | 0.9 | 37 910 | 17.1 | 25.8 | 23.6 |
| Owen | NA | NA | 4 865 | 9.8 | 65.6 | 9.1 | 26.8 | 9 196 | 21 028 | 43 553 | -11.7 | 1.2 | 41 004 | 15.3 | 25.2 | 22.0 |
| Parke | 98 | 511 | 3 469 | 11.9 | 57.7 | 13.9 | 23.8 | 10 298 | 20 000 | 42 441 | -12.0 | 1.7 | 40 790 | 17.8 | 28.4 | 26.4 |
| Perry | NA | NA | 3 697 | 11.2 | 64.5 | 8.9 | 27.9 | 9 222 | 21 298 | 45 808 | -6.4 | 0.8 | 45 234 | 13.5 | 17.9 | 16.0 |

1. Data for serious crimes have not been adjusted for underreporting; this may affect comparability between geographic areas and over time.   2. Per 100,000 population estimated by the FBI.   3. All persons 3 years old and over enrolled in nursery school through college.   4. Persons 25 years old and over.   5. Elementary and secondary education expenditures.   6. Based on population estimated by the American Community Survey, 2007–2011.

# Table B. States and Counties — Personal Income

| STATE County | Personal income, 2011 | | | | | | | | | | | | |
|---|---|---|---|---|---|---|---|---|---|---|---|---|---|
| | | | Per capita¹ | | Wages and salaries² (mil dol) | Proprietors' income (mil dol) | Dividends, interest, and rent (mil dol) | Transfer payments (mil dol) | | | | | |
| | | | | | | | | | Government payments to individuals | | | | |
| | Total (mil dol) | Percent change, 2010–2011 | Dollars | Rank | | | | Total | Total | Social Security | Medical payments | Income mainte-nance | Unemploy-ment insurance |
| | 62 | 63 | 64 | 65 | 66 | 67 | 68 | 69 | 70 | 71 | 72 | 73 | 74 |
| ILLINOIS—Cont'd | | | | | | | | | | | | | |
| Winnebago | 10 107 | 3.3 | 34 377 | 1 456 | 7 005 | 568 | 1 636 | 2 129 | 2 064 | 801 | 708 | 305 | 154 |
| Woodford | 1 664 | 6.9 | 42 811 | 519 | 488 | 124 | 313 | 225 | 217 | 102 | 77 | 14 | 13 |
| INDIANA | 232 586 | 5.3 | 35 689 | X | 150 322 | 18 214 | 30 987 | 46 177 | 44 735 | 16 717 | 17 705 | 4 889 | 2 030 |
| Adams | 1 016 | 6.8 | 29 566 | 2 370 | 542 | 130 | 140 | 205 | 198 | 83 | 79 | 17 | 9 |
| Allen | 12 613 | 5.3 | 35 199 | 1 340 | 9 466 | 958 | 1 877 | 2 415 | 2 336 | 869 | 906 | 284 | 114 |
| Bartholomew | 3 087 | 8.4 | 39 645 | 789 | 2 701 | 202 | 429 | 536 | 518 | 219 | 209 | 45 | 21 |
| Benton | 355 | 12.9 | 40 109 | 734 | 108 | 105 | 42 | 60 | 58 | 25 | 22 | 5 | 3 |
| Blackford | 384 | 5.5 | 30 489 | 2 203 | 144 | 41 | 49 | 114 | 111 | 46 | 43 | 12 | 5 |
| Boone | 3 045 | 7.0 | 52 975 | 141 | 1 096 | 432 | 495 | 310 | 298 | 131 | 115 | 21 | 14 |
| Brown | 541 | 5.9 | 35 863 | 1 235 | 108 | 43 | 83 | 109 | 106 | 55 | 32 | 8 | 4 |
| Carroll | 662 | 5.3 | 33 062 | 1 697 | 218 | 103 | 97 | 128 | 124 | 60 | 41 | 10 | 6 |
| Cass | 1 229 | 6.3 | 31 648 | 1 970 | 659 | 82 | 160 | 316 | 308 | 108 | 139 | 29 | 12 |
| Clark | 3 782 | 4.7 | 33 898 | 1 534 | 2 291 | 216 | 412 | 832 | 807 | 297 | 347 | 76 | 34 |
| Clay | 833 | 3.9 | 30 977 | 2 107 | 321 | 75 | 91 | 216 | 210 | 77 | 88 | 22 | 10 |
| Clinton | 1 062 | 7.9 | 32 076 | 1 865 | 526 | 95 | 142 | 235 | 227 | 87 | 92 | 24 | 10 |
| Crawford | 297 | 3.2 | 27 820 | 2 637 | 77 | 16 | 29 | 92 | 89 | 31 | 40 | 9 | 4 |
| Daviess | 1 055 | 6.7 | 32 989 | 1 709 | 462 | 116 | 149 | 216 | 209 | 66 | 99 | 21 | 6 |
| Dearborn | 1 773 | 4.2 | 35 376 | 1 312 | 735 | 114 | 231 | 347 | 336 | 141 | 133 | 27 | 16 |
| Decatur | 891 | 6.1 | 34 354 | 1 463 | 564 | 87 | 129 | 185 | 180 | 72 | 72 | 17 | 9 |
| DeKalb | 1 353 | 5.7 | 31 863 | 1 913 | 1 036 | 75 | 192 | 290 | 281 | 116 | 105 | 27 | 14 |
| Delaware | 3 549 | 4.1 | 30 164 | 2 256 | 2 092 | 252 | 492 | 955 | 929 | 343 | 372 | 106 | 40 |
| Dubois | 1 718 | 6.7 | 40 718 | 686 | 1 276 | 193 | 356 | 274 | 265 | 112 | 114 | 16 | 9 |
| Elkhart | 6 392 | 5.0 | 32 131 | 1 854 | 5 362 | 550 | 905 | 1 230 | 1 186 | 462 | 437 | 148 | 71 |
| Fayette | 694 | 4.2 | 28 590 | 2 526 | 286 | 46 | 99 | 247 | 242 | 86 | 113 | 25 | 9 |
| Floyd | 3 016 | 4.4 | 40 219 | 722 | 1 414 | 188 | 382 | 566 | 549 | 197 | 230 | 57 | 21 |
| Fountain | 575 | 6.8 | 33 382 | 1 631 | 232 | 56 | 74 | 138 | 134 | 55 | 55 | 11 | 6 |
| Franklin | 842 | 5.5 | 36 561 | 1 129 | 168 | 42 | 135 | 165 | 160 | 73 | 55 | 15 | 7 |
| Fulton | 653 | 6.2 | 31 284 | 2 050 | 299 | 65 | 95 | 156 | 152 | 63 | 58 | 15 | 6 |
| Gibson | 1 175 | 6.3 | 35 066 | 1 363 | 1 005 | 105 | 159 | 242 | 234 | 91 | 97 | 18 | 9 |
| Grant | 2 243 | 4.5 | 32 141 | 1 850 | 1 358 | 169 | 264 | 664 | 648 | 229 | 269 | 69 | 25 |
| Greene | 1 022 | 2.7 | 31 059 | 2 082 | 280 | 59 | 125 | 254 | 247 | 90 | 105 | 25 | 10 |
| Hamilton | 14 656 | 7.6 | 51 824 | 167 | 6 902 | 1 304 | 2 175 | 1 136 | 1 074 | 510 | 356 | 64 | 62 |
| Hancock | 3 083 | 8.6 | 43 714 | 457 | 1 012 | 263 | 327 | 441 | 426 | 190 | 157 | 29 | 20 |
| Harrison | 1 264 | 5.0 | 32 122 | 1 856 | 473 | 52 | 162 | 271 | 262 | 105 | 104 | 23 | 12 |
| Hendricks | 5 355 | 5.8 | 36 188 | 1 190 | 2 476 | 429 | 613 | 739 | 706 | 317 | 251 | 44 | 38 |
| Henry | 1 439 | 4.4 | 29 214 | 2 421 | 532 | 95 | 194 | 416 | 405 | 162 | 168 | 38 | 19 |
| Howard | 2 672 | 6.2 | 32 267 | 1 829 | 2 109 | 134 | 351 | 752 | 733 | 295 | 296 | 77 | 30 |
| Huntington | 1 199 | 4.6 | 32 225 | 1 840 | 648 | 64 | 192 | 270 | 262 | 108 | 99 | 22 | 13 |
| Jackson | 1 415 | 5.9 | 32 941 | 1 718 | 915 | 131 | 184 | 308 | 298 | 123 | 121 | 27 | 12 |
| Jasper | 1 203 | 7.6 | 36 012 | 1 208 | 519 | 179 | 135 | 225 | 218 | 96 | 81 | 17 | 10 |
| Jay | 658 | 8.1 | 30 862 | 2 130 | 333 | 92 | 71 | 161 | 156 | 64 | 64 | 15 | 6 |
| Jefferson | 963 | 2.8 | 29 872 | 2 312 | 574 | 66 | 148 | 276 | 269 | 96 | 124 | 24 | 10 |
| Jennings | 886 | 6.6 | 31 435 | 2 010 | 352 | 35 | 76 | 247 | 241 | 79 | 116 | 24 | 11 |
| Johnson | 5 180 | 5.4 | 36 570 | 1 128 | 1 972 | 333 | 665 | 854 | 822 | 356 | 305 | 68 | 39 |
| Knox | 1 398 | 5.7 | 36 312 | 1 165 | 827 | 144 | 180 | 361 | 352 | 106 | 171 | 33 | 10 |
| Kosciusko | 2 903 | 6.5 | 37 541 | 1 022 | 2 098 | 168 | 431 | 484 | 467 | 209 | 169 | 40 | 24 |
| LaGrange | 893 | 7.0 | 23 897 | 3 031 | 507 | 92 | 132 | 183 | 175 | 77 | 62 | 15 | 10 |
| Lake | 17 269 | 3.9 | 34 847 | 1 396 | 11 209 | 959 | 1 973 | 3 960 | 3 851 | 1 316 | 1 591 | 558 | 158 |
| LaPorte | 3 525 | 5.4 | 31 650 | 1 969 | 2 053 | 205 | 465 | 845 | 821 | 319 | 322 | 95 | 37 |
| Lawrence | 1 442 | 4.5 | 31 205 | 2 063 | 585 | 80 | 182 | 385 | 375 | 138 | 165 | 35 | 17 |
| Madison | 3 992 | 3.4 | 30 421 | 2 218 | 1 791 | 233 | 440 | 1 143 | 1 114 | 426 | 462 | 119 | 50 |
| Marion | 34 910 | 4.3 | 38 309 | 934 | 37 064 | 3 271 | 4 191 | 6 914 | 6 712 | 1 948 | 2 522 | 979 | 310 |
| Marshall | 1 512 | 7.7 | 32 137 | 1 851 | 804 | 125 | 225 | 304 | 294 | 128 | 108 | 26 | 15 |
| Martin | 345 | 4.8 | 33 378 | 1 633 | 713 | 21 | 47 | 77 | 75 | 27 | 32 | 8 | 3 |
| Miami | 988 | 6.8 | 27 000 | 2 765 | 451 | 62 | 130 | 271 | 263 | 89 | 104 | 28 | 13 |
| Monroe | 4 337 | 5.4 | 31 021 | 2 094 | 3 177 | 193 | 742 | 740 | 709 | 264 | 275 | 66 | 35 |
| Montgomery | 1 270 | 7.3 | 33 045 | 1 701 | 756 | 140 | 158 | 281 | 272 | 110 | 114 | 24 | 11 |
| Morgan | 2 614 | 4.8 | 37 634 | 1 010 | 655 | 67 | 263 | 486 | 470 | 197 | 178 | 46 | 22 |
| Newton | 468 | 8.9 | 33 054 | 1 700 | 164 | 65 | 53 | 99 | 96 | 41 | 37 | 8 | 5 |
| Noble | 1 445 | 5.5 | 30 378 | 2 226 | 784 | 93 | 167 | 302 | 292 | 121 | 111 | 27 | 16 |
| Ohio | 220 | 5.4 | 36 241 | 1 182 | 66 | 6 | 21 | 42 | 40 | 17 | 16 | 3 | 2 |
| Orange | 599 | 3.6 | 30 007 | 2 289 | 308 | 31 | 74 | 168 | 164 | 57 | 73 | 18 | 7 |
| Owen | 645 | 1.7 | 30 009 | 2 288 | 239 | 30 | 75 | 168 | 163 | 66 | 63 | 18 | 7 |
| Parke | 486 | 2.8 | 28 182 | 2 593 | 128 | 44 | 73 | 130 | 126 | 49 | 54 | 11 | 5 |
| Perry | 586 | 5.6 | 30 253 | 2 245 | 307 | 32 | 74 | 139 | 135 | 54 | 57 | 11 | 6 |

1. Based on the resident population estimated as of July 1 of the year shown.  2. Includes supplements to wages and salaries.

| STATE County | Earnings, 2011 | | | | | | | | | Social Security beneficiaries, December 2011 | | | Housing units, 2010 | |
|---|---|---|---|---|---|---|---|---|---|---|---|---|---|---|
| | | | | Percent by selected industries | | | | | | | | | | |
| | | | Goods-related[1] | | Service-related and health | | | | | | | | | |
| | Total (mil dol) | Farm | Total | Manu-facturing | Infor-mation and profes-sional and technical services | Retail trade | Finance, insur-ance, and real estate | Health care and social services | Govern-ment | Number | Rate[2] | Supple-mental Security Income recipients, December 2011 | Total | Percent change, 2000–2010 |
| | 75 | 76 | 77 | 78 | 79 | 80 | 81 | 82 | 83 | 84 | 85 | 86 | 87 | 88 |
| ILLINOIS—Cont'd | | | | | | | | | | | | | | |
| Winnebago | 7 573 | 0.4 | 28.3 | 23.5 | 5.1 | 6.8 | 5.9 | 17.4 | 12.4 | 57 965 | 197 | 7 009 | 125 965 | 10.1 |
| Woodford | 612 | 13.6 | 29.4 | 21.9 | D | 6.1 | 2.6 | 7.9 | 15.9 | 7 225 | 186 | 261 | 15 145 | 12.3 |
| INDIANA | 168 537 | 1.8 | 27.7 | 21.2 | 6.9 | 6.1 | 5.7 | 12.4 | 14.7 | 1 219 879 | 187 | 122 130 | 2 795 541 | 10.4 |
| Adams | 672 | 6.4 | D | 35.1 | D | 6.2 | 3.2 | 5.2 | 14.3 | 6 055 | 176 | 335 | 13 014 | 4.9 |
| Allen | 10 423 | 0.2 | 24.7 | 18.6 | 7.6 | 6.0 | 7.6 | 16.6 | 10.8 | 62 320 | 174 | 7 250 | 152 184 | 9.6 |
| Bartholomew | 2 903 | 0.6 | D | 44.3 | 4.6 | 4.7 | 4.8 | 7.0 | 11.3 | 15 560 | 200 | 1 212 | 33 098 | 10.9 |
| Benton | 213 | 34.9 | 11.4 | 8.2 | D | 4.1 | 3.3 | D | 13.9 | 1 945 | 220 | 125 | 3 937 | 3.1 |
| Blackford | 185 | 11.5 | D | 29.1 | 3.0 | 10.3 | 2.8 | 8.3 | 15.1 | 3 460 | 275 | 260 | 6 051 | -1.7 |
| Boone | 1 528 | 2.8 | D | 10.2 | 7.8 | 11.9 | 4.4 | 7.4 | 12.2 | 8 965 | 156 | 429 | 22 754 | 26.9 |
| Brown | 150 | 0.8 | D | 7.2 | D | 7.3 | 3.7 | D | 24.6 | 3 925 | 260 | 197 | 8 285 | 15.7 |
| Carroll | 321 | 17.7 | D | 29.3 | 2.8 | 4.9 | 2.9 | D | 12.6 | 4 415 | 220 | 195 | 9 472 | 9.2 |
| Cass | 741 | 6.4 | D | 28.6 | 2.3 | 6.1 | 3.0 | D | 24.6 | 8 225 | 212 | 763 | 16 474 | -0.9 |
| Clark | 2 506 | 0.3 | D | 16.2 | 3.0 | 8.3 | 5.9 | 9.3 | 19.7 | 22 580 | 202 | 2 309 | 47 776 | 16.0 |
| Clay | 396 | 5.8 | D | 28.3 | 2.0 | 7.1 | 2.5 | D | 15.6 | 5 975 | 222 | 611 | 11 703 | 5.4 |
| Clinton | 621 | 12.1 | 40.9 | 36.6 | D | 4.2 | 2.4 | 7.8 | 14.0 | 6 530 | 197 | 489 | 13 321 | 0.4 |
| Crawford | 93 | 0.7 | D | D | D | 5.8 | 4.9 | 5.5 | 26.9 | 2 600 | 244 | 311 | 5 520 | 7.4 |
| Daviess | 578 | 8.6 | 29.3 | 12.8 | 4.1 | 8.1 | 3.2 | D | 16.7 | 5 580 | 174 | 530 | 12 471 | 4.8 |
| Dearborn | 849 | 0.3 | D | 13.7 | 3.7 | 8.0 | 3.4 | 7.1 | 20.2 | 10 170 | 203 | 596 | 20 171 | 13.3 |
| Decatur | 652 | 7.4 | D | 38.7 | D | 4.9 | 3.3 | 3.7 | 13.5 | 5 475 | 211 | 421 | 11 209 | 12.2 |
| DeKalb | 1 111 | 1.5 | D | 44.6 | 3.2 | 4.0 | 2.1 | 6.9 | 9.8 | 8 530 | 201 | 647 | 17 558 | 8.8 |
| Delaware | 2 344 | 1.5 | D | 9.6 | 7.0 | 8.0 | 5.6 | 20.5 | 23.7 | 25 105 | 213 | 2 858 | 52 357 | 2.6 |
| Dubois | 1 469 | 4.0 | D | 35.7 | 3.4 | 7.4 | 2.7 | 10.9 | 7.6 | 8 215 | 195 | 400 | 17 384 | 12.1 |
| Elkhart | 5 911 | 1.0 | 49.4 | 45.3 | 3.2 | 5.0 | 2.9 | 9.1 | 8.0 | 33 115 | 166 | 3 089 | 77 767 | 11.4 |
| Fayette | 333 | 4.7 | D | 20.9 | 3.5 | 8.2 | 3.3 | 19.2 | 19.0 | 6 570 | 271 | 860 | 10 898 | -0.8 |
| Floyd | 1 603 | 0.1 | D | 22.2 | 6.1 | 6.2 | 5.5 | 11.2 | 21.2 | 14 645 | 195 | 1 561 | 31 968 | 9.9 |
| Fountain | 288 | 10.7 | 43.7 | 40.1 | D | 6.6 | 3.0 | D | 14.5 | 4 195 | 244 | 287 | 7 865 | 2.2 |
| Franklin | 210 | 6.9 | D | 15.8 | D | 9.3 | D | D | 23.1 | 5 620 | 244 | 402 | 9 538 | 11.0 |
| Fulton | 364 | 7.8 | D | 27.7 | 2.7 | 7.1 | 4.0 | 5.3 | 18.7 | 4 760 | 228 | 349 | 9 708 | 6.4 |
| Gibson | 1 110 | 3.7 | 54.4 | 44.6 | 2.3 | 4.4 | 1.1 | 5.0 | 6.4 | 6 845 | 204 | 478 | 14 645 | 3.7 |
| Grant | 1 527 | 2.2 | 27.2 | 24.1 | 2.4 | 5.9 | 3.0 | 16.7 | 15.7 | 17 085 | 245 | 1 975 | 30 443 | -0.4 |
| Greene | 339 | 8.0 | 15.0 | 6.2 | 6.6 | 8.6 | 3.6 | D | 28.6 | 7 455 | 227 | 740 | 15 211 | 1.0 |
| Hamilton | 8 206 | 0.4 | 11.7 | 5.0 | 15.2 | 7.1 | 16.7 | 10.7 | 8.9 | 33 265 | 118 | 1 369 | 106 772 | 53.7 |
| Hancock | 1 275 | 2.5 | 23.3 | 15.0 | 15.9 | 6.0 | 3.6 | 8.4 | 16.6 | 13 080 | 185 | 576 | 28 125 | 29.3 |
| Harrison | 525 | 2.5 | 18.2 | 13.1 | D | 7.8 | 3.4 | D | 20.6 | 8 160 | 207 | 616 | 16 534 | 20.7 |
| Hendricks | 2 905 | 1.1 | 14.5 | 8.1 | D | 10.7 | 2.9 | 8.2 | 16.3 | 21 450 | 145 | 834 | 55 454 | 41.4 |
| Henry | 627 | 6.4 | D | 16.6 | 2.6 | 8.2 | 3.9 | D | 24.7 | 12 010 | 244 | 982 | 21 288 | 3.4 |
| Howard | 2 243 | 1.3 | D | 44.0 | 3.3 | 6.1 | 3.3 | 8.8 | 15.7 | 20 570 | 248 | 2 195 | 38 679 | 2.9 |
| Huntington | 712 | 4.9 | D | 30.3 | 4.9 | 5.4 | 4.3 | 8.5 | 11.7 | 8 015 | 215 | 511 | 15 805 | 3.5 |
| Jackson | 1 046 | 4.9 | D | 34.0 | 2.2 | 7.1 | 2.8 | 5.1 | 15.5 | 9 340 | 217 | 756 | 18 202 | 6.2 |
| Jasper | 697 | 16.6 | D | 13.6 | 2.5 | 6.6 | 2.5 | 5.7 | 13.9 | 6 985 | 209 | 347 | 13 168 | 17.2 |
| Jay | 425 | 15.8 | D | 37.2 | 1.7 | 4.4 | 2.3 | D | 16.2 | 4 895 | 230 | 393 | 9 221 | 1.6 |
| Jefferson | 640 | 1.2 | 29.2 | 25.5 | D | 7.8 | 2.4 | D | 18.8 | 7 400 | 229 | 736 | 14 311 | 6.9 |
| Jennings | 386 | 4.8 | D | 22.9 | D | 5.4 | 2.1 | 7.0 | 18.1 | 6 250 | 222 | 710 | 12 069 | 5.2 |
| Johnson | 2 305 | 0.8 | 20.1 | 12.8 | 5.6 | 10.7 | 4.9 | 11.9 | 16.8 | 24 630 | 174 | 1 326 | 56 649 | 25.6 |
| Knox | 972 | 7.8 | 21.6 | 8.4 | 4.0 | 5.7 | 3.9 | 10.5 | 26.0 | 8 430 | 219 | 981 | 17 038 | -1.5 |
| Kosciusko | 2 265 | 2.5 | D | 52.7 | 2.1 | 4.9 | 2.3 | 6.4 | 7.3 | 14 835 | 192 | 815 | 37 038 | 15.1 |
| LaGrange | 599 | 8.1 | D | 44.8 | 1.8 | 5.4 | 2.5 | D | 11.7 | 5 740 | 154 | 300 | 14 094 | 8.9 |
| Lake | 12 168 | 0.2 | 33.5 | 21.7 | 4.2 | 7.4 | 3.3 | 15.1 | 12.5 | 93 020 | 188 | 12 735 | 208 750 | 7.1 |
| LaPorte | 2 258 | 2.8 | 29.0 | 22.3 | 3.2 | 6.9 | 3.2 | 14.0 | 16.8 | 22 925 | 206 | 2 164 | 48 448 | 6.2 |
| Lawrence | 665 | 1.4 | 28.2 | 21.9 | 7.2 | 8.9 | 4.1 | 15.5 | 16.2 | 10 785 | 233 | 931 | 21 074 | 2.5 |
| Madison | 2 024 | 2.7 | D | 15.5 | 3.9 | 6.8 | 4.3 | 16.3 | 16.7 | 30 720 | 234 | 3 159 | 59 068 | 3.7 |
| Marion | 40 335 | 0.0 | 22.0 | 16.2 | 11.0 | 4.6 | 8.2 | 14.2 | 13.9 | 144 065 | 158 | 24 233 | 417 862 | 7.9 |
| Marshall | 929 | 5.3 | D | 37.6 | D | 6.5 | 4.8 | 6.8 | 12.8 | 9 440 | 201 | 656 | 19 845 | 9.6 |
| Martin | 733 | 2.2 | 4.6 | 2.8 | D | 1.2 | D | 0.5 | 75.7 | 2 345 | 227 | 216 | 4 786 | 1.2 |
| Miami | 513 | 7.5 | 24.0 | 18.4 | 1.5 | 5.0 | 3.5 | 7.6 | 32.0 | 6 915 | 189 | 722 | 15 479 | 1.2 |
| Monroe | 3 370 | 0.1 | 17.0 | 12.4 | 6.7 | 5.8 | 3.5 | 14.7 | 33.8 | 19 070 | 136 | 1 713 | 59 107 | 16.2 |
| Montgomery | 896 | 10.4 | D | 39.8 | 2.2 | 5.1 | 2.3 | D | 11.4 | 8 130 | 211 | 577 | 16 535 | 5.5 |
| Morgan | 722 | 2.9 | 24.4 | 16.0 | D | 9.0 | 4.2 | 11.5 | 20.9 | 14 050 | 202 | 962 | 27 754 | 7.1 |
| Newton | 229 | 28.3 | D | 15.1 | D | 3.0 | 3.3 | D | 16.6 | 2 980 | 210 | 198 | 6 030 | 5.3 |
| Noble | 877 | 1.5 | D | 52.0 | D | 5.4 | 2.1 | 5.9 | 11.5 | 9 045 | 190 | 667 | 20 109 | 10.3 |
| Ohio | 72 | 1.1 | D | D | 1.6 | 2.4 | D | 4.1 | 23.4 | 1 265 | 209 | 75 | 2 784 | 14.9 |
| Orange | 339 | 2.6 | D | 16.0 | D | 5.2 | 1.7 | D | 14.8 | 4 745 | 238 | 527 | 9 176 | 9.9 |
| Owen | 268 | 2.8 | D | 48.2 | D | 4.6 | 2.6 | 6.9 | 14.2 | 5 025 | 234 | 396 | 10 091 | 2.4 |
| Parke | 172 | 11.8 | D | 11.8 | D | 5.9 | 3.8 | D | 30.7 | 3 675 | 213 | 254 | 8 085 | 7.3 |
| Perry | 339 | 2.4 | D | 40.0 | 2.2 | 5.5 | 2.9 | D | 23.5 | 4 180 | 216 | 360 | 8 495 | 3.3 |

1. Includes mining, construction, and manufacturing.  2. Per 1,000 resident population enumerated in the 2010 census.

# Table B. States and Counties — Housing, Labor Force, and Employment

| STATE County | Housing units, 2007–2011 | | | | | | | | Civilian labor force, 2012 | | | | Civilian employment,[6] 2007–2011 | | |
|---|---|---|---|---|---|---|---|---|---|---|---|---|---|---|---|
| | Occupied units | | | | | | | | | | Unemployment | | | Percent | |
| | | Owner-occupied | | | | Renter-occupied | | | | | | | | | |
| | | | | Median owner cost as a percent of income | | | | | | | | | | | Con-struction, produc-tion, and mainte-nance occu-pations |
| | Total | Percent | Median value[1] | With a mort-gage | Without a mort-gage[2] | Median rent[3] | Median rent as a per-cent of income | Sub-stand-ard units[4] (percent) | Total | Percent change, 2011–2012 | Total | Rate[5] | Total | Manage-ment, business, science and arts | |
| | 89 | 90 | 91 | 92 | 93 | 94 | 95 | 96 | 97 | 98 | 99 | 100 | 101 | 102 | 103 |
| **ILLINOIS—Cont'd** | | | | | | | | | | | | | | | |
| Winnebago | 113 015 | 69.0 | 129 200 | 23.7 | 13.9 | 708 | 32.1 | 2.1 | 140 140 | -0.6 | 15 977 | 11.4 | 133 237 | 29.8 | 27.0 |
| Woodford | 14 083 | 83.8 | 152 200 | 21.0 | 11.8 | 679 | 28.3 | 1.8 | 21 240 | 0.6 | 1 371 | 6.5 | 18 952 | 36.2 | 24.7 |
| **INDIANA** | 2 472 870 | 71.1 | 123 300 | 21.7 | 11.5 | 704 | 29.7 | 2.0 | 3 149 743 | -0.3 | 263 993 | 8.4 | 2 984 502 | 31.8 | 27.1 |
| Adams | 12 220 | 79.6 | 114 100 | 22.2 | 9.9 | 564 | 24.3 | 9.2 | 14 480 | -2.0 | 1 135 | 7.8 | 15 453 | 23.9 | 37.6 |
| Allen | 136 147 | 70.6 | 113 100 | 20.4 | 10.0 | 646 | 26.5 | 1.8 | 174 207 | -1.1 | 14 497 | 8.3 | 165 039 | 33.9 | 24.1 |
| Bartholomew | 30 037 | 72.5 | 135 400 | 19.9 | 11.4 | 757 | 26.4 | 2.2 | 41 105 | 4.1 | 2 630 | 6.4 | 36 775 | 37.9 | 25.4 |
| Benton | 3 581 | 76.6 | 85 000 | 20.8 | 11.2 | 607 | 24.9 | 0.7 | 4 233 | 1.1 | 355 | 8.4 | 3 971 | 26.9 | 35.9 |
| Blackford | 5 290 | 76.4 | 76 900 | 20.6 | 11.3 | 560 | 29.5 | 1.8 | 5 903 | -1.8 | 623 | 10.6 | 5 321 | 23.5 | 36.1 |
| Boone | 21 111 | 78.4 | 178 300 | 22.0 | 12.7 | 789 | 28.7 | 0.8 | 28 438 | 0.9 | 1 919 | 6.7 | 27 075 | 46.3 | 18.0 |
| Brown | 6 079 | 85.1 | 159 000 | 25.5 | 14.0 | 845 | 30.1 | 2.8 | 7 527 | 0.8 | 594 | 7.9 | 7 140 | 28.8 | 27.8 |
| Carroll | 8 134 | 79.0 | 105 600 | 21.7 | 12.0 | 593 | 26.4 | 3.0 | 9 601 | 0.6 | 718 | 7.5 | 9 374 | 28.4 | 34.9 |
| Cass | 14 813 | 75.3 | 82 400 | 21.1 | 11.0 | 574 | 26.2 | 3.2 | 17 533 | -1.9 | 1 533 | 8.7 | 17 415 | 24.9 | 37.8 |
| Clark | 42 909 | 71.2 | 127 800 | 22.0 | 11.3 | 703 | 28.2 | 2.1 | 55 141 | -0.2 | 4 290 | 7.8 | 53 279 | 29.7 | 24.8 |
| Clay | 10 120 | 79.8 | 87 300 | 20.4 | 11.7 | 642 | 28.1 | 1.1 | 12 487 | -1.1 | 1 264 | 10.1 | 12 205 | 27.4 | 29.7 |
| Clinton | 11 965 | 72.9 | 99 100 | 20.9 | 11.0 | 650 | 30.0 | 2.8 | 16 540 | -0.7 | 1 345 | 8.1 | 15 147 | 22.9 | 39.4 |
| Crawford | 4 242 | 84.2 | 86 200 | 22.5 | 14.0 | 509 | 27.3 | 2.5 | 5 061 | -1.9 | 504 | 10.0 | 4 512 | 19.6 | 42.1 |
| Daviess | 10 944 | 78.3 | 100 200 | 19.5 | 10.5 | 566 | 23.7 | 1.9 | 14 703 | -1.3 | 891 | 6.1 | 13 951 | 24.0 | 41.1 |
| Dearborn | 18 398 | 76.6 | 161 400 | 22.1 | 11.3 | 642 | 29.3 | 1.2 | 25 347 | -0.7 | 2 145 | 8.5 | 24 312 | 27.5 | 29.0 |
| Decatur | 9 992 | 69.3 | 118 000 | 23.0 | 10.8 | 655 | 24.4 | 1.9 | 12 600 | -2.0 | 1 105 | 8.8 | 11 902 | 25.6 | 37.6 |
| DeKalb | 16 140 | 79.7 | 110 500 | 23.4 | 11.1 | 603 | 26.3 | 1.2 | 19 592 | -2.2 | 1 741 | 8.9 | 19 330 | 25.3 | 37.7 |
| Delaware | 46 162 | 65.9 | 92 200 | 21.2 | 12.3 | 650 | 34.9 | 1.3 | 54 245 | 1.1 | 5 161 | 9.5 | 50 644 | 30.7 | 21.3 |
| Dubois | 15 905 | 77.6 | 133 100 | 21.1 | 9.9 | 612 | 23.6 | 2.1 | 21 357 | -1.6 | 1 237 | 5.8 | 21 884 | 26.9 | 35.7 |
| Elkhart | 70 088 | 73.2 | 126 600 | 22.7 | 11.7 | 716 | 30.6 | 3.1 | 91 830 | 1.5 | 8 788 | 9.6 | 89 772 | 25.2 | 37.5 |
| Fayette | 9 604 | 73.2 | 84 600 | 23.4 | 14.6 | 626 | 36.6 | 2.5 | 8 989 | -2.6 | 1 033 | 11.5 | 8 937 | 26.3 | 33.1 |
| Floyd | 29 092 | 72.8 | 150 700 | 21.8 | 10.8 | 704 | 28.3 | 2.0 | 36 651 | 0.3 | 2 769 | 7.6 | 36 847 | 33.9 | 23.6 |
| Fountain | 6 939 | 80.2 | 90 600 | 20.1 | 12.4 | 604 | 28.6 | 0.9 | 8 278 | -2.2 | 720 | 8.7 | 7 717 | 24.6 | 43.0 |
| Franklin | 8 601 | 80.0 | 151 600 | 22.1 | 10.6 | 624 | 27.4 | 3.2 | 11 200 | -1.1 | 933 | 8.3 | 10 805 | 29.4 | 33.0 |
| Fulton | 8 314 | 75.3 | 93 100 | 21.2 | 10.8 | 622 | 30.0 | 2.1 | 9 898 | -2.2 | 852 | 8.6 | 8 998 | 25.2 | 42.4 |
| Gibson | 12 903 | 77.8 | 99 600 | 19.2 | 11.0 | 592 | 27.4 | 2.2 | 16 633 | -1.5 | 1 225 | 7.4 | 15 764 | 23.0 | 40.4 |
| Grant | 27 081 | 70.1 | 82 500 | 20.8 | 10.9 | 596 | 28.8 | 1.2 | 31 881 | -1.8 | 3 165 | 9.9 | 28 862 | 31.0 | 24.9 |
| Greene | 12 886 | 77.9 | 89 100 | 19.3 | 11.6 | 575 | 26.9 | 3.1 | 15 097 | -0.5 | 1 400 | 9.3 | 14 619 | 26.7 | 34.5 |
| Hamilton | 98 959 | 79.8 | 212 800 | 21.0 | 9.9 | 919 | 25.0 | 0.7 | 145 103 | 1.0 | 8 487 | 5.8 | 138 190 | 51.9 | 10.2 |
| Hancock | 25 803 | 81.6 | 157 200 | 22.0 | 9.9 | 783 | 30.1 | 0.7 | 36 521 | 0.6 | 2 598 | 7.1 | 33 292 | 35.5 | 22.7 |
| Harrison | 14 539 | 84.7 | 124 500 | 21.4 | 9.9 | 654 | 31.3 | 1.0 | 19 428 | -0.2 | 1 450 | 7.5 | 18 338 | 26.1 | 34.8 |
| Hendricks | 51 624 | 82.8 | 161 700 | 22.2 | 11.6 | 893 | 26.0 | 1.0 | 76 341 | 0.9 | 5 068 | 6.6 | 70 791 | 39.1 | 21.9 |
| Henry | 18 837 | 75.5 | 94 400 | 20.9 | 12.5 | 621 | 29.7 | 1.6 | 21 839 | -1.1 | 2 166 | 9.9 | 19 249 | 26.4 | 30.8 |
| Howard | 34 215 | 70.7 | 104 200 | 20.2 | 10.2 | 641 | 31.1 | 1.6 | 35 232 | 0.3 | 3 248 | 9.2 | 34 336 | 28.2 | 29.1 |
| Huntington | 14 237 | 78.8 | 98 800 | 21.6 | 13.1 | 634 | 25.8 | 1.5 | 19 422 | -0.5 | 1 631 | 8.4 | 17 746 | 25.3 | 35.1 |
| Jackson | 16 776 | 73.3 | 117 400 | 21.5 | 11.7 | 666 | 29.3 | 2.4 | 20 971 | -1.4 | 1 518 | 7.2 | 19 565 | 26.4 | 36.9 |
| Jasper | 12 175 | 77.8 | 143 200 | 21.3 | 9.9 | 675 | 24.0 | 2.0 | 15 441 | 0.0 | 1 314 | 8.5 | 15 319 | 25.9 | 36.1 |
| Jay | 8 287 | 77.5 | 78 600 | 19.4 | 12.9 | 526 | 26.7 | 2.5 | 10 874 | -2.1 | 794 | 7.3 | 9 803 | 23.9 | 40.3 |
| Jefferson | 12 725 | 70.7 | 109 900 | 22.4 | 11.3 | 608 | 28.5 | 2.4 | 15 754 | -2.3 | 1 292 | 8.2 | 14 510 | 27.7 | 32.5 |
| Jennings | 10 936 | 74.7 | 94 500 | 21.3 | 13.1 | 683 | 25.9 | 3.5 | 13 386 | -0.7 | 1 349 | 10.1 | 12 003 | 25.1 | 39.8 |
| Johnson | 51 420 | 75.2 | 145 000 | 20.9 | 11.0 | 809 | 27.6 | 1.5 | 73 256 | 0.8 | 5 149 | 7.0 | 68 832 | 35.3 | 23.9 |
| Knox | 14 866 | 69.9 | 84 700 | 19.1 | 12.8 | 567 | 30.0 | 1.5 | 20 069 | -1.4 | 1 348 | 6.7 | 17 375 | 26.8 | 30.4 |
| Kosciusko | 30 390 | 77.5 | 133 100 | 22.0 | 10.7 | 683 | 26.2 | 2.4 | 39 966 | -1.9 | 2 970 | 7.4 | 36 925 | 27.3 | 36.7 |
| LaGrange | 12 081 | 82.0 | 148 900 | 25.4 | 12.0 | 656 | 27.5 | 4.9 | 15 476 | -2.5 | 1 223 | 7.9 | 15 431 | 22.7 | 48.0 |
| Lake | 183 198 | 70.7 | 136 400 | 23.5 | 13.4 | 767 | 32.2 | 2.5 | 220 312 | -0.1 | 20 906 | 9.5 | 215 813 | 29.4 | 27.8 |
| LaPorte | 42 255 | 75.0 | 120 500 | 22.1 | 11.4 | 686 | 30.5 | 2.2 | 49 828 | -0.9 | 4 986 | 10.0 | 48 341 | 26.6 | 30.8 |
| Lawrence | 18 659 | 78.4 | 99 500 | 22.1 | 13.0 | 595 | 28.4 | 2.9 | 21 019 | -1.8 | 2 258 | 10.7 | 19 560 | 27.1 | 31.9 |
| Madison | 51 028 | 72.6 | 95 900 | 21.6 | 12.1 | 663 | 30.5 | 1.6 | 60 424 | -0.5 | 5 871 | 9.7 | 55 956 | 28.5 | 26.8 |
| Marion | 357 586 | 57.9 | 120 700 | 22.3 | 12.0 | 735 | 31.3 | 2.3 | 462 847 | 0.8 | 40 495 | 8.7 | 426 675 | 33.6 | 21.4 |
| Marshall | 17 810 | 76.7 | 124 300 | 21.9 | 12.7 | 646 | 25.8 | 2.4 | 21 788 | -2.2 | 1 930 | 8.9 | 21 798 | 26.5 | 37.2 |
| Martin | 4 017 | 85.5 | 85 400 | 20.1 | 10.1 | 540 | 28.3 | 3.4 | 5 325 | -2.2 | 358 | 6.7 | 4 626 | 26.4 | 39.5 |
| Miami | 13 378 | 75.7 | 86 800 | 22.1 | 12.2 | 607 | 30.6 | 2.1 | 15 309 | -1.6 | 1 583 | 10.3 | 15 285 | 24.6 | 35.3 |
| Monroe | 53 108 | 54.6 | 151 000 | 21.7 | 10.6 | 750 | 42.8 | 1.4 | 70 006 | -0.9 | 4 803 | 6.9 | 64 579 | 43.5 | 16.0 |
| Montgomery | 14 446 | 72.6 | 109 500 | 20.3 | 9.9 | 668 | 28.0 | 1.3 | 18 210 | -1.5 | 1 533 | 8.4 | 17 790 | 26.7 | 36.0 |
| Morgan | 25 357 | 78.6 | 143 600 | 22.1 | 10.4 | 724 | 29.7 | 1.4 | 35 306 | 0.6 | 2 863 | 8.1 | 31 734 | 28.1 | 31.5 |
| Newton | 5 370 | 79.8 | 108 800 | 22.0 | 11.7 | 669 | 28.9 | 1.2 | 6 827 | 0.5 | 666 | 9.8 | 6 517 | 22.2 | 41.6 |
| Noble | 17 723 | 78.1 | 114 500 | 23.3 | 11.7 | 606 | 25.8 | 2.9 | 21 412 | -2.4 | 1 968 | 9.2 | 21 493 | 22.4 | 45.1 |
| Ohio | 2 403 | 73.8 | 132 600 | 20.5 | 11.0 | 666 | 26.2 | 2.0 | 3 071 | -0.6 | 261 | 8.5 | 3 095 | 23.1 | 34.4 |
| Orange | 7 677 | 77.0 | 91 400 | 20.8 | 13.4 | 580 | 29.8 | 2.8 | 9 855 | -3.3 | 937 | 9.5 | 8 212 | 23.8 | 35.4 |
| Owen | 8 494 | 80.9 | 98 500 | 23.1 | 11.0 | 659 | 27.3 | 2.8 | 10 253 | -1.1 | 984 | 9.6 | 9 549 | 24.8 | 39.8 |
| Parke | 6 190 | 83.1 | 91 000 | 22.3 | 10.3 | 532 | 24.6 | 3.7 | 7 574 | -1.4 | 740 | 9.8 | 6 932 | 24.2 | 39.9 |
| Perry | 7 580 | 77.7 | 95 400 | 20.8 | 11.7 | 480 | 26.1 | 1.8 | 9 616 | -0.3 | 759 | 7.9 | 8 591 | 18.4 | 44.3 |

1. Specified owner-occupied units.　2. A value of 9.9 represents 9.9 percent or less.　3. Specified renter-occupied units. A value of 10.0 represents 10 percent or less.　4. Overcrowded or lacking complete plumbing facilities.　5. Percent of civilian labor force.　6. Persons 16 years old and over.

# Table B. States and Counties — Nonfarm Employment and Agriculture

| | Private nonfarm establishments, employment and payroll, 2011 | | | | | | | | | Agriculture, 2007 | | | |
| STATE County | | Employment | | | | | | Annual payroll | | Farms | | Percent with: | |
| | Number of establish-ments | Total | Health care and social assistance | Manufac-turing | Retail trade | Finance and insurance | Professional, scientific, and technical services | Total (mil dol) | Average per employee (dollars) | Number | Fewer than 50 acres | 500 acres or more | Farm operators whose principal occu-pation is farming (percent) |
| | 104 | 105 | 106 | 107 | 108 | 109 | 110 | 111 | 112 | 113 | 114 | 115 | 116 |
| **ILLINOIS—Cont'd** | | | | | | | | | | | | | |
| Winnebago | 6 538 | 116 861 | 20 326 | 23 179 | 14 648 | 4 109 | 3 906 | 4 581 | 39 203 | 860 | 55.3 | 11.9 | 44.2 |
| Woodford | 762 | 8 403 | 1 350 | 2 098 | 905 | 235 | 164 | 295 | 35 109 | 932 | 34.5 | 19.5 | 51.8 |
| **INDIANA** | 143 479 | 2 440 507 | 389 176 | 437 203 | 308 277 | 97 992 | 100 796 | 94 651 | 38 783 | 60 938 | 48.0 | 12.6 | 41.9 |
| Adams | 721 | 11 472 | 1 841 | 3 958 | 1 486 | 283 | 197 | 343 | 29 894 | 1 315 | 61.4 | 5.9 | 35.1 |
| Allen | 8 943 | 159 289 | 30 472 | 24 778 | 19 348 | 8 739 | 7 017 | 6 220 | 39 046 | 1 649 | 57.7 | 7.3 | 36.2 |
| Bartholomew | 1 845 | 40 314 | 4 901 | 9 783 | 4 778 | 974 | 3 152 | 1 677 | 41 597 | 668 | 46.0 | 13.6 | 39.7 |
| Benton | 204 | 1 458 | 180 | 308 | 202 | 101 | 51 | 46 | 31 709 | 399 | 21.3 | 39.1 | 54.6 |
| Blackford | 246 | 2 757 | 429 | 995 | 335 | 98 | 108 | 82 | 29 768 | 250 | 52.8 | 15.6 | 46.0 |
| Boone | 1 368 | 16 984 | 2 328 | 1 466 | 2 256 | 338 | 710 | 618 | 36 396 | 582 | 50.7 | 22.2 | 48.5 |
| Brown | 365 | 1 909 | 235 | D | 315 | 46 | 105 | 46 | 24 133 | 169 | 52.7 | 2.4 | 43.2 |
| Carroll | 395 | 4 191 | 268 | D | 402 | 84 | 103 | 131 | 31 331 | 581 | 43.4 | 18.8 | 48.7 |
| Cass | 748 | 13 017 | 2 885 | 3 898 | 1 598 | 329 | 251 | 386 | 29 668 | 868 | 49.3 | 14.4 | 44.2 |
| Clark | 2 367 | 41 651 | 5 915 | 6 893 | 6 759 | 2 008 | 885 | 1 422 | 34 138 | 585 | 48.9 | 6.8 | 41.5 |
| Clay | 478 | 5 330 | 607 | 1 954 | 833 | D | 95 | 159 | 29 876 | 666 | 51.1 | 12.5 | 46.4 |
| Clinton | 593 | 8 562 | 1 204 | 3 571 | 1 038 | D | 121 | 280 | 32 672 | 693 | 46.2 | 23.1 | 49.1 |
| Crawford | 133 | 1 321 | D | D | 236 | D | D | 36 | 27 290 | 354 | 29.1 | 2.8 | 28.0 |
| Daviess | 823 | 9 794 | 1 439 | 1 900 | 1 517 | 252 | 669 | 292 | 29 832 | 969 | 51.1 | 10.2 | 35.4 |
| Dearborn | 956 | 13 719 | 2 404 | 1 434 | 2 087 | 369 | 276 | 424 | 30 876 | 564 | 36.3 | 3.2 | 37.6 |
| Decatur | 622 | 9 794 | 994 | 3 395 | 1 251 | D | 142 | 351 | 35 802 | 639 | 36.0 | 20.7 | 54.3 |
| DeKalb | 978 | 17 014 | 1 590 | 7 656 | 1 578 | 367 | 493 | 661 | 38 869 | 1 144 | 55.4 | 5.9 | 27.0 |
| Delaware | 2 396 | 36 601 | 9 247 | 3 622 | 6 198 | 2 088 | 1 425 | 1 156 | 31 582 | 659 | 58.0 | 11.1 | 48.1 |
| Dubois | 1 285 | 24 980 | 3 063 | 9 416 | 3 076 | 546 | 556 | 916 | 36 665 | 761 | 33.0 | 12.4 | 43.5 |
| Elkhart | 4 830 | 102 109 | 9 733 | 49 226 | 8 774 | 1 837 | 1 925 | 3 669 | 35 932 | 1 617 | 64.1 | 4.5 | 37.3 |
| Fayette | 459 | 5 188 | 1 531 | 951 | 905 | 142 | 233 | 173 | 33 437 | 391 | 40.2 | 14.1 | 41.9 |
| Floyd | 1 742 | 25 761 | 5 287 | 5 007 | 3 171 | 740 | 1 137 | 840 | 32 601 | 279 | 58.1 | 2.9 | 33.7 |
| Fountain | 322 | 4 687 | D | D | 575 | D | 74 | 141 | 30 135 | 503 | 39.8 | 19.3 | 48.5 |
| Franklin | 439 | 5 086 | 1 086 | 583 | 711 | 163 | 54 | 148 | 29 025 | 723 | 30.8 | 7.3 | 44.0 |
| Fulton | 450 | 5 390 | 751 | 1 892 | 794 | 169 | D | 180 | 33 449 | 639 | 44.6 | 16.3 | 46.5 |
| Gibson | 711 | 16 698 | 1 696 | 6 749 | 1 611 | 175 | 322 | 713 | 42 672 | 590 | 37.5 | 21.5 | 50.0 |
| Grant | 1 366 | 26 001 | 5 232 | 4 352 | 3 041 | 609 | 393 | 875 | 33 653 | 524 | 41.8 | 24.2 | 46.6 |
| Greene | 595 | 5 177 | 1 041 | 355 | 1 157 | D | D | 147 | 28 420 | 799 | 40.8 | 8.3 | 44.8 |
| Hamilton | 7 504 | 101 163 | 14 877 | 4 633 | 14 118 | 11 854 | 6 818 | 4 472 | 44 205 | 636 | 65.7 | 8.6 | 42.8 |
| Hancock | 1 364 | 16 545 | 2 464 | 2 711 | 2 097 | 365 | 1 827 | 595 | 35 974 | 686 | 59.5 | 13.0 | 44.6 |
| Harrison | 660 | 8 812 | 1 414 | 1 427 | 1 444 | 289 | 186 | 265 | 30 061 | 1 125 | 47.7 | 5.1 | 38.1 |
| Hendricks | 2 839 | 47 014 | 6 328 | 3 027 | 8 642 | 825 | 1 148 | 1 492 | 31 731 | 714 | 59.8 | 9.4 | 39.6 |
| Henry | 820 | 10 420 | 2 653 | 1 669 | 1 760 | 364 | 191 | 311 | 29 843 | 781 | 54.7 | 11.8 | 38.0 |
| Howard | 1 790 | 28 734 | 5 562 | 7 444 | 4 842 | 657 | 737 | 1 192 | 41 470 | 601 | 48.1 | 16.5 | 52.4 |
| Huntington | 876 | 12 824 | 1 799 | 3 402 | 1 292 | 383 | 192 | 388 | 30 221 | 766 | 53.7 | 14.5 | 35.4 |
| Jackson | 1 016 | 17 669 | 2 326 | 5 590 | 2 273 | 406 | 294 | 610 | 34 521 | 827 | 40.1 | 15.8 | 44.0 |
| Jasper | 725 | 8 353 | 1 560 | 1 283 | 1 234 | 259 | 196 | 280 | 33 464 | 734 | 34.9 | 29.6 | 49.7 |
| Jay | 411 | 6 505 | 940 | 3 013 | 617 | 164 | 85 | 198 | 30 497 | 881 | 49.1 | 12.0 | 37.0 |
| Jefferson | 687 | 10 479 | 2 056 | 2 594 | 1 619 | 232 | 239 | 361 | 34 419 | 694 | 45.7 | 5.2 | 36.5 |
| Jennings | 407 | 6 150 | 920 | 1 725 | 767 | D | 77 | 211 | 34 301 | 613 | 46.5 | 11.6 | 40.3 |
| Johnson | 2 969 | 39 415 | 5 797 | 4 641 | 8 552 | 1 224 | 1 180 | 1 244 | 31 571 | 585 | 59.1 | 14.0 | 45.0 |
| Knox | 958 | 13 300 | 3 311 | 1 579 | 2 143 | 451 | 222 | 418 | 31 454 | 568 | 33.8 | 27.8 | 59.0 |
| Kosciusko | 1 885 | 33 387 | 3 556 | 13 507 | 3 492 | 767 | D | 1 401 | 41 975 | 1 235 | 54.5 | 9.5 | 37.8 |
| LaGrange | 766 | 9 909 | 888 | 4 844 | 1 177 | 213 | 164 | 339 | 34 163 | 1 507 | 56.2 | 4.3 | 37.6 |
| Lake | 9 840 | 163 902 | 33 139 | 23 016 | 23 373 | 4 254 | 6 056 | 6 656 | 40 611 | 441 | 55.3 | 16.8 | 48.1 |
| LaPorte | 2 387 | 33 833 | 5 079 | 7 267 | 5 678 | 802 | 963 | 1 104 | 32 623 | 869 | 51.6 | 18.1 | 44.3 |
| Lawrence | 868 | 11 216 | 2 559 | 1 910 | 2 076 | 327 | 681 | 357 | 31 872 | 820 | 40.1 | 6.5 | 39.4 |
| Madison | 2 295 | 33 864 | 6 684 | 2 972 | 4 911 | 1 132 | 879 | 1 049 | 30 965 | 870 | 55.3 | 14.3 | 49.8 |
| Marion | 22 929 | 492 783 | 79 827 | 43 364 | 47 332 | 27 413 | 33 890 | 24 053 | 48 811 | 263 | 82.1 | 2.3 | 42.2 |
| Marshall | 1 047 | 15 724 | 1 743 | 5 472 | 2 013 | 365 | 336 | 508 | 32 313 | 866 | 44.3 | 10.7 | 42.3 |
| Martin | 191 | 2 174 | 109 | 418 | 342 | 51 | 553 | 67 | 30 773 | 278 | 39.9 | 11.2 | 37.8 |
| Miami | 560 | 6 762 | 1 142 | 1 835 | 846 | 300 | 84 | 196 | 29 011 | 682 | 44.4 | 15.5 | 40.6 |
| Monroe | 2 963 | 47 095 | 8 378 | D | 7 220 | 1 385 | 2 041 | 1 552 | 32 962 | 481 | 49.1 | 3.7 | 36.4 |
| Montgomery | 850 | 12 800 | 1 343 | 5 100 | 1 643 | 298 | 180 | 444 | 34 654 | 745 | 42.0 | 23.2 | 48.3 |
| Morgan | 1 165 | 11 252 | 2 148 | 1 535 | 2 268 | 403 | 417 | 338 | 30 058 | 642 | 60.7 | 7.8 | 36.3 |
| Newton | 264 | 2 365 | 152 | 718 | 310 | 117 | D | 79 | 33 366 | 434 | 39.2 | 25.6 | 47.0 |
| Noble | 893 | 15 020 | 1 347 | 7 940 | 1 397 | 253 | 208 | 480 | 31 947 | 1 196 | 56.0 | 6.6 | 31.8 |
| Ohio | 85 | 1 263 | 103 | D | 108 | 32 | D | 39 | 31 086 | 179 | 39.1 | 2.2 | 31.8 |
| Orange | 370 | 6 794 | 840 | 1 184 | 638 | 94 | D | 215 | 31 616 | 474 | 35.9 | 7.4 | 31.9 |
| Owen | 296 | 3 692 | 338 | 1 765 | 371 | 128 | 67 | 103 | 27 779 | 570 | 42.3 | 5.6 | 38.9 |
| Parke | 254 | 2 058 | 396 | 442 | 349 | D | D | 58 | 28 281 | 477 | 29.8 | 17.6 | 48.8 |
| Perry | 373 | 5 182 | 837 | 2 025 | 776 | 105 | 81 | 176 | 33 939 | 425 | 23.8 | 5.4 | 40.0 |

| | Land in farms | | | | Value of land and buildings (dollars) | | Value of machinery and equipment, average per farm (dollars) | Value of products sold | | | | Percent of farms with sales of: | | Government payments | |
|---|---|---|---|---|---|---|---|---|---|---|---|---|---|---|---|
| | | | Acres | | | | | | | Percent from: | | | | | |
| STATE County | Acreage (1,000) | Percent change, 2002–2007 | Average size of farm | Total irrigated (1,000) | Total cropland (1,000) | Average per farm | Average per acre | | Total (mil dol) | Average per farm (dollars) | Crops | Live-stock and poultry products | $10,000 or more | $100,000 or more | Total ($1,000) | Percent of farms |
| | 117 | 118 | 119 | 120 | 121 | 122 | 123 | 124 | 125 | 126 | 127 | 128 | 129 | 130 | 131 | 132 |

| | | | | | | | | | | | | | | | | |
|---|---|---|---|---|---|---|---|---|---|---|---|---|---|---|---|---|
| ILLINOIS—Cont'd | | | | | | | | | | | | | | | | |
| Winnebago | 184 | -3.7 | 214 | 0.4 | 162.6 | 941 759 | 4 411 | 89 695 | 89.9 | 104 542 | 81.9 | 18.1 | 40.7 | 20.6 | 4 068 | 56.9 |
| Woodford | 288 | -7.1 | 309 | 0.8 | 267.3 | 1 311 286 | 4 238 | 134 004 | 177.5 | 190 492 | 80.6 | 19.4 | 62.1 | 38.2 | 5 461 | 78.6 |
| INDIANA | 14 773 | -1.9 | 242 | 397.1 | 12 716.0 | 868 699 | 3 583 | 103 427 | 8 271.3 | 135 733 | 64.3 | 35.7 | 45.6 | 20.8 | 260 809 | 58.9 |
| Adams | 182 | -20.5 | 139 | 0.2 | 165.8 | 602 154 | 4 339 | 83 042 | 158.8 | 120 760 | 38.9 | 61.1 | 52.5 | 24.6 | 3 446 | 49.4 |
| Allen | 254 | -10.6 | 154 | 0.7 | 230.4 | 620 138 | 4 024 | 78 985 | 117.5 | 71 264 | 76.3 | 23.7 | 43.0 | 14.9 | 5 533 | 61.3 |
| Bartholomew | 166 | 3.1 | 249 | 10.2 | 148.3 | 945 855 | 3 798 | 108 015 | 69.5 | 104 009 | 87.5 | 12.5 | 48.4 | 19.3 | 3 817 | 64.7 |
| Benton | 271 | 9.3 | 679 | 4.0 | 262.6 | 2 297 119 | 3 384 | 232 443 | 138.4 | 346 900 | 94.1 | 5.9 | 81.7 | 50.6 | 5 606 | 91.5 |
| Blackford | 85 | -12.4 | 339 | 0.0 | 77.1 | 928 317 | 2 742 | 118 784 | 38.6 | 154 275 | 79.5 | 20.5 | 45.2 | 22.4 | 1 478 | 70.0 |
| Boone | 223 | -1.3 | 383 | 1.0 | 210.5 | 1 495 547 | 3 908 | 143 000 | 117.1 | 201 175 | 84.8 | 15.2 | 53.4 | 29.7 | 3 717 | 57.6 |
| Brown | 17 | -15.0 | 100 | 0.1 | 8.2 | 431 476 | 4 300 | 41 953 | 2.5 | 14 757 | D | D | 17.2 | 1.2 | 110 | 25.4 |
| Carroll | 192 | -5.0 | 331 | 0.4 | 178.2 | 1 364 641 | 4 122 | 151 749 | 151.4 | 260 518 | 56.1 | 43.9 | 60.9 | 34.8 | 4 118 | 68.2 |
| Cass | 228 | 9.6 | 263 | 3.1 | 208.5 | 939 498 | 3 574 | 113 562 | 131.4 | 151 403 | 75.2 | 24.8 | 49.0 | 23.8 | 4 632 | 74.3 |
| Clark | 87 | -13.9 | 148 | 0.4 | 61.0 | 530 185 | 3 579 | 65 566 | 23.7 | 40 597 | 73.8 | 26.2 | 39.8 | 9.7 | 1 078 | 52.1 |
| Clay | 158 | 3.9 | 237 | 0.1 | 134.1 | 746 315 | 3 155 | 100 679 | 63.9 | 95 878 | 88.1 | 11.9 | 45.6 | 20.0 | 2 706 | 74.8 |
| Clinton | 255 | 4.1 | 368 | 0.8 | 244.8 | 1 523 643 | 4 136 | 168 228 | 174.4 | 251 720 | 67.8 | 32.2 | 59.3 | 34.8 | 5 321 | 63.1 |
| Crawford | 45 | -18.2 | 128 | 0.0 | 17.1 | 372 429 | 2 904 | 35 406 | 4.7 | 13 297 | 34.7 | 65.3 | 20.9 | 2.0 | 252 | 37.9 |
| Daviess | 199 | -3.9 | 206 | 3.7 | 173.8 | 748 465 | 3 638 | 99 028 | 166.8 | 172 137 | 44.0 | 56.0 | 50.6 | 21.4 | 3 049 | 39.5 |
| Dearborn | 66 | -10.8 | 117 | 0.1 | 35.8 | 448 519 | 3 843 | 44 659 | 11.5 | 20 391 | 66.9 | 33.1 | 26.1 | 5.5 | 558 | 41.7 |
| Decatur | 205 | -1.0 | 320 | D | 183.7 | 1 141 402 | 3 563 | 147 662 | 153.3 | 239 871 | 45.7 | 54.3 | 57.9 | 34.7 | 4 444 | 65.3 |
| DeKalb | 161 | -10.1 | 140 | 0.8 | 135.2 | 509 248 | 3 626 | 53 011 | 62.4 | 54 557 | 69.3 | 30.7 | 29.7 | 9.8 | 4 577 | 76.7 |
| Delaware | 154 | -18.9 | 234 | 0.5 | 143.4 | 824 551 | 3 518 | 95 643 | 68.6 | 104 109 | 88.2 | 11.8 | 44.6 | 18.7 | 2 670 | 58.4 |
| Dubois | 182 | -3.7 | 239 | 0.4 | 135.2 | 773 917 | 3 233 | 107 302 | 200.7 | 263 763 | 22.1 | 77.9 | 54.1 | 26.9 | 2 992 | 64.3 |
| Elkhart | 163 | -18.9 | 101 | 22.0 | 141.6 | 560 281 | 5 548 | 72 668 | 205.8 | 127 245 | 26.1 | 73.9 | 49.7 | 26.2 | 1 909 | 26.3 |
| Fayette | 93 | -13.1 | 237 | 0.0 | 75.8 | 773 927 | 3 271 | 95 706 | 34.2 | 87 377 | 80.3 | 19.7 | 48.8 | 21.2 | 1 777 | 63.4 |
| Floyd | 24 | 0.0 | 86 | 0.0 | 13.8 | 398 364 | 4 632 | 45 785 | 4.8 | 17 050 | D | D | 25.4 | 3.9 | 190 | 30.1 |
| Fountain | 189 | -7.8 | 375 | D | 163.1 | 1 294 404 | 3 450 | 124 401 | 76.5 | 152 136 | 93.3 | 6.7 | 52.1 | 24.5 | 3 121 | 64.0 |
| Franklin | 126 | -9.4 | 175 | 0.1 | 85.4 | 642 318 | 3 676 | 74 735 | 35.7 | 49 364 | 65.7 | 34.3 | 42.2 | 13.3 | 2 070 | 60.6 |
| Fulton | 185 | -4.1 | 289 | 19.6 | 165.9 | 969 826 | 3 353 | 125 001 | 88.9 | 139 054 | 77.6 | 22.4 | 50.2 | 26.3 | 3 346 | 67.9 |
| Gibson | 231 | 9.5 | 392 | 4.9 | 209.3 | 1 233 872 | 3 150 | 154 398 | 105.3 | 178 404 | 87.8 | 12.2 | 61.0 | 31.7 | 3 902 | 74.4 |
| Grant | 202 | 2.0 | 386 | D | 191.1 | 1 318 126 | 3 417 | 161 000 | 79.3 | 151 261 | 88.3 | 11.7 | 52.9 | 30.0 | 3 292 | 69.5 |
| Greene | 170 | -0.6 | 212 | 1.3 | 119.1 | 617 546 | 2 907 | 84 421 | 78.8 | 98 579 | 49.3 | 50.7 | 40.6 | 10.9 | 2 288 | 40.4 |
| Hamilton | 124 | -11.4 | 194 | 1.9 | 114.3 | 883 288 | 4 545 | 95 016 | 115.0 | 180 780 | 96.6 | 3.4 | 39.3 | 16.7 | 1 865 | 38.7 |
| Hancock | 172 | 6.2 | 250 | 0.2 | 159.3 | 1 026 073 | 4 100 | 115 124 | 86.8 | 126 545 | 80.5 | 19.5 | 47.1 | 17.2 | 2 924 | 54.5 |
| Harrison | 155 | -3.1 | 138 | 0.1 | 99.1 | 447 746 | 3 250 | 64 697 | 50.2 | 44 587 | 46.3 | 53.7 | 29.9 | 7.9 | 2 201 | 38.4 |
| Hendricks | 172 | -5.5 | 241 | 0.0 | 157.6 | 989 541 | 4 114 | 95 291 | 74.0 | 103 680 | 90.5 | 9.5 | 40.3 | 16.0 | 2 557 | 48.7 |
| Henry | 174 | 0.6 | 223 | D | 157.5 | 770 537 | 3 451 | 99 450 | 86.3 | 110 517 | 75.7 | 24.3 | 43.0 | 18.2 | 3 109 | 58.0 |
| Howard | 162 | 3.8 | 270 | 0.1 | 151.6 | 1 119 988 | 4 148 | 134 320 | 95.6 | 159 044 | 70.0 | 30.0 | 56.2 | 28.1 | 3 371 | 68.6 |
| Huntington | 199 | -0.5 | 260 | 0.3 | 185.0 | 899 850 | 3 463 | 128 411 | 122.4 | 159 804 | 60.5 | 39.5 | 46.7 | 21.5 | 3 716 | 71.8 |
| Jackson | 209 | 1.0 | 253 | 2.0 | 165.5 | 760 401 | 3 005 | 138 912 | 196.9 | 238 141 | 25.1 | 74.9 | 47.3 | 20.0 | 3 979 | 65.2 |
| Jasper | 340 | 21.4 | 464 | 22.6 | 315.6 | 1 550 715 | 3 344 | 181 318 | 293.5 | 399 924 | 50.2 | 49.8 | 67.0 | 42.9 | 5 965 | 74.0 |
| Jay | 197 | 1.0 | 224 | D | 176.8 | 889 772 | 3 975 | 105 379 | 178.7 | 202 797 | 35.8 | 64.2 | 49.6 | 24.6 | 4 112 | 71.9 |
| Jefferson | 103 | -5.5 | 148 | 0.0 | 67.1 | 502 997 | 3 405 | 63 024 | 27.0 | 38 922 | 65.7 | 34.3 | 27.4 | 6.8 | 1 270 | 47.8 |
| Jennings | 138 | -3.5 | 226 | 0.6 | 105.1 | 719 690 | 3 189 | 98 904 | 63.1 | 102 912 | 56.8 | 43.2 | 36.5 | 13.1 | 2 082 | 57.1 |
| Johnson | 142 | 5.2 | 243 | 2.1 | 128.9 | 1 082 177 | 4 453 | 119 630 | 69.8 | 119 297 | 85.3 | 14.7 | 41.0 | 20.7 | 2 754 | 48.7 |
| Knox | 327 | 9.0 | 576 | 30.2 | 308.1 | 1 991 953 | 3 457 | 203 301 | 192.0 | 338 049 | 85.4 | 14.6 | 65.5 | 39.1 | 5 634 | 75.4 |
| Kosciusko | 251 | -4.2 | 204 | 28.0 | 218.7 | 759 172 | 3 730 | 92 697 | 196.1 | 158 823 | 43.9 | 56.1 | 42.8 | 19.9 | 4 684 | 55.4 |
| LaGrange | 162 | -14.3 | 107 | 24.7 | 127.1 | 546 508 | 5 093 | 61 006 | 171.2 | 113 617 | 26.1 | 73.9 | 53.6 | 22.2 | 1 955 | 24.5 |
| Lake | 128 | 0.0 | 291 | 9.7 | 121.4 | 1 153 687 | 3 961 | 111 625 | 62.1 | 140 869 | 90.9 | 9.1 | 48.1 | 25.4 | 2 406 | 55.3 |
| LaPorte | 256 | 5.3 | 295 | 47.8 | 231.9 | 1 077 366 | 3 655 | 131 009 | 152.3 | 175 238 | 67.4 | 32.6 | 49.0 | 26.6 | 5 128 | 59.7 |
| Lawrence | 135 | -8.2 | 164 | 0.3 | 68.1 | 460 299 | 2 803 | 52 993 | 25.9 | 31 596 | 47.1 | 52.9 | 29.6 | 5.5 | 1 597 | 43.8 |
| Madison | 217 | -11.1 | 250 | 1.5 | 204.1 | 933 308 | 3 736 | 115 455 | 115.5 | 132 730 | 87.5 | 12.5 | 50.9 | 21.6 | 4 441 | 61.0 |
| Marion | 17 | -29.2 | 66 | 0.4 | 14.2 | 384 823 | 5 873 | 52 273 | 22.5 | 85 586 | D | D | 24.7 | 9.5 | 210 | 18.6 |
| Marshall | 179 | -12.3 | 207 | 8.6 | 156.0 | 735 013 | 3 556 | 89 027 | 97.0 | 112 048 | 63.6 | 36.4 | 49.4 | 21.6 | 3 058 | 57.5 |
| Martin | 61 | -4.7 | 221 | D | 40.2 | 712 748 | 3 231 | 83 254 | 54.5 | 195 935 | 25.7 | 74.3 | 41.7 | 20.5 | 737 | 39.6 |
| Miami | 178 | -6.8 | 261 | 2.0 | 156.3 | 874 902 | 3 352 | 101 607 | 104.0 | 152 482 | 58.7 | 41.3 | 47.9 | 23.3 | 3 164 | 72.7 |
| Monroe | 54 | -11.5 | 111 | 0.1 | 27.1 | 405 291 | 3 641 | 56 066 | 12.0 | 24 886 | 79.5 | 20.5 | 28.9 | 4.8 | 555 | 30.8 |
| Montgomery | 301 | 10.3 | 404 | 1.6 | 271.1 | 1 518 713 | 3 755 | 140 585 | 165.4 | 221 990 | 79.9 | 20.1 | 57.2 | 31.0 | 5 582 | 71.1 |
| Morgan | 114 | 1.8 | 178 | 0.0 | 93.0 | 694 578 | 3 907 | 83 852 | 56.5 | 87 961 | 84.1 | 15.9 | 31.5 | 13.9 | 1 621 | 45.3 |
| Newton | 190 | 4.4 | 439 | 5.7 | 176.3 | 1 583 756 | 3 609 | 203 045 | 193.4 | 445 553 | 41.7 | 58.3 | 57.8 | 35.7 | 3 540 | 80.0 |
| Noble | 160 | -7.5 | 134 | 8.4 | 130.1 | 494 049 | 3 696 | 65 093 | 80.0 | 66 869 | 55.6 | 44.4 | 36.5 | 12.0 | 3 193 | 63.9 |
| Ohio | 22 | -8.3 | 120 | 0.2 | 10.2 | 428 904 | 3 571 | 58 017 | 3.1 | 17 485 | 64.6 | 35.4 | 21.8 | 3.9 | 134 | 36.3 |
| Orange | 97 | -8.5 | 206 | D | 58.8 | 597 393 | 2 907 | 82 157 | 40.4 | 85 333 | 42.4 | 57.6 | 25.9 | 7.2 | 1 461 | 51.3 |
| Owen | 88 | -11.1 | 154 | 0.1 | 53.5 | 494 654 | 3 211 | 49 358 | 18.2 | 31 965 | 81.8 | 18.2 | 30.7 | 6.5 | 982 | 49.3 |
| Parke | 177 | 7.3 | 372 | 1.6 | 131.6 | 1 151 369 | 3 097 | 129 596 | 65.6 | 137 549 | 85.8 | 14.2 | 50.5 | 29.4 | 2 514 | 61.8 |
| Perry | 70 | -7.9 | 166 | 0.0 | 36.0 | 441 734 | 2 666 | 67 079 | 24.3 | 57 076 | 34.0 | 66.0 | 36.9 | 12.7 | 559 | 44.0 |

**Water Use, Wholesale Trade, Retail Trade, and Real Estate**

| STATE County | Water use, 2005 | | Wholesale trade,[1] 2007 | | | | Retail trade,[2] 2007 | | | | Real estate and rental and leasing,[2] 2007 | | | |
|---|---|---|---|---|---|---|---|---|---|---|---|---|---|---|
| | Total water withdrawn (mil gal/day) | Gallons withdrawn per person | Number of establishments | Number of employees | Sales (mil dol) | Annual payroll (mil dol) | Number of establishments | Number of employees | Sales (mil dol) | Annual payroll (mil dol) | Number of establishments | Number of employees | Receipts (mil dol) | Annual payroll (mil dol) |
| | 133 | 134 | 135 | 136 | 137 | 138 | 139 | 140 | 141 | 142 | 143 | 144 | 145 | 146 |
| ILLINOIS—Cont'd | | | | | | | | | | | | | | |
| Winnebago | 43.9 | 152 | 363 | 4 931 | 2 624.7 | 209.7 | 1 051 | 16 095 | 3 852.0 | 346.4 | 245 | 1 585 | 211.3 | 46.2 |
| Woodford | 14.2 | 378 | 48 | D | D | D | 102 | 1 089 | 278.3 | 21.6 | 30 | D | D | D |
| INDIANA | 9 340.1 | 1 489 | 6 756 | 97 219 | 67 634.9 | 4 295.6 | 23 692 | 333 172 | 78 745.6 | 7 123.1 | 6 389 | 34 272 | 5 448.1 | 1 061.6 |
| Adams | 7.8 | 230 | 36 | D | D | D | 150 | 1 672 | 369.9 | 32.3 | 30 | 99 | 8.0 | 2.3 |
| Allen | 55.1 | 160 | 548 | D | D | D | 1 345 | 21 214 | 4 774.2 | 440.3 | 410 | 1 913 | 323.3 | 54.3 |
| Bartholomew | 21.2 | 289 | 80 | 1 012 | 747.3 | 50.5 | 375 | 5 133 | 1 075.2 | 106.7 | 74 | 319 | 50.1 | 8.9 |
| Benton | 0.9 | 94 | 16 | D | D | D | 43 | 241 | 50.9 | 4.0 | 3 | 6 | 0.3 | 0.2 |
| Blackford | 2.2 | 159 | 11 | 112 | 158.9 | 3.0 | 51 | 435 | 97.9 | 9.3 | 12 | 38 | 2.9 | 0.6 |
| Boone | 4.8 | 92 | 58 | 532 | 386.4 | 22.8 | 176 | 1 769 | 484.5 | 37.7 | 47 | 110 | 20.7 | 3.1 |
| Brown | 0.3 | 21 | 8 | 64 | 4.3 | 1.0 | 93 | 467 | 61.5 | 7.1 | 17 | 47 | 6.0 | 1.6 |
| Carroll | 7.7 | 377 | 21 | D | D | D | 58 | 529 | 102.1 | 8.4 | 14 | 20 | 4.6 | 1.0 |
| Cass | 33.6 | 838 | 42 | 458 | 439.0 | 14.8 | 134 | 1 561 | 340.9 | 34.6 | 21 | 72 | 7.5 | 1.3 |
| Clark | 24.1 | 237 | 101 | 1 375 | 1 062.0 | 67.1 | 446 | 7 214 | 1 729.5 | 157.4 | 100 | 593 | 91.4 | 15.1 |
| Clay | 1.6 | 59 | 15 | D | D | D | 96 | 1 040 | 312.4 | 20.8 | 13 | 41 | 4.7 | 0.5 |
| Clinton | 6.4 | 188 | 29 | D | D | D | 115 | 1 009 | 223.6 | 22.1 | 19 | 90 | 5.9 | 1.5 |
| Crawford | 4.9 | 433 | 2 | D | D | D | 32 | 189 | 40.7 | 3.5 | 6 | D | D | D |
| Daviess | 7.1 | 234 | 28 | 282 | 153.7 | 10.3 | 121 | 1 563 | 381.5 | 33.9 | 16 | 57 | 6.2 | 1.0 |
| Dearborn | 749.2 | 15 263 | 32 | D | D | D | 151 | 1 866 | 509.7 | 43.3 | 39 | 212 | 29.7 | 5.6 |
| Decatur | 5.1 | 203 | 32 | D | D | D | 119 | 1 403 | 315.0 | 29.7 | 21 | 60 | 8.7 | 1.6 |
| DeKalb | 10.0 | 241 | 45 | D | D | D | 147 | 1 744 | 408.9 | 36.8 | 33 | 184 | 18.3 | 5.8 |
| Delaware | 17.7 | 152 | 97 | 984 | 424.1 | 31.6 | 484 | 6 563 | 1 516.8 | 130.8 | 113 | 575 | 89.0 | 17.2 |
| Dubois | 7.3 | 177 | 64 | 846 | 530.6 | 33.3 | 242 | 3 215 | 763.4 | 74.3 | 38 | D | D | D |
| Elkhart | 36.5 | 187 | 371 | 6 096 | 3 231.4 | 255.2 | 727 | 9 710 | 2 416.9 | 219.0 | 180 | 813 | 109.4 | 20.4 |
| Fayette | 3.3 | 134 | 14 | 126 | 85.9 | 5.7 | 84 | 1 018 | 208.9 | 19.7 | 21 | 61 | 7.2 | 1.2 |
| Floyd | 268.5 | 3 729 | 78 | 873 | 1 420.5 | 33.3 | 221 | 3 457 | 787.4 | 71.9 | 81 | 351 | 43.9 | 7.4 |
| Fountain | 2.2 | 125 | 14 | 105 | 124.8 | 3.6 | 72 | 672 | 142.5 | 10.8 | 8 | 29 | 0.9 | 0.3 |
| Franklin | 4.2 | 180 | 8 | 61 | 18.6 | 2.1 | 79 | 614 | 171.3 | 11.2 | 8 | 36 | 2.5 | 0.5 |
| Fulton | 15.1 | 729 | 15 | 125 | 62.1 | 4.1 | 82 | 925 | 200.8 | 17.6 | 19 | 66 | 3.5 | 0.9 |
| Gibson | 52.1 | 1 558 | 20 | D | D | D | 133 | 1 597 | 442.6 | 30.4 | 17 | 58 | 10.3 | 1.4 |
| Grant | 12.8 | 181 | 44 | D | D | D | 282 | 3 380 | 765.8 | 69.7 | 60 | 217 | 23.2 | 5.1 |
| Greene | 4.8 | 144 | 15 | D | D | D | 118 | 1 087 | 226.1 | 18.9 | 14 | 54 | 2.4 | 0.5 |
| Hamilton | 78.5 | 326 | 346 | 4 043 | 2 779.5 | 231.5 | 821 | 14 029 | 3 295.4 | 323.6 | 367 | 2 871 | 558.5 | 129.1 |
| Hancock | 7.1 | 112 | 51 | 826 | 519.9 | 32.6 | 165 | 2 012 | 568.5 | 47.9 | 43 | 137 | 22.1 | 3.1 |
| Harrison | 3.6 | 98 | 27 | 296 | 98.6 | 8.7 | 134 | 1 421 | 400.9 | 32.3 | 19 | 61 | 7.4 | 1.0 |
| Hendricks | 9.7 | 76 | 103 | 2 465 | 2 520.7 | 103.1 | 437 | 8 440 | 2 088.7 | 176.6 | 110 | 350 | 54.5 | 8.4 |
| Henry | 6.7 | 142 | 23 | 280 | 180.2 | 13.3 | 167 | 1 861 | 455.0 | 41.3 | 34 | 83 | 8.2 | 1.5 |
| Howard | 21.0 | 247 | 62 | 510 | 319.5 | 24.1 | 374 | 5 240 | 1 194.7 | 105.6 | 83 | 320 | 47.7 | 7.5 |
| Huntington | 5.4 | 141 | 38 | D | D | D | 136 | 1 539 | 328.0 | 29.2 | 32 | 109 | 8.4 | 1.6 |
| Jackson | 8.3 | 197 | 42 | D | D | D | 199 | 2 193 | 529.5 | 49.2 | 43 | 171 | 20.0 | 3.1 |
| Jasper | 53.8 | 1 687 | 37 | 234 | 163.4 | 9.8 | 127 | 1 425 | 405.5 | 28.1 | 26 | 112 | 36.5 | 3.3 |
| Jay | 4.1 | 190 | 21 | 270 | 413.7 | 8.3 | 68 | 690 | 139.5 | 14.7 | 8 | 20 | 1.8 | 0.4 |
| Jefferson | 1 287.6 | 39 705 | 14 | D | D | D | 162 | 1 754 | 382.7 | 37.2 | 38 | 126 | 15.8 | 2.8 |
| Jennings | 3.6 | 125 | 15 | D | D | D | 80 | 776 | 223.8 | 18.0 | 13 | 26 | 3.6 | 0.8 |
| Johnson | 15.5 | 121 | 108 | 1 181 | 682.3 | 52.8 | 513 | 9 056 | 2 072.9 | 189.7 | 153 | 532 | 90.4 | 13.0 |
| Knox | 54.5 | 1 421 | 59 | 618 | 321.5 | 21.7 | 192 | 2 194 | 471.8 | 44.8 | 39 | 163 | 17.1 | 3.1 |
| Kosciusko | 26.4 | 347 | 87 | D | D | D | 314 | 3 780 | 794.9 | 80.9 | 80 | 196 | 49.4 | 6.3 |
| LaGrange | 14.7 | 400 | 33 | 318 | 104.6 | 7.3 | 166 | 1 212 | 276.9 | 25.1 | 24 | 65 | 9.0 | 1.1 |
| Lake | 1 720.7 | 3 488 | 396 | 5 198 | 3 348.8 | 254.9 | 1 715 | 26 506 | 7 102.4 | 559.8 | 441 | 2 376 | 328.0 | 64.1 |
| LaPorte | 37.3 | 338 | 123 | 1 446 | 856.2 | 54.1 | 495 | 6 054 | 1 363.6 | 114.9 | 102 | 438 | 60.4 | 11.1 |
| Lawrence | 6.2 | 133 | 22 | D | D | D | 169 | 2 041 | 481.6 | 44.7 | 29 | 85 | 12.5 | 1.9 |
| Madison | 15.6 | 119 | 75 | 1 113 | 574.2 | 44.1 | 431 | 5 542 | 1 234.9 | 108.0 | 103 | 434 | 61.5 | 10.2 |
| Marion | 311.2 | 360 | 1 358 | 25 490 | 15 780.3 | 1 254.1 | 3 291 | 53 214 | 12 951.3 | 1 278.7 | 1 297 | 10 411 | 1 935.6 | 390.8 |
| Marshall | 7.7 | 163 | 65 | D | D | D | 191 | 2 164 | 551.0 | 41.0 | 34 | 98 | 11.0 | 1.9 |
| Martin | 1.6 | 153 | 5 | 39 | 51.1 | 1.0 | 34 | 361 | 81.2 | 6.2 | 6 | 14 | 1.7 | 0.2 |
| Miami | 35.1 | 986 | 30 | D | D | D | 109 | 936 | 235.4 | 19.8 | 30 | 103 | 6.8 | 1.8 |
| Monroe | 17.0 | 140 | 83 | 1 331 | 683.2 | 47.0 | 508 | 7 479 | 1 530.8 | 146.7 | 187 | 1 133 | 144.0 | 29.5 |
| Montgomery | 5.7 | 149 | 43 | 338 | 368.6 | 15.1 | 147 | 1 759 | 429.2 | 34.9 | 28 | 113 | 11.8 | 2.0 |
| Morgan | 224.2 | 3 213 | 44 | 310 | 185.0 | 13.6 | 212 | 2 578 | 586.9 | 54.2 | 62 | 179 | 21.7 | 3.7 |
| Newton | 7.4 | 514 | 17 | 128 | 121.6 | 5.7 | 55 | 391 | 96.7 | 7.5 | 10 | 25 | 2.5 | 0.4 |
| Noble | 10.3 | 218 | 36 | D | D | D | 149 | 1 572 | 357.3 | 31.6 | 41 | 121 | 13.2 | 2.3 |
| Ohio | 0.8 | 143 | 2 | D | D | D | 11 | 107 | 23.7 | 1.7 | 4 | 10 | 0.6 | 0.1 |
| Orange | 1.4 | 71 | 12 | 83 | 52.8 | 2.2 | 75 | 729 | 153.2 | 13.9 | 15 | 60 | 5.4 | 1.2 |
| Owen | 2.4 | 106 | 11 | D | D | D | 44 | 427 | 106.3 | 8.8 | 11 | 19 | 2.6 | 0.2 |
| Parke | 2.4 | 137 | 6 | 44 | 24.5 | 1.5 | 50 | 404 | 84.5 | 6.7 | 16 | 50 | 5.5 | 2.1 |
| Perry | 2.3 | 118 | 10 | 65 | 12.9 | 1.8 | 72 | 796 | 153.4 | 13.9 | 16 | 46 | 6.2 | 0.8 |

1. Merchant wholesalers, except manufacturers' sales branches and offices.    2. Employer establishments.

# Professional Services, Manufacturing, and Accommodation and Food Services

| STATE County | Professional, scientific, and technical services,[1] 2007 | | | | Manufacturing, 2007 | | | | Accommodation and food services, 2007 | | | |
|---|---|---|---|---|---|---|---|---|---|---|---|---|
| | Number of establish-ments | Number of employees | Receipts (mil dol) | Annual payroll (mil dol) | Number of establish-ments | Number of employees | Receipts (mil dol) | Annual payroll (mil dol) | Number of establish-ments | Number of employees | Sales (mil dol) | Annual payroll (mil dol) |
| | 147 | 148 | 149 | 150 | 151 | 152 | 153 | 154 | 155 | 156 | 157 | 158 |
| ILLINOIS—Cont'd | | | | | | | | | | | | |
| Winnebago | 654 | D | D | D | 685 | 27 367 | 7 913.4 | 1 354.8 | 591 | 10 526 | 452.2 | 125.1 |
| Woodford | 43 | 137 | 12.0 | 4.6 | 47 | 1 869 | 963.3 | 78.4 | 62 | 746 | 26.0 | 7.2 |
| INDIANA | 12 959 | 95 701 | 12 128.9 | 4 785.9 | 9 015 | 536 907 | 221 877.8 | 24 474.7 | 12 932 | 254 293 | 11 669.8 | 3 175.2 |
| Adams | 48 | 198 | 16.1 | 6.3 | 65 | 5 564 | 2 127.7 | 215.6 | 53 | 948 | 27.1 | 7.8 |
| Allen | 889 | 6 829 | 716.2 | 333.7 | 568 | 30 612 | 19 741.9 | 1 526.0 | 703 | 15 470 | 550.5 | 169.0 |
| Bartholomew | 157 | D | D | D | 143 | 11 711 | 4 843.9 | 502.9 | 160 | 3 416 | 139.7 | 39.9 |
| Benton | 10 | D | D | D | NA | NA | NA | NA | 10 | 81 | 2.6 | 0.5 |
| Blackford | 14 | 92 | 8.6 | 2.7 | 30 | 1 437 | 397.1 | 62.4 | 20 | 213 | 8.0 | 2.0 |
| Boone | 154 | 618 | 133.3 | 28.8 | 74 | 2 131 | D | D | 102 | 1 473 | 54.5 | 15.5 |
| Brown | 40 | D | D | D | NA | NA | NA | NA | 47 | 559 | 19.8 | 6.8 |
| Carroll | 28 | D | D | D | 29 | 2 536 | D | D | 33 | 556 | 18.4 | 5.3 |
| Cass | 48 | 257 | 18.3 | 7.0 | 49 | 4 628 | 1 302.0 | 151.9 | 80 | 1 032 | 33.8 | 9.3 |
| Clark | 177 | 848 | 122.2 | 30.7 | 165 | 8 119 | 2 114.9 | 332.5 | 204 | 4 834 | 197.5 | 60.4 |
| Clay | 29 | D | D | D | 36 | 1 705 | D | D | 46 | 571 | 18.4 | 4.7 |
| Clinton | 43 | 149 | 13.7 | 3.7 | 50 | 3 910 | 2 283.5 | 139.2 | 56 | 759 | 25.1 | 6.9 |
| Crawford | 6 | D | D | D | NA | NA | NA | NA | 19 | D | D | D |
| Daviess | 36 | 346 | 36.4 | 14.2 | 71 | 2 036 | 643.4 | 54.6 | 62 | 772 | 25.9 | 6.9 |
| Dearborn | 76 | 316 | 28.4 | 10.8 | 48 | D | 786.1 | D | 79 | D | D | D |
| Decatur | 38 | 138 | 13.9 | 5.5 | 55 | 4 294 | 1 869.7 | 174.5 | 56 | 836 | 29.9 | 8.4 |
| DeKalb | 72 | 521 | 36.7 | 14.1 | 120 | 8 220 | 3 818.9 | 381.7 | 85 | 1 353 | 47.5 | 13.6 |
| Delaware | 169 | D | D | D | 150 | 5 268 | 1 280.6 | 232.7 | 216 | 4 981 | 160.8 | 48.3 |
| Dubois | 86 | 757 | 42.4 | 42.8 | 125 | D | D | D | 104 | 1 649 | 58.8 | 17.7 |
| Elkhart | 338 | D | D | D | 852 | 64 309 | 15 779.8 | 2 508.4 | 385 | 7 395 | 272.4 | 76.0 |
| Fayette | 29 | D | D | D | 30 | 2 265 | 486.5 | 107.8 | 47 | 594 | 21.6 | 5.6 |
| Floyd | 185 | D | D | D | 119 | 6 166 | 1 558.4 | 250.7 | 119 | D | D | D |
| Fountain | 20 | 90 | 4.2 | 1.4 | 23 | 2 228 | 498.4 | 90.0 | 36 | 387 | 12.0 | 3.6 |
| Franklin | 34 | D | D | D | 17 | D | D | D | 41 | 676 | 28.5 | 7.5 |
| Fulton | 30 | 190 | 14.9 | 5.2 | 51 | 2 248 | 524.3 | 83.6 | 47 | D | D | D |
| Gibson | 46 | D | D | D | 40 | 6 362 | D | D | 71 | 1 134 | 38.5 | 11.0 |
| Grant | 87 | D | D | D | 69 | 4 653 | 1 670.1 | 272.3 | 148 | 2 496 | 88.1 | 24.3 |
| Greene | 41 | D | D | D | NA | NA | NA | NA | 49 | 665 | 19.5 | 5.2 |
| Hamilton | 1 054 | D | D | D | 200 | 6 001 | 1 569.9 | 241.0 | 499 | 10 012 | 437.2 | 127.2 |
| Hancock | 123 | 683 | 59.1 | 50.5 | 67 | 3 118 | 1 256.0 | 129.8 | 97 | 1 823 | 66.3 | 19.0 |
| Harrison | 44 | D | D | D | 46 | 1 522 | 410.7 | 56.4 | 55 | D | D | D |
| Hendricks | 248 | 1 491 | 144.9 | 57.3 | 109 | 3 566 | 2 819.4 | 139.0 | 250 | 5 771 | 227.6 | 66.7 |
| Henry | 55 | D | D | D | 49 | 2 300 | 1 026.6 | 118.6 | 76 | 1 019 | 36.2 | 10.3 |
| Howard | 131 | D | D | D | 76 | 11 980 | 2 923.2 | 877.5 | 186 | 3 921 | 150.5 | 44.5 |
| Huntington | 42 | 186 | 16.3 | 5.2 | 71 | 4 357 | 1 478.6 | 195.1 | 100 | 1 333 | 44.3 | 13.4 |
| Jackson | 64 | 372 | 29.7 | 11.0 | 74 | 7 015 | 2 585.5 | 279.3 | 83 | 1 557 | 58.4 | 17.4 |
| Jasper | 54 | D | D | D | 38 | 1 549 | 601.1 | 62.1 | 65 | 1 051 | 33.9 | 9.3 |
| Jay | 23 | 90 | 5.6 | 1.8 | 33 | 2 523 | 835.1 | 100.5 | 36 | D | D | D |
| Jefferson | 57 | 280 | 18.6 | 6.5 | 60 | 3 881 | 1 477.0 | 165.4 | 77 | 1 152 | 43.2 | 11.3 |
| Jennings | 20 | D | D | D | 43 | 1 995 | 377.2 | 70.5 | 29 | 433 | 16.1 | 4.4 |
| Johnson | 253 | 1 235 | 107.4 | 37.6 | 133 | 5 904 | 1 609.9 | 233.2 | 265 | 5 447 | 208.4 | 62.7 |
| Knox | 57 | 227 | 20.2 | 5.8 | 38 | 1 917 | 774.3 | 68.2 | 83 | 1 502 | 56.8 | 14.9 |
| Kosciusko | 129 | 545 | 48.8 | 15.2 | 198 | 14 469 | 5 705.3 | 706.3 | 151 | 2 342 | 92.3 | 25.8 |
| LaGrange | 35 | 137 | 8.8 | 3.2 | 147 | 6 694 | 1 602.3 | 280.9 | 65 | 761 | 33.9 | 9.4 |
| Lake | 933 | D | D | D | 411 | 26 654 | 21 914.5 | 1 489.0 | 993 | 19 402 | 1 069.2 | 265.5 |
| LaPorte | 169 | D | D | D | 184 | 8 808 | 2 364.0 | 363.9 | 259 | 5 254 | 389.7 | 80.1 |
| Lawrence | 63 | 406 | 42.5 | 16.5 | 71 | 3 016 | 716.5 | 160.7 | 74 | 1 227 | 43.0 | 12.5 |
| Madison | 202 | D | D | D | 118 | 4 652 | 1 046.9 | 191.8 | 246 | 4 343 | 155.1 | 43.6 |
| Marion | 2 816 | D | D | D | 1 016 | 57 069 | 24 333.9 | 3 137.1 | 2 111 | 45 923 | 2 248.4 | 663.8 |
| Marshall | 69 | 386 | 28.9 | 9.9 | 125 | 6 310 | 1 239.4 | 230.3 | 98 | 1 408 | 50.5 | 13.8 |
| Martin | 10 | D | D | D | NA | NA | NA | NA | 25 | D | D | D |
| Miami | 34 | 140 | 9.4 | 3.9 | 50 | 2 576 | 711.3 | 88.0 | 59 | 805 | 25.8 | 6.9 |
| Monroe | 282 | D | D | D | 108 | 6 389 | 1 799.3 | 279.5 | 335 | 7 271 | 287.8 | 79.1 |
| Montgomery | 55 | 242 | 17.9 | 6.3 | 57 | 6 258 | 2 768.4 | 298.5 | 86 | 1 152 | 48.5 | 12.6 |
| Morgan | 103 | 342 | 32.3 | 10.8 | 66 | D | D | 92.5 | 80 | 1 530 | 59.1 | 17.4 |
| Newton | 15 | D | D | D | 27 | 1 108 | 197.5 | 32.0 | 32 | 256 | 8.0 | 2.0 |
| Noble | 56 | 259 | 30.3 | 8.5 | 138 | 9 525 | 2 454.5 | 345.8 | 82 | 1 028 | 35.9 | 9.9 |
| Ohio | 2 | D | D | D | NA | NA | NA | NA | 15 | D | D | D |
| Orange | 22 | 71 | 4.5 | 1.6 | 24 | 1 414 | 201.7 | 45.1 | 28 | D | D | D |
| Owen | 22 | D | D | D | 33 | 2 040 | D | D | 23 | 316 | 10.4 | 3.0 |
| Parke | 12 | D | D | D | 13 | 660 | 137.6 | 21.5 | 36 | D | D | D |
| Perry | 25 | 76 | 8.1 | 2.1 | 29 | 2 003 | 600.2 | 92.4 | 41 | D | D | D |

1. Establishment subject to federal tax.

# Table B. States and Counties — Health Care and Social Assistance, Other Services, and Federal Funds

| | Health care and social assistance, 2007 | | | | Other services, 2007 | | | | Federal funds and grants, 2009–2010 | | | |
| | | | | | | | | | Expenditures (mil dol) | | | |
| | | | | | | | | | | Direct payments for individuals[1] | | |
| STATE County | Number of establish-ments | Number of employees | Receipts (mil dol) | Annual payroll (mil dol) | Number of establish-ments | Number of employees | Receipts (mil dol) | Annual payroll (mil dol) | Total | Social Security and government retirement | Medicare | Food Stamps and Supplemental Security Income |
|---|---|---|---|---|---|---|---|---|---|---|---|---|
| | 159 | 160 | 161 | 162 | 163 | 164 | 165 | 166 | 167 | 168 | 169 | 170 |
| **ILLINOIS—Cont'd** | | | | | | | | | | | | |
| Winnebago | 669 | 19 367 | 1 909.7 | 798.6 | 551 | 3 698 | 305.0 | 89.8 | 1 903.8 | 842.2 | 346.0 | 99.3 |
| Woodford | 42 | 1 252 | 56.4 | 27.8 | 55 | D | D | D | 173.3 | 93.0 | 45.0 | 3.7 |
| **INDIANA** | 14 972 | 370 093 | 34 768.4 | 13 453.8 | 11 458 | 75 292 | 8 451.2 | 1 892.9 | 58 603.4 | 18 937.0 | 8 987.6 | 2 036.4 |
| Adams | 53 | 1 727 | 103.5 | 38.9 | 73 | 307 | 24.5 | 6.4 | 196.3 | 86.3 | 45.7 | 7.0 |
| Allen | 1 011 | 28 617 | 2 769.4 | 1 073.6 | 692 | 5 000 | 403.4 | 127.8 | 3 067.7 | 929.2 | 394.3 | 117.7 |
| Bartholomew | 228 | 5 095 | 439.1 | 178.5 | 120 | 857 | 82.8 | 19.5 | 709.5 | 247.2 | 97.4 | 15.8 |
| Benton | 13 | 114 | 6.5 | 2.9 | 14 | 32 | 3.9 | 0.8 | 62.3 | 29.0 | 16.1 | 1.8 |
| Blackford | 25 | D | D | D | 23 | 65 | 6.5 | 1.3 | 111.6 | 50.2 | 22.9 | 5.2 |
| Boone | 116 | 2 134 | 175.6 | 71.9 | 97 | 563 | 40.9 | 11.6 | 238.5 | 133.1 | 58.3 | 6.0 |
| Brown | 26 | 228 | 12.6 | 5.7 | 20 | 65 | 6.6 | 1.7 | 58.5 | 34.5 | 10.6 | 3.1 |
| Carroll | 29 | 299 | 15.3 | 7.5 | 33 | 87 | 6.4 | 1.8 | 112.5 | 52.9 | 23.9 | 2.9 |
| Cass | 75 | 2 973 | 173.8 | 80.2 | 75 | 492 | 26.6 | 9.2 | 283.8 | 126.3 | 68.0 | 13.2 |
| Clark | 233 | 5 037 | 453.1 | 182.3 | 182 | 1 226 | 105.3 | 30.9 | 990.3 | 360.1 | 168.0 | 30.2 |
| Clay | 56 | D | D | D | 46 | 255 | 12.1 | 3.2 | 233.0 | 101.9 | 51.6 | 8.7 |
| Clinton | 50 | 1 235 | 77.3 | 29.7 | 55 | 314 | 26.9 | 7.3 | 210.1 | 98.3 | 52.5 | 8.2 |
| Crawford | 14 | 166 | 8.3 | 3.6 | 9 | D | D | D | 92.2 | 39.0 | 19.2 | 5.0 |
| Daviess | 79 | 1 468 | 96.7 | 40.4 | 64 | 365 | 65.4 | 8.7 | 208.6 | 94.4 | 49.8 | 6.8 |
| Dearborn | 107 | D | D | D | 71 | 326 | 24.3 | 6.6 | 276.1 | 149.0 | 59.4 | 10.7 |
| Decatur | 58 | 1 026 | 78.0 | 33.1 | 47 | 251 | 19.2 | 4.2 | 159.7 | 76.7 | 35.6 | 5.8 |
| DeKalb | 89 | 1 615 | 121.4 | 47.6 | 79 | 303 | 20.8 | 6.3 | 234.4 | 134.5 | 44.8 | 7.3 |
| Delaware | 316 | 10 078 | 836.1 | 335.6 | 203 | 1 206 | 119.8 | 26.7 | 932.8 | 377.0 | 182.0 | 52.1 |
| Dubois | 125 | 2 965 | 239.4 | 103.7 | 86 | 478 | 56.8 | 10.9 | 260.1 | 118.8 | 53.7 | 3.5 |
| Elkhart | 347 | 9 746 | 1 024.6 | 358.1 | 374 | 2 298 | 195.7 | 60.1 | 913.7 | 486.1 | 182.1 | 45.9 |
| Fayette | 65 | 1 217 | 114.0 | 48.1 | 44 | 190 | 17.8 | 3.9 | 210.7 | 94.1 | 49.5 | 12.0 |
| Floyd | 233 | 5 234 | 437.2 | 172.7 | 140 | 846 | 71.3 | 16.9 | 554.6 | 245.2 | 115.3 | 24.6 |
| Fountain | 25 | 493 | 27.6 | 10.8 | 29 | 90 | 8.9 | 1.8 | 137.8 | 69.2 | 32.4 | 4.6 |
| Franklin | 58 | D | D | D | 37 | D | D | D | 118.1 | 57.4 | 23.8 | 4.4 |
| Fulton | 45 | 838 | 68.0 | 29.8 | 36 | 112 | 11.8 | 2.6 | 128.3 | 65.9 | 32.2 | 4.2 |
| Gibson | 83 | D | D | D | 58 | 267 | 18.1 | 5.1 | 236.6 | 105.8 | 58.7 | 7.7 |
| Grant | 176 | 5 003 | 435.1 | 182.6 | 124 | 549 | 38.1 | 10.4 | 665.4 | 278.2 | 127.7 | 34.5 |
| Greene | 71 | 1 104 | 65.8 | 26.4 | 50 | D | D | D | 257.1 | 126.1 | 53.2 | 10.4 |
| Hamilton | 729 | 12 555 | 1 354.4 | 494.5 | 461 | 3 217 | 218.4 | 68.8 | 807.0 | 499.9 | 113.7 | 15.2 |
| Hancock | 131 | 2 265 | 187.3 | 70.9 | 105 | 472 | 39.4 | 9.4 | 327.4 | 212.6 | 61.6 | 6.7 |
| Harrison | 69 | 1 327 | 88.4 | 36.0 | 46 | 150 | 17.0 | 3.6 | 228.4 | 125.5 | 44.6 | 9.7 |
| Hendricks | 260 | 4 706 | 427.5 | 170.6 | 208 | 1 051 | 84.9 | 24.2 | 570.4 | 336.8 | 94.3 | 8.7 |
| Henry | 92 | 2 418 | 155.5 | 68.2 | 71 | 316 | 32.0 | 5.6 | 370.3 | 174.3 | 87.5 | 16.8 |
| Howard | 223 | 5 618 | 513.4 | 195.6 | 131 | 711 | 53.2 | 14.1 | 692.4 | 353.2 | 144.9 | 33.8 |
| Huntington | 73 | 1 823 | 122.2 | 47.3 | 77 | 341 | 18.8 | 5.6 | 233.1 | 130.4 | 47.8 | 7.1 |
| Jackson | 108 | 2 174 | 158.1 | 69.7 | 80 | 431 | 35.9 | 9.2 | 284.2 | 139.0 | 56.4 | 11.3 |
| Jasper | 56 | 1 432 | 92.1 | 38.3 | 52 | 157 | 14.4 | 3.4 | 206.5 | 107.6 | 42.1 | 6.7 |
| Jay | 35 | 707 | 59.8 | 22.4 | 40 | 123 | 8.6 | 2.0 | 158.7 | 70.2 | 38.8 | 6.1 |
| Jefferson | 86 | 2 209 | 178.0 | 82.7 | 57 | 254 | 19.4 | 4.8 | 271.9 | 123.4 | 54.6 | 11.1 |
| Jennings | 60 | 886 | 69.7 | 29.3 | 27 | D | D | D | 193.5 | 82.6 | 32.3 | 9.6 |
| Johnson | 276 | 5 814 | 446.4 | 176.6 | 216 | 1 434 | 113.7 | 35.6 | 731.2 | 393.2 | 125.5 | 21.8 |
| Knox | 129 | 3 581 | 296.3 | 116.5 | 71 | 491 | 32.2 | 8.8 | 378.3 | 136.0 | 85.9 | 16.6 |
| Kosciusko | 144 | 3 432 | 225.9 | 101.9 | 160 | 877 | 81.6 | 20.2 | 370.8 | 203.8 | 78.1 | 9.8 |
| LaGrange | 45 | 770 | 57.0 | 21.6 | 49 | 217 | 17.7 | 4.8 | 136.1 | 80.3 | 28.6 | 4.1 |
| Lake | 1 220 | 31 776 | 3 101.1 | 1 205.3 | 902 | 6 829 | 548.1 | 167.1 | 4 006.6 | 1 530.8 | 967.5 | 286.9 |
| LaPorte | 236 | 4 900 | 521.2 | 188.2 | 207 | 1 172 | 74.6 | 22.2 | 756.1 | 357.8 | 183.6 | 38.0 |
| Lawrence | 101 | 2 407 | 184.2 | 75.6 | 85 | 417 | 26.1 | 7.6 | 368.0 | 172.2 | 77.4 | 12.6 |
| Madison | 266 | 6 713 | 556.4 | 223.6 | 201 | 1 239 | 83.4 | 24.0 | 1 214.0 | 561.7 | 257.3 | 55.3 |
| Marion | 2 402 | 74 201 | 8 186.4 | 3 168.6 | 1 780 | 16 477 | 2 991.1 | 535.3 | 13 113.6 | 2 379.9 | 1 427.6 | 427.4 |
| Marshall | 80 | 1 947 | 152.3 | 56.3 | 87 | 509 | 45.3 | 14.4 | 244.9 | 130.8 | 52.5 | 8.2 |
| Martin | 12 | D | D | D | 14 | D | D | D | 847.3 | 44.8 | 17.8 | 3.3 |
| Miami | 43 | 1 226 | 77.8 | 29.9 | 56 | 295 | 18.8 | 5.7 | 306.2 | 128.6 | 53.6 | 14.0 |
| Monroe | 304 | 7 565 | 690.6 | 298.4 | 211 | 2 080 | 609.7 | 56.0 | 1 080.3 | 304.2 | 111.1 | 24.8 |
| Montgomery | 87 | 1 367 | 103.3 | 47.0 | 83 | 525 | 50.5 | 13.0 | 259.3 | 124.7 | 57.3 | 8.8 |
| Morgan | 111 | 1 668 | 145.8 | 55.5 | 110 | 480 | 37.5 | 10.0 | 396.8 | 208.7 | 81.2 | 15.6 |
| Newton | 15 | 165 | 7.7 | 4.0 | 16 | 58 | 7.9 | 1.4 | 81.2 | 39.4 | 20.7 | 3.4 |
| Noble | 76 | 1 354 | 97.2 | 40.6 | 82 | 308 | 54.2 | 6.6 | 224.1 | 120.1 | 52.6 | 9.0 |
| Ohio | 8 | D | D | D | 6 | D | D | D | 35.8 | 17.9 | 7.9 | 0.9 |
| Orange | 43 | 951 | 49.1 | 20.3 | 30 | 132 | 9.2 | 1.9 | 148.5 | 63.9 | 32.5 | 6.9 |
| Owen | 23 | 390 | 18.9 | 8.6 | 31 | D | D | D | 124.5 | 65.6 | 22.6 | 6.6 |
| Parke | 27 | 484 | 24.6 | 10.0 | 27 | 84 | 9.7 | 1.8 | 114.6 | 52.7 | 25.1 | 3.9 |
| Perry | 42 | 832 | 69.7 | 22.2 | 30 | 81 | 7.2 | 1.7 | 145.2 | 57.0 | 31.5 | 4.1 |

1. State totals may include programs not allocated by county.

Items 159—170

| | Federal funds and grants, 2009–2010 (cont.) | | | | | | | Value of residential construction authorized by building permits, 2011 | | Local government finances, 2007 | | | | |
| --- | --- | --- | --- | --- | --- | --- | --- | --- | --- | --- | --- | --- | --- | --- |
| | Expenditures (mil dol) (cont.) | | | | | | | | | General revenue | | | | |
| | Procurement contract awards | | | Grants[1] | | | | | | | | Taxes | | |
| STATE County | | | | | | | | | | | | | Per capita[2] (dollars) | |
| | Salaries and wages | Defense | Other | Medicaid and other health-related | Nutrition and family welfare | Education | Other | New construction ($1,000) | Number of housing units | Total (mil dol) | Inter-govern-mental (mil dol) | Total (mil dol) | Total | Property |
| | 171 | 172 | 173 | 174 | 175 | 176 | 177 | 178 | 179 | 180 | 181 | 182 | 183 | 184 |
| ILLINOIS—Cont'd | | | | | | | | | | | | | | |
| Winnebago | 117.1 | 153.3 | 23.4 | 176.0 | 33.5 | 11.0 | 37.6 | 19 773 | 142 | 1 065.2 | 437.3 | 447.8 | 1 499 | 1 317 |
| Woodford | 6.7 | 0.1 | 1.8 | 7.8 | 4.1 | 0.5 | 1.3 | 16 659 | 83 | 114.1 | 45.3 | 52.2 | 1 374 | 1 312 |
| INDIANA | 4 359.7 | 4 369.9 | 1 128.5 | 6 228.9 | 1 304.6 | 977.7 | 3 453.6 | 1 975 556 | 12 618 | X | X | X | X | X |
| Adams | 5.0 | 0.1 | 1.3 | 35.8 | 3.7 | 2.0 | 0.9 | 5 937 | 38 | 126.4 | 44.8 | 34.8 | 1 034 | 916 |
| Allen | 208.3 | 836.9 | 169.0 | 244.6 | 51.5 | 12.0 | 46.7 | 116 691 | 657 | 1 062.8 | 379.5 | 383.3 | 1 097 | 894 |
| Bartholomew | 185.4 | 19.5 | 4.0 | 68.4 | 12.8 | 1.3 | 49.9 | 36 630 | 178 | 398.0 | 87.4 | 73.8 | 988 | 791 |
| Benton | 2.5 | 0.0 | 0.6 | 6.0 | 0.7 | 0.1 | 0.2 | 1 499 | 7 | 38.1 | 17.4 | 13.4 | 1 522 | 1 357 |
| Blackford | 12.5 | 0.0 | 0.6 | 11.9 | 2.4 | 0.3 | 2.2 | 600 | 5 | 33.9 | 17.6 | 10.1 | 765 | 644 |
| Boone | 12.8 | 0.9 | 2.1 | 14.0 | 4.0 | 0.4 | 0.1 | 71 194 | 530 | 212.4 | 58.5 | 55.4 | 1 024 | 806 |
| Brown | 1.3 | 0.0 | 0.3 | 6.0 | 1.9 | 0.2 | 0.0 | 7 343 | 39 | 46.5 | 13.6 | 24.3 | 1 658 | 1 421 |
| Carroll | 10.6 | 0.0 | 0.9 | 9.7 | 2.4 | 0.3 | 1.2 | 5 397 | 39 | 56.8 | 26.4 | 16.5 | 825 | 680 |
| Cass | 22.7 | 0.6 | 1.7 | 34.4 | 8.4 | 0.8 | 1.4 | 1 716 | 16 | 151.7 | 52.5 | 33.0 | 843 | 713 |
| Clark | 257.8 | 9.6 | 35.5 | 94.3 | 17.9 | 2.0 | 4.5 | 40 339 | 271 | 429.6 | 137.3 | 104.8 | 997 | 785 |
| Clay | 20.1 | 0.2 | 1.4 | 37.2 | 3.2 | 0.7 | 2.1 | 3 757 | 60 | 102.1 | 52.5 | 12.9 | 484 | 444 |
| Clinton | 9.2 | 0.0 | 2.9 | 24.6 | 4.9 | 0.8 | 1.4 | 4 955 | 33 | 92.8 | 46.8 | 24.8 | 734 | 614 |
| Crawford | 2.6 | 0.1 | 0.6 | 22.3 | 1.9 | 0.8 | 0.0 | 0 | 0 | 31.3 | 15.0 | 8.0 | 740 | 600 |
| Daviess | 7.8 | 3.8 | 1.5 | 29.0 | 4.4 | 1.0 | 0.5 | 4 151 | 41 | 124.2 | 34.7 | 29.4 | 980 | 848 |
| Dearborn | 10.3 | 0.0 | 1.8 | 32.9 | 7.7 | 0.6 | 1.2 | 7 528 | 36 | 219.0 | 68.9 | 52.8 | 1 060 | 977 |
| Decatur | 5.8 | 0.0 | 1.3 | 23.2 | 3.5 | 0.6 | 0.5 | 5 383 | 26 | 105.6 | 29.3 | 24.6 | 986 | 766 |
| DeKalb | 7.2 | 0.0 | 1.5 | 17.9 | 4.7 | 0.6 | 6.8 | 9 166 | 50 | 187.1 | 59.3 | 52.5 | 1 255 | 1 101 |
| Delaware | 56.0 | 0.4 | 20.6 | 156.3 | 21.6 | 4.4 | 25.1 | 10 358 | 82 | 304.8 | 150.1 | 87.5 | 758 | 697 |
| Dubois | 18.4 | 17.2 | 17.0 | 12.7 | 5.5 | 0.3 | 5.3 | 14 905 | 80 | 140.7 | 52.7 | 52.1 | 1 265 | 1 114 |
| Elkhart | 27.9 | 21.1 | -6.4 | 103.4 | 21.7 | 5.2 | 14.1 | 26 429 | 146 | 585.9 | 266.7 | 200.5 | 1 013 | 835 |
| Fayette | 5.4 | 0.1 | 0.9 | 35.7 | 5.7 | 0.6 | 3.7 | 283 | 4 | 71.1 | 37.0 | 22.2 | 913 | 723 |
| Floyd | 35.0 | 4.2 | 4.5 | 90.0 | 11.8 | 1.1 | 5.4 | 24 784 | 101 | 340.5 | 76.8 | 58.1 | 795 | 605 |
| Fountain | 4.8 | 0.0 | 1.0 | 14.9 | 5.1 | 0.3 | 0.2 | 749 | 6 | 50.9 | 24.7 | 16.3 | 953 | 842 |
| Franklin | 3.6 | 0.4 | 0.8 | 22.5 | 1.9 | 0.3 | 0.3 | 5 559 | 30 | 44.0 | 23.3 | 13.9 | 599 | 485 |
| Fulton | 4.4 | 0.0 | 1.1 | 9.7 | 2.7 | 0.4 | 2.5 | 2 561 | 19 | 97.0 | 22.0 | 15.7 | 772 | 633 |
| Gibson | 7.5 | 0.0 | 1.9 | 26.1 | 4.4 | 1.7 | 4.9 | 7 573 | 48 | 109.4 | 46.1 | 31.0 | 947 | 798 |
| Grant | 46.6 | 0.1 | 37.8 | 91.6 | 14.4 | 2.5 | 4.3 | 5 017 | 33 | 171.3 | 90.2 | 52.2 | 759 | 691 |
| Greene | 14.8 | 3.8 | 1.5 | 33.5 | 4.3 | 1.5 | 1.3 | NA | NA | 98.9 | 40.0 | 20.5 | 628 | 483 |
| Hamilton | 39.4 | 3.3 | 32.8 | 42.3 | 12.6 | 1.6 | 27.5 | 339 128 | 1 891 | 820.1 | 212.6 | 315.5 | 1 206 | 1 080 |
| Hancock | 13.4 | 2.0 | 2.4 | 16.4 | 4.7 | 0.5 | 1.3 | 32 400 | 208 | 249.0 | 65.1 | 59.1 | 891 | 676 |
| Harrison | 8.6 | 0.1 | 2.2 | 28.3 | 4.6 | 0.5 | 0.2 | 20 003 | 48 | 133.9 | 66.9 | 23.4 | 635 | 449 |
| Hendricks | 27.8 | 2.1 | 59.3 | 23.0 | 7.9 | 1.1 | 0.4 | 114 080 | 814 | 533.5 | 132.4 | 187.5 | 1 393 | 1 181 |
| Henry | 10.7 | 0.0 | 2.0 | 59.5 | 9.4 | 0.8 | 2.4 | 4 299 | 23 | 148.3 | 66.4 | 47.4 | 1 004 | 844 |
| Howard | 33.9 | 0.5 | 5.6 | 81.1 | 14.2 | 1.7 | 10.2 | 3 478 | 22 | 409.8 | 113.6 | 113.9 | 1 360 | 1 292 |
| Huntington | 16.4 | 0.8 | 1.7 | 15.6 | 4.5 | 0.5 | 0.6 | 6 522 | 34 | 105.8 | 50.0 | 39.7 | 1 052 | 915 |
| Jackson | 14.4 | 3.5 | 1.9 | 40.2 | 5.7 | 0.7 | 1.2 | 14 583 | 114 | 179.7 | 41.9 | 31.9 | 757 | 681 |
| Jasper | 18.8 | 0.1 | 1.6 | 14.1 | 3.4 | 0.4 | 0.2 | 11 474 | 72 | 123.3 | 37.3 | 29.2 | 906 | 752 |
| Jay | 3.5 | 0.0 | 0.8 | 23.1 | 6.1 | 0.7 | 2.9 | 1 736 | 13 | 91.5 | 32.8 | 22.6 | 1 050 | 814 |
| Jefferson | 15.3 | 4.1 | 1.7 | 45.4 | 7.1 | 1.0 | -0.3 | 5 222 | 44 | 81.5 | 40.5 | 24.4 | 746 | 653 |
| Jennings | 13.5 | 13.9 | 1.0 | 31.3 | 2.5 | 0.7 | 1.5 | 4 646 | 44 | 67.4 | 40.2 | 15.8 | 562 | 464 |
| Johnson | 25.6 | 67.9 | 21.1 | 53.5 | 10.9 | 1.5 | 0.9 | 73 722 | 414 | 444.0 | 136.3 | 141.8 | 1 043 | 742 |
| Knox | 18.3 | 3.3 | 6.7 | 59.5 | 10.3 | 3.2 | 5.2 | 4 565 | 29 | 242.9 | 43.4 | 29.8 | 786 | 674 |
| Kosciusko | 17.8 | 6.6 | 5.7 | 22.3 | 10.8 | 1.1 | 3.0 | 26 690 | 225 | 209.0 | 84.4 | 65.8 | 865 | 783 |
| LaGrange | 5.3 | 0.0 | 1.2 | 9.7 | 2.4 | 0.9 | 0.0 | 13 733 | 106 | 84.4 | 39.4 | 28.3 | 764 | 602 |
| Lake | 155.0 | 31.3 | 26.6 | 709.0 | 103.6 | 19.2 | 95.0 | 116 514 | 626 | 2 093.9 | 902.5 | 805.8 | 1 637 | 1 561 |
| LaPorte | 37.9 | 4.2 | 5.8 | 86.8 | 17.7 | 2.6 | 5.0 | 23 132 | 143 | 386.6 | 163.7 | 106.7 | 972 | 806 |
| Lawrence | 22.4 | 7.9 | 4.2 | 53.7 | 8.8 | 1.6 | 2.9 | 1 844 | 12 | 154.3 | 54.6 | 41.0 | 892 | 768 |
| Madison | 33.7 | 4.5 | 13.0 | 160.5 | 19.5 | 3.3 | 93.3 | 14 735 | 75 | 356.2 | 165.7 | 101.0 | 769 | 650 |
| Marion | 1 693.0 | 1 290.3 | 429.1 | 1 193.1 | 445.1 | 506.0 | 2 430.7 | 142 560 | 1 185 | 3 905.3 | 1 379.3 | 1 439.0 | 1 641 | 1 393 |
| Marshall | 11.9 | 3.8 | 2.0 | 19.5 | 7.2 | 0.7 | 1.1 | 15 903 | 76 | 108.7 | 54.4 | 36.9 | 789 | 734 |
| Martin | 185.5 | 560.8 | 0.7 | 17.1 | 1.8 | 0.4 | 13.5 | 350 | 3 | 29.6 | 15.3 | 7.9 | 785 | 751 |
| Miami | 34.2 | 31.9 | 1.4 | 26.1 | 6.1 | 0.8 | 5.6 | 1 489 | 10 | 167.1 | 67.7 | 30.1 | 823 | 746 |
| Monroe | 74.9 | 4.7 | 14.0 | 393.2 | 14.9 | 11.7 | 87.6 | 33 049 | 236 | 284.9 | 111.5 | 106.3 | 826 | 744 |
| Montgomery | 21.6 | 0.5 | 1.8 | 27.5 | 4.5 | 0.7 | 3.6 | 5 362 | 37 | 115.7 | 45.5 | 39.4 | 1 041 | 937 |
| Morgan | 20.0 | 6.5 | 2.6 | 46.3 | 7.5 | 1.0 | 1.7 | 12 705 | 96 | 192.0 | 74.8 | 46.7 | 669 | 507 |
| Newton | 2.8 | 0.0 | 0.7 | 6.0 | 2.0 | 0.2 | 0.8 | 493 | 4 | 53.0 | 19.6 | 18.6 | 1 324 | 1 201 |
| Noble | 7.5 | 0.0 | 1.5 | 20.3 | 4.3 | 0.8 | 1.9 | 11 285 | 75 | 114.8 | 49.3 | 23.2 | 488 | 431 |
| Ohio | 1.4 | 0.0 | 0.3 | 6.0 | 0.7 | 0.1 | 0.0 | 1 482 | 11 | 27.9 | 12.1 | 4.0 | 691 | 555 |
| Orange | 3.8 | 0.6 | 1.5 | 31.3 | 3.6 | 0.6 | 1.9 | 604 | 4 | 46.4 | 25.5 | 12.0 | 614 | 512 |
| Owen | 5.2 | 0.6 | 0.9 | 17.1 | 2.8 | 0.5 | 0.0 | 0 | 0 | 44.8 | 22.0 | 15.5 | 691 | 571 |
| Parke | 5.2 | 0.1 | 0.9 | 17.9 | 2.9 | 0.5 | 0.6 | 3 556 | 28 | 50.5 | 19.6 | 11.6 | 677 | 521 |
| Perry | 15.0 | 0.1 | 1.6 | 23.8 | 4.7 | 1.4 | 1.5 | 2 819 | 18 | 56.5 | 24.4 | 16.0 | 847 | 714 |

1. State totals may include programs not allocated by county.     2. Based on the resident population estimated as of July 1 of the year shown.

# Table B. States and Counties — Local Government Finances, Government Employment, and Voting

| | Local government finances, 2007 (cont.) | | | | | | | | | Government employment, 2011 | | | Presidential election,[2] 2012 | | |
| | Direct general expenditure | | | | | | | Debt outstanding | | | | | Percent of vote cast: | | |
| STATE County | | | Percent of total for: | | | | | | | | | | | | |
| | Total (mil dol) | Per capita[1] (dollars) | Educa-tion | Health and hospitals | Police protec-tion | Public welfare | High-ways | Total (mil dol) | Per capita[1] (dollars) | Federal civilian | Federal military | State and local | Demo-cratic | Republi-can | All other |
|---|---|---|---|---|---|---|---|---|---|---|---|---|---|---|---|
| | 185 | 186 | 187 | 188 | 189 | 190 | 191 | 192 | 193 | 194 | 195 | 196 | 197 | 198 | 199 |
| **ILLINOIS—Cont'd** | | | | | | | | | | | | | | | |
| Winnebago | 1 071.9 | 3 588 | 44.7 | 1.5 | 6.0 | 2.8 | 5.6 | 805.9 | 2 697 | 995 | 597 | 13 463 | 55.6 | 42.8 | 1.7 |
| Woodford | 106.9 | 2 812 | 66.3 | 1.4 | 4.0 | 0.1 | 6.5 | 53.1 | 1 396 | 77 | 78 | 1 809 | 35.9 | 62.6 | 1.5 |
| **INDIANA** | X | X | X | X | X | X | X | X | X | 38 373 | 22 329 | 389 202 | 49.9 | 48.9 | 1.1 |
| Adams | 124.6 | 3 704 | 40.4 | 28.2 | 2.4 | 1.5 | 4.7 | 129.7 | 3 854 | 56 | 114 | 1 901 | 36.5 | 62.2 | 1.3 |
| Allen | 1 165.0 | 3 333 | 48.8 | 0.8 | 4.6 | 2.9 | 3.1 | 857.2 | 2 453 | 1 854 | 1 230 | 17 253 | 47.4 | 51.8 | 0.8 |
| Bartholomew | 413.6 | 5 533 | 28.0 | 41.7 | 2.3 | 1.9 | 2.1 | 184.1 | 2 463 | 185 | 259 | 6 148 | 43.7 | 55.0 | 1.3 |
| Benton | 45.7 | 5 186 | 62.6 | 1.3 | 1.9 | 2.3 | 6.3 | 13.6 | 1 542 | 31 | 29 | 614 | 41.0 | 57.2 | 1.8 |
| Blackford | 38.9 | 2 952 | 54.9 | 0.7 | 3.3 | 2.4 | 4.6 | 44.7 | 3 388 | 23 | 42 | 557 | 49.2 | 49.4 | 1.4 |
| Boone | 245.7 | 4 538 | 46.4 | 20.5 | 2.2 | 1.1 | 3.0 | 203.1 | 3 752 | 99 | 190 | 3 157 | 36.6 | 62.4 | 1.0 |
| Brown | 43.1 | 2 936 | 54.0 | 1.2 | 1.8 | 4.4 | 7.6 | 35.4 | 2 415 | 15 | 50 | 836 | 47.8 | 50.4 | 1.8 |
| Carroll | 47.8 | 2 394 | 49.6 | 2.7 | 3.4 | 2.6 | 11.2 | 25.8 | 1 289 | 67 | 66 | 766 | 42.8 | 55.6 | 1.6 |
| Cass | 168.7 | 4 305 | 43.3 | 24.6 | 2.6 | 2.8 | 3.4 | 41.0 | 1 046 | 98 | 128 | 3 255 | 44.8 | 53.3 | 1.9 |
| Clark | 491.3 | 4 677 | 32.3 | 28.7 | 1.6 | 1.7 | 1.9 | 179.3 | 1 707 | 2 124 | 371 | 6 127 | 46.0 | 53.1 | 0.9 |
| Clay | 96.2 | 3 610 | 67.1 | 0.4 | 1.6 | 1.1 | 3.5 | 49.1 | 1 843 | 80 | 89 | 1 222 | 43.5 | 55.0 | 1.5 |
| Clinton | 125.9 | 3 725 | 63.3 | 0.9 | 2.8 | 2.0 | 3.4 | 128.8 | 3 811 | 66 | 109 | 1 616 | 42.8 | 55.8 | 1.3 |
| Crawford | 37.0 | 3 428 | 56.1 | 1.8 | 1.1 | 4.6 | 4.6 | 32.1 | 2 975 | 24 | 35 | 570 | 48.2 | 50.4 | 1.4 |
| Daviess | 123.9 | 4 125 | 40.1 | 32.8 | 3.5 | 1.5 | 3.4 | 80.1 | 2 666 | 77 | 106 | 1 722 | 31.8 | 67.1 | 1.1 |
| Dearborn | 305.2 | 6 133 | 30.0 | 20.6 | 1.6 | 0.9 | 1.6 | 87.8 | 1 765 | 112 | 166 | 2 788 | 32.1 | 67.0 | 0.9 |
| Decatur | 110.3 | 4 420 | 33.8 | 31.0 | 1.7 | 1.5 | 3.5 | 57.1 | 2 286 | 75 | 86 | 1 505 | 37.1 | 61.5 | 1.4 |
| DeKalb | 190.4 | 4 555 | 43.1 | 20.5 | 2.4 | 2.0 | 4.3 | 93.4 | 2 235 | 90 | 140 | 1 924 | 41.8 | 57.0 | 1.1 |
| Delaware | 373.1 | 3 232 | 51.4 | 1.3 | 3.9 | 4.7 | 2.7 | 233.5 | 2 023 | 335 | 394 | 10 472 | 56.9 | 41.9 | 1.1 |
| Dubois | 125.8 | 3 052 | 63.1 | 0.8 | 3.3 | 1.3 | 5.6 | 149.3 | 3 621 | 108 | 140 | 2 003 | 47.1 | 51.3 | 1.6 |
| Elkhart | 815.9 | 4 122 | 53.1 | 1.4 | 3.8 | 2.4 | 2.6 | 702.5 | 3 549 | 255 | 659 | 8 153 | 43.9 | 55.1 | 0.9 |
| Fayette | 76.0 | 3 131 | 49.7 | 2.0 | 4.5 | 4.6 | 4.9 | 34.4 | 1 417 | 47 | 80 | 1 168 | 46.4 | 52.0 | 1.6 |
| Floyd | 367.1 | 5 024 | 34.0 | 41.5 | 2.3 | 1.4 | 1.3 | 351.4 | 4 809 | 218 | 248 | 5 839 | 44.5 | 54.6 | 0.9 |
| Fountain | 51.1 | 2 981 | 58.8 | 2.0 | 1.5 | 2.6 | 7.7 | 30.6 | 1 784 | 56 | 57 | 800 | 41.8 | 56.1 | 2.1 |
| Franklin | 49.1 | 2 113 | 54.8 | 0.5 | 1.4 | 2.2 | 11.6 | 20.3 | 875 | 45 | 76 | 939 | 32.1 | 66.1 | 1.8 |
| Fulton | 86.9 | 4 279 | 28.7 | 34.6 | 2.4 | 2.5 | 4.2 | 40.6 | 2 002 | 53 | 69 | 1 232 | 41.1 | 57.2 | 1.7 |
| Gibson | 121.5 | 3 709 | 60.8 | 1.7 | 2.2 | 1.7 | 4.8 | 187.7 | 5 731 | 88 | 111 | 1 247 | 42.8 | 56.0 | 1.3 |
| Grant | 207.2 | 3 010 | 50.0 | 0.7 | 5.8 | 4.0 | 4.2 | 445.1 | 6 465 | 1 050 | 232 | 2 981 | 42.9 | 56.0 | 1.0 |
| Greene | 105.7 | 3 234 | 50.9 | 18.8 | 1.9 | 2.8 | 5.5 | 56.4 | 1 725 | 76 | 109 | 1 781 | 41.9 | 56.4 | 1.7 |
| Hamilton | 1 162.4 | 4 442 | 40.9 | 12.0 | 3.1 | 0.3 | 5.2 | 1 556.9 | 5 950 | 377 | 937 | 12 017 | 38.5 | 60.7 | 0.7 |
| Hancock | 299.3 | 4 515 | 43.3 | 27.5 | 2.2 | 0.9 | 3.0 | 259.8 | 3 918 | 102 | 233 | 3 627 | 34.7 | 64.3 | 1.1 |
| Harrison | 155.0 | 4 210 | 40.9 | 20.7 | 0.6 | 1.9 | 2.3 | 84.5 | 2 294 | 105 | 130 | 1 942 | 40.3 | 58.3 | 1.4 |
| Hendricks | 544.8 | 4 049 | 43.7 | 25.6 | 2.6 | 0.4 | 1.7 | 542.2 | 4 029 | 278 | 489 | 7 968 | 37.8 | 61.2 | 1.0 |
| Henry | 160.2 | 3 396 | 52.5 | 1.7 | 2.7 | 3.0 | 3.8 | 95.1 | 2 015 | 99 | 163 | 2 885 | 47.2 | 51.1 | 1.7 |
| Howard | 415.3 | 4 958 | 35.2 | 32.9 | 4.5 | 1.5 | 2.8 | 244.7 | 2 921 | 252 | 275 | 6 350 | 46.3 | 52.4 | 1.3 |
| Huntington | 93.5 | 2 477 | 58.0 | 0.5 | 3.5 | 2.1 | 5.3 | 84.3 | 2 233 | 86 | 123 | 1 467 | 35.8 | 63.0 | 1.2 |
| Jackson | 177.3 | 4 204 | 32.7 | 41.0 | 2.5 | 1.2 | 1.4 | 226.8 | 5 376 | 86 | 142 | 2 708 | 42.3 | 56.0 | 1.7 |
| Jasper | 126.8 | 3 928 | 47.2 | 25.0 | 2.7 | 1.4 | 3.1 | 173.0 | 5 362 | 83 | 111 | 1 869 | 39.2 | 59.6 | 1.3 |
| Jay | 96.5 | 4 486 | 49.2 | 20.3 | 2.1 | 1.2 | 4.1 | 57.4 | 2 666 | 44 | 70 | 1 322 | 45.1 | 52.9 | 2.0 |
| Jefferson | 94.0 | 2 875 | 61.2 | 1.4 | 2.6 | 4.3 | 4.2 | 71.3 | 2 180 | 82 | 107 | 2 529 | 46.4 | 52.3 | 1.3 |
| Jennings | 75.9 | 2 700 | 61.5 | 1.1 | 2.4 | 2.9 | 4.5 | 60.5 | 2 152 | 79 | 93 | 1 213 | 44.9 | 52.9 | 2.2 |
| Johnson | 551.3 | 4 055 | 50.8 | 13.8 | 2.4 | 0.6 | 2.1 | 499.6 | 3 675 | 377 | 535 | 6 208 | 36.8 | 62.2 | 1.0 |
| Knox | 232.8 | 6 135 | 22.0 | 53.1 | 1.5 | 1.4 | 2.3 | 88.1 | 2 323 | 205 | 127 | 4 619 | 46.1 | 52.6 | 1.3 |
| Kosciusko | 227.2 | 2 985 | 58.0 | 0.8 | 3.1 | 0.9 | 4.1 | 94.7 | 1 245 | 175 | 256 | 2 934 | 30.6 | 68.0 | 1.4 |
| LaGrange | 96.1 | 2 595 | 61.8 | 0.5 | 1.4 | 1.9 | 4.8 | 91.4 | 2 469 | 61 | 124 | 1 268 | 38.6 | 60.1 | 1.3 |
| Lake | 2 234.5 | 4 541 | 42.9 | 0.6 | 6.6 | 5.8 | 2.2 | 2 131.7 | 4 332 | 1 456 | 1 641 | 26 181 | 66.7 | 32.5 | 0.8 |
| LaPorte | 352.4 | 3 210 | 57.1 | 1.3 | 2.1 | 2.0 | 7.3 | 269.9 | 2 459 | 176 | 388 | 7 038 | 60.2 | 38.2 | 1.6 |
| Lawrence | 173.6 | 3 771 | 42.9 | 24.3 | 3.0 | 1.6 | 3.4 | 121.0 | 2 628 | 130 | 153 | 1 994 | 38.9 | 59.4 | 1.7 |
| Madison | 426.4 | 3 247 | 50.8 | 0.3 | 4.1 | 3.0 | 3.4 | 373.2 | 2 842 | 257 | 435 | 5 787 | 52.6 | 46.0 | 1.4 |
| Marion | 4 422.1 | 5 043 | 37.8 | 14.2 | 4.1 | 2.6 | 1.1 | 7 384.5 | 8 422 | 14 801 | 3 366 | 65 572 | 63.8 | 35.4 | 0.8 |
| Marshall | 143.2 | 3 066 | 64.5 | 1.0 | 3.1 | 2.4 | 5.3 | 116.2 | 2 489 | 99 | 156 | 2 250 | 42.5 | 56.1 | 1.4 |
| Martin | 29.4 | 2 921 | 53.0 | 0.6 | 2.0 | 2.3 | 8.4 | 20.9 | 2 077 | 4 336 | 78 | 503 | 34.8 | 63.7 | 1.5 |
| Miami | 161.0 | 4 393 | 44.6 | 19.5 | 1.8 | 1.7 | 4.0 | 68.4 | 1 867 | 687 | 136 | 1 997 | 39.4 | 58.9 | 1.7 |
| Monroe | 286.0 | 2 223 | 47.4 | 0.8 | 4.0 | 4.3 | 4.0 | 302.5 | 2 351 | 334 | 510 | 21 936 | 65.6 | 33.4 | 1.0 |
| Montgomery | 134.2 | 3 543 | 59.5 | 0.5 | 2.6 | 2.9 | 5.4 | 162.5 | 4 289 | 92 | 127 | 1 855 | 39.3 | 59.3 | 1.4 |
| Morgan | 217.5 | 3 113 | 52.0 | 18.1 | 2.9 | 0.9 | 4.0 | 89.5 | 1 281 | 105 | 230 | 2 723 | 35.9 | 62.9 | 1.2 |
| Newton | 51.8 | 3 694 | 48.3 | 2.5 | 2.2 | 3.8 | 6.3 | 39.8 | 2 843 | 33 | 47 | 768 | 43.4 | 54.6 | 2.0 |
| Noble | 147.0 | 3 093 | 50.9 | 0.4 | 0.7 | 1.3 | 13.0 | 142.8 | 3 004 | 76 | 157 | 1 818 | 41.6 | 57.0 | 1.4 |
| Ohio | 35.1 | 6 082 | 23.6 | 0.3 | 1.8 | 1.7 | 4.5 | 21.6 | 3 743 | 13 | 20 | 363 | 39.7 | 58.7 | 1.6 |
| Orange | 50.8 | 2 592 | 61.7 | 0.7 | 2.2 | 1.4 | 7.7 | 46.5 | 2 373 | 45 | 66 | 966 | 41.9 | 56.1 | 2.0 |
| Owen | 45.7 | 2 042 | 62.2 | 3.7 | 1.8 | 2.9 | 6.6 | 50.0 | 2 234 | 38 | 71 | 762 | 43.7 | 54.0 | 2.3 |
| Parke | 41.3 | 2 404 | 59.4 | 1.7 | 3.3 | 1.3 | 8.3 | 631.0 | 36 750 | 54 | 57 | 1 141 | 42.0 | 56.1 | 1.9 |
| Perry | 54.0 | 2 855 | 51.4 | 0.6 | 3.4 | 1.8 | 6.5 | 62.1 | 3 282 | 73 | 64 | 1 441 | 60.6 | 37.7 | 1.7 |

1. Based on the resident population estimated as of July 1 of the year shown.     2. © 2013 Election Data Services, Inc. All rights reserved.

# Table B. States and Counties — Land Area and Population

| STATE/County code | CBSA code[1] | County type[2] | STATE County | Land area,[3] (sq km) 2010 | Population 2012 Total persons | Rank | Per square kilometer | Race alone or in combination, not Hispanic or Latino (percent) White | Black | American Indian, Alaska Native | Asian and Pacific Islander | Percent Hispanic or Latino[4] | Age (percent) Under 5 years | 5 to 17 years | 18 to 24 years | 25 to 34 years | 35 to 44 years | 45 to 54 years |
|---|---|---|---|---|---|---|---|---|---|---|---|---|---|---|---|---|---|---|
| | | | | 1 | 2 | 3 | 4 | 5 | 6 | 7 | 8 | 9 | 10 | 11 | 12 | 13 | 14 | 15 |
| | | | INDIANA—Cont'd | | | | | | | | | | | | | | | |
| 18 125 | 27540 | 6 | Pike | 866 | 12 766 | 2 254 | 14.7 | 98.2 | 0.7 | 0.5 | 0.3 | 1.0 | 5.7 | 16.2 | 7.3 | 10.7 | 12.4 | 15.9 |
| 18 127 | 16980 | 1 | Porter | 1 083 | 165 682 | 379 | 153.0 | 86.7 | 3.6 | 0.7 | 1.7 | 8.6 | 5.7 | 18.0 | 9.3 | 12.4 | 13.2 | 15.0 |
| 18 129 | 21780 | 2 | Posey | 1 061 | 25 599 | 1 581 | 24.1 | 97.3 | 1.6 | 0.5 | 0.6 | 1.0 | 5.6 | 17.6 | 8.2 | 10.3 | 11.9 | 16.9 |
| 18 131 | ... | 6 | Pulaski | 1 123 | 13 124 | 2 234 | 11.7 | 96.1 | 1.1 | 0.6 | 0.5 | 2.5 | 5.7 | 17.9 | 7.2 | 10.8 | 12.2 | 15.5 |
| 18 133 | 26900 | 1 | Putnam | 1 245 | 37 750 | 1 227 | 30.3 | 93.1 | 4.6 | 0.6 | 1.0 | 1.7 | 5.1 | 15.5 | 13.8 | 12.0 | 12.6 | 15.0 |
| 18 135 | ... | 6 | Randolph | 1 172 | 25 815 | 1 573 | 22.0 | 95.6 | 1.1 | 0.6 | 0.5 | 3.1 | 5.8 | 18.2 | 7.6 | 10.6 | 12.3 | 14.6 |
| 18 137 | ... | 6 | Ripley | 1 156 | 28 583 | 1 464 | 24.7 | 97.2 | 0.7 | 0.5 | 0.8 | 1.7 | 6.5 | 19.4 | 7.7 | 10.9 | 12.7 | 15.0 |
| 18 139 | ... | 6 | Rush | 1 057 | 17 095 | 1 972 | 16.2 | 97.2 | 1.3 | 0.5 | 0.5 | 1.2 | 5.6 | 18.6 | 8.0 | 10.5 | 12.5 | 15.5 |
| 18 141 | 43780 | 2 | St. Joseph | 1 186 | 266 344 | 250 | 224.6 | 77.5 | 14.0 | 0.8 | 2.6 | 7.5 | 6.6 | 17.8 | 11.3 | 12.7 | 12.1 | 13.6 |
| 18 143 | 42500 | 6 | Scott | 493 | 23 791 | 1 655 | 48.3 | 97.3 | 0.7 | 0.4 | 0.7 | 1.5 | 6.1 | 17.5 | 8.4 | 11.7 | 13.5 | 15.8 |
| 18 145 | 26900 | 1 | Shelby | 1 065 | 44 471 | 1 076 | 41.8 | 94.3 | 1.6 | 0.5 | 0.8 | 3.7 | 6.0 | 18.1 | 8.0 | 11.4 | 12.9 | 16.3 |
| 18 147 | ... | 8 | Spencer | 1 028 | 20 837 | 1 785 | 20.3 | 96.3 | 1.0 | 0.4 | 0.5 | 2.5 | 5.7 | 18.1 | 7.0 | 10.9 | 12.2 | 16.3 |
| 18 149 | ... | 6 | Starke | 801 | 23 213 | 1 681 | 29.0 | 95.4 | 0.8 | 0.8 | 0.5 | 3.5 | 6.1 | 17.7 | 8.3 | 10.8 | 12.3 | 15.2 |
| 18 151 | 11420 | 7 | Steuben | 800 | 34 124 | 1 325 | 42.7 | 95.5 | 1.0 | 0.6 | 0.8 | 3.0 | 5.2 | 17.0 | 10.8 | 10.1 | 12.2 | 14.9 |
| 18 153 | 45460 | 3 | Sullivan | 1 158 | 21 188 | 1 775 | 18.3 | 93.4 | 5.0 | 0.7 | 0.4 | 1.5 | 5.1 | 15.6 | 8.8 | 13.4 | 13.5 | 15.0 |
| 18 155 | ... | 8 | Switzerland | 571 | 10 424 | 2 402 | 18.3 | 97.7 | 0.7 | 0.6 | 0.4 | 1.4 | 7.4 | 17.6 | 8.1 | 11.5 | 12.5 | 15.3 |
| 18 157 | 29140 | 3 | Tippecanoe | 1 294 | 177 513 | 355 | 137.2 | 81.4 | 5.0 | 0.6 | 7.1 | 7.7 | 6.3 | 14.1 | 25.5 | 14.0 | 10.6 | 10.6 |
| 18 159 | 29020 | 3 | Tipton | 675 | 15 695 | 2 064 | 23.3 | 96.7 | 0.7 | 0.5 | 0.7 | 2.3 | 4.7 | 17.7 | 7.6 | 10.0 | 12.8 | 15.4 |
| 18 161 | ... | 8 | Union | 418 | 7 362 | 2 649 | 17.6 | 97.4 | 1.2 | 0.8 | 0.5 | 1.3 | 5.6 | 19.2 | 7.9 | 10.8 | 12.7 | 15.2 |
| 18 163 | 21780 | 2 | Vanderburgh | 605 | 180 858 | 349 | 298.9 | 87.2 | 10.5 | 0.6 | 1.6 | 2.3 | 6.4 | 15.7 | 11.5 | 13.5 | 11.4 | 14.3 |
| 18 165 | 45460 | 3 | Vermillion | 665 | 16 040 | 2 044 | 24.1 | 98.2 | 0.6 | 0.6 | 0.4 | 1.0 | 5.4 | 17.5 | 7.4 | 10.4 | 12.8 | 14.3 |
| 18 167 | 45460 | 3 | Vigo | 1 045 | 108 428 | 546 | 103.8 | 88.4 | 8.3 | 0.8 | 2.3 | 2.4 | 5.7 | 15.3 | 15.0 | 13.0 | 12.0 | 13.3 |
| 18 169 | 47340 | 6 | Wabash | 1 068 | 32 361 | 1 381 | 30.3 | 96.0 | 1.1 | 1.1 | 0.6 | 2.2 | 5.6 | 16.8 | 10.0 | 10.2 | 11.4 | 14.3 |
| 18 171 | ... | 8 | Warren | 945 | 8 342 | 2 577 | 8.8 | 97.7 | 0.7 | 0.5 | 0.7 | 1.2 | 5.7 | 17.1 | 7.3 | 10.4 | 12.3 | 16.2 |
| 18 173 | 21780 | 2 | Warrick | 997 | 60 463 | 856 | 60.6 | 94.9 | 2.1 | 0.5 | 2.1 | 1.7 | 6.3 | 19.1 | 6.9 | 11.1 | 13.4 | 15.6 |
| 18 175 | 31140 | 1 | Washington | 1 331 | 27 921 | 1 498 | 21.0 | 97.9 | 0.6 | 0.6 | 0.5 | 1.2 | 5.8 | 18.9 | 8.2 | 11.3 | 13.2 | 15.7 |
| 18 177 | 39980 | 5 | Wayne | 1 041 | 68 346 | 778 | 65.7 | 91.1 | 6.5 | 0.7 | 1.4 | 2.7 | 6.3 | 16.6 | 9.4 | 11.4 | 12.2 | 14.3 |
| 18 179 | 23060 | 2 | Wells | 953 | 27 652 | 1 506 | 29.0 | 96.6 | 0.8 | 0.6 | 0.6 | 2.2 | 6.4 | 18.0 | 8.0 | 11.5 | 11.4 | 15.5 |
| 18 181 | ... | 6 | White | 1 308 | 24 426 | 1 629 | 18.7 | 91.8 | 0.7 | 0.7 | 0.6 | 7.3 | 6.1 | 17.8 | 7.1 | 10.2 | 11.9 | 14.8 |
| 18 183 | 23060 | 2 | Whitley | 869 | 33 342 | 1 345 | 38.4 | 97.3 | 0.8 | 0.7 | 0.6 | 1.7 | 6.1 | 18.1 | 7.8 | 11.1 | 12.7 | 15.7 |
| 19 000 | ... | X | IOWA | 144 669 | 3 074 186 | X | 21.2 | 89.7 | 3.7 | 0.7 | 2.3 | 5.2 | 6.5 | 17.1 | 10.1 | 12.7 | 11.8 | 14.1 |
| 19 001 | ... | 8 | Adair | 1 474 | 7 481 | 2 643 | 5.1 | 98.1 | 0.3 | 0.4 | 0.4 | 1.4 | 5.1 | 17.1 | 6.3 | 10.4 | 10.1 | 16.2 |
| 19 003 | ... | 9 | Adams | 1 097 | 3 911 | 2 915 | 3.6 | 97.6 | 0.5 | 0.8 | 0.7 | 1.0 | 5.8 | 15.2 | 7.0 | 10.5 | 9.7 | 16.3 |
| 19 005 | ... | 6 | Allamakee | 1 655 | 14 237 | 2 160 | 8.6 | 92.7 | 1.0 | 0.4 | 0.6 | 5.7 | 6.4 | 16.1 | 7.3 | 10.3 | 10.6 | 14.7 |
| 19 007 | ... | 7 | Appanoose | 1 288 | 12 700 | 2 261 | 9.9 | 97.4 | 0.8 | 0.8 | 0.5 | 1.5 | 6.1 | 15.9 | 7.5 | 10.5 | 10.7 | 14.7 |
| 19 009 | ... | 8 | Audubon | 1 147 | 5 910 | 2 771 | 5.2 | 98.5 | 0.4 | 0.3 | 0.6 | 0.7 | 5.2 | 15.9 | 6.3 | 8.2 | 10.5 | 16.1 |
| 19 011 | 16300 | 3 | Benton | 1 855 | 25 827 | 1 572 | 13.9 | 97.9 | 0.8 | 0.5 | 0.5 | 1.1 | 6.0 | 18.9 | 6.8 | 10.9 | 12.6 | 16.8 |
| 19 013 | 47940 | 3 | Black Hawk | 1 465 | 131 820 | 475 | 90.0 | 85.7 | 9.9 | 0.6 | 2.1 | 3.9 | 6.3 | 15.0 | 16.5 | 13.2 | 10.5 | 12.3 |
| 19 015 | 14340 | 6 | Boone | 1 480 | 26 195 | 1 555 | 17.7 | 96.3 | 1.3 | 0.6 | 0.7 | 2.1 | 5.8 | 18.0 | 7.4 | 12.2 | 11.6 | 15.2 |
| 19 017 | 47940 | 3 | Bremer | 1 128 | 24 479 | 1 622 | 21.7 | 97.1 | 1.2 | 0.3 | 1.1 | 1.2 | 5.5 | 16.7 | 12.5 | 10.4 | 11.3 | 13.2 |
| 19 019 | ... | 6 | Buchanan | 1 479 | 20 942 | 1 780 | 14.2 | 97.8 | 0.7 | 0.5 | 0.7 | 1.2 | 7.2 | 19.4 | 7.1 | 11.7 | 11.4 | 14.7 |
| 19 021 | 44740 | 7 | Buena Vista | 1 489 | 20 592 | 1 805 | 13.8 | 67.5 | 2.7 | 0.4 | 6.7 | 23.6 | 7.1 | 17.9 | 11.9 | 11.6 | 10.6 | 14.1 |
| 19 023 | ... | 8 | Butler | 1 503 | 14 986 | 2 108 | 10.0 | 98.3 | 0.6 | 0.5 | 0.5 | 1.0 | 6.5 | 17.2 | 5.9 | 11.1 | 10.9 | 14.0 |
| 19 025 | ... | 9 | Calhoun | 1 476 | 9 909 | 2 450 | 6.7 | 98.1 | 0.5 | 0.4 | 0.4 | 1.2 | 5.6 | 15.7 | 6.2 | 9.2 | 9.8 | 14.4 |
| 19 027 | ... | 7 | Carroll | 1 475 | 20 631 | 1 803 | 14.0 | 97.2 | 0.9 | 0.3 | 0.7 | 1.7 | 6.8 | 17.6 | 6.6 | 11.1 | 11.1 | 15.2 |
| 19 029 | ... | 6 | Cass | 1 461 | 13 723 | 2 197 | 9.4 | 96.9 | 0.6 | 0.3 | 0.8 | 1.9 | 6.4 | 16.1 | 6.4 | 10.6 | 10.1 | 15.1 |
| 19 031 | ... | 6 | Cedar | 1 501 | 18 416 | 1 900 | 12.3 | 97.3 | 0.8 | 0.4 | 0.8 | 1.6 | 6.0 | 18.2 | 6.4 | 10.6 | 12.0 | 16.1 |
| 19 033 | 32380 | 5 | Cerro Gordo | 1 472 | 43 788 | 1 091 | 29.7 | 93.7 | 2.0 | 0.5 | 1.3 | 3.9 | 5.7 | 15.7 | 8.4 | 11.2 | 10.7 | 15.4 |
| 19 035 | ... | 6 | Cherokee | 1 494 | 11 946 | 2 301 | 8.0 | 95.9 | 1.0 | 0.5 | 0.9 | 2.6 | 5.6 | 15.4 | 6.4 | 10.2 | 9.7 | 15.6 |
| 19 037 | ... | 6 | Chickasaw | 1 306 | 12 276 | 2 288 | 9.4 | 96.9 | 0.4 | 0.3 | 0.5 | 2.4 | 6.3 | 17.7 | 6.8 | 10.1 | 10.4 | 15.4 |
| 19 039 | ... | 6 | Clarke | 1 117 | 9 370 | 2 483 | 8.4 | 88.2 | 0.8 | 0.5 | 0.8 | 10.6 | 7.0 | 17.8 | 7.9 | 11.3 | 11.6 | 14.4 |
| 19 041 | 43980 | 7 | Clay | 1 469 | 16 599 | 2 003 | 11.3 | 95.7 | 0.8 | 0.5 | 1.0 | 2.9 | 6.2 | 16.7 | 7.3 | 11.7 | 10.8 | 14.6 |
| 19 043 | ... | 8 | Clayton | 2 016 | 17 835 | 1 927 | 8.8 | 97.3 | 0.8 | 0.3 | 0.5 | 1.8 | 5.8 | 16.9 | 6.6 | 9.6 | 10.6 | 15.8 |
| 19 045 | 17540 | 4 | Clinton | 1 800 | 48 717 | 1 001 | 27.1 | 93.9 | 3.6 | 0.7 | 0.9 | 2.6 | 6.2 | 17.2 | 8.1 | 11.3 | 11.5 | 15.5 |
| 19 047 | ... | 6 | Crawford | 1 850 | 17 309 | 1 960 | 9.4 | 72.3 | 1.7 | 0.3 | 1.0 | 25.3 | 7.6 | 19.1 | 8.8 | 10.8 | 11.4 | 13.7 |
| 19 049 | 19780 | 2 | Dallas | 1 524 | 71 967 | 748 | 47.2 | 89.2 | 2.1 | 0.5 | 3.1 | 6.2 | 8.5 | 20.4 | 6.1 | 16.2 | 15.6 | 13.4 |
| 19 051 | ... | 9 | Davis | 1 301 | 8 689 | 2 550 | 6.7 | 98.3 | 0.4 | 0.6 | 0.4 | 1.0 | 8.3 | 20.7 | 7.5 | 10.1 | 10.7 | 13.3 |
| 19 053 | ... | 9 | Decatur | 1 378 | 8 253 | 2 589 | 6.0 | 94.5 | 2.0 | 0.8 | 1.4 | 2.3 | 6.1 | 16.4 | 14.6 | 9.7 | 9.6 | 12.7 |
| 19 055 | ... | 6 | Delaware | 1 496 | 17 574 | 1 945 | 11.7 | 98.4 | 0.6 | 0.3 | 0.4 | 0.9 | 6.1 | 18.7 | 6.4 | 10.4 | 11.1 | 16.9 |
| 19 057 | 15460 | 5 | Des Moines | 1 078 | 40 340 | 1 169 | 37.4 | 91.1 | 6.2 | 0.7 | 1.2 | 2.8 | 6.5 | 16.6 | 7.4 | 11.8 | 11.4 | 14.4 |
| 19 059 | 44020 | 7 | Dickinson | 986 | 16 972 | 1 985 | 17.2 | 97.9 | 0.7 | 0.3 | 0.6 | 1.2 | 4.9 | 14.3 | 5.7 | 10.5 | 10.7 | 14.6 |
| 19 061 | 20220 | 3 | Dubuque | 1 576 | 95 097 | 610 | 60.3 | 93.8 | 3.2 | 0.4 | 1.6 | 2.0 | 6.3 | 17.1 | 10.3 | 12.2 | 11.3 | 14.4 |
| 19 063 | ... | 7 | Emmet | 1 025 | 10 120 | 2 433 | 9.9 | 90.0 | 1.1 | 0.7 | 0.7 | 8.2 | 6.2 | 16.7 | 9.6 | 11.1 | 10.2 | 13.5 |
| 19 065 | ... | 6 | Fayette | 1 893 | 20 793 | 1 789 | 11.0 | 96.2 | 1.5 | 0.4 | 0.8 | 2.0 | 6.2 | 16.1 | 9.7 | 10.0 | 10.2 | 14.9 |
| 19 067 | ... | 7 | Floyd | 1 297 | 16 056 | 2 042 | 12.4 | 95.1 | 1.5 | 0.3 | 1.6 | 2.2 | 6.2 | 17.3 | 7.1 | 10.0 | 11.1 | 14.3 |

1. CBSA = Core Based Statistical Area. See Appendix A for explanation. See Appendix B for list of metropolitan areas with component counties.    2. County type code from the Economic Research Service of USDA Rural-Urban Continuum Codes. See Appendix A for definition.    3. Dry land or land partially or temporarily covered by water.    4. May be of any race.

# Table B. States and Counties — **Population and Households**

| | Population, 2011 (cont.) | | | | Population change and components of change, 2000–2012 | | | | | | | Households, 2010 | | | | |
|---|---|---|---|---|---|---|---|---|---|---|---|---|---|---|---|---|
| | Age (percent) (cont.) | | | | Total persons | | Percent change | | Components of change, 2010–2012 | | | | | | Percent | |
| STATE County | 55 to 64 years | 65 to 74 years | 75 years and over | Percent female | 2000 | 2010 | 2000– 2010 | 2010– 2012 | Births | Deaths | Net migration | Number | Percent change, 2000– 2010 | Persons per house- hold | Female family house- holder[1] | One per- son |
| | 16 | 17 | 18 | 19 | 20 | 21 | 22 | 23 | 24 | 25 | 26 | 27 | 28 | 29 | 30 | 31 |
| **INDIANA—Cont'd** | | | | | | | | | | | | | | | | |
| Pike | 14.4 | 9.6 | 7.7 | 50.0 | 12 837 | 12 845 | 0.1 | -0.6 | 322 | 340 | -57 | 5 186 | 1.3 | 2.44 | 8.5 | 25.5 |
| Porter | 13.6 | 7.2 | 5.5 | 50.9 | 146 798 | 164 343 | 12.0 | 0.8 | 3 955 | 3 076 | 498 | 61 998 | 13.4 | 2.60 | 10.4 | 23.3 |
| Posey | 14.8 | 8.3 | 6.5 | 50.3 | 27 061 | 25 910 | -4.3 | -1.2 | 620 | 553 | -383 | 10 171 | -0.3 | 2.52 | 8.5 | 23.3 |
| Pulaski | 13.6 | 9.3 | 7.8 | 49.3 | 13 755 | 13 402 | -2.6 | -2.1 | 347 | 348 | -275 | 5 282 | 2.2 | 2.50 | 9.0 | 25.6 |
| Putnam | 12.2 | 7.7 | 6.1 | 47.0 | 36 019 | 37 963 | 5.4 | -0.6 | 819 | 716 | -310 | 12 917 | 4.4 | 2.52 | 9.0 | 23.9 |
| Randolph | 13.3 | 9.2 | 8.3 | 50.7 | 27 401 | 26 171 | -4.5 | -1.4 | 654 | 643 | -363 | 10 451 | -4.4 | 2.47 | 11.1 | 25.7 |
| Ripley | 12.6 | 8.2 | 7.1 | 50.8 | 26 523 | 28 818 | 8.7 | -0.8 | 843 | 651 | -467 | 10 789 | 9.6 | 2.63 | 10.2 | 22.8 |
| Rush | 13.3 | 8.5 | 7.5 | 50.6 | 18 261 | 17 392 | -4.8 | -1.7 | 377 | 439 | -236 | 6 767 | -2.3 | 2.54 | 10.9 | 24.5 |
| St. Joseph | 12.5 | 6.6 | 6.8 | 51.5 | 265 559 | 266 931 | 0.5 | -0.2 | 7 745 | 5 415 | -2 827 | 103 069 | 2.3 | 2.48 | 13.6 | 29.1 |
| Scott | 13.1 | 8.4 | 5.6 | 50.6 | 22 960 | 24 181 | 5.3 | -1.6 | 610 | 644 | -366 | 9 397 | 6.4 | 2.54 | 13.0 | 24.0 |
| Shelby | 13.3 | 7.8 | 6.3 | 50.4 | 43 445 | 44 436 | 2.3 | 0.1 | 1 132 | 970 | -114 | 17 302 | 4.5 | 2.53 | 10.5 | 24.5 |
| Spencer | 14.5 | 8.7 | 6.6 | 49.6 | 20 391 | 20 952 | 2.8 | -0.5 | 462 | 458 | -159 | 8 082 | 6.8 | 2.55 | 8.1 | 23.2 |
| Starke | 14.0 | 9.4 | 6.2 | 50.5 | 23 556 | 23 363 | -0.8 | -0.6 | 609 | 604 | -156 | 9 038 | 3.4 | 2.58 | 11.7 | 23.5 |
| Steuben | 14.3 | 9.0 | 6.4 | 49.4 | 33 214 | 34 185 | 2.9 | -0.2 | 767 | 660 | -152 | 13 310 | 4.5 | 2.47 | 9.3 | 25.3 |
| Sullivan | 13.2 | 8.5 | 6.9 | 45.6 | 21 751 | 21 475 | -1.3 | -1.3 | 476 | 518 | -239 | 7 823 | 0.1 | 2.45 | 10.8 | 26.7 |
| Switzerland | 12.8 | 9.4 | 5.6 | 49.0 | 9 065 | 10 613 | 17.1 | -1.8 | 304 | 232 | -255 | 4 034 | 17.4 | 2.60 | 10.0 | 24.3 |
| Tippecanoe | 9.4 | 5.1 | 4.5 | 48.9 | 148 955 | 172 780 | 16.0 | 2.7 | 4 875 | 2 378 | 2 258 | 65 532 | 18.7 | 2.42 | 9.8 | 29.2 |
| Tipton | 14.2 | 9.8 | 7.8 | 50.4 | 16 577 | 15 936 | -3.9 | -1.5 | 293 | 380 | -147 | 6 376 | -1.4 | 2.47 | 9.6 | 25.4 |
| Union | 14.0 | 8.5 | 6.2 | 50.5 | 7 349 | 7 516 | 2.3 | -2.0 | 209 | 167 | -200 | 2 938 | 5.2 | 2.54 | 11.7 | 23.9 |
| Vanderburgh | 12.7 | 7.2 | 7.3 | 51.7 | 171 922 | 179 703 | 4.5 | 0.6 | 5 160 | 4 124 | 226 | 74 454 | 5.4 | 2.31 | 13.1 | 32.3 |
| Vermillion | 14.9 | 9.4 | 7.9 | 50.5 | 16 788 | 16 212 | -3.4 | -1.1 | 416 | 465 | -119 | 6 619 | -2.1 | 2.42 | 11.0 | 27.3 |
| Vigo | 12.1 | 7.1 | 6.4 | 49.3 | 105 848 | 107 848 | 1.9 | 0.5 | 2 825 | 2 461 | 273 | 41 361 | 0.9 | 2.38 | 13.1 | 30.6 |
| Wabash | 13.4 | 8.9 | 9.5 | 51.4 | 34 960 | 32 888 | -5.9 | -1.6 | 756 | 943 | -332 | 12 777 | -3.3 | 2.43 | 9.5 | 27.3 |
| Warren | 13.8 | 9.8 | 7.3 | 49.9 | 8 419 | 8 508 | 1.1 | -2.0 | 195 | 175 | -189 | 3 337 | 3.7 | 2.52 | 8.3 | 23.1 |
| Warrick | 13.8 | 8.1 | 5.8 | 50.7 | 52 383 | 59 689 | 13.9 | 1.3 | 1 526 | 1 175 | 407 | 22 505 | 15.8 | 2.62 | 9.2 | 20.7 |
| Washington | 13.2 | 8.0 | 5.7 | 50.1 | 27 223 | 28 262 | 3.8 | -1.2 | 686 | 662 | -361 | 10 850 | 5.7 | 2.58 | 11.1 | 23.7 |
| Wayne | 13.3 | 8.6 | 7.9 | 51.5 | 71 097 | 68 917 | -3.1 | -0.8 | 1 898 | 1 822 | -673 | 27 551 | -3.2 | 2.41 | 13.3 | 28.5 |
| Wells | 13.1 | 8.3 | 7.7 | 50.7 | 27 600 | 27 636 | 0.1 | 0.1 | 741 | 592 | -139 | 10 780 | 3.6 | 2.52 | 8.6 | 24.8 |
| White | 14.4 | 9.3 | 8.3 | 50.6 | 25 267 | 24 643 | -2.5 | -0.9 | 690 | 631 | -289 | 9 741 | 0.1 | 2.50 | 9.3 | 24.8 |
| Whitley | 14.1 | 7.7 | 6.8 | 50.2 | 30 707 | 33 292 | 8.4 | 0.2 | 892 | 670 | -158 | 13 001 | 11.0 | 2.53 | 9.2 | 24.1 |
| **IOWA** | 12.7 | 7.5 | 7.5 | 50.4 | 2 926 324 | 3 046 355 | 4.1 | 0.9 | 85 272 | 63 778 | 5 995 | 1 221 576 | 6.3 | 2.41 | 9.3 | 28.4 |
| Adair | 13.7 | 9.4 | 11.7 | 50.3 | 8 243 | 7 682 | -6.8 | -2.6 | 159 | 224 | -140 | 3 292 | -3.1 | 2.29 | 6.7 | 30.7 |
| Adams | 14.4 | 10.5 | 10.7 | 50.6 | 4 482 | 4 029 | -10.1 | -2.9 | 98 | 110 | -102 | 1 715 | -8.1 | 2.28 | 5.8 | 29.0 |
| Allamakee | 14.9 | 10.1 | 9.5 | 48.8 | 14 675 | 14 330 | -2.4 | -0.6 | 378 | 423 | -37 | 5 845 | 2.1 | 2.39 | 6.9 | 28.3 |
| Appanoose | 14.5 | 9.8 | 10.2 | 51.1 | 13 721 | 12 887 | -6.1 | -1.5 | 333 | 404 | -125 | 5 627 | -2.6 | 2.27 | 9.9 | 32.3 |
| Audubon | 14.3 | 10.8 | 12.6 | 51.8 | 6 830 | 6 119 | -10.4 | -3.4 | 129 | 182 | -162 | 2 617 | -5.6 | 2.29 | 6.3 | 30.3 |
| Benton | 12.4 | 7.8 | 7.8 | 50.1 | 25 308 | 26 076 | 3.0 | -1.0 | 618 | 524 | -335 | 10 302 | 5.7 | 2.50 | 7.7 | 24.0 |
| Black Hawk | 12.4 | 7.0 | 6.9 | 51.3 | 128 012 | 131 090 | 2.4 | 0.6 | 3 713 | 2 589 | -312 | 52 470 | 5.6 | 2.38 | 11.5 | 28.8 |
| Boone | 13.8 | 7.9 | 8.1 | 49.6 | 26 224 | 26 306 | 0.3 | -0.4 | 671 | 673 | -126 | 10 728 | 3.4 | 2.38 | 8.1 | 27.6 |
| Bremer | 12.8 | 9.0 | 8.6 | 51.0 | 23 325 | 24 276 | 4.1 | 0.8 | 534 | 506 | 183 | 9 385 | 5.9 | 2.40 | 6.6 | 25.8 |
| Buchanan | 12.8 | 8.2 | 7.4 | 50.4 | 21 093 | 20 958 | -0.6 | -0.1 | 650 | 441 | -231 | 8 161 | 2.9 | 2.53 | 7.8 | 25.6 |
| Buena Vista | 12.1 | 6.2 | 8.5 | 49.5 | 20 411 | 20 260 | -0.7 | 1.6 | 664 | 418 | 65 | 7 522 | 0.3 | 2.56 | 8.5 | 28.6 |
| Butler | 14.6 | 9.5 | 10.3 | 50.6 | 15 305 | 14 867 | -2.9 | 0.8 | 358 | 406 | 178 | 6 120 | -0.9 | 2.39 | 6.4 | 25.8 |
| Calhoun | 15.4 | 10.6 | 13.2 | 51.4 | 11 115 | 9 670 | -13.0 | 2.5 | 240 | 352 | -158 | 4 242 | -6.0 | 2.22 | 7.0 | 31.5 |
| Carroll | 13.0 | 8.1 | 10.5 | 51.1 | 21 421 | 20 816 | -2.8 | -0.9 | 596 | 600 | -177 | 8 683 | 2.3 | 2.34 | 7.4 | 31.2 |
| Cass | 14.2 | 10.3 | 10.8 | 51.1 | 14 684 | 13 956 | -5.0 | -1.7 | 341 | 463 | -98 | 5 980 | -2.3 | 2.28 | 8.3 | 30.5 |
| Cedar | 13.9 | 8.0 | 8.8 | 50.6 | 18 187 | 18 499 | 1.7 | -0.4 | 436 | 418 | -88 | 7 511 | 5.1 | 2.42 | 7.5 | 26.2 |
| Cerro Gordo | 14.9 | 8.5 | 9.5 | 51.2 | 46 447 | 44 151 | -4.9 | -0.8 | 1 050 | 1 083 | -317 | 19 350 | -0.1 | 2.22 | 9.4 | 33.0 |
| Cherokee | 15.4 | 9.3 | 12.4 | 50.4 | 13 035 | 12 072 | -7.4 | -1.0 | 274 | 383 | -14 | 5 207 | -3.2 | 2.25 | 7.5 | 30.9 |
| Chickasaw | 14.1 | 9.5 | 9.6 | 49.6 | 13 095 | 12 439 | -5.0 | -1.3 | 314 | 290 | -193 | 5 204 | 0.2 | 2.36 | 6.3 | 28.8 |
| Clarke | 13.4 | 8.3 | 8.4 | 50.0 | 9 133 | 9 286 | 1.7 | 0.9 | 287 | 223 | 15 | 3 701 | 3.3 | 2.47 | 8.7 | 27.8 |
| Clay | 14.2 | 8.2 | 10.2 | 50.8 | 17 372 | 16 667 | -4.1 | -0.4 | 431 | 412 | -75 | 7 282 | 0.3 | 2.26 | 8.2 | 31.7 |
| Clayton | 15.0 | 9.5 | 10.2 | 50.0 | 18 678 | 18 129 | -2.9 | -1.6 | 403 | 457 | -243 | 7 599 | 3.0 | 2.35 | 6.4 | 28.9 |
| Clinton | 13.5 | 8.6 | 8.3 | 50.7 | 50 149 | 49 116 | -2.1 | -0.8 | 1 303 | 1 165 | -522 | 20 223 | 0.6 | 2.39 | 10.3 | 29.1 |
| Crawford | 12.2 | 8.0 | 8.4 | 49.3 | 16 942 | 17 096 | 0.9 | 1.2 | 547 | 381 | 50 | 6 413 | -0.4 | 2.57 | 8.4 | 27.0 |
| Dallas | 10.2 | 5.3 | 4.5 | 51.0 | 40 750 | 66 135 | 62.3 | 8.8 | 2 345 | 822 | 4 115 | 25 240 | 62.0 | 2.60 | 8.3 | 23.6 |
| Davis | 12.3 | 8.8 | 8.3 | 50.5 | 8 541 | 8 753 | 2.5 | -0.7 | 307 | 190 | -194 | 3 201 | -0.2 | 2.70 | 6.2 | 24.3 |
| Decatur | 12.5 | 9.1 | 9.3 | 50.1 | 8 689 | 8 457 | -2.7 | -2.4 | 200 | 230 | -178 | 3 223 | -3.4 | 2.42 | 8.6 | 29.1 |
| Delaware | 13.4 | 8.3 | 8.6 | 50.1 | 18 404 | 17 764 | -3.5 | -1.1 | 418 | 402 | -213 | 7 062 | 3.3 | 2.48 | 6.8 | 24.9 |
| Des Moines | 14.1 | 8.9 | 8.8 | 51.3 | 42 351 | 40 325 | -4.8 | 0.0 | 1 054 | 988 | -31 | 17 003 | -1.5 | 2.33 | 12.1 | 30.3 |
| Dickinson | 17.0 | 11.1 | 11.3 | 50.5 | 16 424 | 16 667 | 1.5 | 1.8 | 357 | 405 | 345 | 7 554 | 6.3 | 2.18 | 6.3 | 30.6 |
| Dubuque | 12.9 | 7.6 | 7.7 | 50.6 | 89 143 | 93 653 | 5.1 | 1.5 | 2 616 | 1 949 | 810 | 36 815 | 9.3 | 2.43 | 9.2 | 28.4 |
| Emmet | 13.8 | 8.6 | 10.4 | 49.8 | 11 027 | 10 302 | -6.6 | -1.8 | 244 | 276 | -158 | 4 236 | -4.8 | 2.30 | 8.4 | 31.7 |
| Fayette | 13.6 | 9.4 | 10.0 | 50.1 | 22 008 | 20 880 | -5.1 | -0.4 | 537 | 522 | -95 | 8 634 | -1.6 | 2.33 | 7.6 | 29.7 |
| Floyd | 13.8 | 9.8 | 10.4 | 50.9 | 16 900 | 16 303 | -3.5 | -1.5 | 414 | 469 | -184 | 6 886 | 0.8 | 2.32 | 8.1 | 31.2 |

1. No spouse present.

# Table B. States and Counties — Population, Vital Statistics, Medicare, and Crime

| STATE County | Persons in group quarters, 2010 | Daytime population, 2007–2011 Number | Employment/residence ratio | Births, 2011 Total | Rate[1] | Deaths, 2011 Number | Rate[1] | Persons under 65 with no health insurance, 2010 Number | Percent | Medicare, 2012 Eligible for Medicare | Enrolled in Medicare Advantage | Enrolled in a Medicare prescription drug plan | Serious crimes known to police,[2] 2011 Total Number | Rate[3] |
|---|---|---|---|---|---|---|---|---|---|---|---|---|---|---|
| | 32 | 33 | 34 | 35 | 36 | 37 | 38 | 39 | 40 | 41 | 42 | 43 | 44 | 45 |
| **INDIANA—Cont'd** | | | | | | | | | | | | | | |
| Pike | 213 | 11 080 | 0.67 | 141 | 11.1 | 154 | 12.1 | 1 573 | 15.0 | 2 801 | 497 | 1 309 | 341 | 3 243 |
| Porter | 3 405 | 145 818 | 0.77 | 1 759 | 10.6 | 1 388 | 8.4 | 19 355 | 13.8 | 26 487 | 1 844 | 14 419 | 3 735 | 2 287 |
| Posey | 242 | 22 789 | 0.75 | 280 | 10.9 | 243 | 9.4 | 2 629 | 12.0 | 4 709 | 1 079 | 2 262 | NA | NA |
| Pulaski | 193 | 13 020 | 0.91 | 158 | 11.8 | 139 | 10.4 | 1 908 | 17.4 | 2 800 | 359 | 1 520 | 267 | 1 982 |
| Putnam | 5 424 | 35 950 | 0.86 | 371 | 9.8 | 307 | 8.1 | 4 437 | 16.1 | 6 345 | 1 428 | 2 649 | NA | NA |
| Randolph | 329 | 22 868 | 0.71 | 293 | 11.2 | 280 | 10.7 | 3 618 | 16.8 | 5 420 | 697 | 2 586 | 737 | 2 924 |
| Ripley | 449 | 28 119 | 0.96 | 375 | 13.0 | 296 | 10.3 | 3 938 | 16.2 | 4 726 | 916 | 2 308 | 496 | 1 712 |
| Rush | 178 | 15 246 | 0.72 | 170 | 9.8 | 183 | 10.6 | 2 468 | 17.0 | 3 338 | 424 | 1 818 | 624 | 3 570 |
| St. Joseph | 11 272 | 275 221 | 1.07 | 3 478 | 13.0 | 2 366 | 8.9 | 37 840 | 17.1 | 43 200 | 11 305 | 16 881 | 11 957 | 4 467 |
| Scott | 312 | 20 963 | 0.67 | 282 | 11.8 | 300 | 12.5 | 3 492 | 16.8 | 4 885 | 841 | 2 423 | 869 | 3 575 |
| Shelby | 683 | 41 252 | 0.86 | 492 | 11.1 | 404 | 9.1 | 6 261 | 16.7 | 7 741 | 1 384 | 3 700 | 1 242 | 2 787 |
| Spencer | 368 | 18 644 | 0.77 | 206 | 9.8 | 211 | 10.1 | 2 577 | 14.7 | 3 849 | 497 | 1 896 | 344 | 1 634 |
| Starke | 16 | 19 345 | 0.56 | 273 | 11.8 | 277 | 11.9 | 3 554 | 17.9 | 5 097 | 566 | 2 667 | 445 | 1 895 |
| Steuben | 1 300 | 32 528 | 0.90 | 342 | 10.1 | 301 | 8.8 | 4 781 | 17.2 | 6 564 | 2 473 | 2 539 | 1 056 | 3 073 |
| Sullivan | 2 298 | 19 912 | 0.81 | 203 | 9.5 | 208 | 9.7 | 2 705 | 16.8 | 4 003 | 329 | 2 141 | 214 | 1 236 |
| Switzerland | 107 | 8 628 | 0.59 | 139 | 13.2 | 105 | 9.9 | 1 735 | 19.3 | 1 592 | 157 | 817 | NA | NA |
| Tippecanoe | 14 463 | 181 704 | 1.13 | 2 200 | 12.6 | 1 019 | 5.8 | 26 769 | 18.7 | 20 561 | 3 195 | 10 146 | 5 364 | 3 089 |
| Tipton | 205 | 13 792 | 0.70 | 119 | 7.5 | 163 | 10.3 | 1 908 | 14.7 | 3 213 | 412 | 1 417 | 343 | 2 141 |
| Union | 67 | 5 538 | 0.45 | 101 | 13.4 | 66 | 8.8 | 1 105 | 17.2 | 1 298 | 229 | 715 | NA | NA |
| Vanderburgh | 7 531 | 202 993 | 1.28 | 2 292 | 12.7 | 1 811 | 10.0 | 22 420 | 15.1 | 33 017 | 8 499 | 14 455 | NA | NA |
| Vermillion | 209 | 14 712 | 0.77 | 189 | 11.6 | 204 | 12.6 | 2 016 | 15.1 | 3 398 | 282 | 1 725 | 157 | 963 |
| Vigo | 9 545 | 117 061 | 1.21 | 1 228 | 11.4 | 1 105 | 10.2 | 14 922 | 17.6 | 19 039 | 1 760 | 10 581 | 5 831 | 5 379 |
| Wabash | 1 839 | 31 818 | 0.92 | 338 | 10.4 | 404 | 12.4 | 3 900 | 15.2 | 7 370 | 2 881 | 2 805 | NA | NA |
| Warren | 84 | 7 104 | 0.63 | 87 | 10.3 | 88 | 10.4 | 1 141 | 16.3 | 1 705 | 133 | 941 | NA | NA |
| Warrick | 726 | 47 087 | 0.59 | 663 | 11.0 | 513 | 8.5 | 6 610 | 13.0 | 10 167 | 2 422 | 4 000 | 1 033 | 1 722 |
| Washington | 261 | 22 708 | 0.54 | 311 | 11.0 | 279 | 9.9 | 4 658 | 19.1 | 5 261 | 1 258 | 2 465 | NA | NA |
| Wayne | 2 614 | 70 533 | 1.05 | 870 | 12.7 | 846 | 12.3 | 10 632 | 19.0 | 14 632 | 1 705 | 8 357 | 2 245 | 3 331 |
| Wells | 472 | 25 985 | 0.87 | 321 | 11.6 | 241 | 8.7 | 3 517 | 15.3 | 5 168 | 1 877 | 2 275 | 684 | 2 462 |
| White | 307 | 23 122 | 0.86 | 323 | 13.1 | 280 | 11.3 | 3 928 | 19.4 | 5 084 | 635 | 2 647 | 239 | 965 |
| Whitley | 436 | 29 545 | 0.77 | 400 | 12.0 | 281 | 8.4 | 4 112 | 14.5 | 5 912 | 2 886 | 2 045 | NA | NA |
| **IOWA** | 98 112 | 3 031 307 | 1.00 | 38 324 | 12.5 | 27 895 | 9.1 | 270 219 | 10.7 | 541 350 | 75 529 | 311 854 | 79 187 | 2 586 |
| Adair | 151 | 6 823 | 0.78 | 73 | 9.7 | 93 | 12.4 | 643 | 10.8 | 1 615 | 152 | 1 107 | 59 | 764 |
| Adams | 114 | 3 658 | 0.79 | 48 | 12.0 | 52 | 13.0 | 405 | 12.9 | 989 | 20 | 700 | 51 | 1 259 |
| Allamakee | 332 | 13 162 | 0.84 | 171 | 12.0 | 199 | 13.9 | 2 057 | 18.2 | 3 172 | 358 | 1 942 | NA | NA |
| Appanoose | 126 | 12 714 | 0.96 | 141 | 11.0 | 194 | 15.2 | 1 287 | 12.7 | 3 083 | 391 | 1 911 | 394 | 3 042 |
| Audubon | 136 | 5 289 | 0.72 | 59 | 9.8 | 80 | 13.3 | 658 | 14.2 | 1 511 | 52 | 1 111 | NA | NA |
| Benton | 313 | 19 234 | 0.48 | 285 | 10.9 | 241 | 9.2 | 2 039 | 9.3 | 4 707 | 843 | 2 585 | 260 | 1 099 |
| Black Hawk | 5 967 | 139 930 | 1.16 | 1 684 | 12.8 | 1 159 | 8.8 | 11 655 | 10.8 | 22 583 | 3 181 | 10 447 | 3 602 | 2 733 |
| Boone | 768 | 23 383 | 0.78 | 286 | 10.9 | 301 | 11.5 | 1 966 | 9.1 | 5 192 | 562 | 3 142 | 548 | 2 072 |
| Bremer | 1 718 | 23 066 | 0.90 | 229 | 9.4 | 234 | 9.6 | 1 520 | 8.2 | 4 645 | 398 | 2 675 | 310 | 1 270 |
| Buchanan | 343 | 17 927 | 0.70 | 292 | 14.0 | 185 | 8.8 | 1 986 | 11.4 | 3 798 | 501 | 2 058 | 276 | 1 310 |
| Buena Vista | 1 014 | 20 863 | 1.07 | 300 | 14.7 | 170 | 8.3 | 2 421 | 14.8 | 3 303 | 166 | 2 194 | 399 | 1 959 |
| Butler | 242 | 12 122 | 0.61 | 156 | 10.4 | 193 | 12.9 | 1 281 | 10.8 | 3 315 | 333 | 2 080 | 26 | 174 |
| Calhoun | 238 | 8 821 | 0.78 | 114 | 11.8 | 141 | 14.6 | 837 | 11.5 | 2 459 | 97 | 1 701 | 100 | 1 029 |
| Carroll | 467 | 22 294 | 1.13 | 255 | 12.2 | 258 | 12.4 | 1 595 | 9.5 | 4 393 | 305 | 3 179 | NA | NA |
| Cass | 304 | 13 911 | 1.00 | 159 | 11.5 | 190 | 13.8 | 1 322 | 12.1 | 3 370 | 239 | 2 302 | 243 | 1 732 |
| Cedar | 324 | 14 223 | 0.57 | 198 | 10.8 | 178 | 9.7 | 1 405 | 9.2 | 3 426 | 598 | 1 855 | 139 | 747 |
| Cerro Gordo | 1 158 | 46 828 | 1.12 | 465 | 10.6 | 478 | 10.9 | 3 504 | 9.9 | 9 728 | 265 | 6 259 | 1 726 | 3 889 |
| Cherokee | 371 | 11 996 | 0.99 | 114 | 9.4 | 170 | 14.1 | 1 059 | 11.4 | 2 672 | 389 | 1 715 | 158 | 1 302 |
| Chickasaw | 183 | 11 470 | 0.83 | 138 | 11.1 | 119 | 9.6 | 1 168 | 11.7 | 2 649 | 108 | 1 816 | NA | NA |
| Clarke | 152 | 9 093 | 0.96 | 127 | 13.6 | 98 | 10.5 | 1 038 | 13.6 | 1 803 | 142 | 1 132 | 144 | 1 543 |
| Clay | 234 | 17 786 | 1.13 | 195 | 11.8 | 170 | 10.2 | 1 505 | 11.2 | 3 614 | 80 | 2 503 | 337 | 2 011 |
| Clayton | 287 | 16 628 | 0.83 | 180 | 10.0 | 190 | 10.5 | 1 969 | 13.7 | 4 156 | 683 | 2 671 | 53 | 291 |
| Clinton | 852 | 49 236 | 1.00 | 599 | 12.2 | 500 | 10.2 | 3 757 | 9.3 | 9 850 | 1 276 | 5 817 | 1 750 | 3 544 |
| Crawford | 585 | 16 845 | 0.98 | 247 | 14.3 | 165 | 9.6 | 2 374 | 16.8 | 3 235 | 244 | 2 145 | 74 | 431 |
| Dallas | 516 | 56 199 | 0.76 | 1 006 | 14.5 | 346 | 5.0 | 5 009 | 8.4 | 8 318 | 1 184 | 4 369 | 1 219 | 1 834 |
| Davis | 124 | 7 700 | 0.72 | 141 | 16.0 | 83 | 9.4 | 1 283 | 17.9 | 1 608 | 125 | 944 | 42 | 477 |
| Decatur | 663 | 7 885 | 0.85 | 98 | 11.8 | 98 | 11.8 | 940 | 15.0 | 1 650 | 164 | 1 070 | NA | NA |
| Delaware | 218 | 15 818 | 0.79 | 192 | 10.9 | 185 | 10.5 | 1 693 | 11.5 | 3 193 | 556 | 2 111 | 143 | 801 |
| Des Moines | 685 | 43 191 | 1.16 | 475 | 11.8 | 421 | 10.5 | 3 330 | 10.2 | 8 670 | 720 | 5 352 | 1 640 | 4 046 |
| Dickinson | 211 | 16 722 | 1.00 | 153 | 9.1 | 179 | 10.6 | 1 391 | 10.8 | 4 306 | 161 | 3 066 | 242 | 1 444 |
| Dubuque | 4 268 | 100 539 | 1.15 | 1 187 | 12.5 | 842 | 8.9 | 6 468 | 8.5 | 17 192 | 6 906 | 10 615 | 2 046 | 2 173 |
| Emmet | 540 | 9 917 | 0.92 | 119 | 11.8 | 127 | 12.6 | 1 041 | 13.2 | 2 103 | 46 | 1 522 | 200 | 1 931 |
| Fayette | 782 | 19 883 | 0.89 | 236 | 11.3 | 225 | 10.7 | 1 993 | 12.3 | 4 624 | 509 | 2 941 | 238 | 1 134 |
| Floyd | 304 | 14 867 | 0.82 | 173 | 10.8 | 205 | 12.8 | 1 505 | 11.7 | 3 714 | 99 | 2 516 | 182 | 1 111 |

1. Per 1,000 estimated resident population.  2. Data for serious crimes have not been adjusted for underreporting; this may affect comparability between geographic areas and over time.  3. Per 100,000 population estimated by the FBI.

# Table B. States and Counties — Crime, Education, Money Income, and Poverty

| STATE County | Serious crimes known to police, 2011 (cont.)[1] Rate[2] Violent | Property | Education — School enrollment and attainment, 2007-2011 Enrollment[3] Total | Per cent private | Attainment[4] (percent) High school graduate or less | Bachelor's degree or more | Local government expenditures,[5] 2009-2010 Total current expenditures (mil dol) | Current expenditures per student (dollars) | Money income, 2007-2011 Per capita income[6] (dollars) | Households Median income Dollars | Percent change, 2000 to 2007-2011 (constant 2011 dollars) | Percent with income of $200,000 or more | Income and poverty, 2011 Median household income (dollars) | Percent below poverty level All persons | Children under 18 years | Children 5 to 17 years in families |
|---|---|---|---|---|---|---|---|---|---|---|---|---|---|---|---|---|
| | 46 | 47 | 48 | 49 | 50 | 51 | 52 | 53 | 54 | 55 | 56 | 57 | 58 | 59 | 60 | 61 |
| **INDIANA—Cont'd** | | | | | | | | | | | | | | | | |
| Pike | 352 | 2 891 | 2 656 | 5.2 | 62.9 | 10.2 | 33.3 | 16 328 | 20 756 | 40 525 | -13.6 | 1.3 | 42 482 | 11.7 | 17.1 | 15.1 |
| Porter | 138 | 2 150 | 45 147 | 19.3 | 43.8 | 25.5 | 235.4 | 8 519 | 28 452 | 62 394 | -13.0 | 3.1 | 62 178 | 10.8 | 14.3 | 12.3 |
| Posey | NA | NA | 6 484 | 14.6 | 50.1 | 19.8 | 41.9 | 10 689 | 27 529 | 57 757 | -3.2 | 2.2 | 55 488 | 12.4 | 16.9 | 12.9 |
| Pulaski | 156 | 1 826 | 3 487 | 11.6 | 60.5 | 15.2 | 22.8 | 10 529 | 21 895 | 45 029 | -5.8 | 1.8 | 43 971 | 13.3 | 20.0 | 18.3 |
| Putnam | NA | NA | 10 453 | 26.3 | 55.3 | 16.7 | 64.9 | 10 095 | 20 927 | 50 165 | -4.4 | 1.5 | 46 961 | 13.8 | 17.8 | 16.2 |
| Randolph | 28 | 2 897 | 6 400 | 6.8 | 60.7 | 11.2 | 44.3 | 9 510 | 20 552 | 41 544 | -10.9 | 0.9 | 39 611 | 17.0 | 26.5 | 23.9 |
| Ripley | 110 | 1 602 | 7 453 | 14.0 | 60.8 | 15.1 | 34.0 | 9 825 | 22 995 | 49 358 | -11.8 | 1.8 | 47 900 | 11.7 | 16.7 | 15.4 |
| Rush | 63 | 3 507 | 4 349 | 9.2 | 62.3 | 14.8 | 23.1 | 8 496 | 21 779 | 47 102 | -8.6 | 1.1 | 44 416 | 14.0 | 20.5 | 18.5 |
| St. Joseph | 388 | 4 079 | 79 241 | 32.0 | 45.5 | 26.2 | 420.1 | 10 405 | 23 420 | 45 183 | -17.2 | 2.5 | 43 813 | 19.5 | 29.6 | 27.9 |
| Scott | 321 | 3 254 | 5 747 | 5.3 | 66.2 | 10.1 | 37.1 | 8 682 | 19 766 | 40 532 | -13.4 | 1.0 | 38 826 | 21.3 | 34.0 | 31.9 |
| Shelby | 103 | 2 684 | 10 540 | 11.2 | 57.6 | 15.0 | 68.0 | 8 916 | 26 197 | 52 156 | -11.5 | 2.4 | 49 437 | 12.7 | 18.7 | 17.0 |
| Spencer | 14 | 1 619 | 5 004 | 16.5 | 58.6 | 15.4 | 31.0 | 8 810 | 23 781 | 54 348 | -5.2 | 1.7 | 53 464 | 10.7 | 14.5 | 12.8 |
| Starke | 268 | 1 627 | 5 213 | 9.3 | 65.4 | 11.3 | 34.8 | 8 578 | 18 507 | 38 961 | -22.5 | 0.5 | 42 088 | 16.9 | 25.4 | 21.9 |
| Steuben | 58 | 3 015 | 8 679 | 21.7 | 52.1 | 19.9 | 38.9 | 9 393 | 23 813 | 48 502 | -18.5 | 1.6 | 45 957 | 13.0 | 21.0 | 18.2 |
| Sullivan | 81 | 1 155 | 4 574 | 8.5 | 57.6 | 13.4 | 31.9 | 9 514 | 21 371 | 47 640 | 7.0 | 1.9 | 42 608 | 18.0 | 22.6 | 19.8 |
| Switzerland | NA | NA | 2 206 | 13.9 | 69.6 | 8.9 | 13.4 | 8 922 | 20 974 | 43 628 | -12.9 | 1.3 | 42 285 | 17.6 | 29.4 | 28.0 |
| Tippecanoe | 297 | 2 792 | 68 379 | 8.4 | 38.1 | 35.8 | 202.1 | 9 470 | 22 892 | 43 485 | -16.7 | 2.6 | 43 339 | 21.4 | 20.8 | 19.5 |
| Tipton | 194 | 1 948 | 3 611 | 9.2 | 56.8 | 15.3 | 23.3 | 8 365 | 24 969 | 53 543 | -18.3 | 1.9 | 53 300 | 9.6 | 13.8 | 11.5 |
| Union | NA | NA | 2 045 | 4.7 | 56.5 | 17.0 | 16.6 | 10 262 | 20 279 | 43 912 | -11.3 | 0.3 | 43 540 | 14.6 | 22.7 | 19.8 |
| Vanderburgh | NA | NA | 44 824 | 16.7 | 47.0 | 21.9 | 232.6 | 10 079 | 24 312 | 43 334 | -12.8 | 2.0 | 43 570 | 15.5 | 22.1 | 20.7 |
| Vermillion | 233 | 730 | 3 816 | 6.5 | 58.6 | 13.8 | 24.4 | 8 641 | 22 786 | 43 856 | -6.8 | 2.3 | 45 089 | 13.1 | 20.4 | 17.8 |
| Vigo | 196 | 5 184 | 31 384 | 13.6 | 49.2 | 21.1 | 153.8 | 9 606 | 20 869 | 39 534 | -11.8 | 1.8 | 39 173 | 19.2 | 25.4 | 22.3 |
| Wabash | NA | NA | 8 270 | 18.0 | 57.4 | 17.1 | 55.0 | 10 041 | 20 741 | 44 242 | -18.9 | 1.0 | 42 032 | 16.0 | 23.4 | 19.1 |
| Warren | NA | NA | 1 904 | 13.8 | 60.1 | 13.7 | 11.1 | 8 862 | 25 447 | 49 615 | -12.1 | 3.5 | 49 095 | 9.7 | 15.3 | 13.3 |
| Warrick | 317 | 1 405 | 14 923 | 18.8 | 43.0 | 25.1 | 75.6 | 7 667 | 30 791 | 63 446 | -3.7 | 4.6 | 63 543 | 8.7 | 12.3 | 10.6 |
| Washington | NA | NA | 6 892 | 13.2 | 66.7 | 10.3 | 40.6 | 8 727 | 19 721 | 39 879 | -19.4 | 0.9 | 39 085 | 15.2 | 24.2 | 22.0 |
| Wayne | 303 | 3 029 | 17 243 | 15.2 | 56.4 | 16.6 | 101.7 | 9 411 | 22 082 | 40 427 | -14.2 | 1.5 | 36 559 | 21.1 | 33.5 | 28.1 |
| Wells | 65 | 2 398 | 6 703 | 12.2 | 53.5 | 14.4 | 45.1 | 9 388 | 23 618 | 48 154 | -18.8 | 1.1 | 49 234 | 10.2 | 15.9 | 14.3 |
| White | 89 | 876 | 5 540 | 9.2 | 56.5 | 15.1 | 45.0 | 8 766 | 22 756 | 47 752 | -13.1 | 1.4 | 45 748 | 11.9 | 18.8 | 15.7 |
| Whitley | NA | NA | 8 100 | 17.5 | 51.7 | 15.6 | 44.6 | 9 178 | 24 898 | 51 666 | -15.9 | 1.6 | 48 192 | 9.3 | 13.7 | 12.4 |
| **IOWA** | 256 | 2 330 | 805 059 | 16.3 | 43.5 | 24.9 | 4 796.4 | 9 764 | 26 110 | 50 451 | -5.3 | 2.5 | 49 545 | 12.7 | 17.1 | 15.4 |
| Adair | 65 | 699 | 1 613 | 4.8 | 52.3 | 14.3 | 8.8 | 9 188 | 24 307 | 47 623 | 0.3 | 1.7 | 44 701 | 11.2 | 15.3 | 13.2 |
| Adams | 296 | 963 | 872 | 13.1 | 51.3 | 17.2 | 5.8 | 9 700 | 24 105 | 44 389 | 8.0 | 2.2 | 42 062 | 13.4 | 21.7 | 20.6 |
| Allamakee | NA | NA | 3 216 | 13.4 | 56.9 | 15.3 | 20.9 | 8 842 | 22 411 | 47 096 | 2.7 | 0.8 | 39 670 | 15.1 | 23.4 | 21.0 |
| Appanoose | 317 | 2 725 | 2 860 | 6.4 | 54.8 | 15.3 | 19.6 | 9 280 | 19 907 | 35 230 | -8.8 | 1.2 | 36 693 | 16.3 | 25.2 | 23.7 |
| Audubon | NA | NA | 1 338 | 4.3 | 52.0 | 15.0 | 8.0 | 8 836 | 25 610 | 41 840 | -3.8 | 2.7 | 45 310 | 9.8 | 15.7 | 13.6 |
| Benton | 97 | 1 001 | 6 786 | 12.8 | 47.6 | 17.8 | 33.5 | 8 005 | 26 432 | 55 810 | -2.6 | 1.6 | 54 222 | 9.0 | 12.0 | 10.6 |
| Black Hawk | 368 | 2 365 | 39 047 | 11.0 | 44.1 | 25.2 | 208.0 | 11 492 | 23 721 | 44 567 | -11.4 | 1.9 | 43 037 | 16.4 | 20.5 | 18.0 |
| Boone | 291 | 1 781 | 6 682 | 12.6 | 43.9 | 20.5 | 35.3 | 9 106 | 26 861 | 51 582 | -6.3 | 2.8 | 50 758 | 9.9 | 12.8 | 11.4 |
| Bremer | 275 | 996 | 7 085 | 29.0 | 41.0 | 27.4 | 39.1 | 8 229 | 27 922 | 58 372 | 5.9 | 2.3 | 57 646 | 7.6 | 7.9 | 7.1 |
| Buchanan | 104 | 1 206 | 5 391 | 14.4 | 51.7 | 18.2 | 25.6 | 8 649 | 24 792 | 54 879 | 6.9 | 1.9 | 52 930 | 10.8 | 17.9 | 16.5 |
| Buena Vista | 354 | 1 606 | 5 493 | 23.1 | 51.1 | 22.4 | 36.1 | 9 377 | 22 632 | 46 145 | -3.2 | 2.3 | 46 356 | 10.9 | 16.6 | 16.0 |
| Butler | 7 | 167 | 3 254 | 5.0 | 56.0 | 14.3 | 15.8 | 8 554 | 24 276 | 50 052 | 3.3 | 1.6 | 51 560 | 9.8 | 13.9 | 13.0 |
| Calhoun | 123 | 905 | 2 004 | 2.8 | 48.4 | 18.7 | 20.3 | 10 352 | 24 262 | 44 331 | -1.4 | 2.9 | 46 171 | 12.1 | 17.1 | 15.3 |
| Carroll | NA | NA | 4 939 | 30.0 | 52.3 | 17.9 | 26.9 | 8 616 | 25 429 | 48 038 | -4.5 | 2.1 | 49 251 | 9.5 | 12.0 | 11.3 |
| Cass | 100 | 1 632 | 2 992 | 6.8 | 51.6 | 15.7 | 24.7 | 9 302 | 22 812 | 41 444 | -6.8 | 1.3 | 41 329 | 13.4 | 20.7 | 19.5 |
| Cedar | 59 | 688 | 4 311 | 6.6 | 49.7 | 19.1 | 29.9 | 8 755 | 25 649 | 57 004 | 0.1 | 0.5 | 57 890 | 8.1 | 11.2 | 10.1 |
| Cerro Gordo | 126 | 3 763 | 10 093 | 11.1 | 39.8 | 21.5 | 56.0 | 9 319 | 26 841 | 45 973 | -5.1 | 2.1 | 43 120 | 13.5 | 18.2 | 15.5 |
| Cherokee | 214 | 1 088 | 2 547 | 5.3 | 50.0 | 19.0 | 15.3 | 8 595 | 25 416 | 45 668 | -3.8 | 1.7 | 47 570 | 10.2 | 15.5 | 13.8 |
| Chickasaw | NA | NA | 2 827 | 8.2 | 57.4 | 14.4 | 19.0 | 8 930 | 24 268 | 42 098 | -17.2 | 2.6 | 47 311 | 9.9 | 13.8 | 12.5 |
| Clarke | 96 | 1 446 | 2 388 | 6.1 | 58.6 | 13.2 | 14.6 | 8 427 | 22 463 | 45 610 | -2.0 | 0.8 | 42 670 | 12.9 | 19.4 | 18.0 |
| Clay | 48 | 1 964 | 3 836 | 11.2 | 46.5 | 18.3 | 22.5 | 9 376 | 26 114 | 45 462 | -5.9 | 1.5 | 50 289 | 10.7 | 17.0 | 15.2 |
| Clayton | 44 | 247 | 3 897 | 7.7 | 55.7 | 15.3 | 40.0 | 19 293 | 23 485 | 46 644 | 1.4 | 1.5 | 44 370 | 12.9 | 20.5 | 18.0 |
| Clinton | 334 | 3 210 | 12 066 | 11.4 | 49.0 | 16.4 | 78.3 | 9 309 | 24 553 | 48 063 | -4.9 | 1.6 | 45 600 | 13.6 | 19.2 | 17.5 |
| Crawford | 47 | 384 | 4 308 | 7.3 | 59.6 | 15.3 | 29.3 | 8 779 | 21 422 | 45 423 | -0.8 | 1.7 | 44 197 | 13.3 | 18.6 | 16.7 |
| Dallas | 155 | 1 679 | 17 329 | 19.3 | 30.0 | 41.1 | 110.7 | 8 543 | 34 246 | 71 691 | 9.4 | 6.2 | 72 146 | 6.3 | 8.0 | 7.4 |
| Davis | 148 | 330 | 2 064 | 21.4 | 51.4 | 16.0 | 11.3 | 9 204 | 21 650 | 46 651 | 5.1 | 2.4 | 40 673 | 16.8 | 28.1 | 27.9 |
| Decatur | NA | NA | 2 641 | 39.3 | 56.3 | 16.8 | 10.1 | 9 327 | 17 477 | 34 185 | -7.4 | 0.9 | 33 803 | 21.4 | 30.1 | 27.9 |
| Delaware | 190 | 610 | 4 354 | 16.7 | 55.0 | 14.2 | 25.3 | 8 796 | 23 519 | 49 375 | -1.6 | 1.3 | 50 231 | 10.5 | 14.7 | 12.9 |
| Des Moines | 459 | 3 587 | 9 291 | 10.4 | 46.1 | 18.3 | 58.2 | 9 000 | 23 908 | 43 111 | -13.2 | 1.4 | 43 721 | 15.4 | 24.1 | 21.8 |
| Dickinson | 60 | 1 385 | 3 206 | 6.6 | 39.1 | 27.0 | 23.3 | 8 943 | 30 862 | 52 704 | 0.0 | 3.5 | 52 821 | 7.9 | 12.4 | 11.0 |
| Dubuque | 155 | 2 018 | 24 873 | 34.3 | 47.0 | 25.5 | 132.9 | 9 219 | 25 525 | 49 663 | -7.1 | 2.2 | 52 084 | 10.2 | 13.1 | 11.7 |
| Emmet | 261 | 1 671 | 2 602 | 5.7 | 47.6 | 16.7 | 16.4 | 9 139 | 25 400 | 44 357 | -1.4 | 2.6 | 44 556 | 11.8 | 18.1 | 17.1 |
| Fayette | 186 | 948 | 5 335 | 19.2 | 54.2 | 16.9 | 35.4 | 9 180 | 21 897 | 42 108 | -3.9 | 1.3 | 41 547 | 12.3 | 18.5 | 17.1 |
| Floyd | 85 | 1 025 | 3 502 | 12.8 | 50.9 | 16.1 | 23.8 | 9 521 | 22 812 | 42 247 | -11.2 | 1.5 | 44 478 | 12.1 | 17.5 | 14.8 |

1. Data for serious crimes have not been adjusted for underreporting; this may affect comparability between geographic areas and over time. 2. Per 100,000 population estimated by the FBI. 3. All persons 3 years old and over enrolled in nursery school through college. 4. Persons 25 years old and over. 5. Elementary and secondary education expenditures. 6. Based on population estimated by the American Community Survey, 2007-2011.

# Table B. States and Counties — Personal Income

| | Personal income, 2011 | | | | | | | | | | | | |
|---|---|---|---|---|---|---|---|---|---|---|---|---|---|
| | | | Per capita[1] | | | | | | Transfer payments (mil dol) | | | | |
| | | | | | | | | | | Government payments to individuals | | | |
| STATE County | Total (mil dol) | Percent change, 2010–2011 | Dollars | Rank | Wages and salaries[2] (mil dol) | Proprietors' income (mil dol) | Dividends, interest, and rent (mil dol) | Total | Total | Social Security | Medical payments | Income mainte-nance | Unemploy-ment insurance |
| | 62 | 63 | 64 | 65 | 66 | 67 | 68 | 69 | 70 | 71 | 72 | 73 | 74 |

INDIANA—Cont'd

| | | | | | | | | | | | | | |
|---|---|---|---|---|---|---|---|---|---|---|---|---|---|
| Pike | 401 | 3.0 | 31 525 | 1 998 | 202 | 17 | 46 | 110 | 107 | 40 | 48 | 8 | 3 |
| Porter | 7 118 | 6.0 | 42 999 | 513 | 3 029 | 317 | 834 | 1 056 | 1 019 | 445 | 388 | 77 | 46 |
| Posey | 1 048 | 6.2 | 40 731 | 683 | 615 | 105 | 141 | 183 | 177 | 74 | 72 | 14 | 6 |
| Pulaski | 469 | 8.7 | 35 071 | 1 362 | 208 | 72 | 79 | 103 | 100 | 42 | 40 | 9 | 4 |
| Putnam | 1 206 | 4.8 | 31 817 | 1 928 | 505 | 90 | 135 | 239 | 230 | 98 | 85 | 19 | 13 |
| Randolph | 856 | 6.7 | 32 773 | 1 746 | 331 | 112 | 104 | 213 | 207 | 83 | 83 | 21 | 9 |
| Ripley | 864 | 6.8 | 30 055 | 2 280 | 757 | 32 | 126 | 195 | 189 | 72 | 81 | 16 | 10 |
| Rush | 643 | 8.0 | 37 175 | 1 063 | 208 | 94 | 77 | 134 | 130 | 51 | 55 | 13 | 6 |
| St. Joseph | 9 678 | 4.2 | 36 289 | 1 171 | 6 237 | 1 178 | 1 434 | 1 897 | 1 838 | 675 | 721 | 228 | 91 |
| Scott | 673 | 3.4 | 28 041 | 2 611 | 282 | 25 | 64 | 210 | 204 | 72 | 88 | 26 | 8 |
| Shelby | 1 568 | 4.2 | 35 376 | 1 312 | 802 | 89 | 186 | 321 | 311 | 120 | 131 | 29 | 14 |
| Spencer | 711 | 5.2 | 33 906 | 1 531 | 325 | 47 | 92 | 143 | 138 | 58 | 55 | 11 | 6 |
| Starke | 646 | 7.1 | 27 844 | 2 631 | 174 | 52 | 77 | 197 | 191 | 77 | 75 | 21 | 8 |
| Steuben | 1 065 | 6.5 | 31 284 | 2 050 | 586 | 65 | 182 | 247 | 239 | 103 | 88 | 21 | 12 |
| Sullivan | 623 | 4.1 | 29 175 | 2 425 | 278 | 56 | 74 | 173 | 168 | 60 | 76 | 16 | 6 |
| Switzerland | 301 | 5.0 | 28 435 | 2 553 | 101 | 10 | 23 | 67 | 64 | 23 | 27 | 7 | 3 |
| Tippecanoe | 5 447 | 7.2 | 31 172 | 2 069 | 4 379 | 369 | 822 | 861 | 822 | 322 | 276 | 96 | 45 |
| Tipton | 594 | 7.7 | 37 631 | 1 012 | 187 | 51 | 84 | 123 | 120 | 53 | 46 | 8 | 6 |
| Union | 251 | 4.7 | 33 458 | 1 616 | 59 | 28 | 26 | 52 | 50 | 19 | 21 | 5 | 2 |
| Vanderburgh | 6 961 | 4.2 | 38 608 | 897 | 5 658 | 576 | 1 223 | 1 421 | 1 381 | 497 | 590 | 150 | 51 |
| Vermillion | 546 | 4.5 | 33 665 | 1 571 | 254 | 47 | 68 | 133 | 130 | 52 | 51 | 11 | 6 |
| Vigo | 3 426 | 3.3 | 31 666 | 1 963 | 2 444 | 251 | 513 | 873 | 849 | 280 | 368 | 101 | 36 |
| Wabash | 1 091 | 5.8 | 33 469 | 1 610 | 505 | 107 | 159 | 284 | 277 | 113 | 116 | 22 | 11 |
| Warren | 303 | 11.4 | 35 958 | 1 217 | 91 | 59 | 36 | 58 | 56 | 26 | 20 | 4 | 2 |
| Warrick | 2 515 | 5.5 | 41 726 | 599 | 787 | 128 | 357 | 389 | 375 | 164 | 147 | 25 | 15 |
| Washington | 832 | 5.0 | 29 544 | 2 372 | 240 | 47 | 95 | 210 | 204 | 77 | 82 | 24 | 9 |
| Wayne | 2 122 | 4.1 | 30 909 | 2 122 | 1 332 | 157 | 298 | 608 | 592 | 220 | 251 | 63 | 24 |
| Wells | 952 | 6.2 | 34 321 | 1 469 | 481 | 58 | 146 | 188 | 181 | 81 | 69 | 13 | 8 |
| White | 864 | 9.9 | 34 982 | 1 378 | 385 | 99 | 124 | 197 | 192 | 79 | 79 | 15 | 8 |
| Whitley | 1 134 | 8.0 | 33 958 | 1 519 | 549 | 29 | 139 | 221 | 214 | 95 | 81 | 15 | 11 |
| **IOWA** | 126 032 | 9.1 | 41 156 | X | 74 924 | 18 158 | 18 783 | 22 176 | 21 498 | 7 844 | 8 710 | 2 082 | 852 |
| Adair | 304 | 16.0 | 40 325 | 713 | 113 | 67 | 46 | 54 | 53 | 22 | 22 | 4 | 2 |
| Adams | 174 | 18.6 | 43 553 | 465 | 53 | 53 | 26 | 35 | 35 | 13 | 17 | 3 | 1 |
| Allamakee | 508 | 11.9 | 35 588 | 1 277 | 202 | 114 | 84 | 107 | 104 | 42 | 43 | 10 | 4 |
| Appanoose | 379 | 5.4 | 29 636 | 2 355 | 174 | 37 | 60 | 117 | 114 | 41 | 50 | 14 | 3 |
| Audubon | 317 | 25.9 | 52 562 | 151 | 71 | 140 | 43 | 49 | 47 | 20 | 20 | 3 | 2 |
| Benton | 1 107 | 9.7 | 42 432 | 549 | 252 | 192 | 148 | 171 | 165 | 69 | 65 | 13 | 9 |
| Black Hawk | 4 928 | 7.0 | 37 461 | 1 030 | 3 853 | 398 | 722 | 982 | 953 | 338 | 388 | 113 | 38 |
| Boone | 1 074 | 7.9 | 40 920 | 665 | 454 | 105 | 145 | 244 | 238 | 74 | 130 | 14 | 6 |
| Bremer | 1 048 | 11.5 | 43 157 | 498 | 449 | 126 | 168 | 170 | 165 | 70 | 73 | 8 | 5 |
| Buchanan | 820 | 15.5 | 39 192 | 832 | 262 | 161 | 144 | 145 | 140 | 55 | 61 | 12 | 6 |
| Buena Vista | 846 | 12.8 | 41 466 | 620 | 445 | 222 | 123 | 138 | 134 | 46 | 53 | 15 | 4 |
| Butler | 680 | 18.2 | 45 534 | 363 | 161 | 203 | 89 | 115 | 112 | 47 | 49 | 8 | 4 |
| Calhoun | 471 | 22.4 | 48 966 | 234 | 123 | 172 | 69 | 84 | 82 | 34 | 36 | 6 | 2 |
| Carroll | 942 | 14.8 | 45 157 | 391 | 504 | 229 | 151 | 156 | 152 | 59 | 73 | 11 | 4 |
| Cass | 601 | 13.2 | 43 471 | 470 | 246 | 147 | 92 | 125 | 122 | 46 | 57 | 11 | 4 |
| Cedar | 798 | 12.8 | 43 351 | 479 | 233 | 149 | 125 | 114 | 110 | 50 | 41 | 8 | 6 |
| Cerro Gordo | 1 811 | 7.0 | 41 225 | 642 | 1 135 | 222 | 302 | 370 | 360 | 137 | 148 | 31 | 13 |
| Cherokee | 546 | 13.7 | 45 252 | 383 | 232 | 163 | 85 | 92 | 90 | 38 | 38 | 6 | 3 |
| Chickasaw | 541 | 16.0 | 43 446 | 473 | 211 | 147 | 87 | 91 | 88 | 37 | 38 | 7 | 3 |
| Clarke | 302 | 8.6 | 32 255 | 1 835 | 166 | 47 | 38 | 71 | 69 | 24 | 31 | 8 | 3 |
| Clay | 741 | 12.5 | 44 683 | 406 | 416 | 177 | 115 | 128 | 124 | 51 | 52 | 11 | 5 |
| Clayton | 696 | 15.5 | 38 662 | 886 | 285 | 143 | 130 | 139 | 135 | 54 | 57 | 10 | 7 |
| Clinton | 1 928 | 8.4 | 39 340 | 819 | 1 059 | 223 | 265 | 473 | 462 | 143 | 172 | 43 | 16 |
| Crawford | 740 | 16.2 | 42 843 | 516 | 339 | 229 | 95 | 121 | 117 | 44 | 53 | 12 | 3 |
| Dallas | 3 315 | 11.6 | 47 740 | 273 | 2 039 | 210 | 502 | 307 | 291 | 129 | 109 | 24 | 12 |
| Davis | 239 | 7.0 | 27 254 | 2 728 | 78 | 37 | 33 | 60 | 58 | 22 | 24 | 6 | 3 |
| Decatur | 224 | 12.1 | 27 009 | 2 764 | 81 | 31 | 30 | 65 | 63 | 21 | 26 | 9 | 1 |
| Delaware | 739 | 17.6 | 41 861 | 588 | 285 | 178 | 119 | 113 | 109 | 45 | 45 | 9 | 5 |
| Des Moines | 1 561 | 7.4 | 38 869 | 870 | 1 024 | 190 | 252 | 367 | 358 | 127 | 143 | 41 | 12 |
| Dickinson | 772 | 8.6 | 45 680 | 354 | 347 | 125 | 184 | 140 | 136 | 64 | 52 | 8 | 6 |
| Dubuque | 3 680 | 8.0 | 38 886 | 864 | 2 712 | 321 | 652 | 687 | 666 | 253 | 284 | 60 | 26 |
| Emmet | 400 | 12.7 | 39 635 | 791 | 176 | 89 | 52 | 92 | 89 | 30 | 36 | 8 | 3 |
| Fayette | 778 | 18.2 | 37 074 | 1 069 | 285 | 167 | 121 | 187 | 182 | 62 | 74 | 15 | 7 |
| Floyd | 614 | 10.8 | 38 187 | 943 | 250 | 110 | 110 | 137 | 133 | 53 | 58 | 11 | 5 |

1. Based on the resident population estimated as of July 1 of the year shown.  2. Includes supplements to wages and salaries.

# Table B. States and Counties — Earnings, Social Security, and Housing

| STATE County | Earnings, 2011 | | | | | | | | | Social Security beneficiaries, December 2011 | | | Housing units, 2010 | |
|---|---|---|---|---|---|---|---|---|---|---|---|---|---|---|
| | | | | | Percent by selected industries | | | | | | | | | |
| | | | Goods-related[1] | | Service-related and health | | | | | | | Supplemental Security Income recipients, December 2011 | | |
| | Total (mil dol) | Farm | Total | Manu-facturing | Infor-mation and profes-sional and technical services | Retail trade | Finance, insur-ance, and real estate | Health care and social services | Govern-ment | Number | Rate[2] | | Total | Percent change, 2000–2010 |
| | 75 | 76 | 77 | 78 | 79 | 80 | 81 | 82 | 83 | 84 | 85 | 86 | 87 | 88 |

**INDIANA—Cont'd**

| | | | | | | | | | | | | | | |
|---|---|---|---|---|---|---|---|---|---|---|---|---|---|---|
| Pike | 220 | 1.6 | 29.5 | 4.9 | D | 3.1 | D | D | 15.1 | 3 115 | 245 | 281 | 5 735 | 2.2 |
| Porter | 3 346 | 0.8 | D | 24.1 | 5.7 | 6.5 | 3.3 | 12.2 | 11.5 | 29 935 | 181 | 1 896 | 66 179 | 14.9 |
| Posey | 720 | 6.6 | 50.8 | 44.8 | D | 5.5 | 2.0 | D | 8.6 | 5 395 | 210 | 355 | 11 207 | 1.2 |
| Pulaski | 280 | 21.3 | D | 26.8 | 2.2 | 4.7 | 3.0 | D | 18.0 | 3 250 | 243 | 259 | 6 060 | 2.4 |
| Putnam | 595 | 4.1 | 27.4 | 23.5 | D | 5.4 | 2.9 | D | 21.2 | 7 230 | 191 | 443 | 14 706 | 8.9 |
| Randolph | 443 | 11.8 | D | 28.3 | D | 4.1 | 1.6 | D | 14.1 | 6 320 | 242 | 474 | 11 743 | -0.3 |
| Ripley | 789 | 1.6 | 22.8 | 18.7 | D | 2.8 | 5.7 | D | 8.7 | 5 465 | 190 | 371 | 11 952 | 14.0 |
| Rush | 302 | 24.5 | D | 18.1 | D | 5.6 | 2.8 | 4.2 | 18.3 | 3 920 | 227 | 317 | 7 508 | 2.3 |
| St. Joseph | 7 415 | 0.7 | 23.3 | 19.0 | 8.9 | 5.9 | 6.0 | 14.6 | 10.9 | 48 710 | 183 | 5 406 | 114 849 | 7.3 |
| Scott | 307 | 2.3 | D | 33.7 | 2.6 | 8.7 | 3.3 | 6.8 | 23.7 | 5 880 | 245 | 913 | 10 440 | 7.2 |
| Shelby | 890 | 4.6 | 38.0 | 30.7 | 2.7 | 6.8 | 1.9 | D | 16.0 | 8 835 | 199 | 679 | 19 080 | 8.2 |
| Spencer | 372 | 4.9 | D | 20.5 | D | 4.3 | 1.7 | D | 13.4 | 4 345 | 207 | 295 | 8 872 | 6.5 |
| Starke | 225 | 14.5 | 23.0 | 20.5 | 2.2 | 8.3 | 1.7 | D | 21.4 | 6 005 | 259 | 603 | 10 962 | 7.5 |
| Steuben | 651 | 2.7 | 36.3 | 31.8 | 4.7 | 8.4 | 2.9 | D | 12.2 | 7 490 | 220 | 447 | 19 377 | 11.8 |
| Sullivan | 334 | 9.4 | 24.4 | 11.8 | 3.2 | 6.3 | 2.3 | 4.3 | 27.5 | 4 675 | 219 | 412 | 8 939 | 1.5 |
| Switzerland | 111 | 3.7 | D | 2.2 | D | 3.2 | D | 5.1 | 21.3 | 1 855 | 176 | 181 | 4 969 | 17.6 |
| Tippecanoe | 4 748 | 1.1 | D | 22.4 | 5.2 | 5.6 | 4.8 | 14.2 | 28.4 | 23 100 | 132 | 1 977 | 71 096 | 21.9 |
| Tipton | 239 | 15.4 | 26.3 | 19.4 | 4.1 | 7.9 | 2.9 | D | 16.1 | 3 670 | 232 | 173 | 6 998 | 2.2 |
| Union | 87 | 18.1 | 18.9 | 14.0 | 1.2 | 6.2 | D | D | 25.2 | 1 510 | 201 | 109 | 3 239 | 5.3 |
| Vanderburgh | 6 234 | 0.2 | D | 14.3 | 7.2 | 6.4 | 3.8 | 16.6 | 9.7 | 37 220 | 206 | 4 506 | 83 003 | 8.8 |
| Vermillion | 301 | 10.8 | D | 25.7 | 2.2 | 6.0 | D | 8.9 | 11.4 | 3 880 | 239 | 303 | 7 488 | 1.1 |
| Vigo | 2 695 | 0.5 | 25.8 | 19.7 | 3.8 | 6.8 | 4.4 | 18.3 | 18.9 | 21 505 | 199 | 3 127 | 46 006 | 1.8 |
| Wabash | 612 | 6.2 | D | 28.3 | 3.2 | 6.3 | 4.4 | D | 16.5 | 8 400 | 258 | 603 | 14 171 | 1.0 |
| Warren | 150 | 36.2 | D | 18.5 | D | 3.8 | D | 8.0 | 13.1 | 1 890 | 224 | 100 | 3 680 | 5.8 |
| Warrick | 916 | 0.9 | 32.4 | 23.1 | 5.9 | 5.2 | 5.1 | 19.3 | 12.5 | 11 495 | 191 | 653 | 24 203 | 17.8 |
| Washington | 287 | 8.3 | D | 26.5 | 3.8 | 7.1 | 3.7 | D | 21.1 | 6 280 | 223 | 686 | 12 220 | 9.2 |
| Wayne | 1 489 | 2.2 | 25.3 | 22.3 | D | 8.1 | 4.3 | 19.0 | 16.0 | 16 750 | 244 | 1 990 | 31 242 | 2.5 |
| Wells | 539 | 5.4 | D | 28.3 | D | 5.4 | 3.5 | 12.9 | 12.6 | 5 810 | 209 | 307 | 11 659 | 6.3 |
| White | 484 | 19.3 | D | 24.7 | D | 8.2 | 2.4 | D | 15.3 | 5 870 | 238 | 296 | 12 970 | 7.3 |
| Whitley | 577 | 3.7 | 49.2 | 44.6 | 2.2 | 5.5 | 2.0 | D | 13.4 | 6 720 | 201 | 297 | 14 281 | 13.8 |
| **IOWA** | 93 082 | 10.1 | 21.1 | 15.3 | 6.0 | 6.2 | 9.5 | 9.8 | 15.7 | 592 000 | 193 | 48 927 | 1 336 417 | 8.4 |
| Adair | 181 | 27.6 | D | 13.4 | 1.4 | 4.9 | 3.4 | D | 12.8 | 1 755 | 233 | 91 | 3 698 | 0.2 |
| Adams | 106 | 34.4 | D | 12.8 | 1.8 | 4.4 | D | D | 11.4 | 1 075 | 268 | 88 | 2 010 | -4.7 |
| Allamakee | 316 | 20.6 | 22.7 | 16.1 | 2.0 | 6.8 | 3.7 | 6.9 | 16.0 | 3 490 | 245 | 214 | 7 617 | 6.7 |
| Appanoose | 210 | 3.2 | D | 18.1 | 3.3 | 9.3 | 3.4 | D | 18.2 | 3 380 | 264 | 454 | 6 633 | -1.0 |
| Audubon | 211 | 55.6 | 7.9 | 4.5 | D | 3.5 | D | D | 9.6 | 1 650 | 273 | 66 | 2 972 | -0.8 |
| Benton | 444 | 25.1 | D | 10.7 | 3.3 | 7.1 | 3.6 | D | 17.8 | 5 200 | 199 | 290 | 11 095 | 6.9 |
| Black Hawk | 4 251 | 2.2 | D | 27.0 | 4.5 | 6.3 | 5.7 | 12.5 | 15.7 | 24 915 | 189 | 3 098 | 55 887 | 8.0 |
| Boone | 560 | 13.3 | D | 5.1 | 4.4 | 6.0 | 3.0 | D | 25.6 | 5 590 | 213 | 367 | 11 756 | 7.2 |
| Bremer | 575 | 14.3 | D | 18.9 | 2.5 | 5.9 | 11.5 | D | 16.7 | 5 055 | 208 | 170 | 9 915 | 6.2 |
| Buchanan | 423 | 31.0 | D | 13.1 | D | 6.3 | 3.8 | D | 17.2 | 4 195 | 200 | 318 | 8 968 | 3.1 |
| Buena Vista | 666 | 22.2 | 24.9 | 21.9 | D | 5.2 | 3.4 | D | 13.4 | 3 615 | 177 | 232 | 8 237 | 1.1 |
| Butler | 364 | 47.3 | D | 13.2 | D | 2.8 | 2.5 | D | 9.6 | 3 635 | 243 | 171 | 6 682 | 1.6 |
| Calhoun | 294 | 51.6 | 5.1 | 1.6 | 1.1 | 4.0 | 2.5 | 9.7 | 12.7 | 2 695 | 280 | 130 | 5 108 | -2.1 |
| Carroll | 732 | 23.0 | D | 10.8 | 2.7 | 6.5 | 7.6 | D | 8.9 | 4 705 | 226 | 254 | 9 376 | 3.9 |
| Cass | 393 | 27.7 | D | 8.0 | D | 6.6 | 4.6 | D | 18.9 | 3 635 | 263 | 339 | 6 591 | 0.0 |
| Cedar | 383 | 25.8 | 15.5 | 9.2 | 4.6 | 5.3 | 2.4 | D | 14.0 | 3 775 | 205 | 142 | 8 064 | 6.5 |
| Cerro Gordo | 1 357 | 8.0 | D | 12.4 | 5.7 | 7.9 | 5.5 | 22.8 | 12.1 | 10 555 | 240 | 787 | 22 163 | 3.1 |
| Cherokee | 395 | 32.5 | D | 16.9 | 1.8 | 5.0 | 2.4 | D | 12.9 | 2 865 | 237 | 146 | 5 777 | -1.2 |
| Chickasaw | 358 | 27.5 | D | 21.3 | 1.5 | 5.6 | 2.7 | D | 9.3 | 2 910 | 234 | 151 | 5 679 | 1.5 |
| Clarke | 213 | 12.2 | D | 24.4 | D | 7.1 | 2.8 | 7.4 | 18.4 | 2 030 | 217 | 152 | 4 086 | 3.9 |
| Clay | 593 | 20.8 | D | 11.4 | 4.5 | 11.2 | 3.3 | 8.8 | 15.2 | 3 940 | 237 | 236 | 8 062 | 3.0 |
| Clayton | 428 | 24.7 | D | 9.7 | 2.3 | 5.7 | 3.7 | D | 16.2 | 4 515 | 251 | 253 | 8 999 | 4.4 |
| Clinton | 1 281 | 9.4 | D | 26.3 | 2.2 | 6.5 | 3.8 | 13.0 | 10.7 | 10 930 | 223 | 1 139 | 21 733 | 0.7 |
| Crawford | 568 | 31.3 | 29.3 | 25.1 | D | 4.6 | 2.2 | 4.5 | 12.6 | 3 550 | 205 | 197 | 6 943 | -0.2 |
| Dallas | 2 249 | 5.2 | D | 4.6 | 4.6 | 6.3 | 43.9 | 7.9 | 8.1 | 8 945 | 129 | 441 | 27 260 | 64.7 |
| Davis | 115 | -0.3 | D | 9.0 | 12.1 | 7.9 | 3.6 | D | 25.8 | 1 830 | 208 | 136 | 3 600 | 2.0 |
| Decatur | 112 | 17.0 | D | 3.7 | D | 5.3 | D | D | 24.9 | 1 810 | 218 | 207 | 3 834 | 0.0 |
| Delaware | 463 | 24.3 | D | 22.6 | D | 4.5 | 3.8 | D | 14.0 | 3 595 | 204 | 209 | 8 028 | 4.5 |
| Des Moines | 1 214 | 2.9 | D | 28.1 | 3.6 | 7.3 | 3.4 | 15.2 | 11.7 | 9 395 | 234 | 971 | 18 535 | -0.6 |
| Dickinson | 472 | 13.5 | D | 21.7 | 3.0 | 9.7 | 5.2 | 6.7 | 13.3 | 4 740 | 280 | 213 | 12 849 | 13.0 |
| Dubuque | 3 033 | 3.4 | D | 19.0 | 9.8 | 6.9 | 7.8 | 14.1 | 8.4 | 19 135 | 202 | 1 548 | 38 951 | 9.7 |
| Emmet | 265 | 24.7 | D | 16.4 | 3.0 | 5.5 | 3.0 | D | 16.3 | 2 285 | 226 | 115 | 4 758 | -2.7 |
| Fayette | 453 | 31.7 | D | 4.8 | 2.1 | 5.4 | 3.2 | D | 13.0 | 5 080 | 242 | 445 | 9 558 | 0.5 |
| Floyd | 359 | 21.4 | D | 21.0 | 2.6 | 5.5 | 4.6 | D | 14.7 | 4 110 | 256 | 312 | 7 526 | 2.8 |

1. Includes mining, construction, and manufacturing.     2. Per 1,000 resident population enumerated in the 2010 census.

Table B. States and Counties — **Housing, Labor Force, and Employment**

| STATE County | Housing units, 2007–2011 Occupied units Owner-occupied Total | Percent | Median value[1] | Median owner cost as a percent of income With a mortgage | Without a mortgage[2] | Renter-occupied Median rent[3] | Median rent as a percent of income | Sub-standard units[4] (percent) | Civilian labor force, 2012 Total | Percent change, 2011–2012 | Unemployment Total | Rate[5] | Civilian employment,[6] 2007–2011 Total | Percent Management, business, science and arts | Construction, production, and maintenance occupations |
|---|---|---|---|---|---|---|---|---|---|---|---|---|---|---|---|
| | 89 | 90 | 91 | 92 | 93 | 94 | 95 | 96 | 97 | 98 | 99 | 100 | 101 | 102 | 103 |
| INDIANA—Cont'd | | | | | | | | | | | | | | | |
| Pike | 5 388 | 81.8 | 81 600 | 20.5 | 12.5 | 591 | 26.9 | 1.5 | 5 758 | -1.4 | 443 | 7.7 | 5 621 | 22.1 | 46.9 |
| Porter | 61 399 | 77.3 | 167 000 | 21.2 | 12.3 | 819 | 28.7 | 1.7 | 82 448 | 0.2 | 6 387 | 7.7 | 77 934 | 33.1 | 26.5 |
| Posey | 10 021 | 84.6 | 119 400 | 19.0 | 10.7 | 572 | 30.3 | 2.2 | 12 713 | -0.9 | 911 | 7.2 | 12 834 | 28.8 | 33.1 |
| Pulaski | 5 074 | 78.9 | 97 100 | 20.0 | 11.1 | 590 | 28.0 | 2.9 | 6 617 | -2.2 | 465 | 7.0 | 5 641 | 29.9 | 36.6 |
| Putnam | 12 433 | 80.0 | 120 500 | 22.6 | 12.3 | 688 | 28.1 | 1.6 | 17 291 | 0.1 | 1 576 | 9.1 | 15 873 | 27.8 | 31.1 |
| Randolph | 10 423 | 75.4 | 78 500 | 21.3 | 11.1 | 560 | 28.8 | 2.1 | 12 711 | -1.0 | 1 228 | 9.7 | 11 749 | 27.3 | 37.8 |
| Ripley | 10 813 | 78.0 | 136 300 | 22.9 | 11.8 | 658 | 24.4 | 2.4 | 13 988 | -2.0 | 1 259 | 9.0 | 13 442 | 25.7 | 35.4 |
| Rush | 6 686 | 73.9 | 107 000 | 22.6 | 11.3 | 564 | 27.3 | 1.3 | 8 812 | -1.9 | 699 | 7.9 | 8 034 | 27.3 | 36.6 |
| St. Joseph | 101 071 | 70.7 | 116 600 | 21.6 | 11.4 | 695 | 29.9 | 1.6 | 124 968 | -1.6 | 12 108 | 9.7 | 121 713 | 34.1 | 22.8 |
| Scott | 9 098 | 74.7 | 98 300 | 23.7 | 11.6 | 660 | 31.0 | 2.3 | 10 759 | -2.0 | 1 050 | 9.8 | 9 926 | 23.8 | 40.2 |
| Shelby | 17 381 | 72.2 | 127 100 | 21.3 | 12.0 | 697 | 26.8 | 1.3 | 22 768 | 0.4 | 1 768 | 7.8 | 21 737 | 26.7 | 34.1 |
| Spencer | 8 082 | 83.6 | 110 700 | 19.5 | 11.4 | 553 | 25.4 | 2.9 | 10 254 | -1.4 | 786 | 7.7 | 10 250 | 26.0 | 37.0 |
| Starke | 9 064 | 79.6 | 99 400 | 24.9 | 12.3 | 646 | 31.2 | 1.9 | 10 209 | -2.0 | 1 066 | 10.4 | 9 086 | 21.1 | 40.1 |
| Steuben | 13 943 | 78.7 | 125 600 | 22.9 | 11.3 | 639 | 27.6 | 1.5 | 16 033 | -2.5 | 1 431 | 8.9 | 16 740 | 28.7 | 30.3 |
| Sullivan | 7 855 | 77.8 | 78 300 | 18.7 | 11.4 | 561 | 26.0 | 3.7 | 8 682 | 0.7 | 961 | 11.1 | 8 627 | 28.3 | 31.1 |
| Switzerland | 4 149 | 78.7 | 118 300 | 25.6 | 12.0 | 656 | 22.9 | 5.0 | 5 456 | -1.5 | 376 | 6.9 | 4 640 | 16.6 | 36.6 |
| Tippecanoe | 65 100 | 54.6 | 130 400 | 21.1 | 9.9 | 752 | 35.3 | 1.9 | 84 137 | 1.1 | 6 199 | 7.4 | 82 843 | 39.3 | 21.1 |
| Tipton | 6 637 | 78.9 | 113 000 | 20.4 | 12.0 | 638 | 22.7 | 1.2 | 7 251 | 0.4 | 673 | 9.3 | 7 528 | 30.1 | 32.9 |
| Union | 2 988 | 78.4 | 112 500 | 23.7 | 13.6 | 589 | 28.6 | 1.8 | 3 378 | -2.8 | 292 | 8.6 | 3 570 | 30.1 | 29.2 |
| Vanderburgh | 73 927 | 64.1 | 112 800 | 21.2 | 11.6 | 688 | 31.4 | 2.3 | 91 244 | -0.9 | 6 975 | 7.6 | 86 581 | 29.4 | 25.3 |
| Vermillion | 6 434 | 76.9 | 75 900 | 19.6 | 11.2 | 601 | 24.9 | 2.7 | 7 665 | -0.9 | 855 | 11.2 | 7 162 | 21.9 | 34.2 |
| Vigo | 39 823 | 65.5 | 90 400 | 19.9 | 11.8 | 624 | 30.2 | 2.0 | 49 877 | -0.6 | 5 012 | 10.0 | 46 813 | 31.5 | 24.1 |
| Wabash | 12 968 | 75.4 | 96 700 | 20.3 | 10.7 | 576 | 27.7 | 3.0 | 15 669 | -2.2 | 1 345 | 8.6 | 14 655 | 28.5 | 33.7 |
| Warren | 3 328 | 78.8 | 100 200 | 21.9 | 10.7 | 616 | 24.3 | 1.4 | 4 748 | -1.2 | 308 | 6.5 | 3 905 | 26.5 | 36.4 |
| Warrick | 22 412 | 83.9 | 140 300 | 20.7 | 10.2 | 732 | 29.6 | 1.9 | 31 270 | -1.0 | 2 130 | 6.8 | 29 509 | 33.3 | 23.7 |
| Washington | 10 744 | 79.2 | 101 300 | 24.2 | 12.6 | 570 | 27.7 | 2.7 | 13 296 | -0.2 | 1 148 | 8.6 | 12 388 | 23.8 | 40.3 |
| Wayne | 28 071 | 68.4 | 98 200 | 21.9 | 12.1 | 602 | 29.2 | 2.2 | 29 884 | -2.7 | 3 078 | 10.3 | 29 799 | 28.7 | 29.1 |
| Wells | 10 767 | 78.3 | 108 900 | 20.6 | 9.9 | 565 | 27.3 | 1.4 | 13 651 | -1.3 | 1 012 | 7.4 | 13 050 | 28.3 | 33.9 |
| White | 9 786 | 77.2 | 111 000 | 21.3 | 12.0 | 684 | 29.2 | 2.3 | 12 624 | -0.3 | 1 028 | 8.1 | 11 482 | 26.7 | 33.1 |
| Whitley | 13 159 | 82.9 | 124 200 | 22.0 | 9.9 | 597 | 29.3 | 1.0 | 17 028 | -1.2 | 1 347 | 7.9 | 16 069 | 25.5 | 37.9 |
| IOWA | 1 219 137 | 73.0 | 121 300 | 21.1 | 11.8 | 637 | 27.6 | 1.8 | 1 638 542 | -1.3 | 85 724 | 5.2 | 1 554 416 | 33.4 | 25.8 |
| Adair | 3 323 | 76.6 | 93 300 | 22.2 | 11.9 | 525 | 22.1 | 2.5 | 4 317 | -0.6 | 183 | 4.2 | 3 971 | 29.2 | 34.6 |
| Adams | 1 706 | 81.5 | 81 100 | 18.8 | 14.0 | 412 | 20.0 | 2.3 | 2 090 | -0.4 | 91 | 4.4 | 2 024 | 35.0 | 26.3 |
| Allamakee | 5 860 | 80.3 | 108 100 | 23.0 | 12.3 | 509 | 22.1 | 2.5 | 7 684 | -1.3 | 530 | 6.9 | 7 228 | 27.5 | 35.9 |
| Appanoose | 5 475 | 71.7 | 73 300 | 23.3 | 13.7 | 513 | 28.5 | 3.1 | 5 916 | -1.3 | 410 | 6.9 | 5 693 | 29.5 | 33.2 |
| Audubon | 2 670 | 79.5 | 71 200 | 20.3 | 11.2 | 515 | 17.5 | 0.3 | 3 158 | -3.0 | 163 | 5.2 | 3 090 | 31.8 | 28.3 |
| Benton | 10 255 | 81.2 | 128 700 | 21.6 | 11.2 | 542 | 24.5 | 1.4 | 13 702 | -1.9 | 732 | 5.3 | 13 515 | 29.3 | 32.3 |
| Black Hawk | 52 002 | 68.6 | 121 600 | 20.5 | 11.4 | 640 | 32.3 | 1.9 | 74 075 | -0.3 | 3 997 | 5.4 | 65 149 | 30.7 | 25.3 |
| Boone | 10 565 | 76.7 | 116 300 | 21.8 | 13.3 | 591 | 24.7 | 1.3 | 15 014 | -1.5 | 656 | 4.4 | 13 749 | 31.5 | 28.8 |
| Bremer | 9 429 | 82.4 | 139 400 | 20.8 | 10.9 | 586 | 23.5 | 1.1 | 13 842 | -0.4 | 542 | 3.9 | 12 334 | 35.4 | 23.9 |
| Buchanan | 8 175 | 78.7 | 114 400 | 20.4 | 10.5 | 557 | 24.7 | 3.7 | 10 740 | -1.9 | 551 | 5.1 | 10 429 | 30.8 | 34.1 |
| Buena Vista | 7 641 | 68.4 | 90 800 | 19.2 | 10.5 | 562 | 23.5 | 4.6 | 10 712 | -1.5 | 481 | 4.5 | 10 675 | 28.3 | 38.7 |
| Butler | 6 053 | 80.8 | 92 800 | 19.3 | 11.1 | 540 | 21.8 | 1.6 | 8 628 | 0.6 | 380 | 4.4 | 7 206 | 27.8 | 33.9 |
| Calhoun | 4 205 | 79.7 | 71 800 | 18.1 | 10.6 | 479 | 21.4 | 0.4 | 5 018 | -1.0 | 243 | 4.8 | 4 345 | 32.7 | 22.2 |
| Carroll | 8 663 | 76.0 | 106 100 | 20.6 | 9.9 | 494 | 27.7 | 0.6 | 11 993 | -2.4 | 442 | 3.7 | 11 277 | 28.0 | 27.8 |
| Cass | 6 022 | 71.0 | 84 000 | 20.8 | 12.6 | 539 | 24.7 | 1.0 | 7 385 | -2.1 | 395 | 5.3 | 6 977 | 28.1 | 30.9 |
| Cedar | 7 581 | 79.9 | 129 900 | 20.8 | 12.0 | 648 | 23.0 | 1.3 | 11 049 | -2.4 | 498 | 4.5 | 9 962 | 29.9 | 32.6 |
| Cerro Gordo | 20 103 | 72.0 | 110 200 | 20.4 | 11.6 | 574 | 27.0 | 1.0 | 24 152 | -2.3 | 1 369 | 5.7 | 23 183 | 30.8 | 27.8 |
| Cherokee | 5 429 | 75.1 | 78 000 | 19.8 | 10.4 | 485 | 22.5 | 0.0 | 6 671 | -1.2 | 309 | 4.6 | 6 303 | 27.4 | 34.6 |
| Chickasaw | 5 401 | 82.7 | 92 500 | 20.2 | 12.5 | 516 | 22.6 | 1.8 | 6 566 | -2.9 | 340 | 5.2 | 6 062 | 29.7 | 36.0 |
| Clarke | 3 490 | 78.0 | 91 100 | 19.8 | 16.6 | 565 | 22.5 | 1.3 | 4 658 | -2.2 | 291 | 6.2 | 4 497 | 26.6 | 31.5 |
| Clay | 7 346 | 72.4 | 99 500 | 20.4 | 10.5 | 502 | 25.9 | 1.2 | 9 202 | -3.6 | 460 | 5.0 | 8 671 | 24.6 | 31.0 |
| Clayton | 7 678 | 78.4 | 97 900 | 22.2 | 12.0 | 521 | 24.2 | 2.4 | 9 890 | -1.5 | 613 | 6.2 | 9 202 | 27.4 | 34.9 |
| Clinton | 19 938 | 74.4 | 109 200 | 20.7 | 12.7 | 556 | 26.3 | 1.1 | 26 307 | -3.2 | 1 592 | 6.1 | 24 280 | 27.8 | 32.8 |
| Crawford | 6 411 | 78.7 | 79 600 | 20.7 | 10.9 | 485 | 24.1 | 4.0 | 9 361 | -0.5 | 399 | 4.3 | 8 131 | 23.4 | 42.7 |
| Dallas | 24 678 | 78.8 | 182 800 | 21.1 | 11.8 | 720 | 24.2 | 1.0 | 37 186 | -0.3 | 1 581 | 4.3 | 34 372 | 46.6 | 15.5 |
| Davis | 3 078 | 82.2 | 99 200 | 22.0 | 12.3 | 527 | 18.6 | 7.1 | 3 897 | -2.5 | 251 | 6.4 | 3 807 | 28.7 | 39.5 |
| Decatur | 3 224 | 68.4 | 69 800 | 23.0 | 14.6 | 515 | 36.5 | 1.7 | 4 130 | -2.2 | 195 | 4.7 | 3 869 | 33.2 | 27.1 |
| Delaware | 7 277 | 80.3 | 119 800 | 22.2 | 12.2 | 508 | 21.2 | 0.3 | 10 804 | 0.0 | 474 | 4.4 | 9 477 | 27.0 | 37.7 |
| Des Moines | 17 007 | 72.8 | 92 600 | 21.4 | 12.3 | 585 | 27.9 | 2.1 | 20 360 | -2.3 | 1 309 | 6.4 | 18 707 | 26.9 | 32.3 |
| Dickinson | 8 126 | 77.2 | 157 900 | 23.0 | 11.4 | 561 | 26.2 | 0.6 | 9 167 | -1.4 | 531 | 5.8 | 9 050 | 32.5 | 28.4 |
| Dubuque | 36 984 | 74.4 | 140 200 | 21.2 | 12.5 | 612 | 26.9 | 1.2 | 53 439 | -0.5 | 2 546 | 4.8 | 49 610 | 32.9 | 23.8 |
| Emmet | 4 203 | 78.5 | 80 100 | 19.0 | 11.8 | 600 | 29.3 | 1.8 | 5 718 | -1.1 | 268 | 4.7 | 5 175 | 25.1 | 33.4 |
| Fayette | 8 498 | 78.6 | 81 600 | 21.1 | 12.3 | 490 | 23.7 | 1.0 | 10 909 | -2.2 | 617 | 5.7 | 10 048 | 29.0 | 34.1 |
| Floyd | 6 899 | 75.9 | 88 000 | 20.1 | 11.4 | 475 | 28.0 | 1.7 | 8 055 | -2.5 | 517 | 6.4 | 7 983 | 27.6 | 35.3 |

1. Specified owner-occupied units.　2. A value of 9.9 represents 9.9 percent or less.　3. Specified renter-occupied units. A value of 10.0 represents 10 percent or less.　4. Overcrowded or lacking complete plumbing facilities.　5. Percent of civilian labor force.　6. Persons 16 years old and over.

# Table B. States and Counties — Nonfarm Employment and Agriculture

| STATE County | Private nonfarm establishments, employment and payroll, 2011 | | | | | | | | | Agriculture, 2007 | | | |
| | Number of establishments | Employment | | | | | | Annual payroll | | Farms | | | |
| | | Total | Health care and social assistance | Manufacturing | Retail trade | Finance and insurance | Professional, scientific, and technical services | Total (mil dol) | Average per employee (dollars) | Number | Percent with: | | Farm operators whose principal occupation is farming (percent) |
| | | | | | | | | | | | Fewer than 50 acres | 500 acres or more | |
| | 104 | 105 | 106 | 107 | 108 | 109 | 110 | 111 | 112 | 113 | 114 | 115 | 116 |
| INDIANA—Cont'd | | | | | | | | | | | | | |
| Pike | 198 | 2 356 | 343 | 169 | 244 | D | 27 | 116 | 49 410 | 334 | 43.4 | 12.6 | 34.7 |
| Porter | 3 391 | 49 224 | 5 704 | 9 174 | 7 136 | 1 075 | 1 826 | 1 937 | 39 357 | 517 | 53.4 | 13.7 | 39.5 |
| Posey | 494 | 8 851 | 543 | 2 684 | 706 | 112 | 326 | 453 | 51 148 | 438 | 39.3 | 24.7 | 57.3 |
| Pulaski | 325 | 3 507 | 610 | 1 270 | 414 | D | 55 | 126 | 35 902 | 552 | 37.9 | 23.7 | 49.5 |
| Putnam | 675 | 10 442 | 1 669 | 1 967 | 1 174 | 254 | 178 | 295 | 28 250 | 843 | 54.9 | 10.2 | 40.1 |
| Randolph | 479 | 5 610 | 722 | 2 153 | 627 | 145 | 97 | 182 | 32 421 | 784 | 43.5 | 15.4 | 51.3 |
| Ripley | 634 | 9 867 | 947 | 2 503 | 794 | 554 | D | 442 | 44 778 | 873 | 43.5 | 8.4 | 38.1 |
| Rush | 360 | 3 552 | 472 | D | 495 | D | 113 | 114 | 32 044 | 607 | 33.1 | 22.1 | 58.5 |
| St. Joseph | 5 922 | 112 215 | 18 369 | 14 340 | 14 994 | 4 032 | 4 035 | 4 066 | 36 230 | 712 | 55.2 | 11.9 | 43.1 |
| Scott | 415 | 5 332 | 916 | 1 505 | 970 | 144 | 172 | 156 | 29 180 | 394 | 57.1 | 6.9 | 32.7 |
| Shelby | 908 | 14 756 | 2 068 | 4 397 | 1 427 | 223 | 263 | 533 | 36 098 | 636 | 45.9 | 18.9 | 48.6 |
| Spencer | 410 | 5 369 | 332 | 1 426 | 840 | 148 | 116 | 197 | 36 651 | 632 | 37.3 | 10.9 | 39.7 |
| Starke | 319 | 2 912 | 414 | 822 | 627 | 78 | 65 | 78 | 26 951 | 640 | 53.9 | 14.1 | 33.3 |
| Steuben | 961 | 12 146 | 1 274 | 3 868 | 2 023 | 241 | 288 | 359 | 29 590 | 719 | 51.9 | 6.4 | 29.5 |
| Sullivan | 350 | 4 215 | D | 735 | 587 | D | 99 | 154 | 36 443 | 447 | 35.1 | 23.0 | 51.5 |
| Switzerland | 124 | 1 871 | 162 | D | 81 | 42 | D | 48 | 25 766 | 374 | 39.8 | 3.5 | 38.8 |
| Tippecanoe | 3 294 | 60 099 | 9 319 | 12 691 | 8 954 | 2 732 | 2 244 | 2 291 | 38 127 | 757 | 54.2 | 13.5 | 41.0 |
| Tipton | 299 | 3 036 | D | 704 | 428 | D | 84 | 109 | 35 893 | 458 | 44.5 | 21.2 | 50.2 |
| Union | 116 | 868 | 150 | 43 | 206 | 27 | 23 | 24 | 28 096 | 233 | 26.2 | 21.5 | 60.1 |
| Vanderburgh | 4 957 | 105 865 | 19 126 | 10 699 | 12 991 | 5 110 | 3 939 | 3 819 | 36 077 | 335 | 54.9 | 11.9 | 45.7 |
| Vermillion | 284 | 3 748 | D | D | 610 | D | 94 | 178 | 47 419 | 293 | 39.9 | 22.5 | 45.7 |
| Vigo | 2 561 | 45 210 | 9 234 | 8 554 | 6 679 | 1 251 | 1 188 | 1 545 | 34 170 | 518 | 59.7 | 11.6 | 44.4 |
| Wabash | 747 | 10 555 | 2 169 | 2 664 | 1 415 | 310 | 355 | 310 | 29 386 | 850 | 46.5 | 13.6 | 41.4 |
| Warren | 122 | 1 409 | D | D | 102 | 32 | D | 46 | 32 522 | 391 | 35.0 | 24.0 | 50.6 |
| Warrick | 1 095 | 12 798 | 2 705 | D | 1 684 | 550 | 528 | 493 | 38 551 | 413 | 51.1 | 14.8 | 32.2 |
| Washington | 444 | 4 097 | 516 | 1 478 | 691 | D | 118 | 121 | 29 528 | 893 | 40.3 | 9.9 | 43.0 |
| Wayne | 1 544 | 24 632 | 5 149 | 5 088 | 3 754 | 868 | 472 | 815 | 33 104 | 894 | 45.7 | 9.6 | 38.0 |
| Wells | 628 | 9 514 | 1 529 | 2 281 | 1 103 | 174 | 270 | 309 | 32 487 | 701 | 46.9 | 16.3 | 43.2 |
| White | 638 | 6 787 | 926 | 1 921 | 1 084 | 195 | 111 | 212 | 31 292 | 646 | 43.3 | 27.4 | 56.8 |
| Whitley | 681 | 10 218 | 1 092 | 4 295 | 1 419 | 255 | 189 | 361 | 35 341 | 809 | 55.6 | 8.2 | 32.8 |
| IOWA | 80 113 | 1 263 665 | 206 984 | 199 812 | 174 126 | 90 726 | 47 698 | 46 556 | 36 842 | 92 856 | 28.6 | 20.8 | 52.4 |
| Adair | 178 | 1 635 | D | D | 284 | 67 | 34 | 47 | 28 851 | 766 | 22.5 | 23.8 | 54.7 |
| Adams | 116 | 846 | D | D | 118 | 36 | 24 | 24 | 28 007 | 610 | 17.0 | 21.3 | 48.2 |
| Allamakee | 411 | 4 265 | 954 | 1 039 | 641 | 199 | 95 | 119 | 27 852 | 1 032 | 24.6 | 15.4 | 47.5 |
| Appanoose | 327 | 3 436 | 705 | 768 | 693 | 116 | D | 90 | 26 247 | 731 | 24.5 | 14.9 | 36.7 |
| Audubon | 186 | 1 189 | 305 | 183 | 234 | 51 | 15 | 35 | 29 436 | 666 | 29.9 | 25.4 | 51.5 |
| Benton | 564 | 4 243 | 794 | 646 | 745 | 196 | 74 | 132 | 31 128 | 1 251 | 28.0 | 21.1 | 52.4 |
| Black Hawk | 3 200 | 64 875 | 12 903 | 13 140 | 8 988 | 2 761 | 2 896 | 2 363 | 36 428 | 942 | 31.8 | 19.4 | 51.5 |
| Boone | 570 | 6 642 | 1 671 | D | 962 | 222 | D | 197 | 29 606 | 925 | 35.4 | 22.3 | 45.7 |
| Bremer | 612 | 8 192 | 1 700 | 1 782 | 1 247 | 783 | 190 | 286 | 34 936 | 995 | 34.1 | 14.0 | 51.3 |
| Buchanan | 488 | 5 166 | 1 159 | 1 071 | 897 | 229 | 93 | 164 | 31 773 | 1 174 | 33.6 | 19.3 | 52.7 |
| Buena Vista | 557 | 8 428 | 1 330 | 2 918 | 1 198 | 299 | D | 269 | 31 935 | 924 | 26.4 | 30.7 | 63.2 |
| Butler | 341 | 2 582 | 468 | 749 | 331 | 127 | 72 | 79 | 30 710 | 1 214 | 36.9 | 18.5 | 50.2 |
| Calhoun | 289 | 2 327 | 685 | 115 | 330 | 125 | D | 59 | 25 295 | 845 | 31.1 | 29.6 | 53.1 |
| Carroll | 889 | 10 729 | 2 135 | 1 402 | 1 698 | 831 | 200 | 333 | 31 077 | 978 | 25.8 | 24.0 | 62.0 |
| Cass | 480 | 4 653 | 1 118 | D | 908 | 223 | 126 | 134 | 28 851 | 763 | 20.3 | 28.4 | 51.5 |
| Cedar | 470 | 4 279 | 634 | 619 | 603 | D | D | 129 | 30 060 | 1 036 | 30.2 | 20.5 | 54.0 |
| Cerro Gordo | 1 384 | 21 438 | 4 732 | 3 025 | 3 734 | 1 085 | 626 | 725 | 33 825 | 844 | 32.5 | 29.3 | 54.6 |
| Cherokee | 360 | 4 721 | 946 | 1 073 | 640 | 177 | 70 | 151 | 32 042 | 840 | 23.1 | 25.7 | 59.0 |
| Chickasaw | 394 | 3 704 | 596 | 1 169 | 423 | 128 | 58 | 119 | 32 072 | 1 037 | 32.1 | 16.7 | 53.5 |
| Clarke | 189 | 3 080 | 622 | D | 565 | 83 | 44 | 83 | 26 810 | 690 | 22.3 | 14.3 | 45.5 |
| Clay | 627 | 7 622 | 1 373 | 999 | 1 517 | 277 | 156 | 254 | 33 266 | 798 | 24.8 | 28.6 | 57.9 |
| Clayton | 522 | 4 878 | 1 054 | 631 | 626 | 189 | D | 152 | 31 240 | 1 655 | 24.8 | 13.1 | 50.2 |
| Clinton | 1 196 | 25 437 | 3 478 | 4 435 | 2 753 | 574 | 270 | 823 | 32 357 | 1 314 | 31.1 | 18.3 | 51.8 |
| Crawford | 459 | 6 454 | 1 067 | 2 546 | 847 | 194 | 97 | 203 | 31 501 | 855 | 24.0 | 26.9 | 57.5 |
| Dallas | 1 540 | 31 301 | 2 871 | 1 934 | 5 393 | 11 133 | 1 394 | 1 413 | 45 133 | 912 | 38.0 | 20.0 | 46.3 |
| Davis | 170 | 1 396 | 431 | 145 | 285 | 51 | D | 38 | 26 967 | 910 | 22.7 | 10.7 | 40.2 |
| Decatur | 138 | 1 823 | 365 | D | 214 | D | D | 39 | 21 280 | 738 | 24.4 | 17.6 | 45.5 |
| Delaware | 497 | 5 203 | 950 | 1 479 | 692 | 250 | 107 | 171 | 32 826 | 1 470 | 31.3 | 12.5 | 59.6 |
| Des Moines | 1 123 | 19 516 | 3 529 | 4 660 | 3 060 | 556 | 331 | 651 | 33 338 | 646 | 31.0 | 18.0 | 47.7 |
| Dickinson | 762 | 7 003 | 884 | 1 604 | 1 043 | 611 | 131 | 229 | 32 639 | 566 | 26.1 | 27.7 | 52.8 |
| Dubuque | 2 708 | 51 097 | 7 555 | 8 194 | 6 988 | 2 936 | 2 691 | 1 843 | 36 067 | 1 483 | 26.0 | 11.1 | 53.1 |
| Emmet | 336 | 3 650 | 923 | 937 | 483 | 135 | 85 | 110 | 30 072 | 532 | 26.7 | 33.8 | 68.4 |
| Fayette | 563 | 6 071 | 1 385 | 588 | 836 | 211 | 145 | 162 | 26 615 | 1 398 | 27.3 | 17.6 | 54.9 |
| Floyd | 414 | 4 822 | 960 | 865 | 724 | 217 | 87 | 172 | 35 744 | 991 | 33.4 | 20.0 | 51.5 |

| | | | | | | | | | | | | | | | |
|---|---|---|---|---|---|---|---|---|---|---|---|---|---|---|---|
| | | | | | | | **Agriculture, 2007 (cont.)** | | | | | | | | |
| | Land in farms | | | | Value of land and buildings (dollars) | | | Value of products sold | | | | Percent of farms with sales of: | | Government payments | |
| | | Acres | | | | | | | | Percent from: | | | | | |
| STATE County | Acreage (1,000) | Percent change, 2002–2007 | Average size of farm | Total irrigated (1,000) | Total cropland (1,000) | Average per farm | Average per acre | Value of machinery and equipment, average per farm (dollars) | Total (mil dol) | Average per farm (dollars) | Crops | Live-stock and poultry products | $10,000 or more | $100,000 or more | Total ($1,000) | Percent of farms |
| | 117 | 118 | 119 | 120 | 121 | 122 | 123 | 124 | 125 | 126 | 127 | 128 | 129 | 130 | 131 | 132 |
| INDIANA—Cont'd | | | | | | | | | | | | | | | | |
| Pike | 74 | -2.6 | 220 | 0.0 | 58.8 | 614 145 | 2 787 | 76 570 | 30.6 | 91 567 | 74.5 | 25.5 | 41.0 | 18.6 | 1 221 | 64.7 |
| Porter | 115 | -21.2 | 223 | 8.9 | 106.1 | 926 001 | 4 161 | 99 668 | 53.6 | 103 649 | 89.6 | 10.4 | 44.7 | 21.3 | 2 067 | 58.0 |
| Posey | 204 | 6.3 | 466 | 8.8 | 186.8 | 1 419 223 | 3 047 | 202 096 | 97.9 | 223 479 | 87.4 | 12.6 | 60.5 | 33.8 | 3 248 | 67.4 |
| Pulaski | 232 | 4.0 | 421 | 20.0 | 213.3 | 1 305 431 | 3 103 | 179 033 | 159.2 | 288 425 | 58.7 | 41.3 | 52.7 | 35.1 | 4 329 | 76.8 |
| Putnam | 168 | -7.2 | 200 | D | 130.6 | 718 756 | 3 597 | 74 156 | 69.3 | 82 149 | 74.2 | 25.8 | 34.8 | 13.4 | 2 773 | 50.1 |
| Randolph | 232 | -10.1 | 296 | 0.1 | 210.5 | 931 610 | 3 151 | 120 497 | 113.8 | 145 116 | 69.3 | 30.7 | 56.8 | 26.7 | 3 922 | 68.6 |
| Ripley | 159 | -8.1 | 182 | 0.0 | 120.9 | 633 669 | 3 479 | 76 990 | 54.0 | 61 843 | 73.4 | 26.6 | 41.0 | 11.7 | 2 535 | 65.6 |
| Rush | 217 | -3.1 | 357 | 0.5 | 201.6 | 1 314 403 | 3 679 | 151 157 | 125.8 | 207 281 | 62.4 | 37.6 | 68.4 | 37.4 | 4 265 | 74.0 |
| St. Joseph | 179 | 8.5 | 251 | 25.0 | 163.6 | 915 848 | 3 650 | 114 265 | 89.9 | 126 195 | 83.5 | 16.5 | 49.0 | 21.5 | 3 106 | 62.2 |
| Scott | 62 | -10.1 | 157 | 0.0 | 48.2 | 486 203 | 3 088 | 57 222 | 18.9 | 48 031 | 94.0 | 6.0 | 25.9 | 7.1 | 1 046 | 49.7 |
| Shelby | 205 | 2.5 | 323 | 3.3 | 194.0 | 1 225 616 | 3 794 | 131 092 | 83.6 | 131 518 | 86.6 | 13.4 | 55.8 | 25.5 | 3 642 | 65.1 |
| Spencer | 150 | -3.2 | 238 | 0.4 | 110.8 | 725 113 | 3 050 | 99 922 | 61.6 | 97 474 | 62.7 | 37.3 | 48.1 | 19.0 | 2 302 | 67.2 |
| Starke | 154 | 14.9 | 240 | 17.3 | 132.8 | 728 640 | 3 035 | 93 974 | 59.1 | 92 399 | 97.6 | 2.4 | 30.9 | 18.9 | 4 022 | 84.4 |
| Steuben | 106 | -6.2 | 148 | 1.5 | 85.4 | 579 770 | 3 918 | 78 711 | 40.6 | 56 490 | 60.5 | 39.5 | 27.5 | 9.5 | 2 529 | 74.1 |
| Sullivan | 177 | -1.1 | 397 | 9.7 | 157.9 | 1 189 316 | 2 997 | 149 235 | 74.8 | 167 313 | 95.1 | 4.9 | 56.4 | 31.8 | 2 742 | 70.7 |
| Switzerland | 47 | -21.7 | 127 | 0.1 | 25.4 | 446 818 | 3 521 | 48 251 | 8.3 | 22 321 | 66.3 | 33.7 | 24.6 | 3.2 | 387 | 33.4 |
| Tippecanoe | 218 | -1.4 | 288 | 5.5 | 199.8 | 1 137 312 | 3 944 | 121 160 | 112.8 | 148 957 | 85.9 | 14.1 | 44.8 | 22.1 | 4 096 | 54.3 |
| Tipton | 166 | 9.2 | 362 | 0.1 | 159.4 | 1 492 178 | 4 120 | 140 884 | 97.3 | 212 394 | 79.3 | 20.7 | 67.2 | 31.2 | 3 038 | 82.8 |
| Union | 73 | -14.1 | 314 | 0.0 | 63.7 | 1 180 880 | 3 756 | 122 174 | 30.0 | 128 656 | 79.8 | 20.2 | 63.5 | 28.8 | 1 354 | 72.1 |
| Vanderburgh | 72 | -12.2 | 215 | D | 67.2 | 736 718 | 3 431 | 113 475 | 32.6 | 97 288 | 88.8 | 11.2 | 50.4 | 23.3 | 1 423 | 63.6 |
| Vermillion | 132 | 20.0 | 452 | D | 112.9 | 1 436 115 | 3 179 | 150 311 | 64.1 | 218 703 | 83.4 | 16.6 | 48.8 | 28.0 | 2 452 | 66.2 |
| Vigo | 121 | -1.6 | 234 | 2.1 | 103.0 | 720 485 | 3 073 | 96 017 | 47.2 | 91 150 | 94.6 | 5.4 | 37.1 | 16.4 | 1 585 | 62.5 |
| Wabash | 201 | -6.5 | 236 | 1.1 | 180.4 | 844 871 | 3 578 | 101 014 | 151.3 | 178 016 | 47.9 | 52.1 | 46.7 | 25.6 | 3 948 | 71.6 |
| Warren | 196 | 17.4 | 501 | 4.4 | 178.7 | 1 770 103 | 3 532 | 142 916 | 103.7 | 265 142 | 82.9 | 17.1 | 48.3 | 30.7 | 3 399 | 67.0 |
| Warrick | 110 | 17.0 | 266 | 0.2 | 88.9 | 812 666 | 3 053 | 117 708 | 33.9 | 82 179 | 87.8 | 12.2 | 36.6 | 19.6 | 1 806 | 67.8 |
| Washington | 200 | 10.5 | 224 | 0.1 | 137.9 | 632 380 | 2 824 | 76 019 | 86.7 | 97 035 | 49.7 | 50.3 | 36.1 | 14.1 | 2 820 | 50.3 |
| Wayne | 164 | -4.1 | 184 | 0.2 | 138.0 | 600 840 | 3 273 | 77 139 | 66.2 | 74 067 | 74.6 | 25.4 | 46.2 | 18.9 | 3 451 | 68.7 |
| Wells | 195 | -13.7 | 278 | 0.1 | 184.1 | 961 703 | 3 464 | 119 797 | 112.0 | 159 770 | 64.3 | 35.7 | 58.8 | 31.7 | 3 431 | 69.6 |
| White | 318 | 12.0 | 492 | 3.4 | 301.0 | 1 888 323 | 3 835 | 189 568 | 232.0 | 359 066 | 63.2 | 36.8 | 62.5 | 38.2 | 6 119 | 72.6 |
| Whitley | 137 | -20.3 | 169 | 1.0 | 118.3 | 647 245 | 3 820 | 77 703 | 85.1 | 105 153 | 63.0 | 37.0 | 38.1 | 15.3 | 2 694 | 70.5 |
| IOWA | 30 748 | -3.1 | 331 | 189.5 | 26 316.3 | 1 122 023 | 3 388 | 136 771 | 20 418.1 | 219 890 | 50.7 | 49.3 | 61.4 | 35.6 | 706 286 | 80.7 |
| Adair | 312 | -16.4 | 407 | D | 243.7 | 1 102 777 | 2 710 | 128 558 | 136.8 | 178 591 | 59.4 | 40.6 | 63.3 | 30.9 | 5 826 | 83.0 |
| Adams | 225 | -5.5 | 369 | 0.4 | 167.8 | 941 061 | 2 553 | 102 601 | 77.6 | 127 227 | 57.6 | 42.4 | 53.3 | 25.7 | 5 889 | 86.7 |
| Allamakee | 275 | -15.6 | 266 | 0.3 | 164.4 | 741 749 | 2 785 | 97 243 | 131.6 | 127 524 | 26.2 | 73.8 | 45.5 | 20.3 | 7 231 | 86.8 |
| Appanoose | 198 | -16.1 | 271 | D | 120.4 | 584 408 | 2 159 | 71 067 | 37.9 | 51 821 | 60.8 | 39.2 | 45.7 | 13.3 | 3 872 | 73.9 |
| Audubon | 279 | 6.9 | 419 | 0.0 | 245.2 | 1 453 725 | 3 469 | 149 587 | 200.5 | 301 088 | 46.3 | 53.7 | 58.7 | 36.8 | 6 484 | 79.4 |
| Benton | 401 | 0.0 | 320 | 0.0 | 356.3 | 1 156 555 | 3 609 | 140 267 | 263.1 | 210 329 | 59.1 | 40.9 | 64.4 | 37.1 | 9 472 | 82.1 |
| Black Hawk | 282 | 2.5 | 300 | 0.2 | 263.2 | 1 167 942 | 3 899 | 161 236 | 178.0 | 189 009 | 68.5 | 31.5 | 69.5 | 38.7 | 7 381 | 79.7 |
| Boone | 332 | 6.1 | 359 | 0.1 | 301.7 | 1 348 605 | 3 757 | 148 616 | 174.2 | 188 286 | 78.9 | 21.1 | 59.6 | 35.0 | 6 682 | 79.0 |
| Bremer | 243 | -4.7 | 244 | 0.3 | 223.0 | 966 883 | 3 958 | 136 806 | 158.2 | 158 979 | 61.9 | 38.1 | 63.2 | 33.7 | 6 486 | 81.3 |
| Buchanan | 360 | 5.9 | 307 | 0.2 | 330.8 | 1 156 930 | 3 770 | 154 736 | 254.6 | 216 828 | 55.7 | 44.3 | 70.7 | 41.7 | 11 678 | 74.3 |
| Buena Vista | 363 | 6.1 | 392 | 0.0 | 335.8 | 1 502 243 | 3 829 | 158 413 | 355.3 | 384 563 | 39.8 | 60.2 | 73.9 | 55.4 | 8 657 | 84.4 |
| Butler | 376 | 14.6 | 310 | 0.3 | 343.2 | 1 086 765 | 3 511 | 117 318 | 253.1 | 208 470 | 58.0 | 42.0 | 59.6 | 34.8 | 7 982 | 82.7 |
| Calhoun | 359 | 5.3 | 425 | D | 339.5 | 1 621 138 | 3 811 | 171 574 | 271.9 | 321 732 | 57.2 | 42.8 | 67.2 | 46.3 | 8 348 | 88.2 |
| Carroll | 358 | -1.6 | 366 | 0.2 | 329.6 | 1 347 857 | 3 681 | 169 461 | 442.7 | 452 612 | 30.5 | 69.5 | 75.6 | 50.4 | 7 092 | 83.2 |
| Cass | 318 | -5.6 | 417 | 0.7 | 264.1 | 1 279 235 | 3 070 | 147 966 | 172.9 | 226 574 | 53.4 | 46.6 | 61.6 | 37.7 | 7 019 | 82.1 |
| Cedar | 337 | -0.3 | 325 | 0.2 | 299.7 | 1 195 881 | 3 678 | 151 347 | 198.0 | 191 160 | 67.2 | 32.8 | 62.2 | 39.6 | 8 497 | 80.1 |
| Cerro Gordo | 337 | 4.3 | 399 | 0.5 | 319.7 | 1 431 476 | 3 588 | 168 157 | 182.4 | 216 110 | 77.6 | 22.4 | 63.9 | 44.9 | 8 714 | 83.4 |
| Cherokee | 315 | -6.0 | 375 | D | 275.5 | 1 423 062 | 3 796 | 166 209 | 266.0 | 316 698 | 42.8 | 57.2 | 77.6 | 51.0 | 5 758 | 82.7 |
| Chickasaw | 289 | 6.6 | 279 | 0.1 | 260.5 | 1 010 190 | 3 623 | 159 289 | 226.2 | 218 110 | 43.6 | 56.4 | 66.3 | 39.2 | 8 351 | 84.6 |
| Clarke | 191 | -11.6 | 276 | D | 105.5 | 639 372 | 2 313 | 65 495 | 58.1 | 84 273 | 30.1 | 69.9 | 45.2 | 12.6 | 3 050 | 76.2 |
| Clay | 328 | 5.1 | 411 | 0.5 | 304.8 | 1 484 677 | 3 610 | 148 124 | 257.2 | 322 313 | 48.3 | 51.7 | 70.6 | 47.1 | 6 621 | 82.6 |
| Clayton | 409 | -5.5 | 247 | 0.0 | 296.1 | 768 155 | 3 108 | 98 757 | 230.0 | 138 966 | 37.8 | 62.2 | 51.6 | 31.4 | 12 658 | 86.2 |
| Clinton | 396 | 2.1 | 301 | 0.1 | 355.6 | 1 025 461 | 3 406 | 144 814 | 229.6 | 174 723 | 66.0 | 34.0 | 63.8 | 37.0 | 9 164 | 81.4 |
| Crawford | 432 | -3.1 | 506 | D | 384.7 | 1 575 267 | 3 115 | 164 491 | 274.9 | 321 536 | 57.1 | 42.9 | 69.8 | 43.5 | 6 936 | 80.5 |
| Dallas | 297 | -3.9 | 326 | 0.4 | 263.7 | 1 089 116 | 3 343 | 138 055 | 185.9 | 203 821 | 59.0 | 41.0 | 55.6 | 28.3 | 6 532 | 71.1 |
| Davis | 219 | -24.7 | 240 | 0.1 | 131.0 | 564 142 | 2 347 | 72 447 | 63.0 | 69 248 | 40.7 | 59.3 | 50.1 | 12.6 | 4 370 | 68.1 |
| Decatur | 229 | -17.6 | 310 | D | 116.7 | 638 036 | 2 060 | 74 479 | 59.2 | 80 194 | 40.2 | 59.8 | 48.2 | 15.6 | 3 619 | 71.8 |
| Delaware | 334 | -3.2 | 227 | D | 291.0 | 863 463 | 3 801 | 133 723 | 326.3 | 221 947 | 30.3 | 69.7 | 68.2 | 45.9 | 9 696 | 85.2 |
| Des Moines | 185 | 2.2 | 286 | 2.5 | 157.1 | 941 178 | 3 287 | 127 308 | 81.1 | 125 502 | 78.6 | 21.4 | 58.0 | 28.6 | 3 946 | 84.2 |
| Dickinson | 226 | 11.3 | 400 | 0.8 | 211.5 | 1 414 772 | 3 538 | 149 864 | 134.6 | 237 831 | 65.0 | 35.0 | 66.6 | 38.9 | 5 263 | 86.6 |
| Dubuque | 311 | -1.6 | 210 | D | 237.4 | 711 542 | 3 395 | 119 819 | 271.1 | 182 789 | 23.6 | 76.4 | 65.3 | 37.2 | 7 841 | 81.2 |
| Emmet | 250 | 6.4 | 470 | 0.3 | 233.9 | 1 687 378 | 3 594 | 203 697 | 208.7 | 392 224 | 49.1 | 50.9 | 71.6 | 51.7 | 5 549 | 82.5 |
| Fayette | 417 | 0.5 | 298 | 0.5 | 355.5 | 1 006 861 | 3 374 | 127 904 | 286.2 | 204 740 | 46.9 | 53.1 | 63.1 | 40.3 | 12 072 | 85.8 |
| Floyd | 298 | 2.4 | 301 | 1.1 | 274.1 | 1 122 840 | 3 728 | 147 116 | 176.0 | 177 627 | 64.6 | 35.4 | 56.8 | 35.9 | 7 224 | 83.9 |

| STATE County | Water use, 2005 | | Wholesale trade,[1] 2007 | | | | Retail trade,[2] 2007 | | | | Real estate and rental and leasing,[2] 2007 | | | |
|---|---|---|---|---|---|---|---|---|---|---|---|---|---|---|
| | Total water withdrawn (mil gal/day) | Gallons withdrawn per person | Number of establish-ments | Number of employees | Sales (mil dol) | Annual payroll (mil dol) | Number of establish-ments | Number of employees | Sales (mil dol) | Annual payroll (mil dol) | Number of establish-ments | Number of employees | Receipts (mil dol) | Annual payroll (mil dol) |
| | 133 | 134 | 135 | 136 | 137 | 138 | 139 | 140 | 141 | 142 | 143 | 144 | 145 | 146 |
| **INDIANA—Cont'd** | | | | | | | | | | | | | | |
| Pike | 529.5 | 41 477 | 8 | 41 | 64.7 | 3.2 | 35 | 265 | 55.9 | 4.6 | 3 | D | D | D |
| Porter | 720.9 | 4 569 | 143 | 2 004 | 1 463.1 | 99.8 | 500 | 7 393 | 1 956.3 | 162.9 | 168 | 779 | 89.8 | 18.3 |
| Posey | 23.3 | 869 | 23 | 381 | 346.7 | 12.1 | 74 | 711 | 268.4 | 17.1 | 10 | 30 | 4.5 | 0.6 |
| Pulaski | 9.6 | 693 | 28 | 396 | 262.9 | 14.1 | 67 | 456 | 112.8 | 8.5 | 11 | 15 | 0.9 | 0.2 |
| Putnam | 6.8 | 185 | 19 | 134 | 43.0 | 4.8 | 111 | 1 134 | 310.8 | 25.9 | 23 | 69 | 6.3 | 1.3 |
| Randolph | 4.4 | 163 | 16 | 184 | 113.3 | 6.8 | 84 | 735 | 273.3 | 14.6 | 11 | 27 | 2.0 | 0.3 |
| Ripley | 3.4 | 124 | 18 | 112 | 44.5 | 3.3 | 106 | 1 027 | 255.4 | 21.6 | 22 | D | D | D |
| Rush | 3.1 | 172 | 17 | 119 | 162.3 | 4.8 | 56 | 535 | 113.4 | 10.9 | 10 | 25 | 3.1 | 0.4 |
| St. Joseph | 54.8 | 206 | 345 | D | D | D | 951 | 16 607 | 3 683.4 | 349.9 | 242 | 1 442 | 215.2 | 43.4 |
| Scott | 3.5 | 145 | 14 | D | D | D | 95 | 1 025 | 241.2 | 19.9 | 19 | 73 | 6.4 | 1.0 |
| Shelby | 8.8 | 201 | 40 | 739 | 291.0 | 18.4 | 136 | 1 707 | 487.6 | 41.5 | 44 | 127 | 16.6 | 2.7 |
| Spencer | 35.5 | 1 730 | 13 | 223 | 181.1 | 8.3 | 72 | 908 | 166.0 | 22.2 | 13 | 37 | 3.0 | 0.6 |
| Starke | 6.9 | 301 | 11 | 63 | 61.5 | 2.4 | 76 | 893 | 156.7 | 14.8 | 16 | 36 | 3.1 | 0.6 |
| Steuben | 4.7 | 140 | 33 | 246 | 97.2 | 8.2 | 198 | 2 293 | 575.1 | 40.8 | 46 | 114 | 16.4 | 2.9 |
| Sullivan | 463.4 | 21 295 | 22 | 159 | 201.5 | 4.8 | 65 | 630 | 146.9 | 11.3 | 8 | 24 | 1.5 | 0.3 |
| Switzerland | 2.8 | 285 | 4 | 10 | 3.9 | 0.3 | 13 | 96 | 19.9 | 1.6 | 3 | D | D | D |
| Tippecanoe | 34.2 | 222 | 99 | 1 033 | 413.3 | 44.0 | 567 | 9 881 | 2 079.6 | 193.0 | 196 | 1 073 | 185.3 | 34.5 |
| Tipton | 2.0 | 125 | 10 | 132 | 141.6 | 4.4 | 52 | 425 | 136.0 | 11.8 | 15 | 35 | 2.0 | 0.5 |
| Union | 0.8 | 110 | 4 | D | D | D | 27 | 179 | 31.0 | 3.0 | 4 | 11 | 0.7 | 0.2 |
| Vanderburgh | 33.1 | 191 | 271 | 5 495 | 2 907.8 | 282.2 | 855 | 13 949 | 3 025.8 | 297.7 | 214 | 1 431 | 217.0 | 38.9 |
| Vermillion | 646.1 | 39 013 | 12 | D | D | D | 57 | 687 | 184.6 | 12.8 | 6 | 27 | 1.3 | 0.2 |
| Vigo | 567.4 | 5 531 | 101 | 1 212 | 584.1 | 46.5 | 487 | 7 679 | 1 668.2 | 154.6 | 102 | 628 | 80.5 | 18.4 |
| Wabash | 8.2 | 241 | 30 | 420 | 168.9 | 12.4 | 148 | 1 475 | 325.6 | 31.9 | 29 | 103 | 11.2 | 2.6 |
| Warren | 2.1 | 242 | 13 | 154 | 118.3 | 5.8 | 16 | 106 | 24.0 | 1.5 | 3 | D | D | D |
| Warrick | 759.2 | 13 470 | 41 | 342 | 412.3 | 17.9 | 134 | 1 436 | 331.2 | 29.7 | 39 | 172 | 27.5 | 3.4 |
| Washington | 4.3 | 152 | 12 | 67 | 16.3 | 1.9 | 87 | 750 | 190.7 | 15.0 | 16 | 45 | 3.9 | 0.7 |
| Wayne | 11.6 | 167 | 58 | 517 | 325.2 | 20.8 | 302 | 4 153 | 1 004.3 | 85.8 | 60 | 274 | 30.5 | 6.9 |
| Wells | 4.5 | 162 | 40 | D | D | D | 103 | 1 219 | 221.3 | 22.8 | 26 | 86 | 7.6 | 1.7 |
| White | 5.2 | 211 | 40 | 424 | 235.1 | 11.6 | 108 | 1 205 | 283.4 | 25.4 | 22 | 90 | 7.4 | 1.4 |
| Whitley | 4.2 | 129 | 23 | D | D | D | 121 | 1 644 | 343.5 | 30.8 | 30 | 103 | 12.4 | 2.9 |
| **IOWA** | 3 366.4 | 1 135 | 4 361 | 55 874 | 41 068.3 | 2 276.7 | 13 203 | 177 156 | 39 234.6 | 3 561.1 | 2 969 | 14 667 | 2 556.0 | 473.0 |
| Adair | 2.0 | 254 | 6 | 60 | 29.4 | 2.3 | 31 | 245 | 49.6 | 3.5 | 5 | D | D | D |
| Adams | 1.8 | 410 | 4 | 27 | 14.2 | 0.8 | 25 | 155 | 32.6 | 2.4 | 3 | 5 | 0.7 | 0.1 |
| Allamakee | 214.6 | 14 586 | 35 | 383 | 154.5 | 12.3 | 62 | 586 | 128.7 | 11.0 | 9 | 15 | 2.1 | 0.4 |
| Appanoose | 10.7 | 786 | 11 | 60 | 23.1 | 1.7 | 65 | 681 | 133.5 | 12.5 | 13 | 24 | 1.8 | 0.3 |
| Audubon | 1.7 | 256 | 14 | 81 | 47.8 | 2.8 | 19 | 200 | 37.3 | 3.3 | 5 | 4 | 0.5 | 0.1 |
| Benton | 3.1 | 113 | 30 | 253 | 213.2 | 8.5 | 96 | 844 | 176.4 | 15.9 | 15 | 54 | 5.1 | 1.4 |
| Black Hawk | 37.6 | 299 | 149 | 2 492 | 1 278.5 | 95.1 | 532 | 8 624 | 1 929.4 | 175.3 | 148 | 707 | 114.7 | 19.2 |
| Boone | 3.3 | 125 | 30 | D | D | D | 75 | 960 | 210.6 | 21.5 | 16 | D | D | D |
| Bremer | 3.5 | 146 | 23 | 149 | 105.6 | 6.2 | 94 | 1 112 | 268.4 | 24.6 | 21 | D | D | D |
| Buchanan | 3.6 | 171 | 30 | 357 | 624.5 | 12.5 | 90 | 861 | 214.8 | 18.0 | 13 | D | D | D |
| Buena Vista | 6.4 | 316 | 29 | D | D | D | 104 | 1 100 | 260.8 | 22.2 | 22 | 77 | 9.3 | 2.6 |
| Butler | 2.4 | 160 | 29 | 228 | 288.4 | 7.7 | 66 | 332 | 79.1 | 5.9 | 7 | D | D | D |
| Calhoun | 2.3 | 217 | 21 | 253 | 200.7 | 11.1 | 53 | 316 | 103.5 | 5.9 | 4 | 18 | 1.2 | 0.3 |
| Carroll | 6.1 | 292 | 58 | 1 519 | 1 350.5 | 59.9 | 156 | 1 572 | 298.1 | 32.2 | 23 | 125 | 24.7 | 4.2 |
| Cass | 3.1 | 217 | 26 | 207 | 151.5 | 6.7 | 79 | 927 | 178.2 | 18.1 | 14 | 68 | 11.8 | 2.2 |
| Cedar | 3.5 | 191 | 29 | 290 | 221.8 | 10.6 | 66 | 585 | 131.3 | 10.9 | 16 | 23 | 1.9 | 0.3 |
| Cerro Gordo | 15.3 | 343 | 88 | 800 | 650.5 | 32.7 | 246 | 3 917 | 887.1 | 77.2 | 63 | D | D | D |
| Cherokee | 4.2 | 344 | 13 | 101 | 114.7 | 3.7 | 71 | 660 | 139.4 | 11.8 | 7 | 18 | 1.2 | 0.2 |
| Chickasaw | 2.6 | 203 | 31 | 266 | 210.1 | 10.1 | 52 | 453 | 103.9 | 8.0 | 5 | D | D | D |
| Clarke | 2.5 | 275 | 3 | 16 | 6.3 | 0.5 | 38 | 436 | 95.4 | 8.3 | 7 | D | D | D |
| Clay | 4.0 | 237 | 46 | 542 | 425.1 | 19.4 | 124 | 1 650 | 298.7 | 31.9 | 27 | 102 | 16.9 | 2.4 |
| Clayton | 6.4 | 347 | 33 | 349 | 564.6 | 13.7 | 87 | 682 | 163.6 | 11.6 | 8 | 10 | 1.0 | 0.2 |
| Clinton | 241.3 | 4 854 | 49 | 319 | 190.1 | 11.2 | 219 | 2 789 | 635.7 | 57.5 | 46 | 136 | 27.6 | 3.9 |
| Crawford | 5.1 | 302 | 14 | 126 | 122.0 | 5.3 | 85 | 854 | 162.4 | 14.4 | 10 | 21 | 1.3 | 0.2 |
| Dallas | 4.8 | 92 | 49 | 420 | 218.3 | 17.3 | 263 | 5 073 | 905.7 | 90.7 | 47 | 298 | 68.3 | 15.0 |
| Davis | 1.5 | 171 | 7 | 47 | 17.9 | 1.3 | 32 | 330 | 71.6 | 6.8 | 7 | 13 | 1.4 | 0.2 |
| Decatur | 1.4 | 160 | 9 | 121 | 76.7 | 2.6 | 27 | 223 | 39.6 | 3.3 | 3 | D | D | D |
| Delaware | 6.7 | 373 | 34 | 369 | 302.4 | 14.9 | 82 | 700 | 171.4 | 14.4 | 11 | 27 | 2.0 | 0.4 |
| Des Moines | 105.3 | 2 580 | 47 | D | D | D | 221 | 3 193 | 616.9 | 63.0 | 41 | D | D | D |
| Dickinson | 6.9 | 412 | 20 | D | D | D | 116 | 1 044 | 255.2 | 22.8 | 49 | 88 | 16.4 | 2.6 |
| Dubuque | 86.8 | 947 | 154 | 2 388 | 1 847.7 | 91.6 | 467 | 7 056 | 1 433.5 | 135.0 | 103 | 446 | 73.6 | 16.6 |
| Emmet | 2.5 | 236 | 18 | 105 | 103.9 | 3.1 | 60 | 510 | 92.7 | 9.7 | 5 | D | D | D |
| Fayette | 4.7 | 220 | 39 | 476 | 304.2 | 18.4 | 100 | 830 | 157.2 | 15.4 | 15 | 48 | 9.4 | 1.1 |
| Floyd | 3.2 | 193 | 24 | 143 | 121.9 | 7.4 | 74 | 762 | 149.1 | 12.7 | 10 | 30 | 4.3 | 0.7 |

1. Merchant wholesalers, except manufacturers' sales branches and offices.  2. Employer establishments.

# Table B. States and Counties — Professional Services, Manufacturing, and Accommodation and Food Services

| STATE County | Professional, scientific, and technical services,[1] 2007 | | | | Manufacturing, 2007 | | | | Accommodation and food services, 2007 | | | |
|---|---|---|---|---|---|---|---|---|---|---|---|---|
| | Number of establishments | Number of employees | Receipts (mil dol) | Annual payroll (mil dol) | Number of establishments | Number of employees | Receipts (mil dol) | Annual payroll (mil dol) | Number of establishments | Number of employees | Sales (mil dol) | Annual payroll (mil dol) |
| | 147 | 148 | 149 | 150 | 151 | 152 | 153 | 154 | 155 | 156 | 157 | 158 |
| INDIANA—Cont'd | | | | | | | | | | | | |
| Pike | 7 | 26 | 2.0 | 0.6 | NA | NA | NA | NA | 11 | 164 | 5.6 | 1.6 |
| Porter | 333 | 2 132 | 224.9 | 83.1 | 152 | 9 716 | 7 318.8 | 615.5 | 301 | 5 474 | 211.3 | 58.6 |
| Posey | 45 | D | D | D | 24 | 2 564 | D | 182.9 | 41 | 477 | 17.1 | 5.5 |
| Pulaski | 22 | 64 | 3.9 | 1.0 | 20 | 1 268 | D | 59.4 | 28 | D | D | D |
| Putnam | 47 | 172 | 10.6 | 3.9 | 30 | 3 004 | 676.0 | 99.9 | 79 | 1 224 | 45.9 | 11.6 |
| Randolph | 34 | 90 | 6.6 | 2.0 | 46 | 2 134 | 577.4 | 84.8 | 42 | D | D | D |
| Ripley | 44 | 142 | 10.9 | 3.6 | 44 | 2 574 | 757.4 | 92.2 | 40 | 495 | 18.7 | 5.3 |
| Rush | 31 | 122 | 11.1 | 3.2 | 36 | 1 160 | 523.3 | 47.0 | 27 | D | D | D |
| St. Joseph | 561 | D | D | D | 427 | 17 667 | 8 011.0 | 862.2 | 555 | 11 175 | 439.7 | 126.6 |
| Scott | 31 | 133 | 11.1 | 3.5 | 32 | 2 096 | 978.7 | 78.0 | 44 | 804 | 30.7 | 8.6 |
| Shelby | 69 | 379 | 23.6 | 11.8 | 87 | 5 730 | 2 354.9 | 247.4 | 68 | 1 322 | 46.4 | 13.3 |
| Spencer | 23 | 112 | 9.8 | 3.0 | 26 | 1 346 | D | 58.4 | 29 | 390 | 16.3 | 4.1 |
| Starke | 16 | 54 | 4.5 | 1.4 | 24 | 996 | 243.7 | 32.1 | 32 | D | D | D |
| Steuben | 57 | 185 | 12.7 | 3.8 | 97 | 4 542 | 1 148.0 | 163.1 | 100 | 1 391 | 57.0 | 15.8 |
| Sullivan | 25 | D | D | D | NA | NA | NA | NA | 35 | 396 | 14.3 | 3.9 |
| Switzerland | 8 | D | D | D | NA | NA | NA | NA | 20 | D | D | D |
| Tippecanoe | 296 | D | D | D | 125 | 13 836 | D | 693.0 | 389 | 8 352 | 316.0 | 92.3 |
| Tipton | 23 | D | D | D | 24 | 1 094 | 362.1 | 37.4 | 27 | 299 | 9.8 | 2.8 |
| Union | 6 | D | D | D | NA | NA | NA | NA | 7 | 88 | 3.0 | 0.8 |
| Vanderburgh | 455 | D | D | D | 276 | 14 248 | 6 447.6 | 607.9 | 457 | 11 318 | 516.8 | 146.4 |
| Vermillion | 18 | D | D | D | 12 | 816 | D | 56.3 | 39 | 376 | 16.3 | 3.5 |
| Vigo | 207 | 1 181 | 110.8 | 37.7 | 126 | 8 821 | 3 565.9 | 393.7 | 252 | 4 838 | 195.5 | 54.9 |
| Wabash | 53 | 352 | 24.3 | 7.9 | 62 | 3 950 | 1 045.4 | 153.9 | 62 | 900 | 30.3 | 8.3 |
| Warren | 7 | D | D | D | 15 | 572 | 93.1 | D | 9 | 173 | 8.4 | 2.2 |
| Warrick | 94 | D | D | D | 46 | 2 973 | D | D | 72 | 1 073 | 36.9 | 11.1 |
| Washington | 32 | D | D | D | 41 | 1 763 | 248.3 | 60.7 | 31 | D | D | D |
| Wayne | 86 | 377 | 30.9 | 11.5 | 128 | 6 830 | 2 483.1 | 265.6 | 147 | 3 153 | 107.2 | 31.8 |
| Wells | 42 | 231 | 23.1 | 7.7 | 54 | 2 855 | 699.1 | 107.5 | 42 | 667 | 19.3 | 5.5 |
| White | 31 | 112 | 7.1 | 2.4 | 44 | 2 058 | 715.2 | 76.3 | 70 | 682 | 24.5 | 6.5 |
| Whitley | 47 | 193 | 14.0 | 5.2 | 72 | 4 783 | 2 107.5 | 203.9 | 58 | 860 | 28.3 | 7.7 |
| IOWA | 6 181 | 42 118 | 5 015.6 | 1 883.8 | 3 802 | 223 049 | 97 592.1 | 9 525.7 | 7 014 | 116 838 | 4 737.7 | 1 276.0 |
| Adair | 12 | 44 | 2.7 | 0.8 | NA | NA | NA | NA | 14 | 129 | 4.1 | 1.2 |
| Adams | 5 | D | D | D | NA | NA | NA | NA | 7 | D | D | D |
| Allamakee | 21 | 151 | 9.8 | 2.7 | 33 | 1 557 | D | 50.6 | 37 | 313 | 8.5 | 2.1 |
| Appanoose | 26 | 68 | 4.3 | 1.4 | 14 | 755 | 151.6 | 28.8 | 30 | 297 | 8.0 | 2.2 |
| Audubon | 11 | D | D | D | NA | NA | NA | NA | 8 | D | D | D |
| Benton | 32 | 82 | 6.3 | 2.2 | 30 | 819 | 176.8 | 27.8 | 42 | 348 | 9.6 | 2.6 |
| Black Hawk | 234 | D | D | D | 163 | 12 539 | 5 880.3 | 531.7 | 288 | 6 172 | 194.6 | 59.7 |
| Boone | 40 | 170 | 17.7 | 5.3 | 33 | 782 | 161.3 | 30.1 | 45 | 592 | 16.2 | 4.6 |
| Bremer | 44 | D | D | D | 39 | 1 950 | 699.7 | 99.5 | 46 | 546 | 16.7 | 4.5 |
| Buchanan | 28 | 115 | 9.8 | 2.6 | 41 | 1 216 | 640.8 | 42.8 | 39 | 388 | 11.5 | 3.2 |
| Buena Vista | 40 | 178 | 15.6 | 6.5 | 32 | 2 906 | 1 578.0 | 92.9 | 47 | 796 | 25.5 | 6.9 |
| Butler | 19 | 62 | 5.2 | 1.1 | 26 | 696 | D | 22.9 | 22 | D | D | D |
| Calhoun | 16 | 39 | 3.7 | 0.9 | NA | NA | NA | NA | 19 | D | D | D |
| Carroll | 51 | 224 | 21.2 | 6.7 | 44 | 1 551 | 794.0 | 67.1 | 56 | 637 | 20.8 | 5.7 |
| Cass | 29 | 121 | 10.0 | 3.8 | 23 | 560 | D | 21.6 | 33 | 374 | 11.6 | 3.1 |
| Cedar | 32 | 96 | 7.5 | 2.4 | 34 | 530 | 178.8 | 19.8 | 36 | 326 | 9.5 | 2.6 |
| Cerro Gordo | 96 | D | D | D | 54 | 3 761 | 1 357.5 | 152.3 | 148 | 2 429 | 83.9 | 24.2 |
| Cherokee | 17 | 71 | 10.8 | 1.8 | 21 | 813 | 279.3 | 26.3 | 30 | 259 | 8.7 | 2.7 |
| Chickasaw | 20 | 58 | 5.0 | 1.2 | 35 | 1 170 | 278.3 | 40.8 | 30 | 263 | 7.4 | 1.7 |
| Clarke | 12 | 39 | 3.0 | 0.8 | 15 | 1 054 | 416.6 | 33.8 | 22 | 791 | 84.9 | 12.9 |
| Clay | 36 | 181 | 16.9 | 6.4 | 30 | D | D | D | 49 | 618 | 23.4 | 6.2 |
| Clayton | 27 | 84 | 6.6 | 1.8 | 31 | 1 010 | 206.4 | 31.6 | 57 | 768 | 53.7 | 10.1 |
| Clinton | 64 | 366 | 30.8 | 13.0 | 61 | 4 678 | 3 914.9 | 218.3 | 117 | 1 440 | 54.1 | 14.4 |
| Crawford | 20 | 101 | 7.0 | 2.6 | 26 | 2 477 | 1 266.8 | 91.4 | 35 | 412 | 12.9 | 3.5 |
| Dallas | 133 | 1 072 | 167.9 | 47.8 | 41 | 2 384 | 574.2 | 79.9 | 132 | 2 621 | 110.4 | 31.3 |
| Davis | 11 | 41 | 4.2 | 0.9 | NA | NA | NA | NA | 13 | 128 | 3.1 | 0.9 |
| Decatur | 7 | D | D | D | NA | NA | NA | NA | 13 | 180 | 4.3 | 1.2 |
| Delaware | 30 | 131 | 9.3 | 3.8 | 37 | 1 573 | 326.4 | 59.9 | 34 | 377 | 9.0 | 2.7 |
| Des Moines | 55 | 336 | 30.0 | 15.1 | 67 | D | D | D | 98 | 2 012 | 68.8 | 20.6 |
| Dickinson | 48 | D | D | D | 37 | 1 878 | 647.5 | 66.3 | 104 | 1 284 | 54.6 | 16.2 |
| Dubuque | 168 | D | D | D | 150 | 9 378 | 4 711.2 | 380.3 | 253 | 4 502 | 145.7 | 42.5 |
| Emmet | 17 | 66 | 7.0 | 2.5 | 16 | 1 138 | 331.4 | 40.9 | 23 | 252 | 7.9 | 2.2 |
| Fayette | 39 | 147 | 10.0 | 3.3 | 32 | 735 | 157.7 | 23.9 | 50 | 479 | 14.6 | 3.6 |
| Floyd | 28 | 92 | 6.9 | 1.8 | 19 | 708 | 461.4 | 40.5 | 43 | 378 | 13.7 | 3.1 |

1. Establishment subject to federal tax.

| STATE County | Health care and social assistance, 2007 | | | | Other services, 2007 | | | | Federal funds and grants, 2009–2010 Expenditures (mil dol) | | | |
|---|---|---|---|---|---|---|---|---|---|---|---|---|
| | | | | | | | | | | Direct payments for individuals[1] | | |
| | Number of establishments | Number of employees | Receipts (mil dol) | Annual payroll (mil dol) | Number of establishments | Number of employees | Receipts (mil dol) | Annual payroll (mil dol) | Total | Social Security and government retirement | Medicare | Food Stamps and Supplemental Security Income |
| | 159 | 160 | 161 | 162 | 163 | 164 | 165 | 166 | 167 | 168 | 169 | 170 |
| INDIANA—Cont'd | | | | | | | | | | | | |
| Pike | 14 | 359 | 17.2 | 6.5 | 22 | 78 | 5.8 | 1.6 | 99.3 | 43.7 | 24.9 | 4.0 |
| Porter | 363 | 7 157 | 632.1 | 248.0 | 290 | 1 827 | 155.6 | 44.4 | 874.1 | 496.1 | 183.1 | 25.5 |
| Posey | 44 | D | D | D | 38 | 130 | 12.1 | 2.7 | 170.4 | 72.7 | 39.4 | 6.4 |
| Pulaski | 33 | 619 | 40.4 | 17.7 | 27 | 105 | 9.2 | 1.8 | 99.5 | 46.7 | 21.2 | 3.8 |
| Putnam | 74 | 1 612 | 93.6 | 38.7 | 63 | 273 | 19.9 | 5.3 | 206.1 | 100.4 | 43.6 | 6.0 |
| Randolph | 34 | 591 | 44.0 | 17.0 | 46 | 177 | 13.9 | 3.2 | 208.8 | 96.5 | 45.9 | 10.5 |
| Ripley | 67 | 903 | 43.9 | 20.9 | 55 | 191 | 17.1 | 3.6 | 210.3 | 98.1 | 44.3 | 6.3 |
| Rush | 31 | 528 | 35.5 | 14.3 | 40 | 138 | 12.7 | 2.6 | 122.6 | 52.6 | 32.3 | 4.2 |
| St. Joseph | 668 | D | D | D | 519 | 3 816 | 403.4 | 96.4 | 3 015.5 | 757.3 | 407.0 | 99.4 |
| Scott | 66 | 955 | 68.4 | 25.0 | 23 | 106 | 8.4 | 2.0 | 224.3 | 84.1 | 42.1 | 12.0 |
| Shelby | 86 | 1 604 | 148.4 | 56.2 | 75 | 525 | 40.4 | 11.3 | 320.8 | 128.2 | 63.4 | 9.5 |
| Spencer | 33 | 404 | 17.4 | 7.7 | 35 | 110 | 6.8 | 2.3 | 131.3 | 64.3 | 29.0 | 4.7 |
| Starke | 31 | 663 | 45.7 | 17.4 | 39 | 141 | 10.6 | 2.1 | 157.2 | 78.8 | 30.5 | 9.0 |
| Steuben | 77 | 1 278 | 86.3 | 32.0 | 81 | 580 | 56.3 | 11.5 | 201.3 | 108.2 | 44.8 | 6.6 |
| Sullivan | 40 | D | D | D | 25 | 100 | 6.9 | 1.6 | 169.8 | 69.4 | 46.0 | 6.2 |
| Switzerland | 16 | 125 | 8.9 | 3.4 | 13 | D | D | D | 66.2 | 26.7 | 13.7 | 3.3 |
| Tippecanoe | 322 | 9 181 | 913.3 | 342.8 | 252 | 1 861 | 239.1 | 46.9 | 1 070.3 | 356.6 | 132.6 | 30.5 |
| Tipton | 30 | 575 | 58.0 | 21.3 | 29 | 127 | 13.2 | 3.1 | 105.4 | 54.8 | 28.7 | 2.6 |
| Union | 12 | D | D | D | 10 | D | D | D | 47.3 | 24.2 | 9.7 | 1.8 |
| Vanderburgh | 563 | 17 053 | 1 720.0 | 649.2 | 367 | 3 041 | 274.3 | 82.1 | 1 573.9 | 574.3 | 323.6 | 76.2 |
| Vermillion | 24 | D | D | D | 22 | 48 | 3.7 | 0.6 | 139.1 | 57.7 | 28.9 | 5.1 |
| Vigo | 357 | 8 792 | 917.0 | 305.2 | 191 | 1 408 | 110.4 | 30.8 | 1 006.3 | 334.4 | 213.6 | 43.5 |
| Wabash | 73 | 2 139 | 134.8 | 51.1 | 61 | 242 | 21.2 | 4.8 | 234.2 | 118.6 | 47.2 | 7.0 |
| Warren | 11 | D | D | D | 8 | D | D | D | 48.2 | 21.7 | 11.6 | 1.3 |
| Warrick | 117 | 2 329 | 225.4 | 75.4 | 91 | 440 | 37.1 | 11.0 | 293.5 | 169.5 | 57.2 | 8.7 |
| Washington | 45 | 738 | 55.2 | 27.9 | 31 | 157 | 12.8 | 3.9 | 187.5 | 80.9 | 36.0 | 9.1 |
| Wayne | 184 | 5 306 | 530.7 | 195.2 | 136 | 612 | 52.8 | 13.4 | 597.1 | 245.0 | 123.5 | 36.2 |
| Wells | 51 | 1 419 | 105.3 | 42.5 | 67 | 273 | 22.0 | 4.9 | 146.2 | 77.8 | 34.7 | 4.0 |
| White | 36 | 742 | 58.2 | 24.3 | 46 | 173 | 13.0 | 2.8 | 182.3 | 91.9 | 43.9 | 5.1 |
| Whitley | 52 | 1 115 | 69.5 | 26.1 | 66 | 413 | 31.7 | 8.1 | 243.1 | 103.1 | 39.7 | 3.6 |
| IOWA | 7 857 | 198 285 | 15 371.6 | 6 603.6 | 6 088 | 31 869 | 3 063.2 | 779.2 | 28 378.9 | 9 174.7 | 4 608.9 | 815.2 |
| Adair | 16 | 297 | 15.3 | 6.2 | 15 | D | D | D | 66.2 | 24.2 | 15.7 | 1.7 |
| Adams | 17 | 301 | 18.4 | 8.9 | 8 | 21 | 1.9 | 0.4 | 39.5 | 15.9 | 9.7 | 1.2 |
| Allamakee | 41 | 937 | 41.7 | 19.9 | 34 | 101 | 11.2 | 2.1 | 98.3 | 45.9 | 20.2 | 3.0 |
| Appanoose | 39 | 723 | 42.3 | 17.6 | 27 | 103 | 6.6 | 1.8 | 140.8 | 50.3 | 30.4 | 7.0 |
| Audubon | 14 | 297 | 17.4 | 7.1 | 20 | 61 | 5.4 | 1.4 | 56.6 | 23.3 | 14.8 | 1.2 |
| Benton | 52 | 755 | 39.1 | 18.1 | 52 | 138 | 12.3 | 3.1 | 151.7 | 75.3 | 36.3 | 4.9 |
| Black Hawk | 340 | 10 326 | 850.4 | 362.6 | 212 | 1 670 | 127.4 | 36.5 | 1 013.1 | 377.8 | 219.0 | 54.0 |
| Boone | 57 | 1 538 | 87.6 | 39.8 | 46 | 155 | 15.5 | 4.1 | 209.8 | 86.3 | 40.3 | 6.1 |
| Bremer | 54 | 1 604 | 91.5 | 43.0 | 59 | D | D | D | 173.0 | 80.0 | 38.8 | 3.0 |
| Buchanan | 39 | 1 104 | 61.6 | 33.7 | 31 | 84 | 6.2 | 1.3 | 143.6 | 66.5 | 34.1 | 4.7 |
| Buena Vista | 51 | 1 322 | 76.4 | 33.0 | 35 | D | D | D | 144.7 | 55.2 | 36.3 | 3.6 |
| Butler | 26 | 460 | 19.3 | 9.3 | 24 | 61 | 5.9 | 1.1 | 126.7 | 56.7 | 33.1 | 2.9 |
| Calhoun | 31 | 684 | 39.3 | 17.0 | 16 | 35 | 4.9 | 0.6 | 95.0 | 38.4 | 24.7 | 2.0 |
| Carroll | 108 | 2 280 | 146.4 | 55.0 | 51 | 211 | 17.4 | 3.8 | 172.6 | 71.8 | 37.7 | 3.8 |
| Cass | 41 | 1 180 | 63.3 | 29.2 | 42 | 205 | 15.2 | 3.0 | 122.1 | 53.1 | 33.4 | 4.5 |
| Cedar | 57 | 585 | 23.9 | 11.9 | 37 | 96 | 7.5 | 1.9 | 111.3 | 52.3 | 26.4 | 3.0 |
| Cerro Gordo | 134 | D | D | D | 115 | 526 | 36.3 | 11.0 | 382.7 | 165.5 | 84.0 | 13.2 |
| Cherokee | 36 | 911 | 53.8 | 27.1 | 29 | 61 | 6.2 | 1.5 | 101.7 | 44.0 | 25.5 | 2.3 |
| Chickasaw | 30 | 490 | 28.8 | 10.9 | 40 | 123 | 14.2 | 2.3 | 96.2 | 43.2 | 22.7 | 2.0 |
| Clarke | 30 | 625 | 37.6 | 17.3 | 21 | 67 | 6.1 | 1.0 | 68.4 | 28.8 | 15.2 | 2.8 |
| Clay | 52 | 1 341 | 113.3 | 48.7 | 51 | 239 | 17.0 | 4.4 | 134.0 | 58.4 | 28.1 | 3.6 |
| Clayton | 54 | 897 | 42.0 | 18.8 | 36 | 72 | 6.1 | 1.3 | 147.4 | 62.2 | 34.4 | 3.0 |
| Clinton | 142 | 3 835 | 240.7 | 101.4 | 114 | 563 | 28.6 | 13.5 | 567.8 | 169.2 | 94.6 | 19.3 |
| Crawford | 37 | 943 | 51.8 | 23.3 | 31 | 133 | 8.3 | 2.5 | 152.3 | 49.1 | 31.5 | 4.5 |
| Dallas | 147 | 2 453 | 183.0 | 92.3 | 82 | 888 | 105.8 | 45.0 | 215.0 | 114.5 | 47.9 | 7.0 |
| Davis | 23 | 413 | 25.9 | 10.6 | 13 | 30 | 2.1 | 0.5 | 67.7 | 27.1 | 14.6 | 2.0 |
| Decatur | 23 | 408 | 21.9 | 9.9 | 7 | D | D | D | 79.0 | 27.0 | 14.6 | 3.7 |
| Delaware | 44 | 843 | 48.4 | 21.9 | 31 | 110 | 7.1 | 1.5 | 112.9 | 49.4 | 23.3 | 3.0 |
| Des Moines | 140 | D | D | D | 92 | D | D | D | 465.5 | 153.0 | 78.7 | 16.2 |
| Dickinson | 57 | D | D | D | 43 | 191 | 13.1 | 3.4 | 124.6 | 66.7 | 28.0 | 3.0 |
| Dubuque | 242 | 7 056 | 592.0 | 264.0 | 208 | 1 505 | 102.2 | 27.4 | 640.7 | 284.2 | 148.6 | 20.4 |
| Emmet | 31 | 666 | 37.9 | 16.0 | 27 | 85 | 6.5 | 1.6 | 106.7 | 37.1 | 22.9 | 2.5 |
| Fayette | 62 | 1 251 | 69.1 | 30.2 | 54 | 200 | 21.0 | 5.7 | 188.9 | 70.4 | 40.3 | 6.2 |
| Floyd | 58 | 966 | 55.6 | 23.6 | 35 | 111 | 8.3 | 2.0 | 159.7 | 62.9 | 36.7 | 5.3 |

1. State totals may include programs not allocated by county.

# Table B. States and Counties — Federal Funds, Residential Construction, and Local Government Finances

| | Federal funds and grants, 2009–2010 (cont.) | | | | | | | Value of residential construction authorized by building permits, 2011 | | Local government finances, 2007 | | | | |
| | Expenditures (mil dol) (cont.) | | | | | | | | | General revenue | | | | |
| | Procurement contract awards | | | Grants[1] | | | | | | | | Taxes | | |
| STATE County | | | | | | | | | | | | | Per capita[2] (dollars) | |
| | Salaries and wages | Defense | Other | Medicaid and other health-related | Nutrition and family welfare | Education | Other | New construction ($1,000) | Number of housing units | Total (mil dol) | Inter-governmental (mil dol) | Total (mil dol) | Total | Property |
| | 171 | 172 | 173 | 174 | 175 | 176 | 177 | 178 | 179 | 180 | 181 | 182 | 183 | 184 |
| INDIANA—Cont'd | | | | | | | | | | | | | | |
| Pike | 2.6 | 0.0 | 0.6 | 16.4 | 1.9 | 0.2 | 0.5 | 3 037 | 26 | 30.8 | 11.9 | 9.3 | 741 | 731 |
| Porter | 33.6 | 5.5 | 13.3 | 58.2 | 14.7 | 2.0 | 29.2 | 56 576 | 237 | 704.0 | 164.8 | 184.9 | 1 152 | 1 101 |
| Posey | 5.2 | 8.2 | 1.1 | 18.6 | 3.4 | 1.8 | 1.1 | 5 962 | 36 | 77.6 | 31.1 | 35.6 | 1 357 | 1 348 |
| Pulaski | 3.5 | 0.0 | 0.8 | 9.7 | 1.8 | 0.3 | 2.6 | 1 998 | 15 | 69.9 | 26.3 | 13.9 | 1 010 | 767 |
| Putnam | 17.0 | 0.0 | 1.3 | 21.6 | 7.6 | 0.6 | 1.0 | 5 598 | 34 | 149.6 | 49.0 | 30.7 | 829 | 686 |
| Randolph | 15.0 | 0.0 | 1.2 | 26.8 | 4.8 | 0.7 | 0.7 | 1 556 | 7 | 78.0 | 40.7 | 22.3 | 864 | 706 |
| Ripley | 6.5 | 2.2 | 5.8 | 29.0 | 3.8 | 0.5 | 8.2 | 10 505 | 71 | 86.8 | 38.9 | 29.9 | 1 092 | 678 |
| Rush | 7.4 | 0.0 | 0.9 | 17.2 | 2.6 | 0.3 | 0.0 | 2 375 | 13 | 61.3 | 22.1 | 13.3 | 759 | 625 |
| St. Joseph | 143.5 | 1 122.3 | 28.9 | 264.0 | 33.5 | 8.8 | 83.1 | 55 746 | 392 | 852.3 | 353.9 | 309.5 | 1 163 | 1 098 |
| Scott | 30.1 | 3.4 | 0.8 | 41.7 | 5.2 | 0.7 | 0.3 | 2 484 | 27 | 81.0 | 35.5 | 17.9 | 756 | 625 |
| Shelby | 71.6 | 1.1 | 1.6 | 32.1 | 5.1 | 0.7 | 0.6 | 5 646 | 48 | 110.2 | 49.8 | 38.8 | 882 | 724 |
| Spencer | 5.5 | 0.0 | 1.2 | 18.6 | 2.1 | 0.3 | 0.2 | 5 135 | 36 | 63.1 | 24.0 | 28.1 | 1 381 | 1 147 |
| Starke | 4.5 | 0.0 | 1.1 | 23.1 | 4.3 | 0.7 | 0.2 | 5 403 | 33 | 82.2 | 39.5 | 19.5 | 830 | 784 |
| Steuben | 8.1 | 1.9 | 1.3 | 14.9 | 4.6 | 0.9 | 1.4 | 22 917 | 92 | 125.3 | 67.3 | 28.5 | 852 | 709 |
| Sullivan | 4.5 | 4.0 | 1.1 | 25.3 | 3.1 | 0.5 | 0.4 | 375 | 4 | 78.6 | 24.3 | 15.6 | 731 | 711 |
| Switzerland | 1.9 | 0.0 | 0.5 | 15.6 | 0.8 | 0.3 | 0.8 | 2 389 | 41 | 37.9 | 23.9 | 7.7 | 790 | 643 |
| Tippecanoe | 58.9 | 17.6 | 18.6 | 145.4 | 16.6 | 9.9 | 235.7 | 169 022 | 1 198 | 392.6 | 141.4 | 168.9 | 1 034 | 910 |
| Tipton | 2.7 | 0.0 | 0.6 | 10.4 | 1.7 | 0.2 | 0.1 | 2 144 | 17 | 81.2 | 18.9 | 21.6 | 1 344 | 1 102 |
| Union | 1.5 | 0.0 | 0.4 | 6.0 | 1.6 | 0.2 | 0.1 | 895 | 9 | 22.3 | 11.8 | 7.1 | 988 | 765 |
| Vanderburgh | 110.5 | 135.9 | 13.4 | 235.7 | 34.4 | 6.3 | 33.1 | 27 698 | 226 | 556.5 | 199.5 | 206.5 | 1 184 | 1 026 |
| Vermillion | 4.1 | 17.0 | 1.3 | 17.6 | 2.9 | 0.3 | 1.4 | 1 782 | 10 | 43.1 | 17.6 | 16.1 | 980 | 946 |
| Vigo | 117.4 | 4.3 | 54.5 | 161.2 | 22.5 | 4.7 | 18.2 | 26 675 | 349 | 276.6 | 124.8 | 90.9 | 866 | 716 |
| Wabash | 6.3 | 0.2 | 1.6 | 33.5 | 4.2 | 0.5 | 1.4 | 3 369 | 23 | 164.5 | 50.1 | 38.5 | 1 168 | 949 |
| Warren | 1.8 | 0.0 | 0.4 | 5.2 | 1.1 | 0.1 | 0.2 | 1 960 | 14 | 24.6 | 11.8 | 8.4 | 985 | 857 |
| Warrick | 10.0 | 0.4 | 2.6 | 29.8 | 6.4 | 0.5 | 2.5 | 40 681 | 183 | 124.4 | 47.6 | 43.0 | 754 | 681 |
| Washington | 13.4 | 0.1 | 1.1 | 34.2 | 4.3 | 0.8 | 1.6 | 3 583 | 26 | 79.8 | 32.8 | 16.0 | 575 | 457 |
| Wayne | 31.0 | 3.5 | 4.2 | 116.5 | 15.0 | 4.2 | 3.1 | 5 061 | 33 | 193.9 | 94.5 | 64.8 | 950 | 720 |
| Wells | 5.9 | 0.0 | 1.2 | 12.7 | 3.4 | 0.3 | 0.0 | 5 828 | 29 | 79.6 | 41.9 | 21.5 | 771 | 619 |
| White | 9.2 | -1.8 | 1.3 | 14.1 | 4.9 | 0.4 | 4.2 | 3 893 | 17 | 108.2 | 35.5 | 28.3 | 1 187 | 1 049 |
| Whitley | 6.4 | 68.2 | 2.1 | 11.6 | 3.0 | 0.3 | 0.1 | 10 598 | 57 | 71.5 | 29.7 | 24.6 | 753 | 613 |
| IOWA | 1 902.3 | 1 556.7 | 815.9 | 2 962.1 | 661.9 | 469.7 | 2 300.6 | 1 245 724 | 7 526 | X | X | X | X | X |
| Adair | 2.1 | 0.0 | 0.5 | 13.2 | 1.6 | 0.3 | 1.5 | 214 | 1 | 21.7 | 9.5 | 9.5 | 1 251 | 997 |
| Adams | 3.2 | 0.0 | 0.3 | 4.0 | 0.9 | 0.2 | 0.3 | 639 | 4 | 14.7 | 7.0 | 5.5 | 1 346 | 1 188 |
| Allamakee | 3.6 | 0.2 | 0.8 | 13.2 | 2.8 | 0.9 | 3.0 | 2 867 | 25 | 55.1 | 21.0 | 18.8 | 1 285 | 1 025 |
| Appanoose | 5.2 | 6.7 | 1.3 | 29.8 | 3.0 | 0.8 | 0.3 | 421 | 4 | 35.6 | 18.2 | 14.1 | 1 081 | 793 |
| Audubon | 3.7 | 0.0 | 1.0 | 4.1 | 1.0 | 0.2 | 1.0 | 1 325 | 5 | 22.5 | 8.8 | 10.9 | 1 802 | 1 206 |
| Benton | 6.4 | 0.2 | 1.9 | 12.1 | 3.6 | 0.5 | 0.4 | 3 985 | 18 | 67.0 | 30.0 | 27.6 | 1 041 | 872 |
| Black Hawk | 81.0 | 0.1 | 32.0 | 138.4 | 23.3 | 8.0 | 40.7 | 50 555 | 340 | 489.8 | 202.2 | 182.9 | 1 435 | 1 113 |
| Boone | 43.7 | 0.1 | 1.3 | 17.4 | 4.0 | 0.6 | 1.5 | 5 226 | 42 | 99.7 | 28.8 | 32.6 | 1 237 | 971 |
| Bremer | 5.4 | 15.3 | 1.1 | 11.5 | 3.3 | 0.5 | 4.8 | 13 858 | 53 | 107.9 | 30.1 | 31.8 | 1 342 | 1 076 |
| Buchanan | 5.0 | 0.0 | 1.2 | 13.8 | 2.8 | 1.2 | 1.3 | 3 338 | 19 | 67.2 | 24.1 | 23.2 | 1 111 | 868 |
| Buena Vista | 12.9 | 0.0 | 1.0 | 14.5 | 3.1 | 0.9 | 0.1 | 2 490 | 15 | 103.2 | 36.5 | 27.3 | 1 378 | 1 081 |
| Butler | 3.2 | 0.0 | 0.8 | 14.9 | 2.3 | 0.6 | 2.2 | 2 832 | 18 | 36.6 | 15.7 | 16.1 | 1 098 | 920 |
| Calhoun | 3.1 | 0.0 | 1.0 | 9.2 | 1.9 | 0.3 | 0.6 | 1 141 | 7 | 48.8 | 16.2 | 26.3 | 2 634 | 2 211 |
| Carroll | 10.4 | 0.0 | 7.3 | 19.5 | 5.0 | 0.4 | 7.8 | 7 517 | 30 | 71.7 | 27.1 | 28.9 | 1 379 | 1 098 |
| Cass | 6.1 | 0.1 | 0.9 | 12.7 | 2.9 | 0.5 | 0.8 | 1 550 | 12 | 73.2 | 22.8 | 21.3 | 1 535 | 1 211 |
| Cedar | 6.6 | 0.0 | 2.3 | 9.2 | 2.5 | 0.3 | 0.6 | 5 299 | 28 | 58.2 | 24.2 | 26.3 | 1 462 | 1 185 |
| Cerro Gordo | 25.5 | 3.0 | 2.5 | 47.6 | 8.8 | 2.3 | 11.9 | 8 263 | 36 | 178.8 | 64.3 | 72.8 | 1 654 | 1 250 |
| Cherokee | 5.4 | 0.2 | 1.4 | 10.9 | 2.1 | 0.6 | 2.3 | 1 888 | 11 | 37.0 | 16.0 | 15.5 | 1 326 | 1 104 |
| Chickasaw | 3.7 | 0.2 | 0.8 | 9.2 | 2.1 | 0.3 | 0.6 | 2 295 | 20 | 36.5 | 15.6 | 16.2 | 1 328 | 1 042 |
| Clarke | 2.5 | 0.0 | 0.5 | 8.6 | 2.1 | 0.3 | 0.9 | 197 | 1 | 45.8 | 13.8 | 14.2 | 1 582 | 1 216 |
| Clay | 6.8 | 0.0 | 1.2 | 16.2 | 2.8 | 0.3 | 6.1 | 1 170 | 7 | 127.4 | 24.1 | 25.1 | 1 504 | 1 122 |
| Clayton | 6.3 | 0.5 | 2.9 | 22.4 | 3.6 | 0.4 | 1.9 | 5 264 | 41 | 68.5 | 32.9 | 25.4 | 1 438 | 1 148 |
| Clinton | 11.3 | 0.3 | 2.2 | 33.7 | 7.5 | 1.6 | 9.2 | 7 785 | 40 | 160.5 | 70.5 | 68.5 | 1 397 | 1 044 |
| Crawford | 13.5 | 0.0 | 22.0 | 16.7 | 3.4 | 0.6 | 0.4 | 2 640 | 17 | 65.8 | 25.6 | 19.6 | 1 182 | 931 |
| Dallas | 10.4 | 0.1 | 2.4 | 14.4 | 4.8 | 1.0 | 1.3 | 46 260 | 212 | 186.9 | 66.1 | 84.4 | 1 473 | 1 245 |
| Davis | 2.6 | 0.0 | 0.5 | 10.3 | 1.2 | 0.4 | 3.0 | 27 | 1 | 40.1 | 11.3 | 13.8 | 1 606 | 1 434 |
| Decatur | 3.3 | 0.0 | 0.8 | 14.6 | 4.2 | 1.2 | 0.4 | 3 595 | 28 | 32.1 | 14.4 | 12.5 | 1 488 | 1 040 |
| Delaware | 4.2 | 0.6 | 0.9 | 13.2 | 2.9 | 0.3 | 0.5 | 2 280 | 18 | 72.8 | 22.3 | 23.6 | 1 351 | 1 115 |
| Des Moines | 18.2 | 125.9 | 2.1 | 36.8 | 9.4 | 2.7 | 4.7 | 2 552 | 14 | 164.7 | 73.0 | 57.2 | 1 405 | 1 052 |
| Dickinson | 4.9 | 0.0 | 1.2 | 10.4 | 2.4 | 0.3 | 2.2 | 20 600 | 128 | 88.7 | 13.2 | 42.1 | 2 523 | 2 021 |
| Dubuque | 35.9 | 3.8 | 5.3 | 77.2 | 14.0 | 3.3 | 28.3 | 62 319 | 410 | 300.1 | 111.3 | 128.9 | 1 395 | 1 009 |
| Emmet | 11.1 | 0.0 | 6.3 | 9.8 | 2.1 | 1.8 | 1.1 | 1 498 | 9 | 64.0 | 24.7 | 16.3 | 1 563 | 1 356 |
| Fayette | 11.0 | 0.0 | 1.2 | 19.5 | 4.4 | 0.8 | 2.9 | 3 015 | 29 | 66.1 | 30.7 | 26.2 | 1 281 | 1 013 |
| Floyd | 4.8 | 0.0 | 0.9 | 25.2 | 2.9 | 0.5 | 12.3 | 2 430 | 13 | 70.1 | 22.1 | 22.8 | 1 398 | 1 110 |

1. State totals may include programs not allocated by county.  2. Based on the resident population estimated as of July 1 of the year shown.

# Table B. States and Counties — Local Government Finances, Government Employment, and Voting

| STATE County | Local government finances, 2007 (cont.) Direct general expenditure — Total (mil dol) | Per capita¹ (dollars) | Percent of total for: Education | Health and hospitals | Police protection | Public welfare | Highways | Debt outstanding — Total (mil dol) | Per capita¹ (dollars) | Government employment, 2011 — Federal civilian | Federal military | State and local | Presidential election,² 2012 Percent of vote cast: — Democratic | Republican | All other |
|---|---|---|---|---|---|---|---|---|---|---|---|---|---|---|---|
| | 185 | 186 | 187 | 188 | 189 | 190 | 191 | 192 | 193 | 194 | 195 | 196 | 197 | 198 | 199 |
| **INDIANA—Cont'd** | | | | | | | | | | | | | | | |
| Pike | 36.2 | 2 868 | 55.9 | 0.4 | 1.9 | 4.7 | 8.4 | 31.3 | 2 481 | 32 | 42 | 667 | 44.8 | 53.4 | 1.8 |
| Porter | 746.2 | 4 647 | 45.8 | 25.8 | 1.7 | 0.7 | 2.2 | 512.1 | 3 189 | 445 | 548 | 6 482 | 53.0 | 45.8 | 1.2 |
| Posey | 86.2 | 3 283 | 57.5 | 1.8 | 2.0 | 2.5 | 9.4 | 43.3 | 1 650 | 71 | 85 | 1 116 | 45.6 | 53.3 | 1.1 |
| Pulaski | 70.8 | 5 140 | 48.4 | 22.6 | 2.3 | 2.9 | 4.0 | 37.6 | 2 727 | 41 | 44 | 974 | 41.3 | 56.8 | 1.8 |
| Putnam | 165.0 | 4 457 | 45.1 | 31.7 | 1.3 | 1.6 | 3.4 | 198.6 | 5 365 | 78 | 125 | 2 486 | 43.2 | 55.2 | 1.5 |
| Randolph | 90.9 | 3 514 | 55.4 | 0.6 | 2.7 | 4.4 | 4.9 | 54.1 | 2 090 | 66 | 86 | 1 232 | 44.8 | 53.6 | 1.7 |
| Ripley | 94.2 | 3 444 | 56.1 | 0.5 | 1.2 | 3.4 | 5.3 | 61.9 | 2 262 | 75 | 95 | 1 295 | 34.4 | 63.9 | 1.7 |
| Rush | 57.2 | 3 267 | 38.5 | 19.0 | 3.1 | 2.3 | 8.0 | 13.1 | 746 | 49 | 57 | 1 038 | 42.3 | 56.0 | 1.7 |
| St. Joseph | 903.8 | 3 396 | 51.3 | 0.6 | 4.8 | 4.0 | 2.4 | 916.7 | 3 445 | 1 013 | 958 | 13 823 | 58.0 | 41.0 | 1.0 |
| Scott | 88.8 | 3 749 | 44.9 | 22.0 | 2.8 | 1.9 | 2.7 | 38.4 | 1 620 | 62 | 79 | 1 289 | 48.1 | 50.1 | 1.8 |
| Shelby | 146.7 | 3 329 | 58.1 | 1.7 | 3.8 | 2.5 | 4.1 | 250.0 | 5 674 | 150 | 147 | 2 351 | 39.8 | 58.8 | 1.4 |
| Spencer | 64.7 | 3 184 | 58.2 | 0.5 | 1.9 | 1.1 | 5.3 | 40.9 | 2 010 | 72 | 69 | 968 | 49.5 | 49.1 | 1.4 |
| Starke | 74.3 | 3 155 | 66.1 | 2.2 | 1.7 | 3.0 | 4.0 | 62.3 | 2 644 | 48 | 77 | 921 | 50.5 | 47.3 | 2.3 |
| Steuben | 105.7 | 3 161 | 47.3 | 0.8 | 3.1 | 2.9 | 10.9 | 112.7 | 3 370 | 68 | 113 | 1 570 | 44.4 | 54.2 | 1.3 |
| Sullivan | 84.2 | 3 943 | 41.3 | 24.7 | 0.8 | 2.1 | 5.9 | 88.3 | 4 132 | 52 | 71 | 1 870 | 48.8 | 49.5 | 1.8 |
| Switzerland | 37.7 | 3 897 | 36.0 | 1.5 | 1.2 | 2.0 | 4.1 | 10.3 | 1 065 | 25 | 35 | 427 | 45.0 | 53.3 | 1.7 |
| Tippecanoe | 438.4 | 2 684 | 47.7 | 0.8 | 3.1 | 3.7 | 6.5 | 454.4 | 2 781 | 540 | 630 | 22 875 | 55.2 | 43.6 | 1.2 |
| Tipton | 93.2 | 5 802 | 26.0 | 32.6 | 1.4 | 3.2 | 2.3 | 33.5 | 2 087 | 36 | 52 | 722 | 41.5 | 56.9 | 1.6 |
| Union | 27.7 | 3 847 | 66.1 | 0.4 | 2.1 | 0.9 | 5.0 | 47.3 | 6 564 | 16 | 25 | 464 | 36.6 | 61.6 | 1.9 |
| Vanderburgh | 619.3 | 3 551 | 36.0 | 1.6 | 6.6 | 2.8 | 2.4 | 524.7 | 3 008 | 880 | 605 | 9 628 | 50.8 | 48.3 | 0.9 |
| Vermillion | 48.4 | 2 950 | 54.2 | 0.9 | 2.0 | 1.1 | 6.5 | 38.1 | 2 322 | 36 | 55 | 666 | 56.1 | 42.2 | 1.7 |
| Vigo | 317.6 | 3 027 | 46.8 | 1.1 | 4.0 | 2.5 | 3.0 | 211.8 | 2 019 | 1 178 | 380 | 7 586 | 57.3 | 41.5 | 1.3 |
| Wabash | 169.6 | 5 153 | 39.4 | 33.3 | 1.4 | 2.2 | 3.6 | 50.2 | 1 524 | 74 | 108 | 1 869 | 39.3 | 59.4 | 1.3 |
| Warren | 25.8 | 3 046 | 53.6 | 1.5 | 2.4 | 3.5 | 12.0 | 12.4 | 1 463 | 21 | 37 | 354 | 43.9 | 54.2 | 1.9 |
| Warrick | 155.5 | 2 724 | 51.9 | 1.1 | 2.7 | 1.6 | 3.7 | 170.3 | 2 983 | 127 | 199 | 2 020 | 43.0 | 55.9 | 1.1 |
| Washington | 95.5 | 3 421 | 54.1 | 16.5 | 1.3 | 1.3 | 3.7 | 40.1 | 1 436 | 57 | 93 | 1 077 | 40.4 | 57.7 | 2.0 |
| Wayne | 222.4 | 3 258 | 46.6 | 1.6 | 5.7 | 1.4 | 4.0 | 119.9 | 1 756 | 163 | 228 | 4 670 | 47.1 | 51.0 | 1.9 |
| Wells | 102.7 | 3 676 | 61.9 | 0.5 | 2.8 | 1.9 | 3.7 | 55.6 | 1 990 | 57 | 92 | 1 276 | 33.7 | 65.1 | 1.3 |
| White | 111.2 | 4 670 | 48.4 | 19.2 | 1.9 | 1.1 | 3.5 | 168.6 | 7 078 | 63 | 82 | 1 474 | 44.9 | 53.2 | 1.8 |
| Whitley | 81.7 | 2 502 | 58.7 | 0.8 | 3.4 | 1.3 | 5.0 | 84.1 | 2 575 | 75 | 110 | 1 415 | 38.6 | 60.1 | 1.3 |
| **IOWA** | X | X | X | X | X | X | X | X | X | 18 045 | 13 013 | 236 638 | 53.9 | 44.4 | 1.7 |
| Adair | 21.6 | 2 839 | 44.3 | 1.2 | 4.4 | 0.1 | 21.0 | 12.8 | 1 685 | 28 | 31 | 457 | 47.5 | 50.8 | 1.7 |
| Adams | 17.6 | 4 301 | 36.3 | 5.3 | 4.6 | 0.1 | 19.0 | 23.0 | 5 621 | 23 | 17 | 241 | 50.7 | 47.4 | 1.9 |
| Allamakee | 64.4 | 4 410 | 45.9 | 20.8 | 2.9 | 0.6 | 8.0 | 48.2 | 3 297 | 54 | 59 | 1 064 | 56.2 | 42.0 | 1.8 |
| Appanoose | 35.5 | 2 729 | 60.4 | 3.7 | 5.8 | 0.3 | 12.0 | 14.4 | 1 108 | 59 | 53 | 661 | 48.1 | 49.9 | 2.0 |
| Audubon | 22.5 | 3 703 | 56.4 | 5.1 | 2.9 | 0.3 | 14.1 | 9.4 | 1 549 | 30 | 25 | 403 | 50.6 | 47.6 | 1.8 |
| Benton | 71.8 | 2 703 | 62.0 | 3.3 | 3.6 | 0.2 | 10.8 | 84.0 | 3 166 | 60 | 108 | 1 468 | 51.5 | 47.0 | 1.5 |
| Black Hawk | 527.8 | 4 142 | 54.2 | 4.8 | 4.3 | 0.9 | 7.3 | 355.7 | 2 791 | 515 | 559 | 12 010 | 60.5 | 38.1 | 1.5 |
| Boone | 104.1 | 3 945 | 38.4 | 29.1 | 3.5 | 0.6 | 8.6 | 286.6 | 10 861 | 108 | 109 | 2 508 | 52.8 | 45.2 | 2.0 |
| Bremer | 111.3 | 4 688 | 41.4 | 31.3 | 3.3 | 0.4 | 5.7 | 66.0 | 2 782 | 71 | 101 | 1 767 | 53.9 | 44.6 | 1.5 |
| Buchanan | 64.3 | 3 072 | 42.2 | 23.1 | 4.0 | 0.5 | 9.7 | 25.1 | 1 201 | 49 | 87 | 1 424 | 58.5 | 40.0 | 1.5 |
| Buena Vista | 100.7 | 5 091 | 36.3 | 27.0 | 3.2 | 0.4 | 6.5 | 79.2 | 4 007 | 129 | 85 | 1 565 | 48.4 | 50.2 | 1.4 |
| Butler | 37.1 | 2 530 | 47.0 | 8.5 | 5.0 | 0.8 | 15.7 | 17.6 | 1 201 | 43 | 62 | 709 | 46.9 | 51.6 | 1.4 |
| Calhoun | 39.5 | 3 960 | 53.8 | 11.3 | 4.0 | 2.9 | 12.2 | 7.3 | 729 | 39 | 40 | 743 | 45.1 | 52.8 | 2.2 |
| Carroll | 65.0 | 3 105 | 42.0 | 2.4 | 6.5 | 5.1 | 10.7 | 64.7 | 3 093 | 90 | 87 | 1 246 | 51.0 | 47.3 | 1.6 |
| Cass | 70.5 | 5 079 | 35.1 | 36.5 | 3.5 | 0.2 | 7.9 | 16.4 | 1 178 | 75 | 57 | 1 288 | 43.7 | 54.5 | 1.8 |
| Cedar | 61.8 | 3 436 | 62.7 | 3.9 | 3.8 | 0.1 | 10.3 | 34.5 | 1 920 | 100 | 76 | 1 000 | 54.0 | 44.4 | 1.6 |
| Cerro Gordo | 182.7 | 4 150 | 50.7 | 5.6 | 5.1 | 0.6 | 6.4 | 121.7 | 2 764 | 160 | 183 | 2 788 | 59.7 | 38.8 | 1.5 |
| Cherokee | 36.8 | 3 149 | 47.7 | 3.5 | 4.3 | 0.0 | 14.0 | 30.8 | 2 638 | 46 | 50 | 951 | 45.4 | 53.0 | 1.7 |
| Chickasaw | 34.1 | 2 790 | 57.0 | 2.3 | 4.6 | 1.2 | 13.7 | 7.9 | 647 | 51 | 52 | 633 | 59.6 | 38.8 | 1.6 |
| Clarke | 45.1 | 5 015 | 33.0 | 36.7 | 3.5 | 0.5 | 6.9 | 31.1 | 3 458 | 29 | 39 | 747 | 49.9 | 47.6 | 2.5 |
| Clay | 115.2 | 6 900 | 23.1 | 47.4 | 2.5 | 0.1 | 5.6 | 106.3 | 6 370 | 69 | 69 | 1 601 | 46.7 | 51.8 | 1.5 |
| Clayton | 74.7 | 4 224 | 61.4 | 0.3 | 4.1 | 1.7 | 11.9 | 49.1 | 2 776 | 106 | 75 | 1 222 | 57.8 | 40.6 | 1.6 |
| Clinton | 160.2 | 3 267 | 53.5 | 5.7 | 6.0 | 0.4 | 7.8 | 97.9 | 1 996 | 115 | 204 | 2 568 | 60.7 | 37.7 | 1.5 |
| Crawford | 70.8 | 4 271 | 44.9 | 20.4 | 2.7 | 0.8 | 10.7 | 28.3 | 1 706 | 92 | 72 | 1 214 | 51.7 | 46.5 | 1.8 |
| Dallas | 199.4 | 3 481 | 60.0 | 10.0 | 2.9 | 0.4 | 7.3 | 255.7 | 4 463 | 107 | 289 | 3 236 | 46.4 | 51.9 | 1.7 |
| Davis | 32.6 | 3 804 | 32.7 | 40.5 | 2.8 | 0.2 | 11.0 | 7.5 | 873 | 38 | 37 | 522 | 44.0 | 53.1 | 2.9 |
| Decatur | 29.7 | 3 527 | 55.8 | 3.0 | 4.2 | 1.4 | 15.1 | 13.6 | 1 620 | 45 | 34 | 563 | 48.4 | 49.2 | 2.4 |
| Delaware | 74.2 | 4 249 | 44.2 | 32.0 | 2.5 | 0.1 | 6.8 | 23.6 | 1 351 | 50 | 73 | 1 179 | 52.2 | 46.2 | 1.6 |
| Des Moines | 163.4 | 4 015 | 61.3 | 1.0 | 4.8 | 1.3 | 6.7 | 101.0 | 2 482 | 143 | 170 | 2 543 | 60.6 | 37.5 | 1.9 |
| Dickinson | 93.5 | 5 599 | 32.4 | 23.2 | 3.3 | 0.3 | 8.7 | 94.7 | 5 672 | 64 | 70 | 1 104 | 46.7 | 52.1 | 1.2 |
| Dubuque | 294.8 | 3 192 | 47.5 | 4.1 | 5.2 | 2.1 | 9.1 | 144.0 | 1 559 | 253 | 410 | 4 296 | 59.7 | 38.9 | 1.5 |
| Emmet | 63.6 | 6 103 | 77.8 | 2.3 | 3.2 | 0.4 | 5.5 | 31.3 | 3 008 | 45 | 42 | 876 | 51.2 | 47.3 | 1.4 |
| Fayette | 70.1 | 3 433 | 52.3 | 4.0 | 4.5 | 0.3 | 11.8 | 42.9 | 2 098 | 74 | 87 | 1 151 | 57.6 | 41.0 | 1.5 |
| Floyd | 66.7 | 4 088 | 37.1 | 29.7 | 3.4 | 1.0 | 8.9 | 18.7 | 1 145 | 51 | 67 | 968 | 59.6 | 37.7 | 2.7 |

1. Based on the resident population estimated as of July 1 of the year shown.  2. © 2013 Election Data Services, Inc. All rights reserved.

# Table B. States and Counties — Land Area and Population

| STATE/ County code | CBSA code[1] | County type[2] | STATE County | Land area,[3] (sq km) 2010 | Population 2012 Total persons | Rank | Per square kilometer | Race alone or in combination, not Hispanic or Latino (percent) White | Black | American Indian, Alaska Native | Asian and Pacific Islander | Percent Hispanic or Latino[4] | Age (percent) Under 5 years | 5 to 17 years | 18 to 24 years | 25 to 34 years | 35 to 44 years | 45 to 54 years |
|---|---|---|---|---|---|---|---|---|---|---|---|---|---|---|---|---|---|---|
| | | | | 1 | 2 | 3 | 4 | 5 | 6 | 7 | 8 | 9 | 10 | 11 | 12 | 13 | 14 | 15 |
| | | | IOWA—Cont'd | | | | | | | | | | | | | | | |
| 19 069 | ... | 7 | Franklin | 1 507 | 10 554 | 2 393 | 7.0 | 88.0 | 0.6 | 0.4 | 0.5 | 11.2 | 6.2 | 17.2 | 7.1 | 11.1 | 10.7 | 14.3 |
| 19 071 | ... | 8 | Fremont | 1 324 | 7 147 | 2 668 | 5.4 | 96.3 | 0.9 | 0.9 | 0.4 | 2.5 | 6.2 | 16.4 | 6.5 | 9.5 | 10.5 | 15.6 |
| 19 073 | ... | 6 | Greene | 1 475 | 9 153 | 2 505 | 6.2 | 96.5 | 0.7 | 0.5 | 0.7 | 2.3 | 5.7 | 17.2 | 6.8 | 10.0 | 9.9 | 15.1 |
| 19 075 | 47940 | 3 | Grundy | 1 300 | 12 448 | 2 276 | 9.6 | 98.3 | 0.5 | 0.3 | 0.6 | 1.1 | 6.5 | 17.3 | 6.5 | 10.8 | 11.5 | 14.9 |
| 19 077 | 19780 | 6 | Guthrie | 1 530 | 10 777 | 2 376 | 7.0 | 97.1 | 0.5 | 0.6 | 0.6 | 2.0 | 5.4 | 17.8 | 5.7 | 9.6 | 11.1 | 15.8 |
| 19 079 | ... | 6 | Hamilton | 1 494 | 15 344 | 2 086 | 10.3 | 92.2 | 0.9 | 0.5 | 2.3 | 5.2 | 5.8 | 17.8 | 6.7 | 10.7 | 11.6 | 15.4 |
| 19 081 | ... | 7 | Hancock | 1 479 | 11 134 | 2 351 | 7.5 | 95.3 | 0.8 | 0.3 | 0.8 | 3.5 | 5.6 | 17.6 | 5.8 | 10.7 | 10.4 | 15.6 |
| 19 083 | ... | 6 | Hardin | 1 474 | 17 302 | 1 961 | 11.7 | 94.4 | 1.6 | 0.5 | 0.6 | 3.7 | 5.7 | 17.1 | 8.2 | 10.0 | 10.2 | 14.1 |
| 19 085 | 36540 | 2 | Harrison | 1 805 | 14 548 | 2 139 | 8.1 | 97.9 | 0.5 | 0.6 | 0.5 | 1.2 | 6.2 | 17.3 | 6.9 | 9.9 | 11.8 | 16.0 |
| 19 087 | ... | 7 | Henry | 1 125 | 20 236 | 1 829 | 18.0 | 90.8 | 2.9 | 0.6 | 3.0 | 4.1 | 5.7 | 16.9 | 9.3 | 12.0 | 12.2 | 14.6 |
| 19 089 | ... | 7 | Howard | 1 226 | 9 563 | 2 466 | 7.8 | 97.9 | 0.6 | 0.3 | 0.6 | 1.3 | 7.0 | 18.0 | 6.6 | 11.3 | 10.1 | 15.1 |
| 19 091 | ... | 7 | Humboldt | 1 125 | 9 729 | 2 456 | 8.6 | 95.3 | 0.8 | 0.4 | 0.6 | 3.7 | 6.1 | 16.6 | 7.0 | 11.0 | 9.8 | 15.4 |
| 19 093 | ... | 8 | Ida | 1 118 | 7 108 | 2 673 | 6.4 | 97.5 | 0.6 | 0.3 | 0.6 | 1.7 | 7.2 | 17.1 | 5.8 | 10.7 | 9.9 | 14.8 |
| 19 095 | ... | 8 | Iowa | 1 519 | 16 189 | 2 032 | 10.7 | 96.9 | 0.7 | 0.4 | 0.6 | 2.1 | 6.0 | 17.9 | 6.7 | 10.6 | 12.1 | 16.3 |
| 19 097 | ... | 6 | Jackson | 1 647 | 19 712 | 1 848 | 12.0 | 97.3 | 0.6 | 0.5 | 1.1 | 1.3 | 5.6 | 17.2 | 6.9 | 9.7 | 11.5 | 16.1 |
| 19 099 | 35500 | 2 | Jasper | 1 892 | 36 602 | 1 259 | 19.3 | 96.2 | 1.7 | 0.6 | 0.7 | 1.6 | 5.5 | 16.8 | 7.2 | 11.9 | 12.5 | 15.7 |
| 19 101 | ... | 7 | Jefferson | 1 128 | 16 867 | 1 990 | 15.0 | 87.1 | 1.7 | 0.6 | 9.1 | 2.8 | 4.4 | 13.5 | 11.2 | 12.5 | 9.8 | 13.0 |
| 19 103 | 26980 | 3 | Johnson | 1 590 | 136 317 | 456 | 85.7 | 84.6 | 5.7 | 0.6 | 6.2 | 4.9 | 6.0 | 13.4 | 22.6 | 16.7 | 11.2 | 11.1 |
| 19 105 | 16300 | 3 | Jones | 1 491 | 20 639 | 1 802 | 13.8 | 95.9 | 2.4 | 0.4 | 0.6 | 1.4 | 5.5 | 16.4 | 6.7 | 11.8 | 12.3 | 15.7 |
| 19 107 | ... | 6 | Keokuk | 1 500 | 10 374 | 2 406 | 6.9 | 98.1 | 0.7 | 0.4 | 0.4 | 1.0 | 5.7 | 17.1 | 7.1 | 10.5 | 10.5 | 15.6 |
| 19 109 | ... | 7 | Kossuth | 2 519 | 15 346 | 2 085 | 6.1 | 97.8 | 0.7 | 0.2 | 0.6 | 1.4 | 5.6 | 16.8 | 5.9 | 9.6 | 9.6 | 15.7 |
| 19 111 | 22800 | 5 | Lee | 1 340 | 35 617 | 1 284 | 26.6 | 92.9 | 4.1 | 0.6 | 0.9 | 3.1 | 5.9 | 15.9 | 8.0 | 11.6 | 11.3 | 15.3 |
| 19 113 | 16300 | 3 | Linn | 1 857 | 215 295 | 291 | 115.9 | 90.9 | 5.3 | 0.6 | 2.5 | 2.8 | 6.6 | 17.7 | 9.7 | 13.8 | 12.8 | 14.2 |
| 19 115 | 34700 | 8 | Louisa | 1 041 | 11 278 | 2 339 | 10.8 | 81.5 | 1.0 | 0.5 | 1.7 | 16.1 | 5.9 | 19.4 | 7.4 | 11.5 | 12.1 | 15.7 |
| 19 117 | ... | 6 | Lucas | 1 115 | 8 760 | 2 537 | 7.9 | 98.1 | 0.5 | 0.4 | 0.3 | 1.3 | 6.0 | 18.0 | 6.4 | 9.3 | 10.7 | 15.0 |
| 19 119 | ... | 8 | Lyon | 1 522 | 11 757 | 2 313 | 7.7 | 97.5 | 0.4 | 0.3 | 0.4 | 2.0 | 7.7 | 19.8 | 7.0 | 11.5 | 11.2 | 13.5 |
| 19 121 | 19780 | 2 | Madison | 1 453 | 15 654 | 2 068 | 10.8 | 97.6 | 0.7 | 0.6 | 0.6 | 1.4 | 6.9 | 20.0 | 5.9 | 10.7 | 13.4 | 15.1 |
| 19 123 | 36820 | 7 | Mahaska | 1 479 | 22 443 | 1 712 | 15.2 | 95.7 | 1.6 | 0.5 | 1.5 | 1.8 | 6.5 | 17.6 | 9.6 | 12.0 | 11.4 | 14.0 |
| 19 125 | 37800 | 6 | Marion | 1 436 | 33 419 | 1 342 | 23.3 | 96.2 | 1.1 | 0.5 | 1.5 | 1.7 | 6.5 | 18.1 | 10.5 | 11.0 | 11.4 | 14.3 |
| 19 127 | 32260 | 4 | Marshall | 1 483 | 40 857 | 1 158 | 27.6 | 78.3 | 2.3 | 0.6 | 2.0 | 18.0 | 7.1 | 18.2 | 8.4 | 11.7 | 11.0 | 13.8 |
| 19 129 | 36540 | 2 | Mills | 1 133 | 14 837 | 2 121 | 13.1 | 96.2 | 0.7 | 0.8 | 0.7 | 2.6 | 6.0 | 19.1 | 6.3 | 10.5 | 12.5 | 16.1 |
| 19 131 | ... | 7 | Mitchell | 1 215 | 10 725 | 2 380 | 8.8 | 98.2 | 0.4 | 0.3 | 0.5 | 1.1 | 5.9 | 18.2 | 7.2 | 9.2 | 10.3 | 14.7 |
| 19 133 | ... | 6 | Monona | 1 798 | 9 124 | 2 508 | 5.1 | 96.8 | 0.9 | 1.5 | 0.5 | 1.4 | 5.2 | 16.7 | 6.0 | 9.3 | 10.1 | 15.1 |
| 19 135 | ... | 7 | Monroe | 1 123 | 8 063 | 2 598 | 7.2 | 96.6 | 0.8 | 0.4 | 0.7 | 2.4 | 6.2 | 17.7 | 7.1 | 10.7 | 11.8 | 14.2 |
| 19 137 | ... | 6 | Montgomery | 1 098 | 10 566 | 2 392 | 9.6 | 95.9 | 0.6 | 0.7 | 0.5 | 3.1 | 5.6 | 17.6 | 6.5 | 9.5 | 11.4 | 15.1 |
| 19 139 | 34700 | 4 | Muscatine | 1 133 | 42 879 | 1 114 | 37.8 | 81.3 | 1.7 | 0.6 | 1.2 | 16.2 | 7.3 | 18.8 | 8.0 | 12.2 | 12.4 | 14.6 |
| 19 141 | ... | 7 | O'Brien | 1 484 | 14 172 | 2 164 | 9.5 | 94.5 | 0.7 | 0.4 | 0.8 | 4.2 | 6.1 | 17.2 | 6.8 | 11.1 | 10.3 | 14.5 |
| 19 143 | ... | 7 | Osceola | 1 033 | 6 193 | 2 745 | 6.0 | 92.6 | 0.5 | 0.6 | 0.5 | 6.5 | 5.6 | 16.7 | 7.0 | 10.4 | 11.2 | 15.6 |
| 19 145 | ... | 7 | Page | 1 385 | 15 713 | 2 063 | 11.3 | 93.5 | 2.8 | 1.0 | 1.2 | 2.9 | 5.7 | 16.3 | 6.9 | 11.1 | 11.4 | 14.2 |
| 19 147 | ... | 7 | Palo Alto | 1 460 | 9 275 | 2 496 | 6.4 | 96.8 | 0.8 | 0.5 | 0.7 | 2.0 | 6.2 | 15.7 | 9.0 | 10.6 | 9.4 | 14.1 |
| 19 149 | ... | 6 | Plymouth | 2 235 | 24 907 | 1 611 | 11.1 | 95.7 | 0.9 | 0.4 | 0.8 | 3.1 | 6.4 | 18.9 | 6.8 | 10.6 | 11.6 | 15.3 |
| 19 151 | ... | 9 | Pocahontas | 1 495 | 7 150 | 2 667 | 4.8 | 96.2 | 0.9 | 0.5 | 0.5 | 2.7 | 5.5 | 15.8 | 6.5 | 9.0 | 9.7 | 16.7 |
| 19 153 | 19780 | 2 | Polk | 1 486 | 443 710 | 151 | 298.6 | 82.2 | 7.0 | 0.7 | 4.2 | 7.8 | 7.5 | 17.9 | 9.0 | 15.8 | 13.6 | 13.8 |
| 19 155 | 36540 | 2 | Pottawattamie | 2 461 | 92 913 | 621 | 37.8 | 90.8 | 2.0 | 0.8 | 1.0 | 6.7 | 6.7 | 17.3 | 9.1 | 12.6 | 11.9 | 14.8 |
| 19 157 | ... | 7 | Poweshiek | 1 515 | 18 736 | 1 887 | 12.4 | 94.4 | 1.7 | 0.6 | 2.2 | 2.4 | 5.4 | 15.3 | 13.8 | 9.7 | 10.4 | 13.9 |
| 19 159 | ... | 9 | Ringgold | 1 387 | 5 096 | 2 833 | 3.7 | 97.3 | 0.6 | 0.5 | 0.5 | 1.7 | 6.2 | 17.8 | 6.4 | 9.1 | 9.6 | 13.8 |
| 19 161 | ... | 9 | Sac | 1 489 | 10 153 | 2 430 | 6.8 | 97.1 | 0.8 | 0.3 | 0.4 | 2.2 | 5.6 | 16.5 | 6.0 | 9.4 | 10.0 | 15.3 |
| 19 163 | 19340 | 2 | Scott | 1 186 | 168 799 | 367 | 142.3 | 85.0 | 8.3 | 0.8 | 2.6 | 5.7 | 6.7 | 17.6 | 8.8 | 13.6 | 12.6 | 14.5 |
| 19 165 | ... | 6 | Shelby | 1 530 | 12 069 | 2 296 | 7.9 | 97.2 | 0.6 | 0.4 | 0.6 | 1.9 | 5.4 | 17.5 | 6.1 | 8.7 | 11.1 | 15.8 |
| 19 167 | ... | 6 | Sioux | 1 990 | 34 268 | 1 320 | 17.2 | 89.4 | 0.7 | 0.3 | 1.0 | 9.2 | 7.8 | 19.2 | 13.4 | 12.3 | 10.1 | 12.5 |
| 19 169 | 11180 | 3 | Story | 1 484 | 91 140 | 632 | 61.4 | 87.9 | 3.2 | 0.5 | 6.9 | 3.1 | 5.2 | 12.2 | 30.2 | 13.6 | 9.1 | 10.0 |
| 19 171 | ... | 6 | Tama | 1 867 | 17 536 | 1 948 | 9.4 | 85.1 | 1.1 | 7.0 | 0.6 | 7.8 | 6.0 | 19.3 | 6.8 | 10.1 | 11.7 | 14.5 |
| 19 173 | ... | 9 | Taylor | 1 378 | 6 208 | 2 744 | 4.5 | 93.0 | 0.5 | 0.6 | 0.5 | 6.3 | 5.8 | 17.6 | 6.2 | 10.7 | 10.3 | 14.3 |
| 19 175 | ... | 6 | Union | 1 097 | 12 594 | 2 267 | 11.5 | 96.3 | 1.2 | 0.6 | 0.8 | 2.1 | 6.6 | 17.0 | 8.7 | 11.2 | 11.0 | 13.9 |
| 19 177 | ... | 9 | Van Buren | 1 256 | 7 449 | 2 646 | 5.9 | 97.8 | 0.4 | 0.4 | 0.8 | 1.2 | 6.6 | 17.1 | 6.6 | 10.4 | 10.9 | 14.3 |
| 19 179 | 36900 | 5 | Wapello | 1 118 | 35 366 | 1 293 | 31.6 | 88.2 | 1.9 | 0.7 | 1.3 | 9.2 | 6.5 | 16.3 | 9.4 | 12.1 | 11.8 | 14.1 |
| 19 181 | 19780 | 2 | Warren | 1 476 | 46 891 | 1 029 | 31.8 | 96.6 | 1.1 | 0.6 | 0.9 | 2.0 | 6.2 | 19.3 | 9.3 | 11.1 | 13.0 | 14.9 |
| 19 183 | 26980 | 3 | Washington | 1 473 | 21 914 | 1 736 | 14.9 | 93.4 | 1.2 | 0.5 | 0.7 | 5.1 | 6.3 | 18.5 | 6.7 | 10.9 | 11.6 | 14.9 |
| 19 185 | ... | 9 | Wayne | 1 361 | 6 344 | 2 736 | 4.7 | 98.0 | 0.6 | 0.5 | 0.5 | 1.2 | 6.5 | 16.8 | 7.1 | 9.8 | 9.3 | 15.3 |
| 19 187 | 22700 | 5 | Webster | 1 853 | 37 273 | 1 241 | 20.1 | 91.3 | 4.9 | 0.6 | 0.9 | 3.9 | 5.8 | 16.2 | 11.0 | 12.1 | 10.3 | 14.5 |
| 19 189 | ... | 7 | Winnebago | 1 037 | 10 600 | 2 390 | 10.2 | 94.7 | 1.0 | 0.4 | 1.1 | 3.5 | 5.4 | 15.9 | 9.6 | 9.9 | 10.7 | 14.4 |
| 19 191 | ... | 7 | Winneshiek | 1 787 | 21 061 | 1 778 | 11.8 | 96.1 | 0.6 | 0.2 | 1.4 | 2.1 | 4.9 | 15.0 | 16.7 | 9.3 | 9.7 | 14.5 |
| 19 193 | 43580 | 3 | Woodbury | 2 261 | 102 323 | 571 | 45.3 | 79.4 | 3.5 | 2.3 | 3.1 | 14.0 | 7.7 | 18.8 | 10.2 | 13.1 | 13.1 | 13.4 |
| 19 195 | 32380 | 9 | Worth | 1 036 | 7 519 | 2 641 | 7.3 | 96.9 | 0.7 | 0.6 | 0.6 | 2.0 | 5.4 | 17.4 | 6.5 | 10.6 | 11.6 | 15.6 |
| 19 197 | ... | 7 | Wright | 1 503 | 12 991 | 2 240 | 8.6 | 89.5 | 0.8 | 0.6 | 0.5 | 9.6 | 6.3 | 16.9 | 6.8 | 10.1 | 10.4 | 14.3 |

1. CBSA = Core Based Statistical Area. See Appendix A for explanation. See Appendix B for list of metropolitan areas with component counties. 2. County type code from the Economic Research Service of USDA Rural-Urban Continuum Codes. See Appendix A for definition. 3. Dry land or land partially or temporarily covered by water. 4. May be of any race.

# Table B. States and Counties — **Population and Households**

| | Population, 2011 (cont.) | | | | Population change and components of change, 2000–2012 | | | | | | | Households, 2010 | | | | |
| | Age (percent) (cont.) | | | | Total persons | | Percent change | | Components of change, 2010–2012 | | | | | | Percent | |
| STATE County | 55 to 64 years | 65 to 74 years | 75 years and over | Percent female | 2000 | 2010 | 2000–2010 | 2010–2012 | Births | Deaths | Net migration | Number | Percent change, 2000–2010 | Persons per household | Female family householder[1] | One person |
|---|---|---|---|---|---|---|---|---|---|---|---|---|---|---|---|---|
| | 16 | 17 | 18 | 19 | 20 | 21 | 22 | 23 | 24 | 25 | 26 | 27 | 28 | 29 | 30 | 31 |
| **IOWA—Cont'd** | | | | | | | | | | | | | | | | |
| Franklin | 14.3 | 9.0 | 10.0 | 49.7 | 10 704 | 10 680 | -0.2 | -1.2 | 287 | 274 | -135 | 4 332 | -0.6 | 2.42 | 6.6 | 27.1 |
| Fremont | 15.6 | 9.3 | 10.3 | 50.3 | 8 010 | 7 441 | -7.1 | -4.0 | 178 | 214 | -259 | 3 064 | -4.2 | 2.38 | 8.6 | 27.3 |
| Greene | 14.7 | 9.2 | 11.3 | 50.6 | 10 366 | 9 336 | -9.9 | -2.0 | 202 | 293 | -88 | 3 996 | -5.0 | 2.30 | 7.8 | 31.6 |
| Grundy | 13.8 | 9.1 | 9.6 | 50.7 | 12 369 | 12 453 | 0.7 | 0.0 | 323 | 304 | -26 | 5 131 | 2.9 | 2.40 | 6.3 | 25.8 |
| Guthrie | 14.7 | 10.0 | 10.0 | 50.3 | 11 353 | 10 954 | -3.5 | -1.6 | 236 | 296 | -114 | 4 544 | -2.1 | 2.37 | 6.7 | 27.6 |
| Hamilton | 13.5 | 8.1 | 10.4 | 50.3 | 16 438 | 15 673 | -4.7 | -2.1 | 374 | 390 | -321 | 6 540 | -2.3 | 2.37 | 8.4 | 29.2 |
| Hancock | 15.3 | 8.9 | 10.1 | 50.1 | 12 100 | 11 341 | -6.3 | -1.8 | 216 | 308 | -110 | 4 741 | -1.1 | 2.35 | 6.8 | 28.6 |
| Hardin | 13.5 | 9.5 | 11.6 | 50.5 | 18 812 | 17 534 | -6.8 | -1.3 | 400 | 537 | -82 | 7 296 | -4.4 | 2.28 | 7.5 | 31.2 |
| Harrison | 14.1 | 8.8 | 8.9 | 50.6 | 15 666 | 14 928 | -4.7 | -2.5 | 340 | 442 | -287 | 5 987 | -2.1 | 2.45 | 8.2 | 27.0 |
| Henry | 13.2 | 8.2 | 8.0 | 48.8 | 20 336 | 20 145 | -0.9 | 0.5 | 501 | 460 | 51 | 7 666 | 0.5 | 2.43 | 9.5 | 27.0 |
| Howard | 12.7 | 8.8 | 10.5 | 50.5 | 9 932 | 9 566 | -3.7 | 0.0 | 259 | 288 | 27 | 3 944 | -0.8 | 2.37 | 6.9 | 30.4 |
| Humboldt | 13.4 | 8.9 | 11.6 | 50.6 | 10 381 | 9 815 | -5.5 | -0.9 | 243 | 277 | -41 | 4 209 | -2.0 | 2.30 | 7.1 | 30.2 |
| Ida | 14.3 | 8.6 | 11.7 | 50.1 | 7 837 | 7 089 | -9.5 | 0.3 | 187 | 250 | 81 | 3 052 | -5.0 | 2.28 | 6.9 | 31.5 |
| Iowa | 13.3 | 7.8 | 9.4 | 50.6 | 15 671 | 16 355 | 4.4 | -1.0 | 406 | 416 | -166 | 6 677 | 8.3 | 2.41 | 6.8 | 27.8 |
| Jackson | 14.0 | 9.7 | 9.3 | 50.3 | 20 296 | 19 848 | -2.2 | -0.7 | 460 | 501 | -93 | 8 289 | 2.6 | 2.37 | 8.5 | 28.3 |
| Jasper | 13.5 | 8.5 | 8.3 | 49.1 | 37 213 | 36 842 | -1.0 | -0.7 | 878 | 811 | -303 | 14 806 | 0.8 | 2.38 | 8.9 | 27.7 |
| Jefferson | 20.2 | 8.2 | 7.2 | 46.6 | 16 181 | 16 843 | 4.1 | 0.1 | 315 | 371 | 75 | 6 846 | 3.0 | 2.21 | 8.2 | 33.9 |
| Johnson | 10.2 | 4.8 | 4.0 | 50.0 | 111 006 | 130 882 | 17.9 | 4.2 | 3 849 | 1 409 | 2 950 | 52 715 | 19.6 | 2.33 | 7.6 | 30.3 |
| Jones | 14.1 | 8.6 | 8.8 | 47.9 | 20 221 | 20 638 | 2.1 | 0.0 | 440 | 481 | 41 | 8 181 | 8.2 | 2.36 | 8.0 | 27.0 |
| Keokuk | 13.9 | 9.1 | 10.4 | 50.3 | 11 400 | 10 511 | -7.8 | -1.3 | 265 | 252 | -143 | 4 408 | -3.9 | 2.35 | 7.6 | 28.9 |
| Kossuth | 14.7 | 10.0 | 12.0 | 50.3 | 17 163 | 15 543 | -9.4 | -1.3 | 360 | 384 | -175 | 6 697 | -4.0 | 2.28 | 6.2 | 30.9 |
| Lee | 14.9 | 8.9 | 8.3 | 49.5 | 38 052 | 35 862 | -5.8 | -0.7 | 902 | 928 | -197 | 14 610 | -3.6 | 2.35 | 11.1 | 29.2 |
| Linn | 12.0 | 6.9 | 6.3 | 50.7 | 191 701 | 211 226 | 10.2 | 1.9 | 6 127 | 3 627 | 1 558 | 86 134 | 12.2 | 2.39 | 9.9 | 29.2 |
| Louisa | 12.9 | 8.1 | 7.0 | 49.1 | 12 183 | 11 387 | -6.5 | -1.0 | 269 | 250 | -120 | 4 346 | -3.8 | 2.59 | 9.4 | 24.6 |
| Lucas | 14.2 | 9.9 | 10.4 | 49.7 | 9 422 | 8 898 | -5.6 | -1.6 | 218 | 235 | -129 | 3 689 | -3.2 | 2.39 | 7.5 | 29.6 |
| Lyon | 12.7 | 7.2 | 9.3 | 50.2 | 11 763 | 11 581 | -1.5 | 1.5 | 370 | 277 | 87 | 4 442 | 0.3 | 2.57 | 5.3 | 24.6 |
| Madison | 13.2 | 7.8 | 7.0 | 50.3 | 14 019 | 15 679 | 11.8 | -0.2 | 394 | 370 | -53 | 6 025 | 13.1 | 2.57 | 7.3 | 23.0 |
| Mahaska | 12.8 | 7.7 | 8.4 | 49.6 | 22 335 | 22 381 | 0.2 | 0.3 | 640 | 510 | -70 | 8 975 | 1.1 | 2.42 | 9.0 | 27.4 |
| Marion | 12.4 | 7.9 | 7.9 | 50.5 | 32 052 | 33 309 | 3.9 | 0.3 | 832 | 749 | 19 | 12 723 | 5.9 | 2.48 | 7.7 | 26.4 |
| Marshall | 13.5 | 8.0 | 8.3 | 49.7 | 39 311 | 40 648 | 3.4 | 0.5 | 1 252 | 1 057 | 25 | 15 538 | 1.3 | 2.53 | 10.3 | 27.1 |
| Mills | 15.5 | 7.7 | 6.1 | 49.7 | 14 547 | 15 059 | 3.5 | -1.5 | 340 | 348 | -212 | 5 605 | 5.3 | 2.58 | 8.8 | 22.4 |
| Mitchell | 12.7 | 9.6 | 12.2 | 50.7 | 10 874 | 10 776 | -0.9 | -0.5 | 274 | 300 | -15 | 4 395 | 2.4 | 2.40 | 6.3 | 29.1 |
| Monona | 14.0 | 10.8 | 12.8 | 50.0 | 10 020 | 9 243 | -7.8 | -1.3 | 183 | 366 | 53 | 4 050 | -3.8 | 2.23 | 8.3 | 33.7 |
| Monroe | 13.8 | 9.4 | 9.1 | 50.2 | 8 016 | 7 970 | -0.6 | 1.2 | 189 | 224 | 128 | 3 213 | -0.5 | 2.44 | 8.6 | 26.9 |
| Montgomery | 14.6 | 9.0 | 10.9 | 51.3 | 11 771 | 10 740 | -8.8 | -1.6 | 244 | 344 | -81 | 4 558 | -6.7 | 2.31 | 9.5 | 30.7 |
| Muscatine | 12.9 | 7.4 | 6.5 | 50.4 | 41 722 | 42 745 | 2.5 | 0.3 | 1 249 | 779 | -317 | 16 412 | 3.6 | 2.57 | 10.8 | 24.5 |
| O'Brien | 13.8 | 8.2 | 12.0 | 50.2 | 15 102 | 14 398 | -4.7 | -1.6 | 352 | 432 | -146 | 6 069 | 1.1 | 2.31 | 6.1 | 31.5 |
| Osceola | 13.4 | 9.2 | 11.0 | 49.6 | 7 003 | 6 462 | -7.7 | -4.2 | 132 | 186 | -220 | 2 682 | -3.5 | 2.37 | 5.9 | 29.2 |
| Page | 14.2 | 9.5 | 10.6 | 48.2 | 16 976 | 15 932 | -6.1 | -1.4 | 396 | 490 | -120 | 6 393 | -4.7 | 2.26 | 9.0 | 31.8 |
| Palo Alto | 13.4 | 8.8 | 12.6 | 50.3 | 10 147 | 9 421 | -7.2 | -1.5 | 214 | 272 | -83 | 3 994 | -3.0 | 2.27 | 7.1 | 31.9 |
| Plymouth | 13.6 | 8.0 | 8.8 | 50.5 | 24 849 | 24 986 | 0.6 | -0.3 | 635 | 531 | -176 | 9 875 | 5.4 | 2.49 | 6.6 | 25.8 |
| Pocahontas | 14.8 | 10.6 | 11.5 | 50.2 | 8 662 | 7 310 | -15.6 | -2.2 | 160 | 213 | -105 | 3 233 | -10.6 | 2.22 | 6.2 | 32.4 |
| Polk | 11.3 | 5.9 | 5.1 | 50.9 | 374 601 | 430 640 | 15.0 | 3.0 | 14 484 | 6 898 | 5 517 | 170 197 | 14.1 | 2.48 | 11.0 | 28.3 |
| Pottawattamie | 13.1 | 7.5 | 7.0 | 50.9 | 87 704 | 93 158 | 6.2 | -0.3 | 2 775 | 2 036 | -949 | 36 775 | 8.7 | 2.48 | 12.6 | 27.1 |
| Poweshiek | 13.1 | 9.0 | 9.5 | 50.9 | 18 815 | 18 914 | 0.5 | -0.9 | 423 | 494 | -103 | 7 555 | 2.1 | 2.29 | 8.5 | 30.4 |
| Ringgold | 13.6 | 10.2 | 13.4 | 50.9 | 5 469 | 5 131 | -6.2 | -0.7 | 118 | 147 | -3 | 2 047 | -8.8 | 2.42 | 6.0 | 28.9 |
| Sac | 14.8 | 9.3 | 13.0 | 51.0 | 11 529 | 10 350 | -10.2 | -1.9 | 228 | 295 | -131 | 4 482 | -5.6 | 2.26 | 6.5 | 31.6 |
| Scott | 13.1 | 7.0 | 6.2 | 51.0 | 158 668 | 165 224 | 4.1 | 2.2 | 5 062 | 3 039 | 1 600 | 66 765 | 7.1 | 2.42 | 11.9 | 29.1 |
| Shelby | 14.0 | 9.3 | 11.9 | 51.0 | 13 173 | 12 167 | -7.6 | -0.8 | 257 | 303 | -58 | 5 085 | -1.7 | 2.35 | 7.4 | 29.1 |
| Sioux | 10.7 | 6.3 | 7.7 | 50.1 | 31 589 | 33 704 | 6.7 | 1.7 | 1 144 | 582 | 1 | 11 584 | 8.3 | 2.70 | 4.5 | 22.5 |
| Story | 9.5 | 5.1 | 5.0 | 48.2 | 79 981 | 89 542 | 12.0 | 1.8 | 2 113 | 1 095 | 597 | 34 736 | 18.2 | 2.34 | 6.2 | 28.3 |
| Tama | 13.2 | 8.9 | 9.6 | 50.9 | 18 103 | 17 767 | -1.9 | -1.3 | 463 | 464 | -226 | 6 947 | -1.0 | 2.50 | 8.6 | 26.0 |
| Taylor | 13.9 | 9.9 | 11.3 | 50.2 | 6 958 | 6 317 | -9.2 | -1.7 | 134 | 191 | -65 | 2 679 | -5.1 | 2.32 | 6.7 | 29.7 |
| Union | 13.5 | 8.8 | 9.2 | 51.5 | 12 309 | 12 534 | 1.8 | 0.5 | 313 | 323 | 73 | 5 271 | 0.6 | 2.31 | 9.7 | 31.6 |
| Van Buren | 14.6 | 10.3 | 9.3 | 49.5 | 7 809 | 7 570 | -3.1 | -1.6 | 199 | 238 | -76 | 3 108 | -2.3 | 2.40 | 7.0 | 29.2 |
| Wapello | 13.5 | 8.0 | 8.3 | 51.0 | 36 051 | 35 625 | -1.2 | -0.7 | 1 005 | 903 | -345 | 14 552 | -1.6 | 2.39 | 11.2 | 29.9 |
| Warren | 12.5 | 7.3 | 6.3 | 51.4 | 40 671 | 46 225 | 13.7 | 1.4 | 1 149 | 890 | 404 | 17 262 | 17.4 | 2.58 | 8.9 | 22.1 |
| Washington | 13.5 | 8.3 | 9.2 | 51.0 | 20 670 | 21 704 | 5.0 | 1.0 | 578 | 521 | 164 | 8 741 | 8.5 | 2.45 | 8.1 | 28.0 |
| Wayne | 13.0 | 10.4 | 11.8 | 51.4 | 6 730 | 6 403 | -4.9 | -0.9 | 185 | 227 | -33 | 2 652 | -6.0 | 2.38 | 7.9 | 30.0 |
| Webster | 13.5 | 7.9 | 8.7 | 48.6 | 40 235 | 38 013 | -5.5 | -1.9 | 955 | 999 | -677 | 15 580 | -1.9 | 2.27 | 10.8 | 32.9 |
| Winnebago | 14.7 | 8.6 | 10.8 | 50.6 | 11 723 | 10 866 | -7.3 | -2.4 | 231 | 292 | -215 | 4 597 | -3.2 | 2.26 | 7.4 | 31.7 |
| Winneshiek | 13.0 | 8.1 | 8.9 | 50.5 | 21 310 | 21 056 | -1.2 | 0.0 | 407 | 416 | 24 | 7 997 | 3.4 | 2.35 | 5.6 | 28.8 |
| Woodbury | 12.0 | 6.6 | 6.3 | 50.6 | 103 877 | 102 172 | -1.6 | 0.1 | 3 453 | 2 019 | -1 254 | 39 052 | -0.3 | 2.55 | 12.6 | 28.1 |
| Worth | 14.9 | 8.7 | 9.3 | 50.1 | 7 909 | 7 598 | -3.9 | -1.0 | 157 | 177 | -57 | 3 172 | -3.2 | 2.37 | 7.4 | 27.5 |
| Wright | 14.2 | 9.0 | 12.1 | 50.2 | 14 334 | 13 229 | -7.7 | -1.8 | 329 | 403 | -154 | 5 625 | -5.3 | 2.32 | 8.2 | 30.6 |

1. No spouse present.

# Table B. States and Counties — Population, Vital Statistics, Medicare, and Crime

| STATE County | Persons in group quarters, 2010 | Daytime population, 2007–2011 Number | Daytime population, 2007–2011 Employment/residence ratio | Births, 2011 Total | Births, 2011 Rate[1] | Deaths, 2011 Number | Deaths, 2011 Rate[1] | Persons under 65 with no health insurance, 2010 Number | Persons under 65 with no health insurance, 2010 Percent | Medicare, 2012 Eligible for Medicare | Medicare, 2012 Enrolled in Medicare Advantage | Medicare, 2012 Enrolled in a Medicare prescription drug plan | Serious crimes known to police,[2] 2011 Total Number | Serious crimes known to police,[2] 2011 Total Rate[3] |
|---|---|---|---|---|---|---|---|---|---|---|---|---|---|---|
| | 32 | 33 | 34 | 35 | 36 | 37 | 38 | 39 | 40 | 41 | 42 | 43 | 44 | 45 |
| **IOWA—Cont'd** | | | | | | | | | | | | | | |
| Franklin | 198 | 10 037 | 0.87 | 134 | 12.5 | 112 | 10.4 | 1 313 | 15.4 | 2 232 | 48 | 1 642 | NA | NA |
| Fremont | 135 | 6 833 | 0.82 | 87 | 11.8 | 89 | 12.1 | 632 | 10.7 | 1 676 | 141 | 1 111 | NA | NA |
| Greene | 142 | 8 798 | 0.87 | 98 | 10.6 | 131 | 14.1 | 822 | 11.2 | 2 186 | 243 | 1 430 | 37 | 394 |
| Grundy | 154 | 10 567 | 0.70 | 148 | 11.9 | 132 | 10.6 | 872 | 8.7 | 2 635 | 300 | 1 579 | 109 | 871 |
| Guthrie | 170 | 9 163 | 0.65 | 100 | 9.2 | 128 | 11.7 | 948 | 10.9 | 2 622 | 332 | 1 602 | 50 | 454 |
| Hamilton | 198 | 15 517 | 0.97 | 169 | 10.9 | 172 | 11.1 | 1 287 | 10.1 | 3 255 | 271 | 2 097 | 250 | 1 587 |
| Hancock | 185 | 10 762 | 0.88 | 102 | 9.0 | 139 | 12.3 | 1 024 | 11.3 | 2 309 | 43 | 1 643 | NA | NA |
| Hardin | 870 | 17 515 | 0.99 | 181 | 10.4 | 234 | 13.4 | 1 440 | 10.9 | 3 935 | 213 | 2 729 | 303 | 1 719 |
| Harrison | 283 | 12 037 | 0.61 | 160 | 10.8 | 190 | 12.8 | 1 308 | 10.8 | 3 045 | 180 | 2 017 | 176 | 1 173 |
| Henry | 1 554 | 21 156 | 1.10 | 222 | 10.9 | 192 | 9.5 | 1 641 | 10.6 | 3 884 | 353 | 2 472 | 383 | 2 088 |
| Howard | 213 | 9 247 | 0.93 | 117 | 12.2 | 132 | 13.8 | 983 | 12.9 | 2 046 | 171 | 1 368 | 145 | 1 508 |
| Humboldt | 133 | 9 224 | 0.87 | 106 | 10.8 | 127 | 13.0 | 889 | 11.5 | 2 142 | 98 | 1 442 | 76 | 770 |
| Ida | 122 | 7 585 | 1.13 | 92 | 13.0 | 117 | 16.5 | 574 | 10.3 | 1 608 | 161 | 1 082 | 46 | 646 |
| Iowa | 290 | 16 008 | 0.96 | 186 | 11.4 | 205 | 12.6 | 1 112 | 8.3 | 3 177 | 461 | 1 931 | 135 | 821 |
| Jackson | 201 | 16 786 | 0.69 | 196 | 9.9 | 227 | 11.5 | 1 863 | 11.6 | 4 263 | 894 | 2 720 | NA | NA |
| Jasper | 1 648 | 31 617 | 0.69 | 390 | 10.7 | 362 | 9.9 | 3 039 | 10.4 | 7 297 | 808 | 4 867 | 819 | 2 211 |
| Jefferson | 1 731 | 17 430 | 1.09 | 136 | 8.1 | 164 | 9.8 | 1 856 | 14.4 | 3 181 | 353 | 1 899 | 301 | 1 778 |
| Johnson | 7 857 | 138 861 | 1.13 | 1 723 | 13.0 | 622 | 4.7 | 10 871 | 9.6 | 14 633 | 1 889 | 6 741 | 2 913 | 2 214 |
| Jones | 1 304 | 17 930 | 0.72 | 211 | 10.2 | 217 | 10.5 | 1 694 | 10.6 | 3 992 | 722 | 2 367 | 215 | 1 036 |
| Keokuk | 140 | 8 653 | 0.63 | 110 | 10.6 | 103 | 9.9 | 1 027 | 12.2 | 2 302 | 327 | 1 354 | 21 | 199 |
| Kossuth | 257 | 15 124 | 0.94 | 165 | 10.7 | 156 | 10.1 | 1 292 | 10.8 | 3 839 | 116 | 2 560 | 143 | 915 |
| Lee | 1 594 | 37 909 | 1.13 | 405 | 11.4 | 409 | 11.5 | 3 176 | 11.2 | 7 637 | 697 | 4 961 | 1 329 | 3 687 |
| Linn | 5 166 | 223 227 | 1.12 | 2 766 | 12.9 | 1 568 | 7.3 | 15 857 | 8.8 | 33 895 | 8 736 | 16 543 | 6 308 | 2 971 |
| Louisa | 116 | 10 142 | 0.74 | 119 | 10.5 | 112 | 9.9 | 1 418 | 14.8 | 1 996 | 213 | 1 125 | 80 | 699 |
| Lucas | 78 | 8 832 | 0.95 | 102 | 11.5 | 97 | 11.0 | 828 | 11.8 | 1 922 | 188 | 1 152 | 206 | 2 303 |
| Lyon | 161 | 10 256 | 0.77 | 162 | 13.9 | 129 | 11.1 | 1 124 | 11.8 | 2 055 | 151 | 1 446 | 87 | 958 |
| Madison | 192 | 11 962 | 0.53 | 197 | 12.5 | 163 | 10.3 | 1 263 | 9.5 | 2 696 | 377 | 1 523 | 232 | 1 472 |
| Mahaska | 659 | 20 342 | 0.80 | 288 | 12.8 | 230 | 10.2 | 1 932 | 10.6 | 4 176 | 445 | 2 720 | 416 | 1 849 |
| Marion | 1 693 | 34 549 | 1.07 | 385 | 11.5 | 329 | 9.9 | 2 265 | 8.5 | 6 252 | 490 | 3 763 | NA | NA |
| Marshall | 1 375 | 40 830 | 1.02 | 566 | 13.8 | 478 | 11.7 | 4 388 | 13.2 | 7 919 | 865 | 5 346 | 1 238 | 3 030 |
| Mills | 608 | 12 199 | 0.60 | 157 | 10.5 | 138 | 9.2 | 1 192 | 9.5 | 2 822 | 285 | 1 801 | 438 | 2 893 |
| Mitchell | 247 | 10 559 | 0.95 | 127 | 11.8 | 128 | 11.9 | 978 | 11.7 | 2 361 | 99 | 1 593 | 60 | 617 |
| Monona | 200 | 8 559 | 0.82 | 86 | 9.3 | 168 | 18.2 | 895 | 12.8 | 2 284 | 291 | 1 498 | NA | NA |
| Monroe | 122 | 7 459 | 0.86 | 84 | 10.4 | 94 | 11.7 | 827 | 12.9 | 1 674 | 141 | 1 018 | 104 | 1 298 |
| Montgomery | 213 | 10 704 | 0.98 | 109 | 10.2 | 148 | 13.9 | 942 | 11.1 | 2 459 | 145 | 1 640 | NA | NA |
| Muscatine | 553 | 43 881 | 1.06 | 572 | 13.4 | 329 | 7.7 | 4 311 | 11.8 | 7 301 | 1 077 | 3 813 | 1 190 | 2 769 |
| O'Brien | 366 | 13 812 | 0.93 | 172 | 12.1 | 195 | 13.7 | 1 354 | 12.0 | 3 175 | 186 | 2 251 | 138 | 953 |
| Osceola | 112 | 5 690 | 0.75 | 61 | 9.6 | 82 | 12.9 | 690 | 13.5 | 1 350 | 66 | 911 | 9 | 139 |
| Page | 1 468 | 16 133 | 1.02 | 177 | 11.1 | 217 | 13.6 | 1 269 | 11.1 | 3 618 | 255 | 2 433 | 281 | 1 755 |
| Palo Alto | 344 | 9 198 | 0.94 | 94 | 10.0 | 116 | 12.3 | 853 | 11.9 | 2 043 | 38 | 1 459 | 112 | 1 183 |
| Plymouth | 349 | 23 192 | 0.87 | 281 | 11.3 | 226 | 9.1 | 1 799 | 8.7 | 4 619 | 722 | 2 719 | 337 | 1 342 |
| Pocahontas | 141 | 6 811 | 0.83 | 65 | 9.1 | 90 | 12.5 | 629 | 11.3 | 1 753 | 87 | 1 184 | 85 | 1 157 |
| Polk | 9 356 | 468 423 | 1.19 | 6 482 | 14.8 | 2 998 | 6.9 | 38 572 | 10.2 | 60 246 | 10 562 | 29 714 | 17 159 | 3 964 |
| Pottawattamie | 2 076 | 84 954 | 0.84 | 1 299 | 13.9 | 919 | 9.8 | 8 928 | 11.4 | 16 890 | 3 648 | 8 613 | 5 708 | 6 095 |
| Poweshiek | 1 627 | 20 048 | 1.11 | 190 | 10.1 | 224 | 11.9 | 1 405 | 10.1 | 3 750 | 324 | 2 272 | 249 | 1 310 |
| Ringgold | 179 | 4 868 | 0.88 | 57 | 11.1 | 60 | 11.7 | 598 | 15.5 | 1 277 | 102 | 883 | NA | NA |
| Sac | 223 | 9 046 | 0.74 | 101 | 9.9 | 139 | 13.6 | 1 002 | 12.6 | 2 437 | 84 | 1 720 | 46 | 563 |
| Scott | 3 334 | 167 474 | 1.05 | 2 190 | 13.1 | 1 313 | 7.9 | 14 618 | 10.3 | 27 425 | 5 229 | 11 406 | 6 439 | 3 877 |
| Shelby | 220 | 12 226 | 1.00 | 115 | 9.6 | 129 | 10.7 | 949 | 10.0 | 2 977 | 209 | 1 982 | NA | NA |
| Sioux | 2 410 | 35 572 | 1.11 | 517 | 15.3 | 253 | 7.5 | 3 224 | 12.1 | 5 256 | 499 | 3 575 | NA | NA |
| Story | 8 174 | 89 815 | 1.03 | 948 | 10.6 | 466 | 5.2 | 7 602 | 10.4 | 10 790 | 1 117 | 6 534 | 2 609 | 2 899 |
| Tama | 399 | 15 428 | 0.71 | 205 | 11.6 | 202 | 11.4 | 1 991 | 13.9 | 3 649 | 421 | 2 239 | 110 | 735 |
| Taylor | 96 | 5 695 | 0.77 | 61 | 9.7 | 80 | 12.7 | 641 | 13.0 | 1 515 | 72 | 1 021 | 13 | 205 |
| Union | 352 | 13 389 | 1.14 | 139 | 11.1 | 138 | 11.0 | 1 134 | 11.3 | 2 706 | 237 | 1 796 | 248 | 1 968 |
| Van Buren | 97 | 6 899 | 0.80 | 102 | 13.6 | 110 | 14.6 | 899 | 15.0 | 1 700 | 190 | 1 048 | 73 | 959 |
| Wapello | 867 | 36 534 | 1.07 | 476 | 13.4 | 391 | 11.0 | 3 532 | 12.2 | 7 431 | 719 | 3 973 | 1 075 | 3 002 |
| Warren | 1 742 | 33 108 | 0.48 | 519 | 11.1 | 390 | 8.3 | 3 026 | 7.8 | 7 402 | 1 205 | 3 611 | 775 | 1 668 |
| Washington | 310 | 19 591 | 0.81 | 252 | 11.5 | 229 | 10.5 | 2 253 | 12.7 | 4 397 | 438 | 2 748 | 306 | 1 403 |
| Wayne | 91 | 5 799 | 0.79 | 80 | 12.7 | 100 | 15.9 | 780 | 15.9 | 1 584 | 174 | 967 | 30 | 466 |
| Webster | 2 627 | 39 641 | 1.08 | 435 | 11.6 | 451 | 12.0 | 3 350 | 11.5 | 7 593 | 480 | 4 774 | 1 543 | 4 038 |
| Winnebago | 488 | 12 167 | 1.23 | 111 | 10.3 | 129 | 12.0 | 843 | 10.1 | 2 349 | 101 | 1 605 | 49 | 449 |
| Winneshiek | 2 288 | 21 645 | 1.05 | 178 | 8.5 | 186 | 8.8 | 1 542 | 10.0 | 4 006 | 595 | 2 468 | 137 | 647 |
| Woodbury | 2 636 | 102 249 | 1.01 | 1 543 | 15.1 | 889 | 8.7 | 12 844 | 14.8 | 16 534 | 3 393 | 8 688 | 4 125 | 4 016 |
| Worth | 90 | 6 452 | 0.71 | 71 | 9.4 | 69 | 9.1 | 681 | 11.1 | 1 534 | 102 | 998 | 104 | 1 362 |
| Wright | 198 | 13 165 | 0.98 | 150 | 11.5 | 164 | 12.5 | 1 222 | 11.8 | 2 990 | 97 | 2 114 | NA | NA |

1. Per 1,000 estimated resident population.  2. Data for serious crimes have not been adjusted for underreporting; this may affect comparability between geographic areas and over time.  3. Per 100,000 population estimated by the FBI.

# Table B. States and Counties — Crime, Education, Money Income, and Poverty

| STATE County | Serious crimes known to police, 2011 (cont.)[1] Rate[2] Violent | Property | Education — School enrollment and attainment, 2007–2011 Enrollment[3] Total | Percent private | Attainment[4] (percent) High school graduate or less | Bachelor's degree or more | Local government expenditures,[5] 2009–2010 Total current expenditures (mil dol) | Current expenditures per student (dollars) | Money income, 2007–2011 Per capita income[6] (dollars) | Households Median income Dollars | Percent change, 2000 to 2007–2011 (constant 2011 dollars) | Percent with income of $200,000 or more | Income and poverty, 2011 Households Median household income (dollars) | Percent below poverty level All persons | Children under 18 years | Children 5 to 17 years in families |
|---|---|---|---|---|---|---|---|---|---|---|---|---|---|---|---|---|
| | 46 | 47 | 48 | 49 | 50 | 51 | 52 | 53 | 54 | 55 | 56 | 57 | 58 | 59 | 60 | 61 |
| **IOWA—Cont'd** | | | | | | | | | | | | | | | | |
| Franklin | NA | NA | 2 263 | 4.2 | 51.6 | 15.1 | 17.6 | 8 691 | 23 759 | 46 461 | -4.5 | 2.5 | 47 396 | 12.2 | 19.2 | 18.5 |
| Fremont | NA | NA | 1 690 | 4.0 | 52.7 | 18.0 | 9.5 | 10 015 | 24 180 | 49 934 | -3.6 | 1.5 | 51 410 | 11.8 | 17.6 | 16.5 |
| Greene | 64 | 330 | 2 110 | 4.3 | 48.4 | 18.2 | 15.6 | 9 389 | 26 072 | 44 981 | -1.7 | 2.1 | 44 271 | 14.4 | 21.5 | 19.0 |
| Grundy | 80 | 791 | 3 020 | 8.3 | 43.6 | 20.7 | 22.9 | 8 578 | 28 450 | 55 848 | 5.0 | 3.3 | 54 645 | 6.4 | 8.4 | 7.5 |
| Guthrie | 27 | 427 | 2 558 | 9.7 | 47.6 | 19.3 | 22.7 | 8 333 | 26 981 | 50 000 | 1.5 | 1.5 | 47 762 | 10.4 | 14.4 | 12.7 |
| Hamilton | 216 | 1 371 | 3 630 | 7.2 | 48.1 | 16.6 | 26.0 | 9 413 | 24 530 | 46 603 | -10.7 | 1.7 | 45 331 | 10.4 | 15.8 | 14.3 |
| Hancock | NA | NA | 2 467 | 10.5 | 48.7 | 15.5 | 15.7 | 8 985 | 24 134 | 48 996 | -3.8 | 1.5 | 50 935 | 8.4 | 13.7 | 12.1 |
| Hardin | 91 | 1 628 | 4 352 | 9.9 | 43.2 | 19.8 | 30.4 | 9 831 | 24 482 | 46 930 | -1.9 | 2.3 | 46 708 | 12.0 | 18.0 | 16.4 |
| Harrison | 73 | 1 100 | 3 648 | 7.7 | 49.1 | 15.9 | 27.8 | 9 238 | 25 506 | 53 750 | 4.4 | 1.6 | 49 921 | 10.2 | 14.2 | 12.6 |
| Henry | 174 | 1 913 | 5 060 | 15.8 | 47.1 | 19.7 | 40.7 | 9 193 | 23 767 | 43 510 | -17.6 | 2.8 | 45 330 | 13.8 | 19.5 | 17.4 |
| Howard | 94 | 1 414 | 2 203 | 13.8 | 56.2 | 12.8 | 16.5 | 9 421 | 23 748 | 45 682 | -2.3 | 2.2 | 45 450 | 12.3 | 19.9 | 19.0 |
| Humboldt | 20 | 750 | 2 287 | 13.8 | 50.2 | 16.4 | 15.5 | 9 787 | 25 372 | 48 075 | -6.8 | 1.7 | 48 954 | 9.7 | 15.6 | 14.3 |
| Ida | 28 | 617 | 1 580 | 5.1 | 50.2 | 18.6 | 10.6 | 9 311 | 25 333 | 43 918 | -6.5 | 1.9 | 48 480 | 12.0 | 17.4 | 16.8 |
| Iowa | 128 | 693 | 3 977 | 13.5 | 44.6 | 21.0 | 23.9 | 8 771 | 28 632 | 57 476 | 3.3 | 1.9 | 53 984 | 7.3 | 9.4 | 8.2 |
| Jackson | NA | NA | 4 595 | 14.1 | 59.2 | 14.6 | 30.9 | 9 564 | 23 752 | 45 042 | -3.4 | 1.8 | 44 840 | 11.2 | 16.3 | 15.2 |
| Jasper | 111 | 2 101 | 8 641 | 10.7 | 51.2 | 17.4 | 51.9 | 8 731 | 24 025 | 48 881 | -13.1 | 1.3 | 50 469 | 10.8 | 14.4 | 12.8 |
| Jefferson | 130 | 1 648 | 4 341 | 36.6 | 40.9 | 30.3 | 24.6 | 10 070 | 25 224 | 47 784 | 4.5 | 2.6 | 39 743 | 17.4 | 23.1 | 20.5 |
| Johnson | 229 | 1 985 | 49 313 | 7.9 | 22.6 | 50.6 | 140.4 | 9 212 | 28 746 | 53 703 | -0.7 | 4.0 | 53 570 | 17.5 | 15.9 | 15.5 |
| Jones | 24 | 1 012 | 4 525 | 17.0 | 52.6 | 16.6 | 28.2 | 8 706 | 23 822 | 50 745 | 0.4 | 0.8 | 50 929 | 10.4 | 14.2 | 12.6 |
| Keokuk | 95 | 104 | 2 467 | 3.7 | 55.3 | 13.6 | 12.1 | 9 251 | 22 159 | 42 030 | -8.5 | 0.8 | 42 766 | 12.1 | 17.9 | 15.9 |
| Kossuth | 134 | 781 | 3 366 | 21.2 | 49.3 | 16.6 | 20.4 | 9 631 | 29 231 | 49 548 | 6.2 | 4.1 | 46 294 | 10.7 | 15.0 | 12.9 |
| Lee | 488 | 3 198 | 8 362 | 13.4 | 53.2 | 14.8 | 41.1 | 9 266 | 21 292 | 42 437 | -13.2 | 0.8 | 43 110 | 15.5 | 24.1 | 22.5 |
| Linn | 211 | 2 759 | 57 547 | 19.7 | 34.6 | 30.0 | 383.9 | 10 750 | 29 209 | 55 666 | -10.8 | 3.1 | 55 772 | 10.6 | 13.8 | 12.2 |
| Louisa | 87 | 612 | 2 979 | 4.7 | 60.4 | 12.5 | 27.0 | 9 523 | 22 642 | 50 982 | -3.4 | 0.9 | 48 372 | 12.3 | 17.9 | 16.0 |
| Lucas | 212 | 2 091 | 1 922 | 9.1 | 55.8 | 12.3 | 13.1 | 8 581 | 20 328 | 43 184 | 3.6 | 0.1 | 38 422 | 17.5 | 25.7 | 22.8 |
| Lyon | 187 | 771 | 2 665 | 19.5 | 52.5 | 16.1 | 16.2 | 8 170 | 22 048 | 49 938 | 0.3 | 1.2 | 53 398 | 9.0 | 12.6 | 12.2 |
| Madison | 57 | 1 415 | 4 128 | 11.1 | 49.4 | 20.2 | 28.2 | 8 506 | 26 763 | 56 333 | -0.3 | 3.1 | 56 258 | 8.7 | 11.3 | 10.1 |
| Mahaska | 218 | 1 631 | 6 373 | 28.7 | 53.0 | 18.9 | 36.4 | 9 054 | 22 252 | 46 477 | -7.7 | 1.3 | 47 598 | 13.6 | 17.9 | 16.3 |
| Marion | NA | NA | 9 440 | 34.2 | 45.1 | 23.5 | 47.7 | 8 443 | 25 062 | 53 730 | -6.1 | 2.4 | 51 996 | 10.0 | 12.3 | 11.2 |
| Marshall | 392 | 2 638 | 9 857 | 10.0 | 50.7 | 18.7 | 61.2 | 8 782 | 23 085 | 47 691 | -7.7 | 1.7 | 47 535 | 13.4 | 20.4 | 18.9 |
| Mills | 271 | 2 623 | 3 741 | 11.0 | 42.8 | 24.1 | 27.5 | 8 495 | 27 099 | 61 796 | 7.9 | 2.6 | 57 331 | 9.8 | 13.9 | 11.9 |
| Mitchell | 103 | 514 | 2 596 | 13.5 | 50.2 | 16.5 | 14.0 | 8 742 | 23 561 | 49 389 | 5.0 | 0.5 | 45 430 | 10.3 | 15.7 | 13.7 |
| Monona | NA | NA | 2 009 | 7.0 | 55.9 | 13.9 | 13.3 | 9 589 | 23 126 | 42 283 | -5.8 | 1.5 | 41 458 | 11.8 | 20.3 | 18.5 |
| Monroe | 137 | 1 161 | 1 739 | 7.2 | 54.3 | 16.7 | 10.5 | 8 476 | 22 504 | 43 913 | -6.7 | 0.6 | 42 961 | 11.8 | 18.3 | 17.2 |
| Montgomery | NA | NA | 2 495 | 8.3 | 48.6 | 15.5 | 17.9 | 9 217 | 22 039 | 38 072 | -15.1 | 1.4 | 41 437 | 14.4 | 21.4 | 19.4 |
| Muscatine | 461 | 2 309 | 10 734 | 4.2 | 49.6 | 18.0 | 67.5 | 8 721 | 24 345 | 51 134 | -9.4 | 1.9 | 47 966 | 13.4 | 20.6 | 18.3 |
| O'Brien | 104 | 850 | 3 456 | 17.4 | 48.2 | 18.6 | 20.7 | 8 500 | 26 821 | 45 995 | -4.7 | 2.9 | 46 233 | 8.8 | 12.7 | 11.3 |
| Osceola | 15 | 123 | 1 509 | 8.5 | 56.6 | 13.3 | 7.4 | 9 516 | 23 278 | 45 696 | -1.3 | 1.3 | 47 890 | 9.7 | 14.8 | 13.6 |
| Page | 94 | 1 661 | 3 582 | 8.5 | 51.8 | 15.9 | 23.8 | 9 773 | 22 114 | 41 503 | -13.3 | 2.1 | 42 449 | 15.9 | 24.8 | 22.3 |
| Palo Alto | 190 | 993 | 2 187 | 12.0 | 49.4 | 15.2 | 15.1 | 10 029 | 24 027 | 44 063 | 0.7 | 1.7 | 43 557 | 11.4 | 14.6 | 13.0 |
| Plymouth | 84 | 1 258 | 6 333 | 18.6 | 47.1 | 20.1 | 36.2 | 8 852 | 28 660 | 56 387 | 0.3 | 3.5 | 55 047 | 7.4 | 10.2 | 9.2 |
| Pocahontas | 109 | 1 048 | 1 636 | 10.0 | 48.9 | 17.3 | 31.6 | 34 812 | 23 556 | 42 545 | -5.5 | 0.8 | 43 766 | 12.5 | 18.8 | 16.9 |
| Polk | 328 | 3 636 | 111 088 | 21.4 | 35.8 | 33.8 | 724.6 | 10 449 | 29 673 | 57 473 | -7.7 | 3.5 | 56 091 | 12.5 | 17.5 | 16.4 |
| Pottawattamie | 781 | 5 315 | 22 094 | 12.4 | 48.9 | 17.7 | 172.7 | 10 642 | 24 644 | 49 924 | -7.8 | 1.8 | 48 589 | 14.5 | 21.2 | 19.0 |
| Poweshiek | 79 | 1 231 | 5 406 | 32.9 | 48.7 | 23.1 | 24.5 | 8 505 | 25 472 | 52 413 | 2.6 | 1.7 | 49 853 | 11.5 | 15.2 | 13.7 |
| Ringgold | NA | NA | 1 171 | 14.0 | 48.3 | 21.1 | 8.5 | 11 178 | 22 620 | 42 213 | 7.4 | 1.3 | 38 547 | 14.0 | 26.7 | 24.1 |
| Sac | 73 | 489 | 2 118 | 7.5 | 53.3 | 18.8 | 17.9 | 9 949 | 26 072 | 44 392 | 0.0 | 3.2 | 49 480 | 9.5 | 14.7 | 12.8 |
| Scott | 461 | 3 416 | 43 141 | 18.2 | 36.6 | 30.3 | 282.5 | 10 031 | 28 010 | 51 274 | -11.1 | 3.3 | 50 007 | 13.8 | 20.6 | 19.4 |
| Shelby | NA | NA | 2 951 | 8.7 | 52.5 | 17.4 | 17.5 | 9 903 | 24 628 | 46 257 | -8.5 | 1.7 | 48 572 | 9.5 | 12.6 | 11.0 |
| Sioux | NA | NA | 10 146 | 49.3 | 48.1 | 22.5 | 39.7 | 8 824 | 22 568 | 53 922 | -1.5 | 2.0 | 57 027 | 9.0 | 10.9 | 9.6 |
| Story | 280 | 2 619 | 38 204 | 4.1 | 23.6 | 47.7 | 98.8 | 9 218 | 26 265 | 49 733 | -8.9 | 3.0 | 48 121 | 21.3 | 12.7 | 11.5 |
| Tama | 160 | 575 | 4 424 | 8.0 | 52.1 | 16.0 | 23.3 | 9 260 | 24 089 | 48 836 | -3.3 | 2.3 | 50 034 | 10.9 | 16.5 | 14.4 |
| Taylor | 0 | 205 | 1 445 | 3.5 | 55.5 | 12.7 | 9.7 | 9 525 | 22 977 | 41 554 | -1.7 | 1.8 | 43 155 | 13.4 | 18.5 | 16.8 |
| Union | 190 | 1 778 | 3 122 | 9.5 | 50.1 | 15.8 | 24.8 | 12 485 | 21 332 | 41 782 | -3.0 | 0.2 | 39 922 | 14.5 | 22.2 | 20.2 |
| Van Buren | 184 | 775 | 1 643 | 13.7 | 54.4 | 13.1 | 10.9 | 9 145 | 20 510 | 40 640 | -3.2 | 1.5 | 39 719 | 16.3 | 27.5 | 26.3 |
| Wapello | 240 | 2 762 | 8 500 | 11.7 | 53.4 | 15.5 | 69.4 | 12 536 | 22 570 | 40 269 | -7.3 | 1.5 | 39 999 | 18.9 | 26.4 | 24.1 |
| Warren | 153 | 1 515 | 13 068 | 22.7 | 38.5 | 26.7 | 73.4 | 8 299 | 29 045 | 63 292 | -6.9 | 3.5 | 62 688 | 6.5 | 9.1 | 7.9 |
| Washington | 316 | 1 086 | 5 099 | 15.0 | 48.3 | 19.5 | 33.0 | 8 773 | 24 615 | 51 875 | -1.7 | 0.8 | 50 559 | 11.4 | 17.8 | 15.5 |
| Wayne | 62 | 404 | 1 432 | 7.1 | 57.8 | 11.9 | 11.5 | 10 088 | 20 107 | 36 365 | -8.3 | 0.9 | 37 662 | 17.2 | 27.7 | 26.3 |
| Webster | 413 | 3 625 | 9 973 | 16.3 | 47.6 | 17.9 | 50.2 | 9 484 | 23 718 | 41 695 | -12.6 | 1.6 | 42 178 | 15.4 | 20.2 | 17.7 |
| Winnebago | 73 | 375 | 2 730 | 21.7 | 43.7 | 20.8 | 22.4 | 9 623 | 23 538 | 46 395 | -10.5 | 0.7 | 47 692 | 10.5 | 15.6 | 13.9 |
| Winneshiek | 19 | 628 | 6 612 | 46.7 | 45.5 | 27.1 | 27.7 | 9 779 | 24 170 | 52 042 | -0.9 | 1.7 | 49 148 | 10.7 | 12.8 | 11.4 |
| Woodbury | 376 | 3 640 | 27 696 | 19.7 | 48.7 | 20.3 | 194.4 | 10 662 | 22 652 | 45 844 | -11.8 | 1.6 | 43 362 | 16.7 | 23.9 | 19.3 |
| Worth | 52 | 1 309 | 1 695 | 10.3 | 43.9 | 16.2 | 10.4 | 9 985 | 27 773 | 50 540 | 2.7 | 2.5 | 48 718 | 11.0 | 15.1 | 13.2 |
| Wright | NA | NA | 2 876 | 6.3 | 52.3 | 14.6 | 24.4 | 9 397 | 23 786 | 43 105 | -11.8 | 1.6 | 43 647 | 11.8 | 18.1 | 17.0 |

1. Data for serious crimes have not been adjusted for underreporting; this may affect comparability between geographic areas and over time.   2. Per 100,000 population estimated by the FBI.   3. All persons 3 years old and over enrolled in nursery school through college.   4. Persons 25 years old and over.   5. Elementary and secondary education expenditures.   6. Based on population estimated by the American Community Survey, 2007–2011.

# Table B. States and Counties — **Personal Income**

| | Personal income, 2011 | | | | | | | | | | | | |
|---|---|---|---|---|---|---|---|---|---|---|---|---|---|
| | | | Per capita[1] | | | | | Transfer payments (mil dol) | | | | | |
| | | | | | | | | | Government payments to individuals | | | | |
| STATE County | Total (mil dol) | Percent change, 2010–2011 | Dollars | Rank | Wages and salaries[2] (mil dol) | Proprietors' income (mil dol) | Dividends, interest, and rent (mil dol) | Total | Total | Social Security | Medical payments | Income mainte-nance | Unemploy-ment insurance |
| | 62 | 63 | 64 | 65 | 66 | 67 | 68 | 69 | 70 | 71 | 72 | 73 | 74 |
| **IOWA—Cont'd** | | | | | | | | | | | | | |
| Franklin | 540 | 25.9 | 50 311 | 199 | 185 | 203 | 81 | 77 | 74 | 32 | 31 | 6 | 2 |
| Fremont | 321 | 6.7 | 43 581 | 461 | 141 | 77 | 45 | 63 | 61 | 24 | 27 | 5 | 1 |
| Greene | 436 | 22.5 | 46 956 | 300 | 147 | 123 | 74 | 76 | 74 | 31 | 30 | 7 | 3 |
| Grundy | 620 | 13.8 | 49 783 | 210 | 195 | 135 | 116 | 83 | 81 | 39 | 31 | 5 | 3 |
| Guthrie | 458 | 14.1 | 41 971 | 574 | 139 | 105 | 70 | 86 | 83 | 37 | 33 | 6 | 3 |
| Hamilton | 714 | 17.8 | 45 945 | 338 | 275 | 218 | 109 | 124 | 120 | 46 | 49 | 9 | 10 |
| Hancock | 496 | 17.3 | 43 929 | 444 | 279 | 150 | 73 | 79 | 76 | 33 | 31 | 6 | 3 |
| Hardin | 799 | 17.9 | 45 878 | 342 | 328 | 236 | 120 | 144 | 140 | 56 | 59 | 11 | 5 |
| Harrison | 621 | 12.9 | 41 885 | 583 | 178 | 123 | 73 | 122 | 119 | 41 | 57 | 9 | 3 |
| Henry | 660 | 6.7 | 32 561 | 1 785 | 419 | 75 | 107 | 151 | 147 | 57 | 59 | 15 | 6 |
| Howard | 386 | 16.0 | 40 392 | 709 | 170 | 112 | 62 | 68 | 66 | 26 | 28 | 6 | 2 |
| Humboldt | 446 | 24.5 | 45 462 | 368 | 169 | 131 | 69 | 76 | 74 | 31 | 33 | 5 | 2 |
| Ida | 372 | 15.8 | 52 555 | 152 | 160 | 140 | 55 | 53 | 51 | 22 | 22 | 4 | 1 |
| Iowa | 662 | 10.2 | 40 554 | 700 | 128 | 110 | 110 | 105 | 101 | 46 | 39 | 7 | 5 |
| Jackson | 715 | 10.1 | 36 099 | 1 200 | 233 | 88 | 125 | 164 | 160 | 58 | 72 | 14 | 7 |
| Jasper | 1 259 | 9.1 | 34 457 | 1 439 | 464 | 207 | 181 | 271 | 263 | 110 | 108 | 22 | 12 |
| Jefferson | 564 | 8.7 | 33 544 | 1 594 | 304 | 61 | 138 | 114 | 110 | 42 | 46 | 13 | 4 |
| Johnson | 5 501 | 7.2 | 41 349 | 631 | 4 443 | 442 | 880 | 609 | 580 | 223 | 208 | 69 | 24 |
| Jones | 691 | 9.6 | 33 518 | 1 598 | 274 | 99 | 145 | 142 | 137 | 58 | 55 | 11 | 7 |
| Keokuk | 407 | 19.0 | 39 175 | 836 | 100 | 90 | 66 | 81 | 79 | 31 | 34 | 7 | 3 |
| Kossuth | 806 | 19.6 | 52 330 | 158 | 293 | 291 | 121 | 121 | 118 | 53 | 49 | 8 | 3 |
| Lee | 1 169 | 6.0 | 32 827 | 1 734 | 787 | 70 | 193 | 318 | 310 | 109 | 134 | 34 | 13 |
| Linn | 9 277 | 6.4 | 43 378 | 478 | 7 342 | 675 | 1 423 | 1 411 | 1 364 | 523 | 525 | 134 | 69 |
| Louisa | 404 | 10.5 | 35 508 | 1 291 | 161 | 52 | 53 | 77 | 75 | 30 | 31 | 8 | 3 |
| Lucas | 268 | 9.2 | 30 301 | 2 241 | 143 | 26 | 45 | 71 | 69 | 26 | 31 | 8 | 2 |
| Lyon | 568 | 22.8 | 48 644 | 248 | 177 | 199 | 80 | 64 | 62 | 28 | 25 | 5 | 1 |
| Madison | 597 | 7.5 | 37 816 | 995 | 154 | 82 | 81 | 103 | 99 | 39 | 41 | 7 | 7 |
| Mahaska | 811 | 12.0 | 36 013 | 1 207 | 353 | 110 | 121 | 164 | 159 | 59 | 63 | 18 | 7 |
| Marion | 1 161 | 6.8 | 34 823 | 1 399 | 811 | 89 | 212 | 221 | 214 | 89 | 83 | 16 | 9 |
| Marshall | 1 492 | 7.5 | 36 420 | 1 146 | 891 | 141 | 230 | 340 | 331 | 118 | 140 | 32 | 12 |
| Mills | 670 | 5.4 | 44 674 | 408 | 185 | 73 | 67 | 199 | 195 | 40 | 134 | 9 | 2 |
| Mitchell | 494 | 15.8 | 45 802 | 346 | 171 | 167 | 76 | 79 | 77 | 33 | 33 | 5 | 2 |
| Monona | 388 | 14.2 | 41 972 | 573 | 111 | 111 | 60 | 87 | 85 | 32 | 40 | 6 | 3 |
| Monroe | 287 | 6.9 | 35 680 | 1 267 | 183 | 25 | 37 | 66 | 64 | 23 | 29 | 6 | 3 |
| Montgomery | 403 | 8.9 | 37 834 | 992 | 180 | 81 | 64 | 99 | 96 | 35 | 45 | 10 | 2 |
| Muscatine | 1 631 | 6.6 | 38 104 | 955 | 1 184 | 147 | 286 | 292 | 282 | 112 | 113 | 35 | 12 |
| O'Brien | 674 | 16.9 | 47 412 | 286 | 249 | 189 | 109 | 116 | 113 | 44 | 51 | 8 | 3 |
| Osceola | 303 | 21.5 | 47 738 | 274 | 94 | 115 | 41 | 43 | 42 | 18 | 17 | 3 | 1 |
| Page | 523 | 5.6 | 32 716 | 1 754 | 260 | 63 | 90 | 133 | 129 | 51 | 59 | 12 | 2 |
| Palo Alto | 446 | 21.5 | 47 327 | 288 | 150 | 167 | 60 | 74 | 72 | 28 | 33 | 5 | 2 |
| Plymouth | 1 174 | 12.0 | 47 144 | 292 | 515 | 287 | 191 | 156 | 150 | 65 | 62 | 11 | 6 |
| Pocahontas | 371 | 30.9 | 51 676 | 171 | 127 | 134 | 46 | 62 | 61 | 24 | 28 | 4 | 1 |
| Polk | 19 830 | 5.7 | 45 336 | 379 | 16 310 | 2 559 | 2 571 | 2 795 | 2 698 | 920 | 1 097 | 315 | 148 |
| Pottawattamie | 3 426 | 4.7 | 36 640 | 1 119 | 1 704 | 270 | 408 | 736 | 715 | 231 | 302 | 81 | 16 |
| Poweshiek | 778 | 11.6 | 41 359 | 629 | 468 | 125 | 132 | 135 | 131 | 55 | 52 | 10 | 6 |
| Ringgold | 166 | 16.3 | 32 397 | 1 804 | 58 | 33 | 31 | 41 | 40 | 16 | 18 | 4 | 1 |
| Sac | 519 | 18.8 | 50 675 | 195 | 142 | 183 | 85 | 79 | 77 | 33 | 33 | 5 | 2 |
| Scott | 7 749 | 7.0 | 46 372 | 323 | 4 352 | 689 | 1 074 | 1 587 | 1 550 | 410 | 437 | 156 | 41 |
| Shelby | 585 | 16.5 | 48 595 | 251 | 231 | 148 | 89 | 106 | 103 | 40 | 49 | 7 | 2 |
| Sioux | 1 434 | 15.3 | 42 297 | 557 | 800 | 367 | 248 | 181 | 174 | 72 | 73 | 11 | 6 |
| Story | 3 356 | 6.2 | 37 429 | 1 035 | 2 325 | 399 | 527 | 453 | 433 | 163 | 162 | 39 | 13 |
| Tama | 683 | 10.8 | 38 615 | 896 | 214 | 156 | 103 | 126 | 122 | 52 | 47 | 10 | 6 |
| Taylor | 268 | 18.6 | 42 430 | 550 | 79 | 89 | 31 | 51 | 50 | 19 | 23 | 5 | 1 |
| Union | 443 | 10.3 | 35 339 | 1 319 | 283 | 59 | 59 | 107 | 104 | 36 | 43 | 11 | 3 |
| Van Buren | 226 | 9.1 | 30 057 | 2 279 | 91 | 27 | 39 | 60 | 59 | 23 | 25 | 6 | 2 |
| Wapello | 1 144 | 5.2 | 32 297 | 1 825 | 716 | 66 | 147 | 334 | 326 | 102 | 133 | 40 | 12 |
| Warren | 1 892 | 6.7 | 40 496 | 703 | 424 | 83 | 213 | 278 | 268 | 113 | 104 | 20 | 12 |
| Washington | 893 | 9.1 | 40 837 | 673 | 319 | 127 | 144 | 157 | 153 | 62 | 66 | 13 | 5 |
| Wayne | 196 | 13.4 | 31 029 | 2 092 | 79 | 27 | 31 | 55 | 53 | 20 | 24 | 5 | 1 |
| Webster | 1 486 | 11.5 | 39 467 | 808 | 866 | 273 | 213 | 327 | 319 | 110 | 131 | 31 | 16 |
| Winnebago | 405 | 11.6 | 37 507 | 1 025 | 185 | 78 | 73 | 83 | 80 | 33 | 32 | 6 | 4 |
| Winneshiek | 830 | 10.6 | 39 471 | 807 | 444 | 157 | 145 | 145 | 140 | 54 | 50 | 9 | 5 |
| Woodbury | 3 560 | 3.8 | 34 726 | 1 415 | 2 255 | 408 | 482 | 746 | 724 | 236 | 307 | 93 | 32 |
| Worth | 298 | 13.0 | 39 521 | 803 | 95 | 72 | 47 | 52 | 51 | 21 | 19 | 4 | 3 |
| Wright | 655 | 24.5 | 50 104 | 205 | 263 | 202 | 102 | 113 | 110 | 43 | 48 | 9 | 5 |

1. Based on the resident population estimated as of July 1 of the year shown.    2. Includes supplements to wages and salaries.

# Table B. States and Counties — **Earnings, Social Security, and Housing**

| STATE County | Total (mil dol) | Farm | Goods-related[1] Total | Manu-facturing | Information and professional and technical services | Retail trade | Finance, insurance, and real estate | Health care and social services | Govern-ment | Number | Rate[2] | Supplemental Security Income recipients, December 2011 | Total | Percent change, 2000–2010 |
|---|---|---|---|---|---|---|---|---|---|---|---|---|---|---|
| | 75 | 76 | 77 | 78 | 79 | 80 | 81 | 82 | 83 | 84 | 85 | 86 | 87 | 88 |
| **IOWA—Cont'd** | | | | | | | | | | | | | | |
| Franklin | 388 | 46.6 | D | 11.4 | 1.5 | 3.2 | 2.5 | 3.2 | 9.6 | 2 450 | 228 | 108 | 4 894 | 2.8 |
| Fremont | 217 | 19.5 | 33.9 | 32.5 | 1.6 | 14.1 | 2.6 | 6.4 | 10.1 | 1 915 | 260 | 153 | 3 431 | -2.4 |
| Greene | 270 | 38.4 | D | 13.4 | 3.3 | 3.8 | 3.6 | 4.2 | 15.8 | 2 400 | 258 | 161 | 4 546 | -1.7 |
| Grundy | 329 | 35.9 | 17.6 | 6.5 | 1.8 | 3.7 | 4.8 | D | 9.7 | 2 850 | 229 | 89 | 5 530 | 4.3 |
| Guthrie | 245 | 39.8 | 12.2 | 5.8 | 2.2 | 3.1 | 7.9 | 5.1 | 17.6 | 2 865 | 263 | 160 | 5 756 | 5.3 |
| Hamilton | 493 | 36.8 | D | 17.3 | 2.6 | 3.6 | 3.2 | 4.4 | 12.2 | 3 560 | 229 | 204 | 7 219 | 1.9 |
| Hancock | 429 | 28.2 | D | 35.9 | 1.7 | 2.6 | 1.9 | D | 8.1 | 2 580 | 229 | 121 | 5 330 | 3.2 |
| Hardin | 564 | 37.4 | D | 6.6 | 2.7 | 4.3 | 3.5 | D | 15.1 | 4 255 | 244 | 230 | 8 224 | -1.1 |
| Harrison | 302 | 32.5 | D | 4.5 | 2.2 | 5.8 | 3.4 | D | 15.2 | 3 270 | 221 | 238 | 6 731 | 2.0 |
| Henry | 494 | 6.3 | D | 20.8 | 4.5 | 5.6 | 2.6 | D | 20.3 | 4 365 | 215 | 350 | 8 280 | 0.4 |
| Howard | 282 | 32.1 | 26.1 | 21.4 | D | 6.3 | 3.6 | D | 13.5 | 2 195 | 229 | 100 | 4 367 | 0.9 |
| Humboldt | 300 | 31.6 | D | 18.9 | 1.9 | 4.6 | D | D | 10.9 | 2 395 | 244 | 137 | 4 684 | 0.8 |
| Ida | 299 | 34.2 | 29.2 | 25.0 | 0.9 | 2.9 | 3.5 | 5.9 | 6.3 | 1 730 | 244 | 65 | 3 426 | -2.3 |
| Iowa | 514 | 14.6 | D | 41.3 | 2.2 | 6.0 | 2.0 | 4.2 | 9.9 | 3 460 | 212 | 141 | 7 258 | 10.9 |
| Jackson | 321 | 17.9 | 16.6 | 11.1 | 3.7 | 9.0 | 4.7 | 7.6 | 17.5 | 4 755 | 240 | 401 | 9 415 | 5.2 |
| Jasper | 671 | 22.7 | D | 12.3 | 7.9 | 6.1 | 3.3 | 6.2 | 20.3 | 8 130 | 222 | 499 | 16 181 | 3.3 |
| Jefferson | 365 | 5.3 | D | 15.3 | 10.0 | 8.5 | 11.6 | 5.7 | 16.2 | 3 420 | 203 | 305 | 7 594 | 4.9 |
| Johnson | 4 885 | 2.1 | D | 7.0 | 6.5 | 5.4 | 4.0 | 7.4 | 44.2 | 15 430 | 116 | 1 500 | 55 967 | 22.1 |
| Jones | 373 | 19.8 | D | 12.0 | 2.9 | 9.3 | 3.1 | D | 19.4 | 4 490 | 218 | 238 | 8 911 | 9.7 |
| Keokuk | 190 | 33.0 | D | 4.4 | 2.4 | 6.4 | 3.3 | 5.0 | 14.4 | 2 495 | 240 | 192 | 4 931 | -1.6 |
| Kossuth | 584 | 38.3 | D | 15.4 | 3.2 | 4.2 | 6.2 | D | 9.6 | 4 135 | 269 | 195 | 7 486 | -1.6 |
| Lee | 857 | 1.6 | D | 33.0 | D | 7.1 | 3.2 | 12.5 | 15.1 | 8 285 | 233 | 960 | 16 205 | -2.5 |
| Linn | 8 017 | 1.0 | 29.0 | 23.0 | 9.6 | 7.5 | 10.1 | 10.7 | 10.3 | 37 220 | 174 | 3 151 | 92 251 | 14.5 |
| Louisa | 213 | 17.3 | D | 31.5 | D | 3.2 | 2.8 | 4.4 | 18.7 | 2 220 | 195 | 180 | 5 002 | -2.6 |
| Lucas | 169 | 4.5 | D | 6.0 | 2.2 | 6.1 | 4.6 | D | 21.4 | 2 095 | 237 | 213 | 4 238 | 0.0 |
| Lyon | 376 | 46.1 | D | 9.8 | 6.1 | 2.8 | 2.4 | 4.1 | 8.1 | 2 205 | 189 | 69 | 4 848 | 1.9 |
| Madison | 236 | 22.1 | 18.8 | 8.4 | D | 6.8 | 4.8 | 6.2 | 22.6 | 3 010 | 191 | 136 | 6 554 | 15.8 |
| Mahaska | 462 | 16.0 | D | 19.9 | 3.5 | 6.6 | 2.6 | D | 17.4 | 4 675 | 208 | 447 | 9 766 | 2.3 |
| Marion | 900 | 4.8 | D | 46.2 | D | 5.0 | 2.6 | 10.8 | 10.0 | 6 840 | 205 | 379 | 13 914 | 9.1 |
| Marshall | 1 032 | 8.1 | D | 31.0 | D | 5.6 | 2.8 | 10.5 | 18.2 | 8 665 | 211 | 664 | 16 831 | 3.1 |
| Mills | 258 | 17.6 | D | 4.0 | D | 3.7 | 4.8 | D | 36.6 | 3 130 | 209 | 282 | 6 109 | 7.7 |
| Mitchell | 339 | 35.1 | D | 19.9 | 1.3 | 3.5 | 2.5 | D | 9.9 | 2 575 | 239 | 95 | 4 850 | 5.6 |
| Monona | 221 | 42.8 | 6.0 | 2.1 | D | 5.0 | D | 11.5 | 13.2 | 2 570 | 278 | 152 | 4 697 | 0.8 |
| Monroe | 208 | 4.9 | 49.5 | 43.2 | D | 4.5 | 2.7 | D | 13.6 | 1 890 | 235 | 146 | 3 884 | 8.2 |
| Montgomery | 260 | 24.6 | D | 12.6 | 3.7 | 5.5 | 3.5 | D | 19.3 | 2 730 | 257 | 242 | 5 239 | -3.0 |
| Muscatine | 1 331 | 3.2 | 42.6 | 38.3 | 6.8 | 5.9 | 2.4 | 6.3 | 11.5 | 8 200 | 192 | 708 | 17 910 | 6.7 |
| O'Brien | 438 | 33.7 | 14.0 | 10.1 | D | 4.6 | 3.9 | 10.6 | 11.3 | 3 480 | 245 | 205 | 6 649 | 2.2 |
| Osceola | 210 | 55.2 | D | 7.8 | 1.0 | 2.1 | D | D | 7.7 | 1 465 | 230 | 63 | 2 990 | -0.7 |
| Page | 324 | 10.5 | D | 16.6 | D | 9.8 | 3.5 | D | 23.7 | 4 025 | 252 | 335 | 7 181 | -1.7 |
| Palo Alto | 317 | 47.8 | 11.4 | 9.5 | 1.4 | 4.1 | 2.7 | D | 14.9 | 2 245 | 238 | 133 | 4 628 | -0.1 |
| Plymouth | 802 | 25.9 | D | 18.8 | 2.5 | 4.3 | 3.7 | 4.4 | 9.8 | 5 005 | 201 | 219 | 10 550 | 6.8 |
| Pocahontas | 261 | 48.5 | D | 8.8 | D | 3.1 | D | D | 11.0 | 1 920 | 267 | 101 | 3 794 | -4.9 |
| Polk | 18 869 | 0.3 | D | 5.9 | 9.4 | 5.3 | 23.3 | 10.3 | 13.2 | 65 580 | 150 | 7 193 | 182 262 | 16.5 |
| Pottawattamie | 1 974 | 5.3 | D | 13.0 | 4.0 | 8.7 | 4.1 | 13.6 | 16.4 | 17 840 | 191 | 2 070 | 39 330 | 9.8 |
| Poweshiek | 593 | 15.0 | D | 14.1 | D | 4.2 | 10.0 | D | 7.8 | 4 115 | 219 | 220 | 8 949 | 4.5 |
| Ringgold | 92 | 25.7 | D | 1.9 | D | 5.6 | D | 8.8 | 27.1 | 1 355 | 265 | 100 | 2 613 | -6.3 |
| Sac | 325 | 46.3 | D | 8.6 | D | 2.8 | D | D | 9.3 | 2 605 | 254 | 105 | 5 429 | -0.6 |
| Scott | 5 041 | 1.1 | 23.3 | 16.9 | 10.2 | 8.9 | 5.1 | 13.3 | 10.4 | 30 190 | 181 | 3 704 | 71 835 | 9.4 |
| Shelby | 379 | 31.5 | 13.8 | 9.4 | 5.9 | 4.5 | 3.9 | D | 14.2 | 3 175 | 264 | 185 | 5 542 | 2.4 |
| Sioux | 1 167 | 26.6 | 28.6 | 23.2 | 3.4 | 4.3 | 3.7 | 5.0 | 9.1 | 5 620 | 166 | 192 | 12 279 | 9.0 |
| Story | 2 724 | 3.9 | D | 15.7 | 5.1 | 5.0 | 2.9 | 7.6 | 40.1 | 11 415 | 127 | 655 | 36 789 | 20.1 |
| Tama | 370 | 36.9 | 7.8 | 4.5 | D | 3.5 | 2.3 | D | 26.7 | 4 045 | 229 | 189 | 7 766 | 2.4 |
| Taylor | 167 | 50.8 | D | 11.7 | D | 1.8 | 1.6 | D | 11.5 | 1 630 | 259 | 111 | 3 107 | -2.9 |
| Union | 341 | 10.6 | D | 24.3 | D | 6.7 | 3.6 | 6.6 | 21.2 | 2 945 | 235 | 284 | 5 937 | 4.9 |
| Van Buren | 118 | 16.1 | D | 30.1 | D | 5.1 | 2.9 | D | 22.7 | 1 860 | 248 | 132 | 3 670 | 2.5 |
| Wapello | 782 | 1.3 | D | 28.5 | 2.9 | 8.0 | 3.5 | 15.0 | 17.6 | 8 160 | 230 | 1 102 | 16 098 | 1.4 |
| Warren | 508 | 3.7 | 14.8 | 4.7 | 7.7 | 10.0 | 4.8 | 11.4 | 23.4 | 8 145 | 174 | 378 | 18 371 | 20.2 |
| Washington | 446 | 18.9 | D | 11.7 | 2.6 | 6.9 | 4.4 | 7.2 | 16.3 | 4 780 | 219 | 326 | 9 516 | 11.4 |
| Wayne | 106 | 16.4 | D | 22.5 | 2.7 | 5.1 | D | 4.2 | 27.6 | 1 720 | 273 | 133 | 3 212 | -4.3 |
| Webster | 1 139 | 15.2 | 22.6 | 16.5 | 4.1 | 6.5 | 3.1 | 13.2 | 14.8 | 8 490 | 225 | 757 | 17 035 | 0.4 |
| Winnebago | 263 | 25.1 | D | 15.5 | D | 6.0 | 4.0 | D | 14.0 | 2 530 | 234 | 102 | 5 194 | 2.5 |
| Winneshiek | 601 | 14.5 | D | 16.6 | D | 6.8 | 3.0 | D | 16.3 | 4 295 | 204 | 207 | 8 721 | 6.3 |
| Woodbury | 2 663 | 5.7 | D | 10.1 | 4.7 | 8.6 | 4.6 | 16.6 | 15.9 | 18 370 | 179 | 1 969 | 41 484 | 0.2 |
| Worth | 167 | 36.8 | D | 12.2 | 1.3 | 3.0 | 2.0 | 3.1 | 12.3 | 1 675 | 222 | 73 | 3 548 | 0.4 |
| Wright | 465 | 41.5 | D | 15.9 | 2.9 | 3.1 | 2.2 | D | 16.3 | 3 280 | 251 | 191 | 6 529 | -0.5 |

1. Includes mining, construction, and manufacturing.    2. Per 1,000 resident population enumerated in the 2010 census.

# Table B. States and Counties — Housing, Labor Force, and Employment

| STATE County | Housing units, 2007–2011 | | | | | | | | Civilian labor force, 2012 | | | | Civilian employment,[6] 2007–2011 | | |
| | Occupied units | | | | | | | | | | Unemployment | | | Percent | |
| | | | Owner-occupied | | | Renter-occupied | | Sub-stand-ard units[4] (percent) | | Percent change, 2011–2012 | | | | Manage-ment, business, science and arts | Con-struction, produc-tion, and mainte-nance occu-pations |
| | | | | Median owner cost as a percent of income | | | | | | | | | | | |
| | Total | Percent | Median value[1] | With a mort-gage | Without a mort-gage[2] | Median rent[3] | Median rent as a per-cent of income | | Total | | Total | Rate[5] | Total | | |
| | 89 | 90 | 91 | 92 | 93 | 94 | 95 | 96 | 97 | 98 | 99 | 100 | 101 | 102 | 103 |
| IOWA—Cont'd | | | | | | | | | | | | | | | |
| Franklin | 4 216 | 74.2 | 84 700 | 18.8 | 11.2 | 497 | 22.1 | 1.2 | 5 856 | -2.5 | 274 | 4.7 | 5 406 | 25.1 | 37.4 |
| Fremont | 3 109 | 77.6 | 93 200 | 18.9 | 12.1 | 523 | 25.9 | 2.3 | 3 840 | -0.6 | 217 | 5.7 | 3 673 | 32.6 | 27.6 |
| Greene | 4 146 | 75.3 | 81 100 | 21.1 | 11.4 | 556 | 24.0 | 2.1 | 4 979 | -1.0 | 258 | 5.2 | 4 597 | 32.4 | 28.1 |
| Grundy | 5 075 | 81.5 | 113 700 | 19.9 | 11.5 | 498 | 21.4 | 0.8 | 6 865 | -0.4 | 309 | 4.5 | 6 266 | 31.8 | 31.1 |
| Guthrie | 4 734 | 78.7 | 95 300 | 19.6 | 12.0 | 526 | 23.5 | 1.0 | 5 472 | -0.6 | 310 | 5.7 | 5 353 | 34.8 | 27.2 |
| Hamilton | 6 542 | 75.9 | 89 700 | 19.7 | 13.3 | 593 | 25.8 | 1.7 | 6 721 | -6.7 | 514 | 7.6 | 7 726 | 29.0 | 34.3 |
| Hancock | 4 778 | 81.4 | 84 800 | 20.4 | 11.7 | 496 | 22.0 | 2.2 | 5 637 | -0.3 | 286 | 5.1 | 5 783 | 27.2 | 35.2 |
| Hardin | 7 155 | 75.3 | 87 100 | 19.2 | 12.4 | 543 | 21.1 | 0.9 | 8 846 | -2.5 | 489 | 5.5 | 8 390 | 31.8 | 30.9 |
| Harrison | 6 004 | 78.9 | 113 200 | 20.9 | 12.2 | 546 | 27.4 | 1.5 | 7 003 | -1.3 | 323 | 4.6 | 7 572 | 32.3 | 30.0 |
| Henry | 7 625 | 72.8 | 98 900 | 21.8 | 11.7 | 580 | 30.2 | 2.3 | 9 246 | -2.0 | 614 | 6.6 | 9 421 | 27.7 | 33.4 |
| Howard | 4 056 | 79.5 | 93 600 | 21.6 | 12.4 | 535 | 27.8 | 0.7 | 4 900 | -2.8 | 253 | 5.2 | 4 993 | 26.7 | 38.1 |
| Humboldt | 4 208 | 76.0 | 84 400 | 18.9 | 9.9 | 483 | 20.0 | 1.9 | 5 102 | 0.4 | 224 | 4.4 | 4 852 | 31.8 | 31.7 |
| Ida | 3 180 | 75.1 | 74 400 | 17.1 | 9.9 | 408 | 18.5 | 1.3 | 3 862 | -0.7 | 156 | 4.0 | 3 598 | 32.7 | 33.8 |
| Iowa | 6 677 | 79.1 | 133 700 | 22.1 | 11.7 | 537 | 21.3 | 1.7 | 8 258 | -2.4 | 448 | 5.4 | 8 932 | 34.2 | 28.7 |
| Jackson | 8 286 | 78.2 | 107 900 | 22.2 | 12.8 | 531 | 25.4 | 1.5 | 10 789 | -2.3 | 616 | 5.7 | 10 119 | 26.4 | 35.7 |
| Jasper | 14 787 | 73.8 | 114 000 | 23.4 | 11.9 | 615 | 29.3 | 1.2 | 16 806 | -1.3 | 1 181 | 7.0 | 17 366 | 29.8 | 27.9 |
| Jefferson | 6 831 | 76.4 | 91 400 | 21.4 | 11.2 | 594 | 30.5 | 1.8 | 7 768 | -1.3 | 490 | 6.3 | 8 515 | 38.3 | 22.8 |
| Johnson | 51 772 | 60.3 | 180 200 | 22.0 | 10.9 | 771 | 34.3 | 2.0 | 79 652 | -1.0 | 3 016 | 3.8 | 73 688 | 44.1 | 15.1 |
| Jones | 8 143 | 81.3 | 112 100 | 21.8 | 12.4 | 571 | 25.5 | 0.6 | 10 332 | -1.6 | 593 | 5.7 | 10 059 | 27.2 | 33.1 |
| Keokuk | 4 436 | 80.9 | 74 600 | 21.2 | 12.5 | 510 | 23.4 | 2.2 | 5 458 | -1.8 | 310 | 5.7 | 5 199 | 24.7 | 34.2 |
| Kossuth | 6 764 | 81.1 | 86 200 | 18.8 | 9.9 | 466 | 24.0 | 2.1 | 9 070 | 0.1 | 337 | 3.7 | 8 030 | 33.5 | 25.7 |
| Lee | 14 040 | 72.6 | 79 000 | 19.7 | 11.3 | 528 | 25.9 | 2.4 | 16 822 | -1.3 | 1 345 | 8.0 | 16 321 | 26.3 | 36.2 |
| Linn | 86 027 | 73.1 | 139 700 | 20.7 | 12.1 | 627 | 26.7 | 1.4 | 120 184 | -1.7 | 6 385 | 5.3 | 111 278 | 36.9 | 21.3 |
| Louisa | 4 258 | 81.0 | 90 500 | 21.3 | 12.2 | 581 | 21.1 | 6.0 | 5 769 | -1.5 | 327 | 5.7 | 5 610 | 23.8 | 44.7 |
| Lucas | 3 658 | 74.8 | 87 400 | 21.5 | 12.6 | 446 | 29.5 | 1.8 | 4 558 | -0.8 | 205 | 4.5 | 3 840 | 23.9 | 32.0 |
| Lyon | 4 430 | 82.8 | 101 300 | 20.7 | 10.4 | 569 | 22.5 | 1.1 | 7 614 | 1.2 | 208 | 2.7 | 5 956 | 30.8 | 30.4 |
| Madison | 5 924 | 79.2 | 153 000 | 23.2 | 13.7 | 669 | 24.0 | 1.8 | 8 022 | -0.4 | 474 | 5.9 | 7 791 | 36.0 | 25.9 |
| Mahaska | 8 947 | 74.6 | 97 000 | 19.6 | 12.3 | 530 | 29.1 | 1.1 | 11 400 | -2.0 | 625 | 5.5 | 10 830 | 29.7 | 32.7 |
| Marion | 12 531 | 77.2 | 132 300 | 21.0 | 11.0 | 672 | 25.5 | 1.6 | 16 616 | -0.7 | 846 | 5.1 | 16 462 | 32.9 | 27.9 |
| Marshall | 15 519 | 74.0 | 102 700 | 21.7 | 12.2 | 578 | 26.3 | 3.7 | 19 838 | -1.6 | 1 323 | 6.7 | 18 682 | 29.9 | 32.9 |
| Mills | 5 605 | 82.9 | 147 900 | 21.4 | 10.4 | 724 | 26.7 | 2.1 | 7 453 | -1.2 | 292 | 3.9 | 7 309 | 31.9 | 25.1 |
| Mitchell | 4 358 | 82.8 | 100 300 | 20.0 | 10.3 | 488 | 24.4 | 1.9 | 5 494 | -2.3 | 262 | 4.8 | 5 258 | 29.9 | 36.0 |
| Monona | 4 114 | 72.4 | 75 800 | 18.7 | 10.0 | 478 | 27.5 | 0.9 | 4 326 | -4.5 | 308 | 7.1 | 4 370 | 28.0 | 29.5 |
| Monroe | 3 329 | 80.5 | 85 800 | 19.0 | 13.5 | 518 | 26.7 | 3.2 | 4 157 | -2.2 | 232 | 5.6 | 3 651 | 34.6 | 34.7 |
| Montgomery | 4 570 | 73.7 | 83 500 | 20.6 | 13.1 | 557 | 32.5 | 1.0 | 4 893 | -0.6 | 264 | 5.4 | 4 846 | 28.4 | 28.4 |
| Muscatine | 16 402 | 77.0 | 121 500 | 21.5 | 12.9 | 661 | 29.2 | 2.4 | 22 551 | -1.7 | 1 231 | 5.4 | 20 790 | 26.3 | 35.5 |
| O'Brien | 6 126 | 76.1 | 83 900 | 18.3 | 9.9 | 522 | 26.0 | 0.8 | 7 825 | -1.4 | 317 | 4.1 | 7 496 | 29.7 | 31.1 |
| Osceola | 2 677 | 74.9 | 68 900 | 17.3 | 9.9 | 574 | 24.5 | 1.3 | 3 120 | -3.0 | 148 | 4.7 | 3 336 | 27.8 | 35.9 |
| Page | 6 332 | 74.4 | 79 400 | 18.8 | 12.1 | 510 | 26.5 | 2.7 | 7 214 | -1.9 | 389 | 5.4 | 7 032 | 33.2 | 27.9 |
| Palo Alto | 3 973 | 75.1 | 79 800 | 20.4 | 12.4 | 430 | 21.4 | 1.5 | 5 130 | -0.2 | 210 | 4.1 | 4 593 | 32.9 | 29.6 |
| Plymouth | 9 739 | 79.0 | 124 600 | 18.6 | 9.9 | 563 | 22.7 | 0.3 | 14 424 | -0.3 | 598 | 4.1 | 13 778 | 31.2 | 30.6 |
| Pocahontas | 3 318 | 80.1 | 55 700 | 18.1 | 9.9 | 442 | 21.4 | 0.5 | 4 229 | 2.2 | 174 | 4.1 | 3 676 | 31.4 | 32.1 |
| Polk | 169 246 | 70.2 | 151 800 | 22.0 | 12.2 | 735 | 28.2 | 2.5 | 235 523 | -0.6 | 12 789 | 5.4 | 227 664 | 38.5 | 17.7 |
| Pottawattamie | 36 327 | 70.9 | 127 000 | 21.7 | 12.5 | 708 | 29.4 | 2.3 | 47 024 | -1.3 | 2 148 | 4.6 | 47 427 | 27.7 | 26.2 |
| Poweshiek | 7 675 | 75.2 | 114 600 | 20.6 | 10.8 | 605 | 30.8 | 0.4 | 9 936 | -2.1 | 503 | 5.1 | 9 968 | 34.8 | 25.4 |
| Ringgold | 2 056 | 79.6 | 85 600 | 19.9 | 13.9 | 457 | 19.7 | 2.6 | 2 452 | -2.1 | 117 | 4.8 | 2 339 | 38.4 | 31.2 |
| Sac | 4 502 | 81.6 | 77 900 | 19.0 | 10.4 | 502 | 23.8 | 1.8 | 5 698 | -2.0 | 242 | 4.2 | 5 250 | 29.2 | 28.9 |
| Scott | 66 529 | 70.3 | 138 900 | 21.4 | 11.5 | 649 | 28.6 | 1.3 | 87 584 | -1.5 | 5 605 | 6.4 | 81 388 | 35.2 | 23.3 |
| Shelby | 5 067 | 77.9 | 106 900 | 20.8 | 12.4 | 581 | 27.9 | 1.2 | 8 070 | 3.6 | 273 | 3.4 | 6 063 | 32.9 | 26.0 |
| Sioux | 11 549 | 81.3 | 125 200 | 20.2 | 9.9 | 565 | 24.6 | 1.5 | 19 757 | -0.8 | 677 | 3.4 | 18 199 | 33.8 | 28.5 |
| Story | 34 613 | 54.9 | 159 900 | 21.0 | 10.3 | 714 | 32.8 | 1.4 | 48 064 | -1.1 | 1 898 | 3.9 | 49 190 | 44.5 | 16.7 |
| Tama | 7 041 | 77.6 | 96 200 | 20.3 | 12.0 | 595 | 23.7 | 1.8 | 8 666 | -1.6 | 573 | 6.6 | 8 504 | 27.9 | 32.0 |
| Taylor | 2 683 | 79.4 | 64 400 | 20.2 | 12.0 | 515 | 24.2 | 3.3 | 3 322 | -0.8 | 132 | 4.0 | 2 964 | 30.0 | 33.5 |
| Union | 5 354 | 70.4 | 90 300 | 21.3 | 12.7 | 566 | 35.8 | 2.0 | 6 861 | -2.3 | 351 | 5.1 | 6 372 | 24.8 | 36.9 |
| Van Buren | 3 077 | 80.8 | 67 100 | 22.2 | 12.5 | 493 | 22.5 | 4.9 | 3 687 | -1.6 | 232 | 6.3 | 3 630 | 26.0 | 34.5 |
| Wapello | 14 771 | 75.3 | 76 800 | 20.3 | 13.3 | 570 | 28.6 | 1.8 | 17 899 | -1.9 | 1 298 | 7.3 | 16 727 | 24.9 | 35.9 |
| Warren | 17 222 | 79.4 | 151 300 | 21.7 | 12.1 | 691 | 24.6 | 1.1 | 25 332 | -0.3 | 1 291 | 5.1 | 24 940 | 36.5 | 19.3 |
| Washington | 8 943 | 75.9 | 116 700 | 21.8 | 11.5 | 616 | 29.4 | 2.2 | 11 856 | -1.1 | 528 | 4.5 | 11 426 | 32.4 | 28.2 |
| Wayne | 2 699 | 79.8 | 57 700 | 20.7 | 13.7 | 446 | 25.2 | 2.8 | 3 213 | -1.6 | 157 | 4.9 | 2 772 | 28.9 | 39.2 |
| Webster | 15 855 | 67.4 | 86 000 | 19.0 | 11.2 | 530 | 25.0 | 0.9 | 18 074 | -3.3 | 1 281 | 7.1 | 18 390 | 27.3 | 29.3 |
| Winnebago | 4 670 | 75.5 | 90 500 | 19.1 | 11.8 | 474 | 19.1 | 1.7 | 5 000 | -6.9 | 290 | 5.8 | 5 685 | 31.6 | 31.5 |
| Winneshiek | 7 979 | 76.9 | 152 500 | 22.3 | 12.1 | 542 | 25.9 | 1.4 | 12 111 | -0.9 | 564 | 4.7 | 11 682 | 33.2 | 26.7 |
| Woodbury | 38 716 | 67.8 | 95 900 | 20.4 | 11.8 | 611 | 29.5 | 2.9 | 53 379 | -1.3 | 2 820 | 5.3 | 50 819 | 27.7 | 28.8 |
| Worth | 3 264 | 79.7 | 94 900 | 21.7 | 12.6 | 516 | 21.7 | 2.5 | 4 189 | -2.9 | 229 | 5.5 | 4 030 | 27.3 | 34.6 |
| Wright | 5 503 | 74.8 | 74 300 | 20.0 | 11.2 | 479 | 22.3 | 1.6 | 6 956 | 0.3 | 387 | 5.6 | 6 493 | 28.4 | 34.0 |

1. Specified owner-occupied units.   2. A value of 9.9 represents 9.9 percent or less.   3. Specified renter-occupied units. A value of 10.0 represents 10 percent or less.   4. Overcrowded or lacking complete plumbing facilities.   5. Percent of civilian labor force.   6. Persons 16 years old and over.

# Table B. States and Counties — **Nonfarm Employment and Agriculture**

| | Private nonfarm establishments, employment and payroll, 2011 | | | | | | | | | Agriculture, 2007 | | | |
| | | Employment | | | | | | Annual payroll | | Farms | | | |
| | | | | | | | | | | | | Percent with: | |
| STATE<br>County | Number of<br>establish-<br>ments | Total | Health care<br>and social<br>assistance | Manufac-<br>turing | Retail<br>trade | Finance<br>and<br>insurance | Professional,<br>scientific,<br>and<br>technical<br>services | Total<br>(mil dol) | Average<br>per<br>employee<br>(dollars) | Number | Fewer<br>than<br>50<br>acres | 500<br>acres<br>or<br>more | Farm<br>operators<br>whose<br>principal<br>occu-<br>pation is<br>farming<br>(percent) |
|---|---|---|---|---|---|---|---|---|---|---|---|---|---|
| | 104 | 105 | 106 | 107 | 108 | 109 | 110 | 111 | 112 | 113 | 114 | 115 | 116 |
| IOWA—Cont'd | | | | | | | | | | | | | |
| Franklin | 325 | 3 042 | 601 | 661 | 321 | 110 | D | 110 | 36 321 | 923 | 30.3 | 30.3 | 57.1 |
| Fremont | 187 | 2 196 | 380 | 638 | 448 | D | 50 | 83 | 37 651 | 497 | 19.5 | 31.0 | 61.8 |
| Greene | 260 | 2 556 | D | D | 369 | 126 | 76 | 83 | 32 541 | 820 | 32.2 | 29.4 | 54.3 |
| Grundy | 301 | 2 831 | 399 | 527 | 406 | 208 | D | 114 | 40 179 | 800 | 32.6 | 24.3 | 56.1 |
| Guthrie | 332 | 2 517 | 505 | 302 | 390 | 242 | 70 | 88 | 35 084 | 987 | 26.6 | 18.8 | 42.0 |
| Hamilton | 400 | 5 155 | 614 | 1 442 | 654 | 170 | 101 | 164 | 31 766 | 882 | 36.2 | 23.4 | 55.7 |
| Hancock | 293 | 2 965 | 448 | 826 | 447 | 55 | 97 | 99 | 33 252 | 949 | 30.1 | 25.7 | 58.9 |
| Hardin | 560 | 5 540 | 1 087 | 624 | 799 | 254 | 164 | 185 | 33 353 | 943 | 33.0 | 25.0 | 56.7 |
| Harrison | 354 | 2 954 | 665 | D | 458 | D | 96 | 91 | 30 844 | 817 | 27.2 | 28.4 | 56.8 |
| Henry | 506 | 7 800 | 1 177 | 1 942 | 837 | 170 | 393 | 254 | 32 619 | 880 | 30.0 | 15.8 | 44.9 |
| Howard | 268 | 2 880 | 457 | 1 000 | 381 | D | 44 | 85 | 29 415 | 877 | 28.4 | 17.2 | 53.7 |
| Humboldt | 329 | 3 352 | 500 | 914 | 474 | 109 | 74 | 106 | 31 772 | 632 | 23.4 | 32.3 | 61.2 |
| Ida | 244 | 2 757 | 441 | 890 | 312 | D | D | 102 | 37 000 | 633 | 28.8 | 25.6 | 56.4 |
| Iowa | 482 | 7 945 | 767 | 3 656 | 1 411 | 172 | 83 | 260 | 32 760 | 1 144 | 26.3 | 15.3 | 51.0 |
| Jackson | 546 | 4 683 | 831 | 813 | 855 | 213 | 87 | 133 | 28 387 | 1 214 | 27.8 | 12.5 | 45.2 |
| Jasper | 763 | 7 828 | 1 551 | D | 1 354 | 292 | 452 | 231 | 29 522 | 1 166 | 31.9 | 21.3 | 53.4 |
| Jefferson | 656 | 6 423 | 660 | 1 098 | 853 | 201 | 585 | 224 | 34 812 | 773 | 21.3 | 11.5 | 43.7 |
| Johnson | 3 017 | 58 663 | 16 419 | 4 969 | 8 392 | 2 185 | 1 620 | 2 032 | 34 635 | 1 293 | 29.5 | 14.5 | 53.4 |
| Jones | 503 | 4 538 | 881 | 769 | 910 | 202 | 127 | 136 | 29 930 | 1 117 | 29.2 | 19.2 | 51.9 |
| Keokuk | 246 | 1 928 | 413 | 217 | 247 | 116 | D | 60 | 31 368 | 1 163 | 23.6 | 17.0 | 50.1 |
| Kossuth | 573 | 5 582 | D | 992 | 908 | D | 185 | 188 | 33 645 | 1 395 | 23.9 | 31.4 | 65.8 |
| Lee | 911 | 12 601 | 2 166 | 3 596 | 2 019 | 481 | 277 | 441 | 35 015 | 883 | 27.2 | 17.0 | 45.2 |
| Linn | 5 335 | 113 621 | 14 659 | 17 236 | 13 768 | 8 649 | 5 057 | 4 953 | 43 591 | 1 413 | 34.9 | 13.7 | 47.8 |
| Louisa | 219 | 2 808 | 309 | D | 243 | 92 | D | 91 | 32 456 | 701 | 29.0 | 17.8 | 47.6 |
| Lucas | 182 | 2 427 | 530 | D | 400 | D | D | 78 | 32 241 | 699 | 29.6 | 11.6 | 34.3 |
| Lyon | 389 | 2 764 | 415 | D | 350 | 150 | 113 | 96 | 34 829 | 1 087 | 28.2 | 20.8 | 56.7 |
| Madison | 351 | 2 628 | 719 | 184 | 472 | 133 | 97 | 77 | 29 387 | 956 | 36.3 | 15.9 | 41.4 |
| Mahaska | 561 | 6 816 | 1 084 | 1 183 | 1 217 | 203 | 115 | 207 | 30 340 | 1 031 | 26.7 | 16.8 | 47.2 |
| Marion | 829 | 15 260 | 2 530 | D | 1 646 | 321 | 385 | 599 | 39 267 | 951 | 32.8 | 15.1 | 37.3 |
| Marshall | 823 | 15 039 | 2 040 | D | 2 005 | 346 | 372 | 526 | 34 946 | 928 | 31.3 | 22.0 | 53.0 |
| Mills | 294 | 2 055 | 642 | D | 325 | 114 | 112 | 57 | 27 798 | 511 | 27.2 | 29.5 | 58.7 |
| Mitchell | 331 | 3 166 | 559 | 1 066 | 392 | 125 | 74 | 102 | 32 111 | 893 | 29.1 | 23.3 | 57.2 |
| Monona | 235 | 2 138 | 682 | D | 382 | 120 | 47 | 56 | 26 109 | 649 | 20.0 | 35.9 | 63.8 |
| Monroe | 173 | 1 679 | 446 | 359 | 282 | 70 | 33 | 45 | 26 866 | 660 | 24.1 | 15.0 | 43.3 |
| Montgomery | 320 | 2 974 | 765 | 373 | 484 | 113 | D | 94 | 31 599 | 558 | 22.4 | 27.8 | 54.8 |
| Muscatine | 928 | 18 560 | 1 805 | 6 389 | 2 037 | 459 | 710 | 790 | 42 556 | 838 | 29.0 | 15.5 | 47.7 |
| O'Brien | 516 | 5 178 | 1 429 | 499 | 809 | 256 | D | 146 | 28 115 | 987 | 27.6 | 26.6 | 63.4 |
| Osceola | 181 | 1 481 | 272 | D | 145 | 86 | 28 | 45 | 30 138 | 663 | 22.5 | 27.1 | 65.6 |
| Page | 400 | 5 261 | 1 527 | 1 468 | 736 | 186 | 122 | 169 | 32 106 | 788 | 25.3 | 23.6 | 53.0 |
| Palo Alto | 278 | 2 614 | 747 | D | 345 | 118 | 31 | 69 | 26 480 | 849 | 32.9 | 26.5 | 54.5 |
| Plymouth | 692 | 9 588 | 1 138 | 2 412 | 1 057 | 309 | 324 | 346 | 36 103 | 1 442 | 24.6 | 26.1 | 60.1 |
| Pocahontas | 233 | 1 901 | 351 | 289 | 254 | 102 | 53 | 57 | 30 156 | 806 | 24.4 | 35.6 | 65.1 |
| Polk | 11 719 | 230 072 | 31 568 | 14 696 | 27 763 | 36 238 | 13 929 | 10 340 | 44 943 | 738 | 47.6 | 19.2 | 48.0 |
| Pottawattamie | 2 018 | 30 891 | 4 907 | 4 930 | 6 133 | 851 | 731 | 955 | 30 929 | 1 158 | 30.7 | 27.5 | 59.6 |
| Poweshiek | 548 | 8 669 | 1 107 | 1 488 | 1 044 | D | 149 | 302 | 34 831 | 938 | 30.3 | 20.7 | 48.4 |
| Ringgold | 141 | 975 | 360 | D | 206 | 38 | 42 | 26 | 27 150 | 733 | 17.1 | 19.0 | 40.0 |
| Sac | 344 | 2 380 | 529 | 360 | 382 | 132 | 48 | 74 | 31 152 | 802 | 26.6 | 31.3 | 61.8 |
| Scott | 4 396 | 80 218 | 12 420 | 11 081 | 11 113 | 2 825 | 2 925 | 2 940 | 36 644 | 861 | 32.9 | 18.2 | 58.3 |
| Shelby | 394 | 5 554 | 1 162 | 578 | 638 | 246 | 149 | 177 | 31 795 | 871 | 21.9 | 29.7 | 62.8 |
| Sioux | 1 225 | 17 821 | 2 365 | 5 500 | 1 695 | D | 912 | 566 | 31 755 | 1 664 | 34.5 | 18.9 | 60.8 |
| Story | 2 015 | 28 288 | 4 845 | 4 315 | 4 798 | 822 | 1 210 | 956 | 33 784 | 1 077 | 36.1 | 20.1 | 50.7 |
| Tama | 341 | 3 533 | 485 | 248 | 534 | 129 | D | 118 | 33 412 | 1 210 | 23.1 | 23.4 | 54.8 |
| Taylor | 134 | 1 395 | D | 390 | 105 | 40 | 34 | 53 | 37 662 | 779 | 18.9 | 18.4 | 43.1 |
| Union | 335 | 5 228 | 839 | 1 640 | 724 | 191 | 59 | 162 | 31 037 | 681 | 26.3 | 18.2 | 48.3 |
| Van Buren | 160 | 1 782 | 310 | D | 188 | 58 | D | 58 | 32 685 | 808 | 22.5 | 13.9 | 40.6 |
| Wapello | 769 | 13 994 | 2 408 | 3 973 | 2 278 | 347 | 283 | 467 | 33 372 | 744 | 34.3 | 11.8 | 38.6 |
| Warren | 767 | 8 049 | 1 247 | 364 | 1 530 | 254 | 346 | 219 | 27 243 | 1 189 | 38.7 | 9.8 | 35.7 |
| Washington | 699 | 6 496 | 1 279 | 886 | 1 047 | 207 | D | 185 | 28 488 | 1 257 | 27.5 | 17.1 | 52.1 |
| Wayne | 160 | 1 372 | 349 | 408 | 269 | 40 | 35 | 39 | 28 679 | 814 | 21.1 | 17.6 | 42.8 |
| Webster | 1 042 | 15 410 | 2 874 | 1 927 | 2 640 | 556 | 385 | 529 | 34 347 | 1 103 | 28.5 | 26.7 | 63.0 |
| Winnebago | 332 | 6 101 | 636 | D | 489 | 161 | 245 | 183 | 29 932 | 679 | 31.7 | 27.4 | 56.4 |
| Winneshiek | 623 | 9 799 | 1 460 | 1 395 | 1 267 | 221 | 138 | 289 | 29 518 | 1 418 | 28.9 | 11.1 | 49.9 |
| Woodbury | 2 723 | 45 578 | 8 309 | 4 856 | 7 240 | 1 377 | 1 001 | 1 485 | 32 588 | 1 149 | 27.2 | 22.3 | 48.8 |
| Worth | 171 | 1 700 | 195 | 406 | 160 | 51 | D | 45 | 26 464 | 683 | 33.7 | 25.9 | 50.5 |
| Wright | 397 | 4 195 | 857 | 1 171 | 559 | 175 | 133 | 144 | 34 231 | 771 | 25.3 | 29.3 | 56.4 |

| STATE County | Agriculture, 2007 (cont.) | | | | | | | | | | | | | | | |
|---|---|---|---|---|---|---|---|---|---|---|---|---|---|---|---|---|
| | Land in farms | | | | Value of land and buildings (dollars) | | Value of machinery and equipment, average per farm (dollars) | Value of products sold | | Percent from: | | Percent of farms with sales of: | | Government payments | |
| | | Acres | | | | | | | | | | | | | |
| | Acreage (1,000) | Percent change, 2002–2007 | Average size of farm | Total irrigated (1,000) | Total cropland (1,000) | Average per farm | Average per acre | | Total (mil dol) | Average per farm (dollars) | Crops | Live-stock and poultry products | $10,000 or more | $100,000 or more | Total ($1,000) | Percent of farms |
| | 117 | 118 | 119 | 120 | 121 | 122 | 123 | 124 | 125 | 126 | 127 | 128 | 129 | 130 | 131 | 132 |
| **IOWA—Cont'd** | | | | | | | | | | | | | | | | |
| Franklin | 367 | 8.9 | 397 | D | 346.0 | 1 446 396 | 3 642 | 170 685 | 328.7 | 356 085 | 46.8 | 53.2 | 69.9 | 50.3 | 9 350 | 86.1 |
| Fremont | 245 | -23.0 | 494 | 8.7 | 214.9 | 1 510 774 | 3 061 | 164 699 | 99.1 | 199 424 | 87.0 | 13.0 | 64.8 | 40.0 | 4 068 | 84.7 |
| Greene | 354 | 2.0 | 431 | 0.5 | 321.7 | 1 641 924 | 3 809 | 177 530 | 231.1 | 281 867 | 61.8 | 38.2 | 66.8 | 40.0 | 7 730 | 85.6 |
| Grundy | 316 | -2.5 | 395 | 0.0 | 300.8 | 1 550 364 | 3 925 | 172 202 | 237.1 | 296 432 | 67.8 | 32.2 | 69.1 | 45.6 | 7 770 | 79.9 |
| Guthrie | 355 | 9.6 | 360 | 2.5 | 282.2 | 1 076 917 | 2 995 | 155 513 | 196.2 | 198 822 | 47.3 | 52.7 | 49.0 | 23.8 | 7 892 | 80.9 |
| Hamilton | 347 | -0.3 | 393 | 0.0 | 326.3 | 1 550 641 | 3 946 | 184 248 | 324.1 | 367 497 | 47.9 | 52.1 | 65.9 | 43.1 | 8 141 | 81.3 |
| Hancock | 361 | 12.1 | 380 | 1.0 | 345.6 | 1 360 015 | 3 575 | 173 651 | 288.6 | 304 153 | 52.8 | 47.2 | 70.6 | 44.7 | 8 570 | 87.2 |
| Hardin | 339 | 3.4 | 359 | 0.0 | 307.5 | 1 360 569 | 3 785 | 163 841 | 379.6 | 402 514 | 36.8 | 63.2 | 64.7 | 42.0 | 7 836 | 79.4 |
| Harrison | 365 | -14.7 | 447 | 31.2 | 313.5 | 1 325 527 | 2 966 | 131 420 | 144.4 | 176 801 | 82.4 | 17.6 | 60.0 | 38.8 | 6 566 | 79.8 |
| Henry | 240 | -4.4 | 272 | 0.0 | 192.8 | 831 807 | 3 055 | 98 395 | 121.8 | 138 390 | 57.1 | 42.9 | 47.8 | 27.5 | 6 002 | 78.9 |
| Howard | 279 | 3.7 | 318 | 0.3 | 248.8 | 969 433 | 3 051 | 140 611 | 174.4 | 198 889 | 52.6 | 47.4 | 59.0 | 35.6 | 8 426 | 85.2 |
| Humboldt | 270 | -0.4 | 428 | D | 256.2 | 1 603 916 | 3 751 | 183 973 | 159.1 | 251 816 | 71.7 | 28.3 | 76.4 | 51.3 | 5 949 | 89.9 |
| Ida | 273 | 2.6 | 431 | D | 251.2 | 1 384 465 | 3 215 | 182 692 | 170.3 | 269 095 | 58.7 | 41.3 | 68.9 | 42.5 | 6 043 | 81.4 |
| Iowa | 345 | 1.5 | 302 | 0.3 | 281.1 | 929 623 | 3 081 | 115 089 | 182.6 | 159 648 | 53.4 | 46.6 | 55.4 | 30.0 | 8 753 | 85.8 |
| Jackson | 296 | -15.2 | 244 | 0.0 | 191.5 | 693 239 | 2 839 | 99 232 | 146.2 | 120 430 | 36.9 | 63.1 | 53.0 | 20.6 | 7 306 | 79.2 |
| Jasper | 428 | 4.4 | 367 | 0.6 | 378.8 | 1 267 110 | 3 453 | 166 231 | 254.7 | 218 419 | 71.3 | 28.7 | 63.2 | 36.5 | 8 741 | 76.3 |
| Jefferson | 197 | -15.5 | 255 | 0.0 | 145.0 | 726 498 | 2 846 | 77 123 | 67.2 | 86 990 | 58.3 | 41.7 | 41.0 | 17.7 | 5 874 | 84.2 |
| Johnson | 321 | 6.6 | 248 | 2.9 | 282.0 | 931 742 | 3 751 | 114 199 | 189.7 | 146 681 | 55.5 | 44.5 | 61.0 | 32.9 | 7 964 | 74.6 |
| Jones | 324 | 3.8 | 290 | 0.6 | 271.2 | 1 013 974 | 3 496 | 139 930 | 200.1 | 179 143 | 52.0 | 48.0 | 65.8 | 36.5 | 8 041 | 81.3 |
| Keokuk | 318 | -7.6 | 274 | 0.0 | 255.2 | 813 483 | 2 974 | 108 846 | 145.7 | 125 307 | 59.0 | 41.0 | 52.1 | 25.6 | 9 831 | 86.9 |
| Kossuth | 602 | 1.7 | 431 | 0.6 | 573.3 | 1 553 530 | 3 603 | 193 168 | 467.8 | 335 347 | 53.4 | 46.6 | 75.8 | 52.2 | 13 371 | 85.9 |
| Lee | 238 | -11.9 | 270 | 1.7 | 174.4 | 731 239 | 2 710 | 88 076 | 87.8 | 99 386 | 71.8 | 28.2 | 47.0 | 24.7 | 4 811 | 77.9 |
| Linn | 335 | -4.0 | 237 | 0.6 | 295.2 | 892 921 | 3 762 | 110 495 | 165.6 | 117 202 | 70.8 | 29.2 | 59.6 | 27.2 | 7 794 | 77.3 |
| Louisa | 186 | -7.5 | 265 | 9.4 | 153.5 | 846 682 | 3 191 | 115 591 | 103.6 | 147 838 | 59.1 | 40.9 | 50.6 | 26.7 | 5 730 | 79.9 |
| Lucas | 171 | -23.0 | 245 | D | 91.2 | 532 190 | 2 174 | 54 042 | 34.3 | 49 000 | 41.1 | 58.9 | 38.9 | 12.0 | 3 108 | 73.2 |
| Lyon | 323 | -5.6 | 297 | 1.0 | 290.9 | 1 248 886 | 4 202 | 162 022 | 453.1 | 416 847 | 25.5 | 74.5 | 81.6 | 55.0 | 5 871 | 76.8 |
| Madison | 283 | -6.9 | 296 | 1.8 | 185.2 | 875 822 | 2 955 | 91 832 | 110.8 | 115 895 | 58.6 | 41.4 | 46.0 | 17.1 | 4 450 | 71.0 |
| Mahaska | 295 | -10.3 | 286 | 0.1 | 244.7 | 878 248 | 3 068 | 136 776 | 211.9 | 205 553 | 39.8 | 60.2 | 55.3 | 28.3 | 7 682 | 81.6 |
| Marion | 246 | -11.2 | 259 | 0.7 | 183.3 | 754 717 | 2 915 | 80 451 | 92.7 | 97 493 | 71.4 | 28.6 | 45.0 | 20.6 | 5 586 | 76.6 |
| Marshall | 324 | -3.3 | 349 | 0.8 | 295.3 | 1 301 147 | 3 724 | 147 211 | 189.8 | 204 537 | 73.8 | 26.2 | 62.7 | 36.9 | 7 638 | 80.3 |
| Mills | 197 | -20.2 | 385 | D | 175.0 | 1 283 812 | 3 333 | 133 637 | 71.9 | 140 662 | 93.9 | 6.1 | 59.1 | 35.2 | 3 538 | 77.9 |
| Mitchell | 294 | 1.7 | 329 | 1.3 | 270.8 | 1 179 551 | 3 582 | 152 635 | 245.9 | 275 373 | 47.1 | 52.9 | 73.7 | 47.9 | 6 495 | 80.3 |
| Monona | 394 | 0.5 | 606 | 65.7 | 346.5 | 1 923 705 | 3 172 | 197 756 | 156.9 | 241 779 | 79.1 | 20.9 | 70.9 | 43.5 | 6 340 | 78.6 |
| Monroe | 201 | -20.6 | 305 | 0.0 | 122.9 | 688 899 | 2 260 | 75 532 | 46.0 | 69 696 | 52.8 | 47.2 | 52.6 | 13.9 | 3 566 | 77.3 |
| Montgomery | 220 | -9.5 | 395 | D | 176.1 | 1 153 369 | 2 919 | 125 679 | 112.6 | 201 722 | 62.4 | 37.6 | 64.5 | 35.3 | 4 424 | 84.2 |
| Muscatine | 222 | -3.5 | 265 | 7.3 | 188.5 | 939 422 | 3 548 | 115 133 | 116.2 | 138 646 | 69.5 | 30.5 | 57.3 | 29.2 | 6 455 | 84.1 |
| O'Brien | 346 | -4.4 | 350 | D | 317.5 | 1 473 786 | 4 205 | 155 574 | 362.0 | 366 766 | 37.1 | 62.9 | 81.8 | 58.7 | 6 953 | 82.0 |
| Osceola | 251 | -2.3 | 379 | 2.0 | 237.6 | 1 469 454 | 3 879 | 178 299 | 286.6 | 432 235 | 34.4 | 65.6 | 79.6 | 55.5 | 5 396 | 84.5 |
| Page | 271 | -20.1 | 344 | 0.1 | 215.1 | 933 727 | 2 714 | 102 944 | 92.8 | 117 734 | 77.8 | 22.2 | 59.9 | 30.6 | 5 204 | 80.1 |
| Palo Alto | 353 | 8.0 | 416 | 4.4 | 337.4 | 1 505 757 | 3 618 | 172 807 | 329.6 | 388 218 | 45.8 | 54.2 | 66.2 | 44.8 | 7 565 | 84.6 |
| Plymouth | 517 | -2.6 | 359 | 2.8 | 460.6 | 1 301 406 | 3 628 | 152 681 | 467.3 | 324 065 | 33.7 | 66.3 | 74.1 | 46.7 | 10 164 | 82.0 |
| Pocahontas | 362 | 2.3 | 450 | D | 348.1 | 1 655 945 | 3 683 | 184 427 | 216.4 | 268 499 | 67.2 | 32.8 | 75.8 | 53.8 | 8 538 | 88.7 |
| Polk | 249 | 9.7 | 338 | 0.7 | 232.6 | 1 299 872 | 3 846 | 146 803 | 122.7 | 166 278 | 85.9 | 14.1 | 51.2 | 28.7 | 5 404 | 66.7 |
| Pottawattamie | 486 | -10.0 | 420 | 2.0 | 434.8 | 1 523 228 | 3 630 | 175 050 | 311.5 | 268 985 | 62.1 | 37.9 | 61.8 | 39.4 | 8 676 | 71.9 |
| Poweshiek | 313 | -9.3 | 334 | 0.0 | 267.7 | 1 107 683 | 3 321 | 129 040 | 165.7 | 176 636 | 67.8 | 32.2 | 57.2 | 31.6 | 7 347 | 85.1 |
| Ringgold | 265 | -11.4 | 361 | D | 180.8 | 821 568 | 2 273 | 78 930 | 70.3 | 95 956 | 43.5 | 56.5 | 47.3 | 18.4 | 5 878 | 81.7 |
| Sac | 363 | 7.1 | 453 | 0.7 | 337.9 | 1 747 284 | 3 857 | 182 827 | 386.6 | 482 001 | 36.4 | 63.6 | 76.1 | 52.1 | 7 373 | 86.3 |
| Scott | 249 | 8.7 | 289 | 2.0 | 230.7 | 1 214 686 | 4 206 | 154 580 | 148.3 | 172 271 | 70.5 | 29.5 | 69.2 | 39.8 | 6 581 | 76.3 |
| Shelby | 358 | 2.9 | 411 | D | 333.7 | 1 322 099 | 3 213 | 136 273 | 212.0 | 243 343 | 65.7 | 34.3 | 77.7 | 49.5 | 7 647 | 85.4 |
| Sioux | 479 | -5.1 | 288 | 9.1 | 441.8 | 1 304 456 | 4 534 | 172 473 | 1 121.1 | 673 764 | 16.1 | 83.9 | 83.3 | 57.5 | 10 189 | 71.6 |
| Story | 352 | -2.2 | 327 | 0.3 | 328.1 | 1 163 987 | 3 559 | 162 630 | 200.6 | 186 271 | 80.6 | 19.4 | 64.2 | 34.2 | 7 792 | 73.9 |
| Tama | 431 | 3.1 | 356 | 0.0 | 380.8 | 1 233 812 | 3 465 | 140 953 | 235.1 | 194 337 | 70.2 | 29.8 | 61.9 | 35.3 | 10 270 | 82.3 |
| Taylor | 283 | -8.1 | 363 | D | 209.6 | 902 297 | 2 487 | 99 662 | 119.0 | 152 754 | 44.2 | 55.8 | 48.8 | 18.1 | 6 882 | 82.3 |
| Union | 215 | -9.7 | 315 | 0.0 | 139.5 | 793 544 | 2 518 | 89 810 | 94.0 | 138 075 | 39.7 | 60.3 | 51.2 | 19.8 | 4 414 | 78.7 |
| Van Buren | 222 | -12.3 | 274 | 0.0 | 144.9 | 679 268 | 2 478 | 72 135 | 89.7 | 111 034 | 44.4 | 55.6 | 40.0 | 15.6 | 4 113 | 82.0 |
| Wapello | 166 | -19.4 | 223 | D | 119.3 | 689 369 | 3 086 | 85 364 | 55.2 | 74 247 | 68.9 | 31.1 | 41.8 | 14.2 | 3 381 | 65.3 |
| Warren | 242 | -19.1 | 203 | 0.1 | 160.3 | 636 132 | 3 130 | 71 015 | 75.2 | 63 211 | 73.8 | 26.2 | 40.5 | 12.6 | 5 353 | 66.0 |
| Washington | 326 | -2.7 | 259 | 0.2 | 268.8 | 956 033 | 3 688 | 123 019 | 269.1 | 214 082 | 35.5 | 64.5 | 59.3 | 34.9 | 10 232 | 80.8 |
| Wayne | 273 | -10.5 | 336 | 0.1 | 192.1 | 751 524 | 2 239 | 90 804 | 55.8 | 68 580 | 70.1 | 29.9 | 43.4 | 15.0 | 6 793 | 81.1 |
| Webster | 454 | 8.9 | 412 | 0.0 | 426.6 | 1 487 541 | 3 615 | 174 122 | 270.7 | 245 465 | 70.7 | 29.3 | 69.7 | 43.3 | 10 462 | 88.4 |
| Winnebago | 252 | 5.0 | 370 | D | 235.6 | 1 241 478 | 3 351 | 170 424 | 174.7 | 257 326 | 58.9 | 41.1 | 59.9 | 43.4 | 6 794 | 84.8 |
| Winneshiek | 314 | -17.4 | 221 | D | 244.2 | 719 078 | 3 250 | 110 317 | 199.7 | 140 844 | 35.7 | 64.3 | 53.6 | 29.4 | 9 875 | 85.6 |
| Woodbury | 446 | 0.9 | 388 | 10.6 | 385.3 | 1 155 786 | 2 981 | 136 018 | 244.6 | 212 862 | 57.4 | 42.6 | 58.1 | 31.9 | 8 623 | 78.0 |
| Worth | 232 | 3.6 | 339 | 0.6 | 213.8 | 1 200 627 | 3 541 | 142 303 | 105.0 | 153 778 | 86.3 | 13.7 | 55.1 | 36.7 | 6 199 | 88.5 |
| Wright | 328 | -4.9 | 425 | 0.0 | 309.1 | 1 662 127 | 3 910 | 253 945 | 405.9 | 526 463 | 34.8 | 65.2 | 63.8 | 45.1 | 8 517 | 89.5 |

| STATE County | Water use, 2005 | | Wholesale trade,[1] 2007 | | | | Retail trade,[2] 2007 | | | | Real estate and rental and leasing,[2] 2007 | | | |
|---|---|---|---|---|---|---|---|---|---|---|---|---|---|---|
| | Total water withdrawn (mil gal/day) | Gallons withdrawn per person | Number of establishments | Number of employees | Sales (mil dol) | Annual payroll (mil dol) | Number of establishments | Number of employees | Sales (mil dol) | Annual payroll (mil dol) | Number of establishments | Number of employees | Receipts (mil dol) | Annual payroll (mil dol) |
| | 133 | 134 | 135 | 136 | 137 | 138 | 139 | 140 | 141 | 142 | 143 | 144 | 145 | 146 |
| IOWA—Cont'd | | | | | | | | | | | | | | |
| Franklin | 2.7 | 254 | 29 | 176 | 154.6 | 6.3 | 42 | 353 | 65.9 | 5.6 | 14 | 36 | 3.6 | 0.4 |
| Fremont | 1.8 | 237 | 13 | 93 | 105.5 | 3.4 | 35 | 478 | 102.9 | 8.5 | 2 | D | D | D |
| Greene | 1.8 | 184 | 18 | 380 | 144.9 | 14.9 | 44 | 374 | 87.9 | 6.5 | 6 | 19 | 2.3 | 0.3 |
| Grundy | 2.0 | 164 | 17 | 225 | 269.9 | 9.8 | 57 | 490 | 109.4 | 9.0 | 8 | D | D | D |
| Guthrie | 2.6 | 226 | 18 | D | D | D | 41 | 350 | 91.3 | 5.6 | 7 | 22 | 2.1 | 0.5 |
| Hamilton | 4.2 | 261 | 31 | 772 | 558.3 | 31.8 | 65 | 683 | 149.3 | 11.0 | 10 | 19 | 2.0 | 0.2 |
| Hancock | 3.5 | 298 | 27 | 214 | 171.7 | 7.2 | 52 | 437 | 119.3 | 7.5 | 13 | 37 | 2.4 | 0.6 |
| Hardin | 7.4 | 410 | 42 | 892 | 1 191.0 | 40.6 | 90 | 815 | 161.8 | 14.6 | 17 | 31 | 3.4 | 0.6 |
| Harrison | 7.2 | 456 | 29 | 255 | 130.2 | 7.8 | 55 | 466 | 100.9 | 7.5 | 10 | 29 | 1.7 | 0.4 |
| Henry | 3.1 | 155 | 32 | 207 | 90.6 | 6.0 | 64 | 900 | 214.7 | 17.7 | 20 | 50 | 5.9 | 0.8 |
| Howard | 2.0 | 201 | 15 | 135 | 143.6 | 5.1 | 53 | 375 | 83.2 | 6.8 | 7 | 11 | 3.3 | 0.4 |
| Humboldt | 2.8 | 284 | 38 | 275 | 183.1 | 10.7 | 51 | 467 | 82.0 | 9.3 | 9 | 27 | 1.8 | 0.5 |
| Ida | 2.2 | 295 | 13 | 185 | 147.1 | 7.1 | 41 | 357 | 61.1 | 5.0 | 8 | D | D | D |
| Iowa | 2.8 | 174 | 19 | 115 | 80.2 | 4.0 | 145 | 1 204 | 213.4 | 18.3 | 4 | D | D | D |
| Jackson | 3.9 | 194 | 28 | 200 | 109.1 | 6.1 | 87 | 935 | 210.0 | 15.7 | 16 | 35 | 2.7 | 0.6 |
| Jasper | 7.5 | 200 | 41 | D | D | D | 122 | 1 424 | 274.0 | 25.8 | 31 | 81 | 8.4 | 1.6 |
| Jefferson | 2.2 | 140 | 48 | 319 | 114.6 | 9.7 | 84 | 1 205 | 333.5 | 33.9 | 20 | 43 | 6.2 | 0.8 |
| Johnson | 45.1 | 386 | 81 | 1 183 | 567.6 | 48.4 | 537 | 8 424 | 1 653.1 | 168.8 | 146 | D | D | D |
| Jones | 3.6 | 175 | 33 | 236 | 144.7 | 7.7 | 81 | 1 060 | 257.7 | 23.6 | 11 | 15 | 1.4 | 0.2 |
| Keokuk | 1.8 | 162 | 26 | 215 | 122.3 | 7.3 | 38 | 265 | 66.9 | 3.9 | 2 | D | D | D |
| Kossuth | 4.8 | 297 | 43 | 525 | 318.4 | 17.2 | 107 | 959 | 195.8 | 16.4 | 16 | 51 | 3.6 | 0.7 |
| Lee | 18.4 | 501 | 36 | 400 | 396.3 | 15.3 | 164 | 2 011 | 420.8 | 38.0 | 28 | 80 | 7.7 | 1.5 |
| Linn | 270.1 | 1 358 | 300 | 4 412 | 2 506.1 | 207.7 | 794 | 14 096 | 3 592.8 | 307.0 | 238 | 1 696 | 356.8 | 91.5 |
| Louisa | 10.4 | 880 | 12 | D | D | D | 27 | 237 | 56.5 | 3.7 | 6 | 7 | 0.4 | 0.1 |
| Lucas | 1.2 | 126 | 6 | 30 | 1.5 | 0.2 | 33 | 372 | 84.3 | 6.9 | 4 | 7 | 1.9 | 0.3 |
| Lyon | 5.8 | 489 | 23 | 226 | 215.3 | 7.7 | 54 | 419 | 91.1 | 6.5 | 7 | 7 | 1.0 | 0.1 |
| Madison | 1.7 | 115 | 13 | D | D | D | 52 | 422 | 80.6 | 7.7 | 7 | 16 | 2.1 | 0.2 |
| Mahaska | 4.0 | 181 | 36 | D | D | D | 109 | 1 229 | 242.9 | 22.7 | 12 | 56 | 5.9 | 1.0 |
| Marion | 4.8 | 146 | 41 | D | D | D | 153 | 1 726 | 333.1 | 30.8 | 40 | 92 | 9.9 | 1.5 |
| Marshall | 11.5 | 291 | 43 | 379 | 298.1 | 16.4 | 166 | 2 126 | 407.7 | 41.6 | 40 | 400 | 46.1 | 10.9 |
| Mills | 2.1 | 137 | 10 | 56 | 23.0 | 1.8 | 42 | 339 | 78.6 | 5.8 | 11 | 40 | 10.4 | 0.9 |
| Mitchell | 2.8 | 253 | 26 | 208 | 228.7 | 7.7 | 65 | 394 | 93.1 | 8.0 | 7 | 16 | 1.0 | 0.2 |
| Monona | 11.6 | 1 214 | 15 | 102 | 77.6 | 3.7 | 43 | 386 | 99.2 | 7.0 | 5 | 9 | 0.5 | 0.1 |
| Monroe | 1.8 | 227 | 13 | 162 | 46.2 | 4.9 | 33 | 290 | 62.5 | 5.2 | 2 | D | D | D |
| Montgomery | 2.2 | 197 | 13 | 109 | 150.7 | 4.5 | 56 | 510 | 88.3 | 8.6 | 9 | 49 | 4.9 | 1.1 |
| Muscatine | 306.3 | 7 164 | 52 | 481 | 377.5 | 17.2 | 158 | 2 086 | 448.6 | 42.3 | 49 | 160 | 19.9 | 4.2 |
| O'Brien | 4.4 | 307 | 33 | 407 | 322.7 | 13.9 | 104 | 844 | 169.7 | 14.0 | 7 | 33 | 4.8 | 0.7 |
| Osceola | 4.8 | 722 | 9 | D | D | D | 28 | 162 | 40.5 | 2.8 | 2 | D | D | D |
| Page | 2.8 | 173 | 16 | 155 | 116.4 | 5.6 | 92 | 738 | 163.0 | 12.8 | 11 | 20 | 1.7 | 0.3 |
| Palo Alto | 3.8 | 390 | 15 | 118 | 132.5 | 4.1 | 47 | 378 | 65.8 | 6.1 | 8 | D | D | D |
| Plymouth | 7.6 | 303 | 42 | 345 | 243.0 | 12.8 | 111 | 1 184 | 299.7 | 22.2 | 22 | 112 | 6.9 | 1.4 |
| Pocahontas | 1.8 | 232 | 14 | 229 | 86.9 | 6.4 | 38 | 306 | 79.9 | 3.6 | 1 | D | D | D |
| Polk | 58.0 | 145 | 668 | 11 440 | 6 697.2 | 536.1 | 1 658 | 28 621 | 6 714.4 | 655.9 | 567 | 3 399 | 673.2 | 120.0 |
| Pottawattamie | 509.5 | 5 678 | 91 | 1 618 | 2 256.7 | 64.7 | 326 | 6 025 | 1 503.4 | 117.5 | 95 | 425 | 66.3 | 10.5 |
| Poweshiek | 2.5 | 129 | 24 | 220 | 118.1 | 7.6 | 95 | 1 109 | 241.3 | 22.0 | 15 | 36 | 3.2 | 0.6 |
| Ringgold | 1.1 | 211 | 7 | 49 | 26.0 | 1.7 | 29 | 213 | 63.6 | 4.1 | 2 | D | D | D |
| Sac | 3.8 | 356 | 33 | 223 | 165.0 | 9.5 | 63 | 391 | 92.5 | 6.6 | 6 | 6 | 0.2 | 0.0 |
| Scott | 110.6 | 687 | 265 | D | D | D | 702 | 11 831 | 2 853.0 | 252.6 | 185 | 1 826 | 276.5 | 47.1 |
| Shelby | 2.8 | 218 | 25 | 423 | 158.6 | 11.7 | 66 | 588 | 135.1 | 10.5 | 7 | D | D | D |
| Sioux | 17.6 | 545 | 78 | 1 345 | 753.1 | 44.9 | 173 | 1 674 | 394.4 | 32.6 | 26 | 76 | 13.1 | 3.2 |
| Story | 11.9 | 149 | 80 | 599 | 432.0 | 24.7 | 320 | 4 611 | 968.3 | 91.7 | 96 | 371 | 38.1 | 10.1 |
| Tama | 5.8 | 325 | 27 | 163 | 154.9 | 5.4 | 78 | 548 | 112.5 | 9.3 | 7 | 17 | 0.9 | 0.2 |
| Taylor | 0.9 | 130 | 8 | 72 | 41.0 | 2.4 | 23 | 154 | 25.1 | 1.8 | 4 | D | D | D |
| Union | 5.4 | 449 | 16 | 236 | 384.7 | 8.1 | 60 | 779 | 153.8 | 15.1 | 18 | 46 | 4.8 | 0.9 |
| Van Buren | 0.9 | 116 | 6 | D | D | D | 30 | 243 | 36.9 | 3.0 | 3 | 4 | 0.6 | 0.1 |
| Wapello | 23.6 | 657 | 28 | D | D | D | 160 | 2 461 | 500.7 | 46.1 | 30 | 81 | 13.1 | 2.0 |
| Warren | 2.4 | 56 | 43 | 527 | 628.1 | 21.6 | 104 | 1 438 | 328.4 | 30.4 | 27 | 75 | 8.8 | 1.6 |
| Washington | 4.4 | 204 | 40 | 315 | 185.7 | 10.6 | 102 | 993 | 195.0 | 16.9 | 11 | D | D | D |
| Wayne | 0.8 | 123 | 5 | 36 | 27.0 | 1.4 | 36 | 247 | 49.2 | 3.7 | 1 | D | D | D |
| Webster | 11.3 | 291 | 68 | D | D | D | 194 | 2 723 | 577.5 | 52.3 | 42 | 120 | 18.9 | 2.9 |
| Winnebago | 2.3 | 200 | 19 | 130 | 170.0 | 4.6 | 60 | 538 | 115.0 | 8.2 | 8 | D | D | D |
| Winneshiek | 6.9 | 323 | 30 | 259 | 167.3 | 9.6 | 129 | 1 221 | 289.6 | 24.7 | 13 | 41 | 4.8 | 0.9 |
| Woodbury | 969.2 | 9 446 | 155 | 2 452 | 1 740.0 | 104.2 | 471 | 7 502 | 1 512.0 | 142.8 | 98 | 592 | 92.1 | 15.5 |
| Worth | 4.4 | 568 | 12 | D | D | D | 22 | 154 | 28.7 | 2.9 | 2 | D | D | D |
| Wright | 4.4 | 324 | 22 | 274 | 291.1 | 12.0 | 65 | 554 | 100.2 | 8.7 | 15 | 33 | 2.3 | 0.5 |

1. Merchant wholesalers, except manufacturers' sales branches and offices.    2. Employer establishments.

# Table B. States and Counties — Professional Services, Manufacturing, and Accommodation and Food Services

| STATE County | Professional, scientific, and technical services,[1] 2007 | | | | Manufacturing, 2007 | | | | Accommodation and food services, 2007 | | | |
|---|---|---|---|---|---|---|---|---|---|---|---|---|
| | Number of establish-ments | Number of employees | Receipts (mil dol) | Annual payroll (mil dol) | Number of establish-ments | Number of employees | Receipts (mil dol) | Annual payroll (mil dol) | Number of establish-ments | Number of employees | Sales (mil dol) | Annual payroll (mil dol) |
| | 147 | 148 | 149 | 150 | 151 | 152 | 153 | 154 | 155 | 156 | 157 | 158 |
| **IOWA—Cont'd** | | | | | | | | | | | | |
| Franklin | 19 | 89 | 5.0 | 2.1 | 24 | 798 | 260.0 | 28.8 | 13 | 169 | 4.4 | 1.4 |
| Fremont | 8 | 34 | 2.4 | 0.8 | 7 | D | D | D | 26 | 241 | 14.8 | 2.0 |
| Greene | 24 | 80 | 6.6 | 3.1 | NA | NA | NA | NA | 14 | 145 | 3.9 | 1.1 |
| Grundy | 17 | D | D | D | 13 | 648 | 143.8 | 21.2 | 21 | 167 | 4.3 | 1.0 |
| Guthrie | 23 | 68 | 7.3 | 1.9 | NA | NA | NA | NA | 25 | 259 | 8.3 | 2.2 |
| Hamilton | 31 | 122 | 9.7 | 3.3 | 27 | 2 916 | 1 162.4 | 95.9 | 33 | 308 | 12.2 | 3.1 |
| Hancock | 19 | 109 | 7.3 | 2.4 | 27 | 1 126 | 266.8 | 49.0 | 17 | 159 | 4.1 | 1.0 |
| Hardin | 35 | 158 | 12.2 | 3.6 | 27 | 661 | 743.1 | 23.5 | 33 | 336 | 11.4 | 3.0 |
| Harrison | 21 | D | D | D | NA | NA | NA | NA | 31 | 304 | 10.4 | 2.8 |
| Henry | 39 | D | D | D | 32 | 2 520 | 889.9 | 79.3 | 54 | 693 | 22.2 | 6.1 |
| Howard | 15 | 38 | 2.9 | 1.2 | 26 | 1 562 | 273.0 | D | 21 | 187 | 4.8 | 1.1 |
| Humboldt | 20 | 67 | 5.6 | 1.9 | 27 | 1 214 | 289.8 | 41.4 | 24 | 244 | 7.5 | 2.0 |
| Ida | 12 | 44 | 3.8 | 1.1 | 15 | 1 241 | 373.0 | 53.3 | 14 | D | D | D |
| Iowa | 22 | 70 | 9.2 | 1.3 | 37 | 3 819 | 1 478.9 | 152.4 | 41 | 684 | 25.0 | 8.0 |
| Jackson | 32 | 85 | 4.9 | 1.7 | 34 | 1 047 | 248.0 | 27.0 | 45 | 485 | 14.5 | 3.3 |
| Jasper | 56 | 566 | 134.1 | 18.9 | 34 | 733 | 170.8 | 24.3 | 68 | 960 | 30.1 | 8.4 |
| Jefferson | 122 | D | D | D | 37 | 1 252 | 246.6 | 46.9 | 39 | 468 | 16.6 | 4.3 |
| Johnson | 241 | D | D | D | 83 | 5 598 | D | 230.1 | 329 | 6 906 | 258.8 | 75.7 |
| Jones | 33 | 130 | 10.6 | 4.3 | 30 | 859 | 180.8 | 31.6 | 34 | 359 | 9.8 | 2.8 |
| Keokuk | 6 | 29 | 3.7 | 1.0 | NA | NA | NA | NA | 11 | D | D | D |
| Kossuth | 41 | 193 | 22.8 | 5.5 | 25 | 946 | 474.8 | 38.2 | 40 | 393 | 11.5 | 2.8 |
| Lee | 50 | 255 | 18.9 | 6.7 | 66 | D | D | D | 96 | 1 154 | 37.0 | 9.5 |
| Linn | 503 | 4 587 | 574.9 | 244.7 | 237 | 17 801 | 8 229.2 | 1 123.9 | 488 | 9 343 | 353.6 | 103.2 |
| Louisa | 12 | D | D | D | 11 | 1 389 | D | 41.8 | 20 | 139 | 4.5 | 1.0 |
| Lucas | 12 | D | D | D | NA | NA | NA | NA | 13 | D | D | D |
| Lyon | 20 | 108 | 12.2 | 6.8 | 23 | 645 | 100.9 | 26.6 | 17 | D | D | D |
| Madison | 32 | 112 | 10.1 | 3.9 | NA | NA | NA | NA | 26 | 224 | 7.6 | 2.0 |
| Mahaska | 33 | 149 | 19.8 | 8.3 | 34 | 1 763 | 1 618.5 | 75.9 | 36 | 495 | 16.8 | 4.6 |
| Marion | 52 | 245 | 22.0 | 9.7 | 40 | 7 392 | 1 856.9 | 376.7 | 68 | 936 | 29.0 | 8.2 |
| Marshall | 52 | 340 | 50.4 | 12.0 | 45 | 5 546 | 1 848.0 | 232.3 | 86 | 1 180 | 40.4 | 11.1 |
| Mills | 25 | D | D | D | NA | NA | NA | NA | 16 | 109 | 5.4 | 0.8 |
| Mitchell | 13 | 66 | 5.9 | 1.5 | 20 | 941 | 252.0 | 34.8 | 20 | 186 | 5.1 | 1.1 |
| Monona | 15 | 96 | 5.1 | 1.6 | NA | NA | NA | NA | 28 | 193 | 7.2 | 1.6 |
| Monroe | 13 | 39 | 3.7 | 1.1 | NA | NA | NA | NA | 20 | D | D | D |
| Montgomery | 18 | 81 | 10.4 | 2.1 | 12 | 813 | 180.8 | 36.3 | 26 | 256 | 7.6 | 2.1 |
| Muscatine | 63 | D | D | D | 68 | 7 982 | D | 366.4 | 88 | 1 266 | 44.2 | 12.1 |
| O'Brien | 25 | 103 | 11.8 | 2.9 | 25 | 511 | 305.0 | 18.7 | 34 | 406 | 9.8 | 2.6 |
| Osceola | 7 | 25 | 3.0 | 0.6 | NA | NA | NA | NA | 14 | D | D | D |
| Page | 20 | 158 | 5.8 | 2.5 | 24 | 2 019 | 348.2 | 80.9 | 34 | 439 | 12.6 | 3.6 |
| Palo Alto | 12 | 35 | 3.3 | 1.1 | 21 | 577 | 401.4 | 23.6 | 23 | 566 | 34.6 | 7.3 |
| Plymouth | 40 | 203 | 13.7 | 7.0 | 30 | 2 228 | D | D | 60 | 982 | 22.0 | 6.5 |
| Pocahontas | 19 | 51 | 3.8 | 1.1 | NA | NA | NA | NA | 13 | D | D | D |
| Polk | 1 366 | 11 826 | 1 761.6 | 645.1 | 378 | 17 620 | 7 519.9 | 797.2 | 1 064 | 19 898 | 825.2 | 243.1 |
| Pottawattamie | 143 | D | D | D | 68 | 5 371 | D | D | 193 | 5 771 | 451.5 | 97.0 |
| Poweshiek | 40 | 181 | 18.9 | 5.1 | 34 | 1 997 | 462.2 | 71.6 | 48 | 632 | 17.0 | 4.9 |
| Ringgold | 9 | 25 | 3.7 | 0.7 | NA | NA | NA | NA | 15 | D | D | D |
| Sac | 16 | 54 | 6.4 | 1.1 | NA | NA | NA | NA | 27 | D | D | D |
| Scott | 389 | D | D | D | 189 | 12 506 | 5 745.1 | 590.4 | 421 | 9 171 | 423.9 | 112.7 |
| Shelby | 26 | 150 | 11.4 | 3.7 | NA | NA | NA | NA | 27 | 292 | 8.7 | 2.3 |
| Sioux | 81 | 769 | 67.0 | 18.4 | 95 | 5 479 | 1 152.4 | 179.0 | 78 | 1 187 | 31.7 | 9.2 |
| Story | 193 | D | D | D | 75 | 4 668 | 1 970.8 | 213.4 | 224 | 4 388 | 151.0 | 43.4 |
| Tama | 21 | 90 | 14.7 | 7.7 | NA | NA | NA | NA | 33 | D | D | D |
| Taylor | 9 | D | D | D | NA | NA | NA | NA | 10 | D | D | D |
| Union | 17 | 60 | 5.0 | 1.9 | 12 | 1 450 | 214.3 | 47.7 | 27 | 344 | 11.2 | 2.8 |
| Van Buren | 11 | 23 | 2.3 | 0.7 | 12 | 734 | D | 22.1 | 12 | D | D | D |
| Wapello | 48 | D | D | D | 28 | 4 309 | 1 840.4 | 178.0 | 76 | 1 116 | 41.5 | 11.3 |
| Warren | 62 | 218 | 18.4 | 6.3 | 27 | 545 | D | D | 60 | 792 | 25.1 | 6.5 |
| Washington | 52 | D | D | D | 39 | 1 114 | D | 33.7 | 41 | 1 224 | 114.7 | 21.3 |
| Wayne | 7 | 28 | 2.6 | 0.6 | NA | NA | NA | NA | 10 | D | D | D |
| Webster | 75 | 419 | 31.4 | 15.1 | 50 | 2 483 | 1 909.4 | 122.4 | 81 | 1 399 | 61.9 | 15.7 |
| Winnebago | 21 | 76 | 7.6 | 2.0 | 21 | 4 215 | 1 094.3 | 170.7 | 18 | 231 | 6.4 | 1.4 |
| Winneshiek | 31 | 145 | 15.2 | 5.8 | 31 | 1 721 | 288.7 | 58.0 | 58 | 732 | 21.5 | 6.2 |
| Woodbury | 190 | D | D | D | 98 | 5 073 | 2 827.5 | 210.2 | 262 | 4 699 | 158.4 | 47.3 |
| Worth | 10 | D | D | D | 13 | 593 | 248.9 | 20.7 | 13 | 110 | 4.7 | 1.0 |
| Wright | 24 | 158 | 11.2 | 3.3 | 26 | 1 096 | 863.3 | 49.5 | 37 | 242 | 7.6 | 2.0 |

1. Establishment subject to federal tax.

# Table B. States and Counties — Health Care and Social Assistance, Other Services, and Federal Funds

| STATE County | Health care and social assistance, 2007 | | | | Other services, 2007 | | | | Federal funds and grants, 2009–2010 — Expenditures (mil dol) | | | |
|---|---|---|---|---|---|---|---|---|---|---|---|---|
| | | | | | | | | | | Direct payments for individuals[1] | | |
| | Number of establishments | Number of employees | Receipts (mil dol) | Annual payroll (mil dol) | Number of establishments | Number of employees | Receipts (mil dol) | Annual payroll (mil dol) | Total | Social Security and government retirement | Medicare | Food Stamps and Supplemental Security Income |
| | 159 | 160 | 161 | 162 | 163 | 164 | 165 | 166 | 167 | 168 | 169 | 170 |
| **IOWA—Cont'd** | | | | | | | | | | | | |
| Franklin | 31 | 524 | 28.1 | 13.3 | 27 | 64 | 5.5 | 1.5 | 83.3 | 35.9 | 18.7 | 2.5 |
| Fremont | 16 | 324 | 18.3 | 8.0 | 14 | D | D | D | 80.8 | 33.8 | 19.6 | 2.6 |
| Greene | 27 | 652 | 29.8 | 15.1 | 23 | 92 | 5.6 | 1.3 | 84.9 | 37.1 | 19.6 | 2.6 |
| Grundy | 29 | 387 | 21.1 | 9.2 | 23 | D | D | D | 86.2 | 40.3 | 20.9 | 1.3 |
| Guthrie | 33 | 505 | 27.2 | 12.6 | 25 | D | D | D | 90.4 | 41.2 | 22.0 | 2.3 |
| Hamilton | 36 | 633 | 47.0 | 18.1 | 36 | 118 | 13.1 | 3.5 | 131.9 | 55.7 | 33.6 | 3.1 |
| Hancock | 17 | 453 | 27.1 | 10.7 | 30 | 214 | 25.9 | 8.1 | 87.4 | 38.4 | 19.5 | 2.1 |
| Hardin | 41 | 995 | 48.9 | 23.7 | 49 | 140 | 12.5 | 3.2 | 171.4 | 69.9 | 38.8 | 4.5 |
| Harrison | 36 | 657 | 43.3 | 18.1 | 23 | D | D | D | 125.9 | 54.3 | 31.6 | 3.9 |
| Henry | 60 | 1 081 | 80.3 | 38.6 | 41 | 158 | 8.7 | 3.3 | 138.3 | 65.2 | 28.4 | 4.4 |
| Howard | 24 | 431 | 24.2 | 12.3 | 19 | 47 | 3.4 | 0.8 | 81.9 | 32.5 | 18.6 | 1.9 |
| Humboldt | 22 | 444 | 25.6 | 11.2 | 18 | 38 | 4.0 | 0.7 | 80.0 | 34.2 | 21.2 | 2.6 |
| Ida | 19 | 420 | 23.8 | 10.8 | 16 | 59 | 4.1 | 1.3 | 58.2 | 24.5 | 14.7 | 0.9 |
| Iowa | 38 | 727 | 36.5 | 17.8 | 22 | 52 | 5.5 | 1.1 | 102.1 | 51.0 | 23.6 | 2.3 |
| Jackson | 40 | 896 | 45.3 | 22.1 | 44 | 114 | 13.4 | 2.3 | 158.1 | 67.6 | 38.7 | 6.5 |
| Jasper | 83 | 1 565 | 97.5 | 46.1 | 60 | 249 | 16.5 | 4.2 | 236.6 | 115.9 | 58.9 | 7.2 |
| Jefferson | 50 | 697 | 48.1 | 18.8 | 44 | 152 | 21.6 | 2.9 | 115.4 | 45.1 | 23.3 | 5.8 |
| Johnson | 357 | 15 466 | 1 501.0 | 577.8 | 213 | 1 376 | 173.4 | 35.3 | 1 055.6 | 243.9 | 79.6 | 16.4 |
| Jones | 44 | 794 | 40.3 | 18.4 | 40 | 86 | 10.2 | 2.1 | 128.0 | 63.3 | 28.1 | 4.3 |
| Keokuk | 21 | 373 | 15.5 | 7.6 | 18 | 49 | 4.0 | 0.9 | 105.7 | 40.9 | 25.3 | 3.4 |
| Kossuth | 41 | 864 | 57.4 | 23.1 | 57 | 129 | 17.4 | 2.5 | 143.8 | 58.7 | 30.5 | 3.0 |
| Lee | 114 | D | D | D | 73 | 285 | 22.5 | 5.0 | 305.3 | 123.9 | 76.1 | 15.4 |
| Linn | 540 | 13 371 | 1 173.9 | 491.2 | 402 | 2 594 | 243.7 | 63.2 | 2 581.4 | 575.2 | 228.6 | 50.7 |
| Louisa | 24 | 322 | 11.2 | 5.3 | 14 | D | D | D | 108.2 | 33.8 | 15.8 | 3.6 |
| Lucas | 29 | 550 | 31.0 | 13.3 | 9 | 23 | 2.3 | 0.5 | 91.1 | 32.7 | 19.2 | 4.0 |
| Lyon | 23 | 403 | 18.2 | 7.6 | 31 | 88 | 7.2 | 1.4 | 70.6 | 30.2 | 18.1 | 1.4 |
| Madison | 27 | 598 | 30.4 | 13.6 | 27 | D | D | D | 101.2 | 45.9 | 24.0 | 2.3 |
| Mahaska | 59 | 934 | 61.5 | 28.0 | 41 | 156 | 12.4 | 2.9 | 158.8 | 65.9 | 36.0 | 6.9 |
| Marion | 93 | 2 430 | 170.3 | 73.0 | 65 | 242 | 22.1 | 5.2 | 244.5 | 120.6 | 47.7 | 6.3 |
| Marshall | 84 | 2 143 | 139.6 | 66.8 | 69 | 465 | 33.2 | 10.0 | 317.6 | 139.1 | 60.6 | 12.1 |
| Mills | 29 | 733 | 27.6 | 14.3 | 25 | D | D | D | 121.4 | 57.3 | 25.9 | 4.2 |
| Mitchell | 30 | 561 | 33.9 | 13.4 | 31 | 70 | 6.1 | 1.5 | 85.6 | 41.3 | 21.9 | 1.3 |
| Monona | 23 | 690 | 40.7 | 19.5 | 16 | 40 | 3.2 | 0.9 | 104.6 | 36.1 | 29.5 | 2.9 |
| Monroe | 22 | 485 | 24.8 | 11.1 | 7 | 19 | 2.2 | 0.4 | 77.7 | 29.6 | 20.5 | 2.7 |
| Montgomery | 38 | 849 | 49.6 | 22.4 | 34 | 93 | 8.6 | 1.7 | 110.6 | 43.2 | 29.4 | 3.7 |
| Muscatine | 92 | 1 866 | 111.1 | 50.1 | 77 | D | D | D | 314.5 | 124.9 | 52.1 | 14.8 |
| O'Brien | 49 | 1 391 | 66.5 | 29.4 | 43 | 170 | 16.9 | 3.9 | 123.5 | 50.8 | 30.8 | 2.3 |
| Osceola | 14 | 307 | 16.1 | 6.6 | 15 | 26 | 2.5 | 0.4 | 47.2 | 19.4 | 12.7 | 1.0 |
| Page | 51 | 1 587 | 91.4 | 43.4 | 33 | 102 | 6.6 | 1.5 | 143.2 | 61.9 | 35.4 | 4.7 |
| Palo Alto | 37 | 688 | 40.3 | 16.8 | 20 | 22 | 2.0 | 0.4 | 95.7 | 35.8 | 22.7 | 2.1 |
| Plymouth | 54 | 986 | 65.3 | 25.4 | 55 | 164 | 14.4 | 3.0 | 160.9 | 66.9 | 35.8 | 2.5 |
| Pocahontas | 21 | 318 | 17.9 | 8.0 | 14 | 38 | 2.4 | 0.5 | 78.8 | 29.1 | 20.9 | 2.1 |
| Polk | 1 021 | 32 180 | 3 108.7 | 1 332.6 | 965 | 6 980 | 751.7 | 206.0 | 4 643.2 | 1 071.3 | 503.4 | 124.3 |
| Pottawattamie | 194 | 4 453 | 364.2 | 159.4 | 148 | 678 | 52.0 | 15.7 | 694.2 | 309.5 | 146.0 | 35.1 |
| Poweshiek | 59 | 1 281 | 89.6 | 42.0 | 35 | 113 | 9.3 | 2.5 | 130.3 | 60.1 | 32.2 | 3.8 |
| Ringgold | 15 | 337 | 19.9 | 8.8 | 12 | 32 | 4.0 | 0.9 | 55.0 | 20.5 | 11.5 | 1.6 |
| Sac | 24 | 558 | 28.5 | 14.0 | 24 | 57 | 6.1 | 1.1 | 95.1 | 37.9 | 23.4 | 1.9 |
| Scott | 456 | 10 963 | 944.3 | 414.0 | 342 | 2 063 | 168.0 | 47.5 | 1 462.7 | 539.6 | 200.1 | 75.5 |
| Shelby | 38 | 1 065 | 52.4 | 24.4 | 24 | 85 | 7.4 | 1.6 | 111.2 | 43.0 | 32.1 | 2.7 |
| Sioux | 74 | 2 078 | 119.2 | 49.1 | 87 | 292 | 26.9 | 6.5 | 197.0 | 75.2 | 43.5 | 2.5 |
| Story | 172 | 5 026 | 415.3 | 172.4 | 148 | 1 096 | 212.9 | 28.7 | 1 268.6 | 195.3 | 80.6 | 12.0 |
| Tama | 30 | 314 | 15.3 | 7.6 | 21 | 64 | 5.3 | 1.1 | 134.9 | 60.0 | 31.5 | 3.6 |
| Taylor | 15 | 206 | 7.8 | 3.8 | 12 | 53 | 4.2 | 1.0 | 65.6 | 25.5 | 15.0 | 2.2 |
| Union | 38 | 904 | 55.5 | 24.8 | 30 | 139 | 13.1 | 2.6 | 142.0 | 53.3 | 25.1 | 4.8 |
| Van Buren | 14 | 353 | 17.0 | 8.5 | 11 | D | D | D | 68.1 | 29.5 | 16.0 | 2.0 |
| Wapello | 103 | 2 848 | 199.1 | 88.0 | 58 | 234 | 15.9 | 4.5 | 353.3 | 132.5 | 80.4 | 18.9 |
| Warren | 74 | 1 230 | 67.1 | 31.9 | 58 | 218 | 14.2 | 4.5 | 223.6 | 125.0 | 43.9 | 6.0 |
| Washington | 66 | 1 248 | 61.5 | 29.4 | 50 | 153 | 19.8 | 3.4 | 147.9 | 69.9 | 34.8 | 4.4 |
| Wayne | 19 | 309 | 18.5 | 8.2 | 12 | 31 | 2.7 | 0.5 | 80.8 | 26.3 | 19.1 | 2.4 |
| Webster | 117 | 2 977 | 239.7 | 108.3 | 77 | 404 | 43.4 | 11.0 | 368.9 | 134.3 | 83.6 | 14.6 |
| Winnebago | 41 | 628 | 27.5 | 12.0 | 15 | 37 | 15.7 | 0.7 | 100.2 | 39.0 | 21.6 | 1.8 |
| Winneshiek | 58 | 1 455 | 90.2 | 40.4 | 42 | 177 | 16.2 | 3.1 | 151.9 | 62.5 | 27.1 | 2.4 |
| Woodbury | 333 | 8 054 | 718.5 | 273.3 | 193 | 1 279 | 90.6 | 28.8 | 783.5 | 283.5 | 171.2 | 31.1 |
| Worth | 13 | D | D | D | 13 | 34 | 4.3 | 0.7 | 57.3 | 25.6 | 14.3 | 1.3 |
| Wright | 40 | 915 | 68.4 | 26.0 | 30 | 73 | 5.7 | 1.1 | 124.0 | 53.3 | 31.2 | 3.0 |

1. State totals may include programs not allocated by county.

**Federal Funds, Residential Construction, and Local Government Finances**

| STATE County | Federal funds and grants, 2009–2010 (cont.) | | | | | | | Value of residential construction authorized by building permits, 2011 | | Local government finances, 2007 | | | | |
|---|---|---|---|---|---|---|---|---|---|---|---|---|---|---|
| | Expenditures (mil dol) (cont.) | | | | | | | | | General revenue | | | | |
| | Procurement contract awards | | | Grants[1] | | | | | | | | Taxes | | |
| | | | | | | | | | | | | | Per capita[2] (dollars) | |
| | Salaries and wages | Defense | Other | Medicaid and other health-related | Nutrition and family welfare | Education | Other | New construction ($1,000) | Number of housing units | Total (mil dol) | Inter-governmental (mil dol) | Total (mil dol) | Total | Property |
| | 171 | 172 | 173 | 174 | 175 | 176 | 177 | 178 | 179 | 180 | 181 | 182 | 183 | 184 |
| IOWA—Cont'd | | | | | | | | | | | | | | |
| Franklin | 2.6 | 0.0 | 0.6 | 9.8 | 1.7 | 0.4 | 0.4 | 565 | 3 | 50.1 | 18.4 | 16.5 | 1 560 | 1 325 |
| Fremont | 2.4 | 0.1 | 0.5 | 9.8 | 1.5 | 0.2 | 0.1 | 1 792 | 11 | 26.6 | 12.9 | 11.4 | 1 500 | 1 192 |
| Greene | 3.0 | 0.0 | 0.7 | 11.5 | 1.7 | 0.2 | 0.5 | 2 354 | 11 | 49.2 | 13.4 | 15.2 | 1 604 | 1 397 |
| Grundy | 3.3 | 0.0 | 0.7 | 5.2 | 1.4 | 0.2 | 0.2 | 3 127 | 17 | 49.4 | 16.0 | 18.1 | 1 492 | 1 232 |
| Guthrie | 4.2 | 0.0 | 0.9 | 10.9 | 1.9 | 0.3 | 0.2 | 2 589 | 11 | 53.7 | 20.5 | 19.9 | 1 797 | 1 459 |
| Hamilton | 4.2 | 0.0 | 1.1 | 12.1 | 2.6 | 0.3 | 4.2 | 755 | 4 | 71.7 | 22.9 | 24.6 | 1 580 | 1 352 |
| Hancock | 3.2 | 0.0 | 6.5 | 5.5 | 1.8 | 0.2 | 1.5 | 1 621 | 8 | 46.6 | 15.7 | 17.1 | 1 506 | 1 260 |
| Hardin | 11.5 | 0.1 | 1.4 | 15.5 | 3.2 | 1.0 | 0.4 | 2 392 | 10 | 81.2 | 24.6 | 29.0 | 1 651 | 1 331 |
| Harrison | 5.3 | 0.0 | 3.5 | 14.9 | 2.8 | 0.4 | 0.6 | 3 150 | 18 | 51.2 | 24.4 | 22.6 | 1 464 | 1 219 |
| Henry | 10.2 | 0.0 | 1.3 | 13.9 | 2.6 | 0.9 | 0.6 | 2 050 | 14 | 89.3 | 27.3 | 24.1 | 1 197 | 940 |
| Howard | 2.4 | 0.5 | 0.9 | 12.0 | 2.1 | 0.2 | 0.9 | 963 | 4 | 47.8 | 14.3 | 16.8 | 1 756 | 1 441 |
| Humboldt | 4.3 | 0.0 | 1.0 | 8.1 | 1.7 | 0.4 | 0.6 | 1 457 | 9 | 44.2 | 12.7 | 14.0 | 1 455 | 1 193 |
| Ida | 2.5 | 0.0 | 0.5 | 5.8 | 1.4 | 0.2 | 0.2 | 1 286 | 8 | 21.3 | 9.0 | 8.5 | 1 222 | 1 000 |
| Iowa | 5.1 | 0.2 | 1.1 | 7.5 | 2.0 | 0.3 | 0.4 | 1 830 | 13 | 59.5 | 20.5 | 24.0 | 1 509 | 1 122 |
| Jackson | 5.5 | 4.8 | 1.3 | 22.4 | 3.7 | 1.0 | 0.4 | 3 419 | 25 | 70.1 | 25.4 | 23.0 | 1 148 | 875 |
| Jasper | 8.1 | 0.0 | 1.6 | 24.2 | 4.9 | 0.8 | 3.6 | 4 878 | 28 | 149.7 | 42.4 | 55.8 | 1 518 | 1 268 |
| Jefferson | 12.8 | 0.0 | 1.1 | 10.6 | 2.0 | 0.4 | 4.6 | 200 | 2 | 59.1 | 20.4 | 17.1 | 1 097 | 862 |
| Johnson | 124.4 | 11.9 | 65.3 | 413.4 | 11.9 | 12.2 | 41.8 | 122 724 | 747 | 353.8 | 109.4 | 175.0 | 1 392 | 1 265 |
| Jones | 4.4 | 0.0 | 1.1 | 12.7 | 2.9 | 0.4 | 0.3 | 2 096 | 14 | 57.7 | 25.0 | 24.1 | 1 181 | 930 |
| Keokuk | 5.2 | 0.0 | 2.5 | 12.6 | 1.9 | 0.5 | 2.4 | 1 175 | 5 | 37.6 | 14.7 | 15.5 | 1 437 | 1 210 |
| Kossuth | 16.2 | 0.0 | 1.2 | 16.2 | 2.4 | 0.4 | 1.1 | 3 245 | 13 | 70.4 | 27.6 | 24.6 | 1 576 | 1 278 |
| Lee | 9.9 | 1.8 | 26.9 | 32.2 | 5.5 | 1.9 | 2.1 | 2 526 | 19 | 104.2 | 46.8 | 42.8 | 1 201 | 868 |
| Linn | 96.4 | 1 128.5 | 251.2 | 128.4 | 28.8 | 5.6 | 36.7 | 71 552 | 699 | 818.0 | 309.3 | 305.9 | 1 486 | 1 353 |
| Louisa | 4.2 | 2.6 | 5.8 | 10.3 | 2.0 | 0.3 | 22.5 | 3 217 | 19 | 46.8 | 20.3 | 18.6 | 1 580 | 1 190 |
| Lucas | 5.3 | 5.1 | 0.6 | 14.9 | 2.1 | 0.5 | 1.0 | 200 | 1 | 40.2 | 13.5 | 10.4 | 1 100 | 889 |
| Lyon | 3.1 | 0.0 | 0.7 | 7.5 | 1.8 | 0.2 | 0.2 | 7 670 | 38 | 39.0 | 16.2 | 15.9 | 1 413 | 1 112 |
| Madison | 3.2 | 0.0 | 0.7 | 11.7 | 2.3 | 0.2 | 4.5 | 7 092 | 39 | 64.8 | 23.7 | 21.5 | 1 393 | 1 159 |
| Mahaska | 5.0 | 0.0 | 1.0 | 23.5 | 3.3 | 1.1 | 2.4 | 2 189 | 15 | 84.6 | 22.8 | 29.0 | 1 301 | 1 048 |
| Marion | 13.1 | 13.2 | 1.7 | 24.8 | 4.6 | 2.0 | 1.8 | 7 919 | 42 | 96.2 | 39.4 | 40.8 | 1 244 | 949 |
| Marshall | 19.4 | 0.0 | 3.7 | 35.7 | 9.1 | 3.5 | 20.7 | 3 617 | 18 | 152.1 | 70.7 | 54.4 | 1 384 | 1 056 |
| Mills | 6.5 | 0.0 | 0.8 | 17.2 | 2.2 | 0.3 | 0.7 | 1 165 | 7 | 44.8 | 20.2 | 19.3 | 1 272 | 1 103 |
| Mitchell | 2.9 | 0.0 | 0.8 | 7.5 | 1.5 | 0.4 | 0.9 | 4 064 | 22 | 45.9 | 12.2 | 14.4 | 1 345 | 1 114 |
| Monona | 3.5 | 0.0 | 0.8 | 16.6 | 2.4 | 0.3 | 0.2 | 4 717 | 30 | 34.6 | 12.9 | 13.2 | 1 444 | 1 207 |
| Monroe | 2.7 | 0.2 | 0.5 | 13.2 | 1.7 | 0.3 | 0.6 | 2 320 | 15 | 19.5 | 9.3 | 8.2 | 1 077 | 802 |
| Montgomery | 13.8 | 0.0 | 0.8 | 11.5 | 2.0 | 0.5 | 0.6 | 360 | 2 | 57.4 | 16.1 | 15.8 | 1 432 | 1 165 |
| Muscatine | 9.9 | 50.6 | 15.0 | 25.3 | 6.9 | 1.0 | 4.5 | 5 200 | 29 | 151.3 | 56.6 | 59.2 | 1 395 | 1 102 |
| O'Brien | 7.7 | 0.0 | 1.0 | 18.3 | 2.2 | 0.9 | 0.3 | 1 975 | 8 | 61.6 | 25.3 | 22.2 | 1 577 | 1 245 |
| Osceola | 1.9 | 0.1 | 1.1 | 4.6 | 1.0 | 0.1 | 0.2 | 250 | 1 | 17.2 | 7.8 | 7.2 | 1 108 | 974 |
| Page | 5.7 | 0.0 | 1.3 | 21.2 | 2.9 | 0.8 | 1.9 | 4 211 | 43 | 65.6 | 21.0 | 18.8 | 1 184 | 899 |
| Palo Alto | 3.1 | 0.0 | 0.7 | 16.4 | 5.0 | 0.2 | 1.1 | 1 345 | 5 | 52.1 | 14.0 | 17.8 | 1 888 | 1 398 |
| Plymouth | 18.3 | 4.1 | 2.5 | 13.3 | 5.3 | 0.6 | 0.3 | 8 549 | 43 | 100.1 | 31.0 | 34.5 | 1 416 | 1 118 |
| Pocahontas | 6.7 | 0.0 | 0.6 | 7.5 | 1.6 | 0.2 | 0.9 | 500 | 3 | 30.9 | 10.2 | 10.6 | 1 383 | 1 161 |
| Polk | 618.0 | 83.0 | 176.3 | 398.0 | 181.5 | 238.2 | 1 125.6 | 421 867 | 2 254 | 1 784.5 | 563.4 | 784.3 | 1 875 | 1 581 |
| Pottawattamie | 36.7 | 0.6 | 4.2 | 99.0 | 14.3 | 3.7 | 13.5 | 28 133 | 137 | 380.1 | 153.0 | 153.1 | 1 713 | 1 264 |
| Poweshiek | 4.3 | 4.5 | 1.1 | 11.1 | 2.4 | 0.4 | 0.9 | 2 974 | 21 | 56.8 | 21.7 | 23.8 | 1 276 | 1 057 |
| Ringgold | 2.8 | 0.0 | 0.8 | 7.5 | 1.5 | 0.2 | 1.2 | 1 050 | 9 | 27.5 | 8.6 | 7.5 | 1 462 | 1 339 |
| Sac | 5.1 | 0.0 | 0.8 | 7.5 | 2.2 | 0.4 | 0.5 | 1 230 | 6 | 49.6 | 13.7 | 14.9 | 1 435 | 1 207 |
| Scott | 73.1 | 57.0 | 7.9 | 128.9 | 27.8 | 5.8 | 28.9 | 75 420 | 474 | 609.5 | 239.1 | 265.9 | 1 634 | 1 314 |
| Shelby | 4.3 | 0.0 | 0.9 | 14.9 | 5.5 | 0.3 | 0.2 | 5 187 | 40 | 63.5 | 18.3 | 17.9 | 1 456 | 1 197 |
| Sioux | 7.6 | 0.9 | 6.3 | 33.1 | 3.8 | 0.5 | 6.9 | 15 254 | 69 | 128.2 | 31.9 | 39.5 | 1 220 | 978 |
| Story | 85.6 | 15.0 | 63.0 | 61.0 | 8.3 | 2.6 | 699.8 | 44 503 | 457 | 394.2 | 77.8 | 112.0 | 1 321 | 1 045 |
| Tama | 4.9 | 0.0 | 1.2 | 12.9 | 3.0 | 1.3 | 3.6 | 3 455 | 15 | 63.8 | 30.8 | 25.7 | 1 440 | 1 158 |
| Taylor | 3.0 | 0.0 | 0.6 | 9.7 | 1.8 | 0.3 | 0.5 | 0 | 0 | 21.5 | 10.4 | 8.2 | 1 285 | 1 065 |
| Union | 6.4 | 0.1 | 1.2 | 18.9 | 3.6 | 0.9 | 16.6 | 1 550 | 6 | 88.4 | 37.1 | 17.6 | 1 453 | 1 137 |
| Van Buren | 3.3 | 0.0 | 0.7 | 7.1 | 1.4 | 0.4 | 0.6 | 0 | 0 | 32.2 | 15.5 | 8.6 | 1 117 | 890 |
| Wapello | 17.4 | 0.2 | 2.6 | 63.6 | 9.2 | 2.8 | 4.8 | 1 272 | 14 | 162.8 | 78.5 | 43.6 | 1 228 | 880 |
| Warren | 8.1 | 0.1 | 2.9 | 19.0 | 5.0 | 1.7 | 1.9 | 29 014 | 124 | 124.0 | 56.2 | 49.7 | 1 118 | 955 |
| Washington | 8.8 | 0.0 | 1.0 | 13.9 | 2.6 | 0.8 | 1.0 | 2 197 | 15 | 83.0 | 27.0 | 27.0 | 1 264 | 975 |
| Wayne | 2.6 | 0.0 | 0.6 | 15.5 | 1.9 | 0.3 | 0.7 | 338 | 2 | 28.8 | 10.5 | 7.0 | 1 113 | 967 |
| Webster | 33.1 | 4.5 | 4.7 | 44.8 | 8.2 | 1.4 | 7.6 | 2 081 | 15 | 157.6 | 68.6 | 49.6 | 1 285 | 1 050 |
| Winnebago | 3.5 | 0.0 | 1.0 | 12.2 | 1.8 | 0.4 | 10.7 | 2 569 | 12 | 44.7 | 18.7 | 19.1 | 1 739 | 1 322 |
| Winneshiek | 10.0 | 0.0 | 1.2 | 11.7 | 5.7 | 2.4 | 4.2 | 8 853 | 43 | 127.6 | 41.6 | 29.0 | 1 388 | 1 110 |
| Woodbury | 85.5 | 9.6 | 12.5 | 103.6 | 19.9 | 6.3 | 19.9 | 15 862 | 76 | 418.3 | 184.4 | 161.2 | 1 576 | 1 141 |
| Worth | 2.4 | 0.0 | 0.6 | 5.8 | 1.1 | 0.3 | 0.3 | 490 | 3 | 22.5 | 8.6 | 11.3 | 1 473 | 1 192 |
| Wright | 9.7 | 0.0 | 1.1 | 12.1 | 2.4 | 0.3 | 1.0 | 787 | 5 | 77.7 | 21.7 | 21.7 | 1 658 | 1 381 |

1. State totals may include programs not allocated by county.    2. Based on the resident population estimated as of July 1 of the year shown.

# Table B. States and Counties — Local Government Finances, Government Employment, and Voting

| STATE County | Total (mil dol) | Per capita[1] (dollars) | Educa- tion | Health and hospitals | Police protec- tion | Public welfare | High- ways | Total (mil dol) | Per capita[1] (dollars) | Federal civilian | Federal military | State and local | Demo- cratic | Republi- can | All other |
|---|---|---|---|---|---|---|---|---|---|---|---|---|---|---|---|
| | 185 | 186 | 187 | 188 | 189 | 190 | 191 | 192 | 193 | 194 | 195 | 196 | 197 | 198 | 199 |
| **IOWA—Cont'd** | | | | | | | | | | | | | | | |
| Franklin | 49.9 | 4 718 | 40.1 | 31.5 | 3.8 | 0.2 | 9.6 | 18.4 | 1 739 | 35 | 45 | 744 | 50.0 | 48.6 | 1.4 |
| Fremont | 25.7 | 3 388 | 53.4 | 5.2 | 2.1 | 0.6 | 13.7 | 9.0 | 1 194 | 32 | 31 | 454 | 47.4 | 51.1 | 1.5 |
| Greene | 48.9 | 5 141 | 35.5 | 37.7 | 2.7 | 0.0 | 8.6 | 15.7 | 1 652 | 40 | 39 | 822 | 49.4 | 48.9 | 1.7 |
| Grundy | 50.4 | 4 151 | 43.8 | 17.9 | 3.1 | 0.1 | 10.2 | 29.8 | 2 453 | 42 | 52 | 646 | 40.9 | 57.8 | 1.4 |
| Guthrie | 49.3 | 4 458 | 53.2 | 18.2 | 3.0 | 0.1 | 8.3 | 32.5 | 2 936 | 57 | 45 | 843 | 44.9 | 52.6 | 2.6 |
| Hamilton | 69.2 | 4 437 | 38.6 | 27.5 | 4.3 | 0.5 | 9.8 | 28.0 | 1 792 | 47 | 65 | 1 202 | 49.7 | 48.4 | 1.9 |
| Hancock | 47.4 | 4 168 | 35.3 | 24.1 | 3.7 | 0.3 | 11.4 | 19.1 | 1 676 | 45 | 47 | 694 | 47.3 | 50.9 | 1.8 |
| Hardin | 79.4 | 4 525 | 41.4 | 24.4 | 4.5 | 0.2 | 8.7 | 29.1 | 1 660 | 77 | 72 | 1 795 | 49.6 | 48.7 | 1.7 |
| Harrison | 49.8 | 3 230 | 60.3 | 1.7 | 5.8 | 0.1 | 13.3 | 40.0 | 2 599 | 74 | 62 | 884 | 46.9 | 51.5 | 1.6 |
| Henry | 86.1 | 4 278 | 39.7 | 32.5 | 3.2 | 0.7 | 6.3 | 85.1 | 4 231 | 74 | 84 | 1 798 | 46.4 | 51.4 | 2.2 |
| Howard | 44.0 | 4 608 | 40.6 | 31.7 | 2.4 | 0.2 | 8.8 | 10.2 | 1 071 | 33 | 40 | 869 | 62.2 | 36.4 | 1.4 |
| Humboldt | 45.2 | 4 696 | 34.0 | 25.6 | 3.0 | 0.3 | 9.8 | 19.2 | 1 998 | 56 | 41 | 633 | 42.2 | 56.5 | 1.3 |
| Ida | 20.9 | 3 005 | 54.1 | 3.0 | 4.4 | 0.3 | 14.0 | 8.5 | 1 228 | 34 | 29 | 382 | 41.0 | 57.4 | 1.6 |
| Iowa | 60.7 | 3 817 | 43.1 | 16.6 | 3.7 | 0.4 | 12.8 | 27.4 | 1 723 | 62 | 68 | 954 | 49.2 | 49.0 | 1.8 |
| Jackson | 73.6 | 3 675 | 44.7 | 19.0 | 3.3 | 0.3 | 10.2 | 37.0 | 1 847 | 79 | 82 | 1 040 | 61.3 | 36.9 | 1.8 |
| Jasper | 146.1 | 3 975 | 37.8 | 27.2 | 4.0 | 1.4 | 4.9 | 92.3 | 2 511 | 100 | 152 | 2 327 | 52.8 | 45.3 | 1.9 |
| Jefferson | 66.5 | 4 259 | 29.4 | 29.8 | 3.5 | 0.5 | 10.6 | 50.6 | 3 241 | 71 | 70 | 1 014 | 58.7 | 38.5 | 2.8 |
| Johnson | 413.7 | 3 291 | 32.3 | 4.2 | 4.2 | 0.5 | 4.3 | 678.6 | 5 399 | 1 746 | 612 | 31 717 | 69.9 | 28.4 | 1.7 |
| Jones | 55.2 | 2 708 | 56.0 | 4.5 | 4.3 | 0.6 | 12.8 | 22.8 | 1 116 | 56 | 86 | 1 359 | 54.4 | 44.0 | 1.6 |
| Keokuk | 42.2 | 3 915 | 46.3 | 25.9 | 2.1 | 0.9 | 11.2 | 21.0 | 1 948 | 59 | 43 | 530 | 47.0 | 50.6 | 2.5 |
| Kossuth | 71.1 | 4 558 | 32.6 | 31.1 | 2.7 | 0.2 | 12.2 | 16.1 | 1 030 | 68 | 64 | 1 054 | 50.8 | 47.6 | 1.6 |
| Lee | 102.8 | 2 885 | 50.2 | 4.6 | 6.2 | 3.2 | 7.7 | 56.3 | 1 582 | 95 | 165 | 2 115 | 57.0 | 41.0 | 2.0 |
| Linn | 801.6 | 3 894 | 57.0 | 3.8 | 4.6 | 1.5 | 5.3 | 849.1 | 4 125 | 1 070 | 891 | 12 969 | 60.0 | 38.5 | 1.5 |
| Louisa | 44.0 | 3 733 | 63.3 | 1.3 | 4.3 | 0.2 | 9.9 | 89.9 | 7 623 | 63 | 47 | 719 | 51.3 | 47.0 | 1.7 |
| Lucas | 38.3 | 4 070 | 35.1 | 32.9 | 2.5 | 0.2 | 11.6 | 44.7 | 4 748 | 39 | 37 | 660 | 45.3 | 52.1 | 2.6 |
| Lyon | 38.0 | 3 377 | 53.5 | 4.0 | 4.0 | 0.2 | 13.1 | 20.4 | 1 813 | 43 | 49 | 638 | 26.9 | 71.9 | 1.2 |
| Madison | 61.4 | 3 982 | 43.8 | 27.5 | 3.9 | 0.4 | 9.8 | 105.8 | 6 860 | 46 | 66 | 982 | 44.0 | 54.0 | 2.0 |
| Mahaska | 77.3 | 3 467 | 36.1 | 34.0 | 4.3 | 0.2 | 10.2 | 47.8 | 2 145 | 60 | 94 | 1 396 | 40.8 | 57.4 | 1.8 |
| Marion | 98.6 | 3 009 | 58.2 | 3.9 | 4.2 | 0.5 | 8.6 | 91.3 | 2 784 | 149 | 139 | 1 633 | 43.6 | 54.3 | 2.1 |
| Marshall | 154.5 | 3 930 | 67.9 | 2.7 | 4.9 | 0.5 | 5.3 | 85.2 | 2 167 | 130 | 170 | 3 407 | 53.7 | 44.4 | 1.9 |
| Mills | 45.1 | 2 974 | 59.4 | 4.7 | 5.2 | 1.6 | 11.2 | 39.5 | 2 604 | 44 | 62 | 1 681 | 40.9 | 57.4 | 1.7 |
| Mitchell | 44.7 | 4 164 | 35.9 | 31.6 | 3.1 | 1.1 | 10.6 | 20.1 | 1 868 | 38 | 45 | 671 | 55.1 | 42.8 | 2.0 |
| Monona | 28.5 | 3 121 | 49.3 | 3.3 | 5.6 | 0.4 | 16.4 | 9.8 | 1 070 | 45 | 38 | 599 | 47.8 | 50.3 | 1.9 |
| Monroe | 18.2 | 2 401 | 60.5 | 2.3 | 5.9 | 0.9 | 15.0 | 7.9 | 1 044 | 40 | 33 | 514 | 46.4 | 51.6 | 2.0 |
| Montgomery | 51.7 | 4 699 | 34.1 | 39.8 | 3.9 | 0.0 | 7.1 | 22.4 | 2 037 | 47 | 44 | 943 | 44.0 | 54.6 | 1.4 |
| Muscatine | 132.0 | 3 112 | 50.7 | 1.9 | 5.3 | 1.0 | 7.2 | 134.7 | 3 174 | 97 | 178 | 2 684 | 57.1 | 41.5 | 1.4 |
| O'Brien | 59.7 | 4 245 | 64.3 | 4.2 | 3.9 | 0.3 | 9.3 | 41.2 | 2 930 | 50 | 59 | 1 115 | 31.9 | 66.7 | 1.4 |
| Osceola | 17.4 | 2 686 | 46.1 | 3.9 | 11.6 | 0.8 | 15.2 | 10.5 | 1 629 | 30 | 26 | 302 | 33.1 | 64.8 | 2.1 |
| Page | 61.2 | 3 852 | 39.4 | 30.6 | 3.7 | 0.5 | 7.8 | 32.7 | 2 058 | 72 | 66 | 1 362 | 39.4 | 59.1 | 1.5 |
| Palo Alto | 51.2 | 5 427 | 33.6 | 32.5 | 2.9 | 0.7 | 11.7 | 30.6 | 3 246 | 39 | 39 | 1 048 | 50.5 | 47.7 | 1.8 |
| Plymouth | 96.1 | 3 943 | 38.5 | 24.1 | 3.4 | 2.0 | 9.2 | 55.9 | 2 294 | 81 | 103 | 1 442 | 37.0 | 62.0 | 1.0 |
| Pocahontas | 30.8 | 4 009 | 32.1 | 23.1 | 4.1 | 1.2 | 13.3 | 10.8 | 1 411 | 38 | 30 | 552 | 44.9 | 53.3 | 1.8 |
| Polk | 1 867.4 | 4 464 | 47.8 | 6.6 | 4.7 | 1.3 | 5.0 | 2 111.8 | 5 048 | 5 904 | 1 961 | 29 288 | 56.4 | 41.8 | 1.8 |
| Pottawattamie | 361.8 | 4 047 | 58.7 | 2.3 | 5.3 | 0.5 | 5.2 | 230.1 | 2 573 | 211 | 390 | 5 369 | 48.3 | 50.2 | 1.5 |
| Poweshiek | 55.0 | 2 947 | 53.0 | 2.2 | 4.5 | 0.7 | 10.2 | 42.2 | 2 262 | 55 | 78 | 883 | 55.0 | 43.3 | 1.7 |
| Ringgold | 25.1 | 4 874 | 38.0 | 35.3 | 1.4 | 0.0 | 10.2 | 6.8 | 1 327 | 45 | 21 | 446 | 46.0 | 52.1 | 1.9 |
| Sac | 48.2 | 4 637 | 34.4 | 39.6 | 3.5 | 0.2 | 9.5 | 6.8 | 655 | 51 | 43 | 598 | 44.6 | 53.5 | 1.8 |
| Scott | 630.3 | 3 874 | 54.0 | 2.8 | 5.8 | 0.3 | 4.7 | 500.2 | 3 074 | 578 | 695 | 8 183 | 56.6 | 42.1 | 1.3 |
| Shelby | 60.8 | 4 937 | 34.6 | 36.9 | 3.0 | 0.2 | 9.6 | 21.4 | 1 737 | 55 | 50 | 1 036 | 44.4 | 54.0 | 1.6 |
| Sioux | 129.3 | 3 997 | 35.6 | 30.3 | 3.8 | 0.4 | 8.3 | 109.4 | 3 382 | 101 | 141 | 2 000 | 18.2 | 80.9 | 0.9 |
| Story | 363.8 | 4 292 | 28.6 | 44.0 | 3.1 | 0.7 | 3.6 | 190.7 | 2 251 | 1 123 | 399 | 18 261 | 57.0 | 40.8 | 2.2 |
| Tama | 62.6 | 3 503 | 59.7 | 4.5 | 3.5 | 0.6 | 14.1 | 28.5 | 1 594 | 61 | 74 | 2 088 | 55.3 | 43.2 | 1.5 |
| Taylor | 21.7 | 3 387 | 51.6 | 6.6 | 3.8 | 0.2 | 14.8 | 11.7 | 1 832 | 40 | 26 | 385 | 44.5 | 53.1 | 2.4 |
| Union | 86.7 | 7 136 | 49.4 | 29.9 | 2.2 | 0.1 | 3.8 | 46.4 | 3 824 | 69 | 52 | 1 347 | 50.7 | 47.0 | 2.2 |
| Van Buren | 32.5 | 4 220 | 39.3 | 34.3 | 2.5 | 0.1 | 10.7 | 10.8 | 1 408 | 40 | 31 | 535 | 42.8 | 55.0 | 2.2 |
| Wapello | 170.3 | 4 790 | 64.7 | 1.4 | 2.5 | 0.5 | 5.3 | 50.8 | 1 430 | 122 | 148 | 2 409 | 55.3 | 41.8 | 2.9 |
| Warren | 132.6 | 2 979 | 64.8 | 3.5 | 4.3 | 0.6 | 8.0 | 104.3 | 2 344 | 88 | 194 | 2 126 | 49.4 | 48.8 | 1.8 |
| Washington | 94.8 | 4 443 | 36.8 | 20.7 | 2.8 | 0.6 | 8.6 | 74.8 | 3 502 | 64 | 91 | 1 411 | 48.6 | 49.4 | 2.0 |
| Wayne | 28.8 | 4 584 | 37.6 | 36.5 | 2.3 | 0.4 | 9.9 | 6.8 | 1 083 | 37 | 26 | 546 | 45.5 | 52.5 | 2.0 |
| Webster | 168.9 | 4 378 | 67.0 | 3.6 | 3.0 | 0.6 | 5.6 | 91.4 | 2 368 | 216 | 160 | 2 929 | 53.4 | 44.9 | 1.6 |
| Winnebago | 47.2 | 4 311 | 57.7 | 4.4 | 3.6 | 0.3 | 9.1 | 23.6 | 2 152 | 46 | 45 | 732 | 53.5 | 44.9 | 1.7 |
| Winneshiek | 132.8 | 6 349 | 51.3 | 31.4 | 2.0 | 0.2 | 5.7 | 77.6 | 3 709 | 74 | 87 | 2 185 | 60.5 | 37.9 | 1.6 |
| Woodbury | 414.2 | 4 049 | 55.6 | 2.7 | 5.4 | 0.6 | 8.0 | 329.8 | 3 225 | 733 | 427 | 6 349 | 49.1 | 49.6 | 1.4 |
| Worth | 22.2 | 2 887 | 44.5 | 8.4 | 6.9 | 0.1 | 14.9 | 13.7 | 1 787 | 30 | 31 | 396 | 60.3 | 37.8 | 1.9 |
| Wright | 84.2 | 6 444 | 38.3 | 35.6 | 3.4 | 1.0 | 6.8 | 55.0 | 4 207 | 88 | 54 | 1 227 | 48.5 | 50.0 | 1.5 |

1. Based on the resident population estimated as of July 1 of the year shown.    2. © 2013 Election Data Services, Inc. All rights reserved.

# Table B. States and Counties — Land Area and Population

| STATE/County code | CBSA code[1] | County type[2] | STATE County | Land area[3] (sq km) 2010 | Total persons | Rank | Per square kilometer | White | Black | American Indian, Alaska Native | Asian and Pacific Islander | Percent Hispanic or Latino[4] | Under 5 years | 5 to 17 years | 18 to 24 years | 25 to 34 years | 35 to 44 years | 45 to 54 years |
|---|---|---|---|---|---|---|---|---|---|---|---|---|---|---|---|---|---|---|
| | | | | 1 | 2 | 3 | 4 | 5 | 6 | 7 | 8 | 9 | 10 | 11 | 12 | 13 | 14 | 15 |
| 20 000 | ... | X | KANSAS | 211 754 | 2 885 905 | X | 13.6 | 79.9 | 6.9 | 1.8 | 3.1 | 10.8 | 7.1 | 18.1 | 10.2 | 13.3 | 12.0 | 13.9 |
| 20 001 | ... | 7 | Allen | 1 296 | 13 319 | 2 223 | 10.3 | 93.5 | 2.8 | 2.0 | 0.9 | 3.0 | 6.4 | 17.1 | 9.2 | 11.4 | 10.5 | 13.9 |
| 20 003 | ... | 6 | Anderson | 1 501 | 7 917 | 2 605 | 5.3 | 96.6 | 1.1 | 1.1 | 0.8 | 1.7 | 6.7 | 18.6 | 6.7 | 10.4 | 11.1 | 14.0 |
| 20 005 | 11860 | 6 | Atchison | 1 117 | 16 813 | 1 994 | 15.1 | 91.2 | 6.4 | 1.3 | 1.0 | 2.4 | 6.4 | 17.7 | 14.1 | 10.5 | 10.7 | 13.4 |
| 20 007 | ... | 9 | Barber | 2 937 | 4 861 | 2 847 | 1.7 | 95.7 | 1.2 | 1.0 | 0.7 | 2.7 | 6.4 | 16.1 | 7.2 | 11.2 | 9.3 | 14.8 |
| 20 009 | 24460 | 7 | Barton | 2 319 | 27 557 | 1 511 | 11.9 | 83.9 | 2.0 | 1.0 | 0.5 | 13.9 | 6.9 | 17.7 | 8.8 | 12.1 | 10.0 | 14.6 |
| 20 011 | ... | 6 | Bourbon | 1 646 | 14 897 | 2 117 | 9.1 | 93.5 | 3.8 | 1.7 | 0.9 | 2.3 | 7.3 | 17.8 | 10.0 | 11.2 | 9.9 | 13.1 |
| 20 013 | ... | 6 | Brown | 1 479 | 9 881 | 2 452 | 6.7 | 86.3 | 2.5 | 9.8 | 0.6 | 3.4 | 7.1 | 18.0 | 6.9 | 11.0 | 10.3 | 14.0 |
| 20 015 | 48620 | 2 | Butler | 3 703 | 65 827 | 802 | 17.8 | 92.3 | 2.3 | 2.0 | 1.2 | 4.1 | 6.3 | 20.2 | 9.1 | 11.5 | 12.4 | 15.3 |
| 20 017 | 21380 | 8 | Chase | 2 002 | 2 757 | 2 992 | 1.4 | 93.9 | 1.7 | 1.2 | 0.7 | 3.8 | 5.4 | 16.4 | 6.7 | 8.8 | 11.5 | 14.5 |
| 20 019 | ... | 9 | Chautauqua | 1 655 | 3 571 | 2 940 | 2.2 | 92.2 | 1.5 | 6.6 | 0.8 | 2.6 | 5.0 | 15.6 | 6.2 | 10.1 | 9.2 | 15.3 |
| 20 021 | ... | 6 | Cherokee | 1 522 | 21 226 | 1 773 | 13.9 | 92.4 | 1.4 | 6.7 | 0.9 | 2.2 | 6.1 | 18.6 | 7.6 | 10.9 | 12.2 | 15.2 |
| 20 023 | ... | 9 | Cheyenne | 2 641 | 2 678 | 3 000 | 1.0 | 94.3 | 0.2 | 0.6 | 0.8 | 4.7 | 5.0 | 15.3 | 5.3 | 7.8 | 10.1 | 13.9 |
| 20 025 | ... | 9 | Clark | 2 524 | 2 181 | 3 038 | 0.9 | 90.6 | 0.7 | 2.0 | 1.8 | 7.4 | 6.4 | 18.3 | 5.8 | 9.3 | 9.7 | 14.3 |
| 20 027 | ... | 7 | Clay | 1 671 | 8 531 | 2 561 | 5.1 | 96.3 | 1.0 | 1.1 | 0.7 | 2.2 | 6.6 | 16.8 | 6.3 | 11.5 | 10.9 | 13.5 |
| 20 029 | ... | 9 | Cloud | 1 853 | 9 397 | 2 480 | 5.1 | 95.6 | 1.1 | 1.1 | 0.4 | 3.2 | 6.2 | 15.8 | 10.9 | 10.7 | 9.7 | 13.2 |
| 20 031 | ... | 6 | Coffey | 1 624 | 8 502 | 2 563 | 5.2 | 95.8 | 1.1 | 1.6 | 0.7 | 2.3 | 5.3 | 18.3 | 6.4 | 9.8 | 11.7 | 16.3 |
| 20 033 | ... | 9 | Comanche | 2 042 | 1 913 | 3 066 | 0.9 | 94.7 | 0.7 | 0.8 | 0.4 | 4.4 | 5.6 | 17.8 | 4.8 | 8.8 | 10.6 | 13.7 |
| 20 035 | 49060 | 4 | Cowley | 2 916 | 36 288 | 1 269 | 12.4 | 84.4 | 3.8 | 3.3 | 2.0 | 9.3 | 6.9 | 17.3 | 10.6 | 11.5 | 11.3 | 13.7 |
| 20 037 | 38260 | 4 | Crawford | 1 527 | 39 361 | 1 188 | 25.8 | 90.7 | 3.0 | 2.0 | 2.0 | 4.7 | 6.3 | 15.7 | 18.4 | 12.4 | 10.4 | 11.8 |
| 20 039 | ... | 9 | Decatur | 2 314 | 2 871 | 2 987 | 1.2 | 97.1 | 0.9 | 1.1 | 0.3 | 1.5 | 5.0 | 13.5 | 4.9 | 8.8 | 8.8 | 14.9 |
| 20 041 | ... | 7 | Dickinson | 2 194 | 19 762 | 1 847 | 9.0 | 94.1 | 1.5 | 1.3 | 1.0 | 4.1 | 6.5 | 17.8 | 7.2 | 10.9 | 11.8 | 14.8 |
| 20 043 | 41140 | 3 | Doniphan | 1 019 | 7 864 | 2 608 | 7.7 | 92.9 | 4.3 | 2.0 | 0.6 | 2.3 | 5.6 | 16.3 | 12.4 | 10.3 | 11.8 | 14.0 |
| 20 045 | 29940 | 3 | Douglas | 1 181 | 112 864 | 532 | 95.6 | 83.9 | 5.4 | 3.4 | 5.2 | 5.5 | 5.4 | 13.1 | 26.0 | 15.4 | 10.7 | 10.7 |
| 20 047 | ... | 9 | Edwards | 1 611 | 2 979 | 2 981 | 1.8 | 80.0 | 0.7 | 1.0 | 0.7 | 18.7 | 6.0 | 17.2 | 5.5 | 10.1 | 10.9 | 16.2 |
| 20 049 | ... | 8 | Elk | 1 669 | 2 720 | 2 999 | 1.6 | 95.3 | 0.7 | 2.8 | 0.7 | 2.8 | 5.1 | 15.5 | 5.6 | 8.0 | 9.9 | 14.2 |
| 20 051 | 25700 | 5 | Ellis | 2 331 | 29 053 | 1 449 | 12.5 | 92.4 | 1.6 | 0.6 | 1.7 | 4.9 | 6.6 | 14.2 | 19.5 | 13.5 | 9.7 | 11.9 |
| 20 053 | ... | 7 | Ellsworth | 1 854 | 6 494 | 2 725 | 3.5 | 88.9 | 5.2 | 1.2 | 0.7 | 5.2 | 5.1 | 13.4 | 7.9 | 13.7 | 11.0 | 15.8 |
| 20 055 | 23780 | 5 | Finney | 3 372 | 37 200 | 1 242 | 11.0 | 46.7 | 2.7 | 0.9 | 3.8 | 47.2 | 9.7 | 22.5 | 10.7 | 13.5 | 12.1 | 13.2 |
| 20 057 | 19980 | 5 | Ford | 2 845 | 34 752 | 1 306 | 12.2 | 44.1 | 2.7 | 0.9 | 1.9 | 51.7 | 9.8 | 21.5 | 10.7 | 14.7 | 12.2 | 12.1 |
| 20 059 | 28140 | 1 | Franklin | 1 481 | 25 906 | 1 567 | 17.5 | 93.9 | 2.1 | 2.0 | 0.6 | 3.5 | 6.7 | 18.5 | 8.9 | 11.8 | 11.9 | 15.4 |
| 20 061 | 31740 | 5 | Geary | 996 | 38 013 | 1 221 | 38.2 | 64.7 | 19.8 | 2.0 | 6.0 | 13.1 | 11.4 | 19.5 | 13.5 | 19.0 | 11.6 | 10.0 |
| 20 063 | ... | 9 | Gove | 2 776 | 2 729 | 2 998 | 1.0 | 97.4 | 0.5 | 0.4 | 0.6 | 1.7 | 6.8 | 16.1 | 5.7 | 10.3 | 8.6 | 14.0 |
| 20 065 | ... | 9 | Graham | 2 327 | 2 578 | 3 002 | 1.1 | 92.8 | 4.9 | 1.9 | 0.8 | 2.5 | 6.0 | 13.7 | 5.4 | 9.9 | 8.5 | 15.8 |
| 20 067 | ... | 7 | Grant | 1 489 | 7 923 | 2 603 | 5.3 | 54.1 | 0.8 | 0.9 | 0.5 | 44.5 | 9.1 | 22.7 | 8.4 | 12.6 | 12.3 | 13.2 |
| 20 069 | ... | 9 | Gray | 2 250 | 6 030 | 2 758 | 2.7 | 83.9 | 0.9 | 0.9 | 0.5 | 14.8 | 8.5 | 21.8 | 7.7 | 12.8 | 11.9 | 13.7 |
| 20 071 | ... | 9 | Greeley | 2 016 | 1 298 | 3 096 | 0.6 | 84.7 | 0.7 | 0.7 | 0.4 | 14.5 | 6.7 | 14.1 | 6.4 | 11.4 | 7.9 | 18.8 |
| 20 073 | ... | 6 | Greenwood | 2 961 | 6 454 | 2 728 | 2.2 | 94.9 | 0.8 | 2.3 | 0.4 | 3.5 | 5.7 | 16.3 | 6.0 | 9.4 | 10.3 | 14.8 |
| 20 075 | ... | 9 | Hamilton | 2 581 | 2 639 | 3 001 | 1.0 | 66.9 | 0.6 | 1.4 | 0.6 | 31.5 | 9.4 | 19.1 | 8.4 | 14.0 | 10.7 | 13.3 |
| 20 077 | ... | 8 | Harper | 2 075 | 5 911 | 2 770 | 2.8 | 92.8 | 1.1 | 1.6 | 0.3 | 5.3 | 6.5 | 16.9 | 6.4 | 10.5 | 10.6 | 12.6 |
| 20 079 | 48620 | 2 | Harvey | 1 398 | 34 852 | 1 304 | 24.9 | 86.1 | 2.4 | 1.3 | 1.1 | 10.9 | 6.7 | 18.3 | 8.8 | 11.7 | 10.7 | 13.9 |
| 20 081 | ... | 9 | Haskell | 1 496 | 4 256 | 2 887 | 2.8 | 71.3 | 0.7 | 1.1 | 0.6 | 27.4 | 8.4 | 22.6 | 8.2 | 11.8 | 11.6 | 13.6 |
| 20 083 | ... | 9 | Hodgeman | 2 227 | 1 963 | 3 058 | 0.9 | 91.4 | 2.1 | 0.7 | 0.5 | 6.7 | 6.2 | 16.9 | 6.4 | 9.7 | 9.3 | 17.5 |
| 20 085 | 45820 | 3 | Jackson | 1 700 | 13 449 | 2 216 | 7.9 | 88.1 | 1.4 | 9.0 | 0.7 | 3.6 | 6.5 | 19.7 | 6.7 | 10.2 | 12.7 | 14.9 |
| 20 087 | 45820 | 3 | Jefferson | 1 379 | 18 945 | 1 877 | 13.7 | 96.3 | 1.0 | 1.9 | 0.5 | 1.9 | 5.4 | 18.5 | 6.6 | 10.0 | 11.9 | 17.2 |
| 20 089 | ... | 9 | Jewell | 2 356 | 3 046 | 2 974 | 1.3 | 96.8 | 0.5 | 1.2 | 0.4 | 2.2 | 5.0 | 13.2 | 5.5 | 7.8 | 8.2 | 14.6 |
| 20 091 | 28140 | 1 | Johnson | 1 226 | 559 913 | 111 | 456.7 | 83.5 | 5.3 | 0.9 | 5.1 | 7.3 | 7.0 | 19.0 | 7.1 | 14.6 | 14.1 | 14.8 |
| 20 093 | ... | 9 | Kearny | 2 255 | 3 968 | 2 909 | 1.8 | 68.9 | 1.4 | 1.4 | 0.5 | 29.2 | 8.6 | 21.9 | 8.4 | 11.0 | 11.6 | 13.4 |
| 20 095 | ... | 6 | Kingman | 2 236 | 7 863 | 2 609 | 3.5 | 95.7 | 0.6 | 1.2 | 0.9 | 2.7 | 5.7 | 18.2 | 6.7 | 9.8 | 10.3 | 15.7 |
| 20 097 | ... | 9 | Kiowa | 1 872 | 2 496 | 3 008 | 1.3 | 93.5 | 1.0 | 1.5 | 1.2 | 4.1 | 5.5 | 15.5 | 11.3 | 10.2 | 10.2 | 13.1 |
| 20 099 | 37660 | 7 | Labette | 1 671 | 21 284 | 1 769 | 12.7 | 88.9 | 6.2 | 3.8 | 0.8 | 4.1 | 6.5 | 17.4 | 8.8 | 10.9 | 11.0 | 14.9 |
| 20 101 | ... | 9 | Lane | 1 858 | 1 704 | 3 074 | 0.9 | 93.5 | 1.2 | 1.5 | 0.5 | 4.8 | 4.9 | 17.9 | 5.7 | 8.7 | 12.1 | 14.0 |
| 20 103 | 28140 | 1 | Leavenworth | 1 199 | 77 739 | 703 | 64.8 | 82.3 | 10.6 | 1.7 | 2.4 | 6.0 | 6.6 | 18.0 | 8.1 | 13.5 | 14.8 | 15.3 |
| 20 105 | ... | 9 | Lincoln | 1 863 | 3 174 | 2 963 | 1.7 | 96.3 | 0.7 | 0.8 | 0.4 | 2.7 | 6.4 | 17.4 | 5.2 | 9.5 | 10.1 | 15.6 |
| 20 107 | 28140 | 1 | Linn | 1 539 | 9 441 | 2 477 | 6.1 | 96.2 | 1.1 | 1.5 | 0.6 | 2.1 | 5.4 | 17.6 | 6.0 | 9.7 | 11.4 | 15.1 |
| 20 109 | ... | 9 | Logan | 2 779 | 2 784 | 2 990 | 1.0 | 95.0 | 1.2 | 1.0 | 0.5 | 3.3 | 5.4 | 17.0 | 6.8 | 10.7 | 9.9 | 15.9 |
| 20 111 | 21380 | 5 | Lyon | 2 195 | 33 748 | 1 333 | 15.4 | 74.0 | 3.2 | 1.3 | 2.7 | 20.5 | 6.7 | 16.5 | 17.4 | 12.6 | 10.4 | 12.5 |
| 20 113 | 32700 | 6 | McPherson | 2 327 | 29 356 | 1 438 | 12.6 | 94.2 | 1.8 | 1.0 | 0.9 | 3.7 | 6.1 | 17.2 | 8.6 | 11.4 | 10.4 | 14.4 |
| 20 115 | ... | 6 | Marion | 2 446 | 12 347 | 2 283 | 5.0 | 95.5 | 1.6 | 1.2 | 0.5 | 2.6 | 5.2 | 16.7 | 9.4 | 9.1 | 9.5 | 15.2 |
| 20 117 | ... | 7 | Marshall | 2 331 | 10 022 | 2 442 | 4.3 | 97.1 | 0.8 | 0.8 | 0.6 | 1.9 | 6.3 | 16.2 | 6.2 | 11.2 | 9.2 | 15.5 |
| 20 119 | ... | 9 | Meade | 2 533 | 4 396 | 2 874 | 1.7 | 83.0 | 1.3 | 1.2 | 0.5 | 15.3 | 6.6 | 20.5 | 7.5 | 10.5 | 11.3 | 13.7 |
| 20 121 | 28140 | 1 | Miami | 1 491 | 32 612 | 1 368 | 21.9 | 94.8 | 2.1 | 1.3 | 0.6 | 2.7 | 6.3 | 20.1 | 6.7 | 10.7 | 13.1 | 16.7 |
| 20 123 | ... | 7 | Mitchell | 1 818 | 6 355 | 2 735 | 3.5 | 97.1 | 0.7 | 0.7 | 0.6 | 1.6 | 6.1 | 15.9 | 7.8 | 10.2 | 9.7 | 14.5 |
| 20 125 | 17700 | 5 | Montgomery | 1 667 | 34 459 | 1 313 | 20.7 | 84.9 | 7.0 | 6.0 | 1.2 | 5.3 | 6.7 | 16.8 | 9.6 | 11.5 | 10.8 | 14.0 |
| 20 127 | ... | 9 | Morris | 1 801 | 5 854 | 2 777 | 3.3 | 94.5 | 1.1 | 1.4 | 0.5 | 4.1 | 5.0 | 16.1 | 6.2 | 9.4 | 9.9 | 15.8 |
| 20 129 | ... | 9 | Morton | 1 890 | 3 169 | 2 964 | 1.7 | 77.1 | 1.2 | 1.4 | 2.2 | 19.4 | 6.7 | 19.7 | 7.1 | 10.7 | 12.1 | 14.0 |
| 20 131 | ... | 8 | Nemaha | 1 858 | 10 132 | 2 431 | 5.5 | 97.3 | 1.3 | 0.8 | 0.4 | 1.3 | 6.7 | 19.4 | 5.7 | 10.3 | 10.6 | 15.2 |

1. CBSA = Core Based Statistical Area. See Appendix A for explanation. See Appendix B for list of metropolitan areas with component counties.   2. County type code from the Economic Research Service of USDA Rural-Urban Continuum Codes. See Appendix A for definition.   3. Dry land or land partially or temporarily covered by water.   4. May be of any race.

# Table B. States and Counties — **Population and Households**

| | Population, 2011 (cont.) | | | | Population change and components of change, 2000–2012 | | | | | | | Households, 2010 | | | |
|---|---|---|---|---|---|---|---|---|---|---|---|---|---|---|---|
| | Age (percent) (cont.) | | | | Total persons | | Percent change | | Components of change, 2010–2012 | | | | | | Percent |
| STATE County | 55 to 64 years | 65 to 74 years | 75 years and over | Percent female | 2000 | 2010 | 2000–2010 | 2010–2012 | Births | Deaths | Net migration | Number | Percent change, 2000–2010 | Persons per household | Female family householder[1] | One person |
| | 16 | 17 | 18 | 19 | 20 | 21 | 22 | 23 | 24 | 25 | 26 | 27 | 28 | 29 | 30 | 31 |
| KANSAS | 12.1 | 6.8 | 6.5 | 50.3 | 2 688 418 | 2 853 118 | 6.1 | 1.1 | 91 020 | 54 764 | -3 599 | 1 112 096 | 7.1 | 2.49 | 10.4 | 27.8 |
| Allen | 13.3 | 8.7 | 9.4 | 51.4 | 14 385 | 13 371 | -7.0 | -0.4 | 347 | 418 | 26 | 5 475 | -5.2 | 2.37 | 10.2 | 29.3 |
| Anderson | 12.5 | 10.3 | 9.8 | 50.4 | 8 110 | 8 102 | -0.1 | -2.3 | 225 | 244 | -167 | 3 260 | 1.2 | 2.45 | 7.7 | 28.2 |
| Atchison | 11.9 | 7.8 | 7.6 | 51.3 | 16 774 | 16 924 | 0.9 | -0.7 | 495 | 415 | -193 | 6 241 | -0.5 | 2.49 | 11.2 | 28.1 |
| Barber | 15.1 | 10.1 | 9.8 | 49.5 | 5 307 | 4 861 | -8.4 | 0.0 | 140 | 124 | -16 | 2 139 | -4.3 | 2.25 | 6.6 | 32.2 |
| Barton | 13.1 | 7.9 | 9.0 | 50.8 | 28 205 | 27 674 | -1.9 | -0.4 | 806 | 691 | -246 | 11 283 | -1.0 | 2.39 | 8.9 | 30.3 |
| Bourbon | 13.3 | 8.5 | 8.9 | 50.8 | 15 379 | 15 173 | -1.3 | -1.8 | 470 | 389 | -367 | 5 986 | -2.8 | 2.47 | 10.6 | 28.9 |
| Brown | 14.4 | 9.1 | 9.2 | 51.2 | 10 724 | 9 984 | -6.9 | -1.0 | 307 | 282 | -123 | 4 094 | -5.2 | 2.41 | 10.3 | 28.9 |
| Butler | 12.5 | 6.4 | 6.3 | 49.7 | 59 482 | 65 880 | 10.8 | -0.1 | 1 777 | 1 308 | -537 | 23 992 | 11.5 | 2.65 | 9.6 | 22.8 |
| Chase | 15.6 | 11.2 | 10.0 | 49.1 | 3 030 | 2 790 | -7.9 | -1.2 | 48 | 53 | -26 | 1 150 | -7.7 | 2.30 | 5.8 | 31.2 |
| Chautauqua | 14.8 | 12.5 | 11.4 | 48.7 | 4 359 | 3 669 | -15.8 | -2.7 | 73 | 115 | -50 | 1 612 | -10.2 | 2.23 | 7.4 | 34.0 |
| Cherokee | 13.4 | 9.1 | 7.0 | 50.3 | 22 605 | 21 603 | -4.4 | -1.7 | 549 | 596 | -332 | 8 625 | -2.8 | 2.48 | 10.9 | 26.9 |
| Cheyenne | 16.0 | 10.8 | 15.9 | 49.6 | 3 165 | 2 726 | -13.9 | -1.8 | 67 | 109 | -9 | 1 260 | -7.4 | 2.12 | 5.4 | 36.4 |
| Clark | 13.3 | 10.1 | 12.7 | 51.8 | 2 390 | 2 215 | -7.3 | -1.5 | 52 | 66 | -23 | 923 | -5.7 | 2.34 | 8.3 | 30.4 |
| Clay | 13.7 | 9.8 | 11.0 | 50.6 | 8 822 | 8 535 | -3.3 | 0.0 | 246 | 263 | 12 | 3 559 | -1.6 | 2.36 | 7.2 | 29.2 |
| Cloud | 13.2 | 9.2 | 11.2 | 51.3 | 10 268 | 9 533 | -7.2 | -1.4 | 289 | 332 | -91 | 3 910 | -6.1 | 2.31 | 7.7 | 30.4 |
| Coffey | 14.7 | 9.5 | 8.0 | 50.4 | 8 865 | 8 601 | -3.0 | -1.2 | 184 | 213 | -72 | 3 497 | 0.2 | 2.42 | 8.6 | 26.2 |
| Comanche | 14.8 | 12.6 | 11.4 | 52.3 | 1 967 | 1 891 | -3.9 | 1.2 | 57 | 66 | 31 | 824 | -5.5 | 2.22 | 5.5 | 33.7 |
| Cowley | 12.7 | 8.2 | 7.8 | 50.0 | 36 291 | 36 311 | 0.1 | -0.1 | 1 076 | 932 | -146 | 13 940 | -0.7 | 2.46 | 10.8 | 28.4 |
| Crawford | 11.1 | 6.9 | 7.1 | 50.4 | 38 242 | 39 134 | 2.3 | 0.6 | 1 200 | 883 | -76 | 15 729 | 1.5 | 2.38 | 10.8 | 29.8 |
| Decatur | 17.3 | 10.6 | 16.2 | 49.7 | 3 472 | 2 961 | -14.7 | -3.0 | 53 | 104 | -43 | 1 378 | -7.8 | 2.09 | 5.5 | 36.1 |
| Dickinson | 13.0 | 8.6 | 9.6 | 50.8 | 19 344 | 19 754 | 2.1 | 0.0 | 540 | 504 | -18 | 8 073 | 2.2 | 2.41 | 9.0 | 27.8 |
| Doniphan | 13.2 | 8.3 | 8.1 | 49.6 | 8 249 | 7 945 | -3.7 | -1.0 | 184 | 166 | -97 | 3 136 | -1.2 | 2.40 | 9.4 | 29.0 |
| Douglas | 9.8 | 4.8 | 4.3 | 49.8 | 99 962 | 110 826 | 10.9 | 1.8 | 2 754 | 1 335 | 616 | 43 576 | 13.2 | 2.34 | 8.6 | 29.8 |
| Edwards | 14.7 | 9.9 | 9.6 | 50.2 | 3 449 | 3 037 | -11.9 | -1.9 | 81 | 74 | -66 | 1 302 | -10.5 | 2.31 | 6.3 | 30.9 |
| Elk | 16.5 | 13.0 | 12.3 | 50.9 | 3 261 | 2 882 | -11.6 | -5.6 | 85 | 91 | -164 | 1 284 | -9.1 | 2.21 | 8.8 | 32.2 |
| Ellis | 11.3 | 6.1 | 7.4 | 50.3 | 27 507 | 28 452 | 3.4 | 2.1 | 888 | 538 | 256 | 11 908 | 6.4 | 2.30 | 7.6 | 31.5 |
| Ellsworth | 14.1 | 9.4 | 9.7 | 43.7 | 6 525 | 6 497 | -0.4 | 0.0 | 151 | 213 | 64 | 2 463 | -0.7 | 2.24 | 6.9 | 29.9 |
| Finney | 9.7 | 4.8 | 3.8 | 49.8 | 40 523 | 36 776 | -9.2 | 1.2 | 1 711 | 443 | -854 | 12 359 | -4.5 | 2.93 | 12.7 | 22.6 |
| Ford | 9.3 | 4.8 | 5.0 | 48.2 | 32 458 | 33 848 | 4.3 | 2.7 | 1 560 | 534 | -144 | 11 145 | 2.7 | 2.97 | 11.8 | 22.7 |
| Franklin | 12.5 | 7.8 | 6.5 | 50.3 | 24 784 | 25 992 | 4.9 | -0.3 | 763 | 569 | -283 | 10 104 | 6.9 | 2.53 | 10.2 | 25.8 |
| Geary | 7.6 | 4.0 | 3.4 | 49.8 | 27 947 | 34 362 | 23.0 | 10.6 | 2 266 | 454 | 1 758 | 12 690 | 21.3 | 2.64 | 16.1 | 24.1 |
| Gove | 14.8 | 10.2 | 13.5 | 50.2 | 3 068 | 2 695 | -12.2 | 1.3 | 85 | 91 | 32 | 1 154 | -7.3 | 2.29 | 4.3 | 29.0 |
| Graham | 15.5 | 12.4 | 12.7 | 50.9 | 2 946 | 2 597 | -11.8 | -0.7 | 56 | 76 | 3 | 1 196 | -5.3 | 2.14 | 5.3 | 33.2 |
| Grant | 11.3 | 5.9 | 4.5 | 49.0 | 7 909 | 7 829 | -1.0 | 1.2 | 323 | 89 | -154 | 2 716 | -0.9 | 2.85 | 8.6 | 21.1 |
| Gray | 11.3 | 6.5 | 5.7 | 50.8 | 5 904 | 6 006 | 1.7 | 0.4 | 230 | 103 | -114 | 2 153 | 5.3 | 2.75 | 6.8 | 22.6 |
| Greeley | 13.9 | 8.0 | 12.7 | 52.5 | 1 534 | 1 247 | -18.7 | 4.1 | 51 | 30 | 30 | 525 | -12.8 | 2.33 | 4.2 | 30.3 |
| Greenwood | 15.2 | 11.0 | 11.3 | 50.7 | 7 673 | 6 689 | -12.8 | -3.5 | 146 | 202 | -189 | 2 988 | -7.6 | 2.21 | 7.0 | 34.2 |
| Hamilton | 11.5 | 6.9 | 6.8 | 49.2 | 2 670 | 2 690 | 0.7 | -1.9 | 124 | 49 | -132 | 1 060 | 0.6 | 2.54 | 7.7 | 29.3 |
| Harper | 14.9 | 10.7 | 11.0 | 50.2 | 6 536 | 6 034 | -7.7 | -2.0 | 186 | 235 | -69 | 2 545 | -8.2 | 2.32 | 8.6 | 30.2 |
| Harvey | 12.6 | 7.8 | 9.6 | 51.1 | 32 869 | 34 684 | 5.5 | 0.5 | 1 019 | 809 | -23 | 13 411 | 6.6 | 2.49 | 8.7 | 26.9 |
| Haskell | 12.5 | 5.4 | 5.9 | 50.5 | 4 307 | 4 256 | -1.2 | 0.0 | 163 | 61 | -118 | 1 510 | 2.0 | 2.80 | 6.8 | 21.9 |
| Hodgeman | 13.2 | 10.1 | 10.6 | 49.5 | 2 085 | 1 916 | -8.1 | 2.5 | 56 | 59 | 33 | 803 | 0.9 | 2.37 | 5.4 | 27.5 |
| Jackson | 13.6 | 8.7 | 7.0 | 49.8 | 12 657 | 13 462 | 6.4 | -0.1 | 350 | 294 | -82 | 5 228 | 10.6 | 2.55 | 9.4 | 24.9 |
| Jefferson | 14.4 | 9.0 | 6.9 | 49.3 | 18 426 | 19 126 | 3.8 | -0.9 | 438 | 351 | -253 | 7 366 | 7.8 | 2.56 | 8.0 | 21.6 |
| Jewell | 18.0 | 13.0 | 14.7 | 48.4 | 3 791 | 3 077 | -18.8 | -1.0 | 64 | 97 | 5 | 1 450 | -14.5 | 2.10 | 5.3 | 34.3 |
| Johnson | 12.1 | 6.0 | 5.3 | 51.1 | 451 086 | 544 179 | 20.6 | 2.9 | 16 595 | 7 612 | 6 729 | 212 882 | 21.9 | 2.53 | 8.7 | 25.8 |
| Kearny | 11.3 | 7.4 | 6.5 | 49.2 | 4 531 | 3 977 | -12.2 | -0.2 | 131 | 66 | -80 | 1 400 | -9.2 | 2.78 | 10.4 | 21.1 |
| Kingman | 13.5 | 9.5 | 10.6 | 50.5 | 8 673 | 7 858 | -9.4 | 0.1 | 203 | 227 | 25 | 3 227 | -4.3 | 2.38 | 6.9 | 29.4 |
| Kiowa | 14.9 | 8.7 | 10.6 | 50.5 | 3 278 | 2 553 | -22.1 | -2.2 | 63 | 58 | -64 | 1 014 | -25.7 | 2.37 | 6.1 | 28.4 |
| Labette | 13.4 | 8.8 | 8.1 | 50.4 | 22 835 | 21 607 | -5.4 | -1.5 | 635 | 554 | -394 | 8 822 | -4.0 | 2.39 | 11.5 | 30.2 |
| Lane | 15.3 | 10.1 | 11.3 | 51.6 | 2 155 | 1 750 | -18.8 | -2.6 | 37 | 40 | -50 | 799 | -12.2 | 2.19 | 4.9 | 34.7 |
| Leavenworth | 12.4 | 6.5 | 4.9 | 46.9 | 68 691 | 76 227 | 11.0 | 2.0 | 2 139 | 1 210 | 602 | 26 447 | 14.6 | 2.63 | 10.6 | 22.8 |
| Lincoln | 15.9 | 8.3 | 11.5 | 50.6 | 3 578 | 3 241 | -9.4 | -2.1 | 86 | 90 | -71 | 1 423 | -6.9 | 2.24 | 7.2 | 32.8 |
| Linn | 15.1 | 10.9 | 8.7 | 50.1 | 9 570 | 9 656 | 0.9 | -2.2 | 209 | 269 | -159 | 4 020 | 5.6 | 2.39 | 7.1 | 27.7 |
| Logan | 13.8 | 8.9 | 11.7 | 50.3 | 3 046 | 2 756 | -9.5 | 1.0 | 57 | 59 | 26 | 1 219 | -1.9 | 2.23 | 6.6 | 34.1 |
| Lyon | 11.3 | 6.4 | 6.1 | 51.2 | 35 935 | 33 690 | -6.2 | 0.2 | 1 046 | 604 | -382 | 13 303 | -2.8 | 2.42 | 10.0 | 29.5 |
| McPherson | 13.4 | 8.3 | 10.1 | 50.9 | 29 554 | 29 180 | -1.3 | 0.6 | 768 | 809 | 211 | 11 748 | 4.8 | 2.41 | 6.7 | 28.0 |
| Marion | 13.7 | 10.1 | 11.2 | 49.8 | 13 361 | 12 660 | -5.2 | -2.5 | 245 | 346 | -208 | 5 005 | -2.1 | 2.39 | 6.4 | 27.7 |
| Marshall | 14.4 | 9.2 | 11.7 | 50.5 | 10 965 | 10 117 | -7.7 | -0.9 | 229 | 280 | -40 | 4 300 | -3.5 | 2.31 | 6.2 | 30.6 |
| Meade | 11.7 | 7.4 | 9.8 | 49.2 | 4 631 | 4 575 | -1.2 | -3.9 | 116 | 110 | -189 | 1 713 | -0.9 | 2.60 | 7.4 | 25.4 |
| Miami | 12.9 | 7.5 | 6.0 | 50.6 | 28 351 | 32 787 | 15.6 | -0.5 | 873 | 613 | -434 | 12 161 | 17.3 | 2.64 | 8.9 | 21.3 |
| Mitchell | 14.8 | 9.4 | 11.7 | 49.3 | 6 932 | 6 373 | -8.1 | -0.3 | 175 | 234 | 40 | 2 790 | -2.1 | 2.20 | 6.2 | 33.1 |
| Montgomery | 13.0 | 9.0 | 8.7 | 51.0 | 36 252 | 35 471 | -2.2 | -2.9 | 1 032 | 899 | -1 188 | 14 382 | -3.5 | 2.39 | 11.5 | 29.6 |
| Morris | 15.0 | 10.8 | 11.7 | 50.2 | 6 104 | 5 923 | -3.0 | -1.2 | 125 | 178 | -11 | 2 554 | 0.6 | 2.29 | 6.5 | 28.7 |
| Morton | 12.5 | 8.1 | 9.1 | 50.5 | 3 496 | 3 233 | -7.5 | -2.0 | 100 | 73 | -98 | 1 250 | -4.3 | 2.52 | 8.3 | 27.0 |
| Nemaha | 11.9 | 8.1 | 12.1 | 49.4 | 10 717 | 10 178 | -5.0 | -0.5 | 286 | 254 | -83 | 4 115 | 3.9 | 2.41 | 5.5 | 31.3 |

1. No spouse present.

# Table B. States and Counties — **Population, Vital Statistics, Medicare, and Crime**

| STATE County | Daytime population, 2007–2011 Persons in group quarters, 2010 | Number | Employment/ residence ratio | Births, 2011 Total | Rate[1] | Deaths, 2011 Number | Rate[1] | Persons under 65 with no health insurance, 2010 Number | Percent | Medicare, 2012 Eligible for Medicare | Enrolled in Medicare Advantage | Enrolled in a Medicare prescription drug plan | Serious crimes known to police,[2] 2011 Total Number | Rate[3] |
|---|---|---|---|---|---|---|---|---|---|---|---|---|---|---|
| | 32 | 33 | 34 | 35 | 36 | 37 | 38 | 39 | 40 | 41 | 42 | 43 | 44 | 45 |
| KANSAS | 79 074 | 2 843 008 | 1.01 | 40 132 | 14.0 | 24 038 | 8.4 | 380 567 | 15.8 | 458 142 | 6 284 | 242 889 | 98 600 | 3 434 |
| Allen | 382 | 13 328 | 0.99 | 147 | 11.0 | 179 | 13.4 | 1 708 | 16.1 | 2 851 | 199 | 1 786 | 435 | 3 379 |
| Anderson | 103 | 7 125 | 0.74 | 102 | 12.6 | 109 | 13.5 | 1 085 | 16.9 | 1 776 | 90 | 1 069 | 194 | 2 546 |
| Atchison | 1 375 | 16 112 | 0.90 | 218 | 13.0 | 185 | 11.0 | 1 895 | 14.4 | 2 967 | 195 | 1 856 | 501 | 2 942 |
| Barber | 40 | 4 756 | 0.95 | 64 | 13.1 | 61 | 12.5 | 703 | 18.3 | 1 167 | 29 | 766 | 98 | 2 003 |
| Barton | 672 | 27 679 | 1.01 | 356 | 12.8 | 312 | 11.2 | 4 409 | 19.6 | 5 233 | 106 | 3 648 | 1 106 | 3 971 |
| Bourbon | 409 | 14 812 | 0.96 | 212 | 14.1 | 165 | 11.0 | 1 971 | 16.1 | 3 163 | 211 | 1 836 | 614 | 4 021 |
| Brown | 116 | 10 119 | 1.03 | 134 | 13.4 | 131 | 13.1 | 1 498 | 18.4 | 2 159 | 49 | 1 439 | 171 | 1 702 |
| Butler | 2 309 | 53 813 | 0.62 | 786 | 11.9 | 579 | 8.8 | 7 572 | 13.7 | 10 172 | 1 142 | 5 467 | 1 709 | 2 578 |
| Chase | 145 | 2 377 | 0.66 | 23 | 8.2 | 17 | 6.0 | 456 | 21.8 | 563 | 16 | 345 | 15 | 534 |
| Chautauqua | 79 | 3 224 | 0.68 | 31 | 8.6 | 58 | 16.2 | 599 | 21.7 | 987 | 34 | 640 | 26 | 704 |
| Cherokee | 202 | 18 789 | 0.70 | 239 | 11.2 | 264 | 12.3 | 3 001 | 16.7 | 4 325 | 285 | 2 499 | 615 | 2 948 |
| Cheyenne | 49 | 2 651 | 0.92 | 29 | 10.7 | 51 | 18.8 | 435 | 21.8 | 739 | 28 | 462 | 47 | 1 713 |
| Clark | 57 | 2 089 | 0.91 | 27 | 12.6 | 31 | 14.5 | 280 | 16.4 | 487 | 11 | 342 | 19 | 852 |
| Clay | 140 | 7 934 | 0.84 | 104 | 12.1 | 117 | 13.6 | 1 040 | 15.5 | 1 887 | 110 | 1 185 | 152 | 1 770 |
| Cloud | 498 | 9 374 | 0.97 | 128 | 13.7 | 153 | 16.3 | 1 261 | 17.4 | 2 214 | 127 | 1 508 | 268 | 2 793 |
| Coffey | 130 | 9 005 | 1.11 | 89 | 10.4 | 86 | 10.1 | 967 | 13.7 | 1 873 | 78 | 1 147 | 74 | 915 |
| Comanche | 65 | 1 864 | 0.96 | 24 | 12.7 | 23 | 12.2 | 264 | 18.7 | 486 | D | 334 | NA | NA |
| Cowley | 2 004 | 35 025 | 0.92 | 474 | 13.1 | 417 | 11.5 | 4 632 | 16.0 | 6 926 | 715 | 4 141 | 1 239 | 3 391 |
| Crawford | 1 773 | 39 656 | 1.03 | 517 | 13.2 | 364 | 9.3 | 5 830 | 18.1 | 6 729 | 310 | 4 328 | 1 747 | 4 436 |
| Decatur | 81 | 2 839 | 0.90 | 24 | 8.2 | 47 | 16.1 | 435 | 20.3 | 818 | 56 | 507 | 15 | 503 |
| Dickinson | 307 | 17 963 | 0.81 | 260 | 13.2 | 215 | 10.9 | 2 396 | 15.0 | 3 978 | 297 | 2 171 | 456 | 2 398 |
| Doniphan | 427 | 6 983 | 0.75 | 85 | 10.7 | 74 | 9.3 | 974 | 15.6 | 1 475 | 38 | 869 | 182 | 2 276 |
| Douglas | 8 792 | 104 277 | 0.90 | 1 227 | 10.9 | 567 | 5.1 | 16 404 | 17.7 | 13 176 | 1 319 | 6 969 | 4 946 | 4 435 |
| Edwards | 35 | 2 833 | 0.86 | 37 | 12.3 | 35 | 11.6 | 475 | 19.4 | 666 | 25 | 419 | NA | NA |
| Elk | 40 | 2 554 | 0.71 | 36 | 12.8 | 36 | 12.8 | 507 | 23.4 | 822 | 28 | 541 | 31 | 1 069 |
| Ellis | 1 033 | 28 899 | 1.04 | 381 | 13.3 | 250 | 8.7 | 3 416 | 14.4 | 4 458 | 97 | 2 972 | 805 | 2 811 |
| Ellsworth | 983 | 6 389 | 0.97 | 62 | 9.6 | 83 | 12.8 | 667 | 15.2 | 1 377 | 40 | 899 | 114 | 1 744 |
| Finney | 548 | 36 836 | 1.03 | 752 | 20.3 | 186 | 5.0 | 7 274 | 21.9 | 3 925 | 97 | 2 538 | 1 187 | 3 207 |
| Ford | 708 | 34 060 | 1.05 | 690 | 20.0 | 226 | 6.5 | 6 684 | 22.2 | 3 707 | 87 | 2 408 | 1 182 | 3 470 |
| Franklin | 478 | 23 730 | 0.83 | 339 | 13.1 | 248 | 9.6 | 2 912 | 13.3 | 4 778 | 339 | 2 748 | 629 | 2 405 |
| Geary | 847 | 36 631 | 1.30 | 1 007 | 28.5 | 201 | 5.7 | 4 435 | 14.0 | 3 378 | 239 | 1 180 | 826 | 2 389 |
| Gove | 56 | 2 925 | 1.18 | 33 | 12.2 | 57 | 21.1 | 463 | 22.8 | 681 | 15 | 466 | 17 | 627 |
| Graham | 40 | 2 532 | 0.91 | 25 | 9.5 | 34 | 12.9 | 362 | 18.8 | 731 | 31 | 478 | 54 | 2 067 |
| Grant | 79 | 8 301 | 1.14 | 133 | 16.7 | 27 | 3.4 | 1 420 | 20.4 | 940 | 11 | 606 | 103 | 1 307 |
| Gray | 78 | 5 627 | 0.90 | 96 | 15.7 | 37 | 6.1 | 1 183 | 22.6 | 887 | 19 | 621 | 46 | 761 |
| Greeley | 26 | 1 266 | 1.05 | 18 | 14.3 | 14 | 11.1 | 183 | 18.6 | 289 | D | 216 | 3 | 239 |
| Greenwood | 90 | 5 920 | 0.71 | 62 | 9.3 | 85 | 12.8 | 962 | 18.7 | 1 642 | 53 | 1 082 | 108 | 1 605 |
| Hamilton | 0 | 2 693 | 1.02 | 57 | 21.4 | 23 | 8.6 | 641 | 27.8 | 386 | D | 268 | 0 | 0 |
| Harper | 129 | 5 822 | 0.93 | 76 | 12.7 | 108 | 18.0 | 875 | 18.7 | 1 359 | 35 | 900 | 57 | 1 242 |
| Harvey | 1 311 | 32 992 | 0.91 | 452 | 13.0 | 339 | 9.7 | 4 308 | 15.5 | 6 919 | 1 028 | 4 011 | 769 | 2 203 |
| Haskell | 33 | 4 101 | 0.95 | 68 | 15.9 | 23 | 5.4 | 818 | 21.6 | 538 | D | 352 | NA | NA |
| Hodgeman | 14 | 1 764 | 0.80 | 20 | 10.2 | 25 | 12.7 | 262 | 17.3 | 410 | 12 | 246 | 51 | 2 645 |
| Jackson | 133 | 11 101 | 0.66 | 163 | 12.1 | 132 | 9.8 | 1 805 | 15.9 | 2 710 | 146 | 1 375 | 211 | 1 621 |
| Jefferson | 235 | 13 559 | 0.42 | 195 | 10.3 | 143 | 7.5 | 2 230 | 14.0 | 3 502 | 260 | 1 733 | 416 | 2 161 |
| Jewell | 27 | 2 720 | 0.74 | 25 | 8.1 | 45 | 14.5 | 440 | 20.0 | 884 | 44 | 588 | NA | NA |
| Johnson | 5 166 | 562 350 | 1.08 | 7 309 | 13.2 | 3 296 | 6.0 | 51 044 | 10.6 | 73 219 | 19 271 | 27 353 | 11 821 | 2 159 |
| Kearny | 81 | 3 406 | 0.70 | 60 | 15.0 | 33 | 8.3 | 840 | 24.5 | 586 | D | 400 | 13 | 325 |
| Kingman | 190 | 7 242 | 0.81 | 86 | 11.0 | 102 | 13.0 | 931 | 15.1 | 1 690 | 66 | 1 084 | 154 | 1 947 |
| Kiowa | 149 | 2 694 | 1.10 | 29 | 11.4 | 28 | 11.0 | 351 | 18.1 | 542 | D | 355 | 45 | 1 752 |
| Labette | 480 | 21 931 | 1.02 | 278 | 12.9 | 249 | 11.6 | 2 751 | 15.4 | 4 669 | 247 | 2 966 | 792 | 3 642 |
| Lane | 3 | 1 553 | 1.06 | 16 | 9.1 | 21 | 12.0 | 258 | 18.8 | 432 | D | 308 | 16 | 909 |
| Leavenworth | 6 561 | 68 987 | 0.80 | 934 | 12.1 | 519 | 6.7 | 6 799 | 11.0 | 10 850 | 1 147 | 3 869 | 1 860 | 2 425 |
| Lincoln | 50 | 2 899 | 0.77 | 35 | 10.9 | 39 | 12.1 | 524 | 20.4 | 713 | 11 | 480 | 57 | 1 747 |
| Linn | 63 | 8 431 | 0.69 | 92 | 9.6 | 118 | 12.3 | 1 378 | 17.9 | 2 148 | 393 | 965 | 175 | 2 131 |
| Logan | 41 | 2 904 | 1.09 | 30 | 10.8 | 23 | 8.3 | 404 | 18.6 | 626 | 27 | 426 | 61 | 2 199 |
| Lyon | 1 444 | 34 584 | 1.00 | 442 | 13.1 | 263 | 7.8 | 5 990 | 21.3 | 5 337 | 236 | 3 370 | 1 293 | 3 918 |
| McPherson | 925 | 29 752 | 1.04 | 324 | 11.1 | 366 | 12.5 | 2 910 | 12.5 | 5 808 | 468 | 3 523 | 642 | 2 235 |
| Marion | 723 | 11 150 | 0.76 | 115 | 9.2 | 156 | 12.4 | 1 521 | 16.1 | 2 895 | 148 | 1 900 | 151 | 1 185 |
| Marshall | 164 | 10 478 | 1.07 | 108 | 10.8 | 124 | 12.4 | 1 186 | 15.0 | 2 401 | 121 | 1 559 | 134 | 1 316 |
| Meade | 119 | 4 130 | 0.81 | 50 | 11.0 | 46 | 10.2 | 746 | 20.0 | 784 | 16 | 481 | 28 | 608 |
| Miami | 645 | 25 337 | 0.55 | 389 | 11.9 | 260 | 7.9 | 3 481 | 12.4 | 5 217 | 994 | 2 454 | 697 | 2 112 |
| Mitchell | 246 | 6 898 | 1.16 | 74 | 11.8 | 102 | 16.2 | 667 | 13.7 | 1 432 | 60 | 991 | 85 | 1 325 |
| Montgomery | 1 112 | 37 220 | 1.12 | 444 | 12.7 | 404 | 11.6 | 5 152 | 18.1 | 7 291 | 424 | 4 466 | 1 336 | 3 743 |
| Morris | 66 | 5 167 | 0.74 | 55 | 9.3 | 78 | 13.2 | 811 | 17.8 | 1 377 | 98 | 706 | 109 | 1 829 |
| Morton | 83 | 3 317 | 1.06 | 39 | 12.2 | 34 | 10.6 | 548 | 20.7 | 581 | D | 348 | 42 | 1 291 |
| Nemaha | 259 | 10 300 | 1.02 | 129 | 12.8 | 100 | 9.9 | 1 119 | 13.9 | 2 129 | 48 | 1 391 | 64 | 625 |

1. Per 1,000 estimated resident population.    2. Data for serious crimes have not been adjusted for underreporting; this may affect comparability between geographic areas and over time.    3. Per 100,000 population estimated by the FBI.

# Table B. States and Counties — Crime, Education, Money Income, and Poverty

| STATE County | Serious crimes known to police, 2011 (cont.)[1] Rate[2] Violent | Property | Education: School enrollment and attainment, 2007–2011 Enrollment[3] Total | Percent private | High school graduate or less | Bachelor's degree or more | Local government expenditures,[5] 2009–2010 Total current expenditures (mil dol) | Current expenditures per student (dollars) | Money income, 2007–2011 Per capita income[6] (dollars) | Households Median income Dollars | Percent change, 2000 to 2007–2011 (constant 2011 dollars) | Percent with income of $200,000 or more | Income and poverty, 2011 Median household income (dollars) | Percent below poverty level All persons | Children under 18 years | Children 5 to 17 years in families |
|---|---|---|---|---|---|---|---|---|---|---|---|---|---|---|---|---|
| | 46 | 47 | 48 | 49 | 50 | 51 | 52 | 53 | 54 | 55 | 56 | 57 | 58 | 59 | 60 | 61 |
| KANSAS | 354 | 3 080 | 783 068 | 14.1 | 38.9 | 29.7 | 4 579.5 | 9 651 | 26 545 | 50 594 | -7.8 | 3.2 | 48 844 | 13.8 | 18.8 | 16.2 |
| Allen | 318 | 3 060 | 3 401 | 6.0 | 46.9 | 16.6 | 24.1 | 10 638 | 20 367 | 40 275 | -5.2 | 0.8 | 37 353 | 18.7 | 27.7 | 24.5 |
| Anderson | 289 | 2 258 | 1 865 | 4.7 | 55.3 | 14.7 | 13.3 | 9 856 | 21 022 | 40 753 | -9.2 | 1.6 | 42 185 | 14.5 | 21.2 | 17.9 |
| Atchison | 258 | 2 683 | 5 012 | 24.3 | 54.8 | 21.4 | 24.2 | 9 923 | 21 461 | 44 433 | -4.2 | 1.6 | 42 131 | 17.1 | 21.1 | 17.9 |
| Barber | 164 | 1 840 | 1 002 | 4.0 | 40.1 | 20.0 | 8.1 | 10 841 | 25 082 | 41 677 | -7.6 | 1.9 | 44 118 | 10.7 | 18.3 | 16.8 |
| Barton | 327 | 3 645 | 6 726 | 4.0 | 46.2 | 16.6 | 39.5 | 8 670 | 24 639 | 44 989 | 3.6 | 2.0 | 42 183 | 15.7 | 22.6 | 19.1 |
| Bourbon | 295 | 3 727 | 4 035 | 10.9 | 41.9 | 21.5 | 22.0 | 8 935 | 18 736 | 39 843 | -5.4 | 0.9 | 35 805 | 20.4 | 30.3 | 26.7 |
| Brown | 199 | 1 503 | 2 271 | 6.2 | 52.5 | 16.3 | 16.5 | 11 210 | 19 822 | 36 218 | -16.1 | 1.3 | 40 424 | 16.6 | 24.5 | 20.8 |
| Butler | 226 | 2 352 | 18 656 | 11.1 | 37.0 | 25.2 | 124.0 | 8 446 | 26 710 | 57 573 | -6.2 | 2.5 | 53 217 | 10.8 | 14.1 | 11.6 |
| Chase | 36 | 499 | 638 | 4.1 | 46.9 | 17.7 | 4.8 | 11 463 | 20 530 | 39 095 | -11.3 | 0.4 | 41 217 | 13.8 | 17.5 | 15.1 |
| Chautauqua | 135 | 569 | 696 | 10.5 | 49.2 | 15.5 | 6.1 | 11 876 | 20 836 | 35 791 | -7.7 | 1.1 | 35 952 | 19.3 | 29.5 | 24.9 |
| Cherokee | 283 | 2 665 | 5 121 | 6.0 | 51.0 | 13.4 | 38.7 | 10 329 | 19 661 | 41 513 | 0.8 | 1.2 | 39 696 | 17.6 | 26.5 | 23.7 |
| Cheyenne | 182 | 1 531 | 609 | 5.7 | 45.1 | 18.1 | 5.3 | 12 316 | 21 318 | 36 364 | -12.0 | 0.0 | 36 835 | 12.3 | 18.7 | 15.8 |
| Clark | 135 | 718 | 546 | 10.1 | 41.5 | 23.3 | 5.6 | 11 227 | 27 172 | 42 021 | -8.1 | 2.5 | 42 171 | 12.4 | 17.1 | 14.6 |
| Clay | 128 | 1 642 | 1 846 | 5.0 | 46.7 | 17.3 | 15.5 | 8 960 | 24 719 | 41 829 | -8.8 | 1.2 | 47 692 | 12.2 | 18.0 | 16.1 |
| Cloud | 375 | 2 418 | 2 359 | 8.9 | 48.4 | 15.2 | 14.5 | 10 063 | 19 570 | 37 073 | -13.5 | 0.8 | 39 763 | 13.7 | 19.1 | 17.0 |
| Coffey | 62 | 853 | 2 135 | 8.4 | 44.0 | 20.2 | 18.4 | 11 513 | 25 512 | 49 552 | -3.0 | 1.6 | 54 644 | 10.5 | 14.7 | 12.6 |
| Comanche | NA | NA | 460 | 4.8 | 46.6 | 23.1 | 3.4 | 9 757 | 23 419 | 38 750 | -2.4 | 2.6 | 39 975 | 10.6 | 14.4 | 11.5 |
| Cowley | 353 | 3 038 | 9 514 | 13.1 | 43.7 | 19.5 | 59.3 | 9 742 | 20 855 | 40 924 | -11.9 | 1.6 | 40 248 | 18.4 | 24.6 | 22.1 |
| Crawford | 322 | 4 113 | 13 045 | 11.8 | 40.7 | 27.8 | 58.9 | 9 996 | 20 396 | 36 043 | -9.2 | 1.3 | 34 080 | 22.3 | 27.3 | 24.7 |
| Decatur | 67 | 436 | 509 | 6.7 | 45.9 | 17.7 | 4.1 | 11 019 | 22 673 | 35 887 | -12.2 | 0.0 | 37 986 | 13.5 | 20.0 | 17.4 |
| Dickinson | 137 | 2 261 | 4 707 | 9.9 | 47.5 | 19.5 | 37.1 | 9 528 | 23 035 | 49 003 | 0.9 | 1.3 | 46 894 | 11.1 | 17.5 | 15.3 |
| Doniphan | 213 | 2 064 | 2 228 | 10.4 | 50.4 | 18.3 | 16.6 | 11 097 | 22 051 | 45 000 | 2.4 | 1.1 | 43 092 | 14.0 | 19.6 | 16.9 |
| Douglas | 360 | 4 075 | 45 225 | 11.1 | 25.3 | 48.8 | 128.2 | 9 252 | 25 654 | 47 063 | -7.2 | 3.0 | 47 930 | 16.6 | 13.7 | 12.4 |
| Edwards | NA | NA | 703 | 5.5 | 47.3 | 21.6 | 5.3 | 11 012 | 24 415 | 41 406 | 0.4 | 2.7 | 43 874 | 12.2 | 19.8 | 17.2 |
| Elk | 138 | 931 | 567 | 5.1 | 47.7 | 16.8 | 7.2 | 12 643 | 20 646 | 34 246 | -7.0 | 2.3 | 34 174 | 17.5 | 25.7 | 23.8 |
| Ellis | 300 | 2 511 | 9 165 | 7.7 | 37.2 | 31.8 | 36.9 | 10 211 | 24 441 | 43 713 | 0.1 | 2.3 | 41 774 | 15.7 | 15.6 | 13.5 |
| Ellsworth | 214 | 1 530 | 1 219 | 6.6 | 47.6 | 21.8 | 13.7 | 12 992 | 22 310 | 43 125 | -10.7 | 1.3 | 46 927 | 11.3 | 15.4 | 14.0 |
| Finney | 332 | 2 875 | 10 464 | 5.2 | 52.9 | 19.1 | 81.7 | 10 083 | 21 872 | 51 179 | -1.5 | 3.2 | 44 888 | 16.9 | 24.3 | 21.7 |
| Ford | 370 | 3 100 | 9 106 | 4.9 | 55.4 | 18.0 | 65.2 | 9 759 | 20 104 | 49 061 | -4.0 | 2.0 | 47 542 | 13.8 | 19.5 | 17.7 |
| Franklin | 241 | 2 164 | 6 705 | 15.9 | 48.2 | 19.5 | 44.6 | 9 543 | 23 267 | 50 231 | -4.7 | 0.8 | 46 553 | 14.1 | 21.2 | 19.0 |
| Geary | 440 | 1 949 | 9 150 | 8.3 | 36.1 | 19.9 | 71.3 | 8 823 | 21 153 | 45 649 | 5.9 | 1.3 | 40 224 | 15.8 | 26.3 | 27.8 |
| Gove | 111 | 516 | 513 | 1.6 | 51.0 | 16.3 | 6.2 | 14 499 | 23 672 | 41 853 | -7.5 | 1.9 | 44 351 | 11.2 | 17.0 | 15.2 |
| Graham | 38 | 2 028 | 486 | 2.9 | 45.6 | 21.1 | 4.3 | 10 804 | 25 418 | 41 008 | -2.9 | 2.4 | 40 903 | 12.0 | 16.2 | 14.5 |
| Grant | 216 | 1 092 | 2 064 | 7.9 | 49.9 | 17.5 | 15.2 | 8 764 | 26 633 | 59 127 | 9.9 | 2.8 | 54 230 | 11.8 | 17.9 | 16.0 |
| Gray | 66 | 695 | 1 622 | 14.9 | 53.1 | 20.2 | 13.7 | 11 196 | 23 363 | 55 559 | 2.9 | 1.7 | 59 278 | 9.3 | 12.8 | 10.8 |
| Greeley | 159 | 80 | 250 | 2.8 | 44.6 | 19.1 | 2.6 | 11 294 | 31 525 | 58 971 | 26.2 | 3.8 | 48 606 | 10.2 | 14.6 | 13.5 |
| Greenwood | 178 | 1 426 | 1 436 | 2.2 | 54.2 | 15.4 | 11.0 | 10 867 | 22 032 | 37 543 | -7.8 | 0.8 | 35 765 | 16.5 | 24.1 | 20.2 |
| Hamilton | 0 | 0 | 621 | 2.3 | 51.5 | 13.6 | 5.3 | 10 151 | 21 258 | 41 351 | -4.4 | 1.1 | 43 679 | 13.5 | 21.1 | 20.3 |
| Harper | 109 | 1 133 | 1 264 | 5.3 | 46.0 | 16.7 | 10.8 | 10 076 | 22 805 | 42 021 | 4.5 | 1.1 | 39 104 | 15.5 | 23.1 | 20.6 |
| Harvey | 364 | 1 839 | 9 380 | 19.5 | 42.1 | 25.7 | 53.5 | 8 770 | 23 574 | 48 880 | -11.5 | 1.4 | 50 958 | 13.4 | 18.5 | 15.6 |
| Haskell | NA | NA | 1 129 | 7.4 | 57.6 | 15.8 | 9.7 | 11 355 | 24 075 | 49 760 | -4.6 | 3.4 | 54 340 | 10.7 | 16.7 | 14.5 |
| Hodgeman | 363 | 2 282 | 523 | 3.6 | 36.3 | 23.6 | 4.3 | 15 024 | 22 804 | 44 176 | -9.1 | 0.5 | 45 992 | 10.3 | 14.3 | 12.9 |
| Jackson | 200 | 1 421 | 3 564 | 11.5 | 49.0 | 18.7 | 23.5 | 9 942 | 24 200 | 54 440 | -0.3 | 1.8 | 50 342 | 11.1 | 15.9 | 13.5 |
| Jefferson | 161 | 2 000 | 4 571 | 7.7 | 48.3 | 22.8 | 39.9 | 10 249 | 26 461 | 58 083 | -5.5 | 2.1 | 57 046 | 9.1 | 13.4 | 10.9 |
| Jewell | NA | NA | 555 | 5.9 | 42.9 | 20.0 | 3.8 | 12 228 | 22 497 | 39 713 | -3.7 | 1.3 | 38 865 | 13.2 | 20.4 | 18.2 |
| Johnson | 164 | 1 994 | 148 687 | 20.7 | 20.8 | 51.3 | 846.5 | 9 389 | 38 428 | 74 761 | -9.9 | 7.9 | 70 665 | 6.7 | 8.4 | 6.6 |
| Kearny | 50 | 275 | 1 142 | 2.8 | 44.2 | 14.7 | 10.9 | 11 927 | 21 536 | 50 612 | -6.6 | 0.9 | 51 413 | 12.0 | 19.5 | 17.7 |
| Kingman | 139 | 1 808 | 1 831 | 21.5 | 42.6 | 19.6 | 13.1 | 10 417 | 23 714 | 45 817 | -10.2 | 1.2 | 47 684 | 11.8 | 18.0 | 15.6 |
| Kiowa | 39 | 1 713 | 658 | 32.4 | 40.9 | 22.1 | 6.7 | 9 982 | 21 177 | 39 496 | -7.4 | 1.8 | 39 796 | 14.6 | 20.0 | 16.5 |
| Labette | 464 | 3 178 | 5 595 | 12.3 | 42.3 | 18.0 | 39.6 | 9 991 | 22 137 | 40 587 | -2.6 | 1.3 | 37 879 | 20.6 | 30.4 | 25.3 |
| Lane | 114 | 795 | 314 | 8.9 | 50.0 | 19.6 | 4.2 | 11 510 | 25 997 | 41 536 | -14.7 | 2.0 | 47 900 | 9.2 | 14.9 | 11.9 |
| Leavenworth | 430 | 1 994 | 20 592 | 19.2 | 40.9 | 28.7 | 110.5 | 8 365 | 26 620 | 62 853 | -3.2 | 3.2 | 61 567 | 11.4 | 14.3 | 12.6 |
| Lincoln | 31 | 1 717 | 761 | 8.8 | 42.4 | 18.8 | 5.8 | 12 025 | 23 566 | 41 050 | -1.6 | 1.0 | 39 317 | 13.1 | 21.1 | 18.5 |
| Linn | 207 | 1 924 | 2 012 | 6.3 | 53.1 | 13.9 | 20.2 | 10 693 | 23 329 | 44 408 | -8.4 | 1.2 | 44 615 | 14.7 | 22.9 | 18.8 |
| Logan | 144 | 2 055 | 654 | 16.1 | 45.5 | 19.6 | 5.7 | 10 732 | 24 544 | 41 289 | -4.8 | 1.6 | 43 315 | 10.7 | 16.1 | 13.8 |
| Lyon | 270 | 3 648 | 10 995 | 6.3 | 46.7 | 23.7 | 57.1 | 10 845 | 18 898 | 37 954 | -14.3 | 0.6 | 39 346 | 20.3 | 24.5 | 18.9 |
| McPherson | 209 | 2 026 | 7 620 | 23.5 | 44.0 | 25.0 | 33.4 | 9 244 | 26 357 | 53 332 | -4.0 | 2.2 | 48 130 | 9.9 | 12.4 | 10.5 |
| Marion | 173 | 1 013 | 3 238 | 21.1 | 46.8 | 20.6 | 22.4 | 10 750 | 21 847 | 45 941 | -1.4 | 0.9 | 43 749 | 12.8 | 17.0 | 14.2 |
| Marshall | 147 | 1 169 | 2 171 | 10.5 | 57.8 | 12.8 | 18.7 | 8 861 | 22 094 | 42 464 | -2.0 | 0.8 | 42 619 | 11.8 | 17.0 | 15.1 |
| Meade | 65 | 543 | 1 166 | 9.1 | 48.4 | 22.5 | 7.1 | 10 292 | 24 862 | 49 551 | -0.2 | 1.8 | 49 141 | 9.6 | 14.2 | 11.6 |
| Miami | 164 | 1 949 | 8 584 | 14.5 | 41.3 | 23.3 | 44.4 | 8 769 | 26 945 | 59 668 | -5.3 | 2.7 | 57 580 | 9.3 | 12.4 | 10.5 |
| Mitchell | 281 | 1 045 | 1 502 | 19.2 | 44.1 | 20.7 | 12.7 | 11 045 | 24 499 | 45 237 | 0.4 | 1.5 | 43 511 | 11.6 | 17.2 | 14.9 |
| Montgomery | 420 | 3 323 | 9 120 | 11.2 | 45.4 | 18.6 | 51.1 | 9 125 | 21 013 | 40 925 | -2.2 | 1.4 | 36 670 | 17.6 | 26.0 | 23.2 |
| Morris | 235 | 1 594 | 1 268 | 3.5 | 52.6 | 19.2 | 8.2 | 10 704 | 24 621 | 44 070 | 1.5 | 2.2 | 44 227 | 11.1 | 16.8 | 14.5 |
| Morton | 246 | 1 045 | 802 | 4.7 | 45.8 | 19.4 | 9.9 | 10 151 | 23 022 | 44 263 | -11.9 | 1.9 | 47 006 | 12.7 | 20.7 | 17.6 |
| Nemaha | 68 | 556 | 2 461 | 10.7 | 54.9 | 19.4 | 20.1 | 12 342 | 24 126 | 47 476 | 2.5 | 2.2 | 47 971 | 10.2 | 11.3 | 9.5 |

1. Data for serious crimes have not been adjusted for underreporting; this may affect comparability between geographic areas and over time.   2. Per 100,000 population estimated by the FBI.   3. All persons 3 years old and over enrolled in nursery school through college.   4. Persons 25 years old and over.   5. Elementary and secondary education expenditures.   6. Based on population estimated by the American Community Survey, 2007–2011.

# Table B. States and Counties — Personal Income

| STATE County | Total (mil dol) | Percent change, 2010–2011 | Per capita Dollars | Per capita Rank | Wages and salaries[2] (mil dol) | Proprietors' income (mil dol) | Dividends, interest, and rent (mil dol) | Total | Total | Social Security | Medical payments | Income maintenance | Unemployment insurance |
|---|---|---|---|---|---|---|---|---|---|---|---|---|---|
| | 62 | 63 | 64 | 65 | 66 | 67 | 68 | 69 | 70 | 71 | 72 | 73 | 74 |
| KANSAS............... | 117 386 | 6.5 | 40 883 | X | 74 110 | 13 024 | 18 415 | 19 310 | 18 680 | 6 708 | 7 663 | 2 105 | 839 |
| Allen...................... | 464 | 3.0 | 34 790 | 1 405 | 247 | 62 | 69 | 123 | 120 | 40 | 52 | 14 | 5 |
| Anderson............... | 270 | 5.4 | 33 439 | 1 618 | 87 | 37 | 43 | 67 | 65 | 25 | 28 | 6 | 3 |
| Atchison................ | 529 | 10.4 | 31 499 | 2 001 | 281 | 76 | 78 | 123 | 120 | 41 | 52 | 14 | 5 |
| Barber................... | 208 | 20.8 | 42 528 | 538 | 76 | 69 | 32 | 41 | 39 | 17 | 18 | 3 | 1 |
| Barton................... | 1 080 | 7.6 | 38 785 | 876 | 609 | 165 | 175 | 213 | 207 | 75 | 93 | 21 | 6 |
| Bourbon................ | 460 | 4.3 | 30 693 | 2 156 | 254 | 38 | 73 | 135 | 131 | 43 | 56 | 17 | 5 |
| Brown................... | 410 | 17.0 | 41 002 | 659 | 214 | 78 | 65 | 82 | 80 | 29 | 36 | 9 | 2 |
| Butler.................... | 2 481 | 3.3 | 37 697 | 1 003 | 872 | 305 | 304 | 417 | 402 | 160 | 149 | 37 | 23 |
| Chase.................... | 145 | 3.0 | 51 481 | 177 | 29 | 61 | 16 | 21 | 21 | 8 | 9 | 2 | 1 |
| Chautauqua........... | 128 | 6.6 | 35 669 | 1 271 | 31 | 21 | 26 | 35 | 35 | 13 | 15 | 3 | 1 |
| Cherokee............... | 729 | 2.2 | 34 084 | 1 499 | 278 | 133 | 83 | 186 | 181 | 62 | 82 | 25 | 5 |
| Cheyenne.............. | 116 | 25.5 | 42 519 | 539 | 34 | 43 | 18 | 24 | 23 | 10 | 11 | 1 | 0 |
| Clark..................... | 76 | 6.6 | 35 455 | 1 302 | 34 | 9 | 16 | 18 | 17 | 7 | 8 | 1 | 0 |
| Clay...................... | 383 | 7.4 | 44 657 | 410 | 124 | 73 | 61 | 66 | 64 | 25 | 27 | 5 | 2 |
| Cloud.................... | 333 | 14.3 | 35 515 | 1 288 | 136 | 79 | 41 | 84 | 82 | 30 | 37 | 7 | 2 |
| Coffey................... | 397 | 9.2 | 46 517 | 319 | 299 | 49 | 57 | 75 | 73 | 27 | 33 | 6 | 3 |
| Comanche............. | 69 | 9.0 | 36 405 | 1 148 | 24 | 17 | 13 | 16 | 16 | 7 | 7 | 1 | 0 |
| Cowley.................. | 1 196 | 5.4 | 32 982 | 1 710 | 623 | 119 | 172 | 298 | 290 | 101 | 121 | 32 | 9 |
| Crawford............... | 1 159 | 3.5 | 29 542 | 2 373 | 710 | 10 | 205 | 321 | 312 | 93 | 138 | 41 | 12 |
| Decatur................. | 142 | 22.0 | 48 685 | 245 | 35 | 59 | 24 | 25 | 25 | 11 | 11 | 2 | 0 |
| Dickinson.............. | 748 | 8.8 | 37 910 | 984 | 290 | 83 | 114 | 143 | 138 | 53 | 53 | 12 | 6 |
| Doniphan.............. | 257 | 7.2 | 32 364 | 1 810 | 102 | 31 | 30 | 61 | 59 | 20 | 23 | 5 | 2 |
| Douglas................ | 3 746 | 4.4 | 33 379 | 1 632 | 2 182 | 169 | 631 | 568 | 544 | 198 | 192 | 66 | 29 |
| Edwards................ | 168 | 23.2 | 55 574 | 107 | 45 | 72 | 25 | 25 | 24 | 9 | 11 | 2 | 1 |
| Elk....................... | 96 | 8.5 | 34 099 | 1 495 | 24 | 18 | 14 | 30 | 29 | 11 | 12 | 3 | 1 |
| Ellis..................... | 1 194 | 8.7 | 41 552 | 611 | 717 | 193 | 200 | 178 | 172 | 63 | 73 | 14 | 3 |
| Ellsworth.............. | 228 | 9.2 | 35 125 | 1 353 | 112 | 42 | 36 | 50 | 49 | 19 | 23 | 3 | 1 |
| Finney.................. | 1 239 | 6.8 | 33 417 | 1 622 | 849 | 154 | 166 | 203 | 195 | 55 | 85 | 39 | 6 |
| Ford..................... | 1 117 | 4.7 | 32 309 | 1 821 | 790 | 114 | 157 | 173 | 166 | 52 | 68 | 29 | 5 |
| Franklin................ | 879 | 3.2 | 33 885 | 1 535 | 423 | 56 | 99 | 213 | 207 | 69 | 94 | 21 | 11 |
| Geary................... | 1 463 | 5.0 | 41 409 | 622 | 2 954 | 49 | 163 | 183 | 177 | 47 | 54 | 36 | 10 |
| Gove..................... | 129 | 17.2 | 47 676 | 276 | 46 | 42 | 20 | 23 | 22 | 9 | 11 | 1 | 0 |
| Graham................. | 151 | 22.1 | 57 090 | 94 | 46 | 63 | 18 | 26 | 26 | 10 | 13 | 1 | 0 |
| Grant.................... | 309 | 3.9 | 38 787 | 875 | 183 | 84 | 37 | 40 | 38 | 15 | 17 | 5 | 1 |
| Gray..................... | 288 | 13.4 | 47 114 | 293 | 132 | 94 | 36 | 30 | 29 | 12 | 13 | 3 | 1 |
| Greeley................. | 80 | 21.8 | 63 499 | 45 | 27 | 40 | 9 | 9 | 9 | 4 | 4 | 0 | 0 |
| Greenwood............ | 229 | 4.8 | 34 437 | 1 446 | 71 | 32 | 41 | 63 | 62 | 24 | 28 | 6 | 2 |
| Hamilton............... | 115 | 11.1 | 43 240 | 490 | 45 | 45 | 14 | 16 | 16 | 6 | 7 | 2 | 0 |
| Harper.................. | 278 | 20.6 | 46 355 | 325 | 103 | 91 | 35 | 50 | 48 | 20 | 22 | 4 | 1 |
| Harvey.................. | 1 333 | 4.3 | 38 254 | 938 | 632 | 311 | 173 | 266 | 258 | 96 | 113 | 22 | 8 |
| Haskell................. | 266 | 24.2 | 62 019 | 51 | 83 | 136 | 30 | 20 | 19 | 8 | 8 | 2 | 0 |
| Hodgeman............. | 81 | 10.0 | 41 348 | 632 | 25 | 26 | 14 | 14 | 13 | 6 | 6 | 1 | 0 |
| Jackson................ | 479 | 8.4 | 35 661 | 1 273 | 169 | 75 | 57 | 92 | 89 | 38 | 31 | 9 | 4 |
| Jefferson.............. | 659 | 6.7 | 34 779 | 1 407 | 144 | 34 | 96 | 127 | 123 | 52 | 44 | 10 | 7 |
| Jewell................... | 153 | 44.3 | 49 412 | 223 | 35 | 69 | 18 | 26 | 25 | 12 | 10 | 2 | 0 |
| Johnson................ | 31 271 | 6.5 | 56 550 | 99 | 19 885 | 3 095 | 6 119 | 2 858 | 2 735 | 1 161 | 1 063 | 178 | 147 |
| Kearny.................. | 145 | 10.1 | 36 346 | 1 160 | 58 | 30 | 25 | 24 | 23 | 8 | 10 | 3 | 1 |
| Kingman............... | 338 | 14.9 | 43 017 | 510 | 119 | 82 | 48 | 62 | 60 | 25 | 26 | 4 | 2 |
| Kiowa................... | 112 | 5.2 | 43 801 | 451 | 42 | 30 | 17 | 21 | 20 | 8 | 10 | 1 | 0 |
| Labette................. | 754 | 5.2 | 35 029 | 1 365 | 404 | 72 | 102 | 222 | 217 | 62 | 109 | 24 | 8 |
| Lane..................... | 70 | 1.1 | 40 053 | 741 | 34 | 10 | 16 | 15 | 14 | 6 | 7 | 1 | 0 |
| Leavenworth.......... | 2 652 | 3.8 | 34 360 | 1 461 | 2 042 | 131 | 404 | 458 | 442 | 152 | 175 | 42 | 23 |
| Lincoln................. | 139 | 22.2 | 43 313 | 483 | 39 | 49 | 20 | 22 | 22 | 9 | 9 | 2 | 1 |
| Linn..................... | 302 | 3.2 | 31 382 | 2 020 | 115 | 13 | 44 | 83 | 81 | 31 | 33 | 7 | 5 |
| Logan................... | 138 | 14.8 | 49 477 | 222 | 52 | 54 | 19 | 21 | 20 | 8 | 9 | 2 | 0 |
| Lyon..................... | 996 | 5.1 | 29 493 | 2 378 | 652 | 36 | 156 | 235 | 227 | 74 | 90 | 29 | 9 |
| McPherson............ | 1 212 | 8.2 | 41 457 | 621 | 723 | 206 | 168 | 212 | 205 | 87 | 89 | 14 | 5 |
| Marion.................. | 442 | 8.1 | 35 248 | 1 331 | 144 | 91 | 63 | 97 | 95 | 39 | 41 | 6 | 3 |
| Marshall................ | 466 | 20.4 | 46 600 | 317 | 226 | 118 | 83 | 79 | 76 | 29 | 31 | 6 | 2 |
| Meade................... | 204 | 12.6 | 45 079 | 392 | 67 | 67 | 33 | 28 | 27 | 11 | 12 | 2 | 0 |
| Miami................... | 1 378 | 5.1 | 42 131 | 564 | 353 | 29 | 173 | 231 | 223 | 77 | 103 | 18 | 12 |
| Mitchell................ | 273 | 17.6 | 43 319 | 482 | 145 | 64 | 43 | 55 | 53 | 20 | 26 | 3 | 1 |
| Montgomery.......... | 1 192 | 5.6 | 34 133 | 1 492 | 762 | 89 | 154 | 318 | 310 | 105 | 132 | 37 | 16 |
| Morris................... | 210 | 6.4 | 35 727 | 1 259 | 65 | 8 | 39 | 47 | 45 | 18 | 18 | 4 | 2 |
| Morton.................. | 168 | 17.1 | 52 667 | 150 | 65 | 68 | 20 | 23 | 23 | 8 | 11 | 2 | 0 |
| Nemaha................ | 493 | 23.2 | 48 745 | 243 | 211 | 114 | 124 | 70 | 68 | 28 | 31 | 5 | 1 |

1. Based on the resident population estimated as of July 1 of the year shown.    2. Includes supplements to wages and salaries.

# Table B. States and Counties — Earnings, Social Security, and Housing

| STATE County | Earnings, 2011 | | | | | | | | | Social Security beneficiaries, December 2011 | | | Housing units, 2010 | |
|---|---|---|---|---|---|---|---|---|---|---|---|---|---|---|
| | | | | | Percent by selected industries | | | | | | | | | |
| | | | Goods-related[1] | | Service-related and health | | | | | | | Supple- mental Security Income recipients, December 2011 | | |
| | Total (mil dol) | Farm | Total | Manu- facturing | Infor- mation and profes- sional and technical services | Retail trade | Finance, insur- ance, and real estate | Health care and social services | Govern- ment | Number | Rate[2] | | Total | Percent change, 2000– 2010 |
| | 75 | 76 | 77 | 78 | 79 | 80 | 81 | 82 | 83 | 84 | 85 | 86 | 87 | 88 |
| KANSAS | 87 133 | 4.2 | 20.5 | 14.1 | 8.9 | 5.8 | 6.7 | 10.6 | 19.9 | 498 707 | 174 | 47 336 | 1 233 215 | 9.0 |
| Allen | 309 | 3.1 | D | 33.4 | 2.3 | 6.5 | 2.9 | D | 22.3 | 3 240 | 243 | 380 | 6 226 | -3.5 |
| Anderson | 123 | 7.7 | 22.2 | 10.5 | 2.1 | 11.6 | D | D | 19.4 | 1 975 | 245 | 107 | 3 720 | 3.4 |
| Atchison | 357 | 8.8 | 35.4 | 28.3 | D | 6.2 | 3.8 | D | 12.1 | 3 270 | 195 | 342 | 6 990 | 2.5 |
| Barber | 145 | 27.2 | 28.3 | 5.2 | D | 5.8 | D | D | 18.9 | 1 280 | 262 | 74 | 2 765 | 0.9 |
| Barton | 774 | 3.1 | 30.9 | 6.4 | 3.4 | 8.2 | 7.8 | 12.1 | 13.2 | 5 715 | 205 | 485 | 12 696 | -1.5 |
| Bourbon | 291 | 0.8 | D | 15.3 | 3.8 | 6.8 | 10.1 | 17.9 | 17.2 | 3 585 | 239 | 414 | 7 167 | 0.4 |
| Brown | 292 | 20.1 | D | 14.5 | 3.0 | 5.6 | 5.3 | 10.9 | 25.6 | 2 330 | 233 | 240 | 4 779 | -0.7 |
| Butler | 1 177 | 2.2 | 27.1 | 16.5 | 3.5 | 9.2 | 4.5 | D | 22.1 | 11 450 | 174 | 788 | 26 058 | 12.4 |
| Chase | 90 | 13.0 | D | 2.6 | D | 5.5 | D | D | 11.3 | 640 | 227 | 41 | 1 503 | -1.7 |
| Chautauqua | 52 | 9.3 | D | D | D | 7.6 | D | 11.4 | 20.6 | 1 110 | 310 | 110 | 2 150 | -0.9 |
| Cherokee | 412 | 3.7 | D | 30.1 | D | 6.5 | 2.9 | D | 13.7 | 5 105 | 239 | 700 | 9 890 | -1.4 |
| Cheyenne | 77 | 52.3 | D | 1.0 | D | 2.8 | D | 8.7 | 13.1 | 805 | 296 | 26 | 1 518 | -7.2 |
| Clark | 42 | 14.8 | D | D | D | 5.2 | D | D | 45.8 | 545 | 254 | 27 | 1 135 | 2.2 |
| Clay | 197 | 14.9 | D | 9.0 | 3.1 | 11.4 | 4.0 | D | 20.5 | 2 040 | 238 | 117 | 4 042 | -1.0 |
| Cloud | 215 | 25.8 | D | 11.0 | 4.4 | 7.1 | 3.3 | D | 16.5 | 2 415 | 258 | 180 | 4 659 | -3.7 |
| Coffey | 347 | 2.0 | 8.1 | 1.5 | 3.5 | 3.6 | 1.8 | 2.1 | 15.3 | 2 150 | 252 | 199 | 3 964 | 2.2 |
| Comanche | 41 | 37.8 | 10.2 | 4.3 | D | D | D | D | 24.8 | 515 | 273 | 26 | 1 044 | -4.0 |
| Cowley | 741 | 2.8 | 38.2 | 32.0 | 2.9 | 7.1 | 3.2 | D | 22.2 | 7 675 | 212 | 778 | 16 030 | 2.3 |
| Crawford | 720 | 0.2 | 17.4 | 14.6 | 4.5 | 7.5 | 2.7 | 14.4 | 30.8 | 7 460 | 190 | 1 040 | 17 801 | 3.4 |
| Decatur | 93 | 54.6 | D | D | D | 4.9 | D | 8.1 | 10.3 | 905 | 310 | 37 | 1 818 | -0.2 |
| Dickinson | 372 | 18.3 | D | 16.8 | 2.4 | 7.1 | 2.6 | D | 20.2 | 4 315 | 219 | 260 | 8 972 | 3.3 |
| Doniphan | 133 | 15.5 | D | 19.1 | D | 3.5 | 3.8 | D | 29.8 | 1 610 | 203 | 128 | 3 576 | 2.5 |
| Douglas | 2 351 | 0.2 | 14.8 | 8.8 | 9.6 | 7.0 | 4.8 | 7.4 | 34.8 | 14 085 | 126 | 1 242 | 46 731 | 16.1 |
| Edwards | 117 | 59.6 | D | 5.7 | D | 2.2 | 1.3 | 5.5 | 8.8 | 700 | 232 | 46 | 1 636 | -6.7 |
| Elk | 42 | 31.3 | D | D | D | 3.2 | 2.1 | D | 31.6 | 930 | 331 | 66 | 1 760 | -5.3 |
| Ellis | 910 | 4.4 | 21.7 | 5.8 | 6.5 | 8.4 | 6.2 | 17.9 | 17.3 | 4 825 | 168 | 266 | 12 872 | 6.6 |
| Ellsworth | 154 | 17.7 | 21.3 | 12.3 | 5.4 | 3.9 | 3.5 | D | 27.1 | 1 485 | 229 | 89 | 3 239 | 0.3 |
| Finney | 1 002 | 4.2 | 28.9 | 19.7 | 3.5 | 8.0 | 4.0 | D | 17.5 | 4 320 | 116 | 616 | 13 276 | -3.5 |
| Ford | 905 | 4.1 | D | 31.0 | 3.9 | 6.5 | 2.7 | D | 15.9 | 4 070 | 118 | 459 | 12 005 | 3.0 |
| Franklin | 479 | 3.1 | 15.4 | 9.9 | 3.1 | 6.4 | 2.5 | D | 20.2 | 5 395 | 208 | 516 | 11 147 | 9.0 |
| Geary | 3 003 | 0.2 | 3.3 | 1.3 | D | 1.6 | 1.1 | 0.9 | 86.6 | 4 215 | 119 | 576 | 14 517 | 21.8 |
| Gove | 88 | 37.4 | 11.9 | 6.9 | D | 7.6 | 3.0 | 2.8 | 19.2 | 720 | 267 | 14 | 1 373 | -3.5 |
| Graham | 108 | 35.4 | D | D | D | 4.8 | 4.4 | 4.1 | 14.6 | 805 | 305 | 36 | 1 484 | -4.4 |
| Grant | 267 | 16.9 | 25.2 | 3.7 | D | 4.1 | 3.0 | 5.5 | 12.0 | 1 105 | 139 | 87 | 2 945 | -2.7 |
| Gray | 227 | 38.8 | D | 2.9 | 5.3 | 3.2 | D | 1.9 | 15.4 | 895 | 146 | 33 | 2 340 | 7.3 |
| Greeley | 67 | 63.5 | D | 0.0 | D | 3.4 | 2.4 | D | 9.5 | 295 | 234 | 0 | 629 | -11.7 |
| Greenwood | 103 | 25.5 | 20.1 | 5.7 | 1.7 | 4.1 | D | D | 19.6 | 1 880 | 283 | 172 | 4 068 | -4.8 |
| Hamilton | 90 | 57.4 | D | 0.0 | D | 3.1 | 5.3 | 0.9 | 16.3 | 435 | 163 | 19 | 1 236 | 2.1 |
| Harper | 194 | 29.5 | 19.6 | 9.5 | D | 7.2 | 3.7 | 1.7 | 18.2 | 1 490 | 249 | 96 | 3 116 | -4.7 |
| Harvey | 943 | 4.3 | 30.0 | 21.5 | 4.1 | 6.5 | 6.4 | D | 10.0 | 7 110 | 204 | 453 | 14 527 | 8.6 |
| Haskell | 219 | 62.1 | D | D | D | 1.2 | D | D | 12.0 | 565 | 132 | 27 | 1 666 | 1.6 |
| Hodgeman | 52 | 51.8 | D | 0.0 | D | 4.2 | 2.7 | D | 22.9 | 425 | 216 | 13 | 973 | 3.1 |
| Jackson | 244 | 9.0 | D | 3.8 | 2.9 | 7.6 | 4.7 | D | 39.7 | 3 035 | 226 | 179 | 5 779 | 13.5 |
| Jefferson | 178 | 9.2 | D | 5.1 | D | 5.8 | D | D | 28.2 | 3 935 | 208 | 220 | 8 160 | 8.9 |
| Jewell | 104 | 57.2 | D | D | D | 3.9 | 1.9 | 0.7 | 13.7 | 980 | 317 | 43 | 2 032 | -3.4 |
| Johnson | 22 980 | 0.1 | 13.5 | 8.6 | 20.3 | 5.8 | 13.6 | 10.6 | 7.9 | 75 720 | 137 | 3 644 | 226 571 | 24.6 |
| Kearny | 88 | 37.8 | D | D | D | 2.6 | D | 1.1 | 33.9 | 635 | 159 | 40 | 1 556 | -6.1 |
| Kingman | 201 | 24.6 | 25.7 | 11.2 | 2.4 | 4.2 | D | 8.1 | 12.3 | 1 885 | 240 | 99 | 3 818 | -0.9 |
| Kiowa | 72 | 28.2 | D | D | D | D | 2.5 | D | 20.3 | 625 | 245 | 61 | 1 220 | -25.7 |
| Labette | 476 | 2.7 | D | 21.6 | 3.8 | 6.7 | 3.3 | 9.9 | 27.3 | 5 155 | 240 | 705 | 10 092 | -2.0 |
| Lane | 44 | 25.6 | D | D | D | 5.4 | 4.4 | D | 24.4 | 460 | 263 | 18 | 990 | -7.0 |
| Leavenworth | 2 173 | -0.2 | D | 2.9 | 5.8 | 3.2 | 4.0 | 4.6 | 67.1 | 11 790 | 153 | 878 | 28 697 | 17.6 |
| Lincoln | 89 | 48.3 | D | D | D | 3.2 | 2.5 | 2.9 | 20.2 | 750 | 233 | 38 | 1 864 | 0.6 |
| Linn | 129 | 0.7 | 15.8 | 6.9 | D | 4.8 | D | 1.5 | 24.2 | 2 465 | 256 | 165 | 5 446 | 15.4 |
| Logan | 107 | 44.4 | D | 0.3 | D | 4.7 | 3.3 | D | 27.0 | 660 | 237 | 41 | 1 441 | 1.3 |
| Lyon | 688 | 1.4 | 25.4 | 21.5 | 3.1 | 7.2 | 3.2 | 8.7 | 31.6 | 5 680 | 168 | 658 | 15 237 | 3.3 |
| McPherson | 929 | 7.5 | 44.2 | 32.6 | 2.8 | 4.4 | 3.4 | 9.5 | 10.0 | 6 305 | 216 | 317 | 12 721 | 7.5 |
| Marion | 235 | 25.0 | D | 10.3 | 3.7 | 3.7 | 3.3 | D | 17.1 | 3 065 | 244 | 146 | 5 946 | 1.1 |
| Marshall | 344 | 20.0 | D | 19.2 | 4.1 | 5.6 | 3.6 | 6.3 | 9.1 | 2 440 | 244 | 158 | 4 866 | -2.7 |
| Meade | 135 | 49.0 | 4.9 | 0.6 | D | 2.9 | D | D | 19.9 | 870 | 192 | 32 | 1 998 | 1.5 |
| Miami | 382 | -0.6 | 18.7 | 7.9 | 4.1 | 12.1 | 5.4 | 12.2 | 27.2 | 5 740 | 175 | 420 | 13 190 | 20.1 |
| Mitchell | 209 | 22.0 | D | 12.5 | 2.6 | 6.9 | D | 5.7 | 22.0 | 1 520 | 241 | 76 | 3 296 | -1.3 |
| Montgomery | 851 | 1.2 | 37.5 | 30.4 | D | 6.1 | 2.5 | 13.3 | 14.4 | 8 345 | 239 | 1 080 | 16 578 | -3.7 |
| Morris | 73 | 9.2 | 15.2 | 8.8 | D | 5.4 | 4.8 | D | 28.3 | 1 480 | 251 | 80 | 3 206 | 1.5 |
| Morton | 133 | 52.3 | D | D | D | 3.7 | D | D | 21.5 | 625 | 195 | 45 | 1 467 | -3.4 |
| Nemaha | 325 | 27.6 | D | 20.0 | 2.1 | 4.2 | D | D | 10.9 | 2 340 | 231 | 110 | 4 562 | 5.1 |

1. Includes mining, construction, and manufacturing.  2. Per 1,000 resident population enumerated in the 2010 census.

# Table B. States and Counties — Housing, Labor Force, and Employment

| STATE County | Housing units, 2007–2011 | | | | | | | | Civilian labor force, 2012 | | | | Civilian employment,[6] 2007–2011 | | |
|---|---|---|---|---|---|---|---|---|---|---|---|---|---|---|---|
| | Occupied units | | | | | | | | | | Unemployment | | | Percent | |
| | Owner-occupied | | | | Renter-occupied | | | | | | | | | | |
| | | | | Median owner cost as a percent of income | | | | | | | | | | | Construction, production, and maintenance occupations |
| | Total | Percent | Median value[1] | With a mortgage | Without a mortgage[2] | Median rent[3] | Median rent as a percent of income | Substandard units[4] (percent) | Total | Percent change, 2011–2012 | Total | Rate[5] | Total | Management, business, science and arts | |
| | 89 | 90 | 91 | 92 | 93 | 94 | 95 | 96 | 97 | 98 | 99 | 100 | 101 | 102 | 103 |
| KANSAS | 1 104 479 | 69.0 | 125 500 | 21.6 | 11.9 | 699 | 27.7 | 2.3 | 1 489 320 | -0.6 | 85 454 | 5.7 | 1 393 658 | 35.9 | 23.4 |
| Allen | 5 598 | 77.5 | 64 200 | 19.1 | 11.5 | 473 | 28.9 | 0.6 | 7 507 | -2.7 | 480 | 6.4 | 6 455 | 28.0 | 35.9 |
| Anderson | 3 201 | 81.5 | 81 100 | 26.5 | 11.0 | 552 | 26.6 | 1.7 | 4 248 | -4.3 | 282 | 6.6 | 3 745 | 29.6 | 33.5 |
| Atchison | 6 096 | 69.1 | 87 600 | 21.5 | 13.0 | 544 | 25.2 | 2.9 | 8 536 | -1.5 | 582 | 6.8 | 7 558 | 32.8 | 29.8 |
| Barber | 2 305 | 74.7 | 54 400 | 18.0 | 12.6 | 513 | 22.4 | 1.3 | 2 800 | -1.8 | 104 | 3.7 | 2 521 | 37.9 | 29.4 |
| Barton | 11 241 | 72.2 | 72 500 | 19.5 | 11.1 | 531 | 23.6 | 1.6 | 16 173 | -0.7 | 672 | 4.2 | 14 004 | 30.3 | 26.4 |
| Bourbon | 5 727 | 73.8 | 80 900 | 22.1 | 13.6 | 574 | 24.5 | 1.2 | 8 095 | -2.5 | 508 | 6.3 | 6 651 | 29.3 | 28.1 |
| Brown | 4 133 | 67.3 | 77 000 | 21.8 | 13.1 | 479 | 24.7 | 1.0 | 5 584 | 0.3 | 278 | 5.0 | 4 755 | 30.2 | 25.7 |
| Butler | 24 039 | 77.6 | 122 500 | 20.7 | 12.2 | 690 | 25.1 | 1.4 | 31 138 | -1.0 | 2 050 | 6.6 | 31 109 | 34.5 | 27.2 |
| Chase | 1 151 | 76.5 | 82 000 | 21.9 | 9.9 | 457 | 27.9 | 1.8 | 1 511 | 0.1 | 71 | 4.7 | 1 333 | 27.6 | 33.6 |
| Chautauqua | 1 545 | 77.1 | 46 000 | 19.9 | 12.9 | 559 | 29.8 | 1.5 | 1 832 | -0.7 | 112 | 6.1 | 1 502 | 26.7 | 37.5 |
| Cherokee | 8 189 | 78.8 | 71 400 | 20.2 | 12.5 | 568 | 27.0 | 2.3 | 11 231 | -2.5 | 822 | 7.3 | 9 728 | 27.6 | 32.5 |
| Cheyenne | 1 276 | 77.2 | 68 400 | 20.9 | 15.4 | 559 | 28.0 | 0.4 | 1 489 | 0.1 | 48 | 3.2 | 1 292 | 28.6 | 26.6 |
| Clark | 885 | 74.9 | 59 100 | 18.0 | 11.8 | 565 | 24.4 | 1.1 | 1 249 | -0.9 | 42 | 3.4 | 1 062 | 41.6 | 19.9 |
| Clay | 3 517 | 74.9 | 84 000 | 20.4 | 12.1 | 623 | 25.5 | 0.5 | 4 926 | -2.9 | 215 | 4.4 | 3 918 | 32.3 | 30.1 |
| Cloud | 3 979 | 78.0 | 63 200 | 20.6 | 13.7 | 484 | 24.3 | 1.4 | 5 893 | 0.9 | 228 | 3.9 | 4 408 | 28.8 | 30.0 |
| Coffey | 3 482 | 79.2 | 97 400 | 19.5 | 11.0 | 515 | 23.2 | 1.6 | 5 193 | -3.1 | 311 | 6.0 | 4 165 | 36.4 | 27.3 |
| Comanche | 843 | 82.0 | 44 600 | 23.8 | 9.9 | 426 | 23.9 | 0.0 | 1 084 | 0.9 | 39 | 3.6 | 997 | 36.8 | 30.7 |
| Cowley | 13 489 | 71.5 | 79 900 | 20.7 | 12.6 | 594 | 27.8 | 3.4 | 18 471 | 0.2 | 1 059 | 5.7 | 16 293 | 27.0 | 32.7 |
| Crawford | 15 354 | 63.7 | 85 200 | 20.6 | 13.4 | 651 | 33.7 | 1.9 | 20 388 | -0.5 | 1 281 | 6.3 | 18 044 | 32.7 | 23.0 |
| Decatur | 1 484 | 80.3 | 52 200 | 21.7 | 12.9 | 458 | 27.5 | 1.8 | 1 663 | 0.0 | 63 | 3.8 | 1 365 | 37.0 | 26.2 |
| Dickinson | 7 591 | 74.9 | 102 500 | 21.5 | 11.4 | 577 | 23.6 | 1.2 | 10 880 | 0.0 | 600 | 5.5 | 9 261 | 30.8 | 29.8 |
| Doniphan | 3 108 | 74.0 | 83 100 | 19.6 | 12.8 | 490 | 21.0 | 1.6 | 4 749 | 0.1 | 291 | 6.1 | 3 901 | 30.3 | 31.7 |
| Douglas | 43 238 | 51.9 | 179 900 | 23.3 | 12.3 | 811 | 34.5 | 2.0 | 61 614 | -0.4 | 3 251 | 5.3 | 60 345 | 43.2 | 15.3 |
| Edwards | 1 352 | 77.4 | 55 500 | 18.5 | 11.0 | 516 | 30.9 | 1.3 | 1 821 | -0.4 | 67 | 3.7 | 1 522 | 35.6 | 32.6 |
| Elk | 1 289 | 80.8 | 53 200 | 19.4 | 15.0 | 421 | 28.3 | 2.9 | 1 521 | -2.3 | 91 | 6.0 | 1 222 | 34.0 | 33.0 |
| Ellis | 11 678 | 63.7 | 123 600 | 21.6 | 12.9 | 579 | 29.8 | 0.6 | 19 571 | 0.4 | 614 | 3.1 | 16 641 | 31.1 | 20.5 |
| Ellsworth | 2 560 | 75.5 | 68 900 | 19.6 | 11.4 | 497 | 24.6 | 0.4 | 4 037 | -0.2 | 134 | 3.3 | 2 996 | 33.7 | 28.1 |
| Finney | 12 105 | 67.8 | 105 300 | 22.6 | 10.8 | 637 | 23.1 | 7.6 | 19 994 | -3.6 | 886 | 4.4 | 18 550 | 24.7 | 34.3 |
| Ford | 10 982 | 66.8 | 85 000 | 22.0 | 12.3 | 598 | 24.0 | 6.7 | 20 129 | 2.6 | 721 | 3.6 | 16 077 | 25.5 | 42.3 |
| Franklin | 10 148 | 71.8 | 120 600 | 22.8 | 13.7 | 699 | 25.7 | 2.1 | 13 174 | -0.3 | 998 | 7.6 | 13 081 | 29.2 | 31.4 |
| Geary | 11 868 | 49.4 | 122 000 | 22.4 | 12.1 | 861 | 27.5 | 3.8 | 14 746 | 0.0 | 1 005 | 6.8 | 12 106 | 30.9 | 25.5 |
| Gove | 1 151 | 80.5 | 66 300 | 20.6 | 10.8 | 484 | 21.0 | 0.8 | 1 685 | 1.4 | 45 | 2.7 | 1 325 | 37.0 | 27.2 |
| Graham | 1 183 | 79.9 | 67 500 | 22.7 | 10.8 | 506 | 22.9 | 1.2 | 1 500 | -2.3 | 47 | 3.1 | 1 279 | 41.1 | 23.8 |
| Grant | 2 811 | 74.1 | 86 400 | 18.3 | 9.9 | 477 | 20.5 | 4.2 | 3 955 | -3.1 | 152 | 3.8 | 3 816 | 32.4 | 37.9 |
| Gray | 2 052 | 75.1 | 93 200 | 20.0 | 10.3 | 548 | 17.8 | 5.6 | 3 695 | 0.2 | 110 | 3.0 | 2 985 | 31.9 | 31.5 |
| Greeley | 502 | 76.1 | 75 200 | 21.6 | 9.9 | 506 | 13.2 | 0.0 | 836 | 6.8 | 28 | 3.3 | 672 | 36.8 | 22.5 |
| Greenwood | 2 944 | 76.2 | 51 400 | 18.2 | 12.4 | 454 | 27.5 | 3.0 | 3 508 | -0.5 | 193 | 5.5 | 2 988 | 30.7 | 33.6 |
| Hamilton | 1 071 | 75.6 | 73 300 | 25.2 | 11.8 | 505 | 19.5 | 3.6 | 1 325 | 4.9 | 49 | 3.7 | 1 321 | 29.8 | 29.4 |
| Harper | 2 660 | 72.4 | 64 100 | 19.8 | 11.8 | 520 | 25.7 | 1.4 | 3 744 | 8.4 | 137 | 3.7 | 2 871 | 31.4 | 32.7 |
| Harvey | 13 137 | 74.2 | 106 700 | 20.1 | 10.5 | 622 | 28.8 | 1.7 | 17 105 | -0.7 | 965 | 5.6 | 16 681 | 35.1 | 27.1 |
| Haskell | 1 397 | 76.2 | 90 300 | 18.5 | 9.9 | 588 | 17.9 | 2.8 | 2 405 | 2.9 | 83 | 3.5 | 2 241 | 30.4 | 37.3 |
| Hodgeman | 781 | 78.0 | 68 500 | 14.9 | 11.0 | 506 | 22.9 | 2.0 | 1 026 | 1.7 | 37 | 3.6 | 924 | 45.3 | 27.4 |
| Jackson | 5 336 | 77.5 | 119 300 | 22.4 | 11.7 | 621 | 21.8 | 2.8 | 6 766 | -0.7 | 431 | 6.4 | 6 756 | 30.5 | 25.0 |
| Jefferson | 7 401 | 85.2 | 135 800 | 22.4 | 13.0 | 697 | 24.2 | 2.4 | 9 650 | -1.4 | 619 | 6.4 | 9 732 | 38.4 | 27.2 |
| Jewell | 1 470 | 78.0 | 48 400 | 19.1 | 11.3 | 424 | 15.0 | 2.2 | 1 795 | -4.7 | 62 | 3.5 | 1 532 | 39.5 | 22.8 |
| Johnson | 212 587 | 71.6 | 211 800 | 21.8 | 11.1 | 880 | 26.2 | 1.4 | 300 603 | -0.2 | 14 989 | 5.0 | 293 207 | 48.5 | 12.1 |
| Kearny | 1 385 | 78.1 | 90 700 | 20.6 | 12.7 | 567 | 15.9 | 4.4 | 2 262 | -0.8 | 86 | 3.8 | 1 881 | 27.9 | 40.1 |
| Kingman | 3 357 | 75.3 | 81 300 | 21.0 | 10.8 | 575 | 19.8 | 3.0 | 4 696 | 1.3 | 224 | 4.8 | 3 534 | 34.0 | 34.3 |
| Kiowa | 1 013 | 69.2 | 81 600 | 20.2 | 11.0 | 500 | 25.9 | 1.3 | 1 609 | 4.0 | 55 | 3.4 | 1 182 | 34.9 | 26.4 |
| Labette | 8 781 | 72.5 | 63 500 | 21.0 | 12.0 | 534 | 24.4 | 2.4 | 10 622 | -3.0 | 851 | 8.0 | 10 245 | 26.7 | 30.7 |
| Lane | 737 | 69.5 | 56 500 | 18.8 | 10.3 | 546 | 17.1 | 0.0 | 1 043 | -5.9 | 40 | 3.8 | 719 | 37.3 | 30.2 |
| Leavenworth | 25 932 | 68.2 | 167 300 | 22.2 | 12.2 | 822 | 26.4 | 1.4 | 33 196 | -0.6 | 2 295 | 6.9 | 31 931 | 36.0 | 21.3 |
| Lincoln | 1 444 | 79.2 | 62 900 | 21.0 | 13.8 | 483 | 25.0 | 0.9 | 1 952 | -0.9 | 89 | 4.6 | 1 655 | 33.2 | 30.9 |
| Linn | 4 323 | 82.2 | 98 100 | 24.5 | 14.1 | 542 | 27.9 | 2.0 | 4 543 | -1.5 | 394 | 8.7 | 4 274 | 31.2 | 33.3 |
| Logan | 1 323 | 74.5 | 69 700 | 19.6 | 11.1 | 503 | 22.1 | 2.2 | 1 758 | -1.5 | 53 | 3.0 | 1 528 | 34.1 | 30.3 |
| Lyon | 13 428 | 60.6 | 92 600 | 21.4 | 12.0 | 581 | 28.4 | 3.4 | 18 183 | -0.7 | 1 007 | 5.5 | 17 490 | 25.6 | 30.5 |
| McPherson | 11 541 | 77.4 | 119 000 | 20.2 | 10.3 | 586 | 21.7 | 1.5 | 16 838 | -0.3 | 677 | 4.0 | 14 945 | 30.6 | 29.5 |
| Marion | 5 058 | 80.9 | 83 300 | 20.8 | 12.1 | 539 | 26.0 | 1.4 | 6 493 | -1.5 | 326 | 5.0 | 6 251 | 34.6 | 28.0 |
| Marshall | 4 309 | 76.1 | 76 400 | 20.2 | 11.3 | 508 | 19.7 | 4.3 | 6 278 | 1.4 | 253 | 4.0 | 5 178 | 31.6 | 32.9 |
| Meade | 1 765 | 73.5 | 77 400 | 19.2 | 11.7 | 578 | 18.1 | 2.3 | 2 533 | -0.9 | 84 | 3.3 | 2 111 | 36.1 | 25.2 |
| Miami | 12 034 | 80.9 | 166 000 | 23.9 | 13.3 | 690 | 30.8 | 1.8 | 16 721 | -0.7 | 1 055 | 6.3 | 16 133 | 34.3 | 25.3 |
| Mitchell | 2 710 | 71.7 | 72 100 | 17.2 | 11.2 | 514 | 19.4 | 0.8 | 3 620 | -0.9 | 113 | 3.1 | 3 315 | 36.1 | 25.9 |
| Montgomery | 14 179 | 72.3 | 71 200 | 19.5 | 11.6 | 547 | 28.2 | 1.9 | 18 713 | 0.3 | 1 433 | 7.7 | 15 868 | 27.4 | 30.5 |
| Morris | 2 558 | 75.1 | 76 800 | 20.0 | 10.2 | 500 | 22.9 | 1.1 | 2 966 | -1.7 | 196 | 6.6 | 2 993 | 31.1 | 35.0 |
| Morton | 1 221 | 74.5 | 69 500 | 17.6 | 12.6 | 529 | 19.4 | 1.1 | 1 636 | -1.1 | 63 | 3.9 | 1 610 | 34.2 | 31.2 |
| Nemaha | 4 040 | 79.9 | 89 000 | 19.1 | 10.7 | 436 | 23.5 | 1.3 | 6 196 | 1.6 | 214 | 3.5 | 5 130 | 39.8 | 26.1 |

1. Specified owner-occupied units.   2. A value of 9.9 represents 9.9 percent or less.   3. Specified renter-occupied units. A value of 10.0 represents 10 percent or less.   4. Overcrowded or lacking complete plumbing facilities.   5. Percent of civilian labor force.   6. Persons 16 years old and over.

## Table B. States and Counties — Nonfarm Employment and Agriculture

| STATE County | Private nonfarm establishments, employment and payroll, 2011 | | | | | | | | | Agriculture, 2007 | | | |
| | Number of establish-ments | Employment | | | | | | Annual payroll | | Farms | | | Farm operators whose principal occu-pation is farming (percent) |
| | | Total | Health care and social assistance | Manufac-turing | Retail trade | Finance and insurance | Professional, scientific, and technical services | Total (mil dol) | Average per employee (dollars) | Number | Percent with: | | |
| | | | | | | | | | | | Fewer than 50 acres | 500 acres or more | |
| | 104 | 105 | 106 | 107 | 108 | 109 | 110 | 111 | 112 | 113 | 114 | 115 | 116 |
| KANSAS | 73 598 | 1 113 423 | 189 323 | 153 926 | 146 158 | 57 248 | 56 408 | 43 734 | 39 279 | 65 531 | 18.6 | 30.9 | 47.1 |
| Allen | 377 | 4 697 | 584 | 2 159 | 572 | 119 | 114 | 144 | 30 758 | 611 | 14.9 | 23.2 | 42.2 |
| Anderson | 211 | 1 510 | 337 | 197 | D | 102 | D | 40 | 26 191 | 715 | 18.5 | 25.3 | 47.1 |
| Atchison | 360 | 5 724 | 938 | 1 149 | 708 | D | 75 | 164 | 28 723 | 711 | 20.3 | 20.8 | 46.8 |
| Barber | 217 | 1 340 | 284 | D | 248 | 48 | D | 40 | 29 822 | 427 | 11.2 | 48.0 | 50.6 |
| Barton | 970 | 9 585 | 1 764 | 1 097 | 1 532 | 453 | 325 | 337 | 35 114 | 678 | 15.8 | 37.5 | 54.1 |
| Bourbon | 372 | 4 726 | 1 073 | 1 081 | 641 | 254 | 115 | 129 | 27 395 | 928 | 17.2 | 18.6 | 39.3 |
| Brown | 257 | 3 377 | 807 | 528 | D | 156 | D | 101 | 29 960 | 637 | 18.7 | 27.0 | 54.2 |
| Butler | 1 275 | 12 883 | 3 589 | D | 2 002 | 497 | 466 | 402 | 31 227 | 1 427 | 32.0 | 19.6 | 42.7 |
| Chase | 73 | 410 | D | D | 59 | D | D | 11 | 26 666 | 250 | 14.8 | 42.8 | 55.2 |
| Chautauqua | 83 | 483 | D | D | 126 | D | 5 | 12 | 23 923 | 359 | 9.7 | 32.3 | 51.5 |
| Cherokee | 344 | 5 151 | 863 | 1 801 | 493 | 120 | 100 | 186 | 36 127 | 809 | 26.1 | 20.0 | 51.5 |
| Cheyenne | 106 | 555 | 149 | D | 94 | 31 | D | 15 | 26 766 | 422 | 8.3 | 49.8 | 55.0 |
| Clark | 62 | D | D | D | D | D | 26 | D | D | 278 | 6.1 | 48.2 | 49.3 |
| Clay | 265 | 2 474 | 621 | D | 360 | 100 | 59 | 71 | 28 534 | 583 | 17.0 | 36.0 | 52.0 |
| Cloud | 310 | 2 968 | 702 | D | 529 | D | 78 | 87 | 29 388 | 466 | 12.0 | 44.4 | 54.3 |
| Coffey | 241 | D | 494 | D | 340 | 115 | D | D | D | 681 | 18.2 | 26.7 | 42.4 |
| Comanche | 81 | 423 | 137 | D | 65 | D | D | 9 | 21 700 | 253 | 4.7 | 53.4 | 53.0 |
| Cowley | 753 | 11 320 | 2 229 | 3 354 | 1 475 | 378 | 196 | 351 | 31 039 | 1 027 | 22.2 | 21.8 | 41.6 |
| Crawford | 912 | 14 043 | 2 975 | 2 635 | 1 924 | 316 | 369 | 394 | 28 068 | 911 | 24.8 | 19.6 | 40.4 |
| Decatur | 103 | 666 | D | D | 85 | 32 | D | 14 | 21 524 | 303 | 9.6 | 59.1 | 59.1 |
| Dickinson | 468 | 4 924 | D | 1 056 | 748 | 154 | 133 | 144 | 29 329 | 1 046 | 16.5 | 30.1 | 43.5 |
| Doniphan | 153 | 1 298 | 74 | 414 | 119 | 76 | D | 45 | 34 629 | 573 | 19.9 | 25.0 | 53.2 |
| Douglas | 2 601 | 37 058 | 5 960 | 3 281 | 6 111 | 979 | 1 899 | 1 031 | 27 816 | 1 040 | 38.8 | 9.2 | 35.4 |
| Edwards | 102 | 647 | D | 152 | 91 | D | 25 | 19 | 30 028 | 371 | 6.2 | 44.7 | 56.1 |
| Elk | 73 | 338 | D | D | D | 25 | D | 7 | 21 861 | 361 | 12.7 | 38.8 | 52.4 |
| Ellis | 1 123 | 12 667 | 3 134 | 981 | 2 202 | 676 | 322 | 398 | 31 403 | 687 | 12.7 | 37.0 | 43.8 |
| Ellsworth | 181 | 1 801 | 499 | 323 | 215 | 98 | 67 | 57 | 31 437 | 408 | 12.3 | 40.4 | 47.8 |
| Finney | 992 | 13 937 | 2 014 | D | 2 356 | 479 | 433 | 454 | 32 562 | 516 | 9.9 | 53.5 | 55.8 |
| Ford | 767 | 15 401 | 1 370 | 6 291 | 1 725 | 288 | 507 | 520 | 33 763 | 664 | 13.0 | 41.9 | 43.7 |
| Franklin | 570 | 9 518 | 1 607 | 823 | 1 076 | 172 | 764 | 316 | 33 245 | 1 051 | 29.0 | 13.5 | 40.7 |
| Geary | 599 | 7 897 | 1 558 | D | 1 387 | 293 | 310 | 228 | 28 922 | 229 | 18.3 | 31.9 | 52.4 |
| Gove | 129 | 835 | 243 | D | 107 | D | D | 23 | 27 546 | 413 | 8.7 | 57.4 | 60.0 |
| Graham | 116 | 773 | D | D | 146 | D | 14 | 21 | 27 096 | 475 | 11.2 | 39.4 | 49.1 |
| Grant | 217 | 2 287 | D | 143 | 302 | 121 | D | 84 | 36 712 | 326 | 10.4 | 44.8 | 46.3 |
| Gray | 216 | 1 477 | D | D | 153 | 65 | 32 | 47 | 31 561 | 473 | 10.6 | 45.2 | 48.8 |
| Greeley | 43 | 345 | D | NA | D | D | D | 11 | 30 528 | 303 | 2.3 | 50.5 | 47.9 |
| Greenwood | 181 | 1 150 | D | D | 195 | D | 27 | 35 | 30 045 | 539 | 14.8 | 35.8 | 49.5 |
| Hamilton | 69 | 528 | D | NA | 88 | D | D | 15 | 28 920 | 431 | 6.3 | 47.3 | 46.4 |
| Harper | 203 | 1 661 | 337 | 451 | 200 | 105 | 25 | 55 | 32 874 | 495 | 12.9 | 39.2 | 52.3 |
| Harvey | 788 | 12 369 | 2 893 | 2 927 | 1 328 | 314 | 248 | 413 | 33 373 | 829 | 30.5 | 23.2 | 42.1 |
| Haskell | 117 | 833 | D | D | 79 | D | 34 | 28 | 33 974 | 248 | 7.7 | 54.8 | 60.9 |
| Hodgeman | 52 | 275 | D | NA | D | 56 | D | 7 | 27 062 | 379 | 4.7 | 56.7 | 59.4 |
| Jackson | 267 | 2 900 | 509 | 210 | 388 | 108 | 81 | 79 | 27 296 | 1 127 | 22.8 | 13.9 | 37.7 |
| Jefferson | 311 | 2 160 | 433 | 187 | 306 | 97 | 58 | 63 | 29 048 | 1 137 | 26.2 | 11.3 | 39.9 |
| Jewell | 80 | 519 | D | D | 84 | 44 | D | 14 | 26 137 | 525 | 11.0 | 45.9 | 66.5 |
| Johnson | 16 871 | 296 871 | 35 059 | 20 192 | 35 550 | 24 209 | 26 573 | 14 396 | 48 491 | 610 | 50.7 | 9.0 | 38.7 |
| Kearny | 80 | 595 | D | D | 74 | D | D | 20 | 33 420 | 337 | 5.6 | 49.0 | 54.3 |
| Kingman | 210 | 1 934 | 429 | 363 | 217 | 141 | 44 | 61 | 31 305 | 876 | 14.5 | 32.3 | 44.6 |
| Kiowa | 93 | 806 | 224 | NA | D | D | D | 23 | 28 422 | 399 | 8.8 | 42.1 | 50.6 |
| Labette | 482 | 8 713 | 3 987 | 1 773 | 906 | 260 | 98 | 239 | 27 467 | 1 052 | 22.9 | 16.9 | 43.1 |
| Lane | 73 | 388 | D | D | D | D | D | 14 | 34 876 | 284 | 6.3 | 54.9 | 51.1 |
| Leavenworth | 1 177 | 13 817 | 2 809 | 935 | 2 170 | 1 113 | 885 | 446 | 32 287 | 1 203 | 38.1 | 5.8 | 39.0 |
| Lincoln | 91 | 554 | 147 | D | D | D | D | 14 | 26 031 | 473 | 9.7 | 40.2 | 56.7 |
| Linn | 165 | D | 57 | 136 | 246 | 75 | 46 | D | D | 918 | 18.4 | 13.2 | 37.3 |
| Logan | 117 | 805 | D | D | D | 52 | 26 | 23 | 28 999 | 289 | 6.6 | 61.6 | 51.6 |
| Lyon | 835 | 11 455 | 2 039 | 2 906 | 1 780 | D | 468 | 335 | 29 243 | 930 | 24.3 | 23.4 | 45.2 |
| McPherson | 892 | 13 764 | 2 268 | 4 567 | 1 316 | 664 | 176 | 521 | 37 888 | 1 142 | 15.9 | 30.1 | 51.1 |
| Marion | 299 | 2 804 | 618 | 211 | 337 | 124 | 124 | 64 | 22 924 | 974 | 18.0 | 32.9 | 53.0 |
| Marshall | 371 | 3 998 | 607 | 1 212 | 650 | 190 | 93 | 133 | 33 387 | 913 | 11.5 | 37.3 | 57.9 |
| Meade | 135 | 911 | D | D | 167 | 55 | 26 | 27 | 30 179 | 448 | 5.6 | 54.5 | 49.8 |
| Miami | 711 | 6 308 | 2 114 | 408 | 1 008 | 226 | 207 | 191 | 30 308 | 1 538 | 42.2 | 8.1 | 34.4 |
| Mitchell | 254 | 2 518 | D | 429 | 384 | 125 | 44 | 75 | 29 647 | 396 | 10.4 | 44.7 | 65.2 |
| Montgomery | 876 | 13 174 | 2 418 | 3 478 | 1 498 | 392 | 188 | 445 | 33 810 | 994 | 25.8 | 14.2 | 39.2 |
| Morris | 143 | 1 244 | D | 208 | 167 | D | 60 | 33 | 26 238 | 479 | 17.7 | 34.4 | 51.8 |
| Morton | 103 | 955 | 241 | D | 154 | D | 16 | 34 | 35 687 | 353 | 2.3 | 51.0 | 39.9 |
| Nemaha | 370 | 4 169 | 905 | 1 060 | 665 | 187 | 92 | 131 | 31 337 | 1 054 | 13.2 | 26.6 | 54.8 |

# Table B. States and Counties — **Agriculture**

| STATE County | Land in farms — Acreage (1,000) | Percent change, 2002–2007 | Acres — Average size of farm | Acres — Total irrigated (1,000) | Acres — Total cropland (1,000) | Value of land and buildings (dollars) — Average per farm | Value of land and buildings — Average per acre | Value of machinery and equipment, average per farm (dollars) | Value of products sold — Total (mil dol) | Value of products sold — Average per farm (dollars) | Percent from: Crops | Percent from: Livestock and poultry products | Percent of farms with sales of: $10,000 or more | Percent of farms with sales of: $100,000 or more | Government payments — Total ($1,000) | Government payments — Percent of farms |
|---|---|---|---|---|---|---|---|---|---|---|---|---|---|---|---|---|
| | 117 | 118 | 119 | 120 | 121 | 122 | 123 | 124 | 125 | 126 | 127 | 128 | 129 | 130 | 131 | 132 |
| KANSAS | 46 346 | -1.9 | 707 | 2 762.7 | 28 216.1 | 644 039 | 911 | 114 261 | 14 413.2 | 219 944 | 33.9 | 66.1 | 51.5 | 21.7 | 427 144 | 67.8 |
| Allen | 267 | -4.6 | 438 | 0.0 | 145.4 | 441 021 | 1 008 | 81 903 | 31.0 | 50 725 | 49.9 | 50.1 | 46.6 | 13.4 | 2 057 | 63.0 |
| Anderson | 367 | -3.2 | 514 | 2.6 | 214.9 | 524 621 | 1 022 | 103 751 | 61.1 | 85 461 | 54.1 | 45.9 | 53.4 | 18.7 | 2 651 | 68.1 |
| Atchison | 254 | 11.9 | 357 | D | 172.4 | 488 263 | 1 366 | 88 910 | 64.0 | 89 989 | 66.5 | 33.5 | 60.3 | 24.3 | 2 170 | 62.2 |
| Barber | 611 | -12.3 | 1 432 | 10.0 | 197.7 | 929 757 | 649 | 123 138 | 64.5 | 150 994 | 24.8 | 75.2 | 57.8 | 26.0 | 2 794 | 65.1 |
| Barton | 559 | -14.0 | 824 | 40.5 | 406.2 | 695 645 | 844 | 149 153 | 282.8 | 417 089 | 23.1 | 76.9 | 58.7 | 26.1 | 4 785 | 79.2 |
| Bourbon | 328 | -3.2 | 353 | D | 139.9 | 395 666 | 1 121 | 56 674 | 42.6 | 45 958 | 23.3 | 76.7 | 44.8 | 8.9 | 1 904 | 43.0 |
| Brown | 347 | 7.1 | 544 | 1.5 | 254.5 | 928 119 | 1 705 | 145 148 | 116.4 | 182 682 | 74.4 | 25.6 | 68.3 | 31.7 | 4 081 | 73.5 |
| Butler | 787 | 12.3 | 552 | 6.2 | 314.7 | 601 671 | 1 091 | 81 689 | 235.1 | 164 778 | 17.5 | 82.5 | 36.2 | 15.1 | 2 959 | 39.2 |
| Chase | 320 | -11.6 | 1 280 | 0.2 | 67.9 | 1 240 483 | 969 | 88 836 | 71.4 | 285 752 | 8.7 | 91.3 | 59.6 | 26.8 | 437 | 45.6 |
| Chautauqua | 308 | -21.0 | 859 | D | 51.6 | 757 655 | 882 | 58 504 | 27.5 | 76 683 | 18.1 | 81.9 | 49.0 | 15.0 | 425 | 27.3 |
| Cherokee | 324 | 11.3 | 401 | 0.1 | 235.3 | 497 881 | 1 242 | 108 936 | 88.5 | 109 393 | 60.4 | 39.6 | 51.8 | 19.4 | 3 165 | 49.9 |
| Cheyenne | 577 | 0.2 | 1 367 | 43.7 | 346.8 | 841 579 | 616 | 151 858 | 82.8 | 196 240 | 63.3 | 36.7 | 62.8 | 29.6 | 5 285 | 83.2 |
| Clark | 486 | -1.2 | 1 748 | 5.2 | 165.2 | 1 104 498 | 632 | 105 579 | 123.5 | 444 414 | 12.5 | 87.5 | 45.3 | 23.7 | 2 822 | 84.9 |
| Clay | 351 | -10.7 | 602 | 18.3 | 216.6 | 702 200 | 1 167 | 112 949 | 78.9 | 135 317 | 60.6 | 39.4 | 59.3 | 27.6 | 4 028 | 84.9 |
| Cloud | 384 | -10.9 | 824 | 17.9 | 253.8 | 836 044 | 1 015 | 157 877 | 71.2 | 152 756 | 77.4 | 22.6 | 66.1 | 35.2 | 3 282 | 79.8 |
| Coffey | 325 | -3.3 | 477 | 1.3 | 168.6 | 465 960 | 977 | 76 140 | 48.5 | 71 210 | 52.6 | 47.4 | 44.8 | 17.3 | 2 287 | 67.4 |
| Comanche | 432 | -3.4 | 1 709 | 4.4 | 128.5 | 908 422 | 532 | 98 758 | 53.8 | 212 795 | 24.9 | 75.1 | 58.5 | 31.2 | 2 017 | 80.6 |
| Cowley | 576 | -16.5 | 560 | 3.5 | 225.8 | 536 077 | 957 | 78 995 | 66.2 | 64 473 | 34.9 | 65.1 | 43.8 | 11.6 | 3 220 | 60.2 |
| Crawford | 342 | 0.3 | 376 | 2.6 | 180.3 | 405 629 | 1 079 | 77 023 | 57.4 | 62 976 | 60.1 | 39.9 | 46.2 | 13.0 | 2 854 | 59.2 |
| Decatur | 483 | 3.0 | 1 595 | 8.6 | 283.7 | 1 046 797 | 657 | 148 823 | 139.1 | 459 095 | 35.8 | 64.2 | 74.6 | 41.3 | 2 854 | 82.2 |
| Dickinson | 537 | -2.5 | 513 | 5.0 | 350.4 | 544 571 | 1 061 | 102 985 | 135.3 | 129 343 | 37.0 | 63.0 | 51.6 | 23.2 | 6 404 | 82.1 |
| Doniphan | 248 | 20.4 | 432 | 1.6 | 180.6 | 740 906 | 1 713 | 106 150 | 75.0 | 130 813 | 90.5 | 9.5 | 57.9 | 30.2 | 2 898 | 72.6 |
| Douglas | 221 | 10.0 | 212 | 1.8 | 134.7 | 408 136 | 1 924 | 66 492 | 41.3 | 39 675 | 67.8 | 32.2 | 34.3 | 7.9 | 1 994 | 44.2 |
| Edwards | 439 | 4.5 | 1 184 | 106.4 | 328.0 | 1 038 291 | 877 | 193 502 | 173.0 | 466 280 | 42.6 | 57.4 | 56.6 | 38.8 | 5 086 | 91.1 |
| Elk | 317 | -14.3 | 877 | 0.5 | 65.2 | 861 330 | 982 | 52 378 | 29.9 | 82 706 | D | D | 51.8 | 13.0 | 690 | 47.4 |
| Ellis | 526 | -9.0 | 766 | 2.5 | 278.7 | 592 976 | 774 | 92 726 | 107.8 | 156 895 | 25.7 | 74.3 | 59.5 | 17.6 | 3 617 | 75.1 |
| Ellsworth | 365 | -11.6 | 895 | 0.6 | 180.3 | 675 082 | 755 | 107 044 | 33.0 | 80 771 | 58.8 | 41.2 | 55.9 | 22.3 | 3 521 | 86.0 |
| Finney | 760 | -5.2 | 1 473 | 179.3 | 567.7 | 1 153 579 | 783 | 285 752 | 693.5 | 1 344 046 | 20.3 | 79.7 | 62.6 | 45.0 | 9 060 | 80.0 |
| Ford | 634 | -2.3 | 955 | 81.9 | 491.1 | 680 092 | 712 | 170 110 | 474.1 | 713 970 | 18.4 | 81.6 | 54.7 | 28.9 | 7 550 | 79.1 |
| Franklin | 314 | -7.4 | 298 | 1.6 | 167.6 | 493 012 | 1 653 | 71 393 | 67.2 | 63 947 | 48.1 | 51.9 | 41.5 | 8.7 | 2 028 | 47.7 |
| Geary | 148 | -17.8 | 648 | 3.0 | 60.5 | 813 657 | 1 255 | 100 460 | 25.6 | 111 764 | 43.1 | 56.9 | 52.4 | 21.8 | 959 | 68.1 |
| Gove | 594 | 0.3 | 1 437 | 17.7 | 371.3 | 865 618 | 602 | 174 232 | 184.4 | 446 502 | 32.0 | 68.0 | 72.4 | 39.2 | 5 732 | 82.1 |
| Graham | 515 | -0.4 | 1 084 | 10.4 | 308.2 | 669 871 | 618 | 106 291 | 57.7 | 121 374 | 73.0 | 27.0 | 52.8 | 27.8 | 4 757 | 85.3 |
| Grant | 337 | 11.6 | 1 035 | 87.4 | 272.0 | 827 976 | 800 | 186 057 | 576.9 | 1 769 655 | 11.1 | 88.9 | 54.0 | 39.3 | 4 856 | 80.7 |
| Gray | 546 | 9.0 | 1 155 | 137.1 | 425.9 | 983 325 | 852 | 248 223 | 691.4 | 1 461 694 | 15.8 | 84.2 | 56.7 | 39.7 | 7 427 | 81.4 |
| Greeley | 493 | 8.1 | 1 627 | 23.4 | 445.2 | 1 150 144 | 707 | 162 830 | 115.4 | 380 891 | 55.9 | 44.1 | 49.2 | 31.7 | 5 850 | 93.1 |
| Greenwood | 609 | 2.5 | 1 130 | 0.4 | 108.5 | 1 082 093 | 958 | 78 155 | 87.7 | 162 642 | 9.2 | 90.8 | 55.1 | 17.1 | 874 | 43.2 |
| Hamilton | 611 | 14.0 | 1 417 | 24.8 | 455.2 | 951 306 | 671 | 186 927 | 267.0 | 619 548 | 19.4 | 80.6 | 38.3 | 26.7 | 6 574 | 85.8 |
| Harper | 481 | 2.3 | 972 | 1.8 | 315.8 | 717 911 | 738 | 134 164 | 93.4 | 188 734 | 19.1 | 80.9 | 47.5 | 20.2 | 4 470 | 83.0 |
| Harvey | 339 | -3.7 | 408 | 35.8 | 273.7 | 557 519 | 1 365 | 105 309 | 103.7 | 125 061 | 47.4 | 52.6 | 50.8 | 20.5 | 3 807 | 67.2 |
| Haskell | 399 | -1.7 | 1 608 | 156.5 | 327.6 | 1 708 092 | 1 062 | 367 208 | 718.3 | 2 896 342 | 16.2 | 83.8 | 67.7 | 58.9 | 5 686 | 86.3 |
| Hodgeman | 526 | 11.7 | 1 387 | 29.4 | 334.3 | 824 336 | 594 | 163 440 | 179.3 | 473 178 | 22.9 | 77.1 | 65.4 | 38.8 | 5 918 | 90.8 |
| Jackson | 339 | 0.6 | 301 | D | 146.8 | 355 481 | 1 181 | 52 976 | 52.0 | 46 139 | 40.7 | 59.3 | 42.9 | 9.6 | 2 697 | 48.9 |
| Jefferson | 286 | 2.1 | 251 | 7.6 | 155.6 | 403 989 | 1 607 | 68 357 | 61.3 | 53 952 | 54.5 | 45.5 | 42.5 | 10.3 | 2 406 | 46.4 |
| Jewell | 471 | -5.0 | 898 | 14.0 | 290.8 | 742 214 | 827 | 149 668 | 101.2 | 192 826 | 60.4 | 39.6 | 70.3 | 37.5 | 4 679 | 87.4 |
| Johnson | 114 | -23.5 | 187 | 1.4 | 69.9 | 375 228 | 2 004 | 72 856 | 40.7 | 66 655 | 72.5 | 27.5 | 30.5 | 9.0 | 676 | 26.2 |
| Kearny | 519 | -7.0 | 1 541 | 66.6 | 359.0 | 1 061 954 | 689 | 198 167 | 221.1 | 655 989 | 30.0 | 70.0 | 51.3 | 32.9 | 5 908 | 85.8 |
| Kingman | 546 | -1.8 | 624 | 21.9 | 332.0 | 523 300 | 839 | 97 277 | 52.1 | 59 419 | 49.5 | 50.5 | 48.4 | 14.4 | 7 204 | 85.8 |
| Kiowa | 440 | 1.1 | 1 104 | 38.9 | 228.2 | 695 277 | 630 | 124 883 | 50.5 | 126 471 | 68.7 | 31.3 | 53.1 | 23.6 | 3 909 | 84.7 |
| Labette | 371 | 2.8 | 353 | D | 193.4 | 361 924 | 1 026 | 76 909 | 89.9 | 85 490 | 25.3 | 74.7 | 47.3 | 9.9 | 3 007 | 49.9 |
| Lane | 401 | -12.8 | 1 413 | 14.0 | 284.1 | 845 541 | 598 | 153 133 | 187.0 | 658 474 | 16.6 | 83.4 | 54.2 | 32.4 | 5 022 | 89.8 |
| Leavenworth | 195 | -1.0 | 162 | 0.7 | 102.5 | 315 933 | 1 951 | 49 515 | 33.2 | 27 613 | 63.2 | 36.8 | 34.7 | 5.4 | 1 256 | 32.1 |
| Lincoln | 432 | -3.1 | 914 | 1.4 | 228.8 | 718 894 | 786 | 115 686 | 55.8 | 117 941 | 58.6 | 41.4 | 65.3 | 26.8 | 3 692 | 87.9 |
| Linn | 265 | -14.8 | 289 | D | 133.8 | 387 739 | 1 342 | 66 913 | 32.0 | 34 868 | 40.8 | 59.2 | 35.3 | 6.3 | 2 292 | 52.7 |
| Logan | 567 | -7.0 | 1 960 | 12.7 | 340.9 | 1 196 169 | 610 | 177 752 | 61.5 | 212 771 | 77.3 | 22.7 | 66.4 | 41.5 | 4 095 | 82.4 |
| Lyon | 474 | -4.0 | 509 | 1.1 | 210.2 | 497 850 | 977 | 78 578 | 102.7 | 110 437 | 23.9 | 76.1 | 46.1 | 13.7 | 2 775 | 65.6 |
| McPherson | 566 | -1.6 | 496 | 33.4 | 421.8 | 558 384 | 1 126 | 117 556 | 119.8 | 104 860 | 47.8 | 52.2 | 60.8 | 21.4 | 6 639 | 76.4 |
| Marion | 599 | 1.9 | 615 | 3.1 | 337.6 | 614 495 | 999 | 102 280 | 111.2 | 114 174 | 39.3 | 60.7 | 58.4 | 24.2 | 4 950 | 75.5 |
| Marshall | 515 | -11.4 | 564 | 2.5 | 338.6 | 710 582 | 1 260 | 130 214 | 111.0 | 121 589 | 73.7 | 26.3 | 71.0 | 33.2 | 6 556 | 83.9 |
| Meade | 602 | -1.5 | 1 344 | 105.2 | 380.5 | 952 328 | 708 | 174 018 | 194.6 | 434 356 | 46.9 | 53.1 | 54.9 | 35.0 | 6 330 | 86.8 |
| Miami | 307 | -4.1 | 200 | 1.7 | 155.0 | 410 186 | 2 054 | 58 177 | 62.7 | 40 749 | 44.2 | 55.8 | 31.5 | 5.8 | 1 839 | 29.1 |
| Mitchell | 444 | -1.1 | 1 122 | 7.9 | 302.8 | 1 034 656 | 922 | 193 541 | 128.1 | 323 371 | 48.2 | 51.8 | 71.5 | 39.1 | 3 911 | 85.6 |
| Montgomery | 314 | -9.2 | 316 | 1.3 | 152.4 | 360 615 | 1 142 | 71 188 | 39.9 | 40 157 | 41.6 | 58.4 | 37.5 | 6.4 | 1 715 | 34.4 |
| Morris | 414 | 7.3 | 863 | 0.3 | 154.4 | 758 291 | 878 | 108 849 | 82.8 | 172 946 | 26.3 | 73.7 | 63.3 | 20.5 | 1 920 | 66.6 |
| Morton | 442 | 25.2 | 1 252 | 47.0 | 366.1 | 720 822 | 576 | 159 913 | 119.1 | 337 520 | 35.8 | 64.2 | 41.6 | 25.2 | 5 969 | 89.8 |
| Nemaha | 451 | 8.2 | 427 | 0.3 | 287.9 | 602 277 | 1 409 | 107 998 | 146.9 | 139 370 | 45.7 | 54.3 | 64.7 | 31.2 | 5 313 | 78.1 |

# Table B. States and Counties — Water Use, Wholesale Trade, Retail Trade, and Real Estate

| STATE County | Water use, 2005 | | Wholesale trade,[1] 2007 | | | | Retail trade,[2] 2007 | | | | Real estate and rental and leasing,[2] 2007 | | | |
|---|---|---|---|---|---|---|---|---|---|---|---|---|---|---|
| | Total water withdrawn (mil gal/day) | Gallons withdrawn per person | Number of establishments | Number of employees | Sales (mil dol) | Annual payroll (mil dol) | Number of establishments | Number of employees | Sales (mil dol) | Annual payroll (mil dol) | Number of establishments | Number of employees | Receipts (mil dol) | Annual payroll (mil dol) |
| | 133 | 134 | 135 | 136 | 137 | 138 | 139 | 140 | 141 | 142 | 143 | 144 | 145 | 146 |
| KANSAS | 3 785.3 | 1 379 | 3 747 | 47 285 | 45 863.9 | 2 150.4 | 11 463 | 149 672 | 34 538.3 | 3 133.7 | 3 314 | 15 160 | 2 428.8 | 439.7 |
| Allen | 4.3 | 310 | 21 | 164 | 37.2 | 4.6 | 63 | 541 | 121.7 | 11.2 | 13 | 44 | 2.0 | 0.5 |
| Anderson | 2.1 | 252 | 8 | 56 | 53.5 | 1.7 | 42 | 309 | 87.2 | 6.5 | 6 | 15 | 0.3 | 0.1 |
| Atchison | 4.9 | 290 | 17 | D | D | D | 58 | 730 | 130.1 | 12.4 | 13 | D | D | D |
| Barber | 6.2 | 1 257 | 8 | 39 | 35.6 | 1.9 | 35 | 250 | 70.3 | 4.4 | 3 | D | D | D |
| Barton | 37.2 | 1 324 | 62 | D | D | D | 138 | 1 543 | 339.4 | 33.1 | 29 | 113 | 12.5 | 3.3 |
| Bourbon | 3.4 | 229 | 17 | 541 | 554.9 | 21.9 | 47 | 567 | 120.6 | 11.6 | 14 | 53 | 10.1 | 1.3 |
| Brown | 1.9 | 181 | 16 | 120 | 87.5 | 4.2 | 34 | 369 | 67.9 | 6.6 | 5 | 14 | 0.8 | 0.1 |
| Butler | 14.2 | 227 | 44 | 243 | 130.1 | 8.7 | 194 | 2 050 | 567.5 | 43.5 | 61 | 125 | 18.3 | 2.6 |
| Chase | 1.2 | 393 | 2 | D | D | D | 10 | 60 | 10.9 | 0.7 | 2 | D | D | D |
| Chautauqua | 1.5 | 360 | 2 | D | D | D | 14 | 81 | 15.8 | 1.1 | NA | NA | NA | NA |
| Cherokee | 98.9 | 4 588 | 18 | 162 | 205.5 | 5.5 | 67 | 503 | 121.7 | 9.8 | 4 | D | D | D |
| Cheyenne | 45.4 | 15 407 | 10 | 102 | 54.6 | 2.6 | 22 | 85 | 12.2 | 1.1 | 2 | D | D | D |
| Clark | 5.4 | 2 343 | 2 | D | D | D | 14 | 70 | 9.9 | 0.9 | 1 | D | D | D |
| Clay | 13.8 | 1 597 | 15 | 136 | 99.3 | 5.7 | 44 | 419 | 76.0 | 6.3 | 3 | 10 | 1.7 | 0.2 |
| Cloud | 15.0 | 1 536 | 18 | 241 | 91.8 | 8.3 | 61 | 493 | 109.7 | 10.7 | 7 | D | D | D |
| Coffey | 27.2 | 3 131 | 10 | 90 | 52.3 | 2.6 | 50 | 442 | 103.0 | 7.1 | 4 | 5 | 0.5 | 0.1 |
| Comanche | 7.2 | 3 726 | 2 | D | D | D | 19 | 73 | 10.3 | 1.0 | 1 | D | D | D |
| Cowley | 7.8 | 222 | 28 | D | D | D | 135 | 1 596 | 317.2 | 31.1 | 19 | 78 | 6.3 | 1.2 |
| Crawford | 7.2 | 187 | 37 | D | D | D | 174 | 1 974 | 395.4 | 36.3 | 38 | 118 | 15.2 | 2.3 |
| Decatur | 11.3 | 3 554 | 13 | 80 | 60.5 | 2.6 | 19 | 119 | 17.2 | 1.4 | 4 | D | D | D |
| Dickinson | 7.0 | 362 | 23 | 255 | 232.6 | 8.5 | 77 | 787 | 191.4 | 17.4 | 14 | 21 | 2.4 | 0.3 |
| Doniphan | 0.8 | 104 | 9 | D | D | D | 21 | 132 | 25.2 | 2.2 | 2 | D | D | D |
| Douglas | 22.0 | 213 | 81 | D | D | D | 407 | 6 121 | 1 202.2 | 110.5 | 170 | 711 | 93.4 | 17.5 |
| Edwards | 95.9 | 29 116 | 5 | 81 | 74.7 | 2.9 | 12 | 73 | 12.4 | 1.1 | 1 | D | D | D |
| Elk | 1.0 | 315 | 2 | D | D | D | 7 | 40 | 8.0 | 0.5 | 1 | D | D | D |
| Ellis | 6.1 | 228 | 43 | 322 | 144.9 | 11.1 | 183 | 2 174 | 497.5 | 42.6 | 40 | 109 | 14.5 | 2.5 |
| Ellsworth | 3.3 | 517 | 9 | 47 | 23.0 | 1.4 | 30 | 185 | 31.9 | 2.3 | 2 | D | D | D |
| Finney | 248.0 | 6 361 | 68 | D | D | D | 182 | 2 396 | 504.2 | 47.1 | 34 | 136 | 23.7 | 4.0 |
| Ford | 90.6 | 2 683 | 57 | D | D | D | 139 | 1 632 | 395.7 | 34.2 | 27 | 115 | 18.8 | 2.7 |
| Franklin | 3.4 | 128 | 14 | 172 | 168.7 | 7.7 | 96 | 1 153 | 234.3 | 22.6 | 23 | D | D | D |
| Geary | 8.7 | 352 | 8 | 154 | 70.8 | 2.7 | 96 | 1 292 | 295.1 | 26.0 | 34 | 138 | 17.5 | 2.7 |
| Gove | 19.1 | 6 898 | 13 | 79 | 104.8 | 2.3 | 23 | 96 | 17.1 | 1.4 | NA | NA | NA | NA |
| Graham | 11.6 | 4 245 | 9 | 23 | 23.1 | 0.8 | 24 | 114 | 30.2 | 2.2 | 3 | D | D | D |
| Grant | 91.7 | 12 171 | 17 | 187 | 253.1 | 6.9 | 39 | 284 | 67.0 | 6.2 | 5 | 18 | 3.3 | 0.5 |
| Gray | 179.4 | 30 606 | 20 | 164 | 112.7 | 5.1 | 28 | 175 | 34.8 | 2.6 | 1 | D | D | D |
| Greeley | 19.8 | 14 655 | 1 | D | D | D | 8 | 46 | 9.6 | 0.9 | 1 | D | D | D |
| Greenwood | 2.3 | 313 | 10 | 70 | 14.1 | 1.4 | 37 | 220 | 53.3 | 3.9 | 2 | D | D | D |
| Hamilton | 34.5 | 13 237 | 9 | 60 | 34.4 | 2.4 | 10 | 85 | 25.4 | 1.4 | NA | NA | NA | NA |
| Harper | 3.0 | 493 | 15 | 155 | 91.0 | 3.9 | 38 | 228 | 50.2 | 4.6 | NA | NA | NA | NA |
| Harvey | 42.8 | 1 264 | 30 | 173 | 90.8 | 6.6 | 131 | 1 445 | 274.7 | 26.1 | 30 | 87 | 10.4 | 1.4 |
| Haskell | 164.4 | 38 837 | 14 | 133 | 147.1 | 4.4 | 15 | 70 | 13.7 | 0.7 | 2 | D | D | D |
| Hodgeman | 25.6 | 12 114 | 4 | D | D | D | 5 | 36 | 5.9 | 0.5 | NA | NA | NA | NA |
| Jackson | 2.2 | 160 | 13 | 89 | 34.5 | 2.6 | 44 | 413 | 91.1 | 8.3 | 7 | 18 | 2.5 | 0.5 |
| Jefferson | 4.1 | 212 | 11 | 35 | 9.6 | 0.8 | 58 | 392 | 71.3 | 5.1 | 9 | D | D | D |
| Jewell | 28.3 | 8 455 | 6 | 38 | 16.8 | 1.2 | 19 | 77 | 14.3 | 0.9 | 1 | D | D | D |
| Johnson | 17.9 | 35 | 919 | 13 922 | 16 252.0 | 785.5 | 2 001 | 38 008 | 9 255.3 | 870.3 | 1 032 | 5 454 | 1 067.3 | 196.3 |
| Kearny | 158.2 | 35 022 | 8 | 20 | 19.8 | 0.5 | 10 | 43 | 7.6 | 0.6 | 2 | D | D | D |
| Kingman | 18.2 | 2 229 | 19 | 124 | 57.0 | 4.2 | 32 | 237 | 43.2 | 3.9 | 4 | 6 | 0.2 | 0.1 |
| Kiowa | 50.4 | 16 883 | 8 | 91 | 71.5 | 3.3 | 14 | 77 | 14.6 | 1.1 | NA | NA | NA | NA |
| Labette | 4.5 | 205 | 21 | D | D | D | 109 | 1 004 | 204.3 | 18.3 | 14 | 65 | 6.4 | 1.3 |
| Lane | 15.8 | 8 337 | 5 | 31 | 12.2 | 0.7 | 11 | 57 | 13.6 | 1.0 | NA | NA | NA | NA |
| Leavenworth | 8.2 | 113 | 17 | 56 | 13.2 | 1.7 | 188 | 2 130 | 493.0 | 45.7 | 61 | 240 | 27.8 | 5.7 |
| Lincoln | 1.6 | 481 | 8 | 55 | 24.1 | 1.5 | 18 | 78 | 11.1 | 0.9 | 1 | D | D | D |
| Linn | 11.8 | 1 193 | 5 | 18 | 4.3 | 0.5 | 38 | 269 | 47.8 | 3.7 | 2 | D | D | D |
| Logan | 8.0 | 2 878 | 13 | 73 | 53.6 | 2.3 | 19 | 197 | 78.6 | 4.5 | NA | NA | NA | NA |
| Lyon | 10.7 | 301 | 30 | D | D | D | 169 | 2 028 | 470.7 | 38.0 | 40 | D | D | D |
| McPherson | 32.9 | 1 114 | 32 | D | D | D | 168 | 1 495 | 382.2 | 31.8 | 32 | 70 | 5.8 | 1.1 |
| Marion | 4.0 | 308 | 16 | 182 | 106.7 | 7.3 | 62 | 349 | 70.0 | 5.7 | 8 | D | D | D |
| Marshall | 3.9 | 377 | 26 | 182 | 128.9 | 5.5 | 75 | 707 | 186.0 | 12.5 | 4 | 3 | 0.3 | 0.1 |
| Meade | 125.2 | 27 072 | 14 | 106 | 108.3 | 3.4 | 20 | 125 | 20.3 | 2.1 | NA | NA | NA | NA |
| Miami | 6.9 | 225 | 21 | 48 | 72.7 | 2.3 | 103 | 1 068 | 251.7 | 21.4 | 40 | D | D | D |
| Mitchell | 15.6 | 2 424 | 25 | 212 | 73.3 | 7.4 | 53 | 419 | 98.8 | 7.7 | 4 | 45 | 2.3 | 0.5 |
| Montgomery | 11.3 | 326 | 36 | D | D | D | 167 | 1 772 | 364.6 | 35.4 | 38 | 140 | 20.4 | 3.0 |
| Morris | 1.7 | 274 | 5 | 20 | 9.2 | 0.7 | 34 | 259 | 45.0 | 4.2 | 3 | D | D | D |
| Morton | 31.5 | 9 862 | 10 | 101 | 54.8 | 2.5 | 17 | 103 | 28.6 | 2.4 | NA | NA | NA | NA |
| Nemaha | 3.4 | 321 | 20 | 147 | 79.6 | 5.1 | 83 | 575 | 106.8 | 9.3 | NA | NA | NA | NA |

1. Merchant wholesalers, except manufacturers' sales branches and offices.    2. Employer establishments.

# Table B. States and Counties — Professional Services, Manufacturing, and Accommodation and Food Services

| STATE County | Professional, scientific, and technical services,[1] 2007 | | | | Manufacturing, 2007 | | | | Accommodation and food services, 2007 | | | |
|---|---|---|---|---|---|---|---|---|---|---|---|---|
| | Number of establish-ments | Number of employees | Receipts (mil dol) | Annual payroll (mil dol) | Number of establish-ments | Number of employees | Receipts (mil dol) | Annual payroll (mil dol) | Number of establish-ments | Number of employees | Sales (mil dol) | Annual payroll (mil dol) |
| | 147 | 148 | 149 | 150 | 151 | 152 | 153 | 154 | 155 | 156 | 157 | 158 |
| KANSAS | 7 042 | 55 922 | 7 781.4 | 2 736.5 | 3 170 | 177 659 | 76 751.8 | 7 983.4 | 5 866 | 104 795 | 4 192.3 | 1 173.7 |
| Allen | 25 | 123 | 8.6 | 3.6 | 24 | 1 971 | 434.7 | 65.6 | 29 | 384 | 12.4 | 3.1 |
| Anderson | 14 | 40 | 2.6 | 0.9 | NA | NA | NA | NA | 17 | 193 | 5.6 | 1.3 |
| Atchison | 20 | D | D | D | 23 | 1 994 | D | D | 35 | 540 | 14.9 | 4.2 |
| Barber | 15 | 55 | 7.8 | 1.5 | NA | NA | NA | NA | 14 | 93 | 2.7 | 0.6 |
| Barton | 61 | 324 | 29.9 | 11.5 | 46 | 1 685 | 561.4 | 58.0 | 61 | 921 | 35.4 | 9.3 |
| Bourbon | 28 | 129 | 9.2 | 3.4 | 31 | 1 114 | 179.0 | 35.6 | 34 | 431 | 16.3 | 4.1 |
| Brown | 15 | 74 | 9.3 | 2.7 | 17 | 544 | 91.4 | 19.9 | 24 | 279 | 7.6 | 2.1 |
| Butler | 100 | D | D | D | 44 | 1 535 | D | 78.5 | 100 | 1 479 | 57.4 | 15.0 |
| Chase | 4 | D | D | D | NA | NA | NA | NA | 7 | 67 | 2.3 | 0.8 |
| Chautauqua | 4 | 7 | 0.5 | 0.2 | NA | NA | NA | NA | 10 | D | D | D |
| Cherokee | 28 | 84 | 4.3 | 1.2 | 34 | 2 041 | 512.1 | 68.8 | 25 | 315 | 8.6 | 2.3 |
| Cheyenne | 7 | 17 | 1.4 | 0.5 | NA | NA | NA | NA | 5 | 40 | 0.9 | 0.2 |
| Clark | 6 | 22 | 4.2 | 0.6 | NA | NA | NA | NA | 7 | D | D | D |
| Clay | 15 | 61 | 3.9 | 1.9 | NA | NA | NA | NA | 19 | 196 | 5.5 | 1.3 |
| Cloud | 17 | 75 | 5.3 | 2.3 | NA | NA | NA | NA | 24 | 388 | 13.7 | 3.2 |
| Coffey | 15 | 57 | 2.2 | 0.7 | NA | NA | NA | NA | 19 | 152 | 4.9 | 1.3 |
| Comanche | 5 | D | D | D | NA | NA | NA | NA | 7 | 38 | 1.5 | 0.4 |
| Cowley | 54 | D | D | D | 44 | 3 726 | 2 025.4 | 132.0 | 71 | 980 | 34.2 | 9.0 |
| Crawford | 68 | D | D | D | 64 | 2 736 | 757.2 | 91.5 | 89 | 1 611 | 51.9 | 14.5 |
| Decatur | 6 | 25 | 1.8 | 0.5 | NA | NA | NA | NA | 9 | 69 | 1.5 | 0.4 |
| Dickinson | 32 | D | D | D | 20 | 1 236 | 317.3 | 38.4 | 37 | 454 | 15.3 | 3.8 |
| Doniphan | 8 | D | D | D | 13 | D | D | 33.8 | 8 | 74 | 1.5 | 0.4 |
| Douglas | 285 | D | D | D | 88 | 3 848 | 976.5 | 143.0 | 299 | 5 937 | 213.7 | 60.1 |
| Edwards | 4 | 11 | 0.3 | 0.2 | NA | NA | NA | NA | 6 | D | D | D |
| Elk | 6 | 14 | 1.0 | 0.4 | NA | NA | NA | NA | 6 | D | D | D |
| Ellis | 65 | D | D | D | 38 | 1 003 | D | D | 101 | 1 950 | 72.2 | 19.6 |
| Ellsworth | 7 | 81 | 5.9 | 2.5 | NA | NA | NA | NA | 12 | 136 | 4.6 | 1.1 |
| Finney | 61 | D | D | D | 27 | 3 510 | D | 110.0 | 74 | 1 190 | 54.9 | 13.3 |
| Ford | 46 | D | D | D | 27 | 5 951 | D | 197.1 | 72 | 960 | 40.3 | 10.0 |
| Franklin | 41 | D | D | D | 30 | 1 045 | 384.1 | 48.0 | 56 | 807 | 27.9 | 7.5 |
| Geary | 37 | D | D | D | 7 | 619 | D | 20.0 | 73 | 1 291 | 52.0 | 16.4 |
| Gove | 7 | 14 | 0.7 | 0.2 | NA | NA | NA | NA | 9 | 48 | 2.0 | 0.5 |
| Graham | 7 | 15 | 0.8 | 0.2 | NA | NA | NA | NA | 9 | 52 | 1.3 | 0.3 |
| Grant | 13 | 30 | 3.2 | 0.7 | NA | NA | NA | NA | 18 | 223 | 7.1 | 1.8 |
| Gray | 14 | 33 | 3.2 | 1.0 | NA | NA | NA | NA | 10 | 63 | 1.3 | 0.3 |
| Greeley | 3 | 6 | 0.6 | 0.2 | NA | NA | NA | NA | 2 | D | D | D |
| Greenwood | 13 | 42 | 2.5 | 0.9 | NA | NA | NA | NA | 14 | 106 | 3.0 | 0.7 |
| Hamilton | 3 | 14 | 0.5 | 0.1 | NA | NA | NA | NA | 6 | 35 | 0.6 | 0.2 |
| Harper | 15 | 26 | 1.8 | 0.5 | NA | NA | NA | NA | 18 | 184 | 4.4 | 1.3 |
| Harvey | 44 | D | D | D | 68 | 3 774 | D | 151.0 | 61 | 997 | 29.4 | 8.7 |
| Haskell | 7 | 31 | 3.9 | 1.3 | NA | NA | NA | NA | 6 | D | D | D |
| Hodgeman | 3 | D | D | D | NA | NA | NA | NA | 3 | 9 | 0.2 | 0.1 |
| Jackson | 19 | 80 | 4.2 | 1.2 | NA | NA | NA | NA | 19 | D | D | D |
| Jefferson | 22 | 57 | 4.9 | 1.6 | NA | NA | NA | NA | 22 | 158 | 4.4 | 1.2 |
| Jewell | 4 | 7 | 0.6 | 0.1 | NA | NA | NA | NA | 9 | 55 | 1.2 | 0.3 |
| Johnson | 2 644 | D | D | D | 527 | 20 896 | 7 847.7 | 1 004.5 | 1 099 | 24 556 | 1 083.0 | 328.1 |
| Kearny | 8 | 33 | 1.3 | 0.4 | NA | NA | NA | NA | 6 | 51 | 1.2 | 0.3 |
| Kingman | 12 | 37 | 2.9 | 0.8 | NA | NA | NA | NA | 13 | 169 | 4.5 | 1.2 |
| Kiowa | 2 | D | D | D | NA | NA | NA | NA | 9 | 71 | 0.9 | 0.2 |
| Labette | 26 | 2 328 | 9.6 | 17.5 | 39 | 2 446 | 410.2 | 84.4 | 39 | 496 | 14.2 | 3.8 |
| Lane | 4 | 17 | 1.3 | 0.5 | NA | NA | NA | NA | 1 | D | D | D |
| Leavenworth | 123 | D | D | D | 37 | 1 036 | 107.7 | 28.3 | 86 | 1 384 | 48.3 | 13.2 |
| Lincoln | 8 | 10 | 1.1 | 0.5 | NA | NA | NA | NA | 5 | 49 | 0.8 | 0.3 |
| Linn | 8 | D | D | D | NA | NA | NA | NA | 7 | 50 | 1.3 | 0.3 |
| Logan | 5 | D | D | D | NA | NA | NA | NA | 18 | 124 | 3.5 | 0.9 |
| Lyon | 45 | D | D | D | 37 | D | D | D | 104 | 1 528 | 51.0 | 14.3 |
| McPherson | 52 | 180 | 14.1 | 4.5 | 64 | 4 288 | 4 222.6 | 188.8 | 64 | 972 | 29.8 | 8.6 |
| Marion | 16 | 139 | 24.5 | 4.5 | NA | NA | NA | NA | 23 | 239 | 5.6 | 1.5 |
| Marshall | 17 | 90 | 9.5 | 2.0 | 19 | 1 091 | 257.7 | 46.6 | 27 | 270 | 8.8 | 2.3 |
| Meade | 7 | 42 | 1.5 | 0.6 | NA | NA | NA | NA | 7 | 44 | 1.5 | 0.3 |
| Miami | 66 | D | D | D | 31 | 527 | D | D | 59 | 695 | 24.0 | 6.7 |
| Mitchell | 15 | 56 | 3.6 | 1.0 | NA | NA | NA | NA | 17 | 164 | 5.1 | 1.4 |
| Montgomery | 49 | 206 | 17.3 | 5.7 | 56 | 5 438 | 3 979.7 | 233.2 | 78 | 1 276 | 43.5 | 10.2 |
| Morris | 12 | 63 | 4.1 | 1.7 | NA | NA | NA | NA | 16 | 167 | 4.6 | 1.5 |
| Morton | 7 | 18 | 1.4 | 0.3 | NA | NA | NA | NA | 6 | 72 | 2.3 | 0.6 |
| Nemaha | 27 | D | D | D | 28 | 1 163 | 243.1 | 44.7 | 18 | 168 | 4.2 | 1.0 |

1. Establishment subject to federal tax.

# Table B. States and Counties — Health Care and Social Assistance, Other Services, and Federal Funds

| STATE County | Health care and social assistance, 2007 | | | | Other services, 2007 | | | | Federal funds and grants, 2009–2010 Expenditures (mil dol) | | | |
|---|---|---|---|---|---|---|---|---|---|---|---|---|
| | | | | | | | | | | Direct payments for individuals[1] | | |
| | Number of establishments | Number of employees | Receipts (mil dol) | Annual payroll (mil dol) | Number of establishments | Number of employees | Receipts (mil dol) | Annual payroll (mil dol) | Total | Social Security and government retirement | Medicare | Food Stamps and Supplemental Security Income |
| | 159 | 160 | 161 | 162 | 163 | 164 | 165 | 166 | 167 | 168 | 169 | 170 |
| KANSAS | 7 695 | 178 528 | 15 128.7 | 6 143.8 | 5 498 | 31 665 | 3 326.1 | 803.6 | 29 045.5 | 8 305.6 | 4 125.5 | 683.0 |
| Allen | 41 | 629 | 43.6 | 18.0 | 29 | 85 | 7.9 | 1.8 | 128.6 | 45.8 | 27.1 | 4.4 |
| Anderson | 25 | 372 | 21.8 | 8.6 | 14 | 26 | 1.8 | 0.5 | 61.2 | 27.1 | 16.9 | 1.5 |
| Atchison | 52 | D | D | D | 24 | D | D | D | 142.5 | 52.6 | 31.6 | 5.4 |
| Barber | 14 | 202 | 14.7 | 7.2 | 21 | 51 | 3.7 | 0.9 | 45.9 | 17.5 | 14.6 | 0.8 |
| Barton | 108 | 2 143 | 130.5 | 55.6 | 82 | 300 | 30.7 | 6.9 | 198.4 | 86.9 | 56.3 | 8.0 |
| Bourbon | 44 | 1 105 | 69.5 | 30.9 | 31 | 67 | 6.5 | 1.4 | 132.4 | 48.4 | 36.5 | 6.0 |
| Brown | 30 | 759 | 45.8 | 18.9 | 20 | D | D | D | 123.8 | 34.6 | 22.5 | 3.5 |
| Butler | 152 | D | D | D | 84 | 243 | 21.5 | 5.0 | 348.8 | 179.9 | 69.7 | 12.5 |
| Chase | 2 | D | D | D | 12 | 24 | 1.8 | 0.3 | 27.6 | 9.9 | 6.6 | 0.9 |
| Chautauqua | 10 | 155 | 7.4 | 3.4 | 5 | D | D | D | 38.1 | 14.8 | 11.7 | 1.4 |
| Cherokee | 39 | 619 | 27.2 | 12.3 | 28 | 72 | 5.4 | 1.1 | 189.6 | 68.9 | 45.9 | 10.4 |
| Cheyenne | 12 | 161 | 9.2 | 4.6 | 6 | D | D | D | 37.9 | 14.6 | 9.1 | 0.3 |
| Clark | 9 | 665 | 26.8 | 13.5 | 6 | D | D | D | 19.9 | 7.3 | 6.9 | 0.4 |
| Clay | 31 | 641 | 31.9 | 15.0 | 29 | 77 | 5.7 | 1.3 | 75.4 | 34.6 | 19.5 | 2.0 |
| Cloud | 38 | 775 | 36.1 | 16.8 | 24 | 85 | 6.6 | 1.4 | 98.9 | 34.1 | 28.8 | 2.4 |
| Coffey | 29 | 477 | 30.6 | 18.7 | 14 | 36 | 3.5 | 0.7 | 67.3 | 27.7 | 19.8 | 2.1 |
| Comanche | 7 | D | D | D | 8 | D | D | D | 18.3 | 7.5 | 5.3 | 0.3 |
| Cowley | 120 | 2 091 | 135.5 | 53.2 | 56 | 218 | 15.2 | 4.5 | 352.3 | 107.0 | 62.3 | 11.9 |
| Crawford | 141 | 3 013 | 182.6 | 70.4 | 69 | D | D | D | 334.7 | 124.2 | 77.5 | 14.5 |
| Decatur | 7 | 233 | 10.4 | 5.0 | 6 | 14 | 1.0 | 0.3 | 35.9 | 14.0 | 9.2 | 0.6 |
| Dickinson | 47 | 876 | 44.1 | 19.1 | 45 | 152 | 13.4 | 2.5 | 174.9 | 75.0 | 35.4 | 3.9 |
| Doniphan | 9 | D | D | D | 8 | D | D | D | 71.3 | 24.2 | 15.0 | 2.2 |
| Douglas | 283 | 5 331 | 375.5 | 163.3 | 190 | 1 429 | 277.4 | 33.7 | 689.9 | 246.9 | 76.3 | 18.1 |
| Edwards | 7 | 162 | 8.5 | 3.7 | 8 | 18 | 1.2 | 0.3 | 37.6 | 10.8 | 10.8 | 0.6 |
| Elk | 5 | D | D | D | 6 | D | D | D | 32.9 | 12.2 | 9.2 | 1.0 |
| Ellis | 115 | 3 027 | 252.3 | 98.6 | 81 | 372 | 37.4 | 7.3 | 195.5 | 74.0 | 46.7 | 4.4 |
| Ellsworth | 22 | 508 | 29.8 | 13.2 | 15 | 46 | 3.1 | 0.8 | 54.7 | 21.4 | 17.9 | 0.8 |
| Finney | 96 | 2 155 | 159.9 | 60.1 | 81 | 377 | 36.9 | 8.2 | 178.0 | 69.4 | 32.5 | 8.5 |
| Ford | 89 | 1 362 | 145.7 | 46.7 | 59 | 437 | 29.9 | 8.9 | 180.4 | 67.2 | 37.7 | 7.0 |
| Franklin | 66 | 1 159 | 80.3 | 34.4 | 46 | 298 | 24.9 | 8.4 | 177.3 | 73.0 | 44.7 | 7.0 |
| Geary | 53 | 1 554 | 130.2 | 57.3 | 51 | 261 | 13.9 | 4.1 | 3 295.5 | 109.1 | 19.1 | 12.1 |
| Gove | 11 | 201 | 12.9 | 5.0 | 14 | 38 | 4.2 | 0.6 | 34.1 | 12.4 | 8.3 | 0.2 |
| Graham | 14 | 272 | 12.5 | 6.5 | 9 | 20 | 3.1 | 0.5 | 35.6 | 12.6 | 8.6 | 0.4 |
| Grant | 14 | 191 | 15.9 | 6.8 | 13 | 55 | 6.0 | 1.1 | 41.1 | 18.4 | 8.3 | 1.3 |
| Gray | 13 | 154 | 6.2 | 3.5 | 13 | 25 | 2.4 | 0.5 | 45.0 | 17.1 | 7.0 | 0.6 |
| Greeley | 2 | D | D | D | 6 | D | D | D | 23.2 | 6.5 | 2.3 | 0.1 |
| Greenwood | 13 | 318 | 18.5 | 7.8 | 16 | 25 | 2.2 | 0.4 | 73.2 | 27.3 | 21.7 | 3.1 |
| Hamilton | 9 | D | D | D | 9 | 18 | 1.6 | 0.3 | 29.2 | 11.4 | 6.6 | 0.3 |
| Harper | 16 | 348 | 19.5 | 9.0 | 24 | 40 | 4.4 | 0.6 | 60.9 | 20.0 | 18.0 | 1.4 |
| Harvey | 97 | 2 877 | 208.7 | 86.1 | 67 | 277 | 19.3 | 5.2 | 232.7 | 116.6 | 58.4 | 6.4 |
| Haskell | 13 | 175 | 10.0 | 4.5 | 9 | D | D | D | 31.0 | 11.5 | 4.7 | 0.8 |
| Hodgeman | 5 | D | D | D | 5 | D | D | D | 19.8 | 6.4 | 5.3 | 0.1 |
| Jackson | 28 | 521 | 21.4 | 10.5 | 26 | 94 | 7.4 | 1.5 | 92.7 | 45.6 | 16.5 | 3.1 |
| Jefferson | 27 | 345 | 14.9 | 7.5 | 27 | 91 | 6.4 | 1.9 | 111.9 | 66.0 | 22.2 | 2.5 |
| Jewell | 4 | D | D | D | 7 | D | D | D | 41.8 | 13.6 | 8.4 | 0.6 |
| Johnson | 1 561 | 32 801 | 3 409.3 | 1 365.4 | 999 | 8 126 | 820.0 | 230.6 | 2 538.6 | 1 321.1 | 490.4 | 36.6 |
| Kearny | 7 | D | D | D | 8 | D | D | D | 35.1 | 12.9 | 5.9 | 0.7 |
| Kingman | 24 | 410 | 20.3 | 8.7 | 14 | 21 | 1.4 | 0.4 | 74.1 | 26.3 | 19.5 | 1.7 |
| Kiowa | 9 | 271 | 12.9 | 4.9 | 9 | 19 | 1.3 | 0.4 | 30.4 | 8.4 | 9.7 | 0.7 |
| Labette | 85 | 2 003 | 132.0 | 58.6 | 38 | 164 | 14.8 | 3.6 | 214.2 | 74.5 | 51.2 | 9.9 |
| Lane | 5 | D | D | D | 7 | D | D | D | 27.3 | 9.4 | 5.8 | 0.3 |
| Leavenworth | 122 | 2 682 | 247.8 | 105.6 | 96 | 510 | 40.6 | 11.4 | 2 169.6 | 291.4 | 79.4 | 14.0 |
| Lincoln | 6 | 138 | 6.8 | 3.5 | 8 | 28 | 1.5 | 0.4 | 30.6 | 10.7 | 7.7 | 0.4 |
| Linn | 11 | 84 | 3.5 | 1.4 | 13 | 62 | 4.3 | 1.0 | 83.9 | 34.2 | 22.3 | 2.4 |
| Logan | 8 | 184 | 11.4 | 5.4 | 14 | 31 | 2.0 | 0.5 | 34.7 | 12.5 | 7.3 | 1.0 |
| Lyon | 103 | D | D | D | 75 | 305 | 25.0 | 5.9 | 207.8 | 97.9 | 43.9 | 11.1 |
| McPherson | 86 | 2 275 | 111.7 | 51.9 | 83 | 389 | 31.6 | 8.8 | 185.9 | 92.9 | 47.4 | 2.9 |
| Marion | 30 | 669 | 34.6 | 15.6 | 27 | 108 | 9.3 | 1.8 | 105.6 | 44.2 | 27.2 | 2.1 |
| Marshall | 40 | 542 | 30.2 | 15.6 | 36 | 94 | 6.1 | 1.4 | 107.8 | 39.8 | 24.0 | 2.1 |
| Meade | 9 | D | D | D | 10 | 20 | 1.8 | 0.3 | 34.3 | 13.1 | 10.4 | 0.4 |
| Miami | 51 | 1 813 | 98.6 | 48.6 | 57 | 155 | 11.4 | 2.9 | 159.2 | 77.1 | 43.5 | 5.5 |
| Mitchell | 25 | 596 | 38.6 | 16.0 | 18 | 69 | 4.8 | 1.1 | 63.1 | 22.6 | 16.3 | 0.8 |
| Montgomery | 108 | 2 513 | 157.1 | 67.6 | 65 | 295 | 15.2 | 6.6 | 334.8 | 133.3 | 80.9 | 15.7 |
| Morris | 10 | 232 | 12.8 | 5.2 | 7 | D | D | D | 53.5 | 26.7 | 12.6 | 1.6 |
| Morton | 8 | D | D | D | 10 | D | D | D | 33.7 | 12.0 | 7.0 | 0.4 |
| Nemaha | 38 | 881 | 39.2 | 18.8 | 32 | 92 | 6.5 | 1.6 | 80.9 | 32.8 | 20.7 | 1.1 |

1. State totals may include programs not allocated by county.

# Table B. States and Counties — Federal Funds, Residential Construction, and Local Government Finances

| STATE County | Salaries and wages | Defense | Other | Medicaid and other health-related | Nutrition and family welfare | Education | Other | New construction ($1,000) | Number of housing units | Total (mil dol) | Inter-governmental (mil dol) | Total (mil dol) | Total | Property |
|---|---|---|---|---|---|---|---|---|---|---|---|---|---|---|
| | 171 | 172 | 173 | 174 | 175 | 176 | 177 | 178 | 179 | 180 | 181 | 182 | 183 | 184 |
| KANSAS.......................... | 5 818.5 | 1 940.8 | 1 118.9 | 2 241.5 | 600.2 | 508.5 | 1 386.0 | 860 729 | 5 386 | X | X | X | X | X |
| Allen.................................. | 12.4 | 0.0 | 0.7 | 23.6 | 2.8 | 0.5 | 1.7 | 4 491 | 42 | 55.1 | 27.4 | 16.1 | 1 203 | 947 |
| Anderson.......................... | 3.2 | 0.0 | 0.7 | 4.5 | 1.4 | 0.2 | 0.3 | 1 104 | 11 | 25.2 | 11.5 | 10.8 | 1 368 | 1 209 |
| Atchison........................... | 4.7 | 3.0 | 18.0 | 15.2 | 3.4 | 0.4 | 1.2 | 548 | 6 | 54.6 | 24.2 | 19.7 | 1 188 | 871 |
| Barber.............................. | 1.9 | 0.0 | 0.4 | 3.4 | 0.9 | 0.1 | 1.6 | 0 | 0 | 31.7 | 6.1 | 12.4 | 2 598 | 2 292 |
| Barton.............................. | 10.0 | 0.1 | 2.0 | 12.6 | 5.2 | 2.3 | 1.1 | 1 263 | 9 | 115.5 | 48.0 | 40.9 | 1 473 | 1 144 |
| Bourbon............................ | 6.1 | 0.0 | 3.9 | 19.1 | 2.9 | 1.0 | 1.7 | 90 | 1 | 53.8 | 25.8 | 16.8 | 1 132 | 865 |
| Brown............................... | 20.7 | 0.1 | 6.8 | 10.2 | 6.6 | 0.6 | 6.5 | 0 | 0 | 34.2 | 15.7 | 12.8 | 1 274 | 1 081 |
| Butler............................... | 22.3 | 1.7 | 3.4 | 24.2 | 10.1 | 2.8 | 2.0 | 28 177 | 137 | 265.3 | 124.4 | 84.8 | 1 346 | 1 199 |
| Chase............................... | 1.6 | 0.0 | 4.4 | 2.3 | 0.5 | 0.1 | 0.2 | 0 | 0 | 10.8 | 3.7 | 5.4 | 1 864 | 1 700 |
| Chautauqua....................... | 1.6 | 0.0 | 0.5 | 6.2 | 1.0 | 0.1 | 0.0 | 0 | 0 | 13.1 | 6.6 | 4.7 | 1 247 | 1 094 |
| Cherokee.......................... | 4.5 | 2.2 | 1.8 | 39.9 | 4.9 | 0.8 | 0.5 | 255 | 4 | 63.1 | 33.0 | 18.1 | 850 | 642 |
| Cheyenne......................... | 1.1 | 0.0 | 0.2 | 2.8 | 0.6 | 0.1 | 0.6 | 0 | 0 | 10.4 | 3.9 | 5.0 | 1 793 | 1 566 |
| Clark................................ | 0.5 | 0.0 | 0.2 | 1.1 | 0.4 | 0.1 | 0.0 | 292 | 2 | 23.0 | 4.0 | 7.4 | 3 529 | 3 462 |
| Clay................................. | 2.9 | 0.0 | 0.7 | 5.6 | 3.2 | 0.2 | 0.5 | 1 300 | 10 | 39.2 | 11.0 | 9.8 | 1 125 | 904 |
| Cloud............................... | 4.2 | 0.0 | 0.9 | 15.2 | 1.7 | 0.4 | 0.9 | 0 | 0 | 46.9 | 17.5 | 14.6 | 1 558 | 1 297 |
| Coffey.............................. | 3.4 | 4.4 | 0.6 | 4.5 | 1.5 | 0.2 | -0.8 | 2 866 | 24 | 65.5 | 9.7 | 32.6 | 3 852 | 3 775 |
| Comanche......................... | 0.4 | 0.0 | 0.1 | 1.7 | 0.3 | 0.1 | 0.0 | 0 | 0 | 11.8 | 2.1 | 5.8 | 3 071 | 2 903 |
| Cowley.............................. | 8.0 | 93.7 | 7.9 | 32.6 | 7.0 | 2.0 | 3.6 | 7 149 | 60 | 174.7 | 65.9 | 38.6 | 1 126 | 916 |
| Crawford........................... | 17.5 | 0.1 | 4.1 | 58.5 | 11.6 | 2.4 | 5.0 | 7 889 | 59 | 125.6 | 53.1 | 37.6 | 968 | 720 |
| Decatur............................ | 1.3 | 0.0 | 0.3 | 2.3 | 0.6 | 0.1 | 0.2 | 0 | 0 | 10.2 | 3.5 | 4.6 | 1 568 | 1 465 |
| Dickinson.......................... | 8.7 | 1.3 | 21.4 | 15.8 | 3.5 | 0.4 | 1.0 | 15 886 | 98 | 78.1 | 32.0 | 21.4 | 1 128 | 937 |
| Doniphan.......................... | 2.9 | 0.4 | 1.4 | 10.8 | 1.6 | 0.4 | 1.5 | 1 862 | 7 | 39.6 | 21.2 | 7.4 | 957 | 805 |
| Douglas............................ | 52.4 | 12.5 | 18.6 | 110.8 | 13.8 | 27.9 | 77.8 | 60 365 | 490 | 429.5 | 85.5 | 157.0 | 1 384 | 1 048 |
| Edwards............................ | 1.7 | 0.0 | 0.4 | 5.1 | 0.6 | 0.1 | 0.0 | 0 | 0 | 11.6 | 4.2 | 6.2 | 1 998 | 1 844 |
| Elk................................... | 1.8 | 0.0 | 0.4 | 5.1 | 0.8 | 0.1 | 1.1 | NA | NA | 13.7 | 6.3 | 4.2 | 1 380 | 1 287 |
| Ellis................................. | 22.1 | 0.0 | 1.8 | 18.5 | 4.8 | 1.0 | 3.9 | 15 819 | 96 | 77.1 | 24.3 | 40.4 | 1 470 | 1 077 |
| Ellsworth.......................... | 1.6 | 0.1 | 0.5 | 2.8 | 1.1 | 0.1 | 4.7 | 0 | 0 | 20.6 | 8.2 | 9.6 | 1 520 | 1 318 |
| Finney.............................. | 9.7 | 0.0 | 1.4 | 20.8 | 7.2 | 2.5 | 2.7 | 4 879 | 45 | 159.3 | 67.0 | 63.9 | 1 669 | 1 351 |
| Ford................................. | 20.9 | 0.5 | 2.1 | 14.1 | 7.3 | 1.9 | 4.7 | 7 947 | 83 | 149.7 | 76.6 | 46.8 | 1 404 | 1 063 |
| Franklin............................ | 13.8 | 0.1 | 1.0 | 20.8 | 6.0 | 0.5 | 1.6 | 4 581 | 25 | 107.0 | 37.5 | 34.0 | 1 284 | 1 003 |
| Geary............................... | 2 790.8 | 310.4 | 1.2 | 22.7 | 8.3 | 13.5 | 1.4 | 20 242 | 187 | 159.0 | 71.1 | 33.7 | 1 341 | 820 |
| Gove................................ | 1.4 | 0.0 | 0.3 | 1.1 | 0.4 | 0.1 | 1.1 | 0 | 0 | 20.8 | 9.9 | 5.4 | 2 053 | 1 800 |
| Graham............................. | 1.6 | 0.0 | 0.3 | 3.4 | 0.6 | 0.1 | 0.7 | 0 | 0 | 16.1 | 3.1 | 6.5 | 2 502 | 2 325 |
| Grant............................... | 0.9 | 0.0 | 0.2 | 1.7 | 1.4 | 0.1 | 0.1 | 328 | 3 | 33.6 | 5.6 | 24.4 | 3 250 | 3 104 |
| Gray................................. | 1.6 | 0.0 | 0.3 | 3.4 | 0.9 | 0.2 | 0.1 | 1 226 | 7 | 22.9 | 11.4 | 9.2 | 1 637 | 1 489 |
| Greeley............................. | 0.5 | 0.0 | 0.1 | 2.2 | 0.3 | 0.1 | 0.0 | 0 | 0 | 7.9 | 1.9 | 5.3 | 4 052 | 3 846 |
| Greenwood........................ | 3.1 | 0.5 | 0.7 | 10.1 | 1.4 | 0.2 | 3.5 | 0 | 0 | 22.5 | 10.6 | 9.7 | 1 381 | 1 217 |
| Hamilton........................... | 0.5 | 0.0 | 0.1 | 1.1 | 0.4 | 0.1 | 0.1 | 0 | 0 | 13.7 | 3.3 | 9.2 | 3 483 | 3 291 |
| Harper.............................. | 2.8 | 0.7 | 0.6 | 4.5 | 1.2 | 0.2 | 4.1 | 563 | 4 | 43.2 | 10.6 | 11.6 | 1 999 | 1 788 |
| Harvey.............................. | 7.2 | 0.4 | 2.9 | 12.0 | 4.7 | 1.4 | 13.0 | 7 392 | 39 | 115.0 | 46.4 | 41.8 | 1 249 | 948 |
| Haskell............................. | 0.8 | 0.0 | 0.1 | 1.7 | 0.7 | 0.2 | 0.0 | 2 945 | 14 | 34.0 | 4.3 | 19.3 | 4 775 | 4 607 |
| Hodgeman......................... | 1.0 | 0.0 | 0.2 | 1.1 | 0.3 | 0.1 | 0.0 | NA | NA | 15.8 | 4.2 | 6.3 | 3 209 | 3 181 |
| Jackson............................ | 4.5 | 0.0 | 1.0 | 8.9 | 3.0 | 1.4 | 4.6 | 2 660 | 14 | 40.9 | 22.1 | 13.6 | 1 015 | 830 |
| Jefferson........................... | 4.5 | 2.8 | 1.0 | 6.2 | 2.8 | 0.4 | 0.5 | 2 874 | 24 | 62.8 | 34.7 | 20.7 | 1 122 | 1 020 |
| Jewell.............................. | 2.7 | 0.0 | 0.9 | 5.6 | 0.7 | 0.1 | 0.4 | 0 | 0 | 16.3 | 5.5 | 5.7 | 1 795 | 1 669 |
| Johnson............................ | 233.2 | 72.4 | 152.7 | 84.4 | 40.9 | 5.5 | 30.8 | 295 914 | 1 431 | 2 164.6 | 534.5 | 1 158.8 | 2 202 | 1 581 |
| Kearny.............................. | 0.8 | 0.0 | 0.2 | 2.8 | 0.9 | 0.1 | 0.0 | 0 | 0 | 36.0 | 3.8 | 21.0 | 5 065 | 4 953 |
| Kingman............................ | 11.6 | 2.4 | 0.6 | 3.9 | 1.5 | 0.2 | 0.0 | 2 075 | 10 | 27.4 | 10.2 | 13.6 | 1 735 | 1 628 |
| Kiowa............................... | 1.2 | 0.0 | -3.0 | 2.6 | 0.6 | 0.1 | 5.4 | 167 | 1 | 15.2 | 4.6 | 6.9 | 2 343 | 2 134 |
| Labette............................. | 11.0 | 8.1 | 1.2 | 37.1 | 4.7 | 1.8 | 3.8 | 338 | 4 | 117.9 | 42.8 | 26.6 | 1 211 | 932 |
| Lane................................. | 0.7 | 0.0 | 0.1 | 3.9 | 0.4 | 0.1 | 0.1 | 0 | 0 | 12.2 | 3.2 | 4.9 | 2 818 | 2 727 |
| Leavenworth...................... | 961.8 | 266.1 | 489.9 | 33.2 | 8.6 | 12.5 | 2.5 | 22 467 | 152 | 214.8 | 96.6 | 81.7 | 1 110 | 852 |
| Lincoln............................. | 2.0 | 1.3 | 0.4 | 2.3 | 0.5 | 0.1 | 0.1 | 0 | 0 | 16.9 | 4.7 | 6.6 | 1 996 | 1 862 |
| Linn................................. | 3.4 | 0.0 | 0.7 | 11.8 | 1.8 | 0.2 | 4.0 | 2 329 | 17 | 35.0 | 14.5 | 17.1 | 1 753 | 1 670 |
| Logan............................... | 1.1 | 0.0 | 0.2 | 1.1 | 2.0 | 0.1 | 0.2 | 0 | 0 | 20.9 | 4.0 | 6.0 | 2 301 | 2 087 |
| Lyon................................. | 14.4 | 0.8 | 0.9 | 15.6 | 5.8 | 2.5 | 1.0 | 2 365 | 26 | 155.3 | 51.2 | 39.9 | 1 109 | 849 |
| McPherson........................ | 6.7 | 3.0 | 1.6 | 10.7 | 4.7 | 0.4 | 2.1 | 7 374 | 49 | 98.6 | 34.2 | 42.4 | 1 452 | 1 204 |
| Marion.............................. | 4.4 | 8.2 | 1.0 | 7.9 | 2.1 | 0.3 | 0.1 | 1 845 | 17 | 52.6 | 21.2 | 16.3 | 1 328 | 1 153 |
| Marshall........................... | 11.2 | 2.5 | 1.3 | 11.8 | 2.1 | 0.2 | 1.7 | 619 | 3 | 37.7 | 17.5 | 14.7 | 1 442 | 1 261 |
| Meade.............................. | 0.9 | 0.0 | 0.2 | 2.8 | 0.6 | 0.1 | 0.0 | 85 | 1 | 31.2 | 4.9 | 9.6 | 2 189 | 2 017 |
| Miami............................... | 6.9 | 0.0 | 1.1 | 16.9 | 3.8 | 0.4 | 0.8 | 9 169 | 41 | 90.4 | 32.8 | 42.8 | 1 378 | 1 083 |
| Mitchell............................ | 2.5 | 0.0 | 3.3 | 5.6 | 1.5 | 0.2 | 0.3 | 2 576 | 12 | 38.6 | 18.8 | 11.2 | 1 776 | 1 455 |
| Montgomery...................... | 18.8 | 3.3 | 2.1 | 56.8 | 7.0 | 2.8 | 2.1 | 2 667 | 24 | 120.2 | 48.3 | 43.9 | 1 272 | 931 |
| Morris............................... | 2.9 | 0.9 | 0.5 | 4.5 | 1.1 | 0.1 | 0.0 | 343 | 3 | 15.7 | 6.5 | 7.2 | 1 205 | 1 024 |
| Morton.............................. | 1.2 | 0.0 | 0.2 | 1.1 | 0.6 | 0.1 | 1.9 | 0 | 0 | 43.6 | 6.8 | 15.1 | 4 973 | 4 837 |
| Nemaha............................ | 4.6 | 0.0 | 2.2 | 7.9 | 1.6 | 0.2 | 0.3 | 835 | 5 | 30.9 | 13.8 | 11.5 | 1 123 | 958 |

1. State totals may include programs not allocated by county.　　2. Based on the resident population estimated as of July 1 of the year shown.

| STATE County | \| Direct general expenditure \| Total (mil dol) | Per capita[1] (dollars) | Educa-tion | Health and hospitals | Police protec-tion | Public welfare | High-ways | \| Debt outstanding \| Total (mil dol) | Per capita[1] (dollars) | \| Government employment, 2011 \| Federal civilian | Federal military | State and local | \| Presidential election,[2] 2012 Percent of vote cast: \| Demo-cratic | Republi-can | All other |
|---|---|---|---|---|---|---|---|---|---|---|---|---|---|---|---|
| | 185 | 186 | 187 | 188 | 189 | 190 | 191 | 192 | 193 | 194 | 195 | 196 | 197 | 198 | 199 |
| KANSAS | X | X | X | X | X | X | X | X | X | 27 356 | 37 988 | 234 601 | 41.7 | 56.6 | 1.7 |
| Allen | 58.1 | 4 334 | 66.5 | 1.5 | 3.0 | 0.0 | 4.8 | 30.9 | 2 300 | 59 | 57 | 1 655 | 37.4 | 60.7 | 1.9 |
| Anderson | 24.0 | 3 034 | 57.2 | 1.7 | 4.0 | 0.0 | 11.0 | 27.7 | 3 509 | 38 | 35 | 506 | 32.4 | 65.1 | 2.5 |
| Atchison | 53.5 | 3 226 | 48.0 | 0.9 | 5.7 | 4.3 | 7.0 | 40.7 | 2 456 | 50 | 72 | 883 | 45.1 | 52.7 | 2.2 |
| Barber | 29.8 | 6 217 | 32.1 | 37.7 | 2.7 | 0.2 | 10.5 | 7.2 | 1 508 | 25 | 21 | 675 | 24.3 | 74.5 | 1.3 |
| Barton | 106.4 | 3 833 | 63.7 | 2.0 | 3.4 | 0.0 | 5.8 | 64.2 | 2 310 | 79 | 120 | 2 230 | 27.4 | 70.6 | 2.1 |
| Bourbon | 50.4 | 3 404 | 65.8 | 0.8 | 2.8 | 0.0 | 7.9 | 33.6 | 2 269 | 80 | 64 | 1 091 | 35.3 | 62.5 | 2.2 |
| Brown | 35.2 | 3 492 | 48.5 | 0.6 | 3.7 | 0.0 | 9.4 | 28.7 | 2 849 | 116 | 43 | 1 674 | 30.1 | 68.2 | 1.7 |
| Butler | 244.6 | 3 880 | 66.6 | 1.1 | 2.8 | 0.0 | 5.7 | 450.1 | 7 139 | 129 | 283 | 5 796 | 32.9 | 65.1 | 2.0 |
| Chase | 12.1 | 4 209 | 41.3 | 1.1 | 2.8 | 0.6 | 10.6 | 4.4 | 1 521 | 23 | 12 | 260 | 27.7 | 70.5 | 1.8 |
| Chautauqua | 12.4 | 3 255 | 56.3 | 3.9 | 3.0 | 0.4 | 12.2 | 7.2 | 1 883 | 16 | 15 | 248 | 21.7 | 76.6 | 1.8 |
| Cherokee | 60.8 | 2 848 | 62.4 | 2.1 | 4.4 | 0.0 | 7.9 | 10.2 | 479 | 53 | 92 | 1 301 | 37.2 | 60.9 | 1.9 |
| Cheyenne | 9.5 | 3 397 | 54.5 | 1.2 | 3.7 | 0.0 | 13.8 | 0.0 | 0 | 20 | 12 | 250 | 21.6 | 76.6 | 1.8 |
| Clark | 22.2 | 10 617 | 26.9 | 54.5 | 1.6 | 0.3 | 4.4 | 5.0 | 2 405 | 12 | 0 | 447 | 21.1 | 77.4 | 1.5 |
| Clay | 42.4 | 4 888 | 27.6 | 40.7 | 2.5 | 0.1 | 5.1 | 25.0 | 2 884 | 34 | 37 | 928 | 24.9 | 74.0 | 1.2 |
| Cloud | 48.0 | 5 120 | 57.9 | 2.5 | 2.8 | 0.0 | 6.1 | 10.4 | 1 113 | 42 | 40 | 863 | 27.7 | 70.1 | 2.2 |
| Coffey | 68.4 | 8 087 | 33.0 | 33.0 | 2.6 | 0.0 | 9.9 | 21.0 | 2 488 | 46 | 37 | 1 159 | 26.5 | 72.2 | 1.3 |
| Comanche | 11.4 | 6 044 | 33.4 | 26.9 | 2.4 | 0.0 | 10.1 | 2.6 | 1 399 | 0 | 0 | 259 | 19.9 | 78.5 | 1.5 |
| Cowley | 173.4 | 5 063 | 47.4 | 19.0 | 3.4 | 0.0 | 6.0 | 102.1 | 2 981 | 92 | 156 | 3 488 | 36.4 | 61.6 | 2.1 |
| Crawford | 122.5 | 3 152 | 45.8 | 12.5 | 4.8 | 0.0 | 5.8 | 100.5 | 2 586 | 110 | 172 | 4 658 | 49.5 | 48.1 | 2.4 |
| Decatur | 10.9 | 3 692 | 48.4 | 3.5 | 4.8 | 0.4 | 13.2 | 4.0 | 1 363 | 20 | 13 | 256 | 22.2 | 76.8 | 1.0 |
| Dickinson | 75.5 | 3 981 | 47.3 | 20.2 | 3.6 | 0.0 | 8.0 | 30.0 | 1 581 | 99 | 85 | 1 659 | 27.9 | 70.2 | 1.9 |
| Doniphan | 40.2 | 5 189 | 71.3 | 1.6 | 0.7 | 0.0 | 6.2 | 14.2 | 1 831 | 39 | 34 | 1 005 | 31.3 | 66.6 | 2.2 |
| Douglas | 378.9 | 3 339 | 32.9 | 31.9 | 6.2 | 0.1 | 3.9 | 522.0 | 4 600 | 473 | 527 | 14 179 | 64.4 | 33.6 | 2.0 |
| Edwards | 11.2 | 3 610 | 47.0 | 4.5 | 5.6 | 0.0 | 14.7 | 1.2 | 374 | 22 | 13 | 217 | 24.5 | 73.3 | 2.1 |
| Elk | 13.8 | 4 554 | 47.6 | 2.1 | 2.1 | 12.9 | 12.4 | 4.0 | 1 307 | 19 | 12 | 345 | 25.3 | 72.7 | 2.0 |
| Ellis | 86.1 | 3 133 | 43.3 | 2.8 | 4.2 | 0.2 | 6.2 | 46.1 | 1 677 | 156 | 124 | 3 117 | 32.2 | 65.9 | 1.8 |
| Ellsworth | 21.0 | 3 323 | 52.9 | 5.5 | 4.6 | 0.3 | 11.3 | 21.3 | 3 373 | 24 | 28 | 929 | 29.0 | 68.8 | 2.2 |
| Finney | 155.7 | 4 065 | 64.2 | 1.7 | 5.4 | 0.0 | 2.8 | 104.9 | 2 740 | 128 | 160 | 3 430 | 31.6 | 66.9 | 1.5 |
| Ford | 148.8 | 4 462 | 59.8 | 1.5 | 4.3 | 0.0 | 6.0 | 109.3 | 3 279 | 242 | 149 | 2 686 | 33.7 | 64.6 | 1.6 |
| Franklin | 102.9 | 3 886 | 43.8 | 23.8 | 3.5 | 0.0 | 5.7 | 90.2 | 3 406 | 70 | 112 | 1 870 | 37.8 | 60.3 | 1.9 |
| Geary | 148.8 | 5 917 | 43.5 | 30.3 | 4.7 | 0.0 | 2.6 | 93.0 | 3 699 | 3 664 | 19 173 | 2 685 | 43.1 | 55.5 | 1.4 |
| Gove | 20.2 | 7 671 | 37.9 | 42.1 | 1.6 | 0.0 | 4.9 | 2.5 | 960 | 18 | 12 | 419 | 18.4 | 80.1 | 1.5 |
| Graham | 15.8 | 6 059 | 30.6 | 35.7 | 2.8 | 0.0 | 9.3 | 1.5 | 558 | 29 | 11 | 345 | 22.8 | 74.5 | 2.7 |
| Grant | 31.5 | 4 200 | 49.3 | 3.0 | 5.2 | 0.0 | 13.4 | 7.5 | 996 | 17 | 34 | 742 | 23.9 | 75.0 | 1.2 |
| Gray | 22.5 | 3 990 | 62.4 | 2.2 | 3.4 | 0.0 | 10.7 | 10.4 | 1 851 | 24 | 26 | 909 | 20.6 | 77.5 | 1.9 |
| Greeley | 6.8 | 5 261 | 43.0 | 5.3 | 4.2 | 0.0 | 11.5 | 3.1 | 2 426 | 10 | 0 | 173 | 20.3 | 79.3 | 0.4 |
| Greenwood | 20.5 | 2 926 | 55.2 | 3.0 | 4.0 | 0.3 | 10.8 | 15.2 | 2 176 | 46 | 29 | 483 | 27.3 | 71.0 | 1.7 |
| Hamilton | 10.9 | 4 154 | 44.5 | 2.4 | 6.4 | 0.0 | 14.2 | 5.9 | 2 238 | 12 | 11 | 358 | 21.3 | 77.0 | 1.7 |
| Harper | 37.7 | 6 484 | 30.5 | 43.8 | 1.9 | 0.0 | 5.9 | 13.7 | 2 362 | 35 | 26 | 844 | 26.3 | 71.5 | 2.2 |
| Harvey | 118.7 | 3 544 | 44.8 | 0.9 | 4.0 | 0.2 | 5.0 | 159.1 | 4 749 | 75 | 150 | 1 961 | 40.5 | 57.7 | 1.9 |
| Haskell | 31.8 | 7 878 | 40.9 | 32.1 | 3.6 | 0.0 | 9.0 | 8.2 | 2 028 | 14 | 18 | 586 | 17.7 | 81.3 | 1.0 |
| Hodgeman | 14.3 | 7 270 | 31.4 | 29.9 | 2.3 | 0.0 | 15.0 | 13.2 | 6 687 | 16 | 0 | 293 | 19.3 | 78.9 | 1.8 |
| Jackson | 43.1 | 3 210 | 62.4 | 0.7 | 7.1 | 0.3 | 10.2 | 27.9 | 2 077 | 47 | 58 | 1 994 | 36.9 | 60.9 | 2.1 |
| Jefferson | 58.0 | 3 140 | 68.0 | 3.5 | 4.3 | 0.0 | 7.4 | 42.8 | 2 319 | 65 | 82 | 1 051 | 39.6 | 58.3 | 2.1 |
| Jewell | 15.5 | 4 843 | 40.2 | 23.3 | 2.0 | 0.0 | 11.0 | 1.7 | 537 | 28 | 13 | 348 | 19.8 | 77.7 | 2.5 |
| Johnson | 2 110.0 | 4 009 | 46.5 | 2.3 | 7.8 | 0.8 | 5.0 | 3 523.8 | 6 695 | 1 954 | 2 386 | 28 245 | 44.8 | 53.8 | 1.3 |
| Kearny | 35.9 | 8 652 | 31.8 | 41.0 | 3.0 | 0.0 | 5.7 | 16.2 | 3 906 | 17 | 17 | 711 | 20.9 | 78.2 | 0.9 |
| Kingman | 27.9 | 3 566 | 47.4 | 2.7 | 4.1 | 0.0 | 14.3 | 30.6 | 3 912 | 34 | 34 | 610 | 26.3 | 71.0 | 2.7 |
| Kiowa | 13.3 | 4 515 | 56.9 | 2.7 | 4.0 | 0.0 | 9.0 | 2.3 | 772 | 20 | 11 | 369 | 17.6 | 80.4 | 2.0 |
| Labette | 120.5 | 5 483 | 41.2 | 31.4 | 2.9 | 0.0 | 3.1 | 60.8 | 2 767 | 74 | 93 | 2 755 | 42.5 | 55.4 | 2.1 |
| Lane | 11.7 | 6 715 | 39.3 | 30.7 | 4.8 | 0.0 | 6.5 | 1.4 | 790 | 12 | 0 | 272 | 18.8 | 79.3 | 1.9 |
| Leavenworth | 195.6 | 2 657 | 54.8 | 1.2 | 5.2 | 0.0 | 6.1 | 211.5 | 2 874 | 4 842 | 3 825 | 4 075 | 43.3 | 54.9 | 1.8 |
| Lincoln | 15.7 | 4 777 | 37.9 | 29.0 | 3.2 | 0.0 | 8.9 | 3.9 | 1 177 | 33 | 14 | 411 | 21.9 | 75.9 | 2.2 |
| Linn | 35.7 | 3 659 | 60.8 | 1.6 | 4.4 | 0.0 | 7.8 | 14.3 | 1 462 | 46 | 41 | 680 | 30.9 | 66.8 | 2.3 |
| Logan | 17.7 | 6 744 | 31.8 | 38.8 | 2.8 | 0.1 | 5.9 | 1.0 | 394 | 17 | 12 | 715 | 15.6 | 82.4 | 1.9 |
| Lyon | 152.9 | 4 250 | 42.1 | 28.5 | 3.7 | 0.0 | 3.8 | 134.1 | 3 727 | 114 | 146 | 4 477 | 45.9 | 51.9 | 2.2 |
| McPherson | 95.3 | 3 264 | 46.6 | 2.8 | 4.0 | 0.0 | 9.5 | 86.8 | 2 974 | 87 | 126 | 1 999 | 31.5 | 66.8 | 1.7 |
| Marion | 54.1 | 4 422 | 43.7 | 18.5 | 2.6 | 0.1 | 13.4 | 34.1 | 2 783 | 61 | 54 | 998 | 29.7 | 68.6 | 1.6 |
| Marshall | 36.8 | 3 612 | 59.5 | 1.7 | 3.4 | 0.0 | 10.9 | 9.4 | 920 | 53 | 43 | 795 | 35.4 | 62.7 | 1.9 |
| Meade | 32.1 | 7 295 | 24.7 | 43.6 | 2.2 | 3.8 | 7.8 | 24.0 | 5 447 | 13 | 19 | 648 | 18.5 | 79.8 | 1.8 |
| Miami | 89.7 | 2 887 | 47.8 | 0.9 | 5.7 | 0.0 | 8.3 | 164.5 | 5 294 | 68 | 141 | 2 041 | 37.3 | 61.0 | 1.6 |
| Mitchell | 32.9 | 5 209 | 57.3 | 4.4 | 4.1 | 0.2 | 7.9 | 4.6 | 721 | 34 | 27 | 1 069 | 21.9 | 76.2 | 1.9 |
| Montgomery | 127.8 | 3 702 | 59.7 | 1.8 | 3.5 | 0.0 | 3.9 | 86.3 | 2 501 | 119 | 150 | 2 705 | 31.2 | 66.9 | 1.9 |
| Morris | 15.5 | 2 590 | 53.2 | 2.5 | 3.6 | 0.0 | 14.0 | 7.2 | 1 203 | 38 | 25 | 446 | 31.9 | 66.0 | 2.1 |
| Morton | 36.3 | 11 945 | 33.7 | 41.9 | 0.6 | 0.0 | 5.1 | 14.0 | 4 592 | 22 | 14 | 611 | 16.3 | 82.2 | 1.4 |
| Nemaha | 29.8 | 2 917 | 52.3 | 1.3 | 4.4 | 0.0 | 10.7 | 21.0 | 2 059 | 58 | 44 | 815 | 26.7 | 71.2 | 2.1 |

1. Based on the resident population estimated as of July 1 of the year shown.    2. © 2013 Election Data Services, Inc. All rights reserved.

# Table B. States and Counties — **Land Area and Population**

| STATE/ County code | CBSA code[1] | County type[2] | STATE County | Land area,[3] (sq km) 2010 | Population 2012 Total persons | Rank | Per square kilometer | Population characteristics[6], 2011 — Race alone or in combination, not Hispanic or Latino (percent) — White | Black | American Indian, Alaska Native | Asian and Pacific Islander | Percent Hispanic or Latino[4] | Age (percent) Under 5 years | 5 to 17 years | 18 to 24 years | 25 to 34 years | 35 to 44 years | 45 to 54 years |
|---|---|---|---|---|---|---|---|---|---|---|---|---|---|---|---|---|---|---|
| | | | | 1 | 2 | 3 | 4 | 5 | 6 | 7 | 8 | 9 | 10 | 11 | 12 | 13 | 14 | 15 |
| | | | **KANSAS—Cont'd** | | | | | | | | | | | | | | | |
| 20 133 | ... | 7 | Neosho | 1 480 | 16 406 | 2 018 | 11.1 | 92.7 | 1.9 | 1.8 | 0.9 | 4.4 | 6.8 | 17.7 | 8.8 | 11.0 | 11.0 | 14.1 |
| 20 135 | ... | 9 | Ness | 2 784 | 3 068 | 2 973 | 1.1 | 90.4 | 0.9 | 0.8 | 0.3 | 8.5 | 5.4 | 17.0 | 4.7 | 9.6 | 9.6 | 16.1 |
| 20 137 | ... | 7 | Norton | 2 274 | 5 612 | 2 796 | 2.5 | 91.6 | 3.5 | 0.9 | 1.1 | 4.4 | 5.0 | 14.9 | 7.4 | 13.0 | 12.4 | 16.6 |
| 20 139 | 45820 | 3 | Osage | 1 827 | 16 142 | 2 035 | 8.8 | 96.2 | 1.0 | 1.5 | 0.6 | 2.3 | 6.0 | 18.6 | 6.7 | 10.0 | 11.2 | 16.3 |
| 20 141 | ... | 9 | Osborne | 2 312 | 3 806 | 2 920 | 1.6 | 97.7 | 0.4 | 0.8 | 0.6 | 1.2 | 5.1 | 15.5 | 6.2 | 9.0 | 9.2 | 15.4 |
| 20 143 | 41460 | 9 | Ottawa | 1 867 | 6 072 | 2 755 | 3.3 | 96.1 | 1.5 | 0.9 | 0.4 | 2.2 | 6.1 | 18.9 | 5.4 | 10.6 | 11.1 | 16.5 |
| 20 145 | ... | 7 | Pawnee | 1 954 | 6 928 | 2 691 | 3.5 | 87.5 | 5.7 | 1.1 | 0.8 | 6.6 | 5.6 | 16.2 | 7.8 | 11.9 | 10.6 | 15.5 |
| 20 147 | ... | 7 | Phillips | 2 294 | 5 519 | 2 804 | 2.4 | 96.0 | 0.8 | 0.6 | 1.0 | 2.3 | 6.0 | 17.7 | 6.0 | 9.5 | 9.8 | 14.9 |
| 20 149 | 31740 | 6 | Pottawatomie | 2 178 | 22 302 | 1 719 | 10.2 | 92.6 | 2.0 | 1.6 | 1.2 | 4.7 | 8.5 | 20.8 | 7.5 | 13.4 | 11.8 | 14.1 |
| 20 151 | ... | 7 | Pratt | 1 904 | 9 728 | 2 457 | 5.1 | 91.9 | 1.9 | 1.3 | 0.8 | 5.9 | 6.5 | 16.1 | 10.6 | 11.3 | 9.7 | 13.5 |
| 20 153 | ... | 9 | Rawlins | 2 770 | 2 560 | 3 003 | 0.9 | 95.6 | 0.7 | 0.5 | 0.3 | 3.7 | 5.1 | 13.5 | 5.5 | 9.2 | 7.8 | 15.5 |
| 20 155 | 26740 | 4 | Reno | 3 251 | 64 438 | 817 | 19.8 | 87.6 | 3.9 | 1.4 | 0.9 | 8.2 | 6.5 | 16.9 | 9.2 | 12.2 | 10.8 | 14.0 |
| 20 157 | ... | 9 | Republic | 1 858 | 4 858 | 2 848 | 2.6 | 97.7 | 0.8 | 0.4 | 0.4 | 1.2 | 5.1 | 14.2 | 5.1 | 8.5 | 8.3 | 15.8 |
| 20 159 | ... | 7 | Rice | 1 881 | 9 985 | 2 445 | 5.3 | 87.0 | 2.1 | 1.4 | 0.8 | 10.5 | 6.3 | 17.2 | 12.0 | 10.7 | 9.9 | 13.5 |
| 20 161 | 31740 | 5 | Riley | 1 579 | 75 508 | 724 | 47.8 | 81.7 | 7.5 | 1.3 | 5.6 | 7.0 | 6.6 | 11.5 | 34.5 | 17.7 | 7.9 | 7.4 |
| 20 163 | ... | 9 | Rooks | 2 306 | 5 223 | 2 824 | 2.3 | 96.4 | 0.9 | 0.6 | 0.7 | 2.3 | 6.6 | 17.0 | 6.8 | 10.3 | 10.7 | 14.8 |
| 20 165 | ... | 9 | Rush | 1 859 | 3 220 | 2 959 | 1.7 | 96.2 | 0.8 | 0.9 | 0.4 | 2.6 | 4.3 | 14.5 | 5.8 | 8.9 | 10.0 | 15.5 |
| 20 167 | ... | 7 | Russell | 2 295 | 6 946 | 2 690 | 3.0 | 95.7 | 1.7 | 1.0 | 0.9 | 2.1 | 5.9 | 15.3 | 6.8 | 10.3 | 10.1 | 14.6 |
| 20 169 | 41460 | 5 | Saline | 1 865 | 55 988 | 903 | 30.0 | 84.0 | 4.6 | 1.2 | 2.6 | 10.0 | 7.1 | 17.7 | 9.2 | 12.7 | 11.8 | 14.3 |
| 20 171 | ... | 7 | Scott | 1 858 | 4 937 | 2 842 | 2.7 | 82.7 | 0.8 | 0.8 | 0.6 | 15.7 | 7.2 | 17.9 | 6.7 | 10.2 | 11.7 | 13.9 |
| 20 173 | 48620 | 2 | Sedgwick | 2 584 | 503 889 | 129 | 195.0 | 72.5 | 10.5 | 2.0 | 4.9 | 13.2 | 7.9 | 19.1 | 9.5 | 14.2 | 12.2 | 13.8 |
| 20 175 | 30580 | 7 | Seward | 1 656 | 23 547 | 1 661 | 14.2 | 36.6 | 3.7 | 1.0 | 3.2 | 57.0 | 10.4 | 22.1 | 12.0 | 14.2 | 12.9 | 11.6 |
| 20 177 | 45820 | 3 | Shawnee | 1 409 | 178 991 | 352 | 127.0 | 78.2 | 10.1 | 2.2 | 1.8 | 11.1 | 6.9 | 17.8 | 8.6 | 13.2 | 11.5 | 14.1 |
| 20 179 | ... | 9 | Sheridan | 2 321 | 2 538 | 3 007 | 1.1 | 96.1 | 0.6 | 0.5 | 0.5 | 3.2 | 5.7 | 17.6 | 5.6 | 8.9 | 9.4 | 15.7 |
| 20 181 | ... | 7 | Sherman | 2 735 | 6 113 | 2 751 | 2.2 | 86.4 | 1.3 | 1.0 | 1.2 | 11.6 | 6.5 | 15.5 | 11.2 | 11.6 | 9.8 | 13.6 |
| 20 183 | ... | 9 | Smith | 2 319 | 3 765 | 2 925 | 1.6 | 97.5 | 0.9 | 1.1 | 0.5 | 1.5 | 4.7 | 14.3 | 5.3 | 8.0 | 8.6 | 16.4 |
| 20 185 | ... | 9 | Stafford | 2 051 | 4 358 | 2 878 | 2.1 | 85.8 | 0.6 | 1.5 | 0.7 | 12.7 | 5.8 | 18.0 | 6.3 | 9.6 | 9.6 | 17.0 |
| 20 187 | ... | 9 | Stanton | 1 762 | 2 175 | 3 039 | 1.2 | 59.8 | 0.9 | 1.4 | 0.6 | 38.5 | 8.5 | 20.4 | 6.8 | 12.4 | 12.3 | 12.2 |
| 20 189 | ... | 7 | Stevens | 1 884 | 5 756 | 2 787 | 3.1 | 65.5 | 0.7 | 1.3 | 0.4 | 33.2 | 8.3 | 21.7 | 8.1 | 11.9 | 12.6 | 14.1 |
| 20 191 | 48620 | 2 | Sumner | 3 061 | 23 674 | 1 657 | 7.7 | 92.9 | 1.6 | 2.5 | 0.5 | 4.6 | 6.6 | 19.2 | 7.2 | 11.0 | 11.0 | 15.5 |
| 20 193 | ... | 7 | Thomas | 2 783 | 7 941 | 2 602 | 2.9 | 93.3 | 1.1 | 0.9 | 1.0 | 4.8 | 6.6 | 15.8 | 15.1 | 11.4 | 10.1 | 13.5 |
| 20 195 | ... | 9 | Trego | 2 304 | 2 986 | 2 980 | 1.3 | 97.0 | 0.7 | 0.6 | 0.5 | 1.8 | 4.4 | 14.7 | 6.3 | 8.6 | 9.0 | 17.5 |
| 20 197 | 45820 | 3 | Wabaunsee | 2 057 | 7 039 | 2 679 | 3.4 | 95.6 | 1.3 | 1.3 | 0.5 | 3.0 | 6.6 | 18.8 | 5.8 | 10.7 | 10.7 | 16.8 |
| 20 199 | ... | 9 | Wallace | 2 366 | 1 517 | 3 082 | 0.6 | 91.6 | 0.7 | 0.8 | 0.4 | 7.4 | 5.2 | 20.8 | 5.4 | 10.5 | 8.5 | 16.0 |
| 20 201 | ... | 9 | Washington | 2 317 | 5 758 | 2 786 | 2.5 | 96.1 | 0.7 | 0.6 | 0.5 | 2.9 | 5.7 | 17.1 | 6.1 | 9.7 | 10.5 | 14.9 |
| 20 203 | ... | 9 | Wichita | 1 861 | 2 256 | 3 031 | 1.2 | 73.5 | 0.9 | 0.5 | 0.4 | 25.4 | 7.0 | 19.3 | 5.5 | 11.9 | 11.2 | 13.5 |
| 20 205 | ... | 7 | Wilson | 1 477 | 9 105 | 2 510 | 6.2 | 95.5 | 0.9 | 2.2 | 0.8 | 2.5 | 6.2 | 17.5 | 6.7 | 10.8 | 10.4 | 14.3 |
| 20 207 | ... | 9 | Woodson | 1 289 | 3 278 | 2 956 | 2.5 | 96.1 | 1.0 | 1.9 | 0.5 | 2.3 | 5.3 | 15.7 | 5.8 | 10.6 | 9.3 | 15.1 |
| 20 209 | 28140 | 1 | Wyandotte | 393 | 159 129 | 396 | 404.9 | 45.7 | 25.6 | 1.6 | 3.0 | 26.7 | 8.7 | 19.5 | 9.4 | 15.1 | 12.4 | 13.2 |
| 21 000 | ... | X | **KENTUCKY** | 102 269 | 4 380 415 | X | 42.8 | 87.5 | 8.7 | 0.7 | 1.5 | 3.2 | 6.4 | 16.9 | 9.6 | 13.0 | 13.0 | 14.6 |
| 21 001 | ... | 7 | Adair | 1 050 | 18 675 | 1 889 | 17.8 | 94.9 | 3.3 | 0.6 | 0.4 | 1.9 | 6.0 | 16.2 | 12.1 | 10.9 | 11.8 | 14.5 |
| 21 003 | ... | 6 | Allen | 892 | 20 210 | 1 831 | 22.7 | 96.9 | 1.4 | 0.8 | 0.4 | 1.6 | 6.4 | 17.7 | 8.5 | 11.4 | 13.3 | 14.6 |
| 21 005 | 23180 | 6 | Anderson | 523 | 21 728 | 1 742 | 41.5 | 95.6 | 3.0 | 0.5 | 0.7 | 1.4 | 6.5 | 18.7 | 7.4 | 12.1 | 14.8 | 15.4 |
| 21 007 | 37140 | 9 | Ballard | 639 | 8 333 | 2 579 | 13.0 | 95.4 | 3.7 | 0.9 | 0.5 | 1.2 | 5.5 | 16.5 | 7.7 | 10.6 | 12.9 | 14.8 |
| 21 009 | 23980 | 6 | Barren | 1 263 | 42 631 | 1 119 | 33.8 | 92.7 | 4.8 | 0.5 | 0.7 | 2.7 | 6.3 | 17.6 | 7.8 | 11.9 | 12.9 | 14.9 |
| 21 011 | 34460 | 8 | Bath | 722 | 11 802 | 2 310 | 16.3 | 96.8 | 2.0 | 0.5 | 0.3 | 1.4 | 6.9 | 17.8 | 7.3 | 11.6 | 13.1 | 14.7 |
| 21 013 | 33180 | 7 | Bell | 930 | 28 183 | 1 485 | 30.3 | 96.3 | 2.9 | 1.0 | 0.5 | 0.8 | 5.8 | 16.1 | 9.0 | 11.6 | 13.0 | 14.8 |
| 21 015 | 17140 | 1 | Boone | 638 | 123 316 | 496 | 193.3 | 91.1 | 3.5 | 0.6 | 2.7 | 3.7 | 7.4 | 20.5 | 7.6 | 13.2 | 15.1 | 14.9 |
| 21 017 | 30460 | 2 | Bourbon | 750 | 19 978 | 1 841 | 26.6 | 86.3 | 7.0 | 0.5 | 0.5 | 7.1 | 6.1 | 17.8 | 7.6 | 10.7 | 13.3 | 15.2 |
| 21 019 | 26580 | 2 | Boyd | 414 | 49 164 | 997 | 118.8 | 94.8 | 3.6 | 0.7 | 0.7 | 1.5 | 5.8 | 15.6 | 7.4 | 12.2 | 13.1 | 14.9 |
| 21 021 | 19220 | 7 | Boyle | 467 | 28 658 | 1 461 | 61.4 | 88.6 | 8.5 | 0.7 | 1.1 | 2.9 | 5.3 | 16.1 | 10.9 | 10.8 | 12.8 | 14.1 |
| 21 023 | 17140 | 1 | Bracken | 533 | 8 494 | 2 564 | 15.9 | 98.1 | 1.0 | 0.6 | 0.2 | 1.2 | 6.9 | 18.3 | 8.3 | 11.3 | 13.0 | 15.4 |
| 21 025 | ... | 7 | Breathitt | 1 275 | 13 635 | 2 205 | 10.7 | 98.2 | 0.6 | 0.4 | 0.7 | 0.7 | 6.0 | 17.0 | 8.5 | 11.8 | 13.1 | 15.4 |
| 21 027 | ... | 8 | Breckinridge | 1 469 | 20 071 | 1 837 | 13.7 | 96.3 | 2.9 | 0.8 | 0.4 | 0.9 | 6.0 | 17.9 | 7.2 | 10.8 | 11.9 | 15.5 |
| 21 029 | 31140 | 1 | Bullitt | 769 | 75 896 | 721 | 98.7 | 96.8 | 1.2 | 0.8 | 0.8 | 1.5 | 6.0 | 18.6 | 8.2 | 12.4 | 14.5 | 15.9 |
| 21 031 | ... | 8 | Butler | 1 104 | 12 840 | 2 250 | 11.6 | 96.0 | 1.0 | 0.6 | 0.3 | 2.9 | 6.6 | 16.6 | 7.7 | 12.3 | 12.4 | 14.6 |
| 21 033 | ... | 6 | Caldwell | 893 | 12 935 | 2 247 | 14.5 | 92.8 | 6.2 | 0.6 | 0.5 | 1.2 | 6.3 | 16.1 | 7.4 | 10.3 | 12.8 | 14.3 |
| 21 035 | 34660 | 7 | Calloway | 997 | 37 655 | 1 228 | 37.8 | 91.3 | 4.7 | 0.6 | 2.2 | 2.5 | 5.2 | 12.6 | 21.8 | 11.7 | 10.0 | 11.9 |
| 21 037 | 17140 | 1 | Campbell | 392 | 90 908 | 633 | 231.9 | 94.6 | 3.4 | 0.6 | 1.2 | 1.7 | 6.3 | 16.3 | 10.8 | 14.1 | 12.3 | 14.9 |
| 21 039 | ... | 9 | Carlisle | 491 | 5 034 | 2 835 | 10.3 | 95.5 | 1.2 | 1.0 | 0.4 | 1.8 | 5.9 | 16.4 | 7.3 | 10.8 | 12.1 | 14.7 |
| 21 041 | ... | 6 | Carroll | 333 | 10 900 | 2 367 | 32.7 | 90.5 | 2.6 | 0.9 | 0.4 | 7.0 | 7.6 | 17.7 | 8.2 | 13.3 | 12.9 | 14.7 |
| 21 043 | ... | 6 | Carter | 1 061 | 27 348 | 1 517 | 25.8 | 97.7 | 0.8 | 0.7 | 0.4 | 1.2 | 6.1 | 16.8 | 9.6 | 11.7 | 12.8 | 14.3 |
| 21 045 | ... | 9 | Casey | 1 151 | 16 082 | 2 041 | 14.0 | 96.4 | 0.9 | 0.6 | 0.3 | 2.6 | 6.4 | 17.0 | 7.7 | 11.8 | 12.6 | 13.9 |
| 21 047 | 17300 | 3 | Christian | 1 858 | 75 427 | 726 | 40.6 | 70.8 | 22.1 | 1.0 | 2.3 | 6.4 | 9.7 | 18.5 | 13.8 | 16.6 | 11.1 | 10.6 |
| 21 049 | 30460 | 2 | Clark | 654 | 35 787 | 1 282 | 54.7 | 91.9 | 5.6 | 0.5 | 0.6 | 2.6 | 6.2 | 16.9 | 7.5 | 11.8 | 13.8 | 15.2 |

1. CBSA = Core Based Statistical Area. See Appendix A for explanation. See Appendix B for list of metropolitan areas with component counties. 2. County type code from the Economic Research Service of USDA Rural-Urban Continuum Codes. See Appendix A for definition. 3. Dry land or land partially or temporarily covered by water. 4. May be of any race.

# Table B. States and Counties — **Population and Households**

| | Population, 2011 (cont.) Age (percent) (cont.) | | | | Population change and components of change, 2000–2012 | | | | | | | Households, 2010 | | | | |
|---|---|---|---|---|---|---|---|---|---|---|---|---|---|---|---|---|
| STATE County | | | | | Total persons | | Percent change | | Components of change, 2010–2012 | | | | | | Percent | |
| | 55 to 64 years | 65 to 74 years | 75 years and over | Percent female | 2000 | 2010 | 2000–2010 | 2010–2012 | Births | Deaths | Net migration | Number | Percent change, 2000–2010 | Persons per house-hold | Female family house-holder[1] | One per-son |
| | 16 | 17 | 18 | 19 | 20 | 21 | 22 | 23 | 24 | 25 | 26 | 27 | 28 | 29 | 30 | 31 |
| **KANSAS—Cont'd** | | | | | | | | | | | | | | | | |
| Neosho | 13.2 | 8.5 | 8.9 | 50.5 | 16 997 | 16 512 | -2.9 | -0.6 | 468 | 412 | -158 | 6 645 | -1.4 | 2.42 | 9.4 | 28.6 |
| Ness | 14.2 | 10.5 | 13.0 | 49.8 | 3 454 | 3 107 | -10.0 | -1.3 | 55 | 94 | 3 | 1 365 | -10.0 | 2.22 | 5.2 | 33.1 |
| Norton | 12.5 | 9.2 | 9.1 | 44.1 | 5 953 | 5 671 | -4.7 | -1.0 | 117 | 150 | -23 | 2 163 | -4.5 | 2.24 | 7.5 | 33.1 |
| Osage | 14.2 | 9.2 | 7.8 | 50.2 | 16 712 | 16 295 | -2.5 | -0.9 | 389 | 445 | -91 | 6 552 | 1.0 | 2.46 | 8.7 | 25.8 |
| Osborne | 14.6 | 10.8 | 14.2 | 50.3 | 4 452 | 3 858 | -13.3 | -1.3 | 76 | 106 | -23 | 1 742 | -10.2 | 2.16 | 7.1 | 35.5 |
| Ottawa | 13.4 | 9.4 | 8.6 | 48.3 | 6 163 | 6 091 | -1.2 | -0.3 | 145 | 155 | -4 | 2 456 | 1.1 | 2.44 | 7.5 | 26.5 |
| Pawnee | 14.8 | 8.4 | 9.0 | 44.5 | 7 233 | 6 973 | -3.6 | -0.6 | 180 | 167 | -74 | 2 665 | -2.7 | 2.23 | 8.7 | 35.6 |
| Phillips | 15.7 | 9.9 | 10.5 | 50.7 | 6 001 | 5 642 | -6.0 | -2.2 | 126 | 167 | -89 | 2 432 | -2.6 | 2.29 | 6.6 | 30.8 |
| Pottawatomie | 11.8 | 6.4 | 5.8 | 50.4 | 18 209 | 21 604 | 18.6 | 3.2 | 811 | 379 | 257 | 7 878 | 16.3 | 2.70 | 7.9 | 23.2 |
| Pratt | 13.6 | 8.5 | 10.3 | 50.4 | 9 647 | 9 656 | 0.1 | 0.7 | 266 | 245 | 54 | 3 956 | -0.2 | 2.34 | 8.9 | 30.8 |
| Rawlins | 17.5 | 11.6 | 14.4 | 50.0 | 2 966 | 2 519 | -15.1 | 1.6 | 59 | 57 | 32 | 1 176 | -7.3 | 2.11 | 4.9 | 35.8 |
| Reno | 13.1 | 8.4 | 8.9 | 49.8 | 64 790 | 64 511 | -0.4 | -0.1 | 1 847 | 1 567 | -325 | 25 794 | 1.2 | 2.38 | 10.4 | 30.0 |
| Republic | 16.2 | 10.7 | 16.2 | 51.2 | 5 835 | 4 980 | -14.7 | -2.4 | 106 | 191 | -34 | 2 274 | -11.1 | 2.14 | 5.7 | 32.8 |
| Rice | 12.6 | 8.6 | 9.0 | 49.7 | 10 761 | 10 083 | -6.3 | -1.0 | 264 | 267 | -91 | 3 906 | -3.6 | 2.42 | 7.6 | 29.0 |
| Riley | 6.9 | 3.6 | 3.7 | 47.7 | 62 843 | 71 115 | 13.2 | 6.2 | 2 479 | 747 | 2 657 | 25 796 | 16.5 | 2.40 | 9.2 | 27.4 |
| Rooks | 14.4 | 9.0 | 10.4 | 51.3 | 5 685 | 5 181 | -8.9 | 0.8 | 153 | 154 | 45 | 2 238 | -5.2 | 2.28 | 8.0 | 31.3 |
| Rush | 16.6 | 10.2 | 14.3 | 50.6 | 3 551 | 3 307 | -6.9 | -2.6 | 59 | 86 | -71 | 1 511 | -2.4 | 2.14 | 6.6 | 34.1 |
| Russell | 14.5 | 10.4 | 12.1 | 50.4 | 7 370 | 6 970 | -5.4 | -0.3 | 179 | 223 | 19 | 3 173 | -1.1 | 2.17 | 8.0 | 34.7 |
| Saline | 12.6 | 7.4 | 7.2 | 50.3 | 53 597 | 55 606 | 3.7 | 0.7 | 1 883 | 1 079 | -406 | 22 416 | 4.6 | 2.42 | 10.8 | 29.7 |
| Scott | 14.0 | 9.3 | 9.1 | 49.8 | 5 120 | 4 936 | -3.6 | 0.0 | 175 | 147 | -27 | 1 983 | -3.0 | 2.44 | 5.7 | 27.3 |
| Sedgwick | 11.7 | 6.1 | 5.6 | 50.6 | 452 869 | 498 365 | 10.0 | 1.1 | 18 053 | 8 929 | -3 527 | 193 502 | 9.7 | 2.54 | 12.4 | 28.7 |
| Seward | 8.5 | 4.4 | 3.9 | 48.5 | 22 510 | 22 952 | 2.0 | 2.6 | 1 220 | 292 | -331 | 7 460 | 0.6 | 3.01 | 12.4 | 21.4 |
| Shawnee | 13.4 | 7.6 | 7.0 | 51.5 | 169 871 | 177 934 | 4.7 | 0.6 | 5 465 | 3 776 | -577 | 72 600 | 5.3 | 2.39 | 12.5 | 30.9 |
| Sheridan | 14.3 | 9.8 | 13.0 | 49.2 | 2 813 | 2 556 | -9.1 | -0.7 | 56 | 59 | -14 | 1 099 | -2.2 | 2.30 | 5.3 | 30.6 |
| Sherman | 13.0 | 9.2 | 9.6 | 49.3 | 6 760 | 6 010 | -11.1 | 1.7 | 151 | 177 | 128 | 2 608 | -5.4 | 2.27 | 8.4 | 33.1 |
| Smith | 15.9 | 10.6 | 16.1 | 50.7 | 4 536 | 3 853 | -15.1 | -2.3 | 81 | 137 | -27 | 1 748 | -10.5 | 2.17 | 4.8 | 32.3 |
| Stafford | 13.4 | 9.2 | 11.1 | 50.2 | 4 789 | 4 437 | -7.4 | -1.8 | 106 | 125 | -58 | 1 907 | -5.1 | 2.29 | 6.8 | 32.9 |
| Stanton | 11.5 | 7.3 | 8.6 | 48.4 | 2 406 | 2 235 | -7.1 | -2.7 | 59 | 39 | -82 | 825 | -3.8 | 2.65 | 6.8 | 24.6 |
| Stevens | 10.3 | 6.2 | 6.8 | 50.5 | 5 463 | 5 724 | 4.8 | 0.6 | 185 | 90 | -66 | 2 044 | 2.8 | 2.77 | 6.8 | 23.6 |
| Sumner | 13.6 | 7.8 | 8.1 | 50.0 | 25 946 | 24 132 | -7.0 | -1.9 | 614 | 602 | -491 | 9 454 | -4.4 | 2.51 | 9.0 | 26.8 |
| Thomas | 12.3 | 7.1 | 8.1 | 50.9 | 8 180 | 7 900 | -3.4 | 0.5 | 253 | 165 | -46 | 3 196 | -0.9 | 2.36 | 7.7 | 30.3 |
| Trego | 16.6 | 10.0 | 13.0 | 50.6 | 3 319 | 3 001 | -9.6 | -0.5 | 72 | 110 | 6 | 1 358 | -3.8 | 2.16 | 6.2 | 32.0 |
| Wabaunsee | 14.8 | 8.7 | 7.1 | 49.0 | 6 885 | 7 053 | 2.4 | -0.2 | 194 | 139 | -68 | 2 737 | 3.9 | 2.54 | 6.1 | 23.5 |
| Wallace | 13.2 | 8.5 | 11.7 | 49.8 | 1 749 | 1 485 | -15.1 | 2.2 | 27 | 36 | 39 | 620 | -8.0 | 2.36 | 5.0 | 31.0 |
| Washington | 13.2 | 10.6 | 12.2 | 49.1 | 6 483 | 5 799 | -10.6 | -0.7 | 159 | 194 | -4 | 2 474 | -7.4 | 2.30 | 4.7 | 32.1 |
| Wichita | 13.6 | 8.3 | 9.6 | 48.7 | 2 531 | 2 234 | -11.7 | 1.0 | 71 | 48 | -1 | 891 | -7.9 | 2.48 | 6.3 | 25.8 |
| Wilson | 14.3 | 10.5 | 9.2 | 50.7 | 10 332 | 9 409 | -8.9 | -3.2 | 249 | 311 | -243 | 3 933 | -6.4 | 2.36 | 9.1 | 29.8 |
| Woodson | 16.5 | 9.6 | 12.1 | 50.3 | 3 788 | 3 309 | -12.6 | -0.9 | 101 | 111 | -20 | 1 524 | -7.2 | 2.15 | 7.3 | 35.2 |
| Wyandotte | 10.8 | 5.8 | 4.9 | 50.6 | 157 882 | 157 505 | -0.2 | 1.0 | 6 182 | 2 931 | -1 639 | 58 399 | -2.2 | 2.67 | 18.5 | 28.5 |
| **KENTUCKY** | 12.8 | 7.7 | 5.9 | 50.8 | 4 041 769 | 4 339 367 | 7.4 | 0.9 | 125 523 | 96 274 | 12 051 | 1 719 965 | 8.1 | 2.45 | 12.7 | 27.5 |
| Adair | 12.8 | 9.1 | 6.6 | 50.6 | 17 244 | 18 656 | 8.2 | 0.1 | 446 | 464 | 45 | 7 285 | 8.0 | 2.42 | 10.4 | 27.4 |
| Allen | 13.1 | 8.9 | 6.1 | 50.7 | 17 800 | 19 956 | 12.1 | 1.3 | 538 | 521 | 225 | 7 848 | 13.6 | 2.52 | 11.3 | 25.2 |
| Anderson | 12.9 | 7.2 | 5.1 | 51.2 | 19 111 | 21 421 | 12.1 | 1.4 | 571 | 417 | 158 | 8 369 | 14.3 | 2.55 | 11.4 | 22.3 |
| Ballard | 14.2 | 10.0 | 7.8 | 50.4 | 8 286 | 8 249 | -0.4 | 1.0 | 215 | 242 | 100 | 3 397 | 0.1 | 2.39 | 9.2 | 25.9 |
| Barren | 13.0 | 8.5 | 6.9 | 51.4 | 38 033 | 42 173 | 10.9 | 1.1 | 1 147 | 1 057 | 342 | 16 999 | 10.8 | 2.44 | 11.8 | 26.8 |
| Bath | 13.6 | 8.8 | 6.1 | 50.6 | 11 085 | 11 591 | 4.6 | 1.8 | 344 | 352 | 217 | 4 587 | 3.2 | 2.50 | 12.1 | 26.4 |
| Bell | 13.9 | 9.5 | 6.5 | 51.4 | 30 060 | 28 691 | -4.6 | -1.8 | 805 | 846 | -470 | 11 787 | -1.8 | 2.35 | 15.8 | 29.8 |
| Boone | 11.3 | 6.0 | 3.9 | 50.5 | 85 991 | 118 811 | 38.2 | 3.8 | 3 822 | 1 727 | 2 394 | 43 216 | 38.3 | 2.73 | 10.9 | 21.3 |
| Bourbon | 13.8 | 8.6 | 6.8 | 51.2 | 19 360 | 19 985 | 3.2 | 0.0 | 504 | 498 | -8 | 7 976 | 3.8 | 2.48 | 13.9 | 26.2 |
| Boyd | 14.2 | 9.1 | 7.8 | 50.3 | 49 752 | 49 542 | -0.4 | -0.8 | 1 290 | 1 332 | -308 | 19 787 | -1.1 | 2.39 | 12.7 | 28.2 |
| Boyle | 13.7 | 8.7 | 7.6 | 51.2 | 27 697 | 28 432 | 2.7 | 0.8 | 645 | 668 | 269 | 11 075 | 4.7 | 2.36 | 12.8 | 28.4 |
| Bracken | 12.9 | 8.2 | 5.7 | 49.9 | 8 279 | 8 488 | 2.5 | 0.1 | 260 | 232 | -25 | 3 317 | 2.8 | 2.55 | 11.0 | 24.7 |
| Breathitt | 14.2 | 8.7 | 5.3 | 50.0 | 16 100 | 13 878 | -13.8 | -1.8 | 362 | 436 | -187 | 5 494 | -11.0 | 2.47 | 13.4 | 26.9 |
| Breckinridge | 14.8 | 9.4 | 6.5 | 50.0 | 18 648 | 20 059 | 7.6 | 0.1 | 493 | 450 | -24 | 7 827 | 6.9 | 2.52 | 9.7 | 25.1 |
| Bullitt | 12.8 | 7.4 | 4.1 | 50.5 | 61 236 | 74 319 | 21.4 | 2.1 | 1 686 | 1 130 | 960 | 27 673 | 24.8 | 2.67 | 11.9 | 19.1 |
| Butler | 13.4 | 9.6 | 6.9 | 50.1 | 13 010 | 12 690 | -2.5 | 1.2 | 365 | 305 | 81 | 5 057 | 0.0 | 2.47 | 11.2 | 25.1 |
| Caldwell | 14.9 | 10.0 | 7.9 | 51.6 | 13 060 | 12 984 | -0.6 | -0.4 | 339 | 390 | 14 | 5 393 | -0.7 | 2.38 | 11.9 | 27.7 |
| Calloway | 11.6 | 8.6 | 6.6 | 51.8 | 34 177 | 37 191 | 8.8 | 1.2 | 926 | 891 | 445 | 15 530 | 12.0 | 2.20 | 8.8 | 33.6 |
| Campbell | 12.5 | 6.8 | 5.9 | 50.9 | 88 616 | 90 336 | 1.9 | 0.6 | 2 698 | 1 846 | -246 | 36 069 | 3.8 | 2.42 | 11.9 | 30.1 |
| Carlisle | 14.0 | 9.5 | 9.2 | 51.1 | 5 351 | 5 104 | -4.6 | -1.4 | 119 | 158 | -32 | 2 116 | -4.2 | 2.38 | 10.1 | 27.4 |
| Carroll | 12.3 | 7.5 | 5.8 | 49.5 | 10 155 | 10 811 | 6.5 | 0.8 | 388 | 277 | -25 | 4 061 | 3.1 | 2.58 | 13.6 | 25.0 |
| Carter | 13.3 | 9.2 | 6.1 | 50.4 | 26 889 | 27 720 | 3.1 | -1.3 | 764 | 739 | -467 | 10 760 | 4.0 | 2.52 | 11.6 | 24.6 |
| Casey | 14.3 | 9.4 | 6.5 | 51.2 | 15 447 | 15 955 | 3.3 | 0.8 | 449 | 454 | 123 | 6 351 | 1.5 | 2.44 | 11.3 | 28.9 |
| Christian | 9.2 | 5.8 | 4.8 | 49.1 | 72 265 | 73 955 | 2.3 | 2.0 | 3 336 | 1 337 | -531 | 26 144 | 5.2 | 2.62 | 16.3 | 25.5 |
| Clark | 13.8 | 8.3 | 6.4 | 51.3 | 33 144 | 35 613 | 7.4 | 0.5 | 961 | 814 | 27 | 14 267 | 9.6 | 2.46 | 13.6 | 25.4 |

1. No spouse present.

# Table B. States and Counties — Population, Vital Statistics, Medicare, and Crime

| STATE County | Persons in group quarters, 2010 | Daytime population, 2007–2011 Number | Employment/residence ratio | Births, 2011 Total | Rate[1] | Deaths, 2011 Number | Rate[1] | Persons under 65 with no health insurance, 2010 Number | Percent | Medicare, 2012 Eligible for Medicare | Enrolled in Medicare Advantage | Enrolled in a Medicare prescription drug plan | Serious crimes known to police,[2] 2011 Total Number | Rate[3] |
|---|---|---|---|---|---|---|---|---|---|---|---|---|---|---|
| | 32 | 33 | 34 | 35 | 36 | 37 | 38 | 39 | 40 | 41 | 42 | 43 | 44 | 45 |
| KANSAS—Cont'd | | | | | | | | | | | | | | |
| Neosho | 450 | 16 927 | 1.05 | 208 | 12.6 | 181 | 11.0 | 2 158 | 16.3 | 3 415 | 186 | 2 210 | 450 | 2 708 |
| Ness | 70 | 3 238 | 1.08 | 29 | 9.3 | 39 | 12.5 | 420 | 18.1 | 765 | 22 | 555 | 23 | 736 |
| Norton | 822 | 5 942 | 1.10 | 49 | 8.7 | 73 | 13.0 | 600 | 15.5 | 1 155 | 68 | 688 | 76 | 1 332 |
| Osage | 194 | 12 055 | 0.46 | 174 | 10.7 | 214 | 13.1 | 1 891 | 14.1 | 3 349 | 224 | 1 738 | 276 | 1 767 |
| Osborne | 100 | 3 690 | 0.91 | 37 | 9.6 | 49 | 12.7 | 519 | 18.2 | 987 | 19 | 652 | NA | NA |
| Ottawa | 98 | 4 908 | 0.58 | 68 | 11.1 | 64 | 10.5 | 772 | 15.6 | 1 262 | 115 | 741 | 133 | 2 170 |
| Pawnee | 1 026 | 7 408 | 1.14 | 77 | 11.0 | 81 | 11.6 | 749 | 15.6 | 1 330 | 28 | 901 | 168 | 2 394 |
| Phillips | 68 | 5 655 | 1.02 | 54 | 9.7 | 76 | 13.7 | 745 | 16.7 | 1 337 | 24 | 882 | 28 | 493 |
| Pottawatomie | 299 | 19 612 | 0.85 | 359 | 16.4 | 175 | 8.0 | 2 356 | 12.5 | 3 226 | 273 | 1 687 | 329 | 1 559 |
| Pratt | 380 | 9 902 | 1.05 | 115 | 11.9 | 100 | 10.3 | 1 358 | 18.0 | 1 959 | 44 | 1 383 | 340 | 3 499 |
| Rawlins | 40 | 2 549 | 0.99 | 23 | 9.2 | 27 | 10.7 | 377 | 20.5 | 714 | 18 | 444 | 20 | 789 |
| Reno | 3 129 | 63 073 | 0.96 | 790 | 12.2 | 690 | 10.7 | 7 696 | 15.1 | 12 930 | 799 | 8 116 | 3 190 | 4 914 |
| Republic | 103 | 4 866 | 0.94 | 43 | 8.8 | 80 | 16.3 | 651 | 18.1 | 1 383 | 76 | 899 | 51 | 1 018 |
| Rice | 648 | 9 419 | 0.85 | 120 | 11.9 | 115 | 11.4 | 1 407 | 18.2 | 1 985 | 60 | 1 304 | 117 | 1 153 |
| Riley | 9 127 | 71 697 | 1.04 | 1 082 | 14.8 | 325 | 4.5 | 7 953 | 13.8 | 6 261 | 375 | 3 272 | 1 714 | 2 395 |
| Rooks | 72 | 5 049 | 0.93 | 68 | 13.1 | 77 | 14.9 | 809 | 19.7 | 1 227 | 23 | 763 | NA | NA |
| Rush | 67 | 3 039 | 0.85 | 27 | 8.3 | 34 | 10.5 | 416 | 16.6 | 862 | 27 | 582 | 48 | 1 442 |
| Russell | 89 | 6 700 | 0.93 | 84 | 12.1 | 94 | 13.5 | 1 029 | 19.2 | 1 750 | 42 | 1 148 | 133 | 1 896 |
| Saline | 1 465 | 58 058 | 1.10 | 820 | 14.7 | 459 | 8.2 | 7 908 | 17.0 | 9 939 | 1 123 | 5 647 | 2 621 | 4 684 |
| Scott | 105 | 5 057 | 0.99 | 70 | 14.3 | 73 | 14.9 | 628 | 15.7 | 919 | 12 | 670 | 62 | 1 248 |
| Sedgwick | 7 252 | 513 136 | 1.09 | 8 002 | 16.0 | 3 924 | 7.8 | 74 425 | 17.1 | 73 078 | 11 533 | 38 199 | 25 058 | 4 996 |
| Seward | 476 | 24 095 | 1.13 | 516 | 22.1 | 135 | 5.8 | 5 169 | 25.1 | 2 291 | 38 | 1 381 | 634 | 2 745 |
| Shawnee | 4 397 | 188 308 | 1.14 | 2 435 | 13.6 | 1 660 | 9.3 | 22 868 | 15.3 | 33 602 | 2 039 | 17 640 | 9 658 | 5 438 |
| Sheridan | 33 | 2 456 | 0.91 | 23 | 9.0 | 29 | 11.4 | 370 | 18.6 | 562 | 14 | 343 | 15 | 583 |
| Sherman | 102 | 6 036 | 1.01 | 70 | 11.6 | 87 | 14.4 | 1 003 | 20.9 | 1 283 | 41 | 888 | 27 | 446 |
| Smith | 56 | 3 815 | 0.96 | 33 | 8.6 | 52 | 13.6 | 506 | 17.9 | 1 107 | 31 | 689 | NA | NA |
| Stafford | 69 | 4 122 | 0.86 | 47 | 10.8 | 56 | 12.8 | 808 | 23.1 | 932 | 18 | 611 | 59 | 1 321 |
| Stanton | 47 | 2 196 | 0.99 | 31 | 13.8 | 19 | 8.4 | 508 | 27.2 | 358 | D | 254 | 15 | 667 |
| Stevens | 72 | 5 085 | 0.82 | 83 | 14.8 | 34 | 6.1 | 1 214 | 24.5 | 805 | 21 | 488 | NA | NA |
| Sumner | 409 | 20 293 | 0.65 | 286 | 12.0 | 263 | 11.1 | 2 949 | 14.7 | 4 497 | 484 | 2 625 | 699 | 3 094 |
| Thomas | 353 | 7 896 | 1.02 | 110 | 13.8 | 66 | 8.3 | 1 105 | 17.2 | 1 327 | 40 | 870 | 144 | 1 811 |
| Trego | 64 | 2 952 | 0.99 | 29 | 9.9 | 48 | 16.4 | 406 | 17.8 | 761 | D | 461 | 23 | 762 |
| Wabaunsee | 90 | 5 150 | 0.46 | 81 | 11.5 | 54 | 7.7 | 852 | 14.6 | 1 320 | 90 | 646 | 106 | 1 693 |
| Wallace | 19 | 1 428 | 0.91 | 14 | 9.2 | 19 | 12.4 | 256 | 21.6 | 332 | 17 | 222 | 1 | 67 |
| Washington | 114 | 5 346 | 0.84 | 63 | 10.8 | 94 | 16.1 | 808 | 18.2 | 1 511 | 55 | 976 | 34 | 583 |
| Wichita | 26 | 2 290 | 1.04 | 31 | 13.6 | 24 | 10.5 | 486 | 26.5 | 420 | D | 300 | 40 | 1 779 |
| Wilson | 121 | 9 494 | 1.00 | 118 | 12.7 | 145 | 15.6 | 1 353 | 18.1 | 2 217 | 88 | 1 466 | 192 | 2 028 |
| Woodson | 39 | 2 932 | 0.72 | 42 | 12.8 | 62 | 18.8 | 527 | 20.7 | 790 | 52 | 512 | 108 | 3 243 |
| Wyandotte | 1 335 | 171 355 | 1.23 | 2 756 | 17.4 | 1 318 | 8.3 | 32 966 | 23.7 | 22 327 | 6 144 | 8 680 | 9 437 | 5 954 |
| KENTUCKY | 125 870 | 4 336 290 | 1.01 | 56 447 | 12.9 | 41 945 | 9.6 | 640 974 | 17.5 | 811 931 | 142 300 | 449 663 | 128 764 | 2 947 |
| Adair | 1 055 | 17 008 | 0.76 | 205 | 11.0 | 220 | 11.8 | 3 402 | 23.0 | 3 877 | 460 | 2 477 | 73 | 389 |
| Allen | 197 | 17 264 | 0.65 | 236 | 11.7 | 233 | 11.6 | 3 310 | 19.6 | 3 992 | 560 | 2 404 | 151 | 751 |
| Anderson | 108 | 16 019 | 0.48 | 265 | 12.2 | 176 | 8.1 | 3 116 | 16.7 | 3 701 | 735 | 1 849 | 218 | 1 011 |
| Ballard | 127 | 7 778 | 0.86 | 96 | 11.6 | 107 | 13.0 | 1 132 | 16.9 | 1 816 | 187 | 987 | 154 | 1 854 |
| Barren | 702 | 42 306 | 1.02 | 509 | 12.0 | 472 | 11.2 | 6 750 | 19.2 | 8 937 | 1 478 | 5 315 | 475 | 1 119 |
| Bath | 103 | 9 895 | 0.56 | 156 | 13.3 | 155 | 13.2 | 1 847 | 18.7 | 2 538 | 610 | 1 426 | NA | NA |
| Bell | 952 | 30 200 | 1.16 | 363 | 12.6 | 362 | 12.6 | 4 669 | 19.9 | 6 785 | 729 | 4 493 | 957 | 3 313 |
| Boone | 835 | 130 864 | 1.23 | 1 710 | 14.0 | 759 | 6.2 | 13 727 | 12.9 | 16 195 | 4 865 | 6 581 | 3 360 | 2 809 |
| Bourbon | 236 | 19 432 | 0.93 | 229 | 11.5 | 221 | 11.1 | 3 427 | 20.6 | 4 016 | 922 | 1 938 | 575 | 2 952 |
| Boyd | 2 338 | 57 715 | 1.46 | 581 | 11.7 | 574 | 11.6 | 6 783 | 17.3 | 11 496 | 1 959 | 5 766 | 1 669 | 3 346 |
| Boyle | 2 301 | 32 216 | 1.32 | 285 | 10.0 | 293 | 10.3 | 3 980 | 18.3 | 6 099 | 885 | 3 486 | 780 | 2 799 |
| Bracken | 41 | 6 617 | 0.47 | 117 | 13.7 | 108 | 12.7 | 1 342 | 18.4 | 1 636 | 344 | 911 | 170 | 2 152 |
| Breathitt | 322 | 13 273 | 0.81 | 165 | 11.9 | 193 | 13.9 | 2 115 | 17.9 | 3 360 | 436 | 2 327 | NA | NA |
| Breckinridge | 301 | 17 043 | 0.58 | 228 | 11.3 | 201 | 9.9 | 3 549 | 21.3 | 4 241 | 464 | 2 540 | 38 | 188 |
| Bullitt | 340 | 57 578 | 0.53 | 738 | 9.8 | 491 | 6.5 | 9 778 | 15.0 | 12 510 | 2 761 | 6 601 | 1 736 | 2 320 |
| Butler | 203 | 10 922 | 0.62 | 180 | 14.0 | 123 | 9.6 | 2 205 | 20.9 | 2 749 | 540 | 1 542 | 59 | 462 |
| Caldwell | 148 | 12 530 | 0.91 | 162 | 12.5 | 170 | 13.1 | 1 991 | 18.8 | 3 175 | 303 | 1 902 | 266 | 2 035 |
| Calloway | 2 952 | 37 440 | 1.03 | 413 | 11.0 | 396 | 10.5 | 5 515 | 19.2 | 7 024 | 1 044 | 4 097 | 1 147 | 3 063 |
| Campbell | 2 963 | 75 519 | 0.68 | 1 232 | 13.5 | 825 | 9.1 | 10 812 | 14.2 | 14 457 | 4 424 | 5 938 | 3 231 | 3 552 |
| Carlisle | 60 | 4 167 | 0.50 | 52 | 10.3 | 70 | 13.9 | 819 | 19.9 | 1 209 | 104 | 700 | 49 | 953 |
| Carroll | 325 | 13 539 | 1.64 | 174 | 15.8 | 121 | 11.0 | 1 729 | 18.9 | 2 105 | 256 | 1 224 | 152 | 1 396 |
| Carter | 626 | 24 401 | 0.68 | 343 | 12.4 | 330 | 12.0 | 4 244 | 18.5 | 6 026 | 1 028 | 3 511 | 179 | 641 |
| Casey | 480 | 14 151 | 0.71 | 209 | 13.1 | 200 | 12.6 | 3 164 | 24.2 | 3 543 | 375 | 2 303 | 113 | 703 |
| Christian | 5 389 | 93 844 | 1.69 | 1 504 | 20.4 | 589 | 8.0 | 10 759 | 17.5 | 10 102 | 1 207 | 5 874 | 2 325 | 3 192 |
| Clark | 458 | 33 531 | 0.87 | 456 | 12.8 | 347 | 9.8 | 5 336 | 17.7 | 7 146 | 1 511 | 3 123 | 1 474 | 4 111 |

1. Per 1,000 estimated resident population.　2. Data for serious crimes have not been adjusted for underreporting; this may affect comparability between geographic areas and over time.　3. Per 100,000 population estimated by the FBI.

# Table B. States and Counties — Crime, Education, Money Income, and Poverty

| STATE County | Violent (46) | Property (47) | Enrollment Total (48) | Percent private (49) | High school graduate or less (50) | Bachelor's degree or more (51) | Total current expenditures (mil dol) (52) | Current expenditures per student (dollars) (53) | Per capita income (dollars) (54) | Median income Dollars (55) | Percent change, 2000 to 2007–2011 (constant 2011 dollars) (56) | Percent with income of $200,000 or more (57) | Median household income (dollars) (58) | All persons (59) | Children under 18 (60) | Children 5 to 17 years in families (61) |
|---|---|---|---|---|---|---|---|---|---|---|---|---|---|---|---|---|
| **KANSAS—Cont'd** | | | | | | | | | | | | | | | | |
| Neosho | 247 | 2 461 | 4 078 | 7.8 | 46.4 | 15.5 | 23.6 | 9 676 | 19 651 | 38 883 | -10.5 | 0.7 | 40 651 | 17.4 | 26.5 | 22.6 |
| Ness | 128 | 608 | 631 | 10.0 | 49.3 | 17.4 | 4.8 | 10 071 | 30 005 | 46 417 | 6.3 | 4.5 | 44 774 | 11.3 | 17.6 | 14.8 |
| Norton | 140 | 1 192 | 1 084 | 4.9 | 48.6 | 16.7 | 9.6 | 11 077 | 20 480 | 37 656 | -10.2 | 1.1 | 41 396 | 14.4 | 17.3 | 15.0 |
| Osage | 275 | 1 492 | 3 894 | 9.3 | 50.5 | 19.8 | 28.4 | 10 260 | 24 319 | 51 878 | 1.3 | 1.8 | 47 318 | 11.7 | 16.6 | 14.2 |
| Osborne | NA | NA | 792 | 5.7 | 49.3 | 18.7 | 5.9 | 12 613 | 25 362 | 36 489 | -7.3 | 3.6 | 37 949 | 13.7 | 21.7 | 19.0 |
| Ottawa | 245 | 1 925 | 1 407 | 9.7 | 41.8 | 19.1 | 12.9 | 10 391 | 23 559 | 53 287 | 3.8 | 1.5 | 48 998 | 10.5 | 14.4 | 12.2 |
| Pawnee | 257 | 2 138 | 1 606 | 4.9 | 39.4 | 21.7 | 12.1 | 10 220 | 22 239 | 43 676 | -8.0 | 2.7 | 41 623 | 14.8 | 17.9 | 15.1 |
| Phillips | 35 | 458 | 1 299 | 4.4 | 46.5 | 16.1 | 8.8 | 10 612 | 22 283 | 43 476 | -8.0 | 0.7 | 40 746 | 12.6 | 16.8 | 14.5 |
| Pottawatomie | 199 | 1 360 | 5 723 | 15.1 | 38.2 | 29.7 | 35.4 | 9 278 | 24 438 | 54 309 | 0.1 | 2.7 | 53 339 | 9.1 | 12.9 | 11.8 |
| Pratt | 288 | 3 211 | 2 471 | 10.1 | 41.9 | 22.2 | 15.1 | 10 588 | 24 855 | 42 825 | -10.7 | 1.8 | 44 964 | 12.6 | 18.2 | 16.4 |
| Rawlins | 79 | 710 | 450 | 4.0 | 40.6 | 22.7 | 3.9 | 12 138 | 25 250 | 40 625 | -6.3 | 1.5 | 40 908 | 12.2 | 15.5 | 13.6 |
| Reno | 394 | 4 519 | 15 702 | 10.5 | 42.0 | 19.5 | 94.8 | 9 486 | 22 578 | 42 207 | -12.0 | 1.6 | 41 892 | 12.8 | 18.5 | 16.1 |
| Republic | 40 | 978 | 923 | 7.2 | 41.2 | 19.4 | 8.1 | 10 646 | 25 647 | 40 538 | -1.5 | 2.4 | 38 132 | 12.9 | 19.3 | 16.9 |
| Rice | 138 | 1 015 | 2 587 | 19.1 | 46.1 | 20.9 | 20.1 | 10 441 | 21 904 | 46 155 | -4.2 | 1.0 | 45 420 | 14.5 | 20.6 | 18.3 |
| Riley | 252 | 2 143 | 29 726 | 5.6 | 23.7 | 45.6 | 68.7 | 9 692 | 21 578 | 41 427 | -4.2 | 2.3 | 45 558 | 20.6 | 16.5 | 16.7 |
| Rooks | NA | NA | 1 140 | 8.1 | 44.6 | 20.1 | 10.0 | 11 666 | 23 846 | 40 000 | -2.7 | 1.5 | 39 326 | 12.7 | 16.8 | 15.4 |
| Rush | 120 | 1 322 | 552 | 2.0 | 48.6 | 17.2 | 5.6 | 11 777 | 24 259 | 40 036 | -5.2 | 1.3 | 37 693 | 13.2 | 19.3 | 16.5 |
| Russell | 399 | 1 497 | 1 375 | 5.8 | 44.4 | 20.2 | 9.8 | 9 959 | 26 249 | 38 168 | -3.5 | 3.4 | 37 140 | 14.6 | 21.3 | 19.3 |
| Saline | 347 | 4 337 | 13 493 | 10.0 | 43.4 | 24.0 | 91.3 | 9 595 | 24 426 | 45 635 | -9.4 | 2.0 | 45 359 | 14.4 | 22.0 | 20.1 |
| Scott | 181 | 1 067 | 1 086 | 8.7 | 43.1 | 19.9 | 8.9 | 9 619 | 26 108 | 58 453 | 6.8 | 3.3 | 49 066 | 8.7 | 13.5 | 12.4 |
| Sedgwick | 650 | 4 347 | 138 197 | 17.2 | 39.9 | 28.0 | 777.9 | 9 696 | 25 832 | 49 451 | -13.8 | 2.8 | 49 526 | 15.2 | 21.3 | 18.8 |
| Seward | 325 | 2 420 | 5 966 | 5.8 | 65.1 | 13.5 | 49.3 | 9 043 | 18 514 | 44 550 | -10.2 | 1.1 | 47 855 | 15.4 | 21.8 | 20.0 |
| Shawnee | 433 | 5 005 | 46 591 | 16.2 | 41.2 | 28.8 | 268.3 | 9 486 | 26 295 | 47 701 | -13.8 | 2.5 | 44 816 | 14.6 | 20.3 | 17.4 |
| Sheridan | 0 | 583 | 561 | 6.4 | 42.1 | 20.9 | 5.9 | 10 428 | 25 245 | 46 821 | 3.4 | 2.6 | 48 498 | 12.6 | 19.4 | 16.1 |
| Sherman | 33 | 413 | 1 209 | 4.8 | 44.5 | 17.2 | 9.1 | 10 181 | 20 799 | 43 012 | -2.5 | 0.5 | 39 660 | 15.8 | 24.9 | 22.5 |
| Smith | NA | NA | 644 | 4.2 | 51.0 | 13.4 | 8.5 | 12 492 | 25 797 | 42 569 | 10.7 | 2.5 | 38 090 | 14.2 | 20.1 | 16.6 |
| Stafford | 112 | 1 209 | 927 | 7.6 | 42.7 | 21.8 | 10.6 | 11 789 | 22 871 | 42 006 | 0.0 | 2.1 | 44 133 | 13.2 | 19.7 | 16.4 |
| Stanton | 133 | 534 | 519 | 11.9 | 53.5 | 15.5 | 5.2 | 10 537 | 21 412 | 49 152 | -9.4 | 1.2 | 49 115 | 12.6 | 20.7 | 18.4 |
| Stevens | NA | NA | 1 424 | 10.5 | 52.4 | 13.1 | 13.3 | 9 976 | 25 826 | 56 019 | -0.8 | 3.3 | 54 901 | 10.9 | 16.7 | 14.4 |
| Sumner | 274 | 2 819 | 6 265 | 12.0 | 45.2 | 18.4 | 40.7 | 10 132 | 22 778 | 48 060 | -9.7 | 1.9 | 47 460 | 13.5 | 19.0 | 16.0 |
| Thomas | 314 | 1 497 | 2 226 | 7.9 | 34.8 | 23.0 | 10.3 | 9 957 | 25 816 | 45 125 | -9.8 | 3.5 | 47 892 | 11.1 | 13.5 | 11.9 |
| Trego | 265 | 497 | 602 | 19.6 | 46.7 | 19.1 | 4.8 | 10 797 | 22 292 | 42 009 | 4.8 | 0.6 | 45 683 | 10.7 | 13.9 | 11.9 |
| Wabaunsee | 160 | 1 533 | 1 741 | 13.1 | 49.9 | 19.8 | 10.9 | 10 722 | 22 987 | 53 292 | -5.4 | 1.2 | 51 666 | 7.9 | 12.5 | 10.8 |
| Wallace | 67 | 0 | 301 | 10.0 | 45.9 | 23.9 | 3.9 | 12 625 | 23 894 | 46 128 | 3.5 | 1.6 | 47 573 | 12.0 | 16.4 | 12.9 |
| Washington | 188 | 394 | 1 224 | 17.1 | 51.0 | 17.3 | 9.0 | 11 335 | 21 391 | 40 469 | 2.1 | 0.5 | 39 962 | 12.0 | 16.0 | 13.6 |
| Wichita | 133 | 1 646 | 574 | 2.3 | 50.2 | 18.0 | 4.7 | 10 136 | 21 734 | 50 324 | 11.4 | 0.5 | 46 929 | 13.2 | 20.5 | 17.7 |
| Wilson | 285 | 1 743 | 2 107 | 6.0 | 57.1 | 11.4 | 17.5 | 10 217 | 19 143 | 40 069 | -0.2 | 0.4 | 37 002 | 17.0 | 24.5 | 21.2 |
| Woodson | 420 | 2 823 | 573 | 8.7 | 51.4 | 16.4 | 5.0 | 11 738 | 22 687 | 31 779 | -7.1 | 1.5 | 33 221 | 17.3 | 27.7 | 23.9 |
| Wyandotte | 632 | 5 322 | 42 562 | 12.1 | 56.7 | 15.2 | 280.5 | 9 775 | 19 214 | 39 812 | -12.7 | 0.8 | 38 016 | 26.0 | 39.7 | 34.1 |
| **KENTUCKY** | 238 | 2 709 | 1 088 379 | 14.5 | 52.6 | 20.6 | 6 083.7 | 8 945 | 23 033 | 42 248 | -7.1 | 2.3 | 41 141 | 19.1 | 27.2 | 25.0 |
| Adair | 37 | 351 | 4 470 | 19.4 | 64.5 | 13.3 | 23.7 | 9 111 | 15 962 | 31 775 | -2.2 | 0.4 | 30 147 | 23.1 | 37.6 | 34.0 |
| Allen | 55 | 697 | 4 791 | 9.8 | 64.1 | 10.9 | 24.2 | 8 062 | 17 582 | 35 357 | -16.2 | 0.5 | 35 614 | 20.5 | 29.4 | 27.5 |
| Anderson | 42 | 969 | 5 563 | 9.6 | 51.5 | 18.4 | 33.3 | 8 169 | 24 910 | 52 447 | -14.5 | 1.1 | 51 817 | 10.8 | 17.2 | 15.6 |
| Ballard | 48 | 1 806 | 1 903 | 8.2 | 59.2 | 11.8 | 13.4 | 9 102 | 24 405 | 41 875 | -3.5 | 2.4 | 40 790 | 16.5 | 24.9 | 22.1 |
| Barren | 80 | 1 039 | 10 055 | 6.8 | 63.4 | 14.2 | 67.4 | 8 768 | 19 991 | 38 616 | -8.4 | 1.4 | 36 298 | 21.7 | 31.0 | 28.6 |
| Bath | NA | NA | 2 683 | 10.0 | 65.1 | 13.3 | 17.1 | 8 264 | 15 630 | 28 776 | -18.1 | 1.1 | 29 857 | 25.6 | 38.0 | 36.5 |
| Bell | 180 | 3 133 | 6 665 | 13.1 | 69.7 | 11.2 | 50.0 | 9 455 | 14 745 | 25 269 | -1.8 | 0.8 | 24 940 | 41.6 | 50.5 | 45.2 |
| Boone | 117 | 2 692 | 33 262 | 18.3 | 39.1 | 28.8 | 165.0 | 8 011 | 28 630 | 68 087 | -5.9 | 3.5 | 64 055 | 8.7 | 12.1 | 10.7 |
| Bourbon | 169 | 2 783 | 4 722 | 15.5 | 57.4 | 16.0 | 33.0 | 9 014 | 22 566 | 42 192 | -10.8 | 1.1 | 40 350 | 18.2 | 28.8 | 26.2 |
| Boyd | 196 | 3 149 | 10 710 | 8.0 | 52.2 | 15.6 | 68.4 | 8 947 | 22 698 | 38 848 | -12.1 | 2.1 | 38 783 | 20.5 | 29.9 | 25.1 |
| Boyle | 194 | 2 605 | 7 387 | 19.2 | 50.4 | 23.3 | 42.7 | 9 183 | 23 499 | 41 035 | -13.8 | 2.7 | 39 663 | 17.6 | 24.8 | 22.0 |
| Bracken | 101 | 2 050 | 1 983 | 4.9 | 67.3 | 13.2 | 12.4 | 8 048 | 19 701 | 39 643 | -15.7 | 0.6 | 41 974 | 14.8 | 25.5 | 23.8 |
| Breathitt | NA | NA | 3 213 | 6.7 | 69.8 | 10.6 | 28.8 | 10 402 | 15 048 | 22 304 | -13.8 | 0.5 | 26 829 | 35.7 | 47.2 | 43.2 |
| Breckinridge | 20 | 168 | 4 547 | 12.8 | 68.5 | 8.1 | 28.4 | 8 991 | 17 872 | 38 325 | -7.1 | 0.8 | 38 028 | 19.3 | 30.6 | 28.8 |
| Bullitt | 94 | 2 226 | 18 868 | 16.0 | 57.8 | 12.0 | 97.6 | 7 528 | 23 357 | 51 857 | -14.9 | 0.8 | 52 033 | 10.8 | 16.7 | 15.0 |
| Butler | 47 | 415 | 2 712 | 4.4 | 69.1 | 8.0 | 18.2 | 8 483 | 17 163 | 32 508 | -18.1 | 0.5 | 32 483 | 20.5 | 30.5 | 29.1 |
| Caldwell | 176 | 1 859 | 2 889 | 4.8 | 62.8 | 14.2 | 17.9 | 8 549 | 20 001 | 37 078 | -4.3 | 1.7 | 36 650 | 19.1 | 30.9 | 30.0 |
| Calloway | 88 | 2 975 | 12 470 | 7.1 | 45.1 | 28.6 | 41.7 | 8 718 | 21 273 | 39 316 | -3.4 | 1.5 | 39 599 | 17.2 | 23.7 | 22.5 |
| Campbell | 162 | 3 391 | 25 173 | 20.6 | 46.2 | 27.4 | 106.0 | 9 036 | 27 501 | 53 018 | -6.3 | 2.8 | 53 501 | 13.1 | 18.3 | 17.2 |
| Carlisle | 78 | 876 | 1 101 | 17.3 | 62.5 | 11.4 | 7.6 | 8 713 | 17 926 | 35 699 | -12.1 | 0.3 | 38 075 | 16.7 | 28.3 | 25.7 |
| Carroll | 46 | 1 350 | 2 363 | 2.3 | 68.7 | 8.1 | 18.8 | 9 262 | 20 966 | 42 063 | -13.3 | 1.3 | 40 685 | 21.2 | 29.7 | 29.2 |
| Carter | 50 | 591 | 6 972 | 14.8 | 66.0 | 10.0 | 42.2 | 8 430 | 19 559 | 35 637 | -0.1 | 1.6 | 35 471 | 20.7 | 33.3 | 30.3 |
| Casey | 44 | 660 | 3 586 | 8.7 | 70.2 | 8.2 | 21.2 | 9 000 | 14 813 | 27 327 | -6.2 | 0.2 | 28 034 | 27.6 | 41.9 | 40.6 |
| Christian | 214 | 2 978 | 19 292 | 12.6 | 52.5 | 13.5 | 79.4 | 8 558 | 18 623 | 37 958 | -9.8 | 1.2 | 35 779 | 23.7 | 34.4 | 35.0 |
| Clark | 421 | 3 689 | 8 267 | 13.0 | 55.3 | 18.2 | 44.8 | 7 803 | 24 022 | 45 726 | -15.2 | 1.8 | 44 494 | 17.4 | 25.4 | 23.0 |

1. Data for serious crimes have not been adjusted for underreporting; this may affect comparability between geographic areas and over time. 2. Per 100,000 population estimated by the FBI. 3. All persons 3 years old and over enrolled in nursery school through college. 4. Persons 25 years old and over. 5. Elementary and secondary education expenditures. 6. Based on population estimated by the American Community Survey, 2007–2011.

# Table B. States and Counties — **Personal Income**

| STATE County | Personal income, 2011 Total (mil dol) | Percent change, 2010–2011 | Per capita[1] Dollars | Per capita[1] Rank | Wages and salaries[2] (mil dol) | Proprietors' income (mil dol) | Dividends, interest, and rent (mil dol) | Transfer payments (mil dol) Total | Government payments to individuals Total | Social Security | Medical payments | Income mainte-nance | Unemploy-ment insurance |
|---|---|---|---|---|---|---|---|---|---|---|---|---|---|
| | 62 | 63 | 64 | 65 | 66 | 67 | 68 | 69 | 70 | 71 | 72 | 73 | 74 |
| **KANSAS—Cont'd** | | | | | | | | | | | | | |
| Neosho | 527 | 5.1 | 32 042 | 1 874 | 294 | 64 | 70 | 143 | 140 | 46 | 61 | 16 | 6 |
| Ness | 138 | -1.8 | 44 307 | 429 | 61 | 23 | 28 | 26 | 25 | 10 | 13 | 1 | 0 |
| Norton | 225 | 15.5 | 39 849 | 763 | 114 | 62 | 32 | 37 | 36 | 16 | 16 | 3 | 0 |
| Osage | 519 | 4.8 | 31 807 | 1 932 | 109 | 15 | 70 | 128 | 125 | 47 | 47 | 12 | 8 |
| Osborne | 169 | 24.1 | 44 023 | 438 | 56 | 54 | 32 | 34 | 33 | 14 | 15 | 3 | 1 |
| Ottawa | 205 | 9.7 | 33 499 | 1 601 | 53 | 35 | 30 | 42 | 40 | 17 | 16 | 3 | 2 |
| Pawnee | 247 | 8.9 | 35 188 | 1 342 | 141 | 36 | 39 | 48 | 46 | 20 | 20 | 4 | 1 |
| Phillips | 248 | 16.4 | 44 602 | 415 | 104 | 67 | 47 | 46 | 45 | 19 | 20 | 3 | 1 |
| Pottawatomie | 792 | 7.8 | 36 131 | 1 196 | 424 | 82 | 115 | 120 | 115 | 45 | 48 | 10 | 5 |
| Pratt | 432 | 17.3 | 44 612 | 412 | 203 | 103 | 73 | 80 | 77 | 29 | 36 | 6 | 2 |
| Rawlins | 161 | 28.0 | 64 186 | 42 | 39 | 82 | 21 | 23 | 22 | 10 | 11 | 1 | 0 |
| Reno | 2 173 | 4.6 | 33 642 | 1 578 | 1 229 | 156 | 387 | 512 | 498 | 189 | 211 | 55 | 17 |
| Republic | 186 | 21.2 | 37 939 | 980 | 76 | 51 | 25 | 42 | 41 | 18 | 17 | 3 | 0 |
| Rice | 319 | 9.2 | 31 654 | 1 968 | 157 | 33 | 50 | 74 | 71 | 30 | 30 | 7 | 2 |
| Riley | 3 423 | 9.1 | 46 890 | 304 | 1 396 | 75 | 454 | 290 | 276 | 90 | 91 | 35 | 10 |
| Rooks | 193 | 23.9 | 37 250 | 1 053 | 81 | 35 | 35 | 43 | 42 | 17 | 20 | 3 | 1 |
| Rush | 121 | 12.0 | 37 344 | 1 045 | 52 | 20 | 22 | 30 | 29 | 11 | 14 | 2 | 0 |
| Russell | 252 | 10.8 | 36 274 | 1 176 | 123 | 26 | 62 | 64 | 62 | 24 | 30 | 5 | 1 |
| Saline | 2 229 | 5.3 | 39 910 | 756 | 1 365 | 347 | 415 | 401 | 389 | 143 | 157 | 44 | 17 |
| Scott | 186 | 8.2 | 37 867 | 989 | 90 | 26 | 45 | 29 | 28 | 14 | 11 | 3 | 0 |
| Sedgwick | 19 368 | 4.7 | 38 653 | 889 | 14 243 | 2 000 | 2 639 | 3 425 | 3 315 | 1 127 | 1 319 | 481 | 198 |
| Seward | 714 | 6.8 | 30 619 | 2 170 | 551 | 92 | 74 | 115 | 110 | 32 | 49 | 21 | 2 |
| Shawnee | 6 963 | 5.2 | 38 913 | 860 | 5 373 | 353 | 1 073 | 1 451 | 1 411 | 470 | 553 | 170 | 60 |
| Sheridan | 157 | 24.9 | 61 365 | 56 | 44 | 75 | 25 | 17 | 17 | 8 | 7 | 1 | 0 |
| Sherman | 306 | 25.1 | 50 602 | 196 | 105 | 128 | 30 | 54 | 52 | 17 | 27 | 5 | 1 |
| Smith | 175 | 31.3 | 45 628 | 356 | 51 | 64 | 26 | 33 | 32 | 15 | 13 | 2 | 0 |
| Stafford | 191 | 22.0 | 43 747 | 453 | 55 | 61 | 34 | 35 | 34 | 13 | 16 | 3 | 1 |
| Stanton | 102 | 14.9 | 45 210 | 386 | 42 | 31 | 20 | 13 | 12 | 5 | 6 | 1 | 0 |
| Stevens | 221 | 4.1 | 39 294 | 823 | 89 | 64 | 45 | 29 | 28 | 12 | 12 | 3 | 0 |
| Sumner | 943 | 7.3 | 39 651 | 785 | 282 | 127 | 103 | 181 | 176 | 66 | 72 | 17 | 8 |
| Thomas | 345 | 16.7 | 43 302 | 484 | 166 | 106 | 45 | 50 | 49 | 19 | 22 | 4 | 1 |
| Trego | 111 | 2.4 | 37 752 | 999 | 52 | 15 | 20 | 26 | 25 | 10 | 12 | 1 | 0 |
| Wabaunsee | 242 | 5.1 | 34 429 | 1 449 | 53 | 10 | 35 | 47 | 46 | 19 | 17 | 3 | 2 |
| Wallace | 100 | 22.8 | 65 411 | 36 | 21 | 60 | 8 | 12 | 12 | 4 | 6 | 1 | 0 |
| Washington | 230 | 23.9 | 39 424 | 812 | 77 | 49 | 46 | 48 | 46 | 20 | 20 | 3 | 1 |
| Wichita | 104 | 19.1 | 45 603 | 358 | 41 | 34 | 18 | 15 | 14 | 6 | 6 | 1 | 0 |
| Wilson | 303 | 2.7 | 32 535 | 1 788 | 150 | 29 | 47 | 89 | 87 | 31 | 38 | 9 | 5 |
| Woodson | 94 | -0.5 | 28 461 | 2 547 | 29 | 15 | 16 | 30 | 29 | 11 | 13 | 3 | 1 |
| Wyandotte | 4 562 | 3.2 | 28 836 | 2 482 | 5 087 | 237 | 390 | 1 255 | 1 220 | 316 | 541 | 219 | 60 |
| **KENTUCKY** | 148 510 | 5.1 | 33 989 | X | 96 276 | 10 585 | 19 955 | 35 720 | 34 760 | 11 385 | 14 335 | 4 488 | 1 377 |
| Adair | 477 | 3.5 | 25 525 | 2 926 | 180 | 22 | 53 | 183 | 179 | 48 | 87 | 21 | 6 |
| Allen | 566 | 4.9 | 28 088 | 2 605 | 175 | 108 | 58 | 157 | 153 | 54 | 64 | 19 | 6 |
| Anderson | 672 | 4.5 | 31 048 | 2 088 | 194 | 23 | 79 | 139 | 134 | 56 | 46 | 14 | 7 |
| Ballard | 299 | 6.5 | 36 228 | 1 185 | 176 | 36 | 29 | 81 | 79 | 26 | 37 | 7 | 3 |
| Barren | 1 231 | 5.0 | 29 128 | 2 433 | 700 | 108 | 178 | 347 | 337 | 119 | 141 | 44 | 14 |
| Bath | 293 | 4.2 | 24 925 | 2 969 | 70 | 9 | 27 | 102 | 100 | 31 | 40 | 18 | 4 |
| Bell | 737 | 2.4 | 25 656 | 2 915 | 378 | 25 | 78 | 339 | 332 | 87 | 157 | 59 | 9 |
| Boone | 4 346 | 6.7 | 35 704 | 1 262 | 4 033 | 256 | 472 | 645 | 618 | 248 | 214 | 52 | 36 |
| Bourbon | 610 | 3.0 | 30 504 | 2 195 | 337 | 30 | 100 | 152 | 148 | 55 | 60 | 18 | 6 |
| Boyd | 1 652 | 2.8 | 33 405 | 1 625 | 1 592 | 105 | 193 | 503 | 492 | 167 | 214 | 56 | 15 |
| Boyle | 876 | 3.5 | 30 686 | 2 158 | 652 | 50 | 165 | 235 | 228 | 84 | 89 | 26 | 10 |
| Bracken | 260 | 4.5 | 30 499 | 2 197 | 59 | 9 | 24 | 68 | 66 | 23 | 26 | 9 | 3 |
| Breathitt | 389 | 2.4 | 28 088 | 2 605 | 142 | 11 | 32 | 180 | 177 | 41 | 83 | 37 | 4 |
| Breckinridge | 555 | 6.2 | 27 404 | 2 701 | 136 | 38 | 76 | 171 | 167 | 57 | 69 | 20 | 7 |
| Bullitt | 2 293 | 5.0 | 30 533 | 2 191 | 781 | 125 | 214 | 494 | 477 | 191 | 167 | 49 | 28 |
| Butler | 340 | 6.1 | 26 519 | 2 820 | 114 | 22 | 39 | 117 | 114 | 36 | 52 | 15 | 4 |
| Caldwell | 393 | 5.7 | 30 328 | 2 232 | 166 | 38 | 52 | 122 | 119 | 43 | 51 | 13 | 4 |
| Calloway | 1 122 | 4.9 | 29 889 | 2 311 | 664 | 89 | 181 | 286 | 278 | 101 | 107 | 24 | 10 |
| Campbell | 3 413 | 4.8 | 37 531 | 1 024 | 1 353 | 124 | 465 | 632 | 612 | 214 | 237 | 60 | 31 |
| Carlisle | 163 | 10.7 | 32 236 | 1 839 | 30 | 29 | 22 | 47 | 46 | 17 | 20 | 4 | 1 |
| Carroll | 352 | -1.4 | 31 945 | 1 898 | 354 | 18 | 38 | 87 | 85 | 29 | 36 | 10 | 4 |
| Carter | 698 | 2.8 | 25 297 | 2 944 | 241 | 30 | 63 | 268 | 262 | 80 | 109 | 41 | 11 |
| Casey | 390 | 3.8 | 24 495 | 3 005 | 128 | 29 | 42 | 147 | 144 | 41 | 66 | 22 | 5 |
| Christian | 2 359 | 4.5 | 32 061 | 1 868 | 5 615 | 167 | 315 | 499 | 487 | 138 | 197 | 81 | 21 |
| Clark | 1 196 | 3.0 | 33 660 | 1 575 | 593 | 153 | 171 | 282 | 274 | 101 | 105 | 36 | 12 |

1. Based on the resident population estimated as of July 1 of the year shown.    2. Includes supplements to wages and salaries.

# Table B. States and Counties — Earnings, Social Security, and Housing

| STATE County | Total (mil dol) | Farm | Goods-related[1] Total | Manu-facturing | Information and profes-sional and technical services | Retail trade | Finance, insur-ance, and real estate | Health care and social services | Govern-ment | Number | Rate[2] | Supple-mental Security Income recipients, December 2011 | Total | Percent change, 2000–2010 |
|---|---|---|---|---|---|---|---|---|---|---|---|---|---|---|
| | 75 | 76 | 77 | 78 | 79 | 80 | 81 | 82 | 83 | 84 | 85 | 86 | 87 | 88 |
| **KANSAS—Cont'd** | | | | | | | | | | | | | | |
| Neosho | 358 | 8.1 | 27.2 | 16.1 | D | 8.1 | 3.8 | D | 26.9 | 3 675 | 223 | 395 | 7 513 | 0.7 |
| Ness | 84 | 6.0 | D | 1.4 | D | 6.2 | D | 0.9 | 22.8 | 815 | 261 | 24 | 1 740 | -5.2 |
| Norton | 176 | 29.4 | D | 5.3 | 3.3 | 5.9 | 5.1 | 7.7 | 23.1 | 1 290 | 229 | 59 | 2 542 | -4.9 |
| Osage | 124 | 4.0 | D | 3.2 | D | 8.6 | D | D | 41.5 | 3 750 | 230 | 334 | 7 503 | 6.9 |
| Osborne | 111 | 33.0 | D | 5.0 | D | 7.0 | 3.7 | 7.5 | 13.1 | 1 125 | 292 | 52 | 2 206 | -8.8 |
| Ottawa | 89 | 32.0 | 5.9 | 3.3 | D | 3.1 | D | 10.1 | 21.5 | 1 350 | 221 | 70 | 2 779 | 0.9 |
| Pawnee | 176 | 15.0 | D | D | D | 3.8 | 3.3 | 5.5 | 48.4 | 1 475 | 210 | 78 | 3 152 | 1.2 |
| Phillips | 171 | 24.9 | 21.1 | 14.8 | 2.4 | 3.5 | D | 6.1 | 17.7 | 1 490 | 268 | 68 | 3 049 | -1.3 |
| Pottawatomie | 506 | 2.2 | 34.2 | 22.5 | D | 8.1 | 4.6 | D | 11.4 | 3 580 | 163 | 219 | 8 626 | 18.0 |
| Pratt | 306 | 22.8 | 17.2 | 1.5 | 2.9 | 7.5 | 4.0 | 12.4 | 16.6 | 2 130 | 220 | 142 | 4 514 | -2.6 |
| Rawlins | 121 | 47.7 | D | 0.9 | D | 4.6 | D | 3.8 | 11.1 | 780 | 311 | 36 | 1 458 | -6.8 |
| Reno | 1 385 | 4.0 | 20.5 | 13.5 | 5.2 | 7.5 | 4.5 | 17.2 | 18.3 | 14 340 | 222 | 1 355 | 28 274 | 2.3 |
| Republic | 128 | 30.7 | D | 6.5 | 2.2 | 5.9 | 5.4 | 10.9 | 16.9 | 1 495 | 305 | 75 | 2 877 | -7.6 |
| Rice | 191 | 12.6 | 20.7 | 10.5 | 3.7 | 4.6 | D | D | 22.8 | 2 245 | 223 | 143 | 4 548 | -1.3 |
| Riley | 1 471 | 1.0 | D | 1.8 | 5.0 | 7.6 | 5.1 | 11.0 | 44.8 | 6 720 | 92 | 513 | 28 212 | 20.4 |
| Rooks | 116 | 27.7 | 12.4 | 3.2 | D | 5.3 | D | 3.0 | 23.2 | 1 355 | 261 | 69 | 2 768 | 0.4 |
| Rush | 72 | 27.3 | D | 19.0 | 5.1 | D | D | 2.9 | 19.9 | 930 | 287 | 59 | 1 869 | -3.1 |
| Russell | 148 | 14.8 | 32.9 | 17.1 | 3.6 | 4.6 | 3.7 | 9.7 | 17.7 | 1 930 | 277 | 133 | 3 910 | 1.0 |
| Saline | 1 713 | 2.4 | D | 18.3 | 6.2 | 7.5 | 3.7 | 14.1 | 12.4 | 10 845 | 194 | 980 | 24 101 | 6.2 |
| Scott | 116 | 25.1 | D | 0.9 | 3.0 | 5.0 | D | D | 14.7 | 1 015 | 207 | 56 | 2 193 | -4.3 |
| Sedgwick | 16 243 | 0.2 | D | 26.4 | 6.2 | 5.9 | 3.9 | 12.1 | 13.8 | 81 340 | 162 | 10 435 | 211 593 | 10.7 |
| Seward | 644 | 3.0 | D | D | D | 7.4 | 3.2 | D | 18.4 | 2 505 | 107 | 339 | 8 061 | 0.4 |
| Shawnee | 5 726 | 0.2 | 12.8 | 7.7 | D | 5.2 | 9.7 | 15.5 | 25.0 | 35 330 | 197 | 4 712 | 79 140 | 7.3 |
| Sheridan | 119 | 47.5 | D | 0.3 | D | 3.5 | 5.0 | D | 10.5 | 590 | 231 | 18 | 1 265 | 0.2 |
| Sherman | 233 | 49.3 | D | 2.7 | 2.1 | 5.7 | D | D | 15.2 | 1 380 | 228 | 110 | 3 148 | -1.1 |
| Smith | 116 | 50.9 | D | 3.4 | D | 4.8 | D | 7.1 | 13.2 | 1 185 | 309 | 44 | 2 232 | -4.0 |
| Stafford | 116 | 54.2 | D | D | D | 1.4 | 2.5 | D | 21.5 | 1 035 | 237 | 46 | 2 319 | -5.7 |
| Stanton | 73 | 47.1 | D | D | D | 2.6 | D | D | 19.0 | 355 | 158 | 0 | 990 | -1.7 |
| Stevens | 153 | 36.0 | D | D | D | 3.5 | D | D | 21.9 | 875 | 156 | 40 | 2 306 | 1.8 |
| Sumner | 410 | 24.5 | 19.1 | 15.6 | 3.5 | 6.3 | 3.8 | D | 20.3 | 4 925 | 207 | 425 | 10 865 | -0.1 |
| Thomas | 272 | 35.4 | D | 0.9 | 2.7 | 8.9 | 3.8 | D | 13.9 | 1 435 | 180 | 91 | 3 536 | -0.7 |
| Trego | 67 | 21.1 | D | 2.0 | D | 5.2 | D | D | 29.4 | 810 | 276 | 32 | 1 682 | -2.4 |
| Wabaunsee | 63 | 5.5 | D | 11.4 | D | 3.4 | 6.0 | D | 31.1 | 1 485 | 211 | 91 | 3 227 | 6.4 |
| Wallace | 81 | 73.2 | D | D | D | 1.6 | D | D | 7.9 | 340 | 223 | 16 | 781 | -1.3 |
| Washington | 126 | 41.5 | D | 4.1 | D | 3.6 | D | 4.0 | 22.4 | 1 655 | 283 | 74 | 2 955 | -6.0 |
| Wichita | 75 | 52.3 | 5.2 | 3.9 | D | 2.5 | D | D | 16.7 | 450 | 198 | 17 | 1 054 | -5.8 |
| Wilson | 179 | 10.3 | 34.7 | 27.2 | 1.6 | 4.5 | 2.9 | 6.5 | 23.1 | 2 490 | 268 | 248 | 4 682 | -5.2 |
| Woodson | 44 | 21.7 | D | 2.0 | D | 7.3 | D | 4.4 | 22.5 | 890 | 270 | 67 | 2 022 | -2.6 |
| Wyandotte | 5 324 | 0.0 | D | 18.3 | 3.1 | 5.2 | 2.0 | 15.3 | 21.3 | 24 905 | 157 | 5 076 | 66 747 | 1.3 |
| **KENTUCKY** | 106 861 | 1.0 | 20.6 | 13.6 | 6.9 | 6.4 | 6.1 | 12.1 | 22.8 | 913 548 | 209 | 192 721 | 1 927 164 | 10.1 |
| Adair | 202 | 0.9 | 14.8 | 7.2 | D | 8.9 | 5.3 | D | 24.4 | 4 475 | 239 | 1 047 | 8 568 | 10.0 |
| Allen | 283 | 4.1 | D | 12.8 | D | 28.4 | 2.9 | D | 14.2 | 4 565 | 227 | 919 | 9 307 | 15.5 |
| Anderson | 217 | -1.8 | D | 28.1 | 3.3 | 9.1 | 4.0 | D | 21.7 | 4 290 | 198 | 431 | 9 127 | 17.7 |
| Ballard | 212 | 10.5 | D | 26.8 | D | 3.1 | 1.5 | 2.7 | 9.8 | 2 085 | 253 | 265 | 3 885 | 1.3 |
| Barren | 808 | 2.7 | 28.9 | 23.1 | D | 10.0 | 3.1 | 15.5 | 14.7 | 10 225 | 242 | 1 906 | 19 188 | 12.2 |
| Bath | 79 | 1.4 | D | 7.4 | D | 6.8 | 5.2 | 6.8 | 34.1 | 2 920 | 249 | 996 | 5 405 | 8.2 |
| Bell | 404 | -0.1 | 25.8 | 10.2 | D | 10.4 | 4.7 | 15.6 | 23.9 | 7 700 | 268 | 3 189 | 13 154 | -1.4 |
| Boone | 4 289 | 0.0 | D | 17.0 | 4.7 | 6.5 | 5.4 | 5.9 | 9.7 | 17 880 | 147 | 1 511 | 46 154 | 38.4 |
| Bourbon | 367 | 5.2 | D | 23.8 | D | 6.7 | 3.7 | D | 14.4 | 4 455 | 223 | 673 | 8 927 | 6.9 |
| Boyd | 1 698 | -0.1 | D | 18.2 | 5.9 | 6.5 | 2.7 | 24.5 | 11.9 | 12 645 | 256 | 2 475 | 21 803 | -0.8 |
| Boyle | 702 | -0.3 | D | 16.4 | D | 9.2 | 3.5 | 23.2 | 13.5 | 6 625 | 232 | 1 147 | 12 312 | 7.8 |
| Bracken | 68 | -2.1 | D | D | D | 4.8 | 3.4 | 5.8 | 28.6 | 1 935 | 227 | 316 | 3 840 | 3.4 |
| Breathitt | 153 | -0.4 | D | D | 2.1 | 10.3 | 4.7 | 22.3 | 36.3 | 3 840 | 277 | 2 310 | 6 231 | -8.5 |
| Breckinridge | 174 | 5.3 | 18.6 | 6.9 | 2.8 | 10.4 | 5.3 | D | 25.3 | 4 980 | 246 | 964 | 10 630 | 7.5 |
| Bullitt | 906 | 0.0 | D | 14.4 | 8.2 | 5.8 | 3.5 | 5.7 | 15.9 | 14 665 | 195 | 1 699 | 29 318 | 26.6 |
| Butler | 136 | 8.8 | D | 25.5 | 1.5 | 4.4 | 3.6 | D | 22.0 | 3 190 | 249 | 639 | 5 877 | 1.1 |
| Caldwell | 204 | 6.9 | 28.8 | 22.9 | D | 11.8 | 3.5 | D | 16.3 | 3 550 | 274 | 581 | 6 292 | 2.7 |
| Calloway | 752 | 2.4 | 22.7 | 16.9 | 3.6 | 8.9 | 3.1 | 5.6 | 33.2 | 7 890 | 210 | 830 | 18 065 | 12.4 |
| Campbell | 1 477 | -0.1 | D | 12.2 | 6.8 | 7.9 | 4.9 | 11.7 | 25.4 | 15 770 | 173 | 1 993 | 39 523 | 7.1 |
| Carlisle | 59 | 35.8 | 10.5 | 4.3 | 1.7 | 5.6 | 8.6 | 4.4 | 19.9 | 1 375 | 272 | 175 | 2 441 | -2.0 |
| Carroll | 373 | -0.5 | D | 51.0 | D | 5.4 | D | D | 9.4 | 2 460 | 223 | 501 | 4 696 | 5.8 |
| Carter | 271 | -0.3 | 21.0 | 11.7 | 4.2 | 11.7 | 4.0 | D | 25.8 | 6 875 | 249 | 1 774 | 12 311 | 6.8 |
| Casey | 157 | 1.6 | D | 18.5 | 2.8 | 8.6 | 3.5 | 13.3 | 21.2 | 3 920 | 246 | 1 161 | 7 487 | 3.4 |
| Christian | 5 783 | 1.0 | D | 4.6 | 2.7 | 1.7 | 0.9 | 2.6 | 79.7 | 11 725 | 159 | 2 536 | 29 459 | 8.3 |
| Clark | 746 | 0.5 | D | 21.1 | 7.7 | 7.9 | 4.1 | 10.5 | 11.5 | 8 015 | 226 | 1 382 | 15 706 | 14.2 |

1. Includes mining, construction, and manufacturing.　　2. Per 1,000 resident population enumerated in the 2010 census.

| STATE County | Housing units, 2007–2011 | | | | | | | | Civilian labor force, 2012 | | | | Civilian employment,[6] 2007–2011 | | |
|---|---|---|---|---|---|---|---|---|---|---|---|---|---|---|---|
| | Occupied units | | | | | | | | | | Unemployment | | | Percent | |
| | | | Owner-occupied | | | Renter-occupied | | | | | | | | | |
| | | | | Median owner cost as a percent of income | | | | | | | | | | | |
| | Total | Percent | Median value[1] | With a mort-gage | Without a mort-gage[2] | Median rent[3] | Median rent as a per-cent of income | Sub-stand-ard units[4] (percent) | Total | Percent change, 2011–2012 | Total | Rate[5] | Total | Manage-ment, business, science and arts | Con-struction, produc-tion, and mainte-nance occu-pations |
| | 89 | 90 | 91 | 92 | 93 | 94 | 95 | 96 | 97 | 98 | 99 | 100 | 101 | 102 | 103 |
| KANSAS—Cont'd | | | | | | | | | | | | | | | |
| Neosho | 6 686 | 75.1 | 68 400 | 19.7 | 13.7 | 470 | 23.4 | 0.9 | 8 103 | -6.6 | 586 | 7.2 | 7 507 | 27.9 | 35.2 |
| Ness | 1 359 | 81.2 | 49 700 | 18.1 | 9.9 | 459 | 20.6 | 1.3 | 1 860 | 1.3 | 53 | 2.8 | 1 547 | 33.0 | 25.9 |
| Norton | 2 255 | 71.1 | 61 100 | 17.8 | 13.6 | 475 | 28.4 | 3.3 | 2 906 | 0.8 | 108 | 3.7 | 2 647 | 35.1 | 24.4 |
| Osage | 6 656 | 78.5 | 99 000 | 21.2 | 13.0 | 624 | 25.2 | 2.2 | 8 296 | -1.6 | 593 | 7.1 | 8 217 | 32.5 | 28.3 |
| Osborne | 1 752 | 80.5 | 42 300 | 20.0 | 11.2 | 496 | 30.0 | 0.9 | 2 256 | -4.0 | 93 | 4.1 | 2 026 | 33.4 | 28.3 |
| Ottawa | 2 354 | 81.9 | 83 500 | 20.0 | 11.8 | 586 | 23.5 | 0.7 | 3 234 | -1.3 | 164 | 5.1 | 2 969 | 30.7 | 31.3 |
| Pawnee | 2 523 | 73.4 | 69 000 | 23.2 | 9.9 | 551 | 26.5 | 0.0 | 3 692 | -1.3 | 154 | 4.2 | 3 372 | 36.0 | 24.0 |
| Phillips | 2 406 | 80.2 | 61 000 | 21.2 | 11.3 | 468 | 17.4 | 1.4 | 3 128 | 0.4 | 132 | 4.2 | 2 783 | 34.9 | 26.6 |
| Pottawatomie | 7 878 | 78.8 | 148 200 | 20.9 | 11.6 | 664 | 23.3 | 2.3 | 11 393 | 0.7 | 550 | 4.8 | 10 554 | 33.5 | 27.3 |
| Pratt | 3 980 | 70.1 | 74 700 | 19.3 | 12.5 | 584 | 23.8 | 0.7 | 6 177 | 0.7 | 244 | 4.0 | 4 848 | 32.9 | 29.0 |
| Rawlins | 1 200 | 74.3 | 58 400 | 22.7 | 11.5 | 482 | 24.2 | 0.3 | 1 391 | 3.7 | 42 | 3.0 | 1 329 | 44.7 | 18.5 |
| Reno | 25 827 | 70.7 | 88 700 | 21.6 | 12.8 | 601 | 25.6 | 2.1 | 34 000 | -1.6 | 1 781 | 5.2 | 30 601 | 28.8 | 26.6 |
| Republic | 2 348 | 82.0 | 47 600 | 20.5 | 12.2 | 381 | 17.9 | 1.2 | 2 804 | -2.1 | 101 | 3.6 | 2 525 | 33.4 | 27.9 |
| Rice | 3 822 | 75.2 | 69 100 | 18.7 | 9.9 | 577 | 26.2 | 2.5 | 6 025 | 0.3 | 241 | 4.0 | 4 901 | 34.4 | 34.1 |
| Riley | 25 375 | 43.8 | 164 500 | 21.3 | 10.2 | 793 | 34.3 | 7.1 | 36 305 | 0.6 | 1 621 | 4.5 | 32 011 | 41.6 | 15.5 |
| Rooks | 2 372 | 76.7 | 63 500 | 19.5 | 11.9 | 488 | 23.5 | 0.5 | 2 703 | 1.7 | 127 | 4.7 | 2 559 | 31.2 | 28.9 |
| Rush | 1 568 | 78.5 | 51 200 | 22.0 | 11.8 | 521 | 19.1 | 2.7 | 1 888 | 3.1 | 89 | 4.7 | 1 680 | 38.6 | 22.0 |
| Russell | 3 270 | 77.2 | 64 200 | 18.5 | 13.6 | 531 | 25.3 | 1.7 | 3 671 | 0.1 | 155 | 4.2 | 3 503 | 31.4 | 23.5 |
| Saline | 22 239 | 66.9 | 116 700 | 21.5 | 11.2 | 629 | 28.4 | 2.4 | 30 492 | -0.7 | 1 768 | 5.8 | 28 848 | 29.3 | 26.5 |
| Scott | 2 051 | 84.8 | 90 600 | 21.7 | 11.1 | 546 | 20.2 | 2.0 | 2 948 | 1.9 | 85 | 2.9 | 2 557 | 39.8 | 27.1 |
| Sedgwick | 191 853 | 66.6 | 120 400 | 21.2 | 11.3 | 662 | 29.0 | 2.4 | 243 429 | -1.2 | 16 807 | 6.9 | 236 402 | 33.6 | 24.9 |
| Seward | 7 426 | 63.7 | 86 500 | 22.4 | 9.9 | 656 | 24.1 | 7.3 | 11 065 | -0.1 | 440 | 4.0 | 10 311 | 19.1 | 46.2 |
| Shawnee | 73 219 | 66.1 | 117 300 | 21.7 | 11.6 | 678 | 28.9 | 2.4 | 92 461 | -1.0 | 5 746 | 6.2 | 85 721 | 34.9 | 19.9 |
| Sheridan | 1 087 | 76.6 | 83 100 | 18.8 | 11.8 | 548 | 27.2 | 1.3 | 1 708 | 2.5 | 42 | 2.5 | 1 298 | 34.5 | 25.2 |
| Sherman | 2 569 | 66.8 | 71 300 | 22.7 | 12.6 | 594 | 25.9 | 0.5 | 3 972 | 0.9 | 125 | 3.1 | 2 942 | 35.8 | 29.1 |
| Smith | 1 769 | 81.7 | 60 200 | 19.9 | 12.7 | 430 | 23.3 | 1.7 | 2 175 | -1.5 | 85 | 3.9 | 1 913 | 37.1 | 25.5 |
| Stafford | 1 853 | 79.9 | 53 000 | 19.0 | 12.6 | 467 | 18.3 | 3.6 | 2 110 | -4.6 | 100 | 4.7 | 2 167 | 36.6 | 28.1 |
| Stanton | 765 | 77.9 | 81 500 | 19.5 | 9.9 | 506 | 23.3 | 3.9 | 1 207 | 0.0 | 37 | 3.1 | 1 071 | 25.6 | 39.0 |
| Stevens | 2 060 | 70.2 | 81 500 | 15.4 | 11.1 | 618 | 29.1 | 4.7 | 2 363 | 3.1 | 98 | 4.1 | 2 616 | 28.5 | 35.7 |
| Sumner | 9 239 | 77.3 | 84 700 | 22.3 | 11.9 | 559 | 26.8 | 1.9 | 10 775 | -1.0 | 690 | 6.4 | 11 264 | 31.0 | 31.0 |
| Thomas | 3 165 | 66.3 | 91 000 | 21.0 | 9.9 | 476 | 23.4 | 0.0 | 4 380 | -1.2 | 163 | 3.7 | 4 387 | 33.8 | 22.8 |
| Trego | 1 220 | 79.6 | 69 600 | 18.2 | 13.4 | 497 | 21.8 | 1.9 | 1 923 | 1.9 | 65 | 3.4 | 1 390 | 31.9 | 27.6 |
| Wabaunsee | 2 768 | 84.8 | 103 300 | 21.3 | 13.5 | 657 | 20.8 | 1.9 | 3 664 | -1.3 | 199 | 5.4 | 3 506 | 33.9 | 30.5 |
| Wallace | 627 | 79.3 | 65 100 | 17.2 | 12.2 | 411 | 25.5 | 3.0 | 895 | -0.2 | 35 | 3.9 | 831 | 38.1 | 33.3 |
| Washington | 2 496 | 79.7 | 52 500 | 18.4 | 12.0 | 404 | 18.8 | 2.1 | 3 297 | -1.7 | 135 | 4.1 | 3 011 | 30.6 | 34.4 |
| Wichita | 862 | 74.6 | 75 300 | 17.8 | 11.9 | 628 | 22.4 | 4.6 | 1 241 | 1.2 | 67 | 5.4 | 1 202 | 30.9 | 32.1 |
| Wilson | 3 830 | 75.6 | 60 300 | 20.3 | 12.8 | 512 | 22.9 | 2.2 | 4 662 | -1.0 | 403 | 8.6 | 4 196 | 29.1 | 34.7 |
| Woodson | 1 562 | 74.6 | 51 500 | 21.9 | 15.1 | 484 | 25.9 | 2.4 | 1 643 | -4.1 | 103 | 6.3 | 1 469 | 28.9 | 32.3 |
| Wyandotte | 57 114 | 62.9 | 97 000 | 25.4 | 15.2 | 714 | 32.3 | 3.9 | 70 383 | -0.5 | 6 068 | 8.6 | 68 067 | 23.2 | 31.6 |
| KENTUCKY | 1 681 085 | 69.5 | 118 700 | 21.8 | 10.9 | 623 | 29.0 | 2.3 | 2 074 806 | 0.2 | 170 926 | 8.2 | 1 865 652 | 31.9 | 26.9 |
| Adair | 7 193 | 73.6 | 78 900 | 21.9 | 10.9 | 465 | 27.3 | 2.7 | 9 631 | 2.2 | 745 | 7.7 | 6 849 | 27.1 | 34.4 |
| Allen | 7 849 | 75.7 | 92 300 | 22.7 | 11.6 | 523 | 26.8 | 3.0 | 8 557 | -0.2 | 743 | 8.7 | 7 594 | 22.0 | 34.6 |
| Anderson | 8 386 | 75.8 | 132 900 | 21.6 | 9.9 | 650 | 24.7 | 1.8 | 10 857 | -0.4 | 801 | 7.4 | 10 283 | 33.6 | 28.8 |
| Ballard | 3 358 | 81.1 | 79 300 | 18.7 | 10.1 | 583 | 27.4 | 2.5 | 4 161 | -1.3 | 353 | 8.5 | 3 467 | 25.0 | 34.5 |
| Barren | 16 708 | 69.4 | 97 600 | 20.2 | 11.8 | 532 | 31.3 | 2.0 | 19 818 | 1.4 | 1 599 | 8.1 | 18 436 | 29.3 | 33.9 |
| Bath | 4 306 | 81.2 | 66 400 | 29.8 | 11.9 | 514 | 42.9 | 2.2 | 5 131 | 2.3 | 519 | 10.1 | 3 953 | 31.1 | 36.2 |
| Bell | 10 632 | 67.8 | 63 900 | 20.2 | 10.6 | 431 | 31.2 | 3.3 | 9 582 | 0.8 | 1 270 | 13.3 | 9 024 | 27.8 | 26.8 |
| Boone | 41 843 | 77.2 | 175 200 | 21.7 | 10.8 | 829 | 27.6 | 2.4 | 66 144 | 0.1 | 4 681 | 7.1 | 59 801 | 36.7 | 21.4 |
| Bourbon | 7 933 | 61.6 | 141 500 | 21.0 | 10.5 | 617 | 29.1 | 1.1 | 9 428 | 0.7 | 726 | 7.7 | 8 783 | 27.7 | 34.2 |
| Boyd | 19 521 | 69.1 | 93 500 | 19.3 | 10.9 | 569 | 29.5 | 1.1 | 22 440 | -1.7 | 1 710 | 7.6 | 18 658 | 31.8 | 23.5 |
| Boyle | 10 916 | 68.9 | 124 300 | 21.7 | 10.7 | 599 | 29.3 | 1.4 | 12 442 | -1.1 | 1 199 | 9.6 | 12 407 | 30.4 | 27.7 |
| Bracken | 3 070 | 78.6 | 89 100 | 23.3 | 11.7 | 528 | 25.6 | 2.2 | 4 187 | -1.2 | 360 | 8.6 | 3 649 | 26.6 | 37.8 |
| Breathitt | 5 314 | 70.2 | 50 600 | 23.7 | 11.9 | 421 | 33.5 | 2.7 | 5 623 | 2.9 | 667 | 11.9 | 4 187 | 22.1 | 29.2 |
| Breckinridge | 7 519 | 78.9 | 79 400 | 21.5 | 9.9 | 495 | 29.0 | 4.9 | 9 697 | 1.0 | 801 | 8.3 | 7 251 | 26.5 | 40.3 |
| Bullitt | 27 705 | 80.8 | 143 400 | 22.9 | 11.7 | 723 | 25.0 | 2.0 | 38 369 | -0.2 | 3 267 | 8.5 | 35 002 | 24.8 | 34.0 |
| Butler | 5 081 | 78.0 | 78 600 | 23.1 | 11.1 | 455 | 30.5 | 1.4 | 5 770 | 2.0 | 492 | 8.5 | 4 920 | 20.1 | 48.2 |
| Caldwell | 5 047 | 76.7 | 73 100 | 20.0 | 10.7 | 509 | 23.9 | 1.1 | 6 652 | 0.1 | 469 | 7.1 | 5 052 | 29.5 | 34.8 |
| Calloway | 14 967 | 67.4 | 112 300 | 21.5 | 10.3 | 548 | 32.6 | 1.7 | 18 335 | 1.0 | 1 311 | 7.2 | 17 460 | 32.2 | 24.4 |
| Campbell | 35 258 | 71.5 | 145 500 | 21.7 | 11.8 | 688 | 29.2 | 1.3 | 46 132 | -0.7 | 3 498 | 7.6 | 45 535 | 35.4 | 20.9 |
| Carlisle | 2 018 | 82.9 | 70 300 | 23.6 | 13.1 | 510 | 22.5 | 1.7 | 2 487 | 1.7 | 185 | 7.4 | 1 927 | 18.2 | 38.9 |
| Carroll | 4 195 | 63.1 | 105 000 | 20.5 | 9.9 | 597 | 26.2 | 5.0 | 5 484 | -0.8 | 526 | 9.6 | 4 417 | 20.2 | 41.7 |
| Carter | 10 407 | 78.7 | 73 900 | 18.8 | 10.3 | 554 | 28.8 | 2.7 | 13 097 | -2.2 | 1 453 | 11.1 | 10 843 | 27.4 | 34.3 |
| Casey | 6 032 | 83.5 | 74 800 | 25.0 | 13.0 | 465 | 32.3 | 3.6 | 7 299 | -0.6 | 576 | 7.9 | 6 263 | 27.4 | 36.6 |
| Christian | 26 117 | 55.7 | 97 700 | 21.8 | 10.8 | 703 | 28.5 | 3.0 | 26 632 | 1.3 | 2 702 | 10.1 | 23 931 | 28.1 | 32.0 |
| Clark | 14 406 | 65.0 | 138 000 | 21.2 | 10.7 | 652 | 28.1 | 2.4 | 16 618 | 0.1 | 1 330 | 8.0 | 15 867 | 31.4 | 27.7 |

1. Specified owner-occupied units.  2. A value of 9.9 represents 9.9 percent or less.  3. Specified renter-occupied units. A value of 10.0 represents 10 percent or less.  4. Overcrowded or lacking complete plumbing facilities.  5. Percent of civilian labor force.  6. Persons 16 years old and over.

# Table B. States and Counties — Nonfarm Employment and Agriculture

| STATE County | Private nonfarm establishments, employment and payroll, 2011 | | | | | | | | | Agriculture, 2007 | | | |
| | Number of establishments | Employment | | | | | | Annual payroll | | Farms | | | |
| | | Total | Health care and social assistance | Manufacturing | Retail trade | Finance and insurance | Professional, scientific, and technical services | Total (mil dol) | Average per employee (dollars) | Number | Percent with: Fewer than 50 acres | Percent with: 500 acres or more | Farm operators whose principal occupation is farming (percent) |
| | 104 | 105 | 106 | 107 | 108 | 109 | 110 | 111 | 112 | 113 | 114 | 115 | 116 |
| **KANSAS—Cont'd** | | | | | | | | | | | | | |
| Neosho | 453 | 5 321 | 1 225 | 1 103 | 873 | 189 | 130 | 162 | 30 392 | 775 | 20.0 | 21.2 | 36.3 |
| Ness | 141 | 1 041 | D | 46 | D | 56 | 19 | 36 | 34 382 | 521 | 5.0 | 52.0 | 48.8 |
| Norton | 178 | 1 799 | 427 | D | 183 | D | 50 | 57 | 31 931 | 388 | 10.3 | 52.1 | 55.2 |
| Osage | 259 | 2 779 | D | D | 368 | 113 | 54 | 49 | 17 691 | 1 092 | 26.2 | 17.5 | 35.0 |
| Osborne | 150 | 1 180 | 308 | 119 | 212 | 79 | D | 31 | 26 296 | 378 | 11.1 | 50.3 | 63.8 |
| Ottawa | 129 | 834 | 260 | D | 79 | 69 | 23 | 23 | 27 826 | 546 | 11.5 | 36.8 | 49.6 |
| Pawnee | 180 | 2 449 | 1 509 | D | 227 | 74 | 81 | 83 | 33 918 | 438 | 9.1 | 43.2 | 46.1 |
| Phillips | 227 | 1 649 | 332 | 175 | 204 | 129 | 99 | 50 | 30 526 | 507 | 18.1 | 41.4 | 50.9 |
| Pottawatomie | 565 | 7 703 | 1 233 | 1 214 | D | 211 | 192 | 262 | 34 005 | 843 | 19.9 | 25.9 | 46.5 |
| Pratt | 368 | 3 457 | 806 | 80 | 738 | 146 | 113 | 110 | 31 911 | 538 | 10.6 | 32.3 | 39.4 |
| Rawlins | 106 | 571 | 186 | 31 | 100 | 40 | D | 19 | 32 786 | 339 | 11.2 | 62.5 | 65.5 |
| Reno | 1 669 | 22 425 | 4 964 | 3 488 | 3 498 | 820 | 659 | 740 | 33 007 | 1 749 | 18.9 | 23.8 | 41.9 |
| Republic | 197 | 1 486 | 336 | 187 | 261 | 98 | D | 38 | 25 598 | 682 | 14.4 | 37.0 | 61.4 |
| Rice | 273 | 2 643 | 402 | 338 | 288 | 149 | 135 | 77 | 29 277 | 580 | 16.9 | 37.4 | 49.3 |
| Riley | 1 533 | 20 347 | 3 377 | 471 | 4 473 | 841 | 880 | 546 | 26 838 | 532 | 23.9 | 25.2 | 43.8 |
| Rooks | 188 | 1 352 | 232 | D | 213 | D | 39 | 41 | 30 652 | 419 | 8.1 | 51.1 | 50.6 |
| Rush | 99 | 891 | D | D | 61 | 43 | D | 28 | 31 396 | 481 | 4.4 | 43.2 | 48.9 |
| Russell | 276 | 1 865 | D | D | D | 76 | 45 | 55 | 29 657 | 522 | 6.3 | 35.4 | 47.1 |
| Saline | 1 594 | 27 146 | 4 618 | 5 646 | 4 421 | 829 | 1 283 | 888 | 32 717 | 749 | 23.5 | 27.4 | 42.7 |
| Scott | 192 | 1 302 | 336 | D | 222 | 96 | D | 43 | 32 906 | 277 | 17.3 | 50.5 | 58.1 |
| Sedgwick | 11 853 | 212 620 | 33 083 | 42 229 | 26 527 | 8 734 | 9 717 | 8 933 | 42 013 | 1 419 | 35.2 | 20.2 | 43.0 |
| Seward | 567 | 9 685 | 1 109 | D | 1 309 | 192 | 158 | 336 | 34 739 | 342 | 7.3 | 44.4 | 46.2 |
| Shawnee | 4 355 | 74 989 | 17 647 | 5 830 | 9 970 | 5 117 | 3 844 | 2 933 | 39 107 | 885 | 38.0 | 11.5 | 41.2 |
| Sheridan | 109 | 629 | D | D | D | D | D | 21 | 33 523 | 380 | 4.2 | 61.3 | 65.0 |
| Sherman | 260 | 1 957 | 410 | D | 371 | 104 | 81 | 51 | 26 035 | 436 | 3.7 | 48.9 | 55.3 |
| Smith | 144 | 1 019 | D | 119 | 186 | 79 | D | 25 | 24 587 | 489 | 10.0 | 46.0 | 57.3 |
| Stafford | 128 | 669 | D | D | D | 51 | D | 18 | 26 792 | 558 | 9.9 | 42.3 | 48.7 |
| Stanton | 63 | 470 | D | D | 41 | 39 | D | 16 | 34 572 | 328 | 3.4 | 51.5 | 51.5 |
| Stevens | 132 | 974 | D | D | 136 | 74 | D | 34 | 34 413 | 425 | 8.0 | 40.7 | 38.4 |
| Sumner | 488 | 4 482 | 964 | 830 | 615 | 308 | 56 | 131 | 29 117 | 1 099 | 19.5 | 31.3 | 51.0 |
| Thomas | 341 | 2 885 | 410 | D | 638 | 138 | 73 | 84 | 28 996 | 464 | 8.8 | 53.9 | 59.1 |
| Trego | 127 | 876 | D | 32 | 151 | D | D | 25 | 28 234 | 380 | 7.4 | 48.2 | 53.7 |
| Wabaunsee | 122 | 882 | 147 | 125 | 101 | 59 | 6 | 22 | 24 895 | 660 | 19.4 | 28.5 | 41.4 |
| Wallace | 58 | 301 | 60 | D | D | 16 | D | 9 | 28 934 | 303 | 6.6 | 58.7 | 51.8 |
| Washington | 213 | 1 553 | 398 | 124 | 236 | 76 | D | 36 | 23 082 | 817 | 12.7 | 35.6 | 52.4 |
| Wichita | 97 | 512 | D | D | 82 | 24 | D | 14 | 27 545 | 323 | 4.0 | 61.9 | 60.1 |
| Wilson | 240 | 3 350 | 703 | 1 004 | 255 | 88 | D | 121 | 36 131 | 553 | 16.3 | 31.8 | 51.0 |
| Woodson | 94 | 501 | 151 | D | D | 29 | D | 13 | 25 533 | 339 | 12.4 | 36.3 | 52.8 |
| Wyandotte | 2 950 | 64 830 | 13 091 | 9 993 | 7 337 | 987 | 1 231 | 2 808 | 43 313 | 191 | 71.2 | 2.6 | 32.5 |
| **KENTUCKY** | 89 770 | 1 463 173 | 243 151 | 205 978 | 216 132 | 64 484 | 63 721 | 54 352 | 37 147 | 85 260 | 35.0 | 5.8 | 39.8 |
| Adair | 312 | 4 234 | 800 | 389 | 682 | 190 | 53 | 99 | 23 272 | 1 424 | 32.0 | 3.4 | 39.7 |
| Allen | 237 | 3 127 | D | D | 415 | 138 | 58 | 81 | 25 841 | 1 208 | 34.9 | 3.7 | 43.4 |
| Anderson | 330 | 3 233 | 319 | 961 | 707 | D | 98 | 104 | 32 045 | 678 | 31.6 | 3.2 | 31.9 |
| Ballard | 135 | 2 065 | D | D | 179 | 56 | D | 101 | 49 032 | 481 | 38.5 | 10.2 | 39.1 |
| Barren | 881 | 13 421 | 2 282 | 3 811 | 2 235 | 396 | 237 | 411 | 30 629 | 2 170 | 40.2 | 3.7 | 43.7 |
| Bath | 129 | 1 010 | 177 | D | 187 | D | 39 | 28 | 27 923 | 789 | 25.9 | 6.6 | 43.9 |
| Bell | 542 | 7 270 | 1 421 | 1 001 | 1 503 | 239 | 136 | 218 | 30 013 | 69 | 40.6 | 5.8 | 40.6 |
| Boone | 2 834 | 62 816 | 4 622 | 10 636 | 8 587 | 3 158 | 1 900 | 2 374 | 37 798 | 682 | 53.1 | 2.8 | 40.5 |
| Bourbon | 371 | 5 865 | 718 | 2 024 | 833 | D | 124 | 218 | 37 094 | 918 | 35.1 | 9.4 | 50.0 |
| Boyd | 1 350 | 24 034 | D | 2 694 | 4 095 | 615 | 719 | 994 | 41 366 | 260 | 41.9 | 1.5 | 29.2 |
| Boyle | 742 | 13 609 | 2 927 | 2 131 | 1 765 | 371 | 335 | 440 | 32 314 | 649 | 39.4 | 6.0 | 40.2 |
| Bracken | 101 | 815 | 112 | D | 126 | D | 26 | 25 | 30 848 | 618 | 24.3 | 5.2 | 38.2 |
| Breathitt | 226 | 2 348 | 846 | 48 | 517 | D | D | 64 | 27 410 | 199 | 25.6 | 10.6 | 29.6 |
| Breckinridge | 290 | 2 264 | 564 | 193 | 524 | 130 | 62 | 59 | 25 894 | 1 509 | 26.8 | 5.3 | 39.9 |
| Bullitt | 1 037 | 15 092 | 1 263 | 2 108 | 2 442 | 312 | 331 | 447 | 29 601 | 519 | 51.3 | 1.7 | 43.0 |
| Butler | 189 | 1 691 | 343 | D | 220 | 73 | 35 | 44 | 26 274 | 778 | 23.7 | 9.9 | 34.8 |
| Caldwell | 279 | 3 674 | 585 | D | 711 | 118 | 45 | 97 | 26 371 | 625 | 26.2 | 8.8 | 33.4 |
| Calloway | 833 | 13 255 | 1 989 | 2 579 | 2 088 | 338 | 288 | 359 | 27 097 | 888 | 47.1 | 7.5 | 34.8 |
| Campbell | 1 615 | 23 892 | 3 268 | 2 417 | 4 336 | 531 | 1 005 | 780 | 32 649 | 535 | 43.6 | 1.3 | 37.4 |
| Carlisle | 72 | 476 | D | 75 | 99 | D | D | 10 | 21 782 | 408 | 35.5 | 8.8 | 37.5 |
| Carroll | 231 | 5 573 | D | 2 246 | 648 | 68 | 92 | 287 | 51 496 | 326 | 22.1 | 5.8 | 45.4 |
| Carter | 394 | 5 551 | 605 | 854 | 926 | D | 192 | 138 | 24 834 | 895 | 29.5 | 4.2 | 36.0 |
| Casey | 221 | 2 625 | 386 | D | 346 | D | D | 64 | 24 440 | 1 286 | 25.7 | 4.4 | 43.1 |
| Christian | 1 318 | 23 677 | 3 594 | 5 360 | 3 097 | 739 | 1 584 | 783 | 33 072 | 1 324 | 28.6 | 9.7 | 43.3 |
| Clark | 746 | 10 790 | 1 410 | 2 343 | 1 687 | 279 | 380 | 368 | 34 144 | 907 | 41.8 | 8.2 | 42.6 |

# Table B. States and Counties — **Agriculture**

| STATE County | Acreage (1,000) [117] | Percent change, 2002–2007 [118] | Average size of farm [119] | Total irrigated (1,000) [120] | Total cropland (1,000) [121] | Average per farm [122] | Average per acre [123] | Value of machinery and equipment, average per farm (dollars) [124] | Total (mil dol) [125] | Average per farm (dollars) [126] | Crops [127] | Live-stock and poultry products [128] | $10,000 or more [129] | $100,000 or more [130] | Total ($1,000) [131] | Percent of farms [132] |
|---|---|---|---|---|---|---|---|---|---|---|---|---|---|---|---|---|
| **KANSAS—Cont'd** | | | | | | | | | | | | | | | | |
| Neosho | 322 | -5.6 | 415 | D | 166.1 | 440 042 | 1 061 | 76 761 | 48.2 | 62 228 | 36.9 | 63.1 | 43.0 | 10.7 | 1 895 | 55.6 |
| Ness | 620 | -5.3 | 1 190 | 2.5 | 389.0 | 642 817 | 540 | 102 326 | 55.8 | 107 082 | 67.5 | 32.5 | 56.8 | 26.1 | 7 662 | 93.5 |
| Norton | 531 | 2.7 | 1 369 | 12.1 | 301.5 | 938 997 | 686 | 159 964 | 105.5 | 271 792 | 40.4 | 59.6 | 62.6 | 33.0 | 4 287 | 80.9 |
| Osage | 380 | 3.5 | 348 | 0.4 | 203.9 | 419 046 | 1 204 | 71 149 | 48.4 | 44 367 | 57.0 | 43.0 | 38.3 | 11.0 | 2 805 | 62.5 |
| Osborne | 420 | -15.8 | 1 111 | 3.0 | 218.7 | 843 491 | 759 | 143 551 | 52.2 | 138 021 | 72.5 | 27.5 | 71.4 | 37.0 | 2 903 | 86.5 |
| Ottawa | 437 | 5.0 | 801 | 4.5 | 263.8 | 662 683 | 827 | 112 362 | 77.0 | 140 936 | 46.2 | 53.8 | 57.0 | 24.5 | 3 373 | 77.5 |
| Pawnee | 487 | -6.3 | 1 113 | 61.6 | 380.9 | 952 707 | 856 | 188 646 | 320.1 | 730 756 | 21.0 | 79.0 | 59.4 | 30.8 | 4 993 | 85.2 |
| Phillips | 495 | -15.7 | 976 | 7.6 | 240.1 | 681 303 | 698 | 110 605 | 75.8 | 149 453 | 54.2 | 45.8 | 59.0 | 29.6 | 2 952 | 75.1 |
| Pottawatomie | 429 | -7.7 | 508 | 20.2 | 164.9 | 606 340 | 1 193 | 80 528 | 85.0 | 100 864 | 35.8 | 64.2 | 51.5 | 15.1 | 2 626 | 65.7 |
| Pratt | 480 | -4.2 | 892 | 71.2 | 321.1 | 798 517 | 895 | 160 420 | 173.6 | 322 687 | 36.3 | 63.7 | 42.6 | 23.8 | 5 258 | 80.3 |
| Rawlins | 591 | -9.2 | 1 742 | 18.7 | 329.7 | 1 111 443 | 638 | 176 909 | 76.8 | 226 430 | 77.4 | 22.6 | 79.4 | 48.1 | 3 403 | 86.7 |
| Reno | 781 | 6.3 | 446 | 42.3 | 547.8 | 452 375 | 1 013 | 88 113 | 171.2 | 97 912 | 40.6 | 59.4 | 44.3 | 14.6 | 11 181 | 75.8 |
| Republic | 407 | -4.0 | 596 | 43.1 | 282.9 | 661 603 | 1 109 | 151 027 | 148.1 | 217 094 | 53.8 | 46.2 | 67.2 | 33.4 | 4 655 | 83.0 |
| Rice | 428 | 2.9 | 739 | 24.7 | 338.8 | 661 906 | 896 | 159 654 | 184.9 | 318 840 | 28.8 | 71.2 | 57.9 | 29.8 | 5 462 | 80.5 |
| Riley | 232 | 4.5 | 436 | 5.2 | 103.1 | 542 879 | 1 245 | 89 015 | 46.8 | 88 003 | 50.5 | 49.5 | 51.1 | 19.0 | 1 738 | 63.5 |
| Rooks | 561 | 0.2 | 1 340 | 1.1 | 314.2 | 880 231 | 657 | 145 996 | 86.8 | 207 254 | 53.8 | 46.2 | 60.9 | 33.2 | 4 400 | 87.4 |
| Rush | 406 | -2.9 | 844 | 11.4 | 287.1 | 590 408 | 700 | 113 270 | 53.7 | 111 574 | 63.1 | 36.9 | 59.0 | 26.0 | 4 810 | 90.0 |
| Russell | 444 | -8.3 | 850 | 0.2 | 226.0 | 560 332 | 659 | 96 309 | 36.9 | 70 777 | 64.0 | 36.0 | 44.6 | 19.3 | 4 036 | 88.9 |
| Saline | 431 | -1.4 | 576 | 2.8 | 246.7 | 618 604 | 1 075 | 106 018 | 55.0 | 73 423 | 48.9 | 51.1 | 48.6 | 15.0 | 3 349 | 75.8 |
| Scott | 453 | -8.5 | 1 636 | 41.6 | 326.5 | 1 218 245 | 744 | 245 594 | 762.7 | 2 753 403 | 9.4 | 90.6 | 69.7 | 47.3 | 3 844 | 78.3 |
| Sedgwick | 510 | -4.5 | 360 | 37.5 | 405.1 | 519 179 | 1 444 | 97 940 | 85.1 | 59 978 | 66.9 | 33.1 | 44.1 | 13.4 | 6 982 | 61.5 |
| Seward | 396 | 9.1 | 1 158 | 114.5 | 293.3 | 842 235 | 727 | 202 410 | 361.7 | 1 057 467 | 22.6 | 77.4 | 48.2 | 35.7 | 4 570 | 80.4 |
| Shawnee | 206 | -5.1 | 233 | 18.5 | 125.1 | 372 351 | 1 598 | 68 821 | 39.7 | 44 828 | 83.1 | 16.9 | 36.9 | 9.9 | 1 703 | 43.2 |
| Sheridan | 522 | 2.2 | 1 374 | 78.7 | 369.3 | 1 064 169 | 775 | 251 818 | 294.9 | 776 121 | 32.4 | 67.6 | 80.8 | 52.9 | 6 197 | 88.2 |
| Sherman | 658 | 8.4 | 1 509 | 103.2 | 530.0 | 1 140 642 | 756 | 190 457 | 161.3 | 370 022 | 67.2 | 32.8 | 63.1 | 37.6 | 7 686 | 90.1 |
| Smith | 457 | -11.8 | 935 | 3.7 | 285.3 | 732 236 | 783 | 140 317 | 80.8 | 165 321 | 66.8 | 33.2 | 71.6 | 35.0 | 3 950 | 82.0 |
| Stafford | 502 | 6.1 | 900 | 104.2 | 386.1 | 780 017 | 867 | 221 555 | 167.8 | 300 767 | 44.5 | 55.5 | 50.5 | 30.1 | 6 887 | 84.1 |
| Stanton | 414 | -5.5 | 1 263 | 84.4 | 358.3 | 966 134 | 765 | 166 328 | 181.8 | 554 116 | 42.1 | 57.9 | 50.6 | 36.0 | 5 372 | 87.2 |
| Stevens | 503 | 2.4 | 1 185 | 167.1 | 402.1 | 935 882 | 790 | 231 921 | 232.9 | 548 037 | 53.3 | 46.7 | 43.5 | 27.5 | 6 031 | 82.6 |
| Sumner | 710 | -3.0 | 646 | 15.0 | 571.2 | 605 771 | 938 | 116 856 | 74.7 | 67 956 | 67.9 | 32.1 | 44.3 | 14.5 | 7 744 | 74.0 |
| Thomas | 657 | -4.8 | 1 417 | 86.1 | 561.3 | 1 157 139 | 817 | 253 121 | 211.0 | 454 799 | 61.4 | 38.6 | 79.1 | 50.9 | 8 815 | 80.4 |
| Trego | 430 | -5.5 | 1 130 | 4.0 | 246.4 | 699 202 | 618 | 107 865 | 44.4 | 116 844 | 67.7 | 32.3 | 58.4 | 28.9 | 3 105 | 87.1 |
| Wabaunsee | 470 | 1.3 | 713 | 7.1 | 127.5 | 695 256 | 975 | 74 138 | 62.0 | 93 969 | 28.0 | 72.0 | 49.7 | 15.6 | 1 842 | 59.5 |
| Wallace | 430 | 3.6 | 1 418 | 43.6 | 287.9 | 883 716 | 623 | 158 099 | 69.0 | 227 634 | 68.4 | 31.6 | 57.8 | 34.7 | 4 860 | 88.1 |
| Washington | 548 | 10.3 | 671 | 9.1 | 326.0 | 693 876 | 1 034 | 127 236 | 151.8 | 185 858 | 43.3 | 56.7 | 68.3 | 31.8 | 5 822 | 79.7 |
| Wichita | 520 | 10.4 | 1 609 | 50.9 | 398.2 | 1 077 030 | 669 | 238 644 | 448.7 | 1 389 261 | D | D | 62.8 | 47.1 | 5 088 | 85.4 |
| Wilson | 333 | -1.2 | 603 | 0.6 | 184.8 | 578 951 | 961 | 120 120 | 44.4 | 80 246 | 60.6 | 39.4 | 53.2 | 17.4 | 2 448 | 61.1 |
| Woodson | 262 | 2.7 | 772 | 0.0 | 107.4 | 716 599 | 929 | 101 224 | 37.4 | 110 230 | 38.8 | 61.2 | 56.6 | 21.5 | 1 719 | 67.8 |
| Wyandotte | 18 | 28.6 | 95 | 0.2 | 12.4 | 230 441 | 2 431 | 36 743 | 5.1 | 26 763 | D | D | 20.4 | 4.7 | 98 | 5.2 |
| **KENTUCKY** | 13 993 | 1.1 | 164 | 58.7 | 7 278.1 | 440 213 | 2 682 | 57 591 | 4 824.6 | 56 586 | 29.1 | 70.9 | 33.5 | 6.9 | 103 104 | 34.6 |
| Adair | 188 | 10.6 | 132 | 0.1 | 85.1 | 326 191 | 2 471 | 52 060 | 47.4 | 33 305 | 16.5 | 83.5 | 35.4 | 6.0 | 991 | 40.1 |
| Allen | 167 | -0.6 | 138 | 0.3 | 69.2 | 385 115 | 2 791 | 45 107 | 52.8 | 43 744 | 14.1 | 85.9 | 38.3 | 3.4 | 1 184 | 38.1 |
| Anderson | 88 | 4.8 | 129 | 0.1 | 43.7 | 351 040 | 2 716 | 45 303 | 11.4 | 16 847 | 15.3 | 84.7 | 25.2 | 3.1 | 245 | 13.4 |
| Ballard | 110 | -2.7 | 229 | 0.1 | 85.0 | 590 043 | 2 575 | 116 385 | 60.4 | 125 580 | 41.6 | 58.4 | 45.3 | 13.3 | 1 469 | 54.7 |
| Barren | 265 | 10.4 | 122 | 0.2 | 151.2 | 339 496 | 2 783 | 52 186 | 105.8 | 48 772 | 19.0 | 81.0 | 42.0 | 8.2 | 1 831 | 29.8 |
| Bath | 129 | 19.4 | 164 | 0.1 | 54.1 | 330 436 | 2 020 | 51 738 | 17.9 | 22 689 | 41.9 | 58.1 | 38.3 | 5.1 | 344 | 25.2 |
| Bell | 10 | 42.9 | 148 | 0.1 | 4.1 | 286 240 | 1 937 | 32 776 | 0.3 | 4 023 | 41.4 | 58.6 | 10.1 | 0.0 | D | 2.9 |
| Boone | 75 | 0.0 | 110 | 0.4 | 35.8 | 539 948 | 4 926 | 55 809 | 17.5 | 25 728 | 51.1 | 48.9 | 26.7 | 4.1 | 193 | 18.2 |
| Bourbon | 184 | -0.5 | 201 | 0.2 | 86.5 | 944 272 | 4 703 | 75 990 | 179.6 | 195 624 | 13.2 | 86.8 | 50.0 | 17.3 | 644 | 21.9 |
| Boyd | 29 | -14.7 | 111 | 0.0 | 7.2 | 287 599 | 2 602 | 47 415 | 1.9 | 7 157 | 12.1 | 87.9 | 11.2 | 0.4 | 12 | 6.5 |
| Boyle | 94 | -5.1 | 145 | 0.1 | 46.5 | 469 769 | 3 235 | 55 041 | 24.3 | 37 517 | 11.1 | 88.9 | 33.1 | 5.7 | 333 | 23.3 |
| Bracken | 101 | 7.4 | 163 | 0.3 | 43.1 | 334 400 | 2 053 | 54 627 | 10.5 | 16 974 | 52.5 | 47.5 | 32.4 | 3.2 | 286 | 23.5 |
| Breathitt | 44 | -13.7 | 219 | 0.0 | 9.4 | 331 771 | 1 516 | 39 100 | 1.6 | 8 097 | 25.0 | 75.0 | 11.6 | 0.5 | 43 | 18.6 |
| Breckinridge | 274 | -0.7 | 182 | 0.0 | 124.9 | 384 909 | 2 116 | 55 561 | 56.1 | 37 164 | 37.2 | 62.8 | 38.2 | 5.6 | 2 440 | 52.0 |
| Bullitt | 51 | -16.4 | 99 | 0.4 | 24.8 | 373 149 | 3 786 | 48 241 | 6.3 | 12 122 | 59.8 | 40.2 | 21.6 | 2.5 | 220 | 18.1 |
| Butler | 174 | 7.4 | 224 | D | 73.6 | 432 624 | 1 935 | 49 124 | 27.7 | 35 629 | 38.4 | 61.6 | 26.0 | 5.1 | 1 536 | 46.3 |
| Caldwell | 143 | -2.7 | 228 | 2.4 | 86.5 | 452 216 | 1 980 | 66 631 | 23.3 | 37 234 | 69.0 | 31.0 | 31.0 | 6.9 | 1 718 | 65.8 |
| Calloway | 158 | -6.5 | 178 | 1.7 | 113.4 | 501 183 | 2 821 | 68 480 | 69.7 | 78 459 | 48.9 | 51.1 | 32.8 | 11.4 | 2 968 | 66.1 |
| Campbell | 47 | -6.0 | 88 | 0.2 | 20.2 | 345 486 | 3 905 | 43 994 | 5.7 | 10 651 | 34.8 | 65.2 | 19.4 | 2.1 | 89 | 12.1 |
| Carlisle | 96 | -10.3 | 235 | 0.4 | 73.9 | 557 075 | 2 375 | 95 525 | 48.4 | 118 526 | 50.6 | 49.4 | 27.7 | 14.5 | 1 498 | 76.2 |
| Carroll | 64 | 4.9 | 195 | 0.1 | 25.7 | 463 198 | 2 370 | 49 696 | 5.4 | 16 424 | 45.3 | 54.7 | 34.4 | 2.5 | 180 | 27.6 |
| Carter | 126 | 5.0 | 140 | 0.0 | 39.0 | 249 326 | 1 778 | 33 228 | 7.9 | 8 774 | 29.9 | 70.1 | 16.0 | 1.2 | 206 | 14.7 |
| Casey | 192 | 0.5 | 149 | 0.2 | 77.9 | 302 017 | 2 027 | 41 100 | 25.8 | 20 056 | 28.6 | 71.4 | 37.0 | 4.7 | 653 | 41.4 |
| Christian | 346 | 1.2 | 262 | 2.7 | 239.4 | 675 113 | 2 580 | 84 335 | 103.0 | 77 795 | 63.9 | 36.1 | 40.6 | 16.6 | 5 958 | 57.5 |
| Clark | 149 | 4.2 | 164 | 0.1 | 69.0 | 550 833 | 3 349 | 51 024 | 32.4 | 35 694 | 23.7 | 76.3 | 37.9 | 9.9 | 452 | 22.1 |

# Table B. States and Counties — Water Use, Wholesale Trade, Retail Trade, and Real Estate

| STATE County | Water use, 2005 | | Wholesale trade,[1] 2007 | | | | Retail trade,[2] 2007 | | | | Real estate and rental and leasing,[2] 2007 | | | |
|---|---|---|---|---|---|---|---|---|---|---|---|---|---|---|
| | Total water withdrawn (mil gal/day) | Gallons withdrawn per person | Number of establishments | Number of employees | Sales (mil dol) | Annual payroll (mil dol) | Number of establishments | Number of employees | Sales (mil dol) | Annual payroll (mil dol) | Number of establishments | Number of employees | Receipts (mil dol) | Annual payroll (mil dol) |
| | 133 | 134 | 135 | 136 | 137 | 138 | 139 | 140 | 141 | 142 | 143 | 144 | 145 | 146 |
| **KANSAS—Cont'd** | | | | | | | | | | | | | | |
| Neosho | 3.9 | 235 | 24 | 262 | 180.2 | 10.0 | 96 | 921 | 199.8 | 18.3 | 6 | 20 | 1.9 | 0.4 |
| Ness | 4.6 | 1 519 | 13 | 74 | 42.4 | 2.3 | 20 | 84 | 16.1 | 1.2 | NA | NA | NA | NA |
| Norton | 10.1 | 1 785 | 11 | 61 | 40.0 | 1.6 | 29 | 180 | 37.0 | 3.0 | 1 | D | D | D |
| Osage | 2.2 | 129 | 11 | 79 | 19.4 | 2.0 | 54 | 369 | 70.6 | 5.7 | 7 | 28 | 2.0 | 0.4 |
| Osborne | 3.5 | 874 | 13 | 97 | 86.2 | 3.3 | 31 | 198 | 38.5 | 2.3 | 1 | D | D | D |
| Ottawa | 3.7 | 598 | 9 | 199 | 48.0 | 5.8 | 17 | 90 | 19.3 | 1.5 | 1 | D | D | D |
| Pawnee | 68.9 | 10 221 | 6 | 92 | 93.8 | 3.8 | 27 | 215 | 48.5 | 4.2 | 3 | 12 | 0.8 | 0.3 |
| Phillips | 6.9 | 1 245 | 8 | 61 | 33.9 | 1.6 | 36 | 243 | 46.6 | 3.6 | 1 | D | D | D |
| Pottawatomie | 43.4 | 2 266 | 20 | 530 | 161.0 | 18.2 | 98 | 1 463 | 283.9 | 30.3 | 21 | 51 | 7.8 | 1.3 |
| Pratt | 79.2 | 8 340 | 22 | 131 | 108.3 | 3.7 | 54 | 690 | 170.2 | 15.4 | 16 | 40 | 3.7 | 0.7 |
| Rawlins | 17.7 | 6 613 | 6 | 54 | 83.5 | 2.9 | 23 | 101 | 16.3 | 1.7 | 2 | D | D | D |
| Reno | 62.8 | 988 | 65 | 749 | 573.3 | 27.1 | 316 | 3 722 | 828.6 | 78.4 | 64 | 166 | 43.2 | 3.9 |
| Republic | 21.4 | 4 134 | 19 | 272 | 97.4 | 4.8 | 40 | 250 | 43.7 | 3.9 | 2 | D | D | D |
| Rice | 24.9 | 2 378 | 17 | 111 | 64.0 | 4.1 | 45 | 279 | 46.9 | 4.2 | 6 | D | D | D |
| Riley | 6.7 | 107 | 35 | 314 | 93.2 | 10.8 | 270 | 4 028 | 728.6 | 66.5 | 105 | 489 | 50.3 | 10.1 |
| Rooks | 2.8 | 527 | 16 | 112 | 120.3 | 4.7 | 33 | 224 | 56.4 | 3.4 | 1 | D | D | D |
| Rush | 8.5 | 2 501 | 10 | 53 | 27.7 | 1.3 | 12 | 80 | 30.7 | 1.9 | NA | NA | NA | NA |
| Russell | 1.1 | 164 | 14 | 107 | 70.3 | 3.2 | 41 | 284 | 68.0 | 4.4 | 9 | 31 | 2.9 | 0.7 |
| Saline | 11.2 | 208 | 84 | 1 178 | 816.4 | 44.4 | 284 | 4 226 | 1 064.6 | 86.3 | 74 | D | D | D |
| Scott | 47.7 | 10 365 | 21 | 114 | 131.5 | 5.1 | 33 | 212 | 46.8 | 3.5 | 3 | 4 | 0.4 | 0.1 |
| Sedgwick | 94.8 | 203 | 599 | 8 304 | 12 449.4 | 383.6 | 1 771 | 26 921 | 6 574.2 | 590.0 | 605 | 3 411 | 501.8 | 93.7 |
| Seward | 132.2 | 5 679 | 42 | 392 | 197.5 | 15.5 | 116 | 1 395 | 314.6 | 29.1 | 27 | 95 | 12.4 | 2.0 |
| Shawnee | 36.1 | 210 | 166 | 1 966 | 915.3 | 81.2 | 747 | 10 406 | 2 310.1 | 216.4 | 241 | D | D | D |
| Sheridan | 73.0 | 28 186 | 11 | 92 | 88.4 | 4.4 | 20 | 96 | 18.4 | 1.5 | NA | NA | NA | NA |
| Sherman | 106.7 | 17 348 | 19 | 116 | 119.1 | 3.7 | 44 | 378 | 110.6 | 7.6 | 11 | 29 | 3.2 | 0.7 |
| Smith | 3.4 | 815 | 11 | 119 | 71.1 | 3.3 | 30 | 170 | 23.6 | 2.1 | 3 | 4 | 0.4 | 0.1 |
| Stafford | 75.9 | 16 914 | 6 | 24 | 18.1 | 0.7 | 19 | 88 | 15.9 | 1.3 | NA | NA | NA | NA |
| Stanton | 81.9 | 36 481 | 11 | D | D | D | 10 | 73 | 16.4 | 1.6 | NA | NA | NA | NA |
| Stevens | 162.8 | 30 085 | 13 | 84 | 113.7 | 3.0 | 25 | 187 | 40.3 | 3.4 | 1 | D | D | D |
| Sumner | 9.3 | 375 | 25 | 152 | 202.2 | 6.1 | 63 | 556 | 131.4 | 10.7 | 16 | 47 | 3.3 | 0.9 |
| Thomas | 95.6 | 12 519 | 34 | 242 | 163.1 | 8.6 | 64 | 633 | 159.4 | 12.2 | 9 | 23 | 3.7 | 0.4 |
| Trego | 6.3 | 2 069 | 9 | 34 | 24.1 | 0.9 | 28 | 127 | 40.4 | 2.5 | 1 | D | D | D |
| Wabaunsee | 4.9 | 707 | 6 | 43 | 13.4 | 1.7 | 23 | 136 | 26.7 | 2.1 | 5 | D | D | D |
| Wallace | 51.0 | 32 416 | 3 | D | D | D | 7 | 47 | 6.3 | 0.7 | 2 | D | D | D |
| Washington | 7.5 | 1 251 | 15 | 185 | 111.3 | 6.4 | 41 | 209 | 34.8 | 2.6 | 2 | D | D | D |
| Wichita | 50.6 | 21 919 | 10 | 60 | 68.2 | 2.3 | 15 | 83 | 18.5 | 1.3 | 1 | D | D | D |
| Wilson | 2.6 | 265 | 5 | D | D | D | 41 | 267 | 54.2 | 4.1 | 6 | D | D | D |
| Woodson | 1.9 | 529 | 5 | 43 | 27.4 | 1.2 | 19 | 79 | 17.2 | 1.6 | 2 | D | D | D |
| Wyandotte | 385.1 | 2 473 | 234 | 5 833 | 4 127.5 | 289.5 | 461 | 7 022 | 1 710.0 | 174.6 | 136 | 791 | 129.4 | 22.7 |
| **KENTUCKY** | 4 329.0 | 1 037 | 3 794 | 59 854 | 74 680.8 | 2 869.5 | 16 404 | 214 782 | 50 405.9 | 4 502.2 | 3 898 | 20 146 | 3 894.3 | 593.4 |
| Adair | 2.9 | 164 | 18 | 131 | 54.7 | 2.8 | 61 | 486 | 137.1 | 9.6 | 11 | 51 | 2.4 | 0.4 |
| Allen | 1.9 | 102 | 11 | 243 | 97.7 | 9.4 | 63 | 533 | 112.1 | 8.6 | 12 | 55 | 3.8 | 0.8 |
| Anderson | 3.8 | 186 | 7 | D | D | D | 58 | 709 | 170.7 | 14.2 | 14 | 52 | 5.3 | 1.1 |
| Ballard | 8.0 | 963 | 6 | D | D | D | 28 | 208 | 52.8 | 3.8 | 2 | D | D | D |
| Barren | 9.1 | 227 | 38 | D | D | D | 193 | 2 319 | 552.9 | 48.5 | 25 | 78 | 9.2 | 1.8 |
| Bath | 5.8 | 501 | NA | NA | NA | NA | 40 | 243 | 51.5 | 3.7 | 6 | D | D | D |
| Bell | 4.7 | 157 | 20 | 195 | 196.1 | 4.7 | 133 | 1 556 | 374.9 | 31.7 | 23 | 67 | 10.6 | 1.7 |
| Boone | 18.8 | 177 | 160 | D | D | D | 493 | 9 371 | 2 439.2 | 206.6 | 133 | 898 | 154.9 | 23.1 |
| Bourbon | 3.0 | 153 | 10 | D | D | D | 66 | 804 | 175.3 | 14.9 | 11 | 40 | 3.1 | 0.6 |
| Boyd | 52.6 | 1 060 | 64 | D | D | D | 271 | 4 016 | 934.6 | 75.1 | 53 | 233 | 41.1 | 6.2 |
| Boyle | 6.7 | 235 | 18 | 120 | 71.2 | 3.8 | 150 | 1 943 | 430.0 | 43.0 | 33 | 99 | 12.6 | 2.1 |
| Bracken | 1.7 | 201 | 3 | D | D | D | 19 | 155 | 25.9 | 2.3 | 2 | D | D | D |
| Breathitt | 10.0 | 629 | 5 | D | D | D | 51 | 501 | 103.7 | 9.2 | 7 | D | D | D |
| Breckinridge | 2.1 | 108 | 8 | 47 | 19.4 | 1.4 | 55 | 445 | 113.8 | 9.2 | 8 | 21 | 2.3 | 0.4 |
| Bullitt | 3.2 | 46 | 29 | 563 | 879.7 | 26.0 | 164 | 1 699 | 500.5 | 31.9 | 33 | 97 | 12.3 | 1.7 |
| Butler | 1.6 | 120 | 6 | D | D | D | 40 | 284 | 58.0 | 4.3 | 6 | 55 | 3.2 | 1.2 |
| Caldwell | 3.6 | 274 | 7 | D | D | D | 61 | 673 | 151.8 | 13.6 | 7 | 58 | 2.8 | 1.6 |
| Calloway | 5.9 | 169 | 39 | D | D | D | 158 | 2 030 | 454.8 | 41.2 | 34 | 129 | 12.1 | 2.2 |
| Campbell | 29.5 | 339 | 55 | D | D | D | 282 | 4 043 | 970.8 | 83.6 | 67 | 468 | 89.2 | 15.2 |
| Carlisle | 0.8 | 148 | 3 | 9 | 2.9 | 0.2 | 14 | 116 | 23.8 | 2.2 | 2 | D | D | D |
| Carroll | 81.7 | 7 810 | 7 | 73 | 13.4 | 1.3 | 55 | 642 | 182.7 | 14.2 | 5 | 22 | 5.8 | 0.7 |
| Carter | 4.3 | 156 | 13 | 406 | 306.2 | 9.7 | 114 | 1 098 | 268.5 | 18.7 | 17 | 53 | 3.7 | 0.7 |
| Casey | 1.9 | 118 | 10 | 95 | 34.9 | 2.6 | 48 | 316 | 71.8 | 5.1 | 2 | D | D | D |
| Christian | 14.5 | 206 | 65 | 1 028 | 878.4 | 38.6 | 270 | 3 263 | 936.1 | 70.7 | 66 | 299 | 29.8 | 5.8 |
| Clark | 187.6 | 5 378 | 34 | D | D | D | 147 | 1 861 | 461.8 | 39.2 | 40 | 135 | 16.6 | 2.5 |

1. Merchant wholesalers, except manufacturers' sales branches and offices.　　2. Employer establishments.

# Table B. States and Counties — Professional Services, Manufacturing, and Accommodation and Food Services

| STATE County | Professional, scientific, and technical services,[1] 2007 | | | | Manufacturing, 2007 | | | | Accommodation and food services, 2007 | | | |
|---|---|---|---|---|---|---|---|---|---|---|---|---|
| | Number of establishments | Number of employees | Receipts (mil dol) | Annual payroll (mil dol) | Number of establishments | Number of employees | Receipts (mil dol) | Annual payroll (mil dol) | Number of establishments | Number of employees | Sales (mil dol) | Annual payroll (mil dol) |
| | 147 | 148 | 149 | 150 | 151 | 152 | 153 | 154 | 155 | 156 | 157 | 158 |
| KANSAS—Cont'd | | | | | | | | | | | | |
| Neosho | 32 | 133 | 11.5 | 4.6 | 36 | 1 395 | 291.0 | 48.8 | 35 | 395 | 13.1 | 3.0 |
| Ness | 6 | 19 | 1.6 | 0.3 | NA | NA | NA | NA | 11 | 71 | 1.5 | 0.4 |
| Norton | 11 | 46 | 2.9 | 0.7 | NA | NA | NA | NA | 13 | 152 | 5.4 | 1.4 |
| Osage | 16 | D | D | D | NA | NA | NA | NA | 21 | D | D | D |
| Osborne | 9 | 51 | 10.4 | 1.6 | NA | NA | NA | NA | 9 | 55 | 1.4 | 0.4 |
| Ottawa | 10 | D | D | D | NA | NA | NA | NA | 8 | 103 | 1.5 | 0.5 |
| Pawnee | 15 | 53 | 4.2 | 1.2 | NA | NA | NA | NA | 13 | 179 | 5.7 | 1.5 |
| Phillips | 16 | 84 | 7.6 | 2.6 | NA | NA | NA | NA | 14 | 146 | 3.7 | 0.8 |
| Pottawatomie | 43 | D | D | D | 33 | 1 626 | 329.6 | 64.9 | 32 | 355 | 11.8 | 3.1 |
| Pratt | 31 | 127 | 9.6 | 3.5 | NA | NA | NA | NA | 25 | 431 | 15.0 | 3.5 |
| Rawlins | 8 | 15 | 1.0 | 0.2 | NA | NA | NA | NA | 9 | 24 | 0.7 | 0.2 |
| Reno | 109 | D | D | D | 93 | 3 672 | 908.7 | 142.1 | 125 | 2 289 | 83.4 | 23.1 |
| Republic | 17 | 25 | 2.7 | 0.5 | NA | NA | NA | NA | 11 | 127 | 3.1 | 0.6 |
| Rice | 19 | 119 | 5.8 | 1.8 | NA | NA | NA | NA | 18 | 231 | 6.6 | 1.9 |
| Riley | 155 | D | D | D | 28 | 795 | D | 24.7 | 158 | 3 493 | 125.4 | 33.4 |
| Rooks | 13 | 41 | 3.5 | 1.3 | NA | NA | NA | NA | 11 | D | D | D |
| Rush | 6 | 16 | 1.4 | 0.6 | NA | NA | NA | NA | 4 | 20 | 0.9 | 0.2 |
| Russell | 14 | 57 | 4.4 | 1.1 | NA | NA | NA | NA | 20 | 300 | 10.0 | 2.3 |
| Saline | 124 | D | D | D | 77 | D | D | 222.7 | 128 | 2 593 | 96.1 | 26.7 |
| Scott | 19 | 67 | 6.3 | 1.4 | NA | NA | NA | NA | 13 | D | D | D |
| Sedgwick | 1 120 | D | D | D | 573 | 53 568 | 21 117.1 | 2 940.1 | 1 066 | 21 268 | 846.9 | 246.6 |
| Seward | 32 | 127 | 11.3 | 4.2 | 9 | D | D | D | 49 | 826 | 32.2 | 8.9 |
| Shawnee | 472 | D | D | D | 121 | 6 097 | D | 274.4 | 370 | D | D | D |
| Sheridan | 4 | 21 | 1.2 | 0.3 | NA | NA | NA | NA | 5 | 31 | 0.8 | 0.1 |
| Sherman | 18 | 79 | 6.6 | 2.4 | NA | NA | NA | NA | 23 | 328 | 11.0 | 3.0 |
| Smith | 9 | 23 | 2.2 | 0.3 | NA | NA | NA | NA | 8 | 79 | 1.4 | 0.3 |
| Stafford | 9 | 15 | 1.8 | 0.6 | NA | NA | NA | NA | 12 | 42 | 1.2 | 0.2 |
| Stanton | 6 | 16 | 1.1 | 0.4 | NA | NA | NA | NA | 4 | 22 | 0.8 | 0.1 |
| Stevens | 11 | 53 | 13.7 | 4.3 | NA | NA | NA | NA | 11 | D | D | D |
| Sumner | 24 | D | D | D | 39 | 1 253 | D | 43.0 | 39 | 537 | 16.8 | 4.8 |
| Thomas | 32 | 76 | 7.7 | 1.6 | NA | NA | NA | NA | 29 | 512 | 18.3 | 5.1 |
| Trego | 8 | 23 | 1.4 | 0.3 | NA | NA | NA | NA | 12 | 106 | 4.0 | 1.1 |
| Wabaunsee | 5 | D | D | D | NA | NA | NA | NA | 10 | D | D | D |
| Wallace | 2 | D | D | D | NA | NA | NA | NA | 3 | D | D | D |
| Washington | 11 | 34 | 3.5 | 0.9 | NA | NA | NA | NA | 14 | 123 | 2.5 | 0.7 |
| Wichita | 3 | D | D | D | NA | NA | NA | NA | 3 | 14 | 0.5 | 0.1 |
| Wilson | 14 | 39 | 4.4 | 0.9 | 22 | 1 428 | D | D | 18 | 191 | 5.8 | 1.4 |
| Woodson | 5 | 18 | 0.8 | 0.3 | NA | NA | NA | NA | 6 | 71 | 1.5 | 0.4 |
| Wyandotte | 158 | D | D | D | 215 | 11 083 | 7 634.5 | 632.0 | 248 | 4 964 | 241.9 | 66.8 |
| KENTUCKY | 8 075 | 61 428 | 7 872.2 | 2 831.6 | 4 165 | 247 096 | 119 105.4 | 10 773.2 | 7 309 | 151 551 | 6 300.9 | 1 787.4 |
| Adair | 16 | D | D | D | NA | NA | NA | NA | 20 | 188 | 9.1 | 1.7 |
| Allen | 11 | 60 | 5.6 | 1.3 | 12 | 592 | 164.8 | 22.1 | 14 | 207 | 8.2 | 2.0 |
| Anderson | 27 | 102 | 9.6 | 3.0 | 21 | 1 102 | 600.9 | 47.9 | 26 | 369 | 11.3 | 3.6 |
| Ballard | 5 | D | D | D | 11 | 727 | D | 43.3 | 10 | 70 | 1.8 | 0.5 |
| Barren | 49 | 292 | 23.2 | 7.3 | 49 | 4 540 | 1 024.9 | 164.9 | 87 | 1 790 | 64.7 | 17.5 |
| Bath | 11 | D | D | D | NA | NA | NA | NA | 10 | D | D | D |
| Bell | 37 | 453 | 31.0 | 17.3 | 21 | 688 | D | D | 47 | 1 044 | 38.1 | 10.5 |
| Boone | 232 | 3 501 | 381.4 | 146.4 | 183 | 13 239 | 4 691.0 | 647.7 | 269 | D | D | D |
| Bourbon | 35 | D | D | D | 26 | 1 769 | D | D | 25 | 327 | 13.5 | 3.6 |
| Boyd | 104 | D | D | D | 33 | 3 024 | D | 229.1 | 112 | 2 820 | 100.5 | 27.7 |
| Boyle | 72 | 437 | 43.7 | 15.3 | 28 | 2 839 | D | D | 63 | 1 539 | 57.7 | 16.8 |
| Bracken | 7 | D | D | D | NA | NA | NA | NA | 10 | D | D | D |
| Breathitt | 11 | D | D | D | NA | NA | NA | NA | 15 | 223 | 8.7 | 2.3 |
| Breckinridge | 12 | 66 | 4.6 | 1.9 | NA | NA | NA | NA | 18 | 273 | 7.9 | 2.5 |
| Bullitt | 76 | 366 | 26.3 | 10.0 | 47 | 2 823 | D | 104.8 | 84 | 1 818 | 73.0 | 20.1 |
| Butler | 6 | 126 | 2.4 | 1.4 | 15 | 573 | 120.5 | 19.5 | 16 | 170 | 5.4 | 1.4 |
| Caldwell | 18 | 50 | 4.0 | 1.0 | 16 | 898 | 213.2 | 27.1 | 24 | 260 | 9.4 | 2.3 |
| Calloway | 55 | 273 | 22.0 | 7.5 | 35 | 2 658 | 729.2 | 96.0 | 70 | 1 548 | 52.5 | 14.2 |
| Campbell | 149 | D | D | D | 85 | 2 338 | 798.2 | 105.8 | 192 | 3 734 | 163.3 | 49.0 |
| Carlisle | 3 | D | D | D | NA | NA | NA | NA | 4 | 42 | 1.1 | 0.3 |
| Carroll | 20 | 98 | 7.7 | 3.8 | 12 | 2 547 | 4 059.7 | 183.7 | 26 | 426 | 18.2 | 5.0 |
| Carter | 28 | 89 | 5.9 | 2.3 | 18 | 712 | D | 19.0 | 39 | 619 | 24.4 | 5.9 |
| Casey | 9 | D | D | D | 28 | 1 019 | 189.1 | 21.1 | 16 | 184 | 6.4 | 1.9 |
| Christian | 89 | 875 | 102.4 | 32.8 | 73 | 5 192 | 1 571.6 | 202.4 | 113 | 2 055 | 80.1 | 21.9 |
| Clark | 57 | 321 | 27.3 | 11.8 | 44 | 3 794 | 1 252.3 | 146.2 | 59 | 1 264 | 51.3 | 13.9 |

1. Establishment subject to federal tax.

# Table B. States and Counties — Health Care and Social Assistance, Other Services, and Federal Funds

| STATE County | Health care and social assistance, 2007 | | | | Other services, 2007 | | | | Federal funds and grants, 2009–2010 Expenditures (mil dol) | | | |
|---|---|---|---|---|---|---|---|---|---|---|---|---|
| | | | | | | | | | | Direct payments for individuals[1] | | |
| | Number of establishments | Number of employees | Receipts (mil dol) | Annual payroll (mil dol) | Number of establishments | Number of employees | Receipts (mil dol) | Annual payroll (mil dol) | Total | Social Security and government retirement | Medicare | Food Stamps and Supplemental Security Income |
| | 159 | 160 | 161 | 162 | 163 | 164 | 165 | 166 | 167 | 168 | 169 | 170 |
| KANSAS—Cont'd | | | | | | | | | | | | |
| Neosho | 58 | 1 256 | 85.1 | 31.8 | 41 | 120 | 11.2 | 2.1 | 135.0 | 54.0 | 34.0 | 6.1 |
| Ness | 11 | 249 | 13.3 | 6.1 | 10 | D | D | D | 34.6 | 12.5 | 12.2 | 0.2 |
| Norton | 23 | 448 | 21.5 | 10.7 | 14 | 40 | 5.0 | 0.7 | 97.6 | 18.5 | 12.5 | 0.9 |
| Osage | 30 | 1 533 | 35.5 | 20.5 | 20 | D | D | D | 114.0 | 60.2 | 25.5 | 3.6 |
| Osborne | 16 | 281 | 11.5 | 5.1 | 10 | D | D | D | 46.8 | 15.6 | 13.5 | 0.8 |
| Ottawa | 9 | D | D | D | 9 | 23 | 3.1 | 0.5 | 43.3 | 18.3 | 10.7 | 1.0 |
| Pawnee | 16 | 1 268 | 72.7 | 49.0 | 15 | 33 | 4.1 | 0.8 | 54.4 | 15.1 | 14.8 | 0.9 |
| Phillips | 21 | 294 | 17.1 | 8.0 | 23 | 64 | 24.8 | 1.2 | 58.8 | 21.3 | 16.0 | 0.6 |
| Pottawatomie | 49 | 1 466 | 56.3 | 28.4 | 46 | 139 | 10.5 | 2.5 | 113.2 | 55.1 | 28.4 | 2.6 |
| Pratt | 38 | 641 | 66.7 | 22.0 | 35 | 122 | 8.7 | 2.3 | 81.6 | 32.0 | 25.0 | 2.0 |
| Rawlins | 7 | D | D | D | 5 | D | D | D | 37.8 | 12.9 | 7.4 | 0.4 |
| Reno | 200 | 4 751 | 420.0 | 173.9 | 132 | 536 | 42.5 | 10.9 | 478.9 | 210.6 | 120.3 | 20.6 |
| Republic | 16 | 306 | 15.5 | 7.2 | 19 | 47 | 3.3 | 0.8 | 54.5 | 20.6 | 13.4 | 0.9 |
| Rice | 25 | 372 | 20.4 | 9.9 | 19 | 62 | 4.7 | 1.2 | 80.7 | 34.9 | 19.8 | 2.6 |
| Riley | 167 | 3 409 | 257.9 | 99.5 | 135 | 1 550 | 279.3 | 49.4 | 446.7 | 141.9 | 41.2 | 8.3 |
| Rooks | 13 | 213 | 11.0 | 4.9 | 15 | 63 | 6.4 | 1.5 | 58.9 | 20.0 | 17.5 | 0.9 |
| Rush | 5 | 128 | 7.2 | 3.3 | 6 | D | D | D | 37.0 | 13.5 | 11.9 | 0.8 |
| Russell | 18 | 420 | 21.9 | 11.0 | 14 | 36 | 3.3 | 0.4 | 66.2 | 27.2 | 22.0 | 1.6 |
| Saline | 180 | D | D | D | 123 | 582 | 55.4 | 13.1 | 438.9 | 170.0 | 83.1 | 13.3 |
| Scott | 12 | 292 | 15.7 | 7.9 | 19 | 65 | 6.0 | 1.0 | 40.1 | 13.8 | 7.9 | 0.3 |
| Sedgwick | 1 298 | 32 662 | 3 447.9 | 1 254.0 | 853 | 6 143 | 554.1 | 168.3 | 4 637.8 | 1 332.7 | 643.9 | 156.9 |
| Seward | 70 | 1 110 | 82.7 | 31.5 | 49 | 226 | 25.6 | 5.2 | 103.0 | 36.6 | 20.6 | 7.7 |
| Shawnee | 502 | 16 040 | 1 388.4 | 610.9 | 410 | 2 872 | 284.2 | 80.6 | 2 879.8 | 651.6 | 244.3 | 59.3 |
| Sheridan | 7 | D | D | D | 6 | D | D | D | 31.5 | 10.1 | 5.6 | 0.3 |
| Sherman | 35 | 390 | 23.0 | 9.3 | 23 | 61 | 5.6 | 1.4 | 76.9 | 25.5 | 15.6 | 1.3 |
| Smith | 9 | 260 | 11.2 | 5.4 | 13 | 30 | 3.0 | 0.5 | 47.1 | 17.0 | 11.7 | 1.0 |
| Stafford | 25 | 244 | 10.8 | 5.0 | 15 | 35 | 1.9 | 0.4 | 49.4 | 20.8 | 12.1 | 0.8 |
| Stanton | 4 | D | D | D | 5 | D | D | D | 31.8 | 12.0 | 2.9 | 0.3 |
| Stevens | 10 | 218 | 13.8 | 7.1 | 7 | D | D | D | 46.3 | 16.2 | 9.0 | 1.0 |
| Sumner | 61 | D | D | D | 42 | 112 | 9.3 | 2.1 | 189.1 | 86.3 | 47.8 | 5.7 |
| Thomas | 37 | 465 | 34.2 | 13.8 | 31 | 124 | 8.4 | 2.3 | 87.0 | 29.2 | 15.0 | 1.1 |
| Trego | 7 | D | D | D | 14 | 26 | 2.2 | 0.4 | 33.2 | 11.4 | 10.1 | 0.4 |
| Wabaunsee | 6 | 121 | 4.9 | 2.2 | 6 | D | D | D | 79.5 | 59.6 | 10.4 | 0.9 |
| Wallace | 5 | D | D | D | 6 | 13 | 0.9 | 0.2 | 23.4 | 7.2 | 4.7 | 0.3 |
| Washington | 26 | 378 | 14.8 | 6.9 | 17 | 55 | 5.3 | 0.8 | 63.4 | 21.9 | 15.5 | 1.3 |
| Wichita | 6 | D | D | D | 10 | 20 | 2.2 | 0.4 | 31.4 | 12.8 | 3.7 | 0.4 |
| Wilson | 35 | 588 | 37.1 | 16.1 | 12 | 26 | 1.6 | 0.5 | 90.5 | 33.9 | 21.9 | 3.0 |
| Woodson | 14 | 110 | 6.8 | 2.4 | 6 | D | D | D | 36.0 | 13.6 | 9.5 | 1.5 |
| Wyandotte | 309 | 10 811 | 1 094.6 | 467.5 | 234 | 1 390 | 232.0 | 34.5 | 1 616.6 | 419.1 | 331.6 | 84.2 |
| KENTUCKY | 10 600 | 235 282 | 22 151.8 | 8 395.1 | 6 150 | 40 956 | 3 751.1 | 1 009.3 | 57 270.5 | 13 649.1 | 11 693.5 | 2 373.7 |
| Adair | 41 | 883 | 49.2 | 24.4 | 15 | 37 | 3.0 | 0.7 | 208.4 | 52.2 | 82.3 | 10.2 |
| Allen | 23 | D | D | D | 13 | 42 | 4.0 | 1.2 | 183.8 | 56.9 | 67.6 | 8.6 |
| Anderson | 33 | 336 | 19.9 | 8.9 | 27 | 91 | 5.2 | 1.5 | 120.0 | 62.9 | 31.3 | 4.7 |
| Ballard | 8 | D | D | D | 9 | D | D | D | 99.1 | 42.3 | 32.6 | 3.6 |
| Barren | 106 | 2 498 | 196.0 | 85.7 | 48 | D | D | D | 362.4 | 124.2 | 116.6 | 17.4 |
| Bath | 13 | 198 | 9.8 | 4.0 | 12 | D | D | D | 122.1 | 33.8 | 40.3 | 11.4 |
| Bell | 80 | 1 525 | 116.8 | 46.1 | 37 | D | D | D | 278.8 | 107.4 | 162.4 | 41.6 |
| Boone | 211 | 3 754 | 311.0 | 123.2 | 184 | 1 641 | 126.9 | 42.9 | 668.0 | 303.8 | 92.7 | 17.3 |
| Bourbon | 39 | D | D | D | 24 | 127 | 6.3 | 1.7 | 168.7 | 62.0 | 53.8 | 8.1 |
| Boyd | 246 | 7 162 | 811.2 | 303.0 | 110 | D | D | D | 605.9 | 223.8 | 186.7 | 33.2 |
| Boyle | 110 | 2 486 | 238.4 | 105.7 | 50 | 219 | 14.2 | 3.9 | 275.3 | 103.9 | 82.6 | 13.3 |
| Bracken | 9 | D | D | D | 6 | D | D | D | 85.5 | 28.4 | 29.0 | 5.9 |
| Breathitt | 40 | 785 | 72.9 | 24.8 | 10 | D | D | D | 318.2 | 52.8 | 105.6 | 26.4 |
| Breckinridge | 30 | 453 | 30.9 | 11.0 | 23 | 49 | 4.4 | 1.0 | 192.2 | 70.0 | 61.0 | 10.7 |
| Bullitt | 90 | 906 | 59.6 | 22.8 | 81 | 1 021 | 27.2 | 23.1 | 340.0 | 175.4 | 74.4 | 18.3 |
| Butler | 19 | 250 | 14.4 | 6.4 | 14 | 51 | 2.8 | 0.8 | 127.7 | 37.5 | 48.6 | 7.6 |
| Caldwell | 30 | 515 | 35.2 | 12.9 | 17 | 62 | 5.4 | 1.3 | 129.4 | 49.9 | 44.8 | 5.3 |
| Calloway | 109 | 1 917 | 152.4 | 56.0 | 49 | 214 | 14.1 | 4.1 | 288.7 | 114.6 | 82.2 | 10.7 |
| Campbell | 160 | 3 393 | 288.9 | 114.6 | 124 | 916 | 111.4 | 26.6 | 648.0 | 255.2 | 200.5 | 30.9 |
| Carlisle | 7 | D | D | D | 3 | D | D | D | 53.3 | 20.7 | 18.9 | 2.0 |
| Carroll | 21 | D | D | D | 15 | 92 | 5.2 | 1.7 | 104.0 | 32.2 | 32.8 | 6.3 |
| Carter | 44 | 572 | 34.8 | 13.6 | 34 | 182 | 11.8 | 3.3 | 316.2 | 76.8 | 105.0 | 24.0 |
| Casey | 24 | 395 | 25.2 | 9.7 | 12 | 30 | 2.9 | 0.6 | 173.6 | 44.6 | 66.5 | 10.9 |
| Christian | 177 | 4 734 | 438.9 | 153.4 | 105 | 739 | 54.2 | 16.0 | 6 240.5 | 196.8 | 158.0 | 34.3 |
| Clark | 111 | 1 459 | 122.5 | 45.9 | 56 | 294 | 17.2 | 4.6 | 279.8 | 126.3 | 77.0 | 16.1 |

1. State totals may include programs not allocated by county.

# Table B. States and Counties — Federal Funds, Residential Construction, and Local Government Finances

| | Federal funds and grants, 2009–2010 (cont.) | | | | | | | Value of residential construction authorized by building permits, 2011 | | Local government finances, 2007 | | | | |
|---|---|---|---|---|---|---|---|---|---|---|---|---|---|---|
| | Expenditures (mil dol) (cont.) | | | | | | | | | General revenue | | | | |
| | Procurement contract awards | | | Grants[1] | | | | | | | | Taxes | | |
| STATE County | Salaries and wages | Defense | Other | Medicaid and other health-related | Nutrition and family welfare | Education | Other | New construction ($1,000) | Number of housing units | Total (mil dol) | Inter-govern-mental (mil dol) | Total (mil dol) | Per capita[2] (dollars) Total | Property |
| | 171 | 172 | 173 | 174 | 175 | 176 | 177 | 178 | 179 | 180 | 181 | 182 | 183 | 184 |
| KANSAS—Cont'd | | | | | | | | | | | | | | |
| Neosho | 4.9 | 1.5 | 1.1 | 16.3 | 3.3 | 1.8 | 2.4 | 4 738 | 61 | 90.3 | 28.0 | 22.7 | 1 398 | 1 059 |
| Ness | 1.8 | 0.0 | 0.6 | 1.7 | 0.6 | 0.1 | 0.0 | 0 | 0 | 23.2 | 3.9 | 7.6 | 2 548 | 2 401 |
| Norton | 3.2 | 0.0 | 0.4 | 3.4 | 1.0 | 0.1 | 50.1 | 300 | 4 | 25.4 | 8.9 | 7.1 | 1 316 | 1 136 |
| Osage | 5.6 | 1.5 | 1.0 | 9.0 | 2.6 | 0.4 | 0.9 | 4 317 | 23 | 55.2 | 29.4 | 15.9 | 964 | 851 |
| Osborne | 2.0 | 0.0 | 0.4 | 6.2 | 0.7 | 0.1 | 0.1 | 0 | 0 | 12.0 | 3.9 | 5.9 | 1 511 | 1 289 |
| Ottawa | 1.6 | 0.0 | 0.4 | 5.1 | 1.0 | 0.1 | 0.1 | 1 064 | 6 | 24.0 | 11.8 | 8.7 | 1 449 | 1 292 |
| Pawnee | 9.3 | 0.0 | 0.6 | 3.9 | 1.1 | 0.1 | 0.5 | 0 | 0 | 24.6 | 10.0 | 10.4 | 1 624 | 1 408 |
| Phillips | 3.6 | 0.0 | 0.7 | 7.3 | 1.0 | 0.1 | 1.1 | 0 | 0 | 26.6 | 11.1 | 8.2 | 1 539 | 1 378 |
| Pottawatomie | 4.6 | 4.3 | 1.0 | 9.0 | 2.7 | 0.4 | 0.6 | 18 484 | 86 | 73.9 | 28.5 | 34.5 | 1 781 | 1 472 |
| Pratt | 4.0 | 0.2 | 0.5 | 3.4 | 1.5 | 0.5 | 1.7 | 403 | 6 | 46.4 | 18.1 | 19.1 | 2 026 | 1 690 |
| Rawlins | 1.4 | 0.0 | 0.5 | 3.9 | 0.5 | 0.1 | 0.0 | 0 | 0 | 9.3 | 3.7 | 4.4 | 1 702 | 1 559 |
| Reno | 33.1 | 0.1 | 3.0 | 48.0 | 13.0 | 2.6 | 3.8 | 9 693 | 51 | 220.8 | 92.7 | 79.1 | 1 253 | 908 |
| Republic | 2.5 | 0.0 | 0.5 | 3.9 | 1.0 | 0.1 | 0.2 | 687 | 8 | 21.5 | 8.5 | 9.9 | 2 018 | 1 787 |
| Rice | 3.5 | 0.0 | 0.8 | 5.1 | 1.9 | 0.2 | 1.2 | 2 003 | 17 | 45.3 | 17.1 | 15.2 | 1 505 | 1 355 |
| Riley | 66.0 | 9.2 | 18.7 | 36.7 | 9.4 | 7.1 | 77.5 | 65 718 | 494 | 151.1 | 48.4 | 74.0 | 1 072 | 765 |
| Rooks | 2.1 | 0.0 | 0.4 | 3.9 | 1.0 | 0.1 | 5.6 | 280 | 2 | 32.0 | 7.3 | 11.8 | 2 285 | 2 115 |
| Rush | 1.9 | 0.0 | 0.4 | 2.8 | 0.7 | 0.1 | 0.0 | 160 | 1 | 16.8 | 4.9 | 6.2 | 1 945 | 1 868 |
| Russell | 3.5 | 0.0 | 0.6 | 5.1 | 1.3 | 0.1 | 0.3 | 827 | 3 | 31.4 | 9.1 | 16.2 | 2 403 | 2 026 |
| Saline | 55.1 | 3.6 | 45.6 | 35.7 | 12.1 | 1.5 | 2.6 | 10 133 | 90 | 181.1 | 70.4 | 74.9 | 1 373 | 946 |
| Scott | 1.4 | 0.0 | 0.3 | 2.8 | 0.8 | 0.1 | 0.7 | 2 884 | 9 | 18.5 | 6.4 | 10.4 | 2 282 | 2 078 |
| Sedgwick | 667.7 | 1 074.6 | 149.5 | 359.7 | 78.5 | 23.7 | 76.1 | 124 735 | 866 | 1 644.2 | 709.8 | 654.3 | 1 375 | 930 |
| Seward | 7.3 | 0.0 | 0.7 | 12.4 | 4.5 | 1.7 | 2.6 | 3 475 | 41 | 136.9 | 38.2 | 39.8 | 1 720 | 1 283 |
| Shawnee | 299.1 | 20.6 | 54.6 | 244.1 | 136.6 | 225.1 | 892.2 | 32 608 | 186 | 671.1 | 224.4 | 285.2 | 1 644 | 1 243 |
| Sheridan | 0.9 | 0.0 | 0.2 | 2.3 | 0.4 | 0.1 | 0.1 | NA | NA | 8.5 | 2.7 | 4.5 | 1 808 | 1 668 |
| Sherman | 6.2 | 0.0 | 0.4 | 4.5 | 1.1 | 0.2 | 0.2 | 100 | 1 | 30.9 | 11.8 | 10.4 | 1 741 | 1 256 |
| Smith | 3.5 | 0.0 | 0.5 | 3.4 | 0.8 | 0.1 | 0.4 | 755 | 7 | 15.4 | 6.1 | 6.8 | 1 730 | 1 630 |
| Stafford | 2.7 | 0.0 | 1.7 | 2.3 | 1.0 | 0.2 | 0.0 | 698 | 6 | 24.5 | 8.2 | 10.1 | 2 293 | 2 172 |
| Stanton | 0.5 | 0.0 | 0.1 | 0.6 | 0.5 | 0.1 | 0.1 | 0 | 0 | 17.6 | 2.2 | 10.6 | 4 888 | 4 730 |
| Stevens | 1.6 | 0.0 | 0.3 | 2.8 | 0.9 | 0.1 | 1.1 | 67 | 1 | 43.7 | 6.0 | 26.1 | 5 164 | 5 055 |
| Sumner | 6.9 | 0.8 | 1.5 | 16.3 | 4.5 | 1.1 | 1.1 | 3 343 | 20 | 91.4 | 37.7 | 30.5 | 1 275 | 1 063 |
| Thomas | 6.2 | 0.0 | 0.6 | 4.5 | 1.3 | 0.7 | 2.4 | 500 | 1 | 41.2 | 18.1 | 11.3 | 1 547 | 1 160 |
| Trego | 1.0 | 0.0 | 0.2 | 3.4 | 0.6 | 0.1 | 0.1 | 0 | 0 | 18.9 | 3.7 | 5.8 | 1 991 | 1 755 |
| Wabaunsee | 2.4 | 0.0 | 0.6 | 2.3 | 1.0 | 0.2 | 0.1 | 2 911 | 17 | 22.0 | 9.6 | 9.3 | 1 347 | 1 263 |
| Wallace | 0.8 | 0.0 | 1.8 | 1.1 | 0.3 | 0.1 | 0.0 | 250 | 1 | 7.4 | 3.1 | 3.5 | 2 387 | 2 342 |
| Washington | 4.2 | 0.0 | 0.9 | 6.8 | 1.2 | 0.2 | 0.1 | 0 | 0 | 29.2 | 12.6 | 9.8 | 1 676 | 1 557 |
| Wichita | 1.0 | 0.0 | 0.2 | 1.8 | 0.5 | 0.1 | 1.2 | 0 | 0 | 15.5 | 4.2 | 5.8 | 2 638 | 2 331 |
| Wilson | 4.2 | 0.0 | 0.8 | 16.3 | 2.3 | 0.3 | 1.7 | 0 | 0 | 37.7 | 16.2 | 12.0 | 1 225 | 1 049 |
| Woodson | 1.4 | 1.8 | 0.3 | 5.1 | 0.7 | 0.1 | 0.0 | 0 | 0 | 10.8 | 4.5 | 5.0 | 1 497 | 1 290 |
| Wyandotte | 200.9 | 18.3 | 52.6 | 405.8 | 39.6 | 8.4 | 29.7 | 13 435 | 81 | 743.6 | 271.8 | 268.2 | 1 742 | 1 216 |
| KENTUCKY | 9 204.7 | 5 180.5 | 2 305.6 | 5 482.6 | 1 065.1 | 784.2 | 2 170.4 | 915 114 | 7 782 | X | X | X | X | X |
| Adair | 3.6 | 0.0 | 0.8 | 42.5 | 3.1 | 1.7 | 2.5 | 680 | 6 | 58.6 | 21.9 | 6.7 | 377 | 235 |
| Allen | 4.0 | 0.0 | 0.9 | 36.1 | 2.5 | 1.3 | 0.2 | NA | NA | 36.6 | 21.1 | 10.3 | 545 | 344 |
| Anderson | 3.3 | 0.2 | 0.7 | 11.5 | 2.2 | 1.2 | 0.0 | 5 233 | 43 | 44.7 | 22.8 | 14.6 | 689 | 492 |
| Ballard | 2.5 | 1.1 | 0.9 | 8.6 | 1.6 | 0.7 | 0.7 | NA | NA | 25.1 | 11.7 | 5.7 | 683 | 449 |
| Barren | 24.5 | 0.6 | 2.0 | 57.2 | 5.1 | 2.4 | 3.6 | 7 410 | 48 | 100.1 | 49.3 | 33.2 | 807 | 450 |
| Bath | 2.2 | 0.2 | 0.5 | 25.3 | 2.4 | 1.2 | 1.0 | 0 | 0 | 21.4 | 14.4 | 4.3 | 369 | 250 |
| Bell | 14.8 | 2.9 | -158.7 | 88.1 | 11.8 | 2.8 | 2.8 | 1 662 | 19 | 74.0 | 48.1 | 15.8 | 545 | 290 |
| Boone | 104.6 | 91.6 | 10.9 | 18.4 | 8.3 | 3.1 | 6.9 | 67 074 | 475 | 290.6 | 80.8 | 167.8 | 1 492 | 954 |
| Bourbon | 3.3 | 0.0 | 0.8 | 21.3 | 4.2 | 2.2 | 3.1 | 6 563 | 56 | 46.4 | 22.9 | 17.3 | 875 | 433 |
| Boyd | 56.9 | 1.1 | 15.0 | 63.1 | 9.7 | 5.0 | 4.9 | 552 | 5 | 127.4 | 59.8 | 46.0 | 948 | 447 |
| Boyle | 10.7 | 0.0 | 1.4 | 37.0 | 3.9 | 3.8 | 14.4 | 5 339 | 44 | 71.0 | 31.2 | 27.3 | 952 | 487 |
| Bracken | 2.5 | 0.0 | 0.6 | 13.8 | 1.4 | 0.8 | 0.1 | NA | NA | 19.4 | 11.5 | 5.1 | 600 | 436 |
| Breathitt | 13.4 | 1.4 | 0.7 | 73.3 | 8.0 | 1.7 | 33.8 | 170 | 1 | 38.2 | 24.9 | 6.5 | 417 | 181 |
| Breckinridge | 4.8 | 0.1 | 1.7 | 29.0 | 4.4 | 1.7 | 3.0 | 994 | 11 | 46.3 | 23.8 | 8.8 | 461 | 305 |
| Bullitt | 6.2 | 25.1 | 1.8 | 23.1 | 7.6 | 3.7 | 0.5 | 43 490 | 410 | 129.1 | 64.0 | 49.5 | 670 | 502 |
| Butler | 2.5 | 0.3 | 1.1 | 24.1 | 2.3 | 1.0 | 0.4 | 0 | 0 | 31.2 | 21.8 | 5.7 | 433 | 178 |
| Caldwell | 2.8 | 0.0 | 0.7 | 18.1 | 1.8 | 1.1 | 1.1 | 365 | 3 | 27.0 | 15.4 | 7.2 | 564 | 283 |
| Calloway | 17.9 | 0.1 | 2.8 | 22.0 | 9.0 | 4.4 | 1.1 | 3 844 | 22 | 209.8 | 31.5 | 21.1 | 582 | 414 |
| Campbell | 49.1 | 2.2 | 3.1 | 56.6 | 11.3 | 6.9 | 9.7 | 22 740 | 162 | 204.2 | 61.6 | 102.4 | 1 179 | 692 |
| Carlisle | 1.3 | 2.4 | 0.3 | 5.8 | 0.9 | 0.5 | -4.6 | NA | NA | 9.9 | 6.3 | 2.4 | 461 | 346 |
| Carroll | 9.9 | 0.0 | 0.5 | 15.1 | 2.3 | 0.9 | 1.7 | 215 | 2 | 154.6 | 12.7 | 11.1 | 1 057 | 453 |
| Carter | 10.5 | 22.2 | 1.1 | 57.8 | 9.2 | 3.2 | 0.5 | 345 | 6 | 52.2 | 37.3 | 8.6 | 315 | 188 |
| Casey | 2.3 | 0.1 | 0.6 | 39.1 | 3.0 | 1.2 | 0.6 | 113 | 1 | 43.9 | 24.3 | 5.3 | 330 | 198 |
| Christian | 5 180.4 | 536.5 | 13.6 | 70.9 | 14.6 | 6.6 | 4.5 | 12 806 | 130 | 126.0 | 69.2 | 37.6 | 465 | 235 |
| Clark | 8.3 | 2.0 | 3.0 | 33.6 | 4.7 | 2.4 | 0.8 | 8 035 | 42 | 88.9 | 41.3 | 29.6 | 833 | 459 |

1. State totals may include programs not allocated by county.  2. Based on the resident population estimated as of July 1 of the year shown.

| STATE County | Total (mil dol)¹ | Per capita¹ (dollars) | Education | Health and hospitals | Police protection | Public welfare | Highways | Total (mil dol) | Per capita¹ (dollars) | Federal civilian | Federal military | State and local | Democratic | Republican | All other |
|---|---|---|---|---|---|---|---|---|---|---|---|---|---|---|---|
| | 185 | 186 | 187 | 188 | 189 | 190 | 191 | 192 | 193 | 194 | 195 | 196 | 197 | 198 | 199 |
| **KANSAS—Cont'd** | | | | | | | | | | | | | | | |
| Neosho | 92.5 | 5 697 | 39.7 | 27.9 | 2.2 | 0.0 | 4.6 | 163.7 | 10 088 | 56 | 71 | 1 917 | 35.6 | 62.2 | 2.2 |
| Ness | 21.5 | 7 182 | 25.4 | 44.1 | 3.0 | 0.0 | 7.6 | 3.5 | 1 157 | 28 | 13 | 443 | 19.0 | 79.1 | 1.9 |
| Norton | 25.8 | 4 764 | 39.6 | 26.7 | 3.0 | 0.0 | 8.1 | 20.3 | 3 737 | 28 | 24 | 877 | 20.6 | 77.8 | 1.7 |
| Osage | 53.0 | 3 222 | 54.3 | 2.1 | 4.6 | 0.2 | 9.1 | 35.2 | 2 140 | 77 | 70 | 1 195 | 33.6 | 63.9 | 2.5 |
| Osborne | 11.5 | 2 978 | 35.5 | 5.5 | 7.2 | 0.0 | 15.0 | 3.7 | 958 | 30 | 17 | 325 | 20.9 | 77.2 | 1.9 |
| Ottawa | 22.9 | 3 818 | 52.2 | 3.7 | 6.2 | 0.0 | 12.1 | 31.7 | 5 282 | 23 | 26 | 448 | 22.8 | 75.3 | 1.9 |
| Pawnee | 22.8 | 3 553 | 54.7 | 3.3 | 4.5 | 0.0 | 10.0 | 4.8 | 744 | 43 | 30 | 1 864 | 30.6 | 67.6 | 1.8 |
| Phillips | 26.1 | 4 877 | 41.7 | 3.9 | 3.0 | 7.6 | 10.4 | 8.1 | 1 508 | 42 | 24 | 785 | 19.7 | 78.9 | 1.4 |
| Pottawatomie | 74.3 | 3 832 | 54.6 | 7.2 | 3.1 | 0.0 | 9.9 | 93.7 | 4 831 | 49 | 94 | 1 300 | 26.4 | 70.4 | 3.1 |
| Pratt | 42.8 | 4 538 | 60.6 | 3.0 | 4.6 | 0.1 | 7.8 | 40.6 | 4 309 | 35 | 42 | 1 192 | 30.9 | 67.4 | 1.8 |
| Rawlins | 7.9 | 3 098 | 50.0 | 3.6 | 4.3 | 0.0 | 11.9 | 2.3 | 890 | 20 | 11 | 330 | 17.6 | 80.5 | 1.9 |
| Reno | 213.8 | 3 385 | 60.6 | 1.7 | 4.3 | 0.1 | 5.9 | 274.0 | 4 339 | 195 | 278 | 5 474 | 37.4 | 60.8 | 1.8 |
| Republic | 20.8 | 4 238 | 42.9 | 4.4 | 2.8 | 0.1 | 11.7 | 13.2 | 2 700 | 34 | 21 | 544 | 24.0 | 74.1 | 2.0 |
| Rice | 43.5 | 4 312 | 46.2 | 19.7 | 3.7 | 0.0 | 10.3 | 22.3 | 2 216 | 46 | 43 | 1 051 | 28.9 | 69.1 | 1.9 |
| Riley | 142.1 | 2 056 | 49.4 | 1.2 | 7.6 | 0.0 | 5.9 | 179.6 | 2 600 | 514 | 322 | 10 773 | 45.6 | 52.7 | 1.7 |
| Rooks | 29.8 | 5 778 | 34.4 | 21.7 | 2.8 | 8.9 | 8.1 | 12.9 | 2 509 | 25 | 22 | 638 | 18.1 | 79.9 | 2.0 |
| Rush | 17.1 | 5 325 | 38.4 | 21.6 | 3.2 | 0.0 | 14.6 | 0.3 | 101 | 25 | 14 | 340 | 28.3 | 68.8 | 2.9 |
| Russell | 27.2 | 4 043 | 43.4 | 4.7 | 4.0 | 0.2 | 12.0 | 13.2 | 1 966 | 39 | 30 | 672 | 22.4 | 76.2 | 1.5 |
| Saline | 175.1 | 3 207 | 49.0 | 1.5 | 4.7 | 0.0 | 4.5 | 140.0 | 2 565 | 272 | 241 | 4 030 | 35.9 | 62.2 | 1.9 |
| Scott | 17.1 | 3 738 | 51.7 | 4.5 | 4.2 | 0.0 | 7.4 | 18.3 | 4 008 | 21 | 21 | 354 | 14.7 | 83.7 | 1.6 |
| Sedgwick | 1 510.6 | 3 173 | 50.7 | 3.9 | 7.5 | 0.6 | 4.4 | 2 929.0 | 6 153 | 5 658 | 4 980 | 25 806 | 42.7 | 55.4 | 1.8 |
| Seward | 131.0 | 5 667 | 44.3 | 27.5 | 2.7 | 0.0 | 3.5 | 70.0 | 3 029 | 95 | 100 | 2 298 | 28.0 | 71.0 | 1.0 |
| Shawnee | 662.5 | 3 819 | 53.2 | 1.7 | 5.9 | 0.3 | 2.9 | 1 077.0 | 6 209 | 3 529 | 1 003 | 19 916 | 49.0 | 49.3 | 1.7 |
| Sheridan | 9.0 | 3 594 | 44.0 | 8.2 | 2.5 | 0.4 | 12.3 | 0.6 | 247 | 15 | 11 | 318 | 18.5 | 80.5 | 1.0 |
| Sherman | 27.9 | 4 675 | 51.3 | 3.5 | 3.1 | 0.2 | 6.9 | 26.1 | 4 375 | 59 | 26 | 680 | 25.4 | 72.4 | 2.1 |
| Smith | 14.1 | 3 568 | 50.6 | 5.1 | 2.7 | 0.1 | 11.4 | 4.7 | 1 198 | 35 | 17 | 347 | 20.2 | 78.0 | 1.8 |
| Stafford | 23.7 | 5 396 | 48.3 | 14.8 | 3.3 | 0.2 | 10.2 | 4.8 | 1 096 | 42 | 19 | 652 | 26.1 | 72.1 | 1.8 |
| Stanton | 14.7 | 6 805 | 34.3 | 27.6 | 2.3 | 0.0 | 11.4 | 1.4 | 636 | 11 | 10 | 312 | 22.7 | 75.9 | 1.3 |
| Stevens | 37.7 | 7 448 | 41.2 | 21.3 | 3.9 | 2.4 | 9.7 | 11.1 | 2 201 | 25 | 24 | 691 | 13.3 | 85.3 | 1.4 |
| Sumner | 92.1 | 3 857 | 44.7 | 17.5 | 1.8 | 0.0 | 9.9 | 98.2 | 4 112 | 81 | 102 | 1 802 | 32.4 | 65.2 | 2.4 |
| Thomas | 39.5 | 5 400 | 62.4 | 1.6 | 3.6 | 0.2 | 4.8 | 8.9 | 1 212 | 38 | 34 | 1 019 | 21.4 | 77.2 | 1.3 |
| Trego | 18.5 | 6 327 | 25.2 | 41.5 | 1.1 | 0.0 | 7.9 | 14.6 | 5 003 | 16 | 13 | 466 | 25.1 | 73.3 | 1.6 |
| Wabaunsee | 19.7 | 2 871 | 54.2 | 1.3 | 4.3 | 0.3 | 10.9 | 25.8 | 3 759 | 28 | 30 | 492 | 29.4 | 68.0 | 2.6 |
| Wallace | 7.0 | 4 815 | 58.0 | 2.5 | 3.5 | 0.0 | 12.6 | 2.1 | 1 408 | 14 | 0 | 156 | 11.9 | 85.8 | 2.2 |
| Washington | 25.9 | 4 441 | 52.5 | 13.4 | 1.3 | 0.3 | 10.6 | 5.7 | 984 | 53 | 25 | 719 | 22.1 | 75.4 | 2.4 |
| Wichita | 15.0 | 6 835 | 34.3 | 34.0 | 3.4 | 0.3 | 9.5 | 3.7 | 1 668 | 15 | 10 | 273 | 16.0 | 82.4 | 1.6 |
| Wilson | 35.8 | 3 647 | 51.8 | 19.5 | 3.9 | 0.2 | 6.6 | 16.8 | 1 711 | 40 | 40 | 899 | 28.4 | 69.2 | 2.5 |
| Woodson | 10.3 | 3 103 | 47.5 | 2.8 | 5.8 | 0.2 | 12.7 | 3.7 | 1 127 | 15 | 14 | 234 | 32.0 | 66.0 | 2.0 |
| Wyandotte | 774.6 | 5 031 | 43.1 | 2.3 | 6.7 | 0.0 | 4.0 | 3 261.3 | 21 183 | 1 849 | 681 | 16 267 | 69.7 | 28.9 | 1.4 |
| **KENTUCKY** | X | X | X | X | X | X | X | X | X | 40 949 | 60 002 | 284 812 | 41.2 | 57.4 | 1.4 |
| Adair | 60.0 | 3 367 | 39.5 | 42.2 | 2.0 | 0.0 | 3.4 | 86.2 | 4 832 | 48 | 61 | 949 | 22.9 | 75.5 | 1.6 |
| Allen | 36.6 | 1 935 | 66.2 | 3.1 | 5.0 | 0.1 | 3.9 | 33.1 | 1 751 | 41 | 66 | 792 | 27.4 | 71.2 | 1.5 |
| Anderson | 55.1 | 2 594 | 73.0 | 2.6 | 3.7 | 0.1 | 2.5 | 89.9 | 4 232 | 35 | 71 | 982 | 32.8 | 65.2 | 1.9 |
| Ballard | 27.7 | 3 336 | 50.5 | 4.7 | 3.2 | 0.0 | 4.8 | 154.2 | 18 567 | 31 | 27 | 408 | 35.1 | 62.5 | 2.4 |
| Barren | 99.2 | 2 409 | 64.9 | 0.9 | 4.2 | 0.1 | 4.4 | 153.2 | 3 719 | 113 | 138 | 2 303 | 32.3 | 66.2 | 1.4 |
| Bath | 21.5 | 1 854 | 70.4 | 4.3 | 2.2 | 0.0 | 2.0 | 18.5 | 1 599 | 27 | 38 | 519 | 48.6 | 49.2 | 2.2 |
| Bell | 69.6 | 2 402 | 62.2 | 1.7 | 3.5 | 0.0 | 3.6 | 45.4 | 1 566 | 159 | 94 | 1 863 | 29.0 | 69.6 | 1.4 |
| Boone | 292.9 | 2 604 | 52.7 | 1.4 | 4.7 | 1.9 | 5.5 | 957.8 | 8 517 | 1 333 | 397 | 5 398 | 32.1 | 66.6 | 1.3 |
| Bourbon | 50.9 | 2 575 | 55.6 | 2.5 | 3.9 | 0.1 | 4.1 | 55.0 | 2 785 | 41 | 65 | 1 040 | 40.6 | 57.9 | 1.5 |
| Boyd | 120.5 | 2 485 | 51.0 | 3.5 | 4.2 | 0.0 | 5.0 | 252.7 | 5 212 | 484 | 161 | 3 346 | 43.0 | 55.3 | 1.7 |
| Boyle | 74.5 | 2 598 | 53.0 | 1.9 | 4.9 | 0.3 | 3.3 | 227.5 | 7 936 | 65 | 93 | 1 842 | 37.7 | 60.9 | 1.3 |
| Bracken | 17.2 | 2 004 | 60.1 | 1.5 | 2.9 | 0.0 | 7.4 | 14.2 | 1 657 | 27 | 28 | 414 | 36.5 | 60.8 | 2.7 |
| Breathitt | 36.6 | 2 338 | 62.9 | 0.1 | 2.6 | 0.0 | 5.0 | 30.7 | 1 964 | 56 | 45 | 1 025 | 43.8 | 53.1 | 3.1 |
| Breckinridge | 43.7 | 2 291 | 52.5 | 0.5 | 2.1 | 0.9 | 5.9 | 237.6 | 12 448 | 66 | 66 | 802 | 36.5 | 62.0 | 1.5 |
| Bullitt | 130.1 | 1 760 | 68.0 | 1.8 | 4.9 | 0.0 | 2.4 | 128.0 | 1 731 | 66 | 245 | 2 485 | 33.1 | 65.4 | 1.5 |
| Butler | 28.5 | 2 151 | 56.3 | 2.0 | 2.6 | 0.0 | 5.1 | 60.5 | 4 562 | 32 | 42 | 627 | 29.3 | 69.6 | 1.1 |
| Caldwell | 24.6 | 1 928 | 58.8 | 1.1 | 4.7 | 0.0 | 5.3 | 46.1 | 3 607 | 36 | 42 | 688 | 35.7 | 62.4 | 2.0 |
| Calloway | 148.0 | 4 090 | 21.9 | 62.6 | 2.3 | 0.0 | 2.0 | 118.2 | 3 266 | 77 | 122 | 5 552 | 40.0 | 58.4 | 1.6 |
| Campbell | 219.3 | 2 524 | 53.0 | 0.5 | 6.8 | 0.2 | 5.1 | 585.2 | 6 737 | 373 | 296 | 6 202 | 38.8 | 59.7 | 1.6 |
| Carlisle | 9.4 | 1 810 | 64.8 | 4.3 | 1.9 | 0.0 | 7.6 | 2.9 | 567 | 16 | 16 | 244 | 33.6 | 64.9 | 1.5 |
| Carroll | 157.5 | 14 966 | 10.3 | 0.4 | 0.6 | 0.0 | 1.0 | 5 108.1 | 485 237 | 36 | 36 | 706 | 44.8 | 53.0 | 2.3 |
| Carter | 56.3 | 2 053 | 73.4 | 4.1 | 3.0 | 0.0 | 3.4 | 51.2 | 1 867 | 59 | 90 | 1 381 | 44.0 | 53.5 | 2.5 |
| Casey | 53.5 | 3 308 | 49.8 | 24.1 | 1.6 | 0.0 | 4.1 | 55.4 | 3 427 | 27 | 52 | 720 | 20.5 | 78.5 | 1.0 |
| Christian | 129.7 | 1 604 | 54.4 | 0.4 | 5.4 | 0.1 | 3.5 | 455.8 | 5 637 | 5 061 | 34 134 | 3 892 | 39.0 | 60.1 | 0.9 |
| Clark | 82.6 | 2 324 | 43.6 | 0.6 | 4.7 | 0.1 | 3.2 | 124.7 | 3 507 | 100 | 116 | 1 567 | 36.8 | 61.8 | 1.4 |

1. Based on the resident population estimated as of July 1 of the year shown.   2. © 2013 Election Data Services, Inc. All rights reserved.

# Table B. States and Counties — Land Area and Population

| STATE/ County code | CBSA code[1] | County type[2] | STATE County | Land area[3] (sq km) 2010 | Total persons | Rank | Per square kilometer | White | Black | American Indian, Alaska Native | Asian and Pacific Islander | Percent Hispanic or Latino[4] | Under 5 years | 5 to 17 years | 18 to 24 years | 25 to 34 years | 35 to 44 years | 45 to 54 years |
|---|---|---|---|---|---|---|---|---|---|---|---|---|---|---|---|---|---|---|
| | | | | 1 | 2 | 3 | 4 | 5 | 6 | 7 | 8 | 9 | 10 | 11 | 12 | 13 | 14 | 15 |
| | | | KENTUCKY—Cont'd | | | | | | | | | | | | | | | |
| 21 051 | ... | 7 | Clay | 1 215 | 21 556 | 1 751 | 17.7 | 93.5 | 4.6 | 0.6 | 0.3 | 1.9 | 6.0 | 15.8 | 8.9 | 14.8 | 15.2 | 14.6 |
| 21 053 | ... | 9 | Clinton | 511 | 10 285 | 2 417 | 20.1 | 96.7 | 0.8 | 0.8 | 0.4 | 2.4 | 6.4 | 17.2 | 7.2 | 11.0 | 12.7 | 14.6 |
| 21 055 | ... | 6 | Crittenden | 932 | 9 280 | 2 495 | 10.0 | 97.9 | 1.2 | 0.8 | 0.4 | 0.5 | 6.4 | 16.0 | 7.0 | 11.1 | 11.7 | 14.6 |
| 21 057 | ... | 9 | Cumberland | 790 | 6 819 | 2 698 | 8.6 | 96.0 | 3.5 | 0.5 | 0.2 | 1.0 | 6.3 | 16.1 | 7.9 | 9.9 | 11.9 | 15.1 |
| 21 059 | 36980 | 3 | Daviess | 1 187 | 97 847 | 599 | 82.4 | 91.5 | 6.0 | 0.4 | 1.0 | 2.6 | 6.9 | 17.4 | 8.7 | 12.5 | 12.3 | 14.7 |
| 21 061 | 14540 | 3 | Edmonson | 784 | 12 071 | 2 294 | 15.4 | 97.0 | 1.9 | 0.8 | 0.4 | 0.8 | 5.5 | 16.3 | 8.8 | 11.4 | 12.5 | 14.3 |
| 21 063 | ... | 9 | Elliott | 607 | 7 780 | 2 618 | 12.8 | 95.4 | 3.6 | 0.4 | 0.2 | 0.8 | 5.4 | 14.6 | 8.4 | 13.9 | 14.8 | 14.8 |
| 21 065 | ... | 6 | Estill | 655 | 14 493 | 2 140 | 22.1 | 98.6 | 0.5 | 0.6 | 0.2 | 0.7 | 5.7 | 16.6 | 7.4 | 11.9 | 13.4 | 15.5 |
| 21 067 | 30460 | 2 | Fayette | 735 | 305 489 | 211 | 415.6 | 75.0 | 15.6 | 0.7 | 4.0 | 7.0 | 6.4 | 14.7 | 14.6 | 16.4 | 13.2 | 13.1 |
| 21 069 | ... | 7 | Fleming | 903 | 14 560 | 2 136 | 16.1 | 97.0 | 1.8 | 0.4 | 0.3 | 1.2 | 6.6 | 17.8 | 7.6 | 11.5 | 13.4 | 14.5 |
| 21 071 | ... | 7 | Floyd | 1 019 | 38 949 | 1 197 | 38.2 | 98.2 | 1.0 | 0.4 | 0.3 | 0.6 | 6.3 | 16.1 | 8.4 | 12.4 | 13.3 | 15.1 |
| 21 073 | 23180 | 4 | Franklin | 538 | 49 804 | 984 | 92.6 | 85.0 | 11.7 | 0.7 | 1.8 | 2.8 | 6.0 | 15.4 | 9.6 | 12.4 | 13.1 | 15.0 |
| 21 075 | 46460 | 7 | Fulton | 532 | 6 525 | 2 720 | 12.3 | 74.9 | 24.4 | 0.7 | 0.9 | 1.0 | 6.2 | 14.5 | 8.5 | 12.0 | 11.8 | 14.1 |
| 21 077 | 17140 | 1 | Gallatin | 262 | 8 479 | 2 566 | 32.4 | 93.5 | 2.5 | 0.7 | 0.5 | 4.5 | 6.9 | 20.0 | 8.2 | 11.4 | 13.6 | 15.7 |
| 21 079 | ... | 6 | Garrard | 596 | 16 913 | 1 989 | 28.4 | 95.1 | 2.5 | 0.4 | 0.3 | 2.4 | 6.0 | 16.7 | 6.9 | 11.5 | 13.4 | 16.4 |
| 21 081 | 17140 | 1 | Grant | 668 | 24 485 | 1 621 | 36.7 | 95.9 | 1.3 | 0.6 | 0.7 | 2.5 | 7.6 | 20.1 | 8.5 | 12.9 | 14.1 | 14.5 |
| 21 083 | 32460 | 7 | Graves | 1 429 | 37 544 | 1 230 | 26.3 | 88.7 | 5.7 | 0.7 | 0.6 | 5.9 | 6.6 | 17.8 | 8.1 | 11.9 | 12.1 | 14.0 |
| 21 085 | ... | 6 | Grayson | 1 286 | 25 964 | 1 565 | 20.2 | 97.3 | 1.5 | 0.7 | 0.4 | 1.1 | 6.2 | 17.4 | 7.9 | 12.1 | 12.7 | 14.5 |
| 21 087 | ... | 8 | Green | 741 | 11 315 | 2 338 | 15.3 | 95.8 | 2.7 | 0.8 | 0.4 | 1.6 | 5.8 | 16.6 | 6.9 | 11.1 | 12.4 | 15.4 |
| 21 089 | 26580 | 2 | Greenup | 892 | 36 707 | 1 255 | 41.2 | 97.5 | 1.1 | 0.7 | 0.7 | 0.9 | 5.4 | 16.6 | 7.3 | 11.0 | 13.2 | 14.3 |
| 21 091 | 36980 | 9 | Hancock | 486 | 8 677 | 2 552 | 17.9 | 97.2 | 1.7 | 0.5 | 0.4 | 1.2 | 6.5 | 19.1 | 7.4 | 10.9 | 13.4 | 15.2 |
| 21 093 | 21060 | 3 | Hardin | 1 614 | 107 025 | 556 | 66.3 | 80.0 | 13.5 | 1.0 | 3.3 | 5.2 | 7.2 | 18.4 | 9.8 | 13.8 | 13.3 | 15.0 |
| 21 095 | ... | 7 | Harlan | 1 206 | 28 543 | 1 466 | 23.7 | 96.4 | 2.7 | 0.5 | 0.5 | 0.8 | 6.4 | 16.4 | 8.4 | 11.8 | 12.7 | 14.6 |
| 21 097 | ... | 6 | Harrison | 793 | 18 624 | 1 892 | 23.5 | 95.5 | 2.9 | 0.5 | 0.5 | 1.8 | 6.1 | 17.6 | 7.6 | 10.8 | 13.2 | 15.8 |
| 21 099 | ... | 8 | Hart | 1 067 | 18 366 | 1 904 | 17.2 | 93.1 | 5.5 | 0.6 | 0.4 | 1.5 | 6.3 | 18.2 | 8.4 | 10.8 | 12.3 | 15.9 |
| 21 101 | 21780 | 2 | Henderson | 1 131 | 46 513 | 1 040 | 41.1 | 89.5 | 8.9 | 0.5 | 0.7 | 1.9 | 6.6 | 16.8 | 8.0 | 12.8 | 12.5 | 15.2 |
| 21 103 | 31140 | 1 | Henry | 741 | 15 318 | 2 087 | 20.7 | 93.4 | 3.5 | 0.7 | 0.5 | 3.2 | 5.9 | 18.6 | 7.2 | 10.9 | 13.2 | 15.4 |
| 21 105 | ... | 9 | Hickman | 627 | 4 754 | 2 856 | 7.6 | 88.4 | 10.3 | 0.6 | 0.5 | 1.4 | 5.2 | 15.8 | 6.9 | 9.9 | 11.3 | 15.1 |
| 21 107 | 31580 | 4 | Hopkins | 1 404 | 46 718 | 1 035 | 33.3 | 91.0 | 7.7 | 0.6 | 0.8 | 1.6 | 6.3 | 16.7 | 7.8 | 12.1 | 12.7 | 14.7 |
| 21 109 | ... | 9 | Jackson | 894 | 13 331 | 2 222 | 14.9 | 98.8 | 0.4 | 0.4 | 0.2 | 0.8 | 6.0 | 17.1 | 7.9 | 12.3 | 13.9 | 15.0 |
| 21 111 | 31140 | 1 | Jefferson | 985 | 750 828 | 78 | 762.3 | 72.2 | 21.8 | 0.7 | 2.8 | 4.5 | 6.6 | 16.4 | 9.0 | 14.2 | 12.8 | 14.6 |
| 21 113 | 30460 | 2 | Jessamine | 446 | 49 635 | 988 | 111.3 | 92.7 | 4.1 | 0.7 | 1.4 | 2.8 | 7.3 | 18.3 | 9.9 | 13.1 | 13.4 | 14.4 |
| 21 115 | ... | 7 | Johnson | 678 | 23 383 | 1 669 | 34.5 | 98.6 | 0.6 | 0.5 | 0.6 | 0.5 | 5.8 | 16.7 | 8.3 | 11.8 | 13.6 | 14.9 |
| 21 117 | 17140 | 1 | Kenton | 415 | 161 711 | 388 | 389.7 | 91.3 | 5.8 | 0.5 | 1.4 | 2.8 | 7.3 | 17.5 | 8.6 | 15.1 | 13.2 | 14.8 |
| 21 119 | ... | 9 | Knott | 910 | 16 124 | 2 037 | 17.7 | 98.3 | 1.0 | 0.4 | 0.2 | 0.7 | 6.0 | 15.2 | 10.1 | 11.1 | 13.1 | 16.3 |
| 21 121 | ... | 7 | Knox | 1 001 | 31 735 | 1 396 | 31.7 | 97.3 | 1.5 | 0.8 | 0.4 | 1.0 | 6.8 | 17.8 | 9.6 | 11.5 | 12.9 | 14.1 |
| 21 123 | 21060 | 3 | Larue | 677 | 14 151 | 2 165 | 20.9 | 93.4 | 4.0 | 0.7 | 0.4 | 2.9 | 6.1 | 17.4 | 8.2 | 12.2 | 12.0 | 15.2 |
| 21 125 | 30940 | 7 | Laurel | 1 124 | 59 462 | 870 | 52.9 | 97.0 | 1.1 | 0.8 | 0.7 | 1.3 | 6.4 | 17.7 | 8.2 | 13.0 | 13.8 | 14.8 |
| 21 127 | ... | 6 | Lawrence | 1 076 | 15 848 | 2 053 | 14.7 | 98.8 | 0.6 | 0.5 | 0.3 | 0.6 | 6.8 | 16.2 | 8.5 | 11.8 | 12.7 | 14.7 |
| 21 129 | ... | 9 | Lee | 541 | 7 706 | 2 626 | 14.2 | 96.1 | 2.7 | 0.7 | 0.3 | 0.9 | 4.4 | 15.3 | 7.9 | 14.5 | 14.4 | 16.2 |
| 21 131 | ... | 9 | Leslie | 1 038 | 11 170 | 2 349 | 10.8 | 99.0 | 0.5 | 0.5 | 0.3 | 0.4 | 6.2 | 15.2 | 8.6 | 12.3 | 13.1 | 16.7 |
| 21 133 | ... | 9 | Letcher | 875 | 23 952 | 1 646 | 27.4 | 98.7 | 0.6 | 0.4 | 0.3 | 0.6 | 6.0 | 16.1 | 7.7 | 12.5 | 12.7 | 15.6 |
| 21 135 | 32500 | 8 | Lewis | 1 251 | 13 835 | 2 185 | 11.1 | 98.8 | 0.6 | 0.4 | 0.2 | 0.6 | 6.2 | 17.1 | 8.0 | 11.2 | 13.1 | 15.5 |
| 21 137 | 19220 | 7 | Lincoln | 865 | 24 461 | 1 626 | 28.3 | 95.7 | 3.0 | 0.7 | 0.4 | 1.6 | 6.5 | 18.1 | 7.8 | 11.6 | 13.3 | 14.7 |
| 21 139 | 37140 | 9 | Livingston | 811 | 9 423 | 2 479 | 11.6 | 97.6 | 0.7 | 0.9 | 0.4 | 1.4 | 5.6 | 14.9 | 7.2 | 10.2 | 11.9 | 15.8 |
| 21 141 | ... | 6 | Logan | 1 430 | 26 646 | 1 541 | 18.6 | 90.4 | 7.5 | 0.6 | 0.5 | 2.4 | 6.1 | 17.8 | 7.8 | 11.8 | 12.1 | 14.9 |
| 21 143 | ... | 8 | Lyon | 554 | 8 351 | 2 574 | 15.1 | 92.9 | 5.8 | 0.6 | 0.5 | 1.3 | 4.1 | 11.3 | 6.5 | 11.2 | 12.8 | 15.7 |
| 21 145 | 37140 | 3 | McCracken | 644 | 65 549 | 806 | 101.8 | 85.8 | 12.0 | 0.7 | 1.2 | 2.2 | 5.8 | 16.3 | 7.3 | 12.1 | 12.4 | 14.8 |
| 21 147 | ... | 9 | McCreary | 1 105 | 18 069 | 1 917 | 16.4 | 91.3 | 6.0 | 1.5 | 0.4 | 2.2 | 6.0 | 16.3 | 9.2 | 14.0 | 15.0 | 14.5 |
| 21 149 | 36980 | 3 | McLean | 654 | 9 506 | 2 472 | 14.5 | 97.7 | 1.1 | 0.5 | 0.2 | 1.2 | 5.8 | 17.4 | 7.4 | 11.0 | 12.7 | 15.1 |
| 21 151 | 40080 | 4 | Madison | 1 133 | 84 786 | 664 | 74.8 | 91.9 | 5.5 | 0.8 | 1.4 | 2.2 | 5.9 | 15.3 | 17.4 | 12.9 | 12.7 | 13.0 |
| 21 153 | ... | 9 | Magoffin | 799 | 13 041 | 2 238 | 16.3 | 98.6 | 0.4 | 0.5 | 0.2 | 0.8 | 5.8 | 17.6 | 8.4 | 12.1 | 13.9 | 15.7 |
| 21 155 | ... | 6 | Marion | 888 | 20 090 | 1 836 | 22.6 | 88.3 | 9.3 | 0.5 | 0.8 | 2.7 | 6.8 | 17.6 | 7.8 | 14.1 | 13.1 | 15.2 |
| 21 157 | ... | 7 | Marshall | 780 | 31 344 | 1 406 | 40.2 | 97.9 | 0.6 | 0.7 | 0.4 | 1.2 | 5.4 | 15.3 | 7.0 | 10.6 | 12.2 | 15.0 |
| 21 159 | ... | 8 | Martin | 595 | 12 743 | 2 257 | 21.4 | 89.3 | 7.2 | 0.7 | 0.2 | 3.1 | 5.4 | 15.7 | 8.6 | 16.7 | 15.4 | 14.6 |
| 21 161 | 32500 | 6 | Mason | 622 | 17 512 | 1 951 | 28.2 | 91.4 | 7.3 | 0.6 | 0.8 | 1.5 | 6.7 | 17.4 | 8.0 | 11.1 | 13.0 | 14.6 |
| 21 163 | 31140 | 1 | Meade | 791 | 29 237 | 1 444 | 37.0 | 91.3 | 4.8 | 1.2 | 1.5 | 3.5 | 7.3 | 19.6 | 9.0 | 14.4 | 13.3 | 14.7 |
| 21 165 | 34460 | 9 | Menifee | 527 | 6 220 | 2 743 | 11.8 | 96.7 | 2.6 | 0.6 | 0.4 | 0.9 | 5.5 | 17.5 | 9.5 | 10.0 | 12.3 | 14.6 |
| 21 167 | ... | 9 | Mercer | 644 | 21 261 | 1 771 | 33.0 | 93.4 | 4.6 | 0.6 | 0.7 | 2.4 | 6.2 | 16.9 | 7.3 | 10.8 | 12.4 | 15.7 |
| 21 169 | 23980 | 9 | Metcalfe | 750 | 9 969 | 2 446 | 13.3 | 96.7 | 1.9 | 0.5 | 0.2 | 1.4 | 6.3 | 17.8 | 8.1 | 10.6 | 12.6 | 14.7 |
| 21 171 | ... | 9 | Monroe | 853 | 10 821 | 2 372 | 12.7 | 94.7 | 2.7 | 0.6 | 0.2 | 2.8 | 5.7 | 17.1 | 7.8 | 10.8 | 12.2 | 15.2 |
| 21 173 | 34460 | 6 | Montgomery | 511 | 26 902 | 1 533 | 52.6 | 93.9 | 3.4 | 0.5 | 0.5 | 2.7 | 6.9 | 17.5 | 8.0 | 12.9 | 14.4 | 14.3 |
| 21 175 | ... | 7 | Morgan | 987 | 13 668 | 2 200 | 13.8 | 94.2 | 4.8 | 0.6 | 0.4 | 0.8 | 5.4 | 14.7 | 8.7 | 15.5 | 14.6 | 14.6 |
| 21 177 | 16420 | 6 | Muhlenberg | 1 210 | 31 181 | 1 408 | 25.8 | 93.7 | 5.2 | 0.5 | 0.3 | 1.2 | 5.4 | 16.2 | 8.5 | 12.0 | 13.1 | 14.7 |
| 21 179 | 31140 | 1 | Nelson | 1 081 | 44 319 | 1 080 | 41.0 | 92.2 | 5.9 | 0.5 | 0.7 | 2.0 | 6.7 | 18.9 | 8.1 | 12.9 | 13.2 | 15.5 |
| 21 181 | ... | 8 | Nicholas | 505 | 7 000 | 2 683 | 13.9 | 97.4 | 0.9 | 0.5 | 0.4 | 1.6 | 6.3 | 17.8 | 6.9 | 11.5 | 13.6 | 15.3 |

1. CBSA = Core Based Statistical Area. See Appendix A for explanation. See Appendix B for list of metropolitan areas with component counties.   2. County type code from the Economic Research Service of USDA Rural-Urban Continuum Codes. See Appendix A for definition.   3. Dry land or land partially or temporarily covered by water.   4. May be of any race.

# Table B. States and Counties — **Population and Households**

| STATE County | Population, 2011 (cont.) Age (percent) (cont.) | | | | Population change and components of change, 2000–2012 | | | | | | | Households, 2010 | | | | |
| | | | | | Total persons | | Percent change | | Components of change, 2010–2012 | | | | | | Percent | |
| | 55 to 64 years | 65 to 74 years | 75 years and over | Percent female | 2000 | 2010 | 2000–2010 | 2010–2012 | Births | Deaths | Net migration | Number | Percent change, 2000–2010 | Persons per house-hold | Female family house-holder[1] | One per-son |
| | 16 | 17 | 18 | 19 | 20 | 21 | 22 | 23 | 24 | 25 | 26 | 27 | 28 | 29 | 30 | 31 |
| KENTUCKY—Cont'd | | | | | | | | | | | | | | | | |
| Clay | 12.1 | 7.7 | 4.9 | 46.5 | 24 556 | 21 730 | -11.5 | -0.8 | 599 | 583 | -191 | 7 732 | -9.6 | 2.52 | 14.8 | 25.3 |
| Clinton | 14.0 | 10.1 | 6.8 | 50.1 | 9 634 | 10 272 | 6.6 | 0.1 | 277 | 268 | -7 | 4 358 | 6.7 | 2.33 | 11.4 | 30.7 |
| Crittenden | 14.5 | 10.9 | 7.6 | 49.9 | 9 384 | 9 315 | -0.7 | -0.4 | 222 | 245 | -8 | 3 781 | -1.3 | 2.41 | 9.9 | 28.3 |
| Cumberland | 13.9 | 10.3 | 8.5 | 51.0 | 7 147 | 6 856 | -4.1 | -0.5 | 181 | 267 | 51 | 2 883 | -3.1 | 2.35 | 11.1 | 29.6 |
| Daviess | 12.9 | 7.8 | 6.9 | 51.5 | 91 545 | 96 656 | 5.6 | 1.2 | 2 979 | 2 177 | 400 | 38 619 | 7.2 | 2.44 | 12.9 | 28.3 |
| Edmonson | 14.5 | 9.9 | 6.7 | 50.0 | 11 644 | 12 161 | 4.4 | -0.7 | 247 | 313 | -56 | 4 857 | 4.5 | 2.44 | 9.7 | 25.0 |
| Elliott | 14.1 | 8.4 | 5.6 | 43.7 | 6 748 | 7 852 | 16.4 | -0.9 | 150 | 144 | -108 | 2 773 | 5.1 | 2.45 | 11.8 | 26.1 |
| Estill | 13.9 | 9.5 | 6.1 | 50.6 | 15 307 | 14 672 | -4.1 | -1.2 | 354 | 411 | -128 | 5 984 | -2.0 | 2.43 | 13.4 | 27.1 |
| Fayette | 11.1 | 5.8 | 4.8 | 50.8 | 260 512 | 295 803 | 13.5 | 3.3 | 8 916 | 4 546 | 5 362 | 123 043 | 13.6 | 2.30 | 12.3 | 32.7 |
| Fleming | 13.6 | 8.9 | 6.2 | 51.0 | 13 792 | 14 348 | 4.0 | 1.5 | 448 | 392 | 149 | 5 729 | 6.7 | 2.50 | 10.2 | 25.4 |
| Floyd | 14.6 | 8.2 | 5.6 | 51.1 | 42 441 | 39 451 | -7.0 | -1.3 | 1 176 | 1 181 | -504 | 16 060 | -4.9 | 2.41 | 13.5 | 27.5 |
| Franklin | 14.3 | 8.1 | 6.2 | 51.4 | 47 687 | 49 285 | 3.4 | 1.1 | 1 311 | 1 067 | 273 | 20 662 | 3.8 | 2.29 | 13.7 | 31.5 |
| Fulton | 14.4 | 10.2 | 8.4 | 49.9 | 7 752 | 6 813 | -12.1 | -4.2 | 184 | 251 | -232 | 2 864 | -11.5 | 2.22 | 16.5 | 34.2 |
| Gallatin | 12.4 | 7.8 | 4.1 | 49.5 | 7 870 | 8 589 | 9.1 | -1.3 | 291 | 198 | -208 | 3 160 | 8.9 | 2.69 | 12.9 | 22.3 |
| Garrard | 13.8 | 8.9 | 6.3 | 50.7 | 14 792 | 16 912 | 14.3 | 0.0 | 395 | 368 | -24 | 6 668 | 16.1 | 2.52 | 9.8 | 22.4 |
| Grant | 11.2 | 7.1 | 4.1 | 49.8 | 22 384 | 24 662 | 10.2 | -0.7 | 781 | 491 | -472 | 8 614 | 5.4 | 2.81 | 13.4 | 19.8 |
| Graves | 13.1 | 8.9 | 7.4 | 50.8 | 37 028 | 37 121 | 0.3 | 1.1 | 1 172 | 973 | 238 | 14 978 | 0.9 | 2.44 | 10.6 | 27.7 |
| Grayson | 13.8 | 9.0 | 6.3 | 49.3 | 24 053 | 25 746 | 7.0 | 0.8 | 755 | 647 | 116 | 10 082 | 5.1 | 2.48 | 10.7 | 25.5 |
| Green | 14.3 | 9.8 | 7.8 | 50.6 | 11 518 | 11 258 | -2.3 | 0.5 | 254 | 300 | 100 | 4 601 | -2.2 | 2.42 | 9.4 | 26.6 |
| Greenup | 14.3 | 9.7 | 7.7 | 51.7 | 36 891 | 36 910 | 0.1 | -0.5 | 812 | 1 006 | 14 | 14 671 | 0.9 | 2.48 | 11.0 | 24.5 |
| Hancock | 13.5 | 8.4 | 5.6 | 49.4 | 8 392 | 8 565 | 2.1 | 1.3 | 249 | 180 | 49 | 3 285 | 2.2 | 2.58 | 9.4 | 22.6 |
| Hardin | 11.4 | 6.3 | 4.9 | 50.2 | 94 174 | 105 543 | 12.1 | 1.4 | 3 666 | 1 897 | -369 | 39 853 | 15.5 | 2.57 | 12.9 | 24.5 |
| Harlan | 15.1 | 8.4 | 6.2 | 51.2 | 33 202 | 29 278 | -11.8 | -2.5 | 853 | 881 | -713 | 11 789 | -11.3 | 2.43 | 13.9 | 27.8 |
| Harrison | 13.7 | 8.8 | 6.6 | 51.1 | 17 983 | 18 846 | 4.8 | -1.2 | 471 | 485 | -201 | 7 343 | 4.7 | 2.53 | 11.8 | 24.1 |
| Hart | 13.3 | 8.9 | 6.0 | 50.6 | 17 445 | 18 199 | 4.3 | 0.9 | 520 | 410 | 63 | 7 097 | 4.8 | 2.53 | 10.9 | 26.2 |
| Henderson | 13.7 | 7.9 | 6.4 | 51.7 | 44 829 | 46 250 | 3.2 | 0.6 | 1 360 | 1 134 | 68 | 18 705 | 3.4 | 2.41 | 13.1 | 28.0 |
| Henry | 14.2 | 8.8 | 5.8 | 50.5 | 15 060 | 15 416 | 2.4 | -0.6 | 410 | 377 | -131 | 5 963 | 2.0 | 2.57 | 11.8 | 23.0 |
| Hickman | 14.2 | 11.1 | 10.0 | 52.4 | 5 262 | 4 902 | -6.8 | -3.0 | 96 | 173 | -73 | 2 028 | -7.3 | 2.31 | 11.5 | 29.9 |
| Hopkins | 13.9 | 8.8 | 6.9 | 51.2 | 46 519 | 46 920 | 0.9 | -0.4 | 1 235 | 1 196 | -220 | 18 980 | 0.9 | 2.41 | 12.6 | 27.0 |
| Jackson | 13.7 | 8.6 | 5.4 | 50.2 | 13 495 | 13 494 | 0.0 | -1.2 | 332 | 367 | -123 | 5 486 | 3.4 | 2.44 | 11.2 | 26.4 |
| Jefferson | 12.8 | 7.0 | 6.5 | 51.8 | 693 604 | 741 096 | 6.8 | 1.3 | 22 860 | 15 716 | 2 965 | 309 175 | 7.7 | 2.35 | 15.4 | 32.0 |
| Jessamine | 11.8 | 6.6 | 5.2 | 51.2 | 39 041 | 48 586 | 24.4 | 2.2 | 1 499 | 820 | 352 | 17 642 | 27.2 | 2.65 | 12.9 | 20.7 |
| Johnson | 14.6 | 8.6 | 5.7 | 50.7 | 23 445 | 23 356 | -0.4 | 0.1 | 640 | 630 | 29 | 9 362 | 2.8 | 2.44 | 11.5 | 26.2 |
| Kenton | 12.2 | 6.2 | 5.1 | 50.5 | 151 464 | 159 720 | 5.5 | 1.2 | 5 411 | 3 001 | -370 | 62 768 | 5.6 | 2.51 | 13.0 | 28.1 |
| Knott | 14.4 | 8.5 | 5.4 | 50.3 | 17 649 | 16 346 | -7.4 | -1.4 | 441 | 429 | -227 | 6 414 | -4.5 | 2.44 | 12.9 | 27.0 |
| Knox | 12.6 | 9.0 | 5.7 | 51.5 | 31 795 | 31 883 | 0.3 | -0.5 | 941 | 894 | -261 | 12 722 | 2.5 | 2.46 | 14.2 | 28.5 |
| Larue | 12.9 | 8.5 | 7.4 | 50.5 | 13 373 | 14 193 | 6.1 | -0.3 | 369 | 374 | -30 | 5 615 | 6.4 | 2.47 | 11.6 | 25.8 |
| Laurel | 13.0 | 7.9 | 5.2 | 51.0 | 52 715 | 58 849 | 11.6 | 1.0 | 1 642 | 1 283 | 266 | 23 014 | 13.1 | 2.53 | 13.0 | 24.3 |
| Lawrence | 14.6 | 8.9 | 5.8 | 50.4 | 15 569 | 15 860 | 1.9 | -0.1 | 485 | 488 | -10 | 6 239 | 4.8 | 2.52 | 10.6 | 24.9 |
| Lee | 13.9 | 7.6 | 5.8 | 45.2 | 7 916 | 7 887 | -0.4 | -2.3 | 152 | 259 | -71 | 2 910 | -2.5 | 2.36 | 13.7 | 28.8 |
| Leslie | 13.8 | 8.3 | 5.8 | 50.4 | 12 401 | 11 310 | -8.8 | -1.2 | 364 | 387 | -134 | 4 555 | -6.8 | 2.43 | 11.6 | 26.8 |
| Letcher | 15.0 | 8.8 | 5.8 | 50.6 | 25 277 | 24 519 | -3.0 | -2.3 | 650 | 663 | -554 | 10 014 | -0.7 | 2.42 | 12.3 | 26.7 |
| Lewis | 13.7 | 9.1 | 6.0 | 50.1 | 14 092 | 13 870 | -1.6 | -0.3 | 358 | 352 | -37 | 5 497 | 1.4 | 2.50 | 10.7 | 23.7 |
| Lincoln | 12.9 | 8.9 | 6.3 | 50.8 | 23 361 | 24 742 | 5.9 | -1.1 | 770 | 623 | -429 | 9 777 | 6.2 | 2.51 | 12.7 | 24.9 |
| Livingston | 16.0 | 10.9 | 7.4 | 51.1 | 9 804 | 9 519 | -2.9 | -1.0 | 217 | 309 | 0 | 3 985 | -0.3 | 2.37 | 9.1 | 26.0 |
| Logan | 13.3 | 9.4 | 6.7 | 51.3 | 26 573 | 26 835 | 1.0 | -0.7 | 759 | 664 | -268 | 10 666 | 1.5 | 2.49 | 11.3 | 25.9 |
| Lyon | 17.2 | 13.0 | 8.0 | 44.7 | 8 080 | 8 314 | 2.9 | 0.4 | 149 | 290 | 184 | 3 287 | 13.4 | 2.19 | 7.7 | 30.0 |
| McCracken | 14.3 | 8.9 | 8.1 | 52.1 | 65 514 | 65 565 | 0.1 | 0.0 | 1 682 | 1 821 | 159 | 28 227 | 1.8 | 2.28 | 12.6 | 31.9 |
| McCreary | 12.2 | 8.0 | 4.7 | 45.6 | 17 080 | 18 306 | 7.2 | -1.3 | 496 | 393 | -340 | 6 477 | -0.7 | 2.50 | 14.0 | 27.1 |
| McLean | 13.4 | 9.9 | 7.4 | 50.9 | 9 938 | 9 531 | -4.1 | -0.3 | 256 | 267 | -15 | 3 833 | -3.8 | 2.47 | 10.4 | 24.5 |
| Madison | 11.3 | 6.6 | 4.9 | 51.5 | 70 872 | 82 916 | 17.0 | 2.3 | 2 186 | 1 454 | 1 116 | 31 973 | 17.8 | 2.42 | 11.7 | 26.3 |
| Magoffin | 13.2 | 8.3 | 4.9 | 50.0 | 13 332 | 13 333 | 0.0 | -2.2 | 350 | 339 | -302 | 5 309 | 5.7 | 2.49 | 11.7 | 25.0 |
| Marion | 12.0 | 7.2 | 6.1 | 48.4 | 18 212 | 19 820 | 8.8 | 1.4 | 610 | 436 | 77 | 7 358 | 11.3 | 2.52 | 13.2 | 26.8 |
| Marshall | 14.9 | 11.2 | 8.5 | 51.0 | 30 125 | 31 448 | 4.4 | -0.3 | 755 | 942 | 103 | 13 073 | 5.3 | 2.37 | 9.6 | 25.4 |
| Martin | 12.4 | 6.4 | 4.9 | 44.8 | 12 578 | 12 929 | 2.8 | -1.4 | 301 | 344 | -158 | 4 516 | -5.4 | 2.50 | 13.0 | 26.8 |
| Mason | 13.8 | 8.5 | 6.8 | 51.7 | 16 800 | 17 490 | 4.1 | 0.1 | 517 | 446 | -53 | 7 031 | 2.7 | 2.45 | 13.5 | 27.7 |
| Meade | 11.3 | 6.4 | 4.1 | 50.0 | 26 349 | 28 602 | 8.6 | 2.2 | 676 | 473 | 417 | 10 471 | 10.6 | 2.71 | 10.8 | 20.8 |
| Menifee | 14.3 | 10.0 | 6.2 | 50.2 | 6 556 | 6 306 | -3.8 | -1.4 | 135 | 193 | -29 | 2 440 | -3.8 | 2.49 | 9.2 | 25.6 |
| Mercer | 14.4 | 9.4 | 6.8 | 51.2 | 20 817 | 21 331 | 2.5 | -0.3 | 566 | 572 | -52 | 8 682 | 3.1 | 2.44 | 11.6 | 26.1 |
| Metcalfe | 13.2 | 9.4 | 7.2 | 50.7 | 10 037 | 10 099 | 0.6 | -1.3 | 312 | 315 | -137 | 4 055 | 1.0 | 2.46 | 10.4 | 26.8 |
| Monroe | 13.7 | 10.5 | 7.0 | 50.4 | 11 756 | 10 963 | -6.7 | -1.3 | 258 | 379 | -13 | 4 509 | -4.9 | 2.40 | 11.0 | 29.8 |
| Montgomery | 12.9 | 7.5 | 5.6 | 51.2 | 22 554 | 26 499 | 17.5 | 1.5 | 904 | 584 | 88 | 10 435 | 17.2 | 2.51 | 12.6 | 25.1 |
| Morgan | 13.3 | 7.6 | 5.6 | 43.3 | 13 948 | 13 923 | -0.2 | -1.8 | 336 | 364 | -225 | 4 860 | 2.3 | 2.46 | 10.1 | 24.6 |
| Muhlenberg | 13.5 | 9.4 | 7.1 | 49.5 | 31 839 | 31 499 | -1.1 | -1.0 | 762 | 889 | -168 | 12 052 | -2.5 | 2.45 | 11.9 | 24.9 |
| Nelson | 12.9 | 6.9 | 4.9 | 50.8 | 37 477 | 43 437 | 15.9 | 2.0 | 1 292 | 828 | 413 | 16 826 | 20.6 | 2.55 | 13.2 | 24.4 |
| Nicholas | 13.0 | 8.7 | 6.9 | 50.7 | 6 813 | 7 135 | 4.7 | -1.9 | 194 | 251 | -79 | 2 809 | 3.7 | 2.51 | 11.1 | 25.6 |

1. No spouse present.

# Table B. States and Counties — Population, Vital Statistics, Medicare, and Crime

| STATE County | Persons in group quarters, 2010 | Daytime population, 2007–2011 Number | Daytime population, 2007–2011 Employ-ment/resi-dence ratio | Births, 2011 Total | Births, 2011 Rate[1] | Deaths, 2011 Number | Deaths, 2011 Rate[1] | Persons under 65 with no health insurance, 2010 Number | Persons under 65 with no health insurance, 2010 Percent | Medicare, 2012 Eligible for Medicare | Medicare, 2012 Enrolled in Medicare Advantage | Medicare, 2012 Enrolled in a Medicare prescription drug plan | Serious crimes known to police,[2] 2011 Total Number | Serious crimes known to police,[2] 2011 Total Rate[3] |
|---|---|---|---|---|---|---|---|---|---|---|---|---|---|---|
| | 32 | 33 | 34 | 35 | 36 | 37 | 38 | 39 | 40 | 41 | 42 | 43 | 44 | 45 |
| KENTUCKY—Cont'd | | | | | | | | | | | | | | |
| Clay | 2 240 | 21 511 | 0.89 | 256 | 11.8 | 233 | 10.7 | 3 036 | 17.8 | 4 648 | 430 | 3 321 | 217 | 992 |
| Clinton | 136 | 11 042 | 1.22 | 133 | 13.0 | 114 | 11.2 | 1 791 | 21.1 | 2 496 | 295 | 1 710 | NA | NA |
| Crittenden | 210 | 8 180 | 0.68 | 114 | 12.2 | 102 | 10.9 | 1 547 | 20.8 | 2 190 | 189 | 1 236 | 99 | 1 056 |
| Cumberland | 86 | 6 512 | 0.86 | 80 | 11.7 | 118 | 17.3 | 1 273 | 23.0 | 1 664 | 246 | 1 098 | 28 | 406 |
| Daviess | 2 581 | 97 668 | 1.04 | 1 323 | 13.6 | 942 | 9.7 | 12 124 | 15.1 | 19 498 | 2 602 | 11 568 | 3 132 | 3 218 |
| Edmonson | 323 | 9 299 | 0.41 | 108 | 8.9 | 147 | 12.2 | 2 218 | 22.0 | 2 631 | 451 | 1 536 | 84 | 686 |
| Elliott | 1 061 | 6 782 | 0.60 | 70 | 9.1 | 66 | 8.6 | 1 138 | 19.7 | 1 559 | 361 | 793 | NA | NA |
| Estill | 118 | 12 721 | 0.57 | 156 | 10.6 | 180 | 12.3 | 2 351 | 19.1 | 3 323 | 512 | 1 952 | 169 | 1 144 |
| Fayette | 12 804 | 324 475 | 1.21 | 3 950 | 13.1 | 1 945 | 6.4 | 46 721 | 18.5 | 40 377 | 8 316 | 20 011 | 14 680 | 4 929 |
| Fleming | 22 | 12 755 | 0.73 | 199 | 13.7 | 177 | 12.2 | 2 668 | 21.8 | 3 176 | 564 | 1 875 | 63 | 436 |
| Floyd | 790 | 40 292 | 1.05 | 529 | 13.5 | 530 | 13.5 | 6 370 | 18.9 | 10 172 | 1 962 | 6 193 | 200 | 511 |
| Franklin | 2 061 | 59 522 | 1.46 | 603 | 12.2 | 446 | 9.0 | 7 043 | 17.4 | 11 275 | 1 237 | 8 067 | 2 001 | 4 032 |
| Fulton | 445 | 6 872 | 1.01 | 82 | 12.1 | 112 | 16.6 | 942 | 18.1 | 1 695 | 111 | 1 003 | NA | NA |
| Gallatin | 85 | 7 376 | 0.69 | 135 | 15.7 | 82 | 9.5 | 1 515 | 20.0 | 1 048 | 210 | 541 | 125 | 1 509 |
| Garrard | 109 | 12 826 | 0.42 | 185 | 11.0 | 165 | 9.8 | 3 118 | 21.7 | 3 437 | 560 | 1 816 | 153 | 898 |
| Grant | 457 | 20 332 | 0.59 | 365 | 14.7 | 218 | 8.8 | 4 022 | 18.7 | 4 525 | 986 | 2 157 | 273 | 1 099 |
| Graves | 548 | 33 986 | 0.79 | 516 | 13.8 | 418 | 11.1 | 6 603 | 21.6 | 8 068 | 925 | 4 813 | 491 | 1 336 |
| Grayson | 768 | 24 580 | 0.89 | 333 | 12.8 | 276 | 10.6 | 4 419 | 20.8 | 5 451 | 638 | 3 509 | 266 | 1 051 |
| Green | 113 | 9 136 | 0.52 | 116 | 10.3 | 132 | 11.8 | 1 955 | 21.1 | 2 624 | 339 | 1 637 | 41 | 362 |
| Greenup | 454 | 33 043 | 0.71 | 360 | 9.8 | 453 | 12.3 | 4 984 | 16.5 | 9 002 | 1 920 | 4 910 | 366 | 1 012 |
| Hancock | 90 | 9 355 | 1.22 | 114 | 13.3 | 79 | 9.2 | 1 100 | 15.1 | 1 681 | 178 | 926 | 33 | 383 |
| Hardin | 3 256 | 110 235 | 1.16 | 1 633 | 15.2 | 834 | 7.8 | 14 376 | 15.7 | 15 865 | 1 304 | 6 991 | 1 887 | 1 776 |
| Harlan | 627 | 29 714 | 1.03 | 372 | 12.8 | 394 | 13.6 | 4 937 | 19.9 | 7 184 | 890 | 4 546 | 229 | 797 |
| Harrison | 275 | 16 271 | 0.68 | 222 | 11.8 | 212 | 11.3 | 2 794 | 17.6 | 3 736 | 660 | 1 999 | 528 | 2 782 |
| Hart | 227 | 16 779 | 0.79 | 224 | 12.3 | 193 | 10.6 | 3 159 | 20.6 | 3 831 | 450 | 2 439 | 50 | 273 |
| Henderson | 1 165 | 44 880 | 0.94 | 606 | 13.1 | 494 | 10.6 | 6 322 | 16.3 | 9 004 | 1 826 | 4 866 | 1 168 | 2 508 |
| Henry | 80 | 12 570 | 0.56 | 183 | 11.9 | 157 | 10.2 | 2 505 | 19.1 | 3 032 | 637 | 1 666 | 80 | 574 |
| Hickman | 212 | 4 798 | 0.94 | 43 | 9.0 | 78 | 16.3 | 718 | 19.3 | 1 249 | 88 | 760 | 8 | 162 |
| Hopkins | 1 086 | 47 220 | 1.02 | 563 | 12.0 | 521 | 11.1 | 7 129 | 18.4 | 9 905 | 1 366 | 5 952 | 1 094 | 2 316 |
| Jackson | 110 | 11 711 | 0.58 | 152 | 11.3 | 151 | 11.2 | 2 386 | 20.6 | 2 797 | 375 | 1 768 | 100 | 736 |
| Jefferson | 14 153 | 816 864 | 1.24 | 10 239 | 13.7 | 6 823 | 9.1 | 101 366 | 16.1 | 129 191 | 26 518 | 67 464 | 38 955 | 5 226 |
| Jessamine | 1 779 | 44 286 | 0.84 | 692 | 14.1 | 347 | 7.1 | 7 643 | 18.4 | 7 434 | 1 577 | 3 613 | 1 997 | 4 082 |
| Johnson | 528 | 21 622 | 0.78 | 292 | 12.5 | 284 | 12.1 | 3 493 | 17.7 | 5 578 | 858 | 3 370 | 299 | 1 271 |
| Kenton | 2 332 | 147 538 | 0.85 | 2 463 | 15.4 | 1 304 | 8.1 | 21 314 | 15.3 | 23 526 | 6 084 | 10 462 | 5 383 | 3 347 |
| Knott | 677 | 15 129 | 0.72 | 199 | 12.2 | 181 | 11.1 | 2 396 | 17.6 | 3 626 | 668 | 2 231 | 2 | 13 |
| Knox | 642 | 30 863 | 0.90 | 426 | 13.4 | 418 | 13.1 | 5 125 | 19.1 | 7 245 | 805 | 4 782 | 513 | 1 598 |
| Larue | 313 | 11 733 | 0.56 | 172 | 12.0 | 159 | 11.1 | 2 334 | 19.9 | 2 936 | 380 | 1 753 | 118 | 826 |
| Laurel | 699 | 60 275 | 1.08 | 724 | 12.2 | 570 | 9.6 | 10 132 | 19.9 | 12 070 | 1 493 | 7 120 | 998 | 1 684 |
| Lawrence | 108 | 14 858 | 0.80 | 217 | 13.5 | 204 | 12.7 | 2 489 | 18.3 | 3 640 | 470 | 2 178 | 107 | 670 |
| Lee | 1 016 | 7 724 | 0.95 | 70 | 9.0 | 124 | 15.9 | 1 080 | 18.4 | 1 687 | 247 | 1 118 | 23 | 290 |
| Leslie | 227 | 10 589 | 0.75 | 166 | 14.8 | 163 | 14.5 | 1 745 | 18.3 | 2 769 | 407 | 1 770 | NA | NA |
| Letcher | 243 | 23 182 | 0.83 | 299 | 12.2 | 283 | 11.6 | 3 772 | 18.0 | 5 826 | 925 | 3 516 | 76 | 308 |
| Lewis | 139 | 11 783 | 0.55 | 166 | 12.0 | 149 | 10.7 | 2 497 | 21.3 | 2 750 | 371 | 1 798 | 60 | 430 |
| Lincoln | 219 | 20 565 | 0.54 | 350 | 14.2 | 265 | 10.7 | 4 168 | 20.0 | 5 336 | 862 | 3 040 | 143 | 605 |
| Livingston | 69 | 8 152 | 0.63 | 102 | 10.7 | 127 | 13.3 | 1 503 | 19.4 | 2 406 | 225 | 1 345 | 81 | 845 |
| Logan | 277 | 25 233 | 0.86 | 321 | 12.0 | 279 | 10.4 | 5 025 | 22.4 | 5 530 | 751 | 3 561 | 507 | 1 938 |
| Lyon | 1 123 | 7 759 | 0.79 | 67 | 8.1 | 131 | 15.8 | 1 014 | 18.4 | 2 170 | 353 | 1 157 | 124 | 1 481 |
| McCracken | 1 189 | 76 351 | 1.39 | 743 | 11.3 | 810 | 12.3 | 8 686 | 16.2 | 14 448 | 1 601 | 7 923 | 1 873 | 2 837 |
| McCreary | 2 111 | 16 939 | 0.74 | 225 | 12.3 | 166 | 9.1 | 3 117 | 21.7 | 3 738 | 505 | 2 470 | 152 | 825 |
| McLean | 82 | 7 879 | 0.55 | 117 | 12.3 | 119 | 12.5 | 1 397 | 17.8 | 2 166 | 446 | 1 142 | 66 | 698 |
| Madison | 5 695 | 78 784 | 0.91 | 995 | 11.8 | 613 | 7.3 | 12 898 | 18.9 | 13 375 | 2 922 | 7 030 | 3 319 | 3 975 |
| Magoffin | 127 | 12 444 | 0.75 | 162 | 12.3 | 158 | 12.0 | 2 038 | 17.6 | 2 953 | 390 | 1 914 | 30 | 223 |
| Marion | 1 297 | 19 790 | 1.01 | 278 | 13.9 | 185 | 9.3 | 3 076 | 19.1 | 3 596 | 435 | 2 443 | 286 | 1 455 |
| Marshall | 464 | 29 509 | 0.86 | 339 | 10.8 | 427 | 13.6 | 4 178 | 16.7 | 7 785 | 866 | 4 084 | 477 | 1 506 |
| Martin | 1 657 | 13 493 | 1.18 | 131 | 10.3 | 152 | 11.9 | 1 555 | 15.8 | 2 727 | 471 | 1 691 | 100 | 768 |
| Mason | 298 | 19 352 | 1.26 | 231 | 13.1 | 195 | 11.0 | 2 701 | 18.5 | 3 635 | 733 | 2 147 | 680 | 3 861 |
| Meade | 212 | 21 997 | 0.43 | 292 | 9.9 | 195 | 6.6 | 4 322 | 17.1 | 4 401 | 542 | 2 177 | 184 | 639 |
| Menifee | 230 | 5 643 | 0.61 | 57 | 9.0 | 84 | 13.3 | 1 108 | 20.9 | 1 563 | 456 | 851 | 51 | 803 |
| Mercer | 128 | 19 846 | 0.84 | 268 | 12.6 | 252 | 11.8 | 3 061 | 17.2 | 4 606 | 875 | 2 280 | 271 | 1 322 |
| Metcalfe | 121 | 8 720 | 0.67 | 141 | 14.0 | 136 | 13.5 | 1 901 | 22.5 | 2 277 | 549 | 1 268 | 71 | 698 |
| Monroe | 143 | 10 306 | 0.84 | 119 | 10.9 | 162 | 14.8 | 2 156 | 23.8 | 2 640 | 380 | 1 807 | 10 | 92 |
| Montgomery | 357 | 26 873 | 1.06 | 388 | 14.5 | 258 | 9.6 | 4 128 | 18.1 | 5 101 | 1 168 | 2 724 | 1 195 | 4 479 |
| Morgan | 1 975 | 13 274 | 0.83 | 154 | 11.0 | 167 | 12.0 | 1 962 | 19.3 | 2 693 | 531 | 1 622 | NA | NA |
| Muhlenberg | 1 951 | 30 138 | 0.88 | 333 | 10.6 | 412 | 13.2 | 4 860 | 19.4 | 7 226 | 910 | 4 756 | 193 | 609 |
| Nelson | 496 | 39 409 | 0.81 | 555 | 12.6 | 363 | 8.3 | 6 316 | 16.6 | 7 815 | 1 171 | 4 637 | 717 | 1 706 |
| Nicholas | 95 | 5 602 | 0.51 | 92 | 13.0 | 114 | 16.1 | 1 248 | 20.9 | 1 550 | 200 | 950 | 59 | 821 |

1. Per 1,000 estimated resident population.   2. Data for serious crimes have not been adjusted for underreporting; this may affect comparability between geographic areas and over time.   3. Per 100,000 population estimated by the FBI.

# Table B. States and Counties — Crime, Education, Money Income, and Poverty

| STATE County | Serious crimes known to police, 2011 (cont.)[1] Rate[2] Violent | Property | Education School enrollment and attainment, 2007-2011 Enrollment[3] Total | Percent private | Attainment[4] (percent) High school graduate or less | Bachelor's degree or more | Local government expenditures,[5] 2009-2010 Total current expenditures (mil dol) | Current expenditures per student (dollars) | Money income, 2007-2011 Per capita income[6] (dollars) | Households Median income Dollars | Percent change, 2000 to 2007-2011 (constant 2011 dollars) | Percent with income of $200,000 or more | Income and poverty, 2011 Median household income (dollars) | Percent below poverty level All persons | Children under 18 years | Children 5 to 17 years in families |
|---|---|---|---|---|---|---|---|---|---|---|---|---|---|---|---|---|
| | 46 | 47 | 48 | 49 | 50 | 51 | 52 | 53 | 54 | 55 | 56 | 57 | 58 | 59 | 60 | 61 |
| **KENTUCKY—Cont'd** | | | | | | | | | | | | | | | | |
| Clay | 41 | 951 | 4 825 | 7.0 | 79.4 | 7.9 | 37.1 | 10 298 | 12 568 | 20 206 | -8.0 | 0.7 | 22 289 | 42.4 | 47.1 | 42.7 |
| Clinton | NA | NA | 2 428 | 0.9 | 70.0 | 7.5 | 18.2 | 10 131 | 15 876 | 27 654 | 4.7 | 2.3 | 27 095 | 27.2 | 39.0 | 36.7 |
| Crittenden | 0 | 1 056 | 1 765 | 7.1 | 65.5 | 9.6 | 11.3 | 8 179 | 20 382 | 32 545 | -17.1 | 0.7 | 33 570 | 20.6 | 32.5 | 31.0 |
| Cumberland | 29 | 377 | 1 419 | 9.8 | 72.9 | 8.7 | 10.3 | 10 027 | 15 546 | 29 528 | 1.4 | 0.0 | 27 570 | 27.4 | 41.0 | 39.7 |
| Daviess | 172 | 3 047 | 24 203 | 17.6 | 52.6 | 18.5 | 144.7 | 9 221 | 22 516 | 44 763 | -9.9 | 1.6 | 44 379 | 16.0 | 24.1 | 23.3 |
| Edmonson | 41 | 645 | 2 669 | 3.3 | 68.6 | 9.6 | 17.8 | 8 534 | 19 588 | 35 217 | 2.6 | 0.7 | 36 321 | 19.1 | 28.0 | 24.6 |
| Elliott | NA | NA | 1 442 | 5.1 | 68.8 | 6.3 | 10.9 | 9 796 | 13 952 | 25 769 | -9.2 | 0.0 | 29 339 | 31.4 | 38.4 | 35.9 |
| Estill | 74 | 1 070 | 3 140 | 9.2 | 74.1 | 6.7 | 21.7 | 8 420 | 16 212 | 28 148 | -10.6 | 0.7 | 28 961 | 28.6 | 40.5 | 37.3 |
| Fayette | 460 | 4 469 | 85 650 | 15.3 | 32.7 | 39.3 | 361.4 | 9 770 | 29 125 | 48 306 | -10.1 | 4.1 | 47 211 | 17.7 | 21.2 | 19.0 |
| Fleming | 21 | 415 | 3 480 | 8.3 | 59.1 | 12.7 | 21.5 | 8 944 | 17 456 | 31 979 | -15.4 | 0.4 | 34 736 | 21.3 | 32.0 | 29.6 |
| Floyd | 36 | 476 | 8 247 | 7.2 | 65.2 | 12.2 | 61.4 | 9 537 | 16 201 | 28 221 | -1.3 | 0.7 | 28 459 | 27.2 | 37.5 | 36.5 |
| Franklin | 256 | 3 776 | 11 704 | 12.5 | 47.6 | 27.5 | 59.7 | 8 571 | 26 714 | 47 062 | -12.9 | 2.1 | 44 241 | 15.2 | 22.4 | 21.1 |
| Fulton | NA | NA | 1 373 | 11.7 | 63.7 | 11.3 | 11.2 | 10 555 | 18 074 | 34 545 | 4.9 | 0.9 | 28 340 | 28.9 | 44.7 | 43.1 |
| Gallatin | 36 | 1 472 | 2 187 | 2.4 | 66.0 | 9.7 | 14.3 | 8 679 | 19 113 | 45 400 | -7.7 | 0.5 | 41 084 | 18.0 | 28.1 | 25.5 |
| Garrard | 53 | 846 | 3 853 | 7.2 | 63.5 | 14.0 | 22.8 | 8 491 | 19 437 | 40 137 | -13.3 | 0.7 | 40 292 | 21.9 | 31.2 | 27.0 |
| Grant | 40 | 1 059 | 6 546 | 10.8 | 59.8 | 11.2 | 39.0 | 7 898 | 20 894 | 43 755 | -15.7 | 1.8 | 44 158 | 15.7 | 25.0 | 23.9 |
| Graves | 120 | 1 217 | 9 128 | 11.0 | 58.3 | 14.6 | 53.6 | 8 256 | 20 326 | 35 514 | -14.8 | 1.5 | 35 690 | 19.7 | 29.4 | 27.2 |
| Grayson | 28 | 1 023 | 6 239 | 8.9 | 69.6 | 7.2 | 35.1 | 8 010 | 17 720 | 32 919 | -11.8 | 0.4 | 32 793 | 26.0 | 39.2 | 35.6 |
| Green | 35 | 326 | 2 452 | 15.0 | 67.7 | 11.2 | 15.4 | 8 915 | 20 981 | 35 313 | 2.7 | 1.5 | 31 189 | 24.6 | 35.2 | 33.0 |
| Greenup | 53 | 960 | 8 038 | 6.6 | 55.9 | 15.6 | 55.4 | 8 555 | 21 565 | 41 902 | -3.4 | 1.5 | 41 676 | 17.4 | 24.1 | 20.0 |
| Hancock | 0 | 383 | 2 190 | 5.5 | 60.0 | 10.9 | 15.2 | 8 844 | 21 352 | 47 895 | -3.9 | 0.3 | 52 049 | 12.9 | 19.9 | 17.8 |
| Hardin | 104 | 1 672 | 27 810 | 10.9 | 46.6 | 19.3 | 139.3 | 8 264 | 23 719 | 48 743 | -4.4 | 2.1 | 47 423 | 14.6 | 24.0 | 21.8 |
| Harlan | 70 | 728 | 6 588 | 6.4 | 66.4 | 11.0 | 46.9 | 8 988 | 15 146 | 26 914 | 6.8 | 0.6 | 28 721 | 31.5 | 41.6 | 37.3 |
| Harrison | 158 | 2 624 | 4 510 | 6.8 | 60.9 | 12.6 | 25.4 | 7 874 | 19 711 | 38 690 | -20.9 | 0.7 | 39 160 | 19.0 | 27.5 | 25.1 |
| Hart | 33 | 240 | 4 277 | 10.1 | 71.3 | 8.6 | 23.3 | 9 729 | 16 796 | 31 858 | -7.0 | 0.4 | 31 677 | 26.3 | 40.4 | 36.4 |
| Henderson | 152 | 2 356 | 10 378 | 10.9 | 53.9 | 16.5 | 62.7 | 8 546 | 22 875 | 41 473 | -14.4 | 1.4 | 41 244 | 16.7 | 24.4 | 23.5 |
| Henry | 79 | 495 | 3 769 | 6.1 | 64.6 | 13.8 | 24.1 | 8 199 | 21 156 | 42 506 | -15.5 | 1.5 | 42 614 | 18.7 | 28.1 | 25.1 |
| Hickman | 0 | 162 | 1 144 | 9.4 | 58.1 | 13.8 | 8.0 | 10 063 | 20 732 | 37 535 | -12.1 | 1.4 | 38 446 | 18.6 | 29.0 | 25.5 |
| Hopkins | 93 | 2 223 | 10 676 | 7.9 | 58.6 | 13.4 | 67.2 | 8 510 | 21 885 | 39 187 | -6.0 | 1.3 | 39 733 | 19.7 | 29.2 | 25.6 |
| Jackson | 0 | 736 | 2 908 | 3.2 | 77.9 | 5.7 | 23.9 | 10 098 | 14 172 | 21 448 | -21.3 | 1.0 | 26 344 | 31.2 | 42.3 | 38.6 |
| Jefferson | 574 | 4 652 | 185 736 | 23.5 | 41.5 | 29.2 | 1 024.6 | 10 324 | 27 301 | 46 298 | -13.1 | 3.6 | 45 407 | 17.3 | 26.6 | 24.3 |
| Jessamine | 196 | 3 886 | 13 291 | 27.8 | 44.5 | 27.2 | 65.5 | 8 461 | 25 006 | 48 547 | -10.3 | 2.9 | 47 280 | 17.2 | 25.3 | 23.4 |
| Johnson | 51 | 1 220 | 4 883 | 4.2 | 66.6 | 10.2 | 44.0 | 9 499 | 19 276 | 32 421 | -3.6 | 2.1 | 35 068 | 25.2 | 35.8 | 32.5 |
| Kenton | 277 | 3 070 | 41 904 | 23.5 | 44.1 | 27.5 | 194.0 | 8 587 | 27 484 | 53 375 | -10.0 | 3.6 | 50 150 | 16.0 | 23.1 | 21.3 |
| Knott | 0 | 13 | 3 938 | 22.9 | 66.8 | 12.1 | 25.4 | 9 750 | 16 857 | 31 735 | 15.4 | 0.4 | 29 791 | 30.5 | 39.3 | 37.2 |
| Knox | 90 | 1 508 | 7 181 | 7.2 | 76.3 | 8.4 | 50.0 | 9 061 | 14 673 | 22 364 | -9.5 | 1.2 | 25 536 | 34.0 | 44.9 | 45.0 |
| Larue | 70 | 756 | 3 383 | 8.3 | 63.5 | 10.9 | 20.6 | 8 584 | 18 499 | 37 920 | -12.4 | 1.0 | 39 174 | 18.3 | 28.2 | 25.8 |
| Laurel | 68 | 1 617 | 13 370 | 11.1 | 62.3 | 13.2 | 78.9 | 7 899 | 19 823 | 37 286 | 2.2 | 1.5 | 35 147 | 22.7 | 33.2 | 30.1 |
| Lawrence | 25 | 645 | 3 406 | 6.1 | 67.2 | 9.0 | 23.1 | 9 317 | 16 839 | 32 279 | 10.6 | 0.9 | 32 275 | 26.3 | 34.6 | 33.8 |
| Lee | 0 | 290 | 1 528 | 4.1 | 72.0 | 6.8 | 10.7 | 9 559 | 14 340 | 24 674 | -1.5 | 0.3 | 24 770 | 35.7 | 48.9 | 43.2 |
| Leslie | NA | NA | 2 540 | 8.7 | 73.3 | 7.7 | 19.0 | 9 805 | 16 345 | 29 050 | 16.0 | 0.3 | 29 645 | 24.5 | 33.9 | 32.2 |
| Letcher | 16 | 292 | 5 152 | 8.7 | 65.4 | 10.3 | 37.9 | 9 755 | 17 203 | 29 564 | 3.7 | 0.5 | 31 146 | 24.3 | 34.9 | 32.8 |
| Lewis | 79 | 351 | 3 137 | 6.7 | 74.3 | 8.8 | 23.2 | 9 518 | 14 898 | 27 181 | -9.4 | 0.6 | 28 740 | 34.2 | 48.0 | 41.2 |
| Lincoln | 34 | 572 | 5 841 | 8.3 | 69.8 | 9.8 | 40.8 | 9 485 | 16 511 | 33 398 | -6.8 | 0.1 | 35 530 | 25.6 | 36.8 | 33.0 |
| Livingston | 52 | 793 | 1 960 | 7.6 | 62.9 | 9.4 | 12.8 | 9 512 | 20 511 | 40 248 | -6.2 | 0.8 | 38 724 | 15.5 | 25.4 | 24.3 |
| Logan | 80 | 1 858 | 6 005 | 7.7 | 68.1 | 10.1 | 40.7 | 8 441 | 19 502 | 35 973 | -18.0 | 1.1 | 39 304 | 20.1 | 30.8 | 28.1 |
| Lyon | 12 | 1 469 | 1 229 | 5.8 | 56.1 | 12.8 | 8.0 | 8 938 | 21 128 | 40 546 | -5.2 | 0.7 | 40 006 | 17.0 | 22.8 | 20.9 |
| McCracken | 197 | 2 640 | 15 170 | 13.3 | 44.5 | 21.4 | 91.7 | 8 950 | 25 676 | 44 054 | -3.7 | 2.6 | 44 115 | 17.2 | 27.2 | 24.0 |
| McCreary | 33 | 792 | 4 137 | 5.5 | 68.5 | 7.6 | 31.5 | 9 705 | 12 425 | 24 292 | -7.0 | 0.0 | 24 640 | 36.6 | 47.8 | 47.5 |
| McLean | 0 | 688 | 2 406 | 7.9 | 62.8 | 11.3 | 13.7 | 8 008 | 21 219 | 40 183 | 0.3 | 1.6 | 38 984 | 19.5 | 28.7 | 23.8 |
| Madison | 182 | 3 793 | 26 626 | 13.7 | 45.7 | 27.4 | 101.0 | 8 296 | 21 737 | 41 876 | -5.6 | 1.5 | 40 034 | 20.8 | 24.4 | 22.2 |
| Magoffin | 7 | 216 | 2 937 | 1.4 | 68.6 | 9.4 | 23.8 | 9 851 | 14 506 | 25 410 | -3.1 | 0.7 | 28 004 | 30.6 | 41.3 | 37.6 |
| Marion | 107 | 1 348 | 4 797 | 12.1 | 63.6 | 13.5 | 28.2 | 8 652 | 18 784 | 38 202 | -6.9 | 1.6 | 36 168 | 21.7 | 27.7 | 27.5 |
| Marshall | 95 | 1 412 | 6 891 | 9.9 | 56.8 | 15.2 | 41.9 | 8 562 | 23 304 | 45 605 | -5.0 | 1.4 | 45 163 | 13.3 | 21.2 | 19.4 |
| Martin | 61 | 707 | 2 917 | 1.5 | 67.7 | 8.4 | 22.3 | 10 421 | 13 759 | 23 920 | -3.1 | 0.0 | 28 880 | 38.6 | 47.0 | 42.4 |
| Mason | 142 | 3 719 | 3 869 | 8.3 | 59.1 | 14.0 | 24.7 | 8 540 | 22 599 | 40 678 | -0.2 | 2.3 | 39 837 | 19.2 | 30.7 | 29.3 |
| Meade | 31 | 608 | 7 853 | 6.7 | 53.1 | 12.9 | 39.3 | 7 661 | 20 188 | 45 007 | -9.8 | 0.3 | 48 485 | 15.4 | 22.0 | 20.4 |
| Menifee | 0 | 803 | 1 466 | 4.8 | 70.6 | 11.0 | 10.7 | 9 077 | 14 069 | 28 279 | -5.1 | 0.0 | 28 773 | 30.0 | 47.2 | 44.7 |
| Mercer | 107 | 1 214 | 5 020 | 11.1 | 57.3 | 18.0 | 32.6 | 8 903 | 23 723 | 47 690 | -0.7 | 1.7 | 40 502 | 16.2 | 24.9 | 23.2 |
| Metcalfe | 10 | 688 | 2 332 | 10.4 | 74.9 | 7.8 | 15.4 | 8 699 | 16 577 | 35 199 | 10.7 | 0.0 | 29 852 | 24.9 | 38.4 | 33.8 |
| Monroe | 18 | 74 | 2 520 | 4.4 | 72.3 | 10.7 | 19.1 | 9 446 | 15 876 | 28 548 | -5.4 | 0.1 | 27 480 | 25.2 | 37.1 | 33.5 |
| Montgomery | 221 | 4 258 | 6 035 | 6.5 | 61.7 | 15.5 | 37.3 | 7 873 | 21 168 | 37 393 | -12.8 | 1.5 | 40 267 | 21.3 | 31.6 | 29.7 |
| Morgan | NA | NA | 3 068 | 6.5 | 70.1 | 10.3 | 18.8 | 8 846 | 19 623 | 29 872 | 1.2 | 2.1 | 29 078 | 31.9 | 38.8 | 35.4 |
| Muhlenberg | 32 | 577 | 6 861 | 5.9 | 64.3 | 9.6 | 50.6 | 9 599 | 19 452 | 37 440 | -2.9 | 1.2 | 35 316 | 21.1 | 30.0 | 26.6 |
| Nelson | 100 | 1 606 | 10 514 | 18.8 | 59.0 | 14.6 | 62.3 | 8 217 | 21 938 | 45 149 | -14.3 | 1.6 | 42 271 | 15.5 | 23.0 | 20.3 |
| Nicholas | 84 | 738 | 1 470 | 13.7 | 66.4 | 11.2 | 10.9 | 8 673 | 18 758 | 39 586 | -1.9 | 0.9 | 34 886 | 18.9 | 30.6 | 28.6 |

1. Data for serious crimes have not been adjusted for underreporting; this may affect comparability between geographic areas and over time.   2. Per 100,000 population estimated by the FBI.   3. All persons 3 years old and over enrolled in nursery school through college.   4. Persons 25 years old and over.   5. Elementary and secondary education expenditures.   6. Based on population estimated by the American Community Survey, 2007-2011.

# Table B. States and Counties — Personal Income

| | Personal income, 2011 | | | | | | | | | | | | |
|---|---|---|---|---|---|---|---|---|---|---|---|---|---|
| | | | Per capita[1] | | | | | Transfer payments (mil dol) | | | | | |
| | | | | | | | | | Government payments to individuals | | | | |
| STATE County | Total (mil dol) | Percent change, 2010–2011 | Dollars | Rank | Wages and salaries[2] (mil dol) | Proprietors' income (mil dol) | Dividends, interest, and rent (mil dol) | Total | Total | Social Security | Medical payments | Income mainte-nance | Unemploy-ment insurance |
| | 62 | 63 | 64 | 65 | 66 | 67 | 68 | 69 | 70 | 71 | 72 | 73 | 74 |

KENTUCKY—Cont'd

| | | | | | | | | | | | | | |
|---|---|---|---|---|---|---|---|---|---|---|---|---|---|
| Clay | 526 | 3.0 | 24 205 | 3 020 | 194 | 18 | 47 | 252 | 247 | 54 | 115 | 58 | 7 |
| Clinton | 270 | 1.9 | 26 424 | 2 835 | 141 | 12 | 26 | 123 | 121 | 27 | 69 | 16 | 3 |
| Crittenden | 268 | 6.2 | 28 682 | 2 509 | 76 | 20 | 31 | 91 | 89 | 32 | 40 | 8 | 3 |
| Cumberland | 178 | 2.7 | 26 104 | 2 871 | 61 | 8 | 22 | 83 | 82 | 20 | 46 | 10 | 2 |
| Daviess | 3 427 | 5.9 | 35 246 | 1 332 | 2 010 | 257 | 530 | 836 | 814 | 285 | 331 | 90 | 28 |
| Edmonson | 310 | 4.8 | 25 668 | 2 913 | 67 | 11 | 33 | 101 | 99 | 34 | 40 | 13 | 4 |
| Elliott | 150 | 2.4 | 19 426 | 3 105 | 37 | 0 | 13 | 67 | 65 | 20 | 26 | 13 | 3 |
| Estill | 353 | 3.3 | 24 043 | 3 028 | 98 | 7 | 33 | 156 | 152 | 39 | 68 | 27 | 5 |
| Fayette | 12 048 | 6.2 | 39 950 | 751 | 9 929 | 1 130 | 1 973 | 1 950 | 1 883 | 589 | 628 | 194 | 80 |
| Fleming | 358 | 2.8 | 24 700 | 2 987 | 124 | 22 | 46 | 123 | 119 | 41 | 49 | 17 | 5 |
| Floyd | 1 226 | 4.2 | 31 270 | 2 058 | 585 | 102 | 104 | 491 | 483 | 141 | 219 | 79 | 11 |
| Franklin | 1 783 | 4.2 | 36 091 | 1 202 | 1 616 | 78 | 249 | 431 | 420 | 157 | 167 | 48 | 14 |
| Fulton | 208 | 10.4 | 30 749 | 2 148 | 110 | 30 | 28 | 76 | 74 | 23 | 32 | 12 | 3 |
| Gallatin | 229 | 2.8 | 26 547 | 2 817 | 120 | 6 | 16 | 57 | 55 | 15 | 27 | 7 | 3 |
| Garrard | 441 | 3.3 | 26 144 | 2 866 | 84 | 37 | 52 | 128 | 125 | 47 | 45 | 17 | 5 |
| Grant | 738 | 4.8 | 29 743 | 2 330 | 204 | 31 | 63 | 194 | 189 | 67 | 73 | 27 | 9 |
| Graves | 1 104 | 4.9 | 29 429 | 2 389 | 468 | 106 | 151 | 347 | 338 | 116 | 150 | 36 | 11 |
| Grayson | 657 | 4.5 | 25 329 | 2 942 | 285 | 40 | 77 | 232 | 226 | 72 | 100 | 31 | 10 |
| Green | 296 | 4.5 | 26 421 | 2 836 | 71 | 28 | 35 | 110 | 107 | 32 | 53 | 13 | 4 |
| Greenup | 1 342 | 4.9 | 36 391 | 1 149 | 404 | 36 | 130 | 373 | 365 | 113 | 141 | 38 | 12 |
| Hancock | 261 | 6.4 | 30 440 | 2 213 | 312 | 13 | 28 | 63 | 61 | 26 | 22 | 6 | 2 |
| Hardin | 4 178 | 9.5 | 38 880 | 869 | 3 787 | 287 | 480 | 778 | 757 | 212 | 308 | 80 | 32 |
| Harlan | 820 | 1.1 | 28 221 | 2 581 | 461 | 16 | 75 | 356 | 350 | 102 | 149 | 62 | 8 |
| Harrison | 540 | 3.2 | 28 778 | 2 491 | 231 | 27 | 68 | 140 | 136 | 51 | 51 | 17 | 6 |
| Hart | 458 | 4.7 | 25 092 | 2 959 | 188 | 27 | 55 | 155 | 151 | 47 | 67 | 23 | 6 |
| Henderson | 1 499 | 6.0 | 32 311 | 1 820 | 913 | 81 | 197 | 391 | 381 | 135 | 164 | 44 | 14 |
| Henry | 477 | 3.9 | 30 890 | 2 125 | 137 | 21 | 63 | 123 | 120 | 43 | 51 | 14 | 5 |
| Hickman | 182 | 9.9 | 38 035 | 965 | 38 | 49 | 23 | 48 | 47 | 17 | 21 | 5 | 1 |
| Hopkins | 1 506 | 5.7 | 32 099 | 1 864 | 900 | 82 | 189 | 414 | 403 | 144 | 163 | 50 | 13 |
| Jackson | 281 | 5.0 | 20 923 | 3 094 | 94 | 6 | 27 | 128 | 125 | 33 | 56 | 24 | 5 |
| Jefferson | 31 241 | 4.7 | 41 828 | 592 | 25 239 | 3 218 | 5 119 | 5 886 | 5 720 | 1 901 | 2 383 | 700 | 264 |
| Jessamine | 1 547 | 4.6 | 31 544 | 1 989 | 702 | 98 | 221 | 297 | 286 | 108 | 96 | 40 | 13 |
| Johnson | 650 | 4.0 | 27 763 | 2 647 | 261 | 28 | 61 | 260 | 255 | 77 | 109 | 41 | 7 |
| Kenton | 6 451 | 5.1 | 40 219 | 722 | 3 718 | 299 | 928 | 1 038 | 1 003 | 351 | 389 | 120 | 54 |
| Knott | 447 | 4.0 | 27 426 | 2 696 | 194 | 19 | 36 | 186 | 183 | 49 | 82 | 33 | 5 |
| Knox | 827 | 3.0 | 25 949 | 2 887 | 340 | 88 | 71 | 343 | 336 | 85 | 143 | 76 | 10 |
| Larue | 522 | 7.2 | 36 474 | 1 141 | 98 | 28 | 53 | 120 | 117 | 39 | 52 | 14 | 4 |
| Laurel | 1 607 | 2.9 | 27 082 | 2 754 | 996 | 113 | 159 | 510 | 496 | 159 | 197 | 79 | 20 |
| Lawrence | 427 | 4.3 | 26 603 | 2 811 | 170 | 15 | 34 | 171 | 167 | 49 | 72 | 28 | 5 |
| Lee | 181 | 2.4 | 23 118 | 3 054 | 71 | 4 | 14 | 87 | 85 | 20 | 40 | 17 | 2 |
| Leslie | 324 | 4.0 | 28 852 | 2 478 | 113 | 12 | 21 | 147 | 144 | 38 | 70 | 26 | 3 |
| Letcher | 708 | 3.5 | 28 942 | 2 458 | 320 | 27 | 51 | 284 | 278 | 83 | 126 | 45 | 6 |
| Lewis | 295 | 3.2 | 21 251 | 3 091 | 79 | 17 | 26 | 129 | 125 | 32 | 54 | 24 | 5 |
| Lincoln | 624 | 3.2 | 25 212 | 2 948 | 179 | 27 | 66 | 213 | 208 | 66 | 87 | 30 | 9 |
| Livingston | 311 | 4.4 | 32 672 | 1 764 | 130 | 17 | 36 | 94 | 92 | 35 | 40 | 8 | 3 |
| Logan | 845 | 6.5 | 31 530 | 1 997 | 391 | 120 | 102 | 239 | 233 | 76 | 109 | 27 | 8 |
| Lyon | 238 | 4.6 | 28 634 | 2 517 | 84 | 13 | 34 | 77 | 75 | 32 | 30 | 5 | 2 |
| McCracken | 2 626 | 5.3 | 39 872 | 759 | 1 946 | 193 | 458 | 595 | 580 | 206 | 243 | 64 | 19 |
| McCreary | 381 | 1.6 | 20 842 | 3 096 | 140 | 14 | 31 | 205 | 201 | 44 | 98 | 39 | 6 |
| McLean | 311 | 7.2 | 32 674 | 1 763 | 76 | 53 | 29 | 86 | 84 | 31 | 37 | 9 | 3 |
| Madison | 2 414 | 4.6 | 28 677 | 2 510 | 1 480 | 106 | 288 | 593 | 574 | 183 | 215 | 71 | 24 |
| Magoffin | 325 | 3.3 | 24 606 | 2 996 | 89 | 14 | 26 | 159 | 156 | 38 | 73 | 33 | 5 |
| Marion | 553 | 5.7 | 27 671 | 2 657 | 321 | 24 | 71 | 154 | 150 | 47 | 66 | 21 | 7 |
| Marshall | 1 043 | 6.1 | 33 315 | 1 652 | 612 | 57 | 148 | 286 | 279 | 117 | 109 | 22 | 10 |
| Martin | 333 | 1.9 | 26 109 | 2 869 | 179 | 11 | 24 | 143 | 140 | 42 | 59 | 28 | 3 |
| Mason | 550 | 4.2 | 31 158 | 2 071 | 388 | 28 | 92 | 144 | 140 | 49 | 56 | 21 | 5 |
| Meade | 1 155 | 10.9 | 39 065 | 848 | 197 | 35 | 108 | 195 | 188 | 62 | 64 | 21 | 11 |
| Menifee | 144 | 2.7 | 22 752 | 3 066 | 39 | 3 | 13 | 68 | 66 | 20 | 28 | 12 | 3 |
| Mercer | 637 | 3.4 | 29 945 | 2 301 | 338 | 33 | 89 | 165 | 161 | 66 | 58 | 18 | 7 |
| Metcalfe | 227 | 2.5 | 22 574 | 3 071 | 79 | 9 | 25 | 93 | 91 | 27 | 43 | 13 | 3 |
| Monroe | 281 | 3.1 | 25 677 | 2 912 | 109 | 20 | 31 | 121 | 118 | 32 | 62 | 16 | 3 |
| Montgomery | 741 | 4.9 | 27 696 | 2 654 | 454 | 39 | 93 | 207 | 201 | 69 | 78 | 31 | 9 |
| Morgan | 311 | 4.7 | 22 309 | 3 078 | 138 | 12 | 30 | 123 | 120 | 34 | 52 | 22 | 4 |
| Muhlenberg | 889 | 7.9 | 28 429 | 2 555 | 477 | 49 | 111 | 294 | 287 | 104 | 120 | 33 | 10 |
| Nelson | 1 454 | 5.6 | 33 071 | 1 696 | 631 | 81 | 184 | 316 | 306 | 112 | 119 | 36 | 17 |
| Nicholas | 200 | 2.4 | 28 332 | 2 569 | 38 | 8 | 19 | 67 | 65 | 21 | 30 | 8 | 2 |

1. Based on the resident population estimated as of July 1 of the year shown.  2. Includes supplements to wages and salaries.

| STATE County | Earnings, 2011 | | | | | | | | | Social Security beneficiaries, December 2011 | | Supplemental Security Income recipients, December 2011 | Housing units, 2010 | |
|---|---|---|---|---|---|---|---|---|---|---|---|---|---|---|
| | | | | | Percent by selected industries | | | | | | | | | |
| | | | Goods-related[1] | | Service-related and health | | | | | | | | | |
| | Total (mil dol) | Farm | Total | Manu-facturing | Infor-mation and profes-sional and technical services | Retail trade | Finance, insur-ance, and real estate | Health care and social services | Govern-ment | Number | Rate[2] | | Total | Percent change, 2000–2010 |
| | 75 | 76 | 77 | 78 | 79 | 80 | 81 | 82 | 83 | 84 | 85 | 86 | 87 | 88 |
| **KENTUCKY—Cont'd** | | | | | | | | | | | | | | |
| Clay | 213 | -0.2 | D | 0.8 | 2.5 | 10.0 | 2.5 | D | 45.0 | 5 265 | 242 | 3 603 | 8 875 | -6.0 |
| Clinton | 153 | 1.7 | 41.6 | 36.3 | D | 4.9 | 2.7 | D | 19.7 | 2 815 | 276 | 954 | 5 311 | 8.7 |
| Crittenden | 97 | 9.0 | D | 18.6 | 4.6 | 6.6 | 4.4 | 16.6 | 19.8 | 2 540 | 272 | 295 | 4 569 | 3.6 |
| Cumberland | 69 | 1.6 | D | 10.6 | D | 9.0 | 6.4 | 26.6 | 24.0 | 1 875 | 274 | 521 | 3 690 | 3.4 |
| Daviess | 2 267 | 2.3 | 20.6 | 14.6 | 4.2 | 8.1 | 6.8 | 10.2 | 22.4 | 22 205 | 228 | 3 642 | 41 452 | 7.9 |
| Edmonson | 78 | 1.0 | D | D | 1.7 | 5.9 | D | D | 51.7 | 3 065 | 254 | 629 | 6 467 | 5.9 |
| Elliott | 36 | -7.5 | D | 0.0 | D | 5.8 | D | 12.8 | 68.0 | 1 795 | 233 | 654 | 3 371 | 8.5 |
| Estill | 105 | -1.6 | D | 12.1 | 2.6 | 8.4 | 3.8 | 17.7 | 31.6 | 3 595 | 245 | 1 364 | 6 865 | 0.6 |
| Fayette | 11 059 | 0.6 | 15.7 | 9.3 | 11.8 | 6.6 | 5.7 | 12.0 | 24.1 | 43 105 | 143 | 6 761 | 135 160 | 16.3 |
| Fleming | 146 | 1.1 | D | 11.9 | 3.0 | 10.4 | 4.1 | 9.3 | 34.0 | 3 750 | 258 | 757 | 6 623 | 8.2 |
| Floyd | 687 | 0.0 | 25.5 | 0.9 | 8.3 | 7.2 | 2.6 | 16.1 | 18.4 | 12 285 | 313 | 4 444 | 18 175 | -2.0 |
| Franklin | 1 694 | 0.1 | D | 8.2 | 5.7 | 4.6 | 4.3 | 7.5 | 53.3 | 12 715 | 257 | 2 897 | 23 164 | 8.2 |
| Fulton | 140 | 14.1 | D | 11.3 | D | 9.7 | 2.8 | D | 18.6 | 1 900 | 281 | 496 | 3 372 | -8.8 |
| Gallatin | 126 | 0.0 | D | D | D | 5.1 | D | D | 17.8 | 1 220 | 142 | 214 | 3 786 | 12.6 |
| Garrard | 121 | 1.2 | D | D | D | 6.5 | 3.9 | 9.2 | 26.0 | 3 970 | 235 | 753 | 7 463 | 16.4 |
| Grant | 235 | -1.5 | 18.7 | 13.1 | D | 13.4 | 4.2 | D | 26.3 | 5 485 | 221 | 893 | 9 942 | 6.8 |
| Graves | 574 | 9.0 | 19.2 | 13.1 | D | 8.6 | 3.4 | D | 18.4 | 9 295 | 248 | 1 549 | 16 777 | 2.7 |
| Grayson | 325 | 1.5 | 29.6 | 21.0 | D | 9.3 | 4.2 | 9.0 | 24.6 | 6 395 | 246 | 1 400 | 13 561 | 5.9 |
| Green | 99 | 14.1 | 6.0 | 2.3 | D | 8.4 | 6.1 | 11.5 | 36.2 | 3 010 | 268 | 647 | 5 324 | -1.7 |
| Greenup | 440 | -0.2 | D | 7.9 | D | 7.8 | 2.8 | 25.2 | 17.9 | 8 815 | 239 | 1 652 | 16 330 | 2.2 |
| Hancock | 326 | 1.5 | D | 70.0 | D | 1.4 | 2.1 | 1.7 | 6.9 | 2 005 | 234 | 247 | 3 734 | 3.7 |
| Hardin | 4 075 | 0.3 | 11.5 | 9.1 | 6.1 | 4.8 | 2.6 | 5.0 | 60.0 | 17 940 | 167 | 2 888 | 43 261 | 14.8 |
| Harlan | 477 | -0.1 | 42.4 | 1.1 | D | 6.3 | 2.7 | D | 19.1 | 8 450 | 291 | 2 933 | 13 513 | -10.0 |
| Harrison | 258 | 0.4 | D | 30.9 | 2.5 | 7.1 | 2.8 | D | 17.4 | 4 205 | 224 | 783 | 8 208 | 7.2 |
| Hart | 215 | 0.4 | D | 37.6 | 1.6 | 6.7 | 2.1 | D | 20.1 | 4 425 | 243 | 1 097 | 8 559 | 6.4 |
| Henderson | 994 | 5.5 | 33.7 | 25.2 | 3.4 | 6.8 | 2.6 | 11.7 | 14.3 | 10 295 | 222 | 1 759 | 20 320 | 4.4 |
| Henry | 158 | 1.6 | D | 18.5 | D | 5.9 | 3.2 | D | 27.2 | 3 475 | 225 | 538 | 6 640 | 4.1 |
| Hickman | 88 | 51.1 | D | D | D | 4.5 | 2.7 | D | 14.2 | 1 355 | 283 | 232 | 2 342 | -3.9 |
| Hopkins | 982 | 2.1 | 33.1 | 17.3 | 3.3 | 7.7 | 3.1 | 14.5 | 18.2 | 11 240 | 240 | 2 119 | 21 180 | 2.5 |
| Jackson | 100 | -3.5 | D | 14.7 | 4.6 | 5.2 | D | D | 35.1 | 3 255 | 242 | 1 465 | 6 523 | 7.6 |
| Jefferson | 28 457 | 0.0 | 16.4 | 11.8 | 9.9 | 5.2 | 11.6 | 15.3 | 12.1 | 140 300 | 188 | 24 640 | 337 616 | 10.4 |
| Jessamine | 800 | 0.7 | D | 19.9 | 4.4 | 15.5 | 3.0 | 4.2 | 15.6 | 8 315 | 170 | 1 339 | 19 331 | 32.0 |
| Johnson | 289 | -0.7 | D | 1.1 | 6.9 | 14.5 | 3.8 | D | 26.6 | 6 560 | 280 | 2 184 | 10 624 | 3.8 |
| Kenton | 4 017 | 0.0 | 15.1 | 8.2 | 9.4 | 4.8 | 9.3 | 15.7 | 19.1 | 25 840 | 161 | 3 865 | 68 975 | 8.5 |
| Knott | 213 | -0.3 | D | D | 3.9 | 3.5 | 1.3 | 8.1 | 19.1 | 4 185 | 257 | 1 813 | 7 461 | -1.6 |
| Knox | 428 | -0.5 | D | 7.9 | 6.4 | 12.7 | 3.3 | D | 21.3 | 8 035 | 252 | 4 226 | 14 485 | 3.5 |
| Larue | 126 | 6.7 | 24.6 | 13.4 | D | 5.7 | 5.2 | 9.3 | 24.5 | 3 360 | 235 | 538 | 6 172 | 5.3 |
| Laurel | 1 109 | 0.1 | 22.6 | 14.2 | D | 10.3 | 3.8 | 14.2 | 14.8 | 13 665 | 230 | 3 733 | 25 446 | 14.0 |
| Lawrence | 185 | -0.7 | D | D | D | 9.2 | 4.2 | 16.5 | 18.6 | 4 130 | 258 | 1 544 | 7 286 | 3.5 |
| Lee | 76 | -2.3 | D | D | D | 10.4 | D | 18.7 | 28.3 | 1 910 | 244 | 902 | 3 436 | 3.5 |
| Leslie | 126 | -0.1 | D | D | 5.2 | 5.3 | D | D | 23.2 | 3 285 | 292 | 1 285 | 5 278 | -4.1 |
| Letcher | 348 | -0.2 | 40.0 | 1.6 | 3.5 | 10.6 | 1.7 | D | 16.9 | 6 895 | 282 | 2 289 | 11 601 | 1.7 |
| Lewis | 96 | 1.2 | D | 13.9 | 1.6 | 6.0 | 3.5 | D | 31.3 | 3 100 | 223 | 1 035 | 6 481 | 5.0 |
| Lincoln | 206 | 2.5 | 25.1 | 18.4 | 5.4 | 8.2 | 4.1 | 12.5 | 25.5 | 6 010 | 243 | 1 544 | 10 819 | 6.8 |
| Livingston | 147 | 4.0 | 34.1 | 3.1 | D | 6.4 | D | 8.6 | 19.8 | 2 700 | 283 | 321 | 4 824 | 1.1 |
| Logan | 510 | 12.3 | D | 34.8 | 2.7 | 5.9 | 2.0 | D | 12.2 | 6 355 | 237 | 973 | 12 339 | 3.9 |
| Lyon | 97 | 4.5 | D | D | D | 4.7 | 1.7 | 7.6 | 46.9 | 2 385 | 287 | 195 | 4 791 | 14.4 |
| McCracken | 2 139 | 0.5 | D | 11.3 | 6.4 | 10.1 | 3.6 | 19.6 | 12.9 | 15 670 | 238 | 2 386 | 31 079 | 2.4 |
| McCreary | 153 | -0.9 | D | 5.5 | 1.9 | 9.3 | 2.9 | D | 56.9 | 4 305 | 235 | 2 094 | 7 507 | 1.4 |
| McLean | 129 | 35.1 | D | 5.4 | D | 7.3 | D | 3.6 | 18.5 | 2 485 | 261 | 353 | 4 264 | -2.9 |
| Madison | 1 586 | 0.2 | D | 17.0 | 7.6 | 7.7 | 2.7 | 10.4 | 31.2 | 14 905 | 177 | 3 051 | 35 043 | 18.4 |
| Magoffin | 103 | -1.1 | D | D | D | 7.6 | D | 11.5 | 31.4 | 3 505 | 265 | 1 851 | 5 950 | 9.2 |
| Marion | 346 | 1.9 | 49.3 | 45.6 | D | 5.6 | 2.4 | D | 13.3 | 4 180 | 209 | 1 047 | 8 182 | 12.4 |
| Marshall | 669 | 0.7 | 52.3 | 36.3 | D | 6.9 | 3.4 | D | 13.3 | 8 860 | 283 | 817 | 15 748 | 6.9 |
| Martin | 190 | -0.1 | D | D | D | 6.7 | D | 5.3 | 36.2 | 3 385 | 265 | 1 531 | 5 164 | -7.0 |
| Mason | 416 | 1.1 | D | 20.3 | 2.4 | 10.1 | 3.0 | D | 15.6 | 4 070 | 231 | 777 | 8 105 | 4.5 |
| Meade | 233 | 2.6 | D | 12.4 | 6.6 | 9.2 | 4.5 | D | 24.0 | 5 175 | 175 | 709 | 11 762 | 14.3 |
| Menifee | 42 | -4.8 | D | 12.7 | D | 6.5 | D | D | 48.7 | 1 800 | 285 | 628 | 3 744 | 0.9 |
| Mercer | 372 | 1.0 | D | 41.3 | D | 7.0 | 1.9 | 6.9 | 12.6 | 5 255 | 247 | 695 | 9 941 | 7.0 |
| Metcalfe | 88 | 1.8 | D | 30.0 | D | 7.9 | 4.1 | 3.9 | 28.9 | 2 595 | 258 | 630 | 4 681 | 1.9 |
| Monroe | 129 | 5.9 | 19.7 | 14.3 | D | 10.0 | 3.9 | 15.4 | 23.8 | 3 030 | 277 | 817 | 5 204 | -1.6 |
| Montgomery | 492 | -0.4 | D | 36.6 | D | 10.2 | 3.5 | 13.5 | 13.0 | 5 935 | 222 | 1 321 | 11 699 | 20.8 |
| Morgan | 150 | -2.9 | D | 7.6 | D | 7.4 | D | 8.3 | 33.0 | 3 180 | 228 | 1 177 | 5 830 | 6.3 |
| Muhlenberg | 526 | 3.1 | 28.2 | 10.4 | D | 7.1 | 2.3 | D | 30.4 | 8 325 | 266 | 1 547 | 13 699 | 0.2 |
| Nelson | 712 | 2.3 | D | 29.2 | D | 8.4 | 3.1 | 11.1 | 13.9 | 9 085 | 207 | 1 309 | 18 075 | 21.0 |
| Nicholas | 45 | 5.3 | 8.5 | 2.8 | D | D | D | 21.3 | 34.0 | 1 820 | 257 | 335 | 3 261 | 6.9 |

1. Includes mining, construction, and manufacturing.  2. Per 1,000 resident population enumerated in the 2010 census.

# Table B. States and Counties — Housing, Labor Force, and Employment

| STATE County | Housing units, 2007–2011 Total | Percent | Median value[1] | Median owner cost as a percent of income With a mortgage | Without a mortgage[2] | Median rent[3] | Median rent as a percent of income | Substandard units[4] (percent) | Civilian labor force, 2012 Total | Percent change, 2011–2012 | Unemployment Total | Rate[5] | Civilian employment,[6] 2007–2011 Total | Percent Management, business, science and arts | Construction, production, and maintenance occupations |
|---|---|---|---|---|---|---|---|---|---|---|---|---|---|---|---|
| | 89 | 90 | 91 | 92 | 93 | 94 | 95 | 96 | 97 | 98 | 99 | 100 | 101 | 102 | 103 |
| KENTUCKY—Cont'd | | | | | | | | | | | | | | | |
| Clay | 6 731 | 75.9 | 56 700 | 23.3 | 14.1 | 425 | 34.5 | 1.8 | 6 987 | -0.8 | 886 | 12.7 | 4 853 | 25.6 | 30.3 |
| Clinton | 3 986 | 76.2 | 64 300 | 22.9 | 11.7 | 448 | 27.6 | 2.9 | 4 862 | 0.2 | 463 | 9.5 | 3 868 | 19.9 | 39.5 |
| Crittenden | 3 855 | 76.9 | 76 700 | 19.4 | 9.9 | 414 | 24.0 | 1.3 | 4 211 | -0.7 | 328 | 7.8 | 3 627 | 24.1 | 38.3 |
| Cumberland | 2 668 | 75.1 | 65 500 | 24.3 | 11.5 | 415 | 29.6 | 3.1 | 3 159 | 2.1 | 341 | 10.8 | 2 787 | 21.2 | 41.9 |
| Daviess | 37 279 | 70.4 | 107 800 | 20.0 | 9.9 | 589 | 26.8 | 1.7 | 50 394 | 1.5 | 3 388 | 6.7 | 42 747 | 28.9 | 29.9 |
| Edmonson | 4 770 | 74.9 | 88 200 | 22.6 | 12.2 | 550 | 29.5 | 1.3 | 5 125 | 0.4 | 484 | 9.4 | 4 957 | 23.5 | 37.6 |
| Elliott | 2 602 | 80.3 | 68 200 | 27.7 | 14.0 | 409 | 40.3 | 1.5 | 3 187 | 0.0 | 354 | 11.1 | 2 108 | 30.4 | 34.4 |
| Estill | 5 680 | 71.9 | 71 700 | 22.2 | 12.6 | 490 | 39.2 | 2.2 | 6 422 | 1.2 | 569 | 8.9 | 4 638 | 22.5 | 41.6 |
| Fayette | 122 075 | 56.9 | 161 100 | 21.6 | 9.9 | 722 | 29.4 | 1.9 | 156 246 | 0.9 | 9 884 | 6.3 | 152 791 | 41.5 | 15.9 |
| Fleming | 5 611 | 79.8 | 83 400 | 24.0 | 12.6 | 536 | 24.8 | 3.6 | 6 448 | 1.0 | 591 | 9.2 | 6 093 | 32.4 | 36.7 |
| Floyd | 15 562 | 71.4 | 68 500 | 24.5 | 11.4 | 538 | 31.0 | 3.7 | 15 194 | 0.3 | 1 604 | 10.6 | 12 185 | 27.4 | 27.1 |
| Franklin | 20 936 | 64.2 | 140 400 | 21.1 | 9.9 | 628 | 28.9 | 2.5 | 24 652 | -0.3 | 1 654 | 6.7 | 22 774 | 35.9 | 21.7 |
| Fulton | 2 876 | 62.8 | 56 800 | 20.5 | 13.9 | 492 | 24.8 | 3.0 | 2 485 | -3.2 | 390 | 15.7 | 2 450 | 23.3 | 46.0 |
| Gallatin | 2 988 | 73.5 | 105 800 | 25.1 | 14.7 | 609 | 28.3 | 1.8 | 4 152 | 0.0 | 352 | 8.5 | 3 703 | 19.4 | 40.5 |
| Garrard | 6 388 | 78.2 | 115 800 | 22.4 | 12.2 | 584 | 36.3 | 2.9 | 7 614 | -0.9 | 661 | 8.7 | 7 382 | 23.0 | 37.7 |
| Grant | 8 755 | 70.5 | 124 300 | 23.4 | 13.2 | 690 | 29.0 | 3.4 | 12 314 | -0.8 | 1 021 | 8.3 | 10 916 | 23.8 | 35.0 |
| Graves | 14 789 | 76.1 | 84 100 | 21.6 | 11.1 | 553 | 31.8 | 2.8 | 16 359 | -1.2 | 1 391 | 8.5 | 15 282 | 25.6 | 34.5 |
| Grayson | 9 939 | 75.2 | 84 700 | 23.5 | 13.2 | 521 | 28.5 | 2.5 | 11 414 | -0.3 | 1 186 | 10.4 | 9 808 | 26.4 | 39.9 |
| Green | 4 422 | 75.4 | 75 600 | 19.3 | 9.9 | 541 | 34.3 | 2.7 | 5 686 | 1.0 | 452 | 7.9 | 4 721 | 30.2 | 35.2 |
| Greenup | 14 309 | 78.5 | 88 300 | 21.5 | 10.6 | 577 | 31.6 | 1.7 | 16 671 | -2.0 | 1 329 | 8.0 | 13 581 | 34.0 | 24.8 |
| Hancock | 3 309 | 83.3 | 86 100 | 17.0 | 9.9 | 549 | 23.0 | 1.6 | 4 292 | 1.5 | 296 | 6.9 | 3 702 | 21.0 | 48.5 |
| Hardin | 37 883 | 64.8 | 135 700 | 20.9 | 9.9 | 675 | 26.5 | 1.8 | 49 952 | -0.2 | 3 950 | 7.9 | 41 189 | 32.6 | 23.8 |
| Harlan | 10 642 | 69.8 | 53 000 | 20.0 | 10.4 | 450 | 25.9 | 5.2 | 10 652 | 0.4 | 1 405 | 13.2 | 8 253 | 28.7 | 34.9 |
| Harrison | 7 172 | 66.7 | 106 300 | 21.2 | 11.2 | 517 | 27.3 | 2.3 | 9 379 | 0.4 | 706 | 7.5 | 8 120 | 24.9 | 36.5 |
| Hart | 6 892 | 75.7 | 78 900 | 21.4 | 12.2 | 488 | 33.1 | 3.4 | 8 616 | 0.6 | 673 | 7.8 | 7 091 | 19.7 | 46.6 |
| Henderson | 18 652 | 69.1 | 100 500 | 21.4 | 9.9 | 558 | 29.4 | 2.0 | 23 257 | -0.9 | 1 726 | 7.4 | 20 916 | 29.5 | 30.8 |
| Henry | 6 023 | 71.7 | 122 800 | 24.4 | 9.9 | 660 | 33.7 | 2.4 | 7 462 | 0.9 | 617 | 8.3 | 6 930 | 26.9 | 33.3 |
| Hickman | 1 983 | 77.8 | 62 700 | 18.1 | 12.5 | 523 | 26.3 | 3.0 | 2 018 | -6.1 | 180 | 8.9 | 1 858 | 30.5 | 31.1 |
| Hopkins | 18 518 | 71.5 | 79 700 | 20.0 | 11.4 | 561 | 26.7 | 2.7 | 23 114 | 0.3 | 1 693 | 7.3 | 20 071 | 28.5 | 31.0 |
| Jackson | 5 569 | 78.4 | 58 700 | 27.6 | 13.9 | 525 | 33.8 | 4.0 | 4 293 | -4.0 | 619 | 14.4 | 4 369 | 20.4 | 41.7 |
| Jefferson | 301 312 | 64.3 | 147 900 | 22.3 | 11.3 | 689 | 29.0 | 1.8 | 365 294 | 0.4 | 31 260 | 8.6 | 348 636 | 35.5 | 21.7 |
| Jessamine | 17 797 | 66.8 | 154 400 | 23.3 | 11.2 | 680 | 29.7 | 2.9 | 23 585 | 0.8 | 1 680 | 7.1 | 22 645 | 33.1 | 23.7 |
| Johnson | 9 397 | 72.8 | 75 300 | 19.5 | 13.1 | 510 | 24.9 | 3.4 | 9 469 | -1.0 | 881 | 9.3 | 7 993 | 23.2 | 31.9 |
| Kenton | 62 054 | 68.7 | 146 700 | 22.1 | 11.6 | 698 | 27.9 | 1.9 | 84 669 | -0.5 | 6 306 | 7.4 | 78 617 | 34.7 | 20.8 |
| Knott | 5 878 | 74.2 | 59 500 | 20.6 | 9.9 | 487 | 23.3 | 1.4 | 6 190 | -1.4 | 817 | 13.2 | 5 093 | 33.6 | 33.3 |
| Knox | 12 541 | 63.5 | 71 900 | 22.2 | 13.1 | 489 | 32.6 | 2.9 | 12 119 | -0.6 | 1 365 | 11.3 | 9 776 | 24.0 | 30.8 |
| Larue | 5 035 | 76.3 | 97 400 | 22.9 | 11.0 | 527 | 30.9 | 1.2 | 6 951 | -0.2 | 523 | 7.5 | 5 615 | 25.9 | 41.2 |
| Laurel | 22 002 | 73.8 | 95 800 | 20.6 | 11.9 | 547 | 28.6 | 1.8 | 26 783 | -0.2 | 2 553 | 9.5 | 22 844 | 28.7 | 27.2 |
| Lawrence | 5 800 | 74.0 | 67 100 | 21.5 | 9.9 | 480 | 31.0 | 2.4 | 6 122 | -2.1 | 607 | 9.9 | 5 313 | 24.2 | 35.6 |
| Lee | 2 827 | 75.8 | 58 200 | 25.3 | 12.6 | 335 | 39.0 | 4.7 | 2 690 | -2.6 | 339 | 12.6 | 2 493 | 27.1 | 34.1 |
| Leslie | 4 428 | 76.2 | 52 100 | 23.3 | 9.9 | 445 | 15.8 | 5.5 | 3 762 | 1.1 | 524 | 13.9 | 3 339 | 25.8 | 35.2 |
| Letcher | 9 300 | 74.4 | 52 300 | 19.3 | 9.9 | 478 | 23.9 | 4.4 | 8 658 | -2.4 | 1 161 | 13.4 | 7 806 | 29.0 | 34.0 |
| Lewis | 4 983 | 82.3 | 56 900 | 24.1 | 12.1 | 411 | 28.4 | 3.4 | 5 388 | -1.9 | 632 | 11.7 | 5 036 | 24.1 | 46.0 |
| Lincoln | 9 793 | 76.3 | 87 100 | 23.2 | 11.9 | 527 | 28.7 | 4.1 | 10 255 | -1.4 | 1 066 | 10.4 | 9 468 | 23.5 | 34.7 |
| Livingston | 3 576 | 83.0 | 80 400 | 18.5 | 9.9 | 521 | 22.2 | 3.6 | 4 750 | -1.1 | 390 | 8.2 | 3 723 | 27.0 | 31.8 |
| Logan | 11 044 | 73.4 | 87 800 | 24.7 | 11.7 | 556 | 28.0 | 3.6 | 12 448 | -1.2 | 930 | 7.5 | 11 587 | 22.7 | 40.3 |
| Lyon | 3 295 | 79.8 | 96 200 | 23.9 | 9.9 | 488 | 18.4 | 3.8 | 3 466 | 0.8 | 302 | 8.7 | 2 818 | 26.6 | 26.7 |
| McCracken | 27 182 | 69.5 | 114 700 | 19.0 | 9.9 | 564 | 27.6 | 1.8 | 31 825 | -0.8 | 2 498 | 7.8 | 28 644 | 31.5 | 23.1 |
| McCreary | 6 333 | 73.6 | 65 800 | 26.7 | 11.4 | 423 | 38.7 | 2.9 | 5 792 | -3.2 | 769 | 13.3 | 5 000 | 23.3 | 36.0 |
| McLean | 3 765 | 77.7 | 75 800 | 21.0 | 10.1 | 472 | 28.5 | 0.8 | 4 636 | 1.7 | 374 | 8.1 | 4 012 | 32.2 | 34.2 |
| Madison | 31 130 | 60.5 | 143 000 | 21.4 | 10.9 | 577 | 29.0 | 2.7 | 45 500 | 1.6 | 3 050 | 6.7 | 38 694 | 33.5 | 21.7 |
| Magoffin | 4 795 | 80.4 | 45 600 | 20.1 | 11.8 | 469 | 48.1 | 2.0 | 4 262 | -2.0 | 705 | 16.5 | 3 658 | 30.2 | 35.7 |
| Marion | 7 206 | 80.4 | 97 200 | 24.3 | 11.7 | 528 | 26.3 | 1.2 | 10 397 | 0.1 | 833 | 8.0 | 7 993 | 27.2 | 38.0 |
| Marshall | 12 434 | 81.1 | 101 300 | 20.5 | 9.9 | 578 | 27.1 | 1.1 | 14 816 | -0.6 | 1 271 | 8.6 | 14 178 | 26.2 | 28.6 |
| Martin | 4 391 | 72.2 | 72 800 | 19.3 | 13.2 | 443 | 36.3 | 2.6 | 3 734 | -0.8 | 383 | 10.3 | 2 912 | 27.8 | 34.2 |
| Mason | 6 568 | 70.6 | 99 500 | 20.0 | 9.9 | 528 | 28.7 | 1.4 | 8 661 | 0.0 | 729 | 8.4 | 7 441 | 28.2 | 27.5 |
| Meade | 10 162 | 71.4 | 111 700 | 21.7 | 10.4 | 745 | 27.1 | 2.1 | 12 384 | -0.6 | 1 253 | 10.1 | 11 431 | 25.5 | 37.3 |
| Menifee | 2 173 | 79.8 | 65 000 | 22.1 | 10.7 | 494 | 50.0 | 3.9 | 2 508 | 1.3 | 311 | 12.4 | 2 000 | 23.7 | 40.0 |
| Mercer | 8 330 | 75.1 | 133 000 | 20.6 | 10.9 | 535 | 30.3 | 3.2 | 10 118 | 0.0 | 848 | 8.4 | 9 512 | 31.2 | 30.7 |
| Metcalfe | 4 019 | 77.1 | 78 300 | 21.6 | 10.7 | 531 | 22.7 | 3.3 | 4 278 | -0.5 | 343 | 8.0 | 4 431 | 23.0 | 47.2 |
| Monroe | 4 358 | 74.2 | 65 600 | 23.8 | 12.2 | 454 | 30.4 | 3.6 | 4 846 | 1.4 | 352 | 7.3 | 4 433 | 27.3 | 32.4 |
| Montgomery | 10 189 | 67.7 | 103 600 | 22.7 | 12.0 | 582 | 25.4 | 1.7 | 12 992 | 2.1 | 1 072 | 8.3 | 10 749 | 27.8 | 39.2 |
| Morgan | 4 627 | 77.5 | 70 300 | 22.7 | 11.4 | 417 | 27.2 | 3.6 | 5 394 | 1.5 | 617 | 11.4 | 4 542 | 25.2 | 33.8 |
| Muhlenberg | 12 117 | 80.6 | 77 200 | 23.0 | 10.7 | 506 | 26.3 | 2.7 | 13 130 | -3.2 | 1 238 | 9.4 | 11 283 | 27.7 | 35.5 |
| Nelson | 16 160 | 76.3 | 120 600 | 22.6 | 9.9 | 629 | 28.9 | 1.6 | 21 375 | -1.1 | 1 857 | 8.7 | 19 424 | 27.0 | 37.8 |
| Nicholas | 2 798 | 75.5 | 84 100 | 20.4 | 10.5 | 413 | 30.1 | 4.7 | 3 186 | -0.3 | 300 | 9.4 | 3 192 | 27.0 | 35.2 |

1. Specified owner-occupied units. 2. A value of 9.9 represents 9.9 percent or less. 3. Specified renter-occupied units. A value of 10.0 represents 10 percent or less. 4. Overcrowded or lacking complete plumbing facilities. 5. Percent of civilian labor force. 6. Persons 16 years old and over.

# Table B. States and Counties — Nonfarm Employment and Agriculture

| | Private nonfarm establishments, employment and payroll, 2011 | | | | | | | | Agriculture, 2007 | | | |
| STATE County | | Employment | | | | | Annual payroll | | Farms | | | |
| | | | | | | | | | | | Percent with: | |
| | Number of establishments | Total | Health care and social assistance | Manufacturing | Retail trade | Finance and insurance | Professional, scientific, and technical services | Total (mil dol) | Average per employee (dollars) | Number | Fewer than 50 acres | 500 acres or more | Farm operators whose principal occupation is farming (percent) |
|---|---|---|---|---|---|---|---|---|---|---|---|---|---|
| | 104 | 105 | 106 | 107 | 108 | 109 | 110 | 111 | 112 | 113 | 114 | 115 | 116 |
| **KENTUCKY—Cont'd** | | | | | | | | | | | | | |
| Clay | 245 | 2 506 | 986 | D | 558 | D | 71 | 67 | 26 645 | 336 | 29.8 | 4.8 | 31.0 |
| Clinton | 189 | 3 239 | 538 | D | 280 | 78 | 32 | 81 | 24 859 | 629 | 35.8 | 4.9 | 38.8 |
| Crittenden | 155 | 1 497 | 395 | 181 | 228 | D | D | 38 | 25 157 | 740 | 22.3 | 8.9 | 35.1 |
| Cumberland | 116 | 1 205 | D | 217 | 207 | D | 19 | 32 | 26 731 | 507 | 25.6 | 9.3 | 38.1 |
| Daviess | 2 261 | 40 582 | 7 917 | 5 439 | 5 846 | 2 381 | 1 375 | 1 352 | 33 304 | 1 008 | 43.8 | 11.9 | 45.1 |
| Edmonson | 137 | 800 | 219 | D | 155 | 70 | 10 | 19 | 23 203 | 712 | 35.4 | 4.1 | 37.9 |
| Elliott | 41 | 310 | 124 | NA | D | D | NA | 8 | 25 097 | 448 | 22.3 | 4.7 | 38.2 |
| Estill | 181 | 1 737 | D | D | 316 | D | 38 | 38 | 21 941 | 456 | 29.6 | 4.6 | 36.0 |
| Fayette | 8 165 | 139 249 | 27 438 | 7 550 | 19 390 | 5 078 | 9 830 | 5 724 | 41 104 | 810 | 50.2 | 8.3 | 52.3 |
| Fleming | 239 | 2 129 | D | 354 | 475 | 100 | D | 59 | 27 742 | 1 129 | 26.3 | 5.8 | 40.9 |
| Floyd | 815 | 8 760 | 2 186 | 148 | 1 674 | 263 | 433 | 323 | 36 895 | 76 | 28.9 | 2.6 | 44.7 |
| Franklin | 1 134 | 14 882 | 2 063 | 2 143 | 2 459 | 964 | 573 | 498 | 33 495 | 625 | 38.2 | 3.2 | 37.1 |
| Fulton | 136 | 2 432 | D | 368 | 203 | D | D | 62 | 25 535 | 156 | 28.2 | 21.8 | 60.3 |
| Gallatin | 91 | 643 | 63 | 50 | 270 | 30 | 28 | 15 | 22 645 | 204 | 30.9 | 7.4 | 46.6 |
| Garrard | 218 | 1 535 | D | 271 | 157 | 53 | D | 41 | 26 560 | 821 | 32.0 | 4.8 | 45.8 |
| Grant | 380 | 4 125 | 546 | D | 938 | 168 | 81 | 108 | 26 279 | 959 | 31.4 | 2.0 | 38.5 |
| Graves | 699 | 9 308 | D | 2 500 | 1 398 | 280 | 317 | 264 | 28 377 | 1 712 | 40.7 | 5.9 | 35.4 |
| Grayson | 476 | 5 855 | D | 1 390 | 1 086 | 233 | 95 | 157 | 26 823 | 1 513 | 27.8 | 3.6 | 37.8 |
| Green | 163 | 1 215 | 460 | D | 255 | D | D | 29 | 23 590 | 1 064 | 32.4 | 4.6 | 41.6 |
| Greenup | 486 | 4 895 | 1 138 | 573 | 784 | 235 | 160 | 157 | 32 002 | 698 | 30.7 | 3.3 | 35.7 |
| Hancock | 131 | 3 385 | 113 | 2 436 | 139 | 79 | D | 181 | 53 374 | 383 | 23.0 | 5.2 | 37.6 |
| Hardin | 2 273 | 34 015 | 6 047 | 4 830 | 5 917 | 1 425 | 1 905 | 1 036 | 30 448 | 1 588 | 43.7 | 5.4 | 40.3 |
| Harlan | 456 | 6 433 | 1 387 | D | 1 081 | 157 | 230 | 268 | 41 591 | 37 | 40.5 | 2.7 | 24.3 |
| Harrison | 287 | 3 956 | 888 | 1 242 | 638 | D | D | 142 | 35 858 | 1 083 | 31.2 | 4.7 | 44.3 |
| Hart | 272 | 3 818 | D | 2 217 | 414 | 100 | 57 | 117 | 30 643 | 1 455 | 32.7 | 3.1 | 40.1 |
| Henderson | 1 025 | 16 126 | 2 446 | 4 496 | 2 148 | 414 | 425 | 581 | 36 053 | 509 | 41.7 | 17.1 | 42.0 |
| Henry | 204 | 1 884 | 102 | 427 | 353 | 97 | D | 58 | 30 839 | 962 | 28.0 | 5.5 | 47.4 |
| Hickman | 79 | 1 211 | D | D | 301 | D | D | 32 | 26 019 | 340 | 30.6 | 14.4 | 45.9 |
| Hopkins | 955 | 14 563 | 2 822 | 2 188 | 2 216 | 393 | 364 | 612 | 42 037 | 661 | 29.0 | 10.1 | 37.5 |
| Jackson | 105 | 1 172 | D | D | 167 | D | D | 35 | 29 646 | 662 | 34.0 | 3.2 | 36.9 |
| Jefferson | 19 173 | 380 789 | 61 575 | 35 925 | 41 321 | 26 798 | 21 270 | 16 234 | 42 633 | 475 | 65.7 | 1.5 | 37.1 |
| Jessamine | 995 | 13 567 | 932 | 2 078 | 2 579 | D | 371 | 417 | 30 758 | 711 | 50.8 | 4.1 | 36.4 |
| Johnson | 417 | 4 307 | 887 | 56 | 1 395 | 216 | D | 118 | 27 332 | 198 | 25.3 | 3.0 | 25.8 |
| Kenton | 3 087 | 68 972 | 9 984 | 4 102 | D | 1 381 | 3 304 | 2 980 | 43 199 | 481 | 46.2 | 1.2 | 34.5 |
| Knott | 184 | 2 006 | 454 | D | 268 | 44 | 42 | 64 | 32 130 | 46 | 23.9 | 2.2 | 30.4 |
| Knox | 479 | 7 373 | 1 158 | D | 1 419 | 228 | 699 | 188 | 25 533 | 376 | 39.6 | 4.3 | 26.6 |
| Larue | 237 | 1 954 | 335 | 584 | 226 | 145 | D | 46 | 23 525 | 811 | 34.8 | 5.2 | 40.3 |
| Laurel | 1 182 | 22 072 | 2 963 | 3 503 | 3 085 | 897 | 601 | 723 | 32 774 | 1 012 | 43.6 | 2.3 | 34.6 |
| Lawrence | 219 | 2 406 | D | D | 610 | 96 | 68 | 79 | 32 787 | 337 | 21.1 | 5.6 | 41.2 |
| Lee | 100 | 1 425 | D | D | 192 | D | D | 32 | 22 126 | 186 | 33.9 | 4.8 | 28.0 |
| Leslie | 118 | 1 095 | 389 | NA | 205 | D | 64 | 35 | 32 196 | 23 | 39.1 | 13.0 | 39.1 |
| Letcher | 341 | 4 511 | 934 | 31 | 680 | D | 170 | 186 | 41 226 | 66 | 62.1 | 0.0 | 24.2 |
| Lewis | 125 | 1 317 | D | 359 | 264 | 81 | D | 37 | 27 900 | 673 | 19.5 | 9.7 | 41.2 |
| Lincoln | 295 | 3 508 | 568 | 753 | 593 | D | D | 85 | 24 284 | 1 278 | 40.1 | 5.6 | 38.3 |
| Livingston | 154 | 1 751 | 350 | 93 | 175 | D | 47 | 65 | 37 109 | 492 | 22.8 | 11.4 | 33.5 |
| Logan | 490 | 6 734 | 774 | D | 932 | 160 | 169 | 257 | 38 222 | 1 172 | 30.7 | 8.5 | 40.8 |
| Lyon | 150 | 1 123 | 238 | D | 202 | D | 42 | 27 | 23 682 | 270 | 23.7 | 6.3 | 39.3 |
| McCracken | 2 138 | 34 524 | 6 856 | 3 095 | 6 218 | 1 170 | 1 338 | 1 256 | 36 376 | 483 | 49.5 | 6.4 | 35.8 |
| McCreary | 155 | 1 552 | 311 | 311 | 361 | D | D | 33 | 21 049 | 139 | 42.4 | 1.4 | 36.0 |
| McLean | 161 | 1 093 | 126 | D | 197 | D | 31 | 31 | 28 729 | 419 | 34.4 | 16.7 | 51.8 |
| Madison | 1 558 | 20 895 | 3 459 | 3 564 | 4 013 | 706 | 689 | 602 | 28 805 | 1 328 | 40.2 | 8.0 | 41.6 |
| Magoffin | 159 | 1 445 | 295 | D | 245 | 60 | 110 | 45 | 31 113 | 470 | 28.9 | 2.3 | 27.0 |
| Marion | 352 | 6 767 | 1 188 | 2 995 | 664 | 150 | 98 | 208 | 30 800 | 1 055 | 33.5 | 5.3 | 39.6 |
| Marshall | 644 | 8 202 | 949 | 2 275 | 1 116 | 356 | 165 | 342 | 41 703 | 867 | 46.6 | 3.2 | 28.0 |
| Martin | 168 | 2 555 | 249 | D | 487 | D | 32 | 106 | 41 429 | 19 | 5.3 | 21.1 | 42.1 |
| Mason | 452 | 7 028 | 1 170 | 1 331 | 1 374 | 179 | 103 | 227 | 32 366 | 753 | 28.4 | 9.0 | 45.6 |
| Meade | 341 | 3 187 | 374 | D | 622 | 109 | 280 | 95 | 29 685 | 887 | 45.2 | 4.3 | 38.7 |
| Menifee | 62 | D | D | D | 125 | D | D | 14 | D | 331 | 29.6 | 4.2 | 34.4 |
| Mercer | 378 | 4 824 | 599 | 1 798 | 715 | 125 | 58 | 193 | 40 071 | 1 111 | 43.1 | 4.4 | 41.3 |
| Metcalfe | 125 | 1 235 | 103 | 605 | 255 | D | D | 33 | 26 534 | 964 | 29.8 | 4.8 | 41.9 |
| Monroe | 212 | 2 324 | 518 | 604 | 489 | 103 | D | 58 | 24 920 | 955 | 27.1 | 8.8 | 46.0 |
| Montgomery | 516 | 9 371 | 1 252 | 3 370 | 1 588 | D | 162 | 273 | 29 101 | 685 | 35.3 | 5.4 | 39.1 |
| Morgan | 164 | 2 025 | 359 | 225 | 404 | D | 60 | 61 | 30 064 | 795 | 23.6 | 7.2 | 32.2 |
| Muhlenberg | 552 | 6 612 | 1 231 | 637 | 1 242 | 204 | 166 | 211 | 31 921 | 636 | 25.5 | 8.6 | 41.4 |
| Nelson | 911 | 12 707 | 1 624 | 3 346 | 1 798 | D | 220 | 404 | 31 773 | 1 406 | 43.0 | 5.0 | 41.8 |
| Nicholas | 77 | 532 | D | D | 137 | 26 | 8 | 13 | 23 699 | 603 | 23.1 | 7.1 | 43.8 |

# Table B. States and Counties — **Agriculture**

| | | | | | | | | | | | | | | | |
|---|---|---|---|---|---|---|---|---|---|---|---|---|---|---|---|
| | | | | | | | Agriculture, 2007 (cont.) | | | | | | | | |
| | Land in farms | | | | Value of land and buildings (dollars) | | | Value of products sold | | | | Percent of farms with sales of: | | Government payments | |
| | | Acres | | | | | | | | Percent from: | | | | | |
| STATE County | Acreage (1,000) | Percent change, 2002–2007 | Average size of farm | Total irrigated (1,000) | Total cropland (1,000) | Average per farm | Average per acre | Value of machinery and equipment, average per farm (dollars) | Total (mil dol) | Average per farm (dollars) | Crops | Live-stock and poultry products | $10,000 or more | $100,000 or more | Total ($1,000) | Percent of farms |
| | 117 | 118 | 119 | 120 | 121 | 122 | 123 | 124 | 125 | 126 | 127 | 128 | 129 | 130 | 131 | 132 |
| **KENTUCKY—Cont'd** | | | | | | | | | | | | | | | | |
| Clay | 51 | -7.3 | 152 | 0.0 | 15.0 | 285 514 | 1 874 | 35 959 | 4.2 | 12 567 | 57.0 | 42.9 | 15.8 | 2.1 | 60 | 14.3 |
| Clinton | 91 | 26.4 | 145 | 0.0 | 33.7 | 332 645 | 2 297 | 49 029 | 30.4 | 48 357 | 10.0 | 90.0 | 39.0 | 6.2 | 359 | 35.9 |
| Crittenden | 160 | 1.9 | 216 | 0.3 | 84.4 | 409 032 | 1 890 | 50 061 | 19.2 | 25 894 | 46.0 | 54.0 | 30.4 | 4.3 | 1 967 | 49.7 |
| Cumberland | 103 | 15.7 | 204 | D | 32.6 | 369 100 | 1 810 | 42 029 | 8.0 | 15 785 | 25.4 | 74.6 | 28.6 | 1.4 | 236 | 40.8 |
| Daviess | 257 | 1.2 | 255 | 3.5 | 209.0 | 770 859 | 3 024 | 100 771 | 117.6 | 116 687 | 75.0 | 25.0 | 41.4 | 16.5 | 2 907 | 51.7 |
| Edmonson | 97 | 3.2 | 136 | 0.0 | 45.1 | 294 407 | 2 169 | 47 761 | 17.5 | 24 562 | 16.0 | 84.0 | 27.7 | 3.2 | 554 | 37.1 |
| Elliott | 67 | 19.6 | 149 | D | 19.3 | 232 597 | 1 559 | 43 887 | 2.4 | 5 426 | 32.1 | 67.8 | 14.5 | 0.0 | 101 | 12.5 |
| Estill | 65 | 1.6 | 142 | 0.0 | 22.5 | 284 049 | 1 999 | 40 149 | 4.5 | 9 784 | 26.7 | 73.3 | 23.7 | 1.5 | 222 | 30.3 |
| Fayette | 136 | 14.3 | 168 | 0.5 | 61.7 | 1 106 925 | 6 594 | 83 203 | 504.1 | 622 377 | 3.1 | 96.9 | 46.7 | 23.5 | 437 | 15.8 |
| Fleming | 182 | -1.1 | 161 | 0.0 | 79.5 | 317 208 | 1 972 | 54 062 | 35.9 | 31 822 | 25.0 | 75.0 | 41.8 | 6.8 | 768 | 53.9 |
| Floyd | 8 | 14.3 | 102 | 0.2 | 2.0 | 237 971 | 2 323 | 27 122 | 0.7 | 9 786 | 84.4 | 15.5 | 10.5 | 2.6 | 2 | 3.9 |
| Franklin | 76 | -7.3 | 122 | 0.4 | 34.9 | 396 506 | 3 248 | 50 598 | 14.0 | 22 449 | 28.6 | 71.4 | 29.9 | 3.2 | 166 | 13.1 |
| Fulton | 91 | -18.8 | 586 | D | 81.5 | 1 325 193 | 2 261 | 152 789 | 37.5 | 240 099 | 69.8 | 30.2 | 48.1 | 29.5 | 1 446 | 79.5 |
| Gallatin | 34 | -10.5 | 166 | 0.1 | 15.6 | 494 116 | 2 981 | 60 543 | 4.9 | 24 081 | 64.6 | 35.4 | 38.2 | 5.4 | 48 | 21.1 |
| Garrard | 122 | 1.7 | 148 | 0.1 | 59.0 | 388 580 | 2 622 | 54 863 | 29.0 | 35 273 | 22.1 | 77.9 | 41.0 | 7.1 | 301 | 22.5 |
| Grant | 115 | -0.9 | 120 | 0.3 | 52.6 | 337 912 | 2 819 | 43 732 | 9.3 | 9 727 | 46.8 | 53.2 | 23.3 | 1.3 | 214 | 16.3 |
| Graves | 278 | -7.3 | 162 | 3.2 | 201.7 | 455 280 | 2 805 | 68 139 | 245.2 | 143 230 | 22.8 | 77.2 | 29.8 | 14.4 | 6 935 | 67.0 |
| Grayson | 216 | -7.3 | 143 | 0.0 | 103.5 | 307 574 | 2 150 | 44 973 | 41.2 | 27 225 | 23.7 | 76.3 | 30.2 | 3.8 | 1 742 | 40.9 |
| Green | 145 | 7.4 | 137 | 0.2 | 66.9 | 317 265 | 2 320 | 52 588 | 31.1 | 29 207 | 26.5 | 73.5 | 42.9 | 7.4 | 1 084 | 45.1 |
| Greenup | 92 | -10.7 | 132 | 0.1 | 29.5 | 260 623 | 1 980 | 41 988 | 4.2 | 5 994 | 40.7 | 59.3 | 15.0 | 0.3 | 181 | 24.9 |
| Hancock | 63 | -8.7 | 165 | 0.2 | 30.5 | 354 193 | 2 151 | 52 149 | 10.6 | 27 634 | 72.5 | 27.5 | 31.1 | 4.7 | 535 | 47.8 |
| Hardin | 222 | -7.5 | 140 | 0.6 | 121.8 | 402 378 | 2 875 | 56 105 | 46.9 | 29 538 | 56.5 | 43.5 | 30.5 | 5.5 | 1 599 | 32.2 |
| Harlan | 3 | 50.0 | 82 | 0.0 | 0.7 | 137 310 | 1 675 | 25 634 | 0.1 | 2 020 | 54.7 | 44.0 | 2.7 | 0.0 | 0 | 0.0 |
| Harrison | 162 | 1.9 | 149 | 1.7 | 74.7 | 400 764 | 2 683 | 57 953 | 24.0 | 22 180 | 46.0 | 54.0 | 37.1 | 4.5 | 627 | 28.6 |
| Hart | 191 | -2.1 | 131 | 0.1 | 82.7 | 316 420 | 2 410 | 45 629 | 34.4 | 23 673 | 28.8 | 71.2 | 36.8 | 5.4 | 1 176 | 44.4 |
| Henderson | 196 | 2.1 | 384 | 4.1 | 164.4 | 1 071 805 | 2 788 | 113 386 | 70.5 | 138 514 | 91.5 | 8.5 | 43.0 | 18.1 | 2 654 | 65.4 |
| Henry | 146 | 2.8 | 152 | 0.9 | 72.7 | 497 292 | 3 268 | 67 967 | 31.2 | 32 455 | 56.1 | 43.9 | 41.2 | 6.3 | 808 | 28.3 |
| Hickman | 130 | 4.0 | 382 | 13.0 | 107.1 | 1 000 739 | 2 622 | 136 946 | 134.2 | 394 693 | 28.3 | 71.7 | 40.0 | 25.6 | 2 383 | 81.8 |
| Hopkins | 159 | -3.0 | 241 | 0.1 | 101.8 | 527 193 | 2 187 | 73 155 | 77.2 | 116 791 | 34.0 | 66.0 | 31.3 | 9.5 | 1 738 | 50.7 |
| Jackson | 83 | 1.2 | 125 | 0.0 | 33.7 | 228 127 | 1 828 | 41 104 | 6.3 | 9 551 | 30.7 | 69.3 | 22.2 | 0.9 | 186 | 19.3 |
| Jefferson | 32 | -22.0 | 68 | 0.2 | 15.4 | 496 480 | 7 302 | 41 150 | 11.1 | 23 403 | 73.8 | 26.2 | 25.1 | 4.8 | 136 | 10.5 |
| Jessamine | 80 | -2.4 | 113 | 0.1 | 37.7 | 529 226 | 4 697 | 49 652 | 123.8 | 174 073 | 3.7 | 96.3 | 34.3 | 7.2 | 277 | 16.9 |
| Johnson | 28 | 16.7 | 140 | D | 6.8 | 299 187 | 2 134 | 35 338 | 1.1 | 5 533 | 49.5 | 50.4 | 13.6 | 0.5 | 27 | 9.6 |
| Kenton | 43 | -6.5 | 88 | 0.0 | 21.5 | 393 811 | 4 452 | 47 431 | 4.6 | 9 512 | 39.3 | 60.7 | 18.9 | 2.3 | 103 | 13.1 |
| Knott | 7 | 75.0 | 151 | 0.0 | 2.7 | 300 696 | 1 994 | 23 662 | 0.3 | 6 735 | D | D | 23.9 | 0.0 | 0 | 0.0 |
| Knox | 51 | 24.4 | 136 | 0.0 | 17.9 | 298 061 | 2 193 | 39 218 | 3.0 | 8 053 | 25.6 | 74.4 | 15.7 | 1.6 | 50 | 12.5 |
| Larue | 125 | -6.7 | 155 | 0.2 | 72.0 | 423 765 | 2 740 | 59 077 | 26.6 | 32 774 | 52.8 | 47.2 | 40.4 | 6.9 | 929 | 40.1 |
| Laurel | 102 | -5.6 | 101 | 0.0 | 43.2 | 289 023 | 2 854 | 40 800 | 14.2 | 14 075 | 31.6 | 68.4 | 23.9 | 2.3 | 171 | 13.3 |
| Lawrence | 60 | 5.3 | 179 | 0.0 | 15.2 | 262 290 | 1 468 | 48 471 | 1.7 | 5 018 | 49.4 | 50.6 | 11.3 | 0.3 | 35 | 12.1 |
| Lee | 29 | 26.1 | 158 | 0.0 | 9.2 | 205 223 | 1 298 | 33 899 | 1.2 | 6 642 | 49.6 | 50.4 | 14.5 | 0.5 | 126 | 27.4 |
| Leslie | 6 | 100.0 | 245 | D | 0.2 | 195 487 | 797 | 21 295 | 0.0 | 1 251 | D | D | 0.0 | 0.0 | 0 | 0.0 |
| Letcher | 4 | 33.3 | 55 | D | 0.8 | 91 932 | 1 678 | 39 957 | 0.2 | 2 547 | 46.4 | 53.6 | 6.1 | 0.0 | D | 6.1 |
| Lewis | 147 | 2.1 | 218 | 0.1 | 41.1 | 333 249 | 1 528 | 44 630 | 9.7 | 14 455 | 47.9 | 52.1 | 28.5 | 2.7 | 330 | 36.8 |
| Lincoln | 178 | 4.1 | 140 | 0.2 | 83.9 | 331 780 | 2 378 | 50 492 | 52.5 | 41 110 | 17.2 | 82.8 | 37.8 | 9.4 | 985 | 33.3 |
| Livingston | 117 | -19.9 | 238 | 0.0 | 61.3 | 467 157 | 1 964 | 54 817 | 12.8 | 26 117 | 42.3 | 57.7 | 26.6 | 4.5 | 1 159 | 53.5 |
| Logan | 290 | 5.1 | 247 | 0.5 | 198.4 | 658 369 | 2 661 | 76 535 | 81.0 | 69 102 | 56.3 | 43.7 | 39.0 | 10.2 | 3 560 | 49.2 |
| Lyon | 54 | -3.6 | 201 | D | 29.4 | 345 058 | 1 720 | 50 969 | 6.7 | 24 697 | 78.8 | 21.2 | 26.3 | 4.1 | 652 | 57.8 |
| McCracken | 75 | -11.8 | 156 | 0.2 | 58.2 | 456 391 | 2 926 | 61 289 | 21.0 | 43 422 | 71.1 | 28.9 | 24.8 | 10.4 | 918 | 57.3 |
| McCreary | 15 | 0.0 | 108 | 0.1 | 5.1 | 258 738 | 2 389 | 42 651 | 0.9 | 6 559 | 16.9 | 83.0 | 14.4 | 0.7 | 15 | 15.1 |
| McLean | 144 | 11.6 | 344 | D | 117.6 | 1 036 508 | 3 012 | 132 390 | 161.1 | 384 390 | 26.3 | 73.7 | 57.8 | 32.0 | 1 712 | 71.8 |
| Madison | 218 | 0.0 | 164 | 0.4 | 108.6 | 484 906 | 2 951 | 51 885 | 42.5 | 31 994 | 18.0 | 82.0 | 39.3 | 6.4 | 680 | 27.3 |
| Magoffin | 62 | 34.8 | 131 | D | 13.9 | 220 451 | 1 681 | 28 809 | 1.8 | 3 878 | 39.6 | 60.4 | 7.0 | 0.6 | 109 | 24.7 |
| Marion | 161 | -5.8 | 152 | 0.4 | 78.8 | 372 658 | 2 447 | 55 914 | 39.7 | 37 586 | 25.5 | 74.5 | 43.9 | 7.8 | 1 119 | 41.8 |
| Marshall | 98 | -19.0 | 113 | 0.1 | 56.0 | 287 521 | 2 551 | 48 562 | 30.4 | 35 074 | 27.7 | 72.3 | 18.5 | 3.9 | 1 407 | 51.6 |
| Martin | 7 | 40.0 | 374 | D | 1.1 | 311 793 | 833 | 26 840 | 0.1 | 4 166 | 22.8 | 77.2 | 10.5 | 0.0 | 0 | 0.0 |
| Mason | 140 | 9.4 | 186 | 0.0 | 78.5 | 469 349 | 2 528 | 57 456 | 28.4 | 37 745 | 39.5 | 60.5 | 47.1 | 8.5 | 798 | 41.6 |
| Meade | 121 | -10.4 | 137 | 0.2 | 65.2 | 403 270 | 2 945 | 67 210 | 28.7 | 32 370 | 42.9 | 57.1 | 31.6 | 4.7 | 1 213 | 46.1 |
| Menifee | 43 | 16.2 | 130 | 0.0 | 15.1 | 245 018 | 1 881 | 33 349 | 2.7 | 8 153 | 34.5 | 65.5 | 22.7 | 0.3 | 106 | 17.8 |
| Mercer | 141 | 5.2 | 127 | 0.1 | 74.9 | 435 542 | 3 421 | 55 937 | 43.2 | 38 865 | 12.4 | 87.6 | 33.8 | 6.6 | 1 173 | 23.4 |
| Metcalfe | 149 | 12.9 | 155 | 0.1 | 69.3 | 361 808 | 2 333 | 54 573 | 33.4 | 34 608 | 19.1 | 80.9 | 40.2 | 7.4 | 708 | 35.9 |
| Monroe | 176 | 8.6 | 184 | 0.1 | 73.2 | 427 772 | 2 324 | 59 660 | 54.3 | 56 809 | 10.1 | 89.9 | 44.6 | 8.9 | 838 | 36.1 |
| Montgomery | 107 | 17.6 | 156 | 0.1 | 53.9 | 394 100 | 2 524 | 50 070 | 18.1 | 26 393 | 35.2 | 64.8 | 37.5 | 5.1 | 614 | 32.6 |
| Morgan | 136 | 17.2 | 171 | 0.1 | 41.3 | 278 108 | 1 622 | 40 588 | 6.8 | 8 516 | 47.1 | 52.9 | 24.7 | 0.3 | 172 | 20.4 |
| Muhlenberg | 141 | 2.2 | 221 | 0.1 | 74.5 | 437 738 | 1 977 | 66 153 | 49.2 | 77 329 | 30.7 | 69.3 | 34.7 | 7.7 | 1 173 | 45.6 |
| Nelson | 196 | 3.7 | 140 | 1.6 | 104.8 | 454 205 | 3 254 | 58 736 | 54.8 | 38 978 | 30.0 | 70.0 | 32.9 | 7.5 | 1 189 | 32.8 |
| Nicholas | 110 | 3.8 | 183 | 0.1 | 55.5 | 361 083 | 1 976 | 63 561 | 15.7 | 26 066 | 42.6 | 57.4 | 40.1 | 6.0 | 226 | 15.3 |

| STATE County | Water use, 2005 | | Wholesale trade,[1] 2007 | | | | Retail trade,[2] 2007 | | | | Real estate and rental and leasing,[2] 2007 | | | |
|---|---|---|---|---|---|---|---|---|---|---|---|---|---|---|
| | Total water withdrawn (mil gal/day) | Gallons withdrawn per person | Number of establishments | Number of employees | Sales (mil dol) | Annual payroll (mil dol) | Number of establishments | Number of employees | Sales (mil dol) | Annual payroll (mil dol) | Number of establishments | Number of employees | Receipts (mil dol) | Annual payroll (mil dol) |
| | 133 | 134 | 135 | 136 | 137 | 138 | 139 | 140 | 141 | 142 | 143 | 144 | 145 | 146 |
| KENTUCKY—Cont'd | | | | | | | | | | | | | | |
| Clay | 4.5 | 187 | 7 | 35 | 13.2 | 0.6 | 72 | 549 | 138.7 | 10.3 | 10 | 19 | 1.7 | 0.3 |
| Clinton | 3.8 | 399 | 11 | 79 | 38.7 | 1.6 | 42 | 232 | 55.3 | 3.7 | 7 | 28 | 3.3 | 0.8 |
| Crittenden | 2.2 | 244 | 5 | 108 | 9.4 | 2.5 | 29 | 286 | 53.4 | 4.9 | 7 | 27 | 31.7 | 0.9 |
| Cumberland | 0.9 | 132 | NA | NA | NA | NA | 34 | 225 | 44.2 | 3.6 | 4 | D | D | D |
| Daviess | 223.2 | 2 398 | 95 | 1 166 | 818.1 | 45.8 | 442 | 5 936 | 1 282.9 | 123.4 | 78 | 518 | 49.7 | 10.9 |
| Edmonson | 1.3 | 110 | 1 | D | D | D | 27 | 171 | 32.5 | 2.7 | NA | NA | NA | NA |
| Elliott | 0.5 | 65 | NA | NA | NA | NA | 14 | 52 | 12.2 | 0.9 | NA | NA | NA | NA |
| Estill | 1.4 | 92 | 3 | D | D | D | 45 | 321 | 84.2 | 6.0 | 6 | 27 | 1.7 | 0.4 |
| Fayette | 49.9 | 186 | 375 | 8 540 | 4 442.4 | 568.5 | 1 249 | 22 335 | 4 778.5 | 510.4 | 476 | 2 268 | 391.2 | 68.2 |
| Fleming | 1.2 | 84 | 19 | 112 | 29.8 | 2.9 | 70 | 539 | 128.5 | 10.8 | 7 | 11 | 1.8 | 0.1 |
| Floyd | 4.4 | 105 | 39 | 497 | 404.4 | 16.8 | 181 | 1 535 | 403.3 | 33.3 | 27 | 99 | 12.1 | 2.1 |
| Franklin | 11.7 | 242 | 23 | 249 | 223.6 | 10.5 | 198 | 2 719 | 622.1 | 59.4 | 47 | 146 | 23.8 | 3.6 |
| Fulton | 1.8 | 242 | 6 | D | D | D | 40 | 268 | 52.2 | 3.5 | 3 | 3 | 0.6 | 0.1 |
| Gallatin | 2.8 | 343 | 3 | D | D | D | 20 | 185 | 37.3 | 2.7 | 5 | D | D | D |
| Garrard | 2.2 | 132 | 5 | 30 | 7.1 | 0.9 | 38 | 179 | 39.6 | 3.0 | 5 | D | D | D |
| Grant | 2.5 | 102 | 9 | D | D | D | 94 | 1 053 | 285.2 | 22.4 | 19 | 51 | 4.5 | 1.0 |
| Graves | 9.9 | 262 | 40 | D | D | D | 130 | 1 427 | 342.5 | 31.5 | 25 | 96 | 6.4 | 1.2 |
| Grayson | 3.7 | 148 | 13 | D | D | D | 101 | 1 097 | 234.9 | 21.8 | 14 | 134 | 5.8 | 1.5 |
| Green | 3.1 | 266 | 5 | 14 | 1.9 | 0.2 | 36 | 242 | 64.4 | 4.0 | 4 | 8 | 1.8 | 0.2 |
| Greenup | 10.8 | 290 | 5 | 22 | 3.6 | 0.4 | 120 | 1 431 | 355.7 | 25.6 | 20 | 72 | 8.3 | 1.3 |
| Hancock | 266.9 | 30 982 | 4 | 15 | 3.3 | 0.3 | 17 | 147 | 28.1 | 2.0 | 5 | D | D | D |
| Hardin | 14.0 | 144 | 54 | 479 | 281.1 | 15.8 | 433 | 6 012 | 1 449.5 | 132.2 | 102 | D | D | D |
| Harlan | 4.3 | 136 | 24 | 227 | 159.3 | 7.5 | 99 | 1 045 | 211.1 | 19.0 | 16 | 50 | 5.8 | 0.9 |
| Harrison | 3.4 | 181 | 10 | 86 | 39.8 | 1.6 | 64 | 724 | 147.0 | 12.8 | 11 | 44 | 5.4 | 0.8 |
| Hart | 4.6 | 253 | 10 | 41 | 21.4 | 1.1 | 69 | 429 | 92.8 | 6.5 | 7 | D | D | D |
| Henderson | 36.2 | 794 | 44 | 687 | 545.0 | 26.3 | 183 | 2 508 | 662.0 | 54.6 | 40 | 218 | 22.0 | 5.1 |
| Henry | 0.9 | 57 | 11 | 136 | 46.5 | 4.8 | 38 | 355 | 153.3 | 6.8 | 3 | 4 | 0.8 | 0.1 |
| Hickman | 1.4 | 274 | 5 | 36 | 29.1 | 0.8 | 20 | 301 | 65.4 | 5.8 | 3 | 7 | 0.3 | 0.0 |
| Hopkins | 13.5 | 289 | 45 | D | D | D | 203 | 2 478 | 560.5 | 50.9 | 33 | 144 | 13.0 | 2.8 |
| Jackson | 1.3 | 93 | 3 | D | D | D | 32 | 221 | 45.2 | 3.0 | 4 | 14 | 1.2 | 0.3 |
| Jefferson | 794.2 | 1 135 | 1 026 | 16 413 | 13 000.6 | 763.2 | 2 775 | 43 687 | 10 002.4 | 978.5 | 991 | 6 888 | 1 995.1 | 263.3 |
| Jessamine | 6.1 | 141 | 37 | D | D | D | 163 | 2 388 | 731.7 | 60.2 | 46 | 202 | 28.1 | 6.4 |
| Johnson | 2.8 | 115 | 19 | 163 | 106.1 | 5.9 | 106 | 1 519 | 350.1 | 28.7 | 16 | 46 | 5.2 | 0.8 |
| Kenton | 6.4 | 42 | 140 | D | D | D | 426 | 6 589 | 1 262.0 | 124.9 | 132 | 856 | 180.0 | 26.6 |
| Knott | 1.9 | 108 | 3 | D | D | D | 34 | 203 | 47.6 | 3.8 | 4 | 11 | 1.0 | 0.2 |
| Knox | 1.1 | 35 | 12 | 85 | 63.7 | 2.6 | 106 | 1 260 | 318.6 | 26.8 | 8 | 75 | 4.4 | 1.8 |
| Larue | 1.2 | 90 | 9 | 39 | 19.8 | 0.9 | 31 | 217 | 49.2 | 4.0 | 4 | D | D | D |
| Laurel | 12.1 | 215 | 60 | D | D | D | 233 | 3 306 | 914.7 | 75.8 | 37 | 179 | 22.5 | 3.4 |
| Lawrence | 14.0 | 864 | 6 | D | D | D | 54 | 528 | 123.6 | 8.9 | 10 | 35 | 4.8 | 0.8 |
| Lee | 0.8 | 101 | 3 | D | D | D | 25 | 212 | 58.6 | 4.4 | 6 | D | D | D |
| Leslie | 1.3 | 107 | NA | NA | NA | NA | 33 | 306 | 59.4 | 4.8 | 2 | D | D | D |
| Letcher | 3.4 | 140 | 13 | 95 | 51.8 | 3.2 | 68 | 621 | 124.0 | 11.4 | 9 | 20 | 3.1 | 0.4 |
| Lewis | 1.8 | 129 | 2 | D | D | D | 38 | 281 | 56.8 | 3.6 | 5 | 14 | 0.6 | 0.1 |
| Lincoln | 3.1 | 124 | 15 | D | D | D | 61 | 659 | 127.2 | 10.8 | 11 | 11 | 2.3 | 0.2 |
| Livingston | 7.8 | 794 | 7 | D | D | D | 25 | 163 | 29.7 | 3.2 | 2 | D | D | D |
| Logan | 1.1 | 42 | 20 | 157 | 132.9 | 5.2 | 101 | 1 008 | 230.6 | 19.8 | 17 | 46 | 5.8 | 1.0 |
| Lyon | 3.1 | 374 | 3 | D | D | D | 29 | 235 | 61.0 | 4.4 | 9 | 16 | 2.1 | 0.4 |
| McCracken | 1 300.5 | 20 101 | 102 | 1 759 | 3 529.6 | 70.4 | 474 | 6 673 | 1 570.8 | 137.6 | 90 | 408 | 62.5 | 10.3 |
| McCreary | 2.0 | 116 | 3 | 9 | 1.3 | 0.2 | 52 | 406 | 82.5 | 6.8 | 6 | 29 | 2.2 | 0.7 |
| McLean | 1.6 | 157 | 7 | 98 | 38.6 | 2.8 | 29 | 215 | 48.0 | 4.4 | 2 | D | D | D |
| Madison | 13.1 | 168 | 45 | 405 | 242.1 | 14.3 | 322 | 4 190 | 976.0 | 82.4 | 75 | 241 | 36.9 | 5.0 |
| Magoffin | 0.9 | 70 | 4 | 28 | 11.6 | 0.7 | 33 | 248 | 52.9 | 4.0 | 3 | 10 | 0.8 | 0.2 |
| Marion | 5.5 | 290 | 11 | 66 | 22.9 | 1.3 | 74 | 625 | 136.2 | 10.5 | 10 | 36 | 4.6 | 0.9 |
| Marshall | 23.0 | 743 | 31 | 284 | 97.2 | 9.3 | 115 | 1 115 | 345.7 | 25.5 | 24 | 69 | 8.3 | 1.1 |
| Martin | 4.9 | 402 | 5 | 59 | 123.7 | 2.8 | 47 | 412 | 108.0 | 7.0 | 8 | 142 | 36.5 | 7.0 |
| Mason | 15.7 | 917 | 17 | D | D | D | 113 | 1 490 | 358.0 | 31.1 | 14 | 43 | 5.6 | 1.1 |
| Meade | 4.7 | 167 | 13 | 72 | 40.8 | 2.3 | 66 | 673 | 170.7 | 11.7 | 18 | 56 | 4.1 | 0.8 |
| Menifee | 0.6 | 93 | NA | NA | NA | NA | 17 | 169 | 24.2 | 1.8 | 4 | D | D | D |
| Mercer | 25.9 | 1 197 | 12 | 45 | 15.0 | 0.8 | 74 | 907 | 157.0 | 18.4 | 17 | 59 | 8.2 | 1.2 |
| Metcalfe | 1.0 | 102 | 1 | D | D | D | 32 | 304 | 58.0 | 5.2 | 5 | 10 | 0.6 | 0.2 |
| Monroe | 2.4 | 208 | 7 | 64 | 28.8 | 1.5 | 50 | 499 | 100.0 | 9.1 | 4 | 5 | 0.8 | 0.1 |
| Montgomery | 3.3 | 136 | 19 | D | D | D | 130 | 1 523 | 355.8 | 31.0 | 25 | 76 | 8.2 | 1.4 |
| Morgan | 0.5 | 36 | 1 | D | D | D | 56 | 408 | 88.1 | 7.7 | 5 | 13 | 1.3 | 0.2 |
| Muhlenberg | 496.7 | 15 745 | 8 | D | D | D | 105 | 1 224 | 265.6 | 24.6 | 22 | 78 | 6.5 | 1.7 |
| Nelson | 7.8 | 190 | 28 | 290 | 217.5 | 9.6 | 173 | 1 926 | 422.3 | 39.2 | 36 | 108 | 14.1 | 2.8 |
| Nicholas | 2.7 | 383 | NA | NA | NA | NA | 19 | 124 | 27.4 | 2.3 | 2 | D | D | D |

1. Merchant wholesalers, except manufacturers' sales branches and offices.   2. Employer establishments.

# Table B. States and Counties — Professional Services, Manufacturing, and Accommodation and Food Services

| STATE<br>County | Professional, scientific, and technical services,[1] 2007 | | | | Manufacturing, 2007 | | | | Accommodation and food services, 2007 | | | |
|---|---|---|---|---|---|---|---|---|---|---|---|---|
| | Number of establishments | Number of employees | Receipts (mil dol) | Annual payroll (mil dol) | Number of establishments | Number of employees | Receipts (mil dol) | Annual payroll (mil dol) | Number of establishments | Number of employees | Sales (mil dol) | Annual payroll (mil dol) |
| | 147 | 148 | 149 | 150 | 151 | 152 | 153 | 154 | 155 | 156 | 157 | 158 |
| KENTUCKY—Cont'd | | | | | | | | | | | | |
| Clay | 22 | 108 | 12.9 | 2.5 | NA | NA | NA | NA | 14 | 361 | 12.4 | 3.5 |
| Clinton | 14 | 34 | 2.5 | 0.8 | 14 | 1 731 | D | 44.4 | 16 | 223 | 7.8 | 1.4 |
| Crittenden | 14 | 42 | 3.6 | 0.7 | NA | NA | NA | NA | 12 | 152 | 5.1 | 1.1 |
| Cumberland | 9 | 24 | 1.4 | 0.4 | NA | NA | NA | NA | 11 | 122 | 4.5 | 1.4 |
| Daviess | 167 | D | D | D | 110 | 6 486 | 2 920.0 | 269.3 | 172 | 3 999 | 147.4 | 44.5 |
| Edmonson | 9 | D | D | D | NA | NA | NA | NA | 13 | 144 | 6.3 | 1.6 |
| Elliott | 1 | D | D | D | NA | NA | NA | NA | 5 | 37 | 3.2 | 0.5 |
| Estill | 9 | 23 | 1.0 | 0.3 | NA | NA | NA | NA | 19 | 223 | 7.9 | 2.0 |
| Fayette | 1 053 | D | D | D | 255 | 9 602 | 3 061.2 | 401.7 | 704 | 17 027 | 785.7 | 230.3 |
| Fleming | 13 | 40 | 3.2 | 1.0 | NA | NA | NA | NA | 12 | 146 | 6.0 | 1.8 |
| Floyd | 68 | D | D | D | NA | NA | NA | NA | 46 | 729 | 34.9 | 8.4 |
| Franklin | 121 | 705 | 88.9 | 31.4 | 41 | 3 566 | 1 400.8 | 141.7 | 95 | 2 121 | 80.5 | 25.5 |
| Fulton | 13 | D | D | D | 10 | 516 | D | D | 13 | D | D | D |
| Gallatin | 8 | D | D | D | NA | NA | NA | NA | 8 | D | D | D |
| Garrard | 17 | 36 | 2.0 | 0.7 | NA | NA | NA | NA | 12 | 126 | 4.5 | 1.1 |
| Grant | 23 | D | D | D | 17 | D | D | 29.1 | 46 | 864 | 30.0 | 8.7 |
| Graves | 36 | D | D | D | 49 | 2 240 | D | 61.8 | 49 | D | D | D |
| Grayson | 19 | 83 | 5.8 | 2.1 | 29 | 2 240 | 692.0 | 62.9 | 30 | 446 | 16.2 | 4.2 |
| Green | 14 | 30 | 2.7 | 0.7 | NA | NA | NA | NA | 10 | 102 | 4.0 | 1.0 |
| Greenup | 34 | D | D | D | 15 | 526 | D | 21.6 | 28 | 504 | 21.0 | 5.7 |
| Hancock | 7 | D | D | D | 14 | 2 709 | D | D | 10 | 71 | 2.2 | 0.5 |
| Hardin | 142 | D | D | D | 79 | 5 423 | 1 792.3 | 224.5 | 180 | 4 566 | 168.6 | 52.9 |
| Harlan | 47 | D | D | D | NA | NA | NA | NA | 28 | 528 | 20.3 | 5.1 |
| Harrison | 18 | 64 | 3.7 | 1.2 | 21 | 1 354 | 549.6 | 67.4 | 19 | 391 | 11.3 | 3.0 |
| Hart | 18 | 69 | 4.0 | 1.4 | 18 | 1 882 | 434.6 | 59.9 | 22 | 337 | 11.5 | 2.5 |
| Henderson | 81 | 404 | 34.9 | 11.1 | 77 | 6 420 | D | D | 88 | 1 348 | 54.7 | 15.1 |
| Henry | 21 | D | D | D | 10 | D | D | D | 13 | D | D | D |
| Hickman | 6 | 17 | 0.7 | 0.3 | NA | NA | NA | NA | 3 | D | D | D |
| Hopkins | 66 | D | D | D | 52 | 2 897 | 896.3 | 128.8 | 64 | 1 406 | 53.7 | 13.9 |
| Jackson | 6 | 12 | 1.1 | 0.5 | NA | NA | NA | NA | 5 | 42 | 2.1 | 0.5 |
| Jefferson | 2 266 | D | D | D | 797 | 45 142 | 25 695.4 | 2 233.8 | 1 561 | 35 897 | 1 629.2 | 480.6 |
| Jessamine | 66 | 224 | 20.6 | 6.4 | 67 | 2 738 | 1 015.6 | 102.8 | 59 | 1 183 | 46.4 | 13.0 |
| Johnson | 33 | 167 | 18.3 | 5.0 | NA | NA | NA | NA | 36 | 848 | 27.2 | 7.6 |
| Kenton | 366 | D | D | D | 123 | 4 637 | 1 236.4 | 210.3 | 307 | 7 033 | 323.3 | 94.2 |
| Knott | 12 | 52 | 5.1 | 1.8 | NA | NA | NA | NA | 4 | 109 | 3.0 | 0.8 |
| Knox | 40 | D | D | D | 18 | 879 | 210.7 | 34.0 | 37 | 580 | 27.5 | 5.7 |
| Larue | 14 | D | D | D | 20 | 783 | 90.0 | 20.6 | 14 | 146 | 5.9 | 1.6 |
| Laurel | 100 | 431 | 36.6 | 11.8 | 58 | 3 668 | D | 124.8 | 91 | 2 146 | 91.0 | 25.0 |
| Lawrence | 14 | 78 | 5.4 | 2.6 | NA | NA | NA | NA | 15 | 319 | 11.5 | 3.1 |
| Lee | 5 | D | D | D | NA | NA | NA | NA | 6 | 64 | 2.5 | 0.6 |
| Leslie | 10 | D | D | D | NA | NA | NA | NA | 6 | 81 | 3.9 | 0.9 |
| Letcher | 23 | 139 | 11.5 | 4.4 | NA | NA | NA | NA | 23 | 347 | 14.1 | 3.8 |
| Lewis | 4 | 16 | 0.8 | 0.4 | NA | NA | NA | NA | 13 | 102 | 3.9 | 0.8 |
| Lincoln | 23 | 128 | 9.8 | 3.3 | 18 | 737 | D | D | 17 | 259 | 9.4 | 2.6 |
| Livingston | 7 | D | D | D | NA | NA | NA | NA | 13 | D | D | D |
| Logan | 30 | 157 | 12.8 | 4.6 | 46 | 3 021 | 2 150.6 | 127.7 | 29 | 379 | 15.3 | 3.7 |
| Lyon | 9 | 132 | 2.9 | 1.3 | NA | NA | NA | NA | 23 | 313 | 12.2 | 3.5 |
| McCracken | 193 | D | D | D | 54 | 3 170 | D | D | 203 | 4 697 | 179.2 | 50.9 |
| McCreary | 7 | 33 | 2.3 | 0.5 | NA | NA | NA | NA | 18 | 247 | 7.1 | 1.9 |
| McLean | 8 | D | D | D | NA | NA | NA | NA | 14 | 101 | 3.1 | 0.8 |
| Madison | 120 | D | D | D | 73 | 5 473 | D | D | 143 | 3 368 | 127.3 | 34.7 |
| Magoffin | 13 | 94 | 13.3 | 6.2 | NA | NA | NA | NA | 11 | 163 | 7.3 | 2.0 |
| Marion | 23 | 110 | 7.7 | 2.9 | 30 | 3 349 | 620.2 | 120.1 | 29 | 417 | 12.3 | 3.6 |
| Marshall | 43 | 169 | 14.3 | 7.3 | 42 | 2 726 | 3 095.3 | 163.9 | 82 | 1 249 | 42.7 | 11.8 |
| Martin | 13 | 47 | 2.8 | 0.8 | NA | NA | NA | NA | 16 | 153 | 4.9 | 1.1 |
| Mason | 29 | 288 | 30.2 | 11.9 | 13 | D | D | D | 48 | 914 | 36.5 | 9.4 |
| Meade | 19 | D | D | D | 5 | D | D | D | 27 | D | D | D |
| Menifee | 2 | D | D | D | NA | NA | NA | NA | 1 | D | D | D |
| Mercer | 34 | 61 | 4.9 | 1.4 | 12 | 2 212 | 1 252.4 | 118.6 | 35 | 536 | 20.7 | 5.7 |
| Metcalfe | 9 | 16 | 1.2 | 0.3 | 9 | 979 | 391.3 | 32.4 | 9 | 101 | 5.1 | 0.7 |
| Monroe | 7 | 20 | 1.3 | 0.3 | 28 | 744 | 146.5 | 22.6 | 17 | 175 | 6.5 | 1.5 |
| Montgomery | 34 | D | D | D | 33 | 3 384 | D | 144.8 | 37 | 764 | 30.9 | 8.3 |
| Morgan | 9 | 42 | 3.0 | 0.8 | NA | NA | NA | NA | 13 | 226 | 8.1 | 1.9 |
| Muhlenberg | 41 | 166 | 7.1 | 2.1 | 26 | 547 | D | 22.6 | 55 | 786 | 27.2 | 7.5 |
| Nelson | 47 | 191 | 15.1 | 4.3 | 65 | 3 572 | 1 348.7 | 144.9 | 59 | D | D | D |
| Nicholas | 7 | D | D | D | NA | NA | NA | NA | 5 | 28 | 0.8 | 0.2 |

1. Establishment subject to federal tax.

# Table B. States and Counties — **Health Care and Social Assistance, Other Services, and Federal Funds**

| STATE County | Health care and social assistance, 2007 | | | | Other services, 2007 | | | | Federal funds and grants, 2009–2010 Expenditures (mil dol) | | | |
|---|---|---|---|---|---|---|---|---|---|---|---|---|
| | | | | | | | | | | Direct payments for individuals[1] | | |
| | Number of establishments | Number of employees | Receipts (mil dol) | Annual payroll (mil dol) | Number of establishments | Number of employees | Receipts (mil dol) | Annual payroll (mil dol) | Total | Social Security and government retirement | Medicare | Food Stamps and Supplemental Security Income |
| | 159 | 160 | 161 | 162 | 163 | 164 | 165 | 166 | 167 | 168 | 169 | 170 |
| KENTUCKY—Cont'd | | | | | | | | | | | | |
| Clay | 33 | 1 068 | 62.3 | 30.9 | 11 | D | D | D | 388.5 | 62.5 | 140.7 | 44.3 |
| Clinton | 24 | 609 | 35.4 | 14.3 | 8 | 17 | 1.2 | 0.3 | 165.7 | 31.3 | 71.4 | 10.4 |
| Crittenden | 17 | 471 | 28.3 | 12.7 | 14 | D | D | D | 93.2 | 33.9 | 34.8 | 4.1 |
| Cumberland | 14 | 382 | 22.4 | 9.7 | 7 | 19 | 1.9 | 0.4 | 105.8 | 21.8 | 46.4 | 5.7 |
| Daviess | 302 | D | D | D | 158 | D | D | D | 797.0 | 316.8 | 219.8 | 46.2 |
| Edmonson | 16 | D | D | D | 6 | 14 | 1.5 | 0.3 | 118.4 | 32.5 | 34.9 | 6.5 |
| Elliott | 9 | D | D | D | 4 | D | D | D | 90.7 | 35.3 | 25.0 | 8.6 |
| Estill | 22 | 388 | 26.7 | 9.5 | 11 | 22 | 2.5 | 0.5 | 203.6 | 55.6 | 76.1 | 16.7 |
| Fayette | 969 | 26 453 | 3 046.9 | 1 172.3 | 590 | 4 928 | 509.8 | 149.5 | 3 036.1 | 707.9 | 434.4 | 86.7 |
| Fleming | 21 | 614 | 42.1 | 16.0 | 14 | 33 | 2.9 | 0.5 | 150.6 | 44.6 | 48.5 | 8.4 |
| Floyd | 127 | 2 271 | 203.1 | 71.4 | 50 | 257 | 25.5 | 6.8 | 580.2 | 173.3 | 187.3 | 64.6 |
| Franklin | 145 | 2 315 | 256.7 | 76.2 | 142 | 797 | 90.9 | 26.5 | 2 671.2 | 197.4 | 220.3 | 18.6 |
| Fulton | 12 | D | D | D | 8 | D | D | D | 118.8 | 30.8 | 43.2 | 7.1 |
| Gallatin | 9 | D | D | D | NA | NA | NA | NA | 60.0 | 21.6 | 17.0 | 3.4 |
| Garrard | 21 | 203 | 13.3 | 5.5 | 14 | 64 | 3.4 | 1.0 | 122.3 | 53.8 | 35.2 | 6.9 |
| Grant | 33 | 519 | 43.1 | 17.5 | 34 | D | D | D | 164.2 | 76.4 | 44.5 | 10.7 |
| Graves | 94 | 1 642 | 113.4 | 39.1 | 31 | 177 | 25.7 | 6.6 | 431.2 | 140.9 | 125.7 | 14.9 |
| Grayson | 53 | 994 | 80.4 | 27.7 | 25 | 78 | 6.9 | 1.1 | 263.2 | 88.8 | 91.0 | 16.1 |
| Green | 27 | 500 | 31.4 | 13.0 | 15 | 47 | 3.2 | 0.7 | 107.2 | 33.6 | 42.0 | 6.1 |
| Greenup | 79 | 983 | 75.9 | 35.0 | 30 | D | D | D | 350.6 | 159.2 | 106.8 | 20.3 |
| Hancock | 13 | 136 | 6.2 | 2.1 | 7 | D | D | D | 64.0 | 27.1 | 19.4 | 3.0 |
| Hardin | 308 | D | D | D | 153 | D | D | D | 2 788.9 | 473.3 | 160.5 | 36.6 |
| Harlan | 54 | 1 362 | 128.9 | 41.6 | 26 | 125 | 8.9 | 2.6 | 639.8 | 130.2 | 148.0 | 196.8 |
| Harrison | 46 | 903 | 71.3 | 27.1 | 22 | 73 | 6.8 | 1.5 | 172.0 | 58.3 | 48.1 | 9.4 |
| Hart | 24 | 408 | 28.4 | 10.9 | 16 | 46 | 3.4 | 1.0 | 168.5 | 51.5 | 60.9 | 11.0 |
| Henderson | 141 | D | D | D | 70 | D | D | D | 360.5 | 150.1 | 117.0 | 22.6 |
| Henry | 21 | D | D | D | 15 | 55 | 4.6 | 1.4 | 131.3 | 45.0 | 46.7 | 7.0 |
| Hickman | 9 | 148 | 8.4 | 3.1 | 2 | D | D | D | 52.1 | 14.7 | 19.2 | 2.6 |
| Hopkins | 113 | 3 152 | 259.2 | 122.7 | 72 | 561 | 51.2 | 14.2 | 523.9 | 172.9 | 129.5 | 28.6 |
| Jackson | 17 | 272 | 15.8 | 6.4 | 4 | D | D | D | 206.2 | 38.8 | 68.8 | 17.1 |
| Jefferson | 2 227 | 58 914 | 6 171.5 | 2 309.4 | 1 402 | 12 526 | 1 315.0 | 317.2 | 9 420.0 | 2 277.8 | 1 886.6 | 172.8 |
| Jessamine | 76 | 726 | 43.7 | 21.6 | 73 | 281 | 19.6 | 5.9 | 243.9 | 120.5 | 54.4 | 15.1 |
| Johnson | 62 | 778 | 86.5 | 23.8 | 32 | 116 | 9.5 | 2.2 | 321.3 | 93.5 | 103.5 | 29.2 |
| Kenton | 337 | 9 485 | 1 026.0 | 418.4 | 249 | 1 848 | 150.4 | 43.6 | 1 195.5 | 415.1 | 309.3 | 57.3 |
| Knott | 17 | 380 | 19.3 | 7.4 | 8 | D | D | D | 236.0 | 50.8 | 83.4 | 23.9 |
| Knox | 71 | 1 071 | 76.4 | 29.5 | 21 | 74 | 6.7 | 1.8 | 453.8 | 79.1 | 148.4 | 48.1 |
| Larue | 15 | D | D | D | 16 | D | D | D | 126.0 | 48.2 | 42.6 | 7.0 |
| Laurel | 128 | 2 861 | 265.9 | 97.5 | 73 | 422 | 37.7 | 10.1 | 497.3 | 172.2 | 136.8 | 40.5 |
| Lawrence | 30 | D | D | D | 15 | D | D | D | 200.1 | 61.0 | 68.2 | 20.2 |
| Lee | 17 | 853 | 16.6 | 9.5 | 1 | D | D | D | 113.4 | 23.4 | 43.5 | 12.8 |
| Leslie | 15 | 431 | 33.1 | 12.9 | 3 | D | D | D | 189.4 | 42.2 | 73.5 | 18.3 |
| Letcher | 44 | 1 097 | 79.9 | 35.5 | 16 | 49 | 5.6 | 1.0 | 321.5 | 97.2 | 111.7 | 32.4 |
| Lewis | 13 | 307 | 25.9 | 10.4 | 3 | D | D | D | 155.7 | 39.5 | 56.5 | 13.3 |
| Lincoln | 34 | 543 | 33.4 | 15.4 | 17 | 45 | 3.9 | 0.8 | 266.1 | 80.8 | 90.7 | 15.8 |
| Livingston | 16 | D | D | D | 6 | 24 | 1.5 | 0.4 | 175.9 | 42.7 | 33.4 | 3.5 |
| Logan | 48 | 703 | 54.6 | 18.3 | 36 | 173 | 12.9 | 3.6 | 280.2 | 87.8 | 105.7 | 11.0 |
| Lyon | 13 | 238 | 10.4 | 4.7 | 10 | 12 | 1.1 | 0.3 | 73.9 | 37.1 | 21.1 | 2.4 |
| McCracken | 264 | 6 501 | 723.3 | 257.3 | 136 | D | D | D | 1 717.4 | 258.6 | 197.9 | 31.9 |
| McCreary | 29 | 360 | 17.3 | 7.3 | 6 | 21 | 1.6 | 0.3 | 265.9 | 54.8 | 77.5 | 27.3 |
| McLean | 9 | D | D | D | 13 | D | D | D | 91.5 | 35.5 | 29.6 | 4.4 |
| Madison | 186 | 3 241 | 238.4 | 91.1 | 89 | 395 | 31.5 | 7.8 | 1 014.7 | 228.8 | 157.4 | 32.4 |
| Magoffin | 14 | 255 | 21.5 | 5.8 | 8 | D | D | D | 203.8 | 41.3 | 78.3 | 22.7 |
| Marion | 43 | 1 019 | 74.2 | 28.1 | 17 | 76 | 7.4 | 1.9 | 176.3 | 52.9 | 62.0 | 10.4 |
| Marshall | 52 | 938 | 54.1 | 22.0 | 42 | 157 | 14.6 | 3.2 | 263.8 | 131.9 | 77.0 | 8.6 |
| Martin | 19 | 227 | 12.7 | 5.0 | 10 | D | D | D | 191.0 | 49.4 | 51.6 | 21.8 |
| Mason | 71 | 1 187 | 107.9 | 37.2 | 45 | D | D | D | 172.6 | 56.0 | 58.4 | 8.1 |
| Meade | 36 | 259 | 15.2 | 6.2 | 24 | 122 | 9.0 | 2.5 | 159.8 | 90.4 | 34.8 | 7.3 |
| Menifee | 7 | 142 | 8.7 | 4.0 | 3 | D | D | D | 141.6 | 25.7 | 23.4 | 7.3 |
| Mercer | 36 | 624 | 41.8 | 17.2 | 25 | D | D | D | 176.1 | 73.4 | 48.7 | 9.0 |
| Metcalfe | 16 | 117 | 6.4 | 2.9 | 6 | D | D | D | 112.8 | 30.7 | 43.0 | 6.9 |
| Monroe | 29 | 475 | 32.0 | 12.6 | 13 | 42 | 3.0 | 0.7 | 181.2 | 35.9 | 77.4 | 10.2 |
| Montgomery | 74 | 1 277 | 76.5 | 28.5 | 32 | D | D | D | 203.6 | 78.0 | 63.9 | 13.1 |
| Morgan | 18 | 445 | 30.4 | 11.4 | 17 | 38 | 3.2 | 0.7 | 198.3 | 37.0 | 59.0 | 13.9 |
| Muhlenberg | 58 | D | D | D | 43 | 160 | 12.4 | 3.0 | 400.9 | 124.5 | 98.9 | 19.3 |
| Nelson | 86 | 1 380 | 113.5 | 40.9 | 50 | 255 | 16.5 | 4.5 | 284.5 | 114.4 | 79.9 | 14.8 |
| Nicholas | 10 | 258 | 13.3 | 6.3 | 7 | 26 | 1.5 | 0.4 | 85.8 | 23.1 | 27.0 | 4.6 |

1. State totals may include programs not allocated by county.

# Federal Funds, Residential Construction, and Local Government Finances

| STATE County | Federal funds and grants, 2009–2010 (cont.) | | | | | | | Value of residential construction authorized by building permits, 2011 | | Local government finances, 2007 | | | | |
| | Expenditures (mil dol) (cont.) | | | | | | | | | General revenue | | | | |
| | Procurement contract awards | | | Grants[1] | | | | | | | | Taxes | | |
| | | | | | | | | | | | | | Per capita[2] (dollars) | |
| | Salaries and wages | Defense | Other | Medicaid and other health-related | Nutrition and family welfare | Education | Other | New con-struction ($1,000) | Number of housing units | Total (mil dol) | Inter-govern-mental (mil dol) | Total (mil dol) | Total | Property |
| | 171 | 172 | 173 | 174 | 175 | 176 | 177 | 178 | 179 | 180 | 181 | 182 | 183 | 184 |
| KENTUCKY—Cont'd | | | | | | | | | | | | | | |
| Clay | 25.1 | 0.0 | 5.3 | 96.6 | 7.8 | 3.6 | 1.1 | 0 | 0 | 46.1 | 33.7 | 6.2 | 262 | 150 |
| Clinton | 3.9 | 2.7 | 0.4 | 38.5 | 2.6 | 2.8 | 0.2 | 0 | 0 | 23.0 | 16.1 | 4.4 | 460 | 228 |
| Crittenden | 2.7 | 0.0 | 0.5 | 12.1 | 1.4 | 0.9 | 0.3 | 60 | 1 | 17.6 | 11.9 | 3.4 | 377 | 253 |
| Cumberland | 1.3 | 0.0 | 0.2 | 25.7 | 1.8 | 0.7 | 0.7 | 0 | 0 | 13.8 | 9.3 | 2.9 | 428 | 205 |
| Daviess | 36.5 | 2.2 | 7.0 | 66.5 | 25.8 | 5.6 | 25.9 | 19 851 | 269 | 278.0 | 107.7 | 81.9 | 873 | 525 |
| Edmonson | 11.1 | 0.9 | 10.3 | 17.5 | 2.1 | 0.9 | 0.0 | NA | NA | 22.5 | 15.6 | 4.1 | 340 | 253 |
| Elliott | 0.7 | 0.0 | 0.2 | 17.5 | 2.1 | 0.7 | 0.1 | NA | NA | 15.0 | 12.2 | 1.6 | 218 | 156 |
| Estill | 7.2 | 0.0 | 0.6 | 39.2 | 3.5 | 1.6 | 2.0 | 0 | 0 | 29.0 | 19.1 | 5.3 | 357 | 229 |
| Fayette | 255.1 | 460.0 | 289.7 | 340.8 | 43.0 | 27.6 | 131.7 | 83 346 | 739 | 671.8 | 148.8 | 426.4 | 1 528 | 594 |
| Fleming | 3.9 | 0.1 | 1.8 | 26.7 | 5.7 | 1.4 | 4.3 | 230 | 3 | 50.8 | 18.0 | 6.6 | 446 | 275 |
| Floyd | 21.0 | 0.7 | 16.9 | 92.4 | 9.8 | 4.0 | 4.6 | 750 | 5 | 85.1 | 53.6 | 21.1 | 503 | 402 |
| Franklin | 117.9 | 0.8 | 3.5 | 224.6 | 215.3 | 351.2 | 1 225.8 | 1 676 | 10 | 134.4 | 38.0 | 58.3 | 1 203 | 567 |
| Fulton | 3.6 | 1.4 | 1.0 | 20.4 | 1.9 | 1.8 | 1.8 | 630 | 9 | 24.6 | 15.4 | 4.7 | 686 | 369 |
| Gallatin | 1.9 | 5.7 | 0.5 | 6.9 | 1.3 | 0.6 | 0.2 | 2 439 | 18 | 26.6 | 10.4 | 7.3 | 903 | 542 |
| Garrard | 2.1 | 0.0 | 0.5 | 15.8 | 2.3 | 1.1 | 0.4 | 85 | 1 | 30.8 | 17.8 | 9.3 | 547 | 377 |
| Grant | 4.4 | 0.1 | 1.0 | 16.7 | 4.6 | 2.0 | 0.7 | 4 939 | 24 | 56.0 | 33.9 | 13.5 | 536 | 402 |
| Graves | 13.1 | 0.0 | 2.6 | 42.8 | 5.9 | 2.3 | 63.3 | 763 | 7 | 76.2 | 40.9 | 20.2 | 538 | 360 |
| Grayson | 7.5 | 1.3 | 1.2 | 44.0 | 6.3 | 1.8 | 0.2 | 650 | 7 | 61.7 | 40.0 | 12.7 | 499 | 255 |
| Green | 1.9 | 0.0 | 0.5 | 16.8 | 1.8 | 0.9 | 0.4 | 0 | 0 | 36.3 | 13.6 | 4.6 | 397 | 255 |
| Greenup | 5.6 | 5.4 | 1.3 | 37.1 | 5.7 | 2.0 | 4.0 | 5 581 | 55 | 76.2 | 40.5 | 22.7 | 610 | 500 |
| Hancock | 1.4 | 0.0 | 0.3 | 9.3 | 1.1 | 0.6 | 0.2 | 1 435 | 8 | 47.8 | 11.5 | 7.8 | 904 | 426 |
| Hardin | 1 611.9 | 316.7 | 92.1 | 56.2 | 15.8 | 5.6 | 1.8 | 60 774 | 687 | 405.5 | 108.8 | 66.8 | 682 | 383 |
| Harlan | 12.3 | 1.3 | 51.7 | 79.0 | 10.2 | 5.3 | 1.8 | 0 | 0 | 65.0 | 47.3 | 12.4 | 400 | 281 |
| Harrison | 12.7 | 0.8 | 2.0 | 22.2 | 2.8 | 1.5 | 9.2 | 3 588 | 20 | 36.0 | 18.8 | 13.4 | 720 | 309 |
| Hart | 3.0 | 0.1 | 0.7 | 31.9 | 2.6 | 1.7 | 1.0 | 6 470 | 61 | 35.6 | 23.2 | 7.5 | 405 | 234 |
| Henderson | 10.6 | 1.1 | 1.8 | 33.3 | 6.2 | 3.0 | 4.8 | 8 101 | 64 | 124.0 | 53.7 | 35.0 | 773 | 417 |
| Henry | 3.5 | 0.0 | 0.8 | 19.7 | 2.6 | 1.0 | 0.2 | 3 415 | 16 | 33.2 | 18.7 | 9.1 | 581 | 404 |
| Hickman | 1.4 | 0.0 | 0.3 | 7.8 | 0.9 | 0.6 | 0.2 | NA | NA | 9.9 | 7.0 | 2.0 | 402 | 300 |
| Hopkins | 20.6 | 6.0 | 89.9 | 50.0 | 7.5 | 5.4 | 6.9 | 7 241 | 55 | 108.5 | 58.7 | 31.3 | 677 | 372 |
| Jackson | 2.6 | 4.9 | 1.9 | 44.9 | 4.2 | 1.7 | 19.5 | 0 | 0 | 25.3 | 20.6 | 3.6 | 267 | 172 |
| Jefferson | 505.4 | 3 079.7 | 177.8 | 701.0 | 113.9 | 95.8 | 186.3 | 139 942 | 1 006 | 2 164.0 | 655.6 | 982.3 | 1 385 | 736 |
| Jessamine | 6.8 | 0.6 | 7.3 | 21.0 | 4.6 | 2.3 | 3.3 | 33 755 | 167 | 101.7 | 39.6 | 47.3 | 1 039 | 612 |
| Johnson | 4.1 | 0.4 | 1.3 | 55.8 | 13.6 | 2.3 | 15.6 | 1 596 | 10 | 62.3 | 38.3 | 14.6 | 609 | 334 |
| Kenton | 205.5 | 2.7 | 27.8 | 91.9 | 22.7 | 7.8 | 43.2 | 35 410 | 241 | 547.8 | 128.7 | 197.8 | 1 263 | 753 |
| Knott | 4.0 | 0.4 | 0.8 | 53.4 | 9.3 | 2.1 | 5.7 | NA | NA | 36.8 | 28.3 | 6.0 | 346 | 283 |
| Knox | 22.3 | 25.7 | 1.1 | 96.8 | 16.6 | 3.5 | 8.3 | 0 | 0 | 80.1 | 48.6 | 14.0 | 432 | 230 |
| Larue | 2.8 | 0.0 | 1.6 | 16.7 | 2.2 | 1.1 | 0.3 | 3 288 | 27 | 29.3 | 20.2 | 5.6 | 409 | 289 |
| Laurel | 30.2 | 0.3 | 22.9 | 72.7 | 9.7 | 4.1 | 5.1 | 280 | 2 | 106.9 | 62.1 | 30.6 | 534 | 286 |
| Lawrence | 3.0 | 0.1 | 0.7 | 40.0 | 3.8 | 1.8 | 0.7 | NA | NA | 45.6 | 22.8 | 6.1 | 371 | 258 |
| Lee | 1.4 | 0.0 | 0.3 | 27.4 | 2.3 | 0.7 | 1.0 | NA | NA | 20.4 | 13.4 | 3.7 | 499 | 285 |
| Leslie | 2.2 | 0.0 | 0.7 | 45.3 | 4.3 | 1.0 | 1.9 | NA | NA | 25.4 | 19.3 | 4.4 | 373 | 291 |
| Letcher | 5.9 | 0.0 | 2.0 | 62.1 | 6.2 | 2.2 | 1.4 | 193 | 8 | 50.8 | 34.7 | 10.4 | 434 | 338 |
| Lewis | 1.8 | 0.0 | 0.4 | 34.1 | 3.1 | 1.2 | 2.1 | NA | NA | 25.2 | 19.4 | 4.3 | 311 | 225 |
| Lincoln | 13.1 | 0.0 | 1.2 | 51.2 | 6.5 | 2.2 | 0.5 | 3 569 | 20 | 47.6 | 34.3 | 9.5 | 375 | 224 |
| Livingston | 3.7 | 61.6 | 15.5 | 10.6 | 1.6 | 0.7 | 0.0 | NA | NA | 18.4 | 11.2 | 5.1 | 526 | 319 |
| Logan | 6.0 | 0.1 | 1.2 | 46.6 | 3.9 | 1.9 | 1.1 | 1 326 | 22 | 66.1 | 37.4 | 18.8 | 694 | 336 |
| Lyon | 2.1 | 0.1 | 0.3 | 6.3 | 0.9 | 0.4 | 1.7 | 1 100 | 6 | 19.3 | 7.8 | 5.9 | 721 | 527 |
| McCracken | 46.5 | 0.5 | 1 078.8 | 61.6 | 11.2 | 4.1 | 6.9 | 31 951 | 156 | 165.6 | 73.2 | 61.3 | 946 | 473 |
| McCreary | 28.0 | 20.5 | 5.4 | 43.0 | 6.0 | 2.6 | 0.3 | 0 | 0 | 39.0 | 28.5 | 7.4 | 429 | 317 |
| McLean | 1.6 | 0.1 | 0.3 | 9.3 | 1.5 | 0.9 | 3.4 | 171 | 1 | 26.1 | 13.9 | 6.4 | 661 | 309 |
| Madison | 125.9 | 315.2 | 3.5 | 76.3 | 14.5 | 9.9 | 6.3 | 16 038 | 239 | 155.5 | 69.1 | 63.2 | 779 | 375 |
| Magoffin | 1.4 | 0.0 | 0.4 | 51.9 | 4.6 | 1.8 | 0.6 | NA | NA | 32.7 | 23.4 | 5.1 | 384 | 212 |
| Marion | 3.9 | 0.0 | 1.1 | 32.2 | 6.8 | 1.6 | 1.1 | 462 | 4 | 45.8 | 22.7 | 12.7 | 668 | 379 |
| Marshall | 14.5 | 0.0 | 3.6 | 18.4 | 4.1 | 1.7 | 0.4 | 4 342 | 62 | 125.3 | 31.8 | 32.4 | 1 038 | 504 |
| Martin | 23.8 | 0.6 | 5.3 | 31.6 | 3.7 | 1.4 | 1.7 | NA | NA | 28.3 | 19.7 | 6.1 | 521 | 332 |
| Mason | 5.9 | 0.0 | 0.9 | 27.3 | 2.8 | 1.6 | 5.9 | 1 945 | 12 | 50.8 | 19.6 | 16.4 | 952 | 426 |
| Meade | 4.8 | 0.7 | 0.8 | 11.5 | 3.7 | 1.3 | 0.0 | 11 884 | 102 | 52.2 | 30.9 | 13.2 | 485 | 368 |
| Menifee | 58.5 | 7.6 | 1.2 | 14.4 | 1.3 | 0.5 | 0.6 | NA | NA | 15.0 | 10.5 | 2.6 | 391 | 257 |
| Mercer | 9.7 | 1.1 | 0.8 | 20.7 | 2.8 | 1.3 | 3.8 | 4 672 | 37 | 44.5 | 21.9 | 16.6 | 761 | 446 |
| Metcalfe | 2.2 | 0.2 | 0.5 | 23.6 | 1.9 | 1.0 | 0.1 | NA | NA | 20.6 | 13.8 | 5.0 | 483 | 231 |
| Monroe | 5.2 | 0.2 | 0.5 | 42.6 | 2.4 | 1.0 | 1.4 | NA | NA | 24.7 | 18.3 | 4.5 | 386 | 232 |
| Montgomery | 5.4 | 0.0 | 1.1 | 30.0 | 3.8 | 2.3 | 1.5 | 3 434 | 24 | 58.9 | 29.5 | 17.8 | 704 | 373 |
| Morgan | 2.6 | 0.0 | 0.6 | 37.7 | 6.0 | 1.2 | 38.7 | 0 | 0 | 33.4 | 25.2 | 4.4 | 311 | 199 |
| Muhlenberg | 19.3 | -3.6 | 94.6 | 36.3 | 5.2 | 1.9 | 1.1 | 538 | 3 | 60.7 | 40.0 | 11.7 | 373 | 288 |
| Nelson | 17.6 | 8.8 | 2.0 | 30.6 | 5.4 | 2.1 | 3.4 | 16 351 | 149 | 94.6 | 45.2 | 27.3 | 643 | 508 |
| Nicholas | 10.3 | 0.0 | 0.3 | 13.5 | 1.5 | 0.6 | 0.3 | 0 | 0 | 13.3 | 8.4 | 2.8 | 411 | 239 |

1. State totals may include programs not allocated by county.  2. Based on the resident population estimated as of July 1 of the year shown.

| | Local government finances, 2007 (cont.) | | | | | | | | | Government employment, 2011 | | | Presidential election,[2] 2012 | | |
| | Direct general expenditure | | | | | | | Debt outstanding | | | | | Percent of vote cast: | | |
| | | | | Percent of total for: | | | | | | | | | | | |
| STATE County | Total (mil dol) | Per capita[1] (dollars) | Education | Health and hospitals | Police protection | Public welfare | Highways | Total (mil dol) | Per capita[1] (dollars) | Federal civilian | Federal military | State and local | Democratic | Republican | All other |
|---|---|---|---|---|---|---|---|---|---|---|---|---|---|---|---|
| | 185 | 186 | 187 | 188 | 189 | 190 | 191 | 192 | 193 | 194 | 195 | 196 | 197 | 198 | 199 |
| **KENTUCKY—Cont'd** | | | | | | | | | | | | | | | |
| Clay | 45.3 | 1 909 | 68.1 | 1.6 | 3.1 | 0.0 | 4.3 | 33.2 | 1 400 | 371 | 71 | 1 218 | 21.1 | 77.5 | 1.4 |
| Clinton | 20.0 | 2 097 | 73.5 | 3.2 | 2.6 | 0.0 | 4.6 | 21.5 | 2 256 | 50 | 33 | 618 | 18.2 | 80.7 | 1.1 |
| Crittenden | 15.8 | 1 729 | 60.8 | 0.9 | 3.8 | 0.0 | 10.6 | 27.4 | 3 004 | 23 | 30 | 421 | 31.9 | 66.3 | 1.8 |
| Cumberland | 13.7 | 1 992 | 66.0 | 0.3 | 4.6 | 0.0 | 7.0 | 23.9 | 3 480 | 0 | 22 | 339 | 24.9 | 73.5 | 1.6 |
| Daviess | 275.0 | 2 933 | 44.7 | 1.7 | 4.5 | 0.1 | 3.2 | 1 042.2 | 11 117 | 269 | 334 | 8 832 | 44.2 | 54.3 | 1.5 |
| Edmonson | 21.2 | 1 773 | 70.1 | 3.9 | 2.5 | 0.0 | 7.0 | 39.0 | 3 252 | 248 | 39 | 527 | 31.3 | 67.6 | 1.1 |
| Elliott | 13.7 | 1 912 | 85.0 | 4.8 | 1.4 | 0.0 | 0.2 | 25.3 | 3 544 | 0 | 25 | 532 | 61.0 | 35.9 | 3.1 |
| Estill | 28.7 | 1 917 | 69.1 | 3.8 | 1.7 | 0.0 | 5.4 | 31.1 | 2 075 | 20 | 48 | 687 | 29.3 | 69.3 | 1.4 |
| Fayette | 637.7 | 2 285 | 44.5 | 3.6 | 7.9 | 1.7 | 0.6 | 1 151.0 | 4 125 | 4 265 | 1 035 | 37 468 | 51.7 | 46.9 | 1.3 |
| Fleming | 48.9 | 3 327 | 37.5 | 34.4 | 1.7 | 0.0 | 3.0 | 194.8 | 13 259 | 51 | 47 | 956 | 39.1 | 58.8 | 2.1 |
| Floyd | 88.5 | 2 106 | 65.7 | 0.1 | 1.9 | 0.0 | 2.4 | 87.0 | 2 070 | 141 | 128 | 2 459 | 48.1 | 49.4 | 2.5 |
| Franklin | 138.8 | 2 867 | 36.2 | 2.5 | 3.8 | 0.4 | 4.4 | 182.3 | 3 765 | 534 | 185 | 14 432 | 48.9 | 49.5 | 1.7 |
| Fulton | 24.8 | 3 652 | 38.1 | 0.6 | 3.5 | 0.1 | 4.3 | 34.9 | 5 141 | 25 | 39 | 526 | 43.8 | 54.2 | 2.0 |
| Gallatin | 36.6 | 4 559 | 63.1 | 1.5 | 2.3 | 0.0 | 2.5 | 179.9 | 22 394 | 31 | 28 | 422 | 40.0 | 57.6 | 2.3 |
| Garrard | 27.9 | 1 637 | 68.2 | 3.1 | 3.3 | 0.0 | 3.1 | 14.1 | 828 | 21 | 55 | 634 | 27.9 | 71.0 | 1.1 |
| Grant | 61.3 | 2 435 | 68.6 | 0.4 | 2.8 | 0.1 | 4.0 | 92.7 | 3 684 | 46 | 81 | 1 184 | 35.5 | 62.9 | 1.5 |
| Graves | 78.6 | 2 093 | 60.4 | 0.2 | 2.6 | 0.0 | 3.6 | 199.7 | 5 316 | 209 | 122 | 1 754 | 36.2 | 62.2 | 1.6 |
| Grayson | 54.5 | 2 150 | 51.0 | 0.3 | 2.9 | 0.7 | 6.4 | 111.2 | 4 387 | 83 | 85 | 1 613 | 31.8 | 66.7 | 1.5 |
| Green | 34.7 | 2 998 | 36.0 | 45.1 | 1.1 | 0.0 | 3.9 | 27.3 | 2 362 | 26 | 37 | 741 | 23.7 | 74.5 | 1.8 |
| Greenup | 74.9 | 2 011 | 63.5 | 1.0 | 3.6 | 0.0 | 3.4 | 55.6 | 1 491 | 60 | 120 | 1 516 | 41.9 | 56.0 | 2.1 |
| Hancock | 46.3 | 5 374 | 25.3 | 1.1 | 1.1 | 0.1 | 2.3 | 690.9 | 80 177 | 19 | 28 | 434 | 51.5 | 46.5 | 2.0 |
| Hardin | 383.8 | 3 919 | 31.5 | 49.9 | 2.1 | 0.1 | 2.0 | 308.9 | 3 154 | 6 910 | 11 811 | 6 766 | 39.1 | 59.8 | 1.1 |
| Harlan | 75.7 | 2 435 | 74.2 | 0.7 | 2.1 | 0.2 | 2.5 | 118.7 | 3 820 | 93 | 95 | 1 838 | 26.1 | 72.3 | 1.6 |
| Harrison | 33.4 | 1 799 | 61.5 | 1.1 | 5.7 | 0.2 | 7.3 | 26.5 | 1 431 | 47 | 61 | 861 | 38.4 | 59.6 | 2.0 |
| Hart | 42.8 | 2 324 | 66.0 | 3.2 | 2.2 | 0.0 | 3.3 | 71.0 | 3 858 | 34 | 59 | 859 | 33.6 | 64.5 | 1.9 |
| Henderson | 115.1 | 2 540 | 41.9 | 0.4 | 4.9 | 0.1 | 4.9 | 569.6 | 12 576 | 122 | 151 | 2 740 | 50.6 | 47.9 | 1.5 |
| Henry | 31.7 | 2 017 | 64.4 | 4.0 | 3.8 | 0.1 | 4.5 | 29.4 | 1 870 | 98 | 50 | 731 | 39.4 | 59.0 | 1.6 |
| Hickman | 10.0 | 2 028 | 63.6 | 0.4 | 3.5 | 0.0 | 6.4 | 9.3 | 1 885 | 19 | 16 | 245 | 36.1 | 62.5 | 1.4 |
| Hopkins | 110.6 | 2 390 | 54.2 | 0.2 | 5.4 | 1.2 | 5.1 | 377.4 | 8 154 | 160 | 153 | 3 474 | 36.7 | 61.6 | 1.7 |
| Jackson | 25.2 | 1 852 | 77.3 | 1.0 | 1.2 | 0.0 | 6.0 | 19.8 | 1 461 | 39 | 44 | 729 | 14.2 | 84.4 | 1.4 |
| Jefferson | 1 894.1 | 2 670 | 45.8 | 3.0 | 6.0 | 0.8 | 3.9 | 4 031.8 | 5 685 | 6 742 | 2 673 | 42 372 | 55.5 | 43.5 | 1.0 |
| Jessamine | 97.2 | 2 133 | 59.4 | 1.8 | 5.3 | 0.0 | 4.0 | 140.7 | 3 088 | 76 | 162 | 2 482 | 30.8 | 67.8 | 1.3 |
| Johnson | 58.2 | 2 422 | 63.7 | 5.7 | 3.2 | 0.1 | 5.3 | 57.2 | 2 382 | 47 | 76 | 1 506 | 28.3 | 69.8 | 1.9 |
| Kenton | 529.9 | 3 382 | 34.7 | 3.1 | 4.9 | 0.3 | 3.9 | 1 949.1 | 12 440 | 4 347 | 532 | 7 324 | 38.8 | 59.7 | 1.5 |
| Knott | 40.7 | 2 357 | 47.0 | 0.1 | 2.8 | 0.2 | 9.3 | 34.4 | 1 991 | 57 | 53 | 766 | 44.9 | 52.7 | 2.4 |
| Knox | 78.1 | 2 402 | 55.9 | 18.2 | 1.9 | 0.1 | 3.6 | 92.4 | 2 841 | 169 | 104 | 1 523 | 27.0 | 71.6 | 1.4 |
| Larue | 35.2 | 2 579 | 72.0 | 1.4 | 2.1 | 0.0 | 3.5 | 48.3 | 3 537 | 38 | 47 | 581 | 31.0 | 67.2 | 1.8 |
| Laurel | 119.1 | 2 077 | 73.2 | 0.3 | 3.8 | 0.0 | 1.9 | 217.6 | 3 794 | 303 | 194 | 2 694 | 20.5 | 78.5 | 1.0 |
| Lawrence | 44.9 | 2 749 | 48.6 | 0.1 | 1.7 | 0.0 | 5.1 | 291.8 | 17 876 | 33 | 52 | 684 | 36.0 | 62.0 | 1.9 |
| Lee | 17.6 | 2 370 | 55.6 | 9.8 | 3.4 | 0.1 | 8.2 | 10.6 | 1 429 | 17 | 25 | 472 | 27.1 | 71.3 | 1.6 |
| Leslie | 24.8 | 2 109 | 65.5 | 0.3 | 0.5 | 0.1 | 5.2 | 17.1 | 1 449 | 24 | 37 | 591 | 17.4 | 81.3 | 1.3 |
| Letcher | 51.7 | 2 151 | 67.8 | 0.2 | 2.5 | 0.1 | 4.4 | 34.3 | 1 426 | 61 | 80 | 1 111 | 31.9 | 65.2 | 3.0 |
| Lewis | 27.1 | 1 952 | 69.4 | 0.0 | 2.2 | 0.0 | 1.2 | 105.7 | 7 610 | 24 | 45 | 648 | 31.5 | 67.1 | 1.4 |
| Lincoln | 46.2 | 1 830 | 72.5 | 0.3 | 2.2 | 0.2 | 4.2 | 43.3 | 1 716 | 56 | 81 | 1 041 | 30.1 | 68.5 | 1.4 |
| Livingston | 18.9 | 1 964 | 56.9 | 5.3 | 2.5 | 0.1 | 6.8 | 17.9 | 1 866 | 94 | 31 | 489 | 35.3 | 62.9 | 1.8 |
| Logan | 65.0 | 2 394 | 57.7 | 14.5 | 4.7 | 0.0 | 3.9 | 48.6 | 1 792 | 64 | 87 | 1 240 | 35.0 | 63.6 | 1.4 |
| Lyon | 16.8 | 2 036 | 40.7 | 5.2 | 3.1 | 0.5 | 6.9 | 16.2 | 1 962 | 32 | 27 | 975 | 40.9 | 57.6 | 1.5 |
| McCracken | 148.2 | 2 288 | 49.0 | 0.2 | 4.1 | 0.1 | 6.7 | 148.7 | 2 296 | 673 | 241 | 4 018 | 36.7 | 61.9 | 1.4 |
| McCreary | 37.8 | 2 183 | 68.8 | 2.2 | 0.8 | 0.0 | 3.1 | 31.3 | 1 807 | 487 | 60 | 915 | 23.3 | 75.4 | 1.3 |
| McLean | 27.1 | 2 784 | 47.8 | 3.4 | 1.7 | 0.3 | 5.5 | 39.1 | 4 022 | 30 | 31 | 537 | 44.4 | 54.0 | 1.7 |
| Madison | 158.3 | 1 951 | 58.7 | 3.0 | 4.1 | 1.4 | 3.8 | 371.4 | 4 580 | 1 278 | 283 | 7 679 | 38.1 | 60.5 | 1.4 |
| Magoffin | 36.6 | 2 779 | 70.3 | 0.2 | 3.0 | 0.0 | 4.5 | 69.0 | 5 235 | 14 | 43 | 686 | 45.3 | 52.3 | 2.4 |
| Marion | 47.2 | 2 492 | 52.5 | 1.7 | 3.6 | 0.0 | 3.8 | 60.0 | 3 171 | 52 | 65 | 891 | 47.2 | 50.5 | 2.3 |
| Marshall | 123.0 | 3 936 | 27.5 | 11.2 | 3.5 | 0.3 | 2.6 | 464.2 | 14 852 | 93 | 102 | 1 684 | 36.7 | 61.4 | 1.9 |
| Martin | 26.4 | 2 270 | 67.3 | 3.3 | 1.8 | 0.6 | 5.8 | 14.4 | 1 235 | 378 | 42 | 720 | 21.9 | 76.5 | 1.6 |
| Mason | 49.6 | 2 887 | 39.4 | 1.1 | 5.4 | 0.0 | 7.8 | 334.8 | 19 477 | 51 | 58 | 1 618 | 40.6 | 57.6 | 1.8 |
| Meade | 62.5 | 2 290 | 74.6 | 1.9 | 1.9 | 0.0 | 2.2 | 80.9 | 2 967 | 39 | 96 | 1 100 | 38.8 | 59.7 | 1.5 |
| Menifee | 14.2 | 2 096 | 62.1 | 3.3 | 4.5 | 0.3 | 5.5 | 17.2 | 2 546 | 52 | 21 | 383 | 51.3 | 46.4 | 2.3 |
| Mercer | 47.1 | 2 159 | 65.5 | 0.4 | 3.9 | 0.0 | 4.7 | 112.4 | 5 155 | 45 | 69 | 893 | 31.4 | 67.4 | 1.2 |
| Metcalfe | 18.3 | 1 783 | 65.3 | 2.5 | 3.4 | 0.0 | 7.8 | 13.7 | 1 333 | 25 | 33 | 542 | 32.2 | 65.1 | 2.7 |
| Monroe | 28.5 | 2 444 | 70.8 | 0.2 | 3.0 | 0.0 | 6.7 | 27.9 | 2 389 | 29 | 36 | 638 | 22.9 | 75.8 | 1.3 |
| Montgomery | 59.9 | 2 376 | 59.1 | 4.1 | 4.9 | 0.0 | 4.4 | 140.7 | 5 576 | 66 | 87 | 1 140 | 41.0 | 57.6 | 1.5 |
| Morgan | 38.2 | 2 684 | 59.9 | 2.9 | 2.3 | 0.0 | 5.5 | 22.9 | 1 608 | 36 | 45 | 1 044 | 42.9 | 54.7 | 2.4 |
| Muhlenberg | 64.3 | 2 053 | 63.0 | 0.2 | 2.7 | 0.2 | 5.3 | 109.7 | 3 499 | 566 | 102 | 1 823 | 48.3 | 50.0 | 1.7 |
| Nelson | 102.9 | 2 420 | 55.6 | 2.0 | 3.8 | 0.3 | 2.5 | 208.2 | 4 897 | 82 | 143 | 1 759 | 42.2 | 55.9 | 1.9 |
| Nicholas | 12.4 | 1 796 | 61.2 | 1.1 | 4.3 | 0.6 | 7.5 | 10.1 | 1 470 | 14 | 23 | 326 | 42.8 | 55.0 | 2.2 |

1. Based on the resident population estimated as of July 1 of the year shown.   2. © 2013 Election Data Services, Inc. All rights reserved.

# Table B. States and Counties — Land Area and Population

| STATE/ County code | CBSA code[1] | County type[2] | STATE County | Land area,[3] (sq km) 2010 | Total persons | Rank | Per square kilometer | White | Black | American Indian, Alaska Native | Asian and Pacific Islander | Percent Hispanic or Latino[4] | Under 5 years | 5 to 17 years | 18 to 24 years | 25 to 34 years | 35 to 44 years | 45 to 54 years |
|---|---|---|---|---|---|---|---|---|---|---|---|---|---|---|---|---|---|---|
| | | | | 1 | 2 | 3 | 4 | 5 | 6 | 7 | 8 | 9 | 10 | 11 | 12 | 13 | 14 | 15 |
| | | | KENTUCKY—Cont'd | | | | | | | | | | | | | | | |
| 21 183 | ... | 6 | Ohio | 1 521 | 24 075 | 1 641 | 15.8 | 95.1 | 1.3 | 0.6 | 0.4 | 3.5 | 6.8 | 18.2 | 7.7 | 12.1 | 12.3 | 14.1 |
| 21 185 | 31140 | 1 | Oldham | 485 | 61 412 | 847 | 126.6 | 90.4 | 5.1 | 0.7 | 1.7 | 3.5 | 5.2 | 21.9 | 6.6 | 10.2 | 15.9 | 17.7 |
| 21 187 | ... | 8 | Owen | 909 | 10 765 | 2 377 | 11.8 | 96.0 | 1.5 | 0.5 | 0.3 | 2.6 | 5.9 | 18.7 | 7.3 | 11.0 | 13.2 | 15.1 |
| 21 189 | ... | 9 | Owsley | 511 | 4 722 | 2 857 | 9.2 | 98.3 | 0.7 | 0.6 | 0.2 | 0.9 | 5.6 | 17.1 | 7.8 | 11.7 | 12.3 | 14.7 |
| 21 191 | 17140 | 1 | Pendleton | 718 | 14 604 | 2 132 | 20.3 | 98.1 | 0.8 | 0.5 | 0.4 | 1.0 | 6.2 | 17.9 | 9.0 | 11.0 | 13.3 | 16.9 |
| 21 193 | ... | 7 | Perry | 880 | 28 241 | 1 482 | 32.1 | 96.9 | 2.2 | 0.5 | 0.7 | 0.7 | 6.2 | 15.7 | 8.6 | 12.7 | 13.7 | 15.4 |
| 21 195 | ... | 7 | Pike | 2 038 | 64 178 | 819 | 31.5 | 98.1 | 0.9 | 0.4 | 0.6 | 0.7 | 5.9 | 15.9 | 8.3 | 12.3 | 13.7 | 15.3 |
| 21 197 | ... | 6 | Powell | 464 | 12 483 | 2 274 | 26.9 | 97.9 | 1.0 | 0.6 | 0.4 | 1.1 | 6.9 | 17.7 | 8.1 | 12.1 | 13.6 | 15.0 |
| 21 199 | 43700 | 5 | Pulaski | 1 705 | 63 593 | 824 | 37.3 | 95.8 | 1.7 | 0.7 | 0.6 | 2.2 | 5.9 | 16.8 | 7.6 | 11.7 | 13.0 | 14.7 |
| 21 201 | ... | 8 | Robertson | 259 | 2 188 | 3 037 | 8.4 | 98.1 | 0.7 | 0.7 | 0.1 | 1.3 | 5.3 | 15.1 | 8.3 | 10.0 | 12.0 | 15.7 |
| 21 203 | 40080 | 7 | Rockcastle | 820 | 17 006 | 1 981 | 20.7 | 98.6 | 0.6 | 0.8 | 0.2 | 0.7 | 5.8 | 17.4 | 8.1 | 11.2 | 13.6 | 15.8 |
| 21 205 | ... | 7 | Rowan | 725 | 23 447 | 1 665 | 32.3 | 95.9 | 2.1 | 0.6 | 1.1 | 1.4 | 5.9 | 13.5 | 22.5 | 11.6 | 11.3 | 12.0 |
| 21 207 | ... | 9 | Russell | 657 | 17 497 | 1 952 | 26.6 | 95.4 | 1.0 | 0.6 | 0.5 | 3.4 | 6.2 | 15.9 | 7.8 | 11.0 | 12.7 | 14.9 |
| 21 209 | 30460 | 2 | Scott | 730 | 49 057 | 999 | 67.2 | 89.2 | 6.1 | 0.5 | 1.3 | 4.3 | 7.2 | 19.4 | 9.3 | 13.4 | 15.5 | 14.4 |
| 21 211 | 31140 | 1 | Shelby | 983 | 43 614 | 1 096 | 44.4 | 82.6 | 8.5 | 0.6 | 0.9 | 9.1 | 6.8 | 17.9 | 7.8 | 12.9 | 13.9 | 15.1 |
| 21 213 | ... | 6 | Simpson | 607 | 17 538 | 1 946 | 28.9 | 87.8 | 10.7 | 0.7 | 0.9 | 1.7 | 6.7 | 17.5 | 8.1 | 12.0 | 12.8 | 15.2 |
| 21 215 | 31140 | 1 | Spencer | 483 | 17 416 | 1 958 | 36.1 | 96.1 | 2.2 | 0.6 | 0.6 | 1.6 | 6.2 | 19.1 | 6.9 | 11.2 | 15.8 | 17.2 |
| 21 217 | 15820 | 7 | Taylor | 690 | 24 691 | 1 617 | 35.8 | 92.4 | 5.9 | 0.6 | 0.8 | 1.8 | 6.3 | 15.9 | 11.4 | 12.0 | 11.0 | 14.2 |
| 21 219 | ... | 8 | Todd | 970 | 12 651 | 2 264 | 13.0 | 87.5 | 8.6 | 0.6 | 0.3 | 4.2 | 7.5 | 19.7 | 8.3 | 12.1 | 12.5 | 14.2 |
| 21 221 | 17300 | 3 | Trigg | 1 143 | 14 447 | 2 142 | 12.6 | 89.8 | 8.9 | 0.9 | 0.6 | 1.3 | 5.6 | 16.3 | 7.0 | 9.2 | 12.2 | 14.6 |
| 21 223 | 31140 | 1 | Trimble | 393 | 8 787 | 2 535 | 22.4 | 96.0 | 1.1 | 0.7 | 0.6 | 2.6 | 6.1 | 18.4 | 7.8 | 11.2 | 14.4 | 15.7 |
| 21 225 | ... | 6 | Union | 888 | 14 850 | 2 119 | 16.7 | 85.2 | 13.1 | 0.6 | 0.7 | 1.8 | 6.2 | 16.5 | 14.8 | 10.9 | 11.1 | 13.3 |
| 21 227 | 14540 | 3 | Warren | 1 403 | 117 110 | 520 | 83.5 | 83.1 | 10.0 | 0.6 | 3.3 | 4.7 | 6.3 | 16.3 | 16.5 | 13.7 | 12.1 | 13.0 |
| 21 229 | ... | 8 | Washington | 770 | 11 833 | 2 308 | 15.4 | 89.8 | 7.1 | 0.5 | 0.5 | 3.5 | 5.8 | 17.3 | 8.9 | 10.3 | 12.6 | 15.8 |
| 21 231 | ... | 7 | Wayne | 1 187 | 20 824 | 1 787 | 17.5 | 95.0 | 2.0 | 0.7 | 0.5 | 3.0 | 5.9 | 16.4 | 8.3 | 11.4 | 12.8 | 14.1 |
| 21 233 | 21780 | 2 | Webster | 860 | 13 583 | 2 209 | 15.8 | 90.4 | 4.9 | 0.6 | 0.7 | 4.7 | 6.8 | 16.5 | 8.3 | 11.8 | 12.9 | 14.2 |
| 21 235 | 18340 | 7 | Whitley | 1 134 | 35 499 | 1 288 | 31.3 | 97.6 | 1.1 | 0.9 | 0.6 | 1.0 | 6.2 | 17.3 | 11.2 | 11.3 | 12.4 | 13.8 |
| 21 237 | ... | 9 | Wolfe | 575 | 7 164 | 2 662 | 12.5 | 98.9 | 0.3 | 0.6 | 0.1 | 0.5 | 6.7 | 17.5 | 6.9 | 11.6 | 11.9 | 15.5 |
| 21 239 | 30460 | 2 | Woodford | 489 | 25 077 | 1 606 | 51.3 | 87.6 | 5.7 | 0.5 | 0.7 | 6.8 | 5.7 | 17.7 | 7.6 | 10.5 | 13.2 | 16.7 |
| 22 000 | ... | X | LOUISIANA | 111 898 | 4 601 893 | X | 41.1 | 61.1 | 32.7 | 1.1 | 2.0 | 4.4 | 6.9 | 17.5 | 10.4 | 14.0 | 12.2 | 14.1 |
| 22 001 | 18940 | 4 | Acadia | 1 697 | 61 912 | 841 | 36.5 | 79.2 | 18.9 | 0.6 | 0.4 | 1.9 | 7.5 | 19.6 | 9.4 | 12.7 | 11.6 | 14.4 |
| 22 003 | ... | 6 | Allen | 1 973 | 25 539 | 1 584 | 12.9 | 71.7 | 24.3 | 3.0 | 0.9 | 1.5 | 6.4 | 16.3 | 8.6 | 15.2 | 14.3 | 14.6 |
| 22 005 | 12940 | 3 | Ascension | 751 | 112 286 | 533 | 149.5 | 71.3 | 23.0 | 0.6 | 1.2 | 4.8 | 7.7 | 20.7 | 8.3 | 13.9 | 15.1 | 14.5 |
| 22 007 | 38200 | 6 | Assumption | 877 | 23 026 | 1 689 | 26.3 | 66.8 | 30.4 | 0.9 | 0.5 | 2.3 | 6.1 | 17.8 | 9.1 | 12.3 | 12.3 | 15.2 |
| 22 009 | ... | 6 | Avoyelles | 2 156 | 41 632 | 1 138 | 19.3 | 67.4 | 30.1 | 1.7 | 0.6 | 1.6 | 6.8 | 17.2 | 8.9 | 13.1 | 12.5 | 14.3 |
| 22 011 | 19760 | 6 | Beauregard | 2 998 | 36 281 | 1 270 | 12.1 | 81.7 | 14.2 | 1.9 | 1.2 | 3.1 | 7.0 | 18.9 | 8.4 | 13.2 | 13.5 | 13.9 |
| 22 013 | ... | 6 | Bienville | 2 101 | 14 076 | 2 170 | 6.7 | 55.4 | 42.7 | 1.0 | 0.5 | 1.7 | 5.5 | 17.4 | 8.9 | 10.9 | 11.1 | 14.4 |
| 22 015 | 43340 | 2 | Bossier | 2 176 | 122 197 | 501 | 56.2 | 70.4 | 21.8 | 1.0 | 2.4 | 6.1 | 7.3 | 18.2 | 9.5 | 15.4 | 12.9 | 13.4 |
| 22 017 | 43340 | 2 | Caddo | 2 275 | 257 093 | 257 | 113.0 | 48.7 | 47.7 | 0.9 | 1.5 | 2.6 | 7.2 | 17.4 | 9.9 | 14.0 | 11.6 | 13.5 |
| 22 019 | 29340 | 3 | Calcasieu | 2 755 | 194 493 | 326 | 70.6 | 70.6 | 25.9 | 1.0 | 1.5 | 2.7 | 7.1 | 18.0 | 10.1 | 13.6 | 11.9 | 14.2 |
| 22 021 | ... | 8 | Caldwell | 1 371 | 10 004 | 2 443 | 7.3 | 79.6 | 18.0 | 0.6 | 0.4 | 2.3 | 6.2 | 16.9 | 8.7 | 12.1 | 13.0 | 14.3 |
| 22 023 | 29340 | 3 | Cameron | 3 328 | 6 702 | 2 708 | 2.0 | 94.1 | 2.8 | 0.8 | 0.3 | 2.8 | 6.0 | 18.6 | 8.1 | 12.6 | 12.0 | 17.8 |
| 22 025 | ... | 9 | Catahoula | 1 834 | 10 292 | 2 416 | 5.6 | 67.1 | 31.7 | 0.6 | 0.2 | 1.0 | 6.5 | 16.2 | 8.9 | 14.4 | 11.0 | 14.6 |
| 22 027 | ... | 7 | Claiborne | 1 955 | 16 828 | 1 992 | 8.6 | 47.6 | 50.8 | 0.7 | 0.6 | 1.2 | 5.2 | 13.9 | 8.9 | 14.7 | 13.1 | 14.7 |
| 22 029 | 35020 | 7 | Concordia | 1 805 | 20 365 | 1 822 | 11.3 | 57.6 | 40.9 | 0.6 | 0.5 | 1.2 | 6.7 | 18.3 | 8.8 | 13.2 | 11.5 | 13.8 |
| 22 031 | 43340 | 2 | De Soto | 2 268 | 26 963 | 1 531 | 11.9 | 57.4 | 39.3 | 1.2 | 0.4 | 2.9 | 6.6 | 18.0 | 8.2 | 11.8 | 11.9 | 15.0 |
| 22 033 | 12940 | 2 | East Baton Rouge | 1 179 | 444 526 | 150 | 377.0 | 47.6 | 45.8 | 0.6 | 3.3 | 3.8 | 6.7 | 16.4 | 15.0 | 15.1 | 11.3 | 12.8 |
| 22 035 | ... | 7 | East Carroll | 1 090 | 7 526 | 2 638 | 6.9 | 29.3 | 68.3 | 0.5 | 0.7 | 1.9 | 7.0 | 18.6 | 10.2 | 15.0 | 12.0 | 13.9 |
| 22 037 | 12940 | 2 | East Feliciana | 1 174 | 20 008 | 1 840 | 17.0 | 53.4 | 45.3 | 0.7 | 0.5 | 1.1 | 5.5 | 15.0 | 9.0 | 13.1 | 12.5 | 16.5 |
| 22 039 | ... | 6 | Evangeline | 1 716 | 33 710 | 1 334 | 19.6 | 68.6 | 28.8 | 0.6 | 0.6 | 2.4 | 7.5 | 19.3 | 9.7 | 12.6 | 11.9 | 13.9 |
| 22 041 | ... | 7 | Franklin | 1 618 | 20 561 | 1 809 | 12.7 | 67.2 | 31.5 | 0.5 | 0.4 | 1.1 | 7.4 | 18.0 | 8.5 | 11.8 | 11.1 | 14.0 |
| 22 043 | 10780 | 3 | Grant | 1 665 | 22 068 | 1 727 | 13.3 | 78.3 | 16.6 | 1.7 | 0.5 | 4.4 | 6.3 | 16.5 | 7.9 | 16.4 | 14.4 | 14.4 |
| 22 045 | 35340 | 4 | Iberia | 1 487 | 73 999 | 737 | 49.8 | 61.6 | 32.8 | 0.7 | 2.8 | 3.4 | 7.7 | 19.4 | 9.5 | 12.9 | 11.8 | 14.8 |
| 22 047 | 12940 | 2 | Iberville | 1 602 | 33 228 | 1 347 | 20.7 | 48.5 | 49.0 | 0.5 | 0.5 | 2.2 | 6.1 | 16.1 | 9.8 | 14.3 | 13.0 | 15.8 |
| 22 049 | 40820 | 6 | Jackson | 1 474 | 16 216 | 2 030 | 11.0 | 68.2 | 30.6 | 0.6 | 0.4 | 1.4 | 6.4 | 16.4 | 8.4 | 13.4 | 12.0 | 13.3 |
| 22 051 | 35380 | 1 | Jefferson | 766 | 433 676 | 156 | 566.2 | 56.7 | 26.7 | 0.8 | 4.4 | 12.7 | 6.5 | 15.8 | 8.9 | 14.4 | 12.4 | 14.8 |
| 22 053 | 27660 | 6 | Jefferson Davis | 1 687 | 31 432 | 1 404 | 18.6 | 79.8 | 18.6 | 0.8 | 0.5 | 1.9 | 7.4 | 19.1 | 8.3 | 12.2 | 11.6 | 14.6 |
| 22 055 | 29180 | 3 | Lafayette | 696 | 227 055 | 283 | 326.2 | 68.2 | 26.5 | 0.7 | 1.9 | 4.0 | 7.1 | 17.2 | 11.9 | 15.7 | 12.5 | 13.9 |
| 22 057 | 26380 | 3 | Lafourche | 2 767 | 97 029 | 602 | 35.1 | 79.0 | 14.1 | 3.3 | 1.0 | 4.0 | 7.0 | 17.2 | 10.3 | 13.6 | 12.5 | 15.1 |
| 22 059 | ... | 6 | La Salle | 1 618 | 14 927 | 2 113 | 9.2 | 84.1 | 12.5 | 1.3 | 0.4 | 2.4 | 6.7 | 16.8 | 9.1 | 14.2 | 12.6 | 13.5 |
| 22 061 | 40820 | 4 | Lincoln | 1 222 | 46 953 | 1 028 | 38.4 | 54.2 | 41.5 | 0.7 | 2.1 | 2.7 | 5.9 | 14.3 | 26.4 | 12.8 | 9.1 | 10.5 |
| 22 063 | 12940 | 6 | Livingston | 1 679 | 131 942 | 474 | 78.6 | 90.0 | 6.2 | 0.9 | 0.7 | 3.1 | 7.4 | 19.8 | 8.7 | 14.4 | 14.3 | 14.1 |
| 22 065 | 45260 | 7 | Madison | 1 617 | 12 154 | 2 290 | 7.5 | 37.4 | 60.8 | 0.6 | 0.4 | 1.7 | 7.0 | 17.8 | 9.7 | 16.0 | 11.9 | 13.7 |
| 22 067 | 12820 | 6 | Morehouse | 2 059 | 27 559 | 1 510 | 13.4 | 51.2 | 47.6 | 0.5 | 0.7 | 1.0 | 7.3 | 17.4 | 8.8 | 12.2 | 11.4 | 13.7 |
| 22 069 | 35060 | 6 | Natchitoches | 3 243 | 39 436 | 1 184 | 12.2 | 54.9 | 42.4 | 1.6 | 0.9 | 1.9 | 6.5 | 17.3 | 16.6 | 11.7 | 10.4 | 11.9 |

1. CBSA = Core Based Statistical Area. See Appendix A for explanation. See Appendix B for list of metropolitan areas with component counties.   2. County type code from the Economic Research Service of USDA Rural-Urban Continuum Codes. See Appendix A for definition.   3. Dry land or land partially or temporarily covered by water.   4. May be of any race.

# Table B. States and Counties — **Population and Households**

| STATE County | Age (percent) (cont.) 55 to 64 years | 65 to 74 years | 75 years and over | Percent female | Total persons 2000 | 2010 | Percent change 2000–2010 | 2010–2012 | Components of change, 2010–2012 Births | Deaths | Net migration | Households, 2010 Number | Percent change, 2000–2010 | Persons per house-hold | Female family house-holder[1] | One per-son |
|---|---|---|---|---|---|---|---|---|---|---|---|---|---|---|---|---|
| | 16 | 17 | 18 | 19 | 20 | 21 | 22 | 23 | 24 | 25 | 26 | 27 | 28 | 29 | 30 | 31 |
| KENTUCKY—Cont'd | | | | | | | | | | | | | | | | |
| Ohio | 13.1 | 9.2 | 6.6 | 50.2 | 22 916 | 23 842 | 4.0 | 1.0 | 704 | 573 | 109 | 9 176 | 3.1 | 2.56 | 10.7 | 24.0 |
| Oldham | 12.9 | 6.4 | 3.3 | 47.4 | 46 178 | 60 316 | 30.6 | 1.8 | 1 120 | 738 | 695 | 19 431 | 30.8 | 2.87 | 9.1 | 15.5 |
| Owen | 13.9 | 9.0 | 5.9 | 50.6 | 10 547 | 10 841 | 2.8 | -0.7 | 241 | 247 | -60 | 4 296 | 5.1 | 2.52 | 9.2 | 25.3 |
| Owsley | 14.8 | 9.3 | 6.7 | 50.4 | 4 858 | 4 755 | -2.1 | -0.7 | 138 | 167 | -2 | 1 914 | 1.1 | 2.44 | 13.7 | 28.4 |
| Pendleton | 13.2 | 7.4 | 5.2 | 50.1 | 14 390 | 14 877 | 3.4 | -1.8 | 419 | 349 | -344 | 5 494 | 6.3 | 2.67 | 10.7 | 21.4 |
| Perry | 14.2 | 8.2 | 5.4 | 50.4 | 29 390 | 28 712 | -2.3 | -1.6 | 876 | 976 | -368 | 11 319 | -1.2 | 2.48 | 14.2 | 26.3 |
| Pike | 14.5 | 8.5 | 5.7 | 51.0 | 68 736 | 65 024 | -5.4 | -1.3 | 1 673 | 1 798 | -693 | 26 728 | -3.2 | 2.39 | 12.5 | 27.2 |
| Powell | 13.2 | 8.3 | 5.1 | 50.3 | 13 237 | 12 613 | -4.7 | -1.0 | 379 | 347 | -159 | 4 834 | -4.2 | 2.57 | 13.6 | 24.8 |
| Pulaski | 13.8 | 9.6 | 7.0 | 51.2 | 56 217 | 63 063 | 12.2 | 0.8 | 1 668 | 1 678 | 558 | 25 722 | 13.2 | 2.41 | 11.9 | 26.7 |
| Robertson | 14.6 | 10.3 | 8.6 | 49.2 | 2 266 | 2 282 | 0.7 | -4.1 | 37 | 77 | -55 | 902 | 4.2 | 2.47 | 9.6 | 24.8 |
| Rockcastle | 13.0 | 9.1 | 6.0 | 50.9 | 16 582 | 17 056 | 2.9 | -0.3 | 373 | 503 | 74 | 6 750 | 3.1 | 2.48 | 12.6 | 25.6 |
| Rowan | 10.7 | 7.2 | 5.3 | 51.2 | 22 094 | 23 333 | 5.6 | 0.5 | 596 | 470 | -21 | 8 864 | 11.8 | 2.36 | 11.2 | 28.6 |
| Russell | 14.0 | 9.9 | 7.7 | 51.1 | 16 315 | 17 565 | 7.7 | -0.4 | 482 | 509 | -33 | 7 401 | 6.6 | 2.35 | 11.8 | 28.7 |
| Scott | 11.3 | 5.8 | 3.8 | 50.8 | 33 061 | 47 173 | 42.7 | 4.0 | 1 433 | 721 | 1 153 | 17 408 | 43.7 | 2.63 | 11.8 | 22.0 |
| Shelby | 13.2 | 7.5 | 4.9 | 51.9 | 33 337 | 42 074 | 26.2 | 3.7 | 1 436 | 669 | 746 | 15 321 | 26.6 | 2.64 | 11.8 | 21.2 |
| Simpson | 12.8 | 8.6 | 6.3 | 51.0 | 16 405 | 17 327 | 5.6 | 1.2 | 474 | 393 | 137 | 6 753 | 5.3 | 2.52 | 12.9 | 25.3 |
| Spencer | 12.6 | 7.1 | 3.8 | 49.4 | 11 766 | 17 061 | 45.0 | 2.1 | 444 | 311 | 228 | 6 165 | 45.0 | 2.75 | 7.9 | 16.0 |
| Taylor | 13.1 | 9.0 | 7.1 | 51.6 | 22 927 | 24 512 | 6.9 | 0.7 | 684 | 656 | 164 | 9 832 | 6.5 | 2.39 | 12.4 | 27.9 |
| Todd | 11.3 | 8.2 | 6.2 | 50.8 | 11 971 | 12 460 | 4.1 | 1.5 | 383 | 314 | 110 | 4 647 | 1.7 | 2.64 | 12.3 | 24.3 |
| Trigg | 15.5 | 12.2 | 7.4 | 50.8 | 12 597 | 14 339 | 13.8 | 0.8 | 357 | 381 | 112 | 5 883 | 12.8 | 2.42 | 10.8 | 25.0 |
| Trimble | 13.1 | 8.0 | 5.3 | 49.2 | 8 125 | 8 809 | 8.4 | -0.2 | 222 | 224 | -17 | 3 420 | 9.0 | 2.56 | 9.7 | 23.6 |
| Union | 13.2 | 7.7 | 6.3 | 48.8 | 15 637 | 15 007 | -4.0 | -1.0 | 386 | 405 | -132 | 5 549 | -2.8 | 2.46 | 11.5 | 26.3 |
| Warren | 10.9 | 6.4 | 4.8 | 51.1 | 92 522 | 113 792 | 23.0 | 2.9 | 3 291 | 1 906 | 1 960 | 43 674 | 23.5 | 2.46 | 12.0 | 27.7 |
| Washington | 13.0 | 8.6 | 7.6 | 51.3 | 10 916 | 11 717 | 7.3 | 1.0 | 287 | 302 | 127 | 4 507 | 9.4 | 2.51 | 10.5 | 24.8 |
| Wayne | 14.5 | 10.2 | 6.5 | 50.4 | 19 923 | 20 813 | 4.5 | 0.1 | 565 | 454 | -87 | 8 646 | 9.3 | 2.37 | 11.5 | 27.7 |
| Webster | 14.2 | 8.3 | 7.0 | 50.5 | 14 120 | 13 621 | -3.5 | -0.3 | 411 | 375 | -65 | 5 272 | -5.2 | 2.51 | 10.8 | 25.4 |
| Whitley | 12.9 | 8.7 | 6.1 | 51.2 | 35 865 | 35 637 | -0.6 | -0.4 | 1 132 | 1 012 | -321 | 13 575 | -1.5 | 2.51 | 14.6 | 26.0 |
| Wolfe | 14.0 | 9.7 | 6.2 | 50.7 | 7 065 | 7 355 | 4.1 | -2.6 | 212 | 259 | -149 | 3 065 | 8.8 | 2.36 | 13.6 | 29.4 |
| Woodford | 15.0 | 8.0 | 5.5 | 51.9 | 23 208 | 24 939 | 7.5 | 0.6 | 636 | 477 | -15 | 9 806 | 10.3 | 2.51 | 11.1 | 23.5 |
| LOUISIANA | 12.2 | 7.0 | 5.5 | 51.1 | 4 468 976 | 4 533 372 | 1.4 | 1.5 | 142 118 | 93 427 | 19 435 | 1 728 360 | 4.4 | 2.55 | 17.2 | 26.9 |
| Acadia | 11.7 | 7.2 | 5.7 | 51.3 | 58 861 | 61 773 | 4.9 | 0.2 | 2 040 | 1 457 | -448 | 22 841 | 8.0 | 2.66 | 16.4 | 24.3 |
| Allen | 11.5 | 7.5 | 5.7 | 43.7 | 25 440 | 25 764 | 1.3 | -0.9 | 717 | 511 | -444 | 8 516 | 5.1 | 2.53 | 15.4 | 26.9 |
| Ascension | 10.8 | 5.7 | 3.4 | 50.7 | 76 627 | 107 215 | 39.9 | 4.7 | 3 721 | 1 589 | 2 867 | 37 790 | 41.6 | 2.82 | 14.2 | 18.9 |
| Assumption | 13.2 | 8.1 | 5.9 | 51.1 | 23 388 | 23 421 | 0.1 | -1.7 | 538 | 498 | -433 | 8 736 | 6.0 | 2.66 | 15.8 | 22.3 |
| Avoyelles | 12.4 | 8.2 | 6.5 | 49.9 | 41 481 | 42 073 | 1.4 | -1.0 | 1 318 | 1 057 | -708 | 15 432 | 4.7 | 2.51 | 17.2 | 27.4 |
| Beauregard | 12.2 | 7.9 | 5.2 | 49.1 | 32 986 | 35 654 | 8.1 | 1.8 | 1 128 | 791 | 295 | 13 159 | 8.7 | 2.61 | 11.6 | 24.1 |
| Bienville | 12.9 | 9.8 | 9.1 | 51.9 | 15 752 | 14 353 | -8.9 | -1.9 | 349 | 483 | -155 | 5 838 | -4.4 | 2.40 | 18.5 | 29.9 |
| Bossier | 11.2 | 6.8 | 5.2 | 50.9 | 98 310 | 116 979 | 19.0 | 4.5 | 3 768 | 2 123 | 3 525 | 45 215 | 23.4 | 2.54 | 14.4 | 25.9 |
| Caddo | 12.7 | 7.2 | 6.5 | 52.5 | 252 161 | 254 969 | 1.1 | 0.8 | 8 647 | 5 946 | -494 | 102 139 | 4.3 | 2.44 | 20.8 | 30.5 |
| Calcasieu | 12.3 | 7.2 | 5.7 | 51.3 | 183 577 | 192 768 | 5.0 | 0.9 | 6 150 | 4 226 | -105 | 73 996 | 7.8 | 2.55 | 15.9 | 26.1 |
| Caldwell | 13.8 | 8.6 | 6.2 | 48.7 | 10 560 | 10 132 | -4.1 | -1.3 | 283 | 285 | -123 | 3 905 | -0.9 | 2.45 | 14.1 | 27.7 |
| Cameron | 12.6 | 7.8 | 4.5 | 50.1 | 9 991 | 6 839 | -31.5 | -2.0 | 174 | 112 | -215 | 2 575 | -28.3 | 2.66 | 8.7 | 20.8 |
| Catahoula | 13.7 | 8.3 | 6.5 | 47.1 | 10 920 | 10 407 | -4.7 | -1.1 | 308 | 283 | -153 | 3 834 | -6.1 | 2.49 | 15.2 | 27.1 |
| Claiborne | 13.2 | 8.7 | 7.7 | 44.1 | 16 851 | 17 195 | 2.0 | -2.1 | 370 | 442 | -299 | 6 017 | -4.0 | 2.37 | 18.7 | 30.2 |
| Concordia | 13.0 | 7.9 | 6.8 | 49.6 | 20 247 | 20 822 | 2.8 | -2.2 | 579 | 577 | -460 | 7 613 | 1.2 | 2.54 | 21.6 | 27.5 |
| De Soto | 13.8 | 8.5 | 6.2 | 51.9 | 25 494 | 26 656 | 4.6 | 1.2 | 736 | 647 | 223 | 10 562 | 9.0 | 2.50 | 18.8 | 26.5 |
| East Baton Rouge | 11.6 | 6.2 | 4.9 | 51.9 | 412 852 | 440 171 | 6.6 | 1.0 | 13 878 | 7 963 | -1 403 | 172 057 | 10.0 | 2.49 | 18.4 | 28.7 |
| East Carroll | 10.9 | 6.7 | 5.7 | 46.1 | 9 421 | 7 759 | -17.6 | -3.0 | 246 | 169 | -310 | 2 552 | -14.0 | 2.62 | 29.3 | 29.8 |
| East Feliciana | 15.0 | 8.3 | 5.0 | 46.3 | 21 360 | 20 267 | -5.1 | -1.3 | 525 | 493 | -308 | 7 022 | 4.8 | 2.55 | 16.6 | 26.4 |
| Evangeline | 11.7 | 7.8 | 5.5 | 49.6 | 35 434 | 33 984 | -4.1 | -0.8 | 1 146 | 841 | -570 | 12 829 | 0.7 | 2.54 | 16.6 | 27.4 |
| Franklin | 12.7 | 8.9 | 7.6 | 51.5 | 21 263 | 20 767 | -2.3 | -1.0 | 675 | 618 | -255 | 7 904 | 1.9 | 2.53 | 17.6 | 27.1 |
| Grant | 11.5 | 7.6 | 5.0 | 44.1 | 18 698 | 22 309 | 19.3 | -1.1 | 560 | 417 | -395 | 7 496 | 6.0 | 2.58 | 13.4 | 24.1 |
| Iberia | 11.8 | 7.0 | 5.3 | 51.1 | 73 266 | 73 240 | 0.0 | 1.0 | 2 598 | 1 549 | -284 | 26 778 | 5.5 | 2.70 | 18.5 | 24.0 |
| Iberville | 12.7 | 7.2 | 5.0 | 49.0 | 33 320 | 33 387 | 0.2 | -0.5 | 923 | 663 | -421 | 11 072 | 3.7 | 2.66 | 20.6 | 25.0 |
| Jackson | 13.3 | 9.4 | 7.4 | 49.2 | 15 397 | 16 274 | 5.7 | -0.4 | 450 | 471 | -36 | 6 261 | 2.9 | 2.43 | 15.1 | 27.2 |
| Jefferson | 13.3 | 7.5 | 6.3 | 51.4 | 455 466 | 432 552 | -5.0 | 0.3 | 12 816 | 8 956 | -2 596 | 169 647 | -3.7 | 2.53 | 16.8 | 27.9 |
| Jefferson Davis | 12.1 | 7.9 | 6.8 | 51.1 | 31 435 | 31 594 | 0.5 | -0.5 | 974 | 862 | -273 | 11 771 | 2.5 | 2.64 | 15.2 | 25.0 |
| Lafayette | 11.3 | 5.7 | 4.7 | 51.3 | 190 503 | 221 578 | 16.3 | 2.5 | 7 301 | 3 691 | 1 952 | 87 027 | 20.2 | 2.49 | 15.0 | 27.8 |
| Lafourche | 11.6 | 7.1 | 5.6 | 50.9 | 89 974 | 96 318 | 7.1 | 0.7 | 2 837 | 1 822 | -547 | 35 486 | 10.7 | 2.67 | 13.8 | 22.1 |
| La Salle | 12.4 | 8.2 | 6.5 | 48.5 | 14 282 | 14 890 | 4.3 | 0.2 | 434 | 383 | -13 | 5 468 | 3.3 | 2.50 | 12.1 | 26.0 |
| Lincoln | 9.8 | 6.0 | 5.3 | 51.3 | 42 509 | 46 735 | 9.9 | 0.5 | 1 302 | 886 | -189 | 17 599 | 15.5 | 2.38 | 15.7 | 29.6 |
| Livingston | 11.1 | 6.4 | 3.9 | 50.5 | 91 814 | 128 026 | 39.4 | 3.1 | 4 112 | 2 098 | 1 847 | 46 007 | 41.0 | 2.76 | 13.1 | 20.1 |
| Madison | 11.7 | 6.7 | 5.5 | 50.5 | 13 728 | 12 093 | -11.9 | 0.5 | 378 | 348 | 31 | 4 025 | -9.9 | 2.61 | 26.4 | 27.3 |
| Morehouse | 13.6 | 8.2 | 7.4 | 52.1 | 31 021 | 27 979 | -9.8 | -1.5 | 918 | 837 | -492 | 10 853 | -4.6 | 2.51 | 21.8 | 27.1 |
| Natchitoches | 11.8 | 7.6 | 6.2 | 52.3 | 39 080 | 39 566 | 1.2 | -0.3 | 1 163 | 865 | -474 | 15 614 | 9.5 | 2.39 | 18.2 | 31.2 |

1. No spouse present.

# Table B. States and Counties — Population, Vital Statistics, Medicare, and Crime

| STATE County | Persons in group quarters, 2010 | Daytime population, 2007–2011 Number | Daytime population, 2007–2011 Employ-ment/ resi-dence ratio | Births, 2011 Total | Births, 2011 Rate[1] | Deaths, 2011 Number | Deaths, 2011 Rate[1] | Persons under 65 with no health insurance, 2010 Number | Persons under 65 with no health insurance, 2010 Percent | Medicare, 2012 Eligible for Medicare | Medicare, 2012 Enrolled in Medicare Advantage | Medicare, 2012 Enrolled in a Medicare prescription drug plan | Serious crimes known to police,[2] 2011 Total Number | Serious crimes known to police,[2] 2011 Total Rate[3] |
|---|---|---|---|---|---|---|---|---|---|---|---|---|---|---|
| | 32 | 33 | 34 | 35 | 36 | 37 | 38 | 39 | 40 | 41 | 42 | 43 | 44 | 45 |
| **KENTUCKY—Cont'd** | | | | | | | | | | | | | | |
| Ohio | 307 | 22 466 | 0.83 | 319 | 13.2 | 253 | 10.5 | 3 532 | 17.7 | 5 108 | 923 | 3 011 | 252 | 1 050 |
| Oldham | 4 568 | 47 587 | 0.55 | 491 | 8.1 | 316 | 5.2 | 5 092 | 10.2 | 7 602 | 1 666 | 3 604 | 710 | 1 169 |
| Owen | 0 | 8 764 | 0.57 | 110 | 10.1 | 104 | 9.6 | 1 720 | 18.7 | 2 223 | 274 | 1 257 | 77 | 705 |
| Owsley | 90 | 4 572 | 0.83 | 61 | 12.7 | 78 | 16.2 | 738 | 18.6 | 1 104 | 99 | 842 | 13 | 276 |
| Pendleton | 215 | 11 453 | 0.47 | 204 | 13.9 | 157 | 10.7 | 2 290 | 17.7 | 2 716 | 616 | 1 361 | 180 | 1 253 |
| Perry | 611 | 32 440 | 1.38 | 384 | 13.4 | 429 | 14.9 | 4 386 | 17.9 | 6 515 | 841 | 4 108 | 412 | 1 425 |
| Pike | 1 100 | 67 446 | 1.11 | 778 | 12.0 | 781 | 12.0 | 9 915 | 18.0 | 16 050 | 2 684 | 9 160 | 491 | 761 |
| Powell | 188 | 11 080 | 0.61 | 167 | 13.2 | 140 | 11.1 | 2 106 | 19.4 | 2 836 | 597 | 1 554 | 197 | 1 551 |
| Pulaski | 962 | 64 199 | 1.06 | 745 | 11.7 | 735 | 11.5 | 10 284 | 19.6 | 15 200 | 2 823 | 8 462 | 1 616 | 2 556 |
| Robertson | 57 | 1 967 | 0.56 | 18 | 8.1 | 29 | 13.0 | 386 | 20.9 | 480 | 77 | 270 | NA | NA |
| Rockcastle | 341 | 15 273 | 0.69 | 164 | 9.6 | 231 | 13.5 | 3 010 | 21.0 | 3 676 | 524 | 2 146 | 137 | 859 |
| Rowan | 2 435 | 24 979 | 1.18 | 281 | 11.9 | 195 | 8.3 | 3 694 | 20.4 | 4 172 | 987 | 2 444 | 316 | 1 345 |
| Russell | 177 | 18 048 | 1.08 | 218 | 12.4 | 213 | 12.1 | 3 090 | 21.4 | 4 108 | 584 | 2 519 | 133 | 752 |
| Scott | 1 316 | 48 471 | 1.11 | 657 | 13.6 | 315 | 6.5 | 5 467 | 13.2 | 6 171 | 1 475 | 2 848 | 1 498 | 3 218 |
| Shelby | 1 696 | 36 987 | 0.76 | 665 | 15.4 | 275 | 6.4 | 6 738 | 18.9 | 6 980 | 1 252 | 4 061 | 863 | 2 041 |
| Simpson | 327 | 18 753 | 1.19 | 208 | 12.0 | 154 | 8.9 | 2 631 | 18.1 | 3 387 | 482 | 1 909 | 569 | 3 261 |
| Spencer | 113 | 11 168 | 0.29 | 203 | 11.7 | 134 | 7.7 | 2 453 | 16.2 | 2 608 | 511 | 1 383 | 205 | 1 193 |
| Taylor | 1 035 | 25 282 | 1.09 | 303 | 12.3 | 301 | 12.2 | 3 933 | 20.0 | 5 633 | 776 | 3 487 | 664 | 2 690 |
| Todd | 195 | 10 243 | 0.57 | 177 | 14.2 | 134 | 10.8 | 2 455 | 23.5 | 2 300 | 239 | 1 497 | 149 | 1 188 |
| Trigg | 78 | 12 904 | 0.75 | 169 | 11.8 | 166 | 11.6 | 2 410 | 20.9 | 3 440 | 576 | 1 765 | 299 | 2 071 |
| Trimble | 41 | 7 280 | 0.57 | 104 | 11.9 | 98 | 11.2 | 1 381 | 18.2 | 1 713 | 271 | 938 | 9 | 101 |
| Union | 1 371 | 14 896 | 0.97 | 171 | 11.3 | 182 | 12.1 | 2 441 | 19.1 | 2 830 | 305 | 1 881 | 197 | 1 304 |
| Warren | 6 210 | 119 439 | 1.14 | 1 469 | 12.7 | 818 | 7.1 | 18 021 | 18.8 | 16 944 | 2 552 | 9 794 | 3 530 | 3 081 |
| Washington | 389 | 9 752 | 0.63 | 126 | 10.6 | 129 | 10.9 | 1 894 | 19.6 | 2 401 | 355 | 1 548 | 67 | 568 |
| Wayne | 331 | 19 870 | 0.86 | 258 | 12.3 | 197 | 9.4 | 3 826 | 22.2 | 4 780 | 886 | 2 890 | 259 | 1 236 |
| Webster | 393 | 12 775 | 0.82 | 180 | 13.2 | 157 | 11.5 | 2 327 | 20.8 | 2 776 | 544 | 1 596 | 30 | 275 |
| Whitley | 1 590 | 36 459 | 1.04 | 501 | 14.0 | 432 | 12.1 | 5 271 | 18.0 | 8 075 | 1 033 | 5 009 | 606 | 1 689 |
| Wolfe | 132 | 6 773 | 0.70 | 94 | 12.8 | 110 | 15.0 | 1 112 | 18.0 | 1 825 | 288 | 1 265 | 26 | 373 |
| Woodford | 329 | 22 765 | 0.84 | 304 | 12.2 | 198 | 7.9 | 3 802 | 17.9 | 4 385 | 1 100 | 1 886 | 788 | 3 138 |
| **LOUISIANA** | 127 427 | 4 500 000 | 1.01 | 63 969 | 14.0 | 40 780 | 8.9 | 793 782 | 20.5 | 735 527 | 188 454 | 316 312 | 194 150 | 4 244 |
| Acadia | 1 050 | 52 601 | 0.64 | 925 | 14.9 | 622 | 10.0 | 11 312 | 21.3 | 10 026 | 787 | 6 045 | 1 665 | 2 884 |
| Allen | 4 200 | 25 318 | 0.94 | 309 | 12.0 | 211 | 8.2 | 3 969 | 21.6 | 4 140 | 401 | 2 472 | NA | NA |
| Ascension | 790 | 91 575 | 0.72 | 1 639 | 14.9 | 681 | 6.2 | 15 351 | 15.8 | 13 422 | 6 668 | 3 433 | 3 980 | 3 679 |
| Assumption | 199 | 18 364 | 0.43 | 239 | 10.3 | 222 | 9.6 | 3 661 | 18.3 | 4 154 | 957 | 2 452 | 507 | 2 145 |
| Avoyelles | 3 343 | 38 490 | 0.77 | 609 | 14.5 | 453 | 10.8 | 6 701 | 20.2 | 8 186 | 973 | 5 137 | 1 045 | 2 897 |
| Beauregard | 1 300 | 30 667 | 0.67 | 501 | 13.9 | 353 | 9.8 | 6 394 | 21.3 | 6 079 | 531 | 3 030 | 545 | 1 515 |
| Bienville | 319 | 14 222 | 0.95 | 155 | 10.8 | 209 | 14.6 | 2 289 | 19.8 | 3 163 | 398 | 1 768 | 249 | 1 719 |
| Bossier | 1 961 | 111 430 | 0.92 | 1 636 | 13.7 | 912 | 7.6 | 18 931 | 18.6 | 17 206 | 2 285 | 5 893 | 3 520 | 3 073 |
| Caddo | 6 247 | 270 118 | 1.15 | 3 858 | 15.0 | 2 594 | 10.1 | 45 788 | 21.2 | 43 920 | 6 876 | 19 096 | 12 056 | 4 754 |
| Calcasieu | 3 796 | 196 836 | 1.07 | 2 785 | 14.3 | 1 816 | 9.4 | 30 076 | 18.2 | 32 450 | 4 109 | 15 157 | 8 392 | 4 496 |
| Caldwell | 584 | 8 660 | 0.60 | 131 | 13.0 | 113 | 11.2 | 1 728 | 21.4 | 1 927 | 245 | 1 114 | 285 | 2 787 |
| Cameron | 0 | 8 532 | 1.44 | 78 | 11.6 | 57 | 8.5 | 1 339 | 22.7 | 973 | 95 | 491 | 167 | 2 420 |
| Catahoula | 866 | 9 430 | 0.70 | 141 | 13.7 | 125 | 12.1 | 1 981 | 24.6 | 2 136 | 173 | 1 363 | 200 | 2 006 |
| Claiborne | 2 917 | 15 862 | 0.79 | 166 | 9.8 | 189 | 11.2 | 2 476 | 21.4 | 3 244 | 361 | 1 878 | 455 | 3 033 |
| Concordia | 1 485 | 19 485 | 0.84 | 256 | 12.3 | 248 | 11.9 | 3 784 | 23.2 | 3 982 | 374 | 2 432 | 509 | 2 422 |
| De Soto | 215 | 23 804 | 0.74 | 328 | 12.2 | 272 | 10.1 | 5 049 | 22.3 | 5 265 | 462 | 2 629 | 818 | 3 263 |
| East Baton Rouge | 11 105 | 486 982 | 1.24 | 6 318 | 14.3 | 3 507 | 7.9 | 70 332 | 18.4 | 62 222 | 21 695 | 20 577 | 25 224 | 5 679 |
| East Carroll | 1 067 | 7 516 | 0.84 | 116 | 15.2 | 77 | 10.1 | 1 278 | 22.6 | 1 364 | 48 | 930 | 161 | 2 056 |
| East Feliciana | 2 391 | 17 787 | 0.65 | 245 | 12.2 | 226 | 11.2 | 2 892 | 18.9 | 3 810 | 983 | 1 623 | 112 | 676 |
| Evangeline | 1 379 | 30 150 | 0.64 | 529 | 15.6 | 357 | 10.5 | 5 442 | 19.3 | 6 348 | 487 | 4 268 | 854 | 2 490 |
| Franklin | 732 | 18 736 | 0.73 | 299 | 14.4 | 271 | 13.0 | 4 194 | 24.8 | 4 209 | 424 | 2 635 | 129 | 646 |
| Grant | 2 937 | 17 715 | 0.46 | 265 | 12.0 | 183 | 8.3 | 3 546 | 21.2 | 3 827 | 514 | 1 912 | 317 | 1 408 |
| Iberia | 944 | 76 828 | 1.11 | 1 192 | 16.2 | 700 | 9.5 | 13 127 | 20.7 | 12 538 | 744 | 7 140 | 2 679 | 3 625 |
| Iberville | 3 979 | 38 249 | 1.38 | 420 | 12.6 | 284 | 8.5 | 4 770 | 18.6 | 5 496 | 2 236 | 1 812 | 1 506 | 4 737 |
| Jackson | 1 038 | 13 987 | 0.67 | 201 | 12.3 | 208 | 12.7 | 2 648 | 20.9 | 3 268 | 433 | 1 845 | NA | NA |
| Jefferson | 3 311 | 424 044 | 0.96 | 5 779 | 13.4 | 3 941 | 9.1 | 84 389 | 22.8 | 74 845 | 39 350 | 18 697 | 18 813 | 4 310 |
| Jefferson Davis | 567 | 28 509 | 0.74 | 459 | 14.5 | 390 | 12.3 | 5 416 | 20.3 | 5 429 | 346 | 3 346 | NA | NA |
| Lafayette | 5 150 | 244 254 | 1.24 | 3 305 | 14.7 | 1 586 | 7.1 | 39 081 | 20.1 | 29 766 | 2 604 | 15 762 | 10 443 | 4 848 |
| Lafourche | 1 625 | 91 061 | 0.88 | 1 305 | 13.5 | 793 | 8.2 | 18 794 | 22.7 | 15 637 | 3 336 | 7 887 | 2 776 | 2 856 |
| La Salle | 1 243 | 13 888 | 0.84 | 202 | 13.5 | 172 | 11.5 | 2 483 | 21.4 | 2 712 | 304 | 1 638 | 214 | 1 424 |
| Lincoln | 4 883 | 47 644 | 1.07 | 590 | 12.6 | 396 | 8.5 | 8 010 | 21.8 | 6 181 | 679 | 3 160 | 1 603 | 3 399 |
| Livingston | 1 192 | 94 073 | 0.44 | 1 839 | 14.1 | 905 | 6.9 | 22 326 | 19.5 | 17 559 | 8 435 | 4 889 | 4 381 | 3 391 |
| Madison | 1 591 | 11 961 | 0.95 | 178 | 14.8 | 159 | 13.2 | 2 160 | 23.6 | 1 853 | 70 | 1 177 | 513 | 4 204 |
| Morehouse | 768 | 25 338 | 0.71 | 446 | 16.2 | 358 | 13.0 | 5 122 | 22.3 | 5 923 | 886 | 3 467 | 1 735 | 6 145 |
| Natchitoches | 2 190 | 38 551 | 0.95 | 513 | 13.0 | 373 | 9.5 | 7 245 | 22.5 | 6 732 | 622 | 3 960 | 2 148 | 5 380 |

1. Per 1,000 estimated resident population.   2. Data for serious crimes have not been adjusted for underreporting; this may affect comparability between geographic areas and over time.   3. Per 100,000 population estimated by the FBI.

# Table B. States and Counties — **Crime, Education, Money Income, and Poverty**

| STATE County | Serious crimes known to police, 2011 (cont.)[1] Rate[2] Violent | Property | School enrollment and attainment, 2007–2011 Enrollment[3] Total | Percent private | Attainment[4] (percent) High school graduate or less | Bachelor's degree or more | Local government expenditures,[5] 2009–2010 Total current expenditures (mil dol) | Current expenditures per student (dollars) | Per capita income[6] (dollars) | Households Median income Dollars | Percent change, 2000 to 2007–2011 (constant 2011 dollars) | Percent with income of $200,000 or more | Median household income (dollars) | Percent below poverty level, 2011 All persons | Children under 18 years | Children 5 to 17 years in families |
|---|---|---|---|---|---|---|---|---|---|---|---|---|---|---|---|---|
| | 46 | 47 | 48 | 49 | 50 | 51 | 52 | 53 | 54 | 55 | 56 | 57 | 58 | 59 | 60 | 61 |
| **KENTUCKY—Cont'd** | | | | | | | | | | | | | | | | |
| Ohio | 87 | 962 | 5 327 | 8.3 | 66.8 | 9.7 | 35.7 | 8 857 | 19 090 | 38 252 | -4.1 | 1.1 | 37 545 | 22.6 | 32.9 | 31.9 |
| Oldham | 49 | 1 120 | 17 593 | 16.1 | 32.1 | 38.3 | 92.3 | 7 699 | 33 366 | 82 578 | -3.3 | 9.7 | 80 872 | 6.4 | 8.0 | 6.8 |
| Owen | 18 | 687 | 2 371 | 9.4 | 60.0 | 19.1 | 17.7 | 9 212 | 22 897 | 45 551 | 1.3 | 0.1 | 40 909 | 17.9 | 28.0 | 25.6 |
| Owsley | 0 | 276 | 973 | 7.7 | 77.7 | 7.6 | 10.0 | 12 403 | 11 883 | 19 344 | -9.4 | 0.0 | 21 865 | 39.0 | 57.0 | 52.8 |
| Pendleton | 35 | 1 218 | 3 792 | 9.8 | 64.0 | 11.9 | 22.8 | 8 330 | 20 758 | 48 354 | -6.1 | 0.4 | 44 853 | 16.2 | 24.6 | 22.2 |
| Perry | 90 | 1 335 | 6 308 | 5.0 | 66.7 | 12.1 | 48.8 | 9 109 | 19 357 | 32 538 | 9.1 | 1.7 | 31 623 | 25.0 | 32.3 | 30.3 |
| Pike | 12 | 749 | 13 920 | 10.3 | 66.4 | 12.0 | 101.4 | 8 955 | 19 326 | 33 148 | 2.6 | 1.4 | 33 881 | 22.5 | 28.4 | 27.0 |
| Powell | 39 | 1 512 | 2 716 | 9.9 | 72.2 | 10.4 | 22.8 | 8 810 | 15 007 | 28 382 | -17.6 | 0.3 | 31 129 | 29.3 | 41.0 | 39.8 |
| Pulaski | 62 | 2 495 | 14 263 | 8.9 | 60.2 | 14.6 | 86.8 | 8 418 | 20 220 | 33 282 | -9.9 | 2.4 | 34 695 | 24.4 | 34.7 | 32.3 |
| Robertson | NA | NA | 656 | 3.0 | 65.1 | 9.8 | 3.9 | 10 448 | 13 749 | 26 544 | -35.7 | 0.0 | 35 504 | 23.1 | 34.2 | 30.7 |
| Rockcastle | 25 | 834 | 4 052 | 7.3 | 67.0 | 11.7 | 27.9 | 9 080 | 15 506 | 26 967 | -14.9 | 0.6 | 30 323 | 28.0 | 38.5 | 36.1 |
| Rowan | 47 | 1 298 | 8 041 | 4.7 | 54.5 | 24.2 | 29.0 | 8 557 | 16 889 | 32 763 | -13.5 | 1.7 | 34 920 | 26.4 | 32.9 | 30.9 |
| Russell | 45 | 707 | 3 423 | 12.3 | 63.7 | 12.7 | 28.3 | 9 342 | 18 626 | 31 087 | 4.5 | 1.4 | 30 691 | 21.9 | 34.9 | 33.0 |
| Scott | 279 | 2 939 | 13 099 | 20.8 | 43.9 | 26.1 | 61.3 | 7 402 | 27 188 | 57 967 | -8.8 | 2.7 | 58 164 | 12.2 | 17.5 | 15.8 |
| Shelby | 114 | 1 927 | 10 678 | 22.8 | 48.2 | 24.5 | 56.5 | 8 348 | 27 655 | 56 417 | -8.2 | 4.5 | 51 021 | 12.7 | 19.0 | 17.7 |
| Simpson | 195 | 3 066 | 4 144 | 7.5 | 59.2 | 17.0 | 24.9 | 8 069 | 20 736 | 41 493 | -15.6 | 1.0 | 40 583 | 16.4 | 25.9 | 24.5 |
| Spencer | 17 | 1 176 | 4 159 | 16.5 | 49.2 | 16.4 | 21.4 | 7 427 | 26 834 | 61 921 | -2.5 | 2.7 | 62 347 | 8.4 | 13.6 | 12.4 |
| Taylor | 166 | 2 524 | 5 575 | 18.5 | 64.6 | 14.5 | 32.1 | 8 353 | 18 087 | 35 054 | -7.6 | 0.5 | 33 348 | 18.8 | 29.5 | 29.0 |
| Todd | 56 | 1 132 | 3 052 | 12.5 | 65.9 | 9.2 | 20.0 | 9 165 | 18 176 | 39 417 | -1.8 | 0.7 | 37 325 | 22.0 | 33.6 | 32.3 |
| Trigg | 69 | 2 002 | 3 158 | 7.7 | 55.3 | 16.8 | 18.3 | 8 587 | 23 489 | 43 331 | -2.8 | 1.3 | 41 699 | 16.4 | 27.1 | 23.7 |
| Trimble | 0 | 101 | 2 442 | 15.7 | 59.4 | 13.1 | 12.5 | 7 735 | 21 996 | 52 224 | 6.9 | 0.1 | 43 677 | 15.1 | 23.7 | 22.0 |
| Union | 73 | 1 231 | 3 498 | 9.1 | 57.0 | 11.3 | 22.9 | 9 649 | 18 681 | 38 651 | -18.3 | 0.9 | 42 059 | 21.4 | 26.6 | 23.6 |
| Warren | 178 | 2 903 | 35 064 | 7.9 | 45.2 | 27.8 | 142.7 | 8 145 | 23 635 | 43 018 | -11.9 | 2.3 | 40 026 | 18.9 | 25.1 | 23.7 |
| Washington | 25 | 542 | 2 975 | 20.5 | 62.2 | 14.6 | 16.3 | 9 443 | 21 206 | 42 516 | -5.0 | 1.9 | 39 023 | 17.1 | 26.0 | 24.2 |
| Wayne | 57 | 1 179 | 4 627 | 3.0 | 69.9 | 9.6 | 32.0 | 9 173 | 15 620 | 26 309 | -6.6 | 0.7 | 27 637 | 31.7 | 47.8 | 37.1 |
| Webster | 9 | 266 | 3 058 | 8.7 | 65.5 | 9.4 | 19.4 | 8 449 | 20 058 | 42 115 | -1.1 | 0.6 | 40 454 | 17.6 | 25.9 | 25.7 |
| Whitley | 78 | 1 611 | 9 523 | 16.9 | 67.1 | 11.7 | 74.2 | 8 863 | 15 430 | 29 280 | -1.8 | 0.4 | 29 870 | 24.8 | 37.0 | 35.5 |
| Wolfe | 0 | 373 | 1 754 | 6.0 | 77.3 | 8.7 | 13.3 | 10 350 | 12 058 | 21 968 | -15.7 | 0.1 | 25 950 | 35.2 | 48.6 | 45.5 |
| Woodford | 104 | 3 035 | 6 080 | 18.3 | 43.6 | 30.4 | 31.1 | 7 490 | 28 816 | 55 124 | -17.5 | 3.9 | 54 930 | 11.0 | 16.8 | 14.9 |
| **LOUISIANA** | 555 | 3 689 | 1 179 387 | 18.9 | 53.0 | 21.1 | 7 317.5 | 10 591 | 23 853 | 44 086 | 0.3 | 2.9 | 41 804 | 20.5 | 28.8 | 27.2 |
| Acadia | 428 | 2 456 | 15 985 | 18.9 | 68.4 | 10.6 | 86.8 | 9 247 | 19 027 | 37 970 | 5.4 | 1.0 | 34 960 | 22.4 | 28.8 | 28.6 |
| Allen | NA | NA | 5 891 | 7.6 | 68.7 | 9.1 | 45.0 | 10 692 | 18 287 | 39 007 | 4.0 | 0.6 | 34 586 | 23.2 | 27.9 | 25.3 |
| Ascension | 386 | 3 292 | 29 510 | 19.9 | 50.0 | 22.8 | 201.2 | 10 337 | 27 756 | 66 173 | 10.7 | 3.7 | 63 305 | 11.5 | 15.4 | 14.1 |
| Assumption | 368 | 1 777 | 5 391 | 18.7 | 72.9 | 8.1 | 45.8 | 11 391 | 21 752 | 46 699 | 11.0 | 2.0 | 44 770 | 18.4 | 25.9 | 23.3 |
| Avoyelles | 463 | 2 434 | 9 644 | 16.1 | 68.6 | 9.6 | 58.6 | 8 588 | 17 497 | 32 321 | 0.4 | 0.9 | 31 733 | 25.5 | 34.2 | 33.3 |
| Beauregard | 250 | 1 265 | 8 621 | 10.2 | 57.9 | 14.8 | 54.4 | 9 011 | 21 808 | 45 113 | 2.5 | 1.4 | 43 673 | 16.9 | 23.8 | 22.2 |
| Bienville | 290 | 1 429 | 3 428 | 6.8 | 61.8 | 13.6 | 31.9 | 13 968 | 18 691 | 30 594 | -4.2 | 2.1 | 30 750 | 26.4 | 37.9 | 33.3 |
| Bossier | 401 | 2 672 | 29 576 | 8.9 | 45.8 | 22.8 | 191.2 | 9 471 | 26 248 | 51 771 | -2.2 | 3.1 | 50 577 | 14.1 | 21.1 | 20.8 |
| Caddo | 648 | 4 106 | 67 083 | 13.0 | 49.7 | 21.9 | 464.3 | 10 878 | 23 743 | 39 086 | -8.0 | 3.0 | 39 948 | 21.6 | 32.9 | 30.3 |
| Calcasieu | 507 | 3 989 | 49 712 | 13.4 | 53.2 | 19.1 | 343.6 | 10 040 | 24 013 | 43 614 | -8.7 | 2.6 | 41 065 | 18.9 | 26.4 | 24.3 |
| Caldwell | 215 | 2 572 | 2 348 | 9.4 | 65.9 | 11.2 | 18.3 | 10 724 | 22 111 | 38 606 | 6.0 | 1.7 | 36 415 | 19.9 | 29.9 | 28.0 |
| Cameron | 217 | 2 202 | 1 897 | 8.3 | 64.7 | 12.4 | NA | NA | 24 649 | 61 679 | 33.4 | 2.9 | 54 318 | 13.0 | 17.7 | 15.8 |
| Catahoula | 782 | 1 224 | 2 074 | 11.9 | 72.1 | 10.2 | 17.4 | 10 758 | 17 245 | 37 115 | 22.0 | 1.0 | 31 678 | 27.3 | 37.4 | 36.2 |
| Claiborne | 567 | 2 466 | 3 659 | 11.3 | 64.7 | 11.7 | 24.4 | 11 070 | 17 654 | 32 972 | -3.6 | 1.6 | 34 084 | 28.7 | 36.1 | 34.2 |
| Concordia | 509 | 1 913 | 5 195 | 8.4 | 67.2 | 11.0 | 36.7 | 9 386 | 16 947 | 28 705 | -6.5 | 0.7 | 29 373 | 27.6 | 40.7 | 38.0 |
| De Soto | 1 241 | 2 022 | 6 354 | 10.4 | 62.5 | 13.3 | 86.9 | 17 783 | 21 122 | 39 213 | 2.8 | 1.4 | 40 507 | 19.0 | 27.1 | 25.0 |
| East Baton Rouge | 712 | 4 967 | 134 094 | 20.9 | 38.6 | 33.4 | 665.2 | 11 386 | 26 714 | 46 838 | -6.8 | 3.8 | 45 924 | 20.2 | 29.3 | 29.2 |
| East Carroll | 690 | 1 367 | 1 864 | 8.5 | 72.1 | 9.7 | 17.7 | 13 712 | 20 767 | 25 267 | -9.7 | 5.0 | 25 163 | 44.0 | 54.3 | 51.4 |
| East Feliciana | 84 | 591 | 4 523 | 25.2 | 61.5 | 11.7 | 23.5 | 10 702 | 19 508 | 37 403 | -12.4 | 2.2 | 38 478 | 20.7 | 28.3 | 26.6 |
| Evangeline | 213 | 2 277 | 8 531 | 18.5 | 70.6 | 12.3 | 58.5 | 9 759 | 18 171 | 34 848 | 25.7 | 1.0 | 32 099 | 26.4 | 33.5 | 30.9 |
| Franklin | 85 | 560 | 4 845 | 14.3 | 67.2 | 11.4 | 33.0 | 10 312 | 19 737 | 34 105 | 10.0 | 1.5 | 29 025 | 27.8 | 42.8 | 40.2 |
| Grant | 58 | 1 350 | 5 060 | 12.5 | 64.1 | 10.6 | 29.1 | 8 568 | 18 427 | 39 988 | 0.0 | 0.9 | 39 539 | 20.9 | 28.4 | 27.1 |
| Iberia | 560 | 3 065 | 18 398 | 16.4 | 66.2 | 12.9 | 131.0 | 9 547 | 21 316 | 42 989 | 2.0 | 2.3 | 40 626 | 21.4 | 30.3 | 28.1 |
| Iberville | 1 217 | 3 520 | 8 402 | 17.2 | 66.7 | 12.0 | 65.9 | 15 874 | 20 624 | 43 195 | 10.2 | 2.3 | 37 832 | 23.0 | 29.9 | 28.5 |
| Jackson | NA | NA | 3 854 | 11.5 | 58.2 | 13.4 | 23.3 | 10 251 | 20 057 | 39 809 | 4.0 | 0.4 | 36 032 | 21.0 | 28.9 | 27.2 |
| Jefferson | 487 | 3 823 | 104 102 | 33.1 | 49.2 | 23.3 | 537.8 | 11 695 | 26 528 | 48 374 | -6.8 | 3.7 | 43 700 | 18.1 | 27.6 | 26.0 |
| Jefferson Davis | NA | NA | 7 918 | 10.8 | 64.1 | 12.0 | 59.6 | 10 170 | 21 208 | 43 585 | 16.4 | 1.2 | 38 723 | 21.6 | 27.8 | 25.4 |
| Lafayette | 602 | 4 246 | 62 506 | 21.4 | 45.5 | 27.3 | 304.4 | 10 178 | 27 808 | 48 591 | -1.4 | 4.8 | 47 138 | 17.5 | 21.2 | 19.7 |
| Lafourche | 155 | 2 701 | 23 800 | 18.2 | 66.3 | 14.8 | 143.9 | 9 699 | 24 324 | 49 262 | 4.5 | 2.7 | 48 180 | 17.1 | 22.8 | 20.9 |
| La Salle | 266 | 1 158 | 3 366 | 9.6 | 62.8 | 13.7 | 26.2 | 10 082 | 21 962 | 42 066 | 10.5 | 1.0 | 42 576 | 18.7 | 23.1 | 21.7 |
| Lincoln | 403 | 2 996 | 18 955 | 8.8 | 42.5 | 32.3 | 65.3 | 9 924 | 19 635 | 34 152 | -6.2 | 2.3 | 34 497 | 29.5 | 31.6 | 28.0 |
| Livingston | 317 | 3 074 | 32 448 | 11.4 | 55.7 | 11.7 | 206.0 | 8 478 | 24 376 | 57 254 | 9.0 | 2.1 | 53 700 | 13.2 | 16.8 | 15.5 |
| Madison | 819 | 3 384 | 3 012 | 15.0 | 64.7 | 11.5 | 24.2 | 12 586 | 14 255 | 26 178 | -5.5 | 1.3 | 23 240 | 41.4 | 54.7 | 47.9 |
| Morehouse | 581 | 5 564 | 6 097 | 10.0 | 67.1 | 11.3 | 49.2 | 10 477 | 15 842 | 31 269 | -7.8 | 0.4 | 26 778 | 28.7 | 40.5 | 39.7 |
| Natchitoches | 706 | 4 673 | 11 894 | 12.3 | 55.9 | 21.6 | 64.9 | 9 096 | 19 144 | 31 830 | -8.3 | 1.6 | 32 203 | 28.9 | 40.0 | 38.4 |

1. Data for serious crimes have not been adjusted for underreporting; this may affect comparability between geographic areas and over time.  2. Per 100,000 population estimated by the FBI.  3. All persons 3 years old and over enrolled in nursery school through college.  4. Persons 25 years old and over.  5. Elementary and secondary education expenditures.  6. Based on population estimated by the American Community Survey, 2007–2011.

# Table B. States and Counties — **Personal Income**

| STATE County | Personal income, 2011 | | | | | | | | | | | | |
|---|---|---|---|---|---|---|---|---|---|---|---|---|---|
| | | | Per capita[1] | | | | | Transfer payments (mil dol) | | | | | |
| | | | | | | | | | Government payments to individuals | | | | |
| | Total (mil dol) | Percent change, 2010–2011 | Dollars | Rank | Wages and salaries[2] (mil dol) | Proprietors' income (mil dol) | Dividends, interest, and rent (mil dol) | Total | Total | Social Security | Medical payments | Income mainte- nance | Unemploy- ment insurance |
| | 62 | 63 | 64 | 65 | 66 | 67 | 68 | 69 | 70 | 71 | 72 | 73 | 74 |
| KENTUCKY—Cont'd | | | | | | | | | | | | | |
| Ohio | 708 | 6.5 | 29 387 | 2 396 | 335 | 39 | 75 | 218 | 213 | 73 | 92 | 27 | 7 |
| Oldham | 2 708 | 6.9 | 44 660 | 409 | 679 | 85 | 431 | 294 | 281 | 120 | 101 | 17 | 15 |
| Owen | 287 | 5.0 | 26 405 | 2 837 | 80 | 9 | 32 | 86 | 84 | 31 | 33 | 12 | 3 |
| Owsley | 119 | 2.8 | 24 593 | 2 997 | 27 | 1 | 8 | 66 | 65 | 12 | 35 | 14 | 1 |
| Pendleton | 411 | 3.0 | 27 961 | 2 621 | 111 | 5 | 41 | 107 | 104 | 38 | 39 | 14 | 5 |
| Perry | 904 | 3.3 | 31 458 | 2 008 | 707 | 50 | 77 | 351 | 345 | 90 | 161 | 59 | 8 |
| Pike | 2 122 | 5.7 | 32 694 | 1 759 | 1 311 | 183 | 211 | 714 | 699 | 236 | 293 | 96 | 16 |
| Powell | 336 | 3.4 | 26 527 | 2 819 | 95 | 25 | 26 | 125 | 122 | 39 | 46 | 24 | 5 |
| Pulaski | 1 849 | 3.0 | 29 043 | 2 445 | 1 027 | 97 | 233 | 666 | 652 | 200 | 311 | 76 | 20 |
| Robertson | 58 | 1.3 | 26 029 | 2 876 | 11 | 2 | 6 | 21 | 20 | 6 | 10 | 3 | 1 |
| Rockcastle | 407 | 3.7 | 23 865 | 3 032 | 131 | 10 | 37 | 163 | 159 | 45 | 72 | 24 | 6 |
| Rowan | 612 | 3.5 | 25 953 | 2 886 | 421 | 22 | 65 | 197 | 191 | 55 | 76 | 25 | 7 |
| Russell | 495 | 4.2 | 28 137 | 2 599 | 253 | 39 | 62 | 175 | 171 | 51 | 79 | 25 | 6 |
| Scott | 1 655 | 6.7 | 34 376 | 1 457 | 1 307 | 71 | 157 | 254 | 243 | 92 | 86 | 31 | 14 |
| Shelby | 1 515 | 7.1 | 35 173 | 1 343 | 605 | 72 | 208 | 260 | 251 | 103 | 91 | 25 | 12 |
| Simpson | 549 | 7.1 | 31 596 | 1 978 | 353 | 63 | 72 | 139 | 135 | 50 | 55 | 16 | 7 |
| Spencer | 605 | 9.1 | 34 806 | 1 402 | 74 | 7 | 50 | 106 | 102 | 39 | 41 | 9 | 6 |
| Taylor | 713 | 5.0 | 28 837 | 2 480 | 416 | 30 | 88 | 237 | 232 | 75 | 103 | 27 | 9 |
| Todd | 346 | 5.8 | 27 761 | 2 649 | 94 | 52 | 47 | 96 | 94 | 30 | 42 | 11 | 4 |
| Trigg | 534 | 7.1 | 37 352 | 1 044 | 133 | 33 | 57 | 125 | 122 | 49 | 47 | 10 | 5 |
| Trimble | 205 | 3.1 | 23 461 | 3 048 | 60 | 3 | 23 | 70 | 68 | 24 | 29 | 8 | 3 |
| Union | 539 | 12.1 | 35 767 | 1 254 | 322 | 81 | 60 | 131 | 127 | 44 | 57 | 13 | 5 |
| Warren | 3 699 | 5.2 | 32 025 | 1 881 | 2 686 | 232 | 525 | 820 | 795 | 242 | 330 | 96 | 33 |
| Washington | 326 | 4.5 | 27 502 | 2 685 | 136 | 23 | 49 | 96 | 94 | 31 | 40 | 11 | 4 |
| Wayne | 483 | 2.5 | 23 020 | 3 057 | 198 | 22 | 52 | 207 | 203 | 57 | 93 | 34 | 8 |
| Webster | 441 | 6.8 | 32 258 | 1 833 | 208 | 55 | 47 | 113 | 110 | 42 | 45 | 12 | 4 |
| Whitley | 1 057 | 2.3 | 29 500 | 2 377 | 549 | 22 | 106 | 441 | 433 | 101 | 210 | 67 | 12 |
| Wolfe | 168 | 2.9 | 22 829 | 3 063 | 45 | 4 | 13 | 90 | 89 | 22 | 42 | 19 | 2 |
| Woodford | 1 042 | 4.7 | 41 755 | 597 | 480 | 71 | 166 | 156 | 151 | 67 | 47 | 14 | 7 |
| LOUISIANA | 176 356 | 4.5 | 38 549 | X | 108 485 | 17 175 | 26 806 | 34 843 | 33 697 | 9 947 | 15 681 | 5 145 | 658 |
| Acadia | 2 038 | 4.1 | 32 883 | 1 727 | 720 | 281 | 261 | 470 | 453 | 131 | 226 | 69 | 7 |
| Allen | 618 | 2.5 | 23 979 | 3 030 | 394 | 65 | 68 | 190 | 184 | 54 | 92 | 24 | 4 |
| Ascension | 4 552 | 6.9 | 41 388 | 625 | 2 294 | 599 | 444 | 648 | 623 | 204 | 295 | 75 | 15 |
| Assumption | 841 | 3.7 | 36 324 | 1 163 | 242 | 64 | 93 | 191 | 186 | 56 | 89 | 28 | 5 |
| Avoyelles | 1 277 | 5.2 | 30 479 | 2 204 | 478 | 145 | 146 | 383 | 374 | 97 | 189 | 63 | 6 |
| Beauregard | 1 073 | 4.4 | 29 705 | 2 337 | 421 | 71 | 132 | 258 | 251 | 83 | 115 | 28 | 5 |
| Bienville | 438 | 2.6 | 30 545 | 2 188 | 200 | 45 | 56 | 140 | 136 | 40 | 67 | 20 | 2 |
| Bossier | 4 394 | 7.9 | 36 697 | 1 112 | 2 840 | 344 | 537 | 788 | 763 | 232 | 336 | 93 | 14 |
| Caddo | 10 490 | 4.7 | 40 810 | 676 | 6 641 | 1 184 | 1 981 | 2 057 | 2 000 | 589 | 862 | 354 | 37 |
| Calcasieu | 7 058 | 5.6 | 36 366 | 1 155 | 4 748 | 497 | 1 091 | 1 460 | 1 415 | 472 | 640 | 186 | 27 |
| Caldwell | 292 | 1.7 | 29 025 | 2 448 | 104 | 18 | 33 | 101 | 99 | 24 | 56 | 12 | 2 |
| Cameron | 236 | 2.7 | 35 114 | 1 355 | 174 | 8 | 44 | 36 | 35 | 14 | 13 | 4 | 1 |
| Catahoula | 317 | 5.8 | 30 655 | 2 161 | 103 | 44 | 30 | 100 | 93 | 26 | 46 | 14 | 2 |
| Claiborne | 499 | 4.0 | 29 515 | 2 375 | 212 | 47 | 80 | 138 | 134 | 41 | 61 | 22 | 3 |
| Concordia | 562 | 4.3 | 26 936 | 2 771 | 250 | 60 | 81 | 176 | 172 | 51 | 74 | 33 | 4 |
| De Soto | 816 | 4.0 | 30 417 | 2 220 | 425 | 50 | 107 | 213 | 207 | 69 | 87 | 35 | 4 |
| East Baton Rouge | 18 529 | 4.2 | 41 974 | 572 | 15 180 | 1 051 | 3 270 | 3 121 | 3 021 | 844 | 1 344 | 520 | 67 |
| East Carroll | 242 | 2.5 | 31 676 | 1 961 | 86 | 39 | 36 | 85 | 82 | 13 | 44 | 20 | 2 |
| East Feliciana | 683 | 3.5 | 33 974 | 1 516 | 252 | 36 | 83 | 190 | 186 | 46 | 102 | 25 | 3 |
| Evangeline | 973 | 3.7 | 28 704 | 2 504 | 379 | 73 | 138 | 303 | 295 | 79 | 148 | 50 | 5 |
| Franklin | 600 | 3.4 | 28 881 | 2 471 | 202 | 107 | 63 | 205 | 201 | 48 | 106 | 33 | 4 |
| Grant | 566 | 1.5 | 25 596 | 2 920 | 189 | 37 | 62 | 167 | 162 | 47 | 76 | 22 | 3 |
| Iberia | 2 775 | 6.2 | 37 805 | 996 | 1 853 | 261 | 421 | 570 | 553 | 173 | 248 | 98 | 10 |
| Iberville | 1 065 | 4.0 | 32 040 | 1 876 | 1 070 | 84 | 140 | 285 | 277 | 73 | 141 | 46 | 6 |
| Jackson | 469 | 2.5 | 28 722 | 2 497 | 181 | 46 | 52 | 151 | 147 | 44 | 75 | 17 | 2 |
| Jefferson | 19 391 | 3.5 | 44 821 | 399 | 11 582 | 2 111 | 3 244 | 3 332 | 3 205 | 1 067 | 1 498 | 403 | 62 |
| Jefferson Davis | 992 | 4.7 | 31 311 | 2 040 | 393 | 86 | 141 | 239 | 232 | 74 | 112 | 29 | 4 |
| Lafayette | 10 560 | 6.1 | 47 060 | 295 | 8 016 | 1 652 | 1 826 | 1 377 | 1 322 | 408 | 570 | 189 | 27 |
| Lafourche | 4 392 | 4.7 | 45 437 | 370 | 2 374 | 900 | 518 | 686 | 658 | 224 | 302 | 82 | 11 |
| La Salle | 451 | 5.0 | 30 066 | 2 277 | 228 | 33 | 57 | 120 | 116 | 37 | 60 | 11 | 2 |
| Lincoln | 1 465 | 2.6 | 31 256 | 2 060 | 849 | 185 | 268 | 316 | 306 | 77 | 130 | 47 | 7 |
| Livingston | 4 146 | 5.3 | 31 832 | 1 924 | 1 076 | 240 | 350 | 796 | 767 | 258 | 357 | 96 | 18 |
| Madison | 309 | 4.6 | 25 709 | 2 908 | 134 | 42 | 31 | 106 | 103 | 21 | 49 | 26 | 2 |
| Morehouse | 822 | 5.4 | 29 775 | 2 326 | 280 | 87 | 106 | 306 | 299 | 79 | 143 | 59 | 7 |
| Natchitoches | 1 195 | 2.6 | 30 307 | 2 238 | 600 | 138 | 160 | 316 | 307 | 80 | 127 | 58 | 6 |

1. Based on the resident population estimated as of July 1 of the year shown.   2. Includes supplements to wages and salaries.

# Table B. States and Counties — Earnings, Social Security, and Housing

| STATE County | Earnings, 2011 | | | | | | | | | Social Security beneficiaries, December 2011 | | | Housing units, 2010 | |
| | Total (mil dol) | Percent by selected industries | | | | | | | | | | Supplemental Security Income recipients, December 2011 | | |
| | | Goods-related[1] | | Service-related and health | | | | | | Number | Rate[2] | | Total | Percent change, 2000–2010 |
| | | Farm | Total | Manu-facturing | Information and professional and technical services | Retail trade | Finance, insurance, and real estate | Health care and social services | Government | | | | | |
| | 75 | 76 | 77 | 78 | 79 | 80 | 81 | 82 | 83 | 84 | 85 | 86 | 87 | 88 |
| KENTUCKY—Cont'd | | | | | | | | | | | | | | |
| Ohio | 374 | 3.5 | D | 27.4 | D | 6.3 | 1.9 | 5.6 | 19.3 | 5 995 | 249 | 1 184 | 10 219 | 3.1 |
| Oldham | 764 | 0.2 | D | 5.9 | 8.6 | 6.7 | 10.4 | 13.3 | 25.2 | 8 255 | 136 | 511 | 20 688 | 31.8 |
| Owen | 89 | 0.9 | D | D | D | 6.9 | D | 12.4 | 28.2 | 2 600 | 239 | 512 | 5 634 | 5.4 |
| Owsley | 28 | -3.6 | D | D | D | 9.9 | 2.8 | 21.8 | 48.1 | 1 285 | 267 | 913 | 2 328 | 3.6 |
| Pendleton | 116 | -4.3 | D | 15.2 | D | 4.9 | D | D | 28.8 | 3 105 | 211 | 536 | 6 339 | 10.1 |
| Perry | 757 | -0.1 | D | 1.1 | 6.1 | 7.9 | 2.6 | D | 16.8 | 7 605 | 265 | 2 892 | 12 791 | 0.3 |
| Pike | 1 494 | 0.0 | 34.9 | 2.5 | 5.5 | 7.8 | 3.5 | 17.1 | 12.6 | 19 200 | 296 | 5 315 | 30 304 | -2.0 |
| Powell | 121 | -0.5 | D | 6.3 | 1.5 | 10.4 | D | 8.5 | 29.4 | 3 480 | 275 | 1 162 | 5 598 | 1.3 |
| Pulaski | 1 123 | 0.5 | D | 13.2 | 4.6 | 9.7 | 3.8 | 22.6 | 17.4 | 17 290 | 272 | 3 880 | 31 443 | 15.7 |
| Robertson | 13 | 2.6 | D | 0.0 | D | D | 1.9 | D | 49.5 | 525 | 236 | 125 | 1 095 | 6.0 |
| Rockcastle | 141 | -2.3 | D | 5.9 | 3.1 | 5.9 | D | 29.2 | 27.8 | 4 225 | 248 | 1 330 | 7 703 | 4.8 |
| Rowan | 442 | -0.1 | D | 9.5 | 2.0 | 9.4 | 3.0 | D | 36.4 | 4 740 | 201 | 1 215 | 10 102 | 12.4 |
| Russell | 292 | 1.6 | D | 26.5 | 3.3 | 10.1 | 3.4 | D | 18.6 | 4 600 | 261 | 1 278 | 9 993 | 10.2 |
| Scott | 1 378 | 1.0 | D | 50.3 | 3.6 | 3.6 | 2.0 | D | 7.8 | 7 000 | 145 | 1 027 | 19 303 | 48.7 |
| Shelby | 677 | 1.4 | D | 27.2 | 5.6 | 8.4 | 4.4 | 8.8 | 15.3 | 7 745 | 180 | 855 | 16 606 | 29.2 |
| Simpson | 416 | 7.5 | 44.0 | 39.9 | D | 8.1 | 2.2 | D | 10.1 | 3 900 | 224 | 555 | 7 435 | 6.0 |
| Spencer | 81 | -1.5 | D | D | D | 8.9 | 5.3 | D | 37.9 | 3 010 | 173 | 342 | 6 704 | 47.2 |
| Taylor | 446 | 1.7 | D | 11.3 | 3.1 | 9.1 | 3.9 | D | 21.9 | 6 395 | 259 | 1 296 | 10 864 | 6.7 |
| Todd | 146 | 24.3 | 14.2 | 7.8 | 2.1 | 5.7 | 3.0 | D | 20.0 | 2 635 | 211 | 425 | 5 286 | 3.2 |
| Trigg | 165 | 7.8 | D | 10.4 | 12.7 | 7.6 | 4.1 | D | 24.9 | 3 850 | 269 | 446 | 7 810 | 16.6 |
| Trimble | 63 | -1.0 | D | D | D | 3.1 | 5.8 | D | 28.1 | 2 000 | 229 | 307 | 3 930 | 14.3 |
| Union | 403 | 13.8 | 41.5 | 7.4 | D | 4.9 | 2.8 | D | 9.3 | 3 340 | 222 | 445 | 6 141 | -1.5 |
| Warren | 2 918 | 0.8 | 24.4 | 17.4 | 4.8 | 7.3 | 5.5 | 13.9 | 17.8 | 19 020 | 165 | 3 347 | 47 223 | 23.1 |
| Washington | 158 | 2.3 | D | 34.9 | D | 5.6 | 5.6 | D | 16.3 | 2 745 | 232 | 488 | 5 044 | 11.1 |
| Wayne | 220 | 4.1 | D | 26.3 | 5.1 | 10.0 | 3.7 | D | 23.2 | 5 385 | 257 | 1 950 | 10 942 | 11.8 |
| Webster | 263 | 14.7 | 40.0 | 3.9 | D | 3.3 | D | D | 12.7 | 3 225 | 236 | 487 | 5 936 | -5.0 |
| Whitley | 571 | -0.2 | 14.1 | 10.1 | 9.0 | 7.5 | 2.1 | D | 19.8 | 8 975 | 251 | 3 160 | 15 166 | -0.8 |
| Wolfe | 49 | -4.5 | D | 2.0 | D | 14.4 | D | D | 40.6 | 2 175 | 296 | 1 217 | 3 660 | 12.1 |
| Woodford | 551 | 9.4 | D | 22.9 | 9.0 | 5.2 | 2.8 | D | 14.9 | 4 850 | 194 | 414 | 10 711 | 14.3 |
| LOUISIANA | 125 660 | 0.8 | 23.0 | 10.1 | 8.2 | 6.4 | 5.9 | 10.9 | 19.1 | 809 450 | 177 | 178 806 | 1 964 981 | 6.4 |
| Acadia | 1 001 | 4.3 | 27.4 | 8.4 | 5.1 | 7.8 | 4.9 | D | 15.3 | 11 530 | 186 | 2 687 | 25 387 | 9.4 |
| Allen | 459 | 0.8 | 10.1 | 7.1 | 2.5 | 5.4 | 2.6 | D | 51.6 | 4 750 | 184 | 917 | 9 733 | 6.3 |
| Ascension | 2 893 | 0.3 | 37.9 | 22.2 | 4.9 | 7.8 | 6.9 | 7.7 | 9.8 | 15 450 | 140 | 2 268 | 40 784 | 39.8 |
| Assumption | 306 | 5.2 | 40.1 | 34.9 | D | 5.3 | 3.2 | 6.5 | 17.8 | 4 705 | 203 | 1 142 | 10 351 | 7.4 |
| Avoyelles | 623 | 6.0 | 18.4 | 4.6 | 4.5 | 8.1 | 4.1 | D | 28.4 | 9 220 | 220 | 2 862 | 18 042 | 8.8 |
| Beauregard | 492 | 0.4 | 28.2 | 17.3 | D | 8.2 | 8.2 | 12.5 | 17.4 | 6 900 | 191 | 1 030 | 15 040 | 3.7 |
| Bienville | 245 | 1.3 | 27.5 | 19.8 | D | 5.3 | 7.3 | 8.4 | 19.6 | 3 455 | 241 | 876 | 7 718 | -1.4 |
| Bossier | 3 183 | 0.1 | 19.6 | 4.7 | 3.5 | 8.6 | 3.5 | 6.6 | 37.3 | 18 725 | 156 | 3 154 | 49 351 | 22.4 |
| Caddo | 7 825 | 0.0 | 20.3 | 7.1 | 6.6 | 6.7 | 5.2 | 17.0 | 20.2 | 47 630 | 185 | 12 776 | 112 028 | 3.5 |
| Calcasieu | 5 245 | 0.1 | 32.7 | 19.9 | 7.4 | 6.2 | 3.7 | 12.3 | 15.5 | 36 320 | 187 | 6 052 | 82 058 | 8.0 |
| Caldwell | 122 | 1.8 | 8.3 | 1.9 | D | 11.3 | 5.1 | 21.3 | 26.0 | 2 085 | 207 | 444 | 4 994 | -0.8 |
| Cameron | 182 | 0.7 | 34.5 | 16.1 | D | D | D | 2.2 | 22.8 | 1 110 | 165 | 105 | 3 593 | -32.7 |
| Catahoula | 146 | 17.1 | D | D | 4.9 | 9.9 | 3.9 | 7.2 | 23.1 | 2 340 | 227 | 630 | 4 877 | -8.8 |
| Claiborne | 259 | 7.6 | 27.6 | 5.9 | 2.0 | 4.8 | 1.8 | D | 27.3 | 3 500 | 207 | 959 | 7 761 | -0.7 |
| Concordia | 310 | 8.5 | 10.0 | 1.3 | D | 8.9 | 3.5 | D | 27.0 | 4 420 | 212 | 1 340 | 9 383 | 2.6 |
| De Soto | 475 | 0.6 | 38.3 | 15.5 | 2.1 | 7.8 | 3.5 | D | 24.4 | 5 765 | 215 | 1 358 | 12 290 | 9.7 |
| East Baton Rouge | 16 231 | 0.0 | 21.1 | 7.9 | 11.4 | 5.8 | 6.6 | 12.5 | 20.5 | 67 115 | 152 | 14 935 | 187 353 | 10.8 |
| East Carroll | 124 | 30.3 | D | D | D | 5.2 | 3.8 | D | 28.4 | 1 410 | 185 | 676 | 2 904 | -12.1 |
| East Feliciana | 288 | 1.0 | D | 6.5 | 1.7 | 4.9 | 3.4 | D | 51.0 | 3 785 | 188 | 925 | 8 014 | 1.3 |
| Evangeline | 453 | 5.1 | 21.0 | 16.0 | 5.2 | 7.5 | 3.9 | 21.3 | 20.0 | 7 180 | 212 | 2 361 | 14 662 | 2.8 |
| Franklin | 309 | 19.8 | D | 2.5 | D | 11.3 | 3.7 | D | 22.9 | 4 465 | 215 | 1 350 | 9 034 | 4.8 |
| Grant | 226 | 1.1 | D | D | 2.2 | 3.9 | D | D | 50.1 | 4 200 | 190 | 868 | 8 886 | 4.2 |
| Iberia | 2 114 | 1.2 | 37.5 | 12.1 | 5.7 | 6.5 | 7.6 | 6.9 | 10.6 | 14 380 | 196 | 3 133 | 29 698 | 6.7 |
| Iberville | 1 153 | 1.8 | 53.8 | 43.3 | 2.4 | 3.2 | 2.9 | D | 15.7 | 6 035 | 182 | 1 499 | 12 707 | 6.3 |
| Jackson | 227 | 1.7 | D | 23.3 | 3.7 | 8.5 | 3.0 | D | 24.3 | 3 480 | 213 | 630 | 7 680 | 4.7 |
| Jefferson | 13 692 | 0.0 | 19.3 | 7.2 | 10.2 | 8.0 | 7.8 | 12.8 | 11.0 | 80 920 | 187 | 13 536 | 189 135 | 0.7 |
| Jefferson Davis | 480 | 4.5 | 15.4 | 5.1 | 4.0 | 8.2 | 7.2 | D | 21.4 | 6 230 | 197 | 1 129 | 13 306 | 3.8 |
| Lafayette | 9 668 | 0.1 | 31.2 | 7.1 | 9.7 | 6.2 | 7.3 | 13.8 | 9.6 | 32 385 | 144 | 5 796 | 93 656 | 20.0 |
| Lafourche | 3 274 | 0.6 | 18.0 | 6.6 | 3.6 | 4.8 | 4.5 | 6.0 | 12.3 | 17 720 | 183 | 3 358 | 38 582 | 10.1 |
| La Salle | 261 | 1.6 | 16.7 | 3.3 | 4.5 | 7.1 | 2.8 | 5.3 | 27.2 | 3 055 | 204 | 496 | 6 560 | 4.6 |
| Lincoln | 1 035 | 1.2 | 17.8 | 8.3 | 6.0 | 9.6 | 4.8 | 19.2 | 23.6 | 6 435 | 137 | 1 447 | 19 479 | 14.6 |
| Livingston | 1 316 | -0.1 | 25.7 | 8.8 | D | 10.2 | 4.7 | 6.9 | 22.5 | 20 100 | 154 | 2 827 | 50 170 | 38.5 |
| Madison | 176 | 20.1 | D | 5.7 | 1.4 | 7.6 | 3.2 | D | 30.3 | 2 025 | 169 | 752 | 4 804 | -3.5 |
| Morehouse | 367 | 15.2 | D | 3.9 | D | 9.4 | 3.7 | D | 20.6 | 6 585 | 239 | 1 848 | 12 423 | -2.3 |
| Natchitoches | 738 | 2.2 | D | 18.2 | 4.5 | 7.9 | 4.7 | D | 29.3 | 7 245 | 184 | 2 174 | 18 587 | 10.0 |

1. Includes mining, construction, and manufacturing.   2. Per 1,000 resident population enumerated in the 2010 census.

# Table B. States and Counties — Housing, Labor Force, and Employment

| | Housing units, 2007–2011 | | | | | | | | Civilian labor force, 2012 | | | | Civilian employment,[6] 2007–2011 | | |
| | Occupied units | | | | | | Sub-stand-ard units[4] (percent) | | | Unemployment | | | | Percent | |
| | Owner-occupied | | | | | Renter-occupied | | | | | | | | | |
| | | | | Median owner cost as a percent of income | | | Median rent as a per-cent of income | | | | | | | | Management, business, science and arts | Con-struction, produc-tion, and mainte-nance occu-pations |
| STATE County | Total | Percent | Median value[1] | With a mort-gage | Without a mort-gage[2] | Median rent[3] | | | Total | Percent change, 2011–2012 | Total | Rate[5] | Total | | |
| | 89 | 90 | 91 | 92 | 93 | 94 | 95 | 96 | 97 | 98 | 99 | 100 | 101 | 102 | 103 |
| **KENTUCKY—Cont'd** | | | | | | | | | | | | | | | |
| Ohio | 8 667 | 79.2 | 79 400 | 21.5 | 10.7 | 500 | 27.9 | 3.2 | 13 252 | 2.9 | 892 | 6.7 | 8 895 | 20.1 | 43.2 |
| Oldham | 19 400 | 85.0 | 240 300 | 21.9 | 9.9 | 717 | 29.5 | 1.8 | 28 665 | 0.8 | 1 904 | 6.6 | 27 305 | 46.0 | 16.9 |
| Owen | 4 713 | 72.3 | 100 800 | 20.0 | 10.6 | 564 | 24.9 | 4.5 | 5 321 | 0.8 | 382 | 7.2 | 5 259 | 24.1 | 38.0 |
| Owsley | 1 650 | 76.5 | 68 900 | 30.4 | 14.3 | 340 | 25.2 | 5.3 | 1 582 | -0.5 | 173 | 10.9 | 1 079 | 21.5 | 27.8 |
| Pendleton | 5 339 | 75.9 | 104 500 | 22.0 | 12.4 | 627 | 24.7 | 3.0 | 7 072 | -1.4 | 609 | 8.6 | 6 461 | 24.6 | 38.3 |
| Perry | 10 849 | 71.4 | 57 800 | 19.8 | 9.9 | 500 | 31.8 | 3.8 | 11 806 | 2.6 | 1 419 | 12.0 | 10 235 | 29.0 | 29.0 |
| Pike | 26 904 | 74.3 | 66 500 | 20.7 | 10.5 | 543 | 29.7 | 2.5 | 25 936 | 0.0 | 2 354 | 9.1 | 21 759 | 25.8 | 31.6 |
| Powell | 4 581 | 68.3 | 76 500 | 23.2 | 14.0 | 579 | 38.8 | 5.9 | 5 580 | 0.0 | 561 | 10.1 | 4 411 | 23.5 | 41.0 |
| Pulaski | 26 199 | 72.5 | 97 600 | 22.1 | 12.0 | 545 | 35.0 | 3.3 | 27 733 | -0.8 | 2 616 | 9.4 | 25 057 | 28.8 | 26.5 |
| Robertson | 776 | 68.9 | 62 900 | 20.2 | 12.8 | 560 | 31.8 | 4.0 | 1 061 | 1.0 | 90 | 8.5 | 665 | 23.9 | 42.6 |
| Rockcastle | 6 474 | 80.5 | 73 200 | 22.8 | 13.6 | 505 | 34.1 | 2.9 | 7 659 | -0.2 | 696 | 9.1 | 6 050 | 24.4 | 31.7 |
| Rowan | 8 206 | 67.5 | 100 400 | 19.2 | 12.3 | 544 | 34.8 | 2.1 | 12 807 | 0.5 | 936 | 7.3 | 9 676 | 32.5 | 22.3 |
| Russell | 7 409 | 76.4 | 84 500 | 23.6 | 11.2 | 472 | 29.0 | 1.8 | 8 678 | 2.1 | 747 | 8.6 | 6 883 | 29.3 | 37.3 |
| Scott | 17 628 | 71.1 | 155 900 | 19.3 | 9.9 | 710 | 26.6 | 3.8 | 23 984 | 0.4 | 1 652 | 6.9 | 21 994 | 36.0 | 27.4 |
| Shelby | 15 030 | 72.4 | 168 400 | 22.7 | 9.9 | 701 | 24.7 | 2.5 | 21 725 | 0.2 | 1 441 | 6.6 | 19 986 | 32.0 | 26.5 |
| Simpson | 6 672 | 70.7 | 115 400 | 23.3 | 12.1 | 675 | 27.6 | 2.2 | 9 709 | 5.2 | 773 | 8.0 | 7 916 | 24.4 | 32.6 |
| Spencer | 6 224 | 87.8 | 166 200 | 22.7 | 9.9 | 614 | 24.0 | 1.8 | 8 809 | -0.3 | 667 | 7.6 | 8 354 | 27.4 | 33.8 |
| Taylor | 9 633 | 69.4 | 94 800 | 22.4 | 9.9 | 513 | 29.9 | 2.0 | 14 122 | -1.9 | 1 103 | 7.8 | 10 206 | 25.4 | 29.7 |
| Todd | 4 665 | 71.9 | 79 600 | 23.2 | 10.9 | 552 | 23.1 | 2.8 | 5 571 | 0.4 | 439 | 7.9 | 4 986 | 20.3 | 40.1 |
| Trigg | 6 149 | 79.0 | 105 800 | 22.8 | 10.8 | 550 | 33.9 | 4.3 | 6 572 | 1.5 | 570 | 8.7 | 5 442 | 27.1 | 37.2 |
| Trimble | 3 420 | 77.7 | 118 600 | 19.2 | 11.3 | 625 | 26.6 | 0.8 | 4 066 | -0.2 | 335 | 8.2 | 3 820 | 23.5 | 39.4 |
| Union | 5 468 | 76.4 | 77 800 | 18.5 | 12.9 | 489 | 31.5 | 3.7 | 7 599 | -7.3 | 533 | 7.0 | 5 621 | 28.5 | 33.9 |
| Warren | 42 910 | 61.2 | 137 800 | 22.1 | 9.9 | 635 | 31.4 | 2.1 | 60 547 | 1.2 | 4 170 | 6.9 | 53 673 | 33.7 | 24.3 |
| Washington | 4 541 | 80.8 | 110 700 | 20.9 | 11.0 | 553 | 24.2 | 1.0 | 5 617 | 1.3 | 482 | 8.6 | 5 343 | 28.8 | 38.9 |
| Wayne | 8 526 | 72.5 | 70 900 | 23.2 | 11.0 | 436 | 30.7 | 3.3 | 8 226 | -0.6 | 1 018 | 12.4 | 7 084 | 23.9 | 44.1 |
| Webster | 4 990 | 77.4 | 68 300 | 18.2 | 10.3 | 551 | 26.1 | 2.7 | 6 392 | 0.0 | 492 | 7.7 | 5 304 | 25.0 | 43.2 |
| Whitley | 13 197 | 70.0 | 67 600 | 22.6 | 11.7 | 541 | 29.3 | 2.2 | 15 714 | 0.2 | 1 496 | 9.5 | 12 357 | 25.4 | 26.0 |
| Wolfe | 2 543 | 76.1 | 53 200 | 27.4 | 11.6 | 505 | 50.0 | 0.9 | 2 430 | 1.7 | 311 | 12.8 | 1 943 | 27.0 | 29.5 |
| Woodford | 9 878 | 71.6 | 190 000 | 22.1 | 9.9 | 701 | 27.7 | 0.8 | 12 958 | 0.5 | 756 | 5.8 | 12 228 | 38.7 | 27.2 |
| **LOUISIANA** | 1 675 097 | 67.9 | 135 400 | 21.5 | 10.1 | 745 | 31.7 | 3.4 | 2 083 710 | 0.7 | 134 361 | 6.4 | 1 974 967 | 31.1 | 25.4 |
| Acadia | 22 083 | 69.0 | 90 900 | 19.1 | 9.9 | 523 | 28.3 | 4.4 | 25 826 | 0.1 | 1 435 | 5.6 | 24 975 | 24.9 | 31.9 |
| Allen | 8 257 | 73.7 | 78 300 | 18.6 | 9.9 | 549 | 26.0 | 3.6 | 8 674 | -1.3 | 741 | 8.5 | 8 722 | 22.5 | 32.5 |
| Ascension | 36 546 | 82.4 | 166 800 | 19.2 | 9.9 | 818 | 31.6 | 4.3 | 53 194 | 1.4 | 3 026 | 5.7 | 50 272 | 35.2 | 26.0 |
| Assumption | 8 590 | 81.9 | 89 100 | 17.7 | 9.9 | 568 | 25.0 | 5.2 | 10 492 | -0.5 | 878 | 8.4 | 9 228 | 25.0 | 40.7 |
| Avoyelles | 15 801 | 69.4 | 85 000 | 20.3 | 11.6 | 566 | 29.4 | 4.3 | 16 425 | -1.2 | 1 189 | 7.2 | 15 261 | 25.1 | 28.3 |
| Beauregard | 12 853 | 78.6 | 84 500 | 18.1 | 9.9 | 604 | 26.7 | 3.5 | 14 403 | 1.0 | 1 013 | 7.0 | 13 852 | 26.0 | 32.8 |
| Bienville | 5 571 | 76.5 | 55 600 | 18.0 | 11.6 | 453 | 36.8 | 2.6 | 6 584 | 1.7 | 489 | 7.4 | 5 114 | 26.5 | 35.1 |
| Bossier | 43 962 | 67.4 | 138 600 | 21.1 | 9.9 | 756 | 28.4 | 3.0 | 56 201 | -0.4 | 3 024 | 5.4 | 52 732 | 31.7 | 25.2 |
| Caddo | 98 270 | 63.1 | 118 400 | 21.8 | 10.8 | 698 | 31.9 | 2.7 | 116 467 | -0.7 | 7 823 | 6.7 | 110 611 | 30.4 | 22.1 |
| Calcasieu | 72 061 | 71.1 | 116 500 | 19.6 | 9.9 | 711 | 29.2 | 2.5 | 92 084 | 1.7 | 5 456 | 5.9 | 84 801 | 28.5 | 26.7 |
| Caldwell | 3 834 | 72.7 | 71 900 | 18.4 | 10.2 | 456 | 28.8 | 3.5 | 4 464 | -2.1 | 329 | 7.4 | 3 928 | 24.4 | 34.9 |
| Cameron | 2 461 | 89.4 | 118 600 | 15.0 | 9.9 | 682 | 16.8 | 3.6 | 3 070 | 2.1 | 162 | 5.3 | 3 396 | 28.0 | 38.8 |
| Catahoula | 3 750 | 78.7 | 68 000 | 20.7 | 9.9 | 394 | 24.0 | 5.5 | 4 077 | -5.0 | 345 | 8.5 | 3 554 | 27.7 | 30.7 |
| Claiborne | 5 702 | 74.1 | 65 900 | 19.5 | 11.7 | 581 | 36.4 | 4.3 | 6 871 | 2.9 | 527 | 7.7 | 6 307 | 23.1 | 31.4 |
| Concordia | 7 710 | 67.4 | 78 100 | 20.9 | 13.5 | 429 | 29.3 | 2.7 | 7 518 | -1.3 | 732 | 9.7 | 7 122 | 24.1 | 27.6 |
| De Soto | 10 326 | 76.9 | 83 100 | 20.0 | 10.3 | 537 | 33.8 | 5.0 | 11 336 | 0.4 | 939 | 8.3 | 11 099 | 24.0 | 33.3 |
| East Baton Rouge | 167 150 | 61.8 | 161 600 | 22.0 | 9.9 | 787 | 33.8 | 2.8 | 218 604 | 1.4 | 13 707 | 6.3 | 215 638 | 36.8 | 18.7 |
| East Carroll | 2 525 | 57.5 | 45 800 | 21.1 | 11.2 | 429 | 41.6 | 5.1 | 2 766 | -7.0 | 434 | 15.7 | 2 214 | 25.8 | 21.5 |
| East Feliciana | 6 978 | 81.5 | 102 200 | 21.7 | 10.9 | 581 | 31.9 | 3.0 | 7 689 | 1.1 | 570 | 7.4 | 7 537 | 21.1 | 30.3 |
| Evangeline | 12 165 | 68.1 | 81 800 | 18.4 | 10.9 | 479 | 27.5 | 4.2 | 12 586 | -1.7 | 905 | 7.2 | 11 679 | 26.9 | 33.4 |
| Franklin | 7 965 | 73.2 | 76 200 | 20.3 | 9.9 | 523 | 30.9 | 2.8 | 7 613 | -3.5 | 755 | 9.9 | 7 657 | 26.4 | 31.5 |
| Grant | 7 231 | 78.8 | 80 700 | 19.8 | 10.7 | 682 | 30.3 | 2.8 | 9 283 | -0.9 | 642 | 6.9 | 8 030 | 26.2 | 33.9 |
| Iberia | 26 370 | 70.5 | 102 600 | 20.5 | 9.9 | 655 | 28.5 | 3.8 | 34 476 | 2.6 | 1 968 | 5.7 | 30 827 | 25.4 | 31.1 |
| Iberville | 11 040 | 76.0 | 89 300 | 19.2 | 9.9 | 547 | 26.4 | 3.8 | 12 540 | 1.0 | 1 192 | 9.5 | 13 143 | 21.9 | 34.1 |
| Jackson | 6 037 | 69.5 | 72 800 | 17.5 | 10.1 | 545 | 25.3 | 2.0 | 6 355 | -2.7 | 461 | 7.3 | 6 573 | 23.7 | 34.1 |
| Jefferson | 165 404 | 63.9 | 176 700 | 23.9 | 11.1 | 889 | 31.6 | 3.1 | 209 855 | 0.8 | 12 974 | 6.2 | 211 488 | 31.5 | 23.8 |
| Jefferson Davis | 11 878 | 76.0 | 85 400 | 18.4 | 10.5 | 579 | 24.9 | 3.5 | 14 587 | 0.9 | 772 | 5.3 | 12 025 | 25.9 | 35.2 |
| Lafayette | 84 594 | 64.8 | 157 300 | 19.9 | 9.9 | 725 | 28.2 | 2.5 | 117 262 | 2.8 | 5 313 | 4.5 | 109 611 | 33.8 | 21.4 |
| Lafourche | 34 474 | 78.1 | 120 200 | 19.1 | 9.9 | 636 | 27.6 | 4.7 | 49 205 | 2.1 | 2 176 | 4.4 | 42 623 | 27.8 | 33.5 |
| La Salle | 5 547 | 84.2 | 74 400 | 17.3 | 9.9 | 484 | 27.3 | 2.5 | 7 267 | 0.1 | 333 | 4.6 | 5 867 | 33.5 | 32.1 |
| Lincoln | 16 594 | 55.6 | 109 700 | 21.1 | 9.9 | 633 | 37.6 | 2.5 | 19 012 | -2.8 | 1 523 | 8.0 | 19 870 | 36.3 | 20.5 |
| Livingston | 44 166 | 80.5 | 152 800 | 20.5 | 9.9 | 722 | 26.2 | 4.1 | 61 297 | 1.4 | 3 616 | 5.9 | 58 269 | 28.5 | 30.3 |
| Madison | 3 938 | 61.0 | 70 200 | 19.2 | 12.2 | 551 | 32.5 | 5.6 | 4 350 | -3.7 | 451 | 10.4 | 4 257 | 28.0 | 29.2 |
| Morehouse | 10 264 | 69.1 | 75 900 | 22.3 | 11.3 | 566 | 29.7 | 4.5 | 11 827 | 1.1 | 1 369 | 11.6 | 9 762 | 22.7 | 28.8 |
| Natchitoches | 15 044 | 61.1 | 94 700 | 20.1 | 10.7 | 608 | 38.5 | 6.0 | 16 672 | -1.5 | 1 320 | 7.9 | 16 120 | 27.8 | 26.4 |

1. Specified owner-occupied units.    2. A value of 9.9 represents 9.9 percent or less.    3. Specified renter-occupied units. A value of 10.0 represents 10 percent or less.    4. Overcrowded or lacking complete plumbing facilities.    5. Percent of civilian labor force.    6. Persons 16 years old and over.

# Table B. States and Counties — Nonfarm Employment and Agriculture

| | Private nonfarm establishments, employment and payroll, 2011 | | | | | | | | Agriculture, 2007 | | | |
| | Employment | | | | | | Annual payroll | | Farms | | | |
| | | | | | | | | | | Percent with: | | |
| STATE County | Number of establishments | Total | Health care and social assistance | Manufacturing | Retail trade | Finance and insurance | Professional, scientific, and technical services | Total (mil dol) | Average per employee (dollars) | Number | Fewer than 50 acres | 500 acres or more | Farm operators whose principal occupation is farming (percent) |
|---|---|---|---|---|---|---|---|---|---|---|---|---|---|
| | 104 | 105 | 106 | 107 | 108 | 109 | 110 | 111 | 112 | 113 | 114 | 115 | 116 |
| **KENTUCKY—Cont'd** | | | | | | | | | | | | | |
| Ohio | 345 | 5 482 | 972 | D | 734 | 135 | D | 142 | 25 868 | 969 | 31.3 | 5.5 | 33.4 |
| Oldham | 1 198 | 10 145 | 2 369 | 775 | 1 330 | 861 | 577 | 326 | 32 115 | 461 | 56.2 | 6.5 | 38.2 |
| Owen | 128 | 1 413 | 262 | D | 210 | D | D | 58 | 41 372 | 864 | 21.8 | 6.7 | 38.9 |
| Owsley | 43 | 348 | 207 | D | D | D | 9 | 9 | 25 115 | 195 | 21.5 | 9.7 | 31.8 |
| Pendleton | 174 | 1 559 | D | 516 | 203 | 70 | 43 | 50 | 32 019 | 910 | 29.1 | 2.7 | 36.2 |
| Perry | 680 | 10 699 | 2 674 | D | 2 040 | 284 | 269 | 425 | 39 681 | 57 | 31.6 | 5.3 | 38.6 |
| Pike | 1 385 | 20 399 | 3 902 | 654 | 3 815 | D | 691 | 828 | 40 588 | 70 | 42.9 | 7.1 | 32.9 |
| Powell | 162 | 1 471 | 206 | 157 | 355 | D | 13 | 35 | 23 734 | 236 | 36.9 | 4.7 | 34.3 |
| Pulaski | 1 378 | 20 144 | 5 275 | 3 326 | 3 252 | 656 | 429 | 609 | 30 254 | 1 808 | 36.5 | 3.2 | 44.0 |
| Robertson | 19 | D | D | NA | D | D | D | 3 | D | 289 | 17.6 | 6.6 | 40.5 |
| Rockcastle | 220 | 2 489 | 810 | 182 | 314 | 90 | 43 | 63 | 25 255 | 727 | 33.8 | 2.8 | 41.5 |
| Rowan | 469 | 7 585 | D | 1 158 | 1 352 | 194 | 101 | 206 | 27 096 | 386 | 37.3 | 4.1 | 35.2 |
| Russell | 370 | 5 152 | 941 | 1 556 | 670 | D | 63 | 144 | 28 013 | 805 | 41.2 | 4.2 | 36.3 |
| Scott | 839 | 19 864 | 1 360 | 8 479 | 1 727 | 281 | 326 | 827 | 41 647 | 930 | 39.7 | 6.0 | 43.1 |
| Shelby | 866 | 11 638 | 1 287 | 3 160 | 1 931 | 329 | 442 | 364 | 31 310 | 1 651 | 47.2 | 3.6 | 41.0 |
| Simpson | 381 | 7 135 | 442 | 2 937 | 979 | 115 | D | 222 | 31 057 | 494 | 45.1 | 9.3 | 43.1 |
| Spencer | 201 | 1 034 | 211 | D | 239 | D | 43 | 23 | 22 644 | 596 | 39.1 | 2.3 | 38.3 |
| Taylor | 611 | 9 598 | 1 159 | 1 329 | 1 491 | 234 | 96 | 245 | 25 527 | 941 | 39.0 | 3.9 | 38.5 |
| Todd | 186 | 1 437 | 227 | 333 | 236 | 72 | 42 | 36 | 25 052 | 759 | 29.5 | 12.3 | 45.6 |
| Trigg | 235 | 2 250 | 353 | 452 | 347 | 67 | 42 | 59 | 26 020 | 458 | 29.3 | 12.2 | 46.9 |
| Trimble | 84 | 647 | D | D | 103 | D | D | 30 | 45 753 | 489 | 32.3 | 3.3 | 40.5 |
| Union | 284 | 4 702 | 1 054 | 464 | 693 | 80 | 63 | 202 | 43 053 | 325 | 29.5 | 28.0 | 50.5 |
| Warren | 2 752 | 46 333 | 7 365 | 7 369 | 7 064 | 1 460 | 2 054 | 1 669 | 36 029 | 1 824 | 45.5 | 4.7 | 34.2 |
| Washington | 245 | 2 590 | 305 | 767 | 267 | 55 | 76 | 55 | 29 442 | 1 119 | 28.3 | 4.0 | 38.1 |
| Wayne | 287 | 3 654 | 546 | 1 352 | 676 | 161 | 59 | 93 | 25 377 | 781 | 31.8 | 7.9 | 41.9 |
| Webster | 215 | 2 406 | 283 | 287 | 355 | 104 | D | 99 | 40 987 | 556 | 26.3 | 12.2 | 37.6 |
| Whitley | 654 | 10 312 | 3 020 | 948 | 1 506 | 279 | 766 | 315 | 30 502 | 565 | 33.6 | 3.9 | 42.8 |
| Wolfe | 81 | 623 | 311 | D | D | D | D | 15 | 23 368 | 342 | 22.5 | 5.3 | 36.0 |
| Woodford | 528 | 6 675 | 598 | 1 834 | 733 | 208 | 511 | 249 | 37 287 | 712 | 44.8 | 8.3 | 49.9 |
| **LOUISIANA** | 103 216 | 1 617 229 | 282 985 | 125 820 | 226 638 | 66 255 | 88 171 | 65 772 | 40 669 | 30 106 | 45.4 | 11.4 | 41.8 |
| Acadia | 1 130 | 12 449 | 2 200 | 1 171 | 2 440 | 439 | 402 | 385 | 30 940 | 905 | 54.4 | 12.8 | 41.7 |
| Allen | 335 | 3 873 | 1 100 | D | 705 | 130 | 52 | 107 | 27 539 | 405 | 47.9 | 10.1 | 41.7 |
| Ascension | 1 986 | 31 087 | 3 032 | 3 988 | 5 623 | 875 | 824 | 1 380 | 44 402 | 277 | 63.5 | 7.9 | 32.1 |
| Assumption | 254 | 2 644 | 747 | 309 | 508 | 95 | 73 | 86 | 32 444 | 114 | 50.0 | 33.3 | 60.5 |
| Avoyelles | 735 | 8 689 | 2 115 | 297 | 1 444 | 444 | 200 | 223 | 25 646 | 947 | 39.0 | 12.9 | 42.8 |
| Beauregard | 581 | 6 719 | 1 189 | 845 | 1 310 | D | 184 | 235 | 34 990 | 909 | 41.3 | 5.0 | 38.1 |
| Bienville | 241 | 3 184 | 436 | D | 351 | D | 22 | 99 | 31 080 | 194 | 35.1 | 5.7 | 42.3 |
| Bossier | 2 430 | 36 106 | 3 877 | 1 751 | 6 805 | 1 165 | 1 126 | 1 124 | 31 140 | 493 | 55.6 | 12.0 | 45.2 |
| Caddo | 6 297 | 109 362 | 27 949 | 6 967 | 14 216 | 3 453 | 4 024 | 4 107 | 37 551 | 625 | 55.5 | 10.7 | 41.3 |
| Calcasieu | 4 212 | 68 049 | 12 233 | 8 062 | 10 571 | 1 881 | 3 378 | 2 601 | 38 225 | 971 | 53.1 | 9.0 | 36.8 |
| Caldwell | 187 | 1 987 | 654 | 38 | 563 | 115 | 72 | 48 | 24 307 | 307 | 34.9 | 8.8 | 34.9 |
| Cameron | 157 | 1 437 | D | D | 100 | D | 77 | 72 | 49 914 | 339 | 36.0 | 22.7 | 41.6 |
| Catahoula | 183 | 1 774 | 545 | D | 271 | 85 | 80 | 47 | 26 409 | 510 | 26.1 | 21.6 | 38.8 |
| Claiborne | 262 | 2 938 | 817 | 221 | 481 | D | D | 98 | 33 381 | 239 | 36.8 | 10.0 | 46.9 |
| Concordia | 375 | 4 178 | 861 | D | 906 | 209 | 109 | 121 | 28 953 | 462 | 22.3 | 24.0 | 39.2 |
| De Soto | 401 | 5 193 | 637 | 740 | 965 | 190 | 72 | 229 | 44 061 | 619 | 38.8 | 9.2 | 45.6 |
| East Baton Rouge | 12 173 | 226 445 | 37 453 | 10 613 | 28 097 | 12 130 | 18 146 | 9 637 | 42 557 | 511 | 55.0 | 5.9 | 37.2 |
| East Carroll | 130 | 1 249 | 327 | 84 | D | 50 | 20 | 40 | 32 097 | 280 | 15.4 | 36.4 | 58.2 |
| East Feliciana | 253 | 3 818 | 2 290 | 287 | 300 | D | D | 125 | 32 820 | 439 | 40.1 | 16.4 | 35.3 |
| Evangeline | 528 | 6 300 | 2 564 | 770 | 1 036 | 282 | 141 | 184 | 29 181 | 806 | 49.5 | 8.7 | 32.0 |
| Franklin | 398 | 4 126 | 1 174 | 225 | 1 056 | 221 | 146 | 97 | 23 456 | 1 273 | 28.6 | 14.4 | 45.2 |
| Grant | 182 | 1 617 | 255 | D | 219 | 83 | D | 42 | 26 074 | 250 | 48.8 | 8.8 | 29.6 |
| Iberia | 1 727 | 29 002 | 3 920 | 4 642 | 3 394 | 964 | 819 | 1 368 | 47 152 | 345 | 61.7 | 17.7 | 45.8 |
| Iberville | 535 | 8 856 | 752 | 3 205 | 1 082 | 272 | 287 | 522 | 58 950 | 175 | 48.0 | 24.0 | 52.0 |
| Jackson | 256 | 2 889 | 651 | D | 540 | 116 | 68 | 101 | 35 096 | 197 | 56.3 | 2.0 | 41.1 |
| Jefferson | 11 697 | 179 200 | 29 001 | 10 823 | 28 846 | 8 417 | 10 560 | 7 478 | 41 729 | 71 | 67.6 | 7.0 | 42.3 |
| Jefferson Davis | 606 | 6 590 | 1 526 | D | 1 462 | 322 | 317 | 204 | 30 963 | 706 | 44.3 | 20.1 | 44.5 |
| Lafayette | 7 992 | 122 637 | 21 278 | 7 849 | 15 646 | 3 556 | 8 281 | 5 223 | 42 589 | 713 | 75.6 | 3.4 | 37.6 |
| Lafourche | 1 867 | 28 269 | 3 989 | 2 343 | 4 205 | 1 150 | 700 | 1 218 | 43 076 | 440 | 47.0 | 9.8 | 45.5 |
| La Salle | 329 | 3 174 | 756 | D | 574 | D | D | 102 | 31 998 | 165 | 39.4 | 3.0 | 38.2 |
| Lincoln | 977 | 14 335 | 3 484 | 1 137 | 2 303 | 680 | 532 | 451 | 31 476 | 321 | 37.7 | 5.6 | 45.8 |
| Livingston | 1 583 | 17 334 | 2 082 | 1 806 | 4 210 | 667 | 651 | 521 | 30 032 | 476 | 70.8 | 1.3 | 33.4 |
| Madison | 211 | 2 379 | 1 066 | D | 457 | 58 | 31 | 56 | 23 339 | 355 | 19.7 | 36.3 | 49.3 |
| Morehouse | 477 | 5 175 | 1 999 | D | 1 087 | 229 | 102 | 129 | 24 995 | 473 | 27.3 | 28.3 | 50.7 |
| Natchitoches | 809 | 10 718 | 1 736 | 2 522 | 1 792 | D | 261 | 300 | 28 012 | 571 | 32.7 | 18.7 | 45.7 |

| STATE County | Land in farms — Acreage (1,000) | Percent change, 2002–2007 | Acres — Average size of farm | Total irrigated (1,000) | Total cropland (1,000) | Value of land and buildings (dollars) — Average per farm | Average per acre | Value of machinery and equipment, average per farm (dollars) | Value of products sold — Total (mil dol) | Average per farm (dollars) | Percent from: Crops | Live-stock and poultry products | Percent of farms with sales of: $10,000 or more | $100,000 or more | Government payments — Total ($1,000) | Percent of farms |
|---|---|---|---|---|---|---|---|---|---|---|---|---|---|---|---|---|
| | 117 | 118 | 119 | 120 | 121 | 122 | 123 | 124 | 125 | 126 | 127 | 128 | 129 | 130 | 131 | 132 |
| KENTUCKY—Cont'd | | | | | | | | | | | | | | | | |
| Ohio | 169 | 1.2 | 174 | D | 84.8 | 348 348 | 2 002 | 53 306 | 72.8 | 75 167 | 27.3 | 72.7 | 28.2 | 6.6 | 1 104 | 40.2 |
| Oldham | 60 | -4.8 | 130 | 0.2 | 29.0 | 795 673 | 6 111 | 63 089 | 19.3 | 41 799 | 39.3 | 60.7 | 31.5 | 6.9 | 223 | 16.1 |
| Owen | 158 | 1.9 | 183 | 0.4 | 69.3 | 416 504 | 2 279 | 50 450 | 17.3 | 20 050 | 40.9 | 59.1 | 34.0 | 3.9 | 466 | 39.8 |
| Owsley | 36 | 9.1 | 184 | 0.1 | 9.9 | 274 202 | 1 491 | 35 100 | 1.2 | 6 262 | 68.6 | 31.4 | 15.9 | 0.5 | 55 | 13.8 |
| Pendleton | 126 | -4.5 | 139 | 1.0 | 55.0 | 351 015 | 2 528 | 54 781 | 12.4 | 13 608 | 58.1 | 41.9 | 21.3 | 2.7 | 376 | 20.3 |
| Perry | 11 | 57.1 | 187 | 0.0 | 2.4 | 227 787 | 1 218 | 48 155 | 0.9 | 15 222 | 5.8 | 94.2 | 22.8 | 7.0 | D | 1.8 |
| Pike | 14 | 100.0 | 203 | 0.0 | 3.0 | 190 309 | 936 | 32 524 | 0.4 | 5 737 | 20.4 | 79.4 | 10.0 | 1.4 | 1 | 4.3 |
| Powell | 33 | -13.2 | 139 | 0.0 | 13.5 | 267 393 | 1 926 | 36 199 | 2.5 | 10 623 | 64.9 | 35.1 | 16.5 | 2.1 | 83 | 26.7 |
| Pulaski | 232 | 0.0 | 128 | 0.2 | 105.0 | 336 474 | 2 625 | 47 179 | 39.7 | 21 980 | 26.2 | 73.8 | 37.9 | 4.6 | 704 | 25.4 |
| Robertson | 51 | 18.6 | 178 | 0.1 | 21.7 | 317 504 | 1 783 | 46 423 | 3.8 | 13 238 | 54.3 | 45.7 | 30.8 | 2.4 | 139 | 16.6 |
| Rockcastle | 90 | -4.3 | 124 | 0.0 | 32.5 | 256 809 | 2 064 | 38 363 | 8.4 | 11 557 | 29.9 | 70.1 | 24.2 | 2.6 | 233 | 21.9 |
| Rowan | 50 | -2.0 | 129 | 0.0 | 19.5 | 256 127 | 1 979 | 47 450 | 4.8 | 12 515 | 37.5 | 62.5 | 21.8 | 1.6 | 89 | 18.4 |
| Russell | 93 | -4.1 | 116 | 0.3 | 46.2 | 358 336 | 3 100 | 51 300 | 43.6 | 54 217 | 10.1 | 89.9 | 41.1 | 9.7 | 633 | 35.9 |
| Scott | 139 | 1.5 | 150 | 1.0 | 62.5 | 575 648 | 3 850 | 60 387 | 67.5 | 72 546 | 15.2 | 84.8 | 34.5 | 8.0 | 358 | 17.5 |
| Shelby | 205 | 1.5 | 124 | 1.5 | 124.2 | 551 127 | 4 432 | 58 291 | 57.0 | 34 520 | 52.0 | 48.0 | 37.7 | 6.7 | 1 689 | 20.7 |
| Simpson | 119 | -7.0 | 241 | 0.1 | 89.1 | 712 528 | 2 955 | 78 935 | 47.4 | 95 976 | 40.9 | 59.1 | 39.3 | 10.5 | 1 243 | 48.6 |
| Spencer | 73 | -6.4 | 123 | 0.6 | 36.1 | 405 163 | 3 295 | 52 129 | 11.5 | 19 361 | 58.3 | 41.7 | 32.2 | 4.0 | 494 | 41.3 |
| Taylor | 119 | 6.3 | 126 | 0.2 | 59.6 | 312 492 | 2 477 | 52 818 | 26.3 | 27 983 | 40.1 | 59.9 | 34.2 | 6.2 | 973 | 41.7 |
| Todd | 198 | 7.6 | 261 | 1.0 | 136.2 | 745 593 | 2 858 | 102 587 | 130.4 | 171 817 | 30.9 | 69.1 | 49.4 | 20.4 | 2 626 | 50.3 |
| Trigg | 136 | 10.6 | 296 | 0.9 | 74.0 | 765 195 | 2 583 | 93 146 | 27.0 | 58 866 | 66.2 | 33.8 | 43.9 | 10.5 | 1 480 | 50.7 |
| Trimble | 65 | 0.0 | 133 | 0.1 | 25.9 | 339 215 | 2 548 | 48 029 | 7.6 | 15 569 | 57.9 | 42.1 | 30.9 | 2.0 | 220 | 22.3 |
| Union | 201 | -3.8 | 618 | 2.3 | 166.9 | 1 596 117 | 2 583 | 219 696 | 78.9 | 242 919 | 92.5 | 7.5 | 59.4 | 31.4 | 3 411 | 64.6 |
| Warren | 265 | 3.9 | 145 | 0.3 | 147.9 | 455 845 | 3 136 | 60 496 | 74.7 | 40 941 | 29.5 | 70.5 | 33.9 | 5.9 | 2 342 | 31.9 |
| Washington | 163 | 8.7 | 146 | 0.7 | 80.6 | 359 002 | 2 465 | 53 052 | 33.0 | 29 491 | 29.8 | 70.2 | 37.0 | 6.3 | 714 | 29.8 |
| Wayne | 143 | 2.9 | 183 | 0.1 | 48.5 | 373 723 | 2 044 | 55 378 | 68.5 | 87 654 | 8.9 | 91.1 | 35.2 | 7.8 | 392 | 24.5 |
| Webster | 155 | -2.5 | 279 | D | 107.5 | 648 343 | 2 326 | 86 349 | 97.0 | 174 497 | 31.7 | 68.3 | 32.9 | 15.8 | 2 592 | 68.9 |
| Whitley | 73 | 14.1 | 130 | D | 27.8 | 319 531 | 2 459 | 41 622 | 4.6 | 8 192 | 29.4 | 70.6 | 18.9 | 1.1 | 81 | 17.9 |
| Wolfe | 58 | -3.3 | 169 | 0.0 | 15.6 | 297 877 | 1 766 | 38 921 | 2.2 | 6 359 | 32.8 | 67.2 | 14.9 | 0.3 | 365 | 37.7 |
| Woodford | 119 | -3.3 | 167 | 0.6 | 50.7 | 1 165 408 | 6 968 | 85 678 | 341.1 | 479 014 | 2.9 | 97.1 | 48.7 | 19.8 | 373 | 14.7 |
| LOUISIANA | 8 110 | 3.6 | 269 | 954.4 | 4 691.3 | 554 270 | 2 058 | 78 998 | 2 618.0 | 86 959 | 61.3 | 38.7 | 30.7 | 10.7 | 169 333 | 35.3 |
| Acadia | 233 | -9.3 | 257 | 72.1 | 185.6 | 475 108 | 1 846 | 78 924 | 69.1 | 76 353 | 87.8 | 12.2 | 30.1 | 12.3 | 7 612 | 56.4 |
| Allen | 83 | -19.4 | 205 | 11.6 | 48.4 | 390 076 | 1 899 | 57 777 | 10.0 | 24 701 | 73.1 | 26.9 | 22.0 | 6.4 | 1 918 | 38.3 |
| Ascension | 45 | -10.0 | 164 | 0.3 | 27.0 | 569 319 | 3 469 | 88 427 | 19.4 | 70 095 | 89.2 | 10.8 | 20.9 | 6.1 | 84 | 4.3 |
| Assumption | 64 | -3.0 | 559 | D | 51.5 | 1 433 380 | 2 565 | 289 435 | 40.9 | 358 505 | 94.4 | 5.6 | 59.6 | 36.0 | 301 | 16.7 |
| Avoyelles | 278 | 2.2 | 294 | 20.2 | 203.1 | 522 377 | 1 776 | 81 807 | 75.2 | 79 378 | 90.1 | 9.9 | 36.0 | 11.9 | 6 185 | 45.5 |
| Beauregard | 179 | 25.2 | 197 | 1.6 | 44.3 | 439 565 | 2 233 | 48 825 | 11.5 | 12 637 | 31.8 | 68.2 | 21.2 | 1.9 | 1 401 | 23.9 |
| Bienville | 41 | -6.8 | 210 | 0.0 | 10.0 | 450 136 | 2 145 | 87 999 | 28.3 | 145 927 | 2.0 | 98.0 | 33.5 | 7.2 | 107 | 10.8 |
| Bossier | 104 | -2.8 | 210 | 0.1 | 37.8 | 583 220 | 2 778 | 57 427 | 13.1 | 26 604 | 37.6 | 62.4 | 28.0 | 6.1 | 1 025 | 13.6 |
| Caddo | 151 | -12.2 | 242 | 9.7 | 77.5 | 516 961 | 2 137 | 78 107 | 33.0 | 52 854 | 78.3 | 21.7 | 26.2 | 7.4 | 3 956 | 12.8 |
| Calcasieu | 368 | 21.5 | 379 | 11.9 | 125.2 | 674 638 | 1 781 | 53 687 | 18.8 | 19 330 | 44.8 | 55.2 | 26.6 | 3.4 | 2 339 | 26.2 |
| Caldwell | 67 | 9.8 | 220 | 4.0 | 28.7 | 414 904 | 1 888 | 60 246 | 8.4 | 27 235 | 83.2 | 16.8 | 30.6 | 4.9 | 1 811 | 50.2 |
| Cameron | 216 | -13.3 | 638 | 12.1 | 55.4 | 1 137 196 | 1 783 | 75 618 | 9.1 | 26 850 | 43.5 | 56.5 | 29.2 | 7.7 | 1 912 | 38.3 |
| Catahoula | 231 | -0.4 | 453 | 22.2 | 172.8 | 741 408 | 1 636 | 110 922 | 57.9 | 113 471 | 94.7 | 5.3 | 34.7 | 16.5 | 8 840 | 68.2 |
| Claiborne | 49 | -12.5 | 203 | D | 13.2 | 529 754 | 2 606 | 70 425 | 76.6 | 320 650 | 3.0 | 97.0 | 46.4 | 20.5 | 109 | 8.4 |
| Concordia | 211 | -0.5 | 456 | 10.7 | 157.7 | 794 055 | 1 742 | 90 152 | 50.0 | 108 188 | 95.0 | 5.0 | 33.8 | 20.8 | 6 772 | 81.0 |
| De Soto | 167 | 21.9 | 270 | 0.6 | 35.9 | 540 986 | 2 000 | 66 155 | 22.1 | 35 664 | 17.2 | 82.8 | 28.8 | 5.2 | 392 | 13.1 |
| East Baton Rouge | 72 | 18.0 | 141 | 0.2 | 30.5 | 569 525 | 4 033 | 50 922 | 10.7 | 21 004 | 28.0 | 72.0 | 28.2 | 5.1 | 179 | 9.4 |
| East Carroll | 261 | 20.3 | 931 | 102.3 | 225.2 | 1 483 695 | 1 594 | 254 233 | 96.0 | 342 990 | 97.9 | 2.1 | 53.6 | 37.9 | 10 101 | 86.1 |
| East Feliciana | 128 | 4.1 | 292 | 1.0 | 33.1 | 757 251 | 2 594 | 49 866 | 8.6 | 19 482 | 17.9 | 82.1 | 31.4 | 3.4 | 349 | 15.9 |
| Evangeline | 172 | -6.5 | 214 | 37.2 | 105.8 | 377 978 | 1 769 | 60 250 | 35.3 | 43 850 | 80.1 | 19.9 | 26.3 | 9.1 | 5 619 | 49.0 |
| Franklin | 347 | 34.5 | 273 | 94.0 | 232.4 | 473 756 | 1 736 | 79 317 | 106.3 | 83 470 | 77.1 | 22.9 | 35.0 | 13.1 | 13 335 | 77.4 |
| Grant | 52 | 44.4 | 207 | 0.7 | 25.4 | 383 287 | 1 852 | 75 144 | 6.0 | 24 115 | 67.0 | 33.0 | 19.6 | 5.2 | 572 | 16.0 |
| Iberia | 116 | 4.5 | 336 | 0.4 | 98.1 | 839 271 | 2 498 | 182 162 | 62.9 | 182 391 | 97.9 | 2.1 | 38.0 | 16.2 | 890 | 18.0 |
| Iberville | 86 | -11.3 | 490 | D | 67.0 | 1 401 691 | 2 861 | 198 841 | 49.4 | 282 014 | 93.9 | 6.1 | 50.3 | 21.1 | 366 | 24.6 |
| Jackson | 20 | -4.8 | 102 | D | 5.1 | 320 200 | 3 141 | 65 834 | 34.7 | 176 385 | 1.1 | 98.9 | 34.5 | 14.7 | 63 | 2.0 |
| Jefferson | 15 | 87.5 | 213 | 1.1 | 5.7 | 440 306 | 2 070 | D | 1.6 | 23 160 | D | D | 32.4 | 7.0 | 242 | 15.5 |
| Jefferson Davis | 288 | -10.8 | 408 | 79.1 | 227.4 | 721 633 | 1 768 | 95 734 | 64.8 | 91 733 | 88.7 | 11.3 | 35.8 | 15.2 | 7 617 | 59.6 |
| Lafayette | 67 | -10.7 | 95 | 3.1 | 49.6 | 322 934 | 3 415 | 57 232 | 30.1 | 42 265 | 91.4 | 8.6 | 17.7 | 3.4 | 647 | 14.2 |
| Lafourche | 106 | -29.8 | 241 | 3.2 | 63.1 | 586 683 | 2 433 | 93 194 | 42.0 | 95 386 | 54.3 | 45.7 | 38.6 | 9.1 | 154 | 5.5 |
| La Salle | 20 | 17.6 | 123 | D | 5.7 | 285 172 | 2 318 | 39 773 | D | D | D | 0.0 | 21.8 | 0.6 | 141 | 17.0 |
| Lincoln | 52 | -21.2 | 164 | 1.0 | 12.9 | 521 181 | 3 187 | 62 247 | 119.7 | 372 981 | 2.4 | 97.6 | 38.0 | 18.7 | 252 | 9.3 |
| Livingston | 30 | -11.8 | 63 | 0.4 | 8.9 | 272 876 | 4 332 | 43 311 | 5.6 | 11 712 | 20.9 | 79.1 | 17.2 | 1.7 | 49 | 3.4 |
| Madison | 235 | -0.8 | 661 | 35.3 | 195.6 | 1 061 834 | 1 607 | 149 597 | 71.2 | 200 681 | 99.0 | 1.0 | 50.4 | 34.9 | 8 604 | 87.3 |
| Morehouse | 274 | 11.8 | 579 | 140.4 | 221.6 | 939 856 | 1 624 | 140 292 | 94.6 | 200 047 | 97.4 | 2.6 | 46.7 | 26.6 | 11 001 | 62.6 |
| Natchitoches | 222 | 15.0 | 388 | 6.1 | 98.0 | 641 833 | 1 653 | 83 520 | 82.4 | 144 395 | 27.4 | 72.6 | 35.0 | 13.5 | 3 673 | 36.1 |

# Table B. States and Counties — Water Use, Wholesale Trade, Retail Trade, and Real Estate

| STATE County | Water use, 2005 | | Wholesale trade,[1] 2007 | | | | Retail trade,[2] 2007 | | | | Real estate and rental and leasing,[2] 2007 | | | |
|---|---|---|---|---|---|---|---|---|---|---|---|---|---|---|
| | Total water withdrawn (mil gal/day) | Gallons withdrawn per person | Number of establishments | Number of employees | Sales (mil dol) | Annual payroll (mil dol) | Number of establishments | Number of employees | Sales (mil dol) | Annual payroll (mil dol) | Number of establishments | Number of employees | Receipts (mil dol) | Annual payroll (mil dol) |
| | 133 | 134 | 135 | 136 | 137 | 138 | 139 | 140 | 141 | 142 | 143 | 144 | 145 | 146 |
| KENTUCKY—Cont'd | | | | | | | | | | | | | | |
| Ohio | 19.1 | 806 | 12 | 363 | 149.5 | 6.6 | 60 | 627 | 142.5 | 12.7 | 7 | 31 | 1.6 | 0.3 |
| Oldham | 5.9 | 110 | 47 | 287 | 95.5 | 11.8 | 135 | 1 483 | 374.8 | 35.3 | 50 | 134 | 24.5 | 3.2 |
| Owen | 2.4 | 208 | 5 | 43 | 10.4 | 0.6 | 26 | 230 | 43.2 | 4.0 | 4 | D | D | D |
| Owsley | 0.3 | 67 | 1 | D | D | D | 11 | 87 | 16.7 | 1.5 | 2 | D | D | D |
| Pendleton | 1.6 | 102 | 8 | D | D | D | 29 | 233 | 47.2 | 4.0 | 8 | 21 | 1.6 | 0.3 |
| Perry | 4.8 | 162 | 32 | 438 | 267.9 | 21.7 | 158 | 1 952 | 463.1 | 39.5 | 21 | 64 | 11.1 | 1.7 |
| Pike | 14.4 | 215 | 59 | 451 | 589.0 | 21.3 | 290 | 3 876 | 894.9 | 80.4 | 42 | 122 | 35.2 | 3.0 |
| Powell | 1.2 | 90 | 5 | 22 | 3.9 | 0.5 | 43 | 382 | 95.0 | 6.1 | 4 | D | D | D |
| Pulaski | 132.8 | 2 242 | 60 | 1 124 | 989.6 | 29.4 | 316 | 3 495 | 884.4 | 73.3 | 51 | 181 | 23.8 | 5.0 |
| Robertson | 0.2 | 75 | NA | NA | NA | NA | 5 | 16 | 1.6 | 0.1 | NA | NA | NA | NA |
| Rockcastle | 2.5 | 149 | 11 | D | D | D | 53 | 316 | 71.6 | 5.1 | 6 | 37 | 2.5 | 0.7 |
| Rowan | 6.8 | 307 | 20 | 177 | 54.1 | 4.2 | 115 | 1 359 | 272.1 | 24.2 | 22 | 69 | 8.4 | 1.4 |
| Russell | 4.1 | 241 | 5 | D | D | D | 89 | 783 | 180.3 | 13.4 | 9 | 57 | 9.9 | 1.2 |
| Scott | 4.2 | 105 | 23 | D | D | D | 132 | 1 779 | 528.6 | 35.8 | 53 | 217 | 39.3 | 6.7 |
| Shelby | 4.7 | 124 | 36 | 618 | 320.8 | 26.8 | 146 | 1 755 | 498.7 | 37.4 | 45 | 169 | 21.5 | 3.8 |
| Simpson | 2.2 | 129 | 11 | 88 | 260.0 | 2.7 | 69 | 1 039 | 415.2 | 22.6 | 19 | 108 | 8.1 | 3.3 |
| Spencer | 0.9 | 58 | 4 | 11 | 1.5 | 0.1 | 23 | 236 | 68.1 | 4.0 | 9 | 28 | 2.7 | 0.4 |
| Taylor | 5.7 | 239 | 24 | D | D | D | 148 | 1 770 | 371.9 | 35.2 | 30 | 157 | 11.9 | 2.7 |
| Todd | 1.0 | 81 | 9 | 47 | 23.2 | 1.3 | 36 | 246 | 58.6 | 3.6 | 3 | 9 | 0.6 | 0.1 |
| Trigg | 6.1 | 454 | 7 | D | D | D | 40 | 364 | 70.9 | 5.9 | 15 | 40 | 5.0 | 1.0 |
| Trimble | 15.7 | 1 740 | NA | NA | NA | NA | 15 | 116 | 32.0 | 1.5 | 3 | 4 | 0.3 | 0.0 |
| Union | 3.8 | 246 | 12 | 103 | 94.0 | 3.7 | 65 | 678 | 144.2 | 12.4 | 7 | 24 | 3.0 | 0.3 |
| Warren | 19.6 | 198 | 134 | D | D | D | 535 | 7 535 | 1 691.2 | 151.0 | 133 | 1 113 | 114.4 | 28.7 |
| Washington | 2.5 | 217 | 10 | 94 | 67.7 | 2.5 | 41 | 262 | 63.3 | 4.6 | 4 | 5 | 0.4 | 0.1 |
| Wayne | 2.7 | 131 | 10 | 76 | 23.6 | 1.6 | 66 | 697 | 152.5 | 13.8 | 10 | 52 | 2.4 | 0.6 |
| Webster | 77.8 | 5 492 | 10 | D | D | D | 42 | 349 | 67.5 | 5.8 | 6 | 14 | 1.1 | 0.2 |
| Whitley | 2.7 | 72 | 22 | D | D | D | 153 | 1 531 | 373.3 | 30.5 | 26 | 78 | 10.5 | 1.9 |
| Wolfe | 0.7 | 93 | 3 | D | D | D | 26 | 187 | 45.3 | 3.3 | 2 | D | D | D |
| Woodford | 54.1 | 2 233 | 15 | D | D | D | 74 | 770 | 225.2 | 18.8 | 21 | 45 | 6.3 | 0.9 |
| LOUISIANA | 11 597.7 | 2 564 | 4 839 | 63 911 | 51 415.6 | 2 808.3 | 17 135 | 231 365 | 56 543.2 | 5 096.1 | 4 625 | 30 922 | 6 014.9 | 1 194.9 |
| Acadia | 293.9 | 4 935 | 40 | D | D | D | 193 | 2 427 | 526.0 | 49.2 | 39 | 122 | 11.2 | 2.3 |
| Allen | 30.0 | 1 188 | 8 | D | D | D | 72 | 741 | 142.9 | 11.7 | 9 | 32 | 2.2 | 0.5 |
| Ascension | 202.8 | 2 241 | 103 | 1 297 | 665.0 | 65.5 | 369 | 5 189 | 1 318.0 | 111.9 | 87 | 488 | 139.5 | 21.7 |
| Assumption | 23.1 | 994 | 12 | D | D | D | 53 | 553 | 100.0 | 8.9 | 7 | 13 | 2.5 | 0.2 |
| Avoyelles | 30.8 | 732 | 22 | 210 | 171.3 | 6.4 | 162 | 1 440 | 310.9 | 25.0 | 18 | 63 | 6.3 | 1.0 |
| Beauregard | 32.9 | 952 | 13 | D | D | D | 100 | 1 412 | 317.4 | 28.6 | 20 | 71 | 7.6 | 1.1 |
| Bienville | 13.7 | 904 | 6 | D | D | D | 45 | 338 | 58.7 | 5.3 | 5 | D | D | D |
| Bossier | 19.0 | 180 | 90 | 1 542 | 1 028.2 | 70.1 | 476 | 6 359 | 1 741.9 | 142.0 | 116 | 554 | 100.6 | 15.0 |
| Caddo | 338.1 | 1 345 | 312 | 4 511 | 5 467.4 | 198.9 | 1 008 | 14 460 | 3 706.8 | 326.5 | 299 | 1 857 | 260.4 | 49.8 |
| Calcasieu | 309.8 | 1 671 | 185 | 2 145 | 1 342.9 | 91.5 | 830 | 11 704 | 2 776.0 | 246.5 | 210 | 948 | 195.1 | 30.7 |
| Caldwell | 3.6 | 344 | 5 | D | D | D | 36 | 459 | 112.9 | 8.0 | 6 | 17 | 2.3 | 0.3 |
| Cameron | 31.8 | 3 322 | 13 | 82 | 62.8 | 3.7 | 23 | 238 | 36.8 | 3.0 | 5 | 105 | 36.4 | 4.9 |
| Catahoula | 25.4 | 2 428 | 15 | 156 | 193.1 | 4.5 | 34 | 244 | 52.7 | 4.2 | 4 | 18 | 5.6 | 0.6 |
| Claiborne | 7.8 | 476 | 9 | 69 | 125.9 | 2.3 | 56 | 444 | 74.2 | 7.3 | 6 | 18 | 1.7 | 0.3 |
| Concordia | 38.6 | 2 003 | 14 | D | D | D | 79 | 871 | 194.9 | 16.6 | 8 | 155 | 6.7 | 3.9 |
| De Soto | 547.0 | 20 732 | 11 | 155 | 22.0 | 5.1 | 73 | 819 | 184.5 | 15.3 | 7 | 21 | 1.5 | 0.3 |
| East Baton Rouge | 168.0 | 408 | 610 | 8 786 | 7 860.1 | 401.7 | 1 930 | 29 228 | 7 043.0 | 664.6 | 583 | 3 137 | 559.9 | 96.5 |
| East Carroll | 45.1 | 5 154 | 12 | D | D | D | 26 | 225 | 34.0 | 3.3 | 7 | 19 | 3.1 | 0.7 |
| East Feliciana | 3.6 | 175 | 9 | D | D | D | 53 | 394 | 72.8 | 6.1 | 5 | D | D | D |
| Evangeline | 141.5 | 3 981 | 17 | D | D | D | 130 | 1 078 | 228.6 | 18.6 | 22 | 65 | 6.0 | 1.3 |
| Franklin | 51.3 | 2 517 | 19 | 191 | 182.7 | 4.8 | 89 | 988 | 215.5 | 18.5 | 21 | 61 | 6.4 | 1.0 |
| Grant | 4.8 | 244 | 4 | D | D | D | 29 | 273 | 74.7 | 6.6 | 2 | D | D | D |
| Iberia | 38.3 | 515 | 84 | D | D | D | 290 | 3 631 | 910.2 | 81.0 | 101 | 2 302 | 553.0 | 164.9 |
| Iberville | 933.8 | 28 833 | 28 | 247 | 149.9 | 8.8 | 95 | 1 103 | 274.4 | 22.6 | 27 | 154 | 26.5 | 3.8 |
| Jackson | 2.3 | 152 | 7 | D | D | D | 47 | 569 | 114.5 | 9.8 | 11 | 33 | 3.8 | 0.5 |
| Jefferson | 1 058.6 | 2 338 | 802 | 10 311 | 6 049.8 | 489.5 | 1 855 | 30 948 | 8 106.2 | 771.5 | 538 | 5 527 | 960.2 | 183.5 |
| Jefferson Davis | 170.6 | 5 455 | 21 | D | D | D | 116 | 1 496 | 338.8 | 28.1 | 19 | 303 | 60.8 | 13.8 |
| Lafayette | 48.2 | 244 | 445 | 6 314 | 2 651.4 | 281.7 | 1 041 | 15 424 | 3 814.3 | 340.3 | 438 | 3 387 | 879.4 | 175.7 |
| Lafourche | 56.5 | 613 | 71 | 1 096 | 888.4 | 44.2 | 304 | 4 103 | 917.5 | 79.0 | 80 | 544 | 116.0 | 23.5 |
| La Salle | 13.5 | 959 | 8 | D | D | D | 58 | 517 | 116.4 | 9.0 | 10 | 42 | 4.5 | 0.9 |
| Lincoln | 8.1 | 191 | 27 | 388 | 171.3 | 14.6 | 184 | 2 482 | 527.8 | 48.1 | 46 | 242 | 51.6 | 6.5 |
| Livingston | 15.8 | 144 | 38 | 308 | 483.0 | 14.5 | 288 | 3 645 | 923.7 | 73.1 | 55 | 177 | 30.5 | 4.3 |
| Madison | 20.2 | 1 622 | 12 | 101 | 153.2 | 3.4 | 39 | 455 | 142.5 | 8.2 | 9 | 30 | 3.7 | 0.5 |
| Morehouse | 131.5 | 4 384 | 18 | 170 | 255.3 | 5.4 | 102 | 1 181 | 241.4 | 24.0 | 24 | 52 | 7.0 | 1.1 |
| Natchitoches | 33.9 | 878 | 25 | D | D | D | 156 | 1 838 | 414.0 | 35.5 | 46 | 175 | 15.3 | 2.4 |

1. Merchant wholesalers, except manufacturers' sales branches and offices.   2. Employer establishments.

# Professional Services, Manufacturing, and Accommodation and Food Services

| STATE County | Professional, scientific, and technical services,[1] 2007 | | | | Manufacturing, 2007 | | | | Accommodation and food services, 2007 | | | |
|---|---|---|---|---|---|---|---|---|---|---|---|---|
| | Number of establish-ments | Number of employees | Receipts (mil dol) | Annual payroll (mil dol) | Number of establish-ments | Number of employees | Receipts (mil dol) | Annual payroll (mil dol) | Number of establish-ments | Number of employees | Sales (mil dol) | Annual payroll (mil dol) |
| | 147 | 148 | 149 | 150 | 151 | 152 | 153 | 154 | 155 | 156 | 157 | 158 |
| KENTUCKY—Cont'd | | | | | | | | | | | | |
| Ohio | 25 | 69 | 5.4 | 1.6 | 27 | 2 377 | 485.5 | 70.5 | 27 | 416 | 15.3 | 4.2 |
| Oldham | 174 | 555 | 60.3 | 24.9 | 46 | 925 | 275.1 | 36.6 | 60 | 1 127 | 47.1 | 12.6 |
| Owen | 8 | 13 | 1.0 | 0.2 | NA | NA | NA | NA | 13 | 178 | 6.6 | 2.0 |
| Owsley | 2 | D | D | D | NA | NA | NA | NA | 2 | D | D | D |
| Pendleton | 9 | D | D | D | 17 | 596 | D | 24.3 | 11 | 182 | 4.5 | 1.2 |
| Perry | 57 | D | D | D | 12 | 690 | 122.2 | 21.4 | 50 | 1 186 | 43.8 | 11.8 |
| Pike | 104 | D | D | D | 28 | 652 | D | 22.2 | 91 | 1 710 | 75.5 | 19.3 |
| Powell | 7 | 8 | 0.6 | 0.1 | NA | NA | NA | NA | 14 | 228 | 9.3 | 2.5 |
| Pulaski | 96 | D | D | D | 85 | 4 129 | 1 088.0 | 139.4 | 92 | 1 862 | 73.5 | 19.3 |
| Robertson | 1 | D | D | D | NA | NA | NA | NA | 1 | D | D | D |
| Rockcastle | 14 | D | D | D | NA | NA | NA | NA | 25 | 351 | 11.3 | 3.3 |
| Rowan | 23 | D | D | D | 20 | 954 | 259.8 | 28.6 | 43 | 971 | 36.1 | 8.4 |
| Russell | 22 | 68 | 5.5 | 1.6 | 25 | 1 182 | D | 36.8 | 31 | 372 | 14.5 | 2.9 |
| Scott | 68 | 414 | 34.7 | 14.1 | 37 | 9 905 | D | D | 79 | 1 815 | 73.1 | 20.8 |
| Shelby | 76 | 317 | 32.0 | 10.6 | 52 | 4 535 | 1 373.1 | 178.2 | 52 | D | D | D |
| Simpson | 17 | 99 | 4.9 | 1.9 | 33 | 3 531 | 1 406.3 | 141.4 | 41 | 654 | 29.7 | 8.2 |
| Spencer | 13 | D | D | D | NA | NA | NA | NA | 13 | D | D | D |
| Taylor | 50 | 115 | 9.3 | 3.3 | 35 | 1 871 | 315.2 | 56.2 | 42 | 831 | 25.4 | 6.4 |
| Todd | 10 | 66 | 3.3 | 1.6 | NA | NA | NA | NA | 12 | 74 | 2.3 | 0.7 |
| Trigg | 11 | 46 | 3.8 | 0.9 | 17 | 1 134 | 235.1 | 39.3 | 21 | 344 | 11.3 | 3.4 |
| Trimble | 4 | D | D | D | NA | NA | NA | NA | 6 | 40 | 1.8 | 0.5 |
| Union | 8 | 28 | 3.2 | 1.1 | 16 | 901 | 250.4 | 40.7 | 22 | 261 | 9.8 | 2.4 |
| Warren | 205 | D | D | D | 118 | D | D | D | 217 | 5 454 | 231.2 | 63.7 |
| Washington | 15 | 46 | 3.3 | 1.0 | 12 | 986 | 259.0 | 35.9 | 12 | 201 | 6.3 | 1.7 |
| Wayne | 23 | 62 | 4.2 | 1.5 | 36 | 2 053 | 378.9 | 52.8 | 26 | 431 | 18.8 | 4.3 |
| Webster | 10 | 23 | 1.8 | 0.3 | NA | NA | NA | NA | 17 | 107 | 4.7 | 1.2 |
| Whitley | 55 | 450 | 53.6 | 15.6 | 27 | 1 233 | D | 40.5 | 58 | 974 | 39.3 | 9.6 |
| Wolfe | 5 | 11 | 0.7 | 0.2 | NA | NA | NA | NA | 5 | 42 | 0.6 | 0.1 |
| Woodford | 68 | D | D | D | 30 | 2 584 | D | 122.8 | 34 | 397 | 15.7 | 4.5 |
| LOUISIANA | 11 128 | 84 666 | 11 856.6 | 4 234.6 | 3 442 | 148 080 | 205 054.7 | 7 564.5 | 8 169 | 180 289 | 9 729.9 | 2 579.0 |
| Acadia | 89 | 307 | 35.1 | 13.3 | 51 | 1 148 | D | 38.5 | 67 | 1 145 | 40.8 | 10.5 |
| Allen | 19 | 59 | 6.0 | 1.7 | 13 | 655 | 167.5 | 27.2 | 28 | 422 | 17.4 | 3.7 |
| Ascension | 150 | D | D | D | 88 | 4 348 | D | 329.2 | 148 | 2 747 | 116.3 | 30.9 |
| Assumption | 26 | 70 | 6.0 | 2.4 | NA | NA | NA | NA | 13 | 135 | 4.1 | 1.0 |
| Avoyelles | 60 | 173 | 18.9 | 5.0 | NA | NA | NA | NA | 52 | 2 423 | 174.7 | 47.0 |
| Beauregard | 40 | 170 | 11.4 | 4.6 | 19 | 935 | D | D | 33 | 550 | 19.5 | 5.2 |
| Bienville | 12 | 31 | 2.7 | 1.3 | 13 | 1 098 | D | 29.3 | 16 | 164 | 6.6 | 1.6 |
| Bossier | 162 | 934 | 96.1 | 31.6 | 73 | 2 200 | D | D | 232 | 9 784 | 711.7 | 174.9 |
| Caddo | 604 | 4 224 | 492.8 | 173.4 | 215 | 9 553 | D | 486.2 | 439 | 12 288 | 675.3 | 175.3 |
| Calcasieu | 440 | D | D | D | 128 | D | D | D | 328 | 10 346 | 878.6 | 181.6 |
| Caldwell | 22 | 66 | 5.3 | 1.1 | NA | NA | NA | NA | 10 | 138 | 5.8 | 1.5 |
| Cameron | 15 | D | D | D | NA | NA | NA | NA | 4 | 20 | 1.4 | 0.2 |
| Catahoula | 22 | 56 | 5.6 | 2.4 | NA | NA | NA | NA | 11 | 127 | 5.0 | 1.3 |
| Claiborne | 14 | 41 | 4.6 | 1.1 | NA | NA | NA | NA | 8 | 52 | 2.3 | 0.6 |
| Concordia | 23 | 108 | 8.1 | 2.2 | NA | NA | NA | NA | 27 | 410 | 17.8 | 4.2 |
| De Soto | 22 | 54 | 5.1 | 1.3 | 15 | 766 | D | D | 21 | 300 | 10.4 | 2.6 |
| East Baton Rouge | 1 684 | D | D | D | 334 | 11 054 | D | 669.1 | 896 | 22 590 | 998.3 | 277.2 |
| East Carroll | 8 | D | D | D | NA | NA | NA | NA | 9 | 59 | 2.1 | 0.5 |
| East Feliciana | 24 | 51 | 4.3 | 1.5 | NA | NA | NA | NA | 17 | 199 | 6.0 | 1.5 |
| Evangeline | 50 | 198 | 18.2 | 4.8 | 20 | 698 | D | 33.4 | 22 | 269 | 9.3 | 2.1 |
| Franklin | 30 | 586 | 12.1 | 6.1 | NA | NA | NA | NA | 23 | 354 | 14.3 | 3.1 |
| Grant | 8 | 21 | 0.8 | 0.2 | NA | NA | NA | NA | 4 | D | D | D |
| Iberia | 161 | 754 | 89.1 | 25.4 | 130 | 6 273 | 1 586.2 | 261.8 | 92 | 1 941 | 73.5 | 18.4 |
| Iberville | 34 | 292 | 30.7 | 19.9 | 31 | 3 461 | 7 694.7 | 283.5 | 35 | 491 | 17.9 | 5.0 |
| Jackson | 20 | 122 | 11.4 | 4.1 | 9 | D | D | D | 18 | 223 | 7.9 | 1.9 |
| Jefferson | 1 401 | D | D | D | 348 | 14 278 | 2 837.2 | 563.6 | 1 032 | 19 590 | 982.9 | 287.8 |
| Jefferson Davis | 59 | 245 | 20.4 | 7.7 | 13 | 530 | 189.2 | 21.2 | 41 | 734 | 26.7 | 6.7 |
| Lafayette | 1 135 | D | D | D | 286 | 8 790 | 2 037.2 | 352.1 | 513 | 12 494 | 584.6 | 156.1 |
| Lafourche | 161 | D | D | D | 59 | 3 265 | 614.3 | 120.5 | 159 | 2 446 | 106.6 | 26.3 |
| La Salle | 31 | 68 | 6.8 | 2.0 | NA | NA | NA | NA | 14 | 175 | 7.6 | 1.9 |
| Lincoln | 80 | 419 | 44.1 | 18.4 | 33 | D | D | D | 80 | 1 674 | 72.5 | 17.6 |
| Livingston | 122 | D | D | D | 68 | 1 884 | 459.9 | 80.3 | 121 | 2 388 | 89.2 | 24.4 |
| Madison | 11 | D | D | D | NA | NA | NA | NA | 19 | 276 | 9.4 | 2.0 |
| Morehouse | 26 | D | D | D | 15 | 741 | D | D | 26 | 490 | 19.8 | 4.7 |
| Natchitoches | 66 | D | D | D | 19 | 2 818 | 1 006.3 | 99.6 | 72 | 1 264 | 52.4 | 13.4 |

1. Establishment subject to federal tax.

# Table B. States and Counties — Health Care and Social Assistance, Other Services, and Federal Funds

| STATE County | Health care and social assistance, 2007 | | | | Other services, 2007 | | | | Federal funds and grants, 2009–2010 Expenditures (mil dol) | | | |
|---|---|---|---|---|---|---|---|---|---|---|---|---|
| | | | | | | | | | | Direct payments for individuals[1] | | |
| | Number of establishments | Number of employees | Receipts (mil dol) | Annual payroll (mil dol) | Number of establishments | Number of employees | Receipts (mil dol) | Annual payroll (mil dol) | Total | Social Security and government retirement | Medicare | Food Stamps and Supplemental Security Income |
| | 159 | 160 | 161 | 162 | 163 | 164 | 165 | 166 | 167 | 168 | 169 | 170 |
| KENTUCKY—Cont'd | | | | | | | | | | | | |
| Ohio | 37 | 842 | 53.3 | 21.7 | 33 | 86 | 8.3 | 2.1 | 204.9 | 79.4 | 65.8 | 15.4 |
| Oldham | 110 | 1 881 | 139.5 | 61.0 | 82 | 431 | 30.3 | 8.8 | 160.8 | 86.1 | 41.2 | 3.8 |
| Owen | 8 | 201 | 15.8 | 6.8 | 12 | 40 | 2.8 | 0.6 | 78.1 | 23.3 | 27.1 | 5.5 |
| Owsley | 10 | 208 | 9.3 | 4.4 | 3 | D | D | D | 104.0 | 14.8 | 42.4 | 12.2 |
| Pendleton | 18 | 219 | 16.2 | 5.2 | 8 | D | D | D | 100.9 | 41.7 | 30.4 | 7.3 |
| Perry | 125 | 2 613 | 285.4 | 96.7 | 29 | 116 | 10.5 | 2.2 | 421.8 | 126.5 | 133.8 | 44.3 |
| Pike | 183 | 3 638 | 381.5 | 139.7 | 78 | 314 | 27.7 | 8.1 | 755.9 | 291.8 | 228.3 | 63.7 |
| Powell | 20 | 246 | 14.4 | 5.9 | 6 | D | D | D | 126.5 | 41.5 | 36.5 | 15.8 |
| Pulaski | 234 | 4 948 | 462.8 | 164.2 | 73 | 378 | 37.0 | 8.0 | 665.2 | 244.3 | 192.8 | 42.7 |
| Robertson | 4 | D | D | D | 1 | D | D | D | 22.0 | 6.6 | 8.2 | 1.4 |
| Rockcastle | 36 | 742 | 56.1 | 23.8 | 13 | 97 | 14.5 | 2.4 | 191.0 | 49.3 | 67.9 | 16.4 |
| Rowan | 74 | 1 718 | 153.8 | 60.1 | 26 | 166 | 6.9 | 2.1 | 226.4 | 62.4 | 62.6 | 14.3 |
| Russell | 47 | 802 | 47.2 | 19.4 | 19 | 54 | 4.3 | 0.9 | 316.5 | 59.9 | 73.9 | 13.1 |
| Scott | 80 | D | D | D | 62 | 277 | 21.1 | 5.8 | 212.1 | 101.3 | 56.5 | 10.2 |
| Shelby | 79 | 1 333 | 114.9 | 44.2 | 59 | 405 | 39.4 | 11.8 | 263.8 | 101.3 | 60.9 | 8.8 |
| Simpson | 37 | 378 | 34.9 | 10.3 | 26 | 126 | 12.3 | 3.2 | 137.5 | 51.0 | 49.2 | 4.9 |
| Spencer | 20 | 259 | 14.9 | 6.0 | 13 | D | D | D | 79.1 | 41.3 | 19.2 | 3.3 |
| Taylor | 79 | 1 249 | 100.7 | 39.8 | 47 | 159 | 10.2 | 2.6 | 264.8 | 90.7 | 76.6 | 16.2 |
| Todd | 13 | 193 | 12.3 | 3.6 | 13 | 50 | 2.8 | 1.0 | 123.0 | 34.1 | 46.4 | 4.8 |
| Trigg | 19 | 308 | 18.0 | 7.3 | 14 | 88 | 6.0 | 1.9 | 142.0 | 62.8 | 39.5 | 4.2 |
| Trimble | 8 | D | D | D | 5 | D | D | D | 58.9 | 24.8 | 17.7 | 3.1 |
| Union | 29 | 1 279 | 66.6 | 26.9 | 16 | D | D | D | 345.5 | 50.6 | 41.2 | 5.6 |
| Warren | 314 | D | D | D | 164 | 1 181 | 83.6 | 24.7 | 841.7 | 295.2 | 215.3 | 41.3 |
| Washington | 16 | 286 | 12.8 | 5.6 | 20 | 69 | 5.4 | 1.4 | 99.8 | 31.0 | 35.3 | 4.6 |
| Wayne | 38 | D | D | D | 25 | 66 | 4.8 | 1.1 | 271.7 | 60.0 | 106.9 | 19.7 |
| Webster | 23 | D | D | D | 22 | D | D | D | 129.7 | 49.9 | 40.0 | 6.7 |
| Whitley | 107 | 2 726 | 235.8 | 85.6 | 34 | 145 | 10.3 | 3.3 | 561.9 | 183.1 | 168.2 | 47.2 |
| Wolfe | 10 | 229 | 17.8 | 5.1 | 4 | D | D | D | 128.5 | 24.6 | 47.3 | 14.1 |
| Woodford | 48 | D | D | D | 39 | 197 | 12.4 | 3.6 | 146.8 | 73.3 | 31.6 | 5.7 |
| LOUISIANA | 11 545 | 256 079 | 23 685.4 | 8 860.6 | 6 637 | 42 223 | 4 664.2 | 1 170.0 | 53 214.2 | 11 959.7 | 8 702.9 | 2 359.5 |
| Acadia | 125 | 2 041 | 148.6 | 55.7 | 68 | 363 | 29.2 | 7.8 | 497.9 | 150.6 | 106.5 | 33.2 |
| Allen | 45 | 801 | 50.0 | 20.5 | 21 | 100 | 6.2 | 1.8 | 233.7 | 65.3 | 49.0 | 10.6 |
| Ascension | 152 | 2 232 | 140.7 | 57.8 | 138 | 940 | 109.6 | 32.1 | 451.4 | 216.4 | 108.3 | 29.2 |
| Assumption | 21 | 612 | 23.4 | 10.5 | 20 | 59 | 8.0 | 1.6 | 176.3 | 57.8 | 50.4 | 13.2 |
| Avoyelles | 91 | 2 066 | 104.9 | 41.9 | 44 | 128 | 10.6 | 2.8 | 408.6 | 119.9 | 91.2 | 29.7 |
| Beauregard | 60 | 1 182 | 78.5 | 31.5 | 39 | 140 | 12.7 | 3.6 | 254.7 | 127.1 | 54.0 | 13.2 |
| Bienville | 15 | D | D | D | 12 | D | D | D | 158.3 | 48.3 | 44.9 | 10.6 |
| Bossier | 207 | 3 397 | 281.4 | 119.5 | 146 | 990 | 66.9 | 20.5 | 1 327.8 | 366.8 | 118.1 | 95.5 |
| Caddo | 801 | D | D | D | 443 | 3 136 | 245.6 | 68.1 | 2 100.8 | 738.0 | 497.9 | 95.6 |
| Calcasieu | 515 | 10 926 | 1 025.2 | 348.4 | 280 | D | D | D | 1 441.4 | 544.6 | 331.7 | 72.1 |
| Caldwell | 23 | 534 | 32.7 | 14.4 | 15 | D | D | D | 103.0 | 31.4 | 33.3 | 5.5 |
| Cameron | 5 | 132 | 12.3 | 4.2 | 4 | D | D | D | 45.5 | 9.6 | 12.9 | 1.6 |
| Catahoula | 14 | 544 | 20.8 | 10.4 | 11 | D | D | D | 140.5 | 34.7 | 26.3 | 7.5 |
| Claiborne | 26 | 780 | 46.7 | 17.8 | 11 | 66 | 3.7 | 0.8 | 146.1 | 44.1 | 36.3 | 11.9 |
| Concordia | 46 | 743 | 48.1 | 20.1 | 25 | 99 | 6.2 | 1.8 | 219.5 | 59.0 | 43.2 | 14.6 |
| De Soto | 25 | D | D | D | 17 | 46 | 3.6 | 0.9 | 211.5 | 76.2 | 51.8 | 19.1 |
| East Baton Rouge | 1 386 | 36 001 | 3 477.8 | 1 247.2 | 909 | 6 732 | 776.3 | 206.2 | 9 253.9 | 991.4 | 663.7 | 189.6 |
| East Carroll | 12 | 300 | 15.7 | 7.4 | 7 | D | D | D | 120.0 | 17.1 | 27.3 | 11.1 |
| East Feliciana | 31 | 1 972 | 120.1 | 64.2 | 21 | 81 | 7.8 | 1.8 | 163.8 | 50.6 | 46.8 | 11.3 |
| Evangeline | 102 | 2 453 | 159.7 | 61.5 | 24 | 45 | 3.5 | 0.6 | 365.4 | 89.0 | 79.2 | 26.0 |
| Franklin | 53 | 1 068 | 65.6 | 26.2 | 20 | 69 | 6.0 | 1.2 | 244.3 | 54.1 | 60.2 | 15.6 |
| Grant | 17 | D | D | D | 6 | 25 | 1.4 | 0.4 | 204.6 | 62.8 | 39.3 | 10.4 |
| Iberia | 214 | 4 177 | 297.5 | 104.4 | 137 | 1 147 | 175.4 | 40.3 | 531.3 | 196.6 | 114.8 | 40.6 |
| Iberville | 47 | D | D | D | 41 | 285 | 25.4 | 8.6 | 356.9 | 88.3 | 82.7 | 21.6 |
| Jackson | 21 | 632 | 35.2 | 13.5 | 17 | D | D | D | 173.1 | 55.6 | 48.3 | 7.2 |
| Jefferson | 1 291 | 29 229 | 3 294.0 | 1 196.7 | 789 | 5 000 | 525.7 | 145.2 | 4 289.2 | 1 166.5 | 919.6 | 172.4 |
| Jefferson Davis | 76 | 1 485 | 106.9 | 42.0 | 39 | 133 | 9.0 | 2.1 | 234.1 | 87.1 | 56.8 | 13.7 |
| Lafayette | 951 | 19 023 | 1 871.8 | 681.0 | 448 | 3 481 | 311.8 | 87.5 | 1 285.4 | 479.2 | 250.5 | 65.5 |
| Lafourche | 185 | 3 167 | 335.1 | 120.8 | 115 | 586 | 57.7 | 15.3 | 987.2 | 235.4 | 155.5 | 40.7 |
| La Salle | 24 | 647 | 44.7 | 17.8 | 8 | D | D | D | 120.3 | 43.8 | 36.5 | 4.5 |
| Lincoln | 123 | 2 598 | 270.8 | 79.8 | 47 | D | D | D | 309.0 | 95.9 | 66.3 | 19.4 |
| Livingston | 131 | 1 632 | 88.1 | 35.0 | 108 | 620 | 55.0 | 14.4 | 520.4 | 272.1 | 128.2 | 29.4 |
| Madison | 35 | 795 | 37.6 | 17.6 | 17 | 33 | 2.6 | 0.4 | 150.7 | 25.5 | 34.7 | 10.4 |
| Morehouse | 85 | 1 709 | 102.7 | 39.4 | 29 | 140 | 9.1 | 2.4 | 357.7 | 94.0 | 86.1 | 23.1 |
| Natchitoches | 101 | 1 602 | 120.0 | 48.0 | 47 | 207 | 18.0 | 4.2 | 374.4 | 103.1 | 66.6 | 26.7 |

1. State totals may include programs not allocated by county.

# Table B. States and Counties — Federal Funds, Residential Construction, and Local Government Finances

| | Federal funds and grants, 2009–2010 (cont.) | | | | | | | Value of residential construction authorized by building permits, 2011 | | Local government finances, 2007 | | | | |
| | Expenditures (mil dol) (cont.) | | | | | | | | | General revenue | | | | |
| STATE County | Procurement contract awards | | | Grants[1] | | | | | | | | Taxes | | |
| | | | | | | | | | | | | | Per capita[2] (dollars) | |
| | Salaries and wages | Defense | Other | Medicaid and other health-related | Nutrition and family welfare | Education | Other | New construction ($1,000) | Number of housing units | Total (mil dol) | Inter-govern-mental (mil dol) | Total (mil dol) | Total | Property |
| | 171 | 172 | 173 | 174 | 175 | 176 | 177 | 178 | 179 | 180 | 181 | 182 | 183 | 184 |

**KENTUCKY—Cont'd**

| | | | | | | | | | | | | | | |
|---|---|---|---|---|---|---|---|---|---|---|---|---|---|---|
| Ohio | 7.0 | 0.0 | 1.1 | 25.7 | 4.3 | 2.2 | 0.2 | 631 | 10 | 58.4 | 33.3 | 11.2 | 474 | 263 |
| Oldham | 7.6 | 0.2 | 1.7 | 9.8 | 4.7 | 2.2 | 0.6 | 29 240 | 144 | 127.2 | 48.9 | 58.2 | 1 041 | 868 |
| Owen | 1.8 | 0.0 | 0.4 | 13.4 | 1.8 | 1.0 | 0.0 | 895 | 13 | 27.7 | 20.2 | 5.7 | 497 | 360 |
| Owsley | 0.8 | 0.0 | 0.2 | 28.6 | 2.6 | 0.7 | 0.6 | NA | NA | 12.5 | 10.2 | 1.2 | 250 | 160 |
| Pendleton | 2.6 | 0.0 | 0.7 | 12.4 | 2.4 | 0.9 | 0.2 | 0 | 0 | 31.6 | 20.4 | 7.3 | 488 | 353 |
| Perry | 15.2 | 0.7 | 10.0 | 74.7 | 7.5 | 4.4 | 3.6 | 1 112 | 12 | 72.7 | 45.8 | 17.8 | 608 | 400 |
| Pike | 28.2 | 0.5 | 6.5 | 100.3 | 12.1 | 5.5 | 10.6 | 5 457 | 33 | 156.8 | 94.5 | 40.4 | 617 | 411 |
| Powell | 2.7 | 0.0 | 0.6 | 23.9 | 3.4 | 1.3 | 0.1 | NA | NA | 28.3 | 19.1 | 5.1 | 369 | 195 |
| Pulaski | 17.4 | 1.3 | 6.6 | 105.2 | 10.6 | 6.2 | 33.0 | 579 | 11 | 132.0 | 71.8 | 41.5 | 690 | 392 |
| Robertson | 0.4 | 0.0 | 0.1 | 3.7 | 0.5 | 0.4 | 0.0 | NA | NA | 5.7 | 4.2 | 1.1 | 518 | 384 |
| Rockcastle | 2.6 | 0.3 | 6.8 | 40.8 | 3.6 | 1.5 | 0.2 | NA | NA | 31.5 | 23.4 | 4.9 | 296 | 176 |
| Rowan | 18.1 | 0.1 | 2.2 | 36.2 | 3.3 | 6.2 | 2.0 | 0 | 0 | 46.9 | 23.5 | 16.2 | 718 | 312 |
| Russell | 4.6 | 107.9 | 0.9 | 40.7 | 9.3 | 1.6 | 2.4 | 500 | 6 | 53.3 | 22.9 | 9.7 | 569 | 334 |
| Scott | 5.4 | 0.6 | 1.3 | 22.3 | 3.5 | 1.8 | 3.1 | 33 496 | 445 | 145.1 | 37.9 | 63.6 | 1 479 | 447 |
| Shelby | 15.5 | 1.4 | 33.1 | 24.6 | 7.4 | 3.9 | 0.2 | 14 794 | 75 | 87.6 | 30.7 | 38.8 | 958 | 669 |
| Simpson | 2.8 | 0.0 | 1.0 | 18.4 | 2.2 | 1.3 | 0.2 | 7 627 | 82 | 46.0 | 23.4 | 14.9 | 871 | 423 |
| Spencer | 2.4 | 0.5 | 0.5 | 7.2 | 1.7 | 0.6 | 0.1 | 9 038 | 49 | 26.5 | 15.4 | 8.4 | 501 | 404 |
| Taylor | 10.5 | 22.1 | 1.6 | 30.0 | 3.2 | 2.0 | 2.8 | 3 939 | 59 | 102.0 | 52.7 | 16.4 | 684 | 343 |
| Todd | 2.5 | 0.0 | 0.5 | 22.4 | 2.1 | 0.9 | 1.1 | 98 | 1 | 26.4 | 17.9 | 4.9 | 403 | 227 |
| Trigg | 7.2 | 0.0 | 3.4 | 14.4 | 1.8 | 1.6 | 1.4 | 2 044 | 20 | 23.7 | 13.9 | 7.5 | 558 | 387 |
| Trimble | 1.3 | 0.0 | 0.3 | 5.9 | 1.9 | 0.7 | 0.3 | NA | NA | 34.0 | 10.6 | 4.7 | 525 | 327 |
| Union | 3.7 | 0.2 | 218.7 | 12.1 | 2.3 | 1.4 | 0.7 | 1 384 | 40 | 34.0 | 20.6 | 8.9 | 588 | 386 |
| Warren | 53.8 | 1.0 | 11.9 | 77.2 | 18.4 | 10.1 | 60.5 | 73 158 | 843 | 235.5 | 96.5 | 107.7 | 1 035 | 465 |
| Washington | 4.1 | 0.0 | 0.5 | 15.6 | 1.9 | 1.0 | 0.5 | 1 200 | 17 | 27.9 | 14.5 | 8.5 | 732 | 427 |
| Wayne | 6.0 | 0.0 | 0.5 | 65.8 | 5.1 | 1.6 | 4.2 | 0 | 0 | 40.7 | 29.6 | 7.9 | 383 | 196 |
| Webster | 3.2 | 0.0 | 6.2 | 14.7 | 2.5 | 0.9 | 1.1 | 219 | 2 | 35.7 | 21.3 | 6.6 | 472 | 351 |
| Whitley | 16.2 | 18.1 | 28.9 | 78.7 | 9.3 | 3.3 | 1.9 | 1 618 | 25 | 99.7 | 65.9 | 21.9 | 572 | 253 |
| Wolfe | 2.0 | 0.0 | 0.5 | 34.2 | 2.4 | 1.1 | 1.3 | NA | NA | 14.8 | 12.1 | 1.9 | 270 | 153 |
| Woodford | 3.6 | 0.0 | 1.0 | 13.4 | 2.5 | 2.2 | 2.4 | 16 189 | 52 | 63.5 | 22.3 | 27.9 | 1 149 | 572 |
| **LOUISIANA** | 4 702.5 | 5 841.7 | 1 448.9 | 6 250.9 | 1 238.6 | 943.3 | 6 654.8 | 1 918 793 | 12 173 | X | X | X | X | X |
| Acadia | 16.4 | 0.1 | 26.6 | 126.2 | 14.7 | 4.7 | 3.9 | 24 068 | 149 | 155.6 | 80.2 | 53.2 | 888 | 282 |
| Allen | 43.2 | 0.0 | 4.2 | 42.7 | 6.8 | 1.7 | 6.8 | 1 200 | 3 | 84.9 | 37.5 | 27.9 | 1 093 | 414 |
| Ascension | 17.4 | 0.4 | 3.8 | 48.8 | 13.3 | 5.1 | 1.6 | 105 254 | 719 | 291.5 | 102.4 | 153.6 | 1 551 | 579 |
| Assumption | 6.9 | 0.0 | 0.9 | 37.6 | 6.3 | 1.9 | 0.6 | 7 498 | 41 | 65.4 | 35.3 | 23.0 | 999 | 410 |
| Avoyelles | 12.4 | 1.9 | 1.9 | 118.4 | 11.9 | 3.4 | 2.8 | 3 837 | 33 | 97.7 | 56.6 | 22.8 | 541 | 116 |
| Beauregard | 8.1 | 0.6 | 1.6 | 37.1 | 5.6 | 2.8 | 0.5 | 2 184 | 11 | 123.0 | 43.9 | 37.9 | 1 090 | 466 |
| Bienville | 4.5 | 3.7 | 0.9 | 38.8 | 3.6 | 1.3 | 0.5 | 0 | 0 | 54.8 | 17.7 | 31.8 | 2 136 | 1 303 |
| Bossier | 461.0 | 154.8 | 6.4 | 60.9 | 18.2 | 7.6 | 11.8 | 155 073 | 1 108 | 374.6 | 123.2 | 192.7 | 1 773 | 566 |
| Caddo | 157.8 | 4.9 | 51.4 | 354.7 | 57.2 | 31.3 | 47.9 | 76 363 | 293 | 919.5 | 335.1 | 450.6 | 1 784 | 851 |
| Calcasieu | 99.9 | 40.8 | 72.3 | 147.8 | 31.9 | 16.3 | 47.5 | 142 554 | 1 149 | 841.8 | 255.5 | 382.9 | 2 075 | 708 |
| Caldwell | 3.5 | 0.1 | 0.3 | 21.3 | 2.8 | 1.2 | 0.6 | 1 664 | 8 | 26.8 | 15.4 | 7.5 | 726 | 288 |
| Cameron | 1.3 | 5.0 | 0.4 | 4.3 | 2.1 | 0.8 | 6.1 | 6 593 | 46 | 67.5 | 21.0 | 27.4 | 3 694 | 3 615 |
| Catahoula | 3.5 | 0.0 | 0.9 | 31.9 | 6.9 | 1.1 | 13.9 | 122 | 2 | 31.7 | 21.2 | 6.7 | 636 | 270 |
| Claiborne | 3.5 | 0.0 | 0.8 | 42.3 | 3.5 | 1.5 | 1.2 | 0 | 0 | 64.5 | 29.6 | 13.5 | 832 | 461 |
| Concordia | 5.0 | 16.4 | 1.1 | 51.8 | 5.5 | 1.9 | 5.9 | 2 440 | 9 | 91.9 | 44.5 | 18.8 | 989 | 504 |
| De Soto | 4.3 | 0.1 | -6.7 | 55.6 | 6.0 | 2.3 | 0.5 | 0 | 0 | 105.8 | 43.2 | 47.5 | 1 810 | 891 |
| East Baton Rouge | 296.5 | 173.7 | -77.1 | 436.1 | 273.4 | 451.3 | 5 712.1 | 241 311 | 1 219 | 1 551.6 | 445.1 | 768.5 | 1 786 | 648 |
| East Carroll | 1.8 | 0.0 | 0.5 | 38.1 | 4.2 | 1.3 | 1.0 | 0 | 0 | 41.1 | 26.1 | 5.5 | 659 | 333 |
| East Feliciana | 3.4 | 0.0 | 0.8 | 41.0 | 4.6 | 1.4 | 2.8 | 7 561 | 41 | 36.7 | 23.0 | 10.0 | 478 | 155 |
| Evangeline | 6.3 | 0.0 | 1.3 | 134.9 | 12.8 | 3.3 | 1.8 | 9 812 | 48 | 88.6 | 49.2 | 30.4 | 846 | 282 |
| Franklin | 15.1 | 0.0 | 1.5 | 69.6 | 6.8 | 2.4 | 0.6 | 4 132 | 22 | 70.2 | 36.9 | 14.6 | 728 | 215 |
| Grant | 46.2 | 0.0 | 5.4 | 31.8 | 4.0 | 1.7 | 0.8 | 4 664 | 26 | 46.4 | 30.6 | 11.3 | 572 | 206 |
| Iberia | 25.7 | 11.8 | 8.9 | 100.9 | 13.8 | 9.0 | 3.5 | 20 220 | 115 | 283.5 | 119.3 | 86.7 | 1 157 | 375 |
| Iberville | 44.3 | 23.1 | 10.0 | 67.0 | 9.4 | 4.9 | 3.3 | 14 481 | 80 | 120.0 | 36.5 | 68.6 | 2 111 | 875 |
| Jackson | 21.9 | 0.0 | 0.7 | 26.8 | 5.4 | 1.2 | 4.9 | 3 961 | 26 | 62.2 | 29.7 | 21.5 | 1 420 | 417 |
| Jefferson | 253.0 | 1 122.5 | 208.1 | 252.7 | 65.9 | 31.5 | 56.2 | 52 478 | 225 | 1 965.7 | 501.8 | 689.0 | 1 627 | 575 |
| Jefferson Davis | 6.7 | 0.1 | 0.9 | 43.3 | 7.7 | 3.0 | 5.0 | 12 900 | 89 | 94.1 | 47.0 | 31.0 | 994 | 436 |
| Lafayette | 133.0 | 9.4 | 31.9 | 150.2 | 34.3 | 24.4 | 43.4 | 102 231 | 739 | 625.8 | 195.8 | 313.3 | 1 530 | 499 |
| Lafourche | 14.9 | 84.7 | 327.2 | 70.4 | 18.5 | 8.4 | 16.6 | 44 209 | 209 | 438.6 | 144.7 | 120.6 | 1 301 | 563 |
| La Salle | 6.6 | 0.0 | 0.7 | 22.3 | 2.4 | 1.0 | 0.7 | 349 | 3 | 79.2 | 28.8 | 12.8 | 915 | 536 |
| Lincoln | 10.3 | 0.2 | 1.7 | 52.6 | 9.1 | 8.9 | 15.3 | 5 753 | 25 | 118.5 | 44.7 | 56.1 | 1 319 | 536 |
| Livingston | 14.5 | 0.0 | 2.4 | 48.3 | 13.9 | 6.1 | 2.9 | 119 838 | 846 | 281.4 | 146.1 | 100.6 | 863 | 266 |
| Madison | 2.5 | 0.0 | 3.3 | 45.1 | 7.4 | 1.7 | 0.7 | 1 502 | 14 | 40.0 | 22.9 | 11.3 | 957 | 466 |
| Morehouse | 7.1 | 1.9 | 1.3 | 90.3 | 9.4 | 3.9 | 9.2 | 1 921 | 20 | 116.8 | 47.6 | 29.6 | 1 028 | 423 |
| Natchitoches | 22.2 | 2.2 | 2.8 | 101.0 | 10.9 | 6.3 | 5.3 | 11 064 | 71 | 164.3 | 68.0 | 45.6 | 1 156 | 402 |

1. State totals may include programs not allocated by county.    2. Based on the resident population estimated as of July 1 of the year shown.

| STATE County | Total (mil dol) 185 | Per capita[1] (dollars) 186 | Education 187 | Health and hospitals 188 | Police protection 189 | Public welfare 190 | Highways 191 | Total (mil dol) 192 | Per capita[1] (dollars) 193 | Federal civilian 194 | Federal military 195 | State and local 196 | Democratic 197 | Republican 198 | All other 199 |
|---|---|---|---|---|---|---|---|---|---|---|---|---|---|---|---|
| **KENTUCKY—Cont'd** | | | | | | | | | | | | | | | |
| Ohio | 53.7 | 2 278 | 53.4 | 2.0 | 3.0 | 0.2 | 3.9 | 185.7 | 7 883 | 96 | 79 | 1 394 | 40.8 | 57.2 | 1.9 |
| Oldham | 130.5 | 2 333 | 66.5 | 2.5 | 4.3 | 0.0 | 3.0 | 459.0 | 8 206 | 70 | 199 | 3 641 | 34.1 | 64.8 | 1.1 |
| Owen | 20.9 | 1 834 | 68.6 | 2.1 | 2.9 | 0.0 | 6.7 | 10.7 | 940 | 24 | 35 | 459 | 35.7 | 62.5 | 1.9 |
| Owsley | 12.4 | 2 690 | 70.6 | 0.7 | 3.3 | 0.0 | 10.2 | 6.8 | 1 483 | 0 | 16 | 315 | 22.6 | 75.9 | 1.5 |
| Pendleton | 31.1 | 2 063 | 71.3 | 2.6 | 2.9 | 0.0 | 5.2 | 42.1 | 2 799 | 32 | 48 | 655 | 34.9 | 63.4 | 1.7 |
| Perry | 74.9 | 2 565 | 56.5 | 2.4 | 2.1 | 0.3 | 6.1 | 245.3 | 8 397 | 147 | 94 | 2 733 | 33.2 | 65.2 | 1.6 |
| Pike | 142.1 | 2 168 | 61.2 | 1.2 | 1.6 | 0.4 | 5.2 | 148.5 | 2 266 | 303 | 211 | 3 127 | 42.1 | 55.9 | 2.0 |
| Powell | 30.9 | 2 241 | 68.8 | 6.6 | 2.4 | 0.0 | 2.5 | 21.0 | 1 524 | 34 | 41 | 801 | 41.5 | 57.1 | 1.4 |
| Pulaski | 131.6 | 2 187 | 56.4 | 3.4 | 4.0 | 0.1 | 5.6 | 180.1 | 2 995 | 183 | 208 | 3 978 | 21.7 | 77.1 | 1.2 |
| Robertson | 5.3 | 2 397 | 66.4 | 0.8 | 2.1 | 0.0 | 8.0 | 3.2 | 1 474 | 0 | 0 | 154 | 44.4 | 52.5 | 3.1 |
| Rockcastle | 38.9 | 2 330 | 75.4 | 1.9 | 2.5 | 0.0 | 4.7 | 37.3 | 2 233 | 32 | 56 | 746 | 22.5 | 75.8 | 1.7 |
| Rowan | 49.2 | 2 180 | 51.6 | 2.1 | 4.3 | 0.2 | 6.9 | 37.0 | 1 640 | 92 | 81 | 3 519 | 50.0 | 47.9 | 2.1 |
| Russell | 56.2 | 3 278 | 49.1 | 29.8 | 2.6 | 0.3 | 2.8 | 63.4 | 3 696 | 86 | 57 | 992 | 21.0 | 77.3 | 1.7 |
| Scott | 136.7 | 3 182 | 44.9 | 1.7 | 4.6 | 5.9 | 2.9 | 717.3 | 16 698 | 56 | 157 | 2 017 | 39.1 | 59.7 | 1.2 |
| Shelby | 85.1 | 2 104 | 52.5 | 2.0 | 3.8 | 0.1 | 3.1 | 188.2 | 4 652 | 76 | 140 | 1 993 | 37.1 | 61.8 | 1.2 |
| Simpson | 45.8 | 2 682 | 54.8 | 2.9 | 3.7 | 1.8 | 3.5 | 73.1 | 4 285 | 35 | 57 | 785 | 38.0 | 60.7 | 1.3 |
| Spencer | 25.3 | 1 503 | 67.6 | 2.1 | 3.4 | 0.2 | 4.2 | 38.3 | 2 273 | 26 | 57 | 568 | 31.3 | 66.8 | 1.9 |
| Taylor | 97.6 | 4 079 | 28.2 | 53.1 | 2.2 | 0.0 | 2.1 | 93.9 | 3 928 | 86 | 81 | 1 760 | 29.1 | 69.7 | 1.2 |
| Todd | 24.4 | 2 023 | 62.6 | 1.9 | 3.3 | 0.0 | 5.8 | 88.0 | 7 309 | 34 | 41 | 628 | 31.2 | 67.5 | 1.3 |
| Trigg | 23.3 | 1 742 | 65.3 | 2.3 | 4.3 | 0.0 | 7.2 | 10.2 | 764 | 126 | 47 | 635 | 34.4 | 64.2 | 1.4 |
| Trimble | 32.5 | 3 614 | 33.6 | 0.9 | 0.6 | 0.0 | 3.3 | 533.2 | 59 351 | 15 | 28 | 353 | 38.9 | 58.7 | 2.3 |
| Union | 34.5 | 2 283 | 60.9 | 0.2 | 5.1 | 0.2 | 3.8 | 30.0 | 1 986 | 46 | 49 | 749 | 46.5 | 51.7 | 1.8 |
| Warren | 236.2 | 2 270 | 50.8 | 0.6 | 7.0 | 0.1 | 4.3 | 810.4 | 7 791 | 437 | 380 | 10 109 | 40.0 | 58.9 | 1.1 |
| Washington | 25.9 | 2 245 | 50.3 | 3.3 | 3.3 | 0.1 | 8.3 | 77.3 | 6 688 | 33 | 39 | 472 | 35.8 | 62.7 | 1.5 |
| Wayne | 47.4 | 2 295 | 72.2 | 2.8 | 2.7 | 0.0 | 4.3 | 55.1 | 2 671 | 36 | 68 | 1 021 | 30.6 | 67.6 | 1.8 |
| Webster | 36.7 | 2 642 | 49.5 | 1.8 | 2.9 | 0.0 | 4.5 | 70.6 | 5 086 | 40 | 45 | 691 | 43.1 | 54.8 | 2.0 |
| Whitley | 97.9 | 2 553 | 70.6 | 1.0 | 2.5 | 0.0 | 2.3 | 110.1 | 2 870 | 95 | 117 | 2 376 | 25.4 | 73.1 | 1.5 |
| Wolfe | 14.4 | 2 040 | 74.0 | 0.1 | 1.6 | 0.1 | 5.0 | 12.6 | 1 796 | 22 | 24 | 418 | 50.3 | 47.4 | 2.3 |
| Woodford | 54.4 | 2 237 | 45.9 | 2.0 | 10.3 | 0.1 | 5.5 | 134.4 | 5 526 | 42 | 81 | 1 525 | 40.9 | 58.0 | 1.1 |
| **LOUISIANA** | X | X | X | X | X | X | X | X | X | 31 621 | 40 854 | 324 867 | 39.9 | 58.6 | 1.5 |
| Acadia | 143.9 | 2 400 | 52.3 | 6.3 | 6.1 | 0.2 | 4.3 | 65.6 | 1 094 | 100 | 293 | 2 725 | 26.3 | 72.0 | 1.7 |
| Allen | 76.8 | 3 010 | 52.5 | 17.0 | 6.1 | 0.0 | 4.9 | 24.5 | 961 | 617 | 122 | 4 051 | 30.5 | 66.9 | 2.6 |
| Ascension | 270.4 | 2 730 | 60.0 | 4.3 | 5.6 | 0.0 | 4.4 | 210.5 | 2 125 | 134 | 520 | 5 252 | 31.4 | 67.1 | 1.5 |
| Assumption | 54.2 | 2 357 | 69.7 | 0.2 | 4.6 | 0.9 | 3.8 | 10.7 | 464 | 29 | 109 | 1 056 | 43.4 | 54.6 | 2.0 |
| Avoyelles | 91.4 | 2 167 | 48.5 | 11.1 | 10.9 | 0.0 | 4.5 | 26.4 | 627 | 84 | 198 | 3 923 | 37.4 | 60.4 | 2.2 |
| Beauregard | 111.6 | 3 209 | 44.3 | 27.3 | 5.7 | 0.0 | 4.8 | 32.9 | 946 | 67 | 170 | 1 625 | 21.8 | 76.2 | 2.0 |
| Bienville | 44.3 | 2 969 | 59.1 | 2.3 | 5.1 | 0.2 | 7.1 | 10.4 | 701 | 54 | 68 | 747 | 48.3 | 50.8 | 0.9 |
| Bossier | 338.9 | 3 118 | 50.1 | 2.1 | 9.5 | 0.0 | 5.9 | 241.0 | 2 217 | 2 021 | 6 238 | 6 956 | 27.7 | 71.4 | 0.9 |
| Caddo | 887.0 | 3 511 | 48.5 | 1.1 | 7.4 | 0.0 | 2.8 | 919.2 | 3 639 | 2 748 | 1 218 | 20 793 | 51.1 | 48.1 | 0.8 |
| Calcasieu | 775.8 | 4 204 | 37.3 | 6.9 | 6.3 | 0.2 | 6.3 | 997.3 | 5 405 | 565 | 1 021 | 14 036 | 36.8 | 61.4 | 1.8 |
| Caldwell | 25.4 | 2 463 | 60.6 | 8.3 | 3.4 | 0.2 | 3.3 | 2.6 | 252 | 28 | 47 | 668 | 22.8 | 75.5 | 1.6 |
| Cameron | 52.0 | 7 010 | 53.0 | 7.8 | 4.7 | 0.1 | 6.8 | 14.0 | 1 885 | 19 | 32 | 770 | 16.2 | 81.4 | 2.4 |
| Catahoula | 33.2 | 3 181 | 44.2 | 7.1 | 5.0 | 0.5 | 6.4 | 3.0 | 289 | 49 | 49 | 679 | 31.8 | 66.7 | 1.5 |
| Claiborne | 61.0 | 3 747 | 39.8 | 25.8 | 3.4 | 0.6 | 2.9 | 27.9 | 1 712 | 42 | 80 | 1 328 | 44.2 | 54.8 | 1.0 |
| Concordia | 90.6 | 4 754 | 40.6 | 14.9 | 6.4 | 0.0 | 2.0 | 17.3 | 910 | 63 | 99 | 1 598 | 39.5 | 59.5 | 1.0 |
| De Soto | 103.6 | 3 942 | 58.3 | 1.2 | 4.1 | 0.5 | 4.5 | 142.9 | 5 438 | 47 | 127 | 1 760 | 42.8 | 56.2 | 1.1 |
| East Baton Rouge | 1 364.3 | 3 171 | 41.2 | 5.4 | 7.2 | 0.2 | 4.8 | 1 905.5 | 4 428 | 2 438 | 2 277 | 50 276 | 50.5 | 48.3 | 1.2 |
| East Carroll | 41.1 | 4 945 | 34.4 | 16.7 | 4.4 | 0.0 | 2.5 | 12.4 | 1 493 | 24 | 36 | 765 | 63.7 | 35.2 | 1.1 |
| East Feliciana | 37.0 | 1 778 | 62.8 | 0.3 | 8.7 | 0.2 | 9.7 | 18.1 | 868 | 35 | 95 | 2 430 | 44.1 | 54.6 | 1.3 |
| Evangeline | 85.6 | 2 385 | 63.1 | 0.4 | 5.1 | 0.0 | 5.0 | 38.6 | 1 075 | 52 | 160 | 1 807 | 36.6 | 61.3 | 2.1 |
| Franklin | 68.4 | 3 412 | 41.0 | 24.5 | 8.7 | 0.3 | 3.5 | 6.0 | 300 | 59 | 98 | 1 325 | 31.6 | 67.1 | 1.3 |
| Grant | 43.8 | 2 216 | 60.6 | 0.5 | 5.3 | 0.0 | 9.5 | 29.2 | 1 477 | 699 | 114 | 918 | 17.2 | 80.7 | 2.1 |
| Iberia | 285.0 | 3 802 | 47.4 | 18.9 | 5.4 | 0.1 | 1.9 | 128.0 | 1 708 | 104 | 347 | 4 334 | 37.7 | 60.7 | 1.7 |
| Iberville | 106.8 | 3 286 | 43.8 | 0.2 | 8.9 | 1.0 | 8.1 | 58.2 | 1 792 | 113 | 157 | 2 968 | 54.9 | 43.8 | 1.3 |
| Jackson | 59.0 | 3 895 | 40.6 | 11.1 | 4.3 | 0.0 | 4.9 | 75.8 | 5 009 | 30 | 77 | 1 096 | 31.7 | 67.1 | 1.2 |
| Jefferson | 1 843.7 | 4 353 | 25.7 | 33.1 | 5.7 | 0.5 | 4.1 | 1 779.5 | 4 202 | 1 342 | 2 522 | 20 449 | 35.9 | 62.5 | 1.6 |
| Jefferson Davis | 89.3 | 2 865 | 61.2 | 1.2 | 8.0 | 0.1 | 3.8 | 54.0 | 1 732 | 94 | 150 | 1 844 | 29.1 | 68.7 | 2.2 |
| Lafayette | 581.3 | 2 838 | 44.0 | 0.5 | 7.3 | 0.0 | 6.5 | 995.1 | 4 858 | 1 024 | 1 093 | 13 671 | 33.6 | 64.9 | 1.5 |
| Lafourche | 423.6 | 4 569 | 34.4 | 33.4 | 3.9 | 0.2 | 4.0 | 206.0 | 2 222 | 143 | 476 | 6 711 | 25.5 | 71.5 | 3.0 |
| La Salle | 73.3 | 5 221 | 38.9 | 35.8 | 4.1 | 0.0 | 2.1 | 5.6 | 397 | 60 | 71 | 1 373 | 13.1 | 85.5 | 1.4 |
| Lincoln | 119.4 | 2 806 | 59.5 | 0.3 | 5.2 | 1.4 | 3.7 | 53.9 | 1 266 | 109 | 231 | 4 684 | 43.2 | 55.7 | 1.1 |
| Livingston | 304.8 | 2 614 | 56.4 | 0.8 | 4.6 | 0.0 | 10.8 | 406.7 | 3 488 | 139 | 615 | 5 430 | 13.1 | 85.0 | 1.9 |
| Madison | 36.2 | 3 049 | 53.7 | 0.1 | 4.4 | 0.4 | 5.6 | 54.0 | 4 554 | 37 | 57 | 1 059 | 58.5 | 40.6 | 0.9 |
| Morehouse | 114.3 | 3 970 | 38.0 | 23.8 | 4.5 | 0.1 | 1.6 | 183.0 | 6 359 | 70 | 130 | 1 325 | 43.9 | 55.0 | 1.1 |
| Natchitoches | 150.7 | 3 816 | 38.8 | 27.3 | 4.4 | 0.5 | 1.3 | 63.5 | 1 609 | 189 | 190 | 3 867 | 45.7 | 53.0 | 1.2 |

1. Based on the resident population estimated as of July 1 of the year shown. 2. © 2013 Election Data Services, Inc. All rights reserved.

| STATE/ County code | CBSA code[1] | County type[2] | STATE County | Land area,[3] (sq km) 2010 | Total persons | Rank | Per square kilometer | White | Black | American Indian, Alaska Native | Asian and Pacific Islander | Percent Hispanic or Latino[4] | Under 5 years | 5 to 17 years | 18 to 24 years | 25 to 34 years | 35 to 44 years | 45 to 54 years |
|---|---|---|---|---|---|---|---|---|---|---|---|---|---|---|---|---|---|---|
| | | | | | Population 2012 | | | Race alone or in combination, not Hispanic or Latino (percent) | | | | | Population characteristics[6], 2011 — Age (percent) | | | | | |
| | | | | 1 | 2 | 3 | 4 | 5 | 6 | 7 | 8 | 9 | 10 | 11 | 12 | 13 | 14 | 15 |
| | | | LOUISIANA—Cont'd | | | | | | | | | | | | | | | |
| 22 071 | 35380 | 1 | Orleans | 439 | 369 250 | 179 | 841.1 | 32.1 | 60.0 | 0.7 | 3.3 | 5.2 | 6.6 | 14.8 | 11.8 | 17.2 | 12.2 | 13.7 |
| 22 073 | 33740 | 3 | Ouachita | 1 581 | 155 363 | 405 | 98.3 | 60.1 | 37.1 | 0.6 | 1.3 | 1.9 | 7.4 | 18.8 | 11.2 | 13.6 | 12.1 | 13.0 |
| 22 075 | 35380 | 1 | Plaquemines | 2 020 | 23 921 | 1 647 | 11.8 | 68.6 | 21.8 | 2.3 | 4.0 | 5.3 | 7.2 | 20.2 | 8.6 | 12.7 | 13.4 | 15.3 |
| 22 077 | 12940 | 2 | Pointe Coupee | 1 444 | 22 726 | 1 699 | 15.7 | 60.7 | 36.8 | 0.4 | 0.5 | 2.4 | 6.3 | 17.8 | 7.8 | 11.3 | 10.9 | 15.4 |
| 22 079 | 10780 | 3 | Rapides | 3 414 | 132 373 | 472 | 38.8 | 63.2 | 32.7 | 1.4 | 1.6 | 2.7 | 7.1 | 18.7 | 9.0 | 13.1 | 11.9 | 14.2 |
| 22 081 | ... | 6 | Red River | 1 008 | 8 983 | 2 523 | 8.9 | 58.3 | 40.1 | 0.6 | 0.3 | 1.4 | 7.0 | 18.8 | 8.6 | 12.4 | 11.6 | 14.7 |
| 22 083 | ... | 6 | Richland | 1 448 | 20 921 | 1 782 | 14.4 | 61.8 | 36.1 | 0.6 | 0.5 | 1.8 | 7.0 | 18.5 | 8.9 | 12.8 | 11.6 | 14.1 |
| 22 085 | ... | 6 | Sabine | 2 245 | 24 325 | 1 632 | 10.8 | 71.7 | 17.7 | 9.6 | 0.6 | 3.4 | 6.7 | 17.5 | 8.1 | 11.3 | 11.3 | 13.5 |
| 22 087 | 35380 | 1 | St. Bernard | 978 | 41 635 | 1 137 | 42.6 | 68.9 | 19.6 | 1.2 | 2.8 | 9.4 | 8.1 | 17.7 | 11.1 | 16.3 | 12.4 | 14.5 |
| 22 089 | 35380 | 1 | St. Charles | 723 | 52 681 | 945 | 72.9 | 67.0 | 27.1 | 0.7 | 1.2 | 5.1 | 6.8 | 19.7 | 8.5 | 12.7 | 13.5 | 16.6 |
| 22 091 | 12940 | 2 | St. Helena | 1 058 | 11 071 | 2 353 | 10.5 | 45.3 | 53.2 | 0.8 | 0.3 | 1.3 | 7.1 | 18.0 | 9.4 | 11.7 | 10.6 | 14.8 |
| 22 093 | ... | 6 | St. James | 626 | 21 722 | 1 743 | 34.7 | 47.9 | 50.6 | 0.4 | 0.3 | 1.4 | 6.8 | 18.5 | 9.5 | 12.4 | 11.2 | 15.5 |
| 22 095 | 35380 | 1 | St. John the Baptist | 552 | 44 758 | 1 073 | 81.1 | 40.8 | 53.6 | 0.6 | 1.2 | 4.9 | 7.2 | 19.4 | 9.4 | 13.1 | 12.7 | 15.3 |
| 22 097 | 36660 | 4 | St. Landry | 2 393 | 83 662 | 669 | 35.0 | 55.9 | 42.1 | 0.6 | 0.7 | 1.7 | 7.8 | 19.4 | 9.1 | 11.9 | 11.4 | 14.1 |
| 22 099 | 29180 | 3 | St. Martin | 1 910 | 52 726 | 943 | 27.6 | 65.6 | 31.4 | 0.7 | 1.0 | 2.3 | 7.2 | 18.9 | 9.1 | 13.0 | 12.6 | 15.0 |
| 22 101 | 34020 | 4 | St. Mary | 1 438 | 53 697 | 928 | 37.3 | 58.3 | 33.2 | 2.3 | 2.0 | 5.6 | 7.0 | 18.2 | 9.5 | 12.5 | 12.1 | 15.5 |
| 22 103 | 35380 | 1 | St. Tammany | 2 190 | 239 453 | 271 | 109.3 | 81.4 | 12.5 | 1.0 | 1.8 | 4.9 | 6.3 | 19.0 | 7.4 | 11.6 | 13.2 | 15.7 |
| 22 105 | 25220 | 4 | Tangipahoa | 2 049 | 123 441 | 495 | 60.2 | 65.2 | 30.5 | 0.8 | 1.0 | 3.6 | 7.3 | 17.7 | 12.4 | 14.0 | 11.5 | 13.2 |
| 22 107 | ... | 9 | Tensas | 1 561 | 4 954 | 2 840 | 3.2 | 42.1 | 56.2 | 0.6 | 0.3 | 1.5 | 6.2 | 18.2 | 7.2 | 10.0 | 9.7 | 14.8 |
| 22 109 | 26380 | 3 | Terrebonne | 3 190 | 111 893 | 538 | 35.1 | 70.2 | 19.9 | 6.3 | 1.5 | 4.2 | 7.3 | 18.5 | 9.9 | 14.1 | 12.4 | 14.8 |
| 22 111 | 33740 | 3 | Union | 2 271 | 22 419 | 1 714 | 9.9 | 68.3 | 27.2 | 0.5 | 0.4 | 4.2 | 6.3 | 16.5 | 8.5 | 11.6 | 11.1 | 14.7 |
| 22 113 | 10020 | 4 | Vermilion | 3 039 | 58 723 | 878 | 19.3 | 80.3 | 15.2 | 0.6 | 2.4 | 2.7 | 7.4 | 19.2 | 8.5 | 13.0 | 12.3 | 14.8 |
| 22 115 | 22860 | 4 | Vernon | 3 439 | 53 869 | 927 | 15.7 | 73.9 | 16.0 | 2.3 | 3.2 | 7.8 | 9.0 | 18.4 | 12.8 | 17.0 | 12.8 | 10.8 |
| 22 117 | 14220 | 6 | Washington | 1 734 | 46 670 | 1 036 | 26.9 | 66.4 | 31.4 | 0.7 | 0.5 | 2.0 | 6.8 | 18.2 | 8.2 | 12.3 | 11.6 | 14.3 |
| 22 119 | 33380 | 6 | Webster | 1 536 | 40 940 | 1 154 | 26.7 | 64.0 | 33.8 | 0.9 | 0.6 | 1.8 | 6.5 | 17.0 | 8.5 | 11.9 | 11.6 | 14.4 |
| 22 121 | 12940 | 2 | West Baton Rouge | 498 | 24 106 | 1 638 | 48.4 | 58.9 | 38.2 | 0.5 | 0.6 | 2.7 | 7.1 | 17.7 | 9.9 | 14.6 | 12.2 | 15.1 |
| 22 123 | ... | 9 | West Carroll | 931 | 11 512 | 2 327 | 12.4 | 80.1 | 16.5 | 0.7 | 0.5 | 2.9 | 6.6 | 17.9 | 8.2 | 11.8 | 11.8 | 14.0 |
| 22 125 | 12940 | 2 | West Feliciana | 1 044 | 15 405 | 2 078 | 14.8 | 51.4 | 46.6 | 0.4 | 0.4 | 1.7 | 4.0 | 12.9 | 5.6 | 14.6 | 18.3 | 19.3 |
| 22 127 | ... | 6 | Winn | 2 461 | 15 000 | 2 107 | 6.1 | 66.6 | 31.1 | 1.1 | 0.6 | 1.7 | 5.9 | 16.5 | 8.5 | 13.5 | 13.0 | 14.7 |
| 23 000 | ... | X | **MAINE** | 79 883 | 1 329 192 | X | 16.6 | 95.7 | 1.6 | 1.3 | 1.5 | 1.4 | 5.1 | 15.2 | 8.7 | 11.0 | 12.5 | 16.2 |
| 23 001 | 30340 | 3 | Androscoggin | 1 212 | 107 609 | 551 | 88.8 | 93.6 | 4.4 | 1.2 | 1.2 | 1.6 | 6.3 | 16.0 | 9.2 | 12.2 | 12.9 | 15.7 |
| 23 003 | ... | 7 | Aroostook | 17 279 | 70 868 | 754 | 4.1 | 96.1 | 0.9 | 2.5 | 0.8 | 1.0 | 4.9 | 14.8 | 8.0 | 9.6 | 11.6 | 15.8 |
| 23 005 | 38860 | 2 | Cumberland | 2 163 | 283 921 | 231 | 131.3 | 93.3 | 2.9 | 0.9 | 2.7 | 1.9 | 5.1 | 15.3 | 9.0 | 12.3 | 13.3 | 16.2 |
| 23 007 | ... | 6 | Franklin | 4 394 | 30 630 | 1 417 | 7.0 | 97.8 | 0.5 | 1.2 | 0.8 | 1.1 | 4.8 | 14.5 | 11.6 | 9.6 | 10.8 | 16.1 |
| 23 009 | ... | 6 | Hancock | 4 110 | 54 558 | 916 | 13.3 | 97.1 | 0.7 | 1.1 | 1.2 | 1.2 | 4.5 | 13.3 | 8.1 | 9.8 | 11.6 | 16.2 |
| 23 011 | 12300 | 4 | Kennebec | 2 247 | 121 853 | 504 | 54.2 | 96.9 | 0.9 | 1.3 | 1.2 | 1.3 | 5.1 | 15.3 | 8.5 | 11.1 | 12.6 | 16.5 |
| 23 013 | 40500 | 7 | Knox | 946 | 39 668 | 1 177 | 41.9 | 97.6 | 0.9 | 1.1 | 0.9 | 1.0 | 4.8 | 14.3 | 6.3 | 10.2 | 12.1 | 15.6 |
| 23 015 | | 8 | Lincoln | 1 181 | 34 180 | 1 324 | 28.9 | 97.8 | 0.6 | 0.9 | 0.8 | 0.9 | 4.5 | 13.7 | 6.2 | 8.9 | 11.3 | 15.6 |
| 23 017 | ... | 6 | Oxford | 5 379 | 57 481 | 887 | 10.7 | 97.5 | 0.8 | 1.2 | 1.0 | 1.1 | 5.0 | 16.0 | 7.2 | 10.0 | 11.8 | 17.0 |
| 23 019 | 12620 | 3 | Penobscot | 8 799 | 153 746 | 411 | 17.5 | 96.0 | 1.3 | 1.8 | 1.3 | 1.1 | 5.1 | 14.4 | 13.0 | 11.6 | 11.9 | 15.5 |
| 23 021 | ... | 8 | Piscataquis | 10 259 | 17 290 | 1 963 | 1.7 | 97.3 | 0.7 | 1.1 | 1.0 | 1.0 | 4.2 | 14.5 | 5.8 | 8.3 | 11.7 | 16.5 |
| 23 023 | 38860 | 2 | Sagadahoc | 657 | 35 191 | 1 297 | 53.6 | 96.7 | 1.4 | 1.0 | 1.3 | 1.3 | 5.1 | 15.2 | 6.6 | 10.5 | 12.9 | 16.8 |
| 23 025 | ... | 6 | Somerset | 10 164 | 51 910 | 956 | 5.1 | 97.6 | 0.8 | 1.2 | 0.9 | 0.8 | 5.0 | 16.0 | 6.9 | 10.4 | 12.9 | 16.4 |
| 23 027 | ... | 6 | Waldo | 1 890 | 38 820 | 1 201 | 20.5 | 97.7 | 0.7 | 1.3 | 0.6 | 1.0 | 5.2 | 15.6 | 5.7 | 10.3 | 12.2 | 15.5 |
| 23 029 | ... | 7 | Washington | 6 637 | 32 462 | 1 378 | 4.9 | 92.6 | 0.8 | 5.9 | 0.8 | 1.6 | 5.0 | 14.6 | 7.3 | 9.9 | 11.3 | 15.4 |
| 23 031 | 38860 | 2 | York | 2 566 | 199 005 | 320 | 77.6 | 96.6 | 1.0 | 0.9 | 1.5 | 1.3 | 5.1 | 15.8 | 7.8 | 10.8 | 12.8 | 16.8 |
| 24 000 | ... | X | **MARYLAND** | 25 142 | 5 884 563 | X | 234.1 | 56.1 | 30.3 | 0.8 | 6.6 | 8.4 | 6.3 | 16.8 | 9.6 | 13.4 | 13.4 | 15.5 |
| 24 001 | 19060 | 3 | Allegany | 1 099 | 74 012 | 736 | 67.3 | 89.2 | 9.2 | 0.5 | 1.2 | 1.5 | 4.6 | 13.0 | 13.3 | 12.0 | 12.0 | 14.0 |
| 24 003 | 12580 | 1 | Anne Arundel | 1 075 | 550 488 | 113 | 512.1 | 73.9 | 16.8 | 0.8 | 4.6 | 6.4 | 6.4 | 16.6 | 9.0 | 13.6 | 13.7 | 15.9 |
| 24 005 | 12580 | 1 | Baltimore | 1 550 | 817 455 | 69 | 527.4 | 63.7 | 27.3 | 0.8 | 6.0 | 4.4 | 6.0 | 15.8 | 10.1 | 13.1 | 12.5 | 14.8 |
| 24 009 | 47900 | 1 | Calvert | 552 | 89 628 | 628 | 162.4 | 81.5 | 14.7 | 1.0 | 2.4 | 2.9 | 5.5 | 19.9 | 8.2 | 10.3 | 13.4 | 18.7 |
| 24 011 | ... | 6 | Caroline | 827 | 32 718 | 1 363 | 39.6 | 79.1 | 15.1 | 0.7 | 1.2 | 5.6 | 6.7 | 18.0 | 8.7 | 11.9 | 12.5 | 15.6 |
| 24 013 | 12580 | 1 | Carroll | 1 159 | 167 217 | 375 | 144.3 | 92.0 | 4.0 | 0.5 | 2.1 | 2.8 | 5.1 | 18.7 | 8.7 | 9.5 | 13.3 | 17.9 |
| 24 015 | 37980 | 1 | Cecil | 897 | 101 696 | 575 | 113.4 | 88.5 | 7.2 | 0.8 | 1.8 | 3.6 | 6.2 | 18.4 | 8.7 | 11.5 | 13.5 | 16.4 |
| 24 017 | 47900 | 1 | Charles | 1 186 | 150 592 | 420 | 127.0 | 50.5 | 42.7 | 1.4 | 4.3 | 4.5 | 6.2 | 19.6 | 9.1 | 11.9 | 15.1 | 17.1 |
| 24 019 | 15700 | 6 | Dorchester | 1 401 | 32 551 | 1 372 | 23.2 | 67.2 | 28.5 | 0.8 | 1.4 | 3.8 | 6.2 | 15.4 | 7.8 | 11.2 | 11.4 | 15.4 |
| 24 021 | 47900 | 1 | Frederick | 1 710 | 239 582 | 270 | 140.1 | 79.3 | 9.9 | 0.6 | 4.9 | 7.6 | 6.2 | 18.6 | 8.5 | 11.9 | 14.4 | 16.8 |
| 24 023 | ... | 6 | Garrett | 1 676 | 29 854 | 1 428 | 17.8 | 97.6 | 1.4 | 0.4 | 0.5 | 0.8 | 5.0 | 16.6 | 8.4 | 10.3 | 12.2 | 15.5 |
| 24 025 | 12580 | 1 | Harford | 1 132 | 248 622 | 265 | 219.6 | 80.6 | 13.9 | 0.7 | 3.4 | 3.7 | 5.9 | 18.1 | 8.4 | 11.8 | 13.4 | 16.5 |
| 24 027 | 12580 | 1 | Howard | 649 | 299 430 | 218 | 461.4 | 61.0 | 19.3 | 0.8 | 16.1 | 6.0 | 6.0 | 19.4 | 7.5 | 12.5 | 14.6 | 17.1 |
| 24 029 | ... | 6 | Kent | 718 | 20 191 | 1 832 | 28.1 | 79.3 | 16.0 | 0.5 | 1.2 | 4.5 | 4.8 | 12.6 | 12.2 | 9.5 | 9.7 | 14.1 |
| 24 031 | 47900 | 1 | Montgomery | 1 272 | 1 004 709 | 40 | 789.9 | 50.8 | 18.2 | 0.7 | 15.6 | 17.5 | 6.5 | 17.2 | 7.6 | 13.7 | 14.2 | 15.5 |
| 24 033 | 47900 | 1 | Prince George's | 1 250 | 881 138 | 58 | 704.9 | 16.6 | 64.6 | 0.9 | 4.9 | 15.2 | 6.8 | 16.7 | 11.6 | 14.7 | 13.9 | 14.8 |
| 24 035 | 12580 | 1 | Queen Anne's | 963 | 48 595 | 1 004 | 50.5 | 88.4 | 7.7 | 0.7 | 1.7 | 3.2 | 5.5 | 17.7 | 7.3 | 9.2 | 13.2 | 17.5 |

1. CBSA = Core Based Statistical Area. See Appendix A for explanation. See Appendix B for list of metropolitan areas with component counties. Service of USDA Rural-Urban Continuum Codes. See Appendix A for definition.   2. County type code from the Economic Research Service of USDA Rural-Urban Continuum Codes. See Appendix A for definition.   3. Dry land or land partially or temporarily covered by water.   4. May be of any race.

# Table B. States and Counties — **Population and Households**

| STATE County | 55 to 64 years | 65 to 74 years | 75 years and over | Percent female | 2000 | 2010 | 2000–2010 | 2010–2012 | Births | Deaths | Net migration | Number | Percent change, 2000–2010 | Persons per house-hold | Female family house-holder[1] | One per-son |
|---|---|---|---|---|---|---|---|---|---|---|---|---|---|---|---|---|
| | 16 | 17 | 18 | 19 | 20 | 21 | 22 | 23 | 24 | 25 | 26 | 27 | 28 | 29 | 30 | 31 |
| **LOUISIANA—Cont'd** | | | | | | | | | | | | | | | | |
| Orleans | 12.5 | 6.3 | 4.9 | 51.8 | 484 674 | 343 829 | -29.1 | 7.4 | 10 983 | 6 624 | 20 500 | 142 158 | -24.5 | 2.33 | 20.9 | 35.9 |
| Ouachita | 11.4 | 6.7 | 5.8 | 52.1 | 147 250 | 153 720 | 4.4 | 1.1 | 5 151 | 3 391 | -47 | 58 691 | 6.3 | 2.52 | 20.0 | 27.9 |
| Plaquemines | 11.4 | 6.3 | 4.9 | 49.8 | 26 757 | 23 042 | -13.9 | 3.8 | 668 | 402 | 579 | 8 077 | -10.5 | 2.82 | 14.8 | 20.1 |
| Pointe Coupee | 14.7 | 8.8 | 6.9 | 51.6 | 22 763 | 22 802 | 0.2 | -0.3 | 664 | 541 | -227 | 9 082 | 8.2 | 2.50 | 15.9 | 26.8 |
| Rapides | 12.3 | 7.7 | 6.1 | 51.8 | 126 337 | 131 613 | 4.2 | 0.6 | 4 155 | 2 966 | -353 | 50 401 | 7.0 | 2.52 | 18.4 | 27.2 |
| Red River | 12.6 | 8.3 | 5.8 | 52.0 | 9 622 | 9 091 | -5.5 | -1.2 | 272 | 229 | -141 | 3 472 | 1.7 | 2.57 | 17.7 | 25.6 |
| Richland | 12.8 | 7.9 | 6.4 | 51.7 | 20 981 | 20 725 | -1.2 | 0.9 | 636 | 583 | 134 | 7 551 | 0.8 | 2.61 | 19.2 | 25.1 |
| Sabine | 14.0 | 10.5 | 7.1 | 50.3 | 23 459 | 24 233 | 3.3 | 0.4 | 681 | 532 | -51 | 9 622 | 4.3 | 2.47 | 13.6 | 26.5 |
| St. Bernard | 10.9 | 5.3 | 3.8 | 49.7 | 67 229 | 35 897 | -46.6 | 16.0 | 1 420 | 669 | 4 854 | 13 221 | -47.4 | 2.69 | 19.5 | 23.7 |
| St. Charles | 12.0 | 5.8 | 4.4 | 50.6 | 48 072 | 52 780 | 9.8 | -0.2 | 1 523 | 888 | -832 | 18 557 | 13.0 | 2.81 | 16.3 | 18.8 |
| St. Helena | 14.1 | 8.4 | 6.0 | 50.8 | 10 525 | 11 203 | 6.4 | -1.2 | 276 | 247 | -183 | 4 333 | 11.9 | 2.56 | 19.3 | 28.7 |
| St. James | 13.0 | 7.6 | 5.5 | 51.1 | 21 216 | 22 102 | 4.2 | -1.7 | 686 | 465 | -641 | 7 717 | 10.4 | 2.84 | 20.5 | 20.5 |
| St. John the Baptist | 12.3 | 6.6 | 4.2 | 51.0 | 43 044 | 45 924 | 6.7 | -2.5 | 1 338 | 921 | -1 523 | 15 965 | 11.8 | 2.85 | 20.9 | 20.1 |
| St. Landry | 12.4 | 7.8 | 6.2 | 52.1 | 87 700 | 83 384 | -4.9 | 0.3 | 3 114 | 2 137 | -686 | 31 857 | -1.5 | 2.58 | 19.2 | 26.8 |
| St. Martin | 12.2 | 7.2 | 4.8 | 50.7 | 48 583 | 52 160 | 7.4 | 1.1 | 1 666 | 1 019 | -89 | 19 216 | 12.0 | 2.68 | 17.0 | 23.1 |
| St. Mary | 12.1 | 7.6 | 5.5 | 50.6 | 53 500 | 54 650 | 2.1 | -1.7 | 1 746 | 1 195 | -1 512 | 20 457 | 5.9 | 2.63 | 18.0 | 25.8 |
| St. Tammany | 13.8 | 7.6 | 5.5 | 51.3 | 191 268 | 233 740 | 22.2 | 2.4 | 6 191 | 4 369 | 3 836 | 87 521 | 26.4 | 2.66 | 12.4 | 22.0 |
| Tangipahoa | 12.1 | 6.9 | 4.8 | 51.5 | 100 588 | 121 097 | 20.4 | 1.9 | 4 053 | 2 582 | 886 | 45 135 | 23.5 | 2.60 | 17.4 | 24.9 |
| Tensas | 16.2 | 9.8 | 7.9 | 52.3 | 6 618 | 5 252 | -20.6 | -5.7 | 138 | 125 | -312 | 2 172 | -10.1 | 2.41 | 23.0 | 32.6 |
| Terrebonne | 11.5 | 6.7 | 4.7 | 50.5 | 104 503 | 111 860 | 7.0 | 0.0 | 3 763 | 2 132 | -1 303 | 40 091 | 11.4 | 2.75 | 15.7 | 21.9 |
| Union | 14.4 | 9.7 | 7.2 | 50.9 | 22 803 | 22 721 | -0.4 | -1.3 | 638 | 551 | -385 | 9 144 | 3.2 | 2.44 | 15.3 | 26.7 |
| Vermilion | 11.8 | 7.0 | 6.0 | 51.4 | 53 807 | 57 999 | 7.8 | 1.2 | 1 825 | 1 193 | 107 | 21 889 | 10.4 | 2.63 | 14.5 | 24.1 |
| Vernon | 9.4 | 5.8 | 3.9 | 48.8 | 52 531 | 52 334 | -0.4 | 2.9 | 2 235 | 766 | 39 | 19 165 | 5.0 | 2.61 | 11.5 | 24.6 |
| Washington | 13.8 | 8.5 | 6.3 | 50.5 | 43 926 | 47 168 | 7.4 | -1.1 | 1 270 | 1 327 | -447 | 18 113 | 10.0 | 2.52 | 18.3 | 28.1 |
| Webster | 13.3 | 9.2 | 7.6 | 51.3 | 41 831 | 41 207 | -1.5 | -0.6 | 1 171 | 1 183 | -244 | 16 537 | 0.2 | 2.42 | 17.6 | 28.7 |
| West Baton Rouge | 12.1 | 6.6 | 4.7 | 50.8 | 21 601 | 23 788 | 10.1 | 1.3 | 781 | 419 | -40 | 8 688 | 13.4 | 2.67 | 18.6 | 23.3 |
| West Carroll | 12.6 | 9.5 | 7.6 | 50.0 | 12 314 | 11 604 | -5.8 | -0.8 | 336 | 349 | -71 | 4 452 | -0.1 | 2.51 | 13.2 | 26.2 |
| West Feliciana | 14.5 | 6.6 | 4.1 | 34.5 | 15 111 | 15 625 | 3.4 | -1.4 | 264 | 248 | -240 | 3 971 | 8.9 | 2.60 | 16.0 | 24.4 |
| Winn | 13.3 | 8.4 | 6.2 | 47.5 | 16 894 | 15 313 | -9.4 | -2.0 | 412 | 415 | -310 | 5 469 | -7.8 | 2.48 | 17.4 | 28.0 |
| **MAINE** | 15.1 | 8.8 | 7.5 | 51.1 | 1 274 923 | 1 328 361 | 4.2 | 0.1 | 29 066 | 28 931 | 1 014 | 557 219 | 7.5 | 2.32 | 10.0 | 28.6 |
| Androscoggin | 13.3 | 7.5 | 6.8 | 51.0 | 103 793 | 107 702 | 3.8 | -0.1 | 2 972 | 2 229 | -808 | 44 315 | 5.4 | 2.37 | 12.0 | 28.3 |
| Aroostook | 15.8 | 10.4 | 9.1 | 50.7 | 73 938 | 71 870 | -2.8 | -1.4 | 1 472 | 1 812 | -632 | 30 961 | 2.0 | 2.26 | 9.4 | 30.8 |
| Cumberland | 14.1 | 7.6 | 7.0 | 51.4 | 265 612 | 281 674 | 6.0 | 0.8 | 6 092 | 5 407 | 1 594 | 117 339 | 8.7 | 2.32 | 9.7 | 29.7 |
| Franklin | 15.4 | 9.8 | 7.4 | 50.9 | 29 467 | 30 768 | 4.4 | -0.4 | 608 | 698 | -35 | 13 000 | 10.1 | 2.28 | 9.4 | 28.9 |
| Hancock | 17.6 | 10.6 | 8.3 | 51.1 | 51 791 | 54 418 | 5.1 | 0.3 | 986 | 1 286 | 447 | 24 221 | 10.8 | 2.20 | 8.2 | 30.3 |
| Kennebec | 15.2 | 8.4 | 7.4 | 51.3 | 117 114 | 122 151 | 4.3 | -0.2 | 2 775 | 2 873 | -169 | 51 128 | 7.2 | 2.32 | 10.6 | 28.8 |
| Knox | 17.1 | 10.5 | 9.3 | 50.6 | 39 618 | 39 736 | 0.3 | -0.2 | 843 | 946 | 32 | 17 258 | 3.9 | 2.22 | 9.4 | 31.0 |
| Lincoln | 17.5 | 12.3 | 10.0 | 50.9 | 33 616 | 34 457 | 2.5 | -0.8 | 649 | 889 | -30 | 15 149 | 7.0 | 2.24 | 8.8 | 28.9 |
| Oxford | 15.8 | 9.4 | 7.9 | 50.5 | 54 755 | 57 833 | 5.6 | -0.6 | 1 174 | 1 381 | -133 | 24 300 | 8.9 | 2.35 | 10.4 | 27.1 |
| Penobscot | 13.9 | 7.8 | 7.0 | 50.7 | 144 919 | 153 923 | 6.2 | -0.1 | 3 384 | 3 224 | -324 | 62 966 | 8.4 | 2.33 | 10.3 | 28.0 |
| Piscataquis | 17.8 | 12.0 | 9.1 | 50.4 | 17 235 | 17 535 | 1.7 | -1.4 | 349 | 513 | -67 | 7 825 | 7.5 | 2.21 | 8.5 | 30.5 |
| Sagadahoc | 15.6 | 9.9 | 7.3 | 51.5 | 35 214 | 35 293 | 0.2 | -0.3 | 879 | 796 | -172 | 15 088 | 6.9 | 2.32 | 10.1 | 27.1 |
| Somerset | 15.4 | 9.6 | 7.3 | 50.5 | 50 888 | 52 228 | 2.6 | -0.6 | 1 153 | 1 210 | -250 | 21 927 | 7.0 | 2.35 | 10.3 | 26.9 |
| Waldo | 17.0 | 9.7 | 6.9 | 51.1 | 36 280 | 38 786 | 6.9 | 0.1 | 851 | 841 | 50 | 16 431 | 11.6 | 2.33 | 9.9 | 27.7 |
| Washington | 16.6 | 11.0 | 8.9 | 50.8 | 33 941 | 32 856 | -3.2 | -1.2 | 650 | 925 | -100 | 14 302 | 1.3 | 2.24 | 9.6 | 31.6 |
| York | 15.1 | 8.5 | 7.2 | 51.3 | 186 742 | 197 131 | 5.6 | 1.0 | 4 229 | 3 901 | 1 611 | 81 009 | 8.6 | 2.40 | 9.7 | 26.5 |
| **MARYLAND** | 12.5 | 6.9 | 5.6 | 51.6 | 5 296 486 | 5 773 552 | 9.0 | 1.9 | 162 714 | 98 598 | 47 519 | 2 156 411 | 8.9 | 2.61 | 14.6 | 26.1 |
| Allegany | 12.9 | 9.3 | 8.8 | 48.1 | 74 930 | 75 087 | 0.2 | -1.4 | 1 555 | 1 999 | -599 | 29 177 | -0.5 | 2.30 | 11.0 | 31.6 |
| Anne Arundel | 12.7 | 7.1 | 5.0 | 50.6 | 489 656 | 537 656 | 9.8 | 2.4 | 15 287 | 8 550 | 6 295 | 199 378 | 11.6 | 2.63 | 12.1 | 23.7 |
| Baltimore | 13.0 | 7.2 | 7.5 | 52.7 | 754 292 | 805 029 | 6.7 | 1.5 | 21 857 | 17 180 | 7 980 | 316 715 | 5.6 | 2.48 | 14.5 | 28.3 |
| Calvert | 12.7 | 6.7 | 4.7 | 50.9 | 74 563 | 88 737 | 19.0 | 1.0 | 2 079 | 1 363 | 204 | 30 873 | 21.3 | 2.85 | 11.3 | 18.1 |
| Caroline | 12.8 | 7.7 | 6.0 | 51.4 | 29 772 | 33 066 | 11.1 | -1.1 | 948 | 706 | -604 | 12 158 | 9.6 | 2.68 | 13.6 | 22.7 |
| Carroll | 13.2 | 7.5 | 6.0 | 50.6 | 150 897 | 167 134 | 10.8 | 0.0 | 3 546 | 3 072 | -440 | 59 786 | 13.9 | 2.74 | 8.6 | 20.0 |
| Cecil | 13.2 | 7.1 | 5.0 | 50.3 | 85 951 | 101 108 | 17.6 | 0.6 | 2 575 | 1 896 | -64 | 36 867 | 18.1 | 2.70 | 12.0 | 21.8 |
| Charles | 11.2 | 6.0 | 3.8 | 51.7 | 120 546 | 146 551 | 21.6 | 2.8 | 4 020 | 2 008 | 2 020 | 51 214 | 22.9 | 2.83 | 16.3 | 19.8 |
| Dorchester | 14.6 | 9.9 | 8.0 | 52.1 | 30 674 | 32 618 | 6.3 | -0.2 | 820 | 821 | -63 | 13 522 | 6.4 | 2.37 | 16.0 | 28.4 |
| Frederick | 12.2 | 6.3 | 5.1 | 50.8 | 195 277 | 233 385 | 19.5 | 2.7 | 6 193 | 3 343 | 3 339 | 84 800 | 21.0 | 2.70 | 10.0 | 22.0 |
| Garrett | 14.4 | 10.1 | 7.6 | 50.4 | 29 846 | 30 097 | 0.8 | -0.8 | 633 | 697 | -176 | 12 057 | 5.1 | 2.45 | 9.3 | 25.5 |
| Harford | 13.1 | 7.4 | 5.5 | 51.1 | 218 590 | 244 826 | 12.0 | 1.6 | 6 056 | 4 099 | 1 900 | 90 218 | 13.2 | 2.68 | 11.3 | 21.5 |
| Howard | 12.4 | 6.4 | 4.2 | 51.0 | 247 842 | 287 085 | 15.8 | 4.3 | 7 477 | 3 139 | 7 997 | 104 749 | 16.3 | 2.72 | 10.5 | 21.9 |
| Kent | 14.6 | 12.0 | 10.4 | 52.3 | 19 197 | 20 197 | 5.2 | 0.0 | 424 | 613 | 184 | 8 165 | 6.5 | 2.29 | 10.9 | 29.6 |
| Montgomery | 12.6 | 6.6 | 5.9 | 51.9 | 873 341 | 971 777 | 11.3 | 3.4 | 29 470 | 12 019 | 15 633 | 357 086 | 10.0 | 2.70 | 11.3 | 25.0 |
| Prince George's | 11.6 | 6.0 | 3.8 | 52.0 | 801 515 | 863 420 | 7.7 | 2.1 | 26 575 | 12 288 | 3 526 | 304 042 | 6.1 | 2.78 | 20.4 | 26.1 |
| Queen Anne's | 14.0 | 9.3 | 6.2 | 50.3 | 40 563 | 47 798 | 17.8 | 1.7 | 1 063 | 767 | 499 | 18 016 | 17.6 | 2.63 | 9.2 | 20.6 |

1. No spouse present.

# Table B. States and Counties — Population, Vital Statistics, Medicare, and Crime

| STATE County | Persons in group quarters, 2010 | Daytime population, 2007–2011 Number | Employ-ment/ resi-dence ratio | Births, 2011 Total | Births, 2011 Rate[1] | Deaths, 2011 Number | Deaths, 2011 Rate[1] | Persons under 65 with no health insurance, 2010 Number | Percent | Medicare, 2012 Eligible for Medicare | Enrolled in Medicare Advantage | Enrolled in a Medicare prescription drug plan | Serious crimes known to police,[2] 2011 Total Number | Rate[3] |
|---|---|---|---|---|---|---|---|---|---|---|---|---|---|---|
| | 32 | 33 | 34 | 35 | 36 | 37 | 38 | 39 | 40 | 41 | 42 | 43 | 44 | 45 |
| LOUISIANA—Cont'd | | | | | | | | | | | | | | |
| Orleans | 13 165 | 381 154 | 1.42 | 4 828 | 13.4 | 2 845 | 7.9 | 67 774 | 22.7 | 50 828 | 20 697 | 17 689 | 17 009 | 4 902 |
| Ouachita | 5 534 | 158 840 | 1.09 | 2 346 | 15.1 | 1 494 | 9.6 | 29 802 | 22.9 | 24 783 | 3 804 | 12 805 | 8 154 | 5 375 |
| Plaquemines | 272 | 31 406 | 1.83 | 296 | 12.5 | 176 | 7.4 | 4 208 | 20.7 | 3 116 | 1 622 | 735 | 428 | 1 841 |
| Pointe Coupee | 116 | 19 667 | 0.67 | 304 | 13.4 | 240 | 10.6 | 3 890 | 20.4 | 4 255 | 1 483 | 1 759 | 554 | 3 055 |
| Rapides | 4 501 | 137 766 | 1.12 | 1 921 | 14.5 | 1 326 | 10.0 | 21 790 | 19.7 | 24 836 | 2 865 | 13 012 | 7 297 | 5 620 |
| Red River | 164 | 8 837 | 0.92 | 120 | 13.5 | 122 | 13.7 | 1 699 | 22.5 | 1 551 | 225 | 827 | 174 | 1 897 |
| Richland | 1 039 | 19 937 | 0.90 | 291 | 13.9 | 248 | 11.8 | 3 999 | 23.7 | 3 854 | 415 | 2 275 | 486 | 2 705 |
| Sabine | 440 | 22 500 | 0.80 | 309 | 12.6 | 212 | 8.6 | 4 631 | 23.4 | 5 026 | 595 | 2 679 | 540 | 2 208 |
| St. Bernard | 293 | 30 443 | 0.86 | 569 | 14.4 | 272 | 6.9 | 8 406 | 25.5 | 4 817 | 2 486 | 1 425 | 1 052 | 2 904 |
| St. Charles | 592 | 52 820 | 1.01 | 709 | 13.5 | 401 | 7.6 | 7 030 | 15.0 | 7 177 | 3 529 | 1 607 | 1 788 | 3 357 |
| St. Helena | 121 | 8 827 | 0.44 | 131 | 12.0 | 100 | 9.1 | 2 229 | 23.4 | 2 599 | 571 | 1 423 | 343 | 3 034 |
| St. James | 204 | 21 884 | 0.98 | 322 | 14.8 | 211 | 9.7 | 3 218 | 16.9 | 3 739 | 1 235 | 1 346 | 711 | 3 188 |
| St. John the Baptist | 471 | 43 051 | 0.84 | 621 | 13.7 | 381 | 8.4 | 7 851 | 19.3 | 6 847 | 3 013 | 1 996 | 1 379 | 2 976 |
| St. Landry | 1 105 | 79 482 | 0.85 | 1 410 | 16.9 | 949 | 11.4 | 13 943 | 19.6 | 16 888 | 1 406 | 10 795 | 3 494 | 4 549 |
| St. Martin | 701 | 42 528 | 0.57 | 771 | 14.6 | 446 | 8.4 | 9 594 | 21.1 | 8 619 | 683 | 4 919 | 1 143 | 2 171 |
| St. Mary | 868 | 59 154 | 1.22 | 799 | 14.7 | 509 | 9.4 | 10 772 | 23.0 | 9 683 | 1 568 | 5 199 | 2 198 | 4 724 |
| St. Tammany | 1 275 | 211 849 | 0.81 | 2 756 | 11.6 | 1 912 | 8.1 | 36 714 | 18.1 | 39 395 | 18 261 | 9 659 | 5 295 | 2 245 |
| Tangipahoa | 3 638 | 112 169 | 0.84 | 1 792 | 14.6 | 1 140 | 9.3 | 21 372 | 20.5 | 18 723 | 4 796 | 8 763 | 9 201 | 7 529 |
| Tensas | 16 | 5 418 | 1.06 | 61 | 12.0 | 58 | 11.4 | 1 160 | 26.9 | 1 103 | 59 | 693 | NA | NA |
| Terrebonne | 1 479 | 118 167 | 1.14 | 1 692 | 15.1 | 947 | 8.5 | 20 926 | 21.3 | 17 877 | 1 983 | 9 955 | 4 840 | 4 288 |
| Union | 415 | 19 738 | 0.66 | 274 | 12.1 | 215 | 9.5 | 4 246 | 22.9 | 4 590 | 668 | 2 399 | 242 | 1 055 |
| Vermilion | 536 | 50 235 | 0.69 | 814 | 14.0 | 527 | 9.0 | 10 411 | 20.7 | 9 666 | 572 | 5 710 | 1 668 | 2 850 |
| Vernon | 2 258 | 52 695 | 1.09 | 983 | 18.9 | 344 | 6.6 | 8 649 | 19.0 | 6 574 | 425 | 2 767 | 1 216 | 2 418 |
| Washington | 1 582 | 44 182 | 0.82 | 576 | 12.2 | 589 | 12.5 | 8 392 | 21.7 | 9 600 | 1 989 | 5 174 | 2 354 | 4 945 |
| Webster | 1 231 | 39 276 | 0.88 | 529 | 12.8 | 511 | 12.4 | 7 109 | 21.4 | 8 830 | 1 145 | 4 524 | 663 | 1 605 |
| West Baton Rouge | 556 | 23 270 | 0.97 | 339 | 14.1 | 186 | 7.7 | 3 618 | 17.5 | 3 571 | 1 583 | 1 071 | 833 | 3 470 |
| West Carroll | 434 | 10 614 | 0.74 | 142 | 12.3 | 155 | 13.4 | 2 213 | 24.1 | 2 451 | 157 | 1 582 | 491 | 4 926 |
| West Feliciana | 5 297 | 16 315 | 1.15 | 114 | 7.4 | 111 | 7.2 | 1 506 | 16.8 | 1 731 | 451 | 679 | 250 | 1 585 |
| Winn | 1 760 | 15 109 | 0.95 | 193 | 12.8 | 190 | 12.6 | 2 544 | 22.1 | 2 806 | 277 | 1 730 | NA | NA |
| MAINE | 35 545 | 1 314 595 | 0.98 | 12 868 | 9.7 | 12 688 | 9.6 | 132 154 | 12.2 | 285 119 | 46 779 | 142 938 | 35 445 | 2 669 |
| Androscoggin | 2 760 | 105 431 | 0.95 | 1 331 | 12.4 | 986 | 9.2 | 10 386 | 11.6 | 21 818 | 4 007 | 11 640 | 3 351 | 3 112 |
| Aroostook | 2 005 | 71 902 | 0.99 | 648 | 9.1 | 795 | 11.1 | 8 243 | 14.5 | 18 365 | 1 772 | 11 507 | 1 305 | 1 816 |
| Cumberland | 9 190 | 307 509 | 1.18 | 2 720 | 9.6 | 2 375 | 8.4 | 25 849 | 11.0 | 52 585 | 10 351 | 23 426 | 7 985 | 2 835 |
| Franklin | 1 110 | 30 150 | 0.96 | 271 | 8.8 | 299 | 9.7 | 3 159 | 13.0 | 6 704 | 1 173 | 3 411 | 874 | 2 841 |
| Hancock | 1 176 | 54 252 | 0.99 | 442 | 8.1 | 576 | 10.6 | 6 661 | 15.4 | 12 556 | 1 750 | 6 173 | 1 022 | 1 878 |
| Kennebec | 3 636 | 124 372 | 1.04 | 1 212 | 9.9 | 1 247 | 10.2 | 10 794 | 10.8 | 27 913 | 5 953 | 13 314 | 4 035 | 3 304 |
| Knox | 1 361 | 41 503 | 1.08 | 369 | 9.3 | 403 | 10.1 | 4 401 | 14.3 | 9 822 | 1 392 | 4 911 | 888 | 2 253 |
| Lincoln | 498 | 31 182 | 0.79 | 290 | 8.5 | 389 | 11.4 | 3 618 | 13.6 | 9 149 | 1 660 | 4 009 | 591 | 1 715 |
| Oxford | 849 | 52 158 | 0.77 | 519 | 9.0 | 634 | 11.0 | 6 368 | 13.5 | 13 209 | 1 816 | 7 473 | 1 474 | 2 549 |
| Penobscot | 7 318 | 156 075 | 1.04 | 1 506 | 9.8 | 1 407 | 9.1 | 15 317 | 12.2 | 31 649 | 5 241 | 16 324 | 4 439 | 2 884 |
| Piscataquis | 220 | 17 027 | 0.93 | 151 | 8.7 | 216 | 12.4 | 1 806 | 13.1 | 4 778 | 537 | 2 664 | 449 | 2 561 |
| Sagadahoc | 265 | 33 820 | 0.90 | 379 | 10.8 | 357 | 10.1 | 3 024 | 10.3 | 7 579 | 1 536 | 3 030 | 809 | 2 293 |
| Somerset | 715 | 49 507 | 0.88 | 503 | 9.7 | 503 | 9.7 | 5 571 | 13.0 | 10 980 | 1 426 | 6 664 | 1 578 | 3 022 |
| Waldo | 501 | 34 158 | 0.74 | 379 | 9.8 | 391 | 10.1 | 4 603 | 14.5 | 8 655 | 1 514 | 4 457 | 716 | 1 846 |
| Washington | 836 | 32 774 | 0.98 | 293 | 9.0 | 399 | 12.2 | 4 204 | 16.5 | 8 547 | 765 | 5 021 | 687 | 2 091 |
| York | 3 105 | 172 775 | 0.75 | 1 855 | 9.4 | 1 711 | 8.6 | 18 150 | 11.0 | 40 810 | 5 886 | 18 914 | 5 156 | 2 616 |
| MARYLAND | 138 375 | 5 458 828 | 0.90 | 72 995 | 12.5 | 43 606 | 7.5 | 630 139 | 12.7 | 853 716 | 73 478 | 336 656 | 195 496 | 3 354 |
| Allegany | 7 924 | 78 583 | 1.12 | 730 | 9.8 | 877 | 11.7 | 6 987 | 12.7 | 16 190 | 559 | 8 452 | 2 768 | 3 652 |
| Anne Arundel | 14 133 | 516 782 | 0.94 | 6 874 | 12.6 | 3 746 | 6.9 | 46 290 | 10.1 | 77 919 | 4 908 | 25 224 | 17 262 | 3 180 |
| Baltimore | 20 781 | 753 891 | 0.88 | 9 740 | 12.0 | 7 751 | 9.6 | 81 610 | 12.1 | 138 856 | 13 930 | 64 064 | 28 394 | 3 494 |
| Calvert | 650 | 66 975 | 0.53 | 905 | 10.1 | 605 | 6.8 | 6 787 | 8.7 | 12 237 | 472 | 3 912 | 2 126 | 2 373 |
| Caroline | 442 | 26 969 | 0.62 | 436 | 13.2 | 311 | 9.4 | 4 601 | 16.1 | 5 789 | 135 | 3 045 | 1 217 | 3 646 |
| Carroll | 3 319 | 137 748 | 0.65 | 1 608 | 9.6 | 1 317 | 7.9 | 12 384 | 8.7 | 27 154 | 1 200 | 12 265 | 2 723 | 1 614 |
| Cecil | 1 551 | 83 683 | 0.65 | 1 165 | 11.5 | 846 | 8.3 | 9 463 | 10.7 | 15 693 | 748 | 6 820 | 4 020 | 3 939 |
| Charles | 1 405 | 111 742 | 0.55 | 1 747 | 11.7 | 874 | 5.9 | 12 850 | 9.8 | 17 683 | 928 | 5 209 | 4 366 | 2 951 |
| Dorchester | 506 | 30 804 | 0.89 | 389 | 11.9 | 379 | 11.6 | 3 665 | 13.6 | 7 118 | 222 | 3 783 | 1 286 | 3 906 |
| Frederick | 4 182 | 215 973 | 0.87 | 2 757 | 11.6 | 1 471 | 6.2 | 19 415 | 9.5 | 32 482 | 1 582 | 12 535 | 4 573 | 1 941 |
| Garrett | 515 | 29 974 | 0.99 | 279 | 9.3 | 307 | 10.2 | 3 891 | 15.7 | 6 265 | 323 | 3 609 | 621 | 2 044 |
| Harford | 2 743 | 210 589 | 0.73 | 2 700 | 11.0 | 1 789 | 7.3 | 19 539 | 9.2 | 38 527 | 2 965 | 14 822 | 4 594 | 1 859 |
| Howard | 2 322 | 280 562 | 0.98 | 3 302 | 11.3 | 1 343 | 4.6 | 21 874 | 8.6 | 35 212 | 2 129 | 12 456 | 7 185 | 2 479 |
| Kent | 1 526 | 20 322 | 1.02 | 192 | 9.5 | 267 | 13.2 | 2 226 | 15.1 | 4 986 | 91 | 2 929 | 457 | 2 242 |
| Montgomery | 8 900 | 926 442 | 0.93 | 13 226 | 13.4 | 5 221 | 5.3 | 111 607 | 13.2 | 130 958 | 11 700 | 43 641 | 20 216 | 2 061 |
| Prince George's | 19 328 | 741 410 | 0.74 | 11 967 | 13.7 | 5 391 | 6.2 | 129 682 | 17.0 | 101 706 | 13 060 | 26 481 | 38 109 | 4 372 |
| Queen Anne's | 426 | 39 283 | 0.65 | 459 | 9.5 | 329 | 6.8 | 4 320 | 10.8 | 8 589 | 194 | 3 509 | 1 099 | 2 278 |

1. Per 1,000 estimated resident population.  2. Data for serious crimes have not been adjusted for underreporting; this may affect comparability between geographic areas and over time.  3. Per 100,000 population estimated by the FBI.

# Table B. States and Counties — Crime, Education, Money Income, and Poverty

| STATE County | Violent (46) | Property (47) | Enrollment Total (48) | Percent private (49) | High school graduate or less (50) | Bachelor's degree or more (51) | Total current expenditures (mil dol) (52) | Current expenditures per student (dollars) (53) | Per capita income (dollars) (54) | Median income Dollars (55) | Percent change, 2000 to 2007–2011 (constant 2011 dollars) (56) | Percent with income of $200,000 or more (57) | Median household income (dollars) (58) | All persons (59) | Children under 18 years (60) | Children 5 to 17 years in families (61) |
|---|---|---|---|---|---|---|---|---|---|---|---|---|---|---|---|---|
| **LOUISIANA—Cont'd** | | | | | | | | | | | | | | | | |
| Orleans | 793 | 4 109 | 85 226 | 34.3 | 41.9 | 32.3 | 478.9 | 12 923 | 25 668 | 37 325 | 1.9 | 4.0 | 34 851 | 28.7 | 41.5 | 40.7 |
| Ouachita | 666 | 4 709 | 42 551 | 9.3 | 49.5 | 23.2 | 283.3 | 10 003 | 22 470 | 39 724 | -8.2 | 2.5 | 35 770 | 26.2 | 41.4 | 36.0 |
| Plaquemines | 176 | 1 664 | 6 618 | 20.2 | 52.8 | 16.8 | 69.4 | 14 836 | 25 015 | 55 301 | 7.3 | 2.3 | 52 259 | 13.0 | 15.9 | 14.4 |
| Pointe Coupee | 673 | 2 382 | 5 432 | 28.8 | 62.1 | 15.6 | 31.1 | 11 643 | 22 693 | 43 030 | 4.1 | 2.1 | 40 052 | 21.9 | 32.8 | 32.0 |
| Rapides | 783 | 4 837 | 33 097 | 12.8 | 53.2 | 18.5 | 213.9 | 8 986 | 21 959 | 40 470 | 0.4 | 1.6 | 36 624 | 23.4 | 31.9 | 30.5 |
| Red River | 741 | 1 155 | 2 388 | 18.4 | 64.7 | 13.0 | 25.9 | 17 011 | 20 300 | 37 159 | 18.9 | 2.3 | 32 650 | 26.8 | 36.5 | 33.7 |
| Richland | 250 | 2 454 | 5 263 | 11.1 | 66.2 | 12.2 | 41.0 | 10 240 | 18 066 | 38 469 | 20.4 | 1.7 | 32 148 | 24.2 | 37.4 | 35.9 |
| Sabine | 196 | 2 012 | 5 609 | 7.2 | 63.9 | 11.9 | 43.5 | 10 100 | 21 643 | 36 959 | 2.7 | 2.2 | 37 875 | 19.1 | 26.4 | 25.5 |
| St. Bernard | 207 | 2 697 | 7 891 | 17.3 | 62.8 | 10.2 | 65.3 | 12 394 | 20 003 | 40 450 | -16.6 | 0.9 | 38 068 | 19.6 | 29.3 | 29.3 |
| St. Charles | 362 | 2 995 | 15 095 | 18.6 | 51.7 | 19.5 | 125.8 | 13 044 | 26 400 | 60 207 | -1.2 | 3.1 | 54 860 | 12.7 | 18.4 | 16.8 |
| St. Helena | 513 | 2 521 | 2 899 | 12.8 | 65.5 | 9.9 | 13.2 | 10 665 | 17 885 | 29 632 | -12.1 | 1.6 | 33 721 | 25.0 | 38.8 | 37.8 |
| St. James | 628 | 2 560 | 5 749 | 15.2 | 66.4 | 11.3 | 50.2 | 12 813 | 23 332 | 52 887 | 11.0 | 2.1 | 43 701 | 20.7 | 28.4 | 27.3 |
| St. John the Baptist | 244 | 2 732 | 13 099 | 28.1 | 54.9 | 15.6 | 82.9 | 13 254 | 21 373 | 49 671 | -6.8 | 1.1 | 50 483 | 17.1 | 25.2 | 23.4 |
| St. Landry | 759 | 3 790 | 20 677 | 17.5 | 67.9 | 12.6 | 144.0 | 9 517 | 18 789 | 34 350 | 11.3 | 2.0 | 33 750 | 25.7 | 35.8 | 34.0 |
| St. Martin | 369 | 1 803 | 13 364 | 17.6 | 68.3 | 12.1 | 76.4 | 9 085 | 21 116 | 40 358 | -2.6 | 1.7 | 38 826 | 21.0 | 32.8 | 30.8 |
| St. Mary | 617 | 4 108 | 12 793 | 13.4 | 68.5 | 9.9 | 101.0 | 10 191 | 20 411 | 40 171 | 6.0 | 1.4 | 38 813 | 20.9 | 27.3 | 25.0 |
| St. Tammany | 206 | 2 039 | 61 923 | 24.4 | 39.4 | 29.8 | 407.2 | 11 305 | 30 133 | 61 442 | -5.0 | 5.1 | 57 694 | 11.8 | 16.2 | 14.3 |
| Tangipahoa | 1 073 | 6 456 | 33 183 | 14.1 | 54.7 | 19.8 | 171.6 | 8 858 | 20 750 | 40 214 | 1.3 | 1.8 | 38 420 | 22.9 | 34.5 | 34.8 |
| Tensas | NA | NA | 1 209 | 15.6 | 66.9 | 11.8 | 10.0 | 14 021 | 16 552 | 28 090 | 5.1 | 0.9 | 26 903 | 33.5 | 48.5 | 43.9 |
| Terrebonne | 449 | 3 838 | 28 463 | 17.3 | 66.2 | 13.3 | 175.1 | 9 227 | 23 553 | 48 166 | 1.2 | 2.4 | 45 054 | 19.3 | 27.7 | 25.7 |
| Union | 179 | 877 | 4 855 | 13.1 | 64.1 | 12.7 | 31.8 | 11 210 | 20 273 | 37 426 | -4.6 | 1.5 | 34 958 | 24.2 | 37.8 | 37.6 |
| Vermilion | 495 | 2 354 | 13 585 | 13.3 | 69.2 | 12.1 | 85.1 | 9 361 | 22 193 | 43 349 | 8.8 | 2.0 | 39 091 | 19.2 | 26.2 | 22.3 |
| Vernon | 322 | 2 096 | 12 815 | 7.8 | 52.9 | 17.2 | 91.2 | 9 128 | 21 081 | 45 292 | 7.5 | 1.0 | 45 726 | 14.9 | 20.7 | 21.0 |
| Washington | 634 | 4 311 | 11 507 | 15.6 | 65.6 | 11.4 | 81.4 | 10 728 | 17 537 | 30 554 | -6.7 | 1.3 | 29 443 | 31.3 | 39.8 | 37.8 |
| Webster | 225 | 1 380 | 9 021 | 9.8 | 63.2 | 13.7 | 68.6 | 9 606 | 20 132 | 36 225 | -5.6 | 1.0 | 35 908 | 22.6 | 32.1 | 30.2 |
| West Baton Rouge | 308 | 3 162 | 6 238 | 20.4 | 58.7 | 17.0 | 43.3 | 11 319 | 23 404 | 49 929 | -0.4 | 1.6 | 46 155 | 15.6 | 23.0 | 21.7 |
| West Carroll | 1 104 | 3 823 | 2 595 | 3.5 | 72.1 | 7.8 | 20.0 | 8 926 | 17 292 | 30 446 | -8.5 | 1.4 | 27 781 | 24.1 | 34.0 | 31.3 |
| West Feliciana | 279 | 1 306 | 3 102 | 8.2 | 64.4 | 15.8 | 26.5 | 11 688 | 19 031 | 50 685 | -5.4 | 2.7 | 49 479 | 22.6 | 20.0 | 17.6 |
| Winn | NA | NA | 3 103 | 7.8 | 66.6 | 12.2 | 25.1 | 9 553 | 15 662 | 30 938 | -10.0 | 0.4 | 33 875 | 25.7 | 33.3 | 30.2 |
| **MAINE** | 123 | 2 545 | 308 811 | 17.0 | 44.2 | 27.1 | 2 319.9 | 12 346 | 26 195 | 47 898 | -4.7 | 2.4 | 46 160 | 14.2 | 19.3 | 16.9 |
| Androscoggin | 156 | 2 956 | 26 169 | 18.2 | 52.3 | 18.6 | 180.5 | 11 411 | 23 663 | 45 699 | -5.4 | 1.4 | 43 899 | 16.1 | 24.3 | 21.2 |
| Aroostook | 82 | 1 734 | 16 197 | 9.1 | 54.9 | 16.4 | 131.1 | 12 713 | 20 659 | 37 138 | -4.6 | 1.1 | 35 572 | 18.3 | 26.7 | 23.5 |
| Cumberland | 138 | 2 697 | 69 866 | 20.6 | 32.3 | 39.9 | 482.7 | 12 813 | 32 277 | 57 267 | -3.7 | 4.7 | 55 459 | 12.1 | 15.1 | 13.2 |
| Franklin | 182 | 2 659 | 7 358 | 9.7 | 48.1 | 23.6 | 53.5 | 13 832 | 21 595 | 40 502 | -4.6 | 1.5 | 39 405 | 17.4 | 24.4 | 20.8 |
| Hancock | 68 | 1 810 | 11 116 | 15.3 | 41.4 | 31.4 | 94.7 | 13 996 | 27 227 | 47 421 | -1.9 | 2.0 | 44 599 | 13.8 | 19.3 | 16.1 |
| Kennebec | 162 | 3 142 | 28 132 | 19.6 | 45.6 | 24.4 | 196.9 | 11 522 | 25 023 | 46 904 | -4.8 | 1.7 | 44 441 | 12.8 | 18.2 | 16.2 |
| Knox | 81 | 2 154 | 7 594 | 13.1 | 46.2 | 28.4 | 85.4 | 13 832 | 26 504 | 46 845 | -5.7 | 2.5 | 46 366 | 13.0 | 20.3 | 17.9 |
| Lincoln | 96 | 1 620 | 6 066 | 18.3 | 39.9 | 31.3 | 52.4 | 12 480 | 28 741 | 48 862 | -6.5 | 3.3 | 45 674 | 12.1 | 19.5 | 17.3 |
| Oxford | 111 | 2 438 | 12 849 | 16.3 | 55.3 | 18.3 | 111.9 | 11 802 | 21 735 | 40 889 | -9.4 | 1.2 | 37 915 | 16.5 | 24.2 | 21.9 |
| Penobscot | 80 | 2 804 | 41 302 | 15.5 | 45.9 | 23.4 | 259.8 | 11 527 | 23 366 | 43 601 | -5.8 | 1.7 | 41 199 | 17.2 | 19.1 | 16.9 |
| Piscataquis | 240 | 2 321 | 3 281 | 20.1 | 55.3 | 16.9 | 28.7 | 11 099 | 20 871 | 35 123 | -7.9 | 1.0 | 36 017 | 19.5 | 29.6 | 25.6 |
| Sagadahoc | 17 | 2 276 | 7 618 | 12.1 | 41.5 | 31.1 | 65.5 | 13 387 | 28 370 | 56 865 | 0.5 | 1.5 | 52 187 | 11.7 | 17.6 | 15.1 |
| Somerset | 98 | 2 924 | 11 225 | 10.3 | 55.7 | 15.4 | 102.9 | 12 264 | 21 105 | 37 875 | -8.7 | 1.2 | 37 339 | 18.6 | 27.0 | 22.4 |
| Waldo | 75 | 1 771 | 8 322 | 15.5 | 48.4 | 24.6 | 55.3 | 13 267 | 22 706 | 41 728 | -9.1 | 1.1 | 41 988 | 16.0 | 24.4 | 19.2 |
| Washington | 201 | 1 890 | 6 848 | 14.5 | 52.8 | 19.2 | 65.8 | 17 927 | 19 527 | 35 272 | 1.0 | 0.5 | 33 637 | 21.7 | 31.2 | 28.3 |
| York | 141 | 2 475 | 44 868 | 18.9 | 42.0 | 28.0 | 352.8 | 11 653 | 28 321 | 56 552 | -4.0 | 2.4 | 55 725 | 10.2 | 13.6 | 12.0 |
| **MARYLAND** | 494 | 2 860 | 1 559 713 | 21.0 | 38.1 | 36.1 | 11 653.6 | 13 736 | 35 751 | 72 419 | 1.5 | 8.1 | 70 075 | 10.2 | 13.9 | 12.7 |
| Allegany | 331 | 3 321 | 17 266 | 11.5 | 56.5 | 15.9 | 130.6 | 14 270 | 21 357 | 39 408 | -5.3 | 1.3 | 38 504 | 19.1 | 25.1 | 23.1 |
| Anne Arundel | 512 | 2 669 | 138 836 | 22.4 | 35.5 | 36.3 | 951.7 | 12 727 | 39 857 | 85 690 | 2.7 | 9.9 | 82 980 | 6.5 | 9.2 | 8.3 |
| Baltimore | 528 | 2 966 | 215 357 | 23.3 | 38.0 | 35.2 | 1 370.1 | 13 260 | 34 304 | 65 411 | -4.4 | 5.9 | 62 309 | 9.6 | 12.5 | 11.6 |
| Calvert | 162 | 2 211 | 25 512 | 12.4 | 41.7 | 29.2 | 217.8 | 12 808 | 37 321 | 92 981 | 4.4 | 8.6 | 88 406 | 6.1 | 8.8 | 7.7 |
| Caroline | 336 | 3 310 | 8 158 | 14.5 | 57.8 | 16.2 | 64.2 | 11 569 | 25 652 | 61 021 | 16.4 | 2.0 | 50 809 | 13.1 | 20.8 | 20.3 |
| Carroll | 152 | 1 462 | 45 537 | 21.1 | 41.2 | 31.5 | 346.6 | 12 502 | 35 098 | 83 325 | 2.8 | 6.8 | 82 553 | 5.5 | 7.3 | 6.1 |
| Cecil | 567 | 3 371 | 25 461 | 18.8 | 50.4 | 21.0 | 194.0 | 11 973 | 29 079 | 66 903 | -1.9 | 3.5 | 61 191 | 9.7 | 15.0 | 13.4 |
| Charles | 397 | 2 554 | 41 456 | 15.4 | 40.0 | 26.3 | 340.9 | 12 731 | 36 519 | 92 135 | 9.7 | 7.5 | 88 575 | 7.7 | 10.7 | 9.6 |
| Dorchester | 431 | 3 474 | 7 042 | 10.2 | 55.4 | 18.0 | 58.8 | 12 697 | 26 208 | 46 683 | 1.5 | 2.4 | 41 936 | 17.5 | 29.9 | 28.7 |
| Frederick | 252 | 1 689 | 63 117 | 19.6 | 35.4 | 36.6 | 489.4 | 12 186 | 36 343 | 82 668 | 1.6 | 7.2 | 77 872 | 6.6 | 8.8 | 7.8 |
| Garrett | 230 | 1 814 | 6 495 | 10.9 | 58.4 | 17.3 | 59.2 | 13 744 | 24 779 | 45 280 | 4.0 | 2.0 | 41 829 | 12.0 | 21.1 | 19.7 |
| Harford | 260 | 1 599 | 65 014 | 20.1 | 38.1 | 30.9 | 479.1 | 12 401 | 34 659 | 79 953 | 3.5 | 6.2 | 77 095 | 8.3 | 12.3 | 10.4 |
| Howard | 209 | 2 270 | 82 965 | 19.6 | 20.2 | 58.7 | 744.6 | 14 704 | 46 594 | 105 692 | 5.5 | 16.9 | 99 040 | 6.0 | 7.5 | 6.6 |
| Kent | 329 | 1 913 | 4 827 | 41.5 | 47.5 | 29.6 | 32.9 | 15 057 | 31 691 | 53 480 | -0.7 | 5.3 | 49 795 | 13.9 | 22.0 | 20.0 |
| Montgomery | 172 | 1 889 | 262 169 | 25.0 | 23.2 | 56.8 | 2 208.3 | 15 582 | 48 357 | 95 660 | -1.0 | 16.3 | 92 288 | 6.7 | 8.8 | 7.9 |
| Prince George's | 593 | 3 779 | 250 319 | 19.5 | 41.9 | 29.7 | 1 781.0 | 14 020 | 32 117 | 73 447 | -1.6 | 5.8 | 70 114 | 9.9 | 12.4 | 11.3 |
| Queen Anne's | 309 | 1 969 | 11 320 | 16.2 | 40.9 | 29.9 | 92.3 | 11 844 | 37 366 | 84 483 | 9.7 | 8.0 | 75 158 | 8.7 | 11.8 | 10.3 |

1. Data for serious crimes have not been adjusted for underreporting; this may affect comparability between geographic areas and over time. 2. Per 100,000 population estimated by the FBI. 3. All persons 3 years old and over enrolled in nursery school through college. 4. Persons 25 years old and over. 5. Elementary and secondary education expenditures. 6. Based on population estimated by the American Community Survey, 2007–2011.

# Table B. States and Counties — Personal Income

| STATE County | Total (mil dol) | Percent change, 2010–2011 | Per capita¹ Dollars | Per capita¹ Rank | Wages and salaries² (mil dol) | Proprietors' income (mil dol) | Dividends, interest, and rent (mil dol) | Transfer payments (mil dol) Total | Government payments to individuals Total | Social Security | Medical payments | Income maintenance | Unemployment insurance |
|---|---|---|---|---|---|---|---|---|---|---|---|---|---|
| | 62 | 63 | 64 | 65 | 66 | 67 | 68 | 69 | 70 | 71 | 72 | 73 | 74 |
| **LOUISIANA—Cont'd** | | | | | | | | | | | | | |
| Orleans | 15 347 | 4.7 | 42 542 | 537 | 12 240 | 2 049 | 2 998 | 2 770 | 2 664 | 622 | 1 214 | 545 | 57 |
| Ouachita | 5 307 | 3.9 | 34 256 | 1 478 | 3 290 | 558 | 801 | 1 253 | 1 218 | 333 | 543 | 221 | 24 |
| Plaquemines | 943 | 2.2 | 39 919 | 755 | 1 191 | 155 | 141 | 154 | 145 | 46 | 72 | 17 | 3 |
| Pointe Coupee | 832 | 4.4 | 36 650 | 1 118 | 289 | 92 | 125 | 177 | 172 | 53 | 80 | 27 | 4 |
| Rapides | 5 113 | 3.8 | 38 624 | 893 | 2 962 | 545 | 755 | 1 288 | 1 259 | 300 | 688 | 164 | 19 |
| Red River | 267 | 4.5 | 30 084 | 2 274 | 142 | 36 | 31 | 73 | 71 | 19 | 33 | 13 | 1 |
| Richland | 649 | 4.8 | 31 005 | 2 101 | 266 | 101 | 66 | 197 | 193 | 47 | 103 | 31 | 4 |
| Sabine | 700 | 5.9 | 28 547 | 2 534 | 247 | 67 | 98 | 203 | 194 | 69 | 87 | 21 | 3 |
| St. Bernard | 1 383 | 3.7 | 34 958 | 1 381 | 723 | 74 | 150 | 262 | 248 | 68 | 116 | 42 | 6 |
| St. Charles | 1 969 | 2.1 | 37 491 | 1 026 | 1 943 | 97 | 236 | 333 | 320 | 109 | 142 | 45 | 7 |
| St. Helena | 382 | 3.4 | 34 856 | 1 394 | 72 | 41 | 35 | 104 | 102 | 32 | 37 | 24 | 2 |
| St. James | 703 | 1.5 | 32 266 | 1 831 | 640 | 46 | 84 | 177 | 172 | 55 | 80 | 26 | 5 |
| St. John the Baptist | 1 653 | 2.1 | 36 548 | 1 132 | 1 039 | 131 | 156 | 360 | 347 | 102 | 153 | 65 | 8 |
| St. Landry | 2 914 | 4.9 | 34 881 | 1 390 | 1 153 | 160 | 379 | 801 | 782 | 209 | 384 | 135 | 13 |
| St. Martin | 1 693 | 5.4 | 31 989 | 1 893 | 571 | 77 | 188 | 376 | 363 | 115 | 161 | 62 | 7 |
| St. Mary | 2 031 | 4.1 | 37 462 | 1 028 | 1 597 | 128 | 367 | 449 | 434 | 140 | 198 | 72 | 9 |
| St. Tammany | 11 249 | 4.6 | 47 508 | 282 | 4 197 | 1 057 | 1 808 | 1 625 | 1 562 | 585 | 708 | 142 | 27 |
| Tangipahoa | 3 889 | 4.4 | 31 732 | 1 950 | 2 093 | 224 | 422 | 1 066 | 1 037 | 244 | 539 | 168 | 21 |
| Tensas | 196 | 13.3 | 38 622 | 895 | 67 | 39 | 38 | 50 | 49 | 12 | 24 | 10 | 1 |
| Terrebonne | 4 450 | 3.5 | 39 764 | 772 | 3 229 | 185 | 628 | 811 | 778 | 257 | 364 | 111 | 12 |
| Union | 706 | 3.2 | 31 051 | 2 087 | 201 | 52 | 84 | 196 | 191 | 63 | 88 | 27 | 3 |
| Vermilion | 1 806 | 4.1 | 30 998 | 2 104 | 754 | 120 | 286 | 404 | 389 | 127 | 182 | 53 | 7 |
| Vernon | 2 287 | 8.8 | 43 887 | 447 | 1 906 | 64 | 200 | 334 | 323 | 81 | 147 | 45 | 9 |
| Washington | 1 298 | 2.4 | 27 527 | 2 681 | 487 | 63 | 156 | 491 | 480 | 127 | 250 | 72 | 7 |
| Webster | 1 416 | 3.3 | 34 292 | 1 471 | 645 | 101 | 190 | 373 | 364 | 116 | 166 | 52 | 7 |
| West Baton Rouge | 896 | 4.9 | 37 160 | 1 064 | 689 | 86 | 91 | 170 | 164 | 48 | 79 | 25 | 4 |
| West Carroll | 275 | 1.1 | 23 753 | 3 036 | 98 | 20 | 31 | 110 | 107 | 29 | 56 | 15 | 3 |
| West Feliciana | 425 | 3.7 | 27 474 | 2 690 | 359 | 30 | 60 | 79 | 75 | 22 | 38 | 9 | 2 |
| Winn | 452 | 2.4 | 30 005 | 2 290 | 223 | 49 | 51 | 134 | 131 | 37 | 64 | 18 | 2 |
| **MAINE** | 50 869 | 4.6 | 38 299 | X | 30 155 | 4 021 | 7 646 | 11 701 | 11 408 | 3 742 | 5 262 | 1 224 | 363 |
| Androscoggin | 3 887 | 3.9 | 36 192 | 1 189 | 2 328 | 259 | 417 | 1 031 | 1 007 | 285 | 491 | 137 | 31 |
| Aroostook | 2 290 | 3.4 | 32 038 | 1 877 | 1 272 | 121 | 273 | 792 | 776 | 226 | 385 | 80 | 24 |
| Cumberland | 13 277 | 5.8 | 47 015 | 298 | 10 118 | 1 098 | 2 190 | 2 182 | 2 120 | 718 | 992 | 199 | 65 |
| Franklin | 946 | 5.0 | 30 757 | 2 146 | 522 | 84 | 138 | 275 | 268 | 89 | 120 | 31 | 9 |
| Hancock | 2 104 | 4.6 | 38 542 | 904 | 1 036 | 220 | 496 | 460 | 448 | 167 | 197 | 39 | 18 |
| Kennebec | 4 506 | 4.2 | 36 958 | 1 081 | 2 969 | 317 | 554 | 1 131 | 1 104 | 349 | 487 | 126 | 31 |
| Knox | 1 540 | 4.9 | 38 777 | 877 | 768 | 193 | 347 | 356 | 348 | 130 | 156 | 35 | 10 |
| Lincoln | 1 387 | 4.5 | 40 534 | 702 | 458 | 150 | 345 | 309 | 301 | 124 | 124 | 27 | 9 |
| Oxford | 1 789 | 3.6 | 30 999 | 2 102 | 747 | 135 | 244 | 551 | 538 | 175 | 250 | 66 | 19 |
| Penobscot | 5 220 | 4.1 | 33 940 | 1 522 | 3 380 | 385 | 632 | 1 375 | 1 341 | 408 | 613 | 156 | 44 |
| Piscataquis | 561 | 4.2 | 32 189 | 1 844 | 238 | 58 | 81 | 186 | 182 | 59 | 81 | 19 | 5 |
| Sagadahoc | 1 445 | 4.1 | 41 044 | 655 | 929 | 76 | 241 | 281 | 273 | 103 | 115 | 26 | 9 |
| Somerset | 1 641 | 4.6 | 31 538 | 1 993 | 824 | 158 | 185 | 503 | 492 | 140 | 240 | 64 | 18 |
| Waldo | 1 256 | 4.6 | 32 416 | 1 799 | 473 | 113 | 197 | 339 | 330 | 111 | 147 | 40 | 11 |
| Washington | 1 068 | 5.2 | 32 738 | 1 752 | 464 | 105 | 145 | 394 | 387 | 107 | 201 | 41 | 11 |
| York | 7 953 | 4.2 | 40 124 | 731 | 3 628 | 549 | 1 160 | 1 537 | 1 494 | 552 | 662 | 137 | 52 |
| **MARYLAND** | 295 236 | 5.0 | 50 656 | X | 182 430 | 20 090 | 46 603 | 39 464 | 38 182 | 11 885 | 17 572 | 4 253 | 1 702 |
| Allegany | 2 454 | 4.3 | 32 855 | 1 731 | 1 490 | 114 | 397 | 807 | 791 | 220 | 394 | 74 | 25 |
| Anne Arundel | 30 634 | 5.2 | 56 270 | 101 | 22 072 | 2 131 | 4 643 | 3 271 | 3 154 | 1 139 | 1 348 | 243 | 150 |
| Baltimore | 41 247 | 4.9 | 50 926 | 188 | 24 430 | 2 735 | 7 301 | 6 032 | 5 853 | 2 091 | 2 693 | 518 | 259 |
| Calvert | 4 238 | 4.4 | 47 483 | 283 | 1 261 | 150 | 628 | 502 | 482 | 177 | 207 | 39 | 22 |
| Caroline | 1 083 | 4.8 | 32 819 | 1 737 | 401 | 90 | 163 | 277 | 270 | 84 | 133 | 31 | 12 |
| Carroll | 7 613 | 4.1 | 45 507 | 367 | 2 857 | 445 | 1 175 | 1 068 | 1 031 | 407 | 461 | 58 | 46 |
| Cecil | 4 036 | 5.2 | 39 689 | 780 | 1 644 | 154 | 511 | 719 | 696 | 236 | 312 | 70 | 36 |
| Charles | 6 678 | 5.2 | 44 778 | 400 | 2 374 | 237 | 813 | 824 | 791 | 233 | 342 | 85 | 38 |
| Dorchester | 1 135 | 4.1 | 34 771 | 1 409 | 536 | 73 | 219 | 332 | 325 | 101 | 153 | 45 | 14 |
| Frederick | 11 035 | 4.7 | 46 610 | 316 | 6 074 | 534 | 1 723 | 1 238 | 1 186 | 464 | 471 | 95 | 61 |
| Garrett | 1 156 | 5.6 | 38 463 | 913 | 500 | 193 | 197 | 276 | 269 | 87 | 125 | 27 | 10 |
| Harford | 12 159 | 5.6 | 49 329 | 224 | 5 906 | 481 | 1 645 | 1 583 | 1 529 | 563 | 644 | 127 | 78 |
| Howard | 19 435 | 6.5 | 66 300 | 32 | 11 852 | 1 129 | 2 721 | 1 342 | 1 278 | 494 | 499 | 94 | 67 |
| Kent | 899 | 4.5 | 44 489 | 421 | 388 | 76 | 283 | 194 | 189 | 75 | 85 | 15 | 7 |
| Montgomery | 69 050 | 4.8 | 69 762 | 24 | 41 344 | 7 015 | 12 833 | 5 069 | 4 851 | 1 709 | 2 145 | 422 | 212 |
| Prince George's | 35 037 | 3.4 | 40 215 | 724 | 22 270 | 1 455 | 4 229 | 4 908 | 4 717 | 1 238 | 2 164 | 577 | 254 |
| Queen Anne's | 2 399 | 6.2 | 49 605 | 217 | 645 | 164 | 439 | 313 | 302 | 130 | 122 | 20 | 15 |

1. Based on the resident population estimated as of July 1 of the year shown.   2. Includes supplements to wages and salaries.

| STATE County | Earnings, 2011 Total (mil dol) | Farm | Goods-related[1] Total | Manu-facturing | Information and profes-sional and technical services | Retail trade | Finance, insur-ance, and real estate | Health care and social services | Govern-ment | Social Security beneficiaries, December 2011 Number | Rate[2] | Supple-mental Security Income recipients, December 2011 | Housing units, 2010 Total | Percent change, 2000-2010 |
|---|---|---|---|---|---|---|---|---|---|---|---|---|---|---|
| | 75 | 76 | 77 | 78 | 79 | 80 | 81 | 82 | 83 | 84 | 85 | 86 | 87 | 88 |
| **LOUISIANA—Cont'd** | | | | | | | | | | | | | | |
| Orleans | 14 289 | 0.0 | 11.6 | 3.3 | 15.6 | 3.4 | 5.9 | 7.3 | 22.8 | 53 240 | 148 | 19 309 | 189 896 | -11.7 |
| Ouachita | 3 848 | 0.3 | 14.7 | 9.4 | 10.5 | 8.4 | 8.0 | 16.6 | 18.3 | 26 875 | 173 | 6 507 | 64 481 | 7.2 |
| Plaquemines | 1 346 | 0.9 | 36.9 | 19.3 | D | D | 5.2 | D | 15.9 | 3 500 | 148 | 572 | 9 596 | -8.4 |
| Pointe Coupee | 381 | 11.9 | 15.8 | 6.6 | D | 7.6 | 5.1 | 5.5 | 16.8 | 4 520 | 199 | 1 068 | 11 130 | 8.1 |
| Rapides | 3 508 | 0.9 | 19.1 | 10.6 | 6.2 | 7.8 | 4.0 | 19.1 | 23.3 | 26 815 | 203 | 7 027 | 55 684 | 7.0 |
| Red River | 178 | 8.6 | 23.3 | 6.7 | 2.0 | 4.7 | 3.3 | D | 21.1 | 1 715 | 193 | 503 | 4 128 | 3.5 |
| Richland | 367 | 12.1 | 15.4 | 7.4 | D | 10.1 | 3.7 | D | 17.5 | 4 195 | 200 | 1 121 | 8 621 | 3.4 |
| Sabine | 314 | 3.8 | 23.3 | 16.6 | 7.3 | 9.7 | 5.6 | D | 23.0 | 5 590 | 228 | 1 060 | 14 130 | 3.4 |
| St. Bernard | 797 | 0.7 | D | 24.9 | 2.3 | 6.2 | 1.4 | D | 16.2 | 5 675 | 143 | 1 465 | 16 794 | -37.3 |
| St. Charles | 2 039 | 0.0 | D | 32.4 | 4.6 | 3.4 | 1.6 | 2.5 | 11.1 | 8 275 | 158 | 1 272 | 19 896 | 14.2 |
| St. Helena | 113 | 2.7 | 23.8 | 13.8 | D | 6.6 | D | D | 26.5 | 3 025 | 276 | 1 040 | 5 150 | 2.3 |
| St. James | 686 | 1.5 | 54.8 | 50.9 | D | 2.8 | 2.5 | 2.9 | 12.8 | 4 250 | 195 | 750 | 8 455 | 11.3 |
| St. John the Baptist | 1 170 | 0.3 | 42.2 | 30.5 | 3.9 | 5.1 | 4.6 | 5.9 | 11.6 | 8 135 | 180 | 1 844 | 17 510 | 12.7 |
| St. Landry | 1 313 | 3.2 | 18.2 | 7.8 | 4.8 | 9.9 | 3.8 | 13.4 | 23.9 | 18 895 | 226 | 5 693 | 35 692 | -1.4 |
| St. Martin | 648 | 1.9 | 28.9 | 13.2 | 3.9 | 8.8 | 7.8 | 8.3 | 18.4 | 9 900 | 187 | 2 027 | 21 941 | 8.4 |
| St. Mary | 1 724 | 0.9 | 37.8 | 19.7 | 3.3 | 4.5 | 6.2 | D | 15.8 | 11 155 | 206 | 2 512 | 23 028 | 6.4 |
| St. Tammany | 5 254 | 0.0 | 17.2 | 4.5 | 9.9 | 9.0 | 6.3 | 13.4 | 17.5 | 43 045 | 182 | 4 807 | 95 412 | 26.5 |
| Tangipahoa | 2 317 | 0.2 | 10.4 | 5.2 | 3.9 | 9.2 | 15.7 | 9.3 | 27.8 | 20 775 | 169 | 5 204 | 50 073 | 22.7 |
| Tensas | 106 | 35.4 | D | 1.3 | D | 3.4 | 4.9 | D | 18.7 | 1 150 | 227 | 430 | 3 357 | -0.1 |
| Terrebonne | 3 414 | 0.4 | 35.8 | 17.4 | 4.6 | 6.6 | 6.9 | 9.5 | 11.0 | 20 585 | 184 | 4 759 | 43 887 | 9.9 |
| Union | 253 | 6.7 | D | D | 3.7 | 9.4 | 2.7 | D | 21.9 | 5 055 | 222 | 900 | 11 346 | 4.4 |
| Vermilion | 874 | 4.0 | 33.7 | 10.7 | 4.4 | 8.2 | 6.0 | D | 19.0 | 10 845 | 186 | 1 873 | 25 235 | 12.0 |
| Vernon | 1 970 | 0.0 | D | 1.7 | 4.4 | 2.6 | 1.2 | 4.0 | 75.2 | 7 430 | 143 | 1 219 | 21 433 | 1.9 |
| Washington | 550 | -0.6 | 23.4 | 15.9 | D | 7.8 | 3.9 | D | 35.2 | 10 960 | 233 | 3 062 | 21 039 | 10.1 |
| Webster | 746 | 0.0 | 33.3 | 13.4 | 2.8 | 9.4 | 5.3 | 13.2 | 16.4 | 9 630 | 233 | 2 055 | 19 336 | 1.8 |
| West Baton Rouge | 774 | 1.7 | D | 23.1 | D | 4.8 | 1.4 | D | 11.3 | 3 960 | 164 | 814 | 9 324 | 11.4 |
| West Carroll | 118 | 8.0 | D | D | 3.2 | 9.3 | 3.4 | D | 35.7 | 2 650 | 229 | 519 | 5 046 | 1.3 |
| West Feliciana | 389 | 0.4 | D | 6.1 | D | 2.6 | 2.2 | 4.7 | 35.7 | 1 765 | 114 | 364 | 5 097 | 13.6 |
| Winn | 272 | 1.0 | 21.5 | 14.8 | D | 5.1 | 4.7 | 20.8 | 14.9 | 3 185 | 211 | 690 | 7 234 | -3.6 |
| **MAINE** | 34 176 | 0.6 | 16.8 | 10.4 | 8.0 | 8.3 | 7.4 | 16.3 | 18.9 | 306 600 | 231 | 36 259 | 721 830 | 10.7 |
| Androscoggin | 2 587 | 0.4 | D | 12.0 | 7.2 | 8.3 | 7.2 | 21.2 | 11.4 | 24 015 | 224 | 3 810 | 49 090 | 6.8 |
| Aroostook | 1 393 | -2.5 | 16.8 | 12.4 | 3.8 | 10.1 | 4.2 | 18.6 | 27.2 | 20 155 | 282 | 2 757 | 39 529 | 2.1 |
| Cumberland | 11 216 | 0.2 | D | 6.7 | 12.0 | 6.7 | 13.4 | 16.6 | 12.9 | 54 615 | 193 | 5 412 | 138 657 | 13.1 |
| Franklin | 606 | 1.2 | D | D | D | 9.7 | 3.7 | D | 16.7 | 7 375 | 240 | 910 | 21 709 | 13.3 |
| Hancock | 1 256 | 1.4 | 18.7 | 8.6 | 12.2 | 10.5 | 4.2 | 14.4 | 14.2 | 13 215 | 242 | 1 025 | 40 184 | 18.4 |
| Kennebec | 3 286 | 0.5 | D | 4.5 | 6.1 | 9.2 | 3.3 | 16.6 | 32.0 | 30 500 | 250 | 4 307 | 60 972 | 8.2 |
| Knox | 961 | 0.8 | 17.9 | 9.3 | 7.2 | 9.0 | 5.7 | 15.0 | 15.9 | 10 400 | 262 | 865 | 23 744 | 9.9 |
| Lincoln | 607 | 7.7 | D | 6.9 | D | 9.4 | 5.2 | 13.9 | 14.3 | 9 680 | 283 | 668 | 23 493 | 12.7 |
| Oxford | 882 | 2.1 | 28.3 | 21.3 | 3.8 | 8.5 | 3.5 | 13.1 | 18.0 | 14 740 | 255 | 1 841 | 36 055 | 11.6 |
| Penobscot | 3 765 | 0.3 | 11.5 | 6.3 | 5.8 | 10.0 | 4.0 | 21.9 | 21.2 | 34 310 | 223 | 5 359 | 73 860 | 10.5 |
| Piscataquis | 296 | 0.8 | D | 26.3 | 2.5 | 9.4 | 1.8 | D | 24.9 | 5 050 | 290 | 696 | 15 340 | 11.3 |
| Sagadahoc | 1 005 | 0.1 | D | D | 7.1 | 6.0 | 3.1 | 5.3 | 13.9 | 7 980 | 227 | 696 | 18 288 | 10.9 |
| Somerset | 982 | 1.7 | D | 22.9 | 3.7 | 7.9 | 2.6 | 13.3 | 14.7 | 12 215 | 235 | 1 889 | 30 569 | 8.3 |
| Waldo | 586 | 2.2 | D | 10.8 | D | 8.5 | 12.1 | 15.9 | 14.3 | 9 400 | 243 | 1 240 | 21 566 | 14.1 |
| Washington | 569 | 4.5 | D | 11.1 | D | 9.7 | 3.7 | 16.4 | 25.8 | 9 420 | 289 | 1 355 | 23 001 | 4.9 |
| York | 4 177 | 0.3 | 18.7 | 11.9 | 5.7 | 8.9 | 4.2 | 12.2 | 29.6 | 43 530 | 220 | 3 429 | 105 773 | 12.2 |
| **MARYLAND** | 202 520 | 0.2 | 12.0 | 5.0 | 16.6 | 5.5 | 7.3 | 11.0 | 26.0 | 872 919 | 150 | 111 494 | 2 378 814 | 10.9 |
| Allegany | 1 604 | 0.2 | 14.7 | 9.3 | D | 7.2 | 3.2 | 21.5 | 26.5 | 17 250 | 231 | 2 208 | 33 311 | 1.0 |
| Anne Arundel | 24 203 | 0.0 | 13.6 | 7.1 | 12.0 | 5.1 | 3.5 | 7.1 | 38.4 | 80 240 | 147 | 5 661 | 212 562 | 13.7 |
| Baltimore | 27 165 | 0.1 | 14.5 | 6.7 | 13.0 | 7.1 | 11.4 | 13.7 | 18.5 | 145 615 | 180 | 14 727 | 335 622 | 7.0 |
| Calvert | 1 412 | 0.2 | 13.4 | 2.7 | 7.5 | 7.0 | 3.8 | 14.9 | 22.4 | 12 765 | 143 | 870 | 33 780 | 22.5 |
| Caroline | 491 | 7.3 | D | 12.5 | 3.9 | 9.3 | 3.0 | D | 19.6 | 6 590 | 200 | 776 | 13 482 | 12.1 |
| Carroll | 3 302 | 1.1 | D | 9.3 | 10.7 | 8.1 | 3.8 | 14.0 | 15.6 | 28 580 | 171 | 1 370 | 62 406 | 15.0 |
| Cecil | 1 797 | 0.9 | D | 22.2 | D | 6.6 | 2.5 | 10.4 | 23.0 | 17 545 | 173 | 1 639 | 41 103 | 19.3 |
| Charles | 2 612 | 0.0 | D | 1.7 | 8.5 | 12.0 | 3.5 | 10.7 | 32.7 | 18 165 | 122 | 1 901 | 54 963 | 25.2 |
| Dorchester | 609 | 2.4 | 23.7 | 17.4 | 3.4 | 5.5 | 4.8 | 12.1 | 24.5 | 7 880 | 241 | 1 162 | 16 554 | 12.8 |
| Frederick | 6 609 | 0.8 | 15.1 | 5.7 | 19.1 | 6.5 | 8.4 | 9.5 | 22.1 | 33 745 | 143 | 2 102 | 90 136 | 23.4 |
| Garrett | 693 | 3.3 | 25.2 | 8.5 | D | 10.1 | 4.6 | D | 14.5 | 6 910 | 230 | 672 | 18 854 | 12.5 |
| Harford | 6 387 | 0.2 | 12.7 | 5.5 | 10.3 | 7.3 | 3.4 | 9.0 | 41.1 | 40 650 | 165 | 3 067 | 95 554 | 14.9 |
| Howard | 12 981 | 0.1 | 13.0 | 4.2 | 32.0 | 5.3 | 7.8 | 6.3 | 10.1 | 33 355 | 114 | 2 811 | 109 282 | 17.7 |
| Kent | 465 | 5.3 | D | 10.8 | 6.7 | 6.9 | 4.3 | 15.5 | 13.3 | 5 315 | 263 | 313 | 10 549 | 12.1 |
| Montgomery | 48 360 | 0.0 | 9.4 | 3.2 | 26.0 | 4.2 | 9.4 | 8.9 | 23.6 | 117 715 | 119 | 13 253 | 375 905 | 12.3 |
| Prince George's | 23 725 | 0.0 | 12.6 | 2.7 | 12.4 | 6.5 | 3.6 | 7.6 | 38.1 | 99 660 | 114 | 13 082 | 328 182 | 8.5 |
| Queen Anne's | 810 | 2.4 | D | 8.7 | 10.0 | 8.8 | 4.0 | 6.7 | 19.6 | 9 050 | 187 | 425 | 20 140 | 20.8 |

1. Includes mining, construction, and manufacturing.  2. Per 1,000 resident population enumerated in the 2010 census.

# Table B. States and Counties — Housing, Labor Force, and Employment

| STATE County | Housing units, 2007–2011 | | | | | | | | Civilian labor force, 2012 | | | | Civilian employment,[6] 2007–2011 | | |
|---|---|---|---|---|---|---|---|---|---|---|---|---|---|---|---|
| | Occupied units | | | | | | | | | | Unemployment | | Percent | | |
| | | | Owner-occupied | | | Renter-occupied | | | | | | | | | |
| | | | | Median owner cost as a percent of income | | | | | | | | | | | |
| | Total | Percent | Median value[1] | With a mortgage | Without a mortgage[2] | Median rent[3] | Median rent as a percent of income | Sub-standard units[4] (percent) | Total | Percent change, 2011–2012 | Total | Rate[5] | Total | Manage-ment, business, science and arts | Con-struction, produc-tion, and mainte-nance occu-pations |
| | 89 | 90 | 91 | 92 | 93 | 94 | 95 | 96 | 97 | 98 | 99 | 100 | 101 | 102 | 103 |
| **LOUISIANA—Cont'd** | | | | | | | | | | | | | | | |
| Orleans | 134 342 | 48.3 | 183 500 | 27.9 | 14.3 | 924 | 39.2 | 4.0 | 151 058 | 0.6 | 11 846 | 7.8 | 143 476 | 38.9 | 17.6 |
| Ouachita | 56 390 | 61.6 | 116 900 | 20.4 | 10.1 | 646 | 31.2 | 2.9 | 71 561 | 1.1 | 4 998 | 7.0 | 67 178 | 32.0 | 20.9 |
| Plaquemines | 8 198 | 71.7 | 203 000 | 24.4 | 9.9 | 1 138 | 32.5 | 2.5 | 9 135 | 0.7 | 556 | 6.1 | 10 154 | 28.4 | 32.7 |
| Pointe Coupee | 8 903 | 79.3 | 108 500 | 19.8 | 10.9 | 541 | 25.9 | 3.3 | 9 566 | 1.0 | 728 | 7.6 | 9 783 | 28.3 | 33.0 |
| Rapides | 47 418 | 67.2 | 113 500 | 21.5 | 10.4 | 687 | 32.6 | 3.4 | 58 085 | -1.3 | 3 685 | 6.3 | 54 214 | 31.8 | 23.0 |
| Red River | 3 174 | 78.2 | 73 500 | 19.3 | 10.1 | 430 | 28.7 | 4.7 | 3 704 | -1.8 | 266 | 7.2 | 3 338 | 24.7 | 32.1 |
| Richland | 7 287 | 70.4 | 69 700 | 19.6 | 9.9 | 530 | 25.9 | 2.9 | 9 113 | -2.0 | 792 | 8.7 | 7 878 | 29.9 | 27.7 |
| Sabine | 9 414 | 77.9 | 78 700 | 18.6 | 10.4 | 474 | 28.7 | 5.7 | 9 373 | -2.2 | 596 | 6.4 | 9 041 | 26.0 | 39.3 |
| St. Bernard | 12 246 | 68.4 | 130 500 | 23.3 | 10.5 | 837 | 34.2 | 3.5 | 18 112 | 1.2 | 1 293 | 7.1 | 13 702 | 22.7 | 37.6 |
| St. Charles | 18 569 | 83.3 | 175 200 | 23.2 | 10.0 | 864 | 34.5 | 2.8 | 24 500 | 0.6 | 1 471 | 6.0 | 24 904 | 33.9 | 25.9 |
| St. Helena | 4 142 | 79.4 | 77 100 | 17.6 | 12.9 | 505 | 25.1 | 6.5 | 4 345 | 0.4 | 482 | 11.1 | 4 164 | 18.1 | 33.4 |
| St. James | 7 578 | 84.3 | 114 000 | 19.0 | 10.0 | 606 | 20.6 | 6.0 | 9 607 | 0.8 | 899 | 9.4 | 9 289 | 23.7 | 34.0 |
| St. John the Baptist | 15 775 | 77.5 | 148 800 | 23.1 | 10.1 | 836 | 32.0 | 4.9 | 19 878 | -0.2 | 1 571 | 7.9 | 21 037 | 24.2 | 30.9 |
| St. Landry | 30 381 | 71.6 | 84 700 | 19.9 | 10.2 | 510 | 32.3 | 3.0 | 37 820 | -0.2 | 2 497 | 6.6 | 31 894 | 25.7 | 30.8 |
| St. Martin | 18 825 | 80.1 | 88 200 | 19.5 | 9.9 | 574 | 28.2 | 3.6 | 23 665 | 2.4 | 1 336 | 5.6 | 22 785 | 22.6 | 30.8 |
| St. Mary | 20 148 | 69.9 | 87 200 | 20.8 | 11.2 | 620 | 27.1 | 3.4 | 23 490 | 0.7 | 1 770 | 7.5 | 22 654 | 22.1 | 38.9 |
| St. Tammany | 86 374 | 79.4 | 201 700 | 23.6 | 10.7 | 985 | 32.9 | 1.9 | 112 202 | 0.9 | 5 878 | 5.2 | 105 314 | 38.4 | 19.4 |
| Tangipahoa | 43 518 | 68.2 | 140 000 | 22.2 | 10.1 | 717 | 30.5 | 3.8 | 53 200 | -0.4 | 4 077 | 7.7 | 51 040 | 29.1 | 27.2 |
| Tensas | 2 205 | 62.8 | 66 600 | 19.2 | 13.2 | 472 | 32.9 | 4.0 | 1 877 | -10.5 | 192 | 10.2 | 1 903 | 25.2 | 27.3 |
| Terrebonne | 39 040 | 73.7 | 124 300 | 20.5 | 9.9 | 752 | 28.8 | 5.2 | 54 664 | 2.1 | 2 494 | 4.6 | 49 059 | 25.8 | 34.6 |
| Union | 8 344 | 79.6 | 79 000 | 17.3 | 9.9 | 512 | 34.4 | 4.6 | 9 803 | 0.8 | 686 | 7.0 | 8 986 | 24.4 | 36.9 |
| Vermilion | 21 737 | 76.8 | 94 900 | 19.6 | 9.9 | 587 | 23.1 | 3.5 | 24 779 | 2.5 | 1 361 | 5.5 | 24 519 | 24.6 | 34.0 |
| Vernon | 18 025 | 56.3 | 87 600 | 18.0 | 9.9 | 801 | 23.6 | 3.2 | 21 770 | -0.4 | 1 425 | 6.5 | 17 547 | 30.1 | 26.6 |
| Washington | 17 444 | 75.0 | 82 900 | 23.3 | 10.7 | 525 | 32.3 | 3.3 | 15 200 | -1.2 | 1 371 | 9.0 | 15 664 | 23.8 | 29.5 |
| Webster | 16 412 | 68.3 | 79 900 | 19.7 | 10.3 | 540 | 31.9 | 3.2 | 19 310 | -1.5 | 1 382 | 7.2 | 16 449 | 24.4 | 34.3 |
| West Baton Rouge | 8 510 | 71.8 | 132 000 | 21.0 | 9.9 | 677 | 30.4 | 3.7 | 11 198 | 1.5 | 757 | 6.8 | 11 148 | 28.0 | 27.2 |
| West Carroll | 4 070 | 72.4 | 76 200 | 20.6 | 12.0 | 481 | 29.2 | 3.8 | 4 349 | -3.2 | 539 | 12.4 | 4 118 | 23.6 | 31.4 |
| West Feliciana | 4 112 | 75.6 | 163 300 | 19.6 | 11.6 | 683 | 31.1 | 6.5 | 4 805 | 1.6 | 360 | 7.5 | 4 773 | 34.1 | 24.5 |
| Winn | 5 375 | 76.3 | 60 600 | 19.0 | 10.1 | 425 | 35.4 | 4.2 | 6 612 | 0.1 | 468 | 7.1 | 4 792 | 28.7 | 30.9 |
| **MAINE** | 551 601 | 72.7 | 176 600 | 24.6 | 14.1 | 736 | 30.3 | 2.0 | 706 097 | 0.4 | 51 596 | 7.3 | 654 300 | 34.7 | 23.2 |
| Androscoggin | 43 968 | 67.2 | 157 100 | 24.5 | 16.4 | 682 | 29.3 | 1.8 | 58 224 | 0.6 | 4 298 | 7.4 | 52 591 | 31.2 | 24.1 |
| Aroostook | 30 459 | 71.7 | 88 400 | 21.2 | 13.1 | 515 | 28.9 | 2.5 | 34 062 | -1.4 | 3 140 | 9.2 | 32 086 | 28.8 | 27.5 |
| Cumberland | 117 138 | 67.8 | 245 900 | 25.4 | 15.2 | 899 | 30.8 | 1.8 | 161 116 | 0.8 | 9 332 | 5.8 | 148 974 | 42.9 | 16.7 |
| Franklin | 12 235 | 75.6 | 134 300 | 22.6 | 11.2 | 579 | 32.2 | 2.7 | 14 313 | -0.3 | 1 337 | 9.3 | 14 320 | 30.7 | 26.3 |
| Hancock | 23 649 | 75.0 | 203 000 | 25.0 | 13.3 | 746 | 30.4 | 2.5 | 29 961 | -0.6 | 2 581 | 8.6 | 27 940 | 34.2 | 26.4 |
| Kennebec | 51 043 | 72.2 | 151 000 | 23.1 | 13.0 | 664 | 30.2 | 1.1 | 63 859 | -0.1 | 4 478 | 7.0 | 59 388 | 34.5 | 22.6 |
| Knox | 16 876 | 79.0 | 202 800 | 26.9 | 15.8 | 758 | 32.9 | 2.5 | 20 984 | 0.9 | 1 426 | 6.8 | 20 109 | 30.8 | 26.0 |
| Lincoln | 15 009 | 84.9 | 206 900 | 27.4 | 13.2 | 804 | 29.0 | 1.8 | 18 391 | 0.7 | 1 246 | 6.8 | 16 427 | 35.5 | 27.4 |
| Oxford | 23 512 | 78.0 | 144 200 | 24.6 | 14.5 | 600 | 29.8 | 2.3 | 28 689 | 0.3 | 2 621 | 9.1 | 25 739 | 26.1 | 31.9 |
| Penobscot | 62 570 | 69.7 | 137 900 | 23.1 | 13.2 | 695 | 31.9 | 2.3 | 79 103 | 0.5 | 6 139 | 7.8 | 74 769 | 32.9 | 21.5 |
| Piscataquis | 7 860 | 79.2 | 106 900 | 23.8 | 15.1 | 554 | 28.5 | 2.3 | 7 366 | -1.2 | 744 | 10.1 | 7 596 | 28.5 | 32.5 |
| Sagadahoc | 14 853 | 76.0 | 192 800 | 24.2 | 13.2 | 793 | 30.9 | 1.6 | 19 077 | 0.1 | 1 256 | 6.6 | 18 058 | 36.0 | 22.8 |
| Somerset | 21 795 | 77.9 | 111 700 | 23.5 | 14.6 | 625 | 31.9 | 3.0 | 24 831 | -0.4 | 2 424 | 9.8 | 22 676 | 28.8 | 31.8 |
| Waldo | 16 204 | 79.2 | 152 700 | 25.9 | 15.2 | 698 | 31.3 | 3.0 | 19 711 | 1.2 | 1 686 | 8.6 | 18 519 | 30.4 | 28.0 |
| Washington | 14 111 | 76.6 | 104 700 | 24.1 | 13.3 | 529 | 28.1 | 3.7 | 14 278 | -1.5 | 1 522 | 10.7 | 13 541 | 27.8 | 31.0 |
| York | 80 319 | 74.8 | 233 500 | 26.3 | 14.8 | 848 | 29.7 | 1.5 | 112 134 | 0.9 | 7 369 | 6.6 | 101 567 | 34.3 | 23.2 |
| **MARYLAND** | 2 128 377 | 68.7 | 319 800 | 25.5 | 12.6 | 1 139 | 30.7 | 2.3 | 3 122 629 | 1.0 | 213 058 | 6.8 | 2 909 466 | 43.5 | 16.3 |
| Allegany | 28 596 | 70.0 | 123 300 | 22.2 | 12.9 | 568 | 28.2 | 1.9 | 36 537 | -0.1 | 3 008 | 8.2 | 31 191 | 28.5 | 24.7 |
| Anne Arundel | 197 348 | 74.9 | 361 700 | 24.6 | 11.9 | 1 369 | 29.7 | 1.5 | 305 158 | 1.5 | 18 665 | 6.1 | 271 913 | 44.1 | 15.9 |
| Baltimore | 315 127 | 67.0 | 269 400 | 24.6 | 12.4 | 1 082 | 30.4 | 2.1 | 452 683 | 1.5 | 32 862 | 7.3 | 409 569 | 42.5 | 15.8 |
| Calvert | 30 381 | 84.0 | 384 500 | 24.6 | 11.1 | 1 321 | 33.5 | 2.0 | 48 093 | 0.5 | 2 761 | 5.7 | 45 240 | 40.4 | 20.6 |
| Caroline | 11 842 | 74.2 | 232 600 | 28.4 | 13.6 | 893 | 25.8 | 3.0 | 16 491 | -1.5 | 1 388 | 8.4 | 16 012 | 31.3 | 28.5 |
| Carroll | 59 314 | 83.9 | 342 900 | 25.0 | 13.2 | 975 | 31.4 | 1.2 | 95 491 | 1.6 | 5 944 | 6.2 | 86 926 | 43.6 | 18.5 |
| Cecil | 35 943 | 74.5 | 262 600 | 25.4 | 13.8 | 968 | 30.6 | 1.9 | 51 078 | -0.4 | 4 268 | 8.4 | 49 188 | 33.1 | 25.6 |
| Charles | 50 305 | 80.1 | 341 200 | 26.2 | 11.9 | 1 370 | 33.4 | 1.6 | 80 600 | 0.7 | 4 807 | 6.0 | 74 603 | 41.3 | 18.6 |
| Dorchester | 13 528 | 69.8 | 202 000 | 27.2 | 15.7 | 753 | 31.8 | 2.9 | 16 945 | -1.0 | 1 779 | 10.5 | 15 120 | 27.3 | 31.0 |
| Frederick | 85 048 | 75.9 | 335 600 | 24.6 | 11.8 | 1 184 | 28.9 | 1.4 | 129 052 | 0.5 | 7 537 | 5.8 | 122 367 | 44.8 | 16.0 |
| Garrett | 12 410 | 76.6 | 168 500 | 23.2 | 11.4 | 582 | 29.1 | 1.6 | 17 085 | -0.6 | 1 284 | 7.5 | 14 199 | 29.5 | 31.8 |
| Harford | 89 260 | 81.5 | 295 900 | 24.6 | 12.6 | 1 044 | 29.3 | 1.0 | 139 513 | 1.5 | 9 711 | 7.0 | 125 020 | 41.4 | 19.0 |
| Howard | 103 547 | 74.2 | 447 000 | 23.6 | 10.1 | 1 388 | 28.8 | 1.7 | 173 703 | 1.7 | 8 675 | 5.0 | 152 515 | 59.7 | 9.3 |
| Kent | 7 605 | 74.7 | 272 900 | 27.1 | 15.0 | 844 | 30.3 | 0.8 | 10 886 | -1.9 | 812 | 7.5 | 9 658 | 33.9 | 23.4 |
| Montgomery | 355 434 | 68.8 | 469 900 | 24.9 | 11.0 | 1 473 | 30.6 | 2.7 | 534 178 | 0.8 | 27 448 | 5.1 | 516 957 | 55.9 | 10.0 |
| Prince George's | 302 091 | 64.1 | 312 800 | 29.1 | 12.6 | 1 180 | 30.1 | 3.5 | 469 150 | 0.5 | 31 990 | 6.8 | 453 409 | 37.8 | 18.2 |
| Queen Anne's | 17 189 | 86.0 | 365 500 | 26.5 | 12.4 | 1 168 | 29.7 | 1.3 | 27 728 | 1.0 | 1 723 | 6.2 | 24 105 | 37.0 | 20.5 |

1. Specified owner-occupied units.   2. A value of 9.9 represents 9.9 percent or less.   3. Specified renter-occupied units. A value of 10.0 represents 10 percent or less.   4. Overcrowded or lacking complete plumbing facilities.   5. Percent of civilian labor force.   6. Persons 16 years old and over.

| | Private nonfarm establishments, employment and payroll, 2011 | | | | | | | | Agriculture, 2007 | | |
|---|---|---|---|---|---|---|---|---|---|---|---|
| | Employment | | | | | | Annual payroll | | Farms | | |
| | | | | | | | | | | Percent with: | |
| STATE County | Number of establishments | Total | Health care and social assistance | Manufacturing | Retail trade | Finance and insurance | Professional, scientific, and technical services | Total (mil dol) | Average per employee (dollars) | Number | Fewer than 50 acres | 500 acres or more | Farm operators whose principal occupation is farming (percent) |
| | 104 | 105 | 106 | 107 | 108 | 109 | 110 | 111 | 112 | 113 | 114 | 115 | 116 |

| STATE County | 104 | 105 | 106 | 107 | 108 | 109 | 110 | 111 | 112 | 113 | 114 | 115 | 116 |
|---|---|---|---|---|---|---|---|---|---|---|---|---|---|
| LOUISIANA—Cont'd | | | | | | | | | | | | | |
| Orleans | 8 386 | 151 821 | 23 558 | 4 792 | 12 473 | 5 694 | 12 815 | 7 204 | 47 452 | 2 | 0.0 | 50.0 | 50.0 |
| Ouachita | 4 145 | 62 418 | 13 075 | 5 119 | 9 198 | 5 193 | 3 904 | 1 951 | 31 253 | 502 | 50.6 | 6.4 | 34.3 |
| Plaquemines | 698 | 11 603 | 363 | 2 002 | 453 | D | 826 | 722 | 62 205 | 177 | 53.1 | 23.7 | 57.1 |
| Pointe Coupee | 375 | 4 135 | 723 | D | 874 | 184 | D | 147 | 35 450 | 441 | 41.0 | 17.0 | 48.3 |
| Rapides | 3 216 | 46 766 | 13 620 | 3 606 | 7 939 | 1 628 | 1 802 | 1 582 | 33 830 | 977 | 54.4 | 7.4 | 46.4 |
| Red River | 130 | 2 014 | 439 | 199 | D | 76 | D | 81 | 40 227 | 251 | 30.7 | 13.9 | 45.0 |
| Richland | 411 | 5 237 | 1 799 | D | 753 | 178 | 88 | 157 | 29 937 | 866 | 29.1 | 15.9 | 34.1 |
| Sabine | 470 | 4 562 | 796 | 819 | 937 | D | 166 | 135 | 29 485 | 366 | 41.5 | 4.9 | 49.5 |
| St. Bernard | 666 | 7 482 | 731 | 1 175 | 1 686 | 179 | 477 | 285 | 38 070 | 45 | 24.4 | 51.1 | 57.8 |
| St. Charles | 942 | 20 632 | 1 453 | 4 262 | 1 379 | 218 | 1 206 | 1 187 | 57 538 | 58 | 43.1 | 6.9 | 44.8 |
| St. Helena | 113 | 1 034 | 267 | D | 175 | D | 17 | 33 | 31 984 | 364 | 38.2 | 3.3 | 42.3 |
| St. James | 324 | 6 556 | 606 | 2 173 | 590 | D | 59 | 426 | 65 036 | 64 | 35.9 | 35.9 | 76.6 |
| St. John the Baptist | 733 | 13 842 | 1 211 | 2 638 | 1 644 | 359 | 273 | 631 | 45 566 | 31 | 45.2 | 25.8 | 71.0 |
| St. Landry | 1 606 | 21 629 | 5 678 | 1 355 | 3 949 | 815 | 560 | 719 | 33 259 | 1 401 | 57.2 | 9.6 | 40.8 |
| St. Martin | 900 | 11 312 | 1 746 | 1 299 | 1 633 | 335 | 372 | 431 | 38 122 | 355 | 65.6 | 12.1 | 40.6 |
| St. Mary | 1 379 | 23 536 | 2 047 | 3 719 | 2 377 | 510 | 690 | 1 108 | 47 085 | 142 | 49.3 | 28.9 | 55.6 |
| St. Tammany | 5 869 | 68 857 | 13 828 | 2 694 | 12 905 | 3 973 | 5 121 | 2 665 | 38 704 | 602 | 74.1 | 2.3 | 42.7 |
| Tangipahoa | 2 261 | 33 304 | 7 912 | 2 270 | 6 434 | 2 599 | 856 | 1 086 | 32 594 | 1 188 | 48.9 | 2.7 | 44.1 |
| Tensas | 92 | 488 | 82 | D | 79 | D | D | 18 | 36 971 | 257 | 21.0 | 36.6 | 42.4 |
| Terrebonne | 2 913 | 47 988 | 6 817 | 5 161 | 7 150 | 1 165 | 2 132 | 2 138 | 44 555 | 169 | 45.6 | 17.8 | 42.6 |
| Union | 334 | 4 055 | 723 | D | 635 | 129 | 57 | 104 | 25 684 | 426 | 34.3 | 5.9 | 53.1 |
| Vermilion | 1 034 | 10 165 | 1 791 | 551 | 2 097 | 487 | 316 | 379 | 37 255 | 1 182 | 47.7 | 10.7 | 44.1 |
| Vernon | 716 | 8 811 | 1 742 | 182 | 1 637 | 316 | 718 | 248 | 28 150 | 479 | 53.9 | 4.2 | 47.0 |
| Washington | 638 | 7 475 | 2 386 | D | 1 237 | 322 | 140 | 233 | 31 130 | 916 | 52.1 | 2.7 | 41.2 |
| Webster | 801 | 10 682 | 2 287 | 1 357 | 2 020 | 398 | 231 | 376 | 35 181 | 430 | 49.5 | 3.3 | 42.6 |
| West Baton Rouge | 514 | 10 451 | 408 | 1 980 | 1 203 | 155 | D | 470 | 44 968 | 128 | 65.6 | 10.9 | 40.6 |
| West Carroll | 182 | 1 760 | 538 | D | 380 | 64 | D | 43 | 24 169 | 1 078 | 29.9 | 7.1 | 31.1 |
| West Feliciana | 193 | 2 531 | 433 | D | 298 | D | D | 127 | 50 130 | 176 | 38.1 | 17.0 | 33.5 |
| Winn | 305 | 4 463 | 1 033 | 621 | 582 | 120 | 55 | 130 | 29 079 | 150 | 40.0 | 5.3 | 34.7 |
| MAINE | 40 112 | 479 728 | 105 689 | 51 068 | 79 525 | 26 696 | 22 730 | 17 764 | 37 030 | 8 136 | 42.1 | 6.3 | 43.5 |
| Androscoggin | 2 749 | 43 155 | 9 557 | 5 317 | 6 188 | 3 108 | 1 879 | 1 545 | 35 801 | 378 | 47.9 | 5.3 | 52.4 |
| Aroostook | 2 005 | 22 038 | 6 140 | 3 455 | 4 255 | 774 | 483 | 685 | 31 087 | 1 246 | 18.9 | 13.3 | 35.1 |
| Cumberland | 10 743 | 153 928 | 31 038 | 8 867 | 21 395 | 13 397 | 9 863 | 6 495 | 42 196 | 630 | 61.6 | 2.5 | 40.2 |
| Franklin | 793 | 9 255 | 1 921 | D | 1 674 | D | 137 | 257 | 27 779 | 388 | 43.8 | 2.1 | 47.4 |
| Hancock | 2 155 | 16 589 | 3 233 | 1 410 | 3 345 | 546 | 1 909 | 628 | 37 852 | 386 | 52.1 | 4.4 | 37.6 |
| Kennebec | 3 242 | 43 377 | 12 777 | 2 366 | 8 365 | 1 177 | 1 875 | 1 530 | 35 278 | 649 | 43.1 | 4.3 | 47.5 |
| Knox | 1 681 | 13 229 | 2 782 | 1 500 | 2 543 | 722 | 467 | 442 | 33 382 | 304 | 53.9 | 3.3 | 49.0 |
| Lincoln | 1 393 | 8 317 | 1 960 | 767 | 1 509 | 307 | 289 | 277 | 33 312 | 363 | 54.3 | 1.4 | 44.1 |
| Oxford | 1 288 | 14 061 | 2 829 | 2 690 | 2 043 | 338 | 295 | 450 | 32 016 | 545 | 45.1 | 4.8 | 44.4 |
| Penobscot | 4 127 | 57 082 | 13 792 | 3 937 | 10 760 | 1 939 | 1 885 | 1 948 | 34 132 | 706 | 41.4 | 9.1 | 49.9 |
| Piscataquis | 436 | 4 445 | D | 956 | 856 | 69 | D | 127 | 28 478 | 190 | 31.6 | 9.5 | 44.2 |
| Sagadahoc | 889 | 13 007 | 1 399 | D | 1 736 | D | 731 | 557 | 42 795 | 183 | 39.9 | 1.6 | 49.2 |
| Somerset | 1 158 | 13 511 | 2 831 | 3 439 | 2 246 | D | 246 | 484 | 35 829 | 564 | 34.6 | 9.8 | 42.2 |
| Waldo | 966 | 8 393 | 1 629 | D | 1 409 | D | 196 | 277 | 33 042 | 424 | 37.7 | 7.8 | 47.4 |
| Washington | 853 | 7 189 | 1 959 | 844 | 1 699 | 292 | 152 | 220 | 30 537 | 472 | 44.5 | 5.9 | 36.9 |
| York | 5 430 | 50 506 | 10 208 | 7 512 | 9 502 | 1 620 | 1 959 | 1 719 | 34 045 | 708 | 53.2 | 1.8 | 45.9 |
| MARYLAND | 133 248 | 2 104 022 | 336 440 | 104 410 | 278 530 | 99 264 | 243 980 | 101 301 | 48 146 | 12 834 | 47.9 | 7.1 | 48.8 |
| Allegany | 1 647 | 24 485 | 6 055 | 2 556 | 3 935 | 1 033 | 692 | 745 | 30 411 | 302 | 29.1 | 1.3 | 36.8 |
| Anne Arundel | 13 370 | 203 465 | 23 961 | 13 117 | 32 602 | 5 935 | 20 828 | 9 448 | 46 435 | 377 | 62.1 | 2.9 | 49.6 |
| Baltimore | 19 627 | 310 726 | 56 674 | 17 740 | 47 560 | 21 489 | 24 843 | 13 900 | 44 733 | 751 | 61.5 | 3.3 | 48.6 |
| Calvert | 1 687 | 17 128 | 3 221 | 418 | 2 978 | 356 | 1 265 | 683 | 39 878 | 274 | 51.1 | 2.6 | 44.9 |
| Caroline | 614 | 6 663 | 914 | D | 940 | 166 | 235 | 213 | 32 037 | 574 | 38.2 | 13.9 | 58.4 |
| Carroll | 4 173 | 47 074 | 9 567 | 3 599 | 8 187 | 1 140 | 2 426 | 1 663 | 35 338 | 1 148 | 53.0 | 4.9 | 49.2 |
| Cecil | 1 771 | 24 366 | 4 460 | D | 3 848 | 471 | 585 | 986 | 40 451 | 583 | 52.7 | 7.2 | 50.8 |
| Charles | 2 627 | 31 333 | 4 450 | 522 | 8 589 | 984 | 2 208 | 1 078 | 34 390 | 418 | 45.7 | 4.8 | 49.8 |
| Dorchester | 736 | 9 185 | 1 790 | 2 652 | 1 029 | 269 | 153 | 292 | 31 761 | 424 | 35.8 | 17.5 | 58.7 |
| Frederick | 5 730 | 79 271 | 10 944 | 5 484 | 11 659 | 6 629 | 7 434 | 3 187 | 40 207 | 1 442 | 46.3 | 5.9 | 49.8 |
| Garrett | 907 | 11 092 | 1 649 | 1 065 | 1 775 | 342 | 259 | 342 | 30 863 | 677 | 26.9 | 3.0 | 45.8 |
| Harford | 5 303 | 65 877 | 9 606 | 4 455 | 12 691 | 1 958 | 8 313 | 2 504 | 38 008 | 704 | 58.1 | 4.1 | 40.9 |
| Howard | 8 547 | 152 384 | 12 813 | 5 099 | 15 403 | 6 702 | 36 475 | 8 905 | 58 438 | 335 | 68.1 | 3.9 | 39.4 |
| Kent | 636 | 7 033 | 1 373 | 801 | 822 | 232 | 222 | 224 | 31 900 | 377 | 31.8 | 15.1 | 53.1 |
| Montgomery | 26 327 | 412 473 | 58 791 | 8 443 | 44 819 | 19 352 | 75 667 | 24 526 | 59 462 | 561 | 64.9 | 4.8 | 43.5 |
| Prince George's | 13 991 | 243 227 | 29 490 | 8 378 | 36 326 | 6 829 | 25 216 | 10 518 | 43 245 | 375 | 61.9 | 2.9 | 42.9 |
| Queen Anne's | 1 316 | 11 184 | 1 082 | 983 | 2 462 | 353 | 713 | 373 | 33 373 | 521 | 35.5 | 18.0 | 51.8 |

# Table B. States and Counties — **Agriculture**

| STATE County | Acreage (1,000) | Percent change, 2002–2007 | Average size of farm | Total irrigated (1,000) | Total cropland (1,000) | Average per farm | Average per acre | Value of machinery and equipment, average per farm (dollars) | Total (mil dol) | Average per farm (dollars) | Crops | Livestock and poultry products | $10,000 or more | $100,000 or more | Total ($1,000) | Percent of farms |
|---|---|---|---|---|---|---|---|---|---|---|---|---|---|---|---|---|
| | 117 | 118 | 119 | 120 | 121 | 122 | 123 | 124 | 125 | 126 | 127 | 128 | 129 | 130 | 131 | 132 |
| LOUISIANA—Cont'd | | | | | | | | | | | | | | | | |
| Orleans | D | D | D | 0.0 | D | 380 479 | 2 238 | 65 946 | D | D | 0.0 | D | 50.0 | 0.0 | 0 | 0.0 |
| Ouachita | 85 | -10.5 | 170 | 7.3 | 50.5 | 380 479 | 2 238 | 65 946 | 33.6 | 67 016 | 38.4 | 61.6 | 24.1 | 8.4 | 2 081 | 24.9 |
| Plaquemines | 121 | 245.7 | 686 | 1.6 | 38.4 | 865 730 | 1 261 | 90 690 | 21.9 | 123 996 | 29.3 | 70.7 | 45.2 | 16.9 | 400 | 15.8 |
| Pointe Coupee | 191 | -4.0 | 432 | 7.3 | 143.4 | 852 053 | 1 972 | 138 232 | 75.5 | 171 314 | 91.3 | 8.7 | 43.8 | 17.9 | 3 545 | 35.6 |
| Rapides | 177 | -11.9 | 181 | 9.7 | 103.1 | 454 947 | 2 507 | 78 127 | 84.5 | 86 539 | 87.2 | 12.8 | 36.3 | 11.8 | 3 917 | 18.0 |
| Red River | 103 | -25.4 | 412 | 0.6 | 37.3 | 690 202 | 1 676 | 78 992 | 20.8 | 82 992 | 45.1 | 54.9 | 33.5 | 8.8 | 1 574 | 36.3 |
| Richland | 291 | 34.7 | 336 | 77.1 | 203.2 | 539 159 | 1 603 | 83 110 | 65.4 | 75 534 | 88.1 | 11.9 | 33.4 | 13.4 | 11 139 | 80.9 |
| Sabine | 51 | -19.0 | 138 | 0.2 | 13.7 | 409 674 | 2 965 | 61 291 | 105.3 | 287 826 | 0.5 | 99.5 | 38.8 | 18.3 | 298 | 7.9 |
| St. Bernard | 32 | NA | 712 | D | 3.2 | 837 797 | 1 176 | 102 260 | 8.2 | 182 815 | 1.5 | 98.5 | 55.6 | 26.7 | 53 | 15.6 |
| St. Charles | D | D | D | 0.0 | D | D | D | 53 973 | D | D | D | D | 46.6 | 3.4 | 13 | 12.1 |
| St. Helena | 52 | 2.0 | 144 | 0.1 | 17.1 | 437 896 | 3 044 | 57 715 | 29.1 | 79 960 | 1.6 | 98.4 | 30.8 | 6.3 | 310 | 19.2 |
| St. James | 43 | -18.9 | 676 | D | 33.6 | 1 755 985 | 2 598 | 279 329 | 22.9 | 357 559 | 99.0 | 1.0 | 64.1 | 40.6 | 144 | 14.1 |
| St. John the Baptist | 14 | -36.4 | 442 | D | 9.8 | 1 273 012 | 2 881 | 174 464 | 6.2 | 199 541 | 98.4 | 1.6 | 41.9 | 25.8 | 55 | 25.8 |
| St. Landry | 298 | 2.8 | 213 | 33.6 | 220.3 | 418 758 | 1 966 | 73 553 | 85.2 | 60 781 | 85.9 | 14.1 | 27.1 | 8.4 | 5 212 | 32.3 |
| St. Martin | 79 | -2.5 | 222 | 8.4 | 58.6 | 534 942 | 2 408 | 100 741 | 31.3 | 88 102 | 88.2 | 11.8 | 34.1 | 12.1 | 1 084 | 17.2 |
| St. Mary | 73 | 0.0 | 512 | 0.0 | 63.7 | 1 146 836 | 2 239 | 220 985 | 43.6 | 307 171 | 97.7 | 2.3 | 37.3 | 26.8 | 147 | 10.6 |
| St. Tammany | 46 | -9.8 | 76 | 0.6 | 10.4 | 408 119 | 5 399 | 48 897 | 11.9 | 19 754 | 59.0 | 41.0 | 23.1 | 3.3 | 278 | 5.5 |
| Tangipahoa | 124 | 5.1 | 104 | 1.6 | 55.9 | 406 142 | 3 895 | 56 686 | 63.3 | 53 260 | 24.2 | 75.8 | 30.8 | 11.3 | 2 461 | 21.5 |
| Tensas | 225 | -0.4 | 877 | 27.0 | 188.8 | 1 414 564 | 1 613 | 202 095 | 85.1 | 331 196 | 99.9 | 0.1 | 40.9 | 31.9 | 11 020 | 90.7 |
| Terrebonne | 178 | 235.8 | 1 056 | 0.4 | 22.2 | 1 256 115 | 1 189 | 138 902 | 27.9 | 165 181 | 30.7 | 69.3 | 42.0 | 12.4 | 38 | 5.3 |
| Union | 67 | -8.2 | 158 | 0.0 | 18.6 | 465 724 | 2 945 | 69 425 | 133.8 | 314 020 | 0.9 | 99.1 | 43.7 | 22.1 | 116 | 4.5 |
| Vermilion | 290 | -19.2 | 246 | 58.9 | 184.3 | 491 297 | 2 000 | 75 512 | 68.2 | 57 703 | 73.2 | 26.8 | 28.8 | 9.5 | 7 386 | 56.7 |
| Vernon | 51 | 2.0 | 106 | 0.0 | 11.8 | 329 409 | 3 116 | 45 438 | 9.1 | 19 073 | 6.3 | 93.7 | 17.7 | 1.7 | 94 | 7.5 |
| Washington | 98 | -3.9 | 107 | 0.3 | 45.0 | 351 400 | 3 295 | 51 482 | 34.1 | 37 211 | 33.4 | 66.6 | 26.1 | 6.4 | 1 054 | 19.5 |
| Webster | 49 | -14.0 | 115 | 0.0 | 16.9 | 295 124 | 2 564 | 50 632 | 9.1 | 21 144 | 11.1 | 88.9 | 17.4 | 2.3 | 147 | 5.1 |
| West Baton Rouge | 26 | 18.2 | 202 | D | 19.9 | 604 352 | 2 996 | 126 362 | 14.4 | 112 580 | 74.8 | 25.2 | 29.7 | 14.1 | 256 | 14.8 |
| West Carroll | 197 | 7.1 | 183 | 36.2 | 113.7 | 335 608 | 1 838 | 51 273 | 34.9 | 32 378 | 90.7 | 9.3 | 18.1 | 6.3 | 7 633 | 88.4 |
| West Feliciana | 67 | -1.5 | 379 | 0.0 | 12.8 | 912 760 | 2 410 | 62 132 | 4.3 | 24 439 | 43.0 | 57.0 | 25.0 | 2.3 | 204 | 22.2 |
| Winn | 21 | 0.0 | 143 | 0.1 | 6.6 | 308 389 | 2 162 | 37 441 | 16.4 | 109 101 | 2.7 | 97.3 | 21.3 | 5.3 | 59 | 8.7 |
| MAINE | 1 348 | -1.6 | 166 | 21.0 | 529.3 | 364 807 | 2 203 | 65 961 | 617.2 | 75 859 | 52.9 | 47.1 | 31.1 | 9.5 | 8 815 | 17.9 |
| Androscoggin | 51 | -8.9 | 135 | 0.5 | 23.1 | 402 339 | 2 991 | 112 469 | 68.4 | 181 071 | 11.2 | 88.8 | 36.2 | 16.4 | 487 | 15.1 |
| Aroostook | 376 | -4.1 | 301 | 10.8 | 200.2 | 348 246 | 1 155 | 95 365 | 146.5 | 117 589 | D | D | 29.1 | 15.2 | 2 779 | 56.6 |
| Cumberland | 52 | -3.7 | 82 | 0.3 | 18.1 | 408 345 | 4 973 | 64 136 | 20.0 | 31 683 | D | D | 28.1 | 7.3 | 357 | 9.0 |
| Franklin | 41 | -18.0 | 105 | 0.1 | 12.2 | 276 055 | 2 629 | 43 546 | 8.4 | 21 708 | 25.2 | 74.8 | 22.9 | 5.7 | 401 | 17.3 |
| Hancock | 53 | 6.0 | 137 | 0.1 | 17.0 | 387 719 | 2 837 | 53 073 | D | D | D | D | 37.3 | 7.3 | 42 | 5.7 |
| Kennebec | 82 | -4.7 | 127 | 0.1 | 38.3 | 345 766 | 2 721 | 65 728 | 63.5 | 97 875 | 13.3 | 86.7 | 29.7 | 8.2 | 1 520 | 11.1 |
| Knox | 30 | 3.4 | 99 | 0.2 | 12.1 | 382 856 | 3 867 | 42 360 | D | D | 0.0 | D | 35.5 | 5.9 | 58 | 4.9 |
| Lincoln | 30 | -3.2 | 83 | 0.1 | 9.5 | 317 823 | 3 846 | 45 310 | D | D | 0.0 | D | 35.5 | 7.4 | 172 | 6.9 |
| Oxford | 69 | 3.0 | 126 | 0.5 | 19.7 | 348 394 | 2 763 | 44 297 | D | D | 0.0 | D | 25.1 | 3.7 | 495 | 13.2 |
| Penobscot | 115 | 7.5 | 162 | 1.8 | 47.1 | 370 924 | 2 285 | 67 340 | 42.5 | 60 231 | 30.2 | 69.8 | 32.7 | 9.1 | 889 | 11.5 |
| Piscataquis | 34 | -12.8 | 179 | 0.1 | 9.3 | 358 841 | 2 002 | 43 773 | 6.5 | 34 177 | 35.2 | 64.8 | 26.8 | 7.9 | 368 | 23.2 |
| Sagadahoc | 19 | -5.0 | 102 | 0.1 | 6.8 | 378 097 | 3 717 | 45 889 | 2.6 | 14 115 | 49.4 | 50.6 | 18.6 | 5.5 | 171 | 7.7 |
| Somerset | 111 | 0.9 | 197 | 0.1 | 34.1 | 371 927 | 1 883 | 80 643 | 53.4 | 94 687 | D | D | 34.0 | 12.9 | 539 | 20.0 |
| Waldo | 68 | -1.4 | 161 | 0.1 | 24.3 | 364 618 | 2 266 | 52 706 | 22.8 | 53 820 | 21.9 | 78.1 | 34.0 | 10.8 | 331 | 10.4 |
| Washington | 158 | 3.9 | 336 | 4.6 | 35.7 | 379 601 | 1 131 | 66 977 | 66.1 | 140 112 | D | D | 40.9 | 9.3 | 94 | 5.7 |
| York | 59 | 3.5 | 84 | 1.3 | 22.0 | 394 389 | 4 706 | 53 327 | 20.7 | 29 254 | D | D | 29.2 | 7.8 | 113 | 6.2 |
| MARYLAND | 2 052 | -1.3 | 160 | 92.8 | 1 405.4 | 1 124 529 | 7 034 | 98 823 | 1 835.1 | 142 987 | 34.3 | 65.7 | 41.5 | 17.6 | 33 386 | 35.7 |
| Allegany | 37 | -5.1 | 121 | 0.3 | 12.5 | 534 085 | 4 402 | 40 200 | 3.2 | 10 461 | 58.3 | 41.7 | 28.5 | 1.0 | 191 | 24.5 |
| Anne Arundel | 29 | -17.1 | 78 | 0.3 | 16.3 | 1 024 267 | 13 204 | 81 946 | 19.1 | 50 636 | 84.8 | 15.2 | 33.2 | 6.1 | 165 | 10.6 |
| Baltimore | 78 | 9.9 | 104 | 0.9 | 50.9 | 959 869 | 9 209 | 90 216 | 68.4 | 91 109 | 82.3 | 17.7 | 37.5 | 11.5 | 541 | 16.6 |
| Calvert | 26 | -13.3 | 97 | 0.1 | 14.4 | 825 428 | 8 553 | 67 111 | 4.1 | 14 788 | 82.6 | 17.4 | 28.5 | 3.3 | 201 | 18.2 |
| Caroline | 131 | 13.9 | 229 | 24.6 | 107.1 | 1 260 068 | 5 510 | 136 800 | 186.0 | 324 109 | 26.3 | 73.7 | 57.3 | 35.9 | 3 028 | 63.4 |
| Carroll | 142 | -3.4 | 124 | 1.0 | 103.2 | 974 324 | 7 881 | 100 900 | 87.4 | 76 138 | 53.4 | 46.6 | 39.5 | 11.5 | 2 921 | 33.0 |
| Cecil | 85 | 10.4 | 146 | 1.1 | 60.1 | 1 121 597 | 7 690 | 103 333 | 95.8 | 164 304 | 46.1 | 53.9 | 43.1 | 16.6 | 1 336 | 30.7 |
| Charles | 52 | 0.0 | 125 | 0.6 | 29.6 | 846 793 | 6 788 | 75 488 | 8.9 | 21 287 | 74.2 | 25.8 | 23.9 | 4.8 | 487 | 21.8 |
| Dorchester | 133 | 6.4 | 314 | 21.0 | 94.9 | 1 538 075 | 4 896 | 155 113 | 166.7 | 393 235 | 26.0 | 74.0 | 49.1 | 33.5 | 2 900 | 71.9 |
| Frederick | 202 | 3.1 | 140 | 1.0 | 143.7 | 1 169 355 | 8 344 | 97 310 | 127.0 | 88 095 | 28.3 | 71.7 | 40.0 | 13.8 | 2 852 | 35.0 |
| Garrett | 96 | -5.0 | 141 | 0.4 | 46.0 | 816 952 | 5 791 | 66 682 | 25.7 | 38 000 | 25.1 | 74.9 | 43.3 | 12.1 | 295 | 18.9 |
| Harford | 75 | -7.4 | 107 | 0.4 | 49.2 | 1 037 882 | 9 721 | 80 025 | 42.9 | 60 888 | 61.1 | 38.9 | 33.2 | 10.8 | 855 | 28.0 |
| Howard | 29 | -23.7 | 88 | 0.2 | 18.7 | 1 158 349 | 13 212 | 66 470 | 22.7 | 67 717 | 78.9 | 21.1 | 29.6 | 7.8 | 246 | 12.8 |
| Kent | 128 | 9.4 | 340 | 7.9 | 101.4 | 2 076 300 | 6 105 | 165 727 | 85.7 | 227 350 | 54.1 | 45.9 | 56.2 | 27.9 | 2 864 | 73.2 |
| Montgomery | 68 | -9.3 | 121 | 1.3 | 48.6 | 1 156 957 | 9 600 | 92 413 | 33.2 | 59 168 | 76.4 | 23.6 | 31.0 | 11.4 | 1 047 | 14.1 |
| Prince George's | 37 | -17.8 | 99 | 0.7 | 17.4 | 933 487 | 9 460 | 67 749 | 18.6 | 49 652 | 92.0 | 8.0 | 27.2 | 4.8 | 208 | 14.1 |
| Queen Anne's | 147 | -5.8 | 282 | 12.9 | 120.3 | 1 631 776 | 5 786 | 132 654 | 113.3 | 217 520 | 42.5 | 57.5 | 51.2 | 30.3 | 3 797 | 68.5 |

# Table B. States and Counties — Water Use, Wholesale Trade, Retail Trade, and Real Estate

| STATE County | Water use, 2005 | | Wholesale trade,[1] 2007 | | | | Retail trade,[2] 2007 | | | | Real estate and rental and leasing,[2] 2007 | | | |
|---|---|---|---|---|---|---|---|---|---|---|---|---|---|---|
| | Total water withdrawn (mil gal/day) | Gallons withdrawn per person | Number of establish-ments | Number of employees | Sales (mil dol) | Annual payroll (mil dol) | Number of establish-ments | Number of employees | Sales (mil dol) | Annual payroll (mil dol) | Number of establish-ments | Number of employees | Receipts (mil dol) | Annual payroll (mil dol) |
| | 133 | 134 | 135 | 136 | 137 | 138 | 139 | 140 | 141 | 142 | 143 | 144 | 145 | 146 |
| **LOUISIANA—Cont'd** | | | | | | | | | | | | | | |
| Orleans | 456.3 | 1 003 | 253 | 3 030 | 1 938.4 | 145.6 | 1 155 | 11 877 | 2 718.0 | 305.5 | 362 | 1 764 | 354.4 | 61.8 |
| Ouachita | 77.2 | 521 | 184 | D | D | D | 738 | 9 569 | 2 221.6 | 195.7 | 193 | 862 | 149.4 | 27.4 |
| Plaquemines | 154.5 | 5 328 | 59 | 711 | 921.0 | 34.0 | 66 | 444 | 113.6 | 10.9 | 36 | 410 | 102.8 | 20.3 |
| Pointe Coupee | 310.7 | 13 883 | 8 | 79 | 177.0 | 3.1 | 89 | 1 016 | 216.3 | 16.6 | 12 | 34 | 11.0 | 1.4 |
| Rapides | 526.6 | 4 099 | 142 | D | D | D | 603 | 7 960 | 1 910.2 | 169.3 | 140 | D | D | D |
| Red River | 2.3 | 239 | 6 | D | D | D | 27 | 186 | 36.7 | 2.8 | 2 | D | D | D |
| Richland | 39.3 | 1 914 | 24 | 213 | 172.6 | 7.7 | 63 | 737 | 228.4 | 14.8 | 23 | 69 | 9.4 | 1.3 |
| Sabine | 3.9 | 164 | 12 | D | D | D | 81 | 824 | 172.7 | 15.4 | 14 | 46 | 6.5 | 1.5 |
| St. Bernard | 292.2 | 4 470 | 26 | 224 | 164.2 | 7.5 | 104 | 1 056 | 291.8 | 22.6 | 18 | 47 | 7.8 | 1.7 |
| St. Charles | 3 131.8 | 61 854 | 78 | 1 896 | 2 137.7 | 95.2 | 120 | 1 510 | 389.2 | 32.0 | 38 | 160 | 52.1 | 8.0 |
| St. Helena | 4.0 | 392 | 2 | D | D | D | 18 | 187 | 35.5 | 2.6 | 2 | D | D | D |
| St. James | 389.4 | 18 412 | 14 | D | D | D | 50 | 627 | 162.9 | 10.8 | 7 | 18 | 1.0 | 0.4 |
| St. John the Baptist | 619.5 | 13 353 | 31 | 672 | 2 540.8 | 36.6 | 114 | 1 742 | 454.8 | 35.5 | 36 | 188 | 53.2 | 7.5 |
| St. Landry | 65.8 | 731 | 59 | D | D | D | 326 | 4 132 | 970.7 | 83.1 | 57 | 184 | 21.2 | 4.2 |
| St. Martin | 56.7 | 1 124 | 45 | 655 | 326.1 | 21.9 | 137 | 1 581 | 407.6 | 34.5 | 42 | 659 | 213.0 | 38.7 |
| St. Mary | 162.4 | 3 158 | 81 | D | D | D | 209 | 2 396 | 508.2 | 46.7 | 90 | 667 | 155.9 | 29.0 |
| St. Tammany | 25.3 | 115 | 236 | 2 118 | 2 363.2 | 106.8 | 897 | 13 585 | 3 481.1 | 318.5 | 240 | 973 | 169.5 | 35.1 |
| Tangipahoa | 19.8 | 186 | 89 | 1 782 | 953.7 | 77.1 | 452 | 6 607 | 1 742.4 | 140.8 | 90 | 417 | 44.6 | 9.0 |
| Tensas | 20.7 | 3 378 | 9 | D | D | D | 18 | 116 | 31.8 | 2.0 | 2 | D | D | D |
| Terrebonne | 11.4 | 106 | 194 | 2 105 | 899.0 | 91.0 | 492 | 7 621 | 1 915.4 | 180.9 | 176 | 1 746 | 372.0 | 79.4 |
| Union | 5.8 | 251 | 6 | D | D | D | 71 | 690 | 148.1 | 12.3 | 5 | 12 | 1.7 | 0.3 |
| Vermilion | 156.9 | 2 842 | 40 | D | D | D | 197 | 2 054 | 518.3 | 43.8 | 43 | 482 | 55.7 | 14.2 |
| Vernon | 8.1 | 165 | 19 | 98 | 51.6 | 3.4 | 156 | 1 535 | 315.7 | 27.3 | 30 | 213 | 17.3 | 8.3 |
| Washington | 37.5 | 840 | 23 | D | D | D | 152 | 1 513 | 326.3 | 29.0 | 13 | 32 | 3.3 | 0.7 |
| Webster | 10.9 | 263 | 27 | D | D | D | 161 | 2 045 | 484.8 | 39.4 | 24 | 216 | 20.9 | 6.2 |
| West Baton Rouge | 14.4 | 664 | 34 | 578 | 602.2 | 27.7 | 78 | 1 202 | 319.7 | 22.4 | 11 | 76 | 2.1 | 0.6 |
| West Carroll | 29.1 | 2 467 | 7 | D | D | D | 29 | 397 | 67.7 | 6.1 | 7 | 24 | 2.4 | 0.4 |
| West Feliciana | 58.4 | 3 840 | 7 | D | D | D | 35 | 301 | 66.0 | 5.4 | 8 | 27 | 3.1 | 0.7 |
| Winn | 13.6 | 853 | 9 | D | D | D | 56 | 579 | 122.5 | 11.6 | 14 | 49 | 5.1 | 0.9 |
| **MAINE** | 604.6 | 458 | 1 439 | 16 939 | 8 823.7 | 686.4 | 6 911 | 83 279 | 20 444.0 | 1 893.7 | 1 771 | 6 942 | 1 054.0 | 209.4 |
| Androscoggin | 15.8 | 146 | 104 | 1 277 | 444.6 | 51.3 | 489 | 6 386 | 1 704.3 | 145.2 | 119 | 509 | 82.0 | 13.4 |
| Aroostook | 18.4 | 252 | 70 | 438 | 230.8 | 17.8 | 388 | 4 657 | 1 105.9 | 92.5 | 74 | 268 | 29.0 | 5.4 |
| Cumberland | 131.3 | 477 | 474 | 6 730 | 3 427.9 | 290.0 | 1 541 | 22 703 | 5 277.2 | 533.9 | 618 | 2 964 | 505.3 | 104.9 |
| Franklin | 3.2 | 107 | 16 | D | D | D | 166 | 1 678 | 381.3 | 35.4 | 29 | 120 | 10.7 | 2.7 |
| Hancock | 65.6 | 1 222 | 70 | 409 | 256.6 | 13.1 | 397 | 3 282 | 820.0 | 81.8 | 86 | 231 | 28.0 | 5.8 |
| Kennebec | 12.5 | 103 | 107 | 2 450 | 1 195.6 | 102.9 | 605 | 8 718 | 2 382.3 | 203.6 | 114 | 476 | 70.4 | 13.8 |
| Knox | 5.4 | 131 | 62 | 356 | 178.0 | 11.5 | 291 | 2 753 | 640.2 | 62.7 | 64 | 156 | 23.5 | 5.3 |
| Lincoln | 2.7 | 77 | 42 | 154 | 65.8 | 4.9 | 226 | 1 773 | 433.2 | 40.7 | 57 | 143 | 14.0 | 3.4 |
| Oxford | 38.6 | 681 | 30 | 470 | 188.3 | 17.9 | 253 | 2 286 | 489.5 | 47.4 | 49 | 172 | 17.6 | 3.7 |
| Penobscot | 45.1 | 307 | 158 | D | D | D | 777 | 10 842 | 2 983.9 | 241.6 | 172 | 782 | 124.9 | 21.8 |
| Piscataquis | 2.6 | 149 | 11 | D | D | D | 102 | 941 | 196.5 | 18.7 | 17 | 39 | 4.6 | 0.8 |
| Sagadahoc | 3.6 | 97 | 29 | 144 | 113.9 | 4.9 | 142 | 1 747 | 415.5 | 37.4 | 44 | 99 | 15.0 | 2.6 |
| Somerset | 87.3 | 1 690 | 27 | 350 | 76.7 | 9.4 | 239 | 2 358 | 577.3 | 49.4 | 35 | 122 | 13.6 | 2.8 |
| Waldo | 4.1 | 106 | 28 | 271 | 522.3 | 10.3 | 169 | 1 476 | 340.3 | 33.9 | 29 | 85 | 8.7 | 2.4 |
| Washington | 50.2 | 1 500 | 51 | 161 | 79.1 | 3.9 | 172 | 1 820 | 405.2 | 37.5 | 26 | 76 | 4.6 | 1.3 |
| York | 118.3 | 585 | 160 | 1 349 | 704.2 | 55.9 | 954 | 9 859 | 2 291.4 | 232.1 | 238 | 700 | 102.1 | 19.3 |
| **MARYLAND** | 7 492.3 | 1 338 | 5 020 | 79 868 | 51 276.8 | 4 158.4 | 19 601 | 294 806 | 75 664.2 | 7 290.8 | 6 768 | 49 766 | 12 391.9 | 2 262.6 |
| Allegany | 44.3 | 602 | 42 | D | D | D | 304 | 4 042 | 865.2 | 72.7 | 58 | D | D | D |
| Anne Arundel | 599.8 | 1 174 | 522 | 10 051 | 6 922.2 | 537.1 | 2 126 | 33 592 | 9 465.0 | 812.4 | 627 | 5 356 | 985.8 | 199.5 |
| Baltimore | 838.9 | 1 067 | 829 | 12 110 | 5 609.3 | 624.5 | 2 991 | 50 468 | 12 074.9 | 1 264.2 | 955 | 7 075 | 2 788.3 | 310.3 |
| Calvert | 3 345.4 | 38 049 | 32 | 151 | 43.7 | 5.5 | 230 | 3 042 | 730.6 | 67.7 | 107 | 465 | 115.1 | 17.1 |
| Caroline | 14.4 | 452 | 26 | 228 | 129.7 | 8.4 | 100 | 1 109 | 406.9 | 27.3 | 24 | D | D | D |
| Carroll | 15.6 | 92 | 139 | 1 604 | 556.1 | 63.8 | 580 | 8 764 | 2 141.8 | 188.9 | 177 | D | D | D |
| Cecil | 10.4 | 107 | 72 | D | D | D | 286 | 3 925 | 1 099.7 | 86.4 | 80 | D | D | D |
| Charles | 985.4 | 7 098 | 59 | D | D | D | 540 | 9 936 | 2 369.8 | 239.0 | 122 | 534 | 74.6 | 19.6 |
| Dorchester | 17.5 | 558 | 31 | D | D | D | 119 | 1 218 | 318.6 | 28.4 | 34 | D | D | D |
| Frederick | 43.1 | 195 | 208 | 2 481 | 1 252.1 | 123.6 | 790 | 12 349 | 3 066.3 | 296.9 | 267 | 1 439 | 231.1 | 50.5 |
| Garrett | 8.4 | 281 | 28 | D | D | D | 160 | 1 754 | 431.4 | 36.0 | 40 | D | D | D |
| Harford | 18.9 | 79 | 191 | 2 439 | 1 871.3 | 95.6 | 774 | 12 630 | 3 380.3 | 308.6 | 246 | 1 017 | 173.2 | 31.7 |
| Howard | 4.5 | 17 | 478 | 11 257 | 7 170.8 | 654.1 | 866 | 16 094 | 4 555.0 | 424.8 | 406 | 3 189 | 1 040.7 | 176.3 |
| Kent | 5.6 | 282 | 26 | D | D | D | 106 | 990 | 197.1 | 20.4 | 39 | D | D | D |
| Montgomery | 649.5 | 700 | 735 | 9 168 | 7 426.6 | 576.9 | 2 952 | 48 390 | 13 255.8 | 1 357.8 | 1 465 | 15 301 | 4 335.6 | 871.7 |
| Prince George's | 720.4 | 851 | 582 | 12 603 | 10 449.8 | 634.4 | 2 265 | 37 623 | 9 209.7 | 944.3 | 740 | 6 315 | 1 118.6 | 246.8 |
| Queen Anne's | 14.3 | 313 | 68 | 509 | 212.9 | 22.6 | 249 | 2 822 | 618.3 | 61.9 | 68 | D | D | D |

1. Merchant wholesalers, except manufacturers' sales branches and offices.   2. Employer establishments.

| STATE County | Professional, scientific, and technical services,[1] 2007 | | | | Manufacturing, 2007 | | | | Accommodation and food services, 2007 | | | |
|---|---|---|---|---|---|---|---|---|---|---|---|---|
| | Number of establishments | Number of employees | Receipts (mil dol) | Annual payroll (mil dol) | Number of establishments | Number of employees | Receipts (mil dol) | Annual payroll (mil dol) | Number of establishments | Number of employees | Sales (mil dol) | Annual payroll (mil dol) |
| | 147 | 148 | 149 | 150 | 151 | 152 | 153 | 154 | 155 | 156 | 157 | 158 |
| LOUISIANA—Cont'd | | | | | | | | | | | | |
| Orleans | 1 290 | D | D | D | 141 | 7 607 | 3 088.9 | 402.0 | 1 058 | 28 356 | 2 148.2 | 602.4 |
| Ouachita | 441 | D | D | D | 135 | D | D | D | 285 | 6 554 | 250.3 | 67.8 |
| Plaquemines | 49 | 691 | 123.1 | 41.4 | 39 | 2 253 | D | 151.0 | 43 | 616 | 43.2 | 14.5 |
| Pointe Coupee | 31 | 120 | 13.3 | 4.3 | NA | NA | NA | NA | 30 | 363 | 14.0 | 3.3 |
| Rapides | 281 | 1 746 | 207.2 | 69.2 | 77 | D | D | 192.7 | 224 | D | D | D |
| Red River | 7 | 26 | 2.3 | 0.7 | NA | NA | NA | NA | 9 | 86 | 3.5 | 1.0 |
| Richland | 31 | 111 | 9.2 | 2.5 | NA | NA | NA | NA | 22 | 359 | 14.6 | 3.4 |
| Sabine | 39 | 165 | 12.8 | 5.5 | 21 | 893 | D | 34.8 | 17 | 282 | 14.0 | 3.2 |
| St. Bernard | 39 | 161 | 13.6 | 3.4 | 34 | 1 371 | D | 105.1 | 61 | 869 | 36.3 | 9.2 |
| St. Charles | 85 | 621 | 68.9 | 28.7 | 38 | 4 864 | 27 354.7 | 440.7 | 81 | 951 | 40.1 | 10.5 |
| St. Helena | 8 | 42 | 2.4 | 0.7 | NA | NA | NA | NA | 9 | 47 | 1.7 | 0.4 |
| St. James | 16 | 46 | 4.0 | 1.3 | 28 | 2 396 | D | 184.1 | 23 | 330 | 12.0 | 3.1 |
| St. John the Baptist | 55 | 341 | 42.9 | 11.7 | 28 | 2 426 | D | 178.5 | 71 | 1 427 | 55.5 | 13.9 |
| St. Landry | 130 | 605 | 66.6 | 23.3 | 55 | 1 732 | D | 68.9 | 97 | 1 454 | 56.6 | 13.9 |
| St. Martin | 78 | D | D | D | 58 | 1 361 | 324.3 | 51.0 | 77 | 983 | 45.1 | 10.9 |
| St. Mary | 106 | 694 | 104.2 | 42.9 | 90 | 4 417 | 2 011.1 | 200.6 | 107 | 1 597 | 60.3 | 15.9 |
| St. Tammany | 791 | D | D | D | 136 | 2 468 | 436.3 | 98.1 | 484 | 8 601 | 370.7 | 105.3 |
| Tangipahoa | 189 | D | D | D | 92 | 2 773 | D | 81.3 | 225 | 4 169 | 164.6 | 41.3 |
| Tensas | 4 | D | D | D | NA | NA | NA | NA | 7 | 19 | 0.5 | 0.2 |
| Terrebonne | 280 | D | D | D | 126 | 5 107 | 1 115.6 | 240.3 | 238 | 4 780 | 233.1 | 68.9 |
| Union | 21 | D | D | D | 11 | D | D | D | 17 | 244 | 10.2 | 2.5 |
| Vermilion | 109 | 288 | 30.7 | 9.7 | 42 | 903 | D | 30.4 | 64 | 1 038 | 51.1 | 10.1 |
| Vernon | 45 | 747 | 64.7 | 26.2 | NA | NA | NA | NA | 62 | 1 150 | 39.8 | 11.5 |
| Washington | 49 | 195 | 23.0 | 6.5 | 35 | 1 383 | D | 75.3 | 61 | 676 | 28.1 | 6.8 |
| Webster | 52 | 274 | 15.8 | 5.2 | 33 | 2 237 | 712.0 | 75.3 | 64 | 801 | 28.7 | 6.3 |
| West Baton Rouge | 28 | 190 | 25.4 | 7.1 | 36 | 2 442 | D | 123.4 | 47 | 753 | 35.2 | 8.2 |
| West Carroll | 11 | 21 | 1.8 | 0.5 | NA | NA | NA | NA | 10 | 76 | 4.1 | 1.0 |
| West Feliciana | 17 | 39 | 4.2 | 1.6 | 6 | D | D | D | 27 | 358 | 11.8 | 3.3 |
| Winn | 15 | D | D | D | 19 | 852 | D | 34.8 | 19 | 316 | 11.2 | 2.4 |
| MAINE | 3 444 | 20 504 | 2 686.1 | 1 004.9 | 1 825 | 58 938 | 16 363.2 | 2 524.5 | 3 938 | 49 363 | 2 515.8 | 747.7 |
| Androscoggin | 182 | D | D | D | 158 | 6 945 | 2 186.2 | 300.2 | 226 | 3 422 | 149.7 | 44.0 |
| Aroostook | 104 | D | D | D | 103 | 2 441 | 621.6 | 82.3 | 151 | 1 833 | 71.8 | 20.9 |
| Cumberland | 1 350 | D | D | D | 423 | 11 005 | D | 479.2 | 898 | 14 351 | 734.9 | 222.3 |
| Franklin | 49 | D | D | D | 32 | 1 721 | 823.5 | 83.7 | 90 | 1 220 | 43.0 | 13.0 |
| Hancock | 136 | D | D | D | 107 | 1 838 | 599.1 | 93.3 | 304 | 2 245 | 167.5 | 45.8 |
| Kennebec | 276 | D | D | D | 113 | 2 557 | 584.1 | 104.6 | 300 | 4 073 | 198.5 | 59.6 |
| Knox | 138 | D | D | D | 97 | 1 676 | 387.0 | 65.0 | 178 | 1 697 | 90.1 | 28.4 |
| Lincoln | 105 | D | D | D | 78 | 762 | 122.6 | 27.6 | 152 | 987 | 72.0 | 20.9 |
| Oxford | 79 | D | D | D | 72 | 2 682 | 865.8 | 132.6 | 144 | 2 402 | 92.6 | 29.9 |
| Penobscot | 333 | D | D | D | 155 | 4 795 | 1 088.5 | 171.9 | 320 | 5 179 | 224.2 | 68.1 |
| Piscataquis | 10 | D | D | D | 27 | 856 | 119.4 | 26.6 | 49 | 321 | 13.6 | 3.6 |
| Sagadahoc | 95 | D | D | D | 41 | D | D | D | 81 | 1 048 | 51.5 | 16.7 |
| Somerset | 63 | 394 | 34.5 | 17.6 | 71 | 3 532 | 1 566.9 | 163.6 | 111 | 1 070 | 45.0 | 13.2 |
| Waldo | 62 | 185 | 18.9 | 6.6 | 54 | 1 487 | 210.3 | 42.8 | 88 | 794 | 37.6 | 10.3 |
| Washington | 39 | D | D | D | 43 | 980 | 444.1 | 42.4 | 92 | 616 | 24.7 | 6.6 |
| York | 423 | D | D | D | 251 | D | 2 904.3 | D | 754 | 8 105 | 499.1 | 144.3 |
| MARYLAND | 19 345 | D | D | D | 3 680 | 127 780 | 41 456.1 | 6 453.7 | 10 802 | 192 619 | 10 758.4 | 2 915.9 |
| Allegany | 108 | D | D | D | 60 | 2 679 | D | 108.9 | 174 | 2 848 | 124.7 | 34.4 |
| Anne Arundel | 2 032 | 19 275 | 3 344.9 | 1 310.5 | 333 | 14 020 | 3 610.1 | 995.5 | 1 052 | 22 159 | 1 288.1 | 344.0 |
| Baltimore | 2 770 | 23 340 | 3 127.1 | 1 295.0 | 512 | 21 919 | 9 247.2 | 1 174.1 | 1 546 | 27 814 | 1 414.1 | 385.4 |
| Calvert | 202 | D | D | D | 49 | D | D | D | 122 | 2 518 | 110.7 | 30.9 |
| Caroline | 39 | D | D | D | 35 | 1 351 | 329.0 | 43.8 | 36 | 466 | 18.9 | 4.5 |
| Carroll | 470 | D | D | D | 155 | 4 369 | 1 095.1 | 203.2 | 251 | 5 293 | 203.8 | 61.2 |
| Cecil | 181 | D | D | D | 55 | 4 006 | 1 301.1 | 229.2 | 171 | 2 648 | 133.4 | 35.7 |
| Charles | 265 | D | D | D | 62 | 910 | 158.0 | 35.3 | 231 | 4 741 | 231.6 | 63.3 |
| Dorchester | 49 | 170 | 16.0 | 6.3 | 56 | 3 077 | 991.9 | 99.3 | 62 | 1 274 | 81.8 | 20.4 |
| Frederick | 815 | D | D | D | 181 | 7 076 | 3 003.7 | 334.7 | 392 | 7 542 | 356.5 | 106.0 |
| Garrett | 58 | 305 | 26.8 | 13.6 | 54 | 909 | 143.2 | 29.1 | 79 | 1 059 | 47.3 | 13.8 |
| Harford | 614 | D | D | D | 161 | 5 578 | 2 016.1 | 256.0 | 367 | 7 942 | 361.9 | 96.7 |
| Howard | 1 700 | D | D | D | 233 | 6 736 | 2 368.3 | 334.6 | 535 | 10 804 | 565.7 | 160.0 |
| Kent | 59 | D | D | D | 29 | 1 065 | 290.2 | 36.9 | 63 | 676 | 36.0 | 10.6 |
| Montgomery | 5 584 | D | D | D | 459 | 10 798 | 3 264.1 | 648.1 | 1 753 | 30 058 | 1 872.8 | 508.1 |
| Prince George's | 1 639 | D | D | D | 347 | 9 985 | 2 504.7 | 494.2 | 1 186 | 20 563 | 1 205.0 | 312.2 |
| Queen Anne's | 174 | D | D | D | 50 | 1 224 | 238.8 | 48.0 | 94 | 1 937 | 103.0 | 30.8 |

1. Establishment subject to federal tax.

# Table B. States and Counties — Health Care and Social Assistance, Other Services, and Federal Funds

| STATE County | Health care and social assistance, 2007 | | | | Other services, 2007 | | | | Federal funds and grants, 2009–2010 Expenditures (mil dol) | | | |
|---|---|---|---|---|---|---|---|---|---|---|---|---|
| | | | | | | | | | | Direct payments for individuals[1] | | |
| | Number of establish-ments | Number of employees | Receipts (mil dol) | Annual payroll (mil dol) | Number of establish-ments | Number of employees | Receipts (mil dol) | Annual payroll (mil dol) | Total | Social Security and government retirement | Medicare | Food Stamps and Supplemental Security Income |
| | 159 | 160 | 161 | 162 | 163 | 164 | 165 | 166 | 167 | 168 | 169 | 170 |
| **LOUISIANA—Cont'd** | | | | | | | | | | | | |
| Orleans | 804 | 16 725 | 2 039.5 | 708.6 | 601 | 3 875 | 654.7 | 107.0 | 8 277.8 | 869.5 | 1 266.8 | 403.7 |
| Ouachita | 587 | 12 571 | 1 137.4 | 400.5 | 227 | 1 524 | 134.4 | 37.2 | 1 174.0 | 388.3 | 284.8 | 82.9 |
| Plaquemines | 25 | D | D | D | 45 | D | D | D | 376.9 | 55.2 | 45.2 | 10.4 |
| Pointe Coupee | 36 | 588 | 36.6 | 15.1 | 26 | D | D | D | 213.1 | 60.2 | 38.0 | 12.8 |
| Rapides | 487 | D | D | D | 228 | 1 192 | 101.7 | 27.8 | 1 407.9 | 438.8 | 270.1 | 75.2 |
| Red River | 17 | 465 | 27.7 | 12.0 | 9 | D | D | D | 94.1 | 23.4 | 22.7 | 5.4 |
| Richland | 65 | 1 633 | 95.4 | 39.5 | 23 | 71 | 5.9 | 1.3 | 228.5 | 53.8 | 56.1 | 14.0 |
| Sabine | 41 | 810 | 42.8 | 15.7 | 25 | 97 | 6.4 | 1.5 | 215.2 | 78.9 | 49.4 | 11.5 |
| St. Bernard | 45 | 374 | 31.6 | 10.5 | 32 | D | D | D | 882.4 | 75.0 | 179.4 | 21.0 |
| St. Charles | 74 | 1 397 | 85.3 | 36.9 | 56 | 344 | 63.0 | 16.2 | 370.1 | 119.1 | 69.5 | 15.6 |
| St. Helena | 15 | 376 | 18.4 | 8.9 | 4 | D | D | D | 83.2 | 18.9 | 19.4 | 7.9 |
| St. James | 29 | 441 | 32.4 | 13.6 | 13 | 42 | 4.1 | 0.9 | 162.9 | 62.1 | 47.0 | 12.5 |
| St. John the Baptist | 73 | D | D | D | 48 | D | D | D | 263.8 | 117.4 | 63.5 | 23.3 |
| St. Landry | 275 | 4 794 | 424.4 | 150.3 | 77 | 363 | 24.1 | 7.6 | 881.1 | 249.7 | 188.4 | 69.7 |
| St. Martin | 69 | 1 334 | 57.6 | 27.9 | 46 | 109 | 12.2 | 2.5 | 364.7 | 117.9 | 70.8 | 22.1 |
| St. Mary | 105 | 1 931 | 136.8 | 50.2 | 91 | 447 | 56.2 | 14.4 | 498.4 | 154.8 | 100.1 | 37.2 |
| St. Tammany | 715 | 12 287 | 1 256.7 | 485.5 | 364 | 2 053 | 168.1 | 51.9 | 1 383.9 | 716.5 | 275.7 | 51.4 |
| Tangipahoa | 269 | 7 321 | 568.5 | 226.1 | 150 | 919 | 86.4 | 21.7 | 928.9 | 307.4 | 224.6 | 70.6 |
| Tensas | 11 | D | D | D | NA | NA | NA | NA | 104.4 | 14.2 | 19.3 | 6.1 |
| Terrebonne | 255 | 6 396 | 619.2 | 253.0 | 173 | 1 575 | 222.5 | 63.2 | 792.9 | 298.0 | 174.8 | 58.9 |
| Union | 29 | 740 | 43.5 | 15.7 | 18 | 49 | 4.1 | 0.8 | 205.0 | 75.9 | 54.3 | 10.8 |
| Vermilion | 104 | 1 458 | 100.3 | 38.8 | 58 | 248 | 22.5 | 5.5 | 381.0 | 140.4 | 99.2 | 27.3 |
| Vernon | 70 | 1 620 | 170.7 | 55.0 | 50 | 324 | 32.7 | 9.3 | 2 271.3 | 171.3 | 67.2 | 16.5 |
| Washington | 89 | 1 933 | 132.1 | 55.3 | 42 | 189 | 13.5 | 3.4 | 493.9 | 152.3 | 160.2 | 34.2 |
| Webster | 92 | 2 374 | 166.5 | 59.4 | 36 | 227 | 20.3 | 5.5 | 411.4 | 146.4 | 106.6 | 24.7 |
| West Baton Rouge | 28 | D | D | D | 32 | 201 | 29.7 | 7.6 | 233.3 | 54.6 | 40.7 | 11.0 |
| West Carroll | 17 | 653 | 32.0 | 12.8 | 15 | 68 | 3.7 | 1.2 | 135.0 | 33.9 | 34.3 | 6.5 |
| West Feliciana | 20 | 321 | 26.0 | 9.4 | 7 | D | D | D | 71.0 | 23.8 | 14.8 | 4.1 |
| Winn | 43 | 820 | 52.6 | 21.9 | 18 | 111 | 10.5 | 4.1 | 142.7 | 43.1 | 41.3 | 9.8 |
| **MAINE** | 4 875 | 104 151 | 8 592.4 | 3 691.6 | 2 840 | 13 297 | 1 279.7 | 328.1 | 14 643.9 | 4 679.4 | 1 837.0 | 569.4 |
| Androscoggin | 421 | 9 495 | 872.4 | 355.7 | 203 | 945 | 69.8 | 21.2 | 874.9 | 352.8 | 171.4 | 57.0 |
| Aroostook | 252 | 6 327 | 419.9 | 188.5 | 134 | 410 | 37.3 | 8.8 | 974.3 | 305.0 | 130.3 | 45.8 |
| Cumberland | 1 316 | 29 849 | 2 669.0 | 1 155.5 | 764 | 4 199 | 398.0 | 107.0 | 2 505.9 | 864.5 | 363.0 | 88.5 |
| Franklin | 100 | 1 888 | 132.8 | 55.7 | 51 | 204 | 19.4 | 4.1 | 221.2 | 93.5 | 43.3 | 14.1 |
| Hancock | 160 | 2 936 | 252.3 | 110.6 | 137 | 749 | 120.8 | 22.8 | 542.7 | 195.6 | 77.1 | 15.4 |
| Kennebec | 496 | 11 949 | 996.5 | 435.9 | 292 | 1 289 | 146.4 | 36.0 | 2 137.6 | 455.5 | 154.2 | 57.8 |
| Knox | 177 | 3 111 | 215.9 | 88.8 | 118 | 545 | 58.5 | 15.1 | 361.0 | 157.9 | 64.3 | 15.5 |
| Lincoln | 102 | 1 878 | 131.4 | 52.9 | 97 | 491 | 38.4 | 12.2 | 298.9 | 146.6 | 53.3 | 10.8 |
| Oxford | 155 | 2 961 | 217.3 | 87.0 | 95 | 354 | 32.9 | 8.1 | 458.3 | 197.9 | 93.1 | 27.6 |
| Penobscot | 563 | 14 538 | 1 318.9 | 561.5 | 276 | 1 350 | 139.8 | 33.6 | 1 644.1 | 537.9 | 207.0 | 75.8 |
| Piscataquis | 44 | 1 420 | 81.8 | 38.9 | 21 | 69 | 6.0 | 1.4 | 170.1 | 78.1 | 30.0 | 10.3 |
| Sagadahoc | 117 | 1 372 | 80.3 | 34.0 | 65 | 326 | 27.0 | 8.3 | 898.4 | 138.9 | 33.2 | 10.7 |
| Somerset | 153 | 3 119 | 202.8 | 88.7 | 94 | 340 | 25.5 | 6.6 | 445.4 | 183.9 | 72.3 | 34.8 |
| Waldo | 111 | 1 526 | 116.3 | 52.0 | 75 | 243 | 23.3 | 5.4 | 333.4 | 131.5 | 42.7 | 20.8 |
| Washington | 110 | 2 256 | 147.2 | 70.0 | 59 | 191 | 18.0 | 5.0 | 455.3 | 136.7 | 61.9 | 24.9 |
| York | 598 | 9 526 | 737.7 | 315.7 | 359 | 1 592 | 118.8 | 32.6 | 1 686.8 | 703.2 | 239.8 | 59.8 |
| **MARYLAND** | 15 304 | 315 781 | 33 826.6 | 13 089.4 | 10 365 | 77 368 | 9 688.6 | 2 487.4 | 96 260.9 | 18 444.1 | 14 530.9 | 1 552.4 |
| Allegany | 256 | 5 848 | 558.7 | 209.7 | 159 | 858 | 63.4 | 17.4 | 961.7 | 292.3 | 379.7 | 33.3 |
| Anne Arundel | 1 184 | 21 198 | 2 092.9 | 851.2 | 1 095 | 7 437 | 691.4 | 232.8 | 8 209.5 | 1 929.3 | 1 024.5 | 78.3 |
| Baltimore | 2 645 | 57 385 | 5 767.6 | 2 276.7 | 1 499 | 10 625 | 1 072.8 | 320.0 | 9 169.4 | 2 530.4 | 1 969.5 | 231.3 |
| Calvert | 173 | 3 200 | 300.6 | 114.6 | 131 | 770 | 58.6 | 19.2 | 569.2 | 317.7 | 126.6 | 10.8 |
| Caroline | 49 | 667 | 33.3 | 17.6 | 52 | 226 | 19.0 | 5.4 | 449.0 | 100.2 | 111.0 | 9.4 |
| Carroll | 457 | 8 597 | 854.7 | 308.0 | 352 | 2 086 | 147.9 | 49.5 | 1 132.3 | 581.5 | 298.5 | 15.7 |
| Cecil | 155 | 5 507 | 637.1 | 280.1 | 152 | 838 | 65.9 | 19.1 | 707.0 | 320.9 | 172.8 | 22.4 |
| Charles | 311 | 4 069 | 384.7 | 150.7 | 231 | 1 471 | 114.6 | 38.3 | 1 367.7 | 543.9 | 209.9 | 27.9 |
| Dorchester | 85 | 1 626 | 130.9 | 56.6 | 63 | 280 | 18.0 | 4.6 | 508.4 | 117.4 | 148.4 | 15.7 |
| Frederick | 531 | 9 326 | 936.8 | 368.8 | 400 | 2 549 | 266.1 | 76.0 | 2 645.5 | 647.9 | 268.1 | 23.6 |
| Garrett | 73 | 1 602 | 95.8 | 42.7 | 77 | 702 | 44.7 | 18.3 | 290.7 | 98.7 | 102.2 | 9.9 |
| Harford | 545 | 8 231 | 782.3 | 297.9 | 436 | 2 714 | 196.2 | 65.0 | 3 147.6 | 824.0 | 372.6 | 36.9 |
| Howard | 804 | 12 295 | 1 131.0 | 458.3 | 524 | 4 238 | 452.0 | 147.4 | 3 351.7 | 695.0 | 204.8 | 23.1 |
| Kent | 72 | 1 333 | 121.6 | 47.2 | 52 | 191 | 21.4 | 5.3 | 222.3 | 98.2 | 75.4 | 4.0 |
| Montgomery | 3 376 | 54 741 | 6 553.4 | 2 574.9 | 1 939 | 17 446 | 3 379.3 | 756.2 | 20 664.2 | 2 851.8 | 1 484.4 | 128.8 |
| Prince George's | 1 763 | 27 511 | 2 588.3 | 1 026.7 | 1 212 | 9 385 | 968.3 | 278.2 | 13 879.8 | 2 979.9 | 1 424.3 | 189.0 |
| Queen Anne's | 67 | 873 | 56.0 | 24.7 | 109 | 596 | 47.2 | 12.5 | 315.3 | 149.3 | 72.7 | 4.9 |

1. State totals may include programs not allocated by county.

| STATE County | Salaries and wages | Defense | Other | Medicaid and other health-related | Nutrition and family welfare | Education | Other | New construction ($1,000) | Number of housing units | Total (mil dol) | Inter-governmental (mil dol) | Total (mil dol) | Per capita Total | Property |
|---|---|---|---|---|---|---|---|---|---|---|---|---|---|---|
| | 171 | 172 | 173 | 174 | 175 | 176 | 177 | 178 | 179 | 180 | 181 | 182 | 183 | 184 |
| LOUISIANA—Cont'd | | | | | | | | | | | | | | |
| Orleans | 774.6 | 2 495.4 | 527.4 | 1 176.9 | 120.2 | 110.8 | 378.1 | 156 896 | 1 094 | 1 569.3 | 514.0 | 609.2 | 2 548 | 1 134 |
| Ouachita | 68.3 | 10.1 | 9.7 | 186.6 | 25.5 | 17.1 | 41.4 | 60 737 | 383 | 523.7 | 232.3 | 226.6 | 1 516 | 474 |
| Plaquemines | 37.9 | 143.9 | 48.8 | 23.0 | 4.8 | 1.7 | 4.7 | 6 930 | 62 | 215.6 | 112.3 | 62.6 | 2 906 | 1 629 |
| Pointe Coupee | 11.9 | 12.2 | 0.9 | 58.4 | 6.4 | 2.0 | 0.2 | 7 401 | 46 | 79.0 | 28.2 | 29.2 | 1 305 | 655 |
| Rapides | 229.9 | 11.0 | 84.6 | 185.5 | 31.6 | 12.3 | 44.9 | 48 251 | 350 | 430.3 | 203.4 | 167.6 | 1 288 | 468 |
| Red River | 8.0 | 0.0 | 0.3 | 28.3 | 2.9 | 0.8 | 0.3 | 0 | 0 | 30.6 | 16.7 | 9.2 | 1 002 | 432 |
| Richland | 8.0 | 0.0 | 1.2 | 64.9 | 5.9 | 2.0 | 3.3 | 5 548 | 38 | 86.3 | 39.5 | 18.7 | 914 | 287 |
| Sabine | 5.4 | 2.0 | 0.9 | 54.6 | 5.7 | 2.9 | 1.1 | 9 407 | 124 | 60.4 | 35.2 | 20.3 | 857 | 326 |
| St. Bernard | 3.9 | 534.6 | 0.2 | 36.7 | 10.7 | 4.8 | 11.0 | 3 195 | 25 | 291.6 | 188.8 | 63.5 | 3 202 | 1 076 |
| St. Charles | 11.6 | 103.0 | 3.0 | 29.3 | 8.5 | 3.0 | 3.9 | 13 993 | 83 | 305.5 | 58.5 | 167.8 | 3 225 | 1 786 |
| St. Helena | 1.2 | 0.0 | 0.2 | 26.1 | 3.2 | 2.8 | 0.8 | 0 | 0 | 33.3 | 16.5 | 6.5 | 614 | 308 |
| St. James | 3.1 | 0.5 | 0.7 | 25.8 | 6.4 | 1.8 | 1.7 | 14 212 | 128 | 111.2 | 32.7 | 51.6 | 2 390 | 1 505 |
| St. John the Baptist | 9.6 | 0.2 | 1.2 | 24.8 | 9.4 | 3.0 | 7.1 | 8 407 | 50 | 156.7 | 52.1 | 67.9 | 1 425 | 594 |
| St. Landry | 17.5 | 9.8 | 3.5 | 273.7 | 27.3 | 11.9 | 6.6 | 24 084 | 143 | 318.6 | 136.2 | 88.5 | 968 | 267 |
| St. Martin | 19.4 | 22.9 | 1.7 | 85.4 | 9.8 | 5.3 | 1.8 | 19 786 | 120 | 130.3 | 70.5 | 39.5 | 764 | 318 |
| St. Mary | 17.1 | 70.1 | 16.3 | 68.4 | 16.6 | 6.2 | 3.4 | 8 821 | 49 | 208.8 | 85.4 | 76.8 | 1 497 | 664 |
| St. Tammany | 78.1 | 93.5 | 13.0 | 81.1 | 33.4 | 8.6 | 17.9 | 140 975 | 789 | 1 134.6 | 348.3 | 419.9 | 1 853 | 720 |
| Tangipahoa | 50.5 | 4.0 | -1.2 | 195.5 | 22.0 | 14.3 | 7.8 | 66 015 | 575 | 514.9 | 184.0 | 114.5 | 992 | 260 |
| Tensas | 1.2 | 9.4 | 0.3 | 27.7 | 2.5 | 1.1 | 1.4 | 565 | 5 | 25.6 | 16.1 | 7.2 | 1 223 | 689 |
| Terrebonne | 35.7 | 39.1 | 41.8 | 90.9 | 19.8 | 10.5 | 14.6 | 49 743 | 181 | 514.7 | 167.9 | 153.2 | 1 413 | 368 |
| Union | 9.1 | 0.0 | 3.6 | 42.0 | 4.3 | 1.6 | 0.8 | 3 648 | 22 | 52.0 | 27.3 | 15.5 | 679 | 239 |
| Vermilion | 17.1 | 0.5 | 2.5 | 65.1 | 9.8 | 4.8 | 4.9 | 31 573 | 221 | 188.2 | 77.7 | 60.0 | 1 078 | 433 |
| Vernon | 1 435.6 | 498.6 | 1.5 | 46.6 | 10.8 | 9.4 | 7.1 | 515 | 5 | 124.3 | 77.2 | 37.1 | 783 | 265 |
| Washington | 18.9 | 0.5 | 3.0 | 101.6 | 9.6 | 4.0 | 3.4 | 15 690 | 86 | 198.2 | 121.6 | 44.7 | 996 | 389 |
| Webster | 23.5 | 5.3 | 1.8 | 76.1 | 10.9 | 3.7 | 4.0 | 4 116 | 21 | 123.1 | 59.8 | 47.3 | 1 155 | 404 |
| West Baton Rouge | 4.4 | 109.7 | -18.9 | 24.5 | 4.7 | 1.5 | 0.0 | 25 634 | 168 | 87.8 | 31.0 | 39.0 | 1 724 | 786 |
| West Carroll | 5.6 | 0.0 | 0.5 | 37.1 | 3.2 | 1.0 | 0.6 | 0 | 0 | 29.8 | 17.3 | 9.6 | 831 | 259 |
| West Feliciana | 1.7 | 7.0 | 0.3 | 14.0 | 3.0 | 0.7 | 0.0 | 5 414 | 16 | 106.8 | 19.2 | 29.3 | 1 941 | 1 385 |
| Winn | 12.7 | 0.0 | 0.8 | 31.8 | 3.7 | 1.8 | -4.2 | 0 | 0 | 38.6 | 22.1 | 12.6 | 812 | 372 |
| MAINE | 1 134.0 | 1 336.2 | 399.5 | 2 186.8 | 340.3 | 229.6 | 1 030.8 | 0 | 69 | X | X | X | X | X |
| Androscoggin | 46.5 | 1.1 | 5.4 | 178.8 | 17.7 | 6.3 | 18.2 | 16 550 | 148 | 330.4 | 146.7 | 142.8 | 1 337 | 1 325 |
| Aroostook | 75.4 | 8.7 | 99.7 | 225.5 | 22.8 | 4.7 | 21.3 | 4 466 | 43 | 253.4 | 109.6 | 74.7 | 1 037 | 1 032 |
| Cumberland | 246.1 | 282.5 | 79.3 | 335.9 | 40.2 | 11.3 | 114.7 | 110 754 | 529 | 998.6 | 258.3 | 529.9 | 1 924 | 1 889 |
| Franklin | 9.0 | 0.6 | 2.3 | 39.0 | 6.7 | 1.7 | 0.9 | 9 438 | 64 | 89.0 | 31.1 | 49.7 | 1 659 | 1 647 |
| Hancock | 25.6 | 4.1 | 24.2 | 165.2 | 10.6 | 1.8 | 17.0 | 28 911 | 169 | 169.3 | 38.0 | 109.3 | 2 052 | 2 036 |
| Kennebec | 157.9 | 5.1 | 69.5 | 292.9 | 88.2 | 118.4 | 670.4 | 32 875 | 260 | 337.7 | 158.7 | 135.1 | 1 118 | 1 109 |
| Knox | 13.6 | 2.1 | 4.8 | 82.2 | 6.8 | 1.9 | 4.5 | 16 831 | 124 | 113.8 | 21.1 | 77.7 | 1 906 | 1 888 |
| Lincoln | 9.3 | 0.0 | 3.5 | 42.8 | 6.7 | 0.9 | 21.8 | 14 531 | 72 | 116.0 | 34.6 | 68.7 | 1 974 | 1 955 |
| Oxford | 16.8 | 0.0 | 7.4 | 85.7 | 15.3 | 1.8 | 4.7 | 23 658 | 123 | 173.7 | 76.3 | 84.1 | 1 482 | 1 473 |
| Penobscot | 173.7 | 131.4 | 69.6 | 254.0 | 28.6 | 10.5 | 90.0 | 36 853 | 369 | 413.1 | 167.1 | 177.0 | 1 190 | 1 173 |
| Piscataquis | 4.6 | 0.7 | 0.9 | 34.5 | 3.7 | 0.7 | 3.3 | 3 827 | 24 | 86.1 | 29.3 | 21.7 | 1 261 | 1 255 |
| Sagadahoc | 29.4 | 647.5 | 1.5 | 26.8 | 6.3 | 0.9 | 1.1 | 9 412 | 60 | 119.0 | 42.1 | 65.7 | 1 806 | 1 791 |
| Somerset | 18.2 | 0.1 | 4.7 | 106.9 | 9.5 | 2.1 | 4.7 | 5 576 | 45 | 171.0 | 85.8 | 72.2 | 1 398 | 1 395 |
| Waldo | 11.5 | 46.0 | 2.4 | 63.7 | 7.1 | 1.2 | 0.9 | 9 971 | 65 | 100.0 | 38.8 | 52.1 | 1 353 | 1 349 |
| Washington | 28.8 | 41.9 | 13.8 | 104.0 | 10.7 | 4.6 | 8.5 | 11 301 | 57 | 94.9 | 43.8 | 42.1 | 1 285 | 1 271 |
| York | 267.8 | 164.4 | 10.3 | 148.6 | 27.1 | 6.5 | 41.3 | 91 551 | 523 | 588.9 | 183.6 | 343.7 | 1 707 | 1 680 |
| MARYLAND | 15 041.5 | 12 017.6 | 14 504.9 | 7 701.5 | 1 138.0 | 1 112.8 | 4 489.1 | 2 204 630 | 13 481 | X | X | X | X | X |
| Allegany | 53.5 | 1.6 | 12.2 | 126.2 | 18.9 | 4.6 | 17.6 | 12 269 | 70 | 294.2 | 150.8 | 73.7 | 1 015 | 592 |
| Anne Arundel | 1 791.7 | 1 879.0 | 252.0 | 321.6 | 66.4 | 446.7 | 294.3 | 277 343 | 2 360 | 1 768.5 | 444.5 | 1 040.4 | 2 032 | 974 |
| Baltimore | 1 572.7 | 857.3 | 915.4 | 542.0 | 86.2 | 17.0 | 394.6 | 93 293 | 487 | 2 559.9 | 799.1 | 1 440.0 | 1 825 | 849 |
| Calvert | 10.6 | 13.0 | 28.3 | 40.3 | 8.2 | 1.3 | 5.6 | 58 350 | 223 | 330.9 | 109.9 | 171.5 | 1 944 | 1 110 |
| Caroline | 160.4 | 1.1 | 1.8 | 49.8 | 5.9 | 0.9 | 0.8 | 3 882 | 29 | 113.0 | 65.2 | 33.6 | 1 022 | 584 |
| Carroll | 39.3 | 40.2 | 19.2 | 66.2 | 14.9 | 2.0 | 40.8 | 42 302 | 183 | 413.7 | 37.1 | 307.7 | 1 818 | 1 009 |
| Cecil | 67.8 | 9.8 | 37.6 | 45.5 | 12.1 | 2.0 | 6.8 | 52 278 | 304 | 336.2 | 144.0 | 146.5 | 1 469 | 856 |
| Charles | 154.3 | 278.3 | 13.2 | 72.3 | 19.8 | 3.2 | 13.6 | 145 400 | 717 | 361.7 | 40.8 | 264.5 | 1 883 | 1 048 |
| Dorchester | 12.6 | 2.3 | 6.0 | 59.0 | 6.5 | 1.6 | 133.9 | 7 727 | 52 | 123.5 | 53.0 | 47.8 | 1 500 | 919 |
| Frederick | 268.1 | 569.7 | 718.7 | 82.2 | 24.1 | 4.1 | 14.5 | 128 601 | 644 | 917.8 | 285.5 | 466.8 | 2 078 | 1 162 |
| Garrett | 6.3 | 7.3 | 4.0 | 41.5 | 11.2 | 1.2 | 2.0 | 26 741 | 93 | 129.9 | 56.0 | 55.1 | 1 859 | 1 198 |
| Harford | 878.2 | 823.5 | 61.3 | 90.3 | 25.3 | 4.5 | 12.8 | 132 843 | 801 | 844.1 | 276.9 | 432.4 | 1 802 | 989 |
| Howard | 63.5 | 1 576.9 | 594.0 | 50.0 | 23.3 | 4.2 | 81.9 | 250 129 | 1 177 | 1 187.3 | 278.0 | 779.7 | 2 849 | 1 403 |
| Kent | 6.2 | 0.0 | 2.2 | 22.4 | 3.6 | 1.4 | 1.4 | 9 577 | 46 | 73.7 | 27.6 | 37.7 | 1 889 | 1 146 |
| Montgomery | 5 128.6 | 2 555.8 | 6 596.2 | 876.8 | 98.2 | 30.2 | 743.9 | 434 450 | 2 512 | 4 656.7 | 909.8 | 3 077.1 | 3 306 | 1 388 |
| Prince George's | 3 133.9 | 750.7 | 4 171.1 | 545.9 | 122.1 | 37.8 | 389.9 | 189 090 | 1 227 | 3 353.2 | 1 185.9 | 1 623.1 | 1 958 | 1 019 |
| Queen Anne's | 7.9 | 31.2 | 8.8 | 21.2 | 5.2 | 0.9 | 6.3 | 30 719 | 156 | 200.8 | 62.7 | 94.7 | 2 034 | 1 024 |

1. State totals may include programs not allocated by county.   2. Based on the resident population estimated as of July 1 of the year shown.

# Table B. States and Counties — Local Government Finances, Government Employment, and Voting

| STATE County | Total (mil dol) | Per capita[1] (dollars) | Education | Health and hospitals | Police protection | Public welfare | Highways | Total (mil dol) | Per capita[1] (dollars) | Federal civilian | Federal military | State and local | Democratic | Republican | All other |
|---|---|---|---|---|---|---|---|---|---|---|---|---|---|---|---|
| | 185 | 186 | 187 | 188 | 189 | 190 | 191 | 192 | 193 | 194 | 195 | 196 | 197 | 198 | 199 |
| **LOUISIANA—Cont'd** | | | | | | | | | | | | | | | |
| Orleans | 1 250.0 | 5 227 | 19.3 | 1.2 | 11.0 | 0.0 | 1.7 | 2 804.5 | 11 728 | 9 599 | 4 074 | 30 770 | 79.4 | 19.1 | 1.5 |
| Ouachita | 493.3 | 3 299 | 49.4 | 2.2 | 5.7 | 0.1 | 4.9 | 386.4 | 2 585 | 481 | 735 | 11 838 | 36.9 | 62.1 | 1.0 |
| Plaquemines | 179.5 | 8 331 | 39.8 | 1.8 | 5.5 | 0.3 | 1.4 | 62.4 | 2 899 | 645 | 519 | 1 956 | 32.3 | 66.0 | 1.7 |
| Pointe Coupee | 74.7 | 3 338 | 39.6 | 19.6 | 6.4 | 0.1 | 1.5 | 45.0 | 2 009 | 65 | 107 | 1 178 | 44.4 | 53.9 | 1.7 |
| Rapides | 409.8 | 3 151 | 49.5 | 0.2 | 9.4 | 0.0 | 4.8 | 342.3 | 2 632 | 2 271 | 627 | 10 489 | 35.0 | 63.6 | 1.4 |
| Red River | 28.1 | 3 054 | 55.6 | 0.0 | 4.8 | 0.0 | 2.7 | 8.5 | 924 | 21 | 42 | 503 | 44.9 | 53.7 | 1.4 |
| Richland | 86.2 | 4 210 | 36.9 | 32.6 | 3.8 | 0.0 | 3.0 | 28.5 | 1 394 | 89 | 99 | 1 161 | 36.1 | 62.6 | 1.3 |
| Sabine | 55.0 | 2 321 | 64.5 | 0.3 | 5.5 | 0.0 | 7.7 | 31.5 | 1 329 | 42 | 116 | 1 372 | 23.3 | 74.9 | 1.9 |
| St. Bernard | 245.5 | 12 382 | 37.6 | 0.2 | 8.9 | 0.2 | 2.5 | 164.7 | 8 308 | 43 | 187 | 2 340 | 25.8 | 71.2 | 3.0 |
| St. Charles | 271.0 | 5 207 | 45.2 | 11.6 | 5.6 | 0.3 | 3.6 | 481.1 | 9 244 | 157 | 248 | 3 585 | 33.6 | 64.8 | 1.6 |
| St. Helena | 31.2 | 2 937 | 39.7 | 33.2 | 4.6 | 0.0 | 7.6 | 8.6 | 807 | 0 | 52 | 608 | 57.7 | 40.8 | 1.5 |
| St. James | 97.9 | 4 539 | 48.9 | 11.3 | 5.7 | 1.7 | 2.6 | 103.6 | 4 800 | 33 | 103 | 1 471 | 55.7 | 43.2 | 1.1 |
| St. John the Baptist | 135.0 | 2 831 | 50.7 | 0.4 | 6.2 | 0.2 | 3.6 | 224.0 | 4 697 | 114 | 213 | 2 108 | 57.4 | 41.2 | 1.5 |
| St. Landry | 302.2 | 3 308 | 42.2 | 27.4 | 5.2 | 0.0 | 2.5 | 112.5 | 1 231 | 179 | 395 | 5 645 | 47.7 | 50.9 | 1.4 |
| St. Martin | 121.9 | 2 360 | 52.8 | 6.5 | 8.5 | 0.1 | 2.6 | 102.7 | 1 988 | 61 | 250 | 2 111 | 38.8 | 59.6 | 1.6 |
| St. Mary | 195.8 | 3 816 | 46.2 | 11.9 | 5.9 | 0.1 | 4.0 | 148.2 | 2 889 | 149 | 378 | 4 904 | 40.8 | 57.6 | 1.6 |
| St. Tammany | 1 020.2 | 4 502 | 38.0 | 27.2 | 3.6 | 0.1 | 4.2 | 758.2 | 3 346 | 511 | 1 116 | 13 631 | 22.5 | 75.8 | 1.7 |
| Tangipahoa | 487.7 | 4 226 | 30.8 | 44.7 | 3.7 | 0.1 | 4.3 | 166.8 | 1 446 | 336 | 580 | 10 905 | 33.8 | 64.7 | 1.5 |
| Tensas | 29.5 | 5 024 | 31.5 | 1.2 | 5.0 | 0.0 | 3.5 | 23.8 | 4 062 | 24 | 24 | 427 | 54.1 | 45.0 | 0.9 |
| Terrebonne | 467.9 | 4 315 | 34.9 | 32.7 | 3.9 | 0.3 | 1.2 | 173.5 | 1 600 | 284 | 566 | 6 333 | 28.5 | 69.3 | 2.2 |
| Union | 50.0 | 2 197 | 51.0 | 9.1 | 4.8 | 0.2 | 4.4 | 10.5 | 462 | 95 | 107 | 937 | 28.6 | 70.1 | 1.3 |
| Vermilion | 177.5 | 3 187 | 44.3 | 23.0 | 5.5 | 0.1 | 3.6 | 30.1 | 540 | 146 | 287 | 2 864 | 25.2 | 72.8 | 2.0 |
| Vernon | 123.4 | 2 605 | 67.5 | 0.4 | 5.5 | 0.0 | 6.0 | 40.2 | 849 | 2 451 | 10 011 | 2 594 | 22.4 | 75.8 | 1.8 |
| Washington | 193.4 | 4 306 | 41.0 | 10.0 | 4.1 | 0.0 | 3.6 | 82.9 | 1 846 | 98 | 223 | 3 422 | 32.9 | 65.6 | 1.5 |
| Webster | 129.6 | 3 168 | 66.5 | 0.3 | 4.6 | 1.6 | 3.4 | 106.5 | 2 601 | 115 | 195 | 2 111 | 36.2 | 62.5 | 1.3 |
| West Baton Rouge | 80.7 | 3 568 | 39.1 | 0.5 | 8.9 | 0.5 | 4.5 | 61.6 | 2 722 | 66 | 114 | 1 485 | 42.5 | 56.1 | 1.4 |
| West Carroll | 28.1 | 2 429 | 62.8 | 5.1 | 4.2 | 0.1 | 6.1 | 7.0 | 609 | 35 | 55 | 804 | 17.6 | 81.1 | 1.3 |
| West Feliciana | 76.3 | 5 049 | 33.8 | 11.5 | 5.2 | 0.2 | 3.6 | 487.8 | 32 278 | 14 | 73 | 2 239 | 43.0 | 56.0 | 1.0 |
| Winn | 40.4 | 2 605 | 65.1 | 0.4 | 5.4 | 0.1 | 4.3 | 22.6 | 1 459 | 60 | 71 | 777 | 30.2 | 68.4 | 1.4 |
| **MAINE** | X | X | X | X | X | X | X | X | X | 14 684 | 7 406 | 86 686 | 57.7 | 40.4 | 1.9 |
| Androscoggin | 325.1 | 3 043 | 50.6 | 0.2 | 3.6 | 0.2 | 4.5 | 321.5 | 3 010 | 291 | 339 | 5 111 | 56.5 | 41.3 | 2.1 |
| Aroostook | 246.6 | 3 422 | 50.3 | 17.2 | 2.5 | 0.3 | 6.6 | 83.0 | 1 151 | 1 274 | 225 | 5 384 | 53.7 | 44.2 | 2.1 |
| Cumberland | 962.9 | 3 497 | 44.0 | 1.2 | 4.8 | 2.7 | 5.2 | 890.9 | 3 235 | 2 168 | 2 565 | 18 315 | 64.1 | 34.2 | 1.7 |
| Franklin | 84.5 | 2 823 | 60.7 | 0.5 | 3.2 | 0.1 | 9.6 | 71.2 | 2 378 | 114 | 97 | 1 824 | 58.9 | 38.6 | 2.5 |
| Hancock | 168.1 | 3 155 | 57.4 | 0.2 | 2.9 | 0.2 | 7.3 | 99.0 | 1 858 | 365 | 282 | 2 927 | 58.7 | 39.4 | 1.8 |
| Kennebec | 349.0 | 2 888 | 63.0 | 0.8 | 3.1 | 0.3 | 5.8 | 231.1 | 1 913 | 2 155 | 420 | 14 507 | 56.4 | 41.6 | 1.9 |
| Knox | 116.8 | 2 864 | 49.4 | 0.5 | 4.5 | 0.2 | 9.0 | 98.4 | 2 413 | 110 | 208 | 2 629 | 59.7 | 38.4 | 1.9 |
| Lincoln | 130.5 | 3 751 | 60.2 | 0.6 | 2.5 | 0.3 | 5.7 | 106.9 | 3 072 | 87 | 133 | 1 627 | 55.1 | 43.0 | 1.9 |
| Oxford | 182.6 | 3 219 | 66.8 | 0.4 | 2.7 | 0.2 | 7.7 | 73.9 | 1 302 | 161 | 182 | 3 145 | 56.7 | 40.6 | 2.7 |
| Penobscot | 434.5 | 2 920 | 52.8 | 0.4 | 4.1 | 0.5 | 4.6 | 271.7 | 1 826 | 1 299 | 497 | 13 170 | 51.7 | 46.6 | 1.7 |
| Piscataquis | 92.4 | 5 381 | 42.2 | 34.7 | 2.0 | 0.2 | 3.6 | 27.2 | 1 580 | 53 | 55 | 1 332 | 47.0 | 50.7 | 2.3 |
| Sagadahoc | 123.7 | 3 400 | 59.1 | 0.3 | 3.9 | 0.2 | 5.9 | 86.9 | 2 389 | 324 | 267 | 1 539 | 57.0 | 40.9 | 2.0 |
| Somerset | 168.8 | 3 267 | 69.6 | 0.5 | 2.8 | 0.3 | 5.8 | 86.9 | 1 682 | 211 | 164 | 2 515 | 51.8 | 46.1 | 2.2 |
| Waldo | 104.8 | 2 721 | 62.1 | 1.0 | 2.1 | 0.4 | 8.5 | 82.4 | 2 139 | 99 | 129 | 1 560 | 54.8 | 43.1 | 2.1 |
| Washington | 95.2 | 2 907 | 62.0 | 0.5 | 3.0 | 0.2 | 7.4 | 24.1 | 735 | 391 | 162 | 2 289 | 49.5 | 48.5 | 2.0 |
| York | 575.5 | 2 858 | 58.2 | 0.3 | 5.6 | 0.3 | 7.0 | 301.6 | 1 498 | 5 582 | 1 681 | 8 812 | 59.4 | 38.8 | 1.8 |
| **MARYLAND** | X | X | X | X | X | X | X | X | X | 176 373 | 48 769 | 345 293 | 61.9 | 36.5 | 1.6 |
| Allegany | 301.8 | 4 157 | 55.9 | 1.8 | 2.8 | 7.2 | 3.9 | 159.8 | 2 201 | 552 | 238 | 6 105 | 36.0 | 61.9 | 2.2 |
| Anne Arundel | 1 783.0 | 3 481 | 55.5 | 2.2 | 5.8 | 0.8 | 3.4 | 1 777.5 | 3 471 | 41 103 | 16 685 | 29 562 | 48.2 | 50.0 | 1.9 |
| Baltimore | 2 748.4 | 3 483 | 54.5 | 1.6 | 6.3 | 0.4 | 2.8 | 2 010.2 | 2 548 | 16 307 | 2 575 | 41 658 | 56.2 | 41.7 | 2.1 |
| Calvert | 331.9 | 3 762 | 57.2 | 1.0 | 3.3 | 1.0 | 6.0 | 217.9 | 2 470 | 144 | 319 | 4 106 | 46.1 | 52.4 | 1.5 |
| Caroline | 120.1 | 3 649 | 56.1 | 2.0 | 4.3 | 0.1 | 4.0 | 70.5 | 2 143 | 81 | 105 | 1 523 | 37.6 | 60.6 | 1.8 |
| Carroll | 513.0 | 3 031 | 60.7 | 1.5 | 3.1 | 0.8 | 6.1 | 412.2 | 2 436 | 292 | 534 | 7 901 | 33.1 | 64.3 | 2.6 |
| Cecil | 331.6 | 3 327 | 62.8 | 1.7 | 3.7 | 0.5 | 6.4 | 189.5 | 1 900 | 1 427 | 322 | 4 338 | 41.6 | 56.1 | 2.3 |
| Charles | 581.7 | 4 142 | 56.7 | 0.7 | 8.0 | 0.7 | 2.9 | 433.9 | 3 089 | 2 280 | 1 069 | 7 053 | 62.2 | 36.7 | 1.1 |
| Dorchester | 131.4 | 4 126 | 41.8 | 0.6 | 8.0 | 1.8 | 5.9 | 46.5 | 1 460 | 200 | 103 | 2 126 | 45.3 | 53.5 | 1.3 |
| Frederick | 907.0 | 4 036 | 54.1 | 1.0 | 4.7 | 3.7 | 4.0 | 789.9 | 3 515 | 4 099 | 1 954 | 11 763 | 48.6 | 49.6 | 1.8 |
| Garrett | 125.9 | 4 250 | 50.1 | 0.9 | 2.4 | 0.0 | 12.5 | 18.3 | 617 | 70 | 95 | 1 654 | 29.0 | 69.2 | 1.8 |
| Harford | 855.8 | 3 566 | 58.7 | 0.5 | 5.6 | 0.8 | 5.7 | 235.5 | 981 | 12 131 | 2 657 | 9 555 | 39.4 | 58.2 | 2.4 |
| Howard | 1 212.9 | 4 432 | 62.6 | 1.0 | 5.7 | 1.4 | 3.3 | 1 105.8 | 4 041 | 653 | 963 | 17 645 | 60.0 | 38.1 | 1.9 |
| Kent | 72.8 | 3 642 | 45.9 | 1.3 | 4.9 | 1.5 | 5.8 | 35.1 | 1 757 | 74 | 64 | 941 | 49.4 | 49.0 | 1.6 |
| Montgomery | 4 525.1 | 4 861 | 50.1 | 3.0 | 4.7 | 3.0 | 3.9 | 3 766.8 | 4 047 | 48 846 | 6 963 | 39 906 | 71.6 | 27.0 | 1.4 |
| Prince George's | 3 180.7 | 3 838 | 54.8 | 2.1 | 6.7 | 0.6 | 2.6 | 2 228.7 | 2 689 | 27 630 | 7 908 | 62 444 | 88.9 | 10.4 | 0.7 |
| Queen Anne's | 201.2 | 4 321 | 58.0 | 1.1 | 2.7 | 0.9 | 3.4 | 143.7 | 3 086 | 86 | 153 | 2 408 | 35.7 | 62.7 | 1.6 |

1. Based on the resident population estimated as of July 1 of the year shown.   2. © 2013 Election Data Services, Inc. All rights reserved.

# Table B. States and Counties — **Land Area and Population**

| STATE/ County code | CBSA code[1] | County type[2] | STATE County | Land area[3] (sq km) 2010 | Total persons | Rank | Per square kilometer | White | Black | American Indian, Alaska Native | Asian and Pacific Islander | Percent Hispanic or Latino[4] | Under 5 years | 5 to 17 years | 18 to 24 years | 25 to 34 years | 35 to 44 years | 45 to 54 years |
|---|---|---|---|---|---|---|---|---|---|---|---|---|---|---|---|---|---|---|
| | | | | | | | | | | | | | | | | | | |
| | | | | | | | | Population 2012 | | | Population characteristics[6], 2011 | | | | | | | |
| | | | | | | | | | | Race alone or in combination, not Hispanic or Latino (percent) | | | Age (percent) | | | | | |
| | | | | 1 | 2 | 3 | 4 | 5 | 6 | 7 | 8 | 9 | 10 | 11 | 12 | 13 | 14 | 15 |
| | | | MARYLAND—Cont'd | | | | | | | | | | | | | | | |
| 24 037 | 30500 | 4 | St. Mary's | 925 | 108 987 | 544 | 117.8 | 78.5 | 15.6 | 1.0 | 3.9 | 4.0 | 7.0 | 18.7 | 9.9 | 13.2 | 13.6 | 16.0 |
| 24 039 | 41540 | 3 | Somerset | 828 | 26 253 | 1 550 | 31.7 | 53.4 | 42.8 | 0.8 | 1.3 | 3.3 | 4.8 | 12.0 | 18.8 | 12.6 | 11.4 | 13.9 |
| 24 041 | 20660 | 6 | Talbot | 696 | 38 098 | 1 216 | 54.7 | 79.7 | 13.8 | 0.4 | 1.6 | 5.8 | 4.9 | 14.2 | 6.7 | 9.3 | 10.7 | 14.5 |
| 24 043 | 25180 | 3 | Washington | 1 186 | 149 180 | 422 | 125.8 | 84.7 | 11.2 | 0.6 | 2.0 | 3.6 | 6.0 | 16.6 | 8.5 | 12.7 | 13.6 | 15.5 |
| 24 045 | 41540 | 3 | Wicomico | 970 | 100 647 | 584 | 103.8 | 67.9 | 25.6 | 0.6 | 3.3 | 4.7 | 6.3 | 15.9 | 14.4 | 12.4 | 11.4 | 14.0 |
| 24 047 | 36180 | 4 | Worcester | 1 213 | 51 578 | 962 | 42.5 | 81.4 | 14.6 | 0.6 | 1.6 | 3.3 | 4.4 | 13.5 | 6.8 | 9.4 | 10.8 | 15.4 |
| 24 510 | 12580 | 1 | Baltimore city | 210 | 621 342 | 104 | 2 958.8 | 29.6 | 64.0 | 0.9 | 3.0 | 4.3 | 6.8 | 14.8 | 12.2 | 17.1 | 12.0 | 13.8 |
| 25 000 | ... | X | MASSACHUSETTS | 20 202 | 6 646 144 | X | 329.0 | 77.8 | 7.2 | 0.6 | 6.3 | 9.9 | 5.6 | 15.8 | 10.3 | 13.2 | 13.1 | 15.3 |
| 25 001 | 12700 | 3 | Barnstable | 1 020 | 215 423 | 290 | 211.2 | 93.7 | 2.8 | 1.1 | 1.7 | 2.3 | 4.1 | 12.8 | 6.8 | 8.5 | 10.0 | 15.5 |
| 25 003 | 38340 | 3 | Berkshire | 2 400 | 130 016 | 480 | 54.2 | 92.2 | 3.6 | 0.6 | 1.9 | 3.5 | 4.5 | 14.6 | 9.6 | 10.0 | 11.2 | 15.8 |
| 25 005 | 39300 | 1 | Bristol | 1 433 | 551 082 | 112 | 384.6 | 87.8 | 4.2 | 0.7 | 2.6 | 6.3 | 5.6 | 16.4 | 9.6 | 11.9 | 13.7 | 15.7 |
| 25 007 | ... | 7 | Dukes | 267 | 17 041 | 1 977 | 63.8 | 91.8 | 4.5 | 2.3 | 1.8 | 2.5 | 5.2 | 13.7 | 6.1 | 11.3 | 12.8 | 16.4 |
| 25 009 | 14460 | 1 | Essex | 1 276 | 755 618 | 77 | 592.2 | 76.8 | 3.5 | 0.3 | 3.6 | 16.9 | 5.8 | 16.9 | 8.9 | 11.5 | 13.1 | 16.1 |
| 25 011 | 44140 | 2 | Franklin | 1 811 | 71 540 | 751 | 39.5 | 93.8 | 1.7 | 0.9 | 2.0 | 3.3 | 4.7 | 14.6 | 8.1 | 11.1 | 12.1 | 16.4 |
| 25 013 | 44140 | 2 | Hampden | 1 598 | 465 923 | 144 | 291.6 | 68.4 | 8.7 | 0.6 | 2.5 | 21.4 | 6.0 | 17.4 | 10.7 | 11.9 | 12.2 | 14.8 |
| 25 015 | 44140 | 2 | Hampshire | 1 366 | 159 795 | 395 | 117.0 | 87.5 | 3.2 | 0.6 | 5.7 | 4.9 | 3.7 | 12.4 | 22.4 | 10.2 | 10.6 | 14.0 |
| 25 017 | 14460 | 1 | Middlesex | 2 118 | 1 537 215 | 23 | 725.8 | 78.6 | 5.3 | 0.4 | 10.7 | 6.8 | 5.7 | 15.4 | 9.5 | 14.8 | 13.8 | 15.4 |
| 25 019 | ... | 7 | Nantucket | 116 | 10 298 | 2 415 | 88.8 | 81.7 | 7.4 | 0.5 | 1.8 | 10.0 | 6.8 | 14.3 | 5.9 | 15.1 | 15.8 | 16.2 |
| 25 021 | 14460 | 1 | Norfolk | 1 026 | 681 845 | 90 | 664.6 | 81.6 | 6.3 | 0.4 | 9.7 | 3.5 | 5.5 | 16.8 | 8.2 | 12.0 | 13.6 | 16.2 |
| 25 023 | 14460 | 1 | Plymouth | 1 707 | 499 759 | 133 | 292.8 | 86.3 | 9.3 | 0.7 | 1.9 | 3.3 | 5.6 | 18.0 | 8.2 | 10.0 | 13.5 | 16.5 |
| 25 025 | 14460 | 1 | Suffolk | 151 | 744 426 | 80 | 4 930.0 | 50.0 | 21.7 | 0.7 | 9.3 | 20.3 | 5.6 | 11.9 | 16.9 | 20.9 | 12.7 | 11.7 |
| 25 027 | 49340 | 2 | Worcester | 3 913 | 806 163 | 73 | 206.0 | 82.2 | 4.5 | 0.6 | 4.8 | 9.6 | 5.8 | 17.2 | 9.7 | 11.8 | 13.7 | 16.3 |
| 26 000 | ... | X | MICHIGAN | 146 435 | 9 883 360 | X | 67.5 | 78.2 | 15.0 | 1.3 | 3.1 | 4.5 | 5.9 | 17.3 | 10.1 | 11.8 | 12.6 | 15.0 |
| 26 001 | ... | 9 | Alcona | 1 747 | 10 635 | 2 386 | 6.1 | 97.6 | 0.5 | 1.2 | 0.4 | 1.2 | 3.1 | 11.3 | 4.7 | 5.9 | 8.5 | 14.9 |
| 26 003 | ... | 9 | Alger | 2 370 | 9 541 | 2 471 | 4.0 | 87.7 | 7.1 | 6.0 | 0.7 | 1.3 | 3.7 | 13.0 | 6.5 | 11.2 | 11.3 | 15.7 |
| 26 005 | 10880 | 4 | Allegan | 2 137 | 112 039 | 536 | 52.4 | 90.8 | 1.9 | 1.1 | 0.9 | 6.8 | 6.5 | 19.3 | 7.8 | 11.0 | 12.9 | 15.9 |
| 26 007 | 10980 | 7 | Alpena | 1 481 | 29 234 | 1 445 | 19.7 | 97.3 | 0.7 | 1.0 | 0.8 | 1.1 | 4.9 | 15.4 | 7.4 | 9.8 | 10.8 | 16.5 |
| 26 009 | ... | 9 | Antrim | 1 232 | 23 406 | 1 667 | 19.0 | 96.5 | 0.8 | 1.7 | 0.5 | 1.8 | 4.8 | 15.3 | 5.9 | 8.8 | 10.4 | 15.3 |
| 26 011 | ... | 8 | Arenac | 941 | 15 477 | 2 075 | 16.4 | 96.5 | 0.7 | 1.9 | 0.5 | 1.6 | 4.3 | 15.2 | 7.0 | 9.6 | 10.6 | 16.5 |
| 26 013 | ... | 9 | Baraga | 2 326 | 8 683 | 2 551 | 3.7 | 78.3 | 8.1 | 16.2 | 0.8 | 1.1 | 4.5 | 15.2 | 7.7 | 12.4 | 13.1 | 14.9 |
| 26 015 | 24340 | 2 | Barry | 1 433 | 58 990 | 875 | 41.2 | 96.3 | 0.9 | 1.1 | 0.6 | 2.4 | 5.7 | 18.1 | 7.6 | 10.4 | 12.2 | 16.4 |
| 26 017 | 13020 | 3 | Bay | 1 146 | 106 935 | 557 | 93.3 | 92.6 | 2.4 | 1.1 | 0.8 | 4.7 | 5.6 | 16.1 | 8.5 | 11.6 | 11.8 | 15.3 |
| 26 019 | 45900 | 9 | Benzie | 828 | 17 465 | 1 955 | 21.1 | 95.8 | 1.0 | 2.1 | 0.4 | 1.9 | 5.0 | 15.3 | 6.1 | 9.5 | 11.1 | 15.7 |
| 26 021 | 35660 | 3 | Berrien | 1 470 | 156 067 | 404 | 106.2 | 77.8 | 16.4 | 1.1 | 2.1 | 4.7 | 6.1 | 17.0 | 8.5 | 11.1 | 11.9 | 14.9 |
| 26 023 | 17740 | 6 | Branch | 1 311 | 43 868 | 1 088 | 33.5 | 91.8 | 3.6 | 1.1 | 0.8 | 4.1 | 6.3 | 17.2 | 8.0 | 12.1 | 12.9 | 15.2 |
| 26 025 | 12980 | 3 | Calhoun | 1 829 | 135 099 | 464 | 73.9 | 82.2 | 12.4 | 1.4 | 2.1 | 4.6 | 6.3 | 17.6 | 9.3 | 11.6 | 12.1 | 14.6 |
| 26 027 | 43780 | 2 | Cass | 1 269 | 52 242 | 951 | 41.2 | 89.8 | 6.8 | 2.0 | 1.1 | 3.1 | 5.6 | 17.5 | 7.5 | 9.9 | 12.3 | 15.7 |
| 26 029 | ... | 7 | Charlevoix | 1 078 | 26 023 | 1 561 | 24.1 | 96.2 | 0.9 | 2.4 | 0.7 | 1.4 | 4.9 | 16.5 | 6.5 | 9.4 | 11.2 | 16.2 |
| 26 031 | ... | 7 | Cheboygan | 1 853 | 25 835 | 1 570 | 13.9 | 95.1 | 1.1 | 4.6 | 0.6 | 1.0 | 4.4 | 15.4 | 6.4 | 8.7 | 11.5 | 14.8 |
| 26 033 | 42300 | 5 | Chippewa | 4 036 | 38 917 | 1 198 | 9.6 | 75.8 | 7.4 | 18.4 | 1.5 | 1.6 | 5.1 | 14.8 | 10.8 | 13.2 | 13.3 | 14.9 |
| 26 035 | ... | 7 | Clare | 1 462 | 30 753 | 1 415 | 21.0 | 96.7 | 1.0 | 1.5 | 0.5 | 1.6 | 5.8 | 15.0 | 7.8 | 9.5 | 10.9 | 15.0 |
| 26 037 | 29620 | 2 | Clinton | 1 467 | 76 001 | 720 | 51.8 | 92.1 | 2.7 | 1.0 | 1.8 | 4.0 | 5.6 | 18.6 | 10.3 | 11.0 | 12.5 | 15.5 |
| 26 039 | ... | 7 | Crawford | 1 441 | 14 009 | 2 175 | 9.7 | 97.1 | 0.8 | 1.2 | 0.6 | 1.5 | 4.7 | 15.0 | 6.4 | 8.9 | 10.4 | 17.3 |
| 26 041 | 21540 | 5 | Delta | 3 033 | 36 884 | 1 251 | 12.2 | 96.0 | 0.7 | 3.7 | 0.8 | 0.9 | 5.2 | 15.3 | 7.3 | 10.0 | 10.9 | 15.3 |
| 26 043 | 27020 | 5 | Dickinson | 1 972 | 26 220 | 1 554 | 13.3 | 97.3 | 0.7 | 1.1 | 0.9 | 1.2 | 4.9 | 15.8 | 6.9 | 10.1 | 11.2 | 16.5 |
| 26 045 | 29620 | 2 | Eaton | 1 490 | 108 008 | 549 | 72.5 | 86.4 | 7.5 | 1.1 | 2.3 | 4.8 | 5.5 | 17.3 | 8.9 | 11.8 | 12.1 | 15.5 |
| 26 047 | ... | 7 | Emmet | 1 211 | 32 915 | 1 359 | 27.2 | 93.8 | 1.1 | 4.8 | 1.0 | 1.4 | 5.0 | 17.0 | 7.4 | 10.4 | 11.7 | 15.5 |
| 26 049 | 22420 | 2 | Genesee | 1 650 | 418 408 | 163 | 253.6 | 74.6 | 21.9 | 1.4 | 1.4 | 3.1 | 6.3 | 18.2 | 9.0 | 11.7 | 12.7 | 15.0 |
| 26 051 | ... | 6 | Gladwin | 1 300 | 25 484 | 1 587 | 19.6 | 97.5 | 0.7 | 1.0 | 0.5 | 1.3 | 4.8 | 15.0 | 6.8 | 8.8 | 10.6 | 14.3 |
| 26 053 | ... | 7 | Gogebic | 2 854 | 16 084 | 2 040 | 5.6 | 92.1 | 4.6 | 3.2 | 0.6 | 0.9 | 4.6 | 11.8 | 8.4 | 10.4 | 11.6 | 15.2 |
| 26 055 | 45900 | 5 | Grand Traverse | 1 203 | 89 112 | 642 | 74.1 | 94.3 | 1.9 | 1.8 | 1.2 | 2.3 | 5.6 | 16.1 | 8.0 | 12.5 | 12.3 | 15.6 |
| 26 057 | 10940 | 6 | Gratiot | 1 472 | 42 063 | 1 129 | 28.6 | 87.9 | 6.1 | 0.9 | 0.6 | 5.5 | 5.4 | 15.8 | 11.4 | 12.7 | 12.9 | 14.8 |
| 26 059 | ... | 6 | Hillsdale | 1 549 | 46 229 | 1 044 | 29.8 | 96.7 | 0.9 | 1.0 | 0.7 | 1.9 | 5.8 | 17.5 | 9.8 | 10.3 | 11.5 | 15.1 |
| 26 061 | 26340 | 5 | Houghton | 2 614 | 36 520 | 1 261 | 14.0 | 94.3 | 1.2 | 1.2 | 3.3 | 1.3 | 5.6 | 14.6 | 21.4 | 10.3 | 9.3 | 11.7 |
| 26 063 | ... | 7 | Huron | 2 164 | 32 463 | 1 377 | 15.0 | 96.7 | 0.7 | 0.7 | 0.7 | 2.0 | 4.8 | 15.4 | 6.6 | 9.3 | 10.7 | 15.5 |
| 26 065 | 29620 | 2 | Ingham | 1 440 | 281 723 | 235 | 195.6 | 75.1 | 13.5 | 1.3 | 6.1 | 7.3 | 5.6 | 14.6 | 20.8 | 13.6 | 10.8 | 12.3 |
| 26 067 | 24340 | 2 | Ionia | 1 480 | 63 941 | 822 | 43.2 | 89.8 | 5.3 | 0.9 | 0.7 | 4.5 | 6.2 | 17.9 | 9.2 | 13.8 | 13.9 | 15.1 |
| 26 069 | ... | 7 | Iosco | 1 422 | 25 357 | 1 596 | 17.8 | 96.2 | 1.1 | 1.4 | 1.0 | 1.7 | 4.0 | 13.2 | 6.1 | 8.0 | 9.3 | 15.3 |
| 26 071 | ... | 7 | Iron | 3 020 | 11 587 | 2 324 | 3.8 | 97.1 | 0.6 | 1.5 | 0.5 | 1.6 | 4.5 | 12.7 | 5.5 | 8.4 | 8.8 | 15.3 |
| 26 073 | 34380 | 5 | Isabella | 1 483 | 70 617 | 757 | 47.6 | 89.2 | 3.6 | 4.0 | 2.3 | 3.4 | 5.0 | 12.5 | 32.9 | 11.1 | 8.8 | 10.4 |
| 26 075 | 27100 | 3 | Jackson | 1 817 | 160 309 | 393 | 88.2 | 87.7 | 9.3 | 1.0 | 1.1 | 3.1 | 5.7 | 17.0 | 9.3 | 11.7 | 12.9 | 15.4 |
| 26 077 | 28020 | 2 | Kalamazoo | 1 455 | 254 580 | 260 | 175.0 | 82.2 | 12.5 | 1.2 | 3.0 | 4.1 | 6.0 | 16.1 | 16.2 | 13.0 | 11.5 | 12.9 |
| 26 079 | 45900 | 7 | Kalkaska | 1 450 | 17 099 | 1 971 | 11.8 | 96.8 | 1.0 | 1.7 | 0.6 | 1.3 | 5.8 | 16.6 | 7.0 | 10.6 | 11.9 | 15.9 |
| 26 081 | 24340 | 2 | Kent | 2 194 | 614 462 | 106 | 280.1 | 77.8 | 10.8 | 0.9 | 2.9 | 9.9 | 7.2 | 18.7 | 10.4 | 14.3 | 12.5 | 14.2 |

1. CBSA = Core Based Statistical Area. See Appendix A for explanation. See Appendix B for list of metropolitan areas with component counties.    2. County type code from the Economic Research Service of USDA Rural-Urban Continuum Codes. See Appendix A for definition.    3. Dry land or land partially or temporarily covered by water.    4. May be of any race.

# Table B. States and Counties — **Population and Households**

| | Population, 2011 (cont.) | | | | Population change and components of change, 2000–2012 | | | | | | | | Households, 2010 | | | | |
| STATE County | Age (percent) (cont.) | | | | Total persons | | Percent change | | Components of change, 2010–2012 | | | | | | | Percent | | |
| | 55 to 64 years | 65 to 74 years | 75 years and over | Percent female | 2000 | 2010 | 2000–2010 | 2010–2012 | Births | Deaths | Net migration | Number | Percent change, 2000–2010 | Persons per household | Female family householder[1] | One person |
| | 16 | 17 | 18 | 19 | 20 | 21 | 22 | 23 | 24 | 25 | 26 | 27 | 28 | 29 | 30 | 31 |

| MARYLAND—Cont'd | | | | | | | | | | | | | | | | |
|---|---|---|---|---|---|---|---|---|---|---|---|---|---|---|---|---|
| St. Mary's | 11.3 | 6.1 | 4.3 | 50.1 | 86 211 | 105 151 | 22.0 | 3.6 | 3 299 | 1 578 | 2 028 | 37 604 | 22.7 | 2.72 | 11.7 | 21.8 |
| Somerset | 12.4 | 7.8 | 6.4 | 46.3 | 24 747 | 26 470 | 7.0 | -0.8 | 555 | 608 | -155 | 8 788 | 5.1 | 2.37 | 15.3 | 31.5 |
| Talbot | 15.4 | 13.3 | 11.1 | 52.3 | 33 812 | 37 782 | 11.7 | 0.8 | 766 | 1 005 | 535 | 16 157 | 12.9 | 2.31 | 10.1 | 28.3 |
| Washington | 12.6 | 7.6 | 6.9 | 49.2 | 131 923 | 147 430 | 11.8 | 1.2 | 3 813 | 3 042 | 1 033 | 55 687 | 12.0 | 2.50 | 12.0 | 26.6 |
| Wicomico | 12.3 | 7.2 | 6.1 | 52.2 | 84 644 | 98 733 | 16.6 | 1.9 | 2 840 | 2 041 | 1 119 | 37 220 | 15.5 | 2.53 | 15.2 | 25.3 |
| Worcester | 16.1 | 13.4 | 10.2 | 51.3 | 46 543 | 51 454 | 10.6 | 0.2 | 987 | 1 384 | 522 | 22 229 | 12.9 | 2.28 | 10.9 | 28.0 |
| Baltimore city | 11.5 | 6.3 | 5.5 | 52.9 | 651 154 | 620 961 | -4.6 | 0.1 | 19 876 | 14 380 | -5 194 | 249 903 | -3.1 | 2.38 | 23.8 | 36.1 |
| | | | | | | | | | | | | | | | | |
| MASSACHUSETTS | 12.7 | 7.2 | 6.8 | 51.6 | 6 349 097 | 6 547 629 | 3.1 | 1.5 | 163 810 | 119 214 | 56 572 | 2 547 075 | 4.2 | 2.48 | 12.5 | 28.7 |
| | | | | | | | | | | | | | | | | |
| Barnstable | 17.0 | 12.8 | 12.6 | 52.4 | 222 230 | 215 888 | -2.9 | -0.2 | 3 903 | 6 222 | 2 078 | 95 755 | 1.0 | 2.21 | 9.6 | 31.8 |
| Berkshire | 15.4 | 9.4 | 9.6 | 51.8 | 134 953 | 131 219 | -2.8 | -0.9 | 2 496 | 3 088 | -514 | 56 091 | 0.2 | 2.23 | 11.5 | 33.0 |
| Bristol | 12.7 | 7.4 | 7.0 | 51.6 | 534 678 | 548 285 | 2.5 | 0.5 | 13 305 | 11 097 | 815 | 213 010 | 3.7 | 2.50 | 14.0 | 27.4 |
| Dukes | 17.8 | 9.3 | 7.4 | 50.4 | 14 987 | 16 535 | 10.3 | 3.1 | 394 | 292 | 405 | 7 368 | 14.7 | 2.22 | 8.9 | 33.4 |
| Essex | 13.3 | 7.3 | 7.1 | 51.9 | 723 419 | 743 159 | 2.7 | 1.7 | 19 117 | 13 876 | 7 538 | 285 956 | 3.8 | 2.54 | 13.5 | 28.1 |
| Franklin | 17.3 | 8.4 | 7.3 | 51.3 | 71 535 | 71 372 | -0.2 | 0.2 | 1 431 | 1 441 | 217 | 30 462 | 3.4 | 2.29 | 10.7 | 30.5 |
| Hampden | 12.7 | 7.1 | 7.2 | 51.9 | 456 228 | 463 490 | 1.6 | 0.5 | 12 366 | 9 367 | -388 | 179 927 | 2.6 | 2.49 | 17.5 | 29.2 |
| Hampshire | 13.6 | 6.7 | 6.2 | 53.1 | 152 251 | 158 080 | 3.8 | 1.1 | 2 432 | 2 656 | 1 941 | 58 702 | 4.8 | 2.34 | 10.3 | 29.7 |
| | | | | | | | | | | | | | | | | |
| Middlesex | 12.3 | 6.8 | 6.5 | 51.3 | 1 465 396 | 1 503 085 | 2.6 | 2.3 | 39 522 | 24 376 | 19 677 | 580 688 | 3.5 | 2.49 | 10.1 | 27.8 |
| Nantucket | 13.5 | 7.0 | 5.5 | 49.0 | 9 520 | 10 172 | 6.8 | 1.2 | 326 | 131 | -72 | 4 229 | 14.3 | 2.39 | 8.3 | 29.7 |
| Norfolk | 13.1 | 7.3 | 7.4 | 52.1 | 650 308 | 670 850 | 3.2 | 1.6 | 15 665 | 12 190 | 7 713 | 257 914 | 3.7 | 2.53 | 10.1 | 27.6 |
| Plymouth | 13.8 | 8.0 | 6.4 | 51.3 | 472 822 | 494 919 | 4.7 | 1.0 | 11 516 | 9 217 | 2 639 | 181 126 | 7.6 | 2.67 | 12.6 | 23.8 |
| Suffolk | 9.6 | 5.6 | 5.0 | 51.8 | 689 807 | 722 023 | 4.7 | 3.1 | 21 338 | 10 570 | 11 947 | 292 767 | 5.0 | 2.30 | 16.3 | 36.3 |
| Worcester | 12.6 | 6.6 | 6.3 | 50.7 | 750 963 | 798 552 | 6.3 | 1.0 | 19 999 | 14 691 | 2 576 | 303 080 | 6.7 | 2.55 | 12.2 | 26.2 |
| | | | | | | | | | | | | | | | | |
| MICHIGAN | 13.2 | 7.5 | 6.5 | 50.9 | 9 938 444 | 9 883 640 | -0.6 | 0.0 | 254 152 | 198 341 | -56 325 | 3 872 508 | 2.3 | 2.49 | 13.2 | 27.9 |
| | | | | | | | | | | | | | | | | |
| Alcona | 19.2 | 19.3 | 13.1 | 49.5 | 11 719 | 10 942 | -6.6 | -2.8 | 148 | 395 | -51 | 5 089 | -0.8 | 2.13 | 6.4 | 29.7 |
| Alger | 17.8 | 11.6 | 9.3 | 45.5 | 9 862 | 9 601 | -2.6 | -0.6 | 143 | 252 | 28 | 3 898 | 3.0 | 2.20 | 7.1 | 31.6 |
| Allegan | 13.4 | 7.6 | 5.7 | 50.2 | 105 665 | 111 408 | 5.4 | 0.6 | 3 133 | 1 935 | -716 | 42 018 | 10.1 | 2.63 | 9.8 | 22.5 |
| Alpena | 15.2 | 10.1 | 9.7 | 51.0 | 31 314 | 29 598 | -5.5 | -1.2 | 596 | 765 | -184 | 12 791 | -0.2 | 2.27 | 9.8 | 30.8 |
| Antrim | 16.7 | 13.1 | 9.6 | 50.5 | 23 110 | 23 580 | 2.0 | -0.7 | 474 | 569 | -95 | 9 890 | 7.2 | 2.36 | 8.3 | 25.5 |
| Arenac | 16.1 | 12.0 | 8.6 | 49.2 | 17 269 | 15 899 | -7.9 | -2.7 | 260 | 464 | -223 | 6 701 | -0.1 | 2.34 | 9.6 | 27.5 |
| Baraga | 15.1 | 10.1 | 7.1 | 45.1 | 8 746 | 8 860 | 1.3 | -2.0 | 158 | 241 | -96 | 3 444 | 2.7 | 2.28 | 10.9 | 31.6 |
| Barry | 14.5 | 8.8 | 6.3 | 49.7 | 56 755 | 59 173 | 4.3 | -0.3 | 1 359 | 1 103 | -451 | 22 551 | 7.2 | 2.60 | 8.6 | 21.7 |
| | | | | | | | | | | | | | | | | |
| Bay | 14.5 | 8.7 | 7.8 | 51.0 | 110 157 | 107 771 | -2.2 | -0.8 | 2 558 | 2 508 | -883 | 44 603 | 1.5 | 2.38 | 11.8 | 29.3 |
| Benzie | 15.9 | 12.1 | 9.3 | 50.6 | 15 998 | 17 525 | 9.5 | -0.3 | 355 | 445 | 10 | 7 298 | 12.3 | 2.37 | 8.4 | 26.2 |
| Berrien | 13.9 | 8.8 | 7.9 | 51.3 | 162 453 | 156 813 | -3.5 | -0.8 | 4 274 | 3 609 | -1 451 | 63 054 | -0.8 | 2.43 | 13.6 | 28.7 |
| Branch | 13.2 | 8.5 | 6.6 | 47.4 | 45 787 | 45 248 | -1.2 | -3.0 | 1 156 | 924 | -1 654 | 16 419 | 0.4 | 2.56 | 11.1 | 25.8 |
| Calhoun | 13.5 | 7.7 | 7.2 | 51.1 | 137 985 | 136 146 | -1.3 | -0.8 | 3 681 | 3 109 | -1 600 | 54 016 | -0.2 | 2.44 | 14.6 | 28.8 |
| Cass | 15.5 | 9.5 | 6.6 | 50.0 | 51 104 | 52 293 | 2.3 | -0.1 | 1 228 | 1 075 | -314 | 20 604 | 4.7 | 2.51 | 10.7 | 24.3 |
| Charlevoix | 16.1 | 10.9 | 8.3 | 50.8 | 26 090 | 25 949 | -0.5 | 0.3 | 520 | 601 | 173 | 10 882 | 4.6 | 2.36 | 9.1 | 27.5 |
| Cheboygan | 16.8 | 12.7 | 9.3 | 50.2 | 26 448 | 26 152 | -1.1 | -1.2 | 433 | 721 | -26 | 11 133 | 2.8 | 2.31 | 8.8 | 27.7 |
| Chippewa | 13.1 | 8.2 | 6.6 | 44.9 | 38 543 | 38 520 | -0.1 | 1.0 | 880 | 697 | 235 | 14 329 | 6.3 | 2.34 | 10.9 | 29.5 |
| | | | | | | | | | | | | | | | | |
| Clare | 15.7 | 12.1 | 8.1 | 50.2 | 31 252 | 30 926 | -1.0 | -0.6 | 762 | 866 | -74 | 12 966 | 2.2 | 2.36 | 10.0 | 28.0 |
| Clinton | 13.3 | 7.5 | 5.7 | 50.8 | 64 753 | 75 382 | 16.4 | 0.8 | 1 556 | 1 145 | 96 | 28 766 | 21.6 | 2.60 | 8.6 | 22.1 |
| Crawford | 16.3 | 12.5 | 8.6 | 49.8 | 14 273 | 14 074 | -1.4 | -0.5 | 308 | 374 | 5 | 6 016 | 7.0 | 2.31 | 9.9 | 27.0 |
| Delta | 16.4 | 9.9 | 9.6 | 50.4 | 38 520 | 37 069 | -3.8 | -0.5 | 846 | 935 | -81 | 15 992 | 1.0 | 2.28 | 8.8 | 29.8 |
| Dickinson | 15.4 | 9.2 | 10.0 | 50.6 | 27 472 | 26 168 | -4.7 | 0.2 | 513 | 702 | 257 | 11 359 | -0.2 | 2.26 | 9.0 | 30.6 |
| Eaton | 14.3 | 8.2 | 6.4 | 51.2 | 103 655 | 107 759 | 4.0 | 0.2 | 2 538 | 2 007 | -253 | 43 494 | 8.3 | 2.44 | 11.1 | 27.1 |
| Emmet | 15.7 | 9.2 | 8.0 | 50.8 | 31 437 | 32 694 | 4.0 | 0.7 | 689 | 686 | 203 | 13 601 | 8.1 | 2.37 | 9.6 | 28.2 |
| Genesee | 13.0 | 7.5 | 6.6 | 51.8 | 436 141 | 425 790 | -2.4 | -1.7 | 11 503 | 9 257 | -9 625 | 169 202 | -0.4 | 2.48 | 17.2 | 28.4 |
| Gladwin | 16.6 | 13.8 | 9.3 | 49.9 | 26 023 | 25 692 | -1.3 | -0.8 | 518 | 786 | 72 | 10 753 | 1.8 | 2.36 | 8.8 | 27.2 |
| | | | | | | | | | | | | | | | | |
| Gogebic | 16.3 | 10.6 | 11.1 | 46.6 | 17 370 | 16 427 | -5.4 | -2.1 | 307 | 533 | -108 | 7 037 | -5.2 | 2.11 | 9.3 | 35.3 |
| Grand Traverse | 14.6 | 8.0 | 7.2 | 50.7 | 77 654 | 86 986 | 12.0 | 2.4 | 2 120 | 1 708 | 1 726 | 35 328 | 16.2 | 2.39 | 9.5 | 27.8 |
| Gratiot | 12.0 | 7.7 | 7.3 | 46.8 | 42 285 | 42 476 | 0.5 | -1.0 | 1 003 | 964 | -464 | 14 852 | 2.4 | 2.49 | 11.4 | 26.0 |
| Hillsdale | 14.0 | 9.1 | 6.9 | 50.3 | 46 527 | 46 688 | 0.3 | -1.0 | 1 139 | 995 | -585 | 17 792 | 2.6 | 2.53 | 9.5 | 24.7 |
| Houghton | 11.8 | 8.1 | 7.0 | 45.9 | 36 016 | 36 628 | 1.7 | -0.3 | 914 | 816 | -222 | 14 232 | 3.2 | 2.38 | 7.7 | 32.2 |
| Huron | 15.7 | 11.3 | 10.8 | 50.5 | 36 079 | 33 118 | -8.2 | -2.0 | 706 | 1 035 | -313 | 14 348 | -1.7 | 2.27 | 8.1 | 30.7 |
| Ingham | 11.5 | 5.8 | 5.0 | 51.5 | 279 320 | 280 895 | 0.6 | 0.3 | 7 339 | 4 448 | -2 096 | 111 162 | 2.4 | 2.36 | 12.7 | 31.3 |
| Ionia | 12.3 | 6.7 | 5.0 | 46.3 | 61 518 | 63 905 | 3.9 | 0.1 | 1 621 | 1 110 | -473 | 22 144 | 7.5 | 2.64 | 10.9 | 22.9 |
| Iosco | 17.4 | 15.0 | 11.7 | 50.5 | 27 339 | 25 887 | -5.3 | -2.0 | 442 | 849 | -111 | 11 757 | 0.3 | 2.17 | 8.8 | 31.8 |
| | | | | | | | | | | | | | | | | |
| Iron | 18.5 | 12.7 | 13.7 | 50.7 | 13 138 | 11 817 | -10.1 | -1.9 | 231 | 445 | -8 | 5 577 | -3.0 | 2.06 | 8.3 | 36.8 |
| Isabella | 9.4 | 5.3 | 4.5 | 51.5 | 63 351 | 70 311 | 11.0 | 0.4 | 1 538 | 950 | -286 | 25 586 | 14.1 | 2.49 | 9.6 | 25.9 |
| Jackson | 13.4 | 7.6 | 6.8 | 49.0 | 158 422 | 160 248 | 1.2 | 0.0 | 4 084 | 3 365 | -598 | 60 771 | 4.5 | 2.48 | 13.3 | 27.1 |
| Kalamazoo | 11.8 | 6.5 | 5.9 | 51.0 | 238 603 | 250 331 | 4.9 | 1.7 | 6 829 | 4 565 | 2 051 | 100 610 | 7.6 | 2.40 | 11.8 | 29.6 |
| Kalkaska | 15.2 | 10.4 | 6.5 | 49.3 | 16 571 | 17 153 | 3.5 | -0.3 | 411 | 383 | -72 | 6 962 | 8.3 | 2.44 | 8.6 | 26.1 |
| Kent | 11.4 | 5.8 | 5.5 | 51.0 | 574 335 | 602 622 | 4.9 | 2.0 | 19 547 | 9 510 | 1 965 | 227 239 | 6.7 | 2.60 | 12.6 | 26.0 |

1. No spouse present.

# Table B. States and Counties — Population, Vital Statistics, Medicare, and Crime

| STATE County | Persons in group quarters, 2010 | Daytime population, 2007–2011 Number | Employment/ residence ratio | Births, 2011 Total | Rate[1] | Deaths, 2011 Number | Rate[1] | Persons under 65 with no health insurance, 2010 Number | Percent | Medicare, 2012 Eligible for Medicare | Enrolled in Medicare Advantage | Enrolled in a Medicare prescription drug plan | Serious crimes known to police,[2] 2011 Total Number | Rate[3] |
|---|---|---|---|---|---|---|---|---|---|---|---|---|---|---|
| | 32 | 33 | 34 | 35 | 36 | 37 | 38 | 39 | 40 | 41 | 42 | 43 | 44 | 45 |
| **MARYLAND—Cont'd** | | | | | | | | | | | | | | |
| St. Mary's | 2 926 | 99 061 | 0.91 | 1 461 | 13.6 | 700 | 6.5 | 9 099 | 9.9 | 13 038 | 179 | 4 494 | 2 957 | 2 786 |
| Somerset | 5 651 | 25 203 | 0.86 | 250 | 9.5 | 260 | 9.9 | 2 649 | 15.0 | 4 353 | 115 | 2 151 | 663 | 2 481 |
| Talbot | 383 | 40 765 | 1.18 | 359 | 9.4 | 434 | 11.4 | 4 013 | 14.0 | 9 940 | 300 | 4 972 | 1 007 | 2 640 |
| Washington | 8 425 | 145 852 | 0.98 | 1 715 | 11.6 | 1 347 | 9.1 | 14 682 | 12.3 | 26 349 | 2 524 | 12 742 | 3 678 | 2 471 |
| Wicomico | 4 403 | 98 483 | 1.01 | 1 259 | 12.7 | 927 | 9.3 | 12 443 | 15.0 | 16 261 | 454 | 8 064 | 3 968 | 3 981 |
| Worcester | 735 | 53 515 | 1.09 | 429 | 8.3 | 601 | 11.7 | 5 706 | 14.6 | 13 358 | 401 | 6 112 | 2 564 | 4 936 |
| Baltimore city | 25 199 | 724 217 | 1.39 | 9 046 | 14.6 | 6 513 | 10.5 | 84 355 | 15.7 | 93 053 | 14 359 | 45 365 | 38 710 | 6 175 |
| **MASSACHUSETTS** | 238 882 | 6 576 971 | 1.02 | 73 368 | 11.1 | 52 355 | 7.9 | 281 724 | 5.2 | 1 134 095 | 206 291 | 494 336 | 177 009 | 2 687 |
| Barnstable | 3 961 | 211 285 | 0.95 | 1 750 | 8.1 | 2 743 | 12.7 | 9 583 | 6.0 | 65 255 | 5 661 | 29 289 | 7 039 | 3 241 |
| Berkshire | 6 159 | 133 770 | 1.04 | 1 110 | 8.5 | 1 365 | 10.5 | 5 247 | 5.1 | 30 253 | 868 | 17 708 | 3 587 | 2 834 |
| Bristol | 15 868 | 500 508 | 0.82 | 6 007 | 10.9 | 4 890 | 8.9 | 25 207 | 5.5 | 104 294 | 14 078 | 51 250 | 16 644 | 3 017 |
| Dukes | 143 | 16 775 | 1.05 | 183 | 10.9 | 127 | 7.6 | 1 144 | 8.3 | 3 628 | 42 | 1 872 | 516 | 3 102 |
| Essex | 16 472 | 688 149 | 0.86 | 8 653 | 11.6 | 6 121 | 8.2 | 34 862 | 5.5 | 132 964 | 21 598 | 62 687 | 18 566 | 2 643 |
| Franklin | 1 481 | 64 170 | 0.80 | 635 | 8.9 | 638 | 8.9 | 2 833 | 4.7 | 14 618 | 2 769 | 6 105 | 1 658 | 2 631 |
| Hampden | 14 791 | 458 750 | 0.98 | 5 571 | 12.0 | 4 102 | 8.8 | 24 417 | 6.3 | 88 893 | 19 149 | 38 903 | 18 201 | 3 966 |
| Hampshire | 20 832 | 150 933 | 0.92 | 1 077 | 6.8 | 1 174 | 7.4 | 5 631 | 4.8 | 26 693 | 4 282 | 10 062 | 3 253 | 2 060 |
| Middlesex | 55 412 | 1 563 942 | 1.09 | 17 581 | 11.6 | 10 644 | 7.0 | 57 135 | 4.5 | 235 049 | 49 458 | 95 124 | 29 725 | 2 046 |
| Nantucket | 58 | 10 759 | 1.11 | 155 | 15.3 | 51 | 5.0 | 716 | 8.1 | 1 567 | 15 | 888 | 344 | 3 361 |
| Norfolk | 17 611 | 658 644 | 0.98 | 6 966 | 10.3 | 5 357 | 7.9 | 20 373 | 3.6 | 114 106 | 18 763 | 45 596 | 11 523 | 1 751 |
| Plymouth | 11 821 | 435 129 | 0.76 | 5 181 | 10.4 | 3 974 | 8.0 | 19 806 | 4.7 | 89 481 | 11 192 | 37 216 | 11 102 | 2 447 |
| Suffolk | 47 228 | 940 919 | 1.63 | 9 430 | 12.9 | 4 669 | 6.4 | 42 137 | 6.9 | 95 503 | 13 869 | 51 213 | 30 296 | 4 171 |
| Worcester | 27 045 | 743 234 | 0.87 | 9 069 | 11.3 | 6 500 | 8.1 | 32 633 | 4.8 | 131 791 | 44 547 | 46 423 | 20 832 | 2 617 |
| **MICHIGAN** | 229 068 | 9 879 521 | 0.99 | 113 894 | 11.5 | 86 988 | 8.8 | 1 193 021 | 14.3 | 1 773 734 | 461 420 | 756 033 | 301 962 | 3 057 |
| Alcona | 127 | 9 982 | 0.67 | 67 | 6.2 | 166 | 15.4 | 1 343 | 18.0 | 4 140 | 728 | 1 778 | 196 | 1 793 |
| Alger | 1 022 | 9 494 | 0.98 | 71 | 7.5 | 120 | 12.6 | 1 050 | 15.5 | 2 357 | 470 | 1 144 | 102 | 1 063 |
| Allegan | 954 | 102 162 | 0.81 | 1 436 | 12.9 | 823 | 7.4 | 13 930 | 14.5 | 18 557 | 7 718 | 6 457 | 1 976 | 1 785 |
| Alpena | 514 | 30 806 | 1.08 | 276 | 9.4 | 336 | 11.4 | 3 506 | 14.8 | 7 903 | 1 117 | 4 365 | 765 | 2 587 |
| Antrim | 226 | 21 553 | 0.76 | 213 | 9.1 | 247 | 10.6 | 3 239 | 17.7 | 6 480 | 1 636 | 3 256 | 465 | 1 974 |
| Arenac | 207 | 15 578 | 0.88 | 120 | 7.7 | 202 | 12.9 | 2 369 | 18.7 | 4 141 | 797 | 2 017 | 160 | 1 007 |
| Baraga | 1 010 | 9 386 | 1.18 | 63 | 7.2 | 113 | 12.8 | 1 157 | 17.8 | 1 749 | 305 | 768 | NA | NA |
| Barry | 603 | 46 602 | 0.51 | 611 | 10.4 | 495 | 8.4 | 6 168 | 12.4 | 11 025 | 3 825 | 4 153 | 1 053 | 1 796 |
| Bay | 1 438 | 98 251 | 0.80 | 1 142 | 10.7 | 1 121 | 10.5 | 12 490 | 13.9 | 23 232 | 4 679 | 9 902 | 2 409 | 2 237 |
| Benzie | 252 | 14 901 | 0.64 | 163 | 9.3 | 199 | 11.4 | 2 441 | 17.7 | 4 575 | 1 139 | 2 164 | 169 | 965 |
| Berrien | 3 527 | 156 218 | 0.99 | 1 901 | 12.1 | 1 588 | 10.1 | 20 054 | 15.5 | 32 144 | 6 467 | 16 769 | 3 673 | 2 380 |
| Branch | 3 148 | 43 452 | 0.87 | 514 | 11.4 | 396 | 8.8 | 5 467 | 15.2 | 8 581 | 1 462 | 4 747 | 878 | 1 942 |
| Calhoun | 4 275 | 142 445 | 1.10 | 1 649 | 12.2 | 1 321 | 9.7 | 17 249 | 15.2 | 27 326 | 4 752 | 14 011 | 5 958 | 4 434 |
| Cass | 474 | 41 179 | 0.51 | 559 | 10.8 | 487 | 9.4 | 7 129 | 16.4 | 10 750 | 2 419 | 5 269 | 646 | 1 393 |
| Charlevoix | 279 | 25 074 | 0.91 | 224 | 8.6 | 267 | 10.3 | 2 896 | 13.8 | 6 141 | 1 503 | 3 233 | 427 | 1 647 |
| Cheboygan | 388 | 24 525 | 0.80 | 211 | 8.1 | 333 | 12.8 | 3 656 | 18.0 | 7 179 | 1 374 | 3 522 | 484 | 1 852 |
| Chippewa | 4 930 | 38 844 | 0.99 | 400 | 10.3 | 318 | 8.2 | 4 918 | 17.2 | 7 331 | 1 390 | 3 260 | 692 | 1 798 |
| Clare | 391 | 28 961 | 0.79 | 349 | 11.2 | 370 | 11.9 | 4 067 | 16.4 | 8 537 | 1 359 | 4 078 | 582 | 1 883 |
| Clinton | 680 | 58 288 | 0.53 | 703 | 9.3 | 484 | 6.4 | 6 422 | 9.9 | 11 755 | 3 169 | 3 969 | 664 | 882 |
| Crawford | 197 | 14 034 | 0.97 | 130 | 9.3 | 153 | 10.9 | 1 688 | 15.2 | 3 494 | 691 | 1 607 | 380 | 2 702 |
| Delta | 623 | 36 713 | 0.97 | 388 | 10.5 | 401 | 10.8 | 4 357 | 14.7 | 9 356 | 2 159 | 4 683 | 1 011 | 2 729 |
| Dickinson | 453 | 27 948 | 1.13 | 225 | 8.6 | 306 | 11.7 | 2 680 | 12.8 | 6 208 | 1 331 | 2 931 | NA | NA |
| Eaton | 1 559 | 103 255 | 0.91 | 1 124 | 10.4 | 860 | 8.0 | 10 252 | 11.3 | 19 435 | 4 933 | 7 012 | 2 391 | 2 221 |
| Emmet | 505 | 35 936 | 1.21 | 307 | 9.3 | 280 | 8.5 | 4 260 | 15.8 | 7 015 | 1 671 | 3 613 | 583 | 1 785 |
| Genesee | 5 973 | 414 570 | 0.91 | 5 222 | 12.4 | 4 102 | 9.7 | 44 805 | 12.3 | 79 974 | 22 869 | 28 955 | 19 615 | 4 620 |
| Gladwin | 289 | 23 298 | 0.70 | 223 | 8.6 | 354 | 13.7 | 3 431 | 17.3 | 7 546 | 1 309 | 3 310 | 397 | 1 546 |
| Gogebic | 1 549 | 16 171 | 0.96 | 133 | 8.2 | 233 | 14.3 | 1 994 | 17.1 | 4 129 | 1 108 | 2 060 | 187 | 1 139 |
| Grand Traverse | 2 642 | 95 974 | 1.22 | 925 | 10.5 | 747 | 8.5 | 9 825 | 13.7 | 17 049 | 4 445 | 7 683 | 1 289 | 1 483 |
| Gratiot | 5 560 | 41 573 | 0.94 | 476 | 11.3 | 426 | 10.1 | 4 455 | 14.2 | 7 711 | 1 379 | 3 928 | 627 | 1 586 |
| Hillsdale | 1 641 | 43 014 | 0.80 | 509 | 10.9 | 436 | 9.4 | 5 993 | 15.7 | 9 003 | 1 893 | 4 833 | 891 | 1 910 |
| Houghton | 2 715 | 36 179 | 0.99 | 406 | 11.1 | 361 | 9.9 | 4 484 | 15.4 | 6 854 | 1 604 | 3 611 | 611 | 1 669 |
| Huron | 524 | 33 046 | 0.98 | 304 | 9.3 | 471 | 14.4 | 4 032 | 15.6 | 8 438 | 1 227 | 4 803 | 468 | 1 508 |
| Ingham | 18 478 | 314 237 | 1.25 | 3 270 | 11.6 | 1 983 | 7.0 | 30 490 | 13.0 | 40 221 | 8 657 | 16 469 | 9 329 | 3 423 |
| Ionia | 5 524 | 57 073 | 0.72 | 729 | 11.4 | 473 | 7.4 | 6 604 | 12.9 | 9 682 | 2 658 | 3 675 | 1 160 | 1 934 |
| Iosco | 400 | 26 725 | 1.07 | 200 | 7.8 | 379 | 14.8 | 3 069 | 16.1 | 8 287 | 1 386 | 3 629 | 543 | 2 099 |
| Iron | 355 | 11 670 | 0.94 | 118 | 10.0 | 204 | 17.3 | 1 415 | 16.3 | 3 557 | 683 | 1 732 | 193 | 2 049 |
| Isabella | 6 540 | 72 168 | 1.08 | 701 | 9.9 | 416 | 5.9 | 9 069 | 15.6 | 9 054 | 1 864 | 4 926 | 1 313 | 1 869 |
| Jackson | 9 672 | 155 570 | 0.92 | 1 815 | 11.4 | 1 496 | 9.4 | 17 963 | 14.0 | 30 074 | 6 482 | 13 727 | 4 111 | 2 602 |
| Kalamazoo | 8 455 | 256 754 | 1.07 | 3 008 | 11.9 | 2 001 | 7.9 | 27 722 | 13.0 | 40 679 | 11 330 | 16 928 | 8 380 | 3 350 |
| Kalkaska | 138 | 14 946 | 0.65 | 183 | 10.7 | 159 | 9.3 | 2 383 | 16.7 | 4 026 | 674 | 1 942 | 434 | 2 657 |
| Kent | 11 353 | 652 127 | 1.18 | 8 675 | 14.3 | 4 162 | 6.8 | 73 488 | 13.9 | 89 590 | 39 506 | 30 167 | 16 917 | 2 809 |

1. Per 1,000 estimated resident population.   2. Data for serious crimes have not been adjusted for underreporting; this may affect comparability between geographic areas and over time.   3. Per 100,000 population estimated by the FBI.

# Table B. States and Counties — Crime, Education, Money Income, and Poverty

| STATE County | Serious crimes known to police, 2011 (cont.)[1] Rate[2] Violent | Property | Education — School enrollment and attainment, 2007–2011 Enrollment[3] Total | Per-cent private | Attainment[4] (percent) High school grad-uate or less | Bach-elor's degree or more | Local government expenditures,[5] 2009–2010 Total current expendi-tures (mil dol) | Current expendi-tures per student (dollars) | Money income, 2007–2011 Per capita income[6] (dollars) | Households Median income Dollars | Percent change, 2000 to 2007–2011 (constant 2011 dollars) | Percent with income of $200,000 or more | Income and poverty, 2011 Median house-hold income (dollars) | Percent below poverty level All per-sons | Children under 18 years | Children 5 to 17 years in families |
|---|---|---|---|---|---|---|---|---|---|---|---|---|---|---|---|---|
| | 46 | 47 | 48 | 49 | 50 | 51 | 52 | 53 | 54 | 55 | 56 | 57 | 58 | 59 | 60 | 61 |
| **MARYLAND—Cont'd** | | | | | | | | | | | | | | | | |
| St. Mary's | 255 | 2 530 | 29 211 | 17.2 | 42.5 | 28.5 | 211.6 | 12 312 | 34 718 | 82 529 | 11.7 | 6.8 | 80 943 | 8.6 | 12.3 | 11.1 |
| Somerset | 307 | 2 174 | 7 878 | 7.3 | 63.9 | 14.3 | 42.0 | 14 492 | 17 599 | 41 420 | 2.6 | 1.2 | 35 426 | 26.2 | 32.1 | 31.9 |
| Talbot | 223 | 2 417 | 7 903 | 26.9 | 40.2 | 32.7 | 53.1 | 11 815 | 38 199 | 63 399 | 7.9 | 7.6 | 55 145 | 10.8 | 17.1 | 15.4 |
| Washington | 302 | 2 169 | 35 297 | 13.4 | 53.0 | 19.0 | 269.7 | 12 314 | 26 392 | 53 180 | -3.0 | 2.6 | 52 028 | 11.8 | 17.7 | 15.6 |
| Wicomico | 585 | 3 396 | 29 688 | 11.3 | 47.8 | 25.6 | 190.3 | 13 019 | 25 929 | 51 739 | -1.8 | 3.1 | 45 788 | 17.7 | 23.7 | 21.6 |
| Worcester | 477 | 4 459 | 10 192 | 16.3 | 44.3 | 27.3 | 106.3 | 15 956 | 32 811 | 57 474 | 4.7 | 4.2 | 48 472 | 13.0 | 22.8 | 21.4 |
| Baltimore city | 1 418 | 4 758 | 168 693 | 24.2 | 51.0 | 25.8 | 1 219.0 | 14 683 | 23 853 | 40 100 | -1.3 | 2.7 | 38 478 | 24.5 | 35.6 | 35.2 |
| **MASSACHUSETTS** | 428 | 2 259 | 1 746 380 | 27.9 | 37.4 | 38.7 | 12 632.7 | 13 200 | 35 051 | 65 981 | -3.2 | 7.2 | 63 126 | 11.6 | 15.3 | 14.1 |
| Barnstable | 454 | 2 787 | 42 693 | 19.4 | 29.9 | 40.5 | 379.8 | 13 954 | 36 000 | 60 525 | -2.4 | 5.0 | 56 167 | 9.8 | 15.2 | 14.0 |
| Berkshire | 415 | 2 419 | 30 545 | 20.3 | 42.6 | 30.2 | 255.6 | 14 267 | 29 387 | 48 705 | -7.6 | 3.3 | 43 813 | 13.5 | 20.2 | 17.3 |
| Bristol | 562 | 2 455 | 137 364 | 18.8 | 49.4 | 25.1 | 980.7 | 12 214 | 28 682 | 55 813 | -5.0 | 3.7 | 53 307 | 11.9 | 16.3 | 15.4 |
| Dukes | 216 | 2 885 | 3 652 | 19.6 | 30.0 | 42.5 | 48.9 | 21 833 | 33 228 | 69 760 | 13.4 | 6.1 | 58 133 | 9.8 | 13.8 | 11.4 |
| Essex | 372 | 2 111 | 194 394 | 23.3 | 38.2 | 36.4 | 1 460.6 | 12 870 | 34 858 | 65 785 | -5.5 | 7.5 | 64 303 | 11.5 | 16.9 | 15.7 |
| Franklin | 432 | 2 199 | 16 628 | 16.9 | 38.3 | 32.3 | 145.5 | 14 998 | 28 313 | 52 246 | -5.1 | 2.2 | 49 940 | 12.3 | 16.6 | 14.3 |
| Hampden | 600 | 3 366 | 124 463 | 18.2 | 48.8 | 23.9 | 968.8 | 12 903 | 25 363 | 48 866 | -8.9 | 2.8 | 47 313 | 16.8 | 25.4 | 22.7 |
| Hampshire | 241 | 1 819 | 57 468 | 21.2 | 32.7 | 42.0 | 254.1 | 12 722 | 29 113 | 60 331 | -3.1 | 4.2 | 54 548 | 13.2 | 12.3 | 10.9 |
| Middlesex | 250 | 1 797 | 401 854 | 32.6 | 30.5 | 49.8 | 2 940.9 | 13 782 | 41 453 | 79 691 | -3.0 | 10.6 | 76 803 | 8.3 | 9.3 | 8.6 |
| Nantucket | 235 | 3 127 | 2 117 | 20.7 | 32.7 | 42.1 | 29.8 | 24 111 | 51 456 | 84 979 | 13.4 | 12.3 | 68 431 | 8.8 | 10.2 | 9.8 |
| Norfolk | 201 | 1 550 | 175 683 | 32.5 | 28.9 | 48.2 | 1 320.8 | 12 963 | 43 685 | 83 733 | -2.2 | 12.1 | 81 590 | 6.4 | 6.7 | 5.8 |
| Plymouth | 436 | 2 012 | 131 798 | 18.7 | 38.6 | 32.9 | 1 012.7 | 11 560 | 34 285 | 74 698 | -0.5 | 7.1 | 67 989 | 8.5 | 10.8 | 10.1 |
| Suffolk | 886 | 3 285 | 211 887 | 47.5 | 41.8 | 39.2 | 1 240.7 | 16 595 | 32 034 | 51 638 | -2.8 | 6.0 | 49 033 | 22.4 | 31.5 | 32.3 |
| Worcester | 439 | 2 177 | 215 834 | 22.7 | 40.1 | 33.3 | 1 593.9 | 12 050 | 31 470 | 65 772 | 1.8 | 5.4 | 60 396 | 11.6 | 16.2 | 14.2 |
| **MICHIGAN** | 445 | 2 612 | 2 743 564 | 13.4 | 42.7 | 25.3 | 17 174.0 | 10 583 | 25 482 | 48 669 | -19.3 | 2.9 | 45 931 | 17.5 | 24.6 | 22.4 |
| Alcona | 110 | 1 683 | 1 828 | 6.2 | 54.9 | 12.8 | 8.5 | 9 324 | 21 003 | 35 490 | -16.2 | 1.5 | 35 407 | 17.9 | 32.6 | 28.2 |
| Alger | 146 | 917 | 1 622 | 14.5 | 57.0 | 17.1 | 11.8 | 10 192 | 19 858 | 38 231 | -21.1 | 1.1 | 39 486 | 16.3 | 22.7 | 19.2 |
| Allegan | 191 | 1 593 | 28 455 | 15.4 | 49.6 | 20.1 | 145.7 | 9 457 | 23 395 | 51 232 | -17.2 | 1.7 | 50 559 | 12.7 | 18.3 | 16.0 |
| Alpena | 189 | 2 397 | 6 577 | 7.6 | 46.6 | 15.4 | 49.3 | 10 647 | 21 867 | 38 081 | -17.5 | 1.2 | 37 270 | 18.6 | 27.4 | 24.4 |
| Antrim | 149 | 1 825 | 5 112 | 7.8 | 46.1 | 23.4 | 37.5 | 8 928 | 23 941 | 42 440 | -17.5 | 2.1 | 41 679 | 16.6 | 30.0 | 26.4 |
| Arenac | 170 | 837 | 3 347 | 6.8 | 59.9 | 10.8 | 22.3 | 8 954 | 19 386 | 36 281 | -18.1 | 1.3 | 38 008 | 18.7 | 31.9 | 29.8 |
| Baraga | NA | NA | 1 763 | 13.2 | 61.9 | 11.3 | 12.7 | 9 666 | 19 076 | 40 115 | -11.8 | 0.8 | 38 119 | 17.2 | 24.9 | 21.5 |
| Barry | 162 | 1 634 | 14 909 | 10.3 | 49.1 | 16.9 | 67.5 | 8 817 | 24 989 | 52 061 | -17.6 | 2.0 | 50 051 | 11.3 | 16.3 | 14.5 |
| Bay | 276 | 1 961 | 26 516 | 13.4 | 46.9 | 18.3 | 160.9 | 10 445 | 23 642 | 45 962 | -11.9 | 1.4 | 43 068 | 13.5 | 21.5 | 19.9 |
| Benzie | 91 | 874 | 3 851 | 9.1 | 43.4 | 25.2 | 21.4 | 8 935 | 24 267 | 47 017 | -6.8 | 1.3 | 45 998 | 12.2 | 20.6 | 18.7 |
| Berrien | 369 | 2 010 | 40 082 | 20.0 | 44.5 | 23.7 | 278.2 | 10 457 | 24 490 | 42 488 | -18.4 | 2.5 | 40 946 | 17.6 | 28.2 | 25.7 |
| Branch | 144 | 1 798 | 11 014 | 12.7 | 54.2 | 14.1 | 77.2 | 10 619 | 19 563 | 42 505 | -18.8 | 1.6 | 40 462 | 18.2 | 26.0 | 25.1 |
| Calhoun | 629 | 3 805 | 35 987 | 12.0 | 47.5 | 18.7 | 249.2 | 11 332 | 22 430 | 42 287 | -19.5 | 1.7 | 39 694 | 19.6 | 29.2 | 25.8 |
| Cass | 106 | 1 287 | 12 909 | 10.8 | 50.9 | 16.7 | 68.7 | 9 192 | 23 045 | 45 432 | -18.5 | 1.6 | 44 626 | 12.9 | 22.1 | 20.0 |
| Charlevoix | 143 | 1 504 | 5 826 | 10.6 | 41.8 | 25.2 | 59.9 | 14 224 | 28 226 | 48 745 | -9.3 | 3.2 | 44 061 | 12.1 | 19.1 | 17.2 |
| Cheboygan | 149 | 1 703 | 5 362 | 11.7 | 51.6 | 17.3 | 39.4 | 11 615 | 22 379 | 37 844 | -16.1 | 1.7 | 37 133 | 18.9 | 31.0 | 26.6 |
| Chippewa | 200 | 1 598 | 9 490 | 7.9 | 48.4 | 17.9 | 62.7 | 11 767 | 20 744 | 41 108 | -11.7 | 1.5 | 39 520 | 18.6 | 24.9 | 23.2 |
| Clare | 155 | 1 728 | 6 483 | 8.4 | 57.0 | 11.0 | 54.2 | 11 416 | 18 413 | 34 431 | -11.6 | 0.6 | 31 443 | 27.0 | 40.0 | 41.6 |
| Clinton | 105 | 777 | 21 909 | 10.2 | 38.0 | 27.2 | 97.7 | 9 488 | 27 723 | 58 244 | -18.3 | 2.8 | 58 286 | 10.3 | 12.7 | 10.9 |
| Crawford | 277 | 2 425 | 3 036 | 10.9 | 54.2 | 15.0 | 15.7 | 8 683 | 21 583 | 39 597 | -12.1 | 1.3 | 37 874 | 17.6 | 29.6 | 27.0 |
| Delta | 143 | 2 586 | 8 332 | 8.6 | 47.8 | 18.3 | 52.4 | 10 587 | 22 208 | 42 932 | -10.5 | 1.1 | 40 982 | 16.8 | 21.0 | 19.4 |
| Dickinson | NA | NA | 5 987 | 8.3 | 47.9 | 19.3 | 44.5 | 10 666 | 24 963 | 43 651 | -7.2 | 1.3 | 44 262 | 12.0 | 18.5 | 16.1 |
| Eaton | 163 | 2 057 | 28 741 | 14.5 | 36.9 | 24.6 | 182.9 | 9 545 | 26 296 | 54 170 | -19.1 | 1.5 | 51 428 | 11.8 | 17.2 | 15.0 |
| Emmet | 104 | 1 680 | 8 002 | 11.6 | 36.9 | 29.6 | 52.1 | 9 382 | 29 465 | 50 269 | -7.4 | 5.2 | 48 285 | 13.1 | 19.2 | 17.3 |
| Genesee | 834 | 3 786 | 119 919 | 10.8 | 45.5 | 18.9 | 796.8 | 10 462 | 22 577 | 43 418 | -23.3 | 1.5 | 40 854 | 20.7 | 30.9 | 27.8 |
| Gladwin | 245 | 1 301 | 5 156 | 10.5 | 55.5 | 11.3 | 28.8 | 8 615 | 20 677 | 38 160 | -11.7 | 1.1 | 34 747 | 22.1 | 35.9 | 33.2 |
| Gogebic | 134 | 1 005 | 2 766 | 7.4 | 46.8 | 18.4 | 18.5 | 9 661 | 20 759 | 34 917 | -5.6 | 1.2 | 33 382 | 20.5 | 30.8 | 28.8 |
| Grand Traverse | 140 | 1 343 | 20 865 | 12.4 | 35.5 | 29.8 | 157.2 | 12 026 | 27 617 | 50 629 | -13.1 | 3.1 | 46 786 | 13.6 | 18.8 | 16.3 |
| Gratiot | 157 | 1 429 | 10 816 | 17.7 | 53.8 | 13.1 | 76.0 | 10 581 | 18 936 | 39 867 | -20.8 | 0.8 | 40 359 | 19.5 | 27.5 | 25.4 |
| Hillsdale | 193 | 1 717 | 11 881 | 20.2 | 55.5 | 14.2 | 69.3 | 10 091 | 20 428 | 43 139 | -20.9 | 1.2 | 41 030 | 18.4 | 28.5 | 25.8 |
| Houghton | 107 | 1 563 | 12 999 | 5.1 | 45.6 | 27.1 | 53.9 | 9 870 | 18 556 | 34 625 | -11.0 | 1.4 | 35 425 | 20.1 | 21.0 | 19.7 |
| Huron | 119 | 1 389 | 7 199 | 10.3 | 59.2 | 14.0 | 54.4 | 11 376 | 21 845 | 40 200 | -15.7 | 1.5 | 39 726 | 14.4 | 22.8 | 20.7 |
| Ingham | 524 | 2 898 | 102 755 | 9.0 | 32.3 | 35.4 | 480.7 | 11 368 | 24 322 | 45 758 | -16.9 | 2.9 | 42 371 | 22.6 | 24.2 | 22.5 |
| Ionia | 180 | 1 754 | 16 771 | 10.4 | 52.0 | 13.4 | 117.3 | 10 414 | 19 994 | 46 958 | -19.3 | 0.9 | 46 072 | 16.6 | 22.8 | 20.6 |
| Iosco | 170 | 1 929 | 4 818 | 9.0 | 54.6 | 13.7 | 46.6 | 10 196 | 21 303 | 36 445 | -13.8 | 0.8 | 33 487 | 22.1 | 36.5 | 31.6 |
| Iron | 127 | 1 922 | 2 161 | 8.3 | 56.3 | 16.3 | 13.0 | 8 738 | 20 099 | 35 390 | -8.2 | 0.8 | 34 384 | 15.1 | 26.6 | 23.4 |
| Isabella | 142 | 1 726 | 30 893 | 5.8 | 43.4 | 25.7 | 58.3 | 8 670 | 18 738 | 36 815 | -20.4 | 1.8 | 38 154 | 30.0 | 23.5 | 21.5 |
| Jackson | 391 | 2 211 | 41 367 | 15.4 | 45.8 | 17.9 | 271.5 | 10 758 | 22 227 | 47 169 | -19.1 | 1.6 | 42 379 | 16.2 | 24.6 | 22.0 |
| Kalamazoo | 370 | 2 980 | 81 655 | 11.3 | 33.3 | 33.6 | 355.1 | 10 110 | 25 620 | 46 019 | -18.9 | 3.0 | 45 798 | 19.3 | 21.8 | 19.0 |
| Kalkaska | 178 | 2 479 | 3 550 | 7.2 | 57.6 | 10.4 | 21.4 | 8 944 | 19 685 | 39 130 | -19.7 | 0.7 | 38 053 | 18.7 | 29.6 | 27.8 |
| Kent | 387 | 2 422 | 173 034 | 21.2 | 38.6 | 30.3 | 1 131.0 | 10 478 | 25 410 | 50 801 | -18.2 | 3.1 | 50 651 | 14.7 | 20.2 | 18.2 |

1. Data for serious crimes have not been adjusted for underreporting; this may affect comparability between geographic areas and over time. 2. Per 100,000 population estimated by the FBI. 3. All persons 3 years old and over enrolled in nursery school through college. 4. Persons 25 years old and over. 5. Elementary and secondary education expenditures. 6. Based on population estimated by the American Community Survey, 2007–2011.

| STATE County | Total (mil dol) | Percent change, 2010–2011 | Dollars | Rank | Wages and salaries[2] (mil dol) | Proprietors' income (mil dol) | Dividends, interest, and rent (mil dol) | Total | Total | Social Security | Medical payments | Income mainte-nance | Unemploy-ment insurance |
|---|---|---|---|---|---|---|---|---|---|---|---|---|---|
| | | | Per capita[1] | | | | | Transfer payments (mil dol) | Government payments to individuals | | | | |
| | 62 | 63 | 64 | 65 | 66 | 67 | 68 | 69 | 70 | 71 | 72 | 73 | 74 |
| MARYLAND—Cont'd | | | | | | | | | | | | | |
| St. Mary's | 4 821 | 6.2 | 44 849 | 398 | 3 871 | 247 | 634 | 615 | 592 | 176 | 269 | 66 | 26 |
| Somerset | 748 | 2.8 | 28 387 | 2 558 | 364 | 49 | 110 | 226 | 220 | 60 | 98 | 32 | 9 |
| Talbot | 2 119 | 5.4 | 55 721 | 104 | 922 | 185 | 708 | 352 | 344 | 149 | 143 | 23 | 11 |
| Washington | 5 485 | 4.9 | 37 008 | 1 076 | 3 373 | 235 | 839 | 1 128 | 1 096 | 379 | 477 | 113 | 53 |
| Wicomico | 3 470 | 3.5 | 34 985 | 1 376 | 2 252 | 200 | 558 | 802 | 781 | 240 | 356 | 97 | 37 |
| Worcester | 2 266 | 5.5 | 43 987 | 440 | 958 | 189 | 667 | 481 | 470 | 198 | 188 | 39 | 27 |
| Baltimore city | 26 041 | 6.3 | 42 036 | 567 | 24 643 | 1 806 | 3 168 | 7 103 | 6 966 | 1 237 | 3 743 | 1 345 | 232 |
| MASSACHUSETTS | 352 243 | 5.1 | 53 471 | X | 239 035 | 29 870 | 58 208 | 55 951 | 54 494 | 15 446 | 26 592 | 6 425 | 3 733 |
| Barnstable | 11 968 | 4.9 | 55 465 | 110 | 4 761 | 851 | 3 418 | 2 306 | 2 259 | 932 | 946 | 149 | 144 |
| Berkshire | 5 803 | 4.4 | 44 483 | 423 | 3 142 | 372 | 1 227 | 1 407 | 1 378 | 425 | 681 | 149 | 77 |
| Bristol | 22 991 | 4.6 | 41 884 | 584 | 11 795 | 1 072 | 2 689 | 5 242 | 5 121 | 1 374 | 2 501 | 640 | 425 |
| Dukes | 1 007 | 6.3 | 60 075 | 67 | 439 | 127 | 368 | 128 | 124 | 51 | 49 | 8 | 12 |
| Essex | 39 850 | 5.3 | 53 209 | 138 | 19 668 | 2 567 | 6 688 | 6 425 | 6 260 | 1 823 | 2 966 | 807 | 435 |
| Franklin | 3 049 | 4.1 | 42 588 | 529 | 1 221 | 192 | 504 | 728 | 712 | 189 | 377 | 74 | 38 |
| Hampden | 18 401 | 3.7 | 39 677 | 782 | 11 017 | 873 | 2 237 | 5 489 | 5 386 | 1 154 | 2 871 | 857 | 303 |
| Hampshire | 6 260 | 3.9 | 39 664 | 783 | 3 153 | 360 | 1 196 | 986 | 951 | 349 | 346 | 100 | 76 |
| Middlesex | 94 619 | 5.3 | 62 324 | 49 | 73 045 | 7 247 | 17 759 | 10 329 | 9 993 | 3 311 | 4 525 | 1 000 | 717 |
| Nantucket | 770 | 7.4 | 75 947 | 12 | 354 | 109 | 307 | 63 | 61 | 24 | 23 | 5 | 8 |
| Norfolk | 45 123 | 5.2 | 66 806 | 31 | 22 889 | 4 213 | 8 352 | 4 616 | 4 466 | 1 630 | 1 931 | 353 | 334 |
| Plymouth | 25 360 | 5.2 | 50 968 | 186 | 10 182 | 2 061 | 3 709 | 4 087 | 3 977 | 1 260 | 1 856 | 390 | 299 |
| Suffolk | 40 546 | 5.2 | 55 472 | 109 | 57 711 | 7 482 | 5 196 | 7 755 | 7 593 | 1 094 | 4 636 | 1 154 | 388 |
| Worcester | 36 494 | 5.0 | 45 548 | 362 | 19 659 | 2 344 | 4 560 | 6 390 | 6 213 | 1 832 | 2 884 | 740 | 478 |
| MICHIGAN | 358 152 | 5.6 | 36 264 | X | 227 396 | 25 069 | 49 359 | 81 711 | 79 526 | 28 284 | 32 247 | 10 459 | 3 875 |
| Alcona | 315 | 3.8 | 29 209 | 2 423 | 67 | 21 | 68 | 137 | 135 | 63 | 50 | 10 | 4 |
| Alger | 243 | 3.5 | 25 518 | 2 927 | 119 | 12 | 39 | 87 | 85 | 36 | 34 | 6 | 4 |
| Allegan | 3 734 | 5.2 | 33 565 | 1 590 | 1 845 | 461 | 505 | 764 | 739 | 295 | 263 | 79 | 37 |
| Alpena | 988 | 4.0 | 33 612 | 1 585 | 531 | 70 | 146 | 342 | 336 | 119 | 151 | 36 | 11 |
| Antrim | 760 | 4.3 | 32 587 | 1 783 | 193 | 56 | 197 | 239 | 233 | 100 | 94 | 20 | 10 |
| Arenac | 475 | 4.9 | 30 335 | 2 231 | 175 | 48 | 66 | 176 | 173 | 64 | 73 | 21 | 7 |
| Baraga | 229 | 1.2 | 25 943 | 2 888 | 133 | 10 | 38 | 76 | 74 | 26 | 29 | 8 | 6 |
| Barry | 1 957 | 5.0 | 33 268 | 1 662 | 537 | 199 | 289 | 398 | 385 | 174 | 129 | 45 | 16 |
| Bay | 3 614 | 5.3 | 33 737 | 1 555 | 1 810 | 191 | 533 | 1 036 | 1 012 | 369 | 405 | 117 | 40 |
| Benzie | 542 | 3.7 | 31 079 | 2 081 | 151 | 33 | 129 | 160 | 156 | 67 | 56 | 16 | 8 |
| Berrien | 5 623 | 3.3 | 35 830 | 1 244 | 3 239 | 372 | 856 | 1 435 | 1 400 | 495 | 590 | 190 | 58 |
| Branch | 1 270 | 5.1 | 28 098 | 2 604 | 631 | 135 | 174 | 356 | 346 | 129 | 142 | 43 | 15 |
| Calhoun | 4 544 | 2.7 | 33 541 | 1 595 | 3 188 | 195 | 589 | 1 241 | 1 211 | 409 | 479 | 187 | 46 |
| Cass | 1 821 | 7.9 | 35 027 | 1 367 | 406 | 139 | 264 | 425 | 413 | 166 | 149 | 54 | 18 |
| Charlevoix | 945 | 4.3 | 36 361 | 1 157 | 485 | 53 | 229 | 221 | 215 | 95 | 80 | 19 | 12 |
| Cheboygan | 765 | 3.9 | 29 533 | 2 374 | 264 | 52 | 161 | 259 | 253 | 107 | 95 | 28 | 10 |
| Chippewa | 1 047 | 2.6 | 26 977 | 2 766 | 630 | 42 | 145 | 317 | 309 | 104 | 125 | 38 | 15 |
| Clare | 878 | 4.6 | 28 297 | 2 571 | 305 | 77 | 110 | 348 | 341 | 126 | 127 | 47 | 13 |
| Clinton | 2 711 | 5.0 | 35 926 | 1 223 | 733 | 243 | 331 | 416 | 400 | 195 | 129 | 36 | 21 |
| Crawford | 385 | 5.0 | 27 501 | 2 686 | 187 | 29 | 55 | 130 | 127 | 52 | 48 | 16 | 5 |
| Delta | 1 194 | 4.0 | 32 175 | 1 849 | 667 | 52 | 174 | 372 | 364 | 137 | 139 | 36 | 15 |
| Dickinson | 984 | 4.8 | 37 594 | 1 016 | 726 | 26 | 157 | 247 | 241 | 89 | 106 | 20 | 10 |
| Eaton | 3 637 | 2.8 | 33 655 | 1 576 | 1 612 | 144 | 474 | 715 | 691 | 322 | 223 | 73 | 32 |
| Emmet | 1 309 | 4.1 | 39 842 | 765 | 765 | 97 | 330 | 302 | 295 | 107 | 124 | 28 | 19 |
| Genesee | 13 108 | 4.6 | 31 057 | 2 084 | 6 908 | 698 | 1 573 | 4 291 | 4 198 | 1 340 | 1 673 | 679 | 169 |
| Gladwin | 694 | 4.3 | 26 853 | 2 784 | 171 | 22 | 109 | 289 | 283 | 118 | 113 | 29 | 10 |
| Gogebic | 480 | 1.5 | 29 454 | 2 385 | 230 | 23 | 79 | 181 | 177 | 60 | 81 | 17 | 6 |
| Grand Traverse | 3 260 | 5.0 | 36 894 | 1 086 | 2 205 | 438 | 612 | 675 | 656 | 262 | 256 | 60 | 34 |
| Gratiot | 1 292 | 7.3 | 30 647 | 2 163 | 611 | 202 | 157 | 347 | 337 | 115 | 151 | 39 | 16 |
| Hillsdale | 1 325 | 7.3 | 28 481 | 2 542 | 588 | 130 | 177 | 365 | 355 | 139 | 138 | 44 | 17 |
| Houghton | 995 | 3.4 | 27 169 | 2 742 | 572 | 35 | 165 | 315 | 307 | 99 | 141 | 31 | 13 |
| Huron | 1 318 | 10.5 | 40 336 | 712 | 532 | 272 | 255 | 322 | 315 | 126 | 136 | 29 | 12 |
| Ingham | 9 701 | 3.1 | 34 450 | 1 442 | 9 259 | 565 | 1 225 | 2 118 | 2 056 | 640 | 839 | 295 | 100 |
| Ionia | 1 713 | 7.3 | 26 781 | 2 791 | 816 | 146 | 184 | 405 | 391 | 149 | 148 | 53 | 23 |
| Iosco | 721 | 3.5 | 28 245 | 2 576 | 282 | 30 | 129 | 322 | 316 | 126 | 134 | 30 | 10 |
| Iron | 389 | 3.6 | 33 002 | 1 708 | 158 | 14 | 68 | 143 | 140 | 51 | 65 | 12 | 4 |
| Isabella | 1 975 | 5.3 | 27 960 | 2 622 | 1 277 | 139 | 254 | 499 | 484 | 138 | 253 | 51 | 22 |
| Jackson | 5 015 | 5.4 | 31 396 | 2 016 | 2 922 | 256 | 677 | 1 313 | 1 278 | 476 | 497 | 161 | 56 |
| Kalamazoo | 9 058 | 4.6 | 35 933 | 1 222 | 6 208 | 468 | 1 565 | 1 829 | 1 773 | 644 | 670 | 245 | 80 |
| Kalkaska | 466 | 6.1 | 27 137 | 2 746 | 208 | 32 | 62 | 151 | 147 | 60 | 54 | 19 | 7 |
| Kent | 22 263 | 6.7 | 36 589 | 1 127 | 17 715 | 2 237 | 3 003 | 3 985 | 3 850 | 1 389 | 1 408 | 577 | 191 |

1. Based on the resident population estimated as of July 1 of the year shown.    2. Includes supplements to wages and salaries.

# Table B. States and Counties — **Earnings, Social Security, and Housing**

| STATE County | Earnings, 2011 Total (mil dol) | Farm | Goods-related[1] Total | Manu-facturing | Service-related and health: Information and professional and technical services | Retail trade | Finance, insurance, and real estate | Health care and social services | Govern-ment | Social Security beneficiaries, December 2011 Number | Rate[2] | Supplemental Security Income recipients, December 2011 | Housing units, 2010 Total | Percent change, 2000–2010 |
|---|---|---|---|---|---|---|---|---|---|---|---|---|---|---|
| | 75 | 76 | 77 | 78 | 79 | 80 | 81 | 82 | 83 | 84 | 85 | 86 | 87 | 88 |
| **MARYLAND—Cont'd** | | | | | | | | | | | | | | |
| St. Mary's | 4 118 | 0.2 | D | 1.0 | 25.3 | 3.5 | 1.4 | 6.2 | 46.3 | 13 680 | 127 | 1 367 | 41 282 | 21.1 |
| Somerset | 413 | 3.0 | 9.8 | 5.8 | 2.6 | 3.5 | 2.2 | 11.0 | 45.6 | 4 925 | 187 | 701 | 11 130 | 10.3 |
| Talbot | 1 107 | 1.8 | 13.0 | 4.8 | 13.0 | 8.7 | 7.5 | 20.4 | 11.3 | 10 340 | 272 | 548 | 19 577 | 18.6 |
| Washington | 3 609 | 1.1 | 19.4 | 13.8 | 5.7 | 10.2 | 11.1 | 15.8 | 15.8 | 28 775 | 194 | 3 134 | 60 814 | 14.8 |
| Wicomico | 2 452 | 0.8 | D | 8.4 | 7.1 | 8.9 | 4.4 | 20.3 | 18.2 | 18 280 | 184 | 2 349 | 41 192 | 19.7 |
| Worcester | 1 147 | 2.2 | D | 3.1 | 4.7 | 15.1 | 5.4 | 9.3 | 20.7 | 14 425 | 280 | 802 | 55 749 | 17.7 |
| Baltimore city | 26 449 | 0.0 | 6.9 | 3.7 | 11.3 | 2.3 | 9.1 | 19.7 | 22.6 | 101 470 | 164 | 36 554 | 296 685 | -1.3 |
| **MASSACHUSETTS** | 268 905 | 0.1 | 14.1 | 9.4 | 18.3 | 4.8 | 12.7 | 13.5 | 11.9 | 1 161 122 | 176 | 197 327 | 2 808 254 | 7.1 |
| Barnstable | 5 612 | 0.1 | 11.4 | 2.4 | 10.2 | 10.2 | 5.7 | 18.2 | 19.1 | 66 520 | 308 | 3 642 | 160 281 | 9.0 |
| Berkshire | 3 514 | 0.0 | 18.3 | 11.4 | 9.2 | 8.2 | 6.6 | 19.6 | 13.6 | 32 465 | 249 | 4 231 | 68 508 | 3.3 |
| Bristol | 12 867 | 0.1 | 22.0 | 16.2 | 6.4 | 8.6 | 3.8 | 16.4 | 14.5 | 111 720 | 204 | 20 348 | 230 535 | 6.3 |
| Dukes | 566 | 0.0 | D | D | D | 10.6 | 5.5 | 10.2 | 16.5 | 3 555 | 212 | 147 | 17 188 | 15.9 |
| Essex | 22 235 | 0.0 | 25.2 | 20.0 | 12.1 | 6.5 | 6.3 | 15.5 | 12.4 | 135 885 | 181 | 23 712 | 306 754 | 6.8 |
| Franklin | 1 413 | 0.7 | D | 14.3 | 6.1 | 8.4 | 3.4 | 12.9 | 18.4 | 15 305 | 214 | 2 312 | 33 758 | 5.7 |
| Hampden | 11 890 | 0.0 | 17.0 | 11.6 | 6.4 | 6.6 | 9.6 | 19.1 | 18.5 | 95 315 | 206 | 30 572 | 192 175 | 3.4 |
| Hampshire | 3 513 | 0.1 | 11.1 | 6.6 | 6.3 | 7.0 | 3.6 | 12.5 | 30.4 | 27 130 | 172 | 3 219 | 62 603 | 6.7 |
| Middlesex | 80 292 | 0.1 | 16.2 | 11.9 | 29.0 | 3.6 | 6.5 | 8.6 | 8.8 | 232 645 | 153 | 27 571 | 612 004 | 6.1 |
| Nantucket | 463 | 0.0 | D | D | D | 9.5 | 5.0 | 7.0 | 14.0 | 1 520 | 150 | 45 | 11 618 | 26.1 |
| Norfolk | 27 102 | 0.0 | 14.2 | 7.8 | 15.1 | 6.3 | 17.5 | 12.7 | 9.0 | 114 040 | 169 | 10 966 | 270 359 | 6.0 |
| Plymouth | 12 243 | 0.2 | 14.7 | 6.6 | 10.3 | 8.0 | 7.1 | 14.4 | 18.0 | 93 030 | 187 | 9 568 | 200 161 | 10.3 |
| Suffolk | 65 193 | 0.0 | D | 1.6 | 19.6 | 2.0 | 26.9 | 16.0 | 10.9 | 92 610 | 127 | 38 107 | 315 522 | 7.9 |
| Worcester | 22 003 | 0.0 | 18.8 | 13.5 | 9.8 | 6.0 | 8.5 | 15.7 | 15.4 | 139 380 | 174 | 22 887 | 326 788 | 9.6 |
| **MICHIGAN** | 252 466 | 1.1 | 21.2 | 16.5 | 11.5 | 6.2 | 6.2 | 12.8 | 15.9 | 2 016 684 | 204 | 264 706 | 4 532 233 | 7.0 |
| Alcona | 88 | 6.2 | 18.5 | 12.5 | D | 9.5 | D | 19.9 | 18.4 | 4 680 | 433 | 287 | 11 073 | 4.6 |
| Alger | 131 | 2.0 | 25.0 | 22.1 | D | 5.4 | D | 7.4 | 36.3 | 2 750 | 289 | 188 | 6 554 | 9.9 |
| Allegan | 2 305 | 7.2 | 44.8 | 37.2 | 3.4 | 4.7 | 4.0 | 5.0 | 11.4 | 21 560 | 194 | 1 770 | 49 426 | 14.2 |
| Alpena | 600 | 2.4 | 22.6 | 16.8 | 3.8 | 9.5 | 4.1 | 13.0 | 28.4 | 9 255 | 315 | 1 182 | 16 053 | 5.0 |
| Antrim | 249 | 3.8 | D | 16.2 | 4.9 | 7.2 | 5.3 | D | 24.3 | 7 235 | 310 | 495 | 17 824 | 18.1 |
| Arenac | 223 | 8.0 | 15.1 | 10.9 | 4.3 | 7.3 | 2.7 | D | 20.3 | 4 910 | 314 | 549 | 9 803 | 2.5 |
| Baraga | 143 | 0.6 | D | 16.4 | 2.6 | 3.8 | D | D | 54.5 | 2 010 | 228 | 170 | 5 270 | 13.8 |
| Barry | 736 | 6.2 | D | 23.6 | D | 5.2 | 7.8 | 10.6 | 15.9 | 12 540 | 213 | 816 | 27 010 | 13.1 |
| Bay | 2 001 | 2.8 | 16.2 | 12.8 | 12.9 | 8.5 | 4.2 | 17.3 | 17.2 | 26 970 | 252 | 3 099 | 48 220 | 3.9 |
| Benzie | 184 | 2.1 | D | 9.7 | 2.9 | 10.1 | 5.8 | D | 19.6 | 4 975 | 285 | 336 | 12 199 | 18.3 |
| Berrien | 3 611 | 1.9 | 33.0 | 29.1 | 4.4 | 5.9 | 4.2 | 11.9 | 13.8 | 36 210 | 231 | 4 993 | 76 922 | 4.7 |
| Branch | 766 | 8.4 | D | 17.9 | D | 7.0 | 5.6 | 5.4 | 23.9 | 9 820 | 217 | 939 | 20 841 | 5.1 |
| Calhoun | 3 383 | 1.3 | D | 23.0 | D | 5.5 | 2.1 | 12.9 | 21.9 | 30 980 | 229 | 4 863 | 61 042 | 4.0 |
| Cass | 545 | 12.4 | 23.7 | 18.6 | D | 5.3 | 4.1 | 6.7 | 20.9 | 12 185 | 234 | 1 145 | 25 887 | 8.4 |
| Charlevoix | 538 | 0.7 | D | 26.8 | D | 5.7 | 4.0 | D | 17.4 | 6 880 | 265 | 444 | 17 249 | 12.2 |
| Cheboygan | 316 | 1.6 | 14.1 | 3.2 | 4.4 | 12.8 | 5.3 | D | 21.4 | 8 280 | 319 | 694 | 18 298 | 10.3 |
| Chippewa | 672 | 0.7 | 7.1 | 3.9 | 2.3 | 7.7 | 2.5 | 5.0 | 60.2 | 8 375 | 216 | 911 | 21 253 | 9.4 |
| Clare | 382 | 2.9 | D | 14.8 | 3.6 | 9.1 | 3.2 | D | 23.0 | 9 690 | 312 | 1 314 | 23 233 | 4.5 |
| Clinton | 975 | 9.5 | 23.8 | 15.5 | D | 7.1 | 5.6 | 7.2 | 14.7 | 13 420 | 178 | 758 | 30 695 | 24.6 |
| Crawford | 216 | 0.0 | D | 13.1 | 4.6 | 7.4 | 3.5 | 26.2 | 22.7 | 3 990 | 285 | 365 | 11 092 | 10.5 |
| Delta | 719 | 0.7 | D | 24.2 | D | 8.1 | 4.2 | 12.8 | 17.3 | 10 550 | 284 | 1 032 | 20 214 | 5.2 |
| Dickinson | 753 | 0.3 | 36.0 | 21.0 | D | 7.3 | 2.3 | 7.1 | 26.7 | 7 020 | 268 | 567 | 13 990 | 2.1 |
| Eaton | 1 756 | 2.3 | 15.3 | 10.1 | D | 7.6 | 19.1 | 6.1 | 20.1 | 22 265 | 206 | 1 573 | 47 050 | 11.7 |
| Emmet | 862 | 0.6 | D | 7.3 | D | 10.3 | 5.3 | 24.1 | 17.0 | 7 805 | 238 | 508 | 21 304 | 14.8 |
| Genesee | 7 606 | 0.2 | 16.2 | 12.3 | 8.6 | 8.4 | 6.1 | 18.6 | 18.6 | 94 095 | 223 | 16 331 | 192 180 | 4.7 |
| Gladwin | 193 | 6.9 | D | 15.2 | 1.8 | 13.9 | 2.5 | D | 22.7 | 8 715 | 337 | 857 | 17 672 | 5.0 |
| Gogebic | 252 | 0.1 | 16.7 | 12.2 | 4.6 | 8.1 | 4.3 | D | 33.7 | 4 800 | 295 | 433 | 10 795 | -0.4 |
| Grand Traverse | 2 643 | 0.5 | 18.4 | 9.4 | 8.9 | 9.2 | 8.0 | 23.1 | 13.7 | 18 925 | 214 | 1 419 | 41 599 | 19.4 |
| Gratiot | 814 | 10.4 | 15.6 | 13.5 | D | 5.2 | 3.7 | D | 17.0 | 8 865 | 210 | 1 006 | 16 339 | 5.3 |
| Hillsdale | 719 | 8.8 | D | 29.6 | D | 6.9 | 4.4 | D | 18.2 | 10 520 | 226 | 1 138 | 21 757 | 7.8 |
| Houghton | 607 | 0.4 | D | 4.1 | 5.2 | 7.5 | 3.5 | D | 40.6 | 7 780 | 212 | 671 | 18 636 | 5.0 |
| Huron | 804 | 26.1 | D | 17.8 | 2.5 | 5.1 | 3.5 | D | 12.0 | 9 540 | 292 | 742 | 21 199 | 3.8 |
| Ingham | 9 824 | 0.5 | 14.5 | 11.1 | 7.5 | 4.9 | 6.6 | 13.9 | 33.8 | 45 225 | 161 | 7 175 | 121 281 | 5.4 |
| Ionia | 963 | 9.9 | D | 21.6 | D | 6.8 | 4.1 | D | 24.7 | 11 240 | 176 | 1 291 | 24 778 | 12.6 |
| Iosco | 312 | 2.0 | D | 10.1 | 3.9 | 11.3 | 4.8 | D | 25.5 | 9 485 | 371 | 772 | 20 443 | 0.1 |
| Iron | 172 | 0.6 | D | 9.8 | 4.7 | 8.2 | 4.3 | 17.4 | 28.2 | 4 030 | 342 | 307 | 9 197 | 4.8 |
| Isabella | 1 416 | 2.6 | 18.0 | 7.2 | 3.3 | 6.7 | 5.8 | 9.0 | 37.8 | 10 455 | 148 | 1 309 | 28 381 | 15.7 |
| Jackson | 3 177 | 1.0 | 21.8 | 18.2 | 4.4 | 6.9 | 3.2 | 14.7 | 17.8 | 34 465 | 216 | 4 288 | 69 458 | 10.4 |
| Kalamazoo | 6 676 | 0.9 | 26.9 | 21.9 | 6.0 | 6.1 | 7.2 | 16.6 | 14.2 | 45 865 | 182 | 6 063 | 110 007 | 10.8 |
| Kalkaska | 240 | 2.8 | 36.3 | 8.5 | 2.6 | 4.8 | 2.3 | 3.8 | 17.7 | 4 610 | 269 | 432 | 12 171 | 12.4 |
| Kent | 19 952 | 0.4 | 24.3 | 19.5 | 9.0 | 6.6 | 8.8 | 14.7 | 8.7 | 100 655 | 165 | 14 678 | 246 901 | 10.2 |

1. Includes mining, construction, and manufacturing.  2. Per 1,000 resident population enumerated in the 2010 census.

# Table B. States and Counties — Housing, Labor Force, and Employment

| STATE County | Housing units, 2007–2011 | | | | | | | | Civilian labor force, 2012 | | | | Civilian employment,[6] 2007–2011 | | |
|---|---|---|---|---|---|---|---|---|---|---|---|---|---|---|---|
| | Total | Occupied units | | | | | | | | | Unemployment | | | Percent | |
| | | Owner-occupied | | | | Renter-occupied | | | | | | | | | |
| | | | | Median owner cost as a percent of income | | | | | | | | | | | Con-struction, produc-tion, and mainte-nance occu-pations |
| | | Percent | Median value[1] | With a mort-gage | Without a mort-gage[2] | Median rent[3] | Median rent as a per-cent of income | Sub-stand-ard units[4] (percent) | Total | Percent change, 2011–2012 | Total | Rate[5] | Total | Manage-ment, business, science and arts | |
| | 89 | 90 | 91 | 92 | 93 | 94 | 95 | 96 | 97 | 98 | 99 | 100 | 101 | 102 | 103 |
| **MARYLAND—Cont'd** | | | | | | | | | | | | | | | |
| St. Mary's | 36 662 | 73.0 | 324 500 | 23.9 | 12.2 | 1 222 | 26.4 | 2.4 | 56 394 | 0.7 | 3 347 | 5.9 | 50 436 | 42.9 | 19.4 |
| Somerset | 8 573 | 66.6 | 162 300 | 28.4 | 16.4 | 686 | 33.6 | 1.7 | 10 914 | 0.2 | 1 125 | 10.3 | 9 259 | 28.2 | 25.3 |
| Talbot | 15 539 | 74.6 | 352 200 | 26.6 | 12.4 | 925 | 30.7 | 1.0 | 18 886 | -0.5 | 1 428 | 7.6 | 18 108 | 36.5 | 17.9 |
| Washington | 55 485 | 66.8 | 230 500 | 25.1 | 12.6 | 802 | 29.4 | 1.4 | 71 196 | 1.2 | 6 029 | 8.5 | 70 473 | 30.5 | 24.0 |
| Wicomico | 36 406 | 64.7 | 195 400 | 24.8 | 13.6 | 969 | 33.2 | 3.1 | 53 135 | -0.2 | 4 572 | 8.6 | 46 983 | 33.2 | 22.9 |
| Worcester | 21 785 | 78.2 | 279 600 | 27.6 | 13.7 | 856 | 29.3 | 1.4 | 28 318 | -0.5 | 3 297 | 11.6 | 23 882 | 32.4 | 20.8 |
| Baltimore city | 238 959 | 49.5 | 163 700 | 26.3 | 15.9 | 889 | 33.7 | 2.8 | 279 416 | 1.3 | 28 598 | 10.2 | 272 333 | 36.8 | 17.2 |
| **MASSACHUSETTS** | 2 522 409 | 63.6 | 343 500 | 26.4 | 15.5 | 1 037 | 30.2 | 2.0 | 3 475 446 | 0.2 | 233 684 | 6.7 | 3 280 503 | 43.1 | 16.2 |
| Barnstable | 96 775 | 79.8 | 384 200 | 29.8 | 16.2 | 1 099 | 34.4 | 1.5 | 121 351 | 0.8 | 8 953 | 7.4 | 102 352 | 37.2 | 18.5 |
| Berkshire | 55 793 | 69.0 | 208 100 | 25.4 | 14.8 | 750 | 30.0 | 1.2 | 71 631 | -1.2 | 4 817 | 6.7 | 62 741 | 35.9 | 18.9 |
| Bristol | 210 536 | 64.0 | 296 400 | 27.1 | 15.8 | 797 | 29.7 | 1.7 | 290 492 | -0.3 | 27 116 | 9.3 | 268 424 | 33.4 | 22.1 |
| Dukes | 5 568 | 81.7 | 679 000 | 36.5 | 18.7 | 1 208 | 40.2 | 2.9 | 11 665 | 0.6 | 805 | 6.9 | 8 479 | 34.3 | 23.7 |
| Essex | 284 940 | 64.9 | 362 300 | 27.3 | 16.0 | 1 001 | 31.6 | 2.1 | 384 950 | 0.4 | 27 467 | 7.1 | 365 415 | 41.1 | 17.0 |
| Franklin | 30 362 | 69.4 | 223 200 | 25.6 | 15.0 | 839 | 30.1 | 1.2 | 38 466 | -0.1 | 2 411 | 6.3 | 37 405 | 39.0 | 23.1 |
| Hampden | 177 954 | 63.0 | 202 500 | 25.1 | 16.3 | 762 | 32.4 | 2.9 | 219 698 | -0.7 | 18 729 | 8.5 | 204 788 | 33.0 | 21.5 |
| Hampshire | 58 921 | 67.2 | 263 600 | 24.4 | 13.6 | 879 | 31.8 | 1.4 | 86 904 | -0.1 | 4 874 | 5.6 | 82 250 | 44.0 | 16.2 |
| Middlesex | 577 349 | 63.4 | 410 100 | 25.8 | 15.2 | 1 243 | 28.5 | 1.9 | 839 137 | 0.5 | 44 620 | 5.3 | 791 260 | 51.8 | 12.6 |
| Nantucket | 3 745 | 70.1 | 993 900 | 37.6 | 14.0 | 1 882 | 29.4 | 1.1 | 8 182 | 4.5 | 487 | 6.0 | 6 035 | 28.1 | 30.4 |
| Norfolk | 255 944 | 70.4 | 398 100 | 25.8 | 15.7 | 1 228 | 29.2 | 1.7 | 366 811 | 0.4 | 20 543 | 5.6 | 342 659 | 50.2 | 12.1 |
| Plymouth | 178 996 | 77.5 | 350 700 | 27.7 | 16.3 | 1 088 | 31.2 | 1.5 | 264 300 | 0.1 | 18 274 | 6.9 | 243 993 | 37.6 | 18.7 |
| Suffolk | 286 437 | 36.1 | 371 300 | 28.2 | 15.9 | 1 221 | 31.5 | 3.5 | 369 620 | 0.5 | 24 392 | 6.6 | 369 431 | 43.0 | 12.5 |
| Worcester | 299 089 | 67.2 | 274 900 | 25.0 | 14.8 | 883 | 29.3 | 1.8 | 402 240 | -0.5 | 30 197 | 7.5 | 395 271 | 40.3 | 19.2 |
| **MICHIGAN** | 3 825 182 | 73.5 | 137 300 | 24.5 | 13.8 | 742 | 32.7 | 2.0 | 4 657 459 | -0.4 | 425 953 | 9.1 | 4 306 814 | 34.0 | 22.9 |
| Alcona | 4 643 | 90.2 | 114 700 | 26.9 | 13.5 | 582 | 38.4 | 1.8 | 3 800 | -0.9 | 477 | 12.6 | 3 479 | 23.6 | 29.7 |
| Alger | 3 606 | 82.4 | 114 700 | 25.2 | 13.1 | 564 | 29.1 | 1.5 | 3 848 | -1.7 | 410 | 10.7 | 3 252 | 26.1 | 28.8 |
| Allegan | 41 914 | 82.8 | 147 600 | 24.7 | 13.2 | 686 | 27.8 | 2.5 | 53 201 | 0.0 | 3 885 | 7.3 | 51 245 | 27.7 | 34.0 |
| Alpena | 13 234 | 79.5 | 102 800 | 23.5 | 13.8 | 505 | 32.1 | 1.0 | 13 384 | -1.3 | 1 239 | 9.3 | 12 456 | 32.0 | 26.0 |
| Antrim | 9 720 | 84.8 | 156 600 | 27.6 | 14.3 | 702 | 36.6 | 1.7 | 10 330 | -0.8 | 1 067 | 10.3 | 9 417 | 28.3 | 28.1 |
| Arenac | 6 526 | 82.7 | 94 900 | 24.8 | 13.5 | 528 | 33.0 | 1.9 | 6 862 | -3.2 | 826 | 12.0 | 5 679 | 27.8 | 29.6 |
| Baraga | 3 308 | 76.1 | 84 700 | 22.8 | 13.0 | 483 | 25.7 | 3.2 | 3 719 | -4.0 | 609 | 16.4 | 3 082 | 29.1 | 24.6 |
| Barry | 22 831 | 84.7 | 142 800 | 24.7 | 12.7 | 659 | 27.5 | 1.3 | 28 898 | 1.7 | 1 818 | 6.3 | 26 995 | 26.3 | 34.5 |
| Bay | 44 005 | 79.5 | 104 600 | 22.8 | 13.4 | 579 | 30.2 | 0.8 | 51 768 | -0.6 | 4 405 | 8.5 | 47 956 | 30.1 | 23.9 |
| Benzie | 7 366 | 85.2 | 156 700 | 26.6 | 12.5 | 732 | 29.9 | 3.1 | 8 291 | -0.8 | 832 | 10.0 | 7 798 | 31.7 | 24.6 |
| Berrien | 61 678 | 73.3 | 135 400 | 23.0 | 12.8 | 619 | 32.9 | 2.0 | 72 468 | -1.4 | 6 528 | 9.0 | 69 139 | 31.7 | 24.2 |
| Branch | 16 078 | 79.2 | 109 800 | 24.3 | 13.3 | 647 | 30.3 | 4.1 | 19 128 | -3.3 | 1 619 | 8.5 | 18 018 | 25.2 | 34.2 |
| Calhoun | 53 481 | 71.1 | 107 000 | 23.8 | 13.8 | 647 | 32.1 | 1.2 | 63 634 | -1.5 | 4 711 | 7.4 | 57 372 | 28.1 | 28.5 |
| Cass | 19 913 | 83.3 | 131 800 | 24.3 | 13.0 | 680 | 29.6 | 2.0 | 25 042 | -1.5 | 1 897 | 7.6 | 23 125 | 27.8 | 34.9 |
| Charlevoix | 11 025 | 83.1 | 158 700 | 26.2 | 12.8 | 622 | 29.7 | 1.2 | 12 797 | -0.2 | 1 379 | 10.8 | 12 090 | 29.8 | 29.1 |
| Cheboygan | 11 536 | 82.0 | 119 100 | 26.5 | 12.9 | 581 | 33.1 | 2.7 | 10 452 | -3.8 | 1 098 | 10.5 | 9 982 | 26.2 | 26.4 |
| Chippewa | 14 699 | 72.5 | 103 700 | 21.7 | 12.9 | 562 | 32.2 | 2.3 | 16 282 | -1.6 | 1 717 | 10.5 | 15 087 | 27.8 | 18.7 |
| Clare | 13 170 | 79.9 | 87 000 | 25.7 | 13.8 | 590 | 34.5 | 3.2 | 12 064 | -1.9 | 1 399 | 11.6 | 10 442 | 25.3 | 29.8 |
| Clinton | 28 565 | 81.4 | 162 400 | 23.2 | 12.5 | 771 | 31.6 | 0.9 | 37 114 | -1.2 | 2 244 | 6.0 | 35 495 | 36.9 | 20.5 |
| Crawford | 5 663 | 83.0 | 102 700 | 25.3 | 11.4 | 628 | 36.4 | 2.9 | 5 866 | -0.9 | 590 | 10.1 | 5 094 | 27.9 | 26.6 |
| Delta | 16 038 | 80.0 | 102 900 | 23.3 | 13.0 | 523 | 33.5 | 2.4 | 18 363 | -1.4 | 1 668 | 9.1 | 16 081 | 27.2 | 28.5 |
| Dickinson | 11 444 | 79.9 | 88 600 | 22.2 | 13.5 | 541 | 31.1 | 0.6 | 13 307 | -1.6 | 1 026 | 7.7 | 11 888 | 28.2 | 25.5 |
| Eaton | 43 416 | 74.2 | 147 900 | 24.0 | 12.2 | 727 | 28.7 | 1.2 | 54 110 | -1.3 | 3 478 | 6.4 | 51 845 | 33.7 | 23.4 |
| Emmet | 13 599 | 75.6 | 181 700 | 25.7 | 13.1 | 739 | 30.0 | 1.4 | 18 480 | -1.6 | 2 130 | 11.5 | 15 854 | 33.0 | 19.0 |
| Genesee | 166 479 | 71.0 | 109 000 | 24.8 | 14.1 | 685 | 34.6 | 1.9 | 184 149 | -1.1 | 17 414 | 9.5 | 164 803 | 30.2 | 24.0 |
| Gladwin | 11 326 | 85.2 | 112 100 | 27.2 | 13.9 | 563 | 34.8 | 2.2 | 9 537 | -1.9 | 1 193 | 12.5 | 8 874 | 23.6 | 32.1 |
| Gogebic | 7 268 | 76.7 | 67 900 | 21.6 | 13.6 | 553 | 32.0 | 0.6 | 6 946 | -2.5 | 711 | 10.2 | 6 363 | 26.1 | 29.8 |
| Grand Traverse | 34 450 | 76.4 | 172 800 | 25.2 | 14.1 | 830 | 30.1 | 1.6 | 46 582 | -0.2 | 3 716 | 8.0 | 42 305 | 34.5 | 19.2 |
| Gratiot | 14 717 | 78.0 | 90 300 | 22.4 | 13.9 | 592 | 31.8 | 2.7 | 18 502 | -1.6 | 1 723 | 9.3 | 17 135 | 25.2 | 27.8 |
| Hillsdale | 17 617 | 81.1 | 113 000 | 24.6 | 13.6 | 629 | 31.6 | 3.1 | 19 203 | -0.1 | 1 815 | 9.5 | 19 158 | 24.8 | 37.3 |
| Houghton | 14 016 | 69.6 | 86 200 | 22.1 | 13.3 | 577 | 36.4 | 2.5 | 16 403 | -2.8 | 1 447 | 8.8 | 15 812 | 35.6 | 17.7 |
| Huron | 14 237 | 82.6 | 102 200 | 24.6 | 13.6 | 544 | 31.4 | 1.1 | 15 783 | 1.1 | 1 282 | 8.1 | 14 352 | 27.4 | 33.8 |
| Ingham | 108 155 | 60.7 | 133 000 | 24.0 | 13.1 | 737 | 34.7 | 1.6 | 141 735 | -1.5 | 11 004 | 7.8 | 133 084 | 39.5 | 16.4 |
| Ionia | 22 420 | 79.0 | 118 600 | 24.8 | 13.1 | 640 | 34.8 | 1.8 | 29 128 | 1.0 | 2 420 | 8.3 | 26 488 | 25.9 | 30.7 |
| Iosco | 10 934 | 84.7 | 98 300 | 26.1 | 12.5 | 552 | 35.4 | 1.2 | 9 892 | -1.5 | 1 116 | 11.3 | 8 741 | 23.9 | 27.0 |
| Iron | 5 248 | 84.7 | 75 400 | 24.7 | 15.8 | 485 | 29.9 | 0.8 | 5 362 | -1.3 | 476 | 8.9 | 4 707 | 25.1 | 27.7 |
| Isabella | 24 746 | 59.2 | 124 100 | 24.2 | 11.8 | 672 | 41.3 | 2.2 | 36 771 | -0.2 | 2 462 | 6.7 | 32 124 | 27.8 | 16.6 |
| Jackson | 60 257 | 75.0 | 123 200 | 23.9 | 13.3 | 708 | 31.6 | 2.0 | 70 432 | -1.4 | 6 012 | 8.5 | 67 007 | 29.0 | 26.7 |
| Kalamazoo | 99 603 | 65.3 | 144 200 | 22.9 | 13.2 | 698 | 34.8 | 1.2 | 124 854 | -1.3 | 8 739 | 7.0 | 116 983 | 37.0 | 19.7 |
| Kalkaska | 7 186 | 82.3 | 105 300 | 26.0 | 14.1 | 684 | 29.5 | 3.2 | 8 003 | -0.4 | 769 | 9.6 | 7 024 | 19.9 | 31.9 |
| Kent | 227 698 | 71.0 | 145 300 | 23.5 | 13.1 | 720 | 31.0 | 2.3 | 311 023 | 1.3 | 20 361 | 6.5 | 287 549 | 34.5 | 23.6 |

1. Specified owner-occupied units, lacking complete plumbing facilities.　2. A value of 9.9 represents 9.9 percent or less.　3. Specified renter-occupied units. A value of 10.0 represents 10 percent or less.　4. Overcrowded or lacking complete plumbing facilities.　5. Percent of civilian labor force.　6. Persons 16 years old and over.

# Table B. States and Counties — Nonfarm Employment and Agriculture

| STATE County | Private nonfarm establishments, employment and payroll, 2011 | | | | | | | | | Agriculture, 2007 | | | |
|---|---|---|---|---|---|---|---|---|---|---|---|---|---|
| | Number of establishments | Employment | | | | | | Annual payroll | | Farms | | | |
| | | Total | Health care and social assistance | Manufacturing | Retail trade | Finance and insurance | Professional, scientific, and technical services | Total (mil dol) | Average per employee (dollars) | Number | Percent with: | | Farm operators whose principal occupation is farming (percent) |
| | | | | | | | | | | | Fewer than 50 acres | 500 acres or more | |
| | 104 | 105 | 106 | 107 | 108 | 109 | 110 | 111 | 112 | 113 | 114 | 115 | 116 |
| MARYLAND—Cont'd | | | | | | | | | | | | | |
| St. Mary's | 1 908 | 28 636 | 3 851 | 225 | 4 434 | 476 | 8 532 | 1 379 | 48 151 | 621 | 49.1 | 3.7 | 45.2 |
| Somerset | 362 | 3 719 | 1 270 | D | 382 | 121 | D | 150 | 40 353 | 329 | 39.8 | 9.7 | 47.1 |
| Talbot | 1 458 | 17 162 | 3 678 | 1 384 | 2 619 | 596 | 1 363 | 605 | 35 230 | 305 | 34.4 | 20.7 | 47.2 |
| Washington | 3 425 | 55 501 | 9 878 | 5 767 | 9 346 | 5 065 | 1 708 | 1 959 | 35 300 | 844 | 46.8 | 4.4 | 51.9 |
| Wicomico | 2 496 | 36 728 | 8 336 | 3 080 | 6 668 | 1 094 | 1 466 | 1 285 | 34 993 | 508 | 50.4 | 9.1 | 53.3 |
| Worcester | 2 100 | 16 881 | 1 930 | 510 | 3 397 | 495 | 559 | 528 | 31 295 | 384 | 42.2 | 12.8 | 56.8 |
| Baltimore city | 12 089 | 271 612 | 70 318 | 12 343 | 15 876 | 15 269 | 18 371 | 14 607 | 53 779 | NA | NA | NA | NA |
| MASSACHUSETTS | 169 146 | 2 960 712 | 573 438 | 225 473 | 350 448 | 196 755 | 249 815 | 165 193 | 55 795 | 7 691 | 66.1 | 1.5 | 48.0 |
| Barnstable | 8 116 | 68 452 | 15 427 | 2 001 | 14 293 | 2 258 | 4 613 | 2 766 | 40 410 | 406 | 93.3 | 0.0 | 53.4 |
| Berkshire | 3 985 | 53 110 | 11 512 | 5 138 | 8 611 | 2 200 | D | 2 085 | 39 265 | 522 | 49.8 | 4.8 | 48.7 |
| Bristol | 12 637 | 192 687 | 39 644 | 27 373 | 34 594 | 5 404 | 5 842 | 7 727 | 40 103 | 777 | 71.3 | 0.9 | 47.4 |
| Dukes | 1 019 | 4 935 | 738 | 99 | 1 064 | D | 216 | 247 | 50 068 | 81 | 82.7 | 1.2 | 45.7 |
| Essex | 17 874 | 267 837 | 57 632 | 37 220 | 37 239 | 11 729 | 13 490 | 12 804 | 47 804 | 531 | 75.7 | 1.9 | 45.2 |
| Franklin | 1 571 | 19 931 | 3 703 | 3 665 | 2 966 | 522 | 513 | 707 | 35 455 | 741 | 51.0 | 3.4 | 47.2 |
| Hampden | 9 652 | 163 486 | 37 520 | 20 583 | 22 481 | 9 694 | 7 123 | 6 569 | 40 180 | 508 | 59.3 | 1.2 | 44.5 |
| Hampshire | 3 459 | 55 451 | 17 625 | 3 326 | 7 421 | 1 414 | 1 664 | 1 708 | 30 802 | 711 | 57.9 | 1.4 | 50.4 |
| Middlesex | 41 961 | 802 736 | 111 697 | 56 691 | 81 339 | 28 218 | 117 307 | 53 711 | 66 910 | 700 | 75.0 | 0.6 | 48.7 |
| Nantucket | 883 | 3 560 | D | D | 742 | 111 | 167 | 229 | 64 462 | 14 | 85.7 | 0.0 | 85.7 |
| Norfolk | 18 987 | 312 576 | 60 939 | 18 223 | 43 511 | 24 766 | 21 131 | 15 537 | 49 708 | 264 | 81.1 | 1.5 | 47.7 |
| Plymouth | 11 740 | 147 825 | 28 903 | 10 563 | 27 196 | 6 817 | 6 649 | 6 213 | 42 029 | 882 | 74.3 | 1.5 | 52.6 |
| Suffolk | 19 436 | 550 649 | 128 160 | 9 114 | 31 061 | 86 714 | 51 987 | 40 712 | 73 934 | 7 | 85.7 | 0.0 | 71.4 |
| Worcester | 17 421 | 270 224 | 58 058 | 31 454 | 37 697 | 15 657 | 15 263 | 12 170 | 45 036 | 1 547 | 59.4 | 0.8 | 44.6 |
| MICHIGAN | 217 344 | 3 379 035 | 571 137 | 477 030 | 443 374 | 146 416 | 240 161 | 145 831 | 43 158 | 56 014 | 44.5 | 8.2 | 44.3 |
| Alcona | 185 | 1 073 | 231 | 170 | 269 | 35 | 27 | 30 | 27 938 | 281 | 32.4 | 7.8 | 52.0 |
| Alger | 244 | 1 716 | 275 | D | 272 | 88 | D | 58 | 33 714 | 86 | 38.4 | 10.5 | 39.5 |
| Allegan | 2 230 | 32 394 | 3 088 | 12 111 | 3 519 | 424 | 1 125 | 1 359 | 41 947 | 1 595 | 51.8 | 7.0 | 43.6 |
| Alpena | 796 | 9 600 | 2 781 | 1 192 | 1 774 | 354 | D | 298 | 31 056 | 573 | 36.8 | 6.5 | 37.9 |
| Antrim | 553 | 3 529 | 430 | 623 | 508 | 95 | 155 | 102 | 28 867 | 411 | 37.7 | 5.8 | 47.2 |
| Arenac | 339 | 2 961 | 625 | 529 | 443 | 76 | D | 85 | 28 709 | 488 | 39.5 | 10.2 | 38.5 |
| Baraga | 201 | 1 741 | 343 | 461 | 268 | D | D | 46 | 26 406 | 76 | 28.9 | 14.5 | 36.8 |
| Barry | 887 | 9 268 | 1 360 | 2 437 | 1 356 | 687 | 195 | 319 | 34 411 | 1 164 | 45.4 | 6.0 | 39.5 |
| Bay | 2 254 | 30 165 | 6 553 | 3 008 | 5 490 | 1 111 | 1 205 | 1 113 | 36 901 | 851 | 40.2 | 12.1 | 48.3 |
| Benzie | 425 | 2 304 | 347 | 435 | 446 | D | D | 71 | 30 956 | 205 | 46.8 | 2.9 | 48.3 |
| Berrien | 3 623 | 51 085 | 8 849 | 7 659 | 6 838 | 1 273 | 2 186 | 1 881 | 36 820 | 1 300 | 57.8 | 5.5 | 49.1 |
| Branch | 799 | 10 632 | 1 588 | 2 381 | 1 585 | 445 | 159 | 352 | 33 116 | 1 129 | 39.1 | 9.9 | 37.2 |
| Calhoun | 2 670 | 47 544 | 9 501 | 10 705 | 5 928 | 968 | 1 193 | 2 015 | 42 379 | 1 178 | 37.6 | 9.3 | 45.3 |
| Cass | 734 | 7 023 | 947 | 1 989 | 834 | 222 | D | 220 | 31 312 | 811 | 43.9 | 9.9 | 42.3 |
| Charlevoix | 812 | 7 203 | 1 126 | 2 088 | 863 | 207 | 238 | 270 | 37 484 | 336 | 42.0 | 4.2 | 35.1 |
| Cheboygan | 757 | 4 495 | 1 009 | 255 | 1 159 | D | 137 | 143 | 31 920 | 347 | 41.2 | 5.8 | 38.6 |
| Chippewa | 805 | 8 353 | 1 883 | 469 | 1 784 | D | 222 | 232 | 27 822 | 401 | 22.2 | 14.2 | 42.1 |
| Clare | 527 | 5 473 | 1 128 | 924 | 1 015 | D | 142 | 165 | 30 085 | 450 | 34.9 | 6.2 | 42.7 |
| Clinton | 1 231 | 15 493 | 4 345 | 1 867 | 1 990 | 665 | 503 | 496 | 32 029 | 1 231 | 42.7 | 9.9 | 43.6 |
| Crawford | 302 | 3 115 | 909 | 455 | 534 | 73 | D | 106 | 34 094 | 39 | 66.7 | 2.6 | 46.2 |
| Delta | 1 100 | 11 593 | 1 755 | D | 2 137 | 422 | 583 | 399 | 34 396 | 290 | 19.3 | 16.6 | 47.6 |
| Dickinson | 893 | 12 405 | 2 492 | 1 934 | 1 956 | 348 | 327 | 542 | 43 731 | 161 | 32.3 | 5.6 | 32.9 |
| Eaton | 2 034 | 38 204 | 3 238 | 8 520 | 5 723 | 3 548 | 1 113 | 1 483 | 38 823 | 1 231 | 43.9 | 9.1 | 42.4 |
| Emmet | 1 460 | 13 313 | 3 166 | 940 | 2 628 | 348 | 438 | 486 | 36 471 | 291 | 37.5 | 5.5 | 41.9 |
| Genesee | 7 810 | 111 270 | 25 591 | 9 658 | 19 288 | 5 219 | 3 383 | 4 137 | 37 179 | 988 | 61.3 | 5.3 | 47.5 |
| Gladwin | 407 | 3 539 | 694 | 847 | 599 | D | 66 | 108 | 30 520 | 557 | 35.5 | 3.8 | 37.2 |
| Gogebic | 412 | 4 260 | 631 | 678 | 775 | 109 | 105 | 103 | 24 184 | 42 | 19.0 | 2.4 | 31.0 |
| Grand Traverse | 3 278 | 39 944 | 8 408 | 3 927 | 7 019 | 2 034 | 2 458 | 1 497 | 37 473 | 522 | 53.1 | 5.0 | 38.5 |
| Gratiot | 737 | 10 674 | 2 545 | 2 296 | 1 293 | 403 | 92 | 356 | 33 306 | 1 036 | 38.6 | 13.2 | 46.5 |
| Hillsdale | 797 | 11 141 | 1 408 | 3 487 | 1 353 | 274 | 189 | 344 | 30 874 | 1 674 | 43.2 | 6.8 | 33.6 |
| Houghton | 900 | 8 721 | 1 981 | 663 | 1 742 | 337 | 405 | 230 | 26 352 | 155 | 35.5 | 6.5 | 40.6 |
| Huron | 952 | 10 037 | 1 778 | 2 890 | 1 525 | 388 | 269 | 336 | 33 439 | 1 394 | 35.9 | 17.5 | 54.1 |
| Ingham | 6 201 | 100 273 | 20 336 | 8 805 | 14 096 | 7 564 | 5 795 | 4 036 | 40 254 | 947 | 58.8 | 7.6 | 45.7 |
| Ionia | 873 | 10 028 | 1 292 | 2 765 | 1 979 | 634 | 178 | 281 | 28 057 | 1 183 | 41.7 | 9.6 | 46.1 |
| Iosco | 619 | 5 746 | 1 093 | 827 | 1 244 | 236 | 126 | 173 | 30 086 | 316 | 43.0 | 8.2 | 40.2 |
| Iron | 363 | 2 568 | 429 | 381 | 461 | D | D | 78 | 30 304 | 111 | 28.8 | 8.1 | 30.6 |
| Isabella | 1 412 | 19 928 | 3 731 | 2 146 | 3 475 | 716 | 843 | 575 | 28 831 | 1 018 | 36.0 | 8.9 | 42.6 |
| Jackson | 2 995 | 46 046 | 9 210 | 7 864 | 7 023 | 1 354 | 2 271 | 1 856 | 40 318 | 1 184 | 50.3 | 6.1 | 40.2 |
| Kalamazoo | 5 567 | 103 970 | 18 566 | 14 329 | 12 928 | 5 880 | 6 282 | 4 402 | 42 339 | 854 | 55.4 | 8.2 | 46.6 |
| Kalkaska | 315 | 3 083 | 516 | 307 | 488 | 68 | D | 127 | 41 103 | 221 | 48.4 | 2.3 | 37.6 |
| Kent | 15 408 | 302 912 | 46 508 | 51 382 | 31 992 | 12 021 | 13 077 | 12 383 | 40 880 | 1 193 | 51.5 | 5.6 | 43.4 |

| STATE County | Acreage (1,000) | Percent change, 2002–2007 | Average size of farm | Total irrigated (1,000) | Total cropland (1,000) | Average per farm | Average per acre | Value of machinery and equipment, average per farm (dollars) | Total (mil dol) | Average per farm (dollars) | Crops | Live-stock and poultry products | $10,000 or more | $100,000 or more | Total ($1,000) | Percent of farms |
|---|---|---|---|---|---|---|---|---|---|---|---|---|---|---|---|---|
| | 117 | 118 | 119 | 120 | 121 | 122 | 123 | 124 | 125 | 126 | 127 | 128 | 129 | 130 | 131 | 132 |
| **MARYLAND—Cont'd** | | | | | | | | | | | | | | | | |
| St. Mary's ........................... | 69 | 1.5 | 111 | 1.1 | 39.8 | 804 658 | 7 279 | 73 148 | 15.9 | 25 680 | 73.3 | 26.7 | 36.6 | 5.6 | 612 | 29.3 |
| Somerset ............................. | 60 | 5.3 | 183 | 0.4 | 35.4 | 1 161 268 | 6 341 | 113 801 | 192.6 | 585 297 | 7.8 | 92.2 | 55.9 | 41.9 | 1 173 | 64.1 |
| Talbot ................................. | 109 | 2.8 | 357 | 3.5 | 87.1 | 2 204 538 | 6 169 | 160 468 | 50.5 | 165 708 | 50.2 | 49.8 | 48.2 | 27.2 | 3 058 | 73.4 |
| Washington .......................... | 114 | -8.8 | 135 | 0.9 | 81.6 | 1 025 346 | 7 587 | 96 240 | 83.7 | 99 160 | 24.4 | 75.6 | 46.4 | 23.6 | 986 | 26.8 |
| Wicomico ............................. | 93 | 5.7 | 183 | 7.0 | 51.7 | 1 058 847 | 5 793 | 89 704 | 197.8 | 389 426 | 20.4 | 79.6 | 54.5 | 36.4 | 1 858 | 51.8 |
| Worcester ............................ | 111 | -15.3 | 289 | 5.2 | 75.4 | 1 272 107 | 4 407 | 144 978 | 185.8 | 483 780 | 13.7 | 86.3 | 60.4 | 45.1 | 1 766 | 54.2 |
| Baltimore city ....................... | NA | NA | NA | NA | NA | NA | NA | NA | NA | NA | NA | NA | NA | NA | NA | NA |
| **MASSACHUSETTS ..........** | 518 | -0.2 | 67 | 23.1 | 187.4 | 829 090 | 12 313 | 56 373 | 489.8 | 63 687 | 74.4 | 25.6 | 35.8 | 10.4 | 4 603 | 7.7 |
| Barnstable ........................... | 5 | -16.7 | 13 | 1.3 | 2.0 | 457 980 | 35 532 | 44 526 | 17.7 | 43 475 | 57.5 | 42.5 | 46.6 | 10.3 | 282 | 9.6 |
| Berkshire ............................. | 66 | -4.3 | 127 | 0.2 | 22.6 | 1 113 751 | 8 762 | 54 632 | 20.6 | 39 465 | 37.5 | 62.5 | 28.4 | 8.2 | 205 | 6.1 |
| Bristol ................................. | 39 | 8.3 | 51 | 1.9 | 15.2 | 806 029 | 15 955 | 55 614 | 44.2 | 56 944 | 82.6 | 17.4 | 36.6 | 10.0 | 555 | 8.0 |
| Dukes .................................. | 8 | 0.0 | 98 | 0.1 | 1.1 | 1 474 733 | 15 090 | 57 758 | 3.3 | 41 193 | 67.8 | 32.2 | 40.7 | 6.2 | D | 1.2 |
| Essex .................................. | 28 | 0.0 | 52 | 0.9 | 12.2 | 971 091 | 18 526 | 59 475 | 25.0 | 47 122 | 75.9 | 24.1 | 33.9 | 10.0 | 276 | 4.0 |
| Franklin ............................... | 79 | 6.8 | 107 | 1.7 | 24.4 | 832 320 | 7 761 | 65 977 | 56.8 | 76 712 | 63.7 | 36.3 | 35.9 | 12.6 | 719 | 13.1 |
| Hampden .............................. | 37 | -2.6 | 73 | 1.2 | 13.0 | 770 017 | 10 618 | 51 866 | 25.7 | 50 659 | 83.2 | 16.8 | 30.9 | 8.7 | 242 | 7.1 |
| Hampshire ........................... | 53 | 3.9 | 74 | 1.0 | 23.8 | 666 331 | 8 980 | 61 033 | 38.6 | 54 314 | 73.8 | 26.2 | 37.1 | 10.7 | 486 | 11.4 |
| Middlesex ............................ | 34 | 3.0 | 48 | 1.5 | 15.4 | 907 619 | 18 745 | 56 824 | 81.7 | 116 726 | 84.2 | 15.8 | 34.3 | 11.7 | D | 2.0 |
| Nantucket ............................ | 1 | NA | 44 | 0.4 | 0.4 | 445 903 | 10 151 | 104 596 | 2.9 | 206 131 | D | D | 50.0 | 21.4 | 0 | 0.0 |
| Norfolk ................................ | 12 | -7.7 | 44 | 0.3 | 3.3 | 915 554 | 20 740 | 40 925 | 14.0 | 52 926 | 92.9 | 7.1 | 29.9 | 9.5 | D | 1.9 |
| Plymouth ............................. | 50 | -15.3 | 56 | 11.9 | 18.3 | 823 166 | 14 634 | 66 646 | 78.4 | 88 935 | 93.2 | 6.8 | 51.1 | 17.2 | 629 | 10.0 |
| Suffolk ................................ | 0 | NA | 14 | 0.0 | 0.0 | 376 684 | 26 634 | 19 045 | 0.2 | 30 214 | D | D | 57.1 | 14.3 | 0 | 0.0 |
| Worcester ............................ | 106 | 1.9 | 69 | 0.9 | 35.6 | 810 727 | 11 792 | 50 355 | 80.6 | 52 069 | 55.5 | 44.5 | 29.2 | 6.9 | 1 034 | 7.6 |
| **MICHIGAN ......................** | 10 032 | -1.1 | 179 | 500.4 | 7 803.6 | 610 556 | 3 409 | 90 742 | 5 753.2 | 102 710 | 57.9 | 42.1 | 38.1 | 14.2 | 118 871 | 41.5 |
| Alcona ................................. | 45 | 9.8 | 162 | 0.1 | 28.3 | 392 702 | 2 431 | 51 035 | 8.7 | 30 890 | 28.3 | 71.7 | 26.7 | 6.0 | 185 | 24.6 |
| Alger ................................... | 18 | 20.0 | 213 | D | 10.4 | 458 926 | 2 150 | 56 784 | 2.8 | 32 231 | 12.2 | 87.8 | 24.4 | 9.3 | 64 | 32.6 |
| Allegan ................................ | 275 | 13.2 | 172 | 21.3 | 226.5 | 721 334 | 4 182 | 110 690 | 397.5 | 249 237 | 37.8 | 62.2 | 42.0 | 18.8 | 3 444 | 29.3 |
| Alpena ................................. | 86 | 16.2 | 150 | 0.0 | 59.6 | 387 180 | 2 581 | 66 222 | 21.5 | 37 449 | 30.0 | 70.0 | 29.0 | 8.2 | 332 | 31.8 |
| Antrim ................................. | 67 | 6.3 | 164 | 1.6 | 37.8 | 632 314 | 3 859 | 71 052 | 23.3 | 56 766 | 73.9 | 26.1 | 34.8 | 11.9 | 233 | 28.0 |
| Arenac ................................. | 95 | 13.1 | 194 | 0.0 | 74.4 | 464 302 | 2 395 | 86 220 | 29.7 | 60 923 | 59.5 | 40.5 | 28.1 | 12.9 | 1 657 | 71.3 |
| Baraga ................................ | 19 | 26.7 | 245 | 0.0 | 9.2 | 502 152 | 2 047 | 57 405 | 1.3 | 17 646 | 56.7 | 43.3 | 28.9 | 3.9 | 13 | 21.1 |
| Barry .................................. | 168 | -7.7 | 144 | 3.1 | 120.0 | 504 427 | 3 491 | 70 091 | 94.4 | 81 088 | 26.9 | 73.1 | 25.8 | 8.2 | 2 204 | 43.9 |
| Bay ..................................... | 186 | 0.0 | 219 | 4.1 | 166.7 | 616 830 | 2 818 | 117 055 | 77.2 | 90 744 | 89.2 | 10.8 | 49.9 | 20.7 | 2 424 | 67.0 |
| Benzie ................................. | 21 | -8.7 | 103 | 0.3 | 9.2 | 470 889 | 4 582 | 68 934 | 8.0 | 38 933 | 68.0 | 32.0 | 30.2 | 10.7 | 74 | 14.1 |
| Berrien ................................ | 169 | -2.9 | 130 | 18.4 | 138.6 | 600 093 | 4 616 | 102 068 | 136.3 | 104 815 | 90.5 | 9.5 | 47.3 | 17.0 | 2 241 | 27.4 |
| Branch ................................ | 250 | -1.6 | 222 | 42.9 | 202.4 | 664 231 | 2 998 | 91 404 | 115.4 | 102 241 | 60.1 | 39.9 | 37.0 | 15.4 | 3 804 | 63.6 |
| Calhoun ............................... | 228 | -5.0 | 194 | 9.3 | 175.1 | 583 048 | 3 012 | 81 935 | 89.8 | 76 245 | 60.6 | 39.4 | 37.4 | 13.1 | 3 170 | 49.6 |
| Cass .................................... | 190 | 0.5 | 235 | 39.0 | 151.9 | 822 259 | 3 504 | 104 890 | 101.5 | 125 214 | 54.8 | 45.2 | 39.0 | 16.8 | 2 807 | 52.7 |
| Charlevoix ............................ | 41 | 5.1 | 123 | 0.2 | 23.9 | 466 944 | 3 788 | 46 592 | 7.6 | 22 762 | 57.7 | 42.3 | 25.0 | 3.6 | 141 | 21.7 |
| Cheboygan ........................... | 48 | -4.0 | 137 | 0.2 | 25.0 | 370 846 | 2 706 | 63 163 | 10.3 | 29 564 | 44.6 | 55.4 | 19.9 | 5.2 | 89 | 21.6 |
| Chippewa ............................. | 99 | 5.3 | 247 | 0.1 | 66.1 | 474 994 | 1 925 | 63 441 | 9.4 | 23 382 | 36.6 | 63.4 | 36.2 | 6.0 | 451 | 28.9 |
| Clare ................................... | 68 | 6.3 | 152 | 0.6 | 37.4 | 435 856 | 2 869 | 60 594 | 18.3 | 40 734 | 14.9 | 85.1 | 31.8 | 8.9 | 383 | 36.7 |
| Clinton ................................ | 272 | 6.3 | 221 | 4.3 | 233.3 | 797 743 | 3 616 | 107 148 | 165.5 | 134 466 | 39.5 | 60.5 | 46.9 | 17.3 | 3 794 | 60.2 |
| Crawford .............................. | 3 | -50.0 | 65 | 0.0 | 0.8 | 262 422 | 4 055 | 49 041 | 0.3 | 8 209 | D | D | 15.4 | 0.0 | D | 5.1 |
| Delta ................................... | 78 | 5.4 | 268 | 0.5 | 40.4 | 612 835 | 2 285 | 72 055 | 11.6 | 40 065 | 37.9 | 62.1 | 40.3 | 12.1 | 299 | 28.3 |
| Dickinson ............................. | 25 | -13.8 | 155 | 0.6 | 12.4 | 381 732 | 2 469 | 59 174 | 4.6 | 28 353 | 43.3 | 56.7 | 21.7 | 4.7 | 159 | 28.6 |
| Eaton .................................. | 222 | -6.7 | 181 | 1.4 | 176.9 | 549 794 | 3 046 | 82 105 | 70.6 | 57 386 | 81.3 | 18.7 | 37.0 | 13.6 | 3 033 | 48.0 |
| Emmet ................................ | 40 | -9.1 | 136 | 0.2 | 21.7 | 487 008 | 3 580 | 61 225 | 7.5 | 25 600 | 38.3 | 61.7 | 28.5 | 5.5 | 91 | 16.8 |
| Genesee ............................... | 129 | -9.8 | 131 | 1.1 | 106.6 | 488 344 | 3 733 | 82 249 | 58.8 | 59 489 | 81.3 | 18.7 | 31.4 | 9.2 | 1 569 | 31.6 |
| Gladwin ............................... | 68 | -5.6 | 121 | 0.2 | 43.7 | 359 504 | 2 961 | 47 614 | 12.1 | 21 732 | 54.3 | 45.7 | 30.2 | 3.2 | 625 | 46.0 |
| Gogebic ............................... | 4 | 0.0 | 93 | D | 1.7 | 317 502 | 3 413 | 33 270 | 0.4 | 9 390 | 31.7 | 68.5 | 14.3 | 0.0 | D | 2.4 |
| Grand Traverse ..................... | 63 | 1.6 | 120 | 1.9 | 41.1 | 668 671 | 5 578 | 65 073 | 19.2 | 36 865 | 80.2 | 19.8 | 37.2 | 10.3 | 284 | 23.6 |
| Gratiot ................................ | 287 | -0.7 | 277 | 6.6 | 254.4 | 819 592 | 2 959 | 131 785 | 189.9 | 183 313 | 45.3 | 54.7 | 49.6 | 21.0 | 4 485 | 72.7 |
| Hillsdale .............................. | 270 | -1.8 | 161 | 4.2 | 212.1 | 485 755 | 3 013 | 66 764 | 120.6 | 72 064 | 54.6 | 45.4 | 28.7 | 9.6 | 6 019 | 65.5 |
| Houghton ............................. | 24 | -7.7 | 153 | 0.1 | 11.2 | 302 836 | 1 985 | 43 628 | 2.7 | 17 476 | 37.4 | 62.6 | 19.4 | 2.6 | 46 | 19.4 |
| Huron .................................. | 441 | 2.1 | 316 | 2.4 | 396.9 | 986 734 | 3 119 | 169 283 | 374.5 | 268 654 | 44.5 | 55.5 | 55.7 | 34.4 | 6 310 | 76.9 |
| Ingham ................................ | 186 | 0.5 | 197 | 2.3 | 155.7 | 751 299 | 3 821 | 104 278 | 84.6 | 89 357 | 61.3 | 38.7 | 35.5 | 12.7 | 2 153 | 29.5 |
| Ionia ................................... | 238 | 3.5 | 202 | 5.1 | 193.4 | 692 622 | 3 436 | 104 217 | 201.2 | 170 098 | 27.0 | 73.0 | 42.9 | 16.6 | 3 349 | 54.6 |
| Iosco .................................. | 48 | 6.7 | 151 | 0.0 | 33.1 | 407 122 | 2 695 | 61 327 | 15.0 | 47 452 | 31.0 | 69.0 | 23.7 | 8.5 | 459 | 32.9 |
| Iron .................................... | 28 | -9.7 | 250 | 0.4 | 10.4 | 681 089 | 2 726 | 52 147 | 1.9 | 17 560 | 73.7 | 26.3 | 25.2 | 2.7 | 44 | 18.9 |
| Isabella ............................... | 196 | 0.5 | 193 | 3.4 | 154.1 | 573 830 | 2 979 | 76 421 | 71.4 | 70 170 | 50.5 | 49.5 | 39.0 | 13.7 | 2 287 | 56.6 |
| Jackson ............................... | 182 | -5.7 | 154 | 3.8 | 135.1 | 534 327 | 3 469 | 73 640 | 56.9 | 48 039 | 55.8 | 44.2 | 31.0 | 8.6 | 2 030 | 32.3 |
| Kalamazoo ............................ | 145 | -2.0 | 170 | 31.3 | 116.0 | 709 610 | 4 183 | 116 842 | 179.3 | 209 900 | 72.0 | 28.0 | 38.3 | 18.4 | 1 974 | 30.1 |
| Kalkaska .............................. | 23 | -4.2 | 106 | 1.3 | 13.7 | 364 828 | 3 436 | 41 075 | 6.1 | 27 397 | 86.8 | 13.2 | 20.8 | 3.6 | 82 | 19.9 |
| Kent .................................... | 170 | -1.7 | 143 | 9.2 | 131.5 | 689 965 | 4 839 | 86 968 | 194.7 | 163 226 | 70.6 | 29.4 | 41.1 | 15.9 | 1 405 | 26.7 |

| STATE County | Water use, 2005 | | Wholesale trade,[1] 2007 | | | | Retail trade,[2] 2007 | | | | Real estate and rental and leasing,[2] 2007 | | | |
|---|---|---|---|---|---|---|---|---|---|---|---|---|---|---|
| | Total water withdrawn (mil gal/day) | Gallons withdrawn per person | Number of establish-ments | Number of employees | Sales (mil dol) | Annual payroll (mil dol) | Number of establish-ments | Number of employees | Sales (mil dol) | Annual payroll (mil dol) | Number of establish-ments | Number of employees | Receipts (mil dol) | Annual payroll (mil dol) |
| | 133 | 134 | 135 | 136 | 137 | 138 | 139 | 140 | 141 | 142 | 143 | 144 | 145 | 146 |
| MARYLAND—Cont'd | | | | | | | | | | | | | | |
| St. Mary's | 11.4 | 118 | 30 | D | D | D | 314 | 4 531 | 1 193.0 | 97.9 | 92 | 466 | 66.1 | 15.0 |
| Somerset | 4.3 | 165 | 17 | D | D | D | 61 | 459 | 105.2 | 8.4 | 21 | 44 | 4.7 | 1.1 |
| Talbot | 6.4 | 178 | 61 | 557 | 252.7 | 23.6 | 262 | 2 750 | 711.9 | 68.0 | 85 | 242 | 45.9 | 9.0 |
| Washington | 71.0 | 500 | 144 | 1 978 | 1 265.3 | 81.8 | 673 | 10 226 | 2 463.3 | 219.5 | 131 | 632 | 136.9 | 17.9 |
| Wicomico | 20.1 | 223 | 112 | D | D | D | 445 | 7 431 | 1 780.8 | 167.2 | 152 | 701 | 107.8 | 22.3 |
| Worcester | 13.1 | 269 | 54 | D | D | D | 458 | 3 979 | 875.1 | 90.8 | 185 | 577 | 75.6 | 16.1 |
| Baltimore city | 29.7 | 47 | 534 | 9 046 | 4 843.4 | 468.9 | 1 950 | 16 682 | 4 348.8 | 401.5 | 647 | 4 677 | 837.5 | 214.9 |
| MASSACHUSETTS | 3 591.4 | 561 | 7 284 | 123 267 | 95 275.7 | 7 644.3 | 25 469 | 360 218 | 88 083.0 | 8 916.5 | 7 053 | 48 576 | 14 029.8 | 2 287.6 |
| Barnstable | 529.6 | 2 338 | 189 | D | D | D | 1 628 | 16 213 | 3 973.2 | 427.7 | 385 | 1 632 | 270.6 | 50.3 |
| Berkshire | 35.6 | 270 | 113 | D | D | D | 766 | 8 942 | 1 901.8 | 208.8 | 128 | 770 | 123.3 | 22.9 |
| Bristol | 1 057.0 | 1 935 | 548 | 10 224 | 7 719.8 | 514.7 | 2 419 | 37 079 | 8 647.7 | 846.5 | 472 | 2 451 | 382.1 | 70.6 |
| Dukes | 4.0 | 257 | 14 | D | D | D | 207 | 1 202 | 349.0 | 42.8 | 61 | 169 | 31.8 | 5.9 |
| Essex | 505.2 | 684 | 806 | 12 176 | 12 405.7 | 806.4 | 2 690 | 38 874 | 9 822.1 | 962.0 | 647 | 3 045 | 584.1 | 109.8 |
| Franklin | 34.4 | 475 | 56 | 579 | 460.1 | 31.6 | 290 | 3 153 | 691.0 | 71.3 | 50 | 127 | 18.2 | 2.9 |
| Hampden | 167.1 | 362 | 408 | 6 818 | 4 991.8 | 321.1 | 1 686 | 24 052 | 5 668.7 | 548.3 | 409 | 2 164 | 356.8 | 69.0 |
| Hampshire | 37.4 | 244 | 91 | 1 638 | 2 021.8 | 68.0 | 584 | 7 705 | 1 546.1 | 169.8 | 128 | 526 | 88.1 | 14.6 |
| Middlesex | 388.9 | 267 | 2 022 | 39 339 | 32 873.3 | 2 847.9 | 5 306 | 80 413 | 19 661.1 | 2 036.6 | 1 690 | 12 621 | 3 802.7 | 571.3 |
| Nantucket | 5.1 | 503 | 12 | 45 | 39.8 | 2.9 | 159 | 920 | 342.8 | 38.9 | 59 | 179 | 51.0 | 6.4 |
| Norfolk | 49.6 | 76 | 974 | 19 035 | 12 398.9 | 1 190.2 | 2 595 | 42 427 | 11 241.4 | 1 107.3 | 841 | 6 719 | 1 538.9 | 297.7 |
| Plymouth | 170.2 | 346 | 531 | 7 002 | 5 253.6 | 456.6 | 2 016 | 27 593 | 6 615.1 | 684.8 | 427 | 1 924 | 493.9 | 68.4 |
| Suffolk | 161.0 | 246 | 689 | 11 905 | 8 914.8 | 683.5 | 2 385 | 31 139 | 7 565.8 | 800.8 | 1 083 | 12 455 | 5 596.1 | 859.4 |
| Worcester | 446.5 | 570 | 831 | 11 876 | 6 913.7 | 603.7 | 2 738 | 40 506 | 10 057.2 | 971.0 | 673 | 3 794 | 692.2 | 138.6 |
| MICHIGAN | 11 659.9 | 1 152 | 9 892 | 137 315 | 107 109.3 | 7 016.1 | 37 619 | 470 794 | 109 102.6 | 10 001.5 | 8 862 | 54 874 | 12 858.6 | 1 685.7 |
| Alcona | 5.7 | 487 | 2 | D | D | D | 45 | 277 | 55.3 | 5.3 | 7 | D | D | D |
| Alger | 7.2 | 740 | 4 | D | D | D | 50 | 318 | 54.4 | 5.1 | 7 | D | D | D |
| Allegan | 29.9 | 264 | 115 | 1 316 | 506.7 | 56.6 | 362 | 3 715 | 881.3 | 77.4 | 77 | 258 | 46.2 | 8.5 |
| Alpena | 122.5 | 4 024 | 31 | D | D | D | 169 | 1 890 | 416.8 | 38.9 | 25 | 143 | 14.3 | 2.7 |
| Antrim | 40.2 | 1 645 | 11 | D | D | D | 103 | 636 | 156.7 | 13.6 | 21 | 77 | 7.0 | 1.7 |
| Arenac | 34.7 | 2 025 | 12 | D | D | D | 72 | 488 | 118.8 | 8.2 | 7 | D | D | D |
| Baraga | 1.8 | 200 | 4 | 5 | 4.6 | 0.2 | 36 | 324 | 67.7 | 5.5 | 5 | D | D | D |
| Barry | 8.8 | 146 | 33 | 210 | 72.3 | 8.4 | 150 | 1 528 | 276.2 | 24.6 | 31 | 100 | 8.3 | 2.9 |
| Bay | 629.6 | 5 774 | 95 | D | D | D | 430 | 5 580 | 1 301.0 | 115.5 | 77 | 316 | 39.9 | 6.0 |
| Benzie | 3.1 | 173 | 7 | 29 | 3.5 | 0.7 | 77 | 558 | 131.3 | 12.2 | 23 | 35 | 6.7 | 1.1 |
| Berrien | 2 327.2 | 14 311 | 143 | 1 836 | 689.1 | 65.2 | 609 | 7 360 | 1 622.8 | 153.9 | 189 | 796 | 105.6 | 19.3 |
| Branch | 32.6 | 702 | 30 | D | D | D | 148 | 1 887 | 396.9 | 38.5 | 33 | 79 | 10.8 | 2.2 |
| Calhoun | 35.6 | 255 | 103 | D | D | D | 531 | 7 074 | 1 571.3 | 136.0 | 95 | 475 | 62.7 | 11.7 |
| Cass | 23.3 | 448 | 44 | D | D | D | 121 | 899 | 183.4 | 17.4 | 25 | 56 | 10.0 | 1.0 |
| Charlevoix | 21.5 | 803 | 14 | 55 | 8.4 | 1.6 | 136 | 995 | 221.2 | 20.8 | 41 | 141 | 29.8 | 6.7 |
| Cheboygan | 3.6 | 133 | 14 | D | D | D | 183 | 1 282 | 316.9 | 28.7 | 31 | 117 | 15.2 | 2.9 |
| Chippewa | 9.3 | 241 | 22 | D | D | D | 169 | 1 654 | 369.5 | 33.0 | 29 | 93 | 12.1 | 2.1 |
| Clare | 4.1 | 130 | 12 | D | D | D | 127 | 1 144 | 246.1 | 22.8 | 16 | 29 | 4.2 | 0.7 |
| Clinton | 11.1 | 159 | 46 | 815 | 562.1 | 31.6 | 186 | 2 123 | 631.9 | 52.4 | 65 | 264 | 41.1 | 8.0 |
| Crawford | 2.5 | 168 | 4 | D | D | D | 74 | 621 | 216.8 | 12.6 | 15 | 28 | 4.0 | 0.6 |
| Delta | 65.4 | 1 704 | 45 | D | D | D | 213 | 2 268 | 459.8 | 46.2 | 31 | 78 | 7.9 | 1.2 |
| Dickinson | 23.7 | 846 | 51 | D | D | D | 181 | 1 975 | 417.3 | 38.8 | 28 | D | D | D |
| Eaton | 11.1 | 103 | 71 | 1 441 | 914.3 | 67.9 | 404 | 5 996 | 1 327.0 | 116.2 | 105 | 488 | 76.7 | 12.7 |
| Emmet | 7.3 | 218 | 34 | D | D | D | 310 | 2 583 | 580.6 | 62.8 | 53 | 195 | 23.9 | 5.5 |
| Genesee | 20.4 | 46 | 296 | 5 871 | 3 554.9 | 382.9 | 1 614 | 21 531 | 4 836.7 | 440.5 | 339 | 1 813 | 270.2 | 47.7 |
| Gladwin | 2.5 | 93 | 6 | 31 | 9.0 | 1.4 | 88 | 627 | 140.2 | 12.6 | 20 | 88 | 8.5 | 2.8 |
| Gogebic | 10.9 | 649 | 10 | D | D | D | 93 | 719 | 138.0 | 13.0 | 16 | 61 | 3.4 | 1.0 |
| Grand Traverse | 14.5 | 172 | 122 | 1 141 | 425.0 | 43.1 | 622 | 7 192 | 1 570.1 | 149.2 | 163 | 546 | 120.9 | 16.8 |
| Gratiot | 9.0 | 213 | 29 | D | D | D | 146 | 1 367 | 316.4 | 27.9 | 20 | 63 | 4.8 | 1.2 |
| Hillsdale | 10.4 | 220 | 37 | 384 | 260.6 | 16.5 | 150 | 1 430 | 323.3 | 31.2 | 27 | 81 | 10.0 | 1.4 |
| Houghton | 4.3 | 119 | 20 | D | D | D | 176 | 1 935 | 335.5 | 34.1 | 28 | D | D | D |
| Huron | 90.9 | 2 624 | 38 | 456 | 253.6 | 17.2 | 188 | 1 585 | 323.1 | 28.5 | 12 | 17 | 4.4 | 0.5 |
| Ingham | 237.6 | 853 | 241 | 3 168 | 4 423.7 | 139.6 | 1 000 | 15 174 | 3 156.2 | 299.6 | 286 | 2 596 | 282.0 | 68.2 |
| Ionia | 11.9 | 184 | 25 | 243 | 118.8 | 8.8 | 163 | 2 021 | 446.7 | 39.8 | 27 | 77 | 7.6 | 1.2 |
| Iosco | 4.2 | 155 | 6 | D | D | D | 137 | 1 294 | 270.6 | 25.0 | 24 | 50 | 5.3 | 0.9 |
| Iron | 2.7 | 223 | 12 | 47 | 18.6 | 1.3 | 73 | 519 | 101.4 | 8.6 | 19 | 65 | 3.9 | 1.2 |
| Isabella | 8.9 | 135 | 44 | D | D | D | 234 | 3 757 | 705.4 | 69.1 | 56 | 729 | 57.4 | 13.8 |
| Jackson | 22.6 | 138 | 146 | D | D | D | 582 | 7 462 | 1 690.9 | 153.6 | 118 | 608 | 64.9 | 12.5 |
| Kalamazoo | 80.3 | 334 | 250 | 3 102 | 1 207.2 | 139.2 | 918 | 14 148 | 2 808.8 | 278.0 | 226 | 2 512 | 219.2 | 69.1 |
| Kalkaska | 4.4 | 253 | 21 | 182 | 83.4 | 10.0 | 57 | 465 | 144.1 | 10.2 | 10 | 55 | 5.0 | 1.1 |
| Kent | 85.6 | 144 | 950 | 21 881 | 13 020.8 | 1 141.5 | 2 216 | 33 139 | 8 058.0 | 715.9 | 649 | 4 013 | 601.0 | 109.0 |

1. Merchant wholesalers, except manufacturers' sales branches and offices.   2. Employer establishments.

# Professional Services, Manufacturing, and Accommodation and Food Services

| STATE County | Professional, scientific, and technical services,[1] 2007 | | | | Manufacturing, 2007 | | | | Accommodation and food services, 2007 | | | |
|---|---|---|---|---|---|---|---|---|---|---|---|---|
| | Number of establish-ments | Number of employees | Receipts (mil dol) | Annual payroll (mil dol) | Number of establish-ments | Number of employees | Receipts (mil dol) | Annual payroll (mil dol) | Number of establish-ments | Number of employees | Sales (mil dol) | Annual payroll (mil dol) |
| | 147 | 148 | 149 | 150 | 151 | 152 | 153 | 154 | 155 | 156 | 157 | 158 |
| MARYLAND—Cont'd | | | | | | | | | | | | |
| St. Mary's | 274 | D | D | D | 35 | D | D | D | 162 | 3 011 | 132.3 | 34.1 |
| Somerset | 23 | D | D | D | NA | NA | NA | NA | 31 | 298 | 9.9 | 2.9 |
| Talbot | 162 | 1 177 | 176.0 | 67.8 | 47 | 2 422 | D | 83.8 | 124 | 1 997 | 104.9 | 31.8 |
| Washington | 235 | D | D | D | 149 | 6 969 | 2 448.7 | 337.4 | 290 | 5 036 | 229.7 | 65.1 |
| Wicomico | 228 | D | D | D | 79 | D | D | 136.1 | 194 | 4 002 | 184.8 | 50.3 |
| Worcester | 158 | D | D | D | 39 | D | 154.6 | D | 406 | 6 477 | 506.8 | 141.6 |
| Baltimore city | 1 506 | D | D | D | 479 | 16 253 | 5 730.9 | 726.5 | 1 481 | 21 456 | 1 434.7 | 372.1 |
| MASSACHUSETTS | 21 773 | 243 374 | 49 085.7 | 20 652.0 | 7 737 | 289 256 | 86 429.0 | 15 712.0 | 16 039 | 257 302 | 14 917.2 | 4 339.7 |
| Barnstable | 753 | D | D | D | 210 | 2 461 | 533.3 | 110.3 | 1 100 | 12 721 | 891.0 | 261.6 |
| Berkshire | 366 | D | D | D | 173 | 6 204 | 1 425.5 | 317.1 | 516 | 7 600 | 401.9 | 125.6 |
| Bristol | 1 110 | D | D | D | 797 | 35 101 | 8 878.1 | 1 659.4 | 1 206 | 20 866 | 885.2 | 261.7 |
| Dukes | 71 | 282 | 38.6 | 14.6 | NA | NA | NA | NA | 125 | 734 | 95.8 | 28.3 |
| Essex | 2 221 | D | D | D | 997 | 47 909 | 17 488.7 | 2 877.4 | 1 708 | 23 927 | 1 301.5 | 377.7 |
| Franklin | 120 | D | D | D | 111 | 4 537 | 1 164.4 | 197.3 | 157 | 1 944 | 80.3 | 24.4 |
| Hampden | 886 | D | D | D | 673 | 24 346 | 6 001.1 | 1 122.1 | 978 | 14 673 | 661.7 | 191.7 |
| Hampshire | 360 | D | D | D | 157 | 3 970 | 1 098.8 | 182.1 | 367 | 5 430 | 225.5 | 67.7 |
| Middlesex | 6 883 | 106 332 | 21 264.5 | 9 828.5 | 1 853 | 72 842 | 22 482.6 | 4 609.2 | 3 372 | 54 344 | 3 250.2 | 932.3 |
| Nantucket | 56 | D | D | D | NA | NA | NA | NA | 104 | 752 | 88.9 | 26.3 |
| Norfolk | 2 704 | D | D | D | 714 | 26 614 | 10 340.8 | 1 434.6 | 1 435 | 24 126 | 1 294.0 | 378.9 |
| Plymouth | 1 288 | D | D | D | 541 | 13 012 | 2 577.2 | 566.5 | 1 023 | 17 051 | 794.6 | 242.1 |
| Suffolk | 3 067 | 52 850 | 13 301.5 | 5 485.4 | 379 | 12 664 | 3 703.4 | 674.8 | 2 257 | 48 978 | 3 795.9 | 1 090.7 |
| Worcester | 1 888 | 14 149 | 2 693.0 | 917.8 | 1 099 | 39 334 | 10 706.1 | 1 953.9 | 1 691 | 24 156 | 1 150.7 | 330.8 |
| MICHIGAN | 22 552 | 249 864 | 29 536.8 | 15 304.5 | 13 675 | 581 739 | 234 455.8 | 29 910.3 | 19 678 | 339 181 | 14 536.6 | 4 207.3 |
| Alcona | 8 | 19 | 1.7 | 0.7 | NA | NA | NA | NA | 26 | 97 | 4.2 | 1.1 |
| Alger | 12 | 36 | 3.0 | 1.0 | 9 | 629 | 193.9 | 28.0 | 41 | 358 | 14.2 | 3.0 |
| Allegan | 169 | 1 012 | 61.7 | 42.4 | 214 | 13 077 | 4 240.7 | 573.6 | 216 | 2 742 | 118.8 | 34.3 |
| Alpena | 48 | D | D | D | 46 | 1 603 | 587.4 | 72.2 | 73 | 882 | 32.2 | 9.2 |
| Antrim | 43 | 135 | 10.5 | 3.9 | 52 | 1 039 | 193.6 | 42.2 | 68 | 1 176 | 35.2 | 14.3 |
| Arenac | 16 | 149 | 8.2 | 4.2 | 27 | 695 | 126.6 | 23.1 | 47 | 398 | 15.6 | 4.1 |
| Baraga | 2 | D | D | D | NA | NA | NA | NA | 14 | 183 | 5.6 | 1.3 |
| Barry | 68 | 266 | 19.6 | 8.6 | 68 | 2 781 | 977.4 | 118.6 | 81 | 929 | 32.3 | 9.8 |
| Bay | 174 | D | D | D | 126 | 3 532 | 1 107.2 | 191.2 | 238 | 3 973 | 134.7 | 41.3 |
| Benzie | 28 | D | D | D | NA | NA | NA | NA | 54 | 1 053 | 44.2 | 12.9 |
| Berrien | 287 | D | D | D | 332 | 10 831 | 2 298.3 | 474.7 | 413 | 5 519 | 219.5 | 64.1 |
| Branch | 46 | 157 | 12.8 | 4.2 | 80 | 2 990 | 1 061.1 | 127.2 | 83 | 990 | 44.7 | 10.7 |
| Calhoun | 209 | D | D | D | 179 | 11 532 | 4 954.0 | 537.5 | 284 | 4 558 | 182.0 | 54.1 |
| Cass | 55 | D | D | D | 85 | 3 114 | 711.3 | 113.6 | 63 | 743 | 27.1 | 7.5 |
| Charlevoix | 71 | 194 | 17.6 | 6.4 | 52 | 2 899 | 698.6 | 134.0 | 87 | 1 570 | 60.2 | 17.4 |
| Cheboygan | 55 | 152 | 14.3 | 4.9 | NA | NA | NA | NA | 116 | 773 | 46.0 | 14.6 |
| Chippewa | 46 | D | D | D | 32 | 578 | D | 19.5 | 114 | 2 428 | 189.9 | 45.0 |
| Clare | 28 | 166 | 12.5 | 6.8 | 31 | 969 | 192.5 | 36.1 | 68 | 736 | 28.9 | 8.0 |
| Clinton | 117 | 574 | 61.1 | 25.2 | 67 | 2 159 | 609.3 | 106.2 | 99 | 1 666 | 50.8 | 14.6 |
| Crawford | 19 | 79 | 9.9 | 2.0 | 18 | 563 | 152.6 | 23.3 | 49 | 600 | 19.6 | 6.4 |
| Delta | 81 | D | D | D | 73 | 2 695 | 712.6 | 124.6 | 110 | 1 342 | 46.4 | 13.3 |
| Dickinson | 54 | D | D | D | 48 | 2 214 | D | 100.4 | 78 | 873 | 28.6 | 8.1 |
| Eaton | 193 | 1 292 | 143.3 | 56.3 | 96 | 8 377 | D | 547.9 | 201 | 4 122 | 155.3 | 48.3 |
| Emmet | 118 | 485 | 56.9 | 22.4 | 51 | 1 026 | 254.4 | 39.9 | 142 | 2 220 | 108.4 | 33.4 |
| Genesee | 694 | D | D | D | 309 | 14 878 | 12 579.5 | 1 099.6 | 762 | 13 583 | 528.7 | 151.9 |
| Gladwin | 21 | 61 | 4.0 | 1.3 | 39 | 811 | 174.1 | 33.6 | 50 | 488 | 17.6 | 5.1 |
| Gogebic | 26 | 110 | 8.2 | 3.7 | 21 | 682 | 80.1 | 20.2 | 61 | 1 188 | 55.7 | 14.5 |
| Grand Traverse | 408 | D | D | D | 179 | 4 727 | 1 160.7 | 202.0 | 236 | 5 267 | 237.7 | 72.0 |
| Gratiot | 37 | 279 | 16.8 | 10.2 | 48 | 2 010 | 357.4 | 73.3 | 66 | 1 152 | 40.1 | 13.0 |
| Hillsdale | 50 | 346 | 20.3 | 8.2 | 92 | 3 917 | 1 330.8 | 145.8 | 80 | 752 | 31.4 | 8.0 |
| Houghton | 68 | D | D | D | 48 | D | D | 28.9 | 111 | 1 427 | 46.5 | 13.6 |
| Huron | 56 | 271 | 23.3 | 13.2 | 68 | 2 692 | 647.3 | 101.9 | 105 | 832 | 33.6 | 8.2 |
| Ingham | 777 | 5 944 | 724.3 | 293.6 | 222 | 9 829 | D | 533.1 | 601 | 11 648 | 446.1 | 131.8 |
| Ionia | 59 | D | D | D | 73 | 3 126 | 1 117.4 | 112.0 | 88 | 980 | 37.4 | 9.5 |
| Iosco | 40 | 169 | 12.5 | 5.6 | 37 | 973 | 190.4 | 33.8 | 77 | 663 | 27.3 | 7.4 |
| Iron | 31 | 199 | 8.6 | 4.0 | NA | NA | NA | NA | 44 | 334 | 11.6 | 3.1 |
| Isabella | 124 | 1 672 | 78.3 | 41.3 | 61 | 2 221 | 528.7 | 85.0 | 125 | 3 431 | 117.8 | 33.8 |
| Jackson | 235 | D | D | D | 284 | 9 250 | 2 783.0 | 403.6 | 300 | 4 999 | 185.4 | 53.5 |
| Kalamazoo | 557 | D | D | D | 334 | 17 261 | 7 145.9 | 904.1 | 507 | 11 678 | 414.6 | 130.6 |
| Kalkaska | 21 | 213 | 17.1 | 9.8 | NA | NA | NA | NA | 29 | 363 | 13.7 | 3.9 |
| Kent | 1 643 | D | D | D | 1 154 | 61 608 | 15 738.3 | 3 034.1 | 1 134 | 24 655 | 925.2 | 283.6 |

1. Establishment subject to federal tax.

| STATE County | Health care and social assistance, 2007 | | | | Other services, 2007 | | | | Federal funds and grants, 2009–2010 Expenditures (mil dol) | | | |
|---|---|---|---|---|---|---|---|---|---|---|---|---|
| | | | | | | | | | | Direct payments for individuals[1] | | |
| | Number of establishments | Number of employees | Receipts (mil dol) | Annual payroll (mil dol) | Number of establishments | Number of employees | Receipts (mil dol) | Annual payroll (mil dol) | Total | Social Security and government retirement | Medicare | Food Stamps and Supplemental Security Income |
| | 159 | 160 | 161 | 162 | 163 | 164 | 165 | 166 | 167 | 168 | 169 | 170 |
| MARYLAND—Cont'd | | | | | | | | | | | | |
| St. Mary's | 159 | 3 563 | 311.3 | 126.3 | 146 | 877 | 83.7 | 27.4 | 3 449.9 | 387.6 | 188.4 | 17.8 |
| Somerset | 40 | 1 267 | 77.2 | 37.7 | 28 | 85 | 11.4 | 1.8 | 288.6 | 74.9 | 99.1 | 10.1 |
| Talbot | 170 | 2 946 | 314.7 | 114.3 | 129 | 833 | 93.2 | 23.7 | 447.4 | 176.5 | 114.6 | 6.9 |
| Washington | 407 | 9 407 | 822.7 | 355.5 | 268 | 1 838 | 159.3 | 43.3 | 1 171.4 | 467.8 | 352.3 | 34.9 |
| Wicomico | 346 | 7 715 | 745.9 | 330.3 | 179 | 1 218 | 100.7 | 30.2 | 766.3 | 277.8 | 240.6 | 28.6 |
| Worcester | 130 | 1 896 | 160.3 | 64.7 | 150 | 925 | 72.2 | 22.6 | 518.0 | 241.3 | 142.5 | 10.8 |
| Baltimore city | 1 506 | 64 978 | 8 368.9 | 2 954.3 | 982 | 9 180 | 1 541.6 | 273.4 | 17 067.5 | 1 736.1 | 4 948.1 | 578.3 |
| MASSACHUSETTS | 17 855 | 511 012 | 51 946.1 | 22 176.0 | 13 516 | 90 268 | 9 841.0 | 2 690.3 | 82 453.6 | 17 313.5 | 13 690.5 | 2 271.0 |
| Barnstable | 807 | 15 247 | 1 466.2 | 620.7 | 601 | 3 279 | 334.9 | 88.2 | 2 650.7 | 1 059.0 | 647.7 | 45.7 |
| Berkshire | 450 | 10 869 | 981.1 | 429.8 | 309 | 1 742 | 142.3 | 38.5 | 1 352.8 | 459.3 | 357.1 | 48.0 |
| Bristol | 1 368 | 36 372 | 2 911.7 | 1 364.1 | 1 052 | 5 898 | 465.7 | 131.5 | 6 187.8 | 1 547.6 | 1 152.2 | 215.8 |
| Dukes | 61 | 590 | 78.1 | 33.0 | 55 | 177 | 26.1 | 6.1 | 126.9 | 50.7 | 29.7 | 1.7 |
| Essex | 2 030 | 47 584 | 4 272.0 | 1 909.5 | 1 470 | 8 644 | 1 096.7 | 254.2 | 9 423.9 | 2 019.7 | 1 518.0 | 274.1 |
| Franklin | 197 | 3 678 | 267.2 | 116.1 | 137 | 572 | 48.5 | 13.3 | 536.9 | 214.7 | 134.6 | 24.3 |
| Hampden | 1 162 | 37 111 | 3 243.2 | 1 423.3 | 834 | 5 453 | 431.5 | 133.2 | 4 304.2 | 1 347.2 | 942.5 | 358.7 |
| Hampshire | 419 | 8 219 | 764.1 | 309.8 | 297 | 1 550 | 147.2 | 38.9 | 1 153.4 | 397.2 | 217.2 | 28.1 |
| Middlesex | 4 386 | 99 055 | 10 192.8 | 4 326.2 | 3 202 | 23 744 | 2 577.2 | 790.2 | 20 144.1 | 3 615.4 | 3 012.9 | 287.1 |
| Nantucket | 34 | 369 | 52.3 | 17.6 | 41 | 173 | 26.3 | 6.2 | 54.3 | 22.7 | 14.4 | 0.4 |
| Norfolk | 2 084 | 53 650 | 4 430.5 | 1 984.8 | 1 535 | 9 656 | 1 036.5 | 297.6 | 4 792.9 | 1 437.3 | 1 466.2 | 80.5 |
| Plymouth | 1 157 | 26 215 | 2 209.8 | 978.5 | 921 | 6 294 | 518.6 | 185.1 | 3 745.4 | 1 414.3 | 855.1 | 110.2 |
| Suffolk | 1 755 | 116 467 | 15 525.9 | 6 462.1 | 1 716 | 15 391 | 2 216.9 | 483.0 | 16 685.5 | 1 699.2 | 1 778.8 | 512.8 |
| Worcester | 1 945 | 55 586 | 5 551.2 | 2 200.6 | 1 346 | 7 695 | 772.5 | 224.3 | 6 321.4 | 2 028.3 | 1 564.3 | 283.5 |
| MICHIGAN | 26 033 | 549 482 | 52 758.4 | 21 588.3 | 17 040 | 101 568 | 10 843.7 | 2 648.1 | 90 921.1 | 30 768.9 | 17 107.6 | 4 443.4 |
| Alcona | 10 | D | D | D | 14 | 36 | 3.1 | 0.5 | 148.1 | 68.2 | 29.6 | 3.5 |
| Alger | 21 | 308 | 18.1 | 7.7 | 14 | D | D | D | 93.3 | 40.3 | 21.0 | 2.2 |
| Allegan | 171 | 3 104 | 208.5 | 88.5 | 182 | 807 | 69.2 | 19.1 | 566.3 | 272.5 | 111.9 | 22.2 |
| Alpena | 92 | 2 734 | 222.1 | 91.5 | 78 | 348 | 29.5 | 7.7 | 338.6 | 139.7 | 67.6 | 14.8 |
| Antrim | 44 | 396 | 23.4 | 11.4 | 34 | 152 | 15.1 | 4.4 | 201.3 | 95.2 | 39.1 | 5.9 |
| Arenac | 32 | 630 | 46.8 | 17.6 | 25 | D | D | D | 163.8 | 76.6 | 38.3 | 9.2 |
| Baraga | 21 | 355 | 26.1 | 11.4 | 18 | 49 | 3.1 | 0.6 | 84.2 | 32.5 | 16.1 | 3.1 |
| Barry | 76 | 1 414 | 104.4 | 43.8 | 94 | 375 | 36.5 | 9.4 | 286.2 | 161.3 | 57.7 | 11.3 |
| Bay | 315 | 5 902 | 513.3 | 209.5 | 196 | 1 068 | 75.9 | 21.8 | 897.4 | 401.0 | 203.4 | 50.5 |
| Benzie | 34 | 355 | 26.4 | 9.7 | 25 | D | D | D | 135.2 | 70.8 | 23.4 | 3.9 |
| Berrien | 394 | 8 821 | 701.7 | 282.8 | 281 | 1 468 | 112.2 | 35.1 | 1 365.2 | 568.7 | 292.2 | 90.6 |
| Branch | 91 | D | D | D | 72 | D | D | D | 278.3 | 131.9 | 67.5 | 12.3 |
| Calhoun | 341 | 8 967 | 898.1 | 372.5 | 225 | 1 249 | 503.8 | 42.5 | 1 481.8 | 503.1 | 252.8 | 76.8 |
| Cass | 60 | D | D | D | 62 | 272 | 27.8 | 6.5 | 296.2 | 128.3 | 62.8 | 18.1 |
| Charlevoix | 75 | 862 | 81.4 | 32.6 | 63 | 251 | 23.8 | 5.9 | 177.2 | 98.3 | 36.1 | 5.7 |
| Cheboygan | 54 | 1 158 | 87.8 | 35.0 | 72 | 206 | 17.9 | 5.0 | 206.8 | 102.7 | 45.7 | 8.8 |
| Chippewa | 78 | 1 546 | 136.9 | 46.6 | 61 | D | D | D | 392.9 | 134.4 | 52.7 | 12.9 |
| Clare | 55 | 947 | 79.6 | 27.1 | 52 | 157 | 12.9 | 2.9 | 290.6 | 133.9 | 69.2 | 17.2 |
| Clinton | 95 | 1 370 | 107.1 | 37.9 | 105 | 592 | 44.7 | 12.6 | 301.2 | 164.6 | 57.9 | 8.9 |
| Crawford | 40 | 1 006 | 90.7 | 35.3 | 25 | 146 | 15.5 | 5.3 | 151.6 | 52.8 | 22.9 | 4.8 |
| Delta | 109 | 1 819 | 147.1 | 53.4 | 95 | 586 | 46.5 | 12.5 | 363.7 | 168.7 | 73.4 | 15.3 |
| Dickinson | 102 | D | D | D | 76 | D | D | D | 267.5 | 117.6 | 43.6 | 7.4 |
| Eaton | 239 | 2 995 | 231.0 | 88.7 | 164 | 1 040 | 118.8 | 38.5 | 736.6 | 255.7 | 100.6 | 19.0 |
| Emmet | 198 | 3 146 | 361.7 | 139.1 | 109 | 508 | 56.0 | 14.9 | 241.0 | 123.1 | 43.3 | 6.6 |
| Genesee | 1 261 | 25 790 | 2 505.1 | 1 005.4 | 648 | 3 695 | 418.1 | 103.4 | 3 751.3 | 1 495.5 | 857.8 | 303.7 |
| Gladwin | 35 | 701 | 55.6 | 18.3 | 32 | 211 | 15.5 | 4.3 | 237.3 | 125.2 | 57.2 | 13.4 |
| Gogebic | 40 | 738 | 62.9 | 24.7 | 43 | 131 | 10.2 | 2.6 | 185.0 | 75.5 | 45.7 | 7.3 |
| Grand Traverse | 382 | 7 736 | 798.1 | 305.0 | 232 | 1 314 | 121.8 | 32.0 | 650.9 | 321.1 | 108.4 | 14.5 |
| Gratiot | 110 | 2 439 | 216.3 | 81.7 | 62 | 255 | 30.3 | 7.2 | 308.3 | 129.9 | 70.4 | 15.0 |
| Hillsdale | 112 | 1 474 | 111.2 | 42.2 | 57 | 416 | 24.4 | 5.0 | 302.2 | 146.0 | 61.9 | 15.0 |
| Houghton | 86 | 2 026 | 146.7 | 61.5 | 69 | D | D | D | 353.5 | 107.4 | 63.7 | 12.1 |
| Huron | 98 | 1 804 | 130.2 | 50.7 | 61 | 212 | 18.2 | 4.0 | 311.3 | 134.3 | 75.5 | 12.0 |
| Ingham | 848 | 20 580 | 1 991.5 | 843.5 | 595 | 5 128 | 584.8 | 158.0 | 6 596.0 | 822.1 | 417.3 | 132.3 |
| Ionia | 108 | 1 287 | 94.2 | 35.9 | 82 | 366 | 24.1 | 5.7 | 326.5 | 154.6 | 72.1 | 18.5 |
| Iosco | 58 | 1 200 | 93.6 | 41.5 | 62 | 223 | 14.1 | 3.7 | 271.5 | 145.5 | 66.1 | 11.1 |
| Iron | 18 | 395 | 37.7 | 14.0 | 22 | D | D | D | 133.0 | 55.8 | 34.4 | 3.8 |
| Isabella | 224 | 3 265 | 193.7 | 86.9 | 101 | 544 | 34.1 | 9.0 | 326.8 | 150.6 | 57.4 | 23.8 |
| Jackson | 379 | 8 717 | 810.5 | 346.6 | 241 | 1 528 | 147.0 | 41.2 | 1 149.7 | 513.5 | 248.9 | 66.6 |
| Kalamazoo | 639 | 18 148 | 1 811.4 | 703.6 | 430 | 3 414 | 480.2 | 91.8 | 2 155.8 | 680.0 | 300.3 | 90.1 |
| Kalkaska | 25 | 466 | 32.7 | 13.6 | 36 | D | D | D | 100.6 | 48.9 | 22.6 | 6.2 |
| Kent | 1 497 | 40 522 | 3 956.9 | 1 564.3 | 1 100 | 7 828 | 721.7 | 198.8 | 3 612.8 | 1 489.9 | 637.8 | 192.0 |

1. State totals may include programs not allocated by county.

# Table B. States and Counties — Federal Funds, Residential Construction, and Local Government Finances

| | Federal funds and grants, 2009–2010 (cont.) | | | | | | | Value of residential construction authorized by building permits, 2011 | | Local government finances, 2007 | | | | | |
| --- | --- | --- | --- | --- | --- | --- | --- | --- | --- | --- | --- | --- | --- | --- | --- |
| | Expenditures (mil dol) (cont.) | | | | | | | | | General revenue | | | | | |
| | Procurement contract awards | | | Grants[1] | | | | | | | | | Taxes | | |
| STATE County | | | | | | | | | | | | | | Per capita[2] (dollars) | |
| | Salaries and wages | Defense | Other | Medicaid and other health-related | Nutrition and family welfare | Education | Other | New construction ($1,000) | Number of housing units | Total (mil dol) | Inter-govern-mental (mil dol) | Total (mil dol) | Total | Property |
| | 171 | 172 | 173 | 174 | 175 | 176 | 177 | 178 | 179 | 180 | 181 | 182 | 183 | 184 |
| MARYLAND—Cont'd | | | | | | | | | | | | | | |
| St. Mary's | 587.9 | 2 123.6 | 23.6 | 70.9 | 11.9 | 4.1 | 20.0 | 120 211 | 784 | 317.6 | 119.3 | 150.9 | 1 503 | 701 |
| Somerset | 9.8 | 0.8 | 2.1 | 50.4 | 5.0 | 7.7 | 14.1 | 9 998 | 62 | 88.4 | 53.0 | 22.2 | 853 | 533 |
| Talbot | 33.0 | 35.0 | 28.8 | 33.9 | 4.8 | 1.0 | 3.9 | 29 731 | 169 | 166.1 | 32.4 | 80.0 | 2 211 | 972 |
| Washington | 58.6 | 18.6 | 46.8 | 120.3 | 23.4 | 6.9 | 20.0 | 31 183 | 168 | 509.0 | 194.6 | 207.2 | 1 428 | 843 |
| Wicomico | 35.9 | 13.3 | 10.4 | 94.1 | 22.3 | 3.7 | 12.6 | 16 034 | 107 | 378.3 | 162.6 | 134.9 | 1 441 | 828 |
| Worcester | 15.7 | 38.2 | 7.0 | 45.6 | 7.8 | 1.4 | 1.1 | 16 736 | 121 | 318.7 | 51.7 | 207.7 | 4 207 | 2 887 |
| Baltimore city | 941.5 | 390.4 | 944.2 | 4 233.1 | 448.6 | 325.6 | 2 204.5 | 85 745 | 989 | 3 324.9 | 1 724.8 | 1 075.5 | 1 687 | 947 |
| MASSACHUSETTS | 4 506.0 | 12 673.5 | 3 313.8 | 14 088.0 | 1 526.5 | 1 343.7 | 5 393.6 | 1 761 071 | 7 725 | X | X | X | X | X |
| Barnstable | 250.1 | 84.7 | 75.5 | 189.4 | 35.0 | 11.3 | 233.0 | 140 861 | 404 | 915.3 | 212.8 | 541.7 | 2 438 | 2 298 |
| Berkshire | 54.6 | 111.3 | 29.3 | 202.4 | 27.1 | 12.7 | 31.0 | 26 265 | 122 | 442.7 | 189.6 | 203.0 | 1 564 | 1 520 |
| Bristol | 153.2 | 1 585.1 | 159.1 | 1 043.2 | 108.7 | 44.9 | 112.4 | 85 784 | 478 | 1 915.3 | 986.2 | 693.1 | 1 276 | 1 225 |
| Dukes | 5.0 | 5.2 | 1.7 | 10.8 | 2.1 | 0.8 | 16.4 | 33 626 | 89 | 120.5 | 27.4 | 74.4 | 4 807 | 4 617 |
| Essex | 269.8 | 3 843.8 | 150.9 | 900.1 | 132.3 | 59.5 | 163.4 | 164 567 | 725 | 2 602.3 | 1 061.9 | 1 210.2 | 1 651 | 1 609 |
| Franklin | 20.4 | 6.7 | 7.5 | 82.8 | 17.8 | 5.2 | 14.4 | 12 885 | 59 | 301.3 | 161.3 | 115.0 | 1 606 | 1 568 |
| Hampden | 379.9 | 64.8 | 91.0 | 755.3 | 108.0 | 48.8 | 102.0 | 58 424 | 309 | 1 722.4 | 980.0 | 586.2 | 1 280 | 1 254 |
| Hampshire | 104.5 | 35.0 | 49.7 | 149.2 | 21.5 | 11.5 | 96.0 | 37 030 | 144 | 431.4 | 177.6 | 194.1 | 1 267 | 1 232 |
| Middlesex | 1 248.1 | 5 847.4 | 1 415.4 | 2 508.9 | 213.3 | 356.0 | 1 452.4 | 454 991 | 1 823 | 6 250.8 | 1 991.3 | 3 083.9 | 2 093 | 2 040 |
| Nantucket | 6.5 | 0.0 | 2.3 | 4.6 | 0.9 | 0.3 | 1.4 | 39 525 | 54 | 92.0 | 7.3 | 57.9 | 5 497 | 5 092 |
| Norfolk | 182.6 | 645.5 | 65.7 | 505.4 | 82.9 | 37.5 | 152.9 | 217 653 | 1 016 | 2 401.7 | 712.8 | 1 366.9 | 2 087 | 2 027 |
| Plymouth | 237.4 | 75.5 | 357.4 | 484.6 | 72.9 | 37.5 | 46.6 | 158 370 | 809 | 1 861.1 | 854.3 | 812.2 | 1 657 | 1 600 |
| Suffolk | 1 280.3 | 203.1 | 795.3 | 5 926.4 | 433.7 | 609.0 | 2 668.5 | 179 973 | 902 | 4 635.6 | 2 563.9 | 1 412.8 | 1 981 | 1 853 |
| Worcester | 313.7 | 165.3 | 113.1 | 1 290.4 | 135.6 | 62.6 | 243.3 | 151 118 | 791 | 2 659.9 | 1 294.8 | 1 073.9 | 1 374 | 1 341 |
| MICHIGAN | 4 798.2 | 4 080.3 | 2 386.4 | 11 165.6 | 2 752.7 | 1 689.6 | 4 969.4 | 0 | 68 | X | X | X | X | X |
| Alcona | 2.5 | 0.0 | 0.6 | 29.5 | 2.4 | 0.9 | 9.9 | 1 909 | 19 | 35.2 | 10.8 | 13.0 | 1 130 | 1 094 |
| Alger | 5.0 | 0.0 | 2.1 | 16.6 | 2.2 | 1.8 | 1.5 | 5 351 | 37 | 35.5 | 19.1 | 8.8 | 916 | 876 |
| Allegan | 17.5 | 2.6 | 4.1 | 64.8 | 19.3 | 6.0 | 2.7 | 28 251 | 145 | 358.5 | 168.6 | 114.4 | 1 014 | 997 |
| Alpena | 26.1 | 13.6 | 4.5 | 33.6 | 24.3 | 2.9 | 1.9 | 1 742 | 11 | 213.3 | 57.8 | 31.9 | 1 075 | 1 055 |
| Antrim | 6.0 | 4.5 | 22.0 | 21.4 | 4.4 | 1.4 | 0.3 | 8 020 | 42 | 98.4 | 30.0 | 44.8 | 1 843 | 1 805 |
| Arenac | 3.9 | 0.5 | 0.9 | 24.8 | 4.1 | 2.9 | 0.2 | 1 131 | 7 | 45.1 | 24.2 | 14.3 | 863 | 851 |
| Baraga | 3.3 | 0.1 | 0.5 | 13.3 | 2.9 | 2.5 | 8.7 | 797 | 8 | 51.5 | 18.2 | 7.9 | 926 | 921 |
| Barry | 7.8 | 1.6 | 2.0 | 30.0 | 8.4 | 1.6 | 0.3 | 11 439 | 71 | 153.2 | 78.4 | 41.5 | 700 | 694 |
| Bay | 40.3 | 1.8 | 13.8 | 103.8 | 22.2 | 5.9 | 6.3 | 14 849 | 91 | 514.5 | 250.3 | 131.3 | 1 221 | 1 199 |
| Benzie | 3.8 | 0.0 | 9.7 | 18.8 | 2.8 | 1.1 | 0.4 | 7 769 | 38 | 57.6 | 19.1 | 22.6 | 1 288 | 1 283 |
| Berrien | 31.8 | 2.9 | 16.0 | 249.9 | 36.3 | 15.7 | 32.6 | 30 856 | 136 | 590.1 | 307.2 | 173.2 | 1 085 | 1 060 |
| Branch | 7.7 | 0.0 | 1.7 | 36.6 | 9.9 | 3.5 | 0.5 | 3 524 | 17 | 216.4 | 80.1 | 40.3 | 872 | 850 |
| Calhoun | 156.6 | 156.0 | 60.6 | 190.7 | 37.0 | 11.3 | 11.6 | 7 704 | 49 | 634.9 | 350.7 | 166.3 | 1 217 | 1 073 |
| Cass | 9.5 | 1.9 | 1.8 | 41.7 | 9.0 | 3.5 | 5.6 | 12 835 | 75 | 172.2 | 93.1 | 40.3 | 797 | 781 |
| Charlevoix | 5.6 | 4.0 | 1.2 | 17.5 | 4.9 | 1.8 | 1.0 | 12 889 | 89 | 141.3 | 43.3 | 67.6 | 2 581 | 2 576 |
| Cheboygan | 9.6 | 0.1 | 3.2 | 28.1 | 5.2 | 1.7 | 0.9 | 7 318 | 42 | 83.2 | 36.1 | 34.8 | 1 301 | 1 281 |
| Chippewa | 44.1 | 12.0 | 11.1 | 57.7 | 18.6 | 6.4 | 20.9 | 3 979 | 43 | 135.2 | 68.4 | 30.8 | 792 | 789 |
| Clare | 6.2 | 0.0 | 1.4 | 35.4 | 9.4 | 4.0 | 0.3 | 3 257 | 35 | 120.5 | 59.2 | 30.1 | 981 | 971 |
| Clinton | 21.6 | 4.5 | 3.5 | 18.1 | 9.6 | 2.9 | 0.8 | 22 340 | 104 | 203.6 | 101.6 | 59.3 | 850 | 826 |
| Crawford | 44.5 | 3.2 | 8.6 | 8.5 | 3.5 | 1.0 | 1.4 | 3 841 | 40 | 42.0 | 19.2 | 16.0 | 1 102 | 1 049 |
| Delta | 19.3 | 7.3 | 6.1 | 45.3 | 12.3 | 2.6 | 1.7 | 5 188 | 43 | 141.9 | 77.0 | 36.3 | 972 | 965 |
| Dickinson | 40.5 | 7.3 | 22.3 | 19.2 | 6.4 | 1.1 | 0.6 | 4 976 | 41 | 178.6 | 60.7 | 30.9 | 1 147 | 1 137 |
| Eaton | 172.5 | 4.2 | 2.6 | 43.3 | 14.2 | 20.2 | 91.9 | 12 826 | 67 | 322.2 | 163.8 | 99.6 | 928 | 906 |
| Emmet | 9.8 | 0.0 | 2.8 | 28.5 | 5.8 | 2.2 | 10.1 | 10 266 | 35 | 233.0 | 110.7 | 74.9 | 2 242 | 2 195 |
| Genesee | 129.6 | 8.1 | 36.2 | 510.6 | 112.4 | 40.8 | 46.5 | 12 723 | 66 | 2 037.0 | 976.1 | 403.5 | 928 | 864 |
| Gladwin | 4.5 | 0.0 | 1.1 | 25.1 | 5.5 | 1.9 | 0.6 | 5 527 | 31 | 64.9 | 32.0 | 21.7 | 824 | 811 |
| Gogebic | 10.3 | 0.0 | 5.3 | 28.5 | 4.5 | 1.9 | -0.6 | 4 778 | 24 | 82.8 | 43.6 | 14.2 | 872 | 866 |
| Grand Traverse | 51.2 | 1.2 | 36.7 | 70.1 | 20.7 | 5.2 | 8.1 | 43 501 | 233 | 460.2 | 201.3 | 144.3 | 1 689 | 1 649 |
| Gratiot | 12.0 | 0.8 | 2.0 | 51.8 | 9.0 | 3.1 | 3.2 | 3 116 | 22 | 149.8 | 99.7 | 30.5 | 724 | 710 |
| Hillsdale | 9.6 | 0.0 | 2.3 | 44.1 | 9.7 | 2.9 | 1.3 | 4 790 | 28 | 135.1 | 74.9 | 31.9 | 681 | 674 |
| Houghton | 30.7 | 16.0 | 10.6 | 52.9 | 12.1 | 2.7 | 33.9 | 4 595 | 42 | 136.7 | 74.5 | 25.3 | 718 | 709 |
| Huron | 9.0 | 1.7 | 2.1 | 45.4 | 8.6 | 2.4 | 0.7 | 7 165 | 38 | 142.2 | 60.6 | 47.0 | 1 412 | 1 390 |
| Ingham | 143.3 | 512.0 | 127.5 | 593.0 | 505.8 | 820.3 | 2 309.0 | 41 988 | 245 | 1 439.6 | 679.0 | 433.6 | 1 552 | 1 424 |
| Ionia | 9.9 | 0.0 | 2.2 | 44.7 | 11.3 | 3.7 | 2.1 | 3 496 | 23 | 203.8 | 130.1 | 46.8 | 731 | 682 |
| Iosco | 9.5 | 7.8 | 2.5 | 17.5 | 7.2 | 2.5 | 0.5 | 4 418 | 28 | 112.1 | 55.5 | 31.8 | 1 212 | 1 200 |
| Iron | 6.6 | 0.0 | 1.0 | 20.7 | 3.1 | 0.9 | 6.0 | 5 669 | 35 | 64.9 | 31.5 | 15.8 | 1 300 | 1 290 |
| Isabella | 14.4 | 0.5 | 4.0 | 46.8 | 10.7 | 3.7 | 5.6 | 6 643 | 70 | 216.0 | 133.1 | 40.7 | 610 | 591 |
| Jackson | 65.1 | 17.2 | 7.3 | 140.0 | 36.5 | 10.9 | 9.0 | 8 432 | 57 | 577.7 | 311.0 | 149.1 | 915 | 851 |
| Kalamazoo | 145.3 | 38.1 | 28.2 | 234.1 | 46.4 | 20.0 | 488.9 | 58 898 | 282 | 905.9 | 446.6 | 294.2 | 1 199 | 1 167 |
| Kalkaska | 2.3 | -0.2 | 0.6 | 15.1 | 3.3 | 1.3 | -0.2 | 5 088 | 27 | 66.1 | 18.1 | 16.5 | 961 | 938 |
| Kent | 302.4 | 87.4 | 98.1 | 441.7 | 93.8 | 38.3 | 104.9 | 142 576 | 761 | 2 388.9 | 1 106.3 | 776.6 | 1 285 | 1 138 |

1. State totals may include programs not allocated by county.    2. Based on the resident population estimated as of July 1 of the year shown.

| | Local government finances, 2007 (cont.) | | | | | | | Government employment, 2011 | | | | Presidential election,[2] 2012 | | |
| --- | --- | --- | --- | --- | --- | --- | --- | --- | --- | --- | --- | --- | --- | --- |
| | Direct general expenditure | | | | | | | Debt outstanding | | | | Percent of vote cast: | | |
| | | | Percent of total for: | | | | | | | | | | | |
| STATE County | Total (mil dol) | Per capita[1] (dollars) | Education | Health and hospitals | Police protection | Public welfare | Highways | Total (mil dol) | Per capita[1] (dollars) | Federal civilian | Federal military | State and local | Democratic | Republican | All other |
| | 185 | 186 | 187 | 188 | 189 | 190 | 191 | 192 | 193 | 194 | 195 | 196 | 197 | 198 | 199 |
| MARYLAND—Cont'd | | | | | | | | | | | | | | | |
| St. Mary's | 286.7 | 2 856 | 62.2 | 0.8 | 6.2 | 0.4 | 2.8 | 208.3 | 2 075 | 8 693 | 2 619 | 4 687 | 42.8 | 55.6 | 1.5 |
| Somerset | 90.1 | 3 465 | 56.5 | 1.0 | 4.7 | 0.1 | 3.9 | 71.1 | 2 732 | 55 | 115 | 3 006 | 48.2 | 50.8 | 1.1 |
| Talbot | 117.6 | 3 249 | 39.6 | 1.9 | 6.2 | 0.7 | 5.9 | 62.1 | 1 715 | 241 | 137 | 1 620 | 44.4 | 54.1 | 1.5 |
| Washington | 453.9 | 3 128 | 57.4 | 0.8 | 4.2 | 0.8 | 5.3 | 337.5 | 2 326 | 725 | 486 | 8 444 | 42.6 | 55.5 | 1.9 |
| Wicomico | 365.4 | 3 904 | 57.8 | 0.9 | 4.8 | 4.9 | 4.4 | 200.1 | 2 137 | 310 | 316 | 7 312 | 46.4 | 52.2 | 1.4 |
| Worcester | 275.7 | 5 583 | 35.5 | 3.9 | 8.7 | 0.6 | 5.3 | 168.8 | 3 419 | 199 | 196 | 3 519 | 41.6 | 57.1 | 1.3 |
| Baltimore city | 3 158.2 | 4 954 | 37.6 | 4.0 | 11.2 | 0.1 | 5.8 | 3 044.0 | 4 775 | 10 175 | 2 193 | 66 017 | 87.2 | 11.7 | 1.2 |
| MASSACHUSETTS | X | X | X | X | X | X | X | X | X | 48 402 | 20 906 | 380 613 | 62.0 | 36.2 | 1.7 |
| Barnstable | 979.9 | 4 411 | 46.8 | 1.1 | 6.2 | 0.3 | 3.2 | 860.0 | 3 871 | 1 708 | 1 228 | 12 384 | 56.1 | 42.4 | 1.5 |
| Berkshire | 500.5 | 3 856 | 60.3 | 0.5 | 3.4 | 0.1 | 5.3 | 347.1 | 2 674 | 389 | 344 | 8 146 | 75.2 | 22.6 | 2.2 |
| Bristol | 1 971.6 | 3 631 | 59.5 | 0.7 | 5.3 | 0.6 | 2.6 | 1 424.2 | 2 623 | 1 175 | 1 444 | 25 700 | 60.7 | 37.5 | 1.8 |
| Dukes | 133.2 | 8 604 | 45.9 | 2.3 | 4.9 | 0.0 | 3.9 | 93.7 | 6 051 | 43 | 44 | 1 349 | 75.1 | 23.2 | 1.6 |
| Essex | 2 691.9 | 3 672 | 57.7 | 0.4 | 4.9 | 0.1 | 2.6 | 2 237.1 | 3 052 | 3 473 | 2 039 | 35 922 | 59.4 | 39.0 | 1.6 |
| Franklin | 314.9 | 4 399 | 63.5 | 0.4 | 2.5 | 0.1 | 4.8 | 156.0 | 2 179 | 197 | 187 | 4 895 | 72.7 | 24.9 | 2.4 |
| Hampden | 1 669.6 | 3 646 | 60.7 | 0.6 | 5.1 | 0.6 | 2.9 | 1 631.0 | 3 562 | 4 089 | 1 394 | 28 807 | 61.5 | 36.4 | 2.1 |
| Hampshire | 468.7 | 3 060 | 59.7 | 0.6 | 4.0 | 0.2 | 4.2 | 272.7 | 1 781 | 1 281 | 426 | 16 318 | 71.8 | 26.0 | 2.3 |
| Middlesex | 6 127.7 | 4 159 | 50.3 | 11.8 | 4.4 | 0.3 | 2.7 | 3 686.3 | 2 502 | 13 699 | 5 270 | 72 788 | 64.2 | 34.1 | 1.7 |
| Nantucket | 100.0 | 9 495 | 27.5 | 0.6 | 3.8 | 3.7 | 0.9 | 156.8 | 14 892 | 66 | 53 | 593 | 67.5 | 31.0 | 1.5 |
| Norfolk | 2 380.8 | 3 635 | 55.8 | 0.5 | 5.2 | 0.1 | 3.5 | 1 506.1 | 2 300 | 1 700 | 1 772 | 31 576 | 58.5 | 40.0 | 1.6 |
| Plymouth | 1 828.7 | 3 730 | 58.3 | 0.5 | 4.7 | 0.2 | 2.7 | 1 192.8 | 2 433 | 3 314 | 1 338 | 27 858 | 53.0 | 45.4 | 1.5 |
| Suffolk | 3 362.6 | 4 716 | 33.8 | 5.1 | 9.5 | 2.7 | 1.7 | 7 558.8 | 10 601 | 14 669 | 3 258 | 65 866 | 77.5 | 21.1 | 1.4 |
| Worcester | 2 872.2 | 3 676 | 59.7 | 0.6 | 4.3 | 0.1 | 3.5 | 2 447.7 | 3 133 | 2 599 | 2 109 | 48 411 | 55.8 | 42.1 | 2.1 |
| MICHIGAN | X | X | X | X | X | X | X | X | X | 53 386 | 20 496 | 558 187 | 57.4 | 41.0 | 1.6 |
| Alcona | 34.5 | 2 989 | 26.6 | 19.4 | 3.1 | 8.4 | 10.7 | 10.3 | 890 | 28 | 20 | 297 | 45.1 | 53.0 | 1.9 |
| Alger | 31.5 | 3 274 | 39.9 | 1.6 | 3.4 | 0.0 | 25.4 | 11.9 | 1 239 | 89 | 18 | 783 | 52.0 | 46.1 | 1.9 |
| Allegan | 374.0 | 3 317 | 60.4 | 6.4 | 3.7 | 3.3 | 5.9 | 1 005.4 | 8 917 | 171 | 206 | 4 817 | 43.7 | 54.4 | 1.9 |
| Alpena | 213.9 | 7 200 | 30.4 | 50.1 | 2.0 | 0.3 | 4.6 | 47.9 | 1 613 | 118 | 57 | 2 808 | 51.1 | 47.2 | 1.7 |
| Antrim | 90.7 | 3 733 | 43.8 | 4.5 | 4.3 | 11.2 | 10.0 | 54.1 | 2 227 | 69 | 43 | 1 090 | 43.9 | 54.2 | 1.9 |
| Arenac | 45.8 | 2 755 | 53.4 | 1.1 | 2.8 | 0.9 | 13.8 | 41.2 | 2 483 | 48 | 29 | 731 | 51.1 | 46.8 | 2.0 |
| Baraga | 50.7 | 5 936 | 25.8 | 40.3 | 2.2 | 0.2 | 13.0 | 34.6 | 4 048 | 29 | 16 | 1 577 | 47.3 | 50.7 | 2.0 |
| Barry | 156.2 | 2 639 | 49.3 | 4.7 | 3.6 | 10.7 | 7.7 | 204.6 | 3 458 | 85 | 108 | 1 936 | 44.0 | 53.8 | 2.2 |
| Bay | 497.3 | 4 625 | 48.5 | 16.6 | 3.8 | 4.2 | 5.0 | 312.7 | 2 909 | 259 | 236 | 5 555 | 56.7 | 41.4 | 1.8 |
| Benzie | 57.5 | 3 281 | 38.6 | 6.2 | 2.9 | 10.2 | 11.1 | 35.4 | 2 021 | 34 | 48 | 606 | 52.9 | 45.5 | 1.7 |
| Berrien | 592.1 | 3 710 | 53.6 | 7.8 | 5.6 | 1.1 | 4.9 | 334.7 | 2 098 | 332 | 312 | 8 674 | 52.0 | 46.5 | 1.5 |
| Branch | 209.8 | 4 542 | 39.7 | 33.3 | 2.2 | 4.2 | 6.2 | 97.1 | 2 102 | 78 | 83 | 2 895 | 46.0 | 52.1 | 1.8 |
| Calhoun | 649.8 | 4 756 | 50.9 | 14.2 | 3.9 | 2.4 | 4.3 | 580.6 | 4 250 | 2 890 | 310 | 7 418 | 53.8 | 44.5 | 1.7 |
| Cass | 182.7 | 3 614 | 55.8 | 6.5 | 3.0 | 3.9 | 4.6 | 159.1 | 3 147 | 78 | 96 | 2 076 | 51.3 | 47.1 | 1.6 |
| Charlevoix | 143.2 | 5 468 | 44.2 | 14.7 | 2.2 | 7.6 | 6.8 | 92.8 | 3 546 | 50 | 69 | 1 590 | 47.4 | 50.9 | 1.7 |
| Cheboygan | 81.2 | 3 035 | 55.6 | 2.1 | 3.5 | 1.5 | 12.4 | 62.7 | 2 342 | 54 | 114 | 968 | 48.3 | 49.8 | 1.9 |
| Chippewa | 134.1 | 3 444 | 43.3 | 9.1 | 2.8 | 0.5 | 12.3 | 132.6 | 3 408 | 471 | 233 | 6 561 | 49.0 | 49.5 | 1.5 |
| Clare | 126.1 | 4 109 | 68.2 | 0.4 | 2.0 | 0.6 | 6.8 | 83.9 | 2 734 | 75 | 57 | 1 606 | 51.5 | 46.6 | 1.9 |
| Clinton | 195.8 | 2 807 | 53.0 | 2.1 | 3.8 | 0.8 | 9.6 | 260.0 | 3 727 | 141 | 217 | 1 925 | 49.5 | 48.8 | 1.6 |
| Crawford | 40.4 | 2 777 | 43.2 | 0.3 | 5.5 | 1.3 | 13.4 | 23.8 | 1 638 | 133 | 26 | 602 | 47.9 | 49.6 | 2.5 |
| Delta | 142.5 | 3 814 | 59.9 | 3.3 | 1.7 | 1.4 | 8.3 | 86.8 | 2 323 | 204 | 68 | 1 936 | 52.3 | 46.0 | 1.7 |
| Dickinson | 173.6 | 6 444 | 27.1 | 46.3 | 1.8 | 0.2 | 5.1 | 151.1 | 5 610 | 819 | 55 | 2 017 | 45.0 | 53.0 | 2.0 |
| Eaton | 342.3 | 3 187 | 52.7 | 3.0 | 4.4 | 4.1 | 6.1 | 470.1 | 4 377 | 197 | 216 | 5 399 | 53.4 | 45.0 | 1.7 |
| Emmet | 229.2 | 6 865 | 28.7 | 36.9 | 1.5 | 5.1 | 4.7 | 191.8 | 5 745 | 101 | 62 | 2 529 | 46.9 | 51.3 | 1.8 |
| Genesee | 2 071.2 | 4 764 | 47.7 | 24.0 | 4.0 | 0.9 | 3.3 | 1 026.1 | 2 360 | 1 282 | 780 | 21 383 | 65.5 | 32.9 | 1.6 |
| Gladwin | 59.2 | 2 251 | 50.6 | 1.6 | 3.5 | 0.5 | 12.5 | 34.3 | 1 305 | 54 | 48 | 804 | 49.8 | 48.3 | 2.0 |
| Gogebic | 80.1 | 4 919 | 37.4 | 11.0 | 3.2 | 10.0 | 10.1 | 57.9 | 3 556 | 176 | 30 | 1 489 | 57.6 | 40.3 | 2.1 |
| Grand Traverse | 461.5 | 5 399 | 47.5 | 15.1 | 2.6 | 5.5 | 3.1 | 515.1 | 6 026 | 490 | 294 | 5 727 | 47.7 | 50.7 | 1.6 |
| Gratiot | 156.9 | 3 724 | 61.6 | 6.5 | 2.8 | 1.3 | 6.6 | 101.2 | 2 401 | 82 | 78 | 2 333 | 51.3 | 46.9 | 1.8 |
| Hillsdale | 135.2 | 2 889 | 52.2 | 0.7 | 3.3 | 10.2 | 8.0 | 159.7 | 3 414 | 114 | 86 | 2 227 | 42.9 | 54.9 | 2.3 |
| Houghton | 131.0 | 3 722 | 42.5 | 5.2 | 1.7 | 10.4 | 7.9 | 99.8 | 2 836 | 179 | 102 | 4 480 | 46.8 | 50.7 | 2.5 |
| Huron | 151.3 | 4 546 | 41.4 | 8.9 | 2.7 | 5.7 | 17.2 | 138.5 | 4 161 | 95 | 74 | 1 695 | 48.8 | 49.2 | 1.9 |
| Ingham | 1 470.4 | 5 265 | 50.4 | 10.0 | 4.6 | 1.8 | 3.4 | 1 557.2 | 5 575 | 1 816 | 666 | 46 877 | 65.9 | 32.6 | 1.6 |
| Ionia | 216.9 | 3 386 | 59.5 | 5.9 | 2.3 | 0.6 | 9.2 | 254.2 | 3 969 | 114 | 118 | 3 511 | 46.0 | 51.8 | 2.2 |
| Iosco | 109.6 | 4 173 | 45.6 | 14.0 | 1.9 | 6.4 | 8.3 | 94.1 | 3 583 | 113 | 71 | 1 495 | 51.5 | 46.4 | 2.1 |
| Iron | 60.7 | 4 997 | 26.3 | 4.3 | 2.7 | 25.2 | 9.8 | 56.4 | 4 645 | 39 | 22 | 927 | 50.0 | 47.8 | 2.2 |
| Isabella | 209.4 | 3 139 | 28.6 | 35.2 | 3.0 | 4.5 | 6.3 | 141.0 | 2 114 | 179 | 135 | 10 953 | 58.8 | 39.6 | 1.6 |
| Jackson | 646.7 | 3 968 | 55.8 | 6.7 | 2.6 | 3.5 | 7.1 | 487.5 | 2 991 | 344 | 295 | 8 596 | 50.3 | 47.9 | 1.8 |
| Kalamazoo | 908.5 | 3 703 | 50.4 | 13.0 | 7.3 | 1.0 | 5.0 | 1 057.9 | 4 312 | 849 | 471 | 13 610 | 58.9 | 39.4 | 1.7 |
| Kalkaska | 54.7 | 3 183 | 26.5 | 36.6 | 4.9 | 1.1 | 10.3 | 19.1 | 1 112 | 25 | 32 | 858 | 44.5 | 53.3 | 2.3 |
| Kent | 2 513.5 | 4 159 | 54.9 | 5.5 | 4.1 | 1.5 | 4.5 | 3 556.9 | 5 886 | 2 933 | 1 192 | 22 257 | 49.4 | 48.9 | 1.6 |

1. Based on the resident population estimated as of July 1 of the year shown.   2. © 2013 Election Data Services, Inc. All rights reserved.

| STATE/ County code | CBSA code[1] | County type[2] | STATE County | Land area,[3] (sq km) 2010 | Population 2012 | | | Population characteristics[6], 2011 | | | | | | | | | | |
|---|---|---|---|---|---|---|---|---|---|---|---|---|---|---|---|---|---|---|
| | | | | | | | | Race alone or in combination, not Hispanic or Latino (percent) | | | | | Age (percent) | | | | | |
| | | | | | Total persons | Rank | Per square kilometer | White | Black | American Indian, Alaska Native | Asian and Pacific Islander | Percent Hispanic or Latino[4] | Under 5 years | 5 to 17 years | 18 to 24 years | 25 to 34 years | 35 to 44 years | 45 to 54 years |
| | | | | 1 | 2 | 3 | 4 | 5 | 6 | 7 | 8 | 9 | 10 | 11 | 12 | 13 | 14 | 15 |
| | | | MICHIGAN—Cont'd | | | | | | | | | | | | | | | |
| 26 083 | 26340 | 9 | Keweenaw | 1 399 | 2 215 | 3 036 | 1.6 | 98.8 | 0.6 | 0.6 | 0.2 | 0.7 | 5.0 | 13.6 | 5.2 | 7.5 | 9.2 | 14.3 |
| 26 085 | ... | 8 | Lake | 1 469 | 11 498 | 2 328 | 7.8 | 87.5 | 10.4 | 1.6 | 0.6 | 2.3 | 4.3 | 13.4 | 5.4 | 8.3 | 10.2 | 15.7 |
| 26 087 | 19820 | 1 | Lapeer | 1 665 | 88 173 | 647 | 53.0 | 93.8 | 1.4 | 1.0 | 0.7 | 4.2 | 5.0 | 18.5 | 7.9 | 9.7 | 13.1 | 17.4 |
| 26 089 | 45900 | 9 | Leelanau | 899 | 21 607 | 1 749 | 24.0 | 92.0 | 0.8 | 3.7 | 0.9 | 3.8 | 4.0 | 14.5 | 6.2 | 7.2 | 9.1 | 15.2 |
| 26 091 | 10300 | 4 | Lenawee | 1 941 | 98 987 | 593 | 51.0 | 88.9 | 3.3 | 0.9 | 0.8 | 7.6 | 5.7 | 17.1 | 9.5 | 11.1 | 12.7 | 15.0 |
| 26 093 | 19820 | 1 | Livingston | 1 464 | 182 838 | 345 | 124.9 | 96.1 | 0.8 | 0.9 | 1.2 | 2.0 | 5.2 | 19.6 | 7.3 | 9.8 | 13.7 | 17.8 |
| 26 095 | ... | 7 | Luce | 2 329 | 6 522 | 2 721 | 2.8 | 82.2 | 12.2 | 6.4 | 0.9 | 1.3 | 4.6 | 12.8 | 7.0 | 13.5 | 14.0 | 15.5 |
| 26 097 | ... | 7 | Mackinac | 2 646 | 11 137 | 2 350 | 4.2 | 80.1 | 1.6 | 21.2 | 0.6 | 1.4 | 4.1 | 14.2 | 5.8 | 8.3 | 10.7 | 16.0 |
| 26 099 | 19820 | 1 | Macomb | 1 241 | 847 383 | 62 | 682.8 | 85.0 | 9.9 | 0.9 | 3.8 | 2.4 | 5.6 | 17.0 | 8.4 | 12.1 | 13.6 | 15.7 |
| 26 101 | ... | 7 | Manistee | 1 404 | 24 672 | 1 618 | 17.6 | 91.7 | 3.7 | 2.9 | 0.8 | 2.7 | 4.3 | 14.4 | 7.1 | 9.8 | 10.8 | 15.4 |
| 26 103 | 32100 | 5 | Marquette | 4 684 | 67 906 | 782 | 14.5 | 94.6 | 2.3 | 2.8 | 1.0 | 1.2 | 5.1 | 13.2 | 15.4 | 12.3 | 10.6 | 13.8 |
| 26 105 | ... | 7 | Mason | 1 282 | 28 680 | 1 460 | 22.4 | 94.0 | 1.2 | 1.6 | 0.7 | 4.0 | 5.5 | 15.6 | 7.5 | 9.8 | 10.8 | 15.5 |
| 26 107 | 13660 | 6 | Mecosta | 1 438 | 43 318 | 1 102 | 30.1 | 93.5 | 4.0 | 1.4 | 1.3 | 1.9 | 5.0 | 14.5 | 22.0 | 9.7 | 9.2 | 12.0 |
| 26 109 | 31940 | 7 | Menominee | 2 704 | 23 815 | 1 653 | 8.8 | 95.3 | 0.8 | 3.3 | 0.6 | 1.3 | 4.7 | 15.8 | 6.5 | 9.6 | 10.7 | 16.5 |
| 26 111 | 33220 | 4 | Midland | 1 337 | 83 822 | 667 | 62.7 | 94.0 | 1.8 | 0.9 | 2.5 | 2.1 | 5.4 | 17.6 | 9.3 | 11.2 | 12.4 | 16.0 |
| 26 113 | 15620 | 9 | Missaukee | 1 463 | 15 031 | 2 104 | 10.3 | 96.5 | 0.8 | 1.2 | 0.6 | 2.2 | 6.0 | 17.8 | 7.3 | 10.6 | 11.0 | 15.5 |
| 26 115 | 33780 | 3 | Monroe | 1 423 | 151 048 | 419 | 106.1 | 93.8 | 2.9 | 0.8 | 0.9 | 3.1 | 5.7 | 18.0 | 8.4 | 10.9 | 12.8 | 16.3 |
| 26 117 | ... | 6 | Montcalm | 1 827 | 63 097 | 826 | 34.5 | 93.4 | 3.0 | 1.0 | 0.8 | 3.1 | 5.7 | 17.9 | 8.2 | 12.3 | 13.1 | 15.4 |
| 26 119 | ... | 9 | Montmorency | 1 416 | 9 476 | 2 473 | 6.7 | 97.9 | 0.7 | 1.3 | 0.4 | 1.0 | 3.8 | 12.6 | 5.2 | 7.8 | 8.7 | 14.8 |
| 26 121 | 34740 | 3 | Muskegon | 1 293 | 170 182 | 365 | 131.6 | 79.3 | 15.6 | 1.6 | 1.0 | 4.9 | 6.5 | 17.9 | 9.1 | 12.4 | 12.2 | 14.9 |
| 26 123 | 24340 | 2 | Newaygo | 2 106 | 47 959 | 1 014 | 22.8 | 92.2 | 1.7 | 1.5 | 0.7 | 5.5 | 6.1 | 18.3 | 8.1 | 10.4 | 11.6 | 15.7 |
| 26 125 | 19820 | 1 | Oakland | 2 247 | 1 220 657 | 32 | 543.2 | 76.3 | 14.7 | 0.8 | 6.6 | 3.6 | 5.6 | 17.4 | 7.7 | 12.0 | 13.8 | 16.2 |
| 26 127 | ... | 8 | Oceana | 1 326 | 26 310 | 1 549 | 19.8 | 84.3 | 1.0 | 1.6 | 0.5 | 14.0 | 6.5 | 18.2 | 7.5 | 10.2 | 11.0 | 14.4 |
| 26 129 | ... | 9 | Ogemaw | 1 459 | 21 437 | 1 758 | 14.7 | 97.0 | 0.6 | 1.5 | 0.6 | 1.5 | 4.6 | 15.0 | 6.9 | 9.1 | 10.1 | 15.1 |
| 26 131 | ... | 9 | Ontonagon | 3 396 | 6 413 | 2 730 | 1.9 | 97.4 | 0.6 | 1.8 | 0.4 | 1.0 | 3.3 | 11.8 | 4.1 | 6.7 | 9.8 | 17.1 |
| 26 133 | ... | 7 | Osceola | 1 467 | 23 276 | 1 676 | 15.9 | 96.8 | 1.4 | 1.4 | 0.5 | 1.6 | 5.9 | 18.5 | 7.4 | 10.3 | 11.1 | 15.1 |
| 26 135 | ... | 9 | Oscoda | 1 465 | 8 592 | 2 557 | 5.9 | 97.9 | 0.6 | 1.2 | 0.5 | 1.1 | 5.2 | 14.6 | 6.6 | 8.0 | 9.1 | 15.5 |
| 26 137 | ... | 3 | Otsego | 1 334 | 24 020 | 1 643 | 18.0 | 96.9 | 0.9 | 1.5 | 0.8 | 1.3 | 5.7 | 16.6 | 7.8 | 9.8 | 11.9 | 16.1 |
| 26 139 | 26100 | 3 | Ottawa | 1 459 | 269 099 | 246 | 184.4 | 86.7 | 2.1 | 0.7 | 3.1 | 8.8 | 6.6 | 19.0 | 12.7 | 11.9 | 12.3 | 14.0 |
| 26 141 | ... | 7 | Presque Isle | 1 706 | 13 129 | 2 233 | 7.7 | 97.6 | 0.8 | 1.1 | 0.5 | 0.9 | 3.8 | 13.1 | 5.3 | 7.7 | 9.1 | 15.5 |
| 26 143 | ... | 7 | Roscommon | 1 346 | 24 106 | 1 638 | 17.9 | 97.2 | 0.8 | 1.3 | 0.6 | 1.2 | 3.8 | 11.7 | 5.5 | 7.4 | 8.7 | 14.6 |
| 26 145 | 40980 | 3 | Saginaw | 2 072 | 198 353 | 323 | 95.7 | 72.0 | 19.6 | 0.8 | 1.5 | 7.8 | 5.9 | 17.2 | 10.6 | 11.1 | 11.7 | 14.4 |
| 26 147 | 19820 | 1 | St. Clair | 1 868 | 160 644 | 391 | 86.0 | 93.6 | 3.3 | 1.0 | 0.9 | 2.9 | 5.5 | 17.6 | 8.1 | 10.3 | 12.8 | 16.5 |
| 26 149 | 44780 | 4 | St. Joseph | 1 297 | 60 796 | 851 | 46.9 | 89.4 | 3.5 | 1.1 | 1.0 | 6.8 | 6.8 | 18.7 | 8.1 | 11.8 | 11.8 | 14.4 |
| 26 151 | ... | 6 | Sanilac | 2 493 | 42 268 | 1 126 | 17.0 | 95.4 | 0.8 | 0.9 | 0.5 | 3.4 | 5.6 | 17.5 | 7.3 | 10.0 | 11.6 | 15.6 |
| 26 153 | ... | 7 | Schoolcraft | 3 034 | 8 343 | 2 576 | 2.7 | 90.0 | 0.8 | 11.0 | 0.5 | 0.9 | 4.6 | 15.1 | 6.0 | 8.1 | 11.2 | 15.8 |
| 26 155 | 37020 | 4 | Shiawassee | 1 374 | 69 232 | 768 | 50.4 | 96.0 | 0.9 | 1.1 | 0.6 | 2.5 | 5.4 | 18.1 | 8.7 | 10.9 | 12.7 | 15.9 |
| 26 157 | ... | 6 | Tuscola | 2 080 | 54 662 | 915 | 26.3 | 95.1 | 1.5 | 1.0 | 0.5 | 2.9 | 5.5 | 17.4 | 8.0 | 10.6 | 12.0 | 15.7 |
| 26 159 | 28020 | 2 | Van Buren | 1 573 | 75 454 | 725 | 48.0 | 84.1 | 5.1 | 1.6 | 0.9 | 10.5 | 6.4 | 18.7 | 7.9 | 11.1 | 12.2 | 15.4 |
| 26 161 | 11460 | 2 | Washtenaw | 1 828 | 350 946 | 189 | 192.0 | 74.4 | 14.1 | 1.0 | 9.4 | 4.2 | 5.3 | 14.8 | 18.4 | 13.8 | 12.3 | 13.2 |
| 26 163 | 19820 | 1 | Wayne | 1 585 | 1 792 365 | 18 | 1 130.8 | 51.4 | 41.1 | 1.0 | 3.3 | 5.4 | 6.5 | 18.4 | 9.9 | 12.1 | 13.1 | 14.6 |
| 26 165 | 15620 | 7 | Wexford | 1 463 | 32 608 | 1 369 | 22.3 | 96.3 | 1.1 | 1.2 | 1.0 | 1.7 | 6.4 | 17.2 | 7.5 | 11.5 | 11.9 | 15.2 |
| 27 000 | ... | X | **MINNESOTA** | 206 232 | 5 379 139 | X | 26.1 | 84.6 | 6.1 | 1.7 | 4.8 | 4.9 | 6.6 | 17.3 | 9.4 | 13.7 | 12.5 | 15.0 |
| 27 001 | ... | 8 | Aitkin | 4 718 | 15 927 | 2 051 | 3.4 | 95.9 | 0.7 | 3.1 | 0.4 | 1.1 | 4.6 | 13.0 | 5.1 | 7.8 | 8.7 | 15.0 |
| 27 003 | 33460 | 1 | Anoka | 1 096 | 336 414 | 194 | 306.9 | 87.2 | 5.3 | 1.3 | 4.8 | 3.8 | 6.6 | 18.9 | 8.0 | 13.2 | 14.2 | 16.8 |
| 27 005 | ... | 6 | Becker | 3 406 | 33 000 | 1 354 | 9.7 | 90.3 | 0.8 | 9.7 | 0.8 | 1.4 | 6.5 | 17.8 | 6.8 | 11.1 | 10.5 | 14.4 |
| 27 007 | 13420 | 7 | Beltrami | 6 488 | 45 375 | 1 060 | 7.0 | 77.2 | 1.3 | 21.4 | 1.3 | 1.8 | 7.6 | 17.6 | 13.9 | 12.6 | 9.9 | 12.8 |
| 27 009 | 41060 | 3 | Benton | 1 057 | 38 865 | 1 200 | 36.8 | 94.5 | 2.8 | 0.9 | 1.6 | 1.8 | 7.1 | 17.5 | 10.3 | 16.0 | 12.6 | 13.8 |
| 27 011 | ... | 9 | Big Stone | 1 292 | 5 164 | 2 829 | 4.0 | 98.3 | 0.5 | 0.8 | 0.4 | 0.9 | 5.8 | 15.1 | 5.9 | 9.5 | 8.6 | 15.3 |
| 27 013 | 31860 | 5 | Blue Earth | 1 937 | 65 091 | 809 | 33.6 | 92.1 | 3.3 | 0.7 | 2.8 | 2.6 | 5.8 | 13.3 | 23.2 | 13.8 | 9.9 | 11.3 |
| 27 015 | 35580 | 7 | Brown | 1 583 | 25 425 | 1 592 | 16.1 | 95.6 | 0.5 | 0.3 | 0.8 | 3.3 | 5.9 | 15.8 | 9.2 | 10.9 | 10.0 | 15.5 |
| 27 017 | 20260 | 2 | Carlton | 2 231 | 35 348 | 1 294 | 15.8 | 90.9 | 1.9 | 7.0 | 1.0 | 1.5 | 6.0 | 17.1 | 7.7 | 12.2 | 12.6 | 15.8 |
| 27 019 | 33460 | 1 | Carver | 918 | 93 707 | 617 | 102.1 | 91.6 | 1.9 | 0.6 | 3.4 | 4.0 | 7.1 | 22.4 | 6.6 | 11.9 | 15.2 | 17.5 |
| 27 021 | 14660 | 8 | Cass | 5 236 | 28 357 | 1 476 | 5.4 | 87.3 | 0.7 | 12.1 | 0.7 | 1.4 | 5.9 | 15.2 | 6.4 | 9.3 | 9.9 | 15.0 |
| 27 023 | ... | 7 | Chippewa | 1 505 | 12 135 | 2 291 | 8.1 | 91.8 | 1.0 | 1.4 | 1.6 | 5.3 | 6.5 | 16.8 | 7.1 | 11.2 | 10.7 | 14.3 |
| 27 025 | 33460 | 1 | Chisago | 1 074 | 53 452 | 931 | 49.8 | 95.5 | 1.6 | 1.1 | 1.3 | 1.7 | 5.8 | 19.2 | 7.4 | 11.7 | 14.4 | 17.4 |
| 27 027 | 22020 | 3 | Clay | 2 707 | 60 155 | 862 | 22.2 | 92.1 | 1.9 | 2.0 | 2.2 | 3.6 | 6.7 | 16.2 | 18.0 | 13.5 | 10.9 | 12.3 |
| 27 029 | ... | 8 | Clearwater | 2 587 | 8 703 | 2 546 | 3.4 | 89.1 | 0.9 | 10.6 | 0.8 | 1.5 | 6.8 | 17.7 | 7.0 | 10.5 | 10.7 | 14.5 |
| 27 031 | ... | 9 | Cook | 3 761 | 5 185 | 2 828 | 1.4 | 89.4 | 0.9 | 9.5 | 1.1 | 1.2 | 4.2 | 12.7 | 5.4 | 9.5 | 10.9 | 16.3 |
| 27 033 | ... | 7 | Cottonwood | 1 654 | 11 597 | 2 323 | 7.0 | 89.6 | 1.1 | 0.6 | 3.0 | 6.6 | 6.0 | 17.7 | 6.8 | 9.9 | 10.5 | 13.9 |
| 27 035 | 14660 | 5 | Crow Wing | 2 588 | 62 882 | 829 | 24.3 | 97.0 | 0.9 | 1.4 | 0.8 | 1.1 | 6.4 | 16.3 | 7.5 | 11.4 | 10.7 | 14.6 |
| 27 037 | 33460 | 1 | Dakota | 1 456 | 405 088 | 168 | 278.2 | 84.1 | 5.8 | 0.9 | 5.4 | 6.1 | 6.8 | 19.0 | 7.7 | 13.7 | 13.9 | 16.4 |
| 27 039 | 40340 | 3 | Dodge | 1 138 | 20 231 | 1 830 | 17.8 | 94.0 | 0.8 | 0.5 | 0.9 | 4.7 | 7.0 | 21.4 | 7.0 | 12.1 | 13.6 | 15.2 |
| 27 041 | 10820 | 7 | Douglas | 1 651 | 36 415 | 1 265 | 22.1 | 97.7 | 0.7 | 0.6 | 0.8 | 1.0 | 5.8 | 15.7 | 8.2 | 11.6 | 10.6 | 14.4 |
| 27 043 | ... | 7 | Faribault | 1 845 | 14 263 | 2 154 | 7.7 | 93.3 | 0.6 | 0.6 | 0.6 | 5.6 | 5.8 | 16.2 | 6.5 | 10.5 | 9.8 | 14.9 |

1. CBSA = Core Based Statistical Area. See Appendix A for explanation. See Appendix B for list of metropolitan areas with component counties. 2. County type code from the Economic Research Service of USDA Rural-Urban Continuum Codes. See Appendix A for definition. 3. Dry land or land partially or temporarily covered by water. 4. May be of any race.

| STATE County | Age (percent) (cont.) | | | | Population change and components of change, 2000–2012 | | | | | | | | Households, 2010 | | | | |
|---|---|---|---|---|---|---|---|---|---|---|---|---|---|---|---|---|---|
| | | | | | Total persons | | Percent change | | Components of change, 2010–2012 | | | | | | | Percent | |
| | 55 to 64 years | 65 to 74 years | 75 years and over | Percent female | 2000 | 2010 | 2000–2010 | 2010–2012 | Births | Deaths | Net migration | Number | Percent change, 2000–2010 | Persons per house-hold | Female family house-holder[1] | One per-son |
| | 16 | 17 | 18 | 19 | 20 | 21 | 22 | 23 | 24 | 25 | 26 | 27 | 28 | 29 | 30 | 31 |
| MICHIGAN—Cont'd | | | | | | | | | | | | | | | | |
| Keweenaw | 20.3 | 15.5 | 9.3 | 48.9 | 2 301 | 2 156 | -6.3 | 2.7 | 47 | 36 | 21 | 1 013 | 1.5 | 2.12 | 4.9 | 34.2 |
| Lake | 18.5 | 15.3 | 9.0 | 49.0 | 11 333 | 11 539 | 1.8 | -0.4 | 223 | 324 | 62 | 5 158 | 9.7 | 2.16 | 9.2 | 32.9 |
| Lapeer | 14.5 | 8.4 | 5.5 | 49.6 | 87 904 | 88 319 | 0.5 | -0.2 | 1 804 | 1 733 | -212 | 32 776 | 6.7 | 2.64 | 9.4 | 21.3 |
| Leelanau | 19.4 | 13.1 | 11.3 | 50.6 | 21 119 | 21 708 | 2.8 | -0.5 | 362 | 472 | -81 | 9 255 | 9.7 | 2.31 | 7.1 | 26.0 |
| Lenawee | 14.0 | 8.1 | 6.9 | 49.4 | 98 890 | 99 892 | 1.0 | -0.9 | 2 275 | 2 084 | -1 078 | 37 514 | 4.4 | 2.52 | 10.8 | 25.1 |
| Livingston | 14.1 | 7.5 | 4.9 | 50.0 | 156 951 | 180 967 | 15.3 | 1.0 | 3 655 | 2 811 | 859 | 67 380 | 21.7 | 2.67 | 8.2 | 20.1 |
| Luce | 14.2 | 10.5 | 7.7 | 42.3 | 7 024 | 6 631 | -5.6 | -1.6 | 124 | 170 | -59 | 2 412 | -2.8 | 2.25 | 9.3 | 31.4 |
| Mackinac | 18.2 | 12.9 | 9.8 | 49.4 | 11 943 | 11 113 | -6.9 | 0.2 | 172 | 295 | 140 | 5 024 | -0.8 | 2.19 | 8.1 | 31.0 |
| Macomb | 13.0 | 7.5 | 7.1 | 51.4 | 788 149 | 840 978 | 6.7 | 0.8 | 20 169 | 17 486 | 4 007 | 331 667 | 7.3 | 2.51 | 12.7 | 28.0 |
| Manistee | 17.2 | 11.6 | 9.4 | 48.2 | 24 527 | 24 733 | 0.8 | -0.2 | 434 | 660 | 174 | 10 308 | 4.5 | 2.27 | 9.3 | 29.9 |
| Marquette | 14.7 | 7.9 | 7.0 | 49.5 | 64 634 | 67 077 | 3.8 | 1.2 | 1 544 | 1 395 | 705 | 27 538 | 6.9 | 2.26 | 8.6 | 30.4 |
| Mason | 16.1 | 11.0 | 8.6 | 50.7 | 28 274 | 28 705 | 1.5 | -0.1 | 666 | 686 | 11 | 11 940 | 4.7 | 2.37 | 9.8 | 28.3 |
| Mecosta | 12.2 | 8.9 | 6.4 | 49.7 | 40 553 | 42 798 | 5.5 | 1.2 | 980 | 770 | 332 | 16 101 | 8.0 | 2.45 | 9.6 | 25.8 |
| Menominee | 16.6 | 10.1 | 9.5 | 49.6 | 25 326 | 24 029 | -5.1 | -0.9 | 446 | 555 | -121 | 10 474 | -0.5 | 2.26 | 9.1 | 30.4 |
| Midland | 13.1 | 7.7 | 7.3 | 50.8 | 82 874 | 83 629 | 0.9 | 0.2 | 1 905 | 1 508 | -169 | 33 437 | 5.3 | 2.46 | 8.9 | 25.8 |
| Missaukee | 14.3 | 10.0 | 7.6 | 49.3 | 14 478 | 14 849 | 2.6 | 1.2 | 385 | 358 | 153 | 5 843 | 7.2 | 2.51 | 8.3 | 24.8 |
| Monroe | 14.1 | 7.6 | 6.2 | 50.7 | 145 945 | 152 021 | 4.2 | -0.6 | 3 641 | 2 856 | -1 772 | 58 230 | 8.3 | 2.59 | 11.1 | 23.5 |
| Montcalm | 12.9 | 8.2 | 6.3 | 48.3 | 61 266 | 63 342 | 3.4 | -0.4 | 1 596 | 1 238 | -584 | 23 432 | 6.1 | 2.57 | 11.4 | 23.8 |
| Montmorency | 19.5 | 15.5 | 12.0 | 49.4 | 10 315 | 9 765 | -5.3 | -3.0 | 155 | 383 | -66 | 4 416 | -0.9 | 2.18 | 8.6 | 30.8 |
| Muskegon | 13.2 | 7.4 | 6.5 | 50.3 | 170 200 | 172 188 | 1.2 | -1.2 | 4 856 | 3 651 | -3 186 | 65 616 | 3.6 | 2.53 | 15.4 | 26.4 |
| Newaygo | 13.9 | 9.2 | 6.7 | 49.8 | 47 874 | 48 460 | 1.2 | -1.0 | 1 234 | 1 082 | -689 | 18 406 | 4.6 | 2.60 | 10.0 | 23.3 |
| Oakland | 13.7 | 7.3 | 6.3 | 51.5 | 1 194 156 | 1 202 362 | 0.7 | 1.5 | 29 222 | 21 720 | 11 085 | 483 698 | 2.7 | 2.46 | 11.1 | 28.6 |
| Oceana | 14.4 | 9.9 | 7.5 | 49.8 | 26 873 | 26 570 | -1.1 | -1.0 | 739 | 568 | -451 | 10 174 | 4.0 | 2.58 | 9.5 | 24.6 |
| Ogemaw | 16.6 | 13.1 | 9.4 | 50.4 | 21 645 | 21 699 | 0.2 | -1.2 | 422 | 636 | -32 | 9 283 | 5.0 | 2.31 | 10.0 | 28.3 |
| Ontonagon | 19.9 | 16.1 | 11.2 | 48.6 | 7 818 | 6 780 | -13.3 | -5.4 | 79 | 239 | -202 | 3 258 | -5.7 | 2.06 | 6.0 | 34.8 |
| Osceola | 14.4 | 9.8 | 7.4 | 50.0 | 23 197 | 23 528 | 1.4 | -1.1 | 595 | 506 | -350 | 9 222 | 4.1 | 2.50 | 9.7 | 25.4 |
| Oscoda | 17.6 | 13.5 | 9.9 | 49.7 | 9 418 | 8 640 | -8.3 | -0.6 | 175 | 285 | 61 | 3 772 | -3.8 | 2.27 | 7.7 | 30.0 |
| Otsego | 14.6 | 9.6 | 7.8 | 50.7 | 23 301 | 24 164 | 3.7 | -0.6 | 569 | 583 | -137 | 9 756 | 8.5 | 2.44 | 9.2 | 25.3 |
| Ottawa | 11.4 | 6.5 | 5.6 | 51.0 | 238 314 | 263 801 | 10.7 | 2.0 | 7 282 | 3 730 | 1 870 | 93 775 | 14.8 | 2.73 | 8.4 | 20.9 |
| Presque Isle | 18.9 | 13.8 | 12.7 | 49.7 | 14 411 | 13 376 | -7.2 | -1.8 | 204 | 440 | -14 | 5 982 | -2.8 | 2.20 | 6.5 | 29.8 |
| Roscommon | 19.7 | 16.3 | 12.2 | 50.1 | 25 469 | 24 449 | -4.0 | -1.4 | 375 | 863 | 143 | 11 433 | 1.6 | 2.11 | 8.0 | 32.2 |
| Saginaw | 13.6 | 8.2 | 7.4 | 51.6 | 210 039 | 200 169 | -4.7 | -0.9 | 5 204 | 4 476 | -2 473 | 79 011 | -1.8 | 2.44 | 16.0 | 28.2 |
| St. Clair | 14.1 | 8.3 | 6.8 | 50.4 | 164 235 | 163 040 | -0.7 | -1.5 | 3 696 | 3 611 | -2 472 | 63 841 | 2.8 | 2.52 | 11.4 | 25.5 |
| St. Joseph | 13.3 | 8.2 | 7.0 | 50.3 | 62 422 | 61 295 | -1.8 | -0.8 | 1 804 | 1 300 | -983 | 23 244 | -0.6 | 2.60 | 11.7 | 24.8 |
| Sanilac | 14.4 | 9.7 | 8.2 | 50.4 | 44 547 | 43 114 | -3.2 | -2.0 | 1 019 | 1 057 | -797 | 17 132 | 1.5 | 2.48 | 9.8 | 26.4 |
| Schoolcraft | 17.7 | 11.3 | 10.3 | 50.4 | 8 903 | 8 485 | -4.7 | -1.7 | 146 | 242 | -53 | 3 759 | 4.2 | 2.22 | 8.1 | 30.9 |
| Shiawassee | 13.7 | 8.2 | 6.5 | 50.5 | 71 687 | 70 648 | -1.4 | -2.0 | 1 545 | 1 533 | -1 436 | 27 481 | 2.2 | 2.54 | 11.6 | 24.2 |
| Tuscola | 14.3 | 9.4 | 7.0 | 49.9 | 58 266 | 55 729 | -4.4 | -1.9 | 1 192 | 1 326 | -929 | 21 590 | 0.6 | 2.52 | 9.9 | 24.0 |
| Van Buren | 14.1 | 8.1 | 6.1 | 50.6 | 76 263 | 76 258 | 0.0 | -1.1 | 2 193 | 1 582 | -1 399 | 28 928 | 3.4 | 2.61 | 12.1 | 24.0 |
| Washtenaw | 11.6 | 5.9 | 4.6 | 50.7 | 322 895 | 344 791 | 6.8 | 1.8 | 8 347 | 4 522 | 2 389 | 137 193 | 9.5 | 2.38 | 9.8 | 30.6 |
| Wayne | 12.6 | 6.6 | 6.2 | 52.1 | 2 061 162 | 1 820 584 | -11.7 | -1.5 | 52 969 | 39 989 | -42 025 | 702 749 | -8.5 | 2.56 | 20.7 | 30.7 |
| Wexford | 14.0 | 8.9 | 7.4 | 50.1 | 30 484 | 32 735 | 7.4 | -0.4 | 882 | 733 | -275 | 13 021 | 10.1 | 2.48 | 11.3 | 25.4 |
| MINNESOTA | 12.4 | 6.9 | 6.3 | 50.3 | 4 919 479 | 5 303 925 | 7.8 | 1.4 | 151 960 | 88 548 | 12 156 | 2 087 227 | 10.1 | 2.48 | 9.5 | 28.0 |
| Aitkin | 18.0 | 16.5 | 11.2 | 49.3 | 15 301 | 16 202 | 5.9 | -1.7 | 282 | 474 | -100 | 7 299 | 9.9 | 2.18 | 6.6 | 31.0 |
| Anoka | 12.1 | 6.1 | 4.0 | 50.0 | 298 084 | 330 844 | 11.0 | 1.7 | 9 089 | 3 682 | 215 | 121 227 | 13.9 | 2.70 | 10.6 | 21.3 |
| Becker | 15.2 | 9.5 | 8.1 | 49.7 | 30 000 | 32 504 | 8.3 | 1.5 | 952 | 812 | 339 | 13 224 | 11.7 | 2.42 | 8.9 | 27.3 |
| Beltrami | 12.4 | 7.0 | 6.2 | 50.0 | 39 650 | 44 442 | 12.1 | 2.1 | 1 567 | 789 | 157 | 16 846 | 17.5 | 2.51 | 13.6 | 27.9 |
| Benton | 10.8 | 5.8 | 6.1 | 49.9 | 34 226 | 38 451 | 12.3 | 1.1 | 1 242 | 663 | -219 | 15 079 | 15.4 | 2.48 | 9.3 | 26.4 |
| Big Stone | 14.7 | 10.9 | 14.3 | 51.3 | 5 820 | 5 269 | -9.5 | -2.0 | 139 | 184 | -62 | 2 293 | -3.5 | 2.24 | 5.7 | 32.4 |
| Blue Earth | 10.5 | 5.8 | 6.2 | 49.7 | 55 941 | 64 013 | 14.4 | 1.7 | 1 672 | 1 040 | 469 | 24 445 | 16.1 | 2.43 | 8.2 | 27.5 |
| Brown | 13.5 | 8.5 | 10.7 | 50.2 | 26 911 | 25 893 | -3.8 | -1.8 | 616 | 650 | -422 | 10 782 | 1.7 | 2.30 | 7.3 | 31.1 |
| Carlton | 13.6 | 7.7 | 7.4 | 47.9 | 31 671 | 35 386 | 11.7 | -0.1 | 867 | 824 | -94 | 13 538 | 12.2 | 2.47 | 9.8 | 26.8 |
| Carver | 10.6 | 4.7 | 3.9 | 50.3 | 70 205 | 91 042 | 29.7 | 2.9 | 2 438 | 974 | 1 166 | 32 891 | 35.0 | 2.74 | 7.6 | 21.0 |
| Cass | 16.4 | 13.4 | 8.5 | 49.1 | 27 150 | 28 567 | 5.2 | -0.7 | 718 | 632 | 632 | 11 948 | 9.7 | 2.37 | 8.6 | 26.4 |
| Chippewa | 14.1 | 8.6 | 10.7 | 50.9 | 13 088 | 12 441 | -4.9 | -2.5 | 349 | 315 | -338 | 5 241 | -2.2 | 2.33 | 8.2 | 30.5 |
| Chisago | 11.8 | 7.0 | 5.4 | 48.4 | 41 101 | 53 887 | 31.1 | -0.8 | 1 262 | 810 | -887 | 19 470 | 34.7 | 2.68 | 7.9 | 20.3 |
| Clay | 10.5 | 5.7 | 6.2 | 50.6 | 51 229 | 58 999 | 15.2 | 2.0 | 1 737 | 934 | 362 | 22 279 | 19.3 | 2.48 | 9.3 | 27.0 |
| Clearwater | 14.0 | 10.0 | 8.9 | 49.8 | 8 423 | 8 695 | 3.2 | 0.1 | 241 | 197 | -42 | 3 527 | 5.9 | 2.43 | 8.8 | 28.6 |
| Cook | 19.5 | 12.8 | 8.6 | 50.5 | 5 168 | 5 176 | 0.2 | 0.2 | 112 | 108 | 7 | 2 494 | 6.1 | 2.05 | 6.4 | 34.6 |
| Cottonwood | 14.0 | 9.5 | 11.8 | 50.7 | 12 167 | 11 687 | -3.9 | -0.8 | 323 | 368 | -55 | 4 857 | -1.2 | 2.36 | 7.2 | 32.1 |
| Crow Wing | 14.3 | 10.5 | 8.5 | 50.1 | 55 099 | 62 500 | 13.4 | 0.6 | 1 672 | 1 373 | 116 | 26 033 | 17.0 | 2.37 | 8.8 | 27.6 |
| Dakota | 12.0 | 5.9 | 4.5 | 50.5 | 355 904 | 398 552 | 12.0 | 1.6 | 11 429 | 4 883 | -72 | 152 060 | 15.9 | 2.60 | 10.1 | 24.1 |
| Dodge | 11.0 | 6.8 | 6.0 | 50.0 | 17 731 | 20 087 | 13.3 | 0.7 | 588 | 292 | -151 | 7 460 | 16.2 | 2.67 | 7.7 | 22.2 |
| Douglas | 13.8 | 10.5 | 9.5 | 49.9 | 32 821 | 36 009 | 9.7 | 1.1 | 885 | 906 | 388 | 15 289 | 15.2 | 2.32 | 6.9 | 28.1 |
| Faribault | 14.5 | 10.0 | 11.7 | 50.3 | 16 181 | 14 553 | -10.1 | -2.0 | 337 | 393 | -239 | 6 236 | -6.3 | 2.28 | 8.1 | 31.0 |

1. No spouse present.

| STATE County | Persons in group quarters, 2010 | Daytime population, 2007–2011 Number | Employ-ment/resi-dence ratio | Births, 2011 Total | Rate[1] | Deaths, 2011 Number | Rate[1] | Persons under 65 with no health insurance, 2010 Number | Percent | Medicare, 2012 Eligible for Medicare | Enrolled in Medicare Advantage | Enrolled in a Medicare prescription drug plan | Serious crimes known to police,[2] 2011 Total Number | Rate[3] |
|---|---|---|---|---|---|---|---|---|---|---|---|---|---|---|
| | 32 | 33 | 34 | 35 | 36 | 37 | 38 | 39 | 40 | 41 | 42 | 43 | 44 | 45 |
| MICHIGAN—Cont'd | | | | | | | | | | | | | | |
| Keweenaw | 10 | 1 719 | 0.49 | 27 | 12.4 | 18 | 8.3 | 287 | 17.3 | 631 | 119 | 298 | 6 | 279 |
| Lake | 397 | 10 566 | 0.70 | 107 | 9.3 | 141 | 12.2 | 1 765 | 20.6 | 3 509 | 612 | 1 770 | 346 | 3 001 |
| Lapeer | 1 716 | 76 621 | 0.66 | 818 | 9.3 | 739 | 8.4 | 10 744 | 14.4 | 15 884 | 3 925 | 6 043 | 1 382 | 1 566 |
| Leelanau | 284 | 19 069 | 0.72 | 173 | 8.1 | 202 | 9.4 | 2 798 | 17.1 | 5 924 | 1 753 | 2 705 | 38 | 175 |
| Lenawee | 5 396 | 90 334 | 0.77 | 1 033 | 10.4 | 917 | 9.2 | 11 797 | 14.7 | 19 625 | 4 043 | 9 597 | 1 893 | 2 018 |
| Livingston | 1 152 | 150 338 | 0.64 | 1 603 | 8.8 | 1 213 | 6.7 | 14 639 | 9.4 | 28 539 | 8 421 | 11 418 | 2 393 | 1 323 |
| Luce | 1 211 | 6 912 | 1.11 | 56 | 8.5 | 86 | 13.1 | 740 | 17.0 | 1 508 | 238 | 634 | 159 | 2 400 |
| Mackinac | 95 | 11 440 | 1.05 | 74 | 6.7 | 126 | 11.4 | 1 875 | 21.7 | 3 044 | 603 | 1 274 | 457 | 4 115 |
| Macomb | 7 432 | 780 269 | 0.84 | 9 036 | 10.7 | 7 669 | 9.1 | 99 424 | 14.0 | 150 640 | 36 394 | 63 464 | 21 335 | 2 539 |
| Manistee | 1 349 | 24 586 | 0.97 | 199 | 8.1 | 289 | 11.7 | 3 007 | 16.2 | 6 444 | 1 375 | 3 119 | 340 | 1 376 |
| Marquette | 4 757 | 66 887 | 1.00 | 692 | 10.2 | 615 | 9.1 | 6 799 | 12.8 | 12 839 | 2 947 | 5 223 | 1 606 | 2 396 |
| Mason | 442 | 28 449 | 0.98 | 293 | 10.2 | 291 | 10.1 | 3 672 | 15.9 | 7 052 | 1 269 | 3 988 | 194 | 676 |
| Mecosta | 3 375 | 42 239 | 0.97 | 451 | 10.4 | 329 | 7.6 | 5 604 | 16.8 | 8 316 | 2 470 | 4 057 | 1 171 | 2 738 |
| Menominee | 382 | 21 764 | 0.77 | 205 | 8.6 | 237 | 9.9 | 3 004 | 15.5 | 5 604 | 1 657 | 2 600 | 246 | 1 063 |
| Midland | 1 272 | 87 367 | 1.10 | 843 | 10.0 | 670 | 8.0 | 7 911 | 11.3 | 15 457 | 2 466 | 5 775 | 986 | 1 180 |
| Missaukee | 194 | 12 830 | 0.65 | 173 | 11.6 | 157 | 10.5 | 2 146 | 17.5 | 3 235 | 579 | 1 612 | 146 | 984 |
| Monroe | 1 462 | 131 438 | 0.68 | 1 658 | 10.9 | 1 246 | 8.2 | 14 322 | 11.0 | 26 714 | 6 701 | 10 736 | 3 972 | 2 769 |
| Montcalm | 3 163 | 57 051 | 0.74 | 683 | 10.8 | 541 | 8.6 | 8 637 | 16.7 | 12 098 | 3 258 | 4 791 | 1 448 | 2 486 |
| Montmorency | 156 | 9 710 | 0.96 | 72 | 7.5 | 170 | 17.6 | 1 318 | 18.4 | 3 474 | 570 | 1 610 | 102 | 1 045 |
| Muskegon | 6 345 | 166 624 | 0.91 | 2 209 | 12.9 | 1 622 | 9.5 | 21 459 | 14.9 | 33 780 | 11 553 | 14 204 | 7 574 | 4 402 |
| Newaygo | 557 | 43 773 | 0.74 | 556 | 11.5 | 469 | 9.7 | 7 060 | 17.3 | 10 124 | 3 894 | 3 534 | 1 107 | 2 302 |
| Oakland | 12 496 | 1 286 605 | 1.15 | 13 022 | 10.8 | 9 463 | 7.8 | 125 062 | 12.2 | 203 115 | 53 634 | 91 827 | 24 837 | 2 067 |
| Oceana | 303 | 24 134 | 0.75 | 333 | 12.6 | 254 | 9.6 | 4 308 | 19.6 | 5 955 | 1 727 | 2 594 | 608 | 2 547 |
| Ogemaw | 244 | 21 849 | 1.01 | 184 | 8.5 | 275 | 12.7 | 3 045 | 18.0 | 6 251 | 801 | 3 057 | 599 | 2 848 |
| Ontonagon | 83 | 6 673 | 0.93 | 38 | 5.8 | 107 | 16.2 | 871 | 17.4 | 2 250 | 429 | 1 150 | 61 | 900 |
| Osceola | 455 | 22 565 | 0.88 | 276 | 11.7 | 226 | 9.6 | 3 112 | 16.0 | 5 343 | 1 211 | 2 562 | 587 | 2 497 |
| Oscoda | 65 | 8 258 | 0.80 | 79 | 9.2 | 114 | 13.2 | 1 397 | 21.0 | 2 662 | 387 | 1 309 | 301 | 3 487 |
| Otsego | 348 | 25 986 | 1.17 | 246 | 10.2 | 259 | 10.8 | 2 988 | 15.0 | 5 324 | 1 160 | 2 769 | 474 | 1 963 |
| Ottawa | 8 261 | 250 834 | 0.90 | 3 154 | 11.8 | 1 595 | 6.0 | 26 637 | 11.9 | 40 141 | 20 938 | 11 336 | 5 225 | 1 982 |
| Presque Isle | 230 | 12 443 | 0.77 | 90 | 6.8 | 189 | 14.4 | 1 710 | 17.4 | 4 168 | 610 | 2 106 | 149 | 1 115 |
| Roscommon | 277 | 24 421 | 0.96 | 172 | 7.0 | 369 | 15.1 | 3 126 | 17.7 | 8 827 | 1 455 | 4 066 | 487 | 1 993 |
| Saginaw | 7 116 | 211 417 | 1.13 | 2 362 | 11.9 | 1 980 | 9.9 | 23 415 | 14.3 | 40 535 | 9 390 | 16 059 | 6 452 | 3 226 |
| St. Clair | 1 999 | 147 550 | 0.75 | 1 705 | 10.5 | 1 572 | 9.7 | 19 766 | 14.3 | 31 294 | 6 957 | 13 934 | 3 969 | 2 436 |
| St. Joseph | 765 | 59 966 | 0.93 | 817 | 13.4 | 548 | 9.0 | 8 067 | 15.5 | 11 599 | 2 107 | 5 889 | 1 342 | 2 191 |
| Sanilac | 566 | 40 044 | 0.79 | 462 | 10.8 | 476 | 11.2 | 6 202 | 17.5 | 9 329 | 1 578 | 4 874 | 685 | 1 646 |
| Schoolcraft | 140 | 8 584 | 1.01 | 69 | 8.1 | 110 | 13.0 | 1 214 | 18.2 | 2 089 | 314 | 993 | 207 | 2 441 |
| Shiawassee | 821 | 60 293 | 0.64 | 693 | 9.9 | 676 | 9.7 | 8 153 | 13.6 | 13 611 | 3 326 | 5 591 | 1 379 | 1 970 |
| Tuscola | 1 235 | 48 522 | 0.66 | 546 | 9.9 | 605 | 10.9 | 6 889 | 14.9 | 11 789 | 2 258 | 4 994 | 829 | 1 605 |
| Van Buren | 877 | 68 528 | 0.76 | 1 002 | 13.2 | 707 | 9.3 | 11 582 | 17.7 | 14 375 | 3 558 | 6 662 | 1 943 | 2 550 |
| Washtenaw | 17 812 | 380 623 | 1.22 | 3 696 | 10.6 | 1 973 | 5.7 | 32 780 | 11.3 | 46 492 | 10 340 | 18 458 | 8 931 | 2 592 |
| Wayne | 23 849 | 1 894 635 | 1.07 | 23 853 | 13.2 | 17 647 | 9.8 | 275 614 | 17.5 | 302 061 | 76 890 | 126 749 | 93 363 | 5 132 |
| Wexford | 389 | 34 923 | 1.17 | 391 | 12.0 | 307 | 9.4 | 4 063 | 14.7 | 7 004 | 1 335 | 3 516 | 1 332 | 4 072 |
| MINNESOTA | 135 395 | 5 295 200 | 1.01 | 68 088 | 12.7 | 38 436 | 7.2 | 468 857 | 10.3 | 842 898 | 401 597 | 333 465 | 148 089 | 2 771 |
| Aitkin | 274 | 15 014 | 0.81 | 133 | 8.2 | 202 | 12.5 | 1 557 | 13.3 | 4 191 | 2 242 | 1 645 | 432 | 2 646 |
| Anoka | 3 009 | 271 871 | 0.66 | 4 123 | 12.4 | 1 535 | 4.6 | 29 059 | 9.8 | 43 947 | 24 369 | 12 734 | 11 089 | 3 326 |
| Becker | 458 | 31 274 | 0.93 | 427 | 13.0 | 362 | 11.0 | 3 300 | 12.3 | 7 212 | 3 479 | 3 285 | 551 | 1 682 |
| Beltrami | 2 079 | 45 098 | 1.04 | 692 | 15.3 | 323 | 7.1 | 5 456 | 14.6 | 7 302 | 2 669 | 3 867 | 1 675 | 3 740 |
| Benton | 1 048 | 35 126 | 0.84 | 557 | 14.4 | 288 | 7.4 | 3 441 | 10.2 | 5 427 | 2 772 | 2 286 | 712 | 1 838 |
| Big Stone | 137 | 5 269 | 0.99 | 66 | 12.6 | 85 | 16.2 | 451 | 11.5 | 1 416 | 584 | 732 | 66 | 1 243 |
| Blue Earth | 4 529 | 66 060 | 1.08 | 746 | 11.6 | 443 | 6.9 | 5 801 | 11.0 | 9 310 | 3 952 | 5 158 | 2 229 | 3 455 |
| Brown | 1 111 | 27 291 | 1.10 | 273 | 10.6 | 295 | 11.5 | 1 826 | 9.0 | 5 611 | 2 149 | 2 839 | 289 | 1 424 |
| Carlton | 1 984 | 32 853 | 0.86 | 388 | 10.9 | 363 | 10.2 | 3 322 | 11.5 | 6 621 | 2 958 | 3 036 | 940 | 2 636 |
| Carver | 836 | 79 981 | 0.79 | 1 136 | 12.3 | 418 | 4.5 | 6 100 | 7.4 | 9 853 | 5 319 | 3 372 | 1 096 | 1 195 |
| Cass | 223 | 27 261 | 0.89 | 312 | 11.0 | 275 | 9.7 | 3 260 | 14.4 | 8 101 | 3 680 | 3 333 | 906 | 3 147 |
| Chippewa | 237 | 12 410 | 1.00 | 163 | 13.2 | 142 | 11.5 | 1 044 | 10.4 | 2 440 | 1 225 | 1 255 | 233 | 1 858 |
| Chisago | 1 673 | 43 604 | 0.62 | 587 | 10.9 | 322 | 6.0 | 4 255 | 9.2 | 7 920 | 4 359 | 2 500 | 1 113 | 2 050 |
| Clay | 3 743 | 48 714 | 0.70 | 787 | 13.2 | 420 | 7.0 | 4 550 | 9.4 | 8 568 | 3 378 | 4 167 | 1 068 | 1 796 |
| Clearwater | 115 | 7 988 | 0.81 | 106 | 12.1 | 90 | 10.3 | 1 078 | 15.2 | 1 829 | 894 | 830 | 214 | 2 442 |
| Cook | 51 | 5 438 | 1.08 | 44 | 8.4 | 51 | 9.8 | 541 | 13.1 | 1 358 | 520 | 588 | 171 | 3 278 |
| Cottonwood | 244 | 12 273 | 1.10 | 135 | 11.6 | 176 | 15.1 | 1 030 | 11.3 | 2 888 | 1 062 | 1 622 | 172 | 1 460 |
| Crow Wing | 750 | 63 880 | 1.06 | 755 | 12.0 | 594 | 9.5 | 6 047 | 11.9 | 14 674 | 7 361 | 6 223 | 1 633 | 2 593 |
| Dakota | 2 853 | 358 199 | 0.82 | 5 187 | 12.9 | 2 070 | 5.1 | 27 614 | 7.7 | 51 753 | 25 719 | 16 898 | 9 100 | 2 266 |
| Dodge | 149 | 15 865 | 0.61 | 267 | 13.2 | 131 | 6.5 | 1 599 | 9.1 | 2 875 | 1 163 | 1 035 | 332 | 1 640 |
| Douglas | 522 | 37 079 | 1.06 | 401 | 11.1 | 402 | 11.1 | 3 121 | 10.9 | 8 700 | 4 903 | 3 991 | 650 | 1 791 |
| Faribault | 336 | 13 931 | 0.89 | 157 | 10.8 | 166 | 11.4 | 1 202 | 10.7 | 3 485 | 1 656 | 1 968 | 124 | 846 |

1. Per 1,000 estimated resident population.   2. Data for serious crimes have not been adjusted for underreporting; this may affect comparability between geographic areas and over time.   3. Per 100,000 population estimated by the FBI.

# Table B. States and Counties — Crime, Education, Money Income, and Poverty

| STATE County | Serious crimes known to police, 2011 (cont.)[1] Rate[2] Violent | Property | Education — School enrollment and attainment, 2007–2011 Enrollment[3] Total | Per cent private | Attainment[4] (percent) High school grad-uate or less | Bach-elor's degree or more | Local government expenditures,[5] 2009–2010 Total current expendi-tures (mil dol) | Current expendi-tures per student (dollars) | Money income, 2007–2011 Per capita income[6] (dollars) | Households Median income Dollars | Percent change, 2000 to 2007–2011 (constant 2011 dollars) | Percent with income of $200,000 or more | Income and poverty, 2011 Median house-hold income (dollars) | Percent below poverty level All per-sons | Children under 18 years | Children 5 to 17 years in families |
|---|---|---|---|---|---|---|---|---|---|---|---|---|---|---|---|---|
| | 46 | 47 | 48 | 49 | 50 | 51 | 52 | 53 | 54 | 55 | 56 | 57 | 58 | 59 | 60 | 61 |
| **MICHIGAN—Cont'd** | | | | | | | | | | | | | | | | |
| Keweenaw | 139 | 139 | 481 | 6.4 | 47.5 | 22.6 | 0.2 | 37 500 | 21 218 | 39 821 | 4.8 | 1.6 | 38 207 | 13.5 | 22.6 | 20.7 |
| Lake | 278 | 2 723 | 2 054 | 7.4 | 60.3 | 9.4 | 7.4 | 13 462 | 16 741 | 30 639 | -14.8 | 0.3 | 28 971 | 26.9 | 48.3 | 44.5 |
| Lapeer | 169 | 1 397 | 23 467 | 10.6 | 48.1 | 17.0 | 146.6 | 9 241 | 24 358 | 54 240 | -22.3 | 1.9 | 50 232 | 12.6 | 19.4 | 16.7 |
| Leelanau | 65 | 111 | 4 458 | 19.8 | 29.6 | 38.6 | 26.1 | 11 765 | 32 311 | 55 247 | -13.1 | 5.0 | 51 267 | 11.9 | 18.3 | 16.6 |
| Lenawee | 256 | 1 763 | 26 413 | 17.5 | 48.6 | 19.5 | 175.7 | 10 632 | 22 449 | 48 595 | -21.3 | 1.2 | 45 512 | 13.2 | 18.0 | 16.6 |
| Livingston | 93 | 1 230 | 50 261 | 10.9 | 33.6 | 31.3 | 269.4 | 9 123 | 31 751 | 71 694 | -21.2 | 4.7 | 68 895 | 6.9 | 8.8 | 7.3 |
| Luce | 272 | 2 128 | 1 254 | 5.1 | 57.9 | 13.7 | 8.6 | 9 854 | 18 294 | 42 083 | -2.7 | 0.6 | 36 515 | 21.0 | 29.9 | 27.1 |
| Mackinac | 243 | 3 872 | 2 087 | 13.9 | 52.3 | 19.8 | 14.9 | 10 154 | 22 195 | 39 055 | -13.3 | 1.3 | 36 393 | 14.5 | 23.8 | 21.5 |
| Macomb | 291 | 2 248 | 219 451 | 13.1 | 43.9 | 22.0 | 1 414.3 | 10 386 | 26 661 | 54 087 | -23.1 | 2.1 | 50 958 | 14.1 | 20.6 | 19.2 |
| Manistee | 210 | 1 165 | 4 722 | 13.9 | 50.5 | 17.6 | 34.2 | 10 496 | 22 258 | 41 169 | -10.9 | 1.3 | 39 347 | 16.8 | 27.4 | 24.5 |
| Marquette | 204 | 2 192 | 18 566 | 6.7 | 41.1 | 28.6 | 86.5 | 10 276 | 23 464 | 45 495 | -5.2 | 1.9 | 41 663 | 18.0 | 20.6 | 18.2 |
| Mason | 213 | 464 | 6 422 | 8.7 | 46.6 | 19.5 | 51.3 | 11 815 | 22 494 | 40 683 | -13.2 | 1.0 | 39 101 | 18.1 | 26.7 | 23.4 |
| Mecosta | 589 | 2 149 | 15 264 | 7.8 | 48.0 | 21.6 | 75.0 | 11 666 | 19 320 | 37 677 | -17.6 | 1.2 | 38 634 | 25.6 | 36.1 | 32.3 |
| Menominee | 99 | 963 | 5 233 | 7.8 | 53.6 | 13.4 | 40.7 | 9 879 | 21 886 | 42 014 | -5.4 | 0.8 | 39 292 | 15.8 | 26.2 | 22.7 |
| Midland | 111 | 1 069 | 23 462 | 18.0 | 37.1 | 31.9 | 134.9 | 9 897 | 29 451 | 52 465 | -14.9 | 5.4 | 53 764 | 13.0 | 17.6 | 15.0 |
| Missaukee | 34 | 950 | 3 404 | 13.2 | 56.4 | 13.4 | 19.4 | 8 701 | 19 740 | 39 735 | -16.5 | 0.7 | 37 616 | 19.0 | 29.0 | 27.4 |
| Monroe | 245 | 2 524 | 39 518 | 13.6 | 49.6 | 17.1 | 261.4 | 9 891 | 25 774 | 55 826 | -20.1 | 1.9 | 54 174 | 12.1 | 18.0 | 14.3 |
| Montcalm | 232 | 2 254 | 16 190 | 10.7 | 53.8 | 13.3 | 101.9 | 9 982 | 19 010 | 40 068 | -20.3 | 0.6 | 41 023 | 17.7 | 26.5 | 23.7 |
| Montmorency | 82 | 963 | 1 635 | 7.6 | 60.9 | 10.4 | 8.2 | 9 655 | 19 264 | 34 490 | -14.9 | 0.8 | 32 241 | 18.9 | 35.3 | 32.7 |
| Muskegon | 426 | 3 976 | 44 454 | 10.2 | 48.3 | 16.8 | 321.3 | 10 444 | 20 222 | 40 298 | -21.5 | 1.2 | 38 482 | 20.0 | 28.4 | 24.6 |
| Newaygo | 233 | 2 069 | 12 164 | 13.5 | 55.7 | 13.1 | 89.8 | 10 060 | 21 120 | 43 864 | -12.5 | 1.9 | 41 674 | 17.9 | 26.9 | 25.1 |
| Oakland | 193 | 1 874 | 328 551 | 17.9 | 28.7 | 42.4 | 2 235.9 | 11 342 | 36 314 | 66 456 | -20.5 | 7.4 | 61 961 | 11.2 | 14.9 | 13.6 |
| Oceana | 180 | 2 367 | 6 064 | 11.4 | 53.4 | 14.8 | 37.5 | 10 494 | 18 916 | 40 422 | -15.2 | 0.9 | 39 670 | 20.7 | 31.5 | 29.3 |
| Ogemaw | 195 | 2 653 | 4 671 | 10.2 | 59.8 | 10.5 | 21.5 | 9 257 | 18 909 | 35 988 | -12.5 | 1.2 | 33 222 | 22.1 | 37.5 | 36.1 |
| Ontonagon | 148 | 753 | 1 071 | 4.5 | 49.5 | 16.9 | 12.2 | 15 556 | 22 195 | 34 786 | -12.8 | 1.0 | 34 352 | 15.7 | 27.0 | 23.4 |
| Osceola | 268 | 2 229 | 5 523 | 11.7 | 56.6 | 12.5 | 42.0 | 9 291 | 18 228 | 39 035 | -15.2 | 0.5 | 38 404 | 17.6 | 27.9 | 25.1 |
| Oscoda | 290 | 3 197 | 1 625 | 14.6 | 61.9 | 9.7 | 9.3 | 9 134 | 18 706 | 32 838 | -13.8 | 1.0 | 31 579 | 19.2 | 33.2 | 31.8 |
| Otsego | 162 | 1 802 | 5 593 | 15.1 | 48.0 | 20.0 | 38.5 | 9 110 | 23 179 | 46 303 | -16.1 | 1.3 | 44 129 | 13.6 | 22.5 | 20.3 |
| Ottawa | 148 | 1 834 | 81 270 | 18.7 | 40.3 | 29.3 | 432.7 | 9 918 | 25 197 | 55 661 | -21.2 | 2.7 | 54 461 | 11.4 | 12.4 | 11.5 |
| Presque Isle | 127 | 988 | 2 439 | 12.0 | 54.1 | 14.3 | 14.6 | 9 228 | 21 926 | 39 240 | -8.2 | 1.1 | 39 483 | 15.5 | 25.5 | 22.3 |
| Roscommon | 184 | 1 809 | 4 322 | 7.9 | 54.2 | 13.8 | 40.6 | 12 627 | 21 637 | 33 286 | -17.9 | 1.2 | 32 742 | 21.2 | 35.8 | 31.8 |
| Saginaw | 780 | 2 446 | 55 007 | 12.1 | 48.8 | 18.6 | 333.4 | 10 365 | 22 257 | 43 258 | -17.1 | 1.9 | 40 411 | 19.9 | 31.1 | 28.8 |
| St. Clair | 256 | 2 180 | 42 498 | 11.5 | 48.5 | 15.6 | 319.0 | 9 985 | 23 960 | 48 869 | -21.8 | 1.7 | 45 858 | 15.7 | 22.1 | 19.5 |
| St. Joseph | 251 | 1 940 | 14 917 | 7.4 | 55.3 | 14.1 | 107.6 | 9 491 | 20 772 | 44 433 | -18.5 | 1.6 | 40 796 | 20.3 | 30.5 | 28.7 |
| Sanilac | 151 | 1 494 | 10 359 | 9.0 | 59.7 | 11.2 | 70.6 | 9 491 | 20 056 | 40 437 | -18.8 | 0.9 | 37 465 | 17.0 | 27.4 | 25.0 |
| Schoolcraft | 212 | 2 229 | 1 603 | 16.3 | 58.0 | 12.1 | 11.1 | 8 899 | 21 134 | 38 367 | -8.7 | 1.1 | 38 366 | 14.8 | 25.2 | 22.4 |
| Shiawassee | 214 | 1 755 | 18 334 | 12.4 | 49.5 | 14.5 | 129.8 | 9 625 | 22 727 | 47 552 | -17.2 | 1.4 | 46 811 | 14.5 | 21.5 | 18.4 |
| Tuscola | 172 | 1 433 | 14 182 | 12.2 | 55.3 | 12.9 | 107.5 | 10 462 | 20 503 | 43 315 | -20.1 | 0.8 | 42 808 | 14.5 | 24.5 | 21.8 |
| Van Buren | 333 | 2 217 | 19 191 | 8.9 | 50.2 | 17.8 | 184.0 | 10 544 | 21 898 | 44 428 | -16.4 | 1.4 | 41 600 | 21.5 | 31.7 | 28.8 |
| Washtenaw | 310 | 2 283 | 125 661 | 10.7 | 22.4 | 51.0 | 527.7 | 11 760 | 32 529 | 59 737 | -14.9 | 6.0 | 56 789 | 16.7 | 17.5 | 14.8 |
| Wayne | 1 048 | 4 084 | 526 320 | 12.6 | 48.1 | 20.6 | 3 524.7 | 10 877 | 22 351 | 41 886 | -23.9 | 2.3 | 38 479 | 26.1 | 37.9 | 35.2 |
| Wexford | 321 | 3 751 | 7 658 | 12.7 | 51.4 | 16.5 | 64.0 | 11 708 | 20 627 | 42 209 | -11.6 | 1.6 | 43 873 | 15.2 | 24.8 | 21.9 |
| **MINNESOTA** | 221 | 2 549 | 1 402 882 | 17.5 | 35.9 | 31.8 | 8 888.0 | 10 656 | 30 310 | 58 476 | -8.1 | 4.2 | 56 944 | 11.8 | 15.3 | 13.6 |
| Aitkin | 141 | 2 505 | 2 771 | 10.4 | 51.3 | 15.1 | 21.2 | 10 429 | 24 694 | 41 301 | -1.8 | 1.1 | 39 958 | 13.2 | 22.9 | 21.2 |
| Anoka | 163 | 3 163 | 89 414 | 15.2 | 37.5 | 25.8 | 659.5 | 10 213 | 29 894 | 69 139 | -11.3 | 3.1 | 63 799 | 8.6 | 11.1 | 9.8 |
| Becker | 82 | 1 600 | 7 439 | 9.4 | 43.1 | 21.4 | 43.0 | 9 678 | 25 233 | 47 959 | 2.1 | 2.2 | 47 819 | 12.9 | 20.4 | 17.7 |
| Beltrami | 259 | 3 481 | 12 943 | 7.1 | 37.5 | 29.1 | 101.9 | 13 385 | 21 753 | 43 989 | -2.4 | 1.5 | 40 657 | 20.4 | 29.6 | 27.9 |
| Benton | 134 | 1 703 | 9 978 | 13.1 | 44.6 | 18.8 | 47.9 | 8 737 | 23 924 | 51 159 | -9.7 | 1.4 | 49 482 | 11.5 | 14.1 | 12.4 |
| Big Stone | 113 | 1 130 | 1 088 | 6.7 | 52.3 | 16.8 | 10.0 | 11 056 | 24 960 | 44 438 | 7.1 | 1.8 | 43 190 | 15.0 | 21.0 | 19.0 |
| Blue Earth | 167 | 3 288 | 21 270 | 7.9 | 35.3 | 29.6 | 104.3 | 10 465 | 23 996 | 48 911 | -7.0 | 1.9 | 46 280 | 18.3 | 17.3 | 15.1 |
| Brown | 30 | 1 394 | 6 648 | 33.3 | 50.2 | 18.5 | 38.3 | 11 070 | 26 046 | 48 194 | -10.4 | 2.0 | 50 339 | 8.0 | 11.5 | 10.4 |
| Carlton | 95 | 2 541 | 8 301 | 13.3 | 41.8 | 22.4 | 61.4 | 9 588 | 24 808 | 53 553 | -0.9 | 1.5 | 49 357 | 12.2 | 13.4 | 11.7 |
| Carver | 68 | 1 127 | 26 957 | 22.7 | 27.0 | 42.9 | 152.7 | 10 007 | 36 807 | 82 710 | -6.5 | 9.0 | 85 314 | 5.4 | 6.2 | 5.1 |
| Cass | 198 | 2 949 | 5 625 | 8.0 | 45.9 | 20.0 | 48.0 | 11 512 | 24 772 | 43 042 | -7.1 | 1.7 | 42 297 | 18.3 | 30.1 | 28.2 |
| Chippewa | 152 | 1 707 | 2 886 | 8.5 | 49.5 | 16.6 | 22.8 | 10 619 | 24 211 | 44 712 | -6.9 | 1.4 | 46 545 | 10.9 | 16.1 | 14.5 |
| Chisago | 92 | 1 958 | 14 020 | 11.2 | 43.1 | 18.3 | 78.5 | 9 634 | 27 626 | 67 075 | -4.5 | 2.4 | 62 776 | 6.7 | 8.8 | 7.5 |
| Clay | 86 | 1 711 | 18 339 | 22.7 | 36.2 | 30.4 | 79.2 | 8 864 | 23 771 | 52 108 | 1.9 | 1.9 | 52 731 | 14.8 | 16.6 | 15.2 |
| Clearwater | 251 | 2 191 | 1 975 | 4.5 | 52.2 | 15.7 | 14.8 | 9 960 | 21 466 | 39 143 | -5.0 | 1.0 | 36 697 | 18.9 | 30.2 | 27.8 |
| Cook | 173 | 3 106 | 854 | 9.6 | 33.6 | 34.4 | 7.4 | 11 700 | 30 501 | 49 496 | 0.1 | 2.4 | 44 278 | 10.9 | 16.6 | 14.1 |
| Cottonwood | 144 | 1 316 | 2 578 | 15.0 | 51.6 | 17.1 | 19.6 | 10 211 | 22 028 | 43 111 | 0.0 | 1.3 | 44 504 | 11.7 | 16.6 | 13.7 |
| Crow Wing | 149 | 2 444 | 14 073 | 10.4 | 40.0 | 22.2 | 93.5 | 9 650 | 25 645 | 45 853 | -9.7 | 1.9 | 45 514 | 13.4 | 19.3 | 18.1 |
| Dakota | 149 | 2 117 | 108 217 | 17.1 | 28.4 | 38.4 | 759.4 | 10 149 | 34 822 | 73 723 | -11.7 | 5.9 | 70 064 | 7.0 | 9.2 | 8.0 |
| Dodge | 183 | 1 457 | 5 330 | 6.8 | 42.1 | 22.1 | 32.9 | 8 086 | 27 776 | 66 216 | 3.4 | 2.0 | 65 423 | 7.4 | 10.1 | 8.7 |
| Douglas | 116 | 1 676 | 7 780 | 10.8 | 39.8 | 22.5 | 51.1 | 9 799 | 26 301 | 48 436 | -4.9 | 2.3 | 49 161 | 10.8 | 13.7 | 12.5 |
| Faribault | 48 | 798 | 3 167 | 13.1 | 50.0 | 16.6 | 19.7 | 9 966 | 23 185 | 43 214 | -7.1 | 1.2 | 43 567 | 13.6 | 20.9 | 18.8 |

1. Data for serious crimes have not been adjusted for underreporting; this may affect comparability between geographic areas and over time.   2. Per 100,000 population estimated by the FBI.   3. All persons 3 years old and over enrolled in nursery school through college.   4. Persons 25 years old and over.   5. Elementary and secondary education expenditures.   6. Based on population estimated by the American Community Survey, 2007–2011.

# Table B. States and Counties — Personal Income

| | | | | | | | | Personal income, 2011 | | | | | |
|---|---|---|---|---|---|---|---|---|---|---|---|---|---|
| | | | Per capita[1] | | | | | | Transfer payments (mil dol) | | | | |
| | | | | | | | | | | Government payments to individuals | | | |
| STATE County | Total (mil dol) | Percent change, 2010–2011 | Dollars | Rank | Wages and salaries[2] (mil dol) | Proprietors' income (mil dol) | Dividends, interest, and rent (mil dol) | Total | Total | Social Security | Medical payments | Income mainte-nance | Unemploy-ment insurance |
| | 62 | 63 | 64 | 65 | 66 | 67 | 68 | 69 | 70 | 71 | 72 | 73 | 74 |
| MICHIGAN—Cont'd | | | | | | | | | | | | | |
| Keweenaw | 80 | 5.7 | 36 886 | 1 087 | 13 | 1 | 17 | 24 | 24 | 9 | 10 | 2 | 1 |
| Lake | 319 | 4.8 | 27 668 | 2 658 | 75 | 19 | 51 | 139 | 137 | 51 | 53 | 22 | 4 |
| Lapeer | 2 803 | 5.0 | 31 825 | 1 927 | 883 | 159 | 348 | 646 | 626 | 268 | 232 | 55 | 43 |
| Leelanau | 944 | 4.9 | 43 978 | 441 | 234 | 52 | 289 | 179 | 174 | 93 | 57 | 9 | 7 |
| Lenawee | 3 243 | 7.5 | 32 611 | 1 777 | 1 299 | 203 | 394 | 793 | 771 | 314 | 303 | 74 | 39 |
| Livingston | 7 392 | 6.9 | 40 677 | 690 | 2 451 | 347 | 909 | 1 062 | 1 022 | 501 | 339 | 59 | 66 |
| Luce | 161 | 2.2 | 24 492 | 3 006 | 77 | 8 | 28 | 65 | 64 | 22 | 29 | 7 | 2 |
| Mackinac | 372 | 2.8 | 33 675 | 1 569 | 175 | 18 | 75 | 109 | 107 | 44 | 42 | 9 | 5 |
| Macomb | 30 079 | 5.1 | 35 717 | 1 260 | 18 400 | 1 408 | 3 797 | 6 433 | 6 246 | 2 476 | 2 517 | 585 | 368 |
| Manistee | 739 | 3.3 | 29 901 | 2 309 | 336 | 35 | 137 | 268 | 263 | 97 | 117 | 26 | 11 |
| Marquette | 2 204 | 4.4 | 32 555 | 1 786 | 1 405 | 78 | 295 | 593 | 578 | 193 | 250 | 50 | 24 |
| Mason | 908 | 3.8 | 31 659 | 1 966 | 443 | 62 | 150 | 287 | 281 | 102 | 113 | 33 | 13 |
| Mecosta | 1 183 | 4.6 | 27 328 | 2 713 | 618 | 91 | 157 | 350 | 340 | 128 | 107 | 46 | 17 |
| Menominee | 763 | 6.0 | 31 871 | 1 912 | 328 | 61 | 128 | 201 | 195 | 81 | 71 | 23 | 8 |
| Midland | 3 652 | 7.4 | 43 446 | 473 | 2 520 | 177 | 613 | 630 | 611 | 245 | 235 | 72 | 26 |
| Missaukee | 397 | 7.5 | 26 591 | 2 813 | 126 | 54 | 57 | 125 | 122 | 48 | 45 | 17 | 6 |
| Monroe | 5 403 | 6.3 | 35 647 | 1 274 | 2 119 | 252 | 658 | 1 127 | 1 093 | 441 | 426 | 110 | 54 |
| Montcalm | 1 590 | 5.9 | 25 160 | 2 954 | 685 | 90 | 201 | 501 | 487 | 183 | 187 | 65 | 24 |
| Montmorency | 270 | 4.6 | 27 993 | 2 614 | 81 | 15 | 51 | 129 | 127 | 53 | 51 | 12 | 5 |
| Muskegon | 5 099 | 4.8 | 29 766 | 2 327 | 2 911 | 243 | 621 | 1 530 | 1 492 | 519 | 582 | 253 | 66 |
| Newaygo | 1 372 | 4.9 | 28 371 | 2 561 | 501 | 95 | 173 | 401 | 391 | 152 | 144 | 59 | 17 |
| Oakland | 64 497 | 9.1 | 53 297 | 137 | 44 469 | 6 609 | 9 718 | 8 673 | 8 405 | 3 431 | 3 375 | 660 | 469 |
| Oceana | 844 | 7.7 | 31 836 | 1 921 | 298 | 50 | 128 | 242 | 236 | 88 | 87 | 37 | 13 |
| Ogemaw | 592 | 3.4 | 27 435 | 2 694 | 219 | 41 | 92 | 248 | 243 | 94 | 95 | 35 | 8 |
| Ontonagon | 195 | -3.6 | 29 514 | 2 376 | 61 | 10 | 31 | 85 | 84 | 33 | 35 | 7 | 4 |
| Osceola | 630 | 6.0 | 26 782 | 2 790 | 320 | 34 | 83 | 211 | 206 | 79 | 79 | 30 | 9 |
| Oscoda | 218 | 4.7 | 25 348 | 2 940 | 61 | 16 | 36 | 99 | 97 | 40 | 35 | 12 | 5 |
| Otsego | 723 | 4.6 | 30 030 | 2 286 | 424 | 70 | 121 | 200 | 195 | 83 | 69 | 22 | 11 |
| Ottawa | 8 995 | 5.7 | 33 777 | 1 552 | 5 482 | 436 | 1 463 | 1 481 | 1 422 | 638 | 477 | 119 | 84 |
| Presque Isle | 387 | 4.1 | 29 450 | 2 386 | 132 | 13 | 69 | 142 | 140 | 63 | 52 | 11 | 7 |
| Roscommon | 731 | 3.4 | 29 948 | 2 300 | 227 | 22 | 138 | 340 | 334 | 136 | 134 | 37 | 10 |
| Saginaw | 6 372 | 5.0 | 32 007 | 1 888 | 4 270 | 374 | 827 | 1 888 | 1 844 | 650 | 744 | 304 | 72 |
| St. Clair | 5 408 | 4.3 | 33 459 | 1 615 | 2 278 | 276 | 707 | 1 356 | 1 321 | 505 | 504 | 152 | 80 |
| St. Joseph | 1 823 | 6.2 | 29 826 | 2 319 | 952 | 157 | 244 | 492 | 478 | 182 | 188 | 64 | 22 |
| Sanilac | 1 372 | 7.0 | 32 193 | 1 842 | 451 | 181 | 195 | 406 | 397 | 139 | 174 | 48 | 18 |
| Schoolcraft | 260 | 2.9 | 30 598 | 2 177 | 136 | 10 | 37 | 95 | 93 | 32 | 44 | 9 | 4 |
| Shiawassee | 2 055 | 4.8 | 29 422 | 2 391 | 718 | 79 | 252 | 596 | 580 | 216 | 243 | 62 | 30 |
| Tuscola | 1 571 | 6.6 | 28 341 | 2 567 | 531 | 110 | 206 | 496 | 484 | 186 | 202 | 52 | 23 |
| Van Buren | 2 361 | 5.0 | 31 013 | 2 096 | 1 049 | 114 | 299 | 645 | 628 | 221 | 259 | 90 | 31 |
| Washtenaw | 14 204 | 6.8 | 40 821 | 674 | 11 879 | 810 | 2 327 | 2 071 | 1 994 | 772 | 759 | 190 | 94 |
| Wayne | 61 293 | 3.5 | 34 012 | 1 507 | 47 120 | 3 684 | 6 760 | 18 312 | 17 913 | 4 799 | 8 067 | 3 344 | 859 |
| Wexford | 905 | 5.2 | 27 661 | 2 659 | 578 | 42 | 125 | 293 | 286 | 103 | 118 | 39 | 14 |
| MINNESOTA | 238 166 | 5.5 | 44 560 | X | 160 186 | 20 444 | 38 934 | 38 651 | 37 469 | 12 129 | 16 755 | 3 768 | 1 846 |
| Aitkin | 502 | 3.8 | 30 949 | 2 111 | 150 | 49 | 102 | 168 | 164 | 59 | 74 | 14 | 7 |
| Anoka | 13 276 | 4.8 | 39 850 | 762 | 6 361 | 553 | 1 569 | 2 024 | 1 950 | 680 | 838 | 174 | 121 |
| Becker | 1 213 | 5.2 | 36 998 | 1 078 | 558 | 149 | 211 | 303 | 296 | 97 | 133 | 34 | 12 |
| Beltrami | 1 441 | 3.5 | 31 834 | 1 923 | 777 | 115 | 232 | 441 | 431 | 97 | 206 | 73 | 18 |
| Benton | 1 325 | 3.9 | 34 270 | 1 475 | 737 | 197 | 185 | 244 | 236 | 73 | 101 | 26 | 15 |
| Big Stone | 208 | 0.8 | 39 621 | 792 | 83 | 29 | 44 | 53 | 52 | 18 | 26 | 4 | 2 |
| Blue Earth | 2 370 | 7.9 | 36 808 | 1 101 | 1 735 | 340 | 390 | 422 | 408 | 129 | 165 | 43 | 20 |
| Brown | 1 009 | 5.8 | 39 204 | 831 | 584 | 151 | 191 | 209 | 203 | 77 | 91 | 15 | 8 |
| Carlton | 1 131 | 3.7 | 31 902 | 1 906 | 616 | 57 | 155 | 307 | 299 | 95 | 133 | 26 | 14 |
| Carver | 5 357 | 7.8 | 57 830 | 85 | 2 030 | 382 | 697 | 419 | 398 | 153 | 168 | 25 | 27 |
| Cass | 1 069 | 4.3 | 37 649 | 1 009 | 355 | 116 | 236 | 336 | 329 | 115 | 141 | 36 | 14 |
| Chippewa | 567 | 6.6 | 46 031 | 336 | 255 | 149 | 89 | 97 | 94 | 32 | 44 | 8 | 4 |
| Chisago | 1 896 | 6.2 | 35 160 | 1 347 | 638 | 89 | 248 | 351 | 339 | 121 | 148 | 25 | 21 |
| Clay | 2 120 | 5.1 | 35 448 | 1 304 | 842 | 158 | 290 | 420 | 407 | 114 | 187 | 46 | 16 |
| Clearwater | 260 | 5.1 | 29 583 | 2 365 | 111 | 30 | 38 | 85 | 83 | 24 | 38 | 11 | 5 |
| Cook | 214 | 5.0 | 41 004 | 658 | 106 | 22 | 54 | 47 | 46 | 19 | 18 | 3 | 2 |
| Cottonwood | 503 | 8.6 | 43 027 | 507 | 212 | 141 | 85 | 102 | 99 | 37 | 45 | 8 | 4 |
| Crow Wing | 2 111 | 4.6 | 33 640 | 1 580 | 1 197 | 84 | 434 | 597 | 584 | 209 | 241 | 52 | 27 |
| Dakota | 18 612 | 4.9 | 46 299 | 328 | 10 526 | 923 | 2 697 | 2 231 | 2 142 | 796 | 870 | 164 | 133 |
| Dodge | 771 | 3.5 | 38 067 | 963 | 250 | 134 | 110 | 121 | 117 | 41 | 54 | 9 | 7 |
| Douglas | 1 364 | 4.8 | 37 703 | 1 001 | 785 | 126 | 280 | 308 | 300 | 117 | 126 | 22 | 12 |
| Faribault | 681 | 13.5 | 46 913 | 303 | 261 | 180 | 116 | 135 | 131 | 46 | 61 | 12 | 5 |

1. Based on the resident population estimated as of July 1 of the year shown.  2. Includes supplements to wages and salaries.

| STATE County | Earnings, 2011 | | | | | | | | | Social Security beneficiaries, December 2011 | | | Housing units, 2010 | |
|---|---|---|---|---|---|---|---|---|---|---|---|---|---|---|
| | | | | Percent by selected industries | | | | | | | | | | |
| | | | Goods-related[1] | | Service-related and health | | | | | | | | | |
| | Total (mil dol) | Farm | Total | Manu-facturing | Infor-mation and profes-sional and technical services | Retail trade | Finance, insur-ance, and real estate | Health care and social services | Govern-ment | Number | Rate[2] | Supple-mental Security Income recipients, December 2011 | Total | Percent change, 2000–2010 |
| | 75 | 76 | 77 | 78 | 79 | 80 | 81 | 82 | 83 | 84 | 85 | 86 | 87 | 88 |
| **MICHIGAN—Cont'd** | | | | | | | | | | | | | | |
| Keweenaw | 15 | 0.0 | D | D | D | 4.9 | D | 0.5 | 42.3 | 720 | 331 | 37 | 2 467 | 6.0 |
| Lake | 95 | 1.9 | 8.7 | 2.8 | D | 5.1 | 3.9 | D | 30.0 | 4 020 | 348 | 604 | 14 966 | 10.9 |
| Lapeer | 1 041 | 3.0 | 29.2 | 23.1 | D | 9.0 | 4.7 | 7.0 | 23.2 | 18 590 | 211 | 1 192 | 36 332 | 11.0 |
| Leelanau | 286 | 5.0 | 14.0 | 3.0 | 6.2 | 4.9 | 6.2 | 9.6 | 31.8 | 6 350 | 296 | 174 | 14 935 | 12.3 |
| Lenawee | 1 502 | 5.1 | D | 26.6 | D | 8.2 | 5.6 | 9.5 | 18.2 | 22 660 | 228 | 1 987 | 43 452 | 9.2 |
| Livingston | 2 798 | 0.7 | 27.3 | 19.7 | 9.0 | 9.2 | 8.6 | 9.1 | 12.8 | 32 350 | 178 | 1 261 | 72 809 | 23.6 |
| Luce | 85 | 0.8 | D | D | D | 7.7 | D | D | 57.0 | 1 740 | 264 | 219 | 4 343 | 8.4 |
| Mackinac | 193 | 1.7 | D | 1.8 | D | 8.1 | 2.9 | D | 27.9 | 3 395 | 308 | 235 | 11 010 | 17.0 |
| Macomb | 19 808 | 0.1 | D | 28.4 | 7.2 | 7.3 | 2.8 | 10.9 | 15.4 | 169 515 | 201 | 17 127 | 356 626 | 11.3 |
| Manistee | 371 | 1.2 | 19.9 | 16.0 | 2.6 | 7.2 | 2.6 | D | 42.8 | 7 360 | 298 | 654 | 15 694 | 10.0 |
| Marquette | 1 483 | 0.3 | 22.0 | 3.1 | 5.3 | 6.7 | 4.6 | 21.7 | 22.9 | 14 520 | 214 | 1 176 | 34 330 | 4.4 |
| Mason | 506 | 3.4 | D | 18.7 | D | 8.3 | 4.0 | 14.4 | 19.6 | 7 810 | 272 | 786 | 17 293 | 7.7 |
| Mecosta | 708 | 4.1 | D | 13.9 | 3.0 | 9.8 | 2.5 | 5.9 | 40.7 | 9 695 | 224 | 1 101 | 21 131 | 7.8 |
| Menominee | 390 | 5.2 | D | 27.1 | D | 5.4 | 3.3 | D | 27.1 | 6 380 | 267 | 456 | 14 227 | 4.3 |
| Midland | 2 698 | 1.0 | D | 26.7 | 5.0 | 4.4 | 3.0 | 10.7 | 7.1 | 17 785 | 212 | 1 578 | 35 960 | 6.4 |
| Missaukee | 180 | 20.2 | D | 19.9 | D | 5.6 | 2.8 | D | 13.8 | 3 765 | 252 | 339 | 9 117 | 5.7 |
| Monroe | 2 371 | 2.0 | D | 17.2 | D | 6.6 | 2.9 | 10.1 | 13.8 | 30 795 | 203 | 2 577 | 62 971 | 11.5 |
| Montcalm | 775 | 7.6 | D | 18.4 | 2.4 | 8.6 | 2.3 | D | 23.0 | 14 200 | 225 | 1 736 | 28 221 | 9.0 |
| Montmorency | 96 | 2.6 | D | 13.4 | 1.7 | 7.2 | 5.4 | D | 18.9 | 4 010 | 415 | 296 | 9 597 | 3.9 |
| Muskegon | 3 154 | 1.1 | D | 25.4 | 4.1 | 10.5 | 3.5 | 17.5 | 16.1 | 39 145 | 229 | 6 221 | 73 561 | 7.3 |
| Newaygo | 596 | 8.7 | D | 17.4 | 3.7 | 10.2 | 9.1 | 10.4 | 21.7 | 11 770 | 243 | 1 447 | 25 075 | 8.1 |
| Oakland | 51 078 | 0.0 | 15.0 | 10.6 | 22.4 | 5.9 | 10.5 | 12.3 | 6.8 | 220 925 | 183 | 21 175 | 527 255 | 7.2 |
| Oceana | 348 | 12.0 | D | 18.9 | D | 4.9 | 2.5 | 2.8 | 25.7 | 6 915 | 261 | 701 | 15 944 | 6.2 |
| Ogemaw | 260 | 6.2 | 10.9 | 4.9 | 2.8 | 16.8 | 3.8 | D | 23.2 | 7 230 | 335 | 843 | 16 047 | 4.2 |
| Ontonagon | 71 | 1.6 | 10.3 | 2.4 | 3.0 | 11.1 | 4.4 | 14.2 | 27.5 | 2 545 | 386 | 149 | 5 672 | 5.0 |
| Osceola | 354 | 3.8 | D | 24.2 | D | 4.3 | D | 10.1 | 15.7 | 6 235 | 265 | 845 | 13 632 | 6.1 |
| Oscoda | 77 | 2.5 | D | 8.3 | D | 8.8 | 3.1 | 6.5 | 24.2 | 3 065 | 356 | 296 | 9 118 | 4.9 |
| Otsego | 494 | 0.4 | 21.5 | 8.0 | 4.1 | 17.1 | 4.8 | D | 15.2 | 6 220 | 258 | 502 | 14 731 | 10.1 |
| Ottawa | 5 918 | 2.4 | 39.5 | 34.8 | 5.1 | 5.1 | 3.8 | 6.9 | 15.3 | 44 880 | 169 | 2 650 | 102 495 | 18.0 |
| Presque Isle | 144 | 4.4 | D | 4.9 | D | 7.8 | 3.8 | 8.8 | 21.1 | 4 775 | 363 | 359 | 10 428 | 5.2 |
| Roscommon | 249 | 0.1 | D | 12.1 | D | 16.5 | 4.3 | D | 31.3 | 10 075 | 413 | 839 | 24 459 | 5.8 |
| Saginaw | 4 644 | 1.7 | 24.1 | 19.9 | 6.5 | 7.5 | 5.5 | 17.4 | 15.6 | 46 925 | 236 | 8 388 | 86 844 | 1.6 |
| St. Clair | 2 554 | 1.1 | D | 14.5 | D | 7.7 | 5.3 | 16.6 | 17.5 | 35 940 | 222 | 3 298 | 71 822 | 7.0 |
| St. Joseph | 1 109 | 9.1 | D | 39.8 | D | 7.0 | 2.8 | 7.0 | 15.4 | 13 385 | 219 | 1 305 | 27 778 | 4.8 |
| Sanilac | 632 | 20.2 | 21.0 | 16.6 | D | 8.3 | 3.5 | 9.0 | 15.9 | 10 625 | 249 | 926 | 22 725 | 6.6 |
| Schoolcraft | 146 | 1.1 | 20.9 | 10.0 | D | 8.6 | D | 4.9 | 39.1 | 2 475 | 292 | 231 | 6 313 | 10.8 |
| Shiawassee | 796 | 4.5 | 18.4 | 14.0 | 4.5 | 10.0 | 3.3 | 12.0 | 22.5 | 15 745 | 225 | 1 628 | 30 319 | 4.2 |
| Tuscola | 640 | 12.1 | D | 13.2 | D | 7.1 | 2.9 | D | 27.2 | 13 725 | 248 | 1 261 | 24 451 | 4.6 |
| Van Buren | 1 163 | 8.2 | D | 12.6 | 7.7 | 5.8 | 4.4 | 5.6 | 24.5 | 16 735 | 220 | 2 117 | 36 785 | 8.3 |
| Washtenaw | 12 689 | 0.2 | D | 9.7 | 14.6 | 4.7 | 4.2 | 11.1 | 35.5 | 50 220 | 144 | 5 129 | 147 573 | 12.7 |
| Wayne | 50 804 | 0.0 | 18.0 | 14.2 | 13.5 | 4.7 | 4.8 | 13.6 | 14.9 | 349 745 | 194 | 81 910 | 821 693 | -0.5 |
| Wexford | 621 | 0.8 | 30.5 | 28.1 | D | 8.6 | 3.4 | 13.0 | 18.0 | 8 100 | 248 | 1 041 | 16 736 | 12.5 |
| **MINNESOTA** | 180 631 | 2.9 | 18.0 | 13.0 | 10.6 | 5.3 | 10.0 | 12.4 | 13.8 | 904 803 | 169 | 88 768 | 2 347 201 | 13.6 |
| Aitkin | 199 | 2.6 | D | 6.6 | D | 11.7 | D | D | 21.7 | 4 590 | 283 | 267 | 16 029 | 13.1 |
| Anoka | 6 913 | 0.2 | 33.6 | 26.2 | 5.5 | 6.9 | 3.9 | 12.7 | 14.1 | 48 055 | 144 | 4 063 | 126 688 | 17.2 |
| Becker | 707 | 6.5 | D | 14.2 | 3.1 | 9.7 | 4.0 | 12.5 | 22.3 | 7 990 | 244 | 697 | 18 784 | 13.1 |
| Beltrami | 892 | 0.4 | D | 8.2 | D | 10.1 | 3.2 | 16.8 | 31.2 | 8 305 | 183 | 1 264 | 20 527 | 20.8 |
| Benton | 935 | 5.5 | D | 25.0 | D | 5.8 | 3.8 | 7.8 | 9.4 | 5 980 | 155 | 587 | 16 140 | 19.9 |
| Big Stone | 112 | 16.6 | D | 1.4 | D | 4.6 | 3.8 | D | 26.7 | 1 550 | 296 | 85 | 3 115 | -1.8 |
| Blue Earth | 2 075 | 7.6 | D | 11.2 | 7.1 | 8.2 | 4.9 | 18.7 | 15.8 | 10 155 | 158 | 1 023 | 26 202 | 19.3 |
| Brown | 736 | 13.3 | D | 22.6 | 6.5 | 5.9 | 3.6 | 12.1 | 11.7 | 6 090 | 237 | 262 | 11 493 | 3.0 |
| Carlton | 673 | 0.5 | D | 15.9 | 2.0 | 6.1 | 3.8 | 10.8 | 37.6 | 7 350 | 207 | 565 | 15 656 | 14.1 |
| Carver | 2 412 | 1.6 | 35.6 | 29.1 | 8.3 | 4.5 | 4.6 | 10.5 | 11.3 | 10 630 | 115 | 465 | 34 536 | 38.8 |
| Cass | 471 | 1.4 | 8.6 | 2.8 | 4.0 | 7.5 | 6.8 | D | 39.2 | 9 140 | 322 | 738 | 24 903 | 17.0 |
| Chippewa | 403 | 24.3 | D | 16.2 | 5.8 | 4.7 | 3.7 | D | 15.1 | 2 640 | 214 | 170 | 5 721 | -2.3 |
| Chisago | 728 | 1.9 | D | 15.8 | 2.4 | 6.3 | 2.9 | 27.0 | 18.9 | 8 810 | 163 | 506 | 21 172 | 36.3 |
| Clay | 1 000 | 7.9 | D | 5.6 | 4.0 | 7.3 | 3.3 | 9.9 | 24.1 | 9 190 | 154 | 997 | 23 959 | 21.3 |
| Clearwater | 142 | 6.7 | D | 19.0 | D | 4.6 | D | 9.1 | 22.4 | 2 090 | 238 | 230 | 4 773 | 16.0 |
| Cook | 128 | 0.0 | D | D | 2.9 | 8.6 | D | 3.8 | 38.9 | 1 425 | 273 | 56 | 5 839 | 24.0 |
| Cottonwood | 353 | 25.9 | 27.9 | 23.9 | 1.7 | 3.7 | 2.5 | D | 12.7 | 3 085 | 264 | 216 | 5 412 | 0.7 |
| Crow Wing | 1 281 | 0.5 | D | 9.6 | 7.1 | 9.7 | 6.8 | 17.5 | 20.8 | 16 045 | 256 | 1 138 | 40 180 | 20.0 |
| Dakota | 11 449 | 0.6 | 19.7 | 13.0 | 14.7 | 6.7 | 9.8 | 7.4 | 12.1 | 55 040 | 137 | 3 940 | 159 598 | 19.3 |
| Dodge | 385 | 18.3 | D | 18.4 | 2.9 | 2.7 | 6.1 | D | 15.9 | 3 155 | 156 | 157 | 7 947 | 19.6 |
| Douglas | 911 | 3.1 | D | 18.0 | 4.9 | 8.7 | 4.4 | 9.8 | 19.2 | 9 480 | 262 | 477 | 19 905 | 19.2 |
| Faribault | 440 | 33.5 | 17.5 | 14.0 | 2.4 | 3.3 | 3.7 | 3.9 | 12.9 | 3 845 | 265 | 236 | 7 090 | -2.2 |

1.  Includes mining, construction, and manufacturing.    2.  Per 1,000 resident population enumerated in the 2010 census.

# Table B. States and Counties — Housing, Labor Force, and Employment

| STATE County | Housing units, 2007–2011 Occupied units Owner-occupied Total | Percent | Median value[1] | Median owner cost as a percent of income With a mortgage | Without a mortgage[2] | Renter-occupied Median rent[3] | Median rent as a percent of income | Sub-stand-ard units[4] (percent) | Civilian labor force, 2012 Total | Percent change, 2011–2012 | Unemployment Total | Rate[5] | Civilian employment,[6] 2007–2011 Total | Percent Management, business, science and arts | Construction, production, and maintenance occupations |
|---|---|---|---|---|---|---|---|---|---|---|---|---|---|---|---|
| | 89 | 90 | 91 | 92 | 93 | 94 | 95 | 96 | 97 | 98 | 99 | 100 | 101 | 102 | 103 |
| **MICHIGAN—Cont'd** | | | | | | | | | | | | | | | |
| Keweenaw | 887 | 85.2 | 87 000 | 23.1 | 13.5 | 417 | 28.3 | 2.9 | 952 | -3.1 | 116 | 12.2 | 839 | 34.6 | 21.7 |
| Lake | 4 192 | 82.7 | 89 600 | 28.3 | 13.3 | 520 | 35.3 | 2.4 | 3 826 | -4.7 | 465 | 12.2 | 3 495 | 20.9 | 31.4 |
| Lapeer | 32 815 | 84.8 | 155 000 | 25.2 | 12.8 | 687 | 31.9 | 2.2 | 39 996 | -0.5 | 4 718 | 11.8 | 37 515 | 31.0 | 31.5 |
| Leelanau | 9 388 | 85.2 | 241 700 | 28.1 | 11.2 | 771 | 30.1 | 2.0 | 10 292 | 0.2 | 765 | 7.4 | 9 725 | 37.5 | 22.9 |
| Lenawee | 37 673 | 79.9 | 133 800 | 24.9 | 14.1 | 663 | 32.4 | 2.2 | 44 053 | -2.1 | 3 910 | 8.9 | 44 217 | 28.7 | 28.5 |
| Livingston | 67 397 | 86.3 | 203 200 | 24.7 | 13.1 | 887 | 31.8 | 1.0 | 88 142 | 0.1 | 7 547 | 8.6 | 87 747 | 38.6 | 21.6 |
| Luce | 2 447 | 79.5 | 84 200 | 21.9 | 10.3 | 550 | 32.0 | 2.2 | 2 509 | -1.2 | 266 | 10.6 | 2 277 | 23.6 | 25.4 |
| Mackinac | 4 917 | 79.8 | 126 600 | 24.1 | 13.8 | 575 | 30.4 | 2.7 | 5 648 | -2.5 | 607 | 10.7 | 4 542 | 26.3 | 25.5 |
| Macomb | 330 452 | 77.7 | 148 600 | 24.8 | 14.7 | 779 | 30.6 | 1.6 | 399 986 | -0.1 | 41 530 | 10.4 | 381 686 | 32.8 | 22.3 |
| Manistee | 10 745 | 80.2 | 120 000 | 25.1 | 13.2 | 657 | 30.0 | 1.8 | 10 753 | -1.2 | 1 092 | 10.2 | 9 554 | 26.6 | 27.1 |
| Marquette | 25 752 | 71.7 | 127 700 | 20.6 | 12.0 | 572 | 32.0 | 1.2 | 34 385 | -0.1 | 2 655 | 7.7 | 30 990 | 33.0 | 20.5 |
| Mason | 12 312 | 75.3 | 121 500 | 25.1 | 13.5 | 657 | 29.0 | 2.4 | 14 532 | 1.0 | 1 314 | 9.0 | 12 496 | 30.7 | 28.3 |
| Mecosta | 15 842 | 73.1 | 117 500 | 25.0 | 11.7 | 672 | 37.1 | 3.0 | 19 872 | -0.8 | 1 847 | 9.3 | 17 112 | 28.5 | 26.1 |
| Menominee | 10 866 | 80.2 | 96 700 | 22.7 | 11.6 | 487 | 28.5 | 2.4 | 12 244 | 0.4 | 879 | 7.2 | 10 771 | 25.8 | 35.8 |
| Midland | 33 658 | 77.1 | 131 900 | 21.5 | 11.8 | 662 | 30.5 | 1.5 | 41 829 | -0.3 | 2 983 | 7.1 | 37 264 | 38.6 | 21.3 |
| Missaukee | 5 861 | 82.2 | 111 800 | 26.0 | 13.2 | 698 | 31.8 | 2.6 | 5 744 | -1.9 | 623 | 10.8 | 6 137 | 26.3 | 33.6 |
| Monroe | 58 200 | 80.4 | 156 600 | 24.1 | 13.2 | 755 | 29.9 | 1.7 | 69 315 | -0.4 | 5 543 | 8.0 | 68 242 | 27.2 | 31.1 |
| Montcalm | 23 332 | 79.6 | 107 000 | 25.8 | 13.6 | 659 | 32.3 | 2.2 | 24 978 | -1.7 | 2 747 | 11.0 | 24 967 | 23.2 | 35.3 |
| Montmorency | 4 204 | 86.9 | 100 200 | 27.2 | 12.5 | 622 | 34.3 | 1.7 | 3 495 | -3.4 | 539 | 15.4 | 3 033 | 24.3 | 30.0 |
| Muskegon | 65 272 | 74.8 | 108 700 | 24.3 | 13.5 | 642 | 34.5 | 1.8 | 83 069 | 0.4 | 7 293 | 8.8 | 68 790 | 26.8 | 30.0 |
| Newaygo | 18 616 | 83.9 | 113 800 | 25.5 | 13.2 | 637 | 30.5 | 2.4 | 21 535 | 0.8 | 1 824 | 8.5 | 19 502 | 24.9 | 37.4 |
| Oakland | 481 449 | 73.6 | 190 500 | 24.3 | 14.4 | 894 | 29.4 | 1.5 | 587 709 | 0.1 | 53 238 | 9.1 | 578 548 | 46.5 | 14.0 |
| Oceana | 9 759 | 84.0 | 110 900 | 24.9 | 13.0 | 644 | 31.8 | 2.5 | 13 575 | 0.8 | 1 506 | 11.1 | 10 936 | 23.4 | 37.3 |
| Ogemaw | 8 291 | 83.6 | 100 800 | 27.4 | 13.7 | 610 | 35.2 | 1.8 | 9 004 | -1.9 | 918 | 10.2 | 7 446 | 24.7 | 27.7 |
| Ontonagon | 3 413 | 85.7 | 75 000 | 23.9 | 13.9 | 444 | 29.4 | 0.8 | 2 603 | -6.0 | 345 | 13.3 | 2 658 | 23.3 | 27.2 |
| Osceola | 9 042 | 80.4 | 99 500 | 24.3 | 13.4 | 534 | 30.6 | 2.9 | 9 032 | -1.1 | 921 | 10.2 | 9 126 | 24.3 | 39.9 |
| Oscoda | 3 987 | 84.0 | 88 800 | 25.9 | 12.6 | 578 | 39.3 | 2.6 | 3 320 | -4.6 | 500 | 15.1 | 2 791 | 24.5 | 29.2 |
| Otsego | 9 692 | 82.2 | 120 500 | 24.7 | 12.7 | 651 | 29.5 | 1.9 | 10 770 | -2.3 | 1 174 | 10.9 | 10 427 | 27.1 | 23.7 |
| Ottawa | 93 777 | 79.1 | 158 900 | 23.5 | 12.5 | 747 | 30.6 | 2.3 | 129 921 | 0.8 | 8 851 | 6.8 | 127 025 | 33.1 | 27.7 |
| Presque Isle | 6 195 | 88.9 | 105 600 | 24.7 | 14.2 | 520 | 25.9 | 1.8 | 5 640 | 0.5 | 787 | 14.0 | 4 816 | 26.9 | 32.2 |
| Roscommon | 11 255 | 84.7 | 102 900 | 31.7 | 12.9 | 593 | 40.7 | 1.4 | 9 319 | -2.9 | 1 071 | 11.5 | 7 531 | 22.8 | 23.9 |
| Saginaw | 76 828 | 73.6 | 106 400 | 23.7 | 13.5 | 697 | 34.6 | 1.5 | 90 451 | -1.1 | 7 761 | 8.6 | 80 749 | 29.6 | 22.2 |
| St. Clair | 63 985 | 78.0 | 141 800 | 25.6 | 14.7 | 723 | 32.3 | 1.3 | 75 028 | 0.0 | 9 155 | 12.2 | 69 706 | 26.4 | 29.5 |
| St. Joseph | 22 319 | 78.3 | 113 800 | 23.1 | 12.4 | 615 | 29.8 | 2.2 | 27 608 | -0.7 | 2 323 | 8.4 | 24 886 | 24.4 | 39.3 |
| Sanilac | 16 657 | 82.7 | 108 900 | 26.6 | 14.1 | 607 | 31.7 | 2.1 | 19 393 | -0.1 | 1 923 | 9.9 | 17 189 | 26.4 | 36.1 |
| Schoolcraft | 3 673 | 87.6 | 85 100 | 23.9 | 12.3 | 489 | 28.9 | 1.7 | 3 588 | -5.1 | 449 | 12.5 | 3 266 | 26.9 | 29.5 |
| Shiawassee | 27 581 | 78.1 | 122 800 | 24.2 | 13.0 | 646 | 31.6 | 1.2 | 32 788 | -1.2 | 3 058 | 9.3 | 30 384 | 28.2 | 29.6 |
| Tuscola | 21 525 | 82.2 | 106 300 | 25.1 | 13.5 | 610 | 31.1 | 1.5 | 25 586 | -1.5 | 2 535 | 9.9 | 22 901 | 25.7 | 29.6 |
| Van Buren | 28 846 | 79.2 | 122 300 | 25.1 | 13.4 | 602 | 33.6 | 1.9 | 35 781 | -1.7 | 3 408 | 9.5 | 33 527 | 26.6 | 33.3 |
| Washtenaw | 134 165 | 62.4 | 208 800 | 24.1 | 13.4 | 879 | 33.1 | 1.2 | 182 258 | 0.5 | 10 346 | 5.7 | 168 734 | 50.1 | 12.5 |
| Wayne | 681 674 | 66.6 | 110 000 | 26.3 | 15.6 | 775 | 36.4 | 3.1 | 816 059 | -0.4 | 95 160 | 11.7 | 704 477 | 31.0 | 22.6 |
| Wexford | 12 426 | 80.0 | 108 400 | 25.6 | 13.1 | 673 | 30.8 | 2.1 | 13 371 | -1.3 | 1 554 | 11.6 | 13 410 | 25.9 | 35.8 |
| **MINNESOTA** | 2 094 265 | 73.6 | 201 400 | 24.2 | 12.0 | 783 | 29.7 | 2.3 | 2 969 367 | 0.0 | 167 696 | 5.6 | 2 734 914 | 38.2 | 21.3 |
| Aitkin | 7 823 | 82.1 | 175 400 | 27.4 | 13.1 | 592 | 26.7 | 3.1 | 7 346 | -3.2 | 568 | 7.7 | 6 816 | 27.0 | 28.1 |
| Anoka | 120 886 | 82.3 | 215 900 | 25.4 | 12.2 | 899 | 29.7 | 1.8 | 190 059 | 0.4 | 11 104 | 5.8 | 175 687 | 36.3 | 22.7 |
| Becker | 13 458 | 78.8 | 169 300 | 24.7 | 12.5 | 586 | 29.2 | 1.8 | 17 931 | 0.2 | 1 043 | 5.8 | 15 889 | 30.6 | 28.4 |
| Beltrami | 16 536 | 71.8 | 148 900 | 24.4 | 12.1 | 627 | 28.1 | 4.1 | 22 105 | -0.1 | 1 621 | 7.3 | 20 255 | 34.6 | 20.7 |
| Benton | 15 139 | 71.4 | 165 800 | 25.3 | 12.7 | 645 | 29.8 | 1.4 | 22 345 | 0.0 | 1 352 | 6.1 | 20 133 | 27.9 | 29.3 |
| Big Stone | 2 395 | 79.2 | 83 300 | 21.9 | 11.3 | 504 | 29.1 | 1.0 | 2 927 | -1.9 | 148 | 5.1 | 2 447 | 36.3 | 27.5 |
| Blue Earth | 24 045 | 66.8 | 161 700 | 23.3 | 11.8 | 688 | 33.3 | 1.2 | 38 393 | -0.6 | 1 866 | 4.9 | 36 229 | 29.3 | 24.1 |
| Brown | 10 861 | 78.6 | 122 400 | 22.3 | 10.9 | 540 | 27.1 | 1.8 | 15 401 | -2.3 | 845 | 5.5 | 13 950 | 26.7 | 33.1 |
| Carlton | 13 820 | 80.2 | 163 300 | 24.3 | 11.7 | 633 | 30.7 | 2.0 | 17 867 | -0.8 | 1 268 | 7.1 | 16 324 | 33.3 | 25.4 |
| Carver | 32 715 | 83.0 | 277 600 | 24.4 | 11.2 | 884 | 30.2 | 1.5 | 51 008 | 0.8 | 2 638 | 5.2 | 48 276 | 44.3 | 17.6 |
| Cass | 12 943 | 82.3 | 185 400 | 25.6 | 13.1 | 637 | 26.7 | 3.5 | 13 890 | -2.9 | 1 238 | 8.9 | 12 358 | 31.3 | 25.9 |
| Chippewa | 5 223 | 73.7 | 94 900 | 20.1 | 11.4 | 623 | 27.9 | 1.7 | 7 404 | -0.3 | 376 | 5.1 | 6 374 | 30.8 | 32.7 |
| Chisago | 19 540 | 85.9 | 224 700 | 27.7 | 12.1 | 776 | 32.4 | 1.9 | 28 748 | 0.1 | 1 924 | 6.7 | 26 512 | 31.5 | 28.7 |
| Clay | 21 928 | 70.8 | 149 900 | 22.5 | 11.4 | 641 | 34.3 | 1.4 | 34 423 | 2.5 | 1 451 | 4.2 | 31 023 | 32.7 | 23.5 |
| Clearwater | 3 684 | 77.7 | 117 300 | 25.8 | 13.3 | 525 | 29.8 | 7.5 | 4 199 | -4.5 | 472 | 11.2 | 3 746 | 29.1 | 31.9 |
| Cook | 2 627 | 72.5 | 240 600 | 27.6 | 9.9 | 613 | 20.0 | 6.9 | 3 203 | -1.1 | 190 | 5.9 | 2 747 | 32.3 | 20.1 |
| Cottonwood | 4 861 | 79.6 | 83 100 | 21.9 | 11.5 | 487 | 27.2 | 2.0 | 6 653 | -3.3 | 385 | 5.8 | 5 680 | 30.4 | 31.3 |
| Crow Wing | 26 906 | 76.5 | 188 600 | 25.5 | 12.3 | 661 | 29.7 | 1.7 | 32 809 | -2.8 | 2 412 | 7.4 | 28 632 | 32.1 | 23.8 |
| Dakota | 151 719 | 78.0 | 238 300 | 23.8 | 11.1 | 906 | 28.5 | 1.7 | 231 946 | 0.5 | 12 179 | 5.3 | 215 668 | 41.6 | 17.5 |
| Dodge | 7 347 | 86.9 | 162 100 | 22.5 | 11.9 | 661 | 27.2 | 1.3 | 11 261 | 1.0 | 595 | 5.3 | 10 673 | 34.7 | 26.7 |
| Douglas | 16 222 | 75.5 | 188 100 | 25.6 | 13.2 | 592 | 28.8 | 0.8 | 21 056 | -0.2 | 1 014 | 4.8 | 18 320 | 34.2 | 24.5 |
| Faribault | 6 274 | 80.3 | 87 300 | 21.5 | 12.2 | 474 | 29.3 | 1.9 | 7 668 | -1.5 | 461 | 6.0 | 7 200 | 30.0 | 32.6 |

1. Specified owner-occupied units. 2. A value of 9.9 represents 9.9 percent or less. 3. Specified renter-occupied units. A value of 10.0 represents 10 percent or less. 4. Overcrowded or lacking complete plumbing facilities. 5. Percent of civilian labor force. 6. Persons 16 years old and over.

# Table B. States and Counties — Nonfarm Employment and Agriculture

| STATE County | Number of establish-ments | Total | Health care and social assistance | Manufac-turing | Retail trade | Finance and insurance | Professional, scientific, and technical services | Total (mil dol) | Average per employee (dollars) | Number | Fewer than 50 acres | 500 acres or more | Farm operators whose principal occupation is farming (percent) |
|---|---|---|---|---|---|---|---|---|---|---|---|---|---|
| | 104 | 105 | 106 | 107 | 108 | 109 | 110 | 111 | 112 | 113 | 114 | 115 | 116 |
| MICHIGAN—Cont'd | | | | | | | | | | | | | |
| Keweenaw | 58 | 170 | NA | D | 19 | D | NA | 4 | 21 024 | 8 | 37.5 | 12.5 | 50.0 |
| Lake | 167 | 1 050 | 238 | 81 | 208 | D | 20 | 28 | 26 432 | 186 | 37.6 | 2.2 | 41.4 |
| Lapeer | 1 541 | 16 091 | 2 507 | 4 112 | 2 888 | 467 | 566 | 515 | 32 002 | 1 317 | 53.5 | 6.3 | 45.5 |
| Leelanau | 705 | 3 823 | 623 | 281 | 551 | 153 | 198 | 130 | 34 001 | 449 | 37.9 | 3.1 | 47.4 |
| Lenawee | 1 827 | 22 482 | 3 330 | 4 387 | 4 121 | 825 | 531 | 680 | 30 241 | 1 686 | 42.9 | 11.0 | 42.2 |
| Livingston | 4 045 | 46 409 | 5 604 | 6 905 | 8 786 | 3 344 | 2 657 | 1 600 | 34 467 | 795 | 60.8 | 5.3 | 45.3 |
| Luce | 163 | 1 252 | D | D | 249 | 67 | D | 40 | 31 802 | 41 | 29.3 | 9.8 | 41.5 |
| Mackinac | 444 | 2 250 | D | D | 376 | 78 | 35 | 115 | 51 014 | 89 | 20.2 | 11.2 | 39.3 |
| Macomb | 17 806 | 263 087 | 36 139 | 53 751 | 39 962 | 6 991 | 28 376 | 11 564 | 43 955 | 475 | 60.0 | 5.9 | 58.5 |
| Manistee | 563 | 5 232 | 768 | 705 | 903 | 167 | 103 | 176 | 33 711 | 358 | 31.6 | 3.1 | 47.2 |
| Marquette | 1 644 | 21 200 | 5 785 | 823 | 3 743 | 868 | 739 | 786 | 37 094 | 144 | 35.4 | 11.1 | 50.7 |
| Mason | 744 | 8 529 | 1 487 | 1 543 | 1 398 | 228 | 149 | 285 | 33 422 | 450 | 33.8 | 7.8 | 43.6 |
| Mecosta | 739 | 8 963 | 1 333 | 1 942 | 2 027 | 211 | 170 | 278 | 31 046 | 845 | 32.8 | 4.5 | 43.8 |
| Menominee | 457 | 5 278 | 338 | 1 637 | 615 | 145 | 70 | 152 | 28 738 | 419 | 27.4 | 13.6 | 45.1 |
| Midland | 1 771 | 36 653 | 6 387 | 6 082 | 4 236 | 940 | 879 | 2 123 | 57 914 | 571 | 46.8 | 7.4 | 40.8 |
| Missaukee | 273 | 1 867 | 268 | 310 | 372 | D | 21 | 52 | 27 888 | 391 | 34.8 | 10.7 | 43.2 |
| Monroe | 2 333 | 34 779 | 5 347 | 6 243 | 5 038 | 867 | 1 822 | 1 360 | 39 104 | 1 119 | 52.4 | 10.0 | 44.2 |
| Montcalm | 1 036 | 11 970 | 2 583 | 2 644 | 2 421 | 348 | 223 | 369 | 30 842 | 1 227 | 39.9 | 7.6 | 47.1 |
| Montmorency | 211 | 1 573 | 283 | 384 | 255 | D | D | 55 | 35 114 | 140 | 25.7 | 5.7 | 47.1 |
| Muskegon | 3 268 | 49 204 | 9 330 | 11 499 | 7 964 | 1 084 | 1 492 | 1 766 | 35 898 | 525 | 52.2 | 5.7 | 45.3 |
| Newaygo | 784 | 8 891 | 1 668 | 1 893 | 1 509 | D | 362 | 299 | 33 655 | 951 | 42.5 | 6.0 | 41.1 |
| Oakland | 38 205 | 609 608 | 94 415 | 42 606 | 69 046 | 40 100 | 78 319 | 32 703 | 53 646 | 588 | 74.7 | 1.0 | 42.0 |
| Oceana | 511 | 4 069 | 522 | 1 230 | 640 | 126 | 75 | 120 | 29 577 | 648 | 38.3 | 8.0 | 47.8 |
| Ogemaw | 584 | 5 785 | 1 472 | 524 | 1 640 | D | 102 | 160 | 27 701 | 321 | 33.6 | 11.8 | 48.3 |
| Ontonagon | 199 | 1 213 | 288 | D | 257 | 72 | 10 | 31 | 25 866 | 104 | 15.4 | 19.2 | 51.9 |
| Osceola | 419 | 5 921 | 966 | 2 139 | 581 | 96 | 82 | 233 | 39 369 | 826 | 34.4 | 5.7 | 36.4 |
| Oscoda | 194 | 1 469 | 196 | 247 | 237 | 41 | D | 37 | 25 524 | 136 | 39.7 | 5.1 | 45.6 |
| Otsego | 762 | 8 101 | 1 369 | 771 | 2 125 | 182 | 207 | 249 | 30 708 | 182 | 38.5 | 13.2 | 45.1 |
| Ottawa | 5 633 | 90 369 | 10 887 | 27 181 | 9 535 | 2 226 | 3 210 | 3 383 | 37 433 | 1 451 | 59.4 | 4.9 | 43.2 |
| Presque Isle | 342 | 2 131 | 274 | 189 | 396 | 92 | D | 63 | 29 420 | 289 | 21.1 | 12.5 | 46.4 |
| Roscommon | 563 | 4 542 | 619 | 374 | 1 540 | 162 | D | 119 | 26 256 | 54 | 46.3 | 1.9 | 48.1 |
| Saginaw | 4 375 | 75 555 | 16 457 | 10 186 | 12 677 | 2 764 | 2 303 | 2 745 | 36 337 | 1 533 | 43.4 | 10.0 | 48.3 |
| St. Clair | 3 123 | 39 572 | 7 678 | 7 929 | 7 195 | 1 304 | 1 138 | 1 364 | 34 460 | 1 072 | 51.5 | 6.7 | 46.9 |
| St. Joseph | 1 182 | 19 492 | 1 985 | 7 441 | 2 294 | 463 | 2 954 | 624 | 32 017 | 1 033 | 45.0 | 10.6 | 39.2 |
| Sanilac | 845 | 7 553 | 1 235 | 2 286 | 1 401 | 402 | 187 | 230 | 30 447 | 1 535 | 32.8 | 14.5 | 56.5 |
| Schoolcraft | 226 | 1 925 | D | D | 381 | D | 42 | 64 | 33 112 | 66 | 25.8 | 16.7 | 36.4 |
| Shiawassee | 1 158 | 12 389 | 2 416 | 2 022 | 2 351 | 395 | 484 | 354 | 28 554 | 1 082 | 45.2 | 10.8 | 45.2 |
| Tuscola | 883 | 9 099 | 2 483 | 1 203 | 1 640 | 312 | D | 289 | 31 784 | 1 372 | 38.7 | 12.8 | 47.7 |
| Van Buren | 1 300 | 15 395 | 2 386 | 2 875 | 2 346 | 325 | 421 | 576 | 37 389 | 1 232 | 49.0 | 3.6 | 46.8 |
| Washtenaw | 7 889 | 134 317 | D | 11 757 | 16 106 | 4 127 | 11 483 | 6 610 | 49 214 | 1 300 | 54.9 | 6.1 | 45.2 |
| Wayne | 32 199 | 579 596 | 101 877 | 69 753 | 64 713 | 22 955 | 46 624 | 27 830 | 48 016 | 313 | 78.0 | 1.9 | 46.6 |
| Wexford | 822 | 12 608 | 1 942 | 3 368 | 1 852 | 295 | 315 | 404 | 32 033 | 371 | 41.5 | 3.0 | 35.0 |
| MINNESOTA | 144 606 | 2 393 746 | 441 665 | 291 463 | 286 361 | 148 501 | 136 937 | 110 751 | 46 267 | 80 992 | 25.5 | 17.9 | 48.9 |
| Aitkin | 399 | 2 979 | 705 | D | 686 | 85 | D | 79 | 26 625 | 538 | 19.0 | 9.7 | 38.1 |
| Anoka | 7 207 | 105 135 | 15 077 | 20 618 | 15 128 | 2 454 | 3 408 | 5 216 | 49 616 | 475 | 58.5 | 3.4 | 37.7 |
| Becker | 955 | 11 146 | 1 950 | 1 671 | 1 898 | 244 | 216 | 313 | 28 077 | 1 202 | 13.6 | 13.0 | 40.3 |
| Beltrami | 1 147 | 13 747 | 3 191 | 816 | 3 004 | 409 | 356 | 443 | 31 684 | 919 | 26.8 | 8.8 | 44.4 |
| Benton | 897 | 14 440 | 2 805 | 3 497 | 1 904 | 214 | 183 | 458 | 31 684 | 452 | 15.7 | 34.3 | 62.2 |
| Big Stone | 178 | 1 587 | 663 | D | 213 | 74 | 26 | 39 | 24 677 | 452 | 15.7 | 34.3 | 62.2 |
| Blue Earth | 1 919 | 34 283 | 9 011 | 3 789 | 5 971 | 1 002 | 1 004 | 1 111 | 32 415 | 1 247 | 29.7 | 21.5 | 52.5 |
| Brown | 765 | 12 145 | 2 388 | 2 972 | 1 601 | 443 | 402 | 376 | 30 939 | 1 129 | 22.1 | 18.6 | 57.9 |
| Carlton | 702 | 7 757 | 1 806 | 1 318 | 1 365 | 412 | 186 | 266 | 34 294 | 485 | 17.9 | 8.5 | 40.8 |
| Carver | 2 328 | 34 145 | 4 373 | 9 974 | 3 305 | 807 | 1 773 | 1 568 | 45 931 | 800 | 38.1 | 8.6 | 50.3 |
| Cass | 817 | 6 467 | 1 107 | 308 | 865 | 203 | 164 | 155 | 24 014 | 563 | 17.6 | 12.3 | 37.8 |
| Chippewa | 429 | 5 137 | 1 157 | 1 173 | 714 | D | 78 | 162 | 31 512 | 720 | 23.9 | 29.2 | 55.4 |
| Chisago | 1 213 | 12 550 | D | 1 880 | 1 867 | 303 | 706 | 422 | 33 605 | 867 | 45.8 | 5.5 | 37.8 |
| Clay | 1 263 | 16 799 | 3 631 | 853 | 2 818 | 444 | 363 | 452 | 26 885 | 921 | 19.4 | 30.7 | 50.8 |
| Clearwater | 200 | 2 291 | 680 | D | 239 | 63 | D | 86 | 37 486 | 601 | 12.1 | 16.3 | 43.3 |
| Cook | 267 | 1 974 | D | D | 307 | 34 | D | 55 | 27 639 | 13 | 38.5 | 7.7 | 38.5 |
| Cottonwood | 351 | 4 554 | 777 | 1 747 | 486 | 122 | 59 | 133 | 29 308 | 865 | 24.6 | 32.3 | 59.5 |
| Crow Wing | 2 026 | 24 886 | 5 875 | 2 263 | 4 371 | 687 | 802 | 801 | 32 172 | 609 | 25.8 | 7.6 | 35.6 |
| Dakota | 9 835 | 163 548 | 20 935 | 16 643 | 21 623 | 10 166 | 9 161 | 7 242 | 44 278 | 1 065 | 48.4 | 12.2 | 46.3 |
| Dodge | 418 | 3 997 | 324 | 1 080 | 461 | 134 | 75 | 151 | 37 658 | 723 | 39.3 | 18.3 | 46.2 |
| Douglas | 1 326 | 16 040 | 3 157 | 2 957 | 2 968 | 427 | 488 | 551 | 34 364 | 1 199 | 25.1 | 9.6 | 39.1 |
| Faribault | 457 | 4 321 | 968 | 1 095 | 581 | D | 75 | 138 | 31 948 | 952 | 22.8 | 31.5 | 65.3 |

# Table B. States and Counties — **Agriculture**

| STATE County | Agriculture, 2007 (cont.) | | | | | | | | | | | | | | |
| | Land in farms | | | | | Value of land and buildings (dollars) | | Value of machinery and equipment, average per farm (dollars) | Value of products sold | | | | Percent of farms with sales of: | | Government payments | |
| | | | Acres | | | | | | | | Percent from: | | | | | |
| | Acreage (1,000) | Percent change, 2002–2007 | Average size of farm | Total irrigated (1,000) | Total cropland (1,000) | Average per farm | Average per acre | | Total (mil dol) | Average per farm (dollars) | Crops | Live-stock and poultry products | $10,000 or more | $100,000 or more | Total ($1,000) | Percent of farms |
|---|---|---|---|---|---|---|---|---|---|---|---|---|---|---|---|---|
| | 117 | 118 | 119 | 120 | 121 | 122 | 123 | 124 | 125 | 126 | 127 | 128 | 129 | 130 | 131 | 132 |
| **MICHIGAN—Cont'd** | | | | | | | | | | | | | | | | |
| Keweenaw | 2 | 100.0 | 200 | 0.0 | 0.4 | 419 412 | 2 094 | 39 254 | 0.0 | 741 | D | D | 0.0 | 0.0 | 0 | 0.0 |
| Lake | 21 | -8.7 | 115 | 0.1 | 10.5 | 334 655 | 2 912 | 53 529 | 2.4 | 13 168 | 28.2 | 71.8 | 15.1 | 2.2 | 112 | 13.4 |
| Lapeer | 176 | -6.9 | 134 | 2.4 | 135.3 | 551 299 | 4 117 | 80 955 | 69.0 | 52 427 | 65.4 | 34.6 | 31.0 | 11.1 | 1 532 | 22.1 |
| Leelanau | 56 | -9.7 | 124 | 1.5 | 33.7 | 877 921 | 7 070 | 81 423 | 35.3 | 78 628 | 89.7 | 10.3 | 54.1 | 17.8 | 231 | 19.6 |
| Lenawee | 349 | -1.1 | 207 | 5.9 | 304.7 | 661 311 | 3 198 | 88 864 | 161.1 | 95 557 | 67.3 | 32.7 | 38.6 | 15.5 | 8 609 | 68.6 |
| Livingston | 96 | 0.0 | 121 | 1.4 | 69.3 | 611 728 | 5 044 | 80 225 | 41.7 | 52 422 | 64.1 | 35.9 | 29.2 | 9.8 | 844 | 18.9 |
| Luce | 9 | -10.0 | 215 | D | 3.4 | 633 653 | 2 946 | 65 537 | 2.6 | 62 208 | 86.9 | 13.1 | 36.6 | 14.6 | D | 7.3 |
| Mackinac | 22 | 10.0 | 244 | D | 13.0 | 515 516 | 2 115 | 63 252 | 4.3 | 48 288 | 9.5 | 90.5 | 39.3 | 6.7 | 43 | 13.5 |
| Macomb | 62 | -8.8 | 131 | 3.0 | 54.8 | 672 691 | 5 154 | 111 424 | 52.7 | 110 915 | 88.7 | 11.3 | 43.6 | 18.9 | 622 | 28.2 |
| Manistee | 46 | 0.0 | 129 | 2.3 | 24.8 | 396 087 | 3 080 | 58 435 | 9.2 | 25 732 | 81.3 | 18.7 | 30.2 | 5.0 | 113 | 14.2 |
| Marquette | 30 | 0.0 | 209 | 0.1 | 10.4 | 504 620 | 2 415 | 61 555 | 3.8 | 26 565 | 36.2 | 63.8 | 16.0 | 6.3 | 40 | 8.3 |
| Mason | 76 | -5.0 | 170 | 3.3 | 55.9 | 542 279 | 3 192 | 82 612 | 34.5 | 76 596 | 59.1 | 40.9 | 37.6 | 15.1 | 574 | 28.9 |
| Mecosta | 115 | -4.2 | 136 | 8.7 | 76.7 | 394 509 | 2 906 | 68 454 | 72.7 | 85 979 | 26.5 | 73.5 | 34.3 | 7.3 | 653 | 37.4 |
| Menominee | 104 | 5.1 | 247 | 0.0 | 59.7 | 551 410 | 2 229 | 75 382 | 33.6 | 80 236 | 10.0 | 90.0 | 37.7 | 15.5 | 699 | 36.5 |
| Midland | 91 | 7.1 | 159 | 0.5 | 69.6 | 476 039 | 3 000 | 72 947 | 48.8 | 85 432 | 45.8 | 54.2 | 31.3 | 10.2 | 1 181 | 39.8 |
| Missaukee | 88 | -10.2 | 226 | 4.6 | 62.9 | 659 931 | 2 920 | 111 648 | 70.6 | 180 652 | 17.0 | 83.0 | 35.8 | 18.9 | 756 | 29.4 |
| Monroe | 208 | -4.1 | 186 | 6.5 | 189.5 | 710 533 | 3 826 | 102 813 | 130.1 | 116 237 | 93.8 | 6.2 | 51.4 | 18.8 | 3 127 | 48.9 |
| Montcalm | 243 | -4.7 | 198 | 40.3 | 189.9 | 566 867 | 2 865 | 89 122 | 139.4 | 113 597 | 63.7 | 36.3 | 35.5 | 12.6 | 2 473 | 49.2 |
| Montmorency | 22 | 4.8 | 156 | D | 12.6 | 370 554 | 2 380 | 85 309 | 4.1 | 29 572 | 33.0 | 67.0 | 22.1 | 7.9 | 64 | 33.6 |
| Muskegon | 80 | 8.1 | 152 | 9.8 | 58.1 | 601 241 | 3 962 | 100 785 | 91.2 | 173 668 | 44.2 | 55.8 | 34.1 | 14.5 | 790 | 23.0 |
| Newaygo | 133 | -1.5 | 140 | 10.3 | 89.5 | 479 025 | 3 415 | 80 344 | 101.2 | 106 382 | 31.4 | 68.6 | 33.4 | 12.6 | 878 | 26.5 |
| Oakland | 33 | -19.5 | 55 | 0.6 | 20.0 | 465 550 | 8 422 | 51 211 | 18.8 | 31 987 | 80.7 | 19.3 | 20.9 | 6.3 | 131 | 6.8 |
| Oceana | 123 | -3.1 | 190 | 6.9 | 83.3 | 719 566 | 3 782 | 92 217 | 78.1 | 120 565 | 58.6 | 41.4 | 40.0 | 13.0 | 1 083 | 21.0 |
| Ogemaw | 61 | -10.3 | 190 | 0.2 | 40.5 | 535 342 | 2 820 | 89 394 | 30.5 | 95 071 | 13.5 | 86.5 | 33.6 | 13.7 | 349 | 40.5 |
| Ontonagon | 31 | -8.8 | 296 | D | 15.2 | 471 379 | 1 590 | 61 361 | 1.9 | 18 610 | 38.9 | 61.2 | 31.7 | 3.8 | 27 | 22.1 |
| Osceola | 122 | 5.2 | 148 | 2.3 | 73.2 | 394 667 | 2 668 | 60 954 | 30.2 | 36 551 | 16.5 | 83.5 | 25.2 | 5.9 | 607 | 22.2 |
| Oscoda | 18 | 5.9 | 129 | 0.0 | 8.4 | 330 846 | 2 560 | 39 659 | 4.9 | 36 054 | 8.3 | 91.7 | 44.9 | 12.5 | 18 | 8.1 |
| Otsego | 34 | -2.9 | 185 | 0.4 | 15.7 | 490 725 | 2 658 | 59 772 | 4.3 | 23 802 | 74.1 | 25.9 | 33.5 | 2.7 | 45 | 30.2 |
| Ottawa | 171 | 3.6 | 118 | 15.2 | 130.0 | 683 668 | 5 817 | 97 890 | 391.1 | 269 533 | 59.3 | 40.7 | 51.8 | 24.7 | 1 463 | 24.9 |
| Presque Isle | 71 | 4.4 | 246 | 1.5 | 45.7 | 554 952 | 2 256 | 94 074 | 13.4 | 46 387 | 60.6 | 39.4 | 33.2 | 10.4 | 284 | 42.9 |
| Roscommon | 5 | -28.6 | 88 | D | 2.3 | 367 438 | 4 169 | 53 978 | 0.4 | 7 016 | 44.9 | 55.1 | 22.2 | 0.0 | 10 | 11.1 |
| Saginaw | 324 | -0.3 | 212 | 1.8 | 287.2 | 599 832 | 2 835 | 100 851 | 142.5 | 92 959 | 88.8 | 11.2 | 49.5 | 17.6 | 5 355 | 70.8 |
| St. Clair | 160 | -12.1 | 150 | 1.3 | 135.4 | 574 011 | 3 834 | 87 841 | 50.8 | 47 365 | 84.7 | 15.3 | 34.1 | 10.4 | 1 621 | 30.8 |
| St. Joseph | 215 | -6.9 | 209 | 102.9 | 181.1 | 705 213 | 3 382 | 119 780 | 136.0 | 131 688 | 77.0 | 23.0 | 41.2 | 17.1 | 3 322 | 46.9 |
| Sanilac | 417 | -4.1 | 272 | 2.0 | 368.2 | 792 375 | 2 916 | 140 989 | 216.7 | 141 197 | 54.5 | 45.5 | 51.1 | 24.6 | 5 412 | 62.9 |
| Schoolcraft | 27 | 92.9 | 405 | 0.0 | 10.8 | 567 778 | 1 404 | 54 036 | 2.4 | 36 343 | 63.4 | 36.6 | 37.9 | 12.1 | 7 | 18.2 |
| Shiawassee | 227 | -3.4 | 209 | 1.6 | 195.5 | 616 615 | 2 945 | 92 640 | 87.8 | 81 189 | 65.9 | 34.1 | 44.7 | 15.5 | 3 176 | 57.7 |
| Tuscola | 343 | 2.1 | 250 | 5.8 | 301.4 | 756 725 | 3 029 | 123 592 | 150.0 | 109 347 | 77.7 | 22.3 | 41.3 | 18.3 | 4 568 | 58.9 |
| Van Buren | 185 | 5.1 | 150 | 30.4 | 135.0 | 643 980 | 4 281 | 96 842 | 173.5 | 140 805 | 82.2 | 17.8 | 42.9 | 16.1 | 1 436 | 21.9 |
| Washtenaw | 167 | -4.6 | 128 | 2.7 | 133.1 | 642 197 | 5 003 | 83 247 | 73.2 | 56 305 | 74.9 | 25.1 | 37.3 | 12.4 | 2 193 | 32.6 |
| Wayne | 17 | -19.0 | 56 | 0.8 | 13.1 | 431 377 | 7 741 | 73 184 | 28.8 | 91 875 | 97.1 | 2.9 | 35.8 | 11.2 | 93 | 10.9 |
| Wexford | 38 | -17.4 | 104 | 1.0 | 24.7 | 330 704 | 3 188 | 43 496 | 6.9 | 18 542 | 42.7 | 57.3 | 25.3 | 4.0 | 110 | 17.5 |
| **MINNESOTA** | 26 918 | -2.2 | 332 | 506.4 | 21 948.6 | 853 968 | 2 569 | 131 698 | 13 180.5 | 162 738 | 53.5 | 46.5 | 50.7 | 27.4 | 445 861 | 70.0 |
| Aitkin | 133 | -23.6 | 247 | 4.4 | 64.4 | 413 719 | 1 678 | 54 510 | 13.5 | 25 157 | 53.1 | 47.0 | 20.4 | 5.2 | 222 | 22.9 |
| Anoka | 46 | -23.3 | 97 | 2.5 | 30.1 | 563 161 | 5 817 | 63 665 | 32.6 | 68 556 | 66.9 | 33.1 | 26.7 | 7.8 | 336 | 24.2 |
| Becker | 396 | -5.0 | 329 | 8.6 | 263.0 | 618 949 | 1 879 | 93 061 | 149.5 | 124 361 | 50.0 | 50.0 | 32.9 | 14.1 | 4 330 | 64.9 |
| Beltrami | 211 | -9.4 | 313 | 2.8 | 101.7 | 486 069 | 1 554 | 57 869 | 21.0 | 31 116 | 46.0 | 54.0 | 33.5 | 6.4 | 1 207 | 33.2 |
| Benton | 186 | -5.1 | 202 | 14.6 | 136.9 | 616 751 | 3 047 | 111 263 | 113.9 | 123 911 | 19.1 | 80.9 | 48.5 | 19.4 | 2 390 | 62.7 |
| Big Stone | 252 | -8.0 | 558 | 2.2 | 223.8 | 1 201 905 | 2 153 | 185 267 | 86.8 | 192 110 | 75.8 | 24.2 | 64.4 | 40.7 | 4 045 | 85.2 |
| Blue Earth | 415 | 2.2 | 333 | 0.6 | 375.7 | 1 183 017 | 3 552 | 163 234 | 327.5 | 262 619 | 47.3 | 52.7 | 60.1 | 40.4 | 8 511 | 79.6 |
| Brown | 355 | 2.0 | 314 | 3.0 | 318.8 | 929 209 | 2 957 | 141 845 | 256.4 | 227 086 | 48.5 | 51.5 | 70.8 | 43.8 | 7 358 | 87.3 |
| Carlton | 98 | -14.0 | 202 | 2.1 | 43.9 | 421 058 | 2 086 | 51 806 | 8.0 | 16 578 | 28.0 | 72.0 | 27.8 | 4.3 | 123 | 13.0 |
| Carver | 169 | -1.7 | 212 | 0.5 | 144.5 | 834 797 | 3 942 | 155 820 | 92.9 | 116 181 | 52.0 | 48.0 | 50.4 | 25.6 | 3 300 | 64.1 |
| Cass | 169 | -14.2 | 300 | 7.6 | 72.2 | 638 582 | 2 125 | 56 372 | 25.6 | 45 525 | 14.5 | 85.5 | 33.2 | 6.2 | 344 | 21.8 |
| Chippewa | 368 | 8.2 | 511 | 2.7 | 337.7 | 1 368 517 | 2 678 | 212 258 | 169.0 | 234 724 | 88.3 | 11.7 | 57.9 | 41.0 | 6 392 | 88.9 |
| Chisago | 115 | -1.7 | 133 | 1.7 | 78.4 | 573 014 | 4 310 | 69 152 | 33.4 | 38 538 | 60.8 | 39.2 | 34.4 | 7.2 | 1 341 | 37.7 |
| Clay | 614 | 2.2 | 666 | 5.9 | 549.6 | 1 232 342 | 1 849 | 178 337 | 201.8 | 219 089 | 84.3 | 15.7 | 48.8 | 30.9 | 10 124 | 77.6 |
| Clearwater | 194 | -14.2 | 323 | D | 91.2 | 480 463 | 1 487 | 68 166 | 23.1 | 38 475 | 37.4 | 62.6 | 38.4 | 6.8 | 943 | 41.9 |
| Cook | 2 | -33.3 | 185 | 0.0 | 0.2 | 794 042 | 4 297 | 27 032 | D | D | D | 0.0 | 15.4 | 7.7 | D | 23.1 |
| Cottonwood | 381 | 1.6 | 441 | 1.1 | 351.5 | 1 307 650 | 2 967 | 192 402 | 240.6 | 278 199 | 57.6 | 42.4 | 69.0 | 49.4 | 6 962 | 84.6 |
| Crow Wing | 122 | -15.9 | 200 | 2.9 | 50.5 | 518 482 | 2 594 | 63 922 | 13.5 | 22 112 | 38.6 | 61.4 | 29.9 | 5.1 | 377 | 26.6 |
| Dakota | 246 | 4.2 | 231 | 57.1 | 217.3 | 899 176 | 3 892 | 117 452 | 184.7 | 173 435 | 63.5 | 36.5 | 58.4 | 25.1 | 4 232 | 53.1 |
| Dodge | 248 | 6.4 | 343 | D | 226.1 | 1 266 667 | 3 691 | 158 083 | 173.0 | 239 228 | 53.2 | 46.8 | 56.3 | 34.2 | 4 465 | 70.7 |
| Douglas | 263 | -3.7 | 219 | 2.0 | 184.2 | 527 933 | 2 410 | 80 248 | 65.3 | 54 459 | 49.1 | 50.9 | 38.3 | 14.9 | 3 726 | 77.0 |
| Faribault | 454 | 5.1 | 477 | 0.4 | 429.2 | 1 514 439 | 3 177 | 232 404 | 290.1 | 304 682 | 67.8 | 32.2 | 73.8 | 53.9 | 9 176 | 82.6 |

| STATE County | Water use, 2005 | | Wholesale trade,[1] 2007 | | | | Retail trade,[2] 2007 | | | | Real estate and rental and leasing,[2] 2007 | | | |
|---|---|---|---|---|---|---|---|---|---|---|---|---|---|---|
| | Total water withdrawn (mil gal/day) | Gallons withdrawn per person | Number of establish- ments | Number of employees | Sales (mil dol) | Annual payroll (mil dol) | Number of establish- ments | Number of employees | Sales (mil dol) | Annual payroll (mil dol) | Number of establish- ments | Number of employees | Receipts (mil dol) | Annual payroll (mil dol) |
| | 133 | 134 | 135 | 136 | 137 | 138 | 139 | 140 | 141 | 142 | 143 | 144 | 145 | 146 |
| MICHIGAN—Cont'd | | | | | | | | | | | | | | |
| Keweenaw | 0.2 | 100 | 1 | D | D | D | 12 | 22 | 3.3 | 0.4 | 3 | D | D | D |
| Lake | 2.2 | 178 | 2 | D | D | D | 32 | 231 | 53.3 | 4.1 | 7 | D | D | D |
| Lapeer | 9.3 | 100 | 54 | 411 | 170.1 | 15.7 | 281 | 3 217 | 799.9 | 62.1 | 68 | 239 | 21.0 | 5.0 |
| Leelanau | 4.5 | 204 | 12 | 83 | 17.1 | 2.3 | 134 | 739 | 128.2 | 13.2 | 28 | 74 | 8.4 | 2.0 |
| Lenawee | 15.1 | 148 | 70 | 526 | 451.9 | 21.2 | 340 | 4 329 | 944.7 | 87.2 | 69 | 231 | 31.4 | 5.1 |
| Livingston | 25.9 | 143 | 208 | 1 475 | 1 293.3 | 78.1 | 611 | 8 734 | 2 059.8 | 186.5 | 139 | 673 | 110.5 | 16.7 |
| Luce | 1.2 | 174 | 7 | D | D | D | 34 | 317 | 74.0 | 5.8 | 4 | D | D | D |
| Mackinac | 10.1 | 894 | 6 | D | D | D | 113 | 462 | 155.8 | 11.0 | 14 | D | D | D |
| Macomb | 12.2 | 15 | 856 | 10 424 | 5 611.1 | 522.4 | 2 941 | 41 513 | 10 007.6 | 950.4 | 674 | 3 569 | 601.9 | 98.4 |
| Manistee | 38.9 | 1 542 | 14 | D | D | D | 117 | 906 | 225.4 | 19.5 | 23 | 76 | 6.1 | 1.1 |
| Marquette | 342.2 | 5 284 | 54 | 437 | 162.4 | 15.3 | 312 | 3 860 | 729.8 | 70.4 | 71 | 313 | 31.2 | 6.4 |
| Mason | 29.0 | 1 001 | 15 | 145 | 148.6 | 5.5 | 143 | 1 562 | 330.4 | 31.5 | 30 | 146 | 20.2 | 3.9 |
| Mecosta | 16.0 | 377 | 21 | D | D | D | 160 | 2 231 | 475.0 | 41.4 | 46 | 162 | 20.4 | 3.4 |
| Menominee | 5.9 | 237 | 18 | D | D | D | 80 | 690 | 166.9 | 12.6 | 16 | 41 | 4.6 | 0.7 |
| Midland | 14.7 | 175 | 49 | D | D | D | 323 | 4 382 | 869.3 | 79.5 | 82 | D | D | D |
| Missaukee | 4.6 | 303 | 17 | D | D | D | 36 | 329 | 91.9 | 7.4 | 6 | 18 | 0.8 | 0.2 |
| Monroe | 1 846.7 | 11 997 | 91 | D | D | D | 427 | 5 637 | 1 465.3 | 120.3 | 95 | 373 | 48.8 | 7.5 |
| Montcalm | 40.1 | 628 | 39 | 221 | 124.8 | 8.6 | 240 | 2 463 | 563.1 | 49.0 | 26 | 81 | 8.0 | 1.5 |
| Montmorency | 1.3 | 128 | 3 | D | D | D | 45 | 303 | 70.1 | 5.2 | 13 | D | D | D |
| Muskegon | 323.1 | 1 840 | 119 | D | D | D | 608 | 7 878 | 1 656.7 | 154.5 | 112 | 484 | 67.0 | 12.0 |
| Newaygo | 12.6 | 252 | 26 | 199 | 71.7 | 8.2 | 169 | 1 577 | 355.3 | 31.1 | 22 | D | D | D |
| Oakland | 62.0 | 51 | 2 150 | 28 244 | 29 825.7 | 1 655.5 | 5 189 | 75 573 | 18 183.7 | 1 798.7 | 1 821 | 16 685 | 2 929.4 | 642.0 |
| Oceana | 7.1 | 250 | 13 | D | D | D | 100 | 714 | 171.5 | 13.5 | 16 | 58 | 5.4 | 1.1 |
| Ogemaw | 3.6 | 162 | 18 | D | D | D | 126 | 1 501 | 364.7 | 31.6 | 27 | 82 | 11.2 | 1.9 |
| Ontonagon | 7.3 | 991 | 6 | 83 | 16.6 | 3.6 | 38 | 311 | 60.9 | 5.6 | 4 | D | D | D |
| Osceola | 7.2 | 304 | 8 | 122 | 57.7 | 4.9 | 80 | 609 | 151.6 | 12.1 | 13 | 20 | 4.3 | 0.6 |
| Oscoda | 1.5 | 158 | 2 | D | D | D | 43 | 264 | 57.1 | 4.7 | 8 | D | D | D |
| Otsego | 4.6 | 186 | 41 | 427 | 290.7 | 21.0 | 157 | 2 137 | 499.8 | 48.0 | 24 | 91 | 15.8 | 3.6 |
| Ottawa | 854.5 | 3 346 | 304 | 3 208 | 2 120.6 | 148.0 | 830 | 10 670 | 2 367.8 | 220.4 | 186 | 891 | 107.9 | 23.9 |
| Presque Isle | 13.6 | 951 | 8 | 37 | 8.3 | 0.9 | 69 | 494 | 101.4 | 9.5 | 7 | D | D | D |
| Roscommon | 3.2 | 124 | 12 | 40 | 6.8 | 0.9 | 133 | 1 610 | 338.4 | 33.1 | 25 | 63 | 6.0 | 1.2 |
| Saginaw | 20.2 | 97 | 184 | 2 319 | 1 070.8 | 92.0 | 973 | 12 584 | 2 534.3 | 243.3 | 149 | 751 | 101.8 | 17.4 |
| St. Clair | 1 668.1 | 9 731 | 86 | 818 | 872.3 | 47.0 | 602 | 7 629 | 1 601.6 | 141.9 | 107 | 408 | 63.0 | 9.7 |
| St. Joseph | 77.8 | 1 235 | 47 | D | D | D | 215 | 2 428 | 559.9 | 50.2 | 40 | 143 | 18.7 | 3.3 |
| Sanilac | 6.9 | 154 | 31 | 309 | 174.9 | 10.9 | 172 | 1 454 | 300.9 | 27.2 | 25 | 119 | 11.7 | 3.5 |
| Schoolcraft | 13.0 | 1 474 | 4 | D | D | D | 61 | 379 | 110.8 | 8.0 | 5 | D | D | D |
| Shiawassee | 8.6 | 118 | 42 | D | D | D | 219 | 2 556 | 614.7 | 54.3 | 39 | 112 | 13.1 | 2.9 |
| Tuscola | 10.3 | 177 | 29 | 387 | 283.1 | 15.4 | 163 | 1 764 | 432.3 | 34.2 | 21 | 77 | 7.4 | 1.3 |
| Van Buren | 146.5 | 1 859 | 55 | D | D | D | 262 | 2 431 | 556.7 | 49.6 | 45 | 189 | 20.0 | 3.0 |
| Washtenaw | 37.9 | 111 | 291 | 3 705 | 3 631.0 | 194.4 | 1 148 | 16 403 | 3 681.1 | 355.3 | 368 | 2 595 | 712.4 | 98.3 |
| Wayne | 1 858.7 | 930 | 1 649 | 26 806 | 26 102.9 | 1 405.1 | 6 361 | 68 272 | 17 275.8 | 1 451.0 | 1 276 | 7 929 | 5 528.0 | 241.0 |
| Wexford | 9.0 | 281 | 30 | 433 | 157.4 | 18.2 | 177 | 2 089 | 525.4 | 42.7 | 32 | 106 | 14.3 | 2.8 |
| MINNESOTA | 4 041.3 | 787 | 6 913 | 110 487 | 82 878.1 | 6 417.8 | 20 777 | 307 034 | 71 384.1 | 6 685.6 | 6 889 | 39 430 | 9 208.0 | 1 317.4 |
| Aitkin | 4.6 | 284 | 7 | 96 | 53.5 | 3.6 | 74 | 750 | 147.5 | 12.4 | 9 | 18 | 1.8 | 0.3 |
| Anoka | 97.9 | 302 | 335 | 8 542 | 7 335.9 | 1 054.6 | 986 | 16 716 | 3 738.9 | 363.0 | 388 | 1 857 | 307.3 | 43.7 |
| Becker | 14.5 | 456 | 31 | 245 | 88.4 | 8.6 | 158 | 1 680 | 373.5 | 32.2 | 45 | 113 | 20.7 | 2.6 |
| Beltrami | 7.7 | 179 | 41 | D | D | D | 228 | 3 236 | 627.4 | 60.8 | 38 | 132 | 15.1 | 2.9 |
| Benton | 24.1 | 626 | 43 | 943 | 513.0 | 41.0 | 118 | 1 989 | 495.2 | 40.3 | 37 | 270 | 16.4 | 7.6 |
| Big Stone | 1.7 | 317 | 8 | 85 | 185.8 | 2.9 | 30 | 244 | 32.9 | 3.2 | 4 | 12 | 0.5 | 0.1 |
| Blue Earth | 32.2 | 555 | 90 | 1 391 | 1 275.9 | 60.6 | 355 | 6 309 | 1 211.5 | 110.9 | 80 | 634 | 74.8 | 13.4 |
| Brown | 4.6 | 173 | 37 | 398 | 547.1 | 14.8 | 126 | 1 754 | 301.2 | 29.6 | 25 | 78 | 5.5 | 1.6 |
| Carlton | 9.8 | 287 | 21 | D | D | D | 130 | 1 490 | 357.4 | 30.8 | 15 | 76 | 9.8 | 1.0 |
| Carver | 10.7 | 126 | 129 | 2 044 | 1 484.3 | 132.0 | 235 | 3 440 | 807.1 | 72.1 | 112 | D | D | D |
| Cass | 6.6 | 228 | 17 | 163 | 44.3 | 5.4 | 160 | 1 122 | 276.8 | 23.1 | 41 | 262 | 22.5 | 5.7 |
| Chippewa | 3.0 | 231 | 18 | 212 | 201.4 | 9.0 | 62 | 697 | 168.3 | 14.2 | 15 | 98 | 4.4 | 1.2 |
| Chisago | 14.8 | 299 | 42 | D | D | D | 167 | 1 864 | 428.6 | 32.9 | 53 | D | D | D |
| Clay | 9.5 | 177 | 69 | D | D | D | 180 | 2 801 | 630.3 | 54.6 | 40 | 179 | 17.4 | 3.2 |
| Clearwater | 5.7 | 675 | 6 | 28 | 14.2 | 0.7 | 35 | 245 | 42.9 | 3.6 | NA | NA | NA | NA |
| Cook | 171.5 | 31 956 | 3 | D | D | D | 45 | 290 | 61.9 | 6.6 | 17 | 48 | 4.2 | 0.7 |
| Cottonwood | 4.7 | 395 | 25 | 224 | 177.2 | 8.5 | 66 | 568 | 90.3 | 7.9 | 8 | 22 | 2.9 | 0.6 |
| Crow Wing | 12.6 | 210 | 67 | 604 | 278.7 | 19.3 | 389 | 4 936 | 1 141.9 | 107.2 | 100 | 236 | 38.2 | 6.9 |
| Dakota | 394.6 | 1 029 | 552 | 9 217 | 4 415.5 | 491.7 | 1 178 | 22 061 | 5 164.0 | 498.1 | 544 | 2 317 | 356.9 | 70.6 |
| Dodge | 2.9 | 145 | 21 | 388 | 244.8 | 16.9 | 63 | 418 | 91.8 | 8.1 | 12 | 18 | 4.9 | 0.5 |
| Douglas | 22.9 | 651 | 45 | D | D | D | 237 | 2 982 | 625.5 | 58.0 | 49 | 167 | 32.2 | 3.9 |
| Faribault | 3.1 | 199 | 29 | 177 | 142.9 | 5.3 | 78 | 610 | 116.7 | 10.9 | 9 | 14 | 0.8 | 0.2 |

1. Merchant wholesalers, except manufacturers' sales branches and offices.    2. Employer establishments.

# Table B. States and Counties — Professional Services, Manufacturing, and Accommodation and Food Services

| STATE County | Professional, scientific, and technical services,[1] 2007 | | | | Manufacturing, 2007 | | | | Accommodation and food services, 2007 | | | |
|---|---|---|---|---|---|---|---|---|---|---|---|---|
| | Number of establish-ments | Number of employees | Receipts (mil dol) | Annual payroll (mil dol) | Number of establish-ments | Number of employees | Receipts (mil dol) | Annual payroll (mil dol) | Number of establish-ments | Number of employees | Sales (mil dol) | Annual payroll (mil dol) |
| | 147 | 148 | 149 | 150 | 151 | 152 | 153 | 154 | 155 | 156 | 157 | 158 |
| **MICHIGAN—Cont'd** | | | | | | | | | | | | |
| Keweenaw | 1 | D | D | D | NA | NA | NA | NA | 15 | 102 | 4.4 | 1.2 |
| Lake | 5 | D | D | D | NA | NA | NA | NA | 31 | 175 | 7.8 | 1.9 |
| Lapeer | 128 | D | D | D | 135 | 4 916 | 1 142.6 | 177.5 | 123 | 1 976 | 72.6 | 21.7 |
| Leelanau | 59 | D | D | D | NA | NA | NA | NA | 75 | 716 | 40.6 | 13.3 |
| Lenawee | 131 | 601 | 43.2 | 20.1 | 152 | 6 797 | 2 230.8 | 303.3 | 178 | 2 680 | 94.2 | 28.3 |
| Livingston | 483 | 2 706 | 327.3 | 155.2 | 268 | 8 278 | 2 715.8 | 377.9 | 263 | 4 955 | 181.0 | 51.3 |
| Luce | 9 | 16 | 0.9 | 0.5 | NA | NA | NA | NA | 22 | 231 | 7.4 | 2.2 |
| Mackinac | 16 | 45 | 3.1 | 1.2 | NA | NA | NA | NA | 106 | 718 | 56.5 | 15.2 |
| Macomb | 1 671 | D | D | D | 1 732 | 65 038 | 23 588.5 | 3 451.5 | 1 547 | 27 891 | 1 120.9 | 332.0 |
| Manistee | 36 | 104 | 9.7 | 3.6 | 24 | 973 | 391.2 | 54.7 | 68 | 654 | 26.8 | 7.4 |
| Marquette | 128 | D | D | D | 45 | 952 | 310.4 | 40.1 | 190 | 3 089 | 100.3 | 32.7 |
| Mason | 52 | 234 | 18.8 | 7.8 | 42 | 2 137 | 518.3 | 87.7 | 90 | 884 | 39.7 | 11.1 |
| Mecosta | 43 | D | D | D | 37 | 1 924 | 668.2 | 78.4 | 76 | 1 289 | 44.1 | 13.2 |
| Menominee | 23 | 89 | 7.4 | 3.2 | 49 | 1 821 | 418.5 | 76.2 | 38 | 495 | 17.2 | 4.8 |
| Midland | 164 | D | D | D | 55 | 5 103 | 2 821.3 | 363.1 | 129 | 2 545 | 108.0 | 30.6 |
| Missaukee | 8 | 19 | 1.3 | 0.6 | NA | NA | NA | NA | 24 | 229 | 9.4 | 2.8 |
| Monroe | 147 | 944 | 84.3 | 39.6 | 143 | 8 555 | 3 503.0 | 440.6 | 274 | 4 682 | 171.5 | 47.8 |
| Montcalm | 61 | D | D | D | 66 | 2 059 | 389.0 | 82.7 | 103 | 1 012 | 45.8 | 10.2 |
| Montmorency | 11 | 31 | 2.9 | 1.1 | NA | NA | NA | NA | 31 | 210 | 7.9 | 2.2 |
| Muskegon | 239 | D | D | D | 290 | 13 271 | 3 675.8 | 609.1 | 344 | 5 763 | 221.0 | 64.6 |
| Newaygo | 51 | D | D | D | 49 | 2 005 | 560.8 | 72.8 | 79 | 873 | 32.1 | 9.4 |
| Oakland | 6 414 | D | D | D | 1 862 | 58 971 | 25 885.2 | 3 228.0 | 2 700 | 48 801 | 2 284.8 | 661.6 |
| Oceana | 28 | 91 | 7.5 | 3.0 | 40 | 1 473 | 364.1 | 40.2 | 78 | 794 | 32.3 | 10.3 |
| Ogemaw | 39 | 139 | 10.9 | 4.2 | 39 | 838 | 151.7 | 27.0 | 60 | 833 | 31.1 | 8.3 |
| Ontonagon | 8 | 9 | 0.8 | 0.2 | NA | NA | NA | NA | 40 | 275 | 6.8 | 1.6 |
| Osceola | 23 | 69 | 5.8 | 2.1 | 44 | 2 038 | 968.0 | 81.2 | 41 | 435 | 19.2 | 5.8 |
| Oscoda | 9 | 24 | 1.4 | 0.7 | NA | NA | NA | NA | 25 | 253 | 9.0 | 2.6 |
| Otsego | 56 | D | D | D | 37 | 874 | 158.0 | 30.7 | 73 | 1 307 | 58.8 | 16.7 |
| Ottawa | 515 | D | D | D | 584 | 31 912 | 9 210.9 | 1 395.5 | 381 | 7 551 | 277.2 | 83.8 |
| Presque Isle | 16 | 36 | 2.1 | 0.7 | NA | NA | NA | NA | 42 | 262 | 9.2 | 2.6 |
| Roscommon | 35 | D | D | D | NA | NA | NA | NA | 80 | 1 063 | 37.3 | 11.7 |
| Saginaw | 355 | 3 009 | 429.9 | 121.3 | 219 | 11 437 | 4 604.6 | 659.0 | 383 | 8 620 | 337.3 | 102.2 |
| St. Clair | 244 | D | D | D | 261 | 9 326 | 2 855.5 | 394.0 | 287 | 4 679 | 178.3 | 52.0 |
| St. Joseph | 80 | 499 | 30.8 | 11.0 | 143 | 9 470 | 3 106.6 | 410.4 | 109 | 1 474 | 53.8 | 15.5 |
| Sanilac | 69 | D | D | D | 87 | 2 921 | 595.1 | 104.5 | 73 | 738 | 30.2 | 7.8 |
| Schoolcraft | 10 | 38 | 2.0 | 0.9 | NA | NA | NA | NA | 32 | 250 | 10.2 | 2.8 |
| Shiawassee | 93 | 475 | 39.2 | 12.5 | 69 | 1 865 | 409.5 | 69.6 | 109 | 1 584 | 57.5 | 15.7 |
| Tuscola | 58 | D | D | D | 55 | 1 953 | 581.5 | 78.8 | 68 | 719 | 24.7 | 7.2 |
| Van Buren | 90 | D | D | D | 100 | 3 838 | 1 312.9 | 160.9 | 168 | 2 089 | 80.5 | 23.1 |
| Washtenaw | 1 215 | 14 248 | 1 788.8 | 1 017.4 | 324 | 15 543 | 5 331.8 | 881.4 | 679 | 13 734 | 613.5 | 180.4 |
| Wayne | 2 880 | D | D | D | 1 729 | 87 991 | 55 896.9 | 5 545.3 | 3 215 | 57 836 | 3 112.4 | 857.5 |
| Wexford | 55 | 438 | 40.1 | 16.9 | 57 | 4 158 | D | D | 88 | 1 344 | 48.8 | 14.2 |
| **MINNESOTA** | 16 595 | 140 786 | 20 473.1 | 8 425.3 | 7 951 | 340 514 | 107 563.1 | 15 999.2 | 11 340 | 221 081 | 10 423.7 | 2 978.4 |
| Aitkin | 17 | 48 | 3.8 | 1.2 | NA | NA | NA | NA | 60 | 488 | 19.7 | 5.6 |
| Anoka | 769 | D | D | D | 675 | 23 959 | 6 460.2 | 1 247.7 | 461 | 9 936 | 374.9 | 112.1 |
| Becker | 56 | 272 | 24.5 | 10.7 | 47 | 1 806 | 284.8 | 59.3 | 88 | 1 130 | 43.4 | 11.4 |
| Beltrami | 66 | D | D | D | 38 | 1 249 | 279.8 | 41.5 | 100 | 1 643 | 65.6 | 18.3 |
| Benton | 48 | D | D | D | 77 | 4 248 | 839.1 | 162.7 | 63 | 1 074 | 42.1 | 11.6 |
| Big Stone | 12 | 31 | 2.2 | 0.9 | NA | NA | NA | NA | 17 | D | D | D |
| Blue Earth | 131 | D | D | D | 87 | 4 181 | 2 728.7 | 172.0 | 167 | 4 053 | 139.0 | 40.9 |
| Brown | 51 | 409 | 40.8 | 14.6 | 42 | 3 570 | 1 596.9 | 128.8 | 74 | 1 134 | 40.5 | 12.6 |
| Carlton | 44 | D | D | D | 33 | 1 635 | D | D | 66 | 856 | 32.6 | 9.6 |
| Carver | 306 | D | D | D | 153 | 12 361 | 3 149.5 | 579.3 | 138 | 2 511 | 91.1 | 26.9 |
| Cass | 45 | D | D | D | NA | NA | NA | NA | 139 | 2 255 | 146.4 | 41.0 |
| Chippewa | 24 | 107 | 9.7 | 3.8 | 29 | 1 069 | 175.8 | 36.4 | 32 | 368 | 11.6 | 3.0 |
| Chisago | 91 | 328 | 29.5 | 12.0 | 88 | 1 851 | 403.1 | 68.1 | 93 | 1 240 | 43.0 | 12.1 |
| Clay | 71 | D | D | D | 48 | 925 | 317.1 | 35.7 | 89 | 1 586 | 58.5 | 16.5 |
| Clearwater | 8 | 35 | 2.7 | 0.9 | 12 | D | D | D | 21 | D | D | D |
| Cook | 12 | 24 | 1.8 | 0.8 | NA | NA | NA | NA | 65 | 806 | 40.4 | 12.5 |
| Cottonwood | 19 | 72 | 7.2 | 1.8 | 19 | 1 590 | 636.1 | 48.2 | 23 | 282 | 9.0 | 2.4 |
| Crow Wing | 134 | D | D | D | 118 | 2 913 | D | 119.6 | 200 | 3 228 | 149.6 | 44.0 |
| Dakota | 1 387 | 8 521 | 971.0 | 469.7 | 490 | 18 815 | 12 930.1 | 929.6 | 645 | 14 819 | 614.3 | 184.9 |
| Dodge | 26 | D | D | D | 30 | 1 475 | D | 68.8 | 28 | 386 | 11.8 | 3.4 |
| Douglas | 74 | D | D | D | 91 | 2 672 | 688.2 | 109.6 | 114 | 2 007 | 71.0 | 20.7 |
| Faribault | 19 | 63 | 6.5 | 2.4 | 30 | 1 063 | 408.6 | 41.2 | 34 | 363 | 10.5 | 2.6 |

1. Establishment subject to federal tax.

# Table B. States and Counties — Health Care and Social Assistance, Other Services, and Federal Funds

| STATE County | Health care and social assistance, 2007 | | | | Other services, 2007 | | | | Federal funds and grants, 2009–2010 | | | |
|---|---|---|---|---|---|---|---|---|---|---|---|---|
| | | | | | | | | | Expenditures (mil dol) | | | |
| | | | | | | | | | | Direct payments for individuals[1] | | |
| | Number of establishments | Number of employees | Receipts (mil dol) | Annual payroll (mil dol) | Number of establishments | Number of employees | Receipts (mil dol) | Annual payroll (mil dol) | Total | Social Security and government retirement | Medicare | Food Stamps and Supplemental Security Income |
| | 159 | 160 | 161 | 162 | 163 | 164 | 165 | 166 | 167 | 168 | 169 | 170 |
| MICHIGAN—Cont'd | | | | | | | | | | | | |
| Keweenaw | NA | NA | NA | NA | 1 | D | D | D | 24.3 | 13.5 | 5.5 | 0.5 |
| Lake | 12 | 236 | 12.2 | 6.4 | 9 | D | D | D | 114.6 | 50.2 | 25.2 | 8.4 |
| Lapeer | 195 | 2 424 | 196.2 | 72.9 | 118 | 488 | 35.1 | 9.7 | 480.9 | 257.8 | 94.6 | 16.4 |
| Leelanau | 56 | 541 | 43.9 | 17.4 | 43 | 86 | 9.6 | 2.0 | 134.9 | 72.8 | 24.7 | 3.3 |
| Lenawee | 252 | 3 345 | 271.9 | 104.2 | 159 | 787 | 52.0 | 12.6 | 688.7 | 336.9 | 157.3 | 29.6 |
| Livingston | 365 | 4 784 | 404.9 | 162.8 | 279 | 1 647 | 131.9 | 41.4 | 677.8 | 406.2 | 128.3 | 14.0 |
| Luce | 16 | D | D | D | 11 | 45 | 2.9 | 0.6 | 67.2 | 24.0 | 15.7 | 3.3 |
| Mackinac | 15 | 283 | 22.6 | 9.9 | 14 | D | D | D | 103.5 | 47.2 | 22.3 | 2.6 |
| Macomb | 2 085 | 35 424 | 3 299.3 | 1 390.3 | 1 450 | 8 269 | 669.0 | 213.7 | 7 930.1 | 2 619.7 | 1 567.3 | 174.8 |
| Manistee | 73 | 876 | 67.4 | 27.5 | 53 | 180 | 15.0 | 4.2 | 219.4 | 104.3 | 49.4 | 10.7 |
| Marquette | 228 | 5 390 | 500.7 | 232.0 | 125 | 711 | 56.9 | 13.1 | 524.3 | 239.5 | 105.6 | 18.0 |
| Mason | 98 | 1 359 | 121.4 | 47.8 | 65 | 245 | 16.9 | 5.1 | 260.7 | 116.4 | 48.2 | 10.9 |
| Mecosta | 79 | 1 424 | 105.1 | 45.7 | 66 | 296 | 23.3 | 5.9 | 286.6 | 137.6 | 48.4 | 16.6 |
| Menominee | 45 | 319 | 19.7 | 8.1 | 30 | D | D | D | 188.9 | 89.6 | 37.5 | 5.5 |
| Midland | 242 | 5 442 | 539.3 | 192.0 | 144 | 947 | 147.4 | 22.3 | 497.1 | 251.5 | 97.3 | 23.2 |
| Missaukee | 24 | 258 | 11.8 | 4.6 | 21 | 60 | 4.9 | 1.1 | 93.2 | 45.5 | 19.7 | 5.1 |
| Monroe | 284 | 4 733 | 381.3 | 158.7 | 195 | 1 172 | 93.7 | 30.3 | 885.2 | 468.7 | 218.6 | 37.2 |
| Montcalm | 105 | 2 392 | 188.0 | 81.3 | 100 | 345 | 28.0 | 6.2 | 470.5 | 202.1 | 95.8 | 25.6 |
| Montmorency | 17 | 236 | 12.5 | 5.8 | 15 | D | D | D | 115.8 | 63.2 | 30.4 | 4.3 |
| Muskegon | 398 | 9 463 | 864.8 | 374.1 | 283 | 1 440 | 116.0 | 27.8 | 1 299.3 | 564.9 | 261.1 | 96.9 |
| Newaygo | 74 | 1 473 | 118.8 | 50.3 | 78 | 308 | 50.4 | 5.4 | 279.4 | 140.9 | 60.2 | 17.4 |
| Oakland | 5 009 | 91 463 | 9 299.4 | 3 883.1 | 2 507 | 16 692 | 2 102.0 | 461.0 | 8 890.3 | 3 895.3 | 2 003.9 | 275.6 |
| Oceana | 45 | 660 | 40.9 | 19.4 | 37 | D | D | D | 198.4 | 94.9 | 40.6 | 12.9 |
| Ogemaw | 75 | 1 289 | 92.4 | 37.9 | 47 | 164 | 10.7 | 2.9 | 196.4 | 101.2 | 45.4 | 12.0 |
| Ontonagon | 24 | 376 | 18.3 | 11.4 | 9 | D | D | D | 83.0 | 37.7 | 19.4 | 2.2 |
| Osceola | 43 | 940 | 67.8 | 29.2 | 31 | 124 | 10.4 | 2.3 | 198.7 | 92.1 | 39.2 | 13.6 |
| Oscoda | 12 | D | D | D | 18 | D | D | D | 69.7 | 34.2 | 17.7 | 4.0 |
| Otsego | 92 | 1 486 | 130.0 | 52.1 | 65 | 229 | 19.6 | 5.3 | 173.1 | 87.9 | 29.8 | 5.4 |
| Ottawa | 500 | 9 536 | 761.6 | 294.0 | 425 | 2 575 | 240.5 | 67.4 | 1 266.2 | 660.2 | 197.4 | 28.4 |
| Presque Isle | 28 | 336 | 20.3 | 8.3 | 26 | D | D | D | 136.4 | 69.9 | 30.0 | 4.6 |
| Roscommon | 48 | 569 | 38.4 | 14.7 | 60 | 178 | 14.7 | 3.8 | 275.4 | 146.5 | 76.4 | 13.9 |
| Saginaw | 584 | 16 811 | 1 512.5 | 605.3 | 369 | 2 191 | 178.2 | 46.5 | 1 822.0 | 749.9 | 366.7 | 145.4 |
| St. Clair | 373 | 7 957 | 645.6 | 286.1 | 221 | 989 | 87.7 | 22.3 | 1 078.8 | 452.7 | 249.2 | 48.6 |
| St. Joseph | 109 | 1 928 | 163.5 | 62.8 | 114 | 494 | 38.8 | 10.4 | 384.3 | 182.2 | 92.5 | 18.7 |
| Sanilac | 97 | 1 354 | 89.9 | 37.9 | 64 | 270 | 20.6 | 5.1 | 340.5 | 146.9 | 86.5 | 14.5 |
| Schoolcraft | 15 | 341 | 27.5 | 13.6 | 21 | D | D | D | 95.2 | 37.7 | 20.9 | 4.7 |
| Shiawassee | 158 | 2 594 | 205.3 | 88.2 | 110 | 515 | 39.5 | 9.8 | 493.3 | 245.4 | 120.4 | 23.7 |
| Tuscola | 121 | 2 284 | 156.8 | 71.9 | 69 | 246 | 17.0 | 4.1 | 417.4 | 202.7 | 93.7 | 19.7 |
| Van Buren | 115 | 2 369 | 167.4 | 73.2 | 93 | 568 | 31.4 | 11.2 | 590.1 | 246.9 | 119.5 | 35.9 |
| Washtenaw | 958 | 34 745 | 3 715.8 | 1 627.0 | 557 | 3 917 | 443.2 | 122.6 | 3 527.0 | 780.4 | 357.0 | 71.1 |
| Wayne | 4 200 | 99 597 | 10 640.0 | 4 241.8 | 2 859 | 18 419 | 2 068.3 | 511.0 | 19 605.8 | 5 484.5 | 4 914.9 | 1 781.8 |
| Wexford | 97 | 2 040 | 172.2 | 68.8 | 64 | 258 | 22.1 | 5.8 | 407.7 | 118.0 | 47.0 | 14.1 |
| MINNESOTA | 13 996 | 386 144 | 33 997.4 | 14 872.0 | 11 137 | 81 829 | 8 301.3 | 2 355.0 | 44 375.7 | 13 726.9 | 7 574.7 | 1 177.8 |
| Aitkin | 25 | 653 | 57.3 | 20.1 | 34 | D | D | D | 174.5 | 78.3 | 41.1 | 5.2 |
| Anoka | 547 | 13 566 | 1 396.4 | 566.1 | 559 | 4 311 | 360.4 | 113.0 | 1 265.1 | 563.9 | 194.7 | 33.0 |
| Becker | 73 | 1 753 | 123.1 | 54.1 | 79 | 411 | 30.7 | 6.2 | 319.2 | 110.1 | 61.7 | 8.8 |
| Beltrami | 124 | 2 971 | 217.7 | 102.7 | 91 | 516 | 44.3 | 10.4 | 429.3 | 127.0 | 78.8 | 20.5 |
| Benton | 76 | 2 060 | 87.3 | 39.0 | 81 | D | D | D | 242.5 | 124.9 | 34.0 | 9.1 |
| Big Stone | 16 | 577 | 31.9 | 12.5 | 17 | D | D | D | 64.1 | 22.4 | 15.6 | 1.1 |
| Blue Earth | 205 | 7 412 | 541.9 | 232.6 | 155 | 953 | 69.9 | 18.8 | 448.3 | 166.9 | 80.2 | 11.3 |
| Brown | 70 | 2 341 | 148.1 | 61.9 | 85 | D | D | D | 192.0 | 85.4 | 45.1 | 3.4 |
| Carlton | 92 | 1 833 | 138.0 | 57.7 | 66 | 249 | 19.8 | 4.8 | 282.5 | 120.1 | 61.7 | 7.5 |
| Carver | 177 | 4 149 | 351.3 | 154.5 | 165 | 1 108 | 87.5 | 23.9 | 304.3 | 143.9 | 50.4 | 5.2 |
| Cass | 78 | 1 275 | 62.5 | 26.2 | 57 | 289 | 23.6 | 5.4 | 349.1 | 115.3 | 72.4 | 10.1 |
| Chippewa | 39 | 1 035 | 54.6 | 25.2 | 42 | D | D | D | 117.2 | 40.7 | 21.1 | 3.0 |
| Chisago | 121 | 3 843 | 332.3 | 163.9 | 91 | D | D | D | 252.6 | 147.6 | 51.5 | 7.5 |
| Clay | 148 | 2 670 | 115.1 | 54.5 | 113 | D | D | D | 425.2 | 144.4 | 74.2 | 17.5 |
| Clearwater | 15 | 419 | 19.6 | 9.6 | 15 | D | D | D | 100.6 | 27.1 | 26.0 | 3.1 |
| Cook | 14 | D | D | D | 10 | D | D | D | 60.0 | 21.7 | 7.8 | 0.6 |
| Cottonwood | 34 | 861 | 40.0 | 16.5 | 29 | D | D | D | 94.5 | 34.5 | 25.8 | 2.7 |
| Crow Wing | 201 | 5 075 | 343.3 | 139.0 | 148 | 764 | 50.8 | 11.7 | 536.9 | 245.3 | 113.3 | 14.0 |
| Dakota | 886 | 16 802 | 1 399.8 | 602.6 | 717 | 5 742 | 551.5 | 161.7 | 2 156.1 | 788.7 | 206.1 | 36.3 |
| Dodge | 29 | D | D | D | 45 | 274 | 24.5 | 7.0 | 100.8 | 43.4 | 25.5 | 2.3 |
| Douglas | 119 | 2 674 | 184.0 | 77.9 | 111 | D | D | D | 291.3 | 132.7 | 61.0 | 5.3 |
| Faribault | 39 | 903 | 51.9 | 23.1 | 31 | D | D | D | 142.4 | 54.5 | 36.2 | 3.1 |

1. State totals may include programs not allocated by county.

# Federal Funds, Residential Construction, and Local Government Finances

| STATE County | Salaries and wages | Defense | Other | Medicaid and other health-related | Nutrition and family welfare | Education | Other | New construction ($1,000) | Number of housing units | Total (mil dol) | Intergovernmental (mil dol) | Total (mil dol) | Per capita (dollars) Total | Property |
|---|---|---|---|---|---|---|---|---|---|---|---|---|---|---|
| | 171 | 172 | 173 | 174 | 175 | 176 | 177 | 178 | 179 | 180 | 181 | 182 | 183 | 184 |
| **MICHIGAN—Cont'd** | | | | | | | | | | | | | | |
| Keweenaw | 0.4 | 0.0 | 0.1 | 1.8 | 0.6 | 0.5 | 0.0 | 1 800 | 9 | 7.3 | 2.6 | 1.8 | 846 | 810 |
| Lake | 4.0 | 0.0 | 1.2 | 18.7 | 3.7 | 1.3 | 1.2 | 1 150 | 40 | 40.4 | 21.4 | 13.3 | 1 189 | 1 185 |
| Lapeer | 23.6 | 2.7 | 3.4 | 57.9 | 13.4 | 4.8 | 0.9 | 6 546 | 34 | 283.2 | 155.3 | 70.8 | 770 | 729 |
| Leelanau | 7.5 | 0.2 | 3.6 | 5.7 | 4.1 | 1.8 | 5.1 | 15 037 | 59 | 63.8 | 14.4 | 34.8 | 1 590 | 1 582 |
| Lenawee | 21.6 | 2.5 | 4.3 | 86.7 | 18.8 | 6.8 | 0.9 | 11 378 | 94 | 352.8 | 191.4 | 100.3 | 991 | 958 |
| Livingston | 33.3 | 5.5 | 9.3 | 41.3 | 20.0 | 6.2 | 3.2 | 41 891 | 174 | 574.5 | 272.6 | 189.8 | 1 036 | 1 019 |
| Luce | 1.4 | 0.0 | 1.1 | 17.7 | 1.8 | 1.0 | 1.0 | 933 | 13 | 53.2 | 13.6 | 5.8 | 856 | 845 |
| Mackinac | 6.5 | 0.5 | 4.6 | 12.2 | 2.8 | 1.3 | 3.0 | 4 276 | 28 | 66.2 | 16.4 | 22.5 | 2 070 | 2 022 |
| Macomb | 523.0 | 2 324.4 | 92.1 | 327.1 | 103.7 | 50.5 | 79.2 | 229 420 | 1 110 | 3 140.2 | 1 386.1 | 1 077.2 | 1 296 | 1 276 |
| Manistee | 13.8 | 0.3 | 1.9 | 17.0 | 4.7 | 6.7 | 7.1 | 1 181 | 7 | 123.8 | 35.8 | 29.9 | 1 204 | 1 188 |
| Marquette | 39.9 | 3.9 | 6.0 | 56.9 | 16.2 | 5.5 | 12.8 | 15 713 | 96 | 229.2 | 105.6 | 60.6 | 930 | 909 |
| Mason | 7.5 | 0.0 | 36.9 | 23.6 | 10.1 | 1.5 | 0.3 | 5 794 | 42 | 126.4 | 48.1 | 51.0 | 1 775 | 1 755 |
| Mecosta | 9.9 | 0.1 | 2.2 | 32.5 | 6.6 | 2.5 | 1.2 | 4 648 | 32 | 172.1 | 75.0 | 42.8 | 1 018 | 966 |
| Menominee | 6.5 | 0.0 | 2.3 | 22.4 | 5.7 | 2.7 | 6.2 | 3 468 | 21 | 67.3 | 39.5 | 17.7 | 729 | 723 |
| Midland | 25.1 | 0.5 | 10.4 | 47.3 | 14.0 | 4.6 | 11.2 | 22 155 | 145 | 318.8 | 137.8 | 120.5 | 1 455 | 1 442 |
| Missaukee | 2.9 | 0.0 | 0.8 | 11.1 | 3.2 | 1.5 | 0.2 | 2 244 | 14 | 48.0 | 28.7 | 10.7 | 712 | 711 |
| Monroe | 23.8 | 1.1 | 5.6 | 72.5 | 25.0 | 10.1 | 4.8 | 19 319 | 110 | 529.2 | 247.3 | 182.9 | 1 191 | 1 160 |
| Montcalm | 24.0 | 0.0 | 3.4 | 62.7 | 19.0 | 5.6 | 20.6 | 5 070 | 46 | 226.2 | 136.9 | 54.1 | 859 | 843 |
| Montmorency | 1.3 | 0.0 | 0.3 | 12.4 | 2.4 | 0.9 | 0.0 | 1 097 | 7 | 28.6 | 10.5 | 9.9 | 963 | 945 |
| Muskegon | 41.1 | 37.2 | 6.6 | 195.6 | 44.5 | 17.7 | 13.4 | 16 817 | 95 | 697.5 | 353.7 | 177.1 | 1 016 | 945 |
| Newaygo | 7.0 | 0.0 | 1.5 | 34.3 | 10.7 | 3.4 | 0.8 | 4 122 | 45 | 165.6 | 98.2 | 44.2 | 899 | 895 |
| Oakland | 481.6 | 251.4 | 458.6 | 568.3 | 166.3 | 68.0 | 525.3 | 299 364 | 1 277 | 5 275.9 | 2 006.3 | 2 211.2 | 1 833 | 1 775 |
| Oceana | 6.1 | 0.0 | 8.6 | 23.6 | 6.7 | 1.9 | 0.1 | 1 326 | 18 | 94.2 | 40.2 | 28.1 | 1 009 | 1 004 |
| Ogemaw | 5.5 | 0.0 | 1.3 | 22.9 | 3.8 | 1.2 | 0.2 | 4 335 | 26 | 91.6 | 30.1 | 18.2 | 852 | 837 |
| Ontonagon | 3.4 | 0.3 | 1.5 | 14.4 | 1.8 | 0.8 | 0.1 | 875 | 6 | 42.5 | 15.9 | 10.1 | 1 448 | 1 444 |
| Osceola | 5.2 | 1.7 | 1.3 | 34.0 | 5.9 | 1.8 | 1.2 | 1 818 | 18 | 73.3 | 43.8 | 19.9 | 860 | 856 |
| Oscoda | 4.3 | 0.0 | 0.5 | 5.3 | 2.0 | 0.8 | 0.3 | 1 250 | 14 | 22.0 | 10.5 | 8.9 | 1 000 | 986 |
| Otsego | 15.6 | 0.1 | 7.3 | 19.9 | 4.1 | 1.2 | 0.3 | 8 038 | 78 | 83.1 | 32.7 | 36.9 | 1 524 | 1 522 |
| Ottawa | 41.7 | 105.5 | 62.4 | 68.2 | 32.7 | 11.3 | 12.0 | 96 405 | 611 | 809.0 | 388.8 | 287.7 | 1 110 | 1 090 |
| Presque Isle | 3.9 | 0.0 | 0.9 | 20.3 | 3.1 | 1.0 | 0.3 | 2 351 | 17 | 43.2 | 23.9 | 14.0 | 1 009 | 1 007 |
| Roscommon | 3.0 | 0.1 | 0.9 | 20.2 | 6.0 | 1.8 | 0.4 | 5 389 | 30 | 98.6 | 35.8 | 42.1 | 1 648 | 1 638 |
| Saginaw | 102.1 | 16.2 | 31.3 | 262.1 | 58.9 | 19.0 | 55.0 | 22 763 | 177 | 749.6 | 432.9 | 168.2 | 831 | 732 |
| St. Clair | 61.2 | 29.9 | 32.5 | 124.4 | 31.1 | 11.4 | 16.6 | 10 753 | 66 | 658.0 | 342.3 | 201.9 | 1 187 | 1 129 |
| St. Joseph | 10.5 | 0.0 | 2.2 | 52.0 | 11.7 | 5.4 | 0.4 | 7 477 | 38 | 295.4 | 119.3 | 58.7 | 939 | 932 |
| Sanilac | 9.6 | 6.0 | 2.6 | 43.9 | 9.6 | 3.1 | 0.2 | 3 740 | 30 | 173.6 | 103.6 | 38.4 | 880 | 863 |
| Schoolcraft | 3.7 | 1.6 | 0.8 | 19.2 | 2.2 | 1.3 | 2.3 | 2 369 | 19 | 55.8 | 13.0 | 8.3 | 980 | 978 |
| Shiawassee | 19.3 | 0.0 | 2.8 | 55.4 | 13.2 | 5.1 | 0.3 | 3 970 | 26 | 239.9 | 146.3 | 52.0 | 725 | 712 |
| Tuscola | 12.0 | 0.2 | 2.8 | 55.7 | 13.2 | 5.3 | 0.6 | 2 990 | 18 | 205.1 | 120.6 | 43.4 | 765 | 750 |
| Van Buren | 18.0 | 0.9 | 4.8 | 110.9 | 24.3 | 4.7 | 15.3 | 12 470 | 69 | 396.4 | 182.4 | 90.3 | 1 158 | 1 145 |
| Washtenaw | 231.6 | 107.4 | 209.4 | 1 191.4 | 49.9 | 31.5 | 388.9 | 65 511 | 477 | 1 351.8 | 485.7 | 589.1 | 1 683 | 1 660 |
| Wayne | 1 265.6 | 104.6 | 779.9 | 3 645.7 | 580.9 | 207.1 | 501.2 | 120 042 | 705 | 10 286.1 | 4 751.5 | 3 099.1 | 1 561 | 1 241 |
| Wexford | 18.9 | 156.4 | 5.4 | 33.6 | 6.7 | 2.0 | 3.2 | 5 868 | 35 | 118.2 | 58.3 | 38.8 | 1 220 | 1 217 |
| **MINNESOTA** | 3 368.3 | 1 520.3 | 1 430.1 | 6 006.5 | 1 249.2 | 755.2 | 2 516.9 | 1 763 836 | 8 890 | X | X | X | X | X |
| Aitkin | 3.9 | 0.0 | 0.8 | 38.4 | 3.5 | 1.0 | 0.3 | 20 281 | 123 | 60.2 | 33.8 | 14.9 | 937 | 923 |
| Anoka | 34.9 | 235.7 | 27.8 | 94.1 | 42.6 | 15.6 | 7.2 | 124 445 | 539 | 1 183.6 | 640.5 | 333.1 | 1 021 | 972 |
| Becker | 18.3 | 0.1 | 7.4 | 64.8 | 14.7 | 3.0 | 8.3 | 17 006 | 137 | 115.4 | 67.0 | 25.5 | 798 | 774 |
| Beltrami | 29.7 | 0.6 | 7.4 | 91.2 | 15.8 | 13.9 | 9.9 | 8 501 | 82 | 203.3 | 126.1 | 30.4 | 698 | 641 |
| Benton | 32.4 | 0.0 | 1.1 | 28.8 | 5.1 | 1.4 | 0.0 | 10 905 | 66 | 118.6 | 66.4 | 31.7 | 802 | 765 |
| Big Stone | 3.9 | 0.0 | 0.6 | 10.7 | 1.7 | 0.5 | 0.4 | 1 767 | 12 | 41.9 | 15.6 | 5.0 | 927 | 904 |
| Blue Earth | 55.6 | 0.5 | 5.8 | 63.1 | 11.8 | 4.3 | 13.0 | 32 700 | 223 | 257.9 | 130.0 | 57.0 | 952 | 840 |
| Brown | 14.9 | 0.1 | 1.8 | 21.5 | 4.2 | 1.4 | 2.8 | 5 132 | 30 | 110.6 | 56.7 | 21.8 | 839 | 776 |
| Carlton | 9.8 | 0.1 | 1.7 | 51.0 | 8.4 | 4.8 | 7.0 | 7 649 | 59 | 155.6 | 77.7 | 27.8 | 819 | 797 |
| Carver | 24.1 | 0.4 | 35.9 | 17.5 | 7.2 | 2.4 | 7.2 | 116 871 | 404 | 352.7 | 144.2 | 117.4 | 1 327 | 1 220 |
| Cass | 15.8 | 0.2 | 5.7 | 81.7 | 11.4 | 8.4 | 13.1 | 26 054 | 149 | 122.5 | 70.5 | 29.1 | 1 012 | 1 000 |
| Chippewa | 15.8 | 3.0 | 0.7 | 13.9 | 5.7 | 0.9 | 2.2 | 1 434 | 7 | 57.2 | 32.7 | 11.3 | 909 | 881 |
| Chisago | 9.5 | 0.4 | 2.3 | 21.4 | 5.9 | 1.8 | 0.5 | 7 746 | 45 | 176.2 | 81.7 | 53.3 | 1 064 | 1 029 |
| Clay | 24.9 | 50.0 | 2.7 | 50.3 | 11.4 | 3.4 | 6.8 | 34 398 | 213 | 239.6 | 129.1 | 34.5 | 628 | 588 |
| Clearwater | 2.6 | 0.0 | 0.6 | 34.1 | 3.0 | 1.3 | 0.5 | 200 | 2 | 35.6 | 21.7 | 8.5 | 1 032 | 1 028 |
| Cook | 7.8 | 0.0 | 1.5 | 6.0 | 1.1 | 0.5 | 12.7 | 5 615 | 38 | 37.4 | 12.6 | 8.0 | 1 483 | 1 196 |
| Cottonwood | 4.7 | 0.0 | 1.0 | 12.8 | 2.5 | 1.1 | 1.5 | 1 070 | 6 | 62.8 | 29.1 | 10.4 | 920 | 910 |
| Crow Wing | 34.0 | 3.0 | 4.5 | 84.3 | 11.8 | 3.7 | 10.9 | 34 584 | 219 | 303.6 | 124.4 | 74.4 | 1 207 | 1 141 |
| Dakota | 468.3 | 405.0 | 57.4 | 70.7 | 39.5 | 15.9 | 34.0 | 126 862 | 636 | 1 549.7 | 719.4 | 460.5 | 1 179 | 1 126 |
| Dodge | 3.5 | 0.0 | 0.8 | 12.8 | 3.0 | 1.0 | 0.7 | 5 518 | 27 | 78.5 | 40.4 | 15.8 | 810 | 794 |
| Douglas | 16.1 | 0.4 | 2.4 | 48.0 | 7.1 | 1.8 | 5.4 | 17 019 | 96 | 181.2 | 62.4 | 34.6 | 959 | 908 |
| Faribault | 4.5 | 0.0 | 1.4 | 20.3 | 3.4 | 1.1 | 6.0 | 3 246 | 16 | 76.1 | 30.9 | 11.5 | 772 | 745 |

1. State totals may include programs not allocated by county.  2. Based on the resident population estimated as of July 1 of the year shown.

# Table B. States and Counties — Local Government Finances, Government Employment, and Voting

| | Local government finances, 2007 (cont.) | | | | | | | | | Government employment, 2011 | | | Presidential election,[2] 2012 | | |
| | Direct general expenditure | | | | | | | Debt outstanding | | | | | Percent of vote cast: | | |
| | | | Percent of total for: | | | | | | | | | | | | |
| STATE County | Total (mil dol) | Per capita[1] (dollars) | Educa-tion | Health and hospitals | Police protec-tion | Public welfare | High-ways | Total (mil dol) | Per capita[1] (dollars) | Federal civilian | Federal military | State and local | Demo-cratic | Republi-can | All other |
| | 185 | 186 | 187 | 188 | 189 | 190 | 191 | 192 | 193 | 194 | 195 | 196 | 197 | 198 | 199 |

| MICHIGAN—Cont'd | | | | | | | | | | | | | | | |
| Keweenaw | 7.6 | 3 522 | 1.7 | 0.9 | 5.7 | 2.6 | 34.8 | 2.0 | 917 | 32 | 0 | 123 | 43.3 | 53.6 | 3.1 |
| Lake | 32.5 | 2 914 | 35.8 | 1.8 | 4.0 | 1.7 | 15.5 | 34.0 | 3 050 | 65 | 21 | 474 | 55.2 | 42.9 | 2.0 |
| Lapeer | 277.5 | 3 016 | 50.7 | 6.6 | 4.0 | 5.9 | 8.2 | 204.1 | 2 218 | 145 | 163 | 4 071 | 47.3 | 50.3 | 2.4 |
| Leelanau | 60.9 | 2 782 | 39.5 | 2.8 | 3.4 | 0.8 | 8.8 | 44.4 | 2 027 | 140 | 40 | 1 764 | 50.9 | 48.0 | 1.2 |
| Lenawee | 365.4 | 3 610 | 56.4 | 6.0 | 3.3 | 4.2 | 6.8 | 373.6 | 3 690 | 206 | 183 | 4 531 | 51.6 | 46.6 | 1.8 |
| Livingston | 583.8 | 3 187 | 57.4 | 5.5 | 3.1 | 0.4 | 5.3 | 1 146.7 | 6 260 | 281 | 336 | 5 302 | 42.5 | 55.8 | 1.7 |
| Luce | 53.5 | 7 955 | 19.9 | 57.8 | 0.9 | 0.2 | 7.8 | 15.4 | 2 283 | 15 | 12 | 781 | 43.5 | 54.4 | 2.2 |
| Mackinac | 65.3 | 6 007 | 24.4 | 31.6 | 2.5 | 0.1 | 13.4 | 58.0 | 5 330 | 57 | 65 | 971 | 47.3 | 51.1 | 1.6 |
| Macomb | 3 218.2 | 3 872 | 55.3 | 6.3 | 6.7 | 2.1 | 4.5 | 3 339.8 | 4 019 | 8 329 | 1 927 | 28 156 | 53.4 | 44.8 | 1.9 |
| Manistee | 118.4 | 4 773 | 31.0 | 30.9 | 2.1 | 7.2 | 5.7 | 87.8 | 3 540 | 95 | 64 | 2 756 | 55.6 | 42.4 | 2.0 |
| Marquette | 222.1 | 3 405 | 43.5 | 2.7 | 3.3 | 5.8 | 10.9 | 152.3 | 2 335 | 299 | 146 | 5 552 | 59.2 | 38.9 | 1.9 |
| Mason | 131.3 | 4 567 | 61.4 | 0.9 | 2.5 | 6.0 | 7.1 | 61.9 | 2 151 | 92 | 68 | 1 814 | 51.3 | 46.9 | 1.7 |
| Mecosta | 166.3 | 3 951 | 44.4 | 26.0 | 3.2 | 0.6 | 5.0 | 90.2 | 2 142 | 91 | 80 | 4 928 | 48.8 | 49.5 | 1.7 |
| Menominee | 62.1 | 2 560 | 54.5 | 3.8 | 6.2 | 0.6 | 10.2 | 23.4 | 963 | 73 | 44 | 2 275 | 54.0 | 43.8 | 2.1 |
| Midland | 281.0 | 3 392 | 53.7 | 2.5 | 3.8 | 1.8 | 6.9 | 271.3 | 3 276 | 141 | 155 | 3 004 | 47.4 | 50.9 | 1.7 |
| Missaukee | 52.7 | 3 517 | 36.7 | 24.7 | 3.1 | 0.7 | 18.3 | 8.1 | 541 | 29 | 27 | 474 | 38.7 | 59.7 | 1.7 |
| Monroe | 519.5 | 3 382 | 55.8 | 6.3 | 3.9 | 0.7 | 7.7 | 565.9 | 3 684 | 239 | 280 | 5 231 | 51.3 | 46.9 | 1.8 |
| Montcalm | 232.1 | 3 688 | 60.2 | 3.0 | 2.2 | 0.6 | 5.7 | 188.6 | 2 996 | 130 | 116 | 2 911 | 48.8 | 49.1 | 2.0 |
| Montmorency | 26.2 | 2 539 | 33.7 | 0.9 | 4.2 | 0.7 | 10.5 | 14.9 | 1 442 | 14 | 18 | 361 | 44.8 | 53.0 | 2.2 |
| Muskegon | 748.6 | 4 293 | 53.1 | 10.7 | 3.7 | 2.9 | 4.2 | 815.1 | 4 674 | 338 | 340 | 7 823 | 63.9 | 34.6 | 1.5 |
| Newaygo | 165.2 | 3 360 | 60.4 | 7.4 | 2.5 | 4.9 | 6.0 | 148.8 | 3 027 | 138 | 89 | 2 170 | 46.7 | 51.3 | 2.0 |
| Oakland | 5 346.4 | 4 433 | 54.0 | 5.3 | 5.8 | 0.4 | 5.5 | 5 480.4 | 4 544 | 4 525 | 2 351 | 45 389 | 56.5 | 42.0 | 1.4 |
| Oceana | 88.3 | 3 175 | 42.3 | 5.3 | 3.4 | 14.9 | 11.0 | 248.8 | 8 951 | 164 | 49 | 1 467 | 51.2 | 46.8 | 2.0 |
| Ogemaw | 93.7 | 4 391 | 24.7 | 46.1 | 2.8 | 1.4 | 8.9 | 43.5 | 2 040 | 58 | 40 | 1 098 | 50.1 | 47.7 | 2.3 |
| Ontonagon | 41.1 | 5 894 | 34.7 | 29.5 | 1.5 | 0.1 | 16.6 | 27.7 | 3 964 | 43 | 12 | 331 | 50.6 | 46.9 | 2.5 |
| Osceola | 74.5 | 3 221 | 58.7 | 2.8 | 3.4 | 0.5 | 9.7 | 55.4 | 2 394 | 53 | 43 | 938 | 44.0 | 54.2 | 1.8 |
| Oscoda | 21.7 | 2 425 | 47.9 | 3.3 | 4.1 | 1.6 | 16.3 | 5.5 | 616 | 58 | 16 | 305 | 43.6 | 53.6 | 2.8 |
| Otsego | 79.3 | 3 275 | 46.7 | 2.4 | 2.4 | 1.0 | 11.8 | 65.4 | 2 700 | 180 | 45 | 938 | 44.7 | 53.5 | 1.8 |
| Ottawa | 823.2 | 3 176 | 56.8 | 5.0 | 3.3 | 1.0 | 7.2 | 1 132.8 | 4 370 | 418 | 558 | 14 475 | 37.3 | 61.2 | 1.5 |
| Presque Isle | 41.6 | 3 004 | 37.2 | 0.8 | 3.2 | 1.1 | 13.8 | 16.3 | 1 174 | 50 | 24 | 559 | 49.6 | 48.0 | 2.4 |
| Roscommon | 100.7 | 3 946 | 60.3 | 2.3 | 3.5 | 1.0 | 7.9 | 30.0 | 1 177 | 31 | 45 | 1 364 | 50.4 | 47.9 | 1.7 |
| Saginaw | 770.9 | 3 811 | 48.9 | 13.1 | 4.2 | 0.7 | 5.5 | 503.7 | 2 490 | 1 513 | 388 | 9 919 | 57.9 | 40.6 | 1.5 |
| St. Clair | 648.9 | 3 815 | 47.3 | 12.8 | 3.9 | 0.9 | 7.7 | 468.1 | 2 752 | 643 | 372 | 6 061 | 50.3 | 47.6 | 2.1 |
| St. Joseph | 304.3 | 4 873 | 44.3 | 33.5 | 2.2 | 0.4 | 3.7 | 269.0 | 4 308 | 103 | 113 | 3 091 | 47.9 | 50.1 | 1.9 |
| Sanilac | 175.3 | 4 017 | 42.5 | 12.0 | 2.6 | 5.1 | 10.3 | 155.3 | 3 558 | 115 | 78 | 1 710 | 44.9 | 52.9 | 2.2 |
| Schoolcraft | 56.4 | 6 621 | 26.4 | 35.6 | 1.8 | 12.1 | 9.0 | 26.1 | 3 067 | 48 | 16 | 1 069 | 50.5 | 47.6 | 1.9 |
| Shiawassee | 256.4 | 3 573 | 62.3 | 6.3 | 2.7 | 5.4 | 6.5 | 152.9 | 2 131 | 136 | 129 | 3 194 | 53.3 | 44.7 | 2.1 |
| Tuscola | 209.4 | 3 686 | 62.3 | 2.0 | 2.9 | 5.8 | 8.5 | 163.4 | 2 876 | 130 | 103 | 2 897 | 48.6 | 49.4 | 2.0 |
| Van Buren | 395.8 | 5 079 | 48.3 | 26.6 | 2.2 | 0.7 | 6.3 | 452.0 | 5 799 | 147 | 140 | 4 924 | 53.5 | 44.7 | 1.9 |
| Washtenaw | 1 453.7 | 4 153 | 53.1 | 3.4 | 5.9 | 0.9 | 5.5 | 1 701.4 | 4 861 | 3 691 | 708 | 70 580 | 69.8 | 28.8 | 1.4 |
| Wayne | 10 151.2 | 5 114 | 39.6 | 3.2 | 6.4 | 4.6 | 3.5 | 17 567.5 | 8 850 | 14 759 | 3 834 | 84 981 | 74.1 | 24.7 | 1.2 |
| Wexford | 110.1 | 3 463 | 55.0 | 0.0 | 3.6 | 1.5 | 8.3 | 58.2 | 1 832 | 135 | 61 | 1 807 | 47.0 | 51.2 | 1.8 |
| MINNESOTA | X | X | X | X | X | X | X | X | X | 32 404 | 20 786 | 360 360 | 54.1 | 43.8 | 2.1 |
| Aitkin | 60.6 | 3 809 | 34.9 | 1.3 | 3.9 | 8.3 | 18.9 | 38.5 | 2 421 | 54 | 61 | 759 | 48.8 | 48.8 | 2.4 |
| Anoka | 1 243.9 | 3 813 | 56.4 | 1.5 | 4.8 | 5.3 | 5.7 | 1 269.8 | 3 892 | 392 | 1 251 | 14 812 | 47.7 | 50.1 | 2.1 |
| Becker | 115.1 | 3 601 | 35.8 | 0.9 | 4.1 | 13.4 | 17.5 | 65.1 | 2 036 | 244 | 123 | 2 682 | 45.3 | 52.2 | 2.5 |
| Beltrami | 209.5 | 4 804 | 50.9 | 1.0 | 3.5 | 7.5 | 8.2 | 197.0 | 4 517 | 264 | 171 | 4 609 | 54.1 | 43.9 | 2.0 |
| Benton | 106.3 | 2 692 | 46.4 | 0.8 | 4.2 | 7.9 | 13.6 | 247.7 | 6 271 | 79 | 146 | 1 536 | 43.7 | 53.5 | 2.8 |
| Big Stone | 40.2 | 7 474 | 24.3 | 36.8 | 3.2 | 5.6 | 11.9 | 322.1 | 59 808 | 43 | 20 | 604 | 51.9 | 45.6 | 2.5 |
| Blue Earth | 263.0 | 4 397 | 42.1 | 0.5 | 4.1 | 6.7 | 15.1 | 240.4 | 4 020 | 317 | 284 | 5 038 | 55.1 | 42.1 | 2.7 |
| Brown | 105.1 | 4 040 | 35.2 | 10.2 | 5.0 | 7.4 | 14.7 | 121.8 | 4 683 | 75 | 96 | 1 587 | 42.7 | 54.7 | 2.6 |
| Carlton | 163.0 | 4 809 | 38.6 | 22.3 | 7.3 | 7.5 | 7.9 | 189.5 | 5 591 | 78 | 133 | 4 992 | 62.3 | 35.5 | 2.2 |
| Carver | 432.6 | 4 890 | 49.9 | 0.7 | 3.4 | 4.4 | 8.4 | 753.1 | 8 513 | 230 | 348 | 4 359 | 41.6 | 56.7 | 1.8 |
| Cass | 122.9 | 4 280 | 45.2 | 2.3 | 4.5 | 7.8 | 10.8 | 85.6 | 2 979 | 235 | 106 | 3 778 | 44.6 | 53.1 | 2.3 |
| Chippewa | 61.4 | 4 925 | 47.6 | 0.5 | 4.8 | 13.1 | 13.2 | 39.0 | 3 129 | 62 | 46 | 1 126 | 51.6 | 45.7 | 2.7 |
| Chisago | 192.6 | 3 841 | 42.0 | 1.2 | 4.1 | 6.5 | 13.9 | 265.2 | 5 291 | 108 | 202 | 2 327 | 43.6 | 53.9 | 2.5 |
| Clay | 257.0 | 4 688 | 32.2 | 2.3 | 4.1 | 7.3 | 10.5 | 467.4 | 8 523 | 128 | 224 | 4 214 | 57.0 | 40.9 | 2.1 |
| Clearwater | 37.5 | 4 543 | 43.6 | 0.0 | 3.9 | 10.2 | 17.7 | 36.9 | 4 477 | 33 | 33 | 614 | 44.1 | 53.8 | 2.2 |
| Cook | 35.3 | 6 542 | 18.6 | 28.9 | 5.1 | 5.1 | 12.1 | 24.9 | 4 615 | 147 | 20 | 787 | 60.3 | 37.0 | 2.7 |
| Cottonwood | 66.7 | 5 881 | 31.9 | 21.9 | 2.8 | 6.7 | 10.4 | 59.8 | 5 266 | 61 | 44 | 831 | 45.7 | 52.3 | 2.0 |
| Crow Wing | 314.2 | 5 097 | 31.5 | 16.4 | 4.0 | 5.9 | 9.5 | 389.3 | 6 314 | 195 | 244 | 4 251 | 45.1 | 52.8 | 2.1 |
| Dakota | 1 608.1 | 4 118 | 52.4 | 0.7 | 4.8 | 5.7 | 7.0 | 2 275.4 | 5 827 | 2 225 | 1 514 | 17 341 | 51.8 | 46.3 | 1.9 |
| Dodge | 76.8 | 3 930 | 44.6 | 1.3 | 5.0 | 14.8 | 11.4 | 71.7 | 3 669 | 43 | 76 | 1 142 | 43.7 | 53.5 | 2.8 |
| Douglas | 178.7 | 4 954 | 29.6 | 34.2 | 2.8 | 4.2 | 7.3 | 117.2 | 3 248 | 130 | 136 | 3 002 | 44.2 | 53.7 | 2.0 |
| Faribault | 76.1 | 5 119 | 31.0 | 23.5 | 3.7 | 1.7 | 13.7 | 42.0 | 2 823 | 55 | 54 | 1 093 | 45.8 | 51.5 | 2.7 |

1. Based on the resident population estimated as of July 1 of the year shown.   2. © 2013 Election Data Services, Inc. All rights reserved.

# Table B. States and Counties — Land Area and Population

| STATE/ County code | CBSA code[1] | County type[2] | STATE County | Land area,[3] (sq km) 2010 | Total persons | Rank | Per square kilometer | White | Black | American Indian, Alaska Native | Asian and Pacific Islander | Percent Hispanic or Latino[4] | Under 5 years | 5 to 17 years | 18 to 24 years | 25 to 34 years | 35 to 44 years | 45 to 54 years |
|---|---|---|---|---|---|---|---|---|---|---|---|---|---|---|---|---|---|---|
| | | | | 1 | 2 | 3 | 4 | 5 | 6 | 7 | 8 | 9 | 10 | 11 | 12 | 13 | 14 | 15 |
| | | | MINNESOTA—Cont'd | | | | | | | | | | | | | | | |
| 27 045 | ... | 8 | Fillmore | 2 231 | 20 834 | 1 786 | 9.3 | 98.2 | 0.5 | 0.4 | 0.6 | 1.0 | 6.6 | 17.1 | 6.6 | 10.9 | 10.9 | 14.6 |
| 27 047 | 10660 | 7 | Freeborn | 1 831 | 31 054 | 1 410 | 17.0 | 89.3 | 1.1 | 0.6 | 1.4 | 8.7 | 6.0 | 15.8 | 7.3 | 10.6 | 10.9 | 15.2 |
| 27 049 | 39860 | 4 | Goodhue | 1 960 | 46 336 | 1 043 | 23.6 | 94.1 | 1.5 | 1.6 | 1.1 | 3.1 | 6.2 | 17.1 | 7.1 | 11.3 | 11.5 | 16.0 |
| 27 051 | ... | 9 | Grant | 1 420 | 5 944 | 2 765 | 4.2 | 97.4 | 0.8 | 0.6 | 0.5 | 1.8 | 6.1 | 15.2 | 6.3 | 10.7 | 10.2 | 15.0 |
| 27 053 | 33460 | 1 | Hennepin | 1 434 | 1 184 576 | 35 | 826.1 | 74.0 | 13.3 | 1.5 | 7.3 | 6.9 | 6.6 | 15.9 | 9.5 | 16.6 | 13.1 | 14.6 |
| 27 055 | 29100 | 3 | Houston | 1 430 | 18 837 | 1 883 | 13.2 | 97.9 | 1.1 | 0.5 | 0.8 | 0.8 | 5.6 | 16.8 | 7.0 | 10.5 | 10.9 | 16.5 |
| 27 057 | ... | 7 | Hubbard | 2 397 | 20 347 | 1 823 | 8.5 | 94.9 | 0.8 | 3.8 | 0.6 | 1.7 | 5.9 | 15.5 | 6.0 | 9.2 | 10.2 | 15.4 |
| 27 059 | 33460 | 1 | Isanti | 1 129 | 38 248 | 1 212 | 33.9 | 96.2 | 1.1 | 1.2 | 1.4 | 1.7 | 6.8 | 18.7 | 7.9 | 12.8 | 12.9 | 16.1 |
| 27 061 | ... | 6 | Itasca | 6 909 | 45 221 | 1 063 | 6.5 | 94.7 | 0.7 | 4.8 | 0.7 | 1.1 | 5.4 | 16.2 | 6.9 | 10.2 | 10.5 | 15.0 |
| 27 063 | ... | 7 | Jackson | 1 821 | 10 281 | 2 418 | 5.6 | 94.8 | 0.8 | 0.6 | 1.6 | 3.0 | 5.8 | 16.5 | 7.2 | 10.7 | 11.0 | 15.3 |
| 27 065 | ... | 6 | Kanabec | 1 351 | 16 005 | 2 047 | 11.8 | 97.1 | 0.9 | 1.3 | 0.8 | 1.5 | 5.8 | 17.5 | 7.0 | 10.7 | 12.1 | 16.0 |
| 27 067 | 48820 | 4 | Kandiyohi | 2 064 | 42 379 | 1 123 | 20.5 | 85.4 | 2.8 | 0.6 | 0.8 | 11.2 | 6.7 | 17.0 | 9.4 | 11.8 | 10.7 | 14.4 |
| 27 069 | ... | 9 | Kittson | 2 846 | 4 493 | 2 869 | 1.6 | 97.5 | 0.4 | 0.3 | 0.4 | 1.8 | 5.0 | 16.6 | 5.4 | 8.0 | 10.6 | 15.5 |
| 27 071 | ... | 7 | Koochiching | 8 040 | 13 208 | 2 230 | 1.6 | 95.2 | 1.2 | 3.3 | 0.7 | 1.2 | 4.7 | 16.0 | 6.8 | 9.2 | 10.9 | 16.3 |
| 27 073 | ... | 9 | Lac qui Parle | 1 981 | 7 109 | 2 671 | 3.6 | 97.3 | 0.8 | 0.4 | 0.5 | 1.7 | 5.3 | 15.6 | 5.4 | 8.9 | 9.4 | 15.8 |
| 27 075 | ... | 6 | Lake | 5 463 | 10 818 | 2 373 | 2.0 | 98.1 | 0.6 | 1.2 | 0.6 | 0.7 | 5.3 | 13.5 | 6.2 | 9.9 | 9.9 | 15.8 |
| 27 077 | ... | 9 | Lake of the Woods | 3 361 | 3 973 | 2 908 | 1.2 | 96.9 | 1.2 | 1.6 | 1.1 | 1.2 | 4.8 | 14.9 | 5.4 | 8.8 | 9.3 | 18.2 |
| 27 079 | ... | 6 | Le Sueur | 1 162 | 27 677 | 1 504 | 23.8 | 93.1 | 0.8 | 0.7 | 0.9 | 5.4 | 6.4 | 18.6 | 6.8 | 12.1 | 12.8 | 15.6 |
| 27 081 | ... | 9 | Lincoln | 1 390 | 5 818 | 2 779 | 4.2 | 97.7 | 0.5 | 0.4 | 0.4 | 1.7 | 6.0 | 16.1 | 5.6 | 10.3 | 10.2 | 13.5 |
| 27 083 | 32140 | 7 | Lyon | 1 851 | 25 543 | 1 583 | 13.8 | 88.5 | 2.9 | 0.7 | 3.3 | 6.0 | 7.4 | 16.8 | 13.0 | 13.8 | 10.6 | 13.4 |
| 27 085 | 26780 | 6 | McLeod | 1 273 | 36 053 | 1 275 | 28.3 | 93.3 | 0.8 | 0.5 | 1.1 | 5.1 | 6.5 | 18.4 | 7.3 | 12.2 | 12.6 | 15.0 |
| 27 087 | ... | 8 | Mahnomen | 1 445 | 5 536 | 2 802 | 3.8 | 58.3 | 1.4 | 45.7 | 0.8 | 2.4 | 9.2 | 20.5 | 7.5 | 10.8 | 10.4 | 12.9 |
| 27 089 | ... | 8 | Marshall | 4 597 | 9 449 | 2 476 | 2.1 | 95.3 | 0.7 | 0.9 | 0.4 | 3.6 | 5.9 | 17.0 | 6.4 | 10.8 | 10.8 | 15.5 |
| 27 091 | 21860 | 7 | Martin | 1 845 | 20 475 | 1 816 | 11.1 | 95.0 | 0.6 | 0.5 | 0.7 | 3.7 | 5.8 | 16.0 | 6.7 | 10.4 | 10.2 | 15.0 |
| 27 093 | ... | 6 | Meeker | 1 575 | 23 061 | 1 688 | 14.6 | 95.8 | 0.6 | 0.4 | 0.5 | 3.3 | 6.7 | 18.3 | 6.7 | 10.9 | 11.4 | 15.1 |
| 27 095 | ... | 6 | Mille Lacs | 1 482 | 25 740 | 1 577 | 17.4 | 91.8 | 1.0 | 6.5 | 0.8 | 1.6 | 6.9 | 18.2 | 7.5 | 11.8 | 12.0 | 15.1 |
| 27 097 | ... | 6 | Morrison | 2 914 | 33 052 | 1 352 | 11.3 | 97.6 | 0.8 | 0.7 | 0.7 | 1.3 | 6.7 | 17.6 | 7.4 | 12.0 | 11.2 | 15.4 |
| 27 099 | 12380 | 4 | Mower | 1 842 | 39 372 | 1 187 | 21.4 | 84.3 | 3.0 | 0.5 | 2.4 | 11.0 | 7.4 | 17.9 | 8.0 | 12.2 | 11.3 | 13.7 |
| 27 101 | ... | 9 | Murray | 1 825 | 8 577 | 2 559 | 4.7 | 95.7 | 0.6 | 0.5 | 1.1 | 2.9 | 5.9 | 16.0 | 5.9 | 9.7 | 9.8 | 14.4 |
| 27 103 | 31860 | 5 | Nicollet | 1 162 | 32 929 | 1 358 | 28.3 | 92.2 | 2.8 | 0.6 | 1.9 | 3.8 | 6.3 | 15.8 | 15.5 | 13.5 | 11.0 | 13.3 |
| 27 105 | 49380 | 7 | Nobles | 1 852 | 21 487 | 1 754 | 11.6 | 67.1 | 4.0 | 0.6 | 6.2 | 23.3 | 8.2 | 17.8 | 8.7 | 12.8 | 11.4 | 13.6 |
| 27 107 | ... | 8 | Norman | 2 261 | 6 634 | 2 713 | 2.9 | 94.3 | 0.9 | 3.0 | 0.6 | 4.3 | 5.5 | 18.3 | 5.8 | 9.5 | 10.5 | 15.4 |
| 27 109 | 40340 | 3 | Olmsted | 1 692 | 147 066 | 429 | 86.9 | 84.8 | 5.6 | 0.6 | 6.5 | 4.3 | 7.3 | 17.7 | 7.7 | 15.3 | 12.3 | 15.1 |
| 27 111 | 22260 | 6 | Otter Tail | 5 108 | 57 288 | 889 | 11.2 | 95.3 | 1.2 | 1.0 | 0.8 | 2.7 | 5.7 | 16.6 | 6.8 | 10.0 | 9.8 | 15.4 |
| 27 113 | ... | 6 | Pennington | 1 597 | 14 074 | 2 171 | 8.8 | 93.2 | 2.1 | 2.3 | 1.1 | 3.0 | 6.8 | 16.7 | 9.2 | 12.7 | 11.8 | 14.1 |
| 27 115 | ... | 6 | Pine | 3 655 | 29 218 | 1 447 | 8.0 | 91.9 | 2.6 | 3.9 | 0.9 | 2.5 | 5.7 | 15.9 | 7.1 | 12.7 | 12.3 | 16.1 |
| 27 117 | ... | 6 | Pipestone | 1 204 | 9 345 | 2 486 | 7.8 | 93.3 | 1.2 | 1.8 | 1.3 | 3.9 | 6.8 | 17.9 | 6.9 | 10.2 | 10.9 | 14.7 |
| 27 119 | 24220 | 3 | Polk | 5 105 | 31 416 | 1 405 | 6.2 | 91.4 | 1.3 | 2.3 | 1.1 | 5.5 | 6.3 | 17.1 | 10.2 | 11.4 | 10.8 | 14.6 |
| 27 121 | ... | 8 | Pope | 1 735 | 10 892 | 2 368 | 6.3 | 98.0 | 0.7 | 0.6 | 0.6 | 1.0 | 5.8 | 15.0 | 6.4 | 11.0 | 10.6 | 14.3 |
| 27 123 | 33460 | 1 | Ramsey | 394 | 520 152 | 126 | 1 320.2 | 69.1 | 12.3 | 1.4 | 12.9 | 7.2 | 7.0 | 16.2 | 11.7 | 16.7 | 11.8 | 13.5 |
| 27 125 | ... | 8 | Red Lake | 1 120 | 4 087 | 2 895 | 3.6 | 95.6 | 0.8 | 2.0 | 0.4 | 2.5 | 7.2 | 17.0 | 5.9 | 12.6 | 10.1 | 15.4 |
| 27 127 | ... | 7 | Redwood | 2 275 | 15 847 | 2 054 | 7.0 | 89.4 | 1.0 | 5.6 | 3.6 | 2.2 | 6.4 | 18.1 | 6.9 | 10.4 | 10.9 | 14.2 |
| 27 129 | ... | 9 | Renville | 2 546 | 15 369 | 2 083 | 6.0 | 91.8 | 0.6 | 1.0 | 0.8 | 6.8 | 5.8 | 16.7 | 6.7 | 10.5 | 10.7 | 15.8 |
| 27 131 | 22060 | 4 | Rice | 1 284 | 64 854 | 813 | 50.5 | 86.2 | 3.7 | 0.7 | 2.7 | 8.0 | 6.1 | 17.0 | 14.5 | 11.9 | 12.3 | 14.3 |
| 27 133 | ... | 6 | Rock | 1 250 | 9 553 | 2 469 | 7.6 | 95.9 | 1.2 | 0.9 | 1.0 | 2.3 | 6.6 | 19.2 | 6.3 | 10.7 | 11.1 | 14.2 |
| 27 135 | ... | 7 | Roseau | 4 329 | 15 476 | 2 076 | 3.6 | 95.1 | 0.7 | 2.0 | 2.9 | 0.8 | 6.2 | 19.6 | 6.5 | 10.2 | 13.0 | 16.8 |
| 27 137 | 20260 | 2 | St. Louis | 16 181 | 200 319 | 315 | 12.4 | 90.4 | 2.2 | 3.3 | 1.5 | 1.3 | 5.3 | 14.1 | 13.0 | 11.7 | 10.6 | 14.5 |
| 27 139 | 33460 | 1 | Scott | 923 | 135 152 | 463 | 146.4 | 86.1 | 3.3 | 1.3 | 6.6 | 4.6 | 7.8 | 21.9 | 6.5 | 13.6 | 16.7 | 16.0 |
| 27 141 | 33460 | 1 | Sherburne | 1 121 | 89 455 | 639 | 79.8 | 94.0 | 2.5 | 1.1 | 1.9 | 2.2 | 7.3 | 21.2 | 8.4 | 13.9 | 15.3 | 15.2 |
| 27 143 | ... | 8 | Sibley | 1 525 | 15 123 | 2 098 | 9.9 | 91.3 | 0.7 | 0.5 | 0.9 | 7.6 | 6.5 | 18.6 | 6.8 | 11.6 | 11.8 | 15.7 |
| 27 145 | 41060 | 3 | Stearns | 3 479 | 151 606 | 415 | 43.6 | 91.5 | 3.8 | 0.7 | 2.6 | 2.9 | 6.3 | 16.4 | 16.2 | 13.0 | 11.1 | 13.7 |
| 27 147 | 36940 | 5 | Steele | 1 113 | 36 322 | 1 268 | 32.6 | 89.6 | 3.2 | 0.6 | 1.2 | 6.5 | 7.2 | 18.9 | 7.1 | 12.4 | 12.5 | 14.8 |
| 27 149 | ... | 7 | Stevens | 1 460 | 9 663 | 2 459 | 6.6 | 91.8 | 2.1 | 2.1 | 2.1 | 4.0 | 5.8 | 14.4 | 21.4 | 10.7 | 8.7 | 11.5 |
| 27 151 | ... | 7 | Swift | 1 922 | 9 594 | 2 464 | 5.0 | 94.6 | 1.0 | 0.6 | 0.5 | 4.1 | 5.9 | 16.2 | 7.5 | 10.2 | 11.2 | 14.8 |
| 27 153 | ... | 6 | Todd | 2 447 | 24 509 | 1 619 | 10.0 | 93.2 | 0.6 | 0.9 | 1.0 | 5.4 | 6.7 | 17.8 | 7.6 | 10.5 | 10.5 | 15.2 |
| 27 155 | ... | 9 | Traverse | 1 486 | 3 451 | 2 944 | 2.3 | 94.0 | 0.9 | 4.1 | 0.5 | 1.6 | 4.7 | 16.4 | 6.3 | 8.8 | 9.5 | 14.8 |
| 27 157 | 40340 | 3 | Wabasha | 1 355 | 21 476 | 1 755 | 15.8 | 96.3 | 0.7 | 0.5 | 0.7 | 2.7 | 5.9 | 17.0 | 6.7 | 10.7 | 12.0 | 15.8 |
| 27 159 | ... | 7 | Wadena | 1 389 | 13 767 | 2 190 | 9.9 | 96.9 | 1.4 | 1.3 | 0.7 | 1.3 | 6.3 | 17.4 | 7.1 | 10.1 | 10.4 | 14.0 |
| 27 161 | ... | 7 | Waseca | 1 096 | 19 237 | 1 865 | 17.6 | 91.0 | 2.5 | 1.2 | 1.2 | 5.3 | 6.2 | 17.3 | 7.3 | 13.9 | 12.4 | 14.9 |
| 27 163 | 33460 | 1 | Washington | 995 | 244 088 | 269 | 245.3 | 87.2 | 4.5 | 0.9 | 5.9 | 3.5 | 6.2 | 19.8 | 7.3 | 12.2 | 13.9 | 16.8 |
| 27 165 | ... | 7 | Watonwan | 1 127 | 11 187 | 2 347 | 9.9 | 77.1 | 1.0 | 0.4 | 0.9 | 21.1 | 6.9 | 17.8 | 7.3 | 11.1 | 10.9 | 14.0 |
| 27 167 | 47420 | 6 | Wilkin | 1 945 | 6 585 | 2 716 | 3.4 | 96.1 | 0.6 | 1.4 | 0.7 | 2.3 | 5.7 | 18.2 | 6.8 | 10.3 | 11.1 | 16.4 |
| 27 169 | 49100 | 4 | Winona | 1 622 | 51 629 | 961 | 31.8 | 93.4 | 1.6 | 0.7 | 2.8 | 2.6 | 5.0 | 13.8 | 22.2 | 10.9 | 9.6 | 12.7 |
| 27 171 | 33460 | 1 | Wright | 1 713 | 127 336 | 483 | 74.3 | 94.7 | 1.6 | 0.8 | 1.7 | 2.6 | 8.3 | 21.2 | 6.7 | 13.6 | 15.2 | 14.8 |
| 27 173 | ... | 9 | Yellow Medicine | 1 966 | 10 158 | 2 429 | 5.2 | 92.1 | 0.5 | 3.6 | 0.8 | 4.2 | 6.1 | 17.3 | 7.3 | 11.0 | 10.4 | 15.0 |

1. CBSA = Core Based Statistical Area. See Appendix A for explanation. See Appendix B for list of metropolitan areas with component counties.  2. County type code from the Economic Research Service of USDA Rural-Urban Continuum Codes. See Appendix A for definition.  3. Dry land or land partially or temporarily covered by water.  4. May be of any race.

# Table B. States and Counties — Population and Households

| STATE County | 55 to 64 years | 65 to 74 years | 75 years and over | Percent female | Total persons 2000 | Total persons 2010 | Percent change 2000–2010 | Percent change 2010–2012 | Births | Deaths | Net migration | Households Number | Percent change, 2000–2010 | Persons per household | Female family householder[1] | One person |
|---|---|---|---|---|---|---|---|---|---|---|---|---|---|---|---|---|
| | 16 | 17 | 18 | 19 | 20 | 21 | 22 | 23 | 24 | 25 | 26 | 27 | 28 | 29 | 30 | 31 |
| MINNESOTA—Cont'd | | | | | | | | | | | | | | | | |
| Fillmore | 13.8 | 9.2 | 10.4 | 50.3 | 21 122 | 20 866 | -1.2 | -0.2 | 535 | 547 | -38 | 8 545 | 3.9 | 2.40 | 7.0 | 28.3 |
| Freeborn | 13.9 | 9.9 | 10.3 | 50.4 | 32 584 | 31 255 | -4.1 | -0.6 | 775 | 811 | -144 | 13 177 | -1.3 | 2.32 | 8.5 | 30.1 |
| Goodhue | 13.9 | 8.4 | 8.5 | 50.3 | 44 127 | 46 183 | 4.7 | 0.3 | 1 226 | 1 061 | -57 | 18 730 | 10.3 | 2.42 | 8.3 | 27.1 |
| Grant | 14.6 | 10.3 | 11.6 | 50.5 | 6 289 | 6 018 | -4.3 | -1.2 | 143 | 172 | -43 | 2 601 | 2.6 | 2.27 | 6.3 | 30.4 |
| Hennepin | 12.1 | 6.0 | 5.6 | 50.8 | 1 116 200 | 1 152 425 | 3.2 | 2.8 | 35 500 | 17 271 | 14 289 | 475 913 | 4.3 | 2.37 | 10.3 | 32.7 |
| Houston | 14.7 | 8.5 | 9.4 | 50.2 | 19 718 | 19 027 | -3.5 | -1.0 | 428 | 432 | -198 | 7 849 | 2.8 | 2.39 | 8.2 | 26.9 |
| Hubbard | 16.3 | 12.3 | 9.1 | 49.6 | 18 376 | 20 428 | 11.2 | -0.4 | 479 | 416 | -136 | 8 661 | 16.5 | 2.34 | 7.4 | 26.8 |
| Isanti | 11.9 | 7.4 | 5.5 | 49.9 | 31 287 | 37 816 | 20.9 | 1.1 | 1 044 | 620 | -16 | 13 972 | 24.4 | 2.67 | 8.9 | 21.5 |
| Itasca | 16.6 | 10.4 | 8.8 | 49.5 | 43 992 | 45 058 | 2.4 | 0.4 | 1 008 | 1 044 | 228 | 18 773 | 5.5 | 2.35 | 8.2 | 28.2 |
| Jackson | 13.8 | 8.8 | 11.0 | 49.4 | 11 268 | 10 266 | -8.9 | 0.1 | 217 | 294 | 98 | 4 429 | -2.8 | 2.29 | 7.1 | 30.9 |
| Kanabec | 14.2 | 9.6 | 7.1 | 49.4 | 14 996 | 16 239 | 8.3 | -1.4 | 340 | 346 | -232 | 6 413 | 11.4 | 2.49 | 8.5 | 24.9 |
| Kandiyohi | 13.5 | 8.2 | 8.3 | 50.1 | 41 203 | 42 239 | 2.5 | 0.3 | 1 212 | 819 | -244 | 16 732 | 5.0 | 2.46 | 8.6 | 26.7 |
| Kittson | 16.3 | 10.2 | 12.3 | 49.9 | 5 285 | 4 552 | -13.9 | -1.3 | 98 | 163 | 4 | 1 986 | -8.4 | 2.24 | 5.1 | 33.7 |
| Koochiching | 16.7 | 10.1 | 9.3 | 50.0 | 14 355 | 13 311 | -7.3 | -0.8 | 264 | 339 | -20 | 5 874 | -2.7 | 2.23 | 8.8 | 32.4 |
| Lac qui Parle | 16.3 | 10.3 | 13.2 | 49.6 | 8 067 | 7 259 | -10.0 | -2.1 | 157 | 227 | -85 | 3 155 | -4.9 | 2.25 | 5.9 | 30.7 |
| Lake | 16.5 | 11.4 | 11.4 | 49.6 | 11 058 | 10 866 | -1.7 | -0.4 | 249 | 332 | 27 | 4 825 | 3.9 | 2.21 | 6.7 | 30.5 |
| Lake of the Woods | 18.4 | 11.3 | 8.9 | 48.9 | 4 522 | 4 045 | -10.5 | -1.8 | 78 | 100 | -48 | 1 784 | -6.3 | 2.24 | 6.0 | 29.8 |
| Le Sueur | 13.3 | 7.9 | 6.4 | 49.5 | 25 426 | 27 703 | 9.0 | -0.1 | 763 | 496 | -311 | 10 758 | 11.7 | 2.55 | 7.3 | 23.8 |
| Lincoln | 13.7 | 11.0 | 13.6 | 49.8 | 6 429 | 5 896 | -8.3 | -1.3 | 144 | 205 | -34 | 2 574 | -3.0 | 2.24 | 5.1 | 34.0 |
| Lyon | 11.4 | 6.3 | 7.5 | 50.3 | 25 425 | 25 857 | 1.7 | -1.2 | 820 | 531 | -614 | 10 227 | 5.3 | 2.42 | 7.9 | 29.6 |
| McLeod | 12.1 | 8.1 | 7.7 | 50.2 | 34 898 | 36 651 | 5.0 | -1.6 | 981 | 735 | -879 | 14 639 | 8.8 | 2.47 | 7.7 | 27.1 |
| Mahnomen | 13.3 | 8.2 | 7.2 | 49.7 | 5 190 | 5 413 | 4.3 | 2.3 | 238 | 118 | -4 | 2 019 | 2.5 | 2.64 | 16.6 | 26.3 |
| Marshall | 14.3 | 9.4 | 9.9 | 49.3 | 10 155 | 9 439 | -7.1 | 0.1 | 219 | 216 | 9 | 3 981 | -2.9 | 2.35 | 6.3 | 28.8 |
| Martin | 15.0 | 9.3 | 11.6 | 50.9 | 21 802 | 20 840 | -4.4 | -1.8 | 486 | 549 | -302 | 9 035 | -0.4 | 2.27 | 7.9 | 31.4 |
| Meeker | 14.0 | 8.6 | 8.4 | 49.2 | 22 644 | 23 300 | 2.9 | -1.0 | 647 | 486 | -402 | 9 176 | 6.8 | 2.50 | 7.0 | 25.6 |
| Mille Lacs | 12.1 | 8.6 | 7.7 | 49.7 | 22 330 | 26 097 | 16.9 | -1.4 | 710 | 613 | -447 | 10 166 | 17.7 | 2.52 | 10.6 | 26.6 |
| Morrison | 13.4 | 8.3 | 8.1 | 49.5 | 31 712 | 33 198 | 4.7 | -0.4 | 862 | 738 | -260 | 13 080 | 10.7 | 2.50 | 8.2 | 26.4 |
| Mower | 12.3 | 7.3 | 9.8 | 50.1 | 38 603 | 39 163 | 1.5 | 0.5 | 1 180 | 823 | -146 | 15 828 | 1.6 | 2.43 | 9.6 | 30.0 |
| Murray | 15.7 | 10.5 | 12.1 | 50.4 | 9 165 | 8 725 | -4.8 | -1.7 | 197 | 211 | -133 | 3 717 | -0.1 | 2.30 | 5.4 | 29.5 |
| Nicollet | 12.3 | 6.4 | 5.8 | 50.2 | 29 771 | 32 727 | 9.9 | 0.6 | 872 | 502 | -179 | 12 201 | 14.6 | 2.46 | 9.0 | 26.3 |
| Nobles | 11.6 | 7.4 | 8.4 | 48.6 | 20 832 | 21 378 | 2.6 | 0.5 | 787 | 423 | -243 | 7 946 | 0.1 | 2.64 | 8.4 | 26.7 |
| Norman | 13.6 | 9.7 | 11.8 | 49.9 | 7 442 | 6 852 | -7.9 | -3.2 | 145 | 243 | -127 | 2 863 | -4.9 | 2.34 | 7.2 | 32.0 |
| Olmsted | 11.6 | 6.8 | 6.2 | 51.1 | 124 277 | 144 248 | 16.1 | 2.0 | 4 800 | 2 103 | 62 | 57 080 | 19.4 | 2.48 | 8.9 | 27.2 |
| Otter Tail | 15.3 | 11.0 | 10.3 | 49.8 | 57 159 | 57 303 | 0.3 | 0.0 | 1 304 | 1 527 | 227 | 24 055 | 6.1 | 2.33 | 6.5 | 28.3 |
| Pennington | 12.7 | 8.0 | 8.0 | 50.7 | 13 584 | 13 930 | 2.5 | 1.0 | 435 | 313 | 18 | 5 836 | 5.6 | 2.33 | 10.0 | 31.0 |
| Pine | 13.6 | 9.5 | 7.1 | 46.5 | 26 530 | 29 750 | 12.1 | -1.8 | 680 | 572 | -634 | 11 373 | 14.4 | 2.46 | 9.1 | 26.7 |
| Pipestone | 12.6 | 8.3 | 11.6 | 51.4 | 9 895 | 9 596 | -3.0 | -2.6 | 252 | 279 | -221 | 4 054 | -0.4 | 2.32 | 7.6 | 32.2 |
| Polk | 13.2 | 7.9 | 8.5 | 49.9 | 31 369 | 31 600 | 0.7 | -0.6 | 857 | 792 | -236 | 12 704 | 5.3 | 2.38 | 9.2 | 30.1 |
| Pope | 15.5 | 10.7 | 10.7 | 49.5 | 11 236 | 10 995 | -2.1 | -0.9 | 263 | 307 | -56 | 4 736 | 4.9 | 2.28 | 6.7 | 29.5 |
| Ramsey | 12.0 | 6.1 | 6.0 | 51.5 | 511 035 | 508 640 | -0.5 | 2.3 | 16 556 | 8 604 | 3 805 | 202 691 | 0.7 | 2.42 | 12.6 | 33.1 |
| Red Lake | 14.1 | 9.5 | 8.1 | 49.8 | 4 299 | 4 089 | -4.9 | 0.0 | 118 | 77 | -44 | 1 737 | 0.6 | 2.33 | 6.3 | 30.5 |
| Redwood | 13.4 | 9.2 | 10.5 | 50.3 | 16 815 | 16 059 | -4.5 | -1.3 | 425 | 424 | -239 | 6 580 | -1.4 | 2.38 | 8.0 | 31.4 |
| Renville | 14.2 | 9.0 | 10.5 | 49.2 | 17 154 | 15 730 | -8.3 | -2.3 | 438 | 469 | -335 | 6 564 | -3.2 | 2.34 | 7.4 | 29.6 |
| Rice | 11.3 | 6.7 | 6.0 | 48.9 | 56 665 | 64 142 | 13.2 | 1.1 | 1 608 | 1 001 | 82 | 22 315 | 18.1 | 2.55 | 9.0 | 25.9 |
| Rock | 13.2 | 8.1 | 10.6 | 50.6 | 9 721 | 9 687 | -0.3 | -1.4 | 241 | 284 | -99 | 3 918 | 2.0 | 2.41 | 6.8 | 29.1 |
| Roseau | 13.0 | 7.7 | 7.0 | 48.9 | 16 338 | 15 629 | -4.3 | -1.0 | 403 | 290 | -268 | 6 300 | 1.8 | 2.45 | 7.0 | 27.1 |
| St. Louis | 14.8 | 8.0 | 8.0 | 49.9 | 200 528 | 200 226 | -0.2 | 0.0 | 4 580 | 4 590 | 216 | 84 783 | 2.6 | 2.25 | 9.5 | 32.9 |
| Scott | 9.5 | 4.8 | 3.2 | 50.2 | 89 498 | 129 928 | 45.2 | 4.0 | 4 196 | 1 174 | 2 169 | 45 108 | 47.0 | 2.85 | 8.3 | 17.9 |
| Sherburne | 9.9 | 5.0 | 3.7 | 48.9 | 64 417 | 88 499 | 37.4 | 1.1 | 2 660 | 1 071 | -662 | 30 212 | 40.0 | 2.86 | 8.1 | 17.7 |
| Sibley | 12.6 | 7.8 | 8.5 | 49.9 | 15 356 | 15 226 | -0.8 | -0.7 | 428 | 323 | -212 | 6 034 | 4.5 | 2.49 | 7.4 | 27.2 |
| Stearns | 11.0 | 6.4 | 6.1 | 49.5 | 133 166 | 150 642 | 13.1 | 0.6 | 4 278 | 1 992 | -1 291 | 56 232 | 18.1 | 2.53 | 8.2 | 25.1 |
| Steele | 12.4 | 7.2 | 7.4 | 50.5 | 33 680 | 36 576 | 8.6 | -0.7 | 1 062 | 664 | -661 | 14 330 | 11.6 | 2.51 | 9.1 | 26.1 |
| Stevens | 11.3 | 6.6 | 9.6 | 50.8 | 10 053 | 9 726 | -3.3 | -0.6 | 268 | 211 | -117 | 3 717 | -0.7 | 2.37 | 5.7 | 29.6 |
| Swift | 14.1 | 8.8 | 11.3 | 49.4 | 11 956 | 9 783 | -18.2 | -1.9 | 239 | 247 | -170 | 4 236 | -2.7 | 2.27 | 7.0 | 32.8 |
| Todd | 14.1 | 9.6 | 7.9 | 48.7 | 24 426 | 24 895 | 1.9 | -1.6 | 701 | 480 | -603 | 9 756 | 4.4 | 2.52 | 6.9 | 26.4 |
| Traverse | 13.7 | 10.2 | 15.6 | 50.3 | 4 134 | 3 558 | -13.9 | -3.0 | 86 | 100 | -91 | 1 524 | -11.2 | 2.27 | 6.4 | 33.0 |
| Wabasha | 14.4 | 9.4 | 8.1 | 50.0 | 21 610 | 21 676 | 0.3 | -0.9 | 632 | 417 | -425 | 8 822 | 6.6 | 2.43 | 6.8 | 25.4 |
| Wadena | 13.2 | 10.2 | 11.3 | 50.7 | 13 713 | 13 843 | 0.9 | -0.5 | 483 | 434 | -119 | 5 705 | 5.1 | 2.34 | 8.7 | 32.2 |
| Waseca | 13.0 | 7.2 | 7.8 | 52.9 | 19 526 | 19 136 | -2.0 | 0.5 | 506 | 332 | -77 | 7 281 | 3.1 | 2.44 | 8.7 | 26.9 |
| Washington | 12.7 | 6.4 | 4.6 | 50.5 | 201 130 | 238 136 | 18.4 | 2.5 | 6 213 | 2 996 | 2 719 | 87 859 | 22.9 | 2.67 | 9.4 | 21.2 |
| Watonwan | 13.0 | 8.5 | 10.4 | 49.9 | 11 876 | 11 211 | -5.6 | -0.2 | 341 | 283 | -81 | 4 520 | -2.3 | 2.45 | 8.6 | 29.5 |
| Wilkin | 13.3 | 8.6 | 9.6 | 49.2 | 7 138 | 6 576 | -7.9 | 0.1 | 156 | 207 | 61 | 2 690 | -2.3 | 2.39 | 6.4 | 28.6 |
| Winona | 12.1 | 7.0 | 6.7 | 50.8 | 49 985 | 51 461 | 3.0 | 0.3 | 1 057 | 966 | 81 | 19 554 | 4.3 | 2.40 | 8.0 | 29.0 |
| Wright | 10.1 | 5.8 | 4.2 | 49.7 | 89 986 | 124 700 | 38.6 | 2.1 | 4 116 | 1 565 | 60 | 44 473 | 41.3 | 2.78 | 8.1 | 20.2 |
| Yellow Medicine | 13.2 | 9.0 | 10.7 | 48.9 | 11 080 | 10 438 | -5.8 | -2.7 | 257 | 268 | -268 | 4 292 | -3.3 | 2.36 | 6.7 | 29.4 |

1. No spouse present.

# Table B. States and Counties — Population, Vital Statistics, Medicare, and Crime

| STATE County | Persons in group quarters, 2010 | Daytime population, 2007–2011 Number | Employment/residence ratio | Births, 2011 Total | Births Rate[1] | Deaths, 2011 Number | Deaths Rate[1] | Persons under 65 with no health insurance, 2010 Number | Percent | Medicare, 2012 Eligible for Medicare | Enrolled in Medicare Advantage | Enrolled in a Medicare prescription drug plan | Serious crimes known to police,[2] 2011 Total Number | Rate[3] |
|---|---|---|---|---|---|---|---|---|---|---|---|---|---|---|
| | 32 | 33 | 34 | 35 | 36 | 37 | 38 | 39 | 40 | 41 | 42 | 43 | 44 | 45 |
| MINNESOTA—Cont'd | | | | | | | | | | | | | | |
| Fillmore | 359 | 17 641 | 0.68 | 250 | 12.0 | 233 | 11.2 | 2 235 | 13.3 | 4 399 | 1 808 | 2 093 | 41 | 195 |
| Freeborn | 637 | 29 774 | 0.90 | 362 | 11.6 | 367 | 11.8 | 2 780 | 11.3 | 7 328 | 3 269 | 3 531 | 613 | 1 946 |
| Goodhue | 901 | 45 765 | 0.99 | 541 | 11.7 | 453 | 9.8 | 3 892 | 10.2 | 8 833 | 4 416 | 3 467 | 1 060 | 2 278 |
| Grant | 110 | 5 512 | 0.81 | 65 | 10.9 | 74 | 12.4 | 540 | 11.6 | 1 612 | 755 | 808 | 94 | 1 550 |
| Hennepin | 25 084 | 1 367 484 | 1.37 | 15 811 | 13.5 | 7 532 | 6.4 | 114 837 | 11.4 | 162 568 | 81 635 | 55 278 | 44 004 | 3 797 |
| Houston | 257 | 15 227 | 0.61 | 176 | 9.3 | 192 | 10.2 | 1 451 | 9.3 | 3 979 | 1 407 | 1 936 | 231 | 1 295 |
| Hubbard | 154 | 18 416 | 0.78 | 217 | 10.7 | 177 | 8.7 | 2 076 | 12.9 | 5 096 | 2 268 | 2 404 | 483 | 2 346 |
| Isanti | 465 | 30 764 | 0.60 | 473 | 12.4 | 265 | 6.9 | 3 457 | 10.5 | 5 935 | 3 236 | 2 058 | 752 | 1 973 |
| Itasca | 1 021 | 43 792 | 0.94 | 424 | 9.4 | 449 | 10.0 | 4 001 | 11.1 | 10 690 | 4 202 | 4 682 | 989 | 2 178 |
| Jackson | 110 | 10 220 | 0.98 | 98 | 9.6 | 129 | 12.6 | 810 | 9.9 | 2 248 | 493 | 1 469 | 86 | 831 |
| Kanabec | 246 | 13 620 | 0.63 | 162 | 10.0 | 159 | 9.8 | 1 560 | 11.6 | 3 482 | 1 608 | 1 207 | 482 | 2 945 |
| Kandiyohi | 1 058 | 42 803 | 1.04 | 546 | 12.9 | 337 | 8.0 | 3 668 | 10.5 | 8 324 | 4 341 | 4 280 | 762 | 1 790 |
| Kittson | 111 | 4 256 | 0.85 | 45 | 10.0 | 76 | 16.8 | 397 | 11.3 | 1 109 | 417 | 595 | 38 | 828 |
| Koochiching | 241 | 13 361 | 1.00 | 116 | 8.8 | 142 | 10.7 | 1 174 | 11.1 | 3 239 | 1 523 | 1 727 | 242 | 1 804 |
| Lac qui Parle | 154 | 6 787 | 0.86 | 65 | 9.0 | 94 | 13.1 | 563 | 10.3 | 1 773 | 846 | 944 | 81 | 1 107 |
| Lake | 224 | 10 657 | 0.96 | 116 | 10.7 | 132 | 12.2 | 845 | 10.1 | 2 762 | 918 | 1 338 | 92 | 840 |
| Lake of the Woods | 53 | 3 837 | 0.88 | 34 | 8.5 | 46 | 11.5 | 407 | 12.7 | 972 | 383 | 415 | 8 | 196 |
| Le Sueur | 270 | 22 580 | 0.64 | 344 | 12.4 | 225 | 8.1 | 2 535 | 10.8 | 4 520 | 2 233 | 2 125 | 231 | 969 |
| Lincoln | 135 | 5 108 | 0.74 | 61 | 10.5 | 88 | 15.1 | 513 | 11.6 | 1 441 | 461 | 874 | 20 | 337 |
| Lyon | 1 092 | 27 641 | 1.14 | 362 | 14.0 | 240 | 9.3 | 2 170 | 10.1 | 4 311 | 1 371 | 2 718 | 468 | 1 960 |
| McLeod | 476 | 35 893 | 0.96 | 463 | 12.7 | 319 | 8.8 | 2 900 | 9.4 | 6 621 | 3 646 | 3 181 | 641 | 1 736 |
| Mahnomen | 79 | 6 144 | 1.34 | 101 | 18.5 | 54 | 9.9 | 655 | 14.1 | 872 | 344 | 432 | 144 | 2 640 |
| Marshall | 76 | 7 995 | 0.67 | 100 | 10.5 | 95 | 10.0 | 846 | 11.2 | 1 993 | 769 | 1 125 | 116 | 1 220 |
| Martin | 348 | 21 044 | 1.02 | 228 | 11.0 | 244 | 11.8 | 1 827 | 11.1 | 5 058 | 2 046 | 2 709 | 350 | 1 667 |
| Meeker | 354 | 20 273 | 0.73 | 299 | 12.9 | 203 | 8.7 | 2 112 | 11.0 | 4 423 | 2 669 | 1 909 | 367 | 1 563 |
| Mille Lacs | 523 | 25 220 | 0.93 | 328 | 12.6 | 255 | 9.8 | 2 778 | 12.8 | 5 393 | 2 934 | 1 936 | 680 | 2 586 |
| Morrison | 528 | 30 660 | 0.84 | 407 | 12.2 | 335 | 10.1 | 3 204 | 11.6 | 6 530 | 3 637 | 2 937 | 395 | 1 181 |
| Mower | 632 | 37 341 | 0.91 | 558 | 14.2 | 370 | 9.4 | 3 912 | 12.2 | 8 018 | 2 377 | 3 225 | 1 003 | 2 541 |
| Murray | 163 | 7 772 | 0.78 | 88 | 10.2 | 99 | 11.5 | 726 | 10.8 | 2 055 | 587 | 1 276 | 65 | 739 |
| Nicollet | 2 720 | 31 473 | 0.94 | 376 | 11.5 | 228 | 6.9 | 2 228 | 8.3 | 4 878 | 2 246 | 2 585 | 736 | 2 232 |
| Nobles | 385 | 22 217 | 1.10 | 369 | 17.2 | 185 | 8.6 | 2 820 | 15.8 | 3 821 | 990 | 2 278 | 337 | 1 564 |
| Norman | 149 | 6 126 | 0.78 | 70 | 10.2 | 102 | 14.8 | 667 | 12.4 | 1 562 | 624 | 803 | NA | NA |
| Olmsted | 2 770 | 158 218 | 1.20 | 2 118 | 14.5 | 885 | 6.1 | 10 410 | 8.4 | 22 194 | 6 293 | 7 737 | 3 014 | 2 073 |
| Otter Tail | 1 188 | 55 051 | 0.91 | 590 | 10.3 | 691 | 12.1 | 5 077 | 11.3 | 13 692 | 7 295 | 6 262 | 852 | 1 475 |
| Pennington | 327 | 16 079 | 1.30 | 188 | 13.4 | 142 | 10.1 | 1 160 | 10.0 | 2 613 | 1 153 | 1 340 | 337 | 2 401 |
| Pine | 1 797 | 26 664 | 0.77 | 304 | 10.3 | 244 | 8.2 | 3 031 | 13.0 | 5 716 | 3 054 | 2 042 | 652 | 2 175 |
| Pipestone | 205 | 9 670 | 1.02 | 126 | 13.3 | 129 | 13.6 | 871 | 11.4 | 1 934 | 501 | 1 187 | 71 | 734 |
| Polk | 1 330 | 29 194 | 0.86 | 377 | 12.0 | 358 | 11.4 | 2 496 | 9.8 | 6 090 | 2 408 | 3 149 | 492 | 1 545 |
| Pope | 184 | 10 163 | 0.85 | 117 | 10.7 | 134 | 12.3 | 1 018 | 11.8 | 2 513 | 1 224 | 1 261 | 65 | 587 |
| Ramsey | 18 384 | 568 454 | 1.25 | 7 264 | 14.1 | 3 759 | 7.3 | 50 179 | 11.5 | 76 374 | 38 477 | 25 432 | 21 171 | 4 130 |
| Red Lake | 34 | 3 228 | 0.59 | 53 | 12.9 | 34 | 8.3 | 366 | 10.9 | 790 | 495 | 466 | 26 | 631 |
| Redwood | 373 | 15 806 | 0.97 | 190 | 11.9 | 180 | 11.3 | 1 434 | 11.2 | 3 434 | 1 401 | 1 904 | 243 | 1 502 |
| Renville | 342 | 14 919 | 0.88 | 193 | 12.5 | 203 | 13.1 | 1 395 | 11.1 | 3 294 | 1 261 | 1 833 | 198 | 1 249 |
| Rice | 7 278 | 58 937 | 0.86 | 720 | 11.2 | 440 | 6.8 | 5 349 | 10.8 | 9 609 | 4 822 | 4 408 | 1 206 | 1 866 |
| Rock | 260 | 8 489 | 0.76 | 114 | 11.9 | 113 | 11.8 | 787 | 10.1 | 2 084 | 674 | 1 224 | 111 | 1 137 |
| Roseau | 191 | 16 370 | 1.07 | 191 | 12.3 | 130 | 8.4 | 1 388 | 10.5 | 2 660 | 1 451 | 1 103 | 78 | 495 |
| St. Louis | 9 433 | 207 757 | 1.09 | 2 056 | 10.3 | 2 046 | 10.2 | 17 186 | 10.6 | 40 750 | 15 716 | 18 271 | 6 955 | 3 447 |
| Scott | 1 287 | 105 406 | 0.66 | 1 897 | 14.3 | 496 | 3.7 | 9 964 | 8.4 | 13 125 | 6 846 | 4 753 | 2 707 | 2 068 |
| Sherburne | 2 174 | 67 792 | 0.54 | 1 223 | 13.7 | 455 | 5.1 | 7 462 | 9.4 | 10 124 | 5 274 | 3 540 | 1 626 | 1 823 |
| Sibley | 230 | 12 643 | 0.67 | 188 | 12.4 | 135 | 8.9 | 1 581 | 12.5 | 2 850 | 1 466 | 1 385 | 5 | 33 |
| Stearns | 8 213 | 156 902 | 1.10 | 1 928 | 12.7 | 864 | 5.7 | 12 959 | 10.3 | 22 661 | 10 703 | 10 053 | 4 064 | 2 798 |
| Steele | 594 | 38 521 | 1.11 | 480 | 13.1 | 293 | 8.0 | 2 744 | 8.9 | 6 187 | 3 156 | 2 769 | 650 | 1 865 |
| Stevens | 892 | 10 646 | 1.20 | 124 | 12.8 | 89 | 9.2 | 771 | 10.5 | 1 666 | 631 | 950 | 177 | 1 806 |
| Swift | 150 | 9 841 | 1.00 | 105 | 10.9 | 110 | 11.4 | 881 | 11.4 | 2 122 | 822 | 1 160 | 165 | 1 674 |
| Todd | 346 | 21 803 | 0.74 | 313 | 12.6 | 197 | 7.9 | 3 072 | 15.0 | 5 158 | 3 001 | 2 160 | 431 | 1 718 |
| Traverse | 100 | 3 636 | 1.02 | 36 | 10.2 | 32 | 9.1 | 361 | 13.9 | 947 | 357 | 522 | 74 | 2 064 |
| Wabasha | 246 | 18 269 | 0.70 | 240 | 11.1 | 175 | 8.1 | 1 884 | 10.6 | 4 225 | 1 931 | 1 599 | 237 | 1 283 |
| Wadena | 482 | 14 713 | 1.15 | 168 | 12.2 | 191 | 13.9 | 1 235 | 11.4 | 3 456 | 1 808 | 1 563 | 245 | 1 756 |
| Waseca | 1 344 | 18 169 | 0.90 | 237 | 12.3 | 138 | 7.2 | 1 379 | 9.1 | 3 560 | 1 775 | 1 887 | 329 | 1 706 |
| Washington | 3 570 | 196 996 | 0.68 | 2 769 | 11.5 | 1 271 | 5.3 | 14 494 | 6.9 | 32 372 | 17 098 | 9 248 | 5 607 | 2 337 |
| Watonwan | 150 | 10 254 | 0.83 | 156 | 13.9 | 122 | 10.9 | 1 426 | 15.8 | 2 176 | 862 | 1 181 | 119 | 1 053 |
| Wilkin | 152 | 5 862 | 0.77 | 72 | 10.9 | 106 | 16.1 | 501 | 9.4 | 1 381 | 548 | 711 | 104 | 1 569 |
| Winona | 4 499 | 51 225 | 0.99 | 465 | 9.1 | 436 | 8.5 | 4 954 | 12.2 | 8 117 | 2 824 | 3 840 | 757 | 1 460 |
| Wright | 1 104 | 99 768 | 0.63 | 1 878 | 14.9 | 664 | 5.3 | 9 939 | 8.9 | 15 381 | 8 600 | 5 549 | 2 326 | 1 851 |
| Yellow Medicine | 290 | 9 873 | 0.89 | 111 | 10.8 | 122 | 11.8 | 866 | 10.4 | 2 317 | 798 | 1 267 | 89 | 846 |

1. Per 1,000 estimated resident population. 2. Data for serious crimes have not been adjusted for underreporting; this may affect comparability between geographic areas and over time. 3. Per 100,000 population estimated by the FBI.

# Table B. States and Counties — Crime, Education, Money Income, and Poverty

| STATE County | Serious crimes known to police, 2011 (cont.)[1] Rate[2] Violent | Property | Education — School enrollment and attainment, 2007–2011 — Enrollment[3] Total | Percent private | Attainment[4] (percent) High school graduate or less | Bachelor's degree or more | Local government expenditures,[5] 2009–2010 Total current expenditures (mil dol) | Current expenditures per student (dollars) | Money income, 2007–2011 Per capita income[6] (dollars) | Households — Median income Dollars | Percent change, 2000 to 2007–2011 (constant 2011 dollars) | Percent with income of $200,000 or more | Income and poverty, 2011 Median household income (dollars) | Percent below poverty level All persons | Children under 18 years | Children 5 to 17 years in families |
|---|---|---|---|---|---|---|---|---|---|---|---|---|---|---|---|---|
| | 46 | 47 | 48 | 49 | 50 | 51 | 52 | 53 | 54 | 55 | 56 | 57 | 58 | 59 | 60 | 61 |
| **MINNESOTA—Cont'd** | | | | | | | | | | | | | | | | |
| Fillmore | 19 | 176 | 4 586 | 11.3 | 50.0 | 18.7 | 23.2 | 8 990 | 24 318 | 47 940 | -3.1 | 1.5 | 47 241 | 12.2 | 17.9 | 16.6 |
| Freeborn | 114 | 1 832 | 6 747 | 8.9 | 51.4 | 14.2 | 41.8 | 10 181 | 24 409 | 43 447 | -12.9 | 2.0 | 44 352 | 12.4 | 17.3 | 16.0 |
| Goodhue | 116 | 2 162 | 10 920 | 11.0 | 42.0 | 22.2 | 78.7 | 11 239 | 27 996 | 56 099 | -11.5 | 2.2 | 54 724 | 9.2 | 12.8 | 12.0 |
| Grant | 0 | 1 550 | 1 191 | 6.5 | 45.3 | 17.2 | 10.3 | 9 365 | 24 169 | 43 777 | -4.0 | 1.2 | 43 715 | 10.4 | 16.3 | 14.8 |
| Hennepin | 418 | 3 379 | 305 388 | 19.4 | 27.1 | 44.7 | 1 808.5 | 11 642 | 36 858 | 62 966 | -9.8 | 7.2 | 60 811 | 13.6 | 17.7 | 16.1 |
| Houston | 73 | 1 222 | 4 326 | 16.0 | 45.5 | 22.7 | 39.1 | 9 067 | 25 791 | 53 017 | -3.5 | 1.8 | 52 325 | 9.5 | 12.6 | 11.2 |
| Hubbard | 83 | 2 264 | 4 075 | 6.8 | 42.0 | 22.3 | 23.2 | 9 858 | 24 869 | 45 733 | -4.1 | 2.3 | 41 196 | 14.1 | 22.8 | 21.4 |
| Isanti | 73 | 1 900 | 9 828 | 11.9 | 48.0 | 16.5 | 57.8 | 9 521 | 25 184 | 58 721 | -13.2 | 2.1 | 57 860 | 8.8 | 12.5 | 11.6 |
| Itasca | 214 | 1 964 | 9 787 | 9.1 | 41.3 | 21.2 | 83.6 | 12 810 | 24 067 | 47 106 | -3.7 | 1.8 | 44 957 | 14.1 | 20.7 | 18.0 |
| Jackson | 68 | 764 | 2 263 | 10.7 | 45.8 | 15.9 | 13.8 | 9 276 | 25 744 | 47 455 | -4.4 | 1.8 | 47 337 | 11.2 | 17.3 | 15.4 |
| Kanabec | 251 | 2 695 | 3 878 | 10.2 | 54.1 | 13.2 | 20.5 | 8 387 | 21 350 | 46 863 | -9.9 | 0.5 | 44 691 | 14.4 | 22.0 | 20.0 |
| Kandiyohi | 155 | 1 635 | 10 321 | 10.8 | 42.7 | 21.4 | 55.4 | 9 811 | 27 053 | 49 915 | -7.0 | 2.9 | 49 543 | 12.7 | 18.6 | 17.1 |
| Kittson | 0 | 828 | 908 | 6.7 | 46.1 | 21.4 | 9.4 | 13 169 | 25 973 | 50 049 | 14.0 | 1.4 | 45 740 | 10.7 | 15.6 | 13.4 |
| Koochiching | 89 | 1 715 | 2 720 | 13.7 | 48.7 | 17.2 | 21.9 | 11 084 | 24 829 | 41 135 | -16.0 | 1.6 | 42 771 | 14.0 | 21.5 | 18.6 |
| Lac qui Parle | 68 | 1 039 | 1 507 | 6.4 | 50.1 | 16.2 | 15.6 | 11 426 | 25 519 | 48 269 | 9.6 | 2.5 | 49 670 | 10.4 | 14.6 | 12.9 |
| Lake | 82 | 758 | 1 895 | 6.0 | 44.0 | 20.0 | 13.7 | 9 559 | 26 675 | 47 450 | -13.0 | 1.0 | 48 683 | 10.5 | 17.0 | 15.2 |
| Lake of the Woods | 74 | 123 | 765 | 3.4 | 47.3 | 15.9 | 5.9 | 10 681 | 25 999 | 43 523 | -1.9 | 2.6 | 39 777 | 12.8 | 18.1 | 16.2 |
| Le Sueur | 29 | 940 | 6 893 | 12.8 | 46.0 | 21.3 | 37.4 | 8 624 | 26 481 | 58 074 | -6.4 | 1.5 | 54 468 | 9.0 | 11.2 | 10.0 |
| Lincoln | 168 | 168 | 1 267 | 4.4 | 51.5 | 13.1 | 10.1 | 10 667 | 25 570 | 46 270 | 8.4 | 2.2 | 43 996 | 9.8 | 12.7 | 11.8 |
| Lyon | 138 | 1 822 | 7 512 | 11.9 | 43.5 | 25.8 | 67.9 | 16 264 | 24 125 | 47 254 | -10.3 | 1.5 | 50 031 | 12.1 | 16.3 | 14.8 |
| McLeod | 116 | 1 619 | 8 869 | 15.9 | 46.2 | 18.3 | 49.3 | 9 045 | 27 704 | 57 323 | -7.6 | 1.8 | 52 120 | 8.2 | 11.2 | 9.9 |
| Mahnomen | 403 | 2 236 | 1 328 | 8.7 | 54.0 | 13.7 | 16.1 | 11 584 | 18 533 | 39 385 | -2.9 | 1.2 | 37 593 | 24.3 | 37.4 | 35.5 |
| Marshall | 74 | 1 146 | 2 046 | 7.2 | 51.4 | 16.6 | 18.2 | 13 325 | 25 828 | 49 636 | 5.6 | 1.7 | 44 760 | 10.1 | 12.9 | 10.3 |
| Martin | 67 | 1 600 | 4 775 | 16.9 | 48.4 | 19.1 | 37.7 | 12 253 | 25 354 | 44 791 | -4.7 | 2.4 | 44 597 | 12.5 | 18.7 | 17.2 |
| Meeker | 102 | 1 461 | 5 572 | 10.0 | 49.3 | 16.1 | 30.9 | 8 685 | 24 766 | 51 929 | -6.0 | 1.6 | 51 299 | 9.3 | 12.8 | 11.8 |
| Mille Lacs | 156 | 2 430 | 6 301 | 12.1 | 51.0 | 14.7 | 56.6 | 8 669 | 22 221 | 46 100 | -7.7 | 0.8 | 43 155 | 13.2 | 18.9 | 17.5 |
| Morrison | 60 | 1 121 | 7 529 | 11.9 | 53.2 | 14.8 | 51.7 | 9 925 | 23 154 | 46 054 | -7.9 | 1.4 | 44 928 | 12.1 | 16.8 | 15.9 |
| Mower | 195 | 2 346 | 9 342 | 9.5 | 48.1 | 16.1 | 59.6 | 10 016 | 24 170 | 45 596 | -7.9 | 1.4 | 46 860 | 13.7 | 19.6 | 18.7 |
| Murray | 11 | 728 | 1 785 | 13.6 | 49.9 | 15.7 | 12.2 | 10 670 | 25 344 | 47 833 | 1.3 | 1.7 | 52 281 | 9.4 | 13.5 | 12.3 |
| Nicollet | 97 | 2 135 | 9 917 | 37.4 | 33.7 | 33.2 | 31.9 | 13 978 | 26 108 | 59 877 | -3.9 | 1.9 | 55 360 | 10.3 | 12.0 | 10.0 |
| Nobles | 162 | 1 402 | 5 051 | 9.6 | 54.5 | 15.6 | 37.6 | 9 577 | 21 634 | 45 552 | -5.5 | 2.0 | 44 945 | 14.5 | 20.8 | 18.7 |
| Norman | NA | NA | 1 522 | 5.8 | 51.3 | 14.9 | 12.2 | 10 697 | 23 463 | 43 333 | -1.4 | 1.2 | 44 576 | 12.5 | 18.5 | 15.5 |
| Olmsted | 167 | 1 906 | 36 756 | 18.4 | 28.5 | 40.4 | 203.6 | 9 148 | 33 850 | 66 204 | -4.5 | 5.6 | 66 997 | 8.0 | 10.8 | 10.5 |
| Otter Tail | 99 | 1 377 | 11 840 | 10.7 | 44.5 | 21.2 | 122.5 | 15 901 | 24 740 | 45 494 | -4.8 | 1.4 | 47 879 | 11.4 | 15.7 | 14.1 |
| Pennington | 171 | 2 230 | 3 262 | 10.1 | 46.7 | 15.4 | 77.1 | 34 835 | 23 142 | 45 007 | -2.6 | 0.9 | 41 986 | 12.6 | 16.5 | 15.6 |
| Pine | 117 | 2 058 | 6 319 | 10.2 | 55.6 | 12.8 | 37.4 | 9 537 | 21 769 | 44 463 | -11.9 | 1.0 | 42 447 | 15.9 | 24.0 | 22.3 |
| Pipestone | 62 | 672 | 2 260 | 19.6 | 48.7 | 16.7 | 11.8 | 10 050 | 23 310 | 42 217 | -2.0 | 1.8 | 43 726 | 12.7 | 17.8 | 16.2 |
| Polk | 157 | 1 388 | 8 032 | 10.7 | 43.5 | 21.7 | 50.5 | 9 945 | 24 274 | 49 257 | 3.9 | 1.4 | 49 978 | 14.5 | 20.4 | 15.8 |
| Pope | 45 | 542 | 2 092 | 12.1 | 47.0 | 18.5 | 15.0 | 11 809 | 27 727 | 49 599 | 3.1 | 2.8 | 47 165 | 10.3 | 14.0 | 13.3 |
| Ramsey | 427 | 3 704 | 142 881 | 26.7 | 33.7 | 38.8 | 1 036.1 | 12 515 | 29 437 | 52 713 | -14.6 | 4.2 | 51 719 | 17.7 | 25.6 | 23.0 |
| Red Lake | 97 | 534 | 834 | 9.8 | 52.3 | 13.9 | 8.4 | 11 460 | 22 408 | 47 719 | 10.3 | 0.6 | 44 658 | 11.4 | 16.1 | 15.1 |
| Redwood | 142 | 1 359 | 3 743 | 14.7 | 51.4 | 16.4 | 25.5 | 9 363 | 24 493 | 45 177 | -10.4 | 2.1 | 47 858 | 10.4 | 14.5 | 13.3 |
| Renville | 82 | 1 167 | 3 562 | 12.3 | 51.8 | 15.9 | 17.9 | 9 023 | 24 317 | 48 442 | -4.7 | 1.4 | 49 153 | 11.1 | 17.1 | 15.1 |
| Rice | 135 | 1 731 | 20 207 | 37.1 | 43.0 | 26.9 | 79.2 | 9 343 | 24 783 | 59 533 | -9.4 | 2.4 | 56 781 | 11.2 | 13.8 | 12.5 |
| Rock | 697 | 440 | 2 369 | 9.3 | 49.6 | 17.2 | 13.9 | 8 866 | 23 094 | 44 510 | -13.5 | 1.6 | 49 920 | 10.9 | 14.6 | 13.1 |
| Roseau | 57 | 438 | 3 990 | 8.7 | 51.7 | 17.5 | 31.7 | 10 321 | 23 730 | 48 612 | -9.7 | 1.7 | 48 344 | 12.1 | 15.4 | 12.3 |
| St. Louis | 226 | 3 220 | 51 232 | 13.8 | 37.7 | 25.5 | 285.2 | 11 273 | 25 586 | 45 399 | -7.4 | 2.0 | 44 475 | 17.5 | 21.3 | 18.9 |
| Scott | 112 | 1 956 | 37 043 | 18.7 | 30.4 | 36.3 | 186.1 | 8 752 | 34 532 | 83 415 | -7.3 | 7.0 | 81 586 | 5.8 | 7.1 | 6.6 |
| Sherburne | 99 | 1 725 | 25 086 | 11.9 | 36.2 | 24.3 | 164.1 | 8 514 | 27 444 | 71 819 | -6.7 | 2.3 | 68 646 | 7.6 | 9.2 | 7.9 |
| Sibley | 0 | 33 | 3 542 | 10.9 | 54.2 | 13.7 | 21.3 | 9 123 | 24 563 | 52 482 | -6.2 | 1.7 | 53 047 | 11.6 | 16.9 | 14.2 |
| Stearns | 198 | 2 601 | 46 751 | 19.5 | 41.2 | 23.9 | 236.9 | 10 292 | 25 329 | 53 035 | -7.4 | 2.4 | 52 053 | 13.5 | 13.0 | 11.2 |
| Steele | 126 | 1 739 | 9 401 | 16.3 | 44.5 | 23.7 | 58.7 | 9 054 | 26 114 | 57 290 | -8.0 | 2.2 | 54 971 | 9.6 | 13.6 | 12.9 |
| Stevens | 112 | 1 694 | 3 138 | 7.6 | 41.8 | 25.0 | 14.0 | 9 524 | 25 855 | 47 712 | -5.2 | 2.0 | 46 892 | 13.3 | 12.2 | 10.3 |
| Swift | 71 | 1 603 | 2 081 | 6.1 | 54.3 | 14.1 | 14.3 | 9 523 | 22 699 | 43 846 | -6.7 | 1.3 | 46 209 | 10.5 | 15.0 | 13.1 |
| Todd | 84 | 1 634 | 5 588 | 15.5 | 52.8 | 11.8 | 48.5 | 13 473 | 21 406 | 44 202 | 1.4 | 1.5 | 41 290 | 16.7 | 24.5 | 20.2 |
| Traverse | 195 | 1 869 | 735 | 4.4 | 49.5 | 16.3 | 5.8 | 10 652 | 25 743 | 44 773 | 8.3 | 2.2 | 45 815 | 12.4 | 18.8 | 16.0 |
| Wabasha | 54 | 1 229 | 5 064 | 8.3 | 48.1 | 16.3 | 38.6 | 8 424 | 27 339 | 52 346 | -7.9 | 2.1 | 53 899 | 9.3 | 13.1 | 11.7 |
| Wadena | 136 | 1 620 | 3 194 | 5.0 | 49.9 | 13.8 | 24.3 | 8 598 | 19 812 | 35 307 | -14.7 | 0.7 | 36 097 | 18.2 | 25.5 | 23.1 |
| Waseca | 156 | 1 551 | 4 461 | 12.4 | 45.7 | 19.0 | 35.1 | 9 764 | 24 408 | 52 357 | -8.6 | 1.2 | 52 660 | 9.9 | 13.5 | 12.1 |
| Washington | 68 | 2 269 | 67 548 | 19.1 | 27.8 | 40.0 | 349.2 | 9 071 | 36 786 | 79 571 | -11.1 | 7.5 | 77 069 | 5.9 | 7.1 | 5.9 |
| Watonwan | 62 | 991 | 2 590 | 9.2 | 55.6 | 14.9 | 19.2 | 9 801 | 24 187 | 49 307 | 3.0 | 1.9 | 46 565 | 11.8 | 17.6 | 16.2 |
| Wilkin | 75 | 1 494 | 1 577 | 11.4 | 41.5 | 17.3 | 11.0 | 9 732 | 25 118 | 51 957 | 1.0 | 1.1 | 50 004 | 9.6 | 12.9 | 11.3 |
| Winona | 137 | 1 323 | 17 152 | 20.7 | 41.9 | 25.3 | 65.2 | 11 669 | 22 327 | 44 848 | -14.2 | 1.6 | 46 028 | 14.6 | 14.6 | 12.6 |
| Wright | 78 | 1 773 | 33 659 | 13.6 | 39.3 | 25.4 | 239.7 | 9 352 | 29 231 | 69 674 | -4.3 | 3.6 | 68 387 | 6.9 | 8.6 | 7.5 |
| Yellow Medicine | 124 | 723 | 2 426 | 8.5 | 49.0 | 18.1 | 21.1 | 12 484 | 23 718 | 50 740 | 9.3 | 1.2 | 46 586 | 11.1 | 15.0 | 13.6 |

1. Data for serious crimes have not been adjusted for underreporting; this may affect comparability between geographic areas and over time. 2. Per 100,000 population estimated by the FBI. 3. All persons 3 years old and over enrolled in nursery school through college. 4. Persons 25 years old and over. 5. Elementary and secondary education expenditures. 6. Based on population estimated by the American Community Survey, 2007–2011.

# Table B. States and Counties — **Personal Income**

| STATE County | Personal income, 2011 | | | | | | | Transfer payments (mil dol) | | | | | |
|---|---|---|---|---|---|---|---|---|---|---|---|---|---|
| | | | Per capita[1] | | | | | | Government payments to individuals | | | | |
| | Total (mil dol) | Percent change, 2010–2011 | Dollars | Rank | Wages and salaries[2] (mil dol) | Proprietors' income (mil dol) | Dividends, interest, and rent (mil dol) | Total | Total | Social Security | Medical payments | Income mainte-nance | Unemploy-ment insurance |
| | 62 | 63 | 64 | 65 | 66 | 67 | 68 | 69 | 70 | 71 | 72 | 73 | 74 |
| **MINNESOTA—Cont'd** | | | | | | | | | | | | | |
| Fillmore | 797 | 6.4 | 38 185 | 944 | 238 | 159 | 132 | 170 | 165 | 57 | 80 | 13 | 7 |
| Freeborn | 1 217 | 6.9 | 39 052 | 851 | 543 | 177 | 217 | 271 | 264 | 101 | 113 | 24 | 11 |
| Goodhue | 1 959 | 6.1 | 42 377 | 553 | 1 103 | 236 | 345 | 339 | 328 | 128 | 144 | 21 | 16 |
| Grant | 242 | 0.6 | 40 436 | 707 | 79 | 54 | 50 | 57 | 56 | 21 | 26 | 5 | 2 |
| Hennepin | 67 157 | 5.6 | 57 476 | 89 | 64 352 | 6 525 | 11 994 | 8 607 | 8 349 | 2 422 | 3 931 | 970 | 385 |
| Houston | 767 | 4.5 | 40 554 | 700 | 187 | 70 | 137 | 148 | 144 | 54 | 62 | 10 | 7 |
| Hubbard | 650 | 4.9 | 32 013 | 1 886 | 225 | 42 | 135 | 197 | 192 | 71 | 83 | 19 | 8 |
| Isanti | 1 399 | 5.6 | 36 544 | 1 133 | 484 | 125 | 171 | 272 | 264 | 90 | 107 | 21 | 16 |
| Itasca | 1 513 | 5.0 | 33 604 | 1 586 | 764 | 72 | 279 | 446 | 436 | 155 | 187 | 41 | 20 |
| Jackson | 507 | 9.8 | 49 666 | 213 | 217 | 155 | 75 | 79 | 77 | 28 | 36 | 6 | 3 |
| Kanabec | 500 | 4.5 | 30 917 | 2 119 | 153 | 52 | 70 | 140 | 137 | 49 | 57 | 13 | 8 |
| Kandiyohi | 1 804 | 4.1 | 42 769 | 522 | 971 | 291 | 345 | 347 | 338 | 110 | 145 | 36 | 14 |
| Kittson | 198 | 3.9 | 43 914 | 445 | 65 | 48 | 37 | 42 | 41 | 15 | 19 | 3 | 2 |
| Koochiching | 474 | 1.4 | 35 855 | 1 238 | 277 | 18 | 70 | 133 | 130 | 46 | 58 | 12 | 6 |
| Lac qui Parle | 341 | 1.9 | 47 448 | 285 | 99 | 109 | 62 | 66 | 64 | 22 | 32 | 5 | 2 |
| Lake | 449 | 5.6 | 41 505 | 616 | 222 | 32 | 75 | 109 | 106 | 38 | 44 | 8 | 4 |
| Lake of the Woods | 133 | 7.7 | 33 091 | 1 693 | 56 | 16 | 29 | 37 | 37 | 13 | 17 | 3 | 1 |
| Le Sueur | 1 040 | 5.8 | 37 608 | 1 015 | 364 | 117 | 179 | 192 | 185 | 65 | 83 | 14 | 11 |
| Lincoln | 242 | 6.8 | 41 559 | 610 | 69 | 57 | 45 | 52 | 50 | 17 | 26 | 3 | 2 |
| Lyon | 1 045 | 4.6 | 40 343 | 711 | 682 | 168 | 178 | 190 | 184 | 57 | 88 | 17 | 8 |
| McLeod | 1 325 | 4.2 | 36 359 | 1 158 | 811 | 125 | 230 | 260 | 252 | 94 | 111 | 19 | 15 |
| Mahnomen | 167 | 5.1 | 30 580 | 2 183 | 78 | 21 | 24 | 58 | 57 | 10 | 31 | 10 | 2 |
| Marshall | 398 | 7.8 | 41 968 | 575 | 118 | 76 | 69 | 80 | 78 | 25 | 38 | 6 | 4 |
| Martin | 942 | 4.1 | 45 532 | 364 | 408 | 206 | 180 | 191 | 187 | 68 | 84 | 16 | 7 |
| Meeker | 821 | 4.8 | 35 304 | 1 325 | 288 | 118 | 139 | 175 | 170 | 61 | 76 | 13 | 9 |
| Mille Lacs | 752 | 4.1 | 28 941 | 2 459 | 366 | 33 | 110 | 245 | 239 | 76 | 114 | 24 | 12 |
| Morrison | 1 129 | 6.8 | 33 985 | 1 511 | 480 | 161 | 176 | 271 | 264 | 84 | 119 | 25 | 15 |
| Mower | 1 584 | 5.5 | 40 268 | 717 | 844 | 172 | 261 | 339 | 330 | 110 | 152 | 31 | 11 |
| Murray | 435 | 10.6 | 50 384 | 198 | 124 | 149 | 71 | 71 | 70 | 26 | 32 | 5 | 3 |
| Nicollet | 1 268 | 5.9 | 38 630 | 892 | 634 | 102 | 210 | 198 | 191 | 70 | 71 | 17 | 10 |
| Nobles | 889 | 8.7 | 41 549 | 612 | 458 | 223 | 145 | 152 | 147 | 49 | 69 | 16 | 6 |
| Norman | 292 | 3.4 | 42 495 | 542 | 81 | 74 | 54 | 66 | 64 | 20 | 32 | 6 | 2 |
| Olmsted | 6 665 | 0.4 | 45 721 | 350 | 5 766 | 338 | 1 051 | 956 | 923 | 324 | 418 | 84 | 41 |
| Otter Tail | 2 106 | 6.0 | 36 781 | 1 105 | 946 | 203 | 432 | 520 | 507 | 185 | 214 | 40 | 19 |
| Pennington | 602 | 7.5 | 42 781 | 520 | 458 | 53 | 98 | 121 | 118 | 34 | 50 | 11 | 6 |
| Pine | 850 | 3.7 | 28 707 | 2 503 | 325 | 41 | 125 | 251 | 245 | 81 | 103 | 27 | 13 |
| Pipestone | 410 | 4.3 | 43 131 | 500 | 163 | 115 | 71 | 76 | 73 | 24 | 36 | 7 | 3 |
| Polk | 1 221 | 5.4 | 38 824 | 874 | 528 | 133 | 181 | 278 | 271 | 79 | 134 | 29 | 11 |
| Pope | 469 | 8.2 | 43 039 | 506 | 179 | 87 | 84 | 94 | 92 | 32 | 44 | 7 | 3 |
| Ramsey | 23 349 | 4.7 | 45 365 | 376 | 22 125 | 1 677 | 3 933 | 4 405 | 4 291 | 1 089 | 2 136 | 574 | 174 |
| Red Lake | 147 | 11.7 | 35 695 | 1 263 | 56 | 19 | 22 | 33 | 32 | 10 | 15 | 3 | 2 |
| Redwood | 683 | 4.2 | 42 779 | 521 | 274 | 180 | 131 | 131 | 127 | 45 | 58 | 11 | 5 |
| Renville | 664 | 2.5 | 42 832 | 517 | 252 | 155 | 126 | 128 | 124 | 43 | 56 | 12 | 6 |
| Rice | 2 102 | 4.4 | 32 631 | 1 773 | 1 122 | 137 | 360 | 398 | 384 | 141 | 161 | 34 | 22 |
| Rock | 437 | 9.9 | 45 457 | 369 | 136 | 129 | 75 | 74 | 72 | 28 | 32 | 6 | 2 |
| Roseau | 632 | 12.3 | 40 638 | 693 | 438 | 70 | 97 | 106 | 102 | 35 | 48 | 9 | 4 |
| St. Louis | 7 622 | 5.7 | 38 059 | 964 | 4 918 | 443 | 1 233 | 1 865 | 1 820 | 574 | 803 | 194 | 82 |
| Scott | 6 018 | 7.8 | 45 400 | 373 | 2 343 | 260 | 782 | 588 | 559 | 202 | 217 | 42 | 42 |
| Sherburne | 2 990 | 7.5 | 33 474 | 1 608 | 1 178 | 130 | 364 | 446 | 426 | 155 | 165 | 36 | 34 |
| Sibley | 595 | 5.5 | 39 205 | 830 | 163 | 97 | 103 | 112 | 109 | 38 | 50 | 9 | 5 |
| Stearns | 5 373 | 5.6 | 35 504 | 1 292 | 4 003 | 399 | 899 | 1 025 | 991 | 303 | 391 | 92 | 52 |
| Steele | 1 445 | 3.5 | 39 554 | 798 | 1 039 | 108 | 226 | 254 | 246 | 90 | 108 | 23 | 13 |
| Stevens | 422 | 3.7 | 43 547 | 467 | 237 | 87 | 86 | 69 | 67 | 21 | 32 | 5 | 3 |
| Swift | 385 | 5.1 | 39 923 | 753 | 166 | 74 | 65 | 88 | 86 | 27 | 44 | 7 | 4 |
| Todd | 766 | 5.8 | 30 838 | 2 133 | 258 | 100 | 121 | 209 | 204 | 64 | 92 | 21 | 9 |
| Traverse | 163 | -1.6 | 46 368 | 324 | 46 | 49 | 39 | 36 | 35 | 12 | 18 | 3 | 1 |
| Wabasha | 852 | 4.1 | 39 457 | 809 | 287 | 68 | 144 | 161 | 156 | 59 | 71 | 10 | 7 |
| Wadena | 419 | 4.3 | 30 456 | 2 211 | 241 | 23 | 74 | 146 | 143 | 43 | 71 | 16 | 6 |
| Waseca | 735 | 7.8 | 38 159 | 950 | 352 | 115 | 122 | 136 | 132 | 49 | 55 | 14 | 6 |
| Washington | 11 949 | 6.3 | 49 523 | 220 | 3 830 | 346 | 2 068 | 1 258 | 1 205 | 515 | 438 | 84 | 77 |
| Watonwan | 438 | 10.9 | 39 074 | 847 | 163 | 113 | 69 | 87 | 84 | 29 | 38 | 8 | 4 |
| Wilkin | 280 | 4.7 | 42 437 | 548 | 97 | 56 | 51 | 58 | 56 | 18 | 29 | 5 | 2 |
| Winona | 1 801 | 5.6 | 35 049 | 1 364 | 1 143 | 115 | 339 | 355 | 343 | 114 | 143 | 32 | 16 |
| Wright | 4 703 | 9.7 | 37 196 | 1 059 | 1 750 | 280 | 537 | 668 | 640 | 233 | 269 | 48 | 47 |
| Yellow Medicine | 443 | 6.4 | 42 986 | 514 | 190 | 92 | 79 | 99 | 97 | 30 | 44 | 7 | 3 |

1. Based on the resident population estimated as of July 1 of the year shown.  2. Includes supplements to wages and salaries.

# Table B. States and Counties — Earnings, Social Security, and Housing

| STATE County | Earnings, 2011 | | | | | | | | | Social Security beneficiaries, December 2011 | | Housing units, 2010 | | |
| | Total (mil dol) | Farm | Goods-related[1] | | Service-related and health | | | | | Number | Rate[2] | Supplemental Security Income recipients, December 2011 | Total | Percent change, 2000–2010 |
| | | | Total | Manufacturing | Information and professional and technical services | Retail trade | Finance, insurance, and real estate | Health care and social services | Government | | | | | |
| | 75 | 76 | 77 | 78 | 79 | 80 | 81 | 82 | 83 | 84 | 85 | 86 | 87 | 88 |
| **MINNESOTA—Cont'd** | | | | | | | | | | | | | | |
| Fillmore | 397 | 24.9 | D | 14.1 | 2.6 | 5.8 | 3.8 | D | 14.6 | 4 795 | 230 | 202 | 9 732 | 9.3 |
| Freeborn | 721 | 15.2 | D | 19.6 | D | 7.9 | 4.9 | D | 11.6 | 7 915 | 254 | 506 | 14 231 | 1.7 |
| Goodhue | 1 339 | 8.3 | D | 18.0 | 3.1 | 5.3 | 3.0 | 10.8 | 16.5 | 9 565 | 207 | 446 | 20 337 | 13.7 |
| Grant | 133 | 30.8 | 13.0 | 2.3 | 3.7 | 3.7 | D | D | 14.1 | 1 730 | 289 | 75 | 3 324 | 7.3 |
| Hennepin | 70 877 | 0.0 | 12.6 | 9.6 | 16.5 | 4.3 | 16.3 | 9.3 | 9.7 | 167 745 | 144 | 24 779 | 509 469 | 8.7 |
| Houston | 258 | 13.4 | D | 8.3 | D | 5.0 | 2.9 | 11.1 | 21.5 | 4 285 | 227 | 213 | 8 601 | 5.3 |
| Hubbard | 267 | 8.5 | D | 17.5 | D | 8.5 | 4.0 | D | 21.5 | 5 660 | 279 | 398 | 14 622 | 19.6 |
| Isanti | 609 | 1.8 | 19.5 | 13.2 | D | 9.9 | 4.6 | 21.3 | 17.5 | 6 720 | 176 | 364 | 15 321 | 27.0 |
| Itasca | 836 | 0.5 | D | 9.2 | 2.9 | 8.2 | 3.3 | 15.5 | 22.1 | 12 010 | 267 | 934 | 27 065 | 10.3 |
| Jackson | 372 | 35.7 | 26.1 | 23.2 | 2.2 | 2.0 | 2.1 | D | 8.9 | 2 405 | 236 | 104 | 4 990 | -2.0 |
| Kanabec | 205 | 5.9 | 24.1 | 9.1 | 3.1 | 8.1 | 4.3 | D | 27.9 | 3 960 | 245 | 281 | 7 849 | 14.7 |
| Kandiyohi | 1 262 | 6.9 | D | 20.2 | D | 7.5 | 3.6 | D | 17.9 | 8 880 | 211 | 704 | 19 476 | 5.8 |
| Kittson | 113 | 36.7 | D | 3.8 | D | 3.9 | D | D | 18.8 | 1 225 | 271 | 53 | 2 605 | -4.2 |
| Koochiching | 294 | 0.6 | 33.7 | 28.8 | 2.3 | 6.7 | 6.7 | D | 21.5 | 3 570 | 270 | 301 | 7 900 | 2.3 |
| Lac qui Parle | 208 | 38.9 | 14.1 | 8.8 | D | 4.4 | 3.8 | 6.1 | 16.1 | 1 920 | 267 | 105 | 3 692 | -2.2 |
| Lake | 253 | 0.0 | D | 13.4 | 1.5 | 5.3 | 3.1 | D | 17.2 | 2 905 | 268 | 154 | 7 681 | 12.3 |
| Lake of the Woods | 72 | 10.8 | 11.8 | 9.5 | D | 6.8 | D | 14.2 | 20.7 | 1 110 | 277 | 42 | 3 672 | 13.4 |
| Le Sueur | 481 | 8.7 | D | 27.9 | 2.7 | 4.4 | 4.5 | 5.6 | 13.0 | 4 935 | 178 | 233 | 12 416 | 14.3 |
| Lincoln | 125 | 33.7 | D | 0.4 | 2.3 | 4.3 | 2.4 | 13.8 | 10.4 | 1 530 | 263 | 61 | 3 108 | 2.1 |
| Lyon | 850 | 11.7 | 21.1 | 14.3 | 4.9 | 6.5 | 7.8 | 5.7 | 17.9 | 4 690 | 181 | 414 | 11 098 | 7.8 |
| McLeod | 936 | 4.7 | D | 38.3 | 2.5 | 5.5 | 3.8 | D | 10.6 | 7 225 | 198 | 333 | 15 760 | 11.9 |
| Mahnomen | 99 | 16.6 | D | D | D | 3.3 | D | D | 52.8 | 980 | 180 | 150 | 2 786 | 3.2 |
| Marshall | 194 | 30.4 | D | 7.4 | 2.1 | 4.3 | D | 5.2 | 17.1 | 2 190 | 231 | 100 | 4 812 | 0.4 |
| Martin | 614 | 26.5 | 15.4 | 12.6 | D | 5.7 | 4.3 | D | 10.5 | 5 525 | 267 | 354 | 10 009 | 2.1 |
| Meeker | 406 | 12.8 | 28.7 | 20.4 | 3.8 | 6.2 | D | D | 16.1 | 4 895 | 210 | 224 | 10 674 | 8.7 |
| Mille Lacs | 399 | 2.0 | D | 7.2 | 7.2 | 5.8 | 3.0 | D | 42.1 | 6 095 | 235 | 399 | 12 750 | 21.8 |
| Morrison | 641 | 18.1 | D | 11.9 | 5.6 | 6.8 | 2.8 | D | 20.3 | 7 315 | 220 | 532 | 15 731 | 13.4 |
| Mower | 1 017 | 11.2 | 21.8 | 18.5 | D | 5.4 | 2.8 | 11.9 | 13.9 | 8 785 | 223 | 719 | 17 027 | 4.8 |
| Murray | 273 | 46.0 | 11.6 | 5.2 | 2.3 | 3.7 | 3.3 | D | 11.5 | 2 205 | 256 | 94 | 4 556 | 4.6 |
| Nicollet | 736 | 11.8 | D | 26.8 | D | 3.2 | 2.3 | D | 22.5 | 5 210 | 159 | 297 | 12 873 | 14.5 |
| Nobles | 682 | 25.2 | 25.4 | 22.5 | 3.3 | 6.5 | 2.5 | D | 11.4 | 4 100 | 192 | 283 | 8 535 | 0.8 |
| Norman | 156 | 41.1 | D | D | D | 4.6 | D | 8.1 | 14.0 | 1 755 | 255 | 138 | 3 421 | -1.0 |
| Olmsted | 6 104 | 0.9 | 15.5 | 11.8 | 3.7 | 4.8 | 2.9 | 52.1 | 8.8 | 23 595 | 162 | 2 131 | 60 495 | 22.4 |
| Otter Tail | 1 150 | 7.4 | 24.0 | 16.6 | 4.9 | 7.5 | 3.4 | 13.8 | 16.6 | 15 025 | 262 | 851 | 35 594 | 5.1 |
| Pennington | 510 | 5.7 | 17.2 | 14.0 | 1.9 | 5.3 | 2.1 | D | 15.1 | 2 810 | 200 | 211 | 6 297 | 4.4 |
| Pine | 366 | 3.8 | D | 2.1 | D | 6.9 | 2.7 | 9.1 | 46.3 | 6 485 | 219 | 520 | 17 276 | 12.5 |
| Pipestone | 278 | 27.4 | D | 5.9 | 8.7 | 5.4 | D | D | 16.5 | 2 075 | 218 | 138 | 4 483 | 1.1 |
| Polk | 661 | 15.6 | 19.0 | 13.9 | 3.6 | 5.9 | 2.6 | 13.6 | 20.6 | 6 600 | 210 | 616 | 14 610 | 4.3 |
| Pope | 266 | 22.1 | 22.1 | 17.1 | 1.5 | 4.2 | 3.1 | D | 15.6 | 2 610 | 240 | 127 | 6 435 | 10.4 |
| Ramsey | 23 802 | 0.0 | D | 12.2 | 9.3 | 4.1 | 8.7 | 12.8 | 17.3 | 78 950 | 153 | 15 710 | 217 197 | 5.2 |
| Red Lake | 75 | 24.2 | D | D | D | 4.0 | D | D | 35.3 | 865 | 211 | 40 | 1 948 | 3.5 |
| Redwood | 454 | 30.8 | D | 14.0 | 2.2 | 4.4 | 3.6 | 6.2 | 19.3 | 3 755 | 235 | 225 | 7 272 | 0.6 |
| Renville | 407 | 37.0 | D | 16.3 | 2.9 | 2.7 | 2.5 | D | 13.8 | 3 565 | 230 | 213 | 7 355 | -0.8 |
| Rice | 1 259 | 4.2 | 25.9 | 18.5 | 3.3 | 6.0 | 2.8 | 9.4 | 19.6 | 10 435 | 162 | 709 | 24 453 | 21.9 |
| Rock | 265 | 41.8 | 10.1 | 7.5 | 1.7 | 4.0 | 7.0 | 10.7 | 12.8 | 2 300 | 239 | 120 | 4 262 | 3.0 |
| Roseau | 508 | 9.8 | 56.3 | 55.3 | 1.1 | 3.6 | 2.3 | D | 12.1 | 2 910 | 187 | 162 | 7 469 | 5.2 |
| St. Louis | 5 360 | 0.1 | 18.3 | 5.7 | 5.5 | 6.9 | 6.5 | 23.3 | 19.1 | 44 360 | 222 | 5 333 | 103 058 | 7.6 |
| Scott | 2 603 | 1.7 | 25.7 | 16.2 | 9.3 | 5.6 | 2.8 | 8.3 | 21.0 | 14 045 | 106 | 1 023 | 47 124 | 49.1 |
| Sherburne | 1 308 | 1.5 | D | 14.3 | 3.8 | 7.2 | 3.5 | 13.8 | 18.8 | 11 430 | 128 | 673 | 32 379 | 41.9 |
| Sibley | 260 | 35.0 | 18.1 | 10.7 | 1.3 | 2.5 | 1.9 | D | 16.4 | 3 120 | 206 | 136 | 6 582 | 9.3 |
| Stearns | 4 403 | 4.3 | 20.6 | 13.7 | 5.3 | 7.5 | 5.6 | 17.6 | 17.5 | 24 590 | 162 | 2 024 | 61 974 | 23.2 |
| Steele | 1 147 | 5.2 | D | 26.6 | D | 8.4 | 17.3 | 9.9 | 10.1 | 6 800 | 186 | 462 | 15 343 | 15.3 |
| Stevens | 324 | 23.5 | D | 16.2 | 3.8 | 4.2 | 3.0 | 10.7 | 20.0 | 1 785 | 184 | 105 | 4 160 | 2.1 |
| Swift | 240 | 24.0 | D | 18.9 | 2.0 | 3.3 | 2.9 | D | 18.2 | 2 285 | 237 | 147 | 4 835 | 0.3 |
| Todd | 359 | 13.4 | D | 27.9 | 1.8 | 5.7 | 2.6 | 10.6 | 19.4 | 5 550 | 223 | 417 | 12 917 | 8.6 |
| Traverse | 94 | 48.0 | 3.6 | 1.0 | D | 3.7 | D | 5.0 | 17.8 | 1 015 | 288 | 45 | 2 073 | -5.7 |
| Wabasha | 355 | 14.2 | D | 25.9 | 2.0 | 6.0 | 3.9 | 8.8 | 15.7 | 4 595 | 213 | 194 | 9 997 | 10.3 |
| Wadena | 263 | 4.1 | 10.8 | 7.8 | 2.0 | 7.5 | 3.2 | D | 24.0 | 3 755 | 273 | 390 | 6 899 | 8.9 |
| Waseca | 467 | 20.5 | D | 29.0 | 4.4 | 4.4 | 3.6 | 8.3 | 16.8 | 3 905 | 203 | 233 | 7 903 | 6.4 |
| Washington | 4 177 | 0.6 | 20.5 | 14.7 | 7.3 | 8.5 | 10.1 | 13.2 | 15.9 | 34 905 | 145 | 1 821 | 92 374 | 25.5 |
| Watonwan | 276 | 37.0 | D | 18.1 | D | 3.0 | 3.1 | 6.7 | 13.7 | 2 370 | 212 | 141 | 5 047 | 0.2 |
| Wilkin | 153 | 28.8 | D | 0.2 | D | 3.4 | 3.9 | 13.0 | 13.7 | 1 465 | 222 | 87 | 3 078 | -0.9 |
| Winona | 1 257 | 4.8 | 31.4 | 27.9 | D | 6.4 | 3.2 | 8.8 | 16.2 | 8 845 | 172 | 658 | 20 760 | 6.2 |
| Wright | 2 031 | 2.5 | D | 13.5 | 3.7 | 8.4 | 3.3 | 8.5 | 17.4 | 17 030 | 135 | 828 | 49 000 | 42.6 |
| Yellow Medicine | 282 | 31.2 | D | 3.5 | 1.7 | 2.9 | 2.1 | D | 24.3 | 2 500 | 243 | 147 | 4 760 | -2.3 |

1. Includes mining, construction, and manufacturing.   2. Per 1,000 resident population enumerated in the 2010 census.

| STATE County | Housing units, 2007–2011 | | | | | | | | Civilian labor force, 2012 | | | | Civilian employment,[6] 2007–2011 | | |
|---|---|---|---|---|---|---|---|---|---|---|---|---|---|---|---|
| | Occupied units | | | | | | | | | | | | | | |
| | Owner-occupied | | | | | Renter-occupied | | Substandard units[4] (percent) | | | Unemployment | | | Percent | |
| | | | | Median owner cost as a percent of income | | | | | | | | | | | |
| | Total | Percent | Median value[1] | With a mortgage | Without a mortgage[2] | Median rent[3] | Median rent as a percent of income | | Total | Percent change, 2011–2012 | Total | Rate[5] | Total | Management, business, science and arts | Construction, production, and maintenance occupations |
| | 89 | 90 | 91 | 92 | 93 | 94 | 95 | 96 | 97 | 98 | 99 | 100 | 101 | 102 | 103 |
| MINNESOTA—Cont'd | | | | | | | | | | | | | | | |
| Fillmore | 8 507 | 80.1 | 137 000 | 23.5 | 13.3 | 552 | 26.7 | 2.7 | 11 476 | -0.6 | 629 | 5.5 | 10 453 | 33.3 | 29.3 |
| Freeborn | 13 210 | 79.0 | 109 500 | 23.4 | 12.8 | 559 | 27.7 | 1.4 | 16 484 | -2.7 | 975 | 5.9 | 15 727 | 25.0 | 32.7 |
| Goodhue | 18 686 | 78.5 | 188 000 | 24.6 | 13.4 | 668 | 30.4 | 1.1 | 25 907 | -1.1 | 1 400 | 5.4 | 23 975 | 32.3 | 28.5 |
| Grant | 2 646 | 77.6 | 102 600 | 22.2 | 14.1 | 546 | 29.9 | 1.0 | 3 304 | 0.2 | 207 | 6.3 | 2 955 | 32.7 | 28.2 |
| Hennepin | 475 737 | 64.8 | 244 100 | 24.4 | 12.6 | 877 | 29.9 | 2.8 | 660 996 | 0.5 | 34 871 | 5.3 | 614 323 | 45.4 | 14.1 |
| Houston | 7 810 | 81.7 | 151 000 | 22.3 | 13.7 | 567 | 25.7 | 1.3 | 10 663 | 0.0 | 667 | 6.3 | 10 089 | 33.1 | 28.9 |
| Hubbard | 8 640 | 83.3 | 173 400 | 25.6 | 12.9 | 662 | 31.4 | 2.7 | 9 332 | -0.5 | 778 | 8.3 | 8 948 | 31.3 | 27.2 |
| Isanti | 13 778 | 82.4 | 196 400 | 27.0 | 12.5 | 820 | 29.8 | 1.8 | 20 830 | -0.3 | 1 404 | 6.7 | 18 457 | 28.1 | 31.8 |
| Itasca | 18 761 | 81.6 | 151 900 | 24.8 | 11.6 | 598 | 29.9 | 2.2 | 23 475 | -0.3 | 1 767 | 7.5 | 19 770 | 32.2 | 26.9 |
| Jackson | 4 526 | 78.6 | 97 000 | 19.2 | 11.2 | 493 | 22.6 | 1.9 | 7 355 | 0.8 | 280 | 3.8 | 5 390 | 33.5 | 31.7 |
| Kanabec | 6 316 | 82.5 | 162 000 | 28.7 | 13.7 | 729 | 31.3 | 2.6 | 8 193 | 0.2 | 806 | 9.8 | 7 489 | 24.9 | 34.9 |
| Kandiyohi | 17 270 | 74.3 | 162 000 | 23.6 | 11.8 | 590 | 30.7 | 2.4 | 24 687 | -2.8 | 1 249 | 5.1 | 21 899 | 33.4 | 27.8 |
| Kittson | 1 954 | 84.4 | 65 600 | 17.9 | 9.9 | 487 | 23.2 | 1.1 | 2 718 | 0.4 | 145 | 5.3 | 2 242 | 34.0 | 34.9 |
| Koochiching | 6 194 | 76.0 | 102 500 | 20.7 | 12.4 | 508 | 29.8 | 2.6 | 6 659 | -1.6 | 543 | 8.2 | 5 968 | 23.5 | 34.9 |
| Lac qui Parle | 3 072 | 83.2 | 80 300 | 20.2 | 10.2 | 489 | 24.3 | 1.0 | 4 250 | -2.2 | 191 | 4.5 | 3 641 | 33.5 | 27.8 |
| Lake | 5 180 | 80.2 | 142 500 | 22.7 | 12.3 | 563 | 27.3 | 2.0 | 6 365 | -1.0 | 360 | 5.7 | 5 339 | 27.0 | 27.6 |
| Lake of the Woods | 1 728 | 88.7 | 130 100 | 26.8 | 12.8 | 575 | 37.8 | 2.5 | 2 345 | -0.7 | 142 | 6.1 | 2 046 | 23.4 | 36.1 |
| Le Sueur | 10 938 | 82.8 | 190 900 | 25.9 | 12.4 | 614 | 27.7 | 1.7 | 14 557 | -0.3 | 1 027 | 7.1 | 14 562 | 29.5 | 31.9 |
| Lincoln | 2 570 | 83.6 | 77 400 | 20.1 | 12.8 | 482 | 25.0 | 1.2 | 3 604 | 0.6 | 160 | 4.4 | 3 028 | 34.9 | 26.9 |
| Lyon | 10 174 | 67.8 | 137 600 | 20.4 | 11.6 | 568 | 27.2 | 1.8 | 14 993 | -0.9 | 684 | 4.6 | 14 170 | 32.8 | 28.0 |
| McLeod | 14 871 | 77.3 | 166 200 | 24.2 | 13.3 | 657 | 25.2 | 1.3 | 19 786 | -3.2 | 1 366 | 6.9 | 19 048 | 32.7 | 30.6 |
| Mahnomen | 2 007 | 74.3 | 89 600 | 22.0 | 13.1 | 450 | 29.0 | 4.6 | 2 520 | -1.7 | 176 | 7.0 | 2 262 | 27.5 | 24.0 |
| Marshall | 4 116 | 82.5 | 87 500 | 18.9 | 10.5 | 507 | 23.6 | 1.2 | 5 598 | -1.8 | 426 | 7.6 | 4 797 | 33.5 | 30.5 |
| Martin | 8 943 | 77.1 | 98 800 | 20.4 | 11.1 | 540 | 27.8 | 1.2 | 11 414 | -4.4 | 614 | 5.4 | 10 315 | 32.7 | 31.9 |
| Meeker | 9 400 | 81.6 | 165 600 | 26.0 | 12.7 | 693 | 30.5 | 2.5 | 12 674 | -2.1 | 841 | 6.6 | 11 551 | 28.7 | 35.1 |
| Mille Lacs | 10 594 | 76.6 | 163 100 | 27.5 | 14.7 | 624 | 30.2 | 2.3 | 12 532 | 1.4 | 1 109 | 8.8 | 12 147 | 27.6 | 31.6 |
| Morrison | 13 573 | 79.8 | 157 600 | 26.1 | 12.4 | 586 | 27.7 | 1.5 | 17 718 | -4.4 | 1 270 | 7.2 | 16 028 | 27.5 | 34.8 |
| Mower | 16 042 | 73.1 | 108 300 | 21.6 | 11.8 | 645 | 31.6 | 4.0 | 21 848 | -1.0 | 1 051 | 4.9 | 19 187 | 29.1 | 34.5 |
| Murray | 3 914 | 83.8 | 88 000 | 21.7 | 12.1 | 545 | 33.2 | 1.7 | 6 046 | -1.3 | 257 | 4.3 | 4 473 | 38.0 | 28.3 |
| Nicollet | 12 247 | 73.9 | 170 000 | 23.2 | 11.6 | 696 | 25.8 | 1.2 | 19 555 | -0.6 | 924 | 4.7 | 18 379 | 36.9 | 22.1 |
| Nobles | 8 035 | 72.1 | 100 100 | 21.6 | 10.9 | 571 | 27.0 | 6.6 | 11 575 | -3.2 | 489 | 4.2 | 10 733 | 23.6 | 39.4 |
| Norman | 2 852 | 80.1 | 81 400 | 21.6 | 12.0 | 469 | 23.9 | 1.6 | 3 724 | -3.5 | 204 | 5.5 | 3 288 | 33.7 | 27.7 |
| Olmsted | 56 601 | 75.9 | 173 000 | 22.2 | 10.4 | 769 | 28.0 | 1.7 | 82 032 | 1.1 | 3 692 | 4.5 | 77 399 | 47.8 | 15.7 |
| Otter Tail | 24 560 | 79.0 | 161 400 | 24.0 | 11.9 | 554 | 28.9 | 1.7 | 30 997 | -1.4 | 1 730 | 5.6 | 27 674 | 32.1 | 28.4 |
| Pennington | 5 825 | 76.9 | 94 100 | 21.1 | 11.7 | 508 | 29.0 | 1.0 | 9 514 | 0.4 | 570 | 6.0 | 7 468 | 27.3 | 27.8 |
| Pine | 11 862 | 81.2 | 158 200 | 26.7 | 14.1 | 642 | 28.0 | 4.2 | 14 491 | -2.0 | 1 174 | 8.1 | 13 136 | 25.0 | 29.9 |
| Pipestone | 3 929 | 75.0 | 87 100 | 20.7 | 12.0 | 601 | 24.6 | 1.1 | 5 736 | -2.0 | 247 | 4.3 | 4 785 | 33.1 | 26.9 |
| Polk | 12 442 | 73.4 | 118 800 | 20.9 | 11.8 | 574 | 30.2 | 1.6 | 18 131 | 1.4 | 948 | 5.2 | 15 772 | 32.5 | 26.7 |
| Pope | 4 823 | 77.7 | 150 500 | 23.2 | 11.7 | 570 | 22.6 | 1.2 | 6 600 | 1.8 | 279 | 4.2 | 5 652 | 32.8 | 28.5 |
| Ramsey | 204 342 | 61.1 | 217 600 | 24.4 | 12.0 | 809 | 31.2 | 3.9 | 274 598 | 0.4 | 15 830 | 5.8 | 255 263 | 42.7 | 16.7 |
| Red Lake | 1 718 | 82.3 | 78 500 | 18.7 | 12.4 | 463 | 21.9 | 1.2 | 2 420 | -2.5 | 170 | 7.0 | 2 111 | 30.2 | 30.3 |
| Redwood | 6 594 | 78.0 | 85 100 | 21.2 | 11.4 | 546 | 28.5 | 2.0 | 8 442 | -1.3 | 453 | 5.4 | 7 722 | 33.8 | 29.1 |
| Renville | 6 491 | 78.8 | 97 700 | 21.6 | 11.9 | 545 | 28.7 | 1.0 | 8 687 | -5.7 | 555 | 6.4 | 7 891 | 30.0 | 32.7 |
| Rice | 22 117 | 77.2 | 204 200 | 25.6 | 12.1 | 762 | 30.2 | 2.3 | 32 768 | -0.2 | 2 090 | 6.4 | 32 772 | 33.7 | 25.4 |
| Rock | 3 942 | 76.1 | 104 100 | 21.4 | 11.3 | 559 | 28.2 | 1.9 | 5 458 | -1.5 | 208 | 3.8 | 4 870 | 29.3 | 28.1 |
| Roseau | 6 357 | 79.7 | 101 300 | 22.3 | 11.6 | 560 | 24.7 | 1.8 | 9 114 | -0.6 | 409 | 4.5 | 8 361 | 24.5 | 44.2 |
| St. Louis | 86 446 | 71.4 | 141 800 | 22.4 | 11.9 | 639 | 32.5 | 1.9 | 104 058 | -0.8 | 6 930 | 6.7 | 94 742 | 33.7 | 20.8 |
| Scott | 44 593 | 85.8 | 263 100 | 25.0 | 11.0 | 922 | 28.1 | 1.4 | 75 008 | 0.5 | 3 917 | 5.2 | 69 450 | 40.9 | 19.1 |
| Sherburne | 29 572 | 82.6 | 218 600 | 25.7 | 11.0 | 813 | 31.0 | 1.4 | 49 556 | 0.4 | 3 149 | 6.4 | 44 657 | 32.7 | 28.0 |
| Sibley | 6 103 | 80.7 | 148 100 | 24.8 | 13.3 | 593 | 25.7 | 2.2 | 10 270 | 2.9 | 498 | 4.8 | 7 902 | 29.9 | 35.0 |
| Stearns | 56 469 | 72.6 | 172 600 | 23.8 | 12.0 | 703 | 30.6 | 1.9 | 85 749 | 0.3 | 4 755 | 5.5 | 79 870 | 30.8 | 26.3 |
| Steele | 14 053 | 78.0 | 158 800 | 24.2 | 11.7 | 674 | 30.4 | 1.7 | 21 381 | 0.0 | 1 180 | 5.5 | 19 040 | 31.6 | 28.2 |
| Stevens | 3 739 | 70.1 | 119 100 | 19.5 | 10.9 | 551 | 29.0 | 1.1 | 6 547 | 3.8 | 241 | 3.7 | 4 907 | 37.8 | 25.1 |
| Swift | 4 192 | 73.4 | 94 600 | 21.1 | 10.3 | 464 | 25.4 | 0.9 | 5 281 | -5.4 | 310 | 5.9 | 4 702 | 31.4 | 26.8 |
| Todd | 9 994 | 82.6 | 135 400 | 26.1 | 13.2 | 589 | 29.0 | 3.6 | 12 656 | -3.0 | 762 | 6.0 | 11 764 | 24.8 | 39.1 |
| Traverse | 1 604 | 80.8 | 69 200 | 19.9 | 12.4 | 457 | 26.3 | 0.4 | 1 760 | -6.3 | 89 | 5.1 | 1 768 | 35.8 | 26.8 |
| Wabasha | 8 751 | 83.5 | 160 300 | 24.7 | 12.5 | 585 | 32.1 | 1.5 | 11 911 | 1.0 | 612 | 5.1 | 11 664 | 31.5 | 27.9 |
| Wadena | 5 968 | 75.2 | 117 600 | 27.1 | 13.3 | 529 | 34.9 | 1.6 | 6 376 | -1.1 | 494 | 7.7 | 5 993 | 29.2 | 30.8 |
| Waseca | 7 303 | 80.6 | 142 700 | 24.2 | 12.7 | 557 | 25.0 | 1.4 | 10 331 | -3.3 | 604 | 5.8 | 9 742 | 30.3 | 30.4 |
| Washington | 87 446 | 83.0 | 257 200 | 24.3 | 10.4 | 1 048 | 29.2 | 1.4 | 133 730 | 0.5 | 7 121 | 5.3 | 123 575 | 43.9 | 16.6 |
| Watonwan | 4 396 | 79.4 | 93 400 | 20.8 | 11.2 | 546 | 22.7 | 1.8 | 5 608 | -1.1 | 348 | 6.2 | 5 691 | 28.3 | 40.0 |
| Wilkin | 2 658 | 82.7 | 103 300 | 20.1 | 10.6 | 523 | 23.8 | 0.7 | 3 800 | -0.3 | 156 | 4.1 | 3 304 | 32.0 | 30.2 |
| Winona | 19 292 | 71.0 | 160 200 | 24.2 | 11.6 | 580 | 32.5 | 1.2 | 29 505 | 1.0 | 1 485 | 5.0 | 28 291 | 30.1 | 25.3 |
| Wright | 44 683 | 84.9 | 213 900 | 25.6 | 12.6 | 807 | 29.4 | 1.8 | 69 717 | 0.3 | 4 245 | 6.1 | 64 309 | 34.0 | 25.1 |
| Yellow Medicine | 4 157 | 79.0 | 98 500 | 19.9 | 9.9 | 540 | 28.2 | 1.8 | 5 694 | -0.6 | 286 | 5.0 | 5 256 | 32.9 | 30.0 |

1. Specified owner-occupied units, lacking complete plumbing facilities.   2. A value of 9.9 represents 9.9 percent or less.   3. Specified renter-occupied units. A value of 10.0 represents 10 percent or less.   4. Overcrowded or
5. Percent of civilian labor force.   6. Persons 16 years old and over.

# Table B. States and Counties — **Nonfarm Employment and Agriculture**

| STATE County | Private nonfarm establishments, employment and payroll, 2011 | | | | | | | | | Agriculture, 2007 | | | |
|---|---|---|---|---|---|---|---|---|---|---|---|---|---|
| | | Employment | | | | | | Annual payroll | | Farms | | | |
| | | | | | | | | | | | Percent with: | | |
| | Number of establishments | Total | Health care and social assistance | Manufacturing | Retail trade | Finance and insurance | Professional, scientific, and technical services | Total (mil dol) | Average per employee (dollars) | Number | Fewer than 50 acres | 500 acres or more | Farm operators whose principal occupation is farming (percent) |
| | 104 | 105 | 106 | 107 | 108 | 109 | 110 | 111 | 112 | 113 | 114 | 115 | 116 |
| **MINNESOTA—Cont'd** | | | | | | | | | | | | | |
| Fillmore | 624 | 4 680 | 1 011 | 831 | 712 | 238 | 174 | 132 | 28 145 | 1 667 | 25.1 | 15.1 | 50.0 |
| Freeborn | 812 | 11 148 | D | 2 518 | 1 763 | 469 | 247 | 357 | 31 998 | 1 257 | 35.3 | 21.4 | 53.1 |
| Goodhue | 1 312 | 19 227 | 3 417 | 4 314 | 2 559 | 480 | 410 | 700 | 36 430 | 1 644 | 31.9 | 11.6 | 48.2 |
| Grant | 203 | 1 427 | 541 | 84 | 191 | 90 | 43 | 49 | 34 446 | 675 | 22.5 | 24.7 | 48.3 |
| Hennepin | 38 620 | 797 765 | 126 191 | 69 452 | 72 133 | 76 683 | 76 096 | 46 468 | 58 248 | 582 | 57.0 | 5.5 | 46.7 |
| Houston | 437 | 4 028 | 1 062 | 374 | 631 | 127 | D | 101 | 25 159 | 1 041 | 17.8 | 10.3 | 44.7 |
| Hubbard | 564 | 4 319 | 850 | 887 | 948 | D | 80 | 128 | 29 602 | 468 | 15.4 | 10.9 | 36.1 |
| Isanti | 775 | 8 171 | 2 041 | 1 268 | 1 728 | 333 | 176 | 286 | 35 034 | 910 | 45.8 | 5.8 | 34.3 |
| Itasca | 1 170 | 13 124 | 3 282 | D | 2 428 | 384 | 555 | 451 | 34 393 | 419 | 23.6 | 7.9 | 39.9 |
| Jackson | 321 | 5 145 | 1 368 | D | 351 | 106 | 52 | 150 | 29 137 | 969 | 20.8 | 30.5 | 60.7 |
| Kanabec | 295 | 3 188 | 1 061 | 560 | 501 | 131 | 92 | 96 | 30 183 | 701 | 21.8 | 8.3 | 39.8 |
| Kandiyohi | 1 399 | 19 035 | 5 585 | 2 545 | 3 011 | 575 | 514 | 600 | 31 545 | 1 386 | 26.4 | 16.1 | 44.4 |
| Kittson | 147 | 1 018 | 334 | 90 | 180 | 61 | D | 30 | 29 301 | 677 | 6.8 | 40.5 | 45.6 |
| Koochiching | 413 | 4 330 | 734 | D | 736 | D | 77 | 143 | 33 108 | 214 | 14.0 | 15.0 | 36.0 |
| Lac qui Parle | 191 | 1 945 | D | 374 | 291 | D | 22 | 58 | 29 712 | 932 | 17.7 | 29.8 | 51.4 |
| Lake | 289 | 3 246 | D | D | 340 | 109 | 30 | 111 | 34 266 | 34 | 32.4 | 2.9 | 41.2 |
| Lake of the Woods | 155 | 1 357 | 305 | D | 206 | 29 | D | 32 | 23 779 | 225 | 8.9 | 20.0 | 32.9 |
| Le Sueur | 659 | 6 263 | 842 | 1 919 | 816 | 210 | 144 | 212 | 33 891 | 1 091 | 35.9 | 11.1 | 42.8 |
| Lincoln | 214 | 1 533 | 527 | 23 | 255 | 56 | 43 | 39 | 25 523 | 784 | 18.1 | 22.4 | 52.6 |
| Lyon | 820 | 13 061 | 2 167 | 1 904 | 2 092 | 1 090 | D | 449 | 34 415 | 1 011 | 22.7 | 32.1 | 62.0 |
| McLeod | 993 | 16 574 | 3 999 | 5 370 | 2 089 | 413 | 247 | 598 | 36 062 | 1 021 | 34.6 | 13.9 | 54.2 |
| Mahnomen | 97 | 1 597 | D | D | 128 | 60 | D | 43 | 26 805 | 374 | 9.6 | 28.3 | 48.1 |
| Marshall | 271 | 1 643 | 283 | 263 | 248 | 118 | D | 59 | 35 995 | 1 405 | 8.4 | 31.5 | 41.9 |
| Martin | 622 | 8 422 | D | 1 583 | 1 309 | 408 | 186 | 313 | 37 220 | 960 | 21.5 | 32.2 | 63.4 |
| Meeker | 578 | 6 095 | 1 134 | 1 736 | 808 | 171 | 147 | 187 | 30 666 | 1 146 | 33.9 | 14.4 | 44.2 |
| Mille Lacs | 647 | 7 602 | 1 858 | 827 | 986 | 209 | 88 | 207 | 27 241 | 762 | 30.4 | 6.7 | 42.9 |
| Morrison | 874 | 8 434 | 1 639 | 1 300 | 1 555 | 398 | 187 | 241 | 28 556 | 1 867 | 28.9 | 8.9 | 47.9 |
| Mower | 874 | 14 279 | 2 785 | 3 936 | 1 946 | 342 | 279 | 540 | 37 801 | 1 088 | 35.8 | 21.2 | 53.3 |
| Murray | 306 | 2 333 | 439 | D | 305 | 143 | D | 70 | 30 092 | 1 023 | 25.3 | 28.6 | 57.0 |
| Nicollet | 645 | 11 363 | D | 3 210 | 831 | 226 | 188 | 453 | 39 865 | 827 | 23.2 | 20.0 | 60.1 |
| Nobles | 611 | 9 327 | 1 437 | D | 1 625 | 295 | 298 | 294 | 31 542 | 1 094 | 22.4 | 25.0 | 59.2 |
| Norman | 196 | 1 341 | 388 | D | 259 | D | D | 43 | 31 934 | 692 | 14.6 | 38.3 | 50.0 |
| Olmsted | 3 386 | 76 509 | D | D | 10 288 | 1 763 | 2 462 | 3 288 | 42 978 | 1 384 | 37.3 | 10.0 | 45.5 |
| Otter Tail | 1 690 | 18 472 | 4 497 | 3 493 | 2 890 | 551 | 408 | 572 | 30 984 | 3 296 | 16.7 | 13.7 | 41.3 |
| Pennington | 387 | 7 996 | 1 180 | 610 | 1 031 | 152 | D | 288 | 36 071 | 630 | 12.1 | 27.0 | 40.6 |
| Pine | 575 | 6 730 | 1 167 | D | 1 119 | D | 92 | 164 | 24 419 | 945 | 20.1 | 9.3 | 45.0 |
| Pipestone | 336 | 3 673 | 710 | D | 496 | 101 | D | 97 | 26 374 | 676 | 23.4 | 22.9 | 59.3 |
| Polk | 768 | 9 781 | 2 402 | 1 724 | 1 328 | 259 | 228 | 300 | 30 667 | 1 609 | 13.5 | 34.0 | 47.9 |
| Pope | 375 | 3 477 | 661 | 663 | 306 | 125 | D | 121 | 34 872 | 1 055 | 20.3 | 17.2 | 41.6 |
| Ramsey | 13 132 | 287 971 | 56 050 | 23 074 | 26 420 | 18 682 | 13 483 | 14 486 | 50 302 | 30 | 90.0 | 0.0 | 80.0 |
| Red Lake | 105 | 664 | D | D | 133 | 49 | D | 20 | 30 446 | 382 | 9.7 | 31.7 | 45.8 |
| Redwood | 519 | 5 468 | 1 008 | 840 | 745 | 214 | 69 | 157 | 28 669 | 1 215 | 17.0 | 34.3 | 68.5 |
| Renville | 479 | 4 529 | 969 | 955 | 560 | 207 | 160 | 148 | 32 680 | 1 119 | 21.4 | 33.5 | 60.8 |
| Rice | 1 496 | 22 468 | 2 961 | 3 749 | 2 572 | 479 | 496 | 740 | 32 950 | 1 494 | 40.5 | 6.8 | 37.7 |
| Rock | 252 | 2 480 | 640 | 275 | 390 | 252 | 85 | 71 | 28 623 | 696 | 26.6 | 26.1 | 65.4 |
| Roseau | 405 | 7 099 | 818 | 3 957 | 862 | 186 | D | 221 | 31 129 | 1 182 | 10.5 | 25.8 | 40.0 |
| St. Louis | 5 367 | 82 204 | 23 615 | 4 199 | 12 427 | 3 481 | 3 071 | 2 985 | 36 318 | 761 | 24.7 | 7.4 | 45.3 |
| Scott | 3 111 | 37 992 | 4 327 | 5 463 | 4 823 | 716 | D | 1 618 | 42 596 | 795 | 48.7 | 5.0 | 42.6 |
| Sherburne | 1 895 | 19 383 | 4 628 | 3 155 | 2 703 | 439 | 538 | 674 | 34 766 | 549 | 45.7 | 9.1 | 44.3 |
| Sibley | 358 | 3 131 | 585 | D | 394 | 136 | 56 | 97 | 31 092 | 1 029 | 25.6 | 18.4 | 57.4 |
| Stearns | 4 267 | 75 490 | 14 517 | 10 975 | 10 731 | 3 618 | 3 627 | 2 804 | 37 143 | 3 368 | 25.4 | 8.0 | 56.5 |
| Steele | 996 | 18 568 | 2 434 | 4 983 | 2 787 | D | 265 | 766 | 41 241 | 934 | 37.0 | 13.6 | 43.8 |
| Stevens | 336 | 4 019 | 1 294 | D | 502 | D | 112 | 128 | 31 769 | 639 | 24.6 | 34.3 | 59.0 |
| Swift | 300 | 3 128 | 618 | D | 383 | 114 | 129 | 102 | 32 705 | 888 | 22.1 | 27.0 | 51.8 |
| Todd | 541 | 4 801 | D | 1 741 | 718 | 189 | 104 | 135 | 28 130 | 1 910 | 18.1 | 6.3 | 44.9 |
| Traverse | 128 | 844 | 247 | 50 | 250 | 47 | 9 | 22 | 25 803 | 479 | 23.0 | 36.3 | 55.5 |
| Wabasha | 572 | 5 705 | 855 | D | 801 | 177 | 101 | 180 | 31 594 | 976 | 22.6 | 14.1 | 57.6 |
| Wadena | 407 | 5 202 | 2 350 | 367 | 787 | 147 | 62 | 153 | 29 319 | 657 | 16.6 | 8.5 | 39.6 |
| Waseca | 494 | 6 267 | 1 104 | D | 696 | 174 | 166 | 212 | 33 834 | 848 | 30.8 | 19.1 | 53.4 |
| Washington | 5 313 | 67 716 | 9 428 | 7 218 | 12 320 | 5 350 | 3 431 | 2 619 | 38 671 | 729 | 59.8 | 4.7 | 44.0 |
| Watonwan | 304 | 3 356 | D | 1 195 | 345 | 158 | D | 95 | 28 384 | 604 | 24.2 | 27.3 | 58.3 |
| Wilkin | 173 | 2 032 | D | D | 155 | 44 | D | 60 | 29 567 | 428 | 18.0 | 48.8 | 65.7 |
| Winona | 1 182 | 21 396 | 3 237 | 4 714 | 2 824 | D | 426 | 713 | 33 325 | 1 203 | 21.7 | 12.0 | 53.8 |
| Wright | 3 009 | 31 821 | 5 073 | 4 601 | 6 743 | 735 | 915 | 1 131 | 35 550 | 1 531 | 39.8 | 7.4 | 42.0 |
| Yellow Medicine | 320 | 4 189 | 1 114 | D | 423 | 119 | 48 | 176 | 41 965 | 986 | 21.4 | 30.6 | 55.0 |

# Table B. States and Counties — **Agriculture**

| | Agriculture, 2007 (cont.) | | | | | | | | | | | | | | |
|---|---|---|---|---|---|---|---|---|---|---|---|---|---|---|---|
| | Land in farms | | | | Value of land and buildings (dollars) | | | Value of products sold | | | | Percent of farms with sales of: | | Government payments | |
| | | Acres | | | | | | | | Percent from: | | | | | |
| STATE County | Acreage (1,000) | Percent change, 2002–2007 | Average size of farm | Total irrigated (1,000) | Total cropland (1,000) | Average per farm | Average per acre | Value of machinery and equipment, average per farm (dollars) | Total (mil dol) | Average per farm (dollars) | Crops | Live-stock and poultry products | $10,000 or more | $100,000 or more | Total ($1,000) | Percent of farms |
| | 117 | 118 | 119 | 120 | 121 | 122 | 123 | 124 | 125 | 126 | 127 | 128 | 129 | 130 | 131 | 132 |
| MINNESOTA—Cont'd | | | | | | | | | | | | | | | |
| Fillmore | 446 | 1.1 | 268 | 0.0 | 330.4 | 771 600 | 2 882 | 120 697 | 223.1 | 133 838 | 47.7 | 52.3 | 55.8 | 27.5 | 9 213 | 72.2 |
| Freeborn | 388 | -1.5 | 309 | 1.4 | 359.6 | 960 388 | 3 107 | 163 464 | 256.1 | 203 773 | 62.8 | 37.2 | 61.7 | 37.5 | 8 345 | 78.3 |
| Goodhue | 397 | 3.4 | 241 | 2.8 | 322.8 | 861 849 | 3 571 | 135 327 | 264.0 | 160 566 | 47.1 | 52.9 | 60.3 | 29.3 | 7 038 | 68.2 |
| Grant | 322 | 1.6 | 476 | 4.0 | 292.1 | 1 064 207 | 2 234 | 151 436 | 103.3 | 153 057 | 86.7 | 13.3 | 43.4 | 28.6 | 6 105 | 93.3 |
| Hennepin | 67 | 3.1 | 114 | 0.6 | 49.1 | 627 606 | 5 488 | 91 035 | 51.4 | 88 364 | 83.4 | 16.6 | 39.5 | 12.9 | 940 | 36.1 |
| Houston | 244 | -3.9 | 235 | 0.2 | 127.6 | 628 865 | 2 679 | 92 548 | 91.0 | 87 415 | 30.5 | 69.5 | 47.6 | 19.4 | 4 096 | 79.9 |
| Hubbard | 126 | -10.0 | 270 | 22.2 | 70.8 | 624 765 | 2 317 | 73 567 | 32.6 | 69 702 | 84.6 | 15.4 | 30.6 | 7.3 | 525 | 28.2 |
| Isanti | 126 | -9.4 | 139 | 1.3 | 87.7 | 554 566 | 3 999 | 60 956 | 27.1 | 29 795 | 59.8 | 40.2 | 24.3 | 5.7 | 1 398 | 43.3 |
| Itasca | 93 | -22.5 | 223 | D | 43.9 | 442 079 | 1 986 | 56 386 | 7.4 | 17 706 | 49.6 | 50.4 | 28.6 | 3.3 | 70 | 14.1 |
| Jackson | 401 | 0.8 | 413 | 0.6 | 371.2 | 1 258 129 | 3 044 | 173 834 | 267.3 | 275 827 | 57.2 | 42.8 | 74.9 | 48.4 | 7 720 | 83.4 |
| Kanabec | 142 | -10.7 | 202 | 0.4 | 70.8 | 496 715 | 2 454 | 62 147 | 19.7 | 28 086 | 37.3 | 62.7 | 31.5 | 6.8 | 680 | 30.7 |
| Kandiyohi | 417 | 2.2 | 301 | 17.5 | 349.0 | 855 562 | 2 843 | 133 113 | 309.1 | 222 992 | 37.1 | 62.9 | 42.7 | 25.5 | 8 249 | 81.5 |
| Kittson | 542 | -2.5 | 801 | 1.4 | 439.6 | 948 150 | 1 184 | 165 001 | 105.4 | 155 619 | 95.8 | 4.2 | 39.7 | 27.3 | 9 536 | 88.3 |
| Koochiching | 55 | -25.7 | 258 | 0.0 | 26.0 | 348 110 | 1 352 | 60 052 | 4.6 | 21 331 | 29.0 | 71.0 | 27.6 | 4.7 | 126 | 19.2 |
| Lac qui Parle | 412 | -5.3 | 442 | 5.0 | 362.1 | 1 014 997 | 2 296 | 151 422 | 157.6 | 169 089 | 72.7 | 27.3 | 59.5 | 35.2 | 8 032 | 90.6 |
| Lake | 3 | -40.0 | 101 | D | 1.2 | 335 244 | 3 324 | 31 748 | 0.3 | 7 546 | D | D | 11.8 | 2.9 | 0 | 0.0 |
| Lake of the Woods | 97 | -36.2 | 431 | D | 58.3 | 515 267 | 1 196 | 71 663 | 7.4 | 32 951 | 86.1 | 13.9 | 28.4 | 7.1 | 512 | 55.1 |
| Le Sueur | 251 | 5.5 | 230 | 1.3 | 211.0 | 805 168 | 3 504 | 112 952 | 139.6 | 127 993 | 52.0 | 48.0 | 48.6 | 26.1 | 5 605 | 81.5 |
| Lincoln | 286 | 5.5 | 365 | 0.7 | 246.3 | 824 131 | 2 257 | 121 826 | 135.1 | 172 323 | 53.2 | 46.8 | 54.2 | 30.4 | 5 794 | 88.0 |
| Lyon | 429 | 6.2 | 424 | 0.0 | 389.5 | 1 164 716 | 2 747 | 167 766 | 305.7 | 302 397 | 45.7 | 54.3 | 64.2 | 48.3 | 7 804 | 84.3 |
| McLeod | 244 | -7.2 | 239 | 0.0 | 218.7 | 812 093 | 3 399 | 154 659 | 125.4 | 122 859 | 62.7 | 37.3 | 60.6 | 26.4 | 4 385 | 74.2 |
| Mahnomen | 191 | -2.1 | 510 | D | 144.7 | 710 387 | 1 392 | 107 799 | 43.9 | 117 432 | 83.1 | 16.9 | 45.2 | 25.1 | 2 883 | 79.9 |
| Marshall | 911 | -2.6 | 648 | 0.4 | 786.3 | 837 318 | 1 292 | 152 148 | 189.8 | 135 124 | 94.8 | 5.2 | 38.9 | 24.4 | 17 581 | 87.3 |
| Martin | 450 | 6.4 | 468 | 1.0 | 426.7 | 1 442 048 | 3 079 | 206 965 | 403.0 | 419 783 | 45.8 | 54.2 | 77.9 | 55.1 | 9 969 | 81.3 |
| Meeker | 322 | -5.6 | 281 | 9.1 | 273.9 | 844 406 | 3 007 | 129 037 | 204.0 | 178 043 | 40.4 | 59.6 | 47.1 | 23.5 | 5 707 | 77.9 |
| Mille Lacs | 125 | -5.3 | 164 | 0.4 | 76.5 | 456 157 | 2 782 | 71 842 | 27.3 | 35 807 | 30.7 | 69.3 | 34.1 | 9.4 | 954 | 45.1 |
| Morrison | 431 | -4.6 | 231 | 18.5 | 250.7 | 536 832 | 2 324 | 109 015 | 261.0 | 139 810 | 10.6 | 89.4 | 46.8 | 20.2 | 4 598 | 61.8 |
| Mower | 420 | 1.9 | 386 | 1.1 | 391.6 | 1 227 730 | 3 181 | 172 683 | 287.6 | 264 341 | 57.9 | 42.1 | 65.3 | 42.6 | 7 847 | 73.7 |
| Murray | 429 | 5.4 | 419 | D | 390.7 | 1 112 129 | 2 653 | 162 878 | 237.1 | 231 812 | 56.6 | 43.4 | 64.4 | 43.5 | 8 860 | 86.5 |
| Nicollet | 274 | 6.6 | 331 | D | 250.0 | 1 116 870 | 3 371 | 173 257 | 236.8 | 286 292 | 40.5 | 59.5 | 72.7 | 47.0 | 5 489 | 81.5 |
| Nobles | 422 | 4.5 | 386 | D | 389.6 | 1 212 829 | 3 142 | 177 674 | 343.8 | 314 272 | 43.5 | 56.5 | 75.2 | 44.1 | 7 727 | 85.6 |
| Norman | 513 | -2.7 | 741 | 0.6 | 465.2 | 1 161 374 | 1 567 | 176 120 | 168.3 | 243 178 | 89.8 | 10.2 | 50.6 | 35.8 | 8 071 | 85.0 |
| Olmsted | 296 | -5.4 | 214 | 0.1 | 227.6 | 768 778 | 3 594 | 107 327 | 154.9 | 111 939 | 53.6 | 46.4 | 48.4 | 22.1 | 5 508 | 70.5 |
| Otter Tail | 899 | 2.0 | 273 | 56.0 | 597.8 | 548 339 | 2 011 | 87 495 | 300.1 | 91 041 | 44.5 | 55.5 | 36.1 | 16.0 | 11 652 | 75.2 |
| Pennington | 325 | -2.1 | 516 | 0.1 | 265.3 | 709 612 | 1 374 | 87 299 | 41.8 | 66 388 | 88.2 | 11.8 | 36.7 | 15.6 | 6 477 | 85.2 |
| Pine | 208 | -18.4 | 220 | 0.8 | 103.0 | 474 096 | 2 158 | 69 700 | 49.7 | 52 585 | 23.0 | 77.0 | 36.5 | 8.0 | 1 389 | 36.4 |
| Pipestone | 245 | -1.6 | 362 | 2.5 | 211.6 | 982 841 | 2 715 | 150 618 | 176.5 | 261 049 | 36.0 | 64.0 | 67.9 | 39.6 | 3 804 | 79.0 |
| Polk | 1 100 | -1.0 | 684 | 10.4 | 976.4 | 1 026 875 | 1 502 | 193 256 | 341.4 | 212 193 | 93.1 | 6.9 | 45.1 | 28.9 | 20 228 | 84.5 |
| Pope | 360 | 2.9 | 341 | 38.1 | 285.2 | 748 080 | 2 192 | 119 598 | 116.9 | 110 774 | 62.6 | 37.4 | 42.1 | 21.6 | 6 256 | 83.3 |
| Ramsey | 1 | NA | 31 | 0.1 | 0.3 | 262 658 | 8 374 | 56 302 | D | D | D | D | 80.0 | 26.7 | D | 3.3 |
| Red Lake | 223 | -1.8 | 585 | 0.2 | 186.1 | 789 273 | 1 349 | 119 195 | 42.7 | 111 670 | 82.1 | 17.9 | 45.3 | 23.0 | 4 165 | 87.7 |
| Redwood | 554 | 1.7 | 456 | 0.0 | 508.7 | 1 379 768 | 3 027 | 194 731 | 364.1 | 299 637 | 55.7 | 44.3 | 75.9 | 55.6 | 10 378 | 86.7 |
| Renville | 620 | -6.6 | 554 | D | 587.5 | 1 613 409 | 2 913 | 223 829 | 420.5 | 375 784 | 63.3 | 36.7 | 72.8 | 52.5 | 9 440 | 85.3 |
| Rice | 253 | 1.6 | 169 | 0.5 | 205.6 | 714 669 | 4 219 | 100 601 | 137.2 | 91 832 | 48.4 | 51.6 | 41.4 | 15.9 | 5 490 | 71.2 |
| Rock | 279 | -6.7 | 401 | 1.2 | 251.3 | 1 303 843 | 3 252 | 173 081 | 282.9 | 406 468 | 34.8 | 65.2 | 78.6 | 55.0 | 4 533 | 76.6 |
| Roseau | 591 | -15.9 | 500 | 0.0 | 462.2 | 552 170 | 1 104 | 91 271 | 84.8 | 71 736 | 75.4 | 24.6 | 32.8 | 14.0 | 9 852 | 80.2 |
| St. Louis | 149 | -14.9 | 195 | 0.2 | 70.7 | 383 167 | 1 961 | 47 155 | 13.6 | 17 813 | 46.5 | 53.5 | 23.7 | 4.3 | 120 | 5.4 |
| Scott | 118 | -9.9 | 148 | 0.4 | 94.8 | 741 776 | 5 017 | 101 196 | 63.3 | 79 663 | 45.0 | 55.0 | 44.9 | 16.0 | 2 293 | 54.2 |
| Sherburne | 106 | -15.9 | 193 | 30.7 | 78.5 | 743 910 | 3 848 | 106 346 | 63.9 | 116 465 | 78.4 | 21.6 | 31.7 | 11.4 | 1 294 | 41.3 |
| Sibley | 346 | 2.1 | 336 | 0.3 | 313.7 | 1 115 472 | 3 320 | 178 970 | 244.0 | 237 103 | 50.9 | 49.1 | 69.5 | 40.5 | 5 784 | 77.6 |
| Stearns | 708 | 4.0 | 210 | 41.5 | 527.6 | 595 214 | 2 830 | 130 988 | 519.4 | 154 226 | 14.2 | 85.8 | 57.7 | 32.0 | 12 639 | 70.7 |
| Steele | 266 | -5.7 | 285 | 0.5 | 242.1 | 960 446 | 3 370 | 133 080 | 184.8 | 197 809 | 60.2 | 39.8 | 52.0 | 30.2 | 5 635 | 78.7 |
| Stevens | 340 | 8.6 | 533 | 16.5 | 319.0 | 1 325 623 | 2 489 | 275 467 | 244.0 | 381 846 | 44.2 | 55.8 | 61.0 | 43.0 | 5 623 | 85.3 |
| Swift | 388 | -6.7 | 437 | 31.4 | 348.2 | 1 091 685 | 2 496 | 173 531 | 206.1 | 232 081 | 55.2 | 44.8 | 54.6 | 33.8 | 7 878 | 87.3 |
| Todd | 379 | 2.4 | 198 | 15.6 | 228.7 | 433 841 | 2 188 | 85 346 | 148.6 | 77 805 | 20.9 | 79.1 | 40.9 | 13.9 | 4 042 | 63.3 |
| Traverse | 328 | -4.7 | 684 | D | 311.7 | 1 493 667 | 2 184 | 245 120 | 111.3 | 232 276 | 89.3 | 10.7 | 57.0 | 43.4 | 5 492 | 93.3 |
| Wabasha | 262 | -1.9 | 269 | 0.2 | 181.7 | 786 131 | 2 926 | 143 312 | 144.2 | 147 758 | 36.2 | 63.8 | 61.8 | 32.7 | 4 647 | 76.8 |
| Wadena | 151 | -9.0 | 230 | 18.4 | 81.3 | 441 947 | 1 920 | 83 045 | 39.9 | 60 798 | 35.7 | 64.3 | 31.4 | 10.5 | 1 420 | 59.8 |
| Waseca | 255 | 10.4 | 300 | 0.1 | 229.6 | 1 042 991 | 3 475 | 156 845 | 201.8 | 237 983 | 49.6 | 50.4 | 62.4 | 39.5 | 5 602 | 82.5 |
| Washington | 81 | -15.6 | 111 | 3.4 | 57.5 | 638 102 | 5 726 | 79 429 | 69.9 | 95 857 | 88.7 | 11.3 | 38.8 | 12.5 | 856 | 25.7 |
| Watonwan | 269 | -1.1 | 446 | 1.6 | 252.9 | 1 332 434 | 2 991 | 184 735 | 184.7 | 305 812 | 57.6 | 42.4 | 68.0 | 47.0 | 5 534 | 86.9 |
| Wilkin | 425 | 0.0 | 993 | 1.6 | 407.6 | 1 945 976 | 1 960 | 278 651 | 130.5 | 304 910 | 98.3 | 1.7 | 66.6 | 44.0 | 5 541 | 88.3 |
| Winona | 306 | -1.6 | 254 | 0.0 | 191.3 | 757 355 | 2 982 | 123 159 | 187.2 | 155 608 | 25.2 | 74.8 | 56.5 | 27.1 | 5 219 | 68.5 |
| Wright | 265 | -0.4 | 173 | 2.7 | 207.3 | 696 111 | 4 016 | 95 428 | 140.1 | 91 481 | 44.7 | 55.3 | 44.1 | 15.8 | 3 714 | 56.4 |
| Yellow Medicine | 409 | -8.7 | 415 | 0.6 | 371.3 | 1 050 878 | 2 532 | 178 186 | 209.0 | 212 014 | 63.6 | 36.4 | 62.3 | 43.4 | 7 587 | 87.4 |

| STATE County | Water use, 2005 | | Wholesale trade,[1] 2007 | | | | Retail trade,[2] 2007 | | | | Real estate and rental and leasing,[2] 2007 | | | |
|---|---|---|---|---|---|---|---|---|---|---|---|---|---|---|
| | Total water withdrawn (mil gal/day) | Gallons withdrawn per person | Number of establishments | Number of employees | Sales (mil dol) | Annual payroll (mil dol) | Number of establishments | Number of employees | Sales (mil dol) | Annual payroll (mil dol) | Number of establishments | Number of employees | Receipts (mil dol) | Annual payroll (mil dol) |
| | 133 | 134 | 135 | 136 | 137 | 138 | 139 | 140 | 141 | 142 | 143 | 144 | 145 | 146 |
| MINNESOTA—Cont'd | | | | | | | | | | | | | | |
| Fillmore | 5.3 | 246 | 26 | 197 | 116.1 | 8.4 | 107 | 728 | 176.8 | 13.8 | 12 | 23 | 1.9 | 0.4 |
| Freeborn | 5.5 | 171 | 47 | 541 | 412.1 | 21.3 | 154 | 2 137 | 492.1 | 41.9 | 23 | 49 | 4.2 | 0.8 |
| Goodhue | 619.3 | 13 586 | 42 | 603 | 313.9 | 24.3 | 241 | 2 664 | 595.8 | 53.4 | 46 | D | D | D |
| Grant | 1.7 | 276 | 11 | 177 | 293.8 | 7.7 | 37 | 259 | 56.4 | 4.5 | 5 | 3 | 0.4 | 0.0 |
| Hennepin | 320.8 | 287 | 2 280 | 39 155 | 34 472.5 | 2 340.5 | 4 405 | 80 179 | 22 278.8 | 2 080.8 | 2 318 | 18 498 | 6 322.6 | 746.8 |
| Houston | 2.9 | 146 | 20 | D | D | D | 77 | 597 | 152.5 | 11.5 | 6 | 10 | 1.5 | 0.2 |
| Hubbard | 13.9 | 738 | 7 | 29 | 35.3 | 0.9 | 120 | 1 071 | 200.9 | 18.1 | 15 | 61 | 3.7 | 0.7 |
| Isanti | 4.6 | 122 | 18 | D | D | D | 108 | 1 560 | 405.2 | 34.2 | 27 | D | D | D |
| Itasca | 185.0 | 4 168 | 31 | 274 | 160.6 | 13.8 | 227 | 2 414 | 521.6 | 47.2 | 36 | 100 | 13.6 | 2.1 |
| Jackson | 2.2 | 194 | 13 | 182 | 151.7 | 6.6 | 51 | 399 | 80.3 | 6.0 | 3 | 13 | 0.7 | 0.1 |
| Kanabec | 1.9 | 115 | 4 | 15 | 4.9 | 0.4 | 54 | 582 | 150.5 | 10.4 | 6 | 59 | 2.5 | 0.9 |
| Kandiyohi | 22.0 | 533 | 77 | D | D | D | 231 | 2 921 | 597.6 | 56.7 | 51 | 198 | 27.2 | 5.8 |
| Kittson | 1.4 | 292 | 19 | 131 | 217.5 | 3.9 | 31 | 206 | 41.3 | 3.0 | 4 | 7 | 0.3 | 0.0 |
| Koochiching | 47.5 | 3 418 | 10 | 55 | 16.8 | 1.6 | 83 | 698 | 165.0 | 14.6 | 15 | 47 | 5.5 | 1.2 |
| Lac qui Parle | 4.5 | 589 | 12 | 121 | 96.2 | 4.4 | 47 | 302 | 61.6 | 4.8 | 7 | 30 | 2.3 | 0.7 |
| Lake | 130.9 | 11 733 | 4 | D | D | D | 46 | 384 | 119.8 | 8.9 | 10 | 67 | 3.1 | 1.3 |
| Lake of the Woods | 1.4 | 310 | 5 | 24 | 11.6 | 0.6 | 29 | 229 | 39.9 | 3.3 | 3 | 7 | 0.5 | 0.1 |
| Le Sueur | 19.7 | 716 | 23 | 299 | 132.0 | 11.4 | 108 | 884 | 206.2 | 16.5 | 24 | 91 | 3.8 | 3.0 |
| Lincoln | 1.8 | 302 | 9 | 64 | 77.6 | 2.3 | 40 | 274 | 53.1 | 3.9 | 7 | 11 | 0.8 | 0.1 |
| Lyon | 6.5 | 266 | 46 | D | D | D | 142 | 1 907 | 378.9 | 36.1 | 35 | 120 | 8.6 | 2.6 |
| McLeod | 6.7 | 183 | 31 | D | D | D | 170 | 2 263 | 477.1 | 43.1 | 38 | D | D | D |
| Mahnomen | 3.3 | 653 | 4 | 23 | 9.9 | 1.2 | 20 | 187 | 20.2 | 2.5 | 3 | 8 | 0.6 | 0.1 |
| Marshall | 1.3 | 127 | 24 | 214 | 246.7 | 8.4 | 43 | 271 | 118.6 | 5.8 | 2 | D | D | D |
| Martin | 17.8 | 846 | 46 | D | D | D | 109 | 1 343 | 268.2 | 22.9 | 16 | 42 | 4.4 | 0.9 |
| Meeker | 7.8 | 335 | 19 | 197 | 98.6 | 7.5 | 90 | 737 | 174.1 | 14.3 | 14 | 39 | 2.2 | 0.6 |
| Mille Lacs | 3.1 | 122 | 20 | 207 | 160.1 | 5.2 | 115 | 1 229 | 251.8 | 21.5 | 18 | 46 | 3.8 | 0.9 |
| Morrison | 17.9 | 547 | 26 | 280 | 249.7 | 11.0 | 130 | 1 501 | 361.2 | 31.2 | 13 | 34 | 4.5 | 0.5 |
| Mower | 9.2 | 238 | 28 | 198 | 229.8 | 9.7 | 171 | 1 946 | 347.7 | 33.9 | 25 | 138 | 8.3 | 1.9 |
| Murray | 2.0 | 227 | 15 | 149 | 283.2 | 5.3 | 44 | 321 | 46.6 | 4.3 | 9 | 49 | 1.7 | 0.7 |
| Nicollet | 6.5 | 212 | 31 | 349 | 194.3 | 14.0 | 86 | 790 | 164.9 | 15.5 | 25 | 132 | 10.1 | 2.7 |
| Nobles | 5.1 | 248 | 38 | 680 | 478.2 | 25.6 | 122 | 1 495 | 303.6 | 27.7 | 15 | 49 | 3.9 | 0.6 |
| Norman | 0.8 | 110 | 17 | 95 | 58.4 | 3.6 | 33 | 260 | 44.4 | 3.4 | 4 | 7 | 0.5 | 0.1 |
| Olmsted | 48.0 | 355 | 111 | 1 141 | 777.9 | 51.6 | 605 | 10 543 | 2 182.1 | 227.4 | 160 | 821 | 114.7 | 21.5 |
| Otter Tail | 150.6 | 2 612 | 67 | 432 | 322.5 | 13.2 | 287 | 3 177 | 704.5 | 61.9 | 67 | 137 | 22.2 | 2.9 |
| Pennington | 2.7 | 196 | 23 | D | D | D | 89 | 1 076 | 209.5 | 21.5 | 11 | 26 | 4.1 | 0.6 |
| Pine | 3.6 | 126 | 13 | 24 | 6.8 | 0.7 | 108 | 1 180 | 243.5 | 21.4 | 26 | 40 | 4.9 | 0.7 |
| Pipestone | 5.0 | 533 | 21 | 400 | 158.3 | 10.9 | 54 | 460 | 110.9 | 8.2 | 2 | D | D | D |
| Polk | 24.7 | 792 | 47 | 459 | 336.9 | 16.0 | 122 | 1 418 | 297.8 | 27.0 | 17 | 89 | 3.9 | 1.4 |
| Pope | 22.3 | 1 985 | 51 | 553 | 305.5 | 22.4 | 55 | 359 | 103.5 | 7.5 | 5 | 11 | 0.7 | 0.1 |
| Ramsey | 198.5 | 401 | 647 | 14 603 | 9 278.4 | 835.5 | 1 719 | 29 640 | 6 156.5 | 636.5 | 762 | 5 417 | 832.0 | 194.8 |
| Red Lake | 1.7 | 387 | 5 | D | D | D | 23 | 193 | 41.1 | 3.3 | 1 | D | D | D |
| Redwood | 3.0 | 188 | 29 | 371 | 210.7 | 17.7 | 93 | 774 | 156.8 | 14.8 | 16 | 37 | 2.8 | 0.6 |
| Renville | 4.0 | 238 | 29 | 236 | 277.7 | 9.1 | 82 | 582 | 117.0 | 8.4 | 6 | 9 | 0.6 | 0.1 |
| Rice | 9.8 | 161 | 59 | D | D | D | 219 | 2 596 | 599.2 | 55.9 | 51 | 168 | 51.4 | 3.7 |
| Rock | 3.1 | 325 | 15 | 161 | 88.5 | 6.6 | 47 | 416 | 109.1 | 7.9 | 9 | 32 | 1.9 | 0.4 |
| Roseau | 1.9 | 114 | 11 | D | D | D | 89 | 837 | 179.9 | 15.1 | 12 | 32 | 2.0 | 0.4 |
| St. Louis | 287.7 | 1 459 | 200 | 2 095 | 1 128.2 | 89.2 | 1 020 | 13 128 | 2 760.5 | 264.9 | 217 | 974 | 160.2 | 22.7 |
| Scott | 17.8 | 149 | 135 | 1 671 | 1 300.8 | 93.9 | 361 | 4 709 | 1 169.7 | 103.5 | 166 | 428 | 58.0 | 10.4 |
| Sherburne | 92.9 | 1 136 | 66 | 471 | 231.7 | 20.6 | 218 | 3 484 | 844.3 | 73.9 | 80 | D | D | D |
| Sibley | 3.3 | 215 | 14 | 99 | 69.3 | 4.5 | 61 | 426 | 75.5 | 6.4 | 9 | 17 | 1.5 | 0.3 |
| Stearns | 49.5 | 347 | 182 | 4 375 | 1 813.6 | 187.0 | 724 | 11 566 | 2 423.6 | 225.5 | 169 | 856 | 105.0 | 19.8 |
| Steele | 7.8 | 217 | 35 | 474 | 323.5 | 23.6 | 206 | 3 004 | 543.9 | 54.6 | 32 | 264 | 16.6 | 4.7 |
| Stevens | 6.5 | 659 | 19 | 90 | 130.8 | 3.4 | 52 | 594 | 170.1 | 12.1 | 11 | 43 | 2.5 | 0.6 |
| Swift | 12.5 | 1 106 | 18 | 282 | 665.6 | 12.1 | 50 | 376 | 80.6 | 6.8 | 6 | 82 | 2.4 | 1.3 |
| Todd | 12.7 | 515 | 12 | 89 | 18.0 | 2.8 | 100 | 758 | 160.0 | 13.4 | 20 | 31 | 2.0 | 0.4 |
| Traverse | 0.4 | 110 | 10 | 71 | 82.6 | 3.0 | 29 | 233 | 45.5 | 3.6 | 3 | 5 | 0.4 | 0.1 |
| Wabasha | 4.9 | 223 | 20 | 223 | 92.2 | 7.7 | 106 | 899 | 210.8 | 19.0 | 7 | 20 | 1.1 | 0.2 |
| Wadena | 13.0 | 952 | 16 | 487 | 243.4 | 22.4 | 98 | 892 | 177.7 | 17.3 | 7 | 25 | 0.7 | 0.3 |
| Waseca | 3.1 | 158 | 27 | 220 | 105.2 | 7.2 | 68 | 839 | 163.6 | 15.4 | 15 | 35 | 2.1 | 0.4 |
| Washington | 359.9 | 1 633 | 191 | 1 432 | 1 743.6 | 65.7 | 729 | 12 945 | 2 690.7 | 262.1 | 338 | 1 292 | 174.6 | 33.4 |
| Watonwan | 3.7 | 332 | 15 | 99 | 145.9 | 3.6 | 49 | 408 | 70.4 | 6.1 | 4 | 18 | 0.5 | 0.3 |
| Wilkin | 0.9 | 129 | 12 | D | D | D | 25 | 210 | 56.3 | 5.6 | 6 | 6 | 1.8 | 0.2 |
| Winona | 9.0 | 183 | 61 | D | D | D | 198 | 3 157 | 666.1 | 62.9 | 50 | 156 | 19.7 | 3.0 |
| Wright | 334.0 | 3 016 | 96 | 985 | 440.7 | 50.6 | 470 | 6 766 | 1 458.8 | 131.5 | 124 | 342 | 51.3 | 8.3 |
| Yellow Medicine | 3.2 | 307 | 17 | 205 | 302.3 | 8.1 | 50 | 449 | 112.9 | 7.7 | 4 | 10 | 0.9 | 0.2 |

1. Merchant wholesalers, except manufacturers' sales branches and offices.    2. Employer establishments.

# Professional Services, Manufacturing, and Accommodation and Food Services

| STATE County | Professional, scientific, and technical services,[1] 2007 | | | | Manufacturing, 2007 | | | | Accommodation and food services, 2007 | | | |
|---|---|---|---|---|---|---|---|---|---|---|---|---|
| | Number of establishments | Number of employees | Receipts (mil dol) | Annual payroll (mil dol) | Number of establishments | Number of employees | Receipts (mil dol) | Annual payroll (mil dol) | Number of establishments | Number of employees | Sales (mil dol) | Annual payroll (mil dol) |
| | 147 | 148 | 149 | 150 | 151 | 152 | 153 | 154 | 155 | 156 | 157 | 158 |
| MINNESOTA—Cont'd | | | | | | | | | | | | |
| Fillmore | 35 | 145 | 11.1 | 3.5 | 48 | 880 | 377.4 | 32.0 | 62 | 487 | 14.5 | 3.4 |
| Freeborn | 39 | D | D | D | 59 | 2 746 | 767.0 | 100.5 | 82 | 1 076 | 33.8 | 9.8 |
| Goodhue | 87 | 358 | 39.5 | 14.4 | 86 | 4 204 | 1 332.3 | 167.6 | 125 | 3 132 | 254.6 | 62.1 |
| Grant | 12 | 51 | 4.0 | 1.4 | NA | NA | NA | NA | 11 | D | D | D |
| Hennepin | 6 938 | 84 413 | 13 992.3 | 5 782.2 | 1 883 | 82 304 | 20 957.7 | 4 397.5 | 2 640 | 62 847 | 3 279.1 | 1 017.7 |
| Houston | 28 | D | D | D | 23 | 647 | D | 19.3 | 42 | 208 | 8.0 | 1.8 |
| Hubbard | 35 | 102 | 6.7 | 2.3 | 36 | 1 284 | 328.6 | 43.2 | 68 | 468 | 20.6 | 5.3 |
| Isanti | 59 | D | D | D | 70 | 1 515 | 317.7 | 62.1 | 68 | 936 | 30.4 | 9.2 |
| Itasca | 70 | D | D | D | 48 | 1 367 | 627.2 | 63.0 | 116 | 1 298 | 51.0 | 15.4 |
| Jackson | 13 | 50 | 3.8 | 1.1 | 11 | 1 025 | 409.6 | 36.2 | 22 | 454 | 7.8 | 2.1 |
| Kanabec | 17 | 83 | 5.4 | 1.6 | 19 | 647 | 114.5 | 22.3 | 28 | 315 | 10.0 | 2.5 |
| Kandiyohi | 89 | D | D | D | 71 | 2 957 | 818.7 | 104.6 | 96 | 1 481 | 52.0 | 14.7 |
| Kittson | 6 | 30 | 2.4 | 1.0 | NA | NA | NA | NA | 11 | D | D | D |
| Koochiching | 24 | 81 | 5.5 | 2.1 | 22 | 1 053 | D | D | 43 | 463 | 21.3 | 6.0 |
| Lac qui Parle | 13 | 37 | 1.7 | 0.5 | NA | NA | NA | NA | 15 | D | D | D |
| Lake | 15 | 74 | 3.3 | 1.2 | 17 | 612 | 156.8 | 24.6 | 55 | 661 | 33.9 | 8.9 |
| Lake of the Woods | 5 | 8 | 0.4 | 0.2 | NA | NA | NA | NA | 38 | 444 | 20.4 | 5.1 |
| Le Sueur | 46 | 174 | 15.4 | 6.4 | 53 | 2 356 | 623.9 | 91.2 | 47 | 531 | 17.0 | 4.7 |
| Lincoln | 8 | 22 | 2.3 | 0.5 | NA | NA | NA | NA | 11 | D | D | D |
| Lyon | 50 | 600 | 24.7 | 23.7 | 38 | 1 976 | 697.0 | 70.3 | 64 | 1 182 | 37.3 | 11.7 |
| McLeod | 68 | 293 | 24.1 | 9.1 | 75 | 7 486 | 1 603.4 | 362.1 | 67 | 1 111 | 39.8 | 11.3 |
| Mahnomen | 3 | D | D | D | NA | NA | NA | NA | 10 | D | D | D |
| Marshall | 11 | 32 | 6.3 | 1.3 | NA | NA | NA | NA | 20 | D | D | D |
| Martin | 43 | 217 | 21.4 | 6.9 | 45 | 1 398 | 779.4 | 55.9 | 49 | 761 | 24.4 | 7.4 |
| Meeker | 35 | 214 | 12.9 | 6.1 | 60 | 1 500 | 692.6 | 60.3 | 39 | 469 | 13.9 | 4.0 |
| Mille Lacs | 31 | 79 | 9.5 | 2.5 | 43 | 1 038 | 215.1 | 37.7 | 75 | 2 035 | 200.5 | 37.5 |
| Morrison | 33 | 129 | 13.2 | 4.9 | 58 | 1 953 | 504.1 | 72.1 | 92 | 953 | 32.1 | 8.7 |
| Mower | 43 | 267 | 29.1 | 8.9 | 37 | 3 701 | D | 155.4 | 86 | 1 132 | 41.8 | 11.5 |
| Murray | 15 | 76 | 5.7 | 1.5 | NA | NA | NA | NA | 19 | D | D | D |
| Nicollet | 38 | D | D | D | 53 | 4 722 | 872.3 | 136.9 | 47 | 787 | 25.6 | 7.7 |
| Nobles | 30 | D | D | D | 31 | 2 898 | 952.0 | 100.5 | 51 | 730 | 26.1 | 6.8 |
| Norman | 11 | 37 | 4.6 | 1.7 | NA | NA | NA | NA | 17 | D | D | D |
| Olmsted | 275 | D | D | D | 100 | 9 150 | 2 971.4 | 579.2 | 311 | 7 364 | 326.9 | 93.7 |
| Otter Tail | 93 | D | D | D | 84 | 4 005 | 1 054.4 | 119.3 | 157 | 1 456 | 62.7 | 17.5 |
| Pennington | 21 | 325 | 44.4 | 15.8 | 20 | 1 656 | D | 55.5 | 34 | 1 083 | 43.3 | 15.8 |
| Pine | 26 | D | D | D | NA | NA | NA | NA | 63 | D | D | D |
| Pipestone | 17 | 60 | 5.0 | 1.1 | 13 | 620 | D | 15.8 | 20 | D | D | D |
| Polk | 39 | D | D | D | 39 | 1 733 | 954.1 | 67.2 | 61 | 1 010 | 36.7 | 10.1 |
| Pope | 19 | 244 | 23.0 | 11.0 | 30 | 524 | 82.7 | 19.2 | 37 | 325 | 12.6 | 3.0 |
| Ramsey | 1 859 | 13 562 | 1 962.6 | 807.4 | 639 | 27 716 | 7 578.9 | 1 580.0 | 1 114 | 21 976 | 963.5 | 291.7 |
| Red Lake | 5 | 20 | 1.4 | 0.4 | NA | NA | NA | NA | 8 | D | D | D |
| Redwood | 26 | 83 | 6.5 | 2.3 | 30 | 685 | 148.1 | 23.6 | 38 | 1 286 | 81.5 | 21.4 |
| Renville | 27 | 120 | 13.5 | 5.9 | 28 | 908 | D | 40.3 | 31 | D | D | D |
| Rice | 130 | 572 | 61.6 | 27.1 | 78 | 4 215 | 1 397.9 | 179.4 | 114 | 1 936 | 80.6 | 21.1 |
| Rock | 17 | 43 | 6.1 | 1.5 | NA | NA | NA | NA | 14 | D | D | D |
| Roseau | 24 | 93 | 6.2 | 1.9 | 20 | 4 317 | D | 144.4 | 38 | 643 | 24.5 | 8.6 |
| St. Louis | 420 | D | D | D | 228 | 5 670 | D | D | 579 | 9 962 | 498.6 | 118.8 |
| Scott | 393 | D | D | D | 182 | 6 024 | 1 925.0 | 344.1 | 185 | 6 552 | 527.5 | 129.9 |
| Sherburne | 145 | 419 | 43.3 | 17.6 | 150 | 3 592 | 683.3 | 150.9 | 119 | 2 211 | 75.3 | 22.0 |
| Sibley | 25 | 73 | 6.2 | 2.6 | 24 | 928 | 548.5 | 30.9 | 25 | D | D | D |
| Stearns | 303 | D | D | D | 253 | 13 255 | 3 745.5 | 531.3 | 389 | 7 167 | 251.2 | 71.9 |
| Steele | 63 | 193 | 17.0 | 5.6 | 70 | 5 727 | 1 485.0 | 263.8 | 85 | 1 477 | 67.7 | 16.6 |
| Stevens | 15 | 109 | 10.7 | 4.4 | 17 | 687 | 192.9 | 27.9 | 27 | 352 | 11.7 | 2.9 |
| Swift | 15 | 58 | 5.1 | 1.9 | NA | NA | NA | NA | 28 | D | D | D |
| Todd | 25 | 94 | 6.7 | 2.2 | 48 | 1 794 | 648.1 | 65.3 | 46 | 439 | 15.1 | 3.8 |
| Traverse | 4 | D | D | D | NA | NA | NA | NA | 7 | D | D | D |
| Wabasha | 33 | D | D | D | 30 | 1 822 | D | 63.4 | 56 | 464 | 17.0 | 4.6 |
| Wadena | 18 | 49 | 4.5 | 2.3 | NA | NA | NA | NA | 35 | 400 | 10.9 | 3.0 |
| Waseca | 33 | 132 | 8.5 | 4.2 | 29 | 2 365 | 633.9 | 106.0 | 39 | 383 | 13.5 | 3.4 |
| Washington | 785 | D | D | D | 227 | 9 698 | 5 751.8 | 532.2 | 385 | 8 209 | 340.9 | 101.4 |
| Watonwan | 12 | 60 | 8.8 | 2.2 | 20 | 1 283 | 327.5 | 38.6 | 22 | 268 | 9.1 | 2.2 |
| Wilkin | 6 | D | D | D | NA | NA | NA | NA | 16 | 196 | 5.1 | 1.5 |
| Winona | 80 | D | D | D | 103 | 6 754 | 1 711.1 | 223.2 | 109 | 1 924 | 65.4 | 16.6 |
| Wright | 270 | 864 | 86.7 | 32.2 | 217 | 5 625 | 1 124.6 | 229.2 | 188 | 3 362 | 106.7 | 31.9 |
| Yellow Medicine | 12 | 96 | 13.4 | 5.4 | NA | NA | NA | NA | 27 | 577 | 38.3 | 8.8 |

1. Establishment subject to federal tax.

# Table B. States and Counties — Health Care and Social Assistance, Other Services, and Federal Funds

| | Health care and social assistance, 2007 | | | | Other services, 2007 | | | | Federal funds and grants, 2009–2010 | | | |
| | | | | | | | | | Expenditures (mil dol) | | | |
| | | | | | | | | | | Direct payments for individuals[1] | | |
| STATE County | Number of establishments | Number of employees | Receipts (mil dol) | Annual payroll (mil dol) | Number of establishments | Number of employees | Receipts (mil dol) | Annual payroll (mil dol) | Total | Social Security and government retirement | Medicare | Food Stamps and Supplemental Security Income |
|---|---|---|---|---|---|---|---|---|---|---|---|---|
| | 159 | 160 | 161 | 162 | 163 | 164 | 165 | 166 | 167 | 168 | 169 | 170 |
| **MINNESOTA—Cont'd** | | | | | | | | | | | | |
| Fillmore | 50 | 1 005 | 44.6 | 21.0 | 46 | 155 | 16.0 | 3.1 | 182.6 | 69.5 | 49.3 | 3.4 |
| Freeborn | 76 | 2 686 | 192.7 | 84.1 | 74 | D | D | D | 264.7 | 112.9 | 65.0 | 7.6 |
| Goodhue | 134 | 3 093 | 235.5 | 110.5 | 97 | D | D | D | 308.2 | 138.6 | 65.4 | 4.8 |
| Grant | 20 | 601 | 32.6 | 13.6 | 17 | D | D | D | 73.6 | 26.2 | 16.9 | 1.0 |
| Hennepin | 3 556 | 110 510 | 11 773.3 | 5 161.1 | 2 653 | 21 236 | 2 352.2 | 583.1 | 11 103.5 | 2 800.8 | 1 990.1 | 372.4 |
| Houston | 44 | D | D | D | 42 | D | D | D | 131.1 | 61.2 | 31.3 | 2.2 |
| Hubbard | 50 | 942 | 71.8 | 30.9 | 37 | D | D | D | 166.3 | 72.6 | 41.5 | 4.4 |
| Isanti | 76 | 2 104 | 179.4 | 71.1 | 62 | D | D | D | 189.9 | 87.4 | 37.9 | 4.5 |
| Itasca | 140 | 2 936 | 209.2 | 90.0 | 85 | D | D | D | 415.4 | 180.6 | 90.9 | 12.7 |
| Jackson | 25 | 1 425 | 42.4 | 21.3 | 30 | D | D | D | 92.7 | 34.1 | 20.6 | 1.6 |
| Kanabec | 31 | 951 | 69.6 | 26.9 | 26 | D | D | D | 105.8 | 48.0 | 21.6 | 3.8 |
| Kandiyohi | 179 | 5 098 | 293.6 | 146.8 | 92 | D | D | D | 356.7 | 124.5 | 66.5 | 10.2 |
| Kittson | 8 | 297 | 13.9 | 6.7 | 13 | D | D | D | 72.8 | 17.4 | 15.0 | 0.7 |
| Koochiching | 46 | 735 | 41.1 | 18.8 | 30 | D | D | D | 144.4 | 55.5 | 31.0 | 3.8 |
| Lac qui Parle | 18 | 575 | 26.4 | 12.0 | 18 | D | D | D | 87.3 | 31.6 | 17.9 | 1.2 |
| Lake | 31 | 568 | 24.9 | 12.4 | 21 | 219 | 12.1 | 3.6 | 104.3 | 47.8 | 22.2 | 1.7 |
| Lake of the Woods | 10 | D | D | D | 9 | D | D | D | 43.7 | 16.3 | 9.8 | 0.4 |
| Le Sueur | 58 | 812 | 37.3 | 16.5 | 55 | 249 | 15.8 | 3.7 | 177.4 | 84.7 | 40.9 | 3.5 |
| Lincoln | 15 | 553 | 31.6 | 12.5 | 14 | D | D | D | 63.1 | 20.1 | 17.9 | 0.8 |
| Lyon | 80 | 1 941 | 122.4 | 49.4 | 59 | D | D | D | 201.1 | 73.7 | 41.2 | 4.8 |
| McLeod | 107 | 2 595 | 183.7 | 78.2 | 94 | D | D | D | 203.0 | 102.0 | 47.1 | 4.2 |
| Mahnomen | 11 | 189 | 10.0 | 4.5 | 8 | D | D | D | 73.1 | 16.7 | 12.8 | 2.4 |
| Marshall | 18 | 306 | 10.3 | 5.7 | 27 | D | D | D | 118.1 | 32.0 | 26.4 | 1.6 |
| Martin | 61 | 1 954 | 124.6 | 60.0 | 57 | D | D | D | 173.3 | 79.2 | 43.9 | 4.6 |
| Meeker | 52 | 984 | 57.8 | 23.7 | 46 | D | D | D | 149.4 | 65.4 | 34.9 | 3.0 |
| Mille Lacs | 60 | 1 500 | 89.6 | 38.5 | 55 | 224 | 18.6 | 3.0 | 221.0 | 98.0 | 54.9 | 4.9 |
| Morrison | 69 | 1 402 | 96.8 | 40.4 | 82 | 399 | 37.6 | 7.4 | 325.4 | 106.2 | 61.7 | 7.0 |
| Mower | 89 | 2 587 | 169.4 | 79.8 | 97 | D | D | D | 335.4 | 133.5 | 88.1 | 8.9 |
| Murray | 19 | 431 | 35.1 | 10.8 | 22 | D | D | D | 76.8 | 28.3 | 19.4 | 1.1 |
| Nicollet | 65 | 2 111 | 152.9 | 89.2 | 65 | 373 | 135.2 | 9.6 | 146.5 | 64.9 | 26.2 | 3.2 |
| Nobles | 63 | 1 361 | 73.3 | 34.7 | 50 | D | D | D | 161.4 | 53.1 | 38.7 | 3.8 |
| Norman | 17 | 384 | 19.7 | 10.2 | 14 | D | D | D | 89.1 | 24.8 | 18.6 | 2.1 |
| Olmsted | 344 | 18 305 | 1 975.0 | 801.4 | 248 | D | D | D | 765.0 | 328.6 | 149.5 | 26.4 |
| Otter Tail | 171 | 4 370 | 232.5 | 109.3 | 134 | D | D | D | 501.9 | 212.2 | 118.1 | 9.0 |
| Pennington | 43 | 1 255 | 95.8 | 38.7 | 41 | 247 | 11.8 | 3.1 | 148.1 | 40.1 | 30.5 | 2.6 |
| Pine | 62 | 1 240 | 58.3 | 23.0 | 50 | 306 | 18.8 | 4.9 | 233.8 | 97.5 | 47.9 | 7.5 |
| Pipestone | 29 | 722 | 42.7 | 15.1 | 29 | D | D | D | 99.3 | 28.5 | 23.5 | 1.9 |
| Polk | 90 | 2 367 | 124.2 | 60.5 | 62 | D | D | D | 314.6 | 94.1 | 72.7 | 10.9 |
| Pope | 25 | 605 | 33.8 | 15.6 | 28 | D | D | D | 105.9 | 38.5 | 25.8 | 2.1 |
| Ramsey | 1 730 | 51 661 | 4 816.8 | 2 087.2 | 1 150 | 10 015 | 1 313.1 | 301.5 | 6 838.8 | 1 562.5 | 1 050.0 | 230.2 |
| Red Lake | 5 | D | D | D | 7 | D | D | D | 42.9 | 11.4 | 10.4 | 0.7 |
| Redwood | 43 | 959 | 56.3 | 22.6 | 52 | D | D | D | 140.5 | 52.2 | 33.4 | 2.6 |
| Renville | 46 | 1 317 | 50.7 | 24.3 | 37 | D | D | D | 144.8 | 48.3 | 33.8 | 3.8 |
| Rice | 149 | 3 197 | 206.3 | 90.5 | 133 | D | D | D | 341.1 | 150.4 | 71.0 | 7.7 |
| Rock | 15 | 600 | 30.4 | 12.2 | 18 | D | D | D | 72.4 | 30.3 | 18.0 | 0.9 |
| Roseau | 32 | 798 | 50.3 | 20.0 | 41 | D | D | D | 138.1 | 38.5 | 27.4 | 1.6 |
| St. Louis | 681 | 22 334 | 2 078.2 | 971.3 | 427 | 2 581 | 218.6 | 55.2 | 2 056.7 | 737.7 | 447.8 | 67.2 |
| Scott | 214 | 4 023 | 340.3 | 139.1 | 220 | 1 372 | 94.2 | 26.8 | 317.9 | 192.0 | 45.0 | 8.6 |
| Sherburne | 147 | 3 811 | 244.8 | 124.5 | 152 | D | D | D | 232.4 | 133.0 | 38.5 | 6.2 |
| Sibley | 29 | 454 | 22.8 | 9.8 | 31 | D | D | D | 97.2 | 37.0 | 27.6 | 1.9 |
| Stearns | 411 | 13 006 | 1 270.1 | 598.4 | 369 | D | D | D | 974.7 | 388.9 | 166.2 | 20.9 |
| Steele | 120 | 2 225 | 170.1 | 74.0 | 83 | 532 | 45.7 | 10.6 | 197.0 | 95.8 | 44.6 | 5.5 |
| Stevens | 40 | D | D | D | 24 | D | D | D | 102.6 | 26.6 | 22.1 | 1.9 |
| Swift | 20 | 593 | 34.7 | 14.8 | 27 | D | D | D | 115.8 | 35.6 | 26.8 | 2.0 |
| Todd | 51 | 728 | 45.3 | 19.2 | 45 | D | D | D | 211.9 | 72.1 | 50.9 | 5.7 |
| Traverse | 11 | 218 | 12.8 | 4.5 | 9 | D | D | D | 53.2 | 21.4 | 11.1 | 1.1 |
| Wabasha | 48 | D | D | D | 52 | 170 | 13.0 | 2.6 | 171.2 | 73.4 | 38.1 | 2.0 |
| Wadena | 46 | 1 976 | 128.2 | 57.9 | 28 | D | D | D | 149.4 | 51.8 | 38.0 | 4.6 |
| Waseca | 54 | 1 241 | 51.4 | 21.0 | 39 | D | D | D | 132.8 | 50.5 | 26.6 | 2.9 |
| Washington | 511 | 9 218 | 826.0 | 327.4 | 384 | 2 490 | 171.5 | 52.7 | 646.4 | 362.0 | 111.5 | 13.2 |
| Watonwan | 24 | 546 | 36.7 | 15.5 | 27 | D | D | D | 78.5 | 35.0 | 19.1 | 2.2 |
| Wilkin | 23 | D | D | D | 13 | D | D | D | 89.7 | 23.2 | 12.5 | 1.5 |
| Winona | 129 | 3 066 | 187.2 | 80.8 | 90 | D | D | D | 305.0 | 125.8 | 70.6 | 8.3 |
| Wright | 219 | 4 309 | 315.0 | 134.5 | 225 | 1 270 | 89.9 | 22.0 | 459.5 | 242.6 | 88.9 | 9.0 |
| Yellow Medicine | 28 | 1 044 | 59.6 | 27.2 | 24 | D | D | D | 113.6 | 41.6 | 26.8 | 1.8 |

1. State totals may include programs not allocated by county.

# Federal Funds, Residential Construction, and Local Government Finances

| STATE County | Federal funds and grants, 2009–2010 (cont.) — Expenditures (mil dol) (cont.) | | | | | | | Value of residential construction authorized by building permits, 2011 | | Local government finances, 2007 — General revenue | | | | |
|---|---|---|---|---|---|---|---|---|---|---|---|---|---|---|
| | Procurement contract awards | | Grants[1] | | | | | | | | | Taxes | | |
| | | | | | | | | | | | | | Per capita[2] (dollars) | |
| | Salaries and wages | Defense | Other | Medicaid and other health-related | Nutrition and family welfare | Education | Other | New construction ($1,000) | Number of housing units | Total (mil dol) | Inter-govern-mental (mil dol) | Total (mil dol) | Total | Property |
| | 171 | 172 | 173 | 174 | 175 | 176 | 177 | 178 | 179 | 180 | 181 | 182 | 183 | 184 |
| MINNESOTA—Cont'd | | | | | | | | | | | | | | |
| Fillmore | 6.0 | 0.0 | 1.5 | 32.0 | 6.0 | 1.5 | 1.2 | 7 642 | 52 | 71.2 | 39.8 | 15.7 | 747 | 737 |
| Freeborn | 15.0 | 0.3 | 2.3 | 36.4 | 5.6 | 1.9 | 4.2 | 5 323 | 34 | 111.6 | 63.7 | 25.1 | 802 | 726 |
| Goodhue | 11.1 | 32.2 | 3.1 | 31.1 | 7.6 | 2.6 | 2.3 | 7 438 | 39 | 202.0 | 88.7 | 58.3 | 1 273 | 1 225 |
| Grant | 2.3 | 0.0 | 0.5 | 11.7 | 3.4 | 0.4 | 0.5 | 502 | 3 | 35.7 | 23.6 | 6.5 | 1 078 | 1 075 |
| Hennepin | 977.5 | 613.5 | 831.2 | 2 046.6 | 181.6 | 93.8 | 538.4 | 381 933 | 1 615 | 5 614.0 | 2 424.2 | 1 770.6 | 1 558 | 1 400 |
| Houston | 5.0 | 0.6 | 1.0 | 21.4 | 3.1 | 1.1 | 0.5 | 3 889 | 22 | 66.2 | 42.0 | 14.3 | 733 | 725 |
| Hubbard | 3.5 | 0.0 | 0.8 | 34.2 | 4.4 | 1.5 | 1.2 | 2 406 | 18 | 78.2 | 48.0 | 19.8 | 1 052 | 1 036 |
| Isanti | 13.2 | -0.4 | 1.8 | 23.5 | 5.0 | 2.4 | 0.8 | 4 316 | 35 | 119.3 | 69.5 | 30.2 | 775 | 739 |
| Itasca | 13.7 | 4.3 | 4.3 | 73.6 | 13.6 | 4.4 | 12.4 | 14 850 | 89 | 230.5 | 94.9 | 40.8 | 917 | 906 |
| Jackson | 5.5 | 0.0 | 0.6 | 11.7 | 2.3 | 0.7 | 6.9 | 2 476 | 20 | 46.4 | 23.3 | 11.9 | 1 092 | 1 086 |
| Kanabec | 3.2 | 1.5 | 0.7 | 18.3 | 5.7 | 0.8 | 0.0 | 2 583 | 19 | 77.2 | 30.9 | 11.7 | 727 | 712 |
| Kandiyohi | 20.6 | 0.1 | 47.5 | 50.4 | 10.2 | 2.9 | 3.3 | 10 852 | 63 | 262.7 | 92.0 | 38.0 | 933 | 846 |
| Kittson | 3.9 | 0.0 | 1.3 | 11.7 | 1.4 | 0.5 | 5.3 | 665 | 3 | 27.9 | 15.8 | 4.9 | 1 093 | 1 076 |
| Koochiching | 12.2 | 0.1 | 2.3 | 26.8 | 3.7 | 1.2 | 3.1 | 2 158 | 14 | 64.0 | 36.3 | 7.8 | 578 | 559 |
| Lac qui Parle | 10.7 | 0.0 | 0.6 | 8.5 | 1.9 | 0.5 | 5.4 | 1 520 | 5 | 44.9 | 23.5 | 6.2 | 854 | 847 |
| Lake | 2.1 | 0.2 | 0.5 | 13.9 | 2.2 | 0.7 | 12.8 | 7 706 | 47 | 56.3 | 29.0 | 12.0 | 1 121 | 1 081 |
| Lake of the Woods | 2.7 | 0.0 | 0.5 | 9.6 | 1.1 | 0.3 | 1.3 | 2 418 | 12 | 23.2 | 14.1 | 4.2 | 1 032 | 970 |
| Le Sueur | 6.4 | 0.1 | 1.9 | 26.7 | 4.0 | 1.6 | 2.0 | 5 136 | 35 | 90.8 | 48.4 | 22.6 | 806 | 779 |
| Lincoln | 1.9 | 0.0 | 0.5 | 11.7 | 1.5 | 0.5 | 0.3 | 3 030 | 13 | 20.6 | 12.3 | 4.8 | 819 | 811 |
| Lyon | 27.1 | 0.0 | 4.0 | 25.6 | 6.1 | 2.5 | 0.4 | 7 515 | 59 | 149.2 | 62.9 | 23.6 | 954 | 922 |
| McLeod | 11.5 | 0.2 | 1.7 | 19.4 | 4.4 | 1.9 | 1.8 | 4 575 | 21 | 199.4 | 69.5 | 32.4 | 871 | 856 |
| Mahnomen | 1.7 | 0.1 | 0.3 | 17.1 | 2.5 | 4.3 | 4.9 | 0 | 0 | 36.1 | 22.5 | 4.5 | 874 | 869 |
| Marshall | 4.3 | 0.1 | 0.9 | 19.3 | 3.2 | 0.9 | 1.3 | 398 | 2 | 43.4 | 29.4 | 6.9 | 714 | 706 |
| Martin | 6.7 | 0.2 | 1.2 | 17.1 | 4.5 | 1.6 | 2.1 | 2 869 | 16 | 77.5 | 41.0 | 16.5 | 804 | 786 |
| Meeker | 10.1 | 0.0 | 1.3 | 20.3 | 4.6 | 1.4 | 0.5 | 5 285 | 37 | 121.9 | 59.3 | 20.9 | 899 | 882 |
| Mille Lacs | 5.7 | 0.0 | 2.0 | 38.1 | 6.6 | 2.3 | 1.5 | 6 482 | 34 | 105.5 | 67.2 | 22.7 | 861 | 841 |
| Morrison | 67.7 | 2.2 | 1.8 | 54.8 | 10.5 | 2.9 | 1.6 | 6 147 | 53 | 111.2 | 64.3 | 25.2 | 769 | 744 |
| Mower | 18.2 | 0.0 | 2.4 | 48.0 | 6.3 | 2.9 | 6.7 | 6 964 | 36 | 157.0 | 89.4 | 23.2 | 611 | 588 |
| Murray | 3.7 | 0.0 | 0.9 | 10.7 | 1.9 | 0.6 | 0.6 | 2 857 | 18 | 40.8 | 21.1 | 8.1 | 950 | 940 |
| Nicollet | 6.7 | 5.6 | 0.8 | 15.0 | 3.6 | 1.3 | 2.5 | 9 703 | 58 | 94.0 | 37.7 | 22.1 | 697 | 672 |
| Nobles | 7.5 | 5.3 | 4.5 | 28.8 | 5.1 | 1.7 | 2.5 | 2 504 | 14 | 107.2 | 48.9 | 16.2 | 807 | 780 |
| Norman | 3.2 | 0.0 | 0.8 | 12.8 | 2.0 | 0.6 | 6.4 | 1 587 | 12 | 34.4 | 23.7 | 5.6 | 842 | 835 |
| Olmsted | 98.0 | 3.2 | 21.5 | 70.3 | 17.6 | 7.8 | 18.1 | 62 257 | 276 | 567.3 | 246.7 | 157.6 | 1 128 | 990 |
| Otter Tail | 19.4 | 0.8 | 4.0 | 89.7 | 13.1 | 3.3 | 3.3 | 11 710 | 115 | 269.7 | 110.6 | 44.7 | 783 | 759 |
| Pennington | 7.7 | 0.1 | 3.7 | 35.2 | 3.2 | 1.2 | 6.2 | 2 567 | 17 | 122.0 | 37.0 | 12.1 | 876 | 853 |
| Pine | 24.7 | 3.1 | -8.1 | 42.7 | 5.6 | 1.8 | 6.3 | 4 798 | 34 | 91.5 | 54.8 | 21.2 | 752 | 734 |
| Pipestone | 5.9 | 0.0 | 1.1 | 18.1 | 2.4 | 0.7 | 11.2 | 1 734 | 10 | 61.8 | 28.1 | 8.3 | 887 | 868 |
| Polk | 13.7 | 0.8 | 2.3 | 60.2 | 15.4 | 2.2 | 6.0 | 7 591 | 48 | 166.2 | 96.2 | 29.1 | 947 | 876 |
| Pope | 2.9 | 10.6 | 0.8 | 13.9 | 2.7 | 0.7 | 0.1 | 3 570 | 27 | 41.7 | 23.3 | 9.5 | 859 | 846 |
| Ramsey | 533.8 | 80.8 | 126.7 | 853.6 | 265.3 | 385.2 | 1 493.2 | 60 342 | 377 | 2 668.9 | 1 240.7 | 622.0 | 1 244 | 1 114 |
| Red Lake | 1.6 | 0.7 | 0.3 | 7.5 | 3.7 | 0.4 | 0.3 | 0 | 0 | 21.6 | 15.2 | 2.9 | 705 | 691 |
| Redwood | 7.1 | 0.0 | 1.7 | 25.6 | 3.0 | 1.3 | 0.6 | 3 015 | 17 | 85.6 | 39.0 | 15.0 | 965 | 936 |
| Renville | 6.5 | 0.0 | 1.2 | 23.7 | 3.7 | 1.4 | 5.7 | 1 581 | 8 | 81.6 | 42.8 | 15.0 | 931 | 915 |
| Rice | 17.0 | 0.1 | 3.2 | 59.5 | 7.6 | 3.0 | 10.4 | 10 783 | 54 | 305.2 | 98.6 | 47.6 | 768 | 699 |
| Rock | 4.4 | 0.0 | 0.5 | 7.5 | 1.9 | 0.7 | 1.8 | 1 543 | 8 | 41.8 | 24.7 | 7.9 | 829 | 773 |
| Roseau | 7.6 | 8.4 | 7.1 | 22.5 | 5.0 | 1.1 | 0.2 | 502 | 4 | 85.4 | 61.7 | 11.2 | 701 | 691 |
| St. Louis | 160.3 | 28.0 | 42.9 | 369.6 | 50.9 | 19.2 | 84.5 | 51 257 | 308 | 945.8 | 459.1 | 193.9 | 986 | 868 |
| Scott | 14.7 | 0.8 | 7.6 | 16.1 | 13.3 | 3.8 | 3.3 | 104 547 | 387 | 434.5 | 188.5 | 141.8 | 1 120 | 1 041 |
| Sherburne | 12.2 | 0.3 | 3.2 | 22.4 | 7.9 | 2.6 | 0.4 | 13 333 | 86 | 324.7 | 168.4 | 95.2 | 1 103 | 1 071 |
| Sibley | 5.6 | 0.0 | 0.9 | 11.7 | 2.5 | 0.9 | 0.1 | 1 910 | 11 | 72.5 | 31.0 | 15.8 | 1 055 | 1 024 |
| Stearns | 96.1 | 0.9 | 55.6 | 116.5 | 24.4 | 8.0 | 15.5 | 46 739 | 302 | 582.1 | 284.4 | 139.3 | 954 | 836 |
| Steele | 9.5 | 1.7 | 1.6 | 20.4 | 4.8 | 1.8 | 1.1 | 8 107 | 65 | 137.2 | 72.7 | 31.8 | 873 | 838 |
| Stevens | 13.6 | 0.1 | 4.8 | 14.9 | 2.2 | 0.6 | 3.5 | 811 | 7 | 38.1 | 21.9 | 8.5 | 882 | 858 |
| Swift | 15.1 | 0.0 | 0.9 | 18.1 | 2.9 | 0.8 | 1.1 | 2 509 | 15 | 64.2 | 27.1 | 9.9 | 883 | 874 |
| Todd | 8.7 | 0.0 | 1.8 | 53.4 | 6.9 | 2.1 | 2.9 | 6 867 | 45 | 123.2 | 72.3 | 18.2 | 756 | 720 |
| Traverse | 1.5 | 0.4 | 0.3 | 5.3 | 1.3 | 0.3 | 0.3 | 994 | 7 | 33.9 | 11.7 | 5.6 | 1 507 | 1 504 |
| Wabasha | 6.1 | 0.2 | 18.5 | 20.3 | 3.4 | 1.4 | 2.0 | 6 411 | 29 | 86.7 | 45.7 | 20.7 | 949 | 836 |
| Wadena | 7.0 | 0.3 | 0.9 | 38.5 | 3.7 | 1.2 | 0.5 | 3 275 | 24 | 59.4 | 36.4 | 9.4 | 705 | 690 |
| Waseca | 19.0 | 0.5 | 5.9 | 14.9 | 3.4 | 1.4 | 0.4 | 4 035 | 18 | 79.4 | 42.7 | 17.5 | 898 | 819 |
| Washington | 56.8 | 2.8 | 12.5 | 45.1 | 21.5 | 7.6 | 3.1 | 155 987 | 632 | 800.8 | 340.1 | 259.8 | 1 147 | 1 077 |
| Watonwan | 5.9 | 0.0 | 1.4 | 5.3 | 2.4 | 0.8 | 0.6 | 1 241 | 12 | 45.9 | 28.6 | 9.2 | 831 | 821 |
| Wilkin | 2.2 | 6.3 | 0.5 | 9.7 | 1.6 | 0.6 | 0.2 | 665 | 5 | 31.0 | 20.4 | 6.0 | 935 | 925 |
| Winona | 14.6 | 3.3 | 2.3 | 42.8 | 7.2 | 3.1 | 4.9 | 15 800 | 133 | 152.0 | 89.0 | 35.5 | 712 | 670 |
| Wright | 39.9 | 0.5 | 4.5 | 44.4 | 13.5 | 4.0 | 4.3 | 32 081 | 167 | 468.5 | 199.8 | 115.1 | 981 | 922 |
| Yellow Medicine | 3.8 | 0.1 | 1.0 | 17.1 | 2.7 | 1.0 | 1.8 | 2 542 | 15 | 65.5 | 28.2 | 9.8 | 964 | 944 |

1. State totals may include programs not allocated by county.   2. Based on the resident population estimated as of July 1 of the year shown.

| STATE County | Total (mil dol) | Per capita[1] (dollars) | Education | Health and hospitals | Police protection | Public welfare | Highways | Total (mil dol) | Per capita[1] (dollars) | Federal civilian | Federal military | State and local | Democratic | Republican | All other |
|---|---|---|---|---|---|---|---|---|---|---|---|---|---|---|---|
| | **Local government finances, 2007 (cont.)** | | | | | | | | | **Government employment, 2011** | | | **Presidential election,[2] 2012** | | |
| | **Direct general expenditure** | | | | | | | **Debt outstanding** | | | | | **Percent of vote cast:** | | |
| | | | | | Percent of total for: | | | | | | | | | | |
| | 185 | 186 | 187 | 188 | 189 | 190 | 191 | 192 | 193 | 194 | 195 | 196 | 197 | 198 | 199 |
| MINNESOTA—Cont'd | | | | | | | | | | | | | | | |
| Fillmore | 80.4 | 3 822 | 37.4 | 3.1 | 4.1 | 3.9 | 18.8 | 70.6 | 3 354 | 73 | 78 | 1 209 | 52.7 | 44.4 | 2.8 |
| Freeborn | 106.6 | 3 411 | 41.0 | 2.2 | 5.0 | 9.3 | 13.5 | 63.0 | 2 015 | 84 | 117 | 1 431 | 57.4 | 40.2 | 2.4 |
| Goodhue | 201.5 | 4 396 | 40.8 | 7.6 | 4.8 | 4.3 | 11.5 | 176.8 | 3 857 | 122 | 173 | 4 253 | 48.1 | 49.5 | 2.3 |
| Grant | 33.3 | 5 529 | 34.8 | 1.1 | 3.4 | 9.2 | 15.7 | 24.0 | 3 993 | 32 | 22 | 345 | 51.3 | 45.7 | 3.0 |
| Hennepin | 5 718.3 | 5 031 | 33.6 | 13.6 | 5.9 | 8.1 | 5.4 | 7 621.7 | 6 706 | 13 314 | 4 883 | 80 279 | 63.4 | 34.8 | 1.8 |
| Houston | 69.9 | 3 583 | 50.3 | 2.5 | 5.3 | 6.0 | 11.1 | 55.6 | 2 848 | 73 | 71 | 1 070 | 54.3 | 43.6 | 2.2 |
| Hubbard | 69.0 | 3 672 | 38.9 | 0.0 | 3.9 | 15.4 | 14.7 | 75.9 | 4 039 | 41 | 76 | 1 086 | 41.9 | 56.3 | 1.8 |
| Isanti | 126.5 | 3 250 | 47.2 | 1.1 | 5.8 | 7.6 | 15.4 | 184.1 | 4 730 | 74 | 144 | 1 901 | 41.1 | 56.5 | 2.4 |
| Itasca | 238.9 | 5 364 | 30.3 | 22.0 | 3.6 | 9.8 | 11.4 | 197.6 | 4 436 | 188 | 169 | 3 304 | 55.2 | 42.3 | 2.6 |
| Jackson | 47.1 | 4 331 | 30.5 | 5.3 | 3.4 | 11.9 | 16.2 | 56.4 | 5 187 | 36 | 38 | 682 | 46.6 | 50.8 | 2.6 |
| Kanabec | 75.6 | 4 701 | 30.3 | 36.6 | 2.2 | 4.6 | 9.5 | 71.5 | 4 443 | 43 | 61 | 1 113 | 44.0 | 52.7 | 3.3 |
| Kandiyohi | 268.9 | 6 593 | 22.7 | 34.4 | 3.0 | 4.6 | 10.2 | 237.3 | 5 818 | 161 | 158 | 3 761 | 46.2 | 51.7 | 2.1 |
| Kittson | 26.0 | 5 773 | 39.6 | 0.2 | 3.4 | 4.4 | 27.1 | 6.2 | 1 368 | 62 | 17 | 287 | 58.1 | 39.6 | 2.3 |
| Koochiching | 72.7 | 5 401 | 33.9 | 1.7 | 4.3 | 12.8 | 18.8 | 64.6 | 4 803 | 191 | 50 | 849 | 53.6 | 43.5 | 2.8 |
| Lac qui Parle | 47.0 | 6 470 | 37.8 | 20.5 | 3.0 | 3.8 | 15.4 | 16.9 | 2 332 | 35 | 27 | 694 | 51.5 | 45.6 | 2.9 |
| Lake | 59.8 | 5 563 | 28.2 | 4.2 | 4.8 | 11.7 | 12.3 | 142.7 | 13 290 | 26 | 41 | 806 | 59.9 | 37.8 | 2.3 |
| Lake of the Woods | 20.9 | 5 097 | 32.6 | 0.3 | 3.4 | 6.6 | 27.2 | 298.3 | 72 846 | 35 | 15 | 262 | 42.0 | 55.3 | 2.8 |
| Le Sueur | 110.0 | 3 925 | 47.0 | 1.9 | 3.3 | 5.6 | 18.3 | 136.5 | 4 870 | 71 | 104 | 1 212 | 46.6 | 50.9 | 2.5 |
| Lincoln | 21.2 | 3 600 | 28.2 | 0.2 | 5.2 | 7.9 | 23.7 | 11.2 | 1 913 | 26 | 22 | 265 | 48.5 | 47.7 | 3.8 |
| Lyon | 162.9 | 6 594 | 39.8 | 21.8 | 3.6 | 2.4 | 11.5 | 155.2 | 6 286 | 129 | 97 | 2 652 | 48.1 | 49.7 | 2.2 |
| McLeod | 191.2 | 5 136 | 27.0 | 29.5 | 4.1 | 4.3 | 7.0 | 190.8 | 5 125 | 78 | 137 | 1 677 | 39.4 | 57.8 | 2.8 |
| Mahnomen | 40.0 | 7 795 | 43.0 | 16.7 | 5.4 | 5.7 | 13.9 | 31.1 | 6 063 | 30 | 20 | 1 297 | 61.3 | 36.0 | 2.7 |
| Marshall | 44.6 | 4 635 | 45.9 | 0.3 | 3.4 | 2.6 | 21.1 | 11.2 | 1 167 | 58 | 36 | 577 | 48.8 | 48.2 | 3.0 |
| Martin | 89.3 | 4 366 | 49.9 | 0.2 | 4.5 | 5.0 | 13.6 | 69.3 | 3 386 | 64 | 78 | 1 262 | 41.0 | 56.3 | 2.7 |
| Meeker | 124.7 | 5 372 | 47.0 | 15.8 | 3.9 | 7.0 | 7.0 | 116.0 | 4 997 | 72 | 87 | 1 158 | 42.9 | 53.7 | 3.4 |
| Mille Lacs | 107.4 | 4 076 | 58.8 | 0.9 | 3.0 | 5.2 | 7.9 | 107.1 | 4 063 | 59 | 97 | 3 510 | 44.8 | 52.0 | 3.1 |
| Morrison | 118.9 | 3 633 | 43.4 | 1.5 | 5.1 | 7.1 | 17.9 | 116.8 | 3 567 | 411 | 125 | 1 825 | 39.1 | 58.1 | 2.8 |
| Mower | 150.6 | 3 960 | 42.5 | 1.6 | 4.0 | 7.6 | 11.9 | 1 209.8 | 31 803 | 149 | 148 | 2 377 | 60.5 | 36.9 | 2.6 |
| Murray | 44.0 | 5 171 | 34.9 | 14.5 | 3.6 | 2.2 | 17.5 | 16.0 | 1 877 | 42 | 32 | 570 | 48.7 | 48.2 | 3.1 |
| Nicollet | 100.7 | 3 177 | 29.9 | 13.3 | 5.2 | 0.9 | 15.3 | 119.4 | 3 768 | 45 | 123 | 2 915 | 54.2 | 43.7 | 2.1 |
| Nobles | 105.3 | 5 231 | 32.2 | 21.6 | 4.4 | 6.8 | 6.4 | 87.6 | 4 353 | 96 | 80 | 1 385 | 48.2 | 49.6 | 2.3 |
| Norman | 35.4 | 5 297 | 38.2 | 1.0 | 3.6 | 8.2 | 19.1 | 15.1 | 2 258 | 41 | 26 | 451 | 62.0 | 35.1 | 2.9 |
| Olmsted | 603.7 | 4 320 | 37.0 | 1.6 | 4.3 | 9.3 | 5.2 | 1 588.4 | 11 367 | 909 | 550 | 7 013 | 50.6 | 47.3 | 2.0 |
| Otter Tail | 280.7 | 4 922 | 45.3 | 7.9 | 3.1 | 6.0 | 10.8 | 205.0 | 3 594 | 231 | 215 | 3 297 | 42.4 | 55.3 | 2.3 |
| Pennington | 119.5 | 8 687 | 68.0 | 0.0 | 3.2 | 4.4 | 7.4 | 67.4 | 4 902 | 75 | 53 | 1 581 | 49.8 | 47.6 | 2.6 |
| Pine | 93.5 | 3 320 | 40.9 | 1.4 | 4.2 | 8.0 | 17.0 | 108.7 | 3 861 | 319 | 111 | 3 284 | 49.3 | 47.7 | 3.0 |
| Pipestone | 65.4 | 7 031 | 31.1 | 28.8 | 2.4 | 5.9 | 14.0 | 40.4 | 4 346 | 52 | 36 | 913 | 42.1 | 55.2 | 2.6 |
| Polk | 176.2 | 5 737 | 29.6 | 1.0 | 3.8 | 9.4 | 14.7 | 171.2 | 5 576 | 124 | 118 | 2 513 | 51.2 | 46.6 | 2.2 |
| Pope | 39.6 | 3 575 | 36.2 | 4.8 | 5.2 | 6.4 | 18.0 | 19.0 | 1 714 | 42 | 41 | 701 | 50.7 | 47.0 | 2.3 |
| Ramsey | 2 647.8 | 5 297 | 40.0 | 1.8 | 5.9 | 7.5 | 3.6 | 5 096.1 | 10 194 | 3 493 | 1 965 | 53 178 | 66.0 | 32.1 | 2.0 |
| Red Lake | 23.0 | 5 581 | 52.7 | 0.1 | 4.0 | 5.4 | 13.1 | 12.0 | 2 908 | 163 | 15 | 269 | 51.1 | 44.9 | 4.0 |
| Redwood | 83.3 | 5 370 | 31.4 | 19.9 | 4.0 | 7.9 | 14.7 | 85.2 | 5 492 | 65 | 60 | 2 018 | 41.6 | 55.2 | 3.2 |
| Renville | 79.9 | 4 950 | 24.2 | 11.2 | 3.8 | 6.8 | 19.1 | 41.4 | 2 567 | 58 | 58 | 1 032 | 48.0 | 48.6 | 3.4 |
| Rice | 309.8 | 5 001 | 25.3 | 37.9 | 3.2 | 2.8 | 9.6 | 326.9 | 5 277 | 134 | 242 | 4 030 | 54.7 | 43.2 | 2.2 |
| Rock | 39.3 | 4 134 | 36.9 | 0.2 | 3.9 | 6.0 | 22.2 | 59.5 | 6 263 | 30 | 36 | 689 | 41.8 | 55.8 | 2.4 |
| Roseau | 91.8 | 5 757 | 37.1 | 0.3 | 3.7 | 4.5 | 22.9 | 64.4 | 4 042 | 105 | 58 | 979 | 40.2 | 57.6 | 2.1 |
| St. Louis | 967.2 | 4 917 | 29.9 | 7.9 | 4.9 | 8.9 | 9.3 | 946.6 | 4 812 | 1 473 | 883 | 15 210 | 65.1 | 32.6 | 2.3 |
| Scott | 553.1 | 4 368 | 50.4 | 0.3 | 5.5 | 3.2 | 14.6 | 1 011.9 | 7 990 | 146 | 497 | 9 284 | 43.5 | 54.7 | 1.8 |
| Sherburne | 323.8 | 3 752 | 52.6 | 0.5 | 4.2 | 4.1 | 9.1 | 768.1 | 8 902 | 135 | 335 | 3 898 | 39.9 | 58.1 | 2.0 |
| Sibley | 70.7 | 4 713 | 35.5 | 15.6 | 4.0 | 10.1 | 12.2 | 49.6 | 3 304 | 40 | 57 | 827 | 38.8 | 58.1 | 3.1 |
| Stearns | 581.9 | 3 984 | 41.7 | 8.3 | 4.8 | 3.9 | 12.4 | 1 010.5 | 6 919 | 2 061 | 574 | 10 180 | 45.3 | 52.3 | 2.4 |
| Steele | 134.3 | 3 693 | 44.6 | 1.6 | 4.4 | 11.6 | 11.6 | 118.9 | 3 267 | 71 | 137 | 1 964 | 45.9 | 51.2 | 2.9 |
| Stevens | 38.7 | 4 019 | 38.7 | 3.5 | 5.0 | 6.3 | 17.1 | 56.8 | 5 901 | 82 | 36 | 1 181 | 49.4 | 48.1 | 2.5 |
| Swift | 70.1 | 6 262 | 22.5 | 28.0 | 3.6 | 5.9 | 19.6 | 22.1 | 1 971 | 59 | 36 | 831 | 55.4 | 41.6 | 2.9 |
| Todd | 128.1 | 5 333 | 45.1 | 15.2 | 2.7 | 5.6 | 11.4 | 61.8 | 2 570 | 83 | 93 | 1 364 | 43.1 | 54.1 | 2.8 |
| Traverse | 34.4 | 9 265 | 19.3 | 20.6 | 3.1 | 12.5 | 12.2 | 20.3 | 5 466 | 26 | 13 | 351 | 51.3 | 45.8 | 2.9 |
| Wabasha | 93.1 | 4 276 | 38.3 | 2.0 | 5.9 | 4.5 | 11.0 | 76.0 | 3 491 | 62 | 81 | 999 | 47.5 | 49.9 | 2.6 |
| Wadena | 60.1 | 4 490 | 47.6 | 1.6 | 4.3 | 17.7 | 10.8 | 33.0 | 2 465 | 53 | 52 | 1 286 | 40.2 | 57.6 | 2.2 |
| Waseca | 85.3 | 4 366 | 45.6 | 1.6 | 4.1 | 11.3 | 12.2 | 67.6 | 3 460 | 268 | 72 | 1 128 | 44.5 | 52.7 | 2.8 |
| Washington | 816.5 | 3 605 | 49.2 | 1.8 | 5.8 | 3.7 | 8.3 | 1 172.3 | 5 176 | 412 | 905 | 10 278 | 51.3 | 46.9 | 1.8 |
| Watonwan | 50.1 | 4 549 | 41.1 | 1.2 | 5.9 | 7.5 | 18.3 | 38.7 | 3 514 | 54 | 42 | 744 | 48.7 | 48.0 | 3.2 |
| Wilkin | 33.0 | 5 138 | 36.5 | 2.2 | 4.5 | 6.3 | 23.5 | 12.3 | 1 923 | 30 | 25 | 365 | 45.4 | 52.3 | 2.3 |
| Winona | 156.1 | 3 134 | 43.5 | 2.0 | 5.0 | 5.8 | 17.2 | 85.1 | 1 708 | 147 | 193 | 3 468 | 58.4 | 39.3 | 2.3 |
| Wright | 539.7 | 4 598 | 47.7 | 8.4 | 3.6 | 3.2 | 14.1 | 984.7 | 8 389 | 198 | 474 | 6 038 | 40.2 | 57.6 | 2.2 |
| Yellow Medicine | 69.1 | 6 821 | 29.2 | 24.2 | 2.2 | 9.5 | 13.5 | 38.5 | 3 797 | 45 | 39 | 1 518 | 50.6 | 46.3 | 3.1 |

1. Based on the resident population estimated as of July 1 of the year shown.    2. © 2013 Election Data Services, Inc. All rights reserved.

# Table B. States and Counties — Land Area and Population

| | | | | | Population 2012 | | | Population characteristics[6], 2011 | | | | | | | | | | |
| | | | | | | | | Race alone or in combination, not Hispanic or Latino (percent) | | | | | Age (percent) | | | | | |
| STATE/ County code | CBSA code[1] | County type[2] | STATE County | Land area,[3] (sq km) 2010 | Total persons | Rank | Per square kilometer | White | Black | American Indian, Alaska Native | Asian and Pacific Islander | Percent Hispanic or Latino[4] | Under 5 years | 5 to 17 years | 18 to 24 years | 25 to 34 years | 35 to 44 years | 45 to 54 years |
|---|---|---|---|---|---|---|---|---|---|---|---|---|---|---|---|---|---|---|
| | | | | 1 | 2 | 3 | 4 | 5 | 6 | 7 | 8 | 9 | 10 | 11 | 12 | 13 | 14 | 15 |
| 28 000 | ... | X | MISSISSIPPI | 121 531 | 2 984 926 | X | 24.6 | 58.5 | 37.6 | 0.8 | 1.2 | 2.9 | 7.0 | 18.2 | 10.4 | 13.1 | 12.4 | 13.8 |
| 28 001 | 35020 | 5 | Adams | 1 198 | 32 122 | 1 386 | 26.8 | 39.2 | 53.7 | 0.6 | 0.7 | 6.8 | 6.1 | 15.9 | 8.3 | 12.5 | 11.7 | 15.2 |
| 28 003 | 18420 | 7 | Alcorn | 1 036 | 37 164 | 1 243 | 35.9 | 84.7 | 12.3 | 0.5 | 0.5 | 2.8 | 6.5 | 17.7 | 7.9 | 12.3 | 12.9 | 13.8 |
| 28 005 | 32620 | 8 | Amite | 1 891 | 12 957 | 2 243 | 6.9 | 57.3 | 41.7 | 0.5 | 0.2 | 1.0 | 6.6 | 15.4 | 7.8 | 10.7 | 10.5 | 15.4 |
| 28 007 | ... | 6 | Attala | 1 904 | 19 157 | 1 867 | 10.1 | 55.7 | 42.4 | 0.5 | 0.5 | 1.7 | 7.6 | 18.4 | 7.9 | 11.0 | 11.5 | 13.1 |
| 28 009 | ... | 8 | Benton | 1 053 | 8 730 | 2 543 | 8.3 | 60.8 | 37.2 | 0.7 | 0.2 | 1.8 | 6.2 | 17.9 | 8.2 | 12.1 | 12.6 | 15.0 |
| 28 011 | 17380 | 5 | Bolivar | 2 270 | 33 904 | 1 328 | 14.9 | 33.5 | 64.0 | 0.3 | 0.8 | 2.0 | 7.6 | 17.9 | 12.4 | 13.3 | 11.1 | 12.9 |
| 28 013 | ... | 7 | Calhoun | 1 519 | 14 843 | 2 120 | 9.8 | 66.4 | 28.4 | 0.5 | 0.3 | 5.4 | 7.0 | 17.9 | 7.9 | 11.1 | 12.9 | 13.4 |
| 28 015 | 24900 | 9 | Carroll | 1 627 | 10 423 | 2 403 | 6.4 | 65.4 | 33.2 | 0.6 | 0.4 | 1.3 | 5.5 | 15.5 | 7.9 | 10.7 | 11.7 | 15.1 |
| 28 017 | ... | 7 | Chickasaw | 1 300 | 17 416 | 1 958 | 13.4 | 53.4 | 42.7 | 0.4 | 0.5 | 3.7 | 7.3 | 18.9 | 9.0 | 11.7 | 11.7 | 14.2 |
| 28 019 | ... | 9 | Choctaw | 1 083 | 8 346 | 2 575 | 7.7 | 67.8 | 31.2 | 0.5 | 0.3 | 1.0 | 6.1 | 17.6 | 7.6 | 10.3 | 11.3 | 15.2 |
| 28 021 | ... | 6 | Claiborne | 1 262 | 9 349 | 2 484 | 7.4 | 14.8 | 83.9 | 0.4 | 0.6 | 1.0 | 6.5 | 17.2 | 17.5 | 10.9 | 9.9 | 12.2 |
| 28 023 | 32940 | 9 | Clarke | 1 791 | 16 556 | 2 008 | 9.2 | 63.8 | 34.9 | 0.6 | 0.3 | 0.9 | 6.4 | 18.2 | 8.1 | 10.7 | 12.1 | 14.0 |
| 28 025 | 48500 | 7 | Clay | 1 062 | 20 427 | 1 819 | 19.2 | 40.2 | 58.5 | 0.3 | 0.3 | 1.1 | 6.8 | 18.6 | 9.4 | 12.0 | 11.6 | 13.9 |
| 28 027 | 17260 | 5 | Coahoma | 1 431 | 25 709 | 1 579 | 18.0 | 23.3 | 75.0 | 0.3 | 0.6 | 1.3 | 8.5 | 20.6 | 10.9 | 12.3 | 10.8 | 12.9 |
| 28 029 | 27140 | 2 | Copiah | 2 013 | 28 955 | 1 452 | 14.4 | 46.0 | 51.1 | 0.4 | 0.5 | 2.7 | 7.2 | 17.5 | 11.3 | 11.9 | 10.9 | 14.3 |
| 28 031 | ... | 8 | Covington | 1 072 | 19 607 | 1 852 | 18.3 | 62.3 | 35.6 | 0.4 | 0.4 | 2.0 | 7.3 | 18.6 | 9.0 | 12.3 | 11.9 | 13.4 |
| 28 033 | 32820 | 1 | DeSoto | 1 233 | 166 234 | 376 | 134.8 | 70.7 | 23.2 | 0.6 | 1.7 | 5.0 | 6.9 | 20.8 | 8.0 | 13.6 | 15.3 | 14.0 |
| 28 035 | 25620 | 3 | Forrest | 1 208 | 76 894 | 711 | 63.7 | 59.1 | 36.5 | 0.7 | 1.4 | 3.7 | 7.3 | 16.2 | 17.3 | 14.6 | 11.2 | 11.9 |
| 28 037 | ... | 9 | Franklin | 1 460 | 7 918 | 2 604 | 5.4 | 64.0 | 35.1 | 0.5 | 0.2 | 0.9 | 6.4 | 18.5 | 7.1 | 11.3 | 11.9 | 13.9 |
| 28 039 | 37700 | 3 | George | 1 240 | 22 930 | 1 693 | 18.5 | 88.7 | 9.0 | 0.7 | 0.4 | 2.1 | 7.3 | 19.2 | 9.2 | 12.5 | 13.3 | 14.0 |
| 28 041 | ... | 8 | Greene | 1 846 | 14 311 | 2 151 | 7.8 | 71.8 | 27.0 | 0.7 | 0.3 | 1.0 | 5.6 | 15.8 | 9.2 | 16.9 | 15.2 | 14.5 |
| 28 043 | 24980 | 7 | Grenada | 1 093 | 21 682 | 1 744 | 19.8 | 56.6 | 42.1 | 0.5 | 0.6 | 1.1 | 6.6 | 18.0 | 8.7 | 11.4 | 12.4 | 14.3 |
| 28 045 | 25060 | 3 | Hancock | 1 227 | 45 255 | 1 062 | 36.9 | 87.0 | 8.6 | 1.3 | 1.4 | 3.5 | 6.2 | 17.6 | 8.1 | 11.1 | 12.2 | 15.4 |
| 28 047 | 25060 | 3 | Harrison | 1 487 | 194 029 | 328 | 130.5 | 68.3 | 22.5 | 1.0 | 3.7 | 5.5 | 7.4 | 17.1 | 10.6 | 14.5 | 12.5 | 14.3 |
| 28 049 | 27140 | 2 | Hinds | 2 253 | 248 643 | 264 | 110.4 | 28.5 | 69.3 | 0.4 | 1.0 | 1.6 | 7.2 | 18.8 | 12.1 | 14.4 | 11.9 | 13.4 |
| 28 051 | ... | 6 | Holmes | 1 960 | 18 796 | 1 884 | 9.6 | 16.7 | 82.3 | 0.4 | 0.4 | 0.8 | 8.7 | 20.1 | 12.4 | 11.2 | 10.5 | 13.1 |
| 28 053 | ... | 7 | Humphreys | 1 084 | 9 189 | 2 504 | 8.5 | 23.5 | 74.3 | 0.5 | 0.4 | 2.2 | 9.1 | 19.5 | 9.9 | 12.3 | 10.8 | 14.2 |
| 28 055 | ... | 9 | Issaquena | 1 070 | 1 386 | 3 090 | 1.3 | 34.7 | 64.1 | 0.4 | 0.4 | 0.6 | 5.6 | 14.4 | 12.8 | 13.7 | 10.6 | 16.2 |
| 28 057 | 46180 | 7 | Itawamba | 1 380 | 23 340 | 1 672 | 16.9 | 91.4 | 7.0 | 0.5 | 0.4 | 1.3 | 6.1 | 16.7 | 11.2 | 10.9 | 13.2 | 13.6 |
| 28 059 | 37700 | 3 | Jackson | 1 872 | 140 298 | 447 | 74.9 | 70.7 | 22.5 | 0.9 | 2.7 | 4.9 | 6.7 | 18.5 | 8.8 | 13.0 | 13.2 | 14.9 |
| 28 061 | 29860 | 9 | Jasper | 1 751 | 16 523 | 2 010 | 9.4 | 46.0 | 52.9 | 0.4 | 0.3 | 0.9 | 6.8 | 17.5 | 8.4 | 11.1 | 11.6 | 14.4 |
| 28 063 | ... | 7 | Jefferson | 1 347 | 7 638 | 2 632 | 5.7 | 14.6 | 84.7 | 0.4 | 0.2 | 0.5 | 6.1 | 17.3 | 10.2 | 13.7 | 11.2 | 15.4 |
| 28 065 | ... | 8 | Jefferson Davis | 1 058 | 12 032 | 2 297 | 11.4 | 39.3 | 59.5 | 0.5 | 0.4 | 1.0 | 6.5 | 16.6 | 8.6 | 10.6 | 11.9 | 14.3 |
| 28 067 | 29860 | 4 | Jones | 1 800 | 68 641 | 772 | 38.1 | 65.9 | 28.7 | 0.7 | 0.6 | 4.8 | 7.5 | 18.1 | 9.7 | 12.5 | 11.8 | 13.5 |
| 28 069 | 32940 | 9 | Kemper | 1 984 | 10 335 | 2 412 | 5.2 | 35.7 | 60.0 | 4.1 | 0.3 | 0.7 | 6.0 | 16.6 | 10.9 | 11.3 | 12.1 | 13.5 |
| 28 071 | 37060 | 6 | Lafayette | 1 636 | 49 495 | 991 | 30.3 | 71.1 | 24.3 | 0.6 | 2.7 | 2.4 | 5.3 | 13.1 | 27.0 | 13.9 | 10.3 | 10.4 |
| 28 073 | 25620 | 3 | Lamar | 1 287 | 57 786 | 884 | 44.9 | 74.8 | 21.0 | 0.6 | 1.5 | 2.2 | 7.4 | 18.6 | 11.4 | 15.1 | 13.3 | 12.8 |
| 28 075 | 32940 | 5 | Lauderdale | 1 822 | 80 220 | 688 | 44.0 | 54.2 | 43.2 | 0.4 | 1.0 | 1.9 | 7.0 | 17.8 | 10.0 | 12.9 | 12.3 | 13.5 |
| 28 077 | ... | 8 | Lawrence | 1 115 | 12 551 | 2 270 | 11.3 | 66.3 | 31.4 | 0.4 | 0.4 | 2.1 | 7.3 | 17.6 | 7.7 | 11.9 | 11.8 | 14.7 |
| 28 079 | ... | 6 | Leake | 1 510 | 23 297 | 1 675 | 15.4 | 49.1 | 41.5 | 5.5 | 0.4 | 4.3 | 7.8 | 23.0 | 8.7 | 12.3 | 11.5 | 12.2 |
| 28 081 | 46180 | 5 | Lee | 1 165 | 85 042 | 663 | 73.0 | 68.9 | 28.3 | 0.4 | 0.9 | 2.6 | 7.3 | 19.2 | 8.4 | 13.2 | 13.2 | 14.0 |
| 28 083 | 24900 | 5 | Leflore | 1 535 | 30 948 | 1 412 | 20.2 | 24.9 | 72.2 | 0.4 | 0.7 | 2.4 | 8.1 | 19.0 | 12.0 | 13.8 | 11.0 | 12.8 |
| 28 085 | 15020 | 6 | Lincoln | 1 518 | 34 900 | 1 303 | 23.0 | 67.9 | 30.7 | 0.5 | 0.5 | 1.1 | 7.2 | 18.7 | 8.4 | 12.2 | 12.4 | 14.0 |
| 28 087 | 18060 | 5 | Lowndes | 1 309 | 59 670 | 868 | 45.6 | 53.7 | 44.1 | 0.5 | 1.0 | 1.7 | 6.9 | 18.0 | 10.8 | 12.9 | 12.0 | 14.0 |
| 28 089 | 27140 | 2 | Madison | 1 851 | 98 468 | 595 | 53.2 | 56.4 | 38.6 | 0.4 | 2.5 | 3.0 | 7.2 | 19.4 | 8.5 | 13.7 | 13.6 | 14.9 |
| 28 091 | ... | 6 | Marion | 1 405 | 26 442 | 1 546 | 18.8 | 65.4 | 33.0 | 0.5 | 0.5 | 1.4 | 7.3 | 18.1 | 8.4 | 12.6 | 12.1 | 13.8 |
| 28 093 | 32820 | 1 | Marshall | 1 829 | 36 612 | 1 258 | 20.0 | 49.2 | 47.4 | 0.5 | 0.4 | 3.3 | 6.5 | 16.5 | 10.0 | 12.4 | 12.3 | 15.4 |
| 28 095 | ... | 7 | Monroe | 1 982 | 36 421 | 1 264 | 18.4 | 67.8 | 31.2 | 0.5 | 0.4 | 1.0 | 6.3 | 17.5 | 8.8 | 11.4 | 12.5 | 14.2 |
| 28 097 | ... | 7 | Montgomery | 1 054 | 10 614 | 2 388 | 10.1 | 52.7 | 46.0 | 0.4 | 0.5 | 1.0 | 6.8 | 17.0 | 8.7 | 10.7 | 10.9 | 14.6 |
| 28 099 | ... | 7 | Neshoba | 1 477 | 29 785 | 1 432 | 20.2 | 60.7 | 22.4 | 15.7 | 0.7 | 1.8 | 8.3 | 20.3 | 8.6 | 12.4 | 11.8 | 12.8 |
| 28 101 | ... | 7 | Newton | 1 497 | 21 601 | 1 750 | 14.4 | 62.7 | 31.3 | 5.0 | 0.4 | 1.5 | 7.1 | 18.7 | 10.1 | 11.3 | 12.7 | 12.9 |
| 28 103 | ... | 7 | Noxubee | 1 800 | 11 218 | 2 344 | 6.2 | 27.3 | 71.6 | 0.5 | 0.3 | 0.9 | 7.4 | 19.3 | 9.8 | 11.7 | 11.4 | 14.6 |
| 28 105 | 44260 | 5 | Oktibbeha | 1 187 | 48 192 | 1 008 | 40.6 | 58.7 | 36.9 | 0.5 | 3.4 | 1.7 | 5.5 | 12.3 | 32.2 | 13.6 | 8.6 | 9.8 |
| 28 107 | ... | 6 | Panola | 1 775 | 34 473 | 1 312 | 19.4 | 49.2 | 49.2 | 0.5 | 0.4 | 1.6 | 7.6 | 19.3 | 9.5 | 12.0 | 12.0 | 14.3 |
| 28 109 | 38100 | 6 | Pearl River | 2 100 | 55 295 | 909 | 26.3 | 83.0 | 13.4 | 1.3 | 0.8 | 3.0 | 6.8 | 17.5 | 9.2 | 11.4 | 12.3 | 14.1 |
| 28 111 | 25620 | 3 | Perry | 1 676 | 12 086 | 2 293 | 7.2 | 77.8 | 21.2 | 0.6 | 0.2 | 1.1 | 6.9 | 18.1 | 8.7 | 11.4 | 12.5 | 14.6 |
| 28 113 | 32620 | 7 | Pike | 1 059 | 40 100 | 1 171 | 37.9 | 46.1 | 52.0 | 0.6 | 0.8 | 1.3 | 7.5 | 19.3 | 9.1 | 12.1 | 11.6 | 13.3 |
| 28 115 | 46180 | 7 | Pontotoc | 1 289 | 30 594 | 1 420 | 23.7 | 78.9 | 15.1 | 0.7 | 0.4 | 6.1 | 7.2 | 19.5 | 8.4 | 12.9 | 12.9 | 14.4 |
| 28 117 | ... | 7 | Prentiss | 1 075 | 25 390 | 1 594 | 23.6 | 84.0 | 15.0 | 0.4 | 0.3 | 1.2 | 6.6 | 16.2 | 11.2 | 11.5 | 12.2 | 13.8 |
| 28 119 | ... | 6 | Quitman | 1 049 | 7 798 | 2 616 | 7.4 | 29.4 | 69.6 | 0.6 | 0.5 | 0.8 | 7.3 | 19.1 | 9.8 | 10.9 | 11.7 | 13.7 |
| 28 121 | 27140 | 2 | Rankin | 2 008 | 145 165 | 436 | 72.3 | 76.3 | 20.0 | 0.5 | 1.5 | 2.7 | 6.8 | 18.1 | 7.9 | 15.0 | 14.5 | 13.9 |
| 28 123 | ... | 6 | Scott | 1 578 | 28 250 | 1 481 | 17.9 | 51.2 | 38.0 | 0.5 | 0.5 | 10.7 | 8.4 | 18.7 | 9.4 | 13.3 | 12.6 | 13.3 |
| 28 125 | ... | 9 | Sharkey | 1 118 | 4 799 | 2 851 | 4.3 | 28.2 | 70.7 | 0.3 | 0.4 | 1.0 | 7.1 | 18.1 | 9.1 | 11.0 | 10.9 | 14.7 |
| 28 127 | 27140 | 2 | Simpson | 1 526 | 27 374 | 1 516 | 17.9 | 62.6 | 35.6 | 0.4 | 0.7 | 1.6 | 7.3 | 18.7 | 8.7 | 11.9 | 11.9 | 14.0 |
| 28 129 | ... | 8 | Smith | 1 648 | 16 345 | 2 023 | 9.9 | 75.1 | 23.6 | 0.4 | 0.2 | 1.3 | 6.8 | 18.5 | 8.6 | 10.9 | 12.5 | 14.0 |
| 28 131 | 25060 | 3 | Stone | 1 154 | 18 028 | 1 920 | 15.6 | 77.8 | 20.2 | 0.9 | 0.5 | 1.5 | 6.5 | 17.2 | 12.5 | 12.3 | 12.2 | 13.9 |

1. CBSA = Core Based Statistical Area. See Appendix A for explanation. See Appendix B for list of metropolitan areas with component counties. 2. County type code from the Economic Research Service of USDA Rural-Urban Continuum Codes. See Appendix A for definition. 3. Dry land or land partially or temporarily covered by water. 4. May be of any race.

| STATE County | Population, 2011 (cont.) Age (percent) (cont.) 55 to 64 years | 65 to 74 years | 75 years and over | Percent female | Population change and components of change, 2000–2012 Total persons 2000 | 2010 | Percent change 2000–2010 | 2010–2012 | Components of change, 2010–2012 Births | Deaths | Net migration | Households, 2010 Number | Percent change, 2000–2010 | Persons per house-hold | Female family house-holder[1] | One per-son |
|---|---|---|---|---|---|---|---|---|---|---|---|---|---|---|---|---|
| | 16 | 17 | 18 | 19 | 20 | 21 | 22 | 23 | 24 | 25 | 26 | 27 | 28 | 29 | 30 | 31 |
| MISSISSIPPI | 12.1 | 7.4 | 5.7 | 51.4 | 2 844 658 | 2 967 297 | 4.3 | 0.6 | 89 282 | 66 148 | -6 610 | 1 115 768 | 6.6 | 2.58 | 18.5 | 26.3 |
| Adams | 14.4 | 8.4 | 7.4 | 50.0 | 34 340 | 32 297 | -5.9 | -0.5 | 897 | 927 | -148 | 12 643 | -7.6 | 2.37 | 22.2 | 31.8 |
| Alcorn | 12.8 | 9.4 | 6.8 | 51.2 | 34 558 | 37 057 | 7.2 | 0.3 | 974 | 988 | 138 | 15 039 | 5.7 | 2.44 | 13.9 | 28.5 |
| Amite | 15.2 | 10.6 | 7.8 | 51.0 | 13 599 | 13 131 | -3.4 | -1.3 | 326 | 323 | -194 | 5 351 | 1.5 | 2.43 | 15.7 | 29.7 |
| Attala | 13.1 | 9.3 | 8.0 | 52.7 | 19 661 | 19 564 | -0.5 | -2.1 | 612 | 629 | -418 | 7 619 | 0.7 | 2.52 | 18.9 | 28.1 |
| Benton | 12.6 | 8.8 | 6.7 | 50.9 | 8 026 | 8 729 | 8.8 | 0.0 | 219 | 211 | -2 | 3 404 | 13.5 | 2.54 | 17.0 | 26.8 |
| Bolivar | 12.6 | 7.1 | 5.2 | 53.6 | 40 633 | 34 145 | -16.0 | -0.7 | 1 251 | 962 | -540 | 12 727 | -7.6 | 2.56 | 26.9 | 28.4 |
| Calhoun | 13.2 | 8.7 | 7.9 | 52.1 | 15 069 | 14 962 | -0.7 | -0.8 | 415 | 421 | -113 | 5 988 | -0.5 | 2.46 | 17.0 | 27.8 |
| Carroll | 15.4 | 11.0 | 7.0 | 49.7 | 10 769 | 10 597 | -1.6 | -1.6 | 198 | 235 | -161 | 4 188 | 2.9 | 2.45 | 14.9 | 26.1 |
| Chickasaw | 12.6 | 8.0 | 6.6 | 52.5 | 19 440 | 17 392 | -10.5 | 0.1 | 564 | 430 | -101 | 6 639 | -8.5 | 2.59 | 19.7 | 26.6 |
| Choctaw | 14.3 | 10.1 | 7.5 | 51.7 | 9 758 | 8 547 | -12.4 | -2.4 | 212 | 225 | -189 | 3 446 | -6.5 | 2.45 | 15.5 | 29.0 |
| Claiborne | 13.4 | 7.0 | 5.4 | 53.4 | 11 831 | 9 604 | -18.8 | -2.7 | 273 | 218 | -316 | 3 440 | -0.2 | 2.53 | 26.6 | 31.4 |
| Clarke | 14.0 | 9.2 | 7.2 | 52.5 | 17 955 | 16 732 | -6.8 | -1.1 | 443 | 434 | -184 | 6 733 | -3.5 | 2.48 | 17.3 | 27.0 |
| Clay | 13.4 | 7.7 | 6.7 | 52.9 | 21 979 | 20 634 | -6.1 | -1.0 | 545 | 503 | -241 | 8 029 | -1.5 | 2.53 | 24.2 | 26.8 |
| Coahoma | 11.5 | 6.8 | 5.6 | 53.9 | 30 622 | 26 151 | -14.6 | -1.7 | 1 041 | 684 | -810 | 9 461 | -10.3 | 2.69 | 30.2 | 28.4 |
| Copiah | 12.8 | 7.8 | 6.3 | 51.7 | 28 757 | 29 449 | 2.4 | -1.7 | 904 | 718 | -679 | 10 708 | 5.6 | 2.65 | 20.7 | 25.6 |
| Covington | 11.9 | 8.6 | 6.9 | 51.5 | 19 407 | 19 568 | 0.8 | 0.2 | 615 | 494 | -72 | 7 430 | 4.3 | 2.60 | 18.1 | 26.6 |
| DeSoto | 10.8 | 6.4 | 4.1 | 51.4 | 107 199 | 161 252 | 50.4 | 3.1 | 4 586 | 2 598 | 2 922 | 57 748 | 48.9 | 2.78 | 15.1 | 19.8 |
| Forrest | 10.0 | 6.3 | 5.3 | 52.3 | 72 604 | 74 934 | 3.2 | 2.6 | 2 513 | 1 624 | 1 046 | 28 746 | 5.7 | 2.48 | 18.5 | 29.3 |
| Franklin | 14.5 | 8.8 | 7.7 | 51.1 | 8 448 | 8 118 | -3.9 | -2.5 | 200 | 188 | -206 | 3 211 | 0.0 | 2.51 | 14.8 | 27.7 |
| George | 11.5 | 8.5 | 4.6 | 49.4 | 19 144 | 22 578 | 17.9 | 1.6 | 807 | 526 | 76 | 7 982 | 18.4 | 2.76 | 11.1 | 21.5 |
| Greene | 11.1 | 7.2 | 4.6 | 41.1 | 13 299 | 14 400 | 8.3 | -0.6 | 312 | 294 | -104 | 4 306 | 3.8 | 2.64 | 13.3 | 23.9 |
| Grenada | 13.1 | 8.8 | 6.7 | 52.9 | 23 263 | 21 906 | -5.8 | -1.0 | 632 | 573 | -290 | 8 779 | -0.5 | 2.47 | 20.6 | 29.0 |
| Hancock | 14.0 | 9.4 | 6.1 | 50.4 | 42 967 | 43 929 | 2.2 | 3.0 | 1 038 | 895 | 1 154 | 17 380 | 2.9 | 2.50 | 13.3 | 26.2 |
| Harrison | 11.8 | 6.7 | 5.1 | 50.2 | 189 601 | 187 105 | -1.3 | 3.7 | 6 238 | 3 594 | 4 170 | 71 476 | -0.1 | 2.54 | 17.2 | 26.4 |
| Hinds | 11.4 | 6.0 | 4.9 | 52.9 | 250 800 | 245 285 | -2.2 | 1.4 | 7 872 | 4 490 | -25 | 91 351 | 0.4 | 2.60 | 25.4 | 28.3 |
| Holmes | 11.0 | 7.1 | 5.8 | 53.0 | 21 609 | 19 198 | -11.2 | -2.1 | 679 | 521 | -606 | 6 926 | -5.3 | 2.69 | 32.6 | 29.2 |
| Humphreys | 11.3 | 7.1 | 5.6 | 52.9 | 11 206 | 9 375 | -16.3 | -2.0 | 349 | 263 | -279 | 3 373 | -10.4 | 2.75 | 30.7 | 27.1 |
| Issaquena | 12.0 | 8.8 | 5.8 | 42.7 | 2 274 | 1 406 | -38.2 | -1.4 | 37 | 21 | -45 | 472 | -35.0 | 2.45 | 19.3 | 32.6 |
| Itawamba | 12.2 | 9.3 | 6.9 | 51.4 | 22 770 | 23 401 | 2.8 | -0.3 | 588 | 587 | -77 | 8 881 | 1.2 | 2.53 | 11.8 | 24.5 |
| Jackson | 12.3 | 7.6 | 5.0 | 50.7 | 131 420 | 139 668 | 6.3 | 0.5 | 3 760 | 2 778 | -330 | 52 205 | 9.5 | 2.65 | 16.4 | 23.1 |
| Jasper | 14.0 | 9.3 | 7.0 | 51.6 | 18 149 | 17 062 | -6.0 | -3.2 | 486 | 404 | -640 | 6 798 | 1.3 | 2.50 | 18.2 | 28.1 |
| Jefferson | 12.8 | 7.2 | 6.0 | 50.2 | 9 740 | 7 726 | -20.7 | -1.1 | 229 | 172 | -160 | 2 929 | -11.5 | 2.50 | 28.3 | 29.9 |
| Jefferson Davis | 14.2 | 10.2 | 7.1 | 52.3 | 13 962 | 12 487 | -10.6 | -3.6 | 327 | 353 | -432 | 4 977 | -3.9 | 2.49 | 20.8 | 29.2 |
| Jones | 12.3 | 7.9 | 6.7 | 51.3 | 64 958 | 67 761 | 4.3 | 1.3 | 2 223 | 1 661 | 349 | 25 247 | 4.0 | 2.61 | 16.8 | 25.6 |
| Kemper | 13.5 | 8.6 | 7.6 | 50.8 | 10 453 | 10 456 | 0.0 | -1.2 | 208 | 244 | -98 | 3 920 | 0.3 | 2.49 | 20.9 | 30.2 |
| Lafayette | 9.4 | 5.9 | 4.7 | 50.9 | 38 744 | 47 351 | 22.2 | 4.5 | 1 159 | 817 | 1 751 | 18 356 | 27.7 | 2.31 | 11.6 | 31.1 |
| Lamar | 10.3 | 6.5 | 4.6 | 51.7 | 39 070 | 55 658 | 42.5 | 3.8 | 1 721 | 785 | 1 126 | 21 542 | 49.6 | 2.57 | 13.5 | 24.1 |
| Lauderdale | 12.4 | 7.4 | 6.7 | 51.8 | 78 161 | 80 261 | 2.7 | -0.1 | 2 373 | 1 877 | -506 | 31 090 | 3.7 | 2.46 | 20.0 | 29.8 |
| Lawrence | 13.6 | 8.9 | 6.4 | 50.8 | 13 258 | 12 929 | -2.5 | -2.9 | 375 | 341 | -422 | 5 078 | 0.8 | 2.55 | 14.6 | 26.1 |
| Leake | 11.3 | 7.2 | 6.0 | 48.3 | 20 940 | 23 805 | 13.7 | -2.1 | 709 | 640 | -593 | 8 272 | 8.7 | 2.65 | 18.4 | 26.8 |
| Lee | 11.6 | 7.3 | 5.8 | 52.3 | 75 755 | 82 910 | 9.4 | 2.6 | 2 651 | 2 126 | 1 523 | 32 086 | 9.9 | 2.55 | 16.9 | 26.4 |
| Leflore | 11.3 | 6.2 | 5.7 | 52.1 | 37 947 | 32 317 | -14.8 | -4.2 | 1 193 | 819 | -1 770 | 11 577 | -10.6 | 2.59 | 29.2 | 29.9 |
| Lincoln | 13.0 | 7.5 | 6.6 | 52.2 | 33 166 | 34 869 | 5.1 | 0.1 | 1 053 | 871 | -141 | 13 296 | 6.0 | 2.57 | 16.3 | 25.1 |
| Lowndes | 12.1 | 7.3 | 6.1 | 52.6 | 61 586 | 59 779 | -2.9 | -0.2 | 1 758 | 1 244 | -616 | 23 487 | 2.8 | 2.49 | 19.2 | 27.9 |
| Madison | 12.1 | 5.9 | 4.8 | 52.1 | 74 674 | 95 203 | 27.5 | 3.4 | 2 882 | 2 325 | 2 532 | 35 829 | 31.6 | 2.61 | 15.8 | 25.5 |
| Marion | 12.7 | 7.9 | 7.1 | 51.8 | 25 595 | 27 088 | 5.8 | -2.4 | 824 | 796 | -683 | 10 135 | 8.6 | 2.60 | 17.1 | 25.6 |
| Marshall | 13.6 | 7.8 | 5.5 | 50.7 | 34 993 | 37 144 | 6.1 | -1.4 | 1 019 | 950 | -624 | 13 369 | 9.9 | 2.65 | 19.3 | 24.4 |
| Monroe | 13.2 | 9.0 | 7.1 | 52.3 | 38 014 | 36 989 | -2.7 | -1.5 | 931 | 885 | -612 | 14 485 | -0.8 | 2.53 | 18.2 | 26.4 |
| Montgomery | 13.8 | 9.4 | 8.1 | 52.5 | 12 189 | 10 925 | -10.4 | -2.8 | 279 | 308 | -290 | 4 438 | -5.4 | 2.44 | 20.3 | 29.2 |
| Neshoba | 12.4 | 7.2 | 6.3 | 52.2 | 28 684 | 29 676 | 3.5 | 0.4 | 1 022 | 711 | -203 | 10 856 | 1.5 | 2.70 | 19.2 | 25.2 |
| Newton | 12.2 | 8.0 | 7.0 | 52.1 | 21 838 | 21 720 | -0.5 | -0.5 | 694 | 632 | -209 | 8 214 | -0.1 | 2.57 | 16.7 | 26.2 |
| Noxubee | 12.2 | 7.3 | 6.3 | 51.8 | 12 548 | 11 545 | -8.0 | -2.8 | 350 | 308 | -387 | 4 305 | -3.7 | 2.64 | 25.4 | 28.3 |
| Oktibbeha | 8.7 | 5.0 | 4.2 | 50.2 | 42 902 | 47 671 | 11.1 | 1.1 | 1 226 | 696 | -59 | 18 820 | 18.0 | 2.30 | 14.1 | 31.6 |
| Panola | 12.4 | 7.5 | 5.4 | 52.0 | 34 274 | 34 707 | 1.3 | -0.7 | 1 168 | 900 | -487 | 12 839 | 5.0 | 2.68 | 21.2 | 25.7 |
| Pearl River | 13.6 | 9.1 | 6.0 | 50.8 | 48 621 | 55 834 | 14.8 | -1.0 | 1 549 | 1 316 | -784 | 20 816 | 15.1 | 2.63 | 13.5 | 23.1 |
| Perry | 13.5 | 8.9 | 5.4 | 51.3 | 12 138 | 12 250 | 0.9 | -1.3 | 346 | 291 | -261 | 4 674 | 5.7 | 2.60 | 15.5 | 25.3 |
| Pike | 12.9 | 7.7 | 6.6 | 52.2 | 38 940 | 40 404 | 3.8 | -0.8 | 1 367 | 1 151 | -511 | 15 370 | 3.9 | 2.57 | 21.4 | 28.0 |
| Pontotoc | 11.8 | 7.1 | 5.8 | 50.7 | 26 726 | 29 957 | 12.1 | 2.1 | 926 | 543 | 243 | 11 172 | 10.6 | 2.66 | 13.5 | 23.6 |
| Prentiss | 12.2 | 8.9 | 7.0 | 51.0 | 25 556 | 25 276 | -1.1 | 0.5 | 753 | 556 | -106 | 9 812 | -0.1 | 2.49 | 14.5 | 26.3 |
| Quitman | 12.6 | 8.5 | 6.3 | 52.3 | 10 117 | 8 223 | -18.7 | -5.2 | 257 | 255 | -455 | 3 058 | -14.2 | 2.64 | 26.2 | 28.4 |
| Rankin | 12.0 | 7.0 | 4.8 | 51.6 | 115 327 | 141 617 | 22.8 | 2.5 | 4 345 | 2 335 | 1 528 | 52 836 | 25.5 | 2.57 | 13.5 | 24.0 |
| Scott | 11.9 | 6.9 | 5.5 | 51.1 | 28 423 | 28 264 | -0.6 | 0.0 | 1 046 | 670 | -392 | 10 248 | 0.6 | 2.74 | 19.6 | 24.5 |
| Sharkey | 14.5 | 7.1 | 7.6 | 53.9 | 6 580 | 4 916 | -25.3 | -2.4 | 176 | 111 | -189 | 1 834 | -15.2 | 2.62 | 27.1 | 29.7 |
| Simpson | 13.2 | 8.1 | 6.2 | 51.5 | 27 639 | 27 503 | -0.5 | -0.5 | 816 | 653 | -284 | 10 330 | 2.5 | 2.60 | 16.5 | 26.0 |
| Smith | 13.2 | 9.3 | 6.3 | 51.5 | 16 182 | 16 491 | 1.9 | -0.9 | 440 | 381 | -218 | 6 221 | 2.9 | 2.63 | 14.3 | 23.6 |
| Stone | 12.8 | 7.7 | 4.9 | 50.1 | 13 622 | 17 786 | 30.6 | 1.4 | 477 | 378 | 133 | 6 165 | 29.9 | 2.68 | 14.4 | 22.5 |

1. No spouse present.

# Table B. States and Counties — **Population, Vital Statistics, Medicare, and Crime**

| STATE County | Persons in group quarters, 2010 | Daytime population, 2007–2011 Number | Employment/residence ratio | Births, 2011 Total | Rate[1] | Deaths, 2011 Number | Rate[1] | Persons under 65 with no health insurance, 2010 Number | Percent | Medicare, 2012 Eligible for Medicare | Enrolled in Medicare Advantage | Enrolled in a Medicare prescription drug plan | Serious crimes known to police,[2] 2011 Total Number | Rate[3] |
|---|---|---|---|---|---|---|---|---|---|---|---|---|---|---|
| | 32 | 33 | 34 | 35 | 36 | 37 | 38 | 39 | 40 | 41 | 42 | 43 | 44 | 45 |
| MISSISSIPPI ......................... | 91 964 | 2 912 408 | 0.96 | 40 464 | 13.6 | 28 837 | 9.7 | 525 570 | 21.0 | 527 570 | 60 682 | 296 157 | 98 151 | 3 295 |
| Adams............................ | 2 320 | 33 119 | 1.06 | 402 | 12.5 | 402 | 12.5 | 5 479 | 22.0 | 6 736 | 643 | 4 076 | 1 725 | 5 321 |
| Alcorn........................... | 435 | 37 652 | 1.06 | 433 | 11.7 | 437 | 11.8 | 6 537 | 21.2 | 8 614 | 185 | 6 289 | NA | NA |
| Amite............................. | 116 | 10 833 | 0.48 | 139 | 10.6 | 148 | 11.3 | 2 542 | 23.9 | 2 949 | 258 | 1 789 | NA | NA |
| Attala............................ | 343 | 18 116 | 0.79 | 288 | 14.8 | 274 | 14.1 | 3 415 | 21.3 | 4 088 | 360 | 2 356 | NA | NA |
| Benton ........................... | 78 | 7 140 | 0.48 | 98 | 11.2 | 91 | 10.4 | 1 608 | 21.9 | 1 811 | 184 | 1 205 | NA | NA |
| Bolivar........................... | 1 564 | 33 801 | 0.94 | 574 | 17.0 | 429 | 12.7 | 5 570 | 19.5 | 6 501 | 265 | 4 455 | 1 005 | 3 521 |
| Calhoun.......................... | 215 | 13 090 | 0.67 | 199 | 13.3 | 185 | 12.4 | 3 044 | 24.6 | 3 435 | 296 | 2 334 | NA | NA |
| Carroll........................... | 334 | 8 211 | 0.30 | 90 | 8.7 | 102 | 9.8 | 1 972 | 23.3 | 2 456 | 59 | 1 574 | NA | NA |
| Chickasaw ...................... | 206 | 17 375 | 0.98 | 267 | 15.6 | 192 | 11.2 | 3 525 | 23.9 | 3 827 | 524 | 2 425 | NA | NA |
| Choctaw.......................... | 121 | 7 734 | 0.74 | 110 | 13.1 | 95 | 11.3 | 1 560 | 22.3 | 1 681 | 156 | 1 111 | 105 | 1 224 |
| Claiborne........................ | 899 | 9 767 | 1.00 | 131 | 13.7 | 99 | 10.3 | 1 591 | 21.1 | 1 639 | 369 | 944 | 133 | 1 380 |
| Clarke............................ | 52 | 13 749 | 0.52 | 207 | 12.4 | 180 | 10.8 | 3 032 | 21.8 | 3 820 | 344 | 2 231 | NA | NA |
| Clay............................... | 303 | 19 684 | 0.86 | 249 | 12.2 | 220 | 10.8 | 3 841 | 22.1 | 4 090 | 531 | 2 547 | 417 | 2 013 |
| Coahoma.......................... | 667 | 26 851 | 1.06 | 472 | 18.2 | 292 | 11.3 | 4 595 | 20.4 | 4 758 | 211 | 3 446 | NA | NA |
| Copiah............................ | 1 027 | 26 788 | 0.76 | 391 | 13.4 | 298 | 10.2 | 5 433 | 21.9 | 5 550 | 1 111 | 2 731 | NA | NA |
| Covington......................... | 240 | 17 973 | 0.77 | 291 | 14.8 | 215 | 11.0 | 3 700 | 22.3 | 3 841 | 483 | 2 217 | 574 | 3 077 |
| DeSoto............................ | 610 | 130 954 | 0.64 | 2 055 | 12.5 | 1 091 | 6.7 | 26 756 | 18.6 | 22 382 | 2 687 | 10 846 | 3 735 | 2 308 |
| Forrest........................... | 3 601 | 85 946 | 1.34 | 1 142 | 15.1 | 706 | 9.3 | 13 484 | 21.3 | 12 105 | 1 837 | 6 264 | 2 121 | 2 820 |
| Franklin.......................... | 67 | 6 754 | 0.51 | 92 | 11.5 | 73 | 9.1 | 1 505 | 22.2 | 1 756 | 85 | 1 012 | 65 | 798 |
| George............................ | 564 | 19 777 | 0.67 | 367 | 16.0 | 234 | 10.2 | 4 034 | 21.1 | 3 909 | 547 | 2 083 | 124 | 547 |
| Greene............................ | 3 042 | 11 897 | 0.46 | 149 | 10.4 | 130 | 9.1 | 2 242 | 22.9 | 2 282 | 159 | 1 340 | 45 | 321 |
| Grenada........................... | 256 | 22 979 | 1.11 | 273 | 12.6 | 262 | 12.1 | 3 838 | 20.9 | 4 899 | 504 | 3 148 | NA | NA |
| Hancock........................... | 547 | 44 096 | 1.05 | 462 | 10.3 | 375 | 8.4 | 9 143 | 24.8 | 7 924 | 1 479 | 3 432 | NA | NA |
| Harrison.......................... | 5 452 | 201 634 | 1.19 | 2 741 | 14.3 | 1 541 | 8.1 | 36 483 | 22.8 | 30 827 | 3 121 | 12 773 | 8 746 | 4 657 |
| Hinds............................. | 7 843 | 267 943 | 1.21 | 3 557 | 14.3 | 1 974 | 8.0 | 42 448 | 20.0 | 37 121 | 8 023 | 17 397 | 15 808 | 6 522 |
| Holmes............................ | 591 | 17 862 | 0.74 | 322 | 17.1 | 247 | 13.1 | 3 626 | 22.4 | 3 720 | 220 | 2 679 | NA | NA |
| Humphreys ....................... | 83 | 9 393 | 0.96 | 172 | 18.5 | 122 | 13.1 | 1 710 | 21.0 | 1 780 | 70 | 1 298 | NA | NA |
| Issaquena ........................ | 251 | 1 595 | 0.50 | 20 | 14.4 | 13 | 9.3 | 236 | 24.8 | 166 | 12 | 108 | NA | NA |
| Itawamba ......................... | 934 | 19 654 | 0.62 | 261 | 11.2 | 240 | 10.3 | 4 006 | 21.2 | 5 245 | 247 | 3 538 | 368 | 1 567 |
| Jackson........................... | 1 290 | 133 359 | 0.91 | 1 714 | 12.3 | 1 222 | 8.7 | 24 991 | 20.7 | 23 723 | 4 095 | 10 080 | 5 499 | 3 922 |
| Jasper............................ | 87 | 15 780 | 0.77 | 221 | 13.2 | 192 | 11.4 | 3 013 | 21.3 | 3 650 | 477 | 2 156 | NA | NA |
| Jefferson......................... | 393 | 7 457 | 0.80 | 100 | 13.1 | 72 | 9.5 | 1 356 | 21.3 | 1 490 | 135 | 985 | 61 | 994 |
| Jefferson Davis.................. | 116 | 10 592 | 0.57 | 158 | 13.0 | 164 | 13.5 | 2 498 | 24.2 | 2 463 | 134 | 1 562 | NA | NA |
| Jones............................. | 1 810 | 70 510 | 1.11 | 1 025 | 15.1 | 752 | 11.0 | 12 983 | 22.8 | 13 258 | 1 388 | 7 738 | 2 303 | 3 666 |
| Kemper............................ | 708 | 8 941 | 0.61 | 93 | 9.2 | 103 | 10.2 | 1 990 | 24.4 | 1 928 | 147 | 1 097 | 51 | 547 |
| Lafayette......................... | 5 038 | 48 394 | 1.09 | 505 | 10.4 | 364 | 7.5 | 8 834 | 23.5 | 6 266 | 384 | 3 921 | NA | NA |
| Lamar............................. | 338 | 47 837 | 0.75 | 768 | 13.4 | 315 | 5.5 | 9 109 | 18.4 | 7 681 | 1 119 | 3 751 | 887 | 1 588 |
| Lauderdale........................ | 3 847 | 85 741 | 1.18 | 1 074 | 13.3 | 812 | 10.1 | 12 903 | 19.7 | 14 051 | 1 009 | 7 780 | 3 374 | 4 188 |
| Lawrence.......................... | 0 | 11 411 | 0.67 | 174 | 13.7 | 137 | 10.8 | 2 335 | 21.4 | 3 006 | 200 | 1 881 | NA | NA |
| Leake............................. | 1 845 | 22 042 | 0.80 | 337 | 14.3 | 289 | 12.3 | 4 611 | 24.4 | 4 121 | 532 | 2 392 | 59 | 247 |
| Lee............................... | 1 065 | 96 953 | 1.40 | 1 185 | 14.1 | 948 | 11.3 | 13 811 | 19.3 | 15 473 | 1 087 | 9 710 | NA | NA |
| Leflore........................... | 2 279 | 36 476 | 1.39 | 547 | 17.2 | 360 | 11.3 | 5 805 | 21.8 | 5 579 | 162 | 4 075 | 1 651 | 5 090 |
| Lincoln........................... | 714 | 33 844 | 0.93 | 478 | 13.7 | 377 | 10.8 | 5 701 | 19.4 | 6 861 | 650 | 4 148 | 608 | 1 737 |
| Lowndes .......................... | 1 318 | 61 450 | 1.08 | 804 | 13.5 | 539 | 9.0 | 11 537 | 22.6 | 10 491 | 1 023 | 5 866 | 1 898 | 3 163 |
| Madison........................... | 1 765 | 94 341 | 1.01 | 1 289 | 13.3 | 1 013 | 10.4 | 13 261 | 15.9 | 13 571 | 2 005 | 6 881 | 1 486 | 1 805 |
| Marion............................ | 693 | 25 854 | 0.89 | 393 | 14.7 | 350 | 13.1 | 4 976 | 22.1 | 5 376 | 705 | 3 210 | 760 | 2 795 |
| Marshall.......................... | 1 737 | 30 178 | 0.50 | 463 | 12.6 | 398 | 10.8 | 7 029 | 22.9 | 6 593 | 937 | 3 668 | NA | NA |
| Monroe............................ | 408 | 34 112 | 0.79 | 427 | 11.7 | 387 | 10.6 | 6 355 | 20.6 | 7 970 | 683 | 5 079 | NA | NA |
| Montgomery........................ | 99 | 10 010 | 0.73 | 137 | 12.6 | 135 | 12.4 | 1 972 | 21.9 | 2 512 | 45 | 1 741 | NA | NA |
| Neshoba........................... | 386 | 29 772 | 1.01 | 475 | 15.9 | 310 | 10.4 | 6 051 | 23.7 | 5 458 | 347 | 3 445 | NA | NA |
| Newton............................ | 600 | 18 935 | 0.69 | 308 | 14.3 | 290 | 13.5 | 4 029 | 22.4 | 4 522 | 409 | 2 601 | NA | NA |
| Noxubee........................... | 173 | 11 291 | 0.90 | 174 | 15.3 | 142 | 12.5 | 2 575 | 26.2 | 2 280 | 70 | 1 752 | NA | NA |
| Oktibbeha......................... | 4 367 | 47 940 | 1.05 | 540 | 11.3 | 328 | 6.9 | 7 226 | 18.6 | 5 898 | 645 | 3 635 | 1 393 | 2 911 |
| Panola............................ | 315 | 33 465 | 0.89 | 541 | 15.6 | 410 | 11.8 | 6 359 | 21.1 | 6 588 | 831 | 3 909 | 824 | 2 413 |
| Pearl River....................... | 1 124 | 48 833 | 0.66 | 691 | 12.4 | 578 | 10.4 | 10 938 | 23.6 | 11 653 | 1 994 | 5 506 | NA | NA |
| Perry............................. | 102 | 10 579 | 0.65 | 150 | 12.3 | 118 | 9.7 | 2 270 | 21.7 | 2 367 | 265 | 1 513 | NA | NA |
| Pike.............................. | 865 | 42 242 | 1.13 | 625 | 15.5 | 497 | 12.3 | 7 047 | 20.8 | 8 011 | 1 219 | 4 511 | 1 206 | 2 974 |
| Pontotoc.......................... | 236 | 27 871 | 0.85 | 433 | 14.5 | 229 | 7.7 | 5 739 | 22.1 | 5 680 | 582 | 3 524 | 94 | 313 |
| Prentiss.......................... | 864 | 22 719 | 0.73 | 324 | 12.8 | 221 | 8.7 | 4 452 | 21.8 | 5 418 | 147 | 3 695 | NA | NA |
| Quitman........................... | 164 | 7 434 | 0.65 | 122 | 15.0 | 110 | 13.5 | 1 532 | 22.1 | 1 703 | 103 | 1 223 | NA | NA |
| Rankin............................ | 5 629 | 132 188 | 0.88 | 1 914 | 13.3 | 983 | 6.8 | 20 274 | 16.9 | 22 600 | 3 726 | 10 390 | 2 235 | 1 653 |
| Scott............................. | 229 | 28 968 | 1.06 | 476 | 16.8 | 288 | 10.1 | 6 538 | 26.5 | 5 051 | 766 | 3 041 | 481 | 2 122 |
| Sharkey........................... | 108 | 4 849 | 1.10 | 76 | 15.5 | 53 | 10.8 | 887 | 21.2 | 1 014 | 39 | 740 | NA | NA |
| Simpson........................... | 642 | 24 607 | 0.72 | 383 | 14.0 | 283 | 10.4 | 5 101 | 22.0 | 5 104 | 670 | 2 914 | 479 | 1 735 |
| Smith............................. | 107 | 13 844 | 0.59 | 210 | 12.8 | 163 | 9.9 | 3 054 | 22.1 | 3 324 | 380 | 1 810 | NA | NA |
| Stone ............................ | 1 288 | 15 814 | 0.79 | 216 | 12.1 | 163 | 9.1 | 3 229 | 22.3 | 3 094 | 541 | 1 474 | 193 | 1 081 |

1. Per 1,000 estimated resident population.   2. Data for serious crimes have not been adjusted for underreporting; this may affect comparability between geographic areas and over time.   3. Per 100,000 population estimated by the FBI.

# Table B. States and Counties — Crime, Education, Money Income, and Poverty

| STATE County | Serious crimes known to police, 2011 (cont.)[1] Rate[2] Violent | Property | Education — School enrollment, Enrollment[3] Total | Percent private | Attainment[4] (percent) High school graduate or less | Bachelor's degree or more | Local government expenditures,[5] 2009-2010 Total current expenditures (mil dol) | Current expenditures per student (dollars) | Money income, 2007-2011 Per capita income[6] (dollars) | Households Median income Dollars | Percent change, 2000 to 2007-2011 (constant 2011 dollars) | Percent with income of $200,000 or more | Income and poverty, 2011 Median household income (dollars) | Percent below poverty level All persons | Children under 18 years | Children 5 to 17 years in families |
|---|---|---|---|---|---|---|---|---|---|---|---|---|---|---|---|---|
| | 46 | 47 | 48 | 49 | 50 | 51 | 52 | 53 | 54 | 55 | 56 | 57 | 58 | 59 | 60 | 61 |
| MISSISSIPPI | 270 | 3 026 | 806 844 | 13.1 | 50.3 | 19.7 | 3 991.7 | 8 105 | 20 521 | 38 718 | -8.5 | 2.0 | 36 963 | 22.8 | 32.4 | 30.4 |
| Adams | 407 | 4 914 | 8 075 | 16.0 | 54.8 | 18.2 | 38.7 | 9 825 | 17 249 | 26 784 | -21.4 | 1.4 | 26 722 | 34.3 | 50.7 | 46.2 |
| Alcorn | NA | NA | 8 269 | 7.3 | 58.9 | 15.3 | 44.6 | 7 851 | 17 920 | 32 221 | -17.8 | 0.8 | 31 496 | 20.5 | 28.9 | 27.0 |
| Amite | NA | NA | 2 608 | 39.9 | 62.2 | 9.4 | 12.1 | 10 040 | 17 681 | 31 402 | -10.7 | 1.9 | 32 824 | 20.8 | 32.9 | 32.2 |
| Attala | NA | NA | 5 020 | 13.5 | 58.0 | 16.2 | 26.2 | 7 546 | 17 701 | 29 805 | -11.0 | 1.3 | 30 108 | 26.4 | 36.7 | 33.9 |
| Benton | NA | NA | 2 028 | 11.7 | 64.2 | 10.5 | 10.5 | 8 209 | 16 724 | 28 666 | -12.1 | 1.8 | 27 834 | 26.8 | 39.6 | 36.6 |
| Bolivar | 196 | 3 324 | 10 790 | 7.4 | 54.6 | 19.5 | 61.2 | 9 333 | 16 114 | 27 173 | -14.1 | 1.6 | 28 802 | 33.4 | 49.5 | 49.3 |
| Calhoun | NA | NA | 3 410 | 7.5 | 66.4 | 9.9 | 19.2 | 7 383 | 16 034 | 29 893 | -18.3 | 0.7 | 32 453 | 22.4 | 31.1 | 29.2 |
| Carroll | NA | NA | 2 113 | 34.7 | 57.4 | 14.0 | 8.2 | 8 450 | 16 412 | 28 793 | -26.2 | 0.0 | 34 876 | 20.1 | 28.4 | 26.7 |
| Chickasaw | NA | NA | 4 727 | 5.8 | 64.5 | 10.9 | 25.5 | 7 903 | 15 978 | 30 395 | -14.6 | 0.8 | 30 524 | 21.4 | 31.0 | 29.1 |
| Choctaw | 128 | 1 096 | 1 928 | 7.0 | 58.0 | 11.3 | 15.3 | 9 578 | 16 584 | 29 832 | -18.2 | 0.2 | 31 177 | 26.6 | 38.5 | 34.7 |
| Claiborne | 342 | 1 037 | 3 255 | 10.2 | 51.9 | 17.5 | 16.1 | 9 371 | 12 238 | 21 924 | -28.2 | 0.0 | 22 802 | 38.6 | 52.8 | 49.8 |
| Clarke | NA | NA | 4 291 | 11.4 | 61.9 | 9.5 | 24.8 | 8 392 | 18 050 | 31 059 | -13.6 | 0.4 | 32 875 | 23.9 | 35.4 | 31.7 |
| Clay | 241 | 1 772 | 5 835 | 11.1 | 53.5 | 16.5 | 30.3 | 8 569 | 18 057 | 32 919 | -10.9 | 1.4 | 30 243 | 27.0 | 41.6 | 38.1 |
| Coahoma | NA | NA | 8 551 | 9.2 | 53.5 | 16.5 | 46.6 | 8 740 | 16 116 | 26 050 | -13.6 | 1.6 | 27 349 | 37.3 | 51.7 | 51.0 |
| Copiah | NA | NA | 8 273 | 15.7 | 52.7 | 14.4 | 32.9 | 7 458 | 17 823 | 38 154 | 7.2 | 1.0 | 31 971 | 24.8 | 36.0 | 34.8 |
| Covington | 193 | 2 884 | 5 379 | 12.2 | 56.3 | 15.6 | 26.3 | 8 211 | 16 917 | 31 127 | -13.6 | 0.3 | 31 655 | 26.5 | 35.4 | 34.1 |
| DeSoto | 168 | 2 139 | 44 840 | 14.4 | 43.4 | 21.3 | 209.4 | 6 707 | 25 065 | 59 734 | -8.2 | 2.0 | 54 495 | 10.4 | 15.7 | 14.4 |
| Forrest | 128 | 2 692 | 23 795 | 16.1 | 44.3 | 26.2 | 104.7 | 9 131 | 20 238 | 35 805 | -3.3 | 1.8 | 33 203 | 27.9 | 34.4 | 33.0 |
| Franklin | 135 | 663 | 2 032 | 11.3 | 59.4 | 10.1 | 14.3 | 9 406 | 22 138 | 33 250 | -1.0 | 1.5 | 33 979 | 22.6 | 33.0 | 31.3 |
| George | 53 | 494 | 5 396 | 7.7 | 60.7 | 10.6 | 27.9 | 6 590 | 20 529 | 45 365 | -3.3 | 1.3 | 42 596 | 18.2 | 25.6 | 24.6 |
| Greene | 71 | 250 | 3 149 | 10.6 | 66.8 | 8.6 | 16.2 | 7 950 | 14 759 | 40 404 | 5.6 | 1.0 | 37 362 | 22.5 | 24.7 | 22.4 |
| Grenada | NA | NA | 5 810 | 9.5 | 54.4 | 17.2 | 30.9 | 6 994 | 20 116 | 33 123 | -10.4 | 1.2 | 32 543 | 21.0 | 31.3 | 29.2 |
| Hancock | NA | NA | 10 823 | 11.6 | 45.8 | 23.0 | 56.0 | 9 164 | 22 596 | 42 591 | -10.4 | 1.7 | 39 996 | 24.5 | 31.5 | 28.2 |
| Harrison | 257 | 4 400 | 46 227 | 15.0 | 44.2 | 20.5 | 252.0 | 8 898 | 23 111 | 44 550 | -7.4 | 2.1 | 39 046 | 20.5 | 31.1 | 27.7 |
| Hinds | 706 | 5 815 | 77 283 | 17.3 | 41.1 | 27.7 | 339.2 | 8 036 | 20 878 | 39 290 | -14.4 | 2.6 | 35 014 | 26.2 | 36.7 | 34.4 |
| Holmes | NA | NA | 6 171 | 7.7 | 63.7 | 11.8 | 33.1 | 8 706 | 11 966 | 22 259 | -4.3 | 0.2 | 22 623 | 41.0 | 52.7 | 50.0 |
| Humphreys | NA | NA | 2 768 | 10.3 | 64.8 | 10.9 | 14.7 | 8 235 | 13 448 | 25 730 | -7.3 | 1.2 | 23 169 | 37.6 | 53.3 | 53.7 |
| Issaquena | NA | NA | 352 | 17.9 | 79.3 | 4.2 | NA | NA | 10 458 | 22 396 | -16.8 | 0.8 | 27 683 | 40.1 | 53.5 | 51.1 |
| Itawamba | 111 | 1 456 | 5 669 | 5.0 | 59.3 | 11.3 | 26.9 | 7 508 | 18 307 | 37 769 | -10.2 | 0.3 | 37 848 | 17.7 | 26.4 | 24.0 |
| Jackson | 338 | 3 584 | 36 001 | 10.7 | 47.7 | 18.6 | 221.2 | 9 020 | 23 547 | 49 620 | -6.1 | 2.4 | 47 672 | 17.3 | 24.6 | 22.9 |
| Jasper | NA | NA | 4 444 | 13.5 | 60.4 | 11.7 | 22.9 | 8 747 | 18 896 | 28 914 | -12.4 | 1.7 | 30 574 | 24.7 | 33.6 | 31.2 |
| Jefferson | 293 | 701 | 2 001 | 3.4 | 66.1 | 19.5 | 12.3 | 8 379 | 12 857 | 20 375 | -18.2 | 1.1 | 23 420 | 37.5 | 45.9 | 42.9 |
| Jefferson Davis | NA | NA | 2 907 | 7.4 | 58.8 | 11.6 | 14.7 | 8 596 | 15 423 | 25 842 | -12.3 | 0.9 | 27 808 | 29.8 | 42.5 | 40.2 |
| Jones | 255 | 3 411 | 16 342 | 10.3 | 51.2 | 16.1 | 87.6 | 7 661 | 19 494 | 37 643 | -3.1 | 2.2 | 37 030 | 20.1 | 31.8 | 30.2 |
| Kemper | 21 | 525 | 2 629 | 10.6 | 64.4 | 10.9 | 9.9 | 8 273 | 14 432 | 25 584 | -21.0 | 1.2 | 27 601 | 28.9 | 38.7 | 35.1 |
| Lafayette | NA | NA | 19 694 | 5.8 | 33.5 | 39.7 | 52.3 | 8 779 | 21 854 | 41 166 | 6.9 | 4.3 | 39 853 | 23.1 | 23.4 | 21.2 |
| Lamar | 70 | 1 518 | 15 437 | 12.2 | 35.1 | 32.5 | 73.1 | 7 812 | 27 399 | 50 075 | -1.4 | 3.9 | 49 250 | 17.0 | 22.0 | 21.6 |
| Lauderdale | 336 | 3 852 | 21 447 | 10.8 | 47.8 | 17.9 | 108.3 | 8 225 | 20 688 | 35 420 | -14.7 | 2.5 | 36 420 | 23.0 | 34.0 | 33.8 |
| Lawrence | NA | NA | 3 048 | 9.0 | 55.7 | 11.8 | 18.9 | 8 696 | 19 896 | 37 000 | -3.8 | 1.7 | 35 396 | 19.9 | 28.3 | 27.3 |
| Leake | 46 | 201 | 6 537 | 11.5 | 60.2 | 10.3 | 24.2 | 7 224 | 15 559 | 32 537 | -10.9 | 0.7 | 33 007 | 27.1 | 43.1 | 41.3 |
| Lee | NA | NA | 20 836 | 9.3 | 46.1 | 20.9 | 135.1 | 8 156 | 22 358 | 41 150 | -15.7 | 3.0 | 40 983 | 16.6 | 25.4 | 22.3 |
| Leflore | 524 | 4 565 | 10 629 | 10.9 | 60.9 | 16.1 | 49.4 | 8 646 | 12 754 | 22 353 | -23.1 | 1.0 | 24 839 | 43.2 | 62.2 | 63.9 |
| Lincoln | 151 | 1 586 | 8 861 | 14.6 | 52.2 | 17.5 | 43.2 | 6 987 | 21 045 | 38 438 | 4.4 | 1.9 | 36 112 | 24.1 | 35.7 | 35.7 |
| Lowndes | 223 | 2 940 | 16 518 | 13.0 | 49.3 | 19.8 | 87.0 | 8 733 | 21 627 | 37 626 | -13.2 | 1.9 | 38 605 | 24.4 | 33.7 | 30.8 |
| Madison | 113 | 1 692 | 27 264 | 22.9 | 29.5 | 44.6 | 113.7 | 7 556 | 32 223 | 59 730 | -5.8 | 7.7 | 55 692 | 14.2 | 19.4 | 17.6 |
| Marion | 184 | 2 611 | 6 591 | 11.7 | 62.3 | 13.4 | 36.5 | 8 396 | 18 077 | 32 117 | -3.1 | 1.5 | 31 368 | 30.8 | 42.3 | 40.8 |
| Marshall | NA | NA | 8 394 | 22.6 | 65.8 | 10.6 | 36.7 | 7 511 | 17 666 | 33 279 | -14.3 | 2.0 | 32 943 | 23.8 | 35.9 | 34.0 |
| Monroe | NA | NA | 8 387 | 6.5 | 60.5 | 13.0 | 47.8 | 8 501 | 18 573 | 35 102 | -14.2 | 0.8 | 34 735 | 19.3 | 29.7 | 27.6 |
| Montgomery | NA | NA | 2 767 | 16.1 | 57.7 | 15.6 | 15.7 | 9 963 | 16 128 | 33 087 | -3.0 | 0.6 | 31 249 | 27.8 | 42.7 | 39.4 |
| Neshoba | NA | NA | 8 372 | 9.8 | 56.4 | 11.3 | 31.1 | 7 070 | 17 718 | 36 128 | -5.4 | 1.3 | 34 658 | 23.7 | 32.8 | 30.4 |
| Newton | NA | NA | 6 007 | 9.5 | 50.8 | 11.3 | 30.7 | 7 881 | 17 576 | 37 386 | -3.6 | 0.7 | 34 269 | 22.0 | 31.4 | 30.5 |
| Noxubee | NA | NA | 3 542 | 14.0 | 65.2 | 12.1 | 17.8 | 9 245 | 12 508 | 21 798 | -27.7 | 0.0 | 21 929 | 39.0 | 48.2 | 44.2 |
| Oktibbeha | 180 | 2 731 | 21 710 | 7.0 | 33.5 | 41.7 | 46.4 | 9 223 | 19 330 | 29 013 | -13.7 | 2.6 | 31 937 | 33.5 | 31.7 | 30.1 |
| Panola | 228 | 2 185 | 8 502 | 9.7 | 59.2 | 14.0 | 51.6 | 8 143 | 16 449 | 34 592 | -4.3 | 0.5 | 32 764 | 24.3 | 36.1 | 33.5 |
| Pearl River | NA | NA | 13 438 | 14.0 | 53.2 | 14.8 | 72.4 | 8 110 | 20 347 | 42 971 | 3.0 | 1.6 | 38 276 | 24.4 | 34.3 | 34.2 |
| Perry | NA | NA | 2 800 | 14.8 | 58.9 | 9.0 | 16.4 | 8 228 | 17 857 | 39 070 | 6.4 | 0.5 | 34 766 | 21.3 | 31.3 | 29.2 |
| Pike | 261 | 2 712 | 11 115 | 14.4 | 54.0 | 16.2 | 57.9 | 8 036 | 18 454 | 32 751 | -1.2 | 1.6 | 31 142 | 27.4 | 41.6 | 39.9 |
| Pontotoc | 73 | 239 | 7 615 | 4.3 | 61.2 | 10.6 | 42.0 | 7 526 | 17 759 | 38 574 | -10.9 | 0.8 | 38 348 | 16.6 | 25.1 | 23.2 |
| Prentiss | NA | NA | 6 283 | 3.8 | 61.3 | 11.0 | 29.2 | 8 197 | 17 115 | 32 518 | -15.3 | 0.4 | 32 927 | 24.2 | 33.8 | 29.5 |
| Quitman | NA | NA | 2 127 | 14.1 | 61.0 | 11.0 | 12.4 | 9 396 | 13 293 | 24 545 | -11.9 | 0.1 | 24 786 | 37.5 | 50.4 | 48.0 |
| Rankin | 109 | 1 543 | 36 138 | 19.5 | 39.3 | 28.1 | 168.0 | 7 472 | 27 183 | 56 159 | -7.5 | 2.9 | 59 890 | 10.8 | 16.8 | 15.7 |
| Scott | 247 | 1 875 | 6 474 | 10.5 | 66.4 | 9.6 | 39.1 | 7 420 | 17 435 | 36 999 | 2.7 | 2.6 | 32 004 | 25.1 | 34.8 | 32.9 |
| Sharkey | NA | NA | 1 306 | 23.0 | 59.2 | 19.2 | 10.7 | 10 037 | 14 750 | 29 451 | -2.1 | 0.2 | 26 439 | 35.0 | 51.9 | 49.1 |
| Simpson | 246 | 1 489 | 6 666 | 14.4 | 58.8 | 13.4 | 32.7 | 7 758 | 18 305 | 36 606 | -4.3 | 1.1 | 32 348 | 24.2 | 35.0 | 34.2 |
| Smith | NA | NA | 4 093 | 15.5 | 62.6 | 13.3 | 22.3 | 7 356 | 19 545 | 36 791 | -11.6 | 2.0 | 36 311 | 21.2 | 28.6 | 27.2 |
| Stone | 67 | 1 014 | 4 169 | 14.1 | 50.7 | 13.1 | 23.4 | 8 093 | 23 209 | 43 731 | 6.2 | 3.0 | 39 113 | 19.3 | 28.7 | 27.0 |

1. Data for serious crimes have not been adjusted for underreporting; this may affect comparability between geographic areas and over time.   2. Per 100,000 population estimated by the FBI.   3. All persons 3 years old and over enrolled in nursery school through college.   4. Persons 25 years old and over.   5. Elementary and secondary education expenditures.   6. Based on population estimated by the American Community Survey, 2007-2011.

# Table B. States and Counties — **Personal Income**

| STATE County | Personal income, 2011 Total (mil dol) | Percent change, 2010–2011 | Per capita[1] Dollars | Per capita[1] Rank | Wages and salaries[2] (mil dol) | Proprietors' income (mil dol) | Dividends, interest, and rent (mil dol) | Transfer payments (mil dol) Total | Government payments to individuals Total | Social Security | Medical payments | Income mainte-nance | Unemploy-ment insurance |
|---|---|---|---|---|---|---|---|---|---|---|---|---|---|
| | 62 | 63 | 64 | 65 | 66 | 67 | 68 | 69 | 70 | 71 | 72 | 73 | 74 |
| MISSISSIPPI | 95 313 | 4.1 | 32 000 | X | 54 169 | 8 081 | 11 882 | 24 768 | 24 047 | 7 419 | 10 886 | 3 673 | 508 |
| Adams | 1 049 | 5.2 | 32 709 | 1 755 | 502 | 122 | 168 | 307 | 300 | 95 | 135 | 53 | 5 |
| Alcorn | 1 032 | 4.0 | 27 844 | 2 631 | 583 | 56 | 134 | 343 | 334 | 122 | 158 | 36 | 7 |
| Amite | 376 | 4.5 | 28 802 | 2 487 | 80 | 44 | 36 | 128 | 121 | 40 | 55 | 19 | 2 |
| Attala | 515 | 4.0 | 26 452 | 2 830 | 205 | 56 | 59 | 178 | 172 | 52 | 83 | 27 | 3 |
| Benton | 193 | 5.0 | 22 063 | 3 084 | 60 | 9 | 20 | 79 | 77 | 24 | 37 | 12 | 2 |
| Bolivar | 1 084 | 4.5 | 32 106 | 1 862 | 544 | 108 | 125 | 352 | 344 | 86 | 157 | 79 | 6 |
| Calhoun | 398 | 3.9 | 26 712 | 2 802 | 139 | 32 | 45 | 146 | 142 | 46 | 70 | 19 | 2 |
| Carroll | 359 | 7.1 | 34 634 | 1 428 | 54 | 15 | 33 | 92 | 90 | 33 | 38 | 13 | 2 |
| Chickasaw | 492 | 3.5 | 28 711 | 2 500 | 251 | 39 | 64 | 168 | 164 | 51 | 81 | 24 | 4 |
| Choctaw | 217 | 2.8 | 25 845 | 2 894 | 94 | 15 | 26 | 73 | 71 | 22 | 34 | 11 | 1 |
| Claiborne | 267 | 3.6 | 27 804 | 2 640 | 270 | 4 | 21 | 114 | 112 | 23 | 46 | 25 | 2 |
| Clarke | 445 | 4.3 | 26 603 | 2 811 | 134 | 28 | 48 | 161 | 156 | 53 | 74 | 20 | 3 |
| Clay | 602 | 5.1 | 29 915 | 2 393 | 232 | 98 | 85 | 182 | 177 | 58 | 75 | 32 | 5 |
| Coahoma | 845 | 5.3 | 32 607 | 1 778 | 383 | 81 | 110 | 311 | 305 | 60 | 149 | 68 | 6 |
| Copiah | 718 | 1.4 | 24 552 | 3 002 | 342 | 44 | 77 | 284 | 278 | 76 | 124 | 47 | 5 |
| Covington | 553 | 1.9 | 28 192 | 2 592 | 217 | 74 | 58 | 175 | 169 | 52 | 80 | 26 | 3 |
| DeSoto | 5 535 | 7.0 | 33 737 | 1 555 | 2 078 | 501 | 458 | 837 | 800 | 347 | 287 | 88 | 23 |
| Forrest | 2 290 | 2.7 | 30 198 | 2 254 | 1 924 | 346 | 361 | 666 | 648 | 173 | 303 | 90 | 13 |
| Franklin | 213 | 3.7 | 26 564 | 2 815 | 83 | 11 | 23 | 75 | 73 | 24 | 34 | 11 | 1 |
| George | 583 | 1.0 | 25 477 | 2 932 | 198 | 28 | 53 | 180 | 175 | 58 | 88 | 19 | 4 |
| Greene | 329 | 1.5 | 22 950 | 3 060 | 93 | 27 | 26 | 110 | 107 | 31 | 56 | 13 | 2 |
| Grenada | 656 | 4.6 | 30 231 | 2 248 | 423 | 43 | 79 | 232 | 227 | 69 | 115 | 32 | 4 |
| Hancock | 1 496 | -3.2 | 33 515 | 1 599 | 965 | 138 | 252 | 343 | 328 | 113 | 156 | 35 | 7 |
| Harrison | 6 854 | 2.9 | 35 878 | 1 231 | 5 097 | 450 | 1 012 | 1 493 | 1 428 | 421 | 686 | 180 | 31 |
| Hinds | 8 804 | 3.5 | 35 473 | 1 299 | 7 358 | 1 229 | 1 156 | 2 002 | 1 944 | 535 | 794 | 394 | 41 |
| Holmes | 523 | 5.2 | 27 815 | 2 638 | 163 | 38 | 43 | 261 | 257 | 46 | 118 | 60 | 5 |
| Humphreys | 268 | 1.3 | 28 808 | 2 486 | 106 | 38 | 29 | 110 | 108 | 22 | 55 | 27 | 2 |
| Issaquena | 60 | 17.5 | 43 298 | 485 | 10 | 28 | 4 | 10 | 10 | 2 | 5 | 3 | 0 |
| Itawamba | 698 | 5.1 | 29 915 | 2 305 | 242 | 36 | 71 | 217 | 212 | 76 | 73 | 18 | 5 |
| Jackson | 5 001 | 2.4 | 35 748 | 1 256 | 3 231 | 209 | 732 | 1 056 | 1 016 | 364 | 444 | 118 | 25 |
| Jasper | 482 | 0.8 | 28 754 | 2 493 | 207 | 36 | 45 | 162 | 159 | 50 | 77 | 23 | 3 |
| Jefferson | 193 | 2.2 | 25 373 | 2 939 | 57 | 3 | 15 | 85 | 84 | 19 | 39 | 20 | 2 |
| Jefferson Davis | 328 | 2.3 | 27 030 | 2 758 | 90 | 21 | 31 | 120 | 117 | 34 | 53 | 23 | 2 |
| Jones | 2 276 | 4.3 | 33 432 | 1 620 | 1 455 | 190 | 274 | 675 | 660 | 188 | 353 | 72 | 9 |
| Kemper | 278 | 10.5 | 27 363 | 2 705 | 107 | 12 | 27 | 108 | 105 | 23 | 39 | 13 | 2 |
| Lafayette | 1 568 | 5.3 | 32 345 | 1 813 | 941 | 179 | 242 | 314 | 304 | 90 | 144 | 26 | 7 |
| Lamar | 1 974 | 6.6 | 34 386 | 1 452 | 695 | 66 | 257 | 307 | 295 | 116 | 119 | 36 | 8 |
| Lauderdale | 2 622 | 4.1 | 32 582 | 1 784 | 1 747 | 168 | 379 | 682 | 664 | 196 | 308 | 99 | 14 |
| Lawrence | 393 | 2.0 | 30 941 | 2 113 | 145 | 28 | 29 | 135 | 132 | 44 | 63 | 17 | 2 |
| Leake | 571 | -2.3 | 24 224 | 3 017 | 217 | 49 | 50 | 200 | 193 | 56 | 96 | 29 | 4 |
| Lee | 2 898 | 5.1 | 34 432 | 1 447 | 2 421 | 232 | 394 | 640 | 621 | 230 | 272 | 79 | 16 |
| Leflore | 984 | 3.8 | 30 888 | 2 126 | 647 | 118 | 153 | 345 | 338 | 71 | 168 | 73 | 7 |
| Lincoln | 960 | 3.3 | 27 516 | 2 683 | 515 | 79 | 114 | 298 | 291 | 99 | 135 | 39 | 5 |
| Lowndes | 2 023 | 6.4 | 33 905 | 1 532 | 1 470 | 155 | 254 | 474 | 462 | 149 | 196 | 73 | 11 |
| Madison | 4 870 | 7.9 | 50 233 | 201 | 2 459 | 532 | 796 | 584 | 561 | 205 | 226 | 90 | 13 |
| Marion | 761 | 4.2 | 28 384 | 2 559 | 372 | 59 | 90 | 260 | 252 | 75 | 121 | 41 | 4 |
| Marshall | 965 | 3.4 | 26 236 | 2 860 | 280 | 39 | 73 | 295 | 287 | 91 | 121 | 52 | 7 |
| Monroe | 1 044 | 4.5 | 28 516 | 2 537 | 473 | 77 | 123 | 327 | 319 | 112 | 142 | 41 | 7 |
| Montgomery | 309 | 4.3 | 28 464 | 2 546 | 107 | 26 | 37 | 118 | 115 | 33 | 60 | 17 | 2 |
| Neshoba | 1 007 | 0.6 | 33 776 | 1 553 | 577 | 171 | 101 | 251 | 243 | 75 | 116 | 36 | 4 |
| Newton | 598 | 1.9 | 27 802 | 2 641 | 252 | 35 | 55 | 223 | 218 | 61 | 107 | 26 | 3 |
| Noxubee | 294 | 3.3 | 25 904 | 2 891 | 102 | 48 | 29 | 114 | 112 | 27 | 51 | 28 | 2 |
| Oktibbeha | 1 353 | 4.5 | 28 340 | 2 568 | 910 | 89 | 184 | 298 | 288 | 82 | 114 | 43 | 8 |
| Panola | 957 | 4.2 | 27 658 | 2 660 | 496 | 93 | 89 | 297 | 289 | 89 | 127 | 57 | 7 |
| Pearl River | 1 585 | 4.0 | 28 453 | 2 549 | 460 | 93 | 184 | 501 | 488 | 168 | 211 | 58 | 8 |
| Perry | 280 | 2.1 | 22 981 | 3 059 | 124 | 5 | 27 | 105 | 102 | 33 | 46 | 16 | 2 |
| Pike | 1 106 | 2.6 | 27 361 | 2 707 | 606 | 58 | 132 | 392 | 382 | 105 | 174 | 69 | 7 |
| Pontotoc | 801 | 4.9 | 26 798 | 2 788 | 461 | 53 | 83 | 215 | 208 | 80 | 90 | 24 | 5 |
| Prentiss | 630 | 3.8 | 24 871 | 2 975 | 295 | 17 | 80 | 228 | 222 | 72 | 103 | 23 | 5 |
| Quitman | 232 | 3.8 | 28 582 | 2 527 | 54 | 35 | 19 | 95 | 93 | 20 | 48 | 21 | 2 |
| Rankin | 5 219 | 4.8 | 36 317 | 1 164 | 2 838 | 363 | 574 | 955 | 923 | 345 | 429 | 85 | 18 |
| Scott | 739 | 1.2 | 26 026 | 2 878 | 497 | 46 | 63 | 244 | 238 | 69 | 119 | 38 | 4 |
| Sharkey | 153 | 4.3 | 31 188 | 2 066 | 51 | 12 | 20 | 63 | 61 | 13 | 31 | 15 | 1 |
| Simpson | 866 | 0.7 | 31 689 | 1 957 | 292 | 63 | 70 | 277 | 271 | 71 | 153 | 34 | 4 |
| Smith | 414 | -2.0 | 25 192 | 2 950 | 140 | 39 | 39 | 132 | 128 | 46 | 55 | 19 | 2 |
| Stone | 503 | 2.3 | 28 199 | 2 589 | 184 | 15 | 44 | 169 | 164 | 43 | 68 | 17 | 3 |

1. Based on the resident population estimated as of July 1 of the year shown.   2. Includes supplements to wages and salaries.

| STATE County | Earnings, 2011 | | | | | | | | | Social Security beneficiaries, December 2011 | | | Housing units, 2010 | |
|---|---|---|---|---|---|---|---|---|---|---|---|---|---|---|
| | | | | Percent by selected industries | | | | | | | | | | |
| | | | Goods-related[1] | | Service-related and health | | | | | | | Supplemental Security Income recipients, December 2011 | | |
| | Total (mil dol) | Farm | Total | Manufacturing | Information and professional and technical services | Retail trade | Finance, insurance, and real estate | Health care and social services | Government | Number | Rate[2] | | Total | Percent change, 2000–2010 |
| | 75 | 76 | 77 | 78 | 79 | 80 | 81 | 82 | 83 | 84 | 85 | 86 | 87 | 88 |
| MISSISSIPPI | 62 249 | 1.8 | 20.6 | 12.6 | 5.6 | 7.4 | 4.9 | 11.1 | 25.0 | 609 651 | 205 | 126 223 | 1 274 719 | 9.7 |
| Adams | 624 | -0.1 | 21.7 | 4.4 | 4.9 | 10.0 | 4.5 | D | 16.7 | 7 775 | 242 | 1 930 | 14 656 | -3.4 |
| Alcorn | 639 | 0.2 | 25.3 | 21.0 | D | 10.7 | 3.6 | 9.8 | 25.9 | 10 085 | 272 | 1 798 | 17 077 | 8.0 |
| Amite | 124 | 3.3 | D | 10.3 | 3.2 | 9.2 | 3.5 | D | 16.8 | 3 365 | 258 | 769 | 6 635 | 2.9 |
| Attala | 260 | 1.5 | 25.9 | 10.5 | 3.2 | 11.6 | 3.8 | D | 23.2 | 4 560 | 234 | 1 025 | 9 126 | 5.6 |
| Benton | 69 | 1.2 | 15.8 | 10.9 | D | 6.7 | D | 7.4 | 23.2 | 2 120 | 243 | 514 | 4 186 | 21.1 |
| Bolivar | 652 | 11.9 | 17.1 | 13.9 | D | 10.9 | 2.9 | 14.2 | 21.1 | 7 700 | 228 | 3 169 | 14 070 | -5.8 |
| Calhoun | 171 | 8.1 | 23.0 | 21.5 | 2.5 | 9.9 | 3.8 | D | 23.3 | 4 030 | 270 | 835 | 6 913 | 0.2 |
| Carroll | 68 | 6.6 | D | D | D | 4.7 | D | D | 25.9 | 2 780 | 268 | 572 | 5 052 | 3.4 |
| Chickasaw | 290 | 3.0 | 48.8 | 46.3 | 1.6 | 7.1 | 2.2 | D | 15.8 | 4 430 | 259 | 889 | 7 514 | -5.9 |
| Choctaw | 110 | 0.0 | D | 8.3 | D | 4.9 | D | D | 21.3 | 1 985 | 236 | 421 | 4 150 | -2.3 |
| Claiborne | 274 | 0.2 | D | 2.0 | 1.6 | 2.2 | D | D | 28.3 | 2 015 | 210 | 747 | 4 223 | -0.7 |
| Clarke | 162 | 1.3 | 23.8 | 13.0 | 5.7 | 7.3 | D | 12.2 | 22.6 | 4 510 | 269 | 837 | 7 876 | -2.7 |
| Clay | 331 | 17.2 | D | 11.6 | 4.3 | 9.4 | 4.1 | D | 14.5 | 4 745 | 232 | 1 144 | 9 180 | 4.2 |
| Coahoma | 464 | 12.3 | 9.7 | 7.3 | 5.2 | 6.8 | 5.6 | D | 22.1 | 5 605 | 216 | 2 283 | 10 792 | -6.1 |
| Copiah | 385 | 1.4 | 37.5 | 31.9 | D | 7.8 | 2.4 | D | 21.1 | 6 515 | 223 | 1 585 | 12 184 | 9.8 |
| Covington | 291 | 7.0 | 30.7 | 16.3 | D | 6.3 | 2.4 | D | 21.6 | 4 540 | 231 | 1 053 | 8 496 | 5.1 |
| DeSoto | 2 579 | 0.7 | D | 9.1 | 3.4 | 10.4 | 4.2 | 12.1 | 13.6 | 25 210 | 154 | 2 533 | 61 634 | 51.1 |
| Forrest | 2 270 | 0.2 | 11.8 | 5.9 | 4.9 | 7.8 | 4.2 | 17.5 | 31.8 | 14 065 | 185 | 2 922 | 32 289 | 7.9 |
| Franklin | 94 | 2.0 | D | 4.1 | 10.6 | 5.2 | D | D | 37.2 | 2 005 | 250 | 398 | 4 154 | 0.8 |
| George | 226 | 0.6 | D | 8.3 | 4.5 | 12.5 | 3.7 | 5.7 | 32.9 | 4 695 | 205 | 685 | 9 330 | 24.2 |
| Greene | 119 | 3.3 | D | D | D | 6.6 | D | 4.6 | 42.2 | 2 725 | 190 | 464 | 5 123 | 3.6 |
| Grenada | 466 | 1.9 | 29.4 | 27.4 | D | 10.0 | 3.9 | D | 22.5 | 5 725 | 264 | 1 368 | 10 155 | 1.8 |
| Hancock | 1 104 | -0.1 | 16.1 | 7.8 | 11.5 | 4.4 | 2.3 | D | 38.4 | 8 805 | 197 | 1 210 | 21 840 | 3.6 |
| Harrison | 5 547 | 0.0 | D | 5.4 | 5.3 | 6.8 | 3.8 | 7.6 | 38.5 | 34 795 | 182 | 5 628 | 85 181 | 7.0 |
| Hinds | 8 587 | 0.0 | 9.5 | 2.7 | 9.3 | 5.1 | 8.1 | 15.2 | 30.8 | 42 780 | 172 | 10 746 | 103 421 | 3.1 |
| Holmes | 201 | 12.4 | D | 11.1 | D | 6.9 | 5.4 | D | 32.7 | 4 610 | 245 | 2 102 | 8 415 | -0.3 |
| Humphreys | 143 | 16.9 | D | D | D | 5.3 | 6.7 | D | 16.0 | 2 120 | 228 | 1 071 | 3 855 | -6.8 |
| Issaquena | 38 | 71.5 | D | 0.2 | D | D | D | D | 10.7 | 195 | 140 | 64 | 560 | -36.1 |
| Itawamba | 278 | 0.8 | D | 23.9 | 1.4 | 6.9 | 2.4 | D | 24.2 | 6 280 | 269 | 706 | 10 126 | 3.3 |
| Jackson | 3 440 | 0.0 | 47.3 | 37.5 | 5.5 | 4.7 | 2.5 | 6.3 | 20.6 | 27 590 | 197 | 3 240 | 60 067 | 16.2 |
| Jasper | 243 | 3.0 | 40.1 | 27.8 | 6.7 | 5.5 | 3.0 | D | 19.8 | 4 280 | 255 | 950 | 8 212 | 7.1 |
| Jefferson | 60 | 1.3 | D | D | D | D | D | 13.2 | 47.6 | 1 830 | 241 | 768 | 3 673 | -3.8 |
| Jefferson Davis | 111 | 2.9 | D | 1.1 | 3.9 | 7.6 | D | D | 28.3 | 2 990 | 247 | 689 | 5 876 | -0.3 |
| Jones | 1 645 | 1.0 | 40.7 | 18.5 | 3.1 | 6.1 | 3.3 | 5.0 | 21.5 | 15 470 | 227 | 2 852 | 28 424 | 5.6 |
| Kemper | 120 | 0.3 | D | 12.8 | D | 4.3 | D | D | 26.0 | 2 145 | 211 | 589 | 4 722 | 4.2 |
| Lafayette | 1 120 | 0.7 | D | 4.5 | 9.9 | 6.8 | 4.4 | 14.3 | 38.5 | 7 000 | 144 | 1 017 | 22 729 | 37.0 |
| Lamar | 762 | 0.9 | 11.7 | 3.8 | D | 15.0 | 6.7 | 21.0 | 14.8 | 8 965 | 156 | 1 138 | 24 070 | 56.0 |
| Lauderdale | 1 915 | 0.0 | D | 8.2 | 4.5 | 8.8 | 4.8 | 20.4 | 23.8 | 16 045 | 199 | 3 389 | 34 698 | 3.8 |
| Lawrence | 173 | 4.8 | 43.5 | 35.0 | D | 5.9 | D | 4.7 | 20.2 | 3 510 | 277 | 590 | 6 019 | 5.8 |
| Leake | 265 | 7.9 | D | D | D | 9.2 | 4.0 | D | 20.3 | 4 915 | 209 | 1 037 | 9 415 | 9.6 |
| Lee | 2 652 | 0.2 | 23.4 | 19.7 | 6.4 | 8.7 | 5.4 | 20.0 | 11.5 | 18 240 | 217 | 2 866 | 35 872 | 12.5 |
| Leflore | 765 | 7.6 | 16.5 | 9.6 | 5.4 | 6.4 | 3.2 | 9.2 | 29.6 | 6 550 | 206 | 2 739 | 13 199 | -6.4 |
| Lincoln | 594 | 1.0 | 21.5 | 7.9 | D | 10.3 | 4.0 | 14.3 | 14.4 | 7 975 | 229 | 1 543 | 15 255 | 8.6 |
| Lowndes | 1 624 | 0.7 | 28.2 | 18.8 | 3.3 | 8.0 | 3.1 | 10.9 | 25.0 | 12 075 | 202 | 2 451 | 26 556 | 5.8 |
| Madison | 2 991 | 0.2 | 24.6 | 14.0 | 14.1 | 8.4 | 11.5 | 8.5 | 8.3 | 14 775 | 152 | 2 304 | 38 558 | 34.0 |
| Marion | 431 | 1.9 | 28.3 | 6.3 | 3.4 | 9.8 | 4.9 | D | 17.1 | 6 390 | 238 | 1 342 | 11 838 | 13.9 |
| Marshall | 319 | -0.2 | 23.1 | 12.0 | 1.8 | 9.3 | 5.8 | D | 22.0 | 7 595 | 206 | 1 709 | 14 881 | 12.3 |
| Monroe | 550 | 3.1 | 39.8 | 27.2 | 2.0 | 7.2 | 2.7 | D | 15.6 | 9 225 | 252 | 1 518 | 16 455 | 1.3 |
| Montgomery | 133 | 4.4 | 7.3 | 2.3 | 6.4 | 10.0 | D | D | 25.9 | 2 915 | 268 | 668 | 5 194 | -3.9 |
| Neshoba | 747 | 4.3 | D | 3.7 | 1.5 | 6.6 | 2.1 | D | 40.1 | 6 455 | 216 | 1 241 | 12 357 | 3.2 |
| Newton | 287 | 5.4 | D | 16.6 | D | 7.2 | 2.1 | D | 33.6 | 5 230 | 243 | 921 | 9 373 | 1.2 |
| Noxubee | 150 | 19.3 | D | 17.7 | D | 8.4 | 2.1 | D | 26.3 | 2 590 | 228 | 1 065 | 5 170 | -1.1 |
| Oktibbeha | 999 | 0.1 | 11.7 | 8.2 | D | 5.8 | 2.5 | 5.8 | 52.6 | 6 625 | 139 | 1 623 | 20 947 | 20.8 |
| Panola | 588 | 2.9 | 23.2 | 17.2 | 6.7 | 9.8 | 4.5 | D | 19.7 | 7 715 | 223 | 2 096 | 14 697 | 7.0 |
| Pearl River | 553 | -1.2 | 20.9 | 9.2 | 4.4 | 13.2 | 4.5 | D | 30.7 | 13 480 | 242 | 1 935 | 23 968 | 16.3 |
| Perry | 129 | 2.0 | D | 38.6 | 2.4 | 4.8 | 2.0 | 9.0 | 19.3 | 2 890 | 238 | 621 | 5 519 | 8.0 |
| Pike | 664 | -0.8 | 17.5 | 13.4 | 3.3 | 12.1 | 5.3 | D | 29.7 | 9 130 | 226 | 2 321 | 17 861 | 6.8 |
| Pontotoc | 515 | 0.0 | 53.7 | 50.2 | 2.8 | 5.6 | 2.3 | D | 12.1 | 6 720 | 225 | 999 | 12 440 | 15.0 |
| Prentiss | 312 | 0.7 | 29.9 | 24.7 | 4.8 | 7.0 | 3.7 | D | 25.1 | 6 255 | 247 | 924 | 11 054 | 3.5 |
| Quitman | 89 | 30.6 | D | 2.9 | D | 4.3 | 4.1 | D | 20.3 | 1 895 | 233 | 762 | 3 589 | -8.5 |
| Rankin | 3 201 | 0.5 | 17.8 | 7.3 | 4.9 | 9.4 | 8.1 | 12.3 | 16.6 | 25 340 | 176 | 2 809 | 56 487 | 25.3 |
| Scott | 542 | 4.5 | D | 46.0 | D | 6.6 | 2.5 | D | 14.4 | 6 010 | 212 | 1 368 | 11 470 | 3.2 |
| Sharkey | 63 | 25.0 | 1.1 | 0.0 | D | 7.5 | 4.3 | D | 32.6 | 1 210 | 247 | 500 | 2 100 | -13.1 |
| Simpson | 355 | 7.1 | 7.0 | 2.1 | D | 8.9 | 4.6 | D | 23.0 | 5 910 | 216 | 1 278 | 11 934 | 5.5 |
| Smith | 179 | 15.7 | D | 29.6 | 3.2 | 3.9 | 1.6 | 4.3 | 18.0 | 3 890 | 237 | 712 | 7 237 | 3.3 |
| Stone | 199 | -0.4 | D | 18.9 | 4.8 | 9.1 | 2.9 | 11.0 | 30.4 | 3 585 | 201 | 534 | 7 161 | 34.0 |

1. Includes mining, construction, and manufacturing.    2. Per 1,000 resident population enumerated in the 2010 census.

# Table B. States and Counties — Housing, Labor Force, and Employment

| STATE County | Housing units, 2007–2011 | | | | | | | | Civilian labor force, 2012 | | | | Civilian employment,[6] 2007–2011 | | |
| | Occupied units | | | | | | | Sub-stand-ard units[4] (percent) | | | Unemployment | | | Percent | |
| | Owner-occupied | | | | | Renter-occupied | | | | | | | | | Con-struction, produc-tion, and mainte-nance occu-pations |
| | | | | Median owner cost as a percent of income | | | | | | | | | | Manage-ment, business, science and arts | |
| | Total | Percent | Median value[1] | With a mort-gage | Without a mort-gage[2] | Median rent[3] | Median rent as a per-cent of income | | Total | Percent change, 2011–2012 | Total | Rate[5] | Total | | |
| | 89 | 90 | 91 | 92 | 93 | 94 | 95 | 96 | 97 | 98 | 99 | 100 | 101 | 102 | 103 |
| MISSISSIPPI | 1 085 062 | 70.6 | 99 200 | 23.1 | 12.2 | 680 | 32.0 | 3.2 | 1 333 046 | -0.4 | 122 060 | 9.2 | 1 210 301 | 30.3 | 28.1 |
| Adams | 12 074 | 69.0 | 81 100 | 26.0 | 13.9 | 578 | 35.6 | 2.9 | 13 054 | -1.3 | 1 229 | 9.4 | 11 352 | 27.8 | 22.4 |
| Alcorn | 13 867 | 72.5 | 85 500 | 22.3 | 12.0 | 522 | 30.1 | 1.8 | 15 904 | 1.0 | 1 424 | 9.0 | 14 087 | 28.8 | 30.9 |
| Amite | 5 001 | 83.7 | 73 800 | 25.4 | 13.5 | 563 | 36.1 | 2.0 | 4 899 | -1.5 | 509 | 10.4 | 4 656 | 23.9 | 39.6 |
| Attala | 7 308 | 73.6 | 70 800 | 25.2 | 13.2 | 529 | 28.3 | 3.0 | 6 891 | -3.4 | 768 | 11.1 | 7 331 | 27.9 | 35.2 |
| Benton | 3 197 | 78.0 | 82 600 | 26.7 | 16.6 | 579 | 42.2 | 6.8 | 3 036 | -0.8 | 358 | 11.8 | 3 018 | 22.3 | 44.2 |
| Bolivar | 12 396 | 56.9 | 81 000 | 24.9 | 14.1 | 565 | 33.5 | 4.6 | 15 061 | -3.3 | 1 568 | 10.4 | 13 035 | 29.1 | 28.0 |
| Calhoun | 5 988 | 70.4 | 58 700 | 22.3 | 12.7 | 486 | 27.3 | 2.0 | 6 183 | -2.7 | 586 | 9.5 | 5 911 | 23.6 | 42.9 |
| Carroll | 3 958 | 83.8 | 62 200 | 19.4 | 17.1 | 508 | 30.9 | 1.7 | 4 984 | -1.1 | 450 | 9.0 | 3 397 | 23.4 | 29.9 |
| Chickasaw | 6 673 | 72.1 | 62 300 | 25.0 | 9.9 | 488 | 36.7 | 2.4 | 7 643 | -2.0 | 839 | 11.0 | 6 638 | 17.9 | 45.8 |
| Choctaw | 3 383 | 78.2 | 68 800 | 25.4 | 13.7 | 445 | 26.5 | 3.2 | 3 414 | -0.8 | 339 | 9.9 | 3 399 | 27.9 | 35.9 |
| Claiborne | 3 299 | 77.4 | 53 800 | 35.2 | 16.7 | 538 | 30.7 | 4.6 | 4 316 | 8.3 | 559 | 13.0 | 3 348 | 20.4 | 30.0 |
| Clarke | 6 521 | 79.0 | 61 600 | 21.7 | 13.6 | 620 | 34.6 | 4.9 | 6 858 | 1.8 | 758 | 11.1 | 6 545 | 24.2 | 38.7 |
| Clay | 7 917 | 72.6 | 78 200 | 24.9 | 14.1 | 578 | 30.2 | 2.9 | 7 361 | -0.1 | 1 239 | 16.8 | 7 600 | 27.8 | 31.1 |
| Coahoma | 9 367 | 54.1 | 56 000 | 26.0 | 13.9 | 561 | 33.9 | 3.9 | 10 287 | -2.8 | 1 319 | 12.8 | 8 993 | 27.6 | 24.1 |
| Copiah | 10 045 | 77.2 | 75 500 | 21.1 | 11.7 | 564 | 28.7 | 3.6 | 12 499 | -0.5 | 1 275 | 10.2 | 11 249 | 22.7 | 40.0 |
| Covington | 7 040 | 84.7 | 78 900 | 23.0 | 12.7 | 505 | 33.6 | 1.2 | 8 997 | -0.1 | 724 | 8.0 | 7 238 | 27.3 | 36.4 |
| DeSoto | 56 641 | 76.9 | 153 600 | 23.0 | 9.9 | 909 | 28.3 | 2.3 | 81 536 | 0.8 | 5 570 | 6.8 | 77 458 | 33.3 | 25.4 |
| Forrest | 28 032 | 58.5 | 112 200 | 23.5 | 13.1 | 659 | 34.0 | 2.9 | 35 557 | -0.3 | 3 068 | 8.6 | 32 516 | 32.6 | 23.5 |
| Franklin | 3 184 | 81.3 | 69 700 | 21.1 | 11.5 | 516 | 47.8 | 3.3 | 3 064 | -2.9 | 308 | 10.1 | 2 851 | 29.4 | 41.4 |
| George | 8 069 | 81.6 | 96 100 | 21.2 | 10.1 | 565 | 29.0 | 4.4 | 9 132 | -2.1 | 959 | 10.5 | 8 015 | 25.9 | 43.0 |
| Greene | 4 233 | 85.7 | 75 300 | 23.7 | 13.4 | 511 | 27.3 | 2.7 | 4 986 | -1.5 | 587 | 11.8 | 4 504 | 21.3 | 41.4 |
| Grenada | 8 766 | 69.4 | 84 900 | 23.3 | 13.2 | 519 | 32.4 | 3.4 | 9 557 | 1.0 | 921 | 9.6 | 8 856 | 27.2 | 35.7 |
| Hancock | 17 166 | 77.3 | 149 700 | 24.3 | 12.8 | 774 | 31.3 | 4.6 | 19 446 | -1.3 | 1 668 | 8.6 | 17 477 | 32.6 | 26.7 |
| Harrison | 69 384 | 64.5 | 146 600 | 24.8 | 11.8 | 855 | 33.0 | 3.1 | 88 491 | -0.7 | 7 646 | 8.6 | 82 215 | 29.3 | 23.1 |
| Hinds | 88 159 | 60.3 | 108 200 | 23.2 | 11.1 | 770 | 35.9 | 3.6 | 120 845 | 0.1 | 10 147 | 8.4 | 106 633 | 31.9 | 20.5 |
| Holmes | 6 603 | 72.5 | 49 700 | 36.5 | 18.4 | 487 | 28.3 | 4.8 | 6 853 | -3.2 | 1 129 | 16.5 | 5 888 | 22.5 | 42.5 |
| Humphreys | 3 256 | 58.6 | 65 100 | 23.3 | 17.3 | 521 | 36.1 | 5.0 | 3 915 | -6.6 | 623 | 15.9 | 3 110 | 26.0 | 33.1 |
| Issaquena | 508 | 62.8 | 54 400 | 32.9 | 20.4 | 508 | 37.8 | 5.5 | 627 | -6.3 | 86 | 13.7 | 485 | 12.8 | 41.9 |
| Itawamba | 8 870 | 79.3 | 80 500 | 21.3 | 11.2 | 575 | 27.9 | 1.5 | 10 310 | 1.1 | 940 | 9.1 | 9 879 | 25.1 | 41.6 |
| Jackson | 50 185 | 72.2 | 129 100 | 23.0 | 11.2 | 851 | 31.6 | 2.5 | 62 219 | -1.0 | 6 110 | 9.8 | 60 532 | 30.0 | 26.9 |
| Jasper | 6 874 | 82.8 | 68 500 | 28.3 | 14.6 | 523 | 28.9 | 1.6 | 7 039 | -0.4 | 709 | 10.1 | 6 474 | 24.2 | 38.2 |
| Jefferson | 2 735 | 71.7 | 64 300 | 27.6 | 16.8 | 395 | 32.8 | 1.7 | 3 120 | 2.5 | 450 | 14.4 | 1 908 | 32.8 | 31.6 |
| Jefferson Davis | 4 905 | 79.1 | 69 500 | 27.3 | 14.9 | 561 | 43.4 | 4.5 | 5 035 | -1.5 | 579 | 11.5 | 4 500 | 21.5 | 40.0 |
| Jones | 24 589 | 73.1 | 85 000 | 22.8 | 11.7 | 639 | 29.7 | 4.1 | 31 472 | 0.3 | 2 216 | 7.0 | 27 300 | 26.8 | 36.5 |
| Kemper | 3 794 | 75.6 | 63 300 | 23.9 | 15.1 | 426 | 31.0 | 3.9 | 4 210 | 1.6 | 534 | 12.7 | 3 813 | 21.7 | 36.5 |
| Lafayette | 15 944 | 61.7 | 158 000 | 21.8 | 11.6 | 760 | 36.5 | 2.6 | 24 104 | 3.6 | 1 764 | 7.3 | 20 014 | 39.2 | 19.0 |
| Lamar | 21 237 | 69.4 | 158 100 | 21.9 | 9.9 | 805 | 32.1 | 2.7 | 28 137 | 0.6 | 1 951 | 6.9 | 25 441 | 38.2 | 21.0 |
| Lauderdale | 29 762 | 67.6 | 85 200 | 23.1 | 11.9 | 608 | 30.5 | 2.5 | 34 713 | 1.4 | 3 276 | 9.4 | 31 690 | 31.2 | 25.0 |
| Lawrence | 5 006 | 79.3 | 75 000 | 22.0 | 12.7 | 582 | 23.5 | 5.3 | 4 994 | -1.8 | 523 | 10.5 | 4 773 | 31.9 | 36.1 |
| Leake | 7 756 | 76.8 | 74 400 | 23.8 | 15.0 | 587 | 27.8 | 5.0 | 8 063 | -3.8 | 862 | 10.7 | 8 267 | 27.9 | 36.2 |
| Lee | 31 765 | 69.0 | 109 000 | 22.3 | 11.4 | 613 | 30.0 | 3.1 | 40 235 | 1.2 | 3 503 | 8.7 | 36 795 | 29.3 | 27.9 |
| Leflore | 11 062 | 51.0 | 66 100 | 24.0 | 15.5 | 515 | 34.0 | 4.5 | 12 731 | -1.7 | 1 610 | 12.6 | 9 820 | 28.9 | 27.0 |
| Lincoln | 13 220 | 76.4 | 80 600 | 19.9 | 11.0 | 550 | 27.1 | 2.2 | 13 869 | -1.6 | 1 292 | 9.3 | 13 513 | 29.6 | 30.6 |
| Lowndes | 23 243 | 64.0 | 110 400 | 24.3 | 10.6 | 631 | 31.7 | 2.4 | 27 009 | 2.0 | 2 591 | 9.6 | 23 797 | 27.2 | 30.3 |
| Madison | 35 297 | 70.7 | 190 600 | 21.7 | 10.3 | 834 | 28.0 | 3.8 | 50 048 | 0.2 | 3 241 | 6.5 | 44 978 | 47.0 | 14.3 |
| Marion | 9 688 | 80.6 | 82 800 | 21.1 | 14.1 | 564 | 35.4 | 2.1 | 10 541 | -4.2 | 1 107 | 10.5 | 9 470 | 24.8 | 34.4 |
| Marshall | 12 735 | 78.4 | 83 700 | 24.2 | 14.7 | 609 | 33.0 | 3.9 | 15 183 | 0.4 | 1 776 | 11.7 | 13 939 | 19.7 | 40.7 |
| Monroe | 14 493 | 78.4 | 79 000 | 22.9 | 11.6 | 529 | 27.7 | 3.0 | 16 105 | -0.9 | 1 838 | 11.4 | 14 637 | 24.8 | 35.4 |
| Montgomery | 4 286 | 76.7 | 68 800 | 24.4 | 14.3 | 613 | 33.5 | 2.4 | 4 617 | -0.8 | 551 | 11.9 | 3 854 | 27.0 | 32.5 |
| Neshoba | 10 652 | 76.1 | 69 900 | 22.5 | 11.3 | 576 | 27.7 | 4.6 | 13 313 | -1.0 | 988 | 7.4 | 11 537 | 28.4 | 27.8 |
| Newton | 7 978 | 79.8 | 68 400 | 21.6 | 12.4 | 595 | 23.6 | 3.0 | 9 342 | -0.4 | 768 | 8.2 | 9 022 | 28.7 | 31.0 |
| Noxubee | 4 151 | 74.6 | 53 000 | 30.3 | 17.4 | 480 | 37.0 | 4.7 | 3 695 | -1.9 | 564 | 15.3 | 3 618 | 20.3 | 44.4 |
| Oktibbeha | 18 537 | 50.1 | 108 100 | 22.8 | 11.6 | 673 | 43.5 | 2.0 | 21 289 | 0.8 | 1 949 | 9.2 | 19 822 | 41.3 | 15.9 |
| Panola | 12 133 | 76.8 | 78 400 | 22.8 | 14.3 | 640 | 32.8 | 5.2 | 15 431 | -1.1 | 1 778 | 11.5 | 12 449 | 28.6 | 32.1 |
| Pearl River | 20 581 | 78.3 | 119 100 | 24.0 | 11.9 | 753 | 34.0 | 3.5 | 21 824 | -0.9 | 2 042 | 9.4 | 21 623 | 31.8 | 30.8 |
| Perry | 4 709 | 86.1 | 82 200 | 20.8 | 10.4 | 697 | 28.7 | 3.2 | 5 030 | -0.5 | 494 | 9.8 | 4 831 | 24.7 | 38.5 |
| Pike | 14 849 | 71.9 | 82 200 | 24.5 | 12.4 | 594 | 32.3 | 3.0 | 15 215 | -1.8 | 1 646 | 10.8 | 15 313 | 25.2 | 33.5 |
| Pontotoc | 10 028 | 77.7 | 80 600 | 23.1 | 11.3 | 583 | 26.8 | 2.4 | 13 792 | 1.1 | 1 106 | 8.0 | 12 382 | 24.6 | 37.8 |
| Prentiss | 9 638 | 79.1 | 73 800 | 22.5 | 11.4 | 457 | 34.7 | 1.7 | 10 999 | -0.8 | 1 022 | 9.3 | 9 883 | 25.1 | 37.6 |
| Quitman | 3 153 | 67.0 | 47 700 | 28.9 | 13.1 | 434 | 31.6 | 5.2 | 3 388 | -2.1 | 430 | 12.7 | 2 781 | 23.7 | 34.8 |
| Rankin | 52 539 | 76.5 | 144 400 | 21.2 | 9.9 | 836 | 29.8 | 2.3 | 77 046 | 0.3 | 4 389 | 5.7 | 68 292 | 39.1 | 20.2 |
| Scott | 9 791 | 81.9 | 62 700 | 24.4 | 13.1 | 600 | 25.9 | 5.2 | 13 710 | -2.4 | 1 027 | 7.5 | 11 862 | 19.3 | 45.9 |
| Sharkey | 1 644 | 66.5 | 61 900 | 24.8 | 12.3 | 465 | 32.5 | 6.9 | 2 325 | -3.6 | 273 | 11.7 | 1 645 | 32.5 | 24.8 |
| Simpson | 10 324 | 75.3 | 78 600 | 22.7 | 11.4 | 590 | 26.9 | 5.0 | 11 649 | -0.3 | 940 | 8.1 | 10 643 | 26.9 | 34.7 |
| Smith | 6 173 | 89.8 | 74 500 | 21.6 | 13.4 | 622 | 21.6 | 4.1 | 6 276 | -3.3 | 538 | 8.6 | 6 617 | 27.5 | 36.4 |
| Stone | 6 083 | 80.1 | 106 900 | 21.9 | 9.9 | 689 | 27.9 | 3.1 | 8 233 | -0.5 | 733 | 8.9 | 7 173 | 22.9 | 31.4 |

1. Specified owner-occupied units.  2. A value of 9.9 represents 9.9 percent or less.  3. Specified renter-occupied units. A value of 10.0 represents 10 percent or less.  4. Overcrowded or lacking complete plumbing facilities.  5. Percent of civilian labor force.  6. Persons 16 years old and over.

# Table B. States and Counties — Nonfarm Employment and Agriculture

| STATE County | Private nonfarm establishments, employment and payroll, 2011 | | | | | | | | | Agriculture, 2007 | | | |
| | | Employment | | | | | | Annual payroll | | Farms | | | |
| | | | | | | | | | | | | Percent with: | |
| | Number of establishments | Total | Health care and social assistance | Manufacturing | Retail trade | Finance and insurance | Professional, scientific, and technical services | Total (mil dol) | Average per employee (dollars) | Number | Fewer than 50 acres | 500 acres or more | Farm operators whose principal occupation is farming (percent) |
| | 104 | 105 | 106 | 107 | 108 | 109 | 110 | 111 | 112 | 113 | 114 | 115 | 116 |
| MISSISSIPPI | 58 592 | 887 772 | 157 066 | 138 412 | 138 471 | 33 593 | 29 623 | 29 585 | 33 325 | 41 959 | 29.3 | 10.8 | 38.0 |
| Adams | 815 | 10 170 | 2 008 | 339 | 2 193 | D | 244 | 294 | 28 955 | 245 | 35.5 | 13.9 | 38.4 |
| Alcorn | 779 | 11 325 | 2 486 | 2 162 | 2 172 | 305 | 290 | 343 | 30 315 | 540 | 29.6 | 5.9 | 28.7 |
| Amite | 169 | 1 218 | D | 261 | 178 | D | 22 | 34 | 28 242 | 599 | 25.0 | 7.3 | 42.1 |
| Attala | 341 | 4 762 | 687 | 593 | 873 | 225 | D | 142 | 29 740 | 559 | 23.6 | 9.8 | 34.3 |
| Benton | 60 | 990 | D | 278 | 129 | D | D | 25 | 24 936 | 336 | 21.1 | 8.6 | 31.3 |
| Bolivar | 708 | 8 266 | 1 842 | 1 338 | 1 504 | 274 | 187 | 245 | 29 686 | 430 | 23.0 | 45.6 | 66.5 |
| Calhoun | 262 | 2 740 | 514 | 989 | 423 | D | D | 76 | 27 779 | 708 | 19.9 | 11.4 | 33.3 |
| Carroll | 90 | 481 | D | D | 42 | 17 | D | 12 | 25 651 | 581 | 19.6 | 17.2 | 34.3 |
| Chickasaw | 347 | 5 340 | D | 3 163 | 698 | 116 | 57 | 140 | 26 268 | 657 | 21.5 | 13.1 | 32.3 |
| Choctaw | 106 | 1 110 | 189 | 167 | 149 | D | D | 45 | 40 331 | 293 | 15.7 | 10.2 | 28.0 |
| Claiborne | 122 | D | 458 | D | D | D | D | D | D | 261 | 20.3 | 16.1 | 41.4 |
| Clarke | 252 | 2 315 | D | 606 | 333 | 79 | 51 | 63 | 27 178 | 373 | 36.5 | 6.4 | 37.0 |
| Clay | 364 | 4 133 | 664 | 773 | 767 | D | D | 131 | 31 815 | 505 | 19.6 | 13.1 | 39.4 |
| Coahoma | 564 | 6 949 | 1 855 | 801 | 1 113 | 241 | 184 | 208 | 29 977 | 261 | 19.5 | 44.8 | 56.7 |
| Copiah | 414 | 6 081 | 703 | 2 342 | 963 | 179 | 77 | 159 | 26 144 | 642 | 30.2 | 7.2 | 36.8 |
| Covington | 329 | 3 819 | 540 | 1 394 | 510 | 116 | 80 | 104 | 27 206 | 623 | 29.2 | 5.3 | 41.1 |
| DeSoto | 2 543 | 42 540 | 5 322 | 3 310 | 7 772 | 971 | 851 | 1 261 | 29 648 | 490 | 46.9 | 10.2 | 34.5 |
| Forrest | 1 846 | 30 777 | 8 249 | 3 434 | 4 006 | 1 039 | 1 055 | 1 070 | 34 772 | 391 | 44.0 | 2.3 | 36.3 |
| Franklin | 117 | 1 177 | D | D | 122 | D | 34 | 36 | 30 620 | 196 | 26.5 | 11.7 | 36.7 |
| George | 317 | 3 141 | 693 | 255 | 878 | D | 100 | 94 | 29 897 | 604 | 54.6 | 3.3 | 40.1 |
| Greene | 123 | 841 | D | 11 | 187 | D | D | 23 | 27 478 | 398 | 36.7 | 4.3 | 32.7 |
| Grenada | 549 | 7 982 | 1 301 | 2 121 | 1 438 | 329 | 154 | 230 | 28 791 | 356 | 18.3 | 15.2 | 24.2 |
| Hancock | 705 | 12 237 | 1 010 | 769 | 1 451 | 271 | 1 748 | 593 | 48 468 | 286 | 44.8 | 4.5 | 37.4 |
| Harrison | 4 167 | 68 421 | 13 026 | 2 829 | 11 068 | 2 930 | 2 585 | 2 310 | 33 765 | 367 | 70.3 | 0.5 | 37.1 |
| Hinds | 5 550 | 94 530 | 26 270 | 3 736 | 10 802 | 5 163 | 5 293 | 3 807 | 40 274 | 1 071 | 33.7 | 8.9 | 31.7 |
| Holmes | 248 | 1 995 | 284 | 402 | 461 | 93 | 38 | 50 | 25 278 | 556 | 21.8 | 17.3 | 36.3 |
| Humphreys | 157 | 2 078 | 275 | D | 264 | 129 | D | 52 | 24 852 | 213 | 21.6 | 42.7 | 67.1 |
| Issaquena | 10 | 99 | D | NA | NA | D | NA | 2 | 21 566 | 104 | 21.2 | 44.2 | 53.8 |
| Itawamba | 339 | 4 270 | 539 | 1 250 | 618 | 149 | D | 124 | 29 026 | 491 | 22.2 | 7.3 | 25.1 |
| Jackson | 2 225 | 46 652 | 5 407 | D | 5 271 | 1 016 | 1 604 | 2 101 | 45 029 | 454 | 62.8 | 1.8 | 37.2 |
| Jasper | 210 | 3 304 | D | 1 413 | 310 | 100 | 84 | 118 | 35 752 | 528 | 27.5 | 7.2 | 37.7 |
| Jefferson | 57 | 654 | 303 | D | 102 | D | NA | 21 | 32 610 | 356 | 23.3 | 12.9 | 41.6 |
| Jefferson Davis | 149 | 1 222 | D | 15 | 278 | 34 | D | 49 | 40 206 | 437 | 30.4 | 4.6 | 47.6 |
| Jones | 1 357 | 25 488 | 3 232 | D | 3 321 | D | 475 | 821 | 32 230 | 1 027 | 44.4 | 1.5 | 40.3 |
| Kemper | 122 | 1 175 | 157 | 464 | 180 | 55 | D | 30 | 25 373 | 455 | 20.4 | 12.1 | 40.9 |
| Lafayette | 1 046 | 12 724 | 2 473 | 684 | 2 503 | 427 | 915 | 381 | 29 938 | 487 | 16.6 | 9.4 | 27.1 |
| Lamar | 1 301 | 17 001 | 3 166 | 301 | 4 979 | 678 | 642 | 431 | 25 372 | 500 | 43.8 | 4.6 | 36.2 |
| Lauderdale | 1 986 | 30 319 | 8 036 | 2 387 | 5 249 | 1 352 | 723 | 962 | 31 745 | 409 | 34.5 | 7.8 | 36.9 |
| Lawrence | 184 | 1 895 | 207 | 644 | 360 | D | D | 80 | 42 029 | 460 | 25.0 | 7.4 | 41.3 |
| Leake | 301 | 4 627 | 309 | D | 747 | 179 | 45 | 108 | 23 368 | 735 | 27.6 | 5.4 | 44.8 |
| Lee | 2 374 | 45 784 | 7 579 | 10 007 | 7 393 | 2 224 | 1 314 | 1 507 | 32 914 | 590 | 36.4 | 7.5 | 34.2 |
| Leflore | 738 | 12 147 | 2 798 | 2 145 | 1 679 | 370 | 338 | 371 | 30 571 | 296 | 8.8 | 46.3 | 55.4 |
| Lincoln | 769 | 10 223 | 1 634 | 1 080 | 1 888 | 303 | 365 | 343 | 33 572 | 725 | 32.0 | 5.2 | 36.8 |
| Lowndes | 1 500 | 21 016 | 3 075 | 3 531 | 3 610 | 498 | 548 | 705 | 33 558 | 497 | 33.0 | 13.5 | 28.8 |
| Madison | 2 749 | 42 676 | 3 270 | 5 975 | 6 716 | 3 008 | 2 944 | 1 616 | 37 871 | 747 | 30.7 | 11.9 | 31.1 |
| Marion | 610 | 6 546 | 888 | D | 1 234 | 248 | 197 | 200 | 30 559 | 611 | 31.1 | 4.9 | 40.8 |
| Marshall | 420 | 6 114 | 1 375 | 493 | 890 | 283 | 95 | 157 | 25 700 | 577 | 25.8 | 14.6 | 31.9 |
| Monroe | 652 | 8 288 | 1 687 | 2 587 | 1 290 | 257 | 103 | 293 | 35 351 | 730 | 25.5 | 12.6 | 39.3 |
| Montgomery | 223 | 2 396 | 638 | 255 | 497 | 93 | 30 | 61 | 25 541 | 363 | 16.3 | 11.0 | 36.4 |
| Neshoba | 530 | 7 903 | 1 229 | D | 1 287 | D | 114 | 284 | 35 957 | 728 | 28.0 | 5.1 | 47.9 |
| Newton | 316 | 3 520 | 556 | 1 114 | 729 | D | D | 99 | 28 140 | 652 | 25.3 | 7.1 | 47.5 |
| Noxubee | 194 | 1 751 | 286 | 521 | 369 | 68 | D | 45 | 25 432 | 606 | 21.1 | 18.2 | 39.9 |
| Oktibbeha | 847 | 10 782 | 1 665 | 1 222 | 1 958 | 413 | 377 | 283 | 26 218 | 451 | 28.6 | 8.2 | 29.7 |
| Panola | 636 | 9 129 | 1 289 | 2 179 | 1 601 | 319 | 125 | 260 | 28 450 | 767 | 16.3 | 15.9 | 27.5 |
| Pearl River | 813 | 7 310 | 997 | 543 | 1 999 | 341 | 321 | 197 | 26 941 | 878 | 48.4 | 5.2 | 41.7 |
| Perry | 158 | 1 684 | 273 | 675 | 276 | D | D | 70 | 41 752 | 347 | 39.5 | 1.7 | 41.8 |
| Pike | 989 | 12 813 | 2 658 | 2 455 | 2 562 | 406 | 243 | 352 | 27 469 | 593 | 39.3 | 2.7 | 41.3 |
| Pontotoc | 459 | 9 818 | 761 | 6 208 | 923 | 209 | 112 | 268 | 27 299 | 919 | 29.8 | 5.8 | 23.7 |
| Prentiss | 506 | 6 352 | 1 107 | 2 364 | 976 | 176 | 235 | 161 | 25 347 | 576 | 25.9 | 5.2 | 31.3 |
| Quitman | 115 | 759 | D | D | 129 | D | D | 19 | 24 823 | 349 | 14.3 | 31.8 | 40.1 |
| Rankin | 3 400 | 49 893 | 8 350 | 3 500 | 8 516 | 2 556 | 1 464 | 1 696 | 33 993 | 782 | 37.9 | 7.0 | 43.9 |
| Scott | 483 | 9 574 | 884 | 5 218 | 1 217 | 214 | 84 | 269 | 28 077 | 803 | 36.9 | 5.5 | 43.8 |
| Sharkey | 119 | 786 | 233 | NA | 163 | D | D | 22 | 27 487 | 114 | 11.4 | 58.8 | 59.6 |
| Simpson | 411 | 5 902 | 2 357 | 366 | 995 | 464 | 106 | 141 | 23 854 | 727 | 32.3 | 4.3 | 44.2 |
| Smith | 181 | 2 409 | D | 1 088 | 231 | 61 | 125 | 76 | 31 656 | 757 | 27.5 | 3.6 | 48.1 |
| Stone | 265 | 2 839 | 448 | D | 622 | D | 86 | 82 | 28 956 | 323 | 45.5 | 5.0 | 37.5 |

# Table B. States and Counties — **Agriculture**

|  | Agriculture, 2007 (cont.) | | | | | | | | | | | | | | |
|---|---|---|---|---|---|---|---|---|---|---|---|---|---|---|---|
| | Land in farms | | | | | Value of land and buildings (dollars) | | | Value of products sold | | | | Percent of farms with sales of: | | Government payments | |
| | | | Acres | | | | | Value of machinery and equipment, average per farm (dollars) | | Percent from: | | | | | | |
| STATE County | Acreage (1,000) | Percent change, 2002–2007 | Average size of farm | Total irrigated (1,000) | Total cropland (1,000) | Average per farm | Average per acre | | Total (mil dol) | Average per farm (dollars) | Crops | Live-stock and poultry products | $10,000 or more | $100,000 or more | Total ($1,000) | Percent of farms |
| | 117 | 118 | 119 | 120 | 121 | 122 | 123 | 124 | 125 | 126 | 127 | 128 | 129 | 130 | 131 | 132 |
| MISSISSIPPI | 11 456 | 3.2 | 273 | 1 368.7 | 5 530.8 | 510 454 | 1 870 | 73 558 | 4 876.8 | 116 227 | 34.2 | 65.8 | 28.8 | 10.8 | 231 382 | 41.0 |
| Adams | 70 | -23.1 | 285 | 0.0 | 25.9 | 478 041 | 1 675 | 50 718 | 4.9 | 20 087 | 75.9 | 24.2 | 21.2 | 3.3 | 586 | 25.3 |
| Alcorn | 94 | 1.1 | 174 | 0.2 | 43.6 | 289 875 | 1 667 | 54 242 | 8.2 | 15 209 | 69.0 | 31.0 | 17.2 | 2.2 | 1 165 | 55.0 |
| Amite | 110 | -29.9 | 184 | 0.2 | 27.4 | 435 105 | 2 370 | 61 001 | 63.2 | 105 555 | 3.2 | 96.8 | 25.2 | 8.0 | 547 | 28.7 |
| Attala | 137 | 8.7 | 246 | 0.4 | 37.7 | 384 718 | 1 567 | 45 167 | 17.3 | 30 912 | 25.7 | 74.3 | 17.7 | 2.9 | 1 694 | 46.0 |
| Benton | 86 | -14.0 | 256 | D | 27.1 | 367 272 | 1 432 | 55 927 | 7.3 | 21 766 | 45.2 | 54.8 | 19.3 | 3.0 | 958 | 53.3 |
| Bolivar | 428 | -2.7 | 996 | 228.3 | 389.5 | 1 986 810 | 1 995 | 322 868 | 182.9 | 425 263 | 99.3 | 0.7 | 76.5 | 47.2 | 14 569 | 77.4 |
| Calhoun | 202 | 18.8 | 286 | 1.8 | 89.9 | 397 483 | 1 392 | 72 351 | 50.7 | 71 653 | 86.6 | 13.4 | 28.1 | 8.9 | 4 547 | 70.3 |
| Carroll | 190 | 13.1 | 327 | 8.8 | 64.0 | 491 667 | 1 502 | 65 965 | 19.9 | 34 197 | 71.2 | 28.8 | 26.3 | 6.0 | 3 603 | 48.5 |
| Chickasaw | 178 | 3.5 | 271 | 1.7 | 69.3 | 396 016 | 1 459 | 56 640 | 36.7 | 55 798 | 36.6 | 63.4 | 28.2 | 10.2 | 2 868 | 57.7 |
| Choctaw | 72 | 12.5 | 246 | 0.4 | 18.3 | 435 184 | 1 768 | 44 334 | 13.9 | 47 295 | 22.6 | 77.4 | 14.7 | 4.1 | 536 | 48.8 |
| Claiborne | 94 | -6.9 | 360 | D | 26.6 | 576 860 | 1 603 | 53 073 | 9.7 | 37 026 | 62.1 | 37.9 | 19.5 | 5.7 | 1 405 | 44.8 |
| Clarke | 65 | 16.1 | 174 | 0.3 | 15.4 | 322 918 | 1 861 | 41 713 | 20.9 | 56 025 | 20.0 | 80.0 | 27.9 | 3.8 | 169 | 19.3 |
| Clay | 142 | 10.1 | 282 | 0.6 | 41.4 | 412 641 | 1 464 | 56 104 | 80.6 | 159 691 | 5.7 | 94.3 | 30.7 | 9.5 | 1 811 | 47.3 |
| Coahoma | 303 | 11.4 | 1 160 | 130.9 | 265.6 | 2 090 970 | 1 803 | 310 055 | 128.8 | 493 664 | 93.2 | 6.8 | 65.1 | 43.3 | 12 949 | 80.1 |
| Copiah | 131 | -17.1 | 205 | 0.9 | 30.1 | 394 956 | 1 928 | 58 722 | 55.6 | 86 599 | 7.4 | 92.6 | 23.2 | 6.1 | 792 | 21.2 |
| Covington | 116 | 12.6 | 187 | 0.5 | 37.3 | 462 975 | 2 478 | 61 060 | 163.1 | 261 727 | 3.3 | 96.7 | 40.0 | 19.6 | 599 | 27.1 |
| DeSoto | 142 | -0.7 | 289 | 22.0 | 94.0 | 678 017 | 2 346 | 81 087 | 30.3 | 61 866 | 86.9 | 13.1 | 24.3 | 8.4 | 2 659 | 21.8 |
| Forrest | 46 | 2.2 | 116 | 1.0 | 15.1 | 352 027 | 3 023 | 59 200 | 23.2 | 59 281 | 23.0 | 77.0 | 23.3 | 6.1 | 999 | 26.9 |
| Franklin | 47 | 6.8 | 240 | D | 10.0 | 446 787 | 1 863 | 53 535 | 5.9 | 30 145 | 16.2 | 83.8 | 23.5 | 2.6 | 303 | 27.0 |
| George | 68 | 7.9 | 113 | 0.7 | 24.6 | 330 376 | 2 927 | 61 447 | 17.4 | 28 847 | 70.7 | 29.3 | 26.0 | 6.0 | 1 739 | 19.0 |
| Greene | 51 | -13.6 | 128 | 0.1 | 13.0 | 303 572 | 2 365 | 52 010 | 34.0 | 85 520 | D | D | 22.9 | 6.3 | 395 | 9.8 |
| Grenada | 112 | 23.1 | 314 | 3.2 | 36.5 | 503 090 | 1 604 | 50 608 | 8.2 | 23 132 | 76.6 | 23.4 | 14.6 | 2.5 | 1 304 | 60.4 |
| Hancock | 42 | 10.5 | 148 | 0.4 | 10.1 | 441 511 | 2 988 | 49 321 | 3.0 | 10 391 | D | D | 20.3 | 2.8 | 343 | 17.1 |
| Harrison | 21 | -16.0 | 58 | 0.1 | 5.7 | 280 585 | 4 799 | 54 071 | 3.1 | 8 403 | 60.4 | 39.6 | 15.8 | 1.4 | 59 | 6.8 |
| Hinds | 260 | -6.8 | 243 | 0.4 | 74.9 | 452 184 | 1 862 | 53 114 | 65.8 | 61 465 | 22.4 | 77.6 | 20.1 | 2.7 | 3 872 | 36.1 |
| Holmes | 228 | 4.1 | 410 | 33.3 | 125.2 | 687 556 | 1 676 | 81 660 | 47.6 | 85 646 | 93.7 | 6.3 | 22.5 | 9.4 | 7 664 | 60.4 |
| Humphreys | 195 | 7.1 | 914 | 63.3 | 145.4 | 1 545 824 | 1 690 | 284 136 | 101.1 | 474 475 | 61.5 | 38.5 | 72.8 | 47.4 | 7 082 | 72.8 |
| Issaquena | 121 | 3.4 | 1 165 | 15.3 | 79.1 | 2 012 618 | 1 727 | 254 474 | 30.3 | 291 593 | 97.7 | 2.3 | 51.9 | 34.6 | 3 634 | 69.2 |
| Itawamba | 93 | -3.1 | 190 | 0.0 | 35.1 | 285 841 | 1 504 | 53 365 | 21.9 | 44 553 | 21.0 | 78.9 | 21.6 | 6.7 | 967 | 52.1 |
| Jackson | 41 | -4.7 | 91 | 0.2 | 17.2 | 329 620 | 3 611 | 52 171 | 8.0 | 17 572 | 51.8 | 48.2 | 21.8 | 1.8 | 273 | 9.7 |
| Jasper | 91 | 13.8 | 172 | 0.0 | 21.1 | 351 626 | 2 046 | 51 204 | 99.2 | 187 962 | 0.9 | 99.1 | 30.7 | 14.6 | 627 | 30.1 |
| Jefferson | 100 | 9.9 | 282 | D | 35.3 | 507 666 | 1 799 | 47 020 | 26.1 | 73 438 | 31.1 | 68.9 | 25.3 | 8.4 | 1 609 | 29.8 |
| Jefferson Davis | 68 | 6.3 | 155 | 0.1 | 21.7 | 318 553 | 2 049 | 59 945 | 37.1 | 84 975 | 11.3 | 88.7 | 28.4 | 8.7 | 582 | 34.8 |
| Jones | 110 | -16.7 | 107 | 0.4 | 32.2 | 333 008 | 3 114 | 53 341 | 181.0 | 176 229 | 2.8 | 97.2 | 32.2 | 15.1 | 683 | 20.6 |
| Kemper | 136 | 10.6 | 299 | 0.1 | 26.2 | 413 304 | 1 381 | 45 722 | 22.0 | 48 287 | 4.6 | 95.4 | 26.6 | 4.8 | 597 | 33.8 |
| Lafayette | 114 | -15.6 | 235 | 0.2 | 35.0 | 469 020 | 1 997 | 52 238 | 8.1 | 16 653 | 60.0 | 40.0 | 18.9 | 2.1 | 1 390 | 49.5 |
| Lamar | 73 | -2.7 | 146 | 0.3 | 15.2 | 397 566 | 2 721 | 56 395 | 21.8 | 43 624 | 17.1 | 82.9 | 29.6 | 6.2 | 1 080 | 23.0 |
| Lauderdale | 84 | -9.7 | 204 | 0.0 | 25.8 | 350 594 | 1 715 | 43 943 | 5.0 | 12 247 | 46.5 | 53.5 | 20.3 | 1.5 | 327 | 17.6 |
| Lawrence | 80 | 21.2 | 174 | D | 27.0 | 385 626 | 2 219 | 64 128 | 70.3 | 152 816 | 4.5 | 95.5 | 28.9 | 10.0 | 720 | 30.9 |
| Leake | 127 | 15.5 | 173 | 0.3 | 30.6 | 389 175 | 2 244 | 63 652 | 225.0 | 306 180 | 0.6 | 99.4 | 35.1 | 19.2 | 1 031 | 35.2 |
| Lee | 146 | 1.4 | 248 | 0.6 | 82.1 | 441 930 | 1 781 | 58 723 | 25.8 | 43 729 | 62.3 | 37.7 | 25.1 | 5.3 | 1 720 | 43.2 |
| Leflore | 315 | 11.3 | 1 064 | 144.8 | 263.0 | 1 820 563 | 1 711 | 321 857 | 162.1 | 547 508 | 70.6 | 29.4 | 60.5 | 41.2 | 13 073 | 77.4 |
| Lincoln | 125 | 11.6 | 172 | 0.2 | 34.3 | 393 366 | 2 290 | 50 192 | 54.7 | 75 489 | 4.9 | 95.1 | 25.9 | 8.0 | 647 | 18.6 |
| Lowndes | 130 | -13.3 | 262 | 0.5 | 62.9 | 467 721 | 1 785 | 61 277 | 23.7 | 47 738 | 39.0 | 61.0 | 28.2 | 7.8 | 2 245 | 43.7 |
| Madison | 223 | 16.1 | 298 | 2.6 | 81.8 | 583 497 | 1 958 | 59 420 | 19.6 | 26 246 | 75.6 | 24.4 | 19.8 | 5.1 | 4 512 | 46.2 |
| Marion | 92 | -7.1 | 151 | 0.2 | 27.3 | 370 329 | 2 457 | 53 958 | 74.1 | 121 218 | 2.0 | 98.0 | 27.8 | 10.6 | 1 003 | 29.8 |
| Marshall | 193 | 0.0 | 335 | 0.7 | 67.6 | 604 850 | 1 808 | 62 359 | 14.9 | 25 759 | 56.9 | 43.1 | 22.5 | 5.0 | 2 496 | 48.2 |
| Monroe | 199 | 8.7 | 272 | 1.7 | 84.0 | 403 486 | 1 483 | 58 655 | 26.9 | 36 852 | 51.6 | 48.4 | 24.4 | 7.0 | 3 229 | 58.9 |
| Montgomery | 97 | 12.8 | 268 | 0.6 | 25.8 | 408 119 | 1 522 | 56 437 | 10.1 | 27 784 | 56.7 | 43.3 | 28.9 | 5.8 | 1 460 | 59.8 |
| Neshoba | 121 | -17.1 | 166 | 0.5 | 29.8 | 402 260 | 2 428 | 70 614 | 227.0 | 311 871 | 0.7 | 99.3 | 39.8 | 21.4 | 349 | 18.0 |
| Newton | 120 | 0.8 | 185 | 0.2 | 29.7 | 376 253 | 2 038 | 63 432 | 120.9 | 185 464 | 1.7 | 98.3 | 34.4 | 15.0 | 592 | 23.9 |
| Noxubee | 222 | 5.7 | 366 | 4.9 | 98.5 | 561 124 | 1 534 | 93 174 | 66.2 | 109 289 | 27.6 | 72.4 | 44.6 | 23.3 | 4 209 | 59.4 |
| Oktibbeha | 101 | 7.4 | 225 | 0.8 | 26.2 | 401 869 | 1 788 | 47 316 | 13.1 | 29 147 | 9.5 | 90.5 | 24.6 | 3.3 | 995 | 39.5 |
| Panola | 270 | -0.7 | 352 | 25.1 | 138.8 | 541 174 | 1 538 | 61 652 | 42.7 | 55 636 | 73.3 | 26.7 | 20.9 | 6.3 | 6 450 | 61.3 |
| Pearl River | 136 | 13.3 | 155 | 1.3 | 30.6 | 418 301 | 2 707 | 50 349 | 20.8 | 23 679 | 43.6 | 56.3 | 26.4 | 4.6 | 2 159 | 19.2 |
| Perry | 41 | 17.1 | 118 | 0.5 | 12.0 | 289 564 | 2 444 | 49 014 | 16.8 | 48 368 | 14.5 | 85.5 | 25.9 | 4.3 | 663 | 24.8 |
| Pike | 73 | -8.8 | 124 | 0.2 | 25.7 | 335 978 | 2 714 | 59 513 | 73.7 | 124 302 | 2.2 | 97.8 | 30.4 | 10.3 | 494 | 20.1 |
| Pontotoc | 146 | 4.3 | 159 | 1.9 | 61.4 | 262 986 | 1 658 | 41 731 | 17.6 | 19 117 | 46.0 | 54.0 | 18.3 | 3.3 | 2 506 | 61.5 |
| Prentiss | 101 | -1.0 | 176 | 0.2 | 44.6 | 246 792 | 1 401 | 41 611 | 8.1 | 13 983 | 59.0 | 41.0 | 17.5 | 2.4 | 1 724 | 69.1 |
| Quitman | 220 | 20.9 | 631 | 49.8 | 176.5 | 977 714 | 1 548 | 139 386 | 52.2 | 149 647 | 95.8 | 4.2 | 38.1 | 23.5 | 7 979 | 92.0 |
| Rankin | 140 | 6.9 | 179 | 0.4 | 40.6 | 449 109 | 2 504 | 64 390 | 123.2 | 157 561 | 5.1 | 94.9 | 31.6 | 11.5 | 1 575 | 21.5 |
| Scott | 127 | 11.4 | 158 | 0.1 | 34.4 | 327 233 | 2 074 | 66 589 | 231.6 | 288 383 | 1.2 | 98.8 | 35.7 | 18.2 | 842 | 23.0 |
| Sharkey | 180 | 9.1 | 1 576 | 47.6 | 156.2 | 2 461 920 | 1 562 | 393 451 | 73.8 | 647 533 | 94.5 | 5.5 | 62.3 | 51.8 | 7 449 | 82.5 |
| Simpson | 118 | 13.5 | 162 | 0.2 | 29.7 | 391 132 | 2 418 | 62 826 | 185.9 | 255 752 | 1.2 | 98.8 | 36.5 | 17.9 | 518 | 22.1 |
| Smith | 110 | 5.8 | 145 | 0.4 | 25.1 | 360 426 | 2 486 | 62 731 | 238.7 | 315 279 | 1.3 | 98.7 | 41.5 | 25.5 | 415 | 19.6 |
| Stone | 52 | -8.8 | 161 | 0.0 | 10.9 | 439 555 | 2 738 | 43 883 | 7.9 | 24 581 | D | D | 22.3 | 1.9 | 567 | 17.0 |

# Table B. States and Counties — Water Use, Wholesale Trade, Retail Trade, and Real Estate

| | Water use, 2005 | | Wholesale trade,[1] 2007 | | | | Retail trade,[2] 2007 | | | | Real estate and rental and leasing,[2] 2007 | | | |
|---|---|---|---|---|---|---|---|---|---|---|---|---|---|---|
| STATE<br>County | Total water withdrawn (mil gal/day) | Gallons withdrawn per person | Number of establishments | Number of employees | Sales (mil dol) | Annual payroll (mil dol) | Number of establishments | Number of employees | Sales (mil dol) | Annual payroll (mil dol) | Number of establishments | Number of employees | Receipts (mil dol) | Annual payroll (mil dol) |
| | 133 | 134 | 135 | 136 | 137 | 138 | 139 | 140 | 141 | 142 | 143 | 144 | 145 | 146 |
| MISSISSIPPI | 2 927.7 | 1 002 | 2 556 | 32 382 | 23 003.6 | 1 276.0 | 12 452 | 141 426 | 33 751.4 | 2 910.9 | 2 517 | 10 169 | 1 734.6 | 283.7 |
| Adams | 6.9 | 214 | 38 | D | D | D | 191 | 2 037 | 427.7 | 41.5 | 41 | 148 | 18.9 | 4.0 |
| Alcorn | 5.3 | 150 | 37 | D | D | D | 196 | 2 237 | 527.6 | 46.6 | 23 | 200 | 10.7 | 3.5 |
| Amite | 2.4 | 175 | 8 | 29 | 17.9 | 0.8 | 33 | 177 | 36.3 | 3.1 | 2 | D | D | D |
| Attala | 2.9 | 146 | 21 | 87 | 37.0 | 3.1 | 95 | 845 | 171.4 | 16.0 | 9 | 22 | 2.3 | 0.4 |
| Benton | 2.3 | 295 | NA | NA | NA | NA | 15 | 130 | 25.1 | 2.2 | 1 | D | D | D |
| Bolivar | 331.8 | 8 586 | 31 | D | D | D | 167 | 1 558 | 303.4 | 27.8 | 38 | 126 | 15.4 | 2.4 |
| Calhoun | 3.2 | 217 | 11 | 75 | 29.0 | 1.8 | 68 | 443 | 94.1 | 7.6 | 3 | D | D | D |
| Carroll | 7.0 | 669 | 3 | D | D | D | 21 | 159 | 24.2 | 1.7 | 2 | D | D | D |
| Chickasaw | 9.1 | 473 | 18 | 188 | 101.5 | 4.5 | 84 | 681 | 128.0 | 10.6 | 12 | 30 | 3.0 | 0.6 |
| Choctaw | 5.6 | 585 | 2 | D | D | D | 31 | 185 | 30.8 | 2.9 | 2 | D | D | D |
| Claiborne | 29.1 | 2 529 | 3 | D | D | D | 31 | 183 | 39.3 | 3.5 | 1 | D | D | D |
| Clarke | 2.6 | 149 | 6 | D | D | D | 51 | 377 | 58.1 | 4.7 | 5 | 39 | 4.5 | 0.8 |
| Clay | 6.1 | 288 | 14 | D | D | D | 77 | 634 | 126.0 | 10.7 | 9 | 111 | 14.1 | 2.4 |
| Coahoma | 139.7 | 4 817 | 26 | D | D | D | 127 | 1 112 | 260.3 | 22.7 | 38 | 58 | 2.9 | 1.0 |
| Copiah | 5.8 | 198 | 11 | D | D | D | 92 | 733 | 143.1 | 13.0 | 9 | 18 | 1.7 | 0.2 |
| Covington | 7.6 | 374 | 13 | 68 | 66.6 | 2.0 | 74 | 567 | 171.6 | 11.3 | 10 | 434 | 90.0 | 12.1 |
| DeSoto | 32.0 | 234 | 100 | 2 098 | 1 676.8 | 80.1 | 471 | 7 895 | 2 069.5 | 178.0 | 110 | | | |
| Forrest | 32.4 | 431 | 77 | 858 | 424.1 | 31.1 | 382 | 4 496 | 2 121.6 | 104.1 | 99 | D | D | D |
| Franklin | 1.2 | 137 | 3 | D | D | D | 20 | 119 | 20.9 | 1.7 | 2 | 18 | 1.7 | 0.3 |
| George | 3.3 | 154 | 11 | D | D | D | 81 | 888 | 231.5 | 16.4 | 9 | 12 | 1.7 | 0.2 |
| Greene | 2.9 | 222 | 3 | 79 | 27.6 | 2.6 | 29 | 194 | 39.1 | 2.9 | 5 | 92 | 16.3 | 2.4 |
| Grenada | 10.1 | 441 | 29 | D | D | D | 136 | 1 378 | 377.0 | 31.1 | 26 | 69 | 12.5 | 1.6 |
| Hancock | 10.8 | 232 | 21 | D | D | D | 116 | 1 411 | 383.2 | 32.7 | 32 | 968 | 175.6 | 29.3 |
| Harrison | 195.3 | 1 007 | 156 | 1 618 | 839.7 | 70.4 | 821 | 11 071 | 2 903.2 | 254.4 | 252 | 1 689 | 412.2 | 60.1 |
| Hinds | 46.3 | 186 | 292 | 4 183 | 2 118.8 | 188.3 | 962 | 12 358 | 2 992.6 | 279.3 | 286 | D | D | D |
| Holmes | 49.9 | 2 366 | 10 | 121 | 31.1 | 2.9 | 81 | 534 | 114.4 | 8.8 | 14 | D | D | D |
| Humphreys | 122.3 | 11 617 | 6 | 35 | 15.1 | 1.2 | 35 | 298 | 81.4 | 5.2 | 3 | D | D | D |
| Issaquena | 11.1 | 5 825 | 2 | D | D | D | NA | NA | NA | NA | NA | NA | NA | NA |
| Itawamba | 10.9 | 468 | 10 | 222 | 59.4 | 7.0 | 80 | 635 | 135.0 | 12.8 | 2 | D | D | D |
| Jackson | 54.4 | 400 | 51 | D | D | D | 453 | 5 356 | 1 305.0 | 116.0 | 105 | 370 | 48.8 | 9.3 |
| Jasper | 2.5 | 140 | 11 | 89 | 89.5 | 3.4 | 42 | 370 | 68.9 | 7.2 | 4 | 38 | 5.4 | 0.9 |
| Jefferson | 0.7 | 69 | 1 | D | D | D | 13 | 89 | 18.6 | 1.3 | 2 | D | D | D |
| Jefferson Davis | 2.5 | 192 | 2 | D | D | D | 52 | 345 | 57.3 | 5.2 | 5 | D | D | D |
| Jones | 17.2 | 260 | 79 | 664 | 402.7 | 28.0 | 284 | 3 367 | 816.4 | 70.0 | 60 | 314 | 59.4 | 12.9 |
| Kemper | 1.8 | 171 | 3 | D | D | D | 31 | 176 | 46.7 | 2.9 | 1 | D | D | D |
| Lafayette | 3.6 | 88 | 22 | D | D | D | 205 | 2 419 | 507.1 | 48.5 | 54 | 177 | 25.0 | 3.6 |
| Lamar | 21.7 | 485 | 35 | D | D | D | 320 | 4 871 | 991.8 | 90.5 | 64 | D | D | D |
| Lauderdale | 12.0 | 155 | 84 | 1 696 | 1 127.6 | 65.7 | 449 | 5 400 | 1 320.6 | 112.8 | 73 | 294 | 39.3 | 6.1 |
| Lawrence | 38.6 | 2 861 | 3 | D | D | D | 43 | 301 | 46.8 | 5.1 | 2 | D | D | D |
| Leake | 5.8 | 257 | 10 | 93 | 22.7 | 2.6 | 88 | 799 | 180.4 | 15.4 | 5 | 12 | 0.6 | 0.2 |
| Lee | 4.6 | 58 | 159 | 1 859 | 847.9 | 65.3 | 541 | 6 753 | 1 439.5 | 136.4 | 99 | 511 | 88.6 | 14.7 |
| Leflore | 213.6 | 5 862 | 39 | D | D | D | 182 | 1 803 | 438.7 | 34.7 | 47 | D | D | D |
| Lincoln | 5.5 | 161 | 28 | D | D | D | 178 | 1 998 | 502.0 | 41.8 | 28 | 102 | 14.5 | 2.3 |
| Lowndes | 41.7 | 697 | 80 | D | D | D | 349 | 3 950 | 809.3 | 80.4 | 75 | 233 | 33.3 | 5.1 |
| Madison | 13.9 | 164 | 131 | 2 958 | 3 305.9 | 119.5 | 457 | 6 441 | 1 268.4 | 135.6 | 139 | 719 | 159.0 | 24.1 |
| Marion | 5.1 | 201 | 24 | 233 | 155.7 | 7.4 | 132 | 1 253 | 259.0 | 23.4 | 24 | 79 | 18.8 | 2.2 |
| Marshall | 4.1 | 116 | 13 | 68 | 43.5 | 2.3 | 114 | 886 | 166.4 | 17.0 | 17 | 47 | 6.4 | 1.1 |
| Monroe | 27.7 | 734 | 23 | 245 | 111.1 | 7.4 | 146 | 1 432 | 282.0 | 26.1 | 16 | 42 | 3.8 | 0.8 |
| Montgomery | 1.8 | 153 | 7 | 30 | 7.6 | 0.9 | 59 | 526 | 136.6 | 9.1 | 4 | D | D | D |
| Neshoba | 4.8 | 162 | 19 | 197 | 286.9 | 9.2 | 126 | 1 227 | 255.8 | 23.7 | 19 | 53 | 5.7 | 1.1 |
| Newton | 3.1 | 139 | 5 | 32 | 9.2 | 0.7 | 85 | 811 | 146.7 | 14.0 | 7 | 18 | 2.0 | 0.2 |
| Noxubee | 29.9 | 2 450 | 10 | 77 | 26.8 | 1.5 | 52 | 395 | 82.9 | 6.0 | 1 | D | D | D |
| Oktibbeha | 6.4 | 156 | 17 | 416 | 166.2 | 13.4 | 161 | 2 105 | 387.9 | 39.8 | 49 | 170 | 25.6 | 3.5 |
| Panola | 29.0 | 820 | 31 | 572 | 484.5 | 21.1 | 185 | 1 664 | 384.4 | 30.0 | 17 | 72 | 10.2 | 1.8 |
| Pearl River | 6.8 | 129 | 30 | D | D | D | 209 | 2 452 | 615.6 | 52.1 | 25 | 76 | 9.3 | 1.3 |
| Perry | 21.2 | 1 745 | 3 | D | D | D | 37 | 280 | 60.4 | 4.6 | 3 | D | D | D |
| Pike | 8.1 | 206 | 50 | 454 | 188.7 | 12.9 | 235 | 2 583 | 544.7 | 51.1 | 43 | D | D | D |
| Pontotoc | 2.2 | 79 | 16 | 155 | 57.5 | 4.3 | 84 | 886 | 203.6 | 15.3 | 5 | D | D | D |
| Prentiss | 2.3 | 91 | 13 | 43 | 17.8 | 1.0 | 109 | 763 | 162.0 | 14.7 | 43 | 96 | 8.1 | 1.3 |
| Quitman | 80.4 | 8 449 | 6 | 35 | 19.1 | 0.9 | 20 | 158 | 24.7 | 2.2 | 5 | 10 | 1.5 | 0.2 |
| Rankin | 21.6 | 164 | 215 | 3 621 | 2 629.6 | 169.1 | 521 | 8 124 | 2 226.2 | 183.0 | 147 | 646 | 121.9 | 20.6 |
| Scott | 10.9 | 381 | 21 | 71 | 41.2 | 1.9 | 125 | 1 156 | 235.1 | 21.8 | 8 | 30 | 2.5 | 0.6 |
| Sharkey | 32.0 | 5 368 | 13 | 91 | 64.2 | 3.1 | 23 | 199 | 31.0 | 2.8 | 7 | 18 | 2.1 | 0.3 |
| Simpson | 5.3 | 190 | 12 | D | D | D | 93 | 1 044 | 212.6 | 19.8 | 13 | 44 | 4.7 | 0.9 |
| Smith | 4.8 | 298 | 8 | 34 | 12.6 | 0.8 | 36 | 312 | 51.1 | 4.8 | 3 | 7 | 0.4 | 0.1 |
| Stone | 3.2 | 217 | 14 | D | D | D | 65 | 716 | 190.7 | 15.7 | 11 | 38 | 3.1 | 0.6 |

1. Merchant wholesalers, except manufacturers' sales branches and offices.  2. Employer establishments.

# Professional Services, Manufacturing, and Accommodation and Food Services

| STATE County | Professional, scientific, and technical services,[1] 2007 | | | | Manufacturing, 2007 | | | | Accommodation and food services, 2007 | | | |
|---|---|---|---|---|---|---|---|---|---|---|---|---|
| | Number of establishments | Number of employees | Receipts (mil dol) | Annual payroll (mil dol) | Number of establishments | Number of employees | Receipts (mil dol) | Annual payroll (mil dol) | Number of establishments | Number of employees | Sales (mil dol) | Annual payroll (mil dol) |
| | 147 | 148 | 149 | 150 | 151 | 152 | 153 | 154 | 155 | 156 | 157 | 158 |
| MISSISSIPPI | 4 751 | 30 855 | 3 971.9 | 1 350.3 | 2 598 | 159 235 | 59 869.5 | 5 756.6 | 4 817 | 119 626 | 7 045.1 | 1 812.3 |
| Adams | 62 | 248 | 24.6 | 6.6 | NA | NA | NA | NA | 88 | 1 728 | 98.0 | 22.2 |
| Alcorn | 60 | 298 | 26.6 | 8.6 | 49 | 2 994 | 944.6 | 122.4 | 70 | 1 157 | 42.5 | 11.0 |
| Amite | 6 | D | D | D | 10 | 599 | D | 21.9 | 4 | 28 | 1.3 | 0.3 |
| Attala | 23 | 58 | 5.4 | 1.4 | 23 | 984 | 319.5 | 27.8 | 26 | 326 | 13.7 | 3.4 |
| Benton | 2 | D | D | D | NA | NA | NA | NA | NA | NA | NA | NA |
| Bolivar | 50 | 219 | 19.7 | 7.1 | 18 | 1 345 | 287.0 | 48.5 | 44 | 777 | 31.1 | 7.0 |
| Calhoun | 14 | 50 | 5.8 | 1.6 | 21 | 876 | 235.3 | 26.9 | 12 | 90 | 2.5 | 0.6 |
| Carroll | 4 | D | D | D | NA | NA | NA | NA | 5 | 28 | 0.7 | 0.2 |
| Chickasaw | 15 | 47 | 3.5 | 1.1 | 51 | 2 668 | 427.2 | 79.1 | 19 | 253 | 11.5 | 2.2 |
| Choctaw | 6 | 17 | 1.5 | 0.6 | NA | NA | NA | NA | 8 | 43 | 1.7 | 0.3 |
| Claiborne | 7 | 21 | 1.6 | 0.4 | NA | NA | NA | NA | 12 | 181 | 4.7 | 1.4 |
| Clarke | 15 | D | D | D | 22 | 584 | D | 16.8 | 11 | 108 | 4.5 | 1.1 |
| Clay | 22 | D | D | D | 23 | 1 122 | 393.0 | 46.5 | 34 | 465 | 15.8 | 3.8 |
| Coahoma | 47 | D | D | D | 22 | 738 | D | 27.3 | 42 | 1 353 | 120.6 | 21.8 |
| Copiah | 24 | 66 | 6.4 | 1.8 | 26 | 2 644 | D | D | 33 | 484 | 15.7 | 3.8 |
| Covington | 17 | 82 | 7.5 | 2.5 | 12 | 1 505 | D | 34.9 | 21 | 359 | 11.2 | 3.2 |
| DeSoto | 175 | 921 | 77.9 | 28.8 | 133 | 4 822 | 1 663.5 | 208.2 | 260 | 6 230 | 256.8 | 67.1 |
| Forrest | 184 | D | D | D | 72 | D | 883.4 | 137.5 | 176 | 4 078 | 158.8 | 42.8 |
| Franklin | 8 | 36 | 2.9 | 1.3 | NA | NA | NA | NA | 5 | D | D | D |
| George | 18 | D | D | D | NA | NA | NA | NA | 27 | 342 | 13.4 | 3.0 |
| Greene | 4 | 19 | 1.2 | 0.5 | NA | NA | NA | NA | 4 | 42 | 1.7 | 0.4 |
| Grenada | 33 | 151 | 14.0 | 5.6 | 24 | 2 910 | 732.5 | 101.7 | 61 | 875 | 36.2 | 8.5 |
| Hancock | 93 | D | D | D | 32 | 863 | D | 58.5 | 78 | 1 616 | 133.8 | 33.0 |
| Harrison | 393 | D | D | D | 110 | 3 234 | D | 137.4 | 353 | 17 953 | 1 619.1 | 435.9 |
| Hinds | 710 | D | D | D | 160 | 5 610 | 1 406.2 | 243.1 | 451 | 9 284 | 403.8 | 107.2 |
| Holmes | 13 | 59 | 20.1 | 4.7 | 6 | 622 | 208.0 | 17.5 | 25 | 178 | 5.5 | 1.5 |
| Humphreys | 5 | 12 | 1.3 | 0.4 | 4 | D | D | D | 9 | 139 | 4.4 | 1.2 |
| Issaquena | NA | NA | NA | NA | NA | NA | NA | NA | NA | NA | NA | NA |
| Itawamba | 17 | D | D | D | 40 | 1 531 | D | 46.8 | 27 | 365 | 12.3 | 3.2 |
| Jackson | 203 | D | D | D | 82 | D | D | D | 227 | 4 167 | 178.0 | 47.2 |
| Jasper | 18 | 136 | 7.2 | 3.3 | 13 | 1 283 | 256.5 | 41.6 | 13 | 117 | 4.4 | 1.0 |
| Jefferson | 1 | D | D | D | NA | NA | NA | NA | 3 | D | D | D |
| Jefferson Davis | 13 | 14 | 3.8 | 1.4 | NA | NA | NA | NA | 9 | 144 | 6.2 | 1.5 |
| Jones | 97 | 598 | 55.1 | 16.0 | 72 | 8 571 | 1 760.0 | 265.3 | 105 | 5 520 | 442.8 | 106.5 |
| Kemper | 5 | D | D | D | NA | NA | NA | NA | 5 | 36 | 1.4 | 0.4 |
| Lafayette | 113 | D | D | D | 27 | 1 479 | D | 47.5 | 128 | 2 298 | 96.2 | 26.3 |
| Lamar | 102 | 604 | 72.1 | 22.9 | 28 | D | D | 19.7 | 100 | 2 701 | 103.5 | 30.2 |
| Lauderdale | 120 | D | D | D | 66 | 2 880 | 750.9 | 99.6 | 159 | 3 620 | 135.8 | 38.0 |
| Lawrence | 8 | 12 | 1.6 | 0.2 | 12 | 717 | D | 42.1 | 16 | 104 | 4.0 | 0.9 |
| Leake | 14 | 45 | 3.3 | 0.8 | 7 | D | D | D | 23 | 299 | 13.0 | 3.1 |
| Lee | 189 | D | D | D | 149 | 11 736 | 2 986.8 | 427.4 | 195 | 4 096 | 148.2 | 41.3 |
| Leflore | 50 | D | D | D | 34 | D | D | D | 62 | 1 137 | 51.4 | 13.1 |
| Lincoln | 56 | 469 | 44.0 | 15.4 | 33 | 1 146 | 275.7 | 45.4 | 58 | 883 | 41.2 | 9.6 |
| Lowndes | 116 | 617 | 78.4 | 24.7 | 63 | 3 879 | 2 075.5 | 172.6 | 111 | 2 456 | 88.6 | 23.4 |
| Madison | 323 | D | D | D | 75 | 7 495 | 6 471.9 | 320.7 | 228 | 4 619 | 180.6 | 49.6 |
| Marion | 43 | 185 | 16.0 | 6.7 | 23 | 950 | 166.3 | 22.0 | 44 | 529 | 20.1 | 4.6 |
| Marshall | 21 | 71 | 6.6 | 1.8 | 31 | D | D | D | 28 | 422 | 14.2 | 3.8 |
| Monroe | 40 | 121 | 8.7 | 2.5 | 53 | 3 144 | 1 472.7 | 130.0 | 51 | 541 | 21.8 | 4.9 |
| Montgomery | 14 | 27 | 3.7 | 0.7 | NA | NA | NA | NA | 23 | 229 | 7.3 | 1.8 |
| Neshoba | 19 | 90 | 8.2 | 3.8 | 14 | 628 | 192.4 | 23.2 | 42 | 665 | 24.2 | 5.8 |
| Newton | 17 | 48 | 2.9 | 1.0 | 21 | 1 693 | 290.8 | 51.2 | 22 | 356 | 11.2 | 3.0 |
| Noxubee | 6 | 12 | 0.8 | 0.2 | 18 | 792 | 198.9 | 26.1 | 11 | 81 | 4.6 | 1.3 |
| Oktibbeha | 73 | D | D | D | 29 | 1 506 | 514.3 | 63.9 | 100 | 2 129 | 77.3 | 20.5 |
| Panola | 29 | 157 | 15.1 | 3.8 | 41 | 2 083 | 495.3 | 74.2 | 54 | 866 | 32.6 | 9.2 |
| Pearl River | 63 | 281 | 22.1 | 9.8 | 36 | 637 | D | 25.3 | 83 | 1 210 | 43.2 | 10.9 |
| Perry | 6 | D | D | D | 10 | 811 | D | 40.9 | 5 | 34 | 1.2 | 0.4 |
| Pike | 76 | D | D | D | 34 | 2 777 | D | 68.1 | 76 | 1 311 | 50.9 | 13.2 |
| Pontotoc | 22 | D | D | D | 78 | 6 833 | D | 198.6 | 30 | 434 | 14.8 | 3.8 |
| Prentiss | 26 | 165 | 34.4 | 5.8 | 40 | 2 609 | 975.2 | 79.1 | 33 | 507 | 17.5 | 4.8 |
| Quitman | 4 | D | D | D | NA | NA | NA | NA | 5 | 62 | 1.9 | 0.4 |
| Rankin | 314 | 1 450 | 204.0 | 67.5 | 131 | 3 897 | 1 865.8 | 161.8 | 241 | 4 832 | 197.8 | 52.7 |
| Scott | 21 | 93 | 5.2 | 1.9 | 23 | 5 072 | 1 057.5 | 143.6 | 38 | 518 | 19.7 | 4.5 |
| Sharkey | 8 | 18 | 1.2 | 0.3 | NA | NA | NA | NA | 4 | 35 | 1.6 | 0.4 |
| Simpson | 27 | 121 | 8.9 | 2.6 | NA | NA | NA | NA | 37 | 552 | 20.6 | 5.2 |
| Smith | 14 | 94 | 8.1 | 1.8 | 13 | 1 052 | 402.6 | 37.5 | 10 | 73 | 1.8 | 0.5 |
| Stone | 18 | D | D | D | 23 | 616 | D | 23.1 | 27 | 482 | 18.6 | 4.8 |

1. Establishment subject to federal tax.

| STATE County | Health care and social assistance, 2007 | | | | Other services, 2007 | | | | Federal funds and grants, 2009–2010 Expenditures (mil dol) | | | |
|---|---|---|---|---|---|---|---|---|---|---|---|---|
| | | | | | | | | | | Direct payments for individuals[1] | | |
| | Number of establishments | Number of employees | Receipts (mil dol) | Annual payroll (mil dol) | Number of establishments | Number of employees | Receipts (mil dol) | Annual payroll (mil dol) | Total | Social Security and government retirement | Medicare | Food Stamps and Supplemental Security Income |
| | 159 | 160 | 161 | 162 | 163 | 164 | 165 | 166 | 167 | 168 | 169 | 170 |
| MISSISSIPPI | 5 876 | 146 858 | 14 113.8 | 5 371.7 | 3 853 | 20 421 | 1 949.6 | 489.6 | 31 418.9 | 9 042.0 | 4 606.0 | 1 588.6 |
| Adams | 102 | 1 881 | 178.3 | 62.7 | 47 | 213 | 16.9 | 4.3 | 306.1 | 113.5 | 57.3 | 27.1 |
| Alcorn | 101 | 2 008 | 215.4 | 68.5 | 58 | 171 | 12.7 | 3.6 | 325.6 | 134.9 | 66.4 | 15.9 |
| Amite | 10 | D | D | D | 7 | D | D | D | 111.7 | 41.5 | 25.7 | 8.2 |
| Attala | 24 | 579 | 42.6 | 15.4 | 25 | 224 | 11.7 | 2.5 | 188.8 | 68.2 | 43.1 | 11.5 |
| Benton | 9 | D | D | D | 3 | D | D | D | 75.9 | 28.0 | 16.0 | 4.4 |
| Bolivar | 72 | 1 942 | 135.8 | 49.2 | 50 | 218 | 16.6 | 4.2 | 423.2 | 98.9 | 66.8 | 40.7 |
| Calhoun | 23 | 429 | 25.9 | 10.0 | 14 | 34 | 2.4 | 0.6 | 158.1 | 49.2 | 32.8 | 6.9 |
| Carroll | 5 | D | D | D | 5 | D | D | D | 80.8 | 31.0 | 15.6 | 6.3 |
| Chickasaw | 29 | D | D | D | 23 | 50 | 3.4 | 0.8 | 182.8 | 61.2 | 37.4 | 11.0 |
| Choctaw | 9 | D | D | D | 11 | 29 | 2.5 | 0.6 | 79.3 | 24.3 | 12.8 | 5.1 |
| Claiborne | 18 | 368 | 21.4 | 9.2 | 5 | D | D | D | 92.1 | 25.2 | 20.0 | 10.8 |
| Clarke | 21 | 402 | 26.3 | 10.1 | 18 | D | D | D | 151.2 | 62.6 | 32.4 | 8.1 |
| Clay | 27 | 690 | 57.3 | 22.3 | 23 | 88 | 8.4 | 2.0 | 169.8 | 62.5 | 30.5 | 15.4 |
| Coahoma | 77 | 1 897 | 179.5 | 61.3 | 36 | 194 | 8.1 | 2.7 | 382.5 | 71.0 | 66.0 | 34.4 |
| Copiah | 31 | 610 | 53.4 | 14.9 | 33 | 130 | 9.5 | 2.2 | 305.1 | 101.1 | 58.4 | 21.3 |
| Covington | 29 | 506 | 37.1 | 14.6 | 22 | 110 | 8.6 | 2.0 | 165.7 | 62.8 | 33.6 | 12.9 |
| DeSoto | 208 | 4 172 | 424.4 | 157.5 | 171 | 993 | 101.2 | 24.0 | 648.1 | 406.8 | 92.0 | 23.4 |
| Forrest | 188 | 7 667 | 787.3 | 357.7 | 102 | 747 | 52.0 | 15.4 | 1 105.6 | 287.6 | 129.3 | 43.6 |
| Franklin | 10 | 258 | 14.0 | 6.6 | 4 | D | D | D | 70.6 | 25.5 | 15.6 | 4.7 |
| George | 30 | 637 | 52.8 | 24.7 | 23 | 88 | 7.1 | 1.8 | 159.4 | 79.4 | 36.7 | 10.1 |
| Greene | 10 | 99 | 5.9 | 2.2 | 10 | D | D | D | 74.5 | 27.7 | 18.8 | 6.0 |
| Grenada | 69 | 1 053 | 95.7 | 36.1 | 40 | 113 | 10.8 | 2.5 | 244.7 | 83.3 | 55.7 | 15.0 |
| Hancock | 59 | D | D | D | 46 | 174 | 16.7 | 4.7 | 895.0 | 140.0 | 71.1 | 17.0 |
| Harrison | 437 | 12 887 | 1 498.9 | 570.4 | 289 | 1 778 | 181.3 | 47.3 | 2 420.3 | 704.2 | 320.0 | 82.8 |
| Hinds | 735 | 25 347 | 2 673.9 | 985.5 | 462 | 3 256 | 316.5 | 88.2 | 4 018.6 | 686.7 | 382.2 | 171.8 |
| Holmes | 33 | 252 | 17.8 | 6.9 | 18 | 185 | 9.0 | 2.6 | 289.7 | 52.8 | 55.7 | 30.8 |
| Humphreys | 19 | 262 | 15.8 | 6.5 | 14 | 41 | 2.5 | 0.6 | 148.9 | 24.7 | 29.4 | 14.2 |
| Issaquena | 2 | D | D | D | NA | NA | NA | NA | 28.0 | 2.4 | 2.5 | 1.4 |
| Itawamba | 28 | D | D | D | 24 | 64 | 5.1 | 1.2 | 250.0 | 61.7 | 33.5 | 4.7 |
| Jackson | 288 | 5 343 | 569.6 | 219.1 | 152 | 761 | 64.7 | 18.1 | 1 067.0 | 451.9 | 179.4 | 44.1 |
| Jasper | 14 | 289 | 16.4 | 7.9 | 14 | 47 | 3.9 | 1.2 | 158.4 | 58.0 | 32.5 | 10.2 |
| Jefferson | 12 | 210 | 14.1 | 5.9 | 4 | D | D | D | 124.8 | 21.5 | 16.1 | 7.4 |
| Jefferson Davis | 13 | 296 | 18.9 | 7.0 | 12 | 26 | 2.3 | 0.4 | 141.4 | 37.1 | 25.2 | 11.0 |
| Jones | 118 | 3 373 | 257.7 | 116.3 | 98 | 690 | 80.7 | 19.1 | 554.6 | 222.7 | 123.4 | 29.2 |
| Kemper | 7 | 175 | 6.2 | 2.8 | 4 | D | D | D | 109.4 | 28.8 | 16.7 | 6.4 |
| Lafayette | 107 | 2 270 | 243.9 | 82.9 | 66 | 402 | 121.4 | 9.9 | 320.1 | 95.0 | 31.7 | 8.0 |
| Lamar | 121 | 2 445 | 268.5 | 88.9 | 54 | 240 | 18.4 | 4.6 | 193.0 | 96.0 | 38.5 | 13.2 |
| Lauderdale | 207 | 8 113 | 919.1 | 320.4 | 139 | 675 | 59.3 | 14.6 | 744.1 | 268.5 | 144.8 | 44.9 |
| Lawrence | 20 | 200 | 13.0 | 4.4 | 10 | D | D | D | 147.5 | 59.9 | 32.1 | 7.5 |
| Leake | 24 | 521 | 31.2 | 14.9 | 15 | 43 | 4.1 | 1.2 | 192.1 | 68.3 | 48.4 | 10.3 |
| Lee | 254 | 7 385 | 910.0 | 337.6 | 143 | 1 055 | 92.7 | 31.7 | 610.3 | 275.4 | 104.8 | 27.8 |
| Leflore | 77 | D | D | D | 47 | D | D | D | 419.9 | 87.5 | 79.0 | 36.9 |
| Lincoln | 72 | 1 556 | 139.9 | 50.4 | 42 | 274 | 20.1 | 7.4 | 267.4 | 110.0 | 50.7 | 17.5 |
| Lowndes | 166 | 2 987 | 282.4 | 97.3 | 104 | 514 | 36.0 | 10.9 | 684.6 | 202.2 | 73.0 | 32.9 |
| Madison | 198 | 2 810 | 222.5 | 81.4 | 133 | 813 | 94.1 | 26.2 | 812.5 | 231.1 | 75.1 | 34.8 |
| Marion | 43 | 756 | 58.5 | 24.4 | 46 | 159 | 14.5 | 3.1 | 246.4 | 84.8 | 55.1 | 18.6 |
| Marshall | 24 | 1 149 | 76.2 | 24.6 | 19 | D | D | D | 319.3 | 117.6 | 48.8 | 24.5 |
| Monroe | 64 | 1 478 | 119.2 | 49.2 | 48 | 132 | 11.1 | 3.0 | 304.3 | 123.4 | 67.9 | 14.3 |
| Montgomery | 21 | 434 | 28.4 | 12.4 | 16 | 76 | 7.0 | 1.6 | 148.8 | 40.8 | 32.0 | 8.1 |
| Neshoba | 39 | 1 155 | 94.9 | 39.8 | 33 | 191 | 16.0 | 4.3 | 276.1 | 74.1 | 50.2 | 14.1 |
| Newton | 31 | 671 | 46.8 | 18.6 | 29 | 89 | 4.3 | 1.2 | 254.0 | 94.5 | 57.4 | 11.2 |
| Noxubee | 18 | 269 | 18.3 | 7.2 | 15 | D | D | D | 125.2 | 30.3 | 17.9 | 13.5 |
| Oktibbeha | 73 | 1 625 | 116.2 | 50.9 | 66 | 330 | 64.0 | 5.7 | 419.8 | 104.7 | 36.2 | 19.7 |
| Panola | 60 | 1 311 | 84.1 | 38.4 | 25 | 118 | 7.1 | 1.9 | 323.7 | 103.0 | 53.4 | 23.9 |
| Pearl River | 94 | 937 | 64.3 | 25.1 | 58 | 272 | 20.8 | 6.3 | 441.9 | 197.8 | 87.1 | 26.3 |
| Perry | 20 | 289 | 18.8 | 7.1 | 11 | 46 | 2.8 | 0.9 | 88.7 | 36.9 | 16.8 | 7.5 |
| Pike | 120 | D | D | D | 56 | D | D | D | 385.5 | 139.7 | 81.7 | 30.0 |
| Pontotoc | 39 | D | D | D | 32 | 88 | 6.9 | 1.6 | 176.0 | 79.0 | 38.4 | 7.8 |
| Prentiss | 39 | 982 | 51.0 | 18.4 | 32 | D | D | D | 221.8 | 91.3 | 42.9 | 10.3 |
| Quitman | 17 | 299 | 17.0 | 7.3 | 8 | 12 | 0.8 | 0.2 | 123.4 | 24.2 | 23.1 | 11.6 |
| Rankin | 265 | 7 288 | 705.5 | 276.3 | 214 | 1 210 | 112.5 | 32.6 | 776.3 | 363.6 | 111.2 | 23.3 |
| Scott | 46 | 1 040 | 65.6 | 25.7 | 36 | 141 | 10.6 | 3.0 | 240.2 | 85.5 | 55.6 | 11.9 |
| Sharkey | 12 | 207 | 15.2 | 5.5 | 9 | 42 | 1.5 | 0.6 | 80.8 | 15.1 | 14.2 | 7.8 |
| Simpson | 53 | 2 198 | 104.8 | 45.4 | 33 | 139 | 9.8 | 2.6 | 295.5 | 81.7 | 48.5 | 14.5 |
| Smith | 8 | D | D | D | 8 | D | D | D | 113.3 | 41.5 | 23.4 | 6.1 |
| Stone | 19 | D | D | D | 14 | 31 | 3.4 | 1.0 | 145.7 | 61.1 | 27.2 | 7.4 |

1. State totals may include programs not allocated by county.

# Table B. States and Counties — Federal Funds, Residential Construction, and Local Government Finances

| STATE County | Federal funds and grants, 2009–2010 (cont.) | | | | | | | Value of residential construction authorized by building permits, 2011 | | Local government finances, 2007 | | | | |
|---|---|---|---|---|---|---|---|---|---|---|---|---|---|---|
| | Expenditures (mil dol) (cont.) | | | | | | | | | General revenue | | | | |
| | Procurement contract awards | | | Grants[1] | | | | | | | | Taxes | | |
| | | | | | | | | | | | | | Per capita[2] (dollars) | |
| | Salaries and wages | Defense | Other | Medicaid and other health-related | Nutrition and family welfare | Education | Other | New construction ($1,000) | Number of housing units | Total (mil dol) | Inter-governmental (mil dol) | Total (mil dol) | Total | Property |
| | 171 | 172 | 173 | 174 | 175 | 176 | 177 | 178 | 179 | 180 | 181 | 182 | 183 | 184 |
| MISSISSIPPI | 3 016.7 | 1 634.0 | 1 031.9 | 4 459.9 | 856.9 | 632.9 | 1 921.4 | 724 061 | 5 273 | X | X | X | X | X |
| Adams | 11.4 | 0.0 | 6.3 | 67.9 | 14.1 | 2.1 | 1.5 | 228 | 2 | 133.0 | 45.0 | 28.5 | 897 | 798 |
| Alcorn | 17.8 | -0.1 | 1.8 | 52.7 | 4.7 | 3.0 | 10.5 | 1 341 | 21 | 200.6 | 60.6 | 18.6 | 523 | 501 |
| Amite | 3.5 | 0.1 | 0.9 | 27.6 | 2.8 | 0.9 | 0.3 | 0 | 0 | 21.9 | 12.6 | 5.2 | 392 | 380 |
| Attala | 5.3 | 0.2 | 0.9 | 47.6 | 4.6 | 1.8 | 4.6 | 484 | 6 | 56.5 | 26.4 | 12.8 | 653 | 623 |
| Benton | 1.8 | 0.1 | 0.4 | 20.5 | 2.8 | 0.4 | 0.1 | 0 | 0 | 16.1 | 11.4 | 3.8 | 470 | 449 |
| Bolivar | 7.9 | 0.7 | 1.7 | 129.7 | 18.0 | 5.3 | 5.8 | 7 612 | 76 | 106.7 | 61.5 | 29.0 | 771 | 727 |
| Calhoun | 19.8 | 3.1 | 0.6 | 35.5 | 3.0 | 0.6 | 2.6 | 150 | 1 | 42.5 | 19.5 | 7.9 | 539 | 514 |
| Carroll | 1.9 | -0.3 | 0.4 | 19.8 | 1.8 | 0.4 | 0.4 | NA | NA | 20.0 | 8.5 | 6.0 | 579 | 566 |
| Chickasaw | 14.9 | 0.0 | 0.8 | 45.6 | 4.2 | 1.1 | 1.8 | 85 | 1 | 47.3 | 28.6 | 10.5 | 551 | 486 |
| Choctaw | 12.0 | 0.0 | 2.4 | 19.2 | 2.2 | 0.7 | 0.3 | 0 | 0 | 22.0 | 13.6 | 4.4 | 485 | 472 |
| Claiborne | 1.6 | 0.0 | 0.4 | 27.2 | 3.0 | 0.8 | 1.7 | 0 | 0 | 38.9 | 23.1 | 5.0 | 452 | 415 |
| Clarke | 4.0 | 1.9 | 1.8 | 34.7 | 3.5 | 1.0 | 0.3 | 60 | 1 | 36.9 | 23.0 | 9.6 | 549 | 530 |
| Clay | 8.2 | 0.0 | 1.4 | 39.0 | 5.2 | 2.3 | 1.5 | 671 | 7 | 47.6 | 28.1 | 15.2 | 724 | 708 |
| Coahoma | 19.4 | 15.7 | 1.2 | 100.8 | 13.1 | 7.9 | 9.2 | 857 | 12 | 121.4 | 72.3 | 22.7 | 822 | 685 |
| Copiah | 23.2 | 1.2 | 16.2 | 60.2 | 6.3 | 2.6 | 0.6 | 289 | 4 | 92.7 | 46.7 | 15.4 | 524 | 502 |
| Covington | 6.3 | 0.1 | 0.7 | 39.2 | 4.0 | 1.4 | 3.4 | 350 | 2 | 52.6 | 26.4 | 10.1 | 497 | 477 |
| DeSoto | 40.0 | 6.9 | 5.8 | 49.4 | 10.4 | 2.8 | 1.5 | 65 336 | 461 | 349.2 | 162.3 | 135.9 | 910 | 854 |
| Forrest | 305.4 | 87.8 | 12.2 | 87.1 | 18.6 | 7.2 | 74.2 | 6 821 | 54 | 562.4 | 122.3 | 73.4 | 939 | 825 |
| Franklin | 4.2 | 0.0 | 0.7 | 15.4 | 1.9 | 0.4 | 0.6 | 0 | 0 | 22.8 | 14.7 | 5.0 | 597 | 576 |
| George | 11.0 | 0.0 | 2.0 | 13.7 | 4.3 | 0.9 | 0.0 | 387 | 3 | 83.3 | 35.1 | 11.9 | 541 | 523 |
| Greene | 1.4 | 0.0 | 0.3 | 16.8 | 2.2 | 0.5 | 0.0 | 0 | 0 | 36.7 | 25.3 | 7.1 | 541 | 533 |
| Grenada | 23.7 | 11.8 | 2.9 | 39.0 | 4.2 | 1.4 | 1.5 | 1 849 | 16 | 102.4 | 36.7 | 17.6 | 762 | 726 |
| Hancock | 135.9 | 57.2 | 443.7 | 15.9 | 6.3 | 1.6 | 3.8 | 50 524 | 397 | 267.5 | 137.2 | 38.7 | 976 | 854 |
| Harrison | 644.5 | 287.4 | 80.2 | 133.7 | 38.7 | 8.2 | 94.5 | 147 862 | 1 260 | 1 200.9 | 552.7 | 198.2 | 1 126 | 913 |
| Hinds | 332.5 | 35.6 | 127.3 | 472.2 | 219.7 | 314.7 | 1 124.9 | 63 232 | 476 | 848.9 | 432.4 | 259.8 | 1 043 | 980 |
| Holmes | 4.8 | 0.5 | 1.2 | 95.6 | 7.2 | 3.5 | 2.7 | 315 | 2 | 84.0 | 52.6 | 13.9 | 680 | 660 |
| Humphreys | 2.0 | 0.4 | 9.1 | 40.6 | 3.7 | 1.0 | 0.4 | 90 | 1 | 31.4 | 16.6 | 7.8 | 781 | 757 |
| Issaquena | 0.5 | 8.4 | 0.1 | 3.7 | 0.8 | 0.1 | 0.0 | 0 | 0 | 5.4 | 0.6 | 1.3 | 777 | 762 |
| Itawamba | 3.8 | 0.0 | 0.6 | 29.0 | 3.2 | 1.6 | 81.3 | 1 085 | 7 | 92.6 | 46.3 | 19.1 | 831 | 827 |
| Jackson | 102.9 | 118.1 | 46.0 | 45.6 | 22.1 | 7.8 | 37.9 | 46 775 | 300 | 766.3 | 253.9 | 150.1 | 1 153 | 1 077 |
| Jasper | 7.7 | 0.0 | 0.7 | 43.0 | 4.3 | 1.1 | 0.3 | 0 | 0 | 54.4 | 30.4 | 12.3 | 682 | 651 |
| Jefferson | 11.4 | 0.0 | 0.4 | 32.6 | 2.7 | 6.6 | 9.8 | 0 | 0 | 29.7 | 14.1 | 5.5 | 611 | 589 |
| Jefferson Davis | 3.0 | 16.4 | 0.4 | 34.2 | 10.0 | 1.1 | 2.7 | 0 | 0 | 35.0 | 23.6 | 6.9 | 537 | 528 |
| Jones | 34.7 | 0.9 | 17.1 | 88.6 | 11.8 | 4.3 | 3.8 | 4 896 | 75 | 367.1 | 160.7 | 44.3 | 663 | 624 |
| Kemper | 3.5 | 0.1 | 0.5 | 28.9 | 2.5 | 0.7 | 0.6 | NA | NA | 59.5 | 31.6 | 8.2 | 812 | 799 |
| Lafayette | 41.8 | 1.4 | 17.4 | 41.5 | 5.3 | 3.0 | 46.9 | 17 868 | 183 | 91.5 | 42.8 | 34.9 | 817 | 765 |
| Lamar | 9.1 | 0.4 | 1.7 | 24.0 | 4.9 | 1.7 | 0.2 | 629 | 9 | 113.9 | 54.6 | 38.7 | 810 | 791 |
| Lauderdale | 79.1 | 32.5 | 6.4 | 118.3 | 13.6 | 4.7 | 12.6 | 22 675 | 142 | 239.6 | 135.6 | 58.9 | 763 | 719 |
| Lawrence | 14.1 | 0.0 | 0.9 | 25.3 | 2.7 | 1.4 | 1.9 | 175 | 2 | 41.5 | 22.2 | 10.0 | 746 | 737 |
| Leake | 6.2 | 0.0 | 0.8 | 51.1 | 4.1 | 1.6 | 0.2 | 300 | 1 | 42.2 | 27.2 | 9.7 | 426 | 404 |
| Lee | 77.9 | 0.8 | 25.2 | 71.6 | 8.5 | 4.6 | 3.1 | 19 241 | 131 | 230.5 | 123.4 | 71.2 | 886 | 856 |
| Leflore | 28.7 | 7.8 | 7.9 | 98.4 | 10.5 | 10.7 | 5.3 | 998 | 7 | 222.2 | 54.7 | 25.4 | 723 | 686 |
| Lincoln | 32.0 | 0.3 | 2.5 | 43.4 | 5.9 | 1.9 | 0.7 | 1 586 | 11 | 81.2 | 47.0 | 22.3 | 645 | 608 |
| Lowndes | 124.8 | 109.1 | 2.9 | 80.3 | 10.2 | 6.0 | 29.3 | 10 423 | 147 | 186.8 | 89.3 | 43.4 | 727 | 702 |
| Madison | 25.2 | 291.1 | 31.8 | 76.4 | 11.4 | 3.9 | 14.6 | 120 505 | 503 | 249.3 | 112.3 | 99.0 | 1 107 | 1 030 |
| Marion | 10.9 | 0.0 | 6.5 | 52.7 | 13.9 | 1.7 | 0.3 | 506 | 2 | 93.6 | 47.3 | 17.6 | 682 | 574 |
| Marshall | 7.4 | 0.8 | 1.8 | 71.5 | 32.0 | 4.2 | 2.4 | 7 038 | 49 | 64.1 | 39.6 | 19.8 | 540 | 516 |
| Monroe | 10.2 | 1.0 | 6.0 | 57.6 | 6.6 | 2.2 | 8.5 | 263 | 2 | 79.1 | 44.9 | 22.3 | 601 | 557 |
| Montgomery | 12.4 | -0.1 | 0.7 | 40.3 | 9.9 | 0.8 | 1.5 | 2 551 | 50 | 28.1 | 18.2 | 6.7 | 587 | 552 |
| Neshoba | 13.1 | 20.7 | 0.9 | 45.0 | 8.3 | 7.1 | 7.5 | 469 | 3 | 52.8 | 34.4 | 13.3 | 441 | 423 |
| Newton | 19.7 | 0.0 | 1.2 | 42.7 | 4.0 | 0.9 | 10.4 | 0 | 0 | 73.4 | 47.7 | 11.4 | 508 | 475 |
| Noxubee | 3.1 | 0.0 | 1.7 | 48.0 | 3.7 | 1.0 | 0.6 | 242 | 4 | 37.2 | 17.6 | 8.0 | 675 | 662 |
| Oktibbeha | 38.9 | 21.9 | 6.8 | 56.5 | 7.0 | 7.2 | 89.1 | 5 904 | 36 | 135.1 | 45.7 | 25.8 | 589 | 573 |
| Panola | 22.2 | 18.3 | 9.2 | 69.0 | 7.7 | 2.1 | 0.5 | 928 | 8 | 97.3 | 50.9 | 23.9 | 676 | 622 |
| Pearl River | 23.0 | 31.6 | 4.8 | 36.8 | 8.0 | 3.3 | 5.2 | 17 369 | 150 | 246.5 | 177.3 | 36.8 | 645 | 616 |
| Perry | 3.1 | 0.0 | 0.4 | 17.6 | 2.7 | 0.8 | 0.1 | 179 | 1 | 34.7 | 19.6 | 7.9 | 648 | 626 |
| Pike | 27.6 | 0.9 | 1.8 | 70.5 | 8.4 | 3.7 | 10.8 | 523 | 3 | 237.4 | 76.8 | 27.2 | 684 | 655 |
| Pontotoc | 4.8 | 0.0 | 1.8 | 35.5 | 3.7 | 1.1 | 1.0 | 1 206 | 21 | 67.4 | 39.9 | 14.9 | 516 | 489 |
| Prentiss | 11.8 | 0.1 | 0.7 | 45.0 | 3.9 | 1.3 | 0.7 | 1 463 | 10 | 84.7 | 52.1 | 13.0 | 510 | 487 |
| Quitman | 1.9 | 0.0 | -0.6 | 42.1 | 2.9 | 0.7 | 0.4 | 370 | 5 | 22.4 | 14.6 | 6.2 | 696 | 660 |
| Rankin | 155.7 | 27.5 | 6.8 | 49.9 | 12.6 | 4.9 | 5.4 | 64 766 | 352 | 286.7 | 135.9 | 103.0 | 744 | 700 |
| Scott | 18.6 | 0.0 | 10.2 | 48.9 | 6.5 | 1.5 | 0.4 | 85 | 2 | 59.6 | 38.2 | 14.3 | 495 | 455 |
| Sharkey | 2.0 | 0.0 | 0.7 | 19.6 | 1.9 | 0.7 | 0.1 | 458 | 8 | 17.9 | 11.3 | 4.9 | 874 | 832 |
| Simpson | 15.9 | 0.0 | 0.9 | 38.0 | 5.0 | 2.4 | 87.3 | 4 506 | 25 | 52.5 | 33.3 | 11.3 | 406 | 389 |
| Smith | 6.5 | -0.1 | 0.5 | 30.6 | 3.1 | 0.8 | 0.0 | 175 | 2 | 38.5 | 23.2 | 8.3 | 521 | 505 |
| Stone | 7.1 | 0.0 | 3.4 | 10.1 | 2.4 | 0.7 | 2.3 | 1 200 | 12 | 143.2 | 84.7 | 27.0 | 1 719 | 1 683 |

1. State totals may include programs not allocated by county.   2. Based on the resident population estimated as of July 1 of the year shown.

| STATE County | Local government finances, 2007 (cont.) Direct general expenditure | | | | | | | Debt outstanding | | Government employment, 2011 | | | Presidential election,[2] 2012 Percent of vote cast: | | |
|---|---|---|---|---|---|---|---|---|---|---|---|---|---|---|---|
| | Total (mil dol) | Per capita[1] (dollars) | Education | Health and hospitals | Police protection | Public welfare | Highways | Total (mil dol) | Per capita[1] (dollars) | Federal civilian | Federal military | State and local | Democratic | Republican | All other |
| | 185 | 186 | 187 | 188 | 189 | 190 | 191 | 192 | 193 | 194 | 195 | 196 | 197 | 198 | 199 |
| MISSISSIPPI | X | X | X | X | X | X | X | X | X | 26 085 | 30 795 | 222 437 | 43.0 | 56.2 | 0.8 |
| Adams | 122.8 | 3 872 | 30.1 | 33.3 | 5.5 | 0.2 | 3.9 | 157.0 | 4 951 | 123 | 195 | 1 892 | 57.5 | 41.8 | 0.7 |
| Alcorn | 198.8 | 5 582 | 23.4 | 53.7 | 2.3 | 0.0 | 2.6 | 69.0 | 1 939 | 101 | 226 | 2 946 | 27.2 | 71.2 | 1.6 |
| Amite | 20.3 | 1 521 | 59.7 | 1.5 | 4.3 | 0.2 | 13.4 | 0.7 | 53 | 29 | 79 | 390 | 43.8 | 55.5 | 0.7 |
| Attala | 58.2 | 2 970 | 46.9 | 21.5 | 3.0 | 0.1 | 7.6 | 13.0 | 662 | 61 | 118 | 1 192 | 41.9 | 57.4 | 0.7 |
| Benton | 16.7 | 2 080 | 62.8 | 0.9 | 5.5 | 0.0 | 9.0 | 3.0 | 369 | 22 | 53 | 309 | 48.0 | 50.2 | 1.8 |
| Bolivar | 102.6 | 2 727 | 60.2 | 1.8 | 6.6 | 0.2 | 6.5 | 45.1 | 1 199 | 84 | 205 | 2 842 | 67.2 | 31.8 | 1.0 |
| Calhoun | 40.3 | 2 765 | 45.9 | 28.8 | 3.9 | 0.0 | 7.1 | 12.0 | 820 | 36 | 90 | 842 | 35.9 | 63.5 | 0.6 |
| Carroll | 20.8 | 2 015 | 45.0 | 0.9 | 4.5 | 0.2 | 11.7 | 13.6 | 1 325 | 23 | 63 | 333 | 34.1 | 65.4 | 0.4 |
| Chickasaw | 46.9 | 2 473 | 57.3 | 1.6 | 5.4 | 7.4 | 5.1 | 18.4 | 969 | 44 | 104 | 932 | 50.7 | 48.5 | 0.8 |
| Choctaw | 22.6 | 2 495 | 66.6 | 1.0 | 5.2 | 1.2 | 10.6 | 6.7 | 739 | 41 | 51 | 436 | 35.3 | 63.6 | 1.1 |
| Claiborne | 39.5 | 3 590 | 39.4 | 13.4 | 3.7 | 0.2 | 9.9 | 143.5 | 13 045 | 27 | 58 | 1 554 | 85.9 | 13.7 | 0.4 |
| Clarke | 38.4 | 2 204 | 65.9 | 1.3 | 4.2 | 0.1 | 10.4 | 15.9 | 912 | 32 | 102 | 769 | 37.2 | 62.3 | 0.6 |
| Clay | 42.7 | 2 035 | 64.8 | 0.7 | 6.5 | 0.7 | 4.9 | 26.5 | 1 265 | 60 | 124 | 914 | 59.1 | 40.3 | 0.6 |
| Coahoma | 105.8 | 3 839 | 60.1 | 0.7 | 4.3 | 0.1 | 3.6 | 156.2 | 5 670 | 71 | 157 | 1 988 | 71.9 | 27.6 | 0.5 |
| Copiah | 92.4 | 3 152 | 66.1 | 11.5 | 4.2 | 0.1 | 6.5 | 20.0 | 681 | 70 | 177 | 1 646 | 53.2 | 46.2 | 0.6 |
| Covington | 54.9 | 2 695 | 50.0 | 25.6 | 3.3 | 0.2 | 6.7 | 17.3 | 848 | 65 | 119 | 1 244 | 40.7 | 58.4 | 0.9 |
| DeSoto | 366.8 | 2 455 | 54.8 | 1.2 | 7.4 | 0.0 | 7.2 | 496.9 | 3 326 | 213 | 994 | 5 952 | 30.5 | 68.8 | 0.7 |
| Forrest | 539.6 | 6 897 | 20.2 | 62.0 | 2.4 | 0.0 | 2.6 | 361.7 | 4 622 | 759 | 818 | 11 207 | 42.8 | 56.3 | 1.0 |
| Franklin | 22.1 | 2 658 | 64.3 | 2.3 | 3.3 | 0.0 | 15.4 | 2.4 | 288 | 59 | 49 | 613 | 37.0 | 62.1 | 0.9 |
| George | 76.1 | 3 468 | 39.8 | 36.7 | 3.0 | 0.1 | 7.8 | 22.0 | 1 001 | 42 | 139 | 1 380 | 16.4 | 82.5 | 1.1 |
| Greene | 36.9 | 2 813 | 41.1 | 0.8 | 3.9 | 0.0 | 43.8 | 10.7 | 813 | 15 | 87 | 1 089 | 23.6 | 75.3 | 1.1 |
| Grenada | 104.4 | 4 525 | 29.5 | 40.9 | 5.0 | 0.1 | 5.9 | 56.1 | 2 432 | 257 | 132 | 1 626 | 44.4 | 55.1 | 0.5 |
| Hancock | 238.5 | 6 009 | 30.9 | 14.9 | 3.2 | 0.1 | 3.7 | 160.8 | 4 051 | 2 034 | 740 | 1 978 | 22.1 | 76.3 | 1.6 |
| Harrison | 1 110.3 | 6 305 | 27.0 | 23.6 | 4.8 | 0.1 | 3.7 | 889.0 | 5 048 | 6 026 | 10 250 | 12 527 | 36.6 | 62.6 | 0.9 |
| Hinds | 854.5 | 3 429 | 54.2 | 0.6 | 5.5 | 0.6 | 5.2 | 1 048.4 | 4 208 | 4 991 | 1 575 | 35 940 | 69.2 | 30.3 | 0.5 |
| Holmes | 86.3 | 4 217 | 77.2 | 1.4 | 3.5 | 0.3 | 4.8 | 38.2 | 1 866 | 54 | 114 | 1 280 | 81.4 | 18.0 | 0.7 |
| Humphreys | 32.1 | 3 212 | 49.8 | 13.1 | 4.7 | 0.1 | 11.7 | 14.6 | 1 461 | 25 | 56 | 480 | 70.9 | 28.5 | 0.6 |
| Issaquena | 5.1 | 3 034 | 1.1 | 2.0 | 14.3 | 0.0 | 11.8 | 3.6 | 2 173 | 0 | 0 | 98 | 60.9 | 38.3 | 0.7 |
| Itawamba | 83.5 | 3 627 | 83.5 | 1.5 | 2.0 | 0.1 | 2.8 | 46.8 | 2 032 | 49 | 142 | 1 210 | 20.9 | 77.0 | 2.1 |
| Jackson | 699.7 | 5 378 | 32.3 | 35.1 | 2.9 | 0.1 | 3.7 | 479.5 | 3 686 | 919 | 1 179 | 9 404 | 32.7 | 66.3 | 1.0 |
| Jasper | 52.9 | 2 929 | 47.4 | 14.2 | 3.2 | 0.2 | 12.9 | 8.6 | 477 | 55 | 102 | 933 | 54.6 | 44.9 | 0.5 |
| Jefferson | 27.5 | 3 066 | 45.3 | 20.5 | 5.4 | 0.2 | 6.0 | 10.2 | 1 134 | 18 | 48 | 619 | 86.7 | 12.3 | 1.0 |
| Jefferson Davis | 27.3 | 2 131 | 63.1 | 4.9 | 4.8 | 0.1 | 7.8 | 12.7 | 993 | 23 | 74 | 666 | 60.4 | 39.0 | 0.6 |
| Jones | 366.4 | 5 488 | 36.7 | 35.3 | 2.2 | 0.1 | 3.6 | 304.3 | 4 558 | 227 | 413 | 6 984 | 30.2 | 68.9 | 0.9 |
| Kemper | 59.4 | 5 878 | 75.7 | 0.7 | 2.0 | 0.1 | 6.0 | 14.7 | 1 451 | 34 | 62 | 581 | 62.3 | 37.0 | 0.6 |
| Lafayette | 98.3 | 2 302 | 59.7 | 1.0 | 6.0 | 0.1 | 8.1 | 108.4 | 2 538 | 339 | 317 | 6 978 | 43.3 | 55.7 | 1.0 |
| Lamar | 130.1 | 2 728 | 70.2 | 0.4 | 4.1 | 0.2 | 9.1 | 79.7 | 1 671 | 55 | 348 | 2 211 | 21.6 | 77.4 | 1.1 |
| Lauderdale | 244.9 | 3 176 | 56.6 | 2.6 | 5.5 | 0.0 | 4.3 | 181.5 | 2 354 | 817 | 1 405 | 5 565 | 40.3 | 59.1 | 0.6 |
| Lawrence | 40.8 | 3 062 | 49.9 | 16.7 | 3.5 | 0.1 | 9.1 | 3.4 | 254 | 41 | 77 | 698 | 36.9 | 62.3 | 0.8 |
| Leake | 43.3 | 1 898 | 55.0 | 1.4 | 5.5 | 0.2 | 10.1 | 28.9 | 1 267 | 60 | 143 | 1 002 | 44.4 | 55.0 | 0.6 |
| Lee | 229.2 | 2 853 | 55.2 | 1.0 | 7.6 | 0.3 | 8.9 | 215.1 | 2 678 | 509 | 511 | 4 999 | 34.4 | 64.9 | 0.7 |
| Leflore | 206.6 | 5 889 | 23.8 | 53.8 | 3.4 | 0.1 | 2.3 | 266.1 | 7 584 | 111 | 193 | 4 198 | 68.1 | 31.4 | 0.5 |
| Lincoln | 72.5 | 2 101 | 60.0 | 1.5 | 6.5 | 0.0 | 9.9 | 65.2 | 1 889 | 94 | 212 | 1 614 | 33.6 | 65.7 | 0.7 |
| Lowndes | 157.1 | 2 635 | 52.4 | 0.9 | 5.5 | 0.2 | 6.4 | 165.4 | 2 774 | 944 | 1 748 | 3 314 | 48.1 | 51.0 | 1.0 |
| Madison | 259.7 | 2 905 | 47.5 | 0.4 | 10.7 | 0.2 | 8.9 | 324.1 | 3 626 | 233 | 588 | 4 323 | 42.0 | 57.5 | 0.5 |
| Marion | 88.9 | 3 456 | 41.6 | 18.5 | 3.7 | 0.0 | 5.7 | 30.0 | 1 165 | 49 | 163 | 1 495 | 34.0 | 65.4 | 0.6 |
| Marshall | 66.8 | 1 820 | 59.1 | 1.8 | 5.9 | 0.2 | 11.1 | 23.8 | 647 | 79 | 223 | 1 233 | 58.8 | 40.6 | 0.7 |
| Monroe | 81.2 | 2 189 | 57.7 | 0.6 | 7.0 | 0.2 | 9.1 | 43.6 | 1 177 | 136 | 222 | 1 484 | 41.0 | 58.2 | 0.8 |
| Montgomery | 28.2 | 2 452 | 57.9 | 2.4 | 5.0 | 0.2 | 13.8 | 9.6 | 832 | 31 | 66 | 669 | 45.7 | 53.8 | 0.6 |
| Neshoba | 52.2 | 1 725 | 58.2 | 1.6 | 5.7 | 0.2 | 9.6 | 32.8 | 1 086 | 83 | 181 | 6 413 | 27.3 | 72.0 | 0.7 |
| Newton | 77.3 | 3 464 | 64.1 | 0.7 | 4.0 | 0.0 | 9.0 | 13.4 | 600 | 79 | 130 | 1 954 | 32.7 | 66.8 | 0.6 |
| Noxubee | 37.2 | 3 132 | 49.3 | 24.9 | 3.8 | 0.2 | 5.6 | 13.3 | 1 118 | 46 | 69 | 736 | 76.3 | 23.1 | 0.5 |
| Oktibbeha | 135.1 | 3 077 | 35.4 | 36.7 | 4.0 | 0.0 | 5.6 | 35.9 | 817 | 259 | 297 | 9 310 | 49.6 | 49.6 | 0.8 |
| Panola | 92.9 | 2 623 | 53.3 | 17.2 | 5.5 | 0.2 | 7.4 | 41.9 | 1 183 | 117 | 210 | 2 174 | 52.9 | 46.4 | 0.6 |
| Pearl River | 244.8 | 4 289 | 49.1 | 0.4 | 2.3 | 0.1 | 3.2 | 53.4 | 935 | 125 | 338 | 3 198 | 19.2 | 79.7 | 1.1 |
| Perry | 34.7 | 2 847 | 56.5 | 1.5 | 4.6 | 0.0 | 11.6 | 82.5 | 6 759 | 17 | 74 | 569 | 27.1 | 71.8 | 1.1 |
| Pike | 230.3 | 5 787 | 35.6 | 46.1 | 2.3 | 0.0 | 3.4 | 68.1 | 1 711 | 121 | 245 | 3 447 | 51.4 | 47.9 | 0.7 |
| Pontotoc | 70.2 | 2 431 | 57.3 | 1.0 | 5.4 | 0.4 | 5.8 | 35.7 | 1 236 | 45 | 181 | 1 150 | 23.2 | 75.6 | 1.2 |
| Prentiss | 90.1 | 3 551 | 79.0 | 1.0 | 3.6 | 0.0 | 4.0 | 47.0 | 1 850 | 45 | 160 | 1 494 | 27.6 | 70.4 | 2.0 |
| Quitman | 23.5 | 2 641 | 59.4 | 1.1 | 6.5 | 0.0 | 9.2 | 12.5 | 1 405 | 25 | 49 | 376 | 67.3 | 32.0 | 0.7 |
| Rankin | 273.0 | 1 973 | 56.9 | 0.9 | 6.1 | 0.2 | 8.0 | 318.0 | 2 298 | 592 | 874 | 9 474 | 22.8 | 76.3 | 0.9 |
| Scott | 56.9 | 1 971 | 65.9 | 1.5 | 6.7 | 0.3 | 7.0 | 19.1 | 662 | 221 | 172 | 1 180 | 43.1 | 56.4 | 0.5 |
| Sharkey | 17.1 | 3 063 | 67.2 | 1.5 | 5.5 | 0.8 | 7.2 | 3.8 | 683 | 27 | 30 | 403 | 68.2 | 31.2 | 0.5 |
| Simpson | 50.2 | 1 806 | 60.0 | 5.9 | 2.6 | 0.0 | 6.9 | 35.5 | 1 275 | 44 | 166 | 1 608 | 38.2 | 60.6 | 1.2 |
| Smith | 38.5 | 2 408 | 65.0 | 1.0 | 5.1 | 0.0 | 10.9 | 10.5 | 655 | 27 | 100 | 636 | 23.7 | 75.4 | 0.9 |
| Stone | 157.2 | 9 992 | 74.2 | 0.4 | 2.1 | 0.0 | 1.4 | 74.8 | 4 755 | 61 | 108 | 1 134 | 27.5 | 71.1 | 1.4 |

1. Based on the resident population estimated as of July 1 of the year shown.    2. © 2013 Election Data Services, Inc. All rights reserved.

# Table B. States and Counties — Land Area and Population

| | | | | | Population 2012 | | | Population characteristics[6], 2011 | | | | | | | | | | |
| | | | | | | | | Race alone or in combination, not Hispanic or Latino (percent) | | | | | Age (percent) | | | | | |
| STATE/ County code | CBSA code[1] | County type[2] | STATE County | Land area,[3] (sq km) 2010 | Total persons | Rank | Per square kilometer | White | Black | Amer- ican Indian, Alaska Native | Asian and Pacific Islander | Percent Hispanic or Latino[4] | Under 5 years | 5 to 17 years | 18 to 24 years | 25 to 34 years | 35 to 44 years | 45 to 54 years |
| | | | | 1 | 2 | 3 | 4 | 5 | 6 | 7 | 8 | 9 | 10 | 11 | 12 | 13 | 14 | 15 |
| | | | MISSISSIPPI—Cont'd | | | | | | | | | | | | | | | |
| 28 133 | 26940 | 5 | Sunflower | 1 807 | 28 431 | 1 472 | 15.7 | 25.9 | 72.2 | 0.4 | 0.5 | 1.5 | 7.1 | 16.9 | 11.8 | 16.2 | 12.8 | 13.7 |
| 28 135 | ... | 7 | Tallahatchie | 1 671 | 15 111 | 2 099 | 9.0 | 36.7 | 56.7 | 0.6 | 1.1 | 5.7 | 6.8 | 15.4 | 11.6 | 16.0 | 14.0 | 13.2 |
| 28 137 | 32820 | 1 | Tate | 1 048 | 28 490 | 1 468 | 27.2 | 66.6 | 30.9 | 0.6 | 0.5 | 2.4 | 6.6 | 19.0 | 11.4 | 11.5 | 12.1 | 13.8 |
| 28 139 | ... | 7 | Tippah | 1 186 | 22 025 | 1 730 | 18.6 | 78.7 | 16.9 | 0.5 | 0.4 | 4.7 | 6.7 | 18.3 | 9.3 | 11.9 | 12.5 | 14.0 |
| 28 141 | ... | 8 | Tishomingo | 1 099 | 19 591 | 1 854 | 17.8 | 93.4 | 3.5 | 0.6 | 0.3 | 3.0 | 5.9 | 16.8 | 8.0 | 10.4 | 12.6 | 14.4 |
| 28 143 | 32820 | 1 | Tunica | 1 178 | 10 475 | 2 396 | 8.9 | 24.1 | 72.8 | 0.4 | 1.0 | 2.5 | 9.0 | 21.1 | 9.7 | 14.3 | 12.0 | 13.2 |
| 28 145 | ... | 7 | Union | 1 076 | 27 414 | 1 515 | 25.5 | 80.2 | 15.5 | 0.4 | 0.5 | 4.5 | 7.1 | 18.6 | 8.3 | 12.4 | 13.4 | 13.4 |
| 28 147 | ... | 9 | Walthall | 1 046 | 15 100 | 2 100 | 14.4 | 53.1 | 45.0 | 0.8 | 0.4 | 1.6 | 7.0 | 18.8 | 8.3 | 12.0 | 11.6 | 13.0 |
| 28 149 | 46980 | 4 | Warren | 1 524 | 48 084 | 1 011 | 31.6 | 50.0 | 47.1 | 0.5 | 1.2 | 2.0 | 6.8 | 18.7 | 8.2 | 12.7 | 12.0 | 14.7 |
| 28 151 | 24740 | 5 | Washington | 1 877 | 49 750 | 987 | 26.5 | 27.3 | 70.9 | 0.4 | 0.8 | 1.2 | 7.7 | 20.2 | 9.5 | 12.2 | 11.2 | 13.7 |
| 28 153 | ... | 7 | Wayne | 2 100 | 20 661 | 1 800 | 9.8 | 59.4 | 39.2 | 0.5 | 0.4 | 1.3 | 7.1 | 18.6 | 9.2 | 12.4 | 11.7 | 14.6 |
| 28 155 | ... | 9 | Webster | 1 090 | 10 039 | 2 441 | 9.2 | 77.8 | 20.8 | 0.5 | 0.3 | 1.3 | 6.5 | 18.0 | 7.6 | 11.4 | 12.2 | 14.7 |
| 28 157 | ... | 8 | Wilkinson | 1 756 | 9 432 | 2 478 | 5.4 | 29.4 | 70.0 | 0.3 | 0.2 | 0.5 | 6.5 | 16.0 | 9.3 | 15.2 | 11.6 | 14.5 |
| 28 159 | ... | 7 | Winston | 1 573 | 19 029 | 1 873 | 12.1 | 52.1 | 45.8 | 1.3 | 0.4 | 1.1 | 7.2 | 17.5 | 8.0 | 11.9 | 11.5 | 13.5 |
| 28 161 | ... | 7 | Yalobusha | 1 210 | 12 401 | 2 279 | 10.2 | 60.5 | 38.1 | 0.6 | 0.3 | 1.3 | 6.5 | 17.2 | 8.3 | 11.2 | 11.8 | 13.8 |
| 28 163 | 49540 | 6 | Yazoo | 2 390 | 28 195 | 1 483 | 11.8 | 37.8 | 56.9 | 0.5 | 0.7 | 4.8 | 7.4 | 17.8 | 8.5 | 16.2 | 13.8 | 13.6 |
| 29 000 | ... | X | MISSOURI | 178 040 | 6 021 988 | X | 33.8 | 82.5 | 12.4 | 1.1 | 2.3 | 3.7 | 6.4 | 17.1 | 9.8 | 13.1 | 12.2 | 14.6 |
| 29 001 | 28860 | 7 | Adair | 1 469 | 25 581 | 1 582 | 17.4 | 93.6 | 2.2 | 0.7 | 3.0 | 2.1 | 5.2 | 13.1 | 28.6 | 9.7 | 9.1 | 11.2 |
| 29 003 | 41140 | 3 | Andrew | 1 121 | 17 417 | 1 957 | 15.5 | 96.7 | 1.1 | 0.9 | 0.6 | 1.8 | 5.6 | 17.8 | 7.8 | 10.8 | 12.2 | 15.5 |
| 29 005 | ... | 9 | Atchison | 1 418 | 5 517 | 2 805 | 3.9 | 98.1 | 0.6 | 0.4 | 0.4 | 1.1 | 5.4 | 15.2 | 7.0 | 9.3 | 11.2 | 14.6 |
| 29 007 | 33020 | 6 | Audrain | 1 793 | 25 621 | 1 580 | 14.3 | 89.7 | 7.7 | 0.7 | 0.9 | 2.7 | 6.6 | 18.2 | 8.1 | 12.9 | 12.0 | 13.7 |
| 29 009 | ... | 6 | Barry | 2 016 | 35 546 | 1 287 | 17.6 | 89.4 | 0.6 | 1.9 | 1.4 | 8.1 | 6.5 | 17.4 | 7.6 | 10.2 | 11.4 | 14.9 |
| 29 011 | ... | 6 | Barton | 1 533 | 12 337 | 2 285 | 8.0 | 96.0 | 1.0 | 2.4 | 0.8 | 2.1 | 6.5 | 19.1 | 7.4 | 11.1 | 11.1 | 14.5 |
| 29 013 | 28140 | 1 | Bates | 2 167 | 16 709 | 1 997 | 7.7 | 96.4 | 1.4 | 1.4 | 0.4 | 1.7 | 6.3 | 18.4 | 7.2 | 11.3 | 10.9 | 15.1 |
| 29 015 | ... | 9 | Benton | 1 824 | 18 962 | 1 876 | 10.4 | 96.7 | 0.7 | 1.4 | 0.7 | 1.7 | 4.1 | 13.2 | 5.7 | 7.3 | 9.6 | 14.5 |
| 29 017 | 16020 | 9 | Bollinger | 1 600 | 12 382 | 2 281 | 7.7 | 97.9 | 0.6 | 1.2 | 0.4 | 0.8 | 6.1 | 17.1 | 8.0 | 10.4 | 12.0 | 15.5 |
| 29 019 | 17860 | 3 | Boone | 1 775 | 168 535 | 370 | 94.9 | 83.2 | 10.6 | 1.0 | 4.6 | 3.2 | 6.1 | 14.6 | 21.5 | 15.1 | 11.2 | 11.9 |
| 29 021 | 41140 | 3 | Buchanan | 1 057 | 89 706 | 637 | 84.9 | 87.7 | 6.6 | 0.9 | 1.4 | 5.4 | 7.0 | 16.5 | 10.8 | 13.6 | 11.8 | 14.3 |
| 29 023 | 38740 | 7 | Butler | 1 799 | 43 053 | 1 108 | 23.9 | 94.1 | 6.3 | 1.4 | 1.0 | 1.6 | 6.3 | 16.9 | 8.3 | 11.9 | 11.9 | 14.1 |
| 29 025 | 28140 | 1 | Caldwell | 1 104 | 9 145 | 2 507 | 8.3 | 96.9 | 1.4 | 1.1 | 0.5 | 1.7 | 5.9 | 18.9 | 6.9 | 10.5 | 11.6 | 15.3 |
| 29 027 | 27620 | 3 | Callaway | 2 162 | 44 305 | 1 081 | 20.5 | 92.4 | 5.5 | 1.2 | 1.0 | 1.7 | 5.7 | 16.4 | 11.5 | 12.9 | 12.5 | 15.4 |
| 29 029 | ... | 7 | Camden | 1 699 | 43 845 | 1 089 | 25.8 | 96.1 | 0.8 | 1.2 | 0.7 | 2.4 | 4.8 | 14.0 | 6.3 | 9.3 | 9.8 | 15.0 |
| 29 031 | 16020 | 5 | Cape Girardeau | 1 498 | 76 950 | 710 | 51.4 | 89.1 | 8.0 | 0.8 | 1.7 | 2.1 | 6.0 | 15.7 | 14.3 | 12.7 | 11.4 | 13.3 |
| 29 033 | ... | 6 | Carroll | 1 799 | 9 086 | 2 511 | 5.1 | 96.1 | 2.5 | 0.7 | 0.4 | 1.4 | 5.8 | 17.9 | 7.3 | 10.3 | 12.2 | 13.7 |
| 29 035 | ... | 9 | Carter | 1 314 | 6 262 | 2 740 | 4.8 | 96.5 | 0.7 | 2.0 | 0.3 | 1.8 | 6.7 | 17.4 | 7.9 | 11.0 | 11.5 | 14.8 |
| 29 037 | 28140 | 1 | Cass | 1 805 | 100 376 | 586 | 55.6 | 91.0 | 4.3 | 1.2 | 1.2 | 4.0 | 6.6 | 19.5 | 7.6 | 12.0 | 13.1 | 15.2 |
| 29 039 | ... | 6 | Cedar | 1 229 | 13 799 | 2 187 | 11.2 | 97.1 | 0.7 | 1.6 | 0.7 | 1.6 | 5.6 | 17.4 | 6.8 | 9.1 | 10.9 | 13.3 |
| 29 041 | ... | 9 | Chariton | 1 946 | 7 649 | 2 631 | 3.9 | 96.8 | 2.5 | 0.7 | 0.2 | 0.6 | 6.1 | 16.2 | 6.5 | 10.1 | 9.9 | 15.2 |
| 29 043 | 44180 | 2 | Christian | 1 457 | 79 824 | 689 | 54.8 | 95.3 | 1.2 | 1.4 | 1.0 | 2.7 | 7.0 | 19.9 | 7.6 | 13.2 | 13.8 | 14.3 |
| 29 045 | 22800 | 9 | Clark | 1 307 | 6 969 | 2 689 | 5.3 | 98.5 | 0.7 | 0.7 | 0.4 | 0.7 | 6.4 | 17.0 | 7.4 | 10.9 | 11.5 | 14.7 |
| 29 047 | 28140 | 1 | Clay | 1 029 | 227 577 | 282 | 221.2 | 85.8 | 6.2 | 1.2 | 3.0 | 6.0 | 7.0 | 18.5 | 8.1 | 14.4 | 14.2 | 14.6 |
| 29 049 | 28140 | 1 | Clinton | 1 085 | 20 508 | 1 813 | 18.9 | 95.7 | 2.1 | 1.4 | 0.6 | 1.6 | 6.0 | 18.3 | 7.4 | 10.9 | 12.3 | 15.8 |
| 29 051 | 27620 | 3 | Cole | 1 020 | 76 363 | 718 | 74.9 | 84.4 | 12.1 | 0.8 | 1.9 | 2.5 | 6.5 | 16.8 | 9.0 | 14.0 | 13.2 | 14.8 |
| 29 053 | ... | 6 | Cooper | 1 463 | 17 520 | 1 950 | 12.0 | 90.7 | 7.9 | 0.9 | 0.7 | 1.4 | 5.6 | 16.5 | 9.7 | 13.7 | 11.7 | 14.5 |
| 29 055 | ... | 6 | Crawford | 1 923 | 24 832 | 1 614 | 12.9 | 97.0 | 0.8 | 1.2 | 0.5 | 1.7 | 6.6 | 17.7 | 7.9 | 11.7 | 11.6 | 15.2 |
| 29 057 | ... | 8 | Dade | 1 269 | 7 568 | 2 636 | 6.0 | 96.5 | 1.2 | 2.5 | 0.6 | 1.6 | 4.9 | 17.2 | 6.2 | 9.2 | 11.2 | 14.9 |
| 29 059 | 44180 | 2 | Dallas | 1 401 | 16 799 | 1 996 | 12.0 | 96.7 | 0.7 | 2.0 | 0.5 | 1.7 | 6.4 | 18.0 | 7.3 | 10.6 | 11.3 | 15.3 |
| 29 061 | ... | 8 | Daviess | 1 459 | 8 239 | 2 590 | 5.6 | 97.8 | 1.0 | 0.8 | 0.3 | 1.2 | 7.0 | 19.1 | 7.1 | 10.1 | 11.4 | 13.6 |
| 29 063 | 41140 | 3 | DeKalb | 1 091 | 12 940 | 2 245 | 11.9 | 85.6 | 11.9 | 0.7 | 0.6 | 1.9 | 4.7 | 12.8 | 9.1 | 16.0 | 15.8 | 16.6 |
| 29 065 | ... | 7 | Dent | 1 950 | 15 647 | 2 069 | 8.0 | 97.2 | 0.8 | 2.1 | 0.5 | 1.0 | 6.1 | 16.9 | 7.3 | 10.4 | 11.1 | 15.1 |
| 29 067 | ... | 6 | Douglas | 2 107 | 13 585 | 2 208 | 6.4 | 97.6 | 0.7 | 1.9 | 0.5 | 1.1 | 5.6 | 16.6 | 7.1 | 9.7 | 10.6 | 14.9 |
| 29 069 | 28380 | 7 | Dunklin | 1 401 | 31 826 | 1 392 | 22.7 | 83.7 | 10.6 | 0.8 | 0.6 | 5.8 | 6.8 | 18.6 | 8.2 | 11.3 | 12.0 | 13.8 |
| 29 071 | 41180 | 1 | Franklin | 2 390 | 101 412 | 579 | 42.4 | 96.7 | 1.4 | 0.8 | 0.7 | 1.5 | 6.3 | 18.0 | 8.3 | 11.8 | 12.5 | 16.1 |
| 29 073 | ... | 6 | Gasconade | 1 341 | 14 972 | 2 109 | 11.2 | 97.8 | 0.5 | 0.8 | 0.7 | 1.2 | 5.2 | 15.9 | 7.0 | 9.6 | 11.1 | 15.7 |
| 29 075 | ... | 8 | Gentry | 1 273 | 6 777 | 2 700 | 5.3 | 98.3 | 0.7 | 0.7 | 0.4 | 0.6 | 6.8 | 17.9 | 8.0 | 10.5 | 10.6 | 14.6 |
| 29 077 | 44180 | 2 | Greene | 1 749 | 280 626 | 237 | 160.4 | 91.4 | 4.0 | 1.5 | 2.4 | 3.2 | 6.1 | 14.8 | 14.2 | 14.2 | 11.7 | 13.0 |
| 29 079 | ... | 7 | Grundy | 1 127 | 10 338 | 2 411 | 9.2 | 96.5 | 0.9 | 0.9 | 0.6 | 1.9 | 7.2 | 17.1 | 9.1 | 10.3 | 10.3 | 13.3 |
| 29 081 | ... | 7 | Harrison | 1 871 | 8 728 | 2 544 | 4.7 | 97.1 | 0.8 | 0.7 | 0.5 | 1.7 | 6.8 | 17.7 | 7.0 | 10.7 | 10.2 | 13.9 |
| 29 083 | ... | 6 | Henry | 1 805 | 22 153 | 1 726 | 12.3 | 96.0 | 1.7 | 1.2 | 0.6 | 1.9 | 5.9 | 16.2 | 7.4 | 11.0 | 11.4 | 14.5 |
| 29 085 | ... | 8 | Hickory | 1 034 | 9 391 | 2 482 | 9.1 | 97.2 | 0.8 | 1.8 | 0.6 | 1.2 | 4.5 | 12.8 | 5.5 | 7.2 | 9.0 | 13.6 |
| 29 087 | ... | 8 | Holt | 1 198 | 4 655 | 2 861 | 3.9 | 97.4 | 0.5 | 1.4 | 0.5 | 1.0 | 5.5 | 14.5 | 6.1 | 10.7 | 11.1 | 15.9 |
| 29 089 | 17860 | 3 | Howard | 1 201 | 10 169 | 2 428 | 8.5 | 92.4 | 6.1 | 1.2 | 0.7 | 1.4 | 5.9 | 15.8 | 13.4 | 10.6 | 10.5 | 14.8 |
| 29 091 | 48460 | 7 | Howell | 2 402 | 40 629 | 1 162 | 16.9 | 96.5 | 0.7 | 1.6 | 0.9 | 1.7 | 6.8 | 17.8 | 8.3 | 11.4 | 11.6 | 13.5 |
| 29 093 | ... | 6 | Iron | 1 425 | 10 374 | 2 406 | 7.3 | 96.5 | 1.9 | 1.4 | 0.4 | 1.3 | 5.7 | 16.4 | 7.7 | 10.6 | 11.6 | 14.9 |
| 29 095 | 28140 | 1 | Jackson | 1 566 | 677 377 | 91 | 432.6 | 65.5 | 25.0 | 1.2 | 2.4 | 8.4 | 7.1 | 17.4 | 9.1 | 14.8 | 12.6 | 14.4 |

1. CBSA = Core Based Statistical Area. See Appendix A for explanation. See Appendix B for list of metropolitan areas with component counties. 2. County type code from the Economic Research Service of USDA Rural-Urban Continuum Codes. See Appendix A for definition. 3. Dry land or land partially or temporarily covered by water. 4. May be of any race.

# Table B. States and Counties — Population and Households

| STATE County | Age (percent) (cont.) | | | | Population change and components of change, 2000-2012 | | | | | | | Households, 2010 | | | | |
|---|---|---|---|---|---|---|---|---|---|---|---|---|---|---|---|---|
| | | | | | Total persons | | Percent change | | Components of change, 2010-2012 | | | | | | Percent | |
| | 55 to 64 years | 65 to 74 years | 75 years and over | Percent female | 2000 | 2010 | 2000-2010 | 2010-2012 | Births | Deaths | Net migration | Number | Percent change, 2000-2010 | Persons per household | Female family householder[1] | One person |
| | 16 | 17 | 18 | 19 | 20 | 21 | 22 | 23 | 24 | 25 | 26 | 27 | 28 | 29 | 30 | 31 |
| MISSISSIPPI—Cont'd | | | | | | | | | | | | | | | | |
| Sunflower | 11.1 | 5.8 | 4.6 | 46.4 | 34 369 | 29 450 | -14.3 | -3.5 | 825 | 720 | -1 149 | 8 822 | -8.5 | 2.81 | 30.4 | 24.9 |
| Tallahatchie | 11.2 | 6.6 | 5.1 | 44.8 | 14 903 | 15 378 | 3.2 | -1.7 | 399 | 337 | -346 | 4 856 | -7.7 | 2.67 | 25.7 | 27.5 |
| Tate | 12.6 | 7.9 | 5.2 | 52.1 | 25 370 | 28 886 | 13.9 | -1.4 | 807 | 643 | -572 | 10 035 | 13.4 | 2.75 | 17.3 | 22.0 |
| Tippah | 12.3 | 8.7 | 6.4 | 51.1 | 20 826 | 22 232 | 6.8 | -0.9 | 613 | 567 | -261 | 8 597 | 6.0 | 2.55 | 13.4 | 26.6 |
| Tishomingo | 13.8 | 10.4 | 7.9 | 51.6 | 19 163 | 19 593 | 2.2 | 0.0 | 433 | 632 | 190 | 8 148 | 2.9 | 2.37 | 11.0 | 29.5 |
| Tunica | 10.9 | 5.8 | 3.9 | 52.6 | 9 227 | 10 778 | 16.8 | -2.8 | 409 | 210 | -525 | 3 927 | 20.5 | 2.72 | 26.6 | 29.5 |
| Union | 12.3 | 7.9 | 6.6 | 51.2 | 25 362 | 27 134 | 7.0 | 1.0 | 784 | 576 | 65 | 10 317 | 5.4 | 2.60 | 12.8 | 24.2 |
| Walthall | 13.3 | 8.8 | 7.2 | 51.5 | 15 156 | 15 443 | 1.9 | -2.2 | 438 | 431 | -351 | 5 888 | 5.7 | 2.60 | 16.9 | 26.5 |
| Warren | 13.6 | 7.6 | 5.6 | 52.4 | 49 644 | 48 773 | -1.8 | -1.4 | 1 415 | 1 136 | -960 | 18 941 | 1.0 | 2.55 | 20.1 | 27.5 |
| Washington | 13.0 | 7.0 | 5.5 | 53.4 | 62 977 | 51 137 | -18.8 | -2.7 | 1 797 | 1 441 | -1 762 | 18 936 | -14.5 | 2.67 | 28.7 | 26.5 |
| Wayne | 12.3 | 8.3 | 5.9 | 51.9 | 21 216 | 20 747 | -2.2 | -0.4 | 640 | 443 | -281 | 8 104 | 3.1 | 2.54 | 17.6 | 26.7 |
| Webster | 12.7 | 9.3 | 7.5 | 51.4 | 10 294 | 10 253 | -0.4 | -2.1 | 273 | 372 | -126 | 4 060 | 4.0 | 2.51 | 14.4 | 25.8 |
| Wilkinson | 12.7 | 7.5 | 6.6 | 46.9 | 10 312 | 9 878 | -4.2 | -4.5 | 264 | 289 | -432 | 3 455 | -3.4 | 2.52 | 24.9 | 31.1 |
| Winston | 13.5 | 9.0 | 7.7 | 51.7 | 20 160 | 19 198 | -4.8 | -0.9 | 513 | 517 | -155 | 7 494 | -1.1 | 2.51 | 20.1 | 28.0 |
| Yalobusha | 14.2 | 9.9 | 7.1 | 52.0 | 13 051 | 12 678 | -2.9 | -2.2 | 340 | 373 | -247 | 5 166 | -1.8 | 2.42 | 19.0 | 30.0 |
| Yazoo | 10.8 | 6.3 | 5.7 | 45.4 | 28 149 | 28 065 | -0.3 | 0.5 | 874 | 602 | -127 | 8 860 | -3.5 | 2.71 | 26.7 | 26.0 |
| MISSOURI | 12.5 | 7.7 | 6.5 | 51.0 | 5 595 211 | 5 988 927 | 7.0 | 0.6 | 169 040 | 123 646 | -12 326 | 2 375 611 | 8.2 | 2.45 | 12.3 | 28.3 |
| Adair | 10.1 | 6.9 | 5.9 | 52.4 | 24 977 | 25 607 | 2.5 | -0.1 | 600 | 440 | -176 | 9 877 | 2.2 | 2.30 | 8.6 | 32.8 |
| Andrew | 14.5 | 8.7 | 7.2 | 50.8 | 16 492 | 17 291 | 4.8 | 0.7 | 398 | 369 | 52 | 6 700 | 6.8 | 2.55 | 8.3 | 21.9 |
| Atchison | 15.1 | 11.2 | 10.8 | 50.5 | 6 430 | 5 685 | -11.6 | -3.0 | 129 | 207 | -91 | 2 498 | -8.2 | 2.24 | 6.8 | 31.5 |
| Audrain | 12.5 | 8.0 | 8.0 | 53.9 | 25 853 | 25 529 | -1.3 | 0.4 | 808 | 660 | -63 | 9 590 | -2.6 | 2.44 | 12.3 | 28.3 |
| Barry | 13.8 | 10.6 | 7.6 | 50.4 | 34 010 | 35 597 | 4.7 | -0.1 | 959 | 847 | -130 | 14 057 | 4.9 | 2.51 | 9.8 | 24.7 |
| Barton | 13.0 | 8.6 | 8.7 | 50.9 | 12 541 | 12 402 | -1.1 | -0.5 | 307 | 304 | -77 | 4 929 | 0.7 | 2.50 | 9.9 | 26.6 |
| Bates | 13.0 | 9.5 | 8.3 | 50.6 | 16 653 | 17 049 | 2.4 | -2.0 | 429 | 447 | -330 | 6 744 | 3.6 | 2.48 | 8.4 | 27.2 |
| Benton | 18.8 | 16.3 | 10.5 | 49.9 | 17 180 | 19 056 | 10.9 | -0.5 | 369 | 629 | 186 | 8 449 | 13.9 | 2.23 | 7.0 | 28.9 |
| Bollinger | 14.3 | 9.7 | 6.9 | 50.0 | 12 029 | 12 363 | 2.8 | 0.2 | 310 | 322 | 34 | 4 847 | 5.9 | 2.52 | 9.0 | 23.1 |
| Boone | 10.3 | 5.1 | 4.3 | 51.5 | 135 454 | 162 642 | 20.1 | 3.6 | 4 646 | 2 118 | 3 386 | 64 077 | 20.7 | 2.40 | 10.7 | 28.2 |
| Buchanan | 11.9 | 7.2 | 6.8 | 50.0 | 85 998 | 89 201 | 3.7 | 0.6 | 2 783 | 2 003 | -290 | 34 509 | 2.8 | 2.45 | 13.4 | 29.0 |
| Butler | 13.5 | 9.1 | 7.9 | 51.8 | 40 867 | 42 794 | 4.7 | 0.6 | 1 220 | 1 188 | 253 | 17 614 | 5.4 | 2.38 | 13.4 | 29.4 |
| Caldwell | 13.6 | 9.3 | 8.0 | 49.8 | 8 969 | 9 424 | 5.1 | -3.0 | 214 | 237 | -284 | 3 676 | 4.3 | 2.51 | 9.5 | 25.8 |
| Callaway | 12.9 | 7.3 | 5.3 | 48.6 | 40 766 | 44 332 | 8.7 | -0.1 | 1 090 | 817 | -281 | 16 333 | 13.3 | 2.48 | 10.6 | 25.9 |
| Camden | 18.3 | 14.7 | 8.0 | 50.3 | 37 051 | 44 002 | 18.8 | -0.4 | 898 | 993 | -117 | 19 068 | 20.8 | 2.27 | 7.8 | 25.8 |
| Cape Girardeau | 12.2 | 7.3 | 7.1 | 51.7 | 68 693 | 75 674 | 10.2 | 1.7 | 2 051 | 1 536 | 727 | 29 848 | 10.6 | 2.41 | 11.0 | 27.7 |
| Carroll | 13.8 | 9.9 | 9.2 | 51.1 | 10 285 | 9 295 | -9.6 | -2.2 | 247 | 297 | -155 | 3 865 | -7.3 | 2.38 | 9.2 | 29.9 |
| Carter | 13.8 | 10.3 | 6.7 | 51.5 | 5 941 | 6 265 | 5.5 | 0.0 | 160 | 212 | 46 | 2 559 | 7.6 | 2.43 | 11.1 | 28.7 |
| Cass | 12.1 | 7.7 | 6.3 | 51.2 | 82 092 | 99 478 | 21.2 | 0.9 | 2 706 | 1 920 | 102 | 37 150 | 23.1 | 2.65 | 10.8 | 21.7 |
| Cedar | 14.3 | 12.1 | 10.5 | 50.6 | 13 733 | 13 982 | 1.8 | -1.3 | 335 | 454 | -88 | 5 838 | 2.7 | 2.37 | 9.6 | 29.1 |
| Chariton | 14.4 | 10.2 | 11.4 | 50.8 | 8 438 | 7 831 | -7.2 | -2.3 | 180 | 243 | -117 | 3 242 | -6.5 | 2.35 | 7.1 | 29.0 |
| Christian | 11.7 | 7.4 | 5.2 | 51.2 | 54 285 | 77 422 | 42.6 | 3.1 | 2 283 | 1 209 | 1 256 | 29 077 | 42.4 | 2.64 | 10.5 | 20.1 |
| Clark | 14.4 | 9.6 | 8.2 | 49.8 | 7 416 | 7 139 | -3.7 | -2.4 | 168 | 163 | -178 | 2 933 | -1.1 | 2.40 | 8.0 | 27.8 |
| Clay | 11.8 | 6.5 | 5.0 | 51.1 | 184 006 | 221 939 | 20.6 | 2.5 | 6 821 | 3 420 | 2 313 | 87 217 | 20.2 | 2.51 | 11.3 | 26.2 |
| Clinton | 13.1 | 8.9 | 7.3 | 49.7 | 18 979 | 20 743 | 9.3 | -1.1 | 539 | 536 | -240 | 7 951 | 11.2 | 2.55 | 9.3 | 23.2 |
| Cole | 13.1 | 6.7 | 5.8 | 49.5 | 71 397 | 75 990 | 6.4 | 0.5 | 2 020 | 1 367 | -248 | 29 722 | 9.9 | 2.39 | 11.3 | 29.3 |
| Cooper | 12.9 | 7.8 | 7.6 | 47.3 | 16 670 | 17 601 | 5.6 | -0.5 | 437 | 417 | -121 | 6 554 | 10.5 | 2.45 | 10.0 | 27.1 |
| Crawford | 13.2 | 9.2 | 7.1 | 50.9 | 22 804 | 24 696 | 8.3 | 0.6 | 615 | 626 | 146 | 9 831 | 11.0 | 2.48 | 10.8 | 26.4 |
| Dade | 15.7 | 10.8 | 9.9 | 49.9 | 7 923 | 7 883 | -0.5 | -4.0 | 162 | 249 | -230 | 3 271 | 2.2 | 2.37 | 7.3 | 28.5 |
| Dallas | 13.9 | 9.7 | 7.5 | 50.1 | 15 661 | 16 777 | 7.1 | 0.1 | 458 | 431 | -31 | 6 524 | 8.2 | 2.54 | 9.3 | 24.3 |
| Daviess | 14.3 | 10.0 | 7.5 | 50.2 | 8 016 | 8 433 | 5.2 | -2.3 | 246 | 204 | -236 | 3 214 | 1.1 | 2.58 | 8.1 | 24.6 |
| DeKalb | 11.6 | 6.9 | 6.6 | 37.0 | 11 597 | 12 892 | 11.2 | 0.4 | 257 | 232 | -9 | 3 839 | 8.8 | 2.43 | 8.2 | 29.9 |
| Dent | 13.7 | 10.7 | 8.7 | 50.5 | 14 927 | 15 657 | 4.9 | -0.1 | 393 | 463 | 69 | 6 338 | 6.0 | 2.44 | 9.6 | 25.5 |
| Douglas | 15.4 | 11.2 | 8.9 | 50.5 | 13 084 | 13 684 | 4.6 | -0.7 | 309 | 325 | -75 | 5 587 | 7.4 | 2.43 | 8.9 | 25.4 |
| Dunklin | 12.8 | 9.2 | 7.4 | 51.9 | 33 155 | 31 953 | -3.6 | -0.4 | 1 021 | 1 007 | -132 | 12 837 | -4.3 | 2.44 | 15.1 | 29.3 |
| Franklin | 12.7 | 7.9 | 6.3 | 50.4 | 93 807 | 101 492 | 8.2 | -0.1 | 2 827 | 2 118 | -751 | 39 110 | 12.1 | 2.57 | 10.0 | 24.2 |
| Gasconade | 14.7 | 10.8 | 10.1 | 51.1 | 15 342 | 15 222 | -0.8 | -1.6 | 335 | 466 | -116 | 6 250 | 1.3 | 2.40 | 8.5 | 27.9 |
| Gentry | 12.1 | 9.0 | 10.6 | 51.7 | 6 861 | 6 738 | -1.8 | 0.6 | 184 | 220 | 66 | 2 674 | -2.7 | 2.45 | 8.2 | 29.0 |
| Greene | 11.8 | 7.3 | 6.9 | 51.3 | 240 391 | 275 174 | 14.5 | 2.0 | 7 817 | 5 519 | 3 217 | 114 244 | 16.7 | 2.31 | 10.7 | 30.4 |
| Grundy | 12.7 | 10.4 | 9.6 | 52.2 | 10 432 | 10 261 | -1.6 | 0.8 | 302 | 302 | 76 | 4 204 | -4.1 | 2.36 | 8.7 | 31.1 |
| Harrison | 12.8 | 10.5 | 10.4 | 50.2 | 8 850 | 8 957 | 1.2 | -2.6 | 234 | 263 | -211 | 3 669 | 0.3 | 2.40 | 8.3 | 28.3 |
| Henry | 14.0 | 10.6 | 9.1 | 51.1 | 21 997 | 22 272 | 1.3 | -0.5 | 594 | 684 | -27 | 9 405 | 3.0 | 2.34 | 10.4 | 28.9 |
| Hickory | 17.5 | 17.3 | 12.5 | 50.9 | 8 940 | 9 627 | 7.7 | -2.5 | 170 | 321 | -100 | 4 371 | 11.8 | 2.19 | 7.6 | 30.2 |
| Holt | 15.1 | 9.7 | 11.4 | 50.5 | 5 351 | 4 912 | -8.2 | -5.2 | 126 | 174 | -212 | 2 133 | -4.6 | 2.26 | 7.2 | 28.7 |
| Howard | 13.5 | 8.1 | 7.5 | 50.4 | 10 212 | 10 144 | -0.7 | 0.2 | 262 | 199 | -52 | 3 981 | 3.8 | 2.37 | 8.3 | 28.8 |
| Howell | 13.2 | 9.3 | 8.1 | 51.5 | 37 238 | 40 400 | 8.5 | 0.6 | 1 190 | 1 063 | 122 | 16 192 | 9.7 | 2.46 | 10.7 | 27.2 |
| Iron | 14.5 | 10.7 | 7.8 | 50.8 | 10 697 | 10 630 | -0.6 | -2.4 | 243 | 355 | -196 | 4 378 | 4.3 | 2.37 | 10.5 | 30.0 |
| Jackson | 12.0 | 6.7 | 6.0 | 51.6 | 654 880 | 674 158 | 2.9 | 0.5 | 21 599 | 13 390 | -4 885 | 274 804 | 3.2 | 2.41 | 15.7 | 31.8 |

1. No spouse present.

# Table B. States and Counties — Population, Vital Statistics, Medicare, and Crime

| STATE County | Persons in group quarters, 2010 | Daytime population, 2007–2011 Number | Employment/ residence ratio | Births, 2011 Total | Rate[1] | Deaths, 2011 Number | Rate[1] | Persons under 65 with no health insurance, 2010 Number | Percent | Medicare, 2012 Eligible for Medicare | Enrolled in Medicare Advantage | Enrolled in a Medicare prescription drug plan | Serious crimes known to police,[2] 2011 Total Number | Rate[3] |
|---|---|---|---|---|---|---|---|---|---|---|---|---|---|---|
| | 32 | 33 | 34 | 35 | 36 | 37 | 38 | 39 | 40 | 41 | 42 | 43 | 44 | 45 |
| MISSISSIPPI—Cont'd | | | | | | | | | | | | | | |
| Sunflower | 4 654 | 30 571 | 1.06 | 389 | 13.3 | 296 | 10.1 | 4 604 | 21.0 | 4 480 | 231 | 3 206 | NA | NA |
| Tallahatchie | 2 421 | 14 210 | 0.76 | 198 | 12.9 | 158 | 10.3 | 2 717 | 24.3 | 2 677 | 70 | 1 993 | NA | NA |
| Tate | 1 281 | 23 743 | 0.62 | 371 | 12.9 | 276 | 9.6 | 5 240 | 21.6 | 5 095 | 711 | 2 636 | NA | NA |
| Tippah | 287 | 20 772 | 0.85 | 274 | 12.4 | 232 | 10.5 | 4 633 | 24.8 | 5 016 | 229 | 3 525 | 114 | 511 |
| Tishomingo | 280 | 18 667 | 0.87 | 184 | 9.4 | 299 | 15.3 | 3 686 | 23.2 | 4 895 | 108 | 3 385 | 132 | 671 |
| Tunica | 104 | 19 162 | 3.02 | 184 | 17.3 | 93 | 8.8 | 1 984 | 20.6 | 1 623 | 231 | 1 002 | 608 | 5 620 |
| Union | 283 | 25 890 | 0.90 | 354 | 12.9 | 239 | 8.7 | 5 381 | 23.4 | 5 727 | 351 | 3 669 | 327 | 1 201 |
| Walthall | 128 | 13 414 | 0.62 | 196 | 12.7 | 183 | 11.9 | 2 957 | 22.9 | 3 200 | 296 | 1 972 | NA | NA |
| Warren | 524 | 51 470 | 1.14 | 660 | 13.7 | 496 | 10.3 | 8 182 | 19.4 | 8 507 | 1 030 | 3 970 | 2 314 | 4 727 |
| Washington | 548 | 51 882 | 1.01 | 815 | 16.2 | 659 | 13.1 | 9 269 | 20.9 | 9 585 | 1 009 | 6 112 | 3 283 | 6 396 |
| Wayne | 137 | 19 214 | 0.79 | 288 | 14.0 | 193 | 9.4 | 4 111 | 23.2 | 3 882 | 372 | 2 504 | NA | NA |
| Webster | 56 | 8 875 | 0.66 | 130 | 12.6 | 148 | 14.3 | 1 886 | 21.9 | 2 770 | 92 | 1 913 | NA | NA |
| Wilkinson | 1 168 | 9 464 | 0.85 | 123 | 12.7 | 140 | 14.5 | 1 584 | 21.5 | 1 828 | 223 | 1 229 | NA | NA |
| Winston | 408 | 17 848 | 0.80 | 235 | 12.3 | 243 | 12.7 | 3 612 | 23.1 | 4 496 | 537 | 2 593 | 151 | 784 |
| Yalobusha | 155 | 11 765 | 0.77 | 155 | 12.3 | 166 | 13.2 | 2 176 | 20.8 | 3 382 | 246 | 2 161 | NA | NA |
| Yazoo | 4 020 | 26 461 | 0.80 | 404 | 14.5 | 254 | 9.1 | 4 223 | 20.3 | 4 667 | 325 | 3 235 | NA | NA |
| MISSOURI | 174 142 | 5 998 264 | 1.02 | 75 910 | 12.6 | 54 361 | 9.0 | 766 031 | 15.3 | 1 065 826 | 250 303 | 458 265 | 225 771 | 3 756 |
| Adair | 2 900 | 26 496 | 1.10 | 273 | 10.7 | 184 | 7.2 | 3 392 | 17.3 | 4 222 | 194 | 2 631 | 932 | 3 626 |
| Andrew | 192 | 11 521 | 0.37 | 188 | 10.9 | 172 | 10.0 | 2 106 | 14.5 | 2 971 | 162 | 1 675 | 156 | 899 |
| Atchison | 98 | 5 167 | 0.79 | 62 | 11.1 | 93 | 16.7 | 668 | 15.2 | 1 383 | 53 | 878 | 31 | 543 |
| Audrain | 2 100 | 25 798 | 1.02 | 362 | 14.2 | 296 | 11.6 | 3 016 | 15.3 | 4 949 | 494 | 2 893 | 511 | 1 994 |
| Barry | 296 | 37 410 | 1.12 | 432 | 12.2 | 358 | 10.1 | 6 040 | 20.8 | 7 734 | 2 270 | 2 956 | 1 062 | 2 973 |
| Barton | 90 | 11 471 | 0.80 | 132 | 10.7 | 138 | 11.2 | 1 795 | 17.6 | 2 764 | 416 | 1 468 | 259 | 2 081 |
| Bates | 311 | 14 528 | 0.64 | 196 | 11.5 | 191 | 11.2 | 2 548 | 18.5 | 3 747 | 526 | 1 919 | 506 | 2 957 |
| Benton | 244 | 16 948 | 0.69 | 166 | 8.7 | 264 | 13.8 | 2 854 | 20.4 | 6 002 | 996 | 2 802 | 442 | 2 311 |
| Bollinger | 163 | 9 550 | 0.43 | 135 | 10.9 | 140 | 11.3 | 1 812 | 17.8 | 2 741 | 307 | 1 500 | 179 | 1 443 |
| Boone | 8 998 | 165 169 | 1.05 | 2 044 | 13.3 | 942 | 5.7 | 19 630 | 14.1 | 20 620 | 2 238 | 11 023 | 6 211 | 3 805 |
| Buchanan | 4 495 | 96 191 | 1.18 | 1 274 | 14.2 | 871 | 9.7 | 10 242 | 14.1 | 15 707 | 1 082 | 8 587 | 4 641 | 5 184 |
| Butler | 884 | 45 588 | 1.17 | 530 | 12.3 | 529 | 12.3 | 5 803 | 16.6 | 10 188 | 931 | 6 081 | 2 290 | 5 332 |
| Caldwell | 214 | 7 308 | 0.48 | 102 | 11.0 | 100 | 10.7 | 1 226 | 15.9 | 1 870 | 226 | 844 | 126 | 1 332 |
| Callaway | 3 907 | 37 921 | 0.71 | 482 | 10.9 | 356 | 8.0 | 5 067 | 14.4 | 7 630 | 673 | 3 693 | 1 473 | 3 311 |
| Camden | 774 | 44 756 | 1.07 | 412 | 9.4 | 448 | 10.3 | 6 355 | 18.7 | 10 752 | 1 124 | 5 338 | 980 | 2 219 |
| Cape Girardeau | 3 823 | 81 469 | 1.18 | 915 | 11.9 | 648 | 8.5 | 9 278 | 15.0 | 13 404 | 874 | 7 512 | 3 427 | 4 512 |
| Carroll | 88 | 8 304 | 0.75 | 107 | 11.6 | 137 | 14.8 | 1 182 | 15.9 | 2 181 | 233 | 1 288 | 93 | 997 |
| Carter | 40 | 5 546 | 0.72 | 77 | 12.1 | 101 | 15.9 | 1 083 | 20.7 | 1 518 | 148 | 919 | 89 | 1 415 |
| Cass | 1 044 | 75 778 | 0.52 | 1 251 | 12.5 | 811 | 8.1 | 10 706 | 12.6 | 16 543 | 5 609 | 4 757 | 2 339 | 2 343 |
| Cedar | 156 | 13 098 | 0.81 | 155 | 11.1 | 201 | 14.4 | 2 138 | 19.8 | 3 613 | 986 | 1 479 | 360 | 2 565 |
| Chariton | 213 | 6 674 | 0.68 | 84 | 10.9 | 108 | 14.0 | 1 011 | 16.7 | 1 842 | 102 | 1 168 | 99 | 1 260 |
| Christian | 582 | 57 996 | 0.50 | 1 057 | 13.5 | 521 | 6.6 | 10 578 | 15.6 | 13 183 | 5 304 | 4 104 | 1 563 | 2 012 |
| Clark | 90 | 5 779 | 0.56 | 77 | 11.0 | 73 | 10.4 | 1 091 | 18.7 | 1 558 | 100 | 1 015 | 43 | 600 |
| Clay | 2 646 | 197 921 | 0.81 | 3 083 | 13.7 | 1 459 | 6.5 | 21 875 | 11.2 | 33 294 | 6 332 | 13 566 | 10 581 | 4 751 |
| Clinton | 445 | 16 760 | 0.57 | 237 | 11.4 | 224 | 10.8 | 2 427 | 14.0 | 3 345 | 312 | 1 761 | 362 | 1 739 |
| Cole | 4 968 | 89 533 | 1.38 | 912 | 11.9 | 597 | 7.8 | 7 092 | 11.4 | 12 184 | 956 | 5 661 | 2 423 | 3 177 |
| Cooper | 1 533 | 16 171 | 0.81 | 192 | 10.9 | 183 | 10.4 | 2 214 | 16.5 | 3 324 | 488 | 1 761 | 459 | 2 598 |
| Crawford | 332 | 21 911 | 0.71 | 278 | 11.2 | 282 | 11.4 | 3 535 | 17.3 | 5 256 | 966 | 2 560 | 567 | 2 288 |
| Dade | 133 | 7 162 | 0.76 | 74 | 9.5 | 112 | 14.3 | 1 287 | 20.8 | 1 887 | 574 | 724 | 92 | 1 163 |
| Dallas | 199 | 13 925 | 0.55 | 203 | 12.1 | 196 | 11.7 | 2 575 | 18.6 | 3 826 | 1 504 | 1 322 | 361 | 2 144 |
| Daviess | 152 | 6 998 | 0.61 | 114 | 13.7 | 87 | 10.5 | 1 538 | 22.5 | 1 726 | 125 | 927 | 93 | 1 099 |
| DeKalb | 3 560 | 12 501 | 0.93 | 108 | 8.5 | 91 | 7.1 | 1 255 | 16.2 | 1 990 | 109 | 1 073 | 200 | 1 546 |
| Dent | 202 | 14 139 | 0.76 | 186 | 11.9 | 207 | 13.2 | 2 374 | 18.8 | 3 665 | 218 | 2 076 | 312 | 1 985 |
| Douglas | 123 | 12 232 | 0.71 | 127 | 9.4 | 149 | 11.0 | 2 182 | 20.1 | 3 185 | 1 220 | 1 134 | 221 | 1 609 |
| Dunklin | 672 | 30 245 | 0.84 | 442 | 13.8 | 445 | 13.9 | 4 431 | 16.8 | 7 374 | 690 | 4 879 | 1 109 | 3 458 |
| Franklin | 857 | 92 060 | 0.80 | 1 260 | 12.4 | 914 | 9.0 | 12 537 | 14.5 | 18 366 | 6 362 | 6 239 | 2 436 | 2 391 |
| Gasconade | 250 | 14 370 | 0.87 | 145 | 9.6 | 207 | 13.6 | 2 136 | 17.7 | 3 602 | 599 | 1 796 | 295 | 1 931 |
| Gentry | 177 | 6 358 | 0.86 | 88 | 13.0 | 104 | 15.3 | 1 021 | 19.3 | 1 748 | 77 | 1 147 | 31 | 458 |
| Greene | 11 242 | 306 258 | 1.25 | 3 454 | 12.5 | 2 408 | 8.7 | 38 502 | 17.0 | 50 434 | 19 429 | 17 013 | 18 581 | 6 728 |
| Grundy | 350 | 9 905 | 0.93 | 146 | 14.3 | 132 | 12.9 | 1 410 | 17.6 | 2 412 | 105 | 1 521 | 237 | 2 301 |
| Harrison | 145 | 8 512 | 0.88 | 101 | 11.4 | 125 | 14.1 | 1 385 | 19.7 | 2 091 | 93 | 1 366 | 113 | 1 257 |
| Henry | 233 | 21 645 | 0.93 | 261 | 11.7 | 315 | 14.2 | 2 933 | 16.5 | 5 794 | 1 007 | 2 817 | 859 | 3 843 |
| Hickory | 75 | 8 487 | 0.65 | 80 | 8.3 | 141 | 14.6 | 1 519 | 22.5 | 3 110 | 926 | 1 142 | 125 | 1 294 |
| Holt | 101 | 4 306 | 0.74 | 62 | 12.9 | 79 | 16.4 | 678 | 17.7 | 1 094 | 61 | 635 | 102 | 2 069 |
| Howard | 714 | 8 572 | 0.66 | 114 | 11.2 | 72 | 7.1 | 1 361 | 17.3 | 1 979 | 242 | 1 073 | 88 | 864 |
| Howell | 608 | 41 635 | 1.10 | 529 | 13.0 | 474 | 11.7 | 5 967 | 17.9 | 9 622 | 1 687 | 5 113 | 1 569 | 3 870 |
| Iron | 276 | 10 490 | 0.95 | 107 | 10.0 | 158 | 14.8 | 1 459 | 17.2 | 2 567 | 165 | 1 623 | 123 | 1 153 |
| Jackson | 11 219 | 733 055 | 1.20 | 9 849 | 14.6 | 5 925 | 8.8 | 104 865 | 18.0 | 108 528 | 35 277 | 35 492 | 35 705 | 5 277 |

1. Per 1,000 estimated resident population.    2. Data for serious crimes have not been adjusted for underreporting; this may affect comparability between geographic areas and over time.    3. Per 100,000 population estimated by the FBI.

# Table B. States and Counties — Crime, Education, Money Income, and Poverty

| STATE County | Serious crimes known to police, 2011 (cont.)[1] Rate[2] Violent | Property | Education — School enrollment and attainment, 2007–2011 Enrollment[3] Total | Percent private | Attainment[4] (percent) High school graduate or less | Bachelor's degree or more | Local government expenditures,[5] 2009–2010 Total current expenditures (mil dol) | Current expenditures per student (dollars) | Money income, 2007–2011 Per capita income[6] (dollars) | Households — Median income Dollars | Percent change, 2000 to 2007–2011 (constant 2011 dollars) | Percent with income of $200,000 or more | Income and poverty, 2011 Median household income (dollars) | Percent below poverty level All persons | Children under 18 years | Children 5 to 17 years in families |
|---|---|---|---|---|---|---|---|---|---|---|---|---|---|---|---|---|
| | 46 | 47 | 48 | 49 | 50 | 51 | 52 | 53 | 54 | 55 | 56 | 57 | 58 | 59 | 60 | 61 |
| **MISSISSIPPI—Cont'd** | | | | | | | | | | | | | | | | |
| Sunflower | NA | NA | 8 754 | 16.4 | 58.9 | 13.8 | 37.5 | 8 243 | 12 601 | 27 042 | -19.8 | 1.2 | 26 788 | 41.8 | 50.4 | 46.2 |
| Tallahatchie | NA | NA | 4 088 | 23.3 | 68.3 | 9.1 | 20.5 | 9 128 | 13 265 | 27 092 | -9.7 | 0.4 | 27 789 | 35.9 | 45.1 | 42.9 |
| Tate | NA | NA | 7 960 | 14.9 | 52.8 | 14.7 | 34.9 | 7 057 | 19 882 | 41 839 | -13.5 | 1.5 | 42 201 | 18.7 | 26.7 | 24.1 |
| Tippah | 36 | 475 | 5 349 | 5.7 | 62.2 | 11.3 | 30.8 | 7 519 | 18 719 | 35 769 | -9.6 | 1.2 | 33 701 | 21.5 | 28.5 | 26.4 |
| Tishomingo | 76 | 595 | 4 343 | 5.0 | 61.3 | 11.8 | 25.2 | 7 751 | 18 063 | 30 734 | -19.6 | 1.4 | 33 494 | 17.4 | 26.8 | 25.2 |
| Tunica | 619 | 5 000 | 2 921 | 14.1 | 61.0 | 13.7 | 23.1 | 10 193 | 14 963 | 30 470 | -3.0 | 0.7 | 29 631 | 30.0 | 45.6 | 45.2 |
| Union | 55 | 1 146 | 6 679 | 6.9 | 59.6 | 13.6 | 36.9 | 7 472 | 18 636 | 36 661 | -16.9 | 1.2 | 36 925 | 19.2 | 27.4 | 26.4 |
| Walthall | NA | NA | 4 210 | 8.4 | 59.6 | 12.6 | 19.5 | 7 702 | 16 592 | 34 045 | 9.9 | 1.4 | 28 707 | 26.1 | 37.7 | 34.0 |
| Warren | 331 | 4 396 | 13 041 | 11.7 | 44.2 | 23.8 | 70.9 | 7 998 | 22 181 | 40 469 | -14.5 | 2.0 | 38 874 | 22.4 | 36.2 | 35.9 |
| Washington | 273 | 6 123 | 15 134 | 10.8 | 54.4 | 18.8 | 83.8 | 7 999 | 16 856 | 28 591 | -17.8 | 1.5 | 29 287 | 37.4 | 54.8 | 50.8 |
| Wayne | NA | NA | 5 350 | 9.1 | 64.2 | 10.1 | 29.0 | 7 826 | 17 879 | 31 388 | -10.3 | 1.5 | 32 817 | 29.6 | 47.0 | 50.7 |
| Webster | NA | NA | 2 334 | 10.2 | 56.3 | 16.9 | 13.8 | 7 601 | 18 969 | 36 392 | -6.5 | 1.1 | 32 935 | 21.5 | 31.7 | 29.3 |
| Wilkinson | NA | NA | 2 000 | 20.7 | 68.8 | 9.6 | 12.3 | 9 130 | 18 254 | 33 732 | 32.0 | 1.0 | 26 738 | 35.0 | 46.2 | 39.4 |
| Winston | 73 | 711 | 4 461 | 15.2 | 53.8 | 15.3 | 22.7 | 8 406 | 18 313 | 33 007 | -13.5 | 0.5 | 31 826 | 23.5 | 33.3 | 32.5 |
| Yalobusha | NA | NA | 2 970 | 6.5 | 59.4 | 12.1 | 15.5 | 8 024 | 17 640 | 33 076 | -6.9 | 1.4 | 32 022 | 23.8 | 36.5 | 34.6 |
| Yazoo | NA | NA | 7 292 | 18.4 | 59.9 | 13.0 | 37.3 | 8 315 | 14 730 | 27 979 | -16.4 | 1.3 | 28 449 | 33.2 | 41.3 | 39.0 |
| **MISSOURI** | 447 | 3 309 | 1 551 053 | 19.5 | 45.3 | 25.4 | 8 844.3 | 9 636 | 25 371 | 47 202 | -7.8 | 2.7 | 45 231 | 15.8 | 22.3 | 20.1 |
| Adair | 533 | 3 093 | 9 988 | 8.4 | 48.9 | 27.1 | 27.3 | 8 728 | 17 997 | 33 157 | -7.9 | 1.2 | 33 639 | 25.1 | 25.8 | 23.9 |
| Andrew | 46 | 853 | 3 999 | 10.1 | 52.1 | 19.8 | 23.6 | 8 235 | 25 409 | 54 148 | -1.4 | 1.3 | 54 994 | 9.4 | 14.0 | 12.3 |
| Atchison | 35 | 508 | 1 181 | 10.3 | 51.6 | 21.7 | 9.3 | 10 361 | 23 976 | 44 330 | 6.1 | 1.8 | 43 322 | 12.5 | 17.2 | 15.7 |
| Audrain | 141 | 1 854 | 5 796 | 15.6 | 62.4 | 14.4 | 27.6 | 8 160 | 19 275 | 41 567 | -4.0 | 1.1 | 39 554 | 17.3 | 27.6 | 25.5 |
| Barry | 272 | 2 701 | 8 212 | 8.0 | 59.3 | 13.2 | 54.5 | 8 045 | 19 755 | 38 321 | -1.8 | 1.0 | 36 546 | 18.0 | 28.9 | 27.1 |
| Barton | 161 | 1 920 | 2 838 | 10.4 | 58.9 | 14.8 | 17.0 | 8 023 | 19 036 | 39 144 | -1.0 | 1.0 | 36 076 | 18.6 | 28.1 | 24.8 |
| Bates | 380 | 2 577 | 4 057 | 13.7 | 64.8 | 10.4 | 23.8 | 8 723 | 19 882 | 38 966 | -6.1 | 0.7 | 40 376 | 16.8 | 23.5 | 21.6 |
| Benton | 251 | 2 060 | 3 394 | 10.0 | 63.8 | 12.4 | 21.2 | 8 031 | 20 551 | 34 512 | -4.1 | 1.2 | 36 255 | 17.3 | 32.2 | 28.9 |
| Bollinger | 306 | 1 136 | 2 993 | 8.1 | 68.0 | 9.7 | 14.4 | 7 478 | 18 709 | 36 119 | -12.2 | 0.9 | 38 565 | 17.3 | 26.3 | 24.3 |
| Boone | 437 | 3 368 | 58 380 | 12.6 | 30.0 | 45.9 | 202.9 | 9 013 | 25 970 | 47 123 | -6.9 | 2.9 | 46 769 | 19.5 | 19.4 | 18.2 |
| Buchanan | 338 | 4 846 | 22 513 | 14.5 | 52.7 | 19.4 | 109.2 | 8 515 | 22 349 | 43 386 | -7.4 | 1.5 | 42 031 | 17.8 | 23.6 | 21.2 |
| Butler | 428 | 4 903 | 10 199 | 9.8 | 58.3 | 14.2 | 53.2 | 7 972 | 19 464 | 34 080 | -7.3 | 1.2 | 33 480 | 22.1 | 33.9 | 30.8 |
| Caldwell | 264 | 1 068 | 2 108 | 8.5 | 57.8 | 12.8 | 9.9 | 10 322 | 20 225 | 40 522 | -3.9 | 0.8 | 44 206 | 14.0 | 20.4 | 17.9 |
| Callaway | 247 | 3 063 | 11 141 | 23.3 | 51.0 | 22.2 | 43.9 | 8 721 | 23 487 | 50 669 | -4.0 | 1.5 | 45 968 | 14.1 | 19.2 | 16.6 |
| Camden | 179 | 2 040 | 8 515 | 13.4 | 45.9 | 20.6 | 49.9 | 9 368 | 25 068 | 44 961 | -7.1 | 2.7 | 40 370 | 15.5 | 29.3 | 25.6 |
| Cape Girardeau | 383 | 4 129 | 21 018 | 15.1 | 47.4 | 26.7 | 80.3 | 8 245 | 23 445 | 45 795 | -7.0 | 2.2 | 41 755 | 17.1 | 21.2 | 19.5 |
| Carroll | 86 | 911 | 2 090 | 10.9 | 60.6 | 17.3 | 15.0 | 9 223 | 25 546 | 44 015 | 6.4 | 2.6 | 40 035 | 13.1 | 23.3 | 20.1 |
| Carter | 111 | 1 304 | 1 525 | 2.0 | 61.4 | 12.5 | 11.4 | 8 915 | 15 597 | 26 689 | -13.5 | 0.7 | 27 878 | 24.7 | 36.7 | 35.7 |
| Cass | 154 | 2 189 | 25 889 | 14.3 | 44.3 | 21.9 | 159.7 | 8 575 | 27 129 | 60 807 | -9.1 | 2.0 | 54 969 | 10.3 | 15.4 | 14.0 |
| Cedar | 257 | 2 309 | 3 353 | 17.4 | 62.6 | 11.8 | 18.9 | 8 257 | 15 980 | 31 353 | -13.0 | 0.2 | 30 536 | 26.6 | 39.5 | 35.2 |
| Chariton | 293 | 967 | 1 700 | 16.6 | 62.6 | 13.7 | 10.8 | 10 046 | 19 904 | 40 958 | -6.0 | 0.5 | 41 409 | 14.4 | 20.2 | 18.8 |
| Christian | 189 | 1 822 | 20 782 | 15.6 | 39.1 | 26.3 | 106.5 | 7 479 | 24 284 | 51 961 | 1.0 | 2.2 | 50 426 | 11.9 | 17.7 | 16.0 |
| Clark | 167 | 433 | 1 701 | 8.9 | 58.7 | 12.7 | 9.0 | 8 158 | 20 014 | 40 333 | 1.4 | 0.6 | 38 597 | 15.4 | 24.9 | 23.3 |
| Clay | 720 | 4 032 | 57 209 | 18.5 | 36.9 | 30.6 | 354.8 | 9 274 | 29 326 | 60 507 | -7.3 | 2.9 | 59 039 | 8.7 | 11.7 | 9.8 |
| Clinton | 355 | 1 383 | 4 924 | 7.1 | 51.6 | 17.1 | 38.7 | 9 002 | 24 553 | 51 439 | -8.5 | 1.6 | 49 202 | 12.1 | 17.7 | 14.7 |
| Cole | 400 | 2 777 | 19 764 | 26.0 | 41.3 | 30.9 | 92.1 | 7 116 | 26 626 | 55 580 | -4.1 | 2.0 | 54 396 | 12.3 | 17.6 | 15.6 |
| Cooper | 68 | 2 530 | 4 064 | 22.0 | 54.1 | 17.8 | 23.8 | 9 232 | 21 316 | 45 869 | -3.8 | 1.1 | 42 482 | 15.7 | 22.5 | 19.7 |
| Crawford | 226 | 2 062 | 5 810 | 14.6 | 63.8 | 10.2 | 26.9 | 7 901 | 17 416 | 35 947 | -13.7 | 0.5 | 38 215 | 20.5 | 30.5 | 27.0 |
| Dade | 177 | 986 | 1 729 | 10.0 | 61.4 | 9.5 | 11.1 | 9 106 | 17 738 | 32 248 | -17.9 | 0.4 | 33 754 | 19.6 | 30.8 | 26.5 |
| Dallas | 226 | 1 918 | 3 267 | 14.4 | 66.1 | 11.7 | 15.5 | 8 128 | 18 384 | 39 132 | 6.0 | 1.3 | 33 535 | 21.5 | 32.5 | 30.2 |
| Daviess | 83 | 1 016 | 2 013 | 16.0 | 57.8 | 14.6 | 19.3 | 9 780 | 19 714 | 41 133 | -1.3 | 1.6 | 38 820 | 18.4 | 30.4 | 28.3 |
| DeKalb | 185 | 1 360 | 2 656 | 7.8 | 61.9 | 11.3 | 11.1 | 9 578 | 17 754 | 45 252 | 5.9 | 1.2 | 41 264 | 16.2 | 16.4 | 14.6 |
| Dent | 185 | 1 801 | 3 134 | 5.8 | 62.4 | 11.8 | 17.8 | 7 830 | 19 003 | 36 715 | 0.0 | 0.7 | 34 288 | 20.9 | 31.8 | 29.5 |
| Douglas | 277 | 1 332 | 3 234 | 10.2 | 65.3 | 9.7 | 14.6 | 9 107 | 16 175 | 32 300 | -7.7 | 0.5 | 30 071 | 23.7 | 37.0 | 33.6 |
| Dunklin | 355 | 3 103 | 7 415 | 5.1 | 69.5 | 11.3 | 49.8 | 8 432 | 17 904 | 30 806 | -8.3 | 1.1 | 32 018 | 28.1 | 44.2 | 41.9 |
| Franklin | 214 | 2 177 | 25 258 | 18.1 | 50.4 | 16.7 | 141.7 | 8 516 | 24 118 | 50 098 | -14.7 | 1.9 | 47 663 | 10.0 | 13.8 | 13.1 |
| Gasconade | 229 | 1 702 | 3 438 | 15.3 | 57.9 | 14.8 | 24.2 | 8 222 | 21 848 | 40 788 | -13.8 | 1.1 | 39 751 | 14.3 | 21.6 | 19.4 |
| Gentry | 0 | 458 | 1 550 | 3.0 | 61.5 | 12.8 | 11.9 | 10 497 | 19 858 | 36 307 | -6.5 | 1.1 | 37 314 | 17.5 | 23.3 | 20.9 |
| Greene | 544 | 6 184 | 72 923 | 17.5 | 39.7 | 27.8 | 293.2 | 7 913 | 23 956 | 41 622 | -9.7 | 2.1 | 40 423 | 17.5 | 23.8 | 22.6 |
| Grundy | 204 | 2 097 | 2 306 | 9.8 | 56.0 | 14.5 | 13.9 | 8 490 | 19 344 | 36 590 | -0.9 | 0.6 | 35 002 | 19.2 | 28.2 | 26.7 |
| Harrison | 145 | 1 112 | 1 861 | 4.4 | 64.8 | 8.1 | 14.5 | 9 612 | 19 080 | 35 915 | -7.3 | 1.0 | 35 626 | 17.1 | 26.4 | 24.8 |
| Henry | 349 | 3 494 | 4 774 | 13.8 | 55.1 | 15.2 | 29.9 | 8 762 | 22 055 | 36 944 | -11.6 | 1.3 | 38 410 | 18.6 | 27.8 | 25.5 |
| Hickory | 21 | 1 273 | 1 628 | 9.2 | 61.7 | 9.0 | 15.4 | 8 024 | 16 844 | 28 850 | -15.7 | 0.5 | 30 049 | 22.7 | 41.4 | 38.4 |
| Holt | 183 | 1 886 | 908 | 5.5 | 59.5 | 15.5 | 7.2 | 11 338 | 23 815 | 41 737 | 4.9 | 1.5 | 41 054 | 13.0 | 20.9 | 16.2 |
| Howard | 157 | 707 | 2 775 | 34.5 | 54.5 | 23.8 | 11.8 | 8 133 | 23 479 | 46 991 | 10.1 | 1.5 | 42 733 | 16.1 | 22.7 | 20.7 |
| Howell | 276 | 3 593 | 9 629 | 7.4 | 57.0 | 15.7 | 45.1 | 7 947 | 18 056 | 35 625 | 3.0 | 1.3 | 31 645 | 22.9 | 32.2 | 28.8 |
| Iron | 300 | 853 | 2 313 | 4.6 | 62.5 | 10.7 | 19.0 | 9 418 | 18 153 | 32 029 | -9.0 | 0.3 | 32 173 | 23.9 | 36.4 | 32.1 |
| Jackson | 705 | 4 573 | 172 132 | 18.2 | 42.3 | 27.1 | 1 145.0 | 10 804 | 25 605 | 46 874 | -11.6 | 2.5 | 44 508 | 18.7 | 27.2 | 24.2 |

1. Data for serious crimes have not been adjusted for underreporting; this may affect comparability between geographic areas and over time. 2. Per 100,000 population estimated by the FBI. 3. All persons 3 years old and over enrolled in nursery school through college. 4. Persons 25 years old and over. 5. Elementary and secondary education expenditures. 6. Based on population estimated by the American Community Survey, 2007–2011.

# Table B. States and Counties — **Personal Income**

| | Personal income, 2011 | | | | | | | | | | | | |
|---|---|---|---|---|---|---|---|---|---|---|---|---|---|
| | | | Per capita[1] | | | | | Transfer payments (mil dol) | | | | | |
| | | | | | | | | | Government payments to individuals | | | | |
| STATE County | Total (mil dol) | Percent change, 2010–2011 | Dollars | Rank | Wages and salaries[2] (mil dol) | Proprietors' income (mil dol) | Dividends, interest, and rent (mil dol) | Total | Total | Social Security | Medical payments | Income mainte-nance | Unemploy-ment insurance |
| | 62 | 63 | 64 | 65 | 66 | 67 | 68 | 69 | 70 | 71 | 72 | 73 | 74 |
| **MISSISSIPPI—Cont'd** | | | | | | | | | | | | | |
| Sunflower | 790 | 4.3 | 26 969 | 2 767 | 390 | 92 | 93 | 278 | 271 | 58 | 118 | 68 | 6 |
| Tallahatchie | 386 | 6.4 | 25 187 | 2 951 | 122 | 55 | 33 | 130 | 127 | 32 | 61 | 27 | 3 |
| Tate | 823 | 4.0 | 28 643 | 2 515 | 255 | 55 | 69 | 233 | 227 | 73 | 84 | 28 | 5 |
| Tippah | 590 | 5.5 | 26 657 | 2 805 | 255 | 35 | 71 | 214 | 209 | 68 | 106 | 23 | 4 |
| Tishomingo | 484 | 4.1 | 24 681 | 2 991 | 217 | 17 | 68 | 192 | 187 | 68 | 93 | 16 | 4 |
| Tunica | 329 | 7.6 | 30 943 | 2 112 | 467 | 49 | 37 | 92 | 89 | 21 | 38 | 24 | 3 |
| Union | 789 | 9.7 | 28 858 | 2 476 | 415 | 55 | 101 | 214 | 208 | 81 | 90 | 24 | 5 |
| Walthall | 385 | 1.9 | 24 971 | 2 967 | 109 | 29 | 39 | 144 | 139 | 42 | 65 | 24 | 3 |
| Warren | 1 779 | 3.4 | 36 792 | 1 103 | 1 200 | 92 | 240 | 416 | 405 | 114 | 193 | 69 | 10 |
| Washington | 1 583 | 3.4 | 31 412 | 2 013 | 836 | 139 | 212 | 531 | 520 | 128 | 227 | 137 | 13 |
| Wayne | 567 | 2.6 | 27 555 | 2 678 | 243 | 48 | 77 | 177 | 170 | 53 | 76 | 32 | 4 |
| Webster | 259 | 2.7 | 25 098 | 2 958 | 86 | 13 | 31 | 109 | 107 | 37 | 50 | 14 | 2 |
| Wilkinson | 239 | 2.9 | 24 685 | 2 990 | 101 | 11 | 29 | 90 | 88 | 22 | 43 | 18 | 2 |
| Winston | 505 | 4.7 | 26 491 | 2 824 | 207 | 33 | 71 | 185 | 181 | 61 | 78 | 29 | 4 |
| Yalobusha | 380 | 4.8 | 30 303 | 2 240 | 138 | 28 | 42 | 143 | 140 | 46 | 67 | 19 | 2 |
| Yazoo | 733 | 5.2 | 26 280 | 2 853 | 327 | 78 | 82 | 247 | 240 | 61 | 115 | 52 | 5 |
| **MISSOURI** | 228 218 | 4.6 | 37 969 | X | 146 657 | 21 078 | 35 245 | 46 044 | 44 717 | 15 423 | 19 929 | 4 719 | 1 500 |
| Adair | 698 | 2.4 | 27 321 | 2 716 | 395 | 64 | 114 | 195 | 189 | 55 | 97 | 17 | 7 |
| Andrew | 765 | 5.6 | 44 465 | 424 | 101 | 64 | 95 | 104 | 100 | 42 | 41 | 8 | 4 |
| Atchison | 230 | 10.0 | 41 250 | 638 | 67 | 62 | 43 | 45 | 44 | 19 | 19 | 3 | 1 |
| Audrain | 816 | 3.6 | 31 899 | 1 908 | 407 | 127 | 121 | 208 | 202 | 71 | 97 | 20 | 5 |
| Barry | 1 068 | 4.3 | 30 278 | 2 243 | 632 | 125 | 161 | 299 | 292 | 104 | 130 | 34 | 8 |
| Barton | 355 | 0.1 | 28 823 | 2 483 | 134 | 59 | 56 | 105 | 102 | 37 | 45 | 13 | 3 |
| Bates | 552 | 2.8 | 32 429 | 1 794 | 151 | 77 | 80 | 148 | 144 | 52 | 68 | 13 | 5 |
| Benton | 550 | 2.9 | 28 794 | 2 488 | 134 | 51 | 89 | 222 | 218 | 86 | 95 | 18 | 5 |
| Bollinger | 330 | 1.2 | 26 746 | 2 797 | 65 | 31 | 43 | 108 | 105 | 37 | 47 | 12 | 3 |
| Boone | 6 196 | 5.5 | 37 409 | 1 037 | 4 453 | 409 | 1 010 | 1 023 | 986 | 297 | 440 | 101 | 30 |
| Buchanan | 3 025 | 4.4 | 33 732 | 1 559 | 2 365 | 262 | 407 | 729 | 709 | 222 | 335 | 80 | 22 |
| Butler | 1 491 | 5.0 | 34 612 | 1 430 | 820 | 211 | 175 | 478 | 468 | 127 | 227 | 58 | 12 |
| Caldwell | 339 | 6.3 | 36 370 | 1 154 | 67 | 64 | 35 | 69 | 67 | 24 | 30 | 6 | 2 |
| Callaway | 1 275 | 3.0 | 28 697 | 2 506 | 732 | 93 | 166 | 308 | 299 | 109 | 130 | 30 | 10 |
| Camden | 1 434 | 4.0 | 32 827 | 1 734 | 622 | 156 | 296 | 379 | 370 | 164 | 144 | 29 | 12 |
| Cape Girardeau | 2 743 | 4.3 | 35 792 | 1 252 | 1 927 | 262 | 462 | 546 | 529 | 189 | 215 | 55 | 17 |
| Carroll | 338 | 7.3 | 36 552 | 1 131 | 97 | 71 | 60 | 82 | 80 | 29 | 37 | 7 | 3 |
| Carter | 165 | 1.3 | 25 973 | 2 884 | 53 | 16 | 20 | 69 | 67 | 20 | 33 | 9 | 2 |
| Cass | 3 526 | 3.6 | 35 244 | 1 333 | 1 031 | 176 | 449 | 674 | 652 | 250 | 280 | 51 | 31 |
| Cedar | 376 | 2.1 | 26 954 | 2 768 | 117 | 40 | 61 | 140 | 137 | 48 | 64 | 14 | 3 |
| Chariton | 302 | 8.7 | 38 985 | 857 | 87 | 70 | 53 | 68 | 67 | 23 | 33 | 5 | 2 |
| Christian | 2 515 | 6.4 | 32 014 | 1 885 | 600 | 221 | 296 | 501 | 484 | 188 | 183 | 49 | 17 |
| Clark | 223 | 7.8 | 31 779 | 1 937 | 53 | 41 | 32 | 59 | 57 | 22 | 26 | 5 | 2 |
| Clay | 8 604 | 3.7 | 38 213 | 940 | 5 486 | 806 | 951 | 1 352 | 1 303 | 513 | 541 | 106 | 53 |
| Clinton | 741 | 5.3 | 35 628 | 1 276 | 179 | 48 | 86 | 142 | 137 | 52 | 59 | 10 | 6 |
| Cole | 3 069 | 3.4 | 40 147 | 730 | 2 724 | 249 | 477 | 522 | 505 | 185 | 217 | 50 | 15 |
| Cooper | 544 | 5.5 | 30 790 | 2 142 | 234 | 66 | 80 | 133 | 129 | 46 | 59 | 12 | 4 |
| Crawford | 760 | 4.4 | 30 648 | 2 162 | 269 | 114 | 96 | 221 | 215 | 74 | 98 | 25 | 7 |
| Dade | 205 | 3.0 | 26 265 | 2 855 | 67 | 23 | 33 | 66 | 64 | 25 | 27 | 6 | 2 |
| Dallas | 481 | 4.0 | 28 709 | 2 501 | 88 | 61 | 69 | 146 | 142 | 51 | 61 | 17 | 4 |
| Daviess | 245 | 8.2 | 29 450 | 2 386 | 61 | 50 | 38 | 61 | 59 | 24 | 24 | 6 | 2 |
| DeKalb | 315 | 8.0 | 24 697 | 2 988 | 141 | 32 | 38 | 72 | 69 | 28 | 28 | 6 | 3 |
| Dent | 446 | 4.4 | 28 436 | 2 552 | 171 | 34 | 62 | 153 | 150 | 48 | 75 | 16 | 4 |
| Douglas | 345 | 4.5 | 25 460 | 2 933 | 96 | 59 | 44 | 116 | 113 | 40 | 49 | 15 | 3 |
| Dunklin | 1 019 | 7.0 | 31 855 | 1 914 | 336 | 152 | 111 | 380 | 373 | 94 | 203 | 54 | 8 |
| Franklin | 3 651 | 4.8 | 35 811 | 1 250 | 1 686 | 232 | 560 | 729 | 706 | 284 | 291 | 60 | 28 |
| Gasconade | 479 | 3.5 | 31 594 | 1 979 | 196 | 30 | 95 | 128 | 125 | 51 | 54 | 10 | 4 |
| Gentry | 237 | 7.8 | 34 887 | 1 387 | 86 | 40 | 37 | 67 | 65 | 22 | 35 | 4 | 1 |
| Greene | 9 822 | 4.2 | 35 429 | 1 307 | 7 432 | 1 220 | 1 812 | 2 052 | 1 990 | 691 | 824 | 207 | 61 |
| Grundy | 324 | 6.4 | 31 707 | 1 954 | 154 | 42 | 50 | 91 | 89 | 29 | 40 | 8 | 2 |
| Harrison | 278 | 7.9 | 31 304 | 2 042 | 93 | 48 | 51 | 80 | 78 | 26 | 40 | 8 | 2 |
| Henry | 717 | 2.4 | 32 287 | 1 826 | 322 | 47 | 125 | 222 | 217 | 79 | 100 | 20 | 6 |
| Hickory | 220 | 3.5 | 22 819 | 3 064 | 42 | 13 | 35 | 106 | 104 | 43 | 44 | 8 | 2 |
| Holt | 176 | 7.1 | 36 631 | 1 121 | 54 | 33 | 29 | 40 | 39 | 15 | 18 | 3 | 1 |
| Howard | 371 | 7.1 | 36 385 | 1 152 | 90 | 35 | 50 | 89 | 87 | 26 | 42 | 7 | 2 |
| Howell | 1 121 | 3.3 | 27 555 | 2 678 | 618 | 88 | 161 | 381 | 372 | 125 | 162 | 48 | 9 |
| Iron | 291 | 5.6 | 27 272 | 2 720 | 148 | 10 | 32 | 119 | 116 | 35 | 61 | 12 | 3 |
| Jackson | 27 436 | 3.1 | 40 564 | 699 | 22 713 | 3 855 | 3 346 | 5 305 | 5 155 | 1 609 | 2 395 | 606 | 190 |

1. Based on the resident population estimated as of July 1 of the year shown.    2. Includes supplements to wages and salaries.

# Table B. States and Counties — Earnings, Social Security, and Housing

| STATE County | Earnings, 2011 | | | | | | | | | Social Security beneficiaries, December 2011 | | Supplemental Security Income recipients, December 2011 | Housing units, 2010 | |
| | | | Goods-related[1] | | Service-related and health | | | | | | | | | |
| | Total (mil dol) | Farm | Total | Manu-facturing | Information and profes-sional and technical services | Retail trade | Finance, insur-ance, and real estate | Health care and social services | Govern-ment | Number | Rate[2] | | Total | Percent change, 2000–2010 |
| | 75 | 76 | 77 | 78 | 79 | 80 | 81 | 82 | 83 | 84 | 85 | 86 | 87 | 88 |

| MISSISSIPPI—Cont'd | | | | | | | | | | | | | | |
| Sunflower | 482 | 17.0 | 5.9 | 4.1 | 1.6 | 5.0 | 2.8 | 6.1 | 36.6 | 5 330 | 182 | 2 115 | 9 685 | -6.3 |
| Tallahatchie | 177 | 21.8 | 3.4 | 0.9 | D | 7.7 | 2.0 | D | 24.5 | 3 155 | 206 | 1 311 | 5 530 | -3.2 |
| Tate | 310 | 3.5 | D | 9.8 | 6.7 | 9.2 | 3.9 | D | 28.3 | 5 810 | 202 | 883 | 10 947 | 17.0 |
| Tippah | 290 | 0.5 | D | 26.4 | D | 7.4 | 3.1 | D | 19.7 | 5 890 | 266 | 1 102 | 9 696 | 9.3 |
| Tishomingo | 234 | 0.3 | 36.5 | 31.9 | D | 7.1 | 3.2 | D | 18.5 | 5 730 | 292 | 771 | 10 295 | 7.8 |
| Tunica | 516 | 6.9 | 3.4 | 1.8 | D | 2.2 | 1.2 | D | 8.7 | 1 980 | 186 | 795 | 4 803 | 29.6 |
| Union | 470 | 1.1 | 36.8 | 31.4 | D | 7.1 | 2.3 | D | 13.7 | 6 710 | 245 | 938 | 11 520 | 7.7 |
| Walthall | 138 | 3.7 | 23.0 | 14.5 | 2.1 | 10.6 | 4.8 | 7.5 | 26.5 | 3 710 | 241 | 826 | 7 132 | 11.1 |
| Warren | 1 292 | 0.6 | 17.9 | 14.0 | 6.5 | 7.0 | 2.7 | 11.5 | 32.3 | 9 545 | 197 | 2 069 | 21 896 | 5.3 |
| Washington | 975 | 8.2 | D | 7.9 | 5.7 | 8.0 | 3.5 | 8.2 | 27.0 | 11 335 | 225 | 4 674 | 21 708 | -11.0 |
| Wayne | 291 | 6.9 | 27.5 | 11.4 | 2.0 | 9.4 | 3.6 | D | 20.9 | 4 575 | 222 | 1 141 | 9 213 | 1.7 |
| Webster | 99 | 3.1 | 20.0 | 14.8 | D | 7.2 | D | D | 22.1 | 3 200 | 310 | 619 | 4 804 | 10.6 |
| Wilkinson | 112 | 2.5 | 8.9 | 6.9 | D | 6.5 | 2.6 | D | 26.6 | 2 145 | 222 | 750 | 5 037 | -1.4 |
| Winston | 240 | 1.7 | D | 19.3 | 3.1 | 10.5 | 2.6 | D | 16.6 | 5 115 | 268 | 975 | 8 745 | 3.2 |
| Yalobusha | 166 | 5.0 | D | 27.4 | D | 6.1 | 2.8 | 2.4 | 26.2 | 3 890 | 310 | 854 | 6 344 | 1.9 |
| Yazoo | 406 | 9.3 | D | 13.3 | 1.8 | 4.8 | 3.9 | D | 33.7 | 5 350 | 192 | 1 824 | 10 074 | 0.6 |
| MISSOURI | 167 736 | 1.4 | 16.3 | 10.5 | 11.8 | 6.5 | 7.6 | 12.0 | 16.8 | 1 188 437 | 198 | 137 167 | 2 712 729 | 11.1 |
| Adair | 459 | 2.0 | 11.6 | 7.0 | 5.3 | 10.0 | 3.8 | D | 26.3 | 4 650 | 182 | 704 | 11 263 | 4.0 |
| Andrew | 165 | 10.7 | D | 1.0 | D | 12.1 | 3.7 | D | 20.4 | 3 250 | 189 | 215 | 7 306 | 9.7 |
| Atchison | 128 | 37.8 | 2.7 | 0.1 | 3.8 | 4.5 | 3.7 | 8.0 | 14.4 | 1 490 | 268 | 80 | 2 985 | -3.8 |
| Audrain | 534 | 9.4 | 26.5 | 22.6 | D | 8.8 | 3.6 | D | 22.7 | 5 525 | 216 | 529 | 10 852 | -0.3 |
| Barry | 757 | 6.0 | 34.7 | 30.1 | D | 7.5 | 4.0 | 4.8 | 11.3 | 8 780 | 249 | 964 | 17 523 | 9.8 |
| Barton | 193 | 13.6 | D | 7.6 | D | 8.3 | 6.2 | 5.6 | 22.4 | 3 230 | 262 | 353 | 5 600 | 3.5 |
| Bates | 228 | 9.7 | D | 6.0 | 6.1 | 12.3 | 5.5 | 7.0 | 26.8 | 4 260 | 250 | 401 | 7 842 | 8.2 |
| Benton | 185 | 3.6 | D | 7.2 | 2.7 | 11.9 | 9.3 | 7.4 | 27.6 | 6 825 | 357 | 555 | 14 150 | 11.5 |
| Bollinger | 96 | 2.0 | D | 5.6 | 3.3 | 9.5 | D | 10.0 | 22.2 | 3 220 | 261 | 453 | 5 878 | 6.4 |
| Boone | 4 862 | 0.2 | 9.0 | 4.1 | 7.1 | 7.6 | 7.7 | 11.5 | 38.1 | 22 605 | 136 | 2 662 | 69 551 | 22.7 |
| Buchanan | 2 627 | 1.1 | D | 25.6 | 5.6 | 7.0 | 5.2 | 15.5 | 13.8 | 17 375 | 194 | 2 319 | 38 427 | 5.1 |
| Butler | 1 030 | 7.4 | D | 13.8 | 5.0 | 9.4 | 3.6 | 18.6 | 20.0 | 11 560 | 268 | 2 567 | 19 731 | 5.5 |
| Caldwell | 131 | 23.3 | D | 0.9 | 4.2 | 6.6 | D | D | 20.3 | 1 985 | 213 | 168 | 4 605 | 2.5 |
| Callaway | 825 | 4.1 | 18.9 | 11.7 | 3.6 | 4.2 | 2.5 | D | 22.4 | 8 615 | 194 | 811 | 18 522 | 14.6 |
| Camden | 778 | 0.2 | D | 4.1 | 5.8 | 14.6 | 6.8 | 17.0 | 12.5 | 12 030 | 275 | 630 | 41 183 | 23.0 |
| Cape Girardeau | 2 190 | 0.7 | 17.2 | 11.2 | 6.0 | 8.4 | 5.0 | 27.5 | 14.0 | 14 870 | 194 | 1 623 | 32 616 | 10.8 |
| Carroll | 168 | 29.6 | 16.0 | 7.8 | 2.8 | 6.9 | 4.4 | D | 16.9 | 2 425 | 262 | 231 | 4 630 | -5.5 |
| Carter | 69 | -0.3 | D | 8.3 | D | 10.3 | D | 7.3 | 31.8 | 1 800 | 283 | 368 | 3 247 | 7.2 |
| Cass | 1 207 | 1.1 | 14.6 | 3.5 | 4.6 | 12.1 | 4.9 | 9.6 | 22.7 | 18 315 | 183 | 997 | 40 030 | 26.4 |
| Cedar | 157 | 1.7 | D | 6.0 | 2.9 | 11.6 | 4.3 | 9.1 | 26.6 | 4 120 | 295 | 455 | 7 224 | 6.0 |
| Chariton | 158 | 23.3 | D | D | 1.6 | 8.1 | 4.9 | 4.5 | 13.2 | 1 935 | 250 | 149 | 4 167 | -2.0 |
| Christian | 822 | 0.2 | D | 6.4 | 9.6 | 10.1 | 7.2 | 6.9 | 17.8 | 14 885 | 189 | 1 143 | 31 576 | 44.7 |
| Clark | 94 | 20.3 | D | 6.2 | 2.0 | 11.7 | 3.9 | 3.7 | 21.8 | 1 785 | 254 | 135 | 3 473 | -0.3 |
| Clay | 6 292 | 0.2 | 21.1 | 14.8 | 19.0 | 7.4 | 4.0 | 7.6 | 14.5 | 36 310 | 161 | 2 212 | 93 918 | 23.2 |
| Clinton | 227 | 11.6 | D | 2.4 | D | 5.5 | 4.8 | 17.2 | 30.3 | 3 915 | 188 | 271 | 8 876 | 12.7 |
| Cole | 2 973 | 0.2 | 11.0 | 4.6 | 9.7 | 6.6 | 5.3 | 11.5 | 37.9 | 14 420 | 189 | 1 562 | 32 324 | 11.8 |
| Cooper | 300 | 13.5 | D | 12.3 | 2.0 | 7.2 | 6.1 | D | 20.2 | 3 715 | 210 | 293 | 7 463 | 11.8 |
| Crawford | 383 | -0.3 | D | 21.4 | 2.9 | 22.8 | 3.5 | D | 11.8 | 6 200 | 250 | 757 | 11 955 | 10.2 |
| Dade | 89 | 9.7 | D | 9.2 | D | 5.9 | D | 2.2 | 24.7 | 2 110 | 270 | 172 | 3 965 | 5.5 |
| Dallas | 149 | 1.2 | D | 3.7 | 3.2 | 10.8 | 5.1 | D | 21.7 | 4 365 | 261 | 538 | 7 662 | 10.8 |
| Daviess | 111 | 29.4 | D | D | 1.8 | 7.6 | D | 4.2 | 20.6 | 1 945 | 234 | 139 | 4 199 | 9.0 |
| DeKalb | 173 | 13.6 | 4.9 | 1.6 | D | 9.0 | 9.4 | D | 34.3 | 2 210 | 173 | 169 | 4 329 | 12.7 |
| Dent | 205 | -0.6 | 24.8 | 20.2 | 2.8 | 10.5 | 5.4 | D | 22.4 | 4 155 | 265 | 564 | 7 285 | 4.2 |
| Douglas | 155 | -0.1 | D | D | D | 11.3 | 3.4 | D | 16.1 | 3 635 | 268 | 467 | 6 519 | 10.1 |
| Dunklin | 488 | 19.9 | 6.9 | 4.5 | 2.7 | 9.9 | 4.5 | D | 17.2 | 8 565 | 268 | 2 408 | 14 419 | -1.8 |
| Franklin | 1 918 | 0.5 | 32.6 | 24.7 | 4.2 | 7.7 | 4.4 | 11.1 | 12.4 | 21 295 | 209 | 1 567 | 43 419 | 13.4 |
| Gasconade | 226 | 1.4 | D | 27.3 | D | 8.1 | 4.5 | D | 22.3 | 4 070 | 268 | 276 | 8 205 | 5.0 |
| Gentry | 126 | 28.9 | 10.9 | 8.1 | D | 6.6 | D | 16.2 | 17.0 | 1 920 | 283 | 163 | 3 209 | -0.2 |
| Greene | 8 652 | 0.1 | 14.4 | 10.1 | 8.3 | 8.0 | 6.8 | 19.5 | 13.3 | 54 560 | 197 | 6 301 | 125 387 | 20.0 |
| Grundy | 196 | 12.4 | D | 21.0 | 2.6 | 6.1 | 3.4 | 12.4 | 22.4 | 2 510 | 245 | 260 | 5 023 | -1.5 |
| Harrison | 141 | 23.7 | D | 1.2 | 2.5 | 13.7 | 5.2 | 6.5 | 26.1 | 2 265 | 255 | 213 | 4 407 | 2.1 |
| Henry | 369 | 2.9 | D | 17.0 | 2.8 | 9.0 | 5.6 | 9.4 | 24.9 | 6 425 | 289 | 706 | 10 886 | 6.1 |
| Hickory | 55 | 3.0 | D | 1.7 | D | 12.8 | D | 6.9 | 31.1 | 3 525 | 366 | 292 | 6 835 | 10.5 |
| Holt | 86 | 29.0 | D | 9.4 | D | 8.0 | 3.6 | 5.1 | 17.2 | 1 230 | 256 | 72 | 2 806 | -4.3 |
| Howard | 125 | 15.8 | D | 11.5 | 2.9 | 7.0 | D | D | 17.2 | 2 195 | 215 | 257 | 4 582 | 5.4 |
| Howell | 707 | 0.6 | 20.8 | 18.0 | 5.2 | 9.0 | 3.8 | 20.0 | 15.9 | 11 185 | 275 | 1 614 | 18 021 | 10.3 |
| Iron | 158 | -0.9 | D | 2.0 | D | 7.5 | 2.3 | D | 17.9 | 2 935 | 275 | 555 | 5 329 | 8.6 |
| Jackson | 26 568 | 0.1 | 13.2 | 6.9 | 20.2 | 4.9 | 11.0 | 11.0 | 17.0 | 119 405 | 177 | 16 306 | 312 105 | 8.3 |

1. Includes mining, construction, and manufacturing.   2. Per 1,000 resident population enumerated in the 2010 census.

| STATE County | Housing units, 2007–2011 | | | | | | | | Civilian labor force, 2012 | | | | Civilian employment,[6] 2007–2011 | | |
|---|---|---|---|---|---|---|---|---|---|---|---|---|---|---|---|
| | Occupied units | | | | | | | | | | Unemployment | | | Percent | |
| | | | Owner-occupied | | | Renter-occupied | | | | | | | | | |
| | | | | Median owner cost as a percent of income | | | | | | | | | | Manage-ment, business, science and arts | Con-struction, produc-tion, and mainte-nance occu-pations |
| | Total | Percent | Median value[1] | With a mort-gage | Without a mort-gage[2] | Median rent[3] | Median rent as a per-cent of income | Sub-stand-ard units[4] (percent) | Total | Percent change, 2011–2012 | Total | Rate[5] | Total | | |
| | 89 | 90 | 91 | 92 | 93 | 94 | 95 | 96 | 97 | 98 | 99 | 100 | 101 | 102 | 103 |
| MISSISSIPPI—Cont'd | | | | | | | | | | | | | | | |
| Sunflower | 8 459 | 58.5 | 65 500 | 30.2 | 13.1 | 521 | 30.0 | 4.2 | 10 287 | -2.7 | 1 498 | 14.6 | 8 537 | 27.7 | 29.1 |
| Tallahatchie | 4 626 | 74.9 | 57 700 | 26.2 | 14.2 | 458 | 30.3 | 4.1 | 6 225 | -2.9 | 712 | 11.4 | 4 677 | 24.2 | 32.6 |
| Tate | 9 982 | 74.4 | 107 000 | 24.3 | 11.8 | 695 | 32.7 | 3.4 | 12 331 | 0.2 | 1 198 | 9.7 | 12 481 | 24.6 | 32.4 |
| Tippah | 8 322 | 76.6 | 74 300 | 23.4 | 11.2 | 548 | 32.0 | 4.2 | 8 580 | -0.7 | 933 | 10.9 | 8 686 | 22.3 | 40.0 |
| Tishomingo | 7 531 | 79.2 | 75 000 | 23.8 | 10.1 | 456 | 35.3 | 1.8 | 7 871 | -0.5 | 832 | 10.6 | 7 235 | 25.3 | 38.6 |
| Tunica | 3 992 | 49.7 | 57 900 | 23.2 | 12.0 | 666 | 32.8 | 8.1 | 4 544 | -2.9 | 687 | 15.1 | 4 182 | 19.1 | 19.9 |
| Union | 10 128 | 75.1 | 85 000 | 23.8 | 10.7 | 555 | 31.1 | 3.4 | 13 465 | 5.3 | 1 127 | 8.4 | 11 361 | 21.1 | 39.8 |
| Walthall | 5 286 | 84.8 | 81 900 | 26.5 | 14.6 | 627 | 27.5 | 2.5 | 5 634 | -2.3 | 642 | 11.4 | 5 598 | 29.0 | 35.6 |
| Warren | 19 023 | 66.8 | 98 500 | 21.4 | 11.9 | 656 | 32.3 | 2.6 | 21 367 | -2.5 | 2 177 | 10.2 | 20 860 | 33.9 | 26.1 |
| Washington | 18 821 | 54.8 | 73 600 | 23.9 | 13.5 | 590 | 34.7 | 5.6 | 21 246 | -4.5 | 2 989 | 14.1 | 17 780 | 30.3 | 24.0 |
| Wayne | 8 436 | 82.5 | 64 400 | 23.5 | 14.3 | 556 | 28.7 | 3.4 | 8 482 | -1.4 | 951 | 11.2 | 8 086 | 21.1 | 46.0 |
| Webster | 3 950 | 73.4 | 72 100 | 20.3 | 12.4 | 467 | 28.1 | 4.0 | 3 448 | -3.4 | 408 | 11.8 | 3 958 | 29.2 | 36.4 |
| Wilkinson | 3 459 | 75.3 | 58 900 | 29.2 | 10.1 | 511 | 32.8 | 5.3 | 3 903 | -4.9 | 439 | 11.2 | 3 269 | 24.7 | 31.7 |
| Winston | 7 348 | 78.2 | 75 100 | 22.2 | 16.3 | 601 | 32.2 | 2.0 | 7 447 | -2.2 | 927 | 12.4 | 7 471 | 29.3 | 28.7 |
| Yalobusha | 4 737 | 73.4 | 60 700 | 24.1 | 13.4 | 473 | 24.2 | 1.5 | 5 965 | 2.6 | 571 | 9.6 | 4 512 | 23.2 | 43.4 |
| Yazoo | 8 518 | 62.7 | 67 000 | 26.5 | 14.3 | 560 | 35.8 | 4.6 | 10 545 | -2.0 | 1 201 | 11.4 | 8 916 | 28.2 | 28.8 |
| MISSOURI | 2 354 104 | 69.5 | 138 900 | 22.4 | 11.6 | 693 | 29.1 | 2.1 | 2 992 858 | -1.0 | 207 391 | 6.9 | 2 790 203 | 33.9 | 23.1 |
| Adair | 9 636 | 60.3 | 100 800 | 18.9 | 11.3 | 509 | 40.7 | 2.6 | 12 219 | -2.8 | 739 | 6.0 | 11 211 | 38.1 | 19.9 |
| Andrew | 6 634 | 78.5 | 127 300 | 19.4 | 10.2 | 623 | 26.7 | 0.8 | 10 669 | 1.7 | 538 | 5.0 | 8 819 | 31.7 | 27.9 |
| Atchison | 2 447 | 72.2 | 71 200 | 18.6 | 11.6 | 478 | 21.0 | 0.2 | 2 997 | -2.2 | 174 | 5.8 | 2 827 | 31.3 | 29.7 |
| Audrain | 9 426 | 75.2 | 83 900 | 20.9 | 10.1 | 595 | 22.6 | 2.4 | 11 874 | -0.8 | 754 | 6.4 | 10 586 | 26.0 | 31.9 |
| Barry | 13 891 | 75.6 | 102 700 | 22.1 | 9.9 | 560 | 27.0 | 5.5 | 16 253 | -3.0 | 1 028 | 6.3 | 15 151 | 28.4 | 37.1 |
| Barton | 4 995 | 75.8 | 83 400 | 20.0 | 11.8 | 498 | 33.4 | 4.3 | 4 906 | -2.9 | 413 | 8.4 | 5 365 | 25.9 | 35.8 |
| Bates | 6 602 | 76.4 | 103 100 | 23.4 | 13.0 | 580 | 32.6 | 3.0 | 7 743 | -0.8 | 637 | 8.2 | 7 315 | 24.5 | 36.5 |
| Benton | 8 253 | 83.8 | 103 800 | 23.9 | 12.0 | 560 | 31.8 | 3.1 | 7 923 | -1.3 | 636 | 8.0 | 7 131 | 26.6 | 31.9 |
| Bollinger | 4 788 | 81.2 | 96 100 | 21.4 | 9.9 | 566 | 29.0 | 3.8 | 5 473 | -1.2 | 381 | 7.0 | 5 177 | 20.6 | 41.2 |
| Boone | 63 790 | 57.6 | 156 600 | 21.2 | 9.9 | 760 | 32.1 | 1.9 | 92 276 | 1.6 | 4 259 | 4.6 | 85 097 | 43.5 | 14.5 |
| Buchanan | 33 662 | 66.9 | 106 800 | 20.5 | 11.4 | 641 | 28.6 | 1.7 | 51 392 | 1.1 | 2 891 | 5.6 | 41 631 | 28.5 | 27.9 |
| Butler | 17 375 | 67.4 | 86 200 | 21.2 | 11.7 | 554 | 29.7 | 1.3 | 20 586 | -0.7 | 1 511 | 7.3 | 17 932 | 28.1 | 29.0 |
| Caldwell | 3 708 | 74.6 | 100 300 | 22.8 | 11.0 | 604 | 29.0 | 3.3 | 4 287 | 0.0 | 317 | 7.4 | 4 043 | 26.2 | 35.2 |
| Callaway | 16 899 | 76.9 | 127 700 | 21.2 | 9.9 | 597 | 25.1 | 2.1 | 22 122 | -1.7 | 1 350 | 6.1 | 21 440 | 32.4 | 24.5 |
| Camden | 18 104 | 80.7 | 187 100 | 24.2 | 11.0 | 604 | 27.3 | 2.3 | 19 754 | -0.5 | 1 777 | 9.0 | 19 634 | 31.5 | 22.9 |
| Cape Girardeau | 29 452 | 67.0 | 137 100 | 21.3 | 10.1 | 626 | 27.7 | 1.8 | 38 447 | -0.4 | 2 272 | 5.9 | 37 205 | 30.9 | 24.4 |
| Carroll | 3 660 | 79.6 | 77 700 | 19.3 | 12.2 | 529 | 24.5 | 2.7 | 4 688 | -3.4 | 375 | 8.0 | 4 326 | 29.7 | 32.6 |
| Carter | 2 472 | 74.0 | 88 800 | 24.4 | 12.3 | 359 | 25.0 | 2.3 | 2 926 | -4.8 | 234 | 8.0 | 2 416 | 29.2 | 29.5 |
| Cass | 36 864 | 78.8 | 154 700 | 23.2 | 12.0 | 880 | 29.5 | 1.7 | 50 407 | -0.3 | 3 421 | 6.8 | 48 485 | 32.8 | 26.2 |
| Cedar | 6 101 | 75.5 | 93 100 | 26.1 | 11.9 | 603 | 31.9 | 3.1 | 6 077 | -5.4 | 421 | 6.9 | 5 083 | 25.0 | 31.9 |
| Chariton | 3 065 | 79.8 | 75 000 | 19.3 | 11.7 | 430 | 21.5 | 2.1 | 4 206 | -1.9 | 263 | 6.3 | 3 585 | 30.2 | 32.8 |
| Christian | 29 166 | 74.4 | 146 600 | 22.5 | 12.1 | 700 | 28.6 | 2.4 | 40 871 | -0.1 | 2 369 | 5.8 | 36 900 | 35.8 | 21.6 |
| Clark | 2 846 | 77.9 | 68 900 | 18.5 | 10.5 | 447 | 26.3 | 2.3 | 3 481 | 0.2 | 250 | 7.2 | 3 083 | 26.4 | 40.2 |
| Clay | 86 954 | 71.5 | 156 100 | 22.9 | 12.0 | 766 | 25.9 | 1.7 | 120 896 | 0.3 | 7 766 | 6.4 | 113 900 | 37.5 | 20.3 |
| Clinton | 8 085 | 74.8 | 150 700 | 23.1 | 12.1 | 708 | 23.9 | 2.1 | 10 173 | -0.7 | 791 | 7.8 | 9 569 | 26.1 | 29.4 |
| Cole | 29 356 | 66.2 | 139 300 | 19.0 | 9.9 | 578 | 23.4 | 1.1 | 39 479 | -1.4 | 2 089 | 5.3 | 37 808 | 40.0 | 17.4 |
| Cooper | 6 376 | 72.8 | 116 600 | 20.0 | 11.3 | 587 | 24.2 | 1.6 | 8 445 | -2.0 | 577 | 6.8 | 7 870 | 31.9 | 27.1 |
| Crawford | 9 528 | 76.5 | 106 900 | 25.6 | 11.9 | 561 | 28.4 | 3.6 | 11 685 | -1.9 | 927 | 7.9 | 9 978 | 19.6 | 39.3 |
| Dade | 3 222 | 77.5 | 72 200 | 22.1 | 12.8 | 503 | 28.2 | 2.9 | 3 469 | -2.6 | 250 | 7.2 | 3 079 | 24.3 | 36.4 |
| Dallas | 6 368 | 79.9 | 99 100 | 21.0 | 9.9 | 517 | 24.5 | 4.0 | 7 197 | -0.6 | 578 | 8.0 | 6 635 | 24.6 | 40.3 |
| Daviess | 3 179 | 75.7 | 109 500 | 24.3 | 12.9 | 554 | 21.9 | 3.5 | 3 920 | -0.1 | 275 | 7.0 | 3 618 | 28.1 | 31.9 |
| DeKalb | 3 947 | 66.7 | 118 900 | 21.8 | 12.6 | 506 | 26.4 | 0.7 | 5 628 | 0.8 | 350 | 6.2 | 4 872 | 27.2 | 29.5 |
| Dent | 6 063 | 75.9 | 82 500 | 22.8 | 11.0 | 504 | 32.4 | 2.3 | 6 352 | -6.5 | 485 | 7.6 | 6 059 | 26.8 | 32.6 |
| Douglas | 5 096 | 78.5 | 102 900 | 24.8 | 12.3 | 491 | 30.7 | 3.3 | 6 162 | -0.9 | 507 | 8.2 | 5 026 | 22.8 | 39.8 |
| Dunklin | 12 862 | 61.7 | 68 500 | 20.9 | 13.1 | 492 | 29.1 | 2.3 | 14 302 | -1.8 | 1 213 | 8.5 | 11 508 | 25.3 | 33.6 |
| Franklin | 38 817 | 76.9 | 150 300 | 22.8 | 11.2 | 644 | 25.4 | 2.5 | 52 494 | -1.3 | 4 189 | 8.0 | 47 723 | 27.7 | 33.1 |
| Gasconade | 6 368 | 79.3 | 112 000 | 23.9 | 10.9 | 499 | 23.6 | 1.5 | 7 229 | -1.8 | 525 | 7.3 | 7 000 | 28.6 | 34.4 |
| Gentry | 2 731 | 75.2 | 78 800 | 22.9 | 12.0 | 431 | 25.5 | 5.0 | 3 573 | -0.5 | 183 | 5.1 | 3 028 | 30.5 | 31.4 |
| Greene | 113 800 | 60.8 | 128 100 | 21.8 | 10.3 | 656 | 30.0 | 1.7 | 142 209 | 0.1 | 8 383 | 5.9 | 132 993 | 32.9 | 20.0 |
| Grundy | 4 335 | 70.2 | 75 400 | 20.6 | 11.6 | 454 | 26.7 | 2.0 | 4 824 | -1.6 | 309 | 6.4 | 4 538 | 26.3 | 34.3 |
| Harrison | 3 482 | 74.9 | 73 100 | 20.6 | 14.3 | 527 | 23.0 | 1.9 | 4 265 | -1.6 | 283 | 6.6 | 3 777 | 22.8 | 33.9 |
| Henry | 9 458 | 73.5 | 105 100 | 22.5 | 12.5 | 565 | 30.5 | 2.2 | 10 250 | -1.5 | 760 | 7.4 | 9 853 | 27.0 | 32.1 |
| Hickory | 4 301 | 83.4 | 92 200 | 26.9 | 12.0 | 469 | 32.2 | 2.4 | 3 496 | 1.2 | 433 | 12.4 | 3 265 | 24.1 | 28.6 |
| Holt | 2 199 | 77.3 | 77 700 | 19.7 | 11.2 | 452 | 23.7 | 2.3 | 2 746 | -0.7 | 138 | 5.0 | 2 374 | 31.9 | 29.3 |
| Howard | 3 794 | 78.4 | 97 300 | 21.7 | 9.9 | 499 | 24.6 | 1.8 | 5 193 | 1.3 | 315 | 6.1 | 4 665 | 31.7 | 29.7 |
| Howell | 15 538 | 72.0 | 98 600 | 22.6 | 9.9 | 521 | 30.0 | 1.6 | 18 771 | -0.3 | 1 309 | 7.0 | 15 905 | 27.7 | 34.9 |
| Iron | 4 298 | 73.5 | 77 200 | 21.2 | 9.9 | 505 | 30.7 | 2.9 | 5 341 | 5.1 | 424 | 7.9 | 3 705 | 26.4 | 26.9 |
| Jackson | 270 493 | 62.4 | 130 300 | 23.0 | 13.0 | 753 | 31.0 | 2.1 | 332 986 | -0.4 | 25 572 | 7.7 | 320 428 | 35.0 | 20.8 |

1. Specified owner-occupied units.   2. A value of 9.9 represents 9.9 percent or less.   3. Specified renter-occupied units. A value of 10.0 represents 10 percent or less.   4. Overcrowded or lacking complete plumbing facilities.   5. Percent of civilian labor force.   6. Persons 16 years old and over.

# Table B. States and Counties — Nonfarm Employment and Agriculture

| | Private nonfarm establishments, employment and payroll, 2011 | | | | | | | | | Agriculture, 2007 | | | |
|---|---|---|---|---|---|---|---|---|---|---|---|---|---|
| | | Employment | | | | | | Annual payroll | | Farms | | | |
| | | | | | | | | | | | | Percent with: | |
| STATE<br>County | Number of establish-ments | Total | Health care and social assistance | Manufac-turing | Retail trade | Finance and insurance | Professional, scientific, and technical services | Total (mil dol) | Average per employee (dollars) | Number | Fewer than 50 acres | 500 acres or more | Farm operators whose principal occu-pation is farming (percent) |
| | 104 | 105 | 106 | 107 | 108 | 109 | 110 | 111 | 112 | 113 | 114 | 115 | 116 |

| | | | | | | | | | | | | | |
|---|---|---|---|---|---|---|---|---|---|---|---|---|---|
| MISSISSIPPI—Cont'd | | | | | | | | | | | | | |
| Sunflower | 469 | 5 182 | D | 276 | 916 | 232 | 62 | 146 | 28 133 | 370 | 17.8 | 41.9 | 57.6 |
| Tallahatchie | 174 | 1 841 | D | D | 255 | D | D | 55 | 29 732 | 488 | 14.5 | 26.2 | 42.0 |
| Tate | 354 | 3 895 | 552 | 785 | 856 | 196 | D | 109 | 28 078 | 622 | 29.7 | 11.1 | 38.4 |
| Tippah | 343 | 5 391 | 626 | 1 590 | 678 | 145 | 125 | 152 | 28 183 | 691 | 25.3 | 5.6 | 24.6 |
| Tishomingo | 345 | 3 995 | 661 | 1 334 | 570 | D | 87 | 112 | 27 992 | 349 | 19.5 | 3.7 | 26.6 |
| Tunica | 220 | 10 234 | 202 | D | 531 | 86 | 19 | 283 | 27 617 | 103 | 4.9 | 61.2 | 65.0 |
| Union | 490 | 7 349 | 1 224 | 2 101 | 1 088 | 203 | 101 | 217 | 29 504 | 751 | 28.5 | 5.5 | 24.8 |
| Walthall | 225 | 1 996 | 223 | 474 | 350 | 68 | D | 49 | 24 645 | 768 | 30.1 | 5.1 | 42.1 |
| | | | | | | | | | | | | | |
| Warren | 1 037 | 17 935 | 2 800 | 2 603 | 2 555 | 400 | 483 | 566 | 31 547 | 278 | 33.8 | 21.6 | 35.6 |
| Washington | 1 213 | 14 651 | 3 002 | 1 162 | 2 956 | 367 | 382 | 417 | 28 491 | 346 | 21.4 | 43.6 | 62.7 |
| Wayne | 385 | 4 679 | D | 910 | 951 | 200 | 80 | 155 | 33 230 | 521 | 31.5 | 6.3 | 42.8 |
| Webster | 169 | 1 644 | D | 427 | 231 | 46 | 74 | 45 | 27 369 | 392 | 18.6 | 9.9 | 27.8 |
| Wilkinson | 155 | 1 542 | 369 | 171 | 275 | D | D | 42 | 26 955 | 207 | 16.4 | 26.6 | 48.8 |
| Winston | 381 | 4 652 | 619 | 1 335 | 919 | D | 105 | 138 | 29 601 | 536 | 27.8 | 6.3 | 36.4 |
| Yalobusha | 190 | 2 358 | 331 | 911 | 328 | 85 | D | 66 | 28 073 | 377 | 15.4 | 14.1 | 34.2 |
| Yazoo | 399 | 3 950 | 883 | D | 663 | D | 159 | 116 | 29 329 | 668 | 17.2 | 23.4 | 36.7 |
| | | | | | | | | | | | | | |
| MISSOURI | 147 274 | 2 298 295 | 388 172 | 241 838 | 305 550 | 124 766 | 140 721 | 92 602 | 40 292 | 107 825 | 26.9 | 13.0 | 41.8 |
| | | | | | | | | | | | | | |
| Adair | 654 | 8 532 | 2 048 | 832 | 1 511 | 235 | 794 | 222 | 25 997 | 944 | 22.6 | 15.4 | 40.0 |
| Andrew | 342 | 1 737 | 384 | D | 322 | 58 | D | 50 | 28 514 | 988 | 28.9 | 13.6 | 39.2 |
| Atchison | 211 | 1 314 | 241 | D | 386 | 72 | 56 | 32 | 24 443 | 501 | 17.6 | 35.5 | 62.5 |
| Audrain | 574 | 6 996 | D | 1 802 | 1 074 | 266 | 110 | 204 | 29 110 | 1 102 | 22.6 | 22.7 | 50.0 |
| Barry | 738 | 13 142 | 1 482 | 4 904 | 1 640 | 284 | D | 442 | 33 599 | 1 606 | 33.4 | 7.4 | 45.6 |
| Barton | 251 | 2 425 | 374 | 433 | 481 | D | D | 67 | 27 795 | 1 046 | 21.6 | 20.8 | 46.7 |
| Bates | 345 | 2 752 | D | 264 | 558 | 158 | 90 | 70 | 25 481 | 1 345 | 23.6 | 16.2 | 40.8 |
| Benton | 380 | 2 177 | 289 | D | 705 | D | D | 44 | 20 247 | 822 | 19.6 | 12.4 | 49.5 |
| | | | | | | | | | | | | | |
| Bollinger | 192 | 1 301 | 321 | 149 | 310 | D | 23 | 31 | 23 596 | 853 | 17.6 | 11.7 | 44.8 |
| Boone | 4 376 | 66 808 | 15 835 | 3 862 | 11 498 | 6 091 | 3 439 | 2 292 | 34 301 | 1 322 | 39.3 | 8.9 | 29.8 |
| Buchanan | 2 330 | 43 801 | 7 523 | 11 092 | 5 828 | 1 749 | 998 | 1 554 | 35 480 | 881 | 30.8 | 10.7 | 40.2 |
| Butler | 1 219 | 14 942 | 4 086 | D | 2 660 | 487 | 422 | 435 | 29 090 | 607 | 27.2 | 21.9 | 52.1 |
| Caldwell | 160 | 767 | D | D | 185 | 59 | D | 25 | 32 100 | 1 048 | 27.2 | 10.4 | 36.7 |
| Callaway | 750 | 11 326 | 2 272 | 1 517 | 1 328 | 310 | 225 | 419 | 37 036 | 1 503 | 29.9 | 9.5 | 34.6 |
| Camden | 1 403 | 11 896 | 2 173 | 700 | 3 117 | D | 428 | 351 | 29 512 | 544 | 16.5 | 13.1 | 40.4 |
| Cape Girardeau | 2 388 | 36 978 | 10 749 | 3 669 | 5 908 | 1 161 | 973 | 1 225 | 33 123 | 1 449 | 29.4 | 9.5 | 42.4 |
| Carroll | 233 | 1 667 | 377 | 181 | 268 | 109 | 45 | 48 | 28 621 | 1 199 | 18.6 | 16.2 | 36.3 |
| | | | | | | | | | | | | | |
| Carter | 169 | 996 | 249 | 173 | 148 | D | D | 18 | 18 380 | 203 | 21.2 | 12.3 | 33.0 |
| Cass | 1 823 | 17 176 | 2 472 | 1 782 | 3 714 | 628 | 479 | 491 | 28 582 | 1 775 | 45.7 | 8.4 | 38.4 |
| Cedar | 274 | 2 376 | 659 | 300 | 435 | 108 | D | 57 | 23 821 | 840 | 22.9 | 10.4 | 46.3 |
| Chariton | 200 | 1 254 | D | D | 223 | 83 | 28 | 35 | 27 594 | 1 173 | 18.8 | 18.2 | 41.7 |
| Christian | 1 587 | 12 453 | 1 453 | 1 317 | 2 671 | 620 | 474 | 323 | 25 945 | 1 265 | 37.6 | 5.8 | 38.5 |
| Clark | 143 | 958 | D | 122 | 249 | 64 | 11 | 23 | 23 921 | 709 | 12.6 | 18.1 | 45.7 |
| Clay | 4 721 | 82 143 | 12 904 | 9 895 | 11 348 | 2 924 | D | 3 720 | 45 284 | 752 | 52.5 | 8.5 | 35.8 |
| Clinton | 368 | 3 001 | 971 | D | 550 | 142 | D | 81 | 27 144 | 914 | 34.9 | 10.4 | 40.3 |
| Cole | 2 209 | 32 793 | 6 005 | 2 246 | 5 345 | 1 908 | 1 824 | 1 233 | 37 606 | 1 103 | 23.4 | 4.6 | 37.3 |
| | | | | | | | | | | | | | |
| Cooper | 401 | 4 353 | 820 | 552 | 812 | 198 | 80 | 108 | 24 887 | 942 | 20.7 | 18.9 | 42.4 |
| Crawford | 513 | 4 988 | D | 1 612 | 672 | D | 122 | 148 | 29 639 | 679 | 21.5 | 13.1 | 38.9 |
| Dade | 142 | 1 292 | D | D | 163 | 33 | D | 34 | 26 511 | 883 | 24.1 | 16.5 | 47.6 |
| Dallas | 248 | 2 608 | D | D | 518 | 133 | D | 42 | 16 283 | 1 369 | 35.4 | 6.6 | 41.5 |
| Daviess | 164 | 864 | D | D | 215 | 59 | D | 21 | 24 282 | 1 169 | 20.9 | 12.9 | 34.3 |
| DeKalb | 224 | 1 926 | 416 | D | 535 | 261 | D | 51 | 26 678 | 978 | 25.7 | 11.8 | 37.0 |
| Dent | 337 | 3 545 | 701 | 599 | 576 | 149 | 49 | 119 | 33 502 | 651 | 21.8 | 14.3 | 41.0 |
| Douglas | 204 | 2 222 | 249 | D | 445 | 68 | 30 | 48 | 21 378 | 1 124 | 22.4 | 8.7 | 43.9 |
| Dunklin | 764 | 8 412 | 3 127 | D | 1 469 | 269 | 137 | 174 | 20 673 | 453 | 24.9 | 42.2 | 66.9 |
| | | | | | | | | | | | | | |
| Franklin | 2 576 | 31 434 | 3 646 | 7 988 | 4 829 | 1 063 | 1 178 | 1 004 | 31 937 | 2 004 | 36.6 | 4.5 | 35.5 |
| Gasconade | 418 | 4 305 | 886 | 1 138 | 673 | 165 | 121 | 108 | 25 128 | 867 | 14.8 | 9.8 | 41.8 |
| Gentry | 205 | 1 760 | 710 | D | 268 | D | D | 41 | 23 177 | 839 | 19.7 | 15.7 | 35.2 |
| Greene | 7 960 | 138 882 | 27 205 | 11 672 | 18 490 | 7 528 | 5 936 | 4 776 | 34 388 | 1 960 | 49.0 | 4.0 | 36.1 |
| Grundy | 251 | 2 623 | 661 | 645 | 444 | 79 | 60 | 77 | 29 334 | 798 | 23.8 | 13.5 | 38.8 |
| Harrison | 228 | 1 958 | 505 | D | 603 | 112 | D | 44 | 22 449 | 1 160 | 18.0 | 17.2 | 34.2 |
| Henry | 592 | 6 621 | 1 564 | 1 297 | 1 060 | D | 136 | 212 | 32 016 | 1 125 | 26.1 | 16.5 | 44.1 |
| Hickory | 140 | 664 | 106 | 7 | 224 | D | D | 13 | 19 038 | 492 | 17.9 | 13.0 | 47.6 |
| Holt | 131 | 879 | D | 140 | 150 | D | D | 25 | 28 422 | 462 | 16.2 | 27.7 | 54.8 |
| | | | | | | | | | | | | | |
| Howard | 192 | 1 870 | 439 | 276 | 275 | 95 | 39 | 45 | 24 037 | 867 | 16.7 | 15.2 | 37.7 |
| Howell | 1 077 | 12 678 | 3 171 | 2 531 | 2 254 | 400 | 453 | 363 | 28 671 | 1 590 | 30.6 | 9.9 | 40.8 |
| Iron | 342 | 2 107 | 622 | 101 | 352 | D | D | 69 | 32 536 | 299 | 18.1 | 13.4 | 43.5 |
| Jackson | 16 752 | 314 471 | 50 574 | 26 157 | 33 896 | 23 703 | 24 942 | 14 160 | 45 029 | 838 | 58.6 | 6.0 | 40.2 |

| STATE County | Acreage (1,000) | Percent change, 2002-2007 | Average size of farm | Total irrigated (1,000) | Total cropland (1,000) | Average per farm | Average per acre | Value of machinery and equipment, average per farm (dollars) | Total (mil dol) | Average per farm (dollars) | Crops | Live-stock and poultry products | $10,000 or more | $100,000 or more | Total ($1,000) | Percent of farms |
|---|---|---|---|---|---|---|---|---|---|---|---|---|---|---|---|---|
| | 117 | 118 | 119 | 120 | 121 | 122 | 123 | 124 | 125 | 126 | 127 | 128 | 129 | 130 | 131 | 132 |
| MISSISSIPPI—Cont'd | | | | | | | | | | | | | | | | |
| Sunflower | 378 | 12.5 | 1 021 | 187.7 | 330.9 | 1 776 934 | 1 741 | 272 845 | 190.2 | 513 941 | 74.0 | 26.0 | 66.2 | 44.9 | 13 815 | 75.4 |
| Tallahatchie | 316 | 7.8 | 647 | 90.6 | 236.3 | 989 326 | 1 529 | 155 503 | 81.5 | 166 987 | 98.0 | 2.0 | 36.9 | 18.6 | 8 424 | 75.4 |
| Tate | 157 | 1.3 | 252 | 2.2 | 75.0 | 511 056 | 2 026 | 70 526 | 30.3 | 48 644 | 62.7 | 37.3 | 28.1 | 7.4 | 3 289 | 42.3 |
| Tippah | 137 | 13.2 | 199 | 0.2 | 52.8 | 289 384 | 1 455 | 43 082 | 16.8 | 24 322 | 52.2 | 47.8 | 16.2 | 2.9 | 1 720 | 63.1 |
| Tishomingo | 57 | 7.5 | 163 | D | 20.1 | 251 060 | 1 544 | 43 727 | 4.9 | 13 899 | 36.0 | 64.0 | 13.5 | 2.3 | 602 | 57.3 |
| Tunica | 201 | 0.0 | 1 952 | 73.8 | 186.3 | 3 530 822 | 1 809 | 461 482 | 79.4 | 771 143 | D | D | 67.0 | 58.3 | 6 410 | 83.5 |
| Union | 135 | -2.9 | 180 | D | 50.3 | 274 040 | 1 523 | 45 051 | 13.5 | 18 033 | 46.9 | 53.1 | 19.7 | 3.6 | 2 016 | 60.9 |
| Walthall | 128 | 19.6 | 167 | 0.1 | 38.7 | 410 004 | 2 456 | 47 600 | 76.4 | 99 531 | 2.9 | 97.1 | 26.7 | 10.3 | 1 301 | 39.8 |
| Warren | 112 | -2.6 | 403 | 3.9 | 42.1 | 712 095 | 1 769 | 73 859 | 14.5 | 52 274 | 90.0 | 10.0 | 25.5 | 9.7 | 2 460 | 50.7 |
| Washington | 333 | 3.7 | 964 | 166.4 | 310.2 | 1 723 694 | 1 788 | 318 831 | 158.8 | 459 035 | 88.2 | 11.8 | 66.8 | 46.5 | 14 660 | 67.1 |
| Wayne | 86 | 2.4 | 166 | 0.2 | 26.9 | 413 040 | 2 494 | 56 764 | 157.0 | 301 369 | 2.8 | 97.2 | 41.5 | 22.8 | 146 | 13.1 |
| Webster | 84 | 9.1 | 214 | 0.2 | 26.0 | 319 966 | 1 496 | 46 235 | 14.9 | 38 111 | 48.6 | 51.4 | 18.4 | 4.8 | 1 787 | 64.8 |
| Wilkinson | 113 | 7.6 | 547 | 0.3 | 17.6 | 989 648 | 1 809 | 54 488 | 5.4 | 25 858 | 21.6 | 78.4 | 26.6 | 3.9 | 357 | 30.9 |
| Winston | 95 | -5.9 | 178 | 0.2 | 22.4 | 303 787 | 1 705 | 48 693 | 40.3 | 75 185 | 3.0 | 97.0 | 27.2 | 5.2 | 596 | 39.4 |
| Yalobusha | 99 | -1.0 | 263 | D | 36.2 | 405 643 | 1 540 | 64 838 | 8.9 | 23 580 | 71.5 | 28.5 | 25.5 | 4.2 | 1 396 | 56.2 |
| Yazoo | 356 | -1.1 | 532 | 37.5 | 194.3 | 899 793 | 1 691 | 114 685 | 92.6 | 138 629 | 84.9 | 15.1 | 27.2 | 15.0 | 13 798 | 66.5 |
| MISSOURI | 29 027 | -3.1 | 269 | 1 200.0 | 16 405.6 | 586 478 | 2 179 | 68 171 | 7 512.9 | 69 677 | 46.5 | 53.5 | 42.0 | 11.0 | 319 519 | 41.8 |
| Adair | 280 | 4.1 | 296 | 0.1 | 144.4 | 552 068 | 1 862 | 54 312 | 33.4 | 35 395 | 54.0 | 46.0 | 40.1 | 7.6 | 3 309 | 50.0 |
| Andrew | 239 | 7.2 | 241 | D | 169.9 | 584 611 | 2 421 | 70 435 | 54.8 | 55 422 | 74.0 | 26.0 | 44.9 | 12.8 | 3 938 | 67.5 |
| Atchison | 304 | -4.4 | 607 | 9.0 | 264.2 | 1 487 826 | 2 452 | 190 814 | 105.1 | 209 731 | 95.6 | 4.4 | 68.7 | 39.5 | 4 051 | 80.4 |
| Audrain | 425 | 2.4 | 386 | 15.5 | 337.9 | 1 005 728 | 2 609 | 104 907 | 136.6 | 123 967 | 65.4 | 34.6 | 52.8 | 25.0 | 6 482 | 65.0 |
| Barry | 290 | -9.7 | 180 | 0.4 | 114.2 | 465 670 | 2 582 | 54 234 | 332.0 | 206 718 | 1.9 | 98.1 | 45.5 | 15.7 | 730 | 11.0 |
| Barton | 349 | 3.6 | 334 | 13.8 | 237.3 | 620 450 | 1 858 | 86 689 | 90.7 | 86 721 | 53.4 | 46.6 | 52.8 | 16.4 | 5 352 | 64.8 |
| Bates | 474 | 1.3 | 352 | 1.2 | 277.7 | 688 518 | 1 955 | 78 014 | 88.0 | 65 461 | 56.4 | 43.6 | 48.6 | 11.4 | 3 804 | 52.6 |
| Benton | 222 | -14.3 | 270 | 0.3 | 89.0 | 514 178 | 1 901 | 59 288 | 50.0 | 60 802 | 21.0 | 79.0 | 45.0 | 7.9 | 819 | 25.7 |
| Bollinger | 208 | -8.8 | 244 | 12.0 | 94.1 | 456 393 | 1 873 | 53 928 | 24.7 | 28 899 | 45.2 | 54.8 | 40.2 | 5.3 | 1 124 | 42.7 |
| Boone | 259 | -4.1 | 196 | 3.6 | 152.5 | 549 026 | 2 805 | 54 231 | 45.5 | 34 435 | 64.1 | 35.9 | 33.0 | 6.6 | 1 927 | 31.5 |
| Buchanan | 198 | -1.0 | 224 | 0.0 | 143.9 | 605 935 | 2 702 | 64 008 | 50.5 | 57 272 | 85.4 | 14.6 | 44.6 | 12.5 | 2 711 | 67.3 |
| Butler | 251 | 1.2 | 413 | 134.0 | 214.8 | 935 745 | 2 266 | 116 325 | 89.6 | 147 541 | 96.7 | 3.3 | 46.3 | 22.9 | 6 838 | 50.6 |
| Caldwell | 250 | 8.7 | 239 | 0.2 | 155.3 | 477 143 | 1 999 | 49 453 | 43.4 | 41 398 | 44.4 | 55.6 | 31.2 | 7.3 | 4 923 | 72.9 |
| Callaway | 323 | -9.8 | 215 | 4.0 | 166.3 | 547 519 | 2 548 | 57 645 | 69.3 | 46 083 | 42.5 | 57.5 | 35.2 | 7.1 | 2 651 | 37.3 |
| Camden | 144 | -19.1 | 265 | 0.1 | 36.4 | 493 143 | 1 858 | 50 000 | 20.2 | 37 060 | 5.6 | 94.4 | 37.7 | 4.6 | 176 | 11.2 |
| Cape Girardeau | 303 | 16.1 | 209 | 18.3 | 202.9 | 530 425 | 2 540 | 70 527 | 79.6 | 54 937 | 57.1 | 42.9 | 40.7 | 10.4 | 3 835 | 56.6 |
| Carroll | 402 | -3.6 | 335 | 3.0 | 294.7 | 707 980 | 2 114 | 78 746 | 83.5 | 69 654 | 84.1 | 15.9 | 43.3 | 12.7 | 7 550 | 80.9 |
| Carter | 63 | -32.3 | 312 | D | 14.6 | 508 658 | 1 630 | 57 540 | 3.8 | 18 772 | 9.1 | 90.9 | 31.5 | 4.4 | 72 | 10.8 |
| Cass | 327 | 4.1 | 184 | 5.3 | 205.0 | 522 325 | 2 839 | 56 921 | 81.4 | 45 834 | 71.6 | 28.4 | 30.9 | 7.9 | 2 601 | 31.9 |
| Cedar | 191 | -16.2 | 227 | 0.2 | 72.3 | 413 509 | 1 823 | 51 994 | 24.1 | 28 670 | 16.2 | 83.8 | 39.9 | 5.2 | 568 | 21.4 |
| Chariton | 384 | 1.3 | 328 | 2.5 | 261.6 | 645 306 | 1 969 | 86 630 | 105.9 | 90 273 | 64.0 | 36.0 | 50.1 | 17.1 | 5 228 | 71.7 |
| Christian | 189 | -11.3 | 150 | 0.2 | 76.0 | 416 435 | 2 785 | 43 351 | 37.6 | 29 736 | 9.2 | 90.8 | 35.4 | 5.0 | 278 | 8.8 |
| Clark | 263 | 3.5 | 371 | 1.9 | 181.7 | 731 041 | 1 971 | 85 578 | 54.4 | 76 779 | 78.0 | 22.0 | 46.5 | 17.6 | 3 600 | 74.2 |
| Clay | 144 | 12.5 | 191 | 0.0 | 75.1 | 545 272 | 2 850 | 62 280 | 32.7 | 43 528 | 43.5 | 56.5 | 27.4 | 7.7 | 1 125 | 25.1 |
| Clinton | 237 | 4.9 | 260 | D | 154.1 | 605 438 | 2 330 | 66 328 | 62.0 | 67 823 | 52.4 | 47.6 | 38.7 | 10.1 | 3 459 | 51.0 |
| Cole | 181 | -2.7 | 164 | 0.4 | 79.5 | 395 059 | 2 410 | 53 619 | 34.7 | 31 470 | 24.2 | 75.8 | 44.9 | 3.9 | 830 | 31.2 |
| Cooper | 302 | 2.7 | 321 | 0.4 | 189.1 | 714 630 | 2 226 | 80 908 | 82.9 | 88 053 | 51.2 | 48.8 | 53.6 | 16.2 | 3 410 | 61.8 |
| Crawford | 187 | -14.2 | 275 | 0.1 | 49.6 | 512 067 | 1 859 | 53 004 | 11.5 | 16 945 | 15.4 | 84.6 | 35.6 | 2.1 | 125 | 12.2 |
| Dade | 276 | -6.8 | 313 | 8.6 | 127.1 | 568 901 | 1 819 | 65 472 | 51.1 | 57 828 | 38.5 | 61.5 | 44.9 | 9.9 | 1 534 | 29.1 |
| Dallas | 223 | -5.1 | 163 | 0.2 | 84.3 | 361 993 | 2 223 | 43 527 | 46.4 | 33 893 | 6.6 | 93.4 | 37.2 | 6.3 | 381 | 10.7 |
| Daviess | 331 | 0.3 | 283 | 0.6 | 203.7 | 548 197 | 1 937 | 59 182 | 76.8 | 65 678 | 49.1 | 50.9 | 35.3 | 10.9 | 5 850 | 73.2 |
| DeKalb | 260 | 15.6 | 266 | D | 161.4 | 521 522 | 1 958 | 60 644 | 58.7 | 59 996 | 45.0 | 55.0 | 39.8 | 9.9 | 4 432 | 69.3 |
| Dent | 177 | -15.7 | 271 | 0.2 | 41.1 | 456 640 | 1 683 | 38 881 | 11.7 | 17 914 | 10.9 | 89.1 | 38.2 | 3.1 | 118 | 9.4 |
| Douglas | 254 | -18.6 | 226 | 0.3 | 64.9 | 417 328 | 1 845 | 40 944 | 29.4 | 26 131 | 6.4 | 93.6 | 35.7 | 6.1 | 185 | 8.3 |
| Dunklin | 325 | 9.4 | 718 | 159.5 | 317.1 | 1 773 930 | 2 472 | 239 059 | 124.2 | 274 118 | 98.9 | 1.1 | 66.0 | 41.9 | 14 086 | 75.7 |
| Franklin | 300 | 0.0 | 150 | 1.1 | 150.3 | 447 562 | 2 992 | 48 504 | 52.5 | 26 222 | 45.7 | 54.3 | 30.6 | 3.9 | 1 596 | 27.9 |
| Gasconade | 213 | -4.1 | 245 | 0.2 | 81.4 | 540 805 | 2 205 | 59 395 | 22.6 | 26 033 | 35.8 | 64.2 | 42.4 | 5.3 | 668 | 32.2 |
| Gentry | 276 | -5.5 | 329 | 0.0 | 173.7 | 614 719 | 1 869 | 55 826 | 94.1 | 112 146 | 27.8 | 72.2 | 38.0 | 12.9 | 4 798 | 77.0 |
| Greene | 232 | -15.6 | 118 | 0.1 | 105.6 | 387 845 | 3 277 | 40 074 | 36.2 | 18 490 | 15.0 | 85.0 | 28.6 | 3.6 | 519 | 8.5 |
| Grundy | 232 | 9.4 | 291 | 0.3 | 156.2 | 540 989 | 1 861 | 50 575 | 47.9 | 60 007 | 64.9 | 35.1 | 35.3 | 10.0 | 4 283 | 69.2 |
| Harrison | 388 | 0.0 | 335 | 0.0 | 236.8 | 615 154 | 1 837 | 56 790 | 71.0 | 61 206 | 57.9 | 42.1 | 38.5 | 10.0 | 6 966 | 75.9 |
| Henry | 345 | 2.1 | 307 | 0.5 | 184.8 | 552 808 | 1 803 | 66 408 | 59.9 | 53 256 | 43.4 | 56.6 | 48.1 | 10.9 | 2 369 | 39.2 |
| Hickory | 147 | -5.8 | 298 | 0.4 | 52.7 | 465 990 | 1 562 | 56 905 | 15.3 | 31 027 | 12.8 | 87.2 | 45.3 | 6.3 | 336 | 26.8 |
| Holt | 237 | -6.0 | 513 | 23.0 | 199.4 | 1 257 203 | 2 452 | 159 917 | 81.2 | 175 706 | 92.2 | 7.8 | 67.5 | 29.0 | 3 763 | 84.2 |
| Howard | 277 | 2.6 | 319 | 12.0 | 172.3 | 672 799 | 2 109 | 72 927 | 45.1 | 51 973 | 76.4 | 23.6 | 45.1 | 12.6 | 3 596 | 62.5 |
| Howell | 385 | -7.0 | 242 | 0.1 | 83.3 | 419 964 | 1 734 | 43 670 | 57.5 | 36 140 | 3.1 | 96.9 | 38.2 | 6.3 | 449 | 15.0 |
| Iron | 70 | -1.4 | 233 | 0.0 | 19.0 | 398 775 | 1 708 | 46 826 | 6.9 | 22 931 | 6.0 | 94.0 | 30.4 | 2.7 | 35 | 5.7 |
| Jackson | 139 | -4.1 | 166 | 0.3 | 102.8 | 542 557 | 3 266 | 54 414 | 32.1 | 38 267 | 86.5 | 13.5 | 25.3 | 8.1 | 885 | 26.3 |

| STATE County | Water use, 2005 | | Wholesale trade,[1] 2007 | | | | Retail trade,[2] 2007 | | | | Real estate and rental and leasing,[2] 2007 | | | |
|---|---|---|---|---|---|---|---|---|---|---|---|---|---|---|
| | Total water withdrawn (mil gal/day) | Gallons withdrawn per person | Number of establishments | Number of employees | Sales (mil dol) | Annual payroll (mil dol) | Number of establishments | Number of employees | Sales (mil dol) | Annual payroll (mil dol) | Number of establishments | Number of employees | Receipts (mil dol) | Annual payroll (mil dol) |
| | 133 | 134 | 135 | 136 | 137 | 138 | 139 | 140 | 141 | 142 | 143 | 144 | 145 | 146 |
| MISSISSIPPI—Cont'd | | | | | | | | | | | | | | |
| Sunflower | 283.0 | 8 757 | 22 | D | D | D | 106 | 913 | 211.3 | 15.8 | 12 | 36 | 4.7 | 0.7 |
| Tallahatchie | 103.1 | 7 265 | 9 | 85 | 62.4 | 2.7 | 47 | 265 | 56.8 | 5.1 | 6 | 9 | 1.4 | 0.1 |
| Tate | 3.5 | 133 | 13 | 70 | 18.7 | 2.0 | 93 | 974 | 237.7 | 20.0 | 16 | 30 | 2.8 | 0.5 |
| Tippah | 5.2 | 243 | 18 | 137 | 131.8 | 4.6 | 88 | 660 | 130.9 | 11.6 | 4 | D | D | D |
| Tishomingo | 2.8 | 148 | 20 | 196 | 54.7 | 4.4 | 82 | 588 | 112.6 | 10.6 | 12 | 28 | 5.0 | 0.5 |
| Tunica | 127.5 | 12 356 | 6 | 47 | 40.7 | 2.3 | 80 | 581 | 130.7 | 8.7 | 11 | 26 | 6.1 | 0.5 |
| Union | 2.9 | 108 | 17 | 173 | 174.7 | 6.1 | 106 | 998 | 267.3 | 19.4 | 17 | 45 | 2.8 | 0.6 |
| Walthall | 3.3 | 211 | 8 | D | D | D | 44 | 485 | 124.7 | 9.4 | 2 | D | D | D |
| Warren | 257.7 | 5 245 | 42 | D | D | D | 249 | 2 696 | 606.5 | 54.4 | 47 | 186 | 30.6 | 5.3 |
| Washington | 228.3 | 3 855 | 69 | D | D | D | 284 | 3 067 | 577.7 | 57.6 | 62 | 276 | 31.5 | 7.9 |
| Wayne | 3.4 | 159 | 27 | 220 | 221.1 | 12.0 | 89 | 899 | 178.9 | 16.1 | 8 | 29 | 3.0 | 0.4 |
| Webster | 1.7 | 165 | 6 | 13 | 2.0 | 0.4 | 45 | 289 | 69.6 | 5.7 | 3 | D | D | D |
| Wilkinson | 4.2 | 406 | 9 | 65 | 44.2 | 1.8 | 38 | 289 | 59.8 | 5.5 | 3 | 3 | 0.7 | 0.1 |
| Winston | 3.9 | 196 | 15 | 266 | 187.9 | 16.2 | 96 | 879 | 183.2 | 16.7 | 11 | 82 | 3.0 | 1.6 |
| Yalobusha | 4.6 | 340 | 5 | 17 | 14.1 | 0.6 | 42 | 328 | 59.7 | 4.6 | 7 | 6 | 1.0 | 0.1 |
| Yazoo | 46.4 | 1 647 | 20 | D | D | D | 92 | 770 | 230.5 | 15.6 | 21 | 47 | 5.9 | 0.9 |
| MISSOURI | 8 793.4 | 1 516 | 6 903 | 96 451 | 81 032.9 | 4 533.6 | 23 360 | 317 318 | 76 575.2 | 7 155.3 | 7 003 | 39 625 | 7 186.3 | 1 248.8 |
| Adair | 3.2 | 132 | 25 | 178 | 54.7 | 5.4 | 118 | 1 536 | 310.1 | 28.9 | 23 | 95 | 12.0 | 2.1 |
| Andrew | 1.5 | 91 | 12 | 77 | 36.9 | 3.0 | 45 | 362 | 80.0 | 6.4 | 18 | D | D | D |
| Atchison | 6.3 | 1 013 | 10 | 74 | 67.8 | 1.8 | 46 | 364 | 86.6 | 6.4 | 4 | D | D | D |
| Audrain | 13.6 | 528 | 28 | D | D | D | 109 | 1 115 | 247.8 | 21.8 | 18 | 56 | 5.6 | 1.1 |
| Barry | 20.8 | 585 | 24 | 331 | 134.8 | 13.8 | 154 | 1 753 | 413.8 | 35.9 | 33 | 97 | 11.3 | 2.3 |
| Barton | 12.1 | 923 | 11 | 106 | 76.0 | 3.4 | 55 | 726 | 135.1 | 12.4 | 7 | 25 | 2.3 | 0.6 |
| Bates | 4.3 | 250 | 11 | 104 | 77.4 | 3.2 | 62 | 540 | 135.4 | 11.6 | 7 | D | D | D |
| Benton | 3.7 | 197 | 11 | 56 | 18.4 | 1.1 | 79 | 739 | 174.3 | 13.9 | 19 | 40 | 6.1 | 0.7 |
| Bollinger | 14.0 | 1 137 | 13 | D | D | D | 33 | 327 | 59.6 | 6.2 | 6 | D | D | D |
| Boone | 20.4 | 143 | 125 | 1 422 | 610.4 | 56.7 | 646 | 11 317 | 3 012.3 | 239.7 | 243 | D | D | D |
| Buchanan | 102.9 | 1 212 | 101 | 1 393 | 1 015.5 | 55.4 | 382 | 5 943 | 1 438.7 | 128.5 | 108 | 462 | 49.9 | 9.7 |
| Butler | 339.7 | 8 217 | 56 | D | D | D | 242 | 2 705 | 634.8 | 52.7 | 38 | 231 | 24.8 | 6.1 |
| Caldwell | 1.2 | 133 | 6 | 38 | 21.2 | 1.0 | 29 | 228 | 34.1 | 3.1 | 2 | D | D | D |
| Callaway | 34.4 | 807 | 25 | 165 | 70.8 | 5.8 | 133 | 1 336 | 331.1 | 24.6 | 32 | D | D | D |
| Camden | 14.7 | 373 | 43 | 267 | 109.4 | 9.4 | 311 | 3 184 | 677.9 | 72.0 | 90 | 316 | 47.1 | 7.7 |
| Cape Girardeau | 30.0 | 422 | 125 | 2 111 | 1 792.0 | 77.8 | 445 | 6 137 | 1 353.0 | 122.1 | 115 | 427 | 63.0 | 9.8 |
| Carroll | 3.9 | 386 | 16 | 76 | 70.1 | 2.4 | 42 | 279 | 60.6 | 5.1 | 9 | D | D | D |
| Carter | 0.8 | 140 | 9 | 57 | 13.6 | 1.2 | 22 | 157 | 27.7 | 2.1 | 3 | 4 | 0.4 | 0.1 |
| Cass | 5.8 | 62 | 60 | 424 | 351.6 | 15.8 | 270 | 3 715 | 898.7 | 79.0 | 78 | 264 | 36.2 | 7.1 |
| Cedar | 2.2 | 153 | 8 | 54 | 13.7 | 1.1 | 63 | 478 | 119.9 | 8.5 | 12 | 47 | 5.4 | 1.6 |
| Chariton | 1.2 | 145 | 15 | 184 | 198.0 | 7.0 | 44 | 215 | 51.8 | 4.0 | 9 | D | D | D |
| Christian | 8.8 | 131 | 71 | 623 | 166.4 | 21.0 | 236 | 2 971 | 716.8 | 67.2 | 77 | 156 | 24.3 | 3.0 |
| Clark | 1.5 | 210 | 11 | D | D | D | 36 | 269 | 88.7 | 4.8 | 4 | 11 | 0.4 | 0.1 |
| Clay | 178.7 | 884 | 300 | 4 532 | 4 517.3 | 232.9 | 683 | 12 599 | 3 366.9 | 280.9 | 247 | 1 057 | 193.9 | 35.1 |
| Clinton | 2.5 | 121 | 11 | 59 | 96.8 | 1.9 | 64 | 641 | 147.2 | 13.3 | 17 | 41 | 5.0 | 0.8 |
| Cole | 11.3 | 155 | 71 | 2 541 | 706.1 | 76.6 | 359 | 5 504 | 1 203.7 | 115.4 | 73 | 252 | 44.8 | 6.2 |
| Cooper | 2.9 | 169 | 16 | 114 | 75.7 | 3.4 | 73 | 787 | 225.6 | 15.4 | 15 | 48 | 5.2 | 0.8 |
| Crawford | 3.1 | 129 | 16 | 201 | 105.2 | 6.6 | 78 | 726 | 174.3 | 15.0 | 25 | 105 | 9.7 | 2.1 |
| Dade | 5.5 | 699 | 9 | 305 | 62.4 | 6.9 | 29 | 165 | 46.9 | 2.9 | 3 | 2 | 0.3 | 0.1 |
| Dallas | 2.6 | 159 | 7 | 94 | 59.9 | 2.4 | 65 | 540 | 144.7 | 10.5 | 9 | 32 | 2.5 | 0.5 |
| Daviess | 2.3 | 280 | 10 | 73 | 41.8 | 1.6 | 39 | 178 | 45.3 | 3.4 | 1 | D | D | D |
| DeKalb | 0.8 | 68 | 7 | D | D | D | 38 | 569 | 128.0 | 10.7 | 16 | D | D | D |
| Dent | 32.5 | 2 156 | 7 | D | D | D | 56 | 549 | 124.5 | 11.0 | 19 | 106 | 3.7 | 1.0 |
| Douglas | 21.1 | 1 549 | 10 | D | D | D | 44 | 446 | 93.7 | 8.0 | 6 | 6 | 0.9 | 0.1 |
| Dunklin | 89.4 | 2 747 | 35 | 298 | 132.8 | 8.9 | 167 | 1 527 | 371.5 | 29.0 | 32 | 407 | 21.8 | 7.0 |
| Franklin | 1 155.5 | 11 662 | 97 | 937 | 386.4 | 36.3 | 422 | 4 955 | 1 326.7 | 112.0 | 95 | 461 | 34.5 | 8.3 |
| Gasconade | 2.6 | 164 | 18 | 183 | 63.1 | 5.1 | 80 | 683 | 146.0 | 12.8 | 16 | D | D | D |
| Gentry | 2.3 | 352 | 12 | 76 | 35.2 | 2.9 | 42 | 258 | 59.2 | 4.8 | 7 | 152 | 3.0 | 1.8 |
| Greene | 221.2 | 882 | 432 | 7 514 | 5 076.0 | 316.1 | 1 253 | 19 282 | 4 710.4 | 421.0 | 458 | 2 781 | 340.0 | 68.3 |
| Grundy | 2.7 | 263 | 5 | 55 | 76.5 | 2.0 | 51 | 452 | 88.3 | 7.4 | 8 | 18 | 2.4 | 0.4 |
| Harrison | 1.3 | 148 | 10 | 203 | 55.5 | 5.1 | 53 | 720 | 143.5 | 13.1 | 6 | D | D | D |
| Henry | 417.5 | 18 491 | 24 | 194 | 101.1 | 5.9 | 125 | 1 237 | 284.3 | 25.2 | 22 | 84 | 10.0 | 1.9 |
| Hickory | 1.4 | 154 | 2 | D | D | D | 32 | 194 | 50.0 | 3.6 | 3 | D | D | D |
| Holt | 7.5 | 1 468 | 9 | 97 | 84.7 | 3.5 | 20 | 152 | 35.8 | 2.6 | 3 | D | D | D |
| Howard | 3.3 | 335 | 6 | 81 | 19.3 | 2.3 | 43 | 312 | 88.1 | 5.7 | 2 | D | D | D |
| Howell | 4.3 | 113 | 46 | 340 | 180.7 | 11.2 | 260 | 2 356 | 545.8 | 45.5 | 54 | 151 | 17.5 | 3.6 |
| Iron | 4.3 | 421 | 4 | 11 | 1.6 | 0.2 | 48 | 301 | 65.8 | 5.0 | 9 | D | D | D |
| Jackson | 546.8 | 825 | 850 | 13 194 | 11 179.9 | 661.9 | 2 326 | 35 780 | 8 460.8 | 825.3 | 904 | 6 335 | 1 474.2 | 222.6 |

1. Merchant wholesalers, except manufacturers' sales branches and offices.  2. Employer establishments.

# Table B. States and Counties — Professional Services, Manufacturing, and Accommodation and Food Services

| STATE County | Professional, scientific, and technical services,[1] 2007 | | | | Manufacturing, 2007 | | | | Accommodation and food services, 2007 | | | |
|---|---|---|---|---|---|---|---|---|---|---|---|---|
| | Number of establishments | Number of employees | Receipts (mil dol) | Annual payroll (mil dol) | Number of establishments | Number of employees | Receipts (mil dol) | Annual payroll (mil dol) | Number of establishments | Number of employees | Sales (mil dol) | Annual payroll (mil dol) |
| | 147 | 148 | 149 | 150 | 151 | 152 | 153 | 154 | 155 | 156 | 157 | 158 |
| MISSISSIPPI—Cont'd | | | | | | | | | | | | |
| Sunflower | 28 | D | D | D | 18 | 918 | D | D | 31 | 349 | 15.1 | 4.1 |
| Tallahatchie | 14 | 36 | 3.2 | 0.7 | NA | NA | NA | NA | 8 | 106 | 3.6 | 0.9 |
| Tate | 25 | 74 | 6.2 | 2.0 | 15 | 922 | 244.3 | 28.7 | 29 | 384 | 14.6 | 4.2 |
| Tippah | 18 | 103 | 7.3 | 2.8 | 37 | 2 635 | 566.2 | 83.9 | 24 | 291 | 11.8 | 2.9 |
| Tishomingo | 19 | 96 | 4.7 | 1.8 | 34 | 1 856 | 305.4 | 57.9 | 29 | 219 | 9.2 | 2.4 |
| Tunica | 7 | 17 | 2.2 | 0.5 | NA | NA | NA | NA | 34 | 13 817 | 1 308.6 | 349.9 |
| Union | 27 | 88 | 11.5 | 3.3 | 36 | 2 512 | 418.1 | 75.6 | 32 | 629 | 20.8 | 5.4 |
| Walthall | 11 | 22 | 3.0 | 0.7 | 19 | 684 | 167.3 | 20.7 | 16 | D | D | D |
| Warren | 98 | 885 | 77.8 | 31.7 | 48 | 4 399 | 1 856.7 | 165.7 | 105 | 4 199 | 384.6 | 71.9 |
| Washington | 91 | D | D | D | 47 | 1 994 | 840.3 | 75.2 | 86 | 1 529 | 93.8 | 20.2 |
| Wayne | 21 | 66 | 4.6 | 1.2 | 16 | 1 128 | 287.5 | 33.7 | 29 | 355 | 15.3 | 3.8 |
| Webster | 8 | 34 | 3.7 | 1.1 | NA | NA | NA | NA | 12 | 68 | 3.2 | 0.8 |
| Wilkinson | 7 | 22 | 1.3 | 0.3 | NA | NA | NA | NA | 6 | 71 | 3.4 | 0.8 |
| Winston | 24 | 87 | 14.5 | 2.1 | 25 | 1 856 | 483.4 | 76.9 | 28 | 485 | 16.5 | 4.6 |
| Yalobusha | 11 | D | D | D | 7 | 598 | D | D | 12 | 47 | 2.9 | 0.6 |
| Yazoo | 26 | D | D | D | 19 | 801 | 371.8 | 27.9 | 25 | 311 | 12.4 | 3.2 |
| MISSOURI | 13 524 | 130 786 | 19 749.8 | 7 454.7 | 6 886 | 295 313 | 110 907.6 | 12 996.5 | 12 261 | 241 438 | 11 070.6 | 3 109.1 |
| Adair | 40 | D | D | D | 14 | 987 | D | 31.6 | 60 | 1 400 | 38.7 | 11.6 |
| Andrew | 15 | D | D | D | NA | NA | NA | NA | 14 | 125 | 4.5 | 1.2 |
| Atchison | 9 | D | D | D | NA | NA | NA | NA | 14 | 189 | 4.5 | 1.1 |
| Audrain | 24 | 120 | 8.1 | 3.8 | 40 | 1 935 | 1 337.1 | 75.2 | 39 | 471 | 18.6 | 5.0 |
| Barry | 53 | D | D | D | 55 | 5 548 | 1 409.8 | 176.1 | 63 | 795 | 25.8 | 6.1 |
| Barton | 15 | 125 | 6.9 | 2.4 | 26 | 1 041 | 174.3 | 30.6 | 20 | 315 | 8.4 | 2.3 |
| Bates | 18 | D | D | D | NA | NA | NA | NA | 26 | 348 | 12.3 | 2.9 |
| Benton | 19 | D | D | D | NA | NA | NA | NA | 60 | 470 | 13.2 | 3.4 |
| Bollinger | 8 | D | D | D | NA | NA | NA | NA | 14 | D | D | D |
| Boone | 382 | D | D | D | 96 | 4 601 | D | D | 422 | 8 458 | 315.1 | 93.0 |
| Buchanan | 177 | D | D | D | 95 | D | D | D | 197 | 4 175 | 154.5 | 45.6 |
| Butler | 64 | 591 | 53.9 | 18.7 | 49 | 2 657 | 632.7 | 72.8 | 87 | 1 666 | 57.9 | 17.4 |
| Caldwell | 8 | D | D | D | NA | NA | NA | NA | 15 | 73 | 2.1 | 0.5 |
| Callaway | 37 | 161 | 12.2 | 4.3 | 39 | 918 | D | 33.6 | 60 | 845 | 33.2 | 9.5 |
| Camden | 85 | 433 | 53.5 | 14.3 | 54 | 1 117 | 251.1 | 35.5 | 187 | 3 061 | 157.6 | 47.4 |
| Cape Girardeau | 156 | D | D | D | 97 | 4 574 | D | D | 177 | 4 043 | 145.9 | 42.6 |
| Carroll | 15 | D | D | D | NA | NA | NA | NA | 17 | 170 | 5.5 | 1.5 |
| Carter | 4 | D | D | D | NA | NA | NA | NA | 15 | 107 | 3.5 | 1.0 |
| Cass | 164 | D | D | D | 84 | 1 867 | 483.7 | 64.7 | 143 | 2 343 | 82.4 | 25.4 |
| Cedar | 14 | D | D | D | NA | NA | NA | NA | 32 | 340 | 9.8 | 2.7 |
| Chariton | 11 | D | D | D | NA | NA | NA | NA | 10 | 61 | 2.0 | 0.4 |
| Christian | 137 | 606 | 52.2 | 16.4 | 106 | 1 327 | 255.6 | 44.9 | 105 | 1 662 | 59.7 | 18.6 |
| Clark | 9 | 16 | 0.8 | 0.2 | NA | NA | NA | NA | 10 | 73 | 2.1 | 0.5 |
| Clay | 464 | D | D | D | 219 | 12 349 | 10 903.5 | 773.8 | 389 | 11 292 | 822.1 | 192.9 |
| Clinton | 24 | D | D | D | NA | NA | NA | NA | 27 | 430 | 16.2 | 4.3 |
| Cole | 238 | 1 409 | 174.0 | 63.0 | 64 | 3 384 | 1 568.1 | 146.9 | 157 | 3 134 | 127.6 | 37.1 |
| Cooper | 22 | D | D | D | 16 | 594 | 155.3 | 20.2 | 39 | 1 070 | 112.7 | 19.2 |
| Crawford | 27 | D | D | D | 44 | 1 479 | 271.7 | 46.1 | 55 | 496 | 25.5 | 6.3 |
| Dade | 4 | D | D | D | NA | NA | NA | NA | 13 | 48 | 2.1 | 0.5 |
| Dallas | 16 | D | D | D | 19 | 562 | D | 11.1 | 23 | 234 | 8.4 | 2.3 |
| Daviess | 8 | D | D | D | NA | NA | NA | NA | 12 | 80 | 2.2 | 0.6 |
| DeKalb | 9 | D | D | D | NA | NA | NA | NA | 13 | 118 | 5.2 | 1.3 |
| Dent | 13 | D | D | D | 19 | 654 | 246.6 | 25.1 | 20 | 286 | 10.8 | 3.1 |
| Douglas | 9 | D | D | D | 15 | D | D | D | 13 | 211 | 7.7 | 2.1 |
| Dunklin | 40 | 107 | 8.7 | 2.2 | 18 | 626 | D | D | 59 | 739 | 24.9 | 6.5 |
| Franklin | 195 | D | D | D | 227 | 9 233 | 2 432.1 | 350.1 | 184 | 3 096 | 109.3 | 32.7 |
| Gasconade | 36 | 137 | 7.0 | 2.2 | 42 | 1 413 | 172.4 | 45.2 | 44 | 445 | 13.5 | 4.2 |
| Gentry | 7 | D | D | D | NA | NA | NA | NA | 13 | 112 | 2.0 | 0.6 |
| Greene | 792 | D | D | D | 330 | 14 842 | 3 845.4 | 560.0 | 663 | 14 922 | 578.3 | 170.4 |
| Grundy | 13 | D | D | D | 9 | 649 | D | 24.9 | 16 | 174 | 6.2 | 1.8 |
| Harrison | 11 | D | D | D | NA | NA | NA | NA | 19 | 269 | 11.0 | 2.8 |
| Henry | 40 | 127 | 9.5 | 2.5 | 34 | 1 426 | 566.6 | 49.7 | 61 | 718 | 25.0 | 6.8 |
| Hickory | 9 | D | D | D | NA | NA | NA | NA | 14 | 45 | 1.6 | 0.4 |
| Holt | 2 | D | D | D | NA | NA | NA | NA | 18 | 140 | 4.0 | 1.0 |
| Howard | 12 | D | D | D | NA | NA | NA | NA | 15 | 157 | 3.4 | 1.0 |
| Howell | 59 | 325 | 21.7 | 8.9 | 82 | 3 113 | 682.1 | 85.3 | 71 | 1 251 | 47.6 | 13.3 |
| Iron | 11 | D | D | D | NA | NA | NA | NA | 18 | 168 | 5.3 | 1.5 |
| Jackson | 2 115 | D | D | D | 721 | 29 100 | 8 939.0 | 1 337.1 | 1 431 | 29 957 | 1 505.8 | 416.6 |

1. Establishment subject to federal tax.

| STATE County | Health care and social assistance, 2007 | | | | Other services, 2007 | | | | Federal funds and grants, 2009–2010 Expenditures (mil dol) | | | |
|---|---|---|---|---|---|---|---|---|---|---|---|---|
| | | | | | | | | | | Direct payments for individuals[1] | | |
| | Number of establishments | Number of employees | Receipts (mil dol) | Annual payroll (mil dol) | Number of establishments | Number of employees | Receipts (mil dol) | Annual payroll (mil dol) | Total | Social Security and government retirement | Medicare | Food Stamps and Supplemental Security Income |
| | 159 | 160 | 161 | 162 | 163 | 164 | 165 | 166 | 167 | 168 | 169 | 170 |
| MISSISSIPPI—Cont'd | | | | | | | | | | | | |
| Sunflower | 44 | 1 198 | 83.5 | 33.4 | 33 | 176 | 19.6 | 3.9 | 326.9 | 59.6 | 56.9 | 32.2 |
| Tallahatchie | 17 | 353 | 21.6 | 9.3 | 11 | 31 | 2.5 | 0.7 | 176.8 | 34.0 | 29.4 | 12.2 |
| Tate | 35 | 525 | 43.8 | 16.2 | 23 | 148 | 10.2 | 3.2 | 218.2 | 80.1 | 35.0 | 9.4 |
| Tippah | 32 | 603 | 37.6 | 16.6 | 14 | 45 | 2.5 | 0.9 | 194.1 | 77.7 | 46.3 | 9.7 |
| Tishomingo | 29 | 581 | 44.2 | 15.6 | 29 | 110 | 13.2 | 2.0 | 189.9 | 86.4 | 42.4 | 6.4 |
| Tunica | 16 | 192 | 11.7 | 4.4 | 9 | D | D | D | 107.4 | 25.0 | 14.7 | 8.4 |
| Union | 47 | 977 | 90.9 | 30.7 | 23 | 99 | 7.6 | 2.3 | 176.4 | 80.8 | 39.0 | 8.3 |
| Walthall | 24 | 403 | 24.2 | 9.9 | 14 | 41 | 2.5 | 0.6 | 133.6 | 40.0 | 29.2 | 9.8 |
| Warren | 104 | 3 313 | 385.9 | 149.9 | 74 | 342 | 22.1 | 6.2 | 914.3 | 177.5 | 101.5 | 28.1 |
| Washington | 161 | 2 889 | 236.1 | 95.3 | 94 | 477 | 51.0 | 10.8 | 695.6 | 154.0 | 105.3 | 69.4 |
| Wayne | 27 | 646 | 41.6 | 20.9 | 23 | 73 | 4.4 | 1.5 | 142.5 | 51.7 | 27.0 | 13.9 |
| Webster | 11 | 412 | 35.5 | 12.4 | 11 | 26 | 1.9 | 0.6 | 98.5 | 37.5 | 20.6 | 6.1 |
| Wilkinson | 15 | 374 | 27.0 | 11.7 | 8 | 33 | 5.2 | 0.6 | 89.1 | 25.6 | 18.3 | 9.1 |
| Winston | 33 | 577 | 41.6 | 15.2 | 21 | 65 | 5.7 | 1.1 | 170.6 | 60.4 | 32.8 | 11.9 |
| Yalobusha | 17 | 317 | 17.1 | 7.7 | 9 | 15 | 1.2 | 0.3 | 148.0 | 58.9 | 34.7 | 8.5 |
| Yazoo | 46 | 617 | 55.9 | 21.9 | 29 | 83 | 5.8 | 1.6 | 339.0 | 69.1 | 55.4 | 25.0 |
| MISSOURI | 15 984 | 362 340 | 32 886.6 | 12 918.6 | 11 111 | 67 476 | 6 770.7 | 1 799.9 | 70 348.1 | 18 407.8 | 9 846.3 | 2 174.6 |
| Adair | 105 | D | D | D | 72 | D | D | D | 198.3 | 60.0 | 45.9 | 8.3 |
| Andrew | 21 | D | D | D | 19 | D | D | D | 113.3 | 40.5 | 19.9 | 3.3 |
| Atchison | 18 | D | D | D | 20 | 34 | 3.0 | 0.5 | 59.3 | 23.3 | 14.0 | 1.9 |
| Audrain | 83 | 1 602 | 112.6 | 47.8 | 46 | 227 | 18.1 | 5.5 | 204.1 | 79.2 | 60.3 | 8.0 |
| Barry | 77 | 1 193 | 74.3 | 28.8 | 60 | 192 | 13.5 | 3.4 | 279.3 | 131.0 | 60.2 | 12.5 |
| Barton | 30 | 525 | 26.3 | 11.0 | 19 | 46 | 4.1 | 0.8 | 96.6 | 38.1 | 23.2 | 4.5 |
| Bates | 39 | 725 | 49.6 | 18.9 | 22 | D | D | D | 137.8 | 57.6 | 34.5 | 5.7 |
| Benton | 32 | 262 | 15.0 | 6.0 | 37 | 90 | 6.3 | 1.4 | 192.3 | 104.2 | 43.3 | 7.2 |
| Bollinger | 20 | D | D | D | 16 | D | D | D | 107.0 | 38.0 | 19.2 | 5.7 |
| Boone | 562 | 15 933 | 1 695.8 | 615.7 | 323 | D | D | D | 1 173.4 | 360.3 | 160.1 | 43.8 |
| Buchanan | 288 | 7 250 | 708.8 | 284.3 | 195 | 1 259 | 108.1 | 37.6 | 718.2 | 283.2 | 173.5 | 41.1 |
| Butler | 218 | 3 809 | 413.0 | 129.8 | 78 | 310 | 22.4 | 5.7 | 513.5 | 165.9 | 87.3 | 29.3 |
| Caldwell | 12 | 88 | 5.1 | 2.1 | 13 | D | D | D | 72.6 | 32.8 | 18.1 | 2.6 |
| Callaway | 76 | 2 346 | 134.5 | 65.4 | 66 | 300 | 22.3 | 6.3 | 436.7 | 125.5 | 60.0 | 12.0 |
| Camden | 120 | 1 950 | 227.0 | 78.6 | 114 | 384 | 31.8 | 7.6 | 281.5 | 161.9 | 67.2 | 9.1 |
| Cape Girardeau | 279 | 9 550 | 972.9 | 354.9 | 162 | D | D | D | 542.0 | 221.3 | 87.6 | 22.9 |
| Carroll | 24 | 440 | 23.0 | 8.9 | 19 | 43 | 4.3 | 1.2 | 106.1 | 35.0 | 24.7 | 3.8 |
| Carter | 27 | 173 | 5.4 | 2.5 | 7 | 34 | 3.2 | 0.6 | 69.3 | 26.5 | 12.1 | 4.6 |
| Cass | 127 | 2 842 | 187.5 | 76.7 | 130 | 548 | 36.7 | 11.6 | 590.5 | 281.2 | 95.3 | 15.1 |
| Cedar | 44 | 674 | 32.5 | 15.0 | 19 | 34 | 2.2 | 0.6 | 140.1 | 59.8 | 31.8 | 5.8 |
| Chariton | 14 | 198 | 7.0 | 3.0 | 14 | 32 | 4.5 | 1.0 | 83.6 | 27.9 | 20.7 | 2.0 |
| Christian | 110 | 1 174 | 59.8 | 24.8 | 109 | 415 | 28.9 | 7.8 | 353.3 | 216.5 | 50.9 | 12.5 |
| Clark | 11 | D | D | D | 14 | 48 | 4.6 | 0.6 | 63.8 | 24.0 | 13.9 | 2.3 |
| Clay | 515 | 11 678 | 1 189.7 | 480.0 | 362 | 2 009 | 162.9 | 50.6 | 932.1 | 414.1 | 249.6 | 21.5 |
| Clinton | 56 | 956 | 70.2 | 27.6 | 28 | 98 | 6.6 | 1.9 | 146.3 | 69.4 | 32.9 | 5.3 |
| Cole | 244 | 5 943 | 612.2 | 230.3 | 238 | 1 584 | 169.1 | 49.2 | 3 231.6 | 230.9 | 106.5 | 15.8 |
| Cooper | 56 | 652 | 39.0 | 14.9 | 24 | 88 | 6.8 | 1.6 | 128.5 | 52.3 | 30.8 | 3.9 |
| Crawford | 66 | 896 | 64.6 | 24.2 | 30 | 120 | 9.6 | 2.3 | 159.6 | 71.8 | 38.0 | 11.1 |
| Dade | 14 | 67 | 3.4 | 1.4 | 11 | D | D | D | 73.4 | 30.4 | 16.6 | 3.0 |
| Dallas | 26 | 1 112 | 24.3 | 12.8 | 18 | 60 | 2.9 | 0.7 | 125.1 | 53.6 | 25.4 | 7.0 |
| Daviess | 16 | 109 | 5.6 | 2.1 | 11 | 41 | 3.8 | 1.2 | 64.1 | 25.1 | 15.1 | 2.1 |
| DeKalb | 34 | D | D | D | 13 | 54 | 4.4 | 1.3 | 57.0 | 26.6 | 12.6 | 2.3 |
| Dent | 51 | 716 | 35.7 | 14.7 | 21 | 53 | 3.8 | 0.9 | 171.8 | 58.2 | 33.1 | 10.8 |
| Douglas | 18 | 211 | 10.0 | 4.4 | 14 | 43 | 4.4 | 1.0 | 111.5 | 40.1 | 21.2 | 5.7 |
| Dunklin | 122 | 2 179 | 111.2 | 43.4 | 54 | 152 | 10.5 | 2.7 | 460.2 | 111.6 | 81.1 | 33.0 |
| Franklin | 216 | 3 558 | 281.7 | 103.4 | 183 | 796 | 59.8 | 17.4 | 624.2 | 329.5 | 133.8 | 25.5 |
| Gasconade | 41 | 587 | 33.8 | 14.9 | 28 | 85 | 7.4 | 1.7 | 118.9 | 60.2 | 31.6 | 3.1 |
| Gentry | 31 | 675 | 32.5 | 13.8 | 11 | D | D | D | 86.5 | 27.7 | 21.5 | 1.4 |
| Greene | 719 | D | D | D | 632 | 4 597 | 412.5 | 120.8 | 1 963.7 | 845.0 | 342.6 | 88.9 |
| Grundy | 28 | 610 | 46.6 | 15.1 | 27 | 64 | 5.0 | 1.3 | 108.0 | 37.3 | 24.5 | 4.0 |
| Harrison | 21 | 527 | 26.0 | 10.9 | 20 | D | D | D | 95.5 | 33.1 | 24.5 | 2.8 |
| Henry | 51 | 1 376 | 117.0 | 43.9 | 44 | 153 | 9.4 | 2.9 | 212.7 | 97.7 | 52.7 | 9.2 |
| Hickory | 7 | 111 | 5.3 | 2.4 | 5 | D | D | D | 92.8 | 46.2 | 24.0 | 3.8 |
| Holt | 12 | D | D | D | 7 | 8 | 1.1 | 0.2 | 68.0 | 21.7 | 14.0 | 1.5 |
| Howard | 31 | 377 | 14.2 | 6.7 | 11 | D | D | D | 99.0 | 29.2 | 24.1 | 3.4 |
| Howell | 157 | 3 094 | 233.5 | 89.4 | 72 | 283 | 21.7 | 4.9 | 364.3 | 153.4 | 67.4 | 17.5 |
| Iron | 105 | 545 | 30.9 | 10.0 | 36 | 55 | 3.5 | 0.7 | 113.5 | 42.6 | 25.0 | 7.1 |
| Jackson | 1 741 | 46 973 | 4 847.2 | 1 977.2 | 1 413 | 9 953 | 1 641.9 | 295.1 | 8 910.3 | 2 357.9 | 1 298.3 | 238.9 |

1. State totals may include programs not allocated by county.

# Table B. States and Counties — Federal Funds, Residential Construction, and Local Government Finances

| STATE County | Federal funds and grants, 2009–2010 (cont.) | | | | | | | Value of residential construction authorized by building permits, 2011 | | Local government finances, 2007 | | | | |
|---|---|---|---|---|---|---|---|---|---|---|---|---|---|---|
| | Expenditures (mil dol) (cont.) | | | | | | | | | General revenue | | | | |
| | Procurement contract awards | | | Grants[1] | | | | | | | | Taxes | | |
| | | | | | | | | | | | | | Per capita[2] (dollars) | |
| | Salaries and wages | Defense | Other | Medicaid and other health-related | Nutrition and family welfare | Education | Other | New construction ($1,000) | Number of housing units | Total (mil dol) | Inter-govern-mental (mil dol) | Total (mil dol) | Total | Property |
| | 171 | 172 | 173 | 174 | 175 | 176 | 177 | 178 | 179 | 180 | 181 | 182 | 183 | 184 |
| MISSISSIPPI—Cont'd | | | | | | | | | | | | | | |
| Sunflower | 20.4 | 0.0 | 1.0 | 78.2 | 12.7 | 2.9 | 3.4 | 3 081 | 38 | 115.9 | 60.2 | 19.9 | 643 | 614 |
| Tallahatchie | 4.0 | 16.0 | 0.6 | 54.6 | 4.6 | 1.5 | 2.1 | 50 | 1 | 41.4 | 25.2 | 8.3 | 629 | 590 |
| Tate | 17.6 | 0.6 | 1.6 | 39.5 | 4.7 | 1.3 | 0.2 | 5 824 | 61 | 111.2 | 57.3 | 24.9 | 927 | 884 |
| Tippah | 5.4 | 0.0 | 1.2 | 45.4 | 3.7 | 1.1 | 0.7 | 686 | 3 | 55.4 | 29.5 | 9.5 | 448 | 413 |
| Tishomingo | 5.8 | 9.0 | 1.1 | 33.5 | 3.2 | 0.6 | 0.5 | 83 | 1 | 42.8 | 28.9 | 8.6 | 452 | 403 |
| Tunica | 2.0 | 0.4 | 0.4 | 28.9 | 2.9 | 1.2 | 0.9 | 803 | 10 | 79.1 | 55.5 | 20.0 | 1 915 | 1 291 |
| Union | 6.1 | 0.0 | 1.1 | 34.2 | 3.6 | 1.4 | 0.0 | 5 556 | 70 | 55.7 | 35.9 | 13.1 | 488 | 468 |
| Walthall | 11.3 | 0.0 | 0.4 | 37.1 | 3.7 | 0.9 | 0.0 | 0 | 0 | 43.5 | 21.9 | 8.0 | 521 | 503 |
| Warren | 143.5 | 358.9 | 16.1 | 64.2 | 9.1 | 4.0 | 2.0 | 180 | 1 | 147.5 | 69.4 | 57.8 | 1 183 | 958 |
| Washington | 46.8 | 1.1 | 44.2 | 179.8 | 24.8 | 6.4 | 16.4 | 1 049 | 7 | 253.0 | 94.6 | 51.7 | 930 | 845 |
| Wayne | 4.5 | 0.0 | 0.7 | 37.2 | 4.7 | 1.0 | 0.6 | 20 | 1 | 75.1 | 33.5 | 10.9 | 516 | 497 |
| Webster | 4.3 | 1.9 | 0.5 | 21.8 | 2.1 | 0.5 | 0.5 | 55 | 1 | 21.2 | 13.6 | 5.1 | 522 | 510 |
| Wilkinson | 0.7 | 0.0 | 0.2 | 30.8 | 2.7 | 0.7 | 0.1 | 100 | 1 | 35.5 | 13.0 | 5.5 | 537 | 523 |
| Winston | 12.1 | 0.0 | 0.6 | 44.3 | 4.3 | 1.1 | 1.2 | 268 | 1 | 58.8 | 23.3 | 9.2 | 468 | 446 |
| Yalobusha | 5.2 | 0.4 | 0.8 | 32.2 | 2.7 | 0.9 | 1.1 | 274 | 9 | 40.3 | 19.0 | 7.6 | 555 | 536 |
| Yazoo | 39.8 | 25.0 | 8.8 | 73.5 | 6.7 | 1.9 | 2.1 | 134 | 2 | 60.9 | 35.9 | 18.5 | 680 | 657 |
| MISSOURI | 7 320.6 | 10 334.5 | 2 667.9 | 7 868.9 | 1 212.9 | 936.2 | 3 984.6 | 1 425 673 | 9 242 | X | X | X | X | X |
| Adair | 10.5 | 7.6 | 1.1 | 46.2 | 4.7 | 2.4 | 1.1 | 5 003 | 33 | 75.6 | 21.4 | 42.0 | 1 706 | 1 275 |
| Andrew | 15.1 | 0.1 | 0.7 | 10.9 | 1.9 | 0.4 | 15.1 | 500 | 3 | 30.5 | 14.7 | 9.5 | 561 | 435 |
| Atchison | 2.6 | 0.0 | 0.5 | 6.7 | 1.0 | 0.2 | 0.9 | 150 | 1 | 16.9 | 6.5 | 7.9 | 1 298 | 960 |
| Audrain | 7.5 | 0.0 | 1.3 | 24.8 | 3.3 | 1.7 | 5.6 | 1 239 | 14 | 76.3 | 30.2 | 31.2 | 1 203 | 820 |
| Barry | 14.8 | 0.6 | 2.4 | 47.0 | 5.1 | 2.7 | 1.5 | 1 008 | 13 | 81.5 | 37.6 | 27.9 | 772 | 531 |
| Barton | 4.9 | 0.0 | 0.7 | 11.9 | 1.7 | 1.2 | 0.0 | 481 | 2 | 37.9 | 18.2 | 10.5 | 822 | 552 |
| Bates | 4.4 | 0.0 | 0.9 | 22.8 | 2.5 | 0.9 | 0.5 | 511 | 1 | 38.7 | 16.8 | 12.5 | 734 | 526 |
| Benton | 5.9 | 5.0 | 1.2 | 20.0 | 2.4 | 1.0 | 0.1 | 250 | 1 | 42.2 | 18.8 | 14.7 | 796 | 587 |
| Bollinger | 2.6 | 0.0 | 0.6 | 36.5 | 1.8 | 0.8 | 0.0 | 40 | 2 | 18.2 | 10.5 | 5.8 | 479 | 351 |
| Boone | 111.1 | 7.6 | 49.2 | 180.0 | 18.9 | 28.1 | 138.8 | 130 306 | 1 037 | 447.0 | 137.4 | 201.6 | 1 323 | 773 |
| Buchanan | 34.6 | 14.8 | 8.7 | 115.7 | 9.2 | 6.1 | 9.4 | 16 773 | 108 | 268.8 | 89.1 | 113.3 | 1 310 | 843 |
| Butler | 33.6 | 0.1 | 13.8 | 140.3 | 6.9 | 4.0 | 10.1 | 1 366 | 23 | 112.3 | 43.1 | 38.1 | 921 | 469 |
| Caldwell | 3.1 | 0.0 | 0.8 | 8.5 | 1.2 | 0.6 | 0.9 | 3 829 | 19 | 23.3 | 12.5 | 6.7 | 726 | 524 |
| Callaway | 180.9 | 0.3 | 5.3 | 35.2 | 4.0 | 1.7 | 2.9 | 5 975 | 44 | 79.0 | 28.5 | 32.3 | 744 | 527 |
| Camden | 6.6 | 0.4 | 1.5 | 25.3 | 3.9 | 2.2 | 2.4 | 1 256 | 9 | 115.6 | 35.5 | 53.8 | 1 302 | 854 |
| Cape Girardeau | 55.5 | 9.1 | 8.4 | 68.5 | 7.0 | 5.0 | 29.0 | 19 082 | 119 | 165.0 | 58.5 | 79.8 | 1 097 | 578 |
| Carroll | 5.2 | 0.0 | 7.2 | 14.2 | 1.7 | 1.0 | 0.8 | 1 010 | 9 | 23.9 | 12.4 | 7.9 | 804 | 638 |
| Carter | 4.2 | 0.0 | 2.6 | 16.6 | 1.6 | 0.5 | 0.4 | 100 | 2 | 13.4 | 8.3 | 3.2 | 538 | 425 |
| Cass | 120.0 | 4.0 | 3.6 | 24.8 | 7.3 | 5.2 | 25.7 | 34 100 | 169 | 344.0 | 111.2 | 120.8 | 1 244 | 827 |
| Cedar | 3.7 | 8.0 | 0.8 | 26.1 | 1.7 | 0.7 | 0.3 | 325 | 5 | 49.3 | 15.8 | 14.0 | 1 019 | 718 |
| Chariton | 3.7 | 0.0 | 0.9 | 16.1 | 1.1 | 0.6 | 0.6 | 200 | 1 | 15.7 | 6.3 | 6.3 | 798 | 615 |
| Christian | 11.7 | 0.0 | 3.0 | 30.4 | 5.3 | 4.1 | 5.7 | 48 890 | 300 | 156.0 | 65.3 | 59.7 | 816 | 539 |
| Clark | 2.9 | 4.0 | 0.7 | 6.7 | 1.1 | 0.6 | 0.2 | 263 | 4 | 21.8 | 6.4 | 9.8 | 1 352 | 987 |
| Clay | 74.3 | 34.6 | 40.3 | 56.7 | 14.8 | 8.4 | 5.9 | 22 896 | 102 | 1 143.2 | 169.2 | 318.9 | 1 505 | 1 062 |
| Clinton | 5.7 | 0.0 | 1.3 | 19.0 | 2.1 | 1.0 | 5.6 | 3 565 | 20 | 46.4 | 21.0 | 18.3 | 875 | 689 |
| Cole | 27.3 | 9.9 | 13.0 | 183.5 | 243.8 | 403.7 | 1 966.9 | 29 051 | 166 | 171.4 | 50.1 | 91.5 | 1 241 | 748 |
| Cooper | 6.2 | 0.0 | 0.9 | 24.2 | 2.0 | 1.0 | 0.1 | 0 | 0 | 50.8 | 15.0 | 15.9 | 906 | 588 |
| Crawford | 3.6 | 0.0 | 0.9 | 29.0 | 3.1 | 1.5 | 0.1 | 970 | 19 | 52.2 | 20.0 | 14.7 | 611 | 407 |
| Dade | 2.7 | 0.0 | 0.6 | 14.7 | 1.4 | 1.7 | 0.0 | 80 | 1 | 22.8 | 8.6 | 5.4 | 711 | 529 |
| Dallas | 3.0 | 0.0 | 0.7 | 32.2 | 2.1 | 0.9 | 0.0 | 167 | 1 | 24.1 | 13.9 | 7.6 | 453 | 291 |
| Daviess | 3.3 | 1.1 | 0.7 | 9.5 | 1.5 | 0.8 | 0.4 | 625 | 4 | 19.9 | 10.2 | 6.9 | 870 | 659 |
| DeKalb | 2.4 | 0.0 | 0.5 | 4.3 | 1.2 | 0.9 | 1.9 | 0 | 0 | 17.1 | 7.5 | 6.3 | 515 | 368 |
| Dent | 4.5 | 17.7 | 1.0 | 42.2 | 2.5 | 1.2 | 0.2 | 780 | 18 | 52.1 | 15.3 | 8.9 | 592 | 405 |
| Douglas | 3.8 | 0.0 | 0.7 | 36.1 | 2.1 | 1.1 | 0.2 | 0 | 0 | 19.7 | 10.5 | 6.2 | 466 | 327 |
| Dunklin | 9.7 | 1.9 | 2.8 | 165.0 | 8.6 | 3.6 | 4.6 | 2 068 | 14 | 71.6 | 38.4 | 23.8 | 752 | 488 |
| Franklin | 39.4 | 1.1 | 5.6 | 59.4 | 9.8 | 5.5 | 1.1 | 35 531 | 226 | 230.2 | 83.6 | 110.8 | 1 107 | 744 |
| Gasconade | 3.9 | 0.0 | 0.9 | 15.2 | 1.8 | 1.0 | 0.1 | 933 | 7 | 53.0 | 15.1 | 17.8 | 1 157 | 797 |
| Gentry | 11.9 | 0.0 | 0.7 | 13.3 | 1.3 | 0.7 | 0.1 | 400 | 4 | 16.7 | 8.0 | 6.1 | 969 | 758 |
| Greene | 235.9 | 8.7 | 42.1 | 226.3 | 37.2 | 15.1 | 37.3 | 87 038 | 899 | 757.8 | 210.2 | 340.5 | 1 290 | 684 |
| Grundy | 7.2 | 0.0 | 0.8 | 16.7 | 3.2 | 1.3 | 2.4 | 315 | 6 | 45.9 | 22.6 | 8.3 | 824 | 604 |
| Harrison | 6.3 | 0.0 | 1.1 | 14.2 | 1.6 | 1.2 | 1.0 | 0 | 0 | 35.9 | 10.3 | 8.4 | 948 | 656 |
| Henry | 9.3 | 2.4 | 1.5 | 30.1 | 2.8 | 1.4 | 1.4 | 1 212 | 15 | 110.8 | 26.0 | 21.6 | 966 | 542 |
| Hickory | 2.2 | 1.3 | 0.4 | 11.9 | 1.7 | 0.9 | 0.1 | NA | NA | 21.7 | 12.7 | 6.4 | 696 | 536 |
| Holt | 2.9 | 0.0 | 1.0 | 8.1 | 0.8 | 0.2 | 0.2 | 39 | 1 | 13.4 | 5.6 | 5.9 | 1 185 | 896 |
| Howard | 2.8 | 1.3 | 0.6 | 22.3 | 1.3 | 0.9 | 5.3 | 895 | 15 | 20.8 | 9.2 | 7.4 | 751 | 485 |
| Howell | 18.7 | 0.0 | 2.3 | 79.0 | 10.7 | 2.9 | 4.3 | 5 734 | 75 | 92.0 | 44.9 | 28.7 | 744 | 408 |
| Iron | 1.9 | 0.0 | 0.5 | 32.2 | 2.2 | 1.8 | 0.0 | 0 | 0 | 27.0 | 14.4 | 9.8 | 983 | 814 |
| Jackson | 1 254.4 | 953.5 | 1 452.8 | 770.7 | 103.5 | 60.1 | 213.6 | 184 517 | 1 060 | 3 265.6 | 849.9 | 1 543.8 | 2 315 | 1 115 |

1. State totals may include programs not allocated by county.   2. Based on the resident population estimated as of July 1 of the year shown.

# Table B. States and Counties — Local Government Finances, Government Employment, and Voting

| STATE County | Total (mil dol) | Per capita[1] (dollars) | Education | Health and hospitals | Police protection | Public welfare | Highways | Total (mil dol) | Per capita[1] (dollars) | Federal civilian | Federal military | State and local | Democratic | Republican | All other |
|---|---|---|---|---|---|---|---|---|---|---|---|---|---|---|---|
| | 185 | 186 | 187 | 188 | 189 | 190 | 191 | 192 | 193 | 194 | 195 | 196 | 197 | 198 | 199 |
| **MISSISSIPPI—Cont'd** | | | | | | | | | | | | | | | |
| Sunflower | 108.5 | 3 504 | 59.3 | 18.3 | 3.8 | 0.2 | 4.5 | 33.4 | 1 079 | 59 | 178 | 3 522 | 70.0 | 29.0 | 1.0 |
| Tallahatchie | 41.1 | 3 098 | 54.3 | 11.8 | 5.3 | 0.4 | 6.2 | 4.1 | 309 | 39 | 93 | 905 | 59.1 | 40.1 | 0.7 |
| Tate | 112.1 | 4 166 | 78.9 | 0.6 | 3.0 | 0.0 | 4.6 | 62.6 | 2 326 | 85 | 174 | 1 634 | 39.2 | 60.1 | 0.8 |
| Tippah | 57.4 | 2 713 | 54.7 | 23.6 | 3.4 | 0.3 | 6.0 | 7.9 | 373 | 53 | 134 | 1 109 | 27.0 | 71.3 | 1.7 |
| Tishomingo | 46.8 | 2 456 | 58.2 | 1.4 | 4.4 | 0.0 | 10.3 | 11.5 | 601 | 60 | 119 | 849 | 23.3 | 74.2 | 2.5 |
| Tunica | 75.1 | 7 180 | 30.6 | 2.9 | 8.4 | 0.7 | 10.8 | 51.4 | 4 916 | 21 | 64 | 898 | 75.7 | 23.5 | 0.8 |
| Union | 55.6 | 2 065 | 64.1 | 1.3 | 4.6 | 0.2 | 7.9 | 29.0 | 1 078 | 55 | 166 | 1 173 | 24.5 | 74.4 | 1.1 |
| Walthall | 41.8 | 2 722 | 48.6 | 25.8 | 4.0 | 0.1 | 7.1 | 4.6 | 296 | 24 | 93 | 740 | 44.4 | 54.7 | 0.9 |
| Warren | 139.2 | 2 848 | 50.3 | 2.4 | 7.8 | 0.5 | 7.4 | 122.5 | 2 507 | 2 235 | 336 | 2 510 | 48.2 | 51.2 | 0.6 |
| Washington | 250.3 | 4 499 | 35.6 | 37.6 | 4.0 | 0.2 | 4.2 | 100.4 | 1 805 | 516 | 327 | 3 957 | 67.1 | 32.4 | 0.5 |
| Wayne | 65.1 | 3 084 | 44.9 | 33.4 | 2.9 | 0.1 | 4.7 | 19.5 | 924 | 35 | 125 | 1 193 | 38.8 | 60.6 | 0.6 |
| Webster | 20.9 | 2 135 | 62.8 | 1.3 | 6.0 | 0.3 | 10.0 | 6.9 | 703 | 35 | 63 | 430 | 24.7 | 74.6 | 0.7 |
| Wilkinson | 34.7 | 3 382 | 37.5 | 40.5 | 3.8 | 0.2 | 5.6 | 5.5 | 536 | 0 | 59 | 588 | 68.8 | 30.4 | 0.9 |
| Winston | 41.1 | 2 085 | 56.2 | 1.4 | 6.1 | 0.1 | 9.0 | 12.0 | 611 | 35 | 116 | 762 | 45.5 | 53.8 | 0.7 |
| Yalobusha | 39.9 | 2 916 | 39.5 | 25.3 | 5.9 | 0.0 | 5.3 | 16.8 | 1 225 | 82 | 76 | 806 | 46.2 | 53.1 | 0.7 |
| Yazoo | 59.5 | 2 189 | 61.0 | 1.2 | 6.5 | 0.3 | 8.3 | 31.6 | 1 164 | 616 | 169 | 1 526 | 53.3 | 46.1 | 0.6 |
| **MISSOURI** | X | X | X | X | X | X | X | X | X | 60 721 | 37 867 | 384 050 | 49.3 | 49.4 | 1.3 |
| Adair | 86.7 | 3 517 | 68.5 | 1.7 | 2.9 | 0.4 | 4.3 | 32.1 | 1 302 | 82 | 91 | 2 399 | 48.3 | 49.6 | 2.1 |
| Andrew | 37.2 | 2 207 | 61.2 | 3.1 | 2.3 | 0.3 | 3.2 | 41.6 | 2 470 | 41 | 59 | 668 | 38.1 | 60.1 | 1.9 |
| Atchison | 17.2 | 2 823 | 53.7 | 6.4 | 3.3 | 0.0 | 21.2 | 2.2 | 355 | 35 | 19 | 365 | 33.6 | 65.1 | 1.3 |
| Audrain | 78.5 | 3 033 | 64.1 | 1.0 | 5.3 | 5.1 | 6.5 | 37.6 | 1 454 | 89 | 88 | 2 514 | 41.1 | 57.2 | 1.7 |
| Barry | 91.2 | 2 519 | 68.8 | 0.9 | 4.4 | 0.0 | 6.9 | 66.9 | 1 848 | 110 | 122 | 1 657 | 31.6 | 66.6 | 1.7 |
| Barton | 43.1 | 3 385 | 38.3 | 43.7 | 3.1 | 0.0 | 4.9 | 29.3 | 2 305 | 35 | 42 | 888 | 24.5 | 74.2 | 1.3 |
| Bates | 42.6 | 2 501 | 62.2 | 1.1 | 4.0 | 6.3 | 7.0 | 59.9 | 3 516 | 56 | 59 | 1 198 | 39.5 | 58.3 | 2.2 |
| Benton | 42.2 | 2 283 | 56.6 | 3.3 | 4.5 | 11.7 | 3.8 | 36.5 | 1 974 | 104 | 66 | 925 | 37.9 | 60.2 | 1.9 |
| Bollinger | 19.1 | 1 573 | 75.7 | 1.1 | 4.9 | 0.0 | 8.5 | 4.9 | 406 | 33 | 43 | 434 | 29.2 | 68.7 | 2.1 |
| Boone | 473.4 | 3 105 | 47.7 | 2.2 | 4.3 | 1.6 | 7.0 | 527.9 | 3 463 | 2 202 | 602 | 28 572 | 55.2 | 43.2 | 1.6 |
| Buchanan | 260.0 | 3 007 | 45.5 | 1.4 | 5.0 | 0.1 | 6.4 | 452.4 | 5 231 | 502 | 329 | 6 338 | 49.1 | 48.9 | 2.0 |
| Butler | 102.2 | 2 472 | 64.3 | 0.0 | 4.5 | 0.0 | 5.4 | 57.1 | 1 381 | 684 | 148 | 2 865 | 30.7 | 68.1 | 1.3 |
| Caldwell | 22.6 | 2 435 | 71.8 | 1.8 | 2.6 | 3.5 | 6.8 | 13.8 | 1 486 | 37 | 32 | 603 | 39.7 | 58.2 | 2.1 |
| Callaway | 89.8 | 2 069 | 54.1 | 3.5 | 3.9 | 0.0 | 5.7 | 75.2 | 1 731 | 119 | 172 | 3 727 | 39.2 | 58.9 | 1.8 |
| Camden | 123.6 | 3 053 | 50.9 | 5.7 | 4.0 | 0.0 | 7.9 | 94.4 | 2 333 | 76 | 150 | 1 876 | 35.1 | 63.6 | 1.3 |
| Cape Girardeau | 178.6 | 2 456 | 62.1 | 1.4 | 4.2 | 0.0 | 7.5 | 175.1 | 2 407 | 418 | 272 | 5 791 | 32.7 | 66.3 | 1.0 |
| Carroll | 28.1 | 2 855 | 58.7 | 3.7 | 2.7 | 0.0 | 10.1 | 3.9 | 394 | 49 | 32 | 597 | 33.8 | 65.1 | 1.1 |
| Carter | 13.8 | 2 329 | 83.2 | 2.3 | 1.4 | 0.0 | 3.9 | 5.8 | 979 | 107 | 22 | 346 | 34.0 | 63.5 | 2.6 |
| Cass | 333.1 | 3 429 | 56.5 | 9.5 | 5.8 | 0.0 | 6.4 | 418.2 | 4 305 | 283 | 451 | 4 504 | 39.5 | 59.2 | 1.3 |
| Cedar | 46.3 | 3 372 | 38.9 | 12.8 | 3.1 | 0.0 | 30.5 | 28.6 | 2 084 | 62 | 48 | 804 | 32.4 | 66.0 | 1.6 |
| Chariton | 16.8 | 2 138 | 63.2 | 3.3 | 4.9 | 0.0 | 10.6 | 5.7 | 723 | 49 | 27 | 434 | 42.7 | 55.5 | 1.8 |
| Christian | 165.1 | 2 259 | 64.0 | 0.9 | 4.9 | 1.0 | 6.4 | 230.8 | 3 158 | 126 | 270 | 2 663 | 31.5 | 67.3 | 1.1 |
| Clark | 21.5 | 2 972 | 59.5 | 2.3 | 2.4 | 14.9 | 7.4 | 6.2 | 857 | 37 | 24 | 466 | 45.5 | 51.6 | 3.0 |
| Clay | 1 144.5 | 5 400 | 34.7 | 43.4 | 1.9 | 0.0 | 1.7 | 875.4 | 4 130 | 878 | 849 | 14 052 | 49.0 | 49.7 | 1.2 |
| Clinton | 48.9 | 2 339 | 68.7 | 1.7 | 5.6 | 0.0 | 6.2 | 43.0 | 2 058 | 68 | 72 | 1 362 | 43.5 | 54.6 | 1.9 |
| Cole | 168.9 | 2 292 | 53.4 | 1.4 | 8.1 | 0.0 | 7.6 | 190.8 | 2 589 | 639 | 269 | 20 099 | 36.0 | 62.9 | 1.0 |
| Cooper | 58.8 | 3 350 | 40.9 | 20.9 | 3.3 | 4.1 | 5.5 | 47.4 | 2 704 | 50 | 61 | 1 274 | 37.3 | 61.1 | 1.6 |
| Crawford | 58.6 | 2 433 | 66.9 | 4.7 | 4.4 | 0.0 | 6.2 | 34.4 | 1 428 | 35 | 85 | 935 | 38.8 | 59.6 | 1.7 |
| Dade | 19.2 | 2 558 | 55.7 | 1.2 | 2.0 | 13.2 | 14.2 | 7.0 | 927 | 31 | 27 | 530 | 28.8 | 69.6 | 1.6 |
| Dallas | 25.6 | 1 523 | 62.4 | 4.9 | 10.4 | 0.0 | 7.3 | 1.4 | 81 | 36 | 58 | 600 | 34.6 | 63.7 | 1.7 |
| Daviess | 20.0 | 2 518 | 67.9 | 2.3 | 3.2 | 0.1 | 11.4 | 7.6 | 959 | 38 | 29 | 492 | 37.0 | 59.8 | 3.2 |
| DeKalb | 18.1 | 1 477 | 66.1 | 2.6 | 2.6 | 0.0 | 6.6 | 10.0 | 820 | 38 | 44 | 1 258 | 36.1 | 61.7 | 2.2 |
| Dent | 43.8 | 2 906 | 46.7 | 32.1 | 3.8 | 0.0 | 4.3 | 3.3 | 219 | 60 | 54 | 862 | 29.9 | 67.8 | 2.3 |
| Douglas | 20.5 | 1 532 | 70.8 | 1.8 | 3.8 | 0.0 | 3.9 | 20.7 | 1 545 | 53 | 47 | 415 | 31.9 | 65.6 | 2.5 |
| Dunklin | 74.0 | 2 340 | 68.1 | 2.1 | 3.5 | 0.0 | 5.8 | 25.4 | 803 | 101 | 110 | 1 642 | 38.6 | 59.9 | 1.5 |
| Franklin | 250.2 | 2 501 | 60.9 | 3.1 | 5.6 | 0.1 | 8.0 | 238.9 | 2 388 | 229 | 352 | 4 403 | 43.1 | 55.5 | 1.4 |
| Gasconade | 65.5 | 4 256 | 56.2 | 21.3 | 2.6 | 1.0 | 5.4 | 72.7 | 4 723 | 49 | 52 | 1 039 | 37.3 | 61.3 | 1.4 |
| Gentry | 18.3 | 2 933 | 63.0 | 3.9 | 2.1 | 0.0 | 11.1 | 5.3 | 847 | 40 | 23 | 431 | 37.5 | 59.7 | 2.8 |
| Greene | 729.1 | 2 762 | 49.1 | 1.4 | 9.9 | 0.5 | 11.5 | 1 086.4 | 4 115 | 2 202 | 981 | 18 233 | 41.4 | 57.2 | 1.3 |
| Grundy | 41.9 | 4 155 | 70.1 | 3.4 | 2.7 | 6.1 | 3.0 | 26.8 | 2 655 | 51 | 35 | 978 | 33.3 | 63.4 | 3.2 |
| Harrison | 37.0 | 4 170 | 38.4 | 34.2 | 2.0 | 0.1 | 8.1 | 15.5 | 1 745 | 46 | 30 | 722 | 32.9 | 64.2 | 3.0 |
| Henry | 115.9 | 5 173 | 36.6 | 41.5 | 3.7 | 0.1 | 4.1 | 53.2 | 2 376 | 81 | 76 | 1 594 | 43.6 | 54.6 | 1.7 |
| Hickory | 23.6 | 2 588 | 77.9 | 1.6 | 2.1 | 0.0 | 5.4 | 17.3 | 1 892 | 39 | 33 | 309 | 42.4 | 55.7 | 1.8 |
| Holt | 14.1 | 2 835 | 51.0 | 2.8 | 1.7 | 0.3 | 17.6 | 4.1 | 831 | 40 | 17 | 299 | 30.5 | 68.1 | 1.4 |
| Howard | 21.7 | 2 192 | 57.8 | 2.9 | 4.1 | 0.0 | 8.7 | 15.4 | 1 555 | 40 | 35 | 463 | 41.9 | 55.8 | 2.3 |
| Howell | 94.1 | 2 435 | 67.1 | 2.6 | 4.8 | 0.0 | 4.0 | 30.0 | 777 | 108 | 141 | 2 195 | 33.7 | 64.5 | 1.8 |
| Iron | 26.9 | 2 690 | 74.3 | 1.3 | 4.1 | 0.0 | 7.4 | 13.5 | 1 346 | 18 | 37 | 622 | 50.1 | 47.3 | 2.5 |
| Jackson | 3 351.0 | 5 025 | 37.3 | 2.8 | 8.2 | 0.2 | 4.4 | 5 888.0 | 8 829 | 17 841 | 2 441 | 44 847 | 62.1 | 36.8 | 1.1 |

1. Based on the resident population estimated as of July 1 of the year shown.  2. © 2013 Election Data Services, Inc. All rights reserved.

# Table B. States and Counties — **Land Area and Population**

| STATE/ County code | CBSA code[1] | County type[2] | STATE County | Land area,[3] (sq km) 2010 | Total persons | Rank | Per square kilometer | White | Black | American Indian, Alaska Native | Asian and Pacific Islander | Percent Hispanic or Latino[4] | Under 5 years | 5 to 17 years | 18 to 24 years | 25 to 34 years | 35 to 44 years | 45 to 54 years |
|---|---|---|---|---|---|---|---|---|---|---|---|---|---|---|---|---|---|---|
| | | | | 1 | 2 | 3 | 4 | 5 | 6 | 7 | 8 | 9 | 10 | 11 | 12 | 13 | 14 | 15 |
| | | | MISSOURI—Cont'd | | | | | | | | | | | | | | | |
| 29 097 | 27900 | 3 | Jasper.............................. | 1 654 | 115 258 | 524 | 69.7 | 88.4 | 3.0 | 2.7 | 1.6 | 7.0 | 7.5 | 18.1 | 10.1 | 13.8 | 12.3 | 13.1 |
| 29 099 | 41180 | 1 | Jefferson.......................... | 1 701 | 220 209 | 288 | 129.5 | 96.4 | 1.4 | 0.8 | 1.0 | 1.7 | 6.7 | 18.1 | 8.2 | 13.0 | 13.5 | 16.3 |
| 29 101 | 47660 | 4 | Johnson............................ | 2 148 | 54 397 | 920 | 25.3 | 89.5 | 5.6 | 1.2 | 2.8 | 3.4 | 6.7 | 15.6 | 20.9 | 13.4 | 10.4 | 12.4 |
| 29 103 | ... | 9 | Knox................................ | 1 305 | 4 082 | 2 896 | 3.1 | 97.9 | 0.8 | 0.5 | 0.7 | 1.1 | 5.8 | 18.7 | 6.6 | 9.5 | 10.6 | 15.4 |
| 29 105 | 30060 | 6 | Laclede............................ | 1 981 | 35 417 | 1 290 | 17.9 | 95.9 | 1.3 | 1.6 | 1.0 | 2.1 | 6.8 | 18.0 | 8.0 | 12.1 | 12.0 | 14.6 |
| 29 107 | 28140 | 1 | Lafayette........................... | 1 628 | 33 080 | 1 351 | 20.3 | 94.4 | 3.2 | 1.1 | 0.9 | 2.3 | 6.1 | 17.9 | 7.9 | 11.0 | 12.1 | 15.3 |
| 29 109 | ... | 6 | Lawrence.......................... | 1 584 | 38 467 | 1 209 | 24.3 | 92.0 | 0.7 | 1.7 | 0.6 | 6.4 | 6.7 | 19.3 | 7.5 | 11.3 | 12.3 | 14.0 |
| 29 111 | 39500 | 9 | Lewis............................... | 1 308 | 10 174 | 2 427 | 7.8 | 94.4 | 4.1 | 0.7 | 0.6 | 1.6 | 5.9 | 17.1 | 12.1 | 10.7 | 10.9 | 14.5 |
| 29 113 | 41180 | 1 | Lincoln............................. | 1 623 | 53 354 | 932 | 32.9 | 95.1 | 2.8 | 0.9 | 0.7 | 2.1 | 7.4 | 20.2 | 8.1 | 13.2 | 12.9 | 15.6 |
| 29 115 | ... | 7 | Linn................................ | 1 594 | 12 484 | 2 273 | 7.8 | 97.0 | 1.5 | 0.5 | 0.5 | 1.6 | 6.3 | 17.9 | 6.8 | 10.2 | 11.2 | 14.7 |
| 29 117 | ... | 6 | Livingston......................... | 1 379 | 15 037 | 2 103 | 10.9 | 95.3 | 3.4 | 0.7 | 0.7 | 1.3 | 5.9 | 15.8 | 7.7 | 12.9 | 12.6 | 13.7 |
| 29 119 | 22220 | 2 | McDonald.......................... | 1 397 | 22 876 | 1 695 | 16.4 | 82.9 | 1.4 | 4.5 | 2.4 | 11.5 | 7.1 | 20.5 | 8.4 | 11.9 | 12.6 | 14.5 |
| 29 121 | ... | 7 | Macon.............................. | 2 075 | 15 573 | 2 073 | 7.5 | 95.7 | 3.3 | 0.7 | 0.8 | 1.0 | 6.3 | 17.4 | 6.8 | 10.5 | 11.4 | 13.5 |
| 29 123 | ... | 7 | Madison............................ | 1 280 | 12 448 | 2 276 | 9.7 | 96.7 | 0.7 | 0.7 | 0.6 | 2.1 | 6.6 | 17.3 | 8.2 | 11.3 | 11.4 | 14.8 |
| 29 125 | ... | 8 | Maries............................. | 1 365 | 9 014 | 2 520 | 6.6 | 97.8 | 0.8 | 1.3 | 0.3 | 1.0 | 5.6 | 17.3 | 7.5 | 10.4 | 11.5 | 15.8 |
| 29 127 | 25300 | 5 | Marion............................. | 1 132 | 28 745 | 1 457 | 25.4 | 92.4 | 6.3 | 0.7 | 1.0 | 1.5 | 6.6 | 17.2 | 9.2 | 12.2 | 11.9 | 14.2 |
| 29 129 | ... | 9 | Mercer............................. | 1 175 | 3 729 | 2 928 | 3.2 | 97.9 | 0.6 | 1.0 | 0.7 | 0.8 | 6.4 | 18.5 | 6.3 | 9.0 | 10.9 | 15.2 |
| 29 131 | ... | 6 | Miller............................... | 1 535 | 24 817 | 1 615 | 16.2 | 96.8 | 1.0 | 1.4 | 0.7 | 1.5 | 6.4 | 18.1 | 7.9 | 11.4 | 12.1 | 14.8 |
| 29 133 | ... | 7 | Mississippi........................ | 1 066 | 14 322 | 2 148 | 13.4 | 73.7 | 24.6 | 0.6 | 0.3 | 1.7 | 6.3 | 15.8 | 8.5 | 13.6 | 13.5 | 14.4 |
| 29 135 | 27620 | 3 | Moniteau........................... | 1 075 | 15 625 | 2 071 | 14.5 | 91.2 | 4.2 | 0.9 | 0.7 | 4.0 | 6.7 | 18.2 | 8.2 | 13.0 | 13.5 | 14.7 |
| 29 137 | ... | 9 | Monroe............................. | 1 677 | 8 703 | 2 546 | 5.2 | 95.3 | 3.9 | 0.6 | 0.6 | 0.9 | 5.6 | 17.0 | 6.9 | 10.1 | 10.6 | 15.0 |
| 29 139 | ... | 8 | Montgomery....................... | 1 389 | 11 996 | 2 298 | 8.6 | 96.0 | 2.6 | 0.8 | 0.6 | 1.6 | 6.0 | 17.3 | 6.7 | 10.9 | 11.0 | 15.4 |
| 29 141 | ... | 8 | Morgan............................. | 1 548 | 20 117 | 1 833 | 13.0 | 96.4 | 1.3 | 1.5 | 0.6 | 1.8 | 5.9 | 15.7 | 7.0 | 9.1 | 10.0 | 14.1 |
| 29 143 | ... | 7 | New Madrid........................ | 1 748 | 18 488 | 1 897 | 10.6 | 82.2 | 16.4 | 0.8 | 0.8 | 1.3 | 6.5 | 17.2 | 7.9 | 11.7 | 12.4 | 14.5 |
| 29 145 | 27900 | 3 | Newton............................. | 1 618 | 59 069 | 874 | 36.5 | 89.9 | 1.5 | 3.9 | 2.7 | 4.7 | 6.6 | 18.6 | 8.8 | 11.3 | 11.9 | 14.5 |
| 29 147 | 32340 | 6 | Nodaway........................... | 2 271 | 23 419 | 1 666 | 10.3 | 94.1 | 3.1 | 0.5 | 1.8 | 1.4 | 5.0 | 13.1 | 28.2 | 10.9 | 8.8 | 11.1 |
| 29 149 | ... | 9 | Oregon............................. | 2 046 | 10 997 | 2 359 | 5.4 | 96.6 | 0.8 | 2.2 | 0.5 | 1.4 | 5.7 | 16.6 | 7.7 | 8.7 | 10.9 | 15.3 |
| 29 151 | 27620 | 3 | Osage.............................. | 1 565 | 13 858 | 2 182 | 8.9 | 98.6 | 0.6 | 0.5 | 0.2 | 0.7 | 6.2 | 18.1 | 9.5 | 10.9 | 12.8 | 15.3 |
| 29 153 | ... | 9 | Ozark.............................. | 1 929 | 9 601 | 2 462 | 5.0 | 97.4 | 0.6 | 1.4 | 0.4 | 1.5 | 4.8 | 14.7 | 6.3 | 8.6 | 9.8 | 14.8 |
| 29 155 | ... | 7 | Pemiscot........................... | 1 276 | 18 111 | 1 915 | 14.2 | 70.6 | 27.5 | 0.7 | 0.5 | 2.0 | 7.7 | 19.8 | 8.7 | 11.4 | 11.7 | 13.8 |
| 29 157 | ... | 7 | Perry............................... | 1 229 | 19 018 | 1 874 | 15.5 | 96.7 | 0.8 | 0.8 | 0.7 | 2.0 | 6.5 | 18.2 | 8.0 | 12.2 | 12.1 | 14.4 |
| 29 159 | 42740 | 4 | Pettis.............................. | 1 767 | 42 319 | 1 125 | 23.9 | 88.2 | 4.1 | 0.9 | 1.2 | 7.5 | 7.2 | 18.1 | 9.2 | 13.1 | 11.3 | 14.3 |
| 29 161 | 40620 | 5 | Phelps.............................. | 1 740 | 44 987 | 1 069 | 25.9 | 91.7 | 3.1 | 1.5 | 3.5 | 2.2 | 6.0 | 15.5 | 17.6 | 12.0 | 10.5 | 13.2 |
| 29 163 | ... | 6 | Pike................................ | 1 736 | 18 565 | 1 894 | 10.7 | 90.1 | 8.2 | 0.5 | 0.5 | 2.0 | 6.0 | 16.0 | 8.7 | 13.2 | 12.3 | 15.4 |
| 29 165 | 28140 | 1 | Platte.............................. | 1 088 | 92 054 | 628 | 84.6 | 85.7 | 7.0 | 1.1 | 3.2 | 5.1 | 6.2 | 18.0 | 7.8 | 13.3 | 14.0 | 16.1 |
| 29 167 | 44180 | 2 | Polk................................ | 1 646 | 31 017 | 1 411 | 18.8 | 95.9 | 1.3 | 1.4 | 0.7 | 2.1 | 6.2 | 18.1 | 11.3 | 10.9 | 11.2 | 14.0 |
| 29 169 | 22780 | 5 | Pulaski............................. | 1 417 | 53 259 | 904 | 37.6 | 75.1 | 12.9 | 1.7 | 4.9 | 9.4 | 7.5 | 16.3 | 22.8 | 17.2 | 11.5 | 10.1 |
| 29 171 | ... | 9 | Putnam............................ | 1 340 | 4 931 | 2 843 | 3.7 | 98.3 | 0.5 | 0.7 | 0.6 | 0.8 | 5.5 | 17.2 | 6.6 | 9.4 | 10.3 | 14.1 |
| 29 173 | 25300 | 9 | Ralls............................... | 1 217 | 10 277 | 2 419 | 8.4 | 97.1 | 1.7 | 0.5 | 0.6 | 1.0 | 6.2 | 16.7 | 6.1 | 10.2 | 12.1 | 15.8 |
| 29 175 | 33620 | 6 | Randolph........................... | 1 250 | 25 330 | 1 598 | 20.3 | 91.5 | 7.0 | 0.9 | 0.8 | 1.8 | 6.1 | 16.8 | 9.5 | 13.8 | 13.2 | 14.4 |
| 29 177 | 28140 | 1 | Ray................................. | 1 473 | 23 064 | 1 687 | 15.7 | 95.8 | 1.9 | 1.1 | 0.6 | 1.9 | 6.2 | 18.4 | 7.6 | 10.9 | 12.5 | 16.3 |
| 29 179 | ... | 9 | Reynolds........................... | 2 094 | 6 667 | 2 711 | 3.2 | 97.0 | 1.4 | 1.6 | 0.4 | 1.2 | 5.4 | 17.1 | 6.6 | 9.5 | 11.1 | 15.2 |
| 29 181 | ... | 9 | Ripley.............................. | 1 630 | 14 036 | 2 174 | 8.6 | 96.9 | 0.8 | 1.8 | 0.5 | 1.3 | 6.3 | 17.3 | 8.0 | 10.7 | 11.5 | 14.4 |
| 29 183 | 41180 | 1 | St. Charles........................ | 1 452 | 368 666 | 180 | 253.9 | 90.2 | 5.1 | 0.6 | 2.8 | 2.9 | 6.5 | 18.7 | 8.6 | 13.3 | 13.7 | 15.7 |
| 29 185 | ... | 8 | St. Clair............................ | 1 735 | 9 474 | 2 474 | 5.5 | 96.5 | 1.1 | 1.8 | 0.4 | 1.9 | 5.2 | 14.2 | 6.7 | 8.4 | 10.6 | 15.4 |
| 29 186 | ... | 6 | Ste. Genevieve.................... | 1 293 | 17 740 | 1 932 | 13.7 | 97.6 | 1.2 | 0.8 | 0.4 | 0.9 | 5.6 | 17.2 | 7.7 | 10.5 | 11.6 | 16.5 |
| 29 187 | 22100 | 4 | St. Francois........................ | 1 170 | 65 917 | 800 | 56.3 | 93.4 | 4.8 | 0.9 | 0.7 | 1.3 | 6.0 | 15.9 | 9.3 | 14.4 | 13.2 | 15.0 |
| 29 189 | 41180 | 1 | St. Louis........................... | 1 315 | 1 000 438 | 41 | 760.8 | 70.2 | 24.1 | 0.6 | 4.2 | 2.6 | 5.8 | 17.2 | 8.7 | 12.5 | 12.0 | 15.3 |
| 29 195 | 32180 | 6 | Saline.............................. | 1 957 | 23 339 | 1 673 | 11.9 | 84.7 | 6.4 | 0.8 | 1.5 | 8.5 | 6.4 | 16.3 | 11.8 | 11.9 | 11.0 | 13.9 |
| 29 197 | 28860 | 9 | Schuyler........................... | 796 | 4 370 | 2 876 | 5.5 | 98.6 | 0.4 | 0.5 | 0.5 | 0.8 | 5.8 | 19.0 | 7.4 | 9.8 | 10.8 | 14.6 |
| 29 199 | ... | 9 | Scotland........................... | 1 131 | 4 877 | 2 846 | 4.3 | 98.7 | 0.4 | 0.5 | 0.4 | 0.6 | 7.8 | 20.4 | 8.0 | 10.3 | 10.0 | 13.3 |
| 29 201 | 43460 | 5 | Scott............................... | 1 088 | 39 139 | 1 193 | 36.0 | 86.1 | 12.0 | 0.9 | 0.6 | 1.9 | 7.0 | 17.7 | 8.4 | 12.1 | 12.1 | 14.3 |
| 29 203 | ... | 9 | Shannon............................ | 2 600 | 8 318 | 2 580 | 3.2 | 96.8 | 0.7 | 2.5 | 0.5 | 1.8 | 6.0 | 16.9 | 8.1 | 9.4 | 10.7 | 15.7 |
| 29 205 | ... | 9 | Shelby............................. | 1 297 | 6 234 | 2 741 | 4.8 | 97.6 | 1.1 | 0.5 | 0.4 | 1.2 | 6.6 | 18.3 | 6.6 | 10.9 | 9.9 | 14.3 |
| 29 207 | ... | 7 | Stoddard........................... | 2 132 | 29 795 | 1 431 | 14.0 | 96.9 | 1.4 | 0.9 | 0.4 | 1.4 | 5.7 | 16.6 | 8.3 | 11.6 | 12.0 | 14.3 |
| 29 209 | 14700 | 8 | Stone............................... | 1 202 | 31 568 | 1 399 | 26.3 | 96.8 | 0.6 | 1.4 | 0.5 | 1.8 | 4.3 | 13.9 | 5.8 | 8.0 | 10.0 | 14.6 |
| 29 211 | ... | 9 | Sullivan............................ | 1 678 | 6 546 | 2 718 | 3.9 | 79.4 | 0.9 | 0.8 | 0.4 | 19.2 | 6.2 | 17.8 | 7.8 | 10.6 | 12.4 | 14.9 |
| 29 213 | 14700 | 6 | Taney.............................. | 1 638 | 52 956 | 941 | 32.3 | 92.1 | 1.5 | 1.9 | 1.3 | 5.1 | 6.2 | 15.9 | 9.7 | 11.4 | 11.6 | 13.6 |
| 29 215 | ... | 9 | Texas.............................. | 3 049 | 25 810 | 1 574 | 8.5 | 93.5 | 3.9 | 1.8 | 0.6 | 1.9 | 6.1 | 15.7 | 8.2 | 11.9 | 11.1 | 14.9 |
| 29 217 | ... | 7 | Vernon............................. | 2 140 | 20 748 | 1 792 | 9.7 | 96.3 | 1.1 | 1.5 | 0.9 | 1.7 | 6.7 | 18.1 | 8.7 | 11.0 | 11.4 | 14.4 |
| 29 219 | 41180 | 1 | Warren............................. | 1 110 | 32 753 | 1 362 | 29.5 | 94.1 | 2.8 | 1.0 | 0.7 | 3.0 | 6.9 | 17.6 | 7.9 | 12.2 | 11.6 | 16.0 |
| 29 221 | 41180 | 1 | Washington........................ | 1 968 | 25 095 | 1 605 | 12.8 | 95.8 | 2.8 | 1.0 | 0.4 | 1.1 | 6.3 | 17.4 | 8.2 | 12.2 | 13.3 | 15.8 |
| 29 223 | ... | 9 | Wayne.............................. | 1 966 | 13 402 | 2 219 | 6.8 | 97.6 | 0.7 | 1.6 | 0.5 | 1.2 | 5.3 | 15.6 | 7.1 | 9.4 | 10.8 | 15.1 |
| 29 225 | 44180 | 2 | Webster............................ | 1 535 | 36 351 | 1 267 | 23.7 | 96.1 | 1.5 | 1.5 | 0.5 | 1.9 | 7.2 | 20.0 | 7.9 | 11.6 | 13.0 | 14.3 |
| 29 227 | ... | 9 | Worth.............................. | 691 | 2 079 | 3 044 | 3.0 | 97.6 | 0.9 | 0.5 | 0.3 | 1.0 | 4.7 | 15.9 | 6.6 | 9.1 | 9.7 | 15.5 |
| 29 229 | ... | 6 | Wright.............................. | 1 766 | 18 629 | 1 891 | 10.5 | 96.9 | 0.9 | 1.2 | 0.6 | 1.6 | 6.7 | 18.8 | 7.7 | 10.4 | 11.0 | 14.6 |

1. CBSA = Core Based Statistical Area. See Appendix A for explanation. See Appendix B for list of metropolitan areas with component counties. 2. County type code from the Economic Research Service of USDA Rural-Urban Continuum Codes. See Appendix A for definition. 3. Dry land or land partially or temporarily covered by water. 4. May be of any race.

# Table B. States and Counties — Population and Households

| STATE County | 55 to 64 years | 65 to 74 years | 75 years and over | Percent female | Total persons 2000 | Total persons 2010 | Percent change 2000–2010 | Percent change 2010–2012 | Births | Deaths | Net migration | Number | Percent change, 2000–2010 | Persons per household | Female family householder[1] | One person |
|---|---|---|---|---|---|---|---|---|---|---|---|---|---|---|---|---|
| | 16 | 17 | 18 | 19 | 20 | 21 | 22 | 23 | 24 | 25 | 26 | 27 | 28 | 29 | 30 | 31 |
| MISSOURI—Cont'd | | | | | | | | | | | | | | | | |
| Jasper | 11.4 | 7.2 | 6.3 | 51.1 | 104 686 | 117 404 | 12.1 | -1.8 | 3 810 | 2 443 | -3 650 | 45 639 | 10.2 | 2.52 | 12.4 | 27.4 |
| Jefferson | 12.7 | 7.0 | 4.5 | 50.3 | 198 099 | 218 733 | 10.4 | 0.7 | 5 992 | 4 120 | -442 | 81 700 | 14.3 | 2.65 | 11.3 | 20.9 |
| Johnson | 9.8 | 6.1 | 4.8 | 49.4 | 48 258 | 52 595 | 9.0 | 3.4 | 1 624 | 831 | 1 010 | 19 311 | 10.9 | 2.53 | 9.2 | 23.9 |
| Knox | 13.1 | 11.1 | 9.1 | 50.5 | 4 361 | 4 131 | -5.3 | -1.2 | 102 | 109 | -47 | 1 708 | -4.6 | 2.37 | 7.5 | 32.0 |
| Laclede | 12.6 | 9.1 | 6.8 | 50.7 | 32 513 | 35 571 | 9.4 | -0.4 | 1 035 | 786 | -406 | 14 081 | 10.4 | 2.50 | 10.4 | 24.8 |
| Lafayette | 13.0 | 8.7 | 8.0 | 50.6 | 32 960 | 33 381 | 1.3 | -0.9 | 832 | 770 | -357 | 13 022 | 3.6 | 2.51 | 10.4 | 25.2 |
| Lawrence | 12.5 | 8.8 | 7.8 | 50.7 | 35 204 | 38 634 | 9.7 | -0.4 | 1 077 | 926 | -304 | 14 869 | 9.6 | 2.56 | 10.1 | 25.4 |
| Lewis | 12.5 | 8.4 | 7.9 | 49.8 | 10 494 | 10 211 | -2.7 | -0.4 | 268 | 257 | -64 | 3 874 | -2.1 | 2.43 | 8.8 | 28.3 |
| Lincoln | 11.5 | 6.5 | 4.6 | 50.1 | 38 944 | 52 566 | 35.0 | 1.5 | 1 659 | 880 | 16 | 18 906 | 36.5 | 2.75 | 11.2 | 19.8 |
| Linn | 13.7 | 9.9 | 9.4 | 51.9 | 13 754 | 12 761 | -7.2 | -2.2 | 306 | 405 | -171 | 5 299 | -7.0 | 2.38 | 9.2 | 30.3 |
| Livingston | 12.9 | 8.8 | 9.6 | 55.3 | 14 558 | 15 195 | 4.4 | -1.0 | 345 | 430 | -64 | 5 871 | 2.4 | 2.36 | 10.0 | 29.9 |
| McDonald | 11.9 | 8.2 | 5.0 | 49.7 | 21 681 | 23 083 | 6.5 | -0.9 | 676 | 444 | -442 | 8 404 | 3.6 | 2.73 | 11.2 | 22.5 |
| Macon | 13.7 | 10.5 | 9.8 | 51.0 | 15 762 | 15 566 | -1.2 | 0.0 | 406 | 413 | 26 | 6 412 | -1.4 | 2.38 | 9.5 | 29.4 |
| Madison | 13.0 | 9.6 | 7.8 | 50.9 | 11 800 | 12 226 | 3.6 | 1.8 | 321 | 387 | 250 | 4 898 | 4.0 | 2.46 | 10.5 | 27.1 |
| Maries | 13.9 | 10.3 | 7.8 | 49.7 | 8 903 | 9 176 | 3.1 | -1.8 | 197 | 227 | -133 | 3 705 | 5.3 | 2.46 | 8.0 | 26.2 |
| Marion | 13.0 | 7.8 | 8.2 | 51.7 | 28 289 | 28 781 | 1.7 | -0.1 | 802 | 706 | -119 | 11 377 | 2.8 | 2.41 | 12.3 | 28.8 |
| Mercer | 13.5 | 9.8 | 10.2 | 50.1 | 3 757 | 3 785 | 0.7 | -1.5 | 97 | 94 | -63 | 1 560 | -2.5 | 2.39 | 6.9 | 30.6 |
| Miller | 13.6 | 8.5 | 7.3 | 50.3 | 23 564 | 24 748 | 5.0 | 0.3 | 654 | 572 | -43 | 9 917 | 6.8 | 2.47 | 10.4 | 26.9 |
| Mississippi | 12.6 | 8.9 | 6.4 | 46.3 | 13 427 | 14 358 | 6.9 | -0.3 | 398 | 450 | 8 | 5 180 | -3.8 | 2.41 | 18.3 | 29.5 |
| Moniteau | 11.8 | 7.2 | 6.6 | 47.4 | 14 827 | 15 607 | 5.3 | 0.1 | 439 | 354 | -68 | 5 532 | 5.2 | 2.58 | 9.2 | 25.5 |
| Monroe | 15.3 | 11.0 | 8.6 | 50.1 | 9 311 | 8 840 | -5.1 | -1.5 | 213 | 215 | -142 | 3 638 | -0.5 | 2.39 | 8.1 | 28.4 |
| Montgomery | 13.6 | 10.1 | 9.0 | 50.1 | 12 136 | 12 236 | 0.8 | -2.0 | 324 | 352 | -211 | 4 868 | 1.9 | 2.43 | 9.3 | 27.5 |
| Morgan | 15.5 | 13.3 | 9.4 | 50.2 | 19 309 | 20 565 | 6.5 | -2.2 | 547 | 677 | -322 | 8 450 | 7.6 | 2.40 | 8.3 | 27.9 |
| New Madrid | 13.7 | 9.1 | 7.3 | 52.2 | 19 760 | 18 956 | -4.1 | -2.5 | 498 | 523 | -439 | 7 742 | -1.0 | 2.41 | 15.3 | 28.7 |
| Newton | 12.8 | 8.7 | 6.7 | 50.5 | 52 636 | 58 114 | 10.4 | 1.6 | 1 676 | 1 216 | 398 | 22 021 | 9.3 | 2.60 | 10.4 | 23.0 |
| Nodaway | 9.8 | 6.6 | 6.7 | 49.6 | 21 912 | 23 370 | 6.7 | 0.2 | 499 | 417 | -38 | 8 545 | 5.0 | 2.31 | 6.9 | 30.2 |
| Oregon | 15.5 | 11.4 | 8.3 | 50.6 | 10 344 | 10 881 | 5.2 | 1.1 | 291 | 330 | 145 | 4 527 | 6.2 | 2.38 | 9.1 | 27.7 |
| Osage | 12.0 | 7.9 | 7.3 | 48.0 | 13 062 | 13 878 | 6.2 | -0.1 | 344 | 283 | -92 | 5 328 | 8.2 | 2.53 | 7.0 | 26.0 |
| Ozark | 17.1 | 14.1 | 9.8 | 49.6 | 9 542 | 9 723 | 1.9 | -1.3 | 176 | 279 | -13 | 4 194 | 6.2 | 2.29 | 7.4 | 27.8 |
| Pemiscot | 12.2 | 7.7 | 6.9 | 52.6 | 20 047 | 18 296 | -8.7 | -1.0 | 636 | 530 | -285 | 7 350 | -6.4 | 2.46 | 20.1 | 30.1 |
| Perry | 12.8 | 7.9 | 7.8 | 50.1 | 18 132 | 18 971 | 4.6 | 0.2 | 491 | 496 | 26 | 7 357 | 6.6 | 2.54 | 8.6 | 25.1 |
| Pettis | 12.0 | 7.4 | 7.3 | 50.8 | 39 403 | 42 201 | 7.1 | 0.3 | 1 315 | 874 | -318 | 16 428 | 5.5 | 2.52 | 11.3 | 27.4 |
| Phelps | 11.4 | 7.5 | 6.3 | 47.9 | 39 825 | 45 156 | 13.4 | -0.4 | 1 194 | 921 | -429 | 17 564 | 12.0 | 2.40 | 10.3 | 28.9 |
| Pike | 12.5 | 8.8 | 7.0 | 45.1 | 18 351 | 18 516 | 0.9 | 0.3 | 502 | 436 | -16 | 6 560 | 1.7 | 2.49 | 10.7 | 27.1 |
| Platte | 13.0 | 6.8 | 4.8 | 50.7 | 73 781 | 89 322 | 21.1 | 3.1 | 2 520 | 1 261 | 1 471 | 36 103 | 23.3 | 2.45 | 9.7 | 27.0 |
| Polk | 11.8 | 8.7 | 7.8 | 50.8 | 26 992 | 31 137 | 15.4 | -0.4 | 859 | 854 | -123 | 11 677 | 17.7 | 2.54 | 9.3 | 24.7 |
| Pulaski | 7.3 | 4.2 | 3.1 | 44.2 | 41 165 | 52 274 | 27.0 | 1.9 | 1 954 | 584 | -442 | 16 004 | 19.1 | 2.64 | 10.9 | 24.2 |
| Putnam | 14.6 | 12.4 | 9.9 | 49.9 | 5 223 | 4 979 | -4.7 | -1.0 | 110 | 130 | -27 | 2 132 | -4.3 | 2.31 | 6.9 | 30.3 |
| Ralls | 15.7 | 11.0 | 6.1 | 49.5 | 9 626 | 10 167 | 5.6 | 1.1 | 224 | 193 | 67 | 4 091 | 9.5 | 2.47 | 6.9 | 23.1 |
| Randolph | 12.0 | 7.5 | 6.8 | 47.6 | 24 663 | 25 414 | 3.0 | -0.3 | 651 | 553 | -178 | 9 342 | 1.6 | 2.46 | 12.8 | 27.7 |
| Ray | 13.3 | 8.8 | 6.1 | 50.1 | 23 354 | 23 494 | 0.6 | -1.8 | 579 | 576 | -439 | 8 957 | 2.4 | 2.59 | 9.4 | 22.8 |
| Reynolds | 14.4 | 12.0 | 8.6 | 48.8 | 6 689 | 6 696 | 0.1 | -0.4 | 147 | 190 | -21 | 2 778 | 2.1 | 2.37 | 8.4 | 27.8 |
| Ripley | 13.1 | 10.5 | 8.1 | 50.6 | 13 509 | 14 100 | 4.4 | -0.5 | 425 | 462 | -22 | 5 637 | 4.1 | 2.49 | 11.3 | 25.8 |
| St. Charles | 11.9 | 6.6 | 5.1 | 50.9 | 283 883 | 360 485 | 27.0 | 2.3 | 10 098 | 5 064 | 3 178 | 134 274 | 32.1 | 2.64 | 9.8 | 22.0 |
| St. Clair | 15.8 | 13.3 | 10.5 | 49.7 | 9 652 | 9 805 | 1.6 | -3.4 | 186 | 324 | -194 | 4 161 | 3.0 | 2.31 | 8.3 | 29.7 |
| Ste. Genevieve | 14.6 | 8.8 | 7.6 | 49.5 | 17 842 | 18 145 | 1.7 | -2.2 | 388 | 413 | -375 | 7 040 | 6.9 | 2.54 | 8.1 | 23.4 |
| St. Francois | 11.9 | 8.0 | 6.4 | 46.8 | 55 641 | 65 359 | 17.5 | 0.9 | 1 692 | 1 603 | 499 | 23 981 | 15.3 | 2.45 | 12.4 | 27.5 |
| St. Louis | 13.4 | 7.6 | 7.6 | 52.7 | 1 016 315 | 998 954 | -1.7 | 0.1 | 25 913 | 20 680 | -3 310 | 404 765 | 0.1 | 2.42 | 14.2 | 29.5 |
| Saline | 12.8 | 8.0 | 7.9 | 50.5 | 23 756 | 23 370 | -1.6 | -0.1 | 661 | 546 | -132 | 8 883 | -1.5 | 2.46 | 11.5 | 27.9 |
| Schuyler | 12.5 | 10.9 | 9.2 | 51.6 | 4 170 | 4 431 | 6.3 | -1.4 | 118 | 115 | -64 | 1 796 | 4.1 | 2.44 | 8.6 | 30.3 |
| Scotland | 12.5 | 9.0 | 8.7 | 51.0 | 4 983 | 4 843 | -2.8 | 0.7 | 162 | 119 | -4 | 1 880 | -1.2 | 2.54 | 7.7 | 28.8 |
| Scott | 13.1 | 8.6 | 6.7 | 51.8 | 40 422 | 39 191 | -3.0 | -0.1 | 1 205 | 964 | -281 | 15 538 | -0.6 | 2.49 | 14.1 | 26.7 |
| Shannon | 15.4 | 11.2 | 6.7 | 50.1 | 8 324 | 8 441 | 1.4 | -1.5 | 206 | 197 | -126 | 3 448 | 3.9 | 2.42 | 8.9 | 27.8 |
| Shelby | 13.5 | 10.0 | 10.0 | 51.0 | 6 799 | 6 373 | -6.3 | -2.2 | 172 | 166 | -155 | 2 581 | -6.0 | 2.39 | 8.0 | 28.6 |
| Stoddard | 13.2 | 9.7 | 8.5 | 51.3 | 29 705 | 29 968 | 0.9 | -0.6 | 754 | 826 | -81 | 12 255 | 1.6 | 2.39 | 10.9 | 27.4 |
| Stone | 17.8 | 16.1 | 9.4 | 50.9 | 28 658 | 32 202 | 12.4 | -2.0 | 564 | 768 | -398 | 13 690 | 15.8 | 2.33 | 7.2 | 22.8 |
| Sullivan | 13.3 | 8.8 | 8.1 | 49.5 | 7 219 | 6 714 | -7.0 | -2.5 | 207 | 190 | -193 | 2 740 | -6.3 | 2.41 | 9.2 | 29.5 |
| Taney | 13.5 | 10.8 | 7.4 | 51.5 | 39 703 | 51 675 | 30.2 | 2.5 | 1 436 | 1 034 | 898 | 20 755 | 28.5 | 2.41 | 10.9 | 26.2 |
| Texas | 13.8 | 10.1 | 8.1 | 48.1 | 23 003 | 26 008 | 13.1 | -0.8 | 667 | 600 | -249 | 10 057 | 7.2 | 2.40 | 9.5 | 27.4 |
| Vernon | 13.5 | 8.7 | 7.8 | 51.5 | 20 454 | 21 159 | 3.4 | -1.9 | 525 | 511 | -419 | 8 396 | 5.4 | 2.42 | 10.2 | 29.4 |
| Warren | 12.7 | 9.0 | 6.1 | 50.3 | 24 525 | 32 513 | 32.6 | 0.7 | 905 | 610 | -76 | 12 339 | 34.3 | 2.61 | 10.7 | 22.0 |
| Washington | 13.1 | 8.5 | 5.2 | 48.5 | 23 344 | 25 195 | 7.9 | -0.4 | 664 | 560 | -194 | 9 355 | 11.3 | 2.58 | 11.7 | 23.4 |
| Wayne | 14.9 | 13.0 | 8.7 | 49.9 | 13 259 | 13 521 | 2.0 | -0.9 | 314 | 427 | -23 | 5 717 | 3.0 | 2.34 | 9.3 | 27.7 |
| Webster | 11.9 | 8.0 | 5.6 | 49.5 | 31 045 | 36 202 | 16.6 | 0.4 | 1 133 | 728 | -260 | 13 062 | 18.0 | 2.70 | 9.9 | 21.2 |
| Worth | 14.0 | 12.3 | 12.2 | 50.9 | 2 382 | 2 171 | -8.9 | -4.2 | 46 | 70 | -70 | 944 | -6.4 | 2.24 | 6.5 | 28.6 |
| Wright | 13.0 | 10.0 | 7.9 | 51.1 | 17 955 | 18 815 | 4.8 | -1.0 | 537 | 491 | -242 | 7 499 | 5.9 | 2.48 | 10.5 | 27.4 |

1. No spouse present.

# Table B. States and Counties — Population, Vital Statistics, Medicare, and Crime

| STATE County | Persons in group quarters, 2010 | Daytime population, 2007–2011 Number | Daytime population, 2007–2011 Employment/residence ratio | Births, 2011 Total | Births, 2011 Rate[1] | Deaths, 2011 Number | Deaths, 2011 Rate[1] | Persons under 65 with no health insurance, 2010 Number | Persons under 65 with no health insurance, 2010 Percent | Medicare, 2012 Eligible for Medicare | Medicare, 2012 Enrolled in Medicare Advantage | Medicare, 2012 Enrolled in a Medicare prescription drug plan | Serious crimes known to police,[2] 2011 Total Number | Serious crimes known to police,[2] 2011 Total Rate[3] |
|---|---|---|---|---|---|---|---|---|---|---|---|---|---|---|
| | 32 | 33 | 34 | 35 | 36 | 37 | 38 | 39 | 40 | 41 | 42 | 43 | 44 | 45 |
| **MISSOURI—Cont'd** | | | | | | | | | | | | | | |
| Jasper | 2 478 | 122 828 | 1.12 | 1 740 | 14.7 | 1 085 | 9.2 | 20 617 | 20.6 | 20 419 | 3 514 | 10 260 | 5 214 | 4 425 |
| Jefferson | 1 983 | 164 510 | 0.49 | 2 733 | 12.5 | 1 786 | 8.1 | 26 963 | 14.0 | 34 641 | 11 921 | 11 537 | 4 973 | 2 265 |
| Johnson | 3 671 | 49 577 | 0.88 | 723 | 13.5 | 356 | 6.7 | 6 572 | 15.0 | 6 980 | 1 016 | 2 891 | 1 432 | 2 713 |
| Knox | 87 | 3 713 | 0.77 | 35 | 8.5 | 49 | 11.9 | 815 | 25.1 | 951 | 59 | 607 | 51 | 1 230 |
| Laclede | 345 | 35 196 | 0.98 | 451 | 12.7 | 349 | 9.8 | 5 211 | 17.5 | 7 670 | 2 897 | 2 627 | 1 275 | 3 571 |
| Lafayette | 724 | 27 463 | 0.63 | 386 | 11.6 | 335 | 10.1 | 4 166 | 15.2 | 6 777 | 1 375 | 2 891 | 645 | 1 925 |
| Lawrence | 559 | 33 804 | 0.71 | 486 | 12.6 | 409 | 10.6 | 6 198 | 19.4 | 8 018 | 2 658 | 2 980 | 1 462 | 3 771 |
| Lewis | 782 | 8 884 | 0.71 | 85 | 8.4 | 112 | 11.0 | 1 382 | 17.4 | 1 988 | 112 | 1 235 | 151 | 1 473 |
| Lincoln | 632 | 40 751 | 0.51 | 748 | 14.1 | 382 | 7.2 | 6 837 | 14.7 | 8 077 | 1 922 | 3 504 | 885 | 1 678 |
| Linn | 152 | 12 578 | 0.97 | 137 | 10.9 | 184 | 14.6 | 1 685 | 16.4 | 3 023 | 212 | 1 839 | 268 | 2 093 |
| Livingston | 1 340 | 15 808 | 1.12 | 163 | 10.8 | 195 | 12.9 | 1 711 | 15.1 | 3 145 | 165 | 1 996 | 363 | 2 380 |
| McDonald | 157 | 19 976 | 0.69 | 301 | 13.1 | 211 | 9.2 | 4 568 | 22.8 | 3 665 | 872 | 1 614 | 574 | 2 478 |
| Macon | 286 | 14 672 | 0.87 | 184 | 11.8 | 166 | 10.6 | 2 198 | 17.7 | 3 684 | 207 | 2 177 | 350 | 2 240 |
| Madison | 168 | 11 121 | 0.76 | 147 | 12.1 | 192 | 15.7 | 1 871 | 18.9 | 2 982 | 314 | 1 693 | 178 | 1 451 |
| Maries | 67 | 7 234 | 0.50 | 93 | 10.1 | 99 | 10.8 | 1 427 | 19.1 | 1 757 | 153 | 909 | 141 | 1 531 |
| Marion | 1 368 | 30 030 | 1.11 | 324 | 11.3 | 301 | 10.5 | 3 308 | 14.1 | 6 019 | 393 | 3 780 | 1 384 | 4 791 |
| Mercer | 51 | 4 113 | 1.23 | 43 | 11.3 | 37 | 9.7 | 593 | 19.8 | 809 | 43 | 463 | 23 | 605 |
| Miller | 271 | 22 500 | 0.79 | 302 | 12.2 | 254 | 10.3 | 3 758 | 18.2 | 4 666 | 452 | 2 475 | 612 | 2 464 |
| Mississippi | 1 874 | 13 318 | 0.84 | 176 | 12.3 | 201 | 14.1 | 1 868 | 17.9 | 2 889 | 112 | 1 984 | 451 | 3 130 |
| Moniteau | 1 316 | 13 841 | 0.74 | 198 | 12.6 | 158 | 10.1 | 2 315 | 18.9 | 2 622 | 157 | 1 389 | 138 | 881 |
| Monroe | 128 | 7 396 | 0.59 | 91 | 10.4 | 93 | 10.6 | 1 307 | 18.5 | 2 024 | 166 | 1 189 | 124 | 1 398 |
| Montgomery | 394 | 10 518 | 0.68 | 133 | 10.8 | 149 | 12.1 | 1 704 | 17.5 | 2 679 | 260 | 1 537 | 215 | 1 751 |
| Morgan | 302 | 18 874 | 0.76 | 244 | 11.9 | 306 | 14.9 | 3 624 | 22.9 | 5 660 | 544 | 2 938 | 491 | 2 379 |
| New Madrid | 332 | 19 071 | 1.03 | 238 | 12.7 | 230 | 12.2 | 2 538 | 16.2 | 3 712 | 305 | 2 533 | 311 | 1 744 |
| Newton | 880 | 56 412 | 0.94 | 742 | 12.7 | 550 | 9.4 | 9 076 | 18.7 | 11 022 | 1 884 | 5 351 | 1 828 | 3 134 |
| Nodaway | 3 611 | 23 175 | 1.00 | 239 | 10.2 | 181 | 7.7 | 2 411 | 14.2 | 3 483 | 138 | 2 271 | 497 | 2 119 |
| Oregon | 121 | 10 124 | 0.81 | 120 | 10.9 | 151 | 13.7 | 1 841 | 21.1 | 2 726 | 413 | 1 498 | 100 | 916 |
| Osage | 405 | 11 197 | 0.61 | 158 | 11.4 | 132 | 9.5 | 1 784 | 15.6 | 2 323 | 158 | 1 283 | 158 | 1 134 |
| Ozark | 123 | 8 948 | 0.78 | 76 | 7.9 | 133 | 13.9 | 1 721 | 23.2 | 2 682 | 659 | 1 138 | 153 | 1 568 |
| Pemiscot | 202 | 18 095 | 0.95 | 288 | 15.8 | 243 | 13.4 | 2 219 | 14.4 | 3 948 | 601 | 2 427 | 775 | 4 221 |
| Perry | 286 | 19 132 | 1.01 | 222 | 11.7 | 226 | 11.9 | 2 311 | 14.6 | 3 595 | 143 | 2 125 | 329 | 1 728 |
| Pettis | 851 | 43 782 | 1.10 | 585 | 13.9 | 378 | 9.0 | 7 073 | 20.0 | 7 904 | 908 | 4 271 | 2 053 | 4 847 |
| Phelps | 3 001 | 46 472 | 1.10 | 524 | 11.6 | 407 | 9.0 | 6 045 | 16.5 | 8 155 | 689 | 4 215 | 1 549 | 3 418 |
| Pike | 2 162 | 18 503 | 0.99 | 223 | 12.0 | 194 | 10.4 | 2 450 | 18.0 | 3 548 | 309 | 2 066 | 250 | 1 345 |
| Platte | 869 | 86 357 | 0.96 | 1 104 | 12.1 | 534 | 5.9 | 7 267 | 9.2 | 12 530 | 2 391 | 5 149 | 3 868 | 4 315 |
| Polk | 1 511 | 28 886 | 0.83 | 361 | 11.6 | 384 | 12.3 | 4 711 | 18.9 | 6 085 | 2 329 | 2 141 | 786 | 2 515 |
| Pulaski | 9 989 | 54 228 | 1.14 | 893 | 16.8 | 255 | 4.8 | 5 537 | 14.2 | 5 400 | 441 | 1 930 | 1 175 | 2 240 |
| Putnam | 57 | 4 560 | 0.79 | 54 | 10.8 | 56 | 11.2 | 796 | 20.5 | 1 234 | 95 | 791 | 32 | 640 |
| Ralls | 54 | 8 326 | 0.63 | 97 | 9.4 | 85 | 8.3 | 1 271 | 15.0 | 2 162 | 201 | 1 179 | 224 | 2 195 |
| Randolph | 2 455 | 26 682 | 1.12 | 313 | 12.3 | 243 | 9.6 | 3 019 | 15.5 | 4 805 | 665 | 2 815 | 651 | 2 552 |
| Ray | 311 | 17 905 | 0.46 | 274 | 11.8 | 258 | 11.1 | 2 641 | 13.4 | 4 352 | 470 | 1 951 | 574 | 2 434 |
| Reynolds | 101 | 7 057 | 1.16 | 68 | 10.3 | 86 | 13.1 | 990 | 18.8 | 1 686 | 105 | 1 008 | 118 | 1 756 |
| Ripley | 63 | 12 506 | 0.68 | 200 | 14.1 | 216 | 15.3 | 2 198 | 19.3 | 3 447 | 288 | 2 087 | 479 | 3 385 |
| St. Charles | 5 426 | 301 878 | 0.71 | 4 529 | 12.4 | 2 119 | 5.8 | 29 228 | 9.3 | 52 278 | 16 630 | 18 061 | 7 328 | 2 025 |
| St. Clair | 207 | 8 597 | 0.71 | 92 | 9.5 | 148 | 15.4 | 1 439 | 19.5 | 2 588 | 518 | 1 175 | 203 | 2 063 |
| Ste. Genevieve | 277 | 16 156 | 0.76 | 176 | 9.7 | 181 | 10.0 | 2 105 | 14.0 | 3 490 | 239 | 2 082 | 268 | 1 472 |
| St. Francois | 6 652 | 63 965 | 0.97 | 762 | 11.6 | 723 | 11.0 | 7 679 | 15.3 | 13 308 | 915 | 7 562 | 1 904 | 2 903 |
| St. Louis | 19 454 | 1 092 115 | 1.20 | 11 411 | 11.4 | 9 097 | 9.1 | 97 327 | 11.7 | 177 572 | 53 340 | 65 053 | 31 549 | 3 147 |
| Saline | 1 484 | 22 774 | 0.96 | 299 | 12.8 | 247 | 10.6 | 3 182 | 17.1 | 4 581 | 664 | 2 452 | 533 | 2 272 |
| Schuyler | 47 | 3 620 | 0.59 | 54 | 12.3 | 44 | 10.0 | 697 | 19.7 | 977 | 61 | 595 | 43 | 967 |
| Scotland | 76 | 4 500 | 0.85 | 69 | 14.3 | 52 | 10.8 | 999 | 25.5 | 952 | 45 | 619 | 51 | 1 049 |
| Scott | 559 | 38 643 | 0.96 | 552 | 14.1 | 428 | 10.9 | 5 118 | 15.5 | 8 754 | 730 | 5 611 | 1 360 | 3 458 |
| Shannon | 80 | 7 526 | 0.71 | 104 | 12.3 | 88 | 10.4 | 1 537 | 22.2 | 1 956 | 260 | 1 035 | 154 | 1 818 |
| Shelby | 198 | 5 653 | 0.74 | 74 | 11.8 | 70 | 11.1 | 965 | 19.1 | 1 420 | 110 | 883 | 64 | 1 001 |
| Stoddard | 689 | 29 537 | 0.96 | 327 | 11.0 | 373 | 12.5 | 4 361 | 17.9 | 7 200 | 903 | 4 195 | 642 | 2 135 |
| Stone | 300 | 27 931 | 0.66 | 265 | 8.2 | 343 | 10.6 | 4 952 | 20.5 | 8 718 | 2 790 | 3 094 | 756 | 2 339 |
| Sullivan | 108 | 6 849 | 1.05 | 96 | 14.4 | 80 | 12.0 | 1 219 | 22.0 | 1 450 | 77 | 930 | 92 | 1 365 |
| Taney | 1 744 | 56 052 | 1.23 | 645 | 12.2 | 450 | 8.5 | 9 574 | 23.2 | 11 564 | 3 158 | 4 354 | 2 343 | 4 518 |
| Texas | 1 897 | 24 408 | 0.84 | 296 | 11.4 | 262 | 10.1 | 3 784 | 19.3 | 5 300 | 518 | 2 707 | 532 | 2 038 |
| Vernon | 866 | 21 069 | 1.01 | 234 | 11.2 | 219 | 10.4 | 3 056 | 17.9 | 4 214 | 596 | 2 054 | 932 | 4 389 |
| Warren | 317 | 25 546 | 0.56 | 425 | 13.1 | 270 | 8.3 | 3 732 | 13.6 | 5 881 | 1 837 | 2 186 | 871 | 2 669 |
| Washington | 1 091 | 22 013 | 0.64 | 299 | 11.9 | 254 | 10.1 | 3 624 | 17.5 | 4 773 | 472 | 2 696 | 601 | 2 377 |
| Wayne | 133 | 12 073 | 0.72 | 145 | 10.8 | 203 | 15.1 | 1 950 | 18.5 | 3 535 | 438 | 2 011 | 191 | 1 408 |
| Webster | 879 | 28 972 | 0.52 | 528 | 14.5 | 324 | 8.9 | 6 081 | 19.8 | 6 891 | 3 184 | 2 012 | 682 | 1 877 |
| Worth | 52 | 1 778 | 0.65 | 19 | 8.8 | 25 | 11.6 | 352 | 21.5 | 523 | 13 | 316 | 39 | 1 790 |
| Wright | 195 | 18 277 | 0.92 | 247 | 13.2 | 216 | 11.5 | 3 161 | 20.5 | 4 667 | 1 456 | 2 003 | 413 | 2 187 |

1. Per 1,000 estimated resident population.   2. Data for serious crimes have not been adjusted for underreporting; this may affect comparability between geographic areas and over time.   3. Per 100,000 population estimated by the FBI.

# Table B. States and Counties — Crime, Education, Money Income, and Poverty

| STATE County | Serious crimes known to police, 2011 (cont.)[1] Rate[2] | | Education | | | | | | Money income, 2007–2011 | | | | Income and poverty, 2011 | | | |
|---|---|---|---|---|---|---|---|---|---|---|---|---|---|---|---|---|
| | | | School enrollment and attainment, 2007–2011 | | | | Local government expenditures,[5] 2009–2010 | | | Households | | | Percent below poverty level | | | |
| | | | Enrollment[3] | | Attainment[4] (percent) | | | | | Median income | | | | | | |
| | Violent | Property | Total | Percent private | High school graduate or less | Bachelor's degree or more | Total current expenditures (mil dol) | Current expenditures per student (dollars) | Per capita income[6] (dollars) | Dollars | Percent change, 2000 to 2007–2011 (constant 2011 dollars) | Percent with income of $200,000 or more | Median household income (dollars) | All persons | Children under 18 years | Children 5 to 17 years in families |
| | 46 | 47 | 48 | 49 | 50 | 51 | 52 | 53 | 54 | 55 | 56 | 57 | 58 | 59 | 60 | 61 |
| **MISSOURI—Cont'd** | | | | | | | | | | | | | | | | |
| Jasper | 377 | 4 048 | 29 753 | 12.4 | 50.8 | 19.3 | 159.5 | 7 595 | 20 735 | 39 522 | -6.5 | 1.4 | 39 359 | 16.8 | 24.2 | 22.6 |
| Jefferson | 250 | 2 016 | 56 376 | 15.1 | 47.5 | 16.7 | 313.3 | 8 822 | 24 965 | 56 400 | -9.9 | 1.5 | 51 008 | 11.2 | 16.6 | 15.0 |
| Johnson | 144 | 2 569 | 17 770 | 6.7 | 39.8 | 24.4 | 67.8 | 8 752 | 21 292 | 47 268 | -1.1 | 0.8 | 48 483 | 16.4 | 18.9 | 17.8 |
| Knox | 48 | 1 182 | 811 | 23.9 | 60.6 | 17.0 | 5.2 | 9 333 | 21 731 | 34 596 | -5.5 | 3.4 | 33 381 | 21.8 | 35.6 | 30.8 |
| Laclede | 543 | 3 028 | 8 399 | 12.7 | 60.7 | 13.3 | 46.6 | 7 584 | 20 784 | 39 697 | -0.5 | 1.4 | 37 442 | 17.0 | 27.0 | 24.9 |
| Lafayette | 104 | 1 821 | 7 662 | 13.4 | 53.6 | 16.4 | 49.5 | 9 147 | 23 584 | 50 000 | -3.1 | 0.7 | 47 604 | 12.6 | 18.9 | 17.3 |
| Lawrence | 407 | 3 363 | 9 088 | 13.1 | 59.5 | 14.6 | 50.4 | 8 170 | 19 357 | 39 829 | -5.6 | 0.8 | 41 128 | 17.1 | 26.6 | 23.0 |
| Lewis | 20 | 1 454 | 2 559 | 37.6 | 60.1 | 12.8 | 13.2 | 8 399 | 19 283 | 40 579 | -1.9 | 0.6 | 40 795 | 16.7 | 26.1 | 23.4 |
| Lincoln | 220 | 1 458 | 13 790 | 17.9 | 58.3 | 12.5 | 65.5 | 7 329 | 22 092 | 53 726 | -6.6 | 1.0 | 50 523 | 13.2 | 19.2 | 17.6 |
| Linn | 187 | 1 905 | 2 891 | 8.2 | 63.5 | 13.2 | 22.4 | 9 295 | 20 666 | 38 211 | 0.2 | 1.5 | 35 697 | 16.8 | 25.1 | 21.9 |
| Livingston | 269 | 2 111 | 3 273 | 11.6 | 57.0 | 19.1 | 21.5 | 9 495 | 20 203 | 42 260 | -3.1 | 1.0 | 37 956 | 15.6 | 23.2 | 20.0 |
| McDonald | 488 | 1 990 | 6 150 | 6.7 | 60.4 | 9.7 | 33.2 | 8 615 | 17 841 | 37 701 | 3.4 | 1.1 | 34 497 | 22.7 | 32.9 | 29.3 |
| Macon | 211 | 2 029 | 3 386 | 11.3 | 59.6 | 14.8 | 21.3 | 9 048 | 19 357 | 37 889 | -7.1 | 0.7 | 36 969 | 17.3 | 25.8 | 23.6 |
| Madison | 155 | 1 296 | 2 630 | 4.3 | 61.5 | 9.8 | 16.7 | 7 950 | 17 491 | 35 141 | 1.7 | 0.7 | 32 734 | 21.6 | 33.0 | 30.4 |
| Maries | 586 | 945 | 1 958 | 9.7 | 61.4 | 14.2 | 10.9 | 8 025 | 20 392 | 42 018 | -2.5 | 0.4 | 38 568 | 18.2 | 28.1 | 24.5 |
| Marion | 235 | 4 556 | 6 992 | 19.6 | 55.7 | 18.0 | 42.7 | 8 437 | 21 835 | 40 915 | -4.6 | 2.1 | 36 120 | 15.6 | 24.0 | 22.8 |
| Mercer | 237 | 369 | 821 | 6.2 | 61.0 | 13.7 | 5.8 | 10 200 | 19 577 | 34 440 | -13.9 | 0.5 | 35 483 | 16.0 | 24.3 | 22.5 |
| Miller | 382 | 2 081 | 5 971 | 11.0 | 59.9 | 13.0 | 42.5 | 8 192 | 19 133 | 36 411 | -12.9 | 0.9 | 35 573 | 19.4 | 30.6 | 28.8 |
| Mississippi | 430 | 2 700 | 2 790 | 6.2 | 74.0 | 10.7 | 18.3 | 8 096 | 15 532 | 28 474 | -8.4 | 0.0 | 29 533 | 30.8 | 40.2 | 38.5 |
| Moniteau | 77 | 804 | 3 709 | 14.3 | 58.9 | 16.9 | 19.5 | 8 110 | 19 422 | 50 887 | 1.4 | 0.2 | 43 931 | 14.5 | 20.7 | 19.1 |
| Monroe | 259 | 1 138 | 2 117 | 12.8 | 62.8 | 12.0 | 14.1 | 8 819 | 20 048 | 39 495 | -5.2 | 0.4 | 40 176 | 15.6 | 26.7 | 24.4 |
| Montgomery | 138 | 1 612 | 2 795 | 11.8 | 64.7 | 11.5 | 15.3 | 8 557 | 20 142 | 40 175 | -9.2 | 1.0 | 38 722 | 16.9 | 25.6 | 23.5 |
| Morgan | 305 | 2 074 | 3 657 | 22.6 | 59.8 | 14.0 | 18.7 | 8 918 | 18 425 | 36 928 | -10.8 | 0.1 | 34 885 | 22.0 | 34.0 | 32.1 |
| New Madrid | 398 | 1 346 | 4 269 | 8.0 | 66.4 | 13.1 | 28.7 | 10 001 | 20 373 | 34 772 | -4.0 | 1.2 | 35 522 | 22.5 | 34.2 | 29.9 |
| Newton | 178 | 2 956 | 14 603 | 12.9 | 48.1 | 18.3 | 65.1 | 7 458 | 22 054 | 41 873 | -11.5 | 2.1 | 41 722 | 16.1 | 24.7 | 22.3 |
| Nodaway | 294 | 1 825 | 9 028 | 7.9 | 50.2 | 24.0 | 28.8 | 10 487 | 18 971 | 38 680 | -9.9 | 1.0 | 38 478 | 25.0 | 18.0 | 16.2 |
| Oregon | 101 | 815 | 2 327 | 5.7 | 64.3 | 9.4 | 16.1 | 8 209 | 15 396 | 27 885 | -7.6 | 0.6 | 27 616 | 27.2 | 40.3 | 36.8 |
| Osage | 323 | 811 | 3 514 | 26.8 | 60.2 | 13.5 | 13.9 | 8 153 | 22 275 | 47 836 | -10.5 | 1.2 | 49 977 | 10.7 | 12.9 | 11.4 |
| Ozark | 123 | 1 445 | 1 634 | 5.8 | 66.3 | 10.1 | 15.7 | 9 491 | 17 710 | 31 992 | -8.4 | 0.7 | 30 284 | 24.0 | 40.7 | 36.0 |
| Pemiscot | 773 | 3 447 | 4 814 | 3.0 | 68.8 | 10.3 | 40.8 | 10 693 | 16 365 | 28 798 | -2.7 | 0.8 | 26 647 | 30.1 | 44.3 | 43.1 |
| Perry | 95 | 1 633 | 4 490 | 30.2 | 64.7 | 13.0 | 20.4 | 8 065 | 21 693 | 44 383 | -10.3 | 1.7 | 43 899 | 13.4 | 18.7 | 17.2 |
| Pettis | 375 | 4 472 | 10 670 | 12.3 | 51.8 | 15.8 | 53.2 | 8 164 | 19 909 | 38 669 | -10.0 | 1.3 | 38 026 | 18.4 | 27.1 | 25.1 |
| Phelps | 307 | 3 111 | 15 013 | 12.3 | 46.3 | 26.4 | 55.0 | 8 525 | 20 245 | 40 675 | 2.5 | 1.6 | 39 880 | 18.1 | 25.2 | 23.8 |
| Pike | 242 | 1 103 | 3 848 | 20.9 | 65.0 | 12.0 | 23.6 | 8 733 | 18 756 | 42 276 | -3.3 | 1.0 | 38 595 | 20.5 | 28.6 | 27.8 |
| Platte | 694 | 3 621 | 23 917 | 22.3 | 30.0 | 37.7 | 154.7 | 10 351 | 34 918 | 66 487 | -11.8 | 5.6 | 63 676 | 7.3 | 9.8 | 8.2 |
| Polk | 454 | 2 061 | 8 509 | 24.2 | 57.4 | 17.2 | 45.6 | 8 454 | 18 905 | 38 423 | -4.0 | 1.2 | 38 112 | 20.2 | 29.8 | 27.2 |
| Pulaski | 299 | 1 940 | 14 619 | 12.0 | 42.8 | 19.3 | 76.8 | 8 516 | 20 168 | 46 919 | 1.5 | 0.5 | 49 600 | 13.3 | 16.3 | 15.5 |
| Putnam | 0 | 640 | 1 146 | 12.3 | 59.2 | 14.9 | 6.8 | 8 903 | 20 463 | 34 556 | -2.6 | 1.6 | 34 146 | 18.8 | 30.0 | 26.7 |
| Ralls | 98 | 2 097 | 2 236 | 22.2 | 58.5 | 16.1 | 5.6 | 7 288 | 23 255 | 47 286 | -5.6 | 1.4 | 46 640 | 12.0 | 17.2 | 15.3 |
| Randolph | 153 | 2 399 | 5 905 | 14.5 | 57.7 | 12.2 | 35.2 | 8 973 | 17 345 | 36 484 | -14.1 | 1.0 | 36 590 | 18.8 | 26.8 | 24.7 |
| Ray | 187 | 2 248 | 5 813 | 11.4 | 57.0 | 14.2 | 31.1 | 8 883 | 25 759 | 54 670 | -3.3 | 1.7 | 52 222 | 12.1 | 17.9 | 15.1 |
| Reynolds | 446 | 1 310 | 1 327 | 1.8 | 69.4 | 6.9 | 12.3 | 11 101 | 17 560 | 33 382 | -4.4 | 0.2 | 29 475 | 26.9 | 43.9 | 37.7 |
| Ripley | 226 | 3 159 | 3 105 | 7.1 | 68.6 | 9.9 | 17.9 | 7 744 | 14 966 | 30 198 | -1.7 | 0.2 | 27 794 | 25.9 | 39.3 | 35.9 |
| St. Charles | 158 | 1 867 | 98 579 | 25.9 | 33.9 | 34.5 | 526.8 | 9 140 | 31 388 | 71 458 | -7.6 | 3.9 | 67 074 | 6.0 | 7.8 | 6.6 |
| St. Clair | 112 | 1 951 | 1 728 | 8.3 | 65.3 | 12.0 | 9.0 | 9 151 | 18 166 | 32 553 | -4.8 | 0.2 | 30 098 | 24.1 | 36.7 | 33.2 |
| Ste. Genevieve | 362 | 1 109 | 4 217 | 23.8 | 61.0 | 9.7 | 18.8 | 9 227 | 23 442 | 48 110 | -9.1 | 1.1 | 48 217 | 12.1 | 17.8 | 15.3 |
| St. Francois | 277 | 2 625 | 15 181 | 14.0 | 54.7 | 14.8 | 87.7 | 8 159 | 18 844 | 37 630 | -10.7 | 1.2 | 35 252 | 20.6 | 28.6 | 25.4 |
| St. Louis | 306 | 2 841 | 271 875 | 29.9 | 31.7 | 39.3 | 1 842.6 | 12 535 | 34 334 | 58 630 | -14.1 | 6.5 | 55 131 | 11.9 | 16.6 | 14.9 |
| Saline | 281 | 1 991 | 6 142 | 23.9 | 57.7 | 16.6 | 31.8 | 8 772 | 19 239 | 39 727 | -10.1 | 0.7 | 38 379 | 18.2 | 26.1 | 22.7 |
| Schuyler | 22 | 944 | 958 | 8.9 | 63.8 | 10.4 | 5.9 | 8 444 | 18 246 | 32 862 | -11.1 | 0.7 | 33 322 | 20.5 | 31.9 | 28.4 |
| Scotland | 21 | 1 029 | 778 | 35.1 | 61.9 | 18.1 | 6.3 | 10 091 | 19 178 | 36 863 | -0.4 | 1.9 | 36 804 | 17.1 | 29.1 | 26.9 |
| Scott | 778 | 2 680 | 10 093 | 12.2 | 65.7 | 13.7 | 55.6 | 8 020 | 20 088 | 39 113 | -7.6 | 1.5 | 37 793 | 19.2 | 29.2 | 26.8 |
| Shannon | 130 | 1 688 | 1 836 | 4.0 | 64.5 | 12.6 | 18.7 | 8 654 | 16 095 | 31 748 | 12.6 | 0.6 | 25 684 | 28.8 | 45.4 | 41.2 |
| Shelby | 94 | 907 | 1 480 | 10.3 | 55.5 | 13.2 | 10.7 | 10 184 | 18 458 | 35 124 | -11.7 | 0.1 | 35 321 | 18.6 | 25.8 | 23.2 |
| Stoddard | 176 | 1 958 | 6 735 | 9.0 | 67.3 | 11.4 | 41.3 | 7 990 | 21 460 | 34 839 | -4.4 | 1.2 | 35 916 | 16.6 | 24.7 | 21.5 |
| Stone | 282 | 2 058 | 5 928 | 8.7 | 54.9 | 16.2 | 37.5 | 8 501 | 21 149 | 41 069 | -6.8 | 1.5 | 37 302 | 19.8 | 32.0 | 28.5 |
| Sullivan | 193 | 1 172 | 1 413 | 4.2 | 63.4 | 10.8 | 10.9 | 9 879 | 17 599 | 33 193 | -5.8 | 0.7 | 36 039 | 16.4 | 23.6 | 21.1 |
| Taney | 538 | 3 980 | 12 162 | 23.3 | 49.6 | 19.8 | 61.7 | 7 874 | 22 192 | 40 120 | -3.8 | 2.2 | 36 176 | 19.7 | 31.9 | 29.9 |
| Texas | 77 | 1 961 | 5 525 | 10.6 | 63.1 | 11.6 | 33.3 | 8 160 | 17 034 | 33 128 | 0.0 | 1.8 | 32 193 | 21.9 | 34.6 | 31.9 |
| Vernon | 443 | 3 946 | 4 978 | 14.9 | 59.7 | 13.7 | 28.4 | 8 821 | 18 554 | 37 312 | -7.9 | 0.4 | 37 342 | 20.5 | 30.5 | 26.9 |
| Warren | 303 | 2 366 | 7 308 | 24.0 | 54.0 | 15.9 | 36.0 | 7 946 | 25 645 | 50 182 | -9.4 | 3.1 | 50 773 | 12.8 | 20.7 | 19.3 |
| Washington | 178 | 2 199 | 5 523 | 7.8 | 70.4 | 7.5 | 31.2 | 8 052 | 16 841 | 35 148 | -4.0 | 0.5 | 30 896 | 26.6 | 38.5 | 38.1 |
| Wayne | 103 | 1 304 | 2 680 | 6.5 | 66.9 | 8.0 | 15.6 | 8 392 | 17 925 | 29 331 | -9.5 | 0.5 | 28 066 | 25.7 | 39.1 | 36.1 |
| Webster | 102 | 1 775 | 8 612 | 17.6 | 58.9 | 13.8 | 53.6 | 7 388 | 18 709 | 41 764 | -3.1 | 1.0 | 39 261 | 19.7 | 32.8 | 29.6 |
| Worth | 92 | 1 698 | 465 | 9.0 | 61.4 | 15.6 | 3.5 | 8 884 | 19 409 | 39 671 | 7.0 | 0.2 | 38 105 | 15.9 | 24.8 | 21.8 |
| Wright | 207 | 1 981 | 4 331 | 14.2 | 64.5 | 11.6 | 29.6 | 8 167 | 15 706 | 29 212 | -12.4 | 0.4 | 27 007 | 28.7 | 39.0 | 35.7 |

1. Data for serious crimes have not been adjusted for underreporting; this may affect comparability between geographic areas and over time.  2. Per 100,000 population estimated by the FBI.  3. All persons 3 years old and over enrolled in nursery school through college.  4. Persons 25 years old and over.  5. Elementary and secondary education expenditures.  6. Based on population estimated by the American Community Survey, 2007–2011.

# Table B. States and Counties — Personal Income

| STATE County | Personal income, 2011 Total (mil dol) [62] | Percent change, 2010–2011 [63] | Per capita[1] Dollars [64] | Per capita[1] Rank [65] | Wages and salaries[2] (mil dol) [66] | Proprietors' income (mil dol) [67] | Dividends, interest, and rent (mil dol) [68] | Transfer payments (mil dol) Total [69] | Government payments to individuals Total [70] | Social Security [71] | Medical payments [72] | Income maintenance [73] | Unemployment insurance [74] |
|---|---|---|---|---|---|---|---|---|---|---|---|---|---|
| | 62 | 63 | 64 | 65 | 66 | 67 | 68 | 69 | 70 | 71 | 72 | 73 | 74 |
| **MISSOURI—Cont'd** | | | | | | | | | | | | | |
| Jasper | 3 519 | 3.2 | 29 709 | 2 335 | 2 721 | 267 | 537 | 917 | 891 | 282 | 415 | 109 | 25 |
| Jefferson | 7 612 | 4.9 | 34 681 | 1 421 | 2 174 | 447 | 781 | 1 467 | 1 418 | 553 | 594 | 119 | 59 |
| Johnson | 1 584 | 5.6 | 29 639 | 2 354 | 1 058 | 155 | 208 | 328 | 316 | 98 | 134 | 30 | 13 |
| Knox | 129 | 3.9 | 31 360 | 2 030 | 40 | 28 | 22 | 35 | 34 | 12 | 16 | 3 | 1 |
| Laclede | 977 | 4.8 | 27 424 | 2 698 | 509 | 70 | 144 | 299 | 291 | 100 | 124 | 37 | 10 |
| Lafayette | 1 256 | 5.1 | 37 831 | 994 | 354 | 129 | 159 | 297 | 289 | 97 | 145 | 23 | 9 |
| Lawrence | 1 040 | 4.6 | 26 896 | 2 776 | 369 | 58 | 155 | 296 | 287 | 108 | 119 | 34 | 8 |
| Lewis | 295 | 6.4 | 29 094 | 2 439 | 103 | 34 | 42 | 76 | 73 | 27 | 33 | 6 | 2 |
| Lincoln | 1 609 | 5.6 | 30 310 | 2 237 | 476 | 110 | 179 | 360 | 348 | 126 | 157 | 35 | 16 |
| Linn | 406 | 4.4 | 32 343 | 1 814 | 180 | 54 | 68 | 119 | 117 | 37 | 54 | 10 | 4 |
| Livingston | 494 | 6.3 | 32 776 | 1 745 | 255 | 69 | 88 | 128 | 125 | 42 | 62 | 11 | 3 |
| McDonald | 571 | 0.3 | 24 849 | 2 979 | 263 | 35 | 58 | 153 | 148 | 49 | 64 | 24 | 5 |
| Macon | 486 | 3.7 | 31 164 | 2 070 | 199 | 46 | 82 | 141 | 137 | 49 | 65 | 11 | 4 |
| Madison | 332 | 4.7 | 27 258 | 2 727 | 130 | 16 | 44 | 126 | 123 | 41 | 59 | 13 | 3 |
| Maries | 293 | 5.1 | 31 954 | 1 897 | 50 | 53 | 36 | 73 | 71 | 24 | 33 | 6 | 2 |
| Marion | 982 | 4.4 | 34 200 | 1 485 | 635 | 90 | 151 | 275 | 268 | 79 | 139 | 27 | 6 |
| Mercer | 104 | 6.2 | 27 364 | 2 704 | 42 | 17 | 16 | 28 | 27 | 11 | 12 | 2 | 1 |
| Miller | 675 | 3.3 | 27 262 | 2 725 | 234 | 66 | 92 | 206 | 200 | 64 | 95 | 23 | 7 |
| Mississippi | 396 | 2.4 | 27 683 | 2 655 | 151 | 51 | 54 | 135 | 132 | 38 | 64 | 21 | 4 |
| Moniteau | 503 | 4.6 | 32 019 | 1 884 | 159 | 60 | 67 | 102 | 98 | 37 | 43 | 9 | 3 |
| Monroe | 276 | 3.3 | 31 604 | 1 977 | 77 | 50 | 44 | 76 | 74 | 28 | 33 | 6 | 2 |
| Montgomery | 388 | 0.9 | 31 609 | 1 975 | 121 | 37 | 63 | 109 | 106 | 38 | 52 | 10 | 3 |
| Morgan | 606 | 4.1 | 29 580 | 2 366 | 145 | 65 | 133 | 206 | 201 | 79 | 86 | 19 | 6 |
| New Madrid | 602 | 7.7 | 32 065 | 1 866 | 354 | 106 | 57 | 184 | 180 | 50 | 93 | 26 | 5 |
| Newton | 2 036 | 7.0 | 34 854 | 1 395 | 923 | 112 | 276 | 445 | 432 | 153 | 185 | 47 | 13 |
| Nodaway | 636 | 4.6 | 27 114 | 2 752 | 370 | 84 | 102 | 133 | 128 | 46 | 51 | 9 | 4 |
| Oregon | 273 | 5.8 | 24 768 | 2 984 | 91 | 28 | 36 | 114 | 112 | 32 | 54 | 14 | 2 |
| Osage | 488 | 4.3 | 35 100 | 1 357 | 145 | 42 | 66 | 88 | 85 | 32 | 37 | 6 | 3 |
| Ozark | 245 | 7.6 | 25 491 | 2 930 | 52 | 13 | 38 | 108 | 106 | 38 | 50 | 10 | 2 |
| Pemiscot | 617 | 8.9 | 33 937 | 1 523 | 247 | 88 | 61 | 216 | 212 | 49 | 113 | 38 | 5 |
| Perry | 585 | 3.4 | 30 747 | 2 149 | 393 | 34 | 84 | 138 | 134 | 49 | 62 | 13 | 4 |
| Pettis | 1 342 | 3.0 | 31 806 | 1 933 | 811 | 115 | 192 | 356 | 346 | 104 | 158 | 39 | 10 |
| Phelps | 1 409 | 4.3 | 31 287 | 2 046 | 830 | 71 | 198 | 353 | 343 | 106 | 157 | 36 | 10 |
| Pike | 553 | 4.2 | 29 756 | 2 329 | 246 | 57 | 96 | 147 | 143 | 49 | 70 | 13 | 4 |
| Platte | 4 051 | 4.8 | 44 561 | 417 | 2 211 | 224 | 520 | 487 | 467 | 201 | 180 | 31 | 21 |
| Polk | 846 | 6.0 | 27 154 | 2 745 | 333 | 52 | 120 | 271 | 264 | 81 | 130 | 28 | 7 |
| Pulaski | 2 215 | 8.8 | 41 655 | 604 | 2 120 | 48 | 186 | 291 | 282 | 67 | 115 | 35 | 12 |
| Putnam | 140 | 10.6 | 28 131 | 2 601 | 45 | 18 | 26 | 44 | 43 | 16 | 21 | 4 | 1 |
| Ralls | 347 | 4.7 | 33 785 | 1 549 | 120 | 29 | 50 | 75 | 73 | 30 | 31 | 6 | 2 |
| Randolph | 828 | 5.2 | 32 687 | 1 761 | 443 | 109 | 104 | 240 | 234 | 61 | 108 | 23 | 7 |
| Ray | 843 | 3.6 | 36 311 | 1 166 | 179 | 105 | 84 | 176 | 171 | 66 | 75 | 14 | 6 |
| Reynolds | 177 | 2.3 | 26 915 | 2 773 | 80 | 7 | 23 | 77 | 75 | 23 | 39 | 8 | 2 |
| Ripley | 365 | 3.2 | 25 807 | 2 901 | 101 | 30 | 40 | 161 | 158 | 44 | 80 | 21 | 4 |
| St. Charles | 15 065 | 6.4 | 41 257 | 636 | 6 567 | 670 | 1 842 | 2 022 | 1 942 | 847 | 771 | 113 | 83 |
| St. Clair | 262 | 0.7 | 27 128 | 2 747 | 65 | 25 | 45 | 96 | 94 | 35 | 42 | 9 | 2 |
| Ste. Genevieve | 610 | 3.8 | 33 652 | 1 577 | 296 | 21 | 103 | 134 | 130 | 53 | 53 | 11 | 5 |
| St. Francois | 1 829 | 4.5 | 27 886 | 2 629 | 939 | 87 | 225 | 598 | 583 | 187 | 273 | 64 | 18 |
| St. Louis | 52 714 | 4.6 | 52 783 | 147 | 38 969 | 4 274 | 11 648 | 7 263 | 7 043 | 2 782 | 3 055 | 625 | 246 |
| Saline | 865 | 10.1 | 37 154 | 1 066 | 376 | 169 | 112 | 238 | 233 | 62 | 133 | 20 | 5 |
| Schuyler | 113 | 5.8 | 25 902 | 2 892 | 27 | 13 | 19 | 38 | 37 | 12 | 19 | 3 | 1 |
| Scotland | 143 | 5.3 | 29 645 | 2 352 | 45 | 28 | 29 | 34 | 33 | 12 | 16 | 3 | 1 |
| Scott | 1 417 | 5.8 | 36 219 | 1 186 | 642 | 202 | 183 | 393 | 385 | 116 | 183 | 52 | 10 |
| Shannon | 187 | 3.3 | 22 152 | 3 083 | 40 | 24 | 25 | 78 | 76 | 24 | 34 | 11 | 3 |
| Shelby | 216 | 5.9 | 34 336 | 1 466 | 73 | 44 | 36 | 53 | 51 | 18 | 25 | 5 | 1 |
| Stoddard | 1 001 | 7.2 | 33 574 | 1 587 | 439 | 161 | 131 | 291 | 284 | 94 | 135 | 30 | 8 |
| Stone | 1 072 | 4.9 | 33 231 | 1 668 | 228 | 135 | 180 | 295 | 287 | 126 | 110 | 23 | 10 |
| Sullivan | 226 | 5.4 | 33 965 | 1 518 | 120 | 43 | 28 | 60 | 59 | 18 | 31 | 6 | 1 |
| Taney | 1 435 | 4.2 | 27 214 | 2 735 | 1 005 | 67 | 210 | 438 | 426 | 164 | 173 | 43 | 19 |
| Texas | 632 | 5.2 | 24 362 | 3 011 | 238 | 32 | 89 | 213 | 207 | 69 | 90 | 24 | 6 |
| Vernon | 650 | 4.3 | 31 011 | 2 099 | 326 | 79 | 87 | 190 | 185 | 57 | 95 | 20 | 4 |
| Warren | 1 096 | 5.5 | 33 708 | 1 562 | 298 | 42 | 151 | 245 | 238 | 94 | 104 | 21 | 9 |
| Washington | 639 | 4.9 | 25 481 | 2 931 | 186 | 28 | 53 | 236 | 230 | 66 | 114 | 33 | 7 |
| Wayne | 347 | 2.1 | 25 778 | 2 903 | 92 | 18 | 39 | 152 | 149 | 46 | 74 | 17 | 3 |
| Webster | 994 | 4.9 | 27 266 | 2 722 | 272 | 50 | 119 | 260 | 252 | 94 | 107 | 28 | 8 |
| Worth | 64 | 5.4 | 29 600 | 2 362 | 15 | 10 | 12 | 17 | 16 | 6 | 6 | 2 | 0 |
| Wright | 460 | 7.3 | 24 580 | 2 998 | 176 | 10 | 75 | 182 | 178 | 59 | 80 | 24 | 4 |

1. Based on the resident population estimated as of July 1 of the year shown.   2. Includes supplements to wages and salaries.

| STATE County | Earnings, 2011 | | | | | | | | | Social Security beneficiaries, December 2011 | | Housing units, 2010 | |
|---|---|---|---|---|---|---|---|---|---|---|---|---|---|
| | | | | Percent by selected industries | | | | | | | | | |
| | | | Goods-related[1] | | Service-related and health | | | | | | | | |
| | Total (mil dol) | Farm | Total | Manu-facturing | Infor-mation and profes-sional and technical services | Retail trade | Finance, insur-ance, and real estate | Health care and social services | Govern-ment | Number | Rate[2] | Supple-mental Security Income recipients, December 2011 | Total | Percent change, 2000–2010 |
| | 75 | 76 | 77 | 78 | 79 | 80 | 81 | 82 | 83 | 84 | 85 | 86 | 87 | 88 |
| MISSOURI—Cont'd | | | | | | | | | | | | | | |
| Jasper | 2 988 | 0.3 | 22.9 | 18.6 | 4.1 | 8.9 | 4.0 | 10.8 | 12.4 | 23 245 | 196 | 3 162 | 50 668 | 11.2 |
| Jefferson | 2 621 | 0.0 | 22.8 | 10.7 | 4.3 | 8.2 | 4.8 | 11.5 | 18.5 | 40 535 | 185 | 3 056 | 87 626 | 15.9 |
| Johnson | 1 213 | 2.7 | D | 5.7 | 2.3 | 5.3 | 3.7 | 4.4 | 59.7 | 7 775 | 145 | 688 | 21 528 | 14.0 |
| Knox | 68 | 25.0 | D | 8.8 | 6.3 | 4.4 | 4.3 | 2.8 | 19.4 | 1 060 | 257 | 93 | 2 289 | -1.2 |
| Laclede | 579 | 0.5 | 37.4 | 33.0 | 2.7 | 11.7 | 4.0 | 11.2 | 13.6 | 8 815 | 247 | 1 135 | 15 778 | 10.2 |
| Lafayette | 483 | 14.1 | 15.3 | 8.2 | 6.7 | 8.0 | 4.6 | D | 21.6 | 7 530 | 227 | 521 | 14 718 | 7.4 |
| Lawrence | 427 | 7.0 | 20.7 | 14.4 | 3.1 | 9.9 | 3.3 | D | 27.1 | 9 275 | 240 | 907 | 16 649 | 12.6 |
| Lewis | 137 | 18.4 | D | 3.7 | D | 6.2 | D | D | 20.0 | 2 265 | 223 | 179 | 4 535 | -1.4 |
| Lincoln | 586 | 3.8 | 26.9 | 13.5 | 2.8 | 9.9 | 5.8 | 4.7 | 22.1 | 9 570 | 180 | 877 | 21 011 | 35.5 |
| Linn | 234 | 10.2 | D | 12.1 | 6.2 | 8.6 | 6.2 | 9.5 | 16.0 | 3 215 | 256 | 369 | 6 429 | -1.9 |
| Livingston | 323 | 10.6 | D | 7.8 | 3.3 | 10.1 | 5.0 | D | 20.5 | 3 485 | 231 | 346 | 6 730 | 4.1 |
| McDonald | 298 | 2.3 | D | 35.4 | D | 11.9 | 2.4 | D | 17.2 | 4 335 | 189 | 597 | 9 925 | 6.9 |
| Macon | 245 | 5.9 | 17.1 | 11.3 | 6.1 | 7.3 | 3.6 | D | 33.5 | 4 100 | 263 | 314 | 7 665 | 2.2 |
| Madison | 146 | 0.6 | D | 10.5 | D | 12.0 | 2.8 | 9.2 | 26.8 | 3 480 | 285 | 515 | 5 970 | 5.6 |
| Maries | 103 | 2.2 | D | 18.0 | D | 8.5 | D | 6.3 | 14.1 | 2 025 | 221 | 165 | 4 611 | 11.1 |
| Marion | 725 | 3.5 | D | 16.1 | D | 8.1 | 3.9 | D | 13.3 | 6 585 | 229 | 1 028 | 12 826 | 3.1 |
| Mercer | 58 | 40.6 | D | D | D | 3.3 | D | D | 19.4 | 925 | 243 | 97 | 2 135 | 0.5 |
| Miller | 300 | 8.7 | 16.5 | 6.2 | D | 12.0 | 4.8 | D | 22.0 | 5 465 | 221 | 624 | 12 758 | 13.3 |
| Mississippi | 203 | 11.2 | 7.2 | 4.9 | 1.1 | 8.5 | 4.5 | D | 24.7 | 3 365 | 235 | 719 | 5 711 | -2.2 |
| Moniteau | 219 | 15.7 | D | 15.3 | 1.7 | 6.7 | 3.9 | D | 22.4 | 3 040 | 194 | 210 | 6 176 | 7.6 |
| Monroe | 127 | 23.6 | D | 11.7 | 3.1 | 4.9 | D | 4.2 | 24.0 | 2 280 | 261 | 189 | 4 798 | 5.1 |
| Montgomery | 159 | 10.2 | 24.6 | 15.3 | D | 8.2 | 5.5 | 6.6 | 21.8 | 2 995 | 244 | 286 | 6 130 | 7.1 |
| Morgan | 210 | 17.2 | D | 9.9 | D | 12.8 | 4.3 | D | 21.9 | 6 290 | 307 | 575 | 15 517 | 11.7 |
| New Madrid | 460 | 18.7 | 26.1 | 24.3 | D | 9.4 | 1.8 | 5.7 | 10.7 | 4 395 | 234 | 999 | 8 531 | -0.8 |
| Newton | 1 035 | 3.7 | D | 15.3 | 2.6 | 7.8 | 3.2 | 28.2 | 12.7 | 12 670 | 217 | 1 284 | 24 313 | 11.0 |
| Nodaway | 454 | 10.6 | D | 20.6 | 3.1 | 6.8 | 2.9 | 10.9 | 26.4 | 3 770 | 161 | 268 | 9 524 | 6.9 |
| Oregon | 119 | 4.9 | D | 8.7 | D | 11.2 | 3.9 | D | 19.3 | 3 045 | 276 | 658 | 5 486 | 9.8 |
| Osage | 187 | 8.6 | 32.5 | 24.0 | D | 8.2 | 3.8 | 6.2 | 18.8 | 2 655 | 191 | 154 | 6 533 | 10.7 |
| Ozark | 65 | 3.5 | D | 5.3 | D | 9.9 | 8.0 | 5.7 | 31.4 | 3 200 | 334 | 351 | 5 652 | 10.5 |
| Pemiscot | 335 | 19.3 | D | 13.9 | 0.8 | 7.4 | 3.6 | 6.9 | 25.0 | 4 635 | 255 | 1 603 | 8 161 | -7.2 |
| Perry | 427 | 0.9 | D | 33.3 | D | 6.9 | 4.4 | D | 13.6 | 3 945 | 207 | 377 | 8 568 | 9.6 |
| Pettis | 926 | 3.6 | 29.4 | 24.1 | 7.5 | 8.0 | 3.7 | 8.0 | 17.7 | 8 815 | 209 | 1 169 | 18 249 | 7.6 |
| Phelps | 901 | 0.0 | D | 6.1 | 3.6 | 8.2 | 3.4 | 13.2 | 39.4 | 9 105 | 202 | 1 166 | 19 533 | 11.6 |
| Pike | 303 | 10.2 | 14.7 | 8.1 | 4.4 | 11.7 | 2.9 | 5.8 | 26.8 | 3 955 | 213 | 432 | 7 875 | 5.1 |
| Platte | 2 435 | 1.1 | D | 8.3 | 6.8 | 7.9 | 7.0 | 6.5 | 10.6 | 13 715 | 151 | 621 | 39 223 | 26.9 |
| Polk | 384 | 2.1 | 7.0 | 2.4 | D | 9.5 | 4.7 | D | 30.8 | 6 935 | 222 | 786 | 13 304 | 19.0 |
| Pulaski | 2 168 | -0.1 | D | 0.3 | 1.6 | 2.3 | 1.2 | 1.7 | 84.7 | 6 235 | 117 | 771 | 17 904 | 16.2 |
| Putnam | 62 | 21.1 | 8.1 | 5.1 | D | 7.4 | 7.6 | 2.6 | 28.9 | 1 375 | 276 | 139 | 2 982 | 2.4 |
| Ralls | 149 | 14.1 | D | 30.8 | D | 4.5 | 1.9 | D | 14.3 | 2 360 | 230 | 179 | 5 183 | 13.6 |
| Randolph | 552 | 1.4 | D | 11.7 | D | 14.8 | 5.9 | 11.5 | 18.4 | 5 200 | 205 | 749 | 10 714 | -0.2 |
| Ray | 284 | 6.9 | D | 8.3 | 4.2 | 11.6 | 5.5 | D | 23.4 | 4 935 | 212 | 301 | 9 984 | 6.5 |
| Reynolds | 88 | -0.9 | D | 5.7 | D | 4.4 | D | 9.5 | 20.2 | 1 960 | 298 | 269 | 4 033 | 7.3 |
| Ripley | 131 | 4.6 | 17.4 | 14.2 | D | 9.4 | 4.2 | 14.3 | 26.9 | 4 080 | 288 | 846 | 6 597 | 3.2 |
| St. Charles | 7 237 | 0.3 | 18.6 | 10.7 | 12.1 | 8.3 | 9.8 | 10.4 | 12.9 | 57 495 | 157 | 2 465 | 141 016 | 33.6 |
| St. Clair | 90 | 5.8 | D | 1.8 | 2.7 | 9.9 | 3.6 | 9.8 | 31.9 | 2 930 | 304 | 295 | 5 640 | 8.4 |
| Ste. Genevieve | 317 | 2.2 | 40.5 | 27.0 | D | 5.3 | 3.0 | D | 16.8 | 4 050 | 223 | 286 | 8 637 | 7.7 |
| St. Francois | 1 027 | 0.3 | 14.3 | 8.0 | 3.6 | 8.8 | 7.7 | 15.6 | 26.4 | 15 320 | 234 | 2 525 | 28 458 | 16.4 |
| St. Louis | 43 243 | 0.0 | 15.8 | 9.9 | 14.4 | 6.0 | 9.1 | 12.5 | 8.6 | 190 500 | 191 | 16 525 | 438 032 | 3.4 |
| Saline | 545 | 18.1 | 20.4 | 17.7 | D | 5.5 | 2.6 | D | 17.2 | 5 080 | 218 | 641 | 10 117 | 1.0 |
| Schuyler | 40 | 15.5 | D | D | D | 9.8 | D | 3.3 | 34.3 | 1 075 | 245 | 108 | 2 102 | 3.7 |
| Scotland | 74 | 19.7 | D | 3.9 | D | 7.9 | D | D | 36.9 | 1 040 | 215 | 71 | 2 369 | 3.4 |
| Scott | 844 | 5.3 | D | 13.4 | 12.5 | 5.3 | 4.0 | D | 13.9 | 9 875 | 252 | 1 792 | 16 987 | 0.2 |
| Shannon | 65 | 0.6 | D | 15.9 | D | 9.1 | 4.8 | D | 23.7 | 2 305 | 273 | 390 | 4 164 | 7.8 |
| Shelby | 116 | 25.1 | D | 10.9 | 2.1 | 8.0 | 2.8 | D | 20.6 | 1 555 | 248 | 139 | 3 206 | -1.2 |
| Stoddard | 600 | 16.9 | D | 23.3 | 2.5 | 7.6 | 3.8 | 8.7 | 12.4 | 8 180 | 274 | 1 128 | 13 609 | 2.9 |
| Stone | 363 | 0.4 | D | D | D | 12.1 | 9.7 | D | 15.1 | 9 765 | 303 | 522 | 20 373 | 25.4 |
| Sullivan | 163 | 25.4 | D | D | 3.1 | 4.9 | 3.0 | 2.5 | 14.6 | 1 620 | 243 | 195 | 3 358 | -0.2 |
| Taney | 1 072 | -0.1 | D | 2.1 | 4.3 | 11.5 | 5.9 | 11.6 | 11.7 | 13 115 | 249 | 1 010 | 29 255 | 48.6 |
| Texas | 270 | 1.3 | 20.0 | 14.6 | 2.6 | 8.7 | 3.7 | 5.2 | 34.8 | 6 210 | 239 | 828 | 11 685 | 8.6 |
| Vernon | 405 | 10.7 | 25.4 | 21.7 | 2.8 | 6.4 | 5.0 | D | 21.7 | 4 855 | 232 | 658 | 9 495 | 7.0 |
| Warren | 340 | 3.1 | D | 27.0 | D | 8.5 | 3.8 | 5.4 | 18.5 | 6 825 | 210 | 447 | 14 685 | 32.9 |
| Washington | 214 | 0.6 | D | 19.9 | 1.5 | 6.6 | 3.0 | 6.1 | 37.7 | 5 625 | 224 | 1 230 | 11 017 | 11.4 |
| Wayne | 110 | 1.7 | D | 12.7 | D | 9.8 | 3.9 | 7.8 | 28.5 | 4 090 | 304 | 724 | 8 083 | 7.8 |
| Webster | 322 | 1.8 | D | 12.8 | D | 11.1 | 4.4 | 5.2 | 23.3 | 7 900 | 217 | 785 | 14 417 | 19.6 |
| Worth | 25 | 28.5 | D | D | D | 5.5 | 3.0 | 3.3 | 32.4 | 570 | 265 | 49 | 1 281 | 2.9 |
| Wright | 186 | 2.9 | D | 10.6 | D | 12.6 | 4.5 | D | 22.7 | 5 410 | 289 | 838 | 8 700 | 9.3 |

1. Includes mining, construction, and manufacturing.   2. Per 1,000 resident population enumerated in the 2010 census.

# Table B. States and Counties — **Housing, Labor Force, and Employment**

| STATE County | Housing units, 2007–2011 | | | | | | | | Civilian labor force, 2012 | | | | Civilian employment,[6] 2007–2011 | | |
|---|---|---|---|---|---|---|---|---|---|---|---|---|---|---|---|
| | Occupied units | | | | | | | | | | Unemployment | | | Percent | |
| | | Owner-occupied | | | | Renter-occupied | | | | | | | | | |
| | | | | Median owner cost as a percent of income | | | | | | | | | | | Con-struction, produc-tion, and mainte-nance occu-pations |
| | Total | Percent | Median value[1] | With a mort-gage | Without a mort-gage[2] | Median rent[3] | Median rent as a per-cent of income | Sub-stand-ard units[4] (percent) | Total | Percent change, 2011–2012 | Total | Rate[5] | Total | Manage-ment, business, science and arts | |
| | 89 | 90 | 91 | 92 | 93 | 94 | 95 | 96 | 97 | 98 | 99 | 100 | 101 | 102 | 103 |
| **MISSOURI—Cont'd** | | | | | | | | | | | | | | | |
| Jasper | 44 674 | 65.3 | 96 900 | 21.6 | 11.8 | 637 | 30.3 | 3.2 | 57 532 | -0.5 | 3 422 | 5.9 | 53 259 | 27.9 | 28.4 |
| Jefferson | 80 703 | 82.9 | 154 100 | 22.6 | 11.3 | 702 | 27.2 | 1.6 | 115 324 | -1.4 | 8 499 | 7.4 | 106 824 | 28.3 | 29.2 |
| Johnson | 19 435 | 64.3 | 135 700 | 22.5 | 10.1 | 679 | 31.2 | 2.2 | 25 088 | -1.3 | 1 733 | 6.9 | 22 346 | 28.9 | 26.7 |
| Knox | 1 760 | 73.4 | 53 900 | 20.6 | 12.6 | 432 | 24.4 | 4.4 | 2 197 | -1.8 | 108 | 4.9 | 1 853 | 32.3 | 33.7 |
| Laclede | 14 357 | 71.5 | 94 400 | 22.6 | 10.9 | 579 | 26.1 | 3.2 | 15 885 | -1.4 | 1 437 | 9.0 | 15 395 | 21.3 | 40.0 |
| Lafayette | 13 290 | 74.9 | 120 800 | 21.2 | 11.7 | 604 | 22.0 | 2.2 | 16 382 | -1.0 | 1 217 | 7.4 | 16 252 | 29.2 | 31.9 |
| Lawrence | 15 012 | 72.8 | 96 300 | 23.1 | 11.2 | 578 | 28.7 | 3.1 | 18 554 | -0.8 | 1 117 | 6.0 | 16 623 | 27.4 | 34.7 |
| Lewis | 3 795 | 75.2 | 80 100 | 19.7 | 10.5 | 448 | 21.9 | 2.9 | 5 492 | -0.9 | 309 | 5.6 | 4 668 | 24.1 | 34.6 |
| Lincoln | 18 638 | 81.5 | 156 100 | 23.3 | 11.5 | 693 | 31.3 | 2.0 | 26 703 | -1.8 | 2 221 | 8.3 | 23 841 | 24.7 | 33.8 |
| Linn | 4 968 | 74.6 | 68 600 | 20.0 | 12.2 | 513 | 34.4 | 1.6 | 5 697 | -4.0 | 472 | 8.3 | 5 179 | 27.3 | 34.9 |
| Livingston | 5 547 | 69.5 | 93 600 | 18.7 | 11.2 | 600 | 30.3 | 1.7 | 6 949 | 0.3 | 454 | 6.5 | 6 759 | 28.0 | 32.1 |
| McDonald | 8 240 | 69.0 | 88 100 | 20.8 | 12.1 | 548 | 25.3 | 6.3 | 10 842 | 0.9 | 676 | 6.2 | 9 858 | 21.7 | 38.2 |
| Macon | 6 311 | 76.4 | 84 100 | 22.4 | 12.1 | 527 | 27.9 | 2.6 | 7 794 | -2.1 | 495 | 6.4 | 6 874 | 30.5 | 30.2 |
| Madison | 4 774 | 76.6 | 85 600 | 24.0 | 12.3 | 554 | 30.6 | 1.9 | 6 038 | -1.4 | 426 | 7.1 | 4 951 | 21.5 | 38.9 |
| Maries | 3 635 | 80.5 | 116 200 | 22.2 | 9.9 | 528 | 30.8 | 2.9 | 4 701 | -1.4 | 293 | 6.2 | 4 048 | 32.0 | 30.7 |
| Marion | 11 194 | 68.9 | 99 000 | 19.8 | 11.5 | 553 | 27.8 | 1.7 | 14 228 | -1.5 | 860 | 6.0 | 13 029 | 28.4 | 29.6 |
| Mercer | 1 560 | 76.0 | 69 600 | 18.7 | 11.9 | 464 | 25.0 | 2.6 | 1 929 | -0.7 | 93 | 4.8 | 1 544 | 36.2 | 31.2 |
| Miller | 10 320 | 76.2 | 109 300 | 22.1 | 10.7 | 557 | 28.9 | 3.0 | 11 518 | -0.7 | 1 016 | 8.8 | 11 196 | 24.6 | 30.3 |
| Mississippi | 5 289 | 64.7 | 65 200 | 22.4 | 11.4 | 511 | 37.6 | 3.6 | 6 100 | 1.7 | 513 | 8.4 | 5 587 | 22.9 | 33.0 |
| Moniteau | 5 507 | 75.9 | 114 500 | 21.5 | 9.9 | 574 | 24.1 | 2.3 | 7 390 | -1.3 | 484 | 6.5 | 6 565 | 31.4 | 31.7 |
| Monroe | 3 630 | 77.2 | 83 700 | 22.2 | 11.8 | 515 | 24.3 | 2.1 | 3 870 | -1.5 | 317 | 8.2 | 3 948 | 27.5 | 33.2 |
| Montgomery | 4 979 | 76.8 | 107 600 | 24.0 | 9.9 | 567 | 25.9 | 1.9 | 5 682 | -2.8 | 454 | 8.0 | 5 442 | 19.8 | 38.0 |
| Morgan | 8 215 | 83.4 | 116 700 | 24.2 | 11.6 | 513 | 25.3 | 5.9 | 8 686 | -0.9 | 764 | 8.8 | 7 329 | 28.7 | 32.2 |
| New Madrid | 7 620 | 62.8 | 70 700 | 19.0 | 11.4 | 473 | 25.8 | 1.6 | 8 420 | -2.0 | 646 | 7.7 | 7 792 | 25.7 | 34.9 |
| Newton | 21 719 | 75.1 | 106 500 | 21.8 | 10.7 | 578 | 26.0 | 3.4 | 28 747 | -0.5 | 1 783 | 6.2 | 26 038 | 28.6 | 28.8 |
| Nodaway | 8 574 | 58.6 | 98 300 | 19.8 | 9.9 | 529 | 31.1 | 1.3 | 11 895 | 0.7 | 651 | 5.5 | 11 730 | 25.7 | 29.9 |
| Oregon | 4 518 | 76.0 | 70 700 | 23.1 | 13.3 | 518 | 27.8 | 3.4 | 4 528 | -0.4 | 313 | 6.9 | 3 760 | 18.9 | 38.7 |
| Osage | 5 331 | 83.9 | 117 300 | 20.7 | 9.9 | 494 | 24.7 | 1.7 | 7 189 | -1.4 | 371 | 5.2 | 6 723 | 28.6 | 34.1 |
| Ozark | 4 000 | 82.0 | 101 700 | 23.9 | 10.1 | 494 | 33.7 | 3.2 | 4 292 | -0.3 | 346 | 8.1 | 3 400 | 21.6 | 38.6 |
| Pemiscot | 6 842 | 56.1 | 65 100 | 20.9 | 11.9 | 482 | 31.4 | 3.4 | 8 218 | -1.9 | 664 | 8.1 | 6 578 | 22.6 | 31.8 |
| Perry | 7 600 | 78.4 | 120 200 | 21.7 | 11.1 | 590 | 26.9 | 2.9 | 10 608 | 0.4 | 501 | 4.7 | 9 271 | 22.7 | 36.7 |
| Pettis | 16 275 | 71.2 | 97 700 | 22.6 | 11.3 | 620 | 30.8 | 3.4 | 19 917 | -0.8 | 1 383 | 6.9 | 18 901 | 24.8 | 36.0 |
| Phelps | 16 688 | 64.8 | 112 700 | 21.7 | 9.9 | 597 | 29.8 | 1.2 | 21 530 | -1.3 | 1 369 | 6.4 | 19 269 | 34.7 | 21.7 |
| Pike | 6 581 | 72.2 | 93 300 | 19.8 | 10.7 | 542 | 27.7 | 3.5 | 8 857 | -1.2 | 590 | 6.7 | 7 590 | 24.6 | 29.8 |
| Platte | 35 686 | 65.9 | 188 400 | 21.6 | 11.0 | 827 | 25.8 | 1.8 | 50 767 | 0.0 | 2 860 | 5.6 | 46 564 | 40.9 | 18.4 |
| Polk | 11 700 | 71.5 | 113 500 | 22.8 | 12.0 | 577 | 26.4 | 2.5 | 14 274 | 0.1 | 1 058 | 7.4 | 12 478 | 30.0 | 27.5 |
| Pulaski | 15 708 | 55.4 | 122 600 | 22.3 | 9.9 | 908 | 24.9 | 2.3 | 19 431 | -5.5 | 1 595 | 8.2 | 14 866 | 32.0 | 23.4 |
| Putnam | 2 238 | 74.6 | 94 900 | 27.7 | 14.2 | 541 | 32.0 | 2.3 | 2 348 | -2.3 | 134 | 5.7 | 2 173 | 33.4 | 32.8 |
| Ralls | 4 222 | 81.4 | 106 300 | 19.2 | 12.2 | 607 | 28.1 | 1.5 | 5 694 | -1.2 | 358 | 6.3 | 5 072 | 28.5 | 33.9 |
| Randolph | 9 064 | 71.4 | 81 300 | 22.4 | 11.1 | 588 | 27.6 | 3.0 | 12 423 | -1.8 | 924 | 7.4 | 10 245 | 25.4 | 28.9 |
| Ray | 9 041 | 78.8 | 124 000 | 22.6 | 12.4 | 652 | 26.8 | 1.5 | 11 297 | 0.6 | 1 014 | 9.0 | 10 710 | 24.8 | 35.6 |
| Reynolds | 2 856 | 73.8 | 81 300 | 21.8 | 11.6 | 405 | 22.1 | 3.7 | 2 440 | -3.4 | 245 | 10.0 | 2 457 | 19.0 | 45.1 |
| Ripley | 5 556 | 73.9 | 68 100 | 23.8 | 11.1 | 546 | 34.4 | 3.3 | 6 810 | 0.1 | 555 | 8.1 | 5 214 | 21.5 | 35.0 |
| St. Charles | 132 908 | 82.1 | 196 100 | 22.2 | 11.7 | 841 | 26.5 | 1.1 | 199 237 | -1.3 | 11 863 | 6.0 | 188 236 | 40.1 | 17.3 |
| St. Clair | 4 351 | 78.6 | 83 500 | 24.5 | 12.2 | 434 | 28.1 | 2.2 | 3 851 | -3.3 | 309 | 8.0 | 4 040 | 30.3 | 28.6 |
| Ste. Genevieve | 7 214 | 81.9 | 125 800 | 22.8 | 10.8 | 619 | 26.3 | 2.0 | 9 369 | -3.0 | 645 | 6.9 | 8 642 | 23.9 | 38.5 |
| St. Francois | 24 519 | 70.3 | 101 100 | 21.2 | 11.6 | 546 | 28.7 | 2.4 | 28 218 | -3.1 | 2 391 | 8.5 | 24 900 | 30.4 | 24.6 |
| St. Louis | 404 158 | 72.1 | 178 800 | 22.7 | 12.1 | 821 | 29.7 | 1.3 | 513 894 | -1.5 | 34 401 | 6.7 | 489 339 | 42.1 | 15.0 |
| Saline | 8 928 | 70.3 | 82 800 | 20.0 | 12.1 | 518 | 29.2 | 2.6 | 11 260 | -1.5 | 716 | 6.4 | 10 574 | 26.4 | 35.9 |
| Schuyler | 1 944 | 69.1 | 61 100 | 22.4 | 13.6 | 433 | 24.1 | 4.5 | 2 016 | -1.9 | 138 | 6.8 | 1 906 | 26.0 | 32.5 |
| Scotland | 2 020 | 75.9 | 73 500 | 23.1 | 12.4 | 408 | 21.7 | 4.5 | 2 423 | -0.9 | 115 | 4.7 | 2 179 | 31.7 | 30.1 |
| Scott | 15 203 | 68.9 | 95 600 | 19.4 | 10.6 | 559 | 26.4 | 2.6 | 20 308 | 0.5 | 1 343 | 6.6 | 17 755 | 23.8 | 31.4 |
| Shannon | 3 362 | 78.6 | 76 700 | 23.8 | 10.7 | 418 | 32.5 | 4.0 | 3 070 | -1.9 | 324 | 10.6 | 3 250 | 28.7 | 40.0 |
| Shelby | 2 653 | 70.3 | 71 700 | 24.7 | 13.5 | 390 | 21.7 | 2.3 | 3 123 | -1.4 | 189 | 6.1 | 2 908 | 26.5 | 33.1 |
| Stoddard | 12 235 | 69.7 | 83 400 | 19.7 | 11.4 | 521 | 27.7 | 1.8 | 15 034 | -1.6 | 1 122 | 7.5 | 12 375 | 22.9 | 37.2 |
| Stone | 13 297 | 78.1 | 141 300 | 23.3 | 11.1 | 652 | 27.2 | 2.4 | 14 409 | -2.5 | 1 497 | 10.4 | 12 974 | 26.7 | 23.8 |
| Sullivan | 2 605 | 67.6 | 71 800 | 23.8 | 11.7 | 516 | 26.1 | 4.3 | 3 374 | -2.7 | 184 | 5.5 | 2 874 | 23.2 | 39.9 |
| Taney | 20 525 | 67.3 | 136 100 | 24.2 | 11.3 | 665 | 28.0 | 2.0 | 27 042 | -2.9 | 2 780 | 10.3 | 23 853 | 25.3 | 16.0 |
| Texas | 9 560 | 73.8 | 93 800 | 21.7 | 11.4 | 497 | 28.2 | 2.8 | 10 874 | -1.6 | 791 | 7.3 | 8 878 | 23.2 | 33.2 |
| Vernon | 8 137 | 72.0 | 83 200 | 23.7 | 11.5 | 553 | 29.5 | 2.0 | 9 529 | -1.1 | 558 | 5.9 | 9 423 | 29.2 | 27.5 |
| Warren | 12 501 | 79.5 | 159 700 | 23.0 | 12.0 | 685 | 34.6 | 2.3 | 16 881 | -1.3 | 1 298 | 7.7 | 15 101 | 26.5 | 30.5 |
| Washington | 9 161 | 78.4 | 81 500 | 21.9 | 11.1 | 509 | 25.9 | 4.7 | 10 106 | -1.5 | 1 059 | 10.5 | 8 718 | 18.6 | 39.1 |
| Wayne | 5 638 | 73.5 | 74 000 | 20.4 | 12.4 | 456 | 36.6 | 2.5 | 5 790 | -3.7 | 475 | 8.2 | 5 079 | 29.2 | 34.1 |
| Webster | 12 848 | 77.0 | 118 600 | 22.5 | 9.9 | 607 | 26.8 | 5.1 | 16 540 | 0.2 | 1 140 | 6.9 | 15 019 | 22.4 | 36.6 |
| Worth | 977 | 74.7 | 57 500 | 16.0 | 12.0 | 290 | 23.0 | 1.1 | 1 131 | -0.6 | 53 | 4.7 | 1 147 | 31.6 | 29.1 |
| Wright | 7 529 | 69.9 | 90 800 | 26.0 | 10.4 | 461 | 27.8 | 4.0 | 8 543 | 5.4 | 610 | 7.1 | 6 576 | 27.8 | 35.4 |

1. Specified owner-occupied units. lacking complete plumbing facilities.  2. A value of 9.9 represents 9.9 percent or less.  3. Specified renter-occupied units. A value of 10.0 represents 10 percent or less.  4. Overcrowded or
5. Percent of civilian labor force.  6. Persons 16 years old and over.

# Table B. States and Counties — Nonfarm Employment and Agriculture

| STATE County | Private nonfarm establishments, employment and payroll, 2011 | | | | | | | | | Agriculture, 2007 | | | |
| | | Employment | | | | | | Annual payroll | | Farms | | | |
| | | | | | | | | | | | Percent with: | | |
| | Number of establish-ments | Total | Health care and social assistance | Manufac-turing | Retail trade | Finance and insurance | Professional, scientific, and technical services | Total (mil dol) | Average per employee (dollars) | Number | Fewer than 50 acres | 500 acres or more | Farm operators whose principal occu-pation is farming (percent) |
| | 104 | 105 | 106 | 107 | 108 | 109 | 110 | 111 | 112 | 113 | 114 | 115 | 116 |
| MISSOURI—Cont'd | | | | | | | | | | | | | |
| Jasper | 2 925 | 51 571 | 9 698 | 9 192 | 7 610 | 1 214 | 1 144 | 1 738 | 33 707 | 1 369 | 34.8 | 8.0 | 41.5 |
| Jefferson | 3 885 | 39 500 | 6 067 | 4 454 | 6 878 | 1 196 | 873 | 1 214 | 30 737 | 697 | 41.2 | 3.9 | 37.6 |
| Johnson | 1 099 | 9 515 | 2 134 | D | 1 769 | 392 | 307 | 248 | 26 014 | 1 947 | 33.2 | 11.3 | 39.9 |
| Knox | 103 | 690 | 49 | D | 103 | 57 | D | 17 | 23 952 | 696 | 15.9 | 19.0 | 43.1 |
| Laclede | 795 | 11 356 | 1 464 | 4 372 | 1 933 | 319 | 191 | 313 | 27 602 | 1 264 | 25.1 | 11.9 | 39.6 |
| Lafayette | 685 | 5 990 | 1 064 | 778 | 1 123 | 263 | 270 | 159 | 26 618 | 1 299 | 31.6 | 13.6 | 47.2 |
| Lawrence | 686 | 7 116 | 1 498 | 1 363 | 1 325 | 185 | 198 | 210 | 29 444 | 1 873 | 36.0 | 7.5 | 43.2 |
| Lewis | 191 | 1 876 | 269 | D | 260 | 110 | D | 44 | 23 617 | 750 | 20.8 | 17.1 | 41.1 |
| Lincoln | 889 | 7 828 | 1 134 | 1 199 | 1 499 | 308 | 183 | 243 | 31 035 | 1 108 | 33.2 | 11.3 | 40.5 |
| Linn | 299 | 3 290 | 498 | 1 023 | 523 | 162 | 75 | 99 | 30 022 | 1 077 | 20.8 | 16.0 | 37.5 |
| Livingston | 415 | 5 488 | 856 | 557 | 1 190 | 230 | 132 | 148 | 27 058 | 913 | 20.9 | 16.5 | 41.7 |
| McDonald | 310 | 5 445 | D | D | 962 | 126 | D | 144 | 26 374 | 996 | 27.6 | 8.7 | 48.4 |
| Macon | 353 | 3 267 | 543 | D | 623 | 168 | D | 87 | 26 489 | 1 451 | 21.6 | 13.4 | 36.8 |
| Madison | 270 | 2 813 | D | 283 | 578 | D | D | 67 | 23 946 | 376 | 19.1 | 11.4 | 39.1 |
| Maries | 136 | 1 021 | D | 212 | 234 | D | D | 28 | 27 167 | 898 | 18.5 | 13.0 | 48.1 |
| Marion | 835 | 11 183 | 2 871 | 1 417 | 1 836 | 407 | 268 | 361 | 32 287 | 749 | 22.4 | 16.0 | 41.7 |
| Mercer | 74 | 414 | D | D | 54 | D | 5 | 11 | 27 548 | 553 | 14.5 | 17.5 | 35.8 |
| Miller | 695 | 5 669 | 441 | 509 | 1 413 | 254 | 233 | 154 | 27 170 | 1 080 | 17.6 | 10.7 | 41.7 |
| Mississippi | 255 | 2 446 | 490 | 181 | 428 | 127 | 63 | 63 | 25 782 | 228 | 17.1 | 51.3 | 73.7 |
| Moniteau | 327 | 2 728 | 353 | D | 456 | 123 | 59 | 76 | 27 681 | 1 138 | 22.6 | 10.2 | 43.0 |
| Monroe | 180 | 1 347 | 259 | D | 282 | 96 | D | 30 | 22 176 | 1 036 | 20.8 | 12.5 | 37.5 |
| Montgomery | 272 | 2 000 | 396 | D | 294 | 122 | D | 55 | 27 647 | 859 | 22.4 | 16.5 | 41.1 |
| Morgan | 456 | 2 763 | 237 | 476 | 757 | 123 | D | 65 | 23 522 | 1 036 | 27.8 | 8.7 | 43.8 |
| New Madrid | 415 | 6 012 | 797 | D | 1 331 | 142 | 80 | 207 | 34 354 | 350 | 10.9 | 57.1 | 72.6 |
| Newton | 1 271 | 18 603 | 5 798 | 2 592 | 2 114 | 540 | 374 | 619 | 33 267 | 1 590 | 36.2 | 5.2 | 43.5 |
| Nodaway | 491 | 6 722 | 1 141 | 1 841 | 1 209 | 199 | 123 | 193 | 28 662 | 1 540 | 19.7 | 20.6 | 49.5 |
| Oregon | 217 | 1 789 | 450 | D | 442 | 65 | 38 | 32 | 17 803 | 776 | 24.4 | 13.7 | 45.2 |
| Osage | 262 | 2 823 | 365 | 1 018 | 416 | 132 | 25 | 82 | 28 880 | 1 181 | 15.6 | 10.0 | 44.9 |
| Ozark | 168 | 883 | 105 | 100 | 210 | 71 | D | 18 | 20 354 | 742 | 16.3 | 16.4 | 51.9 |
| Pemiscot | 386 | 4 826 | 1 478 | D | 700 | 185 | 47 | 132 | 27 267 | 258 | 17.4 | 56.2 | 70.2 |
| Perry | 485 | 9 300 | 1 078 | D | 1 065 | D | D | 280 | 30 128 | 983 | 22.6 | 9.9 | 39.6 |
| Pettis | 1 043 | 17 117 | 2 676 | 3 856 | 2 364 | 441 | 365 | 537 | 31 346 | 1 398 | 28.5 | 16.0 | 45.8 |
| Phelps | 1 115 | 13 331 | 3 298 | 906 | 2 365 | 404 | 319 | 381 | 28 603 | 826 | 30.0 | 9.0 | 35.7 |
| Pike | 392 | 3 739 | 824 | 543 | 697 | 154 | 74 | 106 | 28 391 | 1 102 | 23.3 | 16.7 | 39.5 |
| Platte | 2 207 | 37 732 | 3 292 | 2 420 | 6 076 | 3 113 | 1 583 | 1 382 | 36 623 | 726 | 36.9 | 10.3 | 36.2 |
| Polk | 580 | 6 991 | 1 772 | D | 1 169 | 212 | 150 | 193 | 27 670 | 1 707 | 31.1 | 9.4 | 41.1 |
| Pulaski | 747 | 8 197 | 1 467 | 104 | 1 725 | 404 | 535 | 226 | 27 581 | 481 | 18.3 | 15.0 | 35.6 |
| Putnam | 96 | 598 | 122 | 85 | 175 | 51 | D | 15 | 25 179 | 663 | 17.3 | 19.8 | 48.0 |
| Ralls | 200 | 2 494 | D | 1 310 | 221 | 47 | 23 | 106 | 42 616 | 803 | 25.9 | 15.8 | 41.0 |
| Randolph | 566 | 7 648 | 1 445 | 955 | 1 124 | 377 | 187 | 236 | 30 836 | 1 000 | 29.5 | 8.6 | 32.4 |
| Ray | 373 | 2 883 | 612 | D | 657 | 131 | 95 | 79 | 27 362 | 1 321 | 31.6 | 8.7 | 36.5 |
| Reynolds | 160 | 1 190 | 171 | 291 | 141 | D | D | 55 | 45 890 | 350 | 23.1 | 14.0 | 39.1 |
| Ripley | 547 | 2 599 | 836 | D | 446 | D | 25 | 47 | 17 952 | 471 | 19.7 | 14.6 | 48.2 |
| St. Charles | 7 911 | 115 882 | 15 279 | 10 089 | 18 979 | 9 399 | 6 306 | 4 255 | 36 716 | 644 | 36.8 | 13.2 | 46.4 |
| St. Clair | 171 | 1 369 | 530 | D | 279 | D | D | 31 | 22 768 | 844 | 22.3 | 18.1 | 47.9 |
| Ste. Genevieve | 397 | 5 096 | D | 1 735 | 437 | 146 | 83 | 186 | 36 508 | 717 | 27.3 | 12.0 | 36.0 |
| St. Francois | 1 416 | 17 628 | 4 828 | 1 572 | 3 096 | 915 | 343 | 472 | 26 798 | 719 | 33.5 | 5.3 | 35.5 |
| St. Louis | 29 618 | 545 858 | 82 924 | 34 813 | 67 397 | 30 958 | 49 901 | 27 078 | 49 606 | 276 | 53.3 | 4.0 | 36.6 |
| Saline | 529 | 7 134 | 1 561 | 1 989 | 1 087 | 253 | 104 | 211 | 29 521 | 995 | 21.5 | 24.8 | 48.0 |
| Schuyler | 87 | 350 | 32 | D | 145 | D | D | 9 | 24 400 | 544 | 18.8 | 14.5 | 40.3 |
| Scotland | 119 | 734 | D | 42 | 161 | 48 | D | 20 | 27 307 | 716 | 18.7 | 18.3 | 41.5 |
| Scott | 1 090 | 14 042 | 3 480 | D | 1 485 | 534 | 442 | 411 | 29 244 | 538 | 31.2 | 21.6 | 47.8 |
| Shannon | 168 | 1 049 | 164 | 464 | 109 | 55 | 8 | 20 | 18 799 | 447 | 25.1 | 13.0 | 39.1 |
| Shelby | 171 | 1 245 | 117 | 277 | 207 | 57 | 46 | 32 | 25 455 | 707 | 18.7 | 21.9 | 40.7 |
| Stoddard | 734 | 8 686 | 1 516 | 2 908 | 1 358 | 327 | 198 | 267 | 30 757 | 1 045 | 32.5 | 21.1 | 47.4 |
| Stone | 685 | 4 697 | 519 | 114 | 802 | 191 | 77 | 115 | 24 460 | 753 | 32.0 | 7.4 | 38.1 |
| Sullivan | 118 | 2 027 | 240 | D | D | 44 | D | 63 | 31 283 | 882 | 13.8 | 21.5 | 43.1 |
| Taney | 1 720 | 22 043 | 2 152 | 476 | 5 060 | 389 | 522 | 580 | 26 295 | 434 | 23.3 | 11.8 | 38.9 |
| Texas | 478 | 4 356 | 941 | 812 | 755 | 214 | 76 | 108 | 24 871 | 1 327 | 21.0 | 11.7 | 46.6 |
| Vernon | 503 | 5 640 | 1 442 | D | 898 | 355 | 122 | 159 | 28 221 | 1 383 | 23.8 | 16.1 | 44.4 |
| Warren | 577 | 5 940 | 561 | 1 268 | 1 011 | 207 | 204 | 182 | 30 641 | 723 | 39.0 | 10.2 | 39.8 |
| Washington | 378 | 2 988 | 609 | D | 539 | D | 31 | 77 | 25 789 | 558 | 29.9 | 11.1 | 40.1 |
| Wayne | 292 | 1 930 | 314 | 400 | 368 | 93 | 37 | 44 | 23 051 | 387 | 11.1 | 12.4 | 41.9 |
| Webster | 606 | 4 700 | 457 | 701 | 1 099 | 229 | 144 | 126 | 26 914 | 1 821 | 35.0 | 5.4 | 41.4 |
| Worth | 48 | 186 | D | D | 69 | D | D | 4 | 21 522 | 455 | 16.9 | 18.9 | 38.9 |
| Wright | 405 | 3 386 | 461 | D | 964 | 177 | D | 83 | 24 635 | 1 206 | 20.5 | 12.8 | 48.8 |

# Table B. States and Counties — **Agriculture**

| STATE County | Land in farms | | | | | Value of land and buildings (dollars) | | Value of machinery and equipment, average per farm (dollars) | Value of products sold | | | | Percent of farms with sales of: | | Government payments | |
|---|---|---|---|---|---|---|---|---|---|---|---|---|---|---|---|---|
| | | | Acres | | | | | | | | Percent from: | | | | | |
| | Acreage (1,000) | Percent change, 2002–2007 | Average size of farm | Total irrigated (1,000) | Total cropland (1,000) | Average per farm | Average per acre | | Total (mil dol) | Average per farm (dollars) | Crops | Live-stock and poultry products | $10,000 or more | $100,000 or more | Total ($1,000) | Percent of farms |
| | 117 | 118 | 119 | 120 | 121 | 122 | 123 | 124 | 125 | 126 | 127 | 128 | 129 | 130 | 131 | 132 |
| **MISSOURI—Cont'd** | | | | | | | | | | | | | | | | |
| Jasper | 259 | -10.4 | 189 | 5.2 | 135.7 | 417 814 | 2 210 | 53 862 | 92.7 | 67 688 | 40.7 | 59.3 | 41.4 | 8.2 | 2 983 | 34.8 |
| Jefferson | 92 | -26.4 | 132 | 0.4 | 39.4 | 407 554 | 3 080 | 47 941 | 11.1 | 15 948 | 50.0 | 50.0 | 22.0 | 2.6 | 280 | 12.9 |
| Johnson | 424 | 2.7 | 218 | 1.4 | 244.7 | 485 494 | 2 227 | 72 306 | 104.1 | 53 460 | 36.7 | 63.3 | 40.8 | 8.3 | 3 575 | 44.1 |
| Knox | 254 | 2.0 | 364 | D | 170.2 | 691 276 | 1 897 | 90 240 | 57.3 | 82 325 | 69.0 | 31.0 | 47.4 | 18.8 | 4 269 | 75.4 |
| Laclede | 289 | -9.4 | 228 | 0.1 | 94.2 | 440 349 | 1 928 | 52 580 | 40.2 | 31 835 | 9.3 | 90.7 | 40.5 | 6.2 | 870 | 16.5 |
| Lafayette | 353 | -2.8 | 272 | 2.1 | 262.4 | 734 948 | 2 705 | 87 125 | 120.6 | 92 830 | 70.5 | 29.5 | 52.6 | 17.8 | 4 684 | 63.0 |
| Lawrence | 323 | 2.2 | 172 | 2.4 | 150.7 | 425 204 | 2 467 | 61 081 | 172.5 | 92 077 | 10.1 | 89.9 | 41.4 | 8.8 | 2 967 | 23.4 |
| Lewis | 261 | -8.1 | 348 | 2.3 | 178.3 | 742 403 | 2 131 | 86 827 | 73.0 | 97 383 | 60.5 | 39.5 | 44.5 | 17.9 | 3 529 | 72.5 |
| Lincoln | 249 | -1.2 | 225 | 3.1 | 167.8 | 704 052 | 3 135 | 77 809 | 69.1 | 62 352 | 56.8 | 43.2 | 38.2 | 10.6 | 3 103 | 57.8 |
| Linn | 330 | -2.9 | 306 | 1.3 | 197.0 | 559 578 | 1 826 | 59 902 | 53.7 | 49 867 | 57.0 | 43.0 | 44.4 | 11.9 | 5 210 | 66.9 |
| Livingston | 309 | 3.0 | 338 | D | 221.1 | 685 568 | 2 025 | 68 844 | 60.1 | 65 843 | 79.1 | 20.9 | 44.7 | 13.7 | 5 144 | 74.4 |
| McDonald | 200 | -7.4 | 201 | 0.3 | 54.9 | 475 350 | 2 370 | 66 772 | 110.9 | 111 352 | 2.2 | 97.8 | 39.3 | 10.0 | 181 | 5.5 |
| Macon | 394 | -3.0 | 272 | 0.1 | 219.6 | 486 951 | 1 792 | 55 367 | 63.5 | 43 746 | 49.7 | 50.3 | 39.5 | 9.0 | 5 303 | 60.0 |
| Madison | 98 | -20.3 | 261 | D | 28.1 | 446 826 | 1 710 | 42 331 | 10.5 | 27 806 | 6.8 | 93.2 | 32.2 | 2.7 | 129 | 10.1 |
| Maries | 240 | 2.6 | 268 | 0.0 | 70.3 | 455 995 | 1 704 | 60 038 | 26.1 | 29 021 | 9.2 | 90.8 | 49.1 | 4.1 | 311 | 16.4 |
| Marion | 237 | 3.0 | 316 | 3.0 | 166.2 | 705 986 | 2 231 | 91 129 | 76.5 | 102 172 | 64.4 | 35.6 | 49.1 | 17.1 | 3 030 | 75.3 |
| Mercer | 201 | -5.2 | 364 | D | 105.8 | 659 442 | 1 811 | 84 188 | 81.5 | 147 386 | 17.4 | 82.6 | 38.7 | 8.0 | 2 921 | 74.1 |
| Miller | 246 | -8.2 | 227 | 1.2 | 77.1 | 453 770 | 1 996 | 57 707 | 95.4 | 88 326 | 4.0 | 96.0 | 46.5 | 9.4 | 354 | 14.5 |
| Mississippi | 258 | -5.1 | 1 134 | 80.2 | 249.4 | 2 681 455 | 2 365 | 350 985 | 108.4 | 475 525 | 96.3 | 3.7 | 77.2 | 56.6 | 4 459 | 87.7 |
| Moniteau | 243 | -5.8 | 213 | 0.2 | 122.6 | 506 981 | 2 375 | 63 334 | 123.0 | 108 126 | 13.9 | 86.1 | 53.2 | 12.7 | 1 727 | 39.3 |
| Monroe | 288 | -8.9 | 278 | 1.5 | 183.3 | 630 118 | 2 264 | 66 285 | 69.9 | 67 478 | 59.9 | 40.1 | 43.0 | 12.0 | 5 014 | 72.7 |
| Montgomery | 248 | -4.2 | 289 | 3.4 | 167.2 | 822 951 | 2 850 | 85 520 | 52.2 | 60 717 | 74.9 | 25.1 | 46.1 | 15.8 | 2 949 | 63.8 |
| Morgan | 217 | -2.3 | 209 | 0.4 | 93.5 | 463 405 | 2 216 | 48 802 | 124.9 | 120 528 | 9.0 | 91.0 | 47.5 | 18.2 | 638 | 18.5 |
| New Madrid | 381 | -3.5 | 1 088 | 198.8 | 373.4 | 2 637 463 | 2 425 | 320 207 | 141.3 | 403 606 | 100.0 | 0.0 | 85.7 | 58.0 | 13 667 | 91.1 |
| Newton | 246 | -8.6 | 155 | 1.2 | 107.9 | 405 698 | 2 623 | 63 521 | 235.6 | 148 163 | 4.6 | 95.4 | 38.4 | 9.1 | 864 | 13.6 |
| Nodaway | 543 | 7.3 | 353 | 0.0 | 377.5 | 741 588 | 2 102 | 81 566 | 124.6 | 80 885 | 70.9 | 29.1 | 57.8 | 21.0 | 8 340 | 75.3 |
| Oregon | 239 | -10.2 | 308 | 0.1 | 46.2 | 526 402 | 1 706 | 47 366 | 26.9 | 34 665 | 4.1 | 95.9 | 37.6 | 5.4 | 453 | 10.7 |
| Osage | 297 | -5.7 | 252 | 0.7 | 100.2 | 488 220 | 1 938 | 65 056 | 66.2 | 56 026 | 11.8 | 88.2 | 52.8 | 9.2 | 771 | 32.9 |
| Ozark | 248 | -12.1 | 334 | 0.2 | 55.3 | 569 530 | 1 705 | 44 506 | 31.4 | 42 372 | 2.6 | 97.4 | 41.5 | 8.9 | 250 | 8.0 |
| Pemiscot | 310 | 4.7 | 1 203 | 121.1 | 304.0 | 2 599 770 | 2 161 | 298 933 | 100.5 | 389 355 | 99.6 | 0.4 | 76.0 | 55.0 | 11 368 | 85.7 |
| Perry | 239 | 7.7 | 243 | D | 129.4 | 528 499 | 2 175 | 69 282 | 47.0 | 47 773 | 54.5 | 45.5 | 43.2 | 9.9 | 1 951 | 61.4 |
| Pettis | 409 | 1.7 | 293 | 0.6 | 262.5 | 691 718 | 2 365 | 82 096 | 166.3 | 118 983 | 31.7 | 68.3 | 48.4 | 17.0 | 3 907 | 50.1 |
| Phelps | 176 | -12.4 | 213 | 0.2 | 51.6 | 439 592 | 2 065 | 43 698 | 11.3 | 13 705 | 13.3 | 86.7 | 28.3 | 1.9 | 244 | 9.7 |
| Pike | 373 | 8.4 | 339 | 1.4 | 245.0 | 801 938 | 2 368 | 85 472 | 79.8 | 72 387 | 62.3 | 37.8 | 46.5 | 14.7 | 4 156 | 61.2 |
| Platte | 179 | -3.2 | 246 | 2.4 | 128.0 | 699 645 | 2 843 | 76 224 | 53.0 | 73 070 | 82.9 | 17.1 | 37.2 | 10.9 | 1 885 | 51.7 |
| Polk | 350 | -5.1 | 205 | 1.3 | 144.1 | 444 350 | 2 165 | 49 062 | 80.4 | 47 120 | 7.5 | 92.5 | 44.2 | 8.0 | 715 | 17.1 |
| Pulaski | 123 | -13.4 | 256 | D | 33.6 | 476 513 | 1 862 | 53 712 | 8.9 | 18 476 | 10.7 | 89.3 | 35.3 | 2.5 | 138 | 13.5 |
| Putnam | 273 | -6.8 | 411 | D | 113.9 | 709 547 | 1 725 | 70 906 | 75.9 | 114 537 | 18.3 | 81.7 | 52.3 | 15.7 | 2 796 | 52.8 |
| Ralls | 246 | -2.8 | 306 | 0.9 | 168.4 | 725 659 | 2 373 | 75 561 | 56.7 | 70 653 | 75.0 | 25.0 | 36.5 | 12.5 | 3 383 | 69.6 |
| Randolph | 222 | -9.8 | 222 | 0.7 | 119.9 | 450 571 | 2 033 | 44 895 | 36.1 | 36 064 | 51.6 | 48.4 | 31.9 | 6.1 | 2 849 | 56.8 |
| Ray | 292 | 0.0 | 221 | 4.1 | 180.5 | 486 006 | 2 200 | 58 551 | 64.5 | 48 837 | 55.5 | 44.5 | 36.6 | 6.7 | 3 475 | 47.8 |
| Reynolds | 107 | -9.3 | 307 | 0.0 | 24.9 | 436 578 | 1 424 | 41 467 | 3.4 | 9 739 | 9.5 | 90.5 | 26.9 | 0.9 | 36 | 10.9 |
| Ripley | 137 | -2.1 | 291 | 8.6 | 47.6 | 503 899 | 1 729 | 52 967 | 13.6 | 28 875 | 48.8 | 51.2 | 36.5 | 6.8 | 521 | 22.7 |
| St. Charles | 156 | -15.7 | 242 | 0.9 | 121.8 | 793 152 | 3 271 | 88 341 | 48.4 | 75 141 | 84.7 | 15.3 | 47.5 | 16.5 | 1 853 | 55.1 |
| St. Clair | 265 | -1.1 | 314 | 0.2 | 126.6 | 561 172 | 1 787 | 66 000 | 34.3 | 40 625 | 45.1 | 54.9 | 46.9 | 9.0 | 1 760 | 39.3 |
| Ste. Genevieve | 189 | 2.7 | 263 | 0.4 | 86.0 | 570 917 | 2 168 | 57 750 | 25.7 | 35 834 | 47.7 | 52.3 | 39.2 | 7.1 | 1 029 | 45.7 |
| St. Francois | 113 | -12.4 | 157 | 0.3 | 44.5 | 412 621 | 2 636 | 46 680 | 12.1 | 16 796 | 22.1 | 77.9 | 27.5 | 2.5 | 218 | 12.4 |
| St. Louis | 32 | -17.9 | 117 | 1.4 | 20.2 | 431 316 | 3 686 | 62 075 | 23.8 | 86 203 | 98.4 | 1.6 | 35.1 | 9.1 | 130 | 21.4 |
| Saline | 449 | 8.7 | 452 | 1.5 | 340.2 | 997 734 | 2 209 | 120 500 | 178.4 | 179 320 | 65.5 | 34.5 | 61.0 | 28.4 | 6 365 | 78.7 |
| Schuyler | 152 | 4.1 | 280 | 0.0 | 79.0 | 476 248 | 1 700 | 54 568 | 20.4 | 37 541 | 32.2 | 67.8 | 46.1 | 9.7 | 1 902 | 66.2 |
| Scotland | 232 | -0.9 | 324 | 0.3 | 148.3 | 635 897 | 1 965 | 80 735 | 53.2 | 74 306 | 58.5 | 41.5 | 47.8 | 17.5 | 4 444 | 76.1 |
| Scott | 228 | 1.8 | 424 | 67.3 | 203.0 | 1 097 463 | 2 585 | 144 494 | 108.7 | 202 062 | 76.7 | 23.3 | 49.4 | 25.7 | 4 998 | 71.4 |
| Shannon | 111 | -17.8 | 248 | 0.1 | 28.1 | 435 741 | 1 756 | 46 021 | 7.7 | 17 332 | 8.2 | 91.8 | 40.5 | 2.9 | 145 | 13.4 |
| Shelby | 289 | -3.3 | 409 | 1.4 | 201.3 | 847 723 | 2 073 | 108 076 | 87.2 | 123 375 | 59.7 | 40.3 | 51.2 | 22.5 | 3 844 | 74.5 |
| Stoddard | 461 | 11.1 | 441 | 228.6 | 418.3 | 1 045 580 | 2 369 | 152 911 | 228.1 | 218 293 | 73.1 | 26.9 | 43.3 | 23.7 | 14 415 | 67.7 |
| Stone | 122 | 7.0 | 162 | 0.1 | 36.8 | 398 716 | 2 465 | 44 398 | 25.3 | 33 625 | 7.1 | 92.9 | 32.8 | 3.7 | 149 | 5.8 |
| Sullivan | 334 | -8.5 | 379 | 0.0 | 151.8 | 592 933 | 1 566 | 96 832 | 131.6 | 149 171 | 9.9 | 90.1 | 46.3 | 9.9 | 4 326 | 64.6 |
| Taney | 107 | -30.5 | 245 | D | 21.0 | 466 897 | 1 902 | 45 112 | 7.2 | 16 552 | 11.0 | 89.0 | 31.6 | 2.8 | 55 | 5.5 |
| Texas | 355 | -24.8 | 268 | 0.1 | 97.3 | 465 063 | 1 737 | 47 457 | 42.0 | 31 667 | 9.3 | 90.7 | 40.8 | 7.4 | 273 | 10.6 |
| Vernon | 456 | 7.0 | 330 | 7.6 | 268.0 | 606 988 | 1 842 | 75 820 | 129.4 | 93 530 | 30.4 | 69.6 | 42.5 | 11.2 | 4 692 | 43.0 |
| Warren | 147 | 3.5 | 203 | 0.9 | 85.2 | 674 902 | 3 324 | 65 961 | 28.8 | 39 898 | 62.9 | 37.1 | 34.6 | 10.5 | 1 586 | 47.2 |
| Washington | 137 | 3.0 | 246 | 0.2 | 41.3 | 458 676 | 1 864 | 40 773 | 8.7 | 15 643 | 8.1 | 91.9 | 29.9 | 2.0 | 80 | 5.7 |
| Wayne | 106 | -7.0 | 274 | 0.0 | 29.2 | 467 545 | 1 706 | 44 728 | 6.8 | 17 535 | 20.5 | 79.5 | 32.3 | 3.9 | 223 | 22.0 |
| Webster | 271 | -15.3 | 149 | 0.2 | 99.1 | 389 098 | 2 613 | 48 426 | 67.0 | 36 767 | 7.5 | 92.5 | 41.5 | 8.7 | 349 | 8.5 |
| Worth | 152 | 8.6 | 334 | 0.0 | 82.1 | 545 475 | 1 635 | 63 513 | 19.1 | 41 973 | 58.0 | 42.0 | 40.7 | 9.9 | 2 655 | 79.3 |
| Wright | 284 | -10.7 | 236 | 0.9 | 91.2 | 426 822 | 1 811 | 52 647 | 50.4 | 41 828 | 3.9 | 96.1 | 45.1 | 11.3 | 261 | 11.5 |

| STATE County | Water use, 2005 | | Wholesale trade,[1] 2007 | | | | Retail trade,[2] 2007 | | | | Real estate and rental and leasing,[2] 2007 | | | |
|---|---|---|---|---|---|---|---|---|---|---|---|---|---|---|
| | Total water withdrawn (mil gal/day) | Gallons withdrawn per person | Number of establishments | Number of employees | Sales (mil dol) | Annual payroll (mil dol) | Number of establishments | Number of employees | Sales (mil dol) | Annual payroll (mil dol) | Number of establishments | Number of employees | Receipts (mil dol) | Annual payroll (mil dol) |
| | 133 | 134 | 135 | 136 | 137 | 138 | 139 | 140 | 141 | 142 | 143 | 144 | 145 | 146 |
| MISSOURI—Cont'd | | | | | | | | | | | | | | |
| Jasper | 28.7 | 259 | 140 | 1 528 | 793.4 | 59.1 | 596 | 8 171 | 1 967.4 | 165.8 | 141 | 654 | 76.4 | 16.1 |
| Jefferson | 793.8 | 3 715 | 143 | 1 438 | 782.8 | 66.2 | 524 | 6 796 | 1 709.8 | 154.1 | 171 | 592 | 69.1 | 13.5 |
| Johnson | 6.2 | 122 | 16 | D | D | D | 157 | 1 958 | 412.9 | 37.0 | 40 | D | D | D |
| Knox | 1.5 | 357 | 9 | 45 | 29.9 | 1.3 | 21 | 107 | 27.8 | 1.8 | 1 | D | D | D |
| Laclede | 17.0 | 494 | 28 | D | D | D | 192 | 2 059 | 469.7 | 43.6 | 38 | 99 | 10.7 | 2.0 |
| Lafayette | 4.6 | 140 | 36 | 277 | 140.6 | 9.1 | 151 | 1 402 | 301.4 | 25.1 | 23 | 99 | 5.2 | 1.7 |
| Lawrence | 6.9 | 185 | 25 | 222 | 63.7 | 5.9 | 138 | 1 257 | 419.5 | 30.9 | 33 | 95 | 9.4 | 1.3 |
| Lewis | 2.6 | 258 | 8 | D | D | D | 38 | 296 | 59.3 | 5.0 | 4 | 7 | 0.6 | 0.0 |
| Lincoln | 6.7 | 140 | 36 | 242 | 91.8 | 8.3 | 138 | 1 500 | 433.2 | 35.9 | 38 | D | D | D |
| Linn | 2.5 | 187 | 14 | 58 | 38.9 | 2.8 | 59 | 554 | 117.7 | 9.7 | 11 | 27 | 1.6 | 0.3 |
| Livingston | 2.8 | 195 | 20 | 218 | 86.2 | 7.1 | 85 | 1 124 | 234.5 | 22.3 | 13 | 54 | 13.3 | 1.2 |
| McDonald | 7.3 | 318 | 13 | D | D | D | 69 | 1 055 | 223.3 | 19.0 | 7 | 9 | 0.5 | 0.1 |
| Macon | 3.5 | 226 | 16 | 189 | 50.6 | 5.1 | 71 | 725 | 156.5 | 12.5 | 16 | 44 | 3.7 | 0.7 |
| Madison | 1.4 | 114 | 9 | 23 | 6.9 | 0.5 | 41 | 536 | 106.6 | 12.2 | 7 | 22 | 1.5 | 0.3 |
| Maries | 1.5 | 167 | 5 | 19 | 7.4 | 0.5 | 26 | 186 | 46.3 | 3.1 | 2 | D | D | D |
| Marion | 7.9 | 278 | 30 | 234 | 114.4 | 7.0 | 149 | 1 901 | 423.0 | 34.5 | 26 | D | D | D |
| Mercer | 2.3 | 651 | 2 | D | D | D | 12 | 58 | 20.2 | 0.8 | NA | NA | NA | NA |
| Miller | 4.6 | 185 | 20 | 122 | 68.9 | 4.1 | 134 | 1 734 | 451.8 | 39.8 | 60 | 155 | 27.0 | 4.7 |
| Mississippi | 82.6 | 6 077 | 17 | 176 | 235.2 | 6.7 | 58 | 458 | 161.5 | 8.4 | 6 | 24 | 1.5 | 0.3 |
| Moniteau | 3.0 | 200 | 13 | 219 | 106.3 | 5.5 | 60 | 490 | 159.7 | 8.6 | 5 | D | D | D |
| Monroe | 5.8 | 614 | 9 | 52 | 36.6 | 1.9 | 35 | 263 | 48.0 | 3.9 | 5 | 13 | 1.1 | 0.1 |
| Montgomery | 2.2 | 178 | 19 | 143 | 117.2 | 4.4 | 44 | 342 | 81.5 | 6.3 | 10 | 14 | 1.3 | 0.2 |
| Morgan | 12.1 | 592 | 18 | 149 | 22.1 | 2.1 | 101 | 948 | 191.5 | 18.2 | 24 | 55 | 7.0 | 1.1 |
| New Madrid | 1 027.2 | 55 326 | 31 | 432 | 288.0 | 14.3 | 85 | 1 479 | 509.8 | 28.1 | 12 | 26 | 2.6 | 0.4 |
| Newton | 10.8 | 194 | 42 | 1 233 | 491.8 | 33.5 | 203 | 1 925 | 605.7 | 42.4 | 41 | 181 | 18.7 | 3.1 |
| Nodaway | 2.8 | 130 | 18 | D | D | D | 83 | 1 099 | 206.8 | 17.6 | 22 | 50 | 6.1 | 0.7 |
| Oregon | 2.0 | 189 | 5 | 85 | 14.2 | 1.8 | 45 | 415 | 90.9 | 8.0 | 9 | 24 | 1.5 | 0.3 |
| Osage | 61.8 | 4 581 | 9 | 62 | 26.7 | 1.7 | 54 | 478 | 132.8 | 10.0 | 6 | 11 | 0.5 | 0.1 |
| Ozark | 26.9 | 2 830 | 8 | D | D | D | 33 | 218 | 46.0 | 3.1 | 7 | 10 | 1.7 | 0.3 |
| Pemiscot | 83.8 | 4 318 | 23 | 224 | 382.6 | 7.6 | 72 | 705 | 209.5 | 11.3 | 17 | 58 | 10.8 | 1.7 |
| Perry | 2.8 | 152 | 14 | 388 | 97.3 | 14.8 | 90 | 1 027 | 263.5 | 22.5 | 16 | 47 | 5.9 | 0.6 |
| Pettis | 9.1 | 228 | 36 | 418 | 169.4 | 15.6 | 202 | 2 398 | 547.3 | 50.9 | 54 | 353 | 38.4 | 9.1 |
| Phelps | 10.0 | 237 | 31 | 329 | 103.5 | 10.9 | 208 | 2 361 | 632.5 | 48.7 | 45 | 140 | 17.0 | 3.1 |
| Pike | 12.6 | 669 | 25 | 289 | 252.2 | 8.7 | 76 | 702 | 161.3 | 13.9 | 9 | 19 | 2.2 | 0.5 |
| Platte | 432.9 | 5 273 | 102 | 1 593 | 3 535.5 | 90.3 | 302 | 5 691 | 1 737.4 | 132.0 | 143 | 1 279 | 197.2 | 33.9 |
| Polk | 5.0 | 173 | 25 | 170 | 43.3 | 4.1 | 105 | 1 249 | 276.0 | 26.0 | 22 | 78 | 7.2 | 1.3 |
| Pulaski | 7.3 | 165 | 11 | 76 | 18.2 | 2.1 | 144 | 1 556 | 376.5 | 32.4 | 39 | 127 | 16.4 | 2.8 |
| Putnam | 1.9 | 375 | 1 | D | D | D | 26 | 152 | 38.6 | 2.8 | 6 | 21 | 4.8 | 0.3 |
| Ralls | 1.7 | 174 | 15 | D | D | D | 31 | 199 | 60.2 | 4.5 | 5 | D | D | D |
| Randolph | 581.0 | 22 931 | 17 | D | D | D | 107 | 1 224 | 293.5 | 24.6 | 26 | 118 | 19.3 | 2.7 |
| Ray | 5.7 | 234 | 15 | 152 | 92.2 | 5.0 | 66 | 695 | 141.7 | 13.1 | 11 | 27 | 1.2 | 0.3 |
| Reynolds | 5.9 | 894 | 5 | 30 | 8.3 | 0.6 | 26 | 150 | 28.7 | 2.4 | 1 | D | D | D |
| Ripley | 31.0 | 2 239 | 5 | 29 | 8.0 | 0.6 | 48 | 475 | 92.4 | 8.0 | 11 | 42 | 5.2 | 0.7 |
| St. Charles | 628.8 | 1 906 | 349 | 3 773 | 9 325.6 | 184.0 | 1 115 | 17 972 | 4 408.5 | 414.5 | 378 | 1 629 | 420.4 | 50.7 |
| St. Clair | 1.8 | 187 | 7 | D | D | D | 36 | 289 | 64.7 | 4.8 | 6 | D | D | D |
| Ste. Genevieve | 5.6 | 307 | 12 | 146 | 73.6 | 5.1 | 64 | 515 | 148.2 | 9.3 | 10 | 19 | 1.4 | 0.3 |
| St. Francois | 7.4 | 120 | 37 | D | D | D | 250 | 3 208 | 685.8 | 63.6 | 61 | 265 | 26.8 | 5.3 |
| St. Louis | 789.6 | 786 | 1 719 | 27 191 | 27 366.6 | 1 590.7 | 4 151 | 72 067 | 17 237.5 | 1 929.5 | 1 537 | 12 311 | 2 477.9 | 474.1 |
| Saline | 4.5 | 197 | 33 | D | D | D | 108 | 1 103 | 230.3 | 19.9 | 21 | 58 | 6.5 | 0.8 |
| Schuyler | 0.5 | 114 | 3 | D | D | D | 27 | 179 | 32.1 | 2.4 | NA | NA | NA | NA |
| Scotland | 0.9 | 172 | 6 | D | D | D | 31 | 168 | 39.4 | 3.0 | 3 | D | D | D |
| Scott | 107.9 | 2 622 | 57 | 538 | 252.4 | 16.0 | 190 | 1 515 | 358.4 | 29.1 | 48 | D | D | D |
| Shannon | 1.1 | 129 | 8 | 59 | 14.3 | 1.0 | 21 | 167 | 26.2 | 1.9 | 7 | 30 | 1.5 | 0.3 |
| Shelby | 2.1 | 308 | 12 | 71 | 30.5 | 2.0 | 35 | 229 | 49.1 | 3.8 | 4 | 7 | 0.4 | 0.0 |
| Stoddard | 334.8 | 11 267 | 31 | 230 | 196.3 | 7.0 | 143 | 1 409 | 436.1 | 29.7 | 23 | 62 | 5.3 | 1.0 |
| Stone | 4.5 | 146 | 15 | 35 | 14.2 | 0.8 | 116 | 1 086 | 222.9 | 21.9 | 53 | 262 | 26.8 | 5.0 |
| Sullivan | 3.6 | 520 | 2 | D | D | D | 28 | 183 | 45.0 | 3.2 | 3 | 3 | 0.3 | 0.0 |
| Taney | 32.7 | 760 | 33 | 199 | 76.0 | 5.7 | 447 | 4 576 | 833.0 | 84.4 | 137 | 1 343 | 295.8 | 52.2 |
| Texas | 4.4 | 179 | 22 | 121 | 50.7 | 3.1 | 92 | 789 | 167.8 | 13.9 | 12 | 30 | 2.4 | 0.7 |
| Vernon | 6.0 | 294 | 18 | 130 | 61.2 | 4.6 | 79 | 839 | 200.6 | 17.0 | 18 | 44 | 5.6 | 0.9 |
| Warren | 2.5 | 88 | 29 | D | D | D | 109 | 1 166 | 318.0 | 22.2 | 27 | 97 | 13.4 | 2.0 |
| Washington | 3.3 | 136 | 14 | D | D | D | 53 | 499 | 124.3 | 9.7 | 5 | D | D | D |
| Wayne | 1.9 | 147 | 8 | 44 | 29.8 | 1.2 | 46 | 388 | 65.8 | 6.4 | 2 | D | D | D |
| Webster | 4.7 | 134 | 31 | 146 | 69.5 | 5.3 | 122 | 1 123 | 294.2 | 23.4 | 23 | 56 | 5.3 | 0.9 |
| Worth | 0.3 | 156 | 5 | 14 | 7.7 | 0.4 | 13 | 64 | 13.2 | 1.0 | 1 | D | D | D |
| Wright | 3.3 | 179 | 16 | 101 | 31.7 | 1.9 | 99 | 989 | 237.9 | 19.7 | 18 | 47 | 4.1 | 0.6 |

1. Merchant wholesalers, except manufacturers' sales branches and offices.  2. Employer establishments.

— **Professional Services, Manufacturing, and Accommodation and Food Services**

| STATE County | Professional, scientific, and technical services,[1] 2007 | | | | Manufacturing, 2007 | | | | Accommodation and food services, 2007 | | | |
|---|---|---|---|---|---|---|---|---|---|---|---|---|
| | Number of establishments | Number of employees | Receipts (mil dol) | Annual payroll (mil dol) | Number of establishments | Number of employees | Receipts (mil dol) | Annual payroll (mil dol) | Number of establishments | Number of employees | Sales (mil dol) | Annual payroll (mil dol) |
| | 147 | 148 | 149 | 150 | 151 | 152 | 153 | 154 | 155 | 156 | 157 | 158 |
| MISSOURI—Cont'd | | | | | | | | | | | | |
| Jasper | 200 | D | D | D | 189 | 10 351 | 3 336.6 | 383.6 | 247 | 4 792 | 182.3 | 52.8 |
| Jefferson | 227 | 976 | 75.8 | 27.1 | 202 | 5 784 | 1 538.1 | 229.5 | 272 | 5 399 | 203.3 | 58.0 |
| Johnson | 70 | D | D | D | 36 | 2 030 | D | D | 94 | 1 797 | 56.7 | 16.8 |
| Knox | 8 | D | D | D | NA | NA | NA | NA | 5 | 26 | 0.6 | 0.2 |
| Laclede | 41 | 169 | 11.1 | 3.7 | 63 | 4 892 | 1 225.6 | 151.8 | 74 | 1 233 | 50.3 | 13.9 |
| Lafayette | 50 | D | D | D | 36 | 1 123 | 225.7 | 32.8 | 67 | 793 | 25.4 | 7.2 |
| Lawrence | 48 | 181 | 11.2 | 3.6 | 48 | 1 622 | 608.7 | 58.5 | 55 | 686 | 20.5 | 6.1 |
| Lewis | 7 | D | D | D | NA | NA | NA | NA | 12 | D | D | D |
| Lincoln | 47 | 190 | 12.6 | 4.5 | 47 | 1 400 | 528.3 | 68.0 | 66 | 1 037 | 31.1 | 8.7 |
| Linn | 23 | 82 | 6.6 | 1.9 | 19 | 1 107 | 166.9 | 37.4 | 21 | 269 | 9.3 | 2.5 |
| Livingston | 30 | 160 | 10.0 | 3.2 | 17 | 610 | 130.3 | 22.4 | 32 | 534 | 17.4 | 5.0 |
| McDonald | 16 | 43 | 2.3 | 0.8 | 24 | 2 413 | D | 60.7 | 29 | 265 | 10.0 | 2.5 |
| Macon | 18 | 79 | 7.2 | 2.8 | NA | NA | NA | NA | 36 | 486 | 15.2 | 4.2 |
| Madison | 11 | D | D | D | NA | NA | NA | NA | 23 | 278 | 6.7 | 2.0 |
| Maries | 6 | D | D | D | NA | NA | NA | NA | 15 | 154 | 2.6 | 0.7 |
| Marion | 48 | D | D | D | 43 | 1 843 | D | 72.9 | 74 | 1 275 | 41.8 | 12.7 |
| Mercer | 3 | D | D | D | NA | NA | NA | NA | 9 | 22 | 0.6 | 0.2 |
| Miller | 42 | 199 | 24.5 | 9.5 | 23 | 699 | 74.8 | 21.2 | 58 | 650 | 30.0 | 9.1 |
| Mississippi | 10 | D | D | D | NA | NA | NA | NA | 23 | 271 | 10.0 | 2.8 |
| Moniteau | 18 | 62 | 4.5 | 1.3 | 26 | 747 | D | 25.2 | 27 | 280 | 8.2 | 2.4 |
| Monroe | 8 | D | D | D | 10 | 731 | D | 20.3 | 21 | 139 | 4.4 | 1.1 |
| Montgomery | 12 | D | D | D | 19 | 561 | 121.7 | 18.2 | 16 | 195 | 6.0 | 2.4 |
| Morgan | 26 | D | D | D | 28 | 537 | 108.1 | 14.7 | 43 | 428 | 13.3 | 3.9 |
| New Madrid | 17 | D | D | D | 17 | 1 768 | D | 87.0 | 28 | 383 | 15.0 | 4.2 |
| Newton | 69 | D | D | D | 80 | 3 434 | 646.7 | 107.1 | 105 | 1 962 | 69.6 | 20.4 |
| Nodaway | 27 | 114 | 8.4 | 3.0 | 19 | 2 064 | 866.6 | 65.7 | 40 | 934 | 28.8 | 8.2 |
| Oregon | 11 | D | D | D | NA | NA | NA | NA | 11 | 178 | 5.9 | 1.6 |
| Osage | 10 | 21 | 1.8 | 0.5 | 31 | 943 | 433.1 | 33.5 | 23 | 167 | 4.1 | 1.1 |
| Ozark | 9 | D | D | D | NA | NA | NA | NA | 22 | 174 | 6.4 | 1.9 |
| Pemiscot | 17 | D | D | D | 12 | D | D | D | 34 | 398 | 14.4 | 3.5 |
| Perry | 28 | 128 | 9.1 | 4.0 | 38 | 3 339 | 711.6 | 105.7 | 43 | 599 | 20.2 | 5.8 |
| Pettis | 69 | 328 | 30.2 | 9.1 | 60 | 5 058 | 1 535.8 | 162.4 | 92 | 1 590 | 55.4 | 17.2 |
| Phelps | 66 | 371 | 33.0 | 12.0 | 51 | 1 224 | 454.8 | 51.5 | 106 | 1 893 | 73.6 | 19.1 |
| Pike | 16 | 77 | 5.4 | 1.6 | 20 | 722 | 308.9 | 32.8 | 28 | 318 | 11.3 | 3.0 |
| Platte | 248 | 1 331 | 180.9 | 60.2 | 65 | 2 816 | 2 077.4 | 128.3 | 198 | 6 301 | 465.6 | 109.4 |
| Polk | 48 | 182 | 13.4 | 4.5 | 35 | 697 | D | 17.9 | 54 | 667 | 23.3 | 5.5 |
| Pulaski | 47 | D | D | D | NA | NA | NA | NA | 87 | 2 033 | 74.3 | 32.2 |
| Putnam | 4 | D | D | D | NA | NA | NA | NA | 4 | 18 | 0.5 | 0.1 |
| Ralls | 9 | D | D | D | 15 | 1 481 | D | 69.9 | 16 | 127 | 3.6 | 1.1 |
| Randolph | 32 | 79 | 9.7 | 1.7 | 30 | 1 165 | 196.9 | 38.5 | 40 | 600 | 21.8 | 5.5 |
| Ray | 24 | 79 | 6.3 | 2.1 | NA | NA | NA | NA | 31 | 329 | 10.2 | 2.8 |
| Reynolds | 6 | D | D | D | NA | NA | NA | NA | 17 | 45 | 4.1 | 0.9 |
| Ripley | 10 | D | D | D | NA | NA | NA | NA | 12 | 140 | 5.7 | 1.6 |
| St. Charles | 761 | D | D | D | 271 | 15 683 | 6 532.8 | 806.9 | 677 | 14 650 | 537.7 | 161.9 |
| St. Clair | 8 | D | D | D | 15 | D | D | NA | 15 | 88 | 5.4 | 0.9 |
| Ste. Genevieve | 22 | 84 | 6.3 | 2.0 | 32 | 1 678 | 368.5 | 68.7 | 37 | 411 | 11.4 | 3.3 |
| St. Francois | 88 | D | D | D | 65 | 2 228 | 341.8 | 69.5 | 116 | D | D | D |
| St. Louis | 3 774 | 42 378 | 6 944.0 | 2 652.2 | 1 098 | 54 752 | 22 654.6 | 3 285.3 | 2 142 | 50 401 | 2 440.7 | 703.9 |
| Saline | 32 | 99 | 6.7 | 2.0 | 20 | 1 768 | 803.5 | 62.2 | 41 | 511 | 15.9 | 5.4 |
| Schuyler | 2 | D | D | D | NA | NA | NA | NA | 5 | 19 | 0.4 | 0.1 |
| Scotland | 7 | D | D | D | NA | NA | NA | NA | 10 | 61 | 2.2 | 0.6 |
| Scott | 75 | 435 | 41.6 | 14.0 | 72 | D | 976.9 | D | 83 | D | D | D |
| Shannon | 5 | D | D | D | NA | NA | NA | NA | 21 | 125 | 4.4 | 1.2 |
| Shelby | 11 | D | D | D | NA | NA | NA | NA | 13 | 76 | 1.7 | 0.5 |
| Stoddard | 28 | 184 | 15.6 | 4.4 | 42 | 2 753 | 888.0 | 99.0 | 39 | 630 | 20.5 | 6.0 |
| Stone | 39 | 139 | 7.7 | 3.0 | NA | NA | NA | NA | 101 | 641 | 47.6 | 10.4 |
| Sullivan | 5 | D | D | D | 6 | D | D | D | 6 | 21 | 0.6 | 0.1 |
| Taney | 110 | 581 | 45.4 | 16.2 | 50 | 535 | D | D | 303 | 6 283 | 360.7 | 106.6 |
| Texas | 25 | D | D | D | 48 | 987 | 214.7 | 28.7 | 38 | 381 | 11.0 | 3.3 |
| Vernon | 29 | 116 | 9.9 | 3.0 | 28 | 1 135 | D | 45.3 | 40 | 498 | 18.7 | 4.4 |
| Warren | 33 | 175 | 15.1 | 5.3 | 44 | 1 039 | 297.4 | 42.7 | 47 | 658 | 22.4 | 6.1 |
| Washington | 14 | D | D | D | 20 | 512 | 104.2 | 16.5 | 17 | 401 | 17.3 | 5.2 |
| Wayne | 10 | D | D | D | NA | NA | NA | NA | 21 | 128 | 4.4 | 1.2 |
| Webster | 40 | D | D | D | 48 | 977 | 161.5 | 30.7 | 36 | 638 | 22.2 | 5.6 |
| Worth | 4 | D | D | D | NA | NA | NA | NA | 5 | 15 | 0.5 | 0.1 |
| Wright | 21 | D | D | D | 24 | 526 | 146.6 | 18.0 | 30 | 301 | 38.0 | 5.8 |

1. Establishment subject to federal tax.

# Table B. States and Counties — Health Care and Social Assistance, Other Services, and Federal Funds

| STATE County | Health care and social assistance, 2007 | | | | Other services, 2007 | | | | Federal funds and grants, 2009–2010 Expenditures (mil dol) | | | |
|---|---|---|---|---|---|---|---|---|---|---|---|---|
| | | | | | | | | | | Direct payments for individuals[1] | | |
| | Number of establish-ments | Number of employees | Receipts (mil dol) | Annual payroll (mil dol) | Number of establish-ments | Number of employees | Receipts (mil dol) | Annual payroll (mil dol) | Total | Social Security and government retirement | Medicare | Food Stamps and Supplemental Security Income |
| | 159 | 160 | 161 | 162 | 163 | 164 | 165 | 166 | 167 | 168 | 169 | 170 |
| MISSOURI—Cont'd | | | | | | | | | | | | |
| Jasper | 396 | 5 138 | 349.6 | 164.1 | 252 | 1 297 | 92.5 | 27.5 | 953.0 | 383.2 | 195.6 | 47.1 |
| Jefferson | 445 | 5 598 | 366.7 | 155.4 | 336 | 1 668 | 139.3 | 42.8 | 1 068.4 | 593.6 | 222.8 | 48.6 |
| Johnson | 112 | 1 779 | 123.5 | 51.0 | 59 | D | D | D | 678.4 | 145.9 | 48.1 | 12.3 |
| Knox | 8 | 59 | 2.8 | 1.1 | 13 | 37 | 3.2 | 0.5 | 51.9 | 15.6 | 14.0 | 1.4 |
| Laclede | 73 | 1 228 | 108.3 | 42.8 | 64 | 223 | 17.7 | 4.3 | 283.1 | 138.5 | 47.3 | 11.3 |
| Lafayette | 65 | 1 130 | 62.7 | 26.3 | 49 | 166 | 10.3 | 2.7 | 260.5 | 112.7 | 66.6 | 8.7 |
| Lawrence | 80 | 1 522 | 97.2 | 45.6 | 42 | 116 | 8.5 | 2.5 | 255.7 | 110.9 | 54.4 | 11.3 |
| Lewis | 18 | 311 | 10.5 | 5.2 | 11 | D | D | D | 99.4 | 33.0 | 19.6 | 3.1 |
| Lincoln | 65 | 1 291 | 67.9 | 28.8 | 76 | 276 | 22.2 | 5.4 | 250.9 | 133.4 | 50.2 | 11.3 |
| Linn | 34 | 549 | 30.3 | 12.4 | 29 | 119 | 8.4 | 1.8 | 135.6 | 52.0 | 40.1 | 4.6 |
| Livingston | 45 | 846 | 58.9 | 22.5 | 39 | 182 | 9.9 | 2.4 | 149.2 | 52.1 | 32.9 | 5.2 |
| McDonald | 26 | D | D | D | 18 | D | D | D | 151.6 | 55.7 | 28.0 | 11.2 |
| Macon | 37 | 528 | 31.5 | 12.7 | 36 | 91 | 7.0 | 1.7 | 143.0 | 56.6 | 39.6 | 4.1 |
| Madison | 29 | 713 | 27.3 | 13.6 | 20 | 42 | 3.6 | 0.6 | 109.5 | 45.4 | 25.4 | 6.7 |
| Maries | 12 | 167 | 5.7 | 2.6 | 6 | D | D | D | 62.2 | 27.3 | 16.1 | 2.6 |
| Marion | 105 | 2 778 | 210.2 | 85.6 | 75 | 352 | 19.4 | 4.8 | 266.1 | 105.7 | 60.2 | 14.3 |
| Mercer | 10 | 86 | 3.7 | 1.7 | 5 | 27 | 2.0 | 0.5 | 89.2 | 13.1 | 8.8 | 1.3 |
| Miller | 34 | 444 | 24.7 | 10.1 | 45 | 261 | 16.6 | 5.8 | 188.8 | 88.2 | 48.7 | 9.2 |
| Mississippi | 30 | 540 | 24.2 | 9.3 | 16 | 43 | 3.3 | 0.9 | 187.1 | 44.2 | 29.0 | 14.6 |
| Moniteau | 33 | 355 | 20.1 | 6.8 | 23 | 68 | 3.5 | 0.8 | 91.9 | 40.1 | 25.6 | 3.0 |
| Monroe | 27 | 251 | 8.6 | 3.2 | 13 | 28 | 4.2 | 0.5 | 97.4 | 36.3 | 22.0 | 2.4 |
| Montgomery | 21 | 357 | 17.0 | 7.2 | 19 | 72 | 7.5 | 2.1 | 110.0 | 45.8 | 26.8 | 4.4 |
| Morgan | 31 | 247 | 10.6 | 4.3 | 34 | 95 | 12.0 | 2.0 | 173.0 | 89.8 | 40.5 | 7.5 |
| New Madrid | 42 | 639 | 32.5 | 12.2 | 27 | 69 | 5.6 | 1.0 | 278.4 | 55.9 | 37.0 | 16.5 |
| Newton | 111 | 7 121 | 739.8 | 271.7 | 92 | 378 | 24.7 | 7.1 | 330.0 | 129.5 | 62.9 | 13.8 |
| Nodaway | 52 | 1 096 | 87.0 | 32.5 | 35 | 127 | 10.0 | 2.6 | 165.5 | 59.1 | 30.9 | 3.8 |
| Oregon | 32 | 358 | 14.2 | 6.8 | 20 | 37 | 3.9 | 0.7 | 113.4 | 41.8 | 20.6 | 6.1 |
| Osage | 21 | 412 | 15.0 | 6.4 | 14 | 35 | 4.9 | 0.5 | 84.7 | 34.7 | 23.1 | 1.9 |
| Ozark | 17 | 104 | 4.6 | 2.2 | 18 | D | D | D | 104.0 | 43.0 | 18.5 | 5.3 |
| Pemiscot | 47 | 1 256 | 66.8 | 26.9 | 17 | 101 | 5.3 | 1.6 | 313.3 | 55.9 | 50.0 | 23.4 |
| Perry | 53 | 1 036 | 59.5 | 24.7 | 30 | D | D | D | 129.7 | 54.5 | 30.4 | 3.8 |
| Pettis | 146 | 2 640 | 182.0 | 75.0 | 98 | D | D | D | 348.9 | 139.7 | 71.8 | 16.1 |
| Phelps | 151 | 3 275 | 288.8 | 101.3 | 86 | 329 | 22.0 | 5.9 | 419.9 | 167.2 | 63.4 | 17.4 |
| Pike | 42 | 744 | 37.7 | 16.5 | 25 | 79 | 6.8 | 1.1 | 153.8 | 55.0 | 35.2 | 5.7 |
| Platte | 172 | 2 586 | 221.3 | 89.4 | 165 | 1 057 | 107.2 | 29.4 | 451.4 | 107.3 | 64.7 | 86.3 |
| Polk | 78 | 1 895 | 124.5 | 55.0 | 50 | 138 | 11.8 | 2.2 | 229.7 | 104.9 | 47.9 | 8.6 |
| Pulaski | 65 | 1 496 | 131.3 | 52.4 | 65 | 334 | 20.8 | 7.0 | 2 245.3 | 170.8 | 40.2 | 14.4 |
| Putnam | 12 | 143 | 8.3 | 4.2 | 9 | D | D | D | 53.8 | 18.5 | 14.4 | 1.8 |
| Ralls | 15 | 189 | 8.6 | 3.8 | 15 | 89 | 10.2 | 2.0 | 75.4 | 25.7 | 14.2 | 2.2 |
| Randolph | 89 | 1 422 | 119.9 | 40.1 | 47 | 139 | 10.3 | 2.8 | 221.2 | 85.4 | 56.6 | 12.3 |
| Ray | 33 | 516 | 33.9 | 13.3 | 28 | 87 | 6.2 | 1.4 | 140.8 | 66.2 | 37.6 | 4.9 |
| Reynolds | 18 | 141 | 5.4 | 2.6 | 3 | D | D | D | 73.2 | 25.4 | 14.7 | 4.4 |
| Ripley | 41 | 544 | 20.3 | 10.7 | 15 | 44 | 3.7 | 0.7 | 161.9 | 54.1 | 28.7 | 12.0 |
| St. Charles | 738 | 12 709 | 1 145.5 | 439.2 | 596 | 3 813 | 272.6 | 90.1 | 1 970.7 | 944.4 | 258.7 | 44.2 |
| St. Clair | 25 | 512 | 26.2 | 14.2 | 9 | D | D | D | 102.9 | 40.5 | 21.2 | 5.0 |
| Ste. Genevieve | 35 | 769 | 45.9 | 18.9 | 36 | 151 | 10.5 | 2.9 | 116.3 | 57.3 | 26.3 | 4.1 |
| St. Francois | 233 | 4 516 | 300.1 | 121.7 | 108 | 885 | 33.7 | 10.9 | 523.0 | 224.4 | 113.3 | 35.0 |
| St. Louis | 3 357 | 78 505 | 7 776.5 | 3 129.0 | 2 050 | 16 511 | 1 702.5 | 517.0 | 12 747.8 | 3 202.5 | 1 860.1 | 253.0 |
| Saline | 69 | 1 467 | 93.4 | 35.5 | 38 | 113 | 10.3 | 2.8 | 213.3 | 70.3 | 51.8 | 7.3 |
| Schuyler | 4 | D | D | D | 8 | D | D | D | 47.4 | 17.0 | 11.7 | 1.4 |
| Scotland | 12 | 223 | 15.1 | 7.7 | 15 | D | D | D | 49.0 | 15.0 | 12.8 | 1.4 |
| Scott | 123 | 2 713 | 175.7 | 73.4 | 77 | D | D | D | 385.6 | 144.4 | 70.8 | 27.2 |
| Shannon | 20 | 90 | 4.6 | 2.0 | 5 | 13 | 1.4 | 0.3 | 77.3 | 26.4 | 13.4 | 5.4 |
| Shelby | 8 | 90 | 4.6 | 1.5 | 12 | 31 | 3.9 | 0.8 | 66.3 | 24.0 | 17.5 | 2.1 |
| Stoddard | 77 | 1 558 | 69.0 | 31.2 | 39 | 165 | 16.4 | 3.8 | 325.1 | 109.7 | 60.9 | 13.7 |
| Stone | 50 | 549 | 43.6 | 15.7 | 52 | 260 | 18.3 | 5.2 | 221.4 | 135.1 | 43.9 | 9.6 |
| Sullivan | 17 | 262 | 14.1 | 5.8 | 12 | 26 | 2.7 | 0.6 | 85.9 | 20.8 | 19.4 | 2.6 |
| Taney | 111 | 2 196 | 243.6 | 93.9 | 110 | 512 | 47.6 | 11.1 | 328.3 | 182.5 | 67.7 | 12.1 |
| Texas | 58 | 954 | 49.9 | 20.6 | 37 | 79 | 6.4 | 1.3 | 212.5 | 96.6 | 37.3 | 12.8 |
| Vernon | 103 | 1 272 | 87.7 | 30.4 | 38 | 184 | 14.1 | 4.1 | 172.6 | 71.7 | 37.0 | 8.8 |
| Warren | 42 | 517 | 26.6 | 10.7 | 42 | 153 | 9.1 | 2.9 | 173.5 | 92.6 | 37.7 | 5.2 |
| Washington | 55 | 676 | 39.2 | 15.2 | 23 | 66 | 4.5 | 1.1 | 200.6 | 73.2 | 32.7 | 18.7 |
| Wayne | 29 | 319 | 12.6 | 4.9 | 10 | D | D | D | 230.6 | 65.7 | 32.9 | 10.3 |
| Webster | 48 | D | D | D | 42 | 136 | 8.9 | 2.3 | 265.1 | 119.4 | 43.5 | 10.7 |
| Worth | 3 | D | D | D | 3 | 13 | 0.9 | 0.2 | 24.6 | 9.5 | 4.6 | 0.9 |
| Wright | 43 | 479 | 25.8 | 10.2 | 29 | 81 | 6.0 | 1.4 | 198.9 | 74.4 | 38.7 | 11.3 |

1. State totals may include programs not allocated by county.

# Table B. States and Counties — Federal Funds, Residential Construction, and Local Government Finances

| STATE County | Federal funds and grants, 2009–2010 (cont.) | | | | | | | Value of residential construction authorized by building permits, 2011 | | Local government finances, 2007 | | | | |
| | Expenditures (mil dol) (cont.) | | | | | | | | | General revenue | | | | |
| | Procurement contract awards | | | Grants[1] | | | | | | | | Taxes | | |
| | | | | | | | | | | | | | Per capita[2] (dollars) | |
| | Salaries and wages | Defense | Other | Medicaid and other health-related | Nutrition and family welfare | Education | Other | New construction ($1,000) | Number of housing units | Total (mil dol) | Inter-governmental (mil dol) | Total (mil dol) | Total | Property |
| | 171 | 172 | 173 | 174 | 175 | 176 | 177 | 178 | 179 | 180 | 181 | 182 | 183 | 184 |
| MISSOURI—Cont'd | | | | | | | | | | | | | | |
| Jasper | 51.4 | 37.7 | 27.8 | 141.4 | 20.1 | 9.6 | 14.8 | 24 393 | 270 | 307.9 | 106.1 | 122.2 | 1 060 | 546 |
| Jefferson | 49.0 | 8.7 | 7.0 | 81.2 | 21.4 | 9.0 | 9.1 | 65 591 | 435 | 479.8 | 196.8 | 217.0 | 1 004 | 731 |
| Johnson | 227.7 | 176.3 | 2.5 | 23.1 | 5.8 | 8.9 | 6.0 | 9 489 | 95 | 166.9 | 48.8 | 43.9 | 845 | 536 |
| Knox | 2.9 | 0.0 | 0.6 | 7.6 | 0.7 | 0.4 | 0.0 | 0 | 0 | 10.6 | 5.1 | 3.7 | 910 | 707 |
| Laclede | 15.4 | 0.1 | 1.4 | 57.9 | 4.7 | 2.3 | 1.9 | 2 850 | 36 | 108.9 | 49.2 | 34.4 | 972 | 607 |
| Lafayette | 22.2 | 5.3 | 1.9 | 21.6 | 3.2 | 2.9 | 2.2 | 5 114 | 26 | 79.3 | 34.6 | 29.3 | 898 | 600 |
| Lawrence | 17.4 | 0.0 | 4.4 | 41.3 | 4.7 | 3.8 | 4.5 | 485 | 5 | 70.2 | 34.5 | 23.6 | 627 | 421 |
| Lewis | 4.0 | 10.2 | 0.8 | 14.7 | 1.6 | 0.9 | 0.9 | 529 | 5 | 26.6 | 11.5 | 7.3 | 727 | 509 |
| Lincoln | 8.8 | 2.2 | 1.9 | 29.5 | 3.7 | 0.8 | 2.5 | 7 249 | 72 | 122.5 | 42.3 | 39.2 | 761 | 538 |
| Linn | 4.7 | 0.0 | 1.1 | 23.2 | 2.2 | 1.1 | 1.1 | 0 | 0 | 37.8 | 17.2 | 13.2 | 1 041 | 659 |
| Livingston | 15.8 | 0.0 | 1.4 | 28.0 | 2.0 | 1.0 | 1.3 | 1 955 | 12 | 66.5 | 28.0 | 15.7 | 1 109 | 849 |
| McDonald | 10.1 | 2.4 | 0.8 | 36.6 | 3.2 | 1.6 | 0.9 | 236 | 4 | 43.0 | 24.2 | 13.7 | 599 | 343 |
| Macon | 9.8 | 0.3 | 1.2 | 22.1 | 2.2 | 1.1 | 0.3 | 600 | 10 | 51.8 | 19.2 | 14.5 | 929 | 595 |
| Madison | 1.7 | 0.0 | 1.6 | 23.7 | 2.0 | 0.9 | 1.1 | 550 | 11 | 33.9 | 11.6 | 6.1 | 497 | 374 |
| Maries | 0.9 | 0.0 | 0.2 | 12.8 | 1.1 | 0.6 | 0.1 | 502 | 3 | 14.0 | 6.1 | 5.9 | 643 | 479 |
| Marion | 7.9 | 0.4 | 2.3 | 52.9 | 8.3 | 2.0 | 1.2 | 8 337 | 48 | 111.8 | 42.3 | 45.1 | 1 601 | 1 036 |
| Mercer | 1.4 | 0.0 | 0.3 | 7.6 | 0.7 | 0.1 | 51.2 | 0 | 0 | 11.4 | 4.5 | 4.6 | 1 315 | 1 033 |
| Miller | 5.3 | 0.0 | 1.2 | 29.4 | 3.5 | 1.7 | 0.2 | 4 177 | 22 | 73.7 | 25.6 | 34.7 | 1 395 | 978 |
| Mississippi | 3.1 | 0.0 | 0.7 | 71.7 | 4.3 | 1.9 | 3.3 | 671 | 9 | 31.6 | 16.8 | 9.7 | 709 | 482 |
| Moniteau | 3.3 | 0.0 | 0.7 | 14.7 | 1.5 | 1.1 | 0.1 | 150 | 1 | 28.2 | 13.3 | 10.4 | 683 | 549 |
| Monroe | 4.4 | 4.0 | 0.8 | 17.1 | 1.3 | 0.9 | 0.7 | 3 141 | 19 | 30.0 | 12.5 | 9.1 | 987 | 760 |
| Montgomery | 4.2 | 0.0 | 1.0 | 19.0 | 1.5 | 1.2 | 0.0 | 3 615 | 27 | 22.7 | 10.1 | 8.9 | 745 | 526 |
| Morgan | 3.8 | 0.0 | 1.0 | 21.8 | 2.4 | 1.2 | 3.6 | 0 | 0 | 34.1 | 13.5 | 14.6 | 700 | 534 |
| New Madrid | 8.6 | 2.5 | 0.9 | 98.6 | 12.9 | 2.4 | 24.7 | 1 796 | 17 | 58.7 | 21.2 | 30.9 | 1 737 | 1 465 |
| Newton | 36.5 | 0.1 | 3.5 | 47.7 | 6.9 | 7.2 | 10.0 | 5 006 | 40 | 104.0 | 51.2 | 33.0 | 588 | 366 |
| Nodaway | 18.2 | 1.3 | 2.1 | 20.9 | 4.2 | 4.2 | 0.9 | 3 947 | 31 | 54.5 | 21.3 | 23.1 | 1 042 | 706 |
| Oregon | 2.6 | 0.0 | 0.6 | 37.9 | 2.3 | 1.0 | 0.2 | 0 | 0 | 25.5 | 14.9 | 5.8 | 559 | 390 |
| Osage | 3.0 | 0.0 | 0.7 | 15.2 | 1.0 | 0.7 | 1.1 | 0 | 0 | 19.0 | 8.1 | 8.0 | 596 | 445 |
| Ozark | 2.2 | 0.0 | 0.6 | 30.8 | 2.0 | 1.4 | 0.1 | 118 | 5 | 21.6 | 13.0 | 5.8 | 633 | 527 |
| Pemiscot | 4.4 | 0.4 | 1.0 | 142.7 | 7.4 | 4.0 | 4.0 | 346 | 9 | 60.2 | 35.5 | 13.7 | 730 | 477 |
| Perry | 5.7 | 7.1 | 0.8 | 20.5 | 2.2 | 0.8 | 0.0 | 4 322 | 28 | 35.8 | 10.4 | 18.2 | 969 | 583 |
| Pettis | 20.6 | 3.9 | 3.1 | 61.1 | 6.6 | 3.5 | 1.7 | 1 014 | 29 | 194.7 | 45.6 | 43.7 | 1 070 | 591 |
| Phelps | 42.9 | 3.2 | 5.5 | 58.0 | 5.4 | 3.0 | 44.5 | 11 140 | 139 | 229.4 | 41.7 | 36.0 | 847 | 429 |
| Pike | 5.1 | 0.1 | 1.9 | 26.1 | 2.4 | 2.1 | 10.7 | 540 | 6 | 37.7 | 16.2 | 14.1 | 765 | 494 |
| Platte | 62.3 | 30.7 | 34.0 | 14.8 | 5.8 | 4.0 | 33.3 | 30 802 | 135 | 241.2 | 55.2 | 132.0 | 1 555 | 1 083 |
| Polk | 8.2 | 0.0 | 1.7 | 44.0 | 3.6 | 4.4 | 0.3 | 5 170 | 41 | 134.5 | 73.7 | 21.8 | 720 | 432 |
| Pulaski | 1 513.7 | 422.1 | 1.3 | 40.7 | 10.5 | 22.1 | 0.2 | 14 045 | 112 | 106.3 | 64.4 | 24.7 | 557 | 354 |
| Putnam | 2.4 | 0.0 | 1.1 | 10.0 | 0.8 | 0.5 | 0.0 | 120 | 2 | 20.2 | 4.9 | 5.8 | 1 178 | 972 |
| Ralls | 5.5 | 2.8 | 1.3 | 7.1 | 1.0 | 0.5 | 9.7 | 260 | 3 | 11.7 | 4.5 | 5.4 | 544 | 411 |
| Randolph | 8.4 | 0.2 | 1.5 | 35.6 | 2.9 | 1.8 | 1.1 | 1 954 | 18 | 88.6 | 29.6 | 38.7 | 1 513 | 1 018 |
| Ray | 5.9 | 0.0 | 0.9 | 12.8 | 3.1 | 1.4 | 1.2 | 1 477 | 8 | 94.9 | 26.1 | 23.4 | 997 | 681 |
| Reynolds | 2.0 | 0.0 | 0.6 | 23.2 | 1.4 | 0.8 | 0.3 | 0 | 0 | 16.7 | 8.3 | 4.9 | 761 | 652 |
| Ripley | 4.6 | 0.0 | 2.7 | 53.5 | 3.4 | 1.2 | 0.2 | 75 | 2 | 23.8 | 14.4 | 6.1 | 453 | 347 |
| St. Charles | 86.5 | 436.8 | 57.3 | 67.8 | 20.2 | 9.7 | 9.4 | 209 993 | 1 064 | 1 051.3 | 252.0 | 579.6 | 1 685 | 1 122 |
| St. Clair | 2.4 | 0.0 | 0.6 | 16.6 | 6.0 | 1.0 | 7.4 | 0 | 0 | 47.8 | 16.7 | 5.7 | 609 | 499 |
| Ste. Genevieve | 3.1 | 7.7 | 0.5 | 12.5 | 1.9 | 0.8 | 0.0 | 0 | 0 | 58.3 | 20.7 | 15.5 | 869 | 659 |
| St. Francois | 21.0 | 0.1 | 4.8 | 81.2 | 11.7 | 5.3 | 13.1 | 26 770 | 331 | 156.0 | 70.0 | 54.0 | 859 | 482 |
| St. Louis | 1 567.0 | 4 569.4 | 372.2 | 511.3 | 88.2 | 57.0 | 162.1 | 212 089 | 728 | 3 322.7 | 890.3 | 1 872.3 | 1 882 | 1 386 |
| Saline | 15.5 | 0.0 | 1.1 | 40.3 | 6.8 | 2.0 | 2.0 | 1 345 | 10 | 77.2 | 35.5 | 27.6 | 1 217 | 911 |
| Schuyler | 4.9 | 0.0 | 0.5 | 8.0 | 0.8 | 0.4 | 0.1 | 168 | 1 | 11.4 | 4.6 | 4.0 | 964 | 736 |
| Scotland | 1.4 | 0.0 | 0.3 | 6.7 | 0.7 | 0.4 | 2.3 | 0 | 0 | 28.4 | 7.6 | 3.9 | 813 | 635 |
| Scott | 6.9 | 0.8 | 1.5 | 101.2 | 6.9 | 3.3 | 5.5 | 5 467 | 52 | 92.0 | 40.8 | 35.2 | 865 | 492 |
| Shannon | 2.5 | 0.0 | 0.6 | 22.7 | 5.2 | 0.5 | 0.1 | 0 | 0 | 63.8 | 7.6 | 53.6 | 6 352 | 6 220 |
| Shelby | 3.3 | 0.5 | 0.8 | 10.0 | 1.0 | 0.6 | 0.1 | 167 | 1 | 22.7 | 9.6 | 6.7 | 1 023 | 746 |
| Stoddard | 12.4 | 0.5 | 7.1 | 85.8 | 5.2 | 2.4 | 3.2 | 2 051 | 30 | 69.6 | 28.8 | 28.3 | 951 | 610 |
| Stone | 3.4 | 0.2 | 0.9 | 21.2 | 3.5 | 2.6 | 0.1 | 19 851 | 97 | 82.0 | 29.0 | 44.0 | 1 395 | 966 |
| Sullivan | 4.1 | 0.0 | 2.2 | 22.3 | 1.5 | 0.4 | 8.9 | 65 | 1 | 23.6 | 9.0 | 7.0 | 1 047 | 706 |
| Taney | 9.9 | 14.9 | 1.4 | 27.1 | 3.9 | 1.5 | 1.0 | 22 192 | 191 | 155.5 | 41.5 | 81.1 | 1 773 | 727 |
| Texas | 6.8 | 0.0 | 1.1 | 46.0 | 4.3 | 3.2 | 0.9 | 55 | 1 | 73.4 | 26.8 | 12.9 | 555 | 351 |
| Vernon | 11.3 | 0.2 | 1.4 | 27.5 | 3.1 | 1.6 | 0.7 | 1 327 | 14 | 44.6 | 21.3 | 16.1 | 805 | 501 |
| Warren | 17.2 | 0.6 | 1.0 | 12.9 | 2.3 | 1.0 | 0.1 | 18 606 | 127 | 60.7 | 20.5 | 30.6 | 1 005 | 624 |
| Washington | 4.9 | 0.0 | 1.4 | 49.5 | 4.9 | 1.8 | 12.9 | 400 | 4 | 62.8 | 23.2 | 18.9 | 778 | 589 |
| Wayne | 4.3 | 70.9 | 0.7 | 40.7 | 3.0 | 1.1 | 0.5 | NA | NA | 22.2 | 12.7 | 6.5 | 514 | 342 |
| Webster | 7.4 | 0.2 | 1.6 | 47.4 | 4.0 | 2.4 | 27.3 | 7 025 | 63 | 57.5 | 26.9 | 19.4 | 539 | 294 |
| Worth | 1.9 | 0.0 | 0.5 | 4.3 | 0.4 | 0.2 | 0.0 | 0 | 0 | 6.7 | 2.8 | 1.7 | 799 | 643 |
| Wright | 4.8 | 0.0 | 1.2 | 60.2 | 3.3 | 1.7 | 1.3 | 125 | 2 | 43.4 | 23.1 | 11.0 | 602 | 448 |

1. State totals may include programs not allocated by county.    2. Based on the resident population estimated as of July 1 of the year shown.

| STATE County | Total (mil dol) | Per capita[1] (dollars) | Education | Health and hospitals | Police protection | Public welfare | Highways | Total (mil dol) | Per capita[1] (dollars) | Federal civilian | Federal military | State and local | Demo-cratic | Republi-can | All other |
|---|---|---|---|---|---|---|---|---|---|---|---|---|---|---|---|
| | **Local government finances, 2007 (cont.)** | | | | | | | | | **Government employment, 2011** | | | **Presidential election,[2] 2012** | | |
| | **Direct general expenditure** | | | | | | | **Debt outstanding** | | | | | **Percent of vote cast:** | | |
| | | | **Percent of total for:** | | | | | | | | | | | | |
| | 185 | 186 | 187 | 188 | 189 | 190 | 191 | 192 | 193 | 194 | 195 | 196 | 197 | 198 | 199 |
| **MISSOURI—Cont'd** | | | | | | | | | | | | | | | |
| Jasper | 307.7 | 2 670 | 53.2 | 9.2 | 6.7 | 0.1 | 7.9 | 280.2 | 2 431 | 318 | 418 | 6 810 | 32.8 | 65.9 | 1.3 |
| Jefferson | 495.6 | 2 294 | 71.2 | 2.3 | 4.9 | 0.0 | 6.3 | 385.0 | 1 782 | 307 | 755 | 8 337 | 50.6 | 48.1 | 1.4 |
| Johnson | 158.5 | 3 052 | 42.5 | 31.9 | 4.8 | 0.0 | 5.1 | 226.6 | 4 364 | 1 350 | 3 692 | 6 118 | 42.9 | 55.2 | 1.9 |
| Knox | 10.3 | 2 534 | 50.0 | 9.2 | 3.8 | 20.6 | 5.7 | 2.2 | 553 | 36 | 14 | 286 | 37.5 | 59.9 | 2.6 |
| Laclede | 112.0 | 3 165 | 67.3 | 0.5 | 2.7 | 0.1 | 8.4 | 49.8 | 1 408 | 85 | 123 | 1 518 | 32.0 | 66.6 | 1.4 |
| Lafayette | 88.2 | 2 699 | 59.4 | 1.5 | 6.9 | 0.0 | 7.0 | 83.4 | 2 552 | 122 | 118 | 2 129 | 41.6 | 56.9 | 1.5 |
| Lawrence | 77.8 | 2 066 | 65.0 | 1.7 | 4.2 | 4.6 | 9.5 | 68.6 | 1 821 | 206 | 133 | 2 013 | 30.6 | 67.7 | 1.7 |
| Lewis | 25.2 | 2 511 | 55.7 | 1.2 | 3.9 | 16.5 | 6.3 | 9.6 | 955 | 52 | 35 | 616 | 40.8 | 57.6 | 1.6 |
| Lincoln | 126.0 | 2 446 | 50.1 | 19.4 | 6.3 | 0.0 | 6.5 | 127.9 | 2 483 | 115 | 183 | 2 269 | 43.5 | 54.9 | 1.7 |
| Linn | 43.3 | 3 412 | 57.2 | 3.3 | 4.2 | 0.0 | 10.7 | 16.1 | 1 272 | 55 | 43 | 770 | 44.5 | 52.9 | 2.6 |
| Livingston | 69.8 | 4 914 | 62.4 | 2.7 | 2.9 | 5.7 | 5.8 | 34.1 | 2 405 | 85 | 52 | 1 327 | 37.2 | 60.9 | 1.9 |
| McDonald | 48.6 | 2 121 | 74.9 | 2.4 | 3.2 | 0.0 | 4.9 | 41.9 | 1 831 | 95 | 79 | 893 | 30.2 | 67.6 | 2.2 |
| Macon | 52.6 | 3 379 | 41.6 | 19.4 | 3.5 | 15.8 | 4.7 | 24.8 | 1 592 | 75 | 54 | 1 708 | 37.2 | 61.4 | 1.4 |
| Madison | 35.9 | 2 947 | 45.4 | 39.8 | 1.5 | 0.0 | 3.8 | 11.0 | 902 | 20 | 42 | 868 | 40.6 | 57.6 | 1.8 |
| Maries | 17.1 | 1 871 | 74.6 | 3.7 | 2.9 | 0.0 | 8.3 | 8.7 | 952 | 11 | 32 | 340 | 35.2 | 62.7 | 2.1 |
| Marion | 120.8 | 4 286 | 70.1 | 3.2 | 3.4 | 4.8 | 3.4 | 116.6 | 4 138 | 107 | 99 | 1 872 | 37.5 | 61.4 | 1.2 |
| Mercer | 12.6 | 3 587 | 62.8 | 4.0 | 2.3 | 0.0 | 15.3 | 7.3 | 2 080 | 24 | 13 | 247 | 29.7 | 66.9 | 3.4 |
| Miller | 74.8 | 3 004 | 63.3 | 4.8 | 3.3 | 3.8 | 4.9 | 55.0 | 2 208 | 49 | 85 | 1 376 | 30.8 | 67.6 | 1.6 |
| Mississippi | 33.2 | 2 425 | 60.9 | 4.8 | 4.3 | 0.4 | 4.2 | 18.0 | 1 316 | 38 | 49 | 1 069 | 42.0 | 56.6 | 1.4 |
| Moniteau | 29.7 | 1 961 | 70.2 | 4.9 | 2.8 | 0.0 | 6.8 | 24.4 | 1 609 | 47 | 54 | 1 026 | 31.3 | 67.0 | 1.7 |
| Monroe | 28.4 | 3 090 | 53.2 | 5.7 | 4.1 | 7.5 | 5.9 | 60.5 | 6 578 | 79 | 30 | 589 | 39.5 | 58.7 | 1.8 |
| Montgomery | 26.1 | 2 190 | 59.2 | 8.0 | 2.9 | 0.0 | 10.4 | 16.5 | 1 388 | 50 | 42 | 676 | 40.1 | 58.5 | 1.4 |
| Morgan | 36.4 | 1 746 | 48.9 | 2.3 | 8.3 | 15.3 | 8.5 | 36.0 | 1 728 | 46 | 71 | 994 | 39.0 | 59.6 | 1.5 |
| New Madrid | 63.0 | 3 541 | 67.8 | 3.0 | 3.8 | 0.0 | 5.8 | 28.3 | 1 592 | 60 | 65 | 979 | 41.6 | 56.8 | 1.6 |
| Newton | 124.9 | 2 228 | 69.7 | 0.5 | 3.5 | 0.0 | 5.5 | 78.9 | 1 408 | 156 | 201 | 2 579 | 29.3 | 69.4 | 1.3 |
| Nodaway | 56.1 | 2 536 | 54.2 | 3.5 | 4.3 | 0.0 | 11.4 | 32.0 | 1 445 | 98 | 81 | 2 576 | 44.0 | 54.5 | 1.5 |
| Oregon | 25.3 | 2 458 | 64.0 | 1.5 | 1.3 | 0.0 | 4.5 | 4.9 | 480 | 30 | 38 | 487 | 39.4 | 57.8 | 2.8 |
| Osage | 20.4 | 1 521 | 69.7 | 5.1 | 3.0 | 0.0 | 6.0 | 10.9 | 815 | 34 | 48 | 769 | 26.9 | 71.5 | 1.6 |
| Ozark | 22.8 | 2 464 | 63.2 | 7.6 | 2.5 | 0.0 | 6.1 | 3.2 | 342 | 20 | 33 | 441 | 35.4 | 62.3 | 2.3 |
| Pemiscot | 62.6 | 3 332 | 68.9 | 1.2 | 4.1 | 0.0 | 4.2 | 14.0 | 744 | 59 | 63 | 1 701 | 43.0 | 56.1 | 0.9 |
| Perry | 35.7 | 1 900 | 55.3 | 3.0 | 6.2 | 0.9 | 6.8 | 31.0 | 1 651 | 50 | 65 | 1 144 | 34.8 | 63.9 | 1.3 |
| Pettis | 193.6 | 4 744 | 37.4 | 44.1 | 2.5 | 0.0 | 4.6 | 58.7 | 1 438 | 138 | 146 | 3 211 | 38.1 | 60.5 | 1.4 |
| Phelps | 232.3 | 5 460 | 25.3 | 55.8 | 2.0 | 0.3 | 3.5 | 95.2 | 2 238 | 412 | 254 | 5 868 | 38.0 | 60.2 | 1.7 |
| Pike | 41.7 | 2 259 | 61.6 | 6.0 | 5.2 | 0.0 | 7.1 | 20.9 | 1 132 | 78 | 64 | 1 733 | 44.2 | 54.2 | 1.6 |
| Platte | 264.2 | 3 113 | 52.7 | 0.8 | 4.9 | 0.0 | 8.0 | 425.7 | 5 015 | 452 | 321 | 3 518 | 46.2 | 52.6 | 1.2 |
| Polk | 131.7 | 4 359 | 34.1 | 51.9 | 2.7 | 0.0 | 5.2 | 57.2 | 1 892 | 83 | 107 | 2 142 | 33.2 | 65.4 | 1.4 |
| Pulaski | 100.5 | 2 267 | 73.7 | 3.9 | 3.7 | 0.1 | 3.3 | 30.5 | 689 | 4 521 | 12 698 | 2 086 | 35.0 | 63.7 | 1.3 |
| Putnam | 18.8 | 3 834 | 35.9 | 35.5 | 0.6 | 0.2 | 5.9 | 21.7 | 4 419 | 28 | 17 | 401 | 29.7 | 68.0 | 2.3 |
| Ralls | 11.1 | 1 127 | 54.3 | 3.7 | 5.7 | 0.2 | 16.1 | 16.2 | 1 647 | 29 | 35 | 425 | 40.1 | 58.8 | 1.1 |
| Randolph | 88.0 | 3 437 | 72.1 | 1.5 | 3.8 | 0.4 | 3.8 | 50.2 | 1 962 | 85 | 87 | 2 139 | 37.5 | 60.8 | 1.7 |
| Ray | 85.4 | 3 638 | 37.7 | 29.5 | 2.6 | 2.8 | 8.6 | 49.7 | 2 118 | 50 | 80 | 1 362 | 47.4 | 50.6 | 2.0 |
| Reynolds | 18.0 | 2 779 | 63.8 | 3.5 | 2.5 | 0.6 | 6.6 | 2.8 | 430 | 21 | 23 | 373 | 43.1 | 54.2 | 2.6 |
| Ripley | 24.9 | 1 834 | 73.0 | 5.9 | 4.7 | 0.0 | 5.3 | 0.9 | 68 | 52 | 49 | 658 | 33.5 | 63.5 | 3.0 |
| St. Charles | 1 063.7 | 3 093 | 52.8 | 1.9 | 5.6 | 0.0 | 10.7 | 1 646.2 | 4 786 | 736 | 1 260 | 14 793 | 44.7 | 54.4 | 1.0 |
| St. Clair | 38.8 | 4 111 | 31.2 | 32.5 | 7.7 | 0.0 | 4.1 | 24.6 | 2 614 | 33 | 33 | 592 | 37.8 | 59.8 | 2.4 |
| Ste. Genevieve | 54.3 | 3 041 | 30.7 | 53.8 | 4.0 | 0.0 | 3.7 | 42.1 | 2 361 | 29 | 62 | 953 | 56.4 | 42.3 | 1.3 |
| St. Francois | 161.0 | 2 563 | 68.0 | 3.1 | 7.3 | 0.3 | 3.8 | 156.1 | 2 485 | 136 | 227 | 5 565 | 47.0 | 51.6 | 1.4 |
| St. Louis | 3 250.1 | 3 266 | 56.9 | 1.6 | 7.2 | 0.7 | 4.8 | 2 992.6 | 3 007 | 6 042 | 3 483 | 51 087 | 59.5 | 39.6 | 0.9 |
| Saline | 79.1 | 3 484 | 72.6 | 3.3 | 4.6 | 0.2 | 4.6 | 14.3 | 628 | 81 | 80 | 1 967 | 47.8 | 50.4 | 1.8 |
| Schuyler | 11.1 | 2 706 | 56.1 | 3.7 | 2.8 | 15.1 | 12.5 | 7.8 | 1 911 | 35 | 15 | 326 | 39.1 | 57.4 | 3.5 |
| Scotland | 27.5 | 5 703 | 22.8 | 44.7 | 0.8 | 14.0 | 0.9 | 6.3 | 1 305 | 22 | 17 | 572 | 37.8 | 59.5 | 2.7 |
| Scott | 100.1 | 2 456 | 62.1 | 2.8 | 9.1 | 0.0 | 3.6 | 219.7 | 5 393 | 86 | 135 | 2 172 | 34.7 | 64.1 | 1.1 |
| Shannon | 14.2 | 1 690 | 53.2 | 7.5 | 2.0 | 0.0 | 19.1 | 4.7 | 558 | 22 | 29 | 319 | 42.7 | 54.1 | 3.3 |
| Shelby | 26.8 | 4 118 | 40.3 | 5.2 | 2.3 | 18.4 | 25.0 | 6.6 | 1 006 | 39 | 22 | 569 | 33.6 | 65.3 | 1.1 |
| Stoddard | 71.1 | 2 391 | 60.8 | 3.7 | 5.4 | 0.0 | 13.4 | 57.7 | 1 941 | 174 | 103 | 1 400 | 29.4 | 69.2 | 1.4 |
| Stone | 79.0 | 2 504 | 68.4 | 0.9 | 3.4 | 0.0 | 7.0 | 57.4 | 1 818 | 40 | 111 | 1 121 | 30.7 | 68.0 | 1.3 |
| Sullivan | 23.5 | 3 527 | 46.3 | 26.3 | 7.2 | 0.0 | 6.1 | 4.5 | 667 | 55 | 23 | 469 | 40.9 | 56.0 | 3.1 |
| Taney | 202.1 | 4 421 | 35.2 | 4.6 | 3.2 | 0.0 | 6.7 | 300.1 | 6 563 | 163 | 181 | 2 190 | 30.8 | 68.0 | 1.1 |
| Texas | 86.9 | 3 724 | 38.7 | 31.9 | 1.9 | 0.0 | 16.9 | 42.8 | 1 836 | 83 | 89 | 1 918 | 31.4 | 66.5 | 2.1 |
| Vernon | 44.8 | 2 240 | 62.8 | 3.2 | 5.2 | 0.0 | 9.4 | 14.1 | 707 | 107 | 72 | 1 691 | 38.1 | 60.1 | 1.8 |
| Warren | 70.9 | 2 327 | 66.5 | 4.0 | 4.9 | 0.0 | 6.2 | 94.2 | 3 091 | 53 | 113 | 1 186 | 43.0 | 55.7 | 1.3 |
| Washington | 58.7 | 2 413 | 51.4 | 32.7 | 3.3 | 0.0 | 3.2 | 34.9 | 1 436 | 56 | 86 | 1 516 | 49.0 | 48.9 | 2.0 |
| Wayne | 23.6 | 1 867 | 65.8 | 7.2 | 3.9 | 0.0 | 9.2 | 13.4 | 1 058 | 90 | 46 | 563 | 36.4 | 61.5 | 2.1 |
| Webster | 56.0 | 1 559 | 64.2 | 1.5 | 3.8 | 6.0 | 7.4 | 32.7 | 911 | 81 | 125 | 1 489 | 34.8 | 63.8 | 1.5 |
| Worth | 6.9 | 3 306 | 53.1 | 1.6 | 1.7 | 23.2 | 9.4 | 4.8 | 2 304 | 23 | 0 | 174 | 36.4 | 60.2 | 3.4 |
| Wright | 46.2 | 2 528 | 67.1 | 1.3 | 2.4 | 8.5 | 5.5 | 14.5 | 793 | 52 | 64 | 870 | 30.0 | 67.9 | 2.0 |

1. Based on the resident population estimated as of July 1 of the year shown.  2. © 2013 Election Data Services, Inc. All rights reserved.

# Table B. States and Counties — Land Area and Population

| | | | | Population 2012 | | | | Population characteristics[6], 2011 | | | | | | | | | | |
| | | | | | | | | Race alone or in combination, not Hispanic or Latino (percent) | | | | | Age (percent) | | | | | |
| STATE/ County code | CBSA code[1] | County type[2] | STATE County | Land area,[3] (sq km) 2010 | Total persons | Rank | Per square kilometer | White | Black | American Indian, Alaska Native | Asian and Pacific Islander | Percent Hispanic or Latino[4] | Under 5 years | 5 to 17 years | 18 to 24 years | 25 to 34 years | 35 to 44 years | 45 to 54 years |
|---|---|---|---|---|---|---|---|---|---|---|---|---|---|---|---|---|---|---|
| | | | | 1 | 2 | 3 | 4 | 5 | 6 | 7 | 8 | 9 | 10 | 11 | 12 | 13 | 14 | 15 |
| | | | MISSOURI—Cont'd | | | | | | | | | | | | | | | |
| 29 510 | 41180 | 1 | St. Louis city | 160 | 318 172 | 205 | 1 988.6 | 45.0 | 49.3 | 0.9 | 3.5 | 3.6 | 6.8 | 14.4 | 11.8 | 18.6 | 12.4 | 13.7 |
| 30 000 | ... | X | MONTANA | 376 962 | 1 005 141 | X | 2.7 | 89.6 | 0.9 | 7.6 | 1.2 | 3.1 | 6.2 | 16.1 | 9.8 | 12.5 | 11.2 | 14.5 |
| 30 001 | ... | 7 | Beaverhead | 14 353 | 9 346 | 2 485 | 0.7 | 93.2 | 0.6 | 2.5 | 1.5 | 3.9 | 4.8 | 14.4 | 14.1 | 10.0 | 9.4 | 13.6 |
| 30 003 | ... | 6 | Big Horn | 12 938 | 13 061 | 2 237 | 1.0 | 33.9 | 0.6 | 62.5 | 1.0 | 4.6 | 10.1 | 22.7 | 10.7 | 11.6 | 10.4 | 12.9 |
| 30 005 | ... | 9 | Blaine | 10 949 | 6 683 | 2 710 | 0.6 | 49.7 | 0.5 | 49.2 | 0.4 | 2.2 | 9.2 | 21.5 | 9.1 | 11.1 | 9.6 | 14.0 |
| 30 007 | ... | 9 | Broadwater | 3 089 | 5 756 | 2 787 | 1.9 | 95.7 | 0.6 | 2.2 | 0.5 | 2.3 | 5.5 | 16.2 | 5.9 | 9.2 | 11.9 | 17.1 |
| 30 009 | 13740 | 3 | Carbon | 5 306 | 10 127 | 2 432 | 1.9 | 96.3 | 0.5 | 1.5 | 0.5 | 2.1 | 4.2 | 15.3 | 5.2 | 9.4 | 10.7 | 17.2 |
| 30 011 | ... | 9 | Carter | 8 653 | 1 177 | 3 102 | 0.1 | 98.3 | 0.3 | 1.3 | 0.1 | 0.6 | 3.9 | 12.8 | 6.4 | 8.6 | 7.6 | 17.0 |
| 30 013 | 24500 | 3 | Cascade | 6 998 | 81 723 | 679 | 11.7 | 90.0 | 2.0 | 5.9 | 1.7 | 3.6 | 6.8 | 15.9 | 10.3 | 13.1 | 10.9 | 14.3 |
| 30 015 | ... | 8 | Chouteau | 10 289 | 5 904 | 2 773 | 0.6 | 77.2 | 0.5 | 21.5 | 0.6 | 1.8 | 6.2 | 19.5 | 7.3 | 9.8 | 10.4 | 13.9 |
| 30 017 | ... | 7 | Custer | 9 799 | 11 888 | 2 305 | 1.2 | 95.3 | 0.6 | 2.6 | 0.6 | 2.3 | 6.1 | 16.6 | 8.3 | 11.6 | 10.8 | 14.9 |
| 30 019 | ... | 9 | Daniels | 3 694 | 1 786 | 3 071 | 0.5 | 95.7 | 0.7 | 2.9 | 0.5 | 1.7 | 6.2 | 14.4 | 5.3 | 9.1 | 8.5 | 15.7 |
| 30 021 | ... | 7 | Dawson | 6 143 | 9 249 | 2 497 | 1.5 | 95.0 | 0.7 | 2.7 | 0.6 | 2.4 | 6.2 | 14.9 | 9.0 | 12.0 | 10.4 | 14.7 |
| 30 023 | ... | 7 | Deer Lodge | 1 908 | 9 227 | 2 498 | 4.8 | 93.4 | 0.8 | 4.3 | 0.7 | 3.0 | 4.5 | 14.2 | 8.8 | 9.6 | 11.6 | 14.8 |
| 30 025 | ... | 9 | Fallon | 4 198 | 3 024 | 2 978 | 0.7 | 97.2 | 0.4 | 1.4 | 0.9 | 1.5 | 7.7 | 16.0 | 6.3 | 13.0 | 10.0 | 14.8 |
| 30 027 | ... | 7 | Fergus | 11 240 | 11 435 | 2 331 | 1.0 | 96.5 | 0.5 | 2.3 | 0.5 | 1.7 | 5.2 | 14.4 | 6.2 | 10.2 | 10.3 | 14.9 |
| 30 029 | 28060 | 5 | Flathead | 13 177 | 91 633 | 630 | 7.0 | 95.5 | 0.5 | 2.4 | 1.1 | 2.4 | 6.1 | 16.8 | 7.3 | 11.9 | 11.7 | 15.4 |
| 30 031 | 14580 | 5 | Gallatin | 6 741 | 92 614 | 624 | 13.7 | 94.3 | 0.7 | 1.7 | 2.0 | 2.9 | 6.3 | 14.3 | 16.6 | 16.6 | 12.4 | 12.7 |
| 30 033 | ... | 9 | Garfield | 12 109 | 1 261 | 3 098 | 0.1 | 98.4 | 0.4 | 0.8 | 0.3 | 0.6 | 6.0 | 18.2 | 4.7 | 11.5 | 9.3 | 13.3 |
| 30 035 | ... | 7 | Glacier | 7 759 | 13 711 | 2 198 | 1.8 | 34.8 | 0.6 | 64.7 | 0.7 | 2.2 | 9.2 | 22.2 | 10.1 | 12.2 | 10.5 | 14.2 |
| 30 037 | ... | 8 | Golden Valley | 3 044 | 839 | 3 116 | 0.3 | 94.2 | 0.8 | 1.5 | 1.3 | 3.6 | 3.2 | 18.7 | 5.3 | 7.1 | 9.6 | 14.5 |
| 30 039 | ... | 8 | Granite | 4 474 | 3 109 | 2 968 | 0.7 | 97.8 | 0.4 | 1.6 | 0.5 | 1.5 | 3.7 | 13.1 | 4.5 | 8.0 | 9.0 | 16.8 |
| 30 041 | 25660 | 7 | Hill | 7 508 | 16 366 | 2 020 | 2.2 | 75.4 | 0.7 | 23.2 | 1.0 | 2.6 | 7.7 | 19.2 | 10.7 | 12.7 | 10.5 | 13.7 |
| 30 043 | 25740 | 9 | Jefferson | 4 290 | 11 401 | 2 335 | 2.7 | 95.7 | 0.5 | 3.1 | 0.7 | 2.1 | 5.0 | 17.1 | 5.8 | 7.9 | 11.4 | 18.0 |
| 30 045 | ... | 8 | Judith Basin | 4 843 | 2 024 | 3 049 | 0.4 | 97.6 | 0.3 | 1.3 | 0.2 | 1.2 | 4.5 | 14.6 | 5.7 | 8.1 | 10.1 | 17.7 |
| 30 047 | ... | 6 | Lake | 3 859 | 28 986 | 1 450 | 7.5 | 74.0 | 0.6 | 27.1 | 1.1 | 3.8 | 7.4 | 17.9 | 7.9 | 10.6 | 9.9 | 13.8 |
| 30 049 | 25740 | 5 | Lewis and Clark | 8 958 | 64 876 | 812 | 7.2 | 94.3 | 0.8 | 3.4 | 1.2 | 2.6 | 6.1 | 16.3 | 8.7 | 12.3 | 11.5 | 15.4 |
| 30 051 | ... | 9 | Liberty | 3 704 | 2 392 | 3 015 | 0.6 | 99.0 | 0.5 | 0.8 | 0.4 | 0.5 | 5.5 | 15.9 | 8.4 | 10.7 | 9.8 | 15.5 |
| 30 053 | ... | 7 | Lincoln | 9 357 | 19 491 | 1 857 | 2.1 | 95.9 | 0.5 | 2.7 | 0.7 | 2.4 | 4.7 | 14.8 | 5.6 | 8.9 | 9.7 | 15.7 |
| 30 055 | ... | 9 | McCone | 6 846 | 1 701 | 3 075 | 0.2 | 98.3 | 0.7 | 1.2 | 0.4 | 0.8 | 5.4 | 15.0 | 5.2 | 8.7 | 8.8 | 15.3 |
| 30 057 | ... | 9 | Madison | 9 292 | 7 733 | 2 625 | 0.8 | 96.1 | 0.7 | 1.3 | 0.5 | 2.6 | 4.2 | 12.6 | 5.5 | 9.3 | 10.3 | 15.2 |
| 30 059 | ... | 9 | Meagher | 6 195 | 1 924 | 3 064 | 0.3 | 97.4 | 0.2 | 1.2 | 0.6 | 1.7 | 5.4 | 14.0 | 6.0 | 8.7 | 8.7 | 14.8 |
| 30 061 | ... | 8 | Mineral | 3 158 | 4 167 | 2 891 | 1.3 | 95.3 | 0.8 | 3.1 | 1.1 | 2.0 | 4.9 | 12.7 | 6.3 | 8.7 | 9.5 | 15.9 |
| 30 063 | 33540 | 3 | Missoula | 6 717 | 110 977 | 542 | 16.5 | 92.9 | 0.9 | 4.0 | 2.0 | 2.8 | 5.6 | 13.9 | 15.6 | 15.8 | 11.5 | 12.9 |
| 30 065 | ... | 8 | Musselshell | 4 838 | 4 665 | 2 860 | 1.0 | 95.2 | 0.7 | 2.3 | 0.5 | 2.7 | 4.9 | 15.9 | 5.6 | 8.3 | 11.1 | 15.9 |
| 30 067 | ... | 7 | Park | 7 260 | 15 567 | 2 074 | 2.1 | 96.1 | 0.5 | 1.9 | 0.6 | 2.3 | 5.0 | 14.2 | 5.2 | 10.9 | 13.0 | 16.6 |
| 30 069 | ... | 9 | Petroleum | 4 286 | 511 | 3 137 | 0.1 | 98.6 | 0.2 | 0.6 | 0.0 | 1.4 | 3.3 | 18.1 | 5.5 | 7.5 | 9.4 | 20.0 |
| 30 071 | ... | 9 | Phillips | 13 313 | 4 128 | 2 892 | 0.3 | 89.2 | 0.7 | 11.1 | 0.7 | 2.0 | 5.6 | 16.6 | 6.1 | 8.7 | 9.1 | 17.0 |
| 30 073 | ... | 7 | Pondera | 4 203 | 6 165 | 2 746 | 1.5 | 84.0 | 0.6 | 15.2 | 0.7 | 1.7 | 6.9 | 17.7 | 7.0 | 10.2 | 10.3 | 14.8 |
| 30 075 | ... | 9 | Powder River | 8 540 | 1 763 | 3 072 | 0.2 | 96.4 | 0.5 | 2.5 | 0.6 | 1.7 | 2.9 | 15.4 | 6.7 | 7.5 | 9.0 | 17.3 |
| 30 077 | ... | 7 | Powell | 6 025 | 7 096 | 2 675 | 1.2 | 92.1 | 1.4 | 5.2 | 0.8 | 1.9 | 4.4 | 12.4 | 7.9 | 12.2 | 12.9 | 17.8 |
| 30 079 | ... | 9 | Prairie | 4 498 | 1 157 | 3 103 | 0.3 | 97.6 | 0.9 | 1.8 | 1.1 | 1.4 | 5.3 | 11.7 | 4.2 | 7.5 | 8.4 | 13.2 |
| 30 081 | ... | 6 | Ravalli | 6 192 | 40 617 | 1 163 | 6.6 | 95.1 | 0.5 | 2.0 | 0.9 | 3.1 | 5.0 | 16.3 | 6.2 | 9.4 | 10.7 | 15.1 |
| 30 083 | ... | 7 | Richland | 5 398 | 10 810 | 2 374 | 2.0 | 94.3 | 0.5 | 3.0 | 0.7 | 3.4 | 6.6 | 16.6 | 8.0 | 12.0 | 12.1 | 15.9 |
| 30 085 | ... | 7 | Roosevelt | 6 099 | 10 927 | 2 365 | 1.8 | 38.9 | 0.5 | 60.9 | 0.9 | 1.7 | 9.5 | 20.0 | 10.4 | 12.2 | 10.3 | 13.3 |
| 30 087 | ... | 9 | Rosebud | 12 977 | 9 396 | 2 481 | 0.7 | 62.4 | 0.7 | 34.5 | 1.1 | 4.0 | 8.5 | 20.9 | 7.9 | 11.2 | 10.9 | 14.9 |
| 30 089 | ... | 8 | Sanders | 7 150 | 11 408 | 2 334 | 1.6 | 92.9 | 0.6 | 6.6 | 0.7 | 2.4 | 4.9 | 15.0 | 5.7 | 8.1 | 9.4 | 14.5 |
| 30 091 | ... | 9 | Sheridan | 4 344 | 3 580 | 2 939 | 0.8 | 95.6 | 0.7 | 3.0 | 0.8 | 1.7 | 4.2 | 15.3 | 5.3 | 9.0 | 9.2 | 16.1 |
| 30 093 | 15580 | 5 | Silver Bow | 1 861 | 34 403 | 1 315 | 18.5 | 93.5 | 0.6 | 3.0 | 1.0 | 3.7 | 5.8 | 15.0 | 10.8 | 11.6 | 11.1 | 15.1 |
| 30 095 | ... | 8 | Stillwater | 4 650 | 9 195 | 2 503 | 2.0 | 96.4 | 0.5 | 1.7 | 0.6 | 2.4 | 5.6 | 16.8 | 5.7 | 9.2 | 11.5 | 16.4 |
| 30 097 | ... | 9 | Sweet Grass | 4 805 | 3 605 | 2 934 | 0.8 | 96.6 | 0.5 | 1.7 | 1.2 | 2.0 | 4.9 | 17.7 | 5.1 | 8.5 | 10.8 | 14.8 |
| 30 099 | ... | 8 | Teton | 5 885 | 6 053 | 2 756 | 1.0 | 96.8 | 0.4 | 2.8 | 0.5 | 1.4 | 5.1 | 17.6 | 6.2 | 9.3 | 10.6 | 15.3 |
| 30 101 | ... | 7 | Toole | 4 962 | 5 220 | 2 825 | 1.1 | 91.3 | 0.8 | 6.1 | 1.1 | 2.7 | 5.0 | 15.0 | 8.0 | 13.3 | 12.4 | 16.3 |
| 30 103 | ... | 8 | Treasure | 2 531 | 736 | 3 125 | 0.3 | 93.9 | 0.1 | 2.6 | 1.1 | 4.1 | 5.5 | 13.3 | 5.0 | 8.1 | 7.7 | 18.7 |
| 30 105 | ... | 7 | Valley | 12 758 | 7 505 | 2 642 | 0.6 | 87.7 | 0.7 | 11.1 | 0.9 | 1.6 | 5.3 | 17.6 | 5.6 | 9.9 | 10.1 | 15.0 |
| 30 107 | ... | 9 | Wheatland | 3 686 | 2 104 | 3 042 | 0.6 | 96.9 | 0.7 | 1.9 | 1.2 | 1.7 | 6.7 | 17.0 | 6.4 | 9.1 | 10.5 | 12.6 |
| 30 109 | ... | 9 | Wibaux | 2 303 | 1 057 | 3 107 | 0.5 | 97.5 | 0.1 | 0.8 | 0.8 | 1.6 | 4.3 | 16.3 | 4.3 | 8.6 | 10.4 | 15.2 |
| 30 111 | 13740 | 3 | Yellowstone | 6 820 | 151 882 | 414 | 22.3 | 90.0 | 1.3 | 5.1 | 1.3 | 4.8 | 6.7 | 16.8 | 8.8 | 13.7 | 11.9 | 14.6 |
| 31 000 | ... | X | NEBRASKA | 198 974 | 1 855 525 | X | 9.3 | 83.2 | 5.3 | 1.3 | 2.4 | 9.5 | 7.1 | 17.8 | 10.0 | 13.5 | 11.9 | 13.8 |
| 31 001 | 25580 | 5 | Adams | 1 459 | 31 459 | 1 402 | 21.6 | 89.1 | 1.1 | 0.8 | 1.8 | 8.2 | 6.5 | 17.2 | 11.9 | 11.3 | 10.7 | 14.1 |
| 31 003 | ... | 9 | Antelope | 2 220 | 6 545 | 2 719 | 2.9 | 96.3 | 0.5 | 0.4 | 0.4 | 2.9 | 6.4 | 17.2 | 6.0 | 9.9 | 8.9 | 15.0 |
| 31 005 | ... | 9 | Arthur | 1 853 | 486 | 3 139 | 0.3 | 95.1 | 0.4 | 0.4 | 0.4 | 4.3 | 9.0 | 19.0 | 4.1 | 11.3 | 11.3 | 12.2 |
| 31 007 | 42420 | 9 | Banner | 1 932 | 760 | 3 123 | 0.4 | 95.8 | 0.1 | 1.0 | 0.1 | 3.7 | 4.5 | 16.2 | 4.8 | 7.6 | 7.5 | 17.7 |

1. CBSA = Core Based Statistical Area. See Appendix A for explanation. See Appendix B for list of metropolitan areas with component counties. 2. County type code from the Economic Research Service of USDA Rural-Urban Continuum Codes. See Appendix A for definition. 3. Dry land or land partially or temporarily covered by water. 4. May be of any race.

# Table B. States and Counties — **Population and Households**

| | Population, 2011 (cont.) | | | | Population change and components of change, 2000–2012 | | | | | | | Households, 2010 | | | | |
|---|---|---|---|---|---|---|---|---|---|---|---|---|---|---|---|---|
| | Age (percent) (cont.) | | | | Total persons | | Percent change | | Components of change, 2010–2012 | | | | | | Percent | |
| STATE County | 55 to 64 years | 65 to 74 years | 75 years and over | Percent female | 2000 | 2010 | 2000–2010 | 2010–2012 | Births | Deaths | Net migration | Number | Percent change, 2000–2010 | Persons per house-hold | Female family house-holder[1] | One per-son |
| | 16 | 17 | 18 | 19 | 20 | 21 | 22 | 23 | 24 | 25 | 26 | 27 | 28 | 29 | 30 | 31 |
| MISSOURI—Cont'd | | | | | | | | | | | | | | | | |
| St. Louis city | 11.5 | 5.5 | 5.3 | 51.6 | 348 189 | 319 294 | -8.3 | -0.4 | 10 821 | 6 718 | -5 344 | 142 057 | -3.4 | 2.16 | 19.4 | 42.6 |
| MONTANA | 14.5 | 8.4 | 6.7 | 49.8 | 902 195 | 989 415 | 9.7 | 1.6 | 26 740 | 19 636 | 8 447 | 409 607 | 14.2 | 2.35 | 9.0 | 29.7 |
| Beaverhead | 16.4 | 10.0 | 7.2 | 48.9 | 9 202 | 9 246 | 0.5 | 1.1 | 212 | 189 | 65 | 4 014 | 9.0 | 2.19 | 6.4 | 33.0 |
| Big Horn | 11.4 | 6.4 | 3.9 | 50.2 | 12 671 | 12 865 | 1.5 | 1.5 | 637 | 165 | -289 | 4 004 | 2.0 | 3.18 | 17.3 | 23.0 |
| Blaine | 12.1 | 7.0 | 6.4 | 50.2 | 7 009 | 6 491 | -7.4 | 3.0 | 260 | 109 | 45 | 2 357 | -5.8 | 2.66 | 16.0 | 28.7 |
| Broadwater | 16.0 | 11.0 | 7.1 | 49.0 | 4 385 | 5 612 | 28.0 | 2.6 | 107 | 102 | 134 | 2 347 | 34.0 | 2.37 | 6.2 | 26.6 |
| Carbon | 18.7 | 11.1 | 8.2 | 49.4 | 9 552 | 10 078 | 5.5 | 0.5 | 173 | 201 | 83 | 4 571 | 12.4 | 2.19 | 6.1 | 31.2 |
| Carter | 19.0 | 12.7 | 12.0 | 49.1 | 1 360 | 1 160 | -14.7 | 1.5 | 25 | 30 | 21 | 532 | -2.0 | 2.16 | 4.3 | 30.3 |
| Cascade | 13.0 | 8.3 | 7.4 | 50.1 | 80 357 | 81 327 | 1.2 | 0.5 | 2 658 | 1 646 | -601 | 33 809 | 3.9 | 2.33 | 10.2 | 30.5 |
| Chouteau | 14.9 | 9.3 | 8.6 | 50.5 | 5 970 | 5 813 | -2.6 | 1.6 | 95 | 134 | 127 | 2 294 | 3.1 | 2.48 | 10.1 | 29.1 |
| Custer | 14.5 | 8.1 | 9.0 | 50.4 | 11 696 | 11 699 | 0.0 | 1.6 | 334 | 335 | 197 | 5 031 | 5.5 | 2.24 | 9.0 | 34.3 |
| Daniels | 16.3 | 11.5 | 13.0 | 49.0 | 2 017 | 1 751 | -13.2 | 2.0 | 46 | 50 | 40 | 798 | -10.5 | 2.14 | 4.6 | 35.1 |
| Dawson | 15.3 | 8.6 | 8.9 | 49.3 | 9 059 | 8 966 | -1.0 | 3.2 | 252 | 230 | 244 | 3 749 | 3.4 | 2.26 | 6.7 | 31.2 |
| Deer Lodge | 17.0 | 10.6 | 9.0 | 47.4 | 9 417 | 9 298 | -1.3 | -0.8 | 180 | 293 | 35 | 4 018 | 0.6 | 2.11 | 9.2 | 36.1 |
| Fallon | 14.6 | 8.1 | 9.4 | 49.8 | 2 837 | 2 890 | 1.9 | 4.6 | 108 | 76 | 101 | 1 233 | 8.2 | 2.32 | 5.7 | 30.1 |
| Fergus | 16.8 | 11.4 | 10.7 | 49.8 | 11 893 | 11 586 | -2.6 | -1.3 | 242 | 360 | -36 | 5 099 | 4.9 | 2.18 | 6.5 | 32.6 |
| Flathead | 15.8 | 8.6 | 6.4 | 50.2 | 74 471 | 90 928 | 22.1 | 0.8 | 2 417 | 1 702 | 44 | 37 504 | 26.8 | 2.40 | 8.7 | 27.2 |
| Gallatin | 11.5 | 5.4 | 4.3 | 48.3 | 67 831 | 89 513 | 32.0 | 3.5 | 2 446 | 1 105 | 1 714 | 36 550 | 38.9 | 2.36 | 6.6 | 27.3 |
| Garfield | 16.8 | 11.5 | 8.6 | 49.1 | 1 279 | 1 206 | -5.7 | 4.6 | 30 | 24 | 38 | 532 | 0.0 | 2.27 | 5.1 | 30.3 |
| Glacier | 10.9 | 6.2 | 4.6 | 50.8 | 13 247 | 13 399 | 1.1 | 2.3 | 568 | 213 | -62 | 4 361 | 1.3 | 2.91 | 19.1 | 24.9 |
| Golden Valley | 17.8 | 12.9 | 10.9 | 47.9 | 1 042 | 884 | -15.2 | -5.1 | 11 | 22 | -34 | 363 | -0.5 | 2.19 | 5.2 | 29.5 |
| Granite | 20.5 | 15.2 | 9.3 | 49.2 | 2 830 | 3 079 | 8.8 | 1.0 | 48 | 72 | 33 | 1 417 | 18.1 | 2.14 | 5.7 | 29.5 |
| Hill | 13.0 | 6.7 | 5.9 | 49.3 | 16 673 | 16 096 | -3.5 | 1.7 | 597 | 337 | -2 | 6 275 | -2.8 | 2.47 | 11.9 | 29.8 |
| Jefferson | 19.8 | 10.2 | 4.9 | 49.1 | 10 049 | 11 406 | 13.5 | 0.0 | 211 | 251 | 8 | 4 512 | 20.4 | 2.48 | 5.4 | 22.6 |
| Judith Basin | 17.3 | 12.6 | 9.3 | 47.9 | 2 329 | 2 072 | -11.0 | -2.3 | 31 | 32 | -51 | 924 | -2.8 | 2.24 | 5.2 | 30.3 |
| Lake | 15.2 | 10.1 | 7.2 | 50.6 | 26 507 | 28 746 | 8.4 | 0.8 | 811 | 544 | -29 | 11 432 | 12.2 | 2.46 | 11.5 | 26.5 |
| Lewis and Clark | 15.7 | 8.0 | 6.1 | 50.7 | 55 716 | 63 395 | 13.8 | 2.3 | 1 697 | 1 263 | 1 073 | 26 694 | 16.8 | 2.30 | 9.4 | 30.7 |
| Liberty | 13.4 | 9.6 | 11.1 | 52.1 | 2 158 | 2 339 | 8.4 | 2.3 | 48 | 48 | 53 | 822 | -1.3 | 2.36 | 4.7 | 32.2 |
| Lincoln | 19.3 | 13.5 | 7.9 | 49.3 | 18 837 | 19 687 | 4.5 | -1.0 | 402 | 513 | -86 | 8 843 | 13.9 | 2.20 | 7.4 | 30.6 |
| McCone | 19.5 | 10.9 | 11.3 | 49.5 | 1 977 | 1 734 | -12.3 | -1.9 | 32 | 42 | -24 | 774 | -4.4 | 2.22 | 3.2 | 31.7 |
| Madison | 21.2 | 12.8 | 8.9 | 48.2 | 6 851 | 7 691 | 12.3 | 0.5 | 135 | 155 | 51 | 3 560 | 20.4 | 2.11 | 4.5 | 32.6 |
| Meagher | 17.9 | 13.4 | 11.0 | 49.1 | 1 932 | 1 891 | -2.1 | 1.7 | 57 | 47 | 22 | 806 | 0.4 | 2.13 | 6.2 | 33.3 |
| Mineral | 19.4 | 14.2 | 8.5 | 48.0 | 3 884 | 4 223 | 8.7 | -1.3 | 92 | 101 | -65 | 1 911 | 20.6 | 2.20 | 7.3 | 29.7 |
| Missoula | 13.0 | 6.7 | 5.1 | 49.6 | 95 802 | 109 299 | 14.1 | 1.5 | 2 657 | 1 696 | 752 | 45 926 | 19.5 | 2.30 | 9.2 | 30.3 |
| Musselshell | 20.4 | 10.6 | 7.2 | 50.3 | 4 497 | 4 538 | 0.9 | 2.8 | 96 | 138 | 163 | 2 046 | 8.9 | 2.19 | 6.5 | 33.5 |
| Park | 17.6 | 10.1 | 7.4 | 50.2 | 15 694 | 15 636 | -0.4 | -0.4 | 319 | 328 | -50 | 7 310 | 7.1 | 2.12 | 7.0 | 35.7 |
| Petroleum | 16.3 | 12.0 | 7.9 | 46.6 | 493 | 494 | 0.2 | 3.4 | 7 | 2 | 7 | 225 | 6.6 | 2.20 | 4.0 | 35.1 |
| Phillips | 16.0 | 10.6 | 10.4 | 50.6 | 4 601 | 4 253 | -7.6 | -2.9 | 94 | 106 | -116 | 1 819 | -1.6 | 2.27 | 7.4 | 32.2 |
| Pondera | 13.5 | 9.5 | 10.1 | 51.6 | 6 424 | 6 153 | -4.2 | 0.2 | 173 | 154 | -5 | 2 285 | -5.2 | 2.41 | 9.4 | 29.9 |
| Powder River | 18.5 | 10.9 | 11.7 | 48.8 | 1 858 | 1 743 | -6.2 | 1.1 | 17 | 38 | 36 | 755 | 2.4 | 2.26 | 5.0 | 28.3 |
| Powell | 15.6 | 10.3 | 6.5 | 38.8 | 7 180 | 7 027 | -2.1 | 1.0 | 128 | 178 | 122 | 2 466 | 1.8 | 2.23 | 8.8 | 32.2 |
| Prairie | 21.7 | 15.3 | 12.6 | 49.4 | 1 199 | 1 179 | -1.7 | -1.9 | 28 | 30 | -25 | 551 | 2.6 | 2.10 | 4.2 | 34.1 |
| Ravalli | 17.3 | 11.8 | 8.3 | 50.3 | 36 070 | 40 212 | 11.5 | 1.0 | 860 | 923 | 458 | 16 933 | 18.5 | 2.35 | 7.7 | 27.1 |
| Richland | 14.4 | 7.7 | 6.8 | 48.2 | 9 667 | 9 746 | 0.8 | 10.9 | 291 | 208 | 964 | 4 167 | 7.5 | 2.33 | 7.6 | 29.8 |
| Roosevelt | 11.6 | 6.0 | 4.9 | 50.4 | 10 620 | 10 425 | -1.8 | 4.8 | 472 | 253 | 274 | 3 553 | -0.8 | 2.88 | 20.5 | 24.2 |
| Rosebud | 14.1 | 7.2 | 4.5 | 49.6 | 9 383 | 9 233 | -1.6 | 1.8 | 368 | 154 | -50 | 3 395 | 2.7 | 2.70 | 10.6 | 27.6 |
| Sanders | 19.9 | 14.1 | 8.5 | 48.7 | 10 227 | 11 413 | 11.6 | 0.0 | 201 | 232 | 23 | 5 121 | 19.8 | 2.19 | 6.2 | 32.8 |
| Sheridan | 17.9 | 10.6 | 12.3 | 49.2 | 4 105 | 3 384 | -17.6 | 5.8 | 65 | 136 | 256 | 1 587 | -8.8 | 2.08 | 5.7 | 37.1 |
| Silver Bow | 14.2 | 8.8 | 7.6 | 49.3 | 34 606 | 34 200 | -1.2 | 0.6 | 892 | 939 | 249 | 14 932 | 3.5 | 2.22 | 10.6 | 35.1 |
| Stillwater | 18.1 | 10.0 | 6.7 | 48.6 | 8 195 | 9 117 | 11.3 | 0.9 | 187 | 182 | 76 | 3 796 | 17.4 | 2.37 | 6.0 | 25.8 |
| Sweet Grass | 16.2 | 11.3 | 10.6 | 50.0 | 3 609 | 3 651 | 1.2 | -1.3 | 58 | 78 | -26 | 1 590 | 7.7 | 2.27 | 6.5 | 30.4 |
| Teton | 14.6 | 11.2 | 10.1 | 50.5 | 6 445 | 6 073 | -5.8 | -0.3 | 146 | 144 | -20 | 2 450 | -3.5 | 2.29 | 6.0 | 29.3 |
| Toole | 14.8 | 7.4 | 7.8 | 44.2 | 5 267 | 5 324 | 1.1 | -2.0 | 120 | 112 | -116 | 2 015 | 2.7 | 2.26 | 7.4 | 34.3 |
| Treasure | 16.8 | 12.0 | 12.9 | 49.5 | 861 | 718 | -16.6 | 2.5 | 15 | 11 | 14 | 335 | -6.2 | 2.14 | 2.1 | 32.5 |
| Valley | 16.0 | 10.0 | 10.5 | 50.0 | 7 675 | 7 369 | -4.0 | 1.8 | 151 | 150 | 134 | 3 198 | 1.5 | 2.26 | 8.0 | 33.4 |
| Wheatland | 16.4 | 11.1 | 10.2 | 50.6 | 2 259 | 2 168 | -4.0 | -3.0 | 58 | 51 | -72 | 887 | 4.0 | 2.28 | 6.4 | 35.4 |
| Wibaux | 16.3 | 11.0 | 13.6 | 49.0 | 1 068 | 1 017 | -4.8 | 3.9 | 14 | 30 | 57 | 457 | 8.6 | 2.17 | 6.1 | 35.4 |
| Yellowstone | 13.2 | 7.5 | 6.8 | 51.1 | 129 352 | 147 972 | 14.4 | 2.6 | 4 361 | 2 972 | 2 493 | 60 672 | 16.5 | 2.38 | 10.5 | 29.7 |
| NEBRASKA | 12.1 | 6.8 | 6.7 | 50.3 | 1 711 263 | 1 826 341 | 6.7 | 1.6 | 59 344 | 34 073 | 3 977 | 721 130 | 8.2 | 2.46 | 9.8 | 28.7 |
| Adams | 12.8 | 7.4 | 8.0 | 50.1 | 31 151 | 31 364 | 0.7 | 0.3 | 929 | 703 | -128 | 12 466 | 2.7 | 2.39 | 9.5 | 30.3 |
| Antelope | 15.8 | 9.8 | 11.1 | 50.4 | 7 452 | 6 685 | -10.3 | -2.1 | 195 | 163 | -168 | 2 841 | -3.8 | 2.33 | 5.9 | 30.0 |
| Arthur | 13.2 | 10.4 | 9.6 | 50.5 | 444 | 460 | 3.6 | 5.7 | 22 | 7 | 11 | 187 | 1.1 | 2.46 | 8.0 | 26.7 |
| Banner | 18.6 | 12.1 | 11.0 | 48.7 | 819 | 690 | -15.8 | 10.1 | 14 | 4 | 29 | 293 | -5.8 | 2.35 | 4.1 | 25.6 |

1. No spouse present.

# Table B. States and Counties — Population, Vital Statistics, Medicare, and Crime

| STATE County | Persons in group quarters, 2010 | Daytime population, 2007–2011 Number | Daytime population, 2007–2011 Employment/residence ratio | Births, 2011 Total | Births, 2011 Rate[1] | Deaths, 2011 Number | Deaths, 2011 Rate[1] | Persons under 65 with no health insurance, 2010 Number | Persons under 65 with no health insurance, 2010 Percent | Medicare, 2012 Eligible for Medicare | Medicare, 2012 Enrolled in Medicare Advantage | Medicare, 2012 Enrolled in a Medicare prescription drug plan | Serious crimes known to police,[2] 2011 Total Number | Serious crimes known to police,[2] 2011 Total Rate[3] |
|---|---|---|---|---|---|---|---|---|---|---|---|---|---|---|
| | 32 | 33 | 34 | 35 | 36 | 37 | 38 | 39 | 40 | 41 | 42 | 43 | 44 | 45 |
| MISSOURI—Cont'd | | | | | | | | | | | | | | |
| St. Louis city | 11 978 | 432 592 | 1.79 | 4 895 | 15.4 | 3 026 | 9.5 | 53 134 | 19.3 | 47 765 | 14 061 | 20 884 | 31 619 | 9 866 |
| MONTANA | 28 849 | 981 800 | 1.00 | 11 911 | 11.9 | 8 629 | 8.6 | 170 509 | 20.7 | 183 551 | 10 550 | 83 096 | 25 825 | 2 587 |
| Beaverhead | 444 | 9 067 | 0.98 | 97 | 10.5 | 86 | 9.3 | 1 946 | 26.9 | 1 912 | 158 | 925 | 136 | 1 458 |
| Big Horn | 137 | 13 171 | 1.08 | 293 | 22.4 | 89 | 6.8 | 3 150 | 27.3 | 1 585 | 80 | 786 | 158 | 1 217 |
| Blaine | 220 | 6 536 | 1.03 | 111 | 16.9 | 39 | 5.9 | 1 652 | 29.6 | 1 014 | 88 | 521 | 28 | 525 |
| Broadwater | 52 | 4 810 | 0.73 | 45 | 7.8 | 48 | 8.3 | 1 036 | 22.6 | 1 163 | 185 | 453 | 73 | 1 289 |
| Carbon | 53 | 8 538 | 0.71 | 72 | 7.2 | 81 | 8.1 | 1 626 | 20.0 | 2 222 | 422 | 1 007 | 109 | 1 072 |
| Carter | 11 | 1 182 | 0.88 | 8 | 6.9 | 14 | 12.2 | 274 | 30.8 | 275 | 33 | 150 | 1 | 85 |
| Cascade | 2 562 | 81 221 | 1.01 | 1 154 | 14.1 | 716 | 8.7 | 12 461 | 18.6 | 15 626 | 3 586 | 6 262 | 3 153 | 3 843 |
| Chouteau | 135 | 5 340 | 0.82 | 39 | 6.7 | 66 | 11.4 | 1 223 | 25.7 | 1 120 | 200 | 629 | 45 | 767 |
| Custer | 413 | 11 499 | 0.98 | 145 | 12.3 | 159 | 13.5 | 1 753 | 18.7 | 2 381 | 297 | 1 220 | 250 | 2 118 |
| Daniels | 41 | 1 786 | 1.08 | 18 | 10.2 | 18 | 10.2 | 267 | 20.3 | 455 | 26 | 277 | 3 | 170 |
| Dawson | 498 | 8 735 | 0.95 | 109 | 12.1 | 99 | 11.0 | 1 127 | 16.3 | 1 692 | 135 | 1 018 | 225 | 2 487 |
| Deer Lodge | 811 | 9 043 | 0.93 | 81 | 8.7 | 130 | 14.0 | 1 302 | 18.8 | 2 210 | 280 | 1 019 | 186 | 1 983 |
| Fallon | 34 | 3 045 | 1.12 | 45 | 15.2 | 33 | 11.2 | 464 | 19.5 | 510 | 17 | 302 | 42 | 1 440 |
| Fergus | 465 | 11 560 | 1.01 | 114 | 9.9 | 164 | 14.3 | 2 163 | 24.3 | 2 805 | 421 | 1 259 | 168 | 1 437 |
| Flathead | 992 | 90 423 | 1.00 | 1 085 | 11.9 | 734 | 8.0 | 17 130 | 22.3 | 17 642 | 3 430 | 7 288 | 2 292 | 2 499 |
| Gallatin | 3 260 | 89 795 | 1.01 | 1 083 | 11.9 | 498 | 5.4 | 13 833 | 17.7 | 10 905 | 1 681 | 4 263 | 2 050 | 2 318 |
| Garfield | 0 | 1 203 | 1.07 | 10 | 8.0 | 12 | 9.6 | 375 | 39.4 | 261 | 20 | 172 | 0 | 0 |
| Glacier | 690 | 13 354 | 1.00 | 250 | 18.3 | 99 | 7.3 | 3 230 | 27.0 | 1 733 | 83 | 868 | 189 | 1 398 |
| Golden Valley | 89 | 737 | 0.65 | 6 | 6.9 | 7 | 8.1 | 210 | 30.2 | 254 | 45 | 115 | 1 | 112 |
| Granite | 40 | 2 709 | 0.74 | 18 | 5.9 | 29 | 9.5 | 632 | 27.3 | 797 | 83 | 336 | 56 | 1 803 |
| Hill | 593 | 16 373 | 1.04 | 256 | 15.6 | 147 | 9.0 | 3 124 | 22.6 | 2 640 | 296 | 1 561 | 656 | 4 040 |
| Jefferson | 230 | 8 873 | 0.54 | 106 | 9.3 | 112 | 9.8 | 1 667 | 17.2 | 2 226 | 276 | 859 | 60 | 521 |
| Judith Basin | 0 | 1 950 | 0.87 | 16 | 8.0 | 16 | 8.0 | 499 | 30.7 | 503 | 129 | 227 | 1 | 48 |
| Lake | 587 | 27 539 | 0.90 | 363 | 12.5 | 231 | 8.0 | 6 872 | 29.0 | 5 928 | 814 | 2 692 | 747 | 2 576 |
| Lewis and Clark | 1 946 | 65 362 | 1.09 | 775 | 12.0 | 553 | 8.6 | 8 282 | 15.4 | 11 425 | 1 727 | 4 141 | 1 518 | 2 373 |
| Liberty | 403 | 2 316 | 1.02 | 19 | 7.9 | 22 | 9.2 | 464 | 25.0 | 418 | 22 | 314 | NA | NA |
| Lincoln | 209 | 19 425 | 0.98 | 183 | 9.4 | 234 | 12.0 | 3 827 | 24.9 | 5 803 | 1 336 | 2 518 | 329 | 1 656 |
| McCone | 19 | 1 773 | 0.96 | 14 | 8.2 | 18 | 10.5 | 395 | 29.3 | 321 | 30 | 210 | 21 | 1 201 |
| Madison | 163 | 7 296 | 0.91 | 59 | 7.7 | 59 | 7.7 | 1 498 | 24.8 | 1 782 | 167 | 818 | 49 | 632 |
| Meagher | 174 | 1 847 | 0.93 | 24 | 12.6 | 16 | 8.4 | 431 | 29.8 | 522 | 32 | 301 | 29 | 1 520 |
| Mineral | 22 | 3 997 | 0.88 | 45 | 10.7 | 42 | 10.0 | 858 | 26.3 | 1 157 | 140 | 572 | 1 | 23 |
| Missoula | 3 634 | 113 055 | 1.08 | 1 177 | 10.7 | 744 | 6.8 | 19 173 | 20.5 | 16 967 | 1 798 | 8 226 | 3 501 | 3 175 |
| Musselshell | 52 | 4 069 | 0.81 | 43 | 9.1 | 61 | 13.0 | 903 | 24.7 | 1 123 | 172 | 555 | 95 | 2 075 |
| Park | 108 | 14 878 | 0.89 | 151 | 9.8 | 152 | 9.8 | 2 997 | 23.2 | 3 167 | 342 | 1 575 | 212 | 1 344 |
| Petroleum | 0 | 613 | 1.18 | 3 | 6.1 | 3 | 6.1 | 136 | 34.1 | 90 | D | 51 | NA | NA |
| Phillips | 127 | 4 118 | 0.94 | 43 | 10.1 | 45 | 10.6 | 908 | 27.1 | 945 | 114 | 555 | 67 | 1 561 |
| Pondera | 645 | 5 974 | 0.93 | 82 | 13.1 | 68 | 10.9 | 1 389 | 28.1 | 1 264 | 207 | 657 | 59 | 950 |
| Powder River | 35 | 1 672 | 1.02 | 10 | 5.8 | 14 | 8.1 | 401 | 30.0 | 365 | 50 | 170 | NA | NA |
| Powell | 1 523 | 7 126 | 1.02 | 60 | 8.5 | 84 | 11.9 | 944 | 21.4 | 1 370 | 137 | 584 | 101 | 1 425 |
| Prairie | 21 | 1 042 | 0.90 | 14 | 12.1 | 8 | 6.9 | 258 | 29.5 | 352 | 36 | 211 | 7 | 589 |
| Ravalli | 478 | 36 255 | 0.77 | 393 | 9.7 | 405 | 10.0 | 7 653 | 23.8 | 9 917 | 1 650 | 3 721 | 708 | 1 786 |
| Richland | 34 | 9 786 | 1.02 | 122 | 12.0 | 99 | 9.8 | 1 740 | 21.0 | 1 730 | 53 | 1 152 | 154 | 1 566 |
| Roosevelt | 186 | 10 511 | 1.05 | 212 | 20.1 | 133 | 12.6 | 2 323 | 25.2 | 1 489 | 65 | 850 | 231 | 2 251 |
| Rosebud | 65 | 9 873 | 1.17 | 174 | 18.6 | 72 | 7.7 | 1 706 | 21.0 | 1 431 | 136 | 714 | 86 | 923 |
| Sanders | 188 | 10 996 | 0.90 | 97 | 8.5 | 98 | 8.6 | 2 592 | 29.7 | 3 238 | 432 | 1 416 | 137 | 1 190 |
| Sheridan | 85 | 3 425 | 1.00 | 24 | 6.9 | 57 | 16.5 | 567 | 21.9 | 901 | 43 | 640 | 76 | 2 226 |
| Silver Bow | 998 | 34 094 | 1.01 | 398 | 11.6 | 416 | 12.1 | 4 811 | 17.3 | 6 908 | 1 077 | 3 330 | 1 136 | 3 292 |
| Stillwater | 112 | 8 442 | 0.87 | 87 | 9.5 | 75 | 8.2 | 1 255 | 16.5 | 1 838 | 331 | 828 | 105 | 1 142 |
| Sweet Grass | 45 | 3 843 | 1.08 | 27 | 7.5 | 35 | 9.7 | 654 | 22.8 | 803 | 92 | 413 | 42 | 1 140 |
| Teton | 462 | 5 900 | 0.92 | 59 | 9.7 | 64 | 10.5 | 1 191 | 25.0 | 1 362 | 408 | 665 | 60 | 979 |
| Toole | 766 | 5 424 | 1.11 | 55 | 10.5 | 46 | 8.8 | 861 | 21.9 | 856 | 66 | 492 | 153 | 2 849 |
| Treasure | 0 | 805 | 0.95 | 8 | 11.0 | 2 | 2.8 | 151 | 27.4 | 211 | 13 | 114 | NA | NA |
| Valley | 126 | 7 443 | 1.01 | 65 | 8.7 | 59 | 7.9 | 1 393 | 24.0 | 1 754 | 90 | 999 | 83 | 1 116 |
| Wheatland | 147 | 2 219 | 1.11 | 27 | 12.6 | 20 | 9.3 | 481 | 28.5 | 474 | 59 | 232 | 5 | 229 |
| Wibaux | 24 | 921 | 0.91 | 8 | 8.1 | 15 | 15.2 | 202 | 26.0 | 229 | 13 | 142 | 3 | 292 |
| Yellowstone | 3 695 | 148 811 | 1.04 | 1 929 | 12.9 | 1 283 | 8.5 | 22 051 | 17.6 | 25 480 | 5 478 | 11 721 | 5 847 | 3 917 |
| NEBRASKA | 51 165 | 1 830 998 | 1.02 | 25 991 | 14.1 | 14 878 | 8.1 | 206 100 | 13.4 | 293 482 | 68 | 162 849 | 55 391 | 3 006 |
| Adams | 1 554 | 31 653 | 1.03 | 417 | 13.4 | 322 | 10.3 | 3 550 | 14.2 | 5 963 | 414 | 3 993 | 1 097 | 3 467 |
| Antelope | 70 | 6 249 | 0.86 | 86 | 13.0 | 67 | 10.1 | 804 | 15.5 | 1 473 | 43 | 1 065 | 23 | 448 |
| Arthur | 0 | 388 | 0.74 | 10 | 21.3 | 2 | 4.3 | 75 | 20.7 | 108 | D | 76 | 0 | 0 |
| Banner | 0 | 573 | 0.66 | 7 | 10.2 | 0 | 0.0 | 113 | 20.2 | 206 | 15 | 108 | NA | NA |

1. Per 1,000 estimated resident population.   2. Data for serious crimes have not been adjusted for underreporting; this may affect comparability between geographic areas and over time.   3. Per 100,000 population estimated by the FBI.

# Table B. States and Counties — **Crime, Education, Money Income, and Poverty**

| STATE County | Serious crimes known to police, 2011 (cont.)[1] Rate[2] Violent | Property | Education School enrollment and attainment, 2007–2011 Enrollment[3] Total | Percent private | Attainment[4] (percent) High school graduate or less | Bachelor's degree or more | Local government expenditures,[5] 2009–2010 Total current expenditures (mil dol) | Current expenditures per student (dollars) | Money income, 2007–2011 Per capita income[6] (dollars) | Households Median income Dollars | Percent change, 2000 to 2007–2011 (constant 2011 dollars) | Percent with income of $200,000 or more | Income and poverty, 2011 Median household income (dollars) | Percent below poverty level All persons | Children under 18 years | Children 5 to 17 years in families |
|---|---|---|---|---|---|---|---|---|---|---|---|---|---|---|---|---|
| | 46 | 47 | 48 | 49 | 50 | 51 | 52 | 53 | 54 | 55 | 56 | 57 | 58 | 59 | 60 | 61 |
| **MISSOURI—Cont'd** | | | | | | | | | | | | | | | | |
| St. Louis city | 1 857 | 8 010 | 86 305 | 33.9 | 44.5 | 27.7 | 479.0 | 13 323 | 22 050 | 34 402 | -6.2 | 1.5 | 32 576 | 27.2 | 38.2 | 36.6 |
| **MONTANA** | 267 | 2 320 | 237 973 | 12.7 | 39.4 | 28.2 | 1 488.2 | 10 491 | 24 640 | 45 324 | 1.7 | 2.1 | 44 011 | 15.2 | 20.9 | 19.0 |
| Beaverhead | 150 | 1 308 | 2 840 | 10.6 | 36.5 | 30.9 | 13.3 | 11 233 | 22 216 | 41 226 | 5.4 | 0.9 | 38 632 | 17.2 | 24.5 | 22.0 |
| Big Horn | 177 | 1 040 | 3 759 | 6.1 | 52.3 | 13.8 | 31.3 | 14 267 | 14 827 | 37 277 | -0.3 | 0.6 | 34 778 | 28.6 | 36.1 | 33.0 |
| Blaine | 244 | 281 | 1 689 | 6.3 | 43.7 | 17.6 | 19.2 | 16 169 | 17 287 | 38 721 | 13.6 | 1.5 | 36 562 | 24.2 | 32.2 | 29.4 |
| Broadwater | 300 | 989 | 1 427 | 6.4 | 54.6 | 16.7 | 6.2 | 8 698 | 20 706 | 44 570 | 1.0 | 0.6 | 44 183 | 12.9 | 18.5 | 17.3 |
| Carbon | 236 | 836 | 2 007 | 9.1 | 42.1 | 28.6 | 16.1 | 11 542 | 25 943 | 46 194 | 6.5 | 1.2 | 43 223 | 12.2 | 17.7 | 14.4 |
| Carter | 0 | 85 | 220 | 15.9 | 47.0 | 13.1 | 2.3 | 17 937 | 20 844 | 35 121 | -1.1 | 0.9 | 35 540 | 17.4 | 29.9 | 26.8 |
| Cascade | 250 | 3 593 | 19 192 | 15.8 | 40.4 | 22.8 | 111.9 | 9 557 | 23 554 | 44 074 | -1.0 | 1.6 | 42 525 | 15.3 | 21.2 | 19.3 |
| Chouteau | 119 | 648 | 1 474 | 9.0 | 45.3 | 22.7 | 10.0 | 15 783 | 20 706 | 40 825 | 3.7 | 1.8 | 38 106 | 17.9 | 27.0 | 23.3 |
| Custer | 169 | 1 949 | 2 693 | 11.8 | 41.7 | 19.4 | 15.1 | 8 940 | 22 858 | 41 373 | 2.1 | 1.3 | 42 308 | 14.2 | 20.3 | 18.4 |
| Daniels | 170 | 0 | 301 | 4.7 | 39.3 | 17.3 | 3.3 | 12 395 | 25 496 | 37 578 | 1.9 | 1.5 | 43 585 | 10.2 | 11.2 | 10.1 |
| Dawson | 232 | 2 255 | 1 945 | 9.8 | 39.2 | 19.9 | 14.8 | 11 979 | 25 675 | 51 761 | 22.1 | 1.3 | 44 925 | 12.2 | 15.9 | 14.6 |
| Deer Lodge | 266 | 1 716 | 1 829 | 10.5 | 49.3 | 18.5 | 11.4 | 10 203 | 20 887 | 34 095 | -4.0 | 1.1 | 34 375 | 17.1 | 24.5 | 22.4 |
| Fallon | 171 | 1 269 | 563 | 2.3 | 51.7 | 15.9 | 8.1 | 18 143 | 26 646 | 49 573 | 22.6 | 1.6 | 50 823 | 8.5 | 11.9 | 11.6 |
| Fergus | 248 | 1 189 | 2 304 | 4.6 | 45.5 | 22.2 | 21.5 | 13 083 | 23 877 | 37 601 | -8.4 | 2.2 | 38 912 | 13.1 | 20.8 | 18.8 |
| Flathead | 295 | 2 203 | 19 627 | 16.0 | 40.0 | 27.6 | 124.2 | 9 287 | 25 317 | 45 588 | -2.0 | 2.5 | 44 006 | 12.3 | 19.1 | 17.9 |
| Gallatin | 185 | 2 133 | 27 335 | 11.6 | 24.4 | 45.1 | 98.4 | 9 016 | 27 769 | 51 391 | -0.2 | 3.1 | 50 042 | 12.5 | 13.1 | 12.2 |
| Garfield | 0 | 0 | 231 | 7.4 | 54.1 | 14.2 | 2.4 | 13 719 | 22 306 | 37 500 | 7.2 | 0.0 | 34 607 | 20.0 | 30.6 | 26.8 |
| Glacier | 281 | 1 117 | 4 174 | 11.4 | 44.9 | 18.4 | 37.1 | 13 586 | 17 779 | 40 109 | 6.4 | 1.4 | 33 766 | 31.2 | 39.2 | 37.6 |
| Golden Valley | 112 | 0 | 190 | 5.8 | 48.8 | 21.4 | 2.6 | 17 153 | 20 363 | 36 250 | -1.7 | 0.6 | 32 236 | 23.5 | 36.5 | 31.2 |
| Granite | 32 | 1 771 | 529 | 9.3 | 45.0 | 26.8 | 4.7 | 12 236 | 26 138 | 38 179 | 1.7 | 1.2 | 38 140 | 15.0 | 26.8 | 23.1 |
| Hill | 456 | 3 584 | 4 259 | 10.7 | 37.6 | 21.8 | 39.1 | 12 723 | 21 618 | 46 724 | 12.4 | 1.0 | 42 014 | 18.9 | 25.8 | 24.0 |
| Jefferson | 139 | 382 | 2 501 | 13.4 | 36.3 | 33.5 | 15.9 | 9 722 | 28 865 | 59 284 | 5.8 | 3.0 | 56 280 | 10.1 | 13.6 | 11.7 |
| Judith Basin | 0 | 48 | 355 | 1.4 | 39.4 | 27.3 | 4.7 | 15 969 | 23 710 | 40 046 | 1.4 | 2.5 | 37 657 | 16.2 | 23.8 | 20.3 |
| Lake | 276 | 2 300 | 6 644 | 11.3 | 40.3 | 25.5 | 45.5 | 10 666 | 20 161 | 38 268 | -1.4 | 0.7 | 37 135 | 22.8 | 33.1 | 32.0 |
| Lewis and Clark | 347 | 2 026 | 14 822 | 21.0 | 30.7 | 36.8 | 88.2 | 9 117 | 27 121 | 53 053 | 5.2 | 1.9 | 52 510 | 10.8 | 15.4 | 14.1 |
| Liberty | NA | NA | 378 | 18.0 | 45.0 | 20.8 | 3.3 | 13 084 | 21 236 | 42 674 | 4.4 | 2.2 | 35 769 | 22.0 | 27.7 | 25.6 |
| Lincoln | 181 | 1 475 | 3 435 | 14.4 | 50.1 | 17.2 | 27.4 | 10 374 | 20 526 | 32 012 | -11.4 | 0.8 | 33 656 | 22.2 | 34.4 | 30.3 |
| McCone | 114 | 1 086 | 357 | 8.1 | 47.8 | 19.9 | 3.3 | 12 504 | 25 169 | 50 774 | 26.5 | 2.3 | 39 993 | 16.1 | 21.8 | 19.0 |
| Madison | 77 | 554 | 1 293 | 15.2 | 37.5 | 33.2 | 11.9 | 12 902 | 33 892 | 45 242 | 10.8 | 4.6 | 42 799 | 12.2 | 18.2 | 16.2 |
| Meagher | 314 | 1 205 | 399 | 15.0 | 54.9 | 16.7 | 3.0 | 12 861 | 18 147 | 33 846 | -14.7 | 0.9 | 35 591 | 19.8 | 30.4 | 28.6 |
| Mineral | 0 | 23 | 700 | 9.9 | 59.8 | 12.4 | 9.2 | 14 340 | 18 974 | 36 261 | -1.1 | 0.2 | 33 416 | 17.7 | 30.3 | 27.9 |
| Missoula | 264 | 2 911 | 31 424 | 10.4 | 31.8 | 38.1 | 130.7 | 9 912 | 25 418 | 43 895 | -5.6 | 2.6 | 42 082 | 17.0 | 19.4 | 17.4 |
| Musselshell | 393 | 1 682 | 842 | 9.7 | 53.1 | 15.1 | 7.4 | 10 757 | 22 193 | 38 669 | 12.2 | 0.7 | 37 495 | 17.6 | 29.6 | 26.6 |
| Park | 241 | 1 103 | 3 281 | 13.6 | 42.0 | 29.3 | 22.3 | 10 939 | 24 466 | 41 232 | -3.8 | 1.7 | 42 332 | 12.0 | 19.2 | 17.1 |
| Petroleum | NA | NA | 110 | 9.1 | 58.8 | 8.8 | 1.4 | 13 255 | 19 873 | 38 162 | 17.2 | 1.6 | 31 891 | 18.3 | 26.7 | 20.2 |
| Phillips | 163 | 1 398 | 1 016 | 7.3 | 50.5 | 17.5 | 10.9 | 14 782 | 23 840 | 38 958 | 0.5 | 0.4 | 37 217 | 16.2 | 23.4 | 21.2 |
| Pondera | 193 | 757 | 1 609 | 18.3 | 42.2 | 20.4 | 12.9 | 13 485 | 21 101 | 38 852 | -5.5 | 1.8 | 37 218 | 12.9 | 24.9 | 23.1 |
| Powder River | NA | NA | 398 | 7.3 | 40.9 | 14.8 | 3.9 | 12 412 | 24 637 | 39 091 | 2.0 | 3.1 | 38 756 | 13.9 | 15.4 | 12.4 |
| Powell | 183 | 1 241 | 1 364 | 14.1 | 48.9 | 19.7 | 11.0 | 12 992 | 18 387 | 41 347 | 0.0 | 0.8 | 37 850 | 19.7 | 23.7 | 21.7 |
| Prairie | 84 | 505 | 184 | 3.3 | 50.1 | 14.5 | 1.9 | 13 521 | 21 832 | 34 440 | 0.2 | 3.1 | 35 144 | 13.4 | 19.6 | 18.7 |
| Ravalli | 250 | 1 536 | 8 443 | 16.3 | 42.4 | 25.0 | 51.9 | 8 962 | 24 641 | 43 512 | 0.7 | 2.4 | 39 421 | 15.3 | 25.0 | 22.3 |
| Richland | 203 | 1 363 | 1 974 | 6.9 | 49.4 | 15.9 | 21.9 | 13 048 | 29 490 | 57 413 | 32.4 | 3.8 | 55 593 | 9.7 | 14.0 | 12.6 |
| Roosevelt | 341 | 1 910 | 2 944 | 4.3 | 52.5 | 15.8 | 37.1 | 16 477 | 17 433 | 37 807 | 12.8 | 1.7 | 33 152 | 26.9 | 36.8 | 34.8 |
| Rosebud | 140 | 784 | 2 545 | 5.6 | 46.8 | 17.0 | 28.0 | 15 981 | 20 758 | 44 449 | -8.3 | 1.3 | 45 838 | 18.8 | 27.2 | 25.0 |
| Sanders | 139 | 1 051 | 2 171 | 15.9 | 54.6 | 16.5 | 19.0 | 13 097 | 18 292 | 30 368 | -16.2 | 0.1 | 30 703 | 18.1 | 32.8 | 30.2 |
| Sheridan | 205 | 2 021 | 632 | 10.9 | 37.2 | 19.6 | 8.6 | 17 171 | 27 924 | 42 148 | 5.8 | 2.6 | 44 992 | 10.8 | 13.6 | 10.9 |
| Silver Bow | 293 | 3 000 | 8 221 | 9.9 | 46.9 | 22.5 | 41.6 | 9 233 | 22 249 | 40 030 | -2.5 | 0.7 | 39 586 | 17.2 | 22.7 | 20.7 |
| Stillwater | 163 | 978 | 1 859 | 9.7 | 47.3 | 21.4 | 16.3 | 11 395 | 27 460 | 56 652 | 7.0 | 1.6 | 49 185 | 10.4 | 14.0 | 12.1 |
| Sweet Grass | 136 | 1 005 | 681 | 26.0 | 46.3 | 26.5 | 6.1 | 10 719 | 22 838 | 41 913 | -4.3 | 1.8 | 40 859 | 11.8 | 15.2 | 12.8 |
| Teton | 114 | 865 | 1 263 | 15.6 | 42.1 | 24.9 | 13.9 | 11 771 | 21 834 | 40 811 | 0.1 | 2.2 | 39 479 | 15.2 | 19.8 | 16.3 |
| Toole | 465 | 2 383 | 1 032 | 16.2 | 45.8 | 17.9 | 9.1 | 11 231 | 23 123 | 44 688 | 9.7 | 0.3 | 38 983 | 18.4 | 21.5 | 18.3 |
| Treasure | NA | NA | 153 | 10.5 | 47.0 | 25.5 | 1.6 | 15 692 | 22 524 | 38 571 | -4.2 | 1.3 | 42 837 | 12.5 | 19.7 | 17.9 |
| Valley | 148 | 969 | 1 485 | 6.9 | 51.7 | 15.2 | 15.7 | 12 576 | 24 128 | 44 641 | 6.7 | 0.8 | 46 566 | 15.3 | 22.4 | 18.9 |
| Wheatland | 137 | 91 | 237 | 9.3 | 58.5 | 17.0 | 4.5 | 13 481 | 18 641 | 32 331 | -2.2 | 0.0 | 28 086 | 19.0 | 27.4 | 26.7 |
| Wibaux | 0 | 292 | 195 | 11.8 | 53.3 | 14.5 | 2.3 | 15 874 | 23 157 | 43 417 | 13.9 | 2.3 | 38 722 | 11.8 | 17.0 | 14.1 |
| Yellowstone | 265 | 3 652 | 34 438 | 13.0 | 39.3 | 29.3 | 202.7 | 9 248 | 27 273 | 50 185 | 1.2 | 2.7 | 47 346 | 13.0 | 16.8 | 14.6 |
| **NEBRASKA** | 253 | 2 753 | 499 740 | 17.7 | 38.9 | 27.6 | 3 165.9 | 10 721 | 26 113 | 50 695 | -4.3 | 2.8 | 50 281 | 12.9 | 17.6 | 15.4 |
| Adams | 161 | 3 306 | 8 356 | 23.6 | 41.6 | 22.4 | 58.7 | 11 963 | 24 390 | 47 469 | -5.4 | 2.7 | 46 321 | 13.7 | 19.7 | 18.1 |
| Antelope | 39 | 409 | 1 501 | 14.1 | 49.5 | 15.5 | 21.4 | 19 691 | 21 982 | 40 474 | -0.5 | 1.1 | 44 394 | 14.1 | 22.4 | 20.8 |
| Arthur | 0 | 0 | 110 | 5.5 | 29.1 | 21.9 | 1.6 | 17 689 | 20 071 | 43 194 | 16.9 | 0.6 | 37 578 | 11.5 | 16.0 | 15.9 |
| Banner | NA | NA | 164 | 9.8 | 36.0 | 23.5 | 2.6 | 14 864 | 21 552 | 27 167 | -35.8 | 1.3 | 29 383 | 12.9 | 23.9 | 20.7 |

1. Data for serious crimes have not been adjusted for underreporting; this may affect comparability between geographic areas and over time.   2. Per 100,000 population estimated by the FBI.   3. All persons 3 years old and over enrolled in nursery school through college.   4. Persons 25 years old and over.   5. Elementary and secondary education expenditures.   6. Based on population estimated by the American Community Survey, 2007–2011.

# Table B. States and Counties — **Personal Income**

| STATE County | Total (mil dol) | Percent change, 2010–2011 | Per capita[1] Dollars | Per capita[1] Rank | Wages and salaries[2] (mil dol) | Proprietors' income (mil dol) | Dividends, interest, and rent (mil dol) | Total | Transfer payments (mil dol) Government payments to individuals Total | Social Security | Medical payments | Income mainte-nance | Unemploy-ment insurance |
|---|---|---|---|---|---|---|---|---|---|---|---|---|---|
| | 62 | 63 | 64 | 65 | 66 | 67 | 68 | 69 | 70 | 71 | 72 | 73 | 74 |
| MISSOURI—Cont'd | | | | | | | | | | | | | |
| St. Louis city........... | 11 842 | 4.2 | 37 232 | 1 055 | 16 088 | 1 328 | 1 431 | 3 131 | 3 061 | 636 | 1 434 | 561 | 99 |
| MONTANA ........ | 35 952 | 5.4 | 36 016 | X | 20 935 | 3 521 | 7 352 | 6 917 | 6 697 | 2 486 | 2 492 | 651 | 248 |
| Beaverhead................ | 308 | 5.3 | 33 476 | 1 605 | 154 | 25 | 77 | 73 | 71 | 25 | 30 | 5 | 2 |
| Big Horn ................. | 351 | 7.5 | 26 805 | 2 787 | 239 | 26 | 43 | 96 | 93 | 20 | 37 | 22 | 5 |
| Blaine.................... | 186 | 8.9 | 28 380 | 2 560 | 70 | 39 | 37 | 48 | 47 | 12 | 20 | 7 | 1 |
| Broadwater............... | 161 | 7.5 | 28 067 | 2 608 | 59 | 20 | 35 | 40 | 39 | 16 | 14 | 3 | 1 |
| Carbon.................... | 360 | 5.0 | 35 892 | 1 228 | 97 | 28 | 95 | 70 | 67 | 31 | 24 | 4 | 2 |
| Carter.................... | 33 | 0.5 | 28 451 | 2 550 | 12 | 3 | 11 | 7 | 7 | 3 | 3 | 0 | 0 |
| Cascade.................. | 3 228 | 4.0 | 39 448 | 810 | 1 965 | 299 | 604 | 630 | 612 | 211 | 240 | 56 | 18 |
| Chouteau................. | 210 | 15.5 | 36 262 | 1 180 | 57 | 51 | 50 | 37 | 36 | 15 | 15 | 2 | 1 |
| Custer.................... | 408 | 1.8 | 34 680 | 1 422 | 248 | 39 | 76 | 82 | 79 | 30 | 30 | 7 | 2 |
| Daniels................... | 88 | 5.5 | 49 635 | 214 | 28 | 32 | 18 | 14 | 14 | 6 | 6 | 1 | 0 |
| Dawson................... | 297 | 5.1 | 33 016 | 1 706 | 188 | 17 | 52 | 63 | 61 | 22 | 22 | 4 | 1 |
| Deer Lodge .............. | 272 | 2.0 | 29 234 | 2 420 | 128 | 14 | 44 | 82 | 80 | 31 | 33 | 7 | 2 |
| Fallon.................... | 123 | 5.4 | 41 468 | 619 | 101 | 9 | 21 | 17 | 17 | 7 | 7 | 1 | 0 |
| Fergus.................... | 396 | 4.6 | 34 428 | 1 450 | 195 | 42 | 97 | 92 | 90 | 36 | 37 | 6 | 3 |
| Flathead.................. | 3 275 | 4.5 | 35 875 | 1 232 | 1 743 | 363 | 794 | 640 | 619 | 245 | 215 | 56 | 34 |
| Gallatin.................. | 3 357 | 6.5 | 36 735 | 1 107 | 2 088 | 392 | 773 | 401 | 380 | 154 | 110 | 31 | 21 |
| Garfield.................. | 37 | 10.7 | 29 842 | 2 316 | 12 | 7 | 12 | 7 | 7 | 3 | 3 | 0 | 0 |
| Glacier................... | 407 | 4.9 | 29 900 | 2 310 | 226 | 49 | 72 | 107 | 104 | 21 | 41 | 25 | 5 |
| Golden Valley............ | 35 | 11.0 | 40 629 | 694 | 7 | 3 | 11 | 7 | 7 | 3 | 2 | 1 | 0 |
| Granite................... | 98 | 8.2 | 31 808 | 1 930 | 33 | 12 | 26 | 25 | 24 | 11 | 8 | 2 | 1 |
| Hill...................... | 630 | 8.4 | 38 444 | 917 | 366 | 69 | 124 | 130 | 127 | 31 | 49 | 16 | 4 |
| Jefferson................. | 446 | 4.2 | 39 223 | 829 | 112 | 61 | 78 | 75 | 72 | 32 | 25 | 5 | 2 |
| Judith Basin............. | 76 | 8.2 | 38 102 | 956 | 18 | 14 | 25 | 15 | 15 | 6 | 6 | 1 | 0 |
| Lake...................... | 797 | 3.4 | 27 536 | 2 680 | 349 | 56 | 178 | 230 | 224 | 80 | 87 | 27 | 8 |
| Lewis and Clark .......... | 2 501 | 4.6 | 38 890 | 863 | 1 851 | 170 | 452 | 422 | 408 | 163 | 136 | 38 | 13 |
| Liberty................... | 88 | 17.9 | 36 590 | 1 125 | 21 | 32 | 24 | 16 | 16 | 5 | 8 | 1 | 0 |
| Lincoln................... | 547 | 2.8 | 27 978 | 2 618 | 236 | 43 | 106 | 191 | 187 | 74 | 70 | 18 | 10 |
| McCone................... | 57 | -3.7 | 33 118 | 1 688 | 28 | 5 | 14 | 10 | 10 | 4 | 4 | 1 | 0 |
| Madison.................. | 274 | 6.7 | 35 821 | 1 246 | 148 | 22 | 73 | 54 | 53 | 25 | 19 | 2 | 2 |
| Meagher.................. | 62 | 7.4 | 32 421 | 1 798 | 20 | 5 | 23 | 17 | 16 | 7 | 7 | 1 | 0 |
| Mineral................... | 117 | 4.5 | 27 895 | 2 628 | 45 | 10 | 19 | 43 | 42 | 16 | 16 | 4 | 2 |
| Missoula................. | 3 876 | 4.1 | 35 190 | 1 341 | 2 598 | 351 | 750 | 686 | 662 | 233 | 237 | 69 | 28 |
| Musselshell.............. | 145 | 5.9 | 30 830 | 2 135 | 66 | 3 | 33 | 41 | 40 | 15 | 16 | 3 | 1 |
| Park...................... | 556 | 6.5 | 35 935 | 1 221 | 210 | 40 | 154 | 109 | 106 | 38 | 37 | 8 | 5 |
| Petroleum................ | 16 | 23.4 | 32 699 | 1 758 | 5 | 4 | 3 | 3 | 3 | 1 | 1 | 0 | 0 |
| Phillips.................. | 146 | 9.6 | 34 455 | 1 440 | 61 | 29 | 31 | 33 | 32 | 12 | 14 | 3 | 1 |
| Pondera.................. | 239 | 10.6 | 38 174 | 945 | 79 | 48 | 68 | 50 | 49 | 16 | 22 | 6 | 1 |
| Powder River............. | 50 | 7.4 | 28 737 | 2 496 | 18 | 4 | 14 | 10 | 9 | 4 | 3 | 1 | 0 |
| Powell.................... | 191 | 4.2 | 27 022 | 2 761 | 112 | 12 | 36 | 49 | 48 | 18 | 18 | 4 | 2 |
| Prairie................... | 38 | 6.5 | 33 206 | 1 672 | 14 | 2 | 12 | 10 | 10 | 4 | 4 | 0 | 0 |
| Ravalli................... | 1 252 | 4.1 | 30 955 | 2 109 | 442 | 104 | 312 | 324 | 315 | 135 | 112 | 27 | 12 |
| Richland................. | 518 | 16.8 | 51 183 | 181 | 344 | 63 | 89 | 62 | 59 | 23 | 25 | 4 | 1 |
| Roosevelt................ | 309 | 3.2 | 29 318 | 2 406 | 168 | 30 | 41 | 91 | 89 | 19 | 42 | 18 | 3 |
| Rosebud.................. | 346 | 7.5 | 36 846 | 1 097 | 284 | 17 | 44 | 66 | 64 | 20 | 23 | 11 | 2 |
| Sanders.................. | 298 | 2.0 | 26 061 | 2 875 | 110 | 26 | 63 | 110 | 107 | 43 | 40 | 9 | 5 |
| Sheridan................. | 150 | 2.1 | 43 298 | 485 | 60 | 32 | 38 | 26 | 26 | 11 | 11 | 1 | 0 |
| Silver Bow............... | 1 329 | 5.2 | 38 666 | 885 | 767 | 202 | 202 | 281 | 273 | 99 | 110 | 27 | 8 |
| Stillwater................ | 337 | 8.8 | 36 866 | 1 092 | 217 | 23 | 58 | 60 | 58 | 25 | 21 | 4 | 2 |
| Sweet Grass.............. | 105 | 8.6 | 28 862 | 2 474 | 76 | 3 | 41 | 24 | 23 | 10 | 8 | 1 | 1 |
| Teton..................... | 245 | 10.6 | 40 181 | 726 | 81 | 50 | 63 | 46 | 45 | 18 | 19 | 3 | 1 |
| Toole..................... | 221 | 14.8 | 42 122 | 565 | 113 | 50 | 53 | 30 | 29 | 11 | 11 | 3 | 1 |
| Treasure................. | 27 | 14.8 | 37 003 | 1 077 | 7 | 5 | 8 | 6 | 6 | 3 | 2 | 0 | 0 |
| Valley.................... | 293 | 9.4 | 39 153 | 839 | 136 | 48 | 63 | 61 | 59 | 21 | 25 | 5 | 1 |
| Wheatland ............... | 67 | 10.8 | 31 128 | 2 075 | 22 | 10 | 20 | 16 | 16 | 5 | 7 | 1 | 0 |
| Wibaux................... | 23 | -7.9 | 23 622 | 3 041 | 13 | -2 | 5 | 7 | 7 | 3 | 3 | 0 | 0 |
| Yellowstone.............. | 5 949 | 5.8 | 39 640 | 790 | 4 091 | 413 | 1 088 | 973 | 940 | 353 | 357 | 87 | 29 |
| NEBRASKA................ | 78 220 | 8.4 | 42 450 | X | 48 628 | 11 725 | 12 847 | 11 897 | 11 490 | 4 095 | 4 760 | 1 152 | 307 |
| Adams.................... | 1 233 | 9.6 | 39 483 | 806 | 677 | 183 | 259 | 226 | 219 | 83 | 92 | 20 | 5 |
| Antelope ................. | 407 | 23.4 | 61 552 | 55 | 90 | 209 | 51 | 51 | 49 | 19 | 22 | 4 | 1 |
| Arthur.................... | 16 | 23.5 | 33 343 | 1 644 | 6 | 2 | 3 | 3 | 3 | 1 | 1 | 0 | 0 |
| Banner.................... | 39 | 43.3 | 56 545 | 100 | 9 | 15 | 5 | 5 | 5 | 3 | 2 | 0 | 0 |

1. Based on the resident population estimated as of July 1 of the year shown.   2. Includes supplements to wages and salaries.

# Table B. States and Counties — Earnings, Social Security, and Housing

| STATE County | Total (mil dol) | Farm | Goods-related[1] Total | Manufacturing | Information and professional and technical services | Retail trade | Finance, insurance, and real estate | Health care and social services | Government | Number | Rate[2] | Supplemental Security Income recipients, December 2011 | Total | Percent change, 2000–2010 |
|---|---|---|---|---|---|---|---|---|---|---|---|---|---|---|
| | 75 | 76 | 77 | 78 | 79 | 80 | 81 | 82 | 83 | 84 | 85 | 86 | 87 | 88 |
| **MISSOURI—Cont'd** | | | | | | | | | | | | | | |
| St. Louis city | 17 416 | 0.0 | D | 10.2 | D | 2.0 | 8.5 | 14.6 | 16.4 | 53 805 | 169 | 17 096 | 176 002 | -0.2 |
| **MONTANA** | 24 455 | 2.5 | 15.1 | 4.3 | 7.9 | 8.2 | 6.0 | 13.5 | 22.6 | 198 230 | 199 | 18 196 | 482 825 | 17.0 |
| Beaverhead | 179 | 5.6 | D | 1.1 | 3.3 | 7.8 | 9.7 | D | 30.2 | 2 040 | 222 | 101 | 5 273 | 15.5 |
| Big Horn | 264 | 8.4 | 22.3 | 1.1 | 1.6 | 3.4 | 1.8 | D | 46.0 | 1 875 | 143 | 344 | 4 695 | 0.9 |
| Blaine | 110 | 29.4 | 4.3 | 0.5 | D | 5.8 | D | D | 38.5 | 1 165 | 177 | 203 | 2 843 | -3.5 |
| Broadwater | 78 | 16.5 | D | D | D | 5.2 | 3.4 | 5.3 | 17.7 | 1 285 | 223 | 77 | 2 695 | 34.7 |
| Carbon | 125 | 2.8 | 15.1 | 1.7 | 6.6 | 7.7 | 5.6 | 8.3 | 25.4 | 2 455 | 245 | 103 | 6 441 | 17.2 |
| Carter | 14 | 23.7 | D | 0.0 | D | 4.9 | D | D | 31.0 | 300 | 260 | 0 | 810 | 0.0 |
| Cascade | 2 264 | 0.6 | 9.8 | 2.8 | 6.4 | 7.8 | 7.4 | 16.3 | 30.2 | 17 085 | 209 | 1 859 | 37 276 | 5.8 |
| Chouteau | 108 | 43.6 | 3.5 | 0.9 | D | 4.0 | D | D | 18.9 | 1 195 | 206 | 55 | 2 879 | 3.7 |
| Custer | 286 | 4.7 | D | 1.1 | 4.9 | 10.4 | 6.3 | 14.7 | 23.5 | 2 580 | 220 | 231 | 5 560 | 3.7 |
| Daniels | 60 | 40.7 | D | D | D | 3.4 | 5.1 | D | 10.5 | 475 | 269 | 16 | 1 111 | -3.8 |
| Dawson | 205 | 3.6 | 8.4 | 1.0 | 4.2 | 8.0 | 4.2 | 14.6 | 18.7 | 1 735 | 193 | 100 | 4 233 | 1.6 |
| Deer Lodge | 142 | -0.4 | D | 3.4 | D | 6.4 | 2.9 | 19.5 | 32.7 | 2 370 | 255 | 259 | 5 122 | 3.3 |
| Fallon | 111 | -2.8 | 53.4 | 0.3 | 2.1 | 4.8 | 2.4 | 5.4 | 12.1 | 560 | 189 | 19 | 1 470 | 4.2 |
| Fergus | 237 | 4.1 | 21.6 | 5.5 | D | 8.4 | 5.9 | D | 21.9 | 2 985 | 259 | 184 | 5 836 | 5.0 |
| Flathead | 2 106 | 0.3 | 17.0 | 7.3 | 7.1 | 9.7 | 7.8 | 16.7 | 14.5 | 19 145 | 210 | 1 331 | 46 963 | 35.1 |
| Gallatin | 2 481 | 1.2 | 16.3 | 5.0 | 13.6 | 10.5 | 7.3 | 9.8 | 19.9 | 11 555 | 126 | 601 | 42 289 | 43.4 |
| Garfield | 18 | 36.6 | D | D | D | 6.1 | D | D | 32.5 | 275 | 220 | 0 | 844 | -12.2 |
| Glacier | 275 | 10.9 | 8.5 | 0.5 | 2.2 | 5.8 | D | 3.8 | 48.5 | 1 920 | 141 | 554 | 5 348 | 2.0 |
| Golden Valley | 10 | 24.0 | D | D | D | D | D | D | 32.2 | 285 | 329 | 20 | 476 | 5.8 |
| Granite | 45 | 1.9 | D | 3.3 | D | 6.1 | D | D | 29.3 | 885 | 288 | 42 | 2 822 | 36.0 |
| Hill | 435 | 8.8 | 8.4 | 0.9 | 7.8 | 7.8 | 3.9 | 9.6 | 28.0 | 2 615 | 159 | 432 | 7 250 | -2.7 |
| Jefferson | 172 | -0.3 | D | 5.5 | 4.6 | 10.1 | 9.5 | 7.3 | 22.9 | 2 480 | 218 | 139 | 5 055 | 20.4 |
| Judith Basin | 31 | 44.7 | D | D | D | 2.2 | D | 0.7 | 25.1 | 530 | 264 | 31 | 1 336 | 0.8 |
| Lake | 405 | 2.3 | 13.9 | 4.9 | 5.9 | 8.7 | 3.8 | 13.3 | 37.3 | 6 605 | 228 | 707 | 16 588 | 21.9 |
| Lewis and Clark | 2 021 | 0.2 | 7.8 | 1.9 | 10.4 | 6.8 | 8.2 | 11.0 | 37.0 | 12 655 | 197 | 1 273 | 30 180 | 17.6 |
| Liberty | 53 | 50.4 | D | D | D | 2.1 | D | D | 12.3 | 410 | 171 | 46 | 1 043 | -2.5 |
| Lincoln | 279 | -0.2 | 18.4 | 3.9 | 3.7 | 8.8 | 3.6 | 14.7 | 30.3 | 5 985 | 306 | 607 | 11 413 | 22.5 |
| McCone | 33 | 14.7 | D | 0.0 | D | 5.0 | D | D | 18.5 | 360 | 210 | 11 | 1 008 | -7.3 |
| Madison | 170 | 2.0 | 12.1 | 2.5 | D | 4.7 | 7.6 | 4.3 | 15.7 | 1 990 | 260 | 59 | 6 940 | 48.5 |
| Meagher | 24 | 6.5 | D | D | D | 9.2 | D | D | 26.6 | 555 | 290 | 57 | 1 432 | 5.1 |
| Mineral | 55 | -0.7 | D | D | D | 11.1 | D | 10.6 | 28.5 | 1 295 | 308 | 136 | 2 446 | 24.7 |
| Missoula | 2 949 | 0.0 | 9.7 | 3.2 | 9.0 | 9.0 | 6.4 | 17.9 | 20.7 | 18 020 | 164 | 2 039 | 50 106 | 21.3 |
| Musselshell | 69 | -4.4 | 53.6 | 0.8 | 3.4 | 3.4 | D | 6.8 | 17.4 | 1 250 | 266 | 101 | 2 654 | 14.5 |
| Park | 250 | 2.3 | 13.4 | 5.3 | 7.3 | 8.6 | 5.8 | 12.5 | 16.5 | 3 175 | 205 | 248 | 9 375 | 13.7 |
| Petroleum | 9 | 51.9 | D | 0.0 | D | D | D | D | 23.0 | 105 | 214 | 0 | 324 | 11.0 |
| Phillips | 90 | 20.9 | D | 1.0 | D | 6.1 | 4.6 | D | 23.9 | 1 015 | 239 | 83 | 2 335 | -6.7 |
| Pondera | 127 | 24.8 | 14.1 | 3.7 | 2.6 | 10.2 | 4.0 | D | 13.7 | 1 285 | 205 | 175 | 2 659 | -6.2 |
| Powder River | 22 | 11.1 | D | D | D | 8.4 | D | 1.1 | 36.4 | 390 | 224 | 0 | 1 022 | 1.5 |
| Powell | 125 | 2.2 | D | D | D | 4.6 | 2.5 | D | 51.7 | 1 460 | 207 | 109 | 3 105 | 6.0 |
| Prairie | 16 | 15.4 | D | D | 7.0 | 1.5 | D | 0.0 | 56.6 | 370 | 319 | 13 | 673 | -6.3 |
| Ravalli | 545 | -0.3 | D | 7.2 | D | 9.0 | 5.6 | 11.6 | 23.9 | 10 920 | 270 | 711 | 19 583 | 22.8 |
| Richland | 407 | 6.8 | 30.9 | 4.2 | 5.3 | 5.1 | 4.8 | 7.3 | 9.8 | 1 875 | 185 | 119 | 4 550 | -0.2 |
| Roosevelt | 198 | 7.8 | 7.3 | 0.9 | 1.8 | 7.0 | 2.6 | D | 48.1 | 1 710 | 162 | 450 | 4 063 | 0.5 |
| Rosebud | 301 | 2.2 | 26.6 | 0.2 | 1.8 | 2.9 | 1.1 | D | 30.6 | 1 605 | 171 | 245 | 4 057 | 3.6 |
| Sanders | 135 | 0.6 | 16.3 | 4.8 | 3.3 | 8.5 | 3.9 | 13.9 | 26.7 | 3 590 | 314 | 279 | 6 678 | 26.7 |
| Sheridan | 92 | 27.3 | 6.3 | 0.1 | 3.0 | 6.3 | 4.5 | D | 22.9 | 940 | 272 | 37 | 2 089 | -3.6 |
| Silver Bow | 969 | 0.0 | 22.2 | 4.8 | 7.8 | 10.7 | 3.1 | 14.5 | 17.4 | 7 650 | 222 | 937 | 16 717 | 3.3 |
| Stillwater | 240 | 1.7 | D | 5.6 | 4.9 | 3.8 | 1.3 | D | 9.6 | 2 010 | 220 | 97 | 4 803 | 21.7 |
| Sweet Grass | 79 | -3.6 | D | 3.5 | 2.6 | 6.0 | 4.3 | D | 19.7 | 860 | 237 | 20 | 2 148 | 15.5 |
| Teton | 131 | 24.2 | D | 1.2 | D | 5.2 | 5.0 | 5.5 | 16.8 | 1 465 | 241 | 115 | 2 892 | -0.6 |
| Toole | 163 | 17.5 | D | D | D | 4.2 | 2.8 | 2.4 | 29.1 | 885 | 169 | 114 | 2 336 | 1.6 |
| Treasure | 12 | 52.0 | D | 0.0 | D | D | D | D | 19.8 | 225 | 309 | 0 | 422 | 0.0 |
| Valley | 184 | 21.2 | D | 0.8 | 3.9 | 6.2 | 3.5 | D | 22.4 | 1 800 | 240 | 152 | 4 879 | 0.7 |
| Wheatland | 32 | 9.3 | 12.9 | 6.3 | D | 4.4 | 2.5 | D | 22.3 | 465 | 217 | 48 | 1 197 | 3.7 |
| Wibaux | 11 | -21.5 | D | D | D | 1.6 | 1.8 | D | 37.5 | 250 | 254 | 12 | 538 | -8.3 |
| Yellowstone | 4 504 | 0.1 | 16.8 | 6.6 | 8.9 | 8.3 | 6.3 | 17.4 | 13.8 | 27 260 | 182 | 2 459 | 63 943 | 17.2 |
| **NEBRASKA** | 60 353 | 9.8 | 15.2 | 9.2 | 8.2 | 5.7 | 8.1 | 10.4 | 17.0 | 313 087 | 170 | 26 501 | 796 793 | 10.3 |
| Adams | 860 | 15.1 | 20.4 | 13.9 | 3.6 | 6.0 | 3.6 | D | 15.2 | 6 425 | 206 | 536 | 13 350 | 2.6 |
| Antelope | 299 | 57.9 | D | 4.0 | 0.8 | 3.1 | D | 3.9 | 7.3 | 1 585 | 239 | 85 | 3 284 | -1.9 |
| Arthur | 8 | 56.2 | D | D | D | D | 0.0 | 0.0 | 22.7 | 120 | 256 | 0 | 254 | -7.0 |
| Banner | 24 | 71.8 | D | 0.0 | D | D | D | 0.0 | 12.9 | 235 | 344 | 0 | 369 | -1.6 |

1. Includes mining, construction, and manufacturing.  2. Per 1,000 resident population enumerated in the 2010 census.

| | Housing units, 2007–2011 | | | | | | | | Civilian labor force, 2012 | | | | Civilian employment,[6] 2007–2011 | | |
| --- | --- | --- | --- | --- | --- | --- | --- | --- | --- | --- | --- | --- | --- | --- | --- |
| | Occupied units | | | | | | | | | | Unemployment | | | Percent | |
| | | | Owner-occupied | | | Renter-occupied | | | | | | | | | |
| | | | | Median owner cost as a percent of income | | | | | | | | | | | |
| STATE County | | | | | | | | | | | | | | | Construction, production, and maintenance occupations |
| | | | | | | Median rent as a percent of income | Sub-standard units[4] (percent) | | Percent change, 2011–2012 | | | | Management, business, science and arts | |
| | Total | Percent | Median value[1] | With a mortgage | Without a mortgage[2] | Median rent[3] | | | Total | | Total | Rate[5] | Total | | |
| | 89 | 90 | 91 | 92 | 93 | 94 | 95 | 96 | 97 | 98 | 99 | 100 | 101 | 102 | 103 |
| **MISSOURI—Cont'd** | | | | | | | | | | | | | | | |
| St. Louis city | 139 693 | 46.4 | 123 300 | 24.3 | 13.8 | 690 | 32.5 | 2.8 | 139 923 | -2.5 | 13 015 | 9.3 | 146 638 | 35.4 | 16.9 |
| **MONTANA** | 403 495 | 68.9 | 179 900 | 24.0 | 11.6 | 649 | 27.8 | 2.5 | 507 565 | 1.7 | 30 515 | 6.0 | 477 082 | 34.5 | 22.7 |
| Beaverhead | 4 004 | 62.7 | 182 200 | 23.1 | 11.0 | 529 | 26.9 | 0.6 | 5 093 | -0.4 | 264 | 5.2 | 4 515 | 39.0 | 19.9 |
| Big Horn | 3 489 | 66.6 | 88 800 | 20.0 | 11.8 | 541 | 20.9 | 11.0 | 5 252 | -1.0 | 673 | 12.8 | 4 852 | 33.8 | 18.9 |
| Blaine | 2 318 | 64.3 | 69 900 | 19.4 | 11.2 | 342 | 18.3 | 3.3 | 2 691 | 0.6 | 152 | 5.6 | 2 352 | 40.3 | 23.8 |
| Broadwater | 1 959 | 78.5 | 160 600 | 25.6 | 13.1 | 623 | 21.8 | 1.7 | 2 327 | -1.1 | 191 | 8.2 | 2 481 | 28.5 | 31.1 |
| Carbon | 4 265 | 72.1 | 202 100 | 23.4 | 13.1 | 697 | 22.9 | 2.8 | 5 284 | 2.1 | 248 | 4.7 | 5 238 | 34.6 | 27.9 |
| Carter | 551 | 73.9 | 69 400 | 16.7 | 12.5 | 438 | 16.4 | 6.2 | 696 | 1.2 | 22 | 3.2 | 704 | 55.7 | 25.4 |
| Cascade | 33 134 | 67.0 | 151 200 | 23.2 | 11.8 | 564 | 24.8 | 2.6 | 40 281 | 0.2 | 2 165 | 5.4 | 36 731 | 31.2 | 22.6 |
| Chouteau | 2 167 | 63.5 | 109 200 | 23.6 | 10.6 | 422 | 20.9 | 2.6 | 2 584 | 1.6 | 104 | 4.0 | 2 486 | 41.2 | 19.6 |
| Custer | 5 122 | 68.6 | 97 700 | 20.2 | 12.9 | 474 | 21.6 | 3.2 | 6 349 | 3.5 | 238 | 3.7 | 5 890 | 31.8 | 22.5 |
| Daniels | 801 | 78.5 | 78 600 | 21.1 | 12.4 | 372 | 17.3 | 0.6 | 770 | 0.9 | 31 | 4.0 | 876 | 41.1 | 18.7 |
| Dawson | 3 749 | 73.3 | 110 900 | 16.9 | 10.4 | 434 | 19.4 | 0.2 | 4 452 | 3.1 | 157 | 3.5 | 4 674 | 34.7 | 27.1 |
| Deer Lodge | 4 041 | 70.6 | 105 700 | 21.7 | 13.5 | 494 | 27.6 | 3.2 | 4 099 | 1.3 | 305 | 7.4 | 3 957 | 27.0 | 22.7 |
| Fallon | 1 216 | 74.9 | 89 200 | 15.4 | 10.7 | 472 | 16.3 | 1.5 | 2 143 | 6.4 | 41 | 1.9 | 1 608 | 32.8 | 36.0 |
| Fergus | 4 881 | 72.2 | 115 000 | 19.2 | 13.6 | 566 | 31.2 | 3.5 | 5 978 | 0.4 | 319 | 5.3 | 5 649 | 37.5 | 25.1 |
| Flathead | 36 697 | 71.6 | 235 200 | 27.9 | 12.6 | 721 | 28.7 | 2.1 | 43 840 | -0.1 | 3 931 | 9.0 | 42 950 | 30.6 | 25.9 |
| Gallatin | 36 528 | 62.1 | 276 000 | 26.3 | 11.2 | 838 | 29.9 | 1.8 | 50 329 | 2.2 | 2 686 | 5.3 | 49 066 | 38.5 | 20.7 |
| Garfield | 472 | 79.0 | 69 100 | 28.6 | 11.1 | 450 | 17.5 | 3.0 | 645 | 1.7 | 22 | 3.4 | 602 | 42.2 | 23.9 |
| Glacier | 4 259 | 59.8 | 74 900 | 16.3 | 9.9 | 468 | 19.4 | 10.6 | 6 116 | 7.3 | 623 | 10.2 | 5 492 | 34.7 | 19.4 |
| Golden Valley | 343 | 75.2 | 97 600 | 27.1 | 11.3 | 708 | 24.4 | 3.5 | 528 | 1.3 | 19 | 3.6 | 397 | 29.2 | 37.0 |
| Granite | 1 537 | 73.2 | 170 800 | 28.1 | 11.5 | 605 | 22.4 | 6.1 | 1 274 | 1.4 | 128 | 10.0 | 1 410 | 34.0 | 27.9 |
| Hill | 6 069 | 68.2 | 109 700 | 21.0 | 9.9 | 503 | 27.1 | 3.1 | 8 494 | 1.6 | 468 | 5.5 | 7 629 | 34.6 | 26.6 |
| Jefferson | 4 517 | 85.1 | 234 700 | 22.6 | 9.9 | 622 | 26.8 | 1.1 | 5 874 | 1.5 | 304 | 5.2 | 5 436 | 43.9 | 21.9 |
| Judith Basin | 911 | 79.0 | 102 900 | 22.1 | 12.0 | 480 | 13.9 | 2.3 | 1 135 | 7.4 | 50 | 4.4 | 891 | 62.5 | 16.0 |
| Lake | 12 017 | 68.4 | 200 600 | 27.4 | 10.9 | 583 | 26.8 | 4.6 | 11 300 | -0.2 | 1 007 | 8.9 | 11 633 | 34.5 | 22.7 |
| Lewis and Clark | 26 549 | 72.1 | 196 700 | 23.7 | 11.2 | 688 | 28.2 | 1.2 | 34 931 | 1.6 | 1 700 | 4.9 | 32 238 | 44.4 | 14.6 |
| Liberty | 822 | 64.6 | 85 700 | 18.2 | 9.9 | 464 | 20.4 | 4.4 | 787 | 4.8 | 42 | 5.3 | 1 018 | 41.2 | 23.0 |
| Lincoln | 8 998 | 76.7 | 162 900 | 27.7 | 12.2 | 500 | 25.9 | 5.5 | 7 722 | 0.6 | 1 043 | 13.5 | 7 478 | 29.5 | 30.1 |
| McCone | 745 | 76.8 | 84 300 | 22.5 | 9.9 | 392 | 21.3 | 2.1 | 1 049 | 1.3 | 32 | 3.1 | 1 025 | 55.0 | 17.0 |
| Madison | 3 672 | 71.2 | 250 300 | 27.2 | 12.0 | 693 | 22.3 | 2.7 | 4 034 | -0.8 | 244 | 6.0 | 3 876 | 39.1 | 24.7 |
| Meagher | 694 | 67.3 | 111 500 | 30.4 | 13.1 | 495 | 23.2 | 2.2 | 857 | 2.5 | 52 | 6.1 | 834 | 26.6 | 30.8 |
| Mineral | 1 713 | 69.6 | 169 100 | 27.0 | 12.6 | 574 | 26.7 | 1.2 | 1 934 | -0.9 | 196 | 10.1 | 1 654 | 19.4 | 31.8 |
| Missoula | 44 946 | 60.5 | 239 000 | 25.7 | 11.3 | 718 | 33.7 | 2.5 | 58 869 | 1.0 | 3 465 | 5.9 | 56 776 | 35.7 | 17.5 |
| Musselshell | 1 983 | 77.7 | 122 200 | 24.5 | 10.8 | 533 | 29.0 | 4.5 | 2 458 | 6.2 | 130 | 5.3 | 1 994 | 25.6 | 36.1 |
| Park | 6 735 | 72.3 | 208 000 | 29.0 | 13.4 | 659 | 26.2 | 0.7 | 8 637 | 2.5 | 549 | 6.4 | 7 695 | 31.5 | 28.9 |
| Petroleum | 253 | 68.4 | 103 000 | 30.4 | 9.9 | 758 | 50.0 | 7.1 | 254 | 6.7 | 13 | 5.1 | 254 | 43.3 | 35.8 |
| Phillips | 1 740 | 80.2 | 77 900 | 17.9 | 9.9 | 429 | 21.9 | 2.7 | 2 125 | -0.9 | 121 | 5.7 | 1 958 | 39.1 | 23.1 |
| Pondera | 2 265 | 70.9 | 85 500 | 20.4 | 13.9 | 486 | 27.3 | 6.0 | 2 591 | 2.3 | 145 | 5.6 | 2 690 | 37.0 | 25.2 |
| Powder River | 702 | 68.8 | 106 800 | 18.8 | 9.9 | 500 | 19.8 | 2.7 | 966 | 2.9 | 39 | 4.0 | 861 | 41.8 | 22.0 |
| Powell | 2 365 | 74.1 | 119 500 | 22.9 | 12.2 | 550 | 20.1 | 3.3 | 2 820 | 0.9 | 220 | 7.8 | 2 725 | 30.0 | 20.6 |
| Prairie | 491 | 84.1 | 64 000 | 17.1 | 11.9 | 479 | 32.5 | 0.8 | 554 | 1.5 | 23 | 4.2 | 496 | 44.6 | 27.4 |
| Ravalli | 16 631 | 76.4 | 241 000 | 29.2 | 13.5 | 686 | 29.1 | 2.8 | 17 958 | 0.7 | 1 437 | 8.0 | 17 726 | 32.8 | 26.4 |
| Richland | 4 083 | 69.1 | 112 100 | 16.6 | 9.9 | 553 | 19.0 | 0.4 | 6 897 | 10.1 | 183 | 2.7 | 5 148 | 29.0 | 36.4 |
| Roosevelt | 3 333 | 62.5 | 60 600 | 13.4 | 10.1 | 392 | 17.8 | 6.0 | 4 335 | 4.8 | 321 | 7.4 | 3 930 | 34.0 | 22.8 |
| Rosebud | 3 276 | 68.4 | 104 900 | 18.2 | 9.9 | 534 | 14.8 | 5.5 | 4 174 | 1.7 | 300 | 7.2 | 4 008 | 30.9 | 31.5 |
| Sanders | 5 078 | 77.0 | 174 600 | 32.3 | 13.0 | 571 | 28.8 | 4.0 | 4 232 | -0.8 | 560 | 13.2 | 4 500 | 30.8 | 29.3 |
| Sheridan | 1 684 | 73.9 | 81 500 | 19.5 | 11.7 | 502 | 18.7 | 0.3 | 2 023 | 11.2 | 60 | 3.0 | 1 699 | 32.2 | 31.1 |
| Silver Bow | 14 981 | 65.5 | 120 700 | 20.9 | 12.2 | 552 | 29.1 | 1.5 | 18 007 | 2.2 | 1 048 | 5.8 | 16 222 | 31.5 | 21.5 |
| Stillwater | 3 754 | 76.0 | 175 800 | 21.4 | 12.3 | 649 | 20.7 | 2.0 | 4 497 | 3.7 | 222 | 4.9 | 4 501 | 27.3 | 37.9 |
| Sweet Grass | 1 517 | 76.8 | 182 400 | 24.2 | 11.4 | 618 | 26.5 | 0.7 | 2 406 | 4.7 | 67 | 2.8 | 1 820 | 28.2 | 35.8 |
| Teton | 2 406 | 77.8 | 138 500 | 27.0 | 13.0 | 585 | 25.6 | 3.9 | 2 953 | 1.2 | 142 | 4.8 | 2 680 | 40.2 | 23.6 |
| Toole | 2 034 | 66.3 | 99 200 | 16.6 | 11.6 | 485 | 26.2 | 1.1 | 2 644 | 7.4 | 114 | 4.3 | 2 339 | 38.8 | 23.8 |
| Treasure | 314 | 69.4 | 76 400 | 25.6 | 12.1 | 675 | 16.5 | 0.0 | 379 | 2.4 | 18 | 4.7 | 380 | 33.9 | 34.2 |
| Valley | 3 221 | 71.4 | 87 900 | 19.1 | 9.9 | 488 | 21.1 | 2.4 | 3 783 | 3.5 | 167 | 4.4 | 3 590 | 31.3 | 24.4 |
| Wheatland | 847 | 76.6 | 75 000 | 23.6 | 15.3 | 527 | 15.0 | 8.6 | 1 066 | 5.0 | 51 | 4.8 | 750 | 35.2 | 30.5 |
| Wibaux | 353 | 76.5 | 71 900 | 15.2 | 9.9 | 356 | 21.9 | 0.0 | 611 | 7.4 | 17 | 2.8 | 494 | 34.8 | 23.7 |
| Yellowstone | 60 263 | 70.2 | 173 500 | 22.5 | 11.5 | 673 | 27.8 | 1.6 | 83 480 | 2.4 | 3 646 | 4.4 | 76 204 | 32.0 | 22.2 |
| **NEBRASKA** | 715 703 | 68.3 | 125 400 | 21.8 | 12.6 | 672 | 26.9 | 2.1 | 1 020 913 | 1.4 | 40 245 | 3.9 | 941 270 | 34.8 | 23.9 |
| Adams | 12 441 | 70.7 | 96 900 | 21.0 | 11.3 | 601 | 24.0 | 1.8 | 17 293 | 2.4 | 629 | 3.6 | 15 994 | 29.7 | 29.0 |
| Antelope | 2 804 | 73.6 | 69 000 | 21.5 | 12.0 | 498 | 30.1 | 2.8 | 3 924 | 1.8 | 115 | 2.9 | 3 325 | 34.9 | 29.7 |
| Arthur | 177 | 65.0 | 78 300 | 20.8 | 12.5 | 569 | 19.3 | 1.1 | 264 | 4.8 | 15 | 5.7 | 225 | 50.2 | 27.6 |
| Banner | 316 | 60.8 | 79 200 | 25.3 | 14.5 | 481 | 22.0 | 0.0 | 374 | 0.5 | 16 | 4.3 | 388 | 46.4 | 21.4 |

1. Specified owner-occupied units. lacking complete plumbing facilities.   2. A value of 9.9 represents 9.9 percent or less.   3. Specified renter-occupied units. A value of 10.0 represents 10 percent or less.   4. Overcrowded or
5. Percent of civilian labor force.   6. Persons 16 years old and over.

# Table B. States and Counties — **Nonfarm Employment and Agriculture**

| STATE County | Private nonfarm establishments, employment and payroll, 2011 | | | | | | | | | Agriculture, 2007 | | | |
|---|---|---|---|---|---|---|---|---|---|---|---|---|---|
| | Number of establish- ments | Employment | | | | | | Annual payroll | | Farms | | | |
| | | Total | Health care and social assistance | Manufac- turing | Retail trade | Finance and insurance | Professional, scientific, and technical services | Total (mil dol) | Average per employee (dollars) | Number | Percent with: | | Farm operators whose principal occu- pation is farming (percent) |
| | | | | | | | | | | | Fewer than 50 acres | 500 acres or more | |
| | 104 | 105 | 106 | 107 | 108 | 109 | 110 | 111 | 112 | 113 | 114 | 115 | 116 |
| MISSOURI—Cont'd | | | | | | | | | | | | | |
| St. Louis city | 8 896 | 228 617 | 35 390 | 17 982 | 10 855 | 11 597 | 16 767 | 11 297 | 49 413 | NA | NA | NA | NA |
| MONTANA | 35 687 | 336 110 | 64 520 | 16 535 | 55 554 | 16 047 | 16 677 | 11 292 | 33 595 | 29 524 | 25.0 | 43.0 | 50.7 |
| Beaverhead | 355 | 2 213 | 489 | 65 | 446 | 99 | 78 | 59 | 26 516 | 431 | 29.5 | 43.4 | 49.7 |
| Big Horn | 221 | 2 267 | D | D | 344 | 65 | D | 102 | 45 175 | 695 | 16.8 | 51.4 | 53.1 |
| Blaine | 148 | 1 078 | 244 | D | 185 | 42 | D | 45 | 41 709 | 655 | 6.1 | 66.0 | 56.3 |
| Broadwater | 135 | 892 | D | D | 131 | D | D | 26 | 29 538 | 302 | 21.5 | 39.7 | 56.6 |
| Carbon | 395 | 2 022 | 268 | 35 | 258 | D | 141 | 50 | 24 654 | 715 | 23.5 | 29.1 | 46.9 |
| Carter | 31 | D | D | D | 32 | NA | D | 3 | D | 308 | 6.2 | 80.5 | 72.4 |
| Cascade | 2 429 | 29 151 | 6 485 | 1 059 | 5 029 | 1 960 | 1 292 | 943 | 32 347 | 1 112 | 30.5 | 33.3 | 44.6 |
| Chouteau | 151 | 725 | D | 20 | 89 | 43 | 21 | 17 | 24 072 | 849 | 4.7 | 72.7 | 67.4 |
| Custer | 415 | 4 172 | 1 056 | 64 | 827 | D | 156 | 132 | 31 620 | 411 | 20.9 | 48.7 | 56.2 |
| Daniels | 69 | D | D | D | 98 | 35 | 9 | D | D | 397 | 5.0 | 70.5 | 57.2 |
| Dawson | 332 | 2 803 | D | D | 523 | D | 72 | 85 | 30 482 | 535 | 8.2 | 66.0 | 60.0 |
| Deer Lodge | 257 | 2 811 | 1 309 | D | 267 | 69 | 79 | 87 | 30 995 | 123 | 35.8 | 29.3 | 47.2 |
| Fallon | 145 | 1 083 | D | D | 131 | D | 9 | 51 | 47 463 | 296 | 9.8 | 63.9 | 55.1 |
| Fergus | 439 | 3 221 | 807 | 329 | 493 | D | 71 | 102 | 31 743 | 898 | 12.9 | 61.6 | 60.2 |
| Flathead | 3 847 | 31 357 | 5 294 | 2 732 | 5 582 | 1 584 | 1 289 | 1 011 | 32 255 | 1 094 | 55.3 | 7.0 | 35.3 |
| Gallatin | 4 752 | 37 258 | 4 464 | 2 280 | 6 985 | 1 212 | 2 412 | 1 224 | 32 839 | 1 071 | 46.3 | 19.8 | 41.8 |
| Garfield | 26 | 127 | D | D | 55 | D | D | 2 | 16 307 | 288 | 3.5 | 85.4 | 76.7 |
| Glacier | 255 | 1 946 | 459 | 22 | 414 | D | D | 76 | 38 867 | 625 | 13.8 | 53.8 | 51.4 |
| Golden Valley | 17 | D | D | D | D | NA | D | 2 | D | 153 | 9.8 | 60.8 | 62.7 |
| Granite | 103 | 489 | D | 30 | D | D | 6 | 14 | 29 219 | 166 | 17.5 | 55.4 | 54.8 |
| Hill | 534 | 5 091 | 1 191 | D | 1 028 | 207 | 209 | 158 | 30 992 | 854 | 6.8 | 59.4 | 50.6 |
| Jefferson | 254 | 1 488 | 220 | D | 176 | D | D | 49 | 33 176 | 370 | 27.8 | 24.9 | 34.3 |
| Judith Basin | 51 | 162 | D | NA | 21 | D | 9 | 4 | 26 265 | 306 | 11.8 | 67.0 | 69.3 |
| Lake | 773 | 5 038 | 1 141 | 282 | 1 024 | 220 | 310 | 142 | 28 269 | 1 280 | 52.9 | 9.9 | 44.1 |
| Lewis and Clark | 2 152 | 23 255 | 4 724 | 685 | 3 752 | 1 791 | 1 703 | 799 | 34 339 | 675 | 48.9 | 19.3 | 39.6 |
| Liberty | 64 | 321 | D | D | D | 24 | D | 8 | 23 393 | 299 | 2.0 | 81.6 | 65.6 |
| Lincoln | 620 | 3 645 | 857 | 130 | 641 | 124 | 93 | 106 | 29 098 | 350 | 49.1 | 5.4 | 33.7 |
| McCone | 57 | 378 | D | D | 76 | 25 | D | 13 | 34 349 | 489 | 2.5 | 75.9 | 68.5 |
| Madison | 347 | 1 217 | 160 | D | 172 | D | 54 | 38 | 31 181 | 585 | 26.0 | 37.6 | 47.2 |
| Meagher | 68 | 267 | 95 | D | D | D | D | 6 | 21 180 | 138 | 18.1 | 51.6 | 58.7 |
| Mineral | 113 | 870 | D | D | 192 | 20 | 31 | 22 | 25 438 | 99 | 44.4 | 14.1 | 37.4 |
| Missoula | 4 081 | 46 175 | 10 255 | 1 366 | 7 908 | 1 924 | 2 971 | 1 427 | 30 896 | 699 | 59.2 | 8.0 | 30.3 |
| Musselshell | 114 | 758 | 170 | D | 170 | 32 | D | 25 | 33 168 | 373 | 12.1 | 41.8 | 50.9 |
| Park | 744 | 4 239 | 766 | 243 | 644 | D | 171 | 124 | 29 135 | 535 | 28.6 | 24.6 | 48.2 |
| Petroleum | 15 | 49 | D | NA | D | NA | D | 1 | 15 347 | 103 | 4.9 | 74.8 | 71.8 |
| Phillips | 143 | 912 | D | 18 | 196 | 48 | D | 23 | 24 761 | 556 | 8.3 | 63.8 | 64.6 |
| Pondera | 181 | 1 363 | 316 | 53 | 240 | 76 | 45 | 41 | 29 752 | 542 | 14.0 | 61.3 | 60.0 |
| Powder River | 79 | 319 | D | D | 132 | D | D | 7 | 21 730 | 319 | 7.5 | 74.0 | 64.9 |
| Powell | 160 | 988 | 191 | D | D | D | D | 28 | 28 701 | 273 | 20.1 | 40.7 | 54.9 |
| Prairie | 39 | 163 | D | D | 29 | D | 5 | 4 | 22 227 | 173 | 6.4 | 73.4 | 67.6 |
| Ravalli | 1 352 | 8 459 | 1 389 | 842 | 1 441 | 394 | 470 | 221 | 26 082 | 1 532 | 67.2 | 4.9 | 43.0 |
| Richland | 502 | 4 854 | D | 457 | 564 | 133 | 203 | 209 | 43 047 | 548 | 10.8 | 65.9 | 57.3 |
| Roosevelt | 202 | 1 816 | 451 | D | 447 | 84 | D | 47 | 25 755 | 728 | 4.7 | 58.9 | 48.4 |
| Rosebud | 193 | 2 606 | 310 | D | 269 | 57 | 14 | 110 | 42 307 | 478 | 11.3 | 51.3 | 58.8 |
| Sanders | 341 | 1 964 | 514 | 192 | 335 | D | D | 49 | 24 722 | 508 | 34.4 | 17.5 | 39.8 |
| Sheridan | 160 | 862 | 273 | 1 | 156 | D | D | 24 | 27 607 | 602 | 2.7 | 67.9 | 53.5 |
| Silver Bow | 1 120 | 13 069 | 3 121 | D | 2 248 | 308 | 679 | 442 | 33 854 | 175 | 25.7 | 24.0 | 32.6 |
| Stillwater | 244 | 2 521 | 237 | 464 | 221 | 56 | D | 158 | 62 816 | 635 | 21.7 | 40.0 | 45.7 |
| Sweet Grass | 157 | 933 | 24 | D | 149 | D | 35 | 44 | 46 957 | 355 | 18.0 | 48.7 | 49.9 |
| Teton | 181 | 1 127 | 242 | D | 170 | D | 39 | 32 | 28 679 | 770 | 14.9 | 48.3 | 55.1 |
| Toole | 197 | 1 514 | 276 | D | 184 | D | 38 | 51 | 33 425 | 428 | 5.4 | 74.3 | 55.8 |
| Treasure | 20 | 76 | D | NA | D | D | D | 2 | 24 632 | 101 | 8.9 | 66.3 | 56.4 |
| Valley | 265 | 2 138 | D | 41 | 329 | D | 69 | 60 | 27 989 | 770 | 5.7 | 60.0 | 58.3 |
| Wheatland | 55 | 329 | D | D | 66 | D | D | 9 | 26 766 | 137 | 13.9 | 65.0 | 54.7 |
| Wibaux | 37 | 206 | D | D | 21 | D | D | 6 | 29 602 | 208 | 5.3 | 58.2 | 62.5 |
| Yellowstone | 5 384 | 66 078 | 12 631 | 3 287 | 10 271 | 3 739 | 3 189 | 2 490 | 37 686 | 1 407 | 42.9 | 23.7 | 38.2 |
| NEBRASKA | 51 553 | 797 681 | 121 072 | 91 190 | 106 642 | 58 455 | 38 959 | 29 969 | 37 570 | 47 712 | 18.6 | 39.7 | 60.5 |
| Adams | 953 | 12 845 | 2 649 | 2 485 | 1 865 | 329 | 289 | 407 | 31 675 | 485 | 18.4 | 47.6 | 69.7 |
| Antelope | 219 | 1 396 | 271 | 103 | 286 | D | 25 | 38 | 26 915 | 716 | 13.1 | 42.7 | 68.7 |
| Arthur | 12 | 67 | NA | D | D | D | D | 1 | 18 716 | 68 | 5.9 | 88.2 | 73.5 |
| Banner | 6 | D | NA | NA | NA | D | NA | 1 | D | 218 | 1.8 | 62.4 | 55.5 |

# Table B. States and Counties — Agriculture

| STATE County | Land in farms — Acreage (1,000) [117] | Percent change, 2002–2007 [118] | Acres — Average size of farm [119] | Total irrigated (1,000) [120] | Total cropland (1,000) [121] | Value of land and buildings — Average per farm [122] | Average per acre [123] | Value of machinery and equipment, average per farm (dollars) [124] | Value of products sold — Total (mil dol) [125] | Average per farm (dollars) [126] | Percent from: Crops [127] | Livestock and poultry products [128] | Percent of farms with sales of: $10,000 or more [129] | $100,000 or more [130] | Government payments — Total ($1,000) [131] | Percent of farms [132] |
|---|---|---|---|---|---|---|---|---|---|---|---|---|---|---|---|---|
| **MISSOURI—Cont'd** | | | | | | | | | | | | | | | | |
| St. Louis city | NA | NA | NA | NA | NA | NA | NA | NA | NA | NA | NA | NA | NA | NA | NA | NA |
| MONTANA | 61 388 | 3.0 | 2 079 | 2 013.2 | 18 241.7 | 1 611 155 | 775 | 103 494 | 2 803.1 | 94 942 | 45.4 | 54.6 | 46.8 | 21.6 | 221 977 | 44.3 |
| Beaverhead | 1 239 | -3.1 | 2 875 | 203.5 | 180.5 | 3 463 155 | 1 205 | 134 772 | 86.1 | 199 829 | 16.5 | 83.5 | 50.1 | 28.1 | 318 | 13.9 |
| Big Horn | 2 900 | 3.2 | 4 172 | 59.7 | 383.6 | 1 702 078 | 408 | 112 582 | 94.9 | 136 480 | 43.6 | 56.4 | 55.5 | 26.3 | 3 182 | 30.9 |
| Blaine | 2 331 | 3.1 | 3 558 | 61.8 | 673.8 | 2 180 686 | 613 | 138 487 | 71.6 | 109 385 | 48.2 | 51.8 | 57.6 | 29.9 | 9 664 | 63.4 |
| Broadwater | 475 | 1.1 | 1 572 | 44.1 | 139.0 | 1 733 015 | 1 102 | 114 051 | 25.5 | 84 539 | 57.6 | 42.4 | 45.0 | 19.9 | 2 000 | 48.0 |
| Carbon | 794 | 5.3 | 1 110 | 73.8 | 138.1 | 1 589 309 | 1 432 | 83 201 | 45.3 | 63 309 | 31.3 | 68.7 | 47.0 | 11.5 | 1 229 | 32.7 |
| Carter | 1 698 | 1.9 | 5 514 | 7.1 | 267.2 | 2 174 291 | 394 | 140 539 | 42.8 | 139 001 | 19.8 | 80.2 | 75.6 | 43.2 | 1 766 | 59.7 |
| Cascade | 1 380 | -0.6 | 1 241 | 35.6 | 506.6 | 1 130 619 | 911 | 85 783 | 83.6 | 75 148 | 49.0 | 51.0 | 37.5 | 15.3 | 5 971 | 52.2 |
| Chouteau | 2 278 | -1.0 | 2 683 | 12.1 | 1 310.4 | 1 803 549 | 672 | 165 019 | 147.2 | 173 432 | 84.0 | 16.0 | 62.9 | 44.5 | 19 766 | 83.4 |
| Custer | 2 127 | 11.7 | 5 175 | 31.4 | 186.7 | 2 708 137 | 523 | 115 823 | 73.2 | 178 113 | 13.0 | 87.0 | 56.9 | 28.5 | 1 500 | 43.1 |
| Daniels | 860 | 5.5 | 2 167 | 1.5 | 591.6 | 1 279 818 | 591 | 139 598 | 51.1 | 128 779 | 79.9 | 20.1 | 55.4 | 32.2 | 7 732 | 88.7 |
| Dawson | 1 379 | -2.3 | 2 577 | 19.7 | 446.4 | 1 316 501 | 511 | 112 011 | 56.6 | 105 835 | 56.0 | 44.0 | 64.1 | 31.2 | 6 290 | 73.6 |
| Deer Lodge | 79 | -41.5 | 645 | 19.7 | 19.1 | 948 727 | 1 471 | 64 555 | 4.0 | 32 727 | 12.3 | 87.7 | 30.9 | 13.8 | 32 | 8.9 |
| Fallon | 979 | 5.0 | 3 307 | 1.5 | 247.8 | 1 922 086 | 581 | 133 305 | 35.9 | 121 412 | 19.4 | 80.6 | 64.2 | 33.4 | 2 548 | 72.0 |
| Fergus | 2 446 | 7.2 | 2 724 | 19.8 | 664.7 | 2 522 967 | 926 | 122 288 | 101.2 | 112 658 | 41.5 | 58.5 | 62.5 | 33.7 | 6 187 | 55.0 |
| Flathead | 252 | 7.2 | 230 | 23.3 | 88.5 | 892 403 | 3 880 | 51 610 | 33.5 | 30 644 | 52.3 | 47.7 | 26.1 | 5.6 | 1 001 | 19.5 |
| Gallatin | 777 | 9.6 | 725 | 81.7 | 283.7 | 1 639 919 | 2 261 | 85 074 | 95.1 | 88 840 | 50.3 | 49.7 | 37.8 | 15.4 | 1 761 | 22.2 |
| Garfield | 2 392 | 9.6 | 8 305 | 4.2 | 409.8 | 3 583 051 | 431 | 170 684 | 41.8 | 145 280 | 38.0 | 62.0 | 75.7 | 44.8 | 4 514 | 65.6 |
| Glacier | 1 700 | 3.3 | 2 720 | 30.7 | 552.4 | 1 547 675 | 569 | 123 194 | 55.4 | 88 666 | 41.1 | 58.9 | 49.4 | 19.8 | 6 205 | 46.9 |
| Golden Valley | 672 | 1.7 | 4 391 | 8.6 | 157.4 | 3 307 409 | 753 | 93 040 | 14.6 | 95 589 | 35.0 | 65.0 | 51.6 | 28.1 | 1 902 | 61.4 |
| Granite | 303 | 7.1 | 1 825 | 31.3 | 35.5 | 2 515 494 | 1 378 | 103 724 | 13.1 | 78 804 | 7.3 | 92.7 | 53.6 | 25.9 | 121 | 13.9 |
| Hill | 1 697 | -6.2 | 1 987 | 9.1 | 1 202.9 | 1 321 231 | 665 | 130 016 | 86.6 | 101 444 | 81.9 | 18.1 | 48.9 | 29.5 | 18 178 | 72.0 |
| Jefferson | 391 | 1.0 | 1 057 | 26.7 | 54.5 | 1 293 519 | 1 223 | 65 666 | 13.7 | 37 037 | 13.2 | 86.8 | 30.5 | 9.5 | 451 | 12.2 |
| Judith Basin | 838 | 1.0 | 2 740 | 16.6 | 285.0 | 2 303 311 | 841 | 148 766 | 54.4 | 177 819 | 36.7 | 63.3 | 70.6 | 39.5 | 2 586 | 64.7 |
| Lake | 637 | 5.8 | 498 | 86.5 | 98.8 | 774 473 | 1 555 | 64 012 | 51.6 | 40 337 | 45.4 | 54.6 | 44.4 | 7.3 | 698 | 15.5 |
| Lewis and Clark | 971 | 15.3 | 1 439 | 50.3 | 104.5 | 1 410 544 | 980 | 73 664 | 32.3 | 47 837 | 32.2 | 67.8 | 28.0 | 8.7 | 998 | 13.8 |
| Liberty | 904 | -0.1 | 3 025 | 11.3 | 637.6 | 1 401 882 | 464 | 195 232 | 49.6 | 165 976 | 75.4 | 24.6 | 67.2 | 46.2 | 10 009 | 89.0 |
| Lincoln | 52 | -3.7 | 148 | 4.3 | 16.6 | 550 718 | 3 715 | 44 123 | 2.7 | 7 728 | 19.7 | 80.3 | 12.9 | 1.1 | 24 | 2.6 |
| McCone | 1 507 | 12.0 | 3 081 | 7.2 | 576.6 | 1 466 376 | 476 | 151 834 | 51.6 | 105 470 | 62.5 | 37.5 | 63.6 | 33.1 | 7 628 | 84.9 |
| Madison | 1 061 | 3.1 | 1 813 | 104.9 | 152.2 | 2 864 249 | 1 579 | 82 009 | 53.2 | 90 917 | 25.4 | 74.6 | 44.6 | 20.9 | 743 | 15.4 |
| Meagher | 812 | -5.3 | 5 887 | 40.5 | 113.1 | 6 879 211 | 1 169 | 154 634 | 25.3 | 183 181 | 11.6 | 88.4 | 53.6 | 33.3 | 572 | 29.7 |
| Mineral | 23 | 43.8 | 229 | 1.3 | 4.8 | 840 038 | 3 671 | 44 871 | 0.9 | 8 714 | 28.9 | 71.1 | 16.2 | 2.0 | 33 | 16.2 |
| Missoula | 282 | 9.3 | 403 | 16.6 | 27.9 | 895 806 | 2 221 | 39 176 | 7.6 | 10 839 | 35.8 | 64.2 | 16.9 | 2.9 | 102 | 6.4 |
| Musselshell | 1 133 | 9.6 | 3 038 | 9.0 | 148.9 | 1 847 667 | 608 | 85 049 | 23.6 | 63 165 | 21.2 | 78.8 | 34.0 | 14.5 | 2 011 | 30.3 |
| Park | 763 | -9.9 | 1 426 | 51.9 | 110.2 | 2 589 171 | 1 816 | 74 336 | 27.7 | 51 814 | 27.2 | 72.8 | 42.1 | 13.6 | 726 | 17.8 |
| Petroleum | 641 | 19.1 | 6 220 | 15.8 | 100.9 | 3 032 164 | 487 | 165 748 | 16.2 | 157 197 | 20.4 | 79.6 | 74.8 | 48.5 | 1 240 | 65.0 |
| Phillips | 2 006 | 5.7 | 3 608 | 48.7 | 610.0 | 1 805 753 | 500 | 140 094 | 60.9 | 109 597 | 33.5 | 66.5 | 58.1 | 31.5 | 7 935 | 68.2 |
| Pondera | 944 | 4.9 | 1 743 | 74.5 | 617.9 | 1 239 958 | 712 | 155 750 | 75.1 | 138 576 | 64.4 | 35.6 | 63.5 | 37.1 | 9 108 | 75.8 |
| Powder River | 1 620 | 6.4 | 5 079 | 10.0 | 178.1 | 3 287 235 | 647 | 130 906 | 41.0 | 128 401 | 12.7 | 87.3 | 72.7 | 38.6 | 925 | 44.8 |
| Powell | 670 | 8.2 | 2 456 | 74.1 | 71.0 | 2 218 812 | 904 | 106 676 | 25.7 | 94 306 | 10.2 | 89.8 | 44.7 | 20.1 | 232 | 16.8 |
| Prairie | 768 | 23.9 | 4 436 | 14.5 | 151.1 | 2 748 958 | 620 | 121 418 | 24.4 | 140 778 | 32.6 | 67.4 | 72.8 | 42.2 | 2 200 | 78.6 |
| Ravalli | 263 | 7.3 | 172 | 72.2 | 63.0 | 664 936 | 3 875 | 44 925 | 34.9 | 22 756 | 23.3 | 76.7 | 25.1 | 4.0 | 164 | 7.7 |
| Richland | 1 279 | 6.5 | 2 334 | 56.0 | 568.3 | 1 637 408 | 701 | 175 695 | 107.0 | 195 177 | 49.7 | 50.3 | 60.2 | 32.8 | 6 194 | 73.0 |
| Roosevelt | 1 452 | 0.8 | 1 994 | 14.1 | 783.9 | 1 416 662 | 710 | 127 540 | 67.8 | 93 117 | 76.9 | 23.1 | 52.3 | 25.3 | 9 791 | 78.2 |
| Rosebud | 2 714 | 6.8 | 5 678 | 34.6 | 238.9 | 2 185 210 | 385 | 88 039 | 56.8 | 118 877 | 24.4 | 75.6 | 54.0 | 22.8 | 2 688 | 32.4 |
| Sanders | 342 | -1.2 | 673 | 16.9 | 38.5 | 1 018 914 | 1 514 | 54 424 | 14.0 | 27 579 | 45.7 | 54.3 | 27.8 | 6.1 | 183 | 13.0 |
| Sheridan | 1 066 | 1.8 | 1 770 | 7.4 | 716.3 | 1 174 858 | 664 | 154 210 | 90.7 | 150 706 | 86.6 | 13.4 | 56.3 | 34.7 | 8 646 | 89.7 |
| Silver Bow | 101 | 36.5 | 578 | 8.8 | 15.8 | 1 252 542 | 2 169 | 61 857 | 4.8 | 27 328 | 8.0 | 92.0 | 30.3 | 9.1 | 30 | 4.0 |
| Stillwater | 857 | -3.7 | 1 350 | 28.7 | 234.6 | 1 381 295 | 1 023 | 69 855 | 43.4 | 68 401 | 20.9 | 79.1 | 42.2 | 12.8 | 2 833 | 38.0 |
| Sweet Grass | 813 | -6.2 | 2 289 | 43.2 | 98.0 | 2 780 320 | 1 214 | 93 463 | 21.7 | 61 169 | 10.0 | 90.0 | 43.7 | 15.5 | 561 | 23.4 |
| Teton | 1 153 | -6.3 | 1 497 | 111.3 | 600.9 | 1 269 349 | 848 | 107 382 | 97.7 | 126 889 | 52.1 | 47.9 | 49.0 | 26.5 | 10 506 | 72.5 |
| Toole | 1 115 | 2.5 | 2 605 | 4.2 | 725.1 | 1 546 725 | 594 | 166 176 | 47.7 | 111 513 | 73.2 | 26.8 | 54.4 | 31.5 | 10 315 | 82.7 |
| Treasure | 462 | -23.9 | 4 572 | 20.3 | 36.1 | 2 270 543 | 497 | 183 532 | 30.4 | 300 765 | 37.6 | 62.4 | 66.3 | 41.6 | 585 | 36.6 |
| Valley | 2 061 | 0.4 | 2 677 | 51.9 | 921.5 | 1 575 621 | 589 | 122 993 | 80.4 | 104 406 | 55.7 | 44.3 | 55.3 | 26.4 | 11 345 | 76.4 |
| Wheatland | 822 | -2.4 | 6 002 | 20.8 | 151.4 | 3 347 775 | 558 | 158 881 | 25.7 | 187 370 | 26.3 | 73.7 | 61.3 | 32.1 | 1 689 | 61.3 |
| Wibaux | 493 | -8.0 | 2 368 | 1.1 | 160.0 | 998 788 | 422 | 112 747 | 18.6 | 89 538 | 52.5 | 47.5 | 61.5 | 25.5 | 2 246 | 83.7 |
| Yellowstone | 1 616 | 3.0 | 1 148 | 77.1 | 344.0 | 891 477 | 776 | 74 338 | 164.6 | 117 020 | 24.8 | 75.2 | 34.9 | 13.9 | 4 109 | 32.1 |
| NEBRASKA | 45 480 | -0.9 | 953 | 8 558.6 | 21 486.0 | 1 104 392 | 1 159 | 157 427 | 15 506.0 | 324 992 | 44.1 | 55.9 | 68.5 | 41.0 | 387 340 | 73.2 |
| Adams | 306 | -11.0 | 632 | 203.5 | 265.4 | 1 409 216 | 2 231 | 222 342 | 249.3 | 513 932 | 52.5 | 47.5 | 76.3 | 57.9 | 5 462 | 76.7 |
| Antelope | 517 | -1.9 | 721 | 261.3 | 369.1 | 1 192 984 | 1 654 | 212 581 | 339.8 | 474 627 | 43.4 | 56.6 | 75.1 | 55.3 | 6 560 | 79.7 |
| Arthur | 454 | 4.1 | 6 671 | 8.2 | 31.0 | 2 226 136 | 334 | 133 787 | 19.3 | 284 278 | D | D | 83.8 | 60.3 | 232 | 32.4 |
| Banner | 395 | -3.9 | 1 811 | 16.1 | 169.4 | 993 859 | 549 | 104 855 | 67.3 | 308 599 | 19.3 | 80.7 | 57.3 | 27.5 | 2 732 | 81.7 |

— **Water Use, Wholesale Trade, Retail Trade, and Real Estate**

| STATE County | Water use, 2005 | | Wholesale trade,[1] 2007 | | | | Retail trade,[2] 2007 | | | | Real estate and rental and leasing,[2] 2007 | | | |
|---|---|---|---|---|---|---|---|---|---|---|---|---|---|---|
| | Total water withdrawn (mil gal/day) | Gallons withdrawn per person | Number of establish-ments | Number of employees | Sales (mil dol) | Annual payroll (mil dol) | Number of establish-ments | Number of employees | Sales (mil dol) | Annual payroll (mil dol) | Number of establish-ments | Number of employees | Receipts (mil dol) | Annual payroll (mil dol) |
| | 133 | 134 | 135 | 136 | 137 | 138 | 139 | 140 | 141 | 142 | 143 | 144 | 145 | 146 |
| MISSOURI—Cont'd | | | | | | | | | | | | | | |
| St. Louis city | 141.0 | 409 | 522 | 9 422 | 5 042.1 | 462.3 | 1 028 | 11 368 | 2 496.7 | 263.5 | 418 | 2 633 | 606.6 | 94.7 |
| MONTANA | 10 115.9 | 10 811 | 1 254 | 12 849 | 8 202.8 | 503.4 | 5 258 | 58 883 | 14 686.9 | 1 317.8 | 1 892 | 6 410 | 848.3 | 153.3 |
| Beaverhead | 1 185.6 | 135 142 | 5 | 64 | 24.3 | 1.9 | 57 | 466 | 122.9 | 10.0 | 16 | 69 | 8.5 | 2.1 |
| Big Horn | 279.0 | 21 217 | 5 | D | D | D | 48 | 433 | 87.4 | 7.1 | 10 | 45 | 2.1 | 0.4 |
| Blaine | 236.5 | 35 675 | 9 | 32 | 27.6 | 0.8 | 25 | 174 | 44.2 | 3.2 | 4 | 10 | 0.6 | 0.1 |
| Broadwater | 241.3 | 53 423 | 6 | 27 | 10.3 | 0.5 | 16 | 157 | 59.2 | 2.9 | 7 | 8 | 0.6 | 0.3 |
| Carbon | 417.6 | 42 177 | 12 | 55 | 21.0 | 2.3 | 59 | 330 | 60.7 | 5.7 | 20 | 31 | 5.0 | 0.7 |
| Carter | 10.8 | 8 167 | NA | NA | NA | NA | 5 | 30 | 11.9 | 0.4 | 2 | D | D | D |
| Cascade | 189.2 | 2 378 | 118 | 1 077 | 672.0 | 42.5 | 388 | 5 507 | 1 302.3 | 121.0 | 137 | 378 | 56.3 | 8.3 |
| Chouteau | 80.3 | 14 695 | 12 | 62 | 38.4 | 1.9 | 19 | 125 | 44.7 | 2.0 | 6 | D | D | D |
| Custer | 121.7 | 10 798 | 17 | 128 | 75.1 | 4.4 | 67 | 847 | 199.9 | 16.5 | 14 | 34 | 3.3 | 0.6 |
| Daniels | 3.1 | 1 661 | 4 | 13 | 9.9 | 0.3 | 12 | 72 | 26.6 | 1.7 | NA | NA | NA | NA |
| Dawson | 53.9 | 6 207 | 15 | 157 | 107.6 | 3.5 | 54 | 506 | 118.3 | 9.6 | 8 | 20 | 1.5 | 0.3 |
| Deer Lodge | 67.3 | 7 520 | 1 | D | D | D | 38 | 264 | 71.5 | 5.9 | 12 | 32 | 2.5 | 0.5 |
| Fallon | 2.2 | 791 | 4 | 33 | 32.9 | 1.7 | 16 | 145 | 26.3 | 2.3 | 2 | D | D | D |
| Fergus | 71.4 | 6 180 | 15 | 155 | 400.2 | 5.8 | 76 | 512 | 135.4 | 10.7 | 19 | 65 | 4.8 | 1.2 |
| Flathead | 74.3 | 894 | 98 | 959 | 863.6 | 40.1 | 550 | 6 076 | 1 581.3 | 147.8 | 269 | 936 | 113.6 | 23.5 |
| Gallatin | 470.1 | 6 011 | 127 | 1 405 | 508.8 | 50.8 | 621 | 7 467 | 1 791.8 | 184.6 | 361 | 1 265 | 193.6 | 33.4 |
| Garfield | 16.0 | 13 336 | 1 | D | D | D | 6 | 63 | 10.2 | 0.8 | NA | NA | NA | NA |
| Glacier | 87.0 | 6 418 | 10 | 59 | 125.2 | 2.3 | 45 | 449 | 106.3 | 9.5 | 7 | 16 | 1.3 | 0.2 |
| Golden Valley | 44.1 | 38 007 | 1 | D | D | D | 1 | D | D | D | NA | NA | NA | NA |
| Granite | 137.8 | 46 459 | 1 | D | D | D | 17 | 120 | 23.8 | 2.0 | 4 | 3 | 0.1 | 0.1 |
| Hill | 20.0 | 1 228 | 26 | 182 | 190.2 | 5.8 | 87 | 1 020 | 231.1 | 19.5 | 18 | 49 | 5.4 | 1.0 |
| Jefferson | 161.5 | 14 456 | 8 | D | D | D | 26 | 177 | 39.9 | 2.9 | 7 | 15 | 0.9 | 0.3 |
| Judith Basin | 71.4 | 32 475 | 5 | 18 | 4.6 | 0.4 | 8 | 25 | 5.5 | 0.3 | 3 | 3 | 0.5 | 0.1 |
| Lake | 291.8 | 10 310 | 20 | 43 | 8.7 | 1.0 | 152 | 1 201 | 277.0 | 26.1 | 49 | 77 | 10.9 | 1.5 |
| Lewis and Clark | 220.3 | 3 770 | 48 | 445 | 199.6 | 16.9 | 302 | 4 070 | 972.9 | 94.0 | 98 | 657 | 83.2 | 14.2 |
| Liberty | 57.5 | 28 727 | 4 | 12 | 10.5 | 0.4 | 13 | 69 | 15.6 | 1.2 | 4 | 10 | 0.4 | 0.1 |
| Lincoln | 34.0 | 1 769 | 10 | 42 | 12.1 | 1.0 | 93 | 721 | 170.6 | 13.3 | 29 | 66 | 7.2 | 0.8 |
| McCone | 26.6 | 14 715 | 1 | D | D | D | 11 | 68 | 18.0 | 1.2 | 1 | D | D | D |
| Madison | 647.7 | 89 042 | 7 | D | D | D | 49 | 184 | 48.9 | 4.0 | 29 | 38 | 4.7 | 0.9 |
| Meagher | 377.2 | 188 704 | NA | NA | NA | NA | 13 | 69 | 16.4 | 1.1 | 1 | D | D | D |
| Mineral | 8.1 | 2 008 | 1 | D | D | D | 23 | 242 | 46.1 | 4.5 | 4 | 3 | 0.4 | 0.1 |
| Missoula | 112.7 | 1 126 | 169 | 1 825 | 860.1 | 69.5 | 587 | 8 668 | 2 179.4 | 194.6 | 227 | 952 | 126.3 | 21.6 |
| Musselshell | 97.8 | 21 741 | 5 | 11 | 5.0 | 0.3 | 24 | 140 | 33.6 | 2.6 | 4 | 6 | 0.7 | 0.1 |
| Park | 508.0 | 31 812 | 15 | 58 | 26.3 | 2.5 | 112 | 723 | 208.9 | 15.4 | 30 | 52 | 8.3 | 1.1 |
| Petroleum | 42.1 | 89 596 | NA | NA | NA | NA | 2 | D | D | D | 1 | D | D | D |
| Phillips | 166.2 | 39 773 | 7 | 65 | 80.8 | 1.6 | 27 | 161 | 34.0 | 3.1 | 3 | 4 | 0.5 | 0.0 |
| Pondera | 239.5 | 39 340 | 13 | 119 | 46.1 | 4.1 | 34 | 262 | 64.7 | 4.9 | 5 | D | D | D |
| Powder River | 39.9 | 23 408 | 1 | D | D | D | 13 | 87 | 13.8 | 1.3 | 2 | D | D | D |
| Powell | 247.4 | 35 346 | 3 | D | D | D | 17 | 168 | 35.0 | 3.1 | 8 | 13 | 2.0 | 0.3 |
| Prairie | 54.1 | 48 968 | 1 | D | D | D | 8 | 32 | 7.4 | 0.5 | 1 | D | D | D |
| Ravalli | 293.5 | 7 349 | 38 | 220 | 165.0 | 7.4 | 185 | 1 567 | 344.8 | 31.2 | 72 | 206 | 16.7 | 4.5 |
| Richland | 374.5 | 41 175 | 19 | 149 | 235.8 | 5.9 | 60 | 598 | 128.6 | 10.9 | 18 | 64 | 8.0 | 1.7 |
| Roosevelt | 93.3 | 8 862 | 11 | 41 | 66.3 | 1.4 | 40 | 359 | 99.9 | 6.5 | 7 | 29 | 1.1 | 0.2 |
| Rosebud | 245.0 | 26 592 | 1 | D | D | D | 32 | 306 | 53.4 | 4.5 | 6 | 33 | 3.0 | 0.6 |
| Sanders | 57.0 | 5 152 | 9 | D | D | D | 53 | 366 | 82.1 | 6.6 | 17 | 41 | 3.4 | 0.6 |
| Sheridan | 13.8 | 3 905 | 5 | 20 | 5.0 | 0.7 | 21 | 167 | 31.5 | 2.5 | 2 | D | D | D |
| Silver Bow | 66.7 | 2 024 | 31 | D | D | D | 189 | 2 183 | 504.7 | 44.3 | 45 | 144 | 14.9 | 3.0 |
| Stillwater | 107.0 | 12 593 | 3 | 9 | 14.2 | 0.5 | 43 | 308 | 103.2 | 4.5 | 7 | 10 | 1.6 | 0.2 |
| Sweet Grass | 292.0 | 79 532 | 2 | D | D | D | 27 | 170 | 42.7 | 3.1 | 11 | 16 | 3.3 | 0.4 |
| Teton | 561.7 | 90 010 | 9 | D | D | D | 29 | 220 | 43.9 | 4.4 | 9 | 21 | 1.7 | 0.3 |
| Toole | 16.0 | 3 184 | 9 | 114 | 96.3 | 3.6 | 26 | 202 | 54.8 | 3.8 | 8 | 17 | 1.5 | 0.2 |
| Treasure | 72.5 | 105 269 | 1 | D | D | D | 4 | D | D | D | 1 | D | D | D |
| Valley | 236.7 | 33 132 | 13 | 148 | 80.4 | 5.1 | 54 | 331 | 81.3 | 6.8 | 3 | D | D | D |
| Wheatland | 123.9 | 60 800 | 1 | D | D | D | 13 | 74 | 18.3 | 1.0 | 1 | D | D | D |
| Wibaux | 2.3 | 2 397 | NA | NA | NA | NA | 4 | 22 | 4.3 | 0.2 | NA | NA | NA | NA |
| Yellowstone | 347.7 | 2 544 | 297 | 4 467 | 2 772.5 | 196.0 | 757 | 10 151 | 2 840.7 | 249.2 | 263 | 907 | 142.3 | 26.5 |
| NEBRASKA | 12 604.4 | 7 167 | 2 668 | 32 329 | 24 019.9 | 1 323.5 | 7 888 | 108 209 | 26 486.6 | 2 230.5 | 2 032 | 9 974 | 1 645.5 | 292.0 |
| Adams | 277.7 | 8 396 | 56 | 783 | 499.7 | 27.1 | 163 | 1 863 | 360.8 | 34.7 | 54 | D | D | D |
| Antelope | 217.7 | 31 088 | 27 | 225 | 136.3 | 6.5 | 45 | 278 | 57.0 | 4.4 | 3 | 3 | 0.8 | 0.0 |
| Arthur | 8.4 | 22 222 | NA | NA | NA | NA | 3 | 7 | 0.9 | 0.1 | NA | NA | NA | NA |
| Banner | 26.4 | 36 003 | NA | NA | NA | NA | NA | NA | NA | NA | NA | NA | NA | NA |

1. Merchant wholesalers, except manufacturers' sales branches and offices.  2. Employer establishments.

# Table B. States and Counties — Professional Services, Manufacturing, and Accommodation and Food Services

| STATE County | Professional, scientific, and technical services,[1] 2007 | | | | Manufacturing, 2007 | | | | Accommodation and food services, 2007 | | | |
|---|---|---|---|---|---|---|---|---|---|---|---|---|
| | Number of establish-ments | Number of employees | Receipts (mil dol) | Annual payroll (mil dol) | Number of establish-ments | Number of employees | Receipts (mil dol) | Annual payroll (mil dol) | Number of establish-ments | Number of employees | Sales (mil dol) | Annual payroll (mil dol) |
| | 147 | 148 | 149 | 150 | 151 | 152 | 153 | 154 | 155 | 156 | 157 | 158 |
| MISSOURI—Cont'd | | | | | | | | | | | | |
| St. Louis city | 1 005 | D | D | D | 543 | 21 432 | 10 920.6 | 998.2 | 934 | 20 372 | 1 059.3 | 311.4 |
| MONTANA | 3 403 | 16 547 | 1 770.9 | 670.6 | 1 324 | 19 525 | 10 638.1 | 808.2 | 3 360 | 46 137 | 2 079.4 | 554.2 |
| Beaverhead | 30 | 78 | 7.3 | 2.0 | NA | NA | NA | NA | 48 | 408 | 16.1 | 3.9 |
| Big Horn | 15 | D | D | D | NA | NA | NA | NA | 27 | 248 | 13.6 | 3.1 |
| Blaine | 10 | D | D | D | NA | NA | NA | NA | 18 | 112 | 2.4 | 0.6 |
| Broadwater | 5 | 25 | 1.9 | 0.7 | NA | NA | NA | NA | 19 | 140 | 5.7 | 1.4 |
| Carbon | 31 | 110 | 13.8 | 4.8 | NA | NA | NA | NA | 50 | 557 | 18.5 | 5.6 |
| Carter | 3 | D | D | D | NA | NA | NA | NA | 1 | D | D | D |
| Cascade | 199 | D | D | D | 81 | 1 094 | 670.9 | 44.8 | 247 | 3 997 | 174.3 | 48.6 |
| Chouteau | 9 | 21 | 2.1 | 0.4 | NA | NA | NA | NA | 19 | 104 | 3.8 | 0.8 |
| Custer | 23 | 143 | 8.9 | 3.6 | NA | NA | NA | NA | 40 | 624 | 22.1 | 5.9 |
| Daniels | 4 | 8 | 0.7 | 0.1 | NA | NA | NA | NA | 7 | 25 | 1.0 | 0.2 |
| Dawson | 16 | 64 | 3.7 | 1.3 | NA | NA | NA | NA | 31 | 396 | 21.2 | 4.1 |
| Deer Lodge | 23 | 51 | 5.1 | 1.5 | NA | NA | NA | NA | 36 | 378 | 16.4 | 4.3 |
| Fallon | 8 | D | D | D | NA | NA | NA | NA | 17 | 99 | 4.0 | 0.7 |
| Fergus | 29 | 93 | 6.5 | 1.7 | NA | NA | NA | NA | 49 | 489 | 14.1 | 4.3 |
| Flathead | 380 | D | D | D | 177 | 3 464 | 919.4 | 149.7 | 347 | 4 617 | 232.9 | 63.0 |
| Gallatin | 631 | 2 552 | 301.5 | 113.3 | 188 | 2 425 | 512.6 | 95.2 | 376 | 6 788 | 325.8 | 89.9 |
| Garfield | NA | NA | NA | NA | NA | NA | NA | NA | 6 | 19 | 0.6 | 0.2 |
| Glacier | 15 | D | D | D | NA | NA | NA | NA | 48 | 265 | 37.6 | 6.4 |
| Golden Valley | 1 | D | D | D | NA | NA | NA | NA | 4 | 12 | 0.4 | 0.1 |
| Granite | 6 | 9 | 0.8 | 0.3 | NA | NA | NA | NA | 15 | 66 | 2.5 | 0.6 |
| Hill | 36 | D | D | D | NA | NA | NA | NA | 49 | 658 | 23.8 | 6.2 |
| Jefferson | 26 | 52 | 5.1 | 1.9 | NA | NA | NA | NA | 31 | 273 | 7.3 | 2.0 |
| Judith Basin | 3 | D | D | D | NA | NA | NA | NA | 9 | 34 | 1.3 | 0.3 |
| Lake | 58 | D | D | D | 44 | 654 | 119.8 | 21.8 | 78 | 817 | 34.7 | 8.0 |
| Lewis and Clark | 243 | 1 713 | 207.8 | 84.6 | 54 | 655 | D | 24.3 | 190 | 2 961 | 118.6 | 32.9 |
| Liberty | 4 | 7 | 0.8 | 0.1 | NA | NA | NA | NA | 6 | 24 | 0.8 | 0.2 |
| Lincoln | 42 | D | D | D | NA | NA | NA | NA | 66 | 501 | 26.5 | 6.7 |
| McCone | 1 | D | D | D | NA | NA | NA | NA | 5 | 17 | 0.7 | 0.1 |
| Madison | 21 | D | D | D | NA | NA | NA | NA | 65 | 221 | 15.0 | 4.2 |
| Meagher | 1 | D | D | D | NA | NA | NA | NA | 13 | 74 | 2.1 | 0.5 |
| Mineral | 8 | 41 | 3.0 | 1.2 | NA | NA | NA | NA | 22 | 139 | 6.7 | 1.6 |
| Missoula | 458 | D | D | D | 112 | 2 159 | 674.9 | 93.8 | 332 | 6 209 | 269.1 | 70.0 |
| Musselshell | 8 | 13 | 1.3 | 0.4 | NA | NA | NA | NA | 9 | 74 | 3.5 | 0.7 |
| Park | 62 | 182 | 20.4 | 6.6 | NA | NA | NA | NA | 120 | 1 083 | 61.9 | 16.9 |
| Petroleum | 1 | D | D | D | NA | NA | NA | NA | 3 | 15 | 0.4 | 0.1 |
| Phillips | 9 | 22 | 1.8 | 0.5 | NA | NA | NA | NA | 16 | 114 | 4.1 | 0.9 |
| Pondera | 13 | 43 | 3.4 | 1.2 | NA | NA | NA | NA | 15 | 168 | 4.2 | 1.1 |
| Powder River | 6 | 22 | 1.4 | 0.3 | NA | NA | NA | NA | 9 | 46 | 2.2 | 0.6 |
| Powell | 9 | 57 | 3.1 | 1.1 | NA | NA | NA | NA | 26 | 177 | 7.3 | 2.0 |
| Prairie | 2 | D | D | D | NA | NA | NA | NA | 5 | 16 | 0.9 | 0.1 |
| Ravalli | 111 | D | D | D | 105 | 1 048 | 130.2 | 38.9 | 105 | 992 | 36.5 | 10.6 |
| Richland | 35 | 156 | 20.1 | 6.0 | NA | NA | NA | NA | 37 | 502 | 19.7 | 4.5 |
| Roosevelt | 11 | D | D | D | NA | NA | NA | NA | 30 | 269 | 9.7 | 2.5 |
| Rosebud | 4 | 15 | 1.0 | 0.2 | NA | NA | NA | NA | 29 | 274 | 9.0 | 2.1 |
| Sanders | 17 | 41 | 2.5 | 1.0 | NA | NA | NA | NA | 36 | 313 | 12.2 | 3.5 |
| Sheridan | 8 | 33 | 1.8 | 0.7 | NA | NA | NA | NA | 17 | 142 | 4.8 | 1.2 |
| Silver Bow | 107 | D | D | D | NA | NA | NA | NA | 133 | 1 946 | 78.3 | 22.7 |
| Stillwater | 27 | 52 | 5.3 | 1.6 | NA | NA | NA | NA | 23 | 220 | 9.8 | 2.6 |
| Sweet Grass | 15 | 34 | 3.4 | 1.0 | NA | NA | NA | NA | 18 | 158 | 6.2 | 1.7 |
| Teton | 9 | D | D | D | NA | NA | NA | NA | 17 | 118 | 3.0 | 0.7 |
| Toole | 18 | 49 | 4.2 | 1.4 | NA | NA | NA | NA | 26 | 180 | 10.6 | 2.8 |
| Treasure | 2 | D | D | D | NA | NA | NA | NA | 2 | D | D | D |
| Valley | 18 | D | D | D | NA | NA | NA | NA | 29 | 268 | 11.0 | 3.0 |
| Wheatland | 2 | D | D | D | NA | NA | NA | NA | 11 | 55 | 1.6 | 0.3 |
| Wibaux | 4 | 12 | 0.8 | 0.2 | NA | NA | NA | NA | 5 | 31 | 1.1 | 0.2 |
| Yellowstone | 566 | 3 170 | 367.2 | 135.7 | 187 | 3 974 | 5 740.0 | D | 368 | 7 687 | 361.7 | 97.3 |
| NEBRASKA | 4 205 | 40 692 | 4 836.4 | 2 011.0 | 1 984 | 99 547 | 40 158.0 | 3 788.6 | 4 241 | 69 142 | 2 685.6 | 749.1 |
| Adams | 61 | 312 | 33.2 | 12.0 | 67 | D | D | D | 79 | 1 185 | 43.7 | 10.9 |
| Antelope | 13 | 22 | 2.4 | 0.6 | NA | NA | NA | NA | 13 | 98 | 2.4 | 0.6 |
| Arthur | 1 | D | D | D | NA | NA | NA | NA | 1 | D | D | D |
| Banner | NA | NA | NA | NA | NA | NA | NA | NA | NA | NA | NA | NA |

1. Establishment subject to federal tax.

# Table B. States and Counties — **Health Care and Social Assistance, Other Services, and Federal Funds**

| STATE County | Health care and social assistance, 2007 | | | | Other services, 2007 | | | | Federal funds and grants, 2009–2010 Expenditures (mil dol) | | | |
|---|---|---|---|---|---|---|---|---|---|---|---|---|
| | | | | | | | | | | Direct payments for individuals[1] | | |
| | Number of establishments | Number of employees | Receipts (mil dol) | Annual payroll (mil dol) | Number of establishments | Number of employees | Receipts (mil dol) | Annual payroll (mil dol) | Total | Social Security and government retirement | Medicare | Food Stamps and Supplemental Security Income |
| | 159 | 160 | 161 | 162 | 163 | 164 | 165 | 166 | 167 | 168 | 169 | 170 |
| **MISSOURI—Cont'd** | | | | | | | | | | | | |
| St. Louis city | 1 036 | 34 294 | 3 510.6 | 1 207.0 | 694 | 5 574 | 635.1 | 165.4 | 10 370.1 | 816.3 | 1 036.9 | 372.6 |
| **MONTANA** | 3 301 | 57 860 | 4 970.8 | 1 983.7 | 2 287 | 10 323 | 995.4 | 245.8 | 10 758.4 | 3 301.0 | 1 153.2 | 279.4 |
| Beaverhead | 38 | 382 | 31.4 | 11.9 | 21 | 65 | 3.8 | 0.8 | 91.2 | 30.5 | 15.6 | 2.1 |
| Big Horn | 19 | D | D | D | 12 | 23 | 2.3 | 0.6 | 147.7 | 27.0 | 12.6 | 7.5 |
| Blaine | 11 | D | D | D | 9 | 40 | 2.7 | 0.6 | 99.4 | 17.8 | 7.3 | 3.2 |
| Broadwater | 7 | 79 | 5.2 | 2.1 | 6 | D | D | D | 40.2 | 22.9 | 5.9 | 1.4 |
| Carbon | 26 | 243 | 13.4 | 6.8 | 16 | 43 | 2.5 | 0.6 | 72.0 | 35.0 | 15.2 | 1.8 |
| Carter | 2 | D | D | D | 1 | D | D | D | 12.9 | 4.8 | 1.6 | 0.2 |
| Cascade | 269 | 6 050 | 517.8 | 206.6 | 166 | 845 | 65.4 | 18.8 | 1 022.7 | 329.7 | 119.7 | 23.9 |
| Chouteau | 17 | 236 | 10.9 | 5.7 | 5 | D | D | D | 74.5 | 18.2 | 8.4 | 0.7 |
| Custer | 48 | 926 | 70.2 | 30.5 | 26 | 112 | 10.9 | 2.4 | 112.9 | 41.6 | 17.3 | 3.3 |
| Daniels | 5 | 153 | 7.2 | 3.0 | 5 | D | D | D | 81.2 | 13.0 | 4.2 | 0.2 |
| Dawson | 26 | 567 | 40.5 | 16.9 | 33 | 122 | 8.4 | 2.2 | 94.7 | 34.9 | 13.7 | 2.0 |
| Deer Lodge | 46 | 1 240 | 68.6 | 39.8 | 14 | 57 | 4.9 | 1.1 | 98.9 | 39.5 | 20.4 | 4.1 |
| Fallon | 5 | D | D | D | 10 | D | D | D | 21.9 | 9.3 | 4.2 | 0.6 |
| Fergus | 51 | 770 | 47.6 | 20.8 | 31 | 107 | 9.7 | 1.4 | 131.5 | 48.3 | 23.8 | 2.1 |
| Flathead | 350 | 5 001 | 471.0 | 166.6 | 222 | 967 | 80.5 | 21.7 | 630.3 | 325.6 | 80.3 | 17.9 |
| Gallatin | 349 | 3 634 | 330.0 | 120.5 | 245 | 1 072 | 133.4 | 30.6 | 526.9 | 189.1 | 42.5 | 7.1 |
| Garfield | 3 | D | D | D | 2 | D | D | D | 11.4 | 3.4 | 2.0 | 0.1 |
| Glacier | 18 | D | D | D | 20 | D | D | D | 210.4 | 31.4 | 14.2 | 10.3 |
| Golden Valley | 2 | D | D | D | NA | NA | NA | NA | 10.6 | 4.2 | 1.6 | 0.3 |
| Granite | 3 | D | D | D | 2 | D | D | D | 21.9 | 11.3 | 3.7 | 0.6 |
| Hill | 45 | 1 016 | 86.8 | 34.9 | 45 | 174 | 14.1 | 3.1 | 221.9 | 53.9 | 24.0 | 6.8 |
| Jefferson | 19 | 205 | 8.9 | 3.5 | 15 | D | D | D | 111.0 | 41.5 | 8.8 | 1.4 |
| Judith Basin | 5 | 23 | 0.3 | 0.2 | 1 | D | D | D | 24.7 | 9.0 | 3.0 | 0.2 |
| Lake | 77 | 1 136 | 84.7 | 36.0 | 45 | 141 | 10.0 | 2.6 | 313.3 | 90.2 | 32.8 | 9.3 |
| Lewis and Clark | 247 | 4 736 | 462.8 | 182.3 | 202 | D | D | D | 1 637.6 | 223.2 | 63.9 | 40.1 |
| Liberty | 2 | D | D | D | 2 | D | D | D | 39.3 | 10.4 | 3.8 | 0.6 |
| Lincoln | 50 | 743 | 48.2 | 21.0 | 39 | 145 | 12.2 | 2.6 | 221.3 | 93.2 | 23.7 | 8.7 |
| McCone | 3 | D | D | D | 3 | D | D | D | 25.4 | 7.3 | 3.7 | 0.6 |
| Madison | 16 | 142 | 8.5 | 4.0 | 16 | 35 | 5.7 | 1.0 | 51.3 | 26.9 | 9.3 | 0.3 |
| Meagher | 5 | D | D | D | 4 | D | D | D | 18.9 | 7.7 | 3.0 | 0.4 |
| Mineral | 14 | 139 | 6.7 | 2.9 | 4 | D | D | D | 41.1 | 22.1 | 5.4 | 1.9 |
| Missoula | 451 | 8 022 | 754.8 | 278.6 | 288 | 1 618 | 150.7 | 37.8 | 818.8 | 299.5 | 93.6 | 28.0 |
| Musselshell | 9 | D | D | D | 8 | 18 | 1.4 | 0.3 | 41.4 | 18.7 | 8.0 | 2.5 |
| Park | 45 | 702 | 61.1 | 25.4 | 53 | 221 | 17.3 | 4.9 | 107.4 | 53.1 | 23.1 | 2.7 |
| Petroleum | 1 | D | D | D | NA | NA | NA | NA | 5.7 | 1.6 | 0.7 | 0.0 |
| Phillips | 10 | 216 | 10.0 | 4.4 | 11 | D | D | D | 61.7 | 15.1 | 8.6 | 1.3 |
| Pondera | 20 | 304 | 16.6 | 7.5 | 11 | 37 | 2.3 | 0.4 | 80.1 | 20.4 | 12.3 | 2.2 |
| Powder River | 1 | D | D | D | 4 | D | D | D | 11.7 | 5.4 | 2.0 | 0.2 |
| Powell | 17 | 178 | 12.1 | 4.6 | 9 | 20 | 2.2 | 0.3 | 48.3 | 23.1 | 8.9 | 1.4 |
| Prairie | 1 | D | D | D | 3 | D | D | D | 13.2 | 6.0 | 2.6 | 0.1 |
| Ravalli | 118 | 1 257 | 80.6 | 32.8 | 86 | 265 | 21.9 | 5.8 | 318.8 | 170.9 | 44.4 | 7.9 |
| Richland | 32 | 687 | 41.9 | 17.9 | 32 | 98 | 9.4 | 2.2 | 81.5 | 31.7 | 17.0 | 2.2 |
| Roosevelt | 15 | D | D | D | 13 | 54 | 3.9 | 0.7 | 271.2 | 30.8 | 15.9 | 9.7 |
| Rosebud | 15 | 259 | 10.4 | 5.0 | 11 | 37 | 3.2 | 1.0 | 106.7 | 24.0 | 8.7 | 3.6 |
| Sanders | 34 | 423 | 25.4 | 11.6 | 18 | 46 | 5.0 | 0.9 | 103.7 | 55.0 | 15.4 | 3.5 |
| Sheridan | 10 | 224 | 12.3 | 6.7 | 8 | D | D | D | 63.4 | 19.7 | 8.5 | 0.5 |
| Silver Bow | 157 | 2 804 | 184.9 | 75.9 | 66 | 346 | 32.6 | 7.7 | 336.1 | 124.4 | 67.3 | 14.5 |
| Stillwater | 19 | 229 | 10.8 | 4.4 | 11 | D | D | D | 55.7 | 31.6 | 10.1 | 0.9 |
| Sweet Grass | 7 | 22 | 0.7 | 0.3 | 10 | 30 | 2.1 | 0.5 | 23.0 | 12.5 | 4.4 | 0.5 |
| Teton | 19 | 228 | 9.4 | 4.9 | 8 | 31 | 4.2 | 1.1 | 69.0 | 22.3 | 10.5 | 1.2 |
| Toole | 10 | 226 | 19.0 | 8.0 | 9 | 19 | 1.8 | 0.3 | 57.5 | 10.7 | 9.2 | 0.8 |
| Treasure | 3 | D | D | D | 1 | D | D | D | 7.4 | 3.0 | 1.4 | 0.1 |
| Valley | 19 | 544 | 34.1 | 13.7 | 21 | 57 | 4.6 | 1.0 | 107.9 | 34.7 | 13.4 | 2.5 |
| Wheatland | 3 | D | D | D | 4 | 5 | 0.3 | 0.1 | 22.1 | 8.2 | 6.2 | 0.4 |
| Wibaux | 3 | D | D | D | NA | NA | NA | NA | 11.3 | 4.3 | 1.3 | 0.2 |
| Yellowstone | 504 | 11 503 | 1 168.5 | 474.6 | 380 | 1 972 | 198.3 | 48.7 | 1 131.6 | 451.3 | 164.2 | 32.6 |
| **NEBRASKA** | 4 920 | 114 928 | 10 081.0 | 4 107.3 | 4 073 | 22 543 | 2 391.3 | 542.8 | 16 531.8 | 5 307.5 | 2 142.1 | 387.3 |
| Adams | 120 | 2 780 | 229.1 | 100.8 | 67 | 369 | 23.9 | 6.5 | 236.7 | 98.2 | 41.8 | 6.4 |
| Antelope | 16 | 268 | 18.2 | 6.7 | 19 | 39 | 3.7 | 0.7 | 86.8 | 23.0 | 12.9 | 1.4 |
| Arthur | NA | NA | NA | NA | 2 | D | D | D | 2.5 | 1.5 | 0.5 | 0.1 |
| Banner | NA | NA | NA | NA | NA | NA | NA | NA | 7.7 | 1.5 | 0.6 | 0.0 |

1. State totals may include programs not allocated by county.

# Table B. States and Counties — Federal Funds, Residential Construction, and Local Government Finances

| | Federal funds and grants, 2009–2010 (cont.) | | | | | | | Value of residential construction authorized by building permits, 2011 | | Local government finances, 2007 | | | | |
| | Expenditures (mil dol) (cont.) | | | | | | | | | General revenue | | | | |
| | | Procurement contract awards | | Grants[1] | | | | | | | | Taxes | | |
| | | | | | | | | | | | | | Per capita[2] (dollars) | |
| STATE County | Salaries and wages | Defense | Other | Medicaid and other health-related | Nutrition and family welfare | Education | Other | New construction ($1,000) | Number of housing units | Total (mil dol) | Inter-govern-mental (mil dol) | Total (mil dol) | Total | Property |
| | 171 | 172 | 173 | 174 | 175 | 176 | 177 | 178 | 179 | 180 | 181 | 182 | 183 | 184 |
| MISSOURI—Cont'd | | | | | | | | | | | | | | |
| St. Louis city | 890.9 | 3 414.6 | 389.6 | 2 094.7 | 120.1 | 63.5 | 923.2 | 26 740 | 218 | 2 068.9 | 636.4 | 759.0 | 2 164 | 918 |
| MONTANA | 1 194.6 | 312.7 | 506.7 | 1 080.2 | 271.7 | 263.5 | 1 324.0 | 285 875 | 1 914 | X | X | X | X | X |
| Beaverhead | 21.3 | 0.1 | 5.1 | 9.6 | 1.4 | 0.6 | 0.7 | 482 | 3 | 40.9 | 10.3 | 7.8 | 888 | 883 |
| Big Horn | 22.1 | 0.0 | 11.3 | 17.3 | 7.0 | 11.5 | 14.2 | 0 | 0 | 49.8 | 31.5 | 10.7 | 838 | 828 |
| Blaine | 10.4 | 0.0 | 2.5 | 15.6 | 3.6 | 9.2 | 8.3 | 0 | 0 | 32.1 | 20.7 | 5.5 | 833 | 826 |
| Broadwater | 2.3 | 0.1 | 0.9 | 3.7 | 0.7 | 0.1 | 0.2 | 115 | 2 | 12.8 | 5.4 | 3.8 | 835 | 802 |
| Carbon | 4.0 | 0.2 | 3.6 | 8.1 | 1.4 | 0.3 | 0.3 | 1 235 | 12 | 28.2 | 12.6 | 11.3 | 1 160 | 1 071 |
| Carter | 1.0 | 0.0 | 0.3 | 1.5 | 0.2 | 0.1 | 0.4 | 150 | 2 | 6.4 | 3.7 | 1.9 | 1 469 | 1 415 |
| Cascade | 238.8 | 90.2 | 17.2 | 136.8 | 15.5 | 7.4 | 11.5 | 25 926 | 144 | 227.1 | 110.8 | 63.8 | 781 | 755 |
| Chouteau | 2.4 | 0.0 | 0.5 | 2.2 | 0.9 | 0.4 | 3.5 | 320 | 1 | 24.0 | 8.3 | 8.5 | 1 609 | 1 606 |
| Custer | 14.8 | 0.1 | 6.3 | 20.5 | 1.9 | 1.5 | 0.9 | 1 165 | 6 | 37.5 | 16.9 | 8.7 | 775 | 773 |
| Daniels | 3.1 | 0.4 | 2.8 | 1.1 | 0.3 | 0.1 | 38.2 | 200 | 1 | 10.3 | 3.4 | 5.4 | 3 253 | 3 010 |
| Dawson | 3.4 | 17.9 | 0.7 | 8.2 | 2.4 | 1.4 | 2.0 | 450 | 2 | 37.0 | 15.0 | 11.1 | 1 294 | 1 286 |
| Deer Lodge | 6.0 | 0.0 | 4.7 | 15.7 | 3.0 | 1.0 | 3.3 | 2 339 | 15 | 22.8 | 13.2 | 6.3 | 711 | 707 |
| Fallon | 0.8 | 0.0 | 0.2 | 1.5 | 0.4 | 0.3 | 1.0 | 700 | 5 | 32.5 | 24.7 | 3.6 | 1 343 | 1 250 |
| Fergus | 11.3 | 1.2 | 8.9 | 16.2 | 2.8 | 1.5 | 3.1 | 58 | 1 | 37.2 | 16.9 | 12.2 | 1 095 | 1 075 |
| Flathead | 64.4 | 4.5 | 40.8 | 52.4 | 11.8 | 5.3 | 11.3 | 24 871 | 98 | 247.7 | 88.9 | 92.9 | 1 070 | 969 |
| Gallatin | 60.6 | 18.0 | 19.4 | 61.8 | 8.5 | 2.9 | 90.9 | 83 754 | 387 | 223.3 | 70.1 | 91.5 | 1 048 | 911 |
| Garfield | 1.4 | 0.0 | 0.2 | 0.8 | 0.2 | 0.2 | 0.2 | 130 | 2 | 5.2 | 2.2 | 1.7 | 1 421 | 1 364 |
| Glacier | 24.2 | 1.4 | 47.8 | 28.6 | 7.8 | 15.6 | 10.7 | 250 | 4 | 47.7 | 32.8 | 9.4 | 700 | 694 |
| Golden Valley | 0.5 | 0.0 | 0.1 | 0.0 | 0.2 | 0.1 | 0.0 | 0 | 0 | 3.6 | 1.6 | 1.6 | 1 449 | 1 441 |
| Granite | 1.8 | 0.0 | 1.3 | 2.3 | 0.4 | 0.1 | 0.0 | 0 | 0 | 13.7 | 4.5 | 4.4 | 1 534 | 1 527 |
| Hill | 18.7 | 0.0 | 5.2 | 25.4 | 8.1 | 12.3 | 25.5 | 3 222 | 24 | 58.0 | 33.8 | 14.1 | 854 | 848 |
| Jefferson | 44.6 | 0.0 | 1.8 | 8.9 | 1.2 | 0.9 | 0.9 | 160 | 1 | 27.1 | 11.4 | 9.0 | 806 | 799 |
| Judith Basin | 1.8 | 0.1 | 0.5 | 2.2 | 0.4 | 0.1 | 0.0 | 0 | 0 | 8.4 | 3.7 | 3.8 | 1 835 | 1 821 |
| Lake | 6.7 | 51.6 | 8.4 | 36.9 | 8.3 | 14.1 | 27.9 | 3 555 | 20 | 78.7 | 38.6 | 24.8 | 870 | 858 |
| Lewis and Clark | 166.3 | 10.9 | 49.8 | 105.8 | 55.6 | 100.7 | 785.7 | 24 249 | 156 | 172.8 | 68.6 | 57.9 | 965 | 946 |
| Liberty | 1.6 | 6.4 | 0.6 | 0.7 | 0.3 | 0.1 | 1.1 | 0 | 0 | 7.9 | 4.0 | 2.9 | 1 615 | 1 610 |
| Lincoln | 23.8 | 27.3 | 12.8 | 20.9 | 4.8 | 2.2 | 3.2 | 395 | 3 | 54.0 | 25.0 | 14.0 | 739 | 696 |
| McCone | 0.9 | 0.0 | 0.2 | 2.2 | 0.2 | 0.1 | 0.0 | 0 | 0 | 6.4 | 2.8 | 2.7 | 1 546 | 1 528 |
| Madison | 3.6 | 0.0 | 0.9 | 3.7 | 0.9 | 0.5 | 3.7 | 666 | 3 | 33.6 | 8.4 | 13.7 | 1 851 | 1 840 |
| Meagher | 1.7 | 0.0 | 1.0 | 2.9 | 0.3 | 0.1 | 0.2 | 0 | 0 | 12.4 | 2.5 | 3.0 | 1 573 | 1 558 |
| Mineral | 2.7 | 0.0 | 3.0 | 3.8 | 0.9 | 0.4 | 0.2 | 454 | 2 | 21.0 | 6.9 | 4.9 | 1 261 | 1 221 |
| Missoula | 103.8 | 5.5 | 52.8 | 117.3 | 17.7 | 8.6 | 58.9 | 40 339 | 563 | 266.9 | 105.7 | 114.6 | 1 085 | 1 048 |
| Musselshell | 1.2 | 0.0 | 0.5 | 4.4 | 0.8 | 0.2 | 2.1 | 250 | 1 | 13.1 | 5.6 | 4.1 | 909 | 907 |
| Park | 4.9 | 0.0 | 1.9 | 14.9 | 2.5 | 1.6 | 1.3 | 2 508 | 15 | 42.2 | 15.3 | 15.2 | 944 | 908 |
| Petroleum | 0.3 | 0.0 | 0.8 | 0.0 | 0.1 | 0.0 | 0.0 | 0 | 0 | 2.2 | 1.2 | 0.6 | 1 470 | 1 468 |
| Phillips | 8.6 | 0.0 | 2.6 | 11.8 | 0.8 | 0.4 | 2.1 | 0 | 0 | 26.4 | 14.8 | 4.9 | 1 229 | 1 218 |
| Pondera | 2.9 | 0.8 | 11.5 | 8.8 | 1.3 | 2.4 | 0.3 | 110 | 1 | 29.0 | 10.8 | 5.7 | 958 | 946 |
| Powder River | 0.8 | 0.0 | 0.2 | 0.8 | 0.3 | 0.5 | 0.0 | 0 | 0 | 8.6 | 3.7 | 2.9 | 1 705 | 1 478 |
| Powell | 4.0 | 0.0 | 1.4 | 5.2 | 1.1 | 1.6 | 0.5 | 76 | 1 | 20.0 | 10.3 | 5.7 | 799 | 793 |
| Prairie | 0.6 | 0.0 | 0.1 | 1.5 | 0.2 | 0.1 | 0.0 | 0 | 0 | 6.2 | 2.2 | 1.5 | 1 417 | 1 368 |
| Ravalli | 37.5 | 0.3 | 19.4 | 24.4 | 7.0 | 2.3 | 2.5 | 1 272 | 41 | 79.2 | 40.2 | 27.7 | 687 | 667 |
| Richland | 7.5 | 0.0 | 1.1 | 9.8 | 1.8 | 0.7 | 1.8 | 9 819 | 59 | 53.9 | 38.9 | 8.1 | 884 | 880 |
| Roosevelt | 12.9 | 65.7 | 5.0 | 15.6 | 5.6 | 11.6 | 80.0 | 820 | 4 | 54.7 | 34.1 | 11.1 | 1 094 | 1 074 |
| Rosebud | 11.5 | 0.0 | 5.3 | 14.6 | 3.9 | 11.8 | 12.3 | 826 | 4 | 56.4 | 24.1 | 14.1 | 1 531 | 1 497 |
| Sanders | 6.1 | 0.3 | 6.9 | 11.8 | 2.0 | 1.4 | 0.2 | 0 | 0 | 32.0 | 15.3 | 12.0 | 1 087 | 1 075 |
| Sheridan | 6.2 | -0.3 | 1.2 | 6.0 | 0.7 | 0.5 | 0.0 | 1 110 | 5 | 17.7 | 10.4 | 4.3 | 1 269 | 1 251 |
| Silver Bow | 26.2 | 3.1 | 10.2 | 58.9 | 8.7 | 3.9 | 10.5 | 4 925 | 51 | 92.0 | 40.7 | 31.1 | 952 | 926 |
| Stillwater | 2.4 | 0.0 | 3.9 | 2.2 | 1.0 | 0.8 | 0.5 | 888 | 4 | 28.1 | 10.3 | 12.8 | 1 479 | 1 474 |
| Sweet Grass | 1.9 | 0.0 | 0.2 | 1.5 | 0.4 | 0.3 | 0.2 | 0 | 0 | 18.3 | 4.8 | 5.4 | 1 428 | 1 424 |
| Teton | 3.2 | 0.4 | 9.7 | 6.6 | 1.1 | 0.3 | 0.1 | 410 | 6 | 29.2 | 10.3 | 7.5 | 1 251 | 1 233 |
| Toole | 12.5 | 0.0 | 2.4 | 4.4 | 0.9 | 0.1 | 2.2 | 320 | 2 | 29.3 | 9.2 | 5.6 | 1 094 | 1 084 |
| Treasure | 0.7 | 0.0 | 0.2 | 0.0 | 0.2 | 0.0 | 0.0 | 0 | 0 | 3.2 | 1.2 | 1.5 | 2 246 | 2 229 |
| Valley | 11.4 | 3.1 | 1.4 | 11.0 | 1.3 | 1.3 | 6.3 | 365 | 3 | 30.7 | 14.2 | 10.6 | 1 539 | 1 517 |
| Wheatland | 1.2 | 0.0 | 0.4 | 2.4 | 0.4 | 0.1 | 0.0 | 0 | 0 | 7.1 | 3.3 | 2.8 | 1 410 | 1 386 |
| Wibaux | 0.6 | 0.0 | 0.1 | 2.2 | 0.2 | 0.0 | 0.0 | 0 | 0 | 5.8 | 4.1 | 0.9 | 1 021 | 958 |
| Yellowstone | 158.4 | 3.3 | 108.5 | 126.8 | 32.1 | 10.4 | 13.5 | 46 990 | 260 | 459.4 | 158.1 | 128.0 | 915 | 841 |
| NEBRASKA | 1 782.8 | 793.2 | 513.6 | 1 703.0 | 411.7 | 308.7 | 1 083.6 | 726 319 | 5 203 | X | X | X | X | X |
| Adams | 20.5 | 4.8 | 2.6 | 33.6 | 8.1 | 2.4 | 3.8 | 19 693 | 126 | 221.2 | 45.8 | 63.9 | 1 937 | 1 488 |
| Antelope | 2.5 | 0.0 | 2.0 | 7.9 | 1.5 | 0.4 | 24.6 | 1 545 | 10 | 26.5 | 8.9 | 13.8 | 2 036 | 1 801 |
| Arthur | 0.2 | 0.0 | 0.0 | 0.0 | 0.0 | 0.1 | 0.0 | NA | NA | 2.7 | 0.9 | 1.6 | 4 596 | 4 438 |
| Banner | 0.2 | 0.0 | 0.0 | 0.0 | 0.1 | 0.1 | 0.0 | NA | NA | 3.4 | 1.2 | 2.0 | 2 768 | 2 514 |

1. State totals may include programs not allocated by county.    2. Based on the resident population estimated as of July 1 of the year shown.

| STATE County | Local government finances, 2007 (cont.) | | | | | | | | | | Government employment, 2011 | | | Presidential election,[2] 2012 | | |
|---|---|---|---|---|---|---|---|---|---|---|---|---|---|---|---|---|
| | Direct general expenditure | | | | | | | Debt outstanding | | | | | | Percent of vote cast: | | |
| | | | Percent of total for: | | | | | | | | | | | | | |
| | Total (mil dol) | Per capita[1] (dollars) | Education | Health and hospitals | Police protection | Public welfare | Highways | Total (mil dol) | Per capita[1] (dollars) | Federal civilian | Federal military | State and local | Democratic | Republican | All other |
| | 185 | 186 | 187 | 188 | 189 | 190 | 191 | 192 | 193 | 194 | 195 | 196 | 197 | 198 | 199 |
| **MISSOURI—Cont'd** | | | | | | | | | | | | | | | |
| St. Louis city | 1 963.2 | 5 597 | 31.2 | 2.2 | 8.4 | 0.0 | 1.0 | 3 967.4 | 11 311 | 14 508 | 1 667 | 21 815 | 83.7 | 15.5 | 0.8 |
| **MONTANA** | X | X | X | X | X | X | X | X | X | 13 878 | 8 224 | 74 137 | 47.3 | 49.5 | 3.2 |
| Beaverhead | 37.0 | 4 198 | 35.9 | 40.0 | 3.3 | 0.0 | 3.6 | 17.3 | 1 965 | 211 | 46 | 793 | 33.9 | 63.2 | 2.9 |
| Big Horn | 50.0 | 3 906 | 70.4 | 1.4 | 3.3 | 0.6 | 4.3 | 3.2 | 252 | 417 | 66 | 1 941 | 67.4 | 31.2 | 1.4 |
| Blaine | 31.6 | 4 828 | 66.0 | 1.5 | 4.1 | 0.0 | 5.8 | 4.0 | 616 | 192 | 33 | 511 | 58.2 | 39.0 | 2.8 |
| Broadwater | 13.3 | 2 907 | 46.5 | 2.0 | 6.0 | 0.6 | 2.5 | 6.1 | 1 329 | 46 | 29 | 203 | 31.8 | 65.8 | 2.4 |
| Carbon | 28.1 | 2 889 | 60.3 | 0.6 | 6.5 | 0.3 | 10.2 | 34.2 | 3 519 | 97 | 50 | 483 | 42.5 | 54.1 | 3.4 |
| Carter | 6.2 | 4 928 | 40.2 | 7.7 | 7.4 | 1.7 | 22.5 | 0.3 | 267 | 18 | 0 | 92 | 15.5 | 80.1 | 4.3 |
| Cascade | 225.3 | 2 755 | 48.3 | 8.2 | 0.6 | 3.2 | 95.4 | | 1 166 | 1 787 | 3 522 | 4 147 | 49.9 | 47.6 | 2.4 |
| Chouteau | 23.2 | 4 421 | 44.9 | 22.8 | 3.4 | 0.3 | 8.6 | 3.2 | 614 | 38 | 29 | 433 | 39.2 | 57.1 | 3.7 |
| Custer | 37.4 | 3 345 | 61.1 | 3.7 | 7.6 | 0.5 | 5.3 | 4.8 | 431 | 212 | 59 | 935 | 41.6 | 55.9 | 2.5 |
| Daniels | 10.1 | 6 129 | 41.2 | 5.0 | 3.9 | 0.0 | 6.1 | 3.1 | 1 899 | 22 | 0 | 114 | 32.0 | 64.7 | 3.4 |
| Dawson | 36.4 | 4 257 | 58.7 | 2.6 | 5.0 | 0.1 | 5.4 | 13.0 | 1 523 | 32 | 45 | 756 | 35.9 | 59.5 | 4.5 |
| Deer Lodge | 20.2 | 2 287 | 56.8 | 1.4 | 9.3 | 0.1 | 2.3 | 6.2 | 698 | 87 | 47 | 859 | 67.0 | 29.6 | 3.4 |
| Fallon | 20.4 | 7 565 | 39.8 | 5.4 | 4.0 | 0.0 | 12.4 | 1.5 | 543 | 13 | 15 | 251 | 22.2 | 74.3 | 3.5 |
| Fergus | 40.0 | 3 578 | 54.1 | 3.3 | 4.6 | 0.0 | 5.8 | 10.6 | 945 | 153 | 58 | 843 | 31.0 | 65.9 | 3.1 |
| Flathead | 276.2 | 3 180 | 57.1 | 3.0 | 5.0 | 0.4 | 5.4 | 149.6 | 1 723 | 829 | 461 | 4 050 | 36.9 | 58.5 | 4.6 |
| Gallatin | 239.6 | 2 743 | 44.0 | 1.3 | 6.2 | 3.6 | 3.8 | 163.4 | 1 871 | 660 | 469 | 8 713 | 50.3 | 46.9 | 2.8 |
| Garfield | 6.0 | 4 902 | 41.3 | 5.7 | 3.7 | 0.0 | 29.7 | 0.5 | 386 | 27 | 0 | 119 | 15.1 | 82.3 | 2.6 |
| Glacier | 51.0 | 3 809 | 76.5 | 1.0 | 3.3 | 0.1 | 2.8 | 4.1 | 308 | 468 | 69 | 1 886 | 68.9 | 29.2 | 1.9 |
| Golden Valley | 3.9 | 3 476 | 71.1 | 1.4 | 3.8 | 0.4 | 6.4 | 0.6 | 562 | 0 | 0 | 73 | 25.3 | 69.9 | 4.9 |
| Granite | 13.2 | 4 617 | 39.4 | 0.7 | 5.4 | 28.3 | 7.2 | 7.2 | 2 540 | 37 | 15 | 214 | 35.0 | 59.1 | 5.9 |
| Hill | 56.9 | 3 432 | 67.4 | 3.0 | 4.6 | 0.9 | 4.9 | 12.4 | 747 | 171 | 83 | 2 050 | 54.3 | 42.1 | 3.6 |
| Jefferson | 27.5 | 2 472 | 56.3 | 2.2 | 6.5 | 0.0 | 5.7 | 6.5 | 587 | 43 | 57 | 724 | 40.7 | 55.8 | 3.5 |
| Judith Basin | 8.8 | 4 297 | 62.1 | 0.2 | 1.4 | 0.7 | 8.7 | 3.8 | 1 835 | 32 | 11 | 148 | 32.1 | 64.8 | 3.1 |
| Lake | 78.3 | 2 752 | 61.5 | 1.9 | 4.1 | 0.3 | 3.5 | 31.6 | 1 112 | 75 | 146 | 2 807 | 48.6 | 46.7 | 4.7 |
| Lewis and Clark | 173.8 | 2 897 | 48.4 | 3.2 | 6.3 | 4.1 | 4.7 | 154.6 | 2 576 | 1 935 | 337 | 8 974 | 52.1 | 45.5 | 2.4 |
| Liberty | 7.4 | 4 115 | 47.1 | 9.5 | 5.3 | 0.0 | 10.3 | 1.7 | 944 | 23 | 12 | 124 | 36.7 | 59.3 | 4.0 |
| Lincoln | 60.1 | 3 183 | 46.3 | 2.5 | 8.7 | 0.0 | 6.9 | 15.7 | 831 | 455 | 99 | 722 | 32.8 | 61.8 | 5.4 |
| McCone | 6.8 | 3 969 | 47.8 | 5.5 | 4.3 | 1.4 | 7.3 | 1.8 | 1 029 | 19 | 0 | 155 | 29.4 | 66.5 | 4.0 |
| Madison | 33.4 | 4 496 | 37.3 | 11.3 | 5.4 | 15.7 | 9.0 | 7.9 | 1 067 | 68 | 39 | 467 | 35.2 | 61.8 | 3.0 |
| Meagher | 12.5 | 6 584 | 25.2 | 2.6 | 4.0 | 0.0 | 5.3 | 0.1 | 27 | 26 | 10 | 109 | 30.8 | 64.6 | 4.6 |
| Mineral | 21.0 | 5 392 | 41.3 | 24.2 | 3.8 | 0.0 | 3.6 | 6.7 | 1 722 | 58 | 21 | 270 | 42.4 | 52.8 | 4.9 |
| Missoula | 281.7 | 2 666 | 46.3 | 3.9 | 5.5 | 0.7 | 4.4 | 200.7 | 1 900 | 1 393 | 560 | 9 205 | 61.8 | 35.1 | 3.0 |
| Musselshell | 13.1 | 2 915 | 55.2 | 2.2 | 5.7 | 0.0 | 5.6 | 1.1 | 249 | 14 | 24 | 266 | 27.6 | 68.6 | 3.9 |
| Park | 44.6 | 2 769 | 50.1 | 2.4 | 8.8 | 0.0 | 4.3 | 9.1 | 563 | 75 | 78 | 687 | 46.9 | 49.2 | 3.9 |
| Petroleum | 2.5 | 5 616 | 55.3 | 3.0 | 2.3 | 0.0 | 15.8 | 0.6 | 1 386 | 0 | 0 | 53 | 22.7 | 75.7 | 1.7 |
| Phillips | 21.7 | 5 491 | 55.5 | 1.9 | 6.0 | 0.0 | 12.0 | 4.9 | 1 253 | 80 | 21 | 317 | 30.1 | 67.0 | 2.9 |
| Pondera | 28.4 | 4 776 | 46.7 | 35.3 | 4.6 | 0.0 | 4.9 | 7.1 | 1 188 | 33 | 32 | 324 | 42.4 | 55.0 | 2.6 |
| Powder River | 8.8 | 5 201 | 44.7 | 1.4 | 5.0 | 21.6 | 8.2 | 0.5 | 285 | 12 | 0 | 183 | 20.0 | 77.3 | 2.7 |
| Powell | 21.0 | 2 953 | 58.2 | 3.0 | 5.7 | 0.2 | 2.3 | 3.1 | 435 | 89 | 36 | 1 050 | 36.3 | 59.8 | 3.9 |
| Prairie | 6.3 | 6 069 | 34.2 | 1.5 | 3.5 | 33.9 | 6.6 | 1.9 | 1 824 | 37 | 0 | 134 | 28.7 | 68.4 | 2.9 |
| Ravalli | 80.5 | 1 992 | 66.7 | 1.7 | 6.3 | 0.0 | 4.4 | 35.7 | 884 | 539 | 204 | 1 439 | 38.0 | 58.9 | 3.1 |
| Richland | 41.7 | 4 542 | 59.7 | 3.1 | 4.1 | 0.2 | 9.1 | 9.2 | 1 004 | 91 | 51 | 637 | 26.6 | 70.5 | 2.9 |
| Roosevelt | 57.1 | 5 622 | 67.9 | 7.7 | 4.2 | 0.1 | 3.4 | 5.8 | 568 | 205 | 53 | 1 545 | 61.8 | 35.5 | 2.7 |
| Rosebud | 48.4 | 5 273 | 56.5 | 1.5 | 5.6 | 0.2 | 3.8 | 339.8 | 37 003 | 240 | 47 | 1 513 | 50.4 | 46.4 | 3.2 |
| Sanders | 33.0 | 2 993 | 58.9 | 1.7 | 5.4 | 0.1 | 6.2 | 5.4 | 490 | 131 | 58 | 528 | 33.7 | 60.9 | 5.4 |
| Sheridan | 15.7 | 4 652 | 57.6 | 3.3 | 6.3 | 0.2 | 9.5 | 3.1 | 929 | 92 | 17 | 257 | 47.5 | 49.2 | 3.3 |
| Silver Bow | 91.2 | 2 793 | 43.6 | 4.5 | 6.0 | 0.2 | 3.3 | 49.7 | 1 522 | 290 | 209 | 2 329 | 68.8 | 28.4 | 2.8 |
| Stillwater | 26.8 | 3 095 | 63.5 | 1.5 | 5.4 | 0.0 | 5.9 | 9.3 | 1 074 | 32 | 46 | 424 | 32.4 | 64.1 | 3.5 |
| Sweet Grass | 19.7 | 5 174 | 32.9 | 2.6 | 4.1 | 29.4 | 3.7 | 2.6 | 696 | 34 | 18 | 317 | 26.0 | 71.7 | 2.3 |
| Teton | 29.9 | 4 965 | 47.9 | 20.5 | 3.1 | 5.5 | 3.3 | 8.6 | 1 432 | 58 | 31 | 424 | 39.5 | 57.3 | 3.2 |
| Toole | 31.8 | 6 183 | 30.2 | 34.0 | 3.9 | 0.4 | 6.4 | 11.1 | 2 161 | 192 | 26 | 542 | 34.7 | 62.1 | 3.2 |
| Treasure | 3.1 | 4 822 | 54.5 | 4.0 | 4.8 | 0.0 | 7.4 | 0.7 | 1 058 | 0 | 0 | 54 | 32.1 | 64.6 | 3.3 |
| Valley | 32.7 | 4 734 | 53.5 | 1.7 | 3.7 | 0.0 | 8.4 | 6.9 | 995 | 140 | 38 | 599 | 42.1 | 54.2 | 3.7 |
| Wheatland | 7.2 | 3 611 | 63.3 | 2.8 | 6.7 | 0.1 | 4.8 | 0.3 | 144 | 22 | 11 | 132 | 29.5 | 67.0 | 3.6 |
| Wibaux | 5.5 | 6 097 | 46.3 | 6.5 | 5.2 | 0.0 | 15.5 | 1.0 | 1 072 | 0 | 0 | 97 | 26.0 | 67.6 | 6.4 |
| Yellowstone | 450.0 | 3 216 | 46.7 | 6.0 | 5.7 | 0.2 | 6.2 | 205.1 | 1 466 | 1 798 | 776 | 7 115 | 45.5 | 51.8 | 2.7 |
| **NEBRASKA** | X | X | X | X | X | X | X | X | X | 16 691 | 13 346 | 145 006 | 41.6 | 56.5 | 1.9 |
| Adams | 230.2 | 6 976 | 46.6 | 35.6 | 2.1 | 0.1 | 3.4 | 61.1 | 1 851 | 103 | 125 | 2 356 | 35.5 | 62.5 | 2.1 |
| Antelope | 27.6 | 4 090 | 67.9 | 0.0 | 1.4 | 0.2 | 14.0 | 5.5 | 807 | 33 | 27 | 448 | 23.8 | 74.8 | 1.4 |
| Arthur | 2.4 | 6 820 | 55.8 | 0.3 | 1.5 | 0.0 | 15.6 | 0.1 | 154 | 0 | 0 | 52 | 14.8 | 82.5 | 2.7 |
| Banner | 3.3 | 4 557 | 73.3 | 0.1 | 1.3 | 0.0 | 11.6 | 0.0 | 0 | 0 | 0 | 70 | 14.9 | 83.7 | 1.4 |

1. Based on the resident population estimated as of July 1 of the year shown.    2. © 2013 Election Data Services, Inc. All rights reserved.

| STATE/ County code | CBSA code[1] | County type[2] | STATE County | Land area,[3] (sq km) 2010 | Population 2012 | | | Race alone or in combination, not Hispanic or Latino (percent) | | | | | Age (percent) | | | | | |
|---|---|---|---|---|---|---|---|---|---|---|---|---|---|---|---|---|---|---|
| | | | | | Total persons | Rank | Per square kilometer | White | Black | American Indian, Alaska Native | Asian and Pacific Islander | Percent Hispanic or Latino[4] | Under 5 years | 5 to 17 years | 18 to 24 years | 25 to 34 years | 35 to 44 years | 45 to 54 years |
| | | | | 1 | 2 | 3 | 4 | 5 | 6 | 7 | 8 | 9 | 10 | 11 | 12 | 13 | 14 | 15 |
| | | | NEBRASKA—Cont'd | | | | | | | | | | | | | | | |
| 31 009 | ... | 9 | Blaine | 1 841 | 514 | 3 136 | 0.3 | 99.6 | 0.6 | 0.4 | 0.0 | 0.0 | 5.9 | 17.5 | 5.7 | 7.6 | 9.3 | 18.2 |
| 31 011 | ... | 9 | Boone | 1 778 | 5 417 | 2 812 | 3.0 | 97.8 | 0.5 | 0.4 | 0.3 | 1.4 | 5.8 | 17.0 | 6.6 | 9.0 | 9.8 | 16.1 |
| 31 013 | ... | 7 | Box Butte | 2 785 | 11 317 | 2 337 | 4.1 | 85.4 | 1.0 | 3.6 | 0.8 | 10.8 | 7.0 | 18.1 | 6.7 | 11.4 | 11.2 | 14.2 |
| 31 015 | ... | 9 | Boyd | 1 398 | 2 054 | 3 046 | 1.5 | 96.8 | 0.3 | 0.8 | 1.0 | 1.7 | 4.9 | 15.9 | 5.1 | 7.5 | 8.9 | 15.2 |
| 31 017 | ... | 9 | Brown | 3 163 | 3 023 | 2 979 | 1.0 | 98.4 | 0.3 | 0.8 | 0.6 | 0.9 | 5.0 | 16.6 | 4.9 | 9.0 | 10.0 | 14.6 |
| 31 019 | 28260 | 5 | Buffalo | 2 507 | 47 463 | 1 021 | 18.9 | 90.0 | 1.2 | 0.5 | 1.7 | 7.6 | 7.1 | 16.5 | 16.2 | 14.0 | 10.8 | 12.1 |
| 31 021 | ... | 8 | Burt | 1 273 | 6 659 | 2 712 | 5.2 | 95.4 | 0.6 | 2.2 | 0.5 | 2.2 | 5.4 | 16.8 | 5.5 | 8.9 | 10.5 | 14.9 |
| 31 023 | ... | 6 | Butler | 1 515 | 8 295 | 2 584 | 5.5 | 96.5 | 0.5 | 0.4 | 0.4 | 2.6 | 5.8 | 18.1 | 5.9 | 9.8 | 10.5 | 16.5 |
| 31 025 | 36540 | 2 | Cass | 1 444 | 25 133 | 1 603 | 17.4 | 96.2 | 0.7 | 0.9 | 0.7 | 2.6 | 6.1 | 18.8 | 6.6 | 10.6 | 12.6 | 16.3 |
| 31 027 | ... | 9 | Cedar | 1 917 | 8 746 | 2 539 | 4.6 | 98.1 | 0.3 | 0.6 | 0.3 | 1.4 | 6.4 | 18.7 | 6.3 | 9.1 | 9.9 | 15.7 |
| 31 029 | ... | 9 | Chase | 2 317 | 4 064 | 2 901 | 1.8 | 88.0 | 0.3 | 0.5 | 0.2 | 11.6 | 7.1 | 16.7 | 6.3 | 11.4 | 10.5 | 14.1 |
| 31 031 | ... | 7 | Cherry | 15 437 | 5 727 | 2 791 | 0.4 | 92.0 | 0.7 | 7.0 | 0.8 | 2.0 | 5.3 | 16.5 | 5.7 | 10.8 | 11.0 | 15.2 |
| 31 033 | ... | 7 | Cheyenne | 3 098 | 10 068 | 2 438 | 3.2 | 91.4 | 0.5 | 1.0 | 1.9 | 6.0 | 6.3 | 17.4 | 6.7 | 12.7 | 12.3 | 15.6 |
| 31 035 | 25580 | 9 | Clay | 1 482 | 6 411 | 2 732 | 4.3 | 91.0 | 0.6 | 0.7 | 0.4 | 8.1 | 6.1 | 18.5 | 6.9 | 10.2 | 10.4 | 15.1 |
| 31 037 | ... | 7 | Colfax | 1 066 | 10 653 | 2 384 | 10.0 | 56.2 | 0.8 | 0.5 | 0.5 | 42.3 | 9.4 | 20.1 | 9.0 | 12.8 | 11.6 | 13.4 |
| 31 039 | ... | 7 | Cuming | 1 478 | 9 072 | 2 512 | 6.1 | 90.6 | 0.6 | 0.6 | 0.5 | 8.6 | 5.9 | 18.7 | 5.8 | 10.1 | 10.7 | 14.7 |
| 31 041 | ... | 7 | Custer | 6 671 | 10 740 | 2 378 | 1.6 | 96.9 | 0.7 | 0.8 | 0.4 | 2.2 | 5.6 | 17.5 | 6.3 | 9.6 | 10.8 | 14.9 |
| 31 043 | 43580 | 3 | Dakota | 684 | 20 918 | 1 783 | 30.6 | 55.7 | 3.5 | 2.4 | 3.5 | 35.9 | 8.8 | 21.2 | 9.6 | 12.8 | 12.0 | 13.1 |
| 31 045 | ... | 7 | Dawes | 3 617 | 9 152 | 2 506 | 2.5 | 89.3 | 2.3 | 4.6 | 2.4 | 3.7 | 5.2 | 13.4 | 25.0 | 10.0 | 8.4 | 10.6 |
| 31 047 | 30420 | 7 | Dawson | 2 624 | 24 220 | 1 634 | 9.2 | 63.6 | 3.3 | 0.7 | 1.0 | 32.1 | 7.9 | 20.7 | 8.3 | 11.9 | 12.1 | 12.9 |
| 31 049 | ... | 9 | Deuel | 1 139 | 1 972 | 3 056 | 1.7 | 95.1 | 0.5 | 0.9 | 0.6 | 4.0 | 4.9 | 15.8 | 6.4 | 7.7 | 11.2 | 15.5 |
| 31 051 | 43580 | 3 | Dixon | 1 233 | 5 918 | 2 768 | 4.8 | 87.7 | 0.7 | 0.7 | 0.4 | 11.1 | 6.8 | 18.7 | 6.6 | 10.2 | 11.4 | 14.1 |
| 31 053 | 23340 | 4 | Dodge | 1 369 | 36 427 | 1 263 | 26.6 | 88.0 | 0.9 | 0.8 | 0.9 | 10.3 | 6.7 | 17.1 | 8.5 | 11.9 | 11.2 | 13.7 |
| 31 055 | 36540 | 2 | Douglas | 851 | 531 265 | 122 | 624.3 | 73.7 | 12.6 | 1.1 | 3.4 | 11.5 | 7.7 | 18.3 | 9.9 | 16.0 | 12.8 | 13.4 |
| 31 057 | ... | 9 | Dundy | 2 382 | 2 021 | 3 050 | 0.8 | 92.8 | 1.0 | 1.1 | 0.4 | 6.0 | 5.0 | 17.5 | 4.0 | 9.0 | 10.8 | 14.6 |
| 31 059 | ... | 9 | Fillmore | 1 490 | 5 771 | 2 783 | 3.9 | 95.5 | 0.6 | 0.6 | 0.3 | 3.4 | 5.3 | 17.6 | 6.0 | 9.4 | 9.5 | 15.2 |
| 31 061 | ... | 9 | Franklin | 1 491 | 3 188 | 2 962 | 2.1 | 98.2 | 0.5 | 1.0 | 0.3 | 1.2 | 5.1 | 15.7 | 5.7 | 8.3 | 9.7 | 16.2 |
| 31 063 | ... | 9 | Frontier | 2 524 | 2 741 | 2 995 | 1.1 | 98.0 | 0.4 | 0.5 | 0.5 | 1.4 | 5.3 | 15.3 | 11.5 | 9.5 | 9.3 | 14.3 |
| 31 065 | ... | 9 | Furnas | 1 863 | 4 907 | 2 844 | 2.6 | 96.0 | 0.6 | 0.9 | 0.4 | 3.1 | 5.1 | 17.8 | 5.6 | 8.3 | 10.4 | 14.3 |
| 31 067 | 13100 | 6 | Gage | 2 205 | 21 806 | 1 739 | 9.9 | 96.9 | 0.7 | 1.0 | 0.6 | 1.9 | 6.0 | 16.5 | 7.1 | 10.0 | 11.2 | 15.6 |
| 31 069 | ... | 9 | Garden | 4 414 | 1 953 | 3 059 | 0.4 | 95.3 | 0.7 | 1.2 | 0.2 | 3.8 | 4.3 | 13.6 | 5.4 | 8.4 | 9.8 | 16.2 |
| 31 071 | ... | 9 | Garfield | 1 476 | 2 007 | 3 052 | 1.4 | 98.6 | 0.4 | 0.1 | 0.2 | 1.0 | 3.6 | 16.8 | 4.8 | 8.0 | 9.1 | 14.7 |
| 31 073 | 30420 | 9 | Gosper | 1 187 | 2 029 | 3 048 | 1.7 | 95.7 | 1.1 | 0.9 | 0.6 | 3.0 | 4.3 | 16.8 | 5.4 | 9.7 | 9.4 | 15.7 |
| 31 075 | ... | 9 | Grant | 2 010 | 629 | 3 133 | 0.3 | 97.9 | 0.8 | 0.6 | 0.3 | 1.1 | 7.8 | 11.7 | 6.5 | 12.2 | 8.4 | 17.9 |
| 31 077 | ... | 9 | Greeley | 1 476 | 2 458 | 3 009 | 1.7 | 96.6 | 0.8 | 0.5 | 0.3 | 2.5 | 6.5 | 16.5 | 6.2 | 9.8 | 9.2 | 14.5 |
| 31 079 | 24260 | 5 | Hall | 1 415 | 60 345 | 859 | 42.6 | 72.7 | 2.1 | 0.7 | 1.4 | 24.0 | 8.0 | 19.2 | 8.2 | 13.4 | 12.3 | 13.5 |
| 31 081 | ... | 7 | Hamilton | 1 406 | 9 011 | 2 521 | 6.4 | 97.1 | 0.5 | 0.5 | 0.4 | 2.2 | 5.5 | 19.3 | 6.3 | 10.1 | 11.7 | 16.1 |
| 31 083 | ... | 9 | Harlan | 1 433 | 3 410 | 2 946 | 2.4 | 97.9 | 0.3 | 0.6 | 0.4 | 1.4 | 5.3 | 15.7 | 5.1 | 8.2 | 10.2 | 15.0 |
| 31 085 | ... | 9 | Hayes | 1 847 | 953 | 3 111 | 0.5 | 95.4 | 0.4 | 0.2 | 0.5 | 3.5 | 5.3 | 16.4 | 5.7 | 10.4 | 7.5 | 17.5 |
| 31 087 | ... | 9 | Hitchcock | 1 839 | 2 887 | 2 986 | 1.6 | 97.3 | 0.6 | 0.9 | 0.4 | 1.8 | 5.2 | 16.0 | 5.5 | 10.6 | 9.1 | 15.0 |
| 31 089 | ... | 7 | Holt | 6 248 | 10 396 | 2 405 | 1.7 | 96.2 | 0.4 | 0.5 | 0.3 | 3.1 | 6.3 | 17.0 | 5.9 | 9.5 | 9.7 | 16.4 |
| 31 091 | ... | 9 | Hooker | 1 868 | 727 | 3 126 | 0.4 | 98.6 | 0.1 | 1.1 | 0.1 | 1.2 | 6.2 | 15.4 | 4.8 | 9.6 | 9.9 | 13.7 |
| 31 093 | 24260 | 9 | Howard | 1 475 | 6 336 | 2 738 | 4.3 | 97.1 | 0.5 | 0.9 | 0.4 | 2.0 | 6.1 | 18.2 | 6.1 | 10.1 | 11.7 | 15.0 |
| 31 095 | ... | 7 | Jefferson | 1 477 | 7 521 | 2 640 | 5.1 | 96.0 | 0.7 | 0.8 | 0.4 | 3.0 | 5.3 | 16.2 | 5.7 | 10.1 | 10.3 | 14.8 |
| 31 097 | ... | 8 | Johnson | 974 | 5 140 | 2 830 | 5.3 | 82.8 | 5.6 | 1.4 | 1.5 | 9.2 | 5.4 | 14.0 | 6.8 | 14.0 | 12.4 | 17.2 |
| 31 099 | 28260 | 7 | Kearney | 1 337 | 6 485 | 2 726 | 4.9 | 94.6 | 0.6 | 0.7 | 0.6 | 4.3 | 6.5 | 17.8 | 6.3 | 11.4 | 10.6 | 15.2 |
| 31 101 | ... | 7 | Keith | 2 750 | 8 220 | 2 591 | 3.0 | 93.0 | 0.6 | 0.8 | 0.8 | 5.9 | 5.2 | 15.5 | 5.9 | 9.3 | 9.9 | 16.0 |
| 31 103 | ... | 9 | Keya Paha | 2 002 | 804 | 3 120 | 0.4 | 98.5 | 0.2 | 0.2 | 0.1 | 1.2 | 5.2 | 16.0 | 3.1 | 8.4 | 9.2 | 16.2 |
| 31 105 | ... | 6 | Kimball | 2 465 | 3 783 | 2 923 | 1.5 | 91.0 | 0.9 | 1.6 | 1.1 | 7.0 | 6.1 | 15.9 | 6.4 | 10.0 | 9.9 | 14.8 |
| 31 107 | ... | 9 | Knox | 2 871 | 8 573 | 2 560 | 3.0 | 89.3 | 0.5 | 9.0 | 0.5 | 2.0 | 6.0 | 17.7 | 5.3 | 8.7 | 9.5 | 15.0 |
| 31 109 | 30700 | 2 | Lancaster | 2 169 | 293 407 | 224 | 135.3 | 86.2 | 4.7 | 1.1 | 4.3 | 6.0 | 7.0 | 15.9 | 15.1 | 15.1 | 11.9 | 12.5 |
| 31 111 | 35820 | 5 | Lincoln | 6 641 | 36 099 | 1 273 | 5.4 | 90.8 | 1.1 | 0.8 | 0.9 | 7.4 | 6.9 | 17.8 | 7.7 | 12.2 | 11.7 | 13.8 |
| 31 113 | 35820 | 9 | Logan | 1 478 | 765 | 3 122 | 0.5 | 96.7 | 0.5 | 1.4 | 0.3 | 1.7 | 5.8 | 19.2 | 4.2 | 11.4 | 11.4 | 14.6 |
| 31 115 | ... | 9 | Loup | 1 472 | 589 | 3 135 | 0.4 | 96.9 | 0.2 | 0.2 | 0.0 | 2.8 | 7.0 | 15.4 | 6.1 | 6.7 | 8.9 | 16.4 |
| 31 117 | 35820 | 9 | McPherson | 2 225 | 509 | 3 138 | 0.2 | 98.4 | 1.1 | 0.9 | 0.0 | 0.7 | 7.8 | 21.4 | 2.9 | 12.0 | 9.1 | 16.1 |
| 31 119 | 35740 | 5 | Madison | 1 483 | 35 031 | 1 300 | 23.6 | 83.9 | 1.7 | 1.4 | 0.7 | 13.3 | 7.5 | 17.5 | 10.3 | 12.5 | 10.6 | 14.8 |
| 31 121 | 24260 | 7 | Merrick | 1 256 | 7 780 | 2 618 | 6.2 | 94.9 | 0.6 | 0.9 | 1.1 | 3.4 | 6.0 | 18.3 | 6.9 | 10.1 | 11.2 | 14.9 |
| 31 123 | ... | 9 | Morrill | 3 688 | 4 889 | 2 845 | 1.3 | 84.3 | 0.6 | 1.2 | 0.5 | 14.3 | 6.2 | 18.1 | 6.2 | 10.5 | 11.2 | 14.4 |
| 31 125 | ... | 9 | Nance | 1 144 | 3 715 | 2 930 | 3.2 | 96.8 | 0.7 | 0.7 | 0.2 | 2.3 | 6.1 | 17.4 | 6.6 | 10.5 | 10.0 | 15.0 |
| 31 127 | ... | 7 | Nemaha | 1 055 | 7 154 | 2 666 | 6.8 | 96.5 | 1.3 | 0.7 | 0.7 | 1.9 | 6.2 | 14.8 | 13.1 | 10.6 | 9.1 | 13.9 |
| 31 129 | ... | 9 | Nuckolls | 1 490 | 4 438 | 2 872 | 3.0 | 97.2 | 0.5 | 0.8 | 0.4 | 2.2 | 4.9 | 15.4 | 4.8 | 9.3 | 9.1 | 15.4 |
| 31 131 | ... | 6 | Otoe | 1 594 | 15 747 | 2 060 | 9.9 | 92.8 | 0.8 | 0.8 | 0.8 | 5.7 | 6.3 | 17.4 | 6.7 | 10.7 | 11.2 | 15.6 |
| 31 133 | ... | 9 | Pawnee | 1 116 | 2 765 | 2 991 | 2.5 | 97.6 | 0.6 | 1.1 | 0.4 | 1.5 | 5.0 | 16.1 | 6.0 | 7.6 | 10.2 | 14.2 |
| 31 135 | ... | 9 | Perkins | 2 288 | 2 931 | 2 984 | 1.3 | 95.8 | 0.6 | 0.2 | 0.2 | 3.5 | 6.6 | 17.5 | 5.5 | 10.9 | 9.9 | 14.1 |
| 31 137 | ... | 7 | Phelps | 1 398 | 9 215 | 2 500 | 6.6 | 94.7 | 0.4 | 0.5 | 0.6 | 4.4 | 6.5 | 17.6 | 6.2 | 10.9 | 11.0 | 15.0 |
| 31 139 | 35740 | 9 | Pierce | 1 485 | 7 166 | 2 661 | 4.8 | 97.7 | 0.5 | 0.6 | 0.3 | 1.6 | 6.2 | 19.2 | 6.1 | 10.4 | 11.1 | 16.1 |

1. CBSA = Core Based Statistical Area. See Appendix A for explanation. See Appendix B for list of metropolitan areas with component counties. Service of USDA Rural-Urban Continuum Codes. See Appendix A for definition. 3. Dry land or land partially or temporarily covered by water. 2. County type code from the Economic Research 4. May be of any race.

# Table B. States and Counties — Population and Households

| STATE County | Population, 2011 (cont.) Age (percent) (cont.) | | | | Population change and components of change, 2000–2012 Total persons | | Percent change | | Components of change, 2010–2012 | | | Households, 2010 | | | Percent | |
|---|---|---|---|---|---|---|---|---|---|---|---|---|---|---|---|---|
| | 55 to 64 years | 65 to 74 years | 75 years and over | Percent female | 2000 | 2010 | 2000–2010 | 2010–2012 | Births | Deaths | Net migration | Number | Percent change, 2000–2010 | Persons per household | Female family householder[1] | One person |
| | 16 | 17 | 18 | 19 | 20 | 21 | 22 | 23 | 24 | 25 | 26 | 27 | 28 | 29 | 30 | 31 |
| NEBRASKA—Cont'd | | | | | | | | | | | | | | | | |
| Blaine | 15.2 | 13.3 | 7.2 | 48.8 | 583 | 478 | -18.0 | 7.5 | 15 | 7 | 18 | 196 | -17.6 | 2.44 | 2.0 | 21.9 |
| Boone | 14.3 | 8.9 | 12.5 | 49.8 | 6 259 | 5 505 | -12.0 | -1.6 | 140 | 169 | -58 | 2 336 | -4.8 | 2.32 | 5.3 | 31.2 |
| Box Butte | 15.8 | 7.2 | 8.3 | 50.7 | 12 158 | 11 308 | -7.0 | 0.1 | 334 | 271 | -56 | 4 738 | -0.9 | 2.35 | 8.8 | 30.6 |
| Boyd | 15.4 | 12.8 | 14.3 | 50.8 | 2 438 | 2 099 | -13.9 | -2.1 | 40 | 57 | -29 | 942 | -7.1 | 2.20 | 4.5 | 35.0 |
| Brown | 15.2 | 11.9 | 12.8 | 51.6 | 3 525 | 3 145 | -10.8 | -3.9 | 68 | 92 | -96 | 1 449 | -5.3 | 2.14 | 6.2 | 34.7 |
| Buffalo | 11.1 | 6.1 | 6.0 | 50.4 | 42 259 | 46 102 | 9.1 | 3.0 | 1 500 | 799 | 672 | 18 037 | 13.2 | 2.43 | 8.5 | 28.1 |
| Burt | 15.2 | 9.9 | 13.1 | 50.9 | 7 791 | 6 858 | -12.0 | -2.9 | 159 | 234 | -120 | 2 906 | -7.9 | 2.32 | 6.2 | 28.9 |
| Butler | 14.0 | 9.1 | 10.4 | 49.5 | 8 767 | 8 395 | -4.2 | -1.2 | 208 | 220 | -100 | 3 391 | -1.0 | 2.42 | 7.1 | 27.3 |
| Cass | 14.5 | 8.1 | 6.4 | 49.7 | 24 334 | 25 241 | 3.7 | -0.4 | 621 | 537 | -180 | 9 698 | 5.9 | 2.57 | 7.7 | 22.2 |
| Cedar | 13.7 | 8.5 | 11.7 | 49.4 | 9 615 | 8 852 | -7.9 | -1.2 | 225 | 249 | -89 | 3 539 | -2.3 | 2.46 | 4.7 | 27.4 |
| Chase | 13.8 | 9.1 | 11.1 | 50.3 | 4 068 | 3 966 | -2.5 | 2.5 | 118 | 116 | 99 | 1 681 | 1.1 | 2.32 | 5.9 | 29.9 |
| Cherry | 14.5 | 10.3 | 10.7 | 50.0 | 6 148 | 5 713 | -7.1 | 0.2 | 137 | 139 | 21 | 2 530 | 0.9 | 2.24 | 6.6 | 33.6 |
| Cheyenne | 13.2 | 7.2 | 8.6 | 50.3 | 9 830 | 9 998 | 1.7 | 0.7 | 266 | 190 | -12 | 4 298 | 5.6 | 2.30 | 8.2 | 31.4 |
| Clay | 14.8 | 8.7 | 9.3 | 49.8 | 7 039 | 6 542 | -7.1 | -2.0 | 167 | 185 | -110 | 2 649 | -3.9 | 2.43 | 7.0 | 28.0 |
| Colfax | 10.4 | 6.0 | 7.3 | 48.0 | 10 441 | 10 515 | 0.7 | 1.3 | 497 | 170 | -194 | 3 618 | -1.7 | 2.88 | 8.0 | 24.8 |
| Cuming | 13.2 | 8.9 | 12.0 | 50.4 | 10 203 | 9 139 | -10.4 | -0.7 | 249 | 214 | -98 | 3 756 | -4.8 | 2.40 | 5.6 | 28.3 |
| Custer | 14.5 | 10.1 | 10.6 | 50.4 | 11 793 | 10 939 | -7.2 | -1.8 | 236 | 336 | -112 | 4 714 | -2.3 | 2.29 | 6.7 | 31.2 |
| Dakota | 10.9 | 6.5 | 5.1 | 49.8 | 20 253 | 21 006 | 3.7 | -0.4 | 872 | 334 | -642 | 7 218 | 1.7 | 2.88 | 13.4 | 22.8 |
| Dawes | 11.1 | 8.1 | 8.3 | 50.4 | 9 060 | 9 182 | 1.3 | -0.3 | 228 | 207 | -57 | 3 684 | 4.9 | 2.19 | 8.1 | 34.9 |
| Dawson | 12.0 | 7.2 | 7.0 | 49.2 | 24 365 | 24 326 | -0.2 | -0.4 | 891 | 479 | -534 | 8 899 | 0.8 | 2.70 | 9.7 | 25.3 |
| Deuel | 15.7 | 11.3 | 11.6 | 50.6 | 2 098 | 1 941 | -7.5 | 1.6 | 30 | 53 | 53 | 867 | -4.5 | 2.21 | 7.4 | 30.0 |
| Dixon | 14.3 | 8.9 | 9.0 | 50.6 | 6 339 | 6 000 | -5.3 | -1.4 | 166 | 143 | -108 | 2 370 | -1.8 | 2.50 | 7.5 | 26.9 |
| Dodge | 12.5 | 8.7 | 9.8 | 50.3 | 36 160 | 36 691 | 1.5 | -0.7 | 1 104 | 929 | -417 | 14 990 | 3.9 | 2.38 | 9.8 | 29.2 |
| Douglas | 11.2 | 5.6 | 5.1 | 50.8 | 463 585 | 517 110 | 11.5 | 2.7 | 19 024 | 7 989 | 3 351 | 202 411 | 11.1 | 2.49 | 12.6 | 30.1 |
| Dundy | 15.7 | 10.3 | 13.3 | 49.5 | 2 292 | 2 008 | -12.4 | 0.6 | 45 | 67 | 30 | 897 | -6.7 | 2.19 | 4.7 | 35.1 |
| Fillmore | 14.5 | 10.1 | 12.3 | 50.8 | 6 634 | 5 890 | -11.2 | -2.0 | 136 | 189 | -60 | 2 483 | -7.7 | 2.28 | 5.8 | 30.6 |
| Franklin | 15.4 | 10.9 | 13.0 | 49.8 | 3 574 | 3 225 | -9.8 | -1.1 | 64 | 86 | -14 | 1 406 | -5.3 | 2.25 | 6.7 | 31.4 |
| Frontier | 14.9 | 9.7 | 10.1 | 49.5 | 3 099 | 2 756 | -11.1 | -0.5 | 55 | 31 | -42 | 1 168 | -2.0 | 2.26 | 5.1 | 30.1 |
| Furnas | 15.9 | 10.6 | 12.0 | 51.3 | 5 324 | 4 959 | -6.9 | -1.0 | 102 | 158 | 9 | 2 185 | -4.1 | 2.23 | 6.0 | 34.9 |
| Gage | 13.9 | 9.1 | 10.5 | 50.9 | 22 993 | 22 311 | -3.0 | -2.3 | 546 | 644 | -397 | 9 422 | 1.1 | 2.31 | 8.4 | 30.3 |
| Garden | 14.2 | 13.1 | 15.1 | 49.2 | 2 292 | 2 057 | -10.3 | -5.1 | 35 | 66 | -82 | 961 | -5.8 | 2.10 | 6.0 | 33.6 |
| Garfield | 15.5 | 13.0 | 14.6 | 51.1 | 1 902 | 2 049 | 7.7 | -2.0 | 33 | 61 | -22 | 935 | 15.0 | 2.16 | 4.5 | 35.2 |
| Gosper | 17.1 | 10.6 | 11.1 | 49.4 | 2 143 | 2 044 | -4.6 | -0.7 | 46 | 57 | -26 | 849 | -1.6 | 2.36 | 5.8 | 26.6 |
| Grant | 17.0 | 10.8 | 7.6 | 45.4 | 747 | 614 | -17.8 | 2.4 | 22 | 9 | 2 | 277 | -5.1 | 2.21 | 2.5 | 28.9 |
| Greeley | 14.7 | 10.5 | 12.1 | 49.3 | 2 714 | 2 538 | -6.5 | -3.2 | 68 | 75 | -73 | 1 069 | -0.7 | 2.32 | 5.4 | 32.2 |
| Hall | 11.8 | 6.7 | 6.8 | 49.9 | 53 534 | 58 607 | 9.5 | 3.0 | 2 206 | 1 194 | 751 | 22 196 | 9.0 | 2.59 | 10.9 | 27.6 |
| Hamilton | 14.4 | 8.3 | 8.5 | 50.0 | 9 403 | 9 124 | -3.0 | -1.2 | 210 | 206 | -117 | 3 563 | 1.7 | 2.53 | 6.9 | 23.0 |
| Harlan | 17.5 | 11.9 | 11.1 | 49.0 | 3 786 | 3 423 | -9.6 | -0.4 | 75 | 94 | 8 | 1 519 | -4.9 | 2.22 | 4.3 | 32.5 |
| Hayes | 16.4 | 11.5 | 9.4 | 46.8 | 1 068 | 967 | -9.5 | -1.4 | 22 | 10 | -36 | 414 | -3.7 | 2.34 | 3.4 | 28.0 |
| Hitchcock | 16.0 | 11.2 | 11.4 | 49.5 | 3 111 | 2 908 | -6.5 | -0.7 | 77 | 100 | 1 | 1 301 | 1.1 | 2.22 | 7.1 | 32.9 |
| Holt | 15.0 | 9.4 | 10.8 | 50.4 | 11 551 | 10 435 | -9.7 | -0.4 | 300 | 297 | -29 | 4 447 | -3.5 | 2.31 | 6.2 | 30.7 |
| Hooker | 15.6 | 9.9 | 15.0 | 52.1 | 783 | 736 | -6.0 | -1.2 | 21 | 19 | -15 | 326 | -2.7 | 2.18 | 5.2 | 32.5 |
| Howard | 14.0 | 9.4 | 9.5 | 49.5 | 6 567 | 6 274 | -4.5 | 1.0 | 171 | 135 | 28 | 2 625 | 3.1 | 2.38 | 6.4 | 28.5 |
| Jefferson | 16.1 | 9.7 | 11.8 | 50.6 | 8 333 | 7 547 | -9.4 | -0.3 | 150 | 224 | 52 | 3 348 | -5.1 | 2.22 | 7.5 | 31.7 |
| Johnson | 12.8 | 8.4 | 9.2 | 41.9 | 4 488 | 5 217 | 16.2 | -1.5 | 117 | 139 | -59 | 1 847 | -2.1 | 2.31 | 7.1 | 29.9 |
| Kearney | 14.0 | 8.8 | 9.4 | 51.0 | 6 882 | 6 489 | -5.7 | -0.1 | 147 | 160 | 6 | 2 681 | 1.4 | 2.39 | 6.3 | 27.1 |
| Keith | 16.1 | 12.2 | 9.9 | 50.3 | 8 875 | 8 368 | -5.7 | -1.8 | 172 | 216 | -109 | 3 753 | 1.2 | 2.22 | 7.1 | 31.7 |
| Keya Paha | 16.1 | 13.0 | 12.8 | 49.7 | 983 | 824 | -16.2 | -2.4 | 21 | 9 | -30 | 381 | -6.8 | 2.16 | 3.4 | 30.4 |
| Kimball | 14.3 | 11.6 | 10.9 | 50.3 | 4 089 | 3 821 | -6.6 | -1.0 | 84 | 94 | -24 | 1 673 | -3.1 | 2.26 | 7.3 | 32.0 |
| Knox | 14.7 | 10.4 | 12.5 | 51.0 | 9 374 | 8 701 | -7.2 | -1.5 | 200 | 255 | -64 | 3 647 | -4.3 | 2.32 | 7.2 | 32.1 |
| Lancaster | 11.4 | 5.8 | 5.3 | 49.9 | 250 291 | 285 407 | 14.0 | 2.8 | 9 261 | 4 126 | 2 904 | 113 373 | 14.3 | 2.40 | 9.7 | 30.0 |
| Lincoln | 14.1 | 7.9 | 7.9 | 50.5 | 34 632 | 36 288 | 4.8 | -0.5 | 1 053 | 782 | -447 | 15 025 | 6.7 | 2.37 | 8.9 | 30.0 |
| Logan | 15.9 | 10.2 | 7.3 | 50.9 | 774 | 763 | -1.4 | 0.3 | 13 | 17 | 8 | 325 | 2.8 | 2.35 | 6.5 | 27.4 |
| Loup | 18.7 | 12.5 | 8.4 | 48.5 | 712 | 632 | -11.2 | -6.8 | 8 | 6 | -39 | 275 | -4.8 | 2.30 | 4.4 | 28.0 |
| McPherson | 12.5 | 9.1 | 9.2 | 49.3 | 533 | 539 | 1.1 | -5.6 | 13 | 6 | -37 | 211 | 4.5 | 2.55 | 3.8 | 23.2 |
| Madison | 12.0 | 6.9 | 7.9 | 50.3 | 35 226 | 34 876 | -1.0 | 0.4 | 1 151 | 820 | -191 | 13 939 | 3.7 | 2.43 | 9.3 | 30.0 |
| Merrick | 14.2 | 9.4 | 8.9 | 50.2 | 8 204 | 7 845 | -4.4 | -0.8 | 185 | 186 | -66 | 3 151 | -1.8 | 2.43 | 6.8 | 26.7 |
| Morrill | 14.6 | 9.2 | 9.6 | 49.4 | 5 440 | 5 042 | -7.3 | -3.0 | 115 | 108 | -190 | 2 085 | -2.5 | 2.38 | 7.1 | 28.7 |
| Nance | 15.6 | 8.0 | 10.7 | 50.4 | 4 038 | 3 735 | -7.5 | -0.5 | 103 | 98 | -24 | 1 525 | -3.3 | 2.36 | 6.5 | 31.0 |
| Nemaha | 14.3 | 8.2 | 9.9 | 50.9 | 7 576 | 7 248 | -4.3 | -1.3 | 156 | 187 | -63 | 2 952 | -3.1 | 2.29 | 7.6 | 31.8 |
| Nuckolls | 14.7 | 12.3 | 14.1 | 50.3 | 5 057 | 4 500 | -11.0 | -1.4 | 85 | 169 | 26 | 2 079 | -6.3 | 2.14 | 5.5 | 34.9 |
| Otoe | 13.3 | 8.6 | 10.2 | 51.1 | 15 396 | 15 740 | 2.2 | 0.0 | 467 | 424 | -35 | 6 362 | 5.0 | 2.42 | 8.5 | 27.4 |
| Pawnee | 15.4 | 11.3 | 14.2 | 49.8 | 3 087 | 2 773 | -10.2 | -0.3 | 44 | 91 | 38 | 1 230 | -8.1 | 2.22 | 6.0 | 34.5 |
| Perkins | 14.9 | 9.3 | 11.3 | 49.5 | 3 200 | 2 970 | -7.2 | -1.3 | 65 | 62 | -45 | 1 239 | -2.8 | 2.36 | 4.4 | 28.9 |
| Phelps | 13.4 | 8.8 | 10.6 | 50.7 | 9 747 | 9 188 | -5.7 | 0.3 | 245 | 232 | 11 | 3 779 | -1.7 | 2.37 | 6.6 | 29.2 |
| Pierce | 12.8 | 9.1 | 9.1 | 49.3 | 7 857 | 7 266 | -7.5 | -1.4 | 174 | 162 | -109 | 2 911 | -2.3 | 2.46 | 5.5 | 25.9 |

1. No spouse present.

| STATE County | Persons in group quarters, 2010 | Daytime population, 2007–2011 Number | Employment/ residence ratio | Births, 2011 Total | Rate[1] | Deaths, 2011 Number | Rate[1] | Persons under 65 with no health insurance, 2010 Number | Percent | Medicare, 2012 Eligible for Medicare | Enrolled in Medicare Advantage | Enrolled in a Medicare prescription drug plan | Serious crimes known to police,[2] 2011 Total Number | Rate[3] |
|---|---|---|---|---|---|---|---|---|---|---|---|---|---|---|
| | 32 | 33 | 34 | 35 | 36 | 37 | 38 | 39 | 40 | 41 | 42 | 43 | 44 | 45 |
| NEBRASKA—Cont'd | | | | | | | | | | | | | | |
| Blaine | 0 | 526 | 0.80 | 6 | 12.7 | 2 | 4.2 | 115 | 29.9 | 108 | D | 69 | NA | NA |
| Boone | 95 | 5 380 | 0.95 | 63 | 11.6 | 73 | 13.5 | 547 | 12.8 | 1 226 | 46 | 855 | NA | NA |
| Box Butte | 186 | 11 550 | 1.03 | 146 | 12.8 | 114 | 10.0 | 1 262 | 13.3 | 2 023 | 128 | 1 343 | 192 | 1 683 |
| Boyd | 27 | 1 940 | 0.85 | 18 | 8.6 | 25 | 12.0 | 327 | 21.4 | 607 | D | 413 | 9 | 425 |
| Brown | 40 | 3 224 | 1.05 | 32 | 10.3 | 43 | 13.8 | 487 | 20.6 | 756 | 25 | 474 | 29 | 914 |
| Buffalo | 2 225 | 46 959 | 1.05 | 654 | 14.0 | 351 | 7.5 | 5 073 | 13.2 | 6 603 | 677 | 3 940 | 1 138 | 2 447 |
| Burt | 122 | 5 960 | 0.71 | 70 | 10.3 | 108 | 15.9 | 737 | 14.2 | 1 685 | 141 | 1 095 | 54 | 1 045 |
| Butler | 173 | 7 410 | 0.77 | 90 | 10.9 | 95 | 11.5 | 757 | 11.3 | 1 754 | 91 | 1 167 | 96 | 1 133 |
| Cass | 297 | 18 417 | 0.47 | 280 | 11.1 | 241 | 9.6 | 2 254 | 10.5 | 4 228 | 566 | 1 996 | 495 | 1 944 |
| Cedar | 144 | 7 907 | 0.79 | 106 | 12.1 | 109 | 12.5 | 1 168 | 16.8 | 1 792 | 369 | 1 025 | 15 | 168 |
| Chase | 66 | 4 201 | 1.13 | 51 | 12.7 | 62 | 15.5 | 509 | 16.3 | 854 | 15 | 624 | 31 | 775 |
| Cherry | 57 | 5 796 | 1.01 | 59 | 10.2 | 60 | 10.4 | 899 | 20.1 | 1 251 | 52 | 781 | 48 | 833 |
| Cheyenne | 102 | 10 872 | 1.15 | 120 | 12.0 | 79 | 7.9 | 1 078 | 12.9 | 1 822 | 83 | 1 185 | NA | NA |
| Clay | 96 | 5 889 | 0.80 | 69 | 10.6 | 87 | 13.4 | 744 | 14.1 | 1 379 | 51 | 928 | NA | NA |
| Colfax | 108 | 9 592 | 0.85 | 203 | 19.1 | 82 | 7.7 | 1 884 | 21.0 | 1 408 | 49 | 968 | NA | NA |
| Cuming | 130 | 8 875 | 0.93 | 105 | 11.4 | 94 | 10.2 | 1 209 | 16.9 | 2 069 | 111 | 1 487 | 38 | 412 |
| Custer | 128 | 10 779 | 0.97 | 102 | 9.4 | 151 | 13.8 | 1 350 | 15.9 | 2 322 | 54 | 1 575 | 108 | 979 |
| Dakota | 249 | 21 506 | 1.07 | 393 | 18.8 | 133 | 6.4 | 3 655 | 20.0 | 2 938 | 843 | 1 347 | 476 | 2 283 |
| Dawes | 1 132 | 9 271 | 1.02 | 103 | 11.2 | 95 | 10.3 | 1 199 | 17.7 | 1 712 | 238 | 884 | 162 | 1 749 |
| Dawson | 299 | 24 592 | 1.03 | 401 | 16.4 | 208 | 8.5 | 3 888 | 18.9 | 3 808 | 519 | 2 413 | 494 | 2 013 |
| Deuel | 22 | 1 821 | 0.85 | 12 | 6.0 | 23 | 11.6 | 254 | 17.3 | 469 | 36 | 285 | 18 | 919 |
| Dixon | 81 | 5 180 | 0.72 | 72 | 12.0 | 70 | 11.7 | 724 | 14.9 | 1 062 | 319 | 516 | 73 | 1 291 |
| Dodge | 1 003 | 36 143 | 0.97 | 491 | 13.4 | 404 | 11.0 | 4 006 | 13.7 | 7 515 | 732 | 4 205 | 938 | 2 534 |
| Douglas | 12 188 | 567 459 | 1.21 | 8 277 | 15.8 | 3 454 | 6.6 | 62 529 | 13.8 | 70 635 | 16 341 | 31 355 | 22 661 | 4 351 |
| Dundy | 41 | 1 950 | 0.96 | 20 | 10.1 | 38 | 19.2 | 318 | 20.7 | 467 | 16 | 335 | NA | NA |
| Fillmore | 222 | 5 596 | 0.89 | 56 | 9.5 | 81 | 13.8 | 550 | 12.4 | 1 460 | 25 | 1 042 | NA | NA |
| Franklin | 59 | 2 913 | 0.80 | 29 | 9.0 | 38 | 11.8 | 348 | 14.4 | 844 | 39 | 559 | 9 | 277 |
| Frontier | 113 | 2 650 | 0.91 | 24 | 8.8 | 13 | 4.8 | 351 | 16.8 | 556 | 42 | 387 | NA | NA |
| Furnas | 81 | 4 823 | 0.96 | 43 | 8.7 | 73 | 14.8 | 557 | 14.8 | 1 296 | 112 | 815 | NA | NA |
| Gage | 523 | 21 213 | 0.89 | 244 | 11.1 | 290 | 13.2 | 1 912 | 10.8 | 5 177 | 310 | 3 395 | 663 | 2 945 |
| Garden | 36 | 1 970 | 0.96 | 18 | 8.7 | 31 | 15.0 | 278 | 18.8 | 585 | 71 | 368 | 4 | 193 |
| Garfield | 30 | 2 245 | 1.13 | 12 | 5.9 | 19 | 9.4 | 314 | 21.4 | 490 | 27 | 282 | NA | NA |
| Gosper | 40 | 1 613 | 0.60 | 19 | 9.5 | 21 | 10.4 | 200 | 12.5 | 471 | 83 | 269 | 6 | 291 |
| Grant | 3 | 680 | 1.03 | 8 | 12.7 | 4 | 6.3 | 106 | 21.2 | 174 | 23 | 109 | NA | NA |
| Greeley | 53 | 2 435 | 0.92 | 32 | 12.7 | 39 | 15.5 | 430 | 22.4 | 571 | 17 | 347 | NA | NA |
| Hall | 1 118 | 62 821 | 1.17 | 949 | 16.0 | 525 | 8.8 | 8 379 | 16.7 | 9 181 | 961 | 5 296 | 2 835 | 4 795 |
| Hamilton | 124 | 8 199 | 0.80 | 94 | 10.4 | 94 | 10.4 | 800 | 10.6 | 1 813 | 184 | 1 072 | 114 | 1 238 |
| Harlan | 47 | 3 167 | 0.84 | 34 | 10.0 | 46 | 13.5 | 391 | 15.1 | 839 | 94 | 511 | NA | NA |
| Hayes | 0 | 841 | 0.74 | 9 | 9.4 | 2 | 2.1 | 225 | 29.2 | 181 | D | 109 | NA | NA |
| Hitchcock | 26 | 2 481 | 0.68 | 34 | 11.9 | 45 | 15.8 | 399 | 18.1 | 727 | 14 | 538 | 28 | 954 |
| Holt | 160 | 10 477 | 1.01 | 127 | 12.2 | 137 | 13.2 | 1 357 | 16.6 | 2 498 | 35 | 1 851 | NA | NA |
| Hooker | 26 | 788 | 1.19 | 8 | 11.0 | 8 | 11.0 | 98 | 18.0 | 210 | D | 148 | 0 | 0 |
| Howard | 35 | 5 033 | 0.60 | 74 | 11.7 | 61 | 9.6 | 781 | 15.5 | 1 300 | 28 | 856 | NA | NA |
| Jefferson | 105 | 7 585 | 0.99 | 67 | 8.9 | 100 | 13.3 | 747 | 12.9 | 1 889 | 132 | 1 294 | NA | NA |
| Johnson | 955 | 4 909 | 0.87 | 48 | 9.2 | 63 | 12.1 | 568 | 16.9 | 897 | 46 | 597 | 26 | 494 |
| Kearney | 84 | 5 630 | 0.74 | 74 | 11.2 | 69 | 10.5 | 564 | 10.8 | 1 198 | 93 | 781 | 83 | 1 268 |
| Keith | 55 | 8 043 | 0.93 | 77 | 9.3 | 83 | 10.0 | 1 175 | 18.0 | 2 022 | 148 | 1 276 | 206 | 2 440 |
| Keya Paha | 0 | 687 | 0.82 | 7 | 8.6 | 8 | 9.8 | 197 | 32.6 | 246 | D | 174 | 1 | 120 |
| Kimball | 48 | 3 703 | 0.95 | 39 | 10.3 | 45 | 11.9 | 467 | 15.9 | 897 | 16 | 613 | NA | NA |
| Knox | 234 | 8 331 | 0.91 | 85 | 9.9 | 119 | 13.9 | 1 254 | 19.0 | 2 100 | 205 | 1 382 | 25 | 285 |
| Lancaster | 13 816 | 289 901 | 1.05 | 4 079 | 14.1 | 1 785 | 6.2 | 28 591 | 11.8 | 38 916 | 3 089 | 21 281 | 11 723 | 4 071 |
| Lincoln | 642 | 37 049 | 1.05 | 464 | 12.8 | 353 | 9.8 | 3 290 | 10.9 | 6 883 | 1 307 | 4 660 | 1 233 | 3 368 |
| Logan | 0 | 678 | 0.90 | 4 | 5.2 | 12 | 15.7 | 135 | 21.9 | 161 | 19 | 122 | NA | NA |
| Loup | 0 | 563 | 0.65 | 4 | 6.6 | 6 | 9.8 | 99 | 20.3 | 141 | 20 | 91 | NA | NA |
| McPherson | 0 | 339 | 0.69 | 5 | 9.1 | 1 | 1.8 | 105 | 24.0 | 88 | 15 | 51 | NA | NA |
| Madison | 1 071 | 37 937 | 1.19 | 510 | 14.6 | 373 | 10.7 | 4 631 | 15.9 | 6 282 | 794 | 3 846 | 816 | 2 319 |
| Merrick | 197 | 6 582 | 0.69 | 83 | 10.7 | 88 | 11.4 | 925 | 14.7 | 1 694 | 156 | 1 036 | 62 | 783 |
| Morrill | 82 | 4 509 | 0.77 | 57 | 11.4 | 44 | 8.8 | 613 | 15.3 | 928 | 70 | 619 | 47 | 924 |
| Nance | 143 | 3 362 | 0.79 | 44 | 11.8 | 38 | 10.2 | 453 | 15.4 | 705 | 29 | 491 | 28 | 743 |
| Nemaha | 486 | 7 912 | 1.20 | 70 | 9.6 | 72 | 9.9 | 700 | 12.7 | 1 462 | 71 | 937 | 49 | 670 |
| Nuckolls | 59 | 4 324 | 0.89 | 39 | 8.7 | 81 | 18.1 | 477 | 14.6 | 1 210 | 43 | 812 | 17 | 374 |
| Otoe | 338 | 14 905 | 0.89 | 198 | 12.5 | 184 | 11.6 | 1 512 | 11.9 | 3 186 | 293 | 1 852 | 266 | 1 675 |
| Pawnee | 39 | 2 467 | 0.78 | 17 | 6.2 | 47 | 17.2 | 327 | 16.2 | 682 | 19 | 461 | 41 | 1 465 |
| Perkins | 44 | 2 982 | 1.01 | 30 | 10.2 | 23 | 7.8 | 321 | 13.7 | 618 | 21 | 429 | 19 | 634 |
| Phelps | 249 | 9 967 | 1.17 | 104 | 11.3 | 94 | 10.2 | 782 | 10.7 | 1 970 | 295 | 1 108 | 179 | 1 931 |
| Pierce | 116 | 5 868 | 0.63 | 82 | 11.4 | 71 | 9.8 | 848 | 14.4 | 1 311 | 20 | 929 | 44 | 793 |

1. Per 1,000 estimated resident population.   2. Data for serious crimes have not been adjusted for underreporting; this may affect comparability between geographic areas and over time.   3. Per 100,000 population estimated by the FBI.

| STATE County | Serious crimes known to police, 2011 (cont.)[1] Rate[2] Violent | Property | Education — School enrollment and attainment, 2007–2011 Enrollment[3] Total | Percent private | Attainment[4] (percent) High school graduate or less | Bachelor's degree or more | Local government expenditures,[5] 2009–2010 Total current expenditures (mil dol) | Current expenditures per student (dollars) | Money income, 2007–2011 Per capita income[6] (dollars) | Households Median income Dollars | Percent change, 2000 to 2007–2011 (constant 2011 dollars) | Percent with income of $200,000 or more | Income and poverty, 2011 Median household income (dollars) | Percent below poverty level All persons | Children under 18 years | Children 5 to 17 years in families |
|---|---|---|---|---|---|---|---|---|---|---|---|---|---|---|---|---|
| | 46 | 47 | 48 | 49 | 50 | 51 | 52 | 53 | 54 | 55 | 56 | 57 | 58 | 59 | 60 | 61 |
| **NEBRASKA—Cont'd** | | | | | | | | | | | | | | | | |
| Blaine | NA | NA | 146 | 0.0 | 51.4 | 14.3 | 2.2 | 18 134 | 17 677 | 39 688 | 16.3 | 0.0 | 35 133 | 17.5 | 27.9 | 24.1 |
| Boone | NA | NA | 1 123 | 11.8 | 51.2 | 12.8 | 11.1 | 12 711 | 24 499 | 41 691 | -1.8 | 3.1 | 46 354 | 11.1 | 13.8 | 11.8 |
| Box Butte | 219 | 1 464 | 2 675 | 11.7 | 46.8 | 21.1 | 21.7 | 11 483 | 24 587 | 44 118 | -17.0 | 1.7 | 50 430 | 16.9 | 23.9 | 19.5 |
| Boyd | 0 | 425 | 350 | 10.0 | 54.4 | 13.7 | 5.3 | 14 910 | 21 353 | 37 375 | 6.2 | 1.2 | 36 181 | 13.8 | 22.0 | 19.1 |
| Brown | 95 | 819 | 664 | 19.0 | 48.7 | 17.8 | 8.6 | 17 105 | 18 881 | 29 856 | -22.0 | 0.6 | 38 011 | 13.7 | 19.9 | 17.0 |
| Buffalo | 120 | 2 326 | 14 288 | 9.8 | 36.8 | 31.5 | 81.9 | 10 842 | 23 780 | 49 851 | 0.4 | 2.0 | 50 346 | 12.0 | 14.7 | 13.9 |
| Burt | 58 | 987 | 1 489 | 5.7 | 49.3 | 18.6 | 13.9 | 10 859 | 25 185 | 45 813 | -0.1 | 2.5 | 46 434 | 10.8 | 16.7 | 14.4 |
| Butler | 35 | 1 098 | 2 082 | 30.0 | 49.2 | 15.5 | 13.3 | 11 866 | 26 770 | 48 804 | -0.5 | 1.8 | 53 928 | 9.3 | 12.5 | 10.7 |
| Cass | 75 | 1 869 | 6 586 | 16.2 | 39.1 | 23.7 | 38.6 | 10 167 | 28 974 | 63 608 | 1.3 | 3.1 | 60 091 | 7.7 | 12.6 | 11.1 |
| Cedar | 34 | 134 | 2 270 | 27.4 | 54.3 | 16.1 | 15.9 | 13 437 | 22 736 | 42 857 | -5.1 | 1.8 | 48 085 | 9.8 | 13.5 | 11.8 |
| Chase | 75 | 700 | 883 | 2.3 | 51.5 | 15.9 | 9.5 | 12 498 | 24 184 | 40 465 | -7.4 | 1.5 | 45 885 | 10.2 | 15.1 | 14.0 |
| Cherry | 87 | 746 | 1 412 | 10.8 | 41.0 | 22.9 | 11.4 | 13 880 | 23 051 | 41 929 | 6.1 | 2.0 | 39 638 | 15.6 | 25.5 | 22.1 |
| Cheyenne | NA | NA | 2 326 | 11.5 | 36.2 | 26.3 | 18.6 | 11 148 | 27 630 | 50 143 | 11.1 | 2.4 | 49 065 | 11.5 | 15.9 | 13.3 |
| Clay | NA | NA | 1 670 | 9.6 | 46.4 | 16.8 | 18.7 | 12 233 | 22 456 | 45 590 | -1.4 | 2.0 | 47 339 | 11.3 | 15.9 | 14.1 |
| Colfax | NA | NA | 2 456 | 7.4 | 58.0 | 12.7 | 22.7 | 9 985 | 20 049 | 46 685 | -3.5 | 0.9 | 45 936 | 12.0 | 17.2 | 16.5 |
| Cuming | 76 | 336 | 2 190 | 26.6 | 52.2 | 17.6 | 17.2 | 10 992 | 24 071 | 46 847 | 4.6 | 1.6 | 47 273 | 9.0 | 12.1 | 10.1 |
| Custer | 100 | 879 | 2 546 | 5.6 | 45.7 | 19.1 | 22.5 | 12 477 | 21 740 | 43 657 | 5.4 | 0.9 | 40 928 | 13.9 | 19.8 | 17.5 |
| Dakota | 125 | 2 158 | 5 198 | 10.5 | 62.9 | 10.8 | 42.5 | 10 099 | 19 844 | 43 294 | -17.4 | 0.8 | 47 067 | 12.9 | 19.7 | 18.2 |
| Dawes | 43 | 1 706 | 2 944 | 3.2 | 31.6 | 37.2 | 13.8 | 10 994 | 18 440 | 36 396 | -8.5 | 0.1 | 38 824 | 20.2 | 22.5 | 19.3 |
| Dawson | 114 | 1 899 | 6 134 | 5.0 | 59.8 | 15.4 | 50.6 | 9 670 | 20 077 | 45 038 | -7.7 | 0.8 | 43 224 | 13.0 | 18.5 | 16.7 |
| Deuel | 102 | 817 | 404 | 1.5 | 45.7 | 18.1 | 6.2 | 15 007 | 23 721 | 37 500 | -15.8 | 1.7 | 40 417 | 13.1 | 21.4 | 19.0 |
| Dixon | 53 | 1 238 | 1 506 | 2.7 | 51.5 | 15.1 | 12.5 | 11 045 | 21 875 | 44 840 | -2.9 | 1.1 | 46 524 | 9.8 | 15.9 | 14.3 |
| Dodge | 140 | 2 393 | 9 108 | 19.6 | 52.2 | 17.3 | 62.5 | 10 395 | 23 009 | 44 744 | -10.9 | 1.6 | 46 246 | 11.6 | 16.4 | 15.0 |
| Douglas | 469 | 3 882 | 147 779 | 23.4 | 33.5 | 35.7 | 894.5 | 10 192 | 28 910 | 52 929 | -9.3 | 4.2 | 51 741 | 14.6 | 20.0 | 17.0 |
| Dundy | NA | NA | 407 | 3.4 | 37.5 | 21.7 | 5.7 | 14 057 | 27 383 | 40 278 | 10.4 | 3.9 | 40 556 | 14.7 | 22.4 | 19.5 |
| Fillmore | NA | NA | 1 429 | 8.7 | 46.2 | 16.8 | 12.1 | 11 655 | 22 882 | 44 031 | -7.3 | 0.9 | 48 192 | 10.0 | 15.0 | 12.9 |
| Franklin | 31 | 246 | 679 | 7.7 | 45.1 | 16.5 | 3.8 | 10 939 | 22 859 | 40 556 | 2.5 | 2.2 | 41 551 | 13.2 | 19.8 | 17.4 |
| Frontier | NA | NA | 693 | 9.8 | 42.3 | 19.4 | 7.6 | 13 927 | 22 689 | 47 552 | 6.6 | 1.5 | 50 811 | 12.0 | 15.3 | 13.6 |
| Furnas | NA | NA | 1 154 | 7.8 | 51.6 | 17.2 | 13.7 | 11 941 | 21 987 | 38 650 | -6.1 | 1.8 | 39 868 | 14.3 | 21.5 | 17.7 |
| Gage | 329 | 2 617 | 5 175 | 11.5 | 46.6 | 19.7 | 36.6 | 11 331 | 22 959 | 45 573 | -3.3 | 1.5 | 45 221 | 10.3 | 15.6 | 14.4 |
| Garden | 0 | 193 | 304 | 11.2 | 46.8 | 19.9 | 3.9 | 13 968 | 22 619 | 35 861 | 0.4 | 0.6 | 36 486 | 15.9 | 27.4 | 24.3 |
| Garfield | NA | NA | 525 | 6.3 | 49.3 | 13.3 | 4.1 | 10 544 | 20 019 | 38 973 | 5.3 | 0.8 | 36 318 | 14.3 | 20.1 | 16.7 |
| Gosper | 0 | 291 | 425 | 9.2 | 40.7 | 16.3 | 3.1 | 11 992 | 23 973 | 42 875 | -13.8 | 2.2 | 48 409 | 9.1 | 12.8 | 10.8 |
| Grant | NA | NA | 145 | 3.4 | 50.2 | 15.5 | 2.3 | 18 870 | 20 677 | 39 531 | -15.9 | 0.0 | 40 482 | 12.1 | 22.8 | 26.0 |
| Greeley | NA | NA | 612 | 13.2 | 51.3 | 14.9 | 7.3 | 15 991 | 22 121 | 42 396 | 10.7 | 0.5 | 37 241 | 15.8 | 25.1 | 23.3 |
| Hall | 259 | 4 536 | 14 093 | 9.7 | 50.1 | 16.6 | 123.9 | 10 905 | 23 468 | 47 469 | -4.9 | 1.8 | 45 043 | 14.4 | 20.2 | 19.1 |
| Hamilton | 152 | 1 086 | 2 277 | 11.6 | 40.4 | 22.3 | 17.6 | 10 681 | 25 587 | 54 980 | 1.1 | 2.4 | 58 591 | 8.2 | 11.7 | 10.1 |
| Harlan | NA | NA | 715 | 5.3 | 43.8 | 17.5 | 3.4 | 10 686 | 23 404 | 45 396 | 9.6 | 1.2 | 44 467 | 12.8 | 20.9 | 18.4 |
| Hayes | NA | NA | 185 | 9.2 | 42.1 | 14.8 | 2.4 | 16 524 | 24 219 | 45 536 | 26.5 | 2.7 | 43 321 | 15.3 | 22.9 | 20.7 |
| Hitchcock | 170 | 784 | 574 | 2.4 | 39.7 | 12.8 | 5.2 | 18 413 | 21 536 | 36 920 | -3.3 | 0.1 | 39 411 | 16.3 | 25.2 | 22.9 |
| Holt | NA | NA | 2 238 | 15.0 | 48.1 | 16.6 | 22.0 | 13 966 | 23 380 | 46 292 | 11.5 | 2.2 | 42 844 | 13.6 | 18.1 | 16.6 |
| Hooker | 0 | 0 | 145 | 2.1 | 37.7 | 26.5 | 2.7 | 13 845 | 23 553 | 39 125 | 4.0 | 1.8 | 38 397 | 10.4 | 13.5 | 12.5 |
| Howard | NA | NA | 1 532 | 7.6 | 50.3 | 15.5 | 12.3 | 9 769 | 22 983 | 46 358 | 3.1 | 0.9 | 45 336 | 10.8 | 15.0 | 13.4 |
| Jefferson | NA | NA | 1 719 | 8.8 | 52.6 | 13.6 | 12.5 | 11 321 | 23 675 | 42 979 | -2.4 | 1.1 | 42 418 | 11.2 | 17.8 | 15.5 |
| Johnson | 19 | 475 | 994 | 11.0 | 58.0 | 11.1 | 9.0 | 12 067 | 19 664 | 43 643 | -0.4 | 0.4 | 43 526 | 12.7 | 14.5 | 13.4 |
| Kearney | 76 | 1 191 | 1 461 | 6.5 | 37.7 | 25.5 | 15.0 | 11 372 | 27 444 | 54 611 | 3.1 | 1.6 | 53 129 | 9.1 | 14.8 | 13.3 |
| Keith | 59 | 2 381 | 1 587 | 12.0 | 45.0 | 19.7 | 19.9 | 16 726 | 26 443 | 42 705 | -2.2 | 2.2 | 40 154 | 13.3 | 21.2 | 18.0 |
| Keya Paha | 0 | 120 | 91 | 1.1 | 48.4 | 14.4 | 1.8 | 17 798 | 22 192 | 38 125 | 13.4 | 0.6 | 35 436 | 21.7 | 36.8 | 32.3 |
| Kimball | NA | NA | 827 | 7.3 | 45.5 | 19.8 | 6.5 | 11 420 | 24 564 | 43 191 | 4.6 | 1.0 | 40 240 | 15.5 | 22.0 | 19.6 |
| Knox | 11 | 273 | 1 979 | 7.6 | 52.4 | 17.7 | 19.7 | 12 951 | 21 687 | 38 965 | 4.7 | 1.6 | 39 178 | 15.2 | 22.1 | 19.6 |
| Lancaster | 340 | 3 731 | 87 581 | 17.9 | 30.0 | 35.9 | 397.0 | 9 951 | 26 557 | 51 059 | -9.6 | 2.8 | 49 046 | 14.5 | 17.8 | 15.2 |
| Lincoln | 194 | 3 174 | 8 925 | 13.7 | 42.4 | 19.2 | 55.4 | 9 694 | 26 648 | 49 521 | 0.3 | 2.9 | 49 139 | 12.8 | 18.9 | 16.7 |
| Logan | NA | NA | 131 | 3.8 | 43.7 | 19.8 | 2.5 | 14 040 | 22 510 | 45 625 | 2.0 | 0.6 | 46 820 | 12.2 | 21.1 | 19.0 |
| Loup | NA | NA | 143 | 24.5 | 48.9 | 14.7 | 1.6 | 15 029 | 21 560 | 36 250 | 2.3 | 1.1 | 37 885 | 18.3 | 31.6 | 29.3 |
| McPherson | NA | NA | 93 | 0.0 | 32.0 | 22.7 | 1.5 | 17 627 | 24 231 | 57 917 | 66.6 | 1.1 | 38 097 | 14.4 | 23.4 | 21.9 |
| Madison | 94 | 2 225 | 9 131 | 17.7 | 43.5 | 20.9 | 56.9 | 10 409 | 23 603 | 45 077 | -6.8 | 2.3 | 46 363 | 15.7 | 21.2 | 18.1 |
| Merrick | 51 | 733 | 1 865 | 8.1 | 49.0 | 14.7 | 10.2 | 9 823 | 22 972 | 49 262 | 4.4 | 0.8 | 50 714 | 10.9 | 15.7 | 13.5 |
| Morrill | 59 | 865 | 1 167 | 8.2 | 49.7 | 21.3 | 11.3 | 12 206 | 21 611 | 42 075 | 3.1 | 1.2 | 42 378 | 16.4 | 23.5 | 20.9 |
| Nance | 27 | 717 | 793 | 5.8 | 51.4 | 12.7 | 8.8 | 10 463 | 23 299 | 43 399 | 2.8 | 1.5 | 42 629 | 14.2 | 20.9 | 18.6 |
| Nemaha | 27 | 643 | 2 017 | 8.4 | 45.3 | 23.6 | 17.3 | 15 185 | 23 724 | 41 424 | -5.9 | 1.2 | 44 705 | 12.7 | 17.2 | 16.5 |
| Nuckolls | 88 | 286 | 943 | 10.9 | 54.7 | 13.0 | 5.8 | 12 605 | 21 350 | 32 444 | -17.0 | 1.9 | 36 861 | 13.0 | 17.6 | 15.3 |
| Otoe | 31 | 1 644 | 3 750 | 17.9 | 46.9 | 22.2 | 25.9 | 10 320 | 24 718 | 50 000 | -0.7 | 1.7 | 48 509 | 9.9 | 14.5 | 12.8 |
| Pawnee | 0 | 1 465 | 520 | 12.5 | 60.8 | 13.7 | 6.5 | 13 222 | 24 053 | 44 477 | 13.6 | 0.6 | 37 006 | 14.3 | 22.4 | 19.8 |
| Perkins | 0 | 634 | 664 | 14.2 | 34.1 | 18.0 | 5.5 | 14 069 | 26 040 | 52 266 | 13.2 | 2.5 | 50 293 | 11.3 | 16.8 | 15.1 |
| Phelps | 108 | 1 823 | 2 152 | 10.6 | 38.5 | 22.1 | 20.8 | 13 152 | 25 471 | 44 570 | -11.5 | 2.2 | 51 371 | 9.8 | 13.4 | 11.6 |
| Pierce | 18 | 775 | 1 745 | 10.4 | 50.7 | 14.5 | 14.7 | 11 301 | 22 499 | 51 205 | 17.6 | 1.1 | 51 019 | 9.9 | 13.5 | 11.3 |

1. Data for serious crimes have not been adjusted for underreporting; this may affect comparability between geographic areas and over time.   2. Per 100,000 population estimated by the FBI.   3. All persons 3 years old and over enrolled in nursery school through college.   4. Persons 25 years old and over.   5. Elementary and secondary education expenditures.   6. Based on population estimated by the American Community Survey, 2007–2011.

| STATE County | Personal income, 2011 | | | | | | | | | | | | |
|---|---|---|---|---|---|---|---|---|---|---|---|---|---|
| | Total (mil dol) | Percent change, 2010–2011 | Per capita[1] | | Wages and salaries[2] (mil dol) | Proprietors' income (mil dol) | Dividends, interest, and rent (mil dol) | Transfer payments (mil dol) | | | | | |
| | | | | | | | | | Government payments to individuals | | | | |
| | | | Dollars | Rank | | | | Total | Total | Social Security | Medical payments | Income mainte-nance | Unemploy-ment insurance |
| | 62 | 63 | 64 | 65 | 66 | 67 | 68 | 69 | 70 | 71 | 72 | 73 | 74 |
| NEBRASKA—Cont'd | | | | | | | | | | | | | |
| Blaine | 19 | 28.2 | 41 044 | 655 | 8 | 4 | 4 | 4 | 4 | 1 | 2 | 0 | 0 |
| Boone | 287 | 21.4 | 53 006 | 140 | 97 | 109 | 42 | 40 | 39 | 16 | 17 | 2 | 1 |
| Box Butte | 439 | 16.1 | 38 572 | 901 | 308 | 59 | 64 | 82 | 79 | 22 | 31 | 8 | 2 |
| Boyd | 95 | 18.4 | 45 714 | 352 | 21 | 39 | 14 | 21 | 21 | 7 | 11 | 1 | 0 |
| Brown | 120 | 12.9 | 38 447 | 916 | 50 | 29 | 22 | 26 | 25 | 10 | 10 | 2 | 0 |
| Buffalo | 1 789 | 6.8 | 38 327 | 932 | 1 177 | 253 | 317 | 270 | 260 | 95 | 103 | 26 | 6 |
| Burt | 294 | 10.1 | 43 196 | 496 | 77 | 65 | 41 | 61 | 60 | 23 | 29 | 4 | 1 |
| Butler | 396 | 18.5 | 47 805 | 271 | 116 | 122 | 54 | 57 | 55 | 24 | 22 | 4 | 1 |
| Cass | 1 058 | 8.3 | 41 991 | 571 | 223 | 117 | 137 | 168 | 163 | 61 | 66 | 11 | 5 |
| Cedar | 473 | 22.2 | 54 235 | 126 | 120 | 217 | 62 | 53 | 51 | 23 | 21 | 3 | 1 |
| Chase | 173 | 0.7 | 43 040 | 505 | 75 | 45 | 36 | 29 | 28 | 12 | 13 | 2 | 0 |
| Cherry | 229 | 17.7 | 39 813 | 767 | 88 | 57 | 45 | 39 | 38 | 15 | 16 | 4 | 1 |
| Cheyenne | 467 | 14.2 | 46 811 | 307 | 326 | 83 | 60 | 64 | 62 | 25 | 26 | 5 | 1 |
| Clay | 330 | 24.5 | 50 910 | 189 | 126 | 118 | 42 | 46 | 45 | 19 | 19 | 3 | 1 |
| Colfax | 406 | 9.9 | 38 217 | 939 | 218 | 87 | 54 | 67 | 64 | 18 | 37 | 5 | 1 |
| Cuming | 476 | 13.9 | 51 821 | 168 | 174 | 179 | 69 | 62 | 60 | 27 | 25 | 4 | 1 |
| Custer | 485 | 19.0 | 44 511 | 420 | 185 | 153 | 74 | 81 | 78 | 30 | 34 | 6 | 1 |
| Dakota | 613 | 2.2 | 29 320 | 2 404 | 556 | 64 | 64 | 125 | 121 | 40 | 51 | 17 | 5 |
| Dawes | 285 | 9.5 | 31 015 | 2 095 | 145 | 42 | 44 | 66 | 64 | 21 | 23 | 6 | 1 |
| Dawson | 813 | 8.4 | 33 320 | 1 650 | 482 | 141 | 106 | 148 | 143 | 53 | 59 | 19 | 4 |
| Deuel | 71 | 16.6 | 35 962 | 1 216 | 22 | 13 | 15 | 16 | 15 | 7 | 6 | 1 | 0 |
| Dixon | 215 | 2.3 | 35 926 | 1 223 | 78 | 43 | 29 | 36 | 35 | 14 | 15 | 3 | 1 |
| Dodge | 1 408 | 7.3 | 38 292 | 935 | 721 | 215 | 216 | 283 | 274 | 108 | 119 | 23 | 6 |
| Douglas | 24 673 | 4.6 | 47 008 | 299 | 19 257 | 3 192 | 4 746 | 3 363 | 3 247 | 1 033 | 1 402 | 405 | 96 |
| Dundy | 113 | 12.8 | 57 082 | 95 | 32 | 41 | 23 | 17 | 17 | 6 | 8 | 1 | 0 |
| Fillmore | 334 | 29.9 | 57 011 | 96 | 102 | 128 | 57 | 47 | 46 | 20 | 18 | 3 | 1 |
| Franklin | 143 | 20.4 | 44 576 | 416 | 33 | 49 | 24 | 28 | 27 | 11 | 12 | 2 | 0 |
| Frontier | 133 | 24.6 | 48 963 | 235 | 36 | 60 | 14 | 18 | 17 | 7 | 7 | 1 | 0 |
| Furnas | 226 | 20.2 | 45 679 | 355 | 84 | 69 | 34 | 44 | 43 | 17 | 20 | 3 | 1 |
| Gage | 902 | 9.4 | 40 942 | 664 | 376 | 181 | 131 | 204 | 199 | 70 | 95 | 14 | 4 |
| Garden | 108 | 36.0 | 52 007 | 162 | 28 | 45 | 16 | 20 | 20 | 8 | 9 | 1 | 0 |
| Garfield | 76 | 16.0 | 37 618 | 1 014 | 29 | 21 | 15 | 16 | 15 | 6 | 7 | 1 | 0 |
| Gosper | 109 | 18.5 | 54 274 | 125 | 22 | 41 | 17 | 15 | 15 | 7 | 6 | 1 | 0 |
| Grant | 19 | 17.9 | 29 465 | 2 382 | 8 | 1 | 5 | 5 | 5 | 2 | 2 | 0 | 0 |
| Greeley | 99 | 22.3 | 39 276 | 826 | 28 | 34 | 18 | 19 | 18 | 7 | 8 | 1 | 0 |
| Hall | 2 220 | 7.0 | 37 324 | 1 046 | 1 573 | 256 | 376 | 389 | 376 | 128 | 147 | 45 | 10 |
| Hamilton | 454 | 18.9 | 50 112 | 204 | 154 | 145 | 73 | 59 | 57 | 26 | 22 | 4 | 1 |
| Harlan | 167 | 25.6 | 48 857 | 240 | 39 | 66 | 22 | 28 | 27 | 11 | 11 | 2 | 0 |
| Hayes | 65 | 26.8 | 67 595 | 30 | 11 | 41 | 6 | 6 | 6 | 2 | 2 | 0 | 0 |
| Hitchcock | 113 | 11.1 | 39 593 | 795 | 39 | 26 | 19 | 25 | 24 | 10 | 10 | 2 | 0 |
| Holt | 520 | 26.5 | 49 972 | 206 | 190 | 193 | 77 | 85 | 83 | 30 | 40 | 7 | 1 |
| Hooker | 24 | 12.8 | 32 956 | 1 716 | 13 | 1 | 4 | 7 | 6 | 3 | 3 | 0 | 0 |
| Howard | 259 | 15.3 | 40 780 | 679 | 60 | 64 | 36 | 45 | 44 | 17 | 17 | 3 | 1 |
| Jefferson | 313 | 17.4 | 41 640 | 606 | 149 | 59 | 58 | 61 | 60 | 24 | 24 | 5 | 1 |
| Johnson | 168 | 2.2 | 32 247 | 1 836 | 74 | 32 | 22 | 29 | 28 | 11 | 12 | 2 | 1 |
| Kearney | 356 | 21.3 | 53 989 | 130 | 100 | 127 | 47 | 51 | 50 | 17 | 28 | 3 | 1 |
| Keith | 312 | 15.1 | 37 553 | 1 021 | 130 | 72 | 52 | 63 | 61 | 28 | 23 | 5 | 1 |
| Keya Paha | 42 | 40.9 | 51 993 | 163 | 7 | 21 | 7 | 7 | 6 | 3 | 2 | 1 | 0 |
| Kimball | 165 | 19.3 | 43 713 | 458 | 66 | 43 | 27 | 30 | 29 | 13 | 12 | 2 | 1 |
| Knox | 341 | 17.8 | 39 745 | 774 | 110 | 98 | 52 | 73 | 71 | 26 | 34 | 6 | 1 |
| Lancaster | 11 254 | 5.9 | 38 833 | 873 | 8 232 | 797 | 1 955 | 1 650 | 1 586 | 562 | 621 | 167 | 46 |
| Lincoln | 1 524 | 11.3 | 42 175 | 563 | 893 | 307 | 185 | 287 | 279 | 76 | 104 | 25 | 7 |
| Logan | 39 | 36.9 | 50 845 | 190 | 9 | 16 | 4 | 6 | 5 | 2 | 2 | 0 | 0 |
| Loup | 17 | 28.6 | 28 421 | 2 556 | 5 | 2 | 4 | 5 | 5 | 2 | 2 | 0 | 0 |
| McPherson | 15 | 42.7 | 26 304 | 2 848 | 3 | 3 | 3 | 3 | 3 | 1 | 1 | 0 | 0 |
| Madison | 1 305 | 7.6 | 37 372 | 1 041 | 942 | 164 | 221 | 240 | 233 | 86 | 99 | 24 | 5 |
| Merrick | 307 | 10.2 | 39 751 | 773 | 97 | 64 | 42 | 61 | 59 | 23 | 25 | 5 | 1 |
| Morrill | 251 | 23.1 | 50 169 | 202 | 71 | 109 | 27 | 36 | 35 | 12 | 16 | 4 | 1 |
| Nance | 169 | 24.1 | 45 194 | 388 | 49 | 61 | 17 | 28 | 28 | 9 | 14 | 2 | 1 |
| Nemaha | 298 | 14.1 | 40 958 | 662 | 199 | 57 | 41 | 58 | 56 | 21 | 24 | 4 | 1 |
| Nuckolls | 212 | 29.0 | 47 318 | 289 | 57 | 80 | 30 | 39 | 38 | 16 | 17 | 3 | 1 |
| Otoe | 606 | 8.4 | 38 340 | 931 | 284 | 87 | 103 | 111 | 107 | 44 | 43 | 8 | 3 |
| Pawnee | 112 | 20.9 | 41 131 | 650 | 35 | 35 | 18 | 21 | 21 | 8 | 9 | 2 | 0 |
| Perkins | 175 | 44.3 | 59 282 | 74 | 56 | 82 | 22 | 22 | 21 | 9 | 9 | 1 | 0 |
| Phelps | 433 | 9.6 | 47 148 | 291 | 218 | 105 | 72 | 70 | 68 | 28 | 30 | 5 | 1 |
| Pierce | 305 | 13.9 | 42 209 | 562 | 87 | 91 | 39 | 44 | 42 | 18 | 18 | 3 | 1 |

1. Based on the resident population estimated as of July 1 of the year shown.  2. Includes supplements to wages and salaries.

# Table B. States and Counties — Earnings, Social Security, and Housing

| STATE County | Earnings, 2011 Total (mil dol) | Farm | Goods-related[1] Total | Manu- facturing | Infor- mation and profes- sional and technical services | Retail trade | Finance, insur- ance, and real estate | Health care and social services | Govern- ment | Social Security beneficiaries, December 2011 Number | Rate[2] | Supple- mental Security Income recipients, December 2011 | Housing units, 2010 Total | Percent change, 2000– 2010 |
|---|---|---|---|---|---|---|---|---|---|---|---|---|---|---|
| | 75 | 76 | 77 | 78 | 79 | 80 | 81 | 82 | 83 | 84 | 85 | 86 | 87 | 88 |
| **NEBRASKA—Cont'd** | | | | | | | | | | | | | | |
| Blaine | 12 | 44.8 | D | 0.0 | D | D | D | 0.0 | 34.3 | 115 | 243 | 0 | 326 | -2.1 |
| Boone | 207 | 50.6 | 7.8 | 5.2 | 0.9 | 3.1 | 2.7 | 3.5 | 14.7 | 1 290 | 238 | 46 | 2 649 | -3.1 |
| Box Butte | 367 | 12.7 | 7.2 | 5.2 | D | 3.9 | 2.6 | D | 16.2 | 1 810 | 159 | 182 | 5 478 | -0.2 |
| Boyd | 60 | 52.1 | 2.3 | 0.8 | D | 2.6 | 3.0 | 3.4 | 15.6 | 650 | 312 | 31 | 1 390 | -1.1 |
| Brown | 80 | 30.1 | 5.9 | 1.5 | D | 7.3 | D | 4.9 | 25.7 | 845 | 271 | 56 | 1 865 | -2.7 |
| Buffalo | 1 430 | 6.9 | 21.0 | 15.6 | 5.7 | 7.7 | 4.5 | 15.9 | 15.4 | 7 165 | 153 | 474 | 19 064 | 13.3 |
| Burt | 142 | 36.6 | 9.5 | 4.9 | D | 3.4 | D | 5.1 | 17.8 | 1 840 | 271 | 98 | 3 467 | -6.9 |
| Butler | 238 | 46.5 | D | 13.6 | D | 3.3 | D | D | 13.6 | 1 880 | 227 | 92 | 4 053 | 0.9 |
| Cass | 340 | 20.5 | 16.8 | 8.0 | 2.9 | 5.6 | 6.1 | D | 20.6 | 4 530 | 180 | 204 | 11 117 | 9.2 |
| Cedar | 337 | 55.1 | 7.5 | 3.1 | 1.7 | 4.3 | 3.4 | 2.4 | 10.3 | 1 930 | 221 | 64 | 4 148 | -1.2 |
| Chase | 121 | 32.7 | D | 1.2 | 4.7 | 9.2 | 3.6 | 1.7 | 19.0 | 910 | 227 | 40 | 1 946 | 1.0 |
| Cherry | 145 | 33.3 | 8.4 | 1.3 | 3.5 | 7.8 | 2.5 | 5.4 | 19.9 | 1 315 | 228 | 81 | 3 157 | -2.0 |
| Cheyenne | 409 | 12.2 | 8.5 | 5.8 | D | 8.5 | 2.5 | 5.8 | 10.0 | 1 940 | 194 | 120 | 4 888 | 7.0 |
| Clay | 245 | 47.0 | D | 8.2 | 1.1 | 2.4 | D | 3.0 | 17.2 | 1 485 | 229 | 79 | 3 001 | -2.1 |
| Colfax | 305 | 22.7 | D | D | 1.7 | 3.0 | 2.5 | 4.0 | 11.4 | 1 485 | 140 | 75 | 4 097 | 0.2 |
| Cuming | 353 | 43.0 | D | 10.1 | 2.0 | 3.1 | 4.6 | 6.1 | 10.1 | 2 180 | 237 | 84 | 4 204 | -1.8 |
| Custer | 339 | 41.9 | 13.9 | 9.3 | 2.2 | 4.9 | 3.2 | 6.9 | 12.6 | 2 485 | 228 | 141 | 5 579 | -0.1 |
| Dakota | 620 | 4.3 | D | 38.6 | D | 4.8 | 8.4 | D | 11.2 | 3 220 | 154 | 269 | 7 631 | 1.4 |
| Dawes | 187 | 10.8 | D | 0.3 | D | 12.4 | 3.5 | 11.1 | 32.1 | 1 775 | 193 | 120 | 4 252 | 6.2 |
| Dawson | 623 | 18.0 | D | 26.2 | D | 6.2 | 3.3 | 4.3 | 18.0 | 4 235 | 174 | 325 | 10 123 | 3.2 |
| Deuel | 35 | 32.3 | 2.3 | 0.0 | D | 4.8 | D | 6.2 | 23.7 | 520 | 262 | 23 | 1 044 | 1.2 |
| Dixon | 121 | 29.2 | D | D | D | 1.6 | D | 2.4 | 16.2 | 1 150 | 192 | 54 | 2 688 | 0.6 |
| Dodge | 936 | 14.9 | 22.2 | 18.0 | D | 8.9 | 3.6 | D | 17.7 | 8 185 | 223 | 483 | 16 584 | 7.2 |
| Douglas | 22 449 | 0.1 | D | 6.0 | 13.4 | 5.3 | 12.1 | 12.4 | 12.2 | 75 330 | 144 | 9 361 | 219 580 | 14.0 |
| Dundy | 73 | 56.4 | 4.1 | 0.7 | D | 2.2 | D | D | 16.0 | 540 | 273 | 25 | 1 125 | -5.9 |
| Fillmore | 230 | 51.3 | 10.8 | 4.1 | D | 2.7 | 4.3 | 2.7 | 13.6 | 1 550 | 264 | 59 | 2 913 | -2.6 |
| Franklin | 82 | 55.8 | 2.3 | 0.0 | D | 3.7 | 2.9 | 2.4 | 19.4 | 915 | 285 | 59 | 1 734 | -0.7 |
| Frontier | 96 | 51.7 | D | D | D | 3.8 | D | 1.3 | 14.8 | 600 | 220 | 30 | 1 574 | 2.1 |
| Furnas | 153 | 45.1 | 6.1 | 3.5 | 5.0 | 3.7 | D | D | 15.7 | 1 400 | 283 | 83 | 2 721 | -0.3 |
| Gage | 557 | 19.8 | D | 16.1 | D | 8.3 | 3.3 | D | 20.1 | 5 660 | 257 | 357 | 10 446 | 4.1 |
| Garden | 73 | 62.5 | D | D | D | 6.1 | 2.3 | 0.3 | 16.7 | 645 | 312 | 28 | 1 314 | 1.2 |
| Garfield | 50 | 33.0 | D | 4.7 | 2.5 | 5.9 | D | 6.6 | 16.1 | 540 | 266 | 17 | 1 178 | 15.4 |
| Gosper | 63 | 64.5 | D | D | D | 0.9 | 6.0 | D | 11.6 | 525 | 261 | 18 | 1 267 | -1.1 |
| Grant | 10 | 29.4 | 2.6 | 0.0 | D | D | D | 0.0 | 32.1 | 185 | 294 | 0 | 391 | -12.9 |
| Greeley | 62 | 49.9 | 4.3 | 1.5 | D | 3.8 | 3.8 | 2.2 | 17.9 | 645 | 256 | 35 | 1 300 | 8.4 |
| Hall | 1 829 | 4.4 | 26.5 | 21.3 | 3.5 | 9.0 | 5.2 | 11.9 | 16.8 | 10 000 | 168 | 905 | 23 549 | 9.1 |
| Hamilton | 298 | 41.5 | 12.4 | 9.0 | 4.3 | 3.9 | 2.8 | D | 9.8 | 1 990 | 219 | 79 | 3 968 | 3.1 |
| Harlan | 104 | 60.0 | D | 0.5 | D | 3.5 | D | 2.8 | 13.3 | 895 | 262 | 50 | 2 375 | 2.1 |
| Hayes | 52 | 84.5 | D | D | D | D | D | 0.0 | 6.9 | 180 | 188 | 0 | 511 | -2.9 |
| Hitchcock | 65 | 29.7 | 24.1 | 16.7 | D | 2.4 | D | D | 19.8 | 785 | 275 | 54 | 1 763 | 5.2 |
| Holt | 383 | 41.0 | 8.9 | 5.7 | 1.5 | 5.1 | 3.5 | D | 10.2 | 2 710 | 261 | 195 | 5 215 | -1.2 |
| Hooker | 14 | 6.4 | D | D | D | 3.0 | 2.1 | D | 27.0 | 230 | 316 | 0 | 431 | -2.0 |
| Howard | 125 | 45.3 | 3.8 | 0.6 | 1.8 | 4.8 | 3.2 | 3.1 | 23.7 | 1 425 | 225 | 61 | 2 951 | 6.1 |
| Jefferson | 207 | 24.3 | 17.4 | 11.3 | 2.9 | 7.5 | 2.7 | 8.5 | 13.2 | 1 965 | 261 | 147 | 3 918 | -0.6 |
| Johnson | 106 | 20.3 | D | 4.3 | D | 4.8 | 4.9 | 6.4 | 39.7 | 945 | 181 | 45 | 2 191 | 3.5 |
| Kearney | 227 | 49.9 | 16.8 | 13.1 | D | 1.5 | 2.2 | D | 10.1 | 1 265 | 192 | 74 | 2 886 | 1.4 |
| Keith | 203 | 25.7 | D | 4.4 | 3.6 | 8.7 | 4.9 | D | 14.1 | 2 175 | 262 | 110 | 5 424 | 4.8 |
| Keya Paha | 28 | 75.9 | D | D | D | D | D | D | 9.3 | 265 | 326 | 14 | 549 | 0.2 |
| Kimball | 109 | 28.7 | 21.9 | 10.8 | D | 5.5 | D | D | 17.2 | 980 | 260 | 50 | 1 963 | -0.5 |
| Knox | 209 | 44.6 | 5.3 | 2.8 | D | 5.1 | 2.8 | 6.1 | 22.2 | 2 325 | 271 | 126 | 4 788 | 0.3 |
| Lancaster | 9 029 | 0.8 | D | 8.6 | 9.2 | 6.1 | 9.4 | 13.9 | 22.8 | 40 790 | 141 | 4 396 | 120 875 | 16.0 |
| Lincoln | 1 200 | 17.7 | D | 1.9 | 2.8 | 6.5 | 3.6 | 13.4 | 14.7 | 6 245 | 173 | 696 | 16 583 | 7.4 |
| Logan | 25 | 70.1 | D | D | D | D | D | D | 12.9 | 155 | 203 | 0 | 395 | 2.3 |
| Loup | 7 | 47.8 | D | 0.0 | D | D | D | 0.0 | 33.3 | 155 | 254 | 0 | 426 | 13.0 |
| McPherson | 6 | 60.7 | 0.0 | 0.0 | D | D | D | 0.0 | 30.0 | 90 | 163 | 0 | 283 | 0.0 |
| Madison | 1 106 | 7.0 | D | 16.1 | 3.9 | 8.6 | 4.9 | 14.4 | 18.2 | 6 865 | 197 | 584 | 15 014 | 4.0 |
| Merrick | 161 | 30.4 | D | 6.9 | 2.1 | 3.6 | 5.7 | D | 16.4 | 1 845 | 239 | 143 | 3 698 | 1.3 |
| Morrill | 179 | 54.6 | D | 1.2 | D | 4.6 | 1.7 | 2.9 | 14.0 | 1 010 | 202 | 89 | 2 442 | -0.7 |
| Nance | 110 | 50.2 | D | 0.0 | 1.7 | 2.5 | D | 5.8 | 15.8 | 785 | 210 | 73 | 1 801 | 0.8 |
| Nemaha | 256 | 16.7 | 7.5 | 5.8 | D | 3.3 | 2.7 | 4.8 | 52.3 | 1 635 | 225 | 120 | 3 498 | 1.7 |
| Nuckolls | 137 | 49.7 | 2.2 | 0.1 | 1.6 | 5.7 | 3.5 | 10.6 | 12.7 | 1 280 | 286 | 69 | 2 465 | -2.6 |
| Otoe | 371 | 17.2 | 24.4 | 19.6 | D | 6.2 | 4.0 | D | 21.4 | 3 415 | 216 | 224 | 7 025 | 7.0 |
| Pawnee | 70 | 44.1 | D | 9.5 | D | 4.2 | 2.8 | 5.8 | 20.1 | 715 | 261 | 43 | 1 588 | 0.1 |
| Perkins | 137 | 51.5 | 9.0 | 3.0 | D | 1.8 | 3.2 | 1.8 | 12.5 | 670 | 227 | 24 | 1 450 | 0.4 |
| Phelps | 323 | 29.0 | D | D | 2.1 | 4.7 | 4.4 | D | 12.1 | 2 105 | 229 | 109 | 4 175 | -0.4 |
| Pierce | 178 | 41.4 | D | 3.2 | 2.0 | 3.9 | D | 4.8 | 13.8 | 1 425 | 197 | 59 | 3 222 | -0.8 |

1. Includes mining, construction, and manufacturing.  2. Per 1,000 resident population enumerated in the 2010 census.

# Table B. States and Counties — Housing, Labor Force, and Employment

| | Housing units, 2007–2011 | | | | | | | | Civilian labor force, 2012 | | | | Civilian employment,[6] 2007–2011 | | |
|---|---|---|---|---|---|---|---|---|---|---|---|---|---|---|---|
| | Occupied units | | | | | | | | | | Unemployment | | | Percent | |
| | | | Owner-occupied | | | Renter-occupied | | | | | | | | | |
| | | | | Median owner cost as a percent of income | | | | | | | | | | | Construction, production, and maintenance occupations |
| STATE County | Total | Percent | Median value[1] | With a mortgage | Without a mortgage[2] | Median rent[3] | Median rent as a percent of income | Substandard units[4] (percent) | Total | Percent change, 2011–2012 | Total | Rate[5] | Total | Management, business, science and arts | |
| | 89 | 90 | 91 | 92 | 93 | 94 | 95 | 96 | 97 | 98 | 99 | 100 | 101 | 102 | 103 |
| NEBRASKA—Cont'd | | | | | | | | | | | | | | | |
| Blaine | 247 | 63.6 | 48 300 | 25.5 | 9.9 | 536 | 29.4 | 3.6 | 283 | 6.4 | 14 | 4.9 | 299 | 37.1 | 37.5 |
| Boone | 2 374 | 75.9 | 73 500 | 22.8 | 11.5 | 445 | 17.4 | 1.5 | 3 527 | 0.9 | 91 | 2.6 | 2 862 | 33.9 | 29.6 |
| Box Butte | 4 803 | 67.8 | 92 100 | 19.6 | 9.9 | 512 | 25.8 | 3.1 | 5 553 | 0.4 | 240 | 4.3 | 5 490 | 30.9 | 39.7 |
| Boyd | 909 | 79.2 | 53 700 | 24.1 | 12.9 | 375 | 14.4 | 2.2 | 1 236 | 4.3 | 43 | 3.5 | 1 063 | 39.1 | 28.1 |
| Brown | 1 395 | 71.0 | 57 100 | 24.6 | 14.9 | 508 | 25.1 | 0.4 | 1 895 | 1.3 | 57 | 3.0 | 1 445 | 32.5 | 30.5 |
| Buffalo | 17 340 | 65.2 | 132 600 | 21.7 | 11.0 | 650 | 26.8 | 1.5 | 28 853 | 1.3 | 874 | 3.0 | 25 208 | 31.1 | 25.2 |
| Burt | 2 909 | 77.2 | 84 000 | 21.1 | 12.8 | 571 | 26.4 | 1.4 | 4 058 | 2.4 | 174 | 4.3 | 3 315 | 31.6 | 26.2 |
| Butler | 3 473 | 76.1 | 91 600 | 19.4 | 11.5 | 564 | 20.3 | 2.4 | 5 013 | 0.5 | 155 | 3.1 | 4 262 | 30.3 | 37.0 |
| Cass | 9 787 | 81.7 | 146 900 | 23.5 | 13.5 | 707 | 23.6 | 1.1 | 13 516 | 1.2 | 627 | 4.6 | 13 052 | 33.6 | 27.3 |
| Cedar | 3 474 | 80.6 | 86 100 | 20.2 | 13.7 | 455 | 23.6 | 1.1 | 5 082 | 1.5 | 136 | 2.7 | 4 482 | 32.5 | 31.0 |
| Chase | 1 698 | 78.0 | 83 000 | 19.9 | 13.4 | 560 | 18.3 | 0.2 | 2 194 | 1.3 | 55 | 2.5 | 2 106 | 33.1 | 25.9 |
| Cherry | 2 462 | 67.8 | 92 900 | 21.9 | 13.0 | 594 | 24.6 | 1.5 | 3 733 | 2.6 | 98 | 2.6 | 3 119 | 40.7 | 18.3 |
| Cheyenne | 4 423 | 68.4 | 96 900 | 19.5 | 13.2 | 565 | 24.2 | 3.0 | 5 158 | 1.4 | 159 | 3.1 | 5 662 | 36.3 | 18.8 |
| Clay | 2 598 | 79.6 | 77 200 | 19.7 | 12.9 | 474 | 21.8 | 0.9 | 3 353 | 2.3 | 125 | 3.7 | 3 222 | 31.6 | 30.1 |
| Colfax | 3 726 | 78.4 | 81 800 | 21.4 | 13.5 | 645 | 24.3 | 5.4 | 5 927 | 0.0 | 199 | 3.4 | 5 058 | 22.0 | 50.8 |
| Cuming | 3 795 | 75.8 | 88 300 | 20.7 | 11.9 | 556 | 21.4 | 2.6 | 5 265 | 0.6 | 150 | 2.8 | 4 716 | 34.2 | 30.7 |
| Custer | 4 545 | 76.8 | 74 600 | 19.1 | 12.3 | 486 | 20.2 | 1.2 | 6 485 | 2.2 | 176 | 2.7 | 5 480 | 31.7 | 31.6 |
| Dakota | 7 301 | 64.4 | 99 700 | 21.3 | 12.9 | 651 | 30.5 | 5.1 | 11 524 | 1.6 | 712 | 6.2 | 10 894 | 19.1 | 39.3 |
| Dawes | 3 601 | 61.9 | 90 900 | 23.8 | 15.8 | 532 | 26.2 | 4.0 | 4 979 | -0.5 | 195 | 3.9 | 4 941 | 29.9 | 24.0 |
| Dawson | 8 899 | 70.8 | 85 400 | 20.2 | 12.9 | 582 | 25.4 | 5.8 | 12 713 | 1.4 | 570 | 4.5 | 12 136 | 22.0 | 45.7 |
| Deuel | 906 | 75.5 | 65 500 | 23.0 | 12.3 | 476 | 23.5 | 0.4 | 1 274 | 18.1 | 37 | 2.9 | 988 | 21.9 | 33.3 |
| Dixon | 2 378 | 77.7 | 76 500 | 20.6 | 12.6 | 483 | 22.4 | 2.5 | 3 218 | 1.3 | 137 | 4.3 | 3 003 | 29.2 | 34.5 |
| Dodge | 15 097 | 67.6 | 110 100 | 21.3 | 13.4 | 631 | 24.8 | 2.4 | 20 173 | 1.0 | 849 | 4.2 | 18 270 | 24.2 | 31.9 |
| Douglas | 199 576 | 64.1 | 142 400 | 22.4 | 13.2 | 748 | 29.1 | 2.2 | 281 254 | 1.4 | 12 795 | 4.5 | 265 601 | 38.3 | 18.2 |
| Dundy | 906 | 71.3 | 71 700 | 19.5 | 12.3 | 369 | 16.5 | 0.0 | 1 160 | 2.8 | 35 | 3.0 | 1 047 | 45.1 | 30.8 |
| Fillmore | 2 532 | 78.2 | 74 700 | 17.9 | 12.9 | 511 | 24.7 | 0.2 | 3 329 | 1.4 | 111 | 3.3 | 3 053 | 34.8 | 28.2 |
| Franklin | 1 370 | 81.8 | 54 800 | 19.0 | 13.9 | 563 | 23.2 | 1.2 | 1 837 | 0.1 | 58 | 3.2 | 1 480 | 33.8 | 31.1 |
| Frontier | 1 145 | 77.1 | 75 100 | 22.0 | 12.3 | 487 | 15.7 | 0.8 | 1 719 | 2.2 | 50 | 2.9 | 1 435 | 37.4 | 25.4 |
| Furnas | 2 153 | 76.3 | 54 800 | 23.9 | 13.1 | 463 | 22.3 | 0.3 | 2 637 | 0.4 | 92 | 3.5 | 2 348 | 29.4 | 27.2 |
| Gage | 9 121 | 72.6 | 99 700 | 21.1 | 13.2 | 565 | 23.7 | 1.2 | 11 923 | 0.5 | 544 | 4.6 | 10 762 | 31.6 | 27.2 |
| Garden | 956 | 71.1 | 63 800 | 27.4 | 12.2 | 484 | 24.3 | 0.0 | 1 156 | 3.8 | 42 | 3.6 | 1 063 | 32.5 | 22.6 |
| Garfield | 892 | 74.7 | 79 600 | 21.0 | 14.6 | 393 | 26.3 | 0.0 | 1 164 | 3.0 | 37 | 3.2 | 1 124 | 28.7 | 30.2 |
| Gosper | 818 | 80.4 | 103 600 | 23.4 | 13.2 | 566 | 23.0 | 0.6 | 1 090 | 1.2 | 31 | 2.8 | 1 092 | 26.9 | 33.1 |
| Grant | 292 | 64.0 | 44 700 | 22.9 | 11.0 | 615 | 25.3 | 1.0 | 437 | 2.6 | 16 | 3.7 | 370 | 39.2 | 38.4 |
| Greeley | 1 024 | 81.2 | 55 500 | 20.9 | 12.5 | 413 | 18.1 | 2.6 | 1 344 | -2.1 | 48 | 3.6 | 1 266 | 38.5 | 30.7 |
| Hall | 21 975 | 66.1 | 110 900 | 21.0 | 13.0 | 611 | 24.7 | 4.1 | 33 626 | 1.2 | 1 263 | 3.8 | 30 481 | 25.4 | 31.7 |
| Hamilton | 3 396 | 79.3 | 109 100 | 19.9 | 11.4 | 645 | 20.3 | 1.0 | 5 697 | 1.0 | 158 | 2.8 | 4 845 | 32.9 | 27.5 |
| Harlan | 1 525 | 81.8 | 67 500 | 19.6 | 11.1 | 446 | 24.0 | 1.2 | 1 898 | 2.9 | 60 | 3.2 | 1 735 | 37.4 | 27.9 |
| Hayes | 443 | 70.2 | 70 300 | 19.7 | 10.8 | 669 | 25.6 | 4.3 | 562 | 3.1 | 19 | 3.4 | 537 | 33.5 | 35.2 |
| Hitchcock | 1 350 | 74.0 | 50 200 | 18.0 | 12.4 | 477 | 18.8 | 3.2 | 1 484 | 0.6 | 53 | 3.6 | 1 360 | 34.1 | 35.5 |
| Holt | 4 269 | 76.0 | 86 800 | 18.6 | 13.2 | 519 | 22.3 | 1.1 | 6 560 | 1.3 | 188 | 2.9 | 5 490 | 35.0 | 27.4 |
| Hooker | 329 | 83.0 | 64 500 | 18.8 | 15.8 | 425 | 22.5 | 1.2 | 498 | 5.5 | 21 | 4.2 | 392 | 39.3 | 32.1 |
| Howard | 2 641 | 77.5 | 93 500 | 22.8 | 12.8 | 557 | 22.7 | 1.6 | 3 598 | 1.3 | 119 | 3.3 | 3 210 | 32.1 | 31.0 |
| Jefferson | 3 233 | 80.9 | 71 000 | 19.3 | 14.2 | 485 | 21.3 | 0.8 | 4 504 | -0.4 | 162 | 3.6 | 3 970 | 32.4 | 27.2 |
| Johnson | 1 984 | 77.0 | 78 300 | 21.5 | 13.6 | 478 | 19.4 | 2.0 | 2 803 | -0.5 | 105 | 3.7 | 2 278 | 23.4 | 38.6 |
| Kearney | 2 616 | 78.8 | 99 100 | 19.4 | 11.8 | 543 | 22.6 | 1.7 | 3 764 | 1.3 | 111 | 2.9 | 3 565 | 31.4 | 31.1 |
| Keith | 3 811 | 73.7 | 91 200 | 19.8 | 13.7 | 552 | 22.1 | 2.0 | 4 681 | 1.3 | 166 | 3.5 | 4 209 | 34.4 | 28.1 |
| Keya Paha | 361 | 82.0 | 68 000 | 32.5 | 12.2 | 472 | 17.5 | 2.2 | 434 | 3.6 | 19 | 4.4 | 437 | 47.1 | 24.7 |
| Kimball | 1 727 | 69.7 | 76 800 | 22.6 | 13.5 | 600 | 26.4 | 2.4 | 2 055 | 2.3 | 72 | 3.5 | 1 950 | 33.3 | 30.8 |
| Knox | 3 834 | 74.1 | 68 400 | 19.7 | 12.5 | 404 | 19.2 | 1.5 | 5 015 | 1.4 | 158 | 3.2 | 4 337 | 32.6 | 28.2 |
| Lancaster | 112 904 | 61.8 | 146 200 | 22.5 | 11.4 | 690 | 28.7 | 2.0 | 166 510 | 2.1 | 5 919 | 3.6 | 154 133 | 38.6 | 19.1 |
| Lincoln | 15 127 | 69.2 | 111 900 | 20.4 | 13.9 | 581 | 25.4 | 1.2 | 21 838 | -0.5 | 748 | 3.4 | 17 806 | 27.9 | 32.8 |
| Logan | 317 | 74.4 | 76 000 | 24.0 | 12.4 | 570 | 20.7 | 3.2 | 469 | -0.6 | 10 | 2.1 | 401 | 35.4 | 32.4 |
| Loup | 262 | 78.2 | 70 400 | 35.7 | 12.2 | 525 | 18.0 | 0.0 | 437 | 22.4 | 14 | 3.2 | 312 | 42.6 | 36.5 |
| McPherson | 175 | 69.7 | 77 500 | 26.6 | 9.9 | 294 | 20.4 | 0.0 | 326 | 0.3 | 10 | 3.1 | 239 | 40.6 | 27.6 |
| Madison | 13 748 | 66.4 | 103 300 | 19.5 | 12.2 | 541 | 26.2 | 2.7 | 19 567 | 0.7 | 703 | 3.6 | 18 304 | 27.6 | 30.6 |
| Merrick | 3 234 | 71.9 | 79 800 | 19.7 | 12.0 | 516 | 22.8 | 1.0 | 4 250 | 1.1 | 150 | 3.5 | 3 934 | 29.0 | 29.6 |
| Morrill | 2 062 | 69.1 | 77 300 | 19.2 | 13.1 | 610 | 23.2 | 2.9 | 2 931 | 3.4 | 85 | 2.9 | 2 486 | 29.5 | 34.5 |
| Nance | 1 516 | 78.4 | 65 100 | 17.3 | 10.9 | 518 | 25.6 | 3.1 | 2 349 | 3.7 | 69 | 2.9 | 1 804 | 37.4 | 33.3 |
| Nemaha | 3 049 | 71.0 | 80 800 | 18.2 | 12.4 | 470 | 23.2 | 1.3 | 3 505 | -1.4 | 190 | 5.4 | 3 452 | 32.3 | 26.4 |
| Nuckolls | 2 024 | 78.6 | 50 500 | 23.8 | 12.8 | 470 | 21.4 | 0.6 | 2 399 | 0.5 | 84 | 3.5 | 2 062 | 25.3 | 32.6 |
| Otoe | 6 406 | 72.4 | 116 700 | 21.0 | 12.5 | 598 | 24.6 | 1.3 | 9 048 | -0.2 | 380 | 4.2 | 8 080 | 32.4 | 28.3 |
| Pawnee | 1 290 | 79.9 | 57 200 | 21.2 | 11.9 | 490 | 19.6 | 2.3 | 1 729 | 1.8 | 53 | 3.1 | 1 337 | 32.2 | 29.8 |
| Perkins | 1 216 | 73.1 | 84 800 | 17.5 | 11.7 | 580 | 19.5 | 0.3 | 1 788 | 3.4 | 47 | 2.6 | 1 587 | 40.2 | 25.0 |
| Phelps | 3 851 | 72.5 | 93 300 | 19.2 | 13.1 | 521 | 23.1 | 1.1 | 5 325 | 1.3 | 148 | 2.8 | 4 688 | 30.0 | 28.6 |
| Pierce | 2 931 | 81.7 | 92 200 | 21.8 | 12.6 | 525 | 22.5 | 0.8 | 3 981 | 0.9 | 136 | 3.4 | 3 878 | 30.7 | 33.9 |

1. Specified owner-occupied units. 2. A value of 9.9 represents 9.9 percent or less. 3. Specified renter-occupied units. A value of 10.0 represents 10 percent or less. 4. Overcrowded or lacking complete plumbing facilities. 5. Percent of civilian labor force. 6. Persons 16 years old and over.

# Table B. States and Counties — Nonfarm Employment and Agriculture

| STATE County | Private nonfarm establishments, employment and payroll, 2011 | | | | | | | | | Agriculture, 2007 | | | |
| | Employment | | | | | | | Annual payroll | | Farms | | | Farm operators whose principal occupation is farming (percent) |
| | | | | | | | Professional, scientific, and technical services | | | | Percent with: | | |
| | Number of establishments | Total | Health care and social assistance | Manufacturing | Retail trade | Finance and insurance | | Total (mil dol) | Average per employee (dollars) | Number | Fewer than 50 acres | 500 acres or more | |
| | 104 | 105 | 106 | 107 | 108 | 109 | 110 | 111 | 112 | 113 | 114 | 115 | 116 |
| NEBRASKA—Cont'd | | | | | | | | | | | | | |
| Blaine | 9 | D | NA | NA | D | D | NA | D | D | 114 | 6.1 | 70.2 | 75.4 |
| Boone | 194 | 1 606 | D | 110 | 271 | 74 | 24 | 49 | 30 818 | 619 | 8.1 | 42.3 | 66.1 |
| Box Butte | 314 | 2 980 | 639 | D | 500 | 125 | 85 | 90 | 30 215 | 466 | 11.8 | 55.4 | 61.6 |
| Boyd | 73 | 368 | D | D | 89 | D | D | 9 | 23 620 | 259 | 8.5 | 52.5 | 66.8 |
| Brown | 140 | 842 | 184 | D | 245 | 47 | D | 20 | 24 312 | 292 | 14.7 | 55.5 | 55.1 |
| Buffalo | 1 518 | 21 204 | 3 917 | 3 404 | 3 599 | 611 | 623 | 687 | 32 396 | 949 | 20.7 | 38.9 | 61.7 |
| Burt | 206 | 1 230 | 195 | D | 184 | D | D | 33 | 26 891 | 549 | 20.6 | 30.6 | 58.8 |
| Butler | 206 | 2 087 | 389 | 596 | D | D | 37 | 64 | 30 883 | 809 | 15.6 | 30.3 | 60.9 |
| Cass | 525 | 3 289 | D | 328 | 620 | 218 | 90 | 104 | 31 721 | 682 | 34.6 | 26.0 | 50.9 |
| Cedar | 306 | 1 814 | D | D | 349 | 124 | D | 53 | 29 174 | 924 | 16.9 | 32.3 | 63.6 |
| Chase | 145 | 1 072 | D | D | 246 | 63 | D | 36 | 33 761 | 347 | 12.7 | 57.1 | 62.8 |
| Cherry | 215 | 1 747 | D | D | 436 | 54 | 56 | 40 | 22 788 | 560 | 10.4 | 70.4 | 70.7 |
| Cheyenne | 286 | 4 626 | D | D | 1 044 | 131 | 70 | 207 | 44 653 | 603 | 8.5 | 56.6 | 58.7 |
| Clay | 184 | 1 136 | 159 | D | 251 | D | D | 33 | 29 467 | 454 | 18.7 | 48.7 | 77.3 |
| Colfax | 251 | 3 483 | 288 | D | 281 | 115 | 70 | 110 | 31 506 | 519 | 24.1 | 29.7 | 61.5 |
| Cuming | 353 | 2 614 | 388 | 403 | 412 | 171 | D | 84 | 32 137 | 863 | 19.7 | 27.7 | 63.5 |
| Custer | 380 | 2 540 | 592 | D | 496 | D | 98 | 74 | 29 315 | 1 187 | 16.3 | 55.5 | 66.0 |
| Dakota | 431 | 10 937 | 567 | D | 870 | D | 66 | 354 | 32 372 | 278 | 26.3 | 23.7 | 57.2 |
| Dawes | 292 | 2 302 | 588 | D | 654 | D | 61 | 57 | 24 949 | 469 | 10.4 | 55.2 | 57.1 |
| Dawson | 693 | 9 232 | 1 084 | D | 1 519 | 265 | 179 | 280 | 30 292 | 728 | 21.2 | 40.9 | 63.5 |
| Deuel | 60 | 351 | D | NA | 72 | 24 | D | 9 | 24 940 | 240 | 8.3 | 52.5 | 62.5 |
| Dixon | 112 | 1 007 | D | D | D | D | D | 31 | 30 897 | 568 | 17.6 | 29.4 | 49.6 |
| Dodge | 1 008 | 14 387 | 2 622 | 3 190 | 2 396 | 480 | 214 | 452 | 31 387 | 715 | 23.6 | 31.3 | 62.7 |
| Douglas | 14 761 | 302 633 | 45 129 | 21 085 | 35 400 | 33 718 | 19 098 | 13 084 | 44 233 | 362 | 54.4 | 15.5 | 43.9 |
| Dundy | 65 | 352 | D | D | 44 | D | D | 11 | 31 955 | 263 | 4.9 | 63.9 | 70.7 |
| Fillmore | 215 | 1 523 | 278 | 184 | 209 | 123 | 25 | 51 | 33 165 | 478 | 9.6 | 51.5 | 78.2 |
| Franklin | 73 | 434 | D | NA | 93 | 43 | D | 11 | 26 012 | 312 | 13.5 | 48.7 | 68.6 |
| Frontier | 73 | 482 | 45 | D | 83 | 31 | 16 | 11 | 22 971 | 283 | 11.0 | 62.9 | 67.5 |
| Furnas | 178 | 1 436 | 322 | 95 | 388 | 113 | D | 43 | 30 108 | 365 | 13.2 | 55.9 | 67.7 |
| Gage | 642 | 6 825 | 1 793 | 1 243 | 1 011 | 199 | 119 | 191 | 28 015 | 1 280 | 21.9 | 23.0 | 52.0 |
| Garden | 51 | 376 | D | D | 71 | 22 | D | 9 | 24 037 | 297 | 9.8 | 63.0 | 60.9 |
| Garfield | 93 | 602 | 106 | 105 | 137 | D | D | 13 | 21 161 | 223 | 9.9 | 51.1 | 69.1 |
| Gosper | 66 | 241 | D | D | D | 30 | D | 7 | 29 921 | 218 | 9.2 | 56.9 | 69.7 |
| Grant | 32 | 101 | NA | D | D | D | D | 2 | 23 079 | 84 | 10.7 | 64.3 | 79.8 |
| Greeley | 69 | 406 | D | D | 91 | 38 | NA | 9 | 22 384 | 334 | 12.3 | 44.3 | 64.7 |
| Hall | 1 824 | 30 143 | 4 202 | 7 173 | 5 553 | 1 253 | 639 | 963 | 31 940 | 608 | 23.0 | 33.6 | 62.7 |
| Hamilton | 298 | 2 501 | 331 | 475 | 305 | 117 | 75 | 82 | 32 944 | 550 | 16.2 | 43.1 | 70.5 |
| Harlan | 96 | 613 | D | D | D | 39 | 32 | 15 | 23 667 | 384 | 19.0 | 47.1 | 65.1 |
| Hayes | 20 | 53 | D | D | D | D | D | 1 | 20 264 | 275 | 5.1 | 53.5 | 62.9 |
| Hitchcock | 67 | 427 | D | 82 | D | D | NA | 15 | 35 660 | 272 | 8.5 | 53.7 | 58.5 |
| Holt | 419 | 3 191 | 743 | 213 | 660 | 161 | 62 | 94 | 29 341 | 1 171 | 10.3 | 55.1 | 70.6 |
| Hooker | 31 | 109 | D | D | D | D | D | 4 | 36 000 | 88 | 9.1 | 79.5 | 73.9 |
| Howard | 143 | 960 | D | D | 261 | 85 | D | 21 | 21 984 | 564 | 24.1 | 31.6 | 57.4 |
| Jefferson | 231 | 2 473 | D | 515 | 478 | 94 | 47 | 70 | 28 344 | 601 | 16.8 | 35.3 | 57.7 |
| Johnson | 124 | 885 | 289 | D | 141 | D | 11 | 22 | 24 375 | 541 | 17.0 | 20.1 | 44.5 |
| Kearney | 167 | 1 869 | 580 | 181 | 168 | 79 | 23 | 51 | 27 247 | 381 | 13.1 | 56.2 | 78.0 |
| Keith | 354 | 2 623 | D | D | 515 | D | D | 72 | 27 562 | 398 | 15.3 | 42.2 | 54.8 |
| Keya Paha | 26 | D | D | D | D | D | D | 1 | D | 206 | 6.3 | 75.7 | 72.8 |
| Kimball | 127 | 1 015 | D | D | 148 | D | 23 | 33 | 32 349 | 372 | 8.3 | 54.0 | 48.1 |
| Knox | 252 | 1 549 | 281 | D | 404 | 147 | 58 | 33 | 21 385 | 863 | 11.4 | 42.6 | 68.9 |
| Lancaster | 7 779 | 125 461 | 22 198 | 11 698 | 16 724 | 10 022 | 9 078 | 4 624 | 36 855 | 1 698 | 45.5 | 13.5 | 41.2 |
| Lincoln | 1 041 | 11 273 | 2 390 | 294 | 2 211 | 465 | 465 | 339 | 30 069 | 1 053 | 19.9 | 48.1 | 57.1 |
| Logan | 21 | 96 | D | D | D | D | D | 2 | 21 021 | 152 | 11.8 | 56.6 | 67.8 |
| Loup | 11 | D | NA | NA | D | D | NA | D | D | 137 | 13.9 | 60.6 | 70.1 |
| McPherson | 4 | 10 | NA | NA | D | D | NA | 0 | 14 400 | 143 | 7.0 | 75.5 | 72.0 |
| Madison | 1 289 | 17 985 | 3 598 | 3 126 | 2 946 | 708 | 659 | 568 | 31 606 | 699 | 22.6 | 28.8 | 58.1 |
| Merrick | 232 | 1 627 | D | 198 | D | 88 | 37 | 52 | 31 854 | 473 | 21.8 | 36.2 | 66.0 |
| Morrill | 113 | 677 | 164 | D | 171 | D | D | 20 | 29 362 | 495 | 13.7 | 52.5 | 58.6 |
| Nance | 96 | 479 | 146 | NA | 89 | 49 | D | 11 | 22 802 | 362 | 15.2 | 40.9 | 64.9 |
| Nemaha | 195 | 1 435 | 355 | D | 253 | 104 | D | 42 | 29 234 | 449 | 18.0 | 29.0 | 55.2 |
| Nuckolls | 172 | 1 212 | 375 | D | 253 | D | D | 30 | 24 555 | 405 | 11.1 | 48.4 | 61.2 |
| Otoe | 476 | 5 905 | D | 2 104 | 770 | 181 | 79 | 211 | 35 794 | 804 | 23.4 | 25.4 | 48.9 |
| Pawnee | 69 | 574 | 126 | D | 55 | 52 | D | 17 | 30 427 | 489 | 12.9 | 29.0 | 46.8 |
| Perkins | 118 | 791 | D | D | 118 | 43 | 23 | 28 | 35 200 | 446 | 7.6 | 54.0 | 60.8 |
| Phelps | 333 | 3 566 | 798 | D | 366 | 162 | D | 122 | 34 152 | 420 | 14.3 | 51.9 | 73.1 |
| Pierce | 212 | 1 417 | 406 | D | 198 | 95 | D | 41 | 28 735 | 645 | 18.8 | 31.3 | 59.7 |

# Table B. States and Counties — Agriculture

| STATE County | Land in farms Acreage (1,000) | Percent change, 2002–2007 | Acres Average size of farm | Total irrigated (1,000) | Total cropland (1,000) | Value of land and buildings (dollars) Average per farm | Average per acre | Value of machinery and equipment, average per farm (dollars) | Value of products sold Total (mil dol) | Average per farm (dollars) | Crops | Live-stock and poultry products | $10,000 or more | $100,000 or more | Government payments Total ($1,000) | Percent of farms |
|---|---|---|---|---|---|---|---|---|---|---|---|---|---|---|---|---|
| | 117 | 118 | 119 | 120 | 121 | 122 | 123 | 124 | 125 | 126 | 127 | 128 | 129 | 130 | 131 | 132 |
| NEBRASKA—Cont'd | | | | | | | | | | | | | | | | |
| Blaine | 443 | 0.5 | 3 888 | 13.7 | 43.2 | 1 759 495 | 453 | 127 929 | 28.7 | 251 544 | 11.7 | 88.3 | 78.1 | 47.4 | 457 | 29.8 |
| Boone | 405 | -6.0 | 655 | 173.1 | 282.7 | 1 213 396 | 1 853 | 221 725 | 300.2 | 484 998 | 35.0 | 65.0 | 83.7 | 53.0 | 5 211 | 84.2 |
| Box Butte | 671 | -0.6 | 1 440 | 143.0 | 384.4 | 1 186 522 | 824 | 196 449 | 188.8 | 405 125 | 51.0 | 49.0 | 68.7 | 43.1 | 4 575 | 75.5 |
| Boyd | 252 | -18.2 | 972 | 4.5 | 90.3 | 759 552 | 781 | 123 492 | 46.9 | 181 042 | 24.3 | 75.7 | 79.2 | 35.1 | 954 | 74.1 |
| Brown | 662 | -3.5 | 2 266 | 51.9 | 114.8 | 1 133 653 | 500 | 172 599 | 165.0 | 565 057 | 12.2 | 87.8 | 67.1 | 42.1 | 1 448 | 47.6 |
| Buffalo | 612 | 1.8 | 645 | 269.1 | 371.6 | 1 083 891 | 1 680 | 164 249 | 259.7 | 273 629 | 58.1 | 41.9 | 70.3 | 43.3 | 6 979 | 67.1 |
| Burt | 275 | -11.3 | 501 | 42.9 | 246.6 | 1 249 668 | 2 494 | 144 533 | 145.9 | 265 707 | 63.2 | 36.8 | 66.8 | 44.1 | 5 191 | 78.9 |
| Butler | 356 | -5.1 | 440 | 118.0 | 295.6 | 1 081 926 | 2 458 | 137 671 | 182.6 | 225 679 | 66.4 | 33.6 | 69.3 | 40.5 | 6 797 | 85.9 |
| Cass | 281 | -12.2 | 412 | 3.0 | 246.9 | 1 057 235 | 2 567 | 122 385 | 98.2 | 143 918 | 89.8 | 10.2 | 59.5 | 33.6 | 4 008 | 70.4 |
| Cedar | 475 | 3.3 | 514 | 112.1 | 366.0 | 1 020 642 | 1 986 | 147 754 | 268.0 | 290 071 | 43.3 | 56.7 | 75.0 | 44.2 | 6 106 | 78.0 |
| Chase | 556 | 3.0 | 1 602 | 185.3 | 309.6 | 1 607 310 | 1 003 | 324 228 | 189.1 | 544 867 | 66.2 | 33.8 | 70.0 | 51.3 | 6 471 | 77.5 |
| Cherry | 3 760 | -0.5 | 6 714 | 44.7 | 414.7 | 2 725 129 | 406 | 126 883 | 142.5 | 254 457 | 9.8 | 90.2 | 75.4 | 50.7 | 1 218 | 22.3 |
| Cheyenne | 755 | -6.0 | 1 251 | 51.3 | 556.0 | 927 431 | 741 | 138 262 | 151.9 | 251 880 | 44.4 | 55.6 | 67.0 | 36.3 | 7 452 | 88.4 |
| Clay | 365 | -2.4 | 804 | 218.1 | 291.5 | 1 841 728 | 2 290 | 270 725 | 261.7 | 576 322 | 49.4 | 50.6 | 79.7 | 61.9 | 6 296 | 76.0 |
| Colfax | 213 | -12.7 | 411 | 62.5 | 187.7 | 1 007 713 | 2 453 | 169 620 | 250.8 | 483 193 | 30.3 | 69.7 | 74.4 | 44.9 | 3 301 | 77.3 |
| Cuming | 360 | -1.6 | 417 | 51.2 | 305.1 | 1 040 286 | 2 493 | 189 440 | 856.6 | 992 599 | 14.5 | 85.5 | 80.8 | 54.3 | 5 279 | 77.4 |
| Custer | 1 614 | 7.5 | 1 360 | 333.4 | 574.1 | 1 386 763 | 1 020 | 184 323 | 513.8 | 432 831 | 38.1 | 61.9 | 72.5 | 42.5 | 8 350 | 58.5 |
| Dakota | 167 | 9.9 | 599 | 20.4 | 147.8 | 1 057 606 | 1 765 | 187 147 | 63.4 | 228 168 | 87.1 | 12.9 | 55.0 | 29.9 | 2 966 | 75.5 |
| Dawes | 849 | 8.0 | 1 810 | 17.6 | 202.9 | 1 019 756 | 563 | 91 765 | 45.8 | 97 732 | 25.2 | 74.8 | 65.9 | 27.3 | 2 527 | 69.1 |
| Dawson | 641 | 2.9 | 880 | 263.9 | 330.7 | 1 176 513 | 1 337 | 199 439 | 588.5 | 808 444 | 25.7 | 74.3 | 72.8 | 47.3 | 6 721 | 60.4 |
| Deuel | 279 | -5.1 | 1 162 | 17.9 | 231.8 | 823 459 | 709 | 146 724 | 53.1 | 221 120 | D | D | 75.0 | 40.8 | 2 716 | 86.3 |
| Dixon | 249 | -10.1 | 438 | 21.6 | 188.7 | 806 327 | 1 843 | 98 801 | 143.3 | 252 301 | 39.6 | 60.4 | 55.3 | 30.3 | 4 759 | 79.8 |
| Dodge | 338 | -0.3 | 473 | 116.1 | 305.1 | 1 256 529 | 2 654 | 180 820 | 250.4 | 350 205 | 51.7 | 48.3 | 76.9 | 46.2 | 5 063 | 77.2 |
| Douglas | 84 | -11.6 | 233 | 13.8 | 72.9 | 848 960 | 3 642 | 130 134 | 46.3 | 128 012 | 94.6 | 5.4 | 46.1 | 23.5 | 1 230 | 48.6 |
| Dundy | 595 | 4.9 | 2 262 | 112.7 | 254.2 | 1 856 209 | 821 | 240 571 | 145.6 | 553 728 | 50.8 | 49.2 | 76.8 | 57.0 | 4 277 | 86.3 |
| Fillmore | 362 | -0.5 | 758 | 223.5 | 323.0 | 1 825 852 | 2 410 | 271 419 | 223.8 | 468 147 | 67.9 | 32.1 | 86.2 | 65.3 | 7 130 | 83.9 |
| Franklin | 292 | -11.8 | 934 | 87.3 | 165.0 | 1 207 777 | 1 293 | 187 213 | 78.3 | 250 944 | 77.3 | 22.7 | 74.7 | 46.2 | 4 072 | 82.7 |
| Frontier | 475 | -2.5 | 1 679 | 53.7 | 189.8 | 1 315 651 | 783 | 173 872 | 97.9 | 346 111 | 55.3 | 44.7 | 75.6 | 50.5 | 3 410 | 72.1 |
| Furnas | 446 | 1.1 | 1 221 | 51.9 | 276.5 | 1 195 189 | 978 | 162 841 | 141.9 | 388 895 | 47.0 | 53.0 | 74.8 | 49.0 | 5 057 | 85.5 |
| Gage | 540 | -2.2 | 422 | 59.3 | 413.2 | 757 853 | 1 796 | 118 186 | 173.8 | 135 785 | 62.4 | 37.6 | 61.3 | 31.3 | 10 711 | 81.6 |
| Garden | 1 049 | -2.1 | 3 530 | 44.9 | 188.0 | 1 646 862 | 466 | 151 788 | 81.1 | 273 185 | 35.9 | 64.1 | 75.8 | 43.1 | 1 995 | 70.7 |
| Garfield | 366 | 24.9 | 1 640 | 20.6 | 78.1 | 913 687 | 557 | 104 819 | 61.1 | 274 071 | 13.1 | 86.9 | 76.2 | 40.4 | 1 076 | 60.1 |
| Gosper | 226 | -13.7 | 1 035 | 81.4 | 130.4 | 1 269 983 | 1 227 | 227 140 | 74.0 | 339 652 | 73.4 | 26.6 | 78.4 | 55.5 | 2 713 | 78.9 |
| Grant | 495 | 1.0 | 5 899 | 1.5 | 45.3 | 1 784 493 | 303 | 121 056 | 16.6 | 197 923 | 0.6 | 99.4 | 73.8 | 53.6 | 25 | 8.3 |
| Greeley | 282 | -3.8 | 845 | 76.4 | 127.6 | 1 004 897 | 1 189 | 164 361 | 111.6 | 333 990 | 36.0 | 64.0 | 67.4 | 41.6 | 2 363 | 73.7 |
| Hall | 328 | 3.8 | 540 | 206.9 | 247.1 | 1 104 247 | 2 045 | 189 582 | 228.9 | 376 545 | 51.4 | 48.6 | 73.2 | 47.2 | 5 315 | 65.6 |
| Hamilton | 319 | -8.3 | 580 | 257.7 | 291.8 | 1 511 457 | 2 605 | 232 598 | 235.5 | 428 170 | 66.1 | 33.9 | 84.4 | 63.1 | 6 941 | 82.2 |
| Harlan | 351 | 13.6 | 914 | 107.6 | 224.5 | 1 047 538 | 1 146 | 180 364 | 134.3 | 349 860 | 59.2 | 40.8 | 73.7 | 45.3 | 4 315 | 76.3 |
| Hayes | 454 | 11.3 | 1 650 | 65.7 | 210.3 | 1 118 669 | 678 | 173 453 | 115.5 | 419 885 | 45.7 | 54.3 | 71.6 | 41.5 | 4 301 | 89.8 |
| Hitchcock | 348 | -19.8 | 1 279 | 19.0 | 192.6 | 982 992 | 768 | 124 248 | 58.8 | 216 017 | 64.7 | 35.3 | 65.4 | 37.9 | 3 521 | 79.0 |
| Holt | 1 533 | 3.5 | 1 309 | 339.1 | 667.6 | 1 172 798 | 896 | 176 114 | 373.6 | 319 063 | 49.5 | 50.5 | 74.4 | 44.9 | 8 615 | 58.0 |
| Hooker | 457 | 7.8 | 5 190 | 3.0 | 22.1 | 1 778 035 | 343 | 65 409 | 11.0 | 124 700 | 0.7 | 99.3 | 72.7 | 37.5 | 157 | 22.7 |
| Howard | 279 | -5.1 | 494 | 104.3 | 157.8 | 770 669 | 1 559 | 120 972 | 145.4 | 257 879 | 37.3 | 62.7 | 67.0 | 37.6 | 3 140 | 70.9 |
| Jefferson | 326 | -10.4 | 542 | 81.0 | 232.7 | 970 708 | 1 792 | 124 799 | 131.7 | 219 132 | 59.2 | 40.8 | 63.1 | 35.8 | 5 722 | 78.7 |
| Johnson | 176 | -14.1 | 324 | 11.3 | 114.0 | 498 010 | 1 535 | 71 863 | 44.0 | 81 323 | 56.9 | 43.1 | 47.3 | 20.1 | 3 804 | 86.0 |
| Kearney | 324 | -2.1 | 851 | 216.3 | 272.2 | 1 708 240 | 2 007 | 302 401 | 264.3 | 693 652 | 50.9 | 49.1 | 85.6 | 66.1 | 5 840 | 78.7 |
| Keith | 582 | -7.3 | 1 461 | 116.1 | 260.2 | 1 251 849 | 857 | 173 593 | 142.1 | 357 112 | 57.7 | 42.3 | 66.8 | 39.9 | 3 319 | 68.8 |
| Keya Paha | 483 | 4.3 | 2 347 | 18.1 | 101.4 | 1 302 181 | 555 | 148 106 | 48.5 | 235 218 | 20.1 | 79.9 | 78.6 | 42.2 | 555 | 46.6 |
| Kimball | 528 | -4.0 | 1 418 | 33.3 | 346.0 | 993 252 | 700 | 113 483 | 35.8 | 96 204 | 80.3 | 19.7 | 41.4 | 20.2 | 4 869 | 82.0 |
| Knox | 536 | -10.5 | 622 | 51.8 | 273.6 | 905 312 | 1 456 | 139 020 | 226.5 | 262 510 | 28.4 | 71.6 | 76.2 | 39.6 | 4 976 | 78.9 |
| Lancaster | 421 | -6.2 | 248 | 15.6 | 323.6 | 629 050 | 2 535 | 82 805 | 125.9 | 74 152 | 78.5 | 21.5 | 39.9 | 17.0 | 6 864 | 66.8 |
| Lincoln | 1 601 | 4.7 | 1 521 | 322.9 | 527.0 | 1 268 708 | 834 | 179 875 | 431.9 | 410 131 | 45.6 | 54.4 | 63.5 | 37.8 | 7 902 | 52.5 |
| Logan | 363 | 1.1 | 2 391 | 24.8 | 70.0 | 1 220 963 | 511 | 129 154 | 31.4 | 206 756 | 44.3 | 55.7 | 73.7 | 39.5 | 872 | 60.5 |
| Loup | 355 | 5.0 | 2 589 | 10.4 | 35.3 | 1 163 578 | 449 | 97 833 | 26.1 | 190 485 | 12.4 | 87.6 | 76.6 | 36.5 | 546 | 62.0 |
| McPherson | 542 | 2.5 | 3 793 | 9.7 | 34.9 | 1 383 080 | 365 | 72 724 | 24.0 | 167 650 | 4.0 | 96.0 | 73.4 | 37.1 | 267 | 24.5 |
| Madison | 315 | -7.9 | 451 | 107.9 | 258.0 | 977 194 | 2 167 | 141 271 | 220.5 | 315 519 | 42.5 | 57.5 | 69.7 | 38.2 | 4 325 | 70.2 |
| Merrick | 248 | -12.4 | 524 | 163.8 | 199.6 | 959 888 | 1 831 | 181 984 | 198.0 | 418 604 | 48.0 | 52.0 | 70.4 | 45.5 | 3 811 | 71.7 |
| Morrill | 902 | 3.4 | 1 822 | 144.6 | 266.3 | 1 177 907 | 646 | 146 539 | 245.4 | 495 780 | 25.4 | 74.6 | 70.7 | 41.4 | 4 865 | 76.6 |
| Nance | 226 | -1.3 | 625 | 69.4 | 138.2 | 910 496 | 1 456 | 157 768 | 99.3 | 274 375 | 52.5 | 47.5 | 75.7 | 47.0 | 2 856 | 78.7 |
| Nemaha | 213 | -16.5 | 474 | 8.4 | 169.5 | 926 483 | 1 956 | 133 302 | 72.1 | 160 652 | 82.6 | 17.4 | 60.1 | 34.7 | 3 097 | 82.6 |
| Nuckolls | 307 | -12.5 | 758 | 61.1 | 205.2 | 1 249 559 | 1 648 | 183 177 | 108.1 | 266 801 | 62.4 | 37.6 | 81.2 | 49.1 | 4 686 | 85.7 |
| Otoe | 322 | -6.1 | 401 | 4.2 | 258.4 | 874 306 | 2 182 | 108 819 | 103.6 | 128 855 | 77.4 | 22.6 | 58.3 | 30.2 | 5 061 | 80.6 |
| Pawnee | 218 | -15.2 | 445 | 4.6 | 139.4 | 583 162 | 1 310 | 92 757 | 47.0 | 96 122 | 70.9 | 29.1 | 50.7 | 20.7 | 4 456 | 85.7 |
| Perkins | 558 | 1.8 | 1 252 | 133.4 | 444.5 | 1 223 128 | 977 | 193 983 | 135.5 | 303 846 | 82.0 | 18.0 | 69.3 | 46.2 | 6 594 | 87.2 |
| Phelps | 340 | -7.1 | 810 | 246.8 | 281.7 | 1 663 392 | 2 053 | 278 688 | 470.2 | 1 119 572 | 30.8 | 69.2 | 86.0 | 70.2 | 5 666 | 79.5 |
| Pierce | 317 | -4.8 | 491 | 128.9 | 247.2 | 979 168 | 1 994 | 162 655 | 178.9 | 277 421 | 47.1 | 52.9 | 73.2 | 42.8 | 4 385 | 74.0 |

# Table B. States and Counties — Water Use, Wholesale Trade, Retail Trade, and Real Estate

| STATE County | Water use, 2005 | | Wholesale trade,[1] 2007 | | | | Retail trade,[2] 2007 | | | | Real estate and rental and leasing,[2] 2007 | | | |
|---|---|---|---|---|---|---|---|---|---|---|---|---|---|---|
| | Total water withdrawn (mil gal/day) | Gallons withdrawn per person | Number of establishments | Number of employees | Sales (mil dol) | Annual payroll (mil dol) | Number of establishments | Number of employees | Sales (mil dol) | Annual payroll (mil dol) | Number of establishments | Number of employees | Receipts (mil dol) | Annual payroll (mil dol) |
| | 133 | 134 | 135 | 136 | 137 | 138 | 139 | 140 | 141 | 142 | 143 | 144 | 145 | 146 |
| NEBRASKA—Cont'd | | | | | | | | | | | | | | |
| Blaine | 9.5 | 19 628 | NA | NA | NA | NA | 4 | D | D | D | NA | NA | NA | NA |
| Boone | 165.5 | 28 664 | 12 | 179 | 92.7 | 5.6 | 45 | 290 | 81.6 | 4.8 | 5 | 25 | 3.2 | 0.4 |
| Box Butte | 193.0 | 16 969 | 19 | 197 | 90.0 | 6.6 | 55 | 474 | 82.2 | 7.6 | 17 | 46 | 9.1 | 1.1 |
| Boyd | 6.0 | 2 645 | 2 | D | D | D | 14 | 120 | 13.2 | 1.0 | 1 | D | D | D |
| Brown | 80.6 | 24 207 | 4 | 50 | 26.3 | 1.4 | 29 | 226 | 48.1 | 4.0 | 1 | D | D | D |
| Buffalo | 258.3 | 5 927 | 66 | 776 | 659.3 | 33.4 | 250 | 3 653 | 739.9 | 67.8 | 62 | 210 | 34.1 | 5.1 |
| Burt | 45.4 | 6 089 | 21 | 183 | 70.4 | 5.2 | 34 | 146 | 40.6 | 2.8 | 3 | 10 | 0.3 | 0.1 |
| Butler | 123.6 | 14 179 | 13 | 107 | 118.8 | 4.5 | 26 | 402 | 72.3 | 5.9 | 1 | D | D | D |
| Cass | 20.4 | 791 | 18 | 103 | 99.1 | 3.6 | 74 | 734 | 183.6 | 13.3 | 24 | 41 | 3.9 | 0.6 |
| Cedar | 84.1 | 9 275 | 22 | 124 | 69.7 | 3.8 | 55 | 348 | 121.8 | 6.4 | 8 | 14 | 1.2 | 0.3 |
| Chase | 170.4 | 44 069 | 15 | 161 | 135.1 | 7.1 | 31 | 307 | 60.4 | 5.4 | 3 | 7 | 1.1 | 0.1 |
| Cherry | 52.4 | 8 600 | 6 | D | D | D | 48 | 468 | 78.3 | 7.6 | 6 | 7 | 1.2 | 0.2 |
| Cheyenne | 77.9 | 7 792 | 15 | 76 | 97.9 | 3.2 | 57 | D | D | D | 10 | 19 | 7.6 | 0.4 |
| Clay | 161.1 | 23 928 | 19 | 141 | 155.6 | 4.1 | 28 | 212 | 60.7 | 4.3 | 2 | D | D | D |
| Colfax | 78.4 | 7 514 | 15 | 99 | 63.6 | 3.9 | 48 | 400 | 107.6 | 8.6 | 3 | 4 | 0.2 | 0.1 |
| Cuming | 51.5 | 5 312 | 29 | 158 | 117.4 | 5.0 | 61 | 429 | 174.6 | 8.1 | 3 | 7 | 1.0 | 0.1 |
| Custer | 258.3 | 22 641 | 14 | 113 | 52.8 | 3.6 | 81 | 511 | 118.0 | 8.8 | 9 | D | D | D |
| Dakota | 22.0 | 1 082 | 19 | D | D | D | 73 | 878 | 170.3 | 16.5 | 16 | D | D | D |
| Dawes | 27.9 | 3 234 | 5 | 33 | 10.0 | 0.7 | 58 | 706 | 164.6 | 12.9 | 12 | 15 | 1.6 | 0.3 |
| Dawson | 319.2 | 12 965 | 32 | 403 | 424.7 | 14.1 | 123 | 1 576 | 345.3 | 32.8 | 22 | 46 | 4.1 | 0.6 |
| Deuel | 28.7 | 14 326 | 3 | D | D | D | 12 | 125 | 102.0 | 2.3 | 1 | D | D | D |
| Dixon | 21.5 | 3 493 | 9 | D | D | D | 18 | 219 | 37.1 | 2.5 | 1 | D | D | D |
| Dodge | 113.7 | 3 151 | 63 | D | D | D | 176 | 2 356 | 665.0 | 53.5 | 45 | 162 | 21.1 | 3.2 |
| Douglas | 789.5 | 1 621 | 760 | 10 589 | 6 079.8 | 494.7 | 1 863 | 36 151 | 8 109.0 | 805.7 | 719 | 5 588 | 961.6 | 186.2 |
| Dundy | 110.4 | 51 749 | 5 | D | D | D | 9 | 51 | 14.0 | 0.9 | 2 | D | D | D |
| Fillmore | 163.1 | 25 551 | 21 | 162 | 113.4 | 5.1 | 38 | 219 | 39.7 | 3.6 | 3 | 4 | 0.2 | 0.0 |
| Franklin | 124.4 | 36 352 | 8 | 68 | 51.2 | 1.8 | 18 | 117 | 17.3 | 1.7 | NA | NA | NA | NA |
| Frontier | 59.2 | 21 163 | 4 | D | D | D | 14 | 90 | 14.8 | 1.1 | 2 | D | D | D |
| Furnas | 57.5 | 11 462 | 12 | 91 | 88.6 | 2.6 | 35 | 224 | 50.2 | 4.0 | 3 | 3 | 0.6 | 0.0 |
| Gage | 102.6 | 4 403 | 32 | D | D | D | 118 | 1 164 | 238.1 | 22.4 | 22 | 69 | 8.1 | 1.3 |
| Garden | 57.5 | 28 778 | 5 | D | D | D | 11 | 72 | 12.4 | 0.9 | NA | NA | NA | NA |
| Garfield | 20.2 | 11 096 | 4 | 64 | 9.2 | 0.9 | 24 | 124 | 27.1 | 1.9 | 1 | D | D | D |
| Gosper | 67.6 | 33 475 | 5 | D | D | D | 7 | 23 | 2.3 | 0.2 | 4 | 13 | 4.3 | 0.5 |
| Grant | 2.9 | 4 358 | 4 | 26 | 8.3 | 0.5 | 6 | D | D | D | NA | NA | NA | NA |
| Greeley | 97.4 | 38 786 | 4 | 45 | 23.8 | 1.1 | 19 | 91 | 25.4 | 1.7 | 1 | D | D | D |
| Hall | 240.2 | 4 358 | 100 | 1 192 | 707.9 | 50.5 | 336 | 5 113 | 1 087.7 | 99.4 | 68 | 261 | 44.6 | 7.2 |
| Hamilton | 293.4 | 30 666 | 13 | 322 | 375.5 | 12.9 | 41 | 308 | 101.1 | 5.1 | 8 | D | D | D |
| Harlan | 80.0 | 23 094 | 11 | 55 | 55.1 | 1.4 | 17 | 96 | 26.0 | 1.8 | 1 | D | D | D |
| Hayes | 52.7 | 51 344 | NA | NA | NA | NA | 2 | D | D | D | NA | NA | NA | NA |
| Hitchcock | 45.9 | 15 465 | 7 | 28 | 18.7 | 0.5 | 10 | D | D | D | NA | NA | NA | NA |
| Holt | 271.2 | 25 145 | 37 | 395 | 149.3 | 8.6 | 87 | 716 | 143.2 | 10.3 | 9 | 25 | 4.2 | 1.1 |
| Hooker | 4.3 | 5 780 | 1 | D | D | D | 7 | D | D | D | NA | NA | NA | NA |
| Howard | 131.2 | 19 557 | 7 | 49 | 38.4 | 1.6 | 30 | 260 | 48.4 | 3.8 | 2 | D | D | D |
| Jefferson | 60.0 | 7 576 | 16 | 132 | 139.0 | 4.8 | 38 | 496 | 124.8 | 9.3 | 10 | 21 | 1.0 | 0.3 |
| Johnson | 13.8 | 2 946 | 4 | D | D | D | 28 | 144 | 34.4 | 2.5 | 2 | D | D | D |
| Kearney | 176.2 | 26 004 | 14 | 154 | 151.7 | 4.4 | 25 | 172 | 29.7 | 2.6 | 3 | 4 | 0.6 | 0.1 |
| Keith | 165.7 | 19 887 | 15 | 100 | 54.7 | 3.9 | 70 | 628 | 203.8 | 12.4 | 14 | 22 | 2.0 | 0.5 |
| Keya Paha | 19.7 | 21 829 | 2 | D | D | D | 4 | D | D | D | NA | NA | NA | NA |
| Kimball | 50.8 | 13 421 | 4 | D | D | D | 29 | 191 | 49.0 | 3.9 | 2 | D | D | D |
| Knox | 53.8 | 6 031 | 10 | 92 | 61.8 | 2.5 | 62 | 395 | 82.4 | 6.4 | 5 | 21 | 0.9 | 0.3 |
| Lancaster | 23.9 | 90 | 272 | 3 823 | 2 729.9 | 166.3 | 1 052 | 17 169 | 3 662.7 | 345.8 | 367 | 1 558 | 250.6 | 43.1 |
| Lincoln | 938.7 | 26 340 | 39 | 356 | 245.4 | 13.4 | 204 | 2 419 | 634.9 | 47.6 | 35 | 152 | 20.7 | 2.9 |
| Logan | 24.0 | 32 365 | 2 | D | D | D | 3 | D | D | D | NA | NA | NA | NA |
| Loup | 15.7 | 22 886 | 1 | D | D | D | 3 | D | D | D | 1 | D | D | D |
| McPherson | 96.0 | 189 428 | NA | NA | NA | NA | 3 | D | D | D | NA | NA | NA | NA |
| Madison | 18.8 | 530 | 65 | 1 797 | 1 880.2 | 61.8 | 230 | 3 067 | 649.7 | 57.8 | 61 | D | D | D |
| Merrick | 201.5 | 24 976 | 18 | 162 | 208.7 | 5.4 | 37 | 195 | 45.6 | 3.3 | 4 | D | D | D |
| Morrill | 228.0 | 44 143 | 13 | 134 | 48.1 | 4.9 | 24 | 152 | 46.2 | 2.7 | 2 | D | D | D |
| Nance | 82.3 | 22 460 | 5 | 24 | 35.0 | 0.9 | 18 | 113 | 22.4 | 1.7 | 2 | D | D | D |
| Nemaha | 1 125.0 | 161 525 | 11 | 56 | 59.9 | 2.1 | 44 | 305 | 59.3 | 4.7 | 4 | 10 | 1.0 | 0.1 |
| Nuckolls | 48.4 | 10 211 | 14 | 81 | 147.0 | 2.6 | 32 | 252 | 53.3 | 4.3 | 3 | D | D | D |
| Otoe | 471.9 | 30 429 | 19 | 139 | 238.0 | 5.4 | 84 | 858 | 146.8 | 14.1 | 16 | 48 | 6.0 | 1.1 |
| Pawnee | 5.2 | 1 803 | 2 | D | D | D | 13 | 73 | 14.4 | 1.1 | 1 | D | D | D |
| Perkins | 125.3 | 40 988 | 15 | 82 | 128.3 | 2.5 | 15 | 114 | 44.7 | 2.7 | 3 | 14 | 0.7 | 0.2 |
| Phelps | 205.0 | 21 693 | 24 | 285 | 152.0 | 10.1 | 50 | 385 | 94.5 | 7.8 | 11 | 34 | 1.5 | 0.3 |
| Pierce | 111.9 | 14 726 | 18 | 162 | 77.6 | 4.7 | 36 | 215 | 41.4 | 3.0 | 4 | D | D | D |

1. Merchant wholesalers, except manufacturers' sales branches and offices.   2. Employer establishments.

Items 133—146

| STATE County | Professional, scientific, and technical services,[1] 2007 | | | | Manufacturing, 2007 | | | | Accommodation and food services, 2007 | | | |
|---|---|---|---|---|---|---|---|---|---|---|---|---|
| | Number of establish-ments | Number of employees | Receipts (mil dol) | Annual payroll (mil dol) | Number of establish-ments | Number of employees | Receipts (mil dol) | Annual payroll (mil dol) | Number of establish-ments | Number of employees | Sales (mil dol) | Annual payroll (mil dol) |
| | 147 | 148 | 149 | 150 | 151 | 152 | 153 | 154 | 155 | 156 | 157 | 158 |
| NEBRASKA—Cont'd | | | | | | | | | | | | |
| Blaine | NA | NA | NA | NA | NA | NA | NA | NA | 1 | D | D | D |
| Boone | 7 | 23 | 4.1 | 0.6 | NA | NA | NA | NA | 17 | 113 | 3.6 | 0.8 |
| Box Butte | 25 | 100 | 7.3 | 2.3 | NA | NA | NA | NA | 34 | 410 | 12.4 | 3.3 |
| Boyd | 3 | D | D | D | NA | NA | NA | NA | 5 | D | D | D |
| Brown | 6 | 32 | 2.3 | 0.7 | NA | NA | NA | NA | 11 | 111 | 2.9 | 0.7 |
| Buffalo | 93 | 527 | 44.2 | 18.6 | 59 | 4 292 | D | D | 137 | 2 585 | 103.1 | 28.3 |
| Burt | 11 | 62 | 13.5 | 2.5 | NA | NA | NA | NA | 12 | 68 | 2.0 | 0.4 |
| Butler | 11 | 98 | 3.7 | 1.8 | 10 | 612 | D | D | 13 | 60 | 2.0 | 0.4 |
| Cass | 35 | D | D | D | NA | NA | NA | NA | 46 | 537 | 14.2 | 4.1 |
| Cedar | 11 | 56 | 5.0 | 1.3 | NA | NA | NA | NA | 17 | 176 | 3.5 | 0.9 |
| Chase | 11 | 20 | 2.5 | 0.5 | NA | NA | NA | NA | 11 | 69 | 2.0 | 0.6 |
| Cherry | 14 | 53 | 5.7 | 1.1 | NA | NA | NA | NA | 21 | 276 | 9.7 | 2.7 |
| Cheyenne | 12 | 32 | 3.4 | 1.0 | NA | NA | NA | NA | 39 | 507 | 21.1 | 5.4 |
| Clay | 6 | 22 | 2.5 | 0.6 | NA | NA | NA | NA | 7 | 36 | 1.4 | 0.3 |
| Colfax | 9 | 39 | 3.9 | 0.7 | 6 | D | D | D | 16 | 124 | 3.5 | 0.8 |
| Cuming | 20 | D | D | D | NA | NA | NA | NA | 20 | 229 | 6.5 | 2.0 |
| Custer | 25 | 81 | 7.1 | 1.8 | NA | NA | NA | NA | 31 | 292 | 8.2 | 2.3 |
| Dakota | 17 | D | D | D | 39 | D | D | D | 35 | 499 | 19.2 | 5.6 |
| Dawes | 21 | 148 | 5.7 | 1.9 | NA | NA | NA | NA | 41 | 538 | 13.7 | 4.1 |
| Dawson | 60 | D | D | D | 31 | D | D | D | 57 | 694 | 24.7 | 6.1 |
| Deuel | 4 | 7 | 0.6 | 0.2 | NA | NA | NA | NA | 7 | 93 | 4.1 | 1.3 |
| Dixon | 2 | D | D | D | 3 | D | D | D | 14 | 35 | 1.9 | 0.3 |
| Dodge | 53 | D | D | D | 61 | 3 299 | 1 233.8 | 121.2 | 98 | 1 454 | 53.0 | 13.9 |
| Douglas | 1 631 | D | D | D | 513 | 23 258 | 10 012.8 | 961.2 | 1 237 | 25 985 | 1 118.9 | 321.6 |
| Dundy | 6 | 14 | 1.3 | 0.3 | NA | NA | NA | NA | 6 | 24 | 0.5 | 0.1 |
| Fillmore | 8 | 20 | 1.3 | 0.3 | NA | NA | NA | NA | 21 | 196 | 3.5 | 0.8 |
| Franklin | 4 | 18 | 0.8 | 0.3 | NA | NA | NA | NA | 5 | 20 | 1.0 | 0.2 |
| Frontier | 2 | D | D | D | NA | NA | NA | NA | 4 | 25 | 0.6 | 0.1 |
| Furnas | 9 | 16 | 1.4 | 0.4 | NA | NA | NA | NA | 14 | D | D | D |
| Gage | 30 | 132 | 11.7 | 3.7 | 44 | 1 994 | 602.6 | 66.8 | 47 | 580 | 23.4 | 4.8 |
| Garden | 2 | D | D | D | NA | NA | NA | NA | 6 | D | D | D |
| Garfield | 5 | 18 | 1.3 | 0.4 | NA | NA | NA | NA | 9 | 66 | 1.3 | 0.3 |
| Gosper | 3 | D | D | D | NA | NA | NA | NA | 4 | 23 | 1.7 | 0.2 |
| Grant | 1 | D | D | D | NA | NA | NA | NA | 2 | D | D | D |
| Greeley | NA | NA | NA | NA | NA | NA | NA | NA | 3 | 9 | 0.4 | 0.1 |
| Hall | 99 | D | D | D | 79 | D | D | D | 136 | 2 551 | 96.9 | 28.1 |
| Hamilton | 19 | 68 | 8.0 | 2.8 | 24 | 617 | 463.4 | 20.6 | 13 | 160 | 5.1 | 1.5 |
| Harlan | 10 | 25 | 2.3 | 0.6 | NA | NA | NA | NA | 12 | 82 | 2.8 | 0.6 |
| Hayes | 2 | D | D | D | NA | NA | NA | NA | 3 | 3 | 0.3 | 0.0 |
| Hitchcock | NA | NA | NA | NA | NA | NA | NA | NA | 6 | 19 | 1.0 | 0.2 |
| Holt | 22 | 72 | 9.3 | 2.6 | NA | NA | NA | NA | 35 | 333 | 10.2 | 2.4 |
| Hooker | NA | NA | NA | NA | NA | NA | NA | NA | 5 | D | D | D |
| Howard | 8 | D | D | D | NA | NA | NA | NA | 12 | 63 | 2.8 | 0.5 |
| Jefferson | 12 | 44 | 3.4 | 1.1 | 13 | 531 | 127.9 | 19.7 | 22 | 187 | 6.4 | 1.5 |
| Johnson | 3 | 8 | 0.6 | 0.1 | NA | NA | NA | NA | 9 | 78 | 3.1 | 0.7 |
| Kearney | 10 | 16 | 1.5 | 0.5 | NA | NA | NA | NA | 14 | 94 | 2.8 | 0.7 |
| Keith | 28 | 114 | 9.2 | 3.1 | NA | NA | NA | NA | 46 | 562 | 22.8 | 5.0 |
| Keya Paha | 2 | D | D | D | NA | NA | NA | NA | 1 | D | D | D |
| Kimball | 9 | 21 | 1.4 | 0.2 | NA | NA | NA | NA | 15 | 82 | 3.1 | 0.7 |
| Knox | 18 | 64 | 5.6 | 1.5 | NA | NA | NA | NA | 23 | 74 | 3.3 | 0.5 |
| Lancaster | 773 | 8 282 | 1 102.6 | 383.8 | 252 | 13 413 | D | 540.6 | 651 | 12 028 | 472.5 | 132.9 |
| Lincoln | 81 | D | D | D | NA | NA | NA | NA | 96 | D | D | D |
| Logan | 1 | D | D | D | NA | NA | NA | NA | NA | NA | NA | NA |
| Loup | NA | NA | NA | NA | NA | NA | NA | NA | NA | NA | NA | NA |
| McPherson | NA | NA | NA | NA | NA | NA | NA | NA | 2 | D | D | D |
| Madison | 85 | D | D | D | 53 | D | D | D | 87 | 1 451 | 48.5 | 14.0 |
| Merrick | 10 | D | D | D | NA | NA | NA | NA | 16 | 176 | 3.9 | 1.1 |
| Morrill | 1 | D | D | D | NA | NA | NA | NA | 13 | 82 | 3.2 | 0.7 |
| Nance | 4 | 13 | 0.4 | 0.2 | NA | NA | NA | NA | 8 | 25 | 0.8 | 0.2 |
| Nemaha | 14 | 45 | 3.5 | 1.3 | NA | NA | NA | NA | 23 | 326 | 7.0 | 2.3 |
| Nuckolls | 10 | 31 | 2.7 | 0.6 | NA | NA | NA | NA | 8 | 81 | 2.1 | 0.5 |
| Otoe | 26 | 77 | 8.6 | 2.8 | 12 | 1 395 | 405.4 | 48.3 | 41 | 612 | 17.0 | 5.1 |
| Pawnee | 4 | D | D | D | NA | NA | NA | NA | 6 | 42 | 0.9 | 0.2 |
| Perkins | 7 | 19 | 1.7 | 0.3 | NA | NA | NA | NA | 4 | 34 | 0.8 | 0.2 |
| Phelps | 31 | 110 | 9.3 | 3.8 | 9 | D | D | D | 20 | 297 | 9.1 | 2.3 |
| Pierce | 10 | D | D | D | NA | NA | NA | NA | 9 | 81 | 1.6 | 0.4 |

1. Establishment subject to federal tax.

# Table B. States and Counties — **Health Care and Social Assistance, Other Services, and Federal Funds**

| STATE County | Health care and social assistance, 2007 | | | | Other services, 2007 | | | | Federal funds and grants, 2009–2010 Expenditures (mil dol) | | | |
|---|---|---|---|---|---|---|---|---|---|---|---|---|
| | | | | | | | | | | Direct payments for individuals[1] | | |
| | Number of establishments | Number of employees | Receipts (mil dol) | Annual payroll (mil dol) | Number of establishments | Number of employees | Receipts (mil dol) | Annual payroll (mil dol) | Total | Social Security and government retirement | Medicare | Food Stamps and Supplemental Security Income |
| | 159 | 160 | 161 | 162 | 163 | 164 | 165 | 166 | 167 | 168 | 169 | 170 |
| NEBRASKA—Cont'd | | | | | | | | | | | | |
| Blaine | NA | NA | NA | NA | NA | NA | NA | NA | 4.1 | 1.5 | 0.7 | 0.0 |
| Boone | 16 | 416 | 24.7 | 11.0 | 10 | 29 | 2.5 | 0.7 | 49.8 | 20.3 | 10.8 | 0.8 |
| Box Butte | 27 | 617 | 40.7 | 17.1 | 35 | 115 | 9.6 | 2.1 | 90.5 | 41.6 | 13.0 | 3.0 |
| Boyd | 9 | 98 | 4.2 | 1.9 | 7 | 12 | 1.1 | 0.2 | 23.6 | 8.2 | 7.3 | 0.3 |
| Brown | 14 | 191 | 9.2 | 4.1 | 15 | 36 | 3.4 | 0.7 | 29.2 | 13.1 | 5.8 | 0.4 |
| Buffalo | 151 | 3 954 | 365.2 | 145.3 | 114 | 553 | 45.3 | 10.9 | 257.0 | 112.8 | 43.0 | 6.9 |
| Burt | 16 | 196 | 12.3 | 5.0 | 15 | 60 | 6.2 | 2.0 | 74.3 | 26.7 | 17.6 | 2.0 |
| Butler | 16 | 360 | 22.6 | 9.4 | 15 | D | D | D | 62.3 | 27.8 | 11.6 | 1.3 |
| Cass | 28 | 350 | 19.1 | 7.9 | 41 | 132 | 9.4 | 2.4 | 159.9 | 93.2 | 29.0 | 4.2 |
| Cedar | 16 | 108 | 6.0 | 2.1 | 22 | 52 | 5.7 | 1.3 | 66.9 | 24.7 | 13.4 | 0.7 |
| Chase | 9 | 176 | 10.0 | 4.7 | 10 | 45 | 3.0 | 0.7 | 53.5 | 15.3 | 7.9 | 0.6 |
| Cherry | 15 | 297 | 22.0 | 8.1 | 18 | 41 | 4.9 | 0.7 | 42.7 | 17.6 | 8.4 | 1.0 |
| Cheyenne | 19 | 392 | 39.7 | 12.0 | 28 | 91 | 9.6 | 1.9 | 86.6 | 30.1 | 17.0 | 2.2 |
| Clay | 11 | 151 | 4.8 | 2.7 | 11 | 28 | 1.4 | 0.4 | 66.1 | 24.1 | 10.3 | 1.0 |
| Colfax | 13 | 254 | 21.3 | 7.8 | 28 | 83 | 6.0 | 1.7 | 69.5 | 24.6 | 23.6 | 1.3 |
| Cuming | 25 | 404 | 37.6 | 13.4 | 34 | 156 | 16.4 | 3.0 | 67.4 | 27.4 | 15.8 | 1.1 |
| Custer | 35 | 684 | 39.2 | 16.7 | 32 | 60 | 5.5 | 0.9 | 101.1 | 39.4 | 20.4 | 2.4 |
| Dakota | 32 | D | D | D | 38 | D | D | D | 103.2 | 36.7 | 23.0 | 4.0 |
| Dawes | 30 | 390 | 27.0 | 11.5 | 26 | 73 | 4.2 | 1.0 | 76.3 | 30.1 | 10.5 | 2.7 |
| Dawson | 67 | D | D | D | 59 | D | D | D | 145.2 | 59.6 | 28.6 | 5.4 |
| Deuel | 4 | D | D | D | 4 | 22 | 0.5 | 0.2 | 22.2 | 8.6 | 4.2 | 0.1 |
| Dixon | 10 | D | D | D | 7 | D | D | D | 54.5 | 26.3 | 10.0 | 0.9 |
| Dodge | 109 | 2 771 | 199.9 | 78.0 | 85 | 381 | 31.3 | 6.5 | 266.7 | 128.4 | 59.2 | 7.0 |
| Douglas | 1 552 | 42 408 | 4 430.8 | 1 793.5 | 1 085 | 8 366 | 1 051.5 | 224.7 | 4 258.6 | 1 462.3 | 631.9 | 157.5 |
| Dundy | 8 | 152 | 7.8 | 4.1 | 1 | D | D | D | 33.9 | 8.3 | 6.0 | 0.2 |
| Fillmore | 15 | 290 | 18.1 | 7.4 | 21 | 71 | 4.3 | 1.0 | 55.4 | 22.8 | 10.9 | 0.7 |
| Franklin | 8 | 138 | 7.7 | 3.5 | 7 | 19 | 1.2 | 0.2 | 32.9 | 12.8 | 7.4 | 0.6 |
| Frontier | 11 | 87 | 2.7 | 1.1 | 6 | D | D | D | 27.8 | 10.2 | 4.4 | 0.2 |
| Furnas | 15 | 282 | 15.9 | 6.5 | 15 | 33 | 3.4 | 0.5 | 57.9 | 21.0 | 12.7 | 0.6 |
| Gage | 62 | 1 697 | 91.0 | 39.6 | 58 | 252 | 13.0 | 3.5 | 188.7 | 89.8 | 31.7 | 4.7 |
| Garden | 1 | D | D | D | 1 | D | D | D | 32.8 | 10.6 | 5.3 | 0.2 |
| Garfield | 7 | 100 | 4.6 | 2.1 | 7 | 29 | 1.8 | 0.4 | 16.5 | 7.6 | 4.4 | 0.3 |
| Gosper | 5 | D | D | D | 2 | D | D | D | 19.3 | 9.9 | 3.2 | 0.2 |
| Grant | NA | NA | NA | NA | 3 | D | D | D | 4.6 | 2.5 | 1.0 | 0.1 |
| Greeley | 4 | D | D | D | 4 | 12 | 1.0 | 0.2 | 23.7 | 9.4 | 4.5 | 0.4 |
| Hall | 171 | 3 816 | 320.6 | 125.5 | 158 | 976 | 68.8 | 16.8 | 416.0 | 172.2 | 65.9 | 14.5 |
| Hamilton | 18 | 388 | 17.5 | 7.8 | 25 | 74 | 8.0 | 2.0 | 65.7 | 29.9 | 11.3 | 1.0 |
| Harlan | 7 | 168 | 8.9 | 4.0 | 6 | D | D | D | 37.5 | 13.4 | 7.1 | 0.8 |
| Hayes | 1 | D | D | D | 1 | D | D | D | 14.6 | 2.6 | 1.7 | 0.1 |
| Hitchcock | 4 | 17 | 0.7 | 0.3 | 3 | D | D | D | 32.2 | 13.1 | 5.5 | 0.3 |
| Holt | 36 | 696 | 49.5 | 20.5 | 33 | 93 | 12.6 | 2.0 | 113.7 | 34.5 | 21.8 | 2.2 |
| Hooker | 2 | D | D | D | 3 | D | D | D | 6.2 | 3.2 | 1.6 | 0.1 |
| Howard | 11 | D | D | D | 17 | 62 | 3.6 | 0.9 | 49.2 | 22.3 | 10.9 | 0.7 |
| Jefferson | 14 | 376 | 23.3 | 9.9 | 20 | 73 | 3.8 | 0.8 | 71.4 | 29.8 | 13.7 | 1.8 |
| Johnson | 14 | 306 | 19.6 | 7.8 | 11 | D | D | D | 33.8 | 14.6 | 7.4 | 0.4 |
| Kearney | 15 | 654 | 22.6 | 10.6 | 13 | 44 | 4.9 | 1.0 | 52.0 | 20.2 | 11.3 | 0.7 |
| Keith | 30 | 330 | 26.8 | 10.1 | 26 | 104 | 7.6 | 2.0 | 63.4 | 30.2 | 11.1 | 1.2 |
| Keya Paha | 1 | D | D | D | 3 | 9 | 0.7 | 0.1 | 6.9 | 2.6 | 1.3 | 0.1 |
| Kimball | 9 | D | D | D | 10 | 26 | 1.4 | 0.4 | 35.6 | 15.7 | 5.7 | 0.4 |
| Knox | 20 | 318 | 15.6 | 6.2 | 13 | 27 | 1.8 | 0.5 | 90.6 | 30.7 | 19.0 | 1.9 |
| Lancaster | 842 | 21 431 | 1 932.6 | 789.3 | 660 | 4 233 | 546.6 | 118.0 | 2 822.6 | 714.2 | 223.3 | 55.0 |
| Lincoln | 120 | D | D | D | 83 | D | D | D | 299.0 | 143.8 | 45.9 | 9.3 |
| Logan | 1 | D | D | D | 2 | D | D | D | 7.6 | 3.0 | 1.3 | 0.1 |
| Loup | NA | NA | NA | NA | 1 | D | D | D | 3.8 | 1.6 | 1.3 | 0.0 |
| McPherson | NA | NA | NA | NA | NA | NA | NA | NA | 5.0 | 1.6 | 0.7 | 0.3 |
| Madison | 158 | D | D | D | 107 | D | D | D | 269.3 | 107.7 | 41.1 | 7.1 |
| Merrick | 13 | D | D | D | 20 | 40 | 4.6 | 0.9 | 60.1 | 27.4 | 13.9 | 1.0 |
| Morrill | 5 | 122 | 8.2 | 3.7 | 5 | D | D | D | 41.1 | 17.0 | 7.9 | 1.3 |
| Nance | 10 | D | D | D | 16 | 33 | 2.7 | 0.5 | 34.8 | 12.3 | 7.3 | 0.6 |
| Nemaha | 23 | 359 | 23.3 | 10.5 | 19 | 61 | 2.9 | 0.7 | 60.2 | 25.1 | 12.2 | 1.6 |
| Nuckolls | 16 | 395 | 18.8 | 9.4 | 20 | 55 | 3.4 | 0.6 | 50.3 | 18.8 | 10.8 | 0.8 |
| Otoe | 41 | 915 | 51.3 | 21.6 | 38 | 186 | 10.3 | 3.7 | 106.9 | 52.6 | 21.8 | 2.5 |
| Pawnee | 8 | 143 | 8.2 | 3.8 | 5 | D | D | D | 32.8 | 11.1 | 7.2 | 0.5 |
| Perkins | 6 | 211 | 11.2 | 4.6 | 12 | D | D | D | 37.1 | 10.5 | 5.9 | 0.2 |
| Phelps | 25 | 743 | 51.3 | 17.5 | 36 | 118 | 16.9 | 3.0 | 78.1 | 32.3 | 14.9 | 1.4 |
| Pierce | 18 | D | D | D | 15 | D | D | D | 47.2 | 19.4 | 11.4 | 1.0 |

1. State totals may include programs not allocated by county.

# Table B. States and Counties — Federal Funds, Residential Construction, and Local Government Finances

| | Federal funds and grants, 2009–2010 (cont.) | | | | | | | Value of residential construction authorized by building permits, 2011 | | Local government finances, 2007 | | | | |
|---|---|---|---|---|---|---|---|---|---|---|---|---|---|---|
| | Expenditures (mil dol) (cont.) | | | | | | | | | General revenue | | | | |
| | Procurement contract awards | | | Grants[1] | | | | | | | | Taxes | | |
| | | | | | | | | | | | | | Per capita[2] (dollars) | |
| STATE County | Salaries and wages | Defense | Other | Medicaid and other health-related | Nutrition and family welfare | Education | Other | New construction ($1,000) | Number of housing units | Total (mil dol) | Inter-govern-mental (mil dol) | Total (mil dol) | Total | Property |
| | 171 | 172 | 173 | 174 | 175 | 176 | 177 | 178 | 179 | 180 | 181 | 182 | 183 | 184 |
| **NEBRASKA—Cont'd** | | | | | | | | | | | | | | |
| Blaine | 0.4 | 0.0 | 0.1 | 0.7 | 0.1 | 0.0 | 0.0 | NA | NA | 3.0 | 1.1 | 1.8 | 3 915 | 3 696 |
| Boone | 2.5 | 0.0 | 0.6 | 5.2 | 1.2 | 0.4 | 0.1 | 540 | 3 | 32.7 | 3.8 | 11.9 | 2 146 | 1 892 |
| Box Butte | 3.2 | 0.0 | 0.8 | 7.2 | 2.1 | 1.0 | 0.7 | 0 | 0 | 57.1 | 14.6 | 18.1 | 1 648 | 1 121 |
| Boyd | 1.4 | 0.0 | 0.3 | 2.6 | 0.6 | 0.3 | 0.2 | 0 | 0 | 12.3 | 3.2 | 6.9 | 3 233 | 2 857 |
| Brown | 1.4 | 0.0 | 0.3 | 4.6 | 0.7 | 0.3 | 0.2 | 30 | 1 | 23.9 | 5.1 | 10.2 | 3 194 | 2 749 |
| Buffalo | 29.2 | 0.0 | 4.4 | 20.3 | 10.6 | 2.7 | 2.1 | 19 159 | 121 | 137.4 | 45.7 | 63.8 | 1 418 | 1 074 |
| Burt | 2.4 | 0.0 | 0.6 | 8.5 | 1.5 | 0.3 | 4.7 | 1 594 | 8 | 30.4 | 7.2 | 15.0 | 2 130 | 1 854 |
| Butler | 3.7 | 0.5 | 0.7 | 7.2 | 1.2 | 0.4 | 0.4 | 820 | 10 | 35.1 | 4.6 | 18.6 | 2 222 | 1 828 |
| Cass | 6.0 | 0.0 | 1.4 | 11.2 | 4.3 | 1.2 | 1.9 | 9 172 | 52 | 77.1 | 22.1 | 38.5 | 1 504 | 1 225 |
| Cedar | 5.2 | 2.8 | 0.8 | 7.2 | 1.9 | 0.6 | 0.2 | 389 | 3 | 29.2 | 7.8 | 15.3 | 1 789 | 1 518 |
| Chase | 1.8 | 0.0 | 0.6 | 2.6 | 0.8 | 0.2 | 0.4 | 195 | 1 | 27.4 | 4.3 | 10.6 | 2 862 | 2 611 |
| Cherry | 3.0 | 0.0 | 0.9 | 5.9 | 1.3 | 0.4 | 0.8 | 860 | 10 | 35.8 | 7.1 | 14.9 | 2 614 | 2 130 |
| Cheyenne | 4.3 | 0.0 | 0.8 | 9.2 | 1.5 | 0.5 | 4.2 | 2 328 | 11 | 36.9 | 11.1 | 17.6 | 1 764 | 1 390 |
| Clay | 12.0 | 0.0 | 2.8 | 3.3 | 1.1 | 0.7 | 0.2 | 846 | 4 | 31.8 | 11.1 | 16.6 | 2 630 | 2 177 |
| Colfax | 5.0 | 0.0 | 0.6 | 7.9 | 1.5 | 0.3 | 0.2 | 4 095 | 25 | 33.1 | 11.5 | 17.1 | 1 718 | 1 543 |
| Cuming | 2.8 | 0.0 | 0.7 | 4.6 | 4.2 | 0.7 | 2.6 | 2 289 | 12 | 32.4 | 7.1 | 16.6 | 1 778 | 1 524 |
| Custer | 5.3 | 0.0 | 1.1 | 14.4 | 2.1 | 0.8 | 0.6 | 0 | 0 | 38.5 | 12.6 | 19.2 | 1 767 | 1 539 |
| Dakota | 5.5 | 0.0 | 1.0 | 22.3 | 4.2 | 1.5 | 1.0 | 3 388 | 22 | 67.9 | 32.3 | 26.8 | 1 318 | 846 |
| Dawes | 10.5 | 0.0 | 2.3 | 6.8 | 3.3 | 1.1 | 2.2 | 1 006 | 6 | 29.3 | 11.2 | 11.7 | 1 327 | 980 |
| Dawson | 8.4 | 1.4 | 1.1 | 19.7 | 4.1 | 0.9 | 1.5 | 3 060 | 20 | 125.4 | 39.4 | 34.6 | 1 400 | 1 124 |
| Deuel | 0.5 | 0.0 | 0.1 | 3.3 | 0.3 | 0.2 | 0.0 | 0 | 0 | 11.2 | 3.3 | 6.9 | 3 649 | 3 077 |
| Dixon | 2.4 | 0.0 | 1.7 | 4.6 | 0.9 | 0.4 | 0.1 | 2 110 | 9 | 25.2 | 7.9 | 11.9 | 1 903 | 1 558 |
| Dodge | 19.5 | 1.0 | 2.1 | 23.6 | 6.1 | 3.1 | 5.2 | 6 162 | 41 | 190.5 | 34.7 | 51.5 | 1 429 | 1 153 |
| Douglas | 458.6 | 226.7 | 257.9 | 663.4 | 94.3 | 44.4 | 142.9 | 230 787 | 2 145 | 1 985.9 | 588.8 | 943.2 | 1 896 | 1 386 |
| Dundy | 0.9 | 0.0 | 0.2 | 2.6 | 0.3 | 0.1 | 0.1 | 0 | 0 | 13.7 | 2.4 | 4.2 | 2 069 | 1 915 |
| Fillmore | 2.6 | 0.0 | 0.8 | 5.9 | 1.1 | 0.2 | 0.3 | 763 | 3 | 32.9 | 5.1 | 14.9 | 2 461 | 2 002 |
| Franklin | 1.6 | 0.0 | 0.4 | 2.6 | 0.6 | 0.3 | 0.6 | 575 | 2 | 13.6 | 3.1 | 4.8 | 1 528 | 1 341 |
| Frontier | 1.4 | 0.0 | 0.4 | 2.6 | 0.5 | 0.1 | 0.0 | 437 | 4 | 14.1 | 4.1 | 7.4 | 2 789 | 2 575 |
| Furnas | 2.5 | 0.0 | 0.6 | 10.5 | 1.0 | 0.4 | 0.5 | 305 | 3 | 27.4 | 8.7 | 11.1 | 2 355 | 1 960 |
| Gage | 15.5 | 0.0 | 1.9 | 25.7 | 3.4 | 1.4 | 1.2 | 1 024 | 8 | 69.4 | 24.4 | 31.0 | 1 336 | 1 068 |
| Garden | 1.2 | 0.0 | 8.6 | 2.6 | 0.4 | 0.1 | 0.0 | 145 | 2 | 16.3 | 1.7 | 7.6 | 4 153 | 3 835 |
| Garfield | 0.7 | 0.0 | 0.1 | 2.1 | 0.3 | 0.1 | 0.2 | 0 | 0 | 7.0 | 2.7 | 2.5 | 1 472 | 1 293 |
| Gosper | 0.7 | 0.0 | 0.1 | 0.0 | 0.2 | 0.1 | 0.0 | 1 510 | 8 | 10.6 | 1.5 | 5.8 | 2 929 | 2 508 |
| Grant | 0.5 | 0.0 | 0.1 | 0.0 | 0.1 | 0.0 | 0.0 | NA | NA | 3.8 | 0.5 | 3.0 | 4 824 | 4 563 |
| Greeley | 1.6 | 0.0 | 0.4 | 2.0 | 0.8 | 0.2 | 0.0 | 167 | 1 | 11.7 | 3.1 | 6.1 | 2 606 | 2 199 |
| Hall | 51.8 | 1.8 | 11.6 | 48.2 | 8.5 | 5.0 | 8.1 | 18 263 | 131 | 203.5 | 73.5 | 81.8 | 1 471 | 1 103 |
| Hamilton | 2.9 | 0.0 | 0.7 | 7.9 | 1.2 | 0.5 | 0.8 | 4 064 | 23 | 30.6 | 7.8 | 16.1 | 1 730 | 1 393 |
| Harlan | 1.8 | 4.3 | 0.3 | 2.6 | 0.5 | 0.3 | 0.0 | 1 230 | 11 | 14.5 | 3.9 | 3.6 | 1 055 | 926 |
| Hayes | 0.4 | 0.0 | 0.0 | 0.7 | 0.2 | 0.1 | 0.0 | 0 | 0 | 4.4 | 1.7 | 2.4 | 2 437 | 2 271 |
| Hitchcock | 1.4 | 1.6 | 0.3 | 3.3 | 0.5 | 0.1 | 0.0 | 0 | 0 | 10.6 | 3.7 | 4.5 | 1 578 | 1 335 |
| Holt | 15.3 | 0.0 | 0.7 | 14.4 | 2.5 | 0.6 | 7.2 | 1 806 | 9 | 38.1 | 11.4 | 21.5 | 2 086 | 1 767 |
| Hooker | 0.3 | 0.0 | 0.0 | 0.7 | 0.2 | 0.0 | 0.1 | 215 | 2 | 5.1 | 0.8 | 2.8 | 3 792 | 3 336 |
| Howard | 2.0 | 0.0 | 0.4 | 4.6 | 1.2 | 0.4 | 0.1 | 2 402 | 30 | 33.9 | 8.0 | 9.2 | 1 389 | 1 243 |
| Jefferson | 2.6 | 0.0 | 0.5 | 10.5 | 4.1 | 0.4 | 0.6 | 330 | 3 | 36.9 | 8.1 | 17.2 | 2 295 | 2 000 |
| Johnson | 2.4 | 0.0 | 0.4 | 3.9 | 0.8 | 0.6 | 0.0 | 445 | 3 | 25.5 | 5.1 | 10.8 | 2 403 | 2 053 |
| Kearney | 2.0 | 0.9 | 0.4 | 3.3 | 0.8 | 0.3 | 0.1 | 3 450 | 21 | 29.8 | 5.2 | 15.6 | 2 365 | 2 146 |
| Keith | 3.3 | 0.0 | 0.8 | 5.2 | 1.3 | 0.4 | 1.0 | 2 469 | 13 | 30.6 | 10.3 | 15.7 | 1 959 | 1 460 |
| Keya Paha | 0.2 | 0.0 | 0.0 | 1.3 | 0.2 | 0.1 | 0.0 | 0 | 0 | 4.0 | 1.3 | 2.4 | 2 812 | 2 636 |
| Kimball | 1.1 | 0.0 | 0.2 | 2.5 | 0.6 | 0.1 | 1.7 | 0 | 0 | 29.2 | 3.6 | 8.7 | 2 413 | 1 721 |
| Knox | 3.6 | 0.3 | 0.8 | 12.9 | 3.1 | 2.2 | 4.0 | 4 135 | 29 | 33.4 | 16.1 | 13.5 | 1 554 | 1 380 |
| Lancaster | 325.3 | 19.0 | 89.3 | 278.9 | 114.3 | 159.7 | 773.3 | 131 838 | 1 022 | 942.0 | 239.2 | 482.6 | 1 751 | 1 304 |
| Lincoln | 27.5 | 0.0 | 3.8 | 32.3 | 5.1 | 2.3 | 6.0 | 6 488 | 41 | 243.3 | 46.7 | 73.2 | 2 062 | 1 275 |
| Logan | 0.2 | 0.0 | 0.1 | 1.3 | 0.2 | 0.1 | 0.0 | NA | NA | 3.2 | 1.1 | 1.8 | 2 459 | 2 136 |
| Loup | 0.2 | 0.0 | 0.0 | 0.0 | 0.1 | 0.0 | 0.0 | 0 | 0 | 2.3 | 0.6 | 1.5 | 2 306 | 2 208 |
| McPherson | 0.2 | 0.0 | 0.0 | 1.3 | 0.0 | 0.1 | 0.0 | NA | NA | 2.3 | 0.4 | 1.7 | 3 430 | 2 827 |
| Madison | 25.3 | 14.2 | 10.7 | 31.5 | 5.3 | 1.8 | 8.7 | 7 916 | 39 | 151.2 | 44.7 | 68.7 | 2 011 | 1 593 |
| Merrick | 2.5 | 0.0 | 0.7 | 6.6 | 1.2 | 0.7 | 0.1 | 2 761 | 17 | 33.6 | 7.4 | 10.4 | 1 354 | 1 166 |
| Morrill | 1.4 | 0.0 | 0.3 | 3.9 | 1.2 | 0.4 | 0.1 | 800 | 10 | 27.1 | 9.6 | 7.9 | 1 560 | 1 268 |
| Nance | 0.8 | 0.0 | 0.2 | 7.2 | 0.8 | 0.1 | 0.1 | 1 917 | 15 | 19.0 | 3.5 | 8.4 | 2 339 | 2 022 |
| Nemaha | 2.1 | 0.0 | 0.4 | 7.3 | 1.1 | 0.7 | 0.5 | 1 460 | 7 | 29.8 | 9.3 | 9.4 | 1 333 | 1 112 |
| Nuckolls | 2.5 | 0.0 | 0.5 | 6.6 | 0.8 | 0.2 | 2.0 | 300 | 2 | 7.8 | 1.7 | 2.9 | 643 | 499 |
| Otoe | 6.3 | 0.2 | 1.1 | 11.2 | 2.1 | 0.7 | 0.3 | 3 920 | 22 | 50.0 | 13.6 | 23.9 | 1 527 | 1 224 |
| Pawnee | 1.6 | 0.0 | 0.4 | 4.6 | 0.6 | 0.2 | 3.1 | 0 | 0 | 19.2 | 6.7 | 4.8 | 1 771 | 1 569 |
| Perkins | 0.9 | 0.0 | 0.2 | 0.0 | 0.4 | 0.3 | 0.0 | 250 | 1 | 21.5 | 3.1 | 7.0 | 2 388 | 1 974 |
| Phelps | 2.8 | 0.1 | 0.8 | 7.2 | 1.3 | 0.8 | 0.6 | 3 211 | 14 | 37.7 | 8.7 | 18.6 | 2 025 | 1 596 |
| Pierce | 2.2 | 0.0 | 0.5 | 3.9 | 1.2 | 0.5 | 0.1 | 1 423 | 9 | 32.1 | 6.2 | 16.1 | 2 213 | 1 764 |

1. State totals may include programs not allocated by county.   2. Based on the resident population estimated as of July 1 of the year shown.

# Table B. States and Counties — Local Government Finances, Government Employment, and Voting

| STATE County | Local government finances, 2007 (cont.) | | | | | | | | | Government employment, 2011 | | | Presidential election,[2] 2012 | | |
|---|---|---|---|---|---|---|---|---|---|---|---|---|---|---|---|
| | Direct general expenditure | | | | | | | Debt outstanding | | | | | Percent of vote cast: | | |
| | | | Percent of total for: | | | | | | | | | | | | |
| | Total (mil dol) | Per capita[1] (dollars) | Education | Health and hospitals | Police protection | Public welfare | Highways | Total (mil dol) | Per capita[1] (dollars) | Federal civilian | Federal military | State and local | Democratic | Republican | All other |
| | 185 | 186 | 187 | 188 | 189 | 190 | 191 | 192 | 193 | 194 | 195 | 196 | 197 | 198 | 199 |
| NEBRASKA—Cont'd | | | | | | | | | | | | | | | |
| Blaine | 2.6 | 5 728 | 72.1 | 0.0 | 1.8 | 0.5 | 9.9 | 0.0 | 0 | 31 | 0 | 54 | 13.6 | 84.2 | 2.2 |
| Boone | 32.5 | 5 879 | 31.7 | 45.1 | 1.7 | 0.0 | 7.5 | 3.1 | 564 | 35 | 22 | 617 | 26.2 | 72.0 | 1.8 |
| Box Butte | 53.4 | 4 855 | 36.5 | 31.9 | 2.6 | 0.2 | 4.0 | 12.9 | 1 173 | 42 | 46 | 1 031 | 37.9 | 58.9 | 3.2 |
| Boyd | 7.8 | 3 702 | 64.7 | 0.0 | 1.8 | 0.0 | 9.2 | 7.9 | 3 725 | 17 | 0 | 229 | 22.5 | 75.6 | 1.9 |
| Brown | 18.9 | 5 884 | 45.8 | 27.1 | 1.8 | 0.3 | 6.5 | 13.8 | 4 297 | 23 | 13 | 385 | 19.8 | 77.1 | 3.1 |
| Buffalo | 138.2 | 3 074 | 54.0 | 0.1 | 6.6 | 0.2 | 9.9 | 107.6 | 2 392 | 150 | 188 | 3 857 | 30.4 | 67.9 | 1.7 |
| Burt | 28.3 | 4 005 | 45.9 | 14.3 | 3.4 | 0.2 | 11.6 | 18.3 | 2 588 | 32 | 27 | 538 | 41.7 | 56.3 | 2.0 |
| Butler | 33.6 | 4 012 | 36.4 | 26.9 | 3.9 | 0.1 | 12.6 | 27.5 | 3 281 | 50 | 33 | 627 | 31.0 | 66.6 | 2.4 |
| Cass | 66.2 | 2 588 | 51.6 | 0.1 | 4.4 | 8.2 | 6.6 | 149.5 | 5 844 | 69 | 101 | 1 308 | 39.2 | 58.7 | 2.1 |
| Cedar | 28.1 | 3 289 | 53.4 | 0.2 | 1.6 | 6.5 | 10.4 | 9.4 | 1 106 | 99 | 35 | 606 | 28.5 | 69.8 | 1.7 |
| Chase | 23.8 | 6 425 | 35.9 | 30.4 | 3.2 | 0.5 | 9.0 | 7.9 | 2 123 | 24 | 16 | 473 | 18.5 | 80.1 | 1.4 |
| Cherry | 30.7 | 5 375 | 36.4 | 30.2 | 2.5 | 0.5 | 11.2 | 3.7 | 649 | 58 | 23 | 529 | 19.6 | 77.1 | 3.3 |
| Cheyenne | 33.5 | 3 363 | 50.4 | 0.6 | 4.5 | 1.0 | 8.0 | 31.4 | 3 148 | 37 | 40 | 795 | 24.2 | 73.8 | 1.9 |
| Clay | 31.2 | 4 934 | 70.4 | 0.6 | 1.8 | 0.5 | 8.6 | 10.6 | 1 671 | 162 | 26 | 598 | 25.7 | 71.8 | 2.5 |
| Colfax | 31.6 | 3 163 | 67.5 | 0.3 | 3.5 | 0.1 | 10.7 | 12.5 | 1 257 | 75 | 43 | 607 | 35.1 | 63.0 | 1.9 |
| Cuming | 32.2 | 3 442 | 50.8 | 0.2 | 2.8 | 6.3 | 14.2 | 45.6 | 4 872 | 38 | 37 | 766 | 31.2 | 66.8 | 2.0 |
| Custer | 37.3 | 3 434 | 62.3 | 0.1 | 2.8 | 0.2 | 13.5 | 14.4 | 1 329 | 54 | 44 | 856 | 21.4 | 77.1 | 1.5 |
| Dakota | 63.2 | 3 113 | 55.5 | 0.3 | 6.4 | 0.1 | 6.1 | 61.7 | 3 035 | 80 | 84 | 1 113 | 46.8 | 51.5 | 1.7 |
| Dawes | 25.4 | 2 875 | 48.3 | 0.5 | 5.1 | 12.5 | 9.3 | 5.9 | 664 | 136 | 37 | 1 048 | 34.0 | 62.9 | 3.0 |
| Dawson | 120.7 | 4 880 | 38.7 | 28.6 | 4.2 | 0.1 | 4.5 | 96.3 | 3 891 | 106 | 98 | 1 982 | 30.0 | 68.4 | 1.6 |
| Deuel | 10.7 | 5 650 | 50.2 | 0.4 | 3.5 | 13.6 | 7.7 | 3.8 | 2 023 | 0 | 0 | 204 | 24.5 | 73.7 | 1.8 |
| Dixon | 27.3 | 4 366 | 63.7 | 0.0 | 3.3 | 8.6 | 8.5 | 10.0 | 1 596 | 41 | 24 | 449 | 33.9 | 63.9 | 2.3 |
| Dodge | 179.9 | 4 996 | 32.6 | 44.4 | 2.6 | 0.2 | 5.1 | 108.7 | 3 018 | 113 | 149 | 2 871 | 43.0 | 55.0 | 2.0 |
| Douglas | 1 879.9 | 3 779 | 49.2 | 2.8 | 5.8 | 0.4 | 3.9 | 4 585.7 | 9 219 | 5 733 | 2 359 | 34 720 | 51.5 | 46.9 | 1.6 |
| Dundy | 13.2 | 6 520 | 32.0 | 44.6 | 3.9 | 0.1 | 8.0 | 0.9 | 429 | 13 | 0 | 228 | 21.4 | 76.8 | 1.8 |
| Fillmore | 32.1 | 5 309 | 36.2 | 27.3 | 3.4 | 7.1 | 12.3 | 11.0 | 1 816 | 35 | 24 | 697 | 32.6 | 64.9 | 2.4 |
| Franklin | 12.6 | 3 979 | 28.7 | 33.7 | 2.1 | 0.4 | 14.2 | 1.4 | 447 | 24 | 13 | 350 | 28.5 | 69.5 | 2.0 |
| Frontier | 14.3 | 5 369 | 63.7 | 0.7 | 3.1 | 0.7 | 10.1 | 1.9 | 701 | 16 | 11 | 333 | 24.9 | 73.6 | 1.5 |
| Furnas | 24.9 | 5 257 | 59.0 | 0.1 | 3.3 | 0.2 | 6.3 | 17.9 | 3 773 | 34 | 20 | 544 | 23.9 | 74.1 | 2.0 |
| Gage | 72.1 | 3 104 | 55.9 | 0.1 | 4.9 | 0.3 | 11.9 | 32.4 | 1 396 | 109 | 89 | 2 019 | 44.0 | 53.5 | 2.5 |
| Garden | 14.5 | 7 915 | 28.0 | 33.5 | 2.6 | 0.0 | 6.5 | 0.2 | 83 | 18 | 0 | 257 | 24.9 | 74.2 | 1.0 |
| Garfield | 6.3 | 3 658 | 57.1 | 0.2 | 3.3 | 0.0 | 9.1 | 2.0 | 1 174 | 0 | 0 | 167 | 20.6 | 77.7 | 1.7 |
| Gosper | 9.2 | 4 681 | 33.3 | 0.6 | 3.2 | 23.1 | 11.3 | 23.0 | 11 657 | 12 | 0 | 165 | 24.8 | 74.0 | 1.1 |
| Grant | 3.8 | 6 117 | 72.2 | 0.6 | 1.7 | 0.1 | 8.3 | 0.1 | 220 | 0 | 0 | 80 | 11.2 | 86.6 | 2.2 |
| Greeley | 10.6 | 4 559 | 59.0 | 0.1 | 3.1 | 11.3 | 10.0 | 3.9 | 1 690 | 17 | 10 | 272 | 38.2 | 59.6 | 2.2 |
| Hall | 221.5 | 3 981 | 51.3 | 0.1 | 4.5 | 0.3 | 6.1 | 233.7 | 4 200 | 710 | 240 | 4 319 | 36.9 | 61.0 | 2.1 |
| Hamilton | 34.3 | 3 688 | 54.5 | 1.7 | 2.7 | 0.5 | 12.1 | 20.0 | 2 156 | 38 | 36 | 580 | 27.8 | 70.6 | 1.6 |
| Harlan | 12.8 | 3 784 | 23.9 | 35.1 | 1.9 | 0.0 | 5.5 | 10.6 | 3 119 | 33 | 14 | 272 | 22.8 | 75.3 | 2.0 |
| Hayes | 6.1 | 6 216 | 74.3 | 0.2 | 1.4 | 0.0 | 12.0 | 1.0 | 1 067 | 11 | 0 | 84 | 15.4 | 83.4 | 1.3 |
| Hitchcock | 12.0 | 4 230 | 63.3 | 0.0 | 1.1 | 0.0 | 11.1 | 3.8 | 1 324 | 14 | 11 | 278 | 25.1 | 72.6 | 2.3 |
| Holt | 35.4 | 3 436 | 56.8 | 0.0 | 3.0 | 0.3 | 12.7 | 11.7 | 1 133 | 51 | 42 | 797 | 21.9 | 75.3 | 2.8 |
| Hooker | 4.7 | 6 418 | 49.3 | 24.4 | 1.5 | 0.1 | 6.2 | 1.9 | 2 635 | 0 | 0 | 107 | 17.1 | 81.1 | 1.8 |
| Howard | 32.6 | 4 925 | 38.3 | 33.5 | 2.1 | 0.2 | 7.6 | 14.5 | 2 189 | 30 | 25 | 590 | 36.1 | 61.6 | 2.2 |
| Jefferson | 28.6 | 3 806 | 57.6 | 2.1 | 4.4 | 0.1 | 10.7 | 4.0 | 535 | 40 | 30 | 582 | 41.1 | 56.9 | 2.0 |
| Johnson | 22.8 | 5 095 | 37.2 | 27.8 | 1.6 | 0.1 | 7.4 | 18.5 | 4 143 | 38 | 21 | 811 | 43.3 | 54.1 | 2.6 |
| Kearney | 27.9 | 4 233 | 49.4 | 20.5 | 2.2 | 0.4 | 8.8 | 10.9 | 1 657 | 26 | 26 | 477 | 27.8 | 70.6 | 1.6 |
| Keith | 31.4 | 3 917 | 56.3 | 0.4 | 4.6 | 1.1 | 7.2 | 10.9 | 1 354 | 33 | 33 | 528 | 24.5 | 74.1 | 1.3 |
| Keya Paha | 4.1 | 4 839 | 50.7 | 0.2 | 1.9 | 0.0 | 21.5 | 0.1 | 165 | 0 | 0 | 65 | 21.6 | 76.7 | 1.7 |
| Kimball | 23.3 | 6 471 | 29.0 | 27.9 | 1.9 | 13.2 | 7.1 | 5.7 | 1 575 | 17 | 15 | 412 | 24.2 | 74.3 | 1.4 |
| Knox | 33.0 | 3 812 | 65.6 | 0.2 | 1.9 | 0.0 | 12.5 | 12.6 | 1 459 | 47 | 34 | 1 064 | 30.7 | 66.8 | 2.5 |
| Lancaster | 1 006.3 | 3 651 | 47.6 | 3.4 | 4.2 | 2.2 | 7.6 | 1 773.4 | 6 433 | 2 878 | 1 217 | 29 795 | 51.6 | 46.6 | 1.8 |
| Lincoln | 221.7 | 6 244 | 34.1 | 37.1 | 3.1 | 0.2 | 3.7 | 88.3 | 2 488 | 252 | 145 | 2 657 | 31.0 | 66.5 | 2.5 |
| Logan | 3.2 | 4 259 | 71.3 | 0.4 | 1.8 | 0.0 | 10.2 | 0.1 | 107 | 0 | 0 | 79 | 19.5 | 78.6 | 1.9 |
| Loup | 2.3 | 3 607 | 60.6 | 0.7 | 3.3 | 0.0 | 10.8 | 0.1 | 132 | 0 | 0 | 60 | 21.9 | 76.8 | 1.3 |
| McPherson | 2.0 | 3 944 | 63.4 | 0.2 | 1.8 | 0.1 | 16.3 | 0.4 | 797 | 0 | 0 | 39 | 15.4 | 81.9 | 2.7 |
| Madison | 156.2 | 4 575 | 62.9 | 1.8 | 4.3 | 3.8 | 5.5 | 99.0 | 2 900 | 213 | 141 | 3 616 | 29.5 | 68.7 | 1.8 |
| Merrick | 26.4 | 3 432 | 34.8 | 32.8 | 2.7 | 0.8 | 10.0 | 20.2 | 2 622 | 31 | 31 | 555 | 28.7 | 69.2 | 2.0 |
| Morrill | 24.6 | 4 868 | 42.3 | 18.5 | 2.4 | 7.5 | 7.1 | 8.3 | 1 641 | 22 | 20 | 471 | 23.7 | 73.4 | 2.9 |
| Nance | 17.2 | 4 806 | 47.9 | 26.8 | 3.5 | 0.0 | 11.6 | 2.8 | 789 | 14 | 15 | 364 | 32.2 | 65.4 | 2.5 |
| Nemaha | 30.9 | 4 391 | 49.7 | 23.7 | 2.3 | 0.1 | 8.2 | 8.2 | 1 160 | 31 | 29 | 1 637 | 35.7 | 61.4 | 2.9 |
| Nuckolls | 6.0 | 1 321 | 0.0 | 1.2 | 8.5 | 0.8 | 36.9 | 16.8 | 3 699 | 34 | 18 | 359 | 29.6 | 67.4 | 3.0 |
| Otoe | 47.2 | 3 015 | 48.4 | 12.8 | 4.4 | 0.6 | 8.5 | 21.4 | 1 367 | 56 | 63 | 1 279 | 41.1 | 56.9 | 2.0 |
| Pawnee | 18.1 | 6 740 | 29.7 | 24.8 | 1.0 | 0.1 | 8.4 | 2.2 | 831 | 23 | 11 | 281 | 34.9 | 62.1 | 3.0 |
| Perkins | 22.6 | 7 727 | 27.2 | 47.5 | 1.7 | 0.3 | 11.7 | 5.9 | 2 014 | 17 | 12 | 359 | 21.8 | 76.9 | 1.3 |
| Phelps | 35.6 | 3 882 | 57.7 | 3.7 | 3.2 | 0.2 | 10.5 | 17.3 | 1 882 | 43 | 37 | 714 | 23.5 | 75.1 | 1.4 |
| Pierce | 28.9 | 3 972 | 46.7 | 18.5 | 1.6 | 0.0 | 12.8 | 7.6 | 1 041 | 30 | 29 | 495 | 24.3 | 73.9 | 1.8 |

1. Based on the resident population estimated as of July 1 of the year shown.   2. © 2013 Election Data Services, Inc. All rights reserved.

# Table B. States and Counties — **Land Area and Population**

| STATE/County code | CBSA code[1] | County type[2] | STATE County | Land area,[3] (sq km) 2010 | Population 2012 Total persons | Rank | Per square kilometer | White | Black | American Indian, Alaska Native | Asian and Pacific Islander | Percent Hispanic or Latino[4] | Under 5 years | 5 to 17 years | 18 to 24 years | 25 to 34 years | 35 to 44 years | 45 to 54 years |
|---|---|---|---|---|---|---|---|---|---|---|---|---|---|---|---|---|---|---|
| | | | | 1 | 2 | 3 | 4 | 5 | 6 | 7 | 8 | 9 | 10 | 11 | 12 | 13 | 14 | 15 |
| | | | NEBRASKA—Cont'd | | | | | | | | | | | | | | | |
| 31 141 | 18100 | 5 | Platte | 1 746 | 32 681 | 1 364 | 18.7 | 84.0 | 0.8 | 0.6 | 0.7 | 14.6 | 7.5 | 19.0 | 8.0 | 12.2 | 11.3 | 14.7 |
| 31 143 | ... | 9 | Polk | 1 135 | 5 320 | 2 816 | 4.7 | 95.8 | 0.3 | 0.7 | 0.5 | 3.6 | 6.0 | 17.9 | 5.5 | 8.8 | 11.6 | 14.5 |
| 31 145 | ... | 7 | Red Willow | 1 857 | 10 975 | 2 360 | 5.9 | 94.0 | 1.3 | 0.8 | 0.5 | 4.3 | 6.1 | 16.8 | 9.1 | 11.0 | 10.3 | 14.5 |
| 31 147 | ... | 7 | Richardson | 1 429 | 8 290 | 2 585 | 5.8 | 94.9 | 0.7 | 4.1 | 0.6 | 1.5 | 5.1 | 16.4 | 6.0 | 9.6 | 10.2 | 15.7 |
| 31 149 | ... | 9 | Rock | 2 612 | 1 376 | 3 091 | 0.5 | 98.6 | 0.2 | 1.0 | 0.3 | 0.2 | 5.1 | 14.9 | 4.1 | 9.3 | 8.8 | 14.7 |
| 31 151 | ... | 6 | Saline | 1 487 | 14 557 | 2 137 | 9.8 | 75.9 | 1.1 | 0.7 | 2.0 | 21.3 | 7.2 | 17.4 | 12.8 | 11.4 | 11.8 | 13.8 |
| 31 153 | 36540 | 2 | Sarpy | 619 | 165 853 | 378 | 267.9 | 85.6 | 5.1 | 0.9 | 3.3 | 7.6 | 8.2 | 20.2 | 8.7 | 15.5 | 14.1 | 14.1 |
| 31 155 | 36540 | 2 | Saunders | 1 943 | 20 823 | 1 788 | 10.7 | 96.7 | 0.6 | 0.7 | 0.7 | 2.2 | 6.4 | 18.9 | 6.5 | 10.3 | 11.9 | 16.4 |
| 31 157 | 42420 | 5 | Scotts Bluff | 1 915 | 36 964 | 1 247 | 19.3 | 76.2 | 0.8 | 1.9 | 0.9 | 21.2 | 7.3 | 17.3 | 8.8 | 12.1 | 10.9 | 13.5 |
| 31 159 | 30700 | 2 | Seward | 1 480 | 16 935 | 1 986 | 11.4 | 96.7 | 0.8 | 0.7 | 0.8 | 1.9 | 5.9 | 17.2 | 14.3 | 9.9 | 10.7 | 14.0 |
| 31 161 | ... | 9 | Sheridan | 6 322 | 5 319 | 2 817 | 0.8 | 85.7 | 1.0 | 11.7 | 1.3 | 3.5 | 5.5 | 17.2 | 5.6 | 9.5 | 10.1 | 13.2 |
| 31 163 | ... | 9 | Sherman | 1 465 | 3 108 | 2 969 | 2.1 | 98.3 | 0.3 | 0.4 | 0.6 | 1.1 | 5.2 | 16.7 | 5.1 | 7.9 | 10.9 | 14.6 |
| 31 165 | ... | 9 | Sioux | 5 353 | 1 315 | 3 094 | 0.2 | 95.4 | 0.4 | 0.8 | 0.5 | 4.1 | 4.9 | 17.0 | 5.4 | 9.9 | 9.2 | 15.2 |
| 31 167 | 35740 | 9 | Stanton | 1 108 | 6 089 | 2 752 | 5.5 | 93.9 | 1.1 | 0.8 | 0.3 | 4.7 | 7.1 | 19.9 | 6.8 | 12.1 | 11.3 | 15.4 |
| 31 169 | ... | 9 | Thayer | 1 486 | 5 134 | 2 831 | 3.5 | 97.6 | 0.7 | 0.6 | 0.5 | 1.6 | 5.3 | 15.3 | 5.7 | 8.0 | 10.0 | 14.1 |
| 31 171 | ... | 9 | Thomas | 1 847 | 676 | 3 131 | 0.4 | 97.1 | 0.4 | 0.4 | 0.4 | 2.1 | 5.4 | 16.6 | 4.7 | 10.2 | 9.9 | 12.4 |
| 31 173 | ... | 8 | Thurston | 1 019 | 7 020 | 2 682 | 6.9 | 41.6 | 0.9 | 54.6 | 0.7 | 3.9 | 10.9 | 24.8 | 9.8 | 10.5 | 9.8 | 12.0 |
| 31 175 | ... | 9 | Valley | 1 471 | 4 229 | 2 889 | 2.9 | 97.6 | 0.4 | 0.5 | 0.6 | 1.8 | 5.6 | 16.4 | 5.7 | 9.8 | 10.4 | 13.9 |
| 31 177 | 36540 | 2 | Washington | 1 010 | 20 252 | 1 828 | 20.1 | 96.5 | 1.0 | 0.6 | 0.6 | 2.2 | 5.6 | 18.9 | 8.3 | 9.9 | 12.1 | 16.6 |
| 31 179 | ... | 6 | Wayne | 1 147 | 9 554 | 2 468 | 8.3 | 92.7 | 1.7 | 0.7 | 1.1 | 4.5 | 5.2 | 13.1 | 29.7 | 9.3 | 8.2 | 11.0 |
| 31 181 | ... | 9 | Webster | 1 489 | 3 725 | 2 929 | 2.5 | 94.8 | 0.9 | 0.9 | 0.8 | 3.8 | 5.8 | 16.2 | 6.1 | 8.3 | 9.9 | 16.2 |
| 31 183 | ... | 9 | Wheeler | 1 490 | 805 | 3 119 | 0.5 | 98.8 | 0.2 | 0.6 | 0.6 | 0.6 | 6.6 | 17.2 | 4.9 | 10.0 | 9.8 | 15.4 |
| 31 185 | ... | 7 | York | 1 483 | 13 746 | 2 193 | 9.3 | 93.7 | 1.5 | 0.8 | 0.8 | 4.1 | 6.5 | 16.0 | 9.1 | 11.6 | 10.5 | 14.4 |
| 32 000 | ... | X | NEVADA | 284 332 | 2 758 931 | X | 9.7 | 56.0 | 8.8 | 1.5 | 9.8 | 27.1 | 6.8 | 17.5 | 9.2 | 14.3 | 13.9 | 13.8 |
| 32 001 | 21980 | 6 | Churchill | 12 770 | 24 375 | 1 631 | 1.9 | 78.0 | 2.5 | 5.2 | 4.8 | 12.7 | 6.7 | 18.1 | 8.6 | 12.2 | 11.4 | 14.2 |
| 32 003 | 29820 | 1 | Clark | 20 439 | 2 000 759 | 14 | 97.9 | 50.0 | 11.2 | 1.0 | 11.5 | 29.7 | 7.0 | 17.8 | 9.2 | 15.0 | 14.5 | 13.5 |
| 32 005 | 23820 | 4 | Douglas | 1 838 | 46 996 | 1 026 | 25.6 | 84.5 | 1.0 | 2.5 | 3.3 | 11.3 | 4.7 | 14.8 | 6.6 | 9.2 | 10.4 | 15.8 |
| 32 007 | 21220 | 5 | Elko | 44 470 | 51 216 | 966 | 1.2 | 70.0 | 1.2 | 5.5 | 1.8 | 23.5 | 8.2 | 20.7 | 9.5 | 13.8 | 12.7 | 14.7 |
| 32 009 | ... | 9 | Esmeralda | 9 277 | 775 | 3 121 | 0.1 | 78.1 | 1.0 | 5.8 | 1.7 | 16.9 | 5.2 | 13.4 | 3.9 | 8.9 | 9.5 | 14.8 |
| 32 011 | 21220 | 9 | Eureka | 10 815 | 2 001 | 3 053 | 0.2 | 83.6 | 0.8 | 3.1 | 1.4 | 12.6 | 6.6 | 17.4 | 8.2 | 9.0 | 12.4 | 17.5 |
| 32 013 | ... | 7 | Humboldt | 24 969 | 17 048 | 1 976 | 0.7 | 69.9 | 1.1 | 4.5 | 1.5 | 24.7 | 7.7 | 19.4 | 8.7 | 13.1 | 12.7 | 15.0 |
| 32 015 | ... | 7 | Lander | 14 219 | 5 941 | 2 766 | 0.4 | 73.1 | 0.9 | 4.2 | 0.7 | 22.3 | 8.2 | 18.8 | 9.5 | 11.8 | 12.2 | 14.9 |
| 32 017 | ... | 8 | Lincoln | 27 540 | 5 405 | 2 813 | 0.2 | 88.7 | 3.0 | 1.8 | 1.6 | 6.6 | 5.3 | 19.8 | 8.5 | 10.2 | 10.5 | 12.5 |
| 32 019 | 22280 | 6 | Lyon | 5 183 | 51 327 | 964 | 9.9 | 79.6 | 1.6 | 3.3 | 2.7 | 15.4 | 6.3 | 17.9 | 6.9 | 11.0 | 11.7 | 14.6 |
| 32 021 | ... | 7 | Mineral | 9 720 | 4 653 | 2 862 | 0.5 | 70.2 | 5.4 | 15.2 | 2.3 | 10.4 | 4.8 | 13.5 | 7.4 | 9.4 | 9.1 | 15.1 |
| 32 023 | 37220 | 6 | Nye | 47 091 | 42 963 | 1 113 | 0.9 | 80.6 | 2.7 | 2.7 | 2.7 | 13.8 | 4.8 | 15.1 | 6.2 | 8.1 | 9.7 | 14.7 |
| 32 027 | ... | 8 | Pershing | 15 635 | 6 749 | 2 703 | 0.4 | 69.4 | 4.3 | 3.5 | 2.0 | 22.5 | 4.3 | 14.2 | 8.0 | 13.5 | 15.4 | 17.6 |
| 32 029 | 39900 | 2 | Storey | 681 | 3 935 | 2 913 | 5.8 | 89.4 | 1.5 | 2.4 | 2.4 | 6.0 | 3.7 | 12.5 | 5.4 | 7.7 | 9.6 | 19.1 |
| 32 031 | 39900 | 2 | Washoe | 16 323 | 429 908 | 160 | 26.3 | 67.7 | 2.9 | 2.0 | 7.2 | 22.7 | 6.5 | 16.8 | 10.5 | 13.6 | 12.8 | 14.2 |
| 32 033 | ... | 7 | White Pine | 22 988 | 10 042 | 2 440 | 0.4 | 76.9 | 4.5 | 4.8 | 1.7 | 14.0 | 6.6 | 14.9 | 7.9 | 14.0 | 12.5 | 15.2 |
| 32 510 | 16180 | 3 | Carson City | 375 | 54 838 | 914 | 146.2 | 71.6 | 2.5 | 2.8 | 3.1 | 22.0 | 5.8 | 15.3 | 8.5 | 12.0 | 12.2 | 15.1 |
| 33 000 | ... | X | NEW HAMPSHIRE | 23 187 | 1 320 718 | X | 57.0 | 93.4 | 1.6 | 0.7 | 2.7 | 2.9 | 5.1 | 16.1 | 9.5 | 11.2 | 13.1 | 16.9 |
| 33 001 | 29060 | 4 | Belknap | 1 037 | 60 327 | 860 | 58.2 | 96.6 | 0.8 | 0.9 | 1.6 | 1.3 | 5.0 | 15.3 | 6.9 | 10.5 | 12.2 | 16.6 |
| 33 003 | ... | 8 | Carroll | 2 411 | 47 567 | 1 019 | 19.7 | 97.7 | 0.6 | 0.9 | 0.9 | 1.0 | 3.9 | 14.1 | 6.0 | 8.2 | 11.3 | 17.1 |
| 33 005 | 28300 | 4 | Cheshire | 1 830 | 76 851 | 712 | 42.0 | 96.5 | 0.9 | 0.8 | 1.6 | 1.5 | 4.8 | 14.4 | 13.7 | 10.4 | 11.5 | 15.3 |
| 33 007 | 13620 | 7 | Coos | 4 648 | 32 096 | 1 388 | 6.9 | 97.2 | 0.8 | 1.1 | 0.9 | 1.3 | 4.3 | 13.9 | 6.9 | 9.8 | 12.1 | 16.5 |
| 33 009 | 30100 | 5 | Grafton | 4 426 | 89 181 | 641 | 20.1 | 93.7 | 1.3 | 1.0 | 3.6 | 1.9 | 4.5 | 13.4 | 14.0 | 10.9 | 11.1 | 15.2 |
| 33 011 | 31700 | 2 | Hillsborough | 2 269 | 402 922 | 169 | 177.6 | 89.0 | 2.5 | 0.6 | 4.0 | 5.5 | 5.8 | 17.2 | 8.6 | 12.4 | 13.9 | 17.0 |
| 33 013 | 18180 | 4 | Merrimack | 2 419 | 146 761 | 431 | 60.7 | 95.3 | 1.5 | 0.8 | 2.0 | 1.7 | 5.0 | 16.2 | 9.0 | 11.2 | 13.1 | 16.9 |
| 33 015 | 14460 | 1 | Rockingham | 1 799 | 297 820 | 222 | 165.5 | 95.1 | 1.1 | 0.6 | 2.3 | 2.2 | 4.8 | 17.3 | 7.5 | 10.1 | 13.9 | 18.7 |
| 33 017 | 14460 | 1 | Strafford | 956 | 124 119 | 494 | 129.8 | 94.2 | 1.5 | 0.8 | 3.3 | 1.9 | 5.3 | 14.8 | 15.7 | 12.1 | 12.5 | 15.4 |
| 33 019 | 17200 | 7 | Sullivan | 1 392 | 43 074 | 1 107 | 30.9 | 97.4 | 0.8 | 1.1 | 0.9 | 1.2 | 5.2 | 15.4 | 6.9 | 10.3 | 12.8 | 16.5 |
| 34 000 | ... | X | NEW JERSEY | 19 047 | 8 864 590 | X | 465.4 | 60.0 | 13.6 | 0.5 | 9.2 | 18.1 | 6.1 | 17.1 | 8.8 | 12.7 | 13.7 | 15.6 |
| 34 001 | 12100 | 2 | Atlantic | 1 439 | 275 422 | 240 | 191.4 | 59.6 | 15.9 | 0.7 | 8.4 | 17.3 | 6.0 | 17.0 | 9.3 | 11.5 | 12.7 | 16.0 |
| 34 003 | 35620 | 1 | Bergen | 603 | 918 888 | 56 | 1 523.9 | 62.7 | 5.9 | 0.3 | 15.7 | 16.8 | 5.4 | 16.8 | 7.5 | 11.7 | 14.0 | 16.2 |
| 34 005 | 37980 | 1 | Burlington | 2 068 | 451 336 | 148 | 218.2 | 72.1 | 17.3 | 0.7 | 5.5 | 6.7 | 5.6 | 17.2 | 8.4 | 11.7 | 13.4 | 16.7 |
| 34 007 | 37980 | 1 | Camden | 573 | 513 539 | 127 | 896.2 | 61.1 | 19.4 | 0.6 | 5.9 | 14.7 | 6.4 | 17.6 | 9.1 | 13.3 | 13.2 | 15.1 |
| 34 009 | 36140 | 3 | Cape May | 651 | 96 304 | 606 | 147.9 | 87.9 | 5.2 | 0.5 | 1.4 | 6.4 | 4.8 | 13.7 | 8.0 | 9.7 | 10.1 | 15.3 |
| 34 011 | 47220 | 3 | Cumberland | 1 253 | 157 785 | 400 | 125.9 | 51.3 | 19.9 | 1.4 | 1.8 | 27.6 | 6.9 | 17.0 | 9.5 | 14.4 | 13.8 | 14.1 |
| 34 013 | 35620 | 1 | Essex | 327 | 787 744 | 75 | 2 409.0 | 34.5 | 40.2 | 0.6 | 5.4 | 20.8 | 6.9 | 17.8 | 9.5 | 13.7 | 14.6 | 14.6 |
| 34 015 | 37980 | 1 | Gloucester | 834 | 289 586 | 226 | 347.2 | 82.1 | 10.8 | 0.5 | 3.3 | 5.0 | 5.9 | 18.0 | 9.3 | 11.6 | 13.8 | 16.2 |
| 34 017 | 35620 | 1 | Hudson | 120 | 652 302 | 94 | 5 435.9 | 31.9 | 12.2 | 0.4 | 14.5 | 42.4 | 6.8 | 13.8 | 9.6 | 21.0 | 15.3 | 13.0 |
| 34 019 | 35620 | 1 | Hunterdon | 1 108 | 127 050 | 486 | 114.7 | 88.1 | 3.0 | 0.3 | 4.0 | 5.5 | 4.4 | 18.3 | 7.4 | 8.3 | 13.2 | 20.0 |

1. CBSA = Core Based Statistical Area. See Appendix A for explanation. See Appendix B for list of metropolitan areas with component counties.   2. County type code from the Economic Research Service of USDA Rural-Urban Continuum Codes. See Appendix A for definition.   3. Dry land or land partially or temporarily covered by water.   4. May be of any race.

# Table B. States and Counties — **Population and Households**

| | Population, 2011 (cont.) | | | | Population change and components of change, 2000–2012 | | | | | | | Households, 2010 | | | | |
|---|---|---|---|---|---|---|---|---|---|---|---|---|---|---|---|---|
| | Age (percent) (cont.) | | | | Total persons | | Percent change | | Components of change, 2010–2012 | | | | | | Percent | |
| STATE County | 55 to 64 years | 65 to 74 years | 75 years and over | Percent female | 2000 | 2010 | 2000–2010 | 2010–2012 | Births | Deaths | Net migration | Number | Percent change, 2000–2010 | Persons per house-hold | Female family house-holder[1] | One per-son |
| | 16 | 17 | 18 | 19 | 20 | 21 | 22 | 23 | 24 | 25 | 26 | 27 | 28 | 29 | 30 | 31 |
| NEBRASKA—Cont'd | | | | | | | | | | | | | | | | |
| Platte | 12.4 | 7.3 | 7.6 | 49.8 | 31 662 | 32 237 | 1.8 | 1.4 | 1 163 | 596 | -144 | 12 658 | 4.8 | 2.51 | 8.5 | 26.8 |
| Polk | 16.2 | 8.7 | 10.7 | 50.2 | 5 639 | 5 406 | -4.1 | -1.6 | 135 | 150 | -66 | 2 212 | -2.1 | 2.39 | 5.8 | 27.5 |
| Red Willow | 13.4 | 8.6 | 10.0 | 50.3 | 11 448 | 11 055 | -3.4 | -0.7 | 274 | 300 | -54 | 4 663 | -1.0 | 2.29 | 8.2 | 31.6 |
| Richardson | 14.0 | 11.0 | 12.1 | 50.6 | 9 531 | 8 363 | -12.3 | -0.9 | 201 | 273 | 0 | 3 718 | -6.9 | 2.21 | 8.0 | 33.6 |
| Rock | 19.0 | 10.7 | 13.4 | 49.7 | 1 756 | 1 526 | -13.1 | -9.8 | 27 | 40 | -157 | 685 | -10.2 | 2.18 | 4.5 | 30.5 |
| Saline | 11.3 | 6.4 | 7.9 | 49.6 | 13 843 | 14 200 | 2.6 | 2.5 | 503 | 312 | 166 | 5 131 | -1.1 | 2.57 | 7.8 | 26.8 |
| Sarpy | 10.2 | 5.3 | 3.6 | 50.3 | 122 595 | 158 840 | 29.6 | 4.4 | 5 932 | 1 776 | 2 818 | 58 102 | 33.8 | 2.71 | 10.2 | 21.4 |
| Saunders | 13.7 | 8.3 | 7.6 | 49.3 | 19 830 | 20 780 | 4.8 | 0.2 | 607 | 437 | -135 | 8 040 | 7.2 | 2.54 | 6.9 | 23.8 |
| Scotts Bluff | 13.3 | 8.3 | 8.7 | 51.7 | 36 951 | 36 970 | 0.1 | 0.0 | 1 225 | 943 | -298 | 14 928 | 0.3 | 2.42 | 11.0 | 29.4 |
| Seward | 12.7 | 7.6 | 7.6 | 48.9 | 16 496 | 16 750 | 1.5 | 1.1 | 439 | 376 | 110 | 6 266 | 4.2 | 2.47 | 5.4 | 26.1 |
| Sheridan | 16.5 | 9.7 | 12.6 | 51.3 | 6 198 | 5 469 | -11.8 | -2.7 | 107 | 143 | -111 | 2 380 | -6.6 | 2.25 | 7.9 | 33.7 |
| Sherman | 16.0 | 11.0 | 12.7 | 50.8 | 3 318 | 3 152 | -5.0 | -1.4 | 53 | 104 | -5 | 1 392 | -0.1 | 2.22 | 5.4 | 32.7 |
| Sioux | 16.5 | 10.6 | 11.4 | 49.1 | 1 475 | 1 311 | -11.1 | 0.3 | 20 | 12 | -3 | 577 | -4.6 | 2.27 | 5.5 | 29.1 |
| Stanton | 13.3 | 7.3 | 6.8 | 50.2 | 6 455 | 6 129 | -5.1 | -0.7 | 170 | 85 | -134 | 2 387 | 3.9 | 2.57 | 7.5 | 24.2 |
| Thayer | 16.0 | 10.9 | 14.6 | 51.3 | 6 055 | 5 228 | -13.7 | -1.8 | 113 | 216 | 5 | 2 296 | -9.6 | 2.21 | 4.7 | 33.0 |
| Thomas | 17.5 | 12.2 | 11.0 | 49.2 | 729 | 647 | -11.2 | 4.5 | 9 | 14 | 30 | 291 | -10.5 | 2.22 | 1.7 | 33.0 |
| Thurston | 9.9 | 5.9 | 6.4 | 50.5 | 7 171 | 6 940 | -3.2 | 1.2 | 387 | 142 | -170 | 2 158 | -4.3 | 3.19 | 20.8 | 21.3 |
| Valley | 14.7 | 11.2 | 12.4 | 50.5 | 4 647 | 4 260 | -8.3 | -0.7 | 113 | 131 | -19 | 1 922 | -2.2 | 2.19 | 4.9 | 35.0 |
| Washington | 14.1 | 7.7 | 6.8 | 50.2 | 18 780 | 20 234 | 7.7 | 0.1 | 452 | 389 | -36 | 7 761 | 11.8 | 2.54 | 7.6 | 23.0 |
| Wayne | 9.9 | 6.3 | 7.4 | 49.9 | 9 851 | 9 595 | -2.6 | -0.4 | 202 | 111 | -137 | 3 507 | 2.0 | 2.38 | 5.6 | 27.8 |
| Webster | 13.9 | 10.7 | 13.0 | 51.9 | 4 061 | 3 812 | -6.1 | -2.3 | 77 | 122 | -41 | 1 604 | -6.1 | 2.28 | 7.1 | 32.4 |
| Wheeler | 16.5 | 10.9 | 8.7 | 48.8 | 886 | 818 | -7.7 | -1.6 | 24 | 5 | -31 | 350 | -0.6 | 2.34 | 2.3 | 27.7 |
| York | 13.7 | 8.8 | 9.5 | 51.2 | 14 598 | 13 665 | -6.4 | 0.6 | 393 | 329 | 14 | 5 564 | -2.8 | 2.32 | 6.6 | 29.1 |
| NEVADA | 12.0 | 7.6 | 4.9 | 49.5 | 1 998 257 | 2 700 551 | 35.1 | 2.2 | 81 640 | 43 829 | 20 711 | 1 006 250 | 34.0 | 2.65 | 12.7 | 25.7 |
| Churchill | 13.1 | 9.3 | 6.3 | 49.9 | 23 982 | 24 877 | 3.7 | -2.0 | 745 | 528 | -730 | 9 671 | 8.5 | 2.53 | 11.3 | 25.2 |
| Clark | 11.3 | 7.2 | 4.6 | 49.7 | 1 375 765 | 1 951 269 | 41.8 | 2.5 | 60 960 | 29 877 | 18 588 | 715 365 | 39.7 | 2.70 | 13.5 | 25.3 |
| Douglas | 17.4 | 12.6 | 8.5 | 50.0 | 41 259 | 46 997 | 13.9 | 0.0 | 873 | 907 | 69 | 19 638 | 19.7 | 2.38 | 8.9 | 24.0 |
| Elko | 11.6 | 5.6 | 3.1 | 48.0 | 45 291 | 48 818 | 7.8 | 4.9 | 1 702 | 613 | 1 274 | 17 442 | 11.5 | 2.77 | 9.1 | 22.5 |
| Esmeralda | 18.1 | 15.2 | 11.0 | 43.7 | 971 | 783 | -19.4 | -1.0 | 12 | 9 | -17 | 389 | -14.5 | 2.01 | 5.9 | 40.6 |
| Eureka | 15.5 | 8.3 | 5.1 | 46.9 | 1 651 | 1 987 | 20.4 | 0.7 | 38 | 25 | 2 | 836 | 25.5 | 2.38 | 4.2 | 33.0 |
| Humboldt | 13.1 | 6.3 | 4.0 | 47.5 | 16 106 | 16 528 | 2.6 | 3.1 | 577 | 244 | 163 | 6 289 | 9.7 | 2.60 | 8.9 | 25.6 |
| Lander | 12.8 | 7.7 | 4.2 | 49.1 | 5 794 | 5 775 | -0.3 | 2.9 | 217 | 68 | 21 | 2 213 | 5.7 | 2.60 | 9.4 | 25.6 |
| Lincoln | 14.4 | 11.6 | 7.1 | 45.9 | 4 165 | 5 345 | 28.3 | 1.1 | 96 | 108 | 68 | 1 988 | 29.1 | 2.57 | 7.7 | 30.4 |
| Lyon | 14.6 | 11.0 | 6.1 | 49.5 | 34 501 | 51 980 | 50.7 | -1.3 | 1 293 | 1 078 | -881 | 19 808 | 52.3 | 2.61 | 10.2 | 22.1 |
| Mineral | 17.9 | 13.2 | 9.5 | 51.4 | 5 071 | 4 772 | -5.9 | -2.5 | 103 | 196 | -33 | 2 240 | 2.0 | 2.11 | 11.2 | 36.7 |
| Nye | 16.8 | 15.7 | 8.9 | 49.4 | 32 485 | 43 946 | 35.3 | -2.2 | 842 | 1 297 | -514 | 18 032 | 35.5 | 2.42 | 9.3 | 26.8 |
| Pershing | 12.6 | 9.6 | 4.6 | 36.5 | 6 693 | 6 753 | 0.9 | -0.1 | 96 | 126 | 21 | 2 018 | 2.9 | 2.51 | 9.1 | 26.6 |
| Storey | 22.2 | 13.7 | 6.1 | 49.0 | 3 399 | 4 010 | 18.0 | -1.9 | 45 | 42 | -99 | 1 742 | 19.2 | 2.30 | 7.6 | 26.0 |
| Washoe | 13.0 | 7.6 | 5.0 | 49.6 | 339 486 | 421 407 | 24.1 | 2.0 | 12 313 | 7 131 | 3 337 | 163 445 | 23.7 | 2.55 | 11.3 | 27.2 |
| White Pine | 13.8 | 9.0 | 6.2 | 43.2 | 9 181 | 10 030 | 9.2 | 0.1 | 261 | 189 | -71 | 3 707 | 12.9 | 2.37 | 8.8 | 30.2 |
| Carson City | 14.0 | 9.1 | 7.9 | 48.2 | 52 457 | 55 274 | 5.4 | -0.8 | 1 467 | 1 391 | -487 | 21 427 | 6.2 | 2.41 | 12.0 | 30.4 |
| NEW HAMPSHIRE | 14.1 | 7.7 | 6.3 | 50.6 | 1 235 786 | 1 316 470 | 6.5 | 0.3 | 28 428 | 23 334 | -389 | 518 973 | 9.3 | 2.46 | 9.7 | 25.6 |
| Belknap | 16.3 | 9.5 | 7.7 | 50.8 | 56 325 | 60 088 | 6.7 | 0.4 | 1 275 | 1 507 | 482 | 24 766 | 10.3 | 2.39 | 9.8 | 25.7 |
| Carroll | 18.0 | 12.1 | 9.3 | 50.4 | 43 666 | 47 818 | 9.5 | -0.5 | 833 | 1 159 | 99 | 21 052 | 14.7 | 2.25 | 8.1 | 28.4 |
| Cheshire | 14.7 | 8.2 | 6.9 | 51.2 | 73 825 | 77 117 | 4.5 | -0.3 | 1 609 | 1 440 | -397 | 30 204 | 6.7 | 2.40 | 9.4 | 26.2 |
| Coos | 16.6 | 10.4 | 9.6 | 48.9 | 33 111 | 33 055 | -0.2 | -2.9 | 587 | 926 | -614 | 14 171 | 1.5 | 2.23 | 9.2 | 30.3 |
| Grafton | 14.9 | 8.7 | 7.3 | 50.5 | 81 743 | 89 118 | 9.0 | 0.1 | 1 716 | 1 632 | 28 | 35 986 | 13.9 | 2.28 | 8.4 | 29.4 |
| Hillsborough | 12.9 | 6.7 | 5.6 | 50.5 | 380 841 | 400 721 | 5.2 | 0.5 | 9 948 | 6 430 | -1 175 | 155 466 | 7.6 | 2.53 | 10.5 | 25.3 |
| Merrimack | 14.6 | 7.4 | 6.6 | 50.7 | 136 225 | 146 445 | 7.5 | 0.2 | 3 055 | 2 625 | -87 | 57 069 | 10.1 | 2.46 | 9.9 | 25.4 |
| Rockingham | 14.5 | 7.6 | 5.7 | 50.6 | 277 359 | 295 223 | 6.4 | 0.9 | 5 624 | 4 695 | 1 787 | 115 033 | 10.0 | 2.54 | 8.9 | 23.5 |
| Strafford | 12.0 | 6.5 | 5.6 | 51.2 | 112 233 | 123 143 | 9.7 | 0.8 | 2 885 | 2 014 | 162 | 47 100 | 10.6 | 2.44 | 10.5 | 26.3 |
| Sullivan | 15.9 | 9.5 | 7.5 | 50.5 | 40 458 | 43 742 | 8.1 | -1.5 | 896 | 906 | -674 | 18 126 | 9.7 | 2.37 | 9.9 | 26.1 |
| NEW JERSEY | 12.3 | 7.2 | 6.5 | 51.3 | 8 414 350 | 8 791 894 | 4.5 | 0.8 | 230 222 | 154 982 | -1 594 | 3 214 360 | 4.9 | 2.68 | 13.3 | 25.2 |
| Atlantic | 13.0 | 7.9 | 6.5 | 51.4 | 252 552 | 274 549 | 8.7 | 0.3 | 7 658 | 5 675 | -1 038 | 102 847 | 8.2 | 2.61 | 15.5 | 26.9 |
| Bergen | 13.1 | 7.6 | 7.6 | 51.7 | 884 118 | 905 116 | 2.4 | 1.5 | 19 578 | 15 020 | 9 497 | 335 730 | 1.5 | 2.66 | 10.9 | 24.6 |
| Burlington | 12.9 | 7.4 | 6.7 | 50.9 | 423 394 | 448 734 | 6.0 | 0.6 | 10 564 | 8 217 | 455 | 166 318 | 7.7 | 2.62 | 12.0 | 24.4 |
| Camden | 12.4 | 6.8 | 6.2 | 51.7 | 508 932 | 513 657 | 0.9 | 0.0 | 14 663 | 9 897 | -4 856 | 190 980 | 2.8 | 2.65 | 16.4 | 26.3 |
| Cape May | 16.3 | 11.7 | 10.3 | 51.4 | 102 326 | 97 265 | -4.9 | -1.0 | 2 069 | 2 822 | -138 | 40 812 | -3.2 | 2.32 | 11.0 | 31.2 |
| Cumberland | 11.4 | 6.9 | 5.9 | 48.6 | 146 438 | 156 898 | 7.1 | 0.6 | 4 982 | 3 114 | -922 | 51 931 | 5.7 | 2.79 | 18.6 | 24.0 |
| Essex | 11.2 | 6.2 | 5.5 | 51.9 | 793 633 | 783 969 | -1.2 | 0.5 | 23 018 | 13 034 | -6 503 | 283 712 | 0.0 | 2.68 | 20.6 | 27.7 |
| Gloucester | 12.5 | 6.9 | 5.8 | 51.5 | 254 673 | 288 288 | 13.2 | 0.5 | 7 049 | 5 326 | -406 | 104 271 | 14.9 | 2.72 | 12.4 | 22.0 |
| Hudson | 10.0 | 5.7 | 4.7 | 50.4 | 608 975 | 634 266 | 4.2 | 2.8 | 20 150 | 8 423 | 6 061 | 246 437 | 6.9 | 2.54 | 16.4 | 29.9 |
| Hunterdon | 15.1 | 7.7 | 5.6 | 50.1 | 121 989 | 128 349 | 5.2 | -1.0 | 2 053 | 1 860 | -1 487 | 47 169 | 8.0 | 2.62 | 7.0 | 22.0 |

1. No spouse present.

Items 16—31

# Table B. States and Counties — Population, Vital Statistics, Medicare, and Crime

| STATE County | Persons in group quarters, 2010 | Daytime population, 2007–2011 Number | Employ-ment/resi-dence ratio | Births, 2011 Total | Rate[1] | Deaths, 2011 Number | Rate[1] | Persons under 65 with no health insurance, 2010 Number | Percent | Medicare, 2012 Eligible for Medicare | Enrolled in Medicare Advantage | Enrolled in a Medicare prescription drug plan | Serious crimes known to police,[2] 2011 Total Number | Rate[3] |
|---|---|---|---|---|---|---|---|---|---|---|---|---|---|---|
| | 32 | 33 | 34 | 35 | 36 | 37 | 38 | 39 | 40 | 41 | 42 | 43 | 44 | 45 |
| NEBRASKA—Cont'd | | | | | | | | | | | | | | |
| Platte | 476 | 34 934 | 1.18 | 496 | 15.2 | 256 | 7.9 | 3 612 | 13.4 | 5 595 | 268 | 3 361 | 661 | 2 032 |
| Polk | 124 | 4 544 | 0.68 | 55 | 10.3 | 63 | 11.8 | 529 | 12.4 | 1 104 | 31 | 748 | 61 | 1 118 |
| Red Willow | 369 | 11 333 | 1.05 | 123 | 11.1 | 131 | 11.9 | 1 138 | 13.2 | 2 345 | 45 | 1 642 | 267 | 2 394 |
| Richardson | 155 | 7 395 | 0.74 | 90 | 10.8 | 123 | 14.7 | 967 | 15.2 | 2 136 | 36 | 1 426 | 69 | 818 |
| Rock | 30 | 1 552 | 0.94 | 14 | 9.4 | 18 | 12.0 | 272 | 23.4 | 174 | D | 151 | 12 | 779 |
| Saline | 1 038 | 14 625 | 1.07 | 217 | 15.1 | 132 | 9.2 | 1 599 | 14.3 | 2 348 | 66 | 1 575 | 305 | 2 129 |
| Sarpy | 1 277 | 130 934 | 0.70 | 2 578 | 15.9 | 750 | 4.6 | 13 466 | 9.2 | 18 242 | 2 835 | 6 546 | 2 733 | 1 705 |
| Saunders | 335 | 15 561 | 0.53 | 268 | 12.8 | 175 | 8.4 | 1 788 | 10.3 | 3 651 | 341 | 2 142 | 241 | 1 150 |
| Scotts Bluff | 847 | 37 222 | 1.03 | 546 | 14.7 | 406 | 11.0 | 4 806 | 15.9 | 7 407 | 904 | 4 459 | 1 141 | 3 128 |
| Seward | 1 296 | 14 817 | 0.79 | 198 | 11.9 | 156 | 9.3 | 1 246 | 9.5 | 2 925 | 104 | 1 933 | NA | NA |
| Sheridan | 113 | 4 956 | 0.79 | 53 | 9.8 | 67 | 12.4 | 801 | 19.1 | 1 256 | 151 | 679 | 110 | 1 993 |
| Sherman | 56 | 2 628 | 0.67 | 26 | 8.4 | 52 | 16.8 | 405 | 17.0 | 792 | 86 | 460 | 20 | 629 |
| Sioux | 0 | 1 060 | 0.59 | 8 | 6.0 | 1 | 0.7 | 212 | 20.7 | 230 | 41 | 138 | NA | NA |
| Stanton | 0 | 4 664 | 0.55 | 79 | 12.8 | 39 | 6.3 | 703 | 13.5 | 925 | 133 | 539 | 65 | 1 051 |
| Thayer | 156 | 5 470 | 1.09 | 47 | 9.1 | 96 | 18.6 | 535 | 14.0 | 1 344 | 30 | 947 | 78 | 1 479 |
| Thomas | 2 | 765 | 1.07 | 6 | 8.4 | 4 | 5.6 | 132 | 25.6 | 143 | D | 94 | NA | NA |
| Thurston | 58 | 7 296 | 1.15 | 166 | 23.7 | 55 | 7.9 | 1 129 | 18.5 | 941 | 80 | 588 | NA | NA |
| Valley | 49 | 4 438 | 1.08 | 49 | 11.6 | 57 | 13.5 | 591 | 18.4 | 1 028 | 24 | 708 | NA | NA |
| Washington | 535 | 18 521 | 0.84 | 200 | 9.9 | 169 | 8.3 | 1 545 | 9.1 | 3 390 | 499 | 1 807 | 220 | 1 078 |
| Wayne | 1 262 | 9 077 | 0.91 | 92 | 9.7 | 48 | 5.1 | 1 033 | 14.7 | 1 421 | 152 | 940 | NA | NA |
| Webster | 156 | 3 453 | 0.78 | 36 | 9.5 | 63 | 16.7 | 422 | 14.9 | 978 | 60 | 654 | 41 | 1 066 |
| Wheeler | 0 | 737 | 1.10 | 11 | 13.4 | 0 | 0.0 | 156 | 23.7 | 144 | D | 98 | 4 | 485 |
| York | 737 | 14 776 | 1.14 | 169 | 12.3 | 139 | 10.1 | 1 247 | 11.9 | 2 861 | 68 | 1 911 | 272 | 1 973 |
| NEVADA | 36 154 | 2 685 761 | 1.01 | 36 772 | 13.5 | 19 373 | 7.1 | 589 059 | 25.1 | 395 282 | 125 342 | 114 202 | 85 040 | 3 123 |
| Churchill | 366 | 24 288 | 0.94 | 341 | 13.8 | 242 | 9.8 | 4 813 | 23.1 | 4 721 | 442 | 1 791 | 637 | 2 539 |
| Clark | 21 992 | 1 941 134 | 1.01 | 27 563 | 14.0 | 13 168 | 6.7 | 435 139 | 25.4 | 262 493 | 95 037 | 69 557 | 63 044 | 3 204 |
| Douglas | 230 | 47 056 | 1.00 | 379 | 8.1 | 441 | 9.4 | 7 703 | 20.9 | 11 606 | 883 | 4 832 | 801 | 1 690 |
| Elko | 570 | 46 291 | 0.91 | 754 | 15.2 | 276 | 5.6 | 10 517 | 23.9 | 5 241 | 322 | 2 396 | 999 | 2 029 |
| Esmeralda | 1 | 862 | 0.90 | 8 | 10.3 | 4 | 5.2 | 199 | 33.5 | 238 | 33 | 95 | 3 | 380 |
| Eureka | 1 | 5 136 | 5.12 | 17 | 8.6 | 5 | 2.5 | 367 | 21.0 | 288 | 15 | 118 | 44 | 2 196 |
| Humboldt | 183 | 16 782 | 1.07 | 250 | 14.9 | 111 | 6.6 | 3 782 | 25.7 | 2 191 | 165 | 1 008 | 195 | 1 170 |
| Lander | 16 | 5 382 | 0.89 | 98 | 16.8 | 37 | 6.3 | 1 131 | 22.2 | 803 | 69 | 329 | 76 | 1 305 |
| Lincoln | 239 | 5 139 | 0.98 | 44 | 8.3 | 53 | 10.0 | 1 124 | 27.0 | 984 | 81 | 459 | 75 | 1 391 |
| Lyon | 358 | 45 350 | 0.67 | 583 | 11.2 | 478 | 9.2 | 10 841 | 24.9 | 11 017 | 2 190 | 3 726 | 899 | 1 715 |
| Mineral | 52 | 4 880 | 1.07 | 50 | 10.9 | 99 | 21.6 | 875 | 23.5 | 1 265 | 167 | 413 | 7 | 145 |
| Nye | 334 | 42 553 | 0.89 | 387 | 8.9 | 577 | 13.3 | 8 230 | 24.6 | 12 846 | 5 728 | 2 426 | 759 | 1 713 |
| Pershing | 1 681 | 6 752 | 1.01 | 45 | 6.7 | 53 | 7.9 | 1 206 | 28.4 | 892 | 84 | 428 | 82 | 1 204 |
| Storey | 5 | 2 846 | 0.34 | 25 | 6.4 | 17 | 4.4 | 821 | 25.1 | 919 | 146 | 296 | 77 | 1 904 |
| Washoe | 5 272 | 419 503 | 1.01 | 5 448 | 12.8 | 3 105 | 7.3 | 90 450 | 24.6 | 66 861 | 19 038 | 20 138 | 11 850 | 2 788 |
| White Pine | 1 229 | 9 960 | 1.02 | 118 | 11.7 | 93 | 9.2 | 1 580 | 21.5 | 1 718 | 104 | 849 | 175 | 1 730 |
| Carson City | 3 625 | 61 847 | 1.28 | 662 | 11.9 | 614 | 11.1 | 10 283 | 24.0 | 11 199 | 838 | 5 341 | 1 423 | 2 553 |
| NEW HAMPSHIRE | 40 104 | 1 272 937 | 0.94 | 12 795 | 9.7 | 9 778 | 7.4 | 143 475 | 13.0 | 240 163 | 11 752 | 113 227 | 32 584 | 2 472 |
| Belknap | 858 | 57 428 | 0.91 | 578 | 9.6 | 677 | 11.2 | 7 491 | 15.1 | 14 225 | 945 | 6 565 | 2 238 | 3 720 |
| Carroll | 437 | 46 783 | 0.95 | 380 | 8.0 | 493 | 10.3 | 6 743 | 17.9 | 12 559 | 477 | 6 123 | 1 181 | 2 824 |
| Cheshire | 4 627 | 74 456 | 0.93 | 725 | 9.4 | 600 | 7.8 | 8 977 | 14.6 | 15 178 | 1 014 | 7 262 | NA | NA |
| Coos | 1 467 | 32 309 | 0.94 | 254 | 7.8 | 374 | 11.4 | 4 482 | 17.4 | 8 832 | 355 | 4 779 | NA | NA |
| Grafton | 7 001 | 100 454 | 1.27 | 767 | 8.6 | 679 | 7.6 | 9 861 | 14.3 | 17 411 | 939 | 7 542 | 1 756 | 2 524 |
| Hillsborough | 7 759 | 383 112 | 0.92 | 4 448 | 11.1 | 2 731 | 6.8 | 41 402 | 11.9 | 64 086 | 2 433 | 31 753 | 10 242 | 2 709 |
| Merrimack | 6 335 | 148 292 | 1.02 | 1 381 | 9.4 | 1 088 | 7.4 | 15 436 | 12.7 | 27 400 | 1 776 | 11 844 | 3 098 | 2 538 |
| Rockingham | 2 498 | 281 884 | 0.92 | 2 544 | 8.6 | 1 916 | 6.5 | 29 003 | 11.4 | 50 756 | 2 220 | 23 319 | 5 993 | 2 115 |
| Strafford | 8 421 | 110 954 | 0.82 | 1 311 | 10.6 | 842 | 6.8 | 15 023 | 14.9 | 20 522 | 1 037 | 9 767 | 3 347 | 2 754 |
| Sullivan | 701 | 37 265 | 0.71 | 407 | 9.4 | 378 | 8.7 | 5 056 | 14.0 | 9 194 | 556 | 4 273 | NA | NA |
| NEW JERSEY | 186 876 | 8 498 393 | 0.94 | 104 343 | 11.8 | 68 372 | 7.8 | 1 124 840 | 15.0 | 1 410 297 | 214 208 | 723 283 | 216 922 | 2 459 |
| Atlantic | 6 046 | 281 872 | 1.07 | 3 411 | 12.4 | 2 555 | 9.3 | 35 980 | 15.5 | 48 213 | 5 279 | 26 583 | 10 788 | 3 916 |
| Bergen | 10 422 | 888 747 | 0.97 | 8 910 | 9.8 | 6 647 | 7.3 | 111 379 | 14.6 | 152 385 | 19 949 | 78 105 | 12 301 | 1 355 |
| Burlington | 13 214 | 428 484 | 0.91 | 4 658 | 10.4 | 3 599 | 8.0 | 38 547 | 10.3 | 76 220 | 13 253 | 36 651 | 9 025 | 2 005 |
| Camden | 7 414 | 478 231 | 0.85 | 6 652 | 13.0 | 4 350 | 8.5 | 64 773 | 14.6 | 83 675 | 15 821 | 42 657 | 20 829 | 4 042 |
| Cape May | 2 628 | 95 455 | 0.96 | 941 | 9.7 | 1 260 | 13.0 | 10 988 | 14.7 | 24 569 | 2 664 | 14 010 | 4 853 | 4 973 |
| Cumberland | 12 111 | 155 401 | 0.99 | 2 297 | 14.6 | 1 360 | 8.7 | 24 925 | 19.6 | 25 707 | 3 591 | 15 969 | 5 995 | 3 808 |
| Essex | 23 772 | 808 895 | 1.08 | 10 491 | 13.4 | 5 744 | 7.3 | 130 032 | 19.1 | 106 993 | 22 071 | 51 903 | 27 374 | 3 480 |
| Gloucester | 4 223 | 252 203 | 0.75 | 3 167 | 11.0 | 2 329 | 8.1 | 28 313 | 11.4 | 46 021 | 7 917 | 23 294 | 8 047 | 2 782 |
| Hudson | 9 378 | 586 417 | 0.87 | 9 057 | 14.1 | 3 779 | 5.9 | 130 116 | 23.0 | 74 933 | 16 029 | 38 252 | 15 507 | 2 437 |
| Hunterdon | 4 569 | 120 468 | 0.88 | 945 | 7.4 | 788 | 6.2 | 8 210 | 7.6 | 20 435 | 1 862 | 11 120 | 1 121 | 871 |

1. Per 1,000 estimated resident population.   2. Data for serious crimes have not been adjusted for underreporting; this may affect comparability between geographic areas and over time.   3. Per 100,000 population estimated by the FBI.

| STATE County | Serious crimes known to police, 2011 (cont.)[1] Rate[2] | | Education School enrollment and attainment, 2007–2011 Enrollment[3] | | Attainment[4] (percent) | | Local government expenditures,[5] 2009–2010 | | Money income, 2007–2011 | Households Median income | | | Income and poverty, 2011 | Percent below poverty level | | |
|---|---|---|---|---|---|---|---|---|---|---|---|---|---|---|---|---|
| | Violent | Property | Total | Percent private | High school graduate or less | Bachelor's degree or more | Total current expenditures (mil dol) | Current expenditures per student (dollars) | Per capita income[6] (dollars) | Dollars | Percent change, 2000 to 2007–2011 (constant 2011 dollars) | Percent with income of $200,000 or more | Median household income (dollars) | All persons | Children under 18 years | Children 5 to 17 years in families |
| | 46 | 47 | 48 | 49 | 50 | 51 | 52 | 53 | 54 | 55 | 56 | 57 | 58 | 59 | 60 | 61 |
| NEBRASKA—Cont'd | | | | | | | | | | | | | | | | |
| Platte | 86 | 1 946 | 8 362 | 23.7 | 45.1 | 17.6 | 51.4 | 11 171 | 23 730 | 51 273 | -3.5 | 1.7 | 51 209 | 10.4 | 16.9 | 14.9 |
| Polk | 0 | 1 118 | 1 243 | 10.5 | 46.1 | 16.1 | 14.4 | 11 429 | 24 650 | 50 298 | -1.5 | 1.6 | 51 981 | 8.7 | 13.2 | 11.6 |
| Red Willow | 90 | 2 304 | 2 522 | 8.1 | 41.1 | 20.4 | 18.5 | 10 360 | 22 331 | 42 627 | -2.2 | 1.3 | 44 250 | 11.4 | 18.3 | 16.2 |
| Richardson | 24 | 794 | 1 929 | 13.7 | 55.6 | 15.4 | 14.6 | 10 933 | 21 687 | 39 512 | -2.1 | 0.5 | 37 197 | 14.4 | 22.0 | 18.8 |
| Rock | 0 | 779 | 313 | 4.8 | 43.3 | 22.1 | 3.3 | 16 799 | 24 853 | 39 977 | 14.8 | 1.9 | 37 225 | 17.3 | 32.4 | 28.4 |
| Saline | 202 | 1 926 | 4 300 | 24.0 | 53.7 | 14.1 | 33.7 | 10 548 | 20 700 | 45 347 | -6.5 | 2.1 | 47 635 | 11.1 | 13.5 | 12.0 |
| Sarpy | 60 | 1 645 | 47 644 | 16.7 | 28.7 | 35.5 | 233.8 | 9 942 | 29 610 | 69 018 | -5.0 | 3.2 | 65 801 | 6.6 | 9.3 | 8.3 |
| Saunders | 52 | 1 097 | 5 278 | 26.0 | 43.0 | 22.8 | 28.3 | 9 999 | 27 760 | 58 348 | 2.5 | 2.9 | 56 466 | 8.2 | 10.7 | 9.1 |
| Scotts Bluff | 159 | 2 969 | 9 186 | 12.3 | 45.6 | 19.6 | 66.1 | 10 588 | 21 898 | 40 939 | -5.3 | 1.4 | 41 905 | 16.9 | 26.0 | 23.5 |
| Seward | NA | NA | 5 137 | 34.0 | 37.0 | 26.5 | 32.7 | 12 661 | 27 596 | 59 088 | 2.5 | 3.2 | 58 898 | 8.0 | 8.7 | 7.5 |
| Sheridan | 199 | 1 794 | 1 180 | 8.5 | 46.2 | 21.2 | 10.8 | 11 645 | 20 802 | 34 588 | -13.1 | 1.0 | 37 695 | 16.6 | 26.6 | 23.3 |
| Sherman | 0 | 629 | 580 | 1.7 | 54.2 | 15.8 | 5.9 | 12 084 | 22 456 | 41 250 | 6.7 | 1.3 | 40 734 | 13.8 | 22.3 | 19.2 |
| Sioux | NA | NA | 293 | 11.9 | 39.0 | 24.7 | 2.2 | 22 949 | 26 628 | 42 386 | 5.2 | 3.1 | 38 646 | 17.2 | 31.6 | 27.4 |
| Stanton | 113 | 938 | 1 521 | 16.9 | 43.8 | 14.1 | 4.6 | 9 833 | 22 461 | 49 236 | -0.6 | 0.9 | 48 448 | 9.4 | 15.3 | 14.1 |
| Thayer | 57 | 1 422 | 1 017 | 9.2 | 48.7 | 16.9 | 12.3 | 15 205 | 22 176 | 43 198 | 4.1 | 0.9 | 44 818 | 11.3 | 16.2 | 14.1 |
| Thomas | NA | NA | 148 | 7.4 | 34.6 | 18.7 | 1.9 | 19 412 | 25 404 | 51 375 | 39.4 | 2.5 | 41 783 | 15.2 | 25.3 | 23.5 |
| Thurston | NA | NA | 2 385 | 5.5 | 49.0 | 13.3 | 22.3 | 14 580 | 16 497 | 39 568 | 4.0 | 1.8 | 38 786 | 23.2 | 32.6 | 30.4 |
| Valley | NA | NA | 788 | 9.4 | 49.5 | 18.4 | 8.4 | 12 441 | 22 579 | 42 897 | 13.8 | 1.8 | 40 802 | 12.6 | 18.0 | 15.9 |
| Washington | 20 | 1 058 | 5 681 | 17.7 | 40.2 | 27.4 | 33.2 | 9 424 | 28 829 | 64 737 | -1.1 | 3.4 | 68 406 | 7.3 | 9.5 | 8.0 |
| Wayne | NA | NA | 3 870 | 2.4 | 38.8 | 29.1 | 23.6 | 15 362 | 20 597 | 46 418 | 6.2 | 0.4 | 46 980 | 14.4 | 14.2 | 12.7 |
| Webster | 52 | 1 014 | 822 | 7.5 | 47.9 | 16.5 | 6.8 | 10 381 | 21 054 | 38 538 | -4.9 | 0.8 | 39 018 | 14.4 | 20.2 | 18.1 |
| Wheeler | 0 | 485 | 116 | 1.7 | 36.2 | 23.5 | 2.2 | 18 647 | 23 544 | 39 653 | 9.7 | 2.2 | 38 340 | 15.4 | 20.4 | 18.2 |
| York | 36 | 1 937 | 3 480 | 22.9 | 44.3 | 22.4 | 19.5 | 10 735 | 26 565 | 48 655 | -2.8 | 2.8 | 47 936 | 11.1 | 16.8 | 14.9 |
| NEVADA | 562 | 2 561 | 656 482 | 10.6 | 44.9 | 22.2 | 3 633.1 | 8 470 | 27 625 | 55 553 | -7.7 | 3.6 | 49 099 | 15.8 | 22.2 | 20.8 |
| Churchill | 116 | 2 424 | 6 091 | 7.8 | 47.0 | 17.8 | 39.4 | 9 376 | 24 689 | 52 589 | -4.6 | 1.7 | 50 620 | 12.9 | 20.9 | 19.3 |
| Clark | 624 | 2 580 | 470 628 | 11.0 | 46.0 | 22.0 | 2 536.8 | 8 262 | 27 330 | 55 961 | -7.1 | 3.7 | 48 343 | 16.8 | 23.4 | 22.2 |
| Douglas | 124 | 1 566 | 10 409 | 13.6 | 35.3 | 25.3 | 60.9 | 9 247 | 35 723 | 60 383 | -13.7 | 6.0 | 54 640 | 9.9 | 16.2 | 14.2 |
| Elko | 370 | 1 660 | 13 028 | 5.3 | 46.7 | 16.1 | 80.5 | 8 539 | 27 233 | 69 459 | 6.3 | 2.6 | 62 937 | 10.7 | 13.8 | 12.5 |
| Esmeralda | 127 | 253 | 136 | 0.0 | 54.0 | 16.2 | 2.1 | 31 896 | 32 021 | 29 438 | -34.3 | 6.5 | 40 536 | 17.9 | 22.1 | 22.3 |
| Eureka | 649 | 1 547 | 371 | 8.6 | 48.9 | 22.6 | 6.7 | 25 726 | 29 996 | 61 908 | 10.7 | 2.4 | 58 985 | 9.6 | 12.9 | 11.9 |
| Humboldt | 282 | 888 | 4 132 | 5.0 | 53.6 | 13.4 | 32.4 | 9 527 | 25 855 | 54 943 | -13.7 | 2.6 | 61 680 | 11.2 | 16.0 | 14.6 |
| Lander | 378 | 927 | 1 213 | 6.7 | 55.8 | 13.0 | 11.3 | 9 933 | 28 459 | 69 814 | 12.2 | 2.0 | 64 392 | 10.4 | 14.0 | 13.4 |
| Lincoln | 167 | 1 224 | 1 513 | 11.4 | 48.4 | 16.4 | 12.2 | 12 125 | 18 298 | 42 662 | -1.2 | 0.0 | 42 724 | 14.1 | 19.1 | 17.1 |
| Lyon | 210 | 1 505 | 12 625 | 11.9 | 48.2 | 13.8 | 80.8 | 9 220 | 21 533 | 46 598 | -15.2 | 0.5 | 44 877 | 12.7 | 18.5 | 16.6 |
| Mineral | 42 | 104 | 723 | 3.6 | 60.9 | 7.8 | 8.2 | 14 382 | 21 729 | 31 108 | -30.0 | 0.0 | 39 705 | 17.8 | 26.4 | 23.3 |
| Nye | 350 | 1 363 | 8 438 | 8.3 | 55.2 | 10.6 | 64.8 | 10 507 | 22 503 | 39 740 | -18.3 | 1.3 | 41 150 | 16.5 | 30.1 | 25.9 |
| Pershing | 455 | 749 | 1 636 | 0.9 | 55.9 | 12.4 | 10.1 | 13 992 | 18 741 | 56 473 | 2.8 | 0.5 | 46 683 | 19.3 | 23.7 | 21.1 |
| Storey | 470 | 1 434 | 743 | 7.9 | 34.3 | 18.1 | 6.6 | 14 817 | 30 512 | 59 386 | -3.3 | 3.2 | 54 582 | 8.9 | 14.2 | 12.3 |
| Washoe | 377 | 2 412 | 109 704 | 9.9 | 38.5 | 27.0 | 555.8 | 8 572 | 30 016 | 55 813 | -9.8 | 4.1 | 50 910 | 13.2 | 18.2 | 16.5 |
| White Pine | 316 | 1 414 | 2 290 | 10.5 | 50.6 | 13.0 | 15.4 | 10 697 | 23 484 | 49 812 | 0.6 | 1.9 | 52 014 | 14.1 | 18.3 | 17.7 |
| Carson City | 266 | 2 287 | 12 802 | 9.7 | 45.1 | 21.0 | 109.0 | 8 486 | 27 704 | 54 235 | -3.9 | 2.8 | 50 689 | 14.8 | 22.3 | 20.0 |
| NEW HAMPSHIRE | 188 | 2 284 | 332 571 | 21.6 | 38.3 | 33.1 | 2 441.1 | 12 414 | 32 357 | 64 664 | -3.2 | 5.0 | 62 436 | 9.0 | 12.2 | 10.6 |
| Belknap | 199 | 3 520 | 12 667 | 13.4 | 41.5 | 28.2 | 130.5 | 12 985 | 29 449 | 56 921 | -3.3 | 3.0 | 55 422 | 10.4 | 16.2 | 14.3 |
| Carroll | 165 | 2 659 | 9 590 | 17.2 | 39.4 | 29.7 | 90.6 | 15 820 | 29 194 | 50 555 | -6.4 | 3.5 | 45 582 | 10.9 | 17.5 | 14.7 |
| Cheshire | NA | NA | 21 555 | 18.0 | 44.1 | 30.2 | 134.1 | 15 012 | 27 459 | 55 241 | -3.5 | 3.2 | 53 111 | 10.6 | 14.3 | 12.6 |
| Coos | NA | NA | 6 534 | 10.4 | 56.4 | 16.4 | 62.5 | 14 237 | 23 580 | 41 087 | -9.4 | 1.4 | 37 677 | 14.6 | 23.6 | 21.5 |
| Grafton | 177 | 2 347 | 24 368 | 31.5 | 39.2 | 36.0 | 184.8 | 16 029 | 29 090 | 53 000 | -6.5 | 4.5 | 51 289 | 11.4 | 14.3 | 13.1 |
| Hillsborough | 265 | 2 443 | 102 227 | 24.6 | 37.1 | 34.6 | 681.9 | 11 390 | 33 653 | 70 591 | -2.1 | 5.7 | 66 275 | 8.4 | 11.6 | 10.3 |
| Merrimack | 181 | 2 357 | 36 845 | 24.8 | 36.9 | 33.4 | 284.9 | 12 105 | 31 403 | 65 722 | 0.3 | 4.2 | 64 482 | 8.8 | 11.8 | 10.1 |
| Rockingham | 127 | 1 987 | 73 867 | 20.3 | 33.7 | 36.8 | 585.4 | 11 732 | 37 470 | 77 470 | -1.3 | 6.9 | 75 285 | 6.4 | 8.2 | 7.0 |
| Strafford | 205 | 2 549 | 35 803 | 14.4 | 39.7 | 30.2 | 197.1 | 12 205 | 29 405 | 59 082 | -2.3 | 3.8 | 54 783 | 11.4 | 14.6 | 12.4 |
| Sullivan | NA | NA | 9 115 | 18.6 | 48.5 | 25.8 | 89.2 | 13 597 | 27 223 | 51 678 | -6.5 | 2.6 | 47 868 | 10.8 | 16.3 | 14.5 |
| NEW JERSEY | 308 | 2 151 | 2 285 952 | 20.3 | 41.9 | 35.0 | 23 378.6 | 16 784 | 35 678 | 71 180 | -4.4 | 8.8 | 67 574 | 10.4 | 14.6 | 13.2 |
| Atlantic | 507 | 3 410 | 70 008 | 15.5 | 50.3 | 23.2 | 792.1 | 16 955 | 27 613 | 55 222 | -6.9 | 3.7 | 49 983 | 13.1 | 18.2 | 16.8 |
| Bergen | 95 | 1 259 | 228 944 | 23.6 | 34.1 | 45.1 | 2 339.2 | 17 178 | 43 012 | 83 443 | -5.3 | 12.9 | 79 037 | 6.6 | 8.2 | 7.5 |
| Burlington | 144 | 1 860 | 118 300 | 19.1 | 38.9 | 33.9 | 1 224.3 | 16 754 | 36 101 | 77 798 | -1.7 | 7.3 | 72 594 | 5.7 | 7.9 | 6.9 |
| Camden | 647 | 3 394 | 137 133 | 18.4 | 46.5 | 28.2 | 1 418.3 | 16 636 | 30 136 | 61 824 | -4.8 | 4.8 | 57 261 | 13.2 | 19.0 | 17.5 |
| Cape May | 317 | 4 656 | 19 181 | 16.8 | 47.3 | 27.1 | 252.7 | 18 802 | 33 796 | 55 315 | -1.5 | 4.0 | 52 312 | 11.8 | 18.6 | 17.0 |
| Cumberland | 494 | 3 314 | 38 055 | 10.5 | 62.8 | 14.0 | 460.8 | 16 950 | 22 636 | 52 004 | -1.6 | 2.5 | 49 465 | 16.7 | 25.7 | 25.0 |
| Essex | 689 | 2 791 | 215 881 | 18.9 | 46.4 | 31.7 | 2 436.1 | 19 074 | 32 149 | 55 876 | -7.9 | 8.4 | 51 021 | 17.2 | 23.4 | 20.8 |
| Gloucester | 147 | 2 635 | 80 272 | 17.5 | 44.9 | 27.4 | 743.6 | 14 977 | 32 067 | 74 830 | 2.1 | 5.5 | 70 618 | 7.4 | 10.4 | 8.7 |
| Hudson | 474 | 1 963 | 147 971 | 20.4 | 45.5 | 35.3 | 1 465.3 | 17 935 | 32 087 | 57 660 | 6.0 | 6.7 | 55 133 | 16.2 | 24.4 | 24.5 |
| Hunterdon | 59 | 811 | 33 834 | 19.0 | 28.7 | 48.0 | 405.9 | 17 837 | 49 521 | 103 879 | -3.7 | 18.6 | 99 216 | 4.3 | 4.5 | 3.7 |

1. Data for serious crimes have not been adjusted for underreporting; this may affect comparability between geographic areas and over time.  2. Per 100,000 population estimated by the FBI.  3. All persons 3 years old and over enrolled in nursery school through college.  4. Persons 25 years old and over.  5. Elementary and secondary education expenditures.  6. Based on population estimated by the American Community Survey, 2007–2011.

Table B. States and Counties — **Personal Income**

| | Personal income, 2011 | | | | | | | | | | | | |
|---|---|---|---|---|---|---|---|---|---|---|---|---|---|
| | | | Per capita[1] | | | | | Transfer payments (mil dol) | | | | | |
| | | | | | | | | | Government payments to individuals | | | | |
| STATE County | Total (mil dol) | Percent change, 2010–2011 | Dollars | Rank | Wages and salaries[2] (mil dol) | Proprietors' income (mil dol) | Dividends, interest, and rent (mil dol) | Total | Total | Social Security | Medical payments | Income maintenance | Unemployment insurance |
| | 62 | 63 | 64 | 65 | 66 | 67 | 68 | 69 | 70 | 71 | 72 | 73 | 74 |
| **NEBRASKA—Cont'd** | | | | | | | | | | | | | |
| Platte | 1 289 | 9.6 | 39 552 | 800 | 914 | 214 | 196 | 172 | 165 | 79 | 55 | 16 | 5 |
| Polk | 279 | 17.6 | 52 414 | 156 | 60 | 115 | 35 | 37 | 36 | 16 | 15 | 2 | 1 |
| Red Willow | 428 | 8.1 | 38 771 | 878 | 236 | 78 | 75 | 87 | 85 | 31 | 37 | 7 | 2 |
| Richardson | 326 | 12.8 | 39 115 | 844 | 101 | 69 | 51 | 75 | 74 | 28 | 32 | 6 | 2 |
| Rock | 62 | 27.1 | 41 390 | 623 | 22 | 24 | 10 | 7 | 7 | 2 | 3 | 1 | 0 |
| Saline | 527 | 12.8 | 36 735 | 1 107 | 331 | 90 | 68 | 88 | 85 | 33 | 35 | 6 | 2 |
| Sarpy | 6 806 | 7.6 | 41 865 | 587 | 3 856 | 161 | 805 | 776 | 741 | 267 | 258 | 58 | 26 |
| Saunders | 878 | 8.7 | 42 072 | 566 | 207 | 117 | 112 | 136 | 132 | 51 | 57 | 8 | 4 |
| Scotts Bluff | 1 347 | 7.4 | 36 372 | 1 153 | 849 | 168 | 188 | 290 | 282 | 100 | 116 | 34 | 7 |
| Seward | 705 | 8.7 | 42 216 | 561 | 291 | 103 | 99 | 101 | 97 | 41 | 38 | 6 | 2 |
| Sheridan | 206 | 18.2 | 38 279 | 936 | 64 | 48 | 40 | 43 | 42 | 16 | 17 | 5 | 1 |
| Sherman | 116 | 22.3 | 37 424 | 1 036 | 31 | 38 | 16 | 26 | 26 | 10 | 11 | 2 | 1 |
| Sioux | 60 | 25.3 | 44 751 | 401 | 12 | 21 | 8 | 6 | 6 | 3 | 1 | 1 | 0 |
| Stanton | 265 | 16.7 | 43 000 | 512 | 93 | 65 | 28 | 28 | 27 | 13 | 9 | 2 | 1 |
| Thayer | 243 | 21.0 | 47 098 | 294 | 108 | 65 | 47 | 44 | 43 | 18 | 20 | 2 | 1 |
| Thomas | 26 | 16.2 | 36 479 | 1 139 | 12 | 4 | 7 | 5 | 4 | 2 | 2 | 0 | 0 |
| Thurston | 282 | 15.1 | 40 302 | 715 | 151 | 75 | 27 | 58 | 56 | 13 | 25 | 14 | 2 |
| Valley | 194 | 18.4 | 46 084 | 335 | 72 | 68 | 27 | 34 | 33 | 13 | 15 | 2 | 1 |
| Washington | 874 | 4.8 | 43 059 | 504 | 495 | 70 | 121 | 122 | 118 | 50 | 48 | 7 | 3 |
| Wayne | 367 | 12.4 | 38 598 | 898 | 166 | 93 | 57 | 55 | 53 | 19 | 20 | 4 | 1 |
| Webster | 151 | 16.9 | 40 093 | 735 | 40 | 40 | 24 | 34 | 33 | 13 | 15 | 2 | 1 |
| Wheeler | 41 | 32.5 | 49 628 | 215 | 15 | 19 | 6 | 5 | 5 | 2 | 2 | 0 | 0 |
| York | 635 | 15.5 | 46 278 | 329 | 341 | 151 | 111 | 102 | 99 | 40 | 43 | 6 | 2 |
| **NEVADA** | 100 665 | 4.0 | 36 964 | X | 64 090 | 7 898 | 19 413 | 16 552 | 15 952 | 5 609 | 5 815 | 1 885 | 1 475 |
| Churchill | 1 042 | 4.4 | 42 281 | 559 | 519 | 209 | 129 | 196 | 190 | 62 | 78 | 19 | 12 |
| Clark | 70 289 | 3.8 | 35 680 | 1 267 | 46 205 | 5 616 | 12 488 | 11 561 | 11 127 | 3 753 | 4 063 | 1 421 | 1 083 |
| Douglas | 2 451 | 3.5 | 52 266 | 159 | 890 | 144 | 823 | 345 | 335 | 168 | 104 | 20 | 25 |
| Elko | 1 987 | 9.1 | 40 150 | 729 | 1 345 | 52 | 222 | 215 | 204 | 71 | 71 | 24 | 17 |
| Esmeralda | 31 | 8.6 | 39 730 | 777 | 16 | 3 | 6 | 6 | 6 | 3 | 2 | 0 | 0 |
| Eureka | 75 | 15.8 | 38 071 | 961 | 466 | 8 | 9 | 8 | 8 | 4 | 3 | 1 | 1 |
| Humboldt | 720 | 9.3 | 43 022 | 508 | 535 | 61 | 88 | 87 | 84 | 30 | 31 | 10 | 6 |
| Lander | 265 | 11.4 | 45 370 | 375 | 257 | 13 | 26 | 32 | 31 | 11 | 13 | 3 | 2 |
| Lincoln | 120 | 5.1 | 22 587 | 3 070 | 74 | 5 | 22 | 35 | 34 | 12 | 15 | 2 | 2 |
| Lyon | 1 444 | 3.4 | 27 835 | 2 633 | 543 | 68 | 234 | 371 | 360 | 156 | 115 | 33 | 32 |
| Mineral | 162 | 2.0 | 35 226 | 1 336 | 89 | 7 | 26 | 48 | 47 | 15 | 22 | 4 | 3 |
| Nye | 1 372 | 1.9 | 31 656 | 1 967 | 640 | 70 | 248 | 434 | 424 | 188 | 146 | 38 | 23 |
| Pershing | 174 | 11.1 | 25 772 | 2 904 | 102 | 12 | 22 | 38 | 37 | 13 | 16 | 3 | 3 |
| Storey | 132 | 0.7 | 33 924 | 1 527 | 175 | 6 | 27 | 24 | 23 | 13 | 4 | 2 | 2 |
| Washoe | 17 790 | 4.5 | 41 790 | 594 | 10 374 | 1 366 | 4 536 | 2 650 | 2 556 | 941 | 929 | 258 | 230 |
| White Pine | 403 | 14.0 | 39 955 | 750 | 264 | 17 | 46 | 66 | 64 | 23 | 27 | 6 | 4 |
| Carson City | 2 208 | 2.7 | 39 833 | 766 | 1 596 | 240 | 462 | 435 | 422 | 146 | 176 | 40 | 30 |
| **NEW HAMPSHIRE** | 60 480 | 4.5 | 45 881 | X | 36 546 | 5 586 | 8 852 | 8 934 | 8 642 | 3 556 | 3 450 | 861 | 223 |
| Belknap | 2 529 | 3.9 | 41 995 | 570 | 1 232 | 212 | 512 | 499 | 486 | 212 | 188 | 47 | 12 |
| Carroll | 2 030 | 4.5 | 42 612 | 528 | 868 | 225 | 483 | 426 | 416 | 182 | 170 | 37 | 8 |
| Cheshire | 3 144 | 4.0 | 40 875 | 670 | 1 698 | 338 | 521 | 549 | 532 | 225 | 211 | 52 | 11 |
| Coos | 1 145 | 2.5 | 35 019 | 1 369 | 552 | 103 | 171 | 358 | 351 | 124 | 158 | 39 | 13 |
| Grafton | 4 048 | 4.3 | 45 522 | 365 | 3 254 | 446 | 738 | 646 | 627 | 253 | 267 | 59 | 8 |
| Hillsborough | 19 274 | 4.6 | 47 981 | 270 | 13 051 | 1 599 | 2 391 | 2 528 | 2 439 | 965 | 957 | 281 | 71 |
| Merrimack | 6 383 | 4.0 | 43 548 | 466 | 4 188 | 532 | 965 | 1 011 | 978 | 405 | 386 | 94 | 27 |
| Rockingham | 15 658 | 5.0 | 52 861 | 144 | 8 257 | 1 712 | 2 191 | 1 777 | 1 712 | 766 | 671 | 124 | 47 |
| Strafford | 4 637 | 4.6 | 37 442 | 1 033 | 2 780 | 282 | 602 | 800 | 772 | 289 | 306 | 94 | 23 |
| Sullivan | 1 632 | 3.6 | 37 559 | 1 020 | 667 | 138 | 279 | 340 | 330 | 134 | 137 | 35 | 3 |
| **NEW JERSEY** | 462 494 | 4.2 | 52 430 | X | 273 352 | 40 181 | 71 603 | 69 895 | 67 945 | 21 875 | 29 244 | 6 476 | 6 316 |
| Atlantic | 11 046 | 3.5 | 40 262 | 719 | 7 389 | 1 096 | 1 648 | 2 519 | 2 459 | 727 | 1 053 | 274 | 259 |
| Bergen | 60 214 | 4.8 | 66 096 | 33 | 32 577 | 6 433 | 11 294 | 6 401 | 6 199 | 2 414 | 2 499 | 357 | 562 |
| Burlington | 21 722 | 3.4 | 48 318 | 259 | 13 445 | 1 640 | 3 033 | 3 414 | 3 316 | 1 224 | 1 310 | 215 | 324 |
| Camden | 22 120 | 3.2 | 43 099 | 503 | 12 189 | 1 471 | 2 921 | 4 703 | 4 589 | 1 262 | 2 085 | 552 | 424 |
| Cape May | 4 704 | 2.9 | 48 694 | 244 | 1 893 | 371 | 1 073 | 1 128 | 1 107 | 385 | 491 | 74 | 107 |
| Cumberland | 5 541 | 4.1 | 35 272 | 1 329 | 3 298 | 406 | 671 | 1 499 | 1 464 | 389 | 662 | 201 | 141 |
| Essex | 41 578 | 3.9 | 52 956 | 142 | 27 140 | 4 318 | 6 165 | 7 220 | 7 047 | 1 568 | 3 384 | 1 130 | 600 |
| Gloucester | 12 208 | 4.2 | 42 228 | 560 | 5 406 | 539 | 1 379 | 2 171 | 2 107 | 730 | 828 | 166 | 231 |
| Hudson | 30 379 | 5.7 | 47 377 | 287 | 20 783 | 2 519 | 3 310 | 4 889 | 4 747 | 956 | 2 268 | 775 | 481 |
| Hunterdon | 8 669 | 3.7 | 67 710 | 29 | 3 359 | 833 | 1 461 | 811 | 783 | 345 | 297 | 25 | 72 |

1. Based on the resident population estimated as of July 1 of the year shown.   2. Includes supplements to wages and salaries.

# Table B. States and Counties — Earnings, Social Security, and Housing

| STATE County | Earnings, 2011 | | | | | | | | | Social Security beneficiaries, December 2011 | | Supplemental Security Income recipients, December 2011 | Housing units, 2010 | |
| | Total (mil dol) | Farm | Goods-related[1] | | Service-related and health | | | | Govern-ment | Number | Rate[2] | | Total | Percent change, 2000–2010 |
| | | | Total | Manu-facturing | Infor-mation and profes-sional and technical services | Retail trade | Finance, insur-ance, and real estate | Health care and social services | | | | | | |
| | 75 | 76 | 77 | 78 | 79 | 80 | 81 | 82 | 83 | 84 | 85 | 86 | 87 | 88 |
| NEBRASKA—Cont'd | | | | | | | | | | | | | | |
| Platte | 1 129 | 13.8 | 35.6 | 30.7 | 3.5 | 5.5 | 3.8 | 6.8 | 13.4 | 5 975 | 183 | 305 | 13 378 | 4.5 |
| Polk | 175 | 59.7 | D | 0.3 | D | 3.6 | D | 4.1 | 13.4 | 1 205 | 226 | 50 | 2 731 | 0.5 |
| Red Willow | 314 | 15.5 | 14.7 | 9.4 | D | 9.0 | 5.0 | 10.1 | 17.0 | 2 470 | 224 | 160 | 5 267 | -0.2 |
| Richardson | 170 | 31.2 | D | 5.8 | D | 6.4 | 3.0 | 9.5 | 15.7 | 2 370 | 284 | 154 | 4 393 | -3.7 |
| Rock | 46 | 53.7 | D | D | D | 3.3 | D | D | 20.2 | 180 | 120 | 0 | 912 | -2.5 |
| Saline | 421 | 18.6 | 37.7 | 36.6 | 1.0 | 3.6 | 2.5 | D | 16.5 | 2 540 | 177 | 145 | 5 762 | 2.7 |
| Sarpy | 4 017 | 0.6 | 9.9 | 4.0 | 10.0 | 5.4 | 7.5 | 4.7 | 33.5 | 19 515 | 120 | 1 152 | 61 938 | 37.7 |
| Saunders | 324 | 27.3 | 17.1 | 4.2 | D | 5.6 | 4.4 | D | 21.9 | 3 850 | 185 | 193 | 9 221 | 11.6 |
| Scotts Bluff | 1 017 | 4.8 | 10.1 | 4.7 | 4.0 | 7.9 | 7.7 | 17.9 | 17.0 | 8 030 | 217 | 818 | 16 408 | 1.8 |
| Seward | 394 | 20.8 | 22.6 | 17.6 | 3.5 | 4.0 | 4.0 | D | 16.1 | 3 035 | 182 | 133 | 6 875 | 7.0 |
| Sheridan | 112 | 38.0 | D | 0.7 | D | 6.2 | D | 1.9 | 26.0 | 1 375 | 255 | 75 | 2 936 | -2.6 |
| Sherman | 68 | 52.0 | 1.9 | 0.8 | D | 3.6 | 2.6 | 4.1 | 17.8 | 840 | 272 | 30 | 1 941 | 5.5 |
| Sioux | 33 | 81.0 | 0.0 | 0.0 | D | 1.0 | D | 0.0 | 11.8 | 265 | 198 | 0 | 815 | 4.5 |
| Stanton | 158 | 37.7 | D | D | D | 0.6 | 2.2 | D | 9.0 | 1 070 | 174 | 29 | 2 633 | 7.4 |
| Thayer | 173 | 32.6 | D | 17.5 | 0.7 | 3.9 | 4.2 | 3.5 | 18.5 | 1 425 | 276 | 77 | 2 731 | -3.4 |
| Thomas | 16 | 29.4 | D | D | D | D | D | 0.0 | 23.7 | 170 | 237 | 0 | 402 | -9.9 |
| Thurston | 226 | 31.2 | 8.3 | 5.1 | 4.4 | D | D | 5.9 | 36.7 | 1 135 | 162 | 215 | 2 408 | -2.4 |
| Valley | 140 | 46.0 | D | 2.4 | 2.7 | 4.0 | 3.2 | 2.3 | 22.5 | 1 090 | 258 | 57 | 2 273 | 0.0 |
| Washington | 565 | 7.5 | D | 17.1 | 5.7 | 8.6 | 4.1 | 7.2 | 24.9 | 3 620 | 178 | 145 | 8 301 | 12.1 |
| Wayne | 258 | 32.7 | 15.6 | 13.4 | D | 3.2 | 5.5 | 7.2 | 22.9 | 1 510 | 159 | 76 | 3 776 | 3.1 |
| Webster | 80 | 47.6 | D | D | D | 4.5 | 3.4 | 5.0 | 18.4 | 1 085 | 287 | 88 | 1 912 | -3.0 |
| Wheeler | 34 | 79.1 | D | 0.0 | D | D | D | 0.0 | 8.5 | 165 | 202 | 0 | 576 | 2.7 |
| York | 492 | 24.7 | D | 10.8 | D | 5.9 | 5.0 | D | 13.4 | 3 010 | 219 | 158 | 6 231 | 1.0 |
| NEVADA | 71 989 | 0.3 | 12.3 | 3.7 | 8.6 | 7.1 | 7.0 | 9.0 | 17.1 | 424 836 | 156 | 44 064 | 1 173 814 | 41.9 |
| Churchill | 728 | 3.7 | D | 2.8 | 7.0 | 6.1 | 7.2 | 7.9 | 31.1 | 5 145 | 209 | 457 | 10 826 | 11.2 |
| Clark | 51 822 | 0.0 | 9.4 | 2.7 | 8.8 | 7.4 | 7.0 | 8.7 | 16.2 | 283 050 | 144 | 33 124 | 840 343 | 50.1 |
| Douglas | 1 034 | 0.6 | D | 11.8 | 8.0 | 6.8 | 6.2 | 8.2 | 14.7 | 12 150 | 259 | 390 | 23 671 | 24.5 |
| Elko | 1 397 | 1.5 | 32.7 | 1.0 | 3.2 | 6.0 | 1.8 | 5.3 | 17.0 | 5 720 | 116 | 490 | 19 566 | 6.0 |
| Esmeralda | 19 | 17.6 | D | D | D | D | 0.0 | 0.0 | 22.7 | 255 | 329 | 17 | 850 | 2.0 |
| Eureka | 474 | 2.2 | D | 0.0 | D | 0.1 | D | D | 2.7 | 320 | 162 | 13 | 1 076 | 5.0 |
| Humboldt | 597 | 4.6 | 48.1 | 2.6 | D | 6.3 | 1.2 | D | 15.9 | 2 445 | 146 | 224 | 7 123 | 2.4 |
| Lander | 271 | 3.6 | D | D | D | 2.6 | D | 0.6 | 12.4 | 855 | 146 | 81 | 2 575 | -7.4 |
| Lincoln | 79 | 3.6 | D | D | D | 5.2 | 2.6 | 2.8 | 46.0 | 1 050 | 198 | 66 | 2 730 | 25.3 |
| Lyon | 611 | 4.8 | 27.8 | 20.6 | 3.5 | 13.8 | 2.4 | D | 21.3 | 12 065 | 233 | 792 | 22 547 | 57.9 |
| Mineral | 97 | 2.1 | D | D | D | 3.3 | D | D | 36.6 | 1 345 | 293 | 135 | 2 830 | -1.3 |
| Nye | 710 | 3.4 | 17.2 | 0.8 | 21.2 | 7.2 | 1.7 | 5.6 | 18.3 | 14 190 | 327 | 988 | 22 350 | 40.1 |
| Pershing | 114 | 12.7 | D | D | D | 4.3 | D | D | 36.1 | 995 | 148 | 87 | 2 464 | 3.1 |
| Storey | 182 | 0.0 | D | 18.7 | D | D | D | D | 8.3 | 975 | 250 | 44 | 1 990 | 24.7 |
| Washoe | 11 739 | 0.1 | 13.6 | 6.6 | 9.5 | 6.9 | 8.9 | 11.6 | 17.2 | 70 835 | 166 | 6 183 | 184 841 | 28.4 |
| White Pine | 281 | 1.8 | 40.1 | 0.4 | 1.4 | 4.9 | 1.6 | D | 34.9 | 1 835 | 182 | 153 | 4 498 | 1.3 |
| Carson City | 1 837 | 0.0 | D | 9.3 | 6.1 | 6.6 | 7.6 | 15.3 | 36.0 | 11 605 | 209 | 820 | 23 534 | 10.6 |
| NEW HAMPSHIRE | 42 133 | 0.1 | 19.2 | 12.9 | 11.2 | 8.9 | 8.9 | 13.1 | 13.3 | 262 952 | 199 | 18 695 | 614 754 | 12.4 |
| Belknap | 1 444 | 0.1 | D | 9.6 | 8.6 | 12.4 | 4.7 | 13.9 | 16.4 | 15 745 | 261 | 991 | 37 386 | 16.4 |
| Carroll | 1 092 | -0.1 | D | D | 7.2 | 12.0 | 6.5 | 13.1 | 14.5 | 13 625 | 286 | 726 | 39 813 | 14.6 |
| Cheshire | 2 035 | 0.1 | D | D | 5.2 | 9.8 | 7.5 | 14.7 | 14.1 | 16 820 | 219 | 1 109 | 34 773 | 9.1 |
| Coos | 655 | 0.6 | D | 6.9 | 3.3 | 10.1 | 3.5 | 18.1 | 22.2 | 9 985 | 305 | 926 | 21 321 | 8.6 |
| Grafton | 3 700 | 0.4 | 14.2 | 10.3 | 8.6 | 7.5 | 3.7 | 24.1 | 11.3 | 18 800 | 211 | 993 | 51 120 | 16.9 |
| Hillsborough | 14 650 | 0.0 | 22.1 | 16.7 | 14.7 | 8.2 | 10.7 | 11.7 | 10.8 | 70 455 | 175 | 6 474 | 166 053 | 10.7 |
| Merrimack | 4 720 | 0.1 | 15.0 | 8.8 | 8.1 | 8.4 | 8.5 | 14.9 | 21.8 | 30 085 | 205 | 2 313 | 63 541 | 13.0 |
| Rockingham | 9 969 | 0.0 | 18.2 | 10.7 | 12.8 | 10.0 | 8.6 | 9.6 | 9.5 | 54 500 | 184 | 2 321 | 126 709 | 12.1 |
| Strafford | 3 061 | 0.0 | D | 12.8 | 7.0 | 7.6 | 14.2 | 13.8 | 22.0 | 22 760 | 184 | 1 969 | 51 697 | 13.5 |
| Sullivan | 805 | 0.3 | D | 22.3 | 6.5 | 11.1 | 5.0 | 9.5 | 17.0 | 10 175 | 234 | 873 | 22 341 | 10.8 |
| NEW JERSEY | 313 533 | 0.1 | 13.4 | 8.5 | 15.2 | 6.4 | 10.6 | 11.2 | 15.4 | 1 500 403 | 170 | 173 000 | 3 553 562 | 7.3 |
| Atlantic | 8 485 | 0.8 | D | 1.9 | 6.0 | 6.9 | 3.8 | 14.1 | 21.7 | 52 965 | 193 | 6 512 | 126 647 | 11.0 |
| Bergen | 39 011 | 0.0 | D | 7.9 | 15.1 | 6.9 | 7.1 | 14.8 | 9.3 | 155 435 | 171 | 11 403 | 352 388 | 3.7 |
| Burlington | 15 085 | 0.2 | D | 9.7 | 11.2 | 7.4 | 12.0 | 11.1 | 18.7 | 82 840 | 184 | 5 492 | 175 615 | 8.9 |
| Camden | 13 661 | 0.1 | D | 8.5 | 11.6 | 7.1 | 5.7 | 18.0 | 18.7 | 91 420 | 178 | 15 473 | 204 943 | 2.9 |
| Cape May | 2 264 | 0.2 | 10.2 | 1.4 | 5.2 | 11.1 | 6.2 | 12.1 | 28.5 | 27 115 | 281 | 1 831 | 98 309 | 8.0 |
| Cumberland | 3 704 | 2.0 | 21.9 | 15.3 | 3.4 | 7.3 | 2.8 | 13.5 | 28.0 | 29 120 | 185 | 5 362 | 55 834 | 5.6 |
| Essex | 31 459 | 0.0 | D | 7.5 | 15.1 | 4.1 | 12.3 | 10.7 | 21.2 | 112 810 | 144 | 27 876 | 312 954 | 4.0 |
| Gloucester | 5 945 | 0.9 | 21.0 | 11.5 | 7.1 | 11.5 | 3.1 | 11.0 | 19.9 | 51 365 | 178 | 1 365 | 109 796 | 14.9 |
| Hudson | 23 303 | 0.0 | D | 2.5 | 14.0 | 4.7 | 32.0 | 6.4 | 14.9 | 77 785 | 121 | 21 937 | 270 335 | 12.4 |
| Hunterdon | 4 192 | 0.1 | 13.4 | 4.9 | 17.1 | 11.1 | 10.7 | 11.0 | 15.6 | 21 410 | 167 | 788 | 49 487 | 9.9 |

1. Includes mining, construction, and manufacturing.    2. Per 1,000 resident population enumerated in the 2010 census.

| STATE County | Housing units, 2007–2011 | | | | | | | | Civilian labor force, 2012 | | | | Civilian employment,[6] 2007–2011 | | |
|---|---|---|---|---|---|---|---|---|---|---|---|---|---|---|---|
| | Occupied units | | | | | | | | | | Unemployment | | | Percent | |
| | | | Owner-occupied | | | Renter-occupied | | | | | | | | | |
| | | | | Median owner cost as a percent of income | | | | | | | | | | | |
| | Total | Percent | Median value[1] | With a mortgage | Without a mortgage[2] | Median rent[3] | Median rent as a percent of income | Substandard units[4] (percent) | Total | Percent change, 2011–2012 | Total | Rate[5] | Total | Management, business, science and arts | Construction, production, and maintenance occupations |
| | 89 | 90 | 91 | 92 | 93 | 94 | 95 | 96 | 97 | 98 | 99 | 100 | 101 | 102 | 103 |
| **NEBRASKA—Cont'd** | | | | | | | | | | | | | | | |
| Platte | 12 333 | 73.8 | 109 900 | 20.1 | 10.3 | 582 | 22.5 | 2.9 | 18 911 | 1.4 | 646 | 3.4 | 16 943 | 25.3 | 34.5 |
| Polk | 2 220 | 73.7 | 89 500 | 21.3 | 13.3 | 561 | 20.7 | 1.2 | 3 074 | 0.6 | 90 | 2.9 | 2 703 | 34.9 | 31.1 |
| Red Willow | 4 698 | 71.1 | 78 800 | 17.4 | 13.9 | 571 | 24.6 | 0.6 | 6 221 | 1.0 | 206 | 3.3 | 5 660 | 26.1 | 27.6 |
| Richardson | 3 769 | 78.5 | 62 800 | 18.4 | 11.3 | 502 | 21.2 | 0.6 | 4 364 | 1.0 | 228 | 5.2 | 3 910 | 31.5 | 28.6 |
| Rock | 673 | 87.8 | 61 000 | 17.8 | 11.7 | 625 | 22.5 | 2.7 | 944 | 1.4 | 23 | 2.4 | 836 | 42.9 | 24.0 |
| Saline | 4 979 | 68.7 | 96 200 | 19.8 | 12.1 | 644 | 26.8 | 1.7 | 8 554 | 0.5 | 309 | 3.6 | 6 527 | 28.9 | 34.4 |
| Sarpy | 57 759 | 71.4 | 160 800 | 22.3 | 11.7 | 832 | 26.4 | 1.7 | 84 010 | 1.4 | 3 445 | 4.1 | 81 370 | 40.5 | 17.0 |
| Saunders | 8 102 | 81.1 | 139 700 | 21.7 | 13.9 | 725 | 22.9 | 0.8 | 11 177 | 1.4 | 468 | 4.2 | 10 886 | 32.1 | 27.6 |
| Scotts Bluff | 14 992 | 65.6 | 95 700 | 22.7 | 15.3 | 616 | 28.6 | 3.5 | 19 591 | 0.2 | 885 | 4.5 | 17 925 | 29.0 | 26.1 |
| Seward | 6 364 | 71.7 | 139 000 | 20.4 | 10.3 | 575 | 22.8 | 0.2 | 9 017 | 2.2 | 300 | 3.3 | 8 731 | 36.4 | 28.6 |
| Sheridan | 2 386 | 71.3 | 60 900 | 22.9 | 13.8 | 492 | 24.7 | 3.6 | 3 114 | 0.4 | 98 | 3.1 | 2 547 | 40.8 | 23.6 |
| Sherman | 1 379 | 85.4 | 61 900 | 22.2 | 13.8 | 564 | 24.6 | 0.4 | 2 024 | 0.6 | 64 | 3.2 | 1 575 | 31.1 | 29.8 |
| Sioux | 587 | 76.8 | 107 400 | 33.6 | 14.1 | 392 | 15.8 | 0.2 | 790 | 5.8 | 29 | 3.7 | 681 | 43.5 | 25.7 |
| Stanton | 2 433 | 77.8 | 88 100 | 22.4 | 10.4 | 571 | 18.7 | 1.8 | 3 477 | 1.0 | 119 | 3.4 | 3 367 | 25.8 | 32.9 |
| Thayer | 2 212 | 82.7 | 58 800 | 20.5 | 13.1 | 427 | 19.9 | 0.8 | 3 091 | 4.0 | 92 | 3.0 | 2 556 | 37.3 | 28.5 |
| Thomas | 318 | 74.2 | 66 000 | 26.6 | 11.6 | 608 | 16.9 | 3.8 | 387 | 4.9 | 17 | 4.4 | 408 | 42.9 | 22.8 |
| Thurston | 2 053 | 68.2 | 64 500 | 17.6 | 12.9 | 448 | 24.4 | 10.6 | 3 278 | 1.3 | 263 | 8.0 | 2 517 | 36.6 | 23.2 |
| Valley | 1 868 | 77.4 | 71 700 | 18.3 | 12.5 | 384 | 24.9 | 0.3 | 2 628 | 1.9 | 75 | 2.9 | 2 224 | 31.7 | 28.7 |
| Washington | 7 454 | 81.9 | 172 900 | 23.3 | 13.0 | 699 | 28.0 | 0.5 | 11 281 | 1.1 | 422 | 3.7 | 10 522 | 37.2 | 25.1 |
| Wayne | 3 315 | 68.4 | 95 700 | 19.6 | 11.9 | 477 | 19.9 | 1.3 | 5 659 | 2.5 | 183 | 3.2 | 5 137 | 32.4 | 25.6 |
| Webster | 1 572 | 79.5 | 63 500 | 19.4 | 13.9 | 470 | 23.1 | 1.3 | 1 891 | 2.6 | 63 | 3.3 | 1 657 | 35.8 | 30.2 |
| Wheeler | 315 | 67.6 | 75 900 | 21.8 | 14.0 | 603 | 23.5 | 0.0 | 484 | 7.3 | 16 | 3.3 | 455 | 52.7 | 24.4 |
| York | 5 653 | 74.4 | 92 200 | 19.4 | 11.7 | 579 | 23.3 | 1.2 | 7 407 | 2.3 | 274 | 3.7 | 7 188 | 32.4 | 26.2 |
| **NEVADA** | 986 741 | 59.1 | 225 400 | 28.7 | 11.8 | 1 011 | 30.8 | 4.6 | 1 378 876 | -0.9 | 152 468 | 11.1 | 1 246 387 | 27.6 | 19.8 |
| Churchill | 8 849 | 65.0 | 175 300 | 23.5 | 11.0 | 802 | 24.3 | 3.5 | 13 175 | -3.1 | 1 213 | 9.2 | 10 320 | 27.0 | 27.5 |
| Clark | 701 836 | 57.0 | 226 200 | 29.4 | 11.6 | 1 049 | 31.0 | 5.0 | 992 403 | -0.7 | 111 425 | 11.2 | 904 125 | 26.5 | 18.6 |
| Douglas | 19 175 | 73.3 | 346 600 | 29.9 | 13.5 | 1 052 | 29.6 | 2.2 | 21 634 | -4.0 | 2 599 | 12.0 | 21 172 | 32.0 | 19.2 |
| Elko | 17 244 | 73.3 | 180 700 | 20.4 | 9.9 | 824 | 22.6 | 4.1 | 30 673 | 1.4 | 1 810 | 5.9 | 24 236 | 26.4 | 32.6 |
| Esmeralda | 509 | 64.0 | 86 400 | 23.6 | 9.9 | 443 | 32.5 | 3.7 | 610 | 9.9 | 32 | 5.2 | 340 | 24.7 | 47.6 |
| Eureka | 719 | 73.7 | 103 400 | 18.5 | 9.9 | 432 | 11.3 | 4.6 | 1 122 | 2.5 | 67 | 6.0 | 819 | 43.6 | 39.2 |
| Humboldt | 6 098 | 72.8 | 144 000 | 20.2 | 10.5 | 638 | 23.3 | 5.1 | 9 644 | 0.4 | 598 | 6.2 | 7 204 | 22.8 | 42.5 |
| Lander | 2 006 | 70.8 | 108 900 | 15.5 | 9.9 | 781 | 18.5 | 3.7 | 4 641 | 3.9 | 244 | 5.3 | 2 530 | 18.5 | 46.2 |
| Lincoln | 1 815 | 72.1 | 156 300 | 20.8 | 11.6 | 706 | 28.9 | 2.4 | 1 788 | -2.4 | 229 | 12.8 | 1 753 | 37.9 | 18.4 |
| Lyon | 18 373 | 69.9 | 166 700 | 27.7 | 12.7 | 951 | 30.2 | 3.2 | 22 376 | -3.9 | 3 321 | 14.8 | 20 198 | 25.4 | 30.1 |
| Mineral | 2 209 | 69.1 | 101 000 | 21.5 | 14.7 | 626 | 28.2 | 3.8 | 2 017 | -15.3 | 256 | 12.7 | 1 761 | 23.4 | 25.6 |
| Nye | 18 348 | 71.6 | 142 800 | 27.9 | 13.3 | 857 | 39.2 | 2.3 | 17 789 | -2.2 | 2 404 | 13.5 | 14 363 | 20.5 | 29.4 |
| Pershing | 2 062 | 73.1 | 153 100 | 19.9 | 12.0 | 646 | 24.5 | 7.2 | 2 767 | -1.4 | 286 | 10.3 | 2 229 | 29.7 | 31.9 |
| Storey | 1 755 | 93.7 | 215 200 | 30.6 | 9.9 | 1 063 | 24.9 | 1.9 | 2 119 | -2.4 | 240 | 11.3 | 1 809 | 26.4 | 31.3 |
| Washoe | 160 889 | 59.6 | 257 400 | 28.5 | 12.6 | 922 | 31.0 | 4.3 | 222 314 | -1.3 | 24 214 | 10.9 | 205 272 | 32.7 | 19.7 |
| White Pine | 3 565 | 73.5 | 116 800 | 18.4 | 10.3 | 748 | 30.1 | 1.8 | 5 837 | 0.2 | 416 | 7.1 | 4 345 | 28.0 | 26.2 |
| Carson City | 21 289 | 61.0 | 244 600 | 25.8 | 11.8 | 926 | 30.6 | 2.9 | 27 968 | -3.0 | 3 114 | 11.1 | 23 911 | 30.9 | 21.1 |
| **NEW HAMPSHIRE** | 514 869 | 72.5 | 250 000 | 26.8 | 16.5 | 956 | 29.5 | 1.9 | 742 448 | 0.6 | 41 133 | 5.5 | 695 066 | 38.9 | 20.5 |
| Belknap | 24 645 | 77.0 | 228 100 | 28.6 | 15.8 | 840 | 27.6 | 1.4 | 32 037 | 0.2 | 1 716 | 5.4 | 30 807 | 34.1 | 23.0 |
| Carroll | 20 564 | 80.5 | 239 200 | 27.9 | 14.2 | 880 | 32.6 | 2.0 | 25 392 | -0.1 | 1 330 | 5.2 | 23 544 | 31.4 | 23.1 |
| Cheshire | 30 141 | 70.8 | 202 600 | 26.9 | 18.1 | 912 | 30.9 | 1.9 | 41 289 | 0.4 | 2 174 | 5.3 | 39 983 | 35.1 | 24.5 |
| Coos | 14 860 | 71.8 | 133 200 | 26.6 | 16.1 | 610 | 29.6 | 2.7 | 15 719 | -2.2 | 1 218 | 7.7 | 15 574 | 28.0 | 29.9 |
| Grafton | 34 498 | 70.2 | 209 900 | 24.7 | 15.9 | 897 | 27.9 | 2.0 | 48 920 | -0.4 | 2 173 | 4.4 | 44 882 | 39.7 | 20.2 |
| Hillsborough | 153 471 | 68.3 | 265 100 | 26.6 | 16.5 | 1 019 | 29.5 | 2.0 | 229 472 | 0.7 | 13 040 | 5.7 | 213 830 | 40.5 | 19.6 |
| Merrimack | 57 045 | 73.1 | 241 900 | 26.9 | 17.5 | 924 | 29.6 | 2.2 | 80 319 | 0.2 | 3 959 | 4.9 | 76 832 | 41.3 | 20.3 |
| Rockingham | 115 105 | 78.4 | 296 500 | 27.0 | 16.3 | 1 048 | 28.9 | 1.4 | 176 597 | 1.4 | 10 615 | 6.0 | 160 848 | 41.1 | 18.7 |
| Strafford | 46 384 | 67.9 | 227 100 | 27.2 | 17.6 | 936 | 31.5 | 1.9 | 69 870 | 0.9 | 3 822 | 5.5 | 66 192 | 36.2 | 19.5 |
| Sullivan | 18 156 | 73.2 | 182 700 | 25.5 | 16.9 | 795 | 28.1 | 2.0 | 22 835 | 0.7 | 1 087 | 4.8 | 22 574 | 33.3 | 25.3 |
| **NEW JERSEY** | 3 180 854 | 66.6 | 349 100 | 28.7 | 18.8 | 1 131 | 31.5 | 3.9 | 4 595 460 | 1.1 | 436 174 | 9.5 | 4 221 383 | 39.8 | 18.0 |
| Atlantic | 101 418 | 70.7 | 256 600 | 31.3 | 19.2 | 995 | 33.8 | 3.0 | 136 125 | 0.7 | 18 377 | 13.5 | 129 740 | 28.4 | 16.5 |
| Bergen | 333 073 | 66.9 | 474 200 | 29.8 | 19.5 | 1 289 | 30.1 | 2.6 | 483 097 | 1.1 | 39 141 | 8.1 | 448 803 | 45.3 | 14.2 |
| Burlington | 165 727 | 78.4 | 266 200 | 26.5 | 17.4 | 1 142 | 31.6 | 1.5 | 242 711 | 0.8 | 22 303 | 9.2 | 220 946 | 41.2 | 16.7 |
| Camden | 190 337 | 68.4 | 224 800 | 27.5 | 18.9 | 927 | 33.2 | 2.4 | 267 608 | 0.5 | 28 316 | 10.6 | 244 570 | 36.9 | 18.6 |
| Cape May | 44 788 | 74.3 | 332 400 | 29.7 | 17.8 | 1 001 | 33.1 | 1.7 | 58 190 | 1.7 | 7 793 | 13.4 | 43 734 | 33.6 | 19.5 |
| Cumberland | 50 868 | 68.4 | 177 800 | 27.2 | 17.1 | 914 | 35.2 | 3.9 | 69 538 | -0.7 | 9 824 | 14.1 | 64 661 | 26.2 | 28.1 |
| Essex | 276 441 | 46.8 | 389 800 | 31.3 | 19.6 | 1 024 | 31.9 | 5.9 | 372 009 | 0.8 | 40 147 | 10.8 | 355 766 | 37.0 | 19.1 |
| Gloucester | 103 548 | 80.4 | 236 100 | 27.0 | 18.0 | 994 | 33.1 | 1.3 | 158 623 | 0.7 | 15 806 | 10.0 | 141 326 | 39.7 | 19.0 |
| Hudson | 240 526 | 34.0 | 374 000 | 32.0 | 20.5 | 1 118 | 28.5 | 7.8 | 316 320 | 1.1 | 33 066 | 10.5 | 322 003 | 37.4 | 19.6 |
| Hunterdon | 47 455 | 85.4 | 437 100 | 27.4 | 16.6 | 1 209 | 31.5 | 2.0 | 71 469 | 1.0 | 5 061 | 7.1 | 65 345 | 50.4 | 12.4 |

1. Specified owner-occupied units. 2. A value of 9.9 represents 9.9 percent or less. 3. Specified renter-occupied units. A value of 10.0 represents 10 percent or less. 4. Overcrowded or lacking complete plumbing facilities. 5. Percent of civilian labor force. 6. Persons 16 years old and over.

| STATE County | Number of establishments | Total | Health care and social assistance | Manufacturing | Retail trade | Finance and insurance | Professional, scientific, and technical services | Total (mil dol) | Average per employee (dollars) | Number | Fewer than 50 acres | 500 acres or more | Farm operators whose principal occupation is farming (percent) |
|---|---|---|---|---|---|---|---|---|---|---|---|---|---|
| | 104 | 105 | 106 | 107 | 108 | 109 | 110 | 111 | 112 | 113 | 114 | 115 | 116 |
| **NEBRASKA—Cont'd** | | | | | | | | | | | | | |
| Platte | 1 023 | 15 345 | 1 510 | 5 175 | 2 152 | 501 | 442 | 529 | 34 447 | 882 | 18.6 | 33.7 | 66.4 |
| Polk | 145 | 871 | 259 | D | 127 | 59 | D | 24 | 27 370 | 505 | 17.0 | 39.2 | 68.3 |
| Red Willow | 418 | 3 889 | 585 | D | 899 | 193 | 138 | 110 | 28 341 | 386 | 18.1 | 47.2 | 56.2 |
| Richardson | 260 | 1 750 | 403 | 209 | 299 | 68 | 62 | 44 | 25 407 | 707 | 14.6 | 23.8 | 48.8 |
| Rock | 46 | 325 | D | D | 45 | D | D | 8 | 23 929 | 237 | 9.3 | 62.9 | 66.2 |
| Saline | 292 | 6 035 | 871 | 2 787 | 619 | 144 | 42 | 201 | 33 295 | 702 | 18.8 | 28.6 | 57.0 |
| Sarpy | 3 098 | 40 331 | 4 481 | 2 367 | 7 387 | 2 006 | 2 933 | 1 468 | 36 399 | 360 | 50.6 | 19.4 | 50.3 |
| Saunders | 507 | 3 371 | 665 | 238 | 551 | 197 | 114 | 97 | 28 735 | 1 131 | 27.4 | 23.7 | 56.1 |
| Scotts Bluff | 1 093 | 12 226 | 2 832 | 818 | 2 381 | 503 | 348 | 389 | 31 848 | 730 | 21.6 | 23.4 | 57.1 |
| Seward | 429 | 5 240 | 780 | 996 | 544 | 229 | D | 154 | 29 375 | 893 | 29.5 | 25.9 | 49.2 |
| Sheridan | 172 | 1 018 | D | D | 255 | 98 | D | 24 | 24 017 | 574 | 13.4 | 56.4 | 61.7 |
| Sherman | 80 | 551 | D | D | 85 | D | D | 13 | 23 461 | 411 | 16.3 | 38.0 | 56.9 |
| Sioux | 15 | D | NA | NA | D | D | D | 1 | D | 366 | 3.3 | 66.7 | 72.4 |
| Stanton | 110 | D | 10 | D | 144 | D | D | D | D | 636 | 17.5 | 23.7 | 55.5 |
| Thayer | 206 | 1 772 | D | D | 190 | 140 | D | 57 | 31 910 | 483 | 10.8 | 46.6 | 61.7 |
| Thomas | 25 | 196 | NA | D | D | D | D | 5 | 24 526 | 103 | 9.7 | 70.9 | 67.0 |
| Thurston | 112 | 1 259 | D | D | 207 | 43 | D | 48 | 38 151 | 372 | 20.2 | 34.1 | 58.9 |
| Valley | 175 | 1 273 | 362 | 57 | 271 | 78 | 62 | 33 | 26 209 | 391 | 14.6 | 48.1 | 71.6 |
| Washington | 530 | 5 881 | 824 | 923 | 987 | D | 187 | 263 | 44 713 | 762 | 39.8 | 19.2 | 50.5 |
| Wayne | 239 | 2 957 | 435 | D | 395 | 243 | 62 | 75 | 25 419 | 573 | 20.1 | 32.3 | 64.4 |
| Webster | 76 | 607 | 175 | NA | 148 | 28 | D | 15 | 24 102 | 430 | 13.3 | 42.3 | 57.4 |
| Wheeler | 16 | 96 | NA | NA | D | D | NA | 2 | 16 250 | 205 | 7.3 | 64.9 | 66.8 |
| York | 501 | 6 015 | 1 074 | 718 | 971 | D | 147 | 184 | 30 639 | 549 | 16.4 | 45.9 | 73.4 |
| **NEVADA** | 58 777 | 1 000 610 | 101 159 | 39 277 | 129 067 | 33 486 | 52 489 | 38 744 | 38 720 | 3 131 | 48.8 | 21.2 | 52.7 |
| Churchill | 512 | 4 939 | 890 | D | 865 | 176 | 356 | 164 | 33 303 | 529 | 56.9 | 8.1 | 49.9 |
| Clark | 39 343 | 730 747 | 68 513 | 18 806 | 94 270 | 24 510 | 39 059 | 27 824 | 38 076 | 193 | 74.6 | 5.2 | 40.4 |
| Douglas | 1 540 | 15 740 | 1 247 | 1 548 | 1 831 | 375 | 713 | 557 | 35 358 | 179 | 60.3 | 13.4 | 49.2 |
| Elko | 1 065 | 18 971 | 1 538 | D | 2 284 | 404 | 539 | 905 | 47 715 | 456 | 32.0 | 36.2 | 59.6 |
| Esmeralda | 17 | 119 | NA | D | D | NA | D | 7 | 56 580 | 19 | 26.3 | 42.1 | 78.9 |
| Eureka | 41 | D | D | D | 23 | D | D | D | D | 86 | 12.8 | 48.8 | 75.6 |
| Humboldt | 396 | 6 525 | 587 | 225 | 1 027 | 69 | D | 317 | 48 634 | 254 | 37.0 | 39.8 | 57.1 |
| Lander | 83 | 1 245 | D | D | 180 | D | D | 71 | 57 415 | 84 | 27.4 | 50.0 | 54.8 |
| Lincoln | 86 | 610 | D | NA | 205 | 43 | D | 16 | 25 466 | 98 | 35.7 | 17.3 | 62.2 |
| Lyon | 729 | 8 395 | D | 1 942 | 1 241 | 152 | 405 | 296 | 35 273 | 325 | 55.7 | 17.2 | 53.5 |
| Mineral | 63 | 488 | D | D | D | D | D | 14 | 29 090 | 84 | 69.0 | 2.4 | 66.7 |
| Nye | 638 | 6 923 | 806 | D | 1 335 | 132 | 178 | 241 | 34 782 | 173 | 50.9 | 19.1 | 49.1 |
| Pershing | 74 | 945 | D | D | D | 14 | D | 41 | 43 538 | 135 | 19.3 | 44.4 | 68.9 |
| Storey | 89 | 345 | D | 7 | 62 | D | D | 8 | 24 043 | 5 | 80.0 | 0.0 | 0.0 |
| Washoe | 11 540 | 163 576 | 22 331 | 12 669 | 21 721 | 6 248 | 9 197 | 6 599 | 40 345 | 393 | 67.4 | 6.1 | 38.2 |
| White Pine | 204 | 2 458 | 336 | D | 387 | D | 46 | 114 | 46 248 | 97 | 26.8 | 36.1 | 50.5 |
| Carson City | 2 067 | 21 836 | 3 645 | 3 386 | 3 412 | 948 | 1 531 | 849 | 38 869 | 21 | 66.7 | 9.5 | 42.9 |
| **NEW HAMPSHIRE** | 37 031 | 554 001 | 86 825 | 66 261 | 94 950 | 24 139 | 30 393 | 24 370 | 43 989 | 4 166 | 51.8 | 3.8 | 46.3 |
| Belknap | 1 788 | 20 765 | 3 884 | 2 394 | 5 036 | 646 | 639 | 745 | 35 858 | 270 | 51.9 | 2.2 | 46.7 |
| Carroll | 1 820 | 17 152 | 2 757 | 850 | 3 776 | 480 | 474 | 506 | 29 514 | 274 | 48.9 | 4.0 | 51.8 |
| Cheshire | 1 907 | 27 870 | 3 930 | 4 896 | 5 628 | 1 550 | 630 | 1 059 | 38 007 | 419 | 49.4 | 5.0 | 47.5 |
| Coos | 891 | 9 606 | 2 418 | 768 | 1 811 | 307 | 112 | 291 | 30 301 | 262 | 32.1 | 8.4 | 34.7 |
| Grafton | 2 896 | 48 525 | 11 143 | 5 360 | 7 776 | 962 | 1 502 | 2 116 | 43 600 | 552 | 40.9 | 6.3 | 45.1 |
| Hillsborough | 10 635 | 176 356 | 27 983 | 25 924 | 26 664 | 6 348 | 10 541 | 8 716 | 49 422 | 615 | 57.9 | 1.8 | 48.1 |
| Merrimack | 4 060 | 58 812 | 11 908 | 5 339 | 9 703 | 4 001 | 3 461 | 2 309 | 39 253 | 583 | 52.8 | 4.1 | 47.7 |
| Rockingham | 9 322 | 124 294 | 14 771 | 13 785 | 25 483 | 5 523 | 8 455 | 5 406 | 43 494 | 594 | 67.3 | 0.8 | 47.3 |
| Strafford | 2 476 | 35 146 | 6 503 | 4 545 | 6 582 | D | 1 415 | 1 532 | 43 592 | 303 | 56.1 | 1.0 | 47.5 |
| Sullivan | 974 | 10 768 | 1 390 | 2 400 | 2 490 | 447 | 202 | 403 | 37 432 | 294 | 45.6 | 6.5 | 42.2 |
| **NEW JERSEY** | 226 878 | 3 377 848 | 535 404 | 234 139 | 434 372 | 188 812 | 316 803 | 183 507 | 54 327 | 10 327 | 75.2 | 2.9 | 44.8 |
| Atlantic | 6 408 | 111 036 | 17 538 | 1 664 | 15 941 | 3 211 | 4 453 | 4 040 | 36 386 | 499 | 75.2 | 1.6 | 45.3 |
| Bergen | 30 997 | 412 514 | 67 181 | 33 560 | 54 731 | 16 227 | 32 882 | 23 643 | 57 316 | 89 | 98.9 | 0.0 | 57.3 |
| Burlington | 10 330 | 173 807 | 24 224 | 16 521 | 25 944 | 14 536 | 16 745 | 8 588 | 49 408 | 922 | 74.6 | 4.7 | 48.0 |
| Camden | 11 621 | 167 467 | 37 896 | 11 618 | 23 357 | 5 284 | 11 380 | 7 238 | 43 220 | 225 | 86.7 | 1.3 | 40.4 |
| Cape May | 3 801 | 24 667 | 4 666 | 415 | 5 904 | 1 138 | 997 | 907 | 36 769 | 201 | 80.6 | 1.0 | 50.7 |
| Cumberland | 2 923 | 44 881 | 8 717 | 7 588 | 7 230 | 1 320 | 1 068 | 1 678 | 37 378 | 615 | 62.0 | 5.7 | 52.7 |
| Essex | 18 681 | 288 475 | 55 539 | 18 407 | 26 546 | 20 516 | 25 861 | 15 872 | 55 020 | 13 | 100.0 | 0.0 | 46.2 |
| Gloucester | 5 780 | 84 157 | 13 573 | 7 620 | 16 687 | 1 770 | 4 233 | 3 283 | 39 012 | 669 | 76.5 | 2.4 | 45.7 |
| Hudson | 12 645 | 204 041 | 25 927 | 7 872 | 22 549 | 31 723 | 12 564 | 13 613 | 66 715 | 0 | 0.0 | 0.0 | 0.0 |
| Hunterdon | 3 853 | 44 265 | 7 649 | 3 643 | 6 770 | 3 175 | 3 893 | 2 573 | 58 137 | 1 623 | 75.8 | 1.8 | 39.4 |

| STATE County | Land in farms Acreage (1,000) | Percent change, 2002–2007 | Acres Average size of farm | Total irrigated (1,000) | Total cropland (1,000) | Value of land and buildings (dollars) Average per farm | Average per acre | Value of machinery and equipment, average per farm (dollars) | Value of products sold Total (mil dol) | Average per farm (dollars) | Percent from: Crops | Livestock and poultry products | Percent of farms with sales of: $10,000 or more | $100,000 or more | Government payments Total ($1,000) | Percent of farms |
|---|---|---|---|---|---|---|---|---|---|---|---|---|---|---|---|---|
| | 117 | 118 | 119 | 120 | 121 | 122 | 123 | 124 | 125 | 126 | 127 | 128 | 129 | 130 | 131 | 132 |
| **NEBRASKA—Cont'd** | | | | | | | | | | | | | | | | |
| Platte | 426 | -2.1 | 483 | 208.4 | 355.3 | 1 098 136 | 2 275 | 212 464 | 413.1 | 468 401 | 34.6 | 65.4 | 79.7 | 54.2 | 6 185 | 79.4 |
| Polk | 269 | 1.9 | 533 | 164.6 | 228.6 | 1 315 269 | 2 467 | 190 828 | 254.7 | 504 435 | 39.0 | 61.0 | 85.3 | 56.8 | 4 564 | 84.6 |
| Red Willow | 446 | 4.0 | 1 157 | 55.1 | 247.1 | 1 218 841 | 1 054 | 167 928 | 166.0 | 430 069 | 40.9 | 59.1 | 69.4 | 42.0 | 4 194 | 71.8 |
| Richardson | 279 | -13.1 | 395 | 2.2 | 209.0 | 749 213 | 1 898 | 100 623 | 97.9 | 138 492 | 67.8 | 32.2 | 59.5 | 27.9 | 4 868 | 85.6 |
| Rock | 632 | 0.5 | 2 666 | 43.6 | 154.6 | 1 360 295 | 510 | 157 509 | 77.2 | 325 558 | 26.2 | 73.8 | 73.0 | 46.4 | 1 876 | 54.0 |
| Saline | 298 | -13.6 | 425 | 81.9 | 241.9 | 891 706 | 2 098 | 143 339 | 116.8 | 166 363 | 78.4 | 21.6 | 68.2 | 38.3 | 5 595 | 85.8 |
| Sarpy | 101 | -3.8 | 280 | 11.8 | 86.7 | 939 807 | 3 355 | 145 436 | 68.1 | 189 178 | 51.6 | 48.4 | 48.6 | 26.9 | 1 631 | 64.4 |
| Saunders | 428 | -6.6 | 378 | 93.4 | 359.9 | 1 010 408 | 2 672 | 129 388 | 230.8 | 204 093 | 59.1 | 40.9 | 63.7 | 32.9 | 7 451 | 79.0 |
| Scotts Bluff | 360 | -15.7 | 494 | 155.6 | 192.8 | 537 511 | 1 089 | 116 047 | 214.5 | 293 848 | 30.9 | 69.1 | 60.8 | 27.8 | 3 019 | 65.3 |
| Seward | 333 | -8.5 | 372 | 127.4 | 272.4 | 943 216 | 2 532 | 141 694 | 221.9 | 248 540 | 53.2 | 46.8 | 58.8 | 32.8 | 6 784 | 77.9 |
| Sheridan | 1 540 | 3.6 | 2 683 | 57.0 | 286.0 | 1 293 556 | 482 | 114 056 | 94.5 | 164 573 | 32.5 | 67.5 | 63.5 | 34.7 | 2 713 | 58.0 |
| Sherman | 270 | -14.6 | 657 | 72.3 | 125.6 | 718 838 | 1 094 | 110 428 | 73.2 | 178 136 | 57.3 | 42.6 | 65.7 | 34.3 | 2 370 | 74.9 |
| Sioux | 1 292 | 17.1 | 3 530 | 51.5 | 119.6 | 1 684 596 | 477 | 142 906 | 108.9 | 297 621 | 12.5 | 87.5 | 77.0 | 44.3 | 2 067 | 58.5 |
| Stanton | 236 | -2.9 | 371 | 31.2 | 177.9 | 686 690 | 1 853 | 114 363 | 134.7 | 211 758 | 41.4 | 58.6 | 59.7 | 33.8 | 4 294 | 78.5 |
| Thayer | 351 | -7.6 | 727 | 131.4 | 266.1 | 1 325 009 | 1 821 | 152 136 | 165.3 | 342 249 | 61.4 | 38.6 | 76.2 | 49.9 | 5 959 | 85.5 |
| Thomas | 425 | 21.8 | 4 125 | 3.2 | 10.2 | 1 405 772 | 341 | 66 827 | 14.7 | 142 407 | D | D | 82.5 | 39.8 | 190 | 21.4 |
| Thurston | 200 | -6.5 | 537 | 7.8 | 173.2 | 1 057 191 | 1 969 | 169 075 | 153.7 | 413 284 | 39.3 | 60.7 | 67.2 | 40.3 | 4 015 | 83.6 |
| Valley | 356 | 13.0 | 911 | 99.3 | 147.8 | 1 022 526 | 1 122 | 182 060 | 138.2 | 353 563 | 35.0 | 65.0 | 77.7 | 44.5 | 3 210 | 79.0 |
| Washington | 217 | -10.3 | 285 | 18.5 | 188.1 | 875 349 | 3 069 | 119 687 | 131.4 | 172 487 | 49.8 | 50.2 | 55.5 | 29.4 | 3 193 | 65.0 |
| Wayne | 277 | -1.4 | 483 | 42.7 | 238.3 | 1 154 595 | 2 392 | 141 598 | 177.9 | 310 491 | 49.6 | 50.4 | 68.4 | 46.1 | 3 849 | 78.4 |
| Webster | 306 | -3.8 | 710 | 62.4 | 178.0 | 896 346 | 1 262 | 144 463 | 140.9 | 327 780 | 37.5 | 62.5 | 66.0 | 37.0 | 4 237 | 77.9 |
| Wheeler | 360 | 6.5 | 1 757 | 44.1 | 113.2 | 1 231 349 | 701 | 173 726 | 196.4 | 957 846 | 8.1 | 91.9 | 78.5 | 50.7 | 2 328 | 64.9 |
| York | 346 | -2.3 | 630 | 254.7 | 314.7 | 1 661 830 | 2 636 | 269 338 | 278.4 | 507 169 | 59.6 | 40.4 | 84.9 | 66.3 | 7 215 | 78.0 |
| **NEVADA** | 5 865 | -7.4 | 1 873 | 691.0 | 753.7 | 1 148 693 | 613 | 111 799 | 513.3 | 163 931 | 42.7 | 57.3 | 43.0 | 19.6 | 4 007 | 10.6 |
| Churchill | 131 | -12.1 | 248 | 40.3 | 36.4 | 496 430 | 1 998 | 73 720 | 66.9 | 126 504 | 20.2 | 79.8 | 44.2 | 12.5 | 494 | 13.6 |
| Clark | 88 | 27.5 | 458 | 6.5 | 6.2 | 1 391 798 | 3 039 | 64 840 | 10.2 | 53 060 | 46.1 | 53.9 | 21.2 | 7.3 | 91 | 6.7 |
| Douglas | 91 | -56.9 | 509 | 31.2 | 20.9 | 1 234 191 | 2 426 | 73 444 | D | D | D | 0.0 | 34.6 | 10.1 | D | 2.2 |
| Elko | 2 085 | -15.7 | 4 573 | 182.2 | 190.9 | 1 407 787 | 308 | 97 535 | 53.6 | 117 541 | 4.5 | 95.5 | 49.1 | 22.6 | 460 | 8.3 |
| Esmeralda | 25 | NA | 1 313 | 13.7 | 12.8 | 1 769 708 | 1 348 | 284 228 | 7.7 | 405 921 | D | D | 84.2 | 68.4 | D | 10.5 |
| Eureka | 783 | 194.4 | 9 110 | 46.2 | 50.9 | 1 305 630 | 143 | 218 521 | 25.0 | 290 877 | D | D | 76.7 | 58.1 | 113 | 8.1 |
| Humboldt | 756 | -0.7 | 2 978 | 116.3 | 153.3 | 1 718 038 | 577 | 187 751 | 74.4 | 292 796 | 62.6 | 37.4 | 54.3 | 36.6 | 682 | 21.7 |
| Lander | 339 | -45.3 | 4 037 | 31.4 | 38.0 | 1 647 807 | 408 | 196 558 | 19.1 | 227 357 | 54.7 | 45.3 | 63.1 | 47.6 | 179 | 16.7 |
| Lincoln | 46 | NA | 472 | 18.3 | 17.9 | 698 218 | 1 479 | 129 086 | 15.3 | 156 518 | 50.1 | 49.9 | 54.1 | 17.3 | D | 2.0 |
| Lyon | 261 | 15.5 | 802 | 81.5 | 78.9 | 1 016 512 | 1 267 | 154 740 | 91.1 | 280 331 | 68.2 | 31.8 | 41.8 | 20.3 | 59 | 3.4 |
| Mineral | D | D | D | D | 6.4 | 2 781 061 | 982 | 30 927 | 2.9 | 35 035 | D | D | 20.2 | 4.8 | 938 | 71.4 |
| Nye | 91 | -7.1 | 525 | 21.5 | 28.1 | 674 881 | 1 285 | 109 264 | 58.2 | 336 638 | 5.6 | 94.4 | 39.9 | 14.5 | 115 | 2.9 |
| Pershing | 244 | 86.3 | 1 809 | 48.4 | 69.2 | 1 288 595 | 712 | 165 140 | 42.4 | 314 097 | 54.3 | 45.7 | 63.7 | 41.5 | 344 | 26.7 |
| Storey | D | D | D | D | 0.0 | 206 200 | 14 123 | 47 212 | D | D | D | 0.0 | 20.0 | 0.0 | 0 | 0.0 |
| Washoe | 486 | -39.4 | 1 236 | 18.7 | 19.0 | 980 996 | 793 | 66 268 | 18.4 | 46 771 | 55.3 | 44.7 | 21.6 | 4.6 | 284 | 2.0 |
| White Pine | D | D | D | 30.9 | 23.8 | 1 685 545 | 830 | 185 911 | 15.2 | 156 412 | 28.6 | 71.4 | 60.8 | 29.9 | 131 | 4.1 |
| Carson City | 3 | -25.0 | 131 | D | 1.2 | 408 435 | 3 112 | 67 740 | 1.1 | 54 131 | D | D | 23.8 | 14.3 | 0 | 0.0 |
| **NEW HAMPSHIRE** | 472 | 6.1 | 113 | 2.5 | 128.9 | 558 385 | 4 929 | 58 413 | 199.1 | 47 780 | 53.5 | 46.5 | 27.9 | 6.9 | 2 474 | 10.2 |
| Belknap | 23 | 0.0 | 87 | 0.1 | 6.1 | 496 272 | 5 732 | 47 338 | 7.7 | 28 400 | 61.3 | 38.7 | 20.7 | 5.2 | 120 | 8.1 |
| Carroll | 32 | 6.7 | 117 | 0.1 | 6.8 | 549 028 | 4 695 | 43 292 | 5.3 | 19 268 | 62.7 | 37.3 | 28.5 | 4.0 | 209 | 13.1 |
| Cheshire | 48 | 17.1 | 115 | 0.1 | 11.8 | 531 220 | 4 614 | 61 699 | 15.4 | 36 768 | 28.6 | 71.4 | 30.1 | 5.7 | 143 | 10.0 |
| Coos | 51 | 15.9 | 194 | 0.0 | 13.9 | 465 518 | 2 396 | 65 407 | 13.0 | 49 630 | 21.2 | 78.8 | 30.5 | 6.9 | 413 | 8.8 |
| Grafton | 100 | 16.3 | 181 | 0.1 | 24.9 | 710 052 | 3 921 | 65 838 | 34.4 | 62 306 | 14.0 | 86.0 | 27.4 | 8.7 | 579 | 18.3 |
| Hillsborough | 50 | 25.0 | 82 | 0.8 | 13.1 | 560 697 | 6 864 | 55 096 | 17.1 | 27 799 | 67.6 | 32.4 | 24.6 | 5.4 | 60 | 9.1 |
| Merrimack | 65 | -17.7 | 111 | 0.7 | 16.3 | 527 966 | 4 762 | 56 192 | 55.3 | 94 831 | 81.8 | 18.2 | 29.2 | 8.6 | 360 | 9.1 |
| Rockingham | 34 | 6.3 | 57 | 0.4 | 13.6 | 541 137 | 9 575 | 61 082 | 26.0 | 43 829 | 75.1 | 24.9 | 27.4 | 7.4 | 118 | 6.2 |
| Strafford | 26 | -23.5 | 85 | 0.2 | 9.0 | 526 318 | 6 195 | 56 796 | 9.9 | 32 712 | 60.5 | 39.5 | 32.0 | 5.9 | 224 | 9.2 |
| Sullivan | 43 | 19.4 | 147 | 0.1 | 13.4 | 584 232 | 3 976 | 65 438 | 15.0 | 50 926 | 28.0 | 72.0 | 31.0 | 8.8 | 249 | 18.0 |
| **NEW JERSEY** | 733 | -9.1 | 71 | 95.3 | 488.7 | 1 089 883 | 15 346 | 68 374 | 986.9 | 95 564 | 86.3 | 13.7 | 32.7 | 11.1 | 6 988 | 8.3 |
| Atlantic | 30 | 0.0 | 61 | 11.7 | 18.6 | 902 470 | 14 827 | 113 651 | 128.3 | 257 193 | 98.0 | 2.0 | 44.9 | 20.6 | 349 | 5.0 |
| Bergen | 1 | 0.0 | 13 | 0.2 | 0.6 | 915 051 | 69 192 | 52 244 | 8.7 | 97 685 | 96.4 | 3.6 | 51.7 | 23.6 | D | 2.2 |
| Burlington | 86 | -22.5 | 93 | 12.6 | 53.7 | 1 114 826 | 11 981 | 73 154 | 86.3 | 93 603 | 93.3 | 6.7 | 38.9 | 13.6 | 958 | 8.7 |
| Camden | 9 | -10.0 | 39 | 2.6 | 5.0 | 602 414 | 15 473 | 52 844 | 18.6 | 82 464 | 99.0 | 1.0 | 36.4 | 10.2 | 62 | 2.2 |
| Cape May | 8 | -20.0 | 40 | 2.3 | 4.3 | 637 097 | 16 055 | 55 369 | 14.6 | 72 567 | 96.2 | 3.8 | 35.8 | 8.0 | 20 | 4.0 |
| Cumberland | 69 | -2.8 | 113 | 18.4 | 52.3 | 1 056 005 | 9 346 | 118 184 | 156.9 | 255 186 | 97.4 | 2.6 | 48.0 | 22.9 | 413 | 9.3 |
| Essex | 0 | NA | 14 | 0.0 | 0.0 | 1 302 885 | 92 052 | 28 014 | 0.7 | 54 631 | 98.7 | 1.4 | 69.2 | 23.1 | 0 | 0.0 |
| Gloucester | 47 | -7.8 | 70 | 12.9 | 34.7 | 1 078 215 | 15 459 | 73 867 | 93.9 | 140 333 | 93.8 | 6.2 | 34.4 | 13.5 | 453 | 9.4 |
| Hudson | 0 | NA | 0 | 0.0 | 0.0 | 0 | 0 | 0 | 0.0 | 0 | 0.0 | 0.0 | 0.0 | 0.0 | 0 | 0.0 |
| Hunterdon | 100 | -8.3 | 62 | 1.5 | 66.6 | 1 243 324 | 20 174 | 49 814 | 69.7 | 42 973 | 87.0 | 13.0 | 23.4 | 4.9 | 729 | 8.4 |

| STATE County | Water use, 2005 | | Wholesale trade,[1] 2007 | | | | Retail trade,[2] 2007 | | | | Real estate and rental and leasing,[2] 2007 | | | |
|---|---|---|---|---|---|---|---|---|---|---|---|---|---|---|
| | Total water withdrawn (mil gal/day) | Gallons withdrawn per person | Number of establish-ments | Number of employees | Sales (mil dol) | Annual payroll (mil dol) | Number of establish-ments | Number of employees | Sales (mil dol) | Annual payroll (mil dol) | Number of establish-ments | Number of employees | Receipts (mil dol) | Annual payroll (mil dol) |
| | 133 | 134 | 135 | 136 | 137 | 138 | 139 | 140 | 141 | 142 | 143 | 144 | 145 | 146 |
| NEBRASKA—Cont'd | | | | | | | | | | | | | | |
| Platte | 229.0 | 7 326 | 49 | 529 | 517.8 | 22.9 | 174 | 2 136 | 494.3 | 41.2 | 38 | 118 | 19.0 | 2.4 |
| Polk | 171.3 | 31 603 | 9 | 109 | 103.3 | 3.5 | 24 | 116 | 35.5 | 2.1 | 2 | D | D | D |
| Red Willow | 53.2 | 4 807 | 20 | 244 | 140.9 | 8.3 | 88 | 789 | 175.9 | 17.3 | 20 | 59 | 3.8 | 0.7 |
| Richardson | 3.2 | 364 | 27 | 130 | 186.9 | 3.8 | 48 | 337 | 70.4 | 6.2 | 6 | 26 | 1.5 | 0.4 |
| Rock | 39.4 | 25 163 | 5 | 66 | 23.4 | 1.6 | 10 | D | D | D | NA | NA | NA | NA |
| Saline | 71.8 | 5 056 | 15 | 139 | 157.0 | 6.1 | 55 | 552 | 102.4 | 10.1 | 8 | 23 | 1.5 | 0.3 |
| Sarpy | 28.3 | 203 | 159 | 2 584 | 3 005.9 | 128.5 | 373 | 6 783 | 2 285.8 | 157.2 | 131 | 543 | 99.7 | 15.6 |
| Saunders | 148.9 | 7 280 | 25 | 145 | 147.8 | 5.1 | 64 | 570 | 149.0 | 10.7 | 13 | 17 | 1.1 | 0.3 |
| Scotts Bluff | 264.1 | 7 186 | 65 | D | D | D | 200 | 2 451 | 519.8 | 49.3 | 42 | 133 | 17.9 | 2.9 |
| Seward | 135.8 | 8 111 | 25 | 182 | 127.1 | 8.0 | 56 | 577 | 109.8 | 10.4 | 9 | 17 | 2.2 | 0.2 |
| Sheridan | 96.5 | 17 027 | 11 | 166 | 64.8 | 3.6 | 46 | 281 | 50.3 | 4.0 | 3 | D | D | D |
| Sherman | 88.4 | 28 419 | 3 | 33 | 11.3 | 0.9 | 15 | 69 | 35.5 | 1.5 | 1 | D | D | D |
| Sioux | 49.8 | 34 156 | 4 | D | D | D | 4 | D | D | D | NA | NA | NA | NA |
| Stanton | 30.2 | 4 620 | 3 | D | D | D | 15 | 136 | 33.0 | 2.7 | 1 | D | D | D |
| Thayer | 107.6 | 19 801 | 19 | 146 | 98.6 | 5.7 | 41 | 254 | 54.9 | 4.0 | 2 | D | D | D |
| Thomas | 2.7 | 4 334 | 2 | D | D | D | 4 | D | D | D | 1 | D | D | D |
| Thurston | 13.4 | 1 822 | 9 | 73 | 115.0 | 2.5 | 24 | 199 | 54.1 | 4.1 | 4 | D | D | D |
| Valley | 139.2 | 31 613 | 12 | 89 | 48.4 | 2.8 | 36 | 316 | 66.8 | 5.9 | 3 | D | D | D |
| Washington | 581.7 | 29 420 | 19 | 159 | 211.4 | 5.9 | 60 | 926 | 642.6 | 35.6 | 15 | 30 | 2.2 | 0.5 |
| Wayne | 36.3 | 3 944 | 11 | 139 | 51.9 | 3.4 | 44 | 394 | 79.5 | 6.7 | 7 | 20 | 1.1 | 0.4 |
| Webster | 49.5 | 13 163 | 15 | 75 | 58.9 | 2.1 | 20 | 155 | 23.7 | 1.8 | 1 | D | D | D |
| Wheeler | 50.6 | 61 671 | 2 | D | D | D | 3 | D | D | D | NA | NA | NA | NA |
| York | 281.5 | 19 551 | 32 | 332 | 239.1 | 12.1 | 77 | 1 045 | 241.3 | 20.8 | 18 | 39 | 3.9 | 0.5 |
| NEVADA | 2 377.5 | 985 | 2 614 | 36 052 | 19 255.9 | 1 698.5 | 8 492 | 139 829 | 37 434.0 | 3 691.7 | 4 613 | 31 603 | 6 187.3 | 1 106.5 |
| Churchill | 179.3 | 7 302 | 19 | 153 | 33.3 | 2.7 | 84 | 1 195 | 265.3 | 28.6 | 38 | 140 | 11.9 | 2.6 |
| Clark | 607.7 | 355 | 1 698 | 23 067 | 11 493.1 | 1 114.8 | 5 744 | 99 817 | 26 676.6 | 2 656.9 | 3 356 | 25 654 | 5 235.4 | 925.5 |
| Douglas | 52.0 | 1 106 | 57 | D | D | D | 198 | 2 817 | 670.4 | 66.1 | 140 | 539 | 94.0 | 19.5 |
| Elko | 356.9 | 7 831 | 58 | D | D | D | 179 | 2 307 | 791.4 | 57.3 | 39 | 297 | 26.7 | 5.9 |
| Esmeralda | 41.7 | 53 037 | NA | NA | NA | NA | 2 | D | D | D | NA | NA | NA | NA |
| Eureka | 84.6 | 59 265 | NA | NA | NA | NA | 6 | 35 | 16.3 | 1.4 | NA | NA | NA | NA |
| Humboldt | 263.9 | 15 405 | 15 | 140 | 71.5 | 7.5 | 76 | 1 042 | 333.6 | 24.9 | 11 | 43 | 5.6 | 0.9 |
| Lander | 107.3 | 20 987 | 3 | D | D | D | 22 | 237 | 55.0 | 4.0 | 3 | 4 | 0.7 | 0.1 |
| Lincoln | 50.9 | 11 601 | 2 | D | D | D | 17 | 247 | 31.1 | 3.0 | 3 | 19 | 0.8 | 0.2 |
| Lyon | 217.8 | 4 583 | 40 | D | D | D | 117 | 1 080 | 371.4 | 25.3 | 45 | 138 | 14.9 | 3.0 |
| Mineral | 13.3 | 2 705 | 2 | D | D | D | 11 | D | D | D | 3 | 5 | 0.3 | 0.0 |
| Nye | 68.6 | 1 694 | 16 | D | D | D | 135 | 1 554 | 396.8 | 37.9 | 52 | 141 | 14.5 | 2.9 |
| Pershing | 131.8 | 20 730 | 2 | D | D | D | 18 | 154 | 43.0 | 3.2 | 3 | 9 | 0.4 | 0.1 |
| Storey | 3.8 | 923 | NA | NA | NA | NA | 22 | 54 | 6.8 | 1.1 | 2 | D | D | D |
| Washoe | 116.9 | 300 | 602 | 10 370 | 6 317.7 | 461.6 | 1 555 | 25 025 | 6 667.4 | 671.0 | 763 | D | D | D |
| White Pine | 71.1 | 7 902 | 8 | D | D | D | 44 | 458 | 88.8 | 8.4 | 8 | 37 | 3.0 | 0.6 |
| Carson City | 9.9 | 177 | 92 | D | D | D | 262 | 3 698 | 991.5 | 99.5 | 147 | 569 | 73.4 | 16.0 |
| NEW HAMPSHIRE | 1 323.7 | 1 010 | 1 561 | 21 457 | 14 564.5 | 1 196.3 | 6 603 | 98 333 | 25 353.9 | 2 380.5 | 1 534 | 7 266 | 1 371.8 | 248.2 |
| Belknap | 8.7 | 141 | 48 | D | D | D | 372 | 5 212 | 1 348.7 | 133.2 | 88 | 399 | 56.6 | 10.2 |
| Carroll | 6.1 | 129 | 34 | D | D | D | 424 | 3 891 | 889.0 | 96.0 | 84 | D | D | D |
| Cheshire | 8.5 | 111 | 66 | D | D | D | 382 | 5 775 | 1 649.0 | 139.3 | 69 | 296 | 49.3 | 10.0 |
| Coos | 40.2 | 1 193 | 21 | D | D | D | 197 | 2 229 | 602.9 | 50.3 | 27 | D | D | D |
| Grafton | 13.1 | 154 | 80 | D | D | D | 592 | 8 158 | 1 961.3 | 195.5 | 140 | 582 | 72.8 | 17.5 |
| Hillsborough | 58.6 | 146 | 515 | 6 535 | 3 873.1 | 386.1 | 1 657 | 27 793 | 7 647.3 | 678.7 | 443 | 2 664 | 554.7 | 96.4 |
| Merrimack | 245.3 | 1 670 | 159 | 3 811 | 2 812.4 | 173.4 | 673 | 10 315 | 2 605.6 | 244.8 | 168 | 900 | 222.5 | 32.8 |
| Rockingham | 916.0 | 3 104 | 520 | 6 810 | 5 844.8 | 426.4 | 1 667 | 25 911 | 6 414.9 | 605.5 | 364 | 1 542 | 284.2 | 58.2 |
| Strafford | 20.7 | 174 | 81 | 856 | 351.1 | 50.2 | 439 | 6 640 | 1 672.9 | 173.9 | 111 | 428 | 65.7 | 10.6 |
| Sullivan | 6.4 | 150 | 37 | D | D | D | 200 | 2 409 | 562.4 | 63.3 | 40 | 136 | 16.4 | 3.1 |
| NEW JERSEY | 7 390.5 | 848 | 14 033 | 221 729 | 233 413.0 | 13 266.6 | 34 482 | 460 843 | 124 813.6 | 12 050.0 | 9 618 | 64 021 | 16 347.6 | 2 939.1 |
| Atlantic | 51.4 | 190 | 196 | 2 916 | 1 342.2 | 127.1 | 1 291 | 17 258 | 4 429.4 | 428.6 | 287 | 1 867 | 378.7 | 56.9 |
| Bergen | 123.8 | 137 | 3 046 | 40 189 | 66 117.9 | 2 584.6 | 4 128 | 55 875 | 16 475.0 | 1 768.6 | 1 441 | 7 655 | 2 294.7 | 412.7 |
| Burlington | 104.9 | 233 | 572 | 11 618 | 15 040.9 | 649.7 | 1 594 | 27 383 | 7 005.1 | 706.9 | 409 | 3 744 | 881.0 | 182.1 |
| Camden | 55.4 | 107 | 645 | D | D | D | 1 911 | 24 858 | 5 859.3 | 601.8 | 457 | 3 080 | 575.7 | 118.0 |
| Cape May | 217.6 | 2 191 | 65 | 561 | 276.1 | 25.3 | 746 | 6 103 | 1 584.9 | 164.8 | 258 | 836 | 177.1 | 27.0 |
| Cumberland | 58.1 | 379 | 160 | D | D | D | 564 | 7 602 | 1 952.7 | 185.4 | 125 | 540 | 88.3 | 16.2 |
| Essex | 32.5 | 41 | 1 081 | 17 340 | 12 622.5 | 1 116.1 | 2 892 | 30 136 | 7 750.6 | 764.8 | 947 | 5 988 | 1 411.3 | 243.8 |
| Gloucester | 75.0 | 271 | 314 | 8 732 | 8 962.5 | 426.2 | 989 | 17 301 | 4 352.5 | 386.0 | 180 | D | D | D |
| Hudson | 609.5 | 1 010 | 829 | 16 313 | 14 524.9 | 885.7 | 2 267 | 22 579 | 6 099.9 | 552.6 | 725 | 4 635 | 1 442.8 | 235.2 |
| Hunterdon | 23.1 | 177 | 157 | 1 283 | 629.5 | 62.0 | 572 | 6 676 | 2 186.6 | 193.2 | 112 | 407 | 102.1 | 17.6 |

1. Merchant wholesalers, except manufacturers' sales branches and offices.    2. Employer establishments.

| STATE County | Professional, scientific, and technical services,[1] 2007 | | | | Manufacturing, 2007 | | | | Accommodation and food services, 2007 | | | |
|---|---|---|---|---|---|---|---|---|---|---|---|---|
| | Number of establish-ments | Number of employees | Receipts (mil dol) | Annual payroll (mil dol) | Number of establish-ments | Number of employees | Receipts (mil dol) | Annual payroll (mil dol) | Number of establish-ments | Number of employees | Sales (mil dol) | Annual payroll (mil dol) |
| | 147 | 148 | 149 | 150 | 151 | 152 | 153 | 154 | 155 | 156 | 157 | 158 |
| NEBRASKA—Cont'd | | | | | | | | | | | | |
| Platte | 59 | D | D | D | 79 | 6 253 | 2 353.6 | 248.9 | 80 | 1 110 | 39.1 | 10.6 |
| Polk | 13 | 25 | 2.0 | 0.3 | NA | NA | NA | NA | 8 | 44 | 1.1 | 0.2 |
| Red Willow | 33 | 139 | 10.8 | 4.3 | NA | NA | NA | NA | 27 | 540 | 16.4 | 4.5 |
| Richardson | 16 | 69 | 3.8 | 1.3 | NA | NA | NA | NA | 23 | 142 | 4.1 | 1.1 |
| Rock | 1 | D | D | D | NA | NA | NA | NA | 3 | 23 | 0.3 | 0.1 |
| Saline | 17 | 55 | 4.1 | 1.0 | 19 | 2 907 | 951.8 | 112.2 | 33 | 340 | 11.3 | 2.8 |
| Sarpy | 255 | D | D | D | 79 | 2 573 | 587.7 | 115.2 | 224 | 4 211 | 160.3 | 47.6 |
| Saunders | 41 | D | D | D | 25 | 645 | D | D | 39 | 361 | 9.2 | 2.3 |
| Scotts Bluff | 70 | D | D | D | 42 | D | 177.9 | 33.7 | 104 | 1 488 | 52.9 | 14.4 |
| Seward | 31 | 79 | 9.7 | 2.4 | 20 | 977 | D | 36.8 | 34 | 438 | 13.5 | 3.4 |
| Sheridan | 9 | 43 | 3.1 | 0.8 | NA | NA | NA | NA | 18 | 104 | 2.9 | 0.8 |
| Sherman | 5 | 7 | 0.6 | 0.1 | NA | NA | NA | NA | 8 | 50 | 2.1 | 0.4 |
| Sioux | 1 | D | D | D | NA | NA | NA | NA | 2 | D | D | D |
| Stanton | 6 | D | D | D | NA | NA | NA | NA | 6 | 46 | 1.6 | 0.4 |
| Thayer | 7 | 16 | 1.0 | 0.3 | NA | NA | NA | NA | 16 | 80 | 1.9 | 0.5 |
| Thomas | 1 | D | D | D | NA | NA | NA | NA | 3 | 31 | 1.0 | 0.3 |
| Thurston | 6 | D | D | D | NA | NA | NA | NA | 8 | D | D | D |
| Valley | 12 | 65 | 5.1 | 1.7 | NA | NA | NA | NA | 13 | 110 | 2.7 | 0.7 |
| Washington | 45 | 418 | 36.6 | 19.4 | 23 | 1 181 | 724.2 | 54.8 | 40 | 393 | 12.5 | 3.2 |
| Wayne | 13 | 188 | 8.3 | 2.6 | 12 | 821 | 180.0 | 22.8 | 21 | 361 | 9.3 | 2.2 |
| Webster | 3 | D | D | D | NA | NA | NA | NA | 7 | D | D | D |
| Wheeler | NA | NA | NA | NA | NA | NA | NA | NA | 7 | D | D | D |
| York | 30 | 156 | 17.6 | 6.2 | 25 | 936 | 353.2 | 37.8 | 40 | 705 | 28.9 | 7.7 |
| NEVADA | 7 895 | 57 357 | 8 881.4 | 3 241.1 | 2 035 | 51 958 | 15 735.8 | 2 290.8 | 5 570 | 325 544 | 28 815.5 | 8 594.6 |
| Churchill | 36 | 500 | 38.5 | 23.5 | NA | NA | NA | NA | 52 | 725 | 33.0 | 8.9 |
| Clark | 5 282 | 43 063 | 6 982.5 | 2 498.8 | 1 096 | 26 478 | 7 180.7 | 1 086.3 | 3 797 | 266 845 | 24 857.8 | 7 431.8 |
| Douglas | 240 | 1 032 | 106.0 | 46.4 | 78 | 2 652 | 751.8 | 140.6 | 130 | 9 342 | 680.4 | 200.0 |
| Elko | 100 | D | D | D | NA | NA | NA | NA | 127 | 5 776 | 474.1 | 122.0 |
| Esmeralda | 1 | D | D | D | NA | NA | NA | NA | 2 | D | D | D |
| Eureka | 5 | D | D | D | NA | NA | NA | NA | 4 | 51 | 2.2 | 0.5 |
| Humboldt | 20 | 123 | 9.5 | 3.6 | NA | NA | NA | NA | 57 | 1 024 | 52.0 | 14.6 |
| Lander | 3 | D | D | D | NA | NA | NA | NA | 17 | 126 | 5.4 | 1.5 |
| Lincoln | 8 | 12 | 1.4 | 0.3 | NA | NA | NA | NA | 16 | D | D | D |
| Lyon | 52 | 288 | 24.8 | 10.7 | 101 | 2 171 | 573.6 | 85.1 | 67 | 798 | 35.0 | 9.5 |
| Mineral | 4 | D | D | D | NA | NA | NA | NA | 13 | 326 | 20.2 | 4.8 |
| Nye | 53 | 214 | 14.9 | 6.1 | NA | NA | NA | NA | 74 | 1 519 | 88.1 | 21.8 |
| Pershing | 4 | 8 | 0.6 | 0.2 | NA | NA | NA | NA | 14 | 226 | 9.2 | 3.3 |
| Storey | 8 | 12 | 1.5 | 0.3 | NA | NA | NA | NA | 13 | 93 | 4.8 | 1.5 |
| Washoe | 1 688 | 10 089 | 1 442.8 | 548.7 | 505 | D | D | D | 990 | 35 447 | 2 399.4 | 729.2 |
| White Pine | 10 | D | D | D | NA | NA | NA | NA | 30 | 472 | 22.0 | 6.5 |
| Carson City | 381 | D | D | D | 143 | 3 528 | 621.6 | 141.7 | 167 | 2 664 | 127.7 | 37.8 |
| NEW HAMPSHIRE | 3 961 | 29 160 | 3 730.8 | 1 570.2 | 2 104 | 81 592 | 18 592.4 | 4 196.2 | 3 508 | 55 268 | 2 631.0 | 799.8 |
| Belknap | 161 | D | D | D | 102 | 3 274 | 687.1 | 142.4 | 229 | 2 742 | 151.6 | 48.3 |
| Carroll | 145 | D | D | D | 86 | 992 | 213.4 | 35.5 | 304 | 3 900 | 214.9 | 63.8 |
| Cheshire | 150 | D | D | D | 150 | 5 483 | 1 095.2 | 258.2 | 161 | 2 643 | 110.3 | 35.0 |
| Coos | 44 | D | D | D | 42 | 1 166 | 295.9 | 43.6 | 117 | 1 747 | 85.7 | 25.0 |
| Grafton | 251 | D | D | D | 130 | 6 138 | 1 314.3 | 272.5 | 356 | 5 844 | 272.8 | 83.7 |
| Hillsborough | 1 347 | D | D | D | 633 | 31 243 | 7 707.6 | 1 944.4 | 875 | 15 987 | 732.3 | 224.9 |
| Merrimack | 456 | 2 625 | 412.7 | 152.0 | 230 | 7 043 | 1 539.6 | 315.1 | 306 | 4 900 | 223.5 | 68.4 |
| Rockingham | 1 101 | D | D | D | 475 | 17 081 | 3 912.6 | 801.3 | 832 | 13 262 | 660.7 | 198.6 |
| Strafford | 234 | D | D | D | 152 | 5 739 | 1 186.0 | 243.3 | 256 | 3 500 | 146.8 | 42.8 |
| Sullivan | 72 | D | D | D | 104 | 3 433 | 640.8 | 140.0 | 72 | 743 | 32.3 | 9.4 |
| NEW JERSEY | 31 040 | 330 133 | 52 442.8 | 23 639.9 | 9 250 | 310 606 | 116 608.1 | 16 399.3 | 19 526 | 291 327 | 19 993.6 | 5 232.4 |
| Atlantic | 648 | D | D | D | 140 | 2 974 | D | 113.8 | 862 | 56 370 | 6 093.0 | 1 505.4 |
| Bergen | 4 367 | D | D | D | 1 313 | 42 288 | 11 973.8 | 2 236.6 | 2 222 | 27 945 | 1 848.3 | 489.0 |
| Burlington | 1 374 | D | D | D | 418 | 20 568 | 6 072.3 | 1 150.1 | 907 | 13 306 | 657.0 | 180.6 |
| Camden | 1 613 | D | D | D | 486 | 17 283 | 4 150.1 | 819.3 | 1 019 | 13 550 | 678.8 | 185.1 |
| Cape May | 250 | D | D | D | 81 | 662 | D | 18.9 | 832 | 5 615 | 517.0 | 144.9 |
| Cumberland | 231 | D | D | D | 175 | 9 037 | 2 591.4 | 341.6 | 262 | 3 263 | 155.1 | 40.0 |
| Essex | 2 443 | D | D | D | 914 | 27 302 | 10 422.7 | 1 472.5 | 1 514 | 19 727 | 1 335.8 | 357.1 |
| Gloucester | 538 | D | D | D | 276 | 10 190 | 15 679.4 | 573.7 | 472 | 8 461 | 379.4 | 104.3 |
| Hudson | 1 255 | D | D | D | 477 | 9 898 | 2 614.2 | 404.6 | 1 297 | 13 289 | 880.7 | 218.3 |
| Hunterdon | 644 | D | D | D | 148 | D | D | 194.1 | 284 | 3 243 | 175.8 | 47.2 |

1. Establishment subject to federal tax.

| | Health care and social assistance, 2007 | | | | Other services, 2007 | | | | Federal funds and grants, 2009–2010 | | | |
|---|---|---|---|---|---|---|---|---|---|---|---|---|
| | | | | | | | | | Expenditures (mil dol) | | | |
| | | | | | | | | | | Direct payments for individuals[1] | | |
| STATE County | Number of establishments | Number of employees | Receipts (mil dol) | Annual payroll (mil dol) | Number of establishments | Number of employees | Receipts (mil dol) | Annual payroll (mil dol) | Total | Social Security and government retirement | Medicare | Food Stamps and Supplemental Security Income |
| | 159 | 160 | 161 | 162 | 163 | 164 | 165 | 166 | 167 | 168 | 169 | 170 |
| NEBRASKA—Cont'd | | | | | | | | | | | | |
| Platte | 84 | 1 587 | 125.4 | 47.5 | 78 | 497 | 25.0 | 8.6 | 195.3 | 88.6 | 25.7 | 5.2 |
| Polk | 7 | 233 | 12.9 | 5.6 | 16 | 24 | 3.1 | 0.6 | 40.4 | 17.1 | 9.9 | 0.4 |
| Red Willow | 36 | D | D | D | 31 | 107 | 7.8 | 2.0 | 88.8 | 42.4 | 18.8 | 3.0 |
| Richardson | 22 | 369 | 24.4 | 9.9 | 22 | 64 | 4.1 | 0.7 | 91.1 | 35.2 | 20.3 | 2.5 |
| Rock | 4 | D | D | D | 5 | 11 | 1.1 | 0.3 | 13.2 | 5.0 | 2.5 | 0.2 |
| Saline | 29 | 583 | 31.8 | 14.0 | 26 | 111 | 6.1 | 1.5 | 133.1 | 41.4 | 17.4 | 1.8 |
| Sarpy | 233 | 3 559 | 246.5 | 105.4 | 206 | 1 307 | 107.8 | 31.8 | 1 457.1 | 332.6 | 45.2 | 8.2 |
| Saunders | 32 | 536 | 30.1 | 13.0 | 28 | 87 | 8.7 | 2.2 | 166.5 | 61.3 | 27.7 | 2.5 |
| Scotts Bluff | 127 | 2 980 | 274.2 | 115.9 | 97 | 459 | 29.8 | 9.3 | 306.1 | 129.7 | 51.2 | 16.6 |
| Seward | 32 | 744 | 45.5 | 21.7 | 40 | 139 | 14.5 | 3.1 | 89.8 | 47.0 | 15.9 | 1.6 |
| Sheridan | 16 | 192 | 11.7 | 5.1 | 19 | 47 | 2.9 | 0.5 | 50.1 | 20.7 | 10.5 | 1.9 |
| Sherman | 6 | D | D | D | 7 | D | D | D | 37.1 | 12.3 | 5.9 | 0.3 |
| Sioux | NA | NA | NA | NA | 2 | D | D | D | 6.6 | 2.4 | 0.7 | 0.0 |
| Stanton | 8 | D | D | D | 5 | D | D | D | 24.6 | 9.9 | 4.4 | 0.6 |
| Thayer | 11 | 446 | 23.6 | 10.7 | 20 | 57 | 7.1 | 1.1 | 52.1 | 22.2 | 10.7 | 1.0 |
| Thomas | NA | NA | NA | NA | 1 | D | D | D | 7.9 | 2.2 | 1.6 | 0.1 |
| Thurston | 10 | 361 | 29.4 | 13.2 | 7 | 30 | 4.1 | 0.9 | 106.1 | 15.7 | 12.6 | 3.4 |
| Valley | 21 | 369 | 21.3 | 9.7 | 14 | 45 | 4.1 | 0.8 | 48.6 | 16.3 | 9.2 | 0.7 |
| Washington | 37 | 733 | 47.9 | 21.5 | 35 | 82 | 7.0 | 2.1 | 103.5 | 57.6 | 20.5 | 1.6 |
| Wayne | 23 | 365 | 23.1 | 10.5 | 20 | D | D | D | 58.8 | 20.3 | 9.1 | 0.9 |
| Webster | 6 | 209 | 9.5 | 4.1 | 4 | 19 | 1.9 | 0.3 | 40.8 | 16.1 | 9.0 | 0.7 |
| Wheeler | NA | NA | NA | NA | NA | NA | NA | NA | 7.7 | 2.4 | 1.3 | 0.0 |
| York | 41 | 952 | 62.2 | 27.7 | 57 | 300 | 19.3 | 4.9 | 98.5 | 45.8 | 20.2 | 2.3 |
| NEVADA | 5 772 | 96 633 | 12 191.2 | 4 398.5 | 3 571 | 27 234 | 2 584.3 | 701.7 | 19 771.0 | 6 993.0 | 2 281.3 | 666.6 |
| Churchill | 45 | 862 | 82.8 | 33.3 | 40 | 160 | 12.6 | 3.7 | 339.5 | 101.5 | 33.0 | 5.6 |
| Clark | 3 978 | 67 163 | 8 517.4 | 3 017.6 | 2 313 | 18 791 | 1 602.5 | 473.7 | 11 254.2 | 4 651.5 | 1 579.7 | 494.2 |
| Douglas | 113 | 1 064 | 117.7 | 39.7 | 70 | 470 | 48.3 | 14.1 | 256.9 | 159.0 | 42.0 | 5.1 |
| Elko | 121 | D | D | D | 81 | 549 | 62.7 | 17.8 | 233.4 | 90.2 | 21.3 | 7.0 |
| Esmeralda | NA | NA | NA | NA | 1 | D | D | D | 13.2 | 3.5 | 0.9 | 0.1 |
| Eureka | 3 | D | D | D | NA | NA | NA | NA | 8.2 | 4.1 | 2.0 | 0.0 |
| Humboldt | 31 | D | D | D | 31 | 166 | 19.9 | 5.8 | 98.5 | 41.4 | 13.0 | 5.2 |
| Lander | 8 | D | D | D | 6 | D | D | D | 35.1 | 12.7 | 5.2 | 0.4 |
| Lincoln | 4 | D | D | D | 2 | D | D | D | 49.9 | 31.1 | 6.4 | 0.6 |
| Lyon | 47 | D | D | D | 38 | 195 | 22.3 | 4.9 | 308.6 | 191.3 | 41.7 | 12.6 |
| Mineral | 6 | D | D | D | 5 | D | D | D | 136.0 | 25.4 | 10.3 | 4.8 |
| Nye | 60 | 848 | 76.2 | 23.1 | 50 | 196 | 13.8 | 3.6 | 355.3 | 252.2 | 43.3 | 12.6 |
| Pershing | 10 | 162 | 14.0 | 6.0 | 6 | D | D | D | 28.3 | 12.3 | 4.9 | 0.5 |
| Storey | 1 | D | D | D | 4 | D | D | D | 11.1 | 7.7 | 1.2 | 0.2 |
| Washoe | 1 112 | D | D | D | 761 | D | D | D | 3 484.5 | 1 159.7 | 381.2 | 98.9 |
| White Pine | 13 | 337 | 31.8 | 15.1 | 14 | 65 | 4.6 | 1.7 | 83.1 | 29.6 | 10.0 | 5.0 |
| Carson City | 220 | 3 407 | 453.3 | 164.1 | 149 | 948 | 83.3 | 25.4 | 1 497.0 | 208.9 | 85.3 | 13.9 |
| NEW HAMPSHIRE | 3 492 | 83 717 | 8 085.7 | 3 377.8 | 2 886 | 16 153 | 1 574.3 | 457.9 | 11 335.3 | 4 198.8 | 1 477.6 | 257.0 |
| Belknap | 146 | 4 011 | 310.9 | 143.1 | 148 | 629 | 54.4 | 15.2 | 458.3 | 239.5 | 91.0 | 16.3 |
| Carroll | 138 | D | D | D | 113 | 407 | 34.1 | 9.7 | 338.5 | 201.3 | 65.2 | 10.6 |
| Cheshire | 166 | 3 980 | 330.1 | 134.0 | 145 | 933 | 73.0 | 26.8 | 515.2 | 254.5 | 93.5 | 16.9 |
| Coos | 105 | D | D | D | 72 | 355 | 26.3 | 8.8 | 325.6 | 141.7 | 74.0 | 10.1 |
| Grafton | 278 | 9 894 | 1 483.6 | 559.2 | 198 | 1 083 | 91.7 | 24.6 | 901.2 | 301.1 | 109.1 | 10.6 |
| Hillsborough | 1 020 | 26 771 | 2 503.8 | 1 065.3 | 828 | 5 317 | 501.5 | 155.6 | 3 353.3 | 1 143.0 | 408.1 | 88.2 |
| Merrimack | 415 | 11 751 | 1 002.1 | 454.0 | 398 | 1 940 | 280.1 | 63.3 | 1 562.7 | 417.8 | 168.1 | 28.2 |
| Rockingham | 803 | 14 595 | 1 324.2 | 540.6 | 702 | 3 817 | 377.6 | 106.8 | 2 031.8 | 902.1 | 284.8 | 33.0 |
| Strafford | 310 | 6 170 | 638.1 | 267.0 | 202 | 1 255 | 103.4 | 34.1 | 869.3 | 377.5 | 123.1 | 28.2 |
| Sullivan | 111 | 1 594 | 107.2 | 47.5 | 80 | 417 | 32.3 | 12.8 | 431.3 | 218.7 | 60.6 | 14.9 |
| NEW JERSEY | 25 777 | 503 370 | 51 913.7 | 21 313.6 | 19 047 | 105 659 | 11 203.7 | 3 003.1 | 80 990.1 | 23 840.6 | 16 833.7 | 2 013.4 |
| Atlantic | 821 | 16 172 | 1 780.0 | 702.6 | 547 | 3 496 | 270.1 | 81.7 | 2 365.5 | 831.2 | 563.0 | 79.3 |
| Bergen | 3 435 | 65 456 | 7 781.4 | 2 953.4 | 2 581 | 12 322 | 1 348.6 | 355.7 | 5 911.9 | 2 552.0 | 1 735.3 | 84.3 |
| Burlington | 1 134 | 21 970 | 2 400.1 | 864.6 | 850 | 4 976 | 384.6 | 128.9 | 5 531.3 | 1 484.5 | 674.0 | 56.1 |
| Camden | 1 580 | 35 383 | 3 701.1 | 1 521.5 | 939 | 6 051 | 479.3 | 157.1 | 4 688.9 | 1 505.8 | 1 107.5 | 207.4 |
| Cape May | 268 | D | D | D | 288 | 1 124 | 91.2 | 29.5 | 961.9 | 429.9 | 310.1 | 20.2 |
| Cumberland | 399 | 8 351 | 820.8 | 333.3 | 273 | 1 439 | 103.0 | 31.1 | 1 295.5 | 434.9 | 354.9 | 63.3 |
| Essex | 2 540 | 56 955 | 5 884.7 | 2 599.3 | 1 720 | 10 832 | 1 188.8 | 341.0 | 8 433.4 | 1 708.7 | 1 899.1 | 450.8 |
| Gloucester | 614 | 11 646 | 980.0 | 422.4 | 530 | 3 301 | 272.0 | 77.5 | 1 616.9 | 802.3 | 433.1 | 43.3 |
| Hudson | 1 337 | 24 006 | 2 231.5 | 898.1 | 1 118 | 4 826 | 463.3 | 126.1 | 5 003.1 | 983.7 | 1 261.1 | 272.4 |
| Hunterdon | 361 | 6 893 | 634.4 | 274.0 | 285 | 1 717 | 127.5 | 40.9 | 613.3 | 342.9 | 150.5 | 5.6 |

1. State totals may include programs not allocated by county.

# Table B. States and Counties — Federal Funds, Residential Construction, and Local Government Finances

| STATE County | Federal funds and grants, 2009–2010 (cont.) | | | | | | | Value of residential construction authorized by building permits, 2011 | | Local government finances, 2007 | | | | |
|---|---|---|---|---|---|---|---|---|---|---|---|---|---|---|
| | Expenditures (mil dol) (cont.) | | | | | | | | | General revenue | | | | |
| | | Procurement contract awards | | Grants[1] | | | | | | | | Taxes | | |
| | | | | | | | | | | | | | Per capita[2] (dollars) | |
| | Salaries and wages | Defense | Other | Medicaid and other health-related | Nutrition and family welfare | Education | Other | New construction ($1,000) | Number of housing units | Total (mil dol) | Inter-govern-mental (mil dol) | Total (mil dol) | Total | Property |
| | 171 | 172 | 173 | 174 | 175 | 176 | 177 | 178 | 179 | 180 | 181 | 182 | 183 | 184 |
| NEBRASKA—Cont'd | | | | | | | | | | | | | | |
| Platte | 33.1 | 3.4 | 6.3 | 15.3 | 4.0 | 1.3 | 1.8 | 13 089 | 60 | 108.5 | 30.7 | 47.7 | 1 497 | 1 017 |
| Polk | 1.8 | 0.0 | 0.4 | 2.6 | 0.7 | 0.3 | 0.9 | 405 | 3 | 26.3 | 3.9 | 13.8 | 2 657 | 2 412 |
| Red Willow | 5.5 | 0.0 | 1.0 | 6.6 | 2.0 | 0.9 | 0.3 | 3 080 | 30 | 52.4 | 28.5 | 15.3 | 1 427 | 1 152 |
| Richardson | 3.0 | 0.0 | 0.8 | 11.1 | 3.3 | 0.5 | 8.1 | 2 280 | 19 | 25.0 | 9.6 | 12.9 | 1 545 | 1 266 |
| Rock | 0.5 | 0.0 | 0.1 | 1.3 | 0.4 | 0.1 | 0.7 | 0 | 0 | 5.9 | 1.5 | 3.6 | 2 372 | 2 211 |
| Saline | 5.3 | 0.0 | 43.5 | 8.9 | 1.8 | 1.1 | 2.9 | 2 745 | 17 | 57.0 | 17.4 | 22.7 | 1 634 | 1 456 |
| Sarpy | 485.7 | 495.6 | 9.2 | 22.4 | 12.6 | 14.6 | 5.0 | 144 691 | 671 | 412.6 | 136.1 | 181.5 | 1 237 | 1 013 |
| Saunders | 41.2 | 13.1 | 1.2 | 7.2 | 2.5 | 0.8 | 0.5 | 10 042 | 63 | 65.6 | 15.7 | 29.8 | 1 476 | 1 251 |
| Scotts Bluff | 19.0 | 0.0 | 5.7 | 47.5 | 11.5 | 3.5 | 5.4 | 3 946 | 27 | 160.1 | 61.4 | 60.4 | 1 660 | 1 113 |
| Seward | 6.4 | 0.0 | 2.1 | 5.3 | 2.0 | 1.0 | 0.1 | 7 969 | 37 | 49.2 | 14.6 | 27.8 | 1 678 | 1 472 |
| Sheridan | 1.5 | 0.0 | 0.5 | 4.6 | 1.4 | 0.4 | 0.3 | 238 | 2 | 28.8 | 8.2 | 8.5 | 1 553 | 1 324 |
| Sherman | 1.2 | 0.0 | 0.3 | 5.2 | 4.9 | 0.2 | 2.1 | 1 048 | 6 | 10.4 | 3.7 | 5.3 | 1 771 | 1 576 |
| Sioux | 0.6 | 0.0 | 0.1 | 0.7 | 0.1 | 0.1 | 0.0 | 1 021 | 8 | 3.6 | 0.9 | 2.4 | 1 807 | 1 651 |
| Stanton | 1.7 | 0.0 | 0.2 | 2.6 | 0.7 | 0.2 | 0.4 | 1 690 | 9 | 10.0 | 3.1 | 5.1 | 793 | 708 |
| Thayer | 2.5 | 0.0 | 0.6 | 6.7 | 1.2 | 0.2 | 0.2 | 1 461 | 10 | 32.5 | 6.0 | 13.8 | 2 679 | 2 369 |
| Thomas | 1.8 | 0.0 | 1.1 | 0.0 | 0.1 | 0.1 | 0.0 | NA | NA | 3.8 | 1.4 | 2.0 | 3 330 | 3 162 |
| Thurston | 10.7 | 0.8 | 9.0 | 20.4 | 5.0 | 10.8 | 9.2 | 507 | 5 | 42.6 | 19.9 | 7.0 | 969 | 728 |
| Valley | 2.1 | 0.0 | 0.8 | 11.1 | 0.8 | 0.3 | 0.6 | 1 275 | 8 | 34.9 | 6.2 | 9.9 | 2 311 | 1 752 |
| Washington | 3.9 | -0.2 | 0.8 | 9.2 | 1.8 | 1.0 | 0.8 | 7 054 | 40 | 59.7 | 20.6 | 31.8 | 1 595 | 1 397 |
| Wayne | 5.2 | 0.2 | 0.5 | 4.6 | 1.2 | 0.7 | 4.7 | 1 345 | 14 | 28.2 | 9.4 | 13.7 | 1 475 | 1 283 |
| Webster | 1.9 | 0.0 | 0.4 | 5.2 | 0.6 | 0.4 | 0.4 | 672 | 5 | 20.6 | 5.0 | 6.4 | 1 779 | 1 407 |
| Wheeler | 0.4 | 0.0 | 0.1 | 0.0 | 0.2 | 0.1 | 0.0 | 38 | 1 | 3.4 | 0.7 | 2.4 | 2 913 | 2 712 |
| York | 7.3 | 0.3 | 0.9 | 6.6 | 1.8 | 1.0 | 0.8 | 5 638 | 23 | 48.1 | 11.1 | 26.1 | 1 820 | 1 390 |
| NEVADA | 1 941.7 | 1 315.0 | 1 092.1 | 1 312.3 | 423.8 | 339.0 | 1 626.7 | 789 438 | 6 163 | X | X | X | X | X |
| Churchill | 42.7 | 99.6 | 3.5 | 36.6 | 3.9 | 3.0 | 5.2 | 729 | 3 | 129.7 | 61.4 | 20.7 | 832 | 600 |
| Clark | 1 452.3 | 443.1 | 893.0 | 790.9 | 162.4 | 87.6 | 466.0 | 582 848 | 5 147 | 9 530.4 | 3 523.8 | 3 157.6 | 1 720 | 1 078 |
| Douglas | 7.5 | 6.4 | 9.1 | 5.1 | 5.8 | 3.3 | 10.9 | 10 715 | 36 | 195.4 | 81.4 | 70.6 | 1 556 | 1 180 |
| Elko | 24.8 | 1.1 | 17.0 | 33.7 | 8.5 | 4.5 | 14.7 | 37 027 | 279 | 200.0 | 114.9 | 46.9 | 998 | 649 |
| Esmeralda | 7.1 | 0.0 | 0.3 | 0.9 | 0.1 | 0.2 | 0.0 | NA | NA | 11.7 | 9.0 | 1.2 | 1 794 | 1 770 |
| Eureka | 0.3 | 0.0 | 0.0 | 0.9 | 0.2 | 0.2 | 0.1 | NA | NA | 31.6 | 14.0 | 13.5 | 8 643 | 8 508 |
| Humboldt | 9.5 | 0.0 | 3.7 | 15.0 | 2.6 | 1.8 | 1.9 | 5 485 | 47 | 96.6 | 41.7 | 19.4 | 1 105 | 870 |
| Lander | 4.8 | 0.0 | 1.7 | 5.3 | 0.8 | 1.1 | 1.1 | 2 554 | 19 | 36.7 | 16.2 | 10.7 | 2 093 | 1 784 |
| Lincoln | 2.3 | 0.2 | 1.3 | 1.8 | 1.4 | 0.5 | 2.2 | 1 803 | 11 | 26.8 | 15.7 | 6.0 | 1 259 | 1 221 |
| Lyon | 16.0 | 7.7 | 1.4 | 18.9 | 4.9 | 2.7 | 7.6 | 9 371 | 48 | 171.6 | 93.5 | 43.5 | 829 | 661 |
| Mineral | 4.1 | 66.0 | 1.1 | 13.2 | 0.9 | 1.1 | 8.0 | 100 | 2 | 29.6 | 11.9 | 5.1 | 1 066 | 854 |
| Nye | 15.7 | 1.3 | 7.9 | 10.1 | 4.0 | 2.8 | 2.7 | NA | NA | 156.7 | 93.1 | 44.4 | 1 006 | 806 |
| Pershing | 0.8 | 0.1 | 0.2 | 4.4 | 0.8 | 0.2 | 0.4 | 109 | 1 | 36.6 | 16.4 | 6.0 | 942 | 851 |
| Storey | 0.4 | 0.0 | 0.4 | 0.0 | 0.3 | 0.4 | 0.3 | 988 | 6 | 16.8 | 6.9 | 7.5 | 1 790 | 1 410 |
| Washoe | 274.3 | 674.8 | 135.1 | 292.3 | 58.3 | 34.9 | 315.5 | 135 165 | 550 | 1 793.8 | 774.2 | 626.1 | 1 542 | 1 086 |
| White Pine | 12.1 | 0.3 | 6.0 | 11.5 | 2.1 | 2.1 | 2.2 | 120 | 1 | 60.4 | 23.6 | 10.7 | 1 167 | 909 |
| Carson City | 66.8 | 14.4 | 10.5 | 71.7 | 107.2 | 177.7 | 730.6 | 2 424 | 13 | 198.2 | 99.8 | 49.3 | 897 | 577 |
| NEW HAMPSHIRE | 880.0 | 1 091.9 | 343.5 | 1 132.7 | 209.8 | 195.7 | 772.8 | 432 254 | 2 346 | X | X | X | X | X |
| Belknap | 15.1 | 6.6 | 4.6 | 60.5 | 7.6 | 3.6 | 8.3 | 50 446 | 144 | 253.8 | 76.7 | 144.7 | 2 370 | 2 340 |
| Carroll | 12.5 | 0.8 | 4.1 | 30.6 | 5.9 | 2.4 | 0.6 | 34 739 | 160 | 186.1 | 63.1 | 105.0 | 2 217 | 2 192 |
| Cheshire | 24.6 | 6.7 | 3.5 | 70.4 | 11.7 | 4.6 | 8.6 | 14 398 | 79 | 282.2 | 100.3 | 147.0 | 1 891 | 1 878 |
| Coos | 11.9 | 3.5 | 6.4 | 51.8 | 9.4 | 3.1 | 8.9 | 6 386 | 36 | 154.0 | 64.0 | 63.3 | 1 933 | 1 917 |
| Grafton | 43.1 | 47.4 | 57.4 | 244.0 | 10.6 | 7.7 | 52.7 | 34 266 | 189 | 359.4 | 103.5 | 208.1 | 2 433 | 2 411 |
| Hillsborough | 369.5 | 700.2 | 111.2 | 271.3 | 39.2 | 22.6 | 101.1 | 102 043 | 702 | 1 330.6 | 420.3 | 697.9 | 1 735 | 1 686 |
| Merrimack | 115.3 | 14.8 | 26.8 | 152.7 | 63.3 | 108.6 | 409.2 | 25 468 | 119 | 497.2 | 157.3 | 284.1 | 1 916 | 1 899 |
| Rockingham | 218.8 | 282.4 | 94.1 | 117.3 | 26.2 | 20.2 | 27.0 | 117 039 | 510 | 1 043.1 | 285.1 | 644.8 | 2 174 | 2 150 |
| Strafford | 60.6 | 7.5 | 16.7 | 86.6 | 14.9 | 10.1 | 119.1 | 34 440 | 354 | 381.0 | 135.4 | 199.5 | 1 641 | 1 600 |
| Sullivan | 8.7 | 21.9 | 18.6 | 47.5 | 6.0 | 3.3 | 26.8 | 13 030 | 53 | 141.6 | 54.6 | 73.3 | 1 716 | 1 705 |
| NEW JERSEY | 5 577.9 | 7 857.5 | 2 378.8 | 8 131.6 | 1 857.8 | 1 236.6 | 4 230.7 | 2 043 169 | 12 952 | X | X | X | X | X |
| Atlantic | 301.1 | 40.6 | 95.9 | 278.6 | 51.5 | 10.0 | 40.2 | 64 738 | 390 | 1 515.6 | 456.0 | 828.2 | 3 060 | 2 999 |
| Bergen | 284.9 | 438.1 | 108.7 | 387.5 | 89.5 | 16.2 | 120.9 | 302 712 | 1 660 | 4 209.5 | 720.4 | 2 890.3 | 3 227 | 3 172 |
| Burlington | 941.0 | 1 769.9 | 204.5 | 217.4 | 56.7 | 19.2 | 15.8 | 80 422 | 665 | 1 895.9 | 572.3 | 1 011.2 | 2 263 | 2 230 |
| Camden | 271.5 | 352.0 | 428.7 | 533.3 | 95.2 | 24.2 | 86.0 | 57 069 | 602 | 2 913.8 | 1 153.9 | 1 079.0 | 2 100 | 2 065 |
| Cape May | 75.3 | 7.4 | 17.1 | 61.7 | 15.9 | 4.0 | 5.8 | 120 273 | 452 | 633.6 | 155.7 | 372.3 | 3 861 | 3 709 |
| Cumberland | 61.2 | 42.0 | 14.4 | 232.9 | 41.0 | 11.5 | 17.7 | 19 117 | 182 | 758.8 | 469.5 | 192.0 | 1 234 | 1 205 |
| Essex | 692.5 | 384.7 | 318.8 | 1 545.9 | 216.6 | 60.0 | 952.9 | 118 888 | 575 | 3 608.7 | 1 368.3 | 1 807.1 | 2 328 | 2 225 |
| Gloucester | 55.7 | 27.9 | 12.5 | 134.2 | 35.0 | 6.6 | 28.8 | 77 860 | 592 | 1 187.7 | 391.9 | 614.0 | 2 149 | 2 116 |
| Hudson | 576.9 | 116.5 | 165.0 | 1 148.0 | 135.7 | 31.3 | 151.7 | 228 318 | 1 581 | 2 391.4 | 1 005.0 | 939.1 | 1 570 | 1 510 |
| Hunterdon | 29.6 | 8.7 | 8.4 | 42.0 | 10.8 | 1.6 | 9.0 | 35 825 | 287 | 611.2 | 99.6 | 432.6 | 3 345 | 3 297 |

1. State totals may include programs not allocated by county.   2. Based on the resident population estimated as of July 1 of the year shown.

| STATE County | Total (mil dol) 185 | Per capita[1] (dollars) 186 | Education 187 | Health and hospitals 188 | Police protection 189 | Public welfare 190 | Highways 191 | Total (mil dol) 192 | Per capita[1] (dollars) 193 | Federal civilian 194 | Federal military 195 | State and local 196 | Democratic 197 | Republican 198 | All other 199 |
|---|---|---|---|---|---|---|---|---|---|---|---|---|---|---|---|
| **NEBRASKA—Cont'd** | | | | | | | | | | | | | | | |
| Platte | 91.8 | 2 883 | 53.8 | 0.3 | 5.4 | 1.3 | 11.7 | 1 832.3 | 57 531 | 83 | 131 | 2 598 | 28.3 | 69.8 | 1.9 |
| Polk | 29.9 | 5 747 | 53.1 | 24.4 | 1.5 | 0.1 | 5.8 | 24.1 | 4 631 | 23 | 21 | 495 | 26.3 | 71.6 | 2.1 |
| Red Willow | 39.8 | 3 706 | 46.8 | 0.4 | 3.3 | 14.1 | 5.6 | 48.1 | 4 479 | 67 | 44 | 1 052 | 24.1 | 74.0 | 1.8 |
| Richardson | 23.8 | 2 855 | 63.3 | 0.0 | 4.3 | 0.2 | 9.9 | 14.5 | 1 735 | 39 | 34 | 553 | 38.1 | 59.0 | 2.8 |
| Rock | 6.6 | 4 327 | 48.7 | 5.1 | 4.1 | 0.1 | 11.8 | 0.4 | 232 | 0 | 0 | 219 | 17.4 | 79.9 | 2.7 |
| Saline | 53.1 | 3 826 | 45.6 | 16.1 | 3.4 | 0.5 | 9.7 | 22.7 | 1 638 | 64 | 58 | 1 402 | 50.9 | 46.4 | 2.7 |
| Sarpy | 441.0 | 3 005 | 49.3 | 1.6 | 4.5 | 0.3 | 6.5 | 630.0 | 4 293 | 3 185 | 6 291 | 6 699 | 41.2 | 57.1 | 1.8 |
| Saunders | 80.8 | 4 004 | 35.9 | 30.3 | 3.8 | 0.5 | 7.4 | 52.9 | 2 622 | 88 | 84 | 1 434 | 36.9 | 60.6 | 2.5 |
| Scotts Bluff | 169.4 | 4 657 | 54.1 | 0.2 | 4.0 | 1.3 | 4.0 | 67.2 | 1 847 | 179 | 150 | 3 078 | 32.2 | 65.9 | 1.9 |
| Seward | 50.2 | 3 033 | 58.8 | 0.0 | 4.6 | 0.6 | 9.0 | 54.9 | 3 316 | 53 | 67 | 1 096 | 35.9 | 61.7 | 2.4 |
| Sheridan | 29.0 | 5 329 | 45.8 | 26.2 | 2.7 | 0.6 | 6.1 | 10.2 | 1 871 | 27 | 22 | 642 | 18.4 | 78.8 | 2.7 |
| Sherman | 10.1 | 3 349 | 53.1 | 0.2 | 4.0 | 1.6 | 15.7 | 9.1 | 3 023 | 11 | 12 | 293 | 37.2 | 60.4 | 2.4 |
| Sioux | 3.3 | 2 429 | 62.0 | 1.9 | 2.7 | 0.0 | 12.2 | 0.0 | 11 | 13 | 0 | 81 | 16.0 | 82.4 | 1.6 |
| Stanton | 11.1 | 1 738 | 44.4 | 0.0 | 4.6 | 0.0 | 6.4 | 20.4 | 3 195 | 24 | 25 | 281 | 26.6 | 71.4 | 2.0 |
| Thayer | 29.2 | 5 650 | 37.5 | 27.6 | 1.6 | 0.1 | 6.7 | 11.5 | 2 220 | 33 | 21 | 640 | 32.3 | 65.8 | 1.9 |
| Thomas | 4.7 | 7 763 | 37.2 | 0.2 | 1.3 | 0.0 | 12.6 | 0.2 | 328 | 0 | 0 | 94 | 13.1 | 84.9 | 2.1 |
| Thurston | 37.5 | 5 202 | 57.5 | 25.5 | 1.9 | 0.0 | 5.0 | 27.3 | 3 789 | 210 | 28 | 1 360 | 52.7 | 45.7 | 1.6 |
| Valley | 33.9 | 7 951 | 21.8 | 40.4 | 1.4 | 0.3 | 6.5 | 14.2 | 3 332 | 32 | 17 | 659 | 29.1 | 68.4 | 2.5 |
| Washington | 64.2 | 3 217 | 49.2 | 0.1 | 4.3 | 0.1 | 14.6 | 48.2 | 2 416 | 46 | 82 | 1 623 | 36.0 | 62.3 | 1.8 |
| Wayne | 26.6 | 2 853 | 55.8 | 0.3 | 4.2 | 0.8 | 11.2 | 13.1 | 1 411 | 33 | 38 | 1 137 | 32.8 | 65.7 | 1.5 |
| Webster | 20.0 | 5 529 | 31.8 | 19.2 | 1.7 | 0.1 | 6.5 | 8.0 | 2 208 | 25 | 15 | 295 | 30.4 | 67.9 | 1.8 |
| Wheeler | 3.6 | 4 433 | 61.4 | 0.0 | 2.4 | 0.1 | 15.7 | 0.1 | 103 | 0 | 0 | 60 | 21.8 | 75.9 | 2.3 |
| York | 52.2 | 3 634 | 46.0 | 0.6 | 3.8 | 0.3 | 10.8 | 53.5 | 3 722 | 55 | 55 | 1 188 | 24.5 | 73.8 | 1.7 |
| **NEVADA** | X | X | X | X | X | X | X | X | X | 17 750 | 17 967 | 130 347 | 55.1 | 42.7 | 2.2 |
| Churchill | 122.7 | 4 930 | 37.3 | 0.6 | 6.2 | 1.3 | 4.5 | 47.6 | 1 913 | 622 | 914 | 1 325 | 32.9 | 64.4 | 2.6 |
| Clark | 8 762.7 | 4 772 | 34.3 | 7.6 | 8.9 | 2.7 | 10.3 | 18 383.2 | 10 011 | 11 751 | 15 034 | 81 839 | 58.5 | 39.5 | 2.0 |
| Douglas | 192.2 | 4 233 | 35.2 | 1.7 | 8.2 | 2.4 | 2.2 | 62.6 | 1 378 | 104 | 123 | 2 122 | 41.2 | 56.5 | 2.3 |
| Elko | 199.3 | 4 240 | 55.8 | 0.7 | 7.2 | 0.6 | 5.0 | 53.7 | 1 143 | 390 | 130 | 3 330 | 28.3 | 68.5 | 3.2 |
| Esmeralda | 6.6 | 9 446 | 29.9 | 2.7 | 15.1 | 0.2 | 9.4 | 0.4 | 550 | 0 | 0 | 88 | 23.7 | 69.0 | 7.3 |
| Eureka | 22.5 | 14 424 | 39.2 | 4.0 | 5.6 | 0.5 | 16.5 | 5.0 | 3 203 | 0 | 0 | 199 | 19.3 | 75.7 | 5.0 |
| Humboldt | 87.8 | 5 013 | 37.9 | 25.4 | 5.9 | 1.2 | 5.6 | 79.7 | 4 548 | 163 | 44 | 1 271 | 33.7 | 63.3 | 3.0 |
| Lander | 30.1 | 5 889 | 41.5 | 24.9 | 6.4 | 0.9 | 4.4 | 14.4 | 2 826 | 77 | 15 | 456 | 27.5 | 69.7 | 2.8 |
| Lincoln | 28.7 | 6 038 | 50.7 | 1.8 | 4.5 | 2.8 | 8.6 | 8.4 | 1 770 | 48 | 14 | 579 | 24.6 | 71.1 | 4.3 |
| Lyon | 177.4 | 3 380 | 57.6 | 1.4 | 6.7 | 4.2 | 5.6 | 211.2 | 4 025 | 75 | 136 | 2 118 | 39.8 | 57.6 | 2.6 |
| Mineral | 26.6 | 5 580 | 33.6 | 36.9 | 6.2 | 0.5 | 5.2 | 7.5 | 1 575 | 79 | 13 | 524 | 46.9 | 49.0 | 4.1 |
| Nye | 148.4 | 3 363 | 43.9 | 2.7 | 14.0 | 0.8 | 6.9 | 78.0 | 1 768 | 138 | 171 | 1 649 | 41.3 | 54.5 | 4.2 |
| Pershing | 33.6 | 5 264 | 34.6 | 35.0 | 7.2 | 1.5 | 4.1 | 13.7 | 2 155 | 14 | 18 | 678 | 36.7 | 58.6 | 4.8 |
| Storey | 20.4 | 4 873 | 47.2 | 0.1 | 11.6 | 0.1 | 5.1 | 14.6 | 3 485 | 0 | 10 | 211 | 45.6 | 51.6 | 2.9 |
| Washoe | 1 635.1 | 4 027 | 33.1 | 1.4 | 7.4 | 3.8 | 6.5 | 3 073.0 | 7 568 | 3 502 | 1 165 | 23 792 | 55.2 | 42.6 | 2.1 |
| White Pine | 56.6 | 6 190 | 32.5 | 33.0 | 6.6 | 0.6 | 5.6 | 46.2 | 5 056 | 226 | 26 | 1 193 | 32.0 | 63.5 | 4.5 |
| Carson City | 199.1 | 3 625 | 39.8 | 3.2 | 11.6 | 1.0 | 5.7 | 200.1 | 3 642 | 547 | 147 | 8 973 | 49.1 | 48.2 | 2.7 |
| **NEW HAMPSHIRE** | X | X | X | X | X | X | X | X | X | 7 427 | 4 658 | 83 856 | 54.1 | 44.5 | 1.4 |
| Belknap | 251.7 | 4 124 | 50.0 | 0.5 | 5.2 | 5.9 | 4.2 | 107.4 | 1 759 | 180 | 200 | 4 177 | 50.0 | 48.8 | 1.2 |
| Carroll | 197.2 | 4 162 | 60.4 | 1.1 | 4.4 | 6.3 | 5.4 | 95.8 | 2 023 | 116 | 158 | 2 900 | 52.4 | 46.1 | 1.5 |
| Cheshire | 286.3 | 3 683 | 59.1 | 0.7 | 4.2 | 7.2 | 5.8 | 120.1 | 1 545 | 167 | 255 | 5 316 | 63.0 | 35.5 | 1.5 |
| Coos | 150.6 | 4 596 | 44.5 | 1.4 | 3.6 | 13.6 | 5.1 | 47.7 | 1 454 | 130 | 108 | 2 785 | 58.3 | 40.1 | 1.6 |
| Grafton | 367.6 | 4 299 | 57.5 | 1.0 | 4.6 | 5.2 | 5.3 | 174.8 | 2 044 | 554 | 298 | 7 004 | 63.0 | 35.5 | 1.5 |
| Hillsborough | 1 345.6 | 3 345 | 51.1 | 0.7 | 5.8 | 3.9 | 4.3 | 1 045.4 | 2 599 | 3 886 | 1 358 | 18 230 | 51.2 | 47.5 | 1.3 |
| Merrimack | 541.2 | 3 650 | 53.3 | 0.4 | 4.6 | 9.7 | 4.5 | 348.5 | 2 350 | 849 | 495 | 15 841 | 56.3 | 42.5 | 1.3 |
| Rockingham | 1 037.4 | 3 498 | 59.0 | 0.5 | 6.1 | 3.7 | 3.2 | 484.7 | 1 635 | 1 135 | 1 216 | 13 488 | 49.9 | 48.8 | 1.3 |
| Strafford | 406.3 | 3 342 | 50.1 | 0.2 | 5.2 | 6.8 | 5.1 | 306.2 | 2 518 | 318 | 426 | 11 530 | 59.5 | 39.2 | 1.3 |
| Sullivan | 144.4 | 3 382 | 48.3 | 0.5 | 3.7 | 12.1 | 6.7 | 42.7 | 999 | 92 | 144 | 2 585 | 58.2 | 40.3 | 1.5 |
| **NEW JERSEY** | X | X | X | X | X | X | X | X | X | 53 901 | 25 798 | 545 933 | 57.3 | 41.7 | 1.0 |
| Atlantic | 1 447.7 | 5 349 | 53.0 | 0.9 | 7.2 | 2.0 | 2.4 | 1 176.7 | 4 348 | 2 795 | 893 | 20 356 | 57.0 | 41.9 | 1.1 |
| Bergen | 4 392.2 | 4 903 | 56.6 | 4.9 | 7.1 | 0.8 | 2.0 | 3 023.0 | 3 375 | 2 731 | 1 888 | 44 300 | 54.3 | 44.9 | 0.8 |
| Burlington | 1 976.6 | 4 424 | 63.4 | 1.4 | 4.2 | 2.0 | 2.6 | 2 020.7 | 4 522 | 5 747 | 5 988 | 24 068 | 58.8 | 40.2 | 1.0 |
| Camden | 2 877.5 | 5 601 | 51.6 | 2.8 | 5.3 | 3.2 | 1.9 | 3 868.2 | 7 529 | 2 578 | 1 077 | 30 460 | 67.6 | 31.3 | 1.1 |
| Cape May | 730.0 | 7 570 | 37.5 | 1.2 | 5.3 | 3.6 | 5.2 | 626.5 | 6 497 | 442 | 1 189 | 8 544 | 45.0 | 53.7 | 1.3 |
| Cumberland | 747.9 | 4 808 | 62.4 | 2.2 | 3.5 | 3.7 | 1.8 | 357.1 | 2 296 | 632 | 326 | 13 662 | 60.1 | 38.5 | 1.4 |
| Essex | 3 931.0 | 5 065 | 39.8 | 2.4 | 8.9 | 3.7 | 1.3 | 3 435.1 | 4 426 | 9 218 | 1 653 | 68 267 | 76.0 | 23.4 | 0.6 |
| Gloucester | 1 246.3 | 4 361 | 60.3 | 0.5 | 4.5 | 2.1 | 1.8 | 1 091.3 | 3 819 | 478 | 600 | 17 401 | 55.4 | 43.3 | 1.3 |
| Hudson | 2 466.9 | 4 124 | 33.5 | 1.5 | 9.0 | 2.4 | 2.0 | 2 717.4 | 4 543 | 5 691 | 1 445 | 36 319 | 72.9 | 26.2 | 0.9 |
| Hunterdon | 638.9 | 4 939 | 64.2 | 0.7 | 2.9 | 0.8 | 5.7 | 535.6 | 4 141 | 270 | 265 | 8 779 | 42.6 | 56.0 | 1.4 |

1. Based on the resident population estimated as of July 1 of the year shown.  2. © 2013 Election Data Services, Inc. All rights reserved.

# Table B. States and Counties — Land Area and Population

| STATE/ County code | CBSA code[1] | County type[2] | STATE County | Land area,[3] (sq km) 2010 | Population 2012 Total persons | Rank | Per square kilometer | White | Black | American Indian, Alaska Native | Asian and Pacific Islander | Percent Hispanic or Latino[4] | Under 5 years | 5 to 17 years | 18 to 24 years | 25 to 34 years | 35 to 44 years | 45 to 54 years |
|---|---|---|---|---|---|---|---|---|---|---|---|---|---|---|---|---|---|---|
| | | | | 1 | 2 | 3 | 4 | 5 | 6 | 7 | 8 | 9 | 10 | 11 | 12 | 13 | 14 | 15 |
| | | | **NEW JERSEY—Cont'd** | | | | | | | | | | | | | | | |
| 34 021 | 45940 | 2 | Mercer | 582 | 368 303 | 181 | 632.8 | 55.3 | 20.2 | 0.5 | 10.0 | 15.5 | 5.9 | 16.5 | 11.0 | 12.7 | 13.8 | 15.1 |
| 34 023 | 35620 | 1 | Middlesex | 800 | 823 041 | 68 | 1 028.8 | 49.6 | 9.7 | 0.5 | 22.8 | 18.9 | 6.1 | 16.6 | 10.2 | 13.8 | 14.3 | 14.9 |
| 34 025 | 35620 | 1 | Monmouth | 1 214 | 629 384 | 100 | 518.4 | 77.6 | 7.7 | 0.4 | 5.8 | 9.9 | 5.3 | 18.0 | 8.0 | 10.4 | 13.2 | 17.5 |
| 34 027 | 35620 | 1 | Morris | 1 192 | 497 999 | 134 | 417.8 | 75.6 | 3.4 | 0.3 | 10.2 | 11.8 | 5.4 | 18.0 | 7.3 | 10.7 | 14.1 | 17.3 |
| 34 029 | 35620 | 1 | Ocean | 1 629 | 580 470 | 109 | 356.3 | 86.4 | 3.4 | 0.4 | 2.3 | 8.6 | 6.7 | 16.6 | 7.5 | 10.7 | 11.2 | 13.5 |
| 34 031 | 35620 | 1 | Passaic | 478 | 502 885 | 131 | 1 052.1 | 45.7 | 11.7 | 0.4 | 5.7 | 37.7 | 6.9 | 17.8 | 10.3 | 13.3 | 13.5 | 14.5 |
| 34 033 | 37980 | 1 | Salem | 860 | 65 774 | 804 | 76.5 | 77.7 | 14.9 | 0.8 | 1.3 | 7.1 | 5.9 | 17.2 | 8.5 | 11.4 | 12.3 | 15.7 |
| 34 035 | 35620 | 1 | Somerset | 782 | 327 707 | 198 | 419.1 | 63.0 | 9.3 | 0.4 | 15.6 | 13.3 | 5.8 | 18.7 | 6.8 | 11.2 | 14.6 | 17.7 |
| 34 037 | 35620 | 1 | Sussex | 1 344 | 147 442 | 427 | 109.7 | 89.5 | 2.1 | 0.4 | 2.4 | 6.7 | 5.0 | 18.1 | 7.8 | 9.6 | 13.7 | 18.6 |
| 34 039 | 35620 | 1 | Union | 266 | 543 976 | 118 | 2 045.0 | 45.9 | 21.6 | 0.4 | 5.4 | 28.1 | 6.6 | 17.6 | 8.6 | 13.0 | 14.3 | 15.5 |
| 34 041 | 10900 | 2 | Warren | 924 | 107 653 | 550 | 116.5 | 86.2 | 4.0 | 0.4 | 3.1 | 7.4 | 5.3 | 17.6 | 8.2 | 10.0 | 13.6 | 17.6 |
| 35 000 | ... | X | **NEW MEXICO** | 314 161 | 2 085 538 | X | 6.6 | 41.4 | 2.3 | 9.2 | 1.9 | 46.7 | 7.0 | 17.9 | 9.9 | 13.2 | 11.9 | 13.8 |
| 35 001 | 10740 | 2 | Bernalillo | 3 007 | 673 460 | 92 | 224.0 | 42.7 | 3.1 | 4.8 | 3.0 | 48.1 | 6.8 | 17.0 | 10.2 | 14.7 | 12.5 | 13.9 |
| 35 003 | ... | 9 | Catron | 17 932 | 3 658 | 2 932 | 0.2 | 78.0 | 0.9 | 3.7 | 0.4 | 18.8 | 3.8 | 11.4 | 4.4 | 6.9 | 6.1 | 14.2 |
| 35 005 | 40740 | 5 | Chaves | 15 709 | 65 784 | 803 | 4.2 | 44.0 | 2.0 | 1.3 | 1.0 | 52.8 | 8.0 | 20.0 | 10.1 | 12.3 | 10.9 | 12.8 |
| 35 006 | 24380 | 6 | Cibola | 11 757 | 27 334 | 1 518 | 2.3 | 22.7 | 1.3 | 38.9 | 0.9 | 37.6 | 7.1 | 17.7 | 9.7 | 13.7 | 12.3 | 14.0 |
| 35 007 | ... | 7 | Colfax | 9 733 | 13 223 | 2 229 | 1.4 | 50.4 | 0.6 | 1.9 | 0.7 | 47.6 | 5.4 | 15.0 | 7.1 | 10.0 | 10.1 | 14.9 |
| 35 009 | 17580 | 5 | Curry | 3 638 | 49 938 | 979 | 13.7 | 52.2 | 6.6 | 1.3 | 2.1 | 39.8 | 8.8 | 19.4 | 11.4 | 15.6 | 11.6 | 12.3 |
| 35 011 | ... | 9 | De Baca | 6 016 | 1 927 | 3 063 | 0.3 | 60.1 | 0.6 | 1.6 | 0.4 | 39.0 | 5.1 | 15.8 | 5.1 | 10.1 | 8.6 | 15.1 |
| 35 013 | 29740 | 3 | Dona Ana | 9 861 | 214 445 | 295 | 21.7 | 30.7 | 1.7 | 1.2 | 1.5 | 65.9 | 7.5 | 19.0 | 12.9 | 13.5 | 11.1 | 12.4 |
| 35 015 | 16100 | 5 | Eddy | 10 815 | 54 419 | 919 | 5.0 | 52.4 | 1.6 | 1.4 | 1.0 | 44.7 | 7.0 | 18.7 | 9.0 | 12.8 | 11.4 | 14.0 |
| 35 017 | 43500 | 7 | Grant | 10 261 | 29 388 | 1 436 | 2.9 | 49.6 | 1.0 | 1.5 | 0.8 | 48.3 | 6.0 | 15.4 | 7.7 | 9.9 | 9.4 | 12.7 |
| 35 019 | ... | 7 | Guadalupe | 7 849 | 4 603 | 2 864 | 0.6 | 16.2 | 1.7 | 1.5 | 1.8 | 79.5 | 5.3 | 15.7 | 8.1 | 14.6 | 11.6 | 16.3 |
| 35 021 | ... | 9 | Harding | 5 505 | 707 | 3 129 | 0.1 | 54.3 | 0.9 | 0.6 | 0.1 | 44.3 | 4.8 | 10.7 | 4.1 | 8.4 | 7.5 | 15.1 |
| 35 023 | ... | 7 | Hidalgo | 8 901 | 4 794 | 2 852 | 0.5 | 42.5 | 0.6 | 0.8 | 0.9 | 56.0 | 6.9 | 18.6 | 8.6 | 10.3 | 11.2 | 14.1 |
| 35 025 | 26020 | 5 | Lea | 11 372 | 66 338 | 792 | 5.8 | 42.8 | 4.1 | 1.2 | 0.7 | 52.1 | 9.2 | 20.3 | 10.1 | 14.6 | 12.0 | 12.7 |
| 35 027 | 40760 | 7 | Lincoln | 12 512 | 20 309 | 1 824 | 1.6 | 66.1 | 0.8 | 2.9 | 0.6 | 30.7 | 5.0 | 13.9 | 6.2 | 8.8 | 9.5 | 15.1 |
| 35 028 | 31060 | 6 | Los Alamos | 283 | 18 159 | 1 912 | 64.2 | 77.0 | 1.2 | 1.4 | 6.9 | 15.3 | 5.2 | 18.3 | 5.0 | 9.9 | 12.7 | 17.7 |
| 35 029 | 19700 | 6 | Luna | 7 680 | 25 041 | 1 607 | 3.3 | 35.5 | 1.0 | 1.1 | 0.6 | 62.5 | 7.6 | 18.9 | 8.9 | 10.7 | 10.4 | 11.5 |
| 35 031 | 23700 | 4 | McKinley | 14 115 | 73 016 | 744 | 5.2 | 12.1 | 1.7 | 72.4 | 1.3 | 14.6 | 9.1 | 22.7 | 11.7 | 12.7 | 11.5 | 12.7 |
| 35 033 | ... | 8 | Mora | 5 002 | 4 705 | 2 858 | 0.9 | 18.6 | 0.4 | 0.6 | 0.4 | 80.4 | 4.6 | 15.7 | 7.2 | 9.1 | 10.9 | 15.4 |
| 35 035 | 10460 | 4 | Otero | 17 128 | 66 041 | 797 | 3.9 | 54.3 | 4.1 | 6.4 | 2.4 | 34.9 | 7.4 | 17.3 | 10.9 | 13.4 | 11.0 | 13.1 |
| 35 037 | ... | 7 | Quay | 7 445 | 8 769 | 2 536 | 1.2 | 53.9 | 1.6 | 1.6 | 1.2 | 43.1 | 5.7 | 15.9 | 6.9 | 10.2 | 10.1 | 14.5 |
| 35 039 | 21580 | 6 | Rio Arriba | 15 179 | 40 318 | 1 170 | 2.7 | 14.2 | 0.5 | 14.4 | 0.5 | 71.0 | 6.9 | 17.5 | 8.8 | 11.6 | 12.0 | 14.6 |
| 35 041 | 38780 | 7 | Roosevelt | 6 339 | 20 419 | 1 820 | 3.2 | 55.8 | 2.2 | 1.6 | 1.4 | 40.3 | 7.9 | 18.6 | 18.1 | 13.0 | 10.8 | 10.6 |
| 35 043 | 10740 | 2 | Sandoval | 9 611 | 135 588 | 460 | 14.1 | 48.6 | 2.6 | 12.5 | 2.1 | 36.0 | 6.5 | 19.5 | 8.1 | 11.9 | 13.2 | 14.8 |
| 35 045 | 22140 | 3 | San Juan | 14 279 | 128 529 | 481 | 9.0 | 43.6 | 1.2 | 36.7 | 0.9 | 19.6 | 8.2 | 20.4 | 9.8 | 13.9 | 11.4 | 13.5 |
| 35 047 | 29780 | 6 | San Miguel | 12 214 | 28 891 | 1 454 | 2.4 | 20.7 | 1.4 | 1.4 | 1.0 | 76.4 | 5.4 | 15.9 | 11.2 | 10.9 | 10.8 | 14.9 |
| 35 049 | 42140 | 3 | Santa Fe | 4 945 | 146 375 | 433 | 29.6 | 44.8 | 1.0 | 3.0 | 1.6 | 50.9 | 5.5 | 15.2 | 7.5 | 11.5 | 12.3 | 15.0 |
| 35 051 | ... | 6 | Sierra | 10 823 | 11 895 | 2 304 | 1.1 | 69.1 | 0.9 | 2.5 | 0.8 | 28.4 | 4.7 | 11.4 | 5.9 | 7.4 | 8.0 | 13.0 |
| 35 053 | ... | 6 | Socorro | 17 215 | 17 603 | 1 942 | 1.0 | 38.8 | 1.2 | 11.2 | 1.6 | 48.3 | 6.6 | 17.2 | 12.5 | 11.6 | 10.7 | 13.5 |
| 35 055 | 45340 | 7 | Taos | 5 706 | 32 779 | 1 361 | 5.7 | 37.3 | 0.7 | 6.1 | 1.0 | 56.1 | 5.5 | 14.7 | 6.9 | 10.3 | 11.6 | 15.0 |
| 35 057 | 10740 | 2 | Torrance | 8 663 | 16 021 | 2 046 | 1.8 | 56.5 | 1.6 | 2.7 | 0.9 | 39.9 | 5.4 | 18.1 | 8.4 | 10.6 | 11.8 | 15.0 |
| 35 059 | ... | 9 | Union | 9 903 | 4 431 | 2 873 | 0.4 | 56.0 | 2.0 | 1.8 | 0.7 | 40.4 | 5.0 | 13.7 | 8.3 | 14.7 | 11.9 | 15.0 |
| 35 061 | 10740 | 2 | Valencia | 2 761 | 76 631 | 715 | 27.8 | 36.7 | 1.4 | 3.5 | 0.8 | 58.6 | 6.8 | 19.1 | 9.0 | 11.7 | 12.1 | 14.8 |
| 36 000 | ... | X | **NEW YORK** | 122 057 | 19 570 261 | X | 160.3 | 59.2 | 15.4 | 0.7 | 8.4 | 18.0 | 6.0 | 16.0 | 10.2 | 13.9 | 13.2 | 14.7 |
| 36 001 | 10580 | 2 | Albany | 1 354 | 305 455 | 212 | 225.6 | 77.2 | 13.2 | 0.6 | 5.8 | 5.2 | 4.9 | 14.5 | 13.9 | 13.0 | 11.8 | 14.6 |
| 36 003 | ... | 7 | Allegany | 2 666 | 48 357 | 1 005 | 18.1 | 96.0 | 1.6 | 0.6 | 1.4 | 1.4 | 5.3 | 15.9 | 15.7 | 10.1 | 10.5 | 13.7 |
| 36 005 | 35620 | 1 | Bronx | 109 | 1 408 473 | 26 | 12 921.8 | 11.9 | 30.8 | 0.5 | 4.1 | 53.8 | 7.6 | 18.8 | 11.7 | 14.7 | 13.2 | 13.4 |
| 36 007 | 13780 | 2 | Broome | 1 828 | 198 060 | 324 | 108.3 | 88.0 | 5.6 | 0.7 | 4.4 | 3.5 | 5.1 | 14.8 | 12.7 | 11.7 | 10.8 | 15.0 |
| 36 009 | 36460 | 4 | Cattaraugus | 3 389 | 79 458 | 691 | 23.4 | 93.1 | 2.0 | 3.6 | 1.1 | 1.8 | 6.2 | 16.9 | 9.7 | 10.8 | 11.4 | 15.2 |
| 36 011 | 12180 | 4 | Cayuga | 1 791 | 79 552 | 690 | 44.4 | 92.5 | 4.9 | 0.8 | 0.9 | 2.5 | 5.2 | 16.0 | 8.8 | 12.0 | 12.4 | 16.2 |
| 36 013 | 27460 | 4 | Chautauqua | 2 746 | 133 539 | 469 | 48.6 | 90.5 | 3.0 | 0.9 | 0.9 | 6.3 | 5.6 | 15.9 | 11.3 | 10.6 | 11.2 | 14.8 |
| 36 015 | 21300 | 3 | Chemung | 1 055 | 88 911 | 643 | 84.3 | 89.2 | 7.9 | 0.7 | 1.8 | 2.7 | 5.9 | 16.2 | 9.1 | 12.0 | 12.1 | 15.4 |
| 36 017 | ... | 6 | Chenango | 2 314 | 49 933 | 980 | 21.6 | 96.4 | 1.2 | 0.9 | 0.8 | 1.9 | 5.4 | 16.9 | 7.8 | 10.4 | 11.9 | 16.2 |
| 36 019 | 38460 | 5 | Clinton | 2 688 | 81 654 | 680 | 30.4 | 92.1 | 4.2 | 0.8 | 1.6 | 2.6 | 4.9 | 14.0 | 13.4 | 12.7 | 12.5 | 16.2 |
| 36 021 | 26460 | 6 | Columbia | 1 644 | 62 499 | 837 | 38.0 | 89.5 | 5.4 | 0.5 | 2.4 | 4.0 | 4.6 | 15.1 | 7.6 | 9.4 | 11.9 | 16.6 |
| 36 023 | 18660 | 4 | Cortland | 1 292 | 49 474 | 992 | 38.3 | 94.6 | 2.3 | 0.8 | 1.4 | 2.4 | 5.3 | 15.3 | 17.9 | 10.8 | 11.0 | 13.9 |
| 36 025 | ... | 6 | Delaware | 3 736 | 47 276 | 1 023 | 12.7 | 93.1 | 2.3 | 0.7 | 1.2 | 3.4 | 5.0 | 14.2 | 10.1 | 9.3 | 10.5 | 15.2 |
| 36 027 | 39100 | 2 | Dutchess | 2 061 | 297 322 | 223 | 144.3 | 75.8 | 10.3 | 0.6 | 4.4 | 10.8 | 5.0 | 16.6 | 11.1 | 10.8 | 12.8 | 16.8 |
| 36 029 | 15380 | 1 | Erie | 2 701 | 919 086 | 54 | 340.3 | 79.2 | 14.0 | 0.9 | 3.2 | 4.7 | 5.3 | 15.9 | 10.5 | 12.2 | 11.8 | 15.2 |
| 36 031 | ... | 6 | Essex | 4 647 | 38 961 | 1 196 | 8.4 | 93.6 | 2.9 | 0.8 | 1.0 | 2.6 | 4.5 | 14.3 | 7.5 | 11.6 | 12.2 | 16.2 |
| 36 033 | 31660 | 5 | Franklin | 4 219 | 51 795 | 959 | 12.3 | 83.5 | 6.1 | 7.8 | 0.8 | 3.0 | 5.3 | 15.1 | 10.5 | 14.0 | 12.8 | 16.0 |
| 36 035 | 24100 | 4 | Fulton | 1 283 | 54 925 | 913 | 42.8 | 94.9 | 2.4 | 0.6 | 1.0 | 2.4 | 5.4 | 16.4 | 8.1 | 11.4 | 12.5 | 15.7 |

1. CBSA = Core Based Statistical Area. See Appendix A for explanation. See Appendix B for list of metropolitan areas with component counties.  2. County type code from the Economic Research Service of USDA Rural-Urban Continuum Codes. See Appendix A for definition.  3. Dry land or land partially or temporarily covered by water.  4. May be of any race.

# Table B. States and Counties — Population and Households

| | Population, 2011 (cont.) | | | | Population change and components of change, 2000–2012 | | | | | | | Households, 2010 | | | | |
|---|---|---|---|---|---|---|---|---|---|---|---|---|---|---|---|---|
| | Age (percent) (cont.) | | | | Total persons | | Percent change | | Components of change, 2010–2012 | | | | | | Percent | |
| STATE County | 55 to 64 years | 65 to 74 years | 75 years and over | Percent female | 2000 | 2010 | 2000– 2010 | 2010– 2012 | Births | Deaths | Net migration | Number | Percent change, 2000– 2010 | Persons per house-hold | Female family house-holder[1] | One per-son |
| | 16 | 17 | 18 | 19 | 20 | 21 | 22 | 23 | 24 | 25 | 26 | 27 | 28 | 29 | 30 | 31 |
| NEW JERSEY—Cont'd | | | | | | | | | | | | | | | | |
| Mercer | 12.1 | 6.7 | 6.3 | 51.1 | 350 761 | 366 513 | 4.5 | 0.5 | 9 548 | 6 295 | -1 516 | 133 155 | 5.8 | 2.61 | 14.2 | 26.9 |
| Middlesex | 11.7 | 6.5 | 6.0 | 50.8 | 750 162 | 809 858 | 8.0 | 1.6 | 21 668 | 12 583 | 4 316 | 281 186 | 5.8 | 2.80 | 11.8 | 22.5 |
| Monmouth | 13.5 | 7.3 | 6.8 | 51.3 | 615 301 | 630 380 | 2.5 | -0.2 | 13 739 | 11 820 | -2 694 | 233 983 | 4.3 | 2.66 | 10.5 | 25.0 |
| Morris | 13.0 | 7.5 | 6.7 | 51.0 | 470 212 | 492 276 | 4.7 | 1.2 | 10 474 | 7 814 | 3 341 | 180 534 | 6.4 | 2.68 | 8.5 | 23.5 |
| Ocean | 12.7 | 10.3 | 10.8 | 52.1 | 510 916 | 576 567 | 12.8 | 0.7 | 17 552 | 15 472 | 2 263 | 221 111 | 10.3 | 2.58 | 9.8 | 27.8 |
| Passaic | 11.4 | 6.6 | 5.7 | 51.4 | 489 049 | 501 226 | 2.5 | 0.3 | 15 665 | 7 774 | -6 284 | 166 785 | 1.8 | 2.94 | 17.5 | 22.6 |
| Salem | 13.9 | 7.9 | 7.2 | 51.1 | 64 285 | 66 083 | 2.8 | -0.5 | 1 672 | 1 586 | -416 | 25 290 | 4.1 | 2.56 | 14.4 | 25.4 |
| Somerset | 12.6 | 6.6 | 6.0 | 51.2 | 297 490 | 323 444 | 8.7 | 1.3 | 7 647 | 4 898 | 1 377 | 117 759 | 8.1 | 2.71 | 9.5 | 23.3 |
| Sussex | 14.7 | 7.5 | 5.1 | 50.4 | 144 166 | 149 265 | 3.5 | -1.2 | 2 975 | 2 525 | -2 263 | 54 752 | 7.7 | 2.69 | 9.0 | 21.0 |
| Union | 11.7 | 6.5 | 6.3 | 51.4 | 522 541 | 536 499 | 2.7 | 1.4 | 15 214 | 8 821 | 970 | 188 118 | 1.1 | 2.82 | 15.6 | 23.6 |
| Warren | 13.3 | 7.5 | 6.9 | 51.3 | 102 437 | 108 692 | 6.1 | -1.0 | 2 284 | 2 006 | -1 351 | 41 480 | 7.3 | 2.57 | 10.2 | 25.0 |
| NEW MEXICO | 12.8 | 7.7 | 5.9 | 50.5 | 1 819 046 | 2 059 179 | 13.2 | 1.3 | 63 673 | 36 198 | -1 069 | 791 395 | 16.7 | 2.55 | 14.0 | 28.0 |
| Bernalillo | 12.4 | 6.8 | 5.6 | 50.9 | 556 678 | 662 564 | 19.0 | 1.6 | 19 871 | 11 348 | 2 548 | 266 000 | 20.4 | 2.45 | 14.1 | 30.4 |
| Catron | 23.9 | 18.7 | 10.6 | 48.3 | 3 543 | 3 725 | 5.1 | -1.8 | 47 | 54 | -69 | 1 787 | 12.8 | 2.03 | 4.8 | 34.8 |
| Chaves | 11.7 | 7.3 | 6.9 | 50.4 | 61 382 | 65 645 | 6.9 | 0.2 | 2 258 | 1 442 | -692 | 23 691 | 5.0 | 2.70 | 14.9 | 25.2 |
| Cibola | 12.4 | 7.5 | 5.7 | 49.2 | 25 595 | 27 213 | 6.3 | 0.4 | 928 | 515 | -315 | 8 860 | 6.4 | 2.79 | 20.8 | 24.9 |
| Colfax | 16.6 | 12.1 | 8.8 | 49.1 | 14 189 | 13 750 | -3.1 | -3.8 | 305 | 333 | -495 | 6 011 | 3.3 | 2.22 | 10.9 | 32.9 |
| Curry | 9.8 | 6.1 | 5.1 | 49.4 | 45 044 | 48 376 | 7.4 | 3.2 | 2 056 | 832 | 309 | 18 015 | 7.4 | 2.63 | 14.2 | 26.4 |
| De Baca | 16.1 | 12.8 | 10.7 | 50.2 | 2 240 | 2 022 | -9.7 | -4.7 | 47 | 49 | -96 | 912 | -1.1 | 2.21 | 8.3 | 32.7 |
| Dona Ana | 11.0 | 7.1 | 5.6 | 50.9 | 174 682 | 209 233 | 19.8 | 2.5 | 7 408 | 3 234 | 1 084 | 75 532 | 26.8 | 2.71 | 16.0 | 24.2 |
| Eddy | 12.9 | 7.3 | 6.8 | 49.9 | 51 658 | 53 829 | 4.2 | 1.1 | 1 685 | 1 218 | 136 | 20 411 | 5.3 | 2.59 | 13.0 | 25.5 |
| Grant | 16.7 | 12.4 | 9.6 | 50.7 | 31 002 | 29 514 | -4.8 | -0.4 | 766 | 716 | -161 | 12 586 | 3.6 | 2.30 | 12.6 | 30.9 |
| Guadalupe | 12.1 | 9.0 | 7.3 | 43.4 | 4 680 | 4 687 | 0.1 | -1.8 | 82 | 88 | -89 | 1 766 | 6.7 | 2.33 | 15.2 | 32.4 |
| Harding | 21.3 | 12.6 | 15.5 | 47.3 | 810 | 695 | -14.2 | 1.7 | 17 | 21 | 16 | 349 | -5.9 | 1.99 | 5.4 | 34.7 |
| Hidalgo | 13.5 | 9.2 | 7.7 | 49.8 | 5 932 | 4 894 | -17.5 | -2.0 | 117 | 86 | -135 | 1 936 | -10.0 | 2.49 | 14.2 | 29.1 |
| Lea | 10.3 | 5.9 | 4.9 | 48.8 | 55 511 | 64 727 | 16.6 | 2.5 | 2 539 | 1 121 | 180 | 22 236 | 12.9 | 2.82 | 13.4 | 22.6 |
| Lincoln | 18.9 | 13.8 | 8.7 | 51.1 | 19 411 | 20 497 | 5.6 | -0.9 | 489 | 403 | -256 | 9 219 | 12.4 | 2.21 | 9.8 | 30.5 |
| Los Alamos | 16.0 | 8.2 | 7.0 | 49.7 | 18 343 | 17 950 | -2.1 | 1.2 | 400 | 244 | 43 | 7 663 | 2.2 | 2.33 | 6.4 | 28.5 |
| Luna | 12.2 | 11.0 | 8.8 | 50.1 | 25 016 | 25 095 | 0.3 | -0.2 | 895 | 630 | -317 | 9 593 | 2.1 | 2.56 | 14.5 | 27.8 |
| McKinley | 10.0 | 5.6 | 4.0 | 51.8 | 74 798 | 71 492 | -4.4 | 2.1 | 3 067 | 1 075 | -512 | 21 968 | 2.3 | 3.22 | 24.5 | 24.0 |
| Mora | 17.6 | 11.3 | 8.2 | 48.9 | 5 180 | 4 881 | -5.8 | -3.6 | 81 | 78 | -179 | 2 114 | 4.8 | 2.31 | 10.9 | 33.2 |
| Otero | 11.9 | 8.6 | 6.4 | 49.3 | 62 298 | 63 797 | 2.4 | 3.5 | 2 194 | 1 218 | 1 266 | 24 464 | 6.4 | 2.51 | 12.7 | 27.1 |
| Quay | 16.0 | 12.0 | 8.8 | 51.1 | 10 155 | 9 041 | -11.0 | -3.0 | 235 | 268 | -249 | 4 072 | -3.1 | 2.21 | 12.7 | 34.2 |
| Rio Arriba | 13.9 | 8.6 | 6.1 | 50.5 | 41 190 | 40 246 | -2.3 | 0.2 | 1 354 | 801 | -475 | 15 768 | 4.8 | 2.53 | 16.0 | 28.2 |
| Roosevelt | 9.6 | 6.2 | 5.3 | 49.6 | 18 018 | 19 846 | 10.1 | 2.9 | 719 | 391 | 225 | 7 299 | 9.9 | 2.57 | 11.7 | 28.3 |
| Sandoval | 13.4 | 7.7 | 5.0 | 51.1 | 89 908 | 131 561 | 46.3 | 3.1 | 3 587 | 1 954 | 2 318 | 47 602 | 51.5 | 2.75 | 12.5 | 22.0 |
| San Juan | 11.4 | 6.3 | 5.0 | 50.3 | 113 801 | 130 044 | 14.3 | -1.2 | 4 464 | 2 008 | -3 991 | 44 404 | 17.7 | 2.89 | 15.6 | 21.9 |
| San Miguel | 14.9 | 9.6 | 6.3 | 50.1 | 30 126 | 29 393 | -2.4 | -1.7 | 714 | 633 | -572 | 11 978 | 7.6 | 2.34 | 14.9 | 32.5 |
| Santa Fe | 17.0 | 9.9 | 6.1 | 51.2 | 129 292 | 144 170 | 11.5 | 1.5 | 3 226 | 2 193 | 1 249 | 61 963 | 18.1 | 2.28 | 11.0 | 33.7 |
| Sierra | 18.7 | 17.0 | 13.8 | 49.9 | 13 270 | 11 988 | -9.7 | -0.8 | 221 | 527 | 197 | 5 917 | -3.2 | 1.98 | 8.9 | 40.8 |
| Socorro | 13.0 | 8.9 | 5.9 | 48.7 | 18 078 | 17 866 | -1.2 | -1.5 | 546 | 359 | -460 | 7 014 | 5.1 | 2.46 | 12.9 | 30.8 |
| Taos | 18.0 | 11.0 | 7.0 | 50.9 | 29 979 | 32 937 | 9.9 | -0.5 | 711 | 607 | -281 | 14 806 | 16.8 | 2.19 | 12.6 | 36.0 |
| Torrance | 16.1 | 9.4 | 5.4 | 48.2 | 16 911 | 16 383 | -3.1 | -2.2 | 362 | 325 | -406 | 6 264 | 4.0 | 2.52 | 12.0 | 27.6 |
| Union | 12.6 | 9.8 | 9.0 | 42.7 | 4 174 | 4 549 | 9.0 | -2.6 | 100 | 87 | -132 | 1 695 | -2.2 | 2.29 | 10.1 | 33.2 |
| Valencia | 13.2 | 8.0 | 5.4 | 49.6 | 66 152 | 76 569 | 15.7 | 0.1 | 2 182 | 1 340 | -758 | 27 500 | 21.2 | 2.73 | 13.9 | 22.1 |
| NEW YORK | 12.3 | 7.2 | 6.5 | 51.5 | 18 976 457 | 19 378 102 | 2.1 | 1.0 | 543 408 | 333 712 | -14 551 | 7 317 755 | 3.7 | 2.57 | 14.9 | 29.1 |
| Albany | 13.2 | 7.0 | 7.1 | 51.6 | 294 565 | 304 204 | 3.3 | 0.4 | 6 794 | 5 789 | 324 | 126 251 | 4.8 | 2.27 | 12.2 | 33.8 |
| Allegany | 13.4 | 8.2 | 7.3 | 49.5 | 49 927 | 48 946 | -2.0 | -1.2 | 1 114 | 1 022 | -656 | 18 208 | 1.1 | 2.44 | 9.5 | 27.9 |
| Bronx | 9.9 | 5.9 | 4.8 | 52.9 | 1 332 650 | 1 385 108 | 3.9 | 1.7 | 50 131 | 20 872 | -6 027 | 483 449 | 4.4 | 2.77 | 31.1 | 28.2 |
| Broome | 13.2 | 8.0 | 8.6 | 51.0 | 200 536 | 200 600 | 0.0 | -1.3 | 4 497 | 4 671 | -2 291 | 82 167 | 1.8 | 2.32 | 12.0 | 32.4 |
| Cattaraugus | 14.3 | 8.3 | 7.4 | 50.6 | 83 955 | 80 317 | -4.3 | -1.1 | 2 143 | 1 853 | -1 128 | 32 263 | 0.7 | 2.41 | 11.3 | 29.5 |
| Cayuga | 13.9 | 8.0 | 7.5 | 49.0 | 81 963 | 80 026 | -2.4 | -0.6 | 1 808 | 1 599 | -651 | 31 445 | 2.9 | 2.41 | 11.6 | 28.5 |
| Chautauqua | 13.9 | 8.4 | 8.4 | 50.7 | 139 750 | 134 905 | -3.5 | -1.0 | 3 185 | 3 144 | -1 374 | 54 244 | -0.5 | 2.37 | 11.8 | 29.9 |
| Chemung | 13.6 | 7.9 | 7.9 | 50.2 | 91 070 | 88 830 | -2.5 | 0.1 | 2 225 | 2 091 | -6 | 35 462 | 1.2 | 2.37 | 13.0 | 30.3 |
| Chenango | 14.4 | 9.4 | 7.6 | 50.2 | 51 401 | 50 477 | -1.8 | -1.1 | 1 136 | 1 223 | -474 | 20 436 | 2.6 | 2.43 | 10.8 | 27.5 |
| Clinton | 12.8 | 7.4 | 6.3 | 48.7 | 79 894 | 82 128 | 2.8 | -0.6 | 1 762 | 1 503 | -756 | 31 582 | 7.3 | 2.37 | 10.6 | 27.5 |
| Columbia | 16.1 | 10.1 | 8.6 | 49.8 | 63 094 | 63 096 | 0.0 | -0.9 | 1 225 | 1 415 | -372 | 25 906 | 4.5 | 2.35 | 10.6 | 28.8 |
| Cortland | 12.4 | 7.1 | 6.2 | 51.1 | 48 599 | 49 336 | 1.5 | 0.3 | 1 166 | 955 | -124 | 18 671 | 2.5 | 2.45 | 10.9 | 28.0 |
| Delaware | 15.8 | 10.9 | 8.9 | 49.7 | 48 055 | 47 980 | -0.2 | -1.5 | 992 | 1 226 | -456 | 19 898 | 3.3 | 2.29 | 9.4 | 30.5 |
| Dutchess | 13.0 | 7.4 | 6.4 | 50.2 | 280 150 | 297 488 | 6.2 | -0.1 | 6 400 | 5 186 | -1 258 | 107 965 | 8.5 | 2.57 | 11.0 | 26.0 |
| Erie | 13.2 | 7.7 | 8.0 | 51.7 | 950 265 | 919 040 | -3.3 | 0.0 | 21 758 | 21 262 | 10 | 383 164 | 0.6 | 2.32 | 13.7 | 33.0 |
| Essex | 15.2 | 9.8 | 8.6 | 48.1 | 38 851 | 39 370 | 1.3 | -1.0 | 757 | 893 | -383 | 16 262 | 8.2 | 2.26 | 8.5 | 30.9 |
| Franklin | 12.7 | 7.4 | 6.2 | 45.1 | 51 134 | 51 599 | 0.9 | 0.4 | 1 137 | 985 | 66 | 19 054 | 6.3 | 2.37 | 11.7 | 29.7 |
| Fulton | 14.0 | 8.6 | 7.8 | 50.6 | 55 073 | 55 531 | 0.8 | -1.1 | 1 221 | 1 309 | -537 | 22 554 | 3.1 | 2.40 | 12.5 | 28.2 |

1. No spouse present.

# Table B. States and Counties — Population, Vital Statistics, Medicare, and Crime

| STATE County | Persons in group quarters, 2010 | Daytime population, 2007–2011 Number | Daytime population Employment/residence ratio | Births, 2011 Total | Births, 2011 Rate[1] | Deaths, 2011 Number | Deaths, 2011 Rate[1] | Persons under 65 with no health insurance, 2010 Number | Persons under 65 ... Percent | Medicare, 2012 Eligible for Medicare | Medicare, 2012 Enrolled in Medicare Advantage | Medicare, 2012 Enrolled in a Medicare prescription drug plan | Serious crimes known to police,[2] 2011 Total Number | Total Rate[3] |
|---|---|---|---|---|---|---|---|---|---|---|---|---|---|---|
| | 32 | 33 | 34 | 35 | 36 | 37 | 38 | 39 | 40 | 41 | 42 | 43 | 44 | 45 |
| **NEW JERSEY—Cont'd** | | | | | | | | | | | | | | |
| Mercer | 18 805 | 416 053 | 1.30 | 4 378 | 11.9 | 2 746 | 7.5 | 41 627 | 13.7 | 59 625 | 8 274 | 34 467 | 9 614 | 2 614 |
| Middlesex | 23 835 | 788 390 | 0.96 | 9 813 | 12.1 | 5 546 | 6.8 | 104 747 | 15.1 | 116 570 | 17 392 | 57 486 | 16 543 | 2 036 |
| Monmouth | 7 670 | 590 024 | 0.87 | 6 295 | 10.0 | 5 217 | 8.3 | 62 536 | 11.6 | 105 226 | 13 671 | 54 553 | 14 991 | 2 370 |
| Morris | 8 866 | 528 591 | 1.15 | 4 770 | 9.6 | 3 378 | 6.8 | 40 933 | 9.8 | 78 523 | 7 769 | 40 027 | 6 144 | 1 244 |
| Ocean | 7 163 | 499 957 | 0.69 | 7 786 | 13.4 | 6 863 | 11.8 | 58 577 | 13.0 | 138 694 | 22 539 | 70 068 | 12 631 | 2 183 |
| Passaic | 11 019 | 454 333 | 0.80 | 7 103 | 14.1 | 3 430 | 6.8 | 87 666 | 20.2 | 73 692 | 13 482 | 37 286 | 13 958 | 2 776 |
| Salem | 1 257 | 60 689 | 0.82 | 767 | 11.6 | 719 | 10.9 | 6 879 | 12.4 | 12 694 | 1 061 | 8 101 | 1 776 | 2 679 |
| Somerset | 3 970 | 333 757 | 1.08 | 3 528 | 10.9 | 2 176 | 6.7 | 28 423 | 10.1 | 46 273 | 3 809 | 23 707 | 4 614 | 1 422 |
| Sussex | 1 742 | 118 697 | 0.59 | 1 368 | 9.2 | 1 096 | 7.4 | 13 874 | 10.7 | 23 437 | 2 264 | 12 627 | 1 766 | 1 179 |
| Union | 6 804 | 517 142 | 0.94 | 6 991 | 13.0 | 3 926 | 7.3 | 85 040 | 18.3 | 77 883 | 14 039 | 36 024 | 15 412 | 2 863 |
| Warren | 1 968 | 94 587 | 0.73 | 1 015 | 9.4 | 864 | 8.0 | 11 275 | 12.2 | 18 529 | 1 472 | 10 393 | 1 771 | 1 624 |
| **NEW MEXICO** | 42 629 | 2 032 020 | 0.99 | 28 511 | 13.7 | 15 760 | 7.6 | 397 890 | 22.6 | 339 860 | 94 472 | 129 235 | 85 351 | 4 099 |
| Bernalillo | 11 945 | 684 968 | 1.10 | 8 990 | 13.4 | 5 015 | 7.5 | 116 535 | 20.3 | 102 512 | 47 765 | 25 113 | 36 083 | 5 386 |
| Catron | 106 | 3 553 | 0.90 | 23 | 6.2 | 19 | 5.1 | 847 | 31.1 | 1 172 | 165 | 443 | 23 | 611 |
| Chaves | 1 784 | 63 165 | 0.93 | 1 026 | 15.6 | 648 | 9.8 | 12 803 | 23.4 | 11 277 | 477 | 7 011 | 3 366 | 5 071 |
| Cibola | 2 531 | 26 739 | 0.93 | 410 | 14.8 | 222 | 8.0 | 5 434 | 25.2 | 4 186 | 396 | 2 024 | 657 | 2 388 |
| Colfax | 408 | 13 810 | 1.01 | 137 | 10.0 | 139 | 10.2 | 2 216 | 20.8 | 3 219 | 405 | 1 612 | 226 | 1 759 |
| Curry | 1 041 | 48 198 | 1.03 | 873 | 17.6 | 358 | 7.2 | 9 308 | 22.0 | 6 794 | 602 | 3 814 | 2 584 | 5 354 |
| De Baca | 9 | 2 020 | 1.00 | 20 | 10.3 | 28 | 14.4 | 411 | 26.1 | 534 | 39 | 321 | NA | NA |
| Dona Ana | 4 581 | 202 060 | 0.96 | 3 281 | 15.4 | 1 387 | 6.5 | 46 450 | 25.9 | 31 650 | 8 023 | 12 972 | 7 564 | 3 575 |
| Eddy | 995 | 55 739 | 1.11 | 754 | 13.9 | 524 | 9.7 | 8 215 | 17.9 | 9 267 | 386 | 5 809 | 2 406 | 4 420 |
| Grant | 590 | 29 640 | 1.00 | 346 | 11.8 | 313 | 10.7 | 4 610 | 20.3 | 7 585 | 1 535 | 3 054 | 794 | 2 661 |
| Guadalupe | 571 | 4 606 | 0.94 | 37 | 8.0 | 40 | 8.7 | 738 | 21.7 | 963 | 114 | 609 | 85 | 1 794 |
| Harding | 0 | 639 | 0.88 | 6 | 8.5 | 11 | 15.6 | 163 | 29.8 | 204 | 19 | 99 | NA | NA |
| Hidalgo | 64 | 4 988 | 1.02 | 57 | 11.7 | 44 | 9.1 | 999 | 24.8 | 1 005 | 203 | 438 | 20 | 404 |
| Lea | 2 057 | 64 332 | 1.03 | 1 179 | 18.0 | 457 | 7.0 | 13 783 | 24.7 | 8 180 | 117 | 5 452 | 2 585 | 3 950 |
| Lincoln | 116 | 20 174 | 0.97 | 225 | 11.0 | 173 | 8.5 | 4 044 | 25.5 | 5 195 | 824 | 2 263 | 630 | 3 278 |
| Los Alamos | 94 | 25 885 | 1.88 | 166 | 9.1 | 109 | 6.0 | 738 | 4.9 | 2 947 | 152 | 512 | NA | NA |
| Luna | 551 | 25 236 | 1.00 | 411 | 16.3 | 279 | 11.0 | 5 491 | 27.9 | 6 190 | 1 568 | 2 645 | 1 071 | 4 221 |
| McKinley | 780 | 71 662 | 1.02 | 1 340 | 18.2 | 462 | 6.3 | 20 570 | 31.4 | 8 962 | 478 | 5 037 | 2 525 | 3 493 |
| Mora | 8 | 4 260 | 0.72 | 34 | 7.1 | 33 | 6.9 | 904 | 22.7 | 1 247 | 178 | 674 | 1 | 20 |
| Otero | 2 306 | 61 674 | 0.93 | 951 | 14.5 | 508 | 7.7 | 12 759 | 24.2 | 11 130 | 1 619 | 3 936 | 1 618 | 2 535 |
| Quay | 22 | 9 013 | 1.00 | 101 | 11.2 | 108 | 12.0 | 1 707 | 23.8 | 2 429 | 298 | 1 269 | 376 | 4 113 |
| Rio Arriba | 425 | 35 553 | 0.71 | 611 | 15.1 | 347 | 8.6 | 7 926 | 23.0 | 7 932 | 1 610 | 3 423 | 892 | 2 192 |
| Roosevelt | 1 083 | 18 981 | 0.92 | 306 | 15.0 | 171 | 8.4 | 4 092 | 24.7 | 2 710 | 82 | 1 741 | 696 | 3 468 |
| Sandoval | 761 | 106 751 | 0.62 | 1 564 | 11.6 | 839 | 6.2 | 20 499 | 17.7 | 20 979 | 9 271 | 4 672 | 2 517 | 1 892 |
| San Juan | 1 754 | 128 123 | 1.00 | 2 098 | 16.4 | 898 | 7.0 | 33 447 | 28.9 | 16 905 | 466 | 9 144 | 3 580 | 2 722 |
| San Miguel | 1 310 | 27 017 | 0.79 | 309 | 10.5 | 267 | 9.1 | 4 684 | 19.6 | 5 977 | 524 | 3 765 | NA | NA |
| Santa Fe | 2 613 | 147 181 | 1.06 | 1 411 | 9.7 | 924 | 6.3 | 27 496 | 22.8 | 27 576 | 7 076 | 10 665 | 5 783 | 3 967 |
| Sierra | 265 | 11 978 | 1.02 | 99 | 8.3 | 245 | 20.5 | 2 036 | 24.7 | 4 020 | 906 | 1 583 | 258 | 2 128 |
| Socorro | 583 | 17 800 | 0.98 | 241 | 13.5 | 161 | 9.0 | 3 794 | 25.7 | 3 099 | 535 | 1 293 | 541 | 2 995 |
| Taos | 470 | 32 345 | 0.97 | 320 | 9.7 | 259 | 7.9 | 6 814 | 25.0 | 7 242 | 1 286 | 3 372 | 839 | 2 519 |
| Torrance | 615 | 14 752 | 0.70 | 159 | 9.7 | 146 | 8.9 | 3 210 | 23.9 | 2 913 | 1 171 | 816 | 316 | 1 908 |
| Union | 662 | 4 541 | 1.06 | 46 | 10.4 | 36 | 8.1 | 758 | 24.3 | 923 | 36 | 540 | 21 | 457 |
| Valencia | 1 529 | 64 637 | 0.62 | 980 | 12.7 | 590 | 7.7 | 14 411 | 22.1 | 12 936 | 6 146 | 3 114 | 3 101 | 4 005 |
| **NEW YORK** | 585 678 | 19 630 048 | 1.04 | 242 972 | 12.5 | 146 864 | 7.5 | 2 245 437 | 13.7 | 3 162 814 | 1 044 649 | 1 053 565 | 449 745 | 2 311 |
| Albany | 17 024 | 378 110 | 1.49 | 3 038 | 10.0 | 2 571 | 8.5 | 25 221 | 10.2 | 52 320 | 19 874 | 11 338 | 10 616 | 3 474 |
| Allegany | 4 584 | 45 309 | 0.82 | 505 | 10.4 | 454 | 9.3 | 4 526 | 12.2 | 9 398 | 3 089 | 2 862 | 895 | 1 820 |
| Bronx | 46 710 | 1 216 456 | 0.70 | 22 695 | 16.3 | 9 344 | 6.7 | 205 992 | 17.0 | 177 369 | 83 725 | 59 146 | (4) | (4) |
| Broome | 10 141 | 208 497 | 1.09 | 2 018 | 10.1 | 2 074 | 10.4 | 18 901 | 11.8 | 41 535 | 11 738 | 15 857 | 6 607 | 3 279 |
| Cattaraugus | 2 679 | 77 629 | 0.92 | 952 | 11.9 | 808 | 10.1 | 9 323 | 14.1 | 16 279 | 6 951 | 4 413 | 1 939 | 2 403 |
| Cayuga | 4 245 | 71 561 | 0.77 | 800 | 10.0 | 683 | 8.6 | 8 263 | 12.9 | 14 476 | 3 228 | 4 939 | 1 706 | 2 122 |
| Chautauqua | 6 514 | 135 575 | 1.01 | 1 449 | 10.8 | 1 348 | 10.0 | 13 103 | 12.1 | 28 415 | 11 980 | 9 059 | 3 654 | 2 696 |
| Chemung | 4 916 | 89 685 | 1.03 | 974 | 11.0 | 942 | 10.6 | 7 539 | 10.7 | 18 422 | 4 828 | 6 253 | 2 278 | 2 553 |
| Chenango | 796 | 47 869 | 0.87 | 522 | 10.4 | 534 | 10.7 | 5 020 | 12.0 | 11 003 | 3 046 | 4 370 | 1 074 | 2 177 |
| Clinton | 7 153 | 81 827 | 0.99 | 768 | 9.4 | 649 | 7.9 | 7 271 | 11.3 | 15 633 | 2 277 | 5 657 | 1 688 | 2 046 |
| Columbia | 2 136 | 57 252 | 0.81 | 531 | 8.5 | 613 | 9.8 | 6 714 | 13.3 | 13 479 | 3 196 | 4 597 | 1 192 | 1 881 |
| Cortland | 3 561 | 47 660 | 0.92 | 542 | 11.0 | 409 | 8.3 | 4 501 | 11.4 | 8 413 | 1 682 | 3 430 | 1 103 | 2 226 |
| Delaware | 2 435 | 47 428 | 0.97 | 434 | 9.1 | 540 | 11.4 | 4 914 | 13.3 | 10 302 | 2 222 | 4 026 | 818 | 1 697 |
| Dutchess | 19 965 | 277 858 | 0.86 | 2 879 | 9.7 | 2 310 | 7.8 | 26 251 | 10.9 | 50 771 | 7 913 | 17 786 | 5 616 | 1 908 |
| Erie | 28 387 | 948 267 | 1.07 | 9 625 | 10.5 | 9 407 | 10.2 | 75 216 | 10.0 | 179 903 | 97 028 | 29 457 | 31 360 | 3 397 |
| Essex | 2 647 | 38 796 | 0.97 | 344 | 8.8 | 392 | 10.0 | 4 075 | 13.5 | 8 230 | 1 074 | 3 537 | 650 | 1 644 |
| Franklin | 6 400 | 52 173 | 1.02 | 513 | 10.0 | 441 | 8.6 | 6 243 | 16.1 | 9 850 | 1 773 | 4 371 | 937 | 1 808 |
| Fulton | 1 474 | 52 078 | 0.86 | 540 | 9.8 | 582 | 10.5 | 5 906 | 12.9 | 11 476 | 4 280 | 4 248 | 1 609 | 2 884 |

1. Per 1,000 estimated resident population.  2. Data for serious crimes have not been adjusted for underreporting; this may affect comparability between geographic areas and over time.  3. Per 100,000 population estimated by the FBI.  4. Bronx, Kings, Queens, and Richmond counties are included with New York county.

# Table B. States and Counties — Crime, Education, Money Income, and Poverty

| STATE County | Serious crimes known to police, 2011 (cont.)[1] Rate[2] | | Education | | | | | | Money income, 2007–2011 | | | | Income and poverty, 2011 | | | |
| | Rate[2] | | School enrollment and attainment, 2007–2011 | | | | Local government expenditures,[5] 2009–2010 | | Households | | | | Percent below poverty level | | | |
| | | | Enrollment[3] | | Attainment[4] (percent) | | | | Per capita income[6] | Median income | | | Median household income | | Children under 18 years | Children 5 to 17 years in families |
| | Violent | Property | Total | Percent private | High school graduate or less | Bachelor's degree or more | Total current expenditures (mil dol) | Current expenditures per student (dollars) | (dollars) | Dollars | Percent change, 2000 to 2007–2011 (constant 2011 dollars) | Percent with income of $200,000 or more | (dollars) | All persons | | |
| | 46 | 47 | 48 | 49 | 50 | 51 | 52 | 53 | 54 | 55 | 56 | 57 | 58 | 59 | 60 | 61 |

| STATE County | 46 | 47 | 48 | 49 | 50 | 51 | 52 | 53 | 54 | 55 | 56 | 57 | 58 | 59 | 60 | 61 |
|---|---|---|---|---|---|---|---|---|---|---|---|---|---|---|---|---|
| **NEW JERSEY—Cont'd** | | | | | | | | | | | | | | | | |
| Mercer | 436 | 2 178 | 104 725 | 24.6 | 39.0 | 38.0 | 1 016.6 | 16 192 | 36 721 | 73 883 | -3.3 | 10.7 | 71 926 | 11.1 | 15.4 | 14.2 |
| Middlesex | 184 | 1 852 | 215 366 | 16.7 | 39.5 | 38.9 | 1 743.8 | 15 653 | 34 153 | 78 622 | -5.2 | 7.9 | 73 914 | 8.5 | 10.8 | 10.3 |
| Monmouth | 181 | 2 189 | 167 578 | 23.0 | 35.5 | 39.6 | 1 876.9 | 16 068 | 42 234 | 83 842 | -3.4 | 12.5 | 79 062 | 6.9 | 9.3 | 7.8 |
| Morris | 77 | 1 167 | 130 144 | 25.2 | 30.4 | 49.0 | 1 335.3 | 16 514 | 48 067 | 98 148 | -6.0 | 16.3 | 91 420 | 5.0 | 5.5 | 5.0 |
| Ocean | 114 | 2 069 | 135 737 | 30.9 | 48.6 | 24.5 | 1 137.7 | 14 928 | 30 257 | 60 712 | -3.2 | 4.2 | 56 851 | 11.3 | 19.6 | 17.5 |
| Passaic | 491 | 2 285 | 133 861 | 16.0 | 53.2 | 25.4 | 1 398.3 | 17 062 | 26 615 | 56 299 | -15.3 | 5.1 | 52 243 | 16.2 | 24.5 | 22.3 |
| Salem | 288 | 2 391 | 16 785 | 14.3 | 53.3 | 18.5 | 194.3 | 16 590 | 27 941 | 57 174 | -7.1 | 3.2 | 53 890 | 11.8 | 17.6 | 15.3 |
| Somerset | 79 | 1 343 | 85 421 | 20.8 | 29.3 | 50.2 | 892.9 | 16 120 | 48 090 | 98 842 | -4.8 | 16.9 | 95 915 | 5.2 | 6.2 | 5.2 |
| Sussex | 49 | 1 130 | 39 922 | 19.2 | 39.5 | 31.6 | 442.6 | 17 482 | 36 986 | 84 860 | -3.7 | 8.0 | 82 987 | 5.8 | 6.9 | 5.7 |
| Union | 436 | 2 427 | 139 033 | 17.2 | 46.1 | 31.6 | 1 515.9 | 17 158 | 34 851 | 68 688 | -8.1 | 9.3 | 65 178 | 10.7 | 14.0 | 12.9 |
| Warren | 98 | 1 526 | 27 801 | 16.5 | 46.0 | 29.2 | 285.8 | 15 466 | 33 616 | 72 615 | -4.1 | 5.6 | 66 857 | 7.7 | 10.1 | 9.0 |
| **NEW MEXICO** | 568 | 3 532 | 554 801 | 11.0 | 43.6 | 25.4 | 3 138.0 | 9 383 | 23 537 | 44 631 | -3.2 | 2.7 | 42 097 | 20.9 | 29.4 | 27.3 |
| Bernalillo | 751 | 4 635 | 182 375 | 14.7 | 37.6 | 31.6 | 889.4 | 8 999 | 26 638 | 48 231 | -7.9 | 3.1 | 44 224 | 19.7 | 27.0 | 25.1 |
| Catron | 27 | 584 | 573 | 14.0 | 44.5 | 18.8 | 6.2 | 17 820 | 22 717 | 37 857 | 17.4 | 0.2 | 37 277 | 21.9 | 42.8 | 39.7 |
| Chaves | 548 | 4 522 | 17 698 | 11.3 | 51.5 | 16.4 | 107.1 | 9 125 | 18 764 | 37 293 | -3.1 | 1.1 | 35 894 | 22.3 | 31.5 | 29.5 |
| Cibola | 810 | 1 577 | 7 276 | 9.0 | 63.5 | 9.2 | 37.7 | 10 208 | 14 859 | 36 020 | -3.9 | 0.5 | 33 345 | 29.9 | 41.4 | 38.8 |
| Colfax | 93 | 1 666 | 2 938 | 3.4 | 47.6 | 19.6 | 24.2 | 11 387 | 21 539 | 38 012 | -8.4 | 1.2 | 33 988 | 19.5 | 28.4 | 25.6 |
| Curry | 466 | 4 888 | 13 287 | 7.4 | 45.4 | 19.2 | 79.6 | 8 271 | 20 553 | 40 397 | 3.5 | 1.3 | 38 423 | 18.5 | 28.3 | 26.5 |
| De Baca | NA | NA | 462 | 0.0 | 52.7 | 20.0 | 4.9 | 15 590 | 21 600 | 33 714 | -1.9 | 0.7 | 30 017 | 22.5 | 37.0 | 34.9 |
| Dona Ana | 367 | 3 208 | 66 132 | 4.7 | 45.5 | 25.5 | 359.0 | 8 852 | 19 077 | 37 223 | -7.5 | 1.9 | 36 136 | 29.2 | 39.5 | 36.5 |
| Eddy | 704 | 3 717 | 13 709 | 8.0 | 51.7 | 15.7 | 100.3 | 9 791 | 26 088 | 47 725 | 10.5 | 2.8 | 46 212 | 15.2 | 22.0 | 20.2 |
| Grant | 429 | 2 232 | 7 244 | 11.6 | 43.0 | 24.5 | 48.3 | 10 624 | 21 726 | 36 925 | -6.1 | 0.8 | 34 686 | 20.6 | 33.0 | 32.2 |
| Guadalupe | 485 | 1 308 | 1 123 | 8.3 | 63.1 | 7.8 | 10.8 | 14 663 | 13 574 | 26 152 | -21.8 | 0.5 | 29 187 | 25.4 | 32.9 | 29.5 |
| Harding | NA | NA | 133 | 0.0 | 51.8 | 16.3 | 3.1 | 32 268 | 19 534 | 30 208 | -14.3 | 1.0 | 32 983 | 15.2 | 25.9 | 26.0 |
| Hidalgo | 141 | 263 | 1 209 | 4.4 | 52.4 | 16.6 | 12.9 | 14 904 | 17 770 | 35 532 | 6.0 | 0.2 | 30 978 | 25.8 | 38.8 | 35.4 |
| Lea | 391 | 3 558 | 17 040 | 9.3 | 57.6 | 13.8 | 109.5 | 8 493 | 20 578 | 46 781 | 16.3 | 1.9 | 46 176 | 18.6 | 24.9 | 22.8 |
| Lincoln | 234 | 3 044 | 4 401 | 8.3 | 39.3 | 24.9 | 34.4 | 10 668 | 25 647 | 44 557 | -2.6 | 2.4 | 40 096 | 17.0 | 31.0 | 28.5 |
| Los Alamos | NA | NA | 4 709 | 11.2 | 12.0 | 63.9 | 37.0 | 10 867 | 49 873 | 104 914 | -1.6 | 13.4 | 110 204 | 3.8 | 4.2 | 3.5 |
| Luna | 694 | 3 527 | 6 399 | 5.0 | 60.3 | 14.0 | 52.5 | 9 677 | 16 281 | 30 921 | 10.2 | 1.1 | 27 566 | 28.1 | 43.0 | 38.6 |
| McKinley | 569 | 2 924 | 22 325 | 7.4 | 62.4 | 11.0 | 153.6 | 11 036 | 13 196 | 31 947 | -5.4 | 1.0 | 29 320 | 31.8 | 41.9 | 39.8 |
| Mora | 0 | 20 | 1 278 | 7.6 | 54.3 | 14.6 | 10.5 | 18 114 | 23 990 | 39 792 | 20.2 | 0.0 | 28 911 | 23.8 | 32.8 | 27.8 |
| Otero | 313 | 2 222 | 16 624 | 6.4 | 44.1 | 17.6 | 69.1 | 9 028 | 20 067 | 38 588 | -7.4 | 1.5 | 35 894 | 19.2 | 30.2 | 28.6 |
| Quay | 416 | 3 697 | 2 105 | 1.7 | 60.9 | 14.9 | 19.4 | 12 435 | 18 137 | 29 772 | -11.4 | 0.5 | 29 895 | 21.9 | 35.7 | 33.5 |
| Rio Arriba | 474 | 1 718 | 9 009 | 18.0 | 53.2 | 16.1 | 75.1 | 12 044 | 19 942 | 40 232 | 1.3 | 0.9 | 37 101 | 22.7 | 30.6 | 29.1 |
| Roosevelt | 254 | 3 214 | 6 473 | 6.5 | 49.8 | 21.4 | 35.5 | 10 014 | 17 689 | 35 841 | -0.2 | 1.6 | 34 055 | 24.7 | 32.9 | 30.8 |
| Sandoval | 276 | 1 616 | 35 753 | 11.7 | 36.6 | 28.3 | 182.8 | 8 682 | 26 757 | 57 651 | -5.0 | 3.8 | 53 948 | 14.9 | 19.3 | 17.0 |
| San Juan | 625 | 2 097 | 33 196 | 6.1 | 51.9 | 15.2 | 216.2 | 9 093 | 21 471 | 49 024 | 7.5 | 2.1 | 46 370 | 17.8 | 24.6 | 24.4 |
| San Miguel | NA | NA | 7 598 | 8.8 | 48.9 | 21.6 | 51.8 | 11 723 | 19 130 | 32 332 | -9.7 | 1.0 | 31 983 | 24.4 | 33.5 | 31.5 |
| Santa Fe | 370 | 3 597 | 33 388 | 22.1 | 33.7 | 39.6 | 145.6 | 8 944 | 32 680 | 53 698 | -5.8 | 5.3 | 50 234 | 16.5 | 23.6 | 21.8 |
| Sierra | 371 | 1 757 | 2 559 | 3.6 | 50.8 | 18.8 | 14.3 | 9 948 | 17 033 | 28 373 | -13.0 | 0.8 | 28 544 | 23.1 | 41.6 | 39.4 |
| Socorro | 493 | 2 502 | 5 094 | 9.0 | 55.1 | 21.1 | 27.7 | 11 742 | 18 206 | 34 148 | 7.9 | 2.1 | 31 371 | 26.8 | 39.5 | 35.8 |
| Taos | 492 | 2 027 | 7 035 | 8.7 | 38.7 | 29.2 | 45.6 | 10 885 | 22 126 | 36 205 | 0.2 | 1.7 | 32 521 | 27.2 | 43.7 | 38.0 |
| Torrance | 133 | 1 775 | 4 105 | 11.8 | 56.0 | 12.5 | 45.0 | 9 785 | 17 083 | 32 435 | -21.1 | 1.0 | 33 193 | 27.0 | 38.2 | 32.9 |
| Union | 0 | 457 | 968 | 5.2 | 55.2 | 17.2 | 9.1 | 13 208 | 20 476 | 42 230 | 11.4 | 3.6 | 33 206 | 19.5 | 28.4 | 25.9 |
| Valencia | 515 | 3 490 | 20 583 | 8.7 | 48.9 | 16.2 | 119.8 | 8 896 | 19 995 | 41 388 | -10.1 | 1.4 | 41 983 | 21.3 | 29.2 | 25.9 |
| **NEW YORK** | 398 | 1 912 | 5 046 122 | 24.4 | 43.1 | 32.5 | 50 352.6 | 18 205 | 31 796 | 56 951 | -2.8 | 6.5 | 55 147 | 16.1 | 22.8 | 21.5 |
| Albany | 382 | 3 093 | 85 633 | 23.2 | 35.2 | 37.8 | 621.0 | 15 129 | 31 728 | 57 715 | -0.4 | 4.2 | 56 602 | 13.6 | 18.9 | 16.7 |
| Allegany | 130 | 1 690 | 14 815 | 29.5 | 53.5 | 17.4 | 129.8 | 17 526 | 20 047 | 41 900 | -3.3 | 1.0 | 39 900 | 18.1 | 24.4 | 22.0 |
| Bronx | (7) | (7) | 398 699 | 20.2 | 58.7 | 17.9 | (7) | (7) | 17 992 | 34 744 | -6.8 | 1.4 | 32 137 | 30.3 | 40.9 | 41.0 |
| Broome | 256 | 3 023 | 54 432 | 8.2 | 44.4 | 25.7 | 465.0 | 16 196 | 24 766 | 45 619 | -4.4 | 2.4 | 43 756 | 17.5 | 24.4 | 21.7 |
| Cattaraugus | 207 | 2 196 | 19 901 | 20.2 | 54.6 | 17.5 | 234.3 | 16 193 | 21 369 | 42 754 | -5.2 | 1.1 | 39 368 | 18.7 | 28.0 | 25.8 |
| Cayuga | 226 | 1 896 | 18 264 | 16.9 | 51.1 | 18.3 | 159.3 | 15 749 | 23 990 | 50 140 | -0.9 | 1.4 | 47 875 | 14.0 | 21.0 | 19.2 |
| Chautauqua | 221 | 2 475 | 33 390 | 8.4 | 49.4 | 20.5 | 328.6 | 15 607 | 21 325 | 41 432 | -8.3 | 0.8 | 40 782 | 19.8 | 30.9 | 28.6 |
| Chemung | 198 | 2 355 | 21 510 | 17.3 | 48.9 | 20.8 | 190.2 | 15 176 | 24 299 | 46 589 | -5.2 | 2.4 | 47 994 | 16.4 | 24.2 | 22.5 |
| Chenango | 134 | 2 043 | 11 931 | 6.8 | 54.0 | 17.5 | 145.0 | 16 899 | 22 786 | 44 662 | -1.8 | 1.4 | 40 693 | 16.6 | 26.0 | 22.9 |
| Clinton | 90 | 1 956 | 20 638 | 8.7 | 52.9 | 21.5 | 207.9 | 17 808 | 23 446 | 49 260 | -1.5 | 1.8 | 49 025 | 15.5 | 19.9 | 18.1 |
| Columbia | 134 | 1 747 | 13 803 | 17.0 | 43.5 | 28.4 | 154.7 | 19 413 | 32 259 | 56 185 | -0.7 | 4.4 | 53 500 | 10.4 | 16.7 | 14.8 |
| Cortland | 149 | 2 076 | 15 530 | 7.4 | 46.3 | 24.0 | 106.0 | 15 394 | 22 322 | 45 956 | -1.0 | 1.2 | 44 397 | 17.7 | 22.3 | 20.8 |
| Delaware | 160 | 1 537 | 10 493 | 8.3 | 51.6 | 18.8 | 130.6 | 19 494 | 23 120 | 43 554 | -0.6 | 1.1 | 38 208 | 17.1 | 26.7 | 25.4 |
| Dutchess | 211 | 1 697 | 84 317 | 28.3 | 40.0 | 32.0 | 757.7 | 16 579 | 32 353 | 71 125 | -0.8 | 6.0 | 67 153 | 10.1 | 11.5 | 10.8 |
| Erie | 455 | 2 942 | 244 719 | 18.7 | 40.5 | 29.8 | 1 888.2 | 14 146 | 27 366 | 48 805 | -6.3 | 3.1 | 47 505 | 15.3 | 22.6 | 19.2 |
| Essex | 124 | 1 520 | 8 068 | 15.2 | 46.2 | 24.8 | 86.6 | 20 781 | 24 915 | 46 629 | -0.8 | 1.9 | 45 668 | 14.6 | 21.6 | 19.8 |
| Franklin | 112 | 1 696 | 10 794 | 14.7 | 55.8 | 17.4 | 139.8 | 17 353 | 20 831 | 43 673 | 2.6 | 1.3 | 40 092 | 20.7 | 29.4 | 26.8 |
| Fulton | 109 | 2 775 | 12 368 | 7.1 | 55.8 | 14.9 | 124.7 | 13 707 | 23 606 | 45 289 | -0.4 | 1.4 | 46 976 | 16.6 | 25.3 | 23.6 |

1. Data for serious crimes have not been adjusted for underreporting; this may affect comparability between geographic areas and over time.  2. Per 100,000 population estimated by the FBI.  3. All persons 3 years old and over enrolled in nursery school through college.  4. Persons 25 years old and over.  5. Elementary and secondary education expenditures.  6. Based on population estimated by the American Community Survey, 2007–2011.  7. Bronx, Kings, Queens, and Richmond counties are included with New York county.

# Table B. States and Counties — Personal Income

| | Personal income, 2011 | | | | | | | | | | | | |
|---|---|---|---|---|---|---|---|---|---|---|---|---|---|
| | | | Per capita[1] | | | | | | Transfer payments (mil dol) | | | | |
| | | | | | | | | | | Government payments to individuals | | | |
| STATE County | Total (mil dol) | Percent change, 2010–2011 | Dollars | Rank | Wages and salaries[2] (mil dol) | Proprietors' income (mil dol) | Dividends, interest, and rent (mil dol) | Total | Total | Social Security | Medical payments | Income mainte-nance | Unemploy-ment insurance |
| | 62 | 63 | 64 | 65 | 66 | 67 | 68 | 69 | 70 | 71 | 72 | 73 | 74 |
| **NEW JERSEY—Cont'd** | | | | | | | | | | | | | |
| Mercer | 19 985 | 4.6 | 54 445 | 122 | 17 518 | 1 965 | 3 178 | 3 086 | 3 005 | 926 | 1 362 | 317 | 239 |
| Middlesex | 40 062 | 4.5 | 49 203 | 228 | 29 226 | 3 165 | 5 189 | 5 555 | 5 375 | 1 814 | 2 185 | 415 | 544 |
| Monmouth | 36 823 | 3.5 | 58 355 | 82 | 15 845 | 2 828 | 6 463 | 4 795 | 4 656 | 1 709 | 1 964 | 291 | 424 |
| Morris | 35 504 | 3.9 | 71 730 | 20 | 24 678 | 4 496 | 6 173 | 3 165 | 3 055 | 1 275 | 1 205 | 119 | 283 |
| Ocean | 23 594 | 3.5 | 40 724 | 685 | 7 737 | 1 466 | 4 224 | 5 738 | 5 609 | 2 227 | 2 400 | 288 | 397 |
| Passaic | 21 691 | 5.1 | 43 209 | 494 | 10 936 | 1 403 | 2 913 | 4 255 | 4 144 | 1 073 | 1 839 | 613 | 404 |
| Salem | 2 692 | 3.9 | 40 847 | 671 | 1 508 | 152 | 360 | 647 | 633 | 204 | 289 | 60 | 51 |
| Somerset | 23 721 | 4.3 | 73 011 | 17 | 16 850 | 2 287 | 4 042 | 1 914 | 1 843 | 764 | 667 | 104 | 190 |
| Sussex | 7 393 | 3.3 | 49 782 | 211 | 1 997 | 431 | 977 | 1 008 | 975 | 387 | 366 | 49 | 113 |
| Union | 27 978 | 5.1 | 51 860 | 165 | 17 469 | 2 128 | 4 449 | 4 125 | 4 006 | 1 197 | 1 737 | 398 | 396 |
| Warren | 4 868 | 4.0 | 44 938 | 395 | 2 107 | 233 | 679 | 850 | 826 | 299 | 352 | 52 | 74 |
| **NEW MEXICO** | 71 073 | 4.4 | 34 133 | X | 43 700 | 5 318 | 10 591 | 15 990 | 15 532 | 4 526 | 6 671 | 2 224 | 640 |
| Bernalillo | 24 311 | 3.6 | 36 233 | 1 183 | 18 337 | 1 526 | 3 801 | 4 831 | 4 683 | 1 410 | 1 951 | 609 | 213 |
| Catron | 109 | 10.1 | 29 113 | 2 436 | 30 | 20 | 22 | 34 | 33 | 16 | 11 | 3 | 1 |
| Chaves | 1 998 | 4.7 | 30 319 | 2 235 | 933 | 311 | 291 | 549 | 534 | 148 | 249 | 92 | 17 |
| Cibola | 718 | 3.6 | 25 965 | 2 885 | 374 | 27 | 70 | 231 | 225 | 56 | 104 | 35 | 8 |
| Colfax | 469 | 7.5 | 34 359 | 1 462 | 218 | 68 | 84 | 134 | 131 | 44 | 57 | 15 | 5 |
| Curry | 1 978 | 10.1 | 39 844 | 764 | 1 197 | 319 | 230 | 381 | 370 | 82 | 170 | 62 | 10 |
| De Baca | 73 | 12.9 | 37 454 | 1 032 | 21 | 16 | 13 | 21 | 21 | 6 | 10 | 2 | 0 |
| Dona Ana | 6 400 | 3.3 | 29 963 | 2 295 | 3 443 | 532 | 833 | 1 631 | 1 584 | 389 | 681 | 290 | 66 |
| Eddy | 2 249 | 2.2 | 41 539 | 614 | 1 572 | 240 | 238 | 442 | 430 | 133 | 206 | 58 | 12 |
| Grant | 965 | 8.0 | 32 854 | 1 732 | 471 | 47 | 164 | 333 | 327 | 107 | 144 | 39 | 9 |
| Guadalupe | 122 | 6.3 | 26 426 | 2 834 | 50 | 17 | 13 | 50 | 49 | 10 | 26 | 7 | 2 |
| Harding | 34 | 25.8 | 48 067 | 267 | 9 | 15 | 5 | 6 | 6 | 2 | 2 | 0 | 0 |
| Hidalgo | 158 | 5.5 | 32 425 | 1 796 | 90 | 15 | 18 | 49 | 48 | 13 | 23 | 8 | 2 |
| Lea | 2 479 | 10.7 | 37 898 | 987 | 1 733 | 271 | 231 | 459 | 445 | 116 | 231 | 60 | 14 |
| Lincoln | 661 | 4.6 | 32 309 | 1 821 | 260 | 70 | 147 | 191 | 186 | 74 | 76 | 19 | 6 |
| Los Alamos | 1 106 | 3.6 | 60 719 | 62 | 1 552 | 41 | 181 | 81 | 77 | 38 | 28 | 2 | 3 |
| Luna | 742 | 3.4 | 29 338 | 2 402 | 351 | 79 | 90 | 260 | 254 | 75 | 103 | 42 | 20 |
| McKinley | 1 774 | 3.1 | 24 079 | 3 026 | 1 002 | 35 | 174 | 607 | 591 | 92 | 262 | 144 | 23 |
| Mora | 133 | 3.7 | 27 908 | 2 627 | 33 | 8 | 18 | 58 | 57 | 15 | 25 | 9 | 3 |
| Otero | 1 981 | 6.0 | 30 154 | 2 259 | 1 290 | 104 | 295 | 461 | 447 | 142 | 179 | 56 | 16 |
| Quay | 301 | 6.5 | 33 385 | 1 630 | 118 | 47 | 41 | 107 | 105 | 30 | 47 | 14 | 3 |
| Rio Arriba | 1 168 | 1.6 | 28 888 | 2 469 | 432 | 69 | 130 | 389 | 380 | 99 | 181 | 56 | 15 |
| Roosevelt | 666 | 7.7 | 32 595 | 1 781 | 273 | 121 | 73 | 169 | 165 | 35 | 75 | 24 | 4 |
| Sandoval | 4 421 | 5.6 | 32 931 | 1 719 | 1 719 | 138 | 575 | 850 | 820 | 300 | 308 | 86 | 44 |
| San Juan | 4 022 | 5.7 | 31 373 | 2 024 | 2 811 | 251 | 488 | 863 | 835 | 234 | 359 | 117 | 40 |
| San Miguel | 919 | 2.5 | 31 366 | 2 027 | 358 | 70 | 99 | 341 | 335 | 71 | 169 | 55 | 10 |
| Santa Fe | 6 310 | 4.2 | 43 325 | 481 | 3 373 | 514 | 1 594 | 1 023 | 991 | 388 | 390 | 98 | 41 |
| Sierra | 394 | 3.5 | 32 974 | 1 711 | 125 | 43 | 69 | 162 | 160 | 52 | 70 | 20 | 3 |
| Socorro | 544 | 4.5 | 30 462 | 2 207 | 271 | 51 | 63 | 164 | 160 | 37 | 68 | 36 | 5 |
| Taos | 1 024 | 3.9 | 31 119 | 2 076 | 428 | 110 | 207 | 310 | 303 | 92 | 131 | 43 | 15 |
| Torrance | 498 | 3.6 | 30 439 | 2 214 | 132 | 32 | 47 | 148 | 145 | 39 | 61 | 26 | 6 |
| Union | 115 | 7.3 | 25 986 | 2 881 | 56 | 0 | 24 | 36 | 35 | 12 | 17 | 4 | 1 |
| Valencia | 2 229 | 3.5 | 28 921 | 2 464 | 637 | 110 | 262 | 618 | 601 | 169 | 257 | 93 | 25 |
| **NEW YORK** | 995 185 | 4.5 | 51 126 | X | 662 290 | 107 108 | 161 174 | 182 843 | 178 541 | 45 840 | 93 403 | 22 178 | 7 544 |
| Albany | 14 657 | 3.5 | 48 284 | 261 | 14 340 | 1 494 | 2 643 | 2 700 | 2 633 | 795 | 994 | 257 | 106 |
| Allegany | 1 376 | 4.1 | 28 206 | 2 588 | 626 | 89 | 197 | 407 | 396 | 135 | 167 | 47 | 20 |
| Bronx | 44 249 | 3.9 | 31 788 | 1 935 | 14 200 | 3 047 | 4 081 | 15 208 | 14 900 | 2 106 | 8 899 | 2 822 | 647 |
| Broome | 7 158 | 3.5 | 35 963 | 1 215 | 4 574 | 440 | 1 301 | 1 804 | 1 760 | 615 | 759 | 219 | 77 |
| Cattaraugus | 2 770 | 3.9 | 34 696 | 1 420 | 1 487 | 213 | 374 | 804 | 786 | 235 | 301 | 75 | 34 |
| Cayuga | 2 716 | 4.0 | 34 061 | 1 501 | 1 275 | 235 | 376 | 644 | 627 | 218 | 267 | 66 | 30 |
| Chautauqua | 4 255 | 3.5 | 31 664 | 1 964 | 2 321 | 258 | 645 | 1 278 | 1 248 | 414 | 538 | 174 | 49 |
| Chemung | 3 155 | 3.8 | 35 517 | 1 287 | 2 044 | 155 | 471 | 811 | 792 | 271 | 347 | 95 | 31 |
| Chenango | 1 696 | 5.4 | 33 838 | 1 543 | 852 | 120 | 260 | 441 | 430 | 157 | 180 | 50 | 20 |
| Clinton | 2 789 | 0.8 | 34 029 | 1 505 | 1 681 | 198 | 382 | 694 | 676 | 223 | 288 | 82 | 37 |
| Columbia | 2 628 | 4.4 | 42 007 | 569 | 976 | 189 | 571 | 570 | 556 | 205 | 238 | 50 | 22 |
| Cortland | 1 578 | 4.3 | 31 972 | 1 894 | 835 | 129 | 239 | 379 | 368 | 121 | 164 | 46 | 20 |
| Delaware | 1 540 | 3.4 | 32 373 | 1 808 | 761 | 150 | 299 | 405 | 395 | 149 | 172 | 37 | 18 |
| Dutchess | 13 565 | 4.7 | 45 521 | 366 | 7 040 | 634 | 2 261 | 2 230 | 2 164 | 811 | 931 | 169 | 105 |
| Erie | 37 864 | 4.3 | 41 245 | 639 | 25 126 | 2 738 | 6 054 | 8 257 | 8 054 | 2 719 | 3 428 | 968 | 358 |
| Essex | 1 347 | 3.2 | 34 381 | 1 454 | 689 | 89 | 283 | 353 | 345 | 121 | 163 | 28 | 16 |
| Franklin | 1 536 | 3.1 | 29 794 | 2 323 | 951 | 89 | 214 | 422 | 410 | 133 | 182 | 49 | 20 |
| Fulton | 1 960 | 3.4 | 35 529 | 1 285 | 853 | 141 | 267 | 555 | 542 | 170 | 257 | 61 | 26 |

1. Based on the resident population estimated as of July 1 of the year shown.   2. Includes supplements to wages and salaries.

**468   NJ(Mercer)—NY(Fulton)**

Items 62—74

# Table B. States and Counties — **Earnings, Social Security, and Housing**

| STATE County | Earnings, 2011 | | | | | | | | | Social Security beneficiaries, December 2011 | | | Housing units, 2010 | |
|---|---|---|---|---|---|---|---|---|---|---|---|---|---|---|
| | | | | Percent by selected industries | | | | | | | | Supplemental Security Income recipients, December 2011 | | |
| | | | Goods-related[1] | | Service-related and health | | | | | | | | | |
| | Total (mil dol) | Farm | Total | Manufacturing | Information and professional and technical services | Retail trade | Finance, insurance, and real estate | Health care and social services | Government | Number | Rate[2] | | Total | Percent change, 2000–2010 |
| | 75 | 76 | 77 | 78 | 79 | 80 | 81 | 82 | 83 | 84 | 85 | 86 | 87 | 88 |
| **NEW JERSEY—Cont'd** | | | | | | | | | | | | | | |
| Mercer | 19 483 | 0.0 | 8.0 | 5.1 | 19.8 | 3.9 | 12.8 | 9.5 | 22.4 | 63 800 | 174 | 8 983 | 143 169 | 7.4 |
| Middlesex | 32 391 | 0.0 | 14.1 | 9.8 | 18.1 | 5.6 | 7.8 | 8.2 | 14.1 | 121 730 | 150 | 12 274 | 294 800 | 7.7 |
| Monmouth | 18 673 | 0.2 | 11.7 | 3.9 | 18.3 | 8.2 | 9.5 | 14.7 | 15.6 | 112 280 | 178 | 7 670 | 258 410 | 7.3 |
| Morris | 29 175 | 0.0 | D | 11.7 | 19.7 | 6.0 | 12.8 | 8.6 | 9.2 | 79 860 | 161 | 4 290 | 189 842 | 8.9 |
| Ocean | 9 204 | 0.0 | 12.3 | 3.2 | 7.0 | 11.3 | 5.2 | 20.5 | 21.9 | 151 175 | 261 | 6 602 | 278 052 | 11.8 |
| Passaic | 12 339 | 0.0 | 18.2 | 12.3 | 8.0 | 8.5 | 5.8 | 12.7 | 18.3 | 78 050 | 155 | 14 532 | 175 966 | 3.5 |
| Salem | 1 660 | 2.5 | 25.1 | 16.0 | 5.0 | 4.6 | 2.2 | 9.8 | 17.2 | 14 515 | 220 | 1 587 | 27 417 | 4.8 |
| Somerset | 19 137 | 0.0 | 16.2 | 12.8 | 24.2 | 5.5 | 10.8 | 6.5 | 7.2 | 47 880 | 147 | 2 925 | 123 127 | 9.9 |
| Sussex | 2 428 | -0.1 | 14.9 | 5.9 | 9.6 | 10.2 | 3.8 | 15.2 | 21.9 | 25 830 | 174 | 1 624 | 62 057 | 9.8 |
| Union | 19 597 | 0.0 | D | 14.3 | 14.8 | 6.1 | 6.4 | 10.4 | 13.2 | 82 635 | 153 | 10 149 | 199 489 | 3.4 |
| Warren | 2 341 | 0.7 | D | 24.7 | 5.4 | 9.2 | 2.2 | 13.0 | 16.7 | 20 385 | 188 | 1 340 | 44 925 | 9.2 |
| **NEW MEXICO** | 49 018 | 2.5 | 14.8 | 4.5 | 12.1 | 6.7 | 4.6 | 11.2 | 28.0 | 370 911 | 178 | 61 806 | 901 388 | 15.5 |
| Bernalillo | 19 863 | 0.0 | 10.7 | 4.3 | 16.3 | 6.7 | 5.7 | 12.5 | 26.9 | 109 960 | 164 | 16 367 | 284 234 | 19.0 |
| Catron | 50 | 29.0 | 5.7 | 1.3 | D | D | D | D | 38.6 | 1 320 | 354 | 73 | 3 289 | 29.1 |
| Chaves | 1 244 | 12.8 | 16.2 | 4.9 | 5.5 | 8.8 | 3.5 | 15.0 | 19.7 | 12 680 | 192 | 2 302 | 26 697 | 4.1 |
| Cibola | 401 | 1.3 | D | 0.8 | D | 7.6 | 1.8 | D | 40.9 | 4 690 | 170 | 955 | 11 101 | 7.5 |
| Colfax | 286 | 14.0 | D | 2.1 | 4.0 | 7.8 | 5.3 | D | 28.2 | 3 565 | 261 | 429 | 10 023 | 11.9 |
| Curry | 1 516 | 17.3 | D | 2.8 | D | 4.9 | 2.3 | 8.5 | 41.5 | 7 200 | 145 | 1 625 | 20 062 | 4.4 |
| De Baca | 37 | 42.3 | D | D | D | 5.7 | D | 6.1 | 24.5 | 570 | 293 | 85 | 1 344 | 2.8 |
| Dona Ana | 3 974 | 4.9 | 9.9 | 4.5 | 8.2 | 5.9 | 3.4 | 13.7 | 34.6 | 34 360 | 161 | 7 422 | 81 492 | 25.0 |
| Eddy | 1 813 | 1.7 | 41.4 | 5.9 | D | 4.9 | 4.1 | 7.7 | 14.8 | 10 490 | 194 | 1 434 | 22 585 | 1.5 |
| Grant | 518 | 1.5 | 27.6 | 0.8 | 3.2 | 6.9 | 2.3 | 8.6 | 36.1 | 8 460 | 288 | 905 | 14 693 | 4.5 |
| Guadalupe | 67 | 22.4 | D | D | D | 9.9 | D | 10.0 | 30.6 | 1 065 | 231 | 287 | 2 393 | 10.8 |
| Harding | 24 | 56.7 | D | D | D | D | D | 0.0 | 19.5 | 215 | 305 | 0 | 526 | -3.5 |
| Hidalgo | 104 | 10.8 | D | D | 3.1 | 5.1 | D | 4.8 | 54.6 | 1 150 | 237 | 166 | 2 393 | -16.0 |
| Lea | 2 004 | 3.2 | 44.5 | 5.2 | 3.5 | 5.5 | 4.3 | 5.3 | 9.8 | 9 275 | 142 | 1 512 | 24 919 | 6.5 |
| Lincoln | 330 | 4.3 | D | 1.1 | 6.9 | 11.0 | 6.5 | 10.6 | 20.8 | 5 660 | 277 | 369 | 17 519 | 14.5 |
| Los Alamos | 1 593 | 0.0 | D | D | 75.6 | 0.9 | 2.0 | 3.3 | 7.7 | 2 835 | 156 | 0 | 8 354 | 5.2 |
| Luna | 430 | 8.8 | D | 8.2 | D | 11.2 | 1.9 | D | 37.3 | 6 935 | 274 | 1 383 | 10 999 | -2.6 |
| McKinley | 1 037 | -0.2 | D | 4.1 | 2.2 | 9.5 | 2.3 | 11.8 | 48.2 | 9 500 | 129 | 4 476 | 25 813 | -3.4 |
| Mora | 41 | 11.3 | D | D | D | 5.2 | 1.5 | D | 39.5 | 1 415 | 296 | 367 | 3 232 | 8.7 |
| Otero | 1 393 | 1.9 | 5.7 | 0.5 | 4.8 | 5.2 | 2.1 | 8.9 | 61.1 | 12 270 | 187 | 1 712 | 30 992 | 5.9 |
| Quay | 166 | 23.0 | D | D | 1.2 | 8.0 | 3.4 | 8.5 | 27.2 | 2 665 | 295 | 426 | 5 569 | -1.7 |
| Rio Arriba | 502 | 3.4 | 7.1 | 1.7 | D | 7.7 | 2.6 | 13.3 | 47.3 | 9 015 | 223 | 1 602 | 19 638 | 9.0 |
| Roosevelt | 394 | 29.8 | D | 4.8 | 2.3 | 5.8 | 2.4 | D | 28.4 | 3 040 | 149 | 652 | 8 163 | 5.4 |
| Sandoval | 1 858 | 0.2 | 36.1 | 28.9 | 6.8 | 6.2 | 4.0 | 4.1 | 21.8 | 23 015 | 171 | 2 570 | 52 287 | 48.8 |
| San Juan | 3 061 | 0.2 | 32.1 | 2.6 | 2.7 | 7.2 | 3.4 | 11.5 | 21.0 | 19 345 | 151 | 4 067 | 49 341 | 14.2 |
| San Miguel | 428 | 6.0 | D | 0.6 | 2.8 | 6.9 | 2.9 | D | 48.2 | 6 635 | 226 | 1 845 | 15 595 | 9.4 |
| Santa Fe | 3 887 | 0.0 | 7.5 | 1.4 | 10.2 | 9.2 | 8.2 | 13.9 | 29.5 | 29 065 | 200 | 2 759 | 71 267 | 23.5 |
| Sierra | 169 | 15.1 | D | 1.6 | 3.8 | 7.6 | 3.0 | D | 29.7 | 4 415 | 370 | 583 | 8 356 | -4.2 |
| Socorro | 322 | 11.4 | D | 2.2 | 8.7 | 4.8 | 2.5 | 9.7 | 48.1 | 3 400 | 190 | 1 091 | 8 059 | 3.2 |
| Taos | 539 | 0.6 | 13.2 | 0.9 | D | 12.0 | 5.3 | 16.9 | 22.3 | 7 985 | 243 | 1 128 | 20 265 | 16.4 |
| Torrance | 164 | 11.5 | D | 3.3 | D | 9.2 | 2.1 | 5.4 | 33.8 | 3 370 | 206 | 585 | 7 798 | 7.5 |
| Union | 56 | -2.4 | D | D | D | 8.0 | D | D | 32.4 | 1 005 | 227 | 113 | 2 305 | 3.6 |
| Valencia | 747 | 4.4 | 11.5 | 4.6 | D | 9.4 | 3.3 | 12.5 | 29.1 | 14 340 | 186 | 2 431 | 30 085 | 22.1 |
| **NEW YORK** | 769 398 | 0.2 | 9.0 | 4.8 | 16.7 | 5.0 | 20.5 | 10.9 | 15.0 | 3 337 276 | 171 | 689 019 | 8 108 103 | 5.6 |
| Albany | 15 834 | 0.0 | 9.5 | 3.6 | 12.8 | 5.7 | 9.3 | 11.5 | 31.4 | 56 905 | 187 | 7 737 | 137 739 | 6.0 |
| Allegany | 716 | 1.7 | 26.7 | 18.9 | 2.9 | 6.0 | 1.7 | 7.6 | 29.5 | 10 800 | 221 | 1 556 | 26 140 | 6.7 |
| Bronx | 17 247 | 0.0 | D | 2.3 | 5.6 | 6.2 | 6.8 | 29.5 | 13.2 | 180 905 | 130 | 107 114 | 511 896 | 4.3 |
| Broome | 5 014 | 0.2 | 20.6 | 14.4 | 6.9 | 7.2 | 5.0 | 16.9 | 23.6 | 46 525 | 234 | 6 935 | 90 563 | 2.0 |
| Cattaraugus | 1 700 | 1.5 | 19.9 | 16.0 | 3.2 | 8.6 | 2.8 | 12.9 | 33.8 | 18 755 | 235 | 2 670 | 41 111 | 3.2 |
| Cayuga | 1 510 | 6.7 | D | 14.6 | 4.7 | 7.9 | 2.1 | 13.2 | 25.8 | 16 605 | 208 | 1 994 | 36 489 | 2.9 |
| Chautauqua | 2 579 | 1.9 | 28.8 | 23.5 | 3.7 | 8.3 | 2.8 | 13.1 | 22.4 | 32 165 | 239 | 4 957 | 66 920 | 3.1 |
| Chemung | 2 199 | 0.2 | 26.9 | 18.5 | 4.1 | 7.4 | 3.8 | 16.0 | 20.9 | 20 950 | 236 | 3 549 | 38 369 | 1.7 |
| Chenango | 972 | 2.9 | D | 23.9 | 5.1 | 7.0 | 9.6 | 8.4 | 23.6 | 12 545 | 250 | 1 736 | 24 710 | 3.4 |
| Clinton | 1 879 | 2.4 | D | 11.0 | 3.7 | 9.3 | 2.3 | 16.8 | 31.0 | 17 785 | 217 | 3 083 | 35 888 | 8.5 |
| Columbia | 1 165 | 1.7 | D | 6.2 | 7.3 | 8.2 | 3.8 | 17.8 | 24.6 | 14 990 | 240 | 1 659 | 32 775 | 8.5 |
| Cortland | 964 | 1.9 | 25.3 | 20.4 | 6.6 | 7.9 | 4.1 | 13.2 | 21.0 | 9 535 | 193 | 1 337 | 20 577 | 2.3 |
| Delaware | 911 | 2.0 | 34.1 | 26.8 | 3.9 | 7.9 | 3.9 | D | 24.3 | 11 565 | 243 | 1 212 | 31 222 | 7.8 |
| Dutchess | 7 674 | 0.1 | 23.4 | 17.9 | 7.0 | 6.5 | 4.7 | 14.8 | 21.9 | 55 665 | 187 | 5 556 | 118 638 | 11.8 |
| Erie | 27 864 | 0.1 | 17.3 | 12.2 | 10.0 | 6.3 | 8.1 | 13.4 | 19.4 | 198 980 | 217 | 29 537 | 419 974 | 1.0 |
| Essex | 778 | 0.1 | 18.7 | 8.3 | 4.0 | 7.7 | 3.1 | 12.0 | 34.2 | 9 290 | 237 | 1 049 | 25 603 | 10.8 |
| Franklin | 1 040 | 2.3 | D | 2.0 | D | 6.7 | 1.9 | 16.5 | 50.7 | 11 055 | 214 | 1 921 | 25 306 | 5.7 |
| Fulton | 994 | 0.2 | D | 8.7 | 5.4 | 9.2 | 3.2 | 17.6 | 26.9 | 13 560 | 246 | 2 169 | 28 562 | 2.8 |

1. Includes mining, construction, and manufacturing.   2. Per 1,000 resident population enumerated in the 2010 census.

| | Housing units, 2007–2011 | | | | | | | | Civilian labor force, 2012 | | | | Civilian employment,[6] 2007–2011 | | |
|---|---|---|---|---|---|---|---|---|---|---|---|---|---|---|---|
| | Occupied units | | | | | | | | | | Unemployment | | | Percent | |
| | | | Owner-occupied | | | Renter-occupied | | | | | | | | | | |
| STATE County | Total | Percent | Median value[1] | Median owner cost as a percent of income | | Median rent[3] | Median rent as a percent of income | Sub-standard units[4] (percent) | Total | Percent change, 2011–2012 | Total | Rate[5] | Total | Manage-ment, business, science and arts | Con-struction, produc-tion, and mainte-nance occu-pations |
| | | | | With a mort-gage | Without a mort-gage[2] | | | | | | | | | | |
| | 89 | 90 | 91 | 92 | 93 | 94 | 95 | 96 | 97 | 98 | 99 | 100 | 101 | 102 | 103 |
| NEW JERSEY—Cont'd | | | | | | | | | | | | | | | |
| Mercer | 129 933 | 67.5 | 302 100 | 25.9 | 16.9 | 1 083 | 30.7 | 2.9 | 210 019 | 1.5 | 16 472 | 7.8 | 175 761 | 42.9 | 15.3 |
| Middlesex | 278 513 | 66.6 | 349 000 | 28.1 | 18.2 | 1 216 | 28.5 | 3.9 | 443 880 | 1.6 | 37 730 | 8.5 | 395 255 | 42.8 | 17.9 |
| Monmouth | 233 120 | 75.7 | 413 500 | 28.6 | 18.3 | 1 178 | 33.4 | 2.2 | 334 808 | 1.8 | 29 904 | 8.9 | 307 983 | 42.8 | 15.4 |
| Morris | 179 581 | 76.1 | 463 200 | 27.3 | 17.0 | 1 256 | 28.0 | 1.9 | 275 962 | 1.1 | 20 055 | 7.3 | 252 188 | 49.0 | 13.0 |
| Ocean | 222 863 | 81.9 | 284 100 | 30.0 | 20.3 | 1 293 | 38.8 | 2.2 | 272 069 | 1.7 | 27 944 | 10.3 | 242 504 | 34.0 | 20.4 |
| Passaic | 161 488 | 55.4 | 372 700 | 32.4 | 22.5 | 1 115 | 36.8 | 10.6 | 246 789 | 1.0 | 27 819 | 11.3 | 227 892 | 31.0 | 24.8 |
| Salem | 25 004 | 73.0 | 198 800 | 26.8 | 18.1 | 929 | 33.6 | 1.4 | 31 455 | -0.1 | 3 457 | 11.0 | 29 657 | 31.8 | 29.1 |
| Somerset | 114 348 | 79.3 | 420 500 | 27.2 | 17.2 | 1 379 | 29.1 | 1.9 | 183 366 | 1.7 | 13 611 | 7.4 | 163 764 | 51.3 | 13.7 |
| Sussex | 55 554 | 85.1 | 312 500 | 28.9 | 18.8 | 1 148 | 36.1 | 1.3 | 83 502 | 0.7 | 7 570 | 9.1 | 76 959 | 37.7 | 20.3 |
| Union | 184 584 | 61.3 | 386 000 | 29.8 | 20.4 | 1 119 | 31.8 | 9.6 | 278 307 | 0.8 | 26 889 | 9.7 | 258 459 | 35.4 | 22.2 |
| Warren | 41 685 | 75.9 | 294 000 | 28.3 | 18.9 | 968 | 31.7 | 1.3 | 59 614 | 0.8 | 4 889 | 8.2 | 54 067 | 37.1 | 21.4 |
| NEW MEXICO | 762 002 | 69.6 | 161 800 | 23.6 | 9.9 | 713 | 29.5 | 4.5 | 935 890 | 0.5 | 64 591 | 6.9 | 886 857 | 34.7 | 21.8 |
| Bernalillo | 261 525 | 64.4 | 191 400 | 24.2 | 10.1 | 741 | 29.9 | 2.8 | 304 440 | 0.0 | 21 665 | 7.1 | 311 433 | 39.4 | 17.3 |
| Catron | 1 786 | 86.8 | 154 600 | 26.8 | 9.9 | 653 | 35.9 | 2.8 | 1 566 | 3.0 | 108 | 6.9 | 1 353 | 21.8 | 32.4 |
| Chaves | 23 740 | 68.4 | 90 000 | 21.0 | 9.9 | 590 | 28.8 | 4.4 | 26 313 | -1.7 | 1 728 | 6.6 | 27 233 | 26.6 | 28.1 |
| Cibola | 8 037 | 71.3 | 81 300 | 19.1 | 9.9 | 534 | 22.5 | 9.4 | 12 321 | 1.5 | 770 | 6.2 | 8 648 | 22.0 | 28.8 |
| Colfax | 5 781 | 66.0 | 108 200 | 25.4 | 9.9 | 570 | 27.9 | 1.9 | 6 421 | -1.7 | 486 | 7.6 | 6 090 | 29.4 | 23.6 |
| Curry | 17 498 | 62.6 | 104 400 | 21.2 | 10.6 | 568 | 28.7 | 2.7 | 21 720 | 1.3 | 1 037 | 4.8 | 20 654 | 26.8 | 28.9 |
| De Baca | 832 | 79.4 | 74 700 | 22.8 | 11.3 | 386 | 27.8 | 3.6 | 798 | -0.6 | 34 | 4.3 | 746 | 37.7 | 28.2 |
| Dona Ana | 72 748 | 66.1 | 141 900 | 23.8 | 11.3 | 657 | 33.7 | 4.4 | 93 195 | 0.9 | 6 653 | 7.1 | 85 170 | 32.2 | 22.0 |
| Eddy | 19 557 | 74.8 | 96 200 | 17.7 | 9.9 | 646 | 24.0 | 3.8 | 30 099 | 2.4 | 1 224 | 4.1 | 24 156 | 30.0 | 30.9 |
| Grant | 12 367 | 75.6 | 133 000 | 22.9 | 9.9 | 561 | 28.9 | 2.4 | 12 157 | 2.9 | 844 | 6.9 | 12 021 | 36.9 | 23.7 |
| Guadalupe | 1 472 | 82.6 | 78 300 | 25.7 | 13.8 | 465 | 29.8 | 1.8 | 1 752 | -1.0 | 171 | 9.8 | 1 379 | 22.0 | 26.3 |
| Harding | 300 | 88.3 | 59 800 | 30.8 | 14.4 | 725 | 37.0 | 4.7 | 391 | 1.3 | 18 | 4.6 | 271 | 33.6 | 34.7 |
| Hidalgo | 1 621 | 66.7 | 90 500 | 15.9 | 9.9 | 419 | 24.9 | 4.8 | 2 632 | -0.8 | 166 | 6.3 | 2 075 | 31.8 | 24.9 |
| Lea | 21 238 | 70.5 | 93 900 | 19.3 | 9.9 | 690 | 25.1 | 7.2 | 30 822 | 5.4 | 1 310 | 4.3 | 26 252 | 26.8 | 37.3 |
| Lincoln | 9 108 | 78.1 | 168 900 | 23.3 | 11.3 | 744 | 24.9 | 4.1 | 10 385 | -1.1 | 566 | 5.5 | 9 512 | 30.7 | 22.7 |
| Los Alamos | 7 484 | 79.0 | 300 700 | 19.6 | 9.9 | 962 | 21.4 | 1.3 | 9 731 | -1.7 | 339 | 3.5 | 9 157 | 66.6 | 8.4 |
| Luna | 9 222 | 69.4 | 91 300 | 24.7 | 9.9 | 500 | 27.2 | 3.7 | 12 644 | 0.2 | 2 181 | 17.2 | 8 896 | 22.1 | 28.3 |
| McKinley | 17 263 | 72.4 | 72 200 | 21.4 | 9.9 | 524 | 21.3 | 20.7 | 26 577 | 0.5 | 2 310 | 8.7 | 24 125 | 25.4 | 26.5 |
| Mora | 1 791 | 83.7 | 105 700 | 19.1 | 9.9 | 583 | 28.6 | 8.2 | 1 929 | -1.0 | 251 | 13.0 | 2 269 | 35.6 | 27.1 |
| Otero | 24 375 | 67.2 | 105 900 | 21.1 | 10.8 | 638 | 26.9 | 3.9 | 26 198 | 1.8 | 1 609 | 6.1 | 23 438 | 28.4 | 25.3 |
| Quay | 3 686 | 76.8 | 68 800 | 23.5 | 11.5 | 579 | 27.7 | 3.0 | 3 800 | -0.3 | 263 | 6.9 | 3 344 | 30.3 | 27.7 |
| Rio Arriba | 14 987 | 80.2 | 134 300 | 21.8 | 9.9 | 639 | 24.1 | 6.3 | 18 647 | -2.0 | 1 498 | 8.0 | 16 879 | 32.1 | 23.0 |
| Roosevelt | 6 888 | 59.4 | 104 300 | 19.9 | 9.9 | 612 | 35.6 | 5.0 | 9 279 | 2.0 | 461 | 5.0 | 8 498 | 29.9 | 27.9 |
| Sandoval | 46 061 | 80.6 | 187 800 | 25.3 | 9.9 | 939 | 29.5 | 4.6 | 56 398 | -0.1 | 4 539 | 8.0 | 57 217 | 37.4 | 18.9 |
| San Juan | 42 215 | 74.5 | 154 200 | 20.8 | 9.9 | 704 | 24.5 | 10.3 | 56 035 | 0.8 | 3 836 | 6.8 | 52 807 | 25.9 | 31.8 |
| San Miguel | 12 010 | 67.0 | 118 000 | 25.7 | 12.6 | 609 | 31.2 | 2.5 | 13 138 | 1.0 | 949 | 7.2 | 11 013 | 34.2 | 20.9 |
| Santa Fe | 60 594 | 70.6 | 293 900 | 26.9 | 10.1 | 892 | 31.8 | 3.9 | 75 698 | 0.7 | 4 158 | 5.5 | 71 194 | 42.1 | 15.5 |
| Sierra | 4 338 | 78.5 | 105 100 | 23.7 | 13.1 | 487 | 31.1 | 1.0 | 5 911 | -0.1 | 367 | 6.2 | 3 269 | 29.3 | 19.6 |
| Socorro | 5 694 | 75.6 | 115 900 | 23.3 | 11.8 | 545 | 32.2 | 2.0 | 9 345 | 1.6 | 457 | 4.9 | 6 140 | 37.5 | 23.4 |
| Taos | 13 014 | 74.5 | 214 000 | 25.2 | 9.9 | 752 | 33.8 | 6.1 | 16 656 | -1.6 | 1 520 | 9.1 | 14 482 | 34.1 | 19.5 |
| Torrance | 5 691 | 78.7 | 96 300 | 27.4 | 14.2 | 635 | 32.8 | 8.8 | 6 381 | -1.1 | 521 | 8.2 | 5 469 | 26.6 | 28.7 |
| Union | 1 690 | 73.3 | 96 900 | 22.3 | 12.9 | 600 | 19.6 | 2.9 | 1 878 | -2.0 | 87 | 4.6 | 1 907 | 37.6 | 27.9 |
| Valencia | 27 389 | 80.4 | 132 700 | 24.9 | 10.9 | 694 | 34.2 | 4.6 | 30 638 | -0.3 | 2 468 | 8.1 | 29 760 | 28.6 | 25.9 |
| NEW YORK | 7 215 687 | 54.8 | 301 000 | 26.3 | 15.4 | 1 025 | 31.3 | 5.3 | 9 587 184 | 0.6 | 814 645 | 8.5 | 9 051 668 | 38.2 | 17.4 |
| Albany | 123 544 | 59.5 | 207 300 | 22.7 | 13.0 | 880 | 29.0 | 1.5 | 155 153 | 0.7 | 11 473 | 7.4 | 154 119 | 43.1 | 13.3 |
| Allegany | 18 936 | 74.4 | 66 800 | 21.3 | 14.4 | 584 | 31.2 | 2.3 | 23 721 | -0.8 | 2 023 | 8.5 | 21 595 | 31.7 | 28.1 |
| Bronx | 471 923 | 20.1 | 391 300 | 32.9 | 13.0 | 966 | 33.5 | 12.0 | 551 847 | 1.3 | 69 848 | 12.7 | 543 122 | 24.0 | 19.0 |
| Broome | 80 257 | 66.7 | 103 100 | 20.7 | 13.6 | 645 | 31.0 | 1.9 | 92 438 | -1.1 | 8 179 | 8.8 | 91 564 | 36.0 | 19.6 |
| Cattaraugus | 32 440 | 72.5 | 78 400 | 22.6 | 13.8 | 617 | 29.5 | 2.5 | 39 991 | -0.9 | 3 577 | 8.9 | 36 037 | 28.5 | 27.9 |
| Cayuga | 31 807 | 72.2 | 100 200 | 21.8 | 14.3 | 643 | 26.7 | 1.8 | 40 557 | -0.1 | 3 300 | 8.1 | 37 547 | 29.4 | 29.7 |
| Chautauqua | 55 499 | 69.2 | 80 900 | 21.2 | 14.4 | 596 | 30.0 | 1.6 | 62 702 | -0.5 | 5 324 | 8.5 | 59 927 | 30.6 | 27.4 |
| Chemung | 35 528 | 67.1 | 89 400 | 19.2 | 13.3 | 673 | 29.8 | 1.2 | 39 964 | -1.0 | 3 462 | 8.7 | 38 820 | 33.2 | 22.3 |
| Chenango | 20 003 | 76.8 | 89 700 | 21.4 | 14.0 | 575 | 28.2 | 3.3 | 24 844 | 0.9 | 2 088 | 8.4 | 22 742 | 31.0 | 28.8 |
| Clinton | 31 527 | 69.3 | 119 600 | 22.2 | 13.3 | 693 | 29.9 | 2.2 | 37 692 | -1.2 | 3 716 | 9.9 | 36 937 | 32.4 | 23.1 |
| Columbia | 25 681 | 73.8 | 224 100 | 25.0 | 16.2 | 800 | 28.2 | 2.1 | 30 667 | 0.7 | 2 284 | 7.4 | 30 543 | 37.9 | 21.8 |
| Cortland | 17 915 | 66.2 | 98 400 | 23.2 | 14.4 | 668 | 28.2 | 2.8 | 24 324 | 0.3 | 2 141 | 8.8 | 22 625 | 33.0 | 21.5 |
| Delaware | 20 177 | 75.8 | 133 000 | 23.5 | 14.0 | 616 | 26.4 | 3.5 | 21 566 | -0.2 | 1 911 | 8.9 | 21 238 | 30.0 | 29.1 |
| Dutchess | 107 151 | 70.3 | 314 500 | 27.9 | 16.6 | 1 067 | 32.2 | 2.5 | 144 874 | -0.1 | 11 461 | 7.9 | 142 125 | 39.4 | 18.8 |
| Erie | 379 478 | 65.9 | 120 600 | 21.8 | 14.4 | 704 | 31.2 | 1.2 | 462 497 | 0.2 | 38 554 | 8.3 | 432 735 | 37.2 | 17.9 |
| Essex | 16 067 | 72.8 | 153 200 | 24.6 | 14.2 | 707 | 28.2 | 1.7 | 17 630 | -0.3 | 1 753 | 9.9 | 17 837 | 33.9 | 24.6 |
| Franklin | 18 940 | 72.1 | 91 400 | 21.8 | 13.6 | 630 | 30.1 | 3.1 | 22 256 | -0.6 | 2 159 | 9.7 | 20 808 | 31.8 | 22.5 |
| Fulton | 22 939 | 70.0 | 98 700 | 22.0 | 13.8 | 654 | 33.4 | 1.7 | 26 698 | -0.4 | 2 826 | 10.6 | 24 396 | 28.8 | 28.0 |

1. Specified owner-occupied units.   2. A value of 9.9 represents 9.9 percent or less.   3. Specified renter-occupied units. A value of 10.0 represents 10 percent or less.   4. Overcrowded or lacking complete plumbing facilities.   5. Percent of civilian labor force.   6. Persons 16 years old and over.

# Table B. States and Counties — Nonfarm Employment and Agriculture

| STATE County | Private nonfarm establishments, employment and payroll, 2011 | | | | | | | | | Agriculture, 2007 | | | |
| | Number of establish-ments | Employment | | | | | | Annual payroll | | Farms | | | |
| | | Total | Health care and social assistance | Manufac-turing | Retail trade | Finance and insurance | Professional, scientific, and technical services | Total (mil dol) | Average per employee (dollars) | Number | Percent with: | | Farm operators whose principal occupation is farming (percent) |
| | | | | | | | | | | | Fewer than 50 acres | 500 acres or more | |
| | 104 | 105 | 106 | 107 | 108 | 109 | 110 | 111 | 112 | 113 | 114 | 115 | 116 |
| **NEW JERSEY—Cont'd** | | | | | | | | | | | | | |
| Mercer | 9 615 | 177 336 | 29 150 | 6 704 | 19 037 | 14 006 | 20 014 | 10 705 | 60 363 | 311 | 70.7 | 2.3 | 40.8 |
| Middlesex | 21 095 | 361 453 | 45 395 | 28 917 | 37 477 | 13 679 | 45 984 | 20 695 | 57 256 | 236 | 78.4 | 3.8 | 44.9 |
| Monmouth | 18 625 | 217 076 | 39 705 | 8 601 | 37 739 | 10 918 | 20 332 | 10 056 | 46 327 | 932 | 86.4 | 2.4 | 47.7 |
| Morris | 16 622 | 272 926 | 33 013 | 14 575 | 28 958 | 17 620 | 37 191 | 19 013 | 69 662 | 422 | 82.0 | 1.7 | 37.4 |
| Ocean | 11 715 | 123 710 | 31 204 | 4 987 | 26 046 | 3 439 | 5 568 | 4 225 | 34 152 | 255 | 85.9 | 1.2 | 44.3 |
| Passaic | 11 550 | 147 536 | 24 777 | 19 824 | 22 472 | 5 063 | 7 089 | 6 781 | 45 965 | 103 | 94.2 | 0.0 | 41.7 |
| Salem | 1 174 | 18 222 | 3 273 | 2 910 | 1 913 | 478 | 409 | 932 | 51 163 | 759 | 61.7 | 7.0 | 52.2 |
| Somerset | 9 677 | 175 150 | 21 403 | 10 963 | 18 796 | 12 994 | 27 443 | 12 740 | 72 739 | 445 | 77.3 | 2.9 | 37.5 |
| Sussex | 3 316 | 30 616 | 6 207 | 1 823 | 5 540 | 1 291 | 1 730 | 1 122 | 36 644 | 1 060 | 73.3 | 1.9 | 40.6 |
| Union | 13 497 | 202 461 | 29 620 | 22 226 | 24 552 | 7 549 | 24 213 | 11 378 | 56 196 | 15 | 100.0 | 0.0 | 66.7 |
| Warren | 2 467 | 28 069 | 5 935 | 3 701 | 5 885 | 616 | 921 | 1 269 | 45 218 | 933 | 68.9 | 3.0 | 47.5 |
| **NEW MEXICO** | 43 860 | 597 568 | 110 555 | 27 434 | 94 946 | 22 169 | 47 649 | 22 038 | 36 879 | 20 930 | 52.0 | 23.1 | 48.0 |
| Bernalillo | 15 756 | 239 337 | 43 539 | 12 562 | 35 149 | 10 625 | 19 739 | 8 963 | 37 449 | 635 | 76.7 | 6.3 | 38.3 |
| Catron | 61 | 385 | 104 | 32 | D | D | D | 10 | 25 766 | 259 | 13.5 | 52.9 | 52.1 |
| Chaves | 1 419 | 16 653 | 3 775 | 1 031 | 3 297 | 630 | 921 | 505 | 30 328 | 584 | 35.8 | 36.6 | 50.2 |
| Cibola | 339 | 5 763 | 1 510 | D | 883 | D | D | 176 | 30 602 | 317 | 44.2 | 30.3 | 41.0 |
| Colfax | 472 | 3 847 | 600 | 133 | 720 | 155 | D | 106 | 27 489 | 302 | 12.3 | 50.7 | 60.3 |
| Curry | 1 069 | 12 759 | 2 351 | D | 2 605 | 458 | 551 | 341 | 26 720 | 681 | 18.5 | 41.7 | 42.9 |
| De Baca | 52 | 265 | D | D | 64 | D | D | 6 | 23 555 | 173 | 31.2 | 45.7 | 55.5 |
| Dona Ana | 3 630 | 49 011 | 12 400 | 2 329 | 7 981 | 1 705 | 3 924 | 1 410 | 28 765 | 1 762 | 80.5 | 5.6 | 41.4 |
| Eddy | 1 262 | 20 150 | 3 017 | 1 330 | 2 682 | 551 | 418 | 904 | 44 841 | 543 | 42.7 | 27.8 | 45.9 |
| Grant | 654 | 6 877 | 1 546 | 135 | 1 201 | 202 | 157 | 227 | 33 056 | 327 | 30.6 | 39.8 | 56.0 |
| Guadalupe | 101 | 1 087 | 79 | D | 285 | D | D | 23 | 21 379 | 258 | 15.9 | 57.8 | 52.3 |
| Harding | 10 | D | D | NA | D | D | NA | D | D | 168 | 3.0 | 70.8 | 56.0 |
| Hidalgo | 90 | 738 | 141 | D | 240 | D | D | 18 | 24 370 | 162 | 9.9 | 58.0 | 51.9 |
| Lea | 1 589 | 21 588 | 2 414 | D | 2 962 | 463 | 622 | 988 | 45 779 | 572 | 31.1 | 38.8 | 40.2 |
| Lincoln | 708 | 5 106 | D | 81 | 1 172 | 220 | 155 | 128 | 25 005 | 361 | 30.2 | 45.2 | 49.9 |
| Los Alamos | 366 | D | 920 | 34 | 457 | D | D | D | D | 7 | 100.0 | 0.0 | 57.1 |
| Luna | 410 | 4 492 | 873 | 617 | 1 081 | D | 92 | 112 | 25 004 | 206 | 26.7 | 33.5 | 59.7 |
| McKinley | 992 | 16 063 | 4 668 | D | 3 668 | 409 | 203 | 468 | 29 109 | 2 624 | 74.1 | 8.5 | 56.9 |
| Mora | 48 | 299 | 122 | D | D | 11 | D | 6 | 20 147 | 589 | 25.1 | 26.1 | 38.5 |
| Otero | 1 003 | 12 504 | 2 406 | 163 | 2 710 | 438 | 660 | 312 | 24 980 | 493 | 62.7 | 15.6 | 43.6 |
| Quay | 238 | 1 979 | D | 51 | 401 | 110 | 47 | 46 | 23 355 | 636 | 12.4 | 51.3 | 47.5 |
| Rio Arriba | 593 | 6 620 | 1 645 | 75 | 1 143 | 231 | 84 | 224 | 33 863 | 1 312 | 57.2 | 14.8 | 45.7 |
| Roosevelt | 342 | 3 980 | 719 | 462 | 705 | 131 | 75 | 106 | 26 691 | 876 | 15.6 | 43.7 | 43.0 |
| Sandoval | 1 598 | 24 934 | 2 027 | 3 318 | 3 426 | 834 | D | 1 102 | 44 191 | 652 | 71.3 | 10.1 | 46.2 |
| San Juan | 2 833 | 37 637 | 6 556 | 1 341 | 6 406 | 1 027 | 1 315 | 1 598 | 42 463 | 1 897 | 85.7 | 2.2 | 55.4 |
| San Miguel | 444 | 5 580 | 2 700 | 48 | 989 | 183 | 138 | 240 | 42 925 | 765 | 23.5 | 37.4 | 45.5 |
| Santa Fe | 4 714 | 45 353 | 8 956 | 679 | 9 100 | 1 953 | 2 463 | 1 741 | 38 382 | 489 | 66.9 | 13.5 | 42.7 |
| Sierra | 223 | 2 598 | 807 | D | 466 | 66 | D | 53 | 20 480 | 265 | 34.0 | 32.8 | 57.7 |
| Socorro | 243 | 2 885 | D | 79 | 490 | D | 359 | 78 | 27 084 | 536 | 52.1 | 26.1 | 49.4 |
| Taos | 1 121 | 8 670 | 1 558 | 105 | 1 501 | 214 | 356 | 221 | 25 517 | 637 | 64.7 | 8.6 | 41.8 |
| Torrance | 230 | 1 748 | D | D | 455 | D | D | 43 | 24 553 | 561 | 19.3 | 41.2 | 47.1 |
| Union | 123 | 976 | D | D | 140 | D | 21 | 27 | 27 673 | 380 | 6.3 | 71.8 | 56.6 |
| Valencia | 882 | 10 712 | 2 802 | 677 | 2 445 | 327 | 306 | 257 | 23 976 | 901 | 82.9 | 4.3 | 41.4 |
| **NEW YORK** | 521 537 | 7 369 731 | 1 416 496 | 434 903 | 884 202 | 528 569 | 571 099 | 435 009 | 59 026 | 36 352 | 32.2 | 8.4 | 54.0 |
| Albany | 9 436 | 168 868 | 32 664 | 7 414 | 21 455 | 13 331 | 15 432 | 7 314 | 43 310 | 498 | 41.2 | 4.4 | 42.8 |
| Allegany | 793 | 12 128 | 1 914 | 2 522 | 1 390 | 208 | 246 | 337 | 27 806 | 847 | 23.3 | 6.0 | 47.2 |
| Bronx | 16 404 | 228 384 | 91 571 | 6 433 | 27 059 | 4 041 | 3 988 | 9 722 | 42 567 | 1 | 100.0 | 0.0 | 100.0 |
| Broome | 4 304 | 71 499 | 15 267 | 8 501 | 11 369 | 2 520 | 4 104 | 2 558 | 35 774 | 580 | 28.8 | 3.6 | 43.4 |
| Cattaraugus | 1 677 | 24 230 | 3 525 | 4 696 | 4 039 | 640 | 512 | 794 | 32 759 | 1 122 | 26.7 | 4.7 | 49.0 |
| Cayuga | 1 626 | 19 542 | 4 211 | 3 183 | 3 614 | 338 | 470 | 651 | 33 330 | 936 | 28.5 | 14.2 | 54.8 |
| Chautauqua | 2 924 | 41 724 | 8 393 | 9 976 | 6 326 | 893 | 1 019 | 1 305 | 31 272 | 1 658 | 35.4 | 4.2 | 53.5 |
| Chemung | 1 834 | 33 442 | 6 814 | 5 893 | 5 289 | 1 163 | 779 | 1 185 | 35 423 | 373 | 22.3 | 7.8 | 49.1 |
| Chenango | 956 | 11 621 | 1 893 | 2 809 | 2 034 | D | 318 | 417 | 35 857 | 908 | 24.8 | 7.7 | 54.6 |
| Clinton | 1 909 | 25 840 | 5 198 | 3 307 | 5 089 | 441 | 1 379 | 850 | 32 883 | 590 | 23.4 | 11.5 | 55.9 |
| Columbia | 1 675 | 15 072 | 4 259 | 1 166 | 2 854 | 468 | 643 | 500 | 33 178 | 554 | 39.7 | 9.6 | 51.8 |
| Cortland | 1 031 | 15 675 | 3 278 | 2 560 | 2 180 | 357 | 943 | 477 | 30 437 | 587 | 25.0 | 11.6 | 51.3 |
| Delaware | 1 021 | 10 937 | 1 988 | 3 468 | 1 491 | 419 | 226 | 417 | 38 143 | 747 | 22.8 | 10.2 | 58.5 |
| Dutchess | 7 423 | 92 645 | 18 418 | D | 13 943 | 3 118 | 3 965 | 4 081 | 44 053 | 656 | 46.2 | 6.3 | 55.5 |
| Erie | 22 313 | 405 981 | 73 338 | 42 420 | 53 130 | 27 532 | 25 519 | 15 983 | 39 369 | 1 215 | 47.8 | 4.4 | 52.3 |
| Essex | 1 159 | 9 974 | 1 935 | D | 1 843 | D | 194 | 318 | 31 843 | 243 | 34.2 | 12.8 | 45.7 |
| Franklin | 1 029 | 11 039 | 3 309 | 488 | 1 925 | 250 | 437 | 344 | 31 119 | 604 | 26.0 | 9.3 | 57.0 |
| Fulton | 1 180 | 13 701 | 3 137 | 2 248 | 2 107 | 322 | 323 | 483 | 35 225 | 222 | 29.7 | 6.8 | 47.7 |

# Table B. States and Counties — Agriculture

| | Land in farms | | Acres | | | Value of land and buildings (dollars) | | Value of machinery and equipment, average per farm (dollars) | Value of products sold | | Percent from: | | Percent of farms with sales of: | | Government payments | |
|---|---|---|---|---|---|---|---|---|---|---|---|---|---|---|---|---|
| STATE County | Acreage (1,000) | Percent change, 2002–2007 | Average size of farm | Total irrigated (1,000) | Total cropland (1,000) | Average per farm | Average per acre | | Total (mil dol) | Average per farm (dollars) | Crops | Live-stock and poultry products | $10,000 or more | $100,000 or more | Total ($1,000) | Percent of farms |
| | 117 | 118 | 119 | 120 | 121 | 122 | 123 | 124 | 125 | 126 | 127 | 128 | 129 | 130 | 131 | 132 |
| **NEW JERSEY—Cont'd** | | | | | | | | | | | | | | | | |
| Mercer | 22 | -12.0 | 70 | 1.0 | 15.4 | 1 314 520 | 18 813 | 64 690 | 18.6 | 59 956 | 80.5 | 19.5 | 41.2 | 11.9 | 286 | 13.2 |
| Middlesex | 19 | -13.6 | 79 | 2.7 | 12.9 | 1 609 071 | 20 289 | 79 639 | 41.9 | 177 346 | 96.1 | 3.9 | 41.9 | 19.5 | 109 | 7.6 |
| Monmouth | 44 | -6.4 | 47 | 6.0 | 28.0 | 1 123 048 | 23 718 | 67 217 | 105.4 | 113 104 | 76.1 | 23.9 | 36.2 | 11.1 | 258 | 3.5 |
| Morris | 17 | 0.0 | 40 | 0.9 | 9.3 | 992 865 | 24 606 | 54 184 | 27.3 | 64 720 | 84.7 | 15.3 | 30.1 | 8.3 | 91 | 3.6 |
| Ocean | 10 | -16.7 | 39 | 1.1 | 4.4 | 698 579 | 18 116 | 48 171 | 11.5 | 45 159 | 80.9 | 19.1 | 31.4 | 7.1 | 128 | 3.1 |
| Passaic | 2 | 0.0 | 19 | 0.1 | 0.4 | 787 880 | 40 965 | 31 834 | 6.3 | 61 343 | 95.8 | 4.2 | 20.4 | 3.9 | D | 2.9 |
| Salem | 97 | 1.0 | 127 | 18.0 | 78.1 | 1 332 268 | 10 475 | 102 704 | 80.0 | 105 351 | 75.9 | 24.1 | 37.2 | 16.3 | 1 624 | 21.7 |
| Somerset | 33 | -8.3 | 74 | 0.4 | 19.9 | 1 505 463 | 20 474 | 59 654 | 18.9 | 42 496 | 50.9 | 49.1 | 24.7 | 5.6 | 213 | 5.8 |
| Sussex | 65 | -13.3 | 62 | 0.5 | 32.9 | 838 636 | 13 625 | 42 621 | 21.2 | 20 040 | 55.6 | 44.4 | 20.3 | 4.9 | 328 | 4.5 |
| Union | 0 | NA | 8 | 0.0 | 0.1 | 1 119 405 | 133 263 | 59 995 | 2.5 | 165 549 | 99.4 | 0.6 | 46.7 | 20.0 | 0 | 0.0 |
| Warren | 75 | -3.8 | 80 | 2.4 | 51.5 | 992 474 | 12 350 | 63 855 | 75.5 | 80 897 | 57.8 | 42.2 | 29.0 | 10.5 | 949 | 13.3 |
| **NEW MEXICO** | 43 238 | -3.5 | 2 066 | 830.0 | 2 334.0 | 696 081 | 337 | 55 457 | 2 175.1 | 103 922 | 25.4 | 74.6 | 27.1 | 8.1 | 43 377 | 15.9 |
| Bernalillo | 238 | NA | 374 | 7.8 | 22.8 | 499 833 | 1 335 | 38 871 | 17.9 | 28 162 | 32.9 | 67.1 | 14.8 | 2.5 | 145 | 3.0 |
| Catron | 1 483 | -9.8 | 5 724 | 3.1 | 5.1 | 1 463 469 | 256 | 50 545 | 11.0 | 42 586 | 2.4 | 97.6 | 39.0 | 11.6 | 95 | 3.1 |
| Chaves | 2 455 | -2.4 | 4 203 | 63.1 | 85.4 | 1 289 541 | 307 | 126 473 | 339.1 | 580 629 | 12.2 | 87.8 | 50.5 | 27.4 | 1 970 | 17.0 |
| Cibola | 1 479 | -12.5 | 4 665 | 2.3 | 17.0 | 843 304 | 181 | 33 189 | D | D | D | D | 18.3 | 2.8 | 232 | 7.9 |
| Colfax | 2 152 | -2.9 | 7 127 | 21.1 | 25.2 | 2 383 502 | 334 | 76 638 | 33.3 | 110 378 | 4.8 | 95.2 | 50.0 | 18.5 | 266 | 13.2 |
| Curry | 887 | -3.2 | 1 303 | 72.9 | 411.5 | 854 927 | 656 | 110 887 | 347.3 | 510 020 | 10.8 | 89.2 | 43.0 | 23.2 | 8 457 | 68.4 |
| De Baca | 1 071 | -24.0 | 6 188 | 11.5 | 16.1 | 1 425 675 | 230 | 68 705 | 19.9 | 115 033 | 26.2 | 73.8 | 59.0 | 22.5 | 683 | 38.2 |
| Dona Ana | 589 | 1.4 | 334 | 79.0 | 95.8 | 636 656 | 1 903 | 77 539 | 388.8 | 220 651 | 43.2 | 56.8 | 36.8 | 9.9 | 2 338 | 13.1 |
| Eddy | 1 108 | -6.3 | 2 040 | 53.0 | 67.5 | 770 228 | 377 | 85 775 | 94.8 | 174 674 | 42.5 | 57.5 | 47.7 | 16.4 | 1 702 | 29.1 |
| Grant | 1 213 | -0.4 | 3 711 | 3.4 | 8.8 | 871 368 | 235 | 41 904 | 7.8 | 23 908 | 1.5 | 98.5 | 30.3 | 5.8 | 134 | 6.4 |
| Guadalupe | 1 405 | -3.9 | 5 446 | 2.3 | 13.2 | 991 767 | 182 | 44 337 | 10.9 | 42 056 | 1.6 | 98.4 | 44.6 | 10.1 | 286 | 15.1 |
| Harding | 944 | -4.8 | 5 621 | D | 19.9 | 1 311 240 | 233 | 67 689 | 13.4 | 79 528 | D | D | 44.6 | 16.1 | 754 | 48.2 |
| Hidalgo | 1 029 | -8.8 | 6 349 | 11.9 | 32.2 | 1 074 236 | 169 | 104 085 | 17.5 | 108 222 | 57.7 | 42.3 | 51.2 | 17.3 | 503 | 29.0 |
| Lea | 2 365 | 4.7 | 4 135 | 39.1 | 128.4 | 926 712 | 224 | 70 813 | 93.6 | 163 713 | 18.2 | 81.8 | 37.1 | 15.7 | 3 237 | 27.1 |
| Lincoln | 1 750 | 9.0 | 4 849 | 3.7 | 9.3 | 1 352 329 | 279 | 56 628 | 13.3 | 36 755 | 4.0 | 96.0 | 39.6 | 10.5 | 499 | 10.8 |
| Los Alamos | 0 | NA | 1 | D | D | 82 734 | 64 349 | 7 891 | D | D | D | D | 0.0 | 0.0 | 0 | 0.0 |
| Luna | 654 | -7.9 | 3 173 | 23.2 | 42.8 | 1 111 198 | 350 | 138 772 | 48.9 | 237 334 | 63.0 | 37.0 | 51.5 | 22.3 | 1 476 | 34.5 |
| McKinley | 3 173 | 0.1 | 1 209 | 4.5 | 31.4 | 157 075 | 130 | 14 709 | 7.9 | 3 004 | 14.8 | 85.2 | 4.4 | 0.2 | 71 | 5.2 |
| Mora | 915 | -4.2 | 1 553 | 12.7 | 52.7 | 807 497 | 520 | 42 796 | 7.6 | 12 843 | 23.9 | 76.1 | 21.7 | 3.6 | 330 | 5.1 |
| Otero | 1 126 | -6.8 | 2 285 | 7.0 | 18.6 | 735 337 | 322 | 43 619 | 15.2 | 30 887 | 60.0 | 40.0 | 37.3 | 5.7 | 406 | 6.1 |
| Quay | 1 490 | -9.8 | 2 342 | 18.8 | 245.9 | 846 037 | 361 | 66 660 | 35.9 | 56 451 | 25.5 | 74.5 | 43.1 | 13.5 | 5 168 | 61.2 |
| Rio Arriba | 1 460 | 2.0 | 1 113 | 30.8 | 80.3 | 523 841 | 471 | 46 275 | 12.8 | 9 728 | 30.5 | 69.5 | 19.8 | 1.1 | 323 | 6.7 |
| Roosevelt | 1 494 | -0.5 | 1 706 | 70.2 | 403.3 | 801 954 | 470 | 95 021 | 254.0 | 289 897 | 14.1 | 85.9 | 39.0 | 18.4 | 8 936 | 65.3 |
| Sandoval | 592 | -22.4 | 908 | 9.0 | 22.8 | 327 487 | 361 | 28 442 | 9.1 | 13 887 | 62.0 | 38.0 | 18.6 | 2.1 | 121 | 3.4 |
| San Juan | 1 631 | -7.2 | 860 | 78.4 | 107.4 | 268 195 | 312 | 37 574 | 57.2 | 30 153 | 82.6 | 17.4 | 8.9 | 1.3 | 900 | 4.6 |
| San Miguel | 2 241 | 7.1 | 2 930 | 8.7 | 61.4 | 953 077 | 325 | 34 935 | 17.2 | 22 465 | 7.5 | 92.5 | 19.1 | 3.1 | 502 | 6.0 |
| Santa Fe | 569 | -16.8 | 1 164 | 50.0 | 21.5 | 778 559 | 669 | 42 309 | 12.6 | 25 795 | 68.1 | 31.9 | 20.2 | 3.5 | 49 | 4.5 |
| Sierra | 1 344 | -1.4 | 5 073 | 6.7 | D | 1 102 667 | 217 | 51 354 | 23.6 | 88 891 | 26.4 | 73.6 | 46.0 | 11.7 | 144 | 8.7 |
| Socorro | 1 430 | -6.1 | 2 668 | 14.8 | 23.8 | 737 418 | 276 | 55 712 | 40.1 | 74 816 | 15.6 | 84.4 | 38.6 | 8.6 | 284 | 6.5 |
| Taos | 457 | -1.9 | 717 | 19.4 | 26.2 | 447 020 | 623 | 38 659 | 6.0 | 9 406 | 38.9 | 61.1 | 14.3 | 1.6 | 81 | 11.0 |
| Torrance | 1 796 | 5.8 | 3 202 | 29.9 | 81.1 | 1 059 220 | 331 | 67 957 | 40.4 | 72 082 | 41.6 | 58.4 | 30.1 | 9.6 | 601 | 12.8 |
| Union | 2 193 | -2.2 | 5 770 | 47.0 | 122.6 | 1 778 268 | 308 | 114 132 | 137.0 | 360 451 | 23.2 | 76.8 | 64.5 | 30.5 | 2 569 | 32.1 |
| Valencia | 506 | 37.1 | 561 | 21.0 | 25.2 | 364 132 | 649 | 48 131 | 36.3 | 40 313 | 17.7 | 82.3 | 17.2 | 3.4 | 113 | 2.0 |
| **NEW YORK** | 7 175 | -6.3 | 197 | 68.0 | 4 315.0 | 449 010 | 2 275 | 97 550 | 4 418.6 | 121 551 | 35.3 | 64.7 | 45.4 | 18.8 | 62 652 | 29.1 |
| Albany | 61 | -11.6 | 123 | 0.4 | 32.0 | 392 854 | 3 206 | 75 116 | 22.4 | 45 010 | 51.6 | 48.4 | 34.9 | 7.6 | 270 | 21.1 |
| Allegany | 151 | -16.1 | 178 | 0.2 | 74.6 | 253 899 | 1 426 | 53 782 | 46.1 | 54 390 | 12.5 | 87.5 | 29.8 | 10.0 | 1 285 | 34.6 |
| Bronx | D | D | D | 0.0 | D | D | D | D | D | D | D | D | 100.0 | 100.0 | 0 | 0.0 |
| Broome | 87 | -11.2 | 149 | 0.2 | 43.6 | 275 676 | 1 846 | 62 296 | 29.9 | 51 526 | 18.6 | 81.4 | 28.8 | 7.1 | 754 | 21.6 |
| Cattaraugus | 183 | -9.4 | 163 | 0.5 | 91.6 | 284 810 | 1 742 | 67 862 | 75.2 | 66 980 | 20.2 | 79.8 | 38.7 | 11.7 | 1 102 | 37.0 |
| Cayuga | 249 | 4.6 | 267 | 0.2 | 193.0 | 566 337 | 2 125 | 147 985 | 214.4 | 229 063 | 22.6 | 77.4 | 53.8 | 25.2 | 2 791 | 41.3 |
| Chautauqua | 236 | -7.8 | 142 | 1.2 | 127.2 | 280 124 | 1 969 | 80 228 | 138.6 | 83 581 | 41.7 | 58.3 | 52.4 | 17.2 | 1 882 | 19.1 |
| Chemung | 65 | -5.8 | 175 | 0.2 | 32.9 | 319 539 | 1 830 | 69 729 | 16.6 | 44 526 | 18.9 | 81.1 | 29.2 | 9.4 | 394 | 27.9 |
| Chenango | 177 | -6.8 | 195 | 0.1 | 86.7 | 351 914 | 1 803 | 76 894 | 65.8 | 72 460 | 11.8 | 88.2 | 44.2 | 19.5 | 2 015 | 34.3 |
| Clinton | 149 | -11.8 | 253 | 0.2 | 70.9 | 442 944 | 1 751 | 108 357 | 124.2 | 210 508 | 19.8 | 80.2 | 40.5 | 19.8 | 1 023 | 26.1 |
| Columbia | 107 | -10.8 | 192 | 2.0 | 63.7 | 823 806 | 4 282 | 103 984 | 65.8 | 118 718 | 38.3 | 61.7 | 46.8 | 16.8 | 945 | 19.9 |
| Cortland | 125 | -1.6 | 213 | 0.0 | 61.5 | 331 184 | 1 557 | 72 069 | 54.9 | 93 500 | 10.0 | 90.0 | 39.2 | 17.4 | 1 514 | 41.1 |
| Delaware | 166 | -13.5 | 222 | 0.1 | 69.0 | 502 668 | 2 268 | 83 894 | 55.1 | 73 820 | 14.3 | 85.7 | 46.6 | 19.0 | 1 247 | 33.6 |
| Dutchess | 102 | -8.9 | 156 | 1.3 | 46.9 | 873 887 | 5 601 | 88 862 | 44.9 | 68 393 | 52.2 | 47.8 | 47.3 | 15.2 | 392 | 11.7 |
| Erie | 149 | -8.0 | 123 | 3.0 | 98.6 | 364 369 | 2 964 | 90 447 | 117.0 | 96 322 | 35.6 | 64.4 | 37.8 | 15.5 | 1 401 | 22.0 |
| Essex | 50 | -9.1 | 207 | 0.2 | 22.2 | 486 131 | 2 352 | 81 258 | 11.5 | 47 156 | 42.1 | 57.9 | 32.5 | 13.2 | 274 | 16.5 |
| Franklin | 131 | -5.1 | 217 | 0.4 | 69.7 | 314 833 | 1 453 | 83 318 | 68.1 | 112 743 | 15.2 | 84.8 | 47.0 | 20.5 | 943 | 29.1 |
| Fulton | 34 | -10.5 | 152 | 0.1 | 18.3 | 331 316 | 2 173 | 71 071 | 9.1 | 40 919 | 24.5 | 75.5 | 38.7 | 10.4 | 136 | 21.6 |

| STATE County | Water use, 2005 | | Wholesale trade,[1] 2007 | | | | Retail trade,[2] 2007 | | | | Real estate and rental and leasing,[2] 2007 | | | |
|---|---|---|---|---|---|---|---|---|---|---|---|---|---|---|
| | Total water withdrawn (mil gal/day) | Gallons withdrawn per person | Number of establish-ments | Number of employees | Sales (mil dol) | Annual payroll (mil dol) | Number of establish-ments | Number of employees | Sales (mil dol) | Annual payroll (mil dol) | Number of establish-ments | Number of employees | Receipts (mil dol) | Annual payroll (mil dol) |
| | 133 | 134 | 135 | 136 | 137 | 138 | 139 | 140 | 141 | 142 | 143 | 144 | 145 | 146 |
| NEW JERSEY—Cont'd | | | | | | | | | | | | | | |
| Mercer | 691.6 | 1 888 | 359 | 9 737 | 8 421.0 | 816.7 | 1 412 | 20 683 | 5 089.1 | 505.0 | 357 | D | D | D |
| Middlesex | 645.1 | 817 | 1 687 | 33 964 | 32 631.8 | 1 994.9 | 2 826 | 40 815 | 11 131.0 | 1 048.5 | 731 | 6 267 | 2 206.4 | 316.6 |
| Monmouth | 82.9 | 130 | 931 | 8 184 | 11 058.9 | 484.6 | 2 860 | 42 007 | 11 225.1 | 1 095.8 | 764 | 3 716 | 750.0 | 139.6 |
| Morris | 76.0 | 155 | 1 011 | 15 352 | 17 440.0 | 989.0 | 2 107 | 31 238 | 8 756.3 | 877.7 | 672 | 7 848 | 2 066.6 | 522.5 |
| Ocean | 1 466.2 | 2 626 | 453 | D | D | D | 1 984 | 27 149 | 7 307.4 | 674.0 | 576 | 2 485 | 460.9 | 83.1 |
| Passaic | 164.0 | 329 | 802 | 10 498 | 7 021.1 | 539.0 | 1 912 | 23 180 | 6 598.0 | 579.0 | 447 | 5 992 | 1 103.1 | 211.4 |
| Salem | 2 700.6 | 40 704 | 36 | D | D | D | 197 | 2 311 | 669.4 | 52.0 | 58 | D | D | D |
| Somerset | 146.8 | 459 | 528 | 11 335 | 14 634.5 | 863.8 | 1 216 | 19 972 | 5 756.0 | 530.3 | 304 | 1 592 | 453.3 | 63.9 |
| Sussex | 16.4 | 107 | 146 | D | D | D | 488 | 5 806 | 1 722.4 | 150.3 | 96 | D | D | D |
| Union | 22.0 | 41 | 908 | 14 610 | 12 948.7 | 823.8 | 2 085 | 25 619 | 7 312.1 | 644.5 | 600 | 3 270 | 988.0 | 135.5 |
| Warren | 27.8 | 252 | 107 | D | D | D | 441 | 6 292 | 1 550.6 | 140.4 | 72 | D | D | D |
| NEW MEXICO | 3 331.9 | 1 728 | 1 763 | 19 891 | 10 589.3 | 805.8 | 7 208 | 97 385 | 24 470.0 | 2 250.8 | 2 525 | 11 678 | 1 954.7 | 355.6 |
| Bernalillo | 149.9 | 248 | 833 | 12 139 | 6 135.0 | 503.5 | 2 253 | 36 900 | 9 396.1 | 903.3 | 1 000 | 5 337 | 898.3 | 155.2 |
| Catron | 19.2 | 5 617 | NA | NA | NA | NA | 13 | 77 | 7.2 | 0.7 | 3 | 7 | 0.4 | 0.2 |
| Chaves | 256.9 | 4 152 | 52 | D | D | D | 260 | 3 271 | 836.1 | 69.7 | 85 | 283 | 43.2 | 8.1 |
| Cibola | 14.0 | 506 | 9 | 35 | 15.9 | 0.8 | 79 | 850 | 217.4 | 18.8 | 15 | 40 | 3.7 | 0.7 |
| Colfax | 51.9 | 3 771 | 12 | 54 | 45.1 | 1.8 | 91 | 719 | 158.8 | 14.3 | 34 | 126 | 14.6 | 2.0 |
| Curry | 130.4 | 2 845 | 49 | 251 | 171.5 | 8.4 | 198 | 2 519 | 591.3 | 52.1 | 49 | 170 | 25.6 | 4.4 |
| De Baca | 45.1 | 22 386 | NA | NA | NA | NA | 11 | 63 | 12.4 | 0.9 | NA | NA | NA | NA |
| Dona Ana | 465.2 | 2 456 | 120 | 1 076 | 448.2 | 34.1 | 536 | 7 881 | 1 925.6 | 159.5 | 229 | 1 009 | 143.2 | 22.2 |
| Eddy | 204.9 | 3 984 | 58 | D | D | D | 208 | 2 384 | 562.8 | 51.7 | 39 | 226 | 30.2 | 7.3 |
| Grant | 50.9 | 1 712 | 19 | D | D | D | 132 | 1 257 | 261.4 | 25.4 | 45 | 121 | 16.4 | 2.6 |
| Guadalupe | 24.8 | 5 672 | 2 | D | D | D | 20 | 290 | 109.9 | 4.9 | NA | NA | NA | NA |
| Harding | 3.5 | 4 716 | NA | NA | NA | NA | 4 | 6 | 1.3 | 0.1 | NA | NA | NA | NA |
| Hidalgo | 89.5 | 17 418 | 2 | D | D | D | 36 | 279 | 113.4 | 4.9 | 1 | D | D | D |
| Lea | 163.0 | 2 874 | 90 | 879 | 376.7 | 40.0 | 213 | 2 759 | 765.9 | 67.6 | 69 | 617 | 138.6 | 32.7 |
| Lincoln | 23.2 | 1 103 | 8 | D | D | D | 150 | 1 162 | 245.6 | 25.1 | 66 | 175 | 23.4 | 3.7 |
| Los Alamos | 3.8 | 203 | 4 | D | D | D | 35 | 490 | 97.9 | 9.7 | 19 | 78 | 14.2 | 2.1 |
| Luna | 182.6 | 6 890 | 19 | D | D | D | 76 | 1 111 | 236.8 | 20.2 | 27 | 83 | 13.0 | 1.6 |
| McKinley | 17.2 | 239 | 45 | D | D | D | 262 | 3 778 | 926.4 | 85.1 | 48 | 162 | 21.7 | 3.0 |
| Mora | 20.4 | 3 991 | NA | NA | NA | NA | 9 | 58 | 14.1 | 0.9 | 1 | D | D | D |
| Otero | 42.0 | 660 | 25 | D | D | D | 193 | 2 385 | 527.8 | 46.2 | 62 | 246 | 27.8 | 4.2 |
| Quay | 41.6 | 4 489 | 4 | 9 | 1.7 | 0.2 | 53 | 450 | 143.9 | 7.2 | 7 | 20 | 0.7 | 0.2 |
| Rio Arriba | 110.1 | 2 698 | 10 | D | D | D | 101 | 1 402 | 313.5 | 32.0 | 24 | 95 | 10.9 | 1.9 |
| Roosevelt | 180.0 | 9 871 | 12 | D | D | D | 56 | 660 | 166.7 | 13.5 | 13 | 46 | 3.4 | 0.6 |
| Sandoval | 69.3 | 645 | 40 | 262 | 113.1 | 12.1 | 197 | 3 168 | 1 117.4 | 78.1 | 85 | 272 | 35.5 | 5.8 |
| San Juan | 332.7 | 2 636 | 146 | 1 454 | 866.4 | 70.4 | 482 | 6 671 | 1 742.0 | 155.5 | 120 | 879 | 211.5 | 45.2 |
| San Miguel | 35.9 | 1 214 | 9 | D | D | D | 103 | 1 187 | 277.2 | 23.4 | 16 | 60 | 4.4 | 0.8 |
| Santa Fe | 47.4 | 336 | 134 | D | D | D | 887 | 9 949 | 2 426.3 | 261.6 | 311 | 1 092 | 206.0 | 40.8 |
| Sierra | 40.6 | 3 167 | NA | NA | NA | NA | 52 | 375 | 82.8 | 6.9 | 13 | 36 | 3.3 | 0.5 |
| Socorro | 145.6 | 8 022 | 2 | D | D | D | 46 | 574 | 126.2 | 10.7 | 17 | 54 | 10.3 | 1.0 |
| Taos | 108.3 | 3 413 | 25 | D | D | D | 245 | 1 624 | 309.2 | 35.7 | 67 | 241 | 23.9 | 4.6 |
| Torrance | 41.0 | 2 345 | 8 | 42 | 13.7 | 1.2 | 42 | 562 | 157.5 | 10.5 | 7 | 36 | 8.7 | 0.9 |
| Union | 48.0 | 12 457 | 1 | D | D | D | 18 | 100 | 27.5 | 1.8 | 3 | D | D | D |
| Valencia | 173.4 | 2 499 | 25 | 110 | 51.6 | 3.3 | 147 | 2 424 | 571.3 | 52.6 | 50 | 162 | 21.5 | 3.5 |
| NEW YORK | 15 175.2 | 788 | 30 863 | 357 459 | 313 461.9 | 19 609.0 | 76 637 | 892 863 | 230 718.1 | 22 336.7 | 32 588 | 171 601 | 49 867.2 | 7 941.7 |
| Albany | 128.5 | 432 | 423 | 6 321 | 3 642.6 | 319.4 | 1 379 | 22 854 | 5 404.4 | 519.3 | 424 | 3 112 | 619.8 | 107.2 |
| Allegany | 7.1 | 141 | 20 | 165 | 51.4 | 4.2 | 157 | 1 457 | 276.7 | 24.7 | 17 | 62 | 6.8 | 1.5 |
| Bronx | 4.1 | 3 | 695 | 10 432 | 8 039.8 | 553.9 | 3 462 | 24 355 | 5 539.8 | 522.1 | 2 274 | 8 916 | 1 703.5 | 270.6 |
| Broome | 117.6 | 597 | 194 | 3 831 | 1 958.8 | 150.2 | 753 | 11 949 | 2 573.0 | 237.6 | 157 | 1 114 | 191.8 | 31.2 |
| Cattaraugus | 19.5 | 237 | 55 | 678 | 465.7 | 22.7 | 372 | 4 040 | 1 009.0 | 84.4 | 56 | 197 | 26.8 | 4.3 |
| Cayuga | 14.8 | 181 | 57 | D | D | D | 273 | 3 852 | 884.0 | 81.6 | 60 | 189 | 27.6 | 4.2 |
| Chautauqua | 461.0 | 3 380 | 99 | 1 610 | 2 621.3 | 60.6 | 555 | 6 699 | 1 364.1 | 133.2 | 87 | 480 | 66.4 | 12.6 |
| Chemung | 15.7 | 175 | 86 | 1 077 | 357.9 | 43.2 | 388 | 5 580 | 1 207.2 | 111.0 | 79 | 410 | 65.6 | 10.7 |
| Chenango | 7.4 | 143 | 28 | 254 | 126.3 | 10.2 | 188 | 2 203 | 518.2 | 47.4 | 33 | 84 | 8.1 | 2.1 |
| Clinton | 13.9 | 169 | 97 | 1 223 | 679.4 | 42.8 | 378 | 4 890 | 1 195.0 | 102.8 | 85 | 315 | 51.1 | 7.8 |
| Columbia | 8.9 | 140 | 62 | D | D | D | 259 | 2 555 | 638.4 | 62.4 | 69 | 180 | 22.6 | 3.8 |
| Cortland | 8.7 | 180 | 29 | D | D | D | 194 | 2 268 | 523.1 | 45.9 | 40 | 285 | 21.5 | 3.6 |
| Delaware | 453.6 | 9 543 | 21 | 361 | 441.0 | 14.7 | 207 | 1 726 | 389.6 | 36.3 | 35 | 106 | 13.7 | 2.3 |
| Dutchess | 38.7 | 131 | 228 | 2 069 | 982.3 | 109.1 | 1 095 | 14 632 | 3 599.2 | 356.2 | 387 | 1 844 | 287.9 | 63.2 |
| Erie | 802.4 | 862 | 1 089 | 20 509 | 19 416.1 | 964.4 | 3 360 | 53 571 | 11 217.1 | 1 096.8 | 831 | 6 025 | 929.8 | 172.6 |
| Essex | 9.0 | 232 | 9 | 95 | 17.9 | 1.9 | 231 | 1 852 | 429.2 | 39.7 | 35 | 99 | 16.5 | 2.5 |
| Franklin | 19.0 | 373 | 30 | D | D | D | 214 | 2 257 | 476.4 | 45.8 | 40 | 125 | 14.9 | 2.7 |
| Fulton | 9.6 | 172 | 67 | D | D | D | 199 | 2 338 | 577.1 | 50.9 | 41 | 152 | 28.4 | 5.0 |

1. Merchant wholesalers, except manufacturers' sales branches and offices.    2. Employer establishments.

| STATE County | Professional, scientific, and technical services,[1] 2007 | | | | Manufacturing, 2007 | | | | Accommodation and food services, 2007 | | | |
|---|---|---|---|---|---|---|---|---|---|---|---|---|
| | Number of establish-ments | Number of employees | Receipts (mil dol) | Annual payroll (mil dol) | Number of establish-ments | Number of employees | Receipts (mil dol) | Annual payroll (mil dol) | Number of establish-ments | Number of employees | Sales (mil dol) | Annual payroll (mil dol) |
| | 147 | 148 | 149 | 150 | 151 | 152 | 153 | 154 | 155 | 156 | 157 | 158 |
| NEW JERSEY—Cont'd | | | | | | | | | | | | |
| Mercer | 1 646 | 30 900 | 5 790.4 | 2 345.3 | 293 | 9 352 | D | 420.1 | 834 | 12 103 | 695.8 | 197.7 |
| Middlesex | 4 053 | D | D | D | 847 | 36 047 | 12 207.3 | 1 840.4 | 1 614 | 21 554 | 1 275.1 | 337.5 |
| Monmouth | 2 754 | D | D | D | 511 | 11 717 | 3 468.4 | 538.0 | 1 642 | 21 953 | 1 153.5 | 316.0 |
| Morris | 2 796 | 43 496 | 7 752.3 | 3 425.8 | 628 | 22 068 | 7 631.7 | 1 181.6 | 1 290 | 18 119 | 1 129.8 | 314.1 |
| Ocean | 1 167 | D | D | D | 315 | D | D | 251.0 | 1 087 | 12 584 | 703.0 | 182.7 |
| Passaic | 1 162 | D | D | D | 872 | 22 028 | 5 178.3 | 1 042.9 | 905 | 9 296 | 538.7 | 133.2 |
| Salem | 84 | D | D | D | 43 | 3 113 | 1 440.4 | 204.7 | 112 | 1 580 | 82.3 | 21.6 |
| Somerset | 1 830 | D | D | D | 337 | 17 673 | 6 401.5 | 1 159.7 | 712 | 10 739 | 656.1 | 180.0 |
| Sussex | 379 | D | D | D | 128 | D | D | 89.0 | 299 | 3 245 | 172.4 | 46.5 |
| Union | 1 546 | D | D | D | 712 | 31 897 | 18 574.7 | 2 106.8 | 1 110 | 12 763 | 748.0 | 199.9 |
| Warren | 260 | D | D | D | 136 | 4 603 | 2 212.2 | 240.2 | 250 | 2 622 | 118.0 | 31.3 |
| NEW MEXICO | 4 789 | 43 001 | 5 975.8 | 2 516.7 | 1 574 | 35 409 | 17 122.7 | 1 560.5 | 4 090 | 80 415 | 3 734.3 | 1 054.8 |
| Bernalillo | 2 248 | D | D | D | 661 | 16 573 | D | 719.8 | 1 319 | 29 908 | 1 398.0 | 410.5 |
| Catron | 3 | D | D | D | NA | NA | NA | NA | 11 | 57 | 2.6 | 0.4 |
| Chaves | 111 | 780 | 108.2 | 34.2 | 45 | 1 098 | 661.5 | 37.7 | 121 | 2 306 | 92.4 | 25.0 |
| Cibola | 21 | D | D | D | NA | NA | NA | NA | 43 | 1 403 | 117.3 | 25.0 |
| Colfax | 37 | D | D | D | NA | NA | NA | NA | 76 | 1 426 | 56.9 | 17.2 |
| Curry | 76 | D | D | D | 28 | 530 | D | 20.6 | 86 | 1 934 | 68.3 | 17.8 |
| De Baca | 1 | D | D | D | NA | NA | NA | NA | 3 | D | D | D |
| Dona Ana | 315 | D | D | D | 141 | 2 349 | 931.9 | 84.2 | 298 | 5 955 | 238.7 | 64.9 |
| Eddy | 76 | D | D | D | 37 | 1 302 | D | 84.5 | 110 | 1 778 | 80.5 | 20.8 |
| Grant | 45 | D | D | D | NA | NA | NA | NA | 76 | 957 | 35.5 | 9.1 |
| Guadalupe | 1 | D | D | D | NA | NA | NA | NA | 29 | 373 | 16.7 | 4.5 |
| Harding | NA | NA | NA | NA | NA | NA | NA | NA | 3 | 16 | 0.3 | 0.1 |
| Hidalgo | 2 | D | D | D | NA | NA | NA | NA | 16 | 275 | 9.9 | 2.6 |
| Lea | 78 | 522 | 60.7 | 24.9 | 38 | 815 | 280.4 | 36.4 | 115 | 1 944 | 85.1 | 21.0 |
| Lincoln | 61 | D | D | D | NA | NA | NA | NA | 103 | 1 114 | 60.2 | 15.1 |
| Los Alamos | 79 | D | D | D | NA | NA | NA | NA | 36 | 467 | 17.7 | 4.8 |
| Luna | 22 | D | D | D | 14 | 759 | D | 21.5 | 57 | 945 | 36.9 | 8.4 |
| McKinley | 50 | D | D | D | 33 | 685 | D | 37.7 | 148 | 2 474 | 109.1 | 27.3 |
| Mora | 1 | D | D | D | NA | NA | NA | NA | 3 | D | D | D |
| Otero | 83 | D | D | D | NA | NA | NA | NA | 103 | 1 798 | 92.4 | 24.3 |
| Quay | 10 | D | D | D | NA | NA | NA | NA | 35 | 555 | 17.9 | 4.9 |
| Rio Arriba | 42 | D | D | D | NA | NA | NA | NA | 79 | 1 184 | 66.8 | 18.3 |
| Roosevelt | 19 | D | D | D | NA | NA | NA | NA | 26 | 607 | 17.6 | 5.0 |
| Sandoval | 174 | D | D | D | 65 | 5 705 | D | 321.5 | 144 | 3 392 | 150.8 | 45.5 |
| San Juan | 239 | D | D | D | 91 | 1 649 | 668.7 | 64.3 | 192 | 4 108 | 173.2 | 45.8 |
| San Miguel | 32 | D | D | D | NA | NA | NA | NA | 66 | 773 | 33.1 | 8.2 |
| Santa Fe | 693 | D | D | D | 153 | 980 | D | 34.5 | 398 | 9 203 | 540.4 | 166.3 |
| Sierra | 17 | D | D | D | NA | NA | NA | NA | 39 | 423 | 14.9 | 4.1 |
| Socorro | 25 | D | D | D | NA | NA | NA | NA | 47 | 673 | 24.2 | 6.5 |
| Taos | 125 | D | D | D | NA | NA | NA | NA | 173 | 2 330 | 100.1 | 31.3 |
| Torrance | 9 | D | D | D | NA | NA | NA | NA | 29 | 309 | 12.9 | 3.1 |
| Union | 8 | D | D | D | NA | NA | NA | NA | 14 | 178 | 6.6 | 1.6 |
| Valencia | 86 | 378 | 26.4 | 9.5 | 35 | 1 114 | D | D | 92 | 1 501 | 55.7 | 14.8 |
| NEW YORK | 58 087 | 539 635 | 112 045.6 | 41 604.5 | 18 629 | 533 835 | 162 720.2 | 24 268.0 | 43 791 | 591 653 | 39 813.5 | 10 956.3 |
| Albany | 1 142 | 11 543 | 1 773.4 | 706.6 | 256 | 8 253 | 3 351.5 | 417.3 | 957 | 14 776 | 738.9 | 207.1 |
| Allegany | 56 | D | D | D | 44 | 2 826 | 965.9 | 115.8 | 94 | 1 151 | 40.2 | 10.9 |
| Bronx | 631 | D | D | D | 393 | 8 668 | D | 315.7 | 1 368 | 10 987 | 743.2 | 180.9 |
| Broome | 327 | D | D | D | 210 | 11 107 | 2 525.4 | D | 511 | 7 795 | 326.4 | 92.6 |
| Cattaraugus | 104 | D | D | D | 91 | 3 972 | 738.7 | 169.0 | 197 | 4 131 | 264.8 | 62.2 |
| Cayuga | 100 | 641 | 45.6 | 20.3 | 92 | 3 338 | 1 109.9 | 150.7 | 174 | 1 897 | 76.4 | 19.7 |
| Chautauqua | 196 | D | D | D | 212 | 11 887 | 4 461.9 | 489.2 | 355 | 4 951 | 181.2 | 55.0 |
| Chemung | 115 | D | D | D | 93 | 6 348 | 1 280.8 | 285.8 | 198 | 3 151 | 123.1 | 35.2 |
| Chenango | 74 | 513 | 31.5 | 25.6 | 86 | 2 489 | 595.6 | 93.2 | 90 | 777 | 32.2 | 9.6 |
| Clinton | 128 | D | D | D | 88 | 3 873 | 1 599.8 | 155.8 | 187 | 2 627 | 126.6 | 35.6 |
| Columbia | 212 | D | D | D | 73 | 1 896 | 619.2 | 82.0 | 165 | 1 392 | 65.1 | 19.5 |
| Cortland | 86 | D | D | D | 65 | 3 201 | 603.7 | 134.6 | 135 | 2 079 | 84.6 | 21.7 |
| Delaware | 73 | D | D | D | 41 | 5 120 | 1 432.9 | 223.6 | 125 | 862 | 41.2 | 11.0 |
| Dutchess | 778 | D | D | D | 217 | 15 948 | 3 823.0 | 1 263.0 | 701 | 8 172 | 424.7 | 117.2 |
| Erie | 2 100 | D | D | D | 1 111 | 48 058 | 15 873.8 | 2 444.8 | 2 112 | 36 944 | 1 462.8 | 434.5 |
| Essex | 65 | D | D | D | 34 | 842 | D | 45.8 | 217 | 2 094 | 125.6 | 39.4 |
| Franklin | 75 | D | D | D | NA | NA | NA | NA | 113 | 927 | 42.7 | 11.3 |
| Fulton | 82 | 325 | 25.3 | 9.0 | 90 | 2 346 | 520.6 | 84.0 | 126 | 1 089 | 46.6 | 12.3 |

1. Establishment subject to federal tax.

| STATE County | Health care and social assistance, 2007 | | | | Other services, 2007 | | | | Federal funds and grants, 2009–2010 | | | |
|---|---|---|---|---|---|---|---|---|---|---|---|---|
| | | | | | | | | | Expenditures (mil dol) | | | |
| | | | | | | | | | Total | Direct payments for individuals[1] | | |
| | Number of establish-ments | Number of employees | Receipts (mil dol) | Annual payroll (mil dol) | Number of establish-ments | Number of employees | Receipts (mil dol) | Annual payroll (mil dol) | | Social Security and government retirement | Medicare | Food Stamps and Supplemental Security Income |
| | 159 | 160 | 161 | 162 | 163 | 164 | 165 | 166 | 167 | 168 | 169 | 170 |
| **NEW JERSEY—Cont'd** | | | | | | | | | | | | |
| Mercer | 1 147 | 26 724 | 2 609.3 | 1 180.7 | 860 | 6 084 | 828.6 | 214.7 | 6 657.9 | 1 020.4 | 810.3 | 91.2 |
| Middlesex | 1 970 | 39 959 | 4 285.8 | 1 742.4 | 1 581 | 10 420 | 1 588.0 | 354.1 | 5 185.6 | 1 838.2 | 1 278.4 | 113.9 |
| Monmouth | 2 300 | 37 165 | 4 035.3 | 1 558.5 | 1 518 | 8 075 | 720.8 | 214.3 | 7 482.7 | 1 946.0 | 1 183.0 | 80.8 |
| Morris | 1 660 | 31 028 | 3 263.2 | 1 484.4 | 1 271 | 7 416 | 1 016.6 | 232.4 | 3 525.7 | 1 327.4 | 660.4 | 31.7 |
| Ocean | 1 497 | 29 082 | 2 698.1 | 1 085.8 | 1 065 | 5 305 | 486.8 | 125.2 | 4 702.5 | 2 430.9 | 1 433.1 | 71.0 |
| Passaic | 1 325 | 24 170 | 2 259.9 | 957.3 | 1 001 | 5 020 | 386.3 | 118.6 | 3 670.4 | 1 115.9 | 963.3 | 157.5 |
| Salem | 164 | 2 988 | 240.8 | 99.2 | 116 | 364 | 28.8 | 7.0 | 519.2 | 215.4 | 158.6 | 15.4 |
| Somerset | 1 081 | 19 020 | 2 016.6 | 793.7 | 713 | 4 064 | 574.1 | 130.4 | 1 673.1 | 799.8 | 342.4 | 24.0 |
| Sussex | 328 | D | D | D | 330 | 1 293 | 112.9 | 31.6 | 754.4 | 418.3 | 190.1 | 12.7 |
| Union | 1 526 | 30 202 | 2 934.9 | 1 280.0 | 1 218 | 6 401 | 626.3 | 175.7 | 3 731.0 | 1 318.7 | 1 113.0 | 118.3 |
| Warren | 290 | 5 884 | 498.8 | 205.5 | 243 | 1 133 | 106.2 | 29.7 | 737.5 | 332.8 | 212.4 | 14.3 |
| **NEW MEXICO** | 4 732 | 105 496 | 8 834.1 | 3 781.1 | 2 953 | 18 061 | 1 689.7 | 449.5 | 27 959.0 | 6 260.7 | 2 011.0 | 909.7 |
| Bernalillo | 1 713 | 42 659 | 3 957.7 | 1 724.2 | 1 089 | 8 015 | 670.7 | 211.2 | 9 573.0 | 2 142.0 | 658.6 | 238.2 |
| Catron | 5 | D | D | D | 4 | D | D | D | 39.5 | 20.6 | 3.4 | 1.1 |
| Chaves | 181 | 3 596 | 342.3 | 122.8 | 90 | 528 | 39.8 | 10.3 | 564.8 | 194.3 | 79.4 | 40.6 |
| Cibola | 45 | 1 043 | 70.7 | 34.1 | 22 | 94 | 7.2 | 1.8 | 302.3 | 70.4 | 0.0 | 16.8 |
| Colfax | 37 | 577 | 51.5 | 22.2 | 29 | 110 | 11.7 | 2.4 | 129.9 | 55.3 | 22.7 | 6.1 |
| Curry | 101 | 2 865 | 190.8 | 97.7 | 85 | 460 | 40.9 | 8.1 | 734.8 | 153.0 | 53.7 | 15.9 |
| De Baca | 5 | D | D | D | 4 | D | D | D | 23.7 | 8.5 | 4.6 | 0.8 |
| Dona Ana | 474 | 10 748 | 798.2 | 323.2 | 230 | 1 237 | 94.1 | 27.7 | 2 062.5 | 567.9 | 160.8 | 130.9 |
| Eddy | 117 | 2 773 | 225.3 | 88.8 | 85 | 461 | 40.5 | 9.3 | 706.6 | 160.7 | 84.7 | 24.4 |
| Grant | 94 | 1 506 | 116.4 | 49.4 | 57 | 207 | 14.7 | 4.1 | 306.3 | 129.8 | 43.4 | 14.4 |
| Guadalupe | 9 | 45 | 5.4 | 0.9 | 9 | 38 | 4.7 | 1.3 | 70.8 | 13.4 | 8.0 | 2.3 |
| Harding | 1 | D | D | D | NA | NA | NA | NA | 8.1 | 3.4 | 1.5 | 0.2 |
| Hidalgo | 10 | 102 | 3.8 | 1.6 | 4 | D | D | D | 96.2 | 16.5 | 7.9 | 4.1 |
| Lea | 116 | 2 483 | 199.9 | 74.8 | 100 | 709 | 134.5 | 23.5 | 392.8 | 135.7 | 86.6 | 31.6 |
| Lincoln | 48 | 634 | 54.9 | 24.5 | 42 | 160 | 16.4 | 3.3 | 152.4 | 87.3 | 22.4 | 6.0 |
| Los Alamos | 59 | 965 | 92.7 | 34.9 | 22 | 151 | 9.0 | 2.7 | 2 347.6 | 46.5 | 16.3 | 0.9 |
| Luna | 46 | 804 | 77.0 | 24.9 | 30 | 109 | 6.8 | 1.5 | 248.0 | 91.0 | 34.5 | 18.8 |
| McKinley | 94 | 4 020 | 292.3 | 155.2 | 83 | 528 | 35.7 | 9.6 | 944.8 | 153.6 | 55.5 | 67.3 |
| Mora | 6 | 230 | 10.0 | 5.6 | 3 | D | D | D | 86.3 | 19.4 | 6.4 | 3.8 |
| Otero | 111 | 2 152 | 174.8 | 70.1 | 66 | 348 | 19.2 | 5.4 | 941.6 | 252.4 | 52.5 | 20.8 |
| Quay | 27 | 448 | 31.4 | 13.0 | 21 | 115 | 13.1 | 2.8 | 114.2 | 40.6 | 18.5 | 8.1 |
| Rio Arriba | 95 | 1 808 | 119.6 | 66.0 | 27 | 134 | 14.4 | 2.8 | 481.7 | 120.8 | 45.4 | 25.3 |
| Roosevelt | 35 | 728 | 43.6 | 18.2 | 15 | 78 | 5.4 | 1.5 | 178.2 | 45.4 | 28.1 | 10.9 |
| Sandoval | 159 | 1 861 | 134.8 | 53.8 | 94 | 498 | 42.3 | 11.8 | 675.6 | 333.7 | 78.6 | 28.2 |
| San Juan | 265 | 6 274 | 534.2 | 226.2 | 192 | 1 363 | 170.4 | 37.1 | 995.9 | 299.9 | 102.4 | 51.5 |
| San Miguel | 84 | 2 532 | 164.2 | 69.9 | 26 | 92 | 7.4 | 2.0 | 402.8 | 94.2 | 40.2 | 26.9 |
| Santa Fe | 518 | 8 465 | 809.4 | 318.0 | 341 | 1 849 | 231.0 | 54.1 | 2 153.9 | 470.9 | 117.4 | 28.7 |
| Sierra | 21 | 538 | 33.1 | 15.9 | 20 | 116 | 7.2 | 2.2 | 160.3 | 70.0 | 31.7 | 6.9 |
| Socorro | 30 | 763 | 45.9 | 27.0 | 15 | 45 | 2.9 | 0.7 | 189.7 | 49.8 | 15.9 | 17.2 |
| Taos | 109 | 1 548 | 112.1 | 48.0 | 68 | 270 | 19.9 | 5.3 | 390.6 | 110.4 | 31.0 | 17.7 |
| Torrance | 20 | 361 | 12.4 | 6.4 | 9 | 23 | 2.3 | 0.5 | 113.4 | 48.0 | 11.6 | 9.7 |
| Union | 9 | D | D | D | 11 | D | D | D | 49.9 | 15.0 | 7.9 | 1.6 |
| Valencia | 88 | 2 682 | 113.5 | 56.1 | 60 | 242 | 20.0 | 5.2 | 504.1 | 239.8 | 79.5 | 32.0 |
| **NEW YORK** | 53 948 | 1 326 039 | 128 595.2 | 54 422.4 | 42 575 | 249 391 | 39 147.4 | 8 073.4 | 202 266.2 | 49 784.8 | 37 802.8 | 9 010.1 |
| Albany | 1 010 | 30 989 | 2 855.4 | 1 165.0 | 792 | 6 198 | 716.3 | 200.7 | 9 559.2 | 842.4 | 463.1 | 92.8 |
| Allegany | 95 | 1 994 | 106.1 | 50.1 | 73 | 265 | 17.5 | 3.8 | 350.7 | 148.8 | 75.7 | 21.3 |
| Bronx | 1 997 | 86 879 | 8 795.8 | 3 868.5 | 1 621 | 7 061 | 680.8 | 184.8 | (2) | (2) | (2) | (2) |
| Broome | 435 | 14 029 | 1 253.0 | 505.5 | 326 | 2 032 | 161.7 | 44.0 | 1 795.6 | 682.4 | 363.4 | 83.6 |
| Cattaraugus | 189 | 3 656 | 263.6 | 110.7 | 127 | 794 | 49.7 | 12.5 | 922.4 | 277.9 | 137.3 | 30.3 |
| Cayuga | 201 | 3 683 | 257.5 | 112.0 | 124 | 487 | 41.2 | 8.9 | 583.8 | 241.0 | 129.4 | 26.0 |
| Chautauqua | 297 | 8 735 | 581.0 | 235.6 | 255 | 1 558 | 110.3 | 23.3 | 1 234.7 | 471.2 | 239.7 | 63.4 |
| Chemung | 221 | 6 722 | 587.1 | 247.0 | 129 | 786 | 59.9 | 15.7 | 754.7 | 306.1 | 159.0 | 39.0 |
| Chenango | 116 | 1 795 | 134.8 | 55.4 | 77 | 270 | 21.0 | 6.0 | 374.1 | 171.5 | 70.0 | 20.1 |
| Clinton | 240 | 5 056 | 399.7 | 180.2 | 123 | 585 | 43.2 | 12.2 | 652.0 | 268.0 | 105.9 | 31.7 |
| Columbia | 170 | 3 928 | 274.7 | 130.3 | 97 | 395 | 38.3 | 9.8 | 518.3 | 219.7 | 106.4 | 17.9 |
| Cortland | 130 | 3 262 | 202.1 | 93.4 | 103 | 557 | 37.9 | 10.7 | 302.6 | 131.3 | 62.5 | 16.1 |
| Delaware | 118 | 2 235 | 146.6 | 55.3 | 83 | 357 | 59.3 | 8.2 | 391.9 | 161.0 | 85.1 | 15.9 |
| Dutchess | 908 | 17 764 | 1 631.3 | 682.5 | 614 | 2 577 | 260.9 | 68.7 | 1 990.3 | 881.2 | 401.9 | 52.9 |
| Erie | 2 709 | 73 571 | 6 357.2 | 2 520.7 | 1 773 | 13 107 | 1 091.7 | 322.8 | 8 851.9 | 3 203.3 | 1 767.1 | 410.1 |
| Essex | 137 | 1 755 | 114.9 | 54.8 | 79 | 374 | 35.7 | 8.7 | 340.6 | 140.2 | 69.4 | 12.4 |
| Franklin | 155 | 3 205 | 236.2 | 102.9 | 84 | 250 | 17.9 | 4.8 | 414.5 | 145.5 | 73.2 | 20.6 |
| Fulton | 187 | 3 419 | 228.8 | 106.1 | 87 | 492 | 37.8 | 12.4 | 405.0 | 171.8 | 86.0 | 20.8 |

1. State totals may include programs not allocated by county.     2. Bronx, Kings, Queens, and Richmond counties are included with New York county.

# Federal Funds, Residential Construction, and Local Government Finances

| STATE County | Federal funds and grants, 2009–2010 (cont.) — Expenditures (mil dol) (cont.) — Salaries and wages | Procurement contract awards — Defense | Procurement contract awards — Other | Grants[1] — Medicaid and other health-related | Grants[1] — Nutrition and family welfare | Grants[1] — Education | Grants[1] — Other | Value of residential construction authorized by building permits, 2011 — New construction ($1,000) | Number of housing units | Local government finances, 2007 — General revenue — Total (mil dol) | Intergovernmental (mil dol) | Taxes — Total (mil dol) | Per capita[2] (dollars) — Total | Property |
|---|---|---|---|---|---|---|---|---|---|---|---|---|---|---|
| | 171 | 172 | 173 | 174 | 175 | 176 | 177 | 178 | 179 | 180 | 181 | 182 | 183 | 184 |
| **NEW JERSEY—Cont'd** | | | | | | | | | | | | | | |
| Mercer | 320.8 | 177.4 | 175.7 | 690.6 | 349.7 | 578.2 | 2 175.8 | 62 982 | 400 | 1 979.0 | 683.1 | 990.7 | 2 711 | 2 675 |
| Middlesex | 337.1 | 165.8 | 246.0 | 665.1 | 88.7 | 16.8 | 260.5 | 153 999 | 1 225 | 3 387.0 | 919.5 | 1 897.9 | 2 407 | 2 350 |
| Monmouth | 544.7 | 2 858.3 | 192.1 | 449.0 | 82.8 | 17.1 | 68.2 | 167 631 | 864 | 3 126.6 | 803.2 | 1 814.6 | 2 826 | 2 770 |
| Morris | 392.5 | 629.8 | 177.4 | 153.9 | 44.8 | 6.7 | 56.5 | 123 836 | 547 | 2 299.5 | 375.6 | 1 571.1 | 3 216 | 3 168 |
| Ocean | 218.1 | 100.2 | 34.4 | 223.0 | 75.3 | 17.9 | 39.7 | 178 486 | 933 | 2 124.3 | 556.3 | 1 255.3 | 2 220 | 2 181 |
| Passaic | 102.0 | 375.7 | 26.4 | 613.7 | 106.7 | 28.2 | 70.6 | 47 449 | 406 | 1 897.2 | 681.0 | 1 034.7 | 2 103 | 2 080 |
| Salem | 23.0 | 2.2 | 12.3 | 65.8 | 11.1 | 2.4 | 3.8 | 7 980 | 82 | 320.1 | 134.6 | 127.5 | 1 931 | 1 887 |
| Somerset | 118.3 | 113.1 | 61.2 | 97.2 | 33.5 | 3.8 | 13.7 | 86 900 | 580 | 1 524.2 | 262.5 | 1 043.1 | 3 224 | 3 180 |
| Sussex | 32.0 | 5.2 | 9.4 | 56.5 | 15.4 | 3.0 | 4.3 | 31 600 | 172 | 660.1 | 181.5 | 395.2 | 2 609 | 2 566 |
| Union | 156.7 | 209.5 | 64.8 | 479.6 | 78.9 | 15.4 | 67.9 | 53 635 | 566 | 2 753.2 | 949.6 | 1 402.5 | 2 673 | 2 609 |
| Warren | 43.1 | 32.6 | 5.3 | 55.5 | 17.4 | 3.7 | 9.0 | 23 446 | 191 | 501.1 | 186.9 | 244.4 | 2 227 | 2 198 |
| **NEW MEXICO** | 2 768.0 | 1 519.7 | 5 979.2 | 3 712.9 | 585.8 | 619.3 | 1 802.3 | 0 | 732 | X | X | X | X | X |
| Bernalillo | 1 221.7 | 755.9 | 2 894.6 | 1 015.6 | 111.6 | 73.7 | 242.7 | 176 219 | 1 093 | 2 368.5 | 1 203.9 | 740.8 | 1 177 | 606 |
| Catron | 4.9 | 0.0 | 1.3 | 5.8 | 0.7 | 0.5 | 1.1 | NA | NA | 12.6 | 10.0 | 1.6 | 465 | 385 |
| Chaves | 45.7 | 4.0 | 18.8 | 143.9 | 13.4 | 6.4 | 11.5 | 9 140 | 33 | 205.0 | 146.6 | 31.1 | 496 | 384 |
| Cibola | 23.7 | 0.0 | 124.5 | 1.5 | 9.9 | 5.4 | 17.5 | NA | NA | 61.9 | 41.8 | 9.6 | 352 | 172 |
| Colfax | 7.3 | 2.9 | 0.8 | 28.0 | 3.6 | 0.6 | 1.1 | 5 194 | 14 | 58.1 | 35.1 | 12.4 | 935 | 651 |
| Curry | 196.4 | 143.3 | 2.9 | 93.0 | 10.9 | 4.2 | 38.6 | 37 335 | 191 | 157.2 | 97.0 | 36.8 | 812 | 227 |
| De Baca | 0.9 | 0.0 | 0.2 | 6.3 | 0.8 | 0.1 | 0.8 | NA | NA | 9.7 | 6.7 | 1.6 | 842 | 568 |
| Dona Ana | 218.7 | 309.3 | 203.7 | 273.0 | 47.7 | 15.0 | 64.9 | 126 380 | 644 | 633.2 | 389.2 | 159.6 | 803 | 331 |
| Eddy | 70.2 | 7.6 | 202.4 | 103.3 | 16.4 | 3.0 | 29.5 | 26 752 | 289 | 206.8 | 116.4 | 63.3 | 1 242 | 588 |
| Grant | 17.3 | 0.0 | 4.9 | 66.4 | 7.8 | 1.6 | 12.2 | NA | NA | 160.0 | 66.6 | 27.5 | 927 | 312 |
| Guadalupe | 3.0 | 2.3 | 0.3 | 37.1 | 1.5 | 0.2 | 2.2 | NA | NA | 24.8 | 15.0 | 6.5 | 1 461 | 822 |
| Harding | 0.7 | 0.0 | 0.2 | 1.5 | 0.2 | 0.0 | 0.2 | NA | NA | 6.8 | 5.1 | 0.9 | 1 278 | 635 |
| Hidalgo | 17.6 | 31.6 | 0.3 | 14.2 | 1.4 | 0.9 | 0.6 | NA | NA | 25.1 | 19.0 | 3.3 | 672 | 546 |
| Lea | 8.7 | 4.5 | 1.5 | 94.5 | 14.7 | 3.5 | 1.4 | 4 454 | 28 | 297.4 | 135.3 | 89.9 | 1 549 | 513 |
| Lincoln | 7.8 | 0.5 | 1.8 | 19.0 | 4.4 | 1.1 | 1.2 | 7 873 | 45 | 82.2 | 48.0 | 21.5 | 1 034 | 641 |
| Los Alamos | 21.3 | 1.4 | 2 215.8 | 19.1 | 1.7 | 0.6 | 22.9 | 2 220 | 7 | 139.4 | 72.8 | 44.6 | 2 405 | 705 |
| Luna | 38.2 | 3.0 | 3.4 | 45.1 | 6.5 | 2.5 | 2.6 | 3 305 | 18 | 91.3 | 57.7 | 18.8 | 697 | 335 |
| McKinley | 142.5 | 6.4 | 116.6 | 287.0 | 26.6 | 65.8 | 10.8 | 495 | 2 | 219.4 | 158.6 | 33.8 | 483 | 231 |
| Mora | 2.5 | 0.0 | 0.7 | 40.0 | 3.2 | 0.3 | 9.3 | NA | NA | 17.4 | 12.9 | 2.6 | 515 | 488 |
| Otero | 316.8 | 174.9 | 9.3 | 67.7 | 12.7 | 4.5 | 10.3 | 222 | 1 | 139.3 | 90.9 | 31.1 | 492 | 247 |
| Quay | 2.9 | 0.1 | 0.7 | 28.3 | 5.4 | 0.6 | 1.6 | NA | NA | 45.9 | 29.8 | 6.1 | 676 | 319 |
| Rio Arriba | 22.6 | 2.4 | 6.7 | 198.7 | 14.0 | 11.2 | 17.3 | 0 | 0 | 147.6 | 91.5 | 37.8 | 925 | 426 |
| Roosevelt | 6.3 | 4.1 | 4.0 | 44.1 | 4.3 | 3.5 | 1.4 | 7 231 | 63 | 59.8 | 42.3 | 11.2 | 585 | 261 |
| Sandoval | 26.2 | 13.8 | 11.3 | 111.4 | 17.3 | 14.4 | 24.8 | 83 349 | 463 | 364.7 | 187.7 | 104.4 | 886 | 422 |
| San Juan | 106.8 | 1.2 | 79.4 | 196.6 | 23.1 | 38.8 | 10.4 | 35 045 | 213 | 501.8 | 314.6 | 117.3 | 958 | 569 |
| San Miguel | 20.5 | 1.2 | 2.3 | 184.3 | 10.2 | 5.5 | 7.0 | NA | NA | 118.7 | 83.0 | 24.3 | 850 | 349 |
| Santa Fe | 136.2 | 45.2 | 43.5 | 254.6 | 123.5 | 151.5 | 743.4 | 12 536 | 94 | 511.3 | 237.0 | 184.0 | 1 287 | 676 |
| Sierra | 6.9 | 0.7 | 1.6 | 32.8 | 2.8 | 0.6 | 4.3 | 467 | 3 | 35.5 | 22.2 | 9.3 | 756 | 413 |
| Socorro | 12.9 | 2.7 | 9.8 | 49.2 | 5.2 | 4.2 | 16.0 | 0 | 0 | 64.9 | 40.4 | 15.7 | 867 | 600 |
| Taos | 29.3 | 0.0 | 9.4 | 115.8 | 9.1 | 10.3 | 52.2 | 7 190 | 56 | 114.6 | 66.8 | 28.7 | 907 | 432 |
| Torrance | 3.7 | 0.0 | 1.4 | 30.6 | 4.0 | 0.6 | 2.8 | NA | NA | 75.5 | 54.0 | 13.0 | 781 | 529 |
| Union | 4.2 | 0.0 | 0.6 | 13.2 | 0.9 | 0.2 | 3.4 | NA | NA | 15.1 | 11.0 | 2.6 | 674 | 306 |
| Valencia | 23.7 | 0.7 | 4.5 | 91.0 | 19.2 | 5.2 | 2.8 | 10 024 | 78 | 190.8 | 140.0 | 36.8 | 516 | 292 |
| **NEW YORK** | 13 936.5 | 8 809.8 | 5 073.4 | 39 959.0 | 6 704.4 | 4 360.8 | 12 079.4 | 3 355 501 | 22 575 | X | X | X | X | X |
| Albany | 498.7 | 45.1 | 198.4 | 725.5 | 152.3 | 2 323.0 | 3 747.0 | 60 314 | 360 | 1 621.8 | 493.0 | 796.5 | 2 661 | 1 767 |
| Allegany | 10.1 | 0.6 | 2.4 | 62.7 | 16.1 | 3.7 | 2.1 | 5 073 | 50 | 258.6 | 146.9 | 84.5 | 1 702 | 1 339 |
| Bronx | (3) | (3) | (3) | (3) | (3) | (3) | (3) | 104 708 | 1 116 | (3) | (3) | (3) | (3) | (3) |
| Broome | 65.2 | 177.3 | 19.2 | 235.1 | 54.8 | 19.7 | 69.9 | 7 549 | 45 | 1 049.2 | 455.6 | 431.0 | 2 200 | 1 429 |
| Cattaraugus | 37.4 | 4.5 | 56.3 | 111.8 | 27.5 | 99.8 | 45.9 | 13 757 | 85 | 460.1 | 242.5 | 147.6 | 1 843 | 1 360 |
| Cayuga | 16.7 | 2.1 | 5.4 | 108.7 | 22.0 | 7.4 | 10.1 | 10 544 | 69 | 386.2 | 180.4 | 133.2 | 1 663 | 1 199 |
| Chautauqua | 67.8 | 86.4 | 16.3 | 192.8 | 43.8 | 11.9 | 15.2 | 23 399 | 129 | 727.8 | 336.1 | 254.1 | 1 897 | 1 369 |
| Chemung | 36.0 | 2.0 | 7.9 | 143.0 | 26.0 | 6.1 | 19.8 | 12 355 | 138 | 422.5 | 199.0 | 150.5 | 1 710 | 1 109 |
| Chenango | 9.8 | 3.2 | 2.3 | 70.0 | 16.7 | 4.5 | 3.0 | 3 454 | 68 | 272.8 | 148.7 | 89.2 | 1 742 | 1 374 |
| Clinton | 67.2 | 7.5 | 10.7 | 107.9 | 23.3 | 8.3 | 9.3 | 12 968 | 94 | 438.0 | 201.5 | 159.5 | 1 940 | 1 355 |
| Columbia | 14.4 | 0.3 | 4.8 | 113.3 | 16.4 | 2.7 | 8.4 | 20 866 | 62 | 321.9 | 113.7 | 166.0 | 2 034 | 2 034 |
| Cortland | 10.1 | 0.2 | 4.4 | 52.2 | 13.9 | 4.5 | 4.1 | 5 803 | 37 | 234.1 | 112.3 | 89.9 | 1 858 | 1 336 |
| Delaware | 22.9 | 4.4 | 2.8 | 72.5 | 14.6 | 2.9 | 7.0 | 9 750 | 60 | 304.1 | 139.4 | 121.0 | 2 614 | 2 127 |
| Dutchess | 85.3 | 2.7 | 51.5 | 362.1 | 59.2 | 17.3 | 36.9 | 86 077 | 297 | 1 442.7 | 464.9 | 773.8 | 2 643 | 2 030 |
| Erie | 651.8 | 231.5 | 213.0 | 1 541.5 | 274.2 | 86.9 | 259.4 | 192 962 | 1 086 | 4 525.9 | 2 169.6 | 1 813.0 | 1 985 | 1 342 |
| Essex | 25.4 | 0.5 | 4.7 | 66.8 | 11.9 | 1.8 | 4.5 | 12 311 | 59 | 231.3 | 73.9 | 116.8 | 3 063 | 2 374 |
| Franklin | 15.6 | 0.1 | 4.0 | 103.4 | 15.9 | 5.2 | 20.4 | 7 405 | 57 | 277.2 | 145.6 | 89.6 | 1 776 | 1 400 |
| Fulton | 11.7 | 2.4 | 3.5 | 74.7 | 14.9 | 4.0 | 6.9 | 13 909 | 88 | 275.6 | 128.9 | 99.4 | 1 804 | 1 283 |

1. State totals may include programs not allocated by county. 2. Based on the resident population estimated as of July 1 of the year shown. 3. Bronx, Kings, Queens, and Richmond counties are included with New York county.

# Table B. States and Counties — **Local Government Finances, Government Employment, and Voting**

| | Local government finances, 2007 (cont.) | | | | | | | | | Government employment, 2011 | | | Presidential election,[2] 2012 | | |
| | Direct general expenditure | | | | | | | Debt outstanding | | | | | Percent of vote cast: | | |
| | | | Percent of total for: | | | | | | | | | | | | |
| STATE County | Total (mil dol) | Per capita[1] (dollars) | Education | Health and hospitals | Police protection | Public welfare | High-ways | Total (mil dol) | Per capita[1] (dollars) | Federal civilian | Federal military | State and local | Demo-cratic | Republi-can | All other |
| | 185 | 186 | 187 | 188 | 189 | 190 | 191 | 192 | 193 | 194 | 195 | 196 | 197 | 198 | 199 |
| NEW JERSEY—Cont'd | | | | | | | | | | | | | | | |
| Mercer | 2 085.4 | 5 706 | 53.1 | 1.0 | 5.4 | 4.4 | 1.3 | 1 899.1 | 5 197 | 2 407 | 794 | 45 697 | 67.4 | 31.4 | 1.2 |
| Middlesex | 3 668.9 | 4 652 | 55.3 | 1.2 | 5.7 | 3.4 | 2.3 | 3 699.0 | 4 690 | 2 794 | 1 803 | 56 075 | 60.4 | 38.5 | 1.1 |
| Monmouth | 3 225.6 | 5 024 | 56.7 | 0.8 | 5.7 | 2.4 | 2.4 | 2 828.7 | 4 406 | 4 239 | 1 853 | 32 030 | 47.6 | 51.3 | 1.1 |
| Morris | 2 404.4 | 4 922 | 59.1 | 0.8 | 5.4 | 1.5 | 2.8 | 2 029.0 | 4 154 | 5 801 | 1 112 | 24 789 | 45.5 | 53.6 | 0.9 |
| Ocean | 2 223.9 | 3 933 | 51.9 | 0.4 | 6.3 | 2.5 | 4.7 | 2 186.1 | 3 866 | 2 951 | 1 407 | 23 718 | 40.2 | 58.6 | 1.3 |
| Passaic | 1 873.1 | 3 806 | 50.1 | 1.0 | 7.1 | 4.1 | 1.7 | 1 286.6 | 2 614 | 1 085 | 1 042 | 27 720 | 60.4 | 38.7 | 0.8 |
| Salem | 333.4 | 5 050 | 57.8 | 1.1 | 3.5 | 4.4 | 3.8 | 454.1 | 6 879 | 168 | 137 | 4 166 | 51.2 | 47.2 | 1.6 |
| Somerset | 1 584.8 | 4 898 | 59.9 | 1.3 | 4.8 | 0.7 | 3.8 | 1 217.0 | 3 761 | 1 741 | 674 | 15 662 | 52.5 | 46.4 | 1.1 |
| Sussex | 647.5 | 4 275 | 66.1 | 1.0 | 3.7 | 1.6 | 3.9 | 697.4 | 4 604 | 328 | 308 | 7 185 | 38.9 | 59.6 | 1.5 |
| Union | 2 808.8 | 5 354 | 54.5 | 1.9 | 6.3 | 1.8 | 2.0 | 2 182.8 | 4 160 | 1 567 | 1 120 | 31 101 | 63.7 | 35.5 | 0.9 |
| Warren | 529.4 | 4 824 | 57.6 | 2.1 | 3.3 | 3.2 | 3.7 | 237.2 | 2 162 | 238 | 224 | 5 634 | 42.2 | 56.2 | 1.7 |
| NEW MEXICO | X | X | X | X | X | X | X | X | X | 32 610 | 18 196 | 163 024 | 56.9 | 41.8 | 1.3 |
| Bernalillo | 2 068.8 | 3 287 | 48.6 | 0.8 | 9.1 | 2.1 | 6.6 | 1 797.5 | 2 856 | 15 152 | 5 540 | 54 155 | 60.0 | 38.7 | 1.3 |
| Catron | 9.9 | 2 886 | 61.8 | 1.5 | 7.0 | 0.0 | 8.4 | 2.4 | 709 | 100 | 10 | 215 | 31.4 | 66.2 | 2.4 |
| Chaves | 201.7 | 3 222 | 50.8 | 0.3 | 5.4 | 2.8 | 4.3 | 120.7 | 1 928 | 309 | 197 | 4 057 | 37.1 | 61.7 | 1.2 |
| Cibola | 62.1 | 2 277 | 61.7 | 0.2 | 3.9 | 1.9 | 3.2 | 30.0 | 1 102 | 336 | 76 | 2 821 | 64.1 | 34.4 | 1.5 |
| Colfax | 52.7 | 3 989 | 51.7 | 6.6 | 5.9 | 0.4 | 6.4 | 11.2 | 846 | 53 | 37 | 1 436 | 54.7 | 43.9 | 1.4 |
| Curry | 146.5 | 3 232 | 64.1 | 0.1 | 5.2 | 0.9 | 5.8 | 42.3 | 933 | 944 | 4 243 | 2 549 | 32.3 | 66.5 | 1.2 |
| De Baca | 9.1 | 4 768 | 53.9 | 1.5 | 3.3 | 0.0 | 14.6 | 3.6 | 1 896 | 14 | 0 | 200 | 34.4 | 64.8 | 0.9 |
| Dona Ana | 605.1 | 3 044 | 58.2 | 3.1 | 4.2 | 0.8 | 2.8 | 401.1 | 2 018 | 4 062 | 600 | 17 062 | 58.1 | 40.5 | 1.3 |
| Eddy | 218.6 | 4 286 | 49.2 | 7.1 | 6.9 | 1.9 | 4.4 | 77.6 | 1 521 | 786 | 148 | 3 076 | 36.6 | 62.2 | 1.2 |
| Grant | 164.1 | 5 525 | 31.7 | 38.6 | 4.7 | 0.0 | 2.0 | 44.3 | 1 493 | 228 | 81 | 3 451 | 59.2 | 39.3 | 1.5 |
| Guadalupe | 22.3 | 5 004 | 49.3 | 0.1 | 2.4 | 1.1 | 2.4 | 6.8 | 1 523 | 26 | 13 | 396 | 70.9 | 28.2 | 0.9 |
| Harding | 6.3 | 8 853 | 52.1 | 0.7 | 1.9 | 0.0 | 16.8 | 2.3 | 3 258 | 17 | 0 | 93 | 41.5 | 57.2 | 1.3 |
| Hidalgo | 21.2 | 4 297 | 57.7 | 0.6 | 10.7 | 0.6 | 4.4 | 5.9 | 1 183 | 297 | 13 | 407 | 50.9 | 48.0 | 1.1 |
| Lea | 288.1 | 4 964 | 49.7 | 10.2 | 6.2 | 1.4 | 5.8 | 87.0 | 1 499 | 94 | 179 | 3 445 | 27.4 | 71.6 | 1.0 |
| Lincoln | 80.4 | 3 871 | 47.4 | 3.1 | 7.1 | 0.9 | 3.5 | 61.7 | 2 966 | 114 | 56 | 1 090 | 36.5 | 61.9 | 1.7 |
| Los Alamos | 134.6 | 7 253 | 29.7 | 0.0 | 5.4 | 0.7 | 3.8 | 137.5 | 7 411 | 294 | 53 | 1 619 | 52.6 | 45.7 | 1.6 |
| Luna | 92.5 | 3 425 | 52.0 | 1.9 | 5.9 | 1.1 | 5.8 | 26.3 | 974 | 576 | 69 | 1 638 | 51.7 | 46.4 | 1.9 |
| McKinley | 236.6 | 3 377 | 71.2 | 0.6 | 4.2 | 1.4 | 3.5 | 121.7 | 1 737 | 2 597 | 202 | 5 178 | 71.4 | 27.5 | 1.1 |
| Mora | 18.6 | 3 668 | 67.8 | 0.0 | 2.5 | 0.0 | 2.6 | 4.8 | 947 | 45 | 13 | 277 | 78.6 | 20.6 | 0.8 |
| Otero | 131.6 | 2 084 | 53.9 | 0.1 | 8.0 | 2.3 | 5.7 | 59.4 | 941 | 2 034 | 4 819 | 4 391 | 39.6 | 58.8 | 1.6 |
| Quay | 39.2 | 4 374 | 70.1 | 1.4 | 1.6 | 0.7 | 3.4 | 6.5 | 728 | 44 | 25 | 874 | 38.7 | 59.2 | 2.1 |
| Rio Arriba | 132.1 | 3 236 | 55.9 | 0.5 | 4.2 | 0.9 | 7.8 | 75.9 | 1 859 | 357 | 111 | 4 563 | 75.0 | 24.1 | 0.9 |
| Roosevelt | 58.6 | 3 061 | 61.2 | 1.0 | 5.6 | 0.0 | 5.3 | 14.1 | 737 | 56 | 56 | 2 268 | 34.3 | 64.2 | 1.6 |
| Sandoval | 382.9 | 3 249 | 45.6 | 0.4 | 6.1 | 1.7 | 7.6 | 585.9 | 4 971 | 396 | 368 | 7 107 | 55.7 | 43.0 | 1.3 |
| San Juan | 519.0 | 4 239 | 59.6 | 0.9 | 5.4 | 1.2 | 4.5 | 941.0 | 7 686 | 1 602 | 356 | 9 228 | 38.8 | 59.9 | 1.3 |
| San Miguel | 118.1 | 4 121 | 61.8 | 0.1 | 4.3 | 0.6 | 4.5 | 65.0 | 2 268 | 150 | 80 | 3 939 | 79.7 | 19.1 | 1.1 |
| Santa Fe | 462.7 | 3 237 | 43.5 | 3.0 | 6.5 | 3.1 | 5.8 | 626.5 | 4 382 | 1 030 | 404 | 16 666 | 76.9 | 21.9 | 1.2 |
| Sierra | 36.1 | 2 927 | 47.1 | 0.9 | 2.2 | 1.5 | 3.8 | 17.6 | 1 430 | 121 | 33 | 762 | 42.9 | 55.0 | 2.1 |
| Socorro | 58.6 | 3 235 | 53.2 | 1.2 | 6.9 | 2.8 | 5.0 | 12.6 | 694 | 223 | 49 | 2 722 | 59.5 | 38.4 | 2.1 |
| Taos | 103.6 | 3 278 | 50.3 | 0.9 | 2.6 | 1.3 | 2.0 | 24.7 | 781 | 301 | 90 | 1 933 | 81.8 | 17.0 | 1.2 |
| Torrance | 68.6 | 4 133 | 69.2 | 0.0 | 3.3 | 0.4 | 3.0 | 28.4 | 1 709 | 81 | 45 | 1 054 | 44.5 | 53.8 | 1.7 |
| Union | 17.9 | 4 724 | 58.8 | 5.5 | 5.3 | 0.0 | 2.8 | 2.2 | 578 | 57 | 12 | 307 | 28.2 | 70.4 | 1.3 |
| Valencia | 192.0 | 2 691 | 66.4 | 0.1 | 4.4 | 1.8 | 2.8 | 103.4 | 1 449 | 114 | 211 | 4 045 | 53.2 | 45.5 | 1.4 |
| NEW YORK | X | X | X | X | X | X | X | X | X | 121 187 | 61 472 | 1 295 149 | 62.9 | 36.0 | 1.0 |
| Albany | 1 653.7 | 5 525 | 40.9 | 3.1 | 4.9 | 12.6 | 3.3 | 2 110.9 | 7 053 | 5 328 | 716 | 57 723 | 63.8 | 34.4 | 1.8 |
| Allegany | 259.4 | 5 227 | 50.2 | 3.5 | 3.2 | 12.3 | 8.0 | 280.0 | 5 641 | 120 | 80 | 3 772 | 38.2 | 60.0 | 1.8 |
| Bronx | (3) | (3) | (3) | (3) | (3) | (3) | (3) | (3) | (3) | 7 334 | 2 328 | 15 093 | 88.7 | 10.9 | 0.4 |
| Broome | 1 130.8 | 5 770 | 46.4 | 2.7 | 2.8 | 11.2 | 4.3 | 954.4 | 4 870 | 602 | 334 | 19 517 | 53.2 | 45.2 | 1.6 |
| Cattaraugus | 475.0 | 5 930 | 52.4 | 4.2 | 2.3 | 12.4 | 7.8 | 363.1 | 4 534 | 245 | 141 | 9 914 | 43.9 | 54.5 | 1.6 |
| Cayuga | 380.6 | 4 753 | 50.0 | 4.6 | 2.5 | 10.5 | 6.3 | 277.7 | 3 468 | 148 | 130 | 5 860 | 53.3 | 44.8 | 1.8 |
| Chautauqua | 728.1 | 5 436 | 50.6 | 2.5 | 2.9 | 12.9 | 5.9 | 534.3 | 3 989 | 344 | 221 | 8 769 | 49.6 | 48.6 | 1.8 |
| Chemung | 429.2 | 4 877 | 43.9 | 2.8 | 3.2 | 18.3 | 6.8 | 316.2 | 3 593 | 239 | 146 | 6 617 | 48.8 | 50.0 | 1.1 |
| Chenango | 262.1 | 5 118 | 54.7 | 5.1 | 2.2 | 8.2 | 8.8 | 162.0 | 3 163 | 101 | 82 | 4 092 | 48.4 | 49.6 | 2.0 |
| Clinton | 431.6 | 5 250 | 50.3 | 5.2 | 1.8 | 11.1 | 6.3 | 375.9 | 4 572 | 748 | 136 | 7 147 | 60.7 | 37.8 | 1.6 |
| Columbia | 311.5 | 4 995 | 50.3 | 3.8 | 2.1 | 13.5 | 7.7 | 140.6 | 2 255 | 166 | 102 | 4 450 | 55.9 | 42.5 | 1.6 |
| Cortland | 241.4 | 4 991 | 44.9 | 5.3 | 3.0 | 10.6 | 9.5 | 145.6 | 3 011 | 108 | 82 | 3 338 | 54.2 | 44.2 | 1.6 |
| Delaware | 300.8 | 6 498 | 39.5 | 3.5 | 1.1 | 12.3 | 14.9 | 181.5 | 3 922 | 136 | 79 | 4 474 | 46.4 | 51.6 | 2.0 |
| Dutchess | 1 461.9 | 4 994 | 53.7 | 4.1 | 3.3 | 7.7 | 4.2 | 1 173.4 | 4 008 | 1 242 | 488 | 20 679 | 53.7 | 45.1 | 1.2 |
| Erie | 4 605.8 | 5 043 | 48.0 | 3.3 | 4.1 | 11.3 | 3.3 | 4 139.9 | 4 533 | 8 854 | 1 767 | 65 519 | 58.0 | 40.5 | 1.6 |
| Essex | 250.1 | 6 562 | 33.9 | 4.4 | 7.8 | 9.7 | 10.1 | 258.6 | 6 785 | 340 | 64 | 3 922 | 55.9 | 42.6 | 1.5 |
| Franklin | 279.0 | 5 530 | 52.7 | 3.5 | 1.3 | 11.9 | 5.3 | 159.2 | 3 156 | 158 | 84 | 8 311 | 60.4 | 38.2 | 1.4 |
| Fulton | 293.9 | 5 332 | 53.6 | 2.4 | 2.4 | 14.2 | 4.9 | 226.0 | 4 101 | 84 | 91 | 4 207 | 44.5 | 53.7 | 1.8 |

1. Based on the resident population estimated as of July 1 of the year shown.   2. © 2013 Election Data Services, Inc. All rights reserved.   3. Bronx, Kings, Queens, and Richmond counties are included with New York county.

# Table B. States and Counties — Land Area and Population

| STATE/ County code | CBSA code[1] | County type[2] | STATE County | Land area,[3] (sq km) 2010 | Population 2012 Total persons | Rank | Per square kilometer | White | Black | American Indian, Alaska Native | Asian and Pacific Islander | Percent Hispanic or Latino[4] | Under 5 years | 5 to 17 years | 18 to 24 years | 25 to 34 years | 35 to 44 years | 45 to 54 years |
|---|---|---|---|---|---|---|---|---|---|---|---|---|---|---|---|---|---|---|
| | | | | 1 | 2 | 3 | 4 | 5 | 6 | 7 | 8 | 9 | 10 | 11 | 12 | 13 | 14 | 15 |
| | | | **NEW YORK—Cont'd** | | | | | | | | | | | | | | | |
| 36 037 | 12860 | 4 | Genesee | 1 277 | 59 977 | 865 | 47.0 | 92.6 | 3.5 | 1.5 | 1.1 | 2.9 | 5.5 | 16.1 | 9.3 | 11.2 | 12.2 | 16.5 |
| 36 039 | ... | 6 | Greene | 1 676 | 48 673 | 1 003 | 29.0 | 88.0 | 6.2 | 0.7 | 1.4 | 5.1 | 4.6 | 14.3 | 9.6 | 10.0 | 12.3 | 16.5 |
| 36 041 | ... | 8 | Hamilton | 4 448 | 4 778 | 2 854 | 1.1 | 97.1 | 1.2 | 0.8 | 0.8 | 1.2 | 3.5 | 12.8 | 5.3 | 7.3 | 10.1 | 17.0 |
| 36 043 | 46540 | 2 | Herkimer | 3 656 | 64 508 | 816 | 17.6 | 96.3 | 1.5 | 0.7 | 0.8 | 1.7 | 5.4 | 16.4 | 9.3 | 10.6 | 11.7 | 15.6 |
| 36 045 | 48060 | 4 | Jefferson | 3 286 | 120 262 | 508 | 36.6 | 86.3 | 6.4 | 1.0 | 2.5 | 6.1 | 8.4 | 16.9 | 12.6 | 16.0 | 12.0 | 12.8 |
| 36 047 | 35620 | 1 | Kings | 183 | 2 565 635 | 8 | 14 019.9 | 36.7 | 32.7 | 0.5 | 11.6 | 20.0 | 7.2 | 16.4 | 10.3 | 17.3 | 13.6 | 12.8 |
| 36 049 | ... | 6 | Lewis | 3 301 | 27 224 | 1 522 | 8.2 | 97.2 | 1.1 | 0.5 | 0.6 | 1.4 | 6.4 | 17.8 | 8.1 | 11.3 | 11.8 | 16.2 |
| 36 051 | 40380 | 1 | Livingston | 1 636 | 64 810 | 814 | 39.6 | 92.9 | 3.0 | 0.7 | 1.7 | 2.9 | 4.7 | 14.8 | 15.1 | 10.2 | 11.6 | 16.0 |
| 36 053 | 45060 | 2 | Madison | 1 696 | 72 382 | 747 | 42.7 | 94.5 | 2.3 | 1.0 | 1.3 | 2.0 | 5.0 | 16.2 | 13.7 | 9.9 | 11.5 | 16.0 |
| 36 055 | 40380 | 1 | Monroe | 1 702 | 747 813 | 79 | 439.4 | 74.2 | 15.6 | 0.7 | 4.0 | 7.5 | 5.8 | 16.4 | 11.3 | 12.6 | 12.1 | 14.9 |
| 36 057 | 11220 | 4 | Montgomery | 1 044 | 49 941 | 978 | 47.8 | 85.6 | 2.2 | 0.6 | 1.1 | 11.7 | 6.1 | 16.9 | 8.3 | 11.4 | 12.0 | 14.6 |
| 36 059 | 35620 | 1 | Nassau | 737 | 1 349 233 | 28 | 1 830.7 | 65.7 | 11.4 | 0.4 | 8.7 | 15.0 | 5.5 | 17.4 | 8.6 | 10.9 | 12.9 | 16.1 |
| 36 061 | 35620 | 1 | New York | 59 | 1 619 090 | 20 | 27 442.2 | 49.4 | 14.1 | 0.5 | 12.4 | 25.6 | 5.0 | 9.8 | 10.6 | 22.1 | 14.6 | 12.7 |
| 36 063 | 15380 | 1 | Niagara | 1 353 | 215 124 | 292 | 159.0 | 88.8 | 7.8 | 1.5 | 1.4 | 2.3 | 5.3 | 15.8 | 9.4 | 11.2 | 12.0 | 16.2 |
| 36 065 | 46540 | 2 | Oneida | 3 140 | 233 556 | 277 | 74.4 | 86.0 | 6.8 | 0.6 | 3.5 | 4.8 | 5.6 | 15.9 | 10.0 | 11.6 | 12.0 | 15.1 |
| 36 067 | 45060 | 2 | Onondaga | 2 016 | 466 852 | 143 | 231.6 | 81.0 | 11.9 | 1.4 | 3.8 | 4.3 | 5.8 | 16.7 | 11.1 | 12.3 | 11.9 | 15.2 |
| 36 069 | 40380 | 1 | Ontario | 1 668 | 108 519 | 545 | 65.1 | 92.7 | 2.9 | 0.6 | 1.6 | 3.7 | 5.2 | 16.8 | 9.2 | 10.1 | 12.2 | 16.0 |
| 36 071 | 39100 | 2 | Orange | 2 102 | 374 512 | 177 | 178.2 | 69.2 | 10.4 | 0.7 | 3.2 | 18.5 | 6.9 | 19.8 | 10.0 | 11.3 | 13.5 | 15.5 |
| 36 073 | 40380 | 1 | Orleans | 1 013 | 42 836 | 1 117 | 42.3 | 88.9 | 6.7 | 0.9 | 0.9 | 4.3 | 5.3 | 16.4 | 9.4 | 11.4 | 12.6 | 16.7 |
| 36 075 | 45060 | 2 | Oswego | 2 465 | 121 700 | 505 | 49.4 | 95.8 | 1.2 | 0.8 | 1.0 | 2.2 | 5.7 | 16.8 | 12.3 | 11.1 | 12.2 | 16.0 |
| 36 077 | 36580 | 6 | Otsego | 2 594 | 61 709 | 842 | 23.8 | 93.5 | 2.3 | 0.7 | 1.6 | 3.2 | 4.2 | 13.6 | 17.0 | 9.2 | 10.3 | 14.5 |
| 36 079 | 35620 | 1 | Putnam | 597 | 99 607 | 591 | 166.8 | 83.4 | 2.7 | 0.4 | 2.6 | 12.0 | 4.9 | 18.1 | 7.6 | 9.7 | 14.0 | 18.8 |
| 36 081 | 35620 | 1 | Queens | 281 | 2 272 771 | 10 | 8 088.2 | 28.7 | 19.2 | 0.8 | 25.4 | 27.8 | 6.1 | 14.5 | 9.5 | 16.3 | 14.5 | 14.4 |
| 36 083 | 10580 | 2 | Rensselaer | 1 690 | 159 835 | 394 | 94.6 | 87.0 | 7.3 | 0.7 | 3.0 | 4.1 | 5.5 | 15.5 | 11.5 | 12.6 | 12.4 | 15.3 |
| 36 085 | 35620 | 1 | Richmond | 151 | 470 728 | 140 | 3 117.4 | 64.7 | 10.3 | 0.5 | 8.4 | 17.6 | 6.0 | 16.9 | 9.5 | 12.8 | 13.7 | 15.2 |
| 36 087 | 35620 | 1 | Rockland | 449 | 317 757 | 206 | 707.7 | 65.8 | 12.0 | 0.5 | 7.1 | 16.1 | 7.6 | 20.2 | 9.0 | 11.4 | 12.0 | 14.2 |
| 36 089 | 36300 | 5 | St. Lawrence | 6 942 | 112 232 | 535 | 16.2 | 93.7 | 2.6 | 1.5 | 1.4 | 2.0 | 5.7 | 15.2 | 14.9 | 11.3 | 11.6 | 14.4 |
| 36 091 | 10580 | 2 | Saratoga | 2 098 | 222 133 | 284 | 105.9 | 93.6 | 2.1 | 0.6 | 2.5 | 2.6 | 5.4 | 16.7 | 8.1 | 11.4 | 14.0 | 16.5 |
| 36 093 | 10580 | 2 | Schenectady | 530 | 155 124 | 407 | 292.7 | 79.9 | 11.1 | 0.9 | 5.0 | 6.0 | 5.8 | 16.6 | 9.4 | 12.2 | 12.6 | 15.4 |
| 36 095 | 10580 | 2 | Schoharie | 1 611 | 32 099 | 1 387 | 19.9 | 94.7 | 1.9 | 0.7 | 1.1 | 2.9 | 4.8 | 14.8 | 11.7 | 10.2 | 11.8 | 15.3 |
| 36 097 | ... | 6 | Schuyler | 850 | 18 514 | 1 895 | 21.8 | 96.8 | 1.5 | 0.8 | 0.6 | 1.5 | 4.8 | 15.6 | 8.1 | 10.2 | 12.3 | 16.5 |
| 36 099 | 42900 | 6 | Seneca | 838 | 35 305 | 1 295 | 42.1 | 91.3 | 5.1 | 0.7 | 1.1 | 3.0 | 5.4 | 15.4 | 9.5 | 12.4 | 12.0 | 15.3 |
| 36 101 | 18500 | 4 | Steuben | 3 602 | 99 063 | 592 | 27.5 | 95.3 | 2.1 | 0.7 | 1.6 | 1.5 | 5.8 | 17.2 | 7.9 | 11.3 | 12.0 | 15.6 |
| 36 103 | 35620 | 1 | Suffolk | 2 362 | 1 499 273 | 24 | 634.7 | 72.0 | 7.6 | 0.5 | 4.1 | 17.0 | 5.6 | 17.8 | 8.9 | 11.2 | 13.8 | 16.5 |
| 36 105 | ... | 4 | Sullivan | 2 507 | 76 793 | 714 | 30.6 | 75.8 | 9.3 | 0.8 | 2.1 | 13.9 | 5.9 | 16.4 | 8.4 | 11.2 | 12.2 | 16.3 |
| 36 107 | 13780 | 2 | Tioga | 1 343 | 50 478 | 971 | 37.6 | 96.6 | 1.2 | 0.6 | 1.1 | 1.5 | 5.6 | 17.2 | 7.3 | 10.6 | 11.8 | 17.4 |
| 36 109 | 27060 | 3 | Tompkins | 1 229 | 102 554 | 570 | 83.4 | 81.3 | 4.8 | 0.9 | 11.2 | 4.6 | 4.1 | 11.4 | 28.8 | 12.8 | 9.6 | 11.2 |
| 36 111 | 28740 | 3 | Ulster | 2 912 | 181 791 | 347 | 62.4 | 83.1 | 6.7 | 0.9 | 2.4 | 9.0 | 4.8 | 14.8 | 10.1 | 11.1 | 12.8 | 16.6 |
| 36 113 | 24020 | 3 | Warren | 2 245 | 65 538 | 807 | 29.2 | 96.0 | 1.5 | 0.7 | 1.1 | 1.9 | 4.9 | 15.2 | 7.7 | 10.6 | 12.2 | 16.4 |
| 36 115 | 24020 | 3 | Washington | 2 153 | 62 934 | 827 | 29.2 | 93.9 | 3.3 | 0.6 | 0.8 | 2.4 | 5.1 | 15.5 | 8.7 | 11.8 | 13.1 | 16.0 |
| 36 117 | 40380 | 1 | Wayne | 1 564 | 92 962 | 620 | 59.4 | 92.1 | 3.9 | 0.7 | 0.9 | 3.9 | 5.8 | 17.4 | 7.8 | 10.5 | 12.8 | 16.8 |
| 36 119 | 35620 | 1 | Westchester | 1 115 | 961 670 | 46 | 862.5 | 58.0 | 14.3 | 0.4 | 6.4 | 22.4 | 5.9 | 17.7 | 8.3 | 11.5 | 13.7 | 15.6 |
| 36 121 | ... | 6 | Wyoming | 1 535 | 41 892 | 1 131 | 27.3 | 90.6 | 5.8 | 0.5 | 0.8 | 3.1 | 4.9 | 15.0 | 8.1 | 13.5 | 13.9 | 16.9 |
| 36 123 | ... | 6 | Yates | 876 | 25 344 | 1 597 | 28.9 | 96.5 | 1.3 | 0.5 | 0.7 | 1.9 | 6.4 | 17.6 | 10.8 | 9.5 | 9.8 | 14.5 |
| 37 000 | ... | X | **NORTH CAROLINA** | 125 920 | 9 752 073 | X | 77.4 | 66.4 | 22.2 | 1.7 | 2.8 | 8.6 | 6.5 | 17.2 | 9.9 | 13.1 | 13.6 | 14.2 |
| 37 001 | 15500 | 3 | Alamance | 1 098 | 153 920 | 410 | 140.2 | 68.1 | 19.5 | 0.9 | 1.6 | 11.4 | 6.2 | 17.1 | 10.5 | 11.3 | 13.4 | 14.4 |
| 37 003 | 25860 | 2 | Alexander | 673 | 36 853 | 1 252 | 54.8 | 88.5 | 6.3 | 0.6 | 1.2 | 4.4 | 5.6 | 16.7 | 7.2 | 11.6 | 14.0 | 15.3 |
| 37 005 | ... | 9 | Alleghany | 609 | 10 927 | 2 365 | 17.9 | 88.6 | 1.7 | 0.6 | 0.7 | 9.2 | 4.9 | 14.8 | 6.8 | 9.6 | 11.9 | 14.4 |
| 37 007 | 16740 | 1 | Anson | 1 376 | 26 351 | 1 547 | 19.2 | 48.4 | 48.9 | 1.0 | 1.3 | 3.2 | 5.4 | 16.1 | 9.2 | 13.2 | 12.4 | 14.7 |
| 37 009 | ... | 9 | Ashe | 1 104 | 27 097 | 1 527 | 24.5 | 93.8 | 1.0 | 0.7 | 0.6 | 4.8 | 5.1 | 13.9 | 6.6 | 10.7 | 12.2 | 14.8 |
| 37 011 | ... | 8 | Avery | 640 | 17 635 | 1 939 | 27.6 | 90.1 | 4.4 | 0.8 | 0.6 | 4.8 | 4.4 | 12.6 | 9.8 | 12.6 | 13.9 | 15.2 |
| 37 013 | 47820 | 6 | Beaufort | 2 142 | 47 507 | 1 020 | 22.2 | 66.9 | 25.9 | 0.6 | 0.7 | 7.0 | 5.8 | 16.0 | 7.2 | 10.3 | 11.6 | 14.1 |
| 37 015 | ... | 9 | Bertie | 1 811 | 20 653 | 1 801 | 11.4 | 35.7 | 62.4 | 0.8 | 0.6 | 1.4 | 5.2 | 15.1 | 8.7 | 11.5 | 11.6 | 15.6 |
| 37 017 | ... | 6 | Bladen | 2 264 | 34 915 | 1 302 | 15.4 | 55.5 | 35.4 | 2.6 | 0.7 | 7.2 | 5.7 | 16.9 | 7.9 | 11.2 | 12.2 | 14.7 |
| 37 019 | 48900 | 2 | Brunswick | 2 194 | 112 257 | 534 | 51.2 | 82.2 | 12.1 | 1.2 | 0.8 | 5.1 | 5.1 | 13.3 | 6.1 | 10.5 | 11.1 | 13.1 |
| 37 021 | 11700 | 2 | Buncombe | 1 701 | 244 490 | 268 | 143.7 | 85.7 | 7.3 | 1.0 | 1.5 | 6.2 | 5.5 | 14.8 | 8.5 | 13.5 | 13.1 | 14.2 |
| 37 023 | 25860 | 2 | Burke | 1 313 | 90 505 | 634 | 68.9 | 83.6 | 7.5 | 0.7 | 4.0 | 5.5 | 5.5 | 16.6 | 9.1 | 10.7 | 12.9 | 15.2 |
| 37 025 | 16740 | 1 | Cabarrus | 937 | 184 498 | 342 | 196.9 | 72.6 | 16.1 | 0.7 | 2.5 | 9.6 | 7.1 | 20.0 | 7.6 | 12.5 | 15.7 | 14.6 |
| 37 027 | 25860 | 2 | Caldwell | 1 221 | 81 930 | 676 | 67.1 | 89.4 | 5.7 | 0.7 | 0.7 | 4.7 | 5.5 | 16.7 | 7.9 | 10.4 | 14.2 | 15.3 |
| 37 029 | 21020 | 8 | Camden | 623 | 10 090 | 2 436 | 16.2 | 81.5 | 14.4 | 1.1 | 2.2 | 2.6 | 5.5 | 19.6 | 7.6 | 9.7 | 14.8 | 17.3 |
| 37 031 | 33980 | 4 | Carteret | 1 311 | 67 632 | 783 | 51.6 | 88.4 | 7.1 | 1.1 | 1.5 | 3.7 | 4.7 | 14.0 | 7.1 | 11.0 | 11.8 | 15.5 |
| 37 033 | ... | 8 | Caswell | 1 101 | 23 217 | 1 680 | 21.1 | 62.2 | 34.4 | 0.9 | 0.7 | 3.3 | 4.6 | 15.2 | 7.6 | 10.9 | 12.7 | 16.5 |
| 37 035 | 25860 | 2 | Catawba | 1 033 | 154 339 | 408 | 149.4 | 79.1 | 9.4 | 0.6 | 3.9 | 8.5 | 6.1 | 17.4 | 8.2 | 11.5 | 14.0 | 15.0 |
| 37 037 | 20500 | 2 | Chatham | 1 767 | 65 976 | 799 | 37.3 | 72.2 | 13.8 | 0.7 | 1.5 | 13.2 | 5.8 | 15.8 | 6.3 | 10.0 | 13.1 | 14.8 |
| 37 039 | ... | 9 | Cherokee | 1 180 | 26 992 | 1 530 | 22.9 | 94.1 | 2.0 | 2.7 | 0.8 | 2.6 | 4.6 | 14.0 | 6.0 | 9.0 | 11.1 | 13.7 |

1. CBSA = Core Based Statistical Area. See Appendix A for explanation. See Appendix B for list of metropolitan areas with component counties.   2. County type code from the Economic Research Service of USDA Rural-Urban Continuum Codes. See Appendix A for definition.   3. Dry land or land partially or temporarily covered by water.   4. May be of any race.

| STATE County | 55 to 64 years (16) | 65 to 74 years (17) | 75 years and over (18) | Percent female (19) | 2000 (20) | 2010 (21) | 2000–2010 (22) | 2010–2012 (23) | Births (24) | Deaths (25) | Net migration (26) | Number (27) | Percent change, 2000–2010 (28) | Persons per household (29) | Female family householder[1] (30) | One person (31) |
|---|---|---|---|---|---|---|---|---|---|---|---|---|---|---|---|---|
| **NEW YORK—Cont'd** | | | | | | | | | | | | | | | | |
| Genesee | 13.2 | 8.2 | 7.7 | 50.3 | 60 370 | 60 079 | -0.5 | -0.2 | 1 450 | 1 397 | -117 | 23 728 | 4.2 | 2.45 | 11.1 | 27.2 |
| Greene | 15.1 | 9.9 | 7.7 | 47.8 | 48 195 | 49 221 | 2.1 | -1.1 | 982 | 1 140 | -417 | 19 823 | 8.6 | 2.31 | 10.6 | 30.7 |
| Hamilton | 19.9 | 13.9 | 10.2 | 49.6 | 5 379 | 4 836 | -10.1 | -1.2 | 75 | 136 | 3 | 2 262 | -4.2 | 2.10 | 6.8 | 32.7 |
| Herkimer | 14.3 | 8.6 | 8.1 | 50.9 | 64 427 | 64 519 | 0.1 | 0.0 | 1 460 | 1 436 | -78 | 26 324 | 2.3 | 2.40 | 11.1 | 29.3 |
| Jefferson | 10.3 | 6.0 | 5.2 | 48.8 | 111 738 | 116 229 | 4.0 | 3.5 | 4 659 | 2 056 | 1 346 | 43 451 | 8.4 | 2.53 | 12.4 | 25.6 |
| Kings | 10.9 | 6.2 | 5.4 | 52.7 | 2 465 326 | 2 504 700 | 1.6 | 2.4 | 93 750 | 35 752 | 2 485 | 916 856 | 4.1 | 2.69 | 20.5 | 29.0 |
| Lewis | 13.4 | 7.8 | 7.2 | 49.5 | 26 944 | 27 087 | 0.5 | 0.5 | 762 | 597 | -43 | 10 514 | 4.7 | 2.55 | 8.5 | 24.5 |
| Livingston | 13.4 | 7.4 | 6.7 | 49.8 | 64 328 | 65 393 | 1.7 | -0.9 | 1 244 | 1 170 | -636 | 24 409 | 10.2 | 2.44 | 10.4 | 26.3 |
| Madison | 13.4 | 7.9 | 6.4 | 51.0 | 69 441 | 73 442 | 5.8 | -1.4 | 1 486 | 1 310 | -1 214 | 27 754 | 9.4 | 2.46 | 10.7 | 26.3 |
| Monroe | 12.8 | 7.2 | 6.9 | 51.7 | 735 343 | 744 344 | 1.2 | 0.5 | 19 087 | 14 104 | -1 346 | 300 422 | 4.9 | 2.39 | 14.1 | 30.5 |
| Montgomery | 14.0 | 7.7 | 9.0 | 51.2 | 49 708 | 50 219 | 1.0 | -0.6 | 1 326 | 1 294 | -282 | 20 272 | 1.2 | 2.43 | 13.2 | 29.7 |
| Nassau | 13.3 | 7.5 | 7.9 | 51.6 | 1 334 544 | 1 339 532 | 0.4 | 0.7 | 32 084 | 24 028 | 2 202 | 448 528 | 0.3 | 2.94 | 11.7 | 20.1 |
| New York | 11.4 | 7.4 | 6.3 | 52.9 | 1 537 195 | 1 585 873 | 3.2 | 2.1 | 44 629 | 22 961 | 11 895 | 763 846 | 3.4 | 1.99 | 11.9 | 46.3 |
| Niagara | 14.0 | 8.1 | 8.0 | 51.4 | 219 846 | 216 469 | -1.5 | -0.6 | 5 005 | 5 200 | -1 033 | 90 556 | 3.1 | 2.34 | 12.9 | 31.4 |
| Oneida | 13.2 | 8.1 | 8.4 | 50.2 | 235 469 | 234 878 | -0.3 | -0.6 | 5 800 | 5 554 | -1 459 | 93 028 | 2.8 | 2.38 | 13.1 | 31.1 |
| Onondaga | 12.8 | 7.0 | 7.2 | 51.8 | 458 336 | 467 026 | 1.9 | 0.0 | 11 962 | 8 963 | -2 980 | 187 686 | 3.6 | 2.40 | 13.7 | 30.7 |
| Ontario | 14.7 | 8.5 | 7.3 | 51.1 | 100 224 | 107 931 | 7.7 | 0.5 | 2 315 | 2 236 | 521 | 43 019 | 12.1 | 2.43 | 10.4 | 26.9 |
| Orange | 11.7 | 6.3 | 5.0 | 50.0 | 341 367 | 372 813 | 9.2 | 0.5 | 11 293 | 5 628 | -3 888 | 125 925 | 9.7 | 2.86 | 12.3 | 22.1 |
| Orleans | 13.6 | 7.9 | 6.7 | 50.5 | 44 171 | 42 883 | -2.9 | -0.1 | 960 | 935 | -74 | 16 119 | 4.9 | 2.50 | 12.4 | 26.2 |
| Oswego | 12.9 | 7.2 | 5.6 | 50.1 | 122 377 | 122 109 | -0.2 | -0.3 | 3 054 | 2 308 | -108 | 46 400 | 1.9 | 2.52 | 11.7 | 25.1 |
| Otsego | 14.1 | 9.1 | 7.9 | 51.7 | 61 676 | 62 259 | 0.9 | -0.9 | 1 081 | 1 416 | -208 | 24 620 | 5.7 | 2.31 | 9.2 | 29.4 |
| Putnam | 14.0 | 7.6 | 5.4 | 50.2 | 95 745 | 99 710 | 4.1 | -0.1 | 1 944 | 1 444 | -579 | 35 041 | 7.1 | 2.77 | 8.9 | 20.3 |
| Queens | 11.8 | 6.9 | 6.1 | 51.5 | 2 229 379 | 2 230 722 | 0.1 | 1.9 | 67 403 | 31 817 | 6 514 | 780 117 | -0.3 | 2.82 | 16.4 | 25.6 |
| Rensselaer | 13.6 | 7.2 | 6.5 | 50.7 | 152 538 | 159 429 | 4.5 | 0.3 | 3 907 | 3 301 | -140 | 64 702 | 8.0 | 2.38 | 12.5 | 29.3 |
| Richmond | 12.9 | 7.3 | 5.7 | 51.5 | 443 728 | 468 730 | 5.6 | 0.4 | 12 577 | 7 801 | -2 626 | 165 516 | 5.9 | 2.78 | 14.7 | 24.2 |
| Rockland | 12.0 | 7.3 | 6.4 | 50.9 | 286 753 | 311 687 | 8.7 | 1.9 | 10 642 | 4 603 | 164 | 99 242 | 7.1 | 3.07 | 11.1 | 21.1 |
| St. Lawrence | 12.8 | 7.7 | 6.4 | 49.2 | 111 931 | 111 944 | 0.0 | 0.3 | 2 643 | 2 281 | -36 | 41 605 | 2.7 | 2.43 | 10.8 | 27.9 |
| Saratoga | 13.9 | 7.9 | 6.1 | 50.8 | 200 635 | 219 607 | 9.5 | 1.2 | 4 916 | 3 842 | 1 486 | 88 296 | 13.0 | 2.44 | 9.1 | 26.1 |
| Schenectady | 12.9 | 7.1 | 7.9 | 51.6 | 146 555 | 154 727 | 5.6 | 0.3 | 4 111 | 3 336 | -441 | 62 886 | 5.4 | 2.39 | 13.8 | 30.6 |
| Schoharie | 15.3 | 9.2 | 7.0 | 49.9 | 31 582 | 32 749 | 3.7 | -2.0 | 623 | 609 | -650 | 13 166 | 9.8 | 2.37 | 9.4 | 27.8 |
| Schuyler | 15.7 | 9.2 | 7.7 | 50.1 | 19 224 | 18 343 | -4.6 | 0.9 | 360 | 438 | 216 | 7 530 | 2.1 | 2.39 | 10.2 | 27.2 |
| Seneca | 14.2 | 8.3 | 7.4 | 47.6 | 33 342 | 35 251 | 5.7 | 0.2 | 838 | 732 | -45 | 13 393 | 6.0 | 2.42 | 10.5 | 27.3 |
| Steuben | 14.1 | 8.5 | 7.6 | 50.4 | 98 726 | 98 990 | 0.3 | 0.1 | 2 536 | 2 219 | -244 | 40 344 | 3.3 | 2.41 | 10.9 | 28.9 |
| Suffolk | 12.4 | 7.5 | 6.4 | 50.8 | 1 419 369 | 1 493 350 | 5.2 | 0.4 | 37 283 | 25 871 | -5 116 | 499 922 | 6.5 | 2.93 | 11.7 | 20.6 |
| Sullivan | 14.4 | 9.0 | 6.2 | 48.9 | 73 966 | 77 547 | 4.8 | -1.0 | 1 867 | 1 588 | -963 | 30 139 | 9.0 | 2.45 | 12.9 | 29.1 |
| Tioga | 14.0 | 8.6 | 7.4 | 50.4 | 51 784 | 51 125 | -1.3 | -1.3 | 1 115 | 943 | -818 | 20 350 | 3.2 | 2.49 | 10.4 | 24.7 |
| Tompkins | 11.1 | 5.9 | 5.2 | 50.7 | 96 501 | 101 564 | 5.2 | 1.0 | 1 953 | 1 399 | 425 | 38 967 | 7.0 | 2.27 | 8.7 | 33.3 |
| Ulster | 14.5 | 8.3 | 7.1 | 50.3 | 177 749 | 182 493 | 2.7 | -0.4 | 3 682 | 3 502 | -905 | 71 049 | 5.3 | 2.40 | 11.4 | 29.0 |
| Warren | 15.4 | 9.4 | 8.1 | 51.2 | 63 303 | 65 707 | 3.8 | -0.3 | 1 419 | 1 428 | -111 | 27 990 | 8.8 | 2.32 | 10.6 | 29.5 |
| Washington | 14.0 | 8.5 | 7.2 | 48.2 | 61 042 | 63 216 | 3.6 | -0.4 | 1 385 | 1 402 | -252 | 24 142 | 7.5 | 2.49 | 11.2 | 25.0 |
| Wayne | 14.1 | 8.2 | 6.6 | 50.4 | 93 765 | 93 772 | 0.0 | -0.9 | 2 305 | 1 821 | -1 255 | 36 585 | 4.8 | 2.53 | 11.0 | 24.5 |
| Westchester | 12.5 | 7.4 | 7.4 | 51.8 | 923 459 | 949 113 | 2.8 | 1.3 | 24 332 | 15 348 | 3 900 | 347 232 | 3.0 | 2.65 | 12.8 | 27.2 |
| Wyoming | 13.7 | 8.0 | 5.9 | 45.5 | 43 424 | 42 155 | -2.9 | -0.6 | 896 | 797 | -356 | 15 501 | 4.0 | 2.46 | 9.5 | 25.7 |
| Yates | 14.3 | 9.4 | 7.7 | 51.5 | 24 621 | 25 348 | 3.0 | 0.0 | 756 | 571 | -195 | 9 517 | 5.4 | 2.53 | 10.2 | 26.9 |
| **NORTH CAROLINA** | 12.3 | 7.5 | 5.7 | 51.3 | 8 049 313 | 9 535 483 | 18.5 | 2.3 | 270 488 | 178 941 | 122 575 | 3 745 155 | 19.6 | 2.48 | 13.7 | 27.0 |
| Alamance | 12.2 | 7.8 | 7.0 | 52.4 | 130 800 | 151 131 | 15.5 | 1.8 | 3 935 | 3 214 | 2 147 | 59 960 | 16.2 | 2.45 | 14.5 | 27.8 |
| Alexander | 13.8 | 9.6 | 6.2 | 49.3 | 33 603 | 37 198 | 10.7 | -0.9 | 787 | 766 | -371 | 14 425 | 9.8 | 2.50 | 10.9 | 24.1 |
| Alleghany | 16.1 | 12.1 | 9.4 | 50.5 | 10 677 | 11 155 | 4.5 | -2.0 | 207 | 296 | -138 | 4 778 | 4.0 | 2.31 | 9.3 | 28.2 |
| Anson | 13.2 | 8.2 | 6.6 | 48.0 | 25 275 | 26 948 | 6.6 | -2.2 | 601 | 675 | -536 | 9 755 | 6.0 | 2.51 | 19.8 | 28.4 |
| Ashe | 15.9 | 11.8 | 9.1 | 50.8 | 24 384 | 27 281 | 11.9 | -0.7 | 548 | 750 | -13 | 11 755 | 12.9 | 2.29 | 9.3 | 27.4 |
| Avery | 14.1 | 9.8 | 7.6 | 45.3 | 17 167 | 17 797 | 3.7 | -0.9 | 339 | 441 | -64 | 6 664 | 2.0 | 2.31 | 8.9 | 28.1 |
| Beaufort | 15.9 | 11.4 | 7.7 | 51.9 | 44 958 | 47 759 | 6.2 | -0.5 | 1 172 | 1 259 | -171 | 19 941 | 8.9 | 2.37 | 13.6 | 28.3 |
| Bertie | 14.6 | 9.3 | 8.5 | 50.3 | 19 773 | 21 282 | 7.6 | -3.0 | 448 | 612 | -525 | 8 359 | 8.0 | 2.39 | 19.9 | 30.8 |
| Bladen | 15.1 | 9.7 | 6.6 | 52.1 | 32 278 | 35 190 | 9.0 | -0.8 | 777 | 895 | -161 | 14 430 | 11.9 | 2.40 | 16.9 | 29.8 |
| Brunswick | 18.3 | 15.0 | 7.5 | 51.1 | 73 143 | 107 431 | 46.9 | 4.5 | 2 318 | 2 522 | 4 852 | 46 297 | 52.1 | 2.30 | 10.4 | 25.0 |
| Buncombe | 14.2 | 8.7 | 7.6 | 51.9 | 206 330 | 238 318 | 15.5 | 2.6 | 5 723 | 5 272 | 5 629 | 100 412 | 17.1 | 2.30 | 11.2 | 30.5 |
| Burke | 13.7 | 9.2 | 7.2 | 50.0 | 89 148 | 90 912 | 2.0 | -0.4 | 1 958 | 2 106 | -240 | 35 804 | 3.7 | 2.45 | 12.3 | 27.3 |
| Cabarrus | 10.9 | 6.6 | 4.9 | 51.2 | 131 063 | 178 011 | 35.8 | 3.6 | 5 245 | 3 159 | 4 352 | 65 666 | 32.6 | 2.69 | 12.6 | 22.1 |
| Caldwell | 14.1 | 9.5 | 6.5 | 50.7 | 77 415 | 83 029 | 7.3 | -1.3 | 1 788 | 1 962 | -917 | 33 388 | 8.5 | 2.46 | 12.5 | 25.4 |
| Camden | 12.4 | 8.0 | 5.1 | 50.3 | 6 885 | 9 980 | 45.0 | 1.1 | 201 | 131 | 29 | 3 675 | 38.1 | 2.71 | 9.9 | 19.1 |
| Carteret | 16.3 | 11.4 | 8.1 | 50.6 | 59 383 | 66 469 | 11.9 | 1.7 | 1 372 | 1 667 | 1 477 | 28 870 | 14.5 | 2.27 | 10.4 | 28.4 |
| Caswell | 15.8 | 9.9 | 6.8 | 48.9 | 23 501 | 23 719 | 0.9 | -2.1 | 451 | 568 | -448 | 9 190 | 6.0 | 2.43 | 14.7 | 26.9 |
| Catawba | 13.2 | 8.3 | 6.3 | 51.0 | 141 685 | 154 358 | 8.9 | 0.0 | 3 959 | 3 427 | -541 | 60 887 | 9.6 | 2.50 | 12.4 | 26.2 |
| Chatham | 15.4 | 10.4 | 8.5 | 51.8 | 49 329 | 63 505 | 28.7 | 3.9 | 1 424 | 1 335 | 1 877 | 25 845 | 30.9 | 2.43 | 9.8 | 25.6 |
| Cherokee | 17.6 | 14.6 | 9.4 | 51.4 | 24 298 | 27 444 | 12.9 | -1.6 | 441 | 728 | -155 | 11 753 | 13.7 | 2.30 | 9.7 | 27.2 |

1. No spouse present.

| STATE County | Persons in group quarters, 2010 | Daytime population, 2007–2011 Number | Employment/ residence ratio | Births, 2011 Total | Rate[1] | Deaths, 2011 Number | Rate[1] | Persons under 65 with no health insurance, 2010 Number | Percent | Medicare, 2012 Eligible for Medicare | Enrolled in Medicare Advantage | Enrolled in a Medicare prescription drug plan | Serious crimes known to police,[2] 2011 Total Number | Rate[3] |
|---|---|---|---|---|---|---|---|---|---|---|---|---|---|---|
| | 32 | 33 | 34 | 35 | 36 | 37 | 38 | 39 | 40 | 41 | 42 | 43 | 44 | 45 |
| **NEW YORK—Cont'd** | | | | | | | | | | | | | | |
| Genesee | 1 908 | 55 259 | 0.84 | 645 | 10.8 | 609 | 10.2 | 5 614 | 11.4 | 11 604 | 6 181 | 2 093 | 1 438 | 2 383 |
| Greene | 3 400 | 45 235 | 0.80 | 430 | 8.8 | 492 | 10.1 | 4 892 | 13.0 | 10 563 | 2 677 | 3 122 | 827 | 1 673 |
| Hamilton | 80 | 4 604 | 0.88 | 35 | 7.3 | 74 | 15.4 | 638 | 17.2 | 1 394 | 274 | 496 | 53 | 1 091 |
| Herkimer | 1 426 | 54 848 | 0.67 | 652 | 10.2 | 659 | 10.3 | 6 674 | 12.7 | 13 740 | 4 152 | 5 399 | 1 356 | 2 251 |
| Jefferson | 6 170 | 119 582 | 1.07 | 2 014 | 17.1 | 910 | 7.7 | 13 077 | 13.4 | 17 823 | 3 846 | 5 964 | 2 447 | 2 115 |
| Kings | 35 609 | 2 195 426 | 0.73 | 41 555 | 16.4 | 15 753 | 6.2 | 358 056 | 16.2 | 324 809 | 117 149 | 137 040 | [4] | [4] |
| Lewis | 313 | 24 039 | 0.75 | 357 | 13.2 | 257 | 9.5 | 3 048 | 13.3 | 4 603 | 1 061 | 1 778 | 415 | 1 525 |
| Livingston | 5 758 | 57 078 | 0.73 | 557 | 8.6 | 490 | 7.5 | 5 353 | 10.5 | 11 405 | 6 503 | 1 979 | 1 059 | 1 612 |
| Madison | 5 133 | 65 255 | 0.76 | 680 | 9.3 | 548 | 7.5 | 6 645 | 11.4 | 12 386 | 3 440 | 4 073 | 1 272 | 1 724 |
| Monroe | 26 283 | 779 557 | 1.11 | 8 440 | 11.3 | 6 194 | 8.3 | 62 342 | 10.0 | 134 568 | 83 390 | 25 355 | 24 611 | 3 292 |
| Montgomery | 920 | 47 442 | 0.88 | 611 | 12.2 | 576 | 11.5 | 5 417 | 13.0 | 11 211 | 3 540 | 4 451 | 1 082 | 2 145 |
| Nassau | 21 666 | 1 260 221 | 0.89 | 14 420 | 10.7 | 10 498 | 7.8 | 129 594 | 11.6 | 234 862 | 51 637 | 83 286 | 19 254 | 1 431 |
| New York | 67 373 | 3 095 659 | 2.82 | 19 820 | 12.4 | 10 152 | 6.3 | 164 516 | 12.4 | 253 262 | 75 960 | 105 404 | [4]193 341 | [4]2 354 |
| Niagara | 4 319 | 193 341 | 0.77 | 2 243 | 10.4 | 2 285 | 10.6 | 19 991 | 11.2 | 44 835 | 21 866 | 7 571 | 7 177 | 3 301 |
| Oneida | 13 405 | 242 674 | 1.08 | 2 563 | 10.9 | 2 421 | 10.3 | 19 374 | 10.4 | 48 397 | 13 450 | 16 067 | 5 918 | 2 508 |
| Onondaga | 17 069 | 498 293 | 1.15 | 5 381 | 11.5 | 3 925 | 8.4 | 45 647 | 11.8 | 83 369 | 22 259 | 24 341 | 12 836 | 2 736 |
| Ontario | 3 329 | 108 321 | 1.02 | 1 020 | 9.4 | 973 | 9.0 | 9 448 | 10.6 | 21 283 | 11 707 | 4 078 | 2 102 | 1 939 |
| Orange | 12 230 | 343 668 | 0.84 | 5 097 | 13.6 | 2 478 | 6.6 | 38 369 | 11.9 | 53 339 | 7 250 | 20 203 | 8 854 | 2 403 |
| Orleans | 2 586 | 38 682 | 0.76 | 429 | 10.1 | 402 | 9.4 | 4 497 | 13.0 | 7 914 | 4 025 | 1 558 | 997 | 2 315 |
| Oswego | 4 954 | 106 040 | 0.69 | 1 385 | 11.3 | 987 | 8.1 | 11 872 | 11.6 | 22 153 | 6 443 | 7 505 | 3 189 | 2 652 |
| Otsego | 5 320 | 62 686 | 1.01 | 478 | 7.7 | 605 | 9.8 | 6 158 | 13.0 | 12 583 | 2 058 | 5 144 | 1 139 | 1 821 |
| Putnam | 2 592 | 79 023 | 0.58 | 866 | 8.7 | 635 | 6.4 | 8 472 | 9.9 | 15 586 | 1 793 | 6 454 | 845 | 861 |
| Queens | 28 000 | 1 862 239 | 0.66 | 30 197 | 13.4 | 14 060 | 6.3 | 401 948 | 20.7 | 310 933 | 120 859 | 112 381 | [4] | [4] |
| Rensselaer | 5 607 | 138 471 | 0.74 | 1 753 | 11.0 | 1 485 | 9.3 | 14 327 | 10.8 | 27 794 | 10 085 | 6 049 | 4 676 | 2 920 |
| Richmond | 7 838 | 386 535 | 0.61 | 5 643 | 12.0 | 3 493 | 7.4 | 39 453 | 9.7 | 75 803 | 29 127 | 23 864 | [4] | [4] |
| Rockland | 7 183 | 282 666 | 0.81 | 4 828 | 15.3 | 2 050 | 6.5 | 32 426 | 12.2 | 50 663 | 7 994 | 19 537 | 4 541 | 1 450 |
| St. Lawrence | 10 751 | 109 019 | 0.94 | 1 163 | 10.4 | 990 | 8.9 | 13 454 | 15.6 | 21 338 | 3 644 | 7 337 | 2 484 | 2 242 |
| Saratoga | 3 950 | 188 818 | 0.73 | 2 145 | 9.7 | 1 685 | 7.6 | 17 080 | 9.2 | 38 416 | 13 964 | 9 276 | 3 053 | 1 384 |
| Schenectady | 4 434 | 145 966 | 0.89 | 1 834 | 11.8 | 1 481 | 9.6 | 15 217 | 11.8 | 28 511 | 11 021 | 9 322 | 5 524 | 3 554 |
| Schoharie | 1 556 | 29 361 | 0.77 | 274 | 8.4 | 281 | 8.6 | 3 133 | 12.1 | 5 901 | 1 274 | 2 124 | 433 | 1 316 |
| Schuyler | 354 | 15 894 | 0.69 | 149 | 8.1 | 180 | 9.8 | 1 912 | 12.8 | 4 150 | 949 | 1 366 | 162 | 879 |
| Seneca | 2 809 | 32 848 | 0.84 | 357 | 10.1 | 327 | 9.3 | 3 660 | 13.4 | 6 822 | 2 725 | 1 808 | 673 | 1 934 |
| Steuben | 1 583 | 99 129 | 1.01 | 1 087 | 11.0 | 959 | 9.7 | 10 579 | 12.8 | 20 139 | 5 023 | 6 018 | 1 678 | 1 688 |
| Suffolk | 29 406 | 1 393 685 | 0.87 | 16 846 | 11.2 | 11 275 | 7.5 | 150 410 | 11.8 | 253 918 | 48 447 | 84 328 | 30 938 | 2 064 |
| Sullivan | 3 825 | 73 281 | 0.87 | 854 | 11.1 | 724 | 9.4 | 10 061 | 15.7 | 15 074 | 1 278 | 6 943 | 1 935 | 2 484 |
| Tioga | 523 | 44 052 | 0.70 | 521 | 10.2 | 417 | 8.2 | 4 716 | 11.0 | 10 055 | 2 870 | 3 317 | 589 | 1 147 |
| Tompkins | 13 232 | 111 396 | 1.21 | 910 | 8.9 | 587 | 5.8 | 9 233 | 11.9 | 13 637 | 2 267 | 4 107 | NA | NA |
| Ulster | 11 773 | 165 550 | 0.80 | 1 631 | 8.9 | 1 523 | 8.3 | 19 515 | 13.1 | 34 889 | 6 879 | 12 468 | 3 770 | 2 057 |
| Warren | 738 | 72 327 | 1.21 | 629 | 9.6 | 615 | 9.3 | 6 469 | 12.0 | 15 086 | 5 188 | 4 087 | 1 479 | 2 241 |
| Washington | 3 164 | 52 843 | 0.63 | 623 | 9.8 | 621 | 9.8 | 6 830 | 13.4 | 11 882 | 4 041 | 3 392 | 857 | 1 350 |
| Wayne | 1 390 | 80 309 | 0.70 | 1 047 | 11.2 | 784 | 8.4 | 9 121 | 11.5 | 19 231 | 10 246 | 4 690 | 1 705 | 1 810 |
| Westchester | 28 704 | 932 255 | 0.97 | 10 927 | 11.4 | 6 720 | 7.0 | 100 338 | 12.7 | 156 776 | 29 867 | 59 887 | 15 769 | 1 658 |
| Wyoming | 3 961 | 39 322 | 0.84 | 398 | 9.5 | 326 | 7.8 | 3 925 | 12.1 | 7 628 | 3 880 | 1 321 | 526 | 1 242 |
| Yates | 1 287 | 23 119 | 0.80 | 349 | 13.7 | 257 | 10.1 | 2 960 | 14.8 | 5 205 | 2 456 | 1 236 | 409 | 1 606 |
| **NORTH CAROLINA** | 257 246 | 9 421 667 | 1.00 | 122 131 | 12.6 | 78 169 | 8.1 | 1 549 918 | 19.1 | 1 617 342 | 312 828 | 714 183 | 374 336 | 3 877 |
| Alamance | 4 229 | 140 829 | 0.88 | 1 836 | 12.0 | 1 424 | 9.3 | 26 845 | 21.3 | 27 822 | 11 764 | 9 142 | 6 647 | 4 343 |
| Alexander | 1 161 | 30 814 | 0.62 | 378 | 10.2 | 330 | 8.9 | 6 158 | 20.2 | 7 162 | 1 226 | 3 571 | 1 106 | 2 936 |
| Alleghany | 111 | 11 059 | 0.99 | 103 | 9.3 | 132 | 11.9 | 2 650 | 30.1 | 2 948 | 633 | 1 387 | NA | NA |
| Anson | 2 484 | 24 894 | 0.81 | 269 | 10.1 | 272 | 10.2 | 3 764 | 18.1 | 4 918 | 209 | 2 999 | 1 281 | 4 884 |
| Ashe | 369 | 25 659 | 0.89 | 257 | 9.5 | 323 | 11.9 | 4 990 | 23.0 | 6 545 | 979 | 3 417 | 553 | 2 002 |
| Avery | 2 414 | 18 998 | 1.17 | 163 | 9.3 | 203 | 11.6 | 3 156 | 25.4 | 3 631 | 492 | 1 837 | 262 | 1 454 |
| Beaufort | 503 | 47 201 | 0.99 | 556 | 11.7 | 566 | 11.9 | 7 312 | 18.9 | 11 771 | 602 | 6 301 | 1 642 | 3 432 |
| Bertie | 1 324 | 20 258 | 0.90 | 209 | 10.0 | 265 | 12.7 | 2 898 | 17.6 | 4 931 | 105 | 3 442 | 442 | 2 051 |
| Bladen | 511 | 34 116 | 0.95 | 364 | 10.4 | 401 | 11.5 | 6 311 | 21.5 | 7 139 | 557 | 4 215 | 1 569 | 4 403 |
| Brunswick | 843 | 97 654 | 0.82 | 1 051 | 9.5 | 1 107 | 10.1 | 16 715 | 19.9 | 30 269 | 3 530 | 13 554 | 3 509 | 3 307 |
| Buncombe | 7 673 | 251 229 | 1.14 | 2 570 | 10.6 | 2 312 | 9.6 | 40 791 | 20.9 | 49 141 | 8 357 | 22 084 | 7 186 | 2 987 |
| Burke | 3 352 | 85 774 | 0.87 | 894 | 9.8 | 895 | 9.8 | 14 835 | 20.1 | 18 221 | 3 173 | 8 770 | 2 672 | 2 952 |
| Cabarrus | 1 480 | 160 926 | 0.83 | 2 382 | 13.1 | 1 348 | 7.4 | 28 769 | 18.4 | 26 416 | 5 057 | 11 510 | 5 315 | 2 952 |
| Caldwell | 968 | 75 977 | 0.81 | 808 | 9.8 | 851 | 10.3 | 13 452 | 19.3 | 16 746 | 4 085 | 8 306 | 3 119 | 3 709 |
| Camden | 17 | 6 752 | 0.29 | 95 | 9.5 | 48 | 4.8 | 1 388 | 16.0 | 1 733 | 87 | 637 | 132 | 1 306 |
| Carteret | 987 | 61 972 | 0.88 | 598 | 8.9 | 732 | 10.9 | 10 166 | 19.1 | 15 385 | 904 | 6 623 | 2 541 | 3 775 |
| Caswell | 1 368 | 18 734 | 0.42 | 188 | 8.0 | 239 | 10.2 | 3 545 | 18.9 | 5 155 | 1 669 | 2 051 | 538 | 2 240 |
| Catawba | 2 408 | 169 343 | 1.22 | 1 809 | 11.7 | 1 484 | 9.6 | 26 710 | 20.4 | 30 636 | 5 831 | 15 230 | 6 785 | 4 351 |
| Chatham | 778 | 52 931 | 0.66 | 650 | 10.1 | 583 | 9.1 | 10 302 | 20.0 | 13 655 | 3 622 | 4 877 | 1 499 | 2 331 |
| Cherokee | 436 | 27 195 | 0.98 | 180 | 6.6 | 315 | 11.6 | 4 594 | 21.9 | 7 758 | 1 550 | 3 512 | 781 | 2 810 |

1. Per 1,000 estimated resident population.   2. Data for serious crimes have not been adjusted for underreporting; this may affect comparability between geographic areas and over time.   3. Per 100,000 population estimated by the FBI.   4. Bronx, Kings, Queens, and Richmond counties are included with New York county.

# Table B. States and Counties — Crime, Education, Money Income, and Poverty

| STATE County | Serious crimes known to police, 2011 (cont.)[1] Rate[2] Violent | Property | Education — Enrollment[3] Total | Percent private | Attainment[4] (percent) High school grad or less | Bachelor's degree or more | Local government expenditures[5] 2009-2010 Total current expenditures (mil dol) | Current expenditures per student (dollars) | Money income, 2007-2011 Per capita income[6] (dollars) | Households Median income Dollars | Percent change, 2000 to 2007-2011 (constant 2011 dollars) | Percent with income of $200,000 or more | Income and poverty, 2011 Median household income (dollars) | Percent below poverty level All persons | Children under 18 years | Children 5 to 17 years in families |
|---|---|---|---|---|---|---|---|---|---|---|---|---|---|---|---|---|
| | 46 | 47 | 48 | 49 | 50 | 51 | 52 | 53 | 54 | 55 | 56 | 57 | 58 | 59 | 60 | 61 |
| **NEW YORK—Cont'd** | | | | | | | | | | | | | | | | |
| Genesee | 186 | 2 197 | 14 163 | 10.8 | 47.8 | 20.4 | 143.9 | 15 505 | 25 022 | 50 861 | -7.1 | 1.5 | 45 955 | 13.0 | 18.1 | 15.2 |
| Greene | 212 | 1 460 | 9 133 | 15.1 | 54.5 | 18.6 | 122.2 | 17 648 | 23 605 | 47 033 | -4.5 | 1.9 | 45 127 | 16.0 | 21.8 | 18.8 |
| Hamilton | 21 | 1 070 | 805 | 7.5 | 46.7 | 25.6 | 17.4 | 30 026 | 29 214 | 51 142 | 17.3 | 2.5 | 43 104 | 10.7 | 19.1 | 15.6 |
| Herkimer | 234 | 2 017 | 15 808 | 8.5 | 49.7 | 18.5 | 154.6 | 14 961 | 22 377 | 42 680 | -4.0 | 1.4 | 40 504 | 16.9 | 24.5 | 21.9 |
| Jefferson | 154 | 1 961 | 27 874 | 12.1 | 47.8 | 20.6 | 253.3 | 13 597 | 22 574 | 45 559 | -0.8 | 1.3 | 45 292 | 17.4 | 26.3 | 26.1 |
| Kings | (7) | (7) | 668 495 | 29.3 | 50.3 | 29.2 | (7) | (7) | 24 398 | 44 593 | 2.8 | 3.9 | 42 437 | 23.6 | 33.8 | 33.3 |
| Lewis | 121 | 1 404 | 6 197 | 11.9 | 60.8 | 13.7 | 67.8 | 15 556 | 21 472 | 44 281 | -4.6 | 1.0 | 44 097 | 12.1 | 20.3 | 18.9 |
| Livingston | 65 | 1 547 | 18 737 | 13.3 | 46.0 | 23.3 | 131.7 | 15 165 | 23 637 | 53 231 | -6.3 | 1.3 | 50 186 | 13.5 | 16.5 | 13.8 |
| Madison | 69 | 1 655 | 20 650 | 24.4 | 45.7 | 24.3 | 164.1 | 14 964 | 24 904 | 53 473 | -1.4 | 2.5 | 49 326 | 11.9 | 17.5 | 15.1 |
| Monroe | 355 | 2 937 | 208 185 | 25.8 | 36.7 | 35.3 | 1 843.0 | 16 142 | 27 712 | 52 260 | -13.8 | 3.3 | 50 247 | 16.4 | 23.5 | 21.9 |
| Montgomery | 115 | 2 030 | 11 772 | 12.9 | 53.4 | 16.4 | 116.8 | 15 276 | 22 847 | 43 254 | -0.3 | 1.3 | 40 160 | 19.0 | 29.3 | 26.7 |
| Nassau | 164 | 1 267 | 359 519 | 27.0 | 35.1 | 41.2 | 4 541.7 | 21 964 | 42 307 | 95 823 | -1.5 | 14.8 | 91 162 | 7.0 | 9.3 | 8.7 |
| New York | (7)625 | (7)1 729 | 339 755 | 45.7 | 27.9 | 57.7 | (7)19 453.2 | (7)19 015 | 61 290 | 67 204 | 5.8 | 16.6 | 65 833 | 18.4 | 26.7 | 28.8 |
| Niagara | 372 | 2 929 | 52 223 | 17.9 | 48.0 | 20.6 | 475.4 | 14 886 | 25 046 | 46 599 | -9.5 | 1.8 | 45 291 | 12.9 | 18.6 | 16.3 |
| Oneida | 232 | 2 276 | 58 430 | 15.7 | 47.0 | 21.9 | 525.8 | 14 965 | 24 459 | 48 382 | -0.2 | 2.1 | 45 957 | 17.1 | 26.5 | 22.5 |
| Onondaga | 353 | 2 383 | 130 543 | 25.4 | 38.3 | 32.5 | 1 167.0 | 15 705 | 27 960 | 52 636 | -4.6 | 3.3 | 53 394 | 15.6 | 22.5 | 20.5 |
| Ontario | 138 | 1 800 | 27 028 | 19.9 | 36.9 | 30.5 | 259.5 | 14 979 | 29 293 | 57 069 | -5.2 | 3.4 | 52 367 | 10.7 | 14.8 | 12.7 |
| Orange | 265 | 2 138 | 109 367 | 22.1 | 42.5 | 28.7 | 1 149.8 | 17 899 | 29 880 | 70 294 | 0.0 | 5.4 | 65 648 | 13.9 | 21.0 | 18.3 |
| Orleans | 188 | 2 126 | 10 369 | 7.9 | 55.3 | 15.0 | 100.1 | 14 345 | 21 085 | 47 788 | -6.8 | 1.0 | 43 870 | 14.5 | 20.6 | 18.8 |
| Oswego | 149 | 2 503 | 34 994 | 8.4 | 55.8 | 15.8 | 348.7 | 15 819 | 22 261 | 47 036 | -4.8 | 1.3 | 43 687 | 19.3 | 26.2 | 23.0 |
| Otsego | 190 | 1 631 | 17 853 | 15.0 | 46.3 | 26.2 | 137.8 | 17 080 | 23 176 | 45 334 | 0.4 | 2.0 | 43 563 | 16.4 | 22.5 | 19.6 |
| Putnam | 67 | 794 | 26 504 | 20.1 | 35.2 | 38.1 | 343.0 | 21 104 | 39 746 | 92 711 | -5.0 | 11.9 | 87 248 | 5.9 | 6.5 | 5.5 |
| Queens | (7) | (7) | 544 780 | 24.1 | 47.9 | 29.8 | (7) | (7) | 26 234 | 56 406 | -1.6 | 3.9 | 53 124 | 16.0 | 21.8 | 22.2 |
| Rensselaer | 303 | 2 617 | 42 023 | 27.6 | 42.1 | 27.4 | 343.5 | 15 751 | 28 719 | 56 271 | -2.9 | 2.8 | 57 059 | 12.0 | 18.7 | 17.0 |
| Richmond | (7) | (7) | 122 680 | 27.0 | 46.0 | 28.9 | (7) | (7) | 31 276 | 72 752 | -2.1 | 6.5 | 69 436 | 12.5 | 18.5 | 16.0 |
| Rockland | 176 | 1 275 | 90 803 | 40.3 | 35.9 | 40.8 | 891.9 | 21 589 | 34 983 | 84 661 | -7.7 | 11.9 | 80 765 | 14.1 | 23.4 | 21.0 |
| St. Lawrence | 128 | 2 114 | 32 861 | 24.6 | 51.4 | 18.9 | 260.2 | 16 053 | 21 013 | 43 390 | -0.7 | 1.1 | 42 609 | 18.8 | 25.0 | 23.3 |
| Saratoga | 59 | 1 325 | 54 164 | 18.0 | 35.6 | 35.4 | 454.8 | 14 218 | 33 490 | 67 186 | 0.6 | 4.8 | 64 298 | 7.1 | 9.0 | 8.3 |
| Schenectady | 440 | 3 114 | 38 600 | 18.3 | 41.7 | 28.8 | 393.3 | 15 003 | 28 001 | 55 587 | -1.4 | 3.0 | 52 283 | 14.1 | 23.4 | 21.6 |
| Schoharie | 46 | 1 271 | 8 230 | 10.4 | 50.9 | 20.5 | 85.8 | 17 231 | 25 362 | 50 795 | 2.8 | 1.8 | 49 610 | 11.4 | 18.7 | 17.0 |
| Schuyler | 87 | 792 | 4 191 | 16.5 | 51.1 | 17.0 | 40.3 | 17 328 | 22 803 | 47 804 | -1.7 | 1.2 | 45 986 | 14.1 | 23.0 | 20.3 |
| Seneca | 181 | 1 753 | 7 570 | 20.7 | 51.4 | 18.3 | 74.6 | 16 834 | 21 980 | 47 266 | -5.7 | 1.1 | 45 951 | 13.3 | 20.8 | 18.9 |
| Steuben | 139 | 1 549 | 23 400 | 10.1 | 49.1 | 19.6 | 265.6 | 16 150 | 24 006 | 44 967 | -6.1 | 1.8 | 43 834 | 18.1 | 28.2 | 25.5 |
| Suffolk | 146 | 1 919 | 395 376 | 15.6 | 40.8 | 32.4 | 5 075.9 | 19 813 | 36 588 | 87 187 | -1.1 | 9.8 | 83 360 | 6.9 | 9.0 | 8.3 |
| Sullivan | 255 | 2 229 | 18 187 | 13.2 | 49.9 | 20.7 | 226.5 | 22 165 | 24 023 | 48 303 | -3.3 | 2.8 | 46 161 | 17.0 | 24.6 | 23.0 |
| Tioga | 64 | 1 083 | 12 570 | 10.8 | 48.5 | 22.4 | 124.8 | 15 453 | 25 719 | 53 789 | -1.1 | 1.8 | 51 675 | 10.9 | 16.5 | 15.3 |
| Tompkins | NA | NA | 42 374 | 56.1 | 28.2 | 49.8 | 201.8 | 17 039 | 26 199 | 49 789 | -1.1 | 3.7 | 49 639 | 20.0 | 18.2 | 16.9 |
| Ulster | 183 | 1 874 | 44 559 | 15.1 | 41.5 | 29.3 | 497.9 | 19 283 | 29 692 | 58 808 | 2.4 | 4.3 | 54 060 | 14.5 | 17.8 | 16.3 |
| Warren | 161 | 2 080 | 14 428 | 16.2 | 42.2 | 27.8 | 163.1 | 16 161 | 28 993 | 53 877 | 1.8 | 3.0 | 50 807 | 13.9 | 19.9 | 17.4 |
| Washington | 150 | 1 200 | 14 497 | 13.3 | 55.8 | 16.9 | 150.8 | 16 101 | 23 252 | 50 117 | -1.5 | 1.5 | 48 555 | 14.1 | 21.8 | 18.9 |
| Wayne | 150 | 1 660 | 22 053 | 12.5 | 47.9 | 20.8 | 250.9 | 16 164 | 24 872 | 54 380 | -8.8 | 1.3 | 51 901 | 12.8 | 20.6 | 17.3 |
| Westchester | 256 | 1 402 | 249 870 | 25.8 | 35.1 | 44.5 | 3 351.7 | 22 351 | 48 306 | 80 725 | -6.0 | 16.4 | 76 728 | 10.0 | 13.6 | 11.9 |
| Wyoming | 87 | 1 155 | 9 020 | 12.9 | 55.4 | 14.6 | 72.7 | 15 095 | 21 762 | 51 312 | -4.7 | 0.9 | 50 192 | 11.6 | 15.5 | 14.3 |
| Yates | 51 | 1 555 | 6 177 | 38.5 | 52.4 | 23.4 | 40.4 | 15 465 | 23 928 | 48 125 | 2.9 | 2.9 | 44 776 | 15.1 | 24.3 | 22.6 |
| **NORTH CAROLINA** | 350 | 3 527 | 2 471 140 | 14.5 | 43.6 | 26.5 | 12 419.2 | 8 372 | 25 256 | 46 291 | -12.5 | 3.1 | 44 028 | 17.8 | 25.4 | 23.3 |
| Alamance | 421 | 3 922 | 38 543 | 19.0 | 48.0 | 21.6 | 181.8 | 7 599 | 23 477 | 44 430 | -16.0 | 2.2 | 41 371 | 17.8 | 26.3 | 24.2 |
| Alexander | 165 | 2 771 | 8 522 | 11.4 | 61.5 | 11.3 | 42.1 | 7 574 | 20 467 | 40 658 | -22.2 | 1.9 | 39 812 | 18.2 | 27.2 | 23.4 |
| Alleghany | NA | NA | 2 205 | 5.0 | 58.3 | 15.9 | 16.7 | 10 470 | 18 974 | 32 478 | -17.7 | 0.6 | 32 673 | 20.3 | 32.7 | 29.5 |
| Anson | 389 | 4 495 | 5 804 | 3.4 | 66.7 | 8.4 | 38.5 | 9 877 | 17 462 | 34 659 | -14.0 | 1.5 | 32 341 | 24.9 | 36.4 | 34.3 |
| Ashe | 112 | 1 889 | 5 225 | 8.1 | 53.0 | 17.7 | 31.1 | 9 319 | 20 870 | 36 498 | -6.2 | 1.1 | 34 333 | 19.5 | 31.3 | 28.1 |
| Avery | 172 | 1 282 | 3 827 | 23.0 | 50.4 | 19.3 | 24.3 | 10 147 | 23 516 | 37 985 | -8.1 | 2.4 | 36 071 | 20.8 | 30.9 | 27.3 |
| Beaufort | 314 | 3 119 | 11 053 | 9.0 | 52.2 | 19.1 | 67.8 | 8 964 | 23 209 | 40 986 | -2.3 | 1.5 | 38 248 | 22.3 | 35.7 | 32.7 |
| Bertie | 181 | 1 870 | 4 410 | 13.2 | 64.1 | 10.8 | 34.4 | 11 503 | 17 880 | 29 326 | -13.7 | 0.7 | 29 615 | 25.1 | 35.0 | 31.6 |
| Bladen | 314 | 4 089 | 8 612 | 6.2 | 59.6 | 9.5 | 50.6 | 9 408 | 18 350 | 30 273 | -16.6 | 1.2 | 33 138 | 23.7 | 33.6 | 30.3 |
| Brunswick | 207 | 3 099 | 19 465 | 11.1 | 44.9 | 23.7 | 117.8 | 9 085 | 26 402 | 45 132 | -6.9 | 2.2 | 42 685 | 18.1 | 29.3 | 26.6 |
| Buncombe | 258 | 2 729 | 53 236 | 18.3 | 37.7 | 32.1 | 267.1 | 8 819 | 26 347 | 44 321 | -10.5 | 2.7 | 41 551 | 18.2 | 26.9 | 23.4 |
| Burke | 167 | 2 785 | 21 885 | 8.3 | 54.7 | 15.8 | 112.8 | 7 963 | 19 508 | 37 440 | -22.2 | 1.1 | 37 719 | 20.7 | 30.4 | 26.3 |
| Cabarrus | 108 | 2 844 | 47 773 | 13.4 | 42.3 | 24.1 | 265.3 | 7 836 | 25 898 | 54 280 | -12.9 | 3.5 | 50 298 | 13.0 | 18.0 | 16.3 |
| Caldwell | 146 | 3 563 | 20 034 | 9.4 | 57.0 | 13.6 | 99.8 | 7 644 | 20 064 | 37 845 | -21.6 | 1.5 | 34 876 | 20.8 | 28.8 | 26.0 |
| Camden | 69 | 1 237 | 2 994 | 14.5 | 39.9 | 20.2 | 16.0 | 8 314 | 25 886 | 63 998 | 20.0 | 0.7 | 57 113 | 9.3 | 14.9 | 12.6 |
| Carteret | 281 | 3 494 | 14 029 | 11.9 | 41.4 | 23.7 | 79.1 | 9 095 | 27 707 | 47 403 | -8.4 | 2.6 | 45 507 | 16.7 | 26.2 | 23.3 |
| Caswell | 216 | 2 023 | 5 549 | 18.0 | 61.4 | 9.4 | 28.2 | 8 982 | 17 643 | 37 926 | -19.8 | 0.9 | 38 495 | 19.8 | 29.4 | 26.4 |
| Catawba | 309 | 4 042 | 37 669 | 12.8 | 49.9 | 19.7 | 196.9 | 7 926 | 23 489 | 43 733 | -20.1 | 2.5 | 44 339 | 14.5 | 22.2 | 19.8 |
| Chatham | 162 | 2 169 | 13 827 | 15.1 | 39.4 | 36.5 | 79.8 | 9 153 | 31 465 | 56 935 | -1.6 | 5.2 | 53 564 | 11.3 | 18.9 | 18.1 |
| Cherokee | 227 | 2 583 | 5 221 | 13.2 | 51.3 | 15.2 | 35.4 | 9 348 | 20 451 | 38 621 | 2.2 | 0.4 | 32 913 | 18.0 | 31.6 | 29.2 |

1. Data for serious crimes have not been adjusted for underreporting; this may affect comparability between geographic areas and over time.  2. Per 100,000 population estimated by the FBI.  3. All persons 3 years old and over enrolled in nursery school through college.  4. Persons 25 years old and over.  5. Elementary and secondary education expenditures.  6. Based on population estimated by the American Community Survey, 2007–2011.  7. Bronx, Kings, Queens, and Richmond counties are included with New York county.

# Table B. States and Counties — **Personal Income**

| STATE County | Total (mil dol) | Percent change, 2010–2011 | Per capita[1] Dollars | Per capita[1] Rank | Wages and salaries[2] (mil dol) | Proprietors' income (mil dol) | Dividends, interest, and rent (mil dol) | Transfer payments (mil dol) Total | Government payments to individuals Total | Social Security | Medical payments | Income mainte-nance | Unemploy-ment insurance |
|---|---|---|---|---|---|---|---|---|---|---|---|---|---|
| | 62 | 63 | 64 | 65 | 66 | 67 | 68 | 69 | 70 | 71 | 72 | 73 | 74 |
| **NEW YORK—Cont'd** | | | | | | | | | | | | | |
| Genesee | 2 029 | 3.0 | 33 826 | 1 546 | 1 084 | 176 | 307 | 488 | 475 | 175 | 194 | 40 | 23 |
| Greene | 1 804 | 3.7 | 36 848 | 1 096 | 737 | 84 | 315 | 444 | 433 | 159 | 182 | 44 | 20 |
| Hamilton | 200 | 2.7 | 41 750 | 598 | 69 | 10 | 56 | 49 | 48 | 21 | 21 | 3 | 2 |
| Herkimer | 2 121 | 3.5 | 33 060 | 1 699 | 718 | 136 | 301 | 595 | 581 | 197 | 263 | 59 | 25 |
| Jefferson | 5 355 | 7.4 | 45 418 | 371 | 4 320 | 223 | 599 | 812 | 790 | 258 | 301 | 109 | 46 |
| Kings | 99 662 | 4.9 | 39 351 | 818 | 26 520 | 4 968 | 11 158 | 26 151 | 25 590 | 3 679 | 15 859 | 4 233 | 1 056 |
| Lewis | 888 | 5.6 | 32 809 | 1 740 | 315 | 106 | 135 | 194 | 188 | 65 | 79 | 20 | 12 |
| Livingston | 2 106 | 3.1 | 32 361 | 1 811 | 941 | 185 | 302 | 497 | 482 | 178 | 208 | 48 | 24 |
| Madison | 2 470 | 3.2 | 33 663 | 1 573 | 1 000 | 190 | 386 | 537 | 521 | 182 | 226 | 52 | 28 |
| Monroe | 32 728 | 4.6 | 43 894 | 446 | 22 029 | 2 798 | 5 682 | 6 723 | 6 558 | 2 100 | 2 967 | 865 | 271 |
| Montgomery | 1 641 | 3.1 | 32 882 | 1 728 | 844 | 67 | 249 | 517 | 506 | 161 | 241 | 61 | 23 |
| Nassau | 91 120 | 3.5 | 67 776 | 28 | 41 534 | 9 620 | 19 252 | 11 042 | 10 744 | 3 895 | 5 069 | 678 | 445 |
| New York | 194 317 | 5.8 | 121 301 | 1 | 294 391 | 52 731 | 33 967 | 18 850 | 18 495 | 3 423 | 10 668 | 2 314 | 671 |
| Niagara | 7 635 | 4.8 | 35 345 | 1 318 | 3 513 | 267 | 1 052 | 1 966 | 1 918 | 697 | 812 | 206 | 91 |
| Oneida | 8 446 | 3.3 | 36 049 | 1 203 | 5 430 | 537 | 1 351 | 2 171 | 2 119 | 678 | 954 | 271 | 86 |
| Onondaga | 19 327 | 3.9 | 41 389 | 624 | 14 053 | 1 403 | 3 067 | 3 909 | 3 806 | 1 287 | 1 628 | 480 | 170 |
| Ontario | 4 540 | 4.4 | 41 834 | 590 | 2 544 | 364 | 744 | 892 | 868 | 326 | 367 | 72 | 39 |
| Orange | 15 019 | 3.9 | 40 066 | 738 | 7 671 | 790 | 2 094 | 2 781 | 2 700 | 847 | 1 254 | 302 | 132 |
| Orleans | 1 265 | 2.5 | 29 691 | 2 342 | 657 | 54 | 168 | 348 | 339 | 123 | 140 | 40 | 17 |
| Oswego | 3 823 | 2.7 | 31 275 | 2 056 | 1 714 | 144 | 453 | 995 | 968 | 343 | 398 | 119 | 57 |
| Otsego | 2 069 | 4.1 | 33 414 | 1 623 | 1 175 | 78 | 398 | 511 | 498 | 182 | 217 | 45 | 23 |
| Putnam | 5 374 | 3.5 | 53 781 | 133 | 1 559 | 241 | 813 | 675 | 653 | 265 | 287 | 25 | 34 |
| Queens | 94 447 | 5.0 | 42 017 | 568 | 30 510 | 4 175 | 12 094 | 23 223 | 22 726 | 4 004 | 13 898 | 3 181 | 876 |
| Rensselaer | 6 331 | 4.0 | 39 716 | 778 | 2 930 | 281 | 905 | 1 298 | 1 262 | 419 | 554 | 134 | 60 |
| Richmond | 22 811 | 3.4 | 48 486 | 254 | 5 049 | 856 | 2 906 | 5 419 | 5 315 | 1 200 | 3 142 | 595 | 191 |
| Rockland | 16 951 | 5.2 | 53 787 | 132 | 7 720 | 1 448 | 2 761 | 2 660 | 2 590 | 813 | 1 319 | 223 | 98 |
| St. Lawrence | 3 268 | 3.9 | 29 256 | 2 416 | 1 763 | 208 | 474 | 956 | 931 | 309 | 403 | 112 | 49 |
| Saratoga | 10 301 | 4.7 | 46 637 | 312 | 4 378 | 713 | 1 853 | 1 505 | 1 456 | 608 | 578 | 101 | 73 |
| Schenectady | 6 721 | 4.9 | 43 348 | 480 | 4 097 | 266 | 1 439 | 1 347 | 1 313 | 429 | 596 | 155 | 54 |
| Schoharie | 1 157 | 5.0 | 35 530 | 1 284 | 405 | 52 | 153 | 247 | 240 | 86 | 104 | 23 | 14 |
| Schuyler | 648 | 4.4 | 35 317 | 1 321 | 223 | 57 | 93 | 160 | 156 | 60 | 63 | 18 | 8 |
| Seneca | 1 189 | 4.1 | 33 783 | 1 551 | 566 | 116 | 166 | 277 | 270 | 100 | 118 | 24 | 13 |
| Steuben | 3 692 | 3.9 | 37 278 | 1 051 | 2 381 | 256 | 526 | 853 | 831 | 293 | 335 | 92 | 40 |
| Suffolk | 78 463 | 3.5 | 52 350 | 157 | 42 094 | 4 689 | 13 341 | 12 060 | 11 729 | 4 136 | 5 448 | 918 | 558 |
| Sullivan | 2 880 | 3.2 | 37 457 | 1 031 | 1 197 | 176 | 480 | 788 | 771 | 225 | 394 | 88 | 30 |
| Tioga | 1 842 | 3.9 | 36 097 | 1 201 | 785 | 94 | 272 | 398 | 387 | 153 | 152 | 42 | 19 |
| Tompkins | 3 689 | 4.2 | 36 263 | 1 179 | 2 870 | 213 | 750 | 602 | 579 | 205 | 220 | 63 | 31 |
| Ulster | 7 223 | 3.7 | 39 589 | 796 | 3 004 | 378 | 1 400 | 1 548 | 1 508 | 531 | 682 | 150 | 69 |
| Warren | 2 676 | 4.3 | 40 649 | 691 | 1 836 | 162 | 619 | 591 | 577 | 228 | 234 | 51 | 28 |
| Washington | 2 125 | 5.3 | 33 639 | 1 581 | 819 | 90 | 291 | 510 | 496 | 175 | 220 | 51 | 23 |
| Wayne | 3 348 | 3.1 | 35 832 | 1 243 | 1 498 | 136 | 428 | 798 | 778 | 291 | 341 | 71 | 37 |
| Westchester | 72 509 | 3.8 | 75 855 | 13 | 33 768 | 7 008 | 16 099 | 7 978 | 7 767 | 2 544 | 3 785 | 664 | 312 |
| Wyoming | 1 315 | 5.5 | 31 359 | 2 031 | 664 | 106 | 190 | 303 | 294 | 115 | 121 | 24 | 17 |
| Yates | 817 | 5.5 | 32 110 | 1 859 | 285 | 45 | 170 | 210 | 204 | 76 | 86 | 18 | 9 |
| **NORTH CAROLINA** | 347 905 | 5.2 | 36 028 | X | 227 690 | 24 656 | 51 690 | 71 211 | 69 101 | 23 515 | 27 985 | 8 636 | 4 113 |
| Alamance | 4 808 | 4.7 | 31 363 | 2 028 | 2 670 | 310 | 760 | 1 160 | 1 126 | 417 | 453 | 130 | 68 |
| Alexander | 1 131 | 4.2 | 30 499 | 2 197 | 360 | 114 | 144 | 286 | 278 | 105 | 114 | 30 | 17 |
| Alleghany | 344 | 3.6 | 31 158 | 2 071 | 121 | 39 | 76 | 106 | 104 | 39 | 47 | 10 | 5 |
| Anson | 650 | -0.6 | 24 417 | 3 009 | 333 | 55 | 76 | 249 | 243 | 68 | 109 | 40 | 11 |
| Ashe | 772 | 2.1 | 28 431 | 2 554 | 300 | 68 | 138 | 247 | 241 | 87 | 107 | 24 | 13 |
| Avery | 509 | 3.9 | 28 939 | 2 461 | 254 | 55 | 104 | 149 | 145 | 50 | 68 | 13 | 7 |
| Beaufort | 1 561 | 5.8 | 32 737 | 1 753 | 770 | 109 | 286 | 476 | 465 | 168 | 193 | 57 | 21 |
| Bertie | 611 | 0.6 | 29 262 | 2 415 | 294 | 49 | 66 | 223 | 218 | 62 | 107 | 35 | 9 |
| Bladen | 1 018 | 1.9 | 29 135 | 2 431 | 534 | 100 | 105 | 340 | 332 | 96 | 143 | 51 | 17 |
| Brunswick | 3 674 | 6.0 | 33 375 | 1 634 | 1 319 | 227 | 722 | 1 093 | 1 069 | 465 | 419 | 84 | 47 |
| Buncombe | 8 321 | 4.5 | 34 467 | 1 438 | 5 525 | 558 | 1 780 | 1 923 | 1 870 | 693 | 776 | 193 | 86 |
| Burke | 2 735 | 3.8 | 30 084 | 2 274 | 1 290 | 306 | 352 | 755 | 735 | 266 | 310 | 83 | 35 |
| Cabarrus | 6 453 | 4.8 | 35 561 | 1 280 | 2 896 | 454 | 712 | 1 182 | 1 142 | 406 | 468 | 126 | 90 |
| Caldwell | 2 246 | 3.3 | 27 261 | 2 726 | 1 054 | 127 | 286 | 716 | 697 | 244 | 287 | 81 | 47 |
| Camden | 374 | 5.2 | 37 353 | 1 043 | 110 | 25 | 44 | 67 | 65 | 23 | 25 | 6 | 4 |
| Carteret | 2 639 | 4.2 | 39 174 | 837 | 886 | 216 | 560 | 581 | 566 | 214 | 219 | 49 | 26 |
| Caswell | 733 | 4.1 | 31 326 | 2 036 | 138 | 30 | 79 | 209 | 204 | 73 | 85 | 26 | 9 |
| Catawba | 5 137 | 5.6 | 33 320 | 1 650 | 3 887 | 242 | 851 | 1 241 | 1 206 | 462 | 460 | 140 | 83 |
| Chatham | 3 094 | 5.3 | 48 191 | 264 | 645 | 298 | 680 | 472 | 458 | 207 | 176 | 35 | 21 |
| Cherokee | 700 | 2.3 | 25 751 | 2 907 | 313 | 48 | 114 | 289 | 283 | 108 | 116 | 25 | 16 |

1. Based on the resident population estimated as of July 1 of the year shown.  2. Includes supplements to wages and salaries.

# Table B. States and Counties — Earnings, Social Security, and Housing

| STATE County | Earnings, 2011 Total (mil dol) [75] | Farm [76] | Goods-related[1] Total [77] | Goods-related[1] Manufacturing [78] | Information and professional and technical services [79] | Retail trade [80] | Finance, insurance, and real estate [81] | Health care and social services [82] | Government [83] | Social Security beneficiaries, Dec 2011 Number [84] | Rate[2] [85] | Supplemental Security Income recipients, December 2011 [86] | Housing units, 2010 Total [87] | Percent change, 2000–2010 [88] |
|---|---|---|---|---|---|---|---|---|---|---|---|---|---|---|
| **NEW YORK—Cont'd** | | | | | | | | | | | | | | |
| Genesee | 1 260 | 5.6 | 21.2 | 15.3 | 3.4 | 7.8 | 2.7 | 9.7 | 27.4 | 13 025 | 217 | 1 195 | 25 589 | 5.8 |
| Greene | 821 | 0.6 | D | 8.4 | 4.7 | 8.7 | 3.0 | 7.2 | 36.0 | 11 895 | 243 | 1 374 | 29 210 | 10.1 |
| Hamilton | 79 | 0.0 | 12.5 | 2.0 | D | 9.1 | D | D | 49.0 | 1 535 | 320 | 83 | 8 694 | 9.2 |
| Herkimer | 854 | 2.4 | 24.0 | 16.8 | 3.1 | 9.4 | 2.6 | 10.4 | 27.5 | 15 625 | 244 | 1 871 | 33 381 | 4.2 |
| Jefferson | 4 544 | 1.3 | 7.1 | 3.2 | 2.2 | 4.9 | 1.9 | 7.5 | 65.9 | 20 975 | 178 | 2 968 | 57 966 | 7.2 |
| Kings | 31 488 | 0.0 | D | 3.2 | 8.5 | 7.6 | 9.7 | 27.7 | 9.7 | 307 215 | 121 | 144 241 | 1 000 293 | 7.5 |
| Lewis | 421 | 13.3 | D | 17.1 | 2.8 | 6.2 | 1.7 | D | 33.4 | 5 335 | 197 | 643 | 15 112 | -0.1 |
| Livingston | 1 125 | 4.7 | D | 8.7 | 3.1 | 8.5 | 2.4 | 8.8 | 36.0 | 12 945 | 199 | 1 240 | 27 123 | 12.9 |
| Madison | 1 190 | 3.0 | D | 12.5 | 6.1 | 7.5 | 4.4 | 12.9 | 21.2 | 13 745 | 187 | 1 393 | 31 757 | 10.9 |
| Monroe | 24 827 | 0.1 | 20.6 | 15.1 | 12.2 | 5.4 | 6.4 | 13.4 | 13.4 | 148 325 | 199 | 25 445 | 320 593 | 5.3 |
| Montgomery | 911 | 3.1 | 22.3 | 17.9 | 2.7 | 10.3 | 2.4 | 21.7 | 18.6 | 12 770 | 256 | 1 985 | 23 063 | 2.4 |
| Nassau | 51 153 | 0.0 | D | 3.3 | 16.3 | 7.5 | 10.7 | 18.0 | 15.9 | 247 330 | 184 | 18 264 | 468 346 | 2.2 |
| New York | 347 122 | 0.0 | 2.3 | 0.9 | 24.6 | 2.7 | 35.3 | 4.8 | 10.4 | 240 350 | 150 | 80 325 | 847 090 | 6.1 |
| Niagara | 3 781 | 1.3 | D | 17.2 | 4.7 | 8.1 | 2.6 | 13.1 | 26.2 | 51 190 | 237 | 6 025 | 99 120 | 3.6 |
| Oneida | 5 966 | 0.7 | 12.5 | 8.9 | 6.9 | 8.3 | 7.8 | 16.5 | 30.3 | 53 720 | 229 | 8 653 | 104 180 | 1.3 |
| Onondaga | 15 456 | 0.4 | 16.3 | 11.1 | 10.8 | 6.2 | 8.3 | 13.1 | 18.4 | 92 925 | 199 | 14 726 | 202 357 | 2.9 |
| Ontario | 2 907 | 2.6 | 22.8 | 14.4 | 6.9 | 10.4 | 2.9 | 12.7 | 18.7 | 23 680 | 218 | 2 020 | 48 193 | 13.0 |
| Orange | 8 462 | 0.2 | 9.8 | 5.4 | 8.1 | 9.6 | 4.0 | 14.6 | 32.2 | 60 160 | 160 | 7 144 | 137 025 | 11.6 |
| Orleans | 712 | 5.7 | 23.1 | 19.9 | 2.7 | 4.6 | 7.2 | D | 38.4 | 9 245 | 217 | 998 | 18 431 | 6.2 |
| Oswego | 1 858 | 0.9 | 18.0 | 13.2 | 2.5 | 7.7 | 2.4 | 11.3 | 27.3 | 26 065 | 213 | 3 330 | 53 598 | 1.4 |
| Otsego | 1 253 | 1.1 | 9.3 | 5.1 | 3.6 | 8.3 | 6.7 | 27.2 | 22.4 | 14 110 | 228 | 1 503 | 30 777 | 8.1 |
| Putnam | 1 801 | 0.0 | 14.8 | 5.9 | 10.5 | 5.9 | 5.1 | 18.6 | 23.4 | 17 000 | 170 | 902 | 38 224 | 9.1 |
| Queens | 34 685 | 0.0 | D | 4.0 | 5.3 | 6.6 | 8.4 | 16.6 | 10.2 | 306 475 | 136 | 76 960 | 835 127 | 2.2 |
| Rensselaer | 3 211 | 0.3 | 14.0 | 6.5 | 10.5 | 6.4 | 5.4 | 13.9 | 23.2 | 30 840 | 193 | 4 098 | 71 475 | 8.1 |
| Richmond | 5 906 | 0.0 | D | D | 9.2 | 8.6 | 5.4 | 28.5 | 10.5 | 83 230 | 177 | 15 067 | 176 656 | 7.7 |
| Rockland | 9 169 | 0.0 | D | 11.4 | 11.0 | 6.1 | 9.3 | 13.8 | 18.8 | 52 930 | 168 | 5 681 | 104 057 | 9.6 |
| St. Lawrence | 1 971 | 2.9 | 15.8 | 10.5 | 2.9 | 8.4 | 2.3 | D | 32.7 | 24 590 | 220 | 4 092 | 52 133 | 4.9 |
| Saratoga | 5 091 | 0.3 | 20.3 | 12.0 | 10.1 | 8.0 | 10.2 | 9.6 | 18.1 | 42 700 | 193 | 3 033 | 98 656 | 13.8 |
| Schenectady | 4 363 | 0.0 | 17.9 | 13.8 | 22.3 | 5.5 | 4.0 | 14.4 | 17.2 | 31 630 | 204 | 5 075 | 68 196 | 4.9 |
| Schoharie | 457 | 2.8 | D | D | 5.3 | 8.0 | 5.7 | 10.0 | 33.8 | 6 635 | 204 | 691 | 17 231 | 8.3 |
| Schuyler | 280 | 4.4 | 25.4 | 12.8 | 3.2 | 8.8 | D | D | 24.2 | 4 630 | 252 | 502 | 9 455 | 3.0 |
| Seneca | 682 | 4.6 | D | 22.7 | D | 9.1 | 2.7 | D | 30.1 | 7 715 | 219 | 793 | 16 043 | 8.4 |
| Steuben | 2 637 | 1.9 | 20.7 | 17.9 | 14.8 | 5.3 | 4.3 | 8.6 | 19.4 | 22 860 | 231 | 3 266 | 48 875 | 5.9 |
| Suffolk | 46 783 | 0.2 | 15.8 | 8.9 | 10.8 | 6.9 | 10.6 | 12.2 | 20.3 | 275 410 | 184 | 22 688 | 569 985 | 9.1 |
| Sullivan | 1 373 | 0.6 | 9.1 | 3.8 | 4.9 | 7.1 | 6.2 | 20.9 | 30.8 | 17 115 | 223 | 2 912 | 49 186 | 10.0 |
| Tioga | 878 | 1.5 | 48.7 | 44.2 | 2.8 | 5.9 | 1.8 | 5.3 | 17.5 | 11 545 | 226 | 1 217 | 22 203 | 3.7 |
| Tompkins | 3 083 | 0.8 | 11.2 | 8.0 | 7.5 | 5.2 | 3.4 | D | 13.3 | 14 545 | 143 | 1 747 | 41 674 | 7.9 |
| Ulster | 3 382 | 0.7 | 11.9 | 6.9 | 6.0 | 10.0 | 4.3 | 13.4 | 30.8 | 38 440 | 211 | 4 554 | 83 638 | 7.8 |
| Warren | 1 998 | 0.0 | D | 13.5 | 7.4 | 9.1 | 5.5 | 17.3 | 14.4 | 16 960 | 258 | 1 726 | 38 726 | 11.1 |
| Washington | 909 | 3.0 | D | 19.8 | D | 6.7 | 1.8 | 7.1 | 35.9 | 13 615 | 216 | 1 617 | 28 844 | 7.7 |
| Wayne | 1 634 | 4.0 | D | 21.2 | 4.0 | 6.5 | 2.3 | 7.2 | 30.5 | 21 780 | 233 | 2 284 | 41 057 | 5.9 |
| Westchester | 40 776 | 0.0 | D | 5.0 | 15.0 | 5.5 | 14.2 | 13.2 | 15.1 | 161 280 | 169 | 17 647 | 370 821 | 6.1 |
| Wyoming | 771 | 10.1 | D | 14.4 | D | 6.9 | 2.2 | D | 37.2 | 8 770 | 209 | 715 | 17 970 | 6.1 |
| Yates | 330 | 12.3 | 18.2 | 14.4 | 2.4 | 6.5 | 3.3 | D | 22.1 | 5 835 | 229 | 555 | 13 491 | 11.8 |
| **NORTH CAROLINA** | 252 346 | 0.9 | 17.6 | 12.3 | 9.7 | 6.3 | 8.2 | 10.3 | 21.9 | 1 808 331 | 187 | 224 962 | 4 327 528 | 22.9 |
| Alamance | 2 980 | 0.3 | 22.2 | 16.6 | 4.8 | 7.9 | 5.4 | 16.4 | 11.7 | 31 320 | 204 | 3 031 | 66 576 | 20.0 |
| Alexander | 474 | 5.6 | D | 29.3 | 4.7 | 4.7 | 4.5 | D | 20.1 | 8 275 | 223 | 637 | 16 189 | 14.8 |
| Alleghany | 160 | 11.7 | D | 13.2 | 3.3 | 6.2 | 3.3 | D | 19.8 | 3 300 | 299 | 328 | 8 094 | 26.0 |
| Anson | 388 | 6.1 | D | 18.7 | D | 5.8 | 2.4 | D | 30.6 | 5 700 | 214 | 1 096 | 11 576 | 13.3 |
| Ashe | 368 | 3.9 | D | 14.8 | D | 9.7 | 3.8 | 12.4 | 16.3 | 7 360 | 271 | 833 | 17 342 | 30.7 |
| Avery | 309 | 3.2 | D | 1.6 | D | 8.5 | 5.4 | 11.3 | 23.8 | 4 120 | 234 | 373 | 13 890 | 16.6 |
| Beaufort | 879 | 4.0 | 29.5 | 25.5 | 3.9 | 7.3 | 3.7 | 11.2 | 16.4 | 13 295 | 279 | 1 914 | 24 688 | 11.5 |
| Bertie | 343 | 11.1 | D | 21.6 | D | 2.7 | D | D | 19.3 | 5 695 | 273 | 1 392 | 9 822 | 8.6 |
| Bladen | 634 | 10.0 | 39.3 | 36.5 | 2.1 | 3.9 | 2.7 | D | 19.8 | 8 260 | 236 | 1 874 | 17 718 | 15.7 |
| Brunswick | 1 546 | 0.6 | D | 4.8 | 7.1 | 8.7 | 7.9 | 8.8 | 18.8 | 33 090 | 301 | 2 209 | 77 482 | 50.7 |
| Buncombe | 6 084 | 0.2 | 16.7 | 11.1 | 7.1 | 8.3 | 5.6 | 20.6 | 17.4 | 53 080 | 220 | 5 556 | 113 365 | 20.7 |
| Burke | 1 596 | 0.5 | D | 24.5 | 3.7 | 6.6 | 4.6 | 17.3 | 22.9 | 21 015 | 231 | 2 057 | 40 879 | 9.2 |
| Cabarrus | 3 350 | 0.4 | D | 9.1 | 6.6 | 10.4 | 4.8 | 7.8 | 21.3 | 29 800 | 164 | 2 590 | 71 937 | 36.1 |
| Caldwell | 1 181 | 0.5 | 26.1 | 21.6 | D | 7.8 | 3.7 | 11.8 | 17.7 | 19 330 | 235 | 1 765 | 37 659 | 12.7 |
| Camden | 135 | 10.2 | 6.4 | 1.7 | D | 7.3 | 3.4 | D | 17.0 | 1 910 | 191 | 150 | 4 104 | 38.0 |
| Carteret | 1 102 | 0.4 | D | 4.0 | 6.3 | 10.7 | 6.8 | 9.8 | 25.2 | 16 700 | 248 | 1 227 | 48 179 | 17.7 |
| Caswell | 168 | 6.7 | D | 6.9 | 2.5 | 5.5 | 3.0 | 13.9 | 38.2 | 5 945 | 254 | 843 | 10 619 | 10.6 |
| Catawba | 4 128 | 0.3 | D | 27.4 | 4.3 | 7.7 | 3.2 | 11.7 | 13.1 | 34 260 | 222 | 2 849 | 67 886 | 13.3 |
| Chatham | 943 | 2.2 | D | 16.6 | 9.5 | 6.8 | 7.7 | 12.1 | 14.0 | 14 505 | 226 | 746 | 28 753 | 34.6 |
| Cherokee | 361 | 1.2 | D | 9.0 | 8.3 | 11.1 | 4.5 | D | 22.1 | 8 825 | 325 | 843 | 17 515 | 29.8 |

1. Includes mining, construction, and manufacturing.  2. Per 1,000 resident population enumerated in the 2010 census.

# Table B. States and Counties — Housing, Labor Force, and Employment

| STATE County | Housing units, 2007–2011 Owner-occupied Total | Percent | Median value[1] | Median owner cost as a percent of income With a mortgage | Without a mortgage[2] | Renter-occupied Median rent[3] | Median rent as a percent of income | Substandard units[4] (percent) | Civilian labor force, 2012 Total | Percent change, 2011–2012 | Unemployment Total | Rate[5] | Civilian employment,[6] 2007–2011 Total | Percent Management, business, science and arts | Construction, production, and maintenance occupations |
|---|---|---|---|---|---|---|---|---|---|---|---|---|---|---|---|
| | 89 | 90 | 91 | 92 | 93 | 94 | 95 | 96 | 97 | 98 | 99 | 100 | 101 | 102 | 103 |
| **NEW YORK—Cont'd** | | | | | | | | | | | | | | | |
| Genesee | 23 965 | 73.4 | 103 400 | 23.0 | 14.6 | 685 | 29.6 | 1.9 | 31 747 | -0.8 | 2 494 | 7.9 | 29 554 | 30.3 | 28.9 |
| Greene | 18 922 | 72.7 | 181 300 | 25.8 | 17.5 | 765 | 32.9 | 1.1 | 23 466 | -0.6 | 2 203 | 9.4 | 20 606 | 32.0 | 22.7 |
| Hamilton | 2 303 | 82.5 | 166 300 | 21.7 | 13.6 | 604 | 19.5 | 0.8 | 2 991 | 2.7 | 258 | 8.6 | 2 326 | 30.6 | 26.6 |
| Herkimer | 26 470 | 72.1 | 89 400 | 20.9 | 14.8 | 599 | 30.4 | 1.6 | 30 291 | -1.0 | 2 721 | 9.0 | 29 217 | 32.0 | 25.3 |
| Jefferson | 44 722 | 57.8 | 124 000 | 22.4 | 14.1 | 823 | 29.6 | 2.9 | 48 149 | -1.4 | 4 882 | 10.1 | 45 009 | 30.2 | 23.5 |
| Kings | 907 785 | 29.9 | 570 800 | 33.2 | 16.9 | 1 076 | 32.3 | 10.8 | 1 138 237 | 1.2 | 113 036 | 9.9 | 1 092 326 | 35.8 | 16.8 |
| Lewis | 10 602 | 77.4 | 103 900 | 21.4 | 13.8 | 627 | 28.8 | 1.6 | 12 208 | -1.7 | 1 238 | 10.1 | 12 142 | 28.6 | 34.0 |
| Livingston | 24 201 | 75.1 | 114 300 | 22.7 | 13.9 | 678 | 32.1 | 1.8 | 32 082 | 0.1 | 2 671 | 8.3 | 30 937 | 32.6 | 25.6 |
| Madison | 26 930 | 75.7 | 114 900 | 22.4 | 14.6 | 712 | 25.1 | 1.5 | 35 839 | -0.4 | 3 106 | 8.7 | 34 019 | 36.3 | 23.2 |
| Monroe | 293 104 | 66.0 | 132 800 | 22.9 | 14.2 | 778 | 33.4 | 1.6 | 368 654 | 0.0 | 29 332 | 8.0 | 350 901 | 41.3 | 16.8 |
| Montgomery | 20 059 | 68.4 | 99 500 | 22.5 | 16.2 | 690 | 30.9 | 2.5 | 23 686 | -0.1 | 2 458 | 10.4 | 21 901 | 31.3 | 27.8 |
| Nassau | 443 315 | 81.8 | 478 600 | 30.2 | 19.5 | 1 447 | 32.9 | 2.7 | 691 336 | 0.9 | 48 873 | 7.1 | 650 324 | 43.3 | 14.0 |
| New York | 733 393 | 22.7 | 842 300 | 21.0 | 9.9 | 1 316 | 27.8 | 6.5 | 936 614 | 1.3 | 72 472 | 7.7 | 846 255 | 57.7 | 6.6 |
| Niagara | 88 589 | 70.3 | 100 200 | 22.0 | 14.9 | 631 | 31.1 | 1.3 | 110 773 | 0.3 | 9 963 | 9.0 | 99 095 | 30.5 | 23.3 |
| Oneida | 91 568 | 68.0 | 106 200 | 21.2 | 13.6 | 658 | 29.3 | 1.6 | 105 982 | -1.0 | 9 138 | 8.6 | 104 674 | 35.1 | 19.9 |
| Onondaga | 183 381 | 65.8 | 128 600 | 21.8 | 13.7 | 734 | 30.3 | 1.5 | 226 856 | -0.5 | 18 392 | 8.1 | 220 889 | 39.8 | 16.6 |
| Ontario | 43 474 | 75.3 | 133 600 | 22.5 | 14.4 | 738 | 29.8 | 1.5 | 56 617 | -0.1 | 4 241 | 7.5 | 53 459 | 37.7 | 21.2 |
| Orange | 124 939 | 70.5 | 299 500 | 28.6 | 18.1 | 1 090 | 33.3 | 3.9 | 174 281 | -0.1 | 14 485 | 8.3 | 171 723 | 35.8 | 20.1 |
| Orleans | 15 896 | 76.9 | 87 700 | 23.4 | 17.2 | 622 | 29.9 | 2.9 | 19 188 | 1.0 | 1 997 | 10.4 | 18 190 | 25.9 | 33.6 |
| Oswego | 45 600 | 73.5 | 90 600 | 22.2 | 14.5 | 691 | 33.8 | 1.9 | 57 345 | -0.6 | 6 055 | 10.6 | 53 869 | 27.1 | 30.6 |
| Otsego | 24 713 | 72.3 | 131 100 | 23.3 | 13.9 | 760 | 35.7 | 2.0 | 31 339 | -0.4 | 2 507 | 8.0 | 29 435 | 35.4 | 21.1 |
| Putnam | 34 998 | 83.4 | 406 000 | 29.1 | 18.1 | 1 268 | 33.1 | 1.6 | 53 785 | -0.2 | 3 616 | 6.7 | 50 615 | 43.5 | 16.2 |
| Queens | 773 130 | 44.9 | 474 000 | 33.0 | 14.9 | 1 235 | 32.2 | 9.7 | 1 132 491 | 1.2 | 93 977 | 8.3 | 1 068 375 | 31.1 | 19.6 |
| Rensselaer | 63 626 | 65.6 | 177 300 | 24.0 | 14.5 | 810 | 28.8 | 1.9 | 82 325 | 0.8 | 6 482 | 7.9 | 80 402 | 38.0 | 18.2 |
| Richmond | 163 747 | 69.8 | 456 100 | 29.3 | 15.2 | 1 143 | 32.4 | 4.1 | 243 318 | 1.2 | 20 666 | 8.5 | 206 836 | 36.4 | 17.3 |
| Rockland | 98 106 | 70.6 | 465 100 | 29.0 | 18.9 | 1 299 | 34.2 | 6.4 | 156 849 | 0.2 | 10 816 | 6.9 | 142 289 | 43.9 | 13.9 |
| St. Lawrence | 41 825 | 71.5 | 80 900 | 21.5 | 14.2 | 634 | 31.3 | 2.4 | 47 957 | -1.5 | 5 016 | 10.5 | 46 611 | 31.8 | 22.4 |
| Saratoga | 87 762 | 73.7 | 224 800 | 23.3 | 13.5 | 903 | 27.7 | 1.0 | 117 508 | 0.8 | 8 193 | 7.0 | 112 102 | 41.5 | 17.0 |
| Schenectady | 58 203 | 68.0 | 165 000 | 24.0 | 14.8 | 817 | 30.5 | 1.4 | 75 068 | 0.8 | 5 935 | 7.9 | 73 941 | 37.9 | 16.2 |
| Schoharie | 12 801 | 76.7 | 147 600 | 22.8 | 14.4 | 681 | 35.2 | 2.3 | 15 450 | 0.6 | 1 472 | 9.5 | 15 268 | 32.0 | 26.8 |
| Schuyler | 7 610 | 79.8 | 89 400 | 22.7 | 12.9 | 583 | 25.1 | 1.5 | 9 963 | -0.6 | 841 | 8.4 | 8 465 | 30.4 | 26.1 |
| Seneca | 13 257 | 75.3 | 90 600 | 23.4 | 14.4 | 664 | 28.5 | 2.3 | 16 995 | 0.7 | 1 345 | 7.9 | 15 399 | 32.2 | 27.1 |
| Steuben | 41 101 | 71.7 | 84 200 | 21.4 | 13.1 | 616 | 29.8 | 1.9 | 44 168 | -0.6 | 4 341 | 9.8 | 43 093 | 33.6 | 27.3 |
| Suffolk | 496 677 | 80.8 | 411 000 | 30.8 | 19.3 | 1 461 | 34.7 | 2.5 | 789 008 | 0.8 | 60 231 | 7.6 | 728 496 | 37.6 | 18.9 |
| Sullivan | 29 432 | 66.8 | 186 000 | 28.2 | 16.1 | 812 | 30.5 | 3.4 | 34 190 | -0.3 | 3 287 | 9.6 | 33 581 | 33.4 | 23.9 |
| Tioga | 20 458 | 79.2 | 105 600 | 21.5 | 13.2 | 592 | 24.7 | 1.5 | 24 709 | -1.1 | 2 079 | 8.4 | 24 878 | 34.5 | 26.5 |
| Tompkins | 38 531 | 55.3 | 165 900 | 22.5 | 13.2 | 888 | 34.1 | 1.9 | 57 036 | 0.5 | 3 416 | 6.0 | 50 316 | 50.0 | 14.4 |
| Ulster | 70 034 | 69.3 | 242 500 | 27.3 | 17.8 | 984 | 32.8 | 2.1 | 87 050 | -0.4 | 7 681 | 8.8 | 88 944 | 37.5 | 19.5 |
| Warren | 28 392 | 69.4 | 190 800 | 24.1 | 13.9 | 804 | 30.3 | 1.4 | 35 581 | -0.1 | 3 073 | 8.6 | 31 844 | 34.3 | 21.3 |
| Washington | 24 682 | 74.2 | 143 000 | 24.6 | 14.5 | 741 | 31.2 | 2.0 | 31 926 | -0.2 | 2 499 | 7.8 | 29 206 | 27.5 | 31.6 |
| Wayne | 36 563 | 77.4 | 108 400 | 22.0 | 14.0 | 676 | 29.4 | 2.4 | 47 248 | 0.1 | 4 053 | 8.6 | 45 190 | 34.1 | 28.5 |
| Westchester | 345 908 | 62.1 | 547 000 | 27.6 | 18.3 | 1 252 | 32.3 | 4.7 | 474 201 | 0.2 | 34 319 | 7.2 | 454 005 | 45.1 | 13.8 |
| Wyoming | 15 549 | 75.8 | 98 700 | 21.6 | 13.2 | 628 | 29.5 | 1.0 | 20 158 | -0.3 | 1 762 | 8.7 | 18 703 | 28.8 | 31.8 |
| Yates | 9 552 | 77.4 | 117 000 | 23.6 | 13.9 | 595 | 29.6 | 2.6 | 13 096 | 0.0 | 944 | 7.2 | 11 541 | 31.8 | 27.8 |
| **NORTH CAROLINA** | 3 664 119 | 67.8 | 152 700 | 23.4 | 11.9 | 744 | 30.1 | 2.6 | 4 723 379 | 1.4 | 447 930 | 9.5 | 4 241 650 | 35.0 | 24.2 |
| Alamance | 59 948 | 68.6 | 136 000 | 23.3 | 11.3 | 728 | 29.4 | 3.1 | 73 885 | 1.4 | 6 978 | 9.4 | 70 846 | 30.7 | 26.4 |
| Alexander | 13 372 | 79.4 | 121 400 | 22.7 | 9.9 | 589 | 29.1 | 3.1 | 17 913 | 0.2 | 1 809 | 10.1 | 16 162 | 21.8 | 42.8 |
| Alleghany | 4 815 | 75.1 | 143 100 | 27.6 | 13.7 | 559 | 38.3 | 1.2 | 4 611 | -0.3 | 489 | 10.6 | 4 527 | 28.3 | 36.8 |
| Anson | 9 688 | 68.5 | 81 600 | 23.8 | 14.1 | 640 | 31.0 | 2.2 | 10 914 | 3.4 | 1 295 | 11.9 | 10 086 | 21.1 | 39.8 |
| Ashe | 11 814 | 80.2 | 154 100 | 26.9 | 11.5 | 565 | 28.6 | 2.5 | 12 318 | -0.7 | 1 421 | 11.5 | 11 946 | 26.0 | 35.5 |
| Avery | 7 089 | 71.8 | 160 700 | 30.0 | 9.9 | 698 | 33.4 | 3.9 | 7 892 | -0.8 | 887 | 11.2 | 7 338 | 25.9 | 28.0 |
| Beaufort | 19 831 | 73.1 | 113 600 | 24.2 | 15.0 | 609 | 31.9 | 2.2 | 21 302 | -1.5 | 2 314 | 10.9 | 19 740 | 30.4 | 32.0 |
| Bertie | 8 018 | 76.7 | 79 200 | 24.8 | 14.1 | 581 | 41.2 | 2.4 | 8 498 | -4.2 | 1 028 | 12.1 | 8 208 | 24.3 | 36.9 |
| Bladen | 13 960 | 69.5 | 78 100 | 24.5 | 16.0 | 585 | 30.1 | 2.7 | 15 281 | -3.0 | 1 892 | 12.4 | 13 448 | 26.2 | 38.0 |
| Brunswick | 46 733 | 77.8 | 189 500 | 26.5 | 12.7 | 806 | 32.5 | 1.9 | 51 149 | 1.6 | 5 413 | 10.6 | 42 923 | 31.4 | 25.1 |
| Buncombe | 100 909 | 66.2 | 192 200 | 24.3 | 11.4 | 763 | 29.7 | 2.1 | 127 249 | 1.5 | 9 585 | 7.5 | 113 650 | 36.9 | 19.9 |
| Burke | 34 996 | 73.7 | 110 500 | 23.0 | 11.7 | 592 | 29.3 | 2.8 | 39 542 | -0.4 | 4 275 | 10.8 | 38 223 | 27.9 | 31.5 |
| Cabarrus | 64 430 | 73.6 | 168 200 | 23.1 | 12.0 | 767 | 29.0 | 2.5 | 91 935 | 2.6 | 8 132 | 8.8 | 82 239 | 36.1 | 23.3 |
| Caldwell | 31 497 | 75.4 | 106 800 | 22.3 | 12.1 | 584 | 31.7 | 1.7 | 38 294 | -0.3 | 4 371 | 11.4 | 35 443 | 24.8 | 37.4 |
| Camden | 3 503 | 85.4 | 225 700 | 24.2 | 11.9 | 901 | 37.0 | 2.2 | 4 531 | -1.3 | 354 | 7.8 | 4 374 | 36.9 | 19.2 |
| Carteret | 28 692 | 72.7 | 208 200 | 24.0 | 12.8 | 704 | 28.1 | 1.4 | 33 433 | 1.8 | 2 875 | 8.6 | 29 748 | 30.7 | 26.9 |
| Caswell | 8 690 | 75.4 | 100 900 | 23.5 | 12.7 | 600 | 37.6 | 1.4 | 10 874 | -1.7 | 1 060 | 9.7 | 8 979 | 25.2 | 33.0 |
| Catawba | 58 850 | 71.4 | 129 000 | 21.6 | 10.4 | 644 | 27.8 | 2.9 | 73 611 | -0.2 | 8 095 | 11.0 | 70 679 | 29.6 | 30.6 |
| Chatham | 25 251 | 79.7 | 204 100 | 23.1 | 12.2 | 769 | 29.2 | 2.6 | 34 168 | 2.6 | 2 532 | 7.4 | 29 263 | 41.9 | 25.0 |
| Cherokee | 11 400 | 83.1 | 155 500 | 25.9 | 10.5 | 577 | 28.3 | 1.6 | 10 243 | -0.8 | 1 307 | 12.8 | 10 582 | 26.8 | 33.7 |

1. Specified owner-occupied units.    2. A value of 9.9 represents 9.9 percent or less.    3. Specified renter-occupied units. A value of 10.0 represents 10 percent or less.    4. Overcrowded or lacking complete plumbing facilities.    5. Percent of civilian labor force.    6. Persons 16 years old and over.

# Table B. States and Counties — Nonfarm Employment and Agriculture

| | Private nonfarm establishments, employment and payroll, 2011 | | | | | | | | | Agriculture, 2007 | | | |
| | | Employment | | | | | | Annual payroll | | Farms | | | |
| STATE County | | | | | | | | | | | | Percent with: | |
| | Number of establish-ments | Total | Health care and social assistance | Manufac-turing | Retail trade | Finance and insurance | Professional, scientific, and technical services | Total (mil dol) | Average per employee (dollars) | Number | Fewer than 50 acres | 500 acres or more | Farm operators whose principal occu-pation is farming (percent) |
| | 104 | 105 | 106 | 107 | 108 | 109 | 110 | 111 | 112 | 113 | 114 | 115 | 116 |

NEW YORK—Cont'd

| | | | | | | | | | | | | | |
|---|---|---|---|---|---|---|---|---|---|---|---|---|---|
| Genesee | 1 332 | 16 714 | 2 889 | 2 896 | 2 700 | 369 | 351 | 549 | 32 866 | 551 | 36.1 | 12.5 | 58.4 |
| Greene | 1 143 | 11 249 | 1 272 | 940 | 2 250 | 335 | 289 | 327 | 29 026 | 286 | 35.7 | 6.3 | 50.7 |
| Hamilton | 196 | 814 | D | D | 169 | D | D | 25 | 30 351 | 20 | 85.0 | 0.0 | 45.0 |
| Herkimer | 1 157 | 11 659 | 2 360 | 2 735 | 2 013 | 265 | 254 | 362 | 31 072 | 672 | 20.4 | 9.5 | 61.8 |
| Jefferson | 2 471 | 29 561 | 5 868 | 2 142 | 6 815 | 803 | 1 147 | 981 | 33 198 | 885 | 21.2 | 14.7 | 54.5 |
| Kings | 49 837 | 513 746 | 182 281 | 20 234 | 62 481 | 15 517 | 17 079 | 19 014 | 37 010 | 1 | 100.0 | 0.0 | 100.0 |
| Lewis | 526 | 4 583 | 885 | 1 206 | 798 | 75 | 124 | 151 | 32 908 | 616 | 18.2 | 12.0 | 63.8 |
| Livingston | 1 252 | 13 042 | 2 001 | 2 062 | 2 655 | 274 | 390 | 388 | 29 771 | 792 | 31.9 | 12.9 | 52.7 |
| Madison | 1 400 | 17 128 | 3 030 | 2 507 | 2 669 | 540 | 738 | 533 | 31 127 | 744 | 23.4 | 14.1 | 55.6 |
| Monroe | 17 144 | 336 504 | 61 158 | 37 981 | 40 440 | 12 110 | 20 343 | 14 065 | 41 798 | 585 | 54.9 | 11.3 | 55.4 |
| Montgomery | 1 098 | 15 311 | 4 079 | 3 366 | 2 675 | 380 | 290 | 485 | 31 668 | 604 | 24.0 | 8.3 | 65.1 |
| Nassau | 47 048 | 513 505 | 102 064 | 17 678 | 75 881 | 34 271 | 41 068 | 25 186 | 49 048 | 59 | 88.1 | 0.0 | 40.7 |
| New York | 103 800 | 1 998 051 | 237 489 | 20 368 | 139 247 | 285 578 | 274 895 | 202 981 | 101 590 | 0 | 0.0 | 0.0 | 0.0 |
| Niagara | 4 500 | 58 099 | 10 337 | 8 164 | 10 340 | 1 179 | 1 761 | 1 879 | 32 348 | 865 | 46.7 | 5.8 | 50.8 |
| Oneida | 4 876 | 86 706 | 20 429 | 10 140 | 11 743 | 6 955 | 3 227 | 2 985 | 34 429 | 1 013 | 27.3 | 8.1 | 55.7 |
| Onondaga | 11 723 | 208 799 | 35 836 | 18 980 | 28 278 | 12 657 | 12 814 | 8 318 | 39 838 | 692 | 42.6 | 11.6 | 53.9 |
| Ontario | 2 792 | 44 248 | 7 824 | 6 519 | 9 355 | 850 | 1 631 | 1 571 | 35 509 | 859 | 39.6 | 11.1 | 53.7 |
| Orange | 9 103 | 106 253 | 20 052 | 6 928 | 22 412 | 3 763 | 5 804 | 3 788 | 35 649 | 642 | 46.4 | 4.0 | 61.2 |
| Orleans | 682 | 8 556 | 1 497 | 2 462 | 1 138 | D | 162 | 270 | 31 499 | 554 | 38.1 | 8.7 | 52.5 |
| Oswego | 2 141 | 23 927 | 4 708 | 3 024 | 4 377 | 621 | 555 | 849 | 35 463 | 639 | 28.5 | 4.7 | 54.6 |
| Otsego | 1 439 | 19 443 | 6 114 | 905 | 3 424 | 1 329 | 577 | 670 | 34 468 | 980 | 22.7 | 6.1 | 54.9 |
| Putnam | 2 855 | 20 488 | 4 902 | 1 377 | 2 910 | 653 | 1 131 | 841 | 41 026 | 72 | 70.8 | 1.4 | 48.6 |
| Queens | 44 067 | 490 435 | 116 565 | 22 583 | 59 507 | 18 141 | 12 512 | 21 477 | 43 793 | 4 | 100.0 | 0.0 | 0.0 |
| Rensselaer | 2 981 | 41 390 | 8 713 | 2 313 | 5 675 | 1 371 | 3 680 | 1 577 | 38 100 | 506 | 35.8 | 6.7 | 53.6 |
| Richmond | 8 604 | 91 590 | 29 849 | 938 | 15 076 | 2 557 | 3 530 | 3 479 | 37 982 | 14 | 100.0 | 0.0 | 28.6 |
| Rockland | 9 198 | 99 498 | 22 162 | 8 395 | 13 198 | 3 179 | 5 322 | 4 353 | 43 749 | 21 | 90.5 | 0.0 | 42.9 |
| St. Lawrence | 2 018 | 26 642 | 6 363 | 2 538 | 5 359 | 724 | 588 | 859 | 32 243 | 1 330 | 14.9 | 12.1 | 52.0 |
| Saratoga | 4 986 | 61 049 | 8 050 | 5 141 | 10 933 | 3 934 | 3 707 | 2 425 | 39 718 | 641 | 51.5 | 3.4 | 54.8 |
| Schenectady | 3 068 | 48 703 | 11 828 | 4 039 | 6 666 | 1 546 | D | 2 011 | 41 281 | 194 | 46.4 | 3.1 | 50.5 |
| Schoharie | 556 | 5 365 | 1 013 | 328 | 978 | 247 | 223 | 165 | 30 690 | 525 | 23.4 | 6.9 | 57.7 |
| Schuyler | 378 | 3 662 | D | 603 | 688 | 59 | 40 | 117 | 31 998 | 394 | 25.9 | 6.9 | 55.8 |
| Seneca | 706 | 8 257 | 1 303 | 1 224 | 2 268 | 168 | 92 | 283 | 34 233 | 513 | 32.7 | 12.5 | 62.4 |
| Steuben | 1 796 | 26 733 | 5 733 | 4 826 | 4 248 | 1 029 | D | 1 323 | 49 501 | 1 578 | 17.2 | 10.3 | 48.9 |
| Suffolk | 47 668 | 538 635 | 93 641 | 53 405 | 78 292 | 23 743 | 41 693 | 26 443 | 49 093 | 585 | 74.2 | 1.2 | 64.4 |
| Sullivan | 1 998 | 18 186 | 5 190 | 1 108 | 2 875 | 801 | 551 | 573 | 31 483 | 323 | 31.0 | 7.1 | 50.8 |
| Tioga | 809 | 11 362 | 1 476 | 1 237 | 1 239 | 226 | D | 524 | 46 086 | 565 | 26.2 | 7.4 | 43.5 |
| Tompkins | 2 326 | 45 545 | 5 223 | 2 736 | 5 058 | 1 071 | 2 562 | 1 657 | 36 375 | 588 | 40.5 | 9.0 | 45.9 |
| Ulster | 4 663 | 44 056 | 8 949 | 3 590 | 8 872 | 2 419 | 1 496 | 1 432 | 32 508 | 501 | 42.1 | 5.0 | 57.1 |
| Warren | 2 331 | 31 304 | 6 711 | 4 362 | 5 828 | 1 299 | 878 | 1 129 | 36 076 | 86 | 59.3 | 2.3 | 37.2 |
| Washington | 1 067 | 9 626 | 1 656 | 2 794 | 1 855 | 184 | 223 | 335 | 34 813 | 843 | 29.9 | 13.4 | 49.7 |
| Wayne | 1 707 | 19 600 | 2 790 | 5 738 | 3 587 | 599 | 577 | 695 | 35 459 | 938 | 39.4 | 7.6 | 58.6 |
| Westchester | 31 515 | 371 385 | 77 036 | 12 392 | 47 607 | 22 263 | 26 909 | 22 585 | 60 813 | 106 | 69.8 | 3.8 | 43.4 |
| Wyoming | 800 | 9 251 | 1 293 | 1 743 | 1 377 | 365 | 324 | 277 | 29 988 | 761 | 30.9 | 13.9 | 59.0 |
| Yates | 545 | 5 162 | 1 008 | 855 | 751 | 107 | 113 | 143 | 27 694 | 864 | 25.6 | 3.8 | 64.0 |
| NORTH CAROLINA | 215 113 | 3 284 592 | 540 739 | 403 297 | 446 456 | 163 441 | 185 488 | 131 631 | 40 075 | 52 913 | 48.7 | 6.7 | 45.8 |
| Alamance | 3 153 | 50 394 | 7 730 | 9 626 | 8 545 | 1 490 | 1 285 | 1 541 | 30 583 | 753 | 42.6 | 3.9 | 43.0 |
| Alexander | 591 | 6 710 | 505 | 3 072 | 799 | 173 | 115 | 185 | 27 520 | 627 | 55.5 | 2.4 | 42.3 |
| Alleghany | 251 | 2 158 | 536 | D | 326 | D | D | 56 | 25 839 | 519 | 49.3 | 7.3 | 47.2 |
| Anson | 389 | 4 334 | 531 | 1 375 | 747 | 82 | 131 | 125 | 28 813 | 487 | 30.2 | 8.6 | 42.1 |
| Ashe | 520 | 6 095 | 1 155 | D | 1 047 | 173 | D | 177 | 29 100 | 1 125 | 51.4 | 3.0 | 42.5 |
| Avery | 508 | 4 317 | 804 | 168 | 721 | 106 | 71 | 112 | 25 932 | 477 | 63.3 | 1.0 | 40.7 |
| Beaufort | 1 149 | 13 456 | 2 401 | 3 081 | 2 330 | 380 | 339 | 432 | 32 097 | 369 | 36.3 | 22.0 | 50.9 |
| Bertie | 342 | 5 132 | 1 409 | D | 379 | 78 | 50 | 115 | 22 456 | 279 | 28.3 | 25.8 | 64.5 |
| Bladen | 532 | 10 680 | 1 345 | D | 840 | D | 142 | 302 | 28 276 | 500 | 41.0 | 14.0 | 50.8 |
| Brunswick | 2 223 | 23 021 | 3 462 | 2 758 | 4 315 | 681 | 598 | 721 | 31 308 | 264 | 59.1 | 6.8 | 54.5 |
| Buncombe | 7 171 | 97 718 | 21 311 | 10 190 | 15 056 | 2 473 | 3 819 | 3 390 | 34 690 | 1 077 | 67.2 | 1.3 | 36.4 |
| Burke | 1 436 | 21 782 | 4 168 | 7 485 | 2 521 | 408 | 441 | 688 | 31 606 | 481 | 65.5 | 1.2 | 45.7 |
| Cabarrus | 3 828 | 54 912 | 9 231 | 4 967 | 11 237 | 896 | 1 474 | 1 847 | 33 635 | 611 | 52.9 | 3.6 | 36.3 |
| Caldwell | 1 372 | 18 997 | 3 475 | 5 977 | 2 901 | 431 | 372 | 549 | 28 918 | 459 | 62.5 | 1.1 | 34.4 |
| Camden | 107 | 570 | D | D | 91 | D | D | 15 | 26 112 | 76 | 35.5 | 30.3 | 53.9 |
| Carteret | 1 944 | 17 562 | 3 229 | 950 | 3 875 | 549 | 522 | 491 | 27 982 | 159 | 78.0 | 4.4 | 33.3 |
| Caswell | 249 | 1 775 | 485 | 149 | 300 | 49 | 38 | 41 | 22 839 | 562 | 29.9 | 8.4 | 47.2 |
| Catawba | 4 077 | 76 028 | 10 738 | 21 702 | 9 462 | 1 379 | 1 597 | 2 752 | 36 201 | 737 | 51.8 | 3.0 | 36.4 |
| Chatham | 1 226 | 12 996 | 2 576 | 3 046 | 1 926 | 247 | 505 | 386 | 29 717 | 1 089 | 47.2 | 1.5 | 44.8 |
| Cherokee | 581 | 6 274 | 1 552 | 1 127 | 1 407 | 200 | 288 | 169 | 26 989 | 288 | 59.4 | 1.4 | 47.9 |

# Table B. States and Counties — Agriculture

| STATE County | Acreage (1,000) [117] | Percent change, 2002-2007 [118] | Average size of farm [119] | Total irrigated (1,000) [120] | Total cropland (1,000) [121] | Average per farm [122] | Average per acre [123] | Value of machinery and equipment, average per farm (dollars) [124] | Total (mil dol) [125] | Average per farm (dollars) [126] | Crops [127] | Live-stock and poultry products [128] | $10,000 or more [129] | $100,000 or more [130] | Total ($1,000) [131] | Percent of farms [132] |
|---|---|---|---|---|---|---|---|---|---|---|---|---|---|---|---|---|
| **NEW YORK—Cont'd** | | | | | | | | | | | | | | | | |
| Genesee | 184 | 4.0 | 333 | 7.8 | 146.0 | 583 415 | 1 751 | 165 883 | 177.8 | 322 703 | 35.4 | 64.6 | 46.5 | 22.1 | 1 989 | 49.5 |
| Greene | 44 | -24.1 | 155 | 0.7 | 22.2 | 452 548 | 2 920 | 77 318 | 16.4 | 57 249 | 43.5 | 56.5 | 36.0 | 9.4 | 225 | 22.0 |
| Hamilton | 0 | -100.0 | 23 | D | 0.2 | 97 714 | 4 343 | D | 0.4 | 18 116 | 97.8 | 2.5 | 25.0 | 10.0 | 0 | 0.0 |
| Herkimer | 140 | -11.9 | 208 | 0.2 | 77.9 | 363 264 | 1 743 | 89 577 | 62.1 | 92 472 | 12.3 | 87.7 | 53.1 | 23.2 | 992 | 37.5 |
| Jefferson | 262 | -20.8 | 296 | 0.3 | 166.2 | 410 806 | 1 386 | 114 803 | 139.2 | 157 335 | 12.2 | 87.8 | 51.2 | 22.7 | 1 906 | 35.1 |
| Kings | D | D | D | D | D | D | D | D | D | D | D | 0.0 | 100.0 | 0.0 | 0 | 0.0 |
| Lewis | 167 | -15.2 | 272 | 0.1 | 92.0 | 435 764 | 1 605 | 119 007 | 112.6 | 182 839 | 5.9 | 94.1 | 60.2 | 39.3 | 1 012 | 39.4 |
| Livingston | 222 | 6.2 | 281 | 0.5 | 165.8 | 565 547 | 2 014 | 126 034 | 153.8 | 194 243 | 30.7 | 69.3 | 40.9 | 19.7 | 2 999 | 49.4 |
| Madison | 188 | 11.9 | 253 | 0.5 | 115.9 | 425 987 | 1 683 | 113 067 | 86.3 | 116 036 | 18.7 | 81.3 | 50.7 | 24.9 | 1 629 | 32.5 |
| Monroe | 133 | 24.3 | 227 | 1.6 | 105.7 | 587 711 | 2 584 | 106 178 | 72.2 | 123 436 | 85.1 | 14.9 | 44.3 | 19.8 | 1 327 | 26.0 |
| Montgomery | 125 | -17.8 | 206 | 0.2 | 84.1 | 445 455 | 2 160 | 106 802 | 73.6 | 121 873 | 16.8 | 83.2 | 53.5 | 20.5 | 1 231 | 38.2 |
| Nassau | 1 | 0.0 | 22 | 0.2 | 0.3 | 2 161 159 | 98 997 | 86 665 | 15.8 | 267 787 | 76.1 | 23.9 | 59.3 | 25.4 | 0 | 0.0 |
| New York | 0 | NA | 0 | 0.0 | 0.0 | 0 | 0 | 0 | 0.0 | 0 | 0.0 | 0.0 | 0.0 | 0.0 | 0 | 0.0 |
| Niagara | 143 | -3.4 | 165 | 2.6 | 113.6 | 351 933 | 2 134 | 109 484 | 103.6 | 119 820 | 58.6 | 41.4 | 39.9 | 12.9 | 1 534 | 28.3 |
| Oneida | 192 | -12.7 | 190 | 0.3 | 108.9 | 367 253 | 1 935 | 92 561 | 90.1 | 88 956 | 27.4 | 72.6 | 46.0 | 20.1 | 2 077 | 32.4 |
| Onondaga | 150 | -3.8 | 217 | 1.6 | 106.2 | 521 122 | 2 396 | 127 052 | 137.4 | 198 515 | 26.6 | 73.4 | 48.8 | 22.8 | 2 104 | 33.2 |
| Ontario | 199 | 2.1 | 232 | 1.0 | 153.1 | 510 387 | 2 204 | 127 424 | 153.8 | 179 101 | 32.2 | 67.8 | 53.0 | 22.1 | 2 293 | 40.0 |
| Orange | 81 | -25.0 | 126 | 4.6 | 46.3 | 649 645 | 5 150 | 102 810 | 73.7 | 114 873 | 69.4 | 30.6 | 50.8 | 21.3 | 769 | 25.7 |
| Orleans | 140 | 5.3 | 252 | 3.5 | 106.3 | 433 158 | 1 717 | 132 141 | 101.0 | 182 357 | 88.1 | 11.9 | 44.6 | 21.1 | 2 135 | 44.0 |
| Oswego | 100 | -2.9 | 157 | 1.1 | 49.0 | 295 224 | 1 883 | 81 275 | 39.3 | 61 568 | 66.2 | 33.8 | 41.9 | 13.5 | 482 | 21.9 |
| Otsego | 176 | -14.6 | 180 | 0.2 | 88.2 | 341 977 | 1 899 | 64 459 | 51.4 | 52 457 | 17.1 | 82.9 | 40.3 | 15.6 | 977 | 24.3 |
| Putnam | 6 | -14.3 | 78 | D | 1.3 | 1 092 842 | 13 964 | 64 379 | 7.2 | D | 0.0 | D | 30.6 | 11.1 | D | 1.4 |
| Queens | D | D | D | 0.0 | D | D | D | D | 0.1 | 29 293 | D | D | 100.0 | 0.0 | 0 | 0.0 |
| Rensselaer | 85 | -7.6 | 168 | 1.0 | 45.2 | 529 827 | 3 153 | 89 289 | 37.5 | 74 133 | 37.6 | 62.4 | 46.4 | 13.4 | 818 | 30.2 |
| Richmond | D | D | D | 0.0 | D | 379 581 | 120 776 | 81 523 | 5.2 | 369 589 | 100.0 | 0.0 | 50.0 | 35.7 | 0 | 0.0 |
| Rockland | D | D | D | 0.0 | 0.1 | 651 265 | 56 515 | 82 463 | 2.6 | 121 890 | D | D | 38.1 | 33.3 | 0 | 0.0 |
| St. Lawrence | 347 | -13.9 | 261 | 0.3 | 176.9 | 351 391 | 1 346 | 81 940 | 140.2 | 105 377 | 10.6 | 89.4 | 41.3 | 14.8 | 1 853 | 23.0 |
| Saratoga | 76 | 1.3 | 118 | 0.5 | 42.9 | 515 230 | 4 365 | 81 832 | 58.2 | 90 836 | 26.0 | 74.0 | 34.2 | 9.0 | 566 | 16.5 |
| Schenectady | 19 | -13.6 | 99 | 0.4 | 10.5 | 354 700 | 3 597 | 57 727 | 3.5 | 18 014 | 73.8 | 26.2 | 25.3 | 5.2 | D | 3.6 |
| Schoharie | 95 | -15.9 | 182 | 0.5 | 53.0 | 389 261 | 2 140 | 79 647 | 35.2 | 66 959 | 27.9 | 72.1 | 49.3 | 14.1 | 596 | 26.1 |
| Schuyler | 66 | -10.8 | 168 | 0.3 | 37.1 | 366 960 | 2 178 | 67 088 | 33.1 | 83 907 | 38.0 | 62.0 | 41.6 | 14.7 | 475 | 20.6 |
| Seneca | 128 | 0.8 | 249 | 0.2 | 102.9 | 502 185 | 2 013 | 129 110 | 84.1 | 163 889 | 39.3 | 60.7 | 63.9 | 35.7 | 1 214 | 34.9 |
| Steuben | 372 | -0.3 | 236 | 1.5 | 211.2 | 370 465 | 1 572 | 88 340 | 135.3 | 85 732 | 28.0 | 72.0 | 39.0 | 14.1 | 2 616 | 35.2 |
| Suffolk | 34 | 0.0 | 59 | 13.6 | 26.3 | 1 065 327 | 18 115 | 183 312 | 242.9 | 415 270 | 92.5 | 7.5 | 70.9 | 38.1 | 253 | 9.4 |
| Sullivan | 50 | -21.9 | 156 | 0.1 | 24.6 | 545 478 | 3 493 | 81 001 | 42.1 | 130 393 | 5.0 | 95.0 | 44.6 | 11.8 | 243 | 20.1 |
| Tioga | 107 | -16.4 | 189 | 0.4 | 53.8 | 331 150 | 1 751 | 70 301 | 36.7 | 64 894 | 13.4 | 86.6 | 33.1 | 15.6 | 1 053 | 34.3 |
| Tompkins | 109 | 7.9 | 185 | 0.3 | 67.3 | 418 353 | 2 262 | 94 081 | 60.2 | 102 356 | 25.4 | 74.6 | 39.6 | 17.0 | 955 | 30.4 |
| Ulster | 75 | -9.6 | 150 | 4.7 | 31.7 | 598 130 | 3 985 | 92 909 | 65.6 | 130 928 | 89.7 | 10.3 | 42.8 | 15.8 | 284 | 11.0 |
| Warren | 9 | 50.0 | 99 | 0.0 | 1.3 | 345 406 | 3 472 | 45 201 | D | D | D | D | 25.6 | 2.3 | 0 | 0.0 |
| Washington | 203 | -1.5 | 241 | 0.5 | 112.0 | 512 622 | 2 130 | 104 900 | 112.3 | 133 166 | 11.9 | 88.1 | 49.6 | 21.4 | 2 189 | 27.5 |
| Wayne | 168 | 1.8 | 180 | 2.2 | 119.7 | 410 385 | 2 285 | 125 569 | 169.0 | 180 131 | 76.0 | 24.0 | 53.0 | 26.2 | 1 535 | 27.2 |
| Westchester | 9 | -10.0 | 80 | 0.2 | 2.5 | 2 557 300 | 31 812 | 105 460 | 11.0 | 103 754 | 50.2 | 49.8 | 45.3 | 22.6 | D | 0.9 |
| Wyoming | 218 | 1.4 | 287 | 3.7 | 157.3 | 509 515 | 1 778 | 158 822 | 229.9 | 302 159 | 12.4 | 87.6 | 47.7 | 26.5 | 2 810 | 40.5 |
| Yates | 126 | 9.6 | 146 | 0.5 | 86.6 | 415 303 | 2 845 | 92 975 | 88.4 | 102 294 | 36.0 | 64.0 | 68.6 | 37.5 | 1 107 | 24.8 |
| **NORTH CAROLINA** | 8 475 | -6.7 | 160 | 232.1 | 4 895.2 | 656 080 | 4 096 | 76 793 | 10 313.6 | 194 917 | 25.3 | 74.7 | 35.2 | 15.7 | 147 334 | 26.2 |
| Alamance | 88 | -10.2 | 117 | 1.6 | 35.9 | 538 124 | 4 610 | 60 524 | 42.6 | 56 598 | 19.2 | 80.8 | 34.3 | 10.5 | 459 | 18.2 |
| Alexander | 55 | -5.2 | 88 | 0.7 | 21.5 | 479 054 | 5 465 | 58 998 | 112.0 | 178 560 | 2.9 | 97.1 | 42.1 | 26.5 | 224 | 8.3 |
| Alleghany | 77 | 5.5 | 148 | 0.4 | 29.2 | 838 316 | 5 676 | 67 003 | 34.0 | 65 500 | 54.5 | 45.5 | 45.5 | 9.6 | 389 | 13.1 |
| Anson | 91 | -9.0 | 186 | 0.5 | 27.8 | 664 850 | 3 567 | 62 579 | 157.7 | 323 815 | 4.5 | 95.5 | 36.6 | 23.6 | 951 | 50.3 |
| Ashe | 108 | 0.0 | 96 | 0.3 | 38.0 | 555 859 | 5 766 | 44 922 | 41.7 | 37 070 | 76.5 | 23.5 | 36.4 | 6.8 | 128 | 2.6 |
| Avery | 28 | -9.7 | 58 | 0.4 | 12.6 | 440 933 | 7 561 | 60 203 | 20.5 | 43 024 | 98.0 | 2.0 | 39.8 | 10.1 | 92 | 3.1 |
| Beaufort | 160 | -5.9 | 435 | 0.9 | 139.0 | 1 115 057 | 2 566 | 146 130 | 99.8 | 267 732 | 65.9 | 34.1 | 48.4 | 29.3 | 4 038 | 64.2 |
| Bertie | 147 | 2.8 | 528 | 8.5 | 92.7 | 1 349 552 | 2 555 | 206 421 | 161.6 | 579 071 | 24.4 | 75.6 | 63.4 | 46.2 | 5 475 | 77.1 |
| Bladen | 127 | -12.4 | 254 | 11.1 | 70.6 | 838 266 | 3 296 | 108 439 | 338.5 | 676 987 | 13.3 | 86.7 | 46.0 | 30.0 | 2 260 | 43.0 |
| Brunswick | 44 | 7.3 | 167 | 2.5 | 27.4 | 714 480 | 4 279 | 95 917 | 45.1 | 170 959 | 44.8 | 55.2 | 31.8 | 11.4 | 335 | 23.1 |
| Buncombe | 72 | -24.2 | 67 | 0.5 | 20.3 | 475 105 | 7 098 | 52 613 | 37.2 | 34 578 | 75.7 | 24.3 | 18.5 | 2.8 | 203 | 9.3 |
| Burke | 29 | -9.4 | 60 | 2.1 | 14.4 | 355 410 | 5 881 | 62 632 | 35.6 | 73 999 | 55.0 | 45.0 | 24.5 | 7.7 | 104 | 8.3 |
| Cabarrus | 67 | -8.2 | 109 | 0.4 | 34.6 | 614 341 | 5 621 | 56 510 | 52.4 | 85 752 | 14.1 | 85.9 | 23.7 | 6.4 | 675 | 17.5 |
| Caldwell | 33 | -5.7 | 71 | 1.5 | 11.4 | 360 485 | 5 077 | 48 611 | 20.8 | 45 208 | 63.3 | 36.7 | 20.9 | 7.2 | 51 | 4.4 |
| Camden | 55 | NA | 726 | 0.0 | 47.6 | 2 138 048 | 2 945 | 251 941 | 28.2 | 371 476 | 98.9 | 1.1 | 53.9 | 31.6 | 681 | 52.6 |
| Carteret | 55 | -8.3 | 348 | 0.2 | 38.0 | 1 070 514 | 3 073 | 99 640 | 20.3 | 127 430 | 95.5 | 4.5 | 33.3 | 10.1 | 376 | 16.4 |
| Caswell | 102 | -12.8 | 182 | 1.5 | 37.9 | 568 243 | 3 122 | 50 942 | 20.7 | 36 839 | 44.9 | 55.1 | 34.0 | 6.4 | 950 | 26.2 |
| Catawba | 72 | -8.9 | 98 | 1.1 | 36.7 | 517 123 | 5 300 | 51 627 | 30.5 | 41 413 | 40.7 | 59.3 | 25.4 | 6.0 | 456 | 16.8 |
| Chatham | 104 | -12.6 | 96 | 0.9 | 32.8 | 535 597 | 5 599 | 49 890 | 171.7 | 157 713 | 4.0 | 96.0 | 36.1 | 14.9 | 530 | 12.3 |
| Cherokee | 20 | -9.1 | 71 | 0.2 | 6.5 | 478 486 | 6 747 | 59 654 | D | D | 0.0 | D | 20.1 | 3.5 | 170 | 10.4 |

— **Water Use, Wholesale Trade, Retail Trade, and Real Estate**

| STATE County | Water use, 2005 | | Wholesale trade,[1] 2007 | | | | Retail trade,[2] 2007 | | | | Real estate and rental and leasing,[2] 2007 | | | |
|---|---|---|---|---|---|---|---|---|---|---|---|---|---|---|
| | Total water withdrawn (mil gal/day) | Gallons withdrawn per person | Number of establishments | Number of employees | Sales (mil dol) | Annual payroll (mil dol) | Number of establishments | Number of employees | Sales (mil dol) | Annual payroll (mil dol) | Number of establishments | Number of employees | Receipts (mil dol) | Annual payroll (mil dol) |
| | 133 | 134 | 135 | 136 | 137 | 138 | 139 | 140 | 141 | 142 | 143 | 144 | 145 | 146 |
| NEW YORK—Cont'd | | | | | | | | | | | | | | |
| Genesee | 11.9 | 200 | 68 | 1 164 | 811.7 | 44.7 | 217 | 2 616 | 705.7 | 55.2 | 47 | 197 | 33.4 | 7.3 |
| Greene | 5.8 | 117 | 18 | 309 | 232.2 | 12.0 | 206 | 2 553 | 623.0 | 58.5 | 49 | 217 | 24.8 | 5.8 |
| Hamilton | 1.1 | 214 | NA | NA | NA | NA | 31 | 191 | 31.9 | 3.2 | 8 | 15 | 1.5 | 0.2 |
| Herkimer | 14.8 | 232 | 37 | 577 | 186.8 | 22.1 | 222 | 2 045 | 503.1 | 45.4 | 44 | 192 | 20.2 | 2.7 |
| Jefferson | 15.6 | 134 | 71 | D | D | D | 506 | 7 188 | 1 867.7 | 163.4 | 122 | 543 | 98.9 | 14.3 |
| Kings | 13.9 | 6 | 3 342 | 26 145 | 13 802.2 | 914.5 | 8 365 | 58 365 | 15 431.9 | 1 347.7 | 4 068 | 13 786 | 2 886.4 | 411.2 |
| Lewis | 8.1 | 304 | 12 | 96 | 33.0 | 3.5 | 77 | 738 | 175.8 | 13.9 | 12 | 49 | 4.8 | 1.0 |
| Livingston | 8.2 | 128 | 42 | 418 | 219.8 | 16.8 | 215 | 2 587 | 586.5 | 56.8 | 48 | 199 | 28.9 | 4.0 |
| Madison | 7.1 | 101 | 32 | 318 | 109.5 | 13.1 | 227 | 2 700 | 665.9 | 61.9 | 60 | 150 | 18.7 | 3.9 |
| Monroe | 226.9 | 309 | 809 | 13 783 | 6 778.3 | 728.2 | 2 376 | 40 062 | 8 496.1 | 845.7 | 803 | 6 215 | 1 025.4 | 193.7 |
| Montgomery | 13.2 | 270 | 45 | D | D | D | 197 | 2 469 | 621.8 | 52.2 | 27 | 112 | 13.1 | 3.3 |
| Nassau | 551.5 | 414 | 3 078 | D | D | D | 6 356 | 84 280 | 24 312.6 | 2 273.8 | 2 501 | D | D | D |
| New York | 287.6 | 181 | 8 941 | 99 779 | 108 757.4 | 6 717.5 | 11 665 | 134 567 | 38 797.5 | 4 490.7 | 9 469 | 68 786 | 28 476.7 | 4 350.0 |
| Niagara | 291.0 | 1 341 | 181 | 2 476 | 1 059.3 | 105.4 | 746 | 9 522 | 2 075.1 | 191.8 | 131 | 614 | 71.4 | 14.5 |
| Oneida | 42.9 | 183 | 176 | 2 098 | 939.4 | 80.7 | 869 | 12 369 | 2 751.0 | 264.4 | 206 | 822 | 151.8 | 19.7 |
| Onondaga | 147.5 | 322 | 668 | 12 250 | 17 121.5 | 571.3 | 1 776 | 28 722 | 6 363.1 | 613.2 | 629 | 3 439 | 663.2 | 124.4 |
| Ontario | 14.2 | 136 | 119 | 1 291 | 536.7 | 60.1 | 556 | 8 689 | 1 894.2 | 180.1 | 98 | 450 | 67.4 | 10.2 |
| Orange | 855.1 | 2 293 | 447 | 7 417 | 6 859.2 | 335.0 | 1 586 | 22 345 | 5 729.2 | 517.4 | 424 | 1 591 | 379.5 | 45.1 |
| Orleans | 5.4 | 125 | 21 | 259 | 88.6 | 9.2 | 111 | 1 282 | 262.6 | 25.9 | 19 | 44 | 9.3 | 1.0 |
| Oswego | 1 255.0 | 10 172 | 55 | 429 | 210.8 | 13.3 | 365 | 4 290 | 994.1 | 87.1 | 74 | 310 | 32.8 | 5.8 |
| Otsego | 6.7 | 107 | 44 | D | D | D | 301 | 3 661 | 932.4 | 86.1 | 47 | 184 | 26.5 | 3.8 |
| Putnam | 111.4 | 1 108 | 119 | 928 | 504.7 | 43.3 | 342 | 3 171 | 922.3 | 84.8 | 110 | 300 | 58.0 | 11.0 |
| Queens | 1 738.3 | 775 | 2 886 | 26 189 | 15 308.5 | 1 249.2 | 6 725 | 54 013 | 14 587.1 | 1 322.4 | 2 839 | 13 751 | 2 943.0 | 522.5 |
| Rensselaer | 26.7 | 172 | 100 | 997 | 1 387.7 | 42.1 | 421 | 5 833 | 1 384.4 | 133.0 | 98 | 481 | 74.1 | 13.1 |
| Richmond | 653.9 | 1 408 | 366 | 1 791 | 1 320.1 | 77.2 | 1 242 | 16 274 | 3 850.1 | 358.9 | 322 | 1 157 | 269.4 | 33.9 |
| Rockland | 1 007.5 | 3 439 | 508 | 5 549 | 3 228.2 | 282.0 | 1 186 | 14 122 | 3 866.8 | 346.8 | 458 | 1 752 | 406.8 | 51.6 |
| St. Lawrence | 16.4 | 147 | 53 | 463 | 116.1 | 13.2 | 447 | 5 183 | 1 238.8 | 105.9 | 66 | 289 | 33.0 | 5.8 |
| Saratoga | 23.9 | 111 | 182 | 2 958 | 2 239.4 | 160.4 | 775 | 11 807 | 4 506.4 | 256.4 | 177 | 988 | 181.6 | 30.5 |
| Schenectady | 28.9 | 194 | 100 | 1 124 | 601.6 | 44.6 | 498 | 7 600 | 1 664.3 | 161.8 | 117 | 668 | 114.3 | 21.0 |
| Schoharie | 170.8 | 5 293 | 18 | 126 | 36.0 | 4.7 | 98 | 1 106 | 268.9 | 23.2 | 21 | 50 | 6.8 | 1.0 |
| Schuyler | 3.3 | 169 | 6 | D | D | D | 66 | 713 | 179.9 | 15.8 | 10 | 43 | 2.9 | 0.7 |
| Seneca | 4.7 | 133 | 26 | D | D | D | 201 | 2 141 | 426.2 | 39.1 | 25 | 106 | 20.4 | 2.4 |
| Steuben | 23.8 | 241 | 36 | D | D | D | 363 | 4 336 | 1 076.9 | 89.5 | 56 | 249 | 29.4 | 7.5 |
| Suffolk | 1 508.0 | 1 022 | 3 039 | 42 142 | 38 208.9 | 2 400.2 | 6 750 | 83 958 | 23 319.9 | 2 217.8 | 1 813 | D | D | D |
| Sullivan | 107.8 | 1 408 | 67 | 714 | 299.1 | 22.3 | 318 | 3 035 | 815.2 | 71.1 | 156 | 507 | 66.3 | 10.1 |
| Tioga | 7.9 | 154 | 23 | D | D | D | 151 | 1 310 | 302.2 | 27.3 | 12 | 24 | 3.4 | 0.4 |
| Tompkins | 254.2 | 2 541 | 54 | 426 | 189.6 | 15.5 | 372 | 5 068 | 1 018.3 | 106.1 | 95 | 748 | 116.2 | 19.8 |
| Ulster | 472.5 | 2 586 | 150 | 1 607 | 946.5 | 86.5 | 794 | 9 242 | 2 241.1 | 216.3 | 209 | 676 | 125.2 | 18.4 |
| Warren | 12.0 | 182 | 72 | 758 | 342.0 | 32.5 | 452 | 5 899 | 1 382.2 | 138.7 | 86 | 377 | 67.9 | 10.4 |
| Washington | 10.3 | 163 | 30 | 246 | 85.1 | 8.5 | 206 | 1 934 | 485.6 | 43.7 | 20 | 58 | 4.8 | 1.1 |
| Wayne | 459.9 | 4 913 | 68 | 484 | 189.4 | 19.1 | 289 | 3 451 | 816.7 | 76.7 | 61 | 273 | 27.3 | 4.5 |
| Westchester | 2 529.0 | 2 688 | 1 419 | 17 179 | 20 059.6 | 1 155.2 | 4 058 | 50 195 | 14 205.1 | 1 423.2 | 2 162 | 9 027 | 2 373.8 | 416.9 |
| Wyoming | 10.3 | 242 | 30 | 288 | 297.2 | 11.5 | 144 | 1 463 | 338.0 | 30.6 | 21 | 72 | 7.7 | 1.7 |
| Yates | 71.2 | 2 874 | 16 | 136 | 42.7 | 4.4 | 105 | 690 | 178.9 | 15.2 | 18 | 105 | 9.6 | 2.4 |
| NORTH CAROLINA | 12 852.2 | 1 480 | 10 049 | 142 342 | 88 795.9 | 6 969.2 | 36 592 | 466 577 | 114 578.2 | 10 342.7 | 11 258 | 53 563 | 11 175.1 | 1 881.4 |
| Alamance | 24.3 | 173 | 153 | 1 839 | 655.8 | 73.3 | 631 | 8 251 | 1 968.8 | 168.1 | 135 | 523 | 83.0 | 14.7 |
| Alexander | 5.1 | 145 | 22 | 157 | 49.8 | 5.9 | 91 | 914 | 216.8 | 19.7 | 14 | 41 | 4.0 | 0.7 |
| Alleghany | 4.1 | 378 | 5 | 21 | 1.5 | 0.4 | 44 | 385 | 73.7 | 6.5 | 11 | 31 | 4.8 | 0.5 |
| Anson | 10.9 | 427 | 14 | 333 | 153.5 | 13.9 | 92 | 825 | 180.0 | 16.2 | 8 | 18 | 2.1 | 0.5 |
| Ashe | 3.3 | 132 | 15 | 155 | 55.9 | 4.2 | 117 | 1 176 | 292.4 | 23.5 | 40 | 83 | 15.7 | 1.8 |
| Avery | 12.4 | 701 | 22 | 132 | 41.6 | 3.9 | 94 | 1 029 | 197.6 | 20.0 | 35 | 119 | 13.0 | 3.2 |
| Beaufort | 84.7 | 1 840 | 58 | 487 | 285.4 | 18.1 | 216 | 2 459 | 573.4 | 49.8 | 39 | 109 | 12.8 | 2.0 |
| Bertie | 10.5 | 540 | 16 | 98 | 51.2 | 3.1 | 59 | 390 | 93.0 | 8.1 | 9 | D | D | D |
| Bladen | 56.6 | 1 719 | 22 | 166 | 174.2 | 5.6 | 98 | 847 | 196.7 | 15.9 | 14 | 52 | 6.5 | 1.5 |
| Brunswick | 1 568.4 | 17 591 | 74 | 578 | 206.7 | 20.5 | 392 | 4 264 | 1 004.2 | 90.1 | 214 | 689 | 113.2 | 22.5 |
| Buncombe | 303.8 | 1 388 | 257 | 2 838 | 1 162.9 | 114.1 | 1 205 | 15 865 | 3 597.9 | 342.4 | 427 | 1 534 | 277.8 | 51.2 |
| Burke | 18.9 | 211 | 65 | 757 | 289.5 | 27.9 | 277 | 2 689 | 661.2 | 57.0 | 53 | 164 | 18.2 | 3.4 |
| Cabarrus | 17.7 | 118 | 188 | 2 962 | 1 412.3 | 131.7 | 732 | 11 058 | 2 807.8 | 239.7 | 214 | 763 | 107.6 | 21.6 |
| Caldwell | 11.6 | 147 | 74 | 577 | 236.8 | 23.0 | 276 | 2 676 | 648.6 | 56.4 | 60 | 193 | 26.1 | 5.2 |
| Camden | 0.9 | 96 | 5 | 31 | 9.5 | 1.2 | 17 | 96 | 27.0 | 1.6 | 2 | D | D | D |
| Carteret | 7.9 | 126 | 66 | 577 | 254.3 | 21.1 | 429 | 4 148 | 979.6 | 91.1 | 134 | 575 | 70.7 | 14.5 |
| Caswell | 3.1 | 130 | 3 | D | D | D | 49 | 260 | 53.0 | 4.9 | 4 | 3 | 0.7 | 0.1 |
| Catawba | 1 182.2 | 7 796 | 253 | 6 524 | 4 087.3 | 263.5 | 797 | 10 577 | 2 683.1 | 233.9 | 193 | 700 | 142.2 | 20.2 |
| Chatham | 159.4 | 2 747 | 46 | 360 | 128.7 | 13.0 | 190 | 2 197 | 559.4 | 47.7 | 42 | 128 | 12.6 | 3.1 |
| Cherokee | 31.5 | 1 222 | 12 | 146 | 60.5 | 3.1 | 153 | 1 675 | 404.0 | 34.7 | 54 | 151 | 18.3 | 2.8 |

1. Merchant wholesalers, except manufacturers' sales branches and offices.  2. Employer establishments.

# Table B. States and Counties — Professional Services, Manufacturing, and Accommodation and Food Services

| STATE County | Professional, scientific, and technical services,[1] 2007 | | | | Manufacturing, 2007 | | | | Accommodation and food services, 2007 | | | |
|---|---|---|---|---|---|---|---|---|---|---|---|---|
| | Number of establishments | Number of employees | Receipts (mil dol) | Annual payroll (mil dol) | Number of establishments | Number of employees | Receipts (mil dol) | Annual payroll (mil dol) | Number of establishments | Number of employees | Sales (mil dol) | Annual payroll (mil dol) |
| | 147 | 148 | 149 | 150 | 151 | 152 | 153 | 154 | 155 | 156 | 157 | 158 |
| NEW YORK—Cont'd | | | | | | | | | | | | |
| Genesee | 83 | D | D | D | 99 | 3 206 | 815.5 | 128.9 | 130 | 1 727 | 79.5 | 20.5 |
| Greene | 75 | 265 | 21.4 | 7.7 | 35 | 1 088 | 591.1 | 56.0 | 195 | 2 556 | 90.6 | 25.0 |
| Hamilton | 4 | D | D | D | NA | NA | NA | NA | 56 | 228 | 22.6 | 4.9 |
| Herkimer | 72 | D | D | D | 68 | 2 839 | 546.4 | 109.7 | 156 | 1 274 | 54.2 | 14.6 |
| Jefferson | 123 | 899 | 103.8 | 37.4 | 73 | 2 624 | 839.9 | 108.5 | 320 | 3 748 | 172.0 | 49.7 |
| Kings | 3 411 | 20 021 | 1 888.6 | 653.2 | 1 932 | 24 955 | 4 555.6 | 893.8 | 3 266 | 23 522 | 1 544.4 | 395.6 |
| Lewis | 21 | D | D | D | 23 | 1 254 | 511.6 | 54.3 | 68 | 480 | 18.0 | 4.8 |
| Livingston | 99 | D | D | D | 68 | 2 292 | 463.9 | 86.0 | 146 | 1 790 | 70.8 | 19.5 |
| Madison | 121 | D | D | D | 61 | 2 696 | 941.4 | 101.1 | 157 | 1 943 | 77.6 | 22.6 |
| Monroe | 1 947 | 22 172 | 2 654.9 | 1 237.9 | 939 | 49 854 | 16 615.4 | 2 345.4 | 1 531 | 24 626 | 1 061.3 | 307.5 |
| Montgomery | 67 | D | D | D | 74 | 3 483 | 719.5 | 132.6 | 120 | 1 073 | 42.0 | 12.0 |
| Nassau | 7 008 | D | D | D | 1 221 | D | D | 1 034.1 | 3 192 | 39 540 | 2 439.4 | 680.0 |
| New York | 17 114 | 263 221 | 72 850.5 | 26 601.0 | 2 731 | 37 037 | 8 315.1 | 1 396.0 | 8 583 | 175 329 | 17 182.6 | 4 753.4 |
| Niagara | 338 | D | D | D | 270 | 10 209 | 3 433.1 | 526.8 | 490 | 8 908 | 662.4 | 150.8 |
| Oneida | 390 | D | D | D | 261 | 10 874 | 3 251.8 | 437.3 | 506 | 5 862 | 260.5 | 74.7 |
| Onondaga | 1 214 | D | D | D | 482 | 23 308 | 7 251.5 | 1 213.7 | 1 112 | 17 535 | 784.3 | 229.2 |
| Ontario | 245 | D | D | D | 156 | 6 949 | 2 097.3 | 295.7 | 281 | 4 645 | 206.3 | 62.0 |
| Orange | 901 | D | D | D | 337 | 7 510 | 2 353.5 | 321.0 | 792 | 8 755 | 454.7 | 123.2 |
| Orleans | 37 | D | D | D | 36 | 1 853 | 465.2 | 67.5 | 64 | 652 | 21.3 | 5.9 |
| Oswego | 127 | D | D | D | 90 | 3 535 | 2 441.3 | 152.4 | 258 | 3 262 | 128.1 | 34.9 |
| Otsego | 105 | D | D | D | 58 | 919 | 177.8 | 34.9 | 193 | 2 170 | 121.7 | 31.0 |
| Putnam | 339 | D | D | D | 92 | 2 030 | D | 103.5 | 209 | 1 704 | 94.4 | 24.5 |
| Queens | 2 858 | D | D | D | 1 433 | 29 325 | 5 654.4 | 1 159.3 | 3 619 | 32 175 | 2 223.4 | 577.7 |
| Rensselaer | 305 | D | D | D | 111 | 3 040 | D | 133.8 | 309 | 3 929 | 171.8 | 47.8 |
| Richmond | 895 | D | D | D | 137 | 1 325 | D | 53.5 | 658 | 7 506 | 401.6 | 101.9 |
| Rockland | 1 225 | D | D | D | 266 | 10 344 | 13 670.4 | 540.7 | 689 | 7 222 | 435.3 | 121.2 |
| St. Lawrence | 122 | D | D | D | 82 | 3 601 | 2 141.6 | 180.7 | 247 | 3 033 | 116.6 | 31.5 |
| Saratoga | 589 | D | D | D | 132 | 5 287 | 1 783.6 | 274.6 | 487 | 6 869 | 333.5 | 99.7 |
| Schenectady | 288 | D | D | D | 120 | 4 317 | 1 702.5 | 207.6 | 293 | 3 421 | 151.8 | 44.1 |
| Schoharie | 36 | D | D | D | NA | NA | NA | NA | 64 | 450 | 21.6 | 5.2 |
| Schuyler | 15 | D | D | D | 29 | D | D | D | 61 | 387 | 25.5 | 6.8 |
| Seneca | 32 | D | D | D | 39 | 1 197 | 428.1 | 58.2 | 70 | 685 | 33.0 | 8.7 |
| Steuben | 151 | D | D | D | 82 | 6 168 | 1 821.2 | 305.7 | 221 | 2 295 | 103.4 | 27.7 |
| Suffolk | 5 588 | D | D | D | 2 356 | 64 453 | 19 089.7 | 3 021.9 | 3 274 | 39 934 | 2 376.4 | 651.5 |
| Sullivan | 171 | D | D | D | 52 | 1 129 | 243.8 | 33.5 | 243 | 2 027 | 120.7 | 33.2 |
| Tioga | 59 | D | D | D | 38 | 1 700 | 535.8 | D | 79 | 868 | 32.7 | 10.2 |
| Tompkins | 273 | D | D | D | 92 | 3 152 | 742.8 | 137.3 | 308 | 3 742 | 177.7 | 51.9 |
| Ulster | 455 | D | D | D | 202 | D | D | 165.3 | 533 | 6 542 | 321.4 | 103.9 |
| Warren | 180 | 944 | 94.7 | 37.4 | 74 | 4 240 | 1 130.5 | 170.1 | 418 | 4 956 | 300.0 | 91.2 |
| Washington | 70 | 252 | 19.0 | 6.4 | 102 | 3 023 | 832.2 | 132.7 | 111 | 623 | 25.0 | 6.6 |
| Wayne | 105 | D | D | D | 134 | 6 009 | 1 889.0 | 242.2 | 148 | 1 406 | 52.3 | 14.8 |
| Westchester | 4 401 | 27 021 | 4 865.8 | 2 046.8 | 697 | 14 835 | 4 122.9 | 669.0 | 2 176 | 25 314 | 1 799.3 | 483.6 |
| Wyoming | 51 | D | D | D | 54 | 2 185 | 457.0 | 77.6 | 78 | 692 | 31.1 | 8.5 |
| Yates | 33 | D | D | D | 32 | 844 | D | 30.6 | 55 | 446 | 24.4 | 6.5 |
| NORTH CAROLINA | 22 385 | 182 224 | 26 003.8 | 10 698.3 | 10 150 | 506 013 | 205 867.3 | 19 589.8 | 18 268 | 343 235 | 16 126.9 | 4 395.1 |
| Alamance | 233 | D | D | D | 236 | 11 733 | 3 163.1 | 445.0 | 281 | 5 080 | 219.4 | 62.8 |
| Alexander | 37 | D | D | D | 80 | 3 931 | 604.8 | 120.1 | 44 | 697 | 22.6 | 6.4 |
| Alleghany | 13 | 56 | 4.6 | 1.2 | 17 | 628 | 109.2 | 18.2 | 21 | 186 | 11.3 | 3.2 |
| Anson | 31 | D | D | D | 25 | 1 449 | D | 49.1 | 27 | D | D | D |
| Ashe | 25 | 105 | 4.7 | 2.6 | 22 | 1 122 | 206.3 | 35.3 | 45 | 634 | 22.6 | 6.5 |
| Avery | 39 | 117 | 11.1 | 3.1 | NA | NA | NA | NA | 49 | 604 | 33.6 | 11.9 |
| Beaufort | 91 | 330 | 25.8 | 9.6 | 56 | 3 317 | 1 215.6 | 147.4 | 80 | 1 450 | 49.9 | 13.1 |
| Bertie | 12 | 57 | 4.7 | 1.4 | 17 | 2 099 | D | 52.2 | 14 | 152 | 5.6 | 1.4 |
| Bladen | 31 | 154 | 18.6 | 4.3 | 31 | 5 738 | 1 530.9 | 164.7 | 41 | 448 | 23.3 | 5.3 |
| Brunswick | 212 | D | D | D | 75 | 2 008 | D | 80.1 | 238 | 3 285 | 150.6 | 42.5 |
| Buncombe | 826 | D | D | D | 310 | 11 987 | 3 211.7 | 470.5 | 658 | 13 930 | 684.3 | 203.1 |
| Burke | 125 | D | D | D | 158 | 9 740 | 2 271.2 | 307.2 | 126 | 2 637 | 107.7 | 28.0 |
| Cabarrus | 347 | D | D | D | 188 | 8 103 | D | 394.6 | 324 | 6 659 | 321.5 | 90.2 |
| Caldwell | 93 | 413 | 39.9 | 14.0 | 142 | 9 418 | 1 558.4 | 255.5 | 117 | 1 623 | 63.7 | 16.4 |
| Camden | 5 | D | D | D | NA | NA | NA | NA | 4 | 30 | 1.4 | 0.4 |
| Carteret | 164 | 666 | 65.1 | 24.7 | 76 | 1 488 | 292.2 | 43.4 | 226 | 3 424 | 151.0 | 45.1 |
| Caswell | 20 | 43 | 4.3 | 1.4 | NA | NA | NA | NA | 17 | 149 | 5.4 | 1.4 |
| Catawba | 329 | 1 780 | 202.9 | 70.0 | 465 | 27 597 | 6 291.1 | 935.4 | 358 | 6 654 | 272.1 | 76.2 |
| Chatham | 135 | D | D | D | 82 | 4 982 | 1 129.7 | 167.6 | 74 | 1 036 | 39.6 | 12.7 |
| Cherokee | 61 | 230 | 14.5 | 5.5 | 28 | 1 258 | 265.4 | 42.1 | 63 | 898 | 36.8 | 9.7 |

1. Establishment subject to federal tax.

| STATE County | Health care and social assistance, 2007 | | | | Other services, 2007 | | | | Federal funds and grants, 2009–2010 Expenditures (mil dol) | | | |
|---|---|---|---|---|---|---|---|---|---|---|---|---|
| | | | | | | | | | | Direct payments for individuals[1] | | |
| | Number of establishments | Number of employees | Receipts (mil dol) | Annual payroll (mil dol) | Number of establishments | Number of employees | Receipts (mil dol) | Annual payroll (mil dol) | Total | Social Security and government retirement | Medicare | Food Stamps and Supplemental Security Income |
| | 159 | 160 | 161 | 162 | 163 | 164 | 165 | 166 | 167 | 168 | 169 | 170 |
| NEW YORK—Cont'd | | | | | | | | | | | | |
| Genesee | 138 | 2 647 | 175.3 | 76.3 | 114 | 697 | 46.0 | 12.6 | 494.5 | 209.5 | 98.9 | 13.1 |
| Greene | 88 | 1 144 | 83.7 | 35.5 | 84 | 378 | 29.5 | 8.3 | 356.3 | 171.7 | 80.2 | 14.8 |
| Hamilton | 7 | D | D | D | 11 | 28 | 2.6 | 0.5 | 44.5 | 22.3 | 11.3 | 0.9 |
| Herkimer | 114 | 2 288 | 136.2 | 57.2 | 101 | 517 | 31.0 | 8.9 | 473.5 | 199.7 | 119.1 | 20.0 |
| Jefferson | 234 | 5 780 | 429.1 | 201.9 | 195 | 898 | 78.3 | 18.3 | 3 939.9 | 353.0 | 132.6 | 37.4 |
| Kings | 5 583 | 161 022 | 14 296.4 | 6 402.9 | 3 728 | 15 019 | 1 389.0 | 367.8 | [2] | [2] | [2] | [2] |
| Lewis | 55 | 855 | 63.8 | 25.6 | 44 | 158 | 15.2 | 3.2 | 234.2 | 80.0 | 33.1 | 8.6 |
| Livingston | 132 | 1 722 | 134.3 | 54.6 | 95 | 341 | 33.1 | 7.9 | 391.1 | 189.2 | 85.2 | 17.8 |
| Madison | 166 | 3 088 | 238.0 | 98.8 | 110 | 377 | 33.0 | 7.8 | 441.0 | 214.5 | 84.5 | 15.7 |
| Monroe | 1 842 | 57 096 | 4 771.0 | 2 015.8 | 1 188 | 7 877 | 802.1 | 210.9 | 8 153.1 | 2 203.1 | 1 242.2 | 302.7 |
| Montgomery | 177 | 3 928 | 341.6 | 131.3 | 93 | 471 | 34.8 | 9.3 | 431.0 | 182.9 | 120.0 | 19.0 |
| Nassau | 5 468 | 93 663 | 10 928.4 | 4 452.3 | 3 837 | 19 915 | 1 990.6 | 549.8 | 11 807.8 | 4 184.1 | 3 074.2 | 168.7 |
| New York | 7 612 | 221 081 | 26 406.6 | 10 594.3 | 8 951 | 77 817 | 22 175.4 | 3 558.5 | [2]84 734.2 | [2]15 179.6 | [2]18 481.9 | [2]5 935.4 |
| Niagara | 525 | 10 180 | 700.6 | 294.5 | 347 | 1 603 | 108.7 | 30.2 | 1 844.5 | 814.0 | 405.1 | 75.4 |
| Oneida | 613 | 19 752 | 1 470.7 | 696.7 | 412 | 3 017 | 192.8 | 57.4 | 2 369.5 | 847.3 | 440.4 | 104.5 |
| Onondaga | 1 276 | 34 330 | 3 449.0 | 1 451.7 | 875 | 6 075 | 549.0 | 157.6 | 4 842.0 | 1 424.2 | 706.8 | 180.3 |
| Ontario | 233 | 6 834 | 523.6 | 257.8 | 213 | 1 115 | 83.8 | 23.1 | 851.6 | 372.2 | 145.8 | 22.6 |
| Orange | 993 | 19 291 | 1 706.1 | 771.0 | 740 | 3 887 | 436.7 | 98.5 | 3 184.7 | 978.8 | 488.2 | 93.8 |
| Orleans | 92 | 1 541 | 92.8 | 40.8 | 63 | 198 | 14.5 | 3.3 | 287.9 | 131.1 | 61.4 | 12.7 |
| Oswego | 216 | 4 739 | 316.5 | 138.8 | 173 | 706 | 47.1 | 12.4 | 950.8 | 382.5 | 157.6 | 43.3 |
| Otsego | 166 | 5 311 | 528.4 | 232.3 | 109 | 599 | 83.4 | 10.4 | 477.8 | 204.0 | 100.2 | 15.7 |
| Putnam | 269 | 4 944 | 483.4 | 199.1 | 244 | 1 081 | 126.3 | 35.3 | 490.4 | 264.3 | 126.8 | 6.9 |
| Queens | 4 492 | 113 126 | 10 607.0 | 4 480.8 | 4 042 | 18 673 | 1 754.2 | 509.4 | [2] | [2] | [2] | [2] |
| Rensselaer | 364 | 8 983 | 702.4 | 317.7 | 241 | 1 427 | 143.4 | 43.5 | 2 796.0 | 485.2 | 249.3 | 50.7 |
| Richmond | 1 155 | 27 313 | 2 449.3 | 1 101.3 | 763 | 3 659 | 309.0 | 82.8 | [2] | [2] | [2] | [2] |
| Rockland | 1 129 | 21 162 | 1 829.5 | 815.0 | 688 | 3 019 | 297.1 | 81.4 | 2 132.0 | 823.8 | 515.7 | 56.9 |
| St. Lawrence | 294 | 6 372 | 455.2 | 200.8 | 147 | 707 | 55.3 | 14.2 | 1 001.0 | 362.4 | 164.2 | 50.1 |
| Saratoga | 500 | 7 674 | 608.5 | 245.7 | 285 | 1 860 | 145.7 | 45.8 | 1 170.4 | 652.3 | 217.7 | 30.5 |
| Schenectady | 451 | 10 861 | 867.2 | 407.5 | 207 | 1 481 | 128.2 | 33.4 | 1 684.8 | 533.0 | 282.0 | 55.1 |
| Schoharie | 62 | 1 202 | 72.4 | 30.4 | 37 | 182 | 15.4 | 4.0 | 229.6 | 102.6 | 47.9 | 8.8 |
| Schuyler | 40 | 828 | 61.1 | 23.0 | 28 | 134 | 12.6 | 2.7 | 135.7 | 62.2 | 24.8 | 6.0 |
| Seneca | 66 | 1 457 | 83.2 | 37.8 | 44 | 193 | 14.3 | 3.8 | 231.8 | 110.1 | 49.4 | 7.3 |
| Steuben | 250 | 5 902 | 447.9 | 194.8 | 152 | 723 | 55.8 | 12.6 | 842.1 | 357.7 | 158.8 | 37.9 |
| Suffolk | 4 546 | 85 581 | 8 923.6 | 3 788.5 | 3 767 | 17 775 | 1 746.8 | 492.8 | 12 110.2 | 4 475.1 | 2 501.9 | 230.0 |
| Sullivan | 257 | 4 674 | 361.5 | 155.5 | 163 | 497 | 165.2 | 14.6 | 728.1 | 243.1 | 166.7 | 25.7 |
| Tioga | 74 | 855 | 49.9 | 20.4 | 67 | 221 | 19.0 | 5.2 | 1 020.2 | 152.3 | 57.5 | 16.5 |
| Tompkins | 250 | 4 919 | 388.7 | 152.9 | 149 | 945 | 129.2 | 21.6 | 939.3 | 220.0 | 84.8 | 21.6 |
| Ulster | 520 | D | D | D | 316 | 1 559 | 117.0 | 30.2 | 1 284.7 | 551.4 | 269.0 | 46.9 |
| Warren | 259 | 6 492 | 526.3 | 243.7 | 145 | 743 | 71.0 | 20.9 | 510.6 | 251.7 | 97.0 | 15.2 |
| Washington | 106 | 1 424 | 84.5 | 39.5 | 75 | 286 | 26.8 | 6.9 | 416.9 | 200.8 | 86.3 | 18.5 |
| Wayne | 155 | 2 322 | 153.3 | 68.8 | 134 | 406 | 33.6 | 8.0 | 719.3 | 308.7 | 138.1 | 24.2 |
| Westchester | 3 543 | 70 365 | 7 454.7 | 3 252.3 | 2 733 | 13 610 | 2 092.1 | 482.3 | 7 147.3 | 2 609.5 | 2 007.8 | 207.9 |
| Wyoming | 66 | 1 294 | 84.9 | 37.6 | 60 | 242 | 19.8 | 5.4 | 286.9 | 121.6 | 56.5 | 8.8 |
| Yates | 55 | D | D | D | 38 | 130 | 11.8 | 2.3 | 181.3 | 88.4 | 37.3 | 7.4 |
| NORTH CAROLINA | 21 712 | 523 397 | 46 688.8 | 19 047.4 | 14 105 | 85 304 | 9 362.1 | 2 216.6 | 90 736.7 | 28 314.0 | 10 370.8 | 3 369.2 |
| Alamance | 335 | 6 483 | 549.1 | 227.9 | 201 | 1 165 | 93.5 | 27.7 | 925.3 | 465.3 | 191.6 | 35.2 |
| Alexander | 45 | 637 | 35.9 | 15.0 | 46 | 200 | 12.3 | 2.5 | 195.1 | 105.1 | 39.4 | 7.2 |
| Alleghany | 29 | 504 | 27.7 | 11.6 | 13 | 26 | 2.7 | 0.6 | 105.0 | 45.0 | 20.6 | 3.4 |
| Anson | 43 | 668 | 36.8 | 15.1 | 24 | 76 | 7.1 | 1.4 | 237.8 | 77.5 | 49.3 | 19.5 |
| Ashe | 53 | 1 151 | 64.3 | 30.9 | 34 | 118 | 10.4 | 2.6 | 256.8 | 96.1 | 41.1 | 10.8 |
| Avery | 42 | 1 137 | 75.6 | 27.1 | 34 | 241 | 15.7 | 5.3 | 153.8 | 64.1 | 33.8 | 7.8 |
| Beaufort | 140 | 2 810 | 170.8 | 79.7 | 90 | 363 | 28.7 | 8.3 | 498.6 | 201.9 | 69.3 | 29.2 |
| Bertie | 68 | 1 684 | 69.8 | 33.2 | 26 | 94 | 8.1 | 1.9 | 242.3 | 71.2 | 40.0 | 19.5 |
| Bladen | 73 | 1 375 | 79.3 | 33.1 | 29 | 136 | 8.7 | 3.3 | 330.6 | 109.7 | 52.3 | 26.2 |
| Brunswick | 189 | 2 834 | 213.6 | 88.0 | 103 | 542 | 41.7 | 10.5 | 913.2 | 531.7 | 112.3 | 35.0 |
| Buncombe | 757 | 20 467 | 2 071.2 | 821.5 | 437 | 2 703 | 222.9 | 64.3 | 1 966.7 | 841.3 | 327.5 | 91.5 |
| Burke | 205 | 4 028 | 380.6 | 148.4 | 97 | 357 | 32.3 | 8.0 | 579.1 | 278.2 | 117.3 | 25.7 |
| Cabarrus | 333 | 9 224 | 692.5 | 325.0 | 246 | 1 272 | 120.1 | 30.7 | 905.2 | 477.0 | 202.2 | 40.0 |
| Caldwell | 128 | 3 262 | 228.5 | 88.4 | 85 | 439 | 35.1 | 10.2 | 517.3 | 260.6 | 106.5 | 25.8 |
| Camden | 6 | D | D | D | 9 | 76 | 5.4 | 2.1 | 72.4 | 42.7 | 10.4 | 2.7 |
| Carteret | 176 | 3 206 | 234.8 | 97.8 | 143 | 657 | 52.6 | 14.3 | 592.4 | 321.3 | 85.5 | 21.6 |
| Caswell | 29 | 463 | 18.1 | 9.9 | 17 | 62 | 4.0 | 1.0 | 188.8 | 72.8 | 29.6 | 12.3 |
| Catawba | 383 | 9 682 | 953.0 | 378.2 | 255 | 1 587 | 177.8 | 46.5 | 932.7 | 504.8 | 163.8 | 41.6 |
| Chatham | 117 | 3 903 | 236.4 | 89.8 | 85 | 377 | 29.3 | 10.2 | 320.3 | 166.7 | 64.4 | 11.5 |
| Cherokee | 84 | 1 489 | 109.2 | 44.9 | 37 | 128 | 8.7 | 2.4 | 258.1 | 125.2 | 42.5 | 11.8 |

1. State totals may include programs not allocated by county.    2. Bronx, Kings, Queens, and Richmond counties are included with New York county.

# Table B. States and Counties — Federal Funds, Residential Construction, and Local Government Finances

| | Federal funds and grants, 2009–2010 (cont.) | | | | | | | Value of residential construction authorized by building permits, 2011 | | Local government finances, 2007 | | | | |
|---|---|---|---|---|---|---|---|---|---|---|---|---|---|---|
| | Expenditures (mil dol) (cont.) | | | | | | | | | General revenue | | | | |
| | Procurement contract awards | | | Grants[1] | | | | | | | | Taxes | | |
| STATE County | | | | | | | | | | | | | Per capita[2] (dollars) | |
| | Salaries and wages | Defense | Other | Medicaid and other health-related | Nutrition and family welfare | Education | Other | New construction ($1,000) | Number of housing units | Total (mil dol) | Inter-govern-mental (mil dol) | Total (mil dol) | Total | Property |
| | 171 | 172 | 173 | 174 | 175 | 176 | 177 | 178 | 179 | 180 | 181 | 182 | 183 | 184 |
| NEW YORK—Cont'd | | | | | | | | | | | | | | |
| Genesee | 32.8 | 1.7 | 36.4 | 58.7 | 14.0 | 5.9 | 5.4 | 3 593 | 19 | 363.9 | 149.6 | 118.5 | 2 039 | 1 336 |
| Greene | 11.7 | 0.1 | 2.8 | 50.0 | 13.1 | 3.9 | 4.3 | 13 414 | 78 | 271.3 | 103.3 | 133.8 | 2 717 | 2 064 |
| Hamilton | 1.8 | 0.0 | 0.4 | 2.9 | 1.3 | 1.4 | 1.8 | 4 702 | 27 | 50.3 | 8.9 | 36.8 | 7 247 | 6 576 |
| Herkimer | 9.7 | 4.7 | 2.8 | 81.5 | 16.9 | 5.8 | 2.0 | 15 083 | 81 | 326.4 | 163.9 | 114.8 | 1 836 | 1 408 |
| Jefferson | 2 943.0 | 230.5 | 12.3 | 140.2 | 33.4 | 25.9 | 9.2 | 31 435 | 293 | 544.9 | 266.1 | 179.5 | 1 532 | 964 |
| Kings | (3) | (3) | (3) | (3) | (3) | (3) | (3) | 144 662 | 1 522 | (3) | (3) | (3) | (3) | (3) |
| Lewis | 6.2 | 50.5 | 1.4 | 40.5 | 8.3 | 1.5 | 0.2 | 8 521 | 84 | 183.5 | 72.8 | 46.4 | 1 754 | 1 346 |
| Livingston | 13.9 | 1.1 | 3.8 | 52.4 | 15.3 | 4.8 | 1.2 | 11 244 | 121 | 316.0 | 138.3 | 118.8 | 1 880 | 1 421 |
| Madison | 12.7 | 0.2 | 3.3 | 69.7 | 18.1 | 5.5 | 8.8 | 10 638 | 65 | 327.5 | 148.0 | 128.8 | 1 845 | 1 521 |
| Monroe | 356.6 | 1 843.6 | 154.8 | 1 221.5 | 188.8 | 136.7 | 282.4 | 173 483 | 982 | 3 806.5 | 1 598.4 | 1 653.3 | 2 266 | 1 679 |
| Montgomery | 9.6 | 5.7 | 3.4 | 64.2 | 14.0 | 3.2 | 4.4 | 12 909 | 123 | 266.7 | 122.6 | 92.5 | 1 900 | 1 334 |
| Nassau | 626.4 | 1 713.7 | 170.4 | 1 205.6 | 243.0 | 64.2 | 112.2 | 207 482 | 853 | 9 563.1 | 2 092.4 | 6 273.3 | 4 802 | 3 885 |
| New York | (3)4 625.6 | (3)611.4 | (3)2 225.2 | (3)25 615.8 | (3)2 238.1 | (3)908.3 | (3)5 772.1 | 225 814 | 2 535 | (3)79 683.6 | (3)27 746.0 | (3)38 163.8 | (3)4 612 | (3)1 595 |
| Niagara | 101.6 | 54.3 | 13.9 | 253.9 | 57.2 | 16.1 | 16.3 | 34 006 | 229 | 1 116.5 | 490.8 | 424.7 | 1 977 | 1 433 |
| Oneida | 226.9 | 157.4 | 21.1 | 408.8 | 64.3 | 21.7 | 38.5 | 27 928 | 173 | 1 130.5 | 557.2 | 409.5 | 1 763 | 1 096 |
| Onondaga | 355.8 | 1 051.3 | 204.8 | 545.7 | 116.8 | 45.5 | 126.7 | 115 631 | 940 | 2 450.7 | 1 091.0 | 970.5 | 2 138 | 1 475 |
| Ontario | 63.8 | 65.7 | 40.6 | 82.7 | 22.8 | 7.4 | 7.4 | 52 743 | 305 | 541.4 | 207.5 | 243.1 | 2 339 | 1 682 |
| Orange | 869.6 | 196.3 | 43.5 | 340.6 | 80.8 | 24.6 | 32.6 | 118 582 | 893 | 2 111.5 | 755.0 | 1 059.5 | 2 809 | 2 125 |
| Orleans | 8.0 | 0.5 | 10.7 | 38.4 | 13.3 | 3.7 | 1.2 | 3 739 | 30 | 197.4 | 103.7 | 66.9 | 1 578 | 1 241 |
| Oswego | 28.4 | 139.5 | 6.3 | 135.5 | 34.9 | 9.5 | 7.5 | 24 542 | 215 | 618.7 | 297.9 | 216.9 | 1 786 | 1 328 |
| Otsego | 13.4 | 2.2 | 17.3 | 94.4 | 18.3 | 3.2 | 3.6 | 6 336 | 37 | 289.3 | 126.9 | 115.0 | 1 843 | 1 240 |
| Putnam | 14.8 | 2.2 | 3.8 | 37.7 | 17.0 | 7.5 | 6.9 | 29 275 | 151 | 558.6 | 147.0 | 356.6 | 3 585 | 3 027 |
| Queens | (3) | (3) | (3) | (3) | (3) | (3) | (3) | 312 483 | 3 182 | (3) | (3) | (3) | (3) | (3) |
| Rensselaer | 65.2 | 7.0 | 12.0 | 584.4 | 1 070.4 | 11.8 | 212.9 | 28 074 | 155 | 831.2 | 336.9 | 320.2 | 2 062 | 1 562 |
| Richmond | (3) | (3) | (3) | (3) | (3) | (3) | (3) | 80 749 | 581 | (3) | (3) | (3) | (3) | (3) |
| Rockland | 76.1 | 70.9 | 28.1 | 349.5 | 70.8 | 20.8 | 49.4 | 39 855 | 289 | 1 909.0 | 467.2 | 1 165.1 | 3 930 | 3 196 |
| St. Lawrence | 51.2 | 32.1 | 32.8 | 205.0 | 33.7 | 9.8 | 43.3 | 16 865 | 160 | 562.7 | 263.3 | 174.0 | 1 584 | 1 193 |
| Saratoga | 44.0 | 29.9 | 11.9 | 106.3 | 44.0 | 7.5 | 15.6 | 189 816 | 1 098 | 906.0 | 308.3 | 471.9 | 2 186 | 1 615 |
| Schenectady | 113.9 | 301.9 | 34.0 | 185.5 | 37.3 | 13.0 | 108.5 | 22 165 | 123 | 805.1 | 299.0 | 370.8 | 2 459 | 1 776 |
| Schoharie | 7.0 | 0.0 | 1.7 | 46.1 | 9.6 | 2.4 | 1.3 | 3 639 | 28 | 173.9 | 83.2 | 76.6 | 2 389 | 1 842 |
| Schuyler | 4.5 | 0.0 | 1.2 | 27.4 | 5.5 | 2.0 | 1.3 | 3 145 | 35 | 85.9 | 40.5 | 33.0 | 1 735 | 1 266 |
| Seneca | 7.6 | 4.1 | 2.6 | 38.6 | 7.2 | 1.6 | 1.5 | 10 606 | 69 | 161.6 | 69.9 | 65.9 | 1 925 | 1 312 |
| Steuben | 48.7 | 31.7 | 28.0 | 122.1 | 28.6 | 8.7 | 3.9 | 30 974 | 310 | 536.4 | 259.9 | 185.7 | 1 917 | 1 402 |
| Suffolk | 931.2 | 744.7 | 1 038.5 | 1 520.4 | 286.3 | 88.0 | 192.9 | 320 571 | 856 | 9 421.8 | 2 747.3 | 5 704.5 | 3 925 | 2 946 |
| Sullivan | 18.9 | 0.1 | 17.5 | 203.7 | 21.7 | 7.8 | 14.4 | 41 794 | 239 | 521.8 | 173.2 | 250.9 | 3 288 | 2 718 |
| Tioga | 13.1 | 725.4 | 2.1 | 33.4 | 14.1 | 3.0 | 1.1 | 7 535 | 72 | 233.9 | 119.7 | 85.8 | 1 700 | 1 210 |
| Tompkins | 39.8 | 18.9 | 15.5 | 210.4 | 23.7 | 11.1 | 260.2 | 23 137 | 153 | 478.3 | 175.8 | 213.9 | 2 117 | 1 557 |
| Ulster | 54.7 | 6.1 | 10.4 | 260.8 | 43.2 | 12.7 | 10.8 | 46 577 | 230 | 984.4 | 317.9 | 535.2 | 2 943 | 2 321 |
| Warren | 22.8 | 1.2 | 5.3 | 78.5 | 17.4 | 3.4 | 7.4 | 24 493 | 133 | 371.8 | 120.3 | 194.9 | 2 947 | 2 031 |
| Washington | 12.1 | 0.4 | 3.0 | 66.2 | 19.1 | 5.5 | 1.2 | 20 742 | 109 | 308.7 | 145.8 | 112.3 | 1 791 | 1 470 |
| Wayne | 18.1 | 28.5 | 43.3 | 114.3 | 24.1 | 7.8 | 4.5 | 13 255 | 85 | 465.3 | 215.0 | 173.6 | 1 902 | 1 566 |
| Westchester | 408.7 | 102.7 | 157.3 | 1 066.0 | 190.4 | 62.2 | 166.8 | 230 660 | 950 | 7 597.5 | 1 831.6 | 4 184.1 | 4 398 | 3 576 |
| Wyoming | 9.3 | 0.8 | 40.1 | 31.7 | 9.8 | 3.4 | 0.2 | 3 439 | 29 | 198.1 | 77.2 | 60.1 | 1 433 | 1 058 |
| Yates | 9.8 | 0.2 | 1.4 | 24.1 | 5.8 | 1.4 | 0.6 | 5 963 | 33 | 104.1 | 40.7 | 49.1 | 2 001 | 1 578 |
| NORTH CAROLINA | 15 349.4 | 3 626.5 | 2 464.0 | 11 594.5 | 2 009.1 | 1 865.6 | 4 629.7 | 5 053 273 | 32 804 | X | X | X | X | X |
| Alamance | 28.0 | 5.2 | 9.0 | 128.2 | 19.4 | 10.3 | 9.6 | 76 728 | 556 | 402.1 | 208.0 | 128.4 | 883 | 667 |
| Alexander | 5.5 | 0.0 | 1.1 | 23.9 | 5.7 | 2.7 | 2.2 | 10 951 | 49 | 70.3 | 40.9 | 20.0 | 550 | 337 |
| Alleghany | 3.4 | 0.0 | 1.2 | 27.3 | 1.8 | 0.9 | 0.5 | 4 360 | 34 | 30.5 | 17.2 | 10.4 | 952 | 714 |
| Anson | 12.1 | 0.1 | 2.2 | 58.4 | 6.2 | 3.4 | 1.5 | 3 044 | 21 | 86.2 | 55.3 | 18.3 | 726 | 556 |
| Ashe | 10.5 | 0.0 | 1.4 | 68.8 | 4.4 | 2.0 | 20.4 | 14 099 | 70 | 61.7 | 33.8 | 21.9 | 858 | 591 |
| Avery | 4.4 | 0.5 | 1.3 | 33.5 | 4.2 | 1.6 | 0.3 | 18 087 | 55 | 52.1 | 24.3 | 22.4 | 1 263 | 954 |
| Beaufort | 15.6 | 25.0 | 2.7 | 90.7 | 9.7 | 6.2 | 19.8 | 28 042 | 308 | 145.2 | 81.7 | 41.0 | 895 | 645 |
| Bertie | 6.1 | 0.0 | 2.2 | 84.0 | 7.2 | 2.3 | 0.1 | 3 142 | 29 | 60.4 | 41.0 | 12.3 | 660 | 478 |
| Bladen | 13.5 | 4.8 | 1.2 | 90.2 | 7.2 | 5.2 | 2.0 | 7 001 | 49 | 148.2 | 61.3 | 26.7 | 826 | 605 |
| Brunswick | 25.6 | 85.6 | 6.9 | 73.1 | 11.0 | 4.0 | 19.0 | 187 984 | 914 | 334.9 | 99.6 | 147.9 | 1 491 | 1 097 |
| Buncombe | 214.1 | 27.9 | 116.1 | 226.2 | 36.9 | 19.2 | 25.9 | 118 976 | 545 | 757.9 | 315.7 | 298.7 | 1 317 | 949 |
| Burke | 13.9 | 6.4 | 5.4 | 89.4 | 14.8 | 13.6 | 1.0 | 18 223 | 84 | 243.3 | 150.0 | 53.0 | 595 | 478 |
| Cabarrus | 41.6 | 1.9 | 8.7 | 88.3 | 18.9 | 9.5 | 9.2 | 89 051 | 710 | 531.3 | 215.0 | 193.4 | 1 185 | 923 |
| Caldwell | 16.4 | 0.0 | 4.0 | 66.2 | 13.4 | 6.8 | 3.9 | 13 944 | 118 | 213.9 | 126.5 | 55.0 | 692 | 498 |
| Camden | 3.7 | 0.0 | 0.4 | 7.9 | 1.3 | 0.4 | 0.1 | 3 967 | 15 | 28.4 | 18.3 | 8.3 | 877 | 628 |
| Carteret | 49.1 | 12.3 | 10.2 | 46.0 | 14.4 | 4.7 | 15.2 | 72 494 | 607 | 308.4 | 95.0 | 86.1 | 1 361 | 958 |
| Caswell | 3.4 | 0.0 | 0.8 | 54.3 | 4.1 | 1.7 | 1.2 | 4 823 | 29 | 51.7 | 31.8 | 13.7 | 590 | 392 |
| Catawba | 68.3 | 2.3 | 14.6 | 75.5 | 18.8 | 11.4 | 12.3 | 36 269 | 129 | 625.4 | 225.5 | 145.7 | 936 | 676 |
| Chatham | 13.9 | 1.1 | 1.7 | 42.1 | 7.1 | 2.7 | 5.3 | 71 374 | 329 | 148.0 | 57.6 | 65.0 | 1 057 | 784 |
| Cherokee | 6.1 | 0.6 | 4.7 | 51.1 | 7.1 | 2.1 | 2.4 | 15 239 | 87 | 80.3 | 43.3 | 25.2 | 951 | 639 |

1. State totals may include programs not allocated by county. 2. Based on the resident population estimated as of July 1 of the year shown. 3. Bronx, Kings, Queens, and Richmond counties are included with New York county.

# Table B. States and Counties — Local Government Finances, Government Employment, and Voting

| | Local government finances, 2007 (cont.) | | | | | | | | | Government employment, 2011 | | | Presidential election,[2] 2012 | | |
| | Direct general expenditure | | | | | | | Debt outstanding | | | | | Percent of vote cast: | | |
| STATE County | Total (mil dol) | Per capita[1] (dollars) | Percent of total for: | | | | | Total (mil dol) | Per capita[1] (dollars) | Federal civilian | Federal military | State and local | Demo-cratic | Republi-can | All other |
| | | | Educa-tion | Health and hospitals | Police protec-tion | Public welfare | High-ways | | | | | | | | |
| | 185 | 186 | 187 | 188 | 189 | 190 | 191 | 192 | 193 | 194 | 195 | 196 | 197 | 198 | 199 |
| **NEW YORK—Cont'd** | | | | | | | | | | | | | | | |
| Genesee | 364.2 | 6 266 | 49.9 | 4.2 | 2.6 | 10.9 | 5.1 | 188.7 | 3 246 | 604 | 99 | 5 136 | 40.1 | 58.5 | 1.5 |
| Greene | 265.5 | 5 392 | 48.1 | 4.6 | 1.6 | 9.3 | 9.3 | 180.5 | 3 665 | 108 | 80 | 4 280 | 44.1 | 54.0 | 1.8 |
| Hamilton | 50.9 | 10 026 | 37.3 | 5.3 | 1.4 | 3.1 | 13.8 | 17.7 | 3 496 | 19 | 0 | 706 | 35.9 | 62.8 | 1.3 |
| Herkimer | 318.3 | 5 089 | 54.6 | 3.1 | 1.7 | 9.8 | 9.5 | 212.3 | 3 393 | 106 | 105 | 4 275 | 44.5 | 53.8 | 1.7 |
| Jefferson | 553.1 | 4 719 | 50.1 | 3.3 | 2.3 | 9.3 | 8.0 | 410.6 | 3 503 | 3 660 | 19 611 | 8 274 | 46.8 | 52.0 | 1.2 |
| Kings | (3) | (3) | (3) | (3) | (3) | (3) | (3) | (3) | (3) | 6 724 | 4 332 | 28 019 | 79.4 | 20.0 | 0.6 |
| Lewis | 170.8 | 6 452 | 37.7 | 24.8 | 1.0 | 6.7 | 8.3 | 80.9 | 3 056 | 57 | 44 | 2 280 | 44.8 | 53.6 | 1.6 |
| Livingston | 307.4 | 4 864 | 44.3 | 5.3 | 2.4 | 18.2 | 7.6 | 285.5 | 4 517 | 146 | 106 | 6 584 | 45.3 | 53.2 | 1.5 |
| Madison | 310.4 | 4 446 | 52.4 | 4.0 | 2.1 | 7.6 | 8.4 | 335.1 | 4 799 | 137 | 120 | 4 304 | 49.3 | 48.5 | 2.2 |
| Monroe | 4 099.3 | 5 618 | 47.3 | 3.7 | 4.0 | 11.2 | 2.6 | 2 659.9 | 3 645 | 2 842 | 1 318 | 44 893 | 58.3 | 40.5 | 1.2 |
| Montgomery | 270.1 | 5 547 | 49.4 | 2.3 | 2.0 | 11.9 | 6.7 | 210.9 | 4 331 | 109 | 82 | 2 636 | 45.0 | 53.1 | 1.9 |
| Nassau | 9 819.3 | 7 516 | 46.5 | 7.1 | 8.4 | 5.4 | 3.2 | 7 779.0 | 5 954 | 5 490 | 2 577 | 77 259 | 53.8 | 45.4 | 0.7 |
| New York | (3)70 161.5 | (3)8 479 | (3)26.7 | (3)9.9 | (3)5.5 | (3)15.2 | (3)2.1 | (3)116 285.7 | (3)14 053 | 22 161 | 2 865 | 421 307 | 85.7 | 13.5 | 0.8 |
| Niagara | 1 117.2 | 5 200 | 50.3 | 2.6 | 3.5 | 9.8 | 3.1 | 984.1 | 4 580 | 1 123 | 381 | 13 411 | 49.7 | 48.7 | 1.6 |
| Oneida | 1 147.4 | 4 939 | 50.3 | 2.4 | 3.3 | 11.4 | 6.4 | 1 212.2 | 5 218 | 2 538 | 450 | 25 024 | 46.1 | 52.2 | 1.6 |
| Onondaga | 2 606.9 | 5 742 | 46.5 | 3.7 | 3.8 | 10.8 | 4.1 | 2 425.0 | 5 341 | 4 335 | 913 | 36 147 | 59.3 | 38.9 | 1.8 |
| Ontario | 554.5 | 5 334 | 56.8 | 3.0 | 2.8 | 7.8 | 6.7 | 484.6 | 4 662 | 1 236 | 179 | 6 982 | 49.2 | 49.3 | 1.5 |
| Orange | 2 169.5 | 5 752 | 54.6 | 3.2 | 3.7 | 9.9 | 3.3 | 1 367.0 | 3 624 | 5 277 | 6 720 | 21 787 | 51.6 | 47.4 | 1.0 |
| Orleans | 190.2 | 4 488 | 52.1 | 4.4 | 2.1 | 15.2 | 5.5 | 135.1 | 3 187 | 89 | 70 | 3 996 | 39.9 | 58.6 | 1.5 |
| Oswego | 600.3 | 4 943 | 57.7 | 2.9 | 2.0 | 9.7 | 5.9 | 464.2 | 3 822 | 260 | 230 | 8 675 | 50.3 | 47.9 | 1.8 |
| Otsego | 280.4 | 4 494 | 49.5 | 3.1 | 1.6 | 13.5 | 8.8 | 236.1 | 3 784 | 140 | 101 | 4 676 | 52.0 | 46.1 | 1.9 |
| Putnam | 568.4 | 5 713 | 58.6 | 2.5 | 3.7 | 3.8 | 5.1 | 391.6 | 3 936 | 151 | 163 | 4 390 | 45.8 | 53.3 | 1.0 |
| Queens | (3) | (3) | (3) | (3) | (3) | (3) | (3) | (3) | (3) | 14 386 | 3 715 | 21 930 | 75.1 | 24.3 | 0.6 |
| Rensselaer | 863.1 | 5 557 | 52.3 | 3.8 | 3.0 | 12.6 | 3.2 | 916.6 | 5 902 | 419 | 275 | 10 547 | 53.7 | 44.4 | 1.9 |
| Richmond | (3) | (3) | (3) | (3) | (3) | (3) | (3) | (3) | (3) | 1 117 | 1 279 | 5 377 | 47.6 | 51.7 | 0.7 |
| Rockland | 1 999.7 | 6 745 | 46.1 | 9.5 | 4.7 | 6.4 | 3.3 | 1 991.3 | 6 716 | 528 | 516 | 20 606 | 52.6 | 46.7 | 0.6 |
| St. Lawrence | 553.7 | 5 043 | 46.8 | 10.1 | 2.3 | 10.5 | 7.7 | 449.1 | 4 090 | 599 | 224 | 9 358 | 57.5 | 41.1 | 1.4 |
| Saratoga | 933.7 | 4 325 | 56.3 | 4.0 | 2.6 | 7.8 | 5.9 | 779.4 | 3 611 | 418 | 1 787 | 11 882 | 50.9 | 47.5 | 1.6 |
| Schenectady | 798.4 | 5 294 | 45.3 | 2.5 | 3.7 | 15.1 | 3.9 | 547.6 | 3 631 | 624 | 276 | 10 109 | 55.3 | 42.6 | 2.0 |
| Schoharie | 165.3 | 5 155 | 52.4 | 4.3 | 1.2 | 8.8 | 10.6 | 111.2 | 3 469 | 82 | 53 | 2 621 | 41.8 | 56.1 | 2.1 |
| Schuyler | 82.5 | 4 336 | 38.9 | 5.1 | 1.8 | 10.7 | 11.5 | 49.1 | 2 581 | 51 | 30 | 1 179 | 45.7 | 52.8 | 1.5 |
| Seneca | 170.3 | 4 976 | 49.5 | 4.0 | 2.6 | 9.3 | 5.3 | 259.1 | 7 571 | 92 | 58 | 3 060 | 50.4 | 47.8 | 1.8 |
| Steuben | 533.0 | 5 502 | 56.0 | 3.7 | 1.6 | 11.4 | 8.4 | 357.9 | 3 694 | 1 061 | 163 | 7 081 | 40.9 | 57.8 | 1.3 |
| Suffolk | 9 396.9 | 6 466 | 53.7 | 3.8 | 5.5 | 5.4 | 3.4 | 6 883.1 | 4 736 | 11 927 | 2 708 | 93 436 | 52.6 | 46.6 | 0.9 |
| Sullivan | 507.4 | 6 649 | 47.4 | 4.6 | 2.7 | 12.4 | 7.8 | 371.8 | 4 873 | 209 | 126 | 5 761 | 54.1 | 44.6 | 1.3 |
| Tioga | 216.4 | 4 290 | 53.9 | 4.1 | 2.0 | 9.1 | 6.3 | 125.5 | 2 488 | 160 | 89 | 2 505 | 44.1 | 54.3 | 1.7 |
| Tompkins | 492.8 | 4 876 | 48.5 | 4.3 | 2.7 | 7.5 | 7.6 | 461.8 | 4 570 | 300 | 186 | 6 295 | 70.2 | 28.1 | 1.7 |
| Ulster | 971.0 | 5 340 | 51.6 | 2.6 | 3.4 | 12.6 | 4.9 | 738.4 | 4 060 | 420 | 318 | 13 491 | 61.0 | 37.4 | 1.7 |
| Warren | 374.5 | 5 662 | 44.0 | 3.9 | 2.6 | 9.9 | 6.4 | 328.4 | 4 965 | 181 | 110 | 4 621 | 50.6 | 47.9 | 1.5 |
| Washington | 313.9 | 5 003 | 57.4 | 3.4 | 1.6 | 11.0 | 8.0 | 175.2 | 2 793 | 136 | 103 | 5 147 | 49.5 | 48.7 | 1.7 |
| Wayne | 454.6 | 4 980 | 57.5 | 4.2 | 2.0 | 10.6 | 5.3 | 264.8 | 2 900 | 188 | 156 | 7 964 | 44.3 | 54.2 | 1.4 |
| Westchester | 7 721.6 | 8 117 | 42.3 | 12.0 | 4.6 | 6.3 | 2.7 | 5 783.0 | 6 079 | 4 505 | 1 564 | 58 260 | 63.4 | 35.8 | 0.8 |
| Wyoming | 194.8 | 4 646 | 36.8 | 25.1 | 2.7 | 7.3 | 8.6 | 106.7 | 2 544 | 106 | 69 | 4 260 | 36.1 | 62.3 | 1.6 |
| Yates | 101.6 | 4 135 | 43.0 | 6.1 | 3.8 | 8.4 | 10.7 | 88.6 | 3 608 | 69 | 42 | 1 214 | 47.6 | 51.3 | 1.0 |
| **NORTH CAROLINA** | X | X | X | X | X | X | X | X | X | 69 699 | 144 936 | 646 446 | 49.7 | 49.4 | 0.9 |
| Alamance | 417.6 | 2 873 | 49.4 | 8.4 | 5.8 | 6.2 | 2.8 | 191.4 | 1 317 | 231 | 397 | 6 801 | 44.9 | 54.2 | 0.9 |
| Alexander | 69.5 | 1 909 | 60.4 | 6.1 | 3.1 | 10.0 | 0.6 | 16.8 | 461 | 48 | 96 | 1 941 | 29.9 | 68.3 | 1.7 |
| Alleghany | 29.8 | 2 729 | 54.7 | 4.1 | 4.0 | 9.2 | 0.2 | 7.3 | 665 | 47 | 29 | 651 | 38.4 | 59.4 | 2.2 |
| Anson | 87.3 | 3 464 | 64.5 | 2.9 | 3.9 | 7.8 | 1.0 | 9.5 | 376 | 53 | 69 | 2 530 | 60.2 | 39.2 | 0.7 |
| Ashe | 57.3 | 2 245 | 52.7 | 2.4 | 3.7 | 12.4 | 0.8 | 16.4 | 643 | 64 | 70 | 1 218 | 37.3 | 60.6 | 2.2 |
| Avery | 48.1 | 2 707 | 46.5 | 4.6 | 4.6 | 7.8 | 3.0 | 23.6 | 1 325 | 49 | 46 | 1 550 | 27.4 | 71.5 | 1.1 |
| Beaufort | 154.8 | 3 382 | 55.9 | 2.6 | 4.2 | 8.8 | 0.9 | 84.3 | 1 841 | 128 | 124 | 2 815 | 41.1 | 58.5 | 0.4 |
| Bertie | 59.2 | 3 180 | 64.4 | 0.9 | 3.9 | 12.0 | 1.1 | 25.4 | 1 363 | 94 | 54 | 1 244 | 65.2 | 34.6 | 0.2 |
| Bladen | 149.6 | 4 631 | 39.2 | 19.9 | 2.9 | 6.4 | 0.7 | 26.2 | 810 | 109 | 90 | 2 457 | 50.7 | 48.7 | 0.6 |
| Brunswick | 345.4 | 3 482 | 32.5 | 11.1 | 5.7 | 5.2 | 1.6 | 231.5 | 2 333 | 417 | 342 | 4 768 | 40.5 | 58.5 | 1.0 |
| Buncombe | 784.7 | 3 460 | 40.5 | 7.5 | 4.3 | 5.9 | 1.5 | 412.7 | 1 820 | 3 413 | 666 | 13 405 | 56.3 | 42.4 | 1.3 |
| Burke | 242.3 | 2 723 | 54.2 | 10.3 | 4.8 | 8.1 | 0.8 | 121.5 | 1 366 | 133 | 235 | 7 334 | 39.8 | 59.0 | 1.2 |
| Cabarrus | 557.8 | 3 416 | 48.5 | 4.9 | 5.4 | 5.7 | 2.6 | 658.2 | 4 031 | 269 | 471 | 13 162 | 40.4 | 58.9 | 0.7 |
| Caldwell | 219.8 | 2 767 | 58.6 | 4.1 | 4.7 | 9.1 | 1.7 | 103.6 | 1 304 | 124 | 213 | 4 354 | 34.4 | 64.1 | 1.6 |
| Camden | 24.2 | 2 554 | 63.0 | 0.3 | 4.5 | 5.7 | 0.0 | 10.8 | 1 143 | 18 | 26 | 453 | 33.1 | 65.1 | 1.7 |
| Carteret | 308.0 | 4 870 | 31.2 | 34.5 | 3.9 | 3.7 | 1.8 | 158.8 | 2 510 | 308 | 378 | 4 618 | 32.2 | 66.9 | 1.0 |
| Caswell | 49.7 | 2 138 | 55.8 | 6.1 | 3.7 | 10.3 | 0.0 | 10.2 | 440 | 44 | 61 | 1 339 | 51.0 | 47.9 | 1.0 |
| Catawba | 617.0 | 3 964 | 38.1 | 30.9 | 3.5 | 6.9 | 1.4 | 248.1 | 1 594 | 513 | 401 | 9 520 | 36.9 | 61.9 | 1.2 |
| Chatham | 144.9 | 2 358 | 55.9 | 3.9 | 4.9 | 8.1 | 0.8 | 112.3 | 1 828 | 128 | 166 | 2 392 | 54.3 | 44.6 | 1.1 |
| Cherokee | 81.1 | 3 061 | 51.9 | 5.7 | 4.1 | 6.2 | 0.5 | 26.2 | 989 | 102 | 70 | 1 515 | 30.1 | 68.7 | 1.3 |

1. Based on the resident population estimated as of July 1 of the year shown.　2. © 2013 Election Data Services, Inc. All rights reserved.　3. Bronx, Kings, Queens, and Richmond counties are included with New York county.

# Table B. States and Counties — **Land Area and Population**

| STATE/ County code | CBSA code[1] | County type[2] | STATE County | Land area,[3] (sq km) 2010 | Total persons | Rank | Per square kilometer | White | Black | American Indian, Alaska Native | Asian and Pacific Islander | Percent Hispanic or Latino[4] | Under 5 years | 5 to 17 years | 18 to 24 years | 25 to 34 years | 35 to 44 years | 45 to 54 years |
|---|---|---|---|---|---|---|---|---|---|---|---|---|---|---|---|---|---|---|
| | | | | 1 | 2 | 3 | 4 | 5 | 6 | 7 | 8 | 9 | 10 | 11 | 12 | 13 | 14 | 15 |
| | | | NORTH CAROLINA—Cont'd | | | | | | | | | | | | | | | |
| 37 041 | ... | 7 | Chowan | 447 | 14 772 | 2 124 | 33.0 | 61.6 | 34.6 | 0.6 | 0.6 | 3.6 | 5.8 | 16.3 | 7.0 | 10.7 | 10.3 | 14.5 |
| 37 043 | ... | 9 | Clay | 556 | 10 618 | 2 387 | 19.1 | 95.8 | 1.4 | 1.0 | 0.6 | 2.6 | 4.1 | 14.3 | 6.0 | 9.0 | 10.9 | 13.5 |
| 37 045 | 43140 | 4 | Cleveland | 1 202 | 97 474 | 600 | 81.1 | 75.2 | 21.5 | 0.6 | 1.0 | 3.0 | 5.9 | 17.1 | 9.3 | 10.6 | 12.9 | 15.0 |
| 37 047 | ... | 6 | Columbus | 2 428 | 57 638 | 885 | 23.7 | 61.2 | 31.1 | 3.6 | 0.6 | 4.7 | 5.9 | 17.2 | 8.6 | 12.0 | 12.4 | 14.5 |
| 37 049 | 35100 | 5 | Craven | 1 836 | 104 770 | 562 | 57.1 | 68.8 | 23.0 | 1.0 | 2.9 | 6.5 | 7.3 | 15.7 | 12.4 | 13.5 | 10.7 | 12.6 |
| 37 051 | 22180 | 2 | Cumberland | 1 689 | 324 049 | 200 | 191.9 | 50.2 | 37.4 | 2.4 | 3.9 | 9.9 | 8.4 | 18.1 | 12.9 | 16.3 | 12.2 | 12.6 |
| 37 053 | 47260 | 1 | Currituck | 678 | 24 077 | 1 640 | 35.5 | 89.5 | 6.7 | 1.1 | 1.0 | 3.2 | 5.5 | 17.7 | 7.2 | 10.4 | 13.9 | 17.9 |
| 37 055 | 28620 | 5 | Dare | 993 | 34 573 | 1 310 | 34.8 | 89.6 | 3.4 | 1.0 | 1.0 | 6.6 | 5.5 | 14.4 | 6.4 | 12.0 | 13.1 | 16.3 |
| 37 057 | 45640 | 4 | Davidson | 1 431 | 163 260 | 383 | 114.1 | 82.7 | 9.6 | 0.9 | 1.5 | 6.5 | 5.9 | 17.6 | 7.5 | 11.2 | 14.1 | 15.6 |
| 37 059 | 49180 | 2 | Davie | 684 | 41 433 | 1 142 | 60.6 | 86.2 | 7.3 | 0.7 | 0.9 | 6.4 | 5.5 | 17.6 | 6.6 | 9.6 | 13.5 | 15.7 |
| 37 061 | ... | 6 | Duplin | 2 114 | 60 033 | 864 | 28.4 | 53.1 | 25.6 | 0.7 | 0.6 | 21.0 | 7.2 | 18.1 | 8.6 | 12.4 | 12.8 | 13.8 |
| 37 063 | 20500 | 2 | Durham | 741 | 279 641 | 238 | 377.4 | 43.8 | 38.5 | 0.9 | 5.2 | 13.5 | 7.5 | 15.2 | 11.4 | 18.3 | 14.2 | 12.6 |
| 37 065 | 40580 | 3 | Edgecombe | 1 309 | 55 954 | 904 | 42.7 | 38.5 | 57.5 | 0.7 | 0.5 | 3.9 | 6.6 | 17.5 | 9.0 | 11.6 | 11.5 | 14.7 |
| 37 067 | 49180 | 2 | Forsyth | 1 057 | 358 137 | 186 | 338.8 | 59.9 | 26.5 | 0.7 | 2.3 | 12.2 | 6.8 | 17.4 | 10.0 | 12.9 | 13.1 | 14.3 |
| 37 069 | 39580 | 2 | Franklin | 1 273 | 61 475 | 845 | 48.3 | 64.5 | 27.1 | 0.9 | 0.9 | 8.0 | 6.2 | 17.9 | 8.2 | 11.5 | 14.0 | 15.5 |
| 37 071 | 16740 | 1 | Gaston | 922 | 208 049 | 303 | 225.6 | 76.9 | 16.1 | 0.9 | 1.6 | 6.1 | 6.4 | 17.3 | 8.6 | 11.9 | 14.5 | 14.8 |
| 37 073 | ... | 8 | Gates | 882 | 11 869 | 2 306 | 13.5 | 63.9 | 34.3 | 1.3 | 0.7 | 1.5 | 5.4 | 17.8 | 7.9 | 9.7 | 12.9 | 16.9 |
| 37 075 | ... | 9 | Graham | 756 | 8 700 | 2 548 | 11.5 | 90.6 | 1.0 | 7.2 | 0.5 | 2.4 | 5.6 | 16.0 | 7.2 | 10.5 | 11.1 | 14.4 |
| 37 077 | ... | 6 | Granville | 1 377 | 60 436 | 857 | 43.9 | 58.6 | 33.2 | 1.0 | 1.0 | 7.7 | 5.4 | 16.2 | 8.8 | 11.7 | 15.4 | 16.5 |
| 37 079 | 24780 | 3 | Greene | 689 | 21 429 | 1 759 | 31.1 | 47.9 | 36.9 | 0.8 | 0.6 | 14.6 | 6.6 | 16.4 | 8.9 | 14.0 | 14.0 | 15.2 |
| 37 081 | 24660 | 2 | Guilford | 1 672 | 500 879 | 132 | 299.6 | 55.5 | 33.5 | 1.0 | 4.6 | 7.3 | 6.2 | 17.0 | 11.6 | 13.3 | 13.5 | 14.1 |
| 37 083 | 40260 | 4 | Halifax | 1 875 | 54 006 | 925 | 28.8 | 40.4 | 53.5 | 4.1 | 1.0 | 2.3 | 5.8 | 16.9 | 8.6 | 10.9 | 11.6 | 15.2 |
| 37 085 | 20380 | 4 | Harnett | 1 541 | 122 135 | 502 | 79.3 | 65.8 | 22.1 | 1.7 | 1.8 | 11.2 | 8.0 | 19.6 | 10.0 | 14.7 | 14.1 | 12.9 |
| 37 087 | 11700 | 2 | Haywood | 1 434 | 58 908 | 877 | 41.1 | 94.3 | 1.6 | 1.0 | 0.6 | 3.4 | 4.8 | 14.2 | 7.2 | 9.9 | 12.2 | 14.9 |
| 37 089 | 11700 | 2 | Henderson | 966 | 108 266 | 547 | 112.1 | 85.2 | 3.9 | 0.9 | 1.5 | 10.0 | 5.4 | 14.9 | 6.2 | 10.5 | 12.1 | 13.5 |
| 37 091 | ... | 7 | Hertford | 914 | 24 438 | 1 628 | 26.7 | 35.1 | 60.9 | 1.6 | 0.8 | 2.8 | 5.6 | 15.5 | 10.4 | 11.4 | 11.6 | 15.1 |
| 37 093 | 22180 | 2 | Hoke | 1 012 | 50 536 | 970 | 49.9 | 44.3 | 34.6 | 9.7 | 2.4 | 12.6 | 9.7 | 20.3 | 8.9 | 18.5 | 13.6 | 12.2 |
| 37 095 | ... | 9 | Hyde | 1 587 | 5 859 | 2 776 | 3.7 | 60.5 | 32.2 | 0.7 | 0.5 | 7.1 | 4.8 | 13.5 | 6.9 | 15.0 | 14.4 | 14.5 |
| 37 097 | 44380 | 4 | Iredell | 1 486 | 162 708 | 385 | 109.5 | 78.7 | 12.8 | 0.7 | 2.3 | 7.0 | 6.0 | 19.0 | 8.0 | 11.3 | 14.5 | 15.8 |
| 37 099 | ... | 6 | Jackson | 1 271 | 40 448 | 1 167 | 31.8 | 82.8 | 2.7 | 10.1 | 1.2 | 5.1 | 5.0 | 12.5 | 19.9 | 11.3 | 10.4 | 11.9 |
| 37 101 | 39580 | 2 | Johnston | 2 049 | 174 938 | 358 | 85.4 | 70.7 | 15.9 | 0.9 | 0.9 | 13.0 | 7.4 | 20.2 | 7.5 | 12.5 | 16.1 | 14.5 |
| 37 103 | 35100 | 8 | Jones | 1 219 | 10 275 | 2 420 | 8.4 | 62.5 | 32.8 | 1.2 | 0.9 | 4.4 | 5.5 | 15.1 | 8.6 | 10.9 | 10.6 | 15.6 |
| 37 105 | 41820 | 4 | Lee | 660 | 59 715 | 867 | 90.5 | 60.2 | 20.5 | 0.9 | 1.3 | 18.6 | 7.3 | 18.5 | 8.5 | 12.9 | 13.1 | 13.8 |
| 37 107 | 28820 | 4 | Lenoir | 1 038 | 59 227 | 873 | 57.1 | 51.9 | 40.9 | 0.6 | 0.9 | 6.8 | 6.3 | 17.6 | 8.2 | 11.0 | 11.6 | 14.9 |
| 37 109 | 30740 | 4 | Lincoln | 772 | 79 313 | 692 | 102.7 | 86.4 | 6.4 | 0.7 | 0.8 | 6.9 | 5.8 | 17.5 | 7.6 | 10.7 | 14.9 | 16.2 |
| 37 111 | ... | 6 | McDowell | 1 141 | 44 998 | 1 068 | 39.4 | 89.5 | 4.4 | 0.8 | 1.0 | 5.5 | 5.6 | 15.8 | 7.5 | 11.5 | 13.6 | 14.7 |
| 37 113 | ... | 7 | Macon | 1 335 | 33 869 | 1 329 | 25.4 | 90.6 | 1.9 | 0.9 | 0.9 | 6.7 | 5.1 | 14.0 | 7.1 | 9.6 | 10.1 | 13.4 |
| 37 115 | 11700 | 2 | Madison | 1 164 | 20 742 | 1 793 | 17.8 | 95.6 | 1.7 | 1.0 | 0.7 | 2.2 | 4.4 | 15.0 | 9.9 | 9.9 | 12.3 | 14.6 |
| 37 117 | ... | 6 | Martin | 1 195 | 23 961 | 1 645 | 20.1 | 52.7 | 43.7 | 0.7 | 0.5 | 3.3 | 5.7 | 16.0 | 7.8 | 9.5 | 11.5 | 15.2 |
| 37 119 | 16740 | 1 | Mecklenburg | 1 357 | 969 031 | 45 | 714.1 | 51.9 | 31.4 | 0.9 | 5.4 | 12.4 | 7.4 | 17.8 | 9.4 | 16.8 | 15.7 | 13.7 |
| 37 121 | ... | 9 | Mitchell | 573 | 15 368 | 2 084 | 26.8 | 94.4 | 0.9 | 0.8 | 0.5 | 4.4 | 4.9 | 14.2 | 6.9 | 10.3 | 12.0 | 15.0 |
| 37 123 | ... | 6 | Montgomery | 1 274 | 27 668 | 1 505 | 21.7 | 64.8 | 19.2 | 0.8 | 1.7 | 14.5 | 6.2 | 17.9 | 7.9 | 11.5 | 12.5 | 14.0 |
| 37 125 | 43860 | 4 | Moore | 1 807 | 90 302 | 635 | 50.0 | 78.6 | 14.2 | 1.3 | 1.3 | 6.1 | 5.6 | 15.9 | 6.4 | 10.3 | 11.7 | 13.4 |
| 37 127 | 40580 | 3 | Nash | 1 400 | 95 708 | 608 | 68.4 | 54.3 | 38.2 | 1.1 | 1.2 | 6.5 | 6.0 | 17.5 | 8.7 | 11.3 | 13.0 | 15.2 |
| 37 129 | 48900 | 2 | New Hanover | 496 | 209 234 | 299 | 421.8 | 78.0 | 15.5 | 1.0 | 1.8 | 5.4 | 5.6 | 14.1 | 12.9 | 14.3 | 13.0 | 13.2 |
| 37 131 | 40260 | 9 | Northampton | 1 390 | 21 428 | 1 760 | 15.4 | 40.0 | 58.3 | 0.8 | 0.4 | 1.5 | 5.4 | 15.1 | 7.9 | 9.4 | 10.8 | 15.4 |
| 37 133 | 27340 | 3 | Onslow | 1 975 | 183 263 | 344 | 92.8 | 71.2 | 17.0 | 1.4 | 3.4 | 10.5 | 9.7 | 15.4 | 22.6 | 17.1 | 10.1 | 9.8 |
| 37 135 | 20500 | 2 | Orange | 1 031 | 137 941 | 453 | 133.8 | 72.2 | 13.0 | 1.0 | 7.9 | 8.1 | 4.9 | 15.5 | 19.1 | 12.3 | 12.4 | 13.8 |
| 37 137 | 35100 | 7 | Pamlico | 872 | 13 074 | 2 236 | 15.0 | 75.4 | 20.9 | 1.1 | 0.7 | 3.2 | 4.6 | 13.4 | 6.7 | 10.1 | 10.6 | 15.0 |
| 37 139 | 21020 | 7 | Pasquotank | 588 | 40 591 | 1 165 | 69.0 | 56.5 | 38.6 | 0.9 | 1.7 | 4.1 | 6.4 | 15.7 | 12.9 | 13.0 | 11.7 | 14.3 |
| 37 141 | 48900 | 2 | Pender | 2 253 | 54 195 | 922 | 24.1 | 74.7 | 18.4 | 1.2 | 0.8 | 6.4 | 5.9 | 16.7 | 7.9 | 11.3 | 13.4 | 15.2 |
| 37 143 | 21020 | 9 | Perquimans | 640 | 13 563 | 2 211 | 21.2 | 72.4 | 25.2 | 0.7 | 0.5 | 2.3 | 5.2 | 14.9 | 6.9 | 10.1 | 10.6 | 14.6 |
| 37 145 | 20500 | 2 | Person | 1 016 | 39 268 | 1 192 | 38.6 | 68.0 | 27.6 | 1.0 | 0.6 | 4.2 | 6.0 | 17.0 | 7.6 | 10.7 | 13.0 | 15.3 |
| 37 147 | 24780 | 3 | Pitt | 1 689 | 172 554 | 361 | 102.2 | 58.3 | 34.9 | 0.7 | 2.2 | 5.6 | 6.6 | 15.6 | 18.9 | 14.1 | 12.0 | 12.1 |
| 37 149 | ... | 8 | Polk | 616 | 20 271 | 1 827 | 32.9 | 89.1 | 5.2 | 0.7 | 0.6 | 5.8 | 4.2 | 14.4 | 6.3 | 7.7 | 11.0 | 14.6 |
| 37 151 | 24660 | 2 | Randolph | 2 027 | 142 466 | 442 | 70.3 | 81.8 | 6.6 | 0.9 | 1.2 | 10.7 | 6.3 | 18.1 | 8.0 | 11.2 | 14.1 | 14.9 |
| 37 153 | 40460 | 4 | Richmond | 1 227 | 46 627 | 1 037 | 38.0 | 59.7 | 31.3 | 3.1 | 1.4 | 6.2 | 6.5 | 17.9 | 9.3 | 11.7 | 12.7 | 14.1 |
| 37 155 | 31300 | 4 | Robeson | 2 458 | 135 496 | 461 | 55.1 | 28.7 | 25.3 | 38.5 | 1.3 | 8.4 | 7.7 | 19.2 | 11.2 | 12.7 | 12.7 | 13.1 |
| 37 157 | 24660 | 2 | Rockingham | 1 465 | 92 720 | 623 | 63.3 | 74.5 | 19.7 | 0.9 | 0.8 | 5.7 | 5.4 | 16.4 | 7.7 | 10.4 | 13.2 | 15.7 |
| 37 159 | 41580 | 4 | Rowan | 1 324 | 138 180 | 451 | 104.4 | 74.6 | 16.7 | 0.8 | 1.4 | 7.9 | 6.3 | 17.1 | 9.0 | 12.1 | 13.0 | 14.7 |
| 37 161 | 22580 | 4 | Rutherford | 1 461 | 67 323 | 786 | 46.1 | 85.4 | 11.0 | 0.8 | 0.7 | 3.7 | 5.7 | 16.4 | 7.7 | 10.2 | 12.9 | 14.7 |
| 37 163 | ... | 6 | Sampson | 2 447 | 63 949 | 821 | 26.1 | 54.1 | 27.6 | 2.1 | 0.7 | 16.9 | 6.8 | 18.6 | 8.2 | 11.9 | 13.3 | 13.9 |
| 37 165 | 29900 | 6 | Scotland | 826 | 36 094 | 1 274 | 43.7 | 47.5 | 39.3 | 11.6 | 1.1 | 2.4 | 6.9 | 17.8 | 9.5 | 11.3 | 12.3 | 14.2 |
| 37 167 | 10620 | 6 | Stanly | 1 023 | 60 576 | 853 | 59.2 | 82.9 | 11.7 | 0.7 | 2.0 | 3.8 | 5.9 | 16.5 | 9.1 | 11.2 | 14.5 | 14.7 |
| 37 169 | 49180 | 2 | Stokes | 1 163 | 46 783 | 1 031 | 40.2 | 92.2 | 4.8 | 0.8 | 0.5 | 2.7 | 5.1 | 16.4 | 7.4 | 9.6 | 13.8 | 16.3 |
| 37 171 | 34340 | 4 | Surry | 1 378 | 73 561 | 740 | 53.4 | 85.4 | 4.3 | 0.7 | 0.6 | 10.0 | 5.9 | 17.2 | 7.7 | 10.4 | 13.5 | 14.7 |

1. CBSA = Core Based Statistical Area. See Appendix A for explanation. See Appendix B for list of metropolitan areas with component counties. 2. County type code from the Economic Research Service of USDA Rural-Urban Continuum Codes. See Appendix A for definition. 3. Dry land or land partially or temporarily covered by water. 4. May be of any race.

# Table B. States and Counties — **Population and Households**

| | Population, 2011 (cont.) | | | | Population change and components of change, 2000–2012 | | | | | | | Households, 2010 | | | | |
|---|---|---|---|---|---|---|---|---|---|---|---|---|---|---|---|---|
| | Age (percent) (cont.) | | | | Total persons | | Percent change | | Components of change, 2010–2012 | | | | | | Percent | |
| STATE County | 55 to 64 years | 65 to 74 years | 75 years and over | Percent female | 2000 | 2010 | 2000–2010 | 2010–2012 | Births | Deaths | Net migration | Number | Percent change, 2000–2010 | Persons per household | Female family householder[1] | One person |
| | 16 | 17 | 18 | 19 | 20 | 21 | 22 | 23 | 24 | 25 | 26 | 27 | 28 | 29 | 30 | 31 |
| **NORTH CAROLINA—Cont'd** | | | | | | | | | | | | | | | | |
| Chowan | 15.5 | 10.9 | 9.0 | 52.3 | 14 526 | 14 793 | 1.8 | -0.1 | 374 | 420 | 33 | 6 059 | 8.6 | 2.40 | 16.3 | 27.4 |
| Clay | 18.1 | 14.1 | 10.0 | 50.6 | 8 775 | 10 587 | 20.6 | 0.3 | 155 | 321 | 192 | 4 660 | 21.1 | 2.25 | 8.2 | 28.2 |
| Cleveland | 13.8 | 8.8 | 6.5 | 51.8 | 96 287 | 98 078 | 1.9 | -0.6 | 2 481 | 2 472 | -625 | 38 555 | 4.1 | 2.49 | 15.0 | 25.8 |
| Columbus | 13.7 | 9.1 | 6.5 | 50.5 | 54 749 | 58 098 | 6.1 | -0.8 | 1 474 | 1 492 | -489 | 22 489 | 5.5 | 2.45 | 17.1 | 28.7 |
| Craven | 12.2 | 8.6 | 7.0 | 50.2 | 91 436 | 103 505 | 13.2 | 1.2 | 3 738 | 2 107 | -334 | 40 299 | 16.5 | 2.45 | 13.4 | 25.5 |
| Cumberland | 9.9 | 5.6 | 4.0 | 51.4 | 302 963 | 319 431 | 5.4 | 1.4 | 13 402 | 4 933 | -3 922 | 122 431 | 14.0 | 2.53 | 19.0 | 26.5 |
| Currituck | 14.0 | 8.3 | 5.0 | 50.4 | 18 190 | 23 547 | 29.5 | 2.3 | 507 | 453 | 467 | 8 880 | 28.7 | 2.64 | 9.6 | 19.7 |
| Dare | 16.6 | 9.8 | 6.0 | 50.4 | 29 967 | 33 920 | 13.2 | 1.9 | 816 | 648 | 496 | 14 335 | 13.0 | 2.36 | 9.2 | 25.4 |
| Davidson | 13.3 | 8.6 | 6.2 | 50.9 | 147 246 | 162 878 | 10.6 | 0.2 | 3 899 | 3 502 | -126 | 64 515 | 10.9 | 2.50 | 12.5 | 24.3 |
| Davie | 14.3 | 9.6 | 7.6 | 51.4 | 34 835 | 41 240 | 18.4 | 0.5 | 902 | 805 | 127 | 16 245 | 18.1 | 2.52 | 10.4 | 22.8 |
| Duplin | 12.7 | 8.1 | 6.2 | 50.7 | 49 063 | 58 505 | 19.2 | 2.6 | 1 780 | 1 157 | 901 | 22 495 | 23.1 | 2.57 | 15.1 | 26.7 |
| Durham | 11.0 | 5.4 | 4.5 | 52.3 | 223 314 | 267 587 | 19.8 | 4.5 | 9 416 | 3 928 | 6 454 | 109 348 | 22.8 | 2.35 | 14.8 | 32.3 |
| Edgecombe | 14.3 | 8.4 | 6.5 | 53.5 | 55 606 | 56 552 | 1.7 | -1.1 | 1 498 | 1 320 | -808 | 21 680 | 6.3 | 2.54 | 23.4 | 27.1 |
| Forsyth | 12.2 | 7.1 | 6.2 | 52.5 | 306 067 | 350 670 | 14.6 | 2.1 | 10 285 | 6 468 | 3 779 | 141 163 | 14.0 | 2.41 | 15.0 | 30.1 |
| Franklin | 13.4 | 7.9 | 5.4 | 50.4 | 47 260 | 60 619 | 28.3 | 1.4 | 1 450 | 1 133 | 491 | 23 023 | 29.0 | 2.56 | 13.4 | 24.2 |
| Gaston | 13.0 | 7.6 | 5.9 | 51.7 | 190 365 | 206 086 | 8.3 | 1.0 | 5 750 | 4 654 | 907 | 79 867 | 8.0 | 2.54 | 15.4 | 24.6 |
| Gates | 14.1 | 9.2 | 6.3 | 50.8 | 10 516 | 12 197 | 16.0 | -2.7 | 214 | 287 | -253 | 4 665 | 19.6 | 2.60 | 13.6 | 23.2 |
| Graham | 15.1 | 11.3 | 8.7 | 50.6 | 7 993 | 8 861 | 10.9 | -1.8 | 200 | 230 | -139 | 3 701 | 10.3 | 2.37 | 10.7 | 26.6 |
| Granville | 13.1 | 7.7 | 5.3 | 46.6 | 48 498 | 59 916 | 23.5 | 0.9 | 1 311 | 1 145 | 286 | 20 628 | 23.9 | 2.57 | 15.1 | 24.2 |
| Greene | 12.7 | 7.0 | 5.4 | 46.1 | 18 974 | 21 362 | 12.6 | 0.3 | 534 | 433 | -52 | 7 313 | 9.2 | 2.60 | 17.4 | 26.0 |
| Guilford | 11.8 | 6.8 | 5.8 | 52.4 | 421 048 | 488 406 | 16.0 | 2.6 | 13 401 | 8 704 | 7 871 | 196 628 | 16.6 | 2.41 | 15.1 | 29.8 |
| Halifax | 14.5 | 8.9 | 7.6 | 52.2 | 57 370 | 54 691 | -4.7 | -1.3 | 1 339 | 1 478 | -550 | 21 970 | -0.7 | 2.42 | 21.6 | 29.9 |
| Harnett | 10.3 | 6.2 | 4.2 | 50.9 | 91 025 | 114 678 | 26.0 | 6.5 | 3 958 | 1 940 | 5 350 | 41 594 | 23.1 | 2.68 | 14.9 | 23.4 |
| Haywood | 15.2 | 12.2 | 9.5 | 51.8 | 54 033 | 59 036 | 9.3 | -0.2 | 1 238 | 1 536 | 185 | 25 563 | 10.7 | 2.28 | 10.4 | 28.5 |
| Henderson | 14.6 | 12.0 | 10.8 | 51.7 | 89 173 | 106 740 | 19.7 | 1.4 | 2 428 | 2 852 | 1 996 | 45 448 | 21.5 | 2.32 | 9.1 | 28.3 |
| Hertford | 14.2 | 9.1 | 7.1 | 51.1 | 22 601 | 24 669 | 9.2 | -0.9 | 569 | 595 | -182 | 9 334 | 4.3 | 2.40 | 20.8 | 29.5 |
| Hoke | 9.3 | 4.5 | 2.9 | 51.1 | 33 646 | 46 952 | 39.5 | 7.6 | 2 175 | 599 | 1 970 | 16 532 | 45.4 | 2.80 | 18.9 | 20.8 |
| Hyde | 15.5 | 8.3 | 7.1 | 44.3 | 5 826 | 5 810 | -0.3 | 0.8 | 105 | 102 | 40 | 2 119 | -3.0 | 2.35 | 13.7 | 31.2 |
| Iredell | 12.3 | 7.6 | 5.5 | 50.8 | 122 660 | 159 437 | 30.0 | 2.1 | 3 994 | 3 110 | 2 378 | 61 215 | 29.3 | 2.58 | 12.2 | 23.2 |
| Jackson | 13.5 | 9.4 | 6.1 | 50.4 | 33 121 | 40 271 | 21.6 | 0.4 | 933 | 674 | -91 | 16 446 | 24.7 | 2.23 | 9.7 | 32.1 |
| Johnston | 11.3 | 6.5 | 4.0 | 50.8 | 121 965 | 168 878 | 38.5 | 3.6 | 5 102 | 2 709 | 3 486 | 61 909 | 32.9 | 2.70 | 12.4 | 22.1 |
| Jones | 16.3 | 9.6 | 7.8 | 51.7 | 10 381 | 10 153 | -2.2 | 1.2 | 234 | 261 | 55 | 4 167 | 2.6 | 2.41 | 14.6 | 27.1 |
| Lee | 12.1 | 7.7 | 6.1 | 51.0 | 49 040 | 57 866 | 18.0 | 3.2 | 1 854 | 1 156 | 1 133 | 22 058 | 19.5 | 2.58 | 15.0 | 25.5 |
| Lenoir | 14.2 | 8.9 | 7.3 | 52.2 | 59 648 | 59 495 | -0.3 | -0.5 | 1 535 | 1 624 | -183 | 24 327 | 1.9 | 2.39 | 19.1 | 30.5 |
| Lincoln | 13.8 | 8.4 | 5.3 | 50.4 | 63 780 | 78 265 | 22.7 | 1.3 | 1 801 | 1 559 | 818 | 30 343 | 26.2 | 2.56 | 11.1 | 22.3 |
| McDowell | 14.3 | 9.7 | 7.3 | 50.1 | 42 151 | 44 996 | 6.7 | 0.0 | 1 026 | 999 | -27 | 17 838 | 7.4 | 2.43 | 11.7 | 25.8 |
| Macon | 16.1 | 13.7 | 11.0 | 51.4 | 29 811 | 33 922 | 13.8 | -0.2 | 701 | 892 | 133 | 14 591 | 13.7 | 2.29 | 9.4 | 28.9 |
| Madison | 15.7 | 10.2 | 7.8 | 50.6 | 19 635 | 20 764 | 5.7 | -0.1 | 387 | 496 | 77 | 8 494 | 6.2 | 2.32 | 9.4 | 27.1 |
| Martin | 16.2 | 10.1 | 7.9 | 53.4 | 25 593 | 24 505 | -4.3 | -2.2 | 569 | 696 | -457 | 10 318 | 3.0 | 2.36 | 16.8 | 29.9 |
| Mecklenburg | 10.1 | 5.1 | 3.9 | 51.7 | 695 454 | 919 628 | 32.2 | 5.4 | 31 074 | 11 881 | 29 889 | 362 213 | 32.5 | 2.49 | 14.6 | 29.2 |
| Mitchell | 15.2 | 12.1 | 9.5 | 51.2 | 15 687 | 15 579 | -0.7 | -1.4 | 306 | 503 | -1 | 6 685 | 2.0 | 2.30 | 9.9 | 28.3 |
| Montgomery | 14.4 | 8.9 | 6.8 | 51.5 | 26 822 | 27 798 | 3.6 | -0.5 | 730 | 556 | -337 | 10 544 | 7.1 | 2.53 | 13.1 | 27.2 |
| Moore | 14.0 | 11.5 | 11.3 | 52.2 | 74 769 | 88 247 | 18.0 | 2.3 | 2 102 | 2 377 | 2 296 | 37 540 | 22.2 | 2.33 | 10.8 | 28.1 |
| Nash | 13.9 | 8.2 | 6.3 | 51.7 | 87 420 | 95 840 | 9.6 | -0.1 | 2 569 | 2 133 | -539 | 37 782 | 12.3 | 2.48 | 16.4 | 27.4 |
| New Hanover | 12.7 | 8.0 | 6.2 | 51.7 | 160 307 | 202 667 | 26.4 | 3.2 | 5 026 | 3 676 | 5 235 | 86 046 | 26.2 | 2.28 | 12.1 | 30.7 |
| Northampton | 15.6 | 11.4 | 9.0 | 51.6 | 22 086 | 22 099 | 0.1 | -3.0 | 419 | 610 | -499 | 9 193 | 5.8 | 2.32 | 19.6 | 32.1 |
| Onslow | 7.6 | 4.5 | 3.2 | 46.2 | 150 355 | 177 772 | 18.2 | 3.1 | 9 499 | 1 931 | -2 172 | 60 092 | 24.9 | 2.66 | 13.1 | 20.3 |
| Orange | 11.8 | 6.0 | 4.1 | 52.3 | 118 227 | 133 801 | 13.2 | 3.1 | 2 791 | 1 618 | 2 862 | 51 457 | 12.2 | 2.41 | 10.0 | 27.9 |
| Pamlico | 17.6 | 12.7 | 9.3 | 49.1 | 12 934 | 13 144 | 1.6 | -0.5 | 228 | 349 | 29 | 5 490 | 6.0 | 2.27 | 11.1 | 27.8 |
| Pasquotank | 11.9 | 7.7 | 6.4 | 51.2 | 34 897 | 40 661 | 16.5 | -0.2 | 1 126 | 869 | -311 | 14 956 | 15.9 | 2.51 | 16.3 | 25.7 |
| Pender | 14.2 | 9.1 | 6.3 | 50.0 | 41 082 | 52 217 | 27.1 | 3.8 | 1 343 | 1 053 | 1 634 | 20 333 | 26.7 | 2.51 | 12.2 | 23.3 |
| Perquimans | 15.7 | 13.4 | 8.6 | 51.9 | 11 368 | 13 453 | 18.3 | 0.8 | 288 | 307 | 129 | 5 598 | 20.5 | 2.39 | 12.2 | 25.4 |
| Person | 14.3 | 8.9 | 6.7 | 51.5 | 35 623 | 39 464 | 10.8 | -0.5 | 958 | 964 | -180 | 15 826 | 12.4 | 2.47 | 15.0 | 25.9 |
| Pitt | 10.6 | 5.6 | 4.4 | 52.8 | 133 798 | 168 148 | 25.7 | 2.6 | 4 852 | 2 629 | 2 180 | 67 577 | 28.6 | 2.39 | 15.6 | 30.0 |
| Polk | 17.2 | 12.5 | 12.2 | 52.0 | 18 324 | 20 510 | 11.9 | -1.2 | 300 | 637 | 77 | 8 989 | 13.7 | 2.24 | 8.8 | 31.2 |
| Randolph | 12.9 | 8.4 | 6.1 | 50.7 | 130 454 | 141 752 | 8.7 | 0.5 | 3 589 | 3 040 | 215 | 55 373 | 9.3 | 2.54 | 12.2 | 24.4 |
| Richmond | 13.3 | 8.3 | 6.2 | 50.7 | 46 564 | 46 639 | 0.2 | 0.0 | 1 323 | 1 198 | -116 | 18 430 | 3.1 | 2.47 | 18.2 | 28.7 |
| Robeson | 11.9 | 6.9 | 4.7 | 51.3 | 123 339 | 134 168 | 8.8 | 1.0 | 4 409 | 2 699 | -357 | 47 997 | 9.9 | 2.71 | 22.3 | 24.4 |
| Rockingham | 14.5 | 9.3 | 7.4 | 51.8 | 91 928 | 93 643 | 1.9 | -1.0 | 2 091 | 2 402 | -563 | 38 693 | 4.6 | 2.39 | 14.4 | 28.1 |
| Rowan | 13.1 | 8.0 | 6.7 | 50.7 | 130 340 | 138 428 | 6.2 | -0.2 | 3 442 | 3 195 | -559 | 53 140 | 6.4 | 2.52 | 14.1 | 25.2 |
| Rutherford | 14.7 | 10.2 | 7.6 | 51.7 | 62 899 | 67 810 | 7.8 | -0.7 | 1 572 | 1 806 | -240 | 27 466 | 9.0 | 2.42 | 13.3 | 27.3 |
| Sampson | 12.8 | 8.2 | 6.4 | 50.9 | 60 161 | 63 431 | 5.4 | 0.8 | 1 886 | 1 408 | 12 | 24 005 | 7.8 | 2.60 | 15.8 | 26.1 |
| Scotland | 13.9 | 8.1 | 6.0 | 51.6 | 35 998 | 36 157 | 0.4 | -0.2 | 1 030 | 824 | -286 | 13 614 | 1.6 | 2.53 | 22.4 | 27.2 |
| Stanly | 13.5 | 8.9 | 7.0 | 50.2 | 58 100 | 60 585 | 4.3 | 0.0 | 1 494 | 1 453 | -15 | 23 589 | 6.1 | 2.48 | 11.8 | 25.8 |
| Stokes | 14.6 | 9.7 | 6.9 | 51.2 | 44 711 | 47 401 | 6.0 | -1.3 | 906 | 1 104 | -449 | 19 416 | 10.4 | 2.42 | 10.9 | 26.0 |
| Surry | 13.7 | 9.4 | 7.6 | 51.1 | 71 219 | 73 673 | 3.4 | -0.2 | 1 784 | 1 845 | -63 | 29 914 | 5.3 | 2.43 | 11.4 | 27.3 |

1. No spouse present.

# Table B. States and Counties — Population, Vital Statistics, Medicare, and Crime

| STATE County | Persons in group quarters, 2010 | Daytime population, 2007–2011 | | Births, 2011 | | Deaths, 2011 | | Persons under 65 with no health insurance, 2010 | | Medicare, 2012 | | | Serious crimes known to police,[2] 2011 Total | |
|---|---|---|---|---|---|---|---|---|---|---|---|---|---|---|
| | | Number | Employment/ residence ratio | Total | Rate[1] | Number | Rate[1] | Number | Percent | Eligible for Medicare | Enrolled in Medicare Advantage | Enrolled in a Medicare prescription drug plan | Number | Rate[3] |
| | 32 | 33 | 34 | 35 | 36 | 37 | 38 | 39 | 40 | 41 | 42 | 43 | 44 | 45 |
| NORTH CAROLINA—Cont'd | | | | | | | | | | | | | | |
| Chowan | 273 | 14 795 | 0.99 | 161 | 10.8 | 176 | 11.8 | 2 164 | 18.4 | 3 608 | 130 | 2 100 | 458 | 3 057 |
| Clay | 91 | 9 663 | 0.78 | 57 | 5.4 | 143 | 13.5 | 1 783 | 22.1 | 3 133 | 420 | 1 452 | 302 | 2 817 |
| Cleveland | 2 050 | 93 611 | 0.89 | 1 134 | 11.6 | 1 122 | 11.5 | 14 418 | 17.6 | 21 039 | 2 399 | 11 581 | 2 922 | 2 963 |
| Columbus | 2 925 | 54 358 | 0.86 | 665 | 11.5 | 647 | 11.2 | 10 015 | 21.5 | 12 410 | 645 | 7 640 | 2 745 | 4 869 |
| Craven | 4 939 | 105 682 | 1.09 | 1 671 | 15.9 | 910 | 8.7 | 14 652 | 17.6 | 19 825 | 610 | 9 293 | 3 771 | 4 554 |
| Cumberland | 10 157 | 338 845 | 1.16 | 5 893 | 18.1 | 2 150 | 6.6 | 48 085 | 17.2 | 42 472 | 6 385 | 13 561 | 20 680 | 6 393 |
| Currituck | 135 | 18 740 | 0.58 | 229 | 9.6 | 187 | 7.8 | 3 672 | 18.0 | 3 810 | 265 | 1 492 | 804 | 3 372 |
| Dare | 152 | 35 724 | 1.11 | 370 | 10.8 | 281 | 8.2 | 6 223 | 21.7 | 6 617 | 286 | 3 069 | 2 167 | 6 587 |
| Davidson | 1 691 | 136 061 | 0.64 | 1 766 | 10.9 | 1 526 | 9.4 | 27 558 | 19.9 | 30 598 | 14 033 | 9 684 | 4 875 | 2 986 |
| Davie | 365 | 34 546 | 0.64 | 414 | 10.0 | 326 | 7.8 | 6 102 | 17.8 | 8 500 | 3 662 | 2 415 | 941 | 2 307 |
| Duplin | 679 | 54 846 | 0.88 | 794 | 13.3 | 504 | 8.5 | 14 144 | 28.4 | 9 508 | 482 | 5 496 | 1 826 | 3 170 |
| Durham | 10 121 | 316 645 | 1.41 | 4 248 | 15.5 | 1 690 | 6.2 | 44 454 | 19.1 | 34 501 | 5 490 | 15 032 | 14 785 | 5 456 |
| Edgecombe | 1 430 | 53 068 | 0.85 | 712 | 12.7 | 567 | 10.1 | 8 898 | 18.8 | 10 819 | 802 | 6 749 | 2 686 | 4 708 |
| Forsyth | 9 851 | 371 960 | 1.16 | 4 680 | 13.2 | 2 822 | 8.0 | 55 075 | 18.6 | 59 236 | 28 051 | 16 112 | 19 962 | 5 621 |
| Franklin | 1 640 | 47 649 | 0.53 | 647 | 10.6 | 497 | 8.1 | 10 482 | 20.3 | 9 615 | 1 770 | 4 392 | 1 659 | 2 702 |
| Gaston | 3 317 | 186 997 | 0.80 | 2 597 | 12.5 | 2 052 | 9.9 | 35 069 | 19.8 | 38 129 | 7 963 | 17 245 | 8 016 | 3 975 |
| Gates | 61 | 8 689 | 0.36 | 105 | 8.7 | 127 | 10.5 | 1 833 | 17.8 | 2 217 | 211 | 1 093 | NA | NA |
| Graham | 93 | 8 325 | 0.87 | 84 | 9.5 | 96 | 10.9 | 1 775 | 24.9 | 1 998 | 305 | 1 014 | NA | NA |
| Granville | 6 948 | 56 127 | 0.88 | 616 | 10.3 | 509 | 8.5 | 8 294 | 17.8 | 9 953 | 1 245 | 4 786 | 2 314 | 3 814 |
| Greene | 2 320 | 18 181 | 0.61 | 245 | 11.4 | 200 | 9.3 | 3 930 | 23.8 | 3 128 | 108 | 1 922 | 661 | 3 056 |
| Guilford | 15 492 | 537 692 | 1.24 | 5 965 | 12.0 | 3 841 | 7.8 | 80 759 | 19.4 | 78 168 | 30 199 | 24 668 | 21 719 | 4 391 |
| Halifax | 1 416 | 53 078 | 0.90 | 621 | 11.5 | 667 | 12.3 | 8 399 | 18.8 | 13 115 | 1 165 | 7 881 | 2 329 | 4 258 |
| Harnett | 3 380 | 92 253 | 0.57 | 1 728 | 14.5 | 867 | 7.3 | 20 523 | 20.4 | 16 200 | 1 420 | 7 948 | 3 527 | 3 038 |
| Haywood | 813 | 54 786 | 0.84 | 542 | 9.2 | 688 | 11.7 | 8 740 | 18.9 | 15 562 | 2 941 | 6 723 | 1 754 | 2 934 |
| Henderson | 1 299 | 101 628 | 0.91 | 1 105 | 10.2 | 1 258 | 11.7 | 17 822 | 21.6 | 27 925 | 5 172 | 12 072 | 2 491 | 2 305 |
| Hertford | 2 297 | 25 259 | 1.09 | 270 | 11.1 | 273 | 11.2 | 3 463 | 18.5 | 4 743 | 130 | 3 110 | 746 | 3 082 |
| Hoke | 670 | 36 845 | 0.53 | 922 | 18.7 | 239 | 4.9 | 9 442 | 21.7 | 5 173 | 881 | 2 399 | 1 363 | 2 867 |
| Hyde | 830 | 5 898 | 1.07 | 49 | 8.4 | 47 | 8.1 | 1 011 | 24.2 | 990 | 20 | 608 | NA | NA |
| Iredell | 1 292 | 155 369 | 0.97 | 1 823 | 11.3 | 1 340 | 8.3 | 25 001 | 18.1 | 26 894 | 5 532 | 12 030 | 5 804 | 3 595 |
| Jackson | 3 574 | 40 492 | 1.05 | 440 | 10.9 | 289 | 7.2 | 8 176 | 26.4 | 7 160 | 878 | 3 116 | 1 221 | 2 994 |
| Johnston | 1 771 | 138 666 | 0.65 | 2 290 | 13.3 | 1 180 | 6.8 | 29 704 | 19.7 | 24 772 | 2 755 | 12 260 | 4 770 | 2 829 |
| Jones | 91 | 8 068 | 0.52 | 95 | 9.5 | 109 | 10.9 | 1 866 | 22.3 | 2 127 | 172 | 1 184 | NA | NA |
| Lee | 999 | 58 786 | 1.08 | 843 | 14.3 | 501 | 8.5 | 10 739 | 21.8 | 10 311 | 1 052 | 5 157 | 1 746 | 3 043 |
| Lenoir | 1 242 | 61 636 | 1.10 | 714 | 12.0 | 727 | 12.3 | 9 992 | 20.2 | 12 797 | 464 | 7 787 | 2 831 | 4 743 |
| Lincoln | 679 | 65 003 | 0.66 | 817 | 10.4 | 692 | 8.8 | 13 914 | 20.6 | 13 211 | 1 643 | 6 893 | 2 117 | 2 671 |
| McDowell | 1 666 | 43 970 | 0.95 | 467 | 10.4 | 456 | 10.1 | 7 091 | 19.3 | 9 998 | 2 098 | 4 494 | 1 336 | 2 932 |
| Macon | 439 | 33 314 | 0.97 | 320 | 9.4 | 377 | 11.1 | 6 379 | 24.8 | 9 787 | 1 030 | 4 715 | 866 | 2 521 |
| Madison | 1 028 | 17 157 | 0.57 | 167 | 8.0 | 220 | 10.6 | 3 186 | 19.5 | 4 896 | 796 | 2 391 | 295 | 1 507 |
| Martin | 156 | 22 161 | 0.77 | 268 | 11.1 | 295 | 12.2 | 3 812 | 18.9 | 5 255 | 145 | 3 333 | 1 000 | 4 030 |
| Mecklenburg | 16 015 | 1 036 908 | 1.29 | 13 971 | 14.8 | 5 173 | 5.5 | 152 458 | 18.4 | 107 418 | 21 436 | 47 047 | 41 348 | 4 440 |
| Mitchell | 204 | 15 308 | 0.95 | 140 | 9.1 | 222 | 14.4 | 2 384 | 19.5 | 4 004 | 712 | 1 856 | NA | NA |
| Montgomery | 1 093 | 26 977 | 0.93 | 317 | 11.5 | 244 | 8.8 | 5 114 | 22.8 | 4 843 | 751 | 2 749 | 1 044 | 3 709 |
| Moore | 848 | 86 843 | 0.99 | 926 | 10.4 | 1 064 | 11.9 | 12 756 | 18.7 | 22 525 | 2 983 | 10 202 | 2 191 | 2 506 |
| Nash | 2 210 | 96 463 | 1.03 | 1 191 | 12.4 | 934 | 9.7 | 14 465 | 17.9 | 18 169 | 1 419 | 10 382 | 4 041 | 4 219 |
| New Hanover | 6 698 | 216 437 | 1.17 | 2 249 | 10.9 | 1 613 | 7.8 | 31 595 | 18.7 | 35 560 | 2 570 | 17 752 | 9 865 | 4 855 |
| Northampton | 752 | 20 700 | 0.82 | 206 | 9.4 | 288 | 13.2 | 2 985 | 17.4 | 5 207 | 418 | 3 132 | 565 | 3 129 |
| Onslow | 17 805 | 173 961 | 1.01 | 4 202 | 23.4 | 848 | 4.7 | 23 749 | 16.0 | 18 319 | 1 017 | 7 182 | 5 846 | 3 247 |
| Orange | 9 557 | 138 742 | 1.11 | 1 238 | 9.1 | 686 | 5.1 | 18 280 | 16.4 | 17 210 | 3 147 | 6 191 | 3 972 | 2 931 |
| Pamlico | 705 | 11 666 | 0.72 | 104 | 7.9 | 150 | 11.4 | 1 886 | 19.6 | 3 413 | 125 | 1 659 | 281 | 2 111 |
| Pasquotank | 3 063 | 41 446 | 1.05 | 515 | 12.7 | 354 | 8.7 | 5 789 | 18.0 | 7 055 | 479 | 3 190 | 1 329 | 3 228 |
| Pender | 1 090 | 42 564 | 0.60 | 588 | 11.0 | 455 | 8.5 | 9 343 | 21.5 | 10 151 | 953 | 5 085 | 1 059 | 2 017 |
| Perquimans | 84 | 10 861 | 0.49 | 133 | 9.9 | 133 | 9.9 | 1 911 | 18.1 | 3 447 | 234 | 1 602 | 238 | 1 747 |
| Person | 442 | 33 876 | 0.68 | 446 | 11.3 | 416 | 10.5 | 5 981 | 18.0 | 7 838 | 1 994 | 3 303 | 1 310 | 3 278 |
| Pitt | 6 526 | 166 307 | 1.02 | 2 200 | 12.9 | 1 157 | 6.8 | 25 995 | 17.8 | 23 355 | 1 036 | 12 671 | NA | NA |
| Polk | 330 | 18 223 | 0.73 | 146 | 7.2 | 288 | 14.2 | 3 348 | 21.8 | 5 479 | 660 | 2 619 | 347 | 1 730 |
| Randolph | 1 298 | 124 817 | 0.75 | 1 650 | 11.6 | 1 366 | 9.6 | 24 611 | 20.3 | 26 202 | 11 007 | 8 935 | 5 291 | 3 692 |
| Richmond | 1 160 | 45 283 | 0.92 | 597 | 12.8 | 526 | 11.3 | 8 608 | 22.1 | 10 347 | 454 | 6 144 | 3 099 | 6 562 |
| Robeson | 4 105 | 129 157 | 0.92 | 2 081 | 15.4 | 1 199 | 8.8 | 31 178 | 26.6 | 21 729 | 1 675 | 12 819 | 9 473 | 6 995 |
| Rockingham | 1 055 | 85 699 | 0.80 | 978 | 10.5 | 1 060 | 11.4 | 15 025 | 19.3 | 20 602 | 8 312 | 6 943 | 3 667 | 3 867 |
| Rowan | 4 286 | 130 105 | 0.87 | 1 574 | 11.4 | 1 428 | 10.3 | 24 125 | 21.0 | 26 909 | 6 981 | 10 453 | 5 136 | 3 705 |
| Rutherford | 1 223 | 64 155 | 0.88 | 708 | 10.5 | 793 | 11.7 | 10 824 | 19.5 | 15 019 | 2 139 | 7 628 | 2 263 | 3 520 |
| Sampson | 1 087 | 58 098 | 0.81 | 873 | 13.7 | 585 | 9.2 | 12 779 | 23.8 | 11 938 | 1 005 | 6 674 | 1 940 | 3 069 |
| Scotland | 1 730 | 37 631 | 1.12 | 483 | 13.5 | 362 | 10.1 | 5 565 | 18.7 | 7 622 | 776 | 4 314 | 1 942 | 5 430 |
| Stanly | 2 051 | 54 051 | 0.75 | 693 | 11.4 | 630 | 10.4 | 9 373 | 18.9 | 12 227 | 1 024 | 6 726 | 1 457 | 2 910 |
| Stokes | 456 | 37 022 | 0.49 | 422 | 8.9 | 476 | 10.1 | 6 766 | 17.1 | 8 952 | 4 860 | 2 374 | 1 437 | 2 994 |
| Surry | 870 | 72 168 | 0.96 | 821 | 11.1 | 810 | 11.0 | 13 422 | 22.0 | 15 878 | 6 500 | 5 658 | 2 567 | 3 441 |

1. Per 1,000 estimated resident population.   2. Data for serious crimes have not been adjusted for underreporting; this may affect comparability between geographic areas and over time.   3. Per 100,000 population estimated by the FBI.

# Table B. States and Counties — Crime, Education, Money Income, and Poverty

| | Serious crimes known to police, 2011 (cont.)[1] | | Education | | | | | | Money income, 2007–2011 | | | | Income and poverty, 2011 | | | |
| | Rate[2] | | School enrollment and attainment, 2007–2011 | | | | Local government expenditures,[5] 2009–2010 | | | Households | | | Percent below poverty level | | | |
| | | | Enrollment[3] | | Attainment[4] (percent) | | | | | Median income | | | | | | |
| STATE County | Violent | Property | Total | Per-cent private | High school grad-uate or less | Bach-elor's degree or more | Total current expendi-tures (mil dol) | Current expendi-tures per student (dollars) | Per capita income[6] (dollars) | Dollars | Percent change, 2000 to 2007–2011 (constant 2011 dollars) | Percent with income of $200,000 or more | Median house-hold income (dollars) | All per-sons | Children under 18 years | Children 5 to 17 years in families |
| | 46 | 47 | 48 | 49 | 50 | 51 | 52 | 53 | 54 | 55 | 56 | 57 | 58 | 59 | 60 | 61 |

**NORTH CAROLINA—Cont'd**

| STATE County | 46 | 47 | 48 | 49 | 50 | 51 | 52 | 53 | 54 | 55 | 56 | 57 | 58 | 59 | 60 | 61 |
|---|---|---|---|---|---|---|---|---|---|---|---|---|---|---|---|---|
| Chowan | 174 | 2 884 | 3 548 | 9.8 | 56.5 | 15.5 | 25.6 | 10 582 | 19 808 | 34 565 | -17.2 | 1.6 | 36 231 | 25.1 | 37.5 | 34.6 |
| Clay | 149 | 2 668 | 2 376 | 8.2 | 49.1 | 19.4 | 12.9 | 9 156 | 20 758 | 36 711 | -13.4 | 0.8 | 35 143 | 22.3 | 37.7 | 30.6 |
| Cleveland | 176 | 2 786 | 24 798 | 11.5 | 54.6 | 15.6 | 140.7 | 8 567 | 19 475 | 38 352 | -19.5 | 1.0 | 37 390 | 20.0 | 31.7 | 29.2 |
| Columbus | 344 | 4 525 | 13 601 | 8.4 | 54.5 | 11.6 | 84.6 | 8 778 | 19 010 | 34 938 | -3.5 | 1.4 | 31 282 | 25.9 | 36.8 | 35.1 |
| Craven | 379 | 4 175 | 24 037 | 11.6 | 40.6 | 21.0 | 116.5 | 7 922 | 25 067 | 46 251 | -4.8 | 2.1 | 47 291 | 15.7 | 25.6 | 24.4 |
| Cumberland | 530 | 5 863 | 94 622 | 12.6 | 38.6 | 21.8 | 456.5 | 8 570 | 22 888 | 44 861 | -11.3 | 1.9 | 43 863 | 19.1 | 26.4 | 26.5 |
| Currituck | 222 | 3 149 | 5 676 | 13.2 | 48.8 | 17.0 | 35.8 | 9 028 | 26 487 | 57 588 | 4.5 | 2.2 | 55 665 | 11.7 | 18.2 | 15.5 |
| Dare | 438 | 6 149 | 6 884 | 13.0 | 35.1 | 31.6 | 52.4 | 10 518 | 31 410 | 54 750 | -4.4 | 3.4 | 50 393 | 11.1 | 20.2 | 18.5 |
| Davidson | 222 | 2 764 | 38 186 | 11.4 | 55.9 | 16.8 | 198.3 | 7 495 | 22 624 | 44 728 | -14.3 | 1.4 | 41 631 | 14.7 | 21.6 | 19.5 |
| Davie | 184 | 2 123 | 9 991 | 13.8 | 48.9 | 23.3 | 51.8 | 7 603 | 26 412 | 50 562 | -6.8 | 3.8 | 50 110 | 11.8 | 17.9 | 16.1 |
| Duplin | 352 | 2 818 | 13 600 | 9.3 | 60.0 | 10.7 | 75.1 | 8 311 | 17 354 | 34 264 | -15.1 | 0.9 | 35 587 | 20.2 | 29.6 | 28.2 |
| Durham | 661 | 4 796 | 76 001 | 27.2 | 31.8 | 44.3 | 336.3 | 9 536 | 27 988 | 50 078 | -14.4 | 3.8 | 47 007 | 19.5 | 27.2 | 26.5 |
| Edgecombe | 515 | 4 192 | 14 690 | 7.1 | 60.0 | 10.6 | 62.8 | 8 265 | 17 808 | 34 198 | -18.3 | 0.8 | 32 901 | 25.6 | 39.9 | 35.9 |
| Forsyth | 547 | 5 074 | 90 555 | 20.3 | 40.6 | 31.3 | 492.3 | 9 012 | 26 424 | 46 417 | -18.3 | 3.6 | 43 804 | 18.6 | 28.0 | 24.7 |
| Franklin | 165 | 2 538 | 14 614 | 18.3 | 54.3 | 15.4 | 67.8 | 7 876 | 21 718 | 44 598 | -15.2 | 1.3 | 42 269 | 16.2 | 23.9 | 21.3 |
| Gaston | 394 | 3 581 | 50 868 | 13.5 | 50.2 | 18.0 | 253.4 | 7 597 | 22 808 | 43 052 | -19.2 | 2.5 | 40 969 | 16.6 | 24.1 | 21.3 |
| Gates | NA | NA | 2 931 | 10.6 | 57.2 | 10.7 | 19.0 | 9 894 | 21 164 | 45 183 | -6.1 | 0.9 | 41 437 | 16.6 | 23.6 | 20.4 |
| Graham | NA | NA | 1 897 | 8.1 | 57.2 | 12.1 | 12.5 | 9 975 | 18 999 | 32 255 | -10.3 | 1.9 | 33 041 | 22.1 | 35.4 | 32.7 |
| Granville | 392 | 3 421 | 14 412 | 12.3 | 52.6 | 15.3 | 70.7 | 7 905 | 22 387 | 49 090 | -9.0 | 1.3 | 48 596 | 16.1 | 20.8 | 18.0 |
| Greene | 222 | 2 834 | 5 258 | 6.9 | 58.5 | 11.2 | 32.5 | 9 583 | 17 617 | 41 073 | -5.2 | 1.2 | 35 013 | 25.8 | 35.5 | 33.6 |
| Guilford | 442 | 3 949 | 134 863 | 13.9 | 39.2 | 32.8 | 665.4 | 8 922 | 26 644 | 46 288 | -19.6 | 3.6 | 44 229 | 18.8 | 24.2 | 22.1 |
| Halifax | 428 | 3 830 | 13 078 | 11.6 | 61.7 | 11.5 | 83.7 | 9 923 | 17 934 | 31 370 | -12.2 | 1.1 | 31 084 | 26.8 | 39.1 | 36.5 |
| Harnett | 294 | 2 744 | 33 729 | 16.9 | 48.1 | 16.9 | 141.6 | 7 342 | 19 749 | 42 965 | -9.4 | 1.0 | 40 617 | 18.5 | 25.5 | 23.9 |
| Haywood | 264 | 2 670 | 11 717 | 11.3 | 45.5 | 22.3 | 66.9 | 8 469 | 24 700 | 41 768 | -8.8 | 1.7 | 40 114 | 18.6 | 32.4 | 29.7 |
| Henderson | 137 | 2 168 | 21 228 | 14.6 | 39.2 | 27.5 | 110.8 | 8 166 | 27 175 | 47 371 | -7.9 | 2.6 | 46 165 | 13.3 | 22.8 | 20.5 |
| Hertford | 252 | 2 830 | 6 322 | 21.9 | 56.7 | 14.7 | 33.4 | 10 105 | 17 425 | 31 969 | -10.4 | 0.9 | 31 581 | 28.3 | 37.5 | 34.8 |
| Hoke | 170 | 2 696 | 13 845 | 13.5 | 45.5 | 16.1 | 66.4 | 8 379 | 18 885 | 46 540 | 3.7 | 0.5 | 42 908 | 18.7 | 28.8 | 29.2 |
| Hyde | NA | NA | 1 338 | 25.3 | 61.2 | 10.7 | 10.9 | 17 279 | 16 397 | 40 753 | 6.1 | 0.3 | 35 810 | 22.5 | 30.5 | 28.8 |
| Iredell | 315 | 3 279 | 39 547 | 11.6 | 45.1 | 22.6 | 224.6 | 7 725 | 26 685 | 51 139 | -9.6 | 4.0 | 49 902 | 13.5 | 20.2 | 17.4 |
| Jackson | 351 | 2 643 | 12 107 | 4.4 | 44.0 | 27.1 | 33.8 | 8 851 | 20 226 | 36 826 | -16.2 | 1.1 | 37 388 | 20.2 | 27.2 | 26.4 |
| Johnston | 189 | 2 640 | 43 876 | 11.0 | 47.3 | 19.8 | 259.2 | 8 034 | 22 731 | 49 888 | -9.6 | 1.6 | 48 380 | 15.3 | 21.7 | 19.3 |
| Jones | NA | NA | 1 963 | 12.0 | 55.1 | 12.5 | 14.9 | 11 798 | 21 099 | 40 687 | -2.4 | 1.8 | 38 230 | 19.0 | 33.4 | 31.2 |
| Lee | 207 | 2 835 | 14 050 | 9.7 | 48.0 | 19.2 | 78.9 | 7 988 | 21 695 | 44 836 | -14.6 | 1.1 | 41 506 | 20.0 | 30.9 | 28.6 |
| Lenoir | 635 | 4 108 | 15 497 | 7.6 | 53.5 | 14.2 | 78.6 | 7 965 | 19 413 | 33 749 | -19.9 | 0.9 | 32 602 | 25.4 | 36.3 | 35.0 |
| Lincoln | 170 | 2 501 | 18 767 | 9.4 | 47.8 | 19.7 | 101.3 | 7 595 | 25 485 | 50 279 | -10.1 | 3.7 | 50 746 | 14.2 | 21.8 | 19.8 |
| McDowell | 123 | 2 809 | 9 736 | 8.5 | 57.2 | 13.9 | 55.2 | 8 242 | 19 377 | 35 230 | -19.5 | 1.4 | 35 627 | 19.5 | 33.5 | 31.5 |
| Macon | 99 | 2 422 | 5 921 | 13.5 | 48.2 | 19.8 | 40.0 | 9 107 | 24 914 | 38 653 | -10.9 | 2.3 | 36 953 | 19.0 | 30.4 | 28.6 |
| Madison | 26 | 1 481 | 4 875 | 24.9 | 56.7 | 16.6 | 23.6 | 8 997 | 19 538 | 38 063 | -9.0 | 0.7 | 36 724 | 21.2 | 29.6 | 27.4 |
| Martin | 459 | 3 570 | 6 008 | 7.7 | 55.3 | 12.9 | 38.9 | 9 718 | 19 286 | 36 345 | -6.5 | 1.0 | 33 305 | 24.8 | 36.9 | 32.8 |
| Mecklenburg | 540 | 3 900 | 248 304 | 20.3 | 31.3 | 40.4 | 1 174.0 | 8 228 | 32 506 | 55 994 | -18.0 | 6.0 | 52 111 | 17.1 | 23.8 | 22.1 |
| Mitchell | NA | NA | 3 322 | 6.9 | 59.8 | 13.7 | 21.7 | 10 107 | 19 133 | 36 165 | -12.2 | 0.9 | 35 322 | 19.2 | 29.7 | 27.3 |
| Montgomery | 220 | 3 488 | 6 600 | 6.1 | 56.8 | 14.5 | 41.4 | 9 406 | 18 816 | 32 946 | -25.8 | 1.9 | 30 684 | 27.3 | 37.7 | 36.2 |
| Moore | 223 | 2 283 | 19 610 | 13.7 | 37.8 | 29.3 | 104.9 | 8 100 | 26 981 | 48 348 | -13.2 | 3.6 | 47 301 | 15.1 | 23.1 | 20.1 |
| Nash | 493 | 3 726 | 24 584 | 13.3 | 51.9 | 18.9 | 157.1 | 8 390 | 23 602 | 45 052 | -10.2 | 2.3 | 43 151 | 19.7 | 29.3 | 26.8 |
| New Hanover | 419 | 4 436 | 53 718 | 13.1 | 32.3 | 36.0 | 223.8 | 8 949 | 29 981 | 48 893 | -9.9 | 4.1 | 45 890 | 17.5 | 24.2 | 22.6 |
| Northampton | 166 | 2 963 | 5 074 | 15.1 | 64.6 | 11.5 | 33.1 | 9 822 | 17 676 | 32 090 | -10.8 | 0.4 | 31 668 | 25.6 | 38.8 | 36.5 |
| Onslow | 237 | 3 011 | 42 507 | 13.4 | 41.3 | 18.0 | 184.0 | 7 642 | 21 391 | 45 457 | -0.3 | 1.5 | 45 434 | 16.0 | 22.4 | 22.8 |
| Orange | 165 | 2 766 | 48 168 | 11.4 | 25.7 | 54.6 | 201.2 | 10 552 | 33 897 | 56 055 | -2.0 | 9.1 | 56 792 | 17.0 | 16.8 | 14.8 |
| Pamlico | 203 | 1 908 | 2 735 | 10.3 | 48.9 | 18.1 | 18.5 | 10 448 | 23 996 | 43 658 | -5.1 | 2.4 | 41 325 | 18.6 | 33.1 | 31.1 |
| Pasquotank | 398 | 2 829 | 11 437 | 12.4 | 47.9 | 19.8 | 55.9 | 9 038 | 23 573 | 45 298 | 10.2 | 3.2 | 40 261 | 21.2 | 30.6 | 26.1 |
| Pender | 276 | 1 741 | 12 077 | 11.4 | 49.0 | 19.3 | 66.6 | 7 969 | 23 189 | 44 568 | -8.1 | 2.4 | 44 171 | 16.4 | 25.9 | 25.3 |
| Perquimans | 110 | 1 637 | 3 255 | 12.7 | 51.8 | 16.7 | 18.2 | 9 968 | 21 435 | 37 862 | -5.1 | 2.2 | 39 112 | 18.6 | 31.2 | 28.3 |
| Person | 320 | 2 958 | 10 021 | 11.5 | 56.2 | 14.0 | 51.9 | 8 425 | 21 962 | 43 271 | -13.8 | 0.6 | 42 303 | 18.1 | 25.2 | 22.6 |
| Pitt | NA | NA | 59 175 | 8.8 | 40.9 | 28.0 | 194.1 | 8 303 | 22 656 | 39 824 | -10.3 | 2.7 | 39 713 | 24.9 | 28.4 | 26.9 |
| Polk | 90 | 1 640 | 4 013 | 11.9 | 44.4 | 26.7 | 25.5 | 9 846 | 24 499 | 43 332 | -11.5 | 1.5 | 41 851 | 16.5 | 25.3 | 22.8 |
| Randolph | 144 | 3 548 | 32 983 | 9.6 | 58.4 | 13.8 | 189.2 | 7 983 | 21 384 | 40 602 | -21.6 | 1.4 | 40 749 | 16.2 | 24.9 | 21.8 |
| Richmond | 531 | 6 030 | 11 855 | 10.7 | 60.3 | 11.2 | 69.1 | 8 724 | 16 610 | 31 847 | -18.2 | 0.7 | 32 932 | 25.2 | 37.8 | 34.7 |
| Robeson | 771 | 6 224 | 37 173 | 3.8 | 63.1 | 12.5 | 207.4 | 8 625 | 15 689 | 30 874 | -18.9 | 1.3 | 30 931 | 30.9 | 43.1 | 41.8 |
| Rockingham | 217 | 3 650 | 21 603 | 8.8 | 58.3 | 13.1 | 119.6 | 8 363 | 20 861 | 38 311 | -16.0 | 1.0 | 36 746 | 16.7 | 25.1 | 23.1 |
| Rowan | 313 | 3 392 | 33 375 | 15.7 | 53.7 | 17.4 | 170.3 | 8 156 | 21 658 | 43 121 | -14.8 | 1.7 | 40 267 | 18.9 | 29.2 | 27.4 |
| Rutherford | 235 | 3 285 | 16 374 | 9.3 | 52.1 | 15.3 | 90.0 | 8 642 | 19 550 | 37 128 | -11.6 | 1.3 | 35 208 | 20.5 | 32.0 | 29.2 |
| Sampson | 172 | 2 896 | 15 892 | 7.9 | 59.2 | 12.6 | 97.8 | 8 342 | 19 442 | 36 832 | -14.2 | 1.1 | 36 471 | 23.8 | 31.3 | 28.2 |
| Scotland | 473 | 4 957 | 9 615 | 10.3 | 59.2 | 14.0 | 71.1 | 10 686 | 16 526 | 30 465 | -27.2 | 0.9 | 32 999 | 27.9 | 44.4 | 41.7 |
| Stanly | 232 | 2 678 | 14 913 | 15.1 | 55.7 | 15.0 | 81.7 | 8 385 | 20 868 | 43 424 | -12.8 | 1.5 | 38 301 | 17.5 | 25.2 | 22.9 |
| Stokes | 358 | 2 635 | 10 197 | 10.7 | 61.5 | 11.3 | 59.9 | 8 408 | 21 021 | 43 099 | -17.7 | 0.7 | 42 147 | 15.9 | 21.0 | 19.0 |
| Surry | 227 | 3 214 | 16 423 | 8.7 | 55.2 | 14.9 | 89.9 | 8 240 | 20 391 | 36 788 | -17.5 | 1.3 | 35 269 | 21.6 | 29.9 | 25.5 |

1. Data for serious crimes have not been adjusted for underreporting; this may affect comparability between geographic areas and over time. 2. Per 100,000 population estimated by the FBI. 3. All persons 3 years old and over enrolled in nursery school through college. 4. Persons 25 years old and over. 5. Elementary and secondary education expenditures. 6. Based on population estimated by the American Community Survey, 2007–2011.

# Table B. States and Counties — Personal Income

| STATE County | Total (mil dol) | Percent change, 2010–2011[2] | Per capita[1] Dollars | Per capita Rank | Wages and salaries[2] (mil dol) | Proprietors' income (mil dol) | Dividends, interest, and rent (mil dol) | Transfer payments (mil dol) Total | Government payments to individuals Total | Social Security | Medical payments | Income mainte-nance | Unemploy-ment insurance |
|---|---|---|---|---|---|---|---|---|---|---|---|---|---|
| | 62 | 63 | 64 | 65 | 66 | 67 | 68 | 69 | 70 | 71 | 72 | 73 | 74 |
| **NORTH CAROLINA—Cont'd** | | | | | | | | | | | | | |
| Chowan | 487 | 4.2 | 32 765 | 1 748 | 204 | 48 | 94 | 144 | 140 | 49 | 60 | 19 | 6 |
| Clay | 292 | 3.5 | 27 642 | 2 665 | 72 | 16 | 62 | 105 | 103 | 43 | 42 | 10 | 3 |
| Cleveland | 3 027 | 4.2 | 31 046 | 2 089 | 1 473 | 134 | 381 | 951 | 929 | 314 | 387 | 120 | 54 |
| Columbus | 1 644 | 2.2 | 28 491 | 2 540 | 681 | 130 | 195 | 622 | 609 | 168 | 296 | 87 | 25 |
| Craven | 3 836 | 4.5 | 36 610 | 1 124 | 3 028 | 199 | 625 | 832 | 811 | 274 | 330 | 93 | 37 |
| Cumberland | 14 515 | 7.0 | 44 678 | 407 | 13 209 | 450 | 1 560 | 2 486 | 2 426 | 587 | 883 | 377 | 141 |
| Currituck | 957 | 6.4 | 39 949 | 752 | 243 | 54 | 114 | 155 | 150 | 55 | 60 | 14 | 8 |
| Dare | 1 325 | 5.3 | 38 633 | 891 | 721 | 129 | 310 | 246 | 239 | 99 | 88 | 19 | 22 |
| Davidson | 5 389 | 4.4 | 33 121 | 1 687 | 1 784 | 427 | 672 | 1 267 | 1 231 | 465 | 483 | 147 | 80 |
| Davie | 1 490 | 4.7 | 35 863 | 1 235 | 410 | 90 | 278 | 325 | 316 | 130 | 128 | 27 | 19 |
| Duplin | 1 676 | 0.4 | 28 142 | 2 596 | 775 | 328 | 165 | 432 | 418 | 121 | 187 | 67 | 18 |
| Durham | 10 568 | 3.8 | 38 654 | 888 | 15 276 | 929 | 1 597 | 1 718 | 1 658 | 512 | 696 | 225 | 103 |
| Edgecombe | 1 525 | 2.1 | 27 218 | 2 734 | 885 | 89 | 203 | 575 | 563 | 146 | 251 | 99 | 31 |
| Forsyth | 13 489 | 5.7 | 38 003 | 970 | 10 323 | 1 082 | 2 475 | 2 603 | 2 525 | 906 | 1 019 | 289 | 152 |
| Franklin | 1 814 | 3.1 | 29 670 | 2 348 | 581 | 138 | 183 | 437 | 424 | 138 | 187 | 51 | 26 |
| Gaston | 6 889 | 3.5 | 33 275 | 1 660 | 3 125 | 423 | 932 | 1 737 | 1 692 | 575 | 729 | 208 | 98 |
| Gates | 325 | 2.8 | 27 020 | 2 762 | 65 | 29 | 39 | 89 | 87 | 31 | 36 | 11 | 3 |
| Graham | 221 | 2.9 | 25 099 | 2 957 | 94 | 19 | 27 | 82 | 80 | 26 | 36 | 9 | 5 |
| Granville | 1 716 | 5.4 | 28 605 | 2 523 | 1 119 | 72 | 226 | 395 | 382 | 138 | 153 | 49 | 23 |
| Greene | 567 | 1.3 | 26 317 | 2 847 | 185 | 69 | 57 | 155 | 150 | 42 | 68 | 25 | 7 |
| Guilford | 18 816 | 5.0 | 37 990 | 973 | 14 946 | 1 423 | 3 197 | 3 522 | 3 413 | 1 184 | 1 288 | 442 | 235 |
| Halifax | 1 608 | 3.7 | 29 674 | 2 347 | 720 | 98 | 221 | 598 | 586 | 172 | 255 | 102 | 26 |
| Harnett | 3 488 | 5.1 | 29 247 | 2 418 | 931 | 283 | 381 | 788 | 762 | 225 | 310 | 109 | 45 |
| Haywood | 1 854 | 3.2 | 31 496 | 2 003 | 733 | 129 | 333 | 574 | 561 | 224 | 220 | 57 | 26 |
| Henderson | 3 869 | 5.3 | 35 853 | 1 239 | 1 601 | 195 | 882 | 961 | 937 | 411 | 379 | 71 | 33 |
| Hertford | 665 | 1.2 | 27 208 | 2 736 | 399 | 36 | 79 | 223 | 217 | 63 | 96 | 35 | 8 |
| Hoke | 1 669 | 12.9 | 33 868 | 1 537 | 310 | 63 | 115 | 309 | 299 | 70 | 113 | 56 | 18 |
| Hyde | 172 | 6.6 | 29 572 | 2 369 | 82 | 33 | 29 | 43 | 42 | 12 | 19 | 6 | 3 |
| Iredell | 5 409 | 6.3 | 33 556 | 1 591 | 3 382 | 256 | 813 | 1 160 | 1 124 | 413 | 472 | 107 | 79 |
| Jackson | 1 137 | 3.5 | 28 218 | 2 582 | 633 | 79 | 201 | 290 | 281 | 100 | 106 | 26 | 16 |
| Johnston | 5 894 | 6.9 | 34 149 | 1 491 | 2 064 | 401 | 573 | 1 135 | 1 096 | 358 | 461 | 144 | 69 |
| Jones | 351 | 4.1 | 34 983 | 1 377 | 79 | 37 | 40 | 97 | 95 | 28 | 43 | 12 | 4 |
| Lee | 1 928 | 3.5 | 32 815 | 1 738 | 1 302 | 144 | 270 | 480 | 467 | 152 | 192 | 56 | 30 |
| Lenoir | 1 900 | 2.7 | 32 022 | 1 882 | 1 173 | 98 | 282 | 623 | 610 | 176 | 289 | 81 | 22 |
| Lincoln | 2 705 | 5.6 | 34 275 | 1 474 | 887 | 65 | 312 | 561 | 543 | 201 | 228 | 58 | 37 |
| McDowell | 1 178 | 4.1 | 26 114 | 2 868 | 629 | 47 | 137 | 392 | 382 | 141 | 149 | 45 | 22 |
| Macon | 1 031 | 4.2 | 30 248 | 2 246 | 447 | 61 | 254 | 331 | 324 | 137 | 131 | 28 | 13 |
| Madison | 595 | 3.3 | 28 579 | 2 528 | 159 | 41 | 82 | 187 | 183 | 63 | 79 | 21 | 7 |
| Martin | 740 | 2.7 | 30 613 | 2 173 | 330 | 50 | 101 | 247 | 242 | 72 | 114 | 32 | 13 |
| Mecklenburg | 43 073 | 7.3 | 45 610 | 357 | 41 191 | 5 287 | 6 009 | 5 379 | 5 170 | 1 637 | 1 924 | 808 | 471 |
| Mitchell | 422 | 3.6 | 27 345 | 2 711 | 222 | 12 | 64 | 148 | 145 | 52 | 63 | 13 | 6 |
| Montgomery | 779 | 4.1 | 28 145 | 2 595 | 370 | 61 | 116 | 229 | 223 | 73 | 95 | 29 | 10 |
| Moore | 3 438 | 5.1 | 38 477 | 911 | 1 467 | 224 | 933 | 808 | 788 | 335 | 306 | 63 | 27 |
| Nash | 3 249 | 3.7 | 33 807 | 1 548 | 1 936 | 202 | 459 | 803 | 782 | 254 | 306 | 115 | 49 |
| New Hanover | 7 445 | 5.6 | 36 108 | 1 199 | 5 223 | 728 | 1 491 | 1 528 | 1 483 | 536 | 595 | 146 | 90 |
| Northampton | 641 | 3.0 | 29 282 | 2 411 | 212 | 43 | 78 | 225 | 220 | 69 | 100 | 35 | 7 |
| Onslow | 8 296 | 5.1 | 46 163 | 333 | 7 095 | 186 | 761 | 1 007 | 978 | 243 | 362 | 134 | 46 |
| Orange | 6 609 | 5.5 | 48 683 | 246 | 4 014 | 254 | 1 316 | 730 | 700 | 257 | 296 | 66 | 31 |
| Pamlico | 487 | 5.2 | 36 883 | 1 088 | 126 | 34 | 88 | 123 | 120 | 48 | 48 | 12 | 3 |
| Pasquotank | 1 167 | 4.0 | 28 673 | 2 511 | 828 | 82 | 169 | 331 | 322 | 93 | 133 | 43 | 14 |
| Pender | 1 650 | 4.9 | 30 907 | 2 123 | 433 | 86 | 217 | 415 | 403 | 146 | 162 | 46 | 24 |
| Perquimans | 407 | 5.3 | 30 207 | 2 253 | 74 | 51 | 69 | 125 | 122 | 47 | 50 | 14 | 5 |
| Person | 1 165 | 2.5 | 29 386 | 2 397 | 453 | 48 | 141 | 332 | 323 | 116 | 131 | 38 | 19 |
| Pitt | 5 620 | 5.5 | 32 841 | 1 733 | 3 648 | 259 | 769 | 1 223 | 1 185 | 329 | 494 | 182 | 64 |
| Polk | 753 | 4.7 | 37 190 | 1 060 | 194 | 58 | 206 | 182 | 177 | 81 | 69 | 14 | 5 |
| Randolph | 4 183 | 3.2 | 29 385 | 2 398 | 1 963 | 217 | 505 | 1 090 | 1 059 | 385 | 430 | 131 | 61 |
| Richmond | 1 285 | 1.2 | 27 560 | 2 677 | 603 | 60 | 142 | 502 | 491 | 134 | 204 | 75 | 24 |
| Robeson | 3 365 | 2.4 | 24 834 | 2 980 | 1 587 | 165 | 322 | 1 284 | 1 254 | 288 | 592 | 235 | 58 |
| Rockingham | 2 881 | 3.7 | 30 868 | 2 129 | 1 205 | 114 | 381 | 861 | 841 | 303 | 362 | 95 | 44 |
| Rowan | 4 112 | 2.4 | 29 792 | 2 324 | 2 350 | 96 | 639 | 1 151 | 1 120 | 395 | 430 | 131 | 68 |
| Rutherford | 1 732 | 3.5 | 25 640 | 2 917 | 752 | 114 | 243 | 602 | 587 | 217 | 231 | 74 | 30 |
| Sampson | 1 875 | 1.2 | 29 426 | 2 390 | 809 | 198 | 219 | 530 | 515 | 159 | 226 | 77 | 22 |
| Scotland | 1 017 | 1.1 | 28 364 | 2 562 | 533 | 59 | 122 | 386 | 378 | 110 | 157 | 70 | 20 |
| Stanly | 1 833 | 3.6 | 30 227 | 2 249 | 781 | 110 | 253 | 496 | 482 | 178 | 198 | 51 | 29 |
| Stokes | 1 420 | 4.0 | 30 062 | 2 278 | 290 | 84 | 152 | 348 | 338 | 134 | 137 | 33 | 20 |
| Surry | 2 209 | 3.2 | 29 962 | 2 296 | 1 171 | 135 | 318 | 658 | 641 | 219 | 291 | 70 | 28 |

1. Based on the resident population estimated as of July 1 of the year shown.   2. Includes supplements to wages and salaries.

# Table B. States and Counties — **Earnings, Social Security, and Housing**

| STATE County | Total (mil dol) | Farm | Total | Manu-facturing | Information and professional and technical services | Retail trade | Finance, insurance, and real estate | Health care and social services | Govern-ment | Number | Rate[2] | Supple-mental Security Income recipients, December 2011 | Total | Percent change, 2000–2010 |
|---|---|---|---|---|---|---|---|---|---|---|---|---|---|---|
| | 75 | 76 | 77 | 78 | 79 | 80 | 81 | 82 | 83 | 84 | 85 | 86 | 87 | 88 |
| **NORTH CAROLINA—Cont'd** | | | | | | | | | | | | | | |
| Chowan | 253 | 9.3 | 13.8 | 8.7 | 4.8 | 7.3 | 4.0 | D | 17.4 | 4 065 | 274 | 579 | 7 289 | 13.1 |
| Clay | 88 | 0.9 | D | 4.4 | 3.6 | 19.7 | 5.8 | D | 28.3 | 3 445 | 326 | 324 | 7 140 | 31.6 |
| Cleveland | 1 607 | 1.2 | 27.5 | 22.5 | 2.9 | 8.4 | 3.4 | D | 17.4 | 24 560 | 252 | 3 154 | 43 373 | 7.7 |
| Columbus | 811 | 3.8 | 21.2 | 17.6 | 4.1 | 8.5 | 5.0 | 16.1 | 22.2 | 14 395 | 249 | 3 250 | 26 042 | 8.2 |
| Craven | 3 227 | 0.6 | 9.6 | 6.4 | 5.1 | 4.5 | 2.9 | 7.4 | 58.3 | 21 630 | 206 | 2 381 | 45 002 | 17.8 |
| Cumberland | 13 658 | 0.1 | D | 3.8 | 3.8 | 3.7 | 1.8 | 4.2 | 68.9 | 49 155 | 151 | 9 512 | 135 524 | 14.4 |
| Currituck | 297 | 2.0 | D | 0.9 | D | 11.1 | 14.1 | D | 20.7 | 4 305 | 180 | 302 | 14 453 | 35.3 |
| Dare | 850 | 0.0 | D | 2.3 | D | 12.5 | 14.0 | 6.5 | 21.0 | 7 205 | 210 | 307 | 33 492 | 25.6 |
| Davidson | 2 211 | 0.5 | 28.5 | 21.2 | 4.6 | 7.3 | 4.2 | 10.4 | 15.5 | 35 330 | 217 | 3 165 | 72 655 | 16.4 |
| Davie | 500 | 1.0 | 23.3 | 16.0 | 4.4 | 10.8 | 5.5 | 9.2 | 16.2 | 9 540 | 230 | 578 | 18 238 | 22.0 |
| Duplin | 1 104 | 16.7 | D | 23.9 | D | 4.7 | 2.0 | D | 15.3 | 10 630 | 179 | 1 879 | 25 728 | 25.4 |
| Durham | 16 205 | 0.0 | D | 26.5 | 15.6 | 2.7 | 6.8 | 15.1 | 9.4 | 37 250 | 136 | 5 723 | 120 217 | 25.9 |
| Edgecombe | 974 | 2.7 | D | 18.1 | D | 8.0 | 2.4 | D | 24.8 | 12 470 | 223 | 2 852 | 24 838 | 3.5 |
| Forsyth | 11 405 | 0.0 | 17.5 | 13.7 | 8.6 | 7.3 | 9.8 | 16.7 | 9.9 | 65 215 | 184 | 7 147 | 156 872 | 17.9 |
| Franklin | 719 | 1.3 | D | 22.1 | 5.3 | 5.8 | 3.3 | 8.7 | 17.4 | 10 935 | 179 | 1 485 | 26 577 | 30.5 |
| Gaston | 3 548 | 0.1 | D | 20.8 | 4.8 | 8.7 | 4.5 | 17.6 | 14.7 | 43 555 | 210 | 5 239 | 88 686 | 12.4 |
| Gates | 95 | 25.6 | D | D | 1.9 | 4.6 | 2.2 | 5.2 | 27.8 | 2 595 | 215 | 313 | 5 208 | 18.6 |
| Graham | 112 | 0.4 | D | D | D | 5.3 | 3.3 | 5.9 | 21.2 | 2 305 | 262 | 312 | 5 930 | 16.7 |
| Granville | 1 191 | 0.9 | D | 26.9 | 1.6 | 4.3 | 1.8 | 4.1 | 45.1 | 11 260 | 188 | 1 492 | 22 827 | 27.5 |
| Greene | 255 | 9.8 | 14.4 | 5.7 | D | 4.1 | 3.3 | 10.2 | 35.2 | 3 635 | 169 | 740 | 8 213 | 11.5 |
| Guilford | 16 370 | 0.1 | 18.9 | 14.2 | 9.5 | 6.6 | 10.1 | 12.0 | 12.3 | 85 920 | 173 | 10 389 | 218 017 | 20.9 |
| Halifax | 818 | 5.6 | 17.4 | 13.5 | 2.1 | 9.1 | 3.5 | 9.9 | 27.8 | 14 875 | 275 | 4 053 | 25 781 | 1.9 |
| Harnett | 1 214 | 2.1 | D | 4.3 | 6.6 | 9.6 | 6.2 | 8.1 | 22.8 | 18 625 | 156 | 2 829 | 46 731 | 21.1 |
| Haywood | 862 | 1.2 | D | 17.7 | 5.5 | 10.9 | 5.3 | 10.5 | 24.1 | 17 355 | 295 | 1 674 | 34 954 | 22.0 |
| Henderson | 1 797 | 2.0 | 25.4 | 18.8 | 4.3 | 8.8 | 5.4 | 15.3 | 16.2 | 30 175 | 280 | 1 823 | 54 710 | 27.2 |
| Hertford | 435 | 3.6 | 24.1 | 19.1 | D | 6.6 | 3.4 | D | 18.2 | 5 385 | 220 | 1 271 | 10 635 | 9.4 |
| Hoke | 373 | 3.3 | D | 20.8 | D | 5.7 | 2.4 | 8.4 | 28.9 | 6 180 | 125 | 1 361 | 18 211 | 45.4 |
| Hyde | 115 | 26.5 | 7.2 | 2.5 | D | 4.6 | 2.4 | 1.7 | 30.8 | 1 080 | 206 | 206 | 3 347 | 1.4 |
| Iredell | 3 637 | 0.8 | D | 15.8 | D | 7.7 | 3.2 | 10.1 | 12.7 | 30 725 | 191 | 2 407 | 69 013 | 32.9 |
| Jackson | 713 | 1.2 | D | 2.3 | D | 6.7 | 3.4 | 13.3 | 42.2 | 7 945 | 197 | 698 | 25 948 | 34.5 |
| Johnston | 2 465 | 1.6 | 31.9 | 22.7 | 4.1 | 9.0 | 4.1 | 7.0 | 18.9 | 28 575 | 166 | 3 996 | 67 682 | 34.9 |
| Jones | 116 | 20.4 | 9.5 | 1.3 | D | 4.6 | D | D | 21.0 | 2 475 | 247 | 364 | 4 838 | 3.3 |
| Lee | 1 446 | 0.3 | 46.6 | 42.0 | D | 6.6 | 3.0 | 8.7 | 11.6 | 11 760 | 200 | 1 297 | 24 136 | 20.8 |
| Lenoir | 1 270 | 1.9 | D | 17.8 | 5.3 | 7.1 | 4.1 | 10.2 | 25.1 | 14 780 | 249 | 2 721 | 27 437 | 0.9 |
| Lincoln | 951 | 1.2 | D | 25.6 | 4.4 | 9.1 | 3.1 | D | 20.2 | 15 025 | 190 | 1 389 | 33 641 | 30.8 |
| McDowell | 675 | 0.9 | 43.0 | 37.9 | D | 8.3 | 2.6 | 9.6 | 17.9 | 11 460 | 254 | 1 317 | 20 808 | 13.3 |
| Macon | 508 | 0.4 | 17.7 | 7.4 | 10.0 | 11.1 | 5.4 | 13.6 | 18.2 | 10 780 | 316 | 835 | 25 245 | 21.7 |
| Madison | 200 | 1.6 | D | 9.9 | D | 5.7 | 2.9 | D | 22.4 | 5 455 | 262 | 800 | 10 608 | 9.1 |
| Martin | 381 | 8.6 | 30.6 | 25.8 | 2.8 | 7.8 | 3.2 | D | 19.8 | 6 010 | 249 | 1 106 | 11 704 | 7.3 |
| Mecklenburg | 46 478 | 0.1 | 11.2 | 6.2 | 15.1 | 5.3 | 18.4 | 6.9 | 10.3 | 117 520 | 124 | 15 883 | 398 510 | 36.1 |
| Mitchell | 234 | 0.8 | D | D | 1.5 | 8.6 | 3.3 | 16.3 | 23.3 | 4 460 | 289 | 491 | 8 713 | 10.1 |
| Montgomery | 431 | 2.7 | D | 30.8 | D | 8.6 | 2.7 | D | 19.8 | 5 855 | 212 | 770 | 15 914 | 12.5 |
| Moore | 1 691 | 1.1 | D | 6.6 | 8.7 | 7.5 | 5.8 | 27.6 | 13.5 | 24 250 | 271 | 1 484 | 43 940 | 25.0 |
| Nash | 2 138 | 2.1 | D | 22.6 | 6.3 | 7.5 | 5.2 | 9.6 | 15.5 | 20 375 | 212 | 3 398 | 42 286 | 14.1 |
| New Hanover | 5 951 | 0.0 | D | 9.8 | 12.5 | 8.6 | 6.9 | 12.7 | 19.0 | 38 820 | 188 | 4 119 | 101 436 | 27.4 |
| Northampton | 254 | 10.1 | D | 8.3 | D | 14.8 | D | 7.6 | 23.7 | 5 945 | 272 | 1 348 | 11 674 | 11.7 |
| Onslow | 7 280 | 0.3 | D | 0.6 | 1.9 | 3.2 | 1.3 | 2.3 | 81.1 | 20 805 | 116 | 2 650 | 68 226 | 22.4 |
| Orange | 4 268 | 0.4 | 4.3 | 2.1 | 7.6 | 5.4 | 6.3 | 5.6 | 58.8 | 17 755 | 131 | 1 644 | 55 597 | 16.5 |
| Pamlico | 160 | 8.9 | D | 3.8 | 4.7 | 7.4 | 3.9 | D | 28.2 | 3 775 | 286 | 311 | 7 534 | 11.1 |
| Pasquotank | 911 | 2.1 | 6.8 | 4.1 | 6.5 | 8.8 | 4.6 | 9.3 | 44.6 | 7 905 | 194 | 1 187 | 16 833 | 17.8 |
| Pender | 519 | 7.4 | 17.9 | 8.4 | 4.0 | 7.2 | 4.1 | D | 24.6 | 11 390 | 213 | 1 120 | 26 724 | 28.6 |
| Perquimans | 125 | 25.4 | 7.6 | 1.5 | D | 4.5 | 5.6 | D | 25.0 | 3 760 | 279 | 377 | 6 986 | 15.7 |
| Person | 501 | 0.8 | D | 16.6 | 2.9 | 9.6 | 3.7 | 9.7 | 19.7 | 9 195 | 232 | 1 086 | 18 193 | 17.3 |
| Pitt | 3 906 | 0.8 | D | 11.2 | 4.4 | 7.3 | 4.6 | 12.6 | 37.4 | 26 490 | 155 | 5 692 | 74 990 | 28.5 |
| Polk | 253 | 3.4 | 14.8 | 4.4 | 6.4 | 6.0 | 9.8 | 24.9 | 16.8 | 5 940 | 293 | 297 | 11 432 | 24.4 |
| Randolph | 2 180 | 1.2 | D | 33.2 | 2.7 | 6.2 | 3.3 | 9.3 | 14.8 | 29 905 | 210 | 2 950 | 61 041 | 12.1 |
| Richmond | 663 | 1.8 | 24.2 | 18.0 | 3.9 | 9.0 | 2.6 | 14.0 | 21.7 | 11 270 | 242 | 2 170 | 20 738 | 4.3 |
| Robeson | 1 752 | 2.5 | 19.4 | 14.6 | 2.5 | 8.4 | 3.6 | 18.9 | 24.8 | 25 955 | 192 | 7 352 | 52 751 | 10.5 |
| Rockingham | 1 319 | 0.5 | D | 27.0 | D | 7.9 | 3.5 | 11.9 | 16.4 | 23 710 | 254 | 2 980 | 43 696 | 8.7 |
| Rowan | 2 446 | 0.4 | 26.5 | 21.1 | D | 6.1 | 2.1 | 10.1 | 22.6 | 30 380 | 220 | 2 958 | 60 211 | 11.5 |
| Rutherford | 866 | 0.6 | D | 17.0 | 5.0 | 10.3 | 4.3 | 15.9 | 19.4 | 17 115 | 253 | 1 952 | 33 878 | 14.7 |
| Sampson | 1 006 | 20.1 | D | 14.6 | D | 5.9 | 2.2 | 6.7 | 21.6 | 13 535 | 212 | 2 252 | 27 234 | 8.3 |
| Scotland | 593 | 3.9 | 23.6 | 20.0 | 2.8 | 7.8 | 3.4 | D | 20.7 | 8 980 | 250 | 2 000 | 15 193 | 3.4 |
| Stanly | 891 | 1.8 | D | 19.5 | 3.2 | 8.9 | 5.4 | 14.2 | 20.4 | 13 810 | 228 | 1 300 | 27 110 | 10.3 |
| Stokes | 374 | 3.1 | 25.2 | 17.0 | D | 7.4 | D | 12.4 | 24.1 | 10 365 | 219 | 942 | 21 924 | 13.8 |
| Surry | 1 306 | 1.9 | 26.9 | 12.5 | D | 9.7 | 4.1 | D | 18.3 | 18 085 | 245 | 2 034 | 33 667 | 8.5 |

1. Includes mining, construction, and manufacturing.    2. Per 1,000 resident population enumerated in the 2010 census.

| STATE County | Housing units, 2007–2011 | | | | | | | | Civilian labor force, 2012 | | Unemployment | | Civilian employment,[6] 2007–2011 | | |
|---|---|---|---|---|---|---|---|---|---|---|---|---|---|---|---|
| | Occupied units | | | | | | | | | | | | Percent | | |
| | | | Owner-occupied | | | Renter-occupied | | | | | | | | | |
| | | | | Median owner cost as a percent of income | | | | | | | | | | | Construction, production, and maintenance occupations |
| | Total | Percent | Median value[1] | With a mortgage | Without a mortgage[2] | Median rent[3] | Median rent as a percent of income | Substandard units[4] (percent) | Total | Percent change, 2011–2012 | Total | Rate[5] | Total | Management, business, science and arts | |
| | 89 | 90 | 91 | 92 | 93 | 94 | 95 | 96 | 97 | 98 | 99 | 100 | 101 | 102 | 103 |

NORTH CAROLINA—Cont'd

| | | | | | | | | | | | | | | | |
|---|---|---|---|---|---|---|---|---|---|---|---|---|---|---|---|
| Chowan | 5 870 | 66.4 | 132 400 | 26.5 | 18.1 | 685 | 36.6 | 2.7 | 6 243 | -1.0 | 651 | 10.4 | 5 432 | 29.0 | 25.9 |
| Clay | 4 464 | 83.5 | 162 100 | 26.0 | 11.6 | 584 | 40.0 | 0.9 | 4 601 | -0.1 | 441 | 9.6 | 3 890 | 29.4 | 27.0 |
| Cleveland | 37 690 | 67.3 | 104 300 | 23.0 | 11.8 | 632 | 30.5 | 3.4 | 50 321 | 0.8 | 5 227 | 10.4 | 40 089 | 27.3 | 29.8 |
| Columbus | 21 656 | 73.0 | 86 100 | 25.2 | 13.1 | 563 | 35.1 | 2.2 | 23 714 | -3.0 | 2 981 | 12.6 | 21 361 | 25.8 | 28.0 |
| Craven | 39 986 | 63.6 | 154 700 | 24.2 | 12.5 | 754 | 29.2 | 2.3 | 43 445 | 1.0 | 4 215 | 9.7 | 39 279 | 30.1 | 26.8 |
| Cumberland | 118 117 | 57.8 | 123 400 | 23.3 | 12.2 | 820 | 28.9 | 2.1 | 141 856 | 0.8 | 14 582 | 10.3 | 117 166 | 32.8 | 21.4 |
| Currituck | 9 322 | 80.4 | 236 500 | 28.7 | 11.8 | 903 | 31.0 | 1.1 | 12 985 | 1.8 | 895 | 6.9 | 11 120 | 28.9 | 25.7 |
| Dare | 15 234 | 71.6 | 321 200 | 30.8 | 12.6 | 1 028 | 32.5 | 1.2 | 23 193 | 3.2 | 2 617 | 11.3 | 18 168 | 34.7 | 22.1 |
| Davidson | 65 052 | 73.3 | 130 200 | 22.8 | 10.9 | 627 | 27.6 | 1.9 | 78 996 | 1.3 | 8 021 | 10.2 | 73 903 | 27.2 | 31.8 |
| Davie | 16 000 | 83.6 | 162 000 | 22.1 | 11.2 | 685 | 25.1 | 2.2 | 20 769 | 1.0 | 1 800 | 8.7 | 18 169 | 33.2 | 26.6 |
| Duplin | 21 545 | 69.1 | 86 300 | 24.0 | 15.3 | 556 | 27.1 | 3.9 | 25 426 | -1.2 | 2 473 | 9.7 | 24 332 | 24.8 | 40.5 |
| Durham | 107 150 | 55.4 | 178 400 | 23.1 | 11.2 | 817 | 30.6 | 3.1 | 146 808 | 2.4 | 11 165 | 7.6 | 131 010 | 48.7 | 15.1 |
| Edgecombe | 21 533 | 63.2 | 81 800 | 24.6 | 16.4 | 632 | 31.9 | 2.2 | 24 941 | -1.0 | 3 669 | 14.7 | 22 510 | 21.1 | 35.4 |
| Forsyth | 137 682 | 65.9 | 150 800 | 22.9 | 10.8 | 689 | 30.6 | 3.2 | 180 366 | 1.6 | 16 228 | 9.0 | 159 470 | 38.4 | 20.6 |
| Franklin | 23 068 | 78.2 | 124 700 | 24.7 | 13.2 | 697 | 31.7 | 3.8 | 28 817 | 2.2 | 2 605 | 9.0 | 26 235 | 31.8 | 29.5 |
| Gaston | 78 571 | 68.5 | 124 300 | 23.5 | 12.3 | 699 | 31.5 | 3.6 | 100 447 | 2.9 | 10 656 | 10.6 | 91 083 | 29.6 | 28.9 |
| Gates | 4 404 | 81.4 | 139 500 | 24.4 | 13.3 | 706 | 26.5 | 3.2 | 4 864 | -0.1 | 357 | 7.3 | 5 383 | 27.5 | 37.1 |
| Graham | 3 664 | 79.7 | 124 400 | 23.1 | 10.0 | 527 | 31.1 | 3.1 | 3 921 | -1.6 | 658 | 16.8 | 3 420 | 18.2 | 32.4 |
| Granville | 19 729 | 77.7 | 131 100 | 23.2 | 13.2 | 710 | 27.0 | 2.6 | 26 904 | 1.1 | 2 590 | 9.6 | 25 372 | 33.0 | 27.7 |
| Greene | 7 069 | 69.9 | 88 600 | 22.8 | 13.9 | 615 | 27.8 | 3.5 | 9 719 | 2.9 | 920 | 9.5 | 8 309 | 22.7 | 34.6 |
| Guilford | 192 064 | 62.9 | 156 200 | 23.6 | 11.0 | 729 | 30.0 | 2.4 | 256 786 | 0.7 | 25 047 | 9.8 | 230 712 | 35.8 | 20.5 |
| Halifax | 21 517 | 62.6 | 86 300 | 24.3 | 16.2 | 619 | 35.5 | 3.2 | 22 787 | -2.0 | 3 017 | 13.2 | 20 166 | 26.7 | 30.4 |
| Harnett | 40 262 | 67.6 | 128 500 | 24.3 | 13.7 | 724 | 31.5 | 3.0 | 49 980 | 1.2 | 5 410 | 10.8 | 44 674 | 28.0 | 30.7 |
| Haywood | 26 659 | 74.9 | 156 800 | 23.1 | 11.1 | 696 | 31.9 | 1.5 | 28 647 | 0.9 | 2 489 | 8.7 | 25 706 | 30.8 | 27.6 |
| Henderson | 45 180 | 76.9 | 190 700 | 23.2 | 10.2 | 705 | 29.8 | 2.6 | 51 401 | 1.2 | 3 727 | 7.3 | 45 686 | 34.1 | 24.8 |
| Hertford | 8 994 | 64.2 | 83 400 | 24.1 | 15.9 | 601 | 30.6 | 2.7 | 9 908 | 0.1 | 1 029 | 10.4 | 8 868 | 24.7 | 33.5 |
| Hoke | 14 808 | 72.7 | 126 700 | 25.1 | 13.0 | 735 | 32.8 | 4.6 | 22 798 | 0.3 | 2 139 | 9.4 | 17 026 | 26.1 | 27.0 |
| Hyde | 2 025 | 75.0 | 93 600 | 23.1 | 13.7 | 625 | 34.0 | 1.4 | 2 820 | -2.4 | 306 | 10.9 | 2 300 | 28.0 | 27.5 |
| Iredell | 58 879 | 74.3 | 168 300 | 23.7 | 9.9 | 746 | 28.9 | 2.0 | 83 173 | 1.5 | 8 075 | 9.7 | 71 755 | 30.7 | 29.7 |
| Jackson | 15 759 | 66.6 | 165 800 | 23.9 | 9.9 | 618 | 33.6 | 2.8 | 21 418 | -0.4 | 1 981 | 9.2 | 17 943 | 31.4 | 19.6 |
| Johnston | 60 115 | 72.8 | 138 800 | 23.3 | 11.5 | 757 | 32.4 | 2.7 | 82 156 | 2.4 | 6 912 | 8.4 | 77 447 | 32.3 | 26.9 |
| Jones | 4 074 | 72.6 | 93 800 | 22.4 | 12.5 | 636 | 24.9 | 3.5 | 4 456 | 1.9 | 467 | 10.5 | 4 238 | 28.1 | 32.6 |
| Lee | 21 069 | 68.8 | 135 500 | 22.3 | 12.5 | 677 | 27.0 | 4.8 | 26 948 | 0.0 | 3 189 | 11.8 | 25 264 | 28.5 | 32.9 |
| Lenoir | 24 280 | 61.2 | 93 000 | 23.8 | 15.0 | 639 | 33.9 | 2.9 | 29 121 | 2.9 | 2 904 | 10.0 | 24 323 | 28.0 | 31.8 |
| Lincoln | 29 507 | 76.9 | 151 900 | 22.4 | 10.3 | 659 | 30.7 | 1.3 | 39 427 | 0.9 | 3 967 | 10.1 | 35 887 | 29.4 | 31.6 |
| McDowell | 17 483 | 71.3 | 100 700 | 20.7 | 11.2 | 533 | 27.5 | 2.7 | 20 933 | 1.1 | 2 333 | 11.1 | 19 064 | 28.4 | 34.3 |
| Macon | 16 024 | 74.2 | 167 000 | 26.1 | 9.9 | 718 | 30.9 | 2.8 | 16 014 | -0.3 | 1 706 | 10.7 | 14 200 | 28.5 | 27.6 |
| Madison | 8 082 | 76.6 | 163 100 | 23.8 | 10.8 | 567 | 28.6 | 1.7 | 10 153 | 1.5 | 930 | 9.2 | 8 469 | 26.9 | 28.4 |
| Martin | 9 884 | 69.4 | 82 400 | 22.3 | 14.0 | 575 | 36.6 | 2.6 | 11 478 | -1.7 | 1 293 | 11.3 | 9 906 | 28.8 | 30.6 |
| Mecklenburg | 356 833 | 61.8 | 187 300 | 23.3 | 11.3 | 857 | 29.2 | 2.5 | 500 118 | 2.7 | 46 928 | 9.4 | 458 269 | 41.0 | 17.6 |
| Mitchell | 6 553 | 74.6 | 111 100 | 24.8 | 10.1 | 520 | 25.8 | 2.2 | 7 131 | 0.6 | 839 | 11.8 | 6 273 | 24.3 | 38.4 |
| Montgomery | 10 166 | 73.1 | 87 800 | 23.6 | 13.5 | 524 | 31.9 | 4.7 | 11 382 | 0.5 | 1 282 | 11.3 | 10 431 | 27.1 | 38.5 |
| Moore | 34 625 | 75.7 | 192 500 | 23.2 | 11.0 | 683 | 29.3 | 1.9 | 38 406 | 0.6 | 3 382 | 8.8 | 34 889 | 34.9 | 20.5 |
| Nash | 37 954 | 63.6 | 119 100 | 23.0 | 12.9 | 719 | 29.1 | 2.5 | 45 987 | -0.7 | 5 530 | 12.0 | 42 472 | 30.8 | 27.8 |
| New Hanover | 84 825 | 60.0 | 227 500 | 25.1 | 12.0 | 863 | 33.0 | 2.9 | 108 011 | 1.7 | 9 886 | 9.2 | 99 388 | 36.7 | 17.7 |
| Northampton | 8 505 | 73.8 | 79 000 | 23.5 | 16.1 | 580 | 30.9 | 2.9 | 8 889 | -2.4 | 976 | 11.0 | 7 964 | 24.7 | 30.5 |
| Onslow | 57 571 | 57.2 | 144 300 | 24.9 | 11.8 | 858 | 29.4 | 2.6 | 68 568 | 1.8 | 5 979 | 8.7 | 57 441 | 29.7 | 23.2 |
| Orange | 50 837 | 60.2 | 270 300 | 22.8 | 11.5 | 840 | 32.3 | 2.5 | 74 133 | 2.6 | 4 603 | 6.2 | 66 014 | 52.5 | 12.1 |
| Pamlico | 5 279 | 82.5 | 146 600 | 24.4 | 14.5 | 718 | 32.9 | 2.3 | 5 450 | 1.7 | 528 | 9.7 | 5 222 | 31.9 | 30.2 |
| Pasquotank | 14 550 | 65.6 | 174 000 | 26.8 | 13.6 | 763 | 32.1 | 3.2 | 17 411 | -0.6 | 1 845 | 10.6 | 17 658 | 31.7 | 24.5 |
| Pender | 20 128 | 78.5 | 152 000 | 25.4 | 13.8 | 754 | 30.5 | 2.8 | 24 479 | 1.3 | 2 635 | 10.8 | 22 251 | 26.2 | 30.8 |
| Perquimans | 5 272 | 77.5 | 161 100 | 28.4 | 14.7 | 728 | 40.6 | 0.8 | 5 405 | -1.0 | 531 | 9.8 | 4 753 | 30.9 | 29.8 |
| Person | 15 523 | 72.8 | 118 900 | 21.8 | 11.8 | 651 | 28.0 | 1.9 | 20 037 | 2.5 | 1 952 | 9.7 | 17 273 | 28.1 | 29.9 |
| Pitt | 64 507 | 55.6 | 131 400 | 23.3 | 14.2 | 695 | 34.3 | 2.5 | 89 351 | 2.7 | 8 319 | 9.3 | 77 703 | 37.7 | 20.4 |
| Polk | 8 937 | 78.5 | 168 800 | 26.2 | 10.9 | 601 | 31.6 | 1.5 | 9 426 | -0.2 | 719 | 7.6 | 7 962 | 25.5 | 33.4 |
| Randolph | 54 897 | 73.8 | 122 400 | 23.7 | 12.1 | 622 | 29.9 | 3.3 | 73 584 | 0.7 | 7 090 | 9.6 | 65 018 | 25.6 | 37.0 |
| Richmond | 17 292 | 69.0 | 74 000 | 23.0 | 14.2 | 535 | 29.1 | 3.4 | 19 664 | -2.4 | 2 514 | 12.8 | 16 079 | 24.9 | 31.5 |
| Robeson | 44 528 | 67.2 | 68 900 | 23.8 | 14.4 | 572 | 31.1 | 5.9 | 55 986 | -1.8 | 7 268 | 13.0 | 48 071 | 25.4 | 36.8 |
| Rockingham | 37 836 | 72.3 | 102 800 | 22.6 | 11.0 | 581 | 29.8 | 2.3 | 44 038 | 0.7 | 4 965 | 11.3 | 39 802 | 24.1 | 36.6 |
| Rowan | 53 009 | 70.6 | 127 200 | 22.4 | 11.0 | 684 | 28.7 | 2.9 | 71 702 | 0.6 | 7 117 | 9.9 | 59 086 | 26.7 | 33.7 |
| Rutherford | 27 229 | 72.7 | 104 400 | 23.0 | 12.5 | 549 | 29.1 | 2.2 | 27 660 | 1.6 | 3 688 | 13.3 | 26 323 | 26.8 | 33.1 |
| Sampson | 23 463 | 68.2 | 88 700 | 23.2 | 13.6 | 555 | 28.9 | 3.5 | 32 372 | -1.7 | 2 792 | 8.6 | 27 263 | 27.4 | 38.7 |
| Scotland | 13 075 | 66.2 | 75 600 | 24.9 | 14.8 | 621 | 32.9 | 3.7 | 13 195 | -3.5 | 2 235 | 16.9 | 11 900 | 31.0 | 27.1 |
| Stanly | 22 629 | 74.8 | 127 800 | 23.2 | 12.6 | 605 | 25.3 | 2.7 | 30 773 | -0.1 | 2 961 | 9.6 | 26 154 | 28.9 | 30.1 |
| Stokes | 18 968 | 79.4 | 120 900 | 21.1 | 9.9 | 592 | 29.3 | 1.8 | 24 203 | 1.7 | 2 154 | 8.9 | 20 807 | 23.1 | 35.7 |
| Surry | 30 072 | 73.4 | 105 000 | 21.9 | 12.2 | 537 | 28.4 | 3.4 | 33 248 | -0.6 | 3 349 | 10.1 | 32 257 | 28.0 | 33.3 |

1. Specified owner-occupied units.  2. A value of 9.9 represents 9.9 percent or less.  3. Specified renter-occupied units. A value of 10.0 represents 10 percent or less.  4. Overcrowded or lacking complete plumbing facilities.  5. Percent of civilian labor force.  6. Persons 16 years old and over.

| STATE County | Number of establishments | Employment Total | Health care and social assistance | Manufacturing | Retail trade | Finance and insurance | Professional, scientific, and technical services | Annual payroll Total (mil dol) | Average per employee (dollars) | Farms Number | Percent with: Fewer than 50 acres | 500 acres or more | Farm operators whose principal occupation is farming (percent) |
|---|---|---|---|---|---|---|---|---|---|---|---|---|---|
| | 104 | 105 | 106 | 107 | 108 | 109 | 110 | 111 | 112 | 113 | 114 | 115 | 116 |
| NORTH CAROLINA—Cont'd | | | | | | | | | | | | | |
| Chowan | 366 | 3 741 | 1 128 | 491 | 518 | 81 | 109 | 109 | 29 247 | 190 | 30.0 | 27.4 | 68.4 |
| Clay | 209 | 1 414 | 285 | D | 395 | D | D | 35 | 24 407 | 137 | 62.0 | 1.5 | 39.4 |
| Cleveland | 1 943 | 27 683 | 5 693 | 5 556 | 3 557 | 662 | 716 | 951 | 34 342 | 1 188 | 44.4 | 2.4 | 34.8 |
| Columbus | 1 048 | 11 593 | 3 288 | 1 892 | 2 104 | 805 | 266 | 344 | 29 663 | 777 | 38.7 | 10.3 | 50.6 |
| Craven | 2 235 | 27 146 | 6 487 | 2 886 | 4 566 | 843 | 1 667 | 923 | 33 994 | 286 | 46.2 | 13.6 | 55.6 |
| Cumberland | 5 613 | 94 128 | 18 628 | 6 109 | 16 088 | 2 583 | 7 303 | 3 058 | 32 483 | 500 | 42.4 | 10.4 | 46.6 |
| Currituck | 574 | 3 796 | 240 | 61 | 910 | D | D | 124 | 32 669 | 80 | 48.8 | 21.3 | 51.3 |
| Dare | 1 864 | 12 849 | 940 | 305 | 3 227 | 444 | 500 | 401 | 31 183 | 7 | 57.1 | 42.9 | 71.4 |
| Davidson | 2 747 | 34 286 | 4 778 | 9 290 | 4 648 | 785 | 741 | 1 083 | 31 580 | 1 074 | 53.0 | 1.7 | 36.3 |
| Davie | 771 | 8 600 | 1 058 | 1 484 | 1 375 | 207 | 276 | 245 | 28 523 | 627 | 45.9 | 2.9 | 44.0 |
| Duplin | 848 | 12 873 | 1 940 | 5 691 | 1 679 | 226 | 206 | 350 | 27 216 | 1 159 | 38.5 | 9.4 | 65.9 |
| Durham | 6 637 | 159 417 | 23 938 | 10 341 | 13 962 | 5 267 | 30 323 | 9 825 | 61 632 | 242 | 63.2 | 5.0 | 48.8 |
| Edgecombe | 791 | 13 873 | 2 505 | 2 796 | 1 500 | 182 | 161 | 470 | 33 886 | 300 | 33.3 | 20.7 | 56.7 |
| Forsyth | 8 197 | 159 288 | 32 423 | 14 253 | 19 841 | 10 602 | 6 995 | 6 871 | 43 134 | 680 | 67.8 | 1.6 | 44.4 |
| Franklin | 919 | 8 983 | 1 244 | 2 153 | 1 252 | 148 | 271 | 332 | 36 957 | 593 | 40.0 | 7.3 | 39.3 |
| Gaston | 3 868 | 58 661 | 11 276 | 11 633 | 9 141 | 1 266 | 1 333 | 2 012 | 34 291 | 516 | 59.7 | 0.8 | 31.2 |
| Gates | 127 | 857 | D | 119 | 146 | D | D | 24 | 27 588 | 181 | 35.4 | 14.4 | 44.2 |
| Graham | 161 | 1 899 | 296 | D | D | 38 | D | 62 | 32 779 | 126 | 67.5 | 0.0 | 38.1 |
| Granville | 809 | 13 764 | D | 4 046 | 1 299 | 173 | 178 | 458 | 33 304 | 673 | 33.6 | 6.7 | 40.1 |
| Greene | 236 | 1 748 | 621 | 98 | 244 | 44 | D | 45 | 25 545 | 292 | 35.6 | 18.8 | 57.9 |
| Guilford | 13 065 | 243 329 | 33 416 | 31 281 | 27 259 | 13 272 | 9 851 | 9 650 | 39 660 | 963 | 55.1 | 3.2 | 45.4 |
| Halifax | 1 016 | 12 624 | 3 070 | 1 633 | 2 538 | 316 | 358 | 352 | 27 856 | 365 | 26.3 | 26.3 | 52.1 |
| Harnett | 1 602 | 18 107 | 3 410 | 1 637 | 3 085 | 478 | 488 | 505 | 27 913 | 727 | 51.3 | 8.9 | 48.7 |
| Haywood | 1 371 | 13 912 | 3 298 | 1 632 | 2 834 | 396 | 586 | 424 | 30 464 | 707 | 60.1 | 1.7 | 37.2 |
| Henderson | 2 514 | 29 509 | 6 329 | 5 709 | 4 829 | 809 | 1 106 | 989 | 33 516 | 557 | 67.5 | 2.3 | 50.3 |
| Hertford | 476 | 6 989 | 2 173 | 859 | 1 098 | 163 | 65 | 213 | 30 509 | 163 | 28.2 | 23.3 | 54.0 |
| Hoke | 405 | 5 443 | 1 079 | 2 036 | 763 | D | 219 | 131 | 24 031 | 249 | 47.4 | 10.8 | 51.8 |
| Hyde | 153 | 859 | D | D | 153 | D | D | 22 | 25 427 | 176 | 38.6 | 25.6 | 47.2 |
| Iredell | 4 231 | 57 570 | 8 618 | 9 380 | 7 940 | 1 184 | 2 113 | 2 279 | 39 587 | 1 201 | 48.7 | 4.7 | 44.5 |
| Jackson | 901 | 7 749 | 1 847 | D | 1 593 | 249 | 342 | 229 | 29 492 | 229 | 70.3 | 0.9 | 40.2 |
| Johnston | 3 011 | 36 519 | 5 005 | 6 468 | 7 615 | 959 | 1 067 | 1 142 | 31 281 | 1 245 | 50.1 | 8.4 | 48.5 |
| Jones | 139 | 912 | 271 | D | 118 | D | D | 26 | 28 943 | 159 | 34.0 | 21.4 | 59.1 |
| Lee | 1 260 | 23 387 | 2 692 | 8 825 | 2 960 | 399 | 1 459 | 817 | 34 931 | 272 | 50.4 | 3.7 | 40.8 |
| Lenoir | 1 286 | 20 306 | 4 120 | 3 410 | 3 274 | 563 | 515 | 599 | 29 508 | 480 | 34.4 | 18.3 | 61.0 |
| Lincoln | 1 509 | 16 299 | 2 274 | 3 505 | 2 819 | 392 | 452 | 522 | 32 004 | 638 | 53.8 | 2.4 | 35.6 |
| McDowell | 732 | 12 021 | 1 444 | 5 371 | 1 534 | 216 | 183 | 363 | 30 196 | 383 | 62.9 | 1.3 | 43.9 |
| Macon | 1 087 | 9 162 | 1 605 | 712 | 1 901 | 311 | 245 | 261 | 28 503 | 346 | 65.0 | 0.6 | 44.8 |
| Madison | 306 | 2 908 | 547 | 389 | 394 | 48 | 36 | 73 | 25 090 | 801 | 51.8 | 1.5 | 40.3 |
| Martin | 457 | 5 529 | 1 577 | 829 | 940 | 181 | 116 | 140 | 25 354 | 320 | 24.4 | 20.0 | 60.0 |
| Mecklenburg | 27 520 | 508 744 | 60 619 | 23 631 | 52 065 | 61 104 | 38 859 | 27 070 | 53 209 | 236 | 61.0 | 1.7 | 47.5 |
| Mitchell | 376 | 3 886 | 881 | 437 | 702 | 95 | D | 119 | 30 659 | 314 | 54.1 | 1.6 | 37.6 |
| Montgomery | 497 | 6 707 | 1 049 | 2 491 | 816 | D | 66 | 199 | 29 601 | 289 | 39.4 | 6.2 | 49.5 |
| Moore | 2 157 | 28 330 | 8 255 | 1 999 | 4 176 | 674 | 1 602 | 952 | 33 589 | 804 | 52.9 | 4.0 | 48.1 |
| Nash | 2 130 | 35 462 | 5 581 | D | 5 506 | 1 810 | 965 | 1 260 | 35 522 | 487 | 42.9 | 15.6 | 50.7 |
| New Hanover | 6 634 | 83 669 | 15 753 | 4 748 | 13 524 | 2 939 | 4 967 | 3 107 | 37 133 | 73 | 69.9 | 1.4 | 42.5 |
| Northampton | 281 | 3 804 | 736 | 420 | 382 | D | 34 | 111 | 29 155 | 340 | 30.6 | 25.3 | 47.6 |
| Onslow | 2 710 | 32 898 | 5 703 | 820 | 7 600 | 1 059 | 1 661 | 852 | 25 884 | 401 | 51.1 | 5.5 | 59.1 |
| Orange | 3 060 | 38 276 | 12 551 | 823 | 5 755 | 2 526 | 2 232 | 1 519 | 39 681 | 604 | 49.8 | 3.0 | 43.5 |
| Pamlico | 252 | 1 805 | 344 | 113 | 318 | D | 35 | 46 | 25 312 | 85 | 52.9 | 29.4 | 56.5 |
| Pasquotank | 952 | 11 074 | 2 546 | 707 | 2 554 | 464 | 369 | 338 | 30 533 | 144 | 37.5 | 27.8 | 66.7 |
| Pender | 905 | 7 258 | 1 187 | 1 202 | 1 242 | 136 | 241 | 191 | 26 372 | 357 | 52.7 | 9.2 | 45.7 |
| Perquimans | 209 | 1 379 | 187 | 51 | 231 | 46 | 29 | 38 | 27 430 | 171 | 31.0 | 28.7 | 68.4 |
| Person | 670 | 8 609 | 1 681 | 1 788 | 1 423 | 174 | 136 | 250 | 29 095 | 403 | 40.4 | 12.4 | 42.2 |
| Pitt | 3 515 | 55 958 | 15 283 | 4 870 | 9 108 | 1 813 | 1 785 | 1 870 | 33 411 | 435 | 37.9 | 20.0 | 60.2 |
| Polk | 477 | 3 693 | 1 490 | 361 | 444 | 108 | 133 | 98 | 26 577 | 309 | 60.2 | 0.6 | 49.8 |
| Randolph | 2 558 | 37 461 | 4 666 | 14 666 | 4 313 | 1 021 | 654 | 1 161 | 30 980 | 1 501 | 49.8 | 3.1 | 44.4 |
| Richmond | 835 | 10 892 | 2 002 | 2 970 | 2 019 | 248 | 174 | 307 | 28 224 | 278 | 37.8 | 4.7 | 44.6 |
| Robeson | 1 857 | 30 669 | 7 830 | 7 005 | 4 775 | 799 | 628 | 828 | 26 992 | 1 017 | 45.6 | 13.1 | 54.0 |
| Rockingham | 1 705 | 22 721 | 3 438 | 6 144 | 3 690 | D | 495 | 742 | 32 665 | 863 | 42.1 | 4.2 | 41.4 |
| Rowan | 2 512 | 39 502 | D | 6 975 | 4 387 | 726 | 880 | 1 483 | 37 545 | 983 | 54.1 | 4.4 | 38.3 |
| Rutherford | 1 285 | 16 110 | 3 203 | 2 823 | 2 513 | 344 | 261 | 495 | 30 718 | 705 | 49.9 | 2.0 | 36.5 |
| Sampson | 989 | 13 410 | 2 770 | 3 240 | 2 242 | D | 209 | 402 | 29 958 | 1 203 | 34.7 | 13.7 | 55.8 |
| Scotland | 660 | 10 582 | 2 512 | 1 886 | 1 635 | 237 | 150 | 307 | 28 999 | 190 | 48.4 | 13.7 | 56.3 |
| Stanly | 1 303 | 15 534 | 3 344 | 3 179 | 2 837 | 394 | 305 | 443 | 28 529 | 713 | 39.6 | 5.5 | 39.1 |
| Stokes | 588 | 5 240 | 1 229 | 996 | 889 | 108 | 122 | 150 | 28 531 | 963 | 46.1 | 2.0 | 43.3 |
| Surry | 1 652 | 26 633 | 4 235 | 4 342 | 4 029 | 591 | 399 | 869 | 32 627 | 1 258 | 51.9 | 2.1 | 42.0 |

| STATE County | Land in farms | | | | | Value of land and buildings (dollars) | | Value of machinery and equipment, average per farm (dollars) | Value of products sold | | | | Percent of farms with sales of: | | Government payments | |
|---|---|---|---|---|---|---|---|---|---|---|---|---|---|---|---|---|
| | | | Acres | | | | | | | | Percent from: | | | | | |
| | Acreage (1,000) | Percent change, 2002–2007 | Average size of farm | Total irrigated (1,000) | Total cropland (1,000) | Average per farm | Average per acre | | Total (mil dol) | Average per farm (dollars) | Crops | Live-stock and poultry products | $10,000 or more | $100,000 or more | Total ($1,000) | Percent of farms |
| | 117 | 118 | 119 | 120 | 121 | 122 | 123 | 124 | 125 | 126 | 127 | 128 | 129 | 130 | 131 | 132 |
| **NORTH CAROLINA—Cont'd** | | | | | | | | | | | | | | | | |
| Chowan | 75 | 25.0 | 393 | 6.2 | 53.3 | 967 227 | 2 461 | 191 638 | 41.1 | 216 238 | 83.4 | 16.6 | 68.4 | 42.1 | 3 441 | 70.0 |
| Clay | 10 | -23.1 | 71 | 0.0 | 3.3 | 502 820 | 7 131 | 42 278 | 1.1 | 8 131 | 38.7 | 61.3 | 23.4 | 0.7 | 71 | 19.0 |
| Cleveland | 116 | -0.9 | 97 | 0.6 | 52.6 | 390 048 | 4 007 | 43 728 | 54.5 | 45 873 | 21.2 | 78.8 | 24.4 | 5.6 | 1 714 | 34.6 |
| Columbus | 152 | -5.0 | 196 | 2.2 | 106.6 | 646 186 | 3 295 | 95 387 | 141.4 | 181 986 | 32.2 | 67.8 | 43.5 | 16.1 | 2 902 | 48.6 |
| Craven | 71 | -10.1 | 248 | 1.2 | 49.5 | 762 422 | 3 076 | 102 097 | 50.5 | 176 676 | 48.6 | 51.4 | 48.6 | 25.2 | 2 218 | 55.2 |
| Cumberland | 88 | -2.2 | 177 | 3.4 | 44.6 | 531 536 | 3 008 | 69 974 | 90.9 | 181 712 | 20.8 | 79.2 | 38.2 | 18.0 | 1 258 | 38.2 |
| Currituck | 28 | -20.0 | 345 | 0.5 | 25.1 | 1 146 012 | 3 325 | 126 564 | 12.2 | 153 038 | 98.9 | 1.1 | 50.0 | 25.0 | 371 | 38.8 |
| Dare | 5 | NA | 703 | 0.0 | 4.7 | 1 584 429 | 2 254 | 132 369 | 1.1 | 162 729 | 100.0 | 0.0 | 100.0 | 100.0 | 263 | 42.9 |
| Davidson | 91 | -13.3 | 85 | 1.5 | 45.3 | 484 438 | 5 688 | 49 149 | 36.4 | 33 879 | 30.1 | 69.9 | 23.3 | 5.0 | 560 | 18.6 |
| Davie | 70 | -7.9 | 111 | 0.3 | 31.2 | 583 812 | 5 239 | 50 271 | 18.3 | 29 193 | 33.1 | 66.9 | 30.5 | 6.1 | 151 | 11.2 |
| Duplin | 248 | 5.5 | 214 | 25.3 | 159.3 | 873 575 | 4 082 | 120 938 | 1 176.3 | 1 014 902 | 5.7 | 94.3 | 70.1 | 55.3 | 3 337 | 32.2 |
| Durham | 26 | 0.0 | 108 | 0.3 | 8.4 | 552 803 | 5 116 | 42 823 | D | D | 0.0 | D | 29.3 | 5.4 | 218 | 26.0 |
| Edgecombe | 140 | -14.6 | 466 | 6.7 | 103.5 | 1 162 841 | 2 495 | 172 090 | 146.3 | 487 781 | 47.3 | 52.7 | 42.3 | 29.0 | 5 253 | 66.3 |
| Forsyth | 44 | -15.4 | 64 | 0.4 | 24.3 | 431 497 | 6 731 | 44 708 | 17.1 | 25 138 | 83.8 | 16.2 | 21.2 | 4.4 | 133 | 13.5 |
| Franklin | 113 | -11.7 | 190 | 5.3 | 49.2 | 710 899 | 3 735 | 87 830 | 48.1 | 81 057 | 54.6 | 45.4 | 29.8 | 10.3 | 852 | 34.2 |
| Gaston | 38 | -9.5 | 73 | 0.1 | 14.6 | 405 779 | 5 574 | 49 354 | 11.2 | 21 745 | 24.1 | 75.9 | 18.8 | 2.9 | 198 | 17.4 |
| Gates | 76 | 18.8 | 419 | 2.7 | 49.8 | 1 059 067 | 2 528 | 137 509 | 47.9 | 264 525 | 47.0 | 53.0 | 34.3 | 23.2 | 2 359 | 71.3 |
| Graham | 7 | -12.5 | 57 | 0.0 | 1.9 | 250 526 | 4 395 | 50 517 | 1.4 | 11 254 | 13.0 | 87.0 | 15.9 | 1.6 | 6 | 7.9 |
| Granville | 128 | -12.9 | 191 | 2.7 | 39.8 | 637 331 | 3 341 | 48 355 | 19.7 | 29 344 | 73.0 | 27.0 | 23.9 | 6.7 | 705 | 37.4 |
| Greene | 92 | -6.1 | 316 | 3.6 | 67.4 | 1 081 617 | 3 426 | 134 917 | 200.3 | 685 846 | 19.2 | 80.8 | 65.1 | 43.5 | 2 894 | 65.1 |
| Guilford | 97 | -12.6 | 100 | 2.4 | 46.0 | 525 659 | 5 245 | 57 354 | 48.4 | 50 274 | 56.5 | 43.5 | 27.5 | 7.8 | 506 | 12.3 |
| Halifax | 198 | 1.5 | 541 | 2.0 | 123.9 | 1 288 434 | 2 379 | 141 233 | 91.5 | 250 791 | 48.9 | 51.1 | 38.1 | 25.5 | 7 578 | 73.7 |
| Harnett | 112 | -1.8 | 154 | 2.5 | 72.1 | 815 320 | 5 303 | 83 238 | 177.2 | 243 760 | 21.3 | 78.7 | 35.5 | 21.7 | 2 812 | 36.0 |
| Haywood | 56 | -13.8 | 80 | 0.5 | 14.7 | 497 582 | 6 258 | 49 005 | 15.5 | 21 953 | 38.0 | 62.0 | 29.0 | 4.0 | 155 | 10.5 |
| Henderson | 38 | -22.4 | 68 | 1.8 | 19.0 | 702 488 | 10 311 | 63 616 | 62.3 | 111 894 | 89.9 | 10.1 | 31.1 | 8.1 | 668 | 8.8 |
| Hertford | 79 | -1.3 | 482 | 6.0 | 52.5 | 990 341 | 2 053 | 172 955 | 84.0 | 515 491 | 33.3 | 66.7 | 49.1 | 35.6 | 2 642 | 79.8 |
| Hoke | 60 | -4.8 | 242 | 0.5 | 35.4 | 818 889 | 3 386 | 98 188 | 67.0 | 269 257 | 11.0 | 89.0 | 31.3 | 19.7 | 1 396 | 39.4 |
| Hyde | 83 | -19.4 | 470 | 0.6 | 67.5 | 1 105 505 | 2 353 | 171 764 | 68.2 | 387 347 | D | D | 35.8 | 22.2 | 2 578 | 80.7 |
| Iredell | 138 | -6.1 | 115 | 1.1 | 69.4 | 663 938 | 5 761 | 65 806 | 117.6 | 97 897 | 10.0 | 90.0 | 36.7 | 16.7 | 578 | 13.4 |
| Jackson | 13 | -18.8 | 58 | 0.1 | 5.4 | 420 926 | 7 227 | 69 679 | D | D | 0.0 | D | 29.3 | 5.7 | 4 | 6.6 |
| Johnston | 194 | 0.0 | 156 | 5.8 | 128.2 | 672 607 | 4 314 | 77 828 | 203.0 | 163 014 | 43.8 | 56.2 | 35.3 | 16.9 | 4 358 | 41.2 |
| Jones | 69 | -9.2 | 434 | 2.0 | 51.8 | 1 213 070 | 2 792 | 164 045 | 101.7 | 639 766 | 20.0 | 80.0 | 59.7 | 44.0 | 2 260 | 45.9 |
| Lee | 36 | -21.7 | 133 | 1.5 | 18.6 | 615 587 | 4 624 | 74 273 | 31.5 | 115 627 | 33.3 | 66.7 | 32.7 | 13.6 | 211 | 23.5 |
| Lenoir | 138 | 13.1 | 287 | 3.6 | 108.7 | 969 173 | 3 382 | 140 949 | 236.3 | 492 282 | 29.6 | 70.4 | 61.9 | 43.1 | 7 394 | 60.6 |
| Lincoln | 59 | 1.7 | 93 | 0.5 | 32.2 | 429 913 | 4 621 | 44 800 | 20.8 | 32 662 | 20.5 | 79.5 | 24.1 | 4.5 | 441 | 23.8 |
| McDowell | 23 | -4.2 | 60 | 0.1 | 6.9 | 355 761 | 5 932 | 44 168 | 24.4 | 63 710 | 64.6 | 35.4 | 19.6 | 5.2 | 56 | 4.4 |
| Macon | 21 | -4.5 | 61 | 0.1 | 6.3 | 533 897 | 8 741 | 42 054 | 5.6 | 16 154 | 40.9 | 59.1 | 22.8 | 2.0 | 10 | 4.0 |
| Madison | 67 | -20.2 | 83 | 0.2 | 17.2 | 439 656 | 5 277 | 34 207 | 7.9 | 9 812 | 47.6 | 52.4 | 18.1 | 1.7 | 120 | 10.0 |
| Martin | 105 | -5.4 | 330 | 1.2 | 74.1 | 968 779 | 2 939 | 136 713 | 55.2 | 172 423 | 79.6 | 20.4 | 58.4 | 30.6 | 4 889 | 80.3 |
| Mecklenburg | 19 | -24.0 | 81 | 0.4 | 8.4 | 1 256 769 | 15 500 | 114 845 | D | D | D | 0.0 | 30.9 | 7.2 | 62 | 13.1 |
| Mitchell | 23 | -11.5 | 73 | 0.1 | 6.6 | 369 209 | 5 088 | 40 580 | 3.6 | 11 363 | 84.1 | 15.9 | 23.9 | 1.6 | 178 | 8.6 |
| Montgomery | 43 | 2.4 | 147 | 1.0 | 11.6 | 546 329 | 3 713 | 63 578 | 94.4 | 326 651 | 6.7 | 93.3 | 43.3 | 23.5 | 142 | 13.1 |
| Moore | 80 | -20.8 | 100 | 2.4 | 26.5 | 522 563 | 5 247 | 55 297 | 138.6 | 172 384 | 13.3 | 86.7 | 30.0 | 18.2 | 227 | 9.0 |
| Nash | 154 | -3.8 | 315 | 6.5 | 94.7 | 1 070 817 | 3 396 | 106 164 | 144.5 | 296 721 | 49.3 | 50.7 | 47.4 | 30.0 | 3 133 | 40.9 |
| New Hanover | 4 | NA | 60 | 0.1 | 3.2 | 484 944 | 8 017 | 64 080 | 5.8 | 79 515 | 95.3 | 4.7 | 41.1 | 11.0 | 36 | 15.1 |
| Northampton | 156 | 3.3 | 458 | 3.0 | 106.2 | 1 154 619 | 2 523 | 176 598 | 97.8 | 287 713 | 34.7 | 65.3 | 51.5 | 32.9 | 8 361 | 80.9 |
| Onslow | 55 | -14.1 | 138 | 5.2 | 38.1 | 628 054 | 4 562 | 84 654 | 159.1 | 396 645 | 11.8 | 88.2 | 44.4 | 32.4 | 1 271 | 34.7 |
| Orange | 60 | -15.5 | 99 | 0.8 | 26.0 | 558 040 | 5 612 | 56 294 | 28.1 | 46 497 | 44.8 | 55.2 | 30.0 | 8.3 | 420 | 21.9 |
| Pamlico | 46 | -11.5 | 543 | 0.9 | 40.5 | 1 336 631 | 2 463 | 203 616 | 23.2 | 272 746 | 86.4 | 13.6 | 52.9 | 40.0 | 978 | 60.0 |
| Pasquotank | 86 | -13.1 | 594 | 0.0 | 80.0 | 1 540 302 | 2 591 | 203 146 | 47.9 | 332 295 | 98.4 | 1.6 | 62.5 | 34.0 | 1 263 | 50.0 |
| Pender | 62 | -1.6 | 172 | 5.4 | 35.5 | 694 613 | 4 027 | 81 762 | 165.0 | 462 179 | 29.1 | 70.9 | 39.8 | 22.7 | 555 | 26.1 |
| Perquimans | 68 | -27.7 | 400 | 1.5 | 63.6 | 1 154 491 | 2 883 | 208 260 | 60.2 | 351 840 | 49.1 | 50.9 | 72.5 | 45.0 | 3 042 | 76.0 |
| Person | 99 | 4.2 | 244 | 1.8 | 52.1 | 832 271 | 3 404 | 87 099 | 19.3 | 47 857 | 73.8 | 26.2 | 29.8 | 12.4 | 730 | 26.6 |
| Pitt | 172 | -7.5 | 394 | 4.9 | 131.4 | 1 338 293 | 3 394 | 154 469 | 168.4 | 387 224 | 46.7 | 53.3 | 56.1 | 32.9 | 5 130 | 49.2 |
| Polk | 21 | -22.2 | 68 | 0.2 | 6.8 | 506 658 | 7 455 | 46 228 | D | D | 0.0 | D | 18.1 | 2.6 | 83 | 6.8 |
| Randolph | 147 | -6.4 | 98 | 1.5 | 63.2 | 475 393 | 4 844 | 58 713 | 205.9 | 137 188 | 5.8 | 94.2 | 33.0 | 16.0 | 418 | 13.1 |
| Richmond | 41 | -16.3 | 147 | 0.7 | 18.5 | 564 009 | 3 833 | 66 819 | 127.7 | 459 461 | 4.2 | 95.8 | 35.3 | 27.7 | 194 | 26.6 |
| Robeson | 268 | -6.6 | 264 | 4.7 | 209.3 | 759 287 | 2 881 | 91 234 | 268.9 | 264 438 | 21.9 | 78.1 | 40.7 | 18.9 | 5 326 | 49.0 |
| Rockingham | 117 | -14.0 | 136 | 3.8 | 44.2 | 526 286 | 3 878 | 61 643 | 31.9 | 36 927 | 67.5 | 32.5 | 27.3 | 8.9 | 425 | 23.9 |
| Rowan | 116 | 0.9 | 118 | 1.1 | 63.8 | 612 721 | 5 195 | 70 311 | 59.9 | 60 900 | 55.0 | 45.0 | 27.0 | 7.2 | 1 012 | 18.2 |
| Rutherford | 66 | -2.9 | 93 | 0.4 | 23.5 | 410 058 | 4 387 | 33 735 | 6.6 | 9 347 | 22.0 | 78.0 | 18.3 | 1.1 | 258 | 15.3 |
| Sampson | 321 | 7.7 | 267 | 29.2 | 210.7 | 998 921 | 3 738 | 148 397 | 1 196.3 | 994 457 | 12.5 | 87.5 | 61.6 | 43.3 | 6 793 | 51.0 |
| Scotland | 66 | 13.8 | 346 | 1.0 | 33.8 | 1 002 375 | 2 895 | 85 969 | 110.3 | 580 464 | 6.1 | 93.9 | 43.4 | 31.1 | 1 560 | 26.8 |
| Stanly | 105 | -2.8 | 147 | 0.7 | 58.2 | 589 246 | 4 020 | 64 731 | 106.7 | 149 618 | 14.1 | 85.9 | 29.5 | 10.7 | 1 916 | 27.3 |
| Stokes | 91 | -15.0 | 95 | 0.4 | 35.2 | 401 084 | 4 244 | 52 049 | 21.5 | 22 327 | 54.2 | 45.8 | 23.4 | 4.2 | 351 | 12.7 |
| Surry | 114 | -11.6 | 91 | 1.5 | 53.5 | 426 646 | 4 688 | 60 597 | 121.8 | 96 783 | 16.6 | 83.4 | 33.1 | 9.2 | 640 | 20.0 |

# Table B. States and Counties — Water Use, Wholesale Trade, Retail Trade, and Real Estate

| STATE County | Water use, 2005 | | Wholesale trade,[1] 2007 | | | | Retail trade,[2] 2007 | | | | Real estate and rental and leasing,[2] 2007 | | | |
|---|---|---|---|---|---|---|---|---|---|---|---|---|---|---|
| | Total water withdrawn (mil gal/day) | Gallons withdrawn per person | Number of establishments | Number of employees | Sales (mil dol) | Annual payroll (mil dol) | Number of establishments | Number of employees | Sales (mil dol) | Annual payroll (mil dol) | Number of establishments | Number of employees | Receipts (mil dol) | Annual payroll (mil dol) |
| | 133 | 134 | 135 | 136 | 137 | 138 | 139 | 140 | 141 | 142 | 143 | 144 | 145 | 146 |
| NORTH CAROLINA—Cont'd | | | | | | | | | | | | | | |
| Chowan | 6.0 | 416 | 12 | 132 | 38.5 | 3.7 | 64 | 613 | 136.1 | 11.8 | 22 | 48 | 7.3 | 0.8 |
| Clay | 1.2 | 121 | 1 | D | D | D | 53 | 377 | 133.7 | 8.6 | 19 | D | D | D |
| Cleveland | 271.6 | 2 764 | 92 | 1 550 | 1 247.0 | 52.1 | 406 | 3 947 | 928.8 | 83.7 | 66 | 308 | 50.5 | 7.0 |
| Columbus | 48.6 | 887 | 43 | 329 | 234.2 | 11.1 | 249 | 2 318 | 527.6 | 46.1 | 34 | 111 | 13.2 | 2.3 |
| Craven | 52.3 | 576 | 64 | 714 | 827.7 | 26.5 | 424 | 4 538 | 1 111.7 | 101.0 | 118 | 413 | 56.0 | 11.0 |
| Cumberland | 41.2 | 135 | 161 | 1 706 | 920.0 | 69.8 | 1 073 | 15 913 | 3 897.4 | 343.3 | 334 | 1 700 | 252.2 | 48.9 |
| Currituck | 3.3 | 141 | 15 | D | D | D | 149 | 1 102 | 263.9 | 23.7 | 54 | 676 | 58.8 | 20.8 |
| Dare | 9.6 | 282 | 40 | D | D | D | 475 | 3 467 | 869.1 | 88.5 | 159 | 1 414 | 127.7 | 48.6 |
| Davidson | 12.0 | 78 | 153 | D | D | D | 507 | 5 128 | 1 264.2 | 110.6 | 111 | 337 | 39.1 | 7.0 |
| Davie | 14.2 | 363 | 31 | 349 | 139.1 | 11.9 | 126 | 1 475 | 407.8 | 34.3 | 25 | 64 | 10.7 | 1.3 |
| Duplin | 43.6 | 838 | 41 | 418 | 350.2 | 14.5 | 192 | 1 697 | 412.6 | 33.5 | 29 | 67 | 6.1 | 0.9 |
| Durham | 40.9 | 169 | 215 | 8 974 | 7 657.3 | 842.9 | 935 | 14 439 | 3 135.3 | 311.5 | 320 | 1 941 | 375.4 | 76.0 |
| Edgecombe | 14.9 | 275 | 25 | D | D | D | 159 | 1 539 | 324.7 | 29.8 | 34 | 117 | 18.9 | 2.6 |
| Forsyth | 54.6 | 168 | 424 | 7 342 | 4 542.0 | 312.0 | 1 442 | 21 315 | 5 202.9 | 479.2 | 432 | D | D | D |
| Franklin | 7.3 | 135 | 37 | 324 | 178.0 | 14.6 | 138 | 1 245 | 371.8 | 29.8 | 23 | 65 | 10.7 | 1.4 |
| Gaston | 1 071.6 | 5 464 | 196 | 2 163 | 1 178.4 | 82.7 | 672 | 9 557 | 2 245.3 | 202.1 | 162 | 1 041 | 167.7 | 29.2 |
| Gates | 3.0 | 267 | 10 | 104 | 81.1 | 3.9 | 22 | 159 | 34.0 | 2.3 | 1 | D | D | D |
| Graham | 42.0 | 5 200 | 3 | D | D | D | 33 | 209 | 46.2 | 3.9 | 5 | D | D | D |
| Granville | 7.2 | 134 | 28 | 286 | 125.2 | 9.6 | 141 | 1 315 | 323.9 | 30.8 | 31 | 68 | 8.1 | 1.5 |
| Greene | 9.1 | 456 | 8 | 31 | 15.9 | 0.8 | 45 | 375 | 97.8 | 6.5 | 4 | D | D | D |
| Guilford | 60.2 | 136 | 1 024 | 14 772 | 11 295.4 | 710.0 | 2 004 | 30 247 | 7 252.6 | 718.7 | 690 | 4 564 | 1 455.5 | 147.4 |
| Halifax | 33.4 | 596 | 27 | 158 | 77.1 | 5.9 | 270 | 3 023 | 610.3 | 58.8 | 41 | 134 | 12.9 | 2.4 |
| Harnett | 14.0 | 135 | 46 | D | D | D | 270 | 3 148 | 872.0 | 65.4 | 51 | D | D | D |
| Haywood | 45.5 | 805 | 47 | 325 | 174.4 | 13.1 | 278 | 3 010 | 821.8 | 69.3 | 87 | 204 | 27.5 | 4.4 |
| Henderson | 13.6 | 140 | 115 | 1 173 | 709.9 | 41.9 | 441 | 5 353 | 1 479.2 | 127.7 | 120 | 346 | 52.3 | 9.3 |
| Hertford | 8.5 | 362 | 14 | 122 | 61.2 | 4.8 | 116 | 1 213 | 252.0 | 24.0 | 15 | 53 | 3.5 | 0.9 |
| Hoke | 5.1 | 124 | 10 | 94 | 33.1 | 2.7 | 67 | 512 | 121.7 | 8.1 | 16 | 23 | 4.3 | 0.5 |
| Hyde | 1.0 | 188 | 10 | 90 | 23.5 | 1.9 | 44 | 190 | 26.7 | 2.8 | 5 | D | D | D |
| Iredell | 19.0 | 135 | 228 | 2 420 | 1 275.9 | 116.5 | 647 | 8 360 | 2 288.9 | 201.7 | 219 | 693 | 119.2 | 22.8 |
| Jackson | 4.5 | 127 | 16 | 148 | 52.9 | 5.1 | 175 | 1 872 | 433.7 | 43.2 | 65 | 275 | 32.1 | 6.4 |
| Johnston | 23.2 | 159 | 111 | 1 055 | 820.9 | 49.7 | 580 | 7 163 | 1 971.7 | 148.1 | 105 | 477 | 77.7 | 12.2 |
| Jones | 5.2 | 502 | 10 | 127 | 41.2 | 4.4 | 29 | 163 | 31.8 | 2.8 | 1 | D | D | D |
| Lee | 14.3 | 257 | 56 | 1 128 | 672.2 | 43.6 | 251 | 2 966 | 764.5 | 65.2 | 63 | 197 | 32.0 | 6.0 |
| Lenoir | 13.5 | 233 | 62 | D | D | D | 276 | 3 537 | 842.8 | 80.8 | 54 | 229 | 28.0 | 4.7 |
| Lincoln | 11.4 | 163 | 73 | 986 | 436.2 | 38.6 | 248 | 2 683 | 713.8 | 60.8 | 71 | 181 | 40.8 | 6.0 |
| McDowell | 8.6 | 198 | 32 | 266 | 78.2 | 8.4 | 144 | 1 722 | 482.4 | 40.0 | 28 | 104 | 9.3 | 2.2 |
| Macon | 323.4 | 10 058 | 19 | 61 | 14.8 | 1.8 | 270 | 2 136 | 476.3 | 48.7 | 89 | 196 | 25.4 | 4.7 |
| Madison | 3.3 | 161 | 9 | 56 | 26.5 | 1.3 | 48 | 381 | 76.0 | 6.3 | 16 | 34 | 3.4 | 1.0 |
| Martin | 160.3 | 6 505 | 29 | 320 | 111.7 | 10.2 | 89 | 955 | 227.8 | 19.9 | 19 | 63 | 6.5 | 1.2 |
| Mecklenburg | 2 664.2 | 3 345 | 1 845 | 27 817 | 17 104.8 | 1 537.0 | 3 525 | 55 782 | 14 114.3 | 1 327.1 | 1 804 | 11 907 | 2 904.8 | 551.9 |
| Mitchell | 4.5 | 283 | 15 | 93 | 32.3 | 2.4 | 65 | 794 | 171.9 | 15.5 | 20 | 56 | 6.2 | 1.1 |
| Montgomery | 7.8 | 287 | 25 | 227 | 116.6 | 7.3 | 96 | 866 | 210.2 | 17.5 | 12 | 39 | 4.0 | 1.0 |
| Moore | 22.6 | 276 | 61 | 410 | 172.4 | 16.5 | 386 | 4 202 | 1 001.1 | 90.2 | 107 | 324 | 56.3 | 9.4 |
| Nash | 22.7 | 248 | 106 | D | D | D | 477 | 5 773 | 1 271.2 | 114.8 | 89 | 416 | 77.2 | 11.3 |
| New Hanover | 39.7 | 221 | 295 | 2 736 | 1 410.1 | 113.1 | 1 107 | 15 150 | 3 825.5 | 355.4 | 432 | 1 968 | 326.8 | 63.7 |
| Northampton | 6.8 | 316 | 19 | 425 | 256.1 | 14.5 | 58 | 435 | 102.0 | 7.6 | 5 | 15 | 1.0 | 0.2 |
| Onslow | 18.6 | 122 | 40 | 259 | 96.9 | 10.7 | 550 | 7 276 | 1 913.9 | 154.2 | 185 | 757 | 108.4 | 17.2 |
| Orange | 15.1 | 127 | 77 | 870 | 580.5 | 58.3 | 390 | 6 181 | 1 195.3 | 142.9 | 153 | 502 | 117.5 | 17.2 |
| Pamlico | 3.3 | 258 | 11 | 79 | 20.7 | 1.9 | 45 | 328 | 68.9 | 6.2 | 15 | D | D | D |
| Pasquotank | 7.2 | 187 | 34 | 447 | 148.8 | 13.5 | 217 | 2 750 | 694.3 | 61.8 | 50 | D | D | D |
| Pender | 9.3 | 201 | 34 | 1 166 | 583.9 | 54.7 | 158 | 1 271 | 331.8 | 26.0 | 57 | 172 | 20.9 | 5.8 |
| Perquimans | 4.5 | 369 | 11 | 84 | 32.4 | 2.4 | 37 | 242 | 69.0 | 5.2 | 9 | D | D | D |
| Person | 1 056.3 | 28 382 | 28 | 383 | 193.3 | 13.9 | 143 | 1 570 | 384.2 | 34.0 | 21 | 115 | 8.8 | 1.9 |
| Pitt | 25.6 | 180 | 137 | 1 700 | 898.9 | 70.5 | 668 | 8 846 | 2 176.0 | 188.8 | 201 | D | D | D |
| Polk | 2.5 | 128 | 17 | 146 | 65.0 | 4.9 | 68 | 506 | 110.3 | 9.5 | 28 | 87 | 10.0 | 2.2 |
| Randolph | 19.9 | 144 | 150 | 1 813 | 746.4 | 75.8 | 438 | 4 465 | 1 156.7 | 95.9 | 73 | 292 | 46.6 | 7.1 |
| Richmond | 12.9 | 276 | 33 | D | D | D | 204 | 2 076 | 424.1 | 40.0 | 34 | 93 | 11.1 | 1.6 |
| Robeson | 33.0 | 258 | 73 | 728 | 627.1 | 26.1 | 431 | 5 144 | 1 337.9 | 103.6 | 51 | 259 | 25.5 | 4.1 |
| Rockingham | 282.0 | 3 044 | 59 | 813 | 611.5 | 27.4 | 340 | 3 682 | 839.6 | 76.3 | 61 | 190 | 15.7 | 3.5 |
| Rowan | 361.0 | 2 672 | 111 | 1 570 | 628.6 | 56.4 | 452 | 4 755 | 1 163.8 | 98.1 | 98 | 293 | 52.2 | 8.8 |
| Rutherford | 13.5 | 211 | 45 | D | D | D | 278 | 2 767 | 640.1 | 59.2 | 61 | 218 | 29.2 | 6.5 |
| Sampson | 42.1 | 667 | 52 | 781 | 382.0 | 29.7 | 226 | 2 403 | 575.8 | 48.7 | 33 | 106 | 16.1 | 2.6 |
| Scotland | 6.5 | 175 | 18 | D | D | D | 153 | 1 711 | 361.7 | 32.9 | 23 | 81 | 9.4 | 1.9 |
| Stanly | 14.5 | 246 | 47 | D | D | D | 237 | 2 596 | 610.0 | 54.4 | 40 | D | D | D |
| Stokes | 1 235.8 | 26 948 | 18 | 73 | 11.7 | 2.2 | 115 | 893 | 226.5 | 18.4 | 27 | D | D | D |
| Surry | 23.9 | 329 | 69 | D | D | D | 350 | 3 963 | 1 054.1 | 82.9 | 73 | 272 | 32.5 | 6.3 |

1. Merchant wholesalers, except manufacturers' sales branches and offices.  2. Employer establishments.

# Table B. States and Counties — Professional Services, Manufacturing, and Accommodation and Food Services

| STATE County | Professional, scientific, and technical services,[1] 2007 | | | | Manufacturing, 2007 | | | | Accommodation and food services, 2007 | | | |
|---|---|---|---|---|---|---|---|---|---|---|---|---|
| | Number of establishments | Number of employees | Receipts (mil dol) | Annual payroll (mil dol) | Number of establishments | Number of employees | Receipts (mil dol) | Annual payroll (mil dol) | Number of establishments | Number of employees | Sales (mil dol) | Annual payroll (mil dol) |
| | 147 | 148 | 149 | 150 | 151 | 152 | 153 | 154 | 155 | 156 | 157 | 158 |
| NORTH CAROLINA—Cont'd | | | | | | | | | | | | |
| Chowan | 23 | 124 | 11.6 | 4.9 | 25 | 899 | 341.7 | 29.6 | 28 | 483 | 19.5 | 5.1 |
| Clay | 16 | 49 | 3.5 | 1.3 | NA | NA | NA | NA | 15 | 217 | 7.4 | 2.4 |
| Cleveland | 127 | 752 | 82.0 | 28.9 | 142 | 7 198 | 2 229.8 | 290.6 | 159 | 2 277 | 96.6 | 25.9 |
| Columbus | 56 | 204 | 18.0 | 5.1 | 41 | 2 487 | 887.7 | 108.8 | 87 | 980 | 41.1 | 9.4 |
| Craven | 223 | D | D | D | 85 | 4 745 | D | D | 178 | 3 824 | 142.1 | 37.9 |
| Cumberland | 495 | D | D | D | 110 | 8 424 | D | 391.0 | 586 | D | D | D |
| Currituck | 40 | 128 | 20.3 | 14.7 | NA | NA | NA | NA | 75 | 512 | 34.5 | 8.5 |
| Dare | 131 | 681 | 58.9 | 24.1 | 45 | 636 | 98.4 | 20.3 | 301 | 3 755 | 248.3 | 77.0 |
| Davidson | 207 | 778 | 76.6 | 26.4 | 281 | 11 982 | 2 696.7 | 413.6 | 211 | 3 621 | 131.8 | 39.7 |
| Davie | 68 | 290 | 21.9 | 8.1 | 54 | 3 503 | 1 001.6 | 134.9 | 59 | 795 | 29.0 | 8.2 |
| Duplin | 59 | 175 | 14.5 | 5.3 | 33 | 5 747 | 1 621.4 | 158.2 | 76 | 1 215 | 42.2 | 11.1 |
| Durham | 970 | D | D | D | 179 | 12 930 | 9 359.6 | 750.8 | 617 | 12 994 | 729.3 | 202.7 |
| Edgecombe | 43 | 244 | 21.7 | 7.2 | 43 | 4 437 | 1 226.9 | 152.8 | 73 | 954 | 36.4 | 9.8 |
| Forsyth | 977 | D | D | D | 350 | 18 381 | 16 881.5 | 858.1 | 712 | 14 261 | 646.8 | 179.3 |
| Franklin | 73 | 245 | 28.2 | 10.7 | 54 | 3 150 | 1 034.1 | 150.9 | 46 | 514 | 21.4 | 6.0 |
| Gaston | 287 | D | D | D | 341 | 14 259 | 4 158.6 | 541.2 | 296 | 5 638 | 253.4 | 67.4 |
| Gates | 10 | 44 | 4.0 | 1.3 | NA | NA | NA | NA | 6 | 100 | 2.3 | 0.7 |
| Graham | 7 | 32 | 2.4 | 0.9 | NA | NA | NA | NA | 22 | 240 | 15.4 | 4.8 |
| Granville | 64 | 184 | 17.9 | 5.5 | 48 | 4 792 | 2 252.1 | 186.8 | 66 | 1 132 | 48.8 | 11.0 |
| Greene | 8 | 28 | 2.3 | 0.8 | NA | NA | NA | NA | 9 | 158 | 6.3 | 1.8 |
| Guilford | 1 533 | D | D | D | 746 | 37 752 | 23 940.4 | 1 616.0 | 1 114 | 22 829 | 1 044.5 | 295.5 |
| Halifax | 61 | 404 | 24.2 | 9.2 | 42 | 2 208 | D | D | 86 | 1 899 | 71.9 | 20.1 |
| Harnett | 126 | 509 | 42.7 | 16.9 | 71 | 2 631 | 464.7 | 96.3 | 121 | D | D | D |
| Haywood | 107 | 575 | 60.3 | 24.7 | 45 | 1 926 | D | D | 156 | 2 341 | 99.1 | 28.6 |
| Henderson | 228 | D | D | D | 145 | 6 752 | 2 129.6 | 286.6 | 198 | 3 449 | 170.5 | 47.5 |
| Hertford | 19 | D | D | D | 17 | 867 | D | 50.6 | 43 | 689 | 25.4 | 7.0 |
| Hoke | 33 | D | D | D | 16 | 2 137 | D | 59.1 | 23 | D | D | D |
| Hyde | 3 | D | D | D | NA | NA | NA | NA | 30 | 233 | 16.9 | 4.3 |
| Iredell | 378 | 2 782 | 321.6 | 112.2 | 285 | 11 898 | 3 167.1 | 446.0 | 332 | 6 039 | 246.7 | 69.9 |
| Jackson | 78 | D | D | D | NA | NA | NA | NA | 96 | 1 556 | 74.0 | 20.1 |
| Johnston | 243 | 1 132 | 109.7 | 43.0 | 125 | 6 409 | 2 418.3 | 284.9 | 268 | 4 718 | 197.2 | 51.1 |
| Jones | 6 | D | D | D | NA | NA | NA | NA | 8 | 31 | 1.2 | 0.3 |
| Lee | 83 | 742 | 30.8 | 39.5 | 81 | 9 028 | 3 521.6 | 361.8 | 95 | 1 796 | 67.3 | 17.6 |
| Lenoir | 74 | 459 | 87.6 | 21.0 | 55 | 4 937 | 1 229.1 | 156.0 | 92 | 1 811 | 69.7 | 19.7 |
| Lincoln | 120 | 601 | 61.6 | 20.2 | 106 | 5 190 | 2 106.0 | 188.7 | 102 | 1 705 | 65.2 | 17.0 |
| McDowell | 37 | 170 | 13.2 | 6.6 | 65 | 6 522 | 1 332.5 | 196.9 | 70 | 1 139 | 42.0 | 10.9 |
| Macon | 76 | 272 | 22.9 | 9.4 | 40 | 821 | 230.5 | 26.8 | 114 | 1 234 | 68.2 | 18.9 |
| Madison | 20 | 43 | 3.7 | 1.0 | NA | NA | NA | NA | 30 | 282 | 12.1 | 3.2 |
| Martin | 26 | 142 | 7.7 | 3.6 | 18 | 945 | 362.6 | 29.7 | 43 | 693 | 26.4 | 6.9 |
| Mecklenburg | 3 689 | D | D | D | 890 | 30 349 | 11 201.0 | 1 354.0 | 2 253 | 47 379 | 2 550.5 | 702.9 |
| Mitchell | 23 | 80 | 5.9 | 2.0 | 27 | 552 | 71.0 | 17.1 | 35 | 311 | 12.6 | 3.4 |
| Montgomery | 15 | 67 | 6.8 | 2.0 | 68 | 3 307 | 750.8 | 108.9 | 33 | 282 | 13.4 | 3.5 |
| Moore | 218 | 1 452 | 151.3 | 60.2 | 85 | 2 129 | 669.6 | 80.3 | 174 | 4 310 | 227.5 | 65.9 |
| Nash | 179 | 988 | 111.3 | 41.0 | 102 | 8 298 | 2 956.2 | 347.9 | 193 | 4 104 | 163.8 | 45.4 |
| New Hanover | 832 | D | D | D | 193 | 5 743 | 2 883.6 | 306.4 | 615 | 12 542 | 525.5 | 152.3 |
| Northampton | 17 | 39 | 3.3 | 0.9 | NA | NA | NA | NA | 19 | 142 | 5.2 | 1.6 |
| Onslow | 210 | D | D | D | 43 | 1 016 | 253.0 | 31.8 | 310 | 6 265 | 287.9 | 71.5 |
| Orange | 507 | D | D | D | 73 | 1 534 | D | 56.5 | 304 | 6 088 | 275.6 | 80.1 |
| Pamlico | 15 | D | D | D | NA | NA | NA | NA | 23 | 355 | 23.8 | 6.6 |
| Pasquotank | 76 | 455 | 50.5 | 14.9 | 31 | 720 | D | 29.1 | 93 | 1 931 | 64.8 | 19.0 |
| Pender | 74 | D | D | D | 44 | 1 416 | D | 55.4 | 70 | 892 | 35.5 | 9.3 |
| Perquimans | 14 | D | D | D | NA | NA | NA | NA | 16 | 167 | 5.8 | 1.8 |
| Person | 43 | D | D | D | 39 | 2 114 | D | 69.9 | 50 | 818 | 37.4 | 9.0 |
| Pitt | 310 | 1 750 | 198.5 | 77.0 | 98 | 6 930 | D | 265.8 | 306 | 7 187 | 293.5 | 79.2 |
| Polk | 40 | 138 | 13.3 | 4.7 | 21 | 605 | 153.1 | 17.9 | 38 | 436 | 15.5 | 4.9 |
| Randolph | 167 | D | D | D | 339 | 17 982 | 4 397.7 | 570.6 | 175 | 3 029 | 131.3 | 35.1 |
| Richmond | 57 | 215 | 16.0 | 5.2 | 50 | 3 690 | 697.3 | 94.5 | 67 | 960 | 37.7 | 9.5 |
| Robeson | 110 | D | D | D | 71 | 8 436 | 2 792.6 | 243.8 | 161 | 3 476 | 128.8 | 31.9 |
| Rockingham | 114 | D | D | D | 109 | 7 771 | 3 118.4 | 274.8 | 143 | 2 124 | 84.6 | 22.6 |
| Rowan | 183 | 1 213 | 90.5 | 35.2 | 200 | 12 036 | 3 724.3 | 428.4 | 195 | 3 283 | 132.1 | 37.0 |
| Rutherford | 74 | 294 | 21.3 | 6.8 | 75 | 3 936 | 901.9 | 140.1 | 110 | 1 401 | 60.2 | 16.7 |
| Sampson | 50 | 182 | 16.8 | 5.6 | 52 | 3 043 | 917.6 | 101.1 | 81 | 996 | 38.6 | 10.7 |
| Scotland | 35 | D | D | D | 39 | 3 122 | 1 061.2 | 119.9 | 48 | 812 | 32.7 | 8.8 |
| Stanly | 77 | 329 | 37.3 | 12.0 | 111 | 3 900 | 925.8 | 137.4 | 103 | 1 570 | 55.7 | 15.7 |
| Stokes | 38 | 147 | 12.5 | 4.6 | 33 | 1 078 | D | 37.3 | 53 | 775 | 28.7 | 8.0 |
| Surry | 111 | 435 | 39.1 | 12.2 | 111 | 5 478 | 1 038.0 | 168.5 | 153 | 2 464 | 84.9 | 24.9 |

1. Establishment subject to federal tax.

# Table B. States and Counties — Health Care and Social Assistance, Other Services, and Federal Funds

| STATE County | Health care and social assistance, 2007 | | | | Other services, 2007 | | | | Federal funds and grants, 2009–2010 Expenditures (mil dol) | | | |
|---|---|---|---|---|---|---|---|---|---|---|---|---|
| | | | | | | | | | | Direct payments for individuals[1] | | |
| | Number of establishments | Number of employees | Receipts (mil dol) | Annual payroll (mil dol) | Number of establishments | Number of employees | Receipts (mil dol) | Annual payroll (mil dol) | Total | Social Security and government retirement | Medicare | Food Stamps and Supplemental Security Income |
| | 159 | 160 | 161 | 162 | 163 | 164 | 165 | 166 | 167 | 168 | 169 | 170 |
| NORTH CAROLINA—Cont'd | | | | | | | | | | | | |
| Chowan | 55 | 1 192 | 83.8 | 35.5 | 22 | 83 | 6.3 | 1.9 | 149.5 | 62.2 | 24.1 | 9.7 |
| Clay | 23 | 249 | 13.9 | 6.1 | 11 | 27 | 2.2 | 0.6 | 96.4 | 48.9 | 16.2 | 3.4 |
| Cleveland | 234 | 5 819 | 490.3 | 202.6 | 153 | 638 | 53.0 | 14.4 | 805.2 | 354.4 | 136.2 | 50.1 |
| Columbus | 179 | 3 658 | 217.6 | 90.8 | 69 | 229 | 18.8 | 4.7 | 612.3 | 202.2 | 121.8 | 43.2 |
| Craven | 270 | 7 199 | 648.9 | 263.3 | 159 | 826 | 66.8 | 16.7 | 1 375.4 | 482.9 | 124.5 | 46.5 |
| Cumberland | 743 | 18 732 | 1 573.8 | 646.8 | 411 | 2 670 | 176.6 | 55.2 | 12 931.5 | 1 259.5 | 239.1 | 170.2 |
| Currituck | 27 | D | D | D | 41 | 156 | 13.2 | 4.0 | 160.6 | 93.1 | 22.4 | 5.7 |
| Dare | 80 | D | D | D | 104 | 469 | 33.4 | 9.9 | 228.0 | 132.2 | 34.2 | 5.2 |
| Davidson | 199 | 4 731 | 325.5 | 145.4 | 190 | 982 | 67.6 | 19.2 | 828.2 | 428.3 | 177.2 | 43.5 |
| Davie | 60 | 1 058 | 67.1 | 25.0 | 58 | 288 | 17.0 | 4.2 | 292.6 | 138.7 | 46.5 | 6.3 |
| Duplin | 100 | 2 002 | 108.4 | 48.0 | 56 | 246 | 19.6 | 6.0 | 465.0 | 148.4 | 75.2 | 24.8 |
| Durham | 725 | 22 856 | 2 828.6 | 960.5 | 443 | 4 038 | 664.4 | 153.1 | 4 398.5 | 618.5 | 268.4 | 96.6 |
| Edgecombe | 92 | 2 468 | 153.9 | 63.4 | 60 | 290 | 122.0 | 6.8 | 537.8 | 116.5 | 122.7 | 52.6 |
| Forsyth | 806 | 28 766 | 2 859.9 | 1 108.0 | 605 | 3 859 | 391.1 | 95.0 | 2 593.2 | 1 071.3 | 423.0 | 121.0 |
| Franklin | 84 | D | D | D | 63 | 191 | 19.9 | 4.8 | 367.4 | 148.9 | 63.9 | 22.9 |
| Gaston | 458 | 10 998 | 937.0 | 410.1 | 287 | 1 815 | 186.1 | 44.0 | 1 328.2 | 643.1 | 286.1 | 81.3 |
| Gates | 10 | D | D | D | 11 | 47 | 3.7 | 0.8 | 98.6 | 43.3 | 16.9 | 5.0 |
| Graham | 13 | 355 | 11.2 | 6.0 | 11 | 36 | 3.1 | 0.7 | 76.6 | 31.2 | 13.8 | 4.7 |
| Granville | 93 | 3 092 | 230.2 | 104.3 | 49 | 176 | 20.4 | 4.8 | 445.7 | 148.5 | 61.8 | 15.6 |
| Greene | 43 | D | D | D | 13 | 24 | 2.1 | 0.5 | 136.4 | 46.4 | 24.6 | 8.8 |
| Guilford | 1 240 | 30 287 | 2 861.8 | 1 177.0 | 878 | 5 437 | 740.5 | 148.8 | 3 543.4 | 1 401.8 | 521.0 | 152.5 |
| Halifax | 147 | 3 611 | 218.3 | 96.3 | 82 | 556 | 35.0 | 12.1 | 654.1 | 212.8 | 110.6 | 64.2 |
| Harnett | 164 | 3 567 | 226.1 | 103.5 | 107 | 465 | 33.0 | 9.3 | 646.1 | 260.0 | 112.7 | 39.3 |
| Haywood | 143 | 3 091 | 230.7 | 99.3 | 107 | 477 | 37.4 | 10.5 | 492.0 | 250.0 | 89.4 | 21.5 |
| Henderson | 258 | 6 122 | 487.6 | 204.4 | 177 | 1 007 | 81.9 | 21.7 | 828.7 | 478.5 | 168.6 | 24.4 |
| Hertford | 92 | 2 191 | 124.1 | 52.4 | 34 | 190 | 10.7 | 3.3 | 284.3 | 80.2 | 37.2 | 21.7 |
| Hoke | 70 | 1 927 | 78.2 | 35.9 | 23 | 117 | 6.2 | 2.0 | 255.0 | 103.5 | 26.2 | 19.2 |
| Hyde | 9 | 118 | 6.7 | 2.8 | 5 | D | D | D | 70.3 | 15.5 | 10.6 | 4.7 |
| Iredell | 424 | 8 552 | 821.5 | 326.2 | 275 | 1 666 | 126.0 | 37.4 | 865.3 | 447.9 | 182.6 | 33.0 |
| Jackson | 95 | 1 971 | 181.1 | 75.7 | 50 | 166 | 12.4 | 3.6 | 257.5 | 111.6 | 39.9 | 13.6 |
| Johnston | 273 | D | D | D | 208 | 934 | 80.2 | 21.0 | 902.5 | 373.8 | 158.3 | 49.7 |
| Jones | 17 | 340 | 28.1 | 12.4 | 5 | 16 | 1.3 | 0.4 | 113.8 | 46.0 | 20.1 | 6.6 |
| Lee | 163 | 2 887 | 196.6 | 80.7 | 96 | 469 | 32.0 | 9.7 | 457.7 | 227.3 | 79.5 | 20.5 |
| Lenoir | 199 | 4 574 | 298.0 | 130.7 | 92 | 624 | 44.7 | 14.6 | 747.1 | 224.7 | 137.2 | 43.9 |
| Lincoln | 133 | 2 130 | 166.7 | 69.0 | 119 | 509 | 39.0 | 10.1 | 387.2 | 214.8 | 74.0 | 17.2 |
| McDowell | 74 | 1 529 | 92.9 | 42.0 | 43 | 273 | 20.8 | 6.2 | 307.6 | 158.1 | 51.5 | 15.9 |
| Macon | 91 | 1 666 | 120.6 | 47.7 | 88 | 341 | 29.1 | 8.4 | 307.3 | 162.8 | 56.7 | 10.6 |
| Madison | 29 | 602 | 33.2 | 15.2 | 15 | 43 | 4.6 | 1.0 | 198.6 | 69.6 | 31.4 | 9.8 |
| Martin | 78 | 1 408 | 83.4 | 33.9 | 24 | 71 | 5.9 | 1.7 | 275.9 | 89.2 | 46.0 | 17.6 |
| Mecklenburg | 2 283 | 55 497 | 6 082.2 | 2 453.1 | 1 613 | 12 728 | 2 085.7 | 371.7 | 4 900.0 | 1 882.3 | 626.8 | 249.8 |
| Mitchell | 33 | 1 041 | 61.4 | 29.9 | 23 | 59 | 5.3 | 1.2 | 162.7 | 58.8 | 27.4 | 6.3 |
| Montgomery | 60 | 1 009 | 52.5 | 22.7 | 30 | 109 | 8.4 | 2.2 | 230.5 | 81.7 | 40.7 | 13.5 |
| Moore | 263 | 7 138 | 705.1 | 303.2 | 139 | 727 | 58.8 | 16.2 | 751.0 | 436.3 | 133.4 | 23.9 |
| Nash | 251 | 6 815 | 557.6 | 243.4 | 153 | 908 | 75.7 | 23.0 | 758.4 | 374.4 | 97.6 | 45.9 |
| New Hanover | 686 | 18 139 | 1 822.5 | 767.7 | 468 | 2 908 | 234.9 | 65.3 | 1 465.8 | 664.8 | 215.7 | 75.9 |
| Northampton | 35 | 782 | 29.4 | 14.3 | 18 | 44 | 4.0 | 0.8 | 272.8 | 83.9 | 40.0 | 21.7 |
| Onslow | 246 | 5 465 | 433.8 | 163.4 | 213 | 1 136 | 68.0 | 21.4 | 2 938.6 | 575.1 | 92.7 | 52.6 |
| Orange | 346 | 11 588 | 1 122.7 | 491.9 | 198 | 1 397 | 316.4 | 46.2 | 1 614.9 | 300.0 | 117.3 | 22.8 |
| Pamlico | 20 | 249 | 12.5 | 6.2 | 16 | 60 | 4.7 | 1.4 | 121.8 | 62.3 | 17.3 | 5.9 |
| Pasquotank | 134 | 2 919 | 242.3 | 101.8 | 75 | 459 | 24.8 | 7.8 | 527.7 | 158.3 | 56.3 | 24.5 |
| Pender | 75 | 1 036 | 69.8 | 27.3 | 55 | 222 | 16.9 | 5.4 | 346.4 | 178.9 | 53.9 | 17.5 |
| Perquimans | 17 | D | D | D | 12 | 49 | 2.6 | 0.9 | 128.4 | 66.8 | 19.1 | 8.2 |
| Person | 75 | 1 144 | 90.0 | 35.7 | 43 | 149 | 15.1 | 3.8 | 303.1 | 109.9 | 50.8 | 12.6 |
| Pitt | 439 | D | D | D | 185 | 1 084 | 108.0 | 21.6 | 1 098.7 | 401.6 | 158.8 | 81.9 |
| Polk | 60 | 1 456 | 89.9 | 38.7 | 30 | 96 | 13.7 | 2.4 | 156.4 | 93.5 | 30.7 | 3.9 |
| Randolph | 223 | 4 468 | 325.3 | 141.7 | 177 | 744 | 66.7 | 18.5 | 738.3 | 366.9 | 147.6 | 30.3 |
| Richmond | 104 | 2 119 | 160.5 | 62.8 | 59 | D | D | D | 439.9 | 179.3 | 83.9 | 33.1 |
| Robeson | 296 | 8 599 | 561.4 | 242.8 | 100 | 368 | 30.8 | 7.8 | 1 234.5 | 376.2 | 188.2 | 100.7 |
| Rockingham | 192 | 3 997 | 291.2 | 118.1 | 131 | 503 | 36.3 | 9.9 | 837.6 | 330.0 | 161.3 | 40.9 |
| Rowan | 241 | 7 413 | 717.6 | 322.1 | 164 | 987 | 59.9 | 18.8 | 1 022.7 | 451.3 | 176.7 | 47.7 |
| Rutherford | 140 | 3 133 | 214.0 | 89.4 | 79 | 509 | 34.9 | 10.2 | 496.5 | 231.4 | 85.4 | 27.5 |
| Sampson | 115 | 2 686 | 173.9 | 74.6 | 72 | D | D | D | 509.5 | 174.4 | 86.7 | 29.8 |
| Scotland | 120 | 2 664 | 202.4 | 87.2 | 39 | D | D | D | 350.6 | 118.6 | 48.8 | 33.0 |
| Stanly | 181 | 3 106 | 221.3 | 87.9 | 94 | 454 | 34.3 | 10.4 | 395.0 | 205.0 | 85.5 | 17.0 |
| Stokes | 54 | 1 233 | 69.0 | 30.2 | 48 | 232 | 17.3 | 5.0 | 263.8 | 143.0 | 44.0 | 12.8 |
| Surry | 172 | 3 892 | 303.4 | 119.7 | 103 | 663 | 52.0 | 16.7 | 574.6 | 260.6 | 124.9 | 24.3 |

1. State totals may include programs not allocated by county.

# Table B. States and Counties — Federal Funds, Residential Construction, and Local Government Finances

| STATE County | Federal funds and grants, 2009–2010 (cont.) | | | | | | | Value of residential construction authorized by building permits, 2011 | | Local government finances, 2007 | | | | |
|---|---|---|---|---|---|---|---|---|---|---|---|---|---|---|
| | Expenditures (mil dol) (cont.) | | | | | | | | | General revenue | | | | |
| | Procurement contract awards | | | Grants[1] | | | | | | | | Taxes | | |
| | | | | | | | | | | | | | Per capita[2] (dollars) | |
| | Salaries and wages | Defense | Other | Medicaid and other health-related | Nutrition and family welfare | Education | Other | New construction ($1,000) | Number of housing units | Total (mil dol) | Inter-governmental (mil dol) | Total (mil dol) | Total | Property |
| | 171 | 172 | 173 | 174 | 175 | 176 | 177 | 178 | 179 | 180 | 181 | 182 | 183 | 184 |
| NORTH CAROLINA—Cont'd | | | | | | | | | | | | | | |
| Chowan | 4.1 | 0.2 | 4.0 | 25.7 | 6.5 | 1.3 | 7.7 | 2 444 | 11 | 45.2 | 23.4 | 13.6 | 932 | 658 |
| Clay | 2.2 | 0.0 | 2.1 | 20.8 | 1.5 | 0.7 | 0.3 | 6 511 | 40 | 25.6 | 14.1 | 9.0 | 881 | 587 |
| Cleveland | 19.6 | 20.8 | 3.9 | 139.6 | 18.0 | 10.7 | 30.5 | 20 633 | 137 | 447.4 | 160.4 | 75.9 | 771 | 591 |
| Columbus | 12.7 | 0.5 | 3.6 | 171.3 | 15.1 | 6.3 | 3.6 | 7 202 | 78 | 187.5 | 120.9 | 40.4 | 747 | 563 |
| Craven | 313.8 | 208.9 | 8.9 | 130.9 | 15.1 | 9.6 | 7.0 | 43 816 | 338 | 304.3 | 154.3 | 80.1 | 828 | 585 |
| Cumberland | 9 417.2 | 1 227.0 | 60.3 | 295.8 | 65.2 | 40.4 | 41.3 | 272 904 | 2 401 | 933.7 | 488.1 | 281.0 | 917 | 694 |
| Currituck | 3.8 | 11.1 | 4.1 | 12.5 | 3.0 | 2.0 | 0.0 | 34 845 | 137 | 88.4 | 30.2 | 46.8 | 1 952 | 1 232 |
| Dare | 19.3 | 2.6 | 14.9 | 9.6 | 3.7 | 1.0 | 0.1 | 38 974 | 151 | 175.9 | 39.5 | 105.7 | 3 129 | 2 067 |
| Davidson | 18.1 | 4.9 | 5.5 | 91.7 | 20.6 | 10.9 | 4.8 | 46 512 | 222 | 363.0 | 207.3 | 111.1 | 709 | 511 |
| Davie | 13.7 | 24.0 | 23.5 | 30.0 | 4.3 | 3.0 | 0.3 | 7 009 | 41 | 106.4 | 44.6 | 35.2 | 868 | 668 |
| Duplin | 17.8 | 28.3 | 9.2 | 112.8 | 13.4 | 6.3 | 5.0 | 8 276 | 51 | 150.9 | 90.2 | 38.0 | 717 | 525 |
| Durham | 362.8 | 107.7 | 819.0 | 1 209.6 | 37.5 | 31.8 | 787.6 | 176 266 | 1 283 | 1 149.4 | 615.6 | 365.7 | 1 426 | 1 128 |
| Edgecombe | 53.8 | 0.6 | 7.6 | 133.8 | 15.4 | 4.6 | 3.7 | 3 156 | 27 | 161.7 | 99.7 | 36.6 | 695 | 525 |
| Forsyth | 127.7 | 28.7 | 52.8 | 528.3 | 43.6 | 35.8 | 71.3 | 130 313 | 1 288 | 1 099.0 | 503.2 | 394.7 | 1 165 | 908 |
| Franklin | 12.7 | 2.1 | 5.1 | 85.6 | 8.1 | 3.7 | 1.9 | 21 596 | 126 | 129.3 | 63.0 | 45.1 | 788 | 576 |
| Gaston | 46.7 | 0.9 | 8.3 | 171.0 | 32.0 | 19.6 | 13.8 | 109 201 | 624 | 649.8 | 347.4 | 200.0 | 987 | 769 |
| Gates | 2.6 | 0.1 | 0.6 | 22.5 | 2.7 | 0.8 | 0.1 | 6 020 | 28 | 29.5 | 19.4 | 7.3 | 622 | 442 |
| Graham | 2.1 | 0.0 | 2.3 | 18.8 | 1.9 | 1.3 | 0.1 | 1 323 | 14 | 29.6 | 15.7 | 10.0 | 1 274 | 989 |
| Granville | 106.7 | 2.4 | 12.6 | 70.1 | 9.0 | 4.4 | 4.5 | 20 758 | 142 | 158.8 | 68.1 | 38.0 | 691 | 495 |
| Greene | 4.6 | 0.2 | 0.7 | 29.3 | 4.8 | 1.7 | 5.7 | 1 613 | 9 | 49.0 | 31.1 | 11.7 | 574 | 396 |
| Guilford | 394.5 | 103.0 | 176.2 | 333.5 | 68.8 | 62.4 | 112.0 | 161 196 | 1 681 | 1 639.0 | 702.0 | 602.1 | 1 292 | 1 030 |
| Halifax | 26.4 | 0.2 | 2.6 | 194.8 | 17.3 | 6.8 | 0.9 | 8 333 | 48 | 187.8 | 110.9 | 48.5 | 880 | 637 |
| Harnett | 29.9 | 13.5 | 3.8 | 124.0 | 15.7 | 7.5 | 2.0 | 123 055 | 824 | 274.5 | 140.3 | 72.3 | 665 | 463 |
| Haywood | 12.1 | 0.1 | 12.3 | 79.7 | 10.0 | 3.7 | 5.3 | 31 152 | 152 | 279.0 | 102.6 | 61.6 | 1 092 | 809 |
| Henderson | 27.6 | 6.7 | 5.0 | 67.4 | 14.1 | 6.1 | 10.4 | 47 609 | 254 | 360.7 | 113.6 | 94.5 | 938 | 694 |
| Hertford | 8.4 | 0.0 | 43.0 | 68.1 | 7.0 | 3.3 | 3.5 | 343 | 2 | 77.9 | 44.8 | 18.7 | 808 | 571 |
| Hoke | 21.8 | 3.4 | 17.0 | 43.6 | 7.8 | 3.6 | 0.2 | 71 980 | 406 | 98.1 | 62.6 | 24.2 | 570 | 386 |
| Hyde | 2.3 | 0.6 | 5.2 | 17.7 | 1.5 | 0.5 | 0.3 | 1 051 | 10 | 24.8 | 13.5 | 7.6 | 1 461 | 1 069 |
| Iredell | 27.3 | 13.7 | 5.6 | 88.6 | 16.8 | 14.7 | 6.8 | 96 403 | 307 | 418.9 | 197.1 | 146.7 | 969 | 718 |
| Jackson | 6.4 | 0.1 | 2.6 | 48.5 | 5.3 | 7.8 | 4.6 | 49 852 | 150 | 99.8 | 48.3 | 37.7 | 1 025 | 700 |
| Johnston | 49.1 | 1.5 | 6.3 | 187.5 | 20.8 | 7.4 | 10.8 | 84 219 | 588 | 558.2 | 231.4 | 144.9 | 920 | 646 |
| Jones | 1.5 | 0.2 | 0.4 | 26.2 | 2.9 | 1.2 | 0.0 | 4 028 | 25 | 26.8 | 17.8 | 6.8 | 671 | 497 |
| Lee | 27.9 | 0.4 | 2.7 | 65.4 | 8.5 | 4.6 | 3.2 | 15 210 | 104 | 185.4 | 98.5 | 57.2 | 987 | 782 |
| Lenoir | 64.4 | 63.7 | 5.4 | 142.7 | 15.2 | 8.1 | 6.6 | 8 015 | 90 | 209.4 | 120.1 | 49.3 | 868 | 648 |
| Lincoln | 19.5 | 3.7 | 2.6 | 37.0 | 8.5 | 3.9 | 3.7 | 25 062 | 147 | 188.2 | 83.6 | 63.7 | 871 | 637 |
| McDowell | 8.0 | 0.0 | 1.9 | 55.4 | 7.8 | 3.5 | 0.5 | 27 165 | 111 | 101.0 | 58.2 | 29.2 | 670 | 434 |
| Macon | 14.1 | 3.3 | 3.9 | 42.8 | 8.5 | 2.2 | 0.8 | 20 931 | 77 | 92.4 | 37.7 | 38.1 | 1 169 | 847 |
| Madison | 3.6 | 0.0 | 1.0 | 63.8 | 4.4 | 2.8 | 6.6 | 7 500 | 50 | 47.3 | 26.7 | 14.1 | 696 | 543 |
| Martin | 26.5 | 0.0 | 1.0 | 65.4 | 10.9 | 2.1 | 5.1 | 0 | 0 | 92.1 | 52.2 | 21.1 | 894 | 653 |
| Mecklenburg | 571.2 | 88.9 | 333.1 | 406.2 | 94.0 | 47.7 | 433.8 | 446 077 | 3 094 | 5 658.9 | 1 289.9 | 1 510.5 | 1 742 | 1 297 |
| Mitchell | 4.2 | 0.0 | 1.6 | 45.2 | 7.2 | 7.8 | 0.8 | 3 495 | 32 | 51.6 | 34.8 | 11.4 | 720 | 471 |
| Montgomery | 4.5 | 33.6 | 1.7 | 41.7 | 5.9 | 2.2 | 0.7 | 11 588 | 108 | 81.2 | 49.6 | 20.2 | 735 | 562 |
| Moore | 20.8 | 11.4 | 3.3 | 77.7 | 11.9 | 7.3 | 8.1 | 77 412 | 396 | 295.3 | 171.4 | 82.0 | 971 | 720 |
| Nash | 7.3 | 15.3 | 2.7 | 137.3 | 23.4 | 8.3 | 13.5 | 23 802 | 165 | 307.5 | 170.2 | 83.5 | 899 | 679 |
| New Hanover | 104.9 | 36.2 | 36.5 | 180.3 | 25.8 | 11.5 | 64.3 | 133 291 | 724 | 1 251.2 | 268.4 | 265.3 | 1 393 | 995 |
| Northampton | 4.8 | 0.0 | 4.9 | 85.9 | 12.6 | 2.2 | 7.2 | 2 410 | 16 | 65.8 | 39.8 | 16.5 | 790 | 625 |
| Onslow | 1 099.6 | 920.0 | 8.7 | 89.1 | 25.9 | 15.1 | 19.2 | 226 082 | 2 031 | 491.5 | 204.5 | 109.0 | 670 | 440 |
| Orange | 34.7 | 3.9 | 69.6 | 804.5 | 21.8 | 29.0 | 184.2 | 63 245 | 260 | 444.6 | 174.9 | 203.8 | 1 639 | 1 389 |
| Pamlico | 4.0 | 0.8 | 1.0 | 22.0 | 2.3 | 1.0 | 0.1 | 8 945 | 36 | 44.1 | 25.6 | 12.2 | 968 | 694 |
| Pasquotank | 97.6 | 6.9 | 90.9 | 42.1 | 8.1 | 11.6 | 5.3 | 7 973 | 54 | 238.0 | 73.2 | 33.7 | 830 | 550 |
| Pender | 8.3 | 2.5 | 2.0 | 55.7 | 8.7 | 4.8 | 7.9 | 28 894 | 193 | 129.3 | 59.5 | 52.1 | 1 044 | 801 |
| Perquimans | 2.6 | -0.2 | 0.6 | 22.6 | 2.7 | 1.1 | 0.5 | 9 096 | 38 | 37.4 | 19.3 | 10.4 | 832 | 619 |
| Person | 6.1 | 29.9 | 1.0 | 64.7 | 6.9 | 3.8 | 0.4 | 11 704 | 52 | 121.8 | 61.8 | 38.1 | 1 020 | 780 |
| Pitt | 50.5 | 13.6 | 8.7 | 234.2 | 24.8 | 16.7 | 22.7 | 47 256 | 336 | 467.9 | 237.2 | 132.8 | 873 | 642 |
| Polk | 3.8 | 0.0 | 0.9 | 17.7 | 2.9 | 1.3 | 0.0 | 9 267 | 41 | 51.4 | 22.8 | 20.0 | 1 052 | 834 |
| Randolph | 36.5 | 17.0 | 10.1 | 76.6 | 19.1 | 11.7 | 9.3 | 41 301 | 261 | 317.4 | 178.5 | 96.0 | 685 | 495 |
| Richmond | 19.0 | 0.1 | 3.5 | 92.4 | 10.8 | 5.4 | 1.6 | 5 863 | 118 | 134.3 | 82.3 | 35.5 | 772 | 554 |
| Robeson | 76.6 | 0.3 | 7.2 | 321.7 | 35.9 | 19.5 | 50.4 | 20 891 | 105 | 428.2 | 262.2 | 82.2 | 641 | 435 |
| Rockingham | 16.8 | 96.2 | 8.7 | 140.2 | 15.3 | 9.2 | 1.6 | 25 182 | 105 | 246.0 | 128.2 | 75.0 | 812 | 621 |
| Rowan | 120.9 | 1.8 | 57.9 | 83.5 | 24.7 | 15.7 | 9.9 | 23 908 | 106 | 361.8 | 189.4 | 110.3 | 803 | 621 |
| Rutherford | 11.7 | 0.7 | 2.4 | 101.4 | 12.0 | 7.1 | 8.1 | 17 683 | 93 | 186.9 | 97.7 | 48.5 | 770 | 534 |
| Sampson | 32.6 | 0.9 | 1.8 | 127.9 | 14.5 | 6.9 | 2.0 | 10 734 | 70 | 194.1 | 120.1 | 45.5 | 716 | 508 |
| Scotland | 7.3 | 0.0 | 1.2 | 90.2 | 18.9 | 4.8 | 18.1 | 2 497 | 19 | 121.1 | 72.4 | 32.2 | 886 | 651 |
| Stanly | 13.6 | 0.8 | 2.0 | 45.0 | 8.1 | 4.7 | 1.9 | 14 398 | 98 | 171.4 | 96.2 | 48.3 | 816 | 615 |
| Stokes | 6.7 | 0.0 | 1.6 | 39.2 | 5.6 | 3.0 | 0.0 | 10 490 | 50 | 101.6 | 57.4 | 32.2 | 698 | 500 |
| Surry | 15.3 | 0.5 | 3.0 | 110.2 | 10.0 | 6.6 | 1.8 | 17 156 | 83 | 237.1 | 138.6 | 61.3 | 847 | 587 |

1. State totals may include programs not allocated by county.  2. Based on the resident population estimated as of July 1 of the year shown.

# Table B. States and Counties — **Local Government Finances, Government Employment, and Voting**

| STATE County | Direct general expenditure Total (mil dol) [185] | Per capita[1] (dollars) [186] | Percent of total for: Education [187] | Health and hospitals [188] | Police protection [189] | Public welfare [190] | Highways [191] | Debt outstanding Total (mil dol) [192] | Per capita[1] (dollars) [193] | Government employment, 2011 Federal civilian [194] | Federal military [195] | State and local [196] | Presidential election,[2] 2012 Percent of vote cast: Democratic [197] | Republican [198] | All other [199] |
|---|---|---|---|---|---|---|---|---|---|---|---|---|---|---|---|
| **NORTH CAROLINA—Cont'd** | | | | | | | | | | | | | | | |
| Chowan | 50.5 | 3 450 | 46.3 | 3.6 | 4.4 | 8.9 | 0.7 | 42.0 | 2 873 | 39 | 38 | 853 | 49.1 | 50.2 | 0.7 |
| Clay | 31.4 | 3 064 | 39.4 | 7.0 | 2.9 | 3.0 | 0.1 | 13.1 | 1 278 | 24 | 27 | 498 | 31.3 | 66.9 | 1.8 |
| Cleveland | 469.4 | 4 768 | 34.1 | 43.7 | 3.1 | 5.6 | 0.6 | 204.2 | 2 074 | 178 | 253 | 5 618 | 39.6 | 59.5 | 0.9 |
| Columbus | 177.0 | 3 275 | 56.1 | 4.2 | 3.6 | 9.2 | 1.1 | 53.8 | 996 | 135 | 150 | 3 729 | 45.6 | 53.5 | 0.9 |
| Craven | 290.3 | 3 001 | 46.9 | 7.3 | 5.4 | 8.0 | 1.6 | 505.2 | 1 648 | 14 512 | 53 482 | 23 159 | 43.4 | 55.8 | 0.8 |
| Cumberland | 930.3 | 3 035 | 51.6 | 4.5 | 7.1 | 8.8 | 1.6 | 505.2 | 1 648 | 14 512 | 53 482 | 23 159 | 58.5 | 40.9 | 0.6 |
| Currituck | 81.0 | 3 382 | 44.1 | 4.4 | 4.8 | 4.9 | 0.0 | 16.8 | 700 | 38 | 62 | 1 159 | 33.7 | 65.2 | 1.2 |
| Dare | 200.8 | 5 945 | 36.5 | 8.2 | 6.8 | 3.5 | 1.4 | 213.4 | 6 319 | 230 | 200 | 2 801 | 44.7 | 54.0 | 1.3 |
| Davidson | 373.8 | 2 388 | 59.0 | 3.0 | 5.0 | 6.8 | 1.1 | 193.2 | 1 234 | 166 | 421 | 6 751 | 32.7 | 66.2 | 1.1 |
| Davie | 100.0 | 2 468 | 59.9 | 6.8 | 3.8 | 6.0 | 1.0 | 61.7 | 1 522 | 59 | 108 | 1 535 | 30.3 | 68.6 | 1.0 |
| Duplin | 148.7 | 2 807 | 57.7 | 4.7 | 4.4 | 9.4 | 1.3 | 21.8 | 412 | 153 | 154 | 3 297 | 45.0 | 54.4 | 0.6 |
| Durham | 1 159.6 | 4 521 | 28.7 | 4.4 | 5.3 | 28.3 | 2.3 | 831.0 | 3 240 | 5 437 | 856 | 14 341 | 75.6 | 23.6 | 0.8 |
| Edgecombe | 158.9 | 3 019 | 51.9 | 5.2 | 4.6 | 12.1 | 1.0 | 31.6 | 600 | 228 | 146 | 4 593 | 67.1 | 32.6 | 0.3 |
| Forsyth | 1 134.6 | 3 349 | 44.9 | 5.7 | 6.0 | 5.1 | 2.4 | 1 264.1 | 3 731 | 1 593 | 961 | 18 728 | 54.8 | 44.3 | 0.8 |
| Franklin | 137.9 | 2 409 | 55.6 | 6.3 | 4.4 | 10.4 | 0.7 | 119.4 | 2 087 | 81 | 158 | 2 369 | 49.1 | 49.8 | 1.1 |
| Gaston | 602.9 | 2 977 | 46.4 | 9.7 | 5.9 | 6.5 | 1.7 | 405.1 | 2 000 | 368 | 538 | 9 461 | 37.2 | 62.2 | 0.6 |
| Gates | 29.6 | 2 520 | 67.8 | 0.8 | 2.7 | 12.6 | 0.0 | 17.7 | 1 504 | 32 | 31 | 532 | 52.2 | 47.0 | 0.8 |
| Graham | 24.6 | 3 134 | 50.6 | 8.2 | 3.3 | 8.2 | 2.7 | 5.0 | 631 | 35 | 23 | 463 | 30.3 | 67.7 | 2.0 |
| Granville | 147.0 | 2 670 | 45.0 | 23.5 | 3.8 | 6.4 | 1.0 | 86.8 | 1 577 | 1 498 | 155 | 6 881 | 52.9 | 46.3 | 0.8 |
| Greene | 48.6 | 2 381 | 62.5 | 4.8 | 3.8 | 11.8 | 0.4 | 15.7 | 768 | 36 | 56 | 1 823 | 46.8 | 52.7 | 0.4 |
| Guilford | 1 774.8 | 3 809 | 43.9 | 4.9 | 6.3 | 5.3 | 2.9 | 1 709.2 | 3 668 | 3 865 | 1 345 | 29 760 | 58.8 | 40.4 | 0.8 |
| Halifax | 210.7 | 3 826 | 45.2 | 4.6 | 3.6 | 8.6 | 0.9 | 130.5 | 2 369 | 123 | 140 | 4 466 | 64.0 | 35.7 | 0.3 |
| Harnett | 253.1 | 2 328 | 52.9 | 4.8 | 4.9 | 8.4 | 1.5 | 220.3 | 2 026 | 112 | 310 | 5 185 | 41.2 | 57.9 | 0.8 |
| Haywood | 278.6 | 4 936 | 34.6 | 34.6 | 3.5 | 4.4 | 1.4 | 112.7 | 1 997 | 123 | 153 | 4 041 | 45.4 | 53.1 | 1.5 |
| Henderson | 354.7 | 3 519 | 34.7 | 31.5 | 3.9 | 7.1 | 0.8 | 165.7 | 1 644 | 214 | 280 | 5 308 | 38.9 | 59.9 | 1.2 |
| Hertford | 78.2 | 3 368 | 51.6 | 8.5 | 4.4 | 9.4 | 1.3 | 83.0 | 3 577 | 66 | 63 | 1 655 | 70.5 | 29.0 | 0.5 |
| Hoke | 100.8 | 2 377 | 59.3 | 2.8 | 4.3 | 8.4 | 0.8 | 59.9 | 1 412 | 51 | 128 | 2 110 | 59.0 | 40.3 | 0.7 |
| Hyde | 34.6 | 6 684 | 31.4 | 6.9 | 2.3 | 5.6 | 0.0 | 3.5 | 683 | 38 | 15 | 687 | 50.3 | 49.1 | 0.6 |
| Iredell | 402.1 | 2 655 | 52.5 | 3.3 | 5.5 | 6.9 | 1.2 | 322.4 | 2 129 | 262 | 419 | 8 512 | 37.3 | 61.7 | 1.0 |
| Jackson | 99.0 | 2 693 | 51.8 | 4.8 | 3.4 | 6.6 | 0.5 | 28.2 | 768 | 55 | 105 | 6 315 | 52.0 | 46.6 | 1.5 |
| Johnston | 575.0 | 3 653 | 48.4 | 23.7 | 2.9 | 6.0 | 0.9 | 389.9 | 2 476 | 212 | 447 | 8 998 | 37.7 | 61.4 | 0.8 |
| Jones | 26.1 | 2 575 | 57.8 | 5.1 | 3.1 | 12.1 | 0.4 | 3.4 | 332 | 21 | 26 | 498 | 45.5 | 53.9 | 0.6 |
| Lee | 176.7 | 3 049 | 60.7 | 2.4 | 5.8 | 6.2 | 1.5 | 169.7 | 2 928 | 154 | 152 | 3 233 | 45.3 | 53.7 | 1.0 |
| Lenoir | 199.5 | 3 515 | 51.6 | 3.0 | 5.8 | 8.7 | 1.3 | 247.7 | 4 364 | 256 | 154 | 6 088 | 49.7 | 49.8 | 0.4 |
| Lincoln | 192.4 | 2 631 | 57.0 | 4.9 | 4.4 | 7.4 | 0.6 | 167.4 | 2 289 | 100 | 204 | 3 706 | 32.7 | 66.0 | 1.3 |
| McDowell | 100.2 | 2 301 | 61.6 | 1.7 | 4.5 | 10.1 | 0.9 | 19.3 | 443 | 81 | 117 | 2 649 | 35.7 | 62.7 | 1.5 |
| Macon | 84.6 | 2 594 | 42.4 | 7.4 | 5.8 | 5.6 | 2.1 | 20.0 | 614 | 168 | 88 | 1 681 | 38.4 | 59.9 | 1.7 |
| Madison | 46.8 | 2 305 | 48.5 | 6.9 | 5.4 | 9.8 | 1.3 | 4.9 | 242 | 45 | 54 | 958 | 48.4 | 50.0 | 1.6 |
| Martin | 89.8 | 3 806 | 51.8 | 9.4 | 4.0 | 8.4 | 1.1 | 29.3 | 1 242 | 49 | 63 | 1 632 | 52.1 | 47.5 | 0.4 |
| Mecklenburg | 5 360.0 | 6 182 | 23.3 | 38.5 | 3.7 | 2.2 | 2.1 | 7 546.9 | 8 704 | 5 557 | 2 565 | 64 326 | 61.8 | 37.4 | 0.7 |
| Mitchell | 50.3 | 3 187 | 68.1 | 1.9 | 3.0 | 7.2 | 0.7 | 2.1 | 133 | 57 | 40 | 1 192 | 28.5 | 70.1 | 1.4 |
| Montgomery | 79.5 | 2 895 | 61.3 | 3.7 | 4.7 | 8.2 | 1.8 | 53.6 | 1 951 | 57 | 72 | 1 724 | 43.9 | 54.9 | 1.2 |
| Moore | 290.3 | 3 438 | 43.3 | 24.6 | 5.2 | 4.8 | 1.9 | 57.7 | 684 | 139 | 231 | 4 401 | 38.9 | 60.3 | 0.9 |
| Nash | 316.3 | 3 403 | 52.3 | 5.9 | 5.7 | 6.1 | 1.6 | 56.4 | 607 | 190 | 249 | 6 237 | 49.0 | 50.4 | 0.6 |
| New Hanover | 1 295.2 | 6 801 | 21.6 | 45.7 | 4.0 | 3.3 | 1.0 | 1 282.9 | 6 737 | 910 | 807 | 17 830 | 48.8 | 50.2 | 1.0 |
| Northampton | 70.7 | 3 395 | 47.2 | 6.4 | 3.1 | 11.6 | 1.4 | 33.8 | 1 623 | 43 | 57 | 1 251 | 65.0 | 34.6 | 0.4 |
| Onslow | 512.9 | 3 152 | 44.1 | 27.9 | 3.7 | 5.4 | 0.7 | 286.7 | 1 762 | 6 891 | 51 050 | 7 953 | 38.8 | 60.3 | 0.8 |
| Orange | 455.7 | 3 666 | 44.7 | 7.0 | 5.5 | 4.4 | 1.6 | 516.8 | 4 157 | 240 | 403 | 36 788 | 71.8 | 27.1 | 1.1 |
| Pamlico | 40.4 | 3 214 | 58.6 | 3.0 | 2.4 | 10.4 | 0.8 | 8.0 | 635 | 30 | 61 | 888 | 42.3 | 57.0 | 0.8 |
| Pasquotank | 257.5 | 6 350 | 28.9 | 41.4 | 2.6 | 4.4 | 0.9 | 250.3 | 6 174 | 730 | 856 | 5 315 | 56.5 | 42.8 | 0.7 |
| Pender | 131.7 | 2 642 | 53.9 | 5.2 | 4.1 | 7.6 | 0.7 | 92.5 | 1 855 | 97 | 145 | 2 322 | 41.7 | 57.3 | 0.9 |
| Perquimans | 36.8 | 2 944 | 47.7 | 2.1 | 3.6 | 7.0 | 0.8 | 34.6 | 2 765 | 29 | 35 | 631 | 42.6 | 56.6 | 0.8 |
| Person | 123.3 | 3 301 | 53.5 | 5.3 | 5.3 | 7.9 | 0.7 | 143.1 | 3 832 | 53 | 103 | 1 996 | 45.3 | 53.8 | 0.8 |
| Pitt | 474.8 | 3 122 | 47.1 | 4.9 | 6.5 | 7.4 | 1.5 | 381.1 | 2 506 | 450 | 464 | 23 386 | 54.1 | 45.3 | 0.6 |
| Polk | 48.5 | 2 549 | 49.7 | 3.2 | 5.2 | 7.8 | 1.7 | 24.9 | 1 307 | 42 | 52 | 865 | 41.6 | 56.7 | 1.7 |
| Randolph | 325.5 | 2 323 | 62.4 | 2.7 | 5.3 | 6.9 | 1.2 | 196.3 | 1 401 | 229 | 370 | 6 345 | 28.2 | 70.5 | 1.3 |
| Richmond | 140.2 | 3 049 | 59.0 | 3.2 | 5.1 | 7.4 | 1.0 | 46.3 | 1 008 | 85 | 121 | 3 034 | 50.3 | 48.8 | 1.0 |
| Robeson | 431.5 | 3 367 | 52.6 | 15.8 | 4.3 | 9.6 | 0.9 | 75.0 | 585 | 278 | 352 | 8 709 | 56.5 | 42.7 | 0.8 |
| Rockingham | 255.7 | 2 767 | 50.9 | 5.5 | 6.0 | 8.4 | 2.0 | 96.5 | 1 044 | 152 | 242 | 4 279 | 41.5 | 57.4 | 1.1 |
| Rowan | 366.0 | 2 664 | 59.0 | 2.6 | 5.2 | 6.8 | 1.9 | 221.8 | 1 614 | 2 140 | 359 | 6 867 | 38.0 | 60.8 | 1.2 |
| Rutherford | 190.8 | 3 029 | 54.2 | 7.0 | 4.9 | 7.8 | 1.5 | 299.6 | 4 754 | 102 | 175 | 3 595 | 33.6 | 65.4 | 1.1 |
| Sampson | 199.9 | 3 141 | 55.7 | 10.8 | 4.1 | 8.0 | 1.3 | 220.9 | 3 471 | 108 | 165 | 4 339 | 45.5 | 53.9 | 0.6 |
| Scotland | 118.1 | 3 246 | 56.9 | 2.7 | 4.6 | 10.0 | 0.7 | 25.0 | 688 | 48 | 93 | 2 478 | 57.3 | 42.2 | 0.4 |
| Stanly | 170.6 | 2 882 | 55.4 | 3.5 | 6.7 | 6.5 | 1.6 | 50.1 | 846 | 134 | 157 | 3 620 | 31.1 | 67.8 | 1.0 |
| Stokes | 96.4 | 2 093 | 60.0 | 5.0 | 4.5 | 8.9 | 0.6 | 21.7 | 471 | 72 | 122 | 1 831 | 31.6 | 66.6 | 1.7 |
| Surry | 234.6 | 3 242 | 53.8 | 14.5 | 3.6 | 6.0 | 1.5 | 87.7 | 1 212 | 157 | 191 | 4 940 | 35.5 | 63.4 | 1.1 |

1. Based on the resident population estimated as of July 1 of the year shown.   2. © 2013 Election Data Services, Inc. All rights reserved.

| STATE/ County code | CBSA code[1] | County type[2] | STATE County | Land area,[3] (sq km) 2010 | Population 2012 | | | Population characteristics[6], 2011 | | | | | | | | | | |
|---|---|---|---|---|---|---|---|---|---|---|---|---|---|---|---|---|---|---|
| | | | | | | | | Race alone or in combination, not Hispanic or Latino (percent) | | | | | Age (percent) | | | | | |
| | | | | | Total persons | Rank | Per square kilometer | White | Black | American Indian, Alaska Native | Asian and Pacific Islander | Percent Hispanic or Latino[4] | Under 5 years | 5 to 17 years | 18 to 24 years | 25 to 34 years | 35 to 44 years | 45 to 54 years |
| | | | | 1 | 2 | 3 | 4 | 5 | 6 | 7 | 8 | 9 | 10 | 11 | 12 | 13 | 14 | 15 |
| | | | NORTH CAROLINA—Cont'd | | | | | | | | | | | | | | | |
| 37 173 | ... | 8 | Swain | 1 368 | 14 141 | 2 166 | 10.3 | 68.6 | 2.0 | 28.4 | 0.8 | 4.2 | 6.2 | 17.0 | 9.0 | 10.6 | 11.9 | 14.2 |
| 37 175 | 14820 | 6 | Transylvania | 980 | 32 849 | 1 360 | 33.5 | 92.1 | 5.0 | 1.0 | 0.8 | 2.9 | 4.4 | 13.1 | 8.2 | 8.8 | 10.2 | 13.3 |
| 37 177 | ... | 9 | Tyrrell | 1 008 | 4 338 | 2 881 | 4.3 | 54.1 | 37.4 | 0.7 | 2.5 | 6.6 | 5.6 | 12.5 | 8.8 | 14.8 | 13.2 | 15.7 |
| 37 179 | 16740 | 1 | Union | 1 636 | 208 520 | 302 | 127.5 | 75.4 | 12.4 | 0.8 | 2.1 | 10.7 | 6.9 | 23.0 | 7.5 | 10.4 | 16.3 | 15.4 |
| 37 181 | 25780 | 4 | Vance | 657 | 45 132 | 1 065 | 68.7 | 42.9 | 49.9 | 0.5 | 0.8 | 7.0 | 6.8 | 18.3 | 9.4 | 11.1 | 12.6 | 13.9 |
| 37 183 | 39580 | 2 | Wake | 2 163 | 952 151 | 48 | 440.2 | 63.6 | 21.4 | 0.9 | 6.2 | 10.0 | 7.1 | 18.7 | 9.5 | 15.1 | 16.0 | 14.5 |
| 37 185 | ... | 8 | Warren | 1 110 | 20 576 | 1 807 | 18.5 | 39.0 | 52.8 | 5.7 | 0.6 | 3.4 | 5.6 | 14.5 | 8.2 | 10.7 | 10.8 | 14.5 |
| 37 187 | ... | 7 | Washington | 902 | 12 736 | 2 258 | 14.1 | 46.5 | 49.6 | 0.6 | 0.5 | 3.8 | 6.2 | 16.3 | 7.7 | 9.4 | 10.7 | 14.5 |
| 37 189 | 14380 | 6 | Watauga | 810 | 51 871 | 958 | 64.0 | 93.2 | 2.4 | 0.8 | 1.3 | 3.5 | 3.7 | 10.1 | 31.5 | 10.4 | 9.2 | 10.9 |
| 37 191 | 24140 | 3 | Wayne | 1 432 | 124 246 | 492 | 86.8 | 56.8 | 32.3 | 0.9 | 1.8 | 10.1 | 6.9 | 17.7 | 10.0 | 13.4 | 12.3 | 14.1 |
| 37 193 | 35900 | 6 | Wilkes | 1 954 | 69 306 | 767 | 35.5 | 89.5 | 4.8 | 0.6 | 0.6 | 5.6 | 5.5 | 16.6 | 7.2 | 10.6 | 12.9 | 15.4 |
| 37 195 | 48980 | 4 | Wilson | 954 | 81 867 | 677 | 85.8 | 50.2 | 39.4 | 0.7 | 1.3 | 9.7 | 6.7 | 17.8 | 8.8 | 11.9 | 12.6 | 14.3 |
| 37 197 | 49180 | 2 | Yadkin | 867 | 38 084 | 1 218 | 43.9 | 86.1 | 3.7 | 0.6 | 0.4 | 10.0 | 5.7 | 17.2 | 7.5 | 10.3 | 13.9 | 15.3 |
| 37 199 | ... | 8 | Yancey | 810 | 17 630 | 1 940 | 21.8 | 94.0 | 1.2 | 0.7 | 0.4 | 4.5 | 4.8 | 15.1 | 6.8 | 9.6 | 12.5 | 14.4 |
| 38 000 | ... | X | NORTH DAKOTA | 178 711 | 699 628 | X | 3.9 | 90.0 | 1.7 | 6.2 | 1.5 | 2.2 | 6.6 | 15.5 | 12.3 | 13.8 | 11.0 | 13.8 |
| 38 001 | ... | 9 | Adams | 2 558 | 2 311 | 3 027 | 0.9 | 97.4 | 0.6 | 1.4 | 0.7 | 1.0 | 5.3 | 13.4 | 6.0 | 8.6 | 9.0 | 15.3 |
| 38 003 | ... | 6 | Barnes | 3 863 | 11 015 | 2 356 | 2.9 | 96.5 | 1.2 | 1.5 | 0.9 | 1.2 | 5.2 | 15.4 | 10.2 | 10.1 | 10.1 | 14.5 |
| 38 005 | ... | 9 | Benson | 3 597 | 6 760 | 2 702 | 1.9 | 45.1 | 0.2 | 54.6 | 0.4 | 1.3 | 9.1 | 24.3 | 9.0 | 10.7 | 10.1 | 12.6 |
| 38 007 | 19860 | 9 | Billings | 2 976 | 905 | 3 113 | 0.3 | 97.2 | 0.0 | 1.5 | 1.0 | 0.9 | 5.1 | 12.4 | 8.6 | 13.2 | 9.6 | 17.5 |
| 38 009 | ... | 9 | Bottineau | 4 321 | 6 579 | 2 717 | 1.5 | 95.6 | 0.9 | 3.4 | 0.6 | 1.4 | 5.6 | 13.9 | 8.2 | 9.4 | 9.8 | 15.2 |
| 38 011 | ... | 9 | Bowman | 3 009 | 3 202 | 2 960 | 1.1 | 96.4 | 0.4 | 0.8 | 0.2 | 2.8 | 6.2 | 15.7 | 6.0 | 11.0 | 9.4 | 15.0 |
| 38 013 | ... | 9 | Burke | 2 858 | 2 171 | 3 040 | 0.8 | 95.6 | 0.5 | 1.4 | 0.8 | 2.2 | 6.4 | 15.2 | 5.5 | 11.1 | 9.4 | 16.4 |
| 38 015 | 13900 | 3 | Burleigh | 4 229 | 85 774 | 659 | 20.3 | 93.3 | 1.0 | 4.7 | 0.8 | 1.4 | 6.6 | 15.8 | 10.2 | 14.6 | 11.9 | 14.4 |
| 38 017 | 22020 | 3 | Cass | 4 571 | 156 157 | 403 | 34.2 | 91.8 | 2.8 | 1.9 | 2.9 | 2.2 | 6.8 | 14.7 | 16.4 | 17.1 | 12.1 | 12.3 |
| 38 019 | ... | 9 | Cavalier | 3 856 | 3 948 | 2 912 | 1.0 | 97.6 | 0.5 | 1.5 | 0.3 | 0.9 | 4.4 | 15.1 | 5.1 | 7.9 | 9.3 | 16.2 |
| 38 021 | ... | 9 | Dickey | 2 930 | 5 268 | 2 822 | 1.8 | 96.1 | 1.1 | 1.3 | 0.7 | 2.0 | 6.6 | 16.6 | 9.1 | 9.8 | 10.4 | 12.8 |
| 38 023 | ... | 9 | Divide | 3 265 | 2 228 | 3 034 | 0.7 | 96.9 | 0.7 | 1.2 | 0.3 | 1.6 | 4.5 | 12.2 | 6.0 | 9.2 | 8.2 | 16.0 |
| 38 025 | ... | 9 | Dunn | 5 202 | 3 967 | 2 910 | 0.8 | 85.5 | 0.9 | 13.1 | 0.5 | 1.7 | 6.1 | 15.5 | 8.1 | 11.4 | 11.1 | 15.4 |
| 38 027 | ... | 9 | Eddy | 1 632 | 2 368 | 3 019 | 1.5 | 94.4 | 0.4 | 3.4 | 0.5 | 2.3 | 5.2 | 15.1 | 5.5 | 8.9 | 9.4 | 15.5 |
| 38 029 | ... | 8 | Emmons | 3 912 | 3 491 | 2 941 | 0.9 | 98.2 | 0.3 | 1.0 | 0.3 | 1.0 | 4.4 | 16.5 | 5.1 | 5.6 | 9.6 | 15.7 |
| 38 031 | ... | 9 | Foster | 1 646 | 3 392 | 2 947 | 2.1 | 98.0 | 0.5 | 0.7 | 0.2 | 1.0 | 5.2 | 15.7 | 6.9 | 8.7 | 10.8 | 16.8 |
| 38 033 | ... | 9 | Golden Valley | 2 592 | 1 804 | 3 070 | 0.7 | 96.3 | 0.9 | 1.1 | 0.3 | 2.1 | 5.3 | 19.3 | 5.6 | 11.1 | 8.7 | 14.1 |
| 38 035 | 24220 | 3 | Grand Forks | 3 720 | 67 472 | 784 | 18.1 | 90.3 | 2.7 | 3.5 | 2.7 | 3.1 | 6.3 | 13.2 | 22.3 | 14.7 | 10.0 | 12.1 |
| 38 037 | ... | 8 | Grant | 4 297 | 2 333 | 3 022 | 0.5 | 98.2 | 0.6 | 1.9 | 0.3 | 0.4 | 4.8 | 13.3 | 4.4 | 7.1 | 9.5 | 15.5 |
| 38 039 | ... | 9 | Griggs | 1 836 | 2 362 | 3 020 | 1.3 | 98.5 | 0.3 | 0.5 | 0.2 | 0.5 | 5.4 | 12.9 | 5.0 | 8.2 | 8.5 | 14.5 |
| 38 041 | ... | 9 | Hettinger | 2 932 | 2 553 | 3 005 | 0.9 | 96.5 | 0.7 | 3.5 | 0.3 | 0.5 | 5.1 | 14.2 | 5.4 | 9.3 | 10.0 | 15.4 |
| 38 043 | ... | 8 | Kidder | 3 500 | 2 426 | 3 012 | 0.7 | 95.2 | 0.5 | 0.2 | 1.2 | 3.3 | 5.1 | 15.8 | 6.4 | 9.4 | 10.7 | 15.3 |
| 38 045 | ... | 9 | LaMoure | 2 968 | 4 114 | 2 893 | 1.4 | 98.3 | 0.5 | 0.8 | 0.2 | 0.9 | 5.1 | 16.0 | 4.8 | 8.7 | 9.8 | 15.7 |
| 38 047 | ... | 9 | Logan | 2 571 | 1 924 | 3 064 | 0.7 | 98.3 | 0.3 | 0.7 | 0.3 | 0.9 | 4.8 | 16.3 | 4.5 | 7.7 | 9.5 | 15.3 |
| 38 049 | 33500 | 9 | McHenry | 4 854 | 5 789 | 2 780 | 1.2 | 96.9 | 0.7 | 1.2 | 0.5 | 1.7 | 5.7 | 15.7 | 6.2 | 10.6 | 10.9 | 15.0 |
| 38 051 | ... | 9 | McIntosh | 2 525 | 2 751 | 2 993 | 1.1 | 97.4 | 0.5 | 1.1 | 0.4 | 1.4 | 5.1 | 13.4 | 3.9 | 8.0 | 8.2 | 14.6 |
| 38 053 | ... | 9 | McKenzie | 7 149 | 7 987 | 2 600 | 1.1 | 76.5 | 0.6 | 21.2 | 0.7 | 2.7 | 7.9 | 18.9 | 8.9 | 12.9 | 10.6 | 14.7 |
| 38 055 | ... | 8 | McLean | 5 467 | 9 309 | 2 493 | 1.7 | 91.8 | 0.5 | 7.6 | 0.3 | 1.4 | 4.7 | 14.4 | 5.4 | 9.4 | 10.5 | 15.5 |
| 38 057 | ... | 6 | Mercer | 2 701 | 8 486 | 2 565 | 3.1 | 95.4 | 0.5 | 2.9 | 0.6 | 1.6 | 5.8 | 15.6 | 5.8 | 10.7 | 10.3 | 19.2 |
| 38 059 | 13900 | 3 | Morton | 4 989 | 28 101 | 1 490 | 5.6 | 94.2 | 0.9 | 4.4 | 0.6 | 1.5 | 6.8 | 16.8 | 7.4 | 13.8 | 12.1 | 14.7 |
| 38 061 | ... | 9 | Mountrail | 4 728 | 8 734 | 2 541 | 1.8 | 67.5 | 0.9 | 29.2 | 0.7 | 4.2 | 7.1 | 16.5 | 10.9 | 14.1 | 11.6 | 14.0 |
| 38 063 | ... | 8 | Nelson | 2 543 | 3 080 | 2 971 | 1.2 | 97.2 | 0.8 | 1.8 | 0.4 | 1.2 | 4.3 | 13.2 | 6.0 | 7.9 | 8.9 | 15.7 |
| 38 065 | ... | 8 | Oliver | 1 871 | 1 838 | 3 069 | 1.0 | 96.6 | 0.7 | 2.0 | 0.5 | 1.0 | 5.4 | 16.4 | 5.5 | 9.7 | 9.8 | 18.0 |
| 38 067 | ... | 9 | Pembina | 2 897 | 7 271 | 2 655 | 2.5 | 94.4 | 0.6 | 3.0 | 0.4 | 2.8 | 5.5 | 15.8 | 6.0 | 10.5 | 9.9 | 15.9 |
| 38 069 | ... | 7 | Pierce | 2 638 | 4 457 | 2 871 | 1.7 | 94.0 | 0.7 | 4.9 | 0.3 | 1.2 | 5.4 | 15.6 | 6.8 | 9.0 | 10.6 | 14.7 |
| 38 071 | ... | 7 | Ramsey | 3 074 | 11 536 | 2 325 | 3.8 | 89.5 | 0.7 | 10.1 | 0.8 | 1.5 | 6.1 | 15.5 | 8.9 | 11.6 | 10.4 | 15.5 |
| 38 073 | ... | 8 | Ransom | 2 233 | 5 444 | 2 830 | 2.4 | 97.2 | 0.7 | 1.0 | 0.6 | 1.4 | 5.3 | 17.8 | 5.8 | 10.0 | 11.4 | 14.8 |
| 38 075 | 33500 | 9 | Renville | 2 272 | 2 559 | 3 004 | 1.1 | 98.0 | 0.4 | 1.4 | 0.4 | 1.1 | 6.2 | 15.7 | 6.7 | 10.8 | 10.6 | 15.1 |
| 38 077 | 47420 | 6 | Richland | 3 719 | 16 217 | 2 029 | 4.4 | 94.6 | 1.1 | 2.8 | 0.8 | 2.0 | 5.8 | 15.9 | 14.6 | 10.2 | 9.9 | 15.4 |
| 38 079 | ... | 9 | Rolette | 2 339 | 14 382 | 2 144 | 6.1 | 23.6 | 0.5 | 76.4 | 0.5 | 1.4 | 10.0 | 22.9 | 9.9 | 12.1 | 10.6 | 13.7 |
| 38 081 | ... | 9 | Sargent | 2 224 | 3 896 | 2 916 | 1.8 | 97.0 | 0.3 | 1.2 | 0.5 | 1.7 | 5.3 | 16.6 | 6.1 | 9.7 | 11.0 | 16.1 |
| 38 083 | ... | 9 | Sheridan | 2 518 | 1 266 | 3 097 | 0.5 | 97.3 | 0.2 | 2.1 | 0.8 | 1.1 | 3.1 | 12.6 | 5.3 | 8.0 | 8.6 | 15.4 |
| 38 085 | ... | 8 | Sioux | 2 834 | 4 347 | 2 879 | 1.5 | 16.9 | 1.0 | 82.6 | 0.7 | 2.1 | 11.0 | 26.1 | 11.5 | 12.9 | 11.8 | 11.8 |
| 38 087 | ... | 9 | Slope | 3 147 | 758 | 3 124 | 0.2 | 97.5 | 0.0 | 1.4 | 0.1 | 1.5 | 6.5 | 15.0 | 4.2 | 10.2 | 7.8 | 18.2 |
| 38 089 | 19860 | 7 | Stark | 3 457 | 26 771 | 1 537 | 7.7 | 94.3 | 1.1 | 1.7 | 1.6 | 2.4 | 6.5 | 15.2 | 11.9 | 14.0 | 10.2 | 14.5 |
| 38 091 | ... | 8 | Steele | 1 845 | 1 989 | 3 055 | 1.1 | 96.7 | 0.4 | 1.8 | 0.3 | 1.4 | 4.8 | 16.1 | 5.1 | 8.8 | 10.6 | 16.1 |
| 38 093 | 27420 | 7 | Stutsman | 5 754 | 20 934 | 1 781 | 3.6 | 95.3 | 1.0 | 2.1 | 0.9 | 1.7 | 5.4 | 14.8 | 10.0 | 12.0 | 10.9 | 15.2 |
| 38 095 | ... | 9 | Towner | 2 654 | 2 318 | 3 026 | 0.9 | 96.5 | 0.3 | 3.3 | 0.3 | 0.6 | 5.5 | 14.5 | 5.6 | 7.2 | 9.7 | 16.8 |
| 38 097 | ... | 8 | Traill | 2 232 | 8 072 | 2 597 | 3.6 | 95.7 | 0.7 | 1.7 | 0.5 | 2.5 | 6.3 | 15.6 | 9.9 | 10.0 | 10.7 | 15.0 |
| 38 099 | ... | 6 | Walsh | 3 320 | 11 046 | 2 354 | 3.3 | 88.8 | 0.6 | 2.0 | 0.6 | 9.0 | 6.2 | 16.0 | 6.6 | 10.0 | 10.1 | 15.8 |

1. CBSA = Core Based Statistical Area. See Appendix A for explanation. See Appendix B for list of metropolitan areas with component counties.    2. County type code from the Economic Research Service of USDA Rural-Urban Continuum Codes. See Appendix A for definition.    3. Dry land or land partially or temporarily covered by water.    4. May be of any race.

— **Population and Households**

| STATE County | Age (percent) (cont.) 55 to 64 years | 65 to 74 years | 75 years and over | Percent female | Total persons 2000 | 2010 | Percent change 2000–2010 | 2010–2012 | Components of change, 2010–2012 Births | Deaths | Net migration | Households, 2010 Number | Percent change, 2000–2010 | Persons per house-hold | Percent Female family house-holder[1] | One per-son |
|---|---|---|---|---|---|---|---|---|---|---|---|---|---|---|---|---|
| | 16 | 17 | 18 | 19 | 20 | 21 | 22 | 23 | 24 | 25 | 26 | 27 | 28 | 29 | 30 | 31 |
| NORTH CAROLINA—Cont'd | | | | | | | | | | | | | | | | |
| Swain | 13.8 | 10.2 | 7.0 | 51.4 | 12 968 | 13 981 | 7.8 | 1.1 | 409 | 392 | 155 | 5 672 | 10.4 | 2.42 | 14.3 | 27.4 |
| Transylvania | 15.6 | 14.3 | 12.1 | 51.8 | 29 334 | 33 090 | 12.8 | -0.7 | 608 | 829 | -16 | 14 394 | 16.8 | 2.22 | 9.2 | 29.1 |
| Tyrrell | 13.0 | 9.1 | 7.3 | 45.2 | 4 149 | 4 407 | 6.2 | -1.6 | 110 | 117 | -63 | 1 595 | 3.8 | 2.37 | 16.7 | 28.2 |
| Union | 10.4 | 6.3 | 3.7 | 50.7 | 123 677 | 201 292 | 62.8 | 3.6 | 5 385 | 2 648 | 4 429 | 67 864 | 56.4 | 2.94 | 10.7 | 16.8 |
| Vance | 13.4 | 8.2 | 6.4 | 53.1 | 42 954 | 45 422 | 5.7 | -0.6 | 1 301 | 1 052 | -531 | 17 395 | 7.4 | 2.56 | 22.2 | 26.2 |
| Wake | 10.2 | 5.2 | 3.7 | 51.3 | 627 846 | 900 993 | 43.5 | 5.7 | 28 060 | 9 982 | 32 753 | 345 645 | 42.8 | 2.55 | 11.5 | 26.3 |
| Warren | 16.3 | 10.9 | 8.5 | 49.4 | 19 972 | 20 972 | 5.0 | -1.9 | 425 | 553 | -255 | 8 321 | 8.0 | 2.38 | 18.0 | 29.6 |
| Washington | 16.3 | 10.3 | 8.6 | 53.0 | 13 723 | 13 228 | -3.6 | -3.7 | 325 | 363 | -448 | 5 526 | 3.0 | 2.37 | 20.2 | 30.1 |
| Watauga | 11.5 | 7.4 | 5.3 | 49.9 | 42 695 | 51 079 | 19.6 | 1.6 | 780 | 780 | 809 | 20 403 | 23.4 | 2.24 | 6.6 | 28.5 |
| Wayne | 12.2 | 7.6 | 5.8 | 51.1 | 113 329 | 122 623 | 8.2 | 1.3 | 3 696 | 2 656 | 636 | 47 831 | 12.2 | 2.50 | 16.7 | 27.4 |
| Wilkes | 14.4 | 10.1 | 7.4 | 50.7 | 65 632 | 69 340 | 5.6 | 0.0 | 1 491 | 1 632 | 17 | 28 360 | 6.4 | 2.41 | 10.5 | 26.7 |
| Wilson | 13.4 | 8.1 | 6.4 | 52.2 | 73 814 | 81 234 | 10.1 | 0.8 | 2 271 | 1 826 | 127 | 31 962 | 11.7 | 2.49 | 17.9 | 27.8 |
| Yadkin | 13.6 | 9.4 | 7.1 | 50.7 | 36 348 | 38 406 | 5.7 | -0.8 | 883 | 893 | -295 | 15 486 | 6.8 | 2.46 | 10.5 | 25.9 |
| Yancey | 15.7 | 11.8 | 9.3 | 50.8 | 17 774 | 17 818 | 0.2 | -1.1 | 378 | 476 | -84 | 7 644 | 2.3 | 2.31 | 8.1 | 28.4 |
| NORTH DAKOTA | 12.6 | 7.0 | 7.4 | 49.4 | 642 200 | 672 591 | 4.7 | 4.0 | 20 393 | 13 299 | 19 506 | 281 192 | 9.3 | 2.30 | 8.2 | 31.5 |
| Adams | 17.8 | 10.8 | 13.9 | 51.9 | 2 593 | 2 343 | -9.6 | -1.4 | 46 | 65 | -17 | 1 098 | -2.1 | 2.09 | 4.8 | 36.6 |
| Barnes | 15.2 | 9.2 | 10.2 | 50.3 | 11 775 | 11 066 | -6.0 | -0.5 | 247 | 291 | 0 | 4 826 | -1.2 | 2.19 | 6.4 | 32.9 |
| Benson | 11.5 | 7.0 | 5.7 | 49.1 | 6 964 | 6 660 | -4.4 | 1.5 | 291 | 126 | -69 | 2 233 | -4.1 | 2.98 | 20.6 | 23.2 |
| Billings | 18.1 | 8.1 | 7.4 | 46.8 | 888 | 783 | -11.8 | 15.6 | 19 | 9 | 111 | 358 | -2.2 | 2.16 | 1.7 | 33.2 |
| Bottineau | 16.7 | 10.8 | 10.3 | 48.1 | 7 149 | 6 429 | -10.1 | 2.3 | 154 | 223 | 220 | 2 832 | -4.4 | 2.17 | 5.6 | 32.2 |
| Bowman | 15.7 | 9.0 | 12.0 | 49.5 | 3 242 | 3 151 | -2.8 | 1.6 | 82 | 100 | 63 | 1 385 | 2.0 | 2.22 | 4.4 | 32.9 |
| Burke | 16.4 | 10.0 | 9.6 | 47.4 | 2 242 | 1 968 | -12.2 | 10.3 | 54 | 49 | 195 | 913 | -9.9 | 2.15 | 5.4 | 33.6 |
| Burleigh | 12.8 | 6.8 | 6.8 | 50.7 | 69 416 | 81 308 | 17.1 | 5.5 | 2 458 | 1 395 | 3 329 | 33 976 | 22.8 | 2.31 | 8.7 | 30.5 |
| Cass | 10.7 | 4.9 | 5.0 | 49.6 | 123 138 | 149 778 | 21.6 | 4.3 | 4 879 | 2 009 | 3 440 | 63 899 | 24.5 | 2.27 | 8.3 | 33.0 |
| Cavalier | 16.4 | 12.1 | 13.6 | 49.2 | 4 831 | 3 993 | -17.3 | -1.1 | 90 | 114 | -18 | 1 818 | -9.9 | 2.15 | 4.0 | 34.2 |
| Dickey | 12.5 | 10.1 | 12.1 | 50.4 | 5 757 | 5 289 | -8.1 | -0.4 | 98 | 170 | 50 | 2 180 | -4.5 | 2.29 | 4.4 | 33.3 |
| Divide | 17.9 | 12.1 | 13.8 | 48.8 | 2 283 | 2 071 | -9.3 | 7.6 | 46 | 44 | 157 | 977 | -2.8 | 2.05 | 4.5 | 36.6 |
| Dunn | 15.8 | 8.3 | 8.3 | 47.0 | 3 600 | 3 536 | -1.8 | 12.2 | 89 | 55 | 387 | 1 401 | 1.7 | 2.43 | 6.6 | 26.5 |
| Eddy | 16.1 | 10.1 | 14.3 | 51.9 | 2 757 | 2 385 | -13.5 | -0.7 | 49 | 117 | 50 | 1 057 | -9.2 | 2.18 | 7.4 | 33.9 |
| Emmons | 15.5 | 12.0 | 15.6 | 48.4 | 4 331 | 3 550 | -18.0 | -1.7 | 55 | 128 | 14 | 1 594 | -10.8 | 2.19 | 3.8 | 34.4 |
| Foster | 13.5 | 9.3 | 12.9 | 49.9 | 3 759 | 3 343 | -11.1 | 1.5 | 61 | 96 | 83 | 1 495 | -2.9 | 2.20 | 5.5 | 33.5 |
| Golden Valley | 15.4 | 9.2 | 11.2 | 50.6 | 1 924 | 1 680 | -12.7 | 7.4 | 43 | 29 | 106 | 774 | 1.7 | 2.10 | 4.3 | 39.4 |
| Grand Forks | 10.8 | 5.5 | 5.1 | 48.6 | 66 109 | 66 861 | 1.1 | 0.9 | 2 044 | 1 020 | -419 | 27 417 | 7.8 | 2.28 | 9.1 | 32.1 |
| Grant | 17.8 | 13.6 | 14.2 | 50.2 | 2 841 | 2 394 | -15.7 | -2.5 | 48 | 70 | -41 | 1 128 | -5.6 | 2.10 | 3.9 | 36.5 |
| Griggs | 18.3 | 11.6 | 15.6 | 49.5 | 2 754 | 2 420 | -12.1 | -2.4 | 46 | 87 | -13 | 1 056 | -8.3 | 2.19 | 4.2 | 36.3 |
| Hettinger | 15.7 | 11.1 | 13.7 | 52.1 | 2 715 | 2 477 | -8.8 | 3.1 | 58 | 63 | 80 | 1 059 | -8.3 | 2.30 | 4.5 | 33.1 |
| Kidder | 16.9 | 9.6 | 10.7 | 49.1 | 2 753 | 2 435 | -11.6 | -0.4 | 60 | 38 | -30 | 1 059 | -8.5 | 2.23 | 5.0 | 28.1 |
| LaMoure | 15.4 | 10.5 | 13.9 | 48.9 | 4 701 | 4 139 | -12.0 | -0.6 | 64 | 107 | 21 | 1 825 | -6.0 | 2.23 | 4.6 | 32.7 |
| Logan | 14.0 | 12.7 | 15.4 | 49.3 | 2 308 | 1 990 | -13.8 | -3.3 | 36 | 54 | -53 | 843 | -12.5 | 2.28 | 3.0 | 30.8 |
| McHenry | 15.3 | 9.9 | 10.8 | 48.2 | 5 987 | 5 395 | -9.9 | 7.3 | 131 | 126 | 376 | 2 377 | -5.9 | 2.25 | 5.8 | 31.3 |
| McIntosh | 12.8 | 13.4 | 20.7 | 51.3 | 3 390 | 2 809 | -17.1 | -2.1 | 51 | 120 | 13 | 1 307 | -10.9 | 2.07 | 3.5 | 36.2 |
| McKenzie | 13.3 | 7.3 | 5.7 | 48.5 | 5 737 | 6 360 | 10.9 | 25.6 | 212 | 115 | 1 500 | 2 410 | 12.0 | 2.58 | 10.2 | 25.3 |
| McLean | 17.9 | 11.8 | 10.2 | 48.8 | 9 311 | 8 962 | -3.7 | 3.9 | 214 | 258 | 379 | 3 897 | 2.1 | 2.25 | 5.1 | 29.0 |
| Mercer | 16.6 | 8.3 | 7.6 | 48.5 | 8 644 | 8 424 | -2.5 | 0.7 | 221 | 174 | 17 | 3 625 | 8.3 | 2.29 | 5.0 | 27.3 |
| Morton | 13.6 | 7.4 | 7.4 | 50.2 | 25 303 | 27 471 | 8.6 | 2.3 | 854 | 527 | 308 | 11 289 | 14.2 | 2.38 | 9.3 | 27.7 |
| Mountrail | 13.0 | 6.8 | 6.0 | 45.2 | 6 631 | 7 673 | 15.7 | 13.8 | 298 | 166 | 901 | 2 793 | 9.1 | 2.55 | 11.4 | 28.3 |
| Nelson | 17.0 | 12.6 | 14.4 | 49.0 | 3 715 | 3 126 | -15.9 | -1.5 | 64 | 140 | 33 | 1 474 | -9.5 | 2.07 | 5.4 | 36.0 |
| Oliver | 18.9 | 8.9 | 7.4 | 47.4 | 2 065 | 1 846 | -10.6 | -0.4 | 38 | 17 | -32 | 756 | -4.4 | 2.44 | 4.8 | 22.6 |
| Pembina | 16.5 | 9.0 | 11.1 | 49.1 | 8 585 | 7 413 | -13.7 | -1.9 | 177 | 209 | -117 | 3 257 | -7.9 | 2.23 | 5.6 | 32.4 |
| Pierce | 14.7 | 9.6 | 13.6 | 49.7 | 4 675 | 4 357 | -6.8 | 2.3 | 90 | 144 | 147 | 1 835 | -6.6 | 2.23 | 5.9 | 34.3 |
| Ramsey | 14.0 | 8.7 | 9.3 | 49.9 | 12 066 | 11 451 | -5.1 | 0.7 | 357 | 312 | 48 | 4 955 | 0.0 | 2.21 | 9.5 | 34.5 |
| Ransom | 14.9 | 8.2 | 11.7 | 49.3 | 5 890 | 5 457 | -7.4 | -0.2 | 130 | 189 | 51 | 2 310 | -1.7 | 2.28 | 5.4 | 32.9 |
| Renville | 15.2 | 8.9 | 10.7 | 48.8 | 2 610 | 2 470 | -5.4 | 3.6 | 69 | 64 | 84 | 1 061 | -2.2 | 2.28 | 5.1 | 30.9 |
| Richland | 13.5 | 6.9 | 7.9 | 48.3 | 17 998 | 16 321 | -9.3 | -0.6 | 352 | 316 | -141 | 6 651 | -3.4 | 2.31 | 7.1 | 30.9 |
| Rolette | 10.5 | 5.8 | 4.4 | 50.8 | 13 674 | 13 937 | 1.9 | 3.2 | 672 | 327 | 97 | 4 783 | 5.0 | 2.89 | 23.2 | 25.0 |
| Sargent | 16.1 | 10.4 | 8.9 | 47.0 | 4 366 | 3 829 | -12.3 | 1.7 | 64 | 85 | 83 | 1 675 | -6.2 | 2.26 | 4.7 | 30.2 |
| Sheridan | 16.3 | 16.2 | 14.4 | 49.7 | 1 710 | 1 321 | -22.7 | -4.2 | 20 | 19 | -56 | 645 | -11.8 | 2.05 | 5.7 | 33.0 |
| Sioux | 7.7 | 4.9 | 2.4 | 49.5 | 4 044 | 4 153 | 2.7 | 4.7 | 210 | 80 | 62 | 1 158 | 5.8 | 3.55 | 31.6 | 17.4 |
| Slope | 19.1 | 9.7 | 9.2 | 46.2 | 767 | 727 | -5.2 | 4.3 | 23 | 5 | 11 | 326 | 4.2 | 2.23 | 4.9 | 29.4 |
| Stark | 12.1 | 6.8 | 8.8 | 49.4 | 22 636 | 24 199 | 6.9 | 10.6 | 736 | 518 | 2 296 | 10 085 | 12.9 | 2.31 | 7.4 | 30.9 |
| Steele | 16.7 | 10.7 | 11.2 | 48.4 | 2 258 | 1 975 | -12.5 | 0.7 | 38 | 26 | -20 | 864 | -6.4 | 2.29 | 4.5 | 27.8 |
| Stutsman | 14.3 | 7.7 | 9.5 | 49.1 | 21 908 | 21 100 | -3.7 | -0.8 | 480 | 546 | -94 | 8 931 | -0.3 | 2.17 | 7.5 | 35.3 |
| Towner | 16.7 | 11.9 | 12.1 | 49.0 | 2 876 | 2 246 | -21.9 | 3.2 | 43 | 55 | 77 | 1 048 | -14.0 | 2.10 | 6.0 | 36.4 |
| Traill | 13.5 | 8.6 | 10.4 | 50.0 | 8 477 | 8 121 | -4.2 | -0.6 | 211 | 214 | -44 | 3 394 | 1.6 | 2.29 | 6.2 | 31.3 |
| Walsh | 14.9 | 9.7 | 10.6 | 49.4 | 12 389 | 11 119 | -10.3 | -0.7 | 264 | 280 | -49 | 4 746 | -5.6 | 2.27 | 7.1 | 32.8 |

1. No spouse present.

# Table B. States and Counties — Population, Vital Statistics, Medicare, and Crime

| | Daytime population, 2007–2011 | | Births, 2011 | | Deaths, 2011 | | Persons under 65 with no health insurance, 2010 | | Medicare, 2012 | | | Serious crimes known to police,[2] 2011 Total | |
|---|---|---|---|---|---|---|---|---|---|---|---|---|---|
| STATE County | Persons in group quarters, 2010 | Number | Employ-ment/resi-dence ratio | Total | Rate[1] | Number | Rate[1] | Number | Percent | Eligible for Medicare | Enrolled in Medicare Advantage | Enrolled in a Medicare prescription drug plan | Number | Rate[3] |
| | 32 | 33 | 34 | 35 | 36 | 37 | 38 | 39 | 40 | 41 | 42 | 43 | 44 | 45 |
| NORTH CAROLINA—Cont'd | | | | | | | | | | | | | | |
| Swain | 244 | 15 345 | 1.27 | 175 | 12.5 | 178 | 12.7 | 2 658 | 22.7 | 3 368 | 268 | 1 584 | 427 | 3 016 |
| Transylvania | 1 070 | 30 690 | 0.85 | 287 | 8.7 | 356 | 10.8 | 5 039 | 21.1 | 9 025 | 1 492 | 4 165 | 639 | 1 907 |
| Tyrrell | 632 | 4 240 | 0.91 | 46 | 10.5 | 47 | 10.8 | 816 | 26.7 | 760 | 23 | 466 | 71 | 1 591 |
| Union | 2 050 | 168 059 | 0.68 | 2 456 | 12.0 | 1 095 | 5.3 | 31 988 | 17.8 | 25 177 | 3 021 | 12 205 | 3 231 | 1 894 |
| Vance | 846 | 44 681 | 0.97 | 607 | 13.4 | 478 | 10.6 | 7 593 | 19.6 | 9 343 | 2 040 | 4 861 | 3 764 | 8 183 |
| Wake | 20 983 | 901 171 | 1.05 | 12 622 | 13.6 | 4 274 | 4.6 | 125 353 | 15.5 | 104 462 | 19 539 | 38 141 | 25 875 | 2 836 |
| Warren | 1 168 | 18 143 | 0.60 | 203 | 9.7 | 252 | 12.1 | 3 502 | 21.8 | 4 148 | 729 | 2 190 | 706 | 3 511 |
| Washington | 151 | 13 102 | 0.98 | 148 | 11.4 | 176 | 13.6 | 2 026 | 18.9 | 3 055 | 109 | 2 019 | 351 | 2 620 |
| Watauga | 5 323 | 53 015 | 1.11 | 344 | 6.7 | 338 | 6.6 | 7 921 | 20.1 | 7 725 | 804 | 3 434 | 1 016 | 1 964 |
| Wayne | 3 219 | 118 492 | 0.95 | 1 615 | 13.1 | 1 192 | 9.6 | 21 224 | 20.4 | 21 170 | 1 402 | 10 320 | 5 612 | 4 624 |
| Wilkes | 967 | 66 626 | 0.91 | 665 | 9.6 | 713 | 10.3 | 12 361 | 21.7 | 16 046 | 4 866 | 6 841 | 2 423 | 3 451 |
| Wilson | 1 593 | 84 770 | 1.13 | 1 040 | 12.8 | 806 | 9.9 | 15 065 | 21.9 | 16 758 | 995 | 9 819 | 3 338 | 4 175 |
| Yadkin | 304 | 32 721 | 0.67 | 404 | 10.6 | 379 | 9.9 | 6 693 | 20.9 | 7 855 | 3 814 | 2 283 | 1 173 | 3 167 |
| Yancey | 165 | 16 256 | 0.77 | 173 | 9.8 | 197 | 11.1 | 3 369 | 24.0 | 4 850 | 872 | 2 203 | 265 | 1 469 |
| NORTH DAKOTA | 25 056 | 687 491 | 1.06 | 8 960 | 13.1 | 5 915 | 8.6 | 63 683 | 11.4 | 112 407 | 3 040 | 71 647 | 14 935 | 2 184 |
| Adams | 52 | 2 376 | 1.03 | 27 | 11.7 | 35 | 15.2 | 274 | 15.6 | 621 | 36 | 451 | 20 | 839 |
| Barnes | 492 | 10 960 | 0.98 | 111 | 10.0 | 139 | 12.6 | 940 | 11.0 | 2 446 | 299 | 1 658 | 113 | 1 004 |
| Benson | 16 | 6 692 | 1.01 | 119 | 17.7 | 53 | 7.9 | 1 025 | 17.6 | 1 028 | 105 | 668 | 17 | 251 |
| Billings | 9 | 899 | 1.02 | 9 | 11.0 | 4 | 4.9 | 119 | 18.8 | 143 | D | 87 | 6 | 754 |
| Bottineau | 270 | 5 986 | 0.86 | 64 | 9.9 | 104 | 16.1 | 625 | 12.9 | 1 517 | 96 | 984 | 24 | 367 |
| Bowman | 82 | 3 161 | 1.02 | 36 | 11.5 | 45 | 14.4 | 331 | 13.5 | 680 | 48 | 463 | NA | NA |
| Burke | 2 | 1 950 | 0.99 | 19 | 9.3 | 30 | 14.8 | 170 | 10.8 | 482 | 27 | 324 | 21 | 1 224 |
| Burleigh | 2 763 | 83 443 | 1.07 | 1 065 | 12.8 | 610 | 7.3 | 6 360 | 9.3 | 13 520 | 2 111 | 8 473 | 2 247 | 2 718 |
| Cass | 5 010 | 159 416 | 1.14 | 2 155 | 14.1 | 871 | 5.7 | 13 609 | 10.4 | 18 757 | 2 859 | 10 648 | 3 855 | 2 531 |
| Cavalier | 83 | 3 989 | 1.00 | 33 | 8.4 | 61 | 15.5 | 330 | 11.2 | 1 052 | 68 | 758 | 60 | 1 478 |
| Dickey | 299 | 5 291 | 0.99 | 70 | 13.2 | 81 | 15.2 | 495 | 12.6 | 1 151 | 92 | 812 | 31 | 576 |
| Divide | 66 | 2 161 | 1.10 | 18 | 8.5 | 24 | 11.3 | 180 | 11.8 | 522 | 32 | 358 | NA | NA |
| Dunn | 127 | 3 560 | 1.01 | 31 | 8.3 | 16 | 4.3 | 546 | 18.7 | 645 | 69 | 420 | NA | NA |
| Eddy | 84 | 2 255 | 0.85 | 25 | 10.5 | 48 | 20.2 | 247 | 13.9 | 597 | 62 | 447 | 19 | 784 |
| Emmons | 53 | 3 488 | 0.95 | 20 | 5.6 | 53 | 14.9 | 447 | 17.6 | 1 000 | 219 | 699 | 20 | 554 |
| Foster | 61 | 3 614 | 1.13 | 31 | 9.3 | 45 | 13.5 | 256 | 10.0 | 796 | 94 | 589 | 11 | 324 |
| Golden Valley | 52 | 1 579 | 1.00 | 16 | 9.1 | 8 | 4.6 | 226 | 17.8 | 389 | 20 | 258 | 12 | 703 |
| Grand Forks | 4 216 | 70 912 | 1.11 | 893 | 13.4 | 449 | 6.7 | 6 161 | 11.0 | 8 536 | 1 047 | 5 027 | 1 980 | 2 991 |
| Grant | 25 | 2 250 | 0.85 | 22 | 9.4 | 34 | 14.5 | 440 | 25.6 | 675 | 93 | 459 | 6 | 247 |
| Griggs | 47 | 2 395 | 0.99 | 26 | 11.0 | 45 | 19.0 | 213 | 12.0 | 658 | 67 | 449 | 7 | 284 |
| Hettinger | 169 | 2 358 | 0.88 | 23 | 9.1 | 24 | 9.5 | 257 | 15.1 | 673 | 81 | 473 | 15 | 595 |
| Kidder | 0 | 2 325 | 0.86 | 23 | 9.5 | 22 | 9.1 | 374 | 19.7 | 578 | 147 | 411 | 11 | 444 |
| LaMoure | 65 | 4 081 | 0.95 | 29 | 7.1 | 48 | 11.7 | 395 | 12.8 | 1 023 | 116 | 743 | 3 | 71 |
| Logan | 72 | 1 894 | 0.89 | 17 | 8.6 | 26 | 13.1 | 319 | 22.7 | 527 | 107 | 358 | 13 | 642 |
| McHenry | 48 | 4 416 | 0.62 | 52 | 9.4 | 65 | 11.8 | 668 | 15.8 | 1 245 | 175 | 784 | 42 | 766 |
| McIntosh | 103 | 2 916 | 1.04 | 26 | 9.4 | 57 | 20.6 | 329 | 18.0 | 956 | 155 | 691 | 7 | 245 |
| McKenzie | 152 | 6 905 | 1.22 | 96 | 13.7 | 43 | 6.1 | 854 | 15.5 | 971 | 39 | 637 | 138 | 2 134 |
| McLean | 196 | 8 503 | 0.90 | 82 | 9.0 | 115 | 12.7 | 864 | 12.3 | 2 122 | 285 | 1 344 | 85 | 933 |
| Mercer | 126 | 9 130 | 1.18 | 109 | 12.9 | 81 | 9.6 | 593 | 8.4 | 1 573 | 232 | 897 | NA | NA |
| Morton | 597 | 22 235 | 0.68 | 391 | 14.1 | 233 | 8.4 | 2 617 | 11.2 | 4 844 | 726 | 3 320 | 672 | 2 406 |
| Mountrail | 564 | 8 666 | 1.33 | 114 | 14.1 | 72 | 8.9 | 985 | 14.7 | 1 293 | 67 | 773 | 114 | 1 461 |
| Nelson | 80 | 2 979 | 0.89 | 28 | 9.2 | 64 | 20.9 | 281 | 12.6 | 939 | 40 | 633 | 25 | 786 |
| Oliver | 2 | 2 125 | 1.39 | 18 | 9.8 | 8 | 4.4 | 209 | 13.6 | 364 | 62 | 244 | 3 | 160 |
| Pembina | 149 | 7 747 | 1.08 | 79 | 10.8 | 105 | 14.3 | 701 | 11.9 | 1 630 | 160 | 1 070 | 73 | 968 |
| Pierce | 261 | 4 314 | 0.98 | 41 | 9.4 | 61 | 13.9 | 444 | 14.0 | 1 015 | 271 | 702 | 63 | 1 422 |
| Ramsey | 492 | 11 724 | 1.05 | 140 | 12.2 | 140 | 12.2 | 1 086 | 12.0 | 2 331 | 99 | 1 557 | 406 | 3 487 |
| Ransom | 185 | 5 364 | 0.93 | 51 | 9.4 | 95 | 17.6 | 465 | 10.8 | 1 156 | 90 | 803 | 53 | 955 |
| Renville | 54 | 2 215 | 0.83 | 35 | 14.1 | 30 | 12.0 | 223 | 11.4 | 537 | 38 | 363 | 29 | 1 154 |
| Richland | 986 | 16 123 | 0.97 | 196 | 12.1 | 130 | 8.0 | 1 449 | 11.1 | 2 747 | 457 | 1 828 | 305 | 1 838 |
| Rolette | 122 | 13 750 | 0.97 | 294 | 20.7 | 149 | 10.5 | 2 201 | 17.5 | 1 833 | 109 | 1 031 | 58 | 420 |
| Sargent | 37 | 4 697 | 1.39 | 31 | 8.2 | 36 | 9.5 | 323 | 10.6 | 801 | 58 | 545 | 28 | 719 |
| Sheridan | 0 | 1 150 | 0.79 | 10 | 7.6 | 7 | 5.3 | 200 | 21.8 | 421 | 53 | 279 | 18 | 1 340 |
| Sioux | 44 | 4 915 | 1.64 | 98 | 22.9 | 35 | 8.2 | 604 | 15.8 | 401 | 20 | 218 | 0 | 0 |
| Slope | 0 | 706 | 0.96 | 16 | 22.3 | 4 | 5.6 | 124 | 20.8 | 150 | D | 94 | 2 | 271 |
| Stark | 909 | 24 640 | 1.05 | 315 | 12.5 | 220 | 8.7 | 2 180 | 11.0 | 4 187 | 459 | 2 893 | 555 | 2 255 |
| Steele | 0 | 1 825 | 0.86 | 14 | 7.2 | 8 | 4.1 | 187 | 12.2 | 437 | 42 | 292 | 6 | 299 |
| Stutsman | 1 733 | 21 572 | 1.06 | 222 | 10.5 | 227 | 10.8 | 1 632 | 10.2 | 4 261 | 827 | 2 805 | 374 | 1 743 |
| Towner | 43 | 2 205 | 0.95 | 21 | 9.3 | 29 | 12.8 | 277 | 16.5 | 631 | 37 | 422 | 12 | 525 |
| Traill | 362 | 7 733 | 0.90 | 90 | 11.0 | 99 | 12.2 | 645 | 10.2 | 1 572 | 176 | 1 048 | 51 | 801 |
| Walsh | 332 | 11 301 | 1.02 | 130 | 11.8 | 137 | 12.4 | 1 122 | 12.8 | 2 516 | 241 | 1 737 | 186 | 1 645 |

1. Per 1,000 estimated resident population.   2. Data for serious crimes have not been adjusted for underreporting; this may affect comparability between geographic areas and over time.   3. Per 100,000 population estimated by the FBI.

Table B. States and Counties — **Crime, Education, Money Income, and Poverty**

| STATE County | Serious crimes known to police, 2011 (cont.)[1] Rate[2] Violent (46) | Property (47) | School enrollment and attainment, 2007–2011 — Enrollment[3] Total (48) | Percent private (49) | Attainment[4] (percent) High school grad or less (50) | Bachelor's degree or more (51) | Local govt expenditures,[5] 2009–2010 Total current expenditures (mil dol) (52) | Current expenditures per student (dollars) (53) | Money income 2007–2011 Households Per capita income[6] (dollars) (54) | Median income Dollars (55) | Percent change, 2000 to 2007–2011 (constant 2011 dollars) (56) | Percent with income of $200,000 or more (57) | Income and poverty, 2011 Median household income (dollars) (58) | Percent below poverty level All persons (59) | Children under 18 years (60) | Children 5 to 17 years in families (61) |
|---|---|---|---|---|---|---|---|---|---|---|---|---|---|---|---|---|
| **NORTH CAROLINA—Cont'd** | | | | | | | | | | | | | | | | |
| Swain | 374 | 2 642 | 3 368 | 11.0 | 49.7 | 17.7 | 20.1 | 9 270 | 19 506 | 40 719 | 5.4 | 0.5 | 36 167 | 19.3 | 29.9 | 27.5 |
| Transylvania | 170 | 1 737 | 6 811 | 20.5 | 42.5 | 27.3 | 35.5 | 9 289 | 24 560 | 41 103 | -21.1 | 1.3 | 41 578 | 16.2 | 30.4 | 27.8 |
| Tyrrell | 157 | 1 434 | 712 | 10.5 | 68.9 | 10.1 | 8.8 | 14 614 | 16 786 | 34 071 | -1.8 | 0.0 | 33 430 | 28.0 | 39.9 | 40.6 |
| Union | 156 | 1 738 | 58 202 | 17.3 | 40.4 | 29.9 | 305.0 | 7 535 | 28 835 | 64 813 | -5.2 | 6.0 | 61 515 | 10.6 | 14.4 | 12.5 |
| Vance | 591 | 7 592 | 12 140 | 10.4 | 60.8 | 11.2 | 69.7 | 8 629 | 17 414 | 34 084 | -19.4 | 1.0 | 33 377 | 25.6 | 39.0 | 33.3 |
| Wake | 258 | 2 578 | 259 012 | 18.6 | 25.5 | 47.9 | 1 128.4 | 7 686 | 33 161 | 65 289 | -12.1 | 6.3 | 62 436 | 11.6 | 16.4 | 15.5 |
| Warren | 179 | 3 332 | 4 658 | 8.4 | 57.3 | 14.5 | 28.1 | 10 552 | 19 113 | 34 495 | -9.9 | 1.3 | 33 218 | 25.5 | 37.2 | 34.7 |
| Washington | 463 | 2 157 | 3 211 | 13.3 | 57.8 | 11.9 | 23.3 | 11 666 | 18 395 | 34 219 | -12.2 | 1.0 | 33 278 | 23.4 | 36.2 | 34.2 |
| Watauga | 110 | 1 854 | 20 848 | 6.2 | 32.0 | 39.3 | 44.0 | 9 698 | 21 266 | 34 497 | -21.7 | 2.2 | 39 168 | 25.9 | 23.0 | 21.8 |
| Wayne | 447 | 4 176 | 31 958 | 12.8 | 49.4 | 16.0 | 153.7 | 7 839 | 21 135 | 41 751 | -8.9 | 1.4 | 39 089 | 21.9 | 32.0 | 28.9 |
| Wilkes | 265 | 3 186 | 14 868 | 8.9 | 59.3 | 11.9 | 97.7 | 8 369 | 19 356 | 33 464 | -27.7 | 1.2 | 34 954 | 24.5 | 35.1 | 31.7 |
| Wilson | 383 | 3 792 | 21 060 | 14.0 | 54.1 | 18.0 | 102.5 | 7 709 | 20 756 | 38 760 | -13.3 | 1.4 | 37 166 | 24.7 | 36.2 | 33.1 |
| Yadkin | 289 | 2 878 | 8 815 | 7.1 | 59.3 | 11.9 | 49.9 | 8 177 | 21 523 | 40 375 | -18.4 | 1.2 | 40 983 | 17.2 | 28.0 | 24.3 |
| Yancey | 100 | 1 369 | 3 579 | 14.4 | 52.2 | 18.8 | 23.3 | 9 747 | 19 609 | 38 950 | -2.8 | 0.9 | 36 440 | 20.3 | 31.3 | 28.0 |
| **NORTH DAKOTA** | 247 | 1 937 | 170 009 | 11.0 | 37.4 | 26.5 | 1 043.4 | 10 980 | 27 305 | 49 415 | 5.8 | 2.7 | 52 135 | 12.0 | 14.8 | 12.3 |
| Adams | 42 | 797 | 382 | 5.0 | 48.9 | 21.4 | 3.2 | 11 077 | 25 292 | 40 236 | 2.5 | 2.7 | 43 836 | 10.4 | 12.3 | 10.3 |
| Barnes | 27 | 978 | 2 726 | 6.7 | 43.6 | 27.4 | 18.5 | 13 229 | 28 178 | 43 730 | 3.9 | 3.1 | 47 839 | 10.6 | 14.1 | 11.5 |
| Benson | 0 | 251 | 1 791 | 4.1 | 52.7 | 10.6 | 13.4 | 16 083 | 16 159 | 32 149 | -10.8 | 1.3 | 38 299 | 27.6 | 37.4 | 29.9 |
| Billings | 251 | 503 | 135 | 5.9 | 44.7 | 21.7 | 1.9 | 41 889 | 35 427 | 53 846 | 22.1 | 6.6 | 60 506 | 9.0 | 11.4 | 9.1 |
| Bottineau | 0 | 367 | 1 254 | 7.1 | 40.7 | 22.5 | 12.3 | 15 401 | 28 573 | 44 399 | 10.2 | 3.4 | 52 360 | 10.4 | 13.6 | 11.0 |
| Bowman | NA | NA | 619 | 2.9 | 45.0 | 20.3 | 6.4 | 11 448 | 28 074 | 50 487 | 17.2 | 3.2 | 56 721 | 8.5 | 9.6 | 8.1 |
| Burke | 175 | 1 049 | 294 | 2.0 | 48.6 | 16.1 | 3.8 | 15 715 | 34 630 | 54 402 | 59.1 | 4.4 | 49 481 | 8.8 | 11.4 | 9.7 |
| Burleigh | 227 | 2 490 | 20 019 | 20.4 | 30.8 | 32.3 | 105.5 | 9 528 | 30 070 | 56 231 | 0.8 | 2.7 | 57 519 | 9.1 | 11.3 | 8.6 |
| Cass | 299 | 2 232 | 43 744 | 11.4 | 26.9 | 36.5 | 201.6 | 10 100 | 29 518 | 49 429 | -4.0 | 3.8 | 52 444 | 12.4 | 12.1 | 10.3 |
| Cavalier | 49 | 1 429 | 741 | 14.8 | 44.7 | 16.8 | 5.9 | 12 684 | 27 129 | 49 293 | 14.6 | 1.5 | 50 572 | 9.3 | 14.8 | 11.4 |
| Dickey | 19 | 558 | 1 335 | 20.4 | 42.9 | 21.0 | 6.9 | 8 360 | 24 105 | 41 776 | 5.9 | 2.6 | 47 501 | 10.4 | 13.1 | 11.0 |
| Divide | NA | NA | 271 | 8.9 | 42.9 | 17.8 | 3.7 | 15 855 | 29 512 | 47 545 | 17.0 | 3.4 | 51 219 | 9.4 | 14.4 | 12.1 |
| Dunn | NA | NA | 694 | 5.6 | 47.1 | 16.6 | 7.4 | 16 831 | 28 816 | 52 861 | 30.4 | 3.9 | 55 353 | 10.8 | 13.2 | 10.9 |
| Eddy | 124 | 660 | 545 | 0.7 | 46.5 | 18.6 | 4.6 | 14 098 | 21 865 | 40 096 | 3.7 | 1.4 | 43 249 | 11.2 | 14.4 | 11.5 |
| Emmons | 55 | 499 | 718 | 2.8 | 54.6 | 14.1 | 6.8 | 11 569 | 22 699 | 36 903 | 4.6 | 1.5 | 40 749 | 12.8 | 17.1 | 12.9 |
| Foster | 29 | 294 | 684 | 5.6 | 45.6 | 19.3 | 5.4 | 9 996 | 34 606 | 47 500 | 9.9 | 4.3 | 49 333 | 8.1 | 10.4 | 8.3 |
| Golden Valley | 234 | 468 | 365 | 6.3 | 38.4 | 21.3 | 4.3 | 13 327 | 26 109 | 35 402 | -12.5 | 1.2 | 44 706 | 12.2 | 21.7 | 18.0 |
| Grand Forks | 228 | 2 763 | 23 105 | 6.9 | 31.0 | 33.2 | 86.8 | 10 154 | 25 807 | 46 050 | -4.7 | 2.9 | 45 541 | 14.2 | 14.6 | 12.3 |
| Grant | 0 | 247 | 444 | 2.9 | 51.5 | 15.3 | 3.7 | 14 800 | 28 219 | 41 821 | 33.7 | 2.4 | 35 744 | 19.2 | 26.7 | 21.8 |
| Griggs | 0 | 284 | 370 | 8.4 | 49.3 | 18.0 | 5.0 | 13 032 | 24 838 | 43 000 | 7.7 | 0.9 | 45 283 | 9.7 | 11.9 | 10.2 |
| Hettinger | 79 | 516 | 441 | 3.6 | 49.4 | 18.9 | 5.1 | 13 434 | 24 717 | 41 179 | 4.4 | 3.2 | 46 793 | 10.9 | 13.4 | 10.9 |
| Kidder | 121 | 323 | 523 | 2.1 | 51.7 | 16.6 | 4.3 | 10 728 | 24 765 | 37 105 | 8.2 | 2.3 | 39 857 | 14.2 | 20.6 | 16.8 |
| LaMoure | 0 | 71 | 803 | 7.5 | 44.3 | 20.0 | 8.9 | 11 409 | 28 230 | 49 922 | 24.5 | 1.8 | 52 244 | 10.3 | 11.6 | 9.2 |
| Logan | 0 | 642 | 398 | 3.5 | 55.8 | 13.4 | 4.3 | 12 919 | 24 022 | 42 069 | 11.3 | 1.9 | 40 760 | 13.1 | 18.1 | 14.4 |
| McHenry | 109 | 656 | 1 061 | 14.3 | 51.9 | 14.8 | 10.8 | 12 338 | 24 398 | 41 989 | 14.0 | 1.7 | 44 981 | 13.5 | 18.0 | 14.4 |
| McIntosh | 140 | 105 | 410 | 1.5 | 58.9 | 16.1 | 4.7 | 12 304 | 23 068 | 35 757 | 0.4 | 1.6 | 36 642 | 13.9 | 20.0 | 17.4 |
| McKenzie | 232 | 1 902 | 1 388 | 4.0 | 39.1 | 20.7 | 12.1 | 15 090 | 29 890 | 53 902 | 36.1 | 4.1 | 59 000 | 12.5 | 16.4 | 14.2 |
| McLean | 44 | 889 | 1 673 | 3.8 | 43.9 | 17.3 | 16.1 | 11 034 | 27 945 | 52 996 | 21.4 | 1.8 | 50 902 | 10.8 | 14.4 | 11.6 |
| Mercer | NA | NA | 1 694 | 2.1 | 42.7 | 18.9 | 14.2 | 11 172 | 30 387 | 62 578 | 9.7 | 1.8 | 67 449 | 7.8 | 9.4 | 7.8 |
| Morton | 208 | 2 198 | 6 382 | 16.5 | 42.5 | 22.3 | 41.7 | 10 093 | 27 347 | 55 196 | 10.4 | 2.4 | 58 330 | 9.8 | 14.9 | 12.8 |
| Mountrail | 77 | 1 384 | 1 781 | 5.1 | 40.1 | 19.1 | 15.2 | 10 534 | 28 998 | 56 593 | 54.7 | 4.3 | 52 930 | 13.7 | 18.2 | 15.0 |
| Nelson | 63 | 723 | 618 | 9.1 | 41.0 | 22.6 | 5.8 | 12 246 | 25 757 | 41 961 | 7.6 | 0.8 | 43 426 | 10.5 | 13.1 | 10.5 |
| Oliver | 0 | 160 | 353 | 4.8 | 46.7 | 16.3 | 2.9 | 14 677 | 29 825 | 61 131 | 23.5 | 0.6 | 59 262 | 11.5 | 20.3 | 16.7 |
| Pembina | 40 | 929 | 1 507 | 7.4 | 46.0 | 18.7 | 13.2 | 12 075 | 27 555 | 52 270 | 6.3 | 1.7 | 54 584 | 8.7 | 11.3 | 9.1 |
| Pierce | 0 | 1 422 | 831 | 12.3 | 48.9 | 15.2 | 6.2 | 9 974 | 22 011 | 40 139 | 12.1 | 0.8 | 41 419 | 12.1 | 15.8 | 12.6 |
| Ramsey | 292 | 3 195 | 2 694 | 9.3 | 40.3 | 21.4 | 22.7 | 11 977 | 26 257 | 44 452 | -7.5 | 2.0 | 46 624 | 12.5 | 18.0 | 15.2 |
| Ransom | 54 | 901 | 1 189 | 4.7 | 48.2 | 17.4 | 8.8 | 9 114 | 23 546 | 47 922 | -5.8 | 0.3 | 51 812 | 8.6 | 10.4 | 8.1 |
| Renville | 40 | 1 115 | 480 | 16.0 | 36.6 | 17.8 | 6.9 | 11 860 | 28 704 | 50 093 | 20.7 | 1.9 | 52 982 | 8.4 | 11.0 | 9.3 |
| Richland | 121 | 1 717 | 4 401 | 6.8 | 38.0 | 22.0 | 27.9 | 12 105 | 25 835 | 48 908 | 0.3 | 2.2 | 51 860 | 10.7 | 12.2 | 9.5 |
| Rolette | 29 | 391 | 2 198 | 2.4 | 42.4 | 17.5 | 39.0 | 12 967 | 14 282 | 27 662 | -21.9 | 0.5 | 33 024 | 38.2 | 46.6 | 42.0 |
| Sargent | 77 | 642 | 890 | 3.9 | 52.7 | 16.5 | 7.3 | 10 254 | 26 258 | 52 154 | 3.8 | 1.3 | 58 138 | 7.5 | 8.8 | 7.0 |
| Sheridan | 74 | 1 266 | 217 | 6.0 | 57.0 | 14.2 | 2.0 | 15 600 | 25 217 | 38 235 | 15.8 | 1.6 | 40 593 | 16.4 | 27.2 | 20.9 |
| Sioux | 0 | 0 | 1 276 | 4.2 | 49.0 | 14.1 | 8.7 | 22 157 | 13 983 | 32 802 | 8.1 | 1.4 | 30 271 | 34.5 | 40.8 | 35.2 |
| Slope | 0 | 271 | 111 | 0.0 | 41.3 | 26.8 | 0.4 | 17 000 | 28 079 | 55 625 | 67.0 | 2.6 | 52 493 | 11.0 | 12.3 | 11.1 |
| Stark | 228 | 2 028 | 6 101 | 13.4 | 43.9 | 22.1 | 31.8 | 9 714 | 26 678 | 54 269 | 23.6 | 2.2 | 55 492 | 10.2 | 11.0 | 9.3 |
| Steele | 0 | 299 | 449 | 0.4 | 44.1 | 16.7 | 3.1 | 11 931 | 30 038 | 49 485 | 2.5 | 4.1 | 54 695 | 8.2 | 14.4 | 11.3 |
| Stutsman | 182 | 1 561 | 4 939 | 27.7 | 49.9 | 23.4 | 29.9 | 12 564 | 26 385 | 47 703 | 7.9 | 4.0 | 52 376 | 10.2 | 16.4 | 13.5 |
| Towner | 44 | 482 | 480 | 0.6 | 44.6 | 20.5 | 3.6 | 11 704 | 24 725 | 48 341 | -4.4 | 1.1 | 53 388 | 9.9 | 11.6 | 9.8 |
| Traill | 47 | 754 | 2 104 | 3.8 | 38.2 | 26.0 | 15.6 | 11 704 | 28 479 | 54 112 | 4.6 | 2.0 | 56 048 | 8.9 | 11.8 | 10.0 |
| Walsh | 150 | 1 495 | 2 218 | 5.8 | 49.9 | 16.2 | 24.8 | 13 141 | 25 377 | 46 453 | 1.7 | 1.6 | 46 802 | 11.2 | 14.0 | 11.2 |

1. Data for serious crimes have not been adjusted for underreporting; this may affect comparability between geographic areas and over time. 2. Per 100,000 population estimated by the FBI. 3. All persons 3 years old and over enrolled in nursery school through college. 4. Persons 25 years old and over. 5. Elementary and secondary education expenditures. 6. Based on population estimated by the American Community Survey, 2007–2011.

# Table B. States and Counties — Personal Income

| STATE County | Total (mil dol) | Percent change, 2010–2011 | Per capita[1] Dollars | Per capita[1] Rank | Wages and salaries[2] (mil dol) | Proprietors' income (mil dol) | Dividends, interest, and rent (mil dol) | Transfer payments (mil dol) Total | Government payments to individuals Total | Social Security | Medical payments | Income maintenance | Unemployment insurance |
|---|---|---|---|---|---|---|---|---|---|---|---|---|---|
| | 62 | 63 | 64 | 65 | 66 | 67 | 68 | 69 | 70 | 71 | 72 | 73 | 74 |
| NORTH CAROLINA—Cont'd | | | | | | | | | | | | | |
| Swain | 395 | 3.5 | 28 132 | 2 600 | 267 | 11 | 54 | 137 | 134 | 44 | 60 | 16 | 8 |
| Transylvania | 1 008 | 3.1 | 30 703 | 2 153 | 340 | 62 | 309 | 306 | 299 | 134 | 117 | 25 | 9 |
| Tyrrell | 110 | 4.8 | 25 193 | 2 949 | 42 | 11 | 14 | 34 | 33 | 10 | 15 | 6 | 2 |
| Union | 7 305 | 6.5 | 35 552 | 1 283 | 2 612 | 355 | 874 | 1 046 | 1 000 | 392 | 357 | 119 | 81 |
| Vance | 1 342 | 3.6 | 29 621 | 2 359 | 634 | 65 | 181 | 452 | 442 | 129 | 185 | 79 | 22 |
| Wake | 39 567 | 6.1 | 42 555 | 535 | 28 435 | 2 667 | 5 793 | 4 635 | 4 430 | 1 578 | 1 697 | 487 | 356 |
| Warren | 520 | 4.7 | 24 921 | 2 970 | 159 | 18 | 77 | 185 | 180 | 55 | 81 | 27 | 8 |
| Washington | 387 | 2.8 | 29 830 | 2 318 | 130 | 31 | 61 | 144 | 141 | 44 | 62 | 21 | 9 |
| Watauga | 1 522 | 4.2 | 29 648 | 2 351 | 956 | 113 | 312 | 287 | 276 | 108 | 99 | 23 | 13 |
| Wayne | 3 865 | 5.8 | 31 245 | 2 061 | 2 421 | 149 | 498 | 992 | 965 | 287 | 413 | 138 | 38 |
| Wilkes | 2 178 | 4.0 | 31 575 | 1 980 | 915 | 149 | 304 | 641 | 626 | 220 | 265 | 77 | 31 |
| Wilson | 2 702 | 4.3 | 33 170 | 1 678 | 1 936 | 131 | 374 | 737 | 719 | 231 | 298 | 104 | 42 |
| Yadkin | 1 154 | 2.8 | 30 142 | 2 262 | 400 | 75 | 142 | 306 | 298 | 114 | 129 | 29 | 16 |
| Yancey | 467 | 4.7 | 26 404 | 2 838 | 154 | 24 | 86 | 170 | 166 | 63 | 69 | 18 | 7 |
| NORTH DAKOTA | 32 306 | 12.8 | 47 236 | X | 21 286 | 5 084 | 4 906 | 4 510 | 4 360 | 1 520 | 1 827 | 414 | 95 |
| Adams | 114 | 9.7 | 49 254 | 227 | 40 | 39 | 15 | 23 | 23 | 8 | 12 | 1 | 0 |
| Barnes | 531 | 3.8 | 48 021 | 269 | 214 | 152 | 92 | 87 | 85 | 33 | 37 | 6 | 2 |
| Benson | 282 | 21.5 | 41 871 | 585 | 122 | 97 | 27 | 60 | 58 | 13 | 23 | 13 | 1 |
| Billings | 63 | 39.8 | 76 798 | 11 | 27 | 18 | 9 | 4 | 4 | 2 | 1 | 0 | 0 |
| Bottineau | 284 | -6.6 | 44 061 | 436 | 137 | 27 | 67 | 56 | 54 | 20 | 24 | 4 | 1 |
| Bowman | 178 | 13.1 | 56 727 | 98 | 86 | 46 | 38 | 23 | 23 | 9 | 11 | 1 | 0 |
| Burke | 93 | 0.4 | 45 780 | 348 | 54 | 4 | 24 | 15 | 15 | 6 | 6 | 1 | 0 |
| Burleigh | 3 636 | 7.3 | 43 731 | 455 | 2 731 | 275 | 587 | 535 | 517 | 189 | 213 | 40 | 13 |
| Cass | 6 948 | 8.5 | 45 602 | 359 | 5 462 | 915 | 1 187 | 750 | 716 | 265 | 250 | 74 | 22 |
| Cavalier | 283 | 33.1 | 71 812 | 19 | 78 | 140 | 42 | 34 | 33 | 14 | 15 | 2 | 0 |
| Dickey | 323 | 28.4 | 60 747 | 61 | 89 | 157 | 38 | 45 | 44 | 15 | 23 | 3 | 0 |
| Divide | 83 | -13.8 | 39 000 | 856 | 44 | 1 | 22 | 17 | 17 | 7 | 8 | 1 | 0 |
| Dunn | 227 | 40.6 | 60 987 | 58 | 132 | 32 | 23 | 23 | 22 | 7 | 10 | 2 | 0 |
| Eddy | 104 | 17.5 | 43 729 | 456 | 28 | 30 | 16 | 24 | 23 | 8 | 12 | 1 | 0 |
| Emmons | 198 | 21.2 | 55 728 | 103 | 42 | 102 | 25 | 33 | 32 | 12 | 15 | 2 | 1 |
| Foster | 163 | 8.0 | 48 799 | 242 | 82 | 39 | 33 | 26 | 25 | 10 | 11 | 2 | 0 |
| Golden Valley | 46 | -13.2 | 26 292 | 2 850 | 28 | -7 | 14 | 12 | 11 | 5 | 5 | 1 | 0 |
| Grand Forks | 2 640 | 6.1 | 39 646 | 787 | 2 035 | 287 | 420 | 379 | 364 | 120 | 140 | 39 | 10 |
| Grant | 139 | 20.9 | 59 324 | 73 | 26 | 67 | 17 | 22 | 21 | 8 | 10 | 2 | 0 |
| Griggs | 113 | 5.5 | 47 530 | 281 | 39 | 31 | 23 | 23 | 22 | 9 | 10 | 1 | 0 |
| Hettinger | 121 | 7.3 | 48 181 | 265 | 33 | 41 | 22 | 22 | 22 | 8 | 11 | 1 | 0 |
| Kidder | 109 | 14.6 | 45 267 | 382 | 28 | 38 | 19 | 22 | 21 | 7 | 11 | 2 | 0 |
| LaMoure | 307 | 27.9 | 74 875 | 14 | 66 | 167 | 42 | 32 | 31 | 13 | 14 | 2 | 0 |
| Logan | 121 | 28.4 | 60 819 | 60 | 23 | 61 | 18 | 19 | 18 | 6 | 10 | 1 | 0 |
| McHenry | 197 | -5.9 | 35 784 | 1 253 | 64 | 20 | 33 | 46 | 44 | 16 | 19 | 4 | 1 |
| McIntosh | 151 | 32.5 | 54 392 | 124 | 41 | 59 | 26 | 33 | 32 | 11 | 19 | 2 | 0 |
| McKenzie | 449 | 32.5 | 63 961 | 43 | 416 | 50 | 49 | 40 | 38 | 13 | 16 | 4 | 0 |
| McLean | 449 | 2.0 | 49 538 | 218 | 198 | 73 | 76 | 79 | 77 | 29 | 35 | 5 | 2 |
| Mercer | 388 | 4.4 | 45 907 | 341 | 343 | 27 | 54 | 57 | 56 | 23 | 23 | 4 | 2 |
| Morton | 1 073 | 10.2 | 38 680 | 882 | 534 | 50 | 153 | 193 | 187 | 64 | 81 | 17 | 6 |
| Mountrail | 512 | 32.4 | 63 207 | 46 | 355 | 13 | 47 | 59 | 57 | 17 | 25 | 6 | 1 |
| Nelson | 186 | 27.7 | 60 893 | 59 | 41 | 79 | 28 | 37 | 36 | 13 | 19 | 2 | 0 |
| Oliver | 103 | 1.9 | 56 062 | 102 | 61 | 28 | 13 | 12 | 11 | 5 | 4 | 1 | 0 |
| Pembina | 400 | 8.0 | 54 451 | 121 | 198 | 114 | 75 | 57 | 56 | 23 | 22 | 4 | 3 |
| Pierce | 198 | 21.9 | 45 351 | 378 | 73 | 72 | 28 | 37 | 36 | 13 | 17 | 3 | 1 |
| Ramsey | 529 | 17.9 | 46 193 | 331 | 258 | 123 | 85 | 99 | 96 | 32 | 44 | 9 | 2 |
| Ransom | 246 | 14.8 | 45 557 | 361 | 95 | 72 | 34 | 45 | 43 | 14 | 21 | 3 | 1 |
| Renville | 113 | -4.6 | 45 209 | 387 | 45 | 13 | 23 | 22 | 21 | 7 | 11 | 1 | 0 |
| Richland | 756 | 12.5 | 46 527 | 318 | 361 | 234 | 110 | 103 | 99 | 37 | 38 | 9 | 2 |
| Rolette | 419 | 7.1 | 29 462 | 2 383 | 221 | 52 | 38 | 142 | 139 | 22 | 58 | 37 | 4 |
| Sargent | 218 | 10.4 | 57 283 | 91 | 123 | 85 | 34 | 26 | 25 | 12 | 10 | 2 | 0 |
| Sheridan | 79 | 12.7 | 60 644 | 64 | 11 | 44 | 9 | 13 | 13 | 5 | 6 | 1 | 0 |
| Sioux | 115 | 13.6 | 26 787 | 2 789 | 90 | 16 | 7 | 41 | 40 | 5 | 17 | 11 | 1 |
| Slope | 40 | -13.4 | 55 670 | 105 | 13 | 17 | 8 | 5 | 4 | 2 | 2 | 0 | 0 |
| Stark | 1 378 | 19.6 | 54 750 | 116 | 993 | 181 | 174 | 161 | 156 | 55 | 71 | 12 | 2 |
| Steele | 121 | 8.1 | 61 834 | 53 | 33 | 51 | 24 | 14 | 13 | 7 | 5 | 1 | 0 |
| Stutsman | 911 | 7.2 | 43 271 | 488 | 484 | 212 | 141 | 158 | 154 | 56 | 67 | 13 | 3 |
| Towner | 138 | 18.2 | 61 108 | 57 | 33 | 60 | 25 | 23 | 22 | 8 | 11 | 1 | 0 |
| Traill | 377 | 4.7 | 46 310 | 327 | 155 | 83 | 63 | 62 | 60 | 22 | 26 | 4 | 1 |
| Walsh | 482 | 12.3 | 43 699 | 459 | 215 | 118 | 80 | 92 | 89 | 34 | 41 | 7 | 2 |

1. Based on the resident population estimated as of July 1 of the year shown.   2. Includes supplements to wages and salaries.

| STATE County | Total (mil dol) | Farm | Goods-related[1] Total | Manu-facturing | Infor-mation and profes-sional and technical services | Retail trade | Finance, insur-ance, and real estate | Health care and social services | Govern-ment | Number | Rate[2] | Supple-mental Security Income recipients, December 2011 | Total | Percent change, 2000–2010 |
|---|---|---|---|---|---|---|---|---|---|---|---|---|---|---|
| | 75 | 76 | 77 | 78 | 79 | 80 | 81 | 82 | 83 | 84 | 85 | 86 | 87 | 88 |
| **NORTH CAROLINA—Cont'd** | | | | | | | | | | | | | | |
| Swain | 278 | 0.4 | D | 6.0 | 1.5 | 7.1 | 1.7 | D | 45.3 | 3 945 | 281 | 351 | 8 723 | 22.8 |
| Transylvania | 402 | 1.1 | D | 4.3 | 6.2 | 10.0 | 4.5 | 18.3 | 18.7 | 9 740 | 297 | 606 | 19 163 | 23.3 |
| Tyrrell | 54 | 13.4 | D | D | D | 7.0 | D | D | 41.7 | 850 | 195 | 138 | 2 068 | 1.8 |
| Union | 2 966 | 2.2 | D | 20.3 | 5.5 | 7.9 | 4.3 | 5.0 | 17.6 | 28 270 | 138 | 2 190 | 72 870 | 59.4 |
| Vance | 699 | 2.9 | D | 14.0 | D | 10.4 | 3.7 | 17.2 | 19.5 | 10 810 | 239 | 2 285 | 20 082 | 10.4 |
| Wake | 31 103 | 0.0 | 11.9 | 5.9 | 19.9 | 6.0 | 9.2 | 9.6 | 16.4 | 111 310 | 120 | 11 427 | 371 836 | 43.6 |
| Warren | 178 | 4.0 | 18.6 | 15.2 | 2.1 | 4.0 | 1.6 | D | 37.5 | 4 775 | 229 | 958 | 11 806 | 11.9 |
| Washington | 161 | 12.6 | 15.9 | 13.9 | D | 6.3 | 3.6 | 8.2 | 30.4 | 3 470 | 267 | 661 | 6 491 | 5.1 |
| Watauga | 1 069 | 0.1 | 8.5 | 2.9 | 4.9 | 9.4 | 4.9 | 16.8 | 31.5 | 8 290 | 161 | 662 | 32 137 | 38.7 |
| Wayne | 2 570 | 2.2 | D | 10.8 | 3.1 | 6.4 | 3.5 | 11.5 | 37.4 | 24 185 | 196 | 4 673 | 52 949 | 11.9 |
| Wilkes | 1 064 | 4.9 | D | 14.1 | D | 8.2 | 4.5 | 7.2 | 20.8 | 18 485 | 268 | 2 094 | 33 065 | 13.0 |
| Wilson | 2 067 | 1.8 | D | 28.6 | 4.0 | 6.2 | 4.9 | 6.8 | 16.7 | 18 545 | 228 | 3 118 | 35 511 | 15.6 |
| Yadkin | 475 | 7.7 | 27.9 | 20.1 | 5.4 | 6.1 | 4.8 | 6.7 | 16.0 | 9 045 | 236 | 772 | 17 341 | 9.6 |
| Yancey | 178 | 0.7 | D | 9.5 | 3.7 | 8.4 | 4.1 | D | 23.4 | 5 415 | 306 | 697 | 11 032 | 13.5 |
| **NORTH DAKOTA** | 26 370 | 12.0 | 19.4 | 5.3 | 5.8 | 5.9 | 5.9 | 10.7 | 17.8 | 121 335 | 177 | 8 349 | 317 498 | 9.6 |
| Adams | 80 | 43.5 | D | 2.2 | D | 5.0 | D | 21.0 | 8.4 | 675 | 293 | 17 | 1 377 | -2.8 |
| Barnes | 366 | 30.5 | D | 8.9 | 3.9 | 4.6 | 3.4 | 9.2 | 14.9 | 2 665 | 241 | 144 | 5 704 | 1.9 |
| Benson | 219 | 39.4 | D | D | D | 1.9 | 1.6 | 0.7 | 34.9 | 1 195 | 178 | 204 | 2 950 | 0.6 |
| Billings | 45 | 36.2 | D | 0.0 | D | D | D | 0.0 | 22.5 | 150 | 184 | 0 | 484 | -8.5 |
| Bottineau | 164 | 0.9 | 33.3 | 3.1 | D | 7.9 | 4.1 | D | 20.9 | 1 660 | 258 | 53 | 4 341 | -1.5 |
| Bowman | 132 | 26.8 | 25.5 | 0.7 | 2.9 | 4.9 | D | 7.8 | 8.9 | 755 | 241 | 26 | 1 683 | 5.5 |
| Burke | 58 | -5.7 | 28.6 | 0.0 | D | D | 3.1 | 0.8 | 36.2 | 510 | 251 | 11 | 1 340 | -5.1 |
| Burleigh | 3 006 | 1.3 | 9.4 | 1.7 | 8.0 | 7.5 | 6.9 | 19.8 | 22.3 | 14 390 | 173 | 896 | 35 754 | 23.3 |
| Cass | 6 377 | 4.2 | D | 8.3 | 11.0 | 6.9 | 10.4 | 13.9 | 13.4 | 19 845 | 130 | 1 648 | 67 938 | 26.3 |
| Cavalier | 218 | 56.6 | D | 1.0 | 2.8 | 2.8 | D | 3.9 | 6.4 | 1 135 | 288 | 24 | 2 309 | -15.3 |
| Dickey | 246 | 60.8 | 6.8 | 4.7 | D | 3.8 | D | 7.2 | 5.9 | 1 240 | 233 | 63 | 2 636 | -0.8 |
| Divide | 45 | -5.1 | D | D | D | 5.4 | 3.8 | D | 22.3 | 575 | 271 | 20 | 1 324 | -9.9 |
| Dunn | 164 | 15.9 | D | D | D | 2.5 | 3.7 | D | 8.0 | 695 | 187 | 30 | 2 132 | 8.5 |
| Eddy | 59 | 45.8 | D | D | D | 3.2 | D | 12.6 | 13.9 | 650 | 273 | 36 | 1 323 | -6.7 |
| Emmons | 143 | 65.5 | D | D | D | 3.2 | D | 5.1 | 8.0 | 1 080 | 305 | 41 | 2 085 | -3.8 |
| Foster | 121 | 28.9 | D | D | D | 6.0 | 3.3 | 11.5 | 11.1 | 825 | 247 | 33 | 1 801 | 0.4 |
| Golden Valley | 22 | -41.4 | D | D | D | 8.9 | 8.8 | 18.9 | 33.5 | 425 | 243 | 12 | 967 | -0.6 |
| Grand Forks | 2 322 | 5.9 | D | 4.0 | 4.9 | 8.6 | 4.4 | 16.2 | 30.2 | 9 130 | 137 | 701 | 29 344 | 7.2 |
| Grant | 93 | 68.2 | D | D | D | 1.5 | 1.7 | 6.9 | 8.3 | 735 | 315 | 32 | 1 690 | -1.9 |
| Griggs | 69 | 31.1 | 14.3 | 9.5 | D | 5.0 | 1.7 | 8.3 | 12.7 | 715 | 301 | 20 | 1 461 | -3.9 |
| Hettinger | 74 | 50.0 | 6.0 | 2.0 | D | 1.9 | 3.9 | 4.5 | 11.9 | 720 | 286 | 18 | 1 414 | -0.4 |
| Kidder | 66 | 54.9 | D | 0.3 | D | 2.4 | 3.3 | 1.4 | 12.6 | 620 | 257 | 25 | 1 674 | 4.4 |
| LaMoure | 232 | 67.1 | 3.3 | 1.7 | 0.7 | 2.2 | D | 1.5 | 7.4 | 1 070 | 261 | 47 | 2 238 | -1.5 |
| Logan | 84 | 65.2 | D | D | D | 2.1 | D | D | 8.1 | 590 | 297 | 18 | 1 144 | -4.3 |
| McHenry | 85 | 15.8 | D | D | 2.8 | 3.3 | 3.7 | 4.4 | 24.3 | 1 350 | 245 | 59 | 2 948 | -1.2 |
| McIntosh | 100 | 57.9 | 5.0 | 3.6 | D | 3.6 | 2.1 | 11.6 | 8.3 | 1 020 | 368 | 41 | 1 858 | 0.3 |
| McKenzie | 466 | 6.1 | 40.5 | 0.3 | D | D | 4.7 | 1.6 | 16.4 | 1 075 | 153 | 47 | 3 090 | 13.6 |
| McLean | 271 | 20.2 | D | 1.3 | D | 2.8 | 3.2 | D | 15.3 | 2 325 | 256 | 111 | 5 590 | 6.2 |
| Mercer | 370 | 2.7 | D | D | D | 3.5 | 1.6 | D | 7.1 | 1 730 | 205 | 79 | 4 450 | 1.1 |
| Morton | 584 | 8.3 | D | 12.4 | 8.0 | 7.2 | 4.2 | D | 14.5 | 5 280 | 190 | 329 | 12 079 | 14.1 |
| Mountrail | 369 | 1.1 | D | D | 5.3 | 4.0 | 2.1 | 2.9 | 9.8 | 1 405 | 174 | 105 | 4 119 | 19.9 |
| Nelson | 120 | 62.8 | D | D | D | 1.5 | 4.2 | D | 9.7 | 1 010 | 330 | 33 | 1 927 | -4.3 |
| Oliver | 89 | 28.9 | D | 0.8 | 0.9 | D | D | 0.5 | 5.7 | 410 | 224 | 11 | 905 | 0.1 |
| Pembina | 312 | 36.3 | D | 12.8 | D | 3.3 | D | 3.1 | 18.2 | 1 745 | 238 | 72 | 3 859 | -6.2 |
| Pierce | 145 | 41.3 | D | D | 1.7 | 4.1 | D | D | 9.4 | 1 100 | 251 | 50 | 2 199 | -3.1 |
| Ramsey | 381 | 23.7 | D | 2.9 | 3.8 | 8.5 | 6.1 | D | 20.3 | 2 590 | 226 | 195 | 5 615 | -2.0 |
| Ransom | 166 | 40.0 | D | 7.4 | 2.3 | 4.1 | 3.4 | 9.0 | 13.9 | 1 200 | 222 | 60 | 2 656 | 2.0 |
| Renville | 58 | 6.7 | D | D | D | 2.1 | D | 5.6 | 17.8 | 585 | 235 | 10 | 1 386 | -1.9 |
| Richland | 596 | 34.1 | D | 18.0 | 2.7 | 3.9 | 2.2 | D | 15.6 | 2 970 | 183 | 156 | 7 503 | -1.0 |
| Rolette | 273 | 10.6 | D | 3.4 | 1.0 | 6.0 | D | D | 60.2 | 2 115 | 149 | 823 | 5 372 | 6.9 |
| Sargent | 209 | 40.6 | D | D | D | 2.8 | D | 0.8 | 6.4 | 915 | 241 | 31 | 2 004 | -0.6 |
| Sheridan | 55 | 79.1 | D | D | D | D | D | D | 7.6 | 415 | 317 | 20 | 894 | -3.2 |
| Sioux | 106 | 13.9 | 0.6 | 0.0 | D | 1.3 | 0.0 | D | 81.5 | 505 | 118 | 219 | 1 311 | 7.8 |
| Slope | 29 | 60.6 | D | 0.0 | D | D | 0.0 | 0.0 | 3.9 | 165 | 230 | 0 | 436 | -3.3 |
| Stark | 1 174 | 5.5 | 40.5 | 6.0 | 4.3 | 5.7 | 4.3 | D | 9.7 | 4 560 | 181 | 268 | 10 735 | 10.4 |
| Steele | 84 | 60.7 | 12.6 | 6.1 | D | 2.8 | D | D | 7.7 | 510 | 262 | 0 | 1 171 | -4.9 |
| Stutsman | 696 | 18.4 | D | 10.6 | 3.5 | 6.1 | 4.3 | D | 15.9 | 4 570 | 217 | 424 | 9 862 | 0.5 |
| Towner | 92 | 60.3 | D | D | D | 2.0 | 3.2 | D | 8.5 | 690 | 305 | 28 | 1 449 | -7.0 |
| Traill | 238 | 32.6 | D | 10.7 | 1.4 | 3.1 | 3.8 | D | 15.1 | 1 715 | 211 | 53 | 3 780 | 1.9 |
| Walsh | 333 | 28.0 | 10.6 | 6.1 | 3.5 | 3.7 | 4.6 | D | 16.5 | 2 720 | 247 | 111 | 5 498 | -4.5 |

1. Includes mining, construction, and manufacturing.    2. Per 1,000 resident population enumerated in the 2010 census.

| STATE County | Total | Percent | Median value[1] | With a mort-gage | Without a mort-gage[2] | Median rent[3] | Median rent as a per-cent of income | Sub-stand-ard units[4] (percent) | Total | Percent change, 2011–2012 | Total | Rate[5] | Total | Manage-ment, business, science and arts | Con-struction, produc-tion, and mainte-nance occu-pations |
|---|---|---|---|---|---|---|---|---|---|---|---|---|---|---|---|
| | 89 | 90 | 91 | 92 | 93 | 94 | 95 | 96 | 97 | 98 | 99 | 100 | 101 | 102 | 103 |
| **NORTH CAROLINA—Cont'd** | | | | | | | | | | | | | | | |
| Swain | 5 455 | 81.4 | 119 700 | 23.5 | 9.9 | 630 | 31.0 | 1.6 | 6 862 | -1.0 | 946 | 13.8 | 5 396 | 33.4 | 19.1 |
| Transylvania | 13 914 | 78.3 | 166 300 | 25.0 | 10.1 | 640 | 34.9 | 1.5 | 12 775 | 0.2 | 1 228 | 9.6 | 13 462 | 29.8 | 27.2 |
| Tyrrell | 1 612 | 81.8 | 109 600 | 25.3 | 16.7 | 433 | 22.3 | 2.0 | 2 421 | -0.1 | 235 | 9.7 | 1 600 | 17.8 | 39.9 |
| Union | 66 720 | 82.9 | 196 400 | 23.1 | 11.3 | 817 | 31.5 | 2.5 | 101 821 | 2.7 | 8 342 | 8.2 | 91 896 | 36.6 | 22.6 |
| Vance | 16 477 | 64.6 | 100 500 | 26.0 | 13.3 | 635 | 36.5 | 5.1 | 19 638 | -0.5 | 2 590 | 13.2 | 17 112 | 26.0 | 28.3 |
| Wake | 334 302 | 66.6 | 227 600 | 22.2 | 9.9 | 869 | 28.5 | 2.4 | 490 419 | 2.9 | 37 004 | 7.5 | 451 282 | 49.0 | 13.6 |
| Warren | 7 999 | 74.4 | 102 600 | 26.5 | 16.1 | 600 | 32.5 | 3.2 | 8 002 | -0.7 | 983 | 12.3 | 7 168 | 28.4 | 29.0 |
| Washington | 5 028 | 73.3 | 94 800 | 23.4 | 16.3 | 548 | 44.1 | 2.9 | 6 313 | -1.9 | 771 | 12.2 | 4 636 | 28.4 | 30.5 |
| Watauga | 20 655 | 54.7 | 234 300 | 23.9 | 10.2 | 751 | 50.0 | 0.9 | 24 555 | -0.1 | 2 035 | 8.3 | 25 205 | 35.2 | 14.4 |
| Wayne | 47 027 | 63.0 | 107 200 | 22.9 | 12.0 | 646 | 28.8 | 2.7 | 55 038 | 1.3 | 4 925 | 8.9 | 50 590 | 29.3 | 30.2 |
| Wilkes | 27 928 | 73.6 | 112 200 | 24.1 | 11.7 | 545 | 30.6 | 2.9 | 30 273 | -1.6 | 3 284 | 10.8 | 28 018 | 24.8 | 32.4 |
| Wilson | 31 830 | 61.1 | 114 600 | 24.5 | 14.9 | 737 | 33.0 | 2.8 | 41 127 | 0.0 | 5 154 | 12.5 | 34 320 | 28.9 | 31.0 |
| Yadkin | 14 958 | 78.3 | 113 000 | 22.4 | 11.6 | 560 | 28.3 | 2.9 | 19 178 | 1.6 | 1 699 | 8.9 | 17 063 | 27.4 | 34.1 |
| Yancey | 7 194 | 76.7 | 135 300 | 24.7 | 9.9 | 535 | 23.6 | 3.3 | 7 972 | 1.9 | 885 | 11.1 | 7 440 | 23.5 | 35.5 |
| **NORTH DAKOTA** | 278 669 | 66.5 | 118 200 | 19.9 | 10.6 | 584 | 25.6 | 1.4 | 392 064 | 2.6 | 12 236 | 3.1 | 358 106 | 34.4 | 24.3 |
| Adams | 1 097 | 70.2 | 86 300 | 22.4 | 9.9 | 429 | 23.2 | 1.2 | 1 112 | -4.5 | 30 | 2.7 | 1 265 | 42.7 | 23.4 |
| Barnes | 4 758 | 70.1 | 84 000 | 17.4 | 11.2 | 462 | 24.2 | 1.4 | 5 678 | -5.2 | 193 | 3.4 | 5 766 | 34.3 | 25.8 |
| Benson | 2 300 | 63.6 | 52 800 | 19.8 | 11.6 | 362 | 22.6 | 7.7 | 2 707 | -6.1 | 184 | 6.8 | 2 533 | 34.1 | 26.0 |
| Billings | 364 | 85.7 | 77 100 | 18.2 | 9.9 | 488 | 12.9 | 3.3 | 653 | 14.0 | 12 | 1.8 | 536 | 48.7 | 24.8 |
| Bottineau | 2 999 | 80.3 | 70 000 | 15.8 | 11.7 | 511 | 26.0 | 1.5 | 3 755 | 1.0 | 113 | 3.0 | 3 020 | 34.1 | 26.0 |
| Bowman | 1 317 | 78.9 | 89 600 | 17.2 | 10.9 | 487 | 17.6 | 0.5 | 1 898 | 1.9 | 35 | 1.8 | 1 646 | 31.2 | 31.6 |
| Burke | 989 | 80.5 | 54 000 | 13.3 | 9.9 | 455 | 23.1 | 0.7 | 1 438 | 13.9 | 26 | 1.8 | 1 023 | 32.6 | 31.2 |
| Burleigh | 33 437 | 70.9 | 159 000 | 21.1 | 11.7 | 601 | 24.6 | 1.3 | 46 584 | -1.5 | 1 277 | 2.7 | 45 058 | 36.8 | 19.5 |
| Cass | 63 901 | 53.8 | 150 700 | 21.7 | 11.3 | 629 | 27.5 | 1.3 | 85 042 | -1.6 | 2 794 | 3.3 | 87 446 | 37.1 | 21.2 |
| Cavalier | 1 713 | 84.1 | 70 800 | 15.7 | 10.5 | 365 | 20.3 | 0.6 | 1 941 | -2.5 | 65 | 3.3 | 1 952 | 42.4 | 23.2 |
| Dickey | 2 156 | 73.2 | 65 200 | 19.0 | 11.0 | 482 | 24.2 | 0.8 | 2 586 | -3.7 | 74 | 2.9 | 2 627 | 31.4 | 27.8 |
| Divide | 1 023 | 82.2 | 59 500 | 17.3 | 10.6 | 344 | 17.7 | 0.0 | 1 259 | 18.4 | 27 | 2.1 | 1 123 | 45.2 | 18.2 |
| Dunn | 1 359 | 85.0 | 81 000 | 15.0 | 9.9 | 432 | 15.6 | 2.1 | 3 673 | 31.3 | 54 | 1.5 | 1 923 | 36.2 | 34.1 |
| Eddy | 997 | 78.6 | 50 700 | 20.3 | 10.2 | 414 | 20.9 | 0.4 | 1 162 | 0.0 | 61 | 5.2 | 1 161 | 37.6 | 30.0 |
| Emmons | 1 618 | 83.1 | 64 400 | 19.0 | 13.7 | 361 | 20.1 | 0.9 | 1 519 | -5.6 | 90 | 5.9 | 1 686 | 39.9 | 24.5 |
| Foster | 1 506 | 76.3 | 77 100 | 17.6 | 10.5 | 391 | 21.0 | 0.4 | 1 596 | -5.1 | 52 | 3.3 | 1 737 | 38.1 | 28.2 |
| Golden Valley | 733 | 77.2 | 59 600 | 14.7 | 10.4 | 463 | 33.7 | 3.4 | 872 | 1.4 | 25 | 2.9 | 807 | 43.1 | 23.9 |
| Grand Forks | 26 760 | 54.6 | 143 700 | 21.3 | 12.3 | 649 | 30.5 | 0.9 | 36 151 | -2.6 | 1 338 | 3.7 | 36 650 | 34.3 | 20.4 |
| Grant | 1 175 | 79.3 | 61 700 | 19.2 | 11.8 | 418 | 23.2 | 0.8 | 1 123 | -6.2 | 41 | 3.7 | 1 374 | 47.5 | 23.9 |
| Griggs | 1 086 | 78.0 | 65 700 | 18.0 | 10.9 | 500 | 22.6 | 0.6 | 1 210 | -1.2 | 32 | 2.6 | 1 242 | 39.9 | 26.8 |
| Hettinger | 1 073 | 82.6 | 61 600 | 20.7 | 9.9 | 381 | 16.7 | 2.0 | 1 174 | -2.2 | 38 | 3.2 | 1 204 | 44.2 | 27.3 |
| Kidder | 1 152 | 77.3 | 61 000 | 18.5 | 10.1 | 466 | 27.4 | 0.9 | 977 | -5.4 | 61 | 6.2 | 1 246 | 42.9 | 29.5 |
| LaMoure | 1 923 | 82.6 | 70 500 | 17.6 | 9.9 | 425 | 22.6 | 0.2 | 2 115 | -3.9 | 54 | 2.6 | 2 147 | 41.9 | 26.1 |
| Logan | 848 | 84.4 | 55 300 | 19.2 | 12.2 | 471 | 27.3 | 0.7 | 900 | -6.0 | 28 | 3.1 | 946 | 39.1 | 26.4 |
| McHenry | 2 515 | 77.3 | 68 800 | 19.9 | 10.7 | 459 | 21.3 | 2.5 | 2 718 | 3.9 | 121 | 4.5 | 2 602 | 27.9 | 34.6 |
| McIntosh | 1 301 | 86.4 | 49 700 | 18.7 | 12.6 | 397 | 21.3 | 0.4 | 1 223 | -3.4 | 40 | 3.3 | 1 364 | 41.1 | 26.3 |
| McKenzie | 2 566 | 69.2 | 88 400 | 15.2 | 9.9 | 469 | 18.1 | 4.2 | 5 820 | 30.4 | 85 | 1.5 | 3 080 | 34.0 | 27.9 |
| McLean | 3 904 | 77.6 | 98 900 | 17.8 | 9.9 | 431 | 17.2 | 0.7 | 4 547 | -5.1 | 199 | 4.4 | 4 462 | 34.4 | 27.3 |
| Mercer | 3 662 | 79.4 | 109 300 | 15.9 | 9.9 | 448 | 19.6 | 1.3 | 4 215 | -4.2 | 214 | 5.1 | 4 301 | 27.4 | 36.6 |
| Morton | 10 918 | 78.2 | 120 400 | 21.1 | 10.2 | 537 | 25.4 | 1.4 | 14 770 | -1.6 | 543 | 3.7 | 15 109 | 32.1 | 25.1 |
| Mountrail | 2 885 | 73.8 | 75 400 | 14.4 | 9.9 | 536 | 21.5 | 3.8 | 6 522 | 16.5 | 115 | 1.8 | 3 908 | 33.3 | 23.1 |
| Nelson | 1 443 | 81.2 | 51 100 | 19.6 | 10.8 | 376 | 23.2 | 0.3 | 1 498 | -7.8 | 62 | 4.1 | 1 487 | 35.6 | 28.8 |
| Oliver | 773 | 82.4 | 91 100 | 16.2 | 9.9 | 426 | 17.9 | 1.9 | 1 064 | -8.5 | 59 | 5.5 | 881 | 38.0 | 28.3 |
| Pembina | 3 304 | 79.1 | 73 000 | 17.6 | 9.9 | 488 | 21.7 | 1.0 | 3 543 | -4.7 | 232 | 6.5 | 3 766 | 30.2 | 31.2 |
| Pierce | 1 951 | 69.9 | 81 700 | 18.7 | 10.9 | 544 | 28.3 | 0.0 | 1 712 | -2.9 | 80 | 4.7 | 2 121 | 30.6 | 32.1 |
| Ramsey | 4 807 | 65.7 | 85 400 | 17.2 | 10.4 | 481 | 22.1 | 1.6 | 5 459 | -4.6 | 236 | 4.3 | 5 970 | 34.3 | 20.6 |
| Ransom | 2 307 | 73.8 | 88 800 | 20.2 | 10.5 | 547 | 24.2 | 1.3 | 2 768 | -3.7 | 84 | 3.0 | 2 731 | 33.6 | 37.2 |
| Renville | 1 098 | 76.5 | 66 200 | 16.6 | 9.9 | 497 | 22.2 | 1.5 | 1 316 | 3.5 | 34 | 2.6 | 1 311 | 37.6 | 29.9 |
| Richland | 6 483 | 73.2 | 99 000 | 19.3 | 11.1 | 473 | 23.0 | 1.1 | 8 196 | -4.4 | 327 | 4.0 | 8 567 | 29.2 | 32.5 |
| Rolette | 4 619 | 72.0 | 61 200 | 17.0 | 13.1 | 337 | 30.9 | 6.9 | 4 672 | -3.1 | 522 | 11.2 | 4 539 | 38.6 | 19.8 |
| Sargent | 1 715 | 79.9 | 72 400 | 19.9 | 9.9 | 481 | 26.1 | 0.2 | 2 127 | 2.2 | 55 | 2.6 | 2 055 | 33.9 | 39.1 |
| Sheridan | 608 | 86.2 | 53 800 | 28.8 | 9.9 | 339 | 28.1 | 0.0 | 626 | -4.7 | 28 | 4.5 | 621 | 39.9 | 27.1 |
| Sioux | 1 067 | 45.5 | 72 900 | 16.0 | 14.1 | 422 | 14.5 | 12.6 | 1 257 | -4.3 | 67 | 5.3 | 1 215 | 34.8 | 22.8 |
| Slope | 306 | 84.6 | 54 800 | 14.2 | 9.9 | 342 | 31.3 | 2.6 | 872 | 19.1 | 11 | 1.3 | 396 | 45.7 | 34.1 |
| Stark | 9 793 | 71.8 | 130 000 | 19.0 | 10.2 | 611 | 23.7 | 1.5 | 19 653 | 14.5 | 321 | 1.6 | 13 276 | 27.8 | 31.9 |
| Steele | 836 | 81.5 | 65 500 | 16.0 | 9.9 | 415 | 20.3 | 1.0 | 1 100 | -3.7 | 27 | 2.5 | 983 | 35.8 | 34.1 |
| Stutsman | 8 574 | 68.0 | 92 800 | 19.8 | 11.2 | 520 | 25.5 | 0.5 | 10 796 | -4.4 | 358 | 3.3 | 11 084 | 31.9 | 24.5 |
| Towner | 992 | 79.6 | 53 000 | 18.5 | 9.9 | 422 | 26.1 | 1.3 | 1 000 | -4.0 | 39 | 3.9 | 1 169 | 40.8 | 21.1 |
| Traill | 3 375 | 75.1 | 90 100 | 20.1 | 12.5 | 550 | 24.8 | 0.7 | 3 986 | -1.4 | 141 | 3.5 | 4 295 | 31.2 | 27.7 |
| Walsh | 4 825 | 75.0 | 66 000 | 18.5 | 10.6 | 465 | 22.7 | 1.7 | 4 981 | -4.7 | 266 | 5.3 | 5 696 | 32.1 | 30.6 |

1. Specified owner-occupied units.　2. A value of 9.9 represents 9.9 percent or less.　3. Specified renter-occupied units. A value of 10.0 represents 10 percent or less.　4. Overcrowded or lacking complete plumbing facilities.　5. Percent of civilian labor force.　6. Persons 16 years old and over.

# Table B. States and Counties — Nonfarm Employment and Agriculture

| | Private nonfarm establishments, employment and payroll, 2011 | | | | | | | | | Agriculture, 2007 | | | |
| | | Employment | | | | | | Annual payroll | | Farms | | | |
| | | | | | | | | | | | Percent with: | | |
| STATE County | Number of establishments | Total | Health care and social assistance | Manufacturing | Retail trade | Finance and insurance | Professional, scientific, and technical services | Total (mil dol) | Average per employee (dollars) | Number | Fewer than 50 acres | 500 acres or more | Farm operators whose principal occupation is farming (percent) |
|---|---|---|---|---|---|---|---|---|---|---|---|---|---|
| | 104 | 105 | 106 | 107 | 108 | 109 | 110 | 111 | 112 | 113 | 114 | 115 | 116 |
| **NORTH CAROLINA—Cont'd** | | | | | | | | | | | | | |
| Swain | 400 | 5 322 | D | D | 506 | 71 | 45 | 154 | 28 965 | 85 | 50.6 | 1.2 | 37.6 |
| Transylvania | 789 | 6 876 | 1 652 | 418 | 1 359 | 222 | 204 | 195 | 28 378 | 279 | 73.5 | 1.1 | 35.5 |
| Tyrrell | 72 | 392 | D | D | 128 | 32 | D | 9 | 24 151 | 68 | 35.3 | 32.4 | 54.4 |
| Union | 3 951 | 43 741 | 5 183 | 9 820 | 6 521 | 815 | 1 105 | 1 467 | 33 529 | 1 107 | 55.5 | 5.2 | 51.5 |
| Vance | 882 | 12 989 | 2 798 | 1 744 | 2 156 | 243 | 245 | 393 | 30 292 | 246 | 28.0 | 10.6 | 45.5 |
| Wake | 24 943 | 373 012 | 49 971 | 14 115 | 50 139 | 20 445 | 35 722 | 17 195 | 46 097 | 827 | 56.8 | 3.5 | 49.0 |
| Warren | 218 | 1 821 | 436 | 370 | 309 | D | 49 | 46 | 25 082 | 294 | 25.2 | 12.9 | 44.2 |
| Washington | 242 | 2 848 | 625 | D | 421 | D | D | 96 | 33 591 | 187 | 31.6 | 21.9 | 58.3 |
| Watauga | 1 584 | 15 982 | 3 345 | 757 | 3 330 | 347 | 580 | 450 | 28 155 | 587 | 55.5 | 1.2 | 34.1 |
| Wayne | 2 169 | 34 069 | 7 727 | 5 151 | 5 546 | 1 130 | 755 | 1 033 | 30 330 | 723 | 42.9 | 13.4 | 58.1 |
| Wilkes | 1 266 | 17 997 | 3 171 | 3 881 | 2 478 | 465 | 430 | 543 | 30 153 | 1 095 | 50.7 | 3.1 | 49.5 |
| Wilson | 1 719 | 31 201 | 4 679 | 7 325 | 3 657 | D | 758 | 1 168 | 37 435 | 304 | 41.4 | 19.1 | 53.9 |
| Yadkin | 602 | 8 091 | D | 2 002 | 802 | 173 | 224 | 229 | 28 263 | 990 | 51.8 | 3.0 | 46.0 |
| Yancey | 344 | 3 250 | 689 | 639 | 529 | 82 | D | 91 | 28 057 | 447 | 60.0 | 1.1 | 40.0 |
| **NORTH DAKOTA** | 22 370 | 306 064 | 56 464 | 23 280 | 45 321 | 16 779 | 11 279 | 12 281 | 40 126 | 31 970 | 8.3 | 51.7 | 57.9 |
| Adams | 104 | 801 | D | D | 135 | 34 | D | 23 | 28 351 | 426 | 8.5 | 56.3 | 54.2 |
| Barnes | 366 | 4 188 | 1 106 | 697 | 635 | 159 | D | 121 | 29 003 | 921 | 9.0 | 43.5 | 56.0 |
| Benson | 102 | 1 079 | D | D | 63 | D | D | 32 | 29 209 | 591 | 8.0 | 56.9 | 61.9 |
| Billings | 53 | 224 | D | D | 12 | D | D | 11 | 50 513 | 243 | 1.6 | 61.7 | 63.8 |
| Bottineau | 272 | 1 964 | 253 | 111 | 416 | 124 | D | 67 | 34 216 | 899 | 7.3 | 50.2 | 57.2 |
| Bowman | 152 | 1 123 | D | D | 226 | 73 | D | 41 | 36 524 | 353 | 4.5 | 60.3 | 55.0 |
| Burke | 85 | 473 | 17 | NA | 58 | 36 | D | 20 | 42 609 | 463 | 2.6 | 57.7 | 57.0 |
| Burleigh | 2 732 | 43 530 | 10 394 | 773 | 6 834 | 2 201 | 1 583 | 1 624 | 37 315 | 1 026 | 20.5 | 34.2 | 43.5 |
| Cass | 5 003 | 91 223 | 15 255 | 8 666 | 12 309 | 6 997 | 4 455 | 3 700 | 40 557 | 913 | 15.9 | 53.0 | 68.3 |
| Cavalier | 158 | 1 216 | 249 | D | 199 | 94 | D | 44 | 35 840 | 650 | 6.5 | 59.1 | 64.5 |
| Dickey | 222 | 1 703 | 416 | D | 329 | D | D | 50 | 29 569 | 545 | 5.7 | 53.0 | 61.3 |
| Divide | 98 | 604 | D | D | 47 | D | 13 | 24 | 39 502 | 503 | 4.8 | 59.8 | 63.0 |
| Dunn | 132 | 1 268 | D | D | 164 | D | D | 55 | 43 469 | 563 | 6.9 | 62.9 | 65.5 |
| Eddy | 75 | 444 | 207 | D | 56 | D | D | 12 | 28 029 | 366 | 5.2 | 52.2 | 53.8 |
| Emmons | 127 | 762 | 193 | D | 101 | 46 | D | 20 | 26 827 | 694 | 3.5 | 62.8 | 62.8 |
| Foster | 147 | 1 403 | 315 | D | D | D | D | 52 | 36 877 | 310 | 8.4 | 53.2 | 66.8 |
| Golden Valley | 71 | 456 | D | NA | D | D | D | 14 | 30 741 | 243 | 4.9 | 64.6 | 59.7 |
| Grand Forks | 1 856 | 30 738 | 6 668 | 1 996 | 5 532 | 941 | 1 239 | 1 045 | 34 002 | 973 | 11.9 | 37.8 | 51.5 |
| Grant | 75 | 445 | 216 | D | 43 | 36 | D | 12 | 26 164 | 528 | 6.8 | 66.1 | 68.9 |
| Griggs | 97 | 690 | D | D | D | D | D | 23 | 33 254 | 479 | 7.9 | 45.3 | 55.1 |
| Hettinger | 94 | 454 | D | D | 103 | 47 | D | 14 | 31 044 | 546 | 6.6 | 50.4 | 46.0 |
| Kidder | 66 | 477 | 68 | D | 77 | 40 | D | 13 | 26 245 | 590 | 6.6 | 58.3 | 60.3 |
| LaMoure | 145 | 980 | 155 | 50 | 162 | 112 | D | 31 | 31 827 | 683 | 5.9 | 47.1 | 60.8 |
| Logan | 72 | 427 | D | D | 45 | 30 | D | 10 | 23 623 | 426 | 4.9 | 54.7 | 57.5 |
| McHenry | 122 | 719 | D | D | D | 55 | D | 23 | 32 025 | 928 | 6.4 | 52.0 | 58.2 |
| McIntosh | 111 | 854 | 320 | D | 130 | 59 | D | 23 | 26 769 | 513 | 3.9 | 53.8 | 57.5 |
| McKenzie | 292 | 2 289 | 204 | D | 177 | 74 | 103 | 151 | 65 826 | 585 | 6.8 | 59.5 | 64.6 |
| McLean | 249 | 2 320 | D | D | 277 | 124 | 19 | 106 | 45 727 | 1 001 | 7.7 | 53.6 | 53.5 |
| Mercer | 229 | D | 462 | 36 | 451 | 118 | 42 | D | D | 455 | 7.7 | 49.0 | 45.5 |
| Morton | 752 | 9 179 | 1 616 | 945 | 1 184 | 346 | D | 330 | 35 922 | 836 | 11.5 | 54.4 | 58.9 |
| Mountrail | 258 | 2 146 | 273 | D | 461 | 98 | 28 | 107 | 49 875 | 659 | 2.9 | 62.2 | 62.1 |
| Nelson | 119 | 785 | 253 | D | 117 | 71 | D | 22 | 28 341 | 651 | 7.2 | 37.3 | 41.6 |
| Oliver | 46 | D | D | D | 30 | D | 10 | D | D | 273 | 5.1 | 51.6 | 55.7 |
| Pembina | 279 | 3 025 | D | D | 420 | 132 | 27 | 101 | 33 386 | 521 | 10.2 | 49.9 | 67.8 |
| Pierce | 163 | 1 392 | D | D | 277 | 89 | D | 41 | 29 488 | 530 | 6.8 | 55.3 | 57.7 |
| Ramsey | 398 | 3 907 | 930 | D | 920 | 248 | D | 115 | 29 513 | 629 | 13.4 | 47.5 | 50.6 |
| Ransom | 195 | 1 608 | 407 | 319 | 271 | D | 42 | 48 | 29 556 | 560 | 8.2 | 39.5 | 46.1 |
| Renville | 105 | 847 | D | D | D | D | D | 32 | 37 406 | 370 | 10.0 | 63.8 | 70.0 |
| Richland | 538 | 5 970 | 644 | 1 534 | 823 | 156 | 112 | 203 | 33 922 | 943 | 13.6 | 49.2 | 68.1 |
| Rolette | 191 | 2 395 | 529 | D | 486 | 89 | D | 61 | 25 678 | 662 | 8.0 | 41.7 | 47.3 |
| Sargent | 125 | 1 918 | 69 | D | 127 | D | D | 89 | 46 360 | 493 | 5.9 | 50.9 | 67.7 |
| Sheridan | 41 | 170 | D | D | D | D | D | 4 | 23 929 | 390 | 3.6 | 57.9 | 57.9 |
| Sioux | 24 | 927 | D | NA | D | D | D | 24 | 26 312 | 204 | 8.3 | 69.1 | 68.1 |
| Slope | 16 | D | NA | NA | D | NA | NA | 9 | D | 238 | 2.1 | 63.9 | 65.5 |
| Stark | 1 032 | 12 243 | 1 994 | 1 005 | 1 742 | 402 | 355 | 535 | 43 682 | 865 | 13.1 | 45.3 | 50.5 |
| Steele | 63 | 567 | D | 167 | 78 | 62 | D | 21 | 36 407 | 342 | 7.3 | 50.9 | 59.9 |
| Stutsman | 653 | 8 882 | 2 532 | 772 | 1 313 | 411 | 202 | 260 | 29 282 | 1 043 | 7.8 | 49.9 | 51.3 |
| Towner | 85 | 539 | D | 38 | 36 | D | 26 | 14 | 26 872 | 496 | 3.2 | 59.3 | 61.7 |
| Traill | 276 | 2 555 | D | D | 303 | 167 | D | 81 | 31 567 | 460 | 13.7 | 56.5 | 69.8 |
| Walsh | 414 | 3 426 | 681 | 504 | 546 | 156 | 83 | 103 | 30 194 | 968 | 9.0 | 40.3 | 55.9 |

| STATE County | Agriculture, 2007 (cont.) | | | | | | | | | | | | | | | |
|---|---|---|---|---|---|---|---|---|---|---|---|---|---|---|---|---|
| | Land in farms | | | | Value of land and buildings (dollars) | | Value of machinery and equipment, average per farm (dollars) | Value of products sold | | | | Percent of farms with sales of: | | Government payments | |
| | | Acres | | | | | | | | Percent from: | | | | | |
| | Acreage (1,000) | Percent change, 2002–2007 | Average size of farm | Total irrigated (1,000) | Total cropland (1,000) | Average per farm | Average per acre | | Total (mil dol) | Average per farm (dollars) | Crops | Live-stock and poultry products | $10,000 or more | $100,000 or more | Total ($1,000) | Percent of farms |
| | 117 | 118 | 119 | 120 | 121 | 122 | 123 | 124 | 125 | 126 | 127 | 128 | 129 | 130 | 131 | 132 |
| NORTH CAROLINA—Cont'd | | | | | | | | | | | | | | | | |
| Swain | 6 | -14.3 | 66 | 0.0 | 1.5 | 403 101 | 6 133 | 50 586 | 1.4 | 16 503 | 86.7 | 13.3 | 17.6 | 3.5 | 12 | 15.3 |
| Transylvania | 16 | -11.1 | 58 | 1.0 | 7.7 | 422 408 | 7 345 | 42 670 | 12.4 | 44 310 | 60.8 | 39.2 | 26.9 | 7.5 | 228 | 8.2 |
| Tyrrell | 54 | -27.0 | 792 | 0.0 | 51.7 | 1 805 736 | 2 279 | 269 674 | 36.2 | 531 765 | D | D | 55.9 | 36.8 | 1 026 | 83.8 |
| Union | 178 | -6.8 | 161 | 0.3 | 121.1 | 837 937 | 5 206 | 93 151 | 410.5 | 370 818 | 11.4 | 88.6 | 43.6 | 27.0 | 1 755 | 19.6 |
| Vance | 55 | -26.7 | 224 | 1.5 | 20.1 | 739 950 | 3 304 | 62 112 | D | D | D | 0.0 | 22.4 | 6.9 | 512 | 50.4 |
| Wake | 85 | -8.6 | 103 | 3.8 | 45.9 | 816 154 | 7 945 | 58 385 | 42.3 | 51 102 | 86.0 | 14.0 | 30.7 | 5.9 | 2 196 | 23.8 |
| Warren | 73 | -2.7 | 247 | 1.4 | 27.9 | 607 782 | 2 458 | 60 519 | 22.9 | 77 832 | 33.6 | 66.4 | 35.0 | 11.9 | 661 | 60.2 |
| Washington | 97 | -14.9 | 518 | 3.2 | 82.7 | 1 159 455 | 2 237 | 159 949 | 68.6 | 366 983 | 63.5 | 36.5 | 44.4 | 27.3 | 2 324 | 73.8 |
| Watauga | 46 | -11.5 | 78 | 0.1 | 11.7 | 553 682 | 7 099 | 45 254 | 11.5 | 19 641 | D | D | 33.9 | 2.6 | 77 | 7.7 |
| Wayne | 175 | 2.3 | 242 | 6.7 | 131.7 | 1 008 378 | 4 160 | 163 067 | 501.2 | 693 190 | 15.0 | 85.0 | 59.2 | 38.0 | 3 902 | 50.5 |
| Wilkes | 110 | -11.3 | 100 | 0.3 | 37.3 | 561 362 | 5 590 | 76 873 | 389.8 | 356 010 | 1.8 | 98.2 | 40.4 | 24.6 | 419 | 3.6 |
| Wilson | 105 | -8.7 | 344 | 2.8 | 81.8 | 1 108 122 | 3 218 | 168 875 | 127.8 | 420 390 | 77.1 | 22.9 | 45.1 | 25.3 | 2 997 | 57.9 |
| Yadkin | 105 | -10.3 | 106 | 0.8 | 59.7 | 551 659 | 5 193 | 58 570 | 97.8 | 98 785 | 17.9 | 82.1 | 30.7 | 12.8 | 489 | 13.2 |
| Yancey | 33 | -15.4 | 75 | 0.1 | 10.0 | 364 053 | 4 868 | 33 914 | 5.2 | 11 573 | 62.1 | 37.9 | 19.5 | 2.5 | 123 | 5.8 |
| NORTH DAKOTA | 39 675 | 1.0 | 1 241 | 236.1 | 27 527.2 | 957 053 | 771 | 174 683 | 6 084.2 | 190 310 | 82.8 | 17.2 | 57.9 | 35.9 | 359 532 | 83.5 |
| Adams | 627 | 3.6 | 1 471 | 0.0 | 407.3 | 856 530 | 582 | 144 619 | 70.5 | 165 590 | 55.6 | 44.4 | 53.8 | 32.9 | 4 711 | 83.6 |
| Barnes | 907 | 5.8 | 985 | 1.8 | 795.0 | 925 992 | 940 | 183 067 | 183.3 | 198 980 | 94.1 | 5.9 | 54.6 | 36.3 | 12 066 | 90.0 |
| Benson | 759 | 3.5 | 1 285 | 3.8 | 603.9 | 932 327 | 726 | 180 433 | 122.6 | 207 393 | 88.1 | 11.9 | 60.2 | 37.7 | 8 024 | 84.4 |
| Billings | 725 | -10.6 | 2 982 | D | 120.2 | 1 404 571 | 471 | 103 502 | 23.8 | 97 736 | 30.6 | 69.4 | 63.0 | 30.9 | 1 130 | 69.1 |
| Bottineau | 1 029 | 8.5 | 1 144 | D | 891.1 | 839 438 | 734 | 168 938 | 167.9 | 186 743 | 94.7 | 5.3 | 56.1 | 35.7 | 10 514 | 85.5 |
| Bowman | 721 | -5.0 | 2 042 | 0.9 | 371.9 | 1 043 421 | 511 | 154 249 | 77.7 | 220 062 | 45.2 | 54.8 | 60.6 | 34.8 | 4 261 | 85.8 |
| Burke | 571 | -4.8 | 1 232 | 0.0 | 425.5 | 771 723 | 626 | 135 643 | 61.6 | 133 017 | 89.7 | 10.3 | 55.5 | 29.8 | 4 556 | 89.8 |
| Burleigh | 880 | 1.6 | 857 | 5.7 | 476.9 | 623 424 | 727 | 90 783 | 82.2 | 80 152 | 61.6 | 38.4 | 41.2 | 16.5 | 6 057 | 63.2 |
| Cass | 1 039 | -7.8 | 1 138 | 11.7 | 986.3 | 1 668 866 | 1 467 | 279 562 | 267.9 | 293 426 | 94.1 | 5.9 | 67.1 | 51.3 | 14 274 | 84.3 |
| Cavalier | 873 | 6.6 | 1 344 | D | 812.3 | 1 276 743 | 950 | 263 511 | 173.7 | 267 289 | 98.6 | 1.4 | 64.0 | 50.9 | 12 447 | 92.6 |
| Dickey | 698 | 16.5 | 1 280 | 16.4 | 535.4 | 1 331 801 | 1 041 | 225 365 | 162.2 | 297 545 | 76.7 | 23.3 | 62.2 | 43.1 | 8 251 | 86.4 |
| Divide | 708 | -7.0 | 1 408 | 2.3 | 538.3 | 880 396 | 625 | 172 566 | 80.9 | 160 889 | 91.4 | 8.6 | 59.6 | 40.8 | 5 998 | 92.0 |
| Dunn | 1 044 | -5.6 | 1 854 | 0.4 | 371.2 | 947 467 | 511 | 146 974 | 68.7 | 122 046 | 45.7 | 54.3 | 71.0 | 34.3 | 2 763 | 71.6 |
| Eddy | 377 | 8.0 | 1 029 | 0.6 | 272.2 | 606 782 | 590 | 134 760 | 47.2 | 129 047 | 81.8 | 18.2 | 50.5 | 29.8 | 4 392 | 83.9 |
| Emmons | 872 | 4.1 | 1 256 | 5.0 | 529.8 | 852 478 | 679 | 145 139 | 121.0 | 174 285 | 71.7 | 28.3 | 67.0 | 42.7 | 7 122 | 88.2 |
| Foster | 400 | 4.4 | 1 290 | 3.3 | 336.1 | 981 190 | 761 | 257 515 | 95.0 | 306 319 | 79.6 | 20.4 | 65.8 | 44.8 | 4 604 | 81.6 |
| Golden Valley | 570 | -1.7 | 2 347 | 0.9 | 231.8 | 1 095 900 | 467 | 161 650 | 43.1 | 177 374 | 62.3 | 37.7 | 58.0 | 35.0 | 2 495 | 84.8 |
| Grand Forks | 826 | 9.3 | 848 | 17.1 | 753.9 | 896 590 | 1 057 | 216 815 | 255.6 | 262 687 | 91.3 | 8.7 | 47.3 | 33.7 | 11 583 | 86.4 |
| Grant | 1 058 | 0.1 | 2 004 | 1.9 | 510.9 | 1 036 806 | 517 | 137 893 | 79.9 | 151 270 | 59.0 | 41.0 | 68.4 | 36.9 | 5 834 | 86.9 |
| Griggs | 406 | 7.1 | 848 | 4.0 | 322.5 | 578 615 | 682 | 122 527 | 63.3 | 132 160 | 89.4 | 10.6 | 47.2 | 26.1 | 5 439 | 86.0 |
| Hettinger | 708 | 4.0 | 1 296 | 0.0 | 582.8 | 968 035 | 747 | 160 776 | 93.6 | 171 356 | 89.4 | 10.6 | 45.1 | 30.2 | 8 128 | 91.2 |
| Kidder | 753 | -5.2 | 1 277 | 18.3 | 420.2 | 732 194 | 573 | 125 638 | 78.5 | 132 977 | 59.6 | 40.4 | 53.4 | 28.5 | 5 172 | 88.3 |
| LaMoure | 688 | 1.6 | 1 007 | 6.6 | 569.0 | 1 059 157 | 1 051 | 198 270 | 153.4 | 224 590 | 80.4 | 19.6 | 61.8 | 40.8 | 8 024 | 85.9 |
| Logan | 577 | -0.2 | 1 355 | 2.4 | 326.0 | 990 035 | 731 | 157 599 | 84.5 | 198 452 | 46.8 | 53.2 | 61.0 | 35.4 | 4 722 | 89.9 |
| McHenry | 1 083 | -3.8 | 1 167 | 8.7 | 692.1 | 764 603 | 655 | 128 138 | 134.0 | 144 353 | 67.4 | 32.6 | 56.7 | 31.5 | 8 585 | 81.5 |
| McIntosh | 550 | -3.3 | 1 072 | D | 372.2 | 777 041 | 725 | 131 842 | 75.9 | 147 880 | 65.9 | 34.1 | 57.7 | 33.1 | 4 133 | 87.3 |
| McKenzie | 1 075 | -9.9 | 1 837 | 24.8 | 430.9 | 948 458 | 516 | 159 762 | 78.1 | 133 539 | 64.2 | 35.8 | 67.4 | 34.7 | 3 543 | 72.5 |
| McLean | 1 163 | 6.2 | 1 162 | 6.7 | 884.7 | 905 983 | 780 | 168 483 | 163.4 | 163 276 | 89.2 | 10.8 | 58.8 | 37.5 | 9 673 | 80.5 |
| Mercer | 510 | -4.9 | 1 120 | 2.3 | 238.9 | 673 266 | 601 | 101 405 | 40.1 | 88 061 | 61.5 | 38.5 | 61.5 | 20.4 | 2 609 | 75.4 |
| Morton | 1 165 | -8.7 | 1 394 | 6.6 | 548.6 | 885 436 | 635 | 129 538 | 117.3 | 140 252 | 51.9 | 48.1 | 64.8 | 31.3 | 5 361 | 71.8 |
| Mountrail | 1 037 | -2.9 | 1 573 | 0.0 | 652.4 | 924 497 | 588 | 200 773 | 108.0 | 163 888 | 85.9 | 14.1 | 64.8 | 36.9 | 7 274 | 85.1 |
| Nelson | 550 | 3.4 | 845 | 0.0 | 457.1 | 592 037 | 701 | 121 228 | 85.4 | 131 135 | 90.6 | 9.4 | 35.3 | 24.0 | 7 997 | 90.8 |
| Oliver | 378 | -6.4 | 1 384 | 5.8 | 176.1 | 890 531 | 643 | 153 764 | 53.4 | 195 563 | 45.6 | 54.4 | 70.7 | 34.1 | 1 692 | 74.4 |
| Pembina | 649 | 5.7 | 1 246 | 3.7 | 601.7 | 1 685 235 | 1 352 | 358 324 | 235.6 | 452 248 | 97.3 | 2.7 | 63.3 | 48.0 | 7 678 | 88.5 |
| Pierce | 581 | 9.4 | 1 097 | D | 452.1 | 707 782 | 645 | 141 540 | 72.7 | 137 195 | 80.7 | 19.3 | 54.0 | 35.8 | 6 997 | 92.8 |
| Ramsey | 715 | 12.4 | 1 136 | D | 656.4 | 800 770 | 705 | 202 264 | 124.6 | 198 045 | 98.0 | 2.0 | 47.7 | 34.8 | 9 947 | 88.6 |
| Ransom | 527 | 5.2 | 942 | 18.5 | 367.8 | 967 866 | 1 028 | 159 340 | 93.4 | 166 710 | 77.2 | 22.8 | 51.4 | 29.5 | 7 192 | 86.4 |
| Renville | 554 | 5.1 | 1 498 | 0.0 | 489.2 | 1 344 082 | 897 | 248 782 | 106.3 | 287 218 | 97.0 | 3.0 | 71.4 | 55.7 | 5 497 | 88.4 |
| Richland | 906 | 1.7 | 961 | 4.6 | 833.2 | 1 325 966 | 1 380 | 266 241 | 261.5 | 277 305 | 87.5 | 12.5 | 69.5 | 50.8 | 11 567 | 82.9 |
| Rolette | 568 | 11.8 | 858 | D | 384.7 | 573 518 | 669 | 104 174 | 66.6 | 100 629 | 79.3 | 20.7 | 47.3 | 23.6 | 5 423 | 72.4 |
| Sargent | 505 | 0.0 | 1 024 | 13.3 | 429.6 | 1 151 242 | 1 124 | 217 100 | 127.7 | 259 109 | 81.7 | 18.3 | 65.3 | 44.8 | 7 187 | 91.1 |
| Sheridan | 500 | 6.6 | 1 282 | 0.0 | 354.8 | 752 167 | 587 | 125 352 | 52.5 | 134 586 | 83.3 | 16.7 | 56.7 | 30.8 | 4 779 | 83.8 |
| Sioux | 730 | 4.0 | 3 580 | D | 148.8 | 1 324 598 | 370 | 125 485 | 32.3 | 158 425 | 34.5 | 65.5 | 73.0 | 44.1 | 1 597 | 74.5 |
| Slope | 769 | 0.8 | 3 231 | 0.5 | 269.6 | 1 552 897 | 481 | 193 792 | 47.6 | 200 188 | 66.0 | 34.0 | 63.4 | 39.5 | 2 522 | 81.5 |
| Stark | 837 | 7.7 | 968 | 1.0 | 529.1 | 690 697 | 714 | 112 700 | 96.8 | 111 922 | 65.8 | 34.2 | 50.5 | 24.4 | 6 162 | 76.0 |
| Steele | 402 | 0.2 | 1 175 | 1.9 | 366.7 | 1 144 258 | 974 | 254 960 | 102.3 | 299 251 | 97.7 | 2.3 | 63.2 | 52.3 | 4 710 | 88.0 |
| Stutsman | 1 193 | -1.8 | 1 144 | 8.7 | 931.7 | 939 366 | 821 | 166 881 | 198.3 | 190 108 | 85.0 | 15.0 | 49.1 | 32.1 | 13 790 | 84.9 |
| Towner | 607 | 10.6 | 1 224 | 0.9 | 550.5 | 912 542 | 745 | 185 671 | 107.5 | 216 678 | 89.6 | 10.4 | 63.5 | 45.2 | 7 833 | 93.3 |
| Traill | 544 | 2.6 | 1 182 | D | 530.3 | 1 623 808 | 1 374 | 301 859 | 182.9 | 397 543 | 96.9 | 3.1 | 72.8 | 59.6 | 7 459 | 87.2 |
| Walsh | 795 | 4.7 | 822 | 2.2 | 713.6 | 914 858 | 1 113 | 189 962 | 222.5 | 229 890 | 98.0 | 2.0 | 48.5 | 33.3 | 12 776 | 90.9 |

# Table B. States and Counties — Water Use, Wholesale Trade, Retail Trade, and Real Estate

| STATE County | Water use, 2005 | | Wholesale trade,[1] 2007 | | | | Retail trade,[2] 2007 | | | | Real estate and rental and leasing,[2] 2007 | | | |
|---|---|---|---|---|---|---|---|---|---|---|---|---|---|---|
| | Total water withdrawn (mil gal/day) | Gallons withdrawn per person | Number of establishments | Number of employees | Sales (mil dol) | Annual payroll (mil dol) | Number of establishments | Number of employees | Sales (mil dol) | Annual payroll (mil dol) | Number of establishments | Number of employees | Receipts (mil dol) | Annual payroll (mil dol) |
| | 133 | 134 | 135 | 136 | 137 | 138 | 139 | 140 | 141 | 142 | 143 | 144 | 145 | 146 |
| **NORTH CAROLINA—Cont'd** | | | | | | | | | | | | | | |
| Swain | 17.2 | 1 306 | 7 | 23 | 2.3 | 0.4 | 104 | 619 | 112.3 | 10.1 | 19 | 45 | 5.4 | 0.8 |
| Transylvania | 523.2 | 17 661 | 11 | D | D | D | 122 | 1 331 | 266.2 | 27.0 | 59 | 173 | 19.8 | 4.6 |
| Tyrrell | 0.7 | 159 | 2 | D | D | D | 19 | 143 | 30.7 | 2.0 | 1 | D | D | D |
| Union | 66.8 | 410 | 264 | 2 640 | 1 232.8 | 112.2 | 515 | 6 568 | 1 699.8 | 148.6 | 179 | 530 | 100.8 | 17.6 |
| Vance | 10.2 | 233 | 30 | D | D | D | 190 | 2 242 | 582.1 | 48.3 | 45 | 164 | 22.9 | 3.9 |
| Wake | 133.5 | 178 | 1 059 | 15 635 | 11 334.3 | 918.8 | 3 181 | 49 828 | 12 598.1 | 1 162.4 | 1 374 | 7 297 | 1 901.6 | 324.0 |
| Warren | 3.2 | 164 | 8 | 32 | 17.7 | 0.9 | 53 | 340 | 62.9 | 6.2 | 6 | 30 | 3.4 | 0.6 |
| Washington | 5.8 | 437 | 13 | 111 | 83.2 | 3.4 | 52 | 467 | 107.7 | 8.6 | 5 | 10 | 1.1 | 0.2 |
| Watauga | 7.4 | 174 | 47 | 343 | 169.3 | 15.6 | 343 | 3 588 | 795.2 | 79.3 | 145 | 505 | 59.3 | 11.5 |
| Wayne | 45.1 | 394 | 102 | 1 843 | 1 094.5 | 71.2 | 501 | 5 759 | 1 388.0 | 113.7 | 70 | 288 | 35.3 | 6.6 |
| Wilkes | 19.5 | 290 | 43 | 546 | 260.6 | 16.6 | 226 | 2 503 | 759.3 | 50.0 | 57 | 229 | 52.4 | 8.6 |
| Wilson | 16.9 | 222 | 93 | 1 060 | 728.8 | 48.9 | 370 | 4 130 | 1 058.6 | 89.8 | 70 | 193 | 29.9 | 4.4 |
| Yadkin | 5.8 | 154 | 24 | 169 | 101.2 | 5.9 | 127 | 897 | 238.6 | 16.8 | 13 | D | D | D |
| Yancey | 2.2 | 121 | 9 | 32 | 7.1 | 0.7 | 64 | 592 | 149.1 | 12.3 | 13 | 30 | 3.0 | 0.7 |
| **NORTH DAKOTA** | 1 339.9 | 2 105 | 1 332 | 14 866 | 13 099.3 | 627.1 | 3 361 | 44 054 | 10 527.3 | 891.4 | 770 | 3 748 | 668.8 | 96.0 |
| Adams | 0.5 | 201 | 8 | 46 | 31.0 | 1.3 | 19 | 147 | 30.7 | 2.5 | 2 | D | D | D |
| Barnes | 2.1 | 189 | 25 | 115 | 142.6 | 4.5 | 57 | 536 | 147.8 | 10.6 | 7 | D | D | D |
| Benson | 2.6 | 367 | 13 | 83 | 125.1 | 3.1 | 18 | 104 | 20.1 | 1.2 | 2 | D | D | D |
| Billings | 1.3 | 1 599 | 1 | D | D | D | 10 | 5 | 1.2 | 0.1 | NA | NA | NA | NA |
| Bottineau | 1.7 | 252 | 16 | 95 | 135.0 | 3.6 | 47 | 317 | 57.0 | 5.2 | 10 | 12 | 0.6 | 0.1 |
| Bowman | 3.8 | 1 257 | 9 | 66 | 80.7 | 2.4 | 25 | 197 | 63.5 | 4.2 | 2 | D | D | D |
| Burke | 0.6 | 315 | 7 | 39 | 131.0 | 1.4 | 14 | 51 | 17.9 | 0.8 | 2 | D | D | D |
| Burleigh | 15.3 | 207 | 132 | 1 613 | 889.1 | 71.9 | 385 | 6 713 | 1 401.0 | 134.8 | 110 | 365 | 53.8 | 8.4 |
| Cass | 15.9 | 121 | 335 | D | D | D | 663 | 12 008 | 2 885.6 | 256.5 | 268 | 1 630 | 226.4 | 45.8 |
| Cavalier | 0.9 | 199 | 13 | 116 | 261.5 | 4.9 | 33 | 186 | 83.2 | 4.1 | 1 | D | D | D |
| Dickey | 4.5 | 820 | 13 | 109 | 151.7 | 3.7 | 46 | 308 | 78.1 | 6.0 | 2 | D | D | D |
| Divide | 2.6 | 1 210 | 5 | 56 | 21.3 | 0.6 | 12 | 74 | 11.8 | 0.9 | 5 | D | D | D |
| Dunn | 2.0 | 578 | 5 | 22 | 6.5 | 0.6 | 13 | 106 | 39.3 | 2.2 | 1 | D | D | D |
| Eddy | 1.3 | 503 | 4 | 19 | 21.0 | 0.7 | 14 | 86 | 32.5 | 1.8 | 2 | D | D | D |
| Emmons | 5.0 | 1 311 | 8 | 65 | 46.8 | 1.7 | 19 | 104 | 26.8 | 2.3 | NA | NA | NA | NA |
| Foster | 2.8 | 793 | 15 | 113 | 101.7 | 4.9 | 27 | 251 | 80.7 | 5.1 | 2 | D | D | D |
| Golden Valley | 0.7 | 374 | 5 | 120 | 89.0 | 5.0 | 14 | 86 | 49.9 | 1.3 | NA | NA | NA | NA |
| Grand Forks | 11.6 | 176 | 89 | 1 169 | 734.3 | 49.4 | 336 | 5 844 | 1 238.2 | 114.6 | 58 | 422 | 58.8 | 9.2 |
| Grant | 13.6 | 5 205 | 6 | 20 | 27.3 | 0.5 | 13 | 47 | 12.4 | 0.9 | 3 | 3 | 0.4 | 0.0 |
| Griggs | 2.3 | 917 | 9 | 62 | 38.0 | 2.3 | 11 | 48 | 11.2 | 1.0 | NA | NA | NA | NA |
| Hettinger | 0.4 | 153 | 4 | D | D | D | 16 | 104 | 46.9 | 1.9 | 3 | D | D | D |
| Kidder | 17.8 | 7 166 | 3 | 15 | 10.5 | 0.4 | 10 | 68 | 28.0 | 1.1 | 4 | 9 | 0.8 | 0.1 |
| LaMoure | 4.0 | 922 | 14 | 124 | 137.8 | 5.6 | 24 | 157 | 37.2 | 2.3 | 2 | D | D | D |
| Logan | 2.4 | 1 175 | 7 | 52 | 62.4 | 1.8 | 9 | 41 | 21.5 | 1.0 | 1 | D | D | D |
| McHenry | 20.2 | 3 667 | 5 | D | D | D | 20 | 128 | 37.1 | 2.4 | 6 | D | D | D |
| McIntosh | 0.9 | 295 | 9 | 59 | 53.3 | 1.7 | 26 | 165 | 48.5 | 3.4 | 3 | 9 | 1.0 | 0.1 |
| McKenzie | 13.9 | 2 476 | 11 | 83 | 94.9 | 3.7 | 21 | 155 | 36.8 | 2.7 | 4 | D | D | D |
| McLean | 22.4 | 2 608 | 16 | 123 | 208.0 | 5.5 | 38 | 290 | 52.8 | 4.2 | 4 | 8 | 0.2 | 0.0 |
| Mercer | 500.1 | 59 788 | 5 | D | D | D | 43 | 393 | 85.7 | 7.0 | 6 | 6 | 0.4 | 0.0 |
| Morton | 63.4 | 2 485 | 39 | 283 | 238.1 | 9.2 | 94 | 1 105 | 342.1 | 27.2 | 33 | 75 | 13.6 | 1.5 |
| Mountrail | 1.6 | 243 | 11 | 80 | 110.9 | 2.8 | 39 | 322 | 118.9 | 6.1 | 3 | 8 | 0.3 | 0.1 |
| Nelson | 0.9 | 275 | 12 | 84 | 138.2 | 3.5 | 21 | 94 | 24.4 | 1.5 | 4 | 6 | 0.2 | 0.0 |
| Oliver | 514.4 | 283 712 | 1 | D | D | D | 4 | 34 | 10.0 | 0.7 | NA | NA | NA | NA |
| Pembina | 2.0 | 250 | 34 | 286 | 367.9 | 9.1 | 51 | 480 | 90.0 | 8.3 | 3 | 2 | 0.2 | 0.0 |
| Pierce | 1.2 | 277 | 11 | 100 | 85.9 | 2.8 | 28 | 286 | 85.7 | 5.2 | 2 | D | D | D |
| Ramsey | 0.4 | 34 | 26 | 212 | 266.3 | 8.0 | 85 | 886 | 234.3 | 20.1 | 5 | 11 | 0.7 | 0.1 |
| Ransom | 10.3 | 1 766 | 8 | 96 | 142.5 | 4.3 | 33 | 303 | 53.9 | 5.0 | 3 | D | D | D |
| Renville | 0.3 | 124 | 13 | D | D | D | 11 | 71 | 23.8 | 1.4 | 3 | D | D | D |
| Richland | 6.0 | 344 | 40 | D | D | D | 70 | 718 | 205.0 | 14.7 | 15 | 49 | 5.0 | 0.9 |
| Rolette | 2.4 | 176 | 10 | 100 | 85.8 | 2.5 | 45 | 476 | 107.1 | 9.1 | 1 | D | D | D |
| Sargent | 4.1 | 990 | 14 | 101 | 152.9 | 3.6 | 22 | 141 | 27.6 | 2.1 | 4 | 9 | 1.8 | 0.2 |
| Sheridan | 0.5 | 357 | 5 | 21 | 22.9 | 0.7 | 4 | 11 | 4.3 | 0.2 | 3 | 3 | 0.1 | 0.0 |
| Sioux | 0.7 | 172 | NA | NA | NA | NA | 7 | 63 | 13.2 | 0.7 | NA | NA | NA | NA |
| Slope | 0.9 | 1 199 | NA | NA | NA | NA | NA | NA | NA | NA | NA | NA | NA | NA |
| Stark | 1.9 | 87 | 46 | D | D | D | 160 | 1 686 | 403.4 | 33.8 | 23 | 76 | 11.4 | 1.9 |
| Steele | 1.0 | 473 | 6 | 39 | 159.8 | 1.9 | 9 | 72 | 25.9 | 1.6 | 2 | D | D | D |
| Stutsman | 12.7 | 609 | 33 | D | D | D | 123 | 1 275 | 309.7 | 24.8 | 23 | 142 | 10.6 | 1.3 |
| Towner | 0.4 | 138 | 7 | D | D | D | 13 | 60 | 7.2 | 0.9 | 2 | D | D | D |
| Traill | 1.2 | 142 | 31 | 238 | 275.7 | 9.1 | 41 | 310 | 72.5 | 5.6 | 9 | 27 | 1.4 | 0.3 |
| Walsh | 2.2 | 190 | 31 | 285 | 296.2 | 10.6 | 70 | 592 | 98.8 | 9.2 | 11 | 19 | 0.9 | 0.2 |

1. Merchant wholesalers, except manufacturers' sales branches and offices.　　2. Employer establishments.

# Table B. States and Counties — Professional Services, Manufacturing, and Accommodation and Food Services

| STATE County | Professional, scientific, and technical services,[1] 2007 | | | | Manufacturing, 2007 | | | | Accommodation and food services, 2007 | | | |
|---|---|---|---|---|---|---|---|---|---|---|---|---|
| | Number of establishments | Number of employees | Receipts (mil dol) | Annual payroll (mil dol) | Number of establishments | Number of employees | Receipts (mil dol) | Annual payroll (mil dol) | Number of establishments | Number of employees | Sales (mil dol) | Annual payroll (mil dol) |
| | 147 | 148 | 149 | 150 | 151 | 152 | 153 | 154 | 155 | 156 | 157 | 158 |
| NORTH CAROLINA—Cont'd | | | | | | | | | | | | |
| Swain | 11 | 60 | 2.5 | 1.6 | NA | NA | NA | NA | 99 | 2 857 | 561.6 | 68.9 |
| Transylvania | 69 | D | D | D | 32 | 532 | 71.9 | 18.2 | 84 | 1 132 | 62.8 | 18.4 |
| Tyrrell | 3 | D | D | D | NA | NA | NA | NA | 5 | D | D | D |
| Union | 352 | 1 204 | 140.3 | 48.1 | 249 | 11 264 | D | 459.4 | 246 | D | D | D |
| Vance | 45 | 206 | 16.7 | 7.7 | 42 | 1 916 | 639.2 | 68.4 | 69 | 1 363 | 53.9 | 15.3 |
| Wake | 4 064 | 34 994 | 5 389.2 | 2 217.3 | 631 | 17 932 | 14 091.7 | 827.9 | 1 773 | 36 260 | 1 726.6 | 480.0 |
| Warren | 17 | 55 | 3.7 | 1.0 | NA | NA | NA | NA | 18 | 120 | 5.7 | 1.6 |
| Washington | 10 | 85 | 5.4 | 1.6 | 14 | 1 499 | 727.9 | D | 24 | 376 | 13.5 | 3.5 |
| Watauga | 160 | D | D | D | 54 | 862 | 129.8 | 26.6 | 159 | 3 289 | 131.4 | 41.8 |
| Wayne | 143 | 825 | 65.7 | 22.8 | 84 | 6 147 | 1 474.8 | 221.7 | 197 | 3 485 | 132.1 | 36.2 |
| Wilkes | 92 | 461 | 38.9 | 15.2 | 98 | 5 839 | 1 503.3 | 173.5 | 104 | 1 569 | 62.1 | 17.2 |
| Wilson | 112 | D | D | D | 100 | 8 193 | 8 357.1 | 336.3 | 131 | 2 582 | 112.8 | 28.7 |
| Yadkin | 40 | 247 | 19.4 | 7.6 | 43 | 1 856 | D | 65.2 | 66 | 883 | 33.6 | 9.2 |
| Yancey | 25 | 86 | 5.6 | 2.4 | 17 | 655 | 127.4 | 21.1 | 22 | 291 | 10.5 | 3.0 |
| NORTH DAKOTA | 1 432 | 9 707 | 1 110.7 | 416.9 | 767 | 26 361 | 11 349.8 | 991.4 | 1 840 | 30 307 | 1 214.2 | 337.8 |
| Adams | 4 | D | D | D | NA | NA | NA | NA | 9 | D | D | D |
| Barnes | 21 | 94 | 5.4 | 3.7 | 14 | 691 | 339.8 | 22.4 | 35 | 439 | 12.1 | 3.2 |
| Benson | 6 | 21 | 1.8 | 0.8 | NA | NA | NA | NA | 14 | 39 | 2.1 | 0.4 |
| Billings | 1 | D | D | D | NA | NA | NA | NA | 9 | 76 | 13.5 | 3.2 |
| Bottineau | 14 | 57 | 4.0 | 1.7 | NA | NA | NA | NA | 32 | 152 | 6.9 | 1.5 |
| Bowman | 8 | 28 | 3.4 | 1.2 | NA | NA | NA | NA | 15 | 95 | 3.9 | 0.9 |
| Burke | 3 | D | D | D | NA | NA | NA | NA | 9 | 59 | 3.3 | 0.5 |
| Burleigh | 260 | D | D | D | 73 | 2 089 | D | 85.3 | 173 | 4 405 | 170.1 | 50.3 |
| Cass | 412 | D | D | D | 201 | 8 266 | 2 480.1 | 310.9 | 363 | 8 796 | 341.2 | 101.0 |
| Cavalier | 7 | 12 | 1.0 | 0.4 | NA | NA | NA | NA | 18 | 103 | 3.1 | 0.7 |
| Dickey | 9 | 36 | 1.8 | 0.6 | NA | NA | NA | NA | 19 | 168 | 4.8 | 1.0 |
| Divide | 5 | 11 | 1.1 | 0.2 | NA | NA | NA | NA | 7 | D | D | D |
| Dunn | 1 | D | D | D | NA | NA | NA | NA | 8 | D | D | D |
| Eddy | 5 | 14 | 1.3 | 0.4 | NA | NA | NA | NA | 8 | D | D | D |
| Emmons | 11 | 148 | 2.0 | 1.2 | NA | NA | NA | NA | 14 | D | D | D |
| Foster | 8 | 12 | 0.8 | 0.2 | NA | NA | NA | NA | 11 | 130 | 3.7 | 1.1 |
| Golden Valley | 4 | 17 | 1.0 | 0.3 | NA | NA | NA | NA | 7 | 26 | 1.0 | 0.2 |
| Grand Forks | 118 | D | D | D | 55 | 2 762 | 565.3 | 85.8 | 186 | 4 180 | 141.1 | 41.2 |
| Grant | 3 | 7 | 0.5 | 0.1 | NA | NA | NA | NA | 7 | D | D | D |
| Griggs | 9 | 57 | 3.4 | 1.2 | NA | NA | NA | NA | 9 | D | D | D |
| Hettinger | 4 | D | D | D | NA | NA | NA | NA | 9 | D | D | D |
| Kidder | 4 | D | D | D | NA | NA | NA | NA | 6 | 30 | 1.2 | 0.2 |
| LaMoure | 3 | D | D | D | NA | NA | NA | NA | 7 | D | D | D |
| Logan | 2 | D | D | D | NA | NA | NA | NA | 15 | 86 | 2.6 | 0.6 |
| McHenry | 3 | D | D | D | NA | NA | NA | NA | 7 | 52 | 1.1 | 0.2 |
| McIntosh | 9 | 19 | 1.5 | 0.4 | NA | NA | NA | NA | 10 | 30 | 1.0 | 0.2 |
| | | | | | | | | | 12 | 61 | 2.1 | 0.4 |
| McKenzie | 13 | 27 | 5.0 | 1.2 | NA | NA | NA | NA | 17 | 97 | 3.5 | 0.8 |
| McLean | 6 | 18 | 1.4 | 0.3 | NA | NA | NA | NA | 34 | 160 | 7.2 | 1.4 |
| Mercer | 11 | 39 | 3.5 | 1.1 | NA | NA | NA | NA | 34 | 277 | 8.2 | 2.1 |
| Morton | 52 | D | D | D | 39 | 919 | D | 43.4 | 50 | 717 | 26.1 | 7.3 |
| Mountrail | 6 | D | D | D | NA | NA | NA | NA | 21 | 102 | 4.8 | 0.9 |
| Nelson | 3 | 6 | 0.3 | 0.1 | NA | NA | NA | NA | 13 | 69 | 2.0 | 0.5 |
| Oliver | 3 | D | D | D | NA | NA | NA | NA | 2 | D | D | D |
| Pembina | 12 | 23 | 4.4 | 0.7 | 21 | 707 | 486.5 | 28.8 | 24 | 177 | 5.6 | 1.3 |
| Pierce | 11 | 33 | 2.5 | 0.9 | NA | NA | NA | NA | 15 | 118 | 3.0 | 0.8 |
| Ramsey | 19 | 47 | 4.5 | 1.5 | NA | NA | NA | NA | 45 | 656 | 21.7 | 6.0 |
| Ransom | 16 | 45 | 3.3 | 0.9 | NA | NA | NA | NA | 18 | 146 | 4.3 | 1.1 |
| Renville | 6 | D | D | D | NA | NA | NA | NA | 11 | 29 | 1.0 | 0.2 |
| Richland | 24 | D | D | D | 34 | 1 788 | 941.6 | 73.8 | 47 | 1 096 | 84.6 | 18.1 |
| Rolette | 6 | 12 | 0.6 | 0.2 | NA | NA | NA | NA | 21 | 429 | 36.1 | 10.5 |
| Sargent | 7 | 15 | 0.8 | 0.3 | 9 | D | D | D | 14 | 74 | 2.2 | 0.5 |
| Sheridan | 1 | D | D | D | NA | NA | NA | NA | 5 | 23 | 0.6 | 0.2 |
| Sioux | NA | NA | NA | NA | NA | NA | NA | NA | 6 | D | D | D |
| Slope | NA | NA | NA | NA | NA | NA | NA | NA | 2 | D | D | D |
| Stark | 51 | D | D | D | 33 | 1 170 | 270.6 | 46.9 | 71 | 1 089 | 40.9 | 11.5 |
| Steele | 3 | 8 | 0.3 | 0.1 | NA | NA | NA | NA | 5 | 14 | 0.6 | 0.1 |
| Stutsman | 30 | 171 | 12.2 | 6.1 | 21 | 867 | 230.4 | 30.4 | 62 | 802 | 30.2 | 8.6 |
| Towner | 6 | 20 | 1.7 | 0.3 | NA | NA | NA | NA | 8 | D | D | D |
| Traill | 10 | 38 | 2.4 | 1.2 | NA | NA | NA | NA | 30 | 233 | 7.0 | 1.8 |
| Walsh | 27 | 91 | 6.8 | 2.0 | 7 | 582 | D | D | 42 | 281 | 9.2 | 2.2 |

1. Establishment subject to federal tax.

# Table B. States and Counties — **Health Care and Social Assistance, Other Services, and Federal Funds**

| STATE County | Health care and social assistance, 2007 | | | | Other services, 2007 | | | | Federal funds and grants, 2009–2010 Expenditures (mil dol) | | | |
|---|---|---|---|---|---|---|---|---|---|---|---|---|
| | | | | | | | | | | Direct payments for individuals[1] | | |
| | Number of establish-ments | Number of employees | Receipts (mil dol) | Annual payroll (mil dol) | Number of establish-ments | Number of employees | Receipts (mil dol) | Annual payroll (mil dol) | Total | Social Security and government retirement | Medicare | Food Stamps and Supplemental Security Income |
| | 159 | 160 | 161 | 162 | 163 | 164 | 165 | 166 | 167 | 168 | 169 | 170 |
| NORTH CAROLINA—Cont'd | | | | | | | | | | | | |
| Swain | 33 | 734 | 66.1 | 30.1 | 22 | 77 | 14.7 | 1.9 | 166.8 | 54.3 | 21.7 | 8.3 |
| Transylvania | 75 | 1 508 | 129.0 | 49.3 | 49 | 260 | 19.8 | 5.8 | 275.3 | 154.8 | 49.7 | 10.1 |
| Tyrrell | 7 | D | D | D | 8 | 44 | 4.0 | 1.5 | 42.9 | 11.2 | 6.1 | 3.1 |
| Union | 245 | 5 091 | 406.8 | 165.8 | 279 | 1 143 | 102.8 | 30.0 | 650.7 | 361.7 | 94.7 | 29.1 |
| Vance | 105 | 2 901 | 199.7 | 80.9 | 52 | 236 | 17.8 | 5.0 | 419.3 | 156.6 | 62.5 | 35.6 |
| Wake | 2 244 | 46 079 | 4 446.4 | 1 865.0 | 1 598 | 12 238 | 1 416.0 | 382.4 | 8 348.5 | 1 895.3 | 530.2 | 151.4 |
| Warren | 27 | 313 | 17.8 | 7.7 | 15 | D | D | D | 188.1 | 64.1 | 29.4 | 12.8 |
| Washington | 36 | 818 | 36.9 | 17.9 | 13 | 43 | 4.6 | 1.3 | 135.9 | 50.9 | 23.1 | 11.7 |
| Watauga | 141 | 3 151 | 479.3 | 119.2 | 75 | 395 | 23.8 | 7.9 | 269.8 | 106.0 | 43.1 | 10.9 |
| Wayne | 294 | 7 587 | 573.0 | 248.6 | 159 | 949 | 70.0 | 20.5 | 1 332.9 | 419.7 | 161.2 | 59.5 |
| Wilkes | 149 | 2 955 | 184.8 | 80.4 | 71 | 456 | 24.3 | 9.3 | 539.2 | 225.7 | 89.9 | 27.7 |
| Wilson | 183 | 4 655 | 332.9 | 143.5 | 116 | 660 | 43.2 | 14.7 | 654.2 | 247.4 | 119.2 | 44.3 |
| Yadkin | 51 | 1 200 | 55.8 | 25.5 | 38 | 170 | 10.5 | 2.6 | 267.2 | 123.0 | 50.2 | 10.9 |
| Yancey | 33 | 527 | 25.1 | 11.8 | 18 | 78 | 6.2 | 1.8 | 186.5 | 71.8 | 26.3 | 8.6 |
| NORTH DAKOTA | 1 748 | 52 197 | 3 906.9 | 1 716.1 | 1 708 | 9 261 | 746.0 | 199.3 | 8 696.5 | 2 159.4 | 921.1 | 140.7 |
| Adams | 13 | 330 | 20.4 | 11.6 | 12 | 24 | 2.0 | 0.4 | 33.4 | 14.0 | 5.7 | 0.3 |
| Barnes | 39 | 1 076 | 41.5 | 21.3 | 33 | 127 | 7.2 | 2.0 | 137.3 | 43.2 | 19.9 | 2.5 |
| Benson | 5 | D | D | D | 2 | D | D | D | 135.8 | 20.0 | 10.9 | 4.3 |
| Billings | NA | NA | NA | NA | 2 | D | D | D | 8.0 | 2.9 | 0.7 | 0.0 |
| Bottineau | 8 | 297 | 13.1 | 6.3 | 12 | 40 | 3.7 | 0.6 | 93.3 | 29.8 | 15.8 | 1.2 |
| Bowman | 11 | 216 | 12.1 | 5.9 | 12 | 27 | 2.3 | 0.4 | 37.9 | 16.9 | 7.5 | 0.4 |
| Burke | 2 | D | D | D | 4 | 9 | 1.1 | 0.2 | 42.3 | 9.7 | 6.9 | 0.4 |
| Burleigh | 236 | 8 903 | 742.0 | 330.0 | 256 | 1 700 | 150.7 | 42.5 | 1 432.4 | 230.8 | 81.1 | 13.9 |
| Cass | 427 | 13 903 | 1 348.8 | 549.8 | 368 | D | D | D | 1 141.1 | 336.9 | 102.5 | 20.8 |
| Cavalier | 11 | 267 | 11.8 | 5.9 | 17 | 54 | 2.7 | 0.6 | 110.7 | 20.4 | 10.2 | 0.5 |
| Dickey | 23 | 363 | 20.2 | 8.9 | 18 | 60 | 4.2 | 0.9 | 93.1 | 25.3 | 12.3 | 1.0 |
| Divide | 8 | D | D | D | 7 | D | D | D | 39.0 | 9.3 | 6.1 | 0.3 |
| Dunn | 6 | D | D | D | 5 | D | D | D | 36.5 | 15.8 | 5.9 | 0.5 |
| Eddy | 8 | 199 | 8.2 | 4.7 | 12 | 32 | 3.8 | 0.7 | 31.5 | 10.6 | 6.8 | 0.4 |
| Emmons | 11 | 200 | 8.8 | 3.8 | 8 | D | D | D | 54.0 | 18.3 | 9.6 | 0.4 |
| Foster | 13 | 239 | 18.6 | 8.7 | 11 | 30 | 1.6 | 0.4 | 141.4 | 13.9 | 7.6 | 0.5 |
| Golden Valley | 5 | D | D | D | 8 | D | D | D | 23.5 | 10.4 | 4.1 | 0.4 |
| Grand Forks | 154 | 6 143 | 522.1 | 221.1 | 153 | D | D | D | 694.8 | 153.1 | 63.1 | 11.6 |
| Grant | 7 | 212 | 9.4 | 4.6 | 4 | D | D | D | 40.6 | 15.0 | 8.8 | 0.5 |
| Griggs | 3 | D | D | D | 4 | D | D | D | 33.5 | 12.5 | 6.5 | 0.4 |
| Hettinger | 7 | 98 | 5.0 | 2.1 | 10 | 22 | 1.5 | 0.3 | 60.1 | 26.1 | 7.6 | 0.5 |
| Kidder | 6 | 105 | 3.6 | 2.0 | 1 | D | D | D | 33.7 | 9.4 | 6.9 | 0.3 |
| LaMoure | 11 | 118 | 4.7 | 3.0 | 14 | 49 | 3.5 | 0.7 | 73.8 | 18.3 | 10.5 | 0.6 |
| Logan | 7 | 97 | 3.3 | 1.6 | 7 | D | D | D | 32.2 | 10.6 | 5.7 | 0.4 |
| McHenry | 6 | D | D | D | 7 | D | D | D | 74.0 | 24.9 | 14.5 | 1.3 |
| McIntosh | 10 | 351 | 15.3 | 8.5 | 8 | D | D | D | 47.8 | 14.4 | 13.2 | 0.4 |
| McKenzie | 6 | D | D | D | 17 | 43 | 2.4 | 0.7 | 48.9 | 19.2 | 7.1 | 1.8 |
| McLean | 14 | 453 | 20.2 | 11.0 | 23 | 58 | 3.7 | 0.8 | 165.9 | 53.8 | 20.6 | 1.7 |
| Mercer | 17 | 395 | 22.9 | 10.6 | 14 | 55 | 3.3 | 0.9 | 63.0 | 29.5 | 13.5 | 1.0 |
| Morton | 41 | 1 197 | 49.4 | 28.3 | 51 | 265 | 27.0 | 7.4 | 193.5 | 89.8 | 38.4 | 5.6 |
| Mountrail | 14 | 297 | 11.8 | 6.5 | 14 | 53 | 4.1 | 1.4 | 149.3 | 27.0 | 12.9 | 1.7 |
| Nelson | 10 | D | D | D | 13 | 34 | 2.8 | 0.5 | 59.5 | 20.0 | 11.9 | 0.6 |
| Oliver | 3 | D | D | D | 2 | D | D | D | 19.5 | 7.9 | 2.6 | 0.1 |
| Pembina | 19 | 367 | 15.9 | 6.6 | 19 | 47 | 3.3 | 0.7 | 155.4 | 27.3 | 16.6 | 1.3 |
| Pierce | 11 | 363 | 18.3 | 9.2 | 14 | 59 | 3.1 | 0.7 | 55.1 | 18.2 | 10.3 | 0.8 |
| Ramsey | 48 | 1 056 | 49.8 | 22.6 | 28 | 122 | 7.5 | 1.8 | 214.3 | 48.1 | 23.3 | 3.6 |
| Ransom | 26 | 364 | 21.5 | 9.6 | 21 | 89 | 5.1 | 1.2 | 85.6 | 21.6 | 11.8 | 0.6 |
| Renville | 5 | D | D | D | 3 | D | D | D | 39.5 | 12.2 | 6.1 | 0.3 |
| Richland | 47 | D | D | D | 35 | D | D | D | 176.1 | 48.6 | 21.8 | 3.2 |
| Rolette | 23 | 610 | 56.0 | 21.9 | 14 | 24 | 2.3 | 0.5 | 218.2 | 34.5 | 16.2 | 15.8 |
| Sargent | 5 | 80 | 3.1 | 1.8 | 12 | 40 | 4.1 | 0.7 | 67.9 | 21.9 | 7.7 | 0.5 |
| Sheridan | 1 | D | D | D | 3 | D | D | D | 26.3 | 6.7 | 4.9 | 0.6 |
| Sioux | 1 | D | D | D | 3 | D | D | D | 123.1 | 8.9 | 3.5 | 4.4 |
| Slope | NA | NA | NA | NA | 2 | D | D | D | 43.4 | 6.1 | 0.7 | 0.0 |
| Stark | 75 | 1 879 | 98.7 | 47.5 | 72 | D | D | D | 190.1 | 84.2 | 36.5 | 5.4 |
| Steele | 2 | D | D | D | 3 | 5 | 0.5 | 0.1 | 45.0 | 10.7 | 4.8 | 0.3 |
| Stutsman | 69 | 2 315 | 113.4 | 58.1 | 61 | 318 | 18.0 | 5.5 | 243.4 | 80.4 | 32.5 | 5.8 |
| Towner | 3 | D | D | D | 6 | D | D | D | 47.3 | 9.8 | 7.2 | 0.4 |
| Traill | 21 | 589 | 26.2 | 13.1 | 22 | 53 | 4.9 | 0.8 | 91.1 | 29.9 | 15.4 | 1.4 |
| Walsh | 31 | 707 | 34.7 | 17.0 | 34 | 95 | 7.0 | 1.9 | 129.5 | 38.9 | 25.4 | 2.7 |

1. State totals may include programs not allocated by county.

# Federal Funds, Residential Construction, and Local Government Finances

| STATE County | Salaries and wages | Defense | Other | Medicaid and other health-related | Nutrition and family welfare | Education | Other | New construction ($1,000) | Number of housing units | Total (mil dol) | Inter-govern-mental (mil dol) | Total (mil dol) | Total | Property |
|---|---|---|---|---|---|---|---|---|---|---|---|---|---|---|
| | 171 | 172 | 173 | 174 | 175 | 176 | 177 | 178 | 179 | 180 | 181 | 182 | 183 | 184 |
| **NORTH CAROLINA—Cont'd** | | | | | | | | | | | | | | |
| Swain | 10.2 | 0.0 | 2.2 | 35.2 | 6.5 | 3.5 | 9.2 | 10 024 | 54 | 34.5 | 21.0 | 8.2 | 598 | 344 |
| Transylvania | 11.2 | 0.1 | 14.3 | 24.5 | 4.1 | 2.0 | 1.8 | 28 618 | 62 | 85.1 | 36.3 | 36.5 | 1 218 | 904 |
| Tyrrell | 1.5 | 0.0 | 1.0 | 12.3 | 1.3 | 0.6 | 2.7 | 795 | 7 | 14.8 | 8.9 | 4.2 | 1 007 | 789 |
| Union | 33.7 | 14.0 | 11.9 | 56.6 | 20.1 | 8.5 | 4.6 | 115 415 | 692 | 491.5 | 226.1 | 180.6 | 978 | 709 |
| Vance | 8.0 | 0.2 | 12.3 | 101.9 | 14.2 | 5.2 | 7.6 | 5 404 | 36 | 178.8 | 110.8 | 35.7 | 831 | 581 |
| Wake | 642.7 | 182.5 | 193.9 | 616.7 | 525.7 | 1 080.8 | 2 266.1 | 931 051 | 5 652 | 2 780.6 | 1 017.2 | 1 057.8 | 1 270 | 953 |
| Warren | 3.3 | 0.0 | 0.8 | 63.2 | 6.1 | 1.5 | 2.1 | 4 485 | 25 | 54.3 | 30.2 | 16.4 | 847 | 655 |
| Washington | 2.1 | 0.0 | 0.5 | 32.1 | 4.1 | 2.1 | 0.9 | 1 777 | 12 | 51.8 | 27.1 | 10.1 | 783 | 559 |
| Watauga | 15.2 | 0.0 | 3.1 | 40.8 | 5.8 | 4.2 | 23.3 | 40 027 | 183 | 123.1 | 47.1 | 54.0 | 1 212 | 863 |
| Wayne | 302.7 | 74.2 | 4.5 | 202.6 | 29.5 | 13.7 | 13.4 | 27 492 | 205 | 330.8 | 188.2 | 88.4 | 779 | 555 |
| Wilkes | 24.8 | 1.1 | 2.9 | 122.7 | 12.5 | 5.4 | 16.6 | 21 819 | 128 | 178.1 | 96.0 | 51.4 | 768 | 519 |
| Wilson | 14.2 | 13.5 | 3.6 | 145.5 | 17.5 | 8.9 | 5.0 | 17 997 | 87 | 256.6 | 128.0 | 77.9 | 1 015 | 784 |
| Yadkin | 5.6 | 0.6 | 1.4 | 45.4 | 7.7 | 2.6 | 11.8 | 5 472 | 33 | 85.5 | 47.1 | 28.6 | 756 | 537 |
| Yancey | 3.5 | 0.4 | 2.0 | 48.3 | 4.1 | 1.5 | 19.0 | 1 981 | 32 | 51.6 | 26.1 | 13.5 | 730 | 492 |
| **NORTH DAKOTA** | 1 083.5 | 288.2 | 397.1 | 630.3 | 202.8 | 202.0 | 1 202.3 | 783 616 | 6 201 | X | X | X | X | X |
| Adams | 1.5 | 0.0 | 0.3 | 4.0 | 0.7 | 0.0 | 0.1 | 316 | 2 | 6.2 | 2.3 | 2.8 | 1 240 | 1 153 |
| Barnes | 11.6 | 0.0 | 1.5 | 10.5 | 2.4 | 0.9 | 4.9 | 2 754 | 12 | 36.4 | 14.4 | 14.6 | 1 350 | 1 068 |
| Benson | 7.4 | 1.5 | 2.2 | 14.3 | 4.9 | 13.8 | 11.4 | 0 | 0 | 20.8 | 13.8 | 4.4 | 627 | 626 |
| Billings | 1.6 | 0.0 | 1.2 | 0.0 | 0.1 | 0.0 | 0.0 | 1 556 | 14 | 8.1 | 4.9 | 1.2 | 1 475 | 1 035 |
| Bottineau | 7.4 | 0.7 | 2.2 | 5.8 | 1.7 | 0.1 | 3.8 | 1 235 | 13 | 24.1 | 12.7 | 6.7 | 1 038 | 960 |
| Bowman | 1.4 | 0.1 | 0.7 | 1.9 | 0.7 | 0.1 | 0.0 | 1 713 | 11 | 21.8 | 8.1 | 5.3 | 1 799 | 1 670 |
| Burke | 8.7 | 0.5 | 2.1 | 2.3 | 0.6 | 0.1 | 0.0 | 952 | 11 | 6.2 | 2.6 | 2.5 | 1 361 | 1 357 |
| Burleigh | 177.3 | 5.0 | 35.0 | 66.5 | 46.9 | 83.9 | 638.4 | 94 656 | 592 | 231.9 | 78.5 | 94.1 | 1 217 | 1 004 |
| Cass | 186.2 | 22.0 | 191.7 | 84.5 | 19.8 | 4.7 | 96.1 | 141 081 | 1 323 | 448.0 | 123.5 | 199.6 | 1 451 | 1 178 |
| Cavalier | 2.7 | 12.1 | 8.7 | 4.6 | 1.4 | 0.1 | 3.4 | 100 | 2 | 14.2 | 5.1 | 6.2 | 1 576 | 1 510 |
| Dickey | 3.2 | 0.0 | 0.5 | 6.3 | 1.5 | 0.2 | 2.7 | 0 | 0 | 14.1 | 5.2 | 6.0 | 1 116 | 1 069 |
| Divide | 2.1 | 0.0 | 2.1 | 4.6 | 0.5 | 0.0 | 0.0 | 6 697 | 70 | 10.6 | 3.9 | 3.1 | 1 559 | 1 397 |
| Dunn | 1.1 | 2.3 | 0.4 | 2.9 | 0.8 | 0.4 | 0.3 | 1 675 | 11 | 11.6 | 5.4 | 4.2 | 1 275 | 1 261 |
| Eddy | 1.8 | 0.0 | 0.3 | 2.9 | 0.7 | 0.1 | 0.2 | 354 | 2 | 8.6 | 3.1 | 4.4 | 1 827 | 1 783 |
| Emmons | 1.6 | 0.1 | 0.3 | 6.3 | 1.6 | 0.2 | 0.2 | 750 | 5 | 11.3 | 5.0 | 4.0 | 1 154 | 1 113 |
| Foster | 3.2 | 0.0 | 10.1 | 1.7 | 0.7 | 0.1 | 90.7 | 480 | 2 | 11.8 | 5.0 | 4.4 | 1 258 | 1 181 |
| Golden Valley | 0.7 | 0.0 | 0.1 | 1.7 | 0.5 | 0.2 | 0.2 | 2 549 | 13 | 8.3 | 3.9 | 2.0 | 1 172 | 1 122 |
| Grand Forks | 159.1 | 68.7 | 26.7 | 58.5 | 13.7 | 10.0 | 80.1 | 44 322 | 343 | 215.4 | 67.7 | 85.6 | 1 278 | 969 |
| Grant | 1.5 | 0.0 | 0.4 | 5.8 | 1.3 | 0.1 | 0.1 | 0 | 0 | 8.2 | 2.2 | 4.7 | 1 911 | 1 887 |
| Griggs | 1.3 | 0.0 | 0.3 | 1.7 | 0.9 | 0.0 | 0.2 | 0 | 0 | 9.9 | 3.5 | 4.4 | 1 847 | 1 788 |
| Hettinger | 2.3 | 0.0 | 0.2 | 7.5 | 0.9 | 0.1 | 0.5 | 537 | 5 | 8.2 | 3.4 | 3.7 | 1 514 | 1 450 |
| Kidder | 1.8 | 0.0 | 0.4 | 3.5 | 0.9 | 0.1 | 2.0 | 0 | 0 | 9.7 | 3.9 | 3.5 | 1 493 | 1 473 |
| LaMoure | 4.5 | 0.4 | 0.6 | 5.8 | 1.5 | 0.1 | 0.4 | 200 | 1 | 31.5 | 17.4 | 10.1 | 2 450 | 2 393 |
| Logan | 1.0 | 0.0 | 0.2 | 4.0 | 0.7 | 0.1 | 0.0 | 350 | 1 | 7.4 | 3.0 | 3.5 | 1 780 | 1 770 |
| McHenry | 3.5 | 0.0 | 3.3 | 6.9 | 3.7 | 0.2 | 0.0 | 4 748 | 34 | 15.2 | 6.1 | 6.8 | 1 306 | 1 279 |
| McIntosh | 2.2 | 0.0 | 0.3 | 5.3 | 1.0 | 0.1 | 0.5 | 0 | 0 | 8.8 | 3.6 | 3.5 | 1 289 | 1 236 |
| McKenzie | 3.7 | -0.3 | 0.8 | 2.3 | 1.0 | 0.3 | 0.5 | 9 678 | 151 | 29.4 | 18.0 | 5.4 | 954 | 889 |
| McLean | 6.7 | 25.8 | 9.4 | 19.0 | 2.0 | 0.3 | 1.9 | 5 764 | 53 | 25.6 | 11.0 | 9.2 | 1 101 | 932 |
| Mercer | 3.5 | 0.3 | 0.8 | 8.1 | 1.5 | 0.1 | 0.2 | 3 470 | 22 | 29.5 | 12.3 | 9.0 | 1 124 | 1 067 |
| Morton | 8.0 | 1.7 | 6.7 | 18.5 | 6.9 | 1.3 | 4.5 | 33 528 | 252 | 82.3 | 32.8 | 29.6 | 1 142 | 1 058 |
| Mountrail | 4.0 | 5.5 | 1.9 | 9.1 | 3.4 | 5.4 | 51.4 | 17 021 | 102 | 26.9 | 15.1 | 5.8 | 900 | 858 |
| Nelson | 2.2 | 0.0 | 0.5 | 5.9 | 1.0 | 0.1 | 0.1 | 700 | 6 | 11.7 | 4.6 | 5.3 | 1 659 | 1 647 |
| Oliver | 0.3 | 0.0 | 0.0 | 2.3 | 0.3 | 0.0 | 2.9 | 105 | 1 | 9.3 | 2.5 | 1.7 | 984 | 947 |
| Pembina | 21.3 | 13.5 | 11.5 | 10.4 | 1.7 | 0.3 | 8.0 | 500 | 1 | 28.0 | 13.3 | 11.5 | 1 524 | 1 477 |
| Pierce | 2.6 | 0.0 | 1.9 | 6.9 | 1.2 | 0.2 | 0.0 | 555 | 5 | 12.7 | 5.1 | 4.9 | 1 188 | 1 118 |
| Ramsey | 35.1 | 28.1 | 1.8 | 14.4 | 2.8 | 1.2 | 1.0 | 6 609 | 37 | 38.0 | 15.3 | 13.2 | 1 180 | 999 |
| Ransom | 3.6 | 0.1 | 0.9 | 4.0 | 1.2 | 0.1 | 18.4 | 708 | 4 | 16.0 | 5.7 | 7.3 | 1 278 | 1 227 |
| Renville | 1.4 | 0.0 | 0.2 | 1.7 | 0.6 | 0.1 | 1.3 | 963 | 6 | 10.3 | 4.9 | 3.6 | 1 564 | 1 545 |
| Richland | 9.4 | 0.7 | 1.3 | 11.5 | 2.9 | 0.3 | 6.2 | 5 340 | 31 | 62.1 | 25.9 | 24.0 | 1 455 | 1 347 |
| Rolette | 35.1 | 0.2 | 13.2 | 36.8 | 8.0 | 10.4 | 21.2 | 150 | 1 | 45.3 | 36.5 | 4.1 | 304 | 279 |
| Sargent | 2.9 | 0.0 | 0.9 | 4.6 | 1.5 | 0.1 | 0.2 | 709 | 5 | 16.2 | 6.1 | 6.2 | 1 509 | 1 490 |
| Sheridan | 0.6 | 0.0 | 0.1 | 5.8 | 0.7 | 0.1 | 0.0 | 228 | 3 | 4.2 | 1.3 | 2.3 | 1 768 | 1 744 |
| Sioux | 9.4 | 0.1 | 4.5 | 9.4 | 4.8 | 7.1 | 48.6 | 0 | 0 | 9.4 | 6.5 | 1.3 | 297 | 297 |
| Slope | 0.1 | 0.0 | 0.1 | 0.6 | 0.1 | 0.0 | 29.0 | 0 | 0 | 2.2 | 0.9 | 0.7 | 1 003 | 995 |
| Stark | 13.3 | 0.2 | 2.0 | 18.7 | 5.9 | 1.4 | 7.9 | 49 759 | 319 | 60.6 | 24.6 | 23.5 | 1 048 | 848 |
| Steele | 0.9 | 0.0 | 8.8 | 0.6 | 0.5 | 0.1 | 0.2 | 0 | 0 | 7.5 | 2.7 | 3.5 | 1 908 | 1 870 |
| Stutsman | 20.4 | 0.3 | 12.1 | 38.6 | 6.0 | 0.4 | 3.3 | 3 598 | 18 | 68.0 | 22.8 | 27.5 | 1 341 | 1 101 |
| Towner | 2.1 | 1.1 | 0.3 | 2.3 | 0.9 | 0.0 | 0.2 | 0 | 0 | 14.2 | 2.8 | 9.2 | 4 005 | 3 969 |
| Traill | 3.3 | 0.0 | 1.9 | 5.2 | 2.8 | 0.5 | 0.3 | 1 550 | 13 | 30.5 | 9.7 | 12.4 | 1 539 | 1 486 |
| Walsh | 4.8 | 0.4 | 1.0 | 9.9 | 2.7 | 0.5 | 2.0 | 1 087 | 6 | 41.1 | 17.5 | 12.5 | 1 138 | 1 087 |

1. State totals may include programs not allocated by county.    2. Based on the resident population estimated as of July 1 of the year shown.

| | Local government finances, 2007 (cont.) | | | | | | | | | Government employment, 2011 | | | Presidential election,[2] 2012 | | |
| | Direct general expenditure | | | | | | | Debt outstanding | | | | | Percent of vote cast: | | |
| | | | Percent of total for: | | | | | | | | | | | | |
| STATE<br>County | Total<br>(mil dol) | Per<br>capita[1]<br>(dollars) | Educa-<br>tion | Health<br>and<br>hospitals | Police<br>protec-<br>tion | Public<br>welfare | High-<br>ways | Total<br>(mil dol) | Per<br>capita[1]<br>(dollars) | Federal<br>civilian | Federal<br>military | State and<br>local | Demo-<br>cratic | Republi-<br>can | All<br>other |
| | 185 | 186 | 187 | 188 | 189 | 190 | 191 | 192 | 193 | 194 | 195 | 196 | 197 | 198 | 199 |
| **NORTH CAROLINA—Cont'd** | | | | | | | | | | | | | | | |
| Swain | 35.2 | 2 579 | 50.9 | 5.0 | 3.3 | 8.0 | 0.3 | 13.1 | 963 | 206 | 36 | 2 258 | 48.4 | 50.0 | 1.6 |
| Transylvania | 78.0 | 2 601 | 42.2 | 5.0 | 7.4 | 8.4 | 1.0 | 36.1 | 1 203 | 146 | 85 | 1 334 | 43.0 | 55.6 | 1.4 |
| Tyrrell | 14.2 | 3 457 | 59.8 | 1.2 | 5.6 | 4.8 | 1.0 | 0.5 | 117 | 21 | 11 | 469 | 48.8 | 50.3 | 0.9 |
| Union | 573.6 | 3 106 | 64.3 | 2.2 | 4.2 | 4.6 | 0.8 | 1 370.9 | 7 424 | 252 | 532 | 9 925 | 36.2 | 62.9 | 0.9 |
| Vance | 174.7 | 4 064 | 57.0 | 13.7 | 3.7 | 7.2 | 0.7 | 48.8 | 1 136 | 88 | 117 | 2 791 | 63.1 | 36.4 | 0.5 |
| Wake | 3 039.8 | 3 649 | 42.2 | 4.3 | 4.8 | 4.1 | 2.9 | 12 582.4 | 15 105 | 5 242 | 3 013 | 75 054 | 56.7 | 42.3 | 1.0 |
| Warren | 55.2 | 2 845 | 47.8 | 7.5 | 3.8 | 11.4 | 0.4 | 13.5 | 696 | 36 | 54 | 1 439 | 69.5 | 30.0 | 0.5 |
| Washington | 49.1 | 3 801 | 45.3 | 14.9 | 4.0 | 9.9 | 1.3 | 13.4 | 1 037 | 28 | 34 | 1 019 | 58.1 | 41.4 | 0.6 |
| Watauga | 114.9 | 2 580 | 35.2 | 6.2 | 6.5 | 4.7 | 3.3 | 54.1 | 1 215 | 102 | 138 | 6 147 | 51.3 | 47.0 | 1.7 |
| Wayne | 315.2 | 2 775 | 55.2 | 3.9 | 4.3 | 8.1 | 1.0 | 122.6 | 1 080 | 1 235 | 5 025 | 8 369 | 45.4 | 54.0 | 0.5 |
| Wilkes | 172.4 | 2 580 | 63.3 | 5.5 | 3.4 | 8.7 | 0.6 | 107.0 | 1 601 | 184 | 179 | 4 428 | 30.1 | 68.3 | 1.7 |
| Wilson | 252.6 | 3 291 | 44.8 | 5.0 | 6.1 | 7.0 | 1.6 | 214.7 | 2 797 | 176 | 211 | 6 393 | 52.8 | 46.7 | 0.4 |
| Yadkin | 81.8 | 2 164 | 62.1 | 5.9 | 5.1 | 10.1 | 1.1 | 13.5 | 358 | 64 | 99 | 1 480 | 26.4 | 72.4 | 1.2 |
| Yancey | 49.4 | 2 676 | 46.3 | 18.0 | 2.8 | 9.7 | 0.4 | 30.6 | 1 660 | 48 | 46 | 847 | 46.2 | 51.9 | 1.9 |
| **NORTH DAKOTA** | X | X | X | X | X | X | X | X | X | 9 691 | 11 668 | 62 969 | 44.6 | 53.3 | 2.1 |
| Adams | 6.4 | 2 828 | 47.9 | 0.0 | 3.6 | 4.7 | 15.7 | 0.4 | 160 | 19 | 17 | 129 | 34.2 | 62.0 | 3.8 |
| Barnes | 38.5 | 3 572 | 40.8 | 2.6 | 3.6 | 2.5 | 12.4 | 19.7 | 1 825 | 85 | 81 | 1 014 | 48.1 | 49.6 | 2.2 |
| Benson | 20.5 | 2 940 | 62.2 | 0.4 | 1.3 | 4.0 | 15.6 | 2.0 | 288 | 161 | 49 | 1 527 | 66.1 | 32.6 | 1.3 |
| Billings | 8.0 | 9 984 | 23.2 | 0.1 | 4.8 | 0.0 | 41.1 | 0.0 | 0 | 63 | 0 | 108 | 22.8 | 75.2 | 2.0 |
| Bottineau | 24.8 | 3 864 | 43.2 | 0.0 | 2.4 | 2.4 | 19.9 | 8.3 | 1 293 | 91 | 47 | 585 | 39.4 | 58.6 | 2.0 |
| Bowman | 19.0 | 6 443 | 36.0 | 0.3 | 1.7 | 0.0 | 19.2 | 0.4 | 129 | 24 | 23 | 215 | 29.1 | 67.5 | 3.4 |
| Burke | 6.6 | 3 529 | 55.4 | 0.0 | 4.9 | 1.6 | 16.8 | 0.7 | 369 | 122 | 15 | 165 | 30.3 | 67.9 | 1.8 |
| Burleigh | 229.8 | 2 972 | 43.1 | 2.1 | 5.4 | 1.5 | 9.3 | 141.1 | 1 825 | 1 126 | 618 | 9 833 | 37.3 | 60.9 | 1.7 |
| Cass | 450.0 | 3 271 | 46.0 | 1.6 | 4.6 | 2.2 | 11.6 | 802.2 | 5 831 | 2 250 | 1 144 | 11 206 | 52.7 | 45.6 | 1.7 |
| Cavalier | 13.6 | 3 484 | 40.7 | 1.2 | 4.0 | 7.3 | 22.3 | 9.1 | 2 316 | 41 | 29 | 210 | 43.7 | 53.0 | 3.4 |
| Dickey | 13.3 | 2 479 | 53.4 | 0.9 | 3.7 | 3.4 | 18.2 | 4.6 | 860 | 26 | 39 | 291 | 39.8 | 58.2 | 1.9 |
| Divide | 13.2 | 6 611 | 23.0 | 21.1 | 2.6 | 1.5 | 19.3 | 2.9 | 1 466 | 33 | 16 | 144 | 41.0 | 55.7 | 3.3 |
| Dunn | 12.0 | 3 635 | 56.8 | 0.4 | 1.4 | 3.8 | 18.1 | 0.0 | 4 | 16 | 27 | 241 | 32.1 | 65.7 | 2.3 |
| Eddy | 7.4 | 3 028 | 62.4 | 0.4 | 5.6 | 2.7 | 9.5 | 2.2 | 886 | 24 | 17 | 154 | 50.0 | 47.0 | 2.9 |
| Emmons | 10.9 | 3 138 | 58.5 | 1.8 | 2.2 | 2.8 | 12.3 | 1.8 | 521 | 25 | 26 | 217 | 29.7 | 67.0 | 3.3 |
| Foster | 11.6 | 3 324 | 53.9 | 1.1 | 3.4 | 2.0 | 14.5 | 4.5 | 1 280 | 28 | 25 | 228 | 41.6 | 55.4 | 3.0 |
| Golden Valley | 8.3 | 4 994 | 54.4 | 2.2 | 4.3 | 3.4 | 17.1 | 0.4 | 243 | 11 | 13 | 174 | 24.0 | 73.4 | 2.6 |
| Grand Forks | 204.5 | 3 054 | 44.1 | 0.7 | 4.4 | 2.5 | 4.9 | 387.1 | 5 779 | 1 178 | 1 811 | 9 083 | 51.7 | 46.6 | 1.7 |
| Grant | 7.4 | 2 979 | 47.0 | 1.5 | 2.5 | 0.0 | 27.3 | 2.3 | 940 | 26 | 17 | 147 | 21.1 | 44.2 | 34.8 |
| Griggs | 9.8 | 4 086 | 49.7 | 2.1 | 3.0 | 3.3 | 10.6 | 2.9 | 1 206 | 19 | 17 | 195 | 45.5 | 51.9 | 2.6 |
| Hettinger | 8.5 | 3 514 | 65.8 | 0.0 | 2.9 | 0.0 | 12.3 | 0.8 | 314 | 22 | 18 | 173 | 30.1 | 66.2 | 3.6 |
| Kidder | 9.5 | 4 055 | 51.7 | 2.4 | 1.5 | 0.9 | 19.8 | 7.1 | 3 026 | 26 | 18 | 164 | 34.4 | 61.2 | 4.4 |
| LaMoure | 40.9 | 9 952 | 24.7 | 0.3 | 0.8 | 0.8 | 4.6 | 3.9 | 960 | 46 | 30 | 294 | 38.7 | 58.5 | 2.8 |
| Logan | 6.3 | 3 238 | 68.9 | 1.0 | 2.6 | 0.1 | 12.7 | 1.5 | 782 | 17 | 15 | 137 | 28.3 | 68.7 | 3.0 |
| McHenry | 15.9 | 3 042 | 60.1 | 1.0 | 2.8 | 2.9 | 14.9 | 2.0 | 373 | 53 | 40 | 385 | 40.6 | 56.9 | 2.5 |
| McIntosh | 8.3 | 3 005 | 57.5 | 0.1 | 2.4 | 3.9 | 9.0 | 0.6 | 215 | 20 | 20 | 166 | 37.8 | 59.8 | 2.4 |
| McKenzie | 25.6 | 4 554 | 53.1 | 5.0 | 2.7 | 1.9 | 17.1 | 0.7 | 120 | 51 | 51 | 1 411 | 34.4 | 64.1 | 1.5 |
| McLean | 25.7 | 3 077 | 59.3 | 0.9 | 5.0 | 2.4 | 7.4 | 6.5 | 783 | 124 | 66 | 682 | 39.4 | 58.4 | 2.2 |
| Mercer | 32.1 | 4 029 | 43.3 | 0.7 | 4.5 | 2.1 | 11.0 | 80.8 | 10 141 | 43 | 62 | 511 | 33.6 | 63.4 | 3.0 |
| Morton | 83.3 | 3 212 | 48.5 | 1.1 | 4.5 | 2.6 | 14.5 | 66.8 | 2 578 | 106 | 203 | 1 556 | 38.3 | 59.3 | 2.4 |
| Mountrail | 24.7 | 3 817 | 59.5 | 1.8 | 3.2 | 2.8 | 7.6 | 8.4 | 1 291 | 53 | 59 | 623 | 50.3 | 47.9 | 1.9 |
| Nelson | 14.3 | 4 447 | 41.9 | 12.7 | 1.8 | 0.2 | 25.1 | 5.5 | 1 698 | 31 | 22 | 224 | 51.8 | 45.7 | 2.6 |
| Oliver | 8.8 | 5 073 | 32.6 | 0.8 | 2.2 | 0.0 | 12.0 | 47.9 | 27 776 | 0 | 13 | 105 | 31.9 | 65.6 | 2.5 |
| Pembina | 29.6 | 3 934 | 55.8 | 0.8 | 3.1 | 2.4 | 8.8 | 12.3 | 1 638 | 259 | 87 | 537 | 45.2 | 52.1 | 2.8 |
| Pierce | 12.6 | 3 065 | 45.5 | 1.0 | 4.5 | 3.1 | 25.4 | 0.9 | 221 | 25 | 32 | 245 | 37.0 | 60.8 | 2.2 |
| Ramsey | 39.6 | 3 543 | 53.3 | 0.5 | 3.1 | 2.7 | 12.6 | 20.6 | 1 844 | 186 | 84 | 1 320 | 48.6 | 49.6 | 1.8 |
| Ransom | 16.0 | 2 809 | 53.6 | 2.0 | 3.0 | 2.5 | 11.5 | 9.9 | 1 738 | 43 | 40 | 485 | 56.4 | 41.0 | 2.6 |
| Renville | 10.1 | 4 379 | 66.8 | 0.1 | 2.7 | 1.8 | 12.8 | 1.3 | 580 | 21 | 18 | 203 | 37.5 | 59.4 | 3.1 |
| Richland | 65.3 | 3 960 | 48.6 | 3.2 | 4.5 | 1.7 | 16.0 | 30.2 | 1 833 | 67 | 127 | 1 894 | 46.4 | 51.6 | 2.0 |
| Rolette | 43.7 | 3 194 | 77.8 | 1.6 | 1.7 | 2.5 | 4.2 | 9.3 | 682 | 877 | 104 | 2 002 | 75.1 | 23.0 | 1.9 |
| Sargent | 14.8 | 3 598 | 45.4 | 1.7 | 2.3 | 2.1 | 18.9 | 8.6 | 2 081 | 42 | 28 | 236 | 57.9 | 40.4 | 1.8 |
| Sheridan | 3.4 | 2 558 | 58.6 | 2.2 | 2.5 | 0.2 | 19.7 | 0.3 | 216 | 13 | 10 | 92 | 28.5 | 69.1 | 2.4 |
| Sioux | 8.7 | 2 071 | 80.3 | 0.2 | 1.3 | 9.6 | 1.7 | 0.6 | 133 | 235 | 31 | 1 396 | 83.1 | 15.6 | 1.3 |
| Slope | 2.0 | 3 064 | 18.4 | 5.0 | 2.9 | 3.3 | 33.9 | 0.5 | 780 | 0 | 0 | 32 | 25.8 | 72.3 | 1.9 |
| Stark | 58.2 | 2 591 | 49.0 | 2.5 | 1.7 | 4.9 | 10.4 | 9.3 | 416 | 187 | 185 | 2 103 | 34.3 | 63.5 | 2.2 |
| Steele | 7.2 | 3 915 | 46.6 | 1.0 | 2.7 | 4.2 | 18.9 | 4.2 | 2 264 | 18 | 14 | 114 | 59.5 | 39.1 | 1.4 |
| Stutsman | 69.4 | 3 388 | 44.0 | 5.8 | 5.0 | 2.4 | 6.2 | 51.7 | 2 523 | 190 | 154 | 1 913 | 41.5 | 56.2 | 2.3 |
| Towner | 10.8 | 4 731 | 38.7 | 28.2 | 2.4 | 1.3 | 10.7 | 6.1 | 2 655 | 25 | 17 | 130 | 51.9 | 44.8 | 3.3 |
| Traill | 29.5 | 3 659 | 53.8 | 2.0 | 2.9 | 1.7 | 11.8 | 46.4 | 5 753 | 40 | 60 | 784 | 52.9 | 45.7 | 1.5 |
| Walsh | 39.4 | 3 581 | 52.6 | 1.9 | 5.1 | 2.1 | 16.5 | 10.8 | 978 | 62 | 81 | 1 148 | 47.6 | 49.5 | 2.9 |

1. Based on the resident population estimated as of July 1 of the year shown.  2. © 2013 Election Data Services, Inc. All rights reserved.

# Table B. States and Counties — Land Area and Population

| | | | | | Population 2012 | | | Population characteristics[6], 2011 | | | | | | | | | | |
| | | | | | | | | Race alone or in combination, not Hispanic or Latino (percent) | | | | | Age (percent) | | | | | |
| STATE/ County code | CBSA code[1] | County type[2] | STATE County | Land area,[3] (sq km) 2010 | Total persons | Rank | Per square kilometer | White | Black | American Indian, Alaska Native | Asian and Pacific Islander | Percent Hispanic or Latino[4] | Under 5 years | 5 to 17 years | 18 to 24 years | 25 to 34 years | 35 to 44 years | 45 to 54 years |
|---|---|---|---|---|---|---|---|---|---|---|---|---|---|---|---|---|---|---|
| | | | | 1 | 2 | 3 | 4 | 5 | 6 | 7 | 8 | 9 | 10 | 11 | 12 | 13 | 14 | 15 |
| | | | NORTH DAKOTA—Cont'd | | | | | | | | | | | | | | | |
| 38 101 | 33500 | 5 | Ward | 5 214 | 64 798 | 815 | 12.4 | 90.1 | 3.6 | 3.6 | 1.8 | 3.4 | 7.9 | 15.7 | 13.8 | 16.3 | 10.9 | 12.2 |
| 38 103 | ... | 9 | Wells | 3 292 | 4 271 | 2 884 | 1.3 | 98.6 | 0.2 | 1.0 | 0.2 | 0.6 | 5.2 | 13.5 | 5.1 | 7.9 | 9.0 | 16.4 |
| 38 105 | 48780 | 7 | Williams | 5 380 | 26 697 | 1 539 | 5.0 | 92.4 | 0.8 | 6.0 | 0.6 | 2.8 | 7.1 | 16.0 | 9.3 | 15.3 | 11.0 | 14.9 |
| 39 000 | ... | X | OHIO | 105 829 | 11 544 225 | X | 109.1 | 82.6 | 13.2 | 0.7 | 2.2 | 3.2 | 6.2 | 17.2 | 9.6 | 12.4 | 12.5 | 14.8 |
| 39 001 | ... | 6 | Adams | 1 512 | 28 350 | 1 477 | 18.8 | 98.1 | 0.8 | 1.2 | 0.3 | 0.9 | 6.5 | 18.2 | 7.9 | 11.0 | 13.2 | 14.7 |
| 39 003 | 30620 | 3 | Allen | 1 042 | 105 141 | 561 | 100.9 | 84.6 | 13.6 | 0.6 | 1.1 | 2.5 | 6.3 | 17.4 | 10.7 | 11.7 | 11.5 | 14.2 |
| 39 005 | 11740 | 4 | Ashland | 1 095 | 52 962 | 940 | 48.4 | 97.2 | 1.3 | 0.5 | 0.9 | 1.0 | 6.0 | 17.4 | 10.3 | 11.1 | 11.7 | 14.0 |
| 39 007 | 11780 | 4 | Ashtabula | 1 818 | 100 389 | 585 | 55.2 | 92.3 | 4.6 | 0.7 | 0.7 | 3.5 | 6.1 | 17.1 | 8.0 | 11.0 | 12.6 | 15.3 |
| 39 009 | 11900 | 4 | Athens | 1 304 | 64 304 | 818 | 49.3 | 92.2 | 3.7 | 1.0 | 3.4 | 1.7 | 4.0 | 11.2 | 33.9 | 11.2 | 9.2 | 10.3 |
| 39 011 | 47540 | 4 | Auglaize | 1 040 | 45 831 | 1 051 | 44.1 | 97.6 | 0.9 | 0.5 | 0.6 | 1.3 | 6.7 | 18.3 | 7.5 | 11.0 | 12.2 | 15.1 |
| 39 013 | 48540 | 3 | Belmont | 1 378 | 69 671 | 763 | 50.6 | 94.6 | 4.8 | 0.5 | 0.6 | 0.7 | 5.0 | 14.5 | 8.3 | 11.9 | 12.2 | 15.3 |
| 39 015 | 17140 | 1 | Brown | 1 269 | 44 381 | 1 077 | 35.0 | 97.8 | 1.4 | 0.7 | 0.4 | 0.7 | 6.0 | 18.2 | 7.6 | 11.3 | 13.0 | 15.7 |
| 39 017 | 17140 | 1 | Butler | 1 210 | 370 589 | 178 | 306.3 | 85.7 | 8.4 | 0.6 | 3.0 | 4.1 | 6.7 | 18.2 | 11.2 | 12.3 | 13.0 | 14.7 |
| 39 019 | 15940 | 2 | Carroll | 1 022 | 28 587 | 1 463 | 28.0 | 98.0 | 1.0 | 0.8 | 0.3 | 0.9 | 5.5 | 17.1 | 7.3 | 10.0 | 11.9 | 16.2 |
| 39 021 | 46500 | 6 | Champaign | 1 110 | 39 565 | 1 180 | 35.6 | 95.6 | 3.4 | 0.9 | 0.7 | 1.2 | 6.1 | 18.5 | 8.5 | 10.7 | 13.0 | 15.4 |
| 39 023 | 44220 | 3 | Clark | 1 029 | 137 206 | 454 | 133.3 | 87.4 | 10.2 | 0.9 | 1.1 | 2.8 | 6.2 | 17.2 | 9.1 | 11.1 | 11.8 | 14.3 |
| 39 025 | 17140 | 1 | Clermont | 1 171 | 199 085 | 319 | 170.0 | 95.8 | 1.8 | 0.6 | 1.4 | 1.6 | 6.6 | 18.5 | 7.9 | 12.1 | 13.5 | 15.8 |
| 39 027 | 48940 | 6 | Clinton | 1 058 | 41 886 | 1 132 | 39.6 | 95.3 | 3.3 | 0.8 | 0.9 | 1.5 | 6.3 | 18.0 | 9.6 | 11.8 | 12.2 | 15.3 |
| 39 029 | 20620 | 4 | Columbiana | 1 378 | 106 507 | 560 | 77.3 | 95.9 | 2.9 | 0.6 | 0.5 | 1.3 | 5.5 | 16.0 | 7.6 | 11.2 | 12.7 | 15.5 |
| 39 031 | 18740 | 6 | Coshocton | 1 461 | 36 779 | 1 253 | 25.2 | 97.5 | 1.8 | 0.6 | 0.4 | 0.8 | 6.1 | 17.7 | 7.8 | 11.2 | 12.0 | 14.7 |
| 39 033 | 15340 | 4 | Crawford | 1 041 | 42 849 | 1 116 | 41.2 | 97.2 | 1.5 | 0.5 | 0.6 | 1.3 | 5.6 | 17.0 | 7.6 | 10.8 | 12.3 | 14.4 |
| 39 035 | 17460 | 1 | Cuyahoga | 1 184 | 1 265 111 | 30 | 1 068.5 | 62.7 | 30.4 | 0.6 | 3.1 | 4.9 | 5.8 | 16.5 | 8.9 | 12.5 | 12.1 | 15.1 |
| 39 037 | 24820 | 6 | Darke | 1 549 | 52 507 | 946 | 33.9 | 97.7 | 1.0 | 0.5 | 0.5 | 1.3 | 6.5 | 18.2 | 7.4 | 10.7 | 12.0 | 14.8 |
| 39 039 | 19580 | 4 | Defiance | 1 066 | 38 677 | 1 205 | 36.3 | 88.8 | 2.5 | 0.5 | 0.5 | 8.8 | 6.2 | 18.0 | 8.7 | 11.6 | 12.1 | 14.2 |
| 39 041 | 18140 | 1 | Delaware | 1 148 | 181 061 | 348 | 157.7 | 89.6 | 4.3 | 0.6 | 5.0 | 2.2 | 6.9 | 21.6 | 6.6 | 10.6 | 16.8 | 15.7 |
| 39 043 | 41780 | 3 | Erie | 652 | 76 398 | 717 | 117.2 | 87.1 | 10.1 | 0.7 | 0.9 | 3.5 | 5.3 | 16.5 | 7.5 | 10.6 | 11.7 | 15.5 |
| 39 045 | 18140 | 1 | Fairfield | 1 306 | 147 474 | 425 | 112.9 | 90.6 | 7.0 | 0.8 | 1.7 | 1.8 | 6.2 | 19.6 | 8.0 | 11.9 | 13.9 | 15.3 |
| 39 047 | 47920 | 6 | Fayette | 1 052 | 28 880 | 1 455 | 27.5 | 94.9 | 3.1 | 0.6 | 1.0 | 1.9 | 6.8 | 17.6 | 8.0 | 11.9 | 12.8 | 14.4 |
| 39 049 | 18140 | 1 | Franklin | 1 378 | 1 195 537 | 34 | 867.6 | 69.6 | 22.7 | 0.9 | 4.7 | 4.9 | 7.2 | 16.6 | 11.6 | 16.7 | 13.4 | 13.5 |
| 39 051 | 45780 | 2 | Fulton | 1 050 | 42 513 | 1 122 | 40.5 | 91.1 | 0.9 | 0.5 | 0.6 | 7.7 | 6.3 | 19.0 | 7.6 | 10.9 | 12.2 | 15.7 |
| 39 053 | 38580 | 6 | Gallia | 1 208 | 30 708 | 1 416 | 25.4 | 95.5 | 3.4 | 0.9 | 0.7 | 1.0 | 6.3 | 17.2 | 8.9 | 11.5 | 11.8 | 15.1 |
| 39 055 | 17460 | 1 | Geauga | 1 036 | 93 680 | 618 | 90.4 | 96.8 | 1.7 | 0.4 | 0.9 | 1.1 | 5.2 | 20.0 | 7.0 | 7.7 | 11.9 | 17.0 |
| 39 057 | 19380 | 2 | Greene | 1 072 | 163 587 | 382 | 152.6 | 86.8 | 8.7 | 0.9 | 3.8 | 2.4 | 5.4 | 15.7 | 15.1 | 12.0 | 11.0 | 14.1 |
| 39 059 | 15740 | 6 | Guernsey | 1 353 | 39 817 | 1 175 | 29.4 | 96.3 | 2.5 | 0.8 | 0.6 | 1.0 | 6.0 | 17.5 | 7.9 | 11.0 | 12.3 | 14.9 |
| 39 061 | 17140 | 1 | Hamilton | 1 051 | 802 038 | 74 | 763.1 | 69.3 | 26.8 | 0.7 | 2.6 | 2.7 | 6.7 | 16.8 | 10.3 | 13.8 | 11.9 | 14.6 |
| 39 063 | 22300 | 4 | Hancock | 1 376 | 75 671 | 722 | 55.0 | 91.8 | 2.3 | 0.6 | 2.1 | 4.6 | 6.2 | 17.0 | 10.2 | 12.4 | 12.1 | 14.7 |
| 39 065 | ... | 6 | Hardin | 1 218 | 31 627 | 1 398 | 26.0 | 96.8 | 1.5 | 0.7 | 0.9 | 1.3 | 6.2 | 17.1 | 15.2 | 11.1 | 11.6 | 13.0 |
| 39 067 | ... | 6 | Harrison | 1 042 | 15 714 | 2 062 | 15.1 | 96.9 | 3.3 | 0.5 | 0.3 | 0.5 | 6.0 | 15.8 | 7.2 | 10.1 | 11.5 | 15.5 |
| 39 069 | ... | 6 | Henry | 1 077 | 28 045 | 1 491 | 26.0 | 92.3 | 1.0 | 0.6 | 0.6 | 6.4 | 6.2 | 18.4 | 7.6 | 11.5 | 12.1 | 15.2 |
| 39 071 | ... | 6 | Highland | 1 432 | 42 998 | 1 111 | 30.0 | 97.1 | 2.3 | 0.8 | 0.4 | 0.8 | 6.5 | 18.4 | 8.0 | 11.5 | 12.9 | 14.3 |
| 39 073 | ... | 6 | Hocking | 1 091 | 29 273 | 1 440 | 26.8 | 97.8 | 1.3 | 0.8 | 0.4 | 0.7 | 5.8 | 17.6 | 7.8 | 10.9 | 12.6 | 15.3 |
| 39 075 | ... | 7 | Holmes | 1 094 | 43 025 | 1 110 | 39.3 | 98.5 | 0.6 | 0.3 | 0.3 | 0.8 | 9.4 | 24.5 | 10.1 | 12.0 | 11.0 | 11.5 |
| 39 077 | 35940 | 4 | Huron | 1 273 | 59 280 | 872 | 46.6 | 92.6 | 1.8 | 0.6 | 0.5 | 5.8 | 6.6 | 19.3 | 7.9 | 11.7 | 12.7 | 14.8 |
| 39 079 | ... | 7 | Jackson | 1 089 | 32 954 | 1 356 | 30.3 | 97.6 | 1.3 | 1.0 | 0.6 | 0.9 | 6.6 | 17.9 | 8.1 | 12.2 | 12.9 | 14.2 |
| 39 081 | 44600 | 3 | Jefferson | 1 058 | 68 389 | 777 | 64.6 | 92.6 | 6.6 | 0.6 | 0.7 | 1.1 | 5.0 | 14.9 | 9.6 | 10.0 | 11.5 | 15.1 |
| 39 083 | 34540 | 4 | Knox | 1 361 | 60 705 | 852 | 44.6 | 96.8 | 1.5 | 0.6 | 0.9 | 1.3 | 6.1 | 17.6 | 11.7 | 10.8 | 11.4 | 14.3 |
| 39 085 | 17460 | 1 | Lake | 589 | 229 582 | 280 | 389.8 | 91.7 | 4.1 | 0.4 | 1.6 | 3.6 | 5.3 | 16.5 | 7.6 | 11.3 | 12.7 | 16.1 |
| 39 087 | 26580 | 2 | Lawrence | 1 174 | 62 109 | 839 | 52.9 | 96.4 | 2.9 | 0.6 | 0.6 | 0.8 | 6.0 | 17.1 | 7.9 | 12.0 | 13.1 | 14.6 |
| 39 089 | 18140 | 1 | Licking | 1 768 | 167 537 | 374 | 94.8 | 93.8 | 4.5 | 0.8 | 1.2 | 1.5 | 6.2 | 18.1 | 8.9 | 11.4 | 13.2 | 15.6 |
| 39 091 | 13340 | 4 | Logan | 1 187 | 45 474 | 1 058 | 38.3 | 96.2 | 2.9 | 0.7 | 0.9 | 1.2 | 6.4 | 18.5 | 7.6 | 11.2 | 12.3 | 15.0 |
| 39 093 | 17460 | 1 | Lorain | 1 272 | 301 478 | 216 | 237.0 | 82.1 | 9.6 | 0.8 | 1.3 | 8.4 | 5.8 | 17.6 | 8.6 | 11.1 | 13.1 | 15.5 |
| 39 095 | 45780 | 2 | Lucas | 883 | 437 998 | 154 | 496.0 | 73.1 | 20.4 | 0.8 | 2.0 | 6.2 | 6.6 | 17.1 | 10.8 | 12.8 | 12.1 | 14.3 |
| 39 097 | 18140 | 1 | Madison | 1 207 | 43 053 | 1 108 | 35.7 | 90.9 | 7.5 | 0.6 | 0.9 | 1.5 | 5.7 | 16.6 | 8.4 | 13.1 | 15.3 | 16.0 |
| 39 099 | 49660 | 2 | Mahoning | 1 066 | 235 145 | 275 | 220.6 | 78.8 | 16.4 | 0.6 | 1.1 | 4.8 | 5.3 | 16.0 | 8.5 | 10.9 | 11.7 | 15.0 |
| 39 101 | 32020 | 4 | Marion | 1 046 | 66 238 | 793 | 63.3 | 91.2 | 6.6 | 0.6 | 0.9 | 2.3 | 5.8 | 16.0 | 8.9 | 12.6 | 13.2 | 15.5 |
| 39 103 | 17460 | 1 | Medina | 1 091 | 173 684 | 359 | 159.2 | 95.8 | 1.8 | 0.5 | 1.3 | 1.7 | 5.7 | 19.0 | 7.0 | 10.5 | 14.1 | 16.4 |
| 39 105 | ... | 6 | Meigs | 1 114 | 23 593 | 1 659 | 21.2 | 98.0 | 1.5 | 0.7 | 0.4 | 0.6 | 5.6 | 16.8 | 7.7 | 11.7 | 12.4 | 15.1 |
| 39 107 | 16380 | 7 | Mercer | 1 198 | 40 875 | 1 156 | 34.1 | 97.2 | 0.6 | 0.6 | 0.8 | 1.5 | 6.9 | 19.0 | 7.8 | 11.1 | 11.3 | 14.6 |
| 39 109 | 19380 | 2 | Miami | 1 053 | 103 060 | 568 | 97.9 | 94.9 | 3.2 | 0.5 | 1.5 | 1.4 | 6.1 | 17.7 | 7.6 | 11.3 | 12.8 | 15.0 |
| 39 111 | ... | 8 | Monroe | 1 180 | 14 549 | 2 138 | 12.3 | 98.7 | 0.9 | 0.8 | 0.3 | 0.5 | 5.3 | 15.6 | 7.1 | 10.0 | 11.7 | 14.9 |
| 39 113 | 19380 | 2 | Montgomery | 1 195 | 534 325 | 121 | 447.1 | 74.7 | 22.1 | 0.8 | 2.4 | 2.4 | 6.2 | 16.4 | 9.5 | 12.7 | 11.8 | 14.4 |
| 39 115 | ... | 6 | Morgan | 1 079 | 14 911 | 2 115 | 13.8 | 95.6 | 5.2 | 1.6 | 0.8 | 0.7 | 5.5 | 17.5 | 7.5 | 10.7 | 11.3 | 15.4 |
| 39 117 | 18140 | 1 | Morrow | 1 052 | 34 938 | 1 301 | 33.2 | 97.8 | 1.0 | 0.9 | 0.5 | 1.2 | 6.0 | 19.2 | 7.4 | 11.0 | 13.3 | 15.6 |
| 39 119 | 49780 | 4 | Muskingum | 1 721 | 85 950 | 656 | 49.9 | 94.7 | 5.6 | 0.9 | 0.6 | 0.8 | 6.1 | 17.7 | 9.2 | 11.5 | 12.3 | 14.5 |
| 39 121 | ... | 6 | Noble | 1 031 | 14 579 | 2 134 | 14.1 | 96.3 | 3.1 | 0.7 | 0.3 | 0.4 | 5.2 | 13.8 | 6.5 | 9.7 | 9.5 | 14.8 |

1. CBSA = Core Based Statistical Area. See Appendix A for explanation. See Appendix B for list of metropolitan areas with component counties.   2. County type code from the Economic Research Service of USDA Rural-Urban Continuum Codes. See Appendix A for definition.   3. Dry land or land partially or temporarily covered by water.   4. May be of any race.

| | Population, 2011 (cont.) | | | | Population change and components of change, 2000–2012 | | | | | | | Households, 2010 | | | | |
| | Age (percent) (cont.) | | | | Total persons | | Percent change | | Components of change, 2010–2012 | | | | | | Percent | |
| STATE County | 55 to 64 years | 65 to 74 years | 75 years and over | Percent female | 2000 | 2010 | 2000– 2010 | 2010– 2012 | Births | Deaths | Net migration | Number | Percent change, 2000– 2010 | Persons per house-hold | Female family house-holder[1] | One per-son |
| | 16 | 17 | 18 | 19 | 20 | 21 | 22 | 23 | 24 | 25 | 26 | 27 | 28 | 29 | 30 | 31 |
| **NORTH DAKOTA—Cont'd** | | | | | | | | | | | | | | | | |
| Ward | 10.5 | 6.1 | 6.5 | 48.9 | 58 795 | 61 675 | 4.9 | 5.1 | 2 361 | 1 160 | 1 924 | 25 029 | 8.6 | 2.36 | 8.4 | 30.0 |
| Wells | 15.0 | 12.2 | 15.6 | 50.8 | 5 102 | 4 207 | -17.5 | 1.5 | 85 | 150 | 123 | 1 943 | -12.3 | 2.10 | 5.6 | 34.3 |
| Williams | 12.6 | 6.5 | 7.2 | 47.8 | 19 761 | 22 398 | 13.3 | 19.2 | 811 | 498 | 3 883 | 9 293 | 14.8 | 2.35 | 7.7 | 31.5 |
| | | | | | | | | | | | | | | | | |
| **OHIO** | 13.1 | 7.5 | 6.7 | 51.2 | 11 353 140 | 11 536 504 | 1.6 | 0.1 | 305 848 | 245 688 | -51 037 | 4 603 435 | 3.5 | 2.44 | 13.1 | 28.9 |
| | | | | | | | | | | | | | | | | |
| Adams | 13.4 | 8.8 | 6.4 | 50.7 | 27 330 | 28 550 | 4.5 | -0.7 | 772 | 727 | -262 | 11 147 | 6.2 | 2.53 | 12.1 | 25.9 |
| Allen | 13.2 | 7.6 | 7.4 | 49.6 | 108 473 | 106 331 | -2.0 | -1.1 | 2 873 | 2 428 | -1 639 | 40 619 | -0.1 | 2.47 | 13.8 | 27.8 |
| Ashland | 13.3 | 8.6 | 7.5 | 51.0 | 52 523 | 53 139 | 1.2 | -0.3 | 1 318 | 1 256 | -235 | 20 196 | 3.4 | 2.53 | 9.4 | 25.3 |
| Ashtabula | 14.0 | 8.5 | 7.4 | 50.0 | 102 728 | 101 497 | -1.2 | -1.1 | 2 535 | 2 492 | -1 111 | 39 363 | -0.1 | 2.50 | 12.4 | 26.9 |
| Athens | 10.0 | 5.8 | 4.5 | 50.1 | 62 223 | 64 757 | 4.1 | -0.7 | 1 184 | 1 075 | -574 | 23 578 | 4.8 | 2.35 | 9.2 | 30.0 |
| Auglaize | 13.6 | 7.8 | 7.9 | 50.4 | 46 611 | 45 949 | -1.4 | -0.3 | 1 227 | 1 080 | -292 | 17 972 | 3.4 | 2.53 | 8.5 | 25.3 |
| Belmont | 15.2 | 8.8 | 8.8 | 49.4 | 70 226 | 70 400 | 0.2 | -1.0 | 1 495 | 1 994 | -187 | 28 679 | 1.3 | 2.32 | 11.4 | 29.9 |
| Brown | 13.3 | 8.6 | 6.3 | 50.5 | 42 285 | 44 846 | 6.1 | -1.0 | 1 152 | 1 031 | -571 | 17 014 | 9.4 | 2.60 | 11.2 | 22.6 |
| | | | | | | | | | | | | | | | | |
| Butler | 12.1 | 6.4 | 5.4 | 51.0 | 332 807 | 368 130 | 10.6 | 0.7 | 10 182 | 6 733 | -1 018 | 135 960 | 10.5 | 2.63 | 12.4 | 23.5 |
| Carroll | 15.2 | 9.7 | 7.2 | 50.1 | 28 836 | 28 836 | 0.0 | -0.9 | 639 | 653 | -251 | 11 385 | 2.3 | 2.50 | 8.8 | 24.3 |
| Champaign | 13.2 | 8.5 | 6.2 | 50.5 | 38 890 | 40 097 | 3.1 | -1.3 | 920 | 861 | -606 | 15 329 | 2.5 | 2.56 | 10.2 | 23.9 |
| Clark | 14.0 | 8.8 | 7.6 | 51.5 | 144 742 | 138 333 | -4.4 | -0.8 | 3 627 | 3 625 | -1 111 | 55 244 | -2.5 | 2.45 | 14.1 | 27.7 |
| Clermont | 13.3 | 7.2 | 5.1 | 50.7 | 177 977 | 197 363 | 10.9 | 0.9 | 5 360 | 3 449 | -88 | 74 828 | 13.4 | 2.61 | 10.9 | 22.5 |
| Clinton | 13.1 | 7.5 | 6.2 | 51.0 | 40 543 | 42 040 | 3.7 | -0.4 | 1 123 | 928 | -331 | 16 210 | 5.2 | 2.52 | 11.9 | 25.1 |
| Columbiana | 14.7 | 8.9 | 7.8 | 49.7 | 112 075 | 107 841 | -3.8 | -1.2 | 2 451 | 2 579 | -1 184 | 42 683 | -0.7 | 2.43 | 11.5 | 26.8 |
| Coshocton | 14.0 | 9.1 | 7.4 | 50.6 | 36 655 | 36 901 | 0.7 | -0.3 | 968 | 845 | -223 | 14 658 | 2.1 | 2.49 | 10.4 | 26.3 |
| Crawford | 14.1 | 9.5 | 8.7 | 51.5 | 46 966 | 43 784 | -6.8 | -2.1 | 1 070 | 1 083 | -908 | 18 099 | -4.5 | 2.39 | 11.5 | 28.4 |
| | | | | | | | | | | | | | | | | |
| Cuyahoga | 13.4 | 7.6 | 8.0 | 52.5 | 1 393 978 | 1 280 122 | -8.2 | -1.2 | 33 059 | 29 938 | -18 139 | 545 056 | -4.6 | 2.29 | 16.7 | 35.5 |
| Darke | 13.3 | 9.0 | 8.1 | 50.9 | 53 309 | 52 959 | -0.7 | -0.9 | 1 351 | 1 248 | -545 | 20 929 | 2.5 | 2.50 | 9.0 | 25.9 |
| Defiance | 13.8 | 8.3 | 7.1 | 50.7 | 39 500 | 39 037 | -1.2 | -0.9 | 1 009 | 863 | -501 | 15 268 | 0.9 | 2.51 | 10.8 | 24.6 |
| Delaware | 11.8 | 5.9 | 4.0 | 50.6 | 109 989 | 174 214 | 58.4 | 3.9 | 4 708 | 2 061 | 4 088 | 62 760 | 58.2 | 2.74 | 7.3 | 19.0 |
| Erie | 15.2 | 9.4 | 8.3 | 51.1 | 79 551 | 77 079 | -3.1 | -0.9 | 1 719 | 1 962 | -406 | 31 860 | 0.4 | 2.37 | 12.9 | 28.6 |
| Fairfield | 12.6 | 7.3 | 5.3 | 50.4 | 122 759 | 146 156 | 19.1 | 0.9 | 3 662 | 2 545 | 123 | 54 310 | 19.6 | 2.64 | 11.2 | 21.9 |
| Fayette | 13.4 | 8.4 | 6.7 | 50.7 | 28 433 | 29 030 | 2.1 | -0.5 | 819 | 714 | -258 | 11 436 | 3.5 | 2.49 | 13.5 | 25.8 |
| Franklin | 10.9 | 5.5 | 4.6 | 51.3 | 1 068 978 | 1 163 414 | 8.8 | 2.8 | 39 727 | 19 532 | 12 336 | 477 235 | 8.8 | 2.38 | 14.4 | 31.9 |
| Fulton | 13.8 | 7.6 | 6.9 | 50.8 | 42 084 | 42 698 | 1.5 | -0.4 | 1 081 | 909 | -402 | 16 188 | 4.6 | 2.61 | 9.3 | 22.3 |
| | | | | | | | | | | | | | | | | |
| Gallia | 13.1 | 9.3 | 6.9 | 50.6 | 31 069 | 30 934 | -0.4 | -0.7 | 837 | 784 | -278 | 12 062 | 0.0 | 2.49 | 11.6 | 27.0 |
| Geauga | 15.1 | 9.0 | 7.2 | 50.9 | 90 895 | 93 389 | 2.7 | 0.3 | 1 982 | 1 652 | -48 | 34 264 | 8.3 | 2.70 | 7.7 | 21.2 |
| Greene | 12.9 | 7.4 | 6.4 | 51.1 | 147 886 | 161 573 | 9.3 | 1.2 | 3 885 | 2 867 | 983 | 62 770 | 13.5 | 2.43 | 10.6 | 26.5 |
| Guernsey | 14.2 | 9.1 | 7.2 | 50.9 | 40 792 | 40 087 | -1.7 | -0.7 | 1 000 | 1 013 | -232 | 16 210 | 0.7 | 2.44 | 12.3 | 27.7 |
| Hamilton | 12.6 | 6.7 | 6.6 | 52.0 | 845 303 | 802 374 | -5.1 | 0.0 | 24 253 | 16 964 | -7 394 | 333 945 | -3.7 | 2.34 | 15.4 | 33.9 |
| Hancock | 13.0 | 7.6 | 6.8 | 51.3 | 71 295 | 74 782 | 4.9 | 1.2 | 1 983 | 1 481 | 351 | 30 197 | 8.2 | 2.42 | 10.0 | 27.9 |
| Hardin | 12.2 | 7.5 | 6.1 | 50.2 | 31 945 | 32 058 | 0.4 | -1.3 | 823 | 725 | -551 | 11 762 | -1.7 | 2.53 | 10.1 | 26.7 |
| Harrison | 15.8 | 9.9 | 8.3 | 50.5 | 15 856 | 15 864 | 0.1 | -0.9 | 342 | 475 | -5 | 6 526 | 2.0 | 2.40 | 9.5 | 27.1 |
| Henry | 13.4 | 7.8 | 7.8 | 50.4 | 29 210 | 28 215 | -3.4 | -0.6 | 722 | 571 | -413 | 10 934 | 0.0 | 2.55 | 9.3 | 23.7 |
| | | | | | | | | | | | | | | | | |
| Highland | 13.0 | 8.7 | 6.8 | 51.0 | 40 875 | 43 589 | 6.6 | -1.4 | 1 197 | 1 046 | -753 | 16 693 | 7.1 | 2.58 | 11.9 | 24.3 |
| Hocking | 14.5 | 9.4 | 6.3 | 50.0 | 28 241 | 29 380 | 4.0 | -0.4 | 702 | 664 | -143 | 11 369 | 4.9 | 2.52 | 10.7 | 24.8 |
| Holmes | 10.0 | 6.1 | 5.4 | 50.1 | 38 943 | 42 366 | 8.8 | 1.6 | 1 795 | 700 | -435 | 12 554 | 10.7 | 3.31 | 6.9 | 17.2 |
| Huron | 13.2 | 7.6 | 6.3 | 50.9 | 59 487 | 59 626 | 0.2 | -0.6 | 1 578 | 1 233 | -698 | 22 820 | 2.3 | 2.59 | 12.2 | 24.4 |
| Jackson | 14.0 | 8.0 | 6.2 | 50.9 | 32 641 | 33 225 | 1.8 | -0.8 | 922 | 836 | -351 | 13 010 | 3.1 | 2.53 | 12.7 | 25.9 |
| Jefferson | 15.5 | 9.6 | 8.3 | 51.9 | 73 894 | 69 709 | -5.7 | -1.9 | 1 386 | 2 110 | -583 | 29 109 | -4.3 | 2.32 | 12.4 | 30.5 |
| Knox | 13.1 | 8.1 | 6.8 | 51.1 | 54 500 | 60 921 | 11.8 | -0.4 | 1 582 | 1 349 | -459 | 22 607 | 13.2 | 2.54 | 9.7 | 25.7 |
| Lake | 14.3 | 8.6 | 7.7 | 51.2 | 227 511 | 230 041 | 1.1 | -0.2 | 5 105 | 5 147 | -298 | 94 156 | 5.0 | 2.41 | 11.2 | 28.3 |
| Lawrence | 13.5 | 9.0 | 6.7 | 51.2 | 62 319 | 62 450 | 0.2 | -0.5 | 1 545 | 1 561 | -286 | 24 974 | 1.0 | 2.47 | 13.2 | 26.1 |
| | | | | | | | | | | | | | | | | |
| Licking | 13.1 | 7.8 | 5.8 | 51.0 | 145 491 | 166 492 | 14.4 | 0.6 | 4 344 | 3 245 | -43 | 63 989 | 15.1 | 2.55 | 11.2 | 23.8 |
| Logan | 14.1 | 8.4 | 6.6 | 50.7 | 46 005 | 45 858 | -0.3 | -0.8 | 1 213 | 1 082 | -497 | 18 111 | 0.9 | 2.51 | 10.5 | 25.5 |
| Lorain | 13.7 | 7.8 | 6.8 | 50.8 | 284 664 | 301 356 | 5.9 | 0.0 | 7 453 | 6 096 | -1 209 | 116 274 | 9.9 | 2.51 | 13.5 | 26.0 |
| Lucas | 12.9 | 6.9 | 6.5 | 51.6 | 455 054 | 441 815 | -2.9 | -0.9 | 12 527 | 9 540 | -6 845 | 180 267 | -1.4 | 2.39 | 16.5 | 31.4 |
| Madison | 12.3 | 7.2 | 5.4 | 45.4 | 40 213 | 43 435 | 8.0 | -0.9 | 976 | 841 | -502 | 14 734 | 7.8 | 2.59 | 11.3 | 23.5 |
| Mahoning | 14.8 | 8.4 | 9.4 | 51.6 | 257 555 | 238 823 | -7.3 | -1.5 | 5 205 | 6 729 | -2 032 | 98 712 | -3.8 | 2.34 | 15.0 | 31.8 |
| Marion | 13.6 | 7.7 | 6.8 | 47.5 | 66 217 | 66 501 | 0.4 | -0.4 | 1 772 | 1 525 | -479 | 24 691 | 0.5 | 2.47 | 13.3 | 26.3 |
| Medina | 13.7 | 7.7 | 5.8 | 50.7 | 151 095 | 172 332 | 14.1 | 0.8 | 3 923 | 2 875 | 309 | 65 143 | 19.4 | 2.63 | 8.7 | 21.6 |
| Meigs | 14.7 | 9.0 | 7.0 | 51.0 | 23 072 | 23 770 | 3.0 | -0.7 | 545 | 595 | -128 | 9 557 | 3.5 | 2.46 | 11.5 | 25.3 |
| | | | | | | | | | | | | | | | | |
| Mercer | 13.6 | 7.7 | 8.0 | 50.0 | 40 924 | 40 814 | -0.3 | 0.1 | 1 187 | 874 | -283 | 15 532 | 5.3 | 2.60 | 7.6 | 24.5 |
| Miami | 13.9 | 8.8 | 6.9 | 50.8 | 98 868 | 102 506 | 3.7 | 0.5 | 2 577 | 2 125 | 107 | 40 917 | 6.5 | 2.48 | 10.5 | 25.3 |
| Monroe | 15.4 | 11.4 | 8.5 | 50.0 | 15 180 | 14 642 | -3.5 | -0.6 | 326 | 455 | -16 | 6 065 | 0.7 | 2.39 | 8.6 | 27.3 |
| Montgomery | 13.1 | 8.1 | 7.7 | 52.0 | 559 062 | 535 153 | -4.3 | -0.2 | 14 755 | 12 677 | -2 551 | 223 943 | -2.3 | 2.33 | 15.3 | 32.2 |
| Morgan | 14.5 | 9.5 | 8.0 | 50.1 | 14 897 | 15 054 | 1.1 | -0.9 | 317 | 344 | -114 | 6 034 | 2.4 | 2.46 | 10.4 | 26.3 |
| Morrow | 13.7 | 8.1 | 5.8 | 50.0 | 31 628 | 34 827 | 10.1 | 0.3 | 862 | 679 | -108 | 12 855 | 11.8 | 2.68 | 9.5 | 20.7 |
| Muskingum | 13.1 | 8.2 | 7.3 | 51.6 | 84 585 | 86 074 | 1.8 | -0.1 | 2 305 | 2 079 | -299 | 34 271 | 5.4 | 2.46 | 13.2 | 26.9 |
| Noble | 19.3 | 13.4 | 7.8 | 42.2 | 14 058 | 14 645 | 4.2 | -0.5 | 343 | 290 | -157 | 4 852 | 6.7 | 2.47 | 8.6 | 25.7 |

1. No spouse present.

# Table B. States and Counties — Population, Vital Statistics, Medicare, and Crime

| STATE County | Persons in group quarters, 2010 | Daytime population, 2007–2011 Number | Daytime population Employment/residence ratio | Births, 2011 Total | Births Rate[1] | Deaths, 2011 Number | Deaths Rate[1] | Persons under 65 with no health insurance, 2010 Number | Percent | Medicare, 2012 Eligible for Medicare | Enrolled in Medicare Advantage | Enrolled in a Medicare prescription drug plan | Serious crimes known to police,[2] 2011 Total Number | Rate[3] |
|---|---|---|---|---|---|---|---|---|---|---|---|---|---|---|
| | 32 | 33 | 34 | 35 | 36 | 37 | 38 | 39 | 40 | 41 | 42 | 43 | 44 | 45 |
| **NORTH DAKOTA—Cont'd** | | | | | | | | | | | | | | |
| Ward | 2 685 | 62 301 | 1.05 | 1 034 | 16.1 | 513 | 8.0 | 5 646 | 10.9 | 8 785 | 930 | 5 455 | 1 101 | 1 756 |
| Wells | 119 | 4 246 | 1.00 | 45 | 10.6 | 65 | 15.3 | 371 | 12.6 | 1 208 | 71 | 914 | 54 | 1 262 |
| Williams | 560 | 24 053 | 1.17 | 300 | 12.3 | 212 | 8.7 | 2 066 | 10.8 | 3 465 | 257 | 2 251 | 627 | 2 753 |
| **OHIO** | 306 266 | 11 535 482 | 1.00 | 140 808 | 12.2 | 107 668 | 9.3 | 1 384 046 | 14.3 | 2 017 509 | 735 288 | 897 137 | 422 781 | 3 662 |
| Adams | 338 | 26 279 | 0.78 | 354 | 12.4 | 331 | 11.6 | 4 070 | 16.7 | 5 778 | 1 642 | 3 403 | 128 | 465 |
| Allen | 5 934 | 113 689 | 1.16 | 1 334 | 12.6 | 1 063 | 10.0 | 12 063 | 14.1 | 19 752 | 4 766 | 10 261 | 4 393 | 4 128 |
| Ashland | 2 144 | 49 827 | 0.85 | 600 | 11.3 | 542 | 10.2 | 7 209 | 16.8 | 9 901 | 3 513 | 4 579 | 1 052 | 1 983 |
| Ashtabula | 3 190 | 94 412 | 0.83 | 1 200 | 11.8 | 1 088 | 10.7 | 13 149 | 15.8 | 20 606 | 5 119 | 11 381 | NA | NA |
| Athens | 9 345 | 65 114 | 1.02 | 531 | 8.2 | 465 | 7.2 | 8 870 | 17.9 | 8 870 | 2 843 | 5 785 | 1 670 | 2 596 |
| Auglaize | 525 | 43 203 | 0.87 | 593 | 12.9 | 469 | 10.2 | 5 089 | 13.3 | 7 969 | 1 877 | 4 519 | NA | NA |
| Belmont | 3 834 | 64 021 | 0.78 | 701 | 10.0 | 860 | 12.3 | 7 742 | 14.1 | 14 916 | 6 577 | 6 245 | 810 | 1 169 |
| Brown | 575 | 35 967 | 0.52 | 527 | 11.8 | 447 | 10.0 | 5 565 | 14.6 | 8 522 | 3 172 | 3 993 | 646 | 1 688 |
| Butler | 10 953 | 344 107 | 0.87 | 4 786 | 12.9 | 2 978 | 8.0 | 41 956 | 13.3 | 55 998 | 21 779 | 21 957 | 16 189 | 4 394 |
| Carroll | 405 | 23 263 | 0.55 | 320 | 11.1 | 281 | 9.8 | 4 051 | 17.0 | 5 715 | 2 554 | 2 249 | 223 | 773 |
| Champaign | 793 | 34 935 | 0.70 | 434 | 10.9 | 372 | 9.3 | 4 625 | 13.8 | 7 112 | 2 819 | 4 236 | 854 | 2 128 |
| Clark | 2 798 | 129 245 | 0.84 | 1 674 | 12.2 | 1 599 | 11.6 | 17 234 | 15.1 | 27 540 | 12 569 | 13 286 | 6 020 | 4 358 |
| Clermont | 1 717 | 161 888 | 0.63 | 2 494 | 12.5 | 1 451 | 7.3 | 22 415 | 13.0 | 31 111 | 12 653 | 11 871 | 6 754 | 3 420 |
| Clinton | 1 145 | 45 074 | 1.15 | 526 | 12.5 | 424 | 10.1 | 4 567 | 13.0 | 7 498 | 2 547 | 3 880 | 934 | 2 220 |
| Columbiana | 3 944 | 94 786 | 0.70 | 1 183 | 11.0 | 1 127 | 10.5 | 13 565 | 15.6 | 22 124 | 7 153 | 10 005 | 1 427 | 1 481 |
| Coshocton | 428 | 34 640 | 0.84 | 433 | 11.7 | 370 | 10.0 | 5 538 | 18.0 | 7 392 | 1 663 | 4 361 | 905 | 2 451 |
| Crawford | 579 | 40 924 | 0.83 | 495 | 11.4 | 473 | 10.9 | 5 567 | 15.6 | 9 726 | 2 572 | 5 323 | NA | NA |
| Cuyahoga | 29 251 | 1 421 289 | 1.24 | 15 077 | 11.9 | 13 215 | 10.4 | 160 828 | 15.2 | 233 427 | 85 282 | 100 100 | 43 076 | 3 708 |
| Darke | 606 | 48 275 | 0.80 | 678 | 12.8 | 570 | 10.8 | 6 451 | 14.8 | 10 622 | 2 830 | 5 263 | 654 | 1 284 |
| Defiance | 720 | 37 617 | 0.92 | 460 | 11.8 | 381 | 9.8 | 4 471 | 13.7 | 7 519 | 1 562 | 3 873 | 951 | 2 434 |
| Delaware | 2 368 | 154 428 | 0.81 | 2 131 | 11.9 | 868 | 4.9 | 11 603 | 7.6 | 21 541 | 8 664 | 9 919 | 2 890 | 1 968 |
| Erie | 1 677 | 78 540 | 1.04 | 769 | 10.0 | 864 | 11.3 | 8 691 | 13.8 | 16 421 | 3 412 | 7 924 | 2 164 | 2 817 |
| Fairfield | 2 872 | 120 558 | 0.63 | 1 660 | 11.3 | 1 118 | 7.6 | 15 316 | 12.3 | 23 628 | 10 277 | 9 606 | 4 713 | 3 256 |
| Fayette | 593 | 28 548 | 0.97 | 418 | 14.4 | 301 | 10.4 | 3 931 | 16.1 | 5 620 | 2 237 | 2 876 | 1 431 | 4 945 |
| Franklin | 25 224 | 1 268 308 | 1.20 | 17 962 | 15.2 | 8 556 | 7.3 | 154 735 | 15.1 | 151 153 | 62 459 | 69 473 | 64 737 | 5 614 |
| Fulton | 391 | 41 141 | 0.92 | 502 | 11.8 | 396 | 9.3 | 5 150 | 14.2 | 7 572 | 2 149 | 4 159 | 754 | 1 765 |
| Gallia | 921 | 32 236 | 1.11 | 397 | 12.8 | 332 | 10.7 | 3 883 | 15.3 | 6 316 | 1 493 | 3 828 | 1 109 | 3 598 |
| Geauga | 864 | 83 429 | 0.77 | 867 | 9.3 | 705 | 7.6 | 9 847 | 12.7 | 16 953 | 5 542 | 7 925 | 368 | 513 |
| Greene | 8 775 | 165 272 | 1.06 | 1 731 | 10.6 | 1 272 | 7.8 | 16 122 | 12.3 | 26 228 | 9 517 | 8 859 | 4 773 | 2 952 |
| Guernsey | 510 | 39 185 | 0.94 | 464 | 11.6 | 441 | 11.0 | 5 085 | 15.2 | 8 549 | 2 091 | 4 955 | 1 163 | 2 932 |
| Hamilton | 19 511 | 922 835 | 1.32 | 11 008 | 13.8 | 7 507 | 9.4 | 96 749 | 14.2 | 131 194 | 48 209 | 52 839 | 39 556 | 4 963 |
| Hancock | 1 694 | 81 813 | 1.19 | 931 | 12.4 | 640 | 8.5 | 8 837 | 14.2 | 12 889 | 3 397 | 6 632 | 2 507 | 3 350 |
| Hardin | 2 259 | 28 559 | 0.73 | 388 | 12.1 | 321 | 10.0 | 3 803 | 14.8 | 5 517 | 1 255 | 3 274 | 938 | 2 924 |
| Harrison | 232 | 13 532 | 0.64 | 173 | 10.9 | 206 | 13.0 | 1 972 | 15.3 | 3 397 | 1 049 | 1 859 | 201 | 1 388 |
| Henry | 346 | 25 856 | 0.81 | 316 | 11.3 | 236 | 8.4 | 3 358 | 14.3 | 5 216 | 1 282 | 2 701 | 713 | 2 921 |
| Highland | 484 | 38 908 | 0.73 | 558 | 12.8 | 467 | 10.8 | 6 363 | 17.3 | 8 432 | 2 462 | 4 554 | 1 432 | 3 302 |
| Hocking | 718 | 24 605 | 0.61 | 321 | 10.9 | 287 | 9.8 | 3 790 | 15.4 | 5 676 | 1 510 | 3 037 | 826 | 2 809 |
| Holmes | 765 | 43 836 | 1.09 | 819 | 19.2 | 305 | 7.1 | 10 088 | 27.0 | 4 290 | 1 696 | 1 820 | 368 | 877 |
| Huron | 578 | 56 727 | 0.88 | 744 | 12.5 | 535 | 9.0 | 7 777 | 15.2 | 10 558 | 2 166 | 5 596 | 695 | 1 286 |
| Jackson | 325 | 31 774 | 0.89 | 445 | 13.4 | 351 | 10.6 | 4 338 | 15.2 | 6 683 | 1 402 | 4 083 | NA | NA |
| Jefferson | 2 212 | 67 725 | 0.93 | 676 | 9.8 | 965 | 14.0 | 7 932 | 14.3 | 15 743 | 5 363 | 7 922 | 1 610 | 2 428 |
| Knox | 3 485 | 55 865 | 0.83 | 743 | 12.1 | 591 | 9.6 | 8 011 | 16.3 | 11 111 | 3 337 | 6 060 | NA | NA |
| Lake | 2 786 | 209 904 | 0.83 | 2 301 | 10.0 | 2 259 | 9.8 | 25 790 | 13.6 | 44 882 | 16 012 | 19 503 | 4 348 | 1 984 |
| Lawrence | 669 | 52 022 | 0.56 | 721 | 11.5 | 688 | 11.0 | 7 869 | 15.0 | 13 561 | 2 661 | 7 488 | 1 316 | 2 189 |
| Licking | 3 448 | 146 454 | 0.76 | 1 976 | 11.8 | 1 412 | 8.4 | 19 538 | 13.9 | 28 692 | 10 934 | 11 265 | 4 952 | 3 102 |
| Logan | 450 | 45 397 | 0.97 | 557 | 12.2 | 488 | 10.7 | 5 500 | 14.2 | 8 538 | 2 331 | 5 171 | 1 691 | 3 872 |
| Lorain | 9 332 | 270 417 | 0.77 | 3 333 | 11.1 | 2 608 | 8.6 | 31 048 | 12.4 | 54 566 | 15 785 | 23 863 | 7 987 | 3 187 |
| Lucas | 10 715 | 460 989 | 1.10 | 5 867 | 13.3 | 4 223 | 9.6 | 57 994 | 15.4 | 74 903 | 26 643 | 35 092 | 17 028 | 4 225 |
| Madison | 5 238 | 39 923 | 0.83 | 487 | 11.2 | 361 | 8.3 | 5 204 | 15.8 | 6 805 | 3 312 | 3 001 | 972 | 2 255 |
| Mahoning | 7 925 | 240 792 | 1.01 | 2 406 | 10.1 | 2 963 | 12.5 | 27 349 | 14.4 | 50 768 | 22 495 | 19 913 | 9 461 | 3 995 |
| Marion | 5 457 | 67 496 | 1.04 | 822 | 12.4 | 672 | 10.1 | 7 549 | 14.5 | 12 584 | 4 049 | 6 494 | 4 132 | 6 209 |
| Medina | 1 198 | 146 355 | 0.71 | 1 793 | 10.3 | 1 240 | 7.2 | 16 289 | 11.1 | 28 267 | 10 780 | 10 730 | 1 253 | 883 |
| Meigs | 212 | 19 130 | 0.47 | 247 | 10.4 | 260 | 11.0 | 3 384 | 16.9 | 4 863 | 1 024 | 2 818 | 352 | 1 480 |
| Mercer | 439 | 38 094 | 0.86 | 566 | 13.9 | 374 | 9.2 | 4 619 | 13.5 | 7 445 | 2 024 | 4 423 | 938 | 2 297 |
| Miami | 1 055 | 96 627 | 0.88 | 1 196 | 11.6 | 920 | 8.9 | 11 955 | 13.9 | 19 558 | 6 807 | 8 864 | 3 155 | 3 076 |
| Monroe | 165 | 13 793 | 0.84 | 139 | 9.5 | 201 | 13.8 | 1 770 | 15.0 | 3 544 | 1 379 | 1 689 | 144 | 983 |
| Montgomery | 14 142 | 558 652 | 1.09 | 6 847 | 12.7 | 5 430 | 10.1 | 66 976 | 15.1 | 99 421 | 44 503 | 34 705 | 22 486 | 4 272 |
| Morgan | 188 | 12 621 | 0.58 | 151 | 10.0 | 155 | 10.3 | 1 991 | 16.0 | 2 939 | 820 | 1 634 | 170 | 1 128 |
| Morrow | 366 | 26 731 | 0.49 | 379 | 10.9 | 288 | 8.3 | 4 529 | 15.2 | 5 886 | 1 928 | 2 978 | 618 | 1 773 |
| Muskingum | 1 898 | 85 302 | 0.98 | 993 | 11.5 | 899 | 10.4 | 10 197 | 14.2 | 17 613 | 4 248 | 10 004 | 3 306 | 3 970 |
| Noble | 2 672 | 13 755 | 0.79 | 153 | 10.4 | 124 | 8.4 | 1 635 | 16.2 | 2 328 | 650 | 1 394 | NA | NA |

1. Per 1,000 estimated resident population. 2. Data for serious crimes have not been adjusted for underreporting; this may affect comparability between geographic areas and over time. 3. Per 100,000 population estimated by the FBI.

# Table B. States and Counties — Crime, Education, Money Income, and Poverty

| STATE County | Serious crimes known to police, 2011 (cont.)[1] Rate[2] Violent | Property | Education School enrollment and attainment, 2007–2011 Enrollment[3] Total | Percent private | Attainment[4] (percent) High school graduate or less | Bachelor's degree or more | Local government expenditures,[5] 2009–2010 Total current expenditures (mil dol) | Current expenditures per student (dollars) | Money income, 2007–2011 Per capita income[6] (dollars) | Households Median income Dollars | Percent change, 2000 to 2007–2011 (constant 2011 dollars) | Percent with income of $200,000 or more | Income and poverty, 2011 Median household income (dollars) | Percent below poverty level All persons | Children under 18 years | Children 5 to 17 years in families |
|---|---|---|---|---|---|---|---|---|---|---|---|---|---|---|---|---|
| | 46 | 47 | 48 | 49 | 50 | 51 | 52 | 53 | 54 | 55 | 56 | 57 | 58 | 59 | 60 | 61 |
| **NORTH DAKOTA—Cont'd** | | | | | | | | | | | | | | | | |
| Ward | 236 | 1 520 | 15 141 | 8.8 | 36.3 | 26.2 | 91.8 | 10 434 | 26 026 | 51 081 | 12.4 | 2.1 | 53 157 | 9.8 | 13.5 | 11.0 |
| Wells | 47 | 1 216 | 673 | 9.2 | 50.0 | 19.1 | 7.0 | 12 667 | 26 145 | 42 035 | -2.4 | 3.0 | 47 328 | 10.9 | 12.7 | 10.4 |
| Williams | 334 | 2 419 | 4 349 | 11.7 | 42.0 | 18.8 | 39.6 | 12 248 | 31 822 | 62 082 | 46.0 | 4.0 | 67 492 | 8.1 | 10.9 | 9.2 |
| **OHIO** | 307 | 3 355 | 3 056 969 | 18.2 | 47.5 | 24.5 | 19 438.7 | 11 018 | 25 618 | 48 071 | -13.1 | 2.8 | 45 803 | 16.3 | 23.9 | 21.5 |
| Adams | 18 | 447 | 6 531 | 8.2 | 69.5 | 10.9 | 51.9 | 10 510 | 18 182 | 34 232 | -13.5 | 0.8 | 34 778 | 22.5 | 33.7 | 31.3 |
| Allen | 469 | 3 659 | 28 494 | 18.3 | 54.4 | 15.7 | 161.0 | 10 479 | 21 878 | 43 323 | -13.4 | 1.5 | 41 453 | 19.2 | 29.2 | 27.3 |
| Ashland | 64 | 1 919 | 13 971 | 32.4 | 56.6 | 18.4 | 91.3 | 9 743 | 21 758 | 45 641 | -13.7 | 1.5 | 44 950 | 13.1 | 20.2 | 18.5 |
| Ashtabula | NA | NA | 24 404 | 12.9 | 60.9 | 13.1 | 161.9 | 10 559 | 20 030 | 41 501 | -13.7 | 0.8 | 38 683 | 20.3 | 29.1 | 26.9 |
| Athens | 89 | 2 508 | 29 088 | 2.6 | 46.1 | 28.4 | 99.4 | 12 962 | 17 312 | 33 546 | -9.1 | 1.6 | 33 943 | 35.0 | 31.3 | 28.4 |
| Auglaize | NA | NA | 11 374 | 10.4 | 54.5 | 16.1 | 80.8 | 10 118 | 26 323 | 52 838 | -9.8 | 1.7 | 51 130 | 9.9 | 13.9 | 11.5 |
| Belmont | 52 | 1 117 | 14 880 | 12.0 | 58.2 | 13.5 | 88.4 | 10 112 | 21 129 | 39 712 | -1.0 | 0.7 | 40 300 | 15.7 | 24.0 | 23.0 |
| Brown | 21 | 1 667 | 10 857 | 8.4 | 66.8 | 10.4 | 78.0 | 10 043 | 20 433 | 46 046 | -11.0 | 0.8 | 43 181 | 15.6 | 24.5 | 22.3 |
| Butler | 343 | 4 052 | 104 946 | 13.0 | 47.0 | 26.5 | 606.9 | 10 250 | 26 397 | 55 497 | -14.2 | 2.7 | 53 275 | 13.9 | 18.2 | 14.8 |
| Carroll | 76 | 697 | 6 535 | 13.6 | 64.5 | 12.0 | 31.8 | 8 824 | 21 772 | 43 323 | -9.6 | 0.8 | 40 896 | 16.4 | 26.9 | 23.5 |
| Champaign | 62 | 2 066 | 10 021 | 15.7 | 59.9 | 14.9 | 83.6 | 10 661 | 23 093 | 48 335 | -17.0 | 1.5 | 48 063 | 14.0 | 23.1 | 21.1 |
| Clark | 294 | 4 064 | 35 562 | 19.4 | 52.5 | 16.6 | 210.6 | 9 731 | 22 434 | 44 037 | -19.1 | 1.4 | 41 704 | 19.1 | 30.3 | 27.4 |
| Clermont | 99 | 3 321 | 50 381 | 18.2 | 47.7 | 25.4 | 271.1 | 9 834 | 28 639 | 60 219 | -9.7 | 4.1 | 55 963 | 10.9 | 15.8 | 14.2 |
| Clinton | 67 | 2 154 | 11 004 | 14.4 | 56.9 | 14.6 | 72.2 | 8 940 | 22 582 | 47 264 | -13.5 | 1.5 | 44 905 | 15.7 | 23.0 | 20.6 |
| Columbiana | 35 | 1 445 | 24 154 | 11.1 | 61.4 | 13.0 | 159.6 | 9 698 | 20 691 | 41 003 | -11.3 | 1.0 | 42 091 | 17.1 | 27.2 | 25.7 |
| Coshocton | 54 | 2 397 | 8 431 | 16.2 | 64.0 | 11.5 | 51.3 | 9 852 | 20 084 | 40 727 | -13.1 | 0.7 | 40 282 | 17.0 | 29.0 | 26.7 |
| Crawford | NA | NA | 10 174 | 12.2 | 61.8 | 11.0 | 66.8 | 9 534 | 20 823 | 41 336 | -15.5 | 0.7 | 39 679 | 17.3 | 28.7 | 24.7 |
| Cuyahoga | 540 | 3 168 | 333 913 | 25.7 | 42.9 | 28.6 | 2 353.4 | 12 829 | 26 810 | 44 088 | -16.6 | 3.3 | 41 609 | 18.8 | 29.0 | 27.4 |
| Darke | 96 | 1 188 | 12 578 | 10.7 | 62.6 | 10.9 | 80.5 | 9 257 | 22 095 | 45 055 | -15.1 | 1.3 | 42 065 | 12.9 | 19.1 | 17.0 |
| Defiance | 59 | 2 375 | 9 968 | 16.6 | 56.2 | 16.5 | 56.6 | 8 681 | 22 862 | 46 864 | -22.8 | 1.4 | 49 360 | 11.7 | 19.1 | 16.3 |
| Delaware | 107 | 1 861 | 50 342 | 26.0 | 24.5 | 50.0 | 253.0 | 10 015 | 41 384 | 90 022 | -0.9 | 11.1 | 86 980 | 4.5 | 5.8 | 5.1 |
| Erie | 245 | 2 572 | 17 846 | 14.0 | 51.7 | 20.0 | 166.5 | 13 402 | 25 704 | 47 466 | -17.8 | 2.5 | 46 613 | 12.8 | 21.4 | 19.3 |
| Fairfield | 156 | 3 100 | 39 425 | 16.8 | 45.3 | 24.9 | 236.1 | 9 450 | 26 693 | 58 249 | -10.0 | 2.4 | 58 829 | 11.3 | 15.7 | 13.0 |
| Fayette | 162 | 4 782 | 6 641 | 10.4 | 63.2 | 13.4 | 43.0 | 8 955 | 20 523 | 39 263 | -20.8 | 1.1 | 36 684 | 18.0 | 25.2 | 23.9 |
| Franklin | 486 | 5 128 | 330 094 | 17.0 | 36.9 | 35.5 | 2 281.6 | 11 895 | 27 646 | 50 045 | -13.3 | 3.7 | 47 174 | 18.8 | 26.5 | 24.7 |
| Fulton | 66 | 1 699 | 11 035 | 10.0 | 54.2 | 15.1 | 102.2 | 12 749 | 23 718 | 51 851 | -12.9 | 0.8 | 49 038 | 9.8 | 14.8 | 13.4 |
| Gallia | 88 | 3 510 | 7 764 | 12.9 | 61.1 | 14.5 | 57.1 | 12 531 | 20 782 | 36 918 | -9.4 | 1.4 | 36 441 | 21.2 | 33.0 | 31.7 |
| Geauga | 24 | 490 | 23 973 | 25.0 | 37.5 | 34.3 | 139.4 | 11 512 | 33 947 | 66 229 | -18.5 | 6.9 | 66 088 | 8.0 | 12.3 | 10.6 |
| Greene | 119 | 2 833 | 51 616 | 22.8 | 35.4 | 34.7 | 249.6 | 11 124 | 29 101 | 57 553 | -12.4 | 3.4 | 56 683 | 15.6 | 19.1 | 17.4 |
| Guernsey | 146 | 2 786 | 9 352 | 12.9 | 61.9 | 11.5 | 57.9 | 11 003 | 19 538 | 38 179 | -6.1 | 0.9 | 36 348 | 19.4 | 32.8 | 28.5 |
| Hamilton | 474 | 4 489 | 220 309 | 24.5 | 39.8 | 32.9 | 1 370.6 | 12 192 | 29 197 | 49 218 | -11.0 | 4.4 | 46 125 | 18.5 | 27.7 | 24.8 |
| Hancock | 128 | 3 222 | 19 329 | 21.4 | 47.3 | 24.2 | 145.1 | 10 169 | 25 314 | 49 888 | -15.7 | 2.0 | 48 258 | 13.3 | 18.0 | 14.3 |
| Hardin | 37 | 2 886 | 9 758 | 34.7 | 65.1 | 13.9 | 46.2 | 10 215 | 19 109 | 39 945 | -14.1 | 1.0 | 37 914 | 19.8 | 24.6 | 22.3 |
| Harrison | 62 | 1 326 | 3 396 | 8.3 | 65.4 | 8.6 | 17.6 | 10 890 | 19 927 | 36 920 | -9.8 | 1.0 | 37 057 | 17.4 | 27.5 | 25.8 |
| Henry | 49 | 2 872 | 7 459 | 14.5 | 55.8 | 14.4 | 61.4 | 13 420 | 23 256 | 48 932 | -15.0 | 1.4 | 48 859 | 10.4 | 15.3 | 13.7 |
| Highland | 164 | 3 138 | 10 794 | 8.3 | 63.6 | 10.4 | 67.0 | 8 711 | 19 202 | 40 423 | -15.2 | 0.9 | 36 865 | 21.5 | 31.1 | 26.9 |
| Hocking | 48 | 2 762 | 7 132 | 9.8 | 59.2 | 12.1 | 37.9 | 9 530 | 20 123 | 42 227 | -8.7 | 0.5 | 42 491 | 17.3 | 27.5 | 24.7 |
| Holmes | 60 | 817 | 9 411 | 36.4 | 76.3 | 9.3 | 39.3 | 9 032 | 17 176 | 44 746 | -10.3 | 1.4 | 45 893 | 15.3 | 23.9 | 21.9 |
| Huron | 31 | 1 255 | 15 146 | 12.9 | 63.0 | 12.3 | 106.1 | 9 057 | 22 005 | 48 358 | -11.7 | 1.0 | 48 196 | 14.6 | 22.2 | 20.2 |
| Jackson | NA | NA | 7 740 | 11.3 | 62.5 | 14.0 | 50.4 | 9 261 | 19 835 | 37 243 | -10.0 | 1.4 | 39 144 | 20.4 | 30.1 | 28.2 |
| Jefferson | 176 | 2 252 | 16 170 | 20.8 | 56.9 | 14.2 | 104.9 | 10 999 | 21 587 | 39 453 | -5.3 | 1.0 | 41 103 | 16.8 | 27.7 | 25.2 |
| Knox | NA | NA | 16 390 | 28.1 | 54.2 | 20.0 | 88.3 | 10 779 | 22 628 | 48 734 | -7.2 | 1.5 | 50 929 | 14.5 | 23.0 | 21.7 |
| Lake | 205 | 1 779 | 56 629 | 19.0 | 43.5 | 24.8 | 378.6 | 11 112 | 28 900 | 55 968 | -15.0 | 2.6 | 53 016 | 10.2 | 14.4 | 13.0 |
| Lawrence | 153 | 2 036 | 14 508 | 7.0 | 60.7 | 13.8 | 110.6 | 10 968 | 19 832 | 38 639 | -1.7 | 0.9 | 37 666 | 18.9 | 28.7 | 27.2 |
| Licking | 311 | 2 791 | 44 212 | 18.2 | 49.4 | 22.4 | 265.3 | 9 967 | 25 977 | 54 699 | -8.2 | 2.2 | 54 298 | 13.0 | 19.5 | 17.3 |
| Logan | 137 | 3 734 | 10 871 | 9.4 | 62.6 | 14.4 | 81.1 | 11 597 | 22 898 | 47 378 | -15.4 | 1.4 | 48 011 | 13.6 | 20.8 | 18.7 |
| Lorain | 241 | 2 946 | 79 879 | 19.0 | 47.7 | 21.0 | 475.3 | 10 179 | 25 558 | 52 194 | -14.2 | 2.5 | 48 733 | 15.3 | 24.2 | 21.0 |
| Lucas | 759 | 3 465 | 124 981 | 17.7 | 45.2 | 23.0 | 821.1 | 11 264 | 23 857 | 41 949 | -18.2 | 2.5 | 38 798 | 23.3 | 33.0 | 28.6 |
| Madison | 79 | 2 176 | 10 438 | 12.9 | 55.4 | 16.4 | 77.7 | 11 235 | 24 522 | 54 366 | -8.9 | 3.0 | 54 107 | 11.8 | 17.8 | 16.4 |
| Mahoning | 313 | 3 682 | 58 730 | 14.2 | 52.5 | 20.9 | 352.6 | 9 947 | 23 261 | 40 570 | -14.8 | 1.6 | 39 447 | 17.7 | 29.8 | 27.6 |
| Marion | 180 | 6 029 | 14 881 | 10.4 | 59.8 | 12.4 | 111.2 | 9 617 | 20 430 | 41 337 | -20.9 | 1.1 | 42 141 | 18.4 | 28.3 | 26.4 |
| Medina | 92 | 791 | 46 204 | 16.9 | 40.0 | 30.1 | 279.7 | 9 855 | 30 528 | 65 578 | -13.0 | 4.1 | 60 527 | 8.9 | 11.8 | 9.1 |
| Meigs | 67 | 1 413 | 5 345 | 9.4 | 62.7 | 10.9 | 35.4 | 9 817 | 18 159 | 33 708 | -8.5 | 0.7 | 33 520 | 22.4 | 34.7 | 30.8 |
| Mercer | 78 | 2 218 | 10 271 | 9.5 | 59.6 | 14.5 | 81.3 | 9 686 | 22 689 | 51 236 | -11.2 | 1.3 | 47 994 | 9.1 | 12.4 | 11.1 |
| Miami | 65 | 3 010 | 24 888 | 15.5 | 51.1 | 19.7 | 173.6 | 11 163 | 25 079 | 51 438 | -13.6 | 1.4 | 48 103 | 13.9 | 21.1 | 18.6 |
| Monroe | 55 | 928 | 3 112 | 10.1 | 66.6 | 9.0 | 25.7 | 9 974 | 20 473 | 38 811 | -5.7 | 1.0 | 39 007 | 16.8 | 27.5 | 24.3 |
| Montgomery | 409 | 3 863 | 151 022 | 22.7 | 41.8 | 24.4 | 901.2 | 11 484 | 25 225 | 44 585 | -17.8 | 2.2 | 41 001 | 18.3 | 27.5 | 25.4 |
| Morgan | 33 | 1 095 | 3 498 | 8.7 | 64.3 | 8.5 | 20.1 | 9 447 | 19 731 | 35 855 | -8.0 | 0.6 | 35 173 | 20.9 | 31.3 | 27.5 |
| Morrow | 32 | 1 742 | 8 396 | 18.7 | 59.4 | 13.9 | 50.1 | 9 323 | 22 060 | 50 252 | -9.0 | 0.5 | 47 431 | 13.7 | 23.1 | 20.2 |
| Muskingum | 192 | 3 778 | 21 762 | 14.1 | 59.0 | 13.9 | 162.2 | 10 676 | 21 069 | 40 590 | -14.6 | 1.1 | 38 652 | 18.9 | 29.9 | 26.8 |
| Noble | NA | NA | 2 924 | 9.6 | 72.4 | 7.9 | 17.7 | 10 057 | 18 790 | 40 239 | -9.5 | 0.6 | 41 151 | 18.1 | 23.2 | 21.4 |

1. Data for serious crimes have not been adjusted for underreporting; this may affect comparability between geographic areas and over time.    2. Per 100,000 population estimated by the FBI.    3. All persons 3 years old and over enrolled in nursery school through college.    4. Persons 25 years old and over.    5. Elementary and secondary education expenditures.    6. Based on population estimated by the American Community Survey, 2007–2011.

# Table B. States and Counties — **Personal Income**

| STATE County | Total (mil dol) | Percent change, 2010–2011 | Per capita[1] Dollars | Rank | Wages and salaries[2] (mil dol) | Proprietors' income (mil dol) | Dividends, interest, and rent (mil dol) | Transfer payments (mil dol) Total | Government payments to individuals Total | Social Security | Medical payments | Income maintenance | Unemployment insurance |
|---|---|---|---|---|---|---|---|---|---|---|---|---|---|
| | 62 | 63 | 64 | 65 | 66 | 67 | 68 | 69 | 70 | 71 | 72 | 73 | 74 |
| **NORTH DAKOTA—Cont'd** | | | | | | | | | | | | | |
| Ward | 2 946 | 11.3 | 45 976 | 337 | 2 132 | 217 | 400 | 386 | 373 | 118 | 155 | 36 | 7 |
| Wells | 251 | 23.1 | 59 198 | 77 | 71 | 103 | 43 | 42 | 41 | 15 | 20 | 3 | 1 |
| Williams | 1 978 | 60.1 | 81 170 | 6 | 1 982 | 58 | 205 | 143 | 138 | 51 | 59 | 11 | 1 |
| **OHIO** | 436 818 | 5.4 | 37 836 | X | 283 910 | 34 430 | 58 789 | 93 528 | 90 974 | 28 633 | 38 965 | 11 120 | 3 350 |
| Adams | 766 | 5.5 | 26 909 | 2 774 | 270 | 75 | 82 | 279 | 273 | 73 | 131 | 42 | 10 |
| Allen | 3 369 | 5.2 | 31 750 | 1 941 | 2 580 | 340 | 452 | 869 | 845 | 283 | 333 | 106 | 32 |
| Ashland | 1 564 | 4.9 | 29 422 | 2 391 | 802 | 123 | 220 | 383 | 371 | 142 | 142 | 37 | 18 |
| Ashtabula | 3 176 | 7.0 | 31 339 | 2 033 | 1 402 | 173 | 341 | 992 | 969 | 279 | 461 | 115 | 33 |
| Athens | 1 768 | 3.8 | 27 296 | 2 718 | 1 054 | 92 | 234 | 500 | 485 | 98 | 189 | 73 | 17 |
| Auglaize | 1 772 | 6.7 | 38 647 | 890 | 894 | 140 | 280 | 341 | 331 | 116 | 150 | 25 | 12 |
| Belmont | 2 195 | 6.4 | 31 286 | 2 047 | 1 018 | 137 | 298 | 642 | 627 | 209 | 276 | 68 | 19 |
| Brown | 1 363 | 5.0 | 30 492 | 2 202 | 380 | 144 | 142 | 379 | 369 | 119 | 163 | 42 | 15 |
| Butler | 13 538 | 4.5 | 36 590 | 1 125 | 7 950 | 960 | 1 669 | 2 578 | 2 496 | 838 | 1 015 | 281 | 107 |
| Carroll | 778 | 3.0 | 27 044 | 2 757 | 234 | 102 | 100 | 224 | 217 | 83 | 86 | 24 | 10 |
| Champaign | 1 246 | 6.9 | 31 300 | 2 043 | 455 | 138 | 134 | 296 | 287 | 104 | 116 | 30 | 12 |
| Clark | 4 788 | 4.7 | 34 777 | 1 408 | 2 282 | 253 | 580 | 1 287 | 1 256 | 385 | 564 | 157 | 41 |
| Clermont | 7 177 | 4.4 | 36 038 | 1 205 | 2 759 | 588 | 841 | 1 321 | 1 277 | 472 | 498 | 125 | 59 |
| Clinton | 1 343 | 3.3 | 32 027 | 1 880 | 820 | 163 | 166 | 333 | 324 | 103 | 141 | 36 | 16 |
| Columbiana | 3 291 | 7.9 | 30 590 | 2 182 | 1 324 | 193 | 368 | 968 | 944 | 314 | 414 | 106 | 36 |
| Coshocton | 1 099 | 4.7 | 29 730 | 2 333 | 507 | 148 | 131 | 315 | 306 | 104 | 132 | 37 | 12 |
| Crawford | 1 357 | 7.3 | 31 286 | 2 047 | 598 | 131 | 182 | 406 | 396 | 138 | 170 | 44 | 15 |
| Cuyahoga | 55 556 | 4.8 | 43 735 | 454 | 45 028 | 6 102 | 8 213 | 11 888 | 11 607 | 3 270 | 5 373 | 1 647 | 354 |
| Darke | 1 813 | 6.1 | 34 325 | 1 468 | 779 | 224 | 256 | 392 | 380 | 152 | 147 | 35 | 16 |
| Defiance | 1 296 | 6.1 | 33 323 | 1 649 | 768 | 140 | 156 | 306 | 297 | 114 | 117 | 31 | 12 |
| Delaware | 10 428 | 9.1 | 58 470 | 81 | 4 815 | 667 | 1 180 | 923 | 884 | 314 | 272 | 60 | 36 |
| Erie | 2 929 | 5.1 | 38 161 | 949 | 1 717 | 243 | 441 | 686 | 669 | 241 | 280 | 64 | 24 |
| Fairfield | 4 937 | 4.4 | 33 569 | 1 588 | 1 799 | 351 | 605 | 992 | 959 | 333 | 391 | 109 | 37 |
| Fayette | 993 | 6.6 | 34 264 | 1 477 | 449 | 136 | 111 | 256 | 249 | 74 | 114 | 32 | 10 |
| Franklin | 46 735 | 4.9 | 39 646 | 787 | 42 149 | 4 269 | 5 597 | 8 294 | 8 033 | 2 035 | 3 557 | 1 286 | 306 |
| Fulton | 1 497 | 6.0 | 35 211 | 1 338 | 815 | 188 | 194 | 319 | 309 | 112 | 126 | 25 | 14 |
| Gallia | 981 | 3.0 | 31 680 | 1 959 | 541 | 58 | 114 | 341 | 334 | 81 | 166 | 47 | 9 |
| Geauga | 4 770 | 5.9 | 51 165 | 182 | 1 644 | 288 | 808 | 608 | 588 | 256 | 215 | 30 | 21 |
| Greene | 6 162 | 5.4 | 37 842 | 991 | 5 079 | 408 | 906 | 1 032 | 997 | 351 | 360 | 99 | 44 |
| Guernsey | 1 196 | 6.0 | 29 955 | 2 298 | 631 | 79 | 137 | 384 | 375 | 112 | 175 | 48 | 13 |
| Hamilton | 37 522 | 4.6 | 46 881 | 306 | 33 599 | 3 286 | 6 732 | 6 623 | 6 446 | 1 856 | 2 839 | 862 | 229 |
| Hancock | 2 966 | 7.0 | 39 523 | 802 | 2 241 | 276 | 393 | 534 | 517 | 193 | 179 | 49 | 20 |
| Hardin | 937 | 8.2 | 29 271 | 2 414 | 374 | 130 | 102 | 228 | 221 | 78 | 89 | 24 | 9 |
| Harrison | 451 | 5.2 | 28 485 | 2 541 | 143 | 17 | 51 | 146 | 142 | 46 | 64 | 16 | 5 |
| Henry | 996 | 7.3 | 35 491 | 1 296 | 531 | 112 | 120 | 218 | 212 | 77 | 93 | 17 | 10 |
| Highland | 1 200 | 4.6 | 27 630 | 2 667 | 430 | 121 | 147 | 385 | 376 | 112 | 163 | 48 | 15 |
| Hocking | 829 | 4.2 | 28 208 | 2 587 | 281 | 40 | 94 | 263 | 256 | 78 | 117 | 34 | 9 |
| Holmes | 1 177 | 7.8 | 27 523 | 2 682 | 712 | 305 | 160 | 183 | 174 | 57 | 71 | 20 | 8 |
| Huron | 1 881 | 5.2 | 31 612 | 1 973 | 1 070 | 179 | 252 | 477 | 464 | 153 | 187 | 49 | 22 |
| Jackson | 936 | 3.7 | 28 212 | 2 583 | 447 | 57 | 109 | 304 | 296 | 85 | 128 | 48 | 10 |
| Jefferson | 2 185 | 4.1 | 31 742 | 1 945 | 1 098 | 114 | 259 | 713 | 698 | 231 | 306 | 80 | 24 |
| Knox | 1 956 | 6.6 | 31 917 | 1 901 | 970 | 149 | 243 | 496 | 483 | 154 | 226 | 47 | 17 |
| Lake | 9 276 | 5.4 | 40 351 | 710 | 5 323 | 411 | 1 161 | 1 811 | 1 760 | 674 | 718 | 126 | 62 |
| Lawrence | 1 912 | 4.7 | 30 595 | 2 178 | 523 | 60 | 172 | 648 | 634 | 179 | 283 | 93 | 18 |
| Licking | 6 270 | 8.5 | 37 491 | 1 026 | 2 548 | 334 | 697 | 1 203 | 1 166 | 400 | 463 | 129 | 44 |
| Logan | 1 574 | 4.6 | 34 452 | 1 441 | 943 | 139 | 173 | 362 | 351 | 122 | 146 | 39 | 14 |
| Lorain | 10 943 | 6.2 | 36 283 | 1 173 | 5 070 | 489 | 1 394 | 2 415 | 2 349 | 800 | 950 | 274 | 94 |
| Lucas | 15 796 | 4.5 | 35 900 | 1 225 | 11 354 | 1 443 | 1 931 | 4 059 | 3 961 | 1 062 | 1 834 | 600 | 134 |
| Madison | 1 533 | 6.7 | 35 311 | 1 323 | 687 | 221 | 156 | 298 | 288 | 93 | 128 | 31 | 11 |
| Mahoning | 8 307 | 5.1 | 35 012 | 1 372 | 4 585 | 689 | 1 246 | 2 359 | 2 307 | 721 | 1 010 | 292 | 91 |
| Marion | 2 131 | 5.0 | 32 179 | 1 846 | 1 222 | 198 | 227 | 566 | 551 | 172 | 236 | 73 | 19 |
| Medina | 7 077 | 6.6 | 40 843 | 672 | 2 867 | 360 | 858 | 1 124 | 1 086 | 429 | 428 | 71 | 43 |
| Meigs | 602 | 4.2 | 25 404 | 2 938 | 152 | 35 | 61 | 218 | 212 | 63 | 93 | 33 | 8 |
| Mercer | 1 551 | 8.6 | 37 992 | 972 | 793 | 203 | 241 | 273 | 264 | 106 | 104 | 22 | 9 |
| Miami | 3 808 | 6.0 | 37 021 | 1 074 | 1 903 | 210 | 514 | 776 | 754 | 289 | 295 | 68 | 30 |
| Monroe | 441 | 6.0 | 30 270 | 2 244 | 194 | 25 | 51 | 138 | 135 | 49 | 57 | 15 | 4 |
| Montgomery | 20 259 | 4.7 | 37 684 | 1 006 | 14 016 | 1 235 | 3 092 | 4 788 | 4 670 | 1 403 | 1 985 | 589 | 160 |
| Morgan | 368 | 6.0 | 24 460 | 3 007 | 109 | 28 | 44 | 127 | 124 | 40 | 53 | 16 | 5 |
| Morrow | 1 068 | 7.1 | 30 646 | 2 164 | 223 | 109 | 96 | 239 | 232 | 85 | 88 | 28 | 10 |
| Muskingum | 2 685 | 5.5 | 31 140 | 2 074 | 1 539 | 140 | 342 | 779 | 760 | 242 | 314 | 109 | 29 |
| Noble | 304 | 5.2 | 20 686 | 3 098 | 125 | 19 | 37 | 93 | 90 | 32 | 36 | 11 | 5 |

1. Based on the resident population estimated as of July 1 of the year shown.   2. Includes supplements to wages and salaries.

# Table B. States and Counties — Earnings, Social Security, and Housing

| STATE County | Earnings, 2011 | | | | | | | | | Social Security beneficiaries, December 2011 | | Housing units, 2010 | | |
| | Total (mil dol) | Percent by selected industries | | | | | | | | Number | Rate[2] | Supplemental Security Income recipients, December 2011 | Total | Percent change, 2000–2010 |
| | | Farm | Goods-related[1] | | Service-related and health | | | | Govern-ment | | | | | |
| | | | Total | Manu-facturing | Information and professional and technical services | Retail trade | Finance, insurance, and real estate | Health care and social services | | | | | | |
| | 75 | 76 | 77 | 78 | 79 | 80 | 81 | 82 | 83 | 84 | 85 | 86 | 87 | 88 |
| NORTH DAKOTA—Cont'd | | | | | | | | | | | | | | |
| Ward | 2 349 | 0.8 | 15.1 | 1.6 | 3.8 | 7.0 | 5.7 | 11.9 | 34.4 | 9 405 | 147 | 595 | 26 744 | 6.6 |
| Wells | 174 | 53.7 | D | 0.9 | 0.8 | D | 3.1 | 7.5 | 7.6 | 1 265 | 299 | 67 | 2 481 | -6.1 |
| Williams | 2 040 | -0.1 | 52.4 | 1.3 | 3.9 | 3.8 | 5.4 | D | 4.5 | 3 940 | 162 | 223 | 10 464 | 8.1 |
| OHIO | 318 341 | 1.1 | 20.7 | 15.3 | 9.6 | 6.2 | 7.6 | 13.0 | 15.7 | 2 166 271 | 188 | 295 042 | 5 127 508 | 7.2 |
| Adams | 345 | 4.1 | D | 16.6 | D | 10.3 | 2.8 | D | 22.5 | 6 550 | 230 | 1 739 | 12 978 | 9.8 |
| Allen | 2 921 | 2.2 | D | 24.8 | 3.7 | 7.1 | 3.0 | 19.8 | 13.3 | 21 615 | 204 | 2 961 | 44 999 | 1.7 |
| Ashland | 925 | 2.6 | 26.0 | 19.8 | 7.8 | 7.1 | 2.8 | D | 15.7 | 10 780 | 203 | 747 | 22 141 | 6.3 |
| Ashtabula | 1 575 | 1.5 | 32.5 | 25.9 | 3.4 | 7.6 | 2.7 | 14.9 | 16.6 | 22 105 | 218 | 3 064 | 46 099 | 5.3 |
| Athens | 1 145 | 0.2 | D | D | 4.1 | 8.0 | 3.4 | 12.1 | 52.1 | 8 940 | 138 | 2 431 | 26 385 | 6.0 |
| Auglaize | 1 034 | 7.4 | D | 39.9 | D | 5.6 | 2.7 | 8.7 | 12.0 | 8 605 | 188 | 481 | 19 585 | 6.0 |
| Belmont | 1 156 | 0.3 | 25.3 | 5.4 | D | 10.9 | 6.6 | 14.6 | 17.9 | 16 405 | 234 | 2 291 | 32 452 | 3.9 |
| Brown | 524 | 8.3 | D | 7.3 | 3.4 | 7.0 | 2.8 | D | 21.5 | 9 675 | 217 | 1 260 | 19 301 | 12.3 |
| Butler | 8 910 | 0.3 | D | 17.8 | 4.0 | 7.2 | 9.9 | 10.9 | 13.8 | 61 175 | 165 | 6 752 | 148 273 | 14.3 |
| Carroll | 335 | 7.7 | D | 20.0 | 2.7 | 10.2 | 2.9 | D | 14.8 | 6 415 | 223 | 605 | 13 698 | 5.2 |
| Champaign | 593 | 11.5 | D | 28.4 | 4.7 | 6.4 | 3.0 | D | 17.4 | 7 865 | 198 | 611 | 16 755 | 5.4 |
| Clark | 2 535 | 2.1 | 20.5 | 16.8 | 3.7 | 7.0 | 6.5 | 15.7 | 15.8 | 29 770 | 216 | 3 777 | 61 419 | 0.6 |
| Clermont | 3 347 | 0.5 | D | 11.2 | 10.1 | 9.4 | 10.9 | 9.2 | 13.8 | 34 340 | 172 | 3 019 | 80 656 | 16.5 |
| Clinton | 983 | 6.4 | 25.3 | 22.6 | 3.3 | 5.6 | 4.6 | D | 14.2 | 8 325 | 199 | 897 | 18 133 | 9.4 |
| Columbiana | 1 517 | 1.7 | 24.4 | 18.6 | 2.7 | 9.9 | 3.1 | 15.0 | 19.0 | 24 295 | 226 | 3 094 | 47 088 | 2.2 |
| Coshocton | 655 | 4.6 | 34.2 | 24.3 | D | 6.9 | 2.8 | 11.1 | 12.7 | 8 250 | 223 | 937 | 16 545 | 2.7 |
| Crawford | 730 | 9.7 | D | 26.7 | 3.3 | 6.3 | 6.0 | D | 14.8 | 10 645 | 245 | 1 136 | 20 167 | -0.1 |
| Cuyahoga | 51 130 | 0.0 | D | 11.9 | 12.8 | 4.5 | 11.0 | 14.6 | 13.9 | 245 075 | 193 | 48 696 | 621 763 | 0.8 |
| Darke | 1 003 | 9.1 | D | 22.5 | D | 6.5 | 4.5 | 10.4 | 11.8 | 11 640 | 220 | 812 | 22 730 | 5.3 |
| Defiance | 908 | 5.9 | 35.9 | 32.5 | 3.4 | 9.2 | 5.2 | D | 12.2 | 8 455 | 217 | 712 | 16 729 | 4.3 |
| Delaware | 5 482 | 0.7 | D | 7.5 | 29.9 | 6.8 | 12.7 | 6.9 | 8.9 | 21 830 | 122 | 1 146 | 66 378 | 56.6 |
| Erie | 1 961 | 0.8 | D | 22.5 | 3.3 | 7.1 | 3.4 | 14.5 | 16.5 | 17 550 | 229 | 1 508 | 37 845 | 5.4 |
| Fairfield | 2 150 | 1.9 | D | 13.5 | 4.7 | 8.9 | 4.4 | 16.3 | 18.3 | 25 620 | 174 | 2 404 | 58 687 | 22.4 |
| Fayette | 585 | 10.8 | 22.2 | 17.5 | D | 12.1 | 4.8 | D | 15.3 | 6 195 | 214 | 926 | 12 693 | 6.6 |
| Franklin | 46 418 | 0.0 | 10.6 | 6.1 | 13.3 | 5.9 | 11.4 | 11.3 | 18.5 | 157 450 | 134 | 30 156 | 527 186 | 11.9 |
| Fulton | 1 003 | 7.0 | D | 35.0 | 2.0 | 5.5 | 2.8 | D | 13.5 | 8 310 | 195 | 467 | 17 407 | 7.2 |
| Gallia | 599 | 0.9 | D | 5.4 | D | 7.7 | 4.5 | D | 17.1 | 6 900 | 223 | 1 656 | 13 925 | 3.2 |
| Geauga | 1 932 | 0.5 | D | 23.7 | 5.3 | 7.8 | 4.2 | 9.5 | 12.4 | 17 290 | 185 | 749 | 36 574 | 11.5 |
| Greene | 5 487 | 0.8 | D | 4.6 | 15.9 | 5.5 | 3.0 | 5.5 | 50.2 | 26 890 | 165 | 2 082 | 68 241 | 17.2 |
| Guernsey | 710 | 1.5 | D | 23.0 | D | 8.2 | 3.3 | 15.0 | 18.8 | 9 415 | 236 | 1 569 | 19 193 | 2.2 |
| Hamilton | 36 885 | 0.0 | D | 11.8 | 12.9 | 4.3 | 9.2 | 13.9 | 10.5 | 139 095 | 174 | 22 717 | 377 364 | 1.1 |
| Hancock | 2 517 | 2.5 | D | 26.1 | 5.3 | 6.5 | 2.6 | 10.6 | 7.9 | 14 195 | 189 | 1 073 | 33 174 | 11.4 |
| Hardin | 504 | 19.2 | 23.2 | 20.9 | 2.3 | 5.8 | 2.7 | D | 14.7 | 6 085 | 190 | 663 | 13 100 | 1.5 |
| Harrison | 160 | 2.3 | 37.0 | 14.6 | 2.3 | 4.4 | 2.9 | D | 22.2 | 3 765 | 238 | 526 | 8 170 | 6.4 |
| Henry | 644 | 10.5 | D | 30.2 | 2.1 | 6.6 | 3.3 | 7.8 | 17.3 | 5 760 | 205 | 330 | 11 963 | 2.9 |
| Highland | 551 | 9.6 | 21.9 | 16.2 | D | 11.6 | 4.9 | 10.0 | 23.6 | 9 500 | 219 | 1 349 | 19 380 | 10.2 |
| Hocking | 321 | 0.7 | 25.8 | 15.7 | 2.6 | 8.2 | 4.1 | D | 32.6 | 6 435 | 219 | 1 001 | 13 417 | 10.5 |
| Holmes | 1 017 | 6.7 | 46.0 | 29.6 | D | 7.1 | 2.7 | D | 8.7 | 4 540 | 106 | 365 | 13 666 | 11.3 |
| Huron | 1 249 | 5.0 | 39.2 | 30.1 | 3.1 | 5.3 | 2.7 | 10.4 | 11.5 | 11 630 | 195 | 1 105 | 25 196 | 6.8 |
| Jackson | 504 | 1.0 | 38.1 | 29.3 | 2.2 | 9.2 | 3.2 | 11.9 | 16.8 | 7 275 | 219 | 1 652 | 14 587 | 4.9 |
| Jefferson | 1 212 | 0.3 | D | 9.4 | 5.0 | 7.4 | 2.7 | D | 14.8 | 17 545 | 255 | 2 598 | 32 826 | -1.4 |
| Knox | 1 120 | 2.8 | D | 29.3 | 3.6 | 6.7 | 2.7 | 12.0 | 13.4 | 12 105 | 198 | 1 151 | 25 118 | 15.3 |
| Lake | 5 734 | 0.5 | D | 31.1 | 5.6 | 7.2 | 3.7 | 10.1 | 12.6 | 47 240 | 205 | 2 545 | 101 202 | 8.3 |
| Lawrence | 583 | 0.2 | D | D | 3.1 | 10.6 | 3.3 | 15.2 | 26.8 | 14 805 | 237 | 3 660 | 27 603 | 1.5 |
| Licking | 2 882 | 1.8 | 20.0 | 12.8 | 6.8 | 11.3 | 7.9 | 11.5 | 17.0 | 31 130 | 186 | 3 063 | 69 291 | 17.8 |
| Logan | 1 083 | 3.7 | 45.2 | 41.4 | 3.6 | 5.1 | 2.4 | 8.2 | 11.9 | 9 280 | 203 | 767 | 23 181 | 7.5 |
| Lorain | 5 559 | 0.8 | 29.4 | 24.6 | 4.1 | 7.9 | 3.8 | 12.1 | 18.5 | 58 500 | 194 | 6 757 | 127 036 | 14.1 |
| Lucas | 12 797 | 0.1 | 20.1 | 13.9 | 8.2 | 7.4 | 5.8 | 17.9 | 15.3 | 80 810 | 184 | 16 990 | 202 630 | 3.2 |
| Madison | 908 | 10.3 | 25.8 | 20.9 | 5.1 | 7.5 | 2.2 | D | 21.1 | 7 215 | 166 | 646 | 15 939 | 10.7 |
| Mahoning | 5 274 | 0.3 | 17.1 | 10.3 | 6.5 | 8.8 | 5.3 | 17.2 | 17.2 | 55 385 | 233 | 8 385 | 111 833 | 0.1 |
| Marion | 1 420 | 4.7 | D | 26.0 | 5.9 | 6.4 | 3.3 | 15.5 | 18.5 | 13 690 | 207 | 2 178 | 27 834 | 5.8 |
| Medina | 3 227 | 0.5 | 25.5 | 17.4 | 6.3 | 9.0 | 4.3 | 9.8 | 13.0 | 30 125 | 174 | 1 321 | 69 181 | 21.8 |
| Meigs | 187 | 7.3 | 20.2 | 2.8 | D | 9.5 | 3.6 | D | 28.2 | 5 325 | 225 | 1 226 | 11 191 | 3.8 |
| Mercer | 995 | 13.1 | D | 27.7 | D | 7.1 | 4.3 | D | 14.2 | 7 985 | 196 | 474 | 17 633 | 11.1 |
| Miami | 2 114 | 3.0 | D | 30.3 | D | 7.2 | 3.2 | 9.9 | 13.5 | 21 315 | 207 | 1 582 | 44 256 | 9.1 |
| Monroe | 219 | 2.0 | D | D | 1.4 | 4.8 | D | D | 17.1 | 3 910 | 268 | 549 | 7 567 | 4.9 |
| Montgomery | 15 251 | 0.2 | 15.8 | 11.7 | 11.9 | 5.2 | 6.6 | 18.7 | 17.2 | 106 050 | 197 | 15 296 | 254 775 | 2.5 |
| Morgan | 138 | 3.4 | 29.3 | 23.7 | D | 6.6 | D | 9.4 | 23.2 | 3 320 | 221 | 532 | 7 892 | 1.6 |
| Morrow | 332 | 18.8 | D | 14.5 | D | 6.4 | 2.8 | D | 24.8 | 6 610 | 190 | 618 | 14 155 | 16.7 |
| Muskingum | 1 679 | 1.2 | 20.4 | 11.8 | 4.3 | 9.0 | 3.8 | 21.4 | 16.0 | 19 840 | 230 | 3 158 | 38 074 | 8.3 |
| Noble | 144 | 1.2 | D | 5.0 | 2.8 | 5.2 | 4.0 | 10.0 | 39.6 | 2 585 | 176 | 302 | 6 053 | 10.5 |

1. Includes mining, construction, and manufacturing.   2. Per 1,000 resident population enumerated in the 2010 census.

# Table B. States and Counties — Housing, Labor Force, and Employment

| STATE County | Housing units, 2007–2011 Occupied units Total | Percent | Owner-occupied Median value[1] | Median owner cost as a percent of income With a mortgage | Without a mortgage[2] | Renter-occupied Median rent[3] | Median rent as a percent of income | Substandard units[4] (percent) | Civilian labor force, 2012 Total | Percent change, 2011–2012 | Unemployment Total | Rate[5] | Civilian employment,[6] 2007–2011 Total | Percent Management, business, science and arts | Construction, production, and maintenance occupations |
|---|---|---|---|---|---|---|---|---|---|---|---|---|---|---|---|
| | 89 | 90 | 91 | 92 | 93 | 94 | 95 | 96 | 97 | 98 | 99 | 100 | 101 | 102 | 103 |
| NORTH DAKOTA—Cont'd | | | | | | | | | | | | | | | |
| Ward | 24 453 | 64.3 | 124 300 | 20.8 | 9.9 | 625 | 24.6 | 1.4 | 31 919 | 3.7 | 896 | 2.8 | 30 574 | 29.3 | 23.7 |
| Wells | 2 032 | 73.5 | 55 600 | 18.2 | 11.7 | 431 | 22.5 | 1.2 | 1 936 | -2.9 | 86 | 4.4 | 2 059 | 33.3 | 31.1 |
| Williams | 9 273 | 70.8 | 110 000 | 14.6 | 9.9 | 565 | 18.3 | 1.1 | 34 648 | 38.4 | 283 | 0.8 | 12 366 | 28.8 | 33.3 |
| OHIO | 4 554 007 | 68.7 | 135 600 | 23.2 | 13.1 | 697 | 30.1 | 1.7 | 5 747 885 | -1.0 | 413 023 | 7.2 | 5 326 405 | 33.8 | 23.8 |
| Adams | 10 905 | 72.2 | 95 800 | 26.1 | 14.0 | 514 | 31.7 | 2.6 | 12 126 | -6.3 | 1 307 | 10.8 | 10 335 | 27.8 | 34.3 |
| Allen | 40 703 | 70.0 | 105 400 | 21.6 | 12.3 | 626 | 31.6 | 1.7 | 48 784 | -2.0 | 3 793 | 7.8 | 47 059 | 26.2 | 27.7 |
| Ashland | 20 125 | 78.1 | 126 500 | 24.3 | 13.0 | 667 | 30.7 | 2.9 | 26 414 | -1.5 | 1 973 | 7.5 | 24 261 | 28.3 | 31.1 |
| Ashtabula | 38 771 | 72.8 | 116 600 | 24.4 | 14.3 | 619 | 31.6 | 2.6 | 47 319 | -2.0 | 4 249 | 9.0 | 42 654 | 25.6 | 35.4 |
| Athens | 22 496 | 56.8 | 117 400 | 22.7 | 12.4 | 673 | 44.6 | 2.8 | 29 420 | 0.0 | 2 257 | 7.7 | 26 191 | 35.8 | 17.2 |
| Auglaize | 18 297 | 75.9 | 124 700 | 21.3 | 10.9 | 647 | 24.1 | 1.6 | 25 580 | -0.7 | 1 422 | 5.6 | 22 684 | 28.3 | 36.6 |
| Belmont | 28 747 | 74.9 | 86 500 | 20.2 | 12.2 | 503 | 26.7 | 0.9 | 33 011 | -1.7 | 2 452 | 7.4 | 29 914 | 25.7 | 27.8 |
| Brown | 16 112 | 79.9 | 124 200 | 24.2 | 13.9 | 642 | 28.7 | 1.8 | 21 396 | -1.7 | 1 875 | 8.8 | 18 691 | 25.4 | 33.0 |
| Butler | 135 104 | 70.9 | 160 400 | 23.0 | 13.2 | 777 | 31.7 | 1.9 | 189 596 | -1.2 | 13 428 | 7.1 | 174 087 | 34.3 | 22.1 |
| Carroll | 11 485 | 80.8 | 112 000 | 24.7 | 10.6 | 578 | 28.1 | 2.8 | 13 620 | -1.3 | 1 026 | 7.5 | 12 732 | 24.6 | 37.3 |
| Champaign | 15 278 | 74.5 | 123 000 | 23.0 | 13.6 | 655 | 27.8 | 1.7 | 19 430 | -1.2 | 1 377 | 7.1 | 17 907 | 26.4 | 36.2 |
| Clark | 54 771 | 69.8 | 110 400 | 22.3 | 13.0 | 642 | 30.8 | 1.7 | 67 726 | -1.9 | 4 934 | 7.3 | 59 996 | 28.4 | 27.7 |
| Clermont | 73 333 | 76.8 | 160 500 | 22.8 | 13.0 | 722 | 28.3 | 1.3 | 104 870 | -1.4 | 7 221 | 6.9 | 95 489 | 34.9 | 23.4 |
| Clinton | 16 190 | 70.8 | 123 800 | 23.1 | 14.0 | 653 | 30.3 | 2.1 | 17 222 | -5.0 | 1 776 | 10.3 | 19 436 | 27.2 | 32.0 |
| Columbiana | 42 235 | 74.5 | 97 700 | 22.5 | 11.9 | 575 | 28.5 | 1.5 | 51 528 | -1.5 | 4 097 | 8.0 | 45 916 | 24.9 | 33.6 |
| Coshocton | 14 375 | 75.1 | 96 400 | 22.3 | 10.8 | 528 | 27.8 | 1.8 | 15 830 | -3.7 | 1 569 | 9.9 | 15 382 | 24.7 | 37.8 |
| Crawford | 17 905 | 70.9 | 92 600 | 23.5 | 12.1 | 626 | 26.8 | 1.5 | 20 391 | -2.3 | 1 774 | 8.7 | 18 631 | 24.8 | 35.7 |
| Cuyahoga | 537 203 | 61.6 | 134 900 | 24.7 | 15.2 | 716 | 31.4 | 1.6 | 625 471 | -0.4 | 45 828 | 7.3 | 586 406 | 36.9 | 18.6 |
| Darke | 20 700 | 76.9 | 113 100 | 22.5 | 12.4 | 581 | 27.3 | 1.8 | 27 097 | -0.6 | 1 822 | 6.7 | 24 004 | 25.5 | 36.6 |
| Defiance | 15 183 | 77.8 | 110 500 | 21.5 | 12.7 | 598 | 28.2 | 2.2 | 19 114 | -1.6 | 1 389 | 7.3 | 17 622 | 26.9 | 36.1 |
| Delaware | 62 618 | 82.6 | 253 400 | 22.8 | 12.0 | 817 | 27.1 | 0.9 | 95 264 | 0.6 | 4 785 | 5.0 | 88 020 | 51.4 | 12.1 |
| Erie | 31 642 | 71.4 | 138 000 | 23.5 | 13.4 | 689 | 28.7 | 1.4 | 40 622 | -3.3 | 2 962 | 7.3 | 35 328 | 30.5 | 25.7 |
| Fairfield | 54 388 | 74.3 | 168 000 | 23.4 | 11.4 | 754 | 29.0 | 1.7 | 74 834 | 0.2 | 4 678 | 6.3 | 68 779 | 35.9 | 20.7 |
| Fayette | 11 543 | 63.0 | 110 000 | 25.0 | 13.1 | 694 | 29.8 | 1.7 | 15 567 | -1.9 | 1 112 | 7.1 | 12 902 | 24.1 | 32.7 |
| Franklin | 460 497 | 56.7 | 155 200 | 23.5 | 13.3 | 787 | 29.8 | 2.5 | 625 762 | 0.3 | 38 437 | 6.1 | 579 432 | 39.9 | 16.5 |
| Fulton | 16 332 | 81.3 | 131 500 | 23.4 | 13.2 | 663 | 27.7 | 1.9 | 21 825 | -1.0 | 1 696 | 7.8 | 20 360 | 26.7 | 36.1 |
| Gallia | 12 009 | 73.1 | 96 900 | 20.9 | 13.1 | 539 | 34.9 | 1.8 | 12 936 | -2.2 | 1 154 | 8.9 | 12 288 | 30.8 | 29.6 |
| Geauga | 34 447 | 86.8 | 228 400 | 24.5 | 14.5 | 749 | 28.1 | 1.8 | 49 347 | -0.3 | 2 944 | 6.0 | 45 072 | 38.0 | 22.7 |
| Greene | 62 558 | 68.4 | 159 700 | 22.2 | 12.2 | 813 | 32.0 | 0.9 | 78 340 | -1.5 | 5 506 | 7.0 | 75 501 | 42.2 | 16.9 |
| Guernsey | 15 913 | 72.9 | 92 300 | 23.0 | 12.2 | 548 | 29.7 | 1.5 | 18 658 | -2.3 | 1 559 | 8.4 | 16 554 | 25.2 | 34.0 |
| Hamilton | 325 766 | 60.9 | 147 800 | 23.3 | 13.5 | 673 | 30.7 | 1.8 | 400 040 | -1.3 | 28 144 | 7.0 | 383 695 | 38.6 | 17.3 |
| Hancock | 30 425 | 71.1 | 130 300 | 22.2 | 11.3 | 639 | 27.4 | 0.8 | 39 657 | -1.2 | 2 430 | 6.1 | 37 044 | 32.7 | 29.7 |
| Hardin | 11 692 | 67.4 | 101 000 | 22.4 | 12.3 | 602 | 32.6 | 2.2 | 14 279 | -2.1 | 1 068 | 7.5 | 13 615 | 23.9 | 36.7 |
| Harrison | 6 298 | 77.5 | 84 200 | 22.9 | 11.8 | 554 | 34.0 | 2.8 | 7 082 | -0.8 | 577 | 8.1 | 6 564 | 21.4 | 33.6 |
| Henry | 11 110 | 78.5 | 119 200 | 22.7 | 14.2 | 629 | 24.8 | 1.1 | 15 143 | -1.7 | 1 181 | 7.8 | 13 246 | 26.7 | 36.8 |
| Highland | 16 841 | 72.8 | 104 300 | 24.0 | 12.0 | 614 | 29.3 | 2.4 | 18 434 | -2.6 | 1 765 | 9.6 | 17 668 | 22.7 | 37.8 |
| Hocking | 11 491 | 77.1 | 115 600 | 23.4 | 12.4 | 565 | 31.6 | 2.5 | 13 698 | -1.5 | 1 080 | 7.9 | 12 718 | 27.3 | 33.4 |
| Holmes | 12 261 | 77.8 | 153 400 | 24.1 | 9.9 | 562 | 20.1 | 5.6 | 20 440 | -0.4 | 968 | 4.7 | 17 353 | 22.3 | 44.4 |
| Huron | 22 684 | 74.0 | 121 400 | 22.6 | 12.7 | 599 | 27.7 | 1.7 | 26 990 | -3.0 | 2 751 | 10.2 | 27 492 | 21.6 | 39.8 |
| Jackson | 13 252 | 66.7 | 91 100 | 23.4 | 13.3 | 571 | 28.8 | 2.8 | 14 778 | -1.0 | 1 365 | 9.2 | 13 110 | 28.8 | 33.0 |
| Jefferson | 28 741 | 73.5 | 85 700 | 21.1 | 11.6 | 559 | 30.6 | 0.9 | 30 815 | -1.2 | 3 176 | 10.3 | 28 808 | 26.6 | 29.0 |
| Knox | 22 495 | 73.9 | 134 600 | 22.9 | 12.1 | 663 | 28.0 | 1.9 | 29 780 | -0.9 | 2 020 | 6.8 | 28 211 | 30.4 | 30.4 |
| Lake | 94 347 | 76.7 | 156 000 | 24.0 | 13.8 | 777 | 29.2 | 1.0 | 128 568 | -0.4 | 8 266 | 6.4 | 117 830 | 34.0 | 23.3 |
| Lawrence | 24 479 | 73.2 | 93 800 | 21.7 | 12.6 | 596 | 27.8 | 2.5 | 27 812 | -1.7 | 2 106 | 7.6 | 24 897 | 28.6 | 27.9 |
| Licking | 63 314 | 74.1 | 152 600 | 22.9 | 12.1 | 692 | 28.6 | 1.9 | 84 829 | 0.1 | 5 526 | 6.5 | 79 294 | 32.7 | 23.9 |
| Logan | 18 095 | 74.5 | 123 200 | 22.3 | 14.4 | 662 | 28.7 | 2.2 | 23 161 | -1.1 | 1 555 | 6.7 | 20 897 | 26.3 | 36.0 |
| Lorain | 115 534 | 73.2 | 146 400 | 23.7 | 13.2 | 698 | 30.7 | 1.6 | 156 103 | 0.0 | 12 072 | 7.7 | 136 208 | 32.3 | 25.4 |
| Lucas | 178 777 | 64.1 | 119 200 | 23.6 | 14.0 | 646 | 32.0 | 1.0 | 209 051 | -0.9 | 16 734 | 8.0 | 196 540 | 32.0 | 23.5 |
| Madison | 14 791 | 71.3 | 149 100 | 22.5 | 14.5 | 675 | 28.3 | 2.4 | 20 041 | -0.1 | 1 325 | 6.6 | 19 219 | 28.4 | 27.0 |
| Mahoning | 98 749 | 71.6 | 97 800 | 23.0 | 13.7 | 598 | 32.5 | 1.1 | 110 913 | -1.9 | 8 656 | 7.8 | 103 600 | 30.6 | 23.8 |
| Marion | 24 851 | 69.0 | 99 200 | 22.3 | 13.6 | 659 | 31.5 | 1.5 | 29 761 | -2.7 | 2 286 | 7.7 | 27 995 | 23.6 | 35.9 |
| Medina | 64 813 | 81.2 | 184 200 | 23.5 | 12.3 | 800 | 30.2 | 1.7 | 95 236 | -0.4 | 5 757 | 6.0 | 86 738 | 37.6 | 22.0 |
| Meigs | 9 644 | 80.1 | 82 400 | 22.5 | 12.4 | 499 | 31.8 | 1.7 | 8 958 | -3.6 | 1 056 | 11.8 | 8 685 | 24.5 | 35.3 |
| Mercer | 15 689 | 81.4 | 124 600 | 21.7 | 12.1 | 644 | 29.5 | 1.4 | 24 831 | -0.2 | 1 081 | 4.4 | 20 142 | 25.1 | 37.9 |
| Miami | 41 364 | 70.8 | 137 900 | 22.2 | 12.1 | 692 | 27.0 | 1.8 | 52 408 | -1.8 | 3 647 | 7.0 | 48 866 | 30.8 | 31.8 |
| Monroe | 6 167 | 81.0 | 88 900 | 20.4 | 10.2 | 487 | 27.3 | 2.0 | 5 500 | -1.8 | 529 | 9.6 | 5 832 | 22.1 | 41.0 |
| Montgomery | 223 546 | 64.0 | 118 600 | 23.3 | 13.9 | 703 | 31.7 | 1.5 | 252 776 | -1.7 | 19 802 | 7.8 | 238 804 | 34.8 | 20.8 |
| Morgan | 6 252 | 78.3 | 87 600 | 22.5 | 10.4 | 530 | 29.6 | 1.5 | 5 798 | -1.7 | 645 | 11.1 | 5 980 | 23.0 | 35.6 |
| Morrow | 13 084 | 81.5 | 131 200 | 25.3 | 13.6 | 672 | 28.9 | 1.6 | 17 342 | -0.5 | 1 246 | 7.2 | 16 260 | 25.3 | 34.6 |
| Muskingum | 34 262 | 69.8 | 111 800 | 22.6 | 12.9 | 596 | 30.5 | 2.0 | 37 033 | -2.6 | 3 588 | 9.7 | 37 388 | 27.3 | 28.8 |
| Noble | 4 771 | 81.0 | 80 300 | 19.9 | 10.5 | 555 | 36.8 | 4.1 | 5 349 | -4.2 | 554 | 10.4 | 4 294 | 25.8 | 37.8 |

1. Specified owner-occupied units. 2. A value of 9.9 represents 9.9 percent or less. 3. Specified renter-occupied units. A value of 10.0 represents 10 percent or less. 4. Overcrowded or lacking complete plumbing facilities. 5. Percent of civilian labor force. 6. Persons 16 years old and over.

# Table B. States and Counties — Nonfarm Employment and Agriculture

| | Private nonfarm establishments, employment and payroll, 2011 | | | | | | | | | Agriculture, 2007 | | | |
| | | Employment | | | | | | Annual payroll | | Farms | | | |
| | | | | | | | | | | | | Percent with: | |
| STATE County | Number of establishments | Total | Health care and social assistance | Manufacturing | Retail trade | Finance and insurance | Professional, scientific, and technical services | Total (mil dol) | Average per employee (dollars) | Number | Fewer than 50 acres | 500 acres or more | Farm operators whose principal occupation is farming (percent) |
|---|---|---|---|---|---|---|---|---|---|---|---|---|---|
| | 104 | 105 | 106 | 107 | 108 | 109 | 110 | 111 | 112 | 113 | 114 | 115 | 116 |
| NORTH DAKOTA—Cont'd | | | | | | | | | | | | | |
| Ward............... | 1 866 | 24 715 | 4 438 | 631 | 4 977 | 1 597 | 640 | 952 | 38 529 | 946 | 11.8 | 51.6 | 60.7 |
| Wells............... | 181 | 1 373 | D | D | 230 | 74 | D | 38 | 27 328 | 618 | 5.5 | 50.2 | 59.5 |
| Williams............ | 1 118 | 14 113 | 1 432 | 259 | 1 694 | 360 | 320 | 942 | 66 727 | 857 | 6.2 | 57.9 | 56.0 |
| OHIO.................. | 250 476 | 4 432 849 | 797 437 | 614 027 | 548 920 | 239 950 | 236 593 | 182 110 | 41 082 | 75 861 | 42.4 | 8.9 | 43.1 |
| Adams................ | 367 | 4 109 | 1 206 | D | 879 | D | 84 | 117 | 28 377 | 1 379 | 37.3 | 5.4 | 40.6 |
| Allen................. | 2 516 | 46 301 | 11 626 | 7 595 | 6 055 | 1 195 | 938 | 1 612 | 34 810 | 946 | 40.7 | 13.1 | 37.8 |
| Ashland.............. | 1 018 | 15 391 | 2 423 | 3 650 | 1 981 | 295 | D | 503 | 32 653 | 1 058 | 42.0 | 5.6 | 43.4 |
| Ashtabula............ | 1 996 | 24 659 | 5 858 | 5 643 | 4 013 | 561 | 497 | 809 | 32 789 | 1 127 | 40.8 | 5.3 | 50.3 |
| Athens............... | 1 071 | 12 759 | 2 989 | 309 | 2 710 | 427 | 622 | 343 | 26 899 | 585 | 32.0 | 4.6 | 37.6 |
| Auglaize............. | 960 | 17 371 | 2 410 | 7 023 | 2 123 | 360 | 439 | 618 | 35 567 | 1 059 | 35.9 | 10.1 | 40.9 |
| Belmont.............. | 1 497 | 19 127 | 4 768 | 1 068 | 3 944 | 833 | 517 | 567 | 29 631 | 681 | 30.4 | 5.6 | 40.1 |
| Brown................ | 534 | 6 310 | 1 554 | 600 | 1 076 | 176 | 114 | 173 | 27 376 | 1 487 | 41.1 | 7.8 | 41.7 |
| Butler............... | 6 875 | 122 438 | 14 042 | 16 799 | 17 338 | 8 406 | 3 486 | 4 870 | 39 772 | 949 | 56.2 | 5.3 | 44.6 |
| Carroll.............. | 457 | 4 827 | 832 | 1 350 | 696 | 84 | 87 | 134 | 27 767 | 774 | 32.6 | 4.8 | 44.2 |
| Champaign............ | 608 | 8 757 | 1 092 | 3 240 | 1 036 | 203 | 267 | 301 | 34 415 | 931 | 47.8 | 12.0 | 41.7 |
| Clark................ | 2 388 | 39 851 | 8 187 | 5 431 | 5 699 | 2 420 | 1 215 | 1 266 | 31 773 | 744 | 53.5 | 14.1 | 42.9 |
| Clermont............. | 3 516 | 44 073 | 5 613 | 4 370 | 8 938 | 2 179 | 2 476 | 1 574 | 35 723 | 898 | 59.2 | 4.7 | 37.4 |
| Clinton.............. | 751 | 14 390 | 3 007 | 3 027 | 1 612 | 482 | D | 493 | 34 282 | 799 | 38.7 | 16.6 | 51.6 |
| Columbiana........... | 2 106 | 25 106 | 5 762 | 5 153 | 4 109 | 608 | 433 | 734 | 29 233 | 1 056 | 44.8 | 4.4 | 39.7 |
| Coshocton............ | 640 | 9 275 | 1 782 | 2 502 | 1 254 | 238 | 134 | 317 | 34 218 | 1 032 | 32.6 | 6.9 | 40.0 |
| Crawford............. | 864 | 11 932 | 2 234 | 3 744 | 1 297 | 627 | 328 | 375 | 31 400 | 682 | 35.3 | 16.7 | 51.6 |
| Cuyahoga............. | 33 255 | 646 638 | 136 661 | 68 266 | 60 444 | 45 754 | 43 216 | 30 528 | 47 210 | 127 | 89.0 | 0.0 | 52.0 |
| Darke................ | 1 147 | 14 616 | 2 371 | D | 1 998 | 567 | 244 | 508 | 34 760 | 1 772 | 42.9 | 10.8 | 45.1 |
| Defiance............. | 814 | 12 847 | 2 441 | 3 046 | 2 305 | 609 | 238 | 474 | 36 914 | 1 141 | 38.5 | 11.6 | 35.0 |
| Delaware............. | 3 890 | 69 069 | 5 585 | 5 659 | 10 675 | 13 048 | 3 235 | 3 170 | 45 903 | 726 | 57.4 | 11.0 | 42.3 |
| Erie................. | 1 879 | 28 036 | 5 163 | 5 603 | 4 461 | 633 | 654 | 1 013 | 36 130 | 403 | 47.9 | 11.7 | 42.7 |
| Fairfield............ | 2 550 | 32 929 | 6 411 | 4 479 | 6 582 | 896 | 1 244 | 1 017 | 30 875 | 1 112 | 49.2 | 7.6 | 40.6 |
| Fayette.............. | 593 | 9 412 | 1 370 | 1 746 | 2 408 | 183 | 80 | 271 | 28 813 | 585 | 38.3 | 22.9 | 53.5 |
| Franklin............. | 26 653 | 561 986 | 94 851 | 28 652 | 64 964 | 52 069 | 40 954 | 25 881 | 46 053 | 429 | 62.7 | 7.0 | 42.2 |
| Fulton............... | 946 | 14 496 | 2 103 | 6 086 | 1 689 | 420 | 262 | 512 | 35 329 | 763 | 43.9 | 14.5 | 41.2 |
| Gallia............... | 540 | 9 628 | D | 507 | 1 403 | 345 | 89 | 331 | 34 385 | 993 | 34.5 | 2.4 | 33.4 |
| Geauga............... | 2 726 | 27 533 | 4 071 | 7 643 | 3 717 | 704 | 1 092 | 1 104 | 40 109 | 888 | 59.6 | 1.6 | 47.0 |
| Greene............... | 2 957 | 47 739 | 5 939 | 3 274 | 9 586 | 1 097 | 9 182 | 1 762 | 36 912 | 776 | 56.7 | 11.6 | 43.9 |
| Guernsey............. | 846 | 12 331 | 2 672 | 2 529 | 1 762 | D | 255 | 385 | 31 208 | 883 | 33.0 | 3.9 | 44.7 |
| Hamilton............. | 21 004 | 449 518 | 83 748 | 47 558 | 43 627 | 31 253 | 40 307 | 22 363 | 49 749 | 291 | 67.7 | 1.7 | 41.6 |
| Hancock.............. | 1 715 | 38 122 | 5 030 | 9 320 | 4 158 | 632 | 805 | 1 536 | 40 281 | 922 | 36.9 | 17.1 | 45.9 |
| Hardin............... | 454 | 6 658 | 591 | 1 519 | 943 | 224 | 78 | 188 | 28 233 | 847 | 30.7 | 16.4 | 47.0 |
| Harrison............. | 269 | 2 474 | 606 | 384 | 285 | 60 | D | 82 | 33 158 | 418 | 21.1 | 7.7 | 37.6 |
| Henry................ | 569 | 8 117 | 1 311 | 2 833 | 945 | 293 | 88 | 299 | 36 776 | 881 | 37.1 | 15.0 | 41.0 |
| Highland............. | 654 | 8 051 | 1 672 | 1 658 | 1 575 | 516 | 123 | 238 | 29 551 | 1 497 | 38.9 | 8.5 | 41.5 |
| Hocking.............. | 478 | 5 114 | 1 082 | 861 | 860 | 168 | 95 | 136 | 26 578 | 387 | 40.3 | 3.1 | 38.2 |
| Holmes............... | 1 096 | 15 788 | 1 489 | 5 937 | 1 892 | 352 | 276 | 462 | 29 237 | 1 573 | 39.9 | 3.2 | 51.2 |
| Huron................ | 1 164 | 16 876 | 2 553 | 5 370 | 2 069 | 417 | 372 | 612 | 36 290 | 793 | 43.3 | 13.6 | 43.4 |
| Jackson.............. | 582 | 8 884 | 1 350 | 3 229 | 1 355 | 297 | 170 | 262 | 29 493 | 462 | 31.4 | 6.3 | 40.7 |
| Jefferson............ | 1 301 | 19 353 | 4 343 | 1 417 | 3 273 | 521 | 330 | 620 | 32 050 | 475 | 26.1 | 5.5 | 45.5 |
| Knox................. | 1 056 | 18 713 | 2 932 | 4 538 | 2 193 | 457 | 321 | 719 | 38 442 | 1 270 | 45.4 | 7.6 | 40.1 |
| Lake................. | 6 136 | 83 423 | 11 346 | 17 843 | 12 602 | 1 955 | 3 483 | 3 509 | 42 065 | 259 | 75.7 | 2.3 | 45.2 |
| Lawrence............. | 818 | 10 078 | 2 715 | 767 | 2 071 | 303 | 253 | 291 | 28 855 | 649 | 36.1 | 1.8 | 39.8 |
| Licking.............. | 2 859 | 45 026 | 6 679 | 7 374 | 6 434 | 3 656 | 1 832 | 1 553 | 34 500 | 1 427 | 50.9 | 6.2 | 42.3 |
| Logan................ | 859 | 15 136 | 2 191 | D | 1 772 | 322 | 815 | 562 | 37 135 | 956 | 44.1 | 10.7 | 36.9 |
| Lorain............... | 5 574 | 80 961 | 14 261 | 15 212 | 12 728 | 1 910 | 2 433 | 2 941 | 36 323 | 873 | 58.4 | 6.5 | 42.0 |
| Lucas................ | 9 794 | 193 232 | 43 274 | 17 871 | 23 011 | 6 032 | 9 253 | 7 322 | 37 892 | 372 | 61.3 | 9.1 | 44.1 |
| Madison.............. | 673 | 9 993 | 1 318 | 2 293 | 1 719 | 149 | D | 338 | 33 777 | 718 | 39.4 | 22.7 | 51.8 |
| Mahoning............. | 5 702 | 84 482 | 18 275 | 8 310 | 12 379 | 3 019 | 3 646 | 2 821 | 33 396 | 578 | 48.3 | 2.6 | 45.5 |
| Marion............... | 1 169 | 21 136 | 4 218 | 6 266 | 2 804 | 482 | 288 | 700 | 33 110 | 654 | 40.2 | 17.1 | 43.3 |
| Medina............... | 3 909 | 51 394 | 7 395 | D | 8 834 | 2 366 | 1 975 | 1 808 | 35 175 | 951 | 63.7 | 3.7 | 44.8 |
| Meigs................ | 310 | 2 461 | D | D | 519 | 129 | D | 66 | 26 942 | 551 | 25.0 | 4.0 | 44.1 |
| Mercer............... | 939 | 13 912 | 1 878 | 3 570 | 1 905 | 604 | 311 | 444 | 31 943 | 1 302 | 35.6 | 12.9 | 51.8 |
| Miami................ | 2 099 | 34 097 | 4 740 | 9 406 | 4 827 | 798 | 770 | 1 197 | 35 096 | 1 048 | 55.9 | 11.8 | 42.9 |
| Monroe............... | 252 | 3 216 | 262 | D | 366 | D | D | 153 | 47 462 | 636 | 22.5 | 2.5 | 46.2 |
| Montgomery .......... | 11 534 | 221 571 | 50 810 | 26 694 | 24 933 | 7 986 | 12 538 | 9 347 | 42 186 | 804 | 64.2 | 7.5 | 39.4 |
| Morgan............... | 157 | 1 710 | 364 | 509 | 283 | 83 | 25 | 52 | 30 557 | 524 | 21.6 | 6.1 | 42.0 |
| Morrow............... | 384 | 3 548 | 893 | D | 498 | 93 | 166 | 105 | 29 581 | 874 | 47.9 | 8.2 | 38.6 |
| Muskingum............ | 1 751 | 26 586 | 6 279 | 3 073 | 4 508 | 729 | 479 | 954 | 35 894 | 1 162 | 33.8 | 5.2 | 39.7 |
| Noble................ | 203 | 1 859 | D | D | 278 | 73 | D | 46 | 24 575 | 534 | 20.4 | 5.8 | 40.1 |

# Table B. States and Counties — **Agriculture**

| STATE County | Acreage (1,000) [117] | Percent change, 2002–2007 [118] | Average size of farm [119] | Total irrigated (1,000) [120] | Total cropland (1,000) [121] | Average per farm [122] | Average per acre [123] | Value of machinery and equipment, average per farm (dollars) [124] | Total (mil dol) [125] | Average per farm (dollars) [126] | Crops [127] | Livestock and poultry products [128] | $10,000 or more [129] | $100,000 or more [130] | Total ($1,000) [131] | Percent of farms [132] |
|---|---|---|---|---|---|---|---|---|---|---|---|---|---|---|---|---|
| **NORTH DAKOTA—Cont'd** | | | | | | | | | | | | | | | | |
| Ward | 1 066 | -3.9 | 1 127 | 0.8 | 843.8 | 953 288 | 846 | 173 444 | 167.6 | 177 164 | 91.6 | 8.4 | 64.6 | 38.5 | 8 642 | 75.6 |
| Wells | 757 | 13.3 | 1 225 | 1.0 | 630.5 | 1 022 755 | 835 | 191 239 | 144.8 | 234 236 | 91.8 | 8.2 | 56.5 | 37.7 | 7 004 | 87.4 |
| Williams | 1 145 | -3.0 | 1 336 | 16.5 | 799.8 | 881 903 | 660 | 157 853 | 127.3 | 148 580 | 91.1 | 8.9 | 59.4 | 31.0 | 7 339 | 76.2 |
| | | | | | | | | | | | | | | | | |
| **OHIO** | 13 957 | -4.3 | 184 | 38.0 | 10 832.8 | 649 130 | 3 528 | 88 352 | 7 070.2 | 93 200 | 58.1 | 41.9 | 43.7 | 15.9 | 232 184 | 50.2 |
| | | | | | | | | | | | | | | | | |
| Adams | 184 | -7.1 | 133 | 0.1 | 95.7 | 380 087 | 2 849 | 55 928 | 29.3 | 21 216 | 50.0 | 50.0 | 30.3 | 4.5 | 2 362 | 48.8 |
| Allen | 187 | -0.5 | 198 | 0.4 | 170.4 | 708 676 | 3 581 | 86 747 | 87.6 | 92 629 | 73.7 | 26.3 | 54.1 | 20.6 | 3 921 | 79.7 |
| Ashland | 151 | -6.2 | 142 | 0.1 | 109.3 | 532 611 | 3 743 | 78 117 | 72.3 | 68 303 | 50.2 | 49.8 | 48.9 | 12.0 | 2 201 | 52.4 |
| Ashtabula | 162 | -4.7 | 143 | 0.4 | 106.3 | 418 008 | 2 913 | 79 881 | 55.2 | 49 009 | 51.9 | 48.1 | 38.4 | 10.5 | 1 284 | 31.8 |
| Athens | 82 | -21.9 | 140 | 0.0 | 26.2 | 364 254 | 2 593 | 50 010 | 8.4 | 14 407 | 41.1 | 58.9 | 20.2 | 2.7 | 204 | 19.8 |
| Auglaize | 213 | -2.3 | 201 | D | 192.2 | 767 779 | 3 812 | 115 681 | 138.6 | 130 885 | 47.5 | 52.5 | 62.0 | 27.3 | 5 060 | 80.3 |
| Belmont | 129 | -9.2 | 190 | 0.0 | 42.6 | 399 103 | 2 105 | 55 131 | 14.6 | 21 370 | 23.2 | 76.8 | 28.2 | 4.0 | 140 | 11.3 |
| Brown | 240 | 8.6 | 162 | 0.1 | 173.2 | 473 499 | 2 929 | 81 338 | 58.0 | 39 014 | 81.1 | 18.9 | 36.0 | 9.9 | 2 679 | 52.8 |
| | | | | | | | | | | | | | | | | |
| Butler | 127 | -8.0 | 134 | 0.2 | 96.4 | 621 828 | 4 639 | 81 096 | 38.8 | 40 880 | 67.0 | 33.0 | 30.1 | 8.1 | 2 415 | 34.8 |
| Carroll | 117 | -5.6 | 151 | 0.6 | 62.2 | 480 676 | 3 184 | 68 140 | 28.7 | 37 112 | 43.0 | 57.0 | 35.7 | 8.9 | 819 | 31.9 |
| Champaign | 205 | -1.4 | 220 | 2.4 | 177.1 | 805 163 | 3 658 | 113 332 | 101.1 | 108 540 | 83.5 | 16.5 | 46.3 | 19.8 | 5 082 | 59.6 |
| Clark | 177 | 7.3 | 238 | 1.5 | 153.5 | 911 967 | 3 826 | 112 592 | 137.0 | 184 200 | 67.1 | 32.9 | 44.9 | 21.5 | 3 093 | 53.4 |
| Clermont | 105 | -9.5 | 117 | 0.1 | 75.8 | 483 575 | 4 148 | 67 694 | 24.9 | 27 702 | 86.9 | 13.1 | 23.2 | 5.9 | 1 101 | 28.5 |
| Clinton | 218 | -8.8 | 273 | 0.1 | 195.9 | 985 240 | 3 603 | 119 509 | 85.6 | 107 126 | 92.0 | 8.0 | 54.7 | 25.8 | 4 231 | 69.3 |
| Columbiana | 131 | -3.7 | 124 | 0.3 | 87.2 | 475 649 | 3 836 | 75 591 | 76.4 | 72 311 | 28.8 | 71.2 | 39.4 | 12.5 | 1 384 | 32.1 |
| Coshocton | 171 | -5.0 | 166 | 0.1 | 91.9 | 490 124 | 2 956 | 75 986 | 58.1 | 56 339 | 38.2 | 61.8 | 35.6 | 10.8 | 1 623 | 38.6 |
| Crawford | 220 | -6.0 | 322 | 0.0 | 200.8 | 1 030 121 | 3 200 | 141 983 | 115.6 | 169 528 | 72.2 | 27.8 | 63.3 | 31.2 | 4 134 | 76.2 |
| | | | | | | | | | | | | | | | | |
| Cuyahoga | 3 | -25.0 | 23 | 0.1 | 1.2 | 511 801 | 22 336 | 48 301 | 14.5 | 114 388 | 94.6 | 5.4 | 29.1 | 8.7 | D | 1.6 |
| Darke | 350 | 3.2 | 198 | 0.4 | 319.9 | 829 604 | 4 195 | 106 475 | 479.8 | 270 741 | 26.7 | 73.3 | 61.9 | 27.4 | 7 497 | 72.6 |
| Defiance | 233 | 11.5 | 204 | D | 202.9 | 609 682 | 2 983 | 84 014 | 87.0 | 76 271 | 74.0 | 26.0 | 47.4 | 16.7 | 5 828 | 88.1 |
| Delaware | 138 | -15.3 | 190 | 0.3 | 122.4 | 851 945 | 4 477 | 101 863 | 85.3 | 117 556 | 81.8 | 18.2 | 42.8 | 16.7 | 2 626 | 47.4 |
| Erie | 84 | -11.6 | 209 | 0.2 | 75.3 | 833 263 | 3 994 | 133 276 | 40.4 | 100 165 | 87.1 | 12.9 | 55.8 | 21.1 | 1 615 | 55.3 |
| Fairfield | 178 | -9.2 | 160 | 0.3 | 140.7 | 676 425 | 4 231 | 84 850 | 71.0 | 63 813 | 75.9 | 24.1 | 37.5 | 13.8 | 4 278 | 55.1 |
| Fayette | 218 | 7.4 | 373 | 0.0 | 197.6 | 1 252 824 | 3 358 | 130 387 | 84.0 | 143 559 | 94.5 | 5.5 | 53.7 | 30.6 | 4 295 | 70.1 |
| Franklin | 60 | -26.8 | 139 | 0.8 | 50.6 | 659 530 | 4 747 | 94 235 | 43.7 | 101 830 | 93.6 | 6.4 | 39.4 | 15.2 | 997 | 37.5 |
| Fulton | 184 | -6.6 | 241 | 0.4 | 172.0 | 864 104 | 3 585 | 112 682 | 134.1 | 175 811 | 58.0 | 42.0 | 58.6 | 29.2 | 4 171 | 72.0 |
| | | | | | | | | | | | | | | | | |
| Gallia | 117 | -0.8 | 118 | 0.1 | 38.1 | 323 579 | 2 748 | 50 056 | 12.9 | 13 037 | 26.3 | 73.7 | 19.2 | 1.7 | 317 | 17.4 |
| Geauga | 57 | -13.6 | 64 | 0.4 | 29.5 | 383 374 | 6 019 | 51 578 | 26.9 | 30 246 | 48.6 | 51.4 | 32.7 | 5.1 | 428 | 9.5 |
| Greene | 163 | -3.6 | 209 | 1.7 | 142.3 | 821 221 | 3 921 | 100 506 | 77.7 | 100 161 | 89.4 | 10.6 | 44.6 | 16.6 | 2 867 | 55.2 |
| Guernsey | 138 | 0.7 | 156 | 0.0 | 49.0 | 406 332 | 2 608 | 55 228 | 17.8 | 20 199 | 25.8 | 74.2 | 25.7 | 4.5 | 277 | 16.1 |
| Hamilton | 21 | -30.0 | 73 | 0.7 | 12.3 | 484 766 | 6 626 | 62 046 | 19.5 | 66 938 | 78.0 | 22.0 | 34.0 | 10.7 | 169 | 11.3 |
| Hancock | 248 | -5.3 | 269 | 0.1 | 228.6 | 874 382 | 3 251 | 111 491 | 101.1 | 109 639 | 83.0 | 17.0 | 63.6 | 25.5 | 4 674 | 80.2 |
| Hardin | 257 | 4.5 | 303 | D | 230.5 | 982 809 | 3 241 | 132 089 | 181.8 | 214 668 | 47.2 | 52.8 | 57.9 | 26.2 | 5 078 | 79.0 |
| Harrison | 93 | -32.6 | 223 | D | 38.7 | 507 665 | 2 273 | 62 901 | 11.8 | 28 132 | 39.9 | 60.1 | 29.9 | 6.7 | 312 | 24.2 |
| Henry | 232 | -1.7 | 264 | 0.6 | 218.8 | 890 427 | 3 378 | 110 156 | 107.4 | 121 878 | 87.0 | 13.0 | 66.7 | 26.3 | 4 400 | 86.2 |
| | | | | | | | | | | | | | | | | |
| Highland | 270 | -1.1 | 180 | 0.2 | 203.2 | 563 365 | 3 126 | 78 274 | 67.4 | 45 006 | 74.8 | 25.2 | 35.8 | 10.6 | 5 694 | 70.2 |
| Hocking | 42 | -16.0 | 109 | 0.0 | 17.0 | 366 000 | 3 373 | 46 715 | 4.3 | 11 213 | 71.0 | 29.0 | 18.9 | 1.8 | 300 | 20.4 |
| Holmes | 188 | -9.2 | 119 | 0.2 | 103.7 | 551 698 | 4 624 | 57 119 | 133.8 | 85 078 | 16.8 | 83.2 | 51.4 | 20.2 | 1 328 | 20.9 |
| Huron | 219 | -3.9 | 277 | 3.0 | 189.5 | 956 062 | 3 456 | 123 835 | 113.0 | 142 501 | 83.5 | 16.5 | 47.8 | 23.2 | 4 820 | 67.1 |
| Jackson | 72 | -2.7 | 156 | 0.0 | 33.8 | 394 199 | 2 534 | 56 542 | 8.5 | 18 317 | 39.4 | 60.6 | 28.6 | 3.5 | 449 | 34.2 |
| Jefferson | 69 | 3.0 | 146 | 0.1 | 31.7 | 343 595 | 2 349 | 59 540 | 9.3 | 19 599 | 37.9 | 62.1 | 30.9 | 5.1 | 372 | 26.5 |
| Knox | 198 | -5.3 | 156 | 0.1 | 142.9 | 555 208 | 3 557 | 75 550 | 79.6 | 62 642 | 59.1 | 40.9 | 39.9 | 13.1 | 2 563 | 44.2 |
| Lake | 16 | -20.0 | 62 | 2.2 | 10.1 | 476 160 | 7 677 | 91 159 | 88.9 | 343 113 | 99.4 | 0.6 | 44.8 | 18.5 | D | 5.0 |
| Lawrence | 66 | 1.5 | 101 | 0.0 | 18.1 | 256 391 | 2 531 | 46 059 | 4.6 | 7 016 | 38.0 | 62.0 | 12.5 | 0.8 | 182 | 15.9 |
| | | | | | | | | | | | | | | | | |
| Licking | 226 | -4.6 | 158 | 0.9 | 169.1 | 638 358 | 4 034 | 81 046 | 155.7 | 109 107 | 42.1 | 57.9 | 33.9 | 10.6 | 3 738 | 31.5 |
| Logan | 201 | -10.7 | 211 | 0.0 | 168.8 | 661 167 | 3 140 | 97 977 | 88.3 | 92 387 | 75.2 | 24.8 | 43.2 | 17.4 | 4 783 | 64.7 |
| Lorain | 124 | -23.5 | 142 | 1.3 | 103.9 | 639 691 | 4 500 | 83 516 | 131.2 | 150 292 | 84.2 | 15.8 | 40.9 | 12.9 | 1 813 | 40.0 |
| Lucas | 63 | -19.2 | 169 | 1.2 | 59.1 | 735 848 | 4 351 | 107 975 | 47.9 | 128 731 | 96.6 | 3.4 | 51.3 | 21.0 | 1 017 | 47.8 |
| Madison | 248 | 0.8 | 345 | 0.2 | 225.4 | 1 337 872 | 3 875 | 144 089 | 122.0 | 169 972 | 78.6 | 21.4 | 55.8 | 34.8 | 5 136 | 67.0 |
| Mahoning | 64 | -16.9 | 111 | 0.6 | 46.4 | 456 868 | 4 121 | 76 812 | 45.1 | 78 088 | 35.1 | 64.9 | 42.9 | 11.2 | 677 | 36.0 |
| Marion | 207 | 0.5 | 316 | 0.0 | 189.6 | 975 300 | 3 084 | 129 995 | 100.2 | 153 257 | 71.4 | 28.6 | 54.3 | 24.3 | 4 804 | 78.9 |
| Medina | 95 | -22.8 | 100 | 0.4 | 73.7 | 553 810 | 5 515 | 68 862 | 48.7 | 51 251 | 70.4 | 29.6 | 37.5 | 8.6 | 1 025 | 20.6 |
| Meigs | 78 | -13.3 | 141 | 0.7 | 28.3 | 360 246 | 2 553 | 55 840 | 17.6 | 31 968 | 62.1 | 37.9 | 29.4 | 5.3 | 1 214 | 24.1 |
| | | | | | | | | | | | | | | | | |
| Mercer | 293 | 8.9 | 225 | 0.1 | 265.8 | 1 098 779 | 4 882 | 150 044 | 535.2 | 411 051 | 17.6 | 82.4 | 75.7 | 43.7 | 6 660 | 79.5 |
| Miami | 197 | 7.1 | 188 | 2.1 | 179.0 | 732 444 | 3 898 | 93 758 | 89.8 | 85 670 | 83.2 | 16.8 | 48.2 | 19.1 | 3 545 | 59.9 |
| Monroe | 99 | -7.5 | 156 | 0.0 | 29.0 | 323 906 | 2 074 | 47 191 | 8.7 | 13 701 | 18.9 | 81.1 | 22.5 | 2.2 | 88 | 12.1 |
| Montgomery | 111 | 8.8 | 138 | 0.2 | 97.5 | 615 634 | 4 459 | 79 936 | 47.9 | 59 588 | 83.6 | 16.4 | 36.8 | 11.6 | 1 791 | 48.3 |
| Morgan | 102 | 2.0 | 195 | 0.0 | 31.3 | 426 845 | 2 187 | 58 123 | 12.5 | 23 805 | 24.5 | 75.5 | 29.0 | 4.8 | 561 | 28.6 |
| Morrow | 165 | -7.8 | 189 | 0.2 | 134.9 | 649 802 | 3 442 | 80 480 | 94.3 | 107 871 | 51.3 | 48.7 | 41.6 | 12.5 | 2 763 | 49.4 |
| Muskingum | 166 | -14.0 | 143 | 0.0 | 76.1 | 401 190 | 2 801 | 65 224 | 35.6 | 30 649 | 41.8 | 58.2 | 29.8 | 5.2 | 1 330 | 28.1 |
| Noble | 89 | -16.8 | 167 | 0.0 | 30.3 | 383 331 | 2 292 | 43 986 | 5.2 | 9 723 | 22.0 | 78.0 | 22.7 | 1.1 | 127 | 8.6 |

| STATE County | Water use, 2005 | | Wholesale trade,[1] 2007 | | | | Retail trade,[2] 2007 | | | | Real estate and rental and leasing,[2] 2007 | | | |
|---|---|---|---|---|---|---|---|---|---|---|---|---|---|---|
| | Total water withdrawn (mil gal/day) | Gallons withdrawn per person | Number of establishments | Number of employees | Sales (mil dol) | Annual payroll (mil dol) | Number of establishments | Number of employees | Sales (mil dol) | Annual payroll (mil dol) | Number of establishments | Number of employees | Receipts (mil dol) | Annual payroll (mil dol) |
| | 133 | 134 | 135 | 136 | 137 | 138 | 139 | 140 | 141 | 142 | 143 | 144 | 145 | 146 |
| NORTH DAKOTA—Cont'd | | | | | | | | | | | | | | |
| Ward | 8.3 | 148 | 86 | 1 139 | 1 379.7 | 48.4 | 294 | 4 738 | 1 119.0 | 96.4 | 70 | D | D | D |
| Wells | 1.1 | 238 | 18 | 166 | 184.6 | 5.6 | 35 | 212 | 64.0 | 3.9 | 3 | D | D | D |
| Williams | 29.0 | 1 505 | 58 | 618 | 442.6 | 28.2 | 119 | 1 400 | 403.3 | 30.7 | 38 | 223 | 93.1 | 12.3 |
| OHIO | 11 469.1 | 1 000 | 12 591 | 192 403 | 135 575.3 | 8 914.0 | 40 075 | 591 237 | 138 816.0 | 12 729.5 | 10 973 | 67 048 | 15 011.3 | 2 339.2 |
| Adams | 599.9 | 21 084 | 9 | 62 | 21.1 | 1.5 | 86 | 941 | 210.3 | 18.1 | 14 | 52 | 3.8 | 1.2 |
| Allen | 27.5 | 259 | 135 | D | D | D | 464 | 6 950 | 1 577.5 | 133.6 | 105 | 481 | 67.1 | 12.2 |
| Ashland | 6.2 | 115 | 38 | 494 | 206.2 | 20.8 | 174 | 2 094 | 418.6 | 41.9 | 33 | 136 | 11.8 | 3.1 |
| Ashtabula | 230.1 | 2 229 | 59 | D | D | D | 384 | 4 298 | 1 077.6 | 84.7 | 82 | 260 | 24.1 | 5.3 |
| Athens | 8.5 | 137 | 31 | D | D | D | 210 | 2 784 | 563.2 | 53.8 | 73 | 265 | 35.3 | 5.5 |
| Auglaize | 14.6 | 308 | 43 | D | D | D | 188 | 2 451 | 493.8 | 45.5 | 43 | 141 | 16.0 | 3.0 |
| Belmont | 262.5 | 3 792 | 43 | D | D | D | 331 | 4 544 | 888.8 | 83.4 | 48 | 272 | 29.8 | 5.5 |
| Brown | 5.4 | 122 | 20 | 107 | 55.0 | 3.0 | 104 | 1 103 | 262.3 | 20.4 | 18 | 65 | 5.0 | 1.1 |
| Butler | 190.4 | 543 | 453 | 9 364 | 7 337.0 | 461.8 | 981 | 16 941 | 4 876.2 | 400.2 | 309 | 1 717 | 345.3 | 53.6 |
| Carroll | 3.2 | 110 | 18 | 208 | 104.2 | 6.7 | 79 | 767 | 163.6 | 15.3 | 11 | 42 | 5.0 | 0.8 |
| Champaign | 8.9 | 225 | 33 | 242 | 146.4 | 8.3 | 119 | 1 204 | 287.6 | 23.3 | 24 | 71 | 6.8 | 1.3 |
| Clark | 27.9 | 196 | 95 | D | D | D | 460 | 6 625 | 1 398.7 | 131.7 | 101 | 485 | 64.0 | 10.9 |
| Clermont | 718.8 | 3 771 | 151 | 1 870 | 1 036.0 | 96.4 | 574 | 10 087 | 2 439.6 | 211.8 | 161 | 776 | 99.1 | 21.4 |
| Clinton | 3.5 | 82 | 31 | D | D | D | 142 | 1 945 | 450.9 | 39.6 | 29 | 125 | 12.4 | 3.2 |
| Columbiana | 11.2 | 101 | 93 | D | D | D | 386 | 4 544 | 1 064.2 | 93.7 | 61 | 274 | 29.4 | 6.6 |
| Coshocton | 208.6 | 5 646 | 19 | D | D | D | 121 | 1 291 | 259.2 | 24.1 | 20 | 48 | 3.7 | 0.7 |
| Crawford | 3.6 | 79 | 34 | D | D | D | 150 | 1 370 | 338.7 | 28.8 | 26 | 83 | 8.2 | 1.5 |
| Cuyahoga | 568.6 | 426 | 2 116 | 34 314 | 18 894.4 | 1 783.4 | 4 767 | 65 431 | 14 478.9 | 1 428.9 | 1 585 | 15 316 | 5 925.5 | 709.0 |
| Darke | 7.9 | 150 | 58 | D | D | D | 190 | 2 166 | 447.2 | 44.7 | 38 | 200 | 16.9 | 6.3 |
| Defiance | 5.9 | 152 | 41 | D | D | D | 176 | 2 624 | 559.5 | 50.4 | 28 | 115 | 15.0 | 2.1 |
| Delaware | 25.1 | 167 | 145 | 1 979 | 998.5 | 95.4 | 575 | 10 155 | 2 331.4 | 213.5 | 168 | 677 | 114.1 | 20.4 |
| Erie | 35.2 | 448 | 64 | D | D | D | 351 | 5 086 | 1 034.9 | 101.8 | 79 | 360 | 40.9 | 8.8 |
| Fairfield | 14.3 | 103 | 82 | D | D | D | 441 | 6 485 | 1 360.6 | 129.2 | 135 | 493 | 62.7 | 11.8 |
| Fayette | 3.2 | 112 | 26 | D | D | D | 199 | 2 495 | 610.7 | 45.4 | 24 | 102 | 21.6 | 2.0 |
| Franklin | 205.1 | 188 | 1 288 | 26 610 | 22 138.4 | 1 251.1 | 3 785 | 71 503 | 19 403.6 | 1 758.9 | 1 558 | 10 816 | 2 221.5 | 414.0 |
| Fulton | 4.7 | 109 | 44 | 416 | 238.8 | 15.8 | 168 | 1 614 | 405.9 | 36.5 | 26 | 94 | 8.0 | 1.6 |
| Gallia | 1 188.8 | 37 906 | 19 | D | D | D | 139 | 1 509 | 356.0 | 30.2 | 21 | 78 | 7.6 | 1.7 |
| Geauga | 7.6 | 80 | 138 | 955 | 424.6 | 52.7 | 320 | 4 005 | 916.7 | 88.8 | 84 | 347 | 43.3 | 9.3 |
| Greene | 17.7 | 116 | 73 | 1 126 | 1 275.5 | 46.9 | 540 | 9 938 | 2 029.3 | 193.0 | 136 | 540 | 93.5 | 13.9 |
| Guernsey | 6.7 | 162 | 29 | D | D | D | 169 | 1 911 | 468.3 | 37.2 | 41 | 235 | 22.1 | 4.5 |
| Hamilton | 377.3 | 468 | 1 199 | 19 282 | 13 030.3 | 993.2 | 3 148 | 49 028 | 10 629.5 | 1 082.2 | 1 066 | 7 462 | 1 577.4 | 296.1 |
| Hancock | 46.9 | 637 | 71 | D | D | D | 316 | 4 752 | 1 092.8 | 97.8 | 68 | 504 | 55.9 | 13.2 |
| Hardin | 4.3 | 135 | 17 | 105 | 112.7 | 3.7 | 91 | 962 | 193.0 | 18.7 | 15 | 36 | 4.8 | 1.0 |
| Harrison | 1.6 | 103 | 11 | 117 | 42.8 | 5.3 | 43 | 323 | 52.9 | 4.9 | 4 | 102 | 3.0 | 1.2 |
| Henry | 11.9 | 404 | 33 | 350 | 317.9 | 11.9 | 92 | 989 | 268.0 | 20.0 | 19 | 70 | 14.4 | 1.7 |
| Highland | 3.4 | 79 | 15 | 166 | 79.8 | 3.6 | 143 | 1 767 | 370.5 | 35.3 | 27 | 83 | 8.7 | 1.7 |
| Hocking | 3.0 | 102 | 7 | D | D | D | 85 | 1 027 | 218.9 | 20.2 | 29 | 91 | 7.4 | 1.7 |
| Holmes | 6.2 | 148 | 51 | 658 | 240.9 | 18.8 | 155 | 1 663 | 360.3 | 35.1 | 16 | 43 | 5.3 | 0.8 |
| Huron | 8.0 | 132 | 54 | D | D | D | 203 | 2 294 | 550.3 | 46.2 | 43 | 143 | 18.6 | 4.1 |
| Jackson | 2.3 | 69 | 19 | 131 | 50.1 | 4.5 | 129 | 1 483 | 336.1 | 29.1 | 26 | 101 | 10.0 | 2.0 |
| Jefferson | 2 146.9 | 30 409 | 55 | D | D | D | 271 | 3 523 | 721.5 | 68.3 | 47 | 237 | 27.3 | 5.0 |
| Knox | 9.4 | 161 | 38 | 362 | 130.8 | 11.2 | 192 | 2 397 | 541.9 | 47.6 | 49 | 164 | 16.6 | 3.6 |
| Lake | 884.0 | 3 803 | 336 | 3 443 | 1 867.8 | 164.5 | 866 | 14 140 | 3 460.9 | 314.5 | 227 | 1 178 | 182.9 | 30.4 |
| Lawrence | 8.0 | 126 | 20 | D | D | D | 179 | 2 312 | 508.8 | 44.5 | 26 | 87 | 9.4 | 1.6 |
| Licking | 22.2 | 143 | 114 | 1 769 | 1 141.4 | 70.9 | 466 | 7 144 | 1 774.7 | 145.2 | 108 | 536 | 62.9 | 13.7 |
| Logan | 6.3 | 135 | 31 | 1 117 | 399.6 | 41.2 | 161 | 1 914 | 420.7 | 40.3 | 38 | 176 | 33.1 | 4.3 |
| Lorain | 622.8 | 2 102 | 262 | 2 745 | 1 822.7 | 120.2 | 895 | 14 057 | 3 225.5 | 286.4 | 222 | 860 | 120.8 | 21.2 |
| Lucas | 880.7 | 1 965 | 514 | 7 283 | 4 943.6 | 319.4 | 1 649 | 25 392 | 5 830.0 | 548.2 | 452 | 2 854 | 961.5 | 103.5 |
| Madison | 4.3 | 105 | 29 | D | D | D | 122 | 1 839 | 958.6 | 41.6 | 33 | 84 | 11.5 | 2.0 |
| Mahoning | 7.2 | 28 | 278 | 4 344 | 1 858.8 | 172.5 | 1 026 | 13 896 | 3 025.7 | 281.4 | 199 | 1 337 | 156.7 | 33.1 |
| Marion | 10.2 | 155 | 42 | 598 | 338.1 | 21.5 | 203 | 2 997 | 674.8 | 62.5 | 59 | 224 | 28.5 | 6.2 |
| Medina | 15.0 | 90 | 233 | 2 592 | 1 303.4 | 116.6 | 548 | 8 390 | 2 113.4 | 185.9 | 140 | 501 | 71.5 | 12.2 |
| Meigs | 5.2 | 224 | 7 | 41 | 11.4 | 1.0 | 75 | 561 | 124.2 | 9.5 | 5 | D | D | D |
| Mercer | 10.6 | 256 | 56 | 1 112 | 655.7 | 39.5 | 174 | 1 876 | 394.4 | 40.1 | 34 | 187 | 14.1 | 2.7 |
| Miami | 20.9 | 206 | 90 | 1 551 | 4 168.9 | 79.6 | 354 | 4 699 | 1 080.5 | 101.0 | 92 | 323 | 48.5 | 8.1 |
| Monroe | 7.9 | 537 | 9 | 47 | 22.8 | 2.1 | 51 | 370 | 62.6 | 5.8 | 1 | D | D | D |
| Montgomery | 261.6 | 478 | 592 | 8 419 | 3 766.7 | 387.5 | 1 778 | 27 154 | 6 844.6 | 588.6 | 576 | 3 882 | 564.5 | 128.9 |
| Morgan | 2.0 | 130 | 5 | D | D | D | 28 | 225 | 52.3 | 3.8 | 4 | D | D | D |
| Morrow | 3.2 | 92 | 14 | D | D | D | 58 | 644 | 167.9 | 10.1 | 13 | 29 | 2.6 | 0.4 |
| Muskingum | 18.9 | 220 | 55 | 884 | 2 222.1 | 37.7 | 385 | 5 125 | 1 125.7 | 96.6 | 71 | 309 | 46.8 | 8.3 |
| Noble | 1.4 | 96 | 8 | 36 | 6.2 | 0.8 | 37 | 324 | 103.3 | 6.3 | 1 | D | D | D |

1. Merchant wholesalers, except manufacturers' sales branches and offices.　2. Employer establishments.

# Table B. States and Counties — Professional Services, Manufacturing, and Accommodation and Food Services

| STATE County | Professional, scientific, and technical services,[1] 2007 | | | | Manufacturing, 2007 | | | | Accommodation and food services, 2007 | | | |
|---|---|---|---|---|---|---|---|---|---|---|---|---|
| | Number of establish-ments | Number of employees | Receipts (mil dol) | Annual payroll (mil dol) | Number of establish-ments | Number of employees | Receipts (mil dol) | Annual payroll (mil dol) | Number of establish-ments | Number of employees | Sales (mil dol) | Annual payroll (mil dol) |
| | 147 | 148 | 149 | 150 | 151 | 152 | 153 | 154 | 155 | 156 | 157 | 158 |
| NORTH DAKOTA—Cont'd | | | | | | | | | | | | |
| Ward | 104 | D | D | D | 54 | 623 | D | 19.9 | 150 | 2 891 | 106.7 | 30.0 |
| Wells | 10 | 19 | 0.9 | 0.3 | NA | NA | NA | NA | 17 | 107 | 3.0 | 0.8 |
| Williams | 61 | 217 | 22.9 | 8.3 | NA | NA | NA | NA | 66 | 913 | 36.6 | 10.7 |
| OHIO | 24 963 | 224 265 | 32 285.4 | 12 304.2 | 16 237 | 760 267 | 295 890.9 | 35 485.5 | 23 959 | 436 598 | 17 779.9 | 5 078.5 |
| Adams | 27 | 87 | 5.8 | 1.6 | 35 | 694 | 133.9 | 28.1 | 43 | 523 | 19.0 | 5.1 |
| Allen | 170 | D | D | D | 136 | 8 661 | 10 009.0 | 475.9 | 219 | 4 469 | 173.2 | 47.4 |
| Ashland | 67 | 984 | 128.0 | 36.1 | 93 | 4 140 | 1 017.4 | 164.5 | 101 | 1 572 | 55.6 | 17.7 |
| Ashtabula | 114 | D | D | D | 161 | 7 218 | 2 201.4 | 296.4 | 219 | 2 745 | 110.6 | 29.7 |
| Athens | 70 | D | D | D | NA | NA | NA | NA | 145 | 2 712 | 81.0 | 23.2 |
| Auglaize | 65 | 400 | 46.1 | 14.1 | 88 | 7 835 | 2 550.6 | 349.6 | 87 | 1 193 | 42.9 | 11.2 |
| Belmont | 103 | 568 | 50.3 | 18.4 | 53 | 1 279 | 500.9 | 53.0 | 128 | 2 517 | 91.2 | 26.8 |
| Brown | 29 | D | D | D | 29 | 736 | 74.2 | 27.6 | 69 | 794 | 29.3 | 7.5 |
| Butler | 605 | D | D | D | 440 | 21 082 | 11 362.0 | 1 035.6 | 630 | 13 512 | 531.1 | 154.3 |
| Carroll | 27 | D | D | D | 49 | 1 700 | 344.6 | 63.8 | 43 | 566 | 18.9 | 5.9 |
| Champaign | 40 | D | D | D | 46 | 3 238 | 1 050.2 | 151.4 | 60 | 717 | 25.9 | 6.5 |
| Clark | 163 | D | D | D | 182 | 7 164 | 2 494.3 | 299.2 | 241 | 4 574 | 173.1 | 49.6 |
| Clermont | 376 | D | D | D | 183 | 5 777 | 1 250.6 | 258.1 | 285 | 6 271 | 239.5 | 71.3 |
| Clinton | 46 | D | D | D | 47 | 3 877 | 1 025.4 | 165.6 | 81 | 1 390 | 62.2 | 15.0 |
| Columbiana | 126 | D | D | D | 197 | 6 535 | 1 572.1 | 239.5 | 189 | 2 561 | 87.5 | 25.6 |
| Coshocton | 35 | 320 | 16.5 | 8.4 | 52 | 2 947 | 1 222.9 | 129.2 | 49 | 633 | 22.7 | 6.4 |
| Crawford | 44 | 409 | 26.8 | 11.1 | 93 | 4 989 | 1 470.9 | 182.8 | 90 | 1 106 | 39.1 | 10.5 |
| Cuyahoga | 4 341 | 41 689 | 6 487.8 | 2 543.7 | 2 172 | 82 169 | 23 131.7 | 4 156.8 | 3 089 | 54 151 | 2 499.2 | 691.0 |
| Darke | 69 | 313 | 25.3 | 8.8 | 82 | 4 404 | 1 517.1 | 185.6 | 97 | 1 088 | 43.7 | 11.5 |
| Defiance | 50 | D | D | D | 53 | 3 940 | 1 048.4 | 281.8 | 81 | 1 194 | 41.3 | 11.2 |
| Delaware | 496 | D | D | D | 133 | 6 065 | 2 314.5 | 282.2 | 361 | 8 335 | 344.2 | 103.5 |
| Erie | 132 | D | D | D | 110 | 7 149 | 2 329.9 | 344.9 | 279 | 5 661 | 254.7 | 69.0 |
| Fairfield | 187 | D | D | D | 131 | 4 804 | 1 061.6 | 210.4 | 228 | 4 636 | 169.5 | 50.3 |
| Fayette | 29 | D | D | D | 33 | 2 795 | 975.5 | 112.5 | 58 | 942 | 38.9 | 10.7 |
| Franklin | 3 545 | D | D | D | 925 | 35 625 | 14 289.4 | 1 605.8 | 2 664 | 56 718 | 2 596.3 | 744.2 |
| Fulton | 49 | 313 | 19.1 | 6.6 | 112 | 9 086 | 3 330.4 | 358.4 | 75 | 987 | 34.7 | 9.3 |
| Gallia | 26 | 90 | 6.3 | 1.7 | NA | NA | NA | NA | 50 | 883 | 33.3 | 9.2 |
| Geauga | 332 | D | D | D | 209 | 11 444 | 2 964.4 | 460.0 | 190 | 2 615 | 94.1 | 26.5 |
| Greene | 428 | D | D | D | 106 | 3 881 | 924.1 | 176.9 | 319 | 7 229 | 283.3 | 86.4 |
| Guernsey | 45 | 271 | 32.0 | 10.5 | 61 | 3 169 | 1 403.2 | 119.8 | 94 | 1 659 | 67.0 | 18.4 |
| Hamilton | 2 601 | D | D | D | 1 155 | 58 305 | 25 048.9 | 3 058.2 | 1 933 | 39 897 | 1 788.4 | 522.8 |
| Hancock | 128 | 947 | 81.3 | 34.7 | 105 | 10 975 | 3 757.2 | 498.2 | 172 | 3 619 | 130.6 | 38.4 |
| Hardin | 22 | 95 | 6.3 | 2.1 | 35 | 2 052 | 560.5 | 79.9 | 51 | 917 | 29.5 | 10.4 |
| Harrison | 16 | 37 | 2.3 | 0.6 | 18 | 740 | 165.2 | 24.3 | 29 | 211 | 6.6 | 1.5 |
| Henry | 20 | 107 | 10.5 | 2.4 | 46 | 3 770 | 2 284.3 | 162.1 | 51 | 609 | 17.8 | 5.1 |
| Highland | 44 | 143 | 10.1 | 3.2 | 43 | 2 879 | 643.0 | 102.7 | 54 | 958 | 36.1 | 9.3 |
| Hocking | 24 | 72 | 4.3 | 1.7 | 23 | 964 | 261.5 | 36.3 | 66 | 1 006 | 40.2 | 11.2 |
| Holmes | 39 | 291 | 31.3 | 10.7 | 265 | 6 123 | 1 366.4 | 190.0 | 58 | 1 057 | 36.4 | 12.0 |
| Huron | 81 | 377 | 27.1 | 11.0 | 104 | 7 206 | 2 375.8 | 284.2 | 108 | 1 450 | 51.7 | 14.4 |
| Jackson | 34 | 185 | 10.9 | 3.2 | 38 | 4 015 | 2 083.9 | 115.7 | 52 | 1 087 | 35.5 | 10.6 |
| Jefferson | 90 | D | D | D | 37 | 2 938 | D | 167.9 | 157 | 1 884 | 66.3 | 18.1 |
| Knox | 66 | 275 | 29.5 | 7.1 | 75 | 4 551 | 1 914.0 | 244.6 | 91 | 1 472 | 53.0 | 14.2 |
| Lake | 612 | D | D | D | 688 | 19 820 | 5 220.9 | 887.6 | 561 | 9 339 | 390.8 | 105.4 |
| Lawrence | 44 | D | D | D | 39 | 835 | D | 32.1 | 68 | 1 066 | 41.2 | 11.1 |
| Licking | 252 | D | D | D | 162 | 8 610 | 3 351.8 | 375.6 | 284 | 5 123 | 194.2 | 54.7 |
| Logan | 50 | D | D | D | 50 | 6 042 | D | 351.6 | 104 | 1 333 | 55.7 | 14.3 |
| Lorain | 469 | D | D | D | 408 | 18 330 | 8 305.3 | 976.6 | 565 | 8 530 | 326.6 | 88.0 |
| Lucas | 911 | D | D | D | 560 | 21 793 | 20 075.5 | 1 275.0 | 1 026 | 19 773 | 728.6 | 211.7 |
| Madison | 44 | D | D | D | 46 | 2 949 | 994.6 | 131.8 | 66 | 1 038 | 38.4 | 12.0 |
| Mahoning | 465 | D | D | D | 385 | 9 874 | 2 475.1 | 376.4 | 544 | 9 489 | 340.7 | 96.4 |
| Marion | 72 | D | D | D | 77 | 7 737 | 3 409.2 | 305.4 | 119 | 2 051 | 79.1 | 22.6 |
| Medina | 409 | 2 246 | 229.9 | 91.4 | 297 | 9 403 | 2 558.8 | 395.6 | 309 | 5 106 | 186.1 | 53.0 |
| Meigs | 20 | 66 | 4.6 | 1.3 | NA | NA | NA | NA | 31 | 500 | 15.3 | 4.6 |
| Mercer | 47 | 319 | 31.6 | 12.5 | 76 | 3 926 | 927.9 | 149.4 | 79 | 1 223 | 39.4 | 11.3 |
| Miami | 162 | D | D | D | 241 | 9 924 | 2 807.3 | 420.5 | 181 | 3 438 | 127.6 | 37.5 |
| Monroe | 15 | 66 | 5.9 | 2.4 | 13 | D | D | D | 21 | 123 | 4.3 | 1.0 |
| Montgomery | 1 213 | 14 942 | 2 031.9 | 829.3 | 811 | 34 993 | 14 049.2 | 1 607.2 | 1 112 | 22 069 | 882.7 | 259.0 |
| Morgan | 11 | 29 | 2.1 | 0.5 | NA | NA | NA | NA | 19 | 264 | 5.8 | 2.0 |
| Morrow | 32 | D | D | D | 32 | 1 150 | D | D | 36 | 381 | 14.0 | 3.5 |
| Muskingum | 103 | D | D | D | 86 | 5 131 | 1 134.2 | 188.0 | 194 | 3 276 | 124.0 | 35.9 |
| Noble | 11 | 32 | 3.5 | 1.3 | NA | NA | NA | NA | 23 | 187 | 7.3 | 2.0 |

1. Establishment subject to federal tax.

# Table B. States and Counties — Health Care and Social Assistance, Other Services, and Federal Funds

| STATE County | Health care and social assistance, 2007 | | | | Other services, 2007 | | | | Federal funds and grants, 2009–2010 Expenditures (mil dol) | | | |
|---|---|---|---|---|---|---|---|---|---|---|---|---|
| | | | | | | | | | | Direct payments for individuals[1] | | |
| | Number of establishments | Number of employees | Receipts (mil dol) | Annual payroll (mil dol) | Number of establishments | Number of employees | Receipts (mil dol) | Annual payroll (mil dol) | Total | Social Security and government retirement | Medicare | Food Stamps and Supplemental Security Income |
| | 159 | 160 | 161 | 162 | 163 | 164 | 165 | 166 | 167 | 168 | 169 | 170 |
| **NORTH DAKOTA—Cont'd** | | | | | | | | | | | | |
| Ward | 145 | 4 360 | 345.9 | 154.2 | 142 | 804 | 60.2 | 14.9 | 799.5 | 196.7 | 73.9 | 11.3 |
| Wells | 15 | 431 | 17.8 | 8.2 | 18 | 63 | 3.8 | 0.8 | 67.8 | 21.6 | 12.1 | 1.0 |
| Williams | 59 | 1 432 | 91.6 | 40.6 | 67 | 300 | 32.1 | 7.7 | 171.2 | 73.2 | 33.0 | 5.1 |
| **OHIO** | 27 965 | 741 194 | 65 882.5 | 27 621.4 | 20 349 | 135 272 | 13 047.5 | 3 463.9 | 106 448.7 | 33 289.5 | 20 459.6 | 4 587.1 |
| Adams | 50 | 1 037 | 62.0 | 25.1 | 34 | 90 | 7.4 | 1.9 | 330.0 | 91.6 | 64.9 | 22.5 |
| Allen | 330 | 11 408 | 999.0 | 417.5 | 213 | 1 448 | 93.3 | 27.9 | 1 079.7 | 526.6 | 182.7 | 48.5 |
| Ashland | 120 | 2 082 | 157.8 | 61.9 | 88 | 601 | 40.6 | 12.3 | 290.0 | 150.1 | 63.9 | 10.0 |
| Ashtabula | 224 | 5 839 | 408.3 | 160.8 | 165 | 656 | 44.9 | 10.3 | 776.9 | 332.9 | 223.0 | 46.3 |
| Athens | 132 | 2 593 | 205.9 | 84.2 | 92 | 453 | 26.1 | 7.0 | 533.4 | 132.0 | 92.9 | 34.2 |
| Auglaize | 94 | 1 995 | 147.5 | 53.5 | 91 | 583 | 38.4 | 11.5 | 299.8 | 124.6 | 82.6 | 6.4 |
| Belmont | 180 | 4 237 | 294.3 | 125.5 | 134 | 648 | 35.1 | 9.4 | 592.2 | 239.3 | 170.2 | 35.9 |
| Brown | 50 | 1 563 | 104.1 | 41.4 | 52 | 182 | 12.5 | 3.4 | 286.9 | 122.4 | 63.1 | 14.0 |
| Butler | 720 | 15 799 | 1 313.6 | 535.8 | 541 | 3 726 | 354.1 | 101.3 | 2 069.9 | 918.3 | 433.9 | 90.3 |
| Carroll | 42 | 753 | 37.9 | 17.0 | 38 | 206 | 12.0 | 2.9 | 156.1 | 72.3 | 33.8 | 8.4 |
| Champaign | 48 | 2 077 | 87.8 | 43.6 | 62 | 335 | 15.3 | 4.1 | 263.0 | 118.4 | 53.2 | 8.1 |
| Clark | 319 | 8 186 | 619.8 | 258.2 | 237 | 1 402 | 188.1 | 38.4 | 1 247.9 | 511.9 | 288.8 | 64.5 |
| Clermont | 299 | 5 104 | 392.2 | 165.2 | 289 | 1 734 | 158.3 | 44.1 | 1 010.0 | 419.7 | 163.6 | 36.7 |
| Clinton | 95 | 2 151 | 205.3 | 80.6 | 72 | 328 | 34.1 | 7.9 | 298.5 | 133.2 | 66.5 | 11.8 |
| Columbiana | 288 | 5 808 | 384.5 | 150.6 | 186 | 1 007 | 73.0 | 18.6 | 868.6 | 375.9 | 227.1 | 47.8 |
| Coshocton | 81 | 1 979 | 132.3 | 52.6 | 61 | 253 | 22.6 | 4.7 | 247.3 | 109.7 | 58.2 | 10.2 |
| Crawford | 106 | 2 166 | 148.3 | 58.0 | 80 | 362 | 27.6 | 6.6 | 337.4 | 158.2 | 93.9 | 16.0 |
| Cuyahoga | 3 734 | 125 281 | 12 200.2 | 5 313.6 | 2 652 | 19 545 | 2 112.5 | 553.2 | 14 453.1 | 3 845.3 | 3 578.0 | 866.4 |
| Darke | 75 | 2 098 | 138.9 | 57.8 | 102 | 445 | 27.1 | 6.9 | 340.4 | 158.3 | 81.5 | 9.3 |
| Defiance | 84 | 2 208 | 196.0 | 68.9 | 71 | 446 | 31.5 | 7.6 | 289.8 | 129.4 | 56.2 | 13.2 |
| Delaware | 313 | 4 655 | 420.9 | 171.9 | 239 | 1 914 | 339.1 | 69.1 | 1 056.5 | 282.8 | 75.5 | 12.8 |
| Erie | 195 | 4 986 | 434.3 | 162.8 | 155 | 815 | 49.6 | 14.5 | 666.7 | 297.9 | 153.9 | 23.6 |
| Fairfield | 303 | 5 804 | 488.6 | 207.0 | 181 | 1 121 | 102.5 | 31.8 | 715.1 | 381.1 | 153.4 | 29.2 |
| Fayette | 62 | 1 289 | 87.9 | 36.6 | 44 | 213 | 13.1 | 3.6 | 200.9 | 80.6 | 46.3 | 9.7 |
| Franklin | 3 020 | 84 476 | 8 383.5 | 3 503.0 | 2 217 | 18 766 | 2 208.7 | 582.1 | 14 415.1 | 2 463.6 | 1 468.3 | 462.6 |
| Fulton | 96 | 2 174 | 147.7 | 58.5 | 80 | 274 | 25.2 | 6.2 | 259.1 | 128.8 | 67.8 | 3.0 |
| Gallia | 64 | 2 853 | 219.5 | 89.5 | 41 | 180 | 12.5 | 3.6 | 313.7 | 104.5 | 67.8 | 24.5 |
| Geauga | 239 | 3 737 | 301.3 | 141.0 | 204 | 1 142 | 105.0 | 33.0 | 375.7 | 228.4 | 85.3 | 7.2 |
| Greene | 316 | 5 995 | 488.2 | 198.0 | 221 | 1 261 | 95.4 | 29.9 | 3 170.8 | 449.5 | 138.2 | 30.7 |
| Guernsey | 126 | 2 427 | 186.0 | 69.5 | 71 | 304 | 23.6 | 4.9 | 333.6 | 130.9 | 82.7 | 21.6 |
| Hamilton | 2 455 | 80 329 | 7 905.8 | 3 420.9 | 1 585 | 11 594 | 1 292.8 | 325.3 | 9 881.0 | 2 328.3 | 1 759.5 | 389.4 |
| Hancock | 190 | 4 688 | 443.2 | 165.7 | 146 | 824 | 77.7 | 21.1 | 394.5 | 183.3 | 82.2 | 13.5 |
| Hardin | 38 | 581 | 47.0 | 15.9 | 40 | 151 | 10.5 | 2.3 | 175.2 | 56.0 | 52.2 | 8.1 |
| Harrison | 32 | 603 | 31.4 | 13.7 | 18 | 59 | 3.1 | 1.0 | 142.8 | 59.1 | 35.2 | 8.9 |
| Henry | 54 | 1 190 | 74.9 | 32.2 | 51 | 312 | 18.6 | 5.2 | 170.3 | 83.3 | 44.5 | 4.5 |
| Highland | 87 | 1 656 | 120.8 | 47.8 | 48 | 210 | 13.9 | 3.0 | 319.6 | 119.9 | 72.0 | 15.6 |
| Hocking | 44 | 956 | 62.4 | 24.2 | 42 | 162 | 14.1 | 3.2 | 188.9 | 83.3 | 46.3 | 11.4 |
| Holmes | 52 | 1 317 | 99.8 | 34.0 | 42 | 198 | 17.5 | 4.5 | 116.4 | 54.8 | 21.4 | 3.1 |
| Huron | 103 | 2 460 | 202.1 | 85.0 | 103 | 523 | 39.8 | 10.3 | 412.8 | 208.6 | 96.1 | 17.8 |
| Jackson | 56 | 1 099 | 115.7 | 43.2 | 52 | 179 | 15.7 | 3.4 | 302.1 | 98.8 | 59.4 | 23.1 |
| Jefferson | 161 | 4 454 | 333.9 | 139.7 | 119 | 627 | 37.2 | 10.5 | 762.6 | 310.4 | 217.5 | 46.0 |
| Knox | 124 | 2 475 | 191.6 | 75.8 | 88 | 591 | 37.7 | 10.9 | 369.7 | 172.5 | 89.5 | 12.7 |
| Lake | 558 | 10 822 | 900.8 | 358.1 | 527 | 3 432 | 252.8 | 76.9 | 1 425.4 | 728.3 | 380.6 | 36.0 |
| Lawrence | 112 | 2 226 | 101.3 | 48.4 | 68 | 271 | 21.7 | 6.1 | 622.7 | 234.3 | 133.6 | 53.1 |
| Licking | 243 | 6 550 | 476.2 | 212.4 | 222 | 1 766 | 267.4 | 63.7 | 1 072.6 | 463.5 | 186.8 | 42.9 |
| Logan | 89 | 1 988 | 150.1 | 60.1 | 81 | 516 | 66.0 | 10.9 | 328.4 | 143.8 | 81.1 | 11.9 |
| Lorain | 613 | 13 174 | 1 097.1 | 440.0 | 510 | 3 049 | 252.6 | 68.6 | 1 999.1 | 877.7 | 477.2 | 103.1 |
| Lucas | 1 272 | 40 299 | 3 669.6 | 1 580.7 | 796 | 5 652 | 509.1 | 131.0 | 3 758.6 | 1 193.4 | 1 009.9 | 289.3 |
| Madison | 67 | 1 103 | 78.5 | 30.0 | 42 | 188 | 9.9 | 2.8 | 253.9 | 115.6 | 60.8 | 8.8 |
| Mahoning | 792 | 15 765 | 1 334.0 | 516.8 | 418 | 2 914 | 216.6 | 61.1 | 2 397.2 | 863.2 | 662.5 | 153.6 |
| Marion | 158 | 4 318 | 356.2 | 157.7 | 115 | 652 | 43.2 | 11.7 | 490.3 | 209.8 | 118.9 | 28.0 |
| Medina | 376 | 6 790 | 475.2 | 207.0 | 302 | 1 636 | 114.7 | 34.9 | 796.4 | 461.0 | 176.0 | 16.9 |
| Meigs | 41 | 532 | 28.4 | 11.6 | 15 | 52 | 4.5 | 1.0 | 200.7 | 70.1 | 44.5 | 19.1 |
| Mercer | 79 | 1 611 | 102.7 | 42.0 | 95 | 430 | 37.7 | 9.3 | 161.3 | 41.5 | 60.4 | 3.3 |
| Miami | 195 | D | D | D | 177 | 953 | 76.1 | 19.4 | 690.9 | 337.4 | 145.7 | 21.3 |
| Monroe | 18 | 203 | 11.5 | 4.4 | 24 | 83 | 5.5 | 1.3 | 132.6 | 50.8 | 31.7 | 7.1 |
| Montgomery | 1 505 | 47 348 | 4 928.7 | 1 955.0 | 954 | 6 992 | 738.6 | 202.7 | 5 460.1 | 2 013.2 | 1 096.3 | 218.4 |
| Morgan | 15 | 250 | 14.2 | 5.5 | 17 | 44 | 2.9 | 0.8 | 125.0 | 42.6 | 24.7 | 7.4 |
| Morrow | 45 | 902 | 60.2 | 20.7 | 24 | 79 | 7.7 | 1.9 | 149.2 | 75.6 | 27.3 | 9.0 |
| Muskingum | 220 | 6 095 | 498.6 | 219.4 | 171 | 1 233 | 81.4 | 23.2 | 698.8 | 288.7 | 147.5 | 47.6 |
| Noble | 19 | 433 | 20.2 | 8.2 | 15 | 37 | 2.5 | 0.4 | 75.1 | 28.0 | 17.0 | 4.6 |

1. State totals may include programs not allocated by county.

# Table B. States and Counties — Federal Funds, Residential Construction, and Local Government Finances

| STATE County | Federal funds and grants, 2009–2010 (cont.) Expenditures (mil dol) (cont.) Procurement contract awards Salaries and wages | Defense | Other | Grants[1] Medicaid and other health-related | Nutrition and family welfare | Education | Other | Value of residential construction authorized by building permits, 2011 New construction ($1,000) | Number of housing units | Local government finances, 2007 General revenue Total (mil dol) | Intergovernmental (mil dol) | Taxes Total (mil dol) | Per capita[2] (dollars) Total | Property |
|---|---|---|---|---|---|---|---|---|---|---|---|---|---|---|
| | 171 | 172 | 173 | 174 | 175 | 176 | 177 | 178 | 179 | 180 | 181 | 182 | 183 | 184 |
| NORTH DAKOTA—Cont'd | | | | | | | | | | | | | | |
| Ward | 281.4 | 96.1 | 20.6 | 38.5 | 13.3 | 15.7 | 9.6 | 140 279 | 1 185 | 151.1 | 65.5 | 61.0 | 1 091 | 851 |
| Wells | 2.3 | 0.0 | 0.5 | 6.3 | 1.2 | 0.1 | 1.6 | 660 | 9 | 15.1 | 5.1 | 6.4 | 1 493 | 1 444 |
| Williams | 8.7 | 0.7 | 1.6 | 13.6 | 4.5 | 0.9 | 3.0 | 193 632 | 1 504 | 65.5 | 26.6 | 24.3 | 1 243 | 1 029 |
| OHIO | 6 974.9 | 6 064.3 | 2 765.1 | 13 659.6 | 3 021.0 | 2 193.6 | 5 524.8 | 2 259 867 | 13 762 | X | X | X | X | X |
| Adams | 6.1 | 0.1 | 1.5 | 126.5 | 8.6 | 2.9 | 1.5 | 0 | 0 | 99.3 | 61.1 | 25.6 | 910 | 745 |
| Allen | 41.1 | 87.4 | 6.3 | 108.5 | 24.3 | 8.3 | 9.2 | 7 851 | 51 | 397.7 | 197.7 | 129.4 | 1 230 | 858 |
| Ashland | 12.0 | 6.5 | 1.9 | 23.8 | 8.2 | 5.1 | 0.7 | 5 082 | 37 | 149.2 | 62.2 | 63.2 | 1 150 | 812 |
| Ashtabula | 20.1 | 20.9 | 5.9 | 83.9 | 22.2 | 7.9 | 5.1 | 10 530 | 64 | 387.2 | 210.0 | 124.0 | 1 226 | 954 |
| Athens | 22.4 | 9.0 | 17.1 | 111.2 | 18.2 | 6.4 | 28.0 | 6 577 | 74 | 206.8 | 101.2 | 68.0 | 1 075 | 776 |
| Auglaize | 15.8 | 0.5 | 2.7 | 19.9 | 6.5 | 2.4 | 30.7 | 9 805 | 58 | 170.1 | 69.8 | 67.8 | 1 461 | 868 |
| Belmont | 19.5 | 0.0 | 4.4 | 83.5 | 14.9 | 5.9 | 4.9 | 706 | 7 | 232.5 | 127.2 | 72.2 | 1 064 | 626 |
| Brown | 7.3 | 0.0 | 1.7 | 50.5 | 10.7 | 3.0 | 4.1 | 6 818 | 43 | 176.2 | 83.9 | 32.5 | 738 | 550 |
| Butler | 83.4 | 110.0 | 26.1 | 255.9 | 51.8 | 17.2 | 40.1 | 77 777 | 401 | 1 364.4 | 530.9 | 559.2 | 1 562 | 1 130 |
| Carroll | 4.2 | 0.0 | 1.0 | 27.5 | 5.0 | 1.8 | 0.6 | 707 | 5 | 60.7 | 32.7 | 18.7 | 655 | 544 |
| Champaign | 6.7 | 24.1 | 1.7 | 34.2 | 5.7 | 2.8 | 0.8 | 3 548 | 22 | 135.7 | 66.0 | 44.6 | 1 129 | 713 |
| Clark | 72.3 | 22.3 | 5.4 | 188.8 | 27.6 | 11.8 | 28.5 | 14 749 | 142 | 580.8 | 303.3 | 164.6 | 1 172 | 789 |
| Clermont | 35.3 | 180.7 | 7.8 | 113.3 | 25.9 | 8.8 | 7.9 | 56 844 | 453 | 602.1 | 230.6 | 262.5 | 1 357 | 1 158 |
| Clinton | 15.5 | 0.1 | 2.6 | 43.0 | 7.7 | 5.5 | 3.2 | 3 895 | 22 | 271.4 | 76.3 | 54.6 | 1 268 | 822 |
| Columbiana | 44.1 | 8.6 | 10.8 | 107.0 | 25.0 | 7.2 | 5.0 | 1 679 | 12 | 301.6 | 170.5 | 86.6 | 797 | 553 |
| Coshocton | 15.1 | 0.0 | 2.8 | 33.2 | 10.5 | 2.5 | 1.7 | 165 | 3 | 117.7 | 62.2 | 36.8 | 1 012 | 769 |
| Crawford | 5.9 | 2.4 | 1.5 | 39.3 | 8.8 | 3.4 | 0.5 | 1 728 | 11 | 170.3 | 88.3 | 50.3 | 1 138 | 762 |
| Cuyahoga | 1 214.1 | 181.2 | 811.3 | 2 549.6 | 316.0 | 123.3 | 613.5 | 102 489 | 476 | 8 286.7 | 3 091.3 | 3 445.2 | 2 658 | 1 618 |
| Darke | 18.7 | 2.4 | 4.1 | 35.6 | 18.5 | 3.1 | 0.2 | 6 159 | 28 | 150.3 | 71.7 | 54.1 | 1 036 | 610 |
| Defiance | 8.8 | 0.0 | 1.8 | 25.4 | 8.3 | 2.7 | 34.0 | 4 455 | 24 | 162.6 | 79.2 | 47.6 | 1 235 | 775 |
| Delaware | 27.0 | 2.0 | 4.6 | 29.1 | 11.7 | 424.0 | 81.3 | 167 375 | 668 | 520.2 | 107.9 | 293.3 | 1 823 | 1 339 |
| Erie | 33.6 | 25.3 | 35.8 | 47.4 | 16.2 | 5.5 | 21.0 | 8 940 | 48 | 382.6 | 124.9 | 143.7 | 1 859 | 1 381 |
| Fairfield | 24.9 | 0.3 | 6.0 | 65.3 | 18.8 | 6.7 | 9.0 | 33 178 | 171 | 457.5 | 187.2 | 191.3 | 1 354 | 957 |
| Fayette | 4.3 | 0.0 | 1.7 | 40.3 | 6.5 | 2.0 | 3.4 | 2 541 | 20 | 125.0 | 65.7 | 37.0 | 1 306 | 892 |
| Franklin | 1 223.8 | 1 129.9 | 378.3 | 1 768.6 | 822.0 | 957.1 | 3 293.4 | 387 539 | 3 375 | 6 008.1 | 2 164.4 | 2 783.9 | 2 490 | 1 528 |
| Fulton | 8.3 | 10.3 | 2.4 | 15.6 | 6.2 | 2.4 | 0.3 | 3 153 | 19 | 181.6 | 71.0 | 74.5 | 1 750 | 1 203 |
| Gallia | 7.1 | 0.0 | 1.5 | 84.2 | 9.0 | 3.1 | 1.1 | 205 | 2 | 119.8 | 70.0 | 29.7 | 964 | 717 |
| Geauga | 10.3 | 2.7 | 3.4 | 17.6 | 10.3 | 4.2 | 3.3 | 27 858 | 102 | 348.9 | 116.3 | 186.2 | 1 960 | 1 698 |
| Greene | 1 140.4 | 1 074.1 | 153.5 | 95.6 | 19.9 | 15.0 | 12.6 | 91 851 | 277 | 559.6 | 181.3 | 262.2 | 1 695 | 1 202 |
| Guernsey | 10.4 | 0.1 | 2.2 | 66.3 | 9.2 | 3.1 | 5.7 | 2 848 | 28 | 129.6 | 75.6 | 34.8 | 860 | 556 |
| Hamilton | 753.8 | 1 792.2 | 392.0 | 1 609.5 | 176.6 | 74.0 | 260.8 | 109 997 | 611 | 4 162.0 | 1 577.2 | 1 861.7 | 2 210 | 1 381 |
| Hancock | 14.1 | 0.2 | 2.6 | 38.3 | 12.4 | 3.9 | 6.0 | 22 311 | 78 | 254.3 | 99.7 | 99.5 | 1 340 | 907 |
| Hardin | 6.5 | 6.0 | 1.5 | 21.7 | 5.7 | 5.1 | 1.0 | 11 331 | 94 | 117.0 | 58.0 | 38.0 | 1 201 | 788 |
| Harrison | 7.9 | 0.1 | 1.0 | 18.4 | 4.2 | 1.8 | 1.3 | 0 | 0 | 50.1 | 28.1 | 13.7 | 884 | 666 |
| Henry | 6.3 | 0.1 | 1.5 | 14.8 | 4.5 | 2.8 | 2.8 | 2 583 | 17 | 118.1 | 51.4 | 47.1 | 1 629 | 1 129 |
| Highland | 9.1 | 5.2 | 1.7 | 66.3 | 10.2 | 2.8 | 0.3 | 1 777 | 17 | 180.3 | 84.2 | 36.3 | 852 | 475 |
| Hocking | 4.3 | 0.0 | 1.3 | 31.7 | 5.6 | 2.0 | 1.7 | 898 | 7 | 125.1 | 57.5 | 25.4 | 876 | 666 |
| Holmes | 6.1 | 1.6 | 1.3 | 16.4 | 5.1 | 2.4 | 2.2 | 4 180 | 39 | 121.0 | 46.3 | 33.8 | 818 | 646 |
| Huron | 19.1 | 0.9 | 2.8 | 38.3 | 10.4 | 4.9 | 4.1 | 5 576 | 31 | 202.8 | 100.2 | 73.4 | 1 228 | 716 |
| Jackson | 5.7 | 0.5 | 1.5 | 93.5 | 10.0 | 2.7 | 4.4 | 5 794 | 38 | 118.4 | 70.7 | 24.3 | 730 | 550 |
| Jefferson | 19.7 | 2.8 | 4.5 | 116.3 | 17.1 | 6.2 | 9.2 | 479 | 3 | 294.3 | 164.5 | 76.4 | 1 112 | 744 |
| Knox | 9.1 | 0.0 | 2.1 | 53.1 | 10.1 | 6.3 | 4.4 | 15 285 | 110 | 186.6 | 89.1 | 72.6 | 1 231 | 900 |
| Lake | 42.1 | 40.0 | 16.4 | 79.6 | 31.4 | 14.9 | 27.2 | 56 105 | 226 | 985.8 | 339.1 | 470.8 | 2 017 | 1 478 |
| Lawrence | 11.0 | 1.4 | 5.7 | 147.8 | 20.8 | 8.6 | 2.3 | 2 238 | 15 | 210.1 | 148.6 | 32.1 | 513 | 367 |
| Licking | 45.1 | 114.3 | 31.5 | 107.4 | 24.7 | 8.5 | 17.4 | 45 449 | 330 | 540.4 | 215.6 | 237.4 | 1 512 | 1 047 |
| Logan | 15.0 | 1.2 | 11.2 | 40.9 | 7.4 | 3.0 | 2.1 | 9 961 | 61 | 166.5 | 73.3 | 63.0 | 1 362 | 1 148 |
| Lorain | 132.1 | 10.6 | 13.0 | 211.9 | 54.4 | 23.1 | 37.4 | 103 482 | 590 | 1 207.7 | 500.0 | 463.9 | 1 535 | 1 102 |
| Lucas | 192.6 | 18.3 | 40.6 | 656.3 | 99.5 | 39.4 | 116.3 | 51 162 | 271 | 2 140.0 | 841.8 | 870.7 | 1 970 | 1 200 |
| Madison | 6.7 | 2.7 | 2.0 | 39.3 | 5.9 | 2.5 | 1.7 | 4 561 | 24 | 145.3 | 56.8 | 62.6 | 1 508 | 1 155 |
| Mahoning | 116.0 | 8.3 | 25.3 | 394.7 | 62.2 | 22.1 | 38.3 | 28 396 | 117 | 947.0 | 493.4 | 324.8 | 1 351 | 928 |
| Marion | 23.6 | 0.1 | 2.4 | 66.0 | 18.6 | 5.1 | 1.5 | 6 377 | 61 | 229.6 | 108.2 | 71.5 | 1 096 | 741 |
| Medina | 35.3 | 17.1 | 7.3 | 39.9 | 18.3 | 7.2 | 9.4 | 70 538 | 373 | 590.0 | 215.0 | 265.0 | 1 560 | 1 260 |
| Meigs | 5.2 | 0.1 | 1.1 | 47.9 | 7.2 | 2.9 | 1.7 | 660 | 7 | 70.7 | 45.4 | 13.2 | 577 | 463 |
| Mercer | 7.9 | 0.3 | 2.6 | 16.8 | 7.3 | 2.4 | 4.5 | 5 464 | 26 | 195.8 | 80.5 | 52.3 | 1 280 | 875 |
| Miami | 24.8 | 56.1 | 4.7 | 60.1 | 14.4 | 5.0 | 7.1 | 19 638 | 77 | 360.7 | 134.1 | 142.3 | 1 409 | 934 |
| Monroe | 3.7 | 0.0 | 0.8 | 31.6 | 4.1 | 1.3 | 0.3 | 0 | 0 | 53.6 | 32.6 | 12.8 | 899 | 751 |
| Montgomery | 312.7 | 415.9 | 168.3 | 692.6 | 125.6 | 48.1 | 175.0 | 59 443 | 373 | 2 607.2 | 1 012.6 | 1 029.5 | 1 913 | 1 244 |
| Morgan | 19.9 | 0.1 | 0.6 | 22.8 | 3.9 | 1.2 | 1.1 | 2 469 | 27 | 54.3 | 33.8 | 13.5 | 924 | 500 |
| Morrow | 4.8 | 0.0 | 1.1 | 17.3 | 5.7 | 2.5 | 1.9 | 3 511 | 23 | 123.6 | 54.4 | 28.1 | 813 | 571 |
| Muskingum | 25.9 | 0.4 | 10.3 | 123.4 | 18.6 | 8.3 | 9.5 | 1 389 | 42 | 371.8 | 220.9 | 93.9 | 1 100 | 726 |
| Noble | 2.4 | 0.0 | 0.7 | 14.8 | 5.9 | 1.0 | 0.5 | 0 | 0 | 35.5 | 23.5 | 7.6 | 539 | 458 |

1. State totals may include programs not allocated by county.   2. Based on the resident population estimated as of July 1 of the year shown.

| STATE County | Direct general expenditure — Total (mil dol) | Per capita[1] (dollars) | Percent of total for: Education | Percent of total for: Health and hospitals | Percent of total for: Police protection | Percent of total for: Public welfare | Percent of total for: Highways | Debt outstanding — Total (mil dol) | Per capita[1] (dollars) | Government employment, 2011 — Federal civilian | Federal military | State and local | Presidential election[2] 2012 — Percent of vote cast: Democratic | Republican | All other |
|---|---|---|---|---|---|---|---|---|---|---|---|---|---|---|---|
| | 185 | 186 | 187 | 188 | 189 | 190 | 191 | 192 | 193 | 194 | 195 | 196 | 197 | 198 | 199 |
| **NORTH DAKOTA—Cont'd** | | | | | | | | | | | | | | | |
| Ward | 151.1 | 2 701 | 64.4 | 0.3 | 5.1 | 2.3 | 6.5 | 59.9 | 1 071 | 1 313 | 5 727 | 4 076 | 39.6 | 58.8 | 1.6 |
| Wells | 15.4 | 3 600 | 47.0 | 2.0 | 3.2 | 3.2 | 14.1 | 2.1 | 488 | 30 | 31 | 270 | 35.4 | 61.8 | 2.9 |
| Williams | 62.6 | 3 206 | 54.2 | 3.4 | 4.5 | 2.8 | 7.3 | 93.4 | 4 782 | 90 | 179 | 1 692 | 31.2 | 67.1 | 1.7 |
| **OHIO** | X | X | X | X | X | X | X | X | X | 80 543 | 36 158 | 700 757 | 51.5 | 46.9 | 1.6 |
| Adams | 90.5 | 3 213 | 60.9 | 2.1 | 2.0 | 10.0 | 5.7 | 108.5 | 3 854 | 66 | 72 | 1 504 | 36.6 | 60.7 | 2.7 |
| Allen | 390.5 | 3 711 | 48.9 | 3.1 | 5.8 | 6.2 | 4.3 | 181.4 | 1 724 | 330 | 272 | 6 172 | 38.8 | 59.6 | 1.6 |
| Ashland | 146.2 | 2 662 | 46.5 | 8.2 | 6.8 | 1.9 | 6.7 | 49.0 | 892 | 99 | 135 | 2 541 | 37.0 | 60.2 | 2.8 |
| Ashtabula | 364.7 | 3 606 | 49.3 | 6.5 | 4.2 | 9.8 | 6.6 | 198.2 | 1 959 | 197 | 277 | 4 713 | 55.8 | 42.2 | 2.0 |
| Athens | 210.7 | 3 330 | 47.0 | 6.2 | 2.3 | 13.2 | 5.0 | 97.8 | 1 545 | 252 | 176 | 10 943 | 66.6 | 31.3 | 2.0 |
| Auglaize | 161.7 | 3 483 | 51.6 | 1.5 | 5.6 | 6.9 | 5.6 | 221.5 | 4 771 | 86 | 116 | 2 270 | 28.6 | 69.8 | 1.5 |
| Belmont | 234.7 | 3 457 | 49.7 | 1.0 | 2.4 | 10.6 | 10.1 | 90.7 | 1 335 | 170 | 179 | 3 846 | 50.3 | 47.6 | 2.1 |
| Brown | 175.6 | 3 995 | 51.8 | 24.7 | 3.1 | 3.2 | 4.7 | 68.3 | 1 553 | 89 | 113 | 2 044 | 37.3 | 60.6 | 2.1 |
| Butler | 1 319.4 | 3 687 | 47.9 | 4.9 | 5.9 | 5.2 | 5.4 | 1 887.2 | 5 273 | 596 | 957 | 21 507 | 38.0 | 60.6 | 1.4 |
| Carroll | 60.3 | 2 115 | 46.4 | 7.5 | 5.2 | 9.8 | 11.6 | 14.9 | 524 | 47 | 73 | 1 006 | 46.0 | 50.9 | 3.1 |
| Champaign | 149.7 | 3 787 | 60.0 | 4.0 | 4.2 | 3.9 | 5.7 | 40.9 | 1 035 | 74 | 101 | 1 878 | 39.1 | 59.0 | 1.9 |
| Clark | 533.2 | 3 795 | 49.5 | 6.3 | 6.0 | 8.4 | 3.9 | 240.3 | 1 711 | 577 | 351 | 6 543 | 47.9 | 50.4 | 1.8 |
| Clermont | 581.4 | 3 005 | 47.0 | 5.4 | 3.7 | 7.6 | 4.3 | 310.3 | 1 604 | 292 | 504 | 7 764 | 33.1 | 65.5 | 1.4 |
| Clinton | 271.5 | 6 304 | 28.1 | 38.9 | 3.5 | 3.2 | 4.0 | 411.1 | 9 545 | 138 | 106 | 2 363 | 34.0 | 64.3 | 1.8 |
| Columbiana | 306.2 | 2 817 | 52.0 | 7.1 | 5.6 | 7.1 | 7.2 | 133.5 | 1 228 | 589 | 273 | 4 604 | 45.1 | 52.8 | 2.1 |
| Coshocton | 113.1 | 3 113 | 47.4 | 7.3 | 6.1 | 9.0 | 8.3 | 62.6 | 1 724 | 85 | 94 | 1 542 | 45.6 | 51.4 | 3.0 |
| Crawford | 174.6 | 3 948 | 59.2 | 3.0 | 4.1 | 6.6 | 6.3 | 132.7 | 3 000 | 85 | 110 | 1 890 | 39.1 | 58.2 | 2.7 |
| Cuyahoga | 7 933.8 | 6 122 | 35.0 | 13.4 | 5.4 | 4.9 | 2.8 | 9 881.7 | 7 625 | 16 829 | 3 684 | 79 647 | 68.9 | 30.0 | 1.1 |
| Darke | 136.5 | 2 614 | 56.4 | 4.7 | 5.9 | 5.9 | 7.4 | 57.3 | 1 097 | 106 | 134 | 2 173 | 30.9 | 67.0 | 2.1 |
| Defiance | 159.8 | 4 147 | 41.0 | 17.1 | 3.7 | 3.0 | 4.9 | 64.7 | 1 678 | 98 | 98 | 1 948 | 43.8 | 54.2 | 2.0 |
| Delaware | 531.5 | 3 304 | 52.8 | 3.2 | 4.6 | 2.2 | 7.2 | 729.1 | 4 532 | 236 | 452 | 7 293 | 39.7 | 59.3 | 1.1 |
| Erie | 363.6 | 4 702 | 49.0 | 2.2 | 5.8 | 6.0 | 4.2 | 235.3 | 3 043 | 306 | 195 | 5 209 | 56.1 | 42.3 | 1.6 |
| Fairfield | 416.9 | 2 950 | 52.1 | 5.4 | 2.7 | 4.5 | 4.9 | 545.8 | 3 862 | 247 | 381 | 6 511 | 40.7 | 57.8 | 1.6 |
| Fayette | 114.7 | 4 051 | 48.7 | 6.1 | 3.8 | 5.8 | 7.6 | 61.0 | 2 156 | 50 | 73 | 1 654 | 37.6 | 60.7 | 1.6 |
| Franklin | 5 819.7 | 5 205 | 37.8 | 5.9 | 7.0 | 5.2 | 3.5 | 6 882.1 | 6 155 | 13 552 | 3 502 | 116 720 | 59.7 | 39.0 | 1.3 |
| Fulton | 203.0 | 4 770 | 53.2 | 1.1 | 5.3 | 6.3 | 7.5 | 194.3 | 4 566 | 95 | 108 | 2 658 | 45.1 | 53.2 | 1.7 |
| Gallia | 113.9 | 3 692 | 57.1 | 0.4 | 4.9 | 11.0 | 5.7 | 110.0 | 3 568 | 85 | 78 | 1 875 | 35.9 | 61.9 | 2.2 |
| Geauga | 338.0 | 3 557 | 48.5 | 6.1 | 5.2 | 4.7 | 7.9 | 133.9 | 1 409 | 148 | 236 | 4 229 | 41.6 | 56.9 | 1.5 |
| Greene | 550.9 | 3 562 | 44.0 | 3.9 | 8.3 | 4.9 | 3.6 | 452.6 | 2 926 | 14 392 | 2 949 | 12 058 | 40.1 | 58.5 | 1.3 |
| Guernsey | 130.1 | 3 221 | 41.8 | 4.7 | 4.1 | 11.4 | 6.4 | 42.2 | 1 043 | 128 | 101 | 2 317 | 44.0 | 53.1 | 2.9 |
| Hamilton | 4 130.4 | 4 903 | 38.1 | 2.7 | 7.0 | 11.3 | 3.0 | 5 036.1 | 5 979 | 9 257 | 2 143 | 47 801 | 53.0 | 46.0 | 1.0 |
| Hancock | 248.8 | 3 352 | 44.6 | 8.3 | 4.8 | 3.7 | 6.9 | 203.1 | 2 737 | 159 | 190 | 3 353 | 37.5 | 60.6 | 1.9 |
| Hardin | 111.2 | 3 515 | 56.2 | 6.8 | 3.8 | 7.3 | 8.3 | 20.7 | 655 | 75 | 81 | 1 497 | 38.2 | 59.1 | 2.7 |
| Harrison | 49.7 | 3 208 | 46.8 | 1.1 | 3.6 | 13.9 | 13.4 | 63.3 | 4 082 | 59 | 40 | 712 | 47.3 | 49.7 | 3.0 |
| Henry | 125.8 | 4 347 | 51.9 | 1.5 | 3.0 | 18.7 | 6.5 | 55.8 | 1 928 | 77 | 71 | 2 120 | 42.6 | 55.5 | 1.9 |
| Highland | 162.3 | 3 804 | 46.2 | 22.2 | 4.7 | 7.1 | 2.5 | 81.1 | 1 902 | 108 | 110 | 2 412 | 35.7 | 62.1 | 2.2 |
| Hocking | 116.9 | 4 036 | 42.7 | 27.5 | 3.8 | 7.3 | 5.3 | 32.6 | 1 126 | 45 | 74 | 1 841 | 48.3 | 49.1 | 2.6 |
| Holmes | 118.1 | 2 856 | 34.3 | 28.0 | 2.1 | 4.8 | 8.4 | 38.9 | 941 | 68 | 108 | 1 616 | 28.3 | 69.5 | 2.3 |
| Huron | 194.5 | 3 253 | 52.5 | 1.9 | 4.2 | 6.1 | 6.3 | 113.8 | 1 904 | 139 | 151 | 2 543 | 47.2 | 50.4 | 2.4 |
| Jackson | 109.1 | 3 275 | 52.7 | 3.7 | 4.9 | 7.5 | 7.3 | 76.3 | 2 289 | 70 | 84 | 1 503 | 38.6 | 58.7 | 2.7 |
| Jefferson | 272.7 | 3 968 | 42.3 | 8.7 | 3.5 | 11.3 | 5.5 | 66.6 | 970 | 200 | 175 | 3 382 | 49.1 | 48.9 | 2.1 |
| Knox | 178.0 | 3 019 | 52.2 | 1.6 | 2.7 | 7.0 | 6.5 | 115.4 | 1 958 | 105 | 155 | 2 749 | 39.0 | 58.9 | 2.0 |
| Lake | 922.8 | 3 954 | 49.3 | 7.2 | 6.7 | 2.5 | 6.1 | 483.7 | 2 073 | 460 | 610 | 11 654 | 49.6 | 48.7 | 1.7 |
| Lawrence | 207.3 | 3 312 | 65.2 | 3.2 | 2.3 | 7.8 | 4.0 | 87.1 | 1 390 | 129 | 158 | 3 058 | 41.4 | 56.7 | 1.9 |
| Licking | 555.1 | 3 536 | 59.3 | 2.7 | 4.6 | 4.4 | 3.9 | 450.9 | 2 872 | 464 | 435 | 7 819 | 41.2 | 57.0 | 1.8 |
| Logan | 156.3 | 3 378 | 51.1 | 1.2 | 6.5 | 5.6 | 8.1 | 131.8 | 2 848 | 138 | 117 | 2 231 | 35.7 | 62.3 | 1.9 |
| Lorain | 1 153.0 | 3 815 | 49.5 | 6.1 | 4.5 | 5.0 | 4.1 | 1 861.6 | 6 159 | 1 159 | 786 | 14 412 | 58.1 | 40.2 | 1.7 |
| Lucas | 2 193.6 | 4 964 | 39.4 | 6.3 | 6.0 | 5.8 | 4.4 | 2 105.6 | 4 765 | 2 005 | 1 212 | 27 608 | 65.0 | 33.5 | 1.5 |
| Madison | 145.3 | 3 502 | 53.9 | 6.4 | 3.5 | 5.2 | 5.3 | 131.1 | 3 159 | 72 | 110 | 3 068 | 37.4 | 60.8 | 1.8 |
| Mahoning | 934.0 | 3 885 | 51.2 | 5.3 | 6.6 | 5.8 | 3.4 | 634.0 | 2 637 | 1 320 | 614 | 13 995 | 62.2 | 35.6 | 2.1 |
| Marion | 222.6 | 3 412 | 47.0 | 5.5 | 5.4 | 5.3 | 4.7 | 318.9 | 4 887 | 125 | 176 | 4 394 | 44.4 | 53.3 | 2.4 |
| Medina | 570.5 | 3 359 | 49.6 | 4.6 | 5.9 | 3.4 | 4.9 | 367.5 | 2 164 | 320 | 448 | 6 717 | 45.2 | 53.3 | 1.5 |
| Meigs | 65.4 | 2 857 | 50.1 | 2.6 | 2.2 | 4.3 | 22.5 | 34.8 | 1 520 | 73 | 60 | 1 052 | 39.5 | 58.1 | 2.4 |
| Mercer | 203.5 | 4 976 | 44.3 | 22.0 | 3.7 | 5.0 | 7.0 | 68.4 | 1 672 | 104 | 103 | 2 684 | 27.5 | 71.0 | 1.5 |
| Miami | 364.8 | 3 610 | 52.6 | 3.2 | 6.0 | 3.3 | 4.3 | 154.8 | 1 532 | 193 | 261 | 4 727 | 34.8 | 63.3 | 1.9 |
| Monroe | 53.6 | 3 761 | 47.3 | 3.6 | 3.6 | 20.8 | 10.7 | 6.0 | 419 | 47 | 37 | 792 | 53.1 | 43.9 | 3.0 |
| Montgomery | 2 455.8 | 4 564 | 46.5 | 4.0 | 6.9 | 6.7 | 4.5 | 2 453.7 | 4 560 | 4 451 | 4 235 | 28 049 | 52.4 | 46.2 | 1.4 |
| Morgan | 47.5 | 3 254 | 43.1 | 4.2 | 2.2 | 13.6 | 11.4 | 17.7 | 1 211 | 35 | 38 | 635 | 44.9 | 52.1 | 3.1 |
| Morrow | 117.2 | 3 394 | 41.8 | 25.0 | 2.8 | 4.7 | 6.4 | 35.7 | 1 035 | 54 | 88 | 1 560 | 37.1 | 60.5 | 2.4 |
| Muskingum | 349.6 | 4 097 | 55.2 | 0.9 | 5.4 | 8.3 | 6.6 | 205.5 | 2 408 | 250 | 218 | 4 963 | 45.4 | 52.6 | 2.0 |
| Noble | 34.8 | 2 469 | 48.4 | 2.6 | 3.6 | 13.8 | 15.4 | 3.2 | 227 | 25 | 37 | 992 | 40.1 | 55.9 | 4.0 |

1. Based on the resident population estimated as of July 1 of the year shown.　2. © 2013 Election Data Services, Inc. All rights reserved.

# Table B. States and Counties — **Land Area and Population**

| STATE/ County code | CBSA code[1] | County type[2] | STATE County | Land area,[3] (sq km) 2010 | Population 2012 Total persons | Rank | Per square kilometer | White | Black | American Indian, Alaska Native | Asian and Pacific Islander | Percent Hispanic or Latino[4] | Under 5 years | 5 to 17 years | 18 to 24 years | 25 to 34 years | 35 to 44 years | 45 to 54 years |
|---|---|---|---|---|---|---|---|---|---|---|---|---|---|---|---|---|---|---|
| | | | | 1 | 2 | 3 | 4 | 5 | 6 | 7 | 8 | 9 | 10 | 11 | 12 | 13 | 14 | 15 |
| | | | OHIO—Cont'd | | | | | | | | | | | | | | | |
| 39 123 | 45780 | 2 | Ottawa | 660 | 41 339 | 1 144 | 62.6 | 94.3 | 1.4 | 0.5 | 0.5 | 4.3 | 4.8 | 15.5 | 6.5 | 9.4 | 11.1 | 16.4 |
| 39 125 | ... | 6 | Paulding | 1 079 | 19 295 | 1 863 | 17.9 | 94.2 | 1.4 | 0.6 | 0.4 | 4.3 | 6.6 | 18.0 | 7.4 | 11.1 | 12.2 | 15.2 |
| 39 127 | ... | 6 | Perry | 1 057 | 36 015 | 1 276 | 34.1 | 98.4 | 0.9 | 0.9 | 0.3 | 0.7 | 6.5 | 19.0 | 8.0 | 11.8 | 13.0 | 15.2 |
| 39 129 | 18140 | 1 | Pickaway | 1 298 | 56 399 | 900 | 43.5 | 94.7 | 4.0 | 0.7 | 0.6 | 1.2 | 5.6 | 17.5 | 8.9 | 12.9 | 14.4 | 15.1 |
| 39 131 | ... | 7 | Pike | 1 140 | 28 480 | 1 469 | 25.0 | 97.4 | 1.6 | 1.4 | 0.5 | 0.8 | 6.3 | 18.3 | 8.3 | 11.4 | 12.7 | 15.1 |
| 39 133 | 10420 | 2 | Portage | 1 262 | 161 451 | 389 | 127.9 | 92.5 | 5.1 | 0.7 | 1.9 | 1.4 | 4.9 | 15.4 | 16.1 | 11.0 | 11.7 | 14.9 |
| 39 135 | 19380 | 2 | Preble | 1 098 | 41 886 | 1 132 | 38.1 | 98.0 | 1.0 | 0.8 | 0.7 | 0.7 | 6.0 | 18.0 | 7.5 | 11.0 | 12.5 | 15.4 |
| 39 137 | ... | 6 | Putnam | 1 250 | 34 198 | 1 322 | 27.4 | 93.7 | 0.6 | 0.3 | 0.4 | 5.5 | 7.3 | 18.9 | 7.9 | 11.4 | 11.6 | 15.8 |
| 39 139 | 31900 | 3 | Richland | 1 283 | 122 673 | 497 | 95.6 | 88.3 | 10.4 | 0.7 | 1.0 | 1.5 | 5.9 | 16.3 | 8.5 | 11.9 | 12.3 | 14.7 |
| 39 141 | 17060 | 4 | Ross | 1 785 | 77 429 | 705 | 43.4 | 91.9 | 7.3 | 1.0 | 0.8 | 1.0 | 5.8 | 16.5 | 7.7 | 12.9 | 14.1 | 16.0 |
| 39 143 | 23380 | 4 | Sandusky | 1 058 | 60 510 | 855 | 57.2 | 87.7 | 4.0 | 0.5 | 0.6 | 8.9 | 6.2 | 17.8 | 7.7 | 11.4 | 12.2 | 15.2 |
| 39 145 | 39020 | 4 | Scioto | 1 580 | 78 477 | 701 | 49.7 | 95.1 | 3.4 | 1.4 | 0.6 | 1.1 | 6.0 | 16.5 | 9.8 | 12.5 | 12.6 | 13.9 |
| 39 147 | 45660 | 4 | Seneca | 1 427 | 56 018 | 902 | 39.3 | 92.5 | 3.3 | 0.5 | 0.8 | 4.4 | 6.1 | 17.2 | 10.6 | 11.6 | 11.2 | 14.6 |
| 39 149 | 43380 | 4 | Shelby | 1 056 | 49 167 | 996 | 46.6 | 95.3 | 3.1 | 0.5 | 1.3 | 1.4 | 6.9 | 20.0 | 7.7 | 11.4 | 12.8 | 15.3 |
| 39 151 | 15940 | 2 | Stark | 1 490 | 374 868 | 176 | 251.6 | 89.6 | 0.8 | 0.8 | 1.1 | 1.7 | 5.7 | 16.8 | 8.8 | 11.1 | 12.0 | 15.0 |
| 39 153 | 10420 | 2 | Summit | 1 069 | 540 811 | 119 | 505.9 | 81.3 | 15.7 | 0.7 | 2.7 | 1.7 | 5.8 | 16.7 | 9.1 | 12.1 | 12.5 | 15.3 |
| 39 155 | 49660 | 2 | Trumbull | 1 601 | 207 406 | 304 | 129.5 | 89.6 | 9.3 | 0.6 | 0.8 | 1.4 | 5.4 | 16.3 | 8.0 | 10.7 | 12.0 | 15.1 |
| 39 157 | 35420 | 4 | Tuscarawas | 1 470 | 92 392 | 627 | 62.9 | 96.5 | 1.4 | 0.5 | 0.6 | 2.0 | 6.1 | 17.3 | 7.6 | 11.6 | 12.0 | 14.8 |
| 39 159 | 18140 | 1 | Union | 1 118 | 52 715 | 944 | 47.2 | 93.1 | 3.2 | 0.7 | 3.0 | 1.3 | 6.5 | 20.5 | 7.3 | 13.3 | 16.4 | 15.7 |
| 39 161 | 46780 | 6 | Van Wert | 1 060 | 28 744 | 1 458 | 27.1 | 96.0 | 1.6 | 0.4 | 0.5 | 2.6 | 6.4 | 18.1 | 7.6 | 11.4 | 11.8 | 14.7 |
| 39 163 | ... | 9 | Vinton | 1 068 | 13 239 | 2 227 | 12.4 | 98.3 | 1.0 | 1.0 | 0.4 | 0.6 | 5.8 | 18.4 | 8.4 | 10.8 | 13.2 | 15.6 |
| 39 165 | 17140 | 1 | Warren | 1 039 | 217 241 | 289 | 209.1 | 89.9 | 3.9 | 0.5 | 4.6 | 2.4 | 6.5 | 20.5 | 6.9 | 11.7 | 15.5 | 16.1 |
| 39 167 | 37620 | 3 | Washington | 1 637 | 61 475 | 845 | 37.6 | 97.1 | 1.8 | 0.9 | 0.9 | 0.8 | 5.0 | 15.5 | 9.0 | 10.7 | 11.8 | 15.2 |
| 39 169 | 49300 | 4 | Wayne | 1 437 | 114 848 | 526 | 79.9 | 95.9 | 2.2 | 0.5 | 1.1 | 1.6 | 6.7 | 18.4 | 9.7 | 11.2 | 11.7 | 14.4 |
| 39 171 | ... | 7 | Williams | 1 090 | 37 513 | 1 232 | 34.4 | 94.4 | 1.4 | 0.5 | 0.8 | 3.7 | 5.8 | 17.6 | 7.8 | 11.6 | 12.1 | 15.4 |
| 39 173 | 45780 | 2 | Wood | 1 599 | 128 200 | 482 | 80.2 | 91.0 | 3.1 | 0.6 | 2.0 | 4.6 | 5.4 | 15.8 | 17.1 | 11.6 | 11.6 | 13.5 |
| 39 175 | ... | 7 | Wyandot | 1 054 | 22 607 | 1 704 | 21.4 | 96.5 | 0.7 | 0.5 | 0.9 | 2.3 | 6.3 | 17.9 | 7.4 | 11.5 | 12.5 | 14.6 |
| 40 000 | ... | X | OKLAHOMA | 177 660 | 3 814 820 | X | 21.5 | 73.0 | 8.6 | 12.2 | 2.5 | 9.2 | 7.0 | 17.7 | 10.2 | 13.6 | 12.1 | 13.6 |
| 40 001 | ... | 6 | Adair | 1 485 | 22 286 | 1 720 | 15.0 | 51.7 | 0.8 | 51.2 | 0.8 | 5.4 | 7.2 | 20.5 | 8.6 | 11.7 | 12.6 | 14.0 |
| 40 003 | ... | 9 | Alfalfa | 2 244 | 5 666 | 2 792 | 2.5 | 87.8 | 4.9 | 4.1 | 0.4 | 4.6 | 4.8 | 12.8 | 5.6 | 9.8 | 15.3 | 18.0 |
| 40 005 | ... | 7 | Atoka | 2 527 | 14 007 | 2 179 | 5.5 | 78.4 | 4.7 | 19.3 | 0.8 | 3.5 | 6.4 | 17.4 | 8.0 | 12.6 | 12.1 | 14.0 |
| 40 007 | ... | 9 | Beaver | 4 700 | 5 591 | 2 798 | 1.2 | 77.4 | 1.1 | 2.4 | 0.3 | 20.5 | 6.6 | 18.8 | 7.7 | 11.1 | 11.4 | 14.9 |
| 40 009 | 21120 | 7 | Beckham | 2 336 | 23 081 | 1 685 | 9.9 | 79.9 | 4.6 | 4.4 | 1.1 | 12.2 | 7.8 | 16.5 | 9.6 | 15.7 | 12.5 | 13.9 |
| 40 011 | ... | 6 | Blaine | 2 405 | 9 785 | 2 455 | 4.1 | 78.8 | 4.4 | 11.2 | 1.0 | 8.4 | 7.9 | 17.5 | 7.6 | 10.5 | 10.5 | 14.1 |
| 40 013 | 20460 | 6 | Bryan | 2 343 | 43 399 | 1 101 | 18.5 | 79.5 | 2.3 | 18.6 | 0.9 | 5.3 | 6.7 | 16.6 | 11.6 | 12.8 | 11.5 | 12.7 |
| 40 015 | ... | 6 | Caddo | 3 311 | 29 678 | 1 433 | 9.0 | 63.3 | 4.5 | 26.5 | 0.8 | 10.4 | 6.9 | 18.2 | 8.6 | 13.4 | 12.0 | 14.2 |
| 40 017 | 36420 | 1 | Canadian | 2 322 | 122 560 | 499 | 52.8 | 82.5 | 3.4 | 7.1 | 3.4 | 7.2 | 7.3 | 19.4 | 7.7 | 14.5 | 14.1 | 14.2 |
| 40 019 | 11620 | 5 | Carter | 2 129 | 48 085 | 1 010 | 22.6 | 77.0 | 8.4 | 13.6 | 1.4 | 5.7 | 7.1 | 18.6 | 7.8 | 12.5 | 12.4 | 14.0 |
| 40 021 | 45140 | 6 | Cherokee | 1 941 | 48 150 | 1 009 | 24.8 | 58.5 | 2.3 | 40.5 | 1.1 | 6.5 | 6.6 | 17.3 | 14.8 | 12.4 | 10.9 | 12.4 |
| 40 023 | ... | 7 | Choctaw | 1 995 | 15 182 | 2 094 | 7.6 | 68.4 | 12.3 | 21.5 | 0.7 | 3.4 | 7.1 | 17.3 | 8.2 | 10.5 | 11.0 | 14.0 |
| 40 025 | ... | 9 | Cimarron | 4 752 | 2 385 | 3 016 | 0.5 | 78.7 | 1.0 | 2.0 | 0.4 | 19.7 | 7.5 | 17.6 | 5.9 | 9.5 | 10.2 | 12.9 |
| 40 027 | 36420 | 1 | Cleveland | 1 395 | 265 638 | 252 | 190.4 | 79.6 | 5.6 | 7.9 | 4.9 | 7.2 | 6.2 | 16.3 | 15.3 | 15.3 | 12.4 | 12.9 |
| 40 029 | ... | 9 | Coal | 1 338 | 5 963 | 2 763 | 4.5 | 79.3 | 1.6 | 23.3 | 0.7 | 2.9 | 6.6 | 19.2 | 7.6 | 10.5 | 10.9 | 13.5 |
| 40 031 | 30020 | 3 | Comanche | 2 769 | 126 390 | 487 | 45.6 | 63.1 | 19.2 | 7.4 | 4.4 | 11.5 | 7.7 | 17.4 | 13.5 | 16.7 | 12.0 | 12.7 |
| 40 033 | ... | 6 | Cotton | 1 639 | 6 155 | 2 748 | 3.8 | 81.9 | 3.4 | 12.3 | 0.9 | 6.4 | 6.1 | 18.1 | 7.8 | 11.4 | 11.8 | 14.7 |
| 40 035 | ... | 6 | Craig | 1 972 | 14 748 | 2 126 | 7.5 | 73.5 | 3.9 | 26.8 | 1.2 | 2.7 | 5.7 | 16.3 | 8.4 | 11.1 | 12.1 | 15.5 |
| 40 037 | 46140 | 2 | Creek | 2 461 | 70 651 | 756 | 28.7 | 83.8 | 3.2 | 15.1 | 0.8 | 3.5 | 6.3 | 18.3 | 7.9 | 11.5 | 12.1 | 14.9 |
| 40 039 | 48220 | 7 | Custer | 2 561 | 28 536 | 1 467 | 11.1 | 74.6 | 3.9 | 8.0 | 1.8 | 14.7 | 6.9 | 16.0 | 18.8 | 13.2 | 9.6 | 11.8 |
| 40 041 | ... | 6 | Delaware | 1 912 | 41 441 | 1 141 | 21.7 | 73.0 | 0.7 | 29.1 | 1.5 | 3.3 | 5.3 | 16.9 | 7.2 | 9.4 | 10.8 | 14.0 |
| 40 043 | ... | 9 | Dewey | 2 589 | 4 783 | 2 853 | 1.8 | 87.5 | 1.2 | 7.7 | 0.9 | 5.6 | 6.0 | 18.6 | 6.0 | 11.0 | 10.7 | 14.0 |
| 40 045 | ... | 9 | Ellis | 3 190 | 4 104 | 2 894 | 1.3 | 90.9 | 0.9 | 2.8 | 0.4 | 6.4 | 6.2 | 17.7 | 5.5 | 10.4 | 11.0 | 13.7 |
| 40 047 | 21420 | 5 | Garfield | 2 741 | 61 189 | 848 | 22.3 | 82.5 | 4.1 | 4.0 | 3.3 | 9.3 | 7.5 | 17.2 | 9.0 | 13.8 | 11.0 | 13.8 |
| 40 049 | ... | 6 | Garvin | 2 077 | 27 297 | 1 521 | 13.1 | 82.6 | 3.4 | 11.4 | 0.8 | 6.4 | 6.8 | 17.8 | 7.9 | 11.7 | 12.2 | 13.7 |
| 40 051 | 36420 | 1 | Grady | 2 850 | 53 118 | 937 | 18.6 | 86.8 | 3.3 | 8.3 | 0.9 | 4.8 | 6.5 | 18.2 | 8.7 | 12.3 | 12.4 | 14.9 |
| 40 053 | ... | 9 | Grant | 2 592 | 4 516 | 2 868 | 1.7 | 93.0 | 1.9 | 3.5 | 0.5 | 3.4 | 5.7 | 16.6 | 6.4 | 10.1 | 10.4 | 15.4 |
| 40 055 | ... | 7 | Greer | 1 656 | 6 082 | 2 753 | 3.7 | 79.3 | 8.0 | 4.1 | 0.5 | 10.1 | 5.3 | 14.2 | 8.1 | 15.8 | 13.7 | 14.4 |
| 40 057 | ... | 9 | Harmon | 1 391 | 2 906 | 2 985 | 2.1 | 64.3 | 8.3 | 3.4 | 0.7 | 26.3 | 8.5 | 17.5 | 8.0 | 11.8 | 10.9 | 13.6 |
| 40 059 | ... | 9 | Harper | 2 691 | 3 676 | 2 931 | 1.4 | 80.9 | 0.5 | 1.6 | 0.3 | 18.0 | 7.2 | 17.8 | 6.6 | 13.2 | 10.2 | 13.8 |
| 40 061 | ... | 6 | Haskell | 1 493 | 12 938 | 2 246 | 8.7 | 79.2 | 1.3 | 22.0 | 0.9 | 3.6 | 6.9 | 18.6 | 8.0 | 11.2 | 11.6 | 12.6 |
| 40 063 | ... | 7 | Hughes | 2 084 | 13 836 | 2 184 | 6.6 | 72.2 | 6.1 | 23.0 | 0.6 | 4.1 | 5.4 | 16.4 | 8.2 | 12.9 | 12.3 | 14.0 |
| 40 065 | 11060 | 5 | Jackson | 2 079 | 26 237 | 1 551 | 12.6 | 67.8 | 8.6 | 3.2 | 2.2 | 21.4 | 7.9 | 18.3 | 10.9 | 14.1 | 11.5 | 13.1 |
| 40 067 | ... | 8 | Jefferson | 1 965 | 6 377 | 2 733 | 3.2 | 83.8 | 1.8 | 9.3 | 0.6 | 8.7 | 6.4 | 17.3 | 7.6 | 10.7 | 10.7 | 14.3 |
| 40 069 | ... | 7 | Johnston | 1 665 | 11 003 | 2 358 | 6.6 | 78.3 | 3.2 | 21.0 | 0.7 | 4.2 | 7.3 | 17.2 | 9.6 | 11.5 | 11.4 | 13.3 |
| 40 071 | 38620 | 5 | Kay | 2 382 | 45 831 | 1 051 | 19.2 | 81.1 | 2.7 | 13.0 | 1.0 | 6.8 | 7.3 | 17.8 | 8.6 | 11.8 | 10.6 | 13.5 |
| 40 073 | ... | 6 | Kingfisher | 2 326 | 15 005 | 2 106 | 6.5 | 81.7 | 1.8 | 5.0 | 0.5 | 13.5 | 7.3 | 18.9 | 7.8 | 12.0 | 12.1 | 14.8 |

1. CBSA = Core Based Statistical Area. See Appendix A for explanation. See Appendix B for list of metropolitan areas with component counties.   2. County type code from the Economic Research Service of USDA Rural-Urban Continuum Codes. See Appendix A for definition.   3. Dry land or land partially or temporarily covered by water.   4. May be of any race.

# Table B. States and Counties — **Population and Households**

| | Population, 2011 (cont.) | | | | Population change and components of change, 2000–2012 | | | | | | | Households, 2010 | | | | |
|---|---|---|---|---|---|---|---|---|---|---|---|---|---|---|---|---|
| | Age (percent) (cont.) | | | | Total persons | | Percent change | | Components of change, 2010–2012 | | | | | | Percent | |
| STATE County | 55 to 64 years | 65 to 74 years | 75 years and over | Percent female | 2000 | 2010 | 2000–2010 | 2010–2012 | Births | Deaths | Net migration | Number | Percent change, 2000–2010 | Persons per house-hold | Female family house-holder[1] | One per-son |
| | 16 | 17 | 18 | 19 | 20 | 21 | 22 | 23 | 24 | 25 | 26 | 27 | 28 | 29 | 30 | 31 |
| **OHIO—Cont'd** | | | | | | | | | | | | | | | | |
| Ottawa | 16.8 | 11.0 | 8.5 | 50.6 | 40 985 | 41 428 | 1.1 | -0.2 | 791 | 1 044 | 146 | 17 503 | 6.2 | 2.34 | 8.9 | 27.4 |
| Paulding | 14.2 | 8.5 | 6.7 | 50.5 | 20 293 | 19 614 | -3.3 | -1.6 | 514 | 437 | -399 | 7 769 | -0.1 | 2.51 | 9.2 | 25.0 |
| Perry | 13.4 | 7.7 | 5.5 | 50.2 | 34 078 | 36 058 | 5.8 | -0.1 | 981 | 803 | -218 | 13 576 | 8.6 | 2.63 | 11.6 | 22.8 |
| Pickaway | 12.5 | 7.7 | 5.5 | 47.6 | 52 727 | 55 698 | 5.6 | 1.3 | 1 291 | 1 138 | 539 | 19 624 | 11.5 | 2.61 | 10.9 | 22.2 |
| Pike | 13.0 | 8.3 | 6.7 | 50.5 | 27 695 | 28 709 | 3.7 | -0.8 | 776 | 764 | -238 | 11 012 | 5.4 | 2.56 | 13.1 | 25.1 |
| Portage | 12.8 | 7.4 | 5.8 | 51.1 | 152 061 | 161 419 | 6.2 | 0.0 | 3 284 | 2 924 | -265 | 62 222 | 10.2 | 2.47 | 10.9 | 25.4 |
| Preble | 14.2 | 8.7 | 6.8 | 50.3 | 42 337 | 42 270 | -0.2 | -0.9 | 978 | 967 | -375 | 16 341 | 2.1 | 2.56 | 10.1 | 23.2 |
| Putnam | 12.8 | 7.1 | 7.2 | 50.0 | 34 726 | 34 499 | -0.7 | -0.9 | 1 027 | 714 | -630 | 12 872 | 5.5 | 2.66 | 7.4 | 22.5 |
| Richland | 13.8 | 8.7 | 7.9 | 49.3 | 128 852 | 124 475 | -3.4 | -1.4 | 3 098 | 2 914 | -1 980 | 48 921 | -1.2 | 2.40 | 12.5 | 28.8 |
| Ross | 13.3 | 7.9 | 5.9 | 47.3 | 73 345 | 78 064 | 6.4 | -0.8 | 1 881 | 1 760 | -734 | 28 919 | 6.6 | 2.48 | 12.6 | 26.2 |
| Sandusky | 13.9 | 8.1 | 7.4 | 50.7 | 61 792 | 60 944 | -1.4 | -0.7 | 1 578 | 1 387 | -610 | 24 182 | 2.0 | 2.48 | 12.1 | 26.3 |
| Scioto | 13.1 | 8.4 | 7.2 | 50.6 | 79 195 | 79 499 | 0.4 | -1.3 | 1 971 | 2 020 | -954 | 30 870 | 0.0 | 2.46 | 13.7 | 27.4 |
| Seneca | 13.6 | 7.5 | 7.5 | 50.0 | 58 683 | 56 745 | -3.3 | -1.3 | 1 333 | 1 230 | -829 | 21 774 | -2.3 | 2.49 | 11.3 | 26.3 |
| Shelby | 12.7 | 7.1 | 6.1 | 50.0 | 47 910 | 49 423 | 3.2 | -0.5 | 1 400 | 908 | -740 | 18 467 | 4.7 | 2.64 | 10.4 | 23.0 |
| Stark | 14.1 | 8.5 | 8.1 | 51.6 | 378 098 | 375 586 | -0.7 | -0.2 | 9 026 | 8 786 | -811 | 151 089 | 1.9 | 2.42 | 12.7 | 28.1 |
| Summit | 13.8 | 7.4 | 7.3 | 51.6 | 542 899 | 541 781 | -0.2 | -0.2 | 13 512 | 12 132 | -2 184 | 222 781 | 2.3 | 2.39 | 13.6 | 30.0 |
| Trumbull | 14.9 | 9.1 | 8.5 | 51.4 | 225 116 | 210 312 | -6.6 | -1.4 | 4 645 | 5 346 | -2 107 | 86 011 | -3.4 | 2.40 | 13.7 | 29.2 |
| Tuscarawas | 14.0 | 8.5 | 8.1 | 50.8 | 90 914 | 92 582 | 1.8 | -0.2 | 2 410 | 2 142 | -447 | 36 965 | 3.7 | 2.47 | 9.8 | 26.6 |
| Union | 10.8 | 5.6 | 4.1 | 52.7 | 40 909 | 52 300 | 27.8 | 0.8 | 1 352 | 694 | -282 | 18 065 | 25.9 | 2.73 | 8.7 | 19.5 |
| Van Wert | 13.5 | 8.4 | 8.0 | 51.2 | 29 659 | 28 744 | -3.1 | 0.0 | 697 | 632 | -97 | 11 439 | -1.3 | 2.48 | 9.2 | 26.6 |
| Vinton | 13.7 | 8.6 | 5.6 | 50.3 | 12 806 | 13 435 | 4.9 | -1.5 | 317 | 338 | -183 | 5 260 | 1.2 | 2.54 | 12.1 | 26.1 |
| Warren | 11.7 | 6.4 | 4.7 | 49.7 | 158 383 | 212 693 | 34.3 | 2.1 | 5 575 | 3 287 | 2 094 | 76 424 | 36.6 | 2.70 | 8.8 | 20.4 |
| Washington | 14.8 | 9.8 | 8.1 | 51.2 | 63 251 | 61 778 | -2.3 | -0.5 | 1 336 | 1 557 | -38 | 25 587 | 1.8 | 2.34 | 10.0 | 28.1 |
| Wayne | 13.1 | 8.0 | 6.9 | 50.5 | 111 564 | 114 520 | 2.6 | 0.3 | 3 320 | 2 339 | -600 | 42 638 | 5.4 | 2.61 | 9.2 | 25.1 |
| Williams | 13.4 | 8.6 | 7.7 | 50.4 | 39 188 | 37 642 | -3.9 | -0.3 | 924 | 841 | -205 | 15 075 | -0.2 | 2.43 | 9.9 | 27.0 |
| Wood | 12.5 | 6.6 | 5.9 | 51.1 | 121 065 | 125 488 | 3.7 | 2.2 | 2 951 | 2 194 | 1 881 | 49 043 | 8.6 | 2.43 | 9.0 | 27.5 |
| Wyandot | 13.5 | 8.4 | 8.0 | 50.7 | 22 908 | 22 615 | -1.3 | 0.0 | 580 | 550 | -36 | 9 091 | 2.4 | 2.46 | 10.2 | 26.5 |
| **OKLAHOMA** | 12.1 | 7.6 | 6.1 | 50.5 | 3 450 654 | 3 751 351 | 8.7 | 1.7 | 114 749 | 79 477 | 27 256 | 1 460 450 | 8.8 | 2.49 | 12.3 | 27.5 |
| Adair | 12.0 | 7.9 | 5.3 | 49.9 | 21 038 | 22 683 | 7.8 | -1.8 | 555 | 478 | -473 | 8 156 | 9.2 | 2.77 | 14.2 | 23.0 |
| Alfalfa | 13.6 | 10.8 | 9.1 | 40.5 | 6 105 | 5 642 | -7.6 | 0.4 | 113 | 136 | 42 | 2 022 | -8.0 | 2.27 | 6.4 | 30.2 |
| Atoka | 12.9 | 9.7 | 6.9 | 47.7 | 13 879 | 14 182 | 2.2 | -1.2 | 365 | 264 | -263 | 5 391 | 8.6 | 2.49 | 11.2 | 27.4 |
| Beaver | 14.1 | 8.3 | 7.2 | 49.3 | 5 857 | 5 636 | -3.8 | -0.8 | 103 | 121 | -26 | 2 192 | -2.4 | 2.55 | 6.1 | 23.4 |
| Beckham | 11.3 | 6.5 | 6.1 | 46.6 | 19 799 | 22 119 | 11.7 | 4.3 | 757 | 562 | 735 | 8 163 | 11.0 | 2.48 | 11.1 | 27.6 |
| Blaine | 13.7 | 9.5 | 8.7 | 50.3 | 11 976 | 11 943 | -0.3 | -18.1 | 306 | 283 | -2 265 | 3 959 | -4.8 | 2.46 | 10.3 | 29.4 |
| Bryan | 12.2 | 8.9 | 6.9 | 51.0 | 36 534 | 42 416 | 16.1 | 2.3 | 1 237 | 915 | 684 | 16 838 | 16.8 | 2.45 | 12.6 | 27.6 |
| Caddo | 12.1 | 8.2 | 6.5 | 48.1 | 30 150 | 29 600 | -1.8 | 0.3 | 967 | 673 | -196 | 10 645 | -2.8 | 2.60 | 13.7 | 26.3 |
| Canadian | 11.8 | 6.5 | 4.5 | 50.5 | 87 697 | 115 541 | 31.8 | 6.1 | 3 516 | 1 807 | 5 157 | 42 434 | 34.8 | 2.66 | 10.5 | 20.9 |
| Carter | 12.7 | 8.1 | 6.8 | 51.2 | 45 621 | 47 557 | 4.2 | 1.1 | 1 381 | 1 278 | 428 | 18 635 | 3.6 | 2.51 | 13.1 | 26.5 |
| Cherokee | 11.8 | 8.1 | 5.7 | 50.6 | 42 521 | 46 987 | 10.5 | 2.5 | 1 422 | 886 | 605 | 17 836 | 10.3 | 2.52 | 12.4 | 26.4 |
| Choctaw | 13.8 | 10.9 | 7.4 | 51.8 | 15 342 | 15 205 | -0.9 | -0.2 | 438 | 430 | -26 | 6 270 | 0.8 | 2.40 | 14.3 | 30.2 |
| Cimarron | 14.3 | 11.5 | 10.5 | 50.4 | 3 148 | 2 475 | -21.4 | -3.6 | 51 | 61 | -83 | 1 047 | -16.7 | 2.36 | 6.6 | 30.4 |
| Cleveland | 11.0 | 6.2 | 4.4 | 50.0 | 208 016 | 255 755 | 22.9 | 3.9 | 6 625 | 3 740 | 6 797 | 98 306 | 24.1 | 2.49 | 10.7 | 25.9 |
| Coal | 13.6 | 9.4 | 8.3 | 50.6 | 6 031 | 5 925 | -1.8 | 0.6 | 159 | 183 | 46 | 2 350 | -1.0 | 2.50 | 12.1 | 28.1 |
| Comanche | 9.7 | 5.7 | 4.6 | 48.4 | 114 996 | 124 098 | 7.9 | 1.8 | 4 546 | 2 124 | -178 | 44 982 | 13.0 | 2.53 | 14.5 | 27.1 |
| Cotton | 13.2 | 9.6 | 7.2 | 50.0 | 6 614 | 6 193 | -6.4 | -0.6 | 130 | 180 | 12 | 2 483 | -5.0 | 2.47 | 11.5 | 27.2 |
| Craig | 13.0 | 9.8 | 7.9 | 49.1 | 14 950 | 15 029 | 0.5 | -1.9 | 377 | 410 | -257 | 5 691 | 1.3 | 2.46 | 11.2 | 27.3 |
| Creek | 13.6 | 8.9 | 6.4 | 50.6 | 67 367 | 69 967 | 3.9 | 1.0 | 1 898 | 1 723 | 504 | 26 539 | 4.9 | 2.60 | 11.6 | 23.1 |
| Custer | 10.5 | 6.6 | 6.7 | 50.5 | 26 142 | 27 469 | 5.1 | 3.9 | 971 | 615 | 710 | 10 698 | 5.5 | 2.43 | 9.8 | 29.4 |
| Delaware | 15.1 | 13.2 | 8.1 | 50.7 | 37 077 | 41 487 | 11.9 | -0.1 | 742 | 1 022 | 224 | 17 093 | 15.2 | 2.41 | 9.8 | 26.4 |
| Dewey | 12.7 | 11.6 | 9.4 | 50.5 | 4 743 | 4 810 | 1.4 | -0.6 | 115 | 189 | 45 | 1 944 | -0.9 | 2.43 | 7.9 | 28.8 |
| Ellis | 16.3 | 10.5 | 8.7 | 51.3 | 4 075 | 4 151 | 1.9 | -1.1 | 94 | 124 | -18 | 1 782 | 0.7 | 2.30 | 7.2 | 31.3 |
| Garfield | 12.4 | 7.7 | 7.6 | 50.7 | 57 813 | 60 580 | 4.8 | 1.0 | 2 068 | 1 450 | 5 | 24 175 | 4.3 | 2.43 | 11.0 | 28.8 |
| Garvin | 12.9 | 9.2 | 7.8 | 51.1 | 27 210 | 27 576 | 1.3 | -1.0 | 785 | 770 | -315 | 11 069 | 1.9 | 2.46 | 11.6 | 27.1 |
| Grady | 12.9 | 8.4 | 5.8 | 50.4 | 45 516 | 52 431 | 15.2 | 1.3 | 1 350 | 1 043 | 388 | 19 892 | 14.7 | 2.58 | 10.1 | 22.7 |
| Grant | 14.1 | 10.4 | 10.9 | 50.4 | 5 144 | 4 527 | -12.0 | -0.2 | 104 | 134 | 12 | 1 910 | -8.6 | 2.33 | 6.9 | 29.9 |
| Greer | 11.7 | 7.8 | 9.1 | 42.8 | 6 061 | 6 239 | 2.9 | -2.5 | 127 | 155 | -134 | 2 181 | -2.5 | 2.34 | 11.1 | 32.0 |
| Harmon | 13.5 | 8.0 | 8.3 | 51.7 | 3 283 | 2 922 | -11.0 | -0.5 | 76 | 87 | -5 | 1 112 | -12.2 | 2.54 | 12.2 | 26.3 |
| Harper | 12.8 | 8.5 | 9.9 | 50.1 | 3 562 | 3 685 | 3.5 | -0.2 | 103 | 145 | 31 | 1 527 | 1.2 | 2.39 | 7.9 | 30.8 |
| Haskell | 13.4 | 10.1 | 7.5 | 50.1 | 11 792 | 12 769 | 8.3 | 1.3 | 289 | 299 | 194 | 5 044 | 9.1 | 2.52 | 10.1 | 25.6 |
| Hughes | 13.2 | 9.4 | 8.3 | 46.4 | 14 154 | 14 003 | -1.1 | -1.2 | 329 | 370 | -161 | 5 050 | -5.1 | 2.46 | 12.8 | 28.3 |
| Jackson | 11.3 | 7.1 | 5.8 | 50.3 | 28 439 | 26 446 | -7.0 | -0.8 | 953 | 514 | -664 | 10 247 | -3.2 | 2.51 | 11.9 | 27.0 |
| Jefferson | 13.8 | 10.4 | 8.7 | 50.1 | 6 818 | 6 472 | -5.1 | -1.5 | 142 | 206 | -35 | 2 634 | -3.0 | 2.40 | 10.5 | 29.3 |
| Johnston | 13.3 | 9.4 | 7.1 | 51.0 | 10 513 | 10 957 | 4.2 | 0.4 | 300 | 335 | 83 | 4 312 | 6.3 | 2.47 | 11.6 | 27.3 |
| Kay | 13.0 | 8.8 | 8.4 | 50.7 | 48 080 | 46 562 | -3.2 | -1.6 | 1 429 | 1 198 | -973 | 18 577 | -3.0 | 2.44 | 11.6 | 29.2 |
| Kingfisher | 12.1 | 7.9 | 7.1 | 50.3 | 13 926 | 15 034 | 8.0 | -0.2 | 399 | 313 | -120 | 5 731 | 9.2 | 2.60 | 9.0 | 24.3 |

1. No spouse present.

# Table B. States and Counties — Population, Vital Statistics, Medicare, and Crime

| STATE County | Persons in group quarters, 2010 | Daytime population, 2007–2011 Number | Employment/residence ratio | Births, 2011 Total | Rate[1] | Deaths, 2011 Number | Rate[1] | Persons under 65 with no health insurance, 2010 Number | Percent | Medicare, 2012 Eligible for Medicare | Enrolled in Medicare Advantage | Enrolled in a Medicare prescription drug plan | Serious crimes known to police,[2] 2011 Total Number | Rate[3] |
|---|---|---|---|---|---|---|---|---|---|---|---|---|---|---|
| | 32 | 33 | 34 | 35 | 36 | 37 | 38 | 39 | 40 | 41 | 42 | 43 | 44 | 45 |
| **OHIO—Cont'd** | | | | | | | | | | | | | | |
| Ottawa | 489 | 37 028 | 0.77 | 370 | 8.9 | 476 | 11.5 | 4 329 | 13.1 | 9 618 | 2 727 | 5 064 | 665 | 1 776 |
| Paulding | 85 | 16 580 | 0.64 | 247 | 12.7 | 191 | 9.8 | 2 418 | 14.6 | 3 728 | 949 | 1 925 | 236 | 1 228 |
| Perry | 307 | 28 223 | 0.48 | 464 | 12.8 | 365 | 10.1 | 4 605 | 14.7 | 6 561 | 1 448 | 3 602 | 341 | 983 |
| Pickaway | 4 455 | 48 349 | 0.68 | 573 | 10.2 | 500 | 8.9 | 5 894 | 13.3 | 9 540 | 3 915 | 4 554 | 2 623 | 4 765 |
| Pike | 496 | 29 681 | 1.10 | 364 | 12.7 | 353 | 12.3 | 3 688 | 15.1 | 5 828 | 1 269 | 3 380 | 336 | 1 170 |
| Portage | 7 914 | 142 826 | 0.77 | 1 514 | 9.4 | 1 277 | 7.9 | 18 928 | 14.3 | 25 821 | 10 933 | 10 545 | 3 146 | 2 146 |
| Preble | 386 | 35 188 | 0.63 | 480 | 11.4 | 417 | 9.9 | 5 404 | 15.2 | 7 917 | 3 139 | 3 394 | 924 | 2 195 |
| Putnam | 303 | 29 198 | 0.69 | 485 | 14.1 | 326 | 9.5 | 3 345 | 11.5 | 5 747 | 1 268 | 3 551 | 122 | 366 |
| Richland | 7 263 | 125 908 | 1.01 | 1 484 | 12.0 | 1 273 | 10.3 | 14 686 | 15.0 | 25 283 | 5 805 | 13 398 | 5 666 | 4 618 |
| Ross | 6 353 | 76 212 | 0.94 | 911 | 11.6 | 765 | 9.8 | 9 419 | 15.2 | 14 061 | 4 613 | 7 108 | 4 202 | 5 379 |
| Sandusky | 901 | 60 125 | 0.97 | 744 | 12.3 | 586 | 9.6 | 7 245 | 14.2 | 11 580 | 2 879 | 6 358 | 1 689 | 3 152 |
| Scioto | 3 642 | 77 335 | 0.93 | 908 | 11.5 | 874 | 11.0 | 10 650 | 16.5 | 15 737 | 3 226 | 9 618 | 3 499 | 4 398 |
| Seneca | 2 534 | 51 894 | 0.80 | 642 | 11.4 | 554 | 9.8 | 6 936 | 15.0 | 10 685 | 2 086 | 6 416 | NA | NA |
| Shelby | 589 | 54 222 | 1.21 | 658 | 13.3 | 404 | 8.2 | 6 018 | 14.1 | 8 089 | 2 444 | 4 548 | 1 521 | 3 238 |
| Stark | 9 264 | 370 576 | 0.97 | 4 156 | 11.1 | 3 812 | 10.2 | 44 582 | 14.5 | 74 685 | 36 035 | 25 995 | 13 459 | 3 623 |
| Summit | 9 967 | 557 645 | 1.06 | 6 172 | 11.4 | 5 381 | 10.0 | 63 291 | 13.9 | 96 669 | 42 510 | 33 838 | 20 517 | 4 115 |
| Trumbull | 3 821 | 201 621 | 0.89 | 2 213 | 10.6 | 2 357 | 11.3 | 25 479 | 14.9 | 45 542 | 20 237 | 17 406 | 7 306 | 3 552 |
| Tuscarawas | 1 250 | 87 903 | 0.89 | 1 125 | 12.2 | 958 | 10.4 | 12 320 | 16.0 | 18 064 | 7 522 | 7 552 | 884 | 1 004 |
| Union | 2 932 | 56 984 | 1.23 | 621 | 11.8 | 296 | 5.6 | 4 773 | 10.8 | 6 599 | 2 602 | 3 111 | 847 | 1 690 |
| Van Wert | 396 | 27 271 | 0.88 | 347 | 12.1 | 295 | 10.3 | 3 485 | 14.7 | 5 827 | 1 519 | 3 073 | 854 | 2 969 |
| Vinton | 68 | 11 017 | 0.49 | 149 | 11.1 | 158 | 11.8 | 1 818 | 15.7 | 2 362 | 562 | 1 467 | 400 | 2 975 |
| Warren | 5 985 | 195 216 | 0.85 | 2 590 | 12.1 | 1 434 | 6.7 | 18 233 | 10.0 | 29 159 | 12 013 | 10 948 | 2 690 | 1 267 |
| Washington | 1 781 | 60 698 | 0.95 | 611 | 9.9 | 687 | 11.1 | 7 216 | 14.6 | 13 200 | 2 141 | 7 730 | 813 | 1 327 |
| Wayne | 3 231 | 111 158 | 0.94 | 1 519 | 13.3 | 1 019 | 8.9 | 15 880 | 16.7 | 19 835 | 7 792 | 8 525 | 2 153 | 1 967 |
| Williams | 990 | 38 409 | 1.02 | 392 | 10.4 | 372 | 9.9 | 4 697 | 15.3 | 7 490 | 2 202 | 4 186 | 604 | 1 678 |
| Wood | 6 230 | 127 153 | 1.03 | 1 362 | 10.8 | 952 | 7.5 | 12 221 | 11.8 | 19 583 | 7 353 | 9 717 | 2 590 | 2 377 |
| Wyandot | 251 | 20 373 | 0.79 | 277 | 12.2 | 251 | 11.1 | 2 894 | 15.4 | 4 386 | 1 253 | 2 628 | 53 | 234 |
| **OKLAHOMA** | 112 017 | 3 698 482 | 0.99 | 53 727 | 14.2 | 34 528 | 9.1 | 691 408 | 21.9 | 639 802 | 79 807 | 300 845 | 144 495 | 3 811 |
| Adair | 92 | 20 596 | 0.77 | 303 | 13.4 | 222 | 9.8 | 4 930 | 24.9 | 4 019 | 217 | 2 341 | 473 | 2 063 |
| Alfalfa | 1 054 | 5 311 | 0.85 | 49 | 8.7 | 58 | 10.2 | 835 | 23.7 | 1 156 | 46 | 761 | 30 | 526 |
| Atoka | 750 | 13 128 | 0.78 | 169 | 11.9 | 117 | 8.2 | 2 903 | 26.0 | 2 835 | 170 | 1 721 | 228 | 1 591 |
| Beaver | 43 | 4 945 | 0.75 | 54 | 9.6 | 50 | 8.9 | 1 174 | 24.7 | 971 | 23 | 591 | 62 | 1 088 |
| Beckham | 1 907 | 23 891 | 1.17 | 338 | 15.2 | 255 | 11.4 | 3 829 | 22.1 | 3 487 | 128 | 2 234 | 486 | 2 174 |
| Blaine | 2 190 | 11 138 | 1.00 | 173 | 17.7 | 117 | 12.0 | 1 747 | 21.5 | 2 012 | 108 | 1 275 | 139 | 1 152 |
| Bryan | 1 134 | 40 779 | 0.94 | 569 | 13.2 | 405 | 9.4 | 8 720 | 24.9 | 8 132 | 428 | 4 377 | 1 357 | 3 165 |
| Caddo | 1 935 | 27 459 | 0.84 | 416 | 14.1 | 303 | 10.3 | 6 136 | 26.1 | 5 453 | 204 | 3 327 | 590 | 1 972 |
| Canadian | 2 488 | 87 775 | 0.54 | 1 548 | 13.0 | 763 | 6.4 | 16 326 | 16.0 | 16 143 | 3 915 | 6 112 | 5 048 | 4 323 |
| Carter | 750 | 50 473 | 1.16 | 676 | 14.1 | 547 | 11.4 | 9 102 | 22.7 | 9 462 | 761 | 5 435 | 2 224 | 4 627 |
| Cherokee | 2 008 | 44 808 | 0.90 | 646 | 13.5 | 384 | 8.0 | 11 605 | 29.5 | 8 084 | 757 | 4 217 | 872 | 1 836 |
| Choctaw | 172 | 14 960 | 0.96 | 227 | 14.9 | 194 | 12.7 | 2 943 | 23.8 | 3 539 | 175 | 2 070 | 230 | 1 497 |
| Cimarron | 7 | 2 417 | 0.94 | 31 | 12.5 | 28 | 11.3 | 629 | 32.5 | 608 | 17 | 382 | 8 | 320 |
| Cleveland | 10 561 | 209 888 | 0.67 | 2 902 | 11.1 | 1 543 | 5.9 | 39 462 | 17.8 | 34 589 | 5 763 | 13 705 | 11 447 | 4 428 |
| Coal | 61 | 5 590 | 0.88 | 77 | 13.0 | 77 | 13.0 | 1 202 | 24.8 | 1 149 | 63 | 615 | 77 | 1 286 |
| Comanche | 10 343 | 125 766 | 1.07 | 2 068 | 16.4 | 930 | 7.4 | 19 859 | 19.3 | 16 061 | 540 | 6 241 | 6 768 | 5 396 |
| Cotton | 48 | 5 443 | 0.72 | 59 | 9.5 | 90 | 14.6 | 1 114 | 21.7 | 1 237 | 64 | 613 | 56 | 895 |
| Craig | 1 050 | 15 549 | 1.09 | 191 | 12.7 | 184 | 12.2 | 2 668 | 22.6 | 3 387 | 325 | 2 000 | 263 | 1 731 |
| Creek | 1 062 | 60 662 | 0.70 | 839 | 11.9 | 744 | 10.6 | 13 461 | 22.7 | 13 684 | 4 495 | 5 269 | 1 510 | 2 135 |
| Custer | 1 516 | 27 247 | 1.01 | 408 | 14.7 | 271 | 9.8 | 5 715 | 25.4 | 4 219 | 223 | 2 617 | 616 | 2 219 |
| Delaware | 356 | 36 645 | 0.70 | 396 | 9.5 | 451 | 10.8 | 8 559 | 26.1 | 9 250 | 1 035 | 4 602 | 641 | 1 559 |
| Dewey | 93 | 4 662 | 0.94 | 55 | 11.3 | 87 | 17.9 | 1 007 | 26.4 | 1 044 | 36 | 650 | 61 | 1 255 |
| Ellis | 46 | 3 955 | 0.94 | 53 | 13.1 | 61 | 15.1 | 752 | 22.4 | 869 | 70 | 520 | 48 | 1 144 |
| Garfield | 1 830 | 60 464 | 1.03 | 972 | 16.0 | 628 | 10.4 | 11 143 | 22.1 | 11 192 | 521 | 6 851 | 2 155 | 3 520 |
| Garvin | 317 | 27 263 | 0.98 | 385 | 14.0 | 339 | 12.3 | 5 378 | 23.9 | 5 903 | 566 | 3 395 | 681 | 2 443 |
| Grady | 1 082 | 43 578 | 0.63 | 626 | 11.8 | 444 | 8.4 | 8 579 | 19.3 | 8 975 | 958 | 4 590 | 1 426 | 2 691 |
| Grant | 73 | 4 208 | 0.83 | 48 | 10.5 | 64 | 14.0 | 811 | 22.9 | 989 | 42 | 656 | 51 | 1 115 |
| Greer | 1 146 | 5 595 | 0.73 | 67 | 10.9 | 70 | 11.4 | 900 | 22.2 | 1 328 | 78 | 855 | 43 | 682 |
| Harmon | 100 | 2 733 | 0.88 | 44 | 15.1 | 44 | 15.1 | 722 | 30.5 | 602 | 17 | 413 | 96 | 3 251 |
| Harper | 41 | 3 555 | 0.95 | 45 | 12.2 | 77 | 20.8 | 804 | 27.0 | 732 | D | 487 | 33 | 886 |
| Haskell | 78 | 11 866 | 0.81 | 174 | 13.6 | 128 | 10.0 | 2 775 | 26.5 | 3 009 | 207 | 1 675 | 226 | 1 751 |
| Hughes | 1 565 | 12 905 | 0.84 | 154 | 11.1 | 151 | 10.9 | 2 630 | 25.8 | 3 081 | 232 | 1 749 | 274 | 1 936 |
| Jackson | 687 | 27 149 | 1.07 | 449 | 17.0 | 213 | 8.1 | 4 599 | 20.5 | 4 056 | 123 | 2 041 | 697 | 2 608 |
| Jefferson | 144 | 5 641 | 0.69 | 61 | 9.4 | 91 | 14.0 | 1 431 | 28.1 | 1 440 | 66 | 899 | 90 | 1 376 |
| Johnston | 292 | 10 443 | 0.88 | 162 | 14.5 | 151 | 13.6 | 2 160 | 24.3 | 2 325 | 99 | 1 390 | 89 | 804 |
| Kay | 1 273 | 47 827 | 1.07 | 715 | 15.5 | 518 | 11.2 | 8 368 | 22.2 | 9 759 | 934 | 6 044 | 1 617 | 3 436 |
| Kingfisher | 155 | 14 473 | 0.94 | 203 | 13.3 | 131 | 8.6 | 3 031 | 23.8 | 2 664 | 276 | 1 554 | 198 | 1 303 |

1. Per 1,000 estimated resident population.　2. Data for serious crimes have not been adjusted for underreporting; this may affect comparability between geographic areas and over time.　3. Per 100,000 population estimated by the FBI.

## Table B. States and Counties — Crime, Education, Money Income, and Poverty

| STATE County | Serious crimes known to police, 2011 (cont.)[1] Rate[2] Violent | Property | Education — School enrollment and attainment, 2007–2011 — Enrollment[3] Total | Percent private | Attainment[4] (percent) High school graduate or less | Bachelor's degree or more | Local government expenditures,[5] 2009–2010 Total current expenditures (mil dol) | Current expenditures per student (dollars) | Money income, 2007–2011 Per capita income[6] (dollars) | Households — Median income Dollars | Percent change, 2000 to 2007–2011 (constant 2011 dollars) | Percent with income of $200,000 or more | Income and poverty, 2011 — Median household income (dollars) | Percent below poverty level All persons | Children under 18 years | Children 5 to 17 years in families |
|---|---|---|---|---|---|---|---|---|---|---|---|---|---|---|---|---|
| | 46 | 47 | 48 | 49 | 50 | 51 | 52 | 53 | 54 | 55 | 56 | 57 | 58 | 59 | 60 | 61 |
| **OHIO—Cont'd** | | | | | | | | | | | | | | | | |
| Ottawa | 40 | 1 736 | 8 945 | 14.4 | 47.6 | 19.8 | 64.0 | 11 576 | 28 404 | 53 614 | -10.2 | 2.3 | 51 641 | 10.9 | 17.0 | 14.8 |
| Paulding | 57 | 1 170 | 4 803 | 8.4 | 63.5 | 11.1 | 42.3 | 11 592 | 20 968 | 43 683 | -19.8 | 0.6 | 41 946 | 13.8 | 19.8 | 17.9 |
| Perry | 29 | 954 | 9 171 | 11.3 | 65.0 | 9.5 | 68.4 | 10 923 | 19 876 | 42 860 | -7.7 | 1.2 | 39 383 | 17.7 | 25.9 | 23.2 |
| Pickaway | 138 | 4 627 | 13 619 | 11.5 | 61.8 | 14.1 | 94.4 | 9 672 | 22 356 | 51 418 | -11.1 | 1.2 | 52 161 | 14.9 | 21.0 | 19.3 |
| Pike | 10 | 1 159 | 7 173 | 6.4 | 65.8 | 12.6 | 62.5 | 12 824 | 18 715 | 39 669 | -7.2 | 0.6 | 37 802 | 22.7 | 36.2 | 32.8 |
| Portage | 88 | 2 058 | 48 900 | 10.0 | 48.9 | 24.5 | 249.2 | 10 425 | 25 483 | 51 441 | -14.1 | 2.4 | 49 712 | 15.8 | 18.3 | 15.6 |
| Preble | 69 | 2 126 | 10 287 | 11.3 | 60.0 | 11.1 | 65.1 | 9 826 | 22 896 | 48 874 | -14.0 | 1.7 | 45 920 | 11.6 | 18.9 | 17.1 |
| Putnam | 39 | 327 | 8 943 | 14.3 | 55.0 | 18.6 | 56.3 | 9 877 | 25 019 | 59 378 | -5.3 | 2.2 | 57 039 | 6.4 | 9.7 | 9.0 |
| Richland | 183 | 4 435 | 29 992 | 19.0 | 56.7 | 15.1 | 201.4 | 12 112 | 21 966 | 43 098 | -14.6 | 1.2 | 40 424 | 17.2 | 26.5 | 22.5 |
| Ross | 183 | 5 196 | 18 746 | 7.9 | 59.8 | 14.1 | 126.6 | 11 047 | 21 423 | 44 577 | -11.0 | 1.8 | 43 118 | 19.4 | 27.8 | 26.2 |
| Sandusky | 310 | 2 842 | 15 046 | 16.8 | 54.5 | 13.4 | 87.7 | 10 272 | 22 713 | 47 277 | -13.7 | 1.1 | 44 016 | 14.2 | 21.0 | 18.4 |
| Scioto | 161 | 4 237 | 19 174 | 9.4 | 58.4 | 13.2 | 132.5 | 10 563 | 18 412 | 33 596 | -11.2 | 1.0 | 31 987 | 26.1 | 37.1 | 33.8 |
| Seneca | NA | NA | 15 444 | 24.6 | 56.5 | 16.0 | 67.8 | 11 359 | 21 365 | 41 761 | -18.7 | 1.5 | 38 349 | 16.6 | 22.0 | 19.5 |
| Shelby | 130 | 3 108 | 13 675 | 10.1 | 60.0 | 14.1 | 83.4 | 9 498 | 22 810 | 50 527 | -15.9 | 1.4 | 53 028 | 11.5 | 15.8 | 14.3 |
| Stark | 313 | 3 310 | 96 881 | 17.8 | 51.8 | 20.7 | 589.2 | 9 859 | 24 212 | 45 347 | -15.7 | 2.2 | 42 190 | 16.3 | 24.8 | 22.4 |
| Summit | 414 | 3 701 | 142 107 | 17.2 | 42.6 | 29.4 | 869.1 | 11 040 | 27 220 | 48 790 | -14.6 | 3.3 | 46 595 | 16.5 | 25.2 | 21.7 |
| Trumbull | 229 | 3 323 | 48 151 | 11.5 | 58.3 | 16.6 | 347.0 | 11 064 | 22 127 | 42 441 | -17.9 | 1.1 | 40 913 | 16.5 | 29.2 | 25.4 |
| Tuscarawas | 48 | 956 | 21 360 | 10.5 | 63.6 | 15.0 | 155.7 | 9 835 | 20 994 | 42 846 | -10.6 | 1.0 | 41 857 | 14.5 | 22.1 | 20.2 |
| Union | 48 | 1 642 | 13 784 | 12.3 | 46.2 | 27.4 | 74.2 | 9 672 | 27 916 | 68 279 | -2.3 | 3.1 | 64 403 | 7.5 | 10.2 | 8.5 |
| Van Wert | 118 | 2 851 | 7 144 | 15.8 | 59.2 | 13.9 | 52.6 | 10 665 | 21 245 | 45 111 | -15.4 | 0.7 | 46 717 | 10.5 | 16.5 | 14.8 |
| Vinton | 156 | 2 819 | 3 271 | 3.1 | 69.2 | 7.9 | 25.5 | 10 679 | 17 301 | 34 399 | -13.5 | 0.2 | 35 298 | 23.5 | 38.6 | 34.3 |
| Warren | 65 | 1 202 | 58 712 | 19.5 | 36.7 | 36.5 | 348.1 | 9 645 | 32 114 | 71 961 | -8.0 | 6.4 | 70 245 | 6.9 | 8.6 | 7.2 |
| Washington | 65 | 1 262 | 14 894 | 19.2 | 56.5 | 15.0 | 83.9 | 9 660 | 23 404 | 43 185 | -6.7 | 1.9 | 42 211 | 14.8 | 21.7 | 19.2 |
| Wayne | 110 | 1 857 | 28 656 | 24.8 | 58.4 | 19.2 | 177.4 | 11 060 | 22 892 | 49 261 | -12.2 | 2.1 | 46 842 | 13.7 | 22.0 | 20.2 |
| Williams | 50 | 1 628 | 8 932 | 10.9 | 58.8 | 12.7 | 57.4 | 9 565 | 21 532 | 44 604 | -18.9 | 0.9 | 40 856 | 12.5 | 18.7 | 16.7 |
| Wood | 77 | 2 300 | 42 574 | 11.0 | 40.5 | 30.1 | 227.5 | 12 699 | 26 696 | 53 610 | -10.7 | 2.9 | 50 624 | 13.9 | 14.0 | 12.4 |
| Wyandot | 35 | 199 | 5 646 | 10.9 | 60.0 | 14.2 | 30.4 | 8 609 | 22 967 | 47 958 | -8.5 | 1.4 | 45 555 | 9.5 | 14.2 | 13.1 |
| **OKLAHOMA** | 455 | 3 356 | 972 153 | 11.3 | 46.2 | 23.0 | 5 165.7 | 7 889 | 23 770 | 44 287 | -1.8 | 2.5 | 43 232 | 17.3 | 23.9 | 21.6 |
| Adair | 362 | 1 701 | 5 955 | 5.3 | 63.7 | 11.2 | 44.1 | 9 086 | 14 547 | 31 038 | -7.6 | 0.3 | 31 680 | 22.2 | 34.1 | 32.8 |
| Alfalfa | 53 | 474 | 963 | 7.5 | 55.5 | 18.4 | 8.6 | 10 574 | 24 080 | 42 730 | 4.6 | 3.6 | 38 852 | 18.3 | 21.6 | 19.7 |
| Atoka | 140 | 1 451 | 3 167 | 6.2 | 62.5 | 15.0 | 31.5 | 12 252 | 16 096 | 33 919 | 1.5 | 1.2 | 34 673 | 24.0 | 33.0 | 30.5 |
| Beaver | 70 | 1 018 | 1 270 | 3.6 | 53.2 | 18.0 | 12.3 | 11 260 | 23 002 | 47 386 | -4.4 | 1.9 | 49 683 | 11.2 | 17.1 | 15.2 |
| Beckham | 201 | 1 973 | 4 676 | 4.5 | 57.1 | 15.2 | 30.5 | 7 928 | 21 470 | 45 726 | 23.6 | 1.7 | 43 565 | 16.7 | 23.2 | 22.8 |
| Blaine | 199 | 953 | 2 527 | 6.4 | 55.7 | 15.9 | 19.3 | 10 051 | 20 029 | 41 306 | 7.9 | 1.9 | 37 882 | 19.3 | 28.3 | 27.0 |
| Bryan | 453 | 2 713 | 10 328 | 7.3 | 51.1 | 20.5 | 61.9 | 8 573 | 19 156 | 36 661 | -2.6 | 1.2 | 34 276 | 20.9 | 28.1 | 27.1 |
| Caddo | 384 | 1 588 | 7 079 | 5.8 | 59.5 | 13.6 | 55.0 | 9 097 | 17 355 | 37 835 | 2.5 | 0.6 | 38 583 | 20.4 | 27.1 | 24.8 |
| Canadian | 479 | 3 844 | 30 379 | 10.5 | 37.9 | 25.6 | 140.1 | 7 142 | 27 536 | 62 355 | 1.6 | 3.0 | 60 225 | 8.3 | 12.2 | 11.4 |
| Carter | 1 157 | 3 470 | 11 640 | 12.6 | 58.5 | 17.1 | 74.9 | 8 166 | 20 046 | 39 722 | 0.1 | 1.4 | 40 122 | 16.2 | 24.2 | 22.9 |
| Cherokee | 139 | 1 697 | 13 871 | 8.4 | 45.8 | 24.5 | 64.2 | 8 561 | 16 996 | 33 990 | -5.1 | 0.7 | 34 968 | 24.6 | 33.3 | 30.7 |
| Choctaw | 156 | 1 340 | 3 525 | 3.7 | 62.9 | 11.3 | 24.0 | 8 940 | 17 509 | 28 039 | -8.7 | 0.6 | 28 598 | 28.1 | 40.7 | 37.4 |
| Cimarron | 80 | 240 | 521 | 8.1 | 54.5 | 18.7 | 5.1 | 12 271 | 19 455 | 35 440 | -14.3 | 0.8 | 38 572 | 17.8 | 28.4 | 26.2 |
| Cleveland | 365 | 4 063 | 78 861 | 9.6 | 36.1 | 31.1 | 298.3 | 7 179 | 26 640 | 53 759 | -4.9 | 2.7 | 51 900 | 13.3 | 15.7 | 13.4 |
| Coal | 67 | 1 219 | 1 356 | 5.7 | 68.7 | 9.8 | 12.9 | 10 363 | 18 758 | 34 217 | 6.9 | 0.2 | 35 475 | 22.9 | 31.2 | 27.9 |
| Comanche | 698 | 4 698 | 33 151 | 6.3 | 45.7 | 20.4 | 175.7 | 7 809 | 21 746 | 45 947 | 0.5 | 1.9 | 44 286 | 17.6 | 23.9 | 23.0 |
| Cotton | 128 | 767 | 1 502 | 13.6 | 58.2 | 15.1 | 9.8 | 8 313 | 21 170 | 46 075 | 25.4 | 1.3 | 38 129 | 18.0 | 25.0 | 21.6 |
| Craig | 184 | 1 547 | 3 236 | 7.9 | 56.4 | 14.7 | 25.2 | 7 264 | 20 092 | 41 010 | -2.0 | 0.9 | 36 996 | 20.3 | 26.5 | 24.6 |
| Creek | 177 | 1 959 | 17 298 | 9.7 | 54.9 | 15.0 | 103.3 | 7 886 | 22 558 | 42 940 | -4.1 | 1.9 | 41 000 | 17.0 | 24.5 | 22.8 |
| Custer | 367 | 1 851 | 8 453 | 5.1 | 47.9 | 23.4 | 35.9 | 7 667 | 22 489 | 43 125 | 12.0 | 1.9 | 41 678 | 17.6 | 20.2 | 19.7 |
| Delaware | 180 | 1 379 | 8 508 | 5.1 | 58.4 | 14.9 | 64.0 | 9 322 | 20 082 | 35 552 | -5.9 | 1.5 | 35 936 | 20.9 | 33.4 | 30.8 |
| Dewey | 62 | 1 193 | 1 128 | 1.6 | 54.7 | 20.1 | 10.8 | 10 570 | 23 009 | 41 500 | 9.1 | 2.7 | 41 124 | 12.6 | 19.1 | 16.6 |
| Ellis | 215 | 930 | 860 | 3.3 | 49.9 | 22.8 | 8.5 | 9 832 | 24 544 | 45 017 | 19.3 | 1.4 | 42 728 | 12.8 | 18.2 | 16.7 |
| Garfield | 377 | 3 142 | 13 789 | 12.3 | 49.4 | 23.1 | 79.4 | 7 725 | 23 862 | 41 688 | -6.5 | 2.0 | 42 800 | 15.3 | 25.3 | 21.8 |
| Garvin | 305 | 2 138 | 6 285 | 6.7 | 62.7 | 15.5 | 41.5 | 7 723 | 21 069 | 39 171 | 3.4 | 1.8 | 37 878 | 18.2 | 24.2 | 21.9 |
| Grady | 396 | 2 295 | 13 164 | 6.9 | 52.5 | 16.6 | 62.8 | 6 920 | 22 593 | 47 456 | 7.7 | 1.3 | 45 688 | 13.8 | 19.5 | 17.5 |
| Grant | 0 | 1 115 | 1 044 | 5.4 | 47.5 | 21.2 | 9.4 | 11 373 | 23 431 | 42 227 | 7.9 | 1.9 | 40 691 | 13.3 | 19.2 | 16.8 |
| Greer | 95 | 587 | 1 038 | 0.3 | 59.4 | 13.0 | 8.6 | 8 279 | 15 804 | 38 882 | 11.6 | 0.1 | 34 350 | 23.8 | 29.8 | 26.9 |
| Harmon | 271 | 2 980 | 575 | 9.9 | 51.9 | 18.4 | 5.0 | 9 449 | 19 022 | 31 211 | 3.4 | 1.8 | 30 329 | 28.0 | 38.8 | 39.1 |
| Harper | 0 | 886 | 856 | 7.0 | 58.5 | 14.0 | 6.7 | 9 084 | 23 910 | 44 850 | -1.4 | 2.3 | 43 198 | 11.8 | 18.1 | 16.5 |
| Haskell | 442 | 1 309 | 2 996 | 2.8 | 60.6 | 11.9 | 17.7 | 7 578 | 19 147 | 37 326 | 12.6 | 2.3 | 33 309 | 20.2 | 31.2 | 30.6 |
| Hughes | 163 | 1 773 | 2 971 | 3.6 | 60.2 | 11.4 | 22.7 | 9 248 | 18 844 | 33 895 | 11.0 | 2.2 | 30 888 | 25.1 | 33.3 | 29.9 |
| Jackson | 206 | 2 402 | 6 885 | 7.7 | 45.5 | 20.7 | 41.1 | 7 765 | 21 248 | 41 391 | -0.3 | 1.1 | 40 129 | 18.7 | 26.0 | 25.5 |
| Jefferson | 92 | 1 284 | 1 301 | 4.2 | 66.7 | 11.3 | 11.1 | 9 268 | 18 215 | 34 256 | 7.2 | 0.6 | 30 755 | 21.6 | 31.3 | 30.3 |
| Johnston | 199 | 605 | 2 985 | 5.0 | 47.9 | 19.8 | 32.0 | 7 057 | 20 297 | 35 789 | 7.8 | 0.7 | 35 713 | 17.4 | 28.6 | 27.7 |
| Kay | 368 | 3 068 | 11 346 | 8.2 | 49.2 | 19.2 | 73.0 | 8 596 | 21 566 | 40 164 | -3.3 | 1.6 | 39 152 | 18.1 | 27.0 | 24.8 |
| Kingfisher | 33 | 1 270 | 3 732 | 7.1 | 49.3 | 19.5 | 27.3 | 8 335 | 25 310 | 52 130 | 5.3 | 2.8 | 53 050 | 11.5 | 17.2 | 15.8 |

1. Data for serious crimes have not been adjusted for underreporting; this may affect comparability between geographic areas and over time.   2. Per 100,000 population estimated by the FBI.   3. All persons 3 years old and over enrolled in nursery school through college.   4. Persons 25 years old and over.   5. Elementary and secondary education expenditures.   6. Based on population estimated by the American Community Survey, 2007–2011.

# Table B. States and Counties — **Personal Income**

| STATE County | Personal income, 2011 Total (mil dol) | Per capita[1] Percent change, 2010–2011 | Per capita[1] Dollars | Per capita[1] Rank | Wages and salaries[2] (mil dol) | Proprietors' income (mil dol) | Dividends, interest, and rent (mil dol) | Transfer payments (mil dol) Total | Government payments to individuals Total | Social Security | Medical payments | Income mainte-nance | Unemploy-ment insurance |
|---|---|---|---|---|---|---|---|---|---|---|---|---|---|
| | 62 | 63 | 64 | 65 | 66 | 67 | 68 | 69 | 70 | 71 | 72 | 73 | 74 |
| **OHIO—Cont'd** | | | | | | | | | | | | | |
| Ottawa | 1 637 | 5.7 | 39 553 | 799 | 703 | 112 | 240 | 387 | 378 | 144 | 161 | 26 | 16 |
| Paulding | 623 | 7.1 | 32 059 | 1 870 | 212 | 59 | 78 | 151 | 147 | 57 | 57 | 16 | 6 |
| Perry | 928 | 5.5 | 25 573 | 2 924 | 277 | 34 | 93 | 309 | 301 | 89 | 136 | 43 | 12 |
| Pickaway | 1 826 | 7.2 | 32 617 | 1 776 | 753 | 154 | 194 | 402 | 389 | 131 | 154 | 48 | 15 |
| Pike | 839 | 4.7 | 29 322 | 2 403 | 516 | 84 | 87 | 286 | 280 | 73 | 128 | 48 | 11 |
| Portage | 5 860 | 5.9 | 36 260 | 1 181 | 2 747 | 343 | 718 | 1 199 | 1 163 | 378 | 446 | 103 | 50 |
| Preble | 1 397 | 6.8 | 33 188 | 1 675 | 446 | 106 | 160 | 330 | 321 | 115 | 137 | 31 | 14 |
| Putnam | 1 257 | 8.0 | 36 656 | 1 116 | 482 | 140 | 167 | 222 | 214 | 84 | 85 | 16 | 9 |
| Richland | 3 794 | 4.2 | 30 714 | 2 152 | 2 352 | 176 | 524 | 1 062 | 1 034 | 363 | 426 | 121 | 41 |
| Ross | 2 356 | 6.5 | 30 110 | 2 267 | 1 449 | 123 | 250 | 647 | 630 | 188 | 264 | 94 | 23 |
| Sandusky | 2 015 | 5.0 | 33 170 | 1 678 | 1 217 | 125 | 240 | 492 | 478 | 168 | 197 | 48 | 19 |
| Scioto | 2 290 | 3.4 | 28 888 | 2 469 | 1 119 | 104 | 253 | 827 | 809 | 190 | 383 | 128 | 26 |
| Seneca | 1 779 | 5.7 | 31 506 | 1 999 | 850 | 127 | 219 | 492 | 480 | 150 | 219 | 46 | 18 |
| Shelby | 1 675 | 6.2 | 33 980 | 1 513 | 1 406 | 151 | 216 | 335 | 324 | 120 | 127 | 36 | 15 |
| Stark | 13 252 | 6.0 | 35 330 | 1 320 | 7 598 | 950 | 1 795 | 3 216 | 3 133 | 1 085 | 1 297 | 354 | 113 |
| Summit | 22 206 | 4.9 | 41 135 | 649 | 14 719 | 1 472 | 3 088 | 4 561 | 4 441 | 1 397 | 1 939 | 524 | 159 |
| Trumbull | 6 660 | 4.9 | 31 826 | 1 926 | 3 716 | 310 | 899 | 2 014 | 1 968 | 698 | 866 | 207 | 66 |
| Tuscarawas | 2 806 | 6.1 | 30 337 | 2 230 | 1 500 | 170 | 369 | 726 | 705 | 252 | 288 | 78 | 27 |
| Union | 1 892 | 7.2 | 35 851 | 1 240 | 1 850 | 100 | 185 | 279 | 267 | 96 | 101 | 26 | 13 |
| Van Wert | 1 036 | 10.3 | 36 207 | 1 188 | 473 | 103 | 122 | 213 | 207 | 83 | 79 | 19 | 9 |
| Vinton | 335 | 6.5 | 25 029 | 2 962 | 109 | 13 | 41 | 121 | 118 | 31 | 53 | 20 | 4 |
| Warren | 9 202 | 6.8 | 42 818 | 518 | 4 120 | 407 | 1 087 | 1 214 | 1 167 | 448 | 444 | 79 | 54 |
| Washington | 2 086 | 5.2 | 33 785 | 1 549 | 1 222 | 118 | 271 | 541 | 527 | 185 | 221 | 54 | 17 |
| Wayne | 3 526 | 5.1 | 30 765 | 2 145 | 2 162 | 221 | 527 | 779 | 754 | 280 | 303 | 79 | 29 |
| Williams | 1 251 | 6.3 | 33 278 | 1 658 | 742 | 127 | 167 | 304 | 296 | 107 | 122 | 30 | 13 |
| Wood | 4 699 | 6.2 | 37 190 | 1 060 | 3 173 | 301 | 610 | 874 | 847 | 274 | 309 | 64 | 35 |
| Wyandot | 768 | 9.4 | 33 865 | 1 538 | 382 | 111 | 100 | 167 | 162 | 62 | 66 | 14 | 7 |
| **OKLAHOMA** | 142 862 | 6.9 | 37 679 | X | 85 026 | 17 201 | 21 512 | 27 882 | 27 048 | 9 141 | 11 225 | 3 274 | 619 |
| Adair | 506 | 0.3 | 22 364 | 3 075 | 227 | 43 | 47 | 199 | 194 | 52 | 89 | 35 | 4 |
| Alfalfa | 177 | 15.1 | 31 281 | 2 052 | 63 | 37 | 31 | 41 | 39 | 17 | 17 | 3 | 1 |
| Atoka | 383 | 3.7 | 26 926 | 2 772 | 141 | 71 | 47 | 114 | 111 | 36 | 47 | 17 | 2 |
| Beaver | 223 | 10.0 | 39 679 | 781 | 82 | 55 | 36 | 34 | 32 | 14 | 14 | 2 | 1 |
| Beckham | 816 | 12.7 | 36 616 | 1 123 | 569 | 97 | 134 | 142 | 137 | 47 | 62 | 17 | 3 |
| Blaine | 312 | 8.7 | 31 914 | 1 902 | 135 | 43 | 54 | 83 | 81 | 28 | 37 | 10 | 2 |
| Bryan | 1 245 | 4.1 | 28 891 | 2 468 | 647 | 80 | 150 | 346 | 337 | 107 | 145 | 42 | 6 |
| Caddo | 821 | 5.3 | 27 785 | 2 643 | 347 | 55 | 124 | 234 | 227 | 71 | 98 | 32 | 5 |
| Canadian | 4 720 | 10.2 | 39 501 | 804 | 1 443 | 228 | 534 | 651 | 625 | 238 | 237 | 57 | 17 |
| Carter | 1 802 | 6.2 | 37 462 | 1 028 | 1 165 | 196 | 287 | 414 | 403 | 139 | 179 | 49 | 8 |
| Cherokee | 1 394 | 3.0 | 29 135 | 2 431 | 705 | 111 | 170 | 394 | 384 | 111 | 159 | 48 | 8 |
| Choctaw | 431 | 3.4 | 28 261 | 2 574 | 188 | 40 | 48 | 157 | 154 | 45 | 71 | 23 | 3 |
| Cimarron | 101 | 11.7 | 40 446 | 706 | 30 | 37 | 16 | 18 | 17 | 8 | 6 | 2 | 0 |
| Cleveland | 9 478 | 7.1 | 36 275 | 1 174 | 3 595 | 675 | 1 347 | 1 436 | 1 379 | 510 | 496 | 149 | 35 |
| Coal | 163 | 8.5 | 27 568 | 2 675 | 54 | 13 | 21 | 52 | 51 | 15 | 24 | 6 | 1 |
| Comanche | 4 653 | 4.6 | 36 985 | 1 079 | 3 596 | 165 | 501 | 850 | 825 | 219 | 281 | 114 | 19 |
| Cotton | 219 | 1.4 | 35 436 | 1 306 | 67 | 20 | 24 | 48 | 47 | 17 | 19 | 5 | 1 |
| Craig | 465 | 2.4 | 30 870 | 2 128 | 247 | 54 | 61 | 145 | 142 | 46 | 68 | 15 | 2 |
| Creek | 2 310 | 4.5 | 32 787 | 1 743 | 883 | 169 | 384 | 582 | 567 | 205 | 246 | 62 | 12 |
| Custer | 1 007 | 12.2 | 36 300 | 1 170 | 645 | 98 | 176 | 194 | 188 | 58 | 83 | 19 | 4 |
| Delaware | 1 274 | 2.7 | 30 595 | 2 178 | 361 | 107 | 207 | 362 | 353 | 130 | 147 | 42 | 7 |
| Dewey | 187 | 16.7 | 38 370 | 928 | 79 | 24 | 32 | 36 | 35 | 14 | 16 | 2 | 1 |
| Ellis | 162 | 15.7 | 40 112 | 733 | 61 | 32 | 28 | 29 | 28 | 12 | 13 | 2 | 0 |
| Garfield | 2 415 | 6.2 | 39 803 | 768 | 1 445 | 190 | 476 | 496 | 483 | 160 | 229 | 52 | 8 |
| Garvin | 959 | 5.6 | 34 929 | 1 382 | 483 | 89 | 133 | 280 | 273 | 84 | 142 | 25 | 4 |
| Grady | 1 642 | 6.9 | 30 979 | 2 106 | 591 | 141 | 239 | 350 | 338 | 125 | 132 | 41 | 8 |
| Grant | 178 | 8.6 | 38 867 | 871 | 67 | 36 | 32 | 35 | 34 | 15 | 15 | 2 | 1 |
| Greer | 168 | 1.8 | 27 442 | 2 691 | 59 | 9 | 23 | 55 | 54 | 17 | 27 | 5 | 1 |
| Harmon | 86 | 2.1 | 29 627 | 2 356 | 34 | 10 | 14 | 27 | 26 | 8 | 13 | 3 | 0 |
| Harper | 122 | 11.4 | 32 965 | 1 713 | 48 | 13 | 32 | 25 | 24 | 10 | 10 | 2 | 0 |
| Haskell | 394 | 4.7 | 30 752 | 2 147 | 140 | 41 | 46 | 127 | 124 | 40 | 53 | 17 | 2 |
| Hughes | 380 | 8.0 | 27 480 | 2 689 | 127 | 46 | 49 | 132 | 129 | 41 | 59 | 14 | 3 |
| Jackson | 855 | 0.3 | 32 331 | 1 817 | 611 | 39 | 122 | 207 | 202 | 53 | 89 | 26 | 4 |
| Jefferson | 179 | 9.1 | 27 564 | 2 676 | 52 | 30 | 22 | 59 | 58 | 20 | 27 | 7 | 1 |
| Johnston | 309 | 4.1 | 27 730 | 2 651 | 126 | 27 | 28 | 106 | 104 | 31 | 43 | 12 | 2 |
| Kay | 1 657 | 4.6 | 35 894 | 1 227 | 967 | 162 | 313 | 397 | 386 | 146 | 152 | 46 | 9 |
| Kingfisher | 587 | 10.3 | 38 596 | 899 | 299 | 71 | 106 | 98 | 95 | 38 | 41 | 8 | 2 |

1. Based on the resident population estimated as of July 1 of the year shown.    2. Includes supplements to wages and salaries.

# Table B. States and Counties — Earnings, Social Security, and Housing

| STATE County | Earnings, 2011 | | | | | | | | | Social Security beneficiaries, December 2011 | | Housing units, 2010 | | |
| | Total (mil dol) | Farm | Goods-related[1] | | Service-related and health | | | | Govern-ment | Number | Rate[2] | Supplemental Security Income recipients, December 2011 | Total | Percent change, 2000–2010 |
| | | | Total | Manu-facturing | Information and professional and technical services | Retail trade | Finance, insurance, and real estate | Health care and social services | | | | | | |
| | 75 | 76 | 77 | 78 | 79 | 80 | 81 | 82 | 83 | 84 | 85 | 86 | 87 | 88 |

OHIO—Cont'd

| | | | | | | | | | | | | | | |
|---|---|---|---|---|---|---|---|---|---|---|---|---|---|---|
| Ottawa | 814 | 3.4 | D | 19.2 | D | 6.9 | 4.1 | 8.7 | 16.8 | 10 430 | 252 | 474 | 27 909 | 9.3 |
| Paulding | 271 | 20.2 | D | 22.7 | 1.5 | 5.8 | 2.7 | D | 20.9 | 4 245 | 219 | 374 | 8 749 | 3.2 |
| Perry | 311 | 4.3 | 32.8 | 12.2 | 2.4 | 6.3 | 2.5 | D | 28.2 | 7 475 | 206 | 1 251 | 15 211 | 11.4 |
| Pickaway | 907 | 10.0 | D | 21.0 | D | 5.7 | 2.7 | 8.9 | 27.5 | 10 350 | 185 | 1 271 | 21 275 | 14.4 |
| Pike | 600 | 2.1 | D | 29.9 | 7.1 | 5.3 | 2.3 | D | 13.4 | 6 440 | 225 | 1 880 | 12 481 | 7.6 |
| Portage | 3 091 | 0.4 | 29.1 | 23.0 | 4.7 | 6.9 | 3.7 | 5.4 | 28.2 | 27 685 | 171 | 2 307 | 67 472 | 12.3 |
| Preble | 552 | 13.0 | 35.3 | 30.7 | D | 7.0 | 2.9 | D | 17.5 | 8 695 | 207 | 672 | 17 888 | 4.1 |
| Putnam | 622 | 14.1 | D | 28.4 | 3.8 | 6.1 | 3.4 | 6.0 | 13.7 | 6 310 | 184 | 299 | 13 731 | 7.7 |
| Richland | 2 528 | 1.2 | 26.6 | 21.5 | 5.1 | 8.9 | 3.6 | 15.1 | 18.9 | 27 500 | 223 | 3 156 | 54 599 | 2.9 |
| Ross | 1 572 | 2.7 | 23.1 | 20.4 | 3.2 | 7.5 | 2.4 | 17.9 | 27.8 | 15 355 | 196 | 2 757 | 32 148 | 9.1 |
| Sandusky | 1 342 | 3.2 | 42.8 | 38.1 | 2.4 | 6.4 | 3.7 | D | 13.1 | 12 630 | 208 | 1 126 | 26 390 | 4.5 |
| Scioto | 1 223 | 0.9 | D | 9.3 | 4.8 | 7.8 | 3.2 | 25.0 | 26.2 | 16 470 | 208 | 5 257 | 34 142 | 0.3 |
| Seneca | 977 | 5.8 | 29.4 | 21.6 | 3.1 | 7.1 | D | 10.1 | 16.0 | 11 690 | 207 | 973 | 24 122 | 1.8 |
| Shelby | 1 557 | 4.9 | 54.6 | 48.1 | D | 4.1 | 2.0 | D | 9.4 | 9 010 | 183 | 771 | 20 173 | 8.0 |
| Stark | 8 548 | 0.3 | 28.2 | 20.6 | 5.2 | 7.8 | 5.9 | 17.3 | 13.1 | 81 010 | 216 | 8 771 | 165 215 | 5.2 |
| Summit | 16 191 | 0.0 | 18.1 | 13.4 | 9.0 | 6.4 | 6.3 | 15.2 | 12.4 | 102 570 | 190 | 13 313 | 245 109 | 6.2 |
| Trumbull | 4 026 | 0.3 | 35.5 | 30.7 | 3.3 | 8.0 | 3.6 | 13.9 | 14.2 | 51 145 | 244 | 5 890 | 96 163 | 1.1 |
| Tuscarawas | 1 669 | 1.5 | 32.9 | 25.0 | 3.9 | 8.3 | 3.4 | 12.6 | 15.7 | 19 810 | 214 | 1 931 | 40 206 | 5.5 |
| Union | 1 950 | 1.9 | D | 43.6 | D | 3.7 | 1.8 | 3.3 | 10.6 | 7 125 | 135 | 482 | 19 429 | 27.7 |
| Van Wert | 575 | 11.7 | D | 28.4 | 1.8 | 6.0 | 8.8 | 11.0 | 13.2 | 6 350 | 222 | 494 | 12 615 | 2.0 |
| Vinton | 122 | 2.0 | D | 20.4 | D | 3.7 | 4.5 | 6.5 | 29.5 | 2 655 | 199 | 612 | 6 291 | 11.3 |
| Warren | 4 526 | 0.4 | 21.4 | 16.4 | 9.9 | 7.9 | 10.9 | 7.5 | 12.7 | 31 275 | 146 | 1 874 | 80 750 | 37.4 |
| Washington | 1 340 | 0.5 | 30.4 | 21.1 | 4.2 | 7.1 | 4.7 | 17.6 | 12.0 | 14 550 | 236 | 1 853 | 28 367 | 2.2 |
| Wayne | 2 383 | 2.0 | 39.2 | 31.5 | 4.7 | 6.2 | 4.2 | D | 15.7 | 21 130 | 184 | 1 772 | 45 847 | 8.4 |
| Williams | 870 | 5.4 | 45.3 | 41.7 | D | 5.6 | 2.3 | 11.0 | 12.6 | 8 000 | 213 | 541 | 16 668 | 3.3 |
| Wood | 3 474 | 2.0 | 34.6 | 28.1 | 4.2 | 5.3 | 3.6 | 7.2 | 19.4 | 20 175 | 160 | 1 381 | 53 376 | 12.4 |
| Wyandot | 493 | 17.7 | 40.1 | 30.3 | D | 4.9 | 3.0 | D | 14.0 | 4 765 | 210 | 296 | 9 870 | 5.9 |
| OKLAHOMA | 102 227 | 0.9 | 23.9 | 9.4 | 7.2 | 6.6 | 5.8 | 10.2 | 21.8 | 717 398 | 189 | 95 644 | 1 664 378 | 9.9 |
| Adair | 270 | 7.6 | D | 28.8 | D | 5.9 | 2.4 | 8.2 | 26.7 | 4 735 | 209 | 962 | 9 142 | 9.5 |
| Alfalfa | 100 | 18.1 | D | D | D | 6.6 | D | 3.1 | 21.0 | 1 320 | 233 | 74 | 2 763 | -2.4 |
| Atoka | 212 | 0.3 | 15.1 | 7.3 | 2.9 | 12.4 | D | 5.0 | 31.4 | 3 305 | 233 | 610 | 6 312 | 11.3 |
| Beaver | 138 | 26.2 | D | D | D | 2.3 | D | D | 15.9 | 1 065 | 189 | 52 | 2 670 | -1.8 |
| Beckham | 667 | -0.2 | 35.2 | 3.1 | D | 10.3 | 7.2 | 8.3 | 8.3 | 3 930 | 176 | 600 | 9 647 | 9.7 |
| Blaine | 178 | 11.1 | 24.9 | 12.0 | D | 5.7 | D | 5.4 | 21.7 | 2 295 | 235 | 274 | 5 193 | -0.3 |
| Bryan | 727 | 1.8 | D | 5.9 | 3.9 | 6.3 | 4.5 | 12.2 | 40.0 | 9 145 | 212 | 1 599 | 19 586 | 17.2 |
| Caddo | 402 | 3.5 | 10.2 | 0.5 | 4.6 | 8.8 | 4.1 | D | 37.7 | 6 330 | 214 | 985 | 13 141 | 0.4 |
| Canadian | 1 670 | 1.3 | 31.7 | 12.4 | 5.6 | 7.5 | 5.2 | 5.8 | 20.9 | 17 655 | 148 | 1 184 | 45 810 | 34.9 |
| Carter | 1 361 | 0.0 | 34.6 | 18.5 | 5.5 | 7.3 | 5.1 | 12.5 | 13.1 | 11 020 | 229 | 1 580 | 21 148 | 2.8 |
| Cherokee | 817 | 4.7 | 5.7 | 1.4 | 2.1 | 7.1 | 3.9 | 7.2 | 54.4 | 9 375 | 196 | 1 549 | 21 455 | 10.0 |
| Choctaw | 228 | 1.8 | 9.7 | 3.2 | 3.1 | 7.9 | 2.8 | 10.7 | 31.8 | 3 985 | 261 | 926 | 7 521 | -0.2 |
| Cimarron | 67 | 51.1 | D | D | D | 4.1 | D | 0.6 | 16.4 | 665 | 267 | 33 | 1 587 | 0.3 |
| Cleveland | 4 270 | 0.1 | 15.1 | 5.4 | 8.8 | 8.9 | 5.1 | 9.6 | 32.1 | 38 080 | 146 | 3 326 | 104 821 | 23.5 |
| Coal | 67 | 0.8 | 17.3 | 3.7 | D | 7.2 | D | 10.2 | 29.9 | 1 310 | 221 | 248 | 2 810 | 2.4 |
| Comanche | 3 761 | 0.0 | D | 7.8 | 2.8 | 4.6 | 3.0 | 4.4 | 62.4 | 18 415 | 146 | 3 077 | 50 739 | 11.7 |
| Cotton | 87 | 11.1 | D | D | D | 3.2 | 3.3 | 3.7 | 51.1 | 1 430 | 231 | 151 | 3 016 | -2.2 |
| Craig | 301 | 2.5 | D | 7.3 | D | 9.2 | 3.7 | D | 30.5 | 3 845 | 255 | 585 | 6 749 | 4.5 |
| Creek | 1 052 | -0.4 | 38.9 | 22.5 | D | 6.9 | 4.2 | 8.7 | 15.8 | 15 705 | 223 | 1 749 | 29 761 | 6.3 |
| Custer | 744 | 0.9 | 33.7 | 11.8 | 3.9 | 7.6 | 4.4 | D | 19.9 | 4 700 | 169 | 561 | 12 204 | 4.5 |
| Delaware | 468 | 5.5 | D | 8.5 | D | 8.7 | 4.3 | D | 26.9 | 10 345 | 248 | 1 226 | 24 818 | 11.3 |
| Dewey | 103 | 1.3 | 37.6 | 4.2 | 6.4 | 6.7 | D | 3.3 | 19.0 | 1 190 | 245 | 76 | 2 445 | 0.8 |
| Ellis | 92 | 18.2 | 10.2 | 0.4 | D | 6.4 | D | 4.7 | 23.3 | 945 | 233 | 41 | 2 285 | 6.5 |
| Garfield | 1 635 | 0.4 | 22.8 | 8.9 | 7.5 | 6.7 | 4.5 | 12.6 | 22.4 | 12 370 | 204 | 1 394 | 26 831 | 3.0 |
| Garvin | 572 | 0.1 | 36.9 | 13.7 | 3.7 | 13.0 | 3.3 | 7.4 | 18.3 | 6 810 | 248 | 858 | 12 827 | 1.5 |
| Grady | 732 | 3.0 | 29.5 | 10.7 | 4.3 | 9.6 | 5.3 | 7.1 | 19.5 | 10 115 | 191 | 1 299 | 22 219 | 14.3 |
| Grant | 104 | 14.1 | 28.0 | 0.3 | D | 2.3 | 7.7 | 3.2 | 15.2 | 1 125 | 245 | 57 | 2 486 | -5.2 |
| Greer | 67 | 8.5 | D | D | D | 6.2 | D | 11.2 | 52.8 | 1 495 | 244 | 208 | 2 738 | -1.8 |
| Harmon | 45 | 19.5 | D | D | D | 6.2 | D | 2.7 | 33.7 | 705 | 242 | 149 | 1 544 | -6.3 |
| Harper | 62 | 23.5 | D | D | D | 4.7 | D | 3.5 | 30.9 | 805 | 218 | 45 | 1 908 | 2.4 |
| Haskell | 181 | 7.7 | 18.9 | 2.3 | D | 8.6 | D | 25.3 | 18.6 | 3 510 | 274 | 553 | 6 028 | 8.2 |
| Hughes | 173 | 12.3 | 14.3 | 5.3 | 2.8 | 7.1 | D | 8.0 | 26.1 | 3 620 | 262 | 513 | 6 183 | -0.9 |
| Jackson | 649 | -0.5 | 9.0 | 6.2 | D | 6.8 | 2.9 | 3.8 | 60.2 | 4 560 | 172 | 753 | 12 077 | -2.4 |
| Jefferson | 82 | 27.8 | 8.2 | 1.4 | 2.9 | 7.9 | 8.4 | D | 25.0 | 1 685 | 259 | 220 | 3 378 | 0.1 |
| Johnston | 153 | 0.4 | 28.1 | 16.5 | D | 5.1 | D | 13.7 | 30.2 | 2 695 | 242 | 461 | 5 126 | 7.2 |
| Kay | 1 129 | 0.6 | 21.6 | 11.3 | D | 7.2 | 4.1 | 8.0 | 19.6 | 11 200 | 243 | 1 097 | 21 708 | -0.4 |
| Kingfisher | 371 | 8.1 | 33.9 | 9.8 | D | 6.7 | 3.6 | D | 11.2 | 2 920 | 192 | 194 | 6 409 | 9.0 |

1. Includes mining, construction, and manufacturing.    2. Per 1,000 resident population enumerated in the 2010 census.

# Table B. States and Counties — Housing, Labor Force, and Employment

| | Housing units, 2007–2011 | | | | | | | | Civilian labor force, 2012 | | | | Civilian employment,[6] 2007–2011 | | |
| STATE County | Total | Occupied units | | | | | | | | | Unemployment | | | Percent | |
| | | | Owner-occupied | | | Renter-occupied | | | | | | | | | |
| | | Percent | Median value[1] | Median owner cost as a percent of income | | Median rent[3] | Median rent as a percent of income | Sub-standard units[4] (percent) | Total | Percent change, 2011–2012 | Total | Rate[5] | Total | Management, business, science and arts | Construction, production, and maintenance occupations |
| | | | | With a mortgage | Without a mortgage[2] | | | | | | | | | | |
| | 89 | 90 | 91 | 92 | 93 | 94 | 95 | 96 | 97 | 98 | 99 | 100 | 101 | 102 | 103 |

OHIO—Cont'd

| | | | | | | | | | | | | | | | |
|---|---|---|---|---|---|---|---|---|---|---|---|---|---|---|---|
| Ottawa | 18 009 | 81.3 | 141 900 | 23.3 | 12.8 | 723 | 31.1 | 1.2 | 20 819 | -1.5 | 2 030 | 9.8 | 19 743 | 28.7 | 30.7 |
| Paulding | 7 571 | 79.2 | 91 800 | 21.6 | 11.1 | 548 | 28.5 | 2.3 | 9 772 | -3.0 | 671 | 6.9 | 8 480 | 23.0 | 42.8 |
| Perry | 13 762 | 72.8 | 97 500 | 22.6 | 11.0 | 579 | 29.1 | 3.6 | 15 888 | -3.1 | 1 505 | 9.5 | 15 212 | 24.4 | 36.7 |
| Pickaway | 19 284 | 75.0 | 148 500 | 24.4 | 12.5 | 708 | 30.0 | 2.0 | 24 389 | -0.3 | 1 851 | 7.6 | 23 156 | 29.3 | 28.2 |
| Pike | 10 816 | 72.2 | 95 900 | 22.3 | 13.3 | 615 | 33.4 | 2.6 | 10 265 | -4.3 | 1 328 | 12.9 | 9 953 | 28.9 | 31.4 |
| Portage | 61 746 | 69.1 | 156 500 | 23.6 | 13.4 | 759 | 32.1 | 0.9 | 90 936 | -1.0 | 6 073 | 6.7 | 80 821 | 30.7 | 25.5 |
| Preble | 16 321 | 78.0 | 117 500 | 23.4 | 13.7 | 701 | 28.8 | 1.5 | 20 437 | -2.4 | 1 558 | 7.6 | 19 908 | 24.4 | 34.3 |
| Putnam | 12 936 | 84.4 | 132 900 | 20.1 | 9.9 | 589 | 22.9 | 1.6 | 17 588 | -2.8 | 1 047 | 6.0 | 17 581 | 31.1 | 35.1 |
| Richland | 48 593 | 70.2 | 110 900 | 22.6 | 12.1 | 609 | 27.5 | 1.6 | 57 622 | -3.3 | 4 803 | 8.3 | 54 088 | 27.1 | 31.0 |
| Ross | 28 158 | 73.4 | 114 800 | 21.7 | 12.5 | 645 | 30.4 | 2.2 | 34 970 | -0.7 | 2 861 | 8.2 | 30 260 | 28.6 | 29.5 |
| Sandusky | 24 031 | 75.5 | 113 100 | 22.2 | 11.7 | 576 | 27.6 | 1.1 | 32 521 | -2.5 | 2 298 | 7.1 | 29 084 | 25.0 | 39.1 |
| Scioto | 29 788 | 68.8 | 87 500 | 22.3 | 12.8 | 533 | 33.6 | 1.7 | 31 867 | -2.4 | 3 416 | 10.7 | 28 315 | 31.3 | 25.9 |
| Seneca | 22 026 | 72.8 | 102 000 | 20.6 | 12.5 | 600 | 26.9 | 1.3 | 28 493 | -3.1 | 2 127 | 7.5 | 25 736 | 26.7 | 35.5 |
| Shelby | 18 507 | 75.7 | 124 300 | 21.8 | 12.3 | 649 | 30.1 | 1.7 | 24 226 | -2.3 | 1 658 | 6.8 | 23 235 | 26.4 | 37.6 |
| Stark | 150 072 | 70.7 | 126 700 | 22.7 | 12.4 | 642 | 29.6 | 1.3 | 184 597 | -0.8 | 13 555 | 7.3 | 172 484 | 31.0 | 24.5 |
| Summit | 221 498 | 69.0 | 140 700 | 23.2 | 13.7 | 731 | 30.7 | 1.3 | 281 241 | -1.0 | 19 195 | 6.8 | 258 042 | 36.8 | 20.6 |
| Trumbull | 86 746 | 73.7 | 100 500 | 22.9 | 13.2 | 604 | 30.1 | 1.5 | 100 367 | -1.5 | 8 142 | 8.1 | 88 818 | 26.4 | 29.8 |
| Tuscarawas | 36 262 | 73.8 | 110 000 | 21.6 | 12.2 | 600 | 28.6 | 1.3 | 46 570 | -0.9 | 3 152 | 6.8 | 42 001 | 26.9 | 33.6 |
| Union | 17 795 | 77.9 | 175 900 | 23.7 | 13.4 | 792 | 26.4 | 1.1 | 27 087 | 0.0 | 1 500 | 5.5 | 24 033 | 35.9 | 26.2 |
| Van Wert | 11 381 | 81.6 | 88 800 | 21.5 | 10.4 | 576 | 24.9 | 0.8 | 13 894 | -1.9 | 1 031 | 7.4 | 13 703 | 24.7 | 36.5 |
| Vinton | 5 305 | 76.2 | 84 800 | 25.5 | 13.4 | 580 | 38.9 | 4.8 | 5 461 | -4.0 | 578 | 10.6 | 4 985 | 27.5 | 39.1 |
| Warren | 75 283 | 79.2 | 193 200 | 23.2 | 12.3 | 909 | 27.6 | 0.9 | 109 079 | -1.0 | 6 854 | 6.3 | 101 697 | 42.4 | 18.0 |
| Washington | 25 184 | 75.7 | 109 300 | 21.2 | 10.6 | 562 | 28.9 | 1.6 | 31 170 | -2.1 | 2 160 | 6.9 | 26 963 | 28.0 | 27.6 |
| Wayne | 42 485 | 75.1 | 138 200 | 23.1 | 11.5 | 629 | 27.1 | 3.0 | 57 199 | -0.3 | 3 465 | 6.1 | 54 307 | 28.3 | 32.6 |
| Williams | 15 139 | 76.6 | 101 800 | 22.1 | 12.6 | 596 | 28.1 | 1.3 | 18 981 | -0.4 | 1 448 | 7.6 | 17 574 | 23.3 | 40.0 |
| Wood | 48 680 | 69.2 | 154 200 | 22.8 | 13.0 | 690 | 28.9 | 1.2 | 65 701 | -0.6 | 4 558 | 6.9 | 62 437 | 36.1 | 23.4 |
| Wyandot | 9 179 | 73.5 | 107 500 | 20.8 | 11.1 | 576 | 25.5 | 0.8 | 11 047 | -0.9 | 804 | 7.3 | 11 163 | 24.8 | 39.3 |
| OKLAHOMA | 1 432 735 | 67.8 | 108 400 | 21.3 | 10.9 | 659 | 28.5 | 3.0 | 1 802 639 | 1.0 | 93 842 | 5.2 | 1 685 029 | 32.4 | 25.3 |
| Adair | 7 909 | 71.3 | 77 100 | 23.2 | 10.6 | 499 | 27.9 | 4.1 | 10 476 | -4.9 | 729 | 7.0 | 8 477 | 22.9 | 39.7 |
| Alfalfa | 2 033 | 80.5 | 54 200 | 16.5 | 9.9 | 533 | 25.4 | 1.2 | 2 915 | 13.7 | 94 | 3.2 | 2 112 | 41.0 | 23.3 |
| Atoka | 5 367 | 77.2 | 69 100 | 22.8 | 11.9 | 523 | 27.0 | 2.3 | 6 088 | -0.5 | 337 | 5.5 | 5 036 | 32.0 | 32.0 |
| Beaver | 2 150 | 71.9 | 75 700 | 23.2 | 9.9 | 597 | 16.6 | 3.2 | 3 646 | 6.9 | 91 | 2.5 | 2 636 | 28.4 | 35.1 |
| Beckham | 7 715 | 66.1 | 89 200 | 20.2 | 9.9 | 612 | 19.6 | 3.1 | 14 746 | 11.1 | 388 | 2.6 | 9 733 | 26.1 | 35.4 |
| Blaine | 4 095 | 69.5 | 67 600 | 16.9 | 11.4 | 562 | 22.7 | 4.9 | 4 559 | -1.7 | 200 | 4.4 | 4 407 | 29.8 | 25.1 |
| Bryan | 16 354 | 65.9 | 87 100 | 21.5 | 12.3 | 609 | 27.4 | 4.4 | 19 900 | -0.6 | 931 | 4.7 | 17 979 | 28.2 | 26.9 |
| Caddo | 10 296 | 70.7 | 69 500 | 18.8 | 11.0 | 499 | 24.7 | 5.3 | 12 837 | 0.1 | 695 | 5.4 | 10 554 | 27.0 | 31.5 |
| Canadian | 41 293 | 77.2 | 135 100 | 20.7 | 10.1 | 777 | 26.1 | 1.9 | 58 055 | 1.7 | 2 434 | 4.2 | 56 196 | 36.6 | 20.3 |
| Carter | 17 603 | 70.5 | 87 700 | 20.9 | 9.9 | 584 | 24.6 | 2.2 | 28 558 | 1.7 | 1 187 | 4.2 | 20 383 | 26.2 | 29.5 |
| Cherokee | 16 501 | 67.2 | 97 100 | 22.7 | 10.3 | 549 | 30.0 | 4.1 | 23 979 | -3.7 | 1 277 | 5.3 | 18 011 | 33.4 | 25.1 |
| Choctaw | 6 103 | 69.7 | 69 500 | 22.5 | 10.8 | 516 | 26.7 | 3.3 | 7 038 | -3.9 | 468 | 6.6 | 5 612 | 24.1 | 35.6 |
| Cimarron | 1 095 | 71.3 | 59 100 | 18.6 | 9.9 | 379 | 22.7 | 2.0 | 1 139 | -6.8 | 41 | 3.6 | 1 135 | 36.2 | 29.9 |
| Cleveland | 94 096 | 68.6 | 136 400 | 21.4 | 10.8 | 751 | 29.6 | 2.1 | 128 843 | 1.8 | 5 653 | 4.4 | 126 265 | 37.6 | 18.8 |
| Coal | 2 390 | 68.7 | 65 600 | 19.0 | 11.0 | 453 | 24.7 | 3.6 | 2 747 | 0.8 | 162 | 5.9 | 2 283 | 23.4 | 40.9 |
| Comanche | 44 179 | 57.6 | 106 300 | 20.8 | 10.1 | 706 | 27.5 | 3.2 | 47 772 | -1.0 | 3 151 | 6.6 | 47 646 | 31.1 | 24.7 |
| Cotton | 2 359 | 73.0 | 74 000 | 19.7 | 10.6 | 528 | 23.4 | 3.1 | 3 355 | -3.0 | 159 | 4.7 | 2 654 | 34.1 | 30.2 |
| Craig | 5 744 | 78.5 | 86 200 | 20.9 | 11.3 | 571 | 22.7 | 2.1 | 7 079 | 0.4 | 361 | 5.1 | 6 569 | 29.3 | 28.3 |
| Creek | 26 373 | 74.4 | 106 200 | 22.1 | 11.4 | 647 | 25.1 | 3.0 | 30 665 | 0.9 | 1 840 | 6.0 | 30 261 | 27.3 | 31.0 |
| Custer | 10 407 | 63.4 | 94 900 | 18.5 | 10.7 | 565 | 28.4 | 4.7 | 17 032 | 3.5 | 554 | 3.3 | 13 370 | 30.0 | 28.9 |
| Delaware | 16 070 | 77.2 | 96 800 | 24.0 | 12.4 | 559 | 26.6 | 5.3 | 19 439 | -1.4 | 1 085 | 5.6 | 15 950 | 26.8 | 31.1 |
| Dewey | 1 802 | 79.4 | 75 100 | 17.7 | 12.6 | 572 | 18.9 | 2.9 | 2 903 | -3.7 | 76 | 2.6 | 1 993 | 34.0 | 31.4 |
| Ellis | 1 735 | 79.1 | 71 600 | 16.8 | 11.9 | 474 | 21.0 | 2.6 | 2 791 | 8.6 | 63 | 2.3 | 1 896 | 35.3 | 31.3 |
| Garfield | 24 022 | 67.5 | 85 500 | 20.3 | 10.2 | 615 | 24.7 | 2.9 | 33 785 | 1.6 | 1 184 | 3.5 | 27 817 | 27.5 | 29.6 |
| Garvin | 10 106 | 76.1 | 79 700 | 19.9 | 11.8 | 582 | 23.4 | 1.9 | 15 269 | 1.6 | 612 | 4.0 | 11 696 | 24.7 | 34.4 |
| Grady | 19 646 | 77.8 | 107 400 | 21.0 | 10.8 | 591 | 24.1 | 2.6 | 23 585 | 1.7 | 1 183 | 5.0 | 23 522 | 30.4 | 30.9 |
| Grant | 1 899 | 77.0 | 59 100 | 20.3 | 9.9 | 523 | 18.1 | 0.8 | 2 759 | 3.1 | 89 | 3.2 | 2 172 | 32.5 | 29.3 |
| Greer | 2 221 | 69.8 | 59 700 | 18.8 | 12.0 | 453 | 21.9 | 3.1 | 1 964 | -2.6 | 121 | 6.2 | 2 217 | 33.5 | 19.0 |
| Harmon | 1 159 | 69.8 | 44 800 | 18.2 | 13.8 | 517 | 36.5 | 4.4 | 1 480 | 6.8 | 64 | 4.3 | 1 224 | 29.2 | 29.1 |
| Harper | 1 542 | 79.8 | 66 500 | 17.3 | 10.4 | 521 | 24.9 | 1.1 | 2 002 | 1.1 | 59 | 2.9 | 1 848 | 28.4 | 39.4 |
| Haskell | 4 734 | 76.7 | 75 500 | 21.5 | 10.8 | 533 | 28.0 | 3.4 | 5 744 | -3.1 | 388 | 6.8 | 4 412 | 29.2 | 38.3 |
| Hughes | 5 155 | 76.5 | 64 200 | 20.3 | 11.5 | 580 | 27.8 | 2.9 | 5 899 | 3.8 | 471 | 8.0 | 4 843 | 30.4 | 35.4 |
| Jackson | 10 470 | 63.3 | 87 600 | 19.1 | 11.5 | 624 | 27.8 | 2.6 | 12 025 | -2.3 | 563 | 4.7 | 11 115 | 31.2 | 25.8 |
| Jefferson | 2 454 | 76.3 | 58 700 | 22.7 | 12.0 | 403 | 24.0 | 2.9 | 2 390 | -3.5 | 129 | 5.4 | 2 653 | 22.4 | 33.7 |
| Johnston | 4 354 | 72.5 | 69 300 | 20.7 | 10.5 | 519 | 25.1 | 3.3 | 4 925 | -0.8 | 268 | 5.4 | 3 966 | 34.6 | 32.5 |
| Kay | 18 510 | 70.0 | 76 900 | 19.5 | 11.4 | 594 | 26.0 | 3.4 | 22 245 | -2.5 | 1 394 | 6.3 | 19 993 | 28.8 | 29.4 |
| Kingfisher | 5 662 | 77.0 | 111 400 | 19.1 | 10.6 | 637 | 23.8 | 2.3 | 8 038 | 1.1 | 255 | 3.2 | 7 619 | 32.7 | 32.2 |

1. Specified owner-occupied units. 2. A value of 9.9 represents 9.9 percent or less. 3. Specified renter-occupied units. A value of 10.0 represents 10 percent or less. 4. Overcrowded or lacking complete plumbing facilities. 5. Percent of civilian labor force. 6. Persons 16 years old and over.

# Table B. States and Counties — Nonfarm Employment and Agriculture

| | Private nonfarm establishments, employment and payroll, 2011 | | | | | | | | Agriculture, 2007 | | | |
| | Employment | | | | | | Annual payroll | | Farms | | | |
| | | | | | | | | | | Percent with: | | |
| STATE County | Number of establishments | Total | Health care and social assistance | Manufacturing | Retail trade | Finance and insurance | Professional, scientific, and technical services | Total (mil dol) | Average per employee (dollars) | Number | Fewer than 50 acres | 500 acres or more | Farm operators whose principal occupation is farming (percent) |
|---|---|---|---|---|---|---|---|---|---|---|---|---|---|
| | 104 | 105 | 106 | 107 | 108 | 109 | 110 | 111 | 112 | 113 | 114 | 115 | 116 |
| **OHIO—Cont'd** | | | | | | | | | | | | | |
| Ottawa | 1 000 | 10 317 | 1 736 | 2 010 | 1 368 | 316 | 182 | 397 | 38 504 | 589 | 43.5 | 10.5 | 46.2 |
| Paulding | 303 | 3 636 | 649 | 1 238 | 402 | 95 | 70 | 103 | 28 439 | 754 | 32.5 | 19.4 | 46.9 |
| Perry | 418 | 3 801 | 764 | 728 | 582 | 179 | D | 106 | 27 834 | 643 | 36.2 | 4.0 | 37.5 |
| Pickaway | 786 | 10 484 | 2 277 | 2 118 | 1 435 | 304 | 201 | 385 | 36 708 | 832 | 44.6 | 18.5 | 48.1 |
| Pike | 409 | 7 035 | 1 664 | 1 996 | 881 | 191 | 161 | 309 | 43 854 | 538 | 28.6 | 3.3 | 36.8 |
| Portage | 2 944 | 41 722 | 5 645 | 9 143 | 7 356 | 835 | 1 305 | 1 499 | 35 921 | 862 | 59.0 | 3.0 | 41.3 |
| Preble | 651 | 8 214 | 1 095 | 2 789 | 1 437 | D | 185 | 270 | 32 828 | 1 181 | 46.0 | 11.5 | 46.2 |
| Putnam | 731 | 9 114 | 1 140 | 2 936 | 1 155 | 241 | 188 | 288 | 31 573 | 1 316 | 29.0 | 12.9 | 40.1 |
| Richland | 2 673 | 42 132 | 7 460 | 7 881 | 6 516 | 1 057 | 1 017 | 1 298 | 30 805 | 1 009 | 43.0 | 4.5 | 41.8 |
| Ross | 1 238 | 21 711 | 5 581 | 3 835 | 3 627 | 490 | 412 | 879 | 40 487 | 1 009 | 37.0 | 9.9 | 43.4 |
| Sandusky | 1 330 | 23 134 | 3 474 | 8 663 | 2 651 | 511 | 409 | 792 | 34 217 | 781 | 42.8 | 13.8 | 45.1 |
| Scioto | 1 281 | 18 052 | 6 619 | 1 518 | 3 075 | 521 | D | 538 | 29 789 | 755 | 39.3 | 4.8 | 38.3 |
| Seneca | 1 182 | 17 234 | 2 903 | 3 802 | 2 059 | 441 | 400 | 519 | 30 131 | 1 147 | 32.2 | 13.2 | 40.4 |
| Shelby | 991 | 20 998 | 1 852 | 9 956 | 1 760 | 387 | 383 | 940 | 44 764 | 1 050 | 34.5 | 11.4 | 39.1 |
| Stark | 8 344 | 134 600 | 27 046 | 22 707 | 20 037 | 6 236 | 4 501 | 4 632 | 34 415 | 1 300 | 56.8 | 3.5 | 47.2 |
| Summit | 13 458 | 235 688 | 44 617 | 26 928 | 29 604 | 9 618 | 15 567 | 10 205 | 43 300 | 334 | 74.3 | 1.2 | 42.5 |
| Trumbull | 4 169 | 71 708 | 12 851 | 14 608 | 9 810 | 1 863 | 1 343 | 2 588 | 36 092 | 970 | 44.4 | 5.1 | 47.3 |
| Tuscarawas | 2 125 | 29 112 | 5 419 | 6 963 | 4 376 | 744 | 866 | 902 | 30 984 | 983 | 40.3 | 5.5 | 43.5 |
| Union | 986 | 24 304 | 1 566 | 5 691 | 1 830 | 313 | 2 336 | 1 159 | 47 680 | 932 | 45.6 | 11.4 | 45.9 |
| Van Wert | 536 | 9 121 | 1 689 | 3 073 | 1 188 | 791 | 169 | 298 | 32 665 | 696 | 26.1 | 25.4 | 48.9 |
| Vinton | 132 | 1 589 | 313 | D | 215 | D | 19 | 58 | 36 512 | 250 | 27.2 | 2.8 | 32.4 |
| Warren | 3 916 | 69 988 | 9 136 | 9 438 | 9 019 | 5 615 | 3 496 | 2 981 | 42 589 | 896 | 65.6 | 3.9 | 40.0 |
| Washington | 1 430 | 21 802 | 4 469 | 3 601 | 2 774 | 767 | 601 | 764 | 35 027 | 856 | 23.7 | 3.9 | 42.2 |
| Wayne | 2 436 | 36 562 | 5 709 | 9 894 | 4 791 | 1 214 | 1 250 | 1 310 | 35 826 | 1 788 | 45.5 | 5.5 | 52.1 |
| Williams | 818 | 14 137 | 1 990 | 6 141 | 1 376 | 276 | 263 | 466 | 32 989 | 1 116 | 39.2 | 9.9 | 34.5 |
| Wood | 2 729 | 47 431 | 4 810 | 10 718 | 6 202 | 928 | 2 147 | 1 881 | 39 647 | 1 169 | 43.4 | 14.3 | 41.1 |
| Wyandot | 495 | 6 950 | 723 | 2 714 | 696 | 228 | 103 | 226 | 32 539 | 632 | 35.6 | 21.7 | 48.4 |
| **OKLAHOMA** | 89 749 | 1 261 590 | 212 273 | 126 613 | 170 855 | 59 236 | 62 030 | 49 374 | 39 136 | 86 565 | 26.0 | 17.6 | 41.6 |
| Adair | 211 | 2 834 | 486 | 1 125 | 540 | 118 | 63 | 84 | 29 517 | 1 202 | 27.5 | 9.0 | 43.8 |
| Alfalfa | 127 | 780 | D | D | 147 | 65 | 67 | 22 | 28 406 | 695 | 8.6 | 42.4 | 52.9 |
| Atoka | 249 | 2 030 | 393 | 163 | 457 | D | 41 | 55 | 27 103 | 1 218 | 18.4 | 16.7 | 47.5 |
| Beaver | 181 | 1 249 | D | D | 94 | 58 | D | 50 | 40 348 | 952 | 6.8 | 37.2 | 35.0 |
| Beckham | 836 | 9 593 | 1 254 | D | 1 605 | 296 | 395 | 420 | 43 734 | 862 | 11.5 | 23.3 | 32.1 |
| Blaine | 289 | 2 204 | 337 | D | 240 | 152 | 59 | 70 | 31 592 | 1 701 | 23.5 | 34.0 | 47.7 |
| Bryan | 732 | 9 306 | 2 090 | 1 051 | 1 488 | 546 | 409 | 260 | 27 945 | 1 584 | 11.9 | 11.9 | 43.6 |
| Caddo | 455 | 4 460 | 744 | D | 857 | 198 | 313 | 141 | 31 638 | | 12.7 | 26.5 | 44.4 |
| Canadian | 2 284 | 23 790 | 2 668 | 2 885 | 3 582 | 814 | 705 | 885 | 37 198 | 1 447 | 31.6 | 19.8 | 45.2 |
| Carter | 1 506 | 20 411 | 3 569 | 3 142 | 3 201 | 677 | 502 | 738 | 36 149 | 1 426 | 29.8 | 11.4 | 33.2 |
| Cherokee | 708 | 8 147 | 2 410 | D | 1 721 | 327 | 68 | 218 | 26 707 | 1 375 | 35.7 | 6.9 | 42.0 |
| Choctaw | 251 | 3 353 | 1 007 | D | D | 105 | D | 85 | 25 375 | 1 134 | 18.6 | 14.1 | 45.8 |
| Cimarron | 70 | 365 | D | NA | 104 | 33 | D | 8 | 23 055 | 557 | 3.2 | 50.3 | 44.0 |
| Cleveland | 5 351 | 66 674 | 11 989 | 3 552 | 11 013 | 2 238 | 3 233 | 2 165 | 32 465 | 1 327 | 54.4 | 4.6 | 35.9 |
| Coal | 79 | 729 | 203 | D | 163 | D | D | 19 | 26 562 | 634 | 13.6 | 21.3 | 44.5 |
| Comanche | 2 194 | 32 151 | 6 357 | 3 459 | 5 396 | 1 851 | 1 293 | 1 008 | 31 355 | 1 126 | 24.5 | 21.0 | 42.6 |
| Cotton | 77 | 1 168 | 70 | D | 81 | 49 | D | 33 | 28 461 | 517 | 10.8 | 34.8 | 46.8 |
| Craig | 343 | 4 280 | 1 348 | D | 716 | D | 81 | 126 | 29 508 | 1 359 | 25.2 | 12.7 | 44.3 |
| Creek | 1 403 | 15 360 | 2 150 | 3 656 | 1 969 | D | 283 | 557 | 36 248 | 1 900 | 41.4 | 7.6 | 32.4 |
| Custer | 898 | 10 134 | 1 546 | 1 257 | 1 917 | 355 | 312 | 351 | 34 633 | 907 | 19.3 | 30.7 | 45.8 |
| Delaware | 685 | 6 592 | 1 193 | 627 | 1 332 | 284 | 161 | 189 | 28 652 | 1 509 | 30.0 | 9.3 | 46.3 |
| Dewey | 142 | 893 | D | 28 | 199 | 66 | 10 | 35 | 39 168 | 756 | 6.5 | 35.7 | 43.8 |
| Ellis | 112 | 825 | 169 | D | 140 | 40 | 81 | 36 | 43 539 | 766 | 5.6 | 38.5 | 38.0 |
| Garfield | 1 650 | 22 214 | 4 142 | 2 489 | 3 598 | 773 | 1 299 | 788 | 35 495 | 1 082 | 20.1 | 31.1 | 45.7 |
| Garvin | 670 | 7 419 | 1 287 | 1 093 | 1 164 | 251 | 173 | 263 | 35 510 | 1 666 | 25.3 | 14.8 | 41.1 |
| Grady | 1 050 | 10 685 | 1 801 | 1 731 | 1 580 | 422 | 267 | 331 | 30 946 | 1 850 | 28.1 | 16.9 | 44.4 |
| Grant | 115 | 867 | 123 | 9 | D | 66 | D | 35 | 40 018 | 847 | 7.7 | 37.3 | 51.5 |
| Greer | 88 | 745 | 376 | D | D | D | D | 20 | 26 984 | 571 | 6.5 | 28.4 | 38.7 |
| Harmon | 51 | 446 | 123 | D | D | D | 12 | 12 | 26 146 | 400 | 5.5 | 40.3 | 43.0 |
| Harper | 103 | 593 | 115 | D | D | D | 38 | 19 | 31 607 | 580 | 6.9 | 42.8 | 39.1 |
| Haskell | 223 | 2 698 | 907 | D | 475 | 71 | 41 | 73 | 26 997 | 914 | 18.8 | 16.0 | 44.2 |
| Hughes | 226 | 2 519 | 827 | D | 449 | 63 | 40 | 61 | 24 357 | 1 026 | 15.8 | 18.6 | 45.8 |
| Jackson | 536 | 7 733 | D | D | 1 339 | 285 | 147 | 303 | 39 183 | 745 | 22.4 | 32.3 | 43.0 |
| Jefferson | 110 | 626 | 40 | D | D | 88 | D | 17 | 27 613 | 514 | 12.5 | 37.4 | 46.9 |
| Johnston | 170 | 1 735 | 512 | D | 226 | D | D | 54 | 30 931 | 706 | 19.5 | 16.9 | 46.9 |
| Kay | 1 105 | 14 377 | 2 228 | 2 647 | 2 203 | 509 | 453 | 500 | 34 812 | 1 050 | 25.7 | 24.3 | 46.5 |
| Kingfisher | 471 | 5 088 | 577 | 423 | 604 | 214 | D | 197 | 38 808 | 1 002 | 12.8 | 31.7 | 48.6 |

# Table B. States and Counties — **Agriculture**

| STATE County | Land in farms Acreage (1,000) | Percent change, 2002-2007 | Acres Average size of farm | Total irrigated (1,000) | Total cropland (1,000) | Value of land and buildings (dollars) Average per farm | Average per acre | Value of machinery and equipment, average per farm (dollars) | Value of products sold Total (mil dol) | Average per farm (dollars) | Percent from: Crops | Live-stock and poultry products | Percent of farms with sales of: $10,000 or more | $100,000 or more | Government payments Total ($1,000) | Percent of farms |
|---|---|---|---|---|---|---|---|---|---|---|---|---|---|---|---|---|
| | 117 | 118 | 119 | 120 | 121 | 122 | 123 | 124 | 125 | 126 | 127 | 128 | 129 | 130 | 131 | 132 |
| **OHIO—Cont'd** | | | | | | | | | | | | | | | | |
| Ottawa | 115 | 0.9 | 195 | 0.2 | 107.1 | 565 167 | 2 891 | 100 476 | 46.1 | 78 309 | 95.1 | 4.9 | 56.9 | 19.2 | 1 855 | 78.3 |
| Paulding | 256 | 7.6 | 339 | D | 236.6 | 1 077 646 | 3 179 | 133 146 | 149.0 | 197 588 | 54.5 | 45.5 | 54.9 | 24.5 | 6 257 | 88.9 |
| Perry | 98 | 6.5 | 152 | 0.0 | 58.5 | 437 701 | 2 873 | 58 127 | 25.4 | 39 472 | 65.5 | 34.5 | 27.8 | 6.2 | 953 | 26.7 |
| Pickaway | 289 | 5.1 | 347 | 0.8 | 257.1 | 1 195 810 | 3 444 | 136 102 | 112.1 | 134 701 | 87.8 | 12.2 | 45.9 | 23.8 | 6 366 | 64.2 |
| Pike | 81 | -3.6 | 150 | 0.1 | 38.1 | 377 217 | 2 517 | 56 922 | 11.3 | 20 936 | 69.0 | 31.0 | 22.1 | 4.1 | 931 | 43.3 |
| Portage | 83 | -14.4 | 96 | 0.4 | 57.5 | 445 918 | 4 645 | 65 977 | 34.0 | 39 474 | 68.8 | 31.2 | 31.6 | 7.1 | 815 | 20.3 |
| Preble | 231 | 16.7 | 195 | 0.2 | 204.0 | 709 890 | 3 635 | 91 753 | 109.5 | 92 739 | 64.5 | 35.5 | 49.7 | 20.2 | 4 542 | 57.4 |
| Putnam | 304 | -8.4 | 231 | 0.5 | 283.6 | 804 912 | 3 487 | 120 551 | 146.8 | 111 517 | 64.9 | 35.1 | 72.8 | 26.1 | 5 430 | 88.4 |
| Richland | 147 | -7.5 | 145 | 0.1 | 110.2 | 525 268 | 3 616 | 77 684 | 72.8 | 72 127 | 52.6 | 47.4 | 41.8 | 18.3 | 1 934 | 41.3 |
| Ross | 224 | -9.3 | 222 | D | 152.6 | 630 849 | 2 846 | 71 947 | 51.2 | 50 741 | 83.5 | 16.5 | 29.9 | 10.3 | 5 917 | 55.8 |
| Sandusky | 181 | -7.7 | 232 | 0.5 | 167.2 | 717 040 | 3 088 | 102 521 | 79.3 | 101 533 | 93.5 | 6.5 | 61.8 | 23.8 | 3 085 | 72.6 |
| Scioto | 102 | 6.3 | 135 | 0.0 | 52.3 | 356 531 | 2 638 | 61 696 | 19.9 | 26 407 | 50.4 | 49.6 | 22.3 | 4.0 | 1 067 | 27.8 |
| Seneca | 269 | -3.9 | 235 | 0.6 | 241.7 | 733 642 | 3 124 | 100 325 | 107.4 | 93 644 | 79.0 | 21.0 | 61.6 | 21.4 | 4 893 | 81.3 |
| Shelby | 218 | 5.3 | 208 | 0.0 | 192.8 | 851 633 | 4 102 | 110 152 | 130.5 | 124 256 | 52.2 | 47.8 | 63.0 | 27.1 | 5 430 | 79.7 |
| Stark | 138 | -4.8 | 106 | 0.8 | 104.6 | 505 443 | 4 759 | 87 944 | 135.7 | 104 363 | 27.5 | 72.5 | 40.9 | 12.5 | 1 556 | 30.0 |
| Summit | 15 | -28.6 | 45 | 0.3 | 9.8 | 360 672 | 7 943 | 53 977 | 9.6 | 28 625 | 82.9 | 17.1 | 35.6 | 4.8 | 73 | 8.1 |
| Trumbull | 125 | -0.8 | 129 | 0.2 | 87.4 | 423 502 | 3 283 | 74 449 | 41.6 | 42 847 | 63.7 | 36.3 | 40.0 | 9.7 | 1 128 | 35.5 |
| Tuscarawas | 143 | -10.6 | 145 | 0.2 | 81.8 | 506 516 | 3 491 | 70 867 | 77.0 | 78 371 | 20.3 | 79.7 | 36.1 | 14.1 | 1 151 | 29.6 |
| Union | 219 | -14.5 | 235 | 0.2 | 197.9 | 784 476 | 3 344 | 118 940 | 96.0 | 103 029 | 82.7 | 17.3 | 49.1 | 20.9 | 4 628 | 65.3 |
| Van Wert | 246 | -1.6 | 354 | D | 235.9 | 1 268 533 | 3 582 | 148 603 | 110.1 | 158 160 | 77.9 | 22.1 | 74.4 | 37.9 | 5 778 | 87.2 |
| Vinton | 37 | -15.9 | 147 | D | 14.6 | 400 253 | 2 718 | 43 631 | 4.0 | 15 998 | 82.1 | 17.9 | 15.6 | 1.6 | 188 | 30.0 |
| Warren | 94 | -25.4 | 105 | 0.3 | 72.0 | 561 696 | 5 334 | 62 901 | 44.2 | 49 379 | 89.0 | 11.0 | 29.5 | 6.6 | 1 095 | 27.0 |
| Washington | 124 | -12.1 | 145 | 0.2 | 50.3 | 371 930 | 2 566 | 64 401 | 24.5 | 28 590 | 41.7 | 58.3 | 30.5 | 5.5 | 572 | 24.8 |
| Wayne | 248 | -7.1 | 139 | 0.7 | 192.9 | 695 790 | 5 008 | 99 331 | 247.3 | 138 287 | 23.4 | 76.6 | 58.8 | 25.3 | 2 999 | 36.9 |
| Williams | 213 | 0.0 | 190 | 0.5 | 179.1 | 583 687 | 3 065 | 76 702 | 102.5 | 91 867 | 53.5 | 46.5 | 36.4 | 13.7 | 5 601 | 80.1 |
| Wood | 276 | -9.8 | 236 | 0.5 | 259.7 | 791 826 | 3 359 | 112 384 | 125.4 | 107 309 | 86.9 | 13.1 | 58.3 | 21.7 | 5 160 | 80.6 |
| Wyandot | 220 | 9.5 | 348 | D | 202.0 | 1 086 393 | 3 126 | 144 224 | 134.9 | 213 516 | 54.7 | 45.3 | 57.9 | 30.1 | 4 417 | 81.5 |
| **OKLAHOMA** | 35 087 | 4.2 | 405 | 534.8 | 13 007.6 | 468 809 | 1 157 | 63 642 | 5 806.1 | 67 072 | 20.5 | 79.5 | 37.1 | 8.3 | 209 465 | 31.2 |
| Adair | 249 | 4.6 | 207 | 0.7 | 66.8 | 397 171 | 1 915 | 58 705 | 132.8 | 110 494 | 1.9 | 98.1 | 36.5 | 9.4 | 271 | 12.5 |
| Alfalfa | 543 | 17.8 | 781 | 2.6 | 358.6 | 724 520 | 928 | 131 468 | 85.0 | 122 269 | 25.4 | 74.6 | 43.0 | 23.6 | 8 538 | 81.7 |
| Atoka | 408 | -17.1 | 335 | 0.7 | 90.8 | 413 406 | 1 233 | 51 851 | 27.1 | 22 278 | 6.6 | 93.4 | 38.4 | 4.5 | 339 | 10.8 |
| Beaver | 1 129 | 10.8 | 1 186 | 28.5 | 394.9 | 747 293 | 630 | 94 719 | 188.5 | 197 965 | 19.2 | 80.8 | 37.8 | 15.4 | 6 993 | 78.0 |
| Beckham | 520 | -2.4 | 493 | 6.9 | 187.7 | 488 747 | 991 | 66 942 | 37.8 | 35 880 | 34.5 | 65.5 | 37.1 | 7.2 | 6 603 | 63.7 |
| Blaine | 586 | 9.1 | 680 | 5.8 | 286.0 | 568 359 | 836 | 94 624 | 126.6 | 146 811 | 19.8 | 80.2 | 37.9 | 18.0 | 4 497 | 68.8 |
| Bryan | 491 | 7.2 | 288 | 9.5 | 167.3 | 460 275 | 1 596 | 55 546 | 64.2 | 37 766 | 24.5 | 75.5 | 37.4 | 5.4 | 1 208 | 20.8 |
| Caddo | 750 | 5.5 | 473 | 33.2 | 328.9 | 516 439 | 1 091 | 77 205 | 102.3 | 64 571 | 29.1 | 70.9 | 51.8 | 12.5 | 9 089 | 62.4 |
| Canadian | 509 | 1.6 | 352 | 4.0 | 278.8 | 527 395 | 1 500 | 83 751 | 101.1 | 69 866 | 26.8 | 73.2 | 45.3 | 13.0 | 3 952 | 44.7 |
| Carter | 403 | -6.5 | 282 | 1.3 | 96.7 | 397 835 | 1 408 | 46 679 | 30.9 | 21 657 | 11.9 | 88.1 | 26.4 | 3.4 | 415 | 10.1 |
| Cherokee | 246 | 11.3 | 179 | 1.0 | 67.3 | 333 829 | 1 863 | 52 880 | 129.8 | 94 411 | 77.1 | 22.9 | 30.5 | 4.3 | 291 | 9.2 |
| Choctaw | 326 | -3.3 | 288 | 0.5 | 83.8 | 386 496 | 1 343 | 53 475 | 37.9 | 33 414 | 11.1 | 88.9 | 41.4 | 4.6 | 476 | 16.8 |
| Cimarron | 1 045 | -6.9 | 1 875 | 45.5 | 413.4 | 939 651 | 501 | 106 426 | 261.9 | 470 144 | 17.9 | 82.1 | 46.1 | 28.0 | 7 176 | 83.5 |
| Cleveland | 160 | -3.0 | 120 | 1.1 | 47.0 | 289 499 | 2 404 | 40 609 | 15.8 | 11 873 | 25.6 | 74.4 | 20.4 | 1.7 | 390 | 8.5 |
| Coal | 269 | 2.3 | 425 | 0.5 | 64.2 | 529 119 | 1 245 | 55 875 | 20.2 | 31 937 | 13.5 | 86.6 | 43.4 | 6.8 | 271 | 13.6 |
| Comanche | 498 | 17.2 | 442 | 1.4 | 160.7 | 506 837 | 1 147 | 52 948 | 38.8 | 34 484 | 22.7 | 77.3 | 36.7 | 6.0 | 3 169 | 40.0 |
| Cotton | 367 | 9.9 | 709 | 0.3 | 196.6 | 689 734 | 973 | 87 679 | 59.5 | 115 141 | 21.5 | 78.5 | 52.8 | 20.7 | 3 928 | 74.7 |
| Craig | 457 | 4.8 | 336 | D | 133.4 | 442 031 | 1 314 | 56 906 | 77.5 | 57 029 | 9.3 | 90.7 | 44.1 | 8.0 | 843 | 19.6 |
| Creek | 377 | 3.0 | 199 | 0.3 | 102.0 | 315 908 | 1 590 | 39 155 | 19.6 | 10 303 | 17.3 | 82.7 | 20.6 | 1.2 | 136 | 6.1 |
| Custer | 569 | 4.4 | 627 | 4.1 | 264.5 | 670 954 | 1 070 | 105 101 | 87.0 | 95 879 | 32.6 | 67.4 | 53.3 | 16.2 | 5 034 | 68.2 |
| Delaware | 309 | 9.6 | 205 | 0.6 | 93.8 | 424 988 | 2 076 | 50 445 | 171.1 | 113 358 | 2.7 | 97.3 | 46.0 | 13.2 | 747 | 13.9 |
| Dewey | 589 | 0.9 | 779 | 3.1 | 173.7 | 655 115 | 841 | 73 903 | 31.3 | 41 375 | 35.0 | 64.9 | 48.8 | 10.1 | 3 740 | 69.3 |
| Ellis | 718 | 6.7 | 937 | 12.8 | 167.1 | 679 751 | 725 | 58 832 | 66.9 | 87 392 | 10.1 | 89.9 | 42.8 | 14.5 | 4 059 | 70.9 |
| Garfield | 663 | 4.9 | 613 | 5.4 | 443.2 | 623 900 | 1 018 | 98 441 | 76.2 | 70 421 | 38.4 | 61.6 | 48.6 | 15.2 | 8 754 | 67.0 |
| Garvin | 501 | 6.8 | 301 | 0.8 | 137.3 | 399 830 | 1 330 | 62 489 | 42.2 | 25 330 | 22.2 | 77.8 | 33.5 | 5.6 | 1 465 | 23.5 |
| Grady | 608 | 1.0 | 329 | 8.5 | 208.2 | 424 959 | 1 292 | 64 241 | 139.2 | 75 245 | 11.9 | 88.1 | 39.0 | 8.0 | 3 296 | 32.8 |
| Grant | 633 | 6.4 | 747 | 1.5 | 455.1 | 664 232 | 889 | 103 528 | 48.8 | 57 590 | 50.0 | 50.0 | 47.9 | 12.9 | 7 564 | 84.9 |
| Greer | 375 | 15.4 | 658 | 3.4 | 146.9 | 471 410 | 717 | 67 968 | 23.7 | 41 509 | 51.1 | 48.9 | 42.0 | 10.0 | 6 470 | 80.9 |
| Harmon | 322 | 8.8 | 806 | 17.8 | 152.2 | 689 885 | 856 | 93 830 | 45.4 | 113 572 | 36.1 | 63.9 | 46.5 | 22.0 | 4 864 | 81.8 |
| Harper | 617 | 2.7 | 1 064 | 6.2 | 203.4 | 740 525 | 696 | 80 949 | 122.7 | 211 622 | 8.5 | 91.5 | 41.0 | 14.5 | 4 194 | 70.2 |
| Haskell | 290 | 5.5 | 318 | 1.7 | 72.3 | 408 490 | 1 286 | 61 540 | 80.4 | 87 950 | 2.4 | 97.6 | 44.4 | 10.1 | 307 | 10.3 |
| Hughes | 441 | 17.9 | 430 | 2.2 | 106.7 | 506 521 | 1 178 | 56 718 | 76.7 | 74 765 | 4.4 | 95.6 | 36.6 | 5.0 | 1 199 | 28.2 |
| Jackson | 475 | 4.6 | 637 | 55.1 | 301.0 | 552 780 | 868 | 111 981 | 89.6 | 120 330 | 72.2 | 27.8 | 45.4 | 20.8 | 11 004 | 66.3 |
| Jefferson | 460 | 13.0 | 895 | 0.3 | 119.1 | 943 589 | 1 054 | 77 038 | 75.1 | 146 108 | 10.2 | 89.8 | 58.8 | 22.4 | 1 511 | 55.4 |
| Johnston | 334 | 2.5 | 473 | 0.7 | 57.8 | 576 144 | 1 218 | 52 811 | 20.3 | 28 688 | 9.1 | 90.9 | 38.0 | 6.2 | 325 | 18.6 |
| Kay | 492 | 2.5 | 469 | 3.6 | 323.0 | 484 835 | 1 034 | 84 095 | 50.8 | 48 354 | 59.6 | 40.4 | 42.2 | 12.0 | 5 661 | 65.1 |
| Kingfisher | 566 | 2.4 | 565 | 5.5 | 337.5 | 634 845 | 1 123 | 117 824 | 116.6 | 116 342 | 21.7 | 78.3 | 57.4 | 20.7 | 3 920 | 69.2 |

| STATE County | Water use, 2005 | | Wholesale trade,[1] 2007 | | | | Retail trade,[2] 2007 | | | | Real estate and rental and leasing,[2] 2007 | | | |
|---|---|---|---|---|---|---|---|---|---|---|---|---|---|---|
| | Total water withdrawn (mil gal/day) | Gallons withdrawn per person | Number of establish-ments | Number of employees | Sales (mil dol) | Annual payroll (mil dol) | Number of establish-ments | Number of employees | Sales (mil dol) | Annual payroll (mil dol) | Number of establish-ments | Number of employees | Receipts (mil dol) | Annual payroll (mil dol) |
| | 133 | 134 | 135 | 136 | 137 | 138 | 139 | 140 | 141 | 142 | 143 | 144 | 145 | 146 |
| OHIO—Cont'd | | | | | | | | | | | | | | |
| Ottawa | 46.4 | 1 115 | 27 | 156 | 71.8 | 5.3 | 168 | 1 623 | 461.2 | 40.9 | 56 | 175 | 15.6 | 4.2 |
| Paulding | 2.3 | 117 | 17 | 147 | 115.5 | 5.4 | 53 | 450 | 97.3 | 7.7 | 6 | 48 | 7.0 | 0.7 |
| Perry | 2.7 | 76 | 16 | 134 | 85.4 | 3.7 | 83 | 644 | 136.1 | 11.0 | 15 | 39 | 3.3 | 0.5 |
| Pickaway | 46.7 | 881 | 34 | D | D | D | 136 | 1 521 | 416.4 | 33.0 | 30 | 93 | 12.5 | 1.8 |
| Pike | 7.6 | 271 | 17 | 119 | 30.1 | 3.2 | 86 | 872 | 197.0 | 18.1 | 14 | 75 | 10.7 | 1.8 |
| Portage | 54.8 | 352 | 155 | 3 035 | 1 875.5 | 173.6 | 469 | 6 734 | 1 657.4 | 143.7 | 128 | 511 | 84.6 | 14.0 |
| Preble | 4.7 | 111 | 23 | 240 | 147.5 | 7.9 | 109 | 1 500 | 443.1 | 34.3 | 26 | 82 | 4.8 | 1.1 |
| Putnam | 5.3 | 152 | 33 | 244 | 172.3 | 8.5 | 111 | 1 225 | 252.3 | 22.4 | 11 | 33 | 2.6 | 0.8 |
| Richland | 16.3 | 128 | 127 | 2 113 | 1 010.6 | 76.7 | 497 | 7 387 | 1 489.5 | 145.8 | 108 | 571 | 59.2 | 12.3 |
| Ross | 38.6 | 514 | 47 | 456 | 226.6 | 17.5 | 260 | 3 640 | 831.2 | 73.4 | 54 | 165 | 26.6 | 3.6 |
| Sandusky | 12.9 | 209 | 50 | D | D | D | 220 | 2 801 | 598.0 | 58.8 | 35 | 166 | 13.9 | 2.6 |
| Scioto | 18.4 | 240 | 34 | D | D | D | 277 | 3 038 | 700.7 | 63.1 | 45 | 243 | 20.5 | 4.8 |
| Seneca | 7.3 | 126 | 55 | D | D | D | 184 | 2 086 | 458.8 | 46.8 | 36 | 114 | 9.9 | 1.8 |
| Shelby | 13.7 | 282 | 49 | D | D | D | 147 | 1 991 | 432.5 | 42.7 | 32 | 107 | 17.4 | 2.9 |
| Stark | 50.2 | 132 | 373 | 5 489 | 2 630.6 | 232.4 | 1 384 | 21 952 | 4 963.7 | 474.3 | 325 | 1 569 | 207.8 | 36.6 |
| Summit | 31.4 | 57 | 847 | 13 957 | 7 063.5 | 674.3 | 1 883 | 30 797 | 7 384.2 | 694.2 | 503 | 2 855 | 465.8 | 85.0 |
| Trumbull | 205.6 | 937 | 179 | D | D | D | 771 | 10 690 | 2 318.4 | 204.0 | 163 | 1 205 | 175.7 | 35.1 |
| Tuscarawas | 31.3 | 340 | 90 | 714 | 251.1 | 20.2 | 399 | 4 730 | 1 077.4 | 94.8 | 73 | 365 | 46.8 | 7.7 |
| Union | 10.8 | 236 | 67 | 925 | 1 881.7 | 43.8 | 129 | 2 022 | 479.1 | 49.9 | 46 | 148 | 26.0 | 4.4 |
| Van Wert | 4.9 | 168 | 28 | 229 | 127.0 | 9.4 | 101 | 1 234 | 242.8 | 25.0 | 13 | 128 | 10.5 | 1.5 |
| Vinton | 0.8 | 62 | 5 | D | D | D | 33 | 223 | 43.3 | 3.3 | 3 | 3 | 0.4 | 0.0 |
| Warren | 21.8 | 111 | 184 | 3 170 | 2 006.8 | 169.3 | 566 | 8 735 | 1 862.6 | 178.0 | 171 | 800 | 123.9 | 25.5 |
| Washington | 960.5 | 15 439 | 71 | D | D | D | 256 | 2 962 | 658.4 | 58.4 | 45 | 198 | 34.6 | 6.4 |
| Wayne | 16.5 | 145 | 124 | D | D | D | 409 | 5 123 | 1 110.2 | 109.3 | 82 | 279 | 48.0 | 7.5 |
| Williams | 5.1 | 131 | 41 | 461 | 229.2 | 14.7 | 143 | 1 575 | 333.9 | 29.5 | 30 | 97 | 18.2 | 2.7 |
| Wood | 12.4 | 100 | 177 | 2 923 | 1 505.1 | 126.0 | 434 | 6 632 | 1 522.5 | 125.5 | 118 | 657 | 135.0 | 21.6 |
| Wyandot | 5.6 | 247 | 28 | 295 | 210.6 | 9.9 | 71 | 922 | 190.2 | 15.8 | 14 | 37 | 4.3 | 1.1 |
| OKLAHOMA | 1 727.9 | 488 | 3 917 | 52 262 | 48 074.7 | 2 312.2 | 13 554 | 170 984 | 43 095.4 | 3 610.4 | 4 003 | 24 887 | 3 852.3 | 806.2 |
| Adair | 9.5 | 433 | 7 | D | D | D | 52 | 528 | 108.4 | 8.2 | 8 | D | D | D |
| Alfalfa | 6.7 | 1 171 | 10 | 53 | 23.3 | 1.5 | 25 | 145 | 33.3 | 2.4 | 2 | D | D | D |
| Atoka | 56.4 | 3 936 | 10 | 41 | 33.1 | 1.1 | 51 | 528 | 136.9 | 10.6 | 8 | 12 | 1.3 | 0.2 |
| Beaver | 27.3 | 5 052 | 8 | 13 | 9.5 | 0.4 | 20 | 103 | 22.0 | 1.5 | 4 | D | D | D |
| Beckham | 9.6 | 512 | 26 | 246 | 146.7 | 9.2 | 141 | 1 480 | 523.6 | 30.6 | 36 | 248 | 57.7 | 13.7 |
| Blaine | 8.4 | 652 | 13 | 105 | 135.3 | 3.2 | 53 | 290 | 74.6 | 4.0 | 7 | 22 | 4.0 | 0.7 |
| Bryan | 20.3 | 538 | 31 | D | D | D | 132 | 1 523 | 318.8 | 26.6 | 24 | 91 | 9.2 | 1.8 |
| Caddo | 53.8 | 1 788 | 23 | 237 | 70.1 | 5.1 | 113 | 970 | 234.4 | 15.6 | 10 | 22 | 2.1 | 0.4 |
| Canadian | 14.3 | 145 | 88 | D | D | D | 260 | 3 385 | 1 110.7 | 74.0 | 119 | 645 | 105.4 | 26.1 |
| Carter | 58.7 | 1 248 | 67 | 686 | 590.4 | 24.2 | 248 | 2 695 | 686.9 | 56.1 | 61 | D | D | D |
| Cherokee | 11.0 | 247 | 18 | D | D | D | 137 | 1 620 | 332.5 | 28.5 | 35 | 135 | 20.8 | 2.0 |
| Choctaw | 10.7 | 696 | 6 | 25 | 15.2 | 0.7 | 46 | 485 | 118.9 | 9.5 | 7 | 37 | 1.6 | 0.5 |
| Cimarron | 51.1 | 18 264 | 6 | 20 | 24.9 | 0.6 | 17 | 91 | 33.2 | 1.5 | NA | NA | NA | NA |
| Cleveland | 34.9 | 156 | 136 | 1 719 | 671.5 | 65.8 | 723 | 10 355 | 2 522.3 | 217.5 | 309 | 1 336 | 233.5 | 39.6 |
| Coal | 2.2 | 385 | 2 | D | D | D | 24 | 133 | 38.1 | 2.5 | NA | NA | NA | NA |
| Comanche | 22.6 | 204 | 56 | D | D | D | 435 | 5 540 | 1 206.8 | 108.0 | 135 | 484 | 66.7 | 10.9 |
| Cotton | 3.1 | 479 | 1 | D | D | D | 15 | 126 | 33.5 | 1.6 | 1 | D | D | D |
| Craig | 2.6 | 174 | 14 | 201 | 87.0 | 5.1 | 60 | 663 | 191.7 | 14.7 | 8 | 138 | 18.1 | 3.2 |
| Creek | 24.1 | 351 | 66 | 997 | 384.5 | 43.4 | 179 | 2 339 | 518.3 | 42.5 | 49 | 213 | 45.7 | 13.9 |
| Custer | 11.5 | 454 | 33 | 325 | 270.9 | 13.1 | 155 | 1 547 | 407.5 | 29.1 | 38 | 184 | 46.5 | 7.1 |
| Delaware | 6.0 | 152 | 20 | 80 | 47.1 | 2.8 | 133 | 1 238 | 292.6 | 25.4 | 26 | D | D | D |
| Dewey | 8.5 | 1 868 | 7 | 25 | 20.4 | 0.7 | 34 | 216 | 43.4 | 2.9 | 2 | D | D | D |
| Ellis | 15.8 | 3 985 | 5 | D | D | D | 24 | 136 | 41.2 | 2.5 | 1 | D | D | D |
| Garfield | 7.8 | 137 | 76 | D | D | D | 259 | 3 293 | 737.1 | 68.1 | 72 | 342 | 43.8 | 8.7 |
| Garvin | 12.4 | 454 | 27 | 179 | 95.8 | 6.6 | 121 | 1 137 | 331.6 | 22.2 | 15 | 50 | 13.6 | 2.5 |
| Grady | 18.1 | 367 | 53 | 550 | 198.9 | 19.2 | 167 | 1 657 | 440.1 | 35.6 | 40 | 140 | 17.7 | 3.5 |
| Grant | 8.0 | 1 656 | 11 | 39 | 29.6 | 1.0 | 12 | 148 | 54.7 | 3.2 | NA | NA | NA | NA |
| Greer | 6.3 | 1 072 | 3 | 12 | 4.0 | 0.2 | 16 | 179 | 28.1 | 2.5 | 3 | 6 | 0.8 | 0.1 |
| Harmon | 26.7 | 8 754 | 3 | D | D | D | 15 | 80 | 17.7 | 1.2 | 3 | D | D | D |
| Harper | 15.2 | 4 560 | 3 | D | D | D | 17 | 117 | 21.0 | 1.7 | 2 | 11 | 0.5 | 0.1 |
| Haskell | 5.5 | 455 | 6 | D | D | D | 36 | 425 | 131.0 | 9.2 | 3 | D | D | D |
| Hughes | 9.2 | 663 | 7 | 25 | 7.9 | 0.5 | 52 | 383 | 87.5 | 6.1 | 7 | D | D | D |
| Jackson | 76.3 | 2 897 | 23 | D | D | D | 115 | 1 365 | 350.2 | 28.6 | 18 | 83 | 11.3 | 1.8 |
| Jefferson | 7.7 | 1 192 | 1 | D | D | D | 28 | 152 | 34.8 | 2.6 | 3 | 2 | 0.3 | 0.1 |
| Johnston | 16.2 | 1 573 | 8 | D | D | D | 44 | 262 | 74.9 | 5.3 | 3 | 7 | 0.6 | 0.1 |
| Kay | 31.4 | 680 | 49 | 407 | 305.1 | 13.7 | 205 | 2 351 | 576.4 | 45.6 | 47 | 158 | 20.8 | 3.0 |
| Kingfisher | 10.8 | 759 | 27 | 388 | 429.2 | 16.3 | 64 | 549 | 185.2 | 12.0 | 9 | 79 | 10.9 | 1.9 |

1. Merchant wholesalers, except manufacturers' sales branches and offices.   2. Employer establishments.

# Table B. States and Counties — Professional Services, Manufacturing, and Accommodation and Food Services

| STATE County | Professional, scientific, and technical services,[1] 2007 | | | | Manufacturing, 2007 | | | | Accommodation and food services, 2007 | | | |
|---|---|---|---|---|---|---|---|---|---|---|---|---|
| | Number of establishments | Number of employees | Receipts (mil dol) | Annual payroll (mil dol) | Number of establishments | Number of employees | Receipts (mil dol) | Annual payroll (mil dol) | Number of establishments | Number of employees | Sales (mil dol) | Annual payroll (mil dol) |
| | 147 | 148 | 149 | 150 | 151 | 152 | 153 | 154 | 155 | 156 | 157 | 158 |
| **OHIO—Cont'd** | | | | | | | | | | | | |
| Ottawa | 53 | D | D | D | 52 | 2 560 | 762.7 | 127.2 | 173 | 1 635 | 101.4 | 27.2 |
| Paulding | 12 | 44 | 4.4 | 1.2 | 37 | 1 755 | 388.7 | 56.9 | 34 | 305 | 7.9 | 2.1 |
| Perry | 27 | 106 | 6.8 | 3.5 | 25 | 933 | 124.5 | 31.4 | 45 | 369 | 13.8 | 3.7 |
| Pickaway | 59 | D | D | D | 37 | 2 342 | D | D | 73 | 1 033 | 40.0 | 10.8 |
| Pike | 21 | 136 | 21.4 | 7.3 | 30 | 1 781 | 620.8 | 57.6 | 51 | 738 | 31.5 | 8.4 |
| Portage | 253 | D | D | D | 263 | 11 370 | 2 969.6 | 484.1 | 297 | 4 583 | 187.7 | 51.5 |
| Preble | 45 | D | D | D | 56 | 3 248 | 1 070.3 | 155.5 | 65 | 940 | 32.2 | 9.6 |
| Putnam | 36 | 203 | 20.4 | 7.3 | 50 | 3 304 | 1 985.0 | 133.2 | 67 | 1 022 | 23.2 | 7.2 |
| Richland | 194 | 1 044 | 110.4 | 41.0 | 192 | 11 080 | 3 563.7 | 555.3 | 277 | 4 802 | 178.9 | 52.5 |
| Ross | 82 | D | D | D | 43 | 4 135 | 2 522.2 | 232.5 | 121 | 2 466 | 90.2 | 26.1 |
| Sandusky | 88 | D | D | D | 121 | 9 457 | 3 373.1 | 382.1 | 131 | 1 853 | 76.3 | 19.6 |
| Scioto | 81 | D | D | D | 52 | 1 874 | 927.1 | 65.7 | 150 | 2 160 | 84.8 | 23.2 |
| Seneca | 76 | 334 | 21.6 | 7.6 | 85 | 5 777 | 1 408.8 | 227.8 | 111 | 1 640 | 46.5 | 13.9 |
| Shelby | 62 | 339 | 33.0 | 16.6 | 147 | 15 057 | 6 238.4 | 707.2 | 81 | 1 351 | 55.2 | 14.0 |
| Stark | 739 | D | D | D | 542 | 27 177 | 10 387.4 | 1 175.2 | 784 | 13 705 | 518.0 | 153.6 |
| Summit | 1 618 | D | D | D | 925 | 32 483 | 9 275.5 | 1 470.3 | 1 231 | 22 475 | 885.0 | 253.4 |
| Trumbull | 300 | D | D | D | 262 | 18 808 | 8 841.0 | 1 138.4 | 434 | 6 588 | 245.2 | 68.7 |
| Tuscarawas | 142 | D | D | D | 224 | 9 223 | 2 206.5 | 380.1 | 215 | 3 448 | 114.4 | 36.4 |
| Union | 92 | 1 863 | 520.2 | 149.5 | 57 | 8 296 | D | 559.4 | 78 | 1 297 | 51.4 | 14.4 |
| Van Wert | 42 | D | D | D | 44 | 3 604 | 1 072.3 | 138.2 | 48 | 734 | 25.5 | 7.0 |
| Vinton | 7 | D | D | D | 21 | 592 | 106.5 | 19.2 | 17 | 69 | 2.8 | 0.6 |
| Warren | 439 | D | D | D | 222 | 13 472 | 4 111.2 | 572.2 | 345 | 8 227 | 329.8 | 99.7 |
| Washington | 99 | D | D | D | 96 | 4 374 | 2 563.7 | 217.1 | 120 | 2 065 | 83.7 | 22.8 |
| Wayne | 155 | 935 | 221.8 | 39.5 | 250 | 11 456 | 2 896.5 | 467.3 | 163 | 3 204 | 111.0 | 31.6 |
| Williams | 33 | 192 | 14.4 | 4.5 | 138 | 7 558 | 3 376.8 | 296.4 | 75 | 1 012 | 33.7 | 9.2 |
| Wood | 238 | D | D | D | 203 | 16 126 | 4 416.4 | 797.4 | 293 | 5 767 | 191.1 | 57.2 |
| Wyandot | 27 | 142 | 10.3 | 3.9 | 41 | 2 644 | 791.2 | 101.2 | 52 | 681 | 21.8 | 5.4 |
| **OKLAHOMA** | 9 128 | D | D | D | 3 964 | 142 351 | 60 681.4 | 5 971.2 | 6 900 | 129 159 | 5 106.6 | 1 401.3 |
| Adair | 13 | D | D | D | 13 | 1 314 | 414.4 | 41.1 | 15 | 269 | 6.1 | 1.8 |
| Alfalfa | 9 | 41 | 3.1 | 0.9 | NA | NA | NA | NA | 6 | 39 | 1.2 | 0.3 |
| Atoka | 13 | 46 | 3.2 | 0.9 | NA | NA | NA | NA | 28 | 317 | 13.9 | 2.9 |
| Beaver | 17 | 33 | 3.1 | 0.7 | NA | NA | NA | NA | 7 | 55 | 1.2 | 0.4 |
| Beckham | 70 | 317 | 32.5 | 12.1 | NA | NA | NA | NA | 69 | 895 | 39.2 | 9.7 |
| Blaine | 25 | 72 | 9.2 | 2.1 | NA | NA | NA | NA | 21 | 190 | 8.9 | 1.6 |
| Bryan | 61 | 944 | 87.3 | 48.4 | 38 | 1 102 | 238.2 | 35.2 | 62 | 1 089 | 40.4 | 10.6 |
| Caddo | 40 | 205 | 14.1 | 7.3 | NA | NA | NA | NA | 43 | 447 | 13.1 | 3.2 |
| Canadian | 214 | 663 | 67.6 | 21.1 | 75 | 3 234 | 1 192.9 | 132.5 | 146 | 2 623 | 102.2 | 26.3 |
| Carter | 118 | D | D | D | 49 | 2 993 | D | 167.2 | 86 | 1 979 | 68.1 | 20.7 |
| Cherokee | 50 | 134 | 11.3 | 3.5 | NA | NA | NA | NA | 84 | 1 092 | 42.1 | 11.2 |
| Choctaw | 19 | D | D | D | NA | NA | NA | NA | 28 | 337 | 10.9 | 2.7 |
| Cimarron | 4 | 12 | 1.5 | 0.2 | NA | NA | NA | NA | 11 | 79 | 3.4 | 0.7 |
| Cleveland | 613 | D | D | D | 151 | 3 299 | 1 223.0 | 138.1 | 447 | 10 104 | 391.8 | 108.8 |
| Coal | 2 | D | D | D | NA | NA | NA | NA | 4 | 70 | 2.2 | 0.7 |
| Comanche | 175 | D | D | D | 48 | 3 549 | 1 232.4 | 171.0 | 204 | 4 330 | 154.5 | 46.4 |
| Cotton | 7 | 12 | 0.7 | 0.3 | NA | NA | NA | NA | 8 | D | D | D |
| Craig | 21 | 83 | 9.2 | 3.2 | 16 | 783 | 139.0 | 26.4 | 28 | 374 | 14.8 | 4.0 |
| Creek | 106 | 320 | 25.6 | 8.0 | 133 | 4 257 | 1 204.4 | 178.6 | 83 | 1 181 | 43.4 | 11.0 |
| Custer | 72 | D | D | D | 33 | 1 346 | 533.9 | 45.2 | 67 | 1 053 | 41.5 | 11.0 |
| Delaware | 45 | D | D | D | 26 | 540 | 102.2 | 18.5 | 62 | 738 | 27.1 | 7.8 |
| Dewey | 9 | 98 | 8.2 | 2.6 | NA | NA | NA | NA | 4 | 24 | 1.2 | 0.2 |
| Ellis | 11 | 32 | 4.0 | 0.7 | NA | NA | NA | NA | 7 | D | D | D |
| Garfield | 128 | 559 | 58.4 | 20.1 | 68 | 2 356 | 1 097.7 | 75.9 | 115 | 1 848 | 74.4 | 19.1 |
| Garvin | 50 | 157 | 11.8 | 4.1 | 31 | 954 | D | 42.6 | 40 | 583 | 20.3 | 5.4 |
| Grady | 78 | D | D | D | 59 | 1 616 | 419.7 | 54.6 | 51 | 1 092 | 38.4 | 9.9 |
| Grant | 7 | 27 | 1.6 | 0.5 | NA | NA | NA | NA | 6 | 17 | 0.6 | 0.1 |
| Greer | 5 | 12 | 0.6 | 0.2 | NA | NA | NA | NA | 5 | 51 | 1.7 | 0.4 |
| Harmon | 4 | D | D | D | NA | NA | NA | NA | 3 | D | D | D |
| Harper | 8 | 30 | 3.6 | 1.1 | NA | NA | NA | NA | 3 | D | D | D |
| Haskell | 23 | 58 | 4.5 | 1.3 | NA | NA | NA | NA | 15 | 138 | 6.0 | 1.1 |
| Hughes | 14 | 40 | 2.6 | 0.8 | NA | NA | NA | NA | 18 | 237 | 9.3 | 2.1 |
| Jackson | 41 | D | D | D | 14 | 961 | 357.0 | 32.6 | 49 | 1 106 | 41.0 | 10.3 |
| Jefferson | 7 | 28 | 3.2 | 0.5 | NA | NA | NA | NA | 9 | D | D | D |
| Johnston | 11 | 20 | 1.9 | 0.8 | NA | NA | NA | NA | 11 | 106 | 3.1 | 0.9 |
| Kay | 96 | 523 | 46.1 | 17.9 | 72 | 4 415 | D | 189.3 | 100 | 1 688 | 61.5 | 15.4 |
| Kingfisher | 25 | 126 | 7.4 | 2.5 | NA | NA | NA | NA | 28 | D | D | D |

1. Establishment subject to federal tax.

# Table B. States and Counties — Health Care and Social Assistance, Other Services, and Federal Funds

| STATE County | Health care and social assistance, 2007 | | | | Other services, 2007 | | | | Federal funds and grants, 2009–2010 Expenditures (mil dol) | | | |
|---|---|---|---|---|---|---|---|---|---|---|---|---|
| | | | | | | | | | | Direct payments for individuals[1] | | |
| | Number of establishments | Number of employees | Receipts (mil dol) | Annual payroll (mil dol) | Number of establishments | Number of employees | Receipts (mil dol) | Annual payroll (mil dol) | Total | Social Security and government retirement | Medicare | Food Stamps and Supplemental Security Income |
| | 159 | 160 | 161 | 162 | 163 | 164 | 165 | 166 | 167 | 168 | 169 | 170 |
| OHIO—Cont'd | | | | | | | | | | | | |
| Ottawa | 81 | 1 637 | 110.7 | 45.6 | 88 | 343 | 29.7 | 8.0 | 318.1 | 163.8 | 81.4 | 7.1 |
| Paulding | 34 | 698 | 42.7 | 15.8 | 20 | 74 | 6.2 | 1.6 | 108.2 | 39.1 | 28.7 | 3.5 |
| Perry | 54 | 635 | 35.1 | 17.3 | 36 | 156 | 9.1 | 2.3 | 260.3 | 109.2 | 60.6 | 19.4 |
| Pickaway | 95 | 2 475 | 169.4 | 69.8 | 52 | 197 | 12.7 | 4.0 | 325.7 | 145.7 | 65.7 | 14.8 |
| Pike | 54 | 1 517 | 108.2 | 38.6 | 27 | 92 | 8.9 | 1.8 | 496.2 | 87.2 | 47.3 | 21.9 |
| Portage | 241 | 5 264 | 393.7 | 166.5 | 248 | 1 440 | 99.7 | 32.6 | 913.6 | 392.2 | 192.9 | 34.4 |
| Preble | 56 | D | D | D | 58 | 211 | 17.2 | 4.8 | 250.4 | 128.5 | 60.8 | 8.8 |
| Putnam | 60 | 839 | 39.3 | 19.8 | 58 | 311 | 21.6 | 5.9 | 144.7 | 53.6 | 45.1 | 4.5 |
| Richland | 354 | 7 670 | 663.5 | 263.1 | 238 | 1 533 | 109.3 | 29.3 | 950.7 | 414.3 | 216.4 | 47.1 |
| Ross | 156 | 5 154 | 523.2 | 252.8 | 96 | 524 | 31.0 | 8.7 | 753.4 | 259.0 | 109.1 | 36.9 |
| Sandusky | 152 | 3 553 | 255.6 | 97.1 | 115 | 796 | 44.3 | 14.1 | 394.5 | 166.3 | 101.1 | 18.2 |
| Scioto | 227 | 6 224 | 459.5 | 192.9 | 92 | 374 | 31.7 | 6.9 | 891.0 | 269.2 | 197.4 | 77.8 |
| Seneca | 158 | 2 914 | 170.9 | 73.5 | 109 | 500 | 33.9 | 8.3 | 413.2 | 188.1 | 109.2 | 16.8 |
| Shelby | 91 | 1 953 | 160.7 | 61.2 | 71 | 510 | 35.2 | 10.4 | 245.8 | 114.8 | 64.1 | 10.4 |
| Stark | 993 | 26 783 | 2 133.6 | 922.1 | 734 | 4 997 | 421.9 | 118.4 | 2 866.5 | 1 274.8 | 699.4 | 138.0 |
| Summit | 1 506 | 40 278 | 3 667.9 | 1 497.1 | 1 137 | 7 859 | 748.5 | 201.0 | 4 510.6 | 1 512.6 | 1 125.9 | 226.1 |
| Trumbull | 581 | 12 548 | 1 071.0 | 422.7 | 352 | 2 030 | 169.6 | 45.8 | 1 806.2 | 815.4 | 496.5 | 98.1 |
| Tuscarawas | 201 | 4 721 | 317.9 | 130.1 | 198 | 1 262 | 111.7 | 28.6 | 606.3 | 286.8 | 136.5 | 26.1 |
| Union | 81 | 1 684 | 128.4 | 53.5 | 75 | 579 | 46.8 | 15.6 | 230.9 | 87.9 | 41.8 | 6.5 |
| Van Wert | 63 | 1 826 | 108.9 | 46.4 | 52 | 270 | 18.6 | 3.7 | 150.9 | 67.6 | 40.7 | 4.2 |
| Vinton | 15 | 259 | 11.0 | 5.9 | 8 | 24 | 1.9 | 0.4 | 98.5 | 35.9 | 19.4 | 7.7 |
| Warren | 359 | 5 727 | 414.5 | 179.5 | 240 | 1 775 | 131.8 | 46.7 | 800.1 | 450.1 | 137.1 | 21.0 |
| Washington | 155 | 4 309 | 327.5 | 129.5 | 122 | 575 | 43.8 | 11.0 | 506.5 | 224.4 | 115.9 | 27.0 |
| Wayne | 221 | 5 004 | 347.5 | 147.0 | 168 | 907 | 73.3 | 19.6 | 717.9 | 316.9 | 140.8 | 23.0 |
| Williams | 69 | 1 680 | 147.8 | 63.1 | 66 | 337 | 25.7 | 5.8 | 228.8 | 115.8 | 62.2 | 6.4 |
| Wood | 249 | 4 637 | 338.3 | 145.9 | 212 | 1 461 | 123.4 | 36.4 | 696.2 | 283.6 | 150.4 | 18.3 |
| Wyandot | 41 | 803 | 50.6 | 21.0 | 57 | 286 | 21.4 | 5.4 | 151.8 | 71.1 | 38.1 | 2.7 |
| OKLAHOMA | 10 332 | 200 777 | 18 363.2 | 6 825.0 | 5 541 | 31 654 | 3 318.1 | 758.8 | 38 475.0 | 11 993.7 | 5 583.6 | 1 477.4 |
| Adair | 20 | 417 | 25.7 | 10.5 | 16 | 32 | 2.8 | 0.5 | 235.1 | 62.3 | 39.3 | 10.8 |
| Alfalfa | 9 | 136 | 4.3 | 2.0 | 8 | D | D | D | 53.6 | 19.3 | 14.5 | 0.8 |
| Atoka | 23 | 400 | 21.8 | 8.9 | 15 | 60 | 4.3 | 0.9 | 124.2 | 40.2 | 26.8 | 7.3 |
| Beaver | 6 | 77 | 5.1 | 1.8 | 9 | D | D | D | 37.5 | 17.1 | 7.6 | 1.0 |
| Beckham | 94 | 1 175 | 97.0 | 35.4 | 34 | D | D | D | 138.8 | 49.0 | 37.0 | 9.6 |
| Blaine | 29 | 397 | 17.0 | 7.4 | 16 | 25 | 2.5 | 0.3 | 133.0 | 32.4 | 25.1 | 5.1 |
| Bryan | 118 | 2 034 | 160.5 | 59.8 | 41 | 205 | 17.1 | 5.0 | 424.6 | 136.7 | 74.4 | 18.6 |
| Caddo | 44 | 693 | 28.0 | 13.3 | 25 | 90 | 9.8 | 2.4 | 330.9 | 104.2 | 58.9 | 19.0 |
| Canadian | 197 | 2 602 | 171.1 | 68.3 | 146 | 685 | 65.2 | 14.4 | 626.9 | 320.2 | 77.9 | 18.6 |
| Carter | 207 | D | D | D | 86 | 775 | 146.3 | 25.7 | 431.5 | 167.6 | 96.7 | 22.8 |
| Cherokee | 105 | 2 168 | 177.3 | 75.2 | 45 | 351 | 16.9 | 4.5 | 432.4 | 135.7 | 62.6 | 24.2 |
| Choctaw | 38 | 995 | 57.6 | 21.8 | 13 | 71 | 3.8 | 0.8 | 237.9 | 60.7 | 41.3 | 13.6 |
| Cimarron | 4 | D | D | D | 4 | D | D | D | 39.0 | 15.4 | 5.0 | 0.6 |
| Cleveland | 652 | 10 521 | 826.9 | 355.0 | 284 | 1 582 | 299.8 | 39.2 | 1 356.4 | 623.9 | 160.5 | 144.6 |
| Coal | 9 | 231 | 9.2 | 4.6 | 5 | 14 | 2.2 | 0.2 | 64.8 | 19.8 | 14.1 | 3.0 |
| Comanche | 274 | 6 219 | 580.1 | 223.7 | 170 | 879 | 63.3 | 15.2 | 3 180.5 | 477.1 | 114.1 | 56.3 |
| Cotton | 13 | 116 | 5.0 | 2.6 | 7 | 26 | 2.1 | 0.5 | 71.3 | 24.2 | 15.1 | 2.8 |
| Craig | 57 | 1 077 | 57.8 | 31.0 | 20 | 72 | 9.0 | 2.5 | 158.4 | 68.4 | 31.8 | 7.3 |
| Creek | 121 | 1 874 | 101.1 | 42.7 | 82 | 271 | 25.8 | 6.0 | 476.4 | 225.6 | 90.4 | 27.6 |
| Custer | 100 | 1 416 | 93.7 | 42.8 | 48 | 328 | 28.9 | 8.2 | 188.4 | 50.5 | 50.3 | 7.1 |
| Delaware | 77 | 1 238 | 98.6 | 37.7 | 52 | 261 | 18.3 | 4.8 | 304.7 | 142.1 | 63.2 | 15.7 |
| Dewey | 6 | D | D | D | 8 | 30 | 3.1 | 0.4 | 47.1 | 18.1 | 14.1 | 1.3 |
| Ellis | 9 | 186 | 14.7 | 5.1 | 11 | D | D | D | 35.1 | 13.7 | 11.6 | 0.9 |
| Garfield | 213 | 3 989 | 367.5 | 133.1 | 129 | 581 | 49.7 | 12.7 | 628.8 | 206.7 | 107.9 | 22.6 |
| Garvin | 65 | 1 101 | 61.4 | 25.3 | 28 | 137 | 17.6 | 2.3 | 389.1 | 110.1 | 79.1 | 12.4 |
| Grady | 82 | 1 524 | 110.5 | 46.8 | 67 | 265 | 18.5 | 5.0 | 337.2 | 161.1 | 59.9 | 20.6 |
| Grant | 7 | 103 | 4.6 | 2.0 | 4 | D | D | D | 56.7 | 18.8 | 14.5 | 1.4 |
| Greer | 13 | 204 | 14.8 | 4.9 | 6 | D | D | D | 70.9 | 22.0 | 21.8 | 3.3 |
| Harmon | 6 | 110 | 8.5 | 3.0 | 5 | D | D | D | 41.8 | 9.4 | 12.2 | 2.3 |
| Harper | 7 | 116 | 4.7 | 2.2 | 9 | D | D | D | 31.6 | 13.0 | 8.9 | 0.5 |
| Haskell | 35 | 915 | 48.8 | 19.5 | 13 | 41 | 3.1 | 0.7 | 148.6 | 50.8 | 29.3 | 8.0 |
| Hughes | 36 | 685 | 24.3 | 10.8 | 7 | D | D | D | 152.1 | 50.3 | 36.0 | 7.1 |
| Jackson | 56 | 1 399 | 96.7 | 40.1 | 40 | 190 | 13.1 | 2.9 | 449.2 | 101.0 | 52.0 | 12.3 |
| Jefferson | 8 | 70 | 3.5 | 1.3 | 3 | D | D | D | 75.8 | 25.6 | 19.1 | 3.4 |
| Johnston | 24 | 462 | 25.9 | 9.4 | 6 | D | D | D | 115.6 | 38.3 | 20.4 | 5.1 |
| Kay | 153 | 2 093 | 170.2 | 55.7 | 86 | 348 | 28.7 | 7.5 | 563.2 | 173.4 | 81.0 | 16.7 |
| Kingfisher | 42 | 586 | 29.0 | 11.3 | 30 | 92 | 8.7 | 2.0 | 138.3 | 43.6 | 24.2 | 3.0 |

1. State totals may include programs not allocated by county.

Items 159—170

| STATE County | Federal funds and grants, 2009–2010 (cont.) Expenditures (mil dol) (cont.) | | | | | | | Value of residential construction authorized by building permits, 2011 | | Local government finances, 2007 General revenue | | | | |
|---|---|---|---|---|---|---|---|---|---|---|---|---|---|---|
| | | Procurement contract awards | | Grants[1] | | | | | | | | Taxes | | |
| | Salaries and wages | Defense | Other | Medicaid and other health-related | Nutrition and family welfare | Education | Other | New con-struction ($1,000) | Number of housing units | Total (mil dol) | Inter-govern-mental (mil dol) | Total (mil dol) | Per capita[2] (dollars) Total | Property |
| | 171 | 172 | 173 | 174 | 175 | 176 | 177 | 178 | 179 | 180 | 181 | 182 | 183 | 184 |
| **OHIO—Cont'd** | | | | | | | | | | | | | | |
| Ottawa | 27.2 | 8.0 | 4.5 | 12.8 | 5.7 | 2.2 | 1.0 | 18 861 | 79 | 174.2 | 54.8 | 67.9 | 1 652 | 1 345 |
| Paulding | 4.1 | 1.5 | 1.0 | 13.3 | 3.2 | 1.5 | 3.9 | 1 347 | 8 | 67.7 | 37.3 | 19.4 | 1 010 | 671 |
| Perry | 5.8 | 0.2 | 1.8 | 48.5 | 7.6 | 2.7 | 1.6 | 2 815 | 20 | 110.8 | 74.9 | 20.5 | 589 | 488 |
| Pickaway | 10.4 | 0.3 | 2.0 | 55.6 | 10.1 | 2.9 | 5.2 | 4 870 | 35 | 238.9 | 83.8 | 58.9 | 1 095 | 790 |
| Pike | 5.9 | 0.0 | 238.2 | 70.3 | 11.7 | 2.7 | 6.3 | 9 136 | 56 | 143.1 | 72.8 | 25.0 | 897 | 690 |
| Portage | 29.0 | 25.5 | 5.7 | 83.1 | 24.8 | 12.0 | 31.1 | 49 160 | 595 | 669.9 | 217.0 | 222.5 | 1 427 | 1 057 |
| Preble | 10.9 | 0.1 | 2.0 | 23.5 | 6.6 | 3.1 | 0.4 | 4 237 | 25 | 132.1 | 58.3 | 48.4 | 1 160 | 698 |
| Putnam | 6.5 | 0.0 | 2.0 | 16.3 | 5.0 | 3.6 | 0.2 | 8 465 | 41 | 121.4 | 60.9 | 37.6 | 1 087 | 697 |
| Richland | 57.7 | 7.8 | 8.2 | 119.8 | 24.8 | 10.7 | 23.4 | 7 097 | 42 | 490.3 | 239.1 | 173.6 | 1 381 | 907 |
| Ross | 65.9 | 14.1 | 38.6 | 118.5 | 17.1 | 5.0 | 73.6 | 1 404 | 18 | 258.7 | 135.9 | 79.5 | 1 054 | 634 |
| Sandusky | 10.9 | 6.4 | 14.6 | 36.6 | 17.6 | 4.1 | 2.9 | 8 105 | 51 | 208.8 | 97.8 | 77.5 | 1 270 | 806 |
| Scioto | 16.6 | 0.0 | 4.1 | 238.9 | 25.9 | 9.0 | 19.9 | 1 377 | 61 | 274.5 | 176.1 | 58.0 | 764 | 567 |
| Seneca | 18.4 | 1.3 | 2.5 | 41.0 | 9.7 | 4.0 | 1.9 | 3 172 | 18 | 194.1 | 98.2 | 62.3 | 1 098 | 701 |
| Shelby | 7.7 | 0.5 | 1.9 | 27.0 | 7.0 | 3.4 | 1.5 | 15 877 | 78 | 182.3 | 76.5 | 72.6 | 1 488 | 880 |
| Stark | 163.9 | 9.2 | 23.1 | 324.1 | 69.0 | 31.1 | 61.1 | 45 056 | 251 | 1 298.5 | 606.9 | 471.2 | 1 244 | 941 |
| Summit | 210.4 | 418.2 | 58.3 | 540.7 | 105.1 | 42.4 | 157.0 | 93 907 | 527 | 2 354.0 | 893.1 | 1 026.1 | 1 888 | 1 270 |
| Trumbull | 74.4 | 38.9 | 8.2 | 171.4 | 43.4 | 21.2 | 20.1 | 9 615 | 53 | 734.1 | 362.9 | 260.6 | 1 221 | 898 |
| Tuscarawas | 20.3 | 18.6 | 4.0 | 73.0 | 18.4 | 10.4 | 6.3 | 5 375 | 42 | 298.2 | 139.7 | 94.8 | 1 038 | 779 |
| Union | 7.5 | 1.6 | 42.4 | 20.9 | 5.2 | 1.9 | 7.7 | 21 575 | 104 | 262.8 | 70.0 | 77.6 | 1 644 | 1 234 |
| Van Wert | 5.5 | 1.2 | 1.4 | 16.1 | 4.8 | 1.5 | 0.3 | 6 248 | 66 | 111.4 | 49.5 | 37.9 | 1 313 | 771 |
| Vinton | 2.5 | 0.0 | 0.6 | 25.0 | 4.2 | 1.2 | 1.4 | 0 | 0 | 67.1 | 53.3 | 7.1 | 534 | 445 |
| Warren | 42.7 | 25.9 | 11.1 | 68.9 | 20.8 | 5.3 | 6.5 | 184 554 | 864 | 739.7 | 207.5 | 387.0 | 1 894 | 1 458 |
| Washington | 17.0 | 2.1 | 6.6 | 74.5 | 13.1 | 7.7 | 5.7 | 1 336 | 14 | 196.9 | 96.0 | 70.1 | 1 139 | 792 |
| Wayne | 28.5 | 82.8 | 5.8 | 67.6 | 21.4 | 7.4 | 14.1 | 21 647 | 129 | 445.6 | 155.7 | 139.9 | 1 232 | 929 |
| Williams | 9.3 | 0.7 | 2.0 | 16.8 | 5.3 | 2.4 | 0.6 | 1 527 | 9 | 136.8 | 55.1 | 48.7 | 1 269 | 772 |
| Wood | 63.9 | 1.8 | 5.4 | 49.7 | 15.2 | 15.5 | 8.5 | 32 282 | 234 | 495.4 | 163.1 | 224.8 | 1 792 | 1 219 |
| Wyandot | 5.2 | 0.1 | 1.5 | 18.9 | 3.5 | 1.2 | 2.7 | 2 718 | 11 | 100.8 | 35.0 | 25.7 | 1 145 | 595 |
| **OKLAHOMA** | 5 575.4 | 2 409.9 | 964.9 | 3 961.4 | 1 023.5 | 703.9 | 2 166.0 | 1 285 644 | 8 782 | X | X | X | X | X |
| Adair | 4.4 | 12.3 | 1.0 | 88.6 | 5.7 | 9.0 | 0.3 | 2 550 | 30 | 64.1 | 42.1 | 6.7 | 304 | 157 |
| Alfalfa | 3.5 | 0.2 | 0.6 | 5.5 | 0.9 | 0.2 | 0.2 | 0 | 0 | 10.6 | 4.6 | 4.0 | 723 | 500 |
| Atoka | 4.2 | 0.0 | 0.5 | 37.8 | 3.4 | 1.9 | 0.8 | 425 | 6 | 37.5 | 20.0 | 6.7 | 460 | 202 |
| Beaver | 2.0 | 0.0 | 0.5 | 1.8 | 1.1 | 0.3 | 0.6 | 0 | 0 | 24.7 | 12.9 | 6.9 | 1 280 | 1 079 |
| Beckham | 3.8 | 0.0 | 0.8 | 29.1 | 4.2 | 1.5 | 0.5 | 4 505 | 40 | 69.8 | 29.1 | 24.2 | 1 226 | 482 |
| Blaine | 4.2 | 36.9 | 1.0 | 12.9 | 7.4 | 1.9 | 0.4 | 152 | 5 | 39.4 | 16.0 | 8.4 | 672 | 363 |
| Bryan | 16.3 | 15.5 | 28.0 | 77.5 | 18.3 | 8.9 | 9.3 | 9 947 | 102 | 100.5 | 53.5 | 28.1 | 710 | 316 |
| Caddo | 28.9 | 12.6 | 12.4 | 56.1 | 11.7 | 7.6 | 7.0 | 1 272 | 16 | 95.7 | 60.2 | 18.7 | 637 | 387 |
| Canadian | 129.4 | 0.7 | 15.8 | 22.4 | 14.6 | 6.9 | 2.4 | 32 383 | 156 | 244.6 | 105.3 | 91.0 | 879 | 574 |
| Carter | 34.3 | 11.4 | 2.4 | 67.3 | 9.1 | 5.0 | 11.8 | 16 521 | 101 | 139.7 | 63.1 | 48.8 | 1 025 | 513 |
| Cherokee | 26.5 | 0.0 | 8.1 | 78.1 | 24.4 | 11.1 | 41.0 | 9 386 | 135 | 310.3 | 154.6 | 44.3 | 977 | 397 |
| Choctaw | 3.6 | 13.7 | 0.7 | 74.6 | 8.3 | 2.5 | 17.0 | 370 | 4 | 37.0 | 23.2 | 8.0 | 534 | 196 |
| Cimarron | 1.1 | 0.0 | 0.2 | 2.5 | 0.7 | 0.3 | 0.4 | 0 | 0 | 10.8 | 4.5 | 3.0 | 1 118 | 961 |
| Cleveland | 121.5 | 28.3 | 70.5 | 49.6 | 32.6 | 22.5 | 61.9 | 115 810 | 662 | 708.8 | 198.3 | 199.8 | 845 | 520 |
| Coal | 1.9 | 0.0 | 0.5 | 22.3 | 1.7 | 0.9 | 0.2 | 0 | 0 | 20.9 | 11.9 | 5.8 | 1 011 | 516 |
| Comanche | 1 851.8 | 466.2 | 26.4 | 87.4 | 25.3 | 20.5 | 22.5 | 44 884 | 280 | 403.3 | 143.2 | 85.4 | 751 | 385 |
| Cotton | 5.5 | 0.0 | 0.3 | 12.0 | 1.2 | 3.6 | 0.2 | 476 | 4 | 14.2 | 9.0 | 2.7 | 436 | 275 |
| Craig | 7.5 | 0.0 | 1.0 | 33.2 | 2.9 | 1.8 | 1.3 | 426 | 3 | 39.6 | 21.4 | 11.9 | 780 | 378 |
| Creek | 20.2 | 7.6 | 2.4 | 60.1 | 12.3 | 4.3 | 22.2 | 7 544 | 55 | 172.8 | 95.8 | 49.6 | 718 | 440 |
| Custer | 24.8 | 0.1 | 4.0 | 18.8 | 5.1 | 3.2 | 9.8 | 9 948 | 76 | 76.1 | 32.8 | 27.3 | 1 046 | 529 |
| Delaware | 6.3 | 2.6 | 1.3 | 54.3 | 9.8 | 6.8 | 0.6 | 2 425 | 19 | 71.1 | 40.6 | 21.9 | 541 | 364 |
| Dewey | 2.6 | 0.0 | 0.6 | 5.4 | 0.9 | 0.4 | 0.5 | 0 | 0 | 25.7 | 11.3 | 8.0 | 1 854 | 1 348 |
| Ellis | 1.9 | 0.0 | 0.5 | 2.5 | 0.7 | 0.5 | 0.7 | 184 | 1 | 14.9 | 8.3 | 4.5 | 1 152 | 888 |
| Garfield | 129.9 | 84.2 | 3.6 | 38.8 | 10.3 | 5.4 | 1.8 | 6 005 | 28 | 144.5 | 63.8 | 58.2 | 1 009 | 483 |
| Garvin | 15.5 | 105.7 | 1.8 | 52.9 | 5.3 | 3.4 | 0.4 | 792 | 6 | 87.6 | 38.8 | 17.7 | 652 | 330 |
| Grady | 19.4 | 0.1 | 1.9 | 52.9 | 10.6 | 3.7 | 0.4 | 10 693 | 66 | 159.1 | 63.2 | 37.9 | 749 | 368 |
| Grant | 2.6 | 0.0 | 0.6 | 3.6 | 0.9 | 0.2 | 0.1 | 0 | 0 | 13.0 | 5.6 | 5.4 | 1 193 | 899 |
| Greer | 1.8 | 0.0 | 0.4 | 15.9 | 1.3 | 0.3 | 0.6 | 192 | 4 | 21.7 | 10.6 | 2.5 | 424 | 238 |
| Harmon | 1.5 | 0.0 | 0.2 | 9.7 | 1.0 | 0.3 | 0.1 | NA | NA | 7.3 | 4.3 | 1.7 | 588 | 358 |
| Harper | 1.6 | 0.0 | 0.3 | 1.8 | 0.6 | 0.2 | 1.2 | 0 | 0 | 14.2 | 7.2 | 4.7 | 1 451 | 908 |
| Haskell | 3.5 | 7.0 | 0.8 | 36.2 | 7.7 | 2.4 | 1.7 | 571 | 5 | 28.7 | 17.0 | 7.9 | 654 | 331 |
| Hughes | 3.5 | 0.0 | 1.0 | 46.0 | 3.6 | 2.2 | 0.9 | 3 210 | 26 | 40.3 | 20.5 | 8.9 | 648 | 419 |
| Jackson | 144.7 | 64.4 | 2.7 | 41.4 | 8.1 | 3.5 | 0.2 | 5 317 | 33 | 127.3 | 35.0 | 16.8 | 651 | 292 |
| Jefferson | 2.2 | 0.3 | 0.4 | 20.9 | 1.5 | 0.7 | 0.5 | 0 | 6 | 19.6 | 10.8 | 2.9 | 469 | 206 |
| Johnston | 3.8 | 0.0 | 0.9 | 32.4 | 4.9 | 1.9 | 0.5 | 405 | 5 | 20.8 | 13.4 | 4.5 | 433 | 283 |
| Kay | 19.9 | 185.6 | 3.5 | 33.9 | 10.4 | 4.8 | 6.6 | 1 002 | 8 | 138.4 | 64.0 | 40.8 | 893 | 505 |
| Kingfisher | 4.3 | 1.1 | 13.5 | 4.7 | 2.8 | 1.9 | 27.0 | 4 957 | 19 | 41.8 | 20.8 | 14.7 | 1 026 | 684 |

1. State totals may include programs not allocated by county.    2. Based on the resident population estimated as of July 1 of the year shown.

# Table B. States and Counties — Local Government Finances, Government Employment, and Voting

| | Local government finances, 2007 (cont.) | | | | | | | | | Government employment, 2011 | | | Presidential election,[2] 2012 | | |
| | Direct general expenditure | | | | | | | Debt outstanding | | | | | Percent of vote cast: | | |
| | | | Percent of total for: | | | | | | | | | | | | |
| STATE County | Total (mil dol) | Per capita[1] (dollars) | Education | Health and hospitals | Police protec-tion | Public welfare | High-ways | Total (mil dol) | Per capita[1] (dollars) | Federal civilian | Federal military | State and local | Demo-cratic | Republi-can | All other |
| | 185 | 186 | 187 | 188 | 189 | 190 | 191 | 192 | 193 | 194 | 195 | 196 | 197 | 198 | 199 |
| **OHIO—Cont'd** | | | | | | | | | | | | | | | |
| Ottawa | 159.6 | 3 886 | 40.1 | 6.2 | 5.6 | 12.0 | 6.9 | 117.0 | 2 847 | 180 | 151 | 2 110 | 52.2 | 46.0 | 1.7 |
| Paulding | 68.7 | 3 582 | 58.8 | 3.6 | 4.1 | 3.7 | 10.8 | 32.8 | 1 711 | 50 | 49 | 1 102 | 42.6 | 54.4 | 2.9 |
| Perry | 115.5 | 3 316 | 56.0 | 3.9 | 3.5 | 9.4 | 7.9 | 24.3 | 697 | 62 | 92 | 1 903 | 47.1 | 50.1 | 2.7 |
| Pickaway | 213.0 | 3 958 | 40.6 | 30.0 | 4.4 | 4.6 | 3.6 | 135.0 | 2 509 | 89 | 142 | 4 113 | 38.3 | 60.0 | 1.8 |
| Pike | 137.3 | 4 917 | 46.1 | 21.9 | 2.1 | 4.6 | 5.8 | 75.6 | 2 706 | 78 | 72 | 1 403 | 48.2 | 49.3 | 2.5 |
| Portage | 642.5 | 4 122 | 40.7 | 24.7 | 3.7 | 4.2 | 3.2 | 348.5 | 2 236 | 298 | 426 | 15 842 | 53.5 | 44.5 | 2.0 |
| Preble | 127.3 | 3 049 | 52.7 | 3.9 | 6.0 | 7.1 | 7.9 | 56.1 | 1 344 | 81 | 107 | 1 852 | 33.3 | 64.6 | 2.1 |
| Putnam | 118.2 | 3 411 | 53.6 | 3.5 | 4.9 | 6.8 | 6.2 | 61.3 | 1 769 | 79 | 87 | 1 682 | 28.3 | 70.0 | 1.8 |
| Richland | 479.8 | 3 818 | 47.7 | 7.1 | 5.3 | 5.5 | 6.8 | 143.1 | 1 139 | 630 | 314 | 7 476 | 42.1 | 55.7 | 2.2 |
| Ross | 277.1 | 3 676 | 54.4 | 9.5 | 3.4 | 6.1 | 4.5 | 159.2 | 2 111 | 1 561 | 199 | 5 044 | 45.4 | 52.6 | 2.0 |
| Sandusky | 199.0 | 3 263 | 54.1 | 0.5 | 7.3 | 10.8 | 5.0 | 93.8 | 1 537 | 110 | 154 | 3 200 | 51.4 | 46.7 | 1.9 |
| Scioto | 266.4 | 3 507 | 58.1 | 4.5 | 2.5 | 7.3 | 3.7 | 343.9 | 4 528 | 179 | 202 | 5 892 | 45.8 | 52.2 | 2.0 |
| Seneca | 192.9 | 3 402 | 50.4 | 5.6 | 4.8 | 5.3 | 6.8 | 82.9 | 1 463 | 120 | 144 | 2 824 | 47.7 | 50.4 | 2.0 |
| Shelby | 169.4 | 3 470 | 49.5 | 4.4 | 4.5 | 7.6 | 8.5 | 103.3 | 2 115 | 89 | 125 | 2 487 | 30.9 | 67.3 | 1.8 |
| Stark | 1 313.0 | 3 467 | 52.8 | 7.2 | 5.0 | 5.8 | 4.8 | 738.5 | 1 950 | 1 087 | 961 | 18 330 | 51.7 | 46.3 | 2.0 |
| Summit | 2 406.5 | 4 428 | 38.5 | 7.1 | 6.4 | 6.2 | 5.9 | 2 048.0 | 3 768 | 1 990 | 1 396 | 30 854 | 57.6 | 41.1 | 1.3 |
| Trumbull | 733.6 | 3 437 | 54.3 | 5.6 | 5.2 | 5.7 | 3.8 | 353.6 | 1 657 | 515 | 548 | 9 299 | 60.0 | 37.6 | 2.4 |
| Tuscarawas | 309.7 | 3 389 | 54.0 | 3.8 | 4.4 | 5.6 | 5.4 | 154.4 | 1 690 | 246 | 234 | 4 806 | 50.1 | 47.6 | 2.3 |
| Union | 269.3 | 5 702 | 34.2 | 31.1 | 3.5 | 2.1 | 3.7 | 396.2 | 8 388 | 64 | 135 | 3 340 | 35.1 | 63.2 | 1.7 |
| Van Wert | 111.0 | 3 843 | 50.4 | 0.4 | 4.7 | 9.2 | 11.0 | 89.5 | 3 097 | 59 | 72 | 1 406 | 35.3 | 62.6 | 2.1 |
| Vinton | 71.8 | 5 366 | 62.6 | 2.1 | 1.3 | 8.1 | 7.9 | 20.5 | 1 536 | 24 | 34 | 716 | 43.6 | 53.5 | 2.9 |
| Warren | 712.4 | 3 485 | 49.6 | 2.7 | 4.9 | 2.8 | 5.2 | 1 029.0 | 5 034 | 287 | 552 | 9 046 | 31.4 | 67.5 | 1.1 |
| Washington | 190.2 | 3 089 | 50.3 | 9.1 | 5.9 | 6.6 | 9.3 | 103.0 | 1 673 | 209 | 156 | 2 857 | 41.3 | 56.9 | 1.8 |
| Wayne | 457.4 | 4 028 | 41.7 | 21.3 | 3.4 | 5.4 | 4.8 | 252.2 | 2 221 | 263 | 291 | 6 673 | 41.6 | 56.3 | 2.1 |
| Williams | 128.1 | 3 338 | 46.3 | 6.6 | 4.8 | 8.8 | 7.5 | 68.1 | 1 773 | 81 | 95 | 2 116 | 44.4 | 53.7 | 1.9 |
| Wood | 523.0 | 4 171 | 51.3 | 10.1 | 3.8 | 3.8 | 4.7 | 393.1 | 3 135 | 220 | 338 | 13 687 | 52.7 | 45.6 | 1.7 |
| Wyandot | 102.4 | 4 557 | 37.6 | 28.1 | 4.1 | 4.0 | 8.0 | 22.9 | 1 017 | 62 | 57 | 1 336 | 40.6 | 57.1 | 2.2 |
| **OKLAHOMA** | X | X | X | X | X | X | X | X | X | 49 211 | 38 193 | 284 491 | 34.4 | 65.6 | 0.0 |
| Adair | 79.1 | 3 611 | 55.2 | 1.1 | 1.8 | 0.0 | 3.1 | 32.2 | 1 468 | 53 | 93 | 1 521 | 30.7 | 69.3 | 0.0 |
| Alfalfa | 10.8 | 1 923 | 66.8 | 1.9 | 4.1 | 0.0 | 2.3 | 5.3 | 956 | 42 | 23 | 410 | 16.9 | 83.1 | 0.0 |
| Atoka | 39.6 | 2 729 | 49.1 | 20.0 | 2.9 | 0.0 | 8.4 | 5.3 | 362 | 56 | 58 | 1 266 | 28.1 | 71.9 | 0.0 |
| Beaver | 22.9 | 4 263 | 55.8 | 2.0 | 2.0 | 0.0 | 27.9 | 3.2 | 603 | 31 | 23 | 430 | 10.8 | 89.2 | 0.0 |
| Beckham | 60.3 | 3 058 | 50.5 | 2.1 | 4.6 | 0.0 | 7.6 | 37.4 | 1 899 | 46 | 91 | 1 031 | 22.0 | 78.0 | 0.0 |
| Blaine | 41.3 | 3 313 | 48.2 | 21.8 | 3.2 | 0.0 | 10.0 | 12.8 | 1 026 | 61 | 40 | 814 | 24.6 | 75.4 | 0.0 |
| Bryan | 97.9 | 2 474 | 62.3 | 1.0 | 2.7 | 0.0 | 6.7 | 17.5 | 442 | 104 | 177 | 5 743 | 32.2 | 67.8 | 0.0 |
| Caddo | 97.2 | 3 318 | 61.8 | 4.5 | 4.0 | 0.2 | 9.0 | 22.8 | 778 | 505 | 121 | 2 422 | 34.7 | 65.3 | 0.0 |
| Canadian | 244.8 | 2 364 | 68.0 | 7.1 | 4.7 | 0.0 | 3.7 | 166.2 | 1 605 | 591 | 637 | 5 139 | 23.9 | 76.1 | 0.0 |
| Carter | 139.9 | 2 940 | 57.2 | 2.5 | 6.0 | 0.1 | 8.1 | 84.7 | 1 780 | 111 | 198 | 3 301 | 29.7 | 70.3 | 0.0 |
| Cherokee | 291.6 | 6 424 | 21.4 | 28.2 | 2.5 | 0.0 | 36.1 | 37.9 | 835 | 334 | 196 | 8 108 | 43.9 | 56.1 | 0.0 |
| Choctaw | 33.4 | 2 226 | 66.4 | 6.4 | 3.9 | 0.2 | 7.5 | 9.0 | 601 | 53 | 63 | 1 500 | 33.3 | 66.7 | 0.0 |
| Cimarron | 10.5 | 3 927 | 52.3 | 28.3 | 2.5 | 0.0 | 6.1 | 1.8 | 682 | 17 | 10 | 258 | 12.0 | 88.0 | 0.0 |
| Cleveland | 811.1 | 3 430 | 41.2 | 31.7 | 3.8 | 0.0 | 3.6 | 585.3 | 2 475 | 741 | 1 148 | 23 313 | 38.0 | 62.0 | 0.0 |
| Coal | 19.0 | 3 332 | 63.6 | 4.4 | 2.3 | 0.0 | 8.8 | 6.5 | 1 146 | 20 | 24 | 397 | 26.4 | 73.6 | 0.0 |
| Comanche | 395.6 | 3 476 | 46.6 | 31.8 | 4.1 | 0.0 | 1.7 | 141.9 | 1 247 | 4 546 | 13 312 | 9 678 | 41.2 | 58.8 | 0.0 |
| Cotton | 15.3 | 2 422 | 60.0 | 1.0 | 1.4 | 0.0 | 9.9 | 4.1 | 659 | 27 | 25 | 888 | 27.8 | 72.2 | 0.0 |
| Craig | 39.5 | 2 597 | 68.5 | 1.1 | 5.8 | 0.0 | 8.7 | 9.8 | 647 | 61 | 62 | 1 662 | 35.0 | 65.0 | 0.0 |
| Creek | 171.0 | 2 476 | 67.2 | 0.8 | 5.2 | 0.0 | 8.1 | 142.7 | 2 066 | 146 | 289 | 2 984 | 29.2 | 70.8 | 0.0 |
| Custer | 65.0 | 2 489 | 60.7 | 0.1 | 5.3 | 0.2 | 8.6 | 53.2 | 2 036 | 201 | 114 | 2 766 | 25.3 | 74.7 | 0.0 |
| Delaware | 82.5 | 2 042 | 74.6 | 0.6 | 2.6 | 0.3 | 3.2 | 42.8 | 1 058 | 71 | 171 | 2 563 | 33.1 | 66.9 | 0.0 |
| Dewey | 24.5 | 5 654 | 59.3 | 14.5 | 2.0 | 0.0 | 12.2 | 3.9 | 896 | 33 | 20 | 405 | 15.7 | 84.3 | 0.0 |
| Ellis | 14.7 | 3 757 | 54.6 | 1.3 | 2.2 | 0.0 | 22.4 | 1.8 | 453 | 24 | 17 | 394 | 14.8 | 85.2 | 0.0 |
| Garfield | 133.0 | 2 306 | 63.0 | 0.8 | 6.4 | 0.1 | 9.0 | 65.6 | 1 138 | 492 | 1 470 | 3 350 | 24.5 | 75.5 | 0.0 |
| Garvin | 85.7 | 3 158 | 51.7 | 22.1 | 3.8 | 0.1 | 6.7 | 29.3 | 1 080 | 86 | 113 | 2 062 | 28.2 | 71.8 | 0.0 |
| Grady | 170.2 | 3 363 | 37.7 | 25.8 | 4.9 | 0.1 | 20.1 | 55.6 | 1 098 | 90 | 218 | 2 557 | 26.6 | 73.4 | 0.0 |
| Grant | 14.2 | 3 163 | 67.6 | 0.6 | 3.9 | 0.0 | 5.6 | 2.7 | 596 | 33 | 19 | 318 | 21.9 | 78.1 | 0.0 |
| Greer | 22.0 | 3 791 | 35.9 | 32.7 | 4.2 | 0.2 | 8.3 | 6.1 | 1 055 | 25 | 25 | 674 | 26.8 | 73.2 | 0.0 |
| Harmon | 7.1 | 2 512 | 71.1 | 3.4 | 6.5 | 0.0 | 0.1 | 0.3 | 91 | 23 | 12 | 300 | 30.6 | 69.4 | 0.0 |
| Harper | 15.0 | 4 598 | 49.1 | 5.9 | 3.6 | 0.0 | 22.2 | 0.8 | 256 | 23 | 15 | 378 | 14.1 | 85.9 | 0.0 |
| Haskell | 27.7 | 2 301 | 67.4 | 2.8 | 4.1 | 0.0 | 12.5 | 1.7 | 139 | 59 | 53 | 632 | 31.5 | 68.5 | 0.0 |
| Hughes | 38.8 | 2 838 | 60.7 | 16.7 | 2.1 | 0.0 | 6.8 | 17.6 | 1 286 | 39 | 57 | 943 | 35.3 | 64.7 | 0.0 |
| Jackson | 127.2 | 4 935 | 32.7 | 46.3 | 4.2 | 0.0 | 2.3 | 46.5 | 1 805 | 1 515 | 1 442 | 2 551 | 25.2 | 74.8 | 0.0 |
| Jefferson | 19.4 | 3 095 | 63.7 | 1.0 | 1.6 | 0.0 | 4.7 | 37.7 | 6 015 | 32 | 27 | 376 | 32.8 | 67.2 | 0.0 |
| Johnston | 20.9 | 2 005 | 77.7 | 2.7 | 3.9 | 0.0 | 2.3 | 7.2 | 694 | 53 | 46 | 914 | 31.6 | 68.4 | 0.0 |
| Kay | 142.5 | 3 122 | 50.2 | 1.5 | 6.0 | 0.0 | 7.9 | 81.8 | 1 793 | 109 | 189 | 4 681 | 29.2 | 70.8 | 0.0 |
| Kingfisher | 43.7 | 3 052 | 66.4 | 1.2 | 4.4 | 0.0 | 11.1 | 15.2 | 1 063 | 49 | 62 | 807 | 15.8 | 84.2 | 0.0 |

1. Based on the resident population estimated as of July 1 of the year shown.    2. © 2013 Election Data Services, Inc. All rights reserved.

# Table B. States and Counties — Land Area and Population

| | | | | Population 2012 | | | | Population characteristics[6], 2011 | | | | | | | | | | |
|---|---|---|---|---|---|---|---|---|---|---|---|---|---|---|---|---|---|---|
| | | | | | | | | Race alone or in combination, not Hispanic or Latino (percent) | | | | | Age (percent) | | | | | |
| STATE/ County code | CBSA code[1] | County type[2] | STATE County | Land area,[3] (sq km) 2010 | Total persons | Rank | Per square kilometer | White | Black | American Indian, Alaska Native | Asian and Pacific Islander | Percent Hispanic or Latino[4] | Under 5 years | 5 to 17 years | 18 to 24 years | 25 to 34 years | 35 to 44 years | 45 to 54 years |
| | | | | 1 | 2 | 3 | 4 | 5 | 6 | 7 | 8 | 9 | 10 | 11 | 12 | 13 | 14 | 15 |
| | | | OKLAHOMA—Cont'd | | | | | | | | | | | | | | | |
| 40 075 | ... | 6 | Kiowa | 2 629 | 9 310 | 2 492 | 3.5 | 79.4 | 5.4 | 8.6 | 0.7 | 9.3 | 5.9 | 17.1 | 7.8 | 10.7 | 10.6 | 15.4 |
| 40 077 | ... | 7 | Latimer | 1 870 | 11 019 | 2 355 | 5.9 | 76.1 | 1.8 | 25.7 | 0.6 | 3.1 | 6.4 | 17.6 | 10.4 | 10.9 | 10.9 | 13.5 |
| 40 079 | 22900 | 2 | Le Flore | 4 116 | 49 873 | 981 | 12.1 | 77.9 | 2.8 | 17.0 | 0.9 | 7.1 | 6.7 | 17.9 | 8.9 | 12.1 | 11.8 | 13.9 |
| 40 081 | 36420 | 1 | Lincoln | 2 466 | 34 189 | 1 323 | 13.9 | 88.5 | 2.8 | 10.2 | 0.5 | 2.7 | 6.4 | 18.9 | 7.3 | 10.9 | 12.1 | 15.3 |
| 40 083 | 36420 | 1 | Logan | 1 927 | 43 666 | 1 093 | 22.7 | 81.2 | 10.3 | 5.8 | 0.9 | 5.4 | 6.3 | 18.3 | 11.0 | 11.7 | 12.2 | 14.8 |
| 40 085 | 11620 | 9 | Love | 1 331 | 9 558 | 2 467 | 7.2 | 78.9 | 2.9 | 8.8 | 0.8 | 12.4 | 6.6 | 17.8 | 7.4 | 11.7 | 11.7 | 14.1 |
| 40 087 | 36420 | 1 | McClain | 1 478 | 35 613 | 1 285 | 24.1 | 85.2 | 1.4 | 10.4 | 0.7 | 7.2 | 7.1 | 19.6 | 7.1 | 11.8 | 13.3 | 15.3 |
| 40 089 | ... | 7 | McCurtain | 4 791 | 33 203 | 1 348 | 6.9 | 70.5 | 10.0 | 19.7 | 0.8 | 5.0 | 7.2 | 18.8 | 8.2 | 11.4 | 12.2 | 13.6 |
| 40 091 | ... | 6 | McIntosh | 1 602 | 20 584 | 1 806 | 12.8 | 75.3 | 4.8 | 24.0 | 0.8 | 2.3 | 5.2 | 15.5 | 6.6 | 9.6 | 10.2 | 14.8 |
| 40 093 | ... | 9 | Major | 2 473 | 7 683 | 2 629 | 3.1 | 89.1 | 1.3 | 3.5 | 0.5 | 7.7 | 7.0 | 17.1 | 7.1 | 11.3 | 10.2 | 14.9 |
| 40 095 | ... | 6 | Marshall | 961 | 15 957 | 2 050 | 16.6 | 73.8 | 2.3 | 14.1 | 0.5 | 14.7 | 6.8 | 17.3 | 7.1 | 10.2 | 10.8 | 14.1 |
| 40 097 | ... | 6 | Mayes | 1 697 | 41 168 | 1 148 | 24.3 | 75.0 | 1.0 | 29.0 | 0.6 | 2.9 | 7.0 | 18.5 | 8.0 | 11.5 | 11.7 | 14.2 |
| 40 099 | ... | 7 | Murray | 1 079 | 13 663 | 2 201 | 12.7 | 80.8 | 2.4 | 16.8 | 0.7 | 5.3 | 6.7 | 17.5 | 7.4 | 11.4 | 11.6 | 14.2 |
| 40 101 | 34780 | 4 | Muskogee | 2 099 | 70 596 | 758 | 33.6 | 64.7 | 13.0 | 23.7 | 1.0 | 5.5 | 7.1 | 17.7 | 9.2 | 13.1 | 11.8 | 13.7 |
| 40 103 | ... | 6 | Noble | 1 896 | 11 522 | 2 326 | 6.1 | 86.2 | 2.7 | 11.5 | 0.8 | 2.7 | 6.5 | 17.9 | 7.0 | 11.6 | 12.2 | 14.8 |
| 40 105 | ... | 6 | Nowata | 1 465 | 10 611 | 2 389 | 7.2 | 76.6 | 3.0 | 26.3 | 0.6 | 2.5 | 6.0 | 18.1 | 7.5 | 10.7 | 11.5 | 15.0 |
| 40 107 | ... | 6 | Okfuskee | 1 602 | 12 358 | 2 282 | 7.7 | 68.3 | 9.2 | 24.6 | 0.9 | 3.2 | 6.6 | 16.7 | 7.9 | 12.5 | 12.2 | 15.0 |
| 40 109 | 36420 | 1 | Oklahoma | 1 836 | 741 781 | 81 | 404.0 | 62.6 | 16.8 | 5.9 | 3.8 | 15.5 | 7.8 | 17.6 | 10.1 | 15.5 | 12.2 | 13.2 |
| 40 111 | 46140 | 2 | Okmulgee | 1 806 | 39 625 | 1 179 | 21.9 | 70.7 | 10.3 | 22.2 | 0.7 | 3.6 | 6.3 | 18.2 | 9.8 | 11.4 | 11.3 | 13.9 |
| 40 113 | 46140 | 2 | Osage | 5 818 | 47 917 | 1 015 | 8.2 | 70.7 | 12.4 | 20.1 | 0.6 | 3.2 | 5.9 | 18.0 | 7.8 | 11.1 | 11.7 | 15.7 |
| 40 115 | 33060 | 6 | Ottawa | 1 219 | 32 236 | 1 384 | 26.4 | 74.3 | 1.5 | 24.8 | 1.8 | 5.0 | 7.0 | 17.7 | 10.1 | 11.1 | 11.6 | 12.9 |
| 40 117 | 46140 | 2 | Pawnee | 1 471 | 16 474 | 2 014 | 11.2 | 84.2 | 1.6 | 16.8 | 0.6 | 2.5 | 6.0 | 18.6 | 7.6 | 10.6 | 12.3 | 14.5 |
| 40 119 | 44660 | 4 | Payne | 1 773 | 78 399 | 702 | 44.2 | 83.3 | 4.9 | 7.8 | 4.7 | 4.2 | 5.7 | 12.8 | 28.3 | 13.8 | 9.4 | 10.3 |
| 40 121 | 32540 | 5 | Pittsburg | 3 381 | 45 048 | 1 067 | 13.3 | 77.9 | 4.7 | 19.8 | 0.9 | 4.2 | 6.2 | 15.9 | 8.1 | 12.9 | 11.7 | 14.1 |
| 40 123 | 10220 | 7 | Pontotoc | 1 866 | 37 958 | 1 224 | 20.3 | 74.7 | 4.0 | 22.9 | 1.1 | 4.4 | 7.1 | 16.5 | 12.8 | 13.2 | 11.0 | 12.9 |
| 40 125 | 43060 | 4 | Pottawatomie | 2 040 | 70 760 | 755 | 34.7 | 79.4 | 4.3 | 16.9 | 1.2 | 4.4 | 6.9 | 17.9 | 10.2 | 12.6 | 11.9 | 13.8 |
| 40 127 | ... | 9 | Pushmataha | 3 615 | 11 205 | 2 345 | 3.1 | 78.4 | 1.5 | 22.1 | 0.5 | 3.1 | 6.3 | 16.2 | 7.3 | 10.3 | 10.5 | 14.4 |
| 40 129 | ... | 9 | Roger Mills | 2 956 | 3 774 | 2 924 | 1.3 | 87.3 | 1.4 | 7.4 | 0.6 | 5.6 | 7.4 | 19.0 | 6.7 | 12.3 | 11.0 | 14.1 |
| 40 131 | 46140 | 2 | Rogers | 1 750 | 88 367 | 645 | 50.5 | 81.0 | 1.6 | 19.6 | 1.5 | 4.1 | 6.1 | 19.5 | 8.7 | 11.4 | 13.1 | 15.1 |
| 40 133 | ... | 7 | Seminole | 1 639 | 25 450 | 1 589 | 15.5 | 72.2 | 6.7 | 23.6 | 0.8 | 3.9 | 6.7 | 19.2 | 8.7 | 11.1 | 11.2 | 14.1 |
| 40 135 | 22900 | 2 | Sequoyah | 1 744 | 41 398 | 1 143 | 23.7 | 73.5 | 2.6 | 28.4 | 0.8 | 3.8 | 6.6 | 19.1 | 8.0 | 11.2 | 12.8 | 14.4 |
| 40 137 | 20340 | 4 | Stephens | 2 254 | 44 779 | 1 071 | 19.9 | 85.9 | 2.6 | 8.3 | 0.9 | 6.5 | 6.5 | 17.4 | 7.7 | 11.2 | 11.2 | 14.2 |
| 40 139 | 25100 | 7 | Texas | 5 287 | 21 498 | 1 753 | 4.1 | 51.6 | 2.2 | 1.8 | 2.1 | 43.7 | 8.8 | 19.9 | 11.9 | 14.4 | 12.8 | 12.0 |
| 40 141 | ... | 6 | Tillman | 2 256 | 7 822 | 2 613 | 3.5 | 66.5 | 7.9 | 4.6 | 0.8 | 22.8 | 6.4 | 18.1 | 8.0 | 11.5 | 11.3 | 14.0 |
| 40 143 | 46140 | 2 | Tulsa | 1 477 | 613 816 | 107 | 415.6 | 69.5 | 12.0 | 9.5 | 3.1 | 11.3 | 7.5 | 18.0 | 9.6 | 14.6 | 12.9 | 13.5 |
| 40 145 | 46140 | 2 | Wagoner | 1 454 | 75 030 | 729 | 51.6 | 79.8 | 4.9 | 15.6 | 1.7 | 5.0 | 6.8 | 19.3 | 7.5 | 12.8 | 13.4 | 14.3 |
| 40 147 | 12780 | 4 | Washington | 1 076 | 51 633 | 960 | 48.0 | 80.5 | 3.5 | 14.7 | 1.5 | 5.4 | 6.3 | 17.0 | 8.6 | 11.4 | 11.3 | 14.1 |
| 40 149 | ... | 7 | Washita | 2 598 | 11 622 | 2 322 | 4.5 | 87.2 | 1.5 | 4.9 | 0.6 | 8.6 | 6.8 | 18.7 | 7.9 | 12.6 | 10.6 | 14.2 |
| 40 151 | ... | 7 | Woods | 3 332 | 8 832 | 2 530 | 2.7 | 87.9 | 4.1 | 4.3 | 1.3 | 4.9 | 5.8 | 12.8 | 19.5 | 12.6 | 9.2 | 11.7 |
| 40 153 | 49260 | 7 | Woodward | 3 218 | 20 548 | 1 810 | 6.4 | 84.0 | 2.1 | 4.2 | 1.0 | 10.7 | 7.1 | 17.2 | 8.5 | 14.9 | 12.3 | 14.4 |
| 41 000 | ... | X | OREGON | 248 608 | 3 899 353 | X | 15.7 | 80.8 | 2.4 | 2.4 | 5.5 | 12.0 | 6.1 | 16.2 | 9.4 | 13.7 | 12.9 | 13.7 |
| 41 001 | ... | 7 | Baker | 7 947 | 15 909 | 2 052 | 2.0 | 94.3 | 0.8 | 2.4 | 1.1 | 3.6 | 5.1 | 14.8 | 6.4 | 9.6 | 10.2 | 14.6 |
| 41 003 | 18700 | 3 | Benton | 1 751 | 86 430 | 655 | 49.4 | 85.8 | 1.6 | 1.7 | 7.6 | 6.7 | 4.3 | 12.8 | 24.6 | 11.7 | 9.7 | 11.7 |
| 41 005 | 38900 | 1 | Clackamas | 4 844 | 383 857 | 175 | 79.2 | 86.6 | 1.3 | 1.5 | 5.3 | 8.0 | 5.6 | 17.6 | 7.8 | 11.4 | 13.0 | 15.5 |
| 41 007 | 11820 | 4 | Clatsop | 2 147 | 37 301 | 1 239 | 17.4 | 89.1 | 1.0 | 2.1 | 2.5 | 7.8 | 5.5 | 14.7 | 8.8 | 11.7 | 10.9 | 14.2 |
| 41 009 | 38900 | 1 | Columbia | 1 703 | 49 286 | 995 | 28.9 | 92.9 | 0.9 | 3.0 | 2.1 | 4.2 | 5.5 | 17.7 | 7.4 | 10.7 | 13.0 | 15.6 |
| 41 011 | 18300 | 5 | Coos | 4 134 | 62 534 | 835 | 15.1 | 90.2 | 0.8 | 5.0 | 2.2 | 5.6 | 5.1 | 13.8 | 7.5 | 10.4 | 9.9 | 14.4 |
| 41 013 | 39260 | 6 | Crook | 7 716 | 20 729 | 1 795 | 2.7 | 90.5 | 0.4 | 2.5 | 1.0 | 7.3 | 5.2 | 15.8 | 6.2 | 9.8 | 10.9 | 14.1 |
| 41 015 | 15060 | 7 | Curry | 4 215 | 22 248 | 1 721 | 5.3 | 91.0 | 0.6 | 4.2 | 1.4 | 5.9 | 3.9 | 11.7 | 5.5 | 8.1 | 8.8 | 14.1 |
| 41 017 | 13460 | 3 | Deschutes | 7 817 | 162 277 | 387 | 20.8 | 90.0 | 0.7 | 1.8 | 2.0 | 7.7 | 5.9 | 16.7 | 7.2 | 12.5 | 13.2 | 14.1 |
| 41 019 | 40700 | 4 | Douglas | 13 043 | 107 164 | 553 | 8.2 | 92.0 | 0.6 | 3.6 | 1.8 | 4.8 | 5.1 | 14.9 | 7.5 | 10.2 | 10.3 | 14.0 |
| 41 021 | ... | 9 | Gilliam | 3 120 | 1 953 | 3 059 | 0.6 | 92.7 | 0.4 | 1.5 | 1.3 | 5.2 | 5.1 | 13.6 | 5.3 | 9.1 | 10.6 | 16.6 |
| 41 023 | ... | 9 | Grant | 11 729 | 7 317 | 2 654 | 0.6 | 95.0 | 0.6 | 2.5 | 0.9 | 3.1 | 4.7 | 14.2 | 5.8 | 8.8 | 9.6 | 13.9 |
| 41 025 | ... | 7 | Harney | 26 245 | 7 212 | 2 659 | 0.3 | 91.5 | 0.8 | 4.7 | 1.2 | 4.5 | 5.6 | 16.6 | 6.9 | 9.9 | 10.6 | 14.2 |
| 41 027 | 26220 | 6 | Hood River | 1 352 | 22 584 | 1 708 | 16.7 | 67.5 | 0.8 | 1.6 | 2.5 | 29.8 | 6.5 | 19.0 | 7.9 | 12.3 | 13.7 | 14.9 |
| 41 029 | 32780 | 3 | Jackson | 7 209 | 206 412 | 305 | 28.6 | 85.6 | 1.1 | 2.3 | 2.5 | 11.2 | 5.8 | 15.7 | 8.6 | 11.6 | 11.2 | 13.7 |
| 41 031 | ... | 6 | Jefferson | 4 612 | 21 749 | 1 740 | 4.7 | 63.6 | 1.0 | 16.7 | 1.1 | 19.8 | 6.9 | 17.9 | 8.4 | 11.1 | 11.8 | 13.7 |
| 41 033 | 24420 | 4 | Josephine | 4 247 | 82 930 | 672 | 19.5 | 90.7 | 0.8 | 2.9 | 1.7 | 6.5 | 5.1 | 15.1 | 6.9 | 9.7 | 10.0 | 13.9 |
| 41 035 | 28900 | 5 | Klamath | 15 387 | 65 912 | 801 | 4.3 | 83.6 | 1.2 | 5.6 | 2.0 | 10.9 | 5.9 | 16.0 | 9.4 | 10.8 | 11.2 | 13.7 |
| 41 037 | ... | 7 | Lake | 21 080 | 7 771 | 2 621 | 0.4 | 89.7 | 1.2 | 4.0 | 1.3 | 6.9 | 4.2 | 14.1 | 6.4 | 10.1 | 11.6 | 15.4 |
| 41 039 | 21660 | 2 | Lane | 11 793 | 354 542 | 188 | 30.1 | 87.5 | 1.7 | 2.6 | 4.3 | 7.6 | 5.1 | 14.3 | 13.4 | 12.8 | 11.4 | 13.1 |
| 41 041 | ... | 4 | Lincoln | 2 538 | 46 151 | 1 045 | 18.2 | 86.8 | 0.9 | 5.3 | 2.0 | 8.1 | 5.1 | 12.4 | 6.4 | 10.1 | 9.8 | 14.1 |
| 41 043 | 10540 | 4 | Linn | 5 931 | 118 360 | 513 | 20.0 | 89.2 | 0.8 | 2.6 | 2.1 | 8.0 | 6.4 | 17.4 | 8.6 | 12.5 | 11.9 | 13.7 |
| 41 045 | 36620 | 6 | Malheur | 25 609 | 30 630 | 1 417 | 1.2 | 64.2 | 1.4 | 1.4 | 2.4 | 32.0 | 7.3 | 18.0 | 9.9 | 13.3 | 12.0 | 12.6 |
| 41 047 | 41420 | 2 | Marion | 3 062 | 319 985 | 204 | 104.5 | 70.5 | 1.5 | 2.1 | 3.7 | 24.8 | 7.4 | 18.9 | 9.8 | 13.7 | 12.4 | 12.8 |

1. CBSA = Core Based Statistical Area. See Appendix A for explanation. See Appendix B for list of metropolitan areas with component counties.   2. County type code from the Economic Research Service of USDA Rural-Urban Continuum Codes. See Appendix A for definition.   3. Dry land or land partially or temporarily covered with water.   4. May be of any race.

| STATE County | 55 to 64 years | 65 to 74 years | 75 years and over | Percent female | 2000 | 2010 | 2000–2010 | 2010–2012 | Births | Deaths | Net migration | Number | Percent change, 2000–2010 | Persons per household | Female family householder[1] | One person |
|---|---|---|---|---|---|---|---|---|---|---|---|---|---|---|---|---|
| | 16 | 17 | 18 | 19 | 20 | 21 | 22 | 23 | 24 | 25 | 26 | 27 | 28 | 29 | 30 | 31 |
| OKLAHOMA—Cont'd | | | | | | | | | | | | | | | | |
| Kiowa | 14.1 | 10.3 | 8.1 | 50.3 | 10 227 | 9 446 | -7.6 | -1.4 | 217 | 301 | -49 | 3 978 | -5.5 | 2.33 | 11.4 | 31.1 |
| Latimer | 12.8 | 9.5 | 8.0 | 49.1 | 10 692 | 11 154 | 4.3 | -1.2 | 291 | 222 | -214 | 4 208 | 6.5 | 2.51 | 11.8 | 25.9 |
| Le Flore | 13.0 | 9.2 | 6.5 | 49.8 | 48 109 | 50 384 | 4.7 | -1.0 | 1 123 | 1 327 | -296 | 18 878 | 5.7 | 2.58 | 12.0 | 24.8 |
| Lincoln | 13.7 | 9.2 | 6.3 | 50.2 | 32 080 | 34 273 | 6.8 | -0.2 | 829 | 727 | -194 | 13 243 | 8.7 | 2.56 | 10.3 | 23.5 |
| Logan | 13.0 | 7.6 | 5.1 | 50.5 | 33 924 | 41 848 | 23.4 | 4.3 | 1 028 | 712 | 1 273 | 15 290 | 23.4 | 2.60 | 9.7 | 22.8 |
| Love | 13.2 | 10.4 | 7.2 | 50.7 | 8 831 | 9 423 | 6.7 | 1.4 | 262 | 267 | 144 | 3 713 | 7.9 | 2.51 | 10.7 | 24.7 |
| McClain | 12.4 | 8.2 | 5.2 | 50.2 | 27 740 | 34 506 | 24.4 | 3.2 | 978 | 667 | 802 | 12 891 | 24.8 | 2.66 | 9.9 | 20.1 |
| McCurtain | 13.0 | 9.1 | 6.5 | 51.0 | 34 402 | 33 151 | -3.6 | 0.2 | 957 | 809 | -69 | 12 958 | -2.0 | 2.52 | 14.9 | 27.2 |
| McIntosh | 15.6 | 12.7 | 9.8 | 50.1 | 19 456 | 20 252 | 4.1 | 1.6 | 443 | 631 | 530 | 8 460 | 4.6 | 2.35 | 11.6 | 27.7 |
| Major | 13.7 | 9.8 | 9.0 | 51.1 | 7 545 | 7 527 | -0.2 | 2.1 | 226 | 179 | 106 | 3 109 | 2.1 | 2.40 | 7.0 | 26.5 |
| Marshall | 13.6 | 11.9 | 8.1 | 50.1 | 13 184 | 15 840 | 20.1 | 0.7 | 410 | 347 | 37 | 6 338 | 18.0 | 2.45 | 9.7 | 27.4 |
| Mayes | 13.1 | 9.5 | 6.5 | 50.4 | 38 369 | 41 259 | 7.5 | -0.2 | 1 098 | 990 | -190 | 16 008 | 8.0 | 2.54 | 10.5 | 24.9 |
| Murray | 13.7 | 9.7 | 7.8 | 50.2 | 12 623 | 13 488 | 6.9 | 1.3 | 343 | 392 | 220 | 5 350 | 6.9 | 2.46 | 10.1 | 26.9 |
| Muskogee | 12.6 | 8.1 | 6.8 | 51.1 | 69 451 | 70 990 | 2.2 | -0.6 | 2 192 | 1 887 | -674 | 27 054 | 2.3 | 2.49 | 14.6 | 27.9 |
| Noble | 13.1 | 9.3 | 7.6 | 50.4 | 11 411 | 11 561 | 1.3 | -0.3 | 304 | 288 | -64 | 4 614 | 2.4 | 2.45 | 10.0 | 26.6 |
| Nowata | 13.2 | 9.9 | 8.0 | 50.8 | 10 569 | 10 536 | -0.3 | 0.7 | 232 | 266 | 114 | 4 224 | 1.9 | 2.46 | 10.7 | 25.9 |
| Okfuskee | 12.2 | 9.8 | 6.9 | 46.7 | 11 814 | 12 191 | 3.2 | 1.4 | 408 | 336 | 83 | 4 354 | 2.0 | 2.52 | 12.0 | 27.3 |
| Oklahoma | 11.5 | 6.4 | 5.6 | 51.0 | 660 448 | 718 633 | 8.8 | 3.2 | 26 798 | 14 627 | 10 829 | 287 598 | 7.8 | 2.45 | 14.3 | 30.7 |
| Okmulgee | 13.1 | 8.8 | 7.2 | 50.5 | 39 685 | 40 069 | 1.0 | -1.1 | 1 119 | 1 006 | -560 | 15 362 | 0.4 | 2.52 | 14.6 | 27.2 |
| Osage | 14.4 | 9.2 | 6.2 | 49.6 | 44 437 | 47 472 | 6.8 | 0.9 | 1 030 | 928 | 180 | 18 205 | 9.6 | 2.53 | 12.0 | 24.8 |
| Ottawa | 12.6 | 9.2 | 7.8 | 51.0 | 33 194 | 31 848 | -4.1 | 1.2 | 899 | 960 | 413 | 12 345 | -4.9 | 2.50 | 12.8 | 27.0 |
| Pawnee | 13.9 | 9.7 | 6.8 | 50.1 | 16 612 | 16 577 | -0.2 | -0.6 | 416 | 398 | -117 | 6 486 | 1.6 | 2.53 | 10.3 | 25.5 |
| Payne | 9.2 | 5.7 | 4.9 | 49.0 | 68 190 | 77 350 | 13.4 | 1.4 | 2 019 | 1 177 | 237 | 30 177 | 13.1 | 2.31 | 8.9 | 30.8 |
| Pittsburg | 13.6 | 9.8 | 7.7 | 49.2 | 43 953 | 45 837 | 4.3 | -1.7 | 1 148 | 1 205 | -687 | 18 012 | 5.0 | 2.41 | 12.1 | 27.8 |
| Pontotoc | 11.6 | 8.1 | 6.9 | 51.4 | 35 143 | 37 492 | 6.7 | 1.2 | 1 249 | 927 | 138 | 14 654 | 4.8 | 2.44 | 12.1 | 28.4 |
| Pottawatomie | 12.0 | 8.3 | 6.2 | 52.1 | 65 521 | 69 442 | 6.0 | 1.9 | 2 135 | 1 564 | 758 | 25 911 | 5.6 | 2.56 | 13.3 | 25.1 |
| Pushmataha | 14.2 | 12.1 | 8.7 | 50.9 | 11 667 | 11 572 | -0.8 | -3.2 | 273 | 343 | -298 | 4 809 | 1.5 | 2.38 | 11.8 | 28.4 |
| Roger Mills | 13.8 | 8.6 | 7.1 | 49.7 | 3 436 | 3 647 | 6.1 | 3.5 | 106 | 65 | 72 | 1 470 | 2.9 | 2.47 | 9.4 | 26.3 |
| Rogers | 12.3 | 8.1 | 5.6 | 50.4 | 70 641 | 86 905 | 23.0 | 1.7 | 2 114 | 1 506 | 806 | 31 884 | 23.9 | 2.69 | 9.6 | 20.2 |
| Seminole | 13.1 | 8.9 | 7.0 | 50.8 | 24 894 | 25 482 | 2.4 | -0.1 | 722 | 659 | -100 | 9 750 | 1.8 | 2.55 | 14.0 | 26.9 |
| Sequoyah | 12.6 | 9.2 | 6.1 | 50.5 | 38 972 | 42 391 | 8.8 | -2.3 | 731 | 1 046 | -676 | 16 208 | 9.8 | 2.59 | 13.1 | 24.1 |
| Stephens | 13.5 | 9.1 | 8.4 | 51.2 | 43 182 | 45 048 | 4.3 | -0.6 | 1 182 | 1 205 | -239 | 18 127 | 3.8 | 2.46 | 10.1 | 26.1 |
| Texas | 10.3 | 5.3 | 4.6 | 47.7 | 20 107 | 20 640 | 2.7 | 4.2 | 736 | 306 | 429 | 7 212 | 0.8 | 2.78 | 9.4 | 23.0 |
| Tillman | 12.6 | 10.1 | 8.1 | 49.8 | 9 287 | 7 992 | -13.9 | -2.1 | 230 | 200 | -201 | 3 216 | -10.5 | 2.40 | 12.3 | 30.3 |
| Tulsa | 11.7 | 6.5 | 5.8 | 51.2 | 563 299 | 603 403 | 7.1 | 1.7 | 20 712 | 12 220 | 2 104 | 241 737 | 6.5 | 2.46 | 13.3 | 29.9 |
| Wagoner | 13.0 | 8.4 | 4.6 | 50.7 | 57 491 | 73 085 | 27.1 | 2.7 | 1 933 | 1 204 | 1 179 | 26 878 | 27.9 | 2.71 | 10.3 | 18.8 |
| Washington | 13.4 | 9.0 | 8.9 | 51.6 | 48 996 | 50 976 | 4.0 | 1.3 | 1 390 | 1 259 | 552 | 21 036 | 4.2 | 2.39 | 11.0 | 28.7 |
| Washita | 12.1 | 8.4 | 8.5 | 51.0 | 11 508 | 11 629 | 1.1 | -0.1 | 303 | 329 | 25 | 4 599 | 2.1 | 2.48 | 9.5 | 27.1 |
| Woods | 11.2 | 8.4 | 8.6 | 46.9 | 9 089 | 8 878 | -2.3 | -0.5 | 214 | 240 | -21 | 3 533 | -4.1 | 2.23 | 7.6 | 32.3 |
| Woodward | 11.4 | 8.3 | 5.9 | 47.5 | 18 486 | 20 081 | 8.6 | 2.3 | 627 | 532 | 364 | 7 654 | 7.2 | 2.46 | 8.5 | 28.0 |
| OREGON | 13.7 | 7.9 | 6.4 | 50.5 | 3 421 399 | 3 831 074 | 12.0 | 1.8 | 101 333 | 71 781 | 38 753 | 1 518 938 | 13.9 | 2.47 | 10.5 | 27.4 |
| Baker | 17.1 | 12.5 | 9.8 | 49.7 | 16 741 | 16 134 | -3.6 | -1.4 | 362 | 466 | -107 | 7 040 | 2.3 | 2.24 | 8.3 | 31.2 |
| Benton | 12.8 | 6.6 | 5.7 | 49.8 | 78 153 | 85 579 | 9.5 | 1.0 | 1 654 | 1 201 | 386 | 34 317 | 13.8 | 2.35 | 7.3 | 28.2 |
| Clackamas | 14.9 | 8.0 | 6.2 | 50.8 | 338 391 | 375 992 | 11.1 | 2.1 | 8 616 | 6 832 | 5 908 | 145 790 | 13.7 | 2.56 | 9.8 | 24.1 |
| Clatsop | 17.1 | 9.8 | 7.4 | 50.4 | 35 630 | 37 039 | 4.0 | 0.7 | 909 | 844 | 218 | 15 742 | 7.1 | 2.29 | 9.6 | 31.5 |
| Columbia | 15.5 | 8.8 | 5.8 | 50.0 | 43 560 | 49 351 | 13.3 | -0.1 | 1 080 | 937 | -202 | 19 183 | 17.1 | 2.55 | 9.8 | 23.3 |
| Coos | 17.2 | 12.2 | 9.6 | 50.7 | 62 779 | 63 043 | 0.4 | -0.8 | 1 349 | 1 873 | 64 | 27 133 | 3.5 | 2.29 | 10.2 | 29.8 |
| Crook | 16.6 | 12.8 | 8.5 | 50.3 | 19 182 | 20 978 | 9.4 | -1.2 | 405 | 503 | -149 | 8 558 | 16.4 | 2.42 | 9.0 | 24.1 |
| Curry | 19.6 | 16.1 | 12.1 | 50.7 | 21 137 | 22 364 | 5.8 | -0.5 | 401 | 779 | 277 | 10 417 | 9.2 | 2.12 | 8.4 | 32.4 |
| Deschutes | 14.7 | 9.2 | 6.4 | 50.6 | 115 367 | 157 733 | 36.7 | 2.9 | 3 810 | 2 747 | 3 362 | 64 090 | 40.6 | 2.44 | 9.4 | 24.1 |
| Douglas | 16.4 | 11.7 | 9.8 | 50.6 | 100 399 | 107 667 | 7.2 | -0.5 | 2 342 | 2 928 | 163 | 44 581 | 12.0 | 2.38 | 10.8 | 26.6 |
| Gilliam | 18.2 | 11.5 | 10.1 | 48.6 | 1 915 | 1 871 | -2.3 | 4.4 | 33 | 57 | 97 | 864 | 5.5 | 2.14 | 6.4 | 35.6 |
| Grant | 18.5 | 13.8 | 10.9 | 50.2 | 7 935 | 7 445 | -6.2 | -1.7 | 135 | 175 | -82 | 3 352 | 3.3 | 2.19 | 7.5 | 30.3 |
| Harney | 16.8 | 10.8 | 8.6 | 49.4 | 7 609 | 7 422 | -2.5 | -2.8 | 172 | 180 | -201 | 3 205 | 5.6 | 2.28 | 8.8 | 30.0 |
| Hood River | 12.8 | 6.5 | 6.5 | 50.0 | 20 411 | 22 346 | 9.5 | 1.1 | 620 | 383 | 13 | 8 173 | 12.8 | 2.64 | 9.3 | 23.8 |
| Jackson | 15.2 | 9.7 | 8.4 | 51.3 | 181 269 | 203 206 | 12.1 | 1.6 | 5 160 | 4 712 | 2 774 | 83 076 | 16.1 | 2.40 | 11.0 | 27.7 |
| Jefferson | 13.9 | 10.2 | 6.1 | 48.2 | 19 009 | 21 720 | 14.3 | 0.1 | 667 | 459 | -179 | 7 790 | 15.8 | 2.68 | 12.6 | 22.2 |
| Josephine | 16.5 | 12.5 | 10.5 | 51.3 | 75 726 | 82 713 | 9.2 | 0.3 | 1 715 | 2 447 | 1 006 | 34 646 | 11.8 | 2.34 | 11.0 | 28.3 |
| Klamath | 15.3 | 10.1 | 7.5 | 50.3 | 63 775 | 66 380 | 4.1 | -0.7 | 1 777 | 1 597 | -612 | 27 280 | 8.2 | 2.40 | 10.7 | 27.3 |
| Lake | 17.5 | 12.0 | 8.7 | 47.0 | 7 422 | 7 895 | 6.4 | -1.6 | 140 | 213 | -45 | 3 378 | 9.5 | 2.20 | 7.4 | 31.3 |
| Lane | 14.5 | 8.4 | 7.0 | 50.9 | 322 959 | 351 715 | 8.9 | 0.8 | 7 719 | 6 932 | 2 143 | 145 966 | 11.9 | 2.35 | 10.6 | 28.9 |
| Lincoln | 19.8 | 13.1 | 9.2 | 51.5 | 44 479 | 46 034 | 3.5 | 0.3 | 972 | 1 225 | 383 | 20 550 | 6.5 | 2.20 | 9.6 | 31.2 |
| Linn | 13.9 | 8.7 | 6.9 | 50.6 | 103 069 | 116 672 | 13.2 | 1.4 | 3 245 | 2 648 | 1 079 | 45 204 | 14.3 | 2.55 | 11.2 | 24.4 |
| Malheur | 11.6 | 8.1 | 7.3 | 45.7 | 31 615 | 31 313 | -1.0 | -2.2 | 992 | 611 | -1 112 | 10 411 | 1.9 | 2.69 | 11.8 | 26.0 |
| Marion | 12.0 | 7.0 | 6.1 | 50.1 | 284 834 | 315 335 | 10.7 | 1.5 | 10 011 | 5 748 | 422 | 112 957 | 11.1 | 2.70 | 12.4 | 25.0 |

1. No spouse present.

# Table B. States and Counties — Population, Vital Statistics, Medicare, and Crime

| STATE County | Daytime population, 2007–2011 Persons in group quarters, 2010 | Number | Employ-ment/resi-dence ratio | Births, 2011 Total | Rate[1] | Deaths, 2011 Number | Rate[1] | Persons under 65 with no health insurance, 2010 Number | Percent | Medicare, 2012 Eligible for Medicare | Enrolled in Medicare Advantage | Enrolled in a Medicare prescription drug plan | Serious crimes known to police,[2] 2011 Total Number | Rate[3] |
|---|---|---|---|---|---|---|---|---|---|---|---|---|---|---|
| | 32 | 33 | 34 | 35 | 36 | 37 | 38 | 39 | 40 | 41 | 42 | 43 | 44 | 45 |
| **OKLAHOMA—Cont'd** | | | | | | | | | | | | | | |
| Kiowa | 171 | 8 690 | 0.81 | 93 | 9.9 | 133 | 14.1 | 1 728 | 22.9 | 2 206 | 104 | 1 384 | 163 | 1 707 |
| Latimer | 574 | 10 976 | 0.98 | 142 | 12.7 | 101 | 9.1 | 2 090 | 23.6 | 2 398 | 143 | 1 222 | 102 | 905 |
| Le Flore | 1 616 | 46 141 | 0.79 | 691 | 13.6 | 602 | 11.9 | 10 755 | 25.9 | 10 095 | 1 142 | 5 425 | 745 | 1 463 |
| Lincoln | 386 | 28 685 | 0.62 | 395 | 11.6 | 310 | 9.1 | 6 418 | 22.3 | 6 545 | 952 | 2 801 | 631 | 1 822 |
| Logan | 2 161 | 31 828 | 0.51 | 440 | 10.4 | 306 | 7.2 | 7 366 | 20.9 | 6 616 | 1 018 | 3 125 | 668 | 1 579 |
| Love | 88 | 10 297 | 1.23 | 111 | 11.8 | 119 | 12.7 | 1 728 | 22.2 | 2 033 | 86 | 1 258 | 102 | 1 071 |
| McClain | 194 | 27 995 | 0.62 | 484 | 13.7 | 272 | 7.7 | 6 368 | 21.2 | 5 999 | 565 | 2 800 | 869 | 2 492 |
| McCurtain | 454 | 32 872 | 0.98 | 476 | 14.3 | 358 | 10.8 | 6 871 | 24.9 | 6 907 | 568 | 4 162 | 1 110 | 3 313 |
| McIntosh | 345 | 18 237 | 0.71 | 208 | 10.2 | 261 | 12.8 | 4 232 | 27.0 | 5 841 | 493 | 3 043 | 445 | 2 174 |
| Major | 77 | 7 044 | 0.87 | 112 | 14.6 | 75 | 9.8 | 1 452 | 24.1 | 1 590 | 43 | 1 030 | 155 | 2 037 |
| Marshall | 329 | 14 604 | 0.84 | 200 | 12.5 | 147 | 9.2 | 3 588 | 28.4 | 3 526 | 175 | 2 015 | 120 | 750 |
| Mayes | 567 | 38 027 | 0.82 | 525 | 12.7 | 456 | 11.0 | 8 086 | 23.4 | 8 060 | 996 | 4 081 | 856 | 2 053 |
| Murray | 313 | 12 519 | 0.85 | 167 | 12.3 | 182 | 13.4 | 2 524 | 23.0 | 2 885 | 253 | 1 572 | 276 | 2 025 |
| Muskogee | 3 526 | 72 590 | 1.07 | 1 042 | 14.7 | 819 | 11.5 | 12 981 | 22.5 | 14 071 | 1 049 | 7 371 | 1 842 | 2 567 |
| Noble | 273 | 11 134 | 0.92 | 132 | 11.4 | 127 | 11.0 | 1 861 | 19.4 | 2 275 | 91 | 1 479 | 120 | 1 027 |
| Nowata | 157 | 8 726 | 0.55 | 108 | 10.2 | 138 | 13.0 | 1 954 | 22.9 | 2 396 | 221 | 1 294 | 238 | 2 235 |
| Okfuskee | 1 228 | 11 015 | 0.74 | 147 | 11.9 | 142 | 11.5 | 2 287 | 24.7 | 2 442 | 209 | 1 377 | 297 | 2 410 |
| Oklahoma | 15 025 | 812 748 | 1.30 | 12 383 | 16.9 | 6 236 | 8.5 | 139 828 | 22.5 | 109 467 | 23 081 | 44 068 | 40 989 | 5 643 |
| Okmulgee | 1 374 | 36 450 | 0.79 | 502 | 12.6 | 453 | 11.3 | 6 809 | 20.8 | 8 340 | 845 | 4 245 | 1 039 | 2 566 |
| Osage | 1 504 | 38 586 | 0.56 | 444 | 9.4 | 415 | 8.8 | 8 105 | 20.9 | 8 220 | 1 602 | 3 646 | 1 221 | 2 545 |
| Ottawa | 968 | 31 336 | 0.95 | 461 | 14.5 | 460 | 14.4 | 6 332 | 24.7 | 7 493 | 533 | 4 010 | 807 | 2 507 |
| Pawnee | 194 | 13 716 | 0.60 | 174 | 10.4 | 170 | 10.2 | 3 460 | 25.1 | 3 480 | 350 | 1 801 | 286 | 1 707 |
| Payne | 7 764 | 77 219 | 1.03 | 960 | 12.3 | 518 | 6.6 | 13 372 | 21.7 | 10 191 | 234 | 6 289 | 2 259 | 2 890 |
| Pittsburg | 2 433 | 47 160 | 1.09 | 551 | 12.1 | 536 | 11.7 | 7 888 | 22.0 | 9 324 | 617 | 4 469 | 1 537 | 3 318 |
| Pontotoc | 1 696 | 38 633 | 1.09 | 576 | 15.2 | 417 | 11.0 | 6 834 | 22.3 | 7 164 | 363 | 3 914 | 1 077 | 2 842 |
| Pottawatomie | 3 053 | 65 902 | 0.88 | 960 | 13.7 | 677 | 9.6 | 11 757 | 20.6 | 13 300 | 2 066 | 5 560 | 3 041 | 4 333 |
| Pushmataha | 110 | 10 955 | 0.87 | 138 | 12.0 | 149 | 13.0 | 2 434 | 26.6 | 2 924 | 219 | 1 591 | 232 | 1 984 |
| Roger Mills | 11 | 3 753 | 1.11 | 45 | 12.2 | 24 | 6.5 | 723 | 24.3 | 718 | 13 | 454 | 59 | 1 601 |
| Rogers | 1 216 | 73 518 | 0.69 | 949 | 10.8 | 646 | 7.4 | 13 033 | 17.3 | 14 658 | 4 303 | 5 393 | 1 401 | 1 595 |
| Seminole | 581 | 24 504 | 0.92 | 335 | 13.2 | 290 | 11.5 | 4 967 | 23.8 | 5 203 | 475 | 2 879 | 876 | 3 401 |
| Sequoyah | 416 | 36 964 | 0.68 | 538 | 12.7 | 461 | 10.9 | 8 544 | 23.8 | 8 712 | 1 175 | 4 396 | 1 012 | 2 362 |
| Stephens | 540 | 43 990 | 0.96 | 546 | 12.1 | 511 | 11.3 | 7 234 | 19.5 | 9 390 | 1 003 | 5 039 | 1 352 | 2 969 |
| Texas | 572 | 20 170 | 1.00 | 419 | 19.7 | 133 | 6.2 | 5 094 | 28.1 | 2 422 | 109 | 1 398 | 409 | 1 961 |
| Tillman | 267 | 7 388 | 0.75 | 107 | 13.3 | 81 | 10.0 | 1 556 | 24.7 | 1 698 | 78 | 1 045 | 200 | 2 476 |
| Tulsa | 9 817 | 660 658 | 1.22 | 9 781 | 16.0 | 5 286 | 8.7 | 114 404 | 21.8 | 94 190 | 27 988 | 35 954 | 31 193 | 5 115 |
| Wagoner | 319 | 51 265 | 0.37 | 892 | 12.0 | 517 | 7.0 | 13 195 | 20.6 | 11 528 | 3 559 | 4 075 | 1 851 | 2 506 |
| Washington | 798 | 50 967 | 1.01 | 624 | 12.1 | 558 | 10.8 | 8 196 | 19.8 | 10 985 | 820 | 6 408 | 1 524 | 2 958 |
| Washita | 206 | 10 441 | 0.77 | 137 | 11.8 | 154 | 13.3 | 2 155 | 22.6 | 2 119 | 93 | 1 340 | 76 | 647 |
| Woods | 1 005 | 8 965 | 1.06 | 109 | 12.4 | 107 | 12.2 | 1 294 | 20.1 | 1 600 | 95 | 1 087 | 99 | 1 103 |
| Woodward | 1 240 | 21 027 | 1.10 | 271 | 13.5 | 251 | 12.5 | 3 891 | 24.4 | 3 346 | 141 | 2 071 | 681 | 3 355 |
| **OREGON** | 86 642 | 3 847 243 | 1.03 | 46 232 | 11.9 | 31 451 | 8.1 | 639 710 | 19.7 | 676 117 | 280 493 | 210 198 | 130 180 | 3 362 |
| Baker | 373 | 16 254 | 1.02 | 149 | 9.3 | 208 | 13.0 | 2 476 | 20.2 | 4 224 | 147 | 2 430 | 219 | 1 343 |
| Benton | 5 043 | 86 218 | 1.03 | 753 | 8.8 | 537 | 6.2 | 12 386 | 17.6 | 12 598 | 5 502 | 4 209 | 2 355 | 2 723 |
| Clackamas | 2 753 | 345 657 | 0.84 | 3 951 | 10.4 | 2 966 | 7.8 | 50 010 | 15.5 | 64 295 | 36 903 | 12 470 | 9 423 | 2 480 |
| Clatsop | 956 | 38 266 | 1.07 | 388 | 10.4 | 375 | 10.1 | 4 466 | 21.2 | 7 781 | 1 667 | 3 454 | 1 167 | 3 118 |
| Columbia | 499 | 40 603 | 0.58 | 496 | 10.0 | 428 | 8.7 | 6 904 | 16.4 | 9 310 | 4 610 | 2 309 | 505 | 1 104 |
| Coos | 1 008 | 63 354 | 1.01 | 598 | 9.5 | 830 | 13.2 | 9 517 | 19.3 | 16 727 | 1 092 | 8 858 | 2 192 | 3 583 |
| Crook | 245 | 20 087 | 0.85 | 211 | 10.1 | 202 | 9.7 | 3 595 | 21.6 | 5 332 | 1 048 | 2 300 | 418 | 1 972 |
| Curry | 318 | 22 024 | 0.96 | 173 | 7.7 | 335 | 14.9 | 3 407 | 21.2 | 7 426 | 602 | 3 538 | 400 | 1 770 |
| Deschutes | 1 244 | 158 319 | 1.02 | 1 773 | 11.1 | 1 154 | 7.2 | 26 582 | 19.9 | 31 185 | 8 672 | 12 368 | 5 453 | 3 421 |
| Douglas | 1 708 | 106 806 | 0.99 | 1 047 | 9.7 | 1 255 | 11.7 | 16 407 | 19.4 | 28 294 | 7 779 | 10 045 | 3 052 | 2 805 |
| Gilliam | 20 | 2 075 | 1.21 | 15 | 7.7 | 31 | 16.0 | 289 | 19.7 | 444 | 12 | 235 | 18 | 952 |
| Grant | 105 | 7 419 | 1.02 | 57 | 7.7 | 78 | 10.5 | 1 227 | 21.6 | 1 930 | 323 | 852 | 62 | 824 |
| Harney | 127 | 7 344 | 0.99 | 79 | 10.7 | 75 | 10.2 | 1 404 | 23.7 | 1 715 | 52 | 1 037 | 175 | 2 333 |
| Hood River | 787 | 22 703 | 1.07 | 275 | 12.2 | 169 | 7.5 | 4 646 | 23.8 | 3 385 | 791 | 1 387 | 230 | 1 018 |
| Jackson | 3 492 | 202 368 | 1.00 | 2 293 | 11.2 | 2 012 | 9.8 | 36 877 | 22.3 | 44 994 | 13 742 | 15 851 | 7 638 | 3 719 |
| Jefferson | 853 | 20 600 | 0.86 | 303 | 13.9 | 214 | 9.8 | 4 875 | 27.7 | 4 238 | 1 046 | 1 812 | 468 | 2 132 |
| Josephine | 1 601 | 81 058 | 0.95 | 790 | 9.5 | 1 087 | 13.1 | 13 064 | 20.4 | 22 516 | 8 402 | 6 576 | 2 888 | 3 455 |
| Klamath | 950 | 66 257 | 0.99 | 759 | 11.4 | 728 | 11.0 | 12 083 | 22.2 | 14 474 | 3 004 | 6 287 | 1 588 | 2 398 |
| Lake | 454 | 8 058 | 1.05 | 54 | 6.8 | 94 | 11.9 | 1 389 | 23.6 | 1 911 | 122 | 917 | NA | NA |
| Lane | 8 530 | 351 128 | 1.01 | 3 481 | 9.8 | 3 060 | 8.7 | 62 772 | 21.4 | 67 786 | 31 357 | 19 943 | 13 640 | 3 837 |
| Lincoln | 762 | 46 291 | 1.02 | 462 | 10.1 | 537 | 11.7 | 8 332 | 23.2 | 12 591 | 2 317 | 5 556 | 1 486 | 3 194 |
| Linn | 1 227 | 110 294 | 0.89 | 1 405 | 11.9 | 1 171 | 9.9 | 18 934 | 19.3 | 23 543 | 11 275 | 6 864 | 3 592 | 3 046 |
| Malheur | 3 351 | 34 059 | 1.25 | 452 | 14.5 | 252 | 8.1 | 6 270 | 26.6 | 5 579 | 149 | 3 552 | 1 199 | 3 789 |
| Marion | 10 429 | 321 074 | 1.06 | 4 620 | 14.5 | 2 560 | 8.0 | 58 252 | 21.8 | 51 484 | 28 860 | 12 487 | 9 650 | 3 028 |

1. Per 1,000 estimated resident population.  2. Data for serious crimes have not been adjusted for underreporting; this may affect comparability between geographic areas and over time.  3. Per 100,000 population estimated by the FBI.

# Table B. States and Counties — Crime, Education, Money Income, and Poverty

| STATE County | Serious crimes known to police, 2011 (cont.)[1] Rate[2] Violent | Property | School enrollment and attainment, 2007–2011 Enrollment[3] Total | Per-cent private | Attainment[4] (percent) High school grad-uate or less | Bach-elor's degree or more | Local government expenditures,[5] 2009–2010 Total current expendi-tures (mil dol) | Current expendi-tures per student (dollars) | Money income, 2007–2011 Per capita income[6] (dollars) | Households Median income Dollars | Percent change, 2000 to 2007–2011 (constant 2011 dollars) | Percent with income of $200,000 or more | Income and poverty, 2011 Median house-hold income (dollars) | Percent below poverty level All per-sons | Children under 18 years | Children 5 to 17 years in families |
|---|---|---|---|---|---|---|---|---|---|---|---|---|---|---|---|---|
| | 46 | 47 | 48 | 49 | 50 | 51 | 52 | 53 | 54 | 55 | 56 | 57 | 58 | 59 | 60 | 61 |
| **OKLAHOMA—Cont'd** | | | | | | | | | | | | | | | | |
| Kiowa | 157 | 1 550 | 2 113 | 6.2 | 54.0 | 17.8 | 15.5 | 9 077 | 20 221 | 33 068 | -6.0 | 1.6 | 35 977 | 21.0 | 29.7 | 26.8 |
| Latimer | 115 | 789 | 2 933 | 7.5 | 50.8 | 14.2 | 14.0 | 9 333 | 20 689 | 42 610 | 31.7 | 2.0 | 35 660 | 19.2 | 28.0 | 24.6 |
| Le Flore | 185 | 1 278 | 11 951 | 3.8 | 58.0 | 11.5 | 82.4 | 8 167 | 17 892 | 36 815 | 0.0 | 0.5 | 34 131 | 20.4 | 26.7 | 24.6 |
| Lincoln | 104 | 1 718 | 8 045 | 7.0 | 58.2 | 12.9 | 42.1 | 7 386 | 20 992 | 41 763 | -0.8 | 1.1 | 38 058 | 17.9 | 23.6 | 21.6 |
| Logan | 113 | 1 466 | 11 178 | 11.5 | 47.1 | 23.1 | 34.9 | 7 671 | 25 496 | 50 249 | 1.2 | 3.4 | 48 346 | 14.4 | 19.4 | 17.7 |
| Love | 73 | 997 | 2 045 | 7.6 | 61.5 | 14.7 | 12.8 | 7 739 | 20 842 | 41 163 | -6.4 | 2.0 | 40 853 | 16.4 | 24.4 | 22.8 |
| McClain | 163 | 2 328 | 8 609 | 6.1 | 48.3 | 18.9 | 49.0 | 7 006 | 24 898 | 56 128 | 11.5 | 2.4 | 54 633 | 14.0 | 20.2 | 14.5 |
| McCurtain | 307 | 3 005 | 8 167 | 6.9 | 60.5 | 12.3 | 60.2 | 8 562 | 17 547 | 31 328 | -4.0 | 0.8 | 29 614 | 30.9 | 40.3 | 35.3 |
| McIntosh | 191 | 1 983 | 3 984 | 5.6 | 58.3 | 12.8 | 25.6 | 7 875 | 17 058 | 32 305 | -7.8 | 0.4 | 32 487 | 24.5 | 33.6 | 31.1 |
| Major | 171 | 1 866 | 1 569 | 11.0 | 57.4 | 16.0 | 10.6 | 10 681 | 26 524 | 48 012 | 14.9 | 2.7 | 45 374 | 12.1 | 18.2 | 17.0 |
| Marshall | 194 | 556 | 3 491 | 4.4 | 59.6 | 15.5 | 21.8 | 7 499 | 19 094 | 39 473 | 10.6 | 0.7 | 35 610 | 17.7 | 27.0 | 25.9 |
| Mayes | 237 | 1 815 | 9 759 | 4.6 | 54.8 | 13.6 | 57.5 | 7 673 | 20 170 | 42 425 | 1.0 | 0.3 | 40 229 | 18.5 | 26.8 | 24.9 |
| Murray | 169 | 1 856 | 2 942 | 7.7 | 56.7 | 14.9 | 16.0 | 6 333 | 21 348 | 41 403 | 1.2 | 1.4 | 39 914 | 15.3 | 22.2 | 20.4 |
| Muskogee | 431 | 2 137 | 17 878 | 7.8 | 49.0 | 17.3 | 112.6 | 7 991 | 19 565 | 37 990 | -1.1 | 1.4 | 35 443 | 24.1 | 33.7 | 29.0 |
| Noble | 51 | 976 | 2 838 | 1.8 | 51.9 | 18.9 | 19.5 | 9 080 | 21 262 | 43 324 | -5.5 | 0.5 | 43 416 | 14.2 | 20.2 | 18.4 |
| Nowata | 319 | 1 916 | 2 553 | 3.2 | 59.8 | 11.3 | 15.8 | 7 970 | 21 279 | 38 459 | -3.3 | 1.1 | 38 453 | 16.9 | 26.5 | 23.8 |
| Okfuskee | 219 | 2 191 | 2 735 | 6.4 | 59.3 | 11.3 | 18.0 | 8 345 | 15 187 | 34 418 | 4.8 | 0.2 | 31 150 | 24.7 | 31.9 | 30.1 |
| Oklahoma | 669 | 4 974 | 189 794 | 14.7 | 39.9 | 29.1 | 915.4 | 7 772 | 26 197 | 44 413 | -6.2 | 3.6 | 43 101 | 19.2 | 26.1 | 22.9 |
| Okmulgee | 279 | 2 287 | 9 997 | 4.0 | 53.5 | 13.6 | 58.2 | 8 230 | 19 683 | 39 324 | 5.3 | 0.8 | 35 226 | 23.6 | 32.8 | 29.6 |
| Osage | 344 | 2 201 | 11 613 | 11.9 | 52.1 | 17.6 | 31.4 | 8 805 | 21 797 | 42 847 | -8.0 | 1.3 | 43 170 | 18.2 | 24.4 | 21.7 |
| Ottawa | 230 | 2 277 | 7 711 | 5.7 | 53.3 | 13.0 | 46.6 | 7 678 | 18 226 | 36 931 | -0.6 | 0.7 | 34 431 | 20.7 | 30.5 | 28.4 |
| Pawnee | 173 | 1 534 | 3 736 | 7.7 | 54.5 | 17.2 | 23.7 | 7 603 | 20 279 | 41 832 | -2.1 | 1.5 | 41 938 | 16.2 | 24.8 | 23.0 |
| Payne | 179 | 2 710 | 31 465 | 4.9 | 38.1 | 34.4 | 86.3 | 8 282 | 20 284 | 35 716 | -7.9 | 2.0 | 37 075 | 23.4 | 24.0 | 22.1 |
| Pittsburg | 212 | 3 106 | 9 439 | 10.6 | 55.0 | 15.2 | 64.7 | 8 094 | 22 060 | 41 317 | 6.7 | 2.4 | 41 712 | 17.4 | 23.4 | 21.0 |
| Pontotoc | 525 | 2 317 | 9 913 | 7.7 | 45.8 | 27.3 | 58.1 | 8 363 | 22 238 | 40 641 | 11.7 | 2.0 | 40 378 | 18.2 | 24.8 | 24.2 |
| Pottawatomie | 455 | 3 878 | 18 148 | 15.9 | 52.2 | 16.7 | 103.1 | 7 681 | 20 700 | 41 332 | -3.0 | 1.5 | 41 520 | 18.5 | 27.5 | 25.3 |
| Pushmataha | 265 | 1 719 | 2 262 | 6.6 | 60.9 | 11.4 | 20.8 | 9 111 | 16 583 | 29 053 | -2.8 | 0.6 | 30 190 | 26.4 | 39.4 | 36.9 |
| Roger Mills | 163 | 1 438 | 797 | 1.5 | 47.1 | 21.2 | 11.3 | 13 998 | 28 350 | 54 352 | 33.8 | 5.0 | 50 761 | 13.2 | 18.9 | 17.6 |
| Rogers | 184 | 1 411 | 23 352 | 11.9 | 44.2 | 22.2 | 103.3 | 7 201 | 26 400 | 58 434 | -2.7 | 2.6 | 54 974 | 10.1 | 14.3 | 12.9 |
| Seminole | 248 | 3 153 | 6 346 | 5.4 | 57.6 | 13.6 | 41.6 | 8 084 | 18 262 | 33 799 | -2.1 | 0.9 | 32 976 | 21.3 | 30.6 | 28.2 |
| Sequoyah | 315 | 2 047 | 10 558 | 5.2 | 59.7 | 12.8 | 66.0 | 7 645 | 18 991 | 38 292 | 2.7 | 1.1 | 36 080 | 20.8 | 32.4 | 30.3 |
| Stephens | 242 | 2 728 | 10 320 | 7.4 | 56.5 | 17.0 | 63.5 | 7 690 | 23 080 | 45 030 | 8.6 | 1.5 | 43 765 | 15.3 | 23.6 | 23.4 |
| Texas | 158 | 1 802 | 5 379 | 8.9 | 55.0 | 19.9 | 34.6 | 8 030 | 22 051 | 46 631 | -3.7 | 1.6 | 44 550 | 14.4 | 20.6 | 18.0 |
| Tillman | 371 | 2 104 | 1 842 | 6.5 | 60.8 | 15.5 | 23.4 | 15 092 | 16 541 | 31 437 | -6.2 | 0.1 | 32 122 | 22.7 | 32.7 | 28.9 |
| Tulsa | 735 | 4 380 | 157 757 | 19.2 | 38.5 | 29.2 | 880.9 | 7 693 | 27 425 | 47 005 | -8.9 | 3.7 | 46 497 | 15.0 | 21.0 | 19.1 |
| Wagoner | 273 | 2 232 | 18 968 | 11.0 | 43.8 | 21.9 | 47.3 | 6 991 | 24 976 | 56 819 | 0.8 | 2.0 | 52 717 | 12.8 | 17.5 | 16.4 |
| Washington | 266 | 2 692 | 11 636 | 12.1 | 45.1 | 26.1 | 65.0 | 7 892 | 28 045 | 47 144 | -2.5 | 3.8 | 47 645 | 15.6 | 24.1 | 20.9 |
| Washita | 77 | 570 | 2 659 | 9.3 | 57.8 | 16.4 | 17.7 | 8 027 | 22 781 | 44 331 | 11.1 | 0.9 | 45 374 | 14.2 | 22.9 | 21.3 |
| Woods | 89 | 1 014 | 2 456 | 10.5 | 43.8 | 27.0 | 12.1 | 9 242 | 22 935 | 47 255 | 21.0 | 1.3 | 38 688 | 18.8 | 23.1 | 22.5 |
| Woodward | 128 | 3 227 | 3 994 | 8.6 | 52.9 | 17.5 | 28.3 | 7 834 | 24 735 | 51 087 | 12.7 | 2.5 | 48 420 | 13.7 | 19.8 | 16.4 |
| **OREGON** | 248 | 3 115 | 946 080 | 15.0 | 36.3 | 29.0 | 5 391.6 | 9 603 | 26 561 | 49 850 | -9.8 | 3.1 | 46 876 | 17.3 | 23.4 | 21.5 |
| Baker | 25 | 1 319 | 3 242 | 9.0 | 45.1 | 19.8 | 22.1 | 9 376 | 22 115 | 40 989 | 0.0 | 1.6 | 36 877 | 20.0 | 32.7 | 27.4 |
| Benton | 120 | 2 603 | 32 263 | 7.6 | 22.3 | 47.4 | 80.8 | 9 026 | 26 370 | 47 716 | -15.6 | 3.7 | 46 272 | 21.8 | 17.1 | 14.4 |
| Clackamas | 98 | 2 382 | 92 534 | 16.9 | 32.2 | 31.6 | 510.1 | 8 703 | 32 382 | 63 790 | -9.3 | 5.3 | 58 496 | 11.0 | 15.9 | 14.4 |
| Clatsop | 96 | 3 021 | 8 424 | 7.8 | 37.8 | 22.1 | 50.8 | 10 275 | 25 395 | 43 670 | -10.9 | 1.8 | 43 544 | 18.6 | 27.6 | 24.3 |
| Columbia | 96 | 1 008 | 11 796 | 10.9 | 46.3 | 16.8 | 69.8 | 8 400 | 25 440 | 56 270 | -9.0 | 1.4 | 55 646 | 12.3 | 17.4 | 14.5 |
| Coos | 255 | 3 328 | 12 107 | 9.3 | 43.5 | 18.5 | 87.4 | 10 272 | 21 771 | 37 789 | -11.3 | 1.2 | 36 567 | 19.8 | 29.2 | 26.5 |
| Crook | 198 | 1 774 | 4 550 | 13.9 | 49.7 | 15.7 | 25.0 | 8 037 | 22 043 | 45 004 | -5.3 | 0.9 | 37 473 | 18.6 | 28.3 | 24.5 |
| Curry | 84 | 1 686 | 3 556 | 13.3 | 40.8 | 19.6 | 24.7 | 10 043 | 24 190 | 39 787 | -2.2 | 0.9 | 39 958 | 17.9 | 26.3 | 23.8 |
| Deschutes | 331 | 3 089 | 35 174 | 15.2 | 31.1 | 29.8 | 219.4 | 9 055 | 27 965 | 52 962 | -6.3 | 3.1 | 47 924 | 13.8 | 20.2 | 18.7 |
| Douglas | 108 | 2 697 | 22 706 | 10.7 | 46.4 | 15.7 | 152.3 | 10 264 | 21 440 | 40 501 | -9.7 | 1.1 | 38 196 | 18.1 | 28.1 | 25.1 |
| Gilliam | 53 | 899 | 307 | 5.5 | 42.1 | 18.1 | 6.1 | 24 720 | 25 629 | 42 260 | -6.9 | 1.0 | 49 378 | 11.8 | 18.4 | 17.2 |
| Grant | 27 | 797 | 1 409 | 10.0 | 45.9 | 17.0 | 15.6 | 15 730 | 22 062 | 34 367 | -21.8 | 1.6 | 37 191 | 17.2 | 27.9 | 24.3 |
| Harney | 93 | 2 240 | 1 547 | 8.9 | 47.4 | 16.4 | 15.6 | 12 091 | 22 228 | 38 702 | -7.4 | 0.2 | 35 141 | 18.6 | 29.7 | 25.7 |
| Hood River | 62 | 956 | 5 235 | 6.7 | 44.5 | 26.5 | 39.9 | 9 909 | 25 030 | 54 109 | 4.6 | 3.6 | 48 516 | 14.7 | 23.2 | 20.3 |
| Jackson | 295 | 3 425 | 45 575 | 10.6 | 39.7 | 23.7 | 262.8 | 9 334 | 24 263 | 43 386 | -11.9 | 2.0 | 40 013 | 19.7 | 27.3 | 24.0 |
| Jefferson | 87 | 2 045 | 4 907 | 10.5 | 52.0 | 16.5 | 39.0 | 10 842 | 20 300 | 42 867 | -11.4 | 0.8 | 40 910 | 20.7 | 33.3 | 30.6 |
| Josephine | 207 | 3 248 | 17 033 | 10.0 | 43.9 | 16.8 | 102.5 | 9 375 | 21 535 | 37 824 | -10.3 | 1.8 | 36 269 | 20.8 | 31.8 | 29.2 |
| Klamath | 204 | 2 194 | 16 101 | 10.4 | 44.5 | 19.4 | 92.9 | 9 485 | 22 169 | 41 787 | -1.9 | 1.6 | 36 765 | 23.0 | 30.8 | 27.9 |
| Lake | NA | NA | 1 445 | 2.8 | 48.1 | 17.7 | 13.1 | 11 702 | 22 151 | 36 583 | -8.2 | 0.8 | 35 517 | 20.6 | 30.1 | 26.5 |
| Lane | 282 | 3 556 | 94 306 | 11.6 | 35.0 | 27.8 | 448.6 | 9 720 | 24 105 | 42 621 | -14.5 | 2.2 | 40 689 | 21.1 | 23.5 | 21.1 |
| Lincoln | 383 | 2 811 | 7 932 | 13.3 | 37.5 | 24.4 | 48.0 | 9 258 | 24 799 | 41 764 | -5.6 | 1.0 | 40 507 | 16.3 | 26.9 | 24.3 |
| Linn | 92 | 2 955 | 28 328 | 11.2 | 43.8 | 16.7 | 172.6 | 8 153 | 22 255 | 46 872 | -7.5 | 1.1 | 42 836 | 19.2 | 27.7 | 24.0 |
| Malheur | 190 | 3 599 | 8 479 | 8.7 | 50.8 | 14.2 | 56.7 | 11 119 | 16 703 | 39 013 | -4.5 | 1.0 | 36 039 | 24.5 | 35.1 | 33.6 |
| Marion | 224 | 2 804 | 80 678 | 15.3 | 44.4 | 20.7 | 600.2 | 10 010 | 22 192 | 46 191 | -15.1 | 2.0 | 44 275 | 20.5 | 30.6 | 29.2 |

1. Data for serious crimes have not been adjusted for underreporting; this may affect comparability between geographic areas and over time. 2. Per 100,000 population estimated by the FBI. 3. All persons 3 years old and over enrolled in nursery school through college. 4. Persons 25 years old and over. 5. Elementary and secondary education expenditures. 6. Based on population estimated by the American Community Survey, 2007–2011.

# Table B. States and Counties — **Personal Income**

| | Personal income, 2011 | | | | | | | | | | | | |
|---|---|---|---|---|---|---|---|---|---|---|---|---|---|
| | | | Per capita[1] | | | | | Transfer payments (mil dol) | | | | | |
| | | | | | | | | | Government payments to individuals | | | | |
| STATE County | Total (mil dol) | Percent change, 2010–2011 | Dollars | Rank | Wages and salaries[2] (mil dol) | Proprietors' income (mil dol) | Dividends, interest, and rent (mil dol) | Total | Total | Social Security | Medical payments | Income mainte-nance | Unemploy-ment insurance |
| | 62 | 63 | 64 | 65 | 66 | 67 | 68 | 69 | 70 | 71 | 72 | 73 | 74 |
| OKLAHOMA—Cont'd | | | | | | | | | | | | | |
| Kiowa | 281 | 4.9 | 29 867 | 2 314 | 109 | 21 | 45 | 89 | 87 | 29 | 40 | 10 | 1 |
| Latimer | 362 | 4.9 | 32 434 | 1 791 | 209 | 28 | 42 | 108 | 106 | 32 | 39 | 12 | 3 |
| Le Flore | 1 388 | 2.3 | 27 423 | 2 699 | 581 | 105 | 148 | 473 | 462 | 136 | 206 | 59 | 10 |
| Lincoln | 1 014 | 5.3 | 29 695 | 2 341 | 309 | 85 | 117 | 241 | 233 | 91 | 89 | 27 | 5 |
| Logan | 1 635 | 10.8 | 38 467 | 912 | 328 | 247 | 196 | 271 | 261 | 95 | 101 | 28 | 6 |
| Love | 369 | 5.8 | 39 308 | 821 | 184 | 15 | 37 | 79 | 77 | 28 | 32 | 9 | 1 |
| McClain | 1 524 | 9.8 | 43 239 | 491 | 359 | 62 | 153 | 237 | 229 | 86 | 89 | 22 | 5 |
| McCurtain | 936 | 4.1 | 28 209 | 2 584 | 466 | 101 | 101 | 330 | 323 | 94 | 151 | 50 | 9 |
| McIntosh | 610 | 6.2 | 29 949 | 2 299 | 167 | 48 | 78 | 233 | 229 | 81 | 97 | 23 | 4 |
| Major | 290 | 16.7 | 37 922 | 981 | 120 | 58 | 46 | 55 | 53 | 22 | 22 | 4 | 1 |
| Marshall | 438 | 6.1 | 27 278 | 2 719 | 183 | 41 | 54 | 143 | 140 | 49 | 64 | 14 | 2 |
| Mayes | 1 186 | 3.3 | 28 643 | 2 515 | 536 | 71 | 163 | 341 | 332 | 121 | 135 | 41 | 8 |
| Murray | 486 | 7.2 | 35 796 | 1 251 | 265 | 27 | 62 | 114 | 111 | 40 | 46 | 11 | 2 |
| Muskogee | 2 246 | 4.2 | 31 639 | 1 971 | 1 507 | 150 | 302 | 669 | 653 | 195 | 278 | 84 | 13 |
| Noble | 357 | 7.6 | 30 858 | 2 132 | 219 | 27 | 55 | 88 | 86 | 32 | 39 | 8 | 2 |
| Nowata | 310 | 6.9 | 29 210 | 2 422 | 78 | 28 | 45 | 89 | 87 | 33 | 35 | 9 | 2 |
| Okfuskee | 294 | 6.2 | 23 822 | 3 035 | 95 | 33 | 35 | 112 | 109 | 30 | 55 | 14 | 2 |
| Oklahoma | 31 111 | 7.2 | 42 480 | 543 | 26 910 | 4 844 | 4 916 | 5 107 | 4 946 | 1 548 | 2 075 | 695 | 114 |
| Okmulgee | 1 181 | 3.6 | 29 574 | 2 368 | 443 | 59 | 145 | 381 | 372 | 117 | 161 | 48 | 9 |
| Osage | 1 684 | 6.2 | 35 513 | 1 290 | 314 | 197 | 186 | 313 | 302 | 127 | 96 | 37 | 11 |
| Ottawa | 1 025 | 3.4 | 32 179 | 1 846 | 504 | 57 | 140 | 324 | 317 | 106 | 139 | 38 | 6 |
| Pawnee | 516 | 4.6 | 30 823 | 2 138 | 176 | 39 | 66 | 143 | 139 | 52 | 60 | 14 | 3 |
| Payne | 2 523 | 4.5 | 32 356 | 1 812 | 1 632 | 244 | 395 | 451 | 434 | 148 | 170 | 46 | 11 |
| Pittsburg | 1 514 | 4.0 | 33 191 | 1 674 | 950 | 94 | 230 | 375 | 365 | 122 | 157 | 41 | 8 |
| Pontotoc | 1 302 | 6.9 | 34 445 | 1 444 | 849 | 80 | 193 | 331 | 322 | 97 | 143 | 37 | 6 |
| Pottawatomie | 2 345 | 6.1 | 33 366 | 1 638 | 940 | 210 | 318 | 537 | 521 | 175 | 209 | 73 | 11 |
| Pushmataha | 330 | 4.6 | 28 790 | 2 489 | 117 | 36 | 38 | 125 | 122 | 37 | 57 | 15 | 2 |
| Roger Mills | 135 | 13.6 | 36 470 | 1 143 | 54 | 15 | 35 | 24 | 23 | 9 | 10 | 2 | 0 |
| Rogers | 3 230 | 5.5 | 36 826 | 1 098 | 1 372 | 254 | 368 | 605 | 585 | 226 | 228 | 54 | 14 |
| Seminole | 774 | 5.8 | 30 602 | 2 176 | 350 | 53 | 130 | 239 | 233 | 69 | 103 | 34 | 5 |
| Sequoyah | 1 171 | 2.5 | 27 649 | 2 662 | 348 | 90 | 143 | 397 | 387 | 120 | 169 | 57 | 9 |
| Stephens | 1 733 | 9.4 | 38 344 | 930 | 836 | 320 | 270 | 354 | 344 | 133 | 137 | 35 | 7 |
| Texas | 729 | 10.8 | 34 214 | 1 483 | 421 | 145 | 97 | 101 | 96 | 35 | 39 | 12 | 2 |
| Tillman | 200 | -9.8 | 24 853 | 2 977 | 88 | 4 | 31 | 70 | 68 | 22 | 30 | 10 | 1 |
| Tulsa | 28 579 | 8.5 | 46 804 | 308 | 20 255 | 5 381 | 4 958 | 4 237 | 4 102 | 1 436 | 1 714 | 485 | 109 |
| Wagoner | 2 496 | 7.1 | 33 686 | 1 565 | 341 | 60 | 298 | 447 | 431 | 180 | 152 | 44 | 12 |
| Washington | 2 272 | 7.4 | 44 131 | 434 | 1 224 | 305 | 527 | 416 | 405 | 166 | 158 | 38 | 9 |
| Washita | 364 | 7.1 | 31 487 | 2 004 | 113 | 31 | 59 | 84 | 81 | 29 | 37 | 7 | 1 |
| Woods | 311 | 17.4 | 35 404 | 1 310 | 161 | 38 | 66 | 63 | 61 | 22 | 25 | 5 | 1 |
| Woodward | 827 | 16.3 | 41 287 | 634 | 535 | 149 | 128 | 129 | 124 | 49 | 53 | 12 | 3 |
| OREGON | 145 300 | 5.4 | 37 527 | X | 93 001 | 11 371 | 26 016 | 29 487 | 28 630 | 9 747 | 10 782 | 3 324 | 2 011 |
| Baker | 489 | 4.5 | 30 608 | 2 174 | 220 | 24 | 118 | 151 | 148 | 58 | 56 | 16 | 7 |
| Benton | 3 323 | 4.5 | 38 677 | 883 | 2 136 | 205 | 795 | 469 | 450 | 186 | 124 | 41 | 23 |
| Clackamas | 17 457 | 5.6 | 45 459 | 340 | 8 119 | 1 283 | 3 115 | 2 436 | 2 352 | 984 | 733 | 191 | 203 |
| Clatsop | 1 301 | 6.4 | 35 021 | 1 368 | 768 | 116 | 228 | 316 | 308 | 117 | 107 | 31 | 18 |
| Columbia | 1 675 | 4.9 | 33 907 | 1 530 | 445 | 62 | 240 | 401 | 390 | 146 | 145 | 38 | 28 |
| Coos | 2 037 | 5.1 | 32 443 | 1 790 | 979 | 153 | 379 | 661 | 647 | 236 | 248 | 74 | 31 |
| Crook | 635 | 5.3 | 30 496 | 2 199 | 288 | 50 | 126 | 209 | 204 | 76 | 80 | 21 | 15 |
| Curry | 716 | 4.6 | 31 907 | 1 904 | 266 | 54 | 186 | 246 | 241 | 104 | 88 | 19 | 10 |
| Deschutes | 5 946 | 4.9 | 37 084 | 1 068 | 2 923 | 751 | 1 383 | 1 291 | 1 256 | 469 | 444 | 122 | 120 |
| Douglas | 3 356 | 3.9 | 31 222 | 2 062 | 1 640 | 208 | 601 | 1 115 | 1 091 | 399 | 390 | 114 | 64 |
| Gilliam | 70 | 5.0 | 36 126 | 1 197 | 53 | 6 | 15 | 15 | 15 | 6 | 5 | 1 | 1 |
| Grant | 226 | 3.5 | 30 473 | 2 205 | 109 | 10 | 49 | 68 | 66 | 26 | 25 | 6 | 5 |
| Harney | 213 | 3.3 | 28 862 | 2 474 | 104 | 16 | 43 | 62 | 61 | 23 | 22 | 7 | 4 |
| Hood River | 797 | 4.9 | 35 441 | 1 305 | 497 | 58 | 184 | 139 | 134 | 49 | 50 | 15 | 10 |
| Jackson | 7 087 | 4.0 | 34 602 | 1 431 | 3 606 | 685 | 1 512 | 1 771 | 1 725 | 634 | 637 | 196 | 117 |
| Jefferson | 607 | 4.7 | 27 875 | 2 630 | 275 | 34 | 99 | 191 | 186 | 61 | 75 | 27 | 10 |
| Josephine | 2 498 | 4.2 | 30 103 | 2 269 | 989 | 191 | 508 | 888 | 869 | 315 | 326 | 103 | 46 |
| Klamath | 1 986 | 4.5 | 29 961 | 2 297 | 1 027 | 121 | 341 | 646 | 631 | 200 | 245 | 74 | 35 |
| Lake | 255 | 10.2 | 32 193 | 1 842 | 115 | 42 | 48 | 67 | 65 | 25 | 23 | 7 | 4 |
| Lane | 12 214 | 4.6 | 34 561 | 1 433 | 6 912 | 795 | 2 468 | 2 888 | 2 810 | 968 | 1 049 | 319 | 180 |
| Lincoln | 1 572 | 4.8 | 34 228 | 1 481 | 748 | 126 | 334 | 440 | 430 | 181 | 152 | 42 | 21 |
| Linn | 3 553 | 4.6 | 30 083 | 2 276 | 1 978 | 183 | 587 | 1 082 | 1 055 | 338 | 433 | 124 | 73 |
| Malheur | 773 | 4.3 | 24 892 | 2 974 | 526 | 53 | 138 | 252 | 245 | 72 | 104 | 38 | 8 |
| Marion | 10 791 | 4.0 | 33 841 | 1 542 | 6 591 | 1 026 | 1 669 | 2 626 | 2 555 | 741 | 1 084 | 366 | 164 |

1. Based on the resident population estimated as of July 1 of the year shown.  2. Includes supplements to wages and salaries.

# Table B. States and Counties — Earnings, Social Security, and Housing

| STATE County | Earnings, 2011 Total (mil dol) | Farm | Goods-related[1] Total | Manu-facturing | Service-related and health Infor-mation and profes-sional and technical services | Retail trade | Finance, insur-ance, and real estate | Health care and social services | Govern-ment | Social Security beneficiaries, December 2011 Number | Rate[2] | Supple-mental Security Income recipients, December 2011 | Housing units, 2010 Total | Percent change, 2000–2010 |
|---|---|---|---|---|---|---|---|---|---|---|---|---|---|---|
| | 75 | 76 | 77 | 78 | 79 | 80 | 81 | 82 | 83 | 84 | 85 | 86 | 87 | 88 |
| **OKLAHOMA—Cont'd** | | | | | | | | | | | | | | |
| Kiowa | 129 | 5.4 | D | D | 3.1 | 7.3 | 4.9 | 7.1 | 29.8 | 2 490 | 264 | 377 | 5 216 | -1.7 |
| Latimer | 237 | 2.4 | D | D | D | 3.5 | 1.9 | 3.3 | 25.8 | 2 800 | 251 | 410 | 4 979 | 5.7 |
| Le Flore | 685 | 4.7 | 21.9 | 8.7 | D | 7.6 | 3.2 | D | 36.2 | 11 735 | 232 | 2 090 | 21 448 | 6.5 |
| Lincoln | 394 | -0.2 | D | 9.2 | 4.2 | 8.3 | 9.1 | D | 22.1 | 7 600 | 223 | 806 | 15 208 | 10.9 |
| Logan | 575 | -0.1 | 23.5 | 4.1 | D | 7.3 | 11.1 | D | 18.8 | 7 355 | 173 | 712 | 17 195 | 23.7 |
| Love | 200 | 3.2 | D | 2.4 | 1.6 | 4.4 | D | D | 63.9 | 2 245 | 239 | 232 | 4 539 | 11.6 |
| McClain | 421 | 1.3 | 27.9 | 2.3 | 5.7 | 14.1 | 4.3 | D | 21.4 | 6 735 | 191 | 571 | 13 996 | 25.1 |
| McCurtain | 566 | 5.1 | 28.6 | 21.1 | D | 6.8 | 2.5 | D | 22.0 | 8 190 | 247 | 1 678 | 15 533 | 0.7 |
| McIntosh | 214 | -1.5 | 10.8 | 2.3 | 4.8 | 17.5 | 4.6 | 12.2 | 25.8 | 6 695 | 329 | 787 | 13 350 | 5.6 |
| Major | 178 | 20.0 | 33.8 | 4.3 | 2.4 | 5.3 | 5.6 | 3.8 | 12.4 | 1 775 | 232 | 96 | 3 671 | 3.7 |
| Marshall | 225 | 1.5 | D | 31.0 | D | 6.6 | 5.4 | 9.2 | 17.0 | 3 995 | 249 | 453 | 10 006 | 17.5 |
| Mayes | 607 | 1.2 | D | 24.8 | D | 10.8 | 3.0 | 6.0 | 22.8 | 9 445 | 228 | 1 210 | 19 239 | 10.4 |
| Murray | 291 | -0.9 | 18.1 | 3.0 | D | 7.3 | 3.1 | D | 45.1 | 3 295 | 243 | 330 | 6 746 | 4.1 |
| Muskogee | 1 656 | 0.0 | 21.0 | 15.6 | 2.8 | 7.4 | 3.3 | D | 33.3 | 16 065 | 226 | 2 909 | 30 908 | 4.5 |
| Noble | 246 | 5.5 | D | D | D | 4.2 | 3.5 | D | 24.5 | 2 540 | 219 | 245 | 5 341 | 5.1 |
| Nowata | 106 | 9.7 | 24.6 | 13.7 | D | 4.0 | 4.1 | 11.4 | 23.1 | 2 710 | 255 | 264 | 4 828 | 2.6 |
| Okfuskee | 128 | 9.1 | 14.4 | 4.6 | D | 6.8 | D | 10.8 | 42.9 | 2 715 | 220 | 602 | 5 282 | 3.3 |
| Oklahoma | 31 754 | 0.0 | 21.8 | 6.4 | 9.0 | 5.8 | 6.8 | 12.0 | 21.6 | 118 920 | 162 | 19 083 | 319 828 | 8.4 |
| Okmulgee | 502 | 1.8 | 23.7 | 18.9 | 2.5 | 8.7 | 3.7 | D | 36.1 | 9 635 | 241 | 1 619 | 17 891 | 3.3 |
| Osage | 511 | 1.8 | 32.3 | 4.6 | 5.1 | 6.7 | 3.4 | D | 25.0 | 9 785 | 206 | 1 105 | 21 143 | 12.3 |
| Ottawa | 562 | 2.5 | 17.9 | 13.5 | 1.9 | 6.8 | 3.2 | D | 40.5 | 8 710 | 273 | 1 352 | 14 060 | -5.3 |
| Pawnee | 215 | 4.7 | 16.3 | 3.6 | D | 7.9 | 3.3 | 10.7 | 30.6 | 4 125 | 247 | 408 | 7 745 | 3.8 |
| Payne | 1 876 | 0.3 | 19.2 | 7.3 | 5.3 | 8.2 | 3.9 | 5.5 | 43.3 | 11 410 | 146 | 1 260 | 33 991 | 15.9 |
| Pittsburg | 1 043 | -0.2 | 24.4 | 12.8 | D | 7.2 | 6.2 | D | 36.8 | 10 465 | 229 | 1 467 | 22 634 | 5.2 |
| Pontotoc | 929 | 0.2 | 15.2 | 7.7 | 7.9 | 6.3 | 4.8 | D | 39.1 | 8 130 | 215 | 1 216 | 16 595 | 6.5 |
| Pottawatomie | 1 150 | 0.7 | 23.3 | 14.0 | D | 8.2 | 3.8 | 11.8 | 24.2 | 14 845 | 211 | 1 971 | 29 139 | 6.7 |
| Pushmataha | 153 | 0.0 | D | 5.1 | D | 9.3 | 4.7 | 15.7 | 32.0 | 3 365 | 293 | 605 | 6 110 | 5.4 |
| Roger Mills | 69 | 8.9 | 19.5 | 0.4 | D | 5.5 | D | D | 30.9 | 780 | 211 | 82 | 1 905 | 8.9 |
| Rogers | 1 627 | 0.1 | 34.2 | 21.8 | D | 5.5 | 3.7 | 7.5 | 21.7 | 16 495 | 188 | 1 243 | 35 160 | 28.0 |
| Seminole | 403 | -0.6 | D | 14.1 | 1.9 | 6.3 | 2.7 | D | 25.3 | 5 980 | 236 | 1 119 | 11 642 | 4.4 |
| Sequoyah | 438 | 1.2 | 5.7 | 1.4 | 6.4 | 12.3 | 3.8 | D | 35.9 | 10 365 | 245 | 1 954 | 18 656 | 10.1 |
| Stephens | 1 156 | 0.4 | 48.2 | 14.1 | D | 7.4 | 5.6 | D | 9.8 | 10 490 | 232 | 1 112 | 20 658 | 4.0 |
| Texas | 566 | 21.0 | 27.4 | 19.6 | 6.1 | 5.1 | 2.7 | 2.6 | 15.5 | 2 640 | 124 | 193 | 8 208 | 2.4 |
| Tillman | 91 | -4.4 | D | D | D | 5.0 | D | 4.4 | 37.4 | 1 925 | 239 | 320 | 4 077 | -6.1 |
| Tulsa | 25 636 | 0.0 | 26.7 | 11.5 | 9.4 | 6.1 | 7.2 | 11.5 | 8.3 | 103 015 | 169 | 13 600 | 268 426 | 10.0 |
| Wagoner | 401 | 1.9 | 29.7 | 19.0 | D | 10.6 | 3.8 | D | 23.9 | 13 310 | 180 | 1 221 | 29 694 | 28.1 |
| Washington | 1 529 | 0.2 | 40.3 | 3.8 | 3.8 | 8.2 | 3.9 | D | 8.6 | 12 330 | 240 | 1 055 | 23 451 | 5.4 |
| Washita | 143 | 8.3 | 21.7 | 3.0 | 7.7 | 5.2 | 7.6 | 4.7 | 26.9 | 2 445 | 211 | 229 | 5 479 | 0.5 |
| Woods | 199 | 8.6 | 25.7 | 2.7 | 4.0 | 7.9 | 5.2 | D | 28.5 | 1 695 | 193 | 105 | 4 478 | -0.3 |
| Woodward | 684 | 4.1 | 41.4 | 5.7 | D | 5.9 | 3.9 | 5.3 | 9.8 | 3 750 | 187 | 284 | 8 838 | 6.0 |
| OREGON | 104 372 | 1.3 | 18.6 | 12.9 | 10.0 | 6.7 | 6.4 | 12.7 | 17.4 | 734 841 | 190 | 78 143 | 1 675 562 | 15.3 |
| Baker | 244 | 2.4 | D | 10.3 | D | 9.0 | 4.1 | 13.9 | 26.8 | 4 735 | 296 | 413 | 8 826 | 5.0 |
| Benton | 2 341 | 1.0 | 17.2 | 14.1 | 10.5 | 4.8 | 3.0 | 15.1 | 30.2 | 13 430 | 156 | 964 | 36 245 | 13.3 |
| Clackamas | 9 402 | 1.4 | 21.0 | 13.1 | 11.1 | 7.3 | 6.9 | 13.4 | 10.8 | 69 330 | 182 | 4 781 | 156 945 | 14.6 |
| Clatsop | 884 | 2.0 | D | 15.4 | D | 9.6 | 3.9 | 13.7 | 20.5 | 8 835 | 238 | 766 | 21 546 | 9.5 |
| Columbia | 506 | 1.0 | 23.4 | 16.9 | 4.7 | 8.8 | 5.5 | 8.2 | 22.6 | 10 640 | 215 | 889 | 20 698 | 17.8 |
| Coos | 1 132 | 1.6 | 12.6 | 7.7 | 4.4 | 9.0 | 3.6 | 11.7 | 30.0 | 18 545 | 295 | 2 168 | 30 593 | 4.6 |
| Crook | 338 | -0.6 | 15.6 | 9.2 | 2.8 | 5.3 | 2.5 | 9.4 | 22.0 | 5 885 | 282 | 408 | 10 202 | 23.4 |
| Curry | 320 | 3.0 | D | 9.8 | 4.7 | 11.0 | 5.4 | D | 22.4 | 8 135 | 363 | 527 | 12 613 | 10.6 |
| Deschutes | 3 674 | -0.3 | 14.7 | 6.2 | 11.7 | 9.3 | 8.7 | 18.8 | 14.2 | 34 545 | 215 | 2 010 | 80 139 | 46.8 |
| Douglas | 1 848 | 0.4 | 19.0 | 13.5 | 4.5 | 7.5 | 4.3 | 13.9 | 25.0 | 31 395 | 292 | 2 870 | 48 915 | 13.0 |
| Gilliam | 59 | 12.6 | D | D | D | 2.1 | 1.0 | 3.3 | 18.7 | 485 | 250 | 42 | 1 156 | 10.8 |
| Grant | 120 | 0.6 | D | D | 3.3 | 7.5 | D | D | 50.3 | 2 155 | 291 | 157 | 4 344 | 8.5 |
| Harney | 120 | 9.8 | 3.5 | 0.2 | 2.9 | 8.2 | 2.7 | D | 48.5 | 1 870 | 254 | 190 | 3 835 | 8.5 |
| Hood River | 555 | 8.6 | 15.2 | 11.1 | 11.5 | 7.4 | 2.7 | 15.2 | 13.5 | 3 770 | 168 | 254 | 9 271 | 18.6 |
| Jackson | 4 291 | 0.3 | 16.3 | 8.2 | 7.1 | 10.9 | 5.4 | 18.4 | 16.1 | 48 955 | 239 | 4 158 | 90 937 | 20.1 |
| Jefferson | 309 | 7.4 | D | 13.6 | D | 5.3 | 2.2 | 4.8 | 46.0 | 4 860 | 223 | 503 | 9 815 | 18.0 |
| Josephine | 1 180 | -0.4 | D | 10.3 | 5.1 | 11.2 | 6.7 | 20.3 | 15.8 | 24 975 | 301 | 2 409 | 38 001 | 14.3 |
| Klamath | 1 148 | 1.8 | 12.4 | 8.1 | D | 9.1 | 4.1 | 14.3 | 25.7 | 16 015 | 242 | 1 882 | 32 774 | 13.5 |
| Lake | 156 | 18.3 | D | 6.0 | 3.6 | 6.0 | 2.7 | D | 38.4 | 2 100 | 266 | 221 | 4 439 | 11.0 |
| Lane | 7 707 | 0.4 | 15.5 | 9.9 | 8.9 | 8.9 | 5.4 | 16.8 | 20.8 | 73 565 | 208 | 8 092 | 156 112 | 12.3 |
| Lincoln | 873 | 2.0 | D | 8.3 | 4.6 | 10.3 | 4.0 | 12.7 | 25.7 | 13 795 | 300 | 1 219 | 30 610 | 13.8 |
| Linn | 2 161 | 2.8 | D | 24.3 | 3.3 | 6.8 | 2.8 | 11.1 | 16.4 | 26 075 | 221 | 3 069 | 48 821 | 14.8 |
| Malheur | 579 | 5.7 | D | 6.0 | D | 10.4 | 2.9 | 13.4 | 31.1 | 6 240 | 201 | 886 | 11 692 | 4.1 |
| Marion | 7 617 | 2.8 | 11.9 | 6.1 | 5.4 | 6.9 | 6.0 | 17.3 | 29.1 | 57 115 | 179 | 7 328 | 120 948 | 11.8 |

1. Includes mining, construction, and manufacturing.   2. Per 1,000 resident population enumerated in the 2010 census.

# Table B. States and Counties — Housing, Labor Force, and Employment

| STATE County | Housing units, 2007–2011 Occupied units Owner-occupied Total | Percent | Median value[1] | Median owner cost as a percent of income With a mortgage | Without a mortgage[2] | Renter-occupied Median rent[3] | Median rent as a percent of income | Substandard units[4] (percent) | Civilian labor force, 2012 Total | Percent change, 2011–2012 | Unemployment Total | Rate[5] | Civilian employment,[6] 2007–2011 Total | Percent Management, business, science and arts | Construction, production, and maintenance occupations |
|---|---|---|---|---|---|---|---|---|---|---|---|---|---|---|---|
| | 89 | 90 | 91 | 92 | 93 | 94 | 95 | 96 | 97 | 98 | 99 | 100 | 101 | 102 | 103 |
| **OKLAHOMA—Cont'd** | | | | | | | | | | | | | | | |
| Kiowa | 3 876 | 67.9 | 51 200 | 18.9 | 11.5 | 453 | 26.3 | 1.6 | 4 025 | -1.3 | 199 | 4.9 | 4 084 | 29.3 | 29.6 |
| Latimer | 4 216 | 74.1 | 67 600 | 19.6 | 9.9 | 480 | 23.7 | 5.1 | 4 422 | 1.7 | 391 | 8.8 | 4 454 | 30.6 | 32.5 |
| Le Flore | 18 672 | 73.4 | 74 900 | 22.1 | 11.7 | 552 | 25.3 | 3.3 | 20 177 | 0.6 | 1 833 | 9.1 | 19 332 | 23.6 | 35.2 |
| Lincoln | 12 912 | 78.2 | 91 400 | 19.4 | 10.3 | 531 | 29.3 | 4.6 | 14 602 | 1.7 | 749 | 5.1 | 14 392 | 25.1 | 32.7 |
| Logan | 14 553 | 77.0 | 121 700 | 22.0 | 10.6 | 614 | 27.2 | 2.5 | 19 587 | 1.7 | 867 | 4.4 | 18 886 | 31.4 | 25.5 |
| Love | 3 534 | 76.1 | 79 600 | 19.4 | 11.7 | 563 | 23.7 | 3.6 | 5 786 | 1.8 | 214 | 3.7 | 4 240 | 27.0 | 32.5 |
| McClain | 12 205 | 81.2 | 125 800 | 19.4 | 9.9 | 663 | 26.7 | 2.3 | 16 108 | 1.6 | 705 | 4.4 | 15 990 | 31.3 | 27.0 |
| McCurtain | 13 103 | 67.9 | 72 000 | 20.3 | 10.7 | 539 | 30.1 | 4.4 | 15 182 | -2.6 | 1 333 | 8.8 | 12 621 | 24.4 | 35.1 |
| McIntosh | 7 870 | 78.6 | 75 500 | 22.3 | 11.7 | 553 | 33.4 | 3.0 | 8 953 | -0.4 | 712 | 8.0 | 6 758 | 30.1 | 28.2 |
| Major | 3 185 | 80.5 | 78 900 | 18.1 | 9.9 | 518 | 22.5 | 0.8 | 4 372 | -1.6 | 140 | 3.2 | 3 671 | 23.4 | 42.1 |
| Marshall | 5 995 | 78.9 | 79 400 | 20.4 | 11.0 | 586 | 22.4 | 2.5 | 6 768 | 2.2 | 388 | 5.7 | 6 683 | 23.0 | 33.3 |
| Mayes | 16 088 | 73.5 | 90 400 | 20.9 | 10.8 | 591 | 25.6 | 4.8 | 18 566 | 1.1 | 1 126 | 6.1 | 17 354 | 27.9 | 35.7 |
| Murray | 5 092 | 81.0 | 78 500 | 19.9 | 9.9 | 579 | 24.6 | 1.6 | 9 602 | 3.1 | 305 | 3.2 | 5 784 | 29.0 | 30.1 |
| Muskogee | 27 056 | 67.8 | 88 000 | 21.9 | 11.7 | 579 | 31.6 | 2.5 | 31 681 | 0.0 | 2 034 | 6.4 | 28 038 | 30.2 | 30.0 |
| Noble | 4 531 | 74.9 | 77 500 | 19.8 | 10.8 | 577 | 33.0 | 2.8 | 6 011 | 1.6 | 239 | 4.0 | 5 479 | 32.4 | 29.8 |
| Nowata | 4 083 | 79.2 | 72 500 | 19.4 | 12.1 | 538 | 24.8 | 2.8 | 5 115 | -0.7 | 329 | 6.4 | 4 501 | 26.9 | 37.5 |
| Okfuskee | 4 329 | 70.3 | 70 600 | 21.7 | 10.8 | 484 | 31.1 | 2.3 | 4 760 | -0.8 | 343 | 7.2 | 4 307 | 26.5 | 27.3 |
| Oklahoma | 281 570 | 61.0 | 121 900 | 22.2 | 11.1 | 706 | 29.9 | 3.1 | 334 021 | 1.6 | 17 184 | 5.1 | 339 111 | 35.0 | 21.1 |
| Okmulgee | 15 193 | 70.5 | 78 800 | 21.2 | 11.4 | 596 | 27.6 | 2.9 | 15 933 | 0.0 | 1 224 | 7.7 | 16 333 | 28.2 | 28.6 |
| Osage | 18 406 | 79.1 | 92 400 | 19.7 | 11.7 | 519 | 26.0 | 2.7 | 20 434 | 0.7 | 1 248 | 6.1 | 20 378 | 28.3 | 30.4 |
| Ottawa | 12 048 | 74.8 | 80 200 | 20.9 | 10.8 | 553 | 27.7 | 4.3 | 18 594 | 1.2 | 1 088 | 5.9 | 13 489 | 25.7 | 27.4 |
| Pawnee | 6 392 | 76.5 | 81 900 | 20.6 | 11.3 | 568 | 28.3 | 2.7 | 7 301 | 0.3 | 469 | 6.4 | 7 232 | 24.2 | 35.1 |
| Payne | 29 731 | 52.2 | 123 100 | 21.8 | 9.9 | 640 | 36.3 | 1.8 | 36 579 | 2.9 | 1 768 | 4.8 | 37 992 | 36.7 | 19.6 |
| Pittsburg | 18 765 | 71.9 | 84 800 | 18.8 | 10.5 | 612 | 27.4 | 3.3 | 23 921 | -0.1 | 1 302 | 5.4 | 18 141 | 26.9 | 28.7 |
| Pontotoc | 14 775 | 65.3 | 97 800 | 20.0 | 9.9 | 557 | 28.1 | 3.3 | 21 232 | 0.9 | 913 | 4.3 | 17 843 | 33.8 | 23.8 |
| Pottawatomie | 25 295 | 72.6 | 92 500 | 20.7 | 10.1 | 619 | 29.3 | 3.1 | 35 209 | 2.3 | 1 685 | 4.8 | 29 643 | 29.7 | 28.6 |
| Pushmataha | 4 796 | 71.1 | 73 200 | 24.0 | 12.9 | 472 | 28.7 | 3.3 | 5 504 | -1.9 | 331 | 6.0 | 4 408 | 27.9 | 29.1 |
| Roger Mills | 1 350 | 77.1 | 79 700 | 17.5 | 9.9 | 542 | 15.3 | 3.3 | 2 371 | 10.0 | 57 | 2.4 | 1 512 | 32.1 | 36.4 |
| Rogers | 32 056 | 79.2 | 141 300 | 20.8 | 10.1 | 752 | 26.1 | 2.7 | 40 818 | 1.1 | 2 214 | 5.4 | 41 187 | 32.5 | 29.0 |
| Seminole | 9 250 | 72.9 | 69 500 | 20.3 | 10.6 | 491 | 29.6 | 3.7 | 11 258 | 0.4 | 761 | 6.8 | 9 749 | 28.0 | 31.1 |
| Sequoyah | 15 520 | 71.9 | 82 300 | 19.3 | 11.3 | 547 | 28.1 | 3.5 | 17 136 | -0.4 | 1 455 | 8.5 | 16 195 | 25.4 | 34.8 |
| Stephens | 17 809 | 72.5 | 84 300 | 20.1 | 10.2 | 582 | 24.5 | 2.6 | 23 066 | 0.5 | 1 004 | 4.4 | 19 014 | 29.9 | 29.9 |
| Texas | 7 122 | 66.9 | 87 400 | 19.6 | 10.7 | 606 | 20.1 | 7.0 | 7 803 | -0.1 | 364 | 4.7 | 9 834 | 25.8 | 41.2 |
| Tillman | 2 809 | 73.7 | 52 300 | 19.3 | 12.4 | 484 | 27.7 | 2.7 | 3 500 | 1.0 | 165 | 4.7 | 2 963 | 35.0 | 31.9 |
| Tulsa | 239 674 | 62.0 | 129 900 | 21.8 | 11.5 | 714 | 29.3 | 3.1 | 295 221 | 0.9 | 16 136 | 5.5 | 291 850 | 35.4 | 21.4 |
| Wagoner | 26 168 | 83.4 | 137 100 | 21.9 | 10.6 | 713 | 29.5 | 3.1 | 34 818 | 1.1 | 1 895 | 5.4 | 33 361 | 31.2 | 26.4 |
| Washington | 21 371 | 73.5 | 105 600 | 20.1 | 10.6 | 622 | 25.5 | 1.6 | 28 733 | 0.8 | 1 178 | 4.1 | 23 211 | 33.3 | 24.9 |
| Washita | 4 604 | 71.8 | 73 900 | 18.8 | 9.9 | 603 | 18.6 | 2.0 | 6 419 | 1.7 | 219 | 3.4 | 5 149 | 31.7 | 32.5 |
| Woods | 3 570 | 66.5 | 77 600 | 16.8 | 9.9 | 556 | 24.3 | 1.9 | 5 272 | 11.0 | 151 | 2.9 | 4 272 | 30.7 | 23.5 |
| Woodward | 7 558 | 71.7 | 97 600 | 18.1 | 9.9 | 617 | 20.7 | 2.9 | 13 112 | 6.5 | 371 | 2.8 | 9 333 | 26.6 | 36.6 |
| **OREGON** | 1 509 554 | 63.1 | 252 600 | 26.9 | 12.8 | 830 | 31.3 | 3.3 | 1 962 908 | -0.6 | 171 178 | 8.7 | 1 753 398 | 35.6 | 22.0 |
| Baker | 6 997 | 69.2 | 157 600 | 23.2 | 12.1 | 602 | 32.3 | 3.4 | 7 451 | -0.9 | 744 | 10.0 | 6 557 | 32.8 | 22.9 |
| Benton | 33 427 | 57.4 | 268 200 | 24.2 | 11.0 | 757 | 38.7 | 2.4 | 44 422 | -0.7 | 2 728 | 6.1 | 40 603 | 46.4 | 16.0 |
| Clackamas | 144 588 | 70.3 | 326 300 | 27.6 | 13.2 | 913 | 29.4 | 2.7 | 199 576 | 0.0 | 15 752 | 7.9 | 179 274 | 36.9 | 21.1 |
| Clatsop | 15 999 | 62.4 | 261 600 | 29.0 | 12.1 | 759 | 31.0 | 3.1 | 20 664 | -0.7 | 1 598 | 7.7 | 17 468 | 25.1 | 26.1 |
| Columbia | 19 173 | 76.8 | 221 200 | 25.0 | 12.5 | 739 | 31.7 | 2.4 | 24 221 | -0.2 | 2 309 | 9.5 | 20 958 | 28.9 | 32.5 |
| Coos | 27 077 | 66.6 | 194 500 | 25.1 | 13.8 | 690 | 31.4 | 2.3 | 28 165 | -2.0 | 3 012 | 10.7 | 25 235 | 29.8 | 22.8 |
| Crook | 8 741 | 72.9 | 220 400 | 29.9 | 12.6 | 780 | 27.0 | 4.0 | 8 846 | -1.2 | 1 246 | 14.1 | 8 329 | 26.6 | 27.2 |
| Curry | 10 350 | 71.4 | 254 800 | 29.0 | 10.3 | 764 | 37.0 | 2.3 | 9 073 | -1.3 | 1 054 | 11.6 | 8 863 | 23.7 | 24.9 |
| Deschutes | 63 935 | 66.9 | 290 400 | 29.3 | 12.2 | 901 | 30.8 | 3.1 | 78 294 | -1.5 | 8 822 | 11.3 | 71 762 | 35.1 | 21.3 |
| Douglas | 43 895 | 70.0 | 186 400 | 26.1 | 12.1 | 714 | 30.0 | 3.1 | 44 859 | -2.2 | 5 463 | 12.2 | 42 110 | 26.1 | 29.5 |
| Gilliam | 901 | 63.0 | 104 700 | 18.5 | 10.4 | 681 | 26.8 | 1.4 | 1 192 | -2.5 | 88 | 7.4 | 987 | 26.6 | 41.8 |
| Grant | 3 380 | 70.8 | 128 000 | 25.0 | 12.3 | 569 | 23.5 | 1.4 | 3 426 | -2.5 | 458 | 13.4 | 3 062 | 31.8 | 24.0 |
| Harney | 3 290 | 65.2 | 137 700 | 21.3 | 11.5 | 528 | 25.2 | 5.7 | 3 299 | -3.7 | 417 | 12.6 | 3 277 | 38.7 | 23.0 |
| Hood River | 8 204 | 67.6 | 326 900 | 28.0 | 12.1 | 713 | 28.7 | 4.6 | 14 497 | 0.4 | 1 010 | 7.0 | 11 351 | 27.5 | 31.5 |
| Jackson | 83 897 | 61.8 | 262 500 | 29.2 | 14.1 | 844 | 34.8 | 2.8 | 100 207 | -0.8 | 10 871 | 10.8 | 87 663 | 30.9 | 21.7 |
| Jefferson | 7 844 | 67.9 | 182 100 | 29.2 | 12.8 | 691 | 24.8 | 3.9 | 9 459 | 1.6 | 1 151 | 12.2 | 8 417 | 22.2 | 35.7 |
| Josephine | 34 482 | 67.7 | 242 600 | 29.1 | 11.9 | 744 | 36.0 | 3.1 | 34 170 | -1.9 | 4 062 | 11.9 | 30 530 | 26.8 | 25.8 |
| Klamath | 27 378 | 68.5 | 172 800 | 25.7 | 11.9 | 701 | 31.7 | 3.3 | 30 057 | -2.2 | 3 504 | 11.7 | 27 931 | 29.8 | 27.7 |
| Lake | 3 516 | 66.1 | 151 500 | 23.2 | 12.5 | 582 | 26.1 | 3.7 | 3 684 | -2.3 | 473 | 12.8 | 3 324 | 34.8 | 25.8 |
| Lane | 144 806 | 60.2 | 230 900 | 26.9 | 12.7 | 793 | 33.6 | 2.1 | 177 073 | -1.7 | 15 225 | 8.6 | 157 787 | 34.1 | 21.7 |
| Lincoln | 20 769 | 66.4 | 253 100 | 27.3 | 13.3 | 731 | 31.5 | 2.2 | 22 592 | -1.6 | 2 100 | 9.3 | 19 574 | 27.8 | 21.7 |
| Linn | 44 787 | 67.0 | 181 600 | 25.8 | 11.4 | 756 | 29.1 | 2.8 | 54 547 | -1.5 | 5 940 | 10.9 | 49 335 | 26.9 | 30.7 |
| Malheur | 10 243 | 65.7 | 143 600 | 23.0 | 11.4 | 584 | 28.8 | 5.8 | 13 064 | -2.6 | 1 279 | 9.8 | 11 433 | 29.9 | 28.2 |
| Marion | 112 841 | 61.0 | 206 700 | 27.4 | 13.2 | 761 | 31.4 | 5.2 | 154 899 | -1.3 | 14 793 | 9.6 | 133 653 | 30.8 | 27.5 |

1. Specified owner-occupied units. lacking complete plumbing facilities.  2. A value of 9.9 represents 9.9 percent or less.  3. Specified renter-occupied units. A value of 10.0 represents 10 percent or less.  4. Overcrowded or 5. Percent of civilian labor force.  6. Persons 16 years old and over.

# Table B. States and Counties — Nonfarm Employment and Agriculture

| STATE County | Number of establish-ments | Total | Health care and social assistance | Manufac-turing | Retail trade | Finance and insurance | Professional, scientific, and technical services | Total (mil dol) | Average per employee (dollars) | Number | Fewer than 50 acres | 500 acres or more | Farm operators whose principal occu-pation is farming (percent) |
|---|---|---|---|---|---|---|---|---|---|---|---|---|---|
| | 104 | 105 | 106 | 107 | 108 | 109 | 110 | 111 | 112 | 113 | 114 | 115 | 116 |
| **OKLAHOMA—Cont'd** | | | | | | | | | | | | | |
| Kiowa | 208 | 1 731 | 565 | D | 268 | D | 35 | 49 | 28 576 | 682 | 11.7 | 38.3 | 47.9 |
| Latimer | 178 | 1 715 | 374 | D | 282 | D | D | 63 | 36 649 | 760 | 26.3 | 11.8 | 37.4 |
| Le Flore | 814 | 8 124 | 2 257 | 641 | 1 535 | 396 | 273 | 236 | 29 004 | 2 043 | 31.8 | 9.1 | 45.0 |
| Lincoln | 568 | 5 316 | 790 | 634 | 772 | 396 | 114 | 166 | 31 179 | 2 300 | 25.4 | 8.4 | 36.3 |
| Logan | 725 | 6 126 | 1 232 | 371 | 932 | 229 | 169 | 163 | 26 563 | 1 241 | 28.0 | 14.4 | 36.7 |
| Love | 147 | 3 484 | 148 | 140 | 156 | D | D | 96 | 27 613 | 696 | 24.0 | 17.0 | 41.8 |
| McClain | 779 | 6 898 | 838 | 306 | 1 451 | 248 | 245 | 224 | 32 523 | 1 318 | 38.1 | 12.9 | 40.1 |
| McCurtain | 545 | 8 113 | 1 567 | 2 410 | 1 135 | 233 | D | 226 | 27 864 | 1 796 | 33.9 | 7.3 | 41.9 |
| McIntosh | 343 | 3 079 | 782 | 94 | 839 | 142 | 114 | 81 | 26 387 | 1 042 | 27.1 | 10.3 | 41.2 |
| Major | 255 | 2 061 | D | 59 | 271 | 78 | 41 | 94 | 45 448 | 967 | 12.0 | 28.0 | 43.8 |
| Marshall | 274 | 4 171 | D | 1 233 | 587 | D | 110 | 114 | 27 338 | 545 | 28.8 | 11.7 | 36.5 |
| Mayes | 776 | 9 086 | 943 | 2 505 | 1 656 | 337 | 232 | 303 | 33 299 | 1 640 | 35.1 | 8.5 | 40.9 |
| Murray | 259 | 3 005 | 546 | 266 | 716 | 141 | 88 | 92 | 30 610 | 530 | 23.0 | 16.6 | 40.8 |
| Muskogee | 1 457 | 23 449 | 5 636 | 3 750 | 3 365 | 637 | 839 | 785 | 33 460 | 1 845 | 33.7 | 8.5 | 38.8 |
| Noble | 204 | 3 409 | 400 | D | 330 | 125 | D | 132 | 38 588 | 838 | 16.8 | 28.5 | 41.8 |
| Nowata | 156 | 1 340 | 315 | 268 | 127 | 86 | D | 35 | 26 260 | 912 | 22.0 | 15.9 | 44.2 |
| Okfuskee | 163 | 1 356 | 454 | D | 238 | D | D | 31 | 22 810 | 950 | 19.4 | 14.0 | 40.7 |
| Oklahoma | 22 354 | 343 066 | 56 181 | 20 272 | 40 817 | 19 795 | 22 775 | 14 622 | 42 621 | 1 289 | 55.7 | 4.8 | 38.1 |
| Okmulgee | 677 | 7 445 | 2 082 | 1 485 | 1 388 | 287 | 173 | 217 | 29 097 | 1 449 | 32.4 | 8.1 | 37.7 |
| Osage | 609 | 5 828 | 825 | 313 | 781 | 186 | D | 168 | 28 833 | 1 481 | 29.4 | 23.1 | 43.4 |
| Ottawa | 628 | 8 903 | 1 407 | D | 1 115 | 294 | 203 | 247 | 27 748 | 1 160 | 38.4 | 8.0 | 42.6 |
| Pawnee | 288 | 2 459 | 637 | 309 | 367 | 120 | 78 | 76 | 30 850 | 862 | 22.4 | 18.7 | 40.5 |
| Payne | 1 692 | 21 208 | 3 431 | 1 782 | 4 104 | 861 | 1 209 | 643 | 30 300 | 1 567 | 35.4 | 11.5 | 32.8 |
| Pittsburg | 954 | 12 088 | 2 822 | 1 425 | 2 180 | 390 | 357 | 379 | 31 362 | 1 761 | 27.8 | 13.3 | 42.2 |
| Pontotoc | 960 | 12 686 | 3 306 | D | 1 764 | 1 233 | 379 | 382 | 30 082 | 1 424 | 26.9 | 11.1 | 41.3 |
| Pottawatomie | 1 301 | 18 979 | 3 015 | 2 653 | 2 921 | 652 | 658 | 535 | 28 190 | 1 777 | 31.2 | 8.3 | 40.8 |
| Pushmataha | 180 | 1 920 | 696 | 116 | 392 | 94 | 29 | 49 | 25 447 | 833 | 19.6 | 13.7 | 45.5 |
| Roger Mills | 88 | 533 | D | D | 124 | D | 19 | 17 | 31 174 | 693 | 5.2 | 42.7 | 48.2 |
| Rogers | 1 612 | 23 514 | 2 780 | 5 619 | 2 541 | 534 | 691 | 1 013 | 43 100 | 1 936 | 47.1 | 7.6 | 39.0 |
| Seminole | 463 | 5 368 | 988 | 639 | 823 | 210 | 85 | 174 | 32 383 | 1 172 | 24.7 | 8.4 | 40.0 |
| Sequoyah | 562 | 6 542 | 2 059 | D | 1 202 | D | 139 | 145 | 22 225 | 1 352 | 36.3 | 7.3 | 40.2 |
| Stephens | 1 055 | 13 134 | 2 163 | 2 268 | 2 040 | 641 | 423 | 451 | 34 320 | 1 310 | 22.8 | 14.2 | 37.8 |
| Texas | 475 | 7 150 | 492 | D | 999 | 245 | D | 273 | 38 212 | 1 038 | 7.8 | 39.1 | 42.1 |
| Tillman | 139 | 1 303 | 305 | D | D | 70 | 22 | 35 | 26 543 | 548 | 7.5 | 40.1 | 51.5 |
| Tulsa | 18 382 | 311 069 | 50 327 | 33 979 | 36 848 | 15 315 | 18 184 | 13 826 | 44 448 | 1 150 | 55.9 | 4.3 | 36.2 |
| Wagoner | 881 | 8 001 | 754 | 1 834 | 1 459 | 241 | D | 256 | 31 962 | 1 138 | 42.6 | 9.9 | 39.8 |
| Washington | 1 192 | 20 007 | 3 206 | 922 | 2 440 | 755 | 1 244 | 974 | 48 672 | 853 | 38.8 | 9.6 | 39.3 |
| Washita | 243 | 1 537 | 181 | 98 | 256 | 124 | 90 | 49 | 31 954 | 975 | 13.4 | 34.6 | 47.9 |
| Woods | 280 | 2 241 | 285 | D | 505 | 151 | 75 | 75 | 33 528 | 840 | 13.1 | 36.2 | 43.8 |
| Woodward | 793 | 7 868 | 1 203 | 397 | 1 259 | 332 | 207 | 330 | 41 966 | 892 | 15.6 | 36.2 | 37.8 |
| **OREGON** | 106 340 | 1 341 841 | 210 294 | 144 220 | 184 589 | 57 455 | 80 462 | 56 092 | 41 802 | 38 553 | 61.4 | 10.6 | 46.2 |
| Baker | 519 | 3 885 | 741 | 527 | 748 | 124 | 172 | 110 | 28 271 | 688 | 33.1 | 27.2 | 54.5 |
| Benton | 2 003 | 25 118 | 5 027 | 3 141 | 3 540 | 605 | 2 202 | 1 012 | 40 283 | 906 | 73.3 | 4.5 | 41.1 |
| Clackamas | 10 690 | 121 901 | 17 213 | 15 779 | 17 281 | 5 053 | 8 294 | 5 221 | 42 831 | 3 989 | 82.1 | 1.2 | 41.3 |
| Clatsop | 1 433 | 13 252 | 1 981 | D | 2 649 | 300 | 338 | 425 | 32 059 | 229 | 60.3 | 3.1 | 51.5 |
| Columbia | 928 | 6 948 | 999 | 1 177 | 1 347 | 292 | 251 | 209 | 30 150 | 805 | 72.9 | 1.9 | 38.5 |
| Coos | 1 641 | 16 731 | 3 528 | 1 321 | 3 017 | 474 | 435 | 522 | 31 182 | 746 | 43.6 | 7.1 | 51.7 |
| Crook | 479 | 3 704 | 485 | 699 | 638 | 83 | 111 | 114 | 30 734 | 622 | 51.1 | 15.1 | 46.9 |
| Curry | 671 | 4 507 | 803 | 535 | 914 | 209 | 116 | 135 | 29 882 | 195 | 35.9 | 19.5 | 61.0 |
| Deschutes | 5 695 | 51 078 | 9 461 | 3 464 | 9 045 | 2 020 | 2 636 | 1 756 | 34 369 | 1 405 | 77.9 | 2.3 | 40.8 |
| Douglas | 2 503 | 27 337 | 4 963 | 4 210 | 4 206 | 856 | 870 | 905 | 33 092 | 2 095 | 53.8 | 8.1 | 47.5 |
| Gilliam | 69 | 534 | D | D | 57 | D | D | 21 | 39 494 | 164 | 2.4 | 77.4 | 56.1 |
| Grant | 241 | 1 386 | D | D | 233 | 77 | 49 | 41 | 29 743 | 398 | 27.1 | 38.7 | 53.0 |
| Harney | 202 | 1 263 | 327 | D | 289 | 51 | 65 | 35 | 27 370 | 523 | 16.6 | 43.0 | 57.7 |
| Hood River | 938 | 8 501 | 1 790 | 1 095 | 1 269 | 142 | 385 | 245 | 28 869 | 553 | 68.7 | 0.5 | 59.5 |
| Jackson | 5 704 | 63 060 | 11 480 | 5 288 | 11 071 | 2 489 | 2 292 | 2 120 | 33 623 | 1 976 | 69.5 | 3.5 | 45.5 |
| Jefferson | 348 | 3 421 | D | 842 | 532 | 70 | D | 106 | 31 084 | 510 | 37.5 | 22.4 | 52.7 |
| Josephine | 1 981 | 19 671 | 4 621 | 2 171 | 3 986 | 713 | 613 | 577 | 29 352 | 675 | 76.6 | 1.8 | 51.1 |
| Klamath | 1 552 | 16 232 | 2 887 | 1 704 | 3 004 | 1 072 | 606 | 544 | 33 500 | 1 207 | 39.4 | 18.1 | 57.4 |
| Lake | 192 | 1 207 | 253 | 185 | 207 | 29 | 48 | 38 | 31 085 | 417 | 20.1 | 41.7 | 68.8 |
| Lane | 9 437 | 112 024 | 21 525 | 11 911 | 18 322 | 4 550 | 5 625 | 3 898 | 34 793 | 3 335 | 75.5 | 2.8 | 37.5 |
| Lincoln | 1 601 | 13 651 | 1 808 | 888 | 2 749 | 274 | D | 394 | 28 890 | 371 | 63.6 | 3.2 | 49.9 |
| Linn | 2 393 | 31 723 | 4 482 | 6 314 | 4 530 | 838 | 990 | 1 091 | 34 404 | 2 325 | 65.1 | 7.9 | 44.0 |
| Malheur | 710 | 8 232 | 1 445 | D | 1 877 | 223 | 222 | 224 | 27 180 | 1 250 | 34.4 | 20.6 | 62.2 |
| Marion | 7 515 | 93 122 | 18 616 | 8 247 | 15 420 | 3 540 | 3 891 | 3 105 | 33 344 | 2 670 | 72.2 | 5.2 | 46.4 |

# Table B. States and Counties — Agriculture

| | Agriculture, 2007 (cont.) | | | | | | | | | | | | | | | |
| STATE County | Land in farms | | | | Value of land and buildings (dollars) | | | Value of products sold | | | | | Percent of farms with sales of: | | Government payments | |
| | Acreage (1,000) | Percent change, 2002–2007 | Acres | | | Average per farm | Average per acre | Value of machinery and equipment, average per farm (dollars) | Total (mil dol) | Average per farm (dollars) | Percent from: | | $10,000 or more | $100,000 or more | Total ($1,000) | Percent of farms |
| | | | Average size of farm | Total irrigated (1,000) | Total cropland (1,000) | | | | | | Crops | Live-stock and poultry products | | | | |
| | 117 | 118 | 119 | 120 | 121 | 122 | 123 | 124 | 125 | 126 | 127 | 128 | 129 | 130 | 131 | 132 |

OKLAHOMA—Cont'd

| STATE County | 117 | 118 | 119 | 120 | 121 | 122 | 123 | 124 | 125 | 126 | 127 | 128 | 129 | 130 | 131 | 132 |
|---|---|---|---|---|---|---|---|---|---|---|---|---|---|---|---|---|
| Kiowa | 565 | -2.6 | 828 | 2.6 | 292.5 | 762 776 | 921 | 103 664 | 76.2 | 111 680 | 46.6 | 53.4 | 60.3 | 20.8 | 7 485 | 74.0 |
| Latimer | 213 | 3.4 | 281 | 0.4 | 42.1 | 353 739 | 1 260 | 51 107 | 20.5 | 26 932 | D | D | 26.7 | 3.4 | 774 | 11.6 |
| Le Flore | 466 | 13.4 | 228 | 9.4 | 155.0 | 380 784 | 1 668 | 66 007 | 213.1 | 104 288 | 8.5 | 91.5 | 37.4 | 12.5 | 2 637 | 15.7 |
| Lincoln | 488 | 3.4 | 212 | 2.2 | 147.2 | 346 917 | 1 636 | 45 887 | 37.8 | 16 442 | 10.4 | 89.6 | 25.4 | 1.8 | 512 | 12.4 |
| Logan | 404 | 10.4 | 325 | 1.6 | 152.4 | 450 107 | 1 383 | 54 289 | 48.8 | 39 317 | 18.2 | 81.8 | 31.6 | 5.0 | 1 313 | 33.8 |
| Love | 262 | 7.4 | 376 | 1.8 | 88.0 | 563 481 | 1 498 | 55 450 | 27.9 | 40 089 | 12.2 | 87.8 | 41.1 | 7.5 | 681 | 24.6 |
| McClain | 337 | 9.8 | 256 | 1.7 | 110.6 | 430 232 | 1 683 | 64 735 | 42.0 | 31 854 | 25.8 | 74.2 | 33.2 | 5.9 | 1 331 | 21.4 |
| McCurtain | 340 | -5.0 | 189 | 0.4 | 104.5 | 299 257 | 1 583 | 52 109 | 186.2 | 103 678 | 4.8 | 95.2 | 35.7 | 11.7 | 576 | 5.8 |
| McIntosh | 247 | -7.1 | 237 | 0.6 | 70.6 | 312 954 | 1 322 | 45 100 | 19.2 | 18 378 | 14.9 | 85.1 | 34.6 | 2.3 | 582 | 17.7 |
| Major | 517 | 1.6 | 535 | 8.2 | 237.4 | 504 607 | 943 | 97 895 | 113.0 | 116 863 | 11.2 | 88.8 | 46.8 | 12.7 | 4 142 | 64.8 |
| Marshall | 158 | -3.7 | 289 | 2.3 | 37.1 | 438 535 | 1 515 | 52 581 | 16.5 | 30 240 | 39.6 | 60.4 | 27.9 | 3.9 | 230 | 14.9 |
| Mayes | 313 | 3.6 | 191 | 0.8 | 117.3 | 375 242 | 1 965 | 53 956 | 73.1 | 44 564 | 7.7 | 92.3 | 34.7 | 7.2 | 773 | 14.8 |
| Murray | 197 | -2.5 | 372 | D | 38.9 | 518 378 | 1 394 | 57 773 | 13.9 | 26 267 | D | D | 37.4 | 3.8 | 312 | 22.1 |
| Muskogee | 374 | 6.3 | 203 | 8.2 | 145.0 | 330 688 | 1 630 | 53 502 | 52.7 | 28 558 | 27.4 | 72.6 | 31.0 | 4.1 | 1 467 | 17.8 |
| Noble | 467 | 18.2 | 557 | 0.8 | 215.8 | 638 752 | 1 146 | 83 646 | 37.7 | 45 026 | 24.5 | 75.5 | 43.8 | 10.0 | 2 991 | 55.8 |
| Nowata | 355 | 14.1 | 389 | 0.1 | 76.3 | 467 676 | 1 203 | 53 118 | 43.9 | 48 115 | 4.3 | 95.7 | 40.6 | 6.1 | 545 | 21.6 |
| Okfuskee | 299 | 3.1 | 315 | 1.3 | 83.7 | 373 034 | 1 186 | 50 706 | 33.1 | 34 809 | 5.7 | 94.3 | 33.6 | 5.4 | 357 | 19.8 |
| Oklahoma | 160 | -7.0 | 124 | 2.9 | 57.5 | 319 281 | 2 575 | 43 790 | 28.8 | 22 376 | 61.5 | 38.5 | 22.0 | 3.3 | 371 | 11.1 |
| Okmulgee | 294 | 1.7 | 203 | 0.9 | 100.0 | 353 951 | 1 743 | 52 121 | 21.2 | 14 646 | 18.1 | 81.9 | 27.6 | 2.1 | 420 | 13.6 |
| Osage | 1 291 | 8.9 | 871 | 0.4 | 156.2 | 818 686 | 939 | 55 830 | 131.2 | 88 574 | 3.5 | 96.5 | 36.6 | 8.8 | 1 107 | 16.8 |
| Ottawa | 238 | 5.3 | 205 | 0.3 | 108.1 | 367 647 | 1 792 | 71 467 | 94.0 | 81 013 | 47.0 | 53.0 | 34.1 | 6.6 | 1 217 | 24.3 |
| Pawnee | 298 | 6.0 | 345 | 0.0 | 60.7 | 430 043 | 1 246 | 49 989 | 25.0 | 29 007 | 8.7 | 91.3 | 31.9 | 6.1 | 630 | 28.9 |
| Payne | 357 | 4.7 | 228 | 0.9 | 117.7 | 377 632 | 1 659 | 48 962 | 38.6 | 24 621 | 13.3 | 86.7 | 29.7 | 3.8 | 998 | 23.6 |
| Pittsburg | 547 | 8.3 | 311 | 1.7 | 125.8 | 379 039 | 1 220 | 45 799 | 36.1 | 20 507 | 13.9 | 86.1 | 30.7 | 3.5 | 875 | 8.9 |
| Pontotoc | 379 | 3.0 | 266 | 0.8 | 112.8 | 374 161 | 1 405 | 47 093 | 26.6 | 18 710 | 14.0 | 86.0 | 31.7 | 2.4 | 423 | 15.5 |
| Pottawatomie | 395 | 15.2 | 222 | 1.4 | 127.4 | 316 605 | 1 424 | 42 626 | 35.1 | 19 726 | 19.6 | 80.4 | 25.1 | 2.6 | 703 | 15.9 |
| Pushmataha | 290 | -6.5 | 349 | 0.5 | 47.7 | 453 298 | 1 300 | 51 248 | 14.9 | 17 859 | D | D | 29.4 | 3.0 | 149 | 11.3 |
| Roger Mills | 719 | -2.7 | 1 038 | 4.6 | 186.4 | 802 738 | 773 | 74 841 | 36.3 | 52 372 | 17.6 | 82.4 | 50.2 | 11.4 | 2 888 | 61.6 |
| Rogers | 371 | 19.7 | 192 | 0.8 | 100.7 | 410 485 | 2 140 | 44 152 | 37.4 | 19 333 | 15.5 | 84.5 | 26.3 | 2.7 | 442 | 11.3 |
| Seminole | 251 | -10.0 | 214 | 0.8 | 70.4 | 296 420 | 1 385 | 45 961 | 19.9 | 16 958 | 12.1 | 87.9 | 27.9 | 2.0 | 436 | 19.5 |
| Sequoyah | 232 | 4.5 | 172 | 1.6 | 73.5 | 289 814 | 1 689 | 52 559 | 59.2 | 43 801 | 9.3 | 90.7 | 30.0 | 3.6 | 521 | 5.9 |
| Stephens | 470 | 11.9 | 359 | 1.2 | 127.8 | 429 999 | 1 199 | 51 054 | 41.2 | 31 464 | 8.9 | 91.1 | 33.1 | 4.9 | 1 269 | 28.2 |
| Texas | 1 206 | 2.1 | 1 162 | 156.0 | 656.4 | 791 501 | 681 | 142 789 | 779.9 | 751 318 | 14.7 | 85.3 | 45.1 | 23.4 | 10 897 | 73.8 |
| Tillman | 464 | -4.3 | 847 | 13.0 | 301.0 | 701 387 | 828 | 111 477 | 86.5 | 157 764 | 49.3 | 50.7 | 63.3 | 27.7 | 8 480 | 79.9 |
| Tulsa | 131 | -13.2 | 114 | 3.9 | 59.5 | 331 281 | 2 905 | 44 479 | 24.5 | 21 294 | 67.1 | 32.9 | 22.2 | 2.3 | 171 | 9.0 |
| Wagoner | 263 | 1.2 | 231 | 5.2 | 114.3 | 410 457 | 1 778 | 49 621 | 29.7 | 26 118 | 55.7 | 44.3 | 32.1 | 3.9 | 828 | 17.6 |
| Washington | 227 | 1.8 | 266 | 0.5 | 67.1 | 390 140 | 1 469 | 50 557 | 23.2 | 27 231 | 15.4 | 84.6 | 30.1 | 4.2 | 389 | 17.9 |
| Washita | 591 | 4.0 | 606 | 7.3 | 347.1 | 606 511 | 1 001 | 109 749 | 104.8 | 107 531 | 35.0 | 65.0 | 61.1 | 21.1 | 8 211 | 74.5 |
| Woods | 834 | 2.2 | 993 | 2.0 | 303.8 | 801 448 | 807 | 91 804 | 56.7 | 67 481 | 20.8 | 79.2 | 45.4 | 14.6 | 5 400 | 69.9 |
| Woodward | 783 | 7.9 | 878 | 7.6 | 183.4 | 727 483 | 829 | 65 327 | 78.7 | 88 202 | D | D | 43.7 | 13.6 | 3 233 | 52.9 |
| OREGON | 16 400 | -4.0 | 425 | 1 845.2 | 5 010.4 | 804 145 | 1 890 | 79 175 | 4 386.1 | 113 769 | 67.9 | 32.1 | 32.5 | 12.1 | 76 491 | 13.3 |
| Baker | 712 | -18.2 | 1 035 | 120.7 | 115.1 | 1 201 324 | 1 161 | 96 150 | 62.1 | 90 316 | 30.7 | 69.3 | 46.8 | 17.4 | 1 275 | 19.0 |
| Benton | 115 | -11.5 | 126 | 23.3 | 79.2 | 675 605 | 5 343 | 81 023 | 74.6 | 82 301 | 84.4 | 15.6 | 23.3 | 7.8 | 342 | 7.7 |
| Clackamas | 183 | -14.9 | 46 | 27.8 | 104.6 | 628 848 | 13 727 | 55 139 | 397.3 | 99 603 | 84.4 | 15.6 | 27.1 | 8.1 | 222 | 2.8 |
| Clatsop | 21 | -4.5 | 93 | 1.0 | 7.2 | 564 265 | 6 096 | 60 048 | 9.6 | 41 801 | 11.2 | 88.8 | 21.0 | 6.1 | 35 | 3.1 |
| Columbia | 58 | -6.5 | 72 | 2.5 | 21.4 | 465 382 | 6 486 | 39 679 | D | D | D | D | 14.7 | 2.2 | 181 | 3.6 |
| Coos | 146 | 1.4 | 195 | 10.8 | 26.8 | 731 998 | 3 749 | 59 398 | 41.3 | 55 369 | 43.9 | 56.1 | 37.7 | 11.3 | 940 | 10.1 |
| Crook | 762 | -18.8 | 1 224 | 73.2 | 79.0 | 1 168 777 | 955 | 100 471 | 31.2 | 50 219 | 34.6 | 65.4 | 34.6 | 10.1 | 264 | 10.8 |
| Curry | 74 | 5.7 | 381 | 2.6 | 10.7 | 1 337 378 | 3 508 | 65 931 | 19.7 | 101 140 | 69.0 | 31.1 | 44.6 | 14.4 | 489 | 19.5 |
| Deschutes | 129 | -6.5 | 92 | 37.8 | 39.9 | 633 973 | 6 885 | 45 880 | 19.8 | 14 063 | 45.8 | 54.2 | 20.4 | 2.4 | 135 | 1.4 |
| Douglas | 397 | 1.8 | 189 | 16.4 | 73.6 | 644 351 | 3 400 | 47 042 | 50.8 | 24 243 | D | D | 24.2 | 3.7 | 925 | 4.8 |
| Gilliam | 733 | 14.0 | 4 472 | 7.5 | 294.6 | 1 982 107 | 443 | 178 524 | 37.0 | 225 902 | 82.4 | 17.6 | 53.0 | 33.5 | 5 327 | 76.2 |
| Grant | 762 | -14.6 | 1 913 | 40.8 | 68.5 | 1 276 764 | 667 | 81 564 | 18.3 | 46 085 | 11.5 | 88.5 | 42.5 | 8.5 | 284 | 9.5 |
| Harney | 1 462 | -7.2 | 2 794 | 150.8 | 244.2 | 1 461 377 | 523 | 104 677 | 51.7 | 98 919 | 25.7 | 74.3 | 54.9 | 22.8 | 535 | 14.9 |
| Hood River | 27 | -6.9 | 49 | 16.4 | 18.4 | 862 157 | 17 690 | 87 283 | 100.4 | 181 633 | 98.2 | 1.8 | 55.9 | 34.2 | 697 | 11.6 |
| Jackson | 244 | -3.2 | 124 | 56.4 | 56.5 | 721 613 | 5 843 | 44 133 | 79.1 | 40 042 | 64.8 | 35.2 | 21.3 | 3.0 | 458 | 2.6 |
| Jefferson | 709 | 1.1 | 1 390 | 48.4 | 97.2 | 1 125 534 | 810 | 126 049 | 56.6 | 110 887 | 69.7 | 30.3 | 46.9 | 18.2 | 1 455 | 38.6 |
| Josephine | 38 | 18.8 | 56 | 8.8 | 17.4 | 494 184 | 8 847 | 40 143 | 13.9 | 20 652 | 47.0 | 53.0 | 19.9 | 2.2 | 41 | 3.0 |
| Klamath | 675 | -4.0 | 559 | 226.3 | 168.1 | 883 784 | 1 580 | 107 258 | 149.7 | 124 038 | 50.3 | 49.7 | 46.6 | 17.1 | 2 665 | 16.1 |
| Lake | 693 | -7.4 | 1 661 | 154.1 | 169.4 | 1 542 658 | 929 | 141 189 | 65.1 | 156 200 | 42.5 | 57.5 | 55.9 | 30.7 | 760 | 18.9 |
| Lane | 246 | 4.7 | 74 | 22.4 | 116.4 | 547 167 | 7 432 | 49 129 | 131.1 | 39 307 | 70.5 | 29.5 | 17.5 | 4.4 | 759 | 4.3 |
| Lincoln | 31 | -6.1 | 84 | 0.8 | 5.7 | 441 004 | 5 248 | 35 662 | 5.9 | 15 897 | 28.8 | 71.2 | 17.0 | 3.5 | 34 | 3.2 |
| Linn | 376 | -2.6 | 162 | 32.2 | 257.3 | 703 825 | 4 347 | 80 435 | 213.2 | 91 690 | 76.3 | 23.7 | 27.7 | 11.1 | 721 | 6.2 |
| Malheur | 1 171 | -0.3 | 937 | 198.7 | 240.1 | 1 028 826 | 1 099 | 133 657 | 306.8 | 245 436 | 37.4 | 62.6 | 61.6 | 25.0 | 2 113 | 35.1 |
| Marion | 308 | -9.7 | 115 | 96.4 | 225.1 | 795 988 | 6 908 | 110 309 | 586.7 | 219 754 | 82.6 | 17.4 | 37.1 | 18.0 | 1 048 | 9.0 |

| STATE County | Water use, 2005 Total water withdrawn (mil gal/day) | Gallons withdrawn per person | Wholesale trade,[1] 2007 Number of establishments | Number of employees | Sales (mil dol) | Annual payroll (mil dol) | Retail trade,[2] 2007 Number of establishments | Number of employees | Sales (mil dol) | Annual payroll (mil dol) | Real estate and rental and leasing,[2] 2007 Number of establishments | Number of employees | Receipts (mil dol) | Annual payroll (mil dol) |
|---|---|---|---|---|---|---|---|---|---|---|---|---|---|---|
| | 133 | 134 | 135 | 136 | 137 | 138 | 139 | 140 | 141 | 142 | 143 | 144 | 145 | 146 |
| OKLAHOMA—Cont'd | | | | | | | | | | | | | | |
| Kiowa | 14.6 | 1 471 | 11 | 67 | 56.8 | 2.2 | 44 | 283 | 55.4 | 5.0 | 7 | 14 | 2.0 | 0.3 |
| Latimer | 2.9 | 276 | 7 | 105 | 90.3 | 3.6 | 24 | 248 | 40.5 | 4.0 | 5 | 43 | 17.1 | 2.7 |
| Le Flore | 21.8 | 441 | 22 | D | D | D | 140 | 1 531 | 376.3 | 28.7 | 15 | 176 | 24.6 | 7.3 |
| Lincoln | 10.9 | 336 | 22 | 138 | 85.5 | 5.3 | 87 | 609 | 161.9 | 11.3 | 14 | D | D | D |
| Logan | 11.2 | 308 | 22 | D | D | D | 95 | 878 | 275.6 | 19.9 | 32 | D | D | D |
| Love | 3.9 | 425 | 4 | 24 | 8.9 | 0.9 | 26 | 181 | 56.4 | 4.0 | 3 | D | D | D |
| McClain | 6.3 | 211 | 17 | D | D | D | 108 | 1 453 | 413.0 | 32.3 | 29 | 94 | 19.3 | 2.7 |
| McCurtain | 9.9 | 291 | 27 | 114 | 95.7 | 3.8 | 116 | 1 075 | 261.1 | 20.9 | 16 | 76 | 6.8 | 1.4 |
| McIntosh | 5.0 | 251 | 7 | 30 | 9.6 | 0.7 | 74 | 820 | 266.4 | 14.6 | 11 | 28 | 2.0 | 0.3 |
| Major | 20.3 | 2 780 | 9 | 71 | 39.5 | 2.2 | 40 | 313 | 78.8 | 5.0 | 7 | 23 | 2.3 | 0.5 |
| Marshall | 7.1 | 497 | 10 | D | D | D | 52 | 567 | 126.8 | 11.2 | 8 | 25 | 2.9 | 0.6 |
| Mayes | 107.2 | 2 719 | 28 | 402 | 301.4 | 19.2 | 160 | 1 490 | 414.6 | 31.2 | 22 | 46 | 5.1 | 0.8 |
| Murray | 22.4 | 1 751 | 5 | 87 | 42.2 | 3.5 | 50 | 627 | 193.6 | 13.4 | 8 | 119 | 12.9 | 4.1 |
| Muskogee | 110.2 | 1 559 | 65 | 994 | 580.7 | 49.8 | 287 | 3 468 | 904.0 | 71.7 | 66 | 548 | 45.6 | 10.3 |
| Noble | 5.1 | 457 | 6 | 37 | 28.0 | 0.9 | 30 | 315 | 86.8 | 6.2 | 6 | 25 | 1.7 | 0.2 |
| Nowata | 5.9 | 542 | 8 | 50 | 16.3 | 1.6 | 23 | 145 | 24.9 | 2.6 | 8 | 22 | 1.4 | 0.5 |
| Okfuskee | 4.2 | 368 | 4 | 17 | 2.8 | 0.2 | 29 | 199 | 64.6 | 3.5 | 2 | D | D | D |
| Oklahoma | 108.9 | 159 | 1 126 | 18 070 | 27 232.3 | 809.9 | 2 951 | 42 806 | 10 760.0 | 980.9 | 1 107 | 8 218 | 1 238.5 | 294.4 |
| Okmulgee | 16.9 | 427 | 20 | 125 | 42.1 | 4.6 | 128 | 1 286 | 329.5 | 25.9 | 19 | D | D | D |
| Osage | 19.7 | 434 | 17 | D | D | D | 98 | 769 | 172.1 | 12.9 | 18 | D | D | D |
| Ottawa | 5.8 | 178 | 24 | D | D | D | 98 | 1 206 | 287.6 | 24.9 | 27 | 106 | 9.3 | 2.3 |
| Pawnee | 17.3 | 1 030 | 8 | D | D | D | 45 | 366 | 82.5 | 6.3 | 10 | D | D | D |
| Payne | 7.8 | 106 | 41 | D | D | D | 307 | 3 890 | 818.4 | 74.3 | 76 | 247 | 33.8 | 5.1 |
| Pittsburg | 11.8 | 264 | 32 | 373 | 230.0 | 10.5 | 189 | 2 198 | 606.9 | 43.6 | 51 | 202 | 33.8 | 5.6 |
| Pontotoc | 24.7 | 701 | 47 | D | D | D | 170 | 1 813 | 409.0 | 34.0 | 38 | 148 | 21.8 | 3.8 |
| Pottawatomie | 17.6 | 259 | 33 | D | D | D | 253 | 2 824 | 682.3 | 55.9 | 47 | 203 | 23.7 | 4.2 |
| Pushmataha | 2.1 | 178 | 8 | 62 | 10.7 | 1.6 | 52 | 385 | 74.8 | 5.3 | 1 | D | D | D |
| Roger Mills | 9.0 | 2 716 | 1 | D | D | D | 20 | 124 | 42.8 | 2.4 | NA | NA | NA | NA |
| Rogers | 81.9 | 1 017 | 59 | 1 075 | 921.9 | 47.3 | 210 | 2 575 | 663.8 | 58.0 | 72 | 392 | 64.2 | 6.9 |
| Seminole | 31.1 | 1 262 | 14 | 73 | 85.1 | 3.1 | 78 | 800 | 192.6 | 16.7 | 14 | 48 | 5.2 | 0.9 |
| Sequoyah | 11.6 | 283 | 13 | D | D | D | 115 | 1 258 | 362.4 | 23.5 | 16 | 43 | 3.4 | 0.6 |
| Stephens | 20.6 | 479 | 42 | D | D | D | 210 | 2 076 | 495.1 | 40.4 | 27 | 107 | 11.0 | 1.7 |
| Texas | 173.8 | 8 634 | 27 | D | D | D | 80 | 814 | 182.6 | 15.7 | 12 | D | D | D |
| Tillman | 9.4 | 1 098 | 8 | 94 | 56.8 | 3.0 | 30 | 231 | 35.8 | 2.4 | 1 | D | D | D |
| Tulsa | 20.4 | 36 | 1 045 | 16 244 | 10 026.2 | 838.5 | 2 386 | 37 579 | 9 580.7 | 830.1 | 970 | 8 195 | 1 347.7 | 274.3 |
| Wagoner | 9.6 | 150 | 34 | 208 | 107.6 | 9.1 | 106 | 1 039 | 276.4 | 20.7 | 31 | 80 | 17.1 | 1.5 |
| Washington | 6.2 | 126 | 28 | D | D | D | 198 | 2 531 | 626.4 | 53.3 | 47 | D | D | D |
| Washita | 8.9 | 773 | 11 | 113 | 38.7 | 3.4 | 40 | 249 | 76.4 | 4.4 | 7 | 77 | 9.6 | 2.3 |
| Woods | 6.7 | 787 | 15 | 362 | 69.0 | 7.1 | 57 | 491 | 99.8 | 7.9 | 10 | 20 | 1.0 | 0.1 |
| Woodward | 16.8 | 883 | 40 | 330 | 140.6 | 9.5 | 120 | 1 238 | 337.4 | 25.8 | 28 | 132 | 16.8 | 4.4 |
| OREGON | 7 218.2 | 1 982 | 4 806 | 67 040 | 51 910.8 | 3 215.5 | 14 991 | 204 793 | 50 370.9 | 4 916.3 | 6 391 | 30 978 | 5 077.2 | 950.3 |
| Baker | 535.0 | 32 851 | 15 | 81 | 19.1 | 2.6 | 92 | 747 | 155.5 | 15.0 | 22 | 45 | 7.3 | 1.2 |
| Benton | 45.1 | 573 | 48 | 537 | 387.1 | 21.2 | 275 | 3 559 | 685.2 | 73.0 | 119 | 543 | 58.1 | 11.3 |
| Clackamas | 334.7 | 908 | 598 | 8 273 | 5 292.4 | 386.7 | 1 269 | 19 910 | 5 095.8 | 496.5 | 693 | 2 795 | 563.1 | 98.3 |
| Clatsop | 57.8 | 1 571 | 24 | 184 | 75.5 | 7.6 | 303 | 2 717 | 604.5 | 60.4 | 68 | 363 | 38.1 | 8.2 |
| Columbia | 56.8 | 1 183 | 25 | 122 | 96.8 | 6.6 | 132 | 1 563 | 357.4 | 33.8 | 41 | 112 | 15.0 | 2.5 |
| Coos | 28.5 | 440 | 41 | 426 | 260.8 | 15.3 | 290 | 3 298 | 716.0 | 79.5 | 69 | 274 | 33.4 | 6.2 |
| Crook | 262.0 | 11 873 | 19 | 160 | 100.5 | 5.1 | 80 | 632 | 139.9 | 13.3 | 36 | 92 | 6.9 | 1.7 |
| Curry | 19.8 | 885 | 15 | D | D | D | 105 | 1 188 | 227.0 | 23.4 | 59 | 107 | 12.7 | 2.0 |
| Deschutes | 206.6 | 1 462 | 234 | 2 089 | 1 222.6 | 93.9 | 867 | 10 952 | 2 809.1 | 271.9 | 452 | 1 782 | 229.7 | 48.2 |
| Douglas | 54.0 | 518 | 69 | D | D | D | 441 | 5 113 | 1 169.2 | 107.6 | 150 | 493 | 55.4 | 10.5 |
| Gilliam | 14.4 | 8 010 | 4 | 20 | 31.6 | 0.8 | 15 | 63 | 13.5 | 1.0 | NA | NA | NA | NA |
| Grant | 175.7 | 24 078 | 4 | D | D | D | 47 | 286 | 72.5 | 6.1 | 14 | D | D | D |
| Harney | 501.2 | 72 654 | 4 | 11 | 3.0 | 0.5 | 31 | 330 | 87.6 | 7.4 | 16 | 36 | 10.7 | 0.6 |
| Hood River | 89.6 | 4 208 | 33 | 754 | 224.4 | 25.8 | 146 | 1 393 | 293.7 | 32.9 | 36 | 62 | 9.3 | 1.5 |
| Jackson | 352.8 | 1 806 | 230 | 2 304 | 1 047.1 | 90.9 | 991 | 12 243 | 3 422.4 | 290.1 | 360 | 1 563 | 205.4 | 36.5 |
| Jefferson | 173.1 | 8 611 | 19 | 154 | 192.4 | 6.2 | 69 | 667 | 165.3 | 15.3 | 19 | D | D | D |
| Josephine | 55.4 | 686 | 60 | D | D | D | 347 | 4 549 | 1 024.3 | 107.4 | 110 | 450 | 47.1 | 9.5 |
| Klamath | 590.4 | 8 919 | 62 | D | D | D | 271 | 3 311 | 788.4 | 73.8 | 89 | 356 | 44.1 | 7.6 |
| Lake | 516.4 | 70 617 | 9 | 92 | 40.3 | 3.5 | 35 | 235 | 52.1 | 4.7 | 13 | D | D | D |
| Lane | 213.9 | 638 | 444 | 5 530 | 2 889.2 | 242.0 | 1 403 | 20 408 | 4 452.2 | 456.9 | 569 | 2 554 | 380.1 | 59.6 |
| Lincoln | 27.5 | 597 | 29 | 171 | 48.4 | 6.4 | 349 | 3 069 | 559.6 | 61.3 | 96 | 461 | 55.9 | 9.3 |
| Linn | 120.6 | 1 108 | 126 | 1 577 | 956.9 | 59.9 | 355 | 4 708 | 1 159.0 | 108.4 | 114 | 470 | 55.0 | 9.7 |
| Malheur | 950.4 | 30 334 | 38 | D | D | D | 143 | 2 095 | 484.6 | 46.7 | 37 | 103 | 10.7 | 1.7 |
| Marion | 277.2 | 908 | 312 | 3 806 | 3 461.7 | 161.2 | 1 109 | 16 819 | 4 016.6 | 399.2 | 485 | 2 686 | 337.4 | 66.2 |

1. Merchant wholesalers, except manufacturers' sales branches and offices.    2. Employer establishments.

| STATE County | Professional, scientific, and technical services,[1] 2007 | | | | Manufacturing, 2007 | | | | Accommodation and food services, 2007 | | | |
|---|---|---|---|---|---|---|---|---|---|---|---|---|
| | Number of establish-ments | Number of employees | Receipts (mil dol) | Annual payroll (mil dol) | Number of establish-ments | Number of employees | Receipts (mil dol) | Annual payroll (mil dol) | Number of establish-ments | Number of employees | Sales (mil dol) | Annual payroll (mil dol) |
| | 147 | 148 | 149 | 150 | 151 | 152 | 153 | 154 | 155 | 156 | 157 | 158 |
| OKLAHOMA—Cont'd | | | | | | | | | | | | |
| Kiowa | 15 | 32 | 2.8 | 0.7 | NA | NA | NA | NA | 19 | 192 | 6.4 | 2.3 |
| Latimer | 15 | 41 | 3.0 | 0.9 | NA | NA | NA | NA | 10 | 125 | 5.1 | 1.2 |
| Le Flore | 56 | D | D | D | 35 | 740 | 147.5 | D | 49 | 675 | 25.8 | 6.7 |
| Lincoln | 46 | D | D | D | 23 | 599 | 198.2 | 22.1 | 40 | 557 | 19.6 | 5.4 |
| Logan | 43 | 138 | 12.9 | 4.3 | NA | NA | NA | NA | 53 | 655 | 27.9 | 7.4 |
| Love | 16 | D | D | D | NA | NA | NA | NA | 12 | 134 | 5.3 | 1.4 |
| McClain | 59 | 224 | 22.8 | 6.4 | NA | NA | NA | NA | 53 | 721 | 30.8 | 8.0 |
| McCurtain | 30 | 371 | 14.1 | 8.5 | 27 | 2 178 | 1 361.7 | 89.3 | 39 | 577 | 21.7 | 5.1 |
| McIntosh | 30 | 114 | 10.7 | 4.0 | NA | NA | NA | NA | 35 | 366 | 15.5 | 3.4 |
| Major | 18 | 38 | 3.6 | 1.0 | NA | NA | NA | NA | 12 | 120 | 3.6 | 0.9 |
| Marshall | 21 | 78 | 5.0 | 2.0 | 21 | 1 228 | 207.7 | 43.7 | 30 | 329 | 12.2 | 3.4 |
| Mayes | 59 | 277 | 16.1 | 6.9 | 64 | 3 085 | 944.0 | 130.1 | 70 | 989 | 36.0 | 9.0 |
| Murray | 23 | 83 | 7.2 | 2.9 | NA | NA | NA | NA | 28 | 278 | 14.0 | 3.8 |
| Muskogee | 107 | D | D | D | 69 | 3 455 | 1 167.5 | 153.0 | 129 | 2 484 | 88.1 | 22.8 |
| Noble | 13 | 35 | 1.9 | 0.6 | 10 | D | D | D | 17 | 186 | 7.1 | 1.8 |
| Nowata | 10 | 37 | 4.7 | 0.8 | NA | NA | NA | NA | 11 | 140 | 4.0 | 1.2 |
| Okfuskee | 7 | 18 | 1.2 | 0.5 | NA | NA | NA | NA | 11 | 113 | 2.3 | 0.6 |
| Oklahoma | 2 783 | D | D | D | 770 | 23 255 | 7 039.4 | 908.1 | 1 638 | 36 363 | 1 500.9 | 422.5 |
| Okmulgee | 38 | 166 | 9.8 | 3.5 | 38 | 971 | 363.2 | 43.3 | 56 | 829 | 29.5 | 7.8 |
| Osage | 49 | 144 | 12.0 | 3.4 | NA | NA | NA | NA | 44 | 606 | 18.2 | 4.8 |
| Ottawa | 39 | D | D | D | 51 | 1 581 | 379.1 | 58.9 | 59 | 778 | 28.0 | 8.0 |
| Pawnee | 25 | 70 | 5.9 | 1.7 | NA | NA | NA | NA | 21 | 289 | 10.4 | 2.7 |
| Payne | 158 | D | D | D | 69 | 2 305 | 1 065.3 | 84.8 | 154 | 3 263 | 117.8 | 31.2 |
| Pittsburg | 82 | D | D | D | 24 | 797 | 223.8 | 31.9 | 85 | 1 430 | 64.5 | 13.5 |
| Pontotoc | 88 | D | D | D | 48 | 1 648 | 501.3 | 52.6 | 62 | 1 204 | 47.1 | 13.7 |
| Pottawatomie | 104 | D | D | D | 62 | 3 105 | 1 024.3 | 130.3 | 125 | 2 706 | 98.9 | 26.8 |
| Pushmataha | 13 | 82 | 10.5 | 2.1 | NA | NA | NA | NA | 12 | 159 | 4.7 | 1.2 |
| Roger Mills | 6 | 12 | 0.5 | 0.1 | NA | NA | NA | NA | 9 | 60 | 1.9 | 0.4 |
| Rogers | 129 | 570 | 49.1 | 19.3 | 145 | 7 179 | 2 856.0 | 335.5 | 96 | 1 756 | 62.4 | 17.1 |
| Seminole | 27 | 89 | 6.5 | 1.9 | 24 | 679 | 124.7 | 24.7 | 33 | 536 | 17.7 | 4.6 |
| Sequoyah | 40 | 147 | 12.0 | 4.1 | 23 | 616 | 272.3 | D | 61 | 797 | 34.9 | 9.1 |
| Stephens | 71 | 389 | 31.8 | 10.8 | 71 | 2 625 | 1 084.9 | 117.8 | 84 | 956 | 38.8 | 9.7 |
| Texas | 34 | D | D | D | 12 | D | D | D | 47 | 720 | 24.4 | 6.1 |
| Tillman | 11 | 35 | 2.2 | 1.0 | NA | NA | NA | NA | 10 | 81 | 2.7 | 0.7 |
| Tulsa | 2 398 | 16 682 | 2 403.2 | 894.7 | 998 | 39 890 | 16 400.1 | 1 834.9 | 1 452 | 29 323 | 1 226.5 | 347.3 |
| Wagoner | 70 | 199 | 22.0 | 6.4 | 76 | 2 040 | 561.4 | 74.7 | 57 | 912 | 30.7 | 8.7 |
| Washington | 90 | D | D | D | 51 | 1 462 | 353.5 | 58.1 | 114 | 1 889 | 72.5 | 17.9 |
| Washita | 16 | 48 | 7.3 | 2.0 | NA | NA | NA | NA | 15 | 113 | 3.3 | 0.9 |
| Woods | 24 | 64 | 4.1 | 1.2 | NA | NA | NA | NA | 23 | 262 | 10.4 | 2.3 |
| Woodward | 54 | D | D | D | NA | NA | NA | NA | 52 | 797 | 34.2 | 8.9 |
| OREGON | 11 363 | 83 190 | 9 750.4 | 4 869.5 | 5 717 | 183 953 | 66 880.7 | 8 138.9 | 10 241 | 150 538 | 7 555.8 | 2 152.9 |
| Baker | 40 | D | D | D | 27 | 605 | 138.0 | 20.5 | 58 | 558 | 25.7 | 6.9 |
| Benton | 282 | D | D | D | 92 | 4 322 | 590.5 | 209.8 | 206 | 3 197 | 134.0 | 37.2 |
| Clackamas | 1 234 | D | D | D | 619 | 17 625 | 5 668.2 | 841.4 | 775 | 12 928 | 607.4 | 176.9 |
| Clatsop | 90 | 317 | 22.4 | 8.1 | 56 | 1 868 | 683.6 | 92.0 | 248 | 3 078 | 160.6 | 45.4 |
| Columbia | 69 | D | D | D | 59 | 2 020 | 826.2 | 95.4 | 97 | 1 005 | 44.2 | 11.8 |
| Coos | 117 | D | D | D | 81 | 1 652 | 279.1 | 53.5 | 187 | 2 021 | 83.5 | 23.3 |
| Crook | 35 | D | D | D | 41 | 1 245 | 209.9 | 42.5 | 48 | 517 | 22.7 | 6.4 |
| Curry | 39 | 130 | 9.5 | 3.2 | 21 | 644 | 190.7 | 30.1 | 113 | 1 073 | 56.2 | 13.7 |
| Deschutes | 650 | D | D | D | 299 | 5 359 | 897.4 | 201.7 | 504 | 8 078 | 416.4 | 121.1 |
| Douglas | 179 | D | D | D | 132 | 6 439 | 1 506.4 | 236.6 | 301 | 4 331 | 228.4 | 62.9 |
| Gilliam | 1 | D | D | D | NA | NA | NA | NA | 8 | 66 | 1.5 | 0.5 |
| Grant | 19 | D | D | D | NA | NA | NA | NA | 25 | 162 | 6.6 | 1.9 |
| Harney | 11 | D | D | D | NA | NA | NA | NA | 27 | 211 | 11.1 | 2.6 |
| Hood River | 108 | 401 | 54.3 | 17.0 | 58 | 1 200 | 245.7 | 38.6 | 88 | 1 371 | 55.7 | 17.7 |
| Jackson | 491 | D | D | D | 324 | 6 115 | 2 037.5 | 228.8 | 590 | 7 946 | 372.9 | 108.9 |
| Jefferson | 24 | 76 | 4.7 | 1.9 | 20 | 1 501 | 242.9 | 50.7 | 45 | 798 | 45.8 | 13.3 |
| Josephine | 134 | D | D | D | 127 | 3 127 | 471.3 | 105.0 | 205 | 2 493 | 108.9 | 33.0 |
| Klamath | 118 | D | D | D | 75 | 2 360 | 539.7 | 92.5 | 176 | 2 259 | 103.0 | 28.9 |
| Lake | 10 | D | D | D | NA | NA | NA | NA | 27 | 159 | 7.2 | 1.7 |
| Lane | 988 | 5 097 | 554.6 | 217.5 | 606 | 20 273 | 6 219.9 | 853.6 | 920 | 13 385 | 607.7 | 171.5 |
| Lincoln | 102 | D | D | D | 57 | 1 108 | 582.7 | 58.0 | 292 | 4 035 | 205.4 | 59.9 |
| Linn | 170 | D | D | D | 198 | 7 814 | 2 737.6 | 393.7 | 200 | 2 746 | 125.4 | 33.1 |
| Malheur | 45 | D | D | D | 36 | 1 237 | D | 42.8 | 84 | 1 077 | 45.3 | 12.7 |
| Marion | 720 | 3 958 | 416.3 | 163.9 | 380 | 10 724 | 2 845.4 | 367.2 | 652 | D | D | D |

1. Establishment subject to federal tax.

# Table B. States and Counties — Health Care and Social Assistance, Other Services, and Federal Funds

| STATE County | Health care and social assistance, 2007 | | | | Other services, 2007 | | | | Federal funds and grants, 2009–2010 Expenditures (mil dol) Direct payments for individuals[1] | | | |
|---|---|---|---|---|---|---|---|---|---|---|---|---|
| | Number of establishments | Number of employees | Receipts (mil dol) | Annual payroll (mil dol) | Number of establishments | Number of employees | Receipts (mil dol) | Annual payroll (mil dol) | Total | Social Security and government retirement | Medicare | Food Stamps and Supplemental Security Income |
| | 159 | 160 | 161 | 162 | 163 | 164 | 165 | 166 | 167 | 168 | 169 | 170 |
| OKLAHOMA—Cont'd | | | | | | | | | | | | |
| Kiowa | 28 | 562 | 24.3 | 11.9 | 11 | D | D | D | 121.2 | 37.7 | 30.1 | 6.0 |
| Latimer | 25 | 368 | 21.0 | 8.5 | 6 | D | D | D | 97.0 | 34.3 | 21.8 | 6.0 |
| Le Flore | 83 | 2 121 | 125.4 | 52.5 | 47 | 208 | 17.8 | 4.5 | 498.4 | 187.1 | 99.4 | 27.8 |
| Lincoln | 53 | 679 | 35.2 | 14.2 | 22 | 74 | 7.0 | 1.7 | 252.2 | 124.2 | 44.7 | 12.2 |
| Logan | 52 | 1 253 | 69.4 | 30.4 | 48 | 157 | 13.4 | 2.9 | 243.2 | 97.7 | 45.4 | 10.8 |
| Love | 10 | D | D | D | 5 | 58 | 2.9 | 0.9 | 72.5 | 31.5 | 17.4 | 3.2 |
| McClain | 59 | 802 | 51.2 | 21.4 | 44 | 124 | 8.9 | 2.5 | 199.5 | 115.5 | 39.4 | 7.3 |
| McCurtain | 69 | 1 380 | 73.5 | 30.1 | 31 | 202 | 12.0 | 3.2 | 456.2 | 112.3 | 82.8 | 28.7 |
| McIntosh | 51 | 760 | 36.8 | 14.8 | 24 | 87 | 8.5 | 1.6 | 230.6 | 103.9 | 48.6 | 11.9 |
| Major | 14 | 297 | 12.9 | 6.6 | 11 | D | D | D | 53.1 | 23.5 | 14.2 | 1.4 |
| Marshall | 28 | 527 | 35.1 | 13.9 | 9 | 25 | 2.3 | 0.6 | 124.4 | 59.5 | 31.5 | 5.4 |
| Mayes | 80 | 939 | 60.0 | 24.5 | 53 | 144 | 9.6 | 2.7 | 294.6 | 137.9 | 61.5 | 18.2 |
| Murray | 31 | 735 | 38.4 | 17.2 | 17 | 50 | 3.0 | 0.6 | 135.4 | 48.0 | 27.2 | 4.8 |
| Muskogee | 204 | 5 438 | 384.1 | 180.9 | 95 | 525 | 35.5 | 10.5 | 895.8 | 293.5 | 143.8 | 41.8 |
| Noble | 18 | 365 | 21.0 | 9.0 | 11 | 49 | 3.4 | 0.8 | 85.6 | 36.6 | 20.2 | 3.5 |
| Nowata | 17 | 307 | 12.4 | 5.6 | 12 | 27 | 2.2 | 0.5 | 85.2 | 38.8 | 19.5 | 3.5 |
| Okfuskee | 40 | 432 | 28.1 | 10.9 | 4 | D | D | D | 129.5 | 45.5 | 27.4 | 6.9 |
| Oklahoma | 2 737 | 55 697 | 6 769.4 | 2 187.6 | 1 423 | 10 026 | 936.1 | 253.2 | 9 795.6 | 2 410.1 | 1 039.6 | 225.0 |
| Okmulgee | 140 | 2 352 | 159.6 | 68.4 | 40 | 147 | 11.2 | 2.7 | 433.2 | 138.9 | 84.8 | 25.7 |
| Osage | 50 | D | D | D | 29 | 76 | 5.9 | 1.3 | 302.6 | 84.4 | 44.0 | 12.7 |
| Ottawa | 77 | 1 537 | 101.7 | 45.9 | 36 | 139 | 9.6 | 2.2 | 331.6 | 125.0 | 85.0 | 14.8 |
| Pawnee | 32 | D | D | D | 12 | 38 | 2.9 | 0.6 | 148.2 | 61.2 | 31.3 | 5.6 |
| Payne | 175 | 3 518 | 266.5 | 103.7 | 128 | 813 | 170.0 | 17.8 | 547.8 | 185.1 | 89.9 | 20.0 |
| Pittsburg | 112 | 2 647 | 187.7 | 81.2 | 55 | 272 | 22.7 | 6.3 | 537.0 | 188.7 | 87.8 | 19.6 |
| Pontotoc | 142 | 3 131 | 253.4 | 92.6 | 52 | 247 | 17.7 | 4.4 | 382.3 | 128.7 | 73.2 | 20.1 |
| Pottawatomie | 160 | 2 846 | 216.8 | 79.4 | 67 | 322 | 22.1 | 6.5 | 692.2 | 264.5 | 89.4 | 31.8 |
| Pushmataha | 22 | 701 | 33.9 | 15.5 | 6 | 25 | 1.8 | 0.3 | 152.2 | 46.4 | 31.7 | 8.1 |
| Roger Mills | 5 | D | D | D | 5 | D | D | D | 32.1 | 10.3 | 9.1 | 0.9 |
| Rogers | 172 | 2 431 | 186.6 | 80.4 | 82 | 353 | 36.0 | 9.0 | 464.3 | 233.5 | 71.6 | 15.2 |
| Seminole | 49 | 1 081 | 63.1 | 22.9 | 21 | 81 | 7.7 | 1.9 | 292.9 | 91.2 | 59.2 | 21.1 |
| Sequoyah | 77 | 1 737 | 70.5 | 32.7 | 33 | 88 | 6.8 | 2.0 | 376.6 | 148.6 | 67.9 | 25.3 |
| Stephens | 104 | 1 988 | 136.6 | 52.6 | 66 | 530 | 67.0 | 11.5 | 426.4 | 172.6 | 85.2 | 17.6 |
| Texas | 44 | D | D | D | 32 | 161 | 11.4 | 2.3 | 122.5 | 39.2 | 27.6 | 3.5 |
| Tillman | 18 | 282 | 15.3 | 6.2 | 11 | 36 | 1.7 | 0.5 | 109.9 | 27.6 | 24.2 | 5.0 |
| Tulsa | 2 035 | 44 983 | 4 548.0 | 1 765.5 | 1 197 | 7 646 | 833.4 | 205.9 | 4 333.1 | 1 817.0 | 890.5 | 225.8 |
| Wagoner | 72 | 713 | 45.0 | 19.9 | 60 | 141 | 11.4 | 2.8 | 268.3 | 132.6 | 56.1 | 15.2 |
| Washington | 167 | 3 108 | 237.6 | 98.9 | 80 | 611 | 85.0 | 15.0 | 350.9 | 195.9 | 85.3 | 15.1 |
| Washita | 16 | 335 | 18.7 | 7.5 | 16 | 46 | 3.6 | 0.8 | 99.0 | 36.5 | 27.0 | 4.4 |
| Woods | 21 | 357 | 18.0 | 8.9 | 19 | 64 | 5.7 | 1.0 | 82.2 | 26.6 | 19.6 | 1.8 |
| Woodward | 84 | 1 194 | 76.0 | 31.7 | 43 | 204 | 27.2 | 5.6 | 118.5 | 53.3 | 29.9 | 6.2 |
| OREGON | 11 261 | 192 233 | 20 159.6 | 7 895.9 | 6 888 | 39 129 | 4 462.4 | 1 090.6 | 33 974.1 | 11 620.2 | 4 615.2 | 1 531.1 |
| Baker | 50 | D | D | D | 41 | 108 | 12.1 | 2.2 | 192.3 | 77.3 | 28.1 | 8.3 |
| Benton | 229 | 4 356 | 504.0 | 201.1 | 128 | 855 | 158.3 | 22.7 | 706.7 | 202.6 | 67.9 | 18.4 |
| Clackamas | 963 | 15 229 | 1 702.2 | 665.4 | 660 | 3 437 | 314.4 | 95.4 | 2 347.4 | 1 004.3 | 361.8 | 182.6 |
| Clatsop | 132 | 1 627 | 144.1 | 62.7 | 84 | 522 | 32.2 | 9.3 | 362.8 | 146.1 | 60.7 | 16.3 |
| Columbia | 107 | 826 | 54.7 | 20.8 | 63 | 218 | 15.4 | 4.5 | 298.0 | 158.2 | 58.7 | 13.9 |
| Coos | 236 | 3 508 | 329.8 | 126.1 | 92 | 481 | 59.7 | 11.1 | 657.4 | 301.3 | 115.1 | 46.7 |
| Crook | 33 | 540 | 47.3 | 18.4 | 38 | 168 | 11.4 | 3.3 | 176.8 | 88.3 | 28.3 | 7.9 |
| Curry | 98 | 865 | 61.8 | 23.0 | 34 | 134 | 10.3 | 2.5 | 236.5 | 125.6 | 52.7 | 12.3 |
| Deschutes | 543 | 8 144 | 974.3 | 351.5 | 322 | 1 761 | 169.5 | 46.5 | 950.9 | 535.6 | 125.8 | 37.1 |
| Douglas | 313 | 5 280 | 511.0 | 215.0 | 150 | 757 | 84.4 | 17.7 | 1 059.3 | 514.9 | 164.4 | 61.3 |
| Gilliam | 7 | D | D | D | 4 | D | D | D | 30.3 | 11.0 | 2.9 | 0.1 |
| Grant | 21 | D | D | D | 20 | 48 | 3.4 | 0.8 | 101.1 | 34.0 | 12.2 | 4.1 |
| Harney | 20 | D | D | D | 10 | 35 | 2.1 | 0.7 | 85.6 | 29.6 | 9.6 | 3.5 |
| Hood River | 95 | 1 595 | 107.6 | 43.6 | 47 | 229 | 20.7 | 6.4 | 160.1 | 57.6 | 22.1 | 6.5 |
| Jackson | 627 | 11 160 | 1 173.9 | 434.7 | 357 | 2 107 | 182.0 | 56.9 | 1 624.4 | 769.7 | 250.3 | 87.8 |
| Jefferson | 21 | D | D | D | 25 | 125 | 8.9 | 2.4 | 143.8 | 67.6 | 20.9 | 9.9 |
| Josephine | 251 | 4 055 | 356.7 | 128.0 | 131 | 605 | 40.6 | 12.5 | 774.4 | 385.5 | 129.6 | 64.9 |
| Klamath | 223 | 3 021 | 286.0 | 113.0 | 119 | 570 | 40.2 | 11.6 | 663.4 | 265.2 | 97.0 | 42.6 |
| Lake | 15 | 270 | 18.4 | 8.1 | 15 | 26 | 2.2 | 0.5 | 85.0 | 35.2 | 11.8 | 4.1 |
| Lane | 993 | 18 660 | 1 947.8 | 735.6 | 684 | 3 684 | 516.8 | 95.3 | 2 802.5 | 1 158.9 | 439.6 | 180.6 |
| Lincoln | 106 | 1 583 | 155.8 | 62.7 | 107 | 475 | 30.8 | 8.8 | 435.7 | 209.7 | 84.7 | 23.0 |
| Linn | 214 | 3 654 | 320.4 | 126.2 | 149 | 1 075 | 112.6 | 34.9 | 891.0 | 423.5 | 150.2 | 58.9 |
| Malheur | 102 | 1 403 | 116.3 | 45.0 | 62 | D | D | D | 245.3 | 89.1 | 38.2 | 21.1 |
| Marion | 911 | 15 212 | 1 453.0 | 599.2 | 514 | 2 628 | 214.1 | 64.3 | 3 954.1 | 935.7 | 377.8 | 146.3 |

1. State totals may include programs not allocated by county.

| STATE County | Salaries and wages | Defense | Other | Medicaid and other health-related | Nutrition and family welfare | Education | Other | New construction ($1,000) | Number of housing units | Total (mil dol) | Inter-governmental (mil dol) | Total (mil dol) | Total | Property |
|---|---|---|---|---|---|---|---|---|---|---|---|---|---|---|
| | 171 | 172 | 173 | 174 | 175 | 176 | 177 | 178 | 179 | 180 | 181 | 182 | 183 | 184 |
| OKLAHOMA—Cont'd | | | | | | | | | | | | | | |
| Kiowa | 5.7 | 0.1 | 0.8 | 25.5 | 2.8 | 1.0 | 1.0 | 0 | 0 | 28.7 | 18.5 | 5.8 | 609 | 363 |
| Latimer | 2.0 | 0.0 | 0.5 | 16.9 | 2.9 | 3.5 | 0.3 | 94 | 3 | 57.7 | 28.9 | 20.5 | 1 952 | 1 582 |
| Le Flore | 23.3 | 7.8 | 3.6 | 110.9 | 11.4 | 8.8 | 6.9 | 7 051 | 62 | 121.0 | 74.4 | 21.0 | 422 | 230 |
| Lincoln | 16.4 | 1.2 | 2.9 | 34.4 | 6.3 | 1.8 | 3.5 | 2 107 | 11 | 58.5 | 33.5 | 15.8 | 490 | 245 |
| Logan | 8.3 | 0.6 | 18.1 | 26.1 | 5.8 | 8.6 | 8.9 | 2 430 | 20 | 67.1 | 28.5 | 15.5 | 424 | 290 |
| Love | 1.5 | 0.6 | 0.3 | 15.1 | 1.9 | 0.7 | 0.1 | 0 | 0 | 17.1 | 10.7 | 4.2 | 459 | 283 |
| McClain | 5.9 | 0.0 | 1.3 | 20.6 | 4.3 | 2.3 | 0.2 | 31 858 | 191 | 90.9 | 37.4 | 42.1 | 1 323 | 996 |
| McCurtain | 10.1 | 9.1 | 1.9 | 127.3 | 10.6 | 24.4 | 42.6 | 1 675 | 18 | 87.2 | 57.0 | 19.6 | 583 | 321 |
| McIntosh | 4.1 | 2.6 | 0.8 | 48.6 | 5.1 | 2.8 | 1.6 | 1 142 | 14 | 50.4 | 33.7 | 10.8 | 550 | 252 |
| Major | 2.7 | 0.0 | 0.8 | 4.3 | 1.4 | 0.2 | 0.1 | 150 | 2 | 25.7 | 12.2 | 5.6 | 780 | 492 |
| Marshall | 2.7 | 0.0 | 0.5 | 19.8 | 2.5 | 1.6 | 0.1 | 925 | 7 | 39.6 | 25.4 | 8.9 | 601 | 323 |
| Mayes | 7.5 | 0.0 | 4.3 | 46.1 | 6.9 | 8.7 | 0.0 | 912 | 8 | 82.1 | 45.4 | 25.6 | 645 | 285 |
| Murray | 14.1 | 0.0 | 7.4 | 26.3 | 2.5 | 0.7 | 3.9 | 1 535 | 13 | 29.5 | 15.6 | 7.2 | 565 | 253 |
| Muskogee | 117.8 | 24.0 | 35.1 | 158.4 | 17.3 | 10.0 | 14.0 | 3 715 | 27 | 289.0 | 90.2 | 77.8 | 1 093 | 574 |
| Noble | 3.3 | 0.0 | 1.0 | 8.5 | 3.0 | 1.4 | 1.1 | 0 | 0 | 36.8 | 13.7 | 10.8 | 975 | 684 |
| Nowata | 2.6 | 0.9 | 0.5 | 15.5 | 1.8 | 1.0 | 0.0 | 0 | 0 | 24.1 | 14.4 | 5.3 | 495 | 286 |
| Okfuskee | 3.4 | 0.0 | 0.6 | 36.7 | 4.8 | 1.6 | 1.5 | 1 126 | 15 | 25.8 | 17.3 | 5.0 | 443 | 253 |
| Oklahoma | 1 950.8 | 956.2 | 384.9 | 724.8 | 301.9 | 307.0 | 1 339.3 | 383 095 | 2 155 | 2 322.8 | 702.5 | 979.6 | 1 396 | 641 |
| Okmulgee | 15.7 | 3.1 | 2.8 | 87.4 | 16.1 | 5.9 | 36.5 | 387 | 3 | 86.7 | 50.4 | 22.0 | 560 | 249 |
| Osage | 101.9 | 0.0 | 9.1 | 29.1 | 9.0 | 3.9 | 3.0 | 16 087 | 126 | 57.4 | 35.7 | 10.8 | 238 | 164 |
| Ottawa | 16.4 | 2.3 | 1.6 | 45.2 | 12.8 | 5.5 | 10.4 | 659 | 8 | 100.6 | 50.8 | 31.4 | 968 | 685 |
| Pawnee | 9.8 | 2.3 | 3.7 | 15.9 | 12.9 | 2.1 | 1.9 | 1 950 | 8 | 35.2 | 20.4 | 7.2 | 437 | 239 |
| Payne | 51.6 | 22.6 | 17.1 | 41.2 | 10.6 | 26.7 | 53.5 | 29 897 | 291 | 175.4 | 67.5 | 73.5 | 920 | 456 |
| Pittsburg | 78.3 | 50.1 | 6.5 | 81.4 | 10.1 | 7.8 | 2.7 | 3 894 | 24 | 185.0 | 55.4 | 45.1 | 1 009 | 432 |
| Pontotoc | 31.8 | 0.0 | 8.3 | 59.8 | 13.7 | 9.5 | 18.3 | 837 | 5 | 96.6 | 51.6 | 27.8 | 760 | 327 |
| Pottawatomie | 22.7 | 4.8 | 3.9 | 81.1 | 18.4 | 7.5 | 145.6 | 22 714 | 223 | 166.1 | 94.0 | 48.3 | 700 | 336 |
| Pushmataha | 3.2 | 7.0 | 0.5 | 41.4 | 3.6 | 5.6 | 3.3 | 172 | 1 | 34.4 | 20.9 | 4.4 | 381 | 193 |
| Roger Mills | 2.8 | 0.0 | 0.6 | 5.8 | 0.8 | 0.3 | 0.2 | 0 | 0 | 22.2 | 11.8 | 4.8 | 1 463 | 782 |
| Rogers | 32.6 | 3.1 | 20.4 | 37.9 | 14.3 | 6.8 | 11.4 | 34 132 | 260 | 159.1 | 71.2 | 57.3 | 690 | 401 |
| Seminole | 16.6 | 0.2 | 3.7 | 64.6 | 11.1 | 6.6 | 10.8 | 2 159 | 37 | 70.6 | 40.6 | 15.4 | 636 | 314 |
| Sequoyah | 11.5 | 12.8 | 2.2 | 89.4 | 9.3 | 6.4 | 1.6 | 4 476 | 44 | 115.3 | 63.0 | 22.0 | 535 | 186 |
| Stephens | 22.8 | 0.0 | 30.4 | 46.4 | 9.3 | 3.0 | 35.9 | 4 624 | 33 | 106.0 | 54.5 | 34.1 | 787 | 421 |
| Texas | 5.4 | 0.2 | 0.9 | 8.2 | 3.3 | 2.4 | 12.3 | 1 210 | 10 | 73.3 | 30.3 | 17.3 | 862 | 493 |
| Tillman | 2.5 | 0.0 | 0.5 | 23.0 | 4.7 | 1.2 | 0.9 | 179 | 1 | 31.2 | 16.2 | 4.3 | 530 | 334 |
| Tulsa | 276.4 | 233.8 | 170.0 | 357.0 | 98.4 | 48.1 | 106.7 | 391 319 | 2 966 | 2 023.4 | 633.7 | 907.0 | 1 550 | 832 |
| Wagoner | 5.3 | 1.8 | 1.1 | 40.7 | 7.8 | 3.5 | 0.3 | 21 720 | 147 | 76.6 | 38.4 | 27.0 | 401 | 200 |
| Washington | 2.7 | 1.1 | 2.7 | 25.6 | 7.0 | 5.1 | 5.0 | 17 546 | 128 | 117.6 | 47.5 | 47.7 | 955 | 572 |
| Washita | 3.4 | 4.6 | 0.7 | 9.4 | 2.4 | 2.3 | 1.0 | 0 | 0 | 37.7 | 19.8 | 11.7 | 1 005 | 762 |
| Woods | 11.4 | 0.0 | 0.6 | 4.3 | 1.6 | 3.6 | 2.2 | 150 | 1 | 32.7 | 9.6 | 16.3 | 1 962 | 1 443 |
| Woodward | 7.4 | 0.4 | 1.1 | 9.8 | 3.5 | 1.5 | 1.4 | 1 365 | 19 | 62.5 | 25.6 | 24.8 | 1 270 | 567 |
| OREGON | 2 568.5 | 891.5 | 1 155.6 | 4 360.1 | 926.3 | 608.0 | 2 800.0 | 0 | 72 | X | X | X | X | X |
| Baker | 18.3 | 0.0 | 12.6 | 39.9 | 2.8 | 1.2 | 0.9 | 6 504 | 31 | 54.0 | 28.2 | 14.5 | 908 | 819 |
| Benton | 57.7 | 49.4 | 45.2 | 85.6 | 10.1 | 5.6 | 129.2 | 48 529 | 364 | 246.0 | 103.0 | 88.2 | 1 083 | 962 |
| Clackamas | 232.4 | 137.9 | 59.2 | 181.6 | 70.0 | 19.1 | 62.5 | 247 744 | 1 172 | 1 287.1 | 497.1 | 519.7 | 1 381 | 1 161 |
| Clatsop | 52.2 | 1.5 | 23.2 | 42.4 | 5.5 | 2.9 | 8.7 | 25 455 | 129 | 156.1 | 55.9 | 60.4 | 1 616 | 1 281 |
| Columbia | 8.2 | 6.3 | 3.7 | 31.6 | 6.4 | 2.8 | 5.0 | 5 992 | 27 | 154.7 | 66.0 | 53.1 | 1 084 | 932 |
| Coos | 39.7 | 11.7 | 21.9 | 80.2 | 13.2 | 6.1 | 9.8 | 2 405 | 16 | 368.2 | 120.9 | 60.4 | 952 | 864 |
| Crook | 20.1 | 0.0 | 7.6 | 17.4 | 2.8 | 1.1 | 1.6 | 13 856 | 57 | 74.6 | 24.6 | 34.6 | 1 513 | 1 379 |
| Curry | 8.5 | 0.0 | 12.1 | 16.9 | 3.1 | 1.4 | 2.9 | 5 263 | 21 | 91.0 | 39.2 | 21.3 | 977 | 863 |
| Deschutes | 84.9 | 4.7 | 24.7 | 59.4 | 15.8 | 6.7 | 33.8 | 105 512 | 459 | 589.4 | 201.9 | 249.0 | 1 617 | 1 353 |
| Douglas | 79.6 | 2.9 | 58.9 | 115.9 | 19.5 | 9.0 | 14.3 | 24 093 | 100 | 392.1 | 219.4 | 79.0 | 759 | 686 |
| Gilliam | 0.6 | 0.0 | 0.1 | 0.8 | 0.2 | 0.2 | 0.0 | NA | NA | 18.3 | 5.0 | 3.1 | 1 824 | 1 751 |
| Grant | 13.6 | 3.0 | 22.5 | 7.4 | 1.3 | 0.7 | 1.1 | NA | NA | 56.8 | 26.7 | 7.0 | 1 016 | 804 |
| Harney | 13.4 | 0.0 | 13.8 | 7.5 | 1.5 | 0.7 | 4.1 | 1 303 | 4 | 45.2 | 19.6 | 5.9 | 873 | 805 |
| Hood River | 10.0 | 30.2 | 3.2 | 18.2 | 7.5 | 1.3 | 0.8 | 10 957 | 72 | 86.6 | 36.4 | 21.6 | 1 014 | 879 |
| Jackson | 132.1 | 13.7 | 104.2 | 176.9 | 31.5 | 14.5 | 25.0 | 62 135 | 362 | 629.4 | 302.0 | 211.7 | 1 062 | 872 |
| Jefferson | 7.6 | 0.3 | 3.3 | 15.4 | 5.0 | 4.5 | 6.4 | 2 903 | 15 | 100.2 | 40.7 | 22.7 | 1 097 | 904 |
| Josephine | 26.8 | 3.6 | 19.2 | 96.9 | 13.5 | 6.4 | 7.7 | 16 548 | 70 | 238.2 | 124.1 | 63.4 | 783 | 668 |
| Klamath | 88.9 | 10.9 | 13.3 | 68.5 | 14.5 | 7.8 | 31.2 | 11 317 | 57 | 245.4 | 132.8 | 54.1 | 814 | 720 |
| Lake | 13.3 | 0.2 | 9.7 | 6.6 | 1.4 | 0.7 | 0.6 | 2 312 | 10 | 43.2 | 18.3 | 6.7 | 921 | 854 |
| Lane | 163.3 | 29.0 | 45.5 | 481.3 | 53.8 | 48.9 | 125.5 | 98 962 | 670 | 1 336.0 | 563.3 | 401.7 | 1 169 | 991 |
| Lincoln | 26.7 | 0.1 | 13.0 | 40.3 | 9.4 | 4.8 | 19.5 | 18 515 | 94 | 180.2 | 54.6 | 90.8 | 1 980 | 1 660 |
| Linn | 46.4 | 7.9 | 11.4 | 124.0 | 19.3 | 10.0 | 18.9 | 30 152 | 180 | 386.2 | 177.1 | 124.5 | 1 099 | 931 |
| Malheur | 18.5 | 0.0 | 11.3 | 37.4 | 8.7 | 3.4 | 3.0 | 2 704 | 13 | 129.3 | 77.3 | 18.1 | 581 | 500 |
| Marion | 240.0 | 29.2 | 36.7 | 429.4 | 259.4 | 289.6 | 1 127.0 | 70 076 | 372 | 1 201.6 | 620.2 | 338.7 | 1 088 | 944 |

1. State totals may include programs not allocated by county.    2. Based on the resident population estimated as of July 1 of the year shown.

| STATE County | Total (mil dol) | Per capita[1] (dollars) | Education | Health and hospitals | Police protection | Public welfare | Highways | Total (mil dol) | Per capita[1] (dollars) | Federal civilian | Federal military | State and local | Democratic | Republican | All other |
|---|---|---|---|---|---|---|---|---|---|---|---|---|---|---|---|
| | 185 | 186 | 187 | 188 | 189 | 190 | 191 | 192 | 193 | 194 | 195 | 196 | 197 | 198 | 199 |
| OKLAHOMA—Cont'd | | | | | | | | | | | | | | | |
| Kiowa | 26.4 | 2 794 | 58.0 | 1.2 | 4.2 | 0.1 | 15.4 | 20.6 | 2 184 | 52 | 39 | 718 | 32.6 | 67.4 | 0.0 |
| Latimer | 55.0 | 5 238 | 77.3 | 0.2 | 1.0 | 0.0 | 9.3 | 16.5 | 1 573 | 25 | 46 | 1 316 | 31.5 | 68.5 | 0.0 |
| Le Flore | 117.3 | 2 359 | 66.4 | 2.1 | 3.9 | 0.2 | 6.6 | 28.4 | 571 | 172 | 208 | 4 796 | 30.7 | 69.3 | 0.0 |
| Lincoln | 56.7 | 1 756 | 72.5 | 0.1 | 5.4 | 0.0 | 4.2 | 21.8 | 674 | 73 | 140 | 1 728 | 25.1 | 74.9 | 0.0 |
| Logan | 66.7 | 1 831 | 49.6 | 20.0 | 3.9 | 0.0 | 7.8 | 26.4 | 724 | 69 | 174 | 1 998 | 31.3 | 68.7 | 0.0 |
| Love | 16.8 | 1 842 | 73.3 | 2.8 | 3.6 | 0.0 | 7.7 | 8.7 | 956 | 24 | 39 | 2 586 | 32.7 | 67.3 | 0.0 |
| McClain | 88.0 | 2 762 | 73.2 | 1.3 | 4.5 | 0.0 | 5.1 | 39.9 | 1 253 | 69 | 145 | 1 610 | 24.1 | 75.9 | 0.0 |
| McCurtain | 84.8 | 2 528 | 71.3 | 3.9 | 2.6 | 1.1 | 5.1 | 38.0 | 1 134 | 145 | 136 | 2 342 | 26.5 | 73.5 | 0.0 |
| McIntosh | 49.6 | 2 515 | 52.5 | 0.8 | 4.5 | 0.1 | 26.6 | 13.2 | 672 | 34 | 84 | 1 072 | 40.4 | 59.6 | 0.0 |
| Major | 25.1 | 3 490 | 42.0 | 22.6 | 2.6 | 0.0 | 17.7 | 10.3 | 1 435 | 33 | 31 | 425 | 14.8 | 85.2 | 0.0 |
| Marshall | 37.9 | 2 553 | 59.0 | 1.8 | 4.9 | 0.0 | 13.7 | 7.5 | 504 | 21 | 66 | 704 | 30.6 | 69.4 | 0.0 |
| Mayes | 83.9 | 2 117 | 65.2 | 0.3 | 6.1 | 0.0 | 5.0 | 38.3 | 967 | 67 | 170 | 2 363 | 36.0 | 64.0 | 0.0 |
| Murray | 29.0 | 2 281 | 57.3 | 3.2 | 5.0 | 0.0 | 11.6 | 5.2 | 412 | 79 | 56 | 2 602 | 29.8 | 70.2 | 0.0 |
| Muskogee | 289.6 | 4 073 | 40.0 | 32.5 | 3.5 | 0.0 | 2.9 | 219.9 | 3 092 | 2 756 | 292 | 5 639 | 42.5 | 57.5 | 0.0 |
| Noble | 36.0 | 3 238 | 52.0 | 18.6 | 3.6 | 0.0 | 10.5 | 26.7 | 2 396 | 35 | 48 | 1 270 | 23.2 | 76.8 | 0.0 |
| Nowata | 24.5 | 2 284 | 70.1 | 0.0 | 3.0 | 0.0 | 10.6 | 7.5 | 698 | 32 | 44 | 492 | 31.8 | 68.2 | 0.0 |
| Okfuskee | 25.9 | 2 307 | 74.5 | 1.9 | 3.6 | 0.0 | 8.1 | 8.9 | 788 | 32 | 51 | 1 107 | 35.9 | 64.1 | 0.0 |
| Oklahoma | 2 306.8 | 3 287 | 40.6 | 0.0 | 8.0 | 0.2 | 5.5 | 2 413.0 | 3 438 | 26 793 | 9 954 | 56 777 | 41.6 | 58.4 | 0.0 |
| Okmulgee | 85.5 | 2 176 | 66.4 | 0.5 | 4.8 | 0.0 | 6.3 | 55.2 | 1 403 | 133 | 164 | 3 332 | 41.5 | 58.5 | 0.0 |
| Osage | 57.4 | 1 262 | 63.0 | 6.5 | 3.0 | 0.1 | 8.2 | 16.5 | 362 | 202 | 246 | 2 072 | 38.1 | 61.9 | 0.0 |
| Ottawa | 100.7 | 3 100 | 64.9 | 1.6 | 4.6 | 0.0 | 4.4 | 28.5 | 877 | 115 | 131 | 4 813 | 38.2 | 61.8 | 0.0 |
| Pawnee | 32.9 | 2 001 | 59.2 | 13.4 | 3.9 | 0.0 | 5.2 | 12.8 | 779 | 247 | 69 | 968 | 31.3 | 68.7 | 0.0 |
| Payne | 177.6 | 2 222 | 50.5 | 1.8 | 7.7 | 0.2 | 6.4 | 98.0 | 1 226 | 290 | 335 | 14 963 | 36.5 | 63.5 | 0.0 |
| Pittsburg | 190.7 | 4 266 | 33.6 | 43.5 | 2.7 | 0.0 | 4.8 | 97.6 | 2 184 | 2 042 | 190 | 3 579 | 31.7 | 68.3 | 0.0 |
| Pontotoc | 89.2 | 2 438 | 66.7 | 0.4 | 4.0 | 0.0 | 7.2 | 79.0 | 2 159 | 175 | 156 | 6 276 | 31.6 | 68.4 | 0.0 |
| Pottawatomie | 172.8 | 2 503 | 64.6 | 0.4 | 4.6 | 0.0 | 6.0 | 78.9 | 1 142 | 150 | 289 | 5 652 | 30.8 | 69.2 | 0.0 |
| Pushmataha | 35.3 | 3 026 | 58.1 | 20.7 | 2.5 | 0.0 | 9.4 | 15.1 | 1 293 | 38 | 47 | 972 | 28.3 | 71.7 | 0.0 |
| Roger Mills | 20.1 | 6 068 | 28.6 | 15.0 | 3.3 | 0.0 | 38.7 | 10.4 | 3 137 | 47 | 15 | 354 | 16.0 | 84.0 | 0.0 |
| Rogers | 161.0 | 1 937 | 62.8 | 1.0 | 2.9 | 0.0 | 4.8 | 98.0 | 1 179 | 453 | 360 | 5 887 | 28.0 | 72.0 | 0.0 |
| Seminole | 64.9 | 2 684 | 61.9 | 10.6 | 3.0 | 0.0 | 4.7 | 49.6 | 2 052 | 166 | 104 | 1 912 | 34.7 | 65.3 | 0.0 |
| Sequoyah | 94.0 | 2 291 | 69.8 | 1.5 | 4.3 | 0.0 | 5.1 | 46.5 | 1 135 | 140 | 191 | 3 047 | 32.0 | 68.0 | 0.0 |
| Stephens | 101.5 | 2 342 | 66.3 | 0.8 | 4.6 | 0.0 | 8.9 | 74.0 | 1 707 | 83 | 185 | 2 047 | 24.0 | 76.0 | 0.0 |
| Texas | 80.5 | 4 017 | 43.6 | 21.2 | 4.3 | 0.1 | 16.8 | 15.7 | 782 | 73 | 87 | 1 666 | 14.7 | 85.3 | 0.0 |
| Tillman | 32.1 | 3 936 | 45.2 | 19.2 | 3.1 | 0.0 | 6.5 | 16.5 | 2 019 | 37 | 33 | 662 | 32.2 | 67.8 | 0.0 |
| Tulsa | 2 039.2 | 3 485 | 48.4 | 3.0 | 5.7 | 1.3 | 2.7 | 3 716.4 | 6 352 | 3 457 | 2 525 | 31 938 | 37.8 | 62.2 | 0.0 |
| Wagoner | 76.2 | 1 133 | 59.0 | 2.7 | 5.4 | 0.0 | 10.7 | 21.9 | 326 | 72 | 307 | 1 612 | 29.1 | 70.9 | 0.0 |
| Washington | 118.1 | 2 368 | 58.8 | 0.6 | 5.5 | 0.1 | 7.9 | 98.8 | 1 981 | 101 | 211 | 2 435 | 27.7 | 72.3 | 0.0 |
| Washita | 37.7 | 3 233 | 64.6 | 0.3 | 4.0 | 0.4 | 19.1 | 5.5 | 471 | 44 | 47 | 735 | 22.0 | 78.0 | 0.0 |
| Woods | 30.0 | 3 603 | 55.2 | 5.3 | 3.2 | 0.0 | 13.5 | 19.4 | 2 338 | 36 | 36 | 1 227 | 22.3 | 77.7 | 0.0 |
| Woodward | 59.7 | 3 062 | 56.1 | 4.5 | 5.9 | 0.0 | 8.3 | 32.8 | 1 681 | 97 | 82 | 1 261 | 17.4 | 82.6 | 0.0 |
| OREGON | X | X | X | X | X | X | X | X | X | 28 837 | 12 391 | 253 494 | 56.7 | 40.4 | 2.9 |
| Baker | 52.2 | 3 277 | 46.6 | 5.8 | 5.3 | 2.1 | 6.1 | 90.4 | 5 678 | 230 | 45 | 893 | 32.0 | 64.4 | 3.7 |
| Benton | 227.5 | 2 794 | 43.3 | 9.9 | 8.6 | 0.0 | 4.9 | 279.5 | 3 432 | 596 | 294 | 13 863 | 64.3 | 32.8 | 2.8 |
| Clackamas | 1 355.6 | 3 603 | 44.0 | 4.8 | 5.9 | 1.1 | 4.5 | 2 190.5 | 5 822 | 1 301 | 1 167 | 14 005 | 53.9 | 43.6 | 2.5 |
| Clatsop | 167.7 | 4 489 | 39.2 | 7.7 | 4.8 | 0.4 | 4.7 | 283.3 | 7 581 | 206 | 530 | 2 429 | 57.7 | 38.8 | 3.5 |
| Columbia | 157.9 | 3 222 | 46.0 | 4.1 | 4.9 | 0.4 | 5.7 | 204.3 | 4 169 | 71 | 138 | 1 856 | 54.1 | 42.0 | 3.9 |
| Coos | 337.6 | 5 316 | 34.5 | 41.0 | 2.5 | 0.2 | 4.7 | 201.1 | 3 166 | 344 | 414 | 5 058 | 46.5 | 49.6 | 3.9 |
| Crook | 76.4 | 3 335 | 35.2 | 0.5 | 5.3 | 0.0 | 33.4 | 63.3 | 2 765 | 314 | 58 | 811 | 35.1 | 61.5 | 3.4 |
| Curry | 81.8 | 3 760 | 33.4 | 23.4 | 2.7 | 4.7 | 4.2 | 70.1 | 3 221 | 96 | 103 | 1 065 | 42.4 | 53.9 | 3.7 |
| Deschutes | 590.3 | 3 832 | 42.3 | 3.4 | 7.3 | 0.5 | 6.4 | 840.1 | 5 454 | 900 | 450 | 7 439 | 48.7 | 49.0 | 2.4 |
| Douglas | 406.4 | 3 903 | 44.0 | 9.5 | 4.2 | 0.3 | 10.6 | 275.8 | 2 649 | 1 432 | 344 | 6 263 | 38.3 | 58.4 | 3.2 |
| Gilliam | 18.1 | 10 688 | 36.8 | 1.0 | 3.9 | 0.0 | 7.9 | 66.3 | 39 212 | 11 | 0 | 218 | 38.7 | 58.4 | 2.9 |
| Grant | 57.2 | 8 285 | 32.6 | 26.3 | 3.1 | 3.6 | 9.7 | 22.8 | 3 307 | 264 | 21 | 738 | 25.7 | 71.2 | 3.0 |
| Harney | 49.2 | 7 273 | 36.3 | 41.6 | 1.8 | 0.0 | 6.5 | 47.0 | 6 945 | 251 | 21 | 755 | 25.8 | 70.5 | 3.7 |
| Hood River | 86.1 | 4 044 | 49.6 | 2.8 | 3.9 | 0.8 | 9.6 | 63.9 | 3 000 | 113 | 63 | 1 106 | 64.1 | 33.2 | 2.7 |
| Jackson | 598.7 | 3 004 | 44.0 | 6.5 | 7.5 | 0.0 | 7.3 | 575.5 | 2 887 | 1 697 | 576 | 9 471 | 48.6 | 48.5 | 2.9 |
| Jefferson | 99.1 | 4 791 | 45.3 | 21.7 | 3.3 | 0.0 | 5.0 | 88.5 | 4 277 | 132 | 61 | 2 406 | 44.3 | 52.9 | 2.8 |
| Josephine | 233.4 | 2 880 | 58.9 | 5.0 | 5.2 | 0.3 | 3.8 | 188.1 | 2 320 | 271 | 233 | 2 975 | 41.4 | 54.6 | 4.0 |
| Klamath | 234.7 | 3 529 | 47.3 | 5.1 | 3.8 | 0.3 | 11.0 | 354.2 | 5 325 | 923 | 197 | 4 256 | 31.9 | 65.0 | 3.1 |
| Lake | 39.9 | 5 476 | 32.3 | 34.8 | 2.5 | 0.0 | 10.4 | 6.4 | 881 | 259 | 22 | 714 | 25.9 | 71.5 | 2.5 |
| Lane | 1 242.2 | 3 615 | 45.9 | 4.6 | 6.9 | 2.5 | 5.0 | 1 385.2 | 4 031 | 1 702 | 1 078 | 27 814 | 62.3 | 34.9 | 2.8 |
| Lincoln | 175.6 | 3 828 | 33.2 | 8.5 | 6.9 | 0.3 | 8.4 | 226.3 | 4 935 | 321 | 206 | 3 440 | 59.7 | 36.8 | 3.5 |
| Linn | 432.9 | 3 822 | 48.7 | 2.4 | 5.4 | 1.6 | 5.2 | 493.3 | 4 355 | 329 | 332 | 6 197 | 42.6 | 54.0 | 3.4 |
| Malheur | 127.5 | 4 094 | 61.9 | 4.7 | 1.6 | 0.2 | 4.1 | 70.8 | 2 274 | 220 | 87 | 2 992 | 28.3 | 68.6 | 3.1 |
| Marion | 1 213.3 | 3 896 | 55.2 | 5.7 | 5.1 | 0.3 | 3.9 | 1 571.6 | 5 046 | 1 413 | 901 | 32 219 | 49.6 | 47.4 | 3.0 |

1. Based on the resident population estimated as of July 1 of the year shown.    2. © 2013 Election Data Services, Inc. All rights reserved.

# Table B. States and Counties — Land Area and Population

| STATE/ County code | CBSA code[1] | County type[2] | STATE County | Land area[3] (sq km) 2010 | Population 2012 Total persons | Rank | Per square kilometer | White | Black | American Indian, Alaska Native | Asian and Pacific Islander | Percent Hispanic or Latino[4] | Under 5 years | 5 to 17 years | 18 to 24 years | 25 to 34 years | 35 to 44 years | 45 to 54 years |
|---|---|---|---|---|---|---|---|---|---|---|---|---|---|---|---|---|---|---|
| | | | | 1 | 2 | 3 | 4 | 5 | 6 | 7 | 8 | 9 | 10 | 11 | 12 | 13 | 14 | 15 |
| | | | OREGON—Cont'd | | | | | | | | | | | | | | | |
| 41 049 | 37820 | 6 | Morrow | 5 262 | 11 244 | 2 341 | 2.1 | 65.3 | 0.9 | 2.0 | 1.5 | 32.1 | 7.2 | 21.1 | 8.3 | 11.1 | 12.7 | 13.7 |
| 41 051 | 38900 | 1 | Multnomah | 1 117 | 759 256 | 76 | 679.7 | 75.4 | 6.6 | 2.0 | 8.9 | 11.1 | 6.3 | 14.1 | 9.3 | 18.7 | 15.5 | 13.2 |
| 41 053 | 41420 | 2 | Polk | 1 919 | 76 353 | 719 | 39.8 | 82.9 | 1.1 | 3.2 | 3.4 | 12.4 | 6.1 | 17.6 | 12.5 | 11.3 | 11.5 | 12.6 |
| 41 055 | ... | 9 | Sherman | 2 133 | 1 732 | 3 073 | 0.8 | 91.6 | 0.3 | 2.0 | 0.6 | 6.6 | 4.1 | 15.1 | 5.8 | 10.4 | 9.9 | 16.9 |
| 41 057 | ... | 6 | Tillamook | 2 856 | 25 287 | 1 599 | 8.9 | 88.3 | 0.6 | 2.1 | 1.7 | 9.3 | 5.4 | 14.3 | 6.7 | 10.1 | 10.5 | 14.0 |
| 41 059 | 37820 | 5 | Umatilla | 8 328 | 76 820 | 713 | 9.2 | 70.5 | 1.3 | 4.1 | 1.6 | 24.4 | 7.3 | 19.2 | 9.4 | 13.3 | 12.6 | 13.1 |
| 41 061 | 29260 | 7 | Union | 5 275 | 25 759 | 1 576 | 4.9 | 92.1 | 1.0 | 2.0 | 2.7 | 4.2 | 6.2 | 16.0 | 12.1 | 11.2 | 9.9 | 12.9 |
| 41 063 | ... | 9 | Wallowa | 8 149 | 6 821 | 2 697 | 0.8 | 96.1 | 0.9 | 1.6 | 1.1 | 2.3 | 5.1 | 13.6 | 5.2 | 9.4 | 8.8 | 14.3 |
| 41 065 | 45520 | 6 | Wasco | 6 168 | 25 487 | 1 586 | 4.1 | 78.4 | 0.8 | 5.0 | 2.1 | 15.6 | 6.4 | 16.6 | 8.0 | 11.7 | 11.0 | 13.2 |
| 41 067 | 38900 | 1 | Washington | 1 876 | 547 672 | 114 | 291.9 | 72.4 | 2.5 | 1.3 | 11.4 | 16.0 | 7.1 | 18.2 | 8.2 | 15.6 | 15.2 | 13.9 |
| 41 069 | ... | 9 | Wheeler | 4 441 | 1 424 | 3 088 | 0.3 | 93.0 | 1.1 | 3.0 | 1.4 | 4.8 | 4.7 | 13.0 | 4.8 | 7.8 | 7.5 | 14.2 |
| 41 071 | 38900 | 1 | Yamhill | 1 854 | 100 255 | 589 | 54.1 | 81.0 | 1.3 | 2.4 | 2.8 | 15.1 | 6.4 | 18.2 | 10.4 | 12.3 | 12.7 | 13.5 |
| 42 000 | ... | X | PENNSYLVANIA | 115 883 | 12 763 536 | X | 110.1 | 80.4 | 11.4 | 0.5 | 3.3 | 5.9 | 5.7 | 16.0 | 9.9 | 12.1 | 12.4 | 15.0 |
| 42 001 | 23900 | 4 | Adams | 1 343 | 101 482 | 578 | 75.6 | 91.2 | 2.0 | 0.4 | 1.1 | 6.2 | 5.4 | 16.4 | 9.7 | 10.3 | 12.7 | 15.6 |
| 42 003 | 38300 | 1 | Allegheny | 1 891 | 1 229 338 | 31 | 650.1 | 82.0 | 14.2 | 0.5 | 3.4 | 1.7 | 5.2 | 14.3 | 10.0 | 13.5 | 11.6 | 14.9 |
| 42 005 | 38300 | 1 | Armstrong | 1 692 | 68 409 | 775 | 40.4 | 98.2 | 1.2 | 0.3 | 0.4 | 0.6 | 5.1 | 15.0 | 7.0 | 10.6 | 12.3 | 16.3 |
| 42 007 | 38300 | 1 | Beaver | 1 126 | 170 245 | 364 | 151.2 | 91.8 | 7.4 | 0.5 | 0.7 | 1.3 | 5.2 | 15.0 | 7.9 | 10.9 | 11.6 | 16.1 |
| 42 009 | ... | 6 | Bedford | 2 622 | 49 324 | 994 | 18.8 | 98.1 | 0.9 | 0.4 | 0.4 | 1.0 | 5.1 | 16.1 | 7.0 | 10.1 | 12.5 | 15.7 |
| 42 011 | 39740 | 1 | Berks | 2 218 | 413 491 | 166 | 186.4 | 77.4 | 4.9 | 0.4 | 1.7 | 16.8 | 6.0 | 17.4 | 10.2 | 11.3 | 12.7 | 15.1 |
| 42 013 | 11020 | 3 | Blair | 1 362 | 127 121 | 485 | 93.3 | 96.5 | 2.3 | 0.4 | 0.9 | 1.0 | 5.7 | 15.3 | 9.3 | 11.2 | 12.0 | 14.5 |
| 42 015 | 42380 | 6 | Bradford | 2 972 | 62 792 | 831 | 21.1 | 97.3 | 0.9 | 0.7 | 0.8 | 1.3 | 6.0 | 16.4 | 7.4 | 10.4 | 11.7 | 15.7 |
| 42 017 | 37980 | 1 | Bucks | 1 565 | 627 053 | 103 | 400.7 | 87.7 | 4.2 | 0.4 | 4.6 | 4.4 | 5.3 | 17.2 | 7.6 | 10.8 | 12.9 | 17.2 |
| 42 019 | 38300 | 1 | Butler | 2 042 | 184 970 | 341 | 90.6 | 96.5 | 1.6 | 0.3 | 1.4 | 1.1 | 5.2 | 16.7 | 9.1 | 10.4 | 12.9 | 16.2 |
| 42 021 | 27780 | 3 | Cambria | 1 783 | 141 584 | 444 | 79.4 | 94.0 | 4.5 | 0.3 | 0.8 | 1.5 | 4.9 | 14.4 | 9.8 | 10.6 | 11.8 | 14.8 |
| 42 023 | ... | 7 | Cameron | 1 026 | 4 939 | 2 841 | 4.8 | 98.6 | 0.8 | 0.7 | 0.4 | 0.4 | 4.3 | 14.2 | 6.5 | 8.7 | 10.5 | 16.4 |
| 42 025 | 10900 | 2 | Carbon | 988 | 65 006 | 811 | 65.8 | 94.2 | 1.8 | 0.5 | 0.9 | 3.4 | 5.2 | 15.2 | 6.9 | 10.7 | 12.9 | 16.3 |
| 42 027 | 44300 | 3 | Centre | 2 875 | 155 171 | 406 | 54.0 | 88.6 | 3.6 | 0.4 | 6.2 | 2.7 | 4.2 | 11.2 | 30.5 | 11.6 | 10.0 | 11.2 |
| 42 029 | 37980 | 1 | Chester | 1 944 | 506 575 | 100 | 260.6 | 83.1 | 6.8 | 0.5 | 4.4 | 6.7 | 6.1 | 18.3 | 9.0 | 11.0 | 13.4 | 16.2 |
| 42 031 | ... | 6 | Clarion | 1 556 | 39 646 | 1 178 | 25.5 | 97.3 | 1.6 | 0.4 | 0.8 | 0.7 | 5.1 | 13.9 | 16.7 | 9.9 | 11.1 | 13.8 |
| 42 033 | 20180 | 4 | Clearfield | 2 965 | 81 184 | 681 | 27.4 | 94.6 | 2.5 | 0.3 | 0.7 | 2.5 | 4.8 | 14.8 | 7.9 | 11.5 | 13.5 | 16.0 |
| 42 035 | 30820 | 6 | Clinton | 2 300 | 39 517 | 1 182 | 17.2 | 96.5 | 2.0 | 0.4 | 0.8 | 1.2 | 5.5 | 15.3 | 14.4 | 10.7 | 11.3 | 13.8 |
| 42 037 | 14100 | 4 | Columbia | 1 251 | 66 887 | 789 | 53.5 | 94.8 | 2.3 | 0.4 | 1.2 | 2.2 | 4.6 | 13.5 | 17.5 | 9.6 | 11.3 | 13.9 |
| 42 039 | 32740 | 4 | Crawford | 2 622 | 87 598 | 649 | 33.4 | 96.4 | 2.4 | 0.5 | 0.7 | 1.0 | 5.6 | 16.4 | 9.6 | 10.4 | 11.9 | 14.8 |
| 42 041 | 25420 | 2 | Cumberland | 1 413 | 238 614 | 273 | 168.9 | 90.6 | 4.0 | 0.5 | 3.7 | 2.8 | 5.2 | 15.0 | 10.8 | 12.2 | 12.6 | 14.8 |
| 42 043 | 25420 | 2 | Dauphin | 1 360 | 269 665 | 245 | 198.3 | 71.9 | 19.0 | 0.6 | 3.7 | 7.3 | 6.2 | 16.7 | 8.4 | 13.3 | 12.5 | 15.2 |
| 42 045 | 37980 | 1 | Delaware | 476 | 561 098 | 110 | 1 178.8 | 72.2 | 20.4 | 0.5 | 5.5 | 3.1 | 6.0 | 17.0 | 10.5 | 12.2 | 12.2 | 15.2 |
| 42 047 | 41260 | 7 | Elk | 2 143 | 31 550 | 1 401 | 14.7 | 98.5 | 0.6 | 0.4 | 0.5 | 0.7 | 4.7 | 15.7 | 6.1 | 9.7 | 12.9 | 17.1 |
| 42 049 | 21500 | 2 | Erie | 2 070 | 280 646 | 236 | 135.6 | 88.1 | 8.1 | 0.5 | 1.5 | 3.5 | 5.9 | 16.5 | 11.7 | 11.9 | 11.7 | 14.4 |
| 42 051 | 38300 | 1 | Fayette | 2 047 | 135 660 | 459 | 66.3 | 93.9 | 5.5 | 0.4 | 0.6 | 0.9 | 4.9 | 15.0 | 7.7 | 11.1 | 12.7 | 15.3 |
| 42 053 | ... | 9 | Forest | 1 106 | 7 667 | 2 630 | 6.9 | 75.7 | 18.6 | 0.5 | 0.3 | 5.5 | 2.3 | 9.7 | 10.7 | 16.7 | 12.7 | 15.0 |
| 42 055 | 16540 | 4 | Franklin | 2 000 | 151 275 | 418 | 75.6 | 91.2 | 4.0 | 0.5 | 1.3 | 4.5 | 6.5 | 17.1 | 7.9 | 11.7 | 12.9 | 14.3 |
| 42 057 | ... | 8 | Fulton | 1 133 | 14 772 | 2 124 | 13.0 | 97.7 | 1.5 | 0.6 | 0.4 | 0.9 | 5.8 | 16.9 | 7.1 | 10.6 | 13.4 | 14.9 |
| 42 059 | ... | 6 | Greene | 1 492 | 38 085 | 1 217 | 25.5 | 94.8 | 3.7 | 0.7 | 0.6 | 1.2 | 4.9 | 14.7 | 10.5 | 11.9 | 13.2 | 14.9 |
| 42 061 | 26500 | 6 | Huntingdon | 2 265 | 45 943 | 1 049 | 20.3 | 92.3 | 5.9 | 0.4 | 0.7 | 1.7 | 5.2 | 14.5 | 9.7 | 12.1 | 13.1 | 14.7 |
| 42 063 | 26860 | 4 | Indiana | 2 142 | 88 218 | 646 | 41.2 | 94.8 | 3.2 | 0.4 | 1.3 | 1.2 | 5.0 | 13.5 | 18.8 | 10.3 | 10.4 | 13.3 |
| 42 065 | ... | 7 | Jefferson | 1 690 | 44 764 | 1 072 | 26.5 | 98.4 | 0.7 | 0.6 | 0.4 | 0.7 | 5.6 | 15.6 | 8.1 | 10.8 | 12.0 | 15.5 |
| 42 067 | ... | 6 | Juniata | 1 014 | 24 904 | 1 612 | 24.6 | 96.3 | 1.0 | 0.4 | 0.6 | 2.6 | 6.2 | 17.6 | 7.7 | 11.3 | 12.5 | 15.2 |
| 42 069 | 42540 | 2 | Lackawanna | 1 189 | 214 477 | 294 | 180.4 | 90.4 | 3.1 | 0.4 | 2.1 | 5.2 | 5.4 | 15.0 | 10.0 | 11.6 | 12.0 | 14.6 |
| 42 071 | 29540 | 2 | Lancaster | 2 444 | 526 823 | 123 | 215.6 | 85.7 | 4.0 | 0.4 | 2.3 | 8.9 | 6.8 | 17.8 | 9.6 | 11.9 | 11.9 | 14.3 |
| 42 073 | 35260 | 4 | Lawrence | 928 | 89 871 | 636 | 96.8 | 94.4 | 4.9 | 0.4 | 0.7 | 1.1 | 5.3 | 15.6 | 8.2 | 10.4 | 11.8 | 15.1 |
| 42 075 | 30140 | 3 | Lebanon | 937 | 135 251 | 462 | 144.3 | 87.2 | 2.2 | 0.4 | 1.5 | 9.7 | 6.2 | 16.5 | 8.4 | 11.3 | 12.3 | 14.6 |
| 42 077 | 10900 | 2 | Lehigh | 894 | 355 245 | 187 | 397.4 | 72.1 | 6.1 | 0.4 | 3.5 | 19.5 | 6.1 | 17.2 | 9.0 | 12.3 | 12.9 | 15.2 |
| 42 079 | 42540 | 2 | Luzerne | 2 306 | 321 027 | 203 | 139.2 | 88.4 | 3.7 | 0.3 | 1.4 | 7.2 | 5.1 | 15.0 | 9.4 | 11.2 | 12.6 | 15.1 |
| 42 081 | 48700 | 3 | Lycoming | 3 182 | 117 168 | 519 | 36.8 | 93.2 | 5.5 | 0.5 | 0.9 | 1.5 | 5.5 | 15.1 | 10.8 | 11.5 | 11.7 | 15.0 |
| 42 083 | 14620 | 7 | McKean | 2 536 | 43 127 | 1 105 | 17.0 | 95.0 | 2.8 | 0.6 | 0.7 | 1.8 | 5.4 | 15.5 | 9.1 | 11.4 | 12.9 | 15.0 |
| 42 085 | 49660 | 2 | Mercer | 1 742 | 115 655 | 522 | 66.4 | 92.3 | 6.6 | 0.5 | 1.0 | 1.1 | 5.0 | 16.3 | 9.6 | 10.0 | 11.6 | 14.9 |
| 42 087 | 30380 | 4 | Mifflin | 1 065 | 46 773 | 1 032 | 43.9 | 97.5 | 1.1 | 0.3 | 0.7 | 1.2 | 6.1 | 16.7 | 7.3 | 10.5 | 12.2 | 14.6 |
| 42 089 | 20700 | 4 | Monroe | 1 575 | 168 798 | 368 | 107.2 | 71.6 | 13.2 | 0.7 | 2.7 | 13.5 | 4.9 | 18.2 | 10.6 | 9.6 | 12.7 | 17.3 |
| 42 091 | 37980 | 1 | Montgomery | 1 251 | 808 460 | 71 | 646.3 | 80.1 | 9.5 | 0.4 | 7.2 | 4.4 | 5.8 | 16.8 | 7.7 | 12.2 | 13.2 | 15.9 |
| 42 093 | 14100 | 6 | Montour | 337 | 18 356 | 1 905 | 54.5 | 94.5 | 2.0 | 0.4 | 2.0 | 2.0 | 5.8 | 15.0 | 7.1 | 11.7 | 11.3 | 15.6 |
| 42 095 | 10900 | 2 | Northampton | 957 | 299 267 | 219 | 312.7 | 81.8 | 5.5 | 0.4 | 3.0 | 10.8 | 5.2 | 16.2 | 10.0 | 10.9 | 12.8 | 15.5 |
| 42 097 | 44980 | 2 | Northumberland | 1 187 | 94 428 | 615 | 79.6 | 94.8 | 2.5 | 0.4 | 0.6 | 2.5 | 5.4 | 15.0 | 7.7 | 11.5 | 12.3 | 15.1 |
| 42 099 | 25420 | 2 | Perry | 1 428 | 45 701 | 1 054 | 32.0 | 97.2 | 1.2 | 0.5 | 0.6 | 1.4 | 5.9 | 16.9 | 7.8 | 11.1 | 13.2 | 15.7 |
| 42 101 | 37980 | 1 | Philadelphia | 347 | 1 547 607 | 22 | 4 460.0 | 38.3 | 43.2 | 0.8 | 7.1 | 12.6 | 6.8 | 15.7 | 12.9 | 16.6 | 12.2 | 12.8 |
| 42 103 | 35620 | 1 | Pike | 1 411 | 56 899 | 893 | 40.3 | 83.8 | 6.2 | 0.9 | 1.5 | 9.2 | 4.6 | 17.8 | 7.6 | 8.5 | 12.5 | 17.8 |

1. CBSA = Core Based Statistical Area. See Appendix A for explanation. See Appendix B for list of metropolitan areas with component counties.   2. County type code from the Economic Research Service of USDA Rural-Urban Continuum Codes. See Appendix A for definition.   3. Dry land or land partially or temporarily covered by water.   4. May be of any race.

# Table B. States and Counties — **Population and Households**

| STATE County | Age (percent) (cont.) 55 to 64 years | 65 to 74 years | 75 years and over | Percent female | Total persons 2000 | 2010 | Percent change 2000–2010 | 2010–2012 | Components of change, 2010–2012 Births | Deaths | Net migration | Households, 2010 Number | Percent change, 2000–2010 | Persons per household | Female family householder[1] | One person |
|---|---|---|---|---|---|---|---|---|---|---|---|---|---|---|---|---|
| | 16 | 17 | 18 | 19 | 20 | 21 | 22 | 23 | 24 | 25 | 26 | 27 | 28 | 29 | 30 | 31 |
| **OREGON—Cont'd** | | | | | | | | | | | | | | | | |
| Morrow | 13.1 | 7.7 | 5.1 | 48.4 | 10 995 | 11 173 | 1.6 | 0.6 | 369 | 187 | -111 | 3 916 | 3.7 | 2.85 | 9.6 | 19.1 |
| Multnomah | 12.3 | 5.8 | 4.9 | 50.5 | 660 486 | 735 334 | 11.3 | 3.3 | 21 510 | 11 976 | 14 321 | 304 540 | 11.9 | 2.35 | 10.7 | 32.6 |
| Polk | 13.2 | 8.1 | 7.0 | 51.4 | 62 380 | 75 403 | 20.9 | 1.3 | 1 943 | 1 398 | 422 | 28 288 | 22.7 | 2.60 | 10.3 | 23.0 |
| Sherman | 16.4 | 11.2 | 10.2 | 49.2 | 1 934 | 1 765 | -8.7 | -1.9 | 35 | 25 | -49 | 777 | -2.5 | 2.27 | 7.5 | 30.5 |
| Tillamook | 17.7 | 12.4 | 8.9 | 49.6 | 24 262 | 25 250 | 4.1 | 0.1 | 566 | 619 | 103 | 10 834 | 6.2 | 2.29 | 8.1 | 29.1 |
| Umatilla | 12.3 | 7.0 | 5.7 | 47.8 | 70 548 | 75 889 | 7.6 | 1.2 | 2 370 | 1 397 | -47 | 26 904 | 6.8 | 2.67 | 12.0 | 24.7 |
| Union | 14.6 | 9.1 | 7.9 | 50.7 | 24 530 | 25 748 | 5.0 | 0.0 | 682 | 618 | -43 | 10 501 | 7.8 | 2.38 | 9.5 | 27.6 |
| Wallowa | 19.8 | 13.0 | 10.8 | 50.7 | 7 226 | 7 008 | -3.0 | -2.7 | 119 | 154 | -154 | 3 133 | 3.4 | 2.20 | 7.1 | 30.0 |
| Wasco | 15.3 | 9.3 | 8.5 | 50.4 | 23 791 | 25 213 | 6.0 | 1.1 | 677 | 628 | 228 | 10 031 | 6.7 | 2.44 | 10.9 | 28.8 |
| Washington | 11.4 | 5.8 | 4.7 | 50.8 | 445 342 | 529 710 | 18.9 | 3.4 | 16 183 | 6 523 | 8 302 | 200 934 | 18.8 | 2.60 | 10.1 | 25.1 |
| Wheeler | 18.2 | 17.3 | 12.6 | 50.6 | 1 547 | 1 441 | -6.9 | -1.2 | 24 | 36 | -7 | 651 | -0.3 | 2.18 | 7.2 | 32.4 |
| Yamhill | 12.6 | 7.3 | 6.4 | 49.7 | 84 992 | 99 193 | 16.7 | 1.1 | 2 569 | 1 723 | 182 | 34 726 | 20.9 | 2.70 | 11.1 | 21.7 |
| **PENNSYLVANIA** | 13.3 | 7.8 | 7.7 | 51.2 | 12 281 054 | 12 702 379 | 3.4 | 0.5 | 320 606 | 283 295 | 26 819 | 5 018 904 | 5.1 | 2.45 | 12.2 | 28.6 |
| Adams | 13.9 | 8.6 | 7.5 | 50.8 | 91 292 | 101 407 | 11.1 | 0.1 | 2 296 | 2 034 | -240 | 38 013 | 13.0 | 2.56 | 9.2 | 21.9 |
| Allegheny | 13.9 | 7.8 | 8.8 | 52.0 | 1 281 666 | 1 223 348 | -4.6 | 0.5 | 29 205 | 30 512 | 8 120 | 533 960 | -0.6 | 2.23 | 12.2 | 35.0 |
| Armstrong | 15.1 | 9.3 | 9.2 | 50.6 | 72 392 | 68 941 | -4.8 | -0.8 | 1 514 | 1 911 | -160 | 28 713 | -1.0 | 2.38 | 9.3 | 28.0 |
| Beaver | 14.8 | 8.9 | 9.6 | 51.7 | 181 412 | 170 539 | -6.0 | -0.2 | 3 857 | 4 575 | 530 | 71 383 | -1.6 | 2.34 | 12.1 | 29.3 |
| Bedford | 14.0 | 10.4 | 9.0 | 50.3 | 49 984 | 49 762 | -0.4 | -0.9 | 1 080 | 1 158 | -440 | 20 233 | 2.4 | 2.43 | 8.2 | 25.7 |
| Berks | 12.6 | 7.4 | 7.3 | 50.9 | 373 638 | 411 442 | 10.1 | 0.5 | 11 060 | 8 098 | -710 | 154 356 | 9.0 | 2.59 | 12.0 | 24.5 |
| Blair | 14.3 | 8.8 | 9.0 | 51.4 | 129 144 | 127 089 | -1.6 | 0.0 | 3 184 | 3 621 | 446 | 52 159 | 1.2 | 2.37 | 11.7 | 29.6 |
| Bradford | 14.6 | 9.9 | 8.0 | 50.7 | 62 761 | 62 622 | -0.2 | 0.3 | 1 618 | 1 562 | 136 | 25 321 | 3.5 | 2.45 | 9.6 | 26.2 |
| Bucks | 14.1 | 7.8 | 7.2 | 51.0 | 597 635 | 625 249 | 4.6 | 0.3 | 13 726 | 12 207 | 310 | 234 849 | 7.4 | 2.63 | 9.6 | 23.0 |
| Butler | 14.0 | 7.9 | 7.6 | 50.7 | 174 083 | 183 862 | 5.6 | 0.6 | 3 998 | 4 105 | 1 201 | 72 835 | 10.6 | 2.45 | 8.4 | 26.5 |
| Cambria | 14.9 | 8.9 | 9.8 | 50.4 | 152 598 | 143 679 | -5.8 | -1.5 | 3 036 | 4 080 | -978 | 58 950 | -2.6 | 2.30 | 10.9 | 31.2 |
| Cameron | 17.8 | 10.6 | 10.8 | 50.9 | 5 974 | 5 085 | -14.9 | -2.9 | 77 | 156 | -65 | 2 273 | -7.8 | 2.20 | 9.5 | 32.8 |
| Carbon | 14.8 | 9.6 | 8.4 | 50.7 | 58 802 | 65 249 | 11.0 | -0.4 | 1 323 | 1 767 | 224 | 26 684 | 12.6 | 2.42 | 10.4 | 26.7 |
| Centre | 9.9 | 6.0 | 5.4 | 48.1 | 135 758 | 153 990 | 13.4 | 0.8 | 2 803 | 2 118 | 562 | 57 573 | 16.7 | 2.38 | 6.4 | 28.7 |
| Chester | 12.8 | 7.1 | 6.1 | 50.9 | 433 501 | 498 886 | 15.1 | 1.5 | 12 658 | 8 068 | 3 097 | 182 900 | 15.8 | 2.65 | 8.5 | 23.0 |
| Clarion | 13.1 | 8.9 | 7.7 | 51.5 | 41 765 | 39 988 | -4.3 | -0.9 | 897 | 961 | -256 | 16 128 | 0.5 | 2.37 | 8.7 | 28.4 |
| Clearfield | 13.9 | 9.0 | 8.5 | 48.2 | 83 382 | 81 642 | -2.1 | -0.6 | 1 568 | 2 050 | 51 | 32 288 | -1.5 | 2.37 | 10.3 | 27.7 |
| Clinton | 12.9 | 8.4 | 7.8 | 50.9 | 37 914 | 39 238 | 3.5 | 0.7 | 892 | 855 | 250 | 15 151 | 2.6 | 2.42 | 10.3 | 26.5 |
| Columbia | 13.2 | 8.4 | 8.0 | 52.0 | 64 151 | 67 295 | 4.9 | -0.6 | 1 373 | 1 570 | -233 | 26 479 | 6.3 | 2.38 | 9.3 | 28.3 |
| Crawford | 14.5 | 9.1 | 7.8 | 51.2 | 90 366 | 88 765 | -1.8 | -1.3 | 2 087 | 2 182 | -1 102 | 35 028 | 1.0 | 2.42 | 9.7 | 28.0 |
| Cumberland | 13.5 | 8.1 | 7.8 | 50.9 | 213 674 | 235 406 | 10.2 | 1.4 | 5 361 | 4 732 | 2 717 | 93 943 | 13.2 | 2.37 | 8.8 | 28.2 |
| Dauphin | 13.7 | 7.3 | 6.7 | 51.6 | 251 798 | 268 100 | 6.5 | 0.6 | 7 583 | 5 271 | -662 | 110 435 | 7.6 | 2.37 | 13.8 | 31.2 |
| Delaware | 12.7 | 6.8 | 7.6 | 52.1 | 550 864 | 558 979 | 1.5 | 0.4 | 15 203 | 12 082 | -774 | 208 700 | 1.2 | 2.57 | 14.6 | 27.6 |
| Elk | 14.9 | 9.3 | 9.7 | 50.2 | 35 112 | 31 946 | -9.0 | -1.2 | 575 | 872 | -104 | 13 693 | -3.1 | 2.31 | 8.9 | 29.8 |
| Erie | 13.2 | 7.4 | 7.3 | 50.8 | 280 843 | 280 566 | -0.1 | 0.0 | 7 199 | 6 059 | -930 | 110 413 | 3.7 | 2.36 | 13.1 | 29.1 |
| Fayette | 15.1 | 9.1 | 9.0 | 50.9 | 148 644 | 136 606 | -8.1 | -0.7 | 2 989 | 4 104 | 244 | 55 997 | -6.6 | 2.36 | 13.2 | 29.3 |
| Forest | 14.6 | 11.4 | 7.0 | 33.0 | 4 946 | 7 716 | 56.0 | -0.6 | 62 | 189 | 55 | 2 511 | 25.6 | 2.08 | 5.7 | 36.2 |
| Franklin | 12.9 | 8.8 | 8.0 | 51.1 | 129 313 | 149 618 | 15.7 | 1.1 | 4 046 | 3 243 | 847 | 58 389 | 15.3 | 2.52 | 9.4 | 24.3 |
| Fulton | 13.7 | 10.6 | 7.2 | 49.7 | 14 261 | 14 845 | 4.1 | -0.5 | 352 | 327 | -100 | 6 014 | 6.3 | 2.45 | 8.4 | 25.0 |
| Greene | 14.5 | 8.1 | 7.3 | 48.4 | 40 672 | 38 686 | -4.9 | -1.6 | 842 | 1 008 | -445 | 14 724 | -2.2 | 2.42 | 10.9 | 27.0 |
| Huntingdon | 14.1 | 9.2 | 7.3 | 46.9 | 45 586 | 45 913 | 0.7 | -0.1 | 978 | 1 000 | 26 | 17 280 | 3.1 | 2.39 | 8.7 | 27.6 |
| Indiana | 13.2 | 8.1 | 7.5 | 50.4 | 89 605 | 88 880 | -0.8 | -0.7 | 1 953 | 1 962 | -634 | 35 005 | 2.6 | 2.39 | 8.4 | 28.1 |
| Jefferson | 14.0 | 9.2 | 9.2 | 50.6 | 45 932 | 45 200 | -1.6 | -1.0 | 1 067 | 1 248 | -228 | 18 561 | 1.0 | 2.39 | 9.4 | 28.2 |
| Juniata | 13.4 | 8.5 | 7.7 | 50.2 | 22 821 | 24 636 | 8.0 | 1.1 | 622 | 533 | 64 | 9 476 | 10.4 | 2.57 | 7.6 | 23.0 |
| Lackawanna | 13.8 | 8.5 | 9.1 | 51.9 | 213 295 | 214 437 | 0.5 | 0.0 | 5 054 | 5 783 | 829 | 87 226 | 1.2 | 2.37 | 12.4 | 31.6 |
| Lancaster | 12.4 | 7.6 | 7.7 | 51.1 | 470 658 | 519 445 | 10.4 | 1.4 | 15 896 | 10 240 | 1 815 | 193 602 | 12.2 | 2.62 | 9.6 | 24.2 |
| Lawrence | 14.7 | 8.9 | 9.9 | 51.8 | 94 643 | 91 108 | -3.7 | -1.4 | 2 026 | 2 481 | -771 | 37 126 | 0.1 | 2.39 | 12.3 | 28.9 |
| Lebanon | 13.5 | 8.6 | 8.5 | 51.2 | 120 327 | 133 568 | 11.0 | 1.3 | 3 639 | 3 127 | 1 212 | 52 258 | 12.3 | 2.49 | 10.1 | 25.9 |
| Lehigh | 12.6 | 7.3 | 7.5 | 51.4 | 312 090 | 349 497 | 12.0 | 1.6 | 9 499 | 7 054 | 3 359 | 133 983 | 9.9 | 2.54 | 12.9 | 26.3 |
| Luzerne | 13.8 | 8.7 | 9.3 | 51.0 | 319 250 | 320 918 | 0.5 | 0.0 | 6 990 | 8 952 | 2 209 | 131 932 | 1.0 | 2.34 | 12.9 | 31.4 |
| Lycoming | 13.8 | 8.2 | 8.3 | 51.0 | 120 044 | 116 111 | -3.3 | 0.9 | 2 737 | 2 883 | 1 261 | 46 700 | -0.6 | 2.37 | 10.8 | 28.2 |
| McKean | 13.7 | 8.6 | 8.5 | 49.0 | 45 936 | 43 450 | -5.4 | -0.7 | 1 022 | 1 162 | -184 | 17 183 | -4.7 | 2.34 | 11.2 | 29.5 |
| Mercer | 14.0 | 9.0 | 9.6 | 51.0 | 120 293 | 116 638 | -3.0 | -0.8 | 2 503 | 3 159 | -280 | 46 442 | -0.6 | 2.37 | 11.6 | 29.4 |
| Mifflin | 13.7 | 9.8 | 9.0 | 51.0 | 46 486 | 46 682 | 0.4 | 0.2 | 1 226 | 1 154 | 26 | 18 743 | 1.8 | 2.46 | 9.3 | 27.1 |
| Monroe | 13.5 | 7.6 | 5.5 | 50.7 | 138 687 | 169 842 | 22.5 | -0.6 | 3 429 | 3 026 | -1 371 | 61 091 | 23.5 | 2.72 | 11.5 | 21.4 |
| Montgomery | 13.1 | 7.5 | 7.8 | 51.5 | 750 097 | 799 874 | 6.6 | 1.1 | 20 354 | 16 093 | 4 622 | 307 750 | 7.6 | 2.53 | 9.5 | 26.3 |
| Montour | 14.5 | 8.8 | 10.0 | 52.0 | 18 236 | 18 267 | 0.2 | 0.5 | 464 | 481 | 113 | 7 393 | 4.3 | 2.36 | 9.0 | 29.4 |
| Northampton | 13.5 | 7.8 | 8.1 | 51.1 | 267 066 | 297 735 | 11.5 | 0.5 | 6 654 | 6 170 | 1 182 | 113 565 | 11.8 | 2.53 | 11.1 | 25.0 |
| Northumberland | 14.5 | 9.4 | 9.3 | 50.1 | 94 556 | 94 528 | 0.0 | -0.1 | 2 173 | 2 532 | 327 | 39 242 | 1.0 | 2.32 | 10.3 | 30.3 |
| Perry | 15.1 | 8.3 | 6.1 | 50.0 | 43 602 | 45 969 | 5.4 | -0.6 | 1 241 | 933 | -584 | 17 903 | 7.2 | 2.53 | 8.7 | 23.0 |
| Philadelphia | 10.9 | 6.3 | 5.8 | 52.8 | 1 517 550 | 1 526 006 | 0.6 | 1.4 | 52 188 | 32 248 | 1 741 | 599 736 | 1.6 | 2.45 | 22.5 | 34.1 |
| Pike | 14.8 | 10.0 | 6.5 | 50.1 | 46 302 | 57 369 | 23.9 | -0.8 | 1 017 | 946 | -718 | 21 925 | 25.8 | 2.59 | 9.5 | 22.4 |

1. No spouse present.

# Table B. States and Counties — Population, Vital Statistics, Medicare, and Crime

| STATE County | Persons in group quarters, 2010 | Daytime population, 2007–2011 Number | Daytime population Employment/residence ratio | Births, 2011 Total | Births Rate[1] | Deaths, 2011 Number | Deaths Rate[1] | Persons under 65 with no health insurance, 2010 Number | Percent | Medicare, 2012 Eligible for Medicare | Enrolled in Medicare Advantage | Enrolled in a Medicare prescription drug plan | Serious crimes known to police,[2] 2011 Total Number | Rate[3] |
|---|---|---|---|---|---|---|---|---|---|---|---|---|---|---|
| | 32 | 33 | 34 | 35 | 36 | 37 | 38 | 39 | 40 | 41 | 42 | 43 | 44 | 45 |
| OREGON—Cont'd | | | | | | | | | | | | | | |
| Morrow | 23 | 10 587 | 0.88 | 158 | 14.1 | 94 | 8.4 | 2 400 | 24.6 | 1 778 | 249 | 880 | 324 | 2 869 |
| Multnomah | 19 583 | 823 345 | 1.27 | 9 890 | 13.2 | 5 254 | 7.0 | 131 915 | 20.3 | 101 634 | 54 937 | 24 489 | 40 107 | 5 397 |
| Polk | 1 885 | 62 526 | 0.61 | 850 | 11.2 | 623 | 8.2 | 10 735 | 17.1 | 13 703 | 7 598 | 3 433 | 2 310 | 3 031 |
| Sherman | 0 | 2 022 | 1.14 | 11 | 6.4 | 13 | 7.6 | 285 | 20.4 | 466 | 71 | 224 | 34 | 1 906 |
| Tillamook | 476 | 25 100 | 0.99 | 257 | 10.1 | 285 | 11.2 | 4 257 | 21.7 | 6 514 | 1 408 | 2 842 | 578 | 2 265 |
| Umatilla | 3 985 | 75 113 | 0.99 | 1 010 | 13.2 | 608 | 7.9 | 14 118 | 22.5 | 12 089 | 1 749 | 6 044 | 2 563 | 3 371 |
| Union | 735 | 25 195 | 0.96 | 306 | 11.9 | 282 | 10.9 | 3 976 | 18.9 | 5 348 | 308 | 3 338 | 1 319 | 5 069 |
| Wallowa | 105 | 6 889 | 0.98 | 49 | 7.0 | 71 | 10.2 | 1 200 | 22.3 | 2 022 | 45 | 1 185 | 54 | 762 |
| Wasco | 741 | 25 431 | 1.05 | 324 | 12.8 | 281 | 11.1 | 5 016 | 24.3 | 5 331 | 1 162 | 2 369 | 711 | 2 790 |
| Washington | 6 788 | 521 690 | 0.99 | 7 545 | 14.0 | 2 819 | 5.2 | 81 015 | 17.2 | 66 617 | 35 614 | 15 374 | 11 027 | 2 060 |
| Wheeler | 25 | 1 245 | 1.01 | 14 | 9.8 | 19 | 13.3 | 274 | 26.3 | 440 | 90 | 182 | 3 | 206 |
| Yamhill | 5 461 | 89 784 | 0.81 | 1 234 | 12.3 | 744 | 7.4 | 16 356 | 20.1 | 16 413 | 7 788 | 4 501 | 2 447 | 2 441 |
| PENNSYLVANIA | 426 113 | 12 584 479 | 0.99 | 143 420 | 11.3 | 125 152 | 9.8 | 1 254 674 | 12.1 | 2 400 244 | 926 547 | 827 691 | 328 419 | 2 577 |
| Adams | 3 993 | 86 439 | 0.71 | 1 041 | 10.3 | 884 | 8.7 | 10 181 | 12.4 | 19 949 | 5 608 | 7 234 | 1 347 | 1 324 |
| Allegheny | 35 054 | 1 318 185 | 1.16 | 12 903 | 10.5 | 13 598 | 11.1 | 102 528 | 10.4 | 240 513 | 147 718 | 40 063 | 30 706 | 2 508 |
| Armstrong | 650 | 59 112 | 0.66 | 679 | 9.9 | 881 | 12.8 | 6 730 | 12.1 | 15 363 | 9 536 | 3 182 | 732 | 1 127 |
| Beaver | 3 382 | 149 508 | 0.73 | 1 724 | 10.1 | 2 063 | 12.1 | 13 922 | 10.2 | 38 853 | 25 102 | 6 114 | 4 642 | 2 743 |
| Bedford | 551 | 46 043 | 0.83 | 493 | 9.9 | 505 | 10.2 | 5 749 | 14.4 | 11 835 | 5 603 | 3 357 | 557 | 1 116 |
| Berks | 12 023 | 388 020 | 0.89 | 4 987 | 12.1 | 3 538 | 8.6 | 42 425 | 12.4 | 73 643 | 24 976 | 29 274 | 10 176 | 2 465 |
| Blair | 3 672 | 132 223 | 1.09 | 1 410 | 11.1 | 1 613 | 12.7 | 12 470 | 12.2 | 28 355 | 13 872 | 8 074 | 2 858 | 2 242 |
| Bradford | 579 | 62 059 | 0.98 | 720 | 11.4 | 694 | 11.0 | 7 040 | 13.8 | 13 639 | 3 178 | 6 725 | 1 206 | 1 966 |
| Bucks | 8 233 | 567 790 | 0.82 | 6 195 | 9.9 | 5 280 | 8.4 | 46 340 | 8.8 | 113 670 | 34 489 | 42 620 | 13 443 | 2 143 |
| Butler | 5 490 | 182 543 | 0.99 | 1 788 | 9.7 | 1 787 | 9.7 | 14 616 | 9.7 | 34 572 | 19 439 | 5 935 | 2 582 | 1 400 |
| Cambria | 8 092 | 141 871 | 0.96 | 1 325 | 9.2 | 1 803 | 12.5 | 13 128 | 12.0 | 33 452 | 19 994 | 7 757 | 3 249 | 2 333 |
| Cameron | 92 | 5 159 | 1.01 | 39 | 7.8 | 73 | 14.6 | 526 | 13.1 | 1 388 | 297 | 770 | 103 | 2 019 |
| Carbon | 699 | 53 236 | 0.59 | 589 | 9.0 | 788 | 12.1 | 7 106 | 13.4 | 14 160 | 2 339 | 7 347 | 1 548 | 2 365 |
| Centre | 16 989 | 159 852 | 1.10 | 1 256 | 8.1 | 907 | 5.9 | 15 163 | 12.6 | 20 403 | 8 939 | 6 785 | 2 640 | 1 709 |
| Chester | 13 336 | 489 685 | 0.98 | 5 761 | 11.4 | 3 520 | 7.0 | 40 315 | 9.5 | 76 658 | 16 563 | 33 198 | 8 016 | 1 627 |
| Clarion | 1 841 | 38 869 | 0.92 | 401 | 10.0 | 421 | 10.5 | 4 380 | 13.8 | 8 317 | 2 275 | 3 772 | 643 | 1 682 |
| Clearfield | 5 115 | 80 421 | 0.95 | 708 | 8.7 | 898 | 11.0 | 8 299 | 13.2 | 17 867 | 6 313 | 7 538 | 2 110 | 2 576 |
| Clinton | 2 623 | 36 733 | 0.86 | 395 | 10.1 | 382 | 9.7 | 4 069 | 13.4 | 7 888 | 3 028 | 3 359 | 936 | 2 378 |
| Columbia | 4 387 | 66 089 | 0.97 | 616 | 9.1 | 703 | 10.4 | 6 267 | 12.0 | 13 176 | 5 254 | 4 964 | 1 409 | 2 260 |
| Crawford | 3 875 | 86 411 | 0.93 | 922 | 10.4 | 947 | 10.7 | 10 327 | 14.6 | 19 164 | 5 079 | 9 131 | 1 396 | 1 568 |
| Cumberland | 12 830 | 245 048 | 1.10 | 2 349 | 9.9 | 2 041 | 8.6 | 18 203 | 9.7 | 43 891 | 15 791 | 13 133 | 3 976 | 1 684 |
| Dauphin | 6 780 | 315 330 | 1.37 | 3 409 | 12.7 | 2 301 | 8.6 | 26 758 | 11.7 | 46 782 | 21 174 | 12 287 | 8 862 | 3 312 |
| Delaware | 23 055 | 507 923 | 0.81 | 6 827 | 12.2 | 5 267 | 9.4 | 50 268 | 10.9 | 94 881 | 25 555 | 37 861 | 17 081 | 3 046 |
| Elk | 355 | 31 649 | 0.96 | 262 | 8.3 | 378 | 11.9 | 2 775 | 10.8 | 7 564 | 1 190 | 4 383 | 726 | 2 265 |
| Erie | 12 875 | 284 438 | 1.04 | 3 185 | 11.3 | 2 685 | 9.6 | 27 235 | 11.9 | 52 228 | 22 892 | 18 247 | 8 260 | 2 935 |
| Fayette | 4 216 | 126 979 | 0.80 | 1 332 | 9.8 | 1 823 | 13.4 | 14 777 | 13.5 | 32 684 | 18 020 | 8 029 | 3 716 | 2 733 |
| Forest | 2 500 | 8 049 | 1.23 | 32 | 4.2 | 94 | 12.4 | 549 | 14.2 | 1 563 | 462 | 643 | 128 | 1 654 |
| Franklin | 2 696 | 138 573 | 0.86 | 1 756 | 11.6 | 1 413 | 9.4 | 17 302 | 14.0 | 30 636 | 6 518 | 12 176 | 2 664 | 1 775 |
| Fulton | 122 | 13 601 | 0.80 | 154 | 10.4 | 137 | 9.3 | 1 616 | 13.3 | 3 297 | 613 | 1 560 | 241 | 1 618 |
| Greene | 3 076 | 38 662 | 0.98 | 381 | 9.9 | 443 | 11.5 | 3 368 | 11.3 | 7 477 | 3 521 | 2 076 | 755 | 1 945 |
| Huntingdon | 4 570 | 42 394 | 0.81 | 443 | 9.7 | 461 | 10.0 | 4 182 | 12.3 | 9 444 | 2 940 | 4 193 | 671 | 1 457 |
| Indiana | 5 357 | 88 018 | 0.97 | 888 | 9.9 | 871 | 9.8 | 9 708 | 13.9 | 16 880 | 9 289 | 3 718 | 1 713 | 1 961 |
| Jefferson | 774 | 43 066 | 0.89 | 472 | 10.5 | 525 | 11.7 | 5 188 | 14.2 | 10 271 | 3 124 | 4 615 | 606 | 1 416 |
| Juniata | 292 | 20 636 | 0.66 | 282 | 11.6 | 230 | 9.4 | 3 176 | 15.6 | 4 821 | 2 032 | 1 812 | 276 | 1 117 |
| Lackawanna | 8 063 | 216 763 | 1.03 | 2 261 | 10.6 | 2 582 | 12.1 | 21 480 | 12.6 | 47 460 | 12 030 | 22 027 | 4 995 | 2 322 |
| Lancaster | 12 638 | 504 605 | 0.95 | 7 141 | 13.6 | 4 511 | 8.6 | 62 229 | 14.4 | 93 711 | 30 137 | 38 606 | 11 495 | 2 206 |
| Lawrence | 2 239 | 85 788 | 0.86 | 940 | 10.4 | 1 103 | 12.2 | 9 167 | 12.7 | 21 064 | 12 040 | 4 756 | 2 990 | 3 363 |
| Lebanon | 3 657 | 120 612 | 0.81 | 1 621 | 12.1 | 1 385 | 10.3 | 13 095 | 12.1 | 27 145 | 9 312 | 9 394 | 2 498 | 1 923 |
| Lehigh | 8 993 | 358 920 | 1.07 | 4 217 | 11.9 | 3 087 | 8.7 | 37 253 | 12.8 | 63 974 | 19 111 | 27 559 | 10 595 | 3 022 |
| Luzerne | 11 791 | 319 138 | 0.99 | 3 103 | 9.7 | 3 993 | 12.5 | 32 855 | 12.9 | 69 826 | 15 369 | 33 871 | 8 675 | 2 707 |
| Lycoming | 5 437 | 117 808 | 1.03 | 1 208 | 10.3 | 1 283 | 11.0 | 11 636 | 12.6 | 23 740 | 6 728 | 11 574 | 2 809 | 2 412 |
| McKean | 3 178 | 42 999 | 0.96 | 465 | 10.8 | 517 | 12.0 | 4 139 | 12.4 | 9 581 | 1 673 | 5 215 | 900 | 2 065 |
| Mercer | 6 714 | 117 991 | 1.02 | 1 111 | 9.6 | 1 413 | 12.2 | 10 793 | 12.1 | 26 801 | 11 598 | 9 280 | 2 729 | 2 332 |
| Mifflin | 559 | 44 582 | 0.89 | 560 | 12.0 | 494 | 10.5 | 5 979 | 15.8 | 10 740 | 4 291 | 4 422 | 962 | 2 054 |
| Monroe | 3 790 | 157 402 | 0.84 | 1 540 | 9.1 | 1 361 | 8.0 | 19 313 | 13.4 | 27 774 | 4 298 | 13 045 | 4 869 | 2 858 |
| Montgomery | 21 006 | 858 565 | 1.16 | 9 129 | 11.4 | 7 108 | 8.8 | 53 988 | 8.1 | 138 892 | 38 069 | 56 003 | 16 420 | 2 046 |
| Montour | 843 | 23 492 | 1.64 | 210 | 11.5 | 226 | 12.4 | 1 456 | 10.0 | 3 934 | 1 912 | 1 217 | 278 | 1 517 |
| Northampton | 10 620 | 268 100 | 0.80 | 2 975 | 10.0 | 2 690 | 9.0 | 26 898 | 11.1 | 57 503 | 14 398 | 26 276 | 6 696 | 2 242 |
| Northumberland | 3 446 | 84 485 | 0.76 | 973 | 10.3 | 1 092 | 11.5 | 9 863 | 13.3 | 21 158 | 6 343 | 9 704 | 1 653 | 1 743 |
| Perry | 657 | 33 565 | 0.45 | 540 | 11.7 | 408 | 8.9 | 5 554 | 14.2 | 8 337 | 3 514 | 2 509 | 871 | 1 991 |
| Philadelphia | 57 383 | 1 626 861 | 1.19 | 23 349 | 15.2 | 14 471 | 9.4 | 214 581 | 16.5 | 236 173 | 98 423 | 80 613 | 77 906 | 5 089 |
| Pike | 478 | 47 266 | 0.57 | 473 | 8.3 | 421 | 7.4 | 6 457 | 13.6 | 11 746 | 935 | 5 899 | 1 189 | 2 066 |

1. Per 1,000 estimated resident population.  2. Data for serious crimes have not been adjusted for underreporting; this may affect comparability between geographic areas and over time.  3. Per 100,000 population estimated by the FBI.

# Table B. States and Counties — Crime, Education, Money Income, and Poverty

| STATE County | Serious crimes known to police, 2011 (cont.)[1] Rate[2] Violent | Property | Education — School enrollment and attainment, 2007–2011 Enrollment[3] Total | Percent private | High school graduate or less | Bachelor's degree or more | Local government expenditures,[5] 2009–2010 Total current expenditures (mil dol) | Current expenditures per student (dollars) | Money income, 2007–2011 Per capita income[6] (dollars) | Households Median income Dollars | Percent change, 2000 to 2007–2011 (constant 2011 dollars) | Percent with income of $200,000 or more | Income and poverty, 2011 Median household income (dollars) | Percent below poverty level All persons | Children under 18 years | Children 5 to 17 years in families |
|---|---|---|---|---|---|---|---|---|---|---|---|---|---|---|---|---|
| | 46 | 47 | 48 | 49 | 50 | 51 | 52 | 53 | 54 | 55 | 56 | 57 | 58 | 59 | 60 | 61 |
| **OREGON—Cont'd** | | | | | | | | | | | | | | | | |
| Morrow | 213 | 2 657 | 2 929 | 4.6 | 55.5 | 10.7 | 23.5 | 9 776 | 20 215 | 46 110 | -9.0 | 1.6 | 46 902 | 16.1 | 23.0 | 20.4 |
| Multnomah | 475 | 4 922 | 179 067 | 20.1 | 31.3 | 38.3 | 957.9 | 10 455 | 29 544 | 50 726 | -9.0 | 4.0 | 46 989 | 19.4 | 26.1 | 25.6 |
| Polk | 232 | 2 799 | 20 842 | 12.1 | 36.0 | 28.2 | 67.7 | 8 880 | 24 794 | 52 865 | -7.5 | 2.1 | 52 277 | 14.1 | 18.7 | 17.0 |
| Sherman | 0 | 1 906 | 395 | 14.7 | 37.7 | 15.9 | 4.1 | 16 361 | 24 123 | 46 453 | -2.1 | 2.8 | 52 263 | 15.0 | 21.3 | 16.8 |
| Tillamook | 90 | 2 175 | 4 799 | 9.9 | 46.9 | 19.3 | 37.3 | 11 383 | 22 706 | 41 400 | -10.5 | 1.6 | 41 246 | 16.2 | 25.1 | 22.0 |
| Umatilla | 246 | 3 125 | 18 952 | 6.8 | 48.8 | 15.6 | 144.5 | 10 622 | 20 904 | 45 911 | -6.2 | 1.8 | 43 231 | 17.7 | 25.9 | 23.0 |
| Union | 192 | 4 877 | 6 568 | 12.5 | 45.5 | 21.7 | 38.0 | 10 075 | 22 359 | 40 974 | -10.1 | 1.6 | 41 510 | 15.8 | 20.5 | 19.2 |
| Wallowa | 28 | 734 | 1 238 | 15.4 | 42.5 | 21.3 | 12.8 | 14 679 | 22 813 | 39 556 | -8.8 | 0.9 | 38 486 | 16.0 | 26.8 | 24.4 |
| Wasco | 55 | 2 735 | 5 160 | 9.8 | 42.7 | 21.2 | 39.4 | 11 098 | 23 246 | 43 742 | -9.9 | 2.0 | 41 144 | 17.1 | 25.8 | 23.6 |
| Washington | 146 | 1 914 | 139 714 | 18.2 | 28.5 | 39.5 | 775.1 | 9 197 | 31 165 | 63 814 | -9.3 | 5.0 | 62 463 | 12.6 | 16.0 | 14.6 |
| Wheeler | 137 | 69 | 217 | 28.1 | 53.4 | 13.0 | 3.9 | 16 698 | 23 050 | 34 338 | -11.5 | 2.5 | 32 491 | 20.1 | 35.9 | 33.0 |
| Yamhill | 123 | 2 318 | 26 565 | 25.4 | 43.6 | 22.5 | 131.4 | 8 252 | 23 759 | 53 819 | -9.6 | 2.5 | 52 103 | 14.1 | 20.3 | 19.3 |
| **PENNSYLVANIA** | 355 | 2 222 | 3 179 333 | 24.5 | 49.7 | 26.7 | 22 883.7 | 12 981 | 27 824 | 51 651 | -4.6 | 3.8 | 50 221 | 13.7 | 19.4 | 17.7 |
| Adams | 137 | 1 187 | 25 354 | 29.0 | 57.8 | 18.8 | 264.7 | 18 383 | 26 326 | 57 097 | -1.0 | 2.2 | 54 460 | 8.7 | 13.1 | 11.8 |
| Allegheny | 412 | 2 096 | 301 796 | 26.0 | 40.0 | 34.5 | 2 126.1 | 14 174 | 30 530 | 49 805 | -3.8 | 4.4 | 49 682 | 13.4 | 19.1 | 17.4 |
| Armstrong | 102 | 1 025 | 14 016 | 11.6 | 63.6 | 13.8 | 85.5 | 13 350 | 22 963 | 44 663 | 4.8 | 1.3 | 41 934 | 13.2 | 19.0 | 17.4 |
| Beaver | 279 | 2 464 | 37 346 | 17.7 | 50.8 | 20.3 | 372.9 | 11 485 | 25 095 | 47 928 | -4.0 | 1.8 | 48 140 | 12.3 | 18.1 | 15.1 |
| Bedford | 106 | 1 010 | 10 185 | 12.8 | 66.8 | 12.0 | 80.6 | 10 521 | 20 922 | 40 710 | -7.9 | 1.0 | 40 240 | 12.7 | 17.9 | 16.5 |
| Berks | 306 | 2 160 | 106 675 | 16.4 | 55.0 | 22.1 | 873.9 | 12 450 | 26 332 | 54 823 | -9.2 | 2.8 | 52 168 | 13.5 | 19.4 | 16.8 |
| Blair | 263 | 1 979 | 27 643 | 14.4 | 58.7 | 17.3 | 220.4 | 12 099 | 23 561 | 43 243 | -2.5 | 1.8 | 42 488 | 14.6 | 21.6 | 19.7 |
| Bradford | 130 | 1 835 | 13 627 | 11.9 | 62.0 | 16.5 | 120.1 | 12 058 | 21 828 | 42 433 | -10.3 | 1.7 | 44 265 | 14.6 | 22.4 | 19.6 |
| Bucks | 118 | 2 025 | 157 572 | 24.7 | 39.5 | 34.7 | 1 283.9 | 14 324 | 36 601 | 76 019 | -5.7 | 8.1 | 70 735 | 6.6 | 8.3 | 7.1 |
| Butler | 123 | 1 277 | 47 411 | 15.9 | 45.5 | 29.3 | 339.8 | 10 280 | 29 604 | 57 474 | 0.6 | 3.7 | 54 888 | 8.9 | 11.2 | 9.4 |
| Cambria | 264 | 2 070 | 32 539 | 20.3 | 59.7 | 17.4 | 206.3 | 10 841 | 21 925 | 41 202 | 1.1 | 1.3 | 39 892 | 14.4 | 21.4 | 18.1 |
| Cameron | 137 | 1 882 | 940 | 6.8 | 65.7 | 14.0 | 8.5 | 11 173 | 21 605 | 40 449 | -7.0 | 0.4 | 38 451 | 14.5 | 22.7 | 20.3 |
| Carbon | 306 | 2 059 | 13 742 | 14.9 | 58.3 | 15.0 | 105.2 | 11 728 | 24 144 | 49 056 | 3.5 | 1.2 | 44 062 | 12.0 | 18.9 | 17.1 |
| Centre | 111 | 1 598 | 61 436 | 8.0 | 40.3 | 39.8 | 174.5 | 12 831 | 24 514 | 48 262 | -1.2 | 3.4 | 47 222 | 19.5 | 13.4 | 12.4 |
| Chester | 167 | 1 459 | 136 561 | 27.3 | 31.2 | 48.1 | 1 168.4 | 14 478 | 42 042 | 86 264 | -2.2 | 12.3 | 79 508 | 7.1 | 8.5 | 7.3 |
| Clarion | 89 | 1 594 | 10 335 | 11.1 | 61.5 | 17.8 | 85.8 | 15 111 | 21 303 | 41 557 | 0.0 | 1.4 | 41 423 | 15.0 | 18.4 | 16.5 |
| Clearfield | 269 | 2 308 | 16 801 | 13.4 | 64.4 | 13.3 | 153.4 | 12 446 | 20 784 | 39 391 | -7.0 | 1.3 | 41 408 | 14.8 | 22.1 | 20.3 |
| Clinton | 213 | 2 164 | 11 008 | 8.7 | 61.3 | 16.4 | 58.1 | 12 388 | 20 803 | 39 696 | -5.4 | 0.9 | 40 281 | 15.3 | 23.1 | 21.5 |
| Columbia | 165 | 2 094 | 19 460 | 7.4 | 59.4 | 18.8 | 77.9 | 11 513 | 22 861 | 44 136 | -4.1 | 1.7 | 40 704 | 15.9 | 18.2 | 16.1 |
| Crawford | 74 | 1 494 | 21 293 | 23.9 | 60.0 | 18.3 | 143.2 | 11 600 | 20 910 | 40 379 | -10.9 | 1.1 | 40 775 | 15.3 | 24.9 | 22.1 |
| Cumberland | 108 | 1 575 | 59 174 | 22.3 | 44.1 | 32.5 | 366.0 | 12 617 | 30 958 | 60 832 | -3.5 | 3.8 | 58 722 | 8.0 | 10.5 | 9.3 |
| Dauphin | 501 | 2 811 | 64 755 | 18.0 | 48.1 | 27.0 | 447.8 | 12 238 | 28 658 | 53 771 | -4.1 | 3.3 | 51 668 | 12.7 | 19.9 | 18.6 |
| Delaware | 565 | 2 481 | 157 624 | 35.9 | 41.2 | 34.5 | 1 052.8 | 14 411 | 32 803 | 63 677 | -5.8 | 6.8 | 59 978 | 10.2 | 14.9 | 13.2 |
| Elk | 115 | 2 150 | 6 789 | 25.3 | 62.7 | 15.1 | 42.0 | 10 672 | 22 903 | 42 854 | -15.5 | 1.5 | 43 181 | 9.8 | 14.5 | 12.5 |
| Erie | 242 | 2 693 | 74 353 | 25.9 | 52.4 | 23.6 | 487.6 | 11 996 | 23 321 | 44 503 | -10.0 | 2.1 | 41 951 | 16.5 | 25.5 | 23.1 |
| Fayette | 204 | 2 528 | 28 328 | 10.8 | 65.5 | 13.7 | 208.3 | 11 442 | 19 717 | 36 605 | -1.2 | 0.9 | 36 300 | 19.7 | 31.6 | 28.9 |
| Forest | 362 | 1 292 | 1 190 | 18.4 | 69.9 | 7.8 | 15.7 | 13 024 | 14 306 | 36 006 | -3.3 | 0.3 | 32 852 | 22.0 | 31.9 | 24.4 |
| Franklin | 121 | 1 654 | 32 950 | 19.3 | 58.7 | 18.7 | 228.2 | 10 170 | 25 298 | 51 171 | -6.4 | 1.9 | 49 545 | 10.4 | 15.1 | 14.2 |
| Fulton | 201 | 1 417 | 3 198 | 12.6 | 69.0 | 10.7 | 28.5 | 12 106 | 22 541 | 45 960 | -2.4 | 1.2 | 44 287 | 12.9 | 18.7 | 17.0 |
| Greene | 149 | 1 796 | 8 049 | 18.8 | 63.6 | 15.0 | 71.2 | 13 095 | 20 636 | 42 565 | 3.9 | 1.4 | 42 049 | 15.5 | 22.2 | 19.9 |
| Huntingdon | 124 | 1 333 | 9 716 | 24.9 | 65.7 | 13.8 | 63.5 | 10 404 | 20 574 | 43 026 | -4.3 | 1.0 | 41 923 | 13.9 | 19.2 | 17.8 |
| Indiana | 324 | 1 637 | 24 925 | 9.0 | 58.1 | 20.8 | 173.3 | 14 526 | 21 686 | 41 424 | 1.5 | 1.6 | 41 707 | 18.2 | 23.3 | 21.7 |
| Jefferson | 122 | 1 295 | 9 251 | 12.4 | 66.7 | 12.3 | 64.3 | 12 654 | 21 365 | 40 058 | -6.5 | 1.2 | 39 051 | 14.5 | 23.2 | 20.0 |
| Juniata | 69 | 1 048 | 5 259 | 21.9 | 71.0 | 11.5 | 29.2 | 9 530 | 20 611 | 45 496 | -2.9 | 0.4 | 44 865 | 13.1 | 21.3 | 19.5 |
| Lackawanna | 220 | 2 102 | 51 519 | 34.6 | 50.5 | 24.6 | 326.1 | 11 593 | 25 085 | 45 185 | -2.8 | 2.5 | 43 886 | 13.7 | 19.4 | 17.4 |
| Lancaster | 180 | 2 026 | 126 925 | 26.4 | 56.0 | 23.2 | 879.7 | 12 872 | 26 141 | 55 816 | -9.2 | 2.9 | 53 408 | 10.8 | 16.3 | 15.1 |
| Lawrence | 404 | 2 959 | 20 695 | 17.9 | 57.9 | 19.0 | 143.3 | 10 765 | 22 052 | 43 821 | -2.1 | 1.3 | 41 447 | 16.1 | 24.5 | 22.5 |
| Lebanon | 172 | 1 750 | 30 301 | 22.7 | 60.4 | 18.7 | 192.8 | 10 262 | 26 238 | 53 474 | -3.0 | 2.3 | 53 625 | 11.1 | 17.7 | 16.1 |
| Lehigh | 262 | 2 760 | 87 258 | 23.6 | 48.0 | 27.3 | 618.5 | 12 258 | 27 801 | 54 312 | -7.4 | 3.9 | 50 737 | 14.1 | 21.9 | 20.6 |
| Luzerne | 321 | 2 386 | 73 172 | 22.9 | 53.5 | 20.2 | 500.8 | 11 147 | 23 956 | 43 296 | -5.0 | 2.0 | 42 584 | 15.2 | 25.5 | 22.8 |
| Lycoming | 179 | 2 233 | 27 977 | 15.4 | 55.3 | 18.8 | 204.5 | 12 444 | 22 301 | 43 788 | -4.7 | 1.5 | 42 163 | 14.3 | 21.0 | 18.1 |
| McKean | 177 | 1 888 | 10 139 | 13.2 | 60.6 | 15.2 | 95.3 | 14 621 | 21 436 | 40 721 | -8.7 | 0.8 | 40 338 | 17.9 | 23.9 | 22.0 |
| Mercer | 228 | 2 104 | 27 712 | 24.7 | 57.1 | 19.5 | 240.6 | 14 165 | 22 303 | 43 504 | -7.1 | 1.5 | 41 535 | 14.3 | 22.6 | 19.5 |
| Mifflin | 128 | 1 926 | 9 201 | 20.6 | 70.3 | 11.3 | 93.3 | 16 834 | 19 758 | 38 892 | -10.5 | 0.7 | 38 544 | 18.0 | 27.9 | 27.1 |
| Monroe | 266 | 2 592 | 48 185 | 15.4 | 48.2 | 23.3 | 423.9 | 13 659 | 25 096 | 57 700 | -7.6 | 2.1 | 52 505 | 13.4 | 17.3 | 15.4 |
| Montgomery | 178 | 1 868 | 206 423 | 32.2 | 33.0 | 44.4 | 1 670.0 | 15 459 | 41 163 | 78 446 | -4.5 | 10.1 | 76 172 | 6.5 | 7.2 | 6.7 |
| Montour | 311 | 1 206 | 3 980 | 17.9 | 51.6 | 25.6 | 28.1 | 10 628 | 27 784 | 46 421 | -9.7 | 4.4 | 48 800 | 11.4 | 17.9 | 16.3 |
| Northampton | 190 | 2 052 | 76 831 | 27.9 | 48.0 | 26.7 | 565.7 | 12 413 | 29 020 | 60 540 | -0.9 | 3.8 | 57 284 | 10.0 | 13.4 | 12.1 |
| Northumberland | 318 | 1 425 | 18 842 | 17.6 | 66.2 | 14.0 | 188.8 | 15 640 | 21 899 | 39 605 | -6.3 | 1.0 | 39 834 | 13.1 | 21.0 | 19.6 |
| Perry | 194 | 1 797 | 9 624 | 13.4 | 63.3 | 14.7 | 71.6 | 10 682 | 24 688 | 54 626 | -3.5 | 1.0 | 52 788 | 10.8 | 17.0 | 15.0 |
| Philadelphia | 1 194 | 3 895 | 424 284 | 34.6 | 55.2 | 22.6 | 2 682.0 | 13 436 | 21 671 | 36 957 | -11.0 | 2.1 | 34 433 | 27.9 | 38.7 | 38.6 |
| Pike | 104 | 1 962 | 14 205 | 13.1 | 44.9 | 23.2 | 112.6 | 12 185 | 27 989 | 58 672 | -2.6 | 3.0 | 56 070 | 10.1 | 14.8 | 12.3 |

1. Data for serious crimes have not been adjusted for underreporting; this may affect comparability between geographic areas and over time.   2. Per 100,000 population estimated by the FBI.   3. All persons 3 years old and over enrolled in nursery school through college.   4. Persons 25 years old and over.   5. Elementary and secondary education expenditures.   6. Based on population estimated by the American Community Survey, 2007–2011.

Items 46—61

# Table B. States and Counties — Personal Income

| STATE County | Personal income, 2011 | | | | | | | | | | | | |
|---|---|---|---|---|---|---|---|---|---|---|---|---|---|
| | | | Per capita[1] | | | | | | Transfer payments (mil dol) | | | | |
| | | | | | | | | | | Government payments to individuals | | | |
| | Total (mil dol) | Percent change, 2010–2011[2] | Dollars | Rank | Wages and salaries[2] (mil dol) | Proprietors' income (mil dol) | Dividends, interest, and rent (mil dol) | Total | Total | Social Security | Medical payments | Income mainte-nance | Unemploy-ment insurance |
| | 62 | 63 | 64 | 65 | 66 | 67 | 68 | 69 | 70 | 71 | 72 | 73 | 74 |
| OREGON—Cont'd | | | | | | | | | | | | | |
| Morrow | 425 | 9.1 | 38 029 | 966 | 233 | 98 | 45 | 76 | 74 | 24 | 31 | 9 | 3 |
| Multnomah | 31 161 | 5.9 | 41 658 | 602 | 28 250 | 3 504 | 5 369 | 5 250 | 5 085 | 1 423 | 1 982 | 712 | 398 |
| Polk | 2 389 | 4.4 | 31 437 | 2 009 | 772 | 94 | 439 | 549 | 532 | 200 | 192 | 56 | 33 |
| Sherman | 95 | 4.4 | 55 157 | 112 | 42 | 28 | 14 | 17 | 17 | 6 | 7 | 1 | 1 |
| Tillamook | 869 | 6.0 | 34 194 | 1 486 | 368 | 86 | 186 | 239 | 233 | 95 | 87 | 20 | 12 |
| Umatilla | 2 356 | 5.5 | 30 701 | 2 155 | 1 421 | 232 | 336 | 557 | 540 | 162 | 216 | 76 | 27 |
| Union | 826 | 6.1 | 32 033 | 1 878 | 445 | 64 | 144 | 229 | 223 | 72 | 84 | 24 | 12 |
| Wallowa | 238 | 6.0 | 34 098 | 1 496 | 96 | 27 | 62 | 68 | 66 | 28 | 24 | 6 | 4 |
| Wasco | 880 | 7.2 | 34 878 | 1 392 | 487 | 80 | 156 | 215 | 210 | 74 | 82 | 25 | 11 |
| Washington | 23 043 | 7.1 | 42 639 | 526 | 18 024 | 764 | 3 547 | 3 104 | 2 984 | 1 000 | 1 123 | 321 | 266 |
| Wheeler | 41 | 7.5 | 28 780 | 2 490 | 11 | 3 | 10 | 15 | 14 | 6 | 6 | 1 | 1 |
| Yamhill | 3 398 | 6.1 | 33 980 | 1 513 | 1 538 | 140 | 543 | 741 | 719 | 240 | 291 | 82 | 49 |
| PENNSYLVANIA | 538 909 | 4.8 | 42 291 | X | 336 565 | 44 925 | 80 802 | 110 439 | 107 620 | 35 674 | 48 884 | 10 190 | 6 567 |
| Adams | 3 384 | 3.4 | 33 360 | 1 640 | 1 512 | 256 | 525 | 695 | 673 | 293 | 260 | 42 | 40 |
| Allegheny | 59 895 | 5.1 | 48 812 | 241 | 45 649 | 6 991 | 8 990 | 11 256 | 10 984 | 3 618 | 5 217 | 931 | 519 |
| Armstrong | 2 338 | 5.5 | 34 094 | 1 497 | 935 | 237 | 299 | 681 | 666 | 228 | 306 | 54 | 48 |
| Beaver | 6 480 | 4.8 | 38 025 | 968 | 2 870 | 292 | 762 | 1 716 | 1 678 | 588 | 776 | 131 | 84 |
| Bedford | 1 570 | 4.8 | 31 564 | 1 987 | 691 | 182 | 206 | 439 | 428 | 161 | 176 | 34 | 35 |
| Berks | 15 552 | 4.5 | 37 675 | 1 007 | 9 259 | 990 | 2 310 | 3 244 | 3 152 | 1 123 | 1 321 | 328 | 205 |
| Blair | 4 386 | 4.8 | 34 511 | 1 436 | 2 824 | 270 | 619 | 1 224 | 1 196 | 363 | 520 | 111 | 75 |
| Bradford | 2 105 | 9.4 | 33 462 | 1 614 | 1 272 | 148 | 277 | 496 | 482 | 194 | 196 | 48 | 18 |
| Bucks | 34 232 | 3.3 | 54 609 | 117 | 15 290 | 2 835 | 6 281 | 4 692 | 4 554 | 1 834 | 2 000 | 213 | 252 |
| Butler | 8 110 | 6.0 | 43 876 | 449 | 4 748 | 400 | 1 136 | 1 498 | 1 457 | 531 | 647 | 91 | 97 |
| Cambria | 4 716 | 4.1 | 32 810 | 1 739 | 2 658 | 272 | 644 | 1 508 | 1 476 | 471 | 691 | 117 | 95 |
| Cameron | 169 | 4.5 | 33 642 | 1 578 | 97 | 7 | 33 | 55 | 54 | 20 | 22 | 5 | 5 |
| Carbon | 2 111 | 4.9 | 32 394 | 1 806 | 687 | 203 | 306 | 577 | 562 | 211 | 234 | 39 | 43 |
| Centre | 5 469 | 5.3 | 35 347 | 1 317 | 4 138 | 398 | 888 | 868 | 834 | 307 | 291 | 47 | 49 |
| Chester | 29 965 | 4.4 | 59 467 | 70 | 19 819 | 3 006 | 5 117 | 3 228 | 3 117 | 1 247 | 1 296 | 136 | 242 |
| Clarion | 1 318 | 3.2 | 32 931 | 1 719 | 609 | 101 | 215 | 397 | 388 | 121 | 179 | 29 | 30 |
| Clearfield | 2 621 | 4.7 | 32 181 | 1 845 | 1 388 | 167 | 358 | 789 | 771 | 257 | 340 | 67 | 62 |
| Clinton | 1 251 | 8.3 | 31 912 | 1 903 | 662 | 92 | 151 | 325 | 316 | 111 | 130 | 27 | 22 |
| Columbia | 2 093 | 4.4 | 31 025 | 2 093 | 1 172 | 193 | 323 | 542 | 527 | 190 | 217 | 41 | 41 |
| Crawford | 2 794 | 5.2 | 31 485 | 2 006 | 1 393 | 233 | 377 | 817 | 797 | 272 | 349 | 80 | 46 |
| Cumberland | 10 123 | 5.0 | 42 552 | 536 | 7 390 | 654 | 1 705 | 1 654 | 1 602 | 647 | 654 | 84 | 83 |
| Dauphin | 11 046 | 4.8 | 41 067 | 653 | 10 978 | 733 | 1 481 | 2 173 | 2 113 | 691 | 899 | 215 | 126 |
| Delaware | 27 860 | 3.8 | 49 795 | 209 | 14 090 | 1 654 | 4 413 | 4 765 | 4 641 | 1 481 | 2 237 | 368 | 276 |
| Elk | 1 158 | 5.0 | 36 472 | 1 142 | 718 | 63 | 180 | 300 | 293 | 117 | 126 | 20 | 18 |
| Erie | 9 756 | 6.4 | 34 721 | 1 418 | 6 345 | 498 | 1 365 | 2 538 | 2 476 | 783 | 1 065 | 299 | 171 |
| Fayette | 4 563 | 3.3 | 33 527 | 1 597 | 1 870 | 308 | 597 | 1 581 | 1 551 | 460 | 740 | 175 | 96 |
| Forest | 182 | 5.4 | 24 014 | 3 029 | 117 | 16 | 31 | 65 | 64 | 22 | 32 | 3 | 3 |
| Franklin | 5 169 | 5.2 | 34 277 | 1 473 | 2 755 | 349 | 876 | 1 078 | 1 045 | 420 | 427 | 78 | 56 |
| Fulton | 471 | 5.3 | 31 808 | 1 930 | 238 | 37 | 75 | 120 | 117 | 45 | 47 | 10 | 10 |
| Greene | 1 371 | 8.3 | 35 499 | 1 293 | 968 | 49 | 153 | 372 | 363 | 109 | 176 | 40 | 17 |
| Huntingdon | 1 335 | 4.6 | 29 108 | 2 437 | 573 | 79 | 182 | 393 | 383 | 131 | 161 | 30 | 40 |
| Indiana | 3 091 | 5.2 | 34 613 | 1 429 | 1 829 | 319 | 428 | 762 | 742 | 246 | 314 | 56 | 53 |
| Jefferson | 1 482 | 5.4 | 32 959 | 1 714 | 732 | 103 | 235 | 440 | 430 | 143 | 194 | 36 | 32 |
| Juniata | 766 | 5.1 | 31 385 | 2 018 | 250 | 121 | 119 | 185 | 179 | 66 | 76 | 14 | 14 |
| Lackawanna | 8 175 | 3.8 | 38 171 | 947 | 4 637 | 558 | 1 259 | 2 159 | 2 112 | 667 | 930 | 171 | 141 |
| Lancaster | 19 653 | 4.1 | 37 535 | 1 023 | 11 350 | 1 934 | 3 390 | 3 681 | 3 566 | 1 428 | 1 467 | 298 | 202 |
| Lawrence | 3 031 | 4.2 | 33 475 | 1 607 | 1 454 | 212 | 437 | 930 | 910 | 306 | 415 | 87 | 51 |
| Lebanon | 5 169 | 5.1 | 38 489 | 910 | 2 422 | 321 | 735 | 1 049 | 1 019 | 400 | 417 | 84 | 59 |
| Lehigh | 14 432 | 4.6 | 40 890 | 669 | 10 625 | 1 038 | 2 213 | 2 895 | 2 817 | 971 | 1 240 | 284 | 187 |
| Luzerne | 11 685 | 4.1 | 36 441 | 1 145 | 6 856 | 685 | 1 679 | 3 036 | 2 965 | 992 | 1 286 | 275 | 224 |
| Lycoming | 4 119 | 8.0 | 35 283 | 1 326 | 2 689 | 224 | 637 | 970 | 944 | 344 | 386 | 91 | 61 |
| McKean | 1 477 | 6.9 | 34 171 | 1 488 | 848 | 91 | 202 | 407 | 397 | 140 | 174 | 42 | 24 |
| Mercer | 3 851 | 4.6 | 33 136 | 1 685 | 2 251 | 179 | 576 | 1 145 | 1 119 | 398 | 519 | 105 | 44 |
| Mifflin | 1 407 | 4.5 | 30 017 | 2 287 | 673 | 137 | 176 | 435 | 424 | 148 | 195 | 40 | 24 |
| Monroe | 5 362 | 3.7 | 31 566 | 1 984 | 3 034 | 263 | 672 | 1 189 | 1 151 | 446 | 456 | 107 | 72 |
| Montgomery | 52 047 | 4.4 | 64 718 | 39 | 36 019 | 5 906 | 9 270 | 6 025 | 5 847 | 2 278 | 2 548 | 257 | 470 |
| Montour | 762 | 3.1 | 41 632 | 607 | 1 113 | 117 | 109 | 153 | 149 | 57 | 68 | 10 | 7 |
| Northampton | 11 664 | 4.2 | 39 078 | 846 | 5 586 | 540 | 1 835 | 2 389 | 2 323 | 894 | 1 007 | 177 | 119 |
| Northumberland | 3 151 | 4.9 | 33 328 | 1 648 | 1 312 | 158 | 450 | 863 | 842 | 296 | 371 | 68 | 61 |
| Perry | 1 582 | 4.3 | 34 367 | 1 460 | 315 | 97 | 192 | 337 | 327 | 120 | 134 | 23 | 22 |
| Philadelphia | 59 986 | 5.0 | 39 041 | 852 | 47 591 | 6 818 | 6 332 | 16 989 | 16 649 | 3 048 | 8 928 | 3 020 | 934 |
| Pike | 2 020 | 4.6 | 35 523 | 1 286 | 434 | 107 | 296 | 419 | 406 | 195 | 143 | 30 | 14 |

1. Based on the resident population estimated as of July 1 of the year shown.    2. Includes supplements to wages and salaries.

# Table B. States and Counties — Earnings, Social Security, and Housing

| STATE County | Earnings, 2011 Total (mil dol) | Farm | Goods-related[1] Total | Manu-facturing | Information and professional and technical services | Retail trade | Finance, insurance, and real estate | Health care and social services | Government | Social Security beneficiaries, December 2011 Number | Rate[2] | Supplemental Security Income recipients, December 2011 | Housing units, 2010 Total | Percent change, 2000–2010 |
|---|---|---|---|---|---|---|---|---|---|---|---|---|---|---|
| | 75 | 76 | 77 | 78 | 79 | 80 | 81 | 82 | 83 | 84 | 85 | 86 | 87 | 88 |
| OREGON—Cont'd | | | | | | | | | | | | | | |
| Morrow | 331 | 34.9 | D | 18.9 | D | 1.8 | 1.6 | 2.0 | 13.9 | 1 940 | 174 | 202 | 4 442 | 3.9 |
| Multnomah | 31 753 | 0.1 | D | 7.8 | 14.5 | 5.0 | 8.6 | 11.5 | 17.4 | 106 290 | 142 | 19 133 | 324 832 | 12.6 |
| Polk | 866 | 5.5 | D | 10.3 | D | 5.2 | 2.6 | 11.0 | 34.1 | 15 235 | 200 | 1 278 | 30 302 | 23.9 |
| Sherman | 69 | 39.6 | D | D | D | 4.3 | D | 0.5 | 33.4 | 480 | 279 | 31 | 918 | -1.8 |
| Tillamook | 454 | 9.0 | 20.2 | 15.0 | 2.8 | 7.1 | 3.9 | 10.8 | 22.4 | 7 275 | 286 | 463 | 18 359 | 15.4 |
| Umatilla | 1 652 | 8.2 | 12.3 | 8.4 | D | 6.6 | 3.0 | 10.1 | 26.1 | 13 070 | 170 | 1 618 | 29 693 | 7.3 |
| Union | 509 | 5.6 | D | 11.4 | 3.8 | 8.7 | 3.1 | 15.5 | 25.9 | 5 745 | 223 | 578 | 11 489 | 8.4 |
| Wallowa | 123 | 9.3 | 10.1 | 4.0 | 4.8 | 8.2 | 6.7 | D | 29.8 | 2 225 | 318 | 137 | 4 108 | 5.3 |
| Wasco | 568 | 11.7 | D | 4.8 | D | 10.2 | 3.0 | 18.4 | 24.9 | 5 795 | 230 | 633 | 11 487 | 7.8 |
| Washington | 18 788 | 0.6 | 32.9 | 27.6 | 10.3 | 5.8 | 5.9 | 8.4 | 7.4 | 70 940 | 131 | 6 368 | 212 450 | 18.7 |
| Wheeler | 14 | 20.4 | D | 0.0 | D | 7.0 | D | D | 35.3 | 490 | 344 | 32 | 895 | 6.3 |
| Yamhill | 1 678 | 4.8 | 28.4 | 22.9 | 4.2 | 6.9 | 4.2 | 13.4 | 15.8 | 17 905 | 179 | 1 464 | 37 110 | 22.6 |
| PENNSYLVANIA | 381 490 | 0.4 | 17.6 | 11.0 | 12.7 | 5.9 | 8.2 | 14.4 | 13.3 | 2 617 879 | 205 | 367 586 | 5 567 315 | 6.0 |
| Adams | 1 768 | 2.2 | D | 19.6 | 5.2 | 7.7 | 3.1 | D | 16.5 | 21 715 | 214 | 1 118 | 40 820 | 13.9 |
| Allegheny | 52 639 | 0.0 | 13.7 | 6.8 | 15.2 | 5.3 | 10.3 | 14.5 | 9.7 | 259 690 | 212 | 35 806 | 589 201 | 1.0 |
| Armstrong | 1 171 | 0.2 | 32.9 | 12.3 | 3.4 | 7.8 | 3.9 | 14.8 | 14.6 | 17 640 | 257 | 2 244 | 32 520 | 0.4 |
| Beaver | 3 162 | -0.2 | 22.5 | 17.0 | 8.9 | 7.6 | 3.4 | 14.9 | 14.5 | 43 210 | 254 | 4 979 | 78 211 | 0.6 |
| Bedford | 873 | 4.0 | D | 12.9 | D | 8.9 | 2.6 | 8.4 | 14.1 | 13 050 | 262 | 1 396 | 23 954 | 1.8 |
| Berks | 10 250 | 0.9 | 26.1 | 19.9 | 7.4 | 7.5 | 5.1 | 13.7 | 13.7 | 80 995 | 196 | 9 957 | 164 827 | 9.7 |
| Blair | 3 094 | 1.1 | D | 13.2 | 6.3 | 9.1 | 4.0 | 19.5 | 16.0 | 29 105 | 229 | 4 913 | 56 276 | 2.2 |
| Bradford | 1 420 | 1.7 | 32.1 | 18.7 | 3.5 | 6.8 | 3.9 | 19.8 | 12.8 | 15 470 | 246 | 1 944 | 29 979 | 4.6 |
| Bucks | 18 125 | 0.1 | 22.0 | 12.1 | 13.2 | 7.7 | 6.2 | 13.1 | 9.7 | 120 110 | 192 | 6 874 | 245 956 | 9.1 |
| Butler | 5 149 | 0.1 | 25.8 | 18.3 | 7.7 | 7.3 | 3.1 | 10.4 | 13.8 | 38 580 | 209 | 3 416 | 78 167 | 11.9 |
| Cambria | 2 930 | 0.3 | 13.9 | 8.4 | 8.3 | 7.9 | 5.5 | 21.6 | 18.6 | 37 310 | 260 | 5 123 | 65 650 | -0.2 |
| Cameron | 104 | 1.1 | D | 52.0 | D | 4.1 | D | 5.2 | 20.5 | 1 560 | 311 | 139 | 4 455 | -3.0 |
| Carbon | 891 | 0.2 | 17.3 | 11.2 | 18.2 | 7.6 | 3.3 | 15.6 | 16.4 | 15 975 | 245 | 1 332 | 34 299 | 12.5 |
| Centre | 4 536 | 0.2 | 12.5 | 5.7 | 9.5 | 5.9 | 3.6 | 9.6 | 45.9 | 21 940 | 142 | 1 574 | 63 297 | 19.1 |
| Chester | 22 825 | 0.7 | 13.6 | 8.7 | 20.2 | 5.6 | 17.1 | 9.1 | 7.3 | 80 095 | 159 | 3 913 | 192 462 | 17.5 |
| Clarion | 710 | 0.7 | 23.0 | 8.5 | 3.7 | 8.7 | 3.3 | 14.9 | 26.9 | 9 325 | 233 | 1 249 | 19 962 | 2.8 |
| Clearfield | 1 555 | 0.0 | 16.6 | 8.2 | 3.7 | 9.0 | 3.4 | 20.8 | 17.6 | 20 260 | 249 | 2 721 | 38 644 | 2.1 |
| Clinton | 754 | 1.5 | 33.1 | 23.8 | 4.2 | 6.7 | 1.9 | 8.8 | 22.5 | 8 680 | 221 | 1 087 | 19 080 | 5.0 |
| Columbia | 1 365 | 0.8 | D | 23.5 | 6.0 | 8.6 | 2.8 | 12.6 | 19.8 | 14 750 | 219 | 1 449 | 29 498 | 6.4 |
| Crawford | 1 626 | 2.1 | 30.4 | 25.1 | 4.2 | 7.6 | 2.9 | 16.8 | 15.7 | 21 245 | 239 | 3 150 | 44 686 | 5.3 |
| Cumberland | 8 043 | 0.5 | 10.8 | 6.3 | 11.2 | 6.3 | 10.4 | 12.9 | 18.2 | 46 540 | 196 | 2 468 | 99 988 | 15.0 |
| Dauphin | 11 710 | 0.2 | 13.0 | 8.5 | 8.4 | 4.2 | 8.4 | 14.9 | 23.7 | 51 215 | 190 | 7 007 | 120 406 | 8.3 |
| Delaware | 15 744 | 0.0 | D | 11.0 | 11.3 | 5.7 | 9.8 | 14.4 | 11.0 | 101 545 | 181 | 12 114 | 222 902 | 2.7 |
| Elk | 781 | 0.7 | 53.7 | 47.2 | 2.2 | 5.0 | 2.1 | 12.8 | 9.6 | 8 615 | 271 | 737 | 17 585 | -2.9 |
| Erie | 6 843 | 0.3 | 27.5 | 23.4 | 5.0 | 7.0 | 7.0 | 17.7 | 15.2 | 59 165 | 211 | 11 092 | 119 138 | 4.2 |
| Fayette | 2 178 | 0.0 | 21.8 | 10.2 | 5.1 | 9.4 | 2.7 | 16.6 | 17.6 | 36 590 | 269 | 8 833 | 62 773 | -5.6 |
| Forest | 133 | 5.6 | D | D | D | 2.2 | D | 14.9 | 47.9 | 1 775 | 234 | 160 | 8 760 | 0.7 |
| Franklin | 3 104 | 3.0 | D | 17.0 | 5.3 | 7.1 | 3.2 | 15.2 | 19.3 | 32 980 | 219 | 2 582 | 63 219 | 17.5 |
| Fulton | 275 | 1.9 | D | 39.0 | 1.7 | 4.5 | 1.7 | D | 14.4 | 3 705 | 250 | 359 | 7 122 | 4.9 |
| Greene | 1 017 | -0.7 | D | 1.9 | 4.3 | 5.2 | 2.5 | D | 15.4 | 8 520 | 221 | 1 872 | 16 460 | -1.3 |
| Huntingdon | 651 | 1.9 | D | 12.6 | 3.5 | 6.6 | 4.1 | 12.2 | 27.8 | 10 575 | 231 | 1 240 | 22 365 | 6.2 |
| Indiana | 2 148 | 1.1 | 26.0 | 6.5 | 4.6 | 7.5 | 3.5 | 10.1 | 20.2 | 18 870 | 211 | 2 551 | 38 236 | 2.6 |
| Jefferson | 835 | 0.4 | 40.4 | 25.1 | 3.6 | 6.6 | 2.2 | 15.3 | 12.9 | 11 400 | 253 | 1 540 | 22 434 | 1.5 |
| Juniata | 370 | 10.4 | D | 26.6 | D | 6.8 | 3.2 | D | 12.5 | 5 375 | 220 | 514 | 10 978 | 9.5 |
| Lackawanna | 5 194 | 0.1 | 16.2 | 11.0 | 8.1 | 8.5 | 7.7 | 19.5 | 13.4 | 52 375 | 245 | 6 712 | 96 832 | 1.5 |
| Lancaster | 13 284 | 2.9 | 27.6 | 17.5 | 7.2 | 7.4 | 5.3 | 14.0 | 9.6 | 101 500 | 194 | 9 551 | 202 952 | 12.8 |
| Lawrence | 1 665 | 0.9 | 27.2 | 15.2 | 5.1 | 7.0 | 5.8 | 15.0 | 15.4 | 23 465 | 259 | 3 550 | 40 975 | 3.4 |
| Lebanon | 2 744 | 2.8 | 23.3 | 18.5 | 5.3 | 7.7 | 2.7 | 13.7 | 20.1 | 29 640 | 221 | 2 330 | 55 592 | 12.7 |
| Lehigh | 11 663 | 0.1 | D | 9.9 | 7.4 | 5.6 | 5.2 | 20.7 | 9.5 | 70 625 | 200 | 10 026 | 142 613 | 10.6 |
| Luzerne | 7 541 | 0.0 | 16.8 | 11.5 | 7.6 | 7.8 | 5.7 | 15.4 | 15.7 | 77 670 | 242 | 9 811 | 148 748 | 2.8 |
| Lycoming | 2 913 | 0.5 | 31.1 | 20.0 | 5.2 | 6.8 | 3.9 | 14.3 | 17.8 | 26 575 | 228 | 3 401 | 52 500 | 0.1 |
| McKean | 939 | -0.2 | 41.2 | 22.6 | D | 5.4 | 2.1 | 13.1 | 16.3 | 10 890 | 252 | 1 708 | 21 225 | -1.9 |
| Mercer | 2 431 | 0.9 | 28.2 | 22.6 | 3.1 | 8.5 | 5.0 | 19.3 | 12.9 | 30 030 | 258 | 4 300 | 51 733 | 3.7 |
| Mifflin | 810 | 2.9 | 32.2 | 26.4 | 2.3 | 9.7 | 3.1 | 16.9 | 12.9 | 11 910 | 254 | 1 677 | 21 537 | 3.8 |
| Monroe | 3 297 | 0.0 | 19.1 | 14.7 | 4.5 | 7.9 | 3.0 | 11.3 | 30.3 | 32 240 | 190 | 2 861 | 80 359 | 18.9 |
| Montgomery | 41 926 | 0.0 | 18.0 | 10.2 | 20.6 | 5.2 | 12.8 | 13.0 | 6.4 | 145 195 | 181 | 7 749 | 325 735 | 9.5 |
| Montour | 1 229 | 0.9 | D | 1.8 | 4.5 | 2.4 | 1.9 | 48.6 | 6.9 | 4 330 | 237 | 442 | 7 965 | 4.4 |
| Northampton | 6 126 | 0.3 | 21.7 | 15.8 | 8.6 | 7.1 | 6.7 | 10.4 | 15.0 | 63 285 | 212 | 5 746 | 120 363 | 12.8 |
| Northumberland | 1 471 | 2.8 | 24.4 | 18.0 | 3.8 | 6.6 | 3.5 | 12.7 | 17.3 | 23 750 | 251 | 2 991 | 45 125 | 4.5 |
| Perry | 411 | 9.4 | D | 4.5 | 3.6 | 9.4 | 4.0 | 8.8 | 26.3 | 9 300 | 202 | 768 | 20 424 | 7.8 |
| Philadelphia | 54 409 | 0.0 | 5.2 | 3.3 | 19.9 | 3.1 | 9.4 | 16.8 | 16.4 | 248 540 | 162 | 108 137 | 670 171 | 1.2 |
| Pike | 540 | -0.1 | D | D | 7.4 | 11.1 | 4.2 | 9.0 | 31.0 | 13 495 | 237 | 722 | 38 350 | 10.6 |

1. Includes mining, construction, and manufacturing.   2. Per 1,000 resident population enumerated in the 2010 census.

# Table B. States and Counties — Housing, Labor Force, and Employment

| STATE County | Housing units, 2007–2011 | | | | | | | | Civilian labor force, 2012 | | Unemployment | | Civilian employment,[6] 2007–2011 | | |
|---|---|---|---|---|---|---|---|---|---|---|---|---|---|---|---|
| | Occupied units | | | | | | | | | | | | | Percent | |
| | | Owner-occupied | | | | Renter-occupied | | | | | | | | | |
| | | | | Median owner cost as a percent of income | | | | | | | | | | | Construction, production, and maintenance occupations |
| | Total | Percent | Median value[1] | With a mortgage | Without a mortgage[2] | Median rent[3] | Median rent as a percent of income | Substandard units[4] (percent) | Total | Percent change, 2011–2012 | Total | Rate[5] | Total | Management, business, science and arts | |
| | 89 | 90 | 91 | 92 | 93 | 94 | 95 | 96 | 97 | 98 | 99 | 100 | 101 | 102 | 103 |
| **OREGON—Cont'd** | | | | | | | | | | | | | | | |
| Morrow | 3 855 | 71.8 | 120 100 | 22.3 | 11.0 | 667 | 30.7 | 4.7 | 5 528 | -0.1 | 454 | 8.2 | 4 737 | 23.0 | 44.5 |
| Multnomah | 302 224 | 55.2 | 281 900 | 27.4 | 14.4 | 858 | 32.0 | 3.8 | 404 357 | 0.1 | 31 342 | 7.8 | 371 276 | 41.2 | 18.0 |
| Polk | 28 111 | 67.2 | 231 900 | 26.1 | 11.3 | 749 | 29.7 | 2.4 | 38 442 | -1.0 | 3 244 | 8.4 | 32 355 | 35.2 | 20.8 |
| Sherman | 835 | 66.5 | 128 800 | 21.8 | 11.9 | 675 | 19.6 | 1.9 | 1 072 | -0.3 | 90 | 8.4 | 834 | 40.0 | 27.7 |
| Tillamook | 10 892 | 69.8 | 242 400 | 28.2 | 12.4 | 727 | 31.6 | 3.3 | 12 504 | -2.4 | 1 064 | 8.5 | 10 764 | 25.4 | 31.2 |
| Umatilla | 26 805 | 64.4 | 143 700 | 22.4 | 11.1 | 639 | 25.9 | 4.9 | 39 736 | -0.3 | 3 324 | 8.4 | 32 735 | 26.7 | 32.0 |
| Union | 10 411 | 65.2 | 154 100 | 23.2 | 12.0 | 632 | 32.0 | 2.2 | 12 454 | -0.4 | 1 141 | 9.2 | 11 030 | 31.0 | 26.3 |
| Wallowa | 3 046 | 74.9 | 186 200 | 24.7 | 15.3 | 642 | 29.4 | 1.3 | 3 700 | -1.3 | 377 | 10.2 | 2 971 | 36.3 | 26.0 |
| Wasco | 9 857 | 66.4 | 189 300 | 25.5 | 12.0 | 698 | 26.6 | 2.5 | 14 584 | 1.2 | 1 156 | 7.9 | 11 274 | 28.5 | 30.6 |
| Washington | 198 593 | 62.3 | 300 200 | 25.8 | 11.9 | 927 | 29.0 | 3.2 | 293 472 | 0.2 | 20 695 | 7.1 | 260 525 | 42.2 | 16.8 |
| Wheeler | 601 | 73.9 | 116 500 | 29.7 | 12.6 | 579 | 22.3 | 2.3 | 709 | 1.6 | 54 | 7.6 | 499 | 29.5 | 38.7 |
| Yamhill | 33 804 | 69.9 | 237 700 | 26.9 | 13.0 | 822 | 31.2 | 3.7 | 48 611 | 0.0 | 4 136 | 8.5 | 44 915 | 31.3 | 27.0 |
| **PENNSYLVANIA** | 4 952 566 | 70.6 | 163 200 | 23.7 | 13.8 | 770 | 29.7 | 1.6 | 6 486 578 | 1.4 | 513 171 | 7.9 | 5 938 507 | 35.5 | 22.5 |
| Adams | 38 431 | 77.0 | 202 800 | 25.5 | 13.0 | 774 | 28.7 | 2.4 | 54 424 | 0.3 | 3 582 | 6.6 | 51 673 | 28.6 | 32.1 |
| Allegheny | 523 175 | 66.4 | 118 700 | 21.7 | 13.8 | 713 | 29.0 | 1.1 | 660 973 | 1.9 | 45 606 | 6.9 | 597 728 | 41.3 | 15.4 |
| Armstrong | 28 807 | 77.2 | 91 600 | 21.7 | 12.6 | 570 | 27.2 | 1.2 | 34 053 | 2.1 | 2 880 | 8.5 | 31 181 | 26.4 | 33.7 |
| Beaver | 70 198 | 74.4 | 113 600 | 22.7 | 13.7 | 607 | 27.6 | 1.2 | 90 805 | 1.9 | 6 656 | 7.3 | 80 853 | 31.0 | 24.3 |
| Bedford | 20 001 | 79.5 | 114 700 | 23.0 | 13.2 | 569 | 28.3 | 2.0 | 24 153 | -0.7 | 2 237 | 9.3 | 22 357 | 23.9 | 35.9 |
| Berks | 153 780 | 72.9 | 174 000 | 24.3 | 14.6 | 782 | 30.3 | 2.1 | 206 060 | 1.0 | 16 556 | 8.0 | 195 640 | 31.2 | 27.4 |
| Blair | 51 771 | 72.3 | 101 500 | 21.1 | 12.8 | 587 | 28.8 | 0.9 | 64 939 | 0.5 | 4 649 | 7.2 | 57 571 | 29.9 | 25.8 |
| Bradford | 24 630 | 75.2 | 108 600 | 22.6 | 13.4 | 573 | 27.4 | 2.5 | 34 686 | 0.5 | 2 248 | 6.5 | 27 270 | 28.1 | 35.7 |
| Bucks | 229 955 | 78.3 | 319 600 | 26.0 | 15.0 | 1 059 | 30.8 | 1.0 | 345 039 | 1.6 | 25 438 | 7.4 | 320 885 | 41.5 | 18.3 |
| Butler | 72 458 | 77.2 | 162 900 | 21.7 | 12.2 | 713 | 29.4 | 1.0 | 101 794 | 1.8 | 6 628 | 6.5 | 89 838 | 34.4 | 23.5 |
| Cambria | 58 428 | 73.7 | 87 600 | 20.4 | 13.5 | 525 | 27.1 | 0.9 | 68 583 | 0.4 | 6 011 | 8.8 | 61 595 | 29.5 | 25.6 |
| Cameron | 2 133 | 72.2 | 73 700 | 19.7 | 13.5 | 495 | 23.9 | 0.9 | 2 257 | -2.3 | 261 | 11.6 | 2 283 | 25.8 | 41.4 |
| Carbon | 26 136 | 80.2 | 146 000 | 25.1 | 14.2 | 685 | 28.2 | 0.7 | 32 456 | 2.0 | 3 200 | 9.9 | 29 207 | 26.2 | 31.2 |
| Centre | 56 134 | 59.4 | 181 400 | 22.6 | 12.0 | 817 | 35.5 | 2.8 | 75 989 | 0.1 | 4 454 | 5.9 | 72 984 | 42.3 | 18.3 |
| Chester | 182 732 | 76.5 | 333 400 | 24.5 | 14.0 | 1 122 | 27.8 | 1.7 | 270 852 | 1.5 | 16 652 | 6.1 | 253 010 | 47.3 | 15.4 |
| Clarion | 15 827 | 71.2 | 99 600 | 20.1 | 10.8 | 573 | 31.5 | 2.2 | 19 956 | -1.1 | 1 788 | 9.0 | 17 790 | 29.1 | 30.0 |
| Clearfield | 32 715 | 77.3 | 84 400 | 22.6 | 14.6 | 552 | 29.0 | 1.4 | 41 360 | 0.7 | 3 652 | 8.8 | 34 720 | 25.8 | 32.6 |
| Clinton | 15 282 | 72.2 | 101 000 | 24.0 | 15.2 | 646 | 30.0 | 1.3 | 20 211 | 1.4 | 1 706 | 8.4 | 16 787 | 23.4 | 33.1 |
| Columbia | 25 906 | 70.9 | 129 000 | 22.4 | 13.6 | 642 | 29.7 | 1.2 | 37 577 | 2.1 | 3 030 | 8.1 | 31 174 | 27.5 | 29.7 |
| Crawford | 35 368 | 73.7 | 100 400 | 23.2 | 13.5 | 568 | 28.5 | 2.8 | 43 080 | 0.2 | 3 308 | 7.7 | 38 009 | 30.0 | 30.8 |
| Cumberland | 94 412 | 71.9 | 179 400 | 22.4 | 12.1 | 804 | 26.4 | 1.3 | 124 657 | 1.2 | 8 208 | 6.6 | 118 301 | 38.6 | 19.5 |
| Dauphin | 108 047 | 65.3 | 157 400 | 22.9 | 12.8 | 801 | 27.4 | 1.2 | 139 263 | 1.2 | 10 682 | 7.7 | 133 193 | 36.4 | 20.2 |
| Delaware | 206 596 | 71.3 | 234 700 | 24.9 | 15.2 | 933 | 32.2 | 1.4 | 282 716 | 1.6 | 22 930 | 8.1 | 267 730 | 41.3 | 16.8 |
| Elk | 13 557 | 79.7 | 94 000 | 22.0 | 13.3 | 547 | 28.3 | 0.5 | 17 483 | 0.4 | 1 190 | 6.8 | 15 157 | 22.9 | 42.3 |
| Erie | 108 303 | 68.7 | 113 300 | 22.5 | 12.8 | 634 | 30.0 | 1.5 | 141 404 | 0.8 | 10 969 | 7.8 | 127 332 | 32.3 | 24.3 |
| Fayette | 54 717 | 73.0 | 83 600 | 22.3 | 13.1 | 549 | 29.7 | 1.0 | 64 660 | 1.8 | 5 983 | 9.3 | 54 727 | 25.3 | 29.0 |
| Forest | 1 990 | 86.0 | 81 300 | 23.3 | 12.6 | 482 | 26.8 | 2.5 | 2 334 | 0.6 | 221 | 9.5 | 2 023 | 20.3 | 32.0 |
| Franklin | 58 032 | 73.3 | 177 800 | 24.3 | 11.8 | 715 | 26.3 | 1.9 | 80 659 | 0.7 | 5 428 | 6.7 | 69 767 | 30.4 | 30.5 |
| Fulton | 5 929 | 77.8 | 161 300 | 24.2 | 11.7 | 571 | 24.8 | 2.9 | 7 818 | 0.7 | 703 | 9.0 | 6 614 | 22.3 | 38.5 |
| Greene | 14 102 | 74.4 | 84 500 | 18.9 | 11.5 | 546 | 28.7 | 1.3 | 22 096 | 6.7 | 1 451 | 6.6 | 15 726 | 27.8 | 33.5 |
| Huntingdon | 16 791 | 77.2 | 111 700 | 22.2 | 12.2 | 510 | 25.5 | 1.9 | 22 336 | -1.5 | 2 129 | 9.5 | 18 795 | 28.8 | 31.5 |
| Indiana | 34 558 | 70.2 | 103 700 | 20.8 | 12.0 | 635 | 32.9 | 3.0 | 48 469 | 1.4 | 3 797 | 7.8 | 39 591 | 27.5 | 30.1 |
| Jefferson | 18 389 | 76.0 | 83 200 | 21.2 | 11.9 | 524 | 27.0 | 2.1 | 23 329 | -0.1 | 1 847 | 7.9 | 19 456 | 24.1 | 36.8 |
| Juniata | 9 103 | 77.1 | 132 800 | 23.7 | 11.8 | 565 | 25.5 | 2.1 | 12 148 | -1.2 | 883 | 7.3 | 11 281 | 25.1 | 40.1 |
| Lackawanna | 86 491 | 66.7 | 142 200 | 23.5 | 15.3 | 652 | 27.3 | 1.2 | 107 986 | 0.7 | 9 680 | 9.0 | 100 584 | 32.6 | 23.0 |
| Lancaster | 192 681 | 70.1 | 187 300 | 24.2 | 12.8 | 828 | 29.2 | 2.2 | 268 804 | 0.7 | 17 824 | 6.6 | 252 430 | 31.1 | 29.2 |
| Lawrence | 36 613 | 77.8 | 94 400 | 22.5 | 14.3 | 610 | 30.6 | 1.7 | 43 169 | 0.4 | 3 515 | 8.1 | 40 551 | 29.4 | 26.7 |
| Lebanon | 51 899 | 73.6 | 160 800 | 22.9 | 12.7 | 672 | 28.5 | 2.4 | 74 910 | 1.7 | 4 813 | 6.4 | 63 590 | 29.3 | 27.7 |
| Lehigh | 133 159 | 68.1 | 206 100 | 24.8 | 14.6 | 859 | 31.7 | 1.7 | 185 533 | 2.1 | 15 765 | 8.5 | 164 314 | 36.0 | 22.5 |
| Luzerne | 131 052 | 68.9 | 116 700 | 22.9 | 14.8 | 630 | 28.6 | 1.3 | 162 321 | 1.2 | 15 780 | 9.7 | 146 965 | 29.6 | 25.7 |
| Lycoming | 46 604 | 69.5 | 125 400 | 23.2 | 14.3 | 629 | 29.8 | 1.3 | 64 026 | 3.1 | 4 988 | 7.8 | 54 441 | 28.4 | 29.4 |
| McKean | 17 180 | 73.4 | 73 500 | 21.5 | 12.4 | 563 | 30.4 | 1.1 | 21 598 | 1.8 | 1 746 | 8.1 | 18 240 | 28.7 | 30.7 |
| Mercer | 46 418 | 75.2 | 101 200 | 22.4 | 13.3 | 596 | 29.0 | 1.9 | 54 280 | 1.5 | 4 591 | 8.5 | 49 825 | 28.8 | 27.0 |
| Mifflin | 18 987 | 74.4 | 93 400 | 23.2 | 14.3 | 541 | 27.9 | 3.0 | 22 343 | -0.8 | 1 854 | 8.3 | 19 271 | 25.2 | 37.7 |
| Monroe | 59 941 | 80.5 | 205 400 | 28.5 | 16.4 | 943 | 32.2 | 1.8 | 81 675 | 0.6 | 8 010 | 9.8 | 76 678 | 32.5 | 23.4 |
| Montgomery | 307 598 | 73.8 | 297 900 | 24.4 | 14.2 | 1 078 | 28.8 | 1.1 | 437 405 | 1.6 | 29 750 | 6.8 | 412 931 | 47.9 | 14.7 |
| Montour | 7 200 | 74.1 | 147 600 | 22.0 | 12.7 | 668 | 25.1 | 1.8 | 9 592 | 1.9 | 573 | 6.0 | 8 475 | 40.3 | 22.6 |
| Northampton | 112 111 | 74.8 | 221 800 | 25.3 | 15.1 | 862 | 29.4 | 2.4 | 155 661 | 2.1 | 13 112 | 8.4 | 141 992 | 34.6 | 24.0 |
| Northumberland | 39 293 | 71.7 | 96 000 | 22.1 | 13.2 | 543 | 27.7 | 1.1 | 46 552 | 0.2 | 4 177 | 9.0 | 41 846 | 25.8 | 32.1 |
| Perry | 18 098 | 80.6 | 150 100 | 23.9 | 12.6 | 660 | 24.5 | 2.7 | 24 396 | 1.2 | 1 894 | 7.8 | 22 724 | 28.5 | 32.6 |
| Philadelphia | 578 125 | 54.9 | 140 700 | 25.9 | 15.6 | 850 | 34.1 | 3.0 | 656 173 | 1.5 | 70 795 | 10.8 | 619 412 | 34.4 | 17.8 |
| Pike | 22 207 | 84.7 | 216 200 | 28.1 | 15.0 | 1 023 | 38.6 | 1.8 | 26 684 | 2.2 | 2 877 | 10.8 | 24 092 | 32.4 | 25.0 |

1. Specified owner-occupied units.    2. A value of 9.9 represents 9.9 percent or less.    3. Specified renter-occupied units. A value of 10.0 represents 10 percent or less.    4. Overcrowded or lacking complete plumbing facilities.    5. Percent of civilian labor force.    6. Persons 16 years old and over.

# Table B. States and Counties — Nonfarm Employment and Agriculture

| | Private nonfarm establishments, employment and payroll, 2011 | | | | | | | | | Agriculture, 2007 | | | |
| | Employment | | | | | | Annual payroll | | Farms | | | |
| | | | | | | | | | | | Percent with: | | |
| STATE County | Number of establishments | Total | Health care and social assistance | Manufacturing | Retail trade | Finance and insurance | Professional, scientific, and technical services | Total (mil dol) | Average per employee (dollars) | Number | Fewer than 50 acres | 500 acres or more | Farm operators whose principal occupation is farming (percent) |
|---|---|---|---|---|---|---|---|---|---|---|---|---|---|
| | 104 | 105 | 106 | 107 | 108 | 109 | 110 | 111 | 112 | 113 | 114 | 115 | 116 |
| OREGON—Cont'd | | | | | | | | | | | | | |
| Morrow | 176 | 2 589 | D | 1 090 | 78 | D | D | 109 | 42 250 | 421 | 26.4 | 53.2 | 53.4 |
| Multnomah | 24 664 | 375 965 | 56 182 | 31 389 | 37 000 | 20 119 | 29 224 | 17 780 | 47 292 | 563 | 81.3 | 2.1 | 45.1 |
| Polk | 1 298 | 10 795 | 2 455 | 1 564 | 1 606 | 245 | 333 | 314 | 29 075 | 1 252 | 62.4 | 5.8 | 43.5 |
| Sherman | 50 | 364 | D | D | D | D | NA | 10 | 28 772 | 208 | 5.3 | 73.6 | 59.6 |
| Tillamook | 687 | 6 099 | D | 1 289 | 866 | 151 | 136 | 183 | 30 050 | 302 | 39.7 | 3.0 | 64.2 |
| Umatilla | 1 521 | 21 189 | 2 946 | 2 603 | 3 050 | 552 | 1 532 | 695 | 32 801 | 1 658 | 51.7 | 24.9 | 45.3 |
| Union | 762 | 6 919 | 1 440 | 986 | 1 435 | 248 | 220 | 205 | 29 667 | 880 | 43.6 | 22.3 | 44.3 |
| Wallowa | 346 | 1 578 | 392 | 126 | 251 | D | 80 | 45 | 28 732 | 526 | 32.3 | 31.7 | 47.5 |
| Wasco | 704 | 6 936 | 1 794 | 291 | 1 518 | D | 206 | 209 | 30 129 | 649 | 40.5 | 24.0 | 47.1 |
| Washington | 14 037 | 223 496 | 24 088 | 26 982 | 28 400 | 9 911 | 16 581 | 12 210 | 54 630 | 1 761 | 74.7 | 3.1 | 45.0 |
| Wheeler | 35 | 157 | D | NA | D | D | NA | 3 | 20 210 | 164 | 3.7 | 53.0 | 52.4 |
| Yamhill | 2 286 | 26 599 | 4 357 | 5 547 | 3 312 | 800 | 614 | 935 | 35 133 | 2 115 | 72.7 | 3.9 | 38.7 |
| PENNSYLVANIA | 295 720 | 5 078 111 | 944 517 | 546 956 | 646 970 | 256 020 | 310 331 | 222 252 | 43 767 | 63 163 | 41.0 | 3.9 | 45.5 |
| Adams | 1 884 | 27 901 | 4 389 | 5 889 | 3 292 | 550 | 547 | 873 | 31 298 | 1 289 | 49.2 | 6.6 | 46.4 |
| Allegheny | 33 339 | 679 125 | 123 315 | 38 029 | 74 389 | 47 204 | 58 271 | 32 027 | 47 159 | 534 | 54.5 | 0.9 | 39.3 |
| Armstrong | 1 245 | 13 144 | 2 997 | 1 326 | 2 163 | 670 | 419 | 438 | 33 351 | 794 | 22.8 | 6.0 | 43.2 |
| Beaver | 3 404 | 49 086 | 9 796 | 7 115 | 7 627 | 972 | 3 276 | 1 720 | 35 050 | 824 | 46.1 | 0.8 | 34.2 |
| Bedford | 1 078 | 12 890 | 1 679 | 2 093 | 2 147 | 314 | 318 | 392 | 30 412 | 1 173 | 24.1 | 7.1 | 50.0 |
| Berks | 8 177 | 144 686 | 24 270 | 28 859 | 20 528 | 6 038 | 6 163 | 5 930 | 40 988 | 1 980 | 49.5 | 4.0 | 54.5 |
| Blair | 3 200 | 50 360 | 10 875 | 6 777 | 8 759 | 1 498 | 1 917 | 1 681 | 33 372 | 523 | 33.8 | 5.9 | 58.1 |
| Bradford | 1 440 | 19 511 | 4 430 | 4 123 | 3 015 | 643 | 441 | 734 | 37 606 | 1 457 | 25.6 | 7.1 | 48.8 |
| Bucks | 18 758 | 242 654 | 40 440 | 25 826 | 38 477 | 8 405 | 15 309 | 10 097 | 41 609 | 934 | 71.2 | 3.2 | 46.6 |
| Butler | 4 669 | 79 098 | 12 907 | 12 981 | 11 123 | 2 219 | 6 541 | 3 217 | 40 672 | 1 116 | 41.0 | 3.3 | 45.1 |
| Cambria | 3 381 | 50 282 | 12 250 | 5 544 | 6 977 | 2 168 | 3 161 | 1 609 | 31 992 | 656 | 37.0 | 5.6 | 38.6 |
| Cameron | 117 | 1 541 | 174 | 885 | 179 | D | D | 48 | 31 192 | 34 | 17.6 | 2.9 | 32.4 |
| Carbon | 1 123 | 13 129 | 2 825 | 2 012 | 2 011 | 338 | 303 | 376 | 28 669 | 207 | 46.9 | 2.4 | 37.2 |
| Centre | 3 169 | 43 808 | 7 532 | 4 100 | 7 963 | 1 402 | 3 380 | 1 481 | 33 808 | 1 146 | 40.2 | 4.3 | 44.2 |
| Chester | 13 689 | 230 867 | 32 416 | 15 218 | 26 557 | 22 629 | 21 969 | 13 914 | 60 268 | 1 733 | 57.3 | 3.6 | 53.8 |
| Clarion | 946 | 10 601 | 2 616 | 1 268 | 1 907 | 286 | 223 | 303 | 28 570 | 872 | 28.1 | 5.2 | 32.3 |
| Clearfield | 1 973 | 25 841 | 5 938 | 2 780 | 4 741 | 697 | 585 | 822 | 31 801 | 473 | 33.0 | 3.2 | 37.4 |
| Clinton | 748 | 10 956 | 1 214 | 3 108 | 1 850 | 211 | 299 | 364 | 33 263 | 537 | 40.0 | 2.2 | 46.9 |
| Columbia | 1 416 | 22 104 | 3 695 | 5 278 | 3 718 | 586 | 712 | 690 | 31 220 | 962 | 36.3 | 3.3 | 38.5 |
| Crawford | 2 049 | 27 013 | 5 222 | 6 845 | 3 587 | 506 | 823 | 839 | 31 067 | 1 468 | 29.8 | 5.5 | 51.4 |
| Cumberland | 5 709 | 113 311 | 15 638 | 7 329 | 15 567 | 9 007 | 7 535 | 4 486 | 39 592 | 1 550 | 52.0 | 3.5 | 44.5 |
| Dauphin | 6 862 | 143 099 | 32 421 | 8 114 | 15 215 | 10 186 | 7 313 | 6 032 | 42 155 | 836 | 49.9 | 2.9 | 40.9 |
| Delaware | 12 629 | 204 707 | 37 491 | 13 781 | 24 890 | 12 535 | 11 433 | 10 721 | 52 373 | 79 | 67.1 | 0.0 | 36.7 |
| Elk | 914 | 14 602 | 2 026 | 7 045 | 1 486 | D | 590 | 513 | 35 120 | 376 | 50.0 | 0.8 | 25.8 |
| Erie | 6 246 | 114 273 | 24 086 | 22 960 | 15 339 | D | 3 196 | 3 994 | 34 947 | 1 609 | 44.0 | 2.9 | 39.7 |
| Fayette | 2 697 | 36 720 | 7 932 | 3 664 | 6 466 | 634 | 1 073 | 1 112 | 30 288 | 1 220 | 40.7 | 2.5 | 37.5 |
| Forest | 111 | 1 414 | D | 242 | 100 | D | D | 40 | 28 575 | 84 | 31.0 | 2.4 | 32.1 |
| Franklin | 3 010 | 45 875 | 7 585 | 7 436 | 7 003 | 1 117 | 2 194 | 1 612 | 35 132 | 1 540 | 37.5 | 5.8 | 54.4 |
| Fulton | 267 | 4 845 | D | D | 360 | 81 | 27 | 232 | 47 862 | 608 | 25.3 | 5.3 | 37.7 |
| Greene | 708 | 13 552 | 1 434 | 467 | 2 495 | 292 | 207 | 654 | 48 276 | 1 245 | 29.3 | 2.1 | 31.0 |
| Huntingdon | 830 | 10 326 | 1 766 | 2 266 | 1 489 | 443 | 253 | 302 | 29 289 | 930 | 28.1 | 4.9 | 40.8 |
| Indiana | 1 921 | 27 039 | 4 457 | 2 825 | 5 066 | D | 852 | 998 | 36 920 | 1 544 | 35.6 | 3.6 | 38.7 |
| Jefferson | 1 179 | 13 465 | 3 053 | 3 786 | 1 762 | 280 | 373 | 437 | 32 482 | 597 | 26.1 | 4.2 | 43.9 |
| Juniata | 465 | 4 938 | 422 | 1 889 | 659 | 180 | 67 | 139 | 28 104 | 788 | 42.0 | 2.8 | 45.8 |
| Lackawanna | 5 325 | 94 979 | 22 046 | 9 232 | 13 149 | 5 626 | 3 578 | 3 107 | 32 707 | 417 | 36.9 | 1.0 | 31.7 |
| Lancaster | 12 041 | 210 772 | 34 089 | 33 619 | 30 183 | 6 710 | 10 343 | 7 903 | 37 494 | 5 462 | 46.6 | 1.7 | 64.1 |
| Lawrence | 1 989 | 26 388 | 6 151 | 3 700 | 3 704 | 1 290 | 636 | 882 | 33 410 | 708 | 34.0 | 5.4 | 46.3 |
| Lebanon | 2 610 | 43 384 | 7 539 | 8 889 | 6 425 | 869 | 1 067 | 1 472 | 33 920 | 1 193 | 52.9 | 1.4 | 54.8 |
| Lehigh | 8 382 | 155 897 | 34 883 | 14 671 | 20 413 | 7 065 | 6 110 | 7 398 | 47 452 | 516 | 57.9 | 6.8 | 50.0 |
| Luzerne | 7 182 | 123 796 | 23 381 | 16 387 | 18 608 | 4 881 | 4 360 | 4 287 | 34 631 | 610 | 39.3 | 2.8 | 40.2 |
| Lycoming | 2 867 | 46 228 | 8 119 | 8 348 | 7 377 | 1 395 | 1 748 | 1 578 | 34 136 | 1 211 | 32.6 | 3.1 | 41.4 |
| McKean | 1 055 | 13 476 | 2 592 | 3 101 | 1 710 | D | 221 | 462 | 34 287 | 313 | 29.7 | 3.2 | 36.4 |
| Mercer | 2 779 | 44 066 | 10 547 | 7 430 | 7 262 | 1 414 | 931 | 1 416 | 32 137 | 1 210 | 29.8 | 4.1 | 47.1 |
| Mifflin | 934 | 13 635 | 3 139 | 3 954 | 2 141 | 370 | 117 | 446 | 32 736 | 1 024 | 45.2 | 1.6 | 46.2 |
| Monroe | 3 400 | 44 013 | 6 283 | 4 851 | 8 836 | 981 | 1 315 | 1 484 | 33 708 | 349 | 59.3 | 2.6 | 41.8 |
| Montgomery | 25 632 | 465 939 | 71 139 | 37 603 | 55 904 | 34 626 | 44 817 | 25 974 | 55 746 | 719 | 71.2 | 1.1 | 42.4 |
| Montour | 414 | 14 025 | 7 113 | D | 696 | D | D | 813 | 57 948 | 583 | 43.2 | 1.2 | 35.8 |
| Northampton | 6 202 | 91 888 | 12 739 | 11 028 | 13 235 | 4 239 | 4 433 | 3 605 | 39 235 | 486 | 59.9 | 7.4 | 46.5 |
| Northumberland | 1 660 | 23 034 | 4 449 | 4 412 | 3 183 | 599 | 535 | 765 | 33 196 | 936 | 40.4 | 6.0 | 44.9 |
| Perry | 781 | 6 005 | 859 | 615 | 1 237 | 252 | D | 145 | 24 207 | 1 002 | 36.6 | 4.5 | 42.9 |
| Philadelphia | 26 772 | 585 909 | 153 100 | 23 141 | 47 652 | 28 619 | 43 743 | 29 041 | 49 566 | 17 | 82.4 | 0.0 | 64.7 |
| Pike | 888 | 7 528 | 903 | D | 1 805 | 197 | 205 | 191 | 25 361 | 54 | 50.0 | 11.1 | 35.2 |

Items 104—116

# Table B. States and Counties — **Agriculture**

| | Agriculture, 2007 (cont.) | | | | | | | | | | | | | | |
| STATE County | Land in farms | | | | | Value of land and buildings (dollars) | | Value of machinery and equipment, average per farm (dollars) | Value of products sold | | | | Percent of farms with sales of: | | Government payments | |
| | Acreage (1,000) | Percent change, 2002–2007 | Acres | | | Average per farm | Average per acre | | Total (mil dol) | Average per farm (dollars) | Percent from: | | $10,000 or more | $100,000 or more | Total ($1,000) | Percent of farms |
| | | | Average size of farm | Total irrigated (1,000) | Total cropland (1,000) | | | | | | Crops | Live-stock and poultry products | | | | |
| | 117 | 118 | 119 | 120 | 121 | 122 | 123 | 124 | 125 | 126 | 127 | 128 | 129 | 130 | 131 | 132 |
| **OREGON—Cont'd** | | | | | | | | | | | | | | | | |
| Morrow | 1 104 | -1.9 | 2 623 | 89.9 | 485.0 | 1 938 823 | 739 | 207 000 | 353.5 | 839 712 | 35.4 | 64.6 | 48.2 | 30.6 | 11 482 | 58.0 |
| Multnomah | 29 | -14.7 | 51 | 7.0 | 20.0 | 640 687 | 12 654 | 73 682 | 84.5 | 150 171 | 96.6 | 3.4 | 34.5 | 14.9 | 227 | 4.1 |
| Polk | 167 | -1.2 | 133 | 16.7 | 120.1 | 728 558 | 5 473 | 80 988 | 146.7 | 117 145 | 76.8 | 23.2 | 29.3 | 13.4 | 1 435 | 17.6 |
| Sherman | 514 | 1.2 | 2 471 | 2.8 | 345.5 | 1 551 001 | 628 | 161 189 | 31.7 | 152 639 | 94.8 | 5.2 | 56.3 | 39.9 | 6 848 | 88.9 |
| Tillamook | 38 | -5.0 | 125 | 7.5 | 17.7 | 780 085 | 6 236 | 134 016 | 110.9 | 367 072 | 1.1 | 98.9 | 54.3 | 39.7 | 724 | 33.1 |
| Umatilla | 1 447 | 8.7 | 873 | 142.3 | 804.1 | 1 010 148 | 1 157 | 115 936 | 320.7 | 193 413 | 76.5 | 23.5 | 38.1 | 20.3 | 18 550 | 33.3 |
| Union | 488 | 2.1 | 554 | 63.3 | 141.4 | 833 720 | 1 505 | 93 959 | 58.2 | 66 186 | 72.6 | 27.4 | 35.9 | 11.8 | 3 138 | 30.8 |
| Wallowa | 528 | 1.9 | 1 004 | 44.8 | 96.0 | 1 154 495 | 1 150 | 75 925 | 32.3 | 61 337 | 37.7 | 62.3 | 47.7 | 16.0 | 2 879 | 39.7 |
| Wasco | 949 | -12.7 | 1 463 | 27.7 | 180.6 | 1 083 291 | 740 | 106 144 | 89.9 | 138 063 | 86.7 | 13.3 | 41.4 | 19.6 | 6 416 | 36.1 |
| Washington | 128 | -2.3 | 73 | 26.2 | 92.6 | 740 180 | 10 185 | 81 575 | 311.4 | 176 820 | 94.7 | 5.3 | 35.7 | 13.7 | 809 | 13.0 |
| Wheeler | 758 | 2.7 | 4 621 | 14.1 | 56.3 | 2 145 451 | 464 | 89 715 | D | D | D | 0.0 | 42.1 | 17.1 | 459 | 28.7 |
| Yamhill | 181 | -7.7 | 86 | 26.8 | 114.8 | 757 162 | 8 855 | 76 165 | 277.6 | 131 235 | 83.2 | 16.8 | 31.2 | 10.9 | 1 818 | 15.4 |
| **PENNSYLVANIA** | 7 809 | 0.8 | 124 | 37.8 | 4 870.3 | 590 376 | 4 775 | 72 988 | 5 808.8 | 91 965 | 32.2 | 67.8 | 38.5 | 16.9 | 75 975 | 27.6 |
| Adams | 175 | -3.3 | 135 | 1.9 | 127.5 | 865 422 | 6 389 | 95 911 | 217.0 | 168 343 | 32.4 | 67.6 | 44.3 | 17.1 | 1 853 | 31.6 |
| Allegheny | 38 | 11.8 | 71 | 0.3 | 18.4 | 411 888 | 5 785 | 47 397 | 9.5 | 17 817 | 85.7 | 14.3 | 18.9 | 5.6 | 57 | 6.6 |
| Armstrong | 122 | -6.9 | 154 | 0.2 | 69.4 | 481 854 | 3 129 | 75 021 | 52.0 | 65 461 | 66.3 | 33.7 | 30.4 | 9.2 | 587 | 22.4 |
| Beaver | 67 | 6.3 | 81 | 0.4 | 35.5 | 398 130 | 4 891 | 47 810 | 15.2 | 18 431 | 44.9 | 55.1 | 19.7 | 4.1 | 276 | 12.1 |
| Bedford | 211 | 9.3 | 180 | 0.3 | 118.7 | 620 452 | 3 449 | 78 274 | 90.9 | 77 458 | 18.6 | 81.4 | 40.9 | 20.3 | 1 861 | 33.8 |
| Berks | 222 | 2.8 | 112 | 1.3 | 170.8 | 772 086 | 6 882 | 101 016 | 367.8 | 185 778 | 45.0 | 55.0 | 52.5 | 24.8 | 3 280 | 33.0 |
| Blair | 87 | 1.2 | 167 | 0.2 | 61.9 | 690 402 | 4 130 | 99 314 | 85.2 | 162 904 | 11.9 | 88.1 | 51.6 | 25.0 | 1 092 | 36.3 |
| Bradford | 267 | -11.6 | 183 | 0.1 | 146.6 | 558 698 | 3 053 | 74 576 | 121.3 | 83 261 | 7.6 | 92.4 | 38.4 | 20.3 | 4 111 | 40.5 |
| Bucks | 76 | -1.3 | 81 | 1.4 | 58.0 | 808 476 | 9 951 | 81 015 | 70.6 | 75 560 | 76.4 | 23.6 | 37.0 | 12.7 | 713 | 16.7 |
| Butler | 130 | -9.7 | 116 | 0.7 | 78.3 | 530 189 | 4 557 | 74 008 | 38.7 | 34 645 | 53.2 | 46.8 | 33.8 | 7.7 | 860 | 29.6 |
| Cambria | 88 | 0.0 | 134 | 0.0 | 54.6 | 466 056 | 3 477 | 62 980 | 23.2 | 35 316 | 47.2 | 52.8 | 26.1 | 6.9 | 756 | 32.0 |
| Cameron | 5 | 25.0 | 150 | 0.0 | 2.0 | 298 606 | 1 994 | 56 445 | 0.8 | 24 356 | D | D | 44.1 | 5.9 | D | 32.4 |
| Carbon | 20 | 5.3 | 97 | 0.1 | 12.7 | 529 262 | 5 468 | 71 656 | 8.9 | 43 206 | 87.5 | 12.5 | 38.2 | 10.1 | 239 | 45.4 |
| Centre | 148 | -10.3 | 130 | 0.6 | 86.1 | 660 008 | 5 095 | 60 906 | 69.7 | 60 786 | 25.1 | 74.9 | 39.4 | 17.2 | 1 266 | 26.8 |
| Chester | 167 | -0.6 | 96 | 1.7 | 117.1 | 1 034 252 | 10 740 | 116 652 | 553.3 | 319 267 | 79.6 | 20.4 | 48.8 | 26.6 | 2 068 | 17.5 |
| Clarion | 132 | 21.1 | 152 | 0.1 | 67.5 | 439 775 | 2 902 | 57 045 | 22.0 | 25 181 | 33.7 | 66.3 | 23.6 | 6.4 | 504 | 26.3 |
| Clearfield | 63 | 3.3 | 133 | 0.1 | 32.5 | 334 959 | 2 526 | 59 056 | 11.1 | 23 472 | 38.6 | 61.4 | 27.5 | 5.7 | 240 | 21.1 |
| Clinton | 57 | 7.5 | 105 | 0.6 | 35.6 | 445 401 | 4 224 | 63 683 | 43.7 | 81 305 | 18.4 | 81.6 | 34.6 | 21.2 | 559 | 30.4 |
| Columbia | 123 | -0.8 | 127 | 0.5 | 88.1 | 536 605 | 4 210 | 69 877 | 45.9 | 47 687 | 59.4 | 40.7 | 30.6 | 10.6 | 2 138 | 57.3 |
| Crawford | 232 | 4.5 | 158 | 0.6 | 139.5 | 455 933 | 2 884 | 69 563 | 101.0 | 68 826 | 25.7 | 74.3 | 37.8 | 14.2 | 2 212 | 28.8 |
| Cumberland | 157 | 9.8 | 102 | 1.2 | 123.1 | 644 525 | 6 347 | 72 552 | 132.8 | 85 680 | 20.0 | 80.0 | 40.9 | 17.7 | 2 282 | 32.3 |
| Dauphin | 90 | -5.3 | 107 | 0.4 | 66.2 | 653 346 | 6 101 | 71 835 | 82.9 | 99 148 | 19.7 | 80.3 | 40.6 | 17.2 | 857 | 34.3 |
| Delaware | 4 | NA | 55 | 0.0 | 1.6 | 718 736 | 13 020 | 66 447 | 9.5 | 119 061 | 97.3 | 2.7 | 22.8 | 8.9 | 5 | 5.1 |
| Elk | 33 | 50.0 | 88 | 0.0 | 13.7 | 302 401 | 3 419 | 43 126 | 3.7 | 9 886 | 37.4 | 62.6 | 12.8 | 2.9 | 63 | 8.5 |
| Erie | 173 | 4.2 | 108 | 1.4 | 101.7 | 430 926 | 4 005 | 62 976 | 71.3 | 44 303 | 69.0 | 31.0 | 31.7 | 11.4 | 1 348 | 16.7 |
| Fayette | 141 | 12.8 | 115 | 0.1 | 74.2 | 420 637 | 3 648 | 60 219 | 26.0 | 21 290 | 40.9 | 59.1 | 23.2 | 4.8 | 556 | 16.4 |
| Forest | 11 | 83.3 | 128 | D | 4.4 | 422 752 | 3 310 | 42 827 | 3.1 | 36 979 | 4.8 | 95.2 | 19.0 | 6.0 | 49 | 13.1 |
| Franklin | 243 | -0.8 | 158 | 1.9 | 185.0 | 957 792 | 6 079 | 107 800 | 304.5 | 197 694 | 11.5 | 88.5 | 55.7 | 35.5 | 2 746 | 34.7 |
| Fulton | 104 | 3.0 | 170 | 0.1 | 52.4 | 594 020 | 3 489 | 80 334 | 38.0 | 62 562 | 9.2 | 90.8 | 33.7 | 10.7 | 1 031 | 53.8 |
| Greene | 150 | 5.6 | 121 | 0.0 | 66.8 | 377 350 | 3 128 | 40 178 | 9.3 | 7 483 | 35.9 | 64.1 | 14.9 | 1.0 | 141 | 5.0 |
| Huntingdon | 148 | 3.5 | 159 | 0.2 | 73.0 | 583 415 | 3 659 | 67 636 | 62.3 | 67 011 | 13.6 | 86.4 | 27.8 | 10.9 | 1 559 | 27.7 |
| Indiana | 188 | 19.7 | 122 | 2.3 | 113.0 | 441 183 | 3 629 | 52 313 | 76.4 | 49 500 | 54.1 | 45.9 | 24.9 | 8.0 | 1 140 | 19.4 |
| Jefferson | 87 | 0.0 | 146 | 0.0 | 52.1 | 397 806 | 2 728 | 65 476 | 25.3 | 42 407 | 59.1 | 40.9 | 30.5 | 7.2 | 480 | 19.3 |
| Juniata | 98 | 14.0 | 124 | 0.3 | 59.1 | 571 345 | 4 609 | 72 986 | 91.7 | 116 318 | 9.1 | 90.9 | 44.4 | 23.7 | 1 515 | 45.9 |
| Lackawanna | 40 | 21.2 | 95 | 0.3 | 21.4 | 470 318 | 4 933 | 63 261 | 16.2 | 38 886 | 70.0 | 30.0 | 22.3 | 6.2 | 166 | 11.8 |
| Lancaster | 425 | 3.2 | 78 | 5.4 | 326.6 | 726 059 | 9 324 | 83 136 | 1 072.2 | 196 293 | 13.9 | 86.1 | 69.5 | 44.3 | 4 547 | 23.0 |
| Lawrence | 92 | 5.7 | 130 | 0.1 | 61.5 | 495 649 | 3 798 | 75 871 | 35.6 | 50 338 | 33.9 | 66.1 | 43.9 | 13.1 | 841 | 31.1 |
| Lebanon | 113 | -9.6 | 95 | 1.3 | 89.6 | 791 376 | 8 319 | 100 682 | 257.1 | 215 505 | 8.6 | 91.4 | 51.6 | 33.4 | 1 495 | 29.2 |
| Lehigh | 85 | -6.6 | 164 | 1.2 | 72.7 | 963 477 | 5 874 | 112 524 | 72.1 | 139 650 | 73.0 | 27.0 | 47.9 | 14.7 | 984 | 25.8 |
| Luzerne | 67 | -8.2 | 109 | 0.4 | 38.6 | 515 986 | 4 728 | 62 107 | 18.2 | 29 756 | 74.0 | 26.0 | 27.9 | 8.4 | 991 | 41.1 |
| Lycoming | 160 | -9.6 | 132 | 1.7 | 88.0 | 458 300 | 3 459 | 61 706 | 53.4 | 44 080 | 38.7 | 61.3 | 33.8 | 11.5 | 1 832 | 39.9 |
| McKean | 41 | -2.4 | 132 | 0.0 | 15.4 | 280 034 | 2 114 | 38 736 | 5.2 | 16 564 | 16.7 | 83.3 | 18.2 | 5.8 | 228 | 20.1 |
| Mercer | 172 | 4.9 | 142 | 0.2 | 111.6 | 453 118 | 3 190 | 70 526 | 60.7 | 50 128 | 37.3 | 62.7 | 42.6 | 13.2 | 1 724 | 38.4 |
| Mifflin | 94 | 4.4 | 92 | 0.1 | 58.8 | 425 397 | 4 628 | 58 769 | 86.8 | 84 783 | 9.1 | 90.9 | 41.5 | 18.5 | 897 | 25.8 |
| Monroe | 29 | -12.1 | 84 | 0.1 | 14.3 | 590 756 | 7 069 | 53 463 | 7.8 | 22 404 | 58.1 | 41.9 | 24.6 | 5.2 | 125 | 9.5 |
| Montgomery | 42 | -12.5 | 58 | 0.7 | 28.6 | 584 297 | 10 025 | 53 301 | 30.0 | 41 764 | 62.8 | 37.2 | 30.0 | 7.5 | 238 | 12.5 |
| Montour | 50 | 25.0 | 86 | 0.1 | 34.3 | 441 064 | 5 117 | 49 379 | 36.2 | 62 081 | 58.4 | 41.6 | 28.6 | 10.5 | 837 | 37.2 |
| Northampton | 68 | -12.8 | 140 | 0.2 | 58.9 | 854 282 | 6 083 | 89 758 | 31.8 | 65 355 | 70.2 | 29.8 | 44.9 | 16.5 | 849 | 27.4 |
| Northumberland | 148 | 24.4 | 158 | 1.1 | 110.3 | 636 980 | 4 038 | 76 163 | 111.0 | 118 566 | 35.0 | 65.0 | 45.0 | 19.8 | 2 390 | 53.6 |
| Perry | 144 | 11.6 | 144 | 0.1 | 92.3 | 636 686 | 4 419 | 77 512 | 105.1 | 104 842 | 12.9 | 87.1 | 34.4 | 17.1 | 1 966 | 37.8 |
| Philadelphia | 0 | NA | 15 | D | 0.2 | 539 894 | 35 031 | 22 075 | 0.5 | 28 629 | D | D | 29.4 | 5.9 | D | 11.8 |
| Pike | 28 | 180.0 | 511 | 0.0 | 2.9 | 849 318 | 1 664 | 55 728 | 2.5 | 46 744 | 92.7 | 7.3 | 20.4 | 9.3 | D | 1.9 |

— **Water Use, Wholesale Trade, Retail Trade, and Real Estate**

| STATE County | Water use, 2005 | | Wholesale trade,[1] 2007 | | | | Retail trade,[2] 2007 | | | | Real estate and rental and leasing,[2] 2007 | | | |
|---|---|---|---|---|---|---|---|---|---|---|---|---|---|---|
| | Total water withdrawn (mil gal/day) | Gallons withdrawn per person | Number of establishments | Number of employees | Sales (mil dol) | Annual payroll (mil dol) | Number of establishments | Number of employees | Sales (mil dol) | Annual payroll (mil dol) | Number of establishments | Number of employees | Receipts (mil dol) | Annual payroll (mil dol) |
| | 133 | 134 | 135 | 136 | 137 | 138 | 139 | 140 | 141 | 142 | 143 | 144 | 145 | 146 |
| OREGON—Cont'd | | | | | | | | | | | | | | |
| Morrow | 320.0 | 27 430 | 12 | 67 | 49.4 | 2.6 | 16 | 80 | 17.4 | 1.6 | 10 | 12 | 1.2 | 0.2 |
| Multnomah | 53.8 | 80 | 1 271 | 22 685 | 22 043.8 | 1 114.4 | 2 945 | 40 269 | 9 868.5 | 1 035.5 | 1 491 | 9 735 | 1 770.9 | 366.4 |
| Polk | 50.2 | 714 | 33 | 206 | 70.3 | 7.4 | 150 | 1 728 | 375.1 | 39.0 | 71 | 238 | 21.7 | 3.6 |
| Sherman | 7.2 | 4 128 | 4 | 25 | 12.0 | 1.0 | 10 | 119 | 56.0 | 2.2 | 1 | D | D | D |
| Tillamook | 40.4 | 1 598 | 17 | 134 | 31.0 | 3.1 | 121 | 1 118 | 224.9 | 23.0 | 34 | 116 | 11.0 | 2.5 |
| Umatilla | 405.8 | 5 493 | 64 | 733 | 284.5 | 27.6 | 263 | 3 024 | 763.6 | 71.6 | 68 | 224 | 24.3 | 4.5 |
| Union | 213.9 | 8 717 | 20 | D | D | D | 125 | 1 483 | 333.8 | 32.7 | 20 | 86 | 9.5 | 1.9 |
| Wallowa | 161.8 | 23 070 | 2 | D | D | D | 56 | 376 | 82.7 | 7.5 | 22 | 51 | 5.3 | 1.0 |
| Wasco | 108.6 | 4 602 | 23 | D | D | D | 133 | 1 749 | 381.9 | 39.5 | 45 | 85 | 9.8 | 1.6 |
| Washington | 86.5 | 173 | 813 | 12 907 | 11 021.8 | 793.3 | 1 718 | 31 456 | 8 754.4 | 792.4 | 843 | 4 645 | 992.7 | 165.9 |
| Wheeler | 30.9 | 21 244 | 1 | D | D | D | 7 | 27 | 10.4 | 0.7 | 2 | D | D | D |
| Yamhill | 80.2 | 869 | 84 | 699 | 396.8 | 27.5 | 282 | 3 509 | 951.1 | 84.9 | 117 | 331 | 42.7 | 7.6 |
| PENNSYLVANIA | 9 471.7 | 762 | 13 161 | 200 151 | 142 859.2 | 10 100.7 | 46 532 | 672 042 | 166 842.8 | 14 862.3 | 9 904 | 68 954 | 13 602.6 | 2 611.8 |
| Adams | 17.5 | 175 | 62 | D | D | D | 376 | 3 798 | 832.4 | 79.9 | 52 | 230 | 42.8 | 5.9 |
| Allegheny | 740.8 | 599 | 1 600 | 21 032 | 18 141.6 | 1 090.2 | 4 795 | 76 658 | 20 075.4 | 1 643.2 | 1 273 | 9 972 | 2 000.7 | 387.3 |
| Armstrong | 181.0 | 2 564 | 32 | D | D | D | 221 | 2 352 | 532.1 | 48.4 | 27 | 281 | 29.5 | 9.7 |
| Beaver | 483.3 | 2 725 | 107 | 1 504 | 1 180.1 | 64.0 | 571 | 7 902 | 1 555.3 | 143.4 | 91 | 424 | 74.0 | 12.5 |
| Bedford | 61.1 | 1 219 | 41 | 387 | 295.5 | 13.0 | 209 | 2 165 | 581.6 | 43.1 | 16 | 164 | 45.2 | 4.8 |
| Berks | 61.0 | 154 | 375 | 6 306 | 4 417.6 | 306.7 | 1 327 | 20 433 | 4 953.2 | 466.8 | 273 | 1 384 | 210.2 | 39.4 |
| Blair | 18.4 | 145 | 123 | 2 160 | 1 511.2 | 87.6 | 619 | 9 366 | 2 038.7 | 179.6 | 82 | 393 | 66.7 | 10.3 |
| Bradford | 12.3 | 197 | 44 | D | D | D | 286 | 2 941 | 727.8 | 59.9 | 26 | 62 | 9.3 | 1.2 |
| Bucks | 113.1 | 182 | 1 167 | 14 880 | 9 859.6 | 803.5 | 2 551 | 41 993 | 13 089.8 | 1 020.0 | 608 | 3 671 | 787.7 | 145.9 |
| Butler | 17.6 | 97 | 237 | 3 604 | 2 580.2 | 171.0 | 719 | 10 950 | 2 527.3 | 224.8 | 141 | 630 | 125.2 | 17.6 |
| Cambria | 18.6 | 125 | 123 | 1 362 | 582.5 | 44.2 | 588 | 7 207 | 1 626.5 | 137.9 | 99 | 584 | 65.8 | 16.7 |
| Cameron | 0.8 | 140 | 2 | D | D | D | 18 | 208 | 29.6 | 2.8 | NA | NA | NA | NA |
| Carbon | 47.4 | 765 | 19 | 137 | 35.8 | 5.7 | 198 | 2 301 | 483.9 | 48.2 | 36 | 117 | 17.5 | 3.7 |
| Centre | 101.6 | 723 | 92 | 1 091 | 572.3 | 70.9 | 548 | 8 014 | 1 604.3 | 151.0 | 129 | 922 | 184.7 | 26.2 |
| Chester | 253.1 | 534 | 769 | 9 902 | 8 571.4 | 771.3 | 1 610 | 30 395 | 11 338.4 | 923.5 | 479 | D | D | D |
| Clarion | 4.4 | 107 | 38 | 669 | 287.4 | 20.4 | 203 | 2 147 | 421.1 | 42.0 | 18 | 50 | 8.7 | 1.1 |
| Clearfield | 353.8 | 4 273 | 66 | D | D | D | 368 | 4 677 | 1 150.1 | 91.9 | 39 | 275 | 26.4 | 6.1 |
| Clinton | 32.4 | 866 | 17 | D | D | D | 139 | 1 862 | 520.7 | 36.8 | 26 | 140 | 14.6 | 2.6 |
| Columbia | 8.8 | 135 | 42 | 461 | 109.9 | 16.0 | 274 | 3 692 | 826.2 | 71.3 | 58 | 206 | 30.7 | 5.6 |
| Crawford | 17.6 | 197 | 76 | 442 | 146.7 | 14.5 | 329 | 3 948 | 877.3 | 86.8 | 51 | 197 | 24.6 | 4.2 |
| Cumberland | 114.4 | 513 | 228 | 3 165 | 3 657.8 | 134.6 | 907 | 15 471 | 3 684.9 | 333.7 | 218 | 1 352 | 288.3 | 50.4 |
| Dauphin | 100.9 | 397 | 277 | 9 815 | 6 456.6 | 493.7 | 1 064 | 16 695 | 3 869.5 | 361.3 | 227 | 2 010 | 515.1 | 72.8 |
| Delaware | 929.7 | 1 673 | 548 | 7 021 | 4 220.0 | 470.4 | 1 861 | 26 462 | 6 358.4 | 617.2 | 449 | 5 011 | 1 168.9 | 196.0 |
| Elk | 22.2 | 661 | 30 | 226 | 69.9 | 7.8 | 130 | 1 536 | 291.2 | 26.0 | 13 | 44 | 4.2 | 0.6 |
| Erie | 55.7 | 199 | 279 | 3 118 | 1 157.2 | 124.0 | 1 051 | 15 831 | 3 428.4 | 314.5 | 187 | 1 115 | 135.3 | 25.9 |
| Fayette | 42.8 | 293 | 106 | 1 042 | 528.1 | 40.6 | 514 | 6 849 | 1 535.5 | 134.9 | 79 | 394 | 54.6 | 8.9 |
| Forest | 0.2 | 40 | 1 | D | D | D | 20 | 75 | 19.3 | 1.5 | 2 | D | D | D |
| Franklin | 22.3 | 162 | 120 | D | D | D | 503 | 7 526 | 1 750.0 | 160.6 | 92 | 485 | 71.2 | 13.7 |
| Fulton | 1.7 | 116 | 14 | 237 | 215.3 | 9.8 | 48 | 390 | 101.4 | 7.7 | 4 | D | D | D |
| Greene | 21.1 | 530 | 20 | 375 | 191.1 | 11.3 | 134 | 1 541 | 432.8 | 29.6 | 11 | 59 | 7.7 | 1.0 |
| Huntingdon | 13.2 | 288 | 25 | D | D | D | 154 | 1 600 | 363.2 | 31.0 | 17 | 59 | 7.7 | 1.0 |
| Indiana | 50.5 | 569 | 63 | 693 | 492.3 | 27.0 | 336 | 5 039 | 1 279.0 | 102.9 | 49 | 248 | 23.9 | 5.5 |
| Jefferson | 6.1 | 134 | 46 | 445 | 235.4 | 16.4 | 183 | 1 927 | 477.4 | 35.0 | 24 | 100 | 14.7 | 2.4 |
| Juniata | 2.9 | 123 | 21 | 169 | 69.8 | 7.3 | 81 | 785 | 197.6 | 14.2 | 10 | D | D | D |
| Lackawanna | 32.1 | 153 | 258 | 4 248 | 3 127.6 | 160.5 | 991 | 14 196 | 3 178.8 | 281.9 | 158 | 913 | 119.1 | 22.3 |
| Lancaster | 102.6 | 209 | 604 | 10 635 | 6 333.6 | 435.7 | 2 000 | 30 083 | 6 542.3 | 644.4 | 348 | 2 223 | 420.1 | 74.3 |
| Lawrence | 161.3 | 1 738 | 91 | D | D | D | 313 | 4 208 | 949.6 | 90.6 | 46 | 290 | 23.1 | 5.6 |
| Lebanon | 124.5 | 992 | 104 | 3 250 | 2 802.6 | 122.3 | 451 | 6 611 | 1 488.6 | 144.1 | 68 | 271 | 43.5 | 7.3 |
| Lehigh | 40.8 | 124 | 429 | D | D | D | 1 273 | 20 590 | 5 081.2 | 466.6 | 314 | 1 860 | 329.1 | 58.8 |
| Luzerne | 113.1 | 361 | 309 | 5 139 | 2 174.7 | 206.4 | 1 279 | 18 777 | 5 223.7 | 389.9 | 226 | 1 687 | 264.5 | 49.6 |
| Lycoming | 14.5 | 123 | 116 | 1 933 | 701.9 | 62.0 | 519 | 6 968 | 1 458.4 | 130.8 | 94 | 444 | 80.7 | 11.4 |
| McKean | 7.5 | 169 | 31 | D | D | D | 176 | 1 917 | 422.3 | 37.9 | 22 | D | D | D |
| Mercer | 32.2 | 269 | 91 | D | D | D | 555 | 7 229 | 1 441.6 | 140.5 | 85 | 394 | 65.8 | 10.3 |
| Mifflin | 11.7 | 254 | 48 | D | D | D | 187 | 2 415 | 526.1 | 48.8 | 21 | 78 | 13.9 | 1.8 |
| Monroe | 64.6 | 396 | 98 | D | D | D | 688 | 9 091 | 2 014.9 | 190.0 | 166 | 583 | 84.7 | 14.8 |
| Montgomery | 122.6 | 158 | 1 367 | 20 029 | 12 012.4 | 1 249.2 | 3 458 | 58 150 | 15 151.3 | 1 443.8 | 1 062 | 9 282 | 2 287.0 | 478.4 |
| Montour | 26.7 | 1 482 | 11 | 131 | 177.3 | 5.8 | 69 | 690 | 156.9 | 14.3 | 8 | 29 | 4.3 | 0.6 |
| Northampton | 399.2 | 1 387 | 245 | 3 915 | 9 815.9 | 174.0 | 908 | 13 201 | 3 405.0 | 302.0 | 187 | D | D | D |
| Northumberland | 25.8 | 279 | 47 | 795 | 587.5 | 33.8 | 318 | 3 286 | 797.0 | 66.7 | 45 | 193 | 19.5 | 4.7 |
| Perry | 4.1 | 92 | 20 | 141 | 85.1 | 5.4 | 154 | 1 537 | 393.4 | 30.1 | 17 | 68 | 4.4 | 0.7 |
| Philadelphia | 395.7 | 270 | 1 067 | 18 338 | 11 566.1 | 956.3 | 4 420 | 50 225 | 11 167.8 | 1 158.1 | 1 088 | 9 813 | 1 956.1 | 433.9 |
| Pike | 26.9 | 477 | 22 | D | D | D | 131 | 1 946 | 401.1 | 43.2 | 50 | D | D | D |

1. Merchant wholesalers, except manufacturers' sales branches and offices.   2. Employer establishments.

## Table B. States and Counties — Professional Services, Manufacturing, and Accommodation and Food Services

| STATE County | Professional, scientific, and technical services,[1] 2007 | | | | Manufacturing, 2007 | | | | Accommodation and food services, 2007 | | | |
|---|---|---|---|---|---|---|---|---|---|---|---|---|
| | Number of establishments | Number of employees | Receipts (mil dol) | Annual payroll (mil dol) | Number of establishments | Number of employees | Receipts (mil dol) | Annual payroll (mil dol) | Number of establishments | Number of employees | Sales (mil dol) | Annual payroll (mil dol) |
| | 147 | 148 | 149 | 150 | 151 | 152 | 153 | 154 | 155 | 156 | 157 | 158 |
| OREGON—Cont'd | | | | | | | | | | | | |
| Morrow | 4 | D | D | D | 10 | 774 | D | D | 18 | 162 | 7.1 | 1.7 |
| Multnomah | 3 324 | D | D | D | 1 153 | 37 545 | 10 527.6 | 1 668.5 | 2 472 | 38 415 | 2 048.6 | 604.2 |
| Polk | 106 | 312 | 29.3 | 8.6 | 68 | 2 059 | 416.7 | 70.8 | 121 | D | D | D |
| Sherman | 1 | D | D | D | NA | NA | NA | NA | 8 | 87 | 5.9 | 1.3 |
| Tillamook | 38 | 156 | 13.0 | 4.8 | 29 | 1 509 | 633.8 | 59.1 | 124 | 1 033 | 53.7 | 15.7 |
| Umatilla | 97 | D | D | D | 69 | 3 335 | D | D | 166 | 2 721 | 159.4 | 40.4 |
| Union | 60 | 236 | 19.3 | 7.1 | 33 | 1 450 | 337.1 | 56.4 | 65 | 831 | 32.9 | 9.0 |
| Wallowa | 22 | 73 | 6.4 | 2.1 | NA | NA | NA | NA | 42 | 224 | 7.4 | 1.9 |
| Wasco | 55 | 196 | 17.2 | 6.8 | NA | NA | NA | NA | 72 | 896 | 47.6 | 13.5 |
| Washington | 1 773 | D | D | D | 770 | 32 506 | 24 049.0 | 1 759.9 | 1 085 | 17 125 | 849.4 | 249.8 |
| Wheeler | NA | NA | NA | NA | NA | NA | NA | NA | 6 | 14 | 0.6 | 0.1 |
| Yamhill | 207 | D | D | D | 205 | 6 265 | 1 885.8 | 291.9 | 186 | 2 305 | 98.9 | 28.4 |
| PENNSYLVANIA | 29 534 | 292 791 | 45 888.3 | 18 184.2 | 15 406 | 650 804 | 234 840.4 | 29 433.0 | 26 910 | 420 209 | 19 625.4 | 5 454.0 |
| Adams | 135 | D | D | D | 126 | 8 038 | 2 498.3 | 297.9 | 206 | 4 098 | 160.1 | 46.1 |
| Allegheny | 3 954 | D | D | D | 1 198 | 43 118 | 15 725.2 | 2 149.5 | 3 153 | 56 803 | 2 540.3 | 735.1 |
| Armstrong | 76 | D | D | D | 78 | 2 086 | 370.9 | 75.0 | 103 | 1 227 | 39.5 | 10.1 |
| Beaver | 243 | D | D | D | 191 | 7 749 | 4 708.8 | 344.4 | 315 | 4 355 | 156.3 | 42.3 |
| Bedford | 52 | D | D | D | 69 | 2 286 | 728.7 | 81.8 | 104 | 1 402 | 70.3 | 19.4 |
| Berks | 735 | 6 289 | 1 449.0 | 389.4 | 550 | 32 597 | 8 461.8 | 1 487.9 | 715 | 11 030 | 446.0 | 124.4 |
| Blair | 228 | D | D | D | 139 | 7 282 | 1 931.2 | 285.6 | 274 | 4 841 | 178.9 | 52.0 |
| Bradford | 80 | D | D | D | 69 | 4 787 | 1 772.4 | 198.6 | 108 | 1 206 | 48.8 | 13.1 |
| Bucks | 2 375 | D | D | D | 1 129 | 31 813 | 9 316.3 | 1 484.6 | 1 307 | 19 756 | 970.2 | 258.4 |
| Butler | 411 | D | D | D | 294 | 14 408 | 5 362.0 | 750.1 | 361 | 6 949 | 269.5 | 74.9 |
| Cambria | 221 | D | D | D | 146 | 5 409 | 1 439.8 | 199.6 | 307 | 4 135 | 156.0 | 40.9 |
| Cameron | 6 | 17 | 1.2 | 0.5 | 26 | 1 180 | 213.8 | 48.8 | 14 | 96 | 2.8 | 0.6 |
| Carbon | 70 | D | D | D | 56 | 2 450 | 514.3 | 95.1 | 127 | 1 491 | 104.7 | 21.7 |
| Centre | 376 | D | D | D | 150 | 4 341 | 1 216.5 | 181.0 | 301 | 5 961 | 240.1 | 68.8 |
| Chester | 2 310 | 20 064 | 3 947.2 | 1 610.7 | 572 | 18 981 | 6 753.0 | 985.9 | 907 | 15 286 | 783.2 | 221.0 |
| Clarion | 36 | D | D | D | 46 | 2 716 | 586.6 | 92.7 | 103 | 1 315 | 51.2 | 13.0 |
| Clearfield | 100 | D | D | D | 112 | 3 213 | D | 108.8 | 177 | 2 316 | 88.0 | 22.5 |
| Clinton | 40 | 182 | 15.4 | 4.8 | 46 | 2 730 | 1 215.0 | 104.5 | 82 | 998 | 43.2 | 11.5 |
| Columbia | 92 | 843 | 50.1 | 27.7 | 90 | 6 569 | D | 245.6 | 152 | 2 252 | 90.6 | 25.1 |
| Crawford | 124 | D | D | D | 282 | 7 686 | 1 632.6 | 308.8 | 199 | 2 438 | 90.1 | 26.7 |
| Cumberland | 614 | D | D | D | 200 | 10 191 | 3 472.6 | 404.8 | 520 | 9 519 | 402.7 | 116.0 |
| Dauphin | 720 | D | D | D | 215 | 9 794 | D | 446.3 | 668 | 12 489 | 676.8 | 194.8 |
| Delaware | 1 603 | D | D | D | 425 | 16 122 | 19 060.4 | 1 158.3 | 1 028 | 15 048 | 779.5 | 206.2 |
| Elk | 36 | 193 | 9.0 | 3.3 | 139 | 6 932 | 1 616.5 | 280.7 | 76 | 634 | 24.1 | 5.3 |
| Erie | 416 | D | D | D | 505 | 24 441 | 6 890.8 | 1 190.2 | 646 | 10 728 | 428.1 | 114.6 |
| Fayette | 154 | D | D | D | 128 | 3 757 | 1 161.4 | 153.0 | 270 | 5 432 | 246.9 | 78.3 |
| Forest | 3 | D | D | D | NA | NA | NA | NA | 25 | 145 | 8.4 | 2.1 |
| Franklin | 227 | D | D | D | 222 | 10 149 | 3 244.4 | 412.7 | 278 | 3 837 | 164.5 | 45.5 |
| Fulton | 12 | 41 | 2.6 | 0.8 | 19 | D | D | D | 23 | 206 | 9.9 | 2.4 |
| Greene | 46 | D | D | D | 25 | D | D | D | 73 | 908 | 36.8 | 10.2 |
| Huntingdon | 49 | D | D | D | 45 | D | D | 85.0 | 86 | 898 | 40.4 | 10.7 |
| Indiana | 112 | D | D | D | 105 | 3 316 | D | 120.8 | 166 | 2 740 | 92.4 | 24.4 |
| Jefferson | 66 | D | D | D | 101 | 4 415 | 953.5 | 171.7 | 91 | 908 | 32.3 | 8.1 |
| Juniata | 20 | 64 | 3.2 | 0.7 | 54 | 2 047 | 392.0 | 63.6 | 34 | 506 | 14.6 | 4.5 |
| Lackawanna | 472 | D | D | D | 267 | 11 834 | D | 439.1 | 546 | 8 601 | 360.5 | 99.6 |
| Lancaster | 939 | D | D | D | 920 | 40 077 | 13 269.9 | 1 735.9 | 935 | 17 060 | 763.9 | 221.2 |
| Lawrence | 119 | D | D | D | 147 | 3 840 | 1 745.2 | 183.6 | 177 | 2 325 | 73.4 | 21.3 |
| Lebanon | 193 | D | D | D | 213 | 9 655 | 2 393.6 | 363.3 | 241 | 3 075 | 125.3 | 35.3 |
| Lehigh | 763 | D | D | D | 419 | 18 331 | 7 031.6 | 835.6 | 740 | 11 730 | 546.3 | 148.6 |
| Luzerne | 594 | D | D | D | 352 | 17 955 | 5 708.3 | 727.4 | 763 | 10 586 | 442.9 | 119.8 |
| Lycoming | 183 | 1 367 | 102.9 | 39.6 | 183 | 10 240 | 3 358.2 | 408.7 | 277 | 3 721 | 147.9 | 40.0 |
| McKean | 65 | D | D | D | 56 | 4 029 | 1 394.4 | 160.6 | 112 | 1 055 | 40.9 | 10.5 |
| Mercer | 172 | D | D | D | 193 | 8 929 | 3 463.6 | 365.1 | 271 | 4 434 | 166.8 | 48.8 |
| Mifflin | 34 | D | D | D | 91 | 3 899 | 950.4 | 162.2 | 80 | 1 055 | 36.1 | 10.3 |
| Monroe | 340 | 1 671 | 198.0 | 53.9 | 131 | 5 322 | 2 656.5 | 317.4 | 386 | 7 491 | 394.4 | 113.0 |
| Montgomery | 3 697 | 45 686 | 7 015.0 | 3 370.4 | 1 110 | 51 179 | 20 398.8 | 2 848.2 | 1 769 | 27 834 | 1 478.0 | 409.4 |
| Montour | 32 | 444 | 32.4 | 25.9 | 18 | 950 | D | 55.4 | 42 | 734 | 27.5 | 7.5 |
| Northampton | 594 | D | D | D | 340 | 13 197 | 3 923.1 | 608.1 | 646 | 8 637 | 384.8 | 103.8 |
| Northumberland | 99 | 520 | 39.6 | 13.0 | 105 | 6 048 | 1 420.5 | 226.3 | 170 | 1 443 | 54.5 | 13.9 |
| Perry | 56 | D | D | D | 35 | 741 | D | 25.0 | 76 | 490 | 21.7 | 5.0 |
| Philadelphia | 2 703 | 44 302 | 9 243.3 | 3 533.1 | 946 | 32 672 | 18 069.4 | 1 396.7 | 3 396 | 48 552 | 3 051.4 | 837.9 |
| Pike | 80 | D | D | D | NA | NA | NA | NA | 98 | 1 300 | 75.8 | 17.6 |

1. Establishment subject to federal tax.

# Table B. States and Counties — Health Care and Social Assistance, Other Services, and Federal Funds

| STATE County | Health care and social assistance, 2007 | | | | Other services, 2007 | | | | Federal funds and grants, 2009–2010 Expenditures (mil dol) | | | |
|---|---|---|---|---|---|---|---|---|---|---|---|---|
| | | | | | | | | | | Direct payments for individuals[1] | | |
| | Number of establishments | Number of employees | Receipts (mil dol) | Annual payroll (mil dol) | Number of establishments | Number of employees | Receipts (mil dol) | Annual payroll (mil dol) | Total | Social Security and government retirement | Medicare | Food Stamps and Supplemental Security Income |
| | 159 | 160 | 161 | 162 | 163 | 164 | 165 | 166 | 167 | 168 | 169 | 170 |
| **OREGON—Cont'd** | | | | | | | | | | | | |
| Morrow | 14 | 119 | 11.2 | 4.8 | 11 | 32 | 2.2 | 0.7 | 97.8 | 36.9 | 12.7 | 2.7 |
| Multnomah | 2 601 | 53 379 | 6 135.2 | 2 471.3 | 1 726 | 11 789 | 1 748.2 | 367.3 | 8 056.3 | 2 026.5 | 1 100.6 | 264.7 |
| Polk | 136 | 2 127 | 127.1 | 56.4 | 82 | 248 | 21.8 | 5.9 | 449.1 | 171.0 | 70.2 | 13.6 |
| Sherman | 3 | 19 | 0.2 | 0.1 | 1 | D | D | D | 58.4 | 11.3 | 4.2 | 1.2 |
| Tillamook | 57 | 739 | 73.7 | 28.6 | 46 | 212 | 15.6 | 3.9 | 219.1 | 111.3 | 47.3 | 9.4 |
| Umatilla | 176 | 2 641 | 240.9 | 94.7 | 103 | 435 | 33.4 | 10.3 | 729.1 | 227.8 | 91.9 | 39.3 |
| Union | 93 | 1 185 | 95.8 | 38.1 | 51 | 168 | 13.3 | 3.2 | 234.9 | 95.6 | 40.4 | 13.7 |
| Wallowa | 33 | 345 | 24.2 | 10.1 | 20 | 72 | 8.6 | 1.7 | 78.3 | 34.1 | 13.0 | 2.8 |
| Wasco | 80 | 1 708 | 137.4 | 58.1 | 43 | 179 | 15.2 | 4.1 | 259.8 | 99.7 | 35.0 | 11.2 |
| Washington | 1 514 | 23 384 | 2 575.1 | 967.1 | 823 | 5 172 | 497.9 | 165.1 | 1 908.2 | 893.5 | 375.9 | 84.2 |
| Wheeler | 3 | D | D | D | 2 | D | D | D | 13.1 | 6.7 | 3.5 | 0.2 |
| Yamhill | 241 | 3 852 | 342.7 | 131.0 | 124 | 541 | 45.5 | 13.4 | 580.8 | 269.0 | 110.3 | 29.6 |
| **PENNSYLVANIA** | 35 156 | 874 743 | 81 977.9 | 33 431.6 | 25 316 | 154 379 | 17 622.1 | 3 932.7 | 145 933.8 | 41 143.6 | 31 745.1 | 4 647.1 |
| Adams | 185 | 3 887 | 313.4 | 130.3 | 165 | 1 004 | 81.8 | 20.2 | 718.6 | 339.8 | 134.9 | 11.6 |
| Allegheny | 4 262 | 122 200 | 12 649.6 | 4 896.5 | 2 985 | 19 550 | 2 504.6 | 520.9 | 17 592.4 | 4 317.2 | 4 292.2 | 494.6 |
| Armstrong | 187 | 3 226 | 201.5 | 90.4 | 101 | 428 | 33.0 | 7.2 | 688.6 | 284.4 | 225.6 | 29.4 |
| Beaver | 462 | 9 722 | 707.9 | 319.0 | 343 | 1 506 | 101.6 | 28.4 | 1 567.8 | 688.6 | 513.8 | 72.3 |
| Bedford | 117 | 1 558 | 121.2 | 45.9 | 97 | 373 | 23.8 | 5.8 | 409.4 | 179.6 | 114.7 | 15.2 |
| Berks | 799 | 21 887 | 2 014.4 | 848.1 | 781 | 4 670 | 398.8 | 108.0 | 2 648.7 | 1 186.8 | 686.4 | 108.4 |
| Blair | 403 | 10 162 | 909.5 | 373.1 | 299 | 1 686 | 115.7 | 33.5 | 1 300.8 | 508.9 | 337.5 | 63.5 |
| Bradford | 151 | 4 300 | 465.5 | 174.1 | 118 | 521 | 31.0 | 7.9 | 479.1 | 216.4 | 119.8 | 23.5 |
| Bucks | 1 925 | 37 382 | 3 395.7 | 1 381.8 | 1 395 | 8 612 | 709.3 | 229.6 | 4 456.9 | 1 957.7 | 1 060.1 | 76.8 |
| Butler | 538 | 11 344 | 839.5 | 338.5 | 370 | 2 184 | 230.6 | 48.0 | 1 529.0 | 619.6 | 392.3 | 38.3 |
| Cambria | 545 | 11 825 | 872.0 | 383.6 | 320 | 1 590 | 114.3 | 28.9 | 2 819.4 | 606.4 | 492.3 | 63.8 |
| Cameron | 19 | D | D | D | 12 | 58 | 2.6 | 0.6 | 54.9 | 21.9 | 16.3 | 1.1 |
| Carbon | 153 | 2 525 | 180.6 | 78.6 | 94 | 352 | 26.4 | 6.6 | 518.9 | 248.0 | 165.6 | 14.2 |
| Centre | 332 | 6 543 | 549.7 | 238.6 | 228 | 1 270 | 100.7 | 27.6 | 1 405.5 | 336.6 | 165.5 | 19.1 |
| Chester | 1 343 | 29 982 | 2 692.4 | 1 136.2 | 977 | 6 655 | 1 590.1 | 229.8 | 5 285.7 | 1 288.5 | 639.9 | 46.6 |
| Clarion | 141 | 2 411 | 155.7 | 62.5 | 85 | 393 | 36.9 | 7.1 | 349.1 | 132.8 | 113.0 | 18.4 |
| Clearfield | 248 | 5 584 | 449.8 | 185.9 | 162 | 945 | 63.1 | 17.4 | 696.0 | 292.4 | 210.6 | 32.5 |
| Clinton | 80 | 1 208 | 90.9 | 36.0 | 56 | 270 | 23.0 | 3.8 | 319.3 | 117.6 | 84.3 | 13.4 |
| Columbia | 165 | D | D | D | 115 | 683 | 49.7 | 14.2 | 490.3 | 220.4 | 142.0 | 15.4 |
| Crawford | 270 | 5 084 | 377.9 | 156.5 | 177 | 867 | 60.3 | 16.1 | 740.9 | 315.1 | 202.4 | 36.8 |
| Cumberland | 602 | 14 452 | 1 308.1 | 541.9 | 539 | 3 906 | 387.1 | 102.6 | 2 421.5 | 922.6 | 339.6 | 21.1 |
| Dauphin | 810 | 28 300 | 2 611.3 | 1 119.7 | 681 | 4 904 | 598.9 | 167.0 | 9 329.5 | 858.5 | 510.0 | 86.6 |
| Delaware | 1 545 | 38 693 | 3 531.7 | 1 521.9 | 1 055 | 6 909 | 1 240.3 | 197.9 | 5 548.0 | 1 719.4 | 1 479.5 | 144.4 |
| Elk | 124 | 2 206 | 134.3 | 63.1 | 78 | 353 | 23.8 | 4.9 | 265.8 | 122.5 | 81.4 | 8.3 |
| Erie | 893 | 21 880 | 1 847.7 | 783.0 | 563 | 3 529 | 242.4 | 70.2 | 2 238.2 | 876.3 | 576.3 | 134.9 |
| Fayette | 410 | 7 904 | 526.2 | 234.4 | 234 | 1 061 | 91.0 | 21.2 | 1 753.7 | 540.1 | 580.3 | 118.1 |
| Forest | 8 | D | D | D | 6 | 18 | 1.0 | 0.2 | 63.3 | 27.3 | 18.6 | 2.4 |
| Franklin | 307 | 7 302 | 640.1 | 267.8 | 297 | 1 653 | 121.0 | 33.1 | 1 332.9 | 550.3 | 208.9 | 24.2 |
| Fulton | 27 | 542 | 34.2 | 15.5 | 31 | 103 | 7.1 | 1.8 | 304.2 | 53.9 | 27.5 | 3.1 |
| Greene | 109 | 1 540 | 121.0 | 46.4 | 68 | 274 | 22.5 | 6.0 | 450.5 | 133.2 | 131.9 | 27.5 |
| Huntingdon | 103 | 1 660 | 111.2 | 44.5 | 69 | 239 | 14.8 | 3.6 | 358.4 | 151.0 | 95.8 | 13.8 |
| Indiana | 259 | 4 492 | 319.7 | 135.2 | 174 | 868 | 76.5 | 20.1 | 806.9 | 288.0 | 233.4 | 34.2 |
| Jefferson | 161 | 3 304 | 179.1 | 77.6 | 99 | 440 | 28.8 | 7.1 | 406.5 | 166.1 | 125.3 | 17.7 |
| Juniata | 29 | 501 | 29.9 | 10.8 | 29 | 101 | 11.5 | 2.9 | 153.2 | 72.7 | 41.7 | 4.5 |
| Lackawanna | 708 | 18 457 | 1 560.5 | 641.5 | 400 | 2 264 | 181.5 | 52.3 | 2 449.9 | 767.7 | 693.6 | 67.7 |
| Lancaster | 1 062 | 32 573 | 2 878.0 | 1 163.1 | 1 042 | 6 812 | 587.2 | 157.1 | 2 993.7 | 1 497.6 | 683.1 | 94.5 |
| Lawrence | 256 | 5 749 | 392.9 | 166.1 | 183 | 789 | 56.7 | 15.6 | 942.8 | 374.3 | 304.9 | 46.1 |
| Lebanon | 266 | 7 662 | 626.6 | 286.9 | 233 | 1 059 | 93.0 | 25.2 | 1 398.6 | 491.7 | 205.8 | 22.5 |
| Lehigh | 1 111 | 32 364 | 3 486.0 | 1 402.0 | 715 | 4 637 | 451.0 | 121.5 | 2 678.2 | 887.0 | 678.4 | 113.3 |
| Luzerne | 983 | 23 418 | 1 986.6 | 809.9 | 582 | 2 996 | 231.0 | 58.1 | 3 227.1 | 1 201.7 | 1 001.1 | 110.6 |
| Lycoming | 285 | 8 065 | 675.8 | 272.5 | 244 | 1 521 | 150.1 | 33.0 | 969.5 | 391.6 | 250.7 | 45.6 |
| McKean | 165 | 2 857 | 191.3 | 87.7 | 104 | 404 | 26.1 | 6.1 | 398.7 | 152.1 | 112.2 | 22.0 |
| Mercer | 395 | 10 499 | 750.1 | 314.8 | 260 | 1 319 | 87.8 | 23.5 | 1 076.2 | 454.9 | 339.1 | 53.3 |
| Mifflin | 115 | 2 731 | 210.0 | 90.3 | 71 | 250 | 19.9 | 4.7 | 407.6 | 162.4 | 118.5 | 16.8 |
| Monroe | 367 | 6 064 | 537.3 | 221.1 | 308 | 1 590 | 119.9 | 36.2 | 2 069.5 | 498.5 | 221.3 | 30.3 |
| Montgomery | 2 746 | 62 216 | 6 560.8 | 2 613.6 | 1 933 | 12 597 | 1 506.0 | 352.9 | 7 173.0 | 2 543.6 | 1 610.3 | 88.8 |
| Montour | 63 | D | D | D | 33 | 170 | 18.8 | 5.0 | 146.1 | 63.0 | 46.2 | 4.9 |
| Northampton | 749 | 11 498 | 979.1 | 394.3 | 545 | 3 094 | 224.8 | 70.6 | 2 482.7 | 1 084.7 | 659.9 | 39.6 |
| Northumberland | 199 | 3 853 | 241.3 | 103.8 | 151 | 809 | 44.5 | 12.4 | 830.0 | 343.0 | 266.7 | 29.3 |
| Perry | 73 | 565 | 40.9 | 13.2 | 70 | 241 | 17.4 | 4.0 | 283.5 | 152.9 | 73.6 | 9.2 |
| Philadelphia | 3 600 | 131 738 | 14 539.8 | 5 888.7 | 2 466 | 17 806 | 2 843.4 | 574.6 | 23 099.4 | 3 785.4 | 6 081.5 | 1 569.2 |
| Pike | 89 | D | D | D | 102 | 701 | 56.6 | 16.3 | 301.6 | 184.6 | 55.6 | 8.7 |

1. State totals may include programs not allocated by county.

Items 159—170

# Table B. States and Counties — Federal Funds, Residential Construction, and Local Government Finances

| | Federal funds and grants, 2009–2010 (cont.) | | | | | | | Value of residential construction authorized by building permits, 2011 | | Local government finances, 2007 | | | | |
| | Expenditures (mil dol) (cont.) | | | | | | | | | General revenue | | | | |
| | Procurement contract awards | | | Grants[1] | | | | | | | | Taxes | | |
| STATE County | | | | | | | | | | | | | Per capita[2] (dollars) | |
| | Salaries and wages | Defense | Other | Medicaid and other health-related | Nutrition and family welfare | Education | Other | New construction ($1,000) | Number of housing units | Total (mil dol) | Inter-govern-mental (mil dol) | Total (mil dol) | Total | Property |
| | 171 | 172 | 173 | 174 | 175 | 176 | 177 | 178 | 179 | 180 | 181 | 182 | 183 | 184 |
| OREGON—Cont'd | | | | | | | | | | | | | | |
| Morrow | 3.7 | 0.3 | 4.0 | 3.8 | 2.8 | 0.8 | 0.6 | 6 624 | 47 | 61.6 | 25.0 | 17.3 | 1 544 | 1 537 |
| Multnomah | 838.7 | 318.6 | 481.1 | 1 707.6 | 132.1 | 73.2 | 878.2 | 205 427 | 1 417 | 4 106.1 | 1 372.1 | 1 506.0 | 2 145 | 1 328 |
| Polk | 24.8 | 0.1 | 2.6 | 71.2 | 8.6 | 11.0 | 62.4 | 12 655 | 59 | 134.8 | 76.1 | 37.3 | 496 | 402 |
| Sherman | 4.4 | 21.1 | 0.2 | 2.4 | 0.3 | 0.2 | 0.0 | NA | NA | 15.0 | 5.7 | 7.3 | 4 356 | 4 326 |
| Tillamook | 10.6 | 0.3 | 4.2 | 21.2 | 3.8 | 2.4 | 4.0 | 16 486 | 76 | 104.5 | 42.1 | 37.3 | 1 492 | 1 301 |
| Umatilla | 60.4 | 120.1 | 11.5 | 77.1 | 18.9 | 7.4 | 9.9 | 10 453 | 60 | 264.4 | 149.0 | 65.8 | 896 | 813 |
| Union | 25.5 | 0.2 | 5.3 | 25.4 | 5.4 | 2.4 | 6.7 | 8 314 | 35 | 76.6 | 40.4 | 20.3 | 820 | 729 |
| Wallowa | 5.2 | 0.2 | 4.1 | 12.9 | 1.3 | 0.5 | 0.0 | NA | NA | 43.6 | 17.5 | 7.2 | 1 065 | 964 |
| Wasco | 22.6 | 22.1 | 9.1 | 22.6 | 4.2 | 3.3 | 7.4 | NA | NA | 91.4 | 43.5 | 28.8 | 1 213 | 1 099 |
| Washington | 126.5 | 55.7 | 47.4 | 173.1 | 46.9 | 26.2 | 52.3 | 282 701 | 1 409 | 1 661.4 | 649.3 | 639.3 | 1 224 | 1 069 |
| Wheeler | 0.4 | 0.0 | 0.1 | 1.4 | 0.2 | 0.2 | 0.1 | NA | NA | 11.0 | 4.8 | 1.2 | 902 | 889 |
| Yamhill | 42.9 | 10.4 | 9.7 | 59.1 | 16.9 | 8.1 | 11.9 | 41 925 | 193 | 303.3 | 141.3 | 87.7 | 908 | 773 |
| PENNSYLVANIA | 8 802.6 | 11 900.9 | 7 451.5 | 16 147.3 | 2 976.8 | 3 813.4 | 6 473.7 | 2 545 786 | 14 967 | X | X | X | X | X |
| Adams | 71.5 | 20.9 | 19.9 | 78.1 | 13.7 | 1.4 | 4.5 | 27 327 | 148 | 326.9 | 140.3 | 137.2 | 1 361 | 1 002 |
| Allegheny | 1 201.2 | 1 885.2 | 1 430.4 | 2 592.3 | 234.4 | 81.3 | 591.7 | 300 119 | 1 300 | 6 457.4 | 2 763.3 | 2 543.3 | 2 086 | 1 470 |
| Armstrong | 20.8 | 4.3 | 3.7 | 88.5 | 14.7 | 2.1 | 10.6 | 5 994 | 43 | 220.2 | 110.1 | 80.6 | 1 168 | 1 005 |
| Beaver | 35.8 | 1.9 | 10.4 | 167.9 | 36.5 | 6.5 | 11.3 | 33 315 | 175 | 714.6 | 310.9 | 212.6 | 1 229 | 991 |
| Bedford | 13.4 | 1.7 | 2.9 | 62.8 | 9.4 | 1.3 | 3.8 | 16 126 | 118 | 141.3 | 65.2 | 42.2 | 850 | 682 |
| Berks | 146.1 | 65.2 | 29.9 | 225.9 | 52.4 | 11.3 | 78.4 | 44 516 | 306 | 1 848.0 | 724.3 | 738.8 | 1 838 | 1 472 |
| Blair | 83.3 | 1.9 | 63.2 | 170.2 | 31.2 | 4.1 | 23.9 | 13 020 | 75 | 389.5 | 217.2 | 109.2 | 870 | 625 |
| Bradford | 17.1 | 0.5 | 3.5 | 77.5 | 12.6 | 2.2 | 1.5 | 12 074 | 87 | 247.6 | 115.3 | 66.8 | 1 087 | 864 |
| Bucks | 119.0 | 778.0 | 84.7 | 212.4 | 67.9 | 6.1 | 43.3 | 82 734 | 454 | 2 538.9 | 654.7 | 1 357.2 | 2 185 | 1 832 |
| Butler | 147.3 | 32.8 | 90.4 | 138.7 | 27.4 | 2.8 | 11.5 | 107 432 | 509 | 564.3 | 233.0 | 226.5 | 1 245 | 955 |
| Cambria | 158.9 | 1 180.9 | 28.1 | 180.3 | 33.8 | 6.0 | 41.5 | 12 027 | 62 | 524.9 | 265.3 | 128.6 | 887 | 691 |
| Cameron | 1.3 | 0.0 | 0.6 | 9.6 | 3.3 | 0.1 | 0.0 | 0 | 0 | 16.3 | 8.4 | 5.7 | 1 073 | 906 |
| Carbon | 12.0 | 12.6 | 9.2 | 41.3 | 8.7 | 1.7 | 2.6 | 17 746 | 97 | 228.3 | 72.4 | 91.7 | 1 450 | 1 180 |
| Centre | 72.0 | 236.8 | 68.0 | 179.8 | 22.9 | 11.9 | 192.3 | 46 699 | 259 | 400.8 | 139.2 | 181.2 | 1 253 | 907 |
| Chester | 225.4 | 1 541.4 | 1 222.7 | 175.9 | 47.5 | 8.5 | 49.9 | 184 928 | 934 | 1 897.5 | 491.6 | 1 084.0 | 2 229 | 1 822 |
| Clarion | 10.9 | 0.1 | 1.9 | 43.4 | 8.9 | 2.3 | 2.7 | 4 594 | 44 | 148.6 | 93.3 | 35.1 | 878 | 680 |
| Clearfield | 28.4 | 0.1 | 5.2 | 88.7 | 18.1 | 2.7 | 5.8 | 9 052 | 62 | 251.0 | 134.7 | 82.4 | 1 012 | 823 |
| Clinton | 25.9 | 4.8 | 12.7 | 37.5 | 7.1 | 1.6 | 1.0 | 4 007 | 35 | 107.9 | 44.2 | 39.3 | 1 056 | 804 |
| Columbia | 22.2 | 1.9 | 4.0 | 50.5 | 11.5 | 2.3 | 3.9 | 12 880 | 89 | 180.8 | 77.6 | 79.6 | 1 229 | 914 |
| Crawford | 57.2 | 1.1 | 5.3 | 84.9 | 20.3 | 3.5 | 4.6 | 8 133 | 60 | 246.9 | 126.0 | 86.8 | 979 | 818 |
| Cumberland | 438.9 | 312.2 | 128.2 | 79.8 | 24.5 | 3.8 | 118.9 | 113 262 | 652 | 808.9 | 280.6 | 382.0 | 1 675 | 1 151 |
| Dauphin | 266.1 | 680.8 | 66.3 | 566.4 | 630.2 | 2 782.6 | 2 601.4 | 71 798 | 385 | 1 386.8 | 528.6 | 466.2 | 1 823 | 1 309 |
| Delaware | 213.9 | 1 289.0 | 35.9 | 404.4 | 76.3 | 19.5 | 74.6 | 42 603 | 190 | 2 406.7 | 773.9 | 1 043.7 | 1 883 | 1 679 |
| Elk | 18.7 | 1.5 | 1.7 | 20.7 | 5.5 | 0.5 | 3.5 | 3 230 | 20 | 93.6 | 38.3 | 33.0 | 1 013 | 753 |
| Erie | 120.8 | 41.5 | 43.0 | 264.1 | 59.0 | 12.5 | 38.0 | 38 019 | 311 | 1 069.7 | 529.9 | 326.3 | 1 169 | 941 |
| Fayette | 44.1 | 35.7 | 10.2 | 341.9 | 38.5 | 7.5 | 24.3 | 33 824 | 159 | 368.8 | 225.0 | 96.3 | 666 | 523 |
| Forest | 4.3 | 1.2 | 0.9 | 7.0 | 1.0 | 0.2 | 0.3 | 1 195 | 7 | 20.2 | 11.2 | 6.5 | 941 | 816 |
| Franklin | 121.3 | 295.4 | 7.8 | 87.4 | 19.0 | 2.8 | 2.8 | 32 731 | 227 | 384.0 | 141.5 | 152.8 | 1 078 | 820 |
| Fulton | 2.9 | 190.3 | 2.5 | 19.4 | 3.2 | 0.4 | 0.0 | 1 750 | 17 | 42.5 | 23.3 | 15.1 | 1 010 | 827 |
| Greene | 13.9 | 0.1 | 42.0 | 85.2 | 8.5 | 1.3 | 0.8 | 6 477 | 37 | 145.2 | 72.1 | 51.4 | 1 301 | 1 132 |
| Huntingdon | 21.3 | 0.6 | 2.1 | 55.4 | 9.8 | 1.0 | 2.4 | 12 191 | 75 | 112.8 | 58.2 | 31.9 | 700 | 539 |
| Indiana | 32.2 | 7.2 | 14.4 | 130.0 | 19.5 | 2.5 | 7.7 | 8 733 | 73 | 265.3 | 150.3 | 81.4 | 929 | 720 |
| Jefferson | 26.2 | 0.2 | 2.3 | 51.4 | 10.1 | 1.3 | 2.1 | 6 881 | 61 | 119.7 | 65.5 | 36.2 | 801 | 609 |
| Juniata | 6.5 | 0.0 | 1.2 | 18.6 | 3.5 | 0.5 | 0.0 | 4 139 | 29 | 45.3 | 21.7 | 19.2 | 830 | 656 |
| Lackawanna | 113.0 | 338.4 | 30.3 | 249.4 | 39.3 | 5.5 | 32.5 | 31 603 | 167 | 746.7 | 279.2 | 308.3 | 1 473 | 1 054 |
| Lancaster | 177.0 | 44.0 | 95.9 | 238.2 | 63.5 | 13.4 | 51.1 | 159 827 | 1 204 | 1 635.2 | 540.9 | 714.1 | 1 433 | 1 148 |
| Lawrence | 40.4 | 1.3 | 17.8 | 109.6 | 22.0 | 3.6 | 7.1 | 7 310 | 35 | 293.5 | 166.0 | 90.5 | 995 | 809 |
| Lebanon | 423.9 | 36.7 | 83.5 | 61.2 | 14.6 | 2.2 | 45.5 | 28 862 | 175 | 428.2 | 136.1 | 157.2 | 1 229 | 937 |
| Lehigh | 102.5 | 58.0 | 37.0 | 198.1 | 50.4 | 12.3 | 496.9 | 69 894 | 409 | 1 490.9 | 565.2 | 590.8 | 1 751 | 1 401 |
| Luzerne | 259.5 | 33.9 | 106.8 | 346.4 | 59.4 | 10.1 | 45.4 | 38 386 | 200 | 923.2 | 370.0 | 391.1 | 1 253 | 922 |
| Lycoming | 64.5 | 20.3 | 16.9 | 107.0 | 24.2 | 4.8 | 20.0 | 17 260 | 156 | 397.9 | 173.9 | 143.6 | 1 229 | 892 |
| McKean | 37.1 | 0.0 | 4.5 | 53.0 | 9.3 | 1.7 | 4.0 | 2 935 | 21 | 175.0 | 94.0 | 42.2 | 968 | 768 |
| Mercer | 41.3 | 5.9 | 9.6 | 115.5 | 25.9 | 4.5 | 9.7 | 16 743 | 86 | 391.5 | 214.7 | 122.6 | 1 050 | 807 |
| Mifflin | 29.4 | 1.6 | 2.1 | 61.1 | 8.9 | 1.5 | 2.2 | 7 458 | 55 | 130.3 | 71.5 | 41.8 | 891 | 676 |
| Monroe | 153.1 | 219.6 | 864.9 | 40.1 | 18.4 | 4.1 | 7.2 | 40 301 | 197 | 618.0 | 176.9 | 356.6 | 2 165 | 1 905 |
| Montgomery | 458.0 | 570.0 | 1 326.0 | 304.7 | 78.9 | 11.4 | 91.1 | 128 658 | 909 | 3 183.4 | 752.0 | 1 824.2 | 2 350 | 1 887 |
| Montour | 3.6 | 0.0 | 2.9 | 19.3 | 3.3 | 0.3 | 0.9 | 4 393 | 24 | 59.8 | 19.2 | 22.3 | 1 254 | 823 |
| Northampton | 132.5 | 26.2 | 35.5 | 180.2 | 33.0 | 5.9 | 246.6 | 68 573 | 436 | 1 249.8 | 426.7 | 555.5 | 1 893 | 1 521 |
| Northumberland | 22.7 | 3.3 | 9.2 | 122.3 | 14.9 | 3.2 | 5.2 | 7 359 | 55 | 274.2 | 145.3 | 78.8 | 866 | 596 |
| Perry | 8.4 | 0.0 | 2.0 | 28.0 | 5.9 | 0.8 | 0.0 | 16 213 | 76 | 116.5 | 53.9 | 53.6 | 1 186 | 837 |
| Philadelphia | 2 201.8 | 437.7 | 1 141.7 | 5 702.6 | 408.3 | 149.6 | 1 204.4 | 192 715 | 1 552 | 10 578.9 | 5 544.4 | 3 600.8 | 2 484 | 663 |
| Pike | 16.3 | 2.6 | 17.9 | 7.2 | 5.0 | 1.4 | 0.5 | 27 201 | 108 | 121.3 | 40.4 | 67.0 | 1 143 | 1 056 |

1. State totals may include programs not allocated by county.　　2. Based on the resident population estimated as of July 1 of the year shown.

# Table B. States and Counties — Local Government Finances, Government Employment, and Voting

| STATE County | Direct general expenditure Total (mil dol) | Per capita[1] (dollars) | Education | Health and hospitals | Police protection | Public welfare | Highways | Debt outstanding Total (mil dol) | Per capita[1] (dollars) | Government employment, 2011 Federal civilian | Federal military | State and local | Presidential election,[2] 2012 Percent of vote cast: Democratic | Republican | All other |
|---|---|---|---|---|---|---|---|---|---|---|---|---|---|---|---|
| | 185 | 186 | 187 | 188 | 189 | 190 | 191 | 192 | 193 | 194 | 195 | 196 | 197 | 198 | 199 |
| OREGON—Cont'd | | | | | | | | | | | | | | | |
| Morrow | 60.1 | 5 366 | 38.6 | 12.7 | 2.4 | 0.0 | 2.2 | 160.7 | 14 352 | 66 | 38 | 765 | 34.7 | 61.8 | 3.4 |
| Multnomah | 3 950.4 | 5 628 | 30.8 | 4.0 | 5.0 | 4.7 | 6.5 | 7 039.1 | 10 027 | 12 269 | 2 490 | 60 288 | 76.7 | 20.6 | 2.7 |
| Polk | 154.5 | 2 052 | 36.8 | 13.5 | 6.6 | 0.8 | 10.9 | 165.0 | 2 192 | 77 | 213 | 5 926 | 48.4 | 48.9 | 2.6 |
| Sherman | 15.5 | 9 236 | 25.7 | 4.0 | 3.3 | 0.1 | 7.8 | 2.1 | 1 252 | 122 | 0 | 185 | 36.8 | 60.6 | 2.7 |
| Tillamook | 102.0 | 4 073 | 46.4 | 5.3 | 4.2 | 0.6 | 6.5 | 125.6 | 5 015 | 117 | 111 | 1 622 | 53.2 | 43.3 | 3.5 |
| Umatilla | 264.5 | 3 599 | 59.0 | 4.2 | 4.0 | 0.1 | 3.1 | 258.6 | 3 519 | 810 | 223 | 6 206 | 37.2 | 59.8 | 3.1 |
| Union | 74.5 | 3 009 | 50.7 | 1.9 | 4.7 | 0.7 | 5.8 | 45.9 | 1 853 | 239 | 72 | 2 454 | 36.6 | 60.2 | 3.2 |
| Wallowa | 53.1 | 7 859 | 22.5 | 48.0 | 3.2 | 0.4 | 9.0 | 36.9 | 5 453 | 99 | 20 | 551 | 33.4 | 63.5 | 3.1 |
| Wasco | 90.9 | 3 826 | 55.4 | 1.7 | 5.2 | 1.8 | 5.7 | 149.4 | 6 289 | 390 | 71 | 1 877 | 51.9 | 44.8 | 3.3 |
| Washington | 1 698.0 | 3 250 | 45.3 | 3.9 | 6.2 | 0.0 | 6.7 | 2 480.0 | 4 746 | 780 | 1 518 | 20 742 | 59.8 | 37.7 | 2.5 |
| Wheeler | 11.5 | 8 441 | 35.0 | 4.1 | 1.9 | 0.0 | 6.7 | 1.5 | 1 126 | 0 | 0 | 104 | 34.6 | 61.3 | 4.1 |
| Yamhill | 283.6 | 2 937 | 48.9 | 6.8 | 6.0 | 0.2 | 7.2 | 516.7 | 5 350 | 466 | 280 | 3 791 | 47.8 | 49.1 | 3.1 |
| PENNSYLVANIA | X | X | X | X | X | X | X | X | X | 103 076 | 35 532 | 664 346 | 54.7 | 44.3 | 1.0 |
| Adams | 389.1 | 3 861 | 70.8 | 3.1 | 1.3 | 5.4 | 2.8 | 320.4 | 3 179 | 729 | 258 | 3 586 | 39.6 | 59.2 | 1.1 |
| Allegheny | 6 106.5 | 5 009 | 43.3 | 8.4 | 4.0 | 6.2 | 3.4 | 11 122.6 | 9 123 | 13 836 | 3 593 | 55 120 | 57.3 | 41.8 | 0.9 |
| Armstrong | 224.0 | 3 243 | 61.6 | 0.2 | 1.1 | 12.1 | 3.5 | 178.3 | 2 582 | 206 | 174 | 2 829 | 37.0 | 61.6 | 1.3 |
| Beaver | 707.9 | 4 090 | 50.0 | 4.7 | 3.0 | 12.4 | 3.1 | 2 412.0 | 13 936 | 310 | 435 | 7 954 | 47.9 | 50.8 | 1.3 |
| Bedford | 157.4 | 3 169 | 58.7 | 0.0 | 0.4 | 1.9 | 5.1 | 249.4 | 5 023 | 124 | 126 | 2 225 | 27.0 | 71.8 | 1.2 |
| Berks | 1 817.4 | 4 521 | 55.4 | 4.1 | 3.6 | 7.3 | 2.6 | 3 268.4 | 8 131 | 1 098 | 1 063 | 22 637 | 53.9 | 44.7 | 1.4 |
| Blair | 382.8 | 3 050 | 55.8 | 0.2 | 2.5 | 7.8 | 5.2 | 430.7 | 3 431 | 1 019 | 324 | 8 002 | 37.3 | 61.6 | 1.1 |
| Bradford | 267.3 | 4 349 | 51.8 | 3.4 | 1.4 | 6.2 | 3.8 | 936.8 | 15 240 | 216 | 160 | 3 176 | 40.0 | 58.4 | 1.6 |
| Bucks | 2 564.0 | 4 128 | 58.8 | 3.5 | 4.8 | 5.4 | 2.5 | 3 298.0 | 5 310 | 1 154 | 1 592 | 23 381 | 53.8 | 45.1 | 1.1 |
| Butler | 585.8 | 3 220 | 52.4 | 3.7 | 2.2 | 7.2 | 3.9 | 921.2 | 5 063 | 2 220 | 471 | 9 020 | 35.7 | 63.1 | 1.2 |
| Cambria | 556.4 | 3 838 | 53.9 | 5.1 | 3.3 | 8.7 | 4.5 | 684.2 | 4 719 | 1 235 | 422 | 8 020 | 49.4 | 48.7 | 1.9 |
| Cameron | 16.8 | 3 132 | 56.5 | 0.0 | 0.9 | 4.4 | 6.2 | 18.5 | 3 452 | 13 | 13 | 409 | 39.2 | 58.9 | 1.9 |
| Carbon | 244.4 | 3 864 | 55.6 | 1.1 | 1.8 | 9.1 | 2.4 | 378.3 | 5 982 | 107 | 165 | 2 637 | 50.0 | 48.1 | 1.9 |
| Centre | 425.6 | 2 942 | 51.8 | 4.4 | 3.0 | 7.7 | 5.2 | 425.5 | 2 942 | 443 | 486 | 45 055 | 55.4 | 43.5 | 1.1 |
| Chester | 2 134.3 | 4 388 | 56.8 | 6.1 | 3.3 | 2.2 | 2.7 | 3 130.1 | 6 436 | 2 985 | 1 281 | 21 856 | 54.2 | 45.0 | 0.8 |
| Clarion | 157.2 | 3 927 | 68.2 | 7.4 | 0.9 | 3.0 | 4.7 | 80.4 | 2 008 | 111 | 102 | 3 532 | 38.0 | 60.4 | 1.5 |
| Clearfield | 287.9 | 3 535 | 55.3 | 2.2 | 3.9 | 2.4 | 3.7 | 267.1 | 3 279 | 261 | 209 | 4 814 | 43.0 | 55.2 | 1.8 |
| Clinton | 103.3 | 2 776 | 52.9 | 0.1 | 1.3 | 3.4 | 5.6 | 92.6 | 2 488 | 133 | 101 | 3 075 | 48.0 | 50.7 | 1.3 |
| Columbia | 182.4 | 2 819 | 65.4 | 0.3 | 2.9 | 2.8 | 4.2 | 184.2 | 2 846 | 155 | 171 | 5 095 | 47.1 | 51.6 | 1.3 |
| Crawford | 241.8 | 2 727 | 53.1 | 5.4 | 1.5 | 8.2 | 5.9 | 214.6 | 2 420 | 304 | 226 | 4 251 | 44.0 | 54.4 | 1.6 |
| Cumberland | 800.2 | 3 509 | 59.0 | 5.1 | 3.3 | 7.5 | 3.0 | 847.9 | 3 718 | 5 082 | 1 321 | 12 436 | 42.6 | 56.3 | 1.1 |
| Dauphin | 1 482.2 | 5 796 | 46.4 | 5.4 | 3.3 | 8.5 | 1.9 | 3 092.0 | 12 092 | 2 591 | 747 | 41 098 | 54.0 | 45.0 | 1.0 |
| Delaware | 2 470.9 | 4 457 | 47.4 | 3.1 | 4.3 | 10.8 | 2.0 | 4 574.7 | 8 252 | 2 056 | 1 461 | 23 516 | 60.2 | 38.8 | 1.0 |
| Elk | 79.8 | 2 448 | 50.6 | 0.1 | 2.5 | 0.0 | 11.5 | 156.6 | 4 801 | 107 | 81 | 1 332 | 51.1 | 46.8 | 2.1 |
| Erie | 1 050.1 | 3 763 | 47.5 | 8.1 | 2.5 | 8.8 | 2.8 | 1 590.5 | 5 699 | 1 570 | 761 | 16 123 | 59.3 | 39.4 | 1.2 |
| Fayette | 380.8 | 2 635 | 56.4 | 7.8 | 1.6 | 2.8 | 3.4 | 430.6 | 2 978 | 399 | 347 | 6 240 | 49.2 | 49.6 | 1.2 |
| Forest | 22.9 | 3 287 | 55.3 | 2.8 | 1.7 | 5.9 | 8.4 | 17.0 | 2 442 | 69 | 19 | 946 | 42.5 | 55.9 | 1.6 |
| Franklin | 410.3 | 2 896 | 54.2 | 4.7 | 1.6 | 5.8 | 5.6 | 451.6 | 3 188 | 2 593 | 386 | 6 395 | 33.3 | 65.8 | 0.9 |
| Fulton | 40.9 | 2 738 | 69.9 | 0.0 | 1.9 | 3.7 | 3.0 | 46.8 | 3 130 | 34 | 38 | 761 | 25.0 | 73.6 | 1.4 |
| Greene | 137.8 | 3 490 | 54.3 | 4.5 | 0.9 | 3.7 | 6.1 | 160.8 | 4 071 | 128 | 98 | 2 575 | 49.0 | 49.4 | 1.6 |
| Huntingdon | 106.0 | 2 326 | 58.1 | 1.8 | 1.2 | 6.3 | 4.1 | 184.5 | 4 049 | 122 | 116 | 3 059 | 35.5 | 63.0 | 1.4 |
| Indiana | 280.4 | 3 197 | 58.5 | 0.8 | 1.0 | 10.8 | 3.6 | 346.6 | 3 952 | 210 | 233 | 7 432 | 45.7 | 52.9 | 1.4 |
| Jefferson | 113.2 | 2 507 | 62.0 | 0.1 | 2.1 | 0.4 | 5.9 | 132.4 | 2 934 | 109 | 114 | 1 906 | 34.3 | 64.1 | 1.6 |
| Juniata | 41.4 | 1 787 | 67.1 | 0.0 | 0.7 | 2.7 | 5.3 | 9.4 | 405 | 76 | 62 | 789 | 31.6 | 66.8 | 1.6 |
| Lackawanna | 810.6 | 3 872 | 41.5 | 0.3 | 3.1 | 5.3 | 2.8 | 880.6 | 4 207 | 1 070 | 551 | 10 216 | 62.6 | 36.6 | 0.8 |
| Lancaster | 1 704.0 | 3 419 | 57.0 | 3.5 | 4.3 | 3.6 | 3.2 | 3 018.1 | 6 055 | 1 307 | 1 331 | 19 732 | 43.7 | 55.5 | 0.9 |
| Lawrence | 306.7 | 3 370 | 50.0 | 0.0 | 2.9 | 14.4 | 4.7 | 275.2 | 3 024 | 348 | 231 | 3 998 | 46.8 | 51.9 | 1.3 |
| Lebanon | 452.1 | 3 535 | 52.0 | 5.2 | 2.3 | 12.1 | 2.9 | 710.8 | 5 558 | 2 583 | 343 | 5 453 | 40.0 | 58.9 | 1.2 |
| Lehigh | 1 487.1 | 4 408 | 47.9 | 2.8 | 2.8 | 11.6 | 2.6 | 3 226.3 | 9 564 | 875 | 936 | 16 813 | 57.1 | 41.6 | 1.3 |
| Luzerne | 954.1 | 3 055 | 56.7 | 0.4 | 3.1 | 2.2 | 5.2 | 1 177.2 | 3 770 | 3 220 | 842 | 15 367 | 53.6 | 45.2 | 1.2 |
| Lycoming | 377.8 | 3 234 | 55.4 | 0.0 | 2.6 | 4.4 | 4.6 | 503.7 | 4 312 | 435 | 296 | 9 455 | 37.3 | 61.5 | 1.2 |
| McKean | 183.3 | 4 201 | 54.0 | 3.4 | 1.7 | 5.1 | 5.0 | 143.5 | 3 289 | 434 | 110 | 2 082 | 40.5 | 57.8 | 1.6 |
| Mercer | 415.3 | 3 556 | 64.2 | 4.5 | 2.6 | 2.6 | 4.8 | 406.2 | 3 477 | 251 | 301 | 5 395 | 49.1 | 49.4 | 1.6 |
| Mifflin | 141.5 | 3 014 | 65.9 | 0.1 | 2.0 | 0.0 | 2.5 | 113.8 | 2 424 | 89 | 119 | 1 783 | 32.6 | 66.2 | 1.2 |
| Monroe | 647.0 | 3 928 | 72.6 | 0.1 | 2.9 | 3.7 | 3.1 | 1 117.5 | 6 784 | 4 455 | 461 | 9 068 | 57.6 | 41.3 | 1.0 |
| Montgomery | 3 308.9 | 4 263 | 54.3 | 1.9 | 4.5 | 7.2 | 3.7 | 4 577.8 | 5 898 | 2 939 | 2 384 | 33 633 | 60.0 | 39.2 | 0.8 |
| Montour | 61.1 | 3 430 | 46.3 | 0.0 | 2.4 | 1.9 | 4.6 | 586.6 | 32 924 | 36 | 46 | 1 433 | 41.9 | 57.0 | 1.1 |
| Northampton | 1 355.9 | 4 619 | 55.3 | 3.0 | 3.4 | 9.5 | 2.8 | 1 935.0 | 6 592 | 1 127 | 759 | 13 827 | 55.5 | 43.2 | 1.3 |
| Northumberland | 270.7 | 2 974 | 48.1 | 0.1 | 3.5 | 18.5 | 3.0 | 242.0 | 2 659 | 183 | 241 | 4 554 | 42.2 | 56.0 | 1.7 |
| Perry | 107.9 | 2 389 | 72.5 | 0.2 | 0.9 | 2.5 | 5.5 | 164.4 | 3 641 | 88 | 117 | 1 981 | 32.4 | 66.1 | 1.5 |
| Philadelphia | 9 207.3 | 6 351 | 32.8 | 14.4 | 5.8 | 5.4 | 0.9 | 18 159.9 | 12 527 | 31 899 | 4 747 | 72 657 | 83.1 | 16.3 | 0.6 |
| Pike | 107.5 | 1 834 | 51.7 | 0.1 | 8.1 | 6.7 | 4.5 | 60.2 | 1 027 | 233 | 144 | 2 409 | 47.3 | 51.5 | 1.1 |

1. Based on the resident population estimated as of July 1 of the year shown.    2. © 2013 Election Data Services, Inc. All rights reserved.

| STATE/ County code | CBSA code[1] | County type[2] | STATE County | Population 2012 | | | | Population characteristics[6], 2011 | | | | | | | | | | |
|---|---|---|---|---|---|---|---|---|---|---|---|---|---|---|---|---|---|---|
| | | | | | | | | Race alone or in combination, not Hispanic or Latino (percent) | | | | | Age (percent) | | | | | |
| | | | | Land area,[3] (sq km) 2010 | Total persons | Rank | Per square kilometer | White | Black | American Indian, Alaska Native | Asian and Pacific Islander | Percent Hispanic or Latino[4] | Under 5 years | 5 to 17 years | 18 to 24 years | 25 to 34 years | 35 to 44 years | 45 to 54 years |
| | | | | 1 | 2 | 3 | 4 | 5 | 6 | 7 | 8 | 9 | 10 | 11 | 12 | 13 | 14 | 15 |
| | | | PENNSYLVANIA—Cont'd | | | | | | | | | | | | | | | |
| 42 105 | ... | 9 | Potter | 2 801 | 17 577 | 1 944 | 6.3 | 97.9 | 0.7 | 0.6 | 0.5 | 1.1 | 5.5 | 16.1 | 7.2 | 9.6 | 11.0 | 15.3 |
| 42 107 | 39060 | 4 | Schuylkill | 2 017 | 147 063 | 430 | 72.9 | 93.7 | 3.1 | 0.4 | 0.8 | 2.9 | 5.0 | 14.8 | 7.3 | 11.7 | 13.3 | 15.5 |
| 42 109 | 42780 | 7 | Snyder | 851 | 39 672 | 1 176 | 46.6 | 96.4 | 1.4 | 0.4 | 0.8 | 1.8 | 5.7 | 16.3 | 12.6 | 10.5 | 12.1 | 14.1 |
| 42 111 | 43740 | 4 | Somerset | 2 783 | 76 957 | 709 | 27.7 | 95.9 | 2.7 | 0.3 | 0.5 | 1.2 | 4.7 | 14.3 | 7.4 | 11.2 | 12.7 | 15.8 |
| 42 113 | ... | 8 | Sullivan | 1 165 | 6 461 | 2 727 | 5.5 | 94.8 | 3.1 | 0.7 | 0.4 | 1.7 | 4.2 | 12.0 | 9.1 | 7.7 | 9.5 | 16.2 |
| 42 115 | ... | 6 | Susquehanna | 2 133 | 42 696 | 1 118 | 20.0 | 97.6 | 0.7 | 0.5 | 0.5 | 1.4 | 5.0 | 15.6 | 7.3 | 9.9 | 11.3 | 17.0 |
| 42 117 | ... | 6 | Tioga | 2 936 | 42 577 | 1 121 | 14.5 | 97.2 | 1.3 | 0.6 | 0.7 | 1.2 | 5.4 | 14.9 | 11.2 | 10.2 | 11.1 | 14.8 |
| 42 119 | 30260 | 4 | Union | 818 | 44 952 | 1 070 | 55.0 | 86.1 | 7.3 | 0.7 | 1.9 | 5.3 | 4.5 | 13.8 | 13.8 | 13.1 | 13.9 | 14.2 |
| 42 121 | 36340 | 4 | Venango | 1 746 | 54 272 | 921 | 31.1 | 97.3 | 1.7 | 0.5 | 0.6 | 0.9 | 5.4 | 15.8 | 7.3 | 10.4 | 11.4 | 15.9 |
| 42 123 | 47620 | 6 | Warren | 2 290 | 41 146 | 1 150 | 18.0 | 98.1 | 0.7 | 0.5 | 0.6 | 0.8 | 4.9 | 15.3 | 7.0 | 10.2 | 11.7 | 16.1 |
| 42 125 | 38300 | 1 | Washington | 2 220 | 208 716 | 301 | 94.0 | 94.6 | 4.2 | 0.4 | 1.0 | 1.2 | 5.0 | 15.2 | 9.0 | 10.1 | 12.2 | 15.7 |
| 42 127 | ... | 6 | Wayne | 1 879 | 51 955 | 955 | 27.7 | 92.7 | 3.5 | 0.6 | 0.7 | 3.5 | 4.1 | 14.3 | 6.8 | 10.0 | 12.3 | 16.5 |
| 42 129 | 38300 | 1 | Westmoreland | 2 661 | 363 395 | 183 | 136.6 | 95.7 | 3.1 | 0.4 | 1.1 | 1.0 | 4.8 | 14.8 | 7.7 | 10.0 | 12.2 | 16.3 |
| 42 131 | 42540 | 2 | Wyoming | 1 029 | 28 125 | 1 488 | 27.3 | 96.8 | 1.2 | 0.5 | 0.6 | 1.7 | 5.1 | 15.8 | 9.0 | 10.5 | 12.1 | 15.4 |
| 42 133 | 49620 | 2 | York | 2 342 | 437 846 | 155 | 187.0 | 87.3 | 6.3 | 0.5 | 1.7 | 5.8 | 6.0 | 17.1 | 8.4 | 11.7 | 13.5 | 15.7 |
| 44 000 | ... | X | RHODE ISLAND | 2 678 | 1 050 292 | X | 392.2 | 78.0 | 6.5 | 1.0 | 3.6 | 12.8 | 5.3 | 15.6 | 11.5 | 12.3 | 12.6 | 15.2 |
| 44 001 | 39300 | 1 | Bristol | 63 | 49 144 | 998 | 780.1 | 95.1 | 1.3 | 0.5 | 2.1 | 2.3 | 4.2 | 15.9 | 12.1 | 9.0 | 11.5 | 16.6 |
| 44 003 | 39300 | 1 | Kent | 436 | 164 843 | 381 | 378.1 | 92.6 | 2.0 | 0.7 | 2.7 | 3.5 | 4.8 | 15.3 | 7.7 | 11.7 | 13.2 | 16.8 |
| 44 005 | 39300 | 1 | Newport | 265 | 82 036 | 674 | 309.6 | 89.6 | 4.7 | 1.0 | 2.5 | 4.5 | 4.6 | 14.5 | 9.7 | 10.7 | 12.2 | 15.7 |
| 44 007 | 39300 | 1 | Providence | 1 061 | 628 323 | 101 | 592.2 | 68.2 | 9.2 | 1.1 | 4.4 | 19.3 | 5.9 | 15.8 | 12.2 | 13.6 | 12.8 | 14.4 |
| 44 009 | 39300 | 1 | Washington | 853 | 125 946 | 488 | 147.7 | 93.4 | 2.0 | 1.5 | 2.3 | 2.6 | 4.1 | 15.2 | 14.0 | 8.5 | 11.2 | 16.3 |
| 45 000 | ... | X | SOUTH CAROLINA | 77 857 | 4 723 723 | X | 60.7 | 65.2 | 28.5 | 0.8 | 1.8 | 5.3 | 6.5 | 16.6 | 10.3 | 12.9 | 12.7 | 14.1 |
| 45 001 | ... | 6 | Abbeville | 1 270 | 25 101 | 1 604 | 19.8 | 70.0 | 28.9 | 0.6 | 0.6 | 1.1 | 5.9 | 16.4 | 10.0 | 9.6 | 11.9 | 14.0 |
| 45 003 | 12260 | 2 | Aiken | 2 774 | 162 812 | 384 | 58.7 | 69.1 | 25.2 | 1.0 | 1.2 | 5.1 | 5.6 | 16.5 | 9.1 | 12.3 | 11.9 | 14.8 |
| 45 005 | ... | 6 | Allendale | 1 057 | 9 988 | 2 444 | 9.4 | 24.3 | 72.8 | 0.5 | 0.6 | 2.6 | 5.5 | 16.1 | 9.3 | 14.0 | 12.8 | 14.1 |
| 45 007 | 11340 | 3 | Anderson | 1 853 | 189 355 | 335 | 102.2 | 79.5 | 17.1 | 0.6 | 1.1 | 3.1 | 6.3 | 17.4 | 8.5 | 11.6 | 13.1 | 14.6 |
| 45 009 | ... | 7 | Bamberg | 1 019 | 15 763 | 2 059 | 15.5 | 36.7 | 61.1 | 0.6 | 0.7 | 1.8 | 5.8 | 16.1 | 14.2 | 9.3 | 10.3 | 13.3 |
| 45 011 | ... | 6 | Barnwell | 1 420 | 22 212 | 1 722 | 15.6 | 56.7 | 44.9 | 0.8 | 0.8 | 2.0 | 6.4 | 18.9 | 8.8 | 11.0 | 11.7 | 14.7 |
| 45 013 | 25940 | 5 | Beaufort | 1 493 | 168 049 | 371 | 112.6 | 67.6 | 19.8 | 0.6 | 1.7 | 11.9 | 6.5 | 14.2 | 10.0 | 12.2 | 10.5 | 11.3 |
| 45 015 | 16700 | 2 | Berkeley | 2 846 | 189 781 | 334 | 66.7 | 65.8 | 26.0 | 1.1 | 3.2 | 6.1 | 7.3 | 17.7 | 10.6 | 14.9 | 13.4 | 14.2 |
| 45 017 | 17900 | 2 | Calhoun | 987 | 14 910 | 2 116 | 15.1 | 53.4 | 43.2 | 0.7 | 0.5 | 3.2 | 5.7 | 15.9 | 8.2 | 10.2 | 11.6 | 15.6 |
| 45 019 | 16700 | 2 | Charleston | 2 373 | 365 162 | 182 | 153.9 | 63.4 | 30.0 | 0.7 | 1.9 | 5.4 | 6.6 | 14.1 | 11.7 | 16.2 | 12.1 | 13.5 |
| 45 021 | 23500 | 4 | Cherokee | 1 017 | 55 662 | 906 | 54.7 | 74.9 | 21.1 | 0.7 | 0.8 | 3.8 | 6.6 | 17.8 | 9.6 | 11.5 | 13.5 | 14.2 |
| 45 023 | 16900 | 6 | Chester | 1 504 | 32 546 | 1 374 | 21.6 | 60.1 | 38.2 | 0.8 | 0.7 | 1.6 | 6.5 | 17.0 | 8.8 | 11.0 | 12.6 | 15.0 |
| 45 025 | ... | 6 | Chesterfield | 2 070 | 46 103 | 1 047 | 22.3 | 62.8 | 33.3 | 0.9 | 0.6 | 3.8 | 6.3 | 17.9 | 8.8 | 11.0 | 13.5 | 14.8 |
| 45 027 | ... | 6 | Clarendon | 1 572 | 34 357 | 1 317 | 21.9 | 46.9 | 49.8 | 0.5 | 0.9 | 2.7 | 5.7 | 16.1 | 10.5 | 10.5 | 10.6 | 14.1 |
| 45 029 | 47500 | 6 | Colleton | 2 736 | 38 153 | 1 214 | 13.9 | 56.9 | 39.5 | 1.2 | 0.8 | 2.9 | 6.5 | 17.4 | 8.3 | 10.7 | 11.5 | 14.6 |
| 45 031 | ... | 3 | Darlington | 1 453 | 68 139 | 779 | 46.9 | 56.2 | 41.8 | 0.6 | 0.6 | 1.8 | 6.2 | 17.6 | 9.1 | 10.8 | 12.6 | 14.4 |
| 45 033 | 19900 | 6 | Dillon | 1 049 | 31 446 | 1 403 | 30.0 | 48.2 | 47.0 | 2.9 | 0.7 | 2.8 | 7.3 | 19.0 | 9.2 | 12.2 | 12.0 | 13.9 |
| 45 035 | 16700 | 2 | Dorchester | 1 485 | 142 496 | 441 | 96.0 | 67.2 | 26.8 | 1.3 | 2.4 | 4.5 | 7.0 | 19.5 | 8.5 | 13.8 | 14.0 | 14.8 |
| 45 037 | 12260 | 2 | Edgefield | 1 296 | 26 347 | 1 648 | 20.3 | 56.8 | 37.4 | 0.6 | 0.6 | 5.5 | 4.5 | 16.2 | 8.6 | 13.0 | 13.7 | 15.8 |
| 45 039 | 17900 | 2 | Fairfield | 1 777 | 23 363 | 1 671 | 13.1 | 39.0 | 59.2 | 0.5 | 0.5 | 1.8 | 5.6 | 16.4 | 8.4 | 10.1 | 11.8 | 16.0 |
| 45 041 | 22500 | 3 | Florence | 2 072 | 137 948 | 452 | 66.6 | 54.6 | 41.8 | 0.7 | 1.6 | 2.3 | 6.7 | 17.8 | 9.7 | 12.5 | 12.7 | 14.0 |
| 45 043 | 23860 | 4 | Georgetown | 2 107 | 60 189 | 861 | 28.6 | 62.7 | 33.8 | 0.5 | 0.7 | 3.1 | 5.4 | 15.7 | 7.0 | 9.5 | 10.8 | 13.8 |
| 45 045 | 24860 | 2 | Greenville | 2 033 | 467 605 | 142 | 230.0 | 71.2 | 18.8 | 0.6 | 2.5 | 8.3 | 7.1 | 17.1 | 9.4 | 13.5 | 13.6 | 14.3 |
| 45 047 | 24940 | 4 | Greenwood | 1 178 | 69 756 | 762 | 59.2 | 61.7 | 31.8 | 0.5 | 1.2 | 5.7 | 6.8 | 16.8 | 10.7 | 12.2 | 12.3 | 13.4 |
| 45 049 | ... | 6 | Hampton | 1 450 | 20 726 | 1 796 | 14.3 | 42.3 | 53.7 | 0.6 | 0.8 | 3.6 | 6.4 | 17.2 | 9.0 | 12.6 | 13.4 | 14.3 |
| 45 051 | 34820 | 3 | Horry | 2 937 | 282 285 | 234 | 96.1 | 78.5 | 14.3 | 0.9 | 1.6 | 6.3 | 5.6 | 14.4 | 9.5 | 12.4 | 12.1 | 13.5 |
| 45 053 | 25940 | 6 | Jasper | 1 697 | 25 833 | 1 571 | 15.2 | 38.9 | 45.9 | 0.6 | 1.0 | 14.6 | 7.4 | 17.1 | 10.3 | 14.9 | 12.6 | 14.7 |
| 45 055 | 17900 | 2 | Kershaw | 1 882 | 62 343 | 838 | 33.1 | 70.2 | 25.6 | 0.8 | 0.8 | 3.9 | 6.5 | 17.8 | 8.0 | 11.2 | 12.5 | 15.1 |
| 45 057 | 29580 | 4 | Lancaster | 1 422 | 79 089 | 696 | 55.6 | 70.7 | 24.2 | 0.6 | 0.9 | 4.6 | 6.5 | 16.3 | 7.7 | 12.0 | 13.8 | 13.7 |
| 45 059 | 24860 | 2 | Laurens | 1 849 | 66 223 | 794 | 35.8 | 69.5 | 26.1 | 0.6 | 0.6 | 4.3 | 6.5 | 16.5 | 10.1 | 10.7 | 12.4 | 14.7 |
| 45 061 | ... | 6 | Lee | 1 062 | 18 654 | 1 890 | 17.6 | 33.7 | 63.8 | 0.5 | 0.7 | 2.0 | 5.8 | 16.4 | 10.3 | 13.4 | 11.0 | 15.2 |
| 45 063 | 17900 | 2 | Lexington | 1 810 | 270 406 | 244 | 149.4 | 77.8 | 15.2 | 0.9 | 1.9 | 5.7 | 6.6 | 17.6 | 8.7 | 13.1 | 13.7 | 14.9 |
| 45 065 | ... | 8 | McCormick | 930 | 9 943 | 2 447 | 10.7 | 49.1 | 49.7 | 0.5 | 0.5 | 1.1 | 3.9 | 10.2 | 6.1 | 10.8 | 11.0 | 14.2 |
| 45 067 | ... | 6 | Marion | 1 267 | 32 457 | 1 379 | 25.6 | 40.8 | 56.0 | 0.7 | 0.9 | 2.7 | 6.9 | 17.2 | 8.8 | 11.2 | 11.6 | 13.9 |
| 45 069 | 13500 | 6 | Marlboro | 1 242 | 28 145 | 1 487 | 22.7 | 41.7 | 51.5 | 4.9 | 0.6 | 3.0 | 5.7 | 15.5 | 8.5 | 14.5 | 13.8 | 15.2 |
| 45 071 | 35140 | 6 | Newberry | 1 632 | 37 576 | 1 229 | 23.0 | 61.2 | 31.2 | 0.5 | 0.5 | 7.4 | 6.6 | 16.1 | 10.2 | 11.0 | 11.8 | 13.9 |
| 45 073 | 42860 | 6 | Oconee | 1 622 | 74 627 | 734 | 46.0 | 86.8 | 8.3 | 0.7 | 0.8 | 4.6 | 5.5 | 15.2 | 8.5 | 10.4 | 11.7 | 14.0 |
| 45 075 | 36700 | 4 | Orangeburg | 2 865 | 91 476 | 631 | 31.9 | 34.6 | 62.5 | 1.0 | 1.1 | 2.0 | 6.8 | 16.2 | 12.4 | 11.3 | 10.6 | 13.7 |
| 45 077 | 24860 | 2 | Pickens | 1 286 | 119 670 | 510 | 93.1 | 87.8 | 7.5 | 0.6 | 2.0 | 3.3 | 5.2 | 14.7 | 19.1 | 11.1 | 11.3 | 13.1 |
| 45 079 | 17900 | 2 | Richland | 1 961 | 393 830 | 170 | 200.8 | 46.7 | 46.5 | 0.8 | 3.0 | 4.9 | 6.3 | 15.0 | 14.9 | 15.3 | 12.7 | 13.3 |
| 45 081 | 17900 | 2 | Saluda | 1 173 | 19 893 | 1 843 | 17.0 | 58.6 | 26.7 | 0.5 | 0.4 | 14.8 | 6.9 | 16.0 | 8.6 | 12.7 | 12.2 | 13.6 |
| 45 083 | 43900 | 2 | Spartanburg | 2 093 | 288 745 | 228 | 138.0 | 70.9 | 21.4 | 0.6 | 2.4 | 6.1 | 6.7 | 17.5 | 10.0 | 11.9 | 13.2 | 14.2 |

1. CBSA = Core Based Statistical Area. See Appendix A for explanation. See Appendix B for list of metropolitan areas with component counties. 2. County type code from the Economic Research Service of USDA Rural-Urban Continuum Codes. See Appendix A for definition. 3. Dry land or land partially or temporarily covered by water. 4. May be of any race.

# Table B. States and Counties — **Population and Households**

| STATE County | 55 to 64 years | 65 to 74 years | 75 years and over | Percent female | 2000 | 2010 | 2000–2010 | 2010–2012 | Births | Deaths | Net migration | Number | Percent change, 2000–2010 | Persons per house-hold | Female family house-holder[1] | One per-son |
|---|---|---|---|---|---|---|---|---|---|---|---|---|---|---|---|---|
| | 16 | 17 | 18 | 19 | 20 | 21 | 22 | 23 | 24 | 25 | 26 | 27 | 28 | 29 | 30 | 31 |
| **PENNSYLVANIA—Cont'd** | | | | | | | | | | | | | | | | |
| Potter | 15.6 | 10.8 | 9.0 | 49.8 | 18 080 | 17 457 | -3.4 | 0.7 | 408 | 474 | 190 | 7 227 | 3.2 | 2.39 | 8.7 | 27.4 |
| Schuylkill | 14.2 | 8.9 | 9.3 | 49.2 | 150 336 | 148 289 | -1.4 | -0.8 | 3 093 | 4 173 | -64 | 60 192 | -0.6 | 2.35 | 10.9 | 30.0 |
| Snyder | 13.2 | 8.3 | 7.3 | 50.8 | 37 546 | 39 702 | 5.7 | -0.1 | 950 | 761 | -244 | 14 750 | 8.0 | 2.53 | 8.1 | 24.1 |
| Somerset | 15.0 | 9.4 | 9.5 | 48.5 | 80 023 | 77 742 | -2.9 | -1.0 | 1 506 | 2 092 | -185 | 31 090 | -0.4 | 2.35 | 8.7 | 28.1 |
| Sullivan | 16.8 | 12.9 | 11.5 | 48.5 | 6 556 | 6 428 | -2.0 | 0.5 | 123 | 237 | 138 | 2 777 | 4.4 | 2.16 | 6.2 | 32.3 |
| Susquehanna | 15.6 | 10.4 | 7.9 | 49.7 | 42 238 | 43 356 | 2.6 | -1.5 | 904 | 996 | -624 | 17 798 | 7.7 | 2.42 | 8.7 | 26.4 |
| Tioga | 14.3 | 10.1 | 8.0 | 50.9 | 41 373 | 41 981 | 1.5 | 1.4 | 986 | 1 020 | 613 | 16 727 | 5.0 | 2.39 | 8.9 | 26.1 |
| Union | 11.7 | 7.4 | 7.5 | 45.1 | 41 624 | 44 947 | 8.0 | 0.0 | 857 | 892 | 69 | 14 765 | 12.0 | 2.43 | 7.9 | 27.6 |
| Venango | 15.6 | 9.4 | 8.8 | 50.9 | 57 565 | 54 984 | -4.5 | -1.3 | 1 237 | 1 458 | -463 | 22 621 | -0.6 | 2.37 | 11.1 | 27.5 |
| Warren | 15.8 | 10.0 | 9.0 | 50.0 | 43 863 | 41 815 | -4.7 | -1.6 | 851 | 1 105 | -392 | 17 767 | 0.4 | 2.31 | 8.6 | 30.1 |
| Washington | 15.1 | 8.9 | 8.8 | 51.4 | 202 897 | 207 820 | 2.4 | 0.4 | 4 456 | 5 521 | 2 010 | 85 089 | 4.9 | 2.37 | 10.5 | 28.1 |
| Wayne | 15.8 | 11.6 | 8.6 | 47.7 | 47 722 | 52 822 | 10.7 | -1.6 | 936 | 1 307 | -701 | 20 625 | 12.4 | 2.38 | 9.2 | 27.2 |
| Westmoreland | 15.4 | 9.4 | 9.6 | 51.3 | 369 993 | 365 169 | -1.3 | -0.5 | 7 224 | 9 727 | 1 008 | 153 650 | 2.6 | 2.32 | 10.0 | 29.0 |
| Wyoming | 15.0 | 10.0 | 7.2 | 49.9 | 28 080 | 28 276 | 0.7 | -0.5 | 625 | 698 | -63 | 11 237 | 4.4 | 2.46 | 9.8 | 26.1 |
| York | 13.3 | 7.7 | 6.6 | 50.6 | 381 751 | 434 972 | 13.9 | 0.7 | 11 254 | 8 190 | -80 | 168 372 | 13.6 | 2.53 | 10.6 | 23.7 |
| **RHODE ISLAND** | 12.9 | 7.3 | 7.4 | 51.7 | 1 048 319 | 1 052 567 | 0.4 | -0.2 | 24 409 | 20 912 | -5 712 | 413 600 | 1.3 | 2.44 | 13.5 | 29.6 |
| Bristol | 13.9 | 8.1 | 8.8 | 52.1 | 50 648 | 49 875 | -1.5 | -1.5 | 786 | 1 108 | -406 | 19 150 | 0.6 | 2.44 | 9.8 | 27.4 |
| Kent | 14.2 | 8.0 | 8.1 | 51.8 | 167 090 | 166 158 | -0.6 | -0.8 | 3 502 | 3 754 | -978 | 68 645 | 2.0 | 2.40 | 11.1 | 29.2 |
| Newport | 15.0 | 9.3 | 8.2 | 51.2 | 85 433 | 82 888 | -3.0 | -1.0 | 1 592 | 1 604 | -832 | 34 911 | -0.9 | 2.27 | 10.2 | 32.2 |
| Providence | 11.8 | 6.5 | 7.0 | 51.7 | 621 602 | 626 667 | 0.8 | 0.3 | 16 486 | 12 081 | -2 835 | 241 717 | 0.7 | 2.48 | 15.8 | 30.2 |
| Washington | 15.0 | 8.5 | 7.1 | 51.5 | 123 546 | 126 979 | 2.8 | -0.8 | 2 043 | 2 365 | -661 | 49 177 | 4.8 | 2.45 | 9.5 | 26.1 |
| **SOUTH CAROLINA** | 13.0 | 8.3 | 5.8 | 51.3 | 4 012 012 | 4 625 364 | 15.3 | 2.1 | 128 897 | 95 175 | 63 360 | 1 801 181 | 17.4 | 2.49 | 15.6 | 26.5 |
| Abbeville | 15.0 | 9.6 | 7.4 | 51.4 | 26 167 | 25 417 | -2.9 | -1.2 | 574 | 602 | -288 | 9 990 | -1.4 | 2.45 | 15.3 | 27.3 |
| Aiken | 13.9 | 9.1 | 6.8 | 51.6 | 142 552 | 160 099 | 12.3 | 1.7 | 3 653 | 3 471 | 2 446 | 64 253 | 15.6 | 2.45 | 14.4 | 26.9 |
| Allendale | 14.5 | 7.8 | 5.8 | 46.5 | 11 211 | 10 419 | -7.1 | -4.1 | 250 | 219 | -472 | 3 706 | -5.3 | 2.45 | 26.9 | 33.7 |
| Anderson | 13.2 | 8.8 | 6.6 | 51.7 | 165 740 | 187 126 | 12.9 | 1.2 | 4 987 | 4 383 | 1 633 | 73 829 | 12.5 | 2.50 | 14.5 | 25.4 |
| Bamberg | 14.4 | 9.3 | 7.4 | 52.3 | 16 658 | 15 987 | -4.0 | -1.4 | 381 | 451 | -145 | 6 048 | -1.2 | 2.44 | 21.6 | 31.8 |
| Barnwell | 13.8 | 8.4 | 6.3 | 52.2 | 23 478 | 22 621 | -3.7 | -1.8 | 605 | 566 | -449 | 8 937 | -0.9 | 2.50 | 20.8 | 28.4 |
| Beaufort | 13.9 | 13.0 | 8.3 | 50.7 | 120 937 | 162 233 | 34.1 | 3.6 | 4 574 | 2 896 | 4 084 | 64 945 | 42.6 | 2.42 | 10.7 | 24.3 |
| Berkeley | 11.6 | 6.7 | 3.6 | 50.0 | 142 651 | 177 843 | 24.7 | 6.7 | 5 642 | 2 583 | 8 439 | 65 419 | 31.0 | 2.66 | 15.3 | 22.0 |
| Calhoun | 16.0 | 10.1 | 6.6 | 51.3 | 15 185 | 15 175 | -0.1 | -1.7 | 345 | 402 | -238 | 6 080 | 2.8 | 2.47 | 15.9 | 26.8 |
| Charleston | 12.6 | 7.4 | 5.6 | 51.5 | 309 969 | 350 209 | 13.0 | 4.3 | 10 745 | 6 576 | 10 645 | 144 309 | 17.0 | 2.36 | 14.7 | 30.1 |
| Cherokee | 12.9 | 8.2 | 5.7 | 51.4 | 52 537 | 55 342 | 5.3 | 0.6 | 1 542 | 1 264 | 63 | 21 519 | 5.0 | 2.54 | 17.4 | 25.8 |
| Chester | 14.1 | 8.7 | 6.3 | 51.6 | 34 068 | 33 140 | -2.7 | -1.8 | 880 | 863 | -611 | 12 876 | 0.0 | 2.56 | 19.8 | 25.9 |
| Chesterfield | 13.8 | 8.4 | 5.6 | 51.4 | 42 768 | 46 734 | 9.3 | -1.4 | 1 146 | 1 133 | -679 | 18 173 | 9.8 | 2.52 | 18.3 | 27.4 |
| Clarendon | 14.9 | 10.8 | 6.8 | 50.7 | 32 502 | 34 971 | 7.6 | -1.8 | 784 | 838 | -553 | 13 132 | 11.2 | 2.54 | 20.6 | 26.1 |
| Colleton | 14.5 | 9.8 | 6.6 | 52.0 | 38 264 | 38 892 | 1.6 | -1.9 | 1 039 | 1 205 | -577 | 15 131 | 4.6 | 2.54 | 18.4 | 26.8 |
| Darlington | 14.5 | 8.8 | 6.0 | 52.7 | 67 394 | 68 681 | 1.9 | -0.8 | 1 749 | 1 749 | -523 | 26 531 | 2.9 | 2.54 | 20.5 | 26.0 |
| Dillon | 13.0 | 7.8 | 5.6 | 52.8 | 30 722 | 32 062 | 4.4 | -1.9 | 968 | 818 | -773 | 11 923 | 6.5 | 2.65 | 23.9 | 26.5 |
| Dorchester | 11.6 | 6.7 | 4.0 | 51.4 | 96 413 | 136 555 | 41.6 | 4.4 | 4 064 | 2 102 | 3 827 | 50 259 | 44.8 | 2.68 | 16.0 | 21.6 |
| Edgefield | 14.3 | 8.6 | 5.2 | 46.0 | 24 595 | 26 985 | 9.7 | -2.4 | 320 | 489 | -486 | 9 348 | 13.0 | 2.56 | 16.0 | 24.9 |
| Fairfield | 16.1 | 9.2 | 6.4 | 52.1 | 23 454 | 23 956 | 2.1 | -2.5 | 528 | 633 | -489 | 9 419 | 7.4 | 2.50 | 21.3 | 26.5 |
| Florence | 13.0 | 8.0 | 5.6 | 53.1 | 125 761 | 136 885 | 8.8 | 0.8 | 4 040 | 3 238 | 339 | 52 653 | 11.7 | 2.54 | 19.6 | 26.3 |
| Georgetown | 16.9 | 12.8 | 7.9 | 52.4 | 55 797 | 60 158 | 7.8 | 0.1 | 1 345 | 1 582 | 178 | 24 524 | 13.2 | 2.43 | 15.6 | 25.4 |
| Greenville | 12.1 | 7.4 | 5.6 | 51.4 | 379 616 | 451 225 | 18.9 | 3.6 | 14 539 | 8 302 | 10 138 | 176 531 | 18.0 | 2.49 | 13.5 | 27.0 |
| Greenwood | 12.5 | 8.2 | 7.2 | 53.1 | 66 271 | 69 661 | 5.1 | 0.1 | 2 017 | 1 603 | -302 | 27 547 | 7.1 | 2.43 | 17.5 | 27.9 |
| Hampton | 13.2 | 8.2 | 5.7 | 48.6 | 21 386 | 21 090 | -1.4 | -1.7 | 538 | 489 | -409 | 7 598 | 2.1 | 2.57 | 19.1 | 28.1 |
| Horry | 14.7 | 11.0 | 6.8 | 51.1 | 196 629 | 269 291 | 37.0 | 4.8 | 6 877 | 5 978 | 11 922 | 112 225 | 37.2 | 2.37 | 12.5 | 26.8 |
| Jasper | 11.5 | 7.1 | 4.4 | 48.2 | 20 678 | 24 777 | 19.8 | 4.3 | 752 | 441 | 670 | 8 517 | 20.9 | 2.73 | 18.6 | 24.8 |
| Kershaw | 14.3 | 8.4 | 6.1 | 51.4 | 52 647 | 61 697 | 17.2 | 1.0 | 1 638 | 1 467 | 500 | 23 928 | 18.5 | 2.56 | 15.1 | 24.5 |
| Lancaster | 13.7 | 10.1 | 6.2 | 50.7 | 61 351 | 76 652 | 24.9 | 3.2 | 1 943 | 1 683 | 2 081 | 29 697 | 28.1 | 2.51 | 15.4 | 24.7 |
| Laurens | 13.7 | 8.7 | 6.7 | 51.4 | 69 567 | 66 537 | -4.4 | -0.5 | 1 817 | 1 739 | -365 | 25 525 | -2.9 | 2.51 | 17.2 | 26.1 |
| Lee | 14.0 | 7.8 | 6.2 | 48.1 | 20 119 | 19 220 | -4.5 | -2.9 | 415 | 576 | -439 | 6 797 | -1.3 | 2.54 | 24.0 | 29.3 |
| Lexington | 12.8 | 7.4 | 5.1 | 51.1 | 216 014 | 262 391 | 21.5 | 3.1 | 7 437 | 4 766 | 5 321 | 102 733 | 23.4 | 2.53 | 13.0 | 24.9 |
| McCormick | 18.1 | 17.1 | 8.5 | 45.5 | 9 958 | 10 233 | 2.8 | -2.8 | 124 | 307 | -113 | 4 027 | 13.2 | 2.22 | 15.2 | 27.4 |
| Marion | 15.2 | 9.0 | 6.1 | 54.2 | 35 466 | 33 062 | -6.8 | -1.8 | 954 | 956 | -601 | 13 058 | -1.8 | 2.52 | 24.9 | 28.5 |
| Marlboro | 13.3 | 8.2 | 5.4 | 47.1 | 28 818 | 28 933 | 0.4 | -2.7 | 665 | 696 | -774 | 10 383 | -0.9 | 2.47 | 24.3 | 30.0 |
| Newberry | 13.9 | 9.4 | 7.1 | 51.3 | 36 108 | 37 508 | 3.9 | 0.2 | 1 030 | 999 | 36 | 14 709 | 4.9 | 2.47 | 17.2 | 27.0 |
| Oconee | 15.0 | 11.7 | 7.9 | 50.7 | 66 215 | 74 273 | 12.2 | 0.5 | 1 804 | 1 846 | 413 | 30 676 | 12.4 | 2.40 | 11.2 | 26.2 |
| Orangeburg | 13.7 | 8.9 | 6.4 | 53.0 | 91 582 | 92 501 | 1.0 | -1.1 | 2 694 | 2 419 | -1 303 | 35 788 | 4.9 | 2.49 | 22.5 | 29.0 |
| Pickens | 11.6 | 7.9 | 5.9 | 50.0 | 110 757 | 119 224 | 7.6 | 0.4 | 2 618 | 2 350 | 203 | 45 228 | 9.5 | 2.48 | 10.8 | 25.2 |
| Richland | 11.1 | 5.7 | 4.3 | 51.4 | 320 677 | 384 504 | 19.9 | 2.4 | 10 841 | 6 071 | 4 569 | 145 194 | 20.9 | 2.43 | 17.7 | 30.2 |
| Saluda | 13.4 | 9.6 | 7.0 | 49.8 | 19 181 | 19 875 | 3.6 | 0.1 | 554 | 431 | -117 | 7 527 | 5.6 | 2.61 | 15.0 | 24.2 |
| Spartanburg | 12.7 | 8.0 | 5.8 | 51.5 | 253 791 | 284 307 | 12.0 | 1.6 | 8 154 | 6 155 | 2 520 | 109 246 | 11.8 | 2.53 | 15.1 | 26.2 |

1. No spouse present.

# Table B. States and Counties — Population, Vital Statistics, Medicare, and Crime

| STATE County | Persons in group quarters, 2010 | Daytime population, 2007–2011 Number | Employ-ment/resi-dence ratio | Births, 2011 Total | Rate[1] | Deaths, 2011 Number | Rate[1] | Persons under 65 with no health insurance, 2010 Number | Percent | Medicare, 2012 Eligible for Medicare | Enrolled in Medicare Advantage | Enrolled in a Medicare prescription drug plan | Serious crimes known to police,[2] 2011 Total Number | Rate[3] |
|---|---|---|---|---|---|---|---|---|---|---|---|---|---|---|
| | 32 | 33 | 34 | 35 | 36 | 37 | 38 | 39 | 40 | 41 | 42 | 43 | 44 | 45 |
| **PENNSYLVANIA—Cont'd** | | | | | | | | | | | | | | |
| Potter | 217 | 17 420 | 0.99 | 184 | 10.5 | 206 | 11.8 | 2 011 | 14.4 | 4 191 | 1 007 | 1 844 | 214 | 1 222 |
| Schuylkill | 6 780 | 137 041 | 0.82 | 1 411 | 9.6 | 1 845 | 12.5 | 13 835 | 12.0 | 33 141 | 8 574 | 15 237 | 2 515 | 1 696 |
| Snyder | 2 317 | 39 043 | 0.97 | 428 | 10.7 | 343 | 8.6 | 4 381 | 14.0 | 7 424 | 3 098 | 2 919 | 859 | 2 157 |
| Somerset | 4 533 | 73 337 | 0.86 | 677 | 8.7 | 935 | 12.1 | 8 904 | 15.0 | 17 525 | 10 160 | 4 182 | 1 091 | 1 538 |
| Sullivan | 434 | 5 896 | 0.79 | 57 | 8.8 | 103 | 15.9 | 764 | 15.9 | 1 767 | 435 | 860 | 121 | 1 877 |
| Susquehanna | 282 | 35 939 | 0.62 | 402 | 9.3 | 415 | 9.6 | 5 215 | 14.8 | 9 335 | 1 649 | 4 467 | 700 | 1 609 |
| Tioga | 1 951 | 40 253 | 0.91 | 423 | 10.0 | 443 | 10.4 | 4 794 | 14.7 | 9 463 | 2 003 | 4 197 | 597 | 1 493 |
| Union | 9 109 | 47 396 | 1.15 | 369 | 8.2 | 382 | 8.5 | 4 063 | 13.7 | 7 325 | 2 439 | 3 037 | 533 | 1 182 |
| Venango | 1 297 | 53 832 | 0.95 | 562 | 10.3 | 650 | 11.9 | 5 740 | 12.9 | 12 863 | 3 953 | 5 635 | 801 | 1 452 |
| Warren | 788 | 40 001 | 0.91 | 381 | 9.2 | 501 | 12.1 | 4 164 | 12.4 | 9 471 | 1 445 | 4 935 | 996 | 2 374 |
| Washington | 5 925 | 196 058 | 0.88 | 2 024 | 9.7 | 2 457 | 11.8 | 17 801 | 10.7 | 45 572 | 27 905 | 8 167 | 3 995 | 1 937 |
| Wayne | 3 820 | 49 295 | 0.85 | 415 | 7.8 | 568 | 10.7 | 5 853 | 14.8 | 12 169 | 1 385 | 6 170 | 792 | 1 495 |
| Westmoreland | 7 962 | 340 800 | 0.85 | 3 240 | 8.9 | 4 341 | 11.9 | 30 301 | 10.5 | 81 492 | 53 159 | 12 756 | 5 772 | 1 576 |
| Wyoming | 602 | 27 132 | 0.91 | 268 | 9.4 | 305 | 10.7 | 2 628 | 11.3 | 5 810 | 1 703 | 2 233 | 361 | 1 417 |
| York | 8 430 | 397 480 | 0.84 | 5 039 | 11.5 | 3 559 | 8.1 | 40 797 | 11.1 | 77 853 | 24 728 | 27 150 | 10 046 | 2 302 |
| **RHODE ISLAND** | 42 663 | 1 034 097 | 0.96 | 11 012 | 10.5 | 9 189 | 8.7 | 120 001 | 13.8 | 192 596 | 67 379 | 70 457 | 30 743 | 2 924 |
| Bristol | 3 242 | 42 067 | 0.66 | 361 | 7.2 | 510 | 10.2 | 4 157 | 10.6 | 10 197 | 3 991 | 3 168 | 781 | 1 568 |
| Kent | 1 536 | 158 667 | 0.90 | 1 571 | 9.5 | 1 619 | 9.8 | 15 098 | 10.8 | 33 709 | 12 880 | 11 008 | 4 043 | 2 436 |
| Newport | 3 576 | 86 994 | 1.10 | 714 | 8.6 | 692 | 8.4 | 6 814 | 10.3 | 17 004 | 3 779 | 6 122 | 2 299 | 2 777 |
| Providence | 27 785 | 629 905 | 1.01 | 7 419 | 11.8 | 5 333 | 8.5 | 83 505 | 16.1 | 107 433 | 39 474 | 41 344 | 21 170 | 3 382 |
| Washington | 6 524 | 116 464 | 0.84 | 947 | 7.5 | 1 035 | 8.2 | 10 426 | 10.1 | 24 253 | 7 255 | 8 815 | 2 174 | 1 714 |
| **SOUTH CAROLINA** | 139 154 | 4 542 644 | 0.98 | 59 522 | 12.7 | 41 144 | 8.8 | 785 961 | 20.3 | 848 217 | 154 547 | 337 277 | 209 445 | 4 476 |
| Abbeville | 901 | 21 479 | 0.58 | 261 | 10.4 | 254 | 10.1 | 4 150 | 20.3 | 5 483 | 1 371 | 2 113 | 605 | 2 353 |
| Aiken | 2 439 | 156 047 | 0.97 | 1 016 | 6.3 | 1 516 | 9.4 | 24 529 | 18.3 | 31 424 | 4 923 | 12 796 | 6 908 | 4 265 |
| Allendale | 1 342 | 10 841 | 1.11 | 102 | 10.0 | 111 | 10.9 | 1 698 | 22.0 | 1 867 | 521 | 738 | 455 | 4 317 |
| Anderson | 2 764 | 173 283 | 0.84 | 2 246 | 11.9 | 1 885 | 10.0 | 29 910 | 19.1 | 38 657 | 9 564 | 15 217 | 10 805 | 5 708 |
| Bamberg | 1 241 | 15 441 | 0.89 | 186 | 11.6 | 185 | 11.6 | 2 438 | 19.5 | 3 121 | 521 | 1 451 | 786 | 4 860 |
| Barnwell | 285 | 21 804 | 0.90 | 229 | 10.2 | 294 | 13.1 | 3 638 | 18.9 | 4 058 | 656 | 1 873 | 1 269 | 5 545 |
| Beaufort | 5 265 | 163 220 | 1.06 | 2 060 | 12.5 | 1 221 | 7.4 | 28 206 | 22.7 | 37 729 | 5 095 | 16 037 | 6 108 | 3 722 |
| Berkeley | 3 742 | 150 430 | 0.70 | 2 522 | 13.7 | 1 082 | 5.9 | 32 246 | 20.6 | 25 878 | 4 122 | 7 556 | 6 437 | 3 588 |
| Calhoun | 153 | 12 145 | 0.52 | 152 | 10.0 | 173 | 11.4 | 2 611 | 20.7 | 3 132 | 708 | 1 238 | 592 | 3 856 |
| Charleston | 10 331 | 400 964 | 1.32 | 4 944 | 13.8 | 2 854 | 8.0 | 58 777 | 19.8 | 57 580 | 8 033 | 19 610 | 14 167 | 4 012 |
| Cherokee | 707 | 53 387 | 0.92 | 688 | 12.4 | 570 | 10.3 | 9 964 | 21.0 | 11 074 | 2 703 | 4 625 | 1 408 | 2 515 |
| Chester | 218 | 30 288 | 0.77 | 416 | 12.6 | 385 | 11.7 | 5 708 | 20.3 | 6 803 | 1 148 | 3 250 | 1 532 | 4 570 |
| Chesterfield | 874 | 43 083 | 0.82 | 522 | 11.2 | 501 | 10.8 | 8 997 | 22.5 | 8 736 | 891 | 4 667 | 1 756 | 3 714 |
| Clarendon | 1 661 | 32 177 | 0.78 | 381 | 11.0 | 355 | 10.2 | 5 915 | 21.5 | 7 695 | 1 478 | 3 213 | 1 616 | 4 568 |
| Colleton | 388 | 35 029 | 0.73 | 505 | 13.1 | 516 | 13.4 | 7 431 | 22.7 | 8 410 | 1 613 | 3 244 | 2 287 | 5 813 |
| Darlington | 1 345 | 64 365 | 0.85 | 790 | 11.6 | 759 | 11.1 | 11 343 | 19.6 | 13 469 | 1 351 | 7 255 | 4 235 | 6 095 |
| Dillon | 451 | 30 142 | 0.85 | 448 | 14.1 | 344 | 10.8 | 6 084 | 22.0 | 5 758 | 665 | 3 199 | 2 241 | 6 909 |
| Dorchester | 2 015 | 108 643 | 0.59 | 1 854 | 13.2 | 862 | 6.1 | 21 960 | 18.1 | 19 924 | 2 906 | 6 257 | 5 611 | 4 121 |
| Edgefield | 3 045 | 23 307 | 0.65 | 111 | 4.2 | 248 | 9.3 | 3 879 | 18.8 | 4 527 | 819 | 1 747 | 617 | 2 260 |
| Fairfield | 397 | 21 331 | 0.72 | 239 | 10.1 | 284 | 12.0 | 3 749 | 18.6 | 4 652 | 1 089 | 1 801 | 1 033 | 4 262 |
| Florence | 3 228 | 144 989 | 1.16 | 1 847 | 13.4 | 1 372 | 10.0 | 21 807 | 18.7 | 24 969 | 1 593 | 13 412 | 7 413 | 5 353 |
| Georgetown | 559 | 59 972 | 0.99 | 652 | 10.9 | 704 | 11.7 | 10 436 | 21.9 | 15 883 | 1 981 | 6 898 | 2 899 | 4 763 |
| Greenville | 11 854 | 476 000 | 1.15 | 7 654 | 16.6 | 3 601 | 7.8 | 78 873 | 20.6 | 77 698 | 20 763 | 29 408 | 19 242 | 4 215 |
| Greenwood | 2 640 | 71 808 | 1.09 | 940 | 13.5 | 702 | 10.1 | 12 657 | 22.3 | 13 812 | 2 597 | 5 544 | 4 794 | 6 803 |
| Hampton | 1 531 | 19 389 | 0.77 | 278 | 13.4 | 229 | 11.0 | 3 531 | 21.0 | 3 934 | 569 | 1 772 | 922 | 4 960 |
| Horry | 2 952 | 268 281 | 1.03 | 3 103 | 11.2 | 2 523 | 9.1 | 57 872 | 26.2 | 62 135 | 6 862 | 26 409 | 17 088 | 6 273 |
| Jasper | 1 488 | 22 154 | 0.80 | 352 | 14.0 | 197 | 7.8 | 6 141 | 29.7 | 3 880 | 817 | 1 485 | 876 | 3 495 |
| Kershaw | 526 | 53 230 | 0.70 | 754 | 12.1 | 640 | 10.3 | 10 455 | 19.9 | 11 783 | 1 507 | 5 393 | 2 293 | 3 674 |
| Lancaster | 2 114 | 66 079 | 0.71 | 900 | 11.6 | 709 | 9.1 | 12 952 | 20.5 | 16 142 | 1 604 | 8 531 | 3 012 | 3 884 |
| Laurens | 2 402 | 60 378 | 0.76 | 840 | 12.6 | 763 | 11.5 | 11 160 | 20.4 | 14 495 | 3 359 | 5 824 | 3 043 | 4 521 |
| Lee | 1 975 | 16 892 | 0.60 | 222 | 11.7 | 271 | 14.3 | 3 306 | 22.4 | 3 638 | 385 | 2 013 | 763 | 3 924 |
| Lexington | 2 320 | 241 810 | 0.87 | 3 445 | 12.9 | 2 006 | 7.5 | 41 284 | 18.0 | 41 782 | 7 472 | 14 461 | 8 883 | 3 346 |
| McCormick | 1 306 | 9 522 | 0.80 | 51 | 5.1 | 130 | 13.0 | 1 195 | 18.4 | 3 068 | 728 | 1 205 | 185 | 1 787 |
| Marion | 203 | 30 617 | 0.79 | 461 | 14.0 | 420 | 12.8 | 5 979 | 21.3 | 6 835 | 652 | 3 848 | 2 323 | 6 945 |
| Marlboro | 3 291 | 28 535 | 0.95 | 311 | 10.9 | 300 | 10.5 | 4 671 | 21.3 | 5 678 | 641 | 3 091 | 1 882 | 6 430 |
| Newberry | 1 168 | 36 495 | 0.95 | 516 | 13.7 | 413 | 10.9 | 6 921 | 22.6 | 7 717 | 1 611 | 2 977 | 1 200 | 3 162 |
| Oconee | 795 | 71 919 | 0.94 | 805 | 10.8 | 815 | 11.0 | 12 725 | 21.3 | 18 316 | 3 040 | 7 545 | 2 611 | 3 481 |
| Orangeburg | 3 300 | 91 675 | 0.98 | 1 306 | 14.2 | 1 036 | 11.3 | 15 900 | 21.0 | 17 776 | 4 101 | 6 900 | 5 433 | 5 945 |
| Pickens | 7 053 | 107 882 | 0.79 | 1 137 | 9.5 | 1 021 | 8.5 | 19 332 | 20.1 | 22 122 | 6 152 | 7 894 | 4 825 | 4 000 |
| Richland | 32 002 | 420 897 | 1.23 | 4 917 | 12.6 | 2 698 | 6.9 | 52 903 | 16.7 | 51 172 | 8 388 | 15 798 | 22 856 | 5 876 |
| Saluda | 239 | 16 631 | 0.62 | 264 | 13.3 | 183 | 9.2 | 4 156 | 25.0 | 3 853 | 744 | 1 544 | 549 | 2 731 |
| Spartanburg | 7 986 | 288 786 | 1.06 | 3 845 | 13.4 | 2 660 | 9.3 | 53 232 | 22.2 | 54 324 | 17 325 | 19 615 | 11 802 | 4 103 |

1. Per 1,000 estimated resident population.   2. Data for serious crimes have not been adjusted for underreporting; this may affect comparability between geographic areas and over time.   3. Per 100,000 population estimated by the FBI.

# Table B. States and Counties — Crime, Education, Money Income, and Poverty

| STATE County | Serious crimes known to police, 2011 (cont.)[1] Rate[2] Violent | Property | Education — School enrollment and attainment, 2007–2011 Enrollment[3] Total | Percent private | Attainment[4] (percent) High school graduate or less | Bachelor's degree or more | Local government expenditures,[5] 2009–2010 Total current expenditures (mil dol) | Current expenditures per student (dollars) | Money income, 2007–2011 Per capita income[6] (dollars) | Households Median income Dollars | Percent change, 2000 to 2007–2011 (constant 2011 dollars) | Percent with income of $200,000 or more | Income and poverty, 2011 Median household income (dollars) | Percent below poverty level All persons | Children under 18 years | Children 5 to 17 years in families |
|---|---|---|---|---|---|---|---|---|---|---|---|---|---|---|---|---|
| | 46 | 47 | 48 | 49 | 50 | 51 | 52 | 53 | 54 | 55 | 56 | 57 | 58 | 59 | 60 | 61 |
| **PENNSYLVANIA—Cont'd** | | | | | | | | | | | | | | | | |
| Potter | 114 | 1 108 | 3 686 | 10.9 | 63.6 | 12.8 | 31.7 | 12 088 | 21 491 | 40 000 | -8.1 | 1.8 | 40 599 | 15.7 | 24.6 | 22.0 |
| Schuylkill | 223 | 1 473 | 29 983 | 14.5 | 63.7 | 14.3 | 227.0 | 11 963 | 22 365 | 44 150 | 0.0 | 1.0 | 45 549 | 12.6 | 18.5 | 16.4 |
| Snyder | 233 | 1 923 | 10 062 | 37.2 | 64.4 | 16.3 | 53.3 | 10 866 | 21 891 | 46 184 | -4.9 | 1.6 | 45 460 | 12.0 | 18.9 | 17.5 |
| Somerset | 171 | 1 367 | 15 208 | 14.1 | 65.6 | 14.5 | 115.2 | 11 151 | 20 909 | 41 102 | -1.5 | 1.5 | 39 042 | 13.7 | 20.9 | 18.8 |
| Sullivan | 62 | 1 815 | 1 037 | 12.3 | 63.4 | 12.7 | 10.6 | 16 989 | 21 703 | 38 732 | -5.3 | 1.0 | 38 608 | 13.7 | 21.7 | 18.9 |
| Susquehanna | 129 | 1 481 | 9 269 | 13.5 | 59.2 | 16.0 | 91.3 | 12 641 | 23 392 | 46 392 | 2.2 | 1.4 | 46 814 | 13.4 | 21.1 | 19.0 |
| Tioga | 78 | 1 415 | 10 160 | 13.3 | 56.4 | 17.6 | 68.7 | 11 890 | 21 420 | 42 027 | -2.8 | 1.5 | 41 010 | 15.7 | 22.3 | 20.0 |
| Union | 98 | 1 084 | 11 889 | 48.0 | 57.4 | 21.6 | 48.3 | 11 780 | 22 135 | 46 269 | -15.0 | 3.5 | 46 992 | 14.5 | 16.7 | 14.6 |
| Venango | 156 | 1 296 | 11 629 | 14.7 | 61.2 | 14.5 | 81.5 | 12 447 | 21 128 | 40 986 | -5.9 | 0.8 | 39 608 | 16.6 | 26.3 | 23.0 |
| Warren | 188 | 2 186 | 8 460 | 18.1 | 58.2 | 16.6 | 65.7 | 12 128 | 23 147 | 42 167 | -13.4 | 1.5 | 40 940 | 14.5 | 24.2 | 21.7 |
| Washington | 196 | 1 740 | 48 335 | 17.6 | 51.1 | 24.7 | 360.8 | 12 426 | 26 987 | 51 965 | 2.3 | 2.9 | 52 384 | 10.6 | 13.8 | 11.8 |
| Wayne | 119 | 1 376 | 10 759 | 17.1 | 56.9 | 17.3 | 69.1 | 13 036 | 23 500 | 49 020 | 6.5 | 2.1 | 47 824 | 14.1 | 20.1 | 17.9 |
| Westmoreland | 158 | 1 418 | 80 367 | 17.3 | 48.7 | 24.3 | 574.0 | 11 316 | 26 963 | 48 979 | -2.2 | 2.5 | 46 630 | 10.6 | 15.4 | 13.4 |
| Wyoming | 43 | 1 374 | 6 563 | 20.0 | 59.0 | 17.3 | 52.4 | 13 093 | 23 375 | 48 063 | -2.1 | 1.2 | 49 011 | 12.4 | 19.7 | 17.9 |
| York | 304 | 1 998 | 103 352 | 19.3 | 54.4 | 21.6 | 769.2 | 11 468 | 28 042 | 58 586 | -4.1 | 2.8 | 55 521 | 10.8 | 15.1 | 12.8 |
| **RHODE ISLAND** | 248 | 2 677 | 283 440 | 26.3 | 43.4 | 30.6 | 2 018.1 | 13 920 | 29 685 | 55 975 | -1.5 | 4.3 | 53 152 | 14.7 | 21.5 | 19.3 |
| Bristol | 76 | 1 492 | 14 411 | 36.2 | 34.8 | 41.7 | 89.8 | 12 888 | 36 382 | 70 553 | 3.0 | 8.5 | 68 483 | 8.7 | 8.9 | 7.5 |
| Kent | 119 | 2 317 | 39 611 | 19.6 | 41.5 | 28.9 | 339.7 | 14 271 | 32 358 | 61 279 | -4.7 | 4.0 | 59 880 | 9.5 | 14.0 | 11.3 |
| Newport | 180 | 2 597 | 21 018 | 32.0 | 31.2 | 44.1 | 145.8 | 14 440 | 37 915 | 69 369 | 1.8 | 6.4 | 65 755 | 10.0 | 13.9 | 12.0 |
| Providence | 333 | 3 049 | 171 242 | 28.4 | 48.9 | 25.8 | 1 192.0 | 13 641 | 25 973 | 49 411 | -1.0 | 3.3 | 46 385 | 18.3 | 27.0 | 25.0 |
| Washington | 84 | 1 630 | 37 158 | 16.5 | 31.1 | 42.5 | 250.8 | 14 994 | 36 501 | 72 163 | 0.6 | 6.8 | 68 539 | 9.3 | 11.5 | 9.9 |
| **SOUTH CAROLINA** | 572 | 3 904 | 1 165 667 | 15.0 | 47.3 | 24.2 | 6 572.6 | 9 089 | 23 854 | 44 587 | -10.9 | 2.5 | 42 477 | 18.8 | 27.5 | 25.4 |
| Abbeville | 498 | 1 855 | 6 375 | 18.6 | 57.0 | 13.9 | 31.6 | 9 733 | 17 424 | 34 670 | -21.3 | 0.3 | 36 787 | 20.4 | 29.4 | 26.6 |
| Aiken | 372 | 3 893 | 38 934 | 13.2 | 47.6 | 23.7 | 189.3 | 7 685 | 24 648 | 43 999 | -14.0 | 2.6 | 42 826 | 20.2 | 31.6 | 27.8 |
| Allendale | 977 | 3 340 | 2 346 | 6.4 | 65.7 | 13.4 | 19.9 | 12 570 | 13 684 | 22 982 | -18.5 | 1.2 | 24 820 | 39.9 | 48.9 | 44.0 |
| Anderson | 585 | 5 123 | 45 563 | 13.8 | 52.2 | 18.1 | 258.4 | 8 319 | 22 494 | 42 854 | -13.8 | 1.6 | 41 000 | 15.7 | 24.1 | 22.2 |
| Bamberg | 526 | 4 334 | 4 759 | 16.2 | 50.2 | 18.0 | 24.6 | 10 240 | 17 589 | 26 697 | -17.6 | 1.2 | 28 467 | 29.5 | 37.4 | 34.2 |
| Barnwell | 765 | 4 781 | 5 977 | 8.9 | 62.9 | 10.8 | 42.4 | 9 768 | 18 141 | 34 546 | -10.5 | 0.7 | 33 178 | 24.1 | 35.4 | 32.5 |
| Beaufort | 513 | 3 209 | 33 647 | 21.0 | 33.7 | 37.5 | 211.8 | 10 705 | 32 891 | 57 133 | -10.0 | 5.7 | 55 018 | 12.9 | 22.8 | 22.7 |
| Berkeley | 412 | 3 176 | 46 009 | 15.7 | 48.6 | 19.2 | 244.3 | 8 393 | 23 109 | 51 093 | -5.2 | 1.6 | 49 516 | 15.5 | 23.4 | 23.1 |
| Calhoun | 482 | 3 374 | 3 632 | 20.0 | 50.7 | 20.3 | 19.8 | 11 429 | 22 203 | 37 318 | -15.6 | 1.3 | 38 417 | 20.0 | 30.0 | 27.5 |
| Charleston | 478 | 3 534 | 89 544 | 18.5 | 35.2 | 37.7 | 393.2 | 9 132 | 29 738 | 50 133 | -1.8 | 4.8 | 49 432 | 19.1 | 25.7 | 23.0 |
| Cherokee | 338 | 2 177 | 13 631 | 10.6 | 64.2 | 11.5 | 75.6 | 8 251 | 17 910 | 35 025 | -23.2 | 0.8 | 36 400 | 22.5 | 32.4 | 31.2 |
| Chester | 728 | 3 842 | 7 705 | 9.0 | 63.7 | 11.1 | 50.9 | 8 999 | 17 929 | 32 112 | -26.7 | 1.5 | 32 857 | 29.4 | 45.7 | 37.2 |
| Chesterfield | 455 | 3 259 | 11 149 | 9.1 | 64.4 | 12.0 | 67.3 | 8 613 | 17 542 | 32 304 | -18.8 | 0.8 | 30 378 | 25.2 | 32.5 | 29.6 |
| Clarendon | 684 | 3 884 | 8 073 | 14.3 | 63.8 | 13.4 | 48.7 | 9 110 | 16 950 | 33 355 | -8.9 | 1.0 | 30 780 | 22.9 | 37.2 | 36.4 |
| Colleton | 579 | 5 233 | 9 622 | 12.8 | 62.4 | 14.4 | 56.6 | 8 963 | 17 702 | 31 700 | -21.0 | 0.8 | 32 963 | 28.1 | 40.1 | 38.0 |
| Darlington | 876 | 5 219 | 16 933 | 15.4 | 58.7 | 15.8 | 92.3 | 8 441 | 20 743 | 38 567 | -8.1 | 1.9 | 36 248 | 23.9 | 35.1 | 32.5 |
| Dillon | 1 273 | 5 636 | 7 537 | 7.4 | 71.2 | 7.8 | 52.4 | 8 521 | 14 135 | 26 067 | -27.5 | 0.6 | 26 308 | 32.9 | 47.7 | 40.8 |
| Dorchester | 463 | 3 658 | 37 589 | 19.5 | 41.2 | 24.6 | 206.3 | 8 372 | 24 787 | 54 875 | -6.2 | 2.2 | 51 332 | 12.9 | 19.1 | 18.4 |
| Edgefield | 154 | 2 106 | 6 281 | 13.4 | 55.5 | 17.9 | 34.7 | 8 649 | 20 549 | 44 090 | -7.1 | 0.6 | 42 289 | 19.6 | 27.8 | 24.4 |
| Fairfield | 582 | 3 681 | 5 792 | 14.7 | 59.5 | 14.8 | 41.1 | 12 602 | 19 445 | 34 117 | -16.8 | 1.1 | 34 700 | 22.8 | 31.7 | 28.9 |
| Florence | 546 | 4 807 | 35 266 | 13.5 | 52.8 | 20.5 | 217.1 | 9 374 | 22 198 | 41 325 | -12.9 | 2.0 | 39 663 | 21.3 | 31.0 | 27.0 |
| Georgetown | 634 | 4 129 | 13 055 | 11.0 | 49.3 | 22.0 | 96.4 | 9 753 | 24 517 | 42 677 | -10.5 | 3.1 | 40 864 | 22.4 | 37.0 | 32.7 |
| Greenville | 561 | 3 654 | 112 948 | 23.2 | 42.1 | 30.3 | 545.6 | 7 688 | 26 412 | 48 518 | -12.7 | 3.3 | 48 480 | 15.8 | 24.8 | 23.0 |
| Greenwood | 1 866 | 4 937 | 17 336 | 7.4 | 52.2 | 21.9 | 105.2 | 8 851 | 21 588 | 39 366 | -16.0 | 1.9 | 37 038 | 20.2 | 28.8 | 26.3 |
| Hampton | 780 | 4 180 | 5 171 | 8.6 | 63.7 | 11.3 | 42.0 | 11 127 | 16 728 | 35 914 | -7.5 | 0.3 | 31 915 | 28.3 | 39.1 | 36.9 |
| Horry | 670 | 5 603 | 55 419 | 8.5 | 47.1 | 21.9 | 375.2 | 9 929 | 24 531 | 42 877 | -12.9 | 2.2 | 38 807 | 18.8 | 31.6 | 29.2 |
| Jasper | 279 | 3 216 | 5 739 | 17.9 | 64.1 | 11.1 | 38.9 | 11 559 | 17 952 | 36 696 | -11.5 | 1.9 | 34 927 | 25.8 | 38.8 | 38.6 |
| Kershaw | 477 | 3 196 | 14 782 | 9.4 | 52.0 | 18.2 | 86.4 | 8 246 | 21 865 | 43 509 | -17.0 | 1.6 | 41 055 | 18.5 | 27.0 | 25.6 |
| Lancaster | 496 | 3 388 | 16 664 | 9.2 | 54.4 | 16.8 | 102.5 | 8 771 | 20 085 | 40 034 | -14.5 | 1.2 | 40 372 | 18.5 | 27.5 | 27.1 |
| Laurens | 770 | 3 751 | 16 011 | 16.9 | 59.1 | 14.9 | 80.5 | 8 760 | 19 330 | 38 713 | -15.5 | 0.9 | 35 839 | 23.1 | 36.6 | 36.0 |
| Lee | 540 | 3 384 | 4 360 | 16.7 | 69.9 | 8.0 | 24.4 | 9 809 | 14 641 | 27 011 | -25.6 | 0.8 | 28 733 | 30.4 | 40.4 | 37.4 |
| Lexington | 401 | 2 946 | 65 620 | 12.7 | 41.0 | 27.3 | 343.9 | 9 325 | 26 842 | 52 857 | -12.3 | 2.6 | 50 738 | 14.5 | 21.4 | 20.3 |
| McCormick | 338 | 1 449 | 1 748 | 9.3 | 50.5 | 17.3 | 10.9 | 12 610 | 20 163 | 36 243 | -15.0 | 0.6 | 35 209 | 19.6 | 34.1 | 33.0 |
| Marion | 834 | 6 111 | 7 837 | 6.7 | 64.3 | 12.7 | 54.2 | 10 008 | 17 072 | 31 762 | -11.3 | 1.4 | 27 726 | 31.6 | 42.4 | 40.4 |
| Marlboro | 1 083 | 5 347 | 6 855 | 6.0 | 71.8 | 8.8 | 44.3 | 9 681 | 14 275 | 28 511 | -20.6 | 0.8 | 28 662 | 32.5 | 43.8 | 39.6 |
| Newberry | 337 | 2 825 | 8 793 | 14.6 | 55.4 | 20.1 | 57.7 | 9 841 | 22 203 | 42 866 | -3.4 | 1.5 | 38 024 | 20.0 | 32.7 | 30.1 |
| Oconee | 547 | 2 935 | 16 448 | 10.9 | 50.9 | 21.3 | 105.0 | 9 755 | 24 075 | 42 641 | -13.9 | 2.3 | 42 142 | 19.0 | 28.4 | 25.9 |
| Orangeburg | 515 | 5 429 | 24 751 | 14.5 | 59.2 | 17.3 | 148.6 | 10 375 | 18 223 | 33 162 | -16.9 | 1.3 | 31 605 | 24.2 | 34.0 | 33.8 |
| Pickens | 335 | 3 665 | 39 113 | 11.1 | 48.9 | 23.1 | 128.7 | 7 754 | 21 036 | 42 241 | -13.6 | 2.0 | 40 221 | 19.8 | 23.5 | 19.7 |
| Richland | 921 | 4 955 | 117 361 | 17.4 | 33.3 | 36.1 | 751.1 | 10 262 | 26 225 | 48 485 | -10.1 | 3.5 | 45 182 | 18.6 | 23.9 | 21.5 |
| Saluda | 532 | 2 198 | 4 610 | 11.4 | 64.0 | 13.5 | 20.0 | 9 357 | 18 563 | 39 095 | -19.1 | 0.8 | 39 689 | 18.9 | 28.2 | 27.1 |
| Spartanburg | 500 | 3 604 | 71 887 | 15.6 | 50.6 | 20.4 | 436.9 | 9 305 | 22 275 | 43 563 | -14.1 | 1.9 | 40 687 | 19.0 | 26.9 | 24.7 |

1. Data for serious crimes have not been adjusted for underreporting; this may affect comparability between geographic areas and over time.   2. Per 100,000 population estimated by the FBI.   3. All persons 3 years old and over enrolled in nursery school through college.   4. Persons 25 years old and over.   5. Elementary and secondary education expenditures.   6. Based on population estimated by the American Community Survey, 2007–2011.

# Table B. States and Counties — **Personal Income**

| STATE County | Total (mil dol) | Percent change, 2010–2011 | Per capita[1] Dollars | Per capita[1] Rank | Wages and salaries[2] (mil dol) | Proprietors' income (mil dol) | Dividends, interest, and rent (mil dol) | Total | Transfer payments (mil dol) Government payments to individuals Total | Social Security | Medical payments | Income maintenance | Unemployment insurance |
|---|---|---|---|---|---|---|---|---|---|---|---|---|---|
| | 62 | 63 | 64 | 65 | 66 | 67 | 68 | 69 | 70 | 71 | 72 | 73 | 74 |
| **PENNSYLVANIA—Cont'd** | | | | | | | | | | | | | |
| Potter | 561 | 6.1 | 32 120 | 1 857 | 264 | 80 | 80 | 159 | 155 | 60 | 64 | 13 | 9 |
| Schuylkill | 4 830 | 3.8 | 32 744 | 1 750 | 2 342 | 247 | 695 | 1 393 | 1 360 | 478 | 575 | 104 | 106 |
| Snyder | 1 236 | 4.2 | 31 031 | 2 091 | 623 | 116 | 178 | 367 | 358 | 107 | 195 | 21 | 20 |
| Somerset | 2 597 | 4.9 | 33 549 | 1 592 | 1 166 | 183 | 393 | 703 | 686 | 245 | 292 | 53 | 57 |
| Sullivan | 205 | 7.5 | 31 566 | 1 984 | 73 | 12 | 42 | 64 | 63 | 25 | 29 | 3 | 2 |
| Susquehanna | 1 338 | 3.7 | 30 975 | 2 108 | 435 | 103 | 216 | 341 | 332 | 137 | 133 | 29 | 15 |
| Tioga | 1 277 | 10.7 | 30 100 | 2 270 | 682 | 61 | 190 | 346 | 337 | 136 | 135 | 29 | 13 |
| Union | 1 423 | 5.4 | 31 721 | 1 951 | 845 | 134 | 222 | 276 | 267 | 108 | 110 | 18 | 16 |
| Venango | 1 839 | 4.6 | 33 628 | 1 582 | 977 | 80 | 257 | 606 | 594 | 189 | 304 | 50 | 28 |
| Warren | 1 379 | 5.7 | 33 268 | 1 662 | 699 | 85 | 208 | 385 | 376 | 144 | 163 | 30 | 21 |
| Washington | 9 630 | 10.8 | 46 237 | 330 | 5 051 | 509 | 1 215 | 1 973 | 1 927 | 704 | 886 | 137 | 96 |
| Wayne | 1 719 | 4.0 | 32 431 | 1 792 | 706 | 100 | 326 | 464 | 453 | 185 | 190 | 33 | 21 |
| Westmoreland | 15 129 | 5.3 | 41 510 | 615 | 6 853 | 730 | 2 100 | 3 515 | 3 435 | 1 247 | 1 561 | 225 | 223 |
| Wyoming | 917 | 4.1 | 32 275 | 1 828 | 551 | 27 | 142 | 233 | 227 | 87 | 95 | 19 | 15 |
| York | 16 326 | 4.9 | 37 380 | 1 040 | 9 565 | 816 | 2 422 | 3 069 | 2 972 | 1 193 | 1 151 | 258 | 202 |
| **RHODE ISLAND** | 46 125 | 4.3 | 43 875 | X | 27 864 | 3 232 | 7 505 | 9 515 | 9 283 | 2 740 | 4 205 | 1 065 | 609 |
| Bristol | 2 735 | 5.0 | 54 919 | 114 | 685 | 176 | 634 | 378 | 367 | 151 | 140 | 22 | 25 |
| Kent | 7 642 | 4.1 | 46 167 | 332 | 4 213 | 388 | 1 126 | 1 463 | 1 426 | 505 | 588 | 109 | 98 |
| Newport | 4 303 | 4.6 | 52 038 | 161 | 2 804 | 195 | 985 | 687 | 669 | 238 | 282 | 54 | 45 |
| Providence | 25 236 | 4.3 | 40 268 | 717 | 17 346 | 2 100 | 3 544 | 5 989 | 5 850 | 1 475 | 2 808 | 820 | 372 |
| Washington | 6 209 | 4.3 | 49 057 | 230 | 2 816 | 374 | 1 216 | 999 | 971 | 372 | 386 | 61 | 70 |
| **SOUTH CAROLINA** | 156 231 | 4.7 | 33 388 | X | 96 784 | 9 965 | 22 107 | 36 270 | 35 242 | 12 459 | 13 592 | 4 572 | 1 232 |
| Abbeville | 684 | 2.8 | 27 169 | 2 742 | 262 | 41 | 74 | 214 | 208 | 77 | 70 | 31 | 8 |
| Aiken | 5 646 | 4.7 | 35 141 | 1 352 | 3 713 | 344 | 783 | 1 359 | 1 324 | 480 | 533 | 156 | 40 |
| Allendale | 266 | 0.4 | 26 164 | 2 863 | 180 | 20 | 27 | 98 | 96 | 24 | 41 | 23 | 3 |
| Anderson | 5 854 | 4.5 | 31 059 | 2 082 | 2 780 | 362 | 716 | 1 494 | 1 453 | 583 | 530 | 179 | 40 |
| Bamberg | 412 | 1.5 | 25 818 | 2 899 | 185 | 29 | 44 | 159 | 155 | 41 | 65 | 27 | 2 |
| Barnwell | 583 | 1.1 | 26 064 | 2 874 | 241 | 32 | 63 | 224 | 219 | 59 | 102 | 37 | 11 |
| Beaufort | 6 861 | 5.2 | 41 662 | 601 | 3 597 | 412 | 2 105 | 1 309 | 1 275 | 585 | 457 | 95 | 29 |
| Berkeley | 6 090 | 7.1 | 33 184 | 1 676 | 2 335 | 531 | 562 | 1 087 | 1 047 | 360 | 357 | 142 | 29 |
| Calhoun | 521 | 4.1 | 34 431 | 1 448 | 217 | 62 | 59 | 126 | 123 | 44 | 46 | 18 | 6 |
| Charleston | 14 900 | 5.2 | 41 656 | 603 | 13 458 | 1 672 | 2 710 | 2 556 | 2 478 | 805 | 1 044 | 290 | 93 |
| Cherokee | 1 492 | 3.7 | 26 856 | 2 783 | 822 | 63 | 158 | 475 | 463 | 166 | 170 | 70 | 21 |
| Chester | 929 | 3.3 | 28 237 | 2 578 | 400 | 47 | 90 | 300 | 293 | 100 | 115 | 47 | 12 |
| Chesterfield | 1 143 | 3.6 | 24 554 | 3 001 | 598 | 47 | 125 | 389 | 379 | 123 | 157 | 65 | 4 |
| Clarendon | 848 | 1.3 | 24 431 | 3 008 | 279 | 47 | 107 | 327 | 320 | 103 | 129 | 61 | 3 |
| Colleton | 1 132 | 2.9 | 29 311 | 2 408 | 426 | 67 | 137 | 383 | 375 | 113 | 157 | 62 | 16 |
| Darlington | 2 005 | 1.8 | 29 355 | 2 400 | 1 055 | 76 | 240 | 613 | 598 | 195 | 231 | 110 | 20 |
| Dillon | 750 | 0.5 | 23 616 | 3 042 | 347 | 32 | 69 | 291 | 284 | 76 | 121 | 61 | 8 |
| Dorchester | 4 715 | 9.7 | 33 468 | 1 611 | 1 379 | 49 | 429 | 914 | 883 | 285 | 337 | 106 | 46 |
| Edgefield | 897 | 6.3 | 33 615 | 1 583 | 274 | 23 | 95 | 173 | 167 | 65 | 60 | 27 | 2 |
| Fairfield | 638 | 0.0 | 27 062 | 2 756 | 445 | 16 | 68 | 227 | 221 | 65 | 92 | 36 | 9 |
| Florence | 4 749 | 3.5 | 34 450 | 1 442 | 3 217 | 291 | 594 | 1 289 | 1 259 | 347 | 554 | 197 | 41 |
| Georgetown | 2 304 | 3.5 | 38 403 | 924 | 1 060 | 176 | 478 | 703 | 690 | 244 | 319 | 72 | 18 |
| Greenville | 17 386 | 5.9 | 37 689 | 1 005 | 13 449 | 1 203 | 2 424 | 3 186 | 3 084 | 1 184 | 1 177 | 341 | 111 |
| Greenwood | 2 123 | 3.2 | 30 398 | 2 221 | 1 430 | 103 | 302 | 601 | 586 | 207 | 211 | 78 | 22 |
| Hampton | 567 | 2.0 | 27 235 | 2 730 | 253 | 34 | 68 | 195 | 190 | 53 | 86 | 33 | 6 |
| Horry | 8 055 | 4.3 | 29 148 | 2 428 | 4 553 | 510 | 1 413 | 2 301 | 2 240 | 927 | 781 | 235 | 108 |
| Jasper | 678 | 4.3 | 26 896 | 2 776 | 322 | 35 | 48 | 178 | 173 | 52 | 68 | 32 | 6 |
| Kershaw | 2 076 | 4.2 | 33 331 | 1 646 | 812 | 122 | 235 | 488 | 474 | 179 | 179 | 55 | 16 |
| Lancaster | 2 049 | 5.9 | 26 302 | 2 849 | 857 | 122 | 269 | 645 | 627 | 248 | 244 | 78 | 19 |
| Laurens | 1 970 | 4.1 | 29 609 | 2 360 | 844 | 35 | 210 | 635 | 620 | 211 | 265 | 80 | 19 |
| Lee | 501 | 1.7 | 26 379 | 2 841 | 162 | 30 | 49 | 186 | 182 | 47 | 76 | 39 | 6 |
| Lexington | 9 406 | 4.0 | 35 211 | 1 338 | 4 798 | 706 | 1 184 | 1 731 | 1 672 | 634 | 634 | 179 | 58 |
| McCormick | 276 | 3.5 | 27 509 | 2 684 | 78 | 12 | 58 | 111 | 109 | 45 | 43 | 13 | 1 |
| Marion | 867 | 0.8 | 26 397 | 2 839 | 291 | 110 | 84 | 346 | 339 | 91 | 150 | 65 | 16 |
| Marlboro | 689 | 2.1 | 24 156 | 3 024 | 363 | 16 | 67 | 271 | 264 | 77 | 105 | 54 | 12 |
| Newberry | 1 120 | 2.6 | 29 697 | 2 340 | 594 | 30 | 144 | 322 | 314 | 112 | 122 | 42 | 11 |
| Oconee | 2 379 | 3.2 | 31 964 | 1 895 | 1 278 | 104 | 444 | 658 | 642 | 274 | 253 | 56 | 17 |
| Orangeburg | 2 662 | 2.8 | 28 965 | 2 453 | 1 422 | 127 | 296 | 870 | 849 | 244 | 305 | 156 | 38 |
| Pickens | 3 328 | 3.3 | 27 833 | 2 634 | 1 673 | 144 | 465 | 879 | 853 | 331 | 336 | 84 | 24 |
| Richland | 14 143 | 4.7 | 36 347 | 1 159 | 12 736 | 787 | 1 831 | 2 632 | 2 548 | 745 | 929 | 341 | 101 |
| Saluda | 687 | 4.5 | 34 544 | 1 434 | 173 | 21 | 63 | 148 | 144 | 55 | 53 | 22 | 2 |
| Spartanburg | 9 085 | 4.2 | 31 670 | 1 962 | 6 418 | 664 | 1 268 | 2 183 | 2 119 | 813 | 803 | 241 | 74 |

1. Based on the resident population estimated as of July 1 of the year shown.　2. Includes supplements to wages and salaries.

| STATE County | Earnings, 2011 | | | | | | | | | Social Security beneficiaries, December 2011 | | | Housing units, 2010 | |
|---|---|---|---|---|---|---|---|---|---|---|---|---|---|---|
| | | | Percent by selected industries | | | | | | | | | | | |
| | | | Goods-related[1] | | Service-related and health | | | | | | | Supplemental Security Income recipients, December 2011 | | |
| | Total (mil dol) | Farm | Total | Manufacturing | Information and professional and technical services | Retail trade | Finance, insurance, and real estate | Health care and social services | Government | Number | Rate[2] | | Total | Percent change, 2000–2010 |
| | 75 | 76 | 77 | 78 | 79 | 80 | 81 | 82 | 83 | 84 | 85 | 86 | 87 | 88 |
| PENNSYLVANIA—Cont'd | | | | | | | | | | | | | | |
| Potter | 344 | 2.1 | 18.0 | 10.5 | D | 5.4 | 2.4 | D | 16.3 | 4 750 | 272 | 479 | 12 932 | 6.4 |
| Schuylkill | 2 589 | 1.1 | 28.0 | 22.4 | 4.2 | 7.2 | 2.9 | 15.5 | 17.5 | 37 495 | 254 | 3 753 | 69 323 | 2.2 |
| Snyder | 739 | 5.3 | D | 21.3 | 3.6 | 11.1 | 2.2 | D | 18.0 | 8 370 | 210 | 696 | 16 027 | 7.6 |
| Somerset | 1 350 | 1.7 | 25.1 | 11.4 | 4.2 | 7.4 | 3.4 | 12.5 | 19.0 | 19 610 | 253 | 2 408 | 38 113 | 2.6 |
| Sullivan | 84 | 0.0 | D | D | 3.5 | 8.0 | D | D | 24.9 | 1 940 | 299 | 132 | 6 304 | 4.8 |
| Susquehanna | 538 | 0.8 | 31.0 | 4.7 | 4.0 | 8.3 | 2.8 | 9.1 | 20.2 | 10 560 | 244 | 948 | 22 968 | 5.2 |
| Tioga | 743 | 0.5 | 27.3 | 15.6 | 4.0 | 7.9 | 5.8 | D | 21.7 | 10 735 | 253 | 1 184 | 21 364 | 7.4 |
| Union | 979 | 3.7 | D | 6.8 | 2.6 | 5.9 | 3.4 | D | 25.6 | 8 100 | 181 | 578 | 16 997 | 15.8 |
| Venango | 1 057 | 1.7 | 33.1 | 29.2 | 2.4 | 7.4 | 3.5 | 14.7 | 18.9 | 14 825 | 271 | 2 170 | 27 464 | 2.1 |
| Warren | 784 | 0.1 | 27.3 | 19.5 | 3.3 | 6.7 | 5.2 | 14.7 | 16.3 | 10 805 | 261 | 983 | 23 560 | 2.2 |
| Washington | 5 560 | -0.2 | 28.8 | 11.0 | 7.8 | 5.9 | 7.0 | 12.0 | 10.7 | 50 860 | 244 | 5 638 | 92 977 | 6.5 |
| Wayne | 806 | 0.2 | 17.5 | 3.5 | 8.5 | 10.3 | 4.5 | 14.3 | 25.4 | 13 770 | 260 | 1 052 | 31 653 | 3.5 |
| Westmoreland | 7 583 | 0.2 | 24.0 | 15.8 | 7.3 | 8.0 | 3.6 | 13.2 | 13.3 | 91 165 | 250 | 8 768 | 168 199 | 4.4 |
| Wyoming | 578 | -0.6 | 44.0 | 32.5 | 3.0 | 6.5 | 2.7 | D | 11.8 | 6 710 | 236 | 665 | 13 254 | 4.3 |
| York | 10 382 | 0.6 | 29.2 | 21.0 | 7.3 | 6.5 | 3.8 | 13.5 | 14.4 | 85 795 | 196 | 8 197 | 178 671 | 14.0 |
| RHODE ISLAND | 31 097 | 0.0 | 0.0 | 9.1 | 10.9 | 5.7 | 9.9 | 14.8 | 18.5 | 207 122 | 197 | 32 218 | 463 388 | 5.4 |
| Bristol | 861 | 0.0 | 17.7 | 11.7 | 7.3 | 5.1 | 5.9 | 12.9 | 16.9 | 10 715 | 215 | 674 | 20 850 | 4.9 |
| Kent | 4 601 | 0.0 | D | 11.8 | 9.5 | 9.3 | 9.9 | 15.1 | 14.0 | 36 790 | 222 | 3 293 | 73 701 | 4.7 |
| Newport | 2 999 | 0.2 | D | 7.5 | 12.0 | 5.2 | 4.2 | 7.2 | 40.4 | 17 560 | 212 | 1 371 | 41 796 | 5.6 |
| Providence | 19 445 | 0.0 | 12.7 | 7.4 | 11.8 | 4.5 | 11.9 | 16.4 | 15.5 | 116 420 | 186 | 25 353 | 264 835 | 4.6 |
| Washington | 3 190 | 0.2 | 20.9 | 15.9 | 7.6 | 8.7 | 4.3 | 12.1 | 23.5 | 25 635 | 203 | 1 527 | 62 206 | 9.5 |
| SOUTH CAROLINA | 106 749 | 0.3 | 19.4 | 13.9 | 8.6 | 7.4 | 6.9 | 9.4 | 22.8 | 956 097 | 204 | 114 974 | 2 137 683 | 21.9 |
| Abbeville | 303 | -0.4 | D | 28.3 | 3.4 | 4.5 | 2.6 | D | 24.7 | 6 120 | 243 | 709 | 12 079 | 3.6 |
| Aiken | 4 057 | -0.4 | 23.2 | 12.6 | 11.3 | 6.2 | 4.0 | 7.0 | 12.3 | 35 485 | 221 | 4 112 | 72 249 | 16.6 |
| Allendale | 201 | 6.7 | D | 27.2 | D | 2.9 | D | D | 28.5 | 2 155 | 212 | 679 | 4 486 | -1.8 |
| Anderson | 3 142 | 0.1 | 30.5 | 24.2 | 3.7 | 9.6 | 3.9 | 8.1 | 21.6 | 44 645 | 237 | 4 170 | 84 774 | 15.8 |
| Bamberg | 214 | 5.6 | 18.2 | 15.2 | 2.9 | 9.7 | D | 8.4 | 25.9 | 3 605 | 226 | 772 | 7 716 | 8.2 |
| Barnwell | 273 | 2.3 | 31.4 | 27.7 | 5.9 | 9.2 | 1.9 | 8.7 | 27.1 | 4 875 | 218 | 1 096 | 10 484 | 2.9 |
| Beaufort | 4 008 | 0.8 | 6.8 | 1.1 | 8.4 | 7.5 | 7.0 | 7.5 | 39.6 | 39 325 | 239 | 1 888 | 93 023 | 53.7 |
| Berkeley | 2 866 | 0.1 | D | 17.6 | 18.7 | 6.0 | 5.1 | 3.9 | 18.9 | 29 215 | 159 | 3 197 | 73 372 | 34.2 |
| Calhoun | 279 | 5.7 | 45.9 | 32.3 | 2.5 | 3.2 | 1.9 | D | 13.7 | 3 575 | 236 | 487 | 7 340 | 7.0 |
| Charleston | 15 129 | 0.0 | 12.7 | 7.6 | 10.9 | 6.8 | 8.2 | 10.6 | 28.4 | 61 640 | 172 | 7 476 | 169 984 | 20.5 |
| Cherokee | 885 | 2.0 | D | 36.0 | D | 7.5 | 3.3 | 6.4 | 13.9 | 13 145 | 237 | 1 642 | 23 997 | 7.1 |
| Chester | 447 | 1.2 | 38.1 | 34.0 | 4.3 | 6.2 | 2.7 | D | 19.6 | 7 990 | 243 | 1 081 | 14 701 | 2.3 |
| Chesterfield | 645 | -1.3 | 40.7 | 36.2 | 2.6 | 8.0 | 2.2 | 8.5 | 16.2 | 10 230 | 220 | 1 658 | 21 482 | 14.2 |
| Clarendon | 326 | 1.1 | 8.9 | 3.6 | 4.3 | 13.0 | 3.8 | 8.1 | 37.3 | 8 730 | 251 | 1 727 | 17 467 | 14.1 |
| Colleton | 494 | 1.6 | D | 8.3 | D | 9.2 | 5.2 | 13.2 | 22.1 | 9 655 | 250 | 1 722 | 19 901 | 9.8 |
| Darlington | 1 130 | 0.6 | 36.2 | 32.4 | 2.3 | 6.7 | 2.5 | 9.5 | 14.1 | 15 605 | 228 | 2 953 | 30 297 | 4.7 |
| Dillon | 379 | 0.9 | 23.6 | 21.6 | 1.8 | 10.5 | 4.0 | D | 20.8 | 6 805 | 214 | 1 725 | 13 742 | 8.4 |
| Dorchester | 1 428 | 0.4 | D | 20.7 | 5.0 | 10.2 | 3.6 | 8.1 | 21.7 | 22 610 | 160 | 2 472 | 55 186 | 48.3 |
| Edgefield | 298 | 4.1 | 18.8 | 15.1 | D | 12.5 | 1.7 | D | 36.2 | 5 080 | 190 | 668 | 10 559 | 14.7 |
| Fairfield | 461 | 0.2 | D | 19.9 | D | 3.8 | D | 5.8 | 17.7 | 5 380 | 228 | 886 | 11 681 | 12.5 |
| Florence | 3 508 | 0.2 | 15.6 | 12.1 | 7.4 | 8.2 | 14.5 | 13.4 | 20.8 | 28 295 | 205 | 5 637 | 58 666 | 13.2 |
| Georgetown | 1 236 | 0.0 | 22.2 | 13.0 | D | 8.5 | 5.3 | 11.1 | 23.7 | 18 015 | 300 | 1 686 | 33 672 | 19.1 |
| Greenville | 14 653 | 0.0 | 19.7 | 14.4 | 12.0 | 6.8 | 6.8 | 9.6 | 12.1 | 86 745 | 188 | 8 904 | 195 462 | 20.1 |
| Greenwood | 1 533 | 0.1 | D | 23.6 | 5.3 | 6.6 | 3.4 | 11.9 | 26.2 | 15 795 | 226 | 1 740 | 31 054 | 9.9 |
| Hampton | 287 | 1.6 | 16.8 | 13.2 | D | 7.4 | D | D | 33.0 | 4 545 | 218 | 921 | 9 140 | 6.5 |
| Horry | 5 062 | -0.2 | 10.9 | 3.5 | 6.4 | 12.0 | 11.2 | 11.1 | 18.0 | 69 015 | 250 | 5 422 | 185 992 | 52.3 |
| Jasper | 357 | 0.2 | 14.8 | 3.4 | D | 14.2 | 4.8 | 12.7 | 22.7 | 4 345 | 172 | 666 | 10 299 | 29.9 |
| Kershaw | 934 | 0.9 | 29.2 | 22.2 | 6.5 | 9.8 | 7.3 | 6.4 | 20.2 | 13 820 | 222 | 1 489 | 27 478 | 21.1 |
| Lancaster | 979 | -0.2 | 19.3 | 14.8 | 13.8 | 7.8 | 5.9 | 15.6 | 18.7 | 18 115 | 233 | 1 638 | 32 687 | 30.9 |
| Laurens | 878 | -2.0 | D | 30.9 | D | 5.9 | 2.1 | D | 22.3 | 16 725 | 251 | 2 177 | 30 709 | 1.6 |
| Lee | 192 | 6.5 | 19.3 | 15.2 | D | 6.2 | D | 11.5 | 31.1 | 4 235 | 223 | 1 040 | 7 775 | 1.4 |
| Lexington | 5 504 | 0.1 | 19.8 | 11.5 | 6.9 | 9.3 | 6.6 | 8.2 | 20.4 | 46 550 | 174 | 4 064 | 113 957 | 25.3 |
| McCormick | 89 | 5.7 | 14.3 | 10.3 | D | 3.6 | D | D | 47.7 | 3 375 | 336 | 298 | 5 453 | 22.3 |
| Marion | 401 | 7.5 | D | 9.2 | D | 12.2 | D | 18.2 | 20.3 | 8 015 | 244 | 1 782 | 14 953 | -1.3 |
| Marlboro | 379 | 0.3 | D | 37.5 | D | 5.9 | 1.7 | D | 30.4 | 6 735 | 236 | 1 532 | 12 072 | 1.5 |
| Newberry | 624 | -0.1 | 45.7 | 40.1 | D | 6.5 | 1.8 | D | 20.1 | 8 735 | 232 | 984 | 17 922 | 6.6 |
| Oconee | 1 382 | 1.7 | D | 26.7 | D | 6.6 | 2.5 | 7.0 | 17.4 | 20 680 | 278 | 1 457 | 38 763 | 19.7 |
| Orangeburg | 1 549 | 1.0 | 24.9 | 22.0 | 2.8 | 9.8 | 3.6 | 7.4 | 27.8 | 20 480 | 223 | 3 909 | 42 504 | 8.2 |
| Pickens | 1 817 | -0.1 | D | 17.0 | 4.3 | 8.9 | 4.0 | 9.1 | 32.4 | 25 095 | 210 | 2 091 | 51 244 | 11.4 |
| Richland | 13 523 | 0.0 | 9.2 | 5.7 | 11.1 | 5.3 | 10.0 | 10.8 | 32.7 | 57 105 | 147 | 8 048 | 161 725 | 24.6 |
| Saluda | 194 | 7.0 | 40.6 | 36.8 | D | 5.2 | 3.5 | 3.8 | 24.4 | 4 405 | 222 | 517 | 9 289 | 8.7 |
| Spartanburg | 7 082 | 0.2 | 30.2 | 25.5 | 5.3 | 6.2 | 5.9 | 8.8 | 17.2 | 62 070 | 216 | 7 049 | 122 628 | 14.6 |

1. Includes mining, construction, and manufacturing.    2. Per 1,000 resident population enumerated in the 2010 census.

# Table B. States and Counties — Housing, Labor Force, and Employment

| STATE County | Total | Percent | Median value[1] | With a mortgage | Without a mortgage[2] | Median rent[3] | Median rent as a percent of income | Substandard units[4] (percent) | Total | Percent change, 2011–2012 | Total | Rate[5] | Total | Management, business, science and arts | Construction, production, and maintenance occupations |
|---|---|---|---|---|---|---|---|---|---|---|---|---|---|---|---|
| | 89 | 90 | 91 | 92 | 93 | 94 | 95 | 96 | 97 | 98 | 99 | 100 | 101 | 102 | 103 |
| **PENNSYLVANIA—Cont'd** | | | | | | | | | | | | | | | |
| Potter | 7 196 | 75.2 | 91 100 | 23.2 | 14.2 | 597 | 30.3 | 2.3 | 7 881 | -0.8 | 720 | 9.1 | 7 118 | 27.8 | 36.7 |
| Schuylkill | 60 029 | 76.6 | 91 200 | 22.3 | 14.7 | 571 | 27.0 | 1.2 | 73 888 | 1.4 | 6 978 | 9.4 | 64 162 | 27.4 | 33.2 |
| Snyder | 14 320 | 75.8 | 128 300 | 22.6 | 12.3 | 622 | 24.9 | 2.3 | 18 859 | -0.9 | 1 540 | 8.2 | 18 897 | 25.0 | 33.9 |
| Somerset | 30 168 | 79.1 | 94 200 | 22.4 | 13.3 | 529 | 26.1 | 1.2 | 38 477 | -1.4 | 3 379 | 8.8 | 34 008 | 27.1 | 33.8 |
| Sullivan | 2 438 | 82.9 | 123 700 | 24.8 | 12.4 | 460 | 27.7 | 1.6 | 3 306 | 1.5 | 244 | 7.4 | 2 722 | 23.1 | 39.9 |
| Susquehanna | 17 273 | 78.5 | 131 700 | 23.9 | 14.1 | 628 | 27.9 | 1.3 | 23 259 | 1.3 | 1 754 | 7.5 | 19 937 | 28.2 | 33.2 |
| Tioga | 17 187 | 75.3 | 111 100 | 24.1 | 13.6 | 628 | 29.7 | 1.8 | 21 946 | 0.8 | 1 671 | 7.6 | 18 233 | 29.8 | 33.2 |
| Union | 15 310 | 75.1 | 148 500 | 24.7 | 13.2 | 654 | 29.5 | 2.3 | 17 457 | -0.3 | 1 348 | 7.7 | 17 665 | 35.3 | 26.2 |
| Venango | 22 482 | 75.1 | 78 500 | 21.1 | 12.3 | 556 | 29.7 | 1.1 | 26 484 | 0.0 | 2 088 | 7.9 | 24 432 | 26.5 | 30.7 |
| Warren | 17 602 | 77.9 | 85 400 | 21.2 | 12.6 | 535 | 26.9 | 1.5 | 21 534 | 0.2 | 1 445 | 6.7 | 19 264 | 27.5 | 32.1 |
| Washington | 83 806 | 77.2 | 136 400 | 21.0 | 12.3 | 604 | 28.4 | 0.8 | 109 282 | 2.0 | 7 997 | 7.3 | 97 513 | 33.3 | 23.2 |
| Wayne | 19 305 | 81.6 | 180 000 | 26.7 | 13.8 | 708 | 31.1 | 1.4 | 25 368 | -0.3 | 1 921 | 7.6 | 22 529 | 29.3 | 28.3 |
| Westmoreland | 152 819 | 76.3 | 130 800 | 21.3 | 13.2 | 601 | 27.1 | 0.9 | 193 828 | 1.9 | 14 277 | 7.4 | 171 543 | 34.0 | 24.8 |
| Wyoming | 11 013 | 77.3 | 147 100 | 23.7 | 13.5 | 636 | 26.7 | 1.9 | 14 557 | 1.2 | 1 404 | 9.6 | 13 182 | 25.6 | 34.1 |
| York | 167 568 | 76.2 | 178 400 | 24.5 | 14.1 | 782 | 28.4 | 1.3 | 228 725 | 1.5 | 17 698 | 7.7 | 216 693 | 31.5 | 28.3 |
| **RHODE ISLAND** | 410 475 | 62.1 | 270 600 | 27.3 | 16.0 | 901 | 30.5 | 2.1 | 560 381 | -0.4 | 58 293 | 10.4 | 513 558 | 36.7 | 19.1 |
| Bristol | 19 289 | 72.3 | 357 500 | 27.0 | 17.8 | 906 | 31.3 | 1.1 | 26 845 | -0.3 | 2 385 | 8.9 | 25 005 | 46.0 | 14.5 |
| Kent | 68 774 | 72.4 | 240 400 | 26.9 | 16.7 | 951 | 29.9 | 1.4 | 94 261 | -0.4 | 9 285 | 9.9 | 85 648 | 36.6 | 19.4 |
| Newport | 34 600 | 63.3 | 380 700 | 26.6 | 14.4 | 1 144 | 28.7 | 0.8 | 44 491 | -0.5 | 4 154 | 9.3 | 41 052 | 44.4 | 14.4 |
| Providence | 238 633 | 55.1 | 247 700 | 28.0 | 16.6 | 866 | 31.0 | 2.9 | 322 757 | -0.4 | 36 068 | 11.2 | 295 654 | 33.8 | 20.7 |
| Washington | 49 179 | 76.7 | 340 500 | 26.2 | 14.2 | 966 | 29.3 | 0.9 | 72 025 | -0.4 | 6 399 | 8.9 | 66 199 | 41.6 | 16.4 |
| **SOUTH CAROLINA** | 1 758 732 | 69.8 | 137 000 | 23.2 | 11.4 | 728 | 30.3 | 2.4 | 2 167 195 | 0.0 | 197 083 | 9.1 | 1 999 063 | 32.0 | 25.1 |
| Abbeville | 9 811 | 77.9 | 89 100 | 22.3 | 12.7 | 557 | 38.4 | 2.0 | 10 861 | -0.9 | 1 104 | 10.2 | 9 814 | 24.4 | 34.6 |
| Aiken | 63 414 | 72.8 | 122 300 | 21.3 | 10.7 | 657 | 29.4 | 2.3 | 76 583 | -1.5 | 6 278 | 8.2 | 67 739 | 33.9 | 26.7 |
| Allendale | 3 348 | 61.3 | 72 400 | 24.3 | 15.0 | 553 | 34.9 | 5.3 | 3 218 | -1.9 | 543 | 16.9 | 2 611 | 26.9 | 37.9 |
| Anderson | 72 519 | 73.5 | 120 500 | 21.6 | 10.2 | 643 | 31.1 | 2.7 | 85 046 | -0.8 | 7 296 | 8.6 | 80 174 | 28.9 | 29.6 |
| Bamberg | 5 742 | 73.9 | 77 400 | 22.4 | 17.1 | 530 | 32.1 | 2.0 | 5 838 | -6.4 | 899 | 15.4 | 5 604 | 28.6 | 27.8 |
| Barnwell | 8 405 | 72.8 | 71 900 | 21.8 | 13.2 | 579 | 35.4 | 4.2 | 8 315 | -1.7 | 1 216 | 14.6 | 8 340 | 27.5 | 36.8 |
| Beaufort | 64 270 | 71.6 | 288 800 | 28.8 | 11.7 | 1 016 | 30.6 | 2.5 | 63 521 | 2.5 | 5 021 | 7.9 | 64 496 | 32.1 | 19.5 |
| Berkeley | 62 447 | 70.2 | 150 600 | 24.4 | 12.1 | 886 | 29.3 | 3.0 | 86 507 | 1.0 | 6 910 | 8.0 | 77 851 | 28.9 | 28.1 |
| Calhoun | 6 155 | 81.4 | 102 000 | 21.4 | 13.0 | 583 | 32.4 | 2.2 | 6 704 | -0.8 | 714 | 10.7 | 6 525 | 30.3 | 30.8 |
| Charleston | 139 262 | 61.8 | 242 000 | 27.0 | 13.3 | 895 | 32.5 | 1.9 | 179 170 | 1.0 | 12 998 | 7.3 | 167 617 | 37.5 | 18.5 |
| Cherokee | 21 012 | 67.9 | 82 300 | 22.5 | 10.1 | 571 | 27.2 | 2.1 | 25 116 | 1.0 | 2 946 | 11.7 | 21 267 | 22.8 | 37.3 |
| Chester | 12 605 | 75.8 | 84 300 | 22.5 | 13.1 | 578 | 32.0 | 2.5 | 14 739 | -0.3 | 2 029 | 13.8 | 12 629 | 21.4 | 37.9 |
| Chesterfield | 17 464 | 71.7 | 77 200 | 21.2 | 11.6 | 580 | 32.7 | 2.5 | 18 770 | 0.1 | 2 332 | 12.4 | 18 735 | 23.3 | 38.6 |
| Clarendon | 12 165 | 71.7 | 91 200 | 23.8 | 10.7 | 570 | 30.2 | 2.8 | 12 208 | -2.0 | 1 706 | 14.0 | 12 276 | 25.8 | 33.5 |
| Colleton | 15 281 | 72.9 | 92 600 | 26.9 | 14.5 | 646 | 35.0 | 2.8 | 16 802 | -0.3 | 1 939 | 11.5 | 14 444 | 25.2 | 33.8 |
| Darlington | 26 279 | 72.7 | 85 900 | 21.0 | 10.5 | 590 | 31.0 | 2.7 | 30 397 | -0.4 | 3 247 | 10.7 | 27 932 | 26.8 | 32.0 |
| Dillon | 11 785 | 62.6 | 62 000 | 24.3 | 13.8 | 552 | 32.4 | 5.3 | 12 795 | -2.5 | 1 827 | 14.3 | 10 990 | 19.3 | 38.7 |
| Dorchester | 48 697 | 73.8 | 172 300 | 24.7 | 12.0 | 930 | 29.6 | 1.6 | 70 205 | 1.3 | 5 134 | 7.3 | 60 990 | 34.2 | 23.9 |
| Edgefield | 9 151 | 77.0 | 104 400 | 20.6 | 13.4 | 550 | 27.0 | 3.0 | 11 196 | -1.2 | 1 016 | 9.1 | 10 322 | 28.7 | 35.4 |
| Fairfield | 9 405 | 74.0 | 93 800 | 24.4 | 13.7 | 577 | 32.0 | 2.2 | 10 554 | 0.1 | 1 262 | 12.0 | 9 654 | 27.1 | 32.6 |
| Florence | 51 508 | 66.1 | 110 200 | 21.5 | 10.2 | 627 | 29.6 | 2.5 | 62 881 | -0.2 | 6 123 | 9.7 | 58 667 | 32.5 | 22.5 |
| Georgetown | 22 329 | 76.7 | 170 500 | 27.8 | 13.4 | 777 | 33.2 | 2.8 | 28 932 | -1.1 | 2 826 | 9.8 | 22 734 | 27.8 | 25.1 |
| Greenville | 173 082 | 67.9 | 150 100 | 22.0 | 10.2 | 710 | 29.1 | 1.7 | 227 728 | -0.3 | 16 220 | 7.1 | 206 722 | 36.0 | 22.0 |
| Greenwood | 26 508 | 70.5 | 104 400 | 21.4 | 10.6 | 622 | 31.7 | 2.8 | 30 589 | -0.5 | 3 168 | 10.4 | 29 297 | 29.5 | 31.1 |
| Hampton | 7 248 | 75.3 | 81 500 | 21.6 | 16.2 | 596 | 25.4 | 6.1 | 7 613 | -1.2 | 939 | 12.3 | 7 670 | 21.1 | 35.2 |
| Horry | 112 358 | 70.9 | 170 600 | 26.5 | 12.1 | 808 | 33.0 | 5.1 | 129 445 | 0.0 | 13 243 | 10.2 | 121 926 | 26.9 | 19.8 |
| Jasper | 7 811 | 73.3 | 104 700 | 27.2 | 13.1 | 770 | 32.9 | 3.8 | 10 321 | 2.1 | 885 | 8.6 | 10 462 | 19.1 | 29.9 |
| Kershaw | 23 992 | 78.6 | 112 000 | 22.3 | 10.5 | 654 | 29.9 | 1.7 | 29 640 | -0.3 | 2 495 | 8.4 | 26 659 | 30.0 | 28.0 |
| Lancaster | 29 024 | 74.0 | 133 200 | 24.0 | 11.3 | 637 | 30.4 | 2.8 | 32 140 | 3.5 | 3 777 | 11.8 | 30 168 | 24.4 | 31.0 |
| Laurens | 24 839 | 71.7 | 85 600 | 21.7 | 10.6 | 599 | 29.5 | 2.6 | 30 403 | -0.7 | 2 781 | 9.1 | 27 431 | 23.3 | 38.0 |
| Lee | 6 542 | 72.5 | 63 900 | 24.8 | 12.8 | 468 | 27.1 | 3.5 | 8 027 | -1.6 | 970 | 12.1 | 6 511 | 23.2 | 31.7 |
| Lexington | 102 751 | 74.6 | 138 000 | 21.5 | 10.2 | 784 | 28.7 | 1.5 | 134 532 | 0.0 | 9 312 | 6.9 | 125 974 | 35.5 | 22.5 |
| McCormick | 4 266 | 78.8 | 108 100 | 25.6 | 12.1 | 478 | 32.0 | 1.6 | 3 336 | -1.2 | 431 | 12.9 | 3 428 | 22.1 | 29.0 |
| Marion | 12 086 | 67.1 | 83 000 | 21.5 | 13.6 | 529 | 29.8 | 3.2 | 11 603 | -4.5 | 2 098 | 18.1 | 12 943 | 25.5 | 32.7 |
| Marlboro | 9 830 | 64.5 | 58 800 | 23.4 | 14.7 | 527 | 31.2 | 4.4 | 11 470 | -1.0 | 1 911 | 16.7 | 9 153 | 19.1 | 42.7 |
| Newberry | 14 236 | 73.0 | 104 200 | 21.0 | 11.8 | 619 | 30.6 | 2.7 | 18 182 | -1.2 | 1 565 | 8.6 | 16 856 | 28.2 | 34.2 |
| Oconee | 29 941 | 76.0 | 134 600 | 21.5 | 10.1 | 620 | 29.0 | 1.9 | 31 357 | 0.8 | 2 854 | 9.1 | 29 593 | 31.4 | 29.3 |
| Orangeburg | 34 616 | 68.4 | 81 300 | 22.9 | 13.1 | 621 | 33.3 | 3.4 | 40 242 | -1.8 | 5 480 | 13.6 | 35 688 | 27.6 | 31.1 |
| Pickens | 44 127 | 70.2 | 126 400 | 21.0 | 10.2 | 667 | 34.4 | 1.7 | 57 790 | 0.0 | 4 724 | 8.2 | 51 775 | 33.1 | 27.1 |
| Richland | 142 773 | 60.8 | 150 600 | 22.9 | 11.0 | 809 | 30.9 | 1.6 | 182 705 | 0.1 | 15 438 | 8.4 | 175 564 | 39.6 | 16.4 |
| Saluda | 6 821 | 74.0 | 101 700 | 21.0 | 12.0 | 572 | 28.8 | 3.0 | 8 957 | -0.5 | 681 | 7.6 | 8 286 | 25.2 | 40.0 |
| Spartanburg | 106 055 | 70.6 | 118 800 | 22.2 | 9.9 | 650 | 29.6 | 2.2 | 136 513 | 1.9 | 12 279 | 9.0 | 122 472 | 30.3 | 28.7 |

1. Specified owner-occupied units.   2. A value of 9.9 represents 9.9 percent or less.   3. Specified renter-occupied units. A value of 10.0 represents 10 percent or less.   4. Overcrowded or lacking complete plumbing facilities.   5. Percent of civilian labor force.   6. Persons 16 years old and over.

| STATE County | Private nonfarm establishments, employment and payroll, 2011 | | | | | | | | | Agriculture, 2007 | | | |
| | | Employment | | | | | | Annual payroll | | Farms | | | |
| | | | | | | | | | | | Percent with: | | Farm operators whose principal occupation is farming (percent) |
| | Number of establishments | Total | Health care and social assistance | Manufacturing | Retail trade | Finance and insurance | Professional, scientific, and technical services | Total (mil dol) | Average per employee (dollars) | Number | Fewer than 50 acres | 500 acres or more | |
| | 104 | 105 | 106 | 107 | 108 | 109 | 110 | 111 | 112 | 113 | 114 | 115 | 116 |
| PENNSYLVANIA—Cont'd | | | | | | | | | | | | | |
| Potter | 384 | 4 526 | 922 | 687 | 615 | 78 | 111 | 156 | 34 516 | 378 | 20.9 | 11.6 | 46.3 |
| Schuylkill | 2 842 | 41 211 | 7 583 | 9 790 | 6 004 | 977 | 1 039 | 1 374 | 33 335 | 966 | 45.9 | 4.7 | 35.3 |
| Snyder | 830 | 13 485 | 906 | 3 129 | 3 077 | 262 | 268 | 355 | 26 346 | 998 | 45.5 | 2.6 | 47.7 |
| Somerset | 1 743 | 20 104 | 3 526 | 3 275 | 2 824 | 695 | 625 | 702 | 34 903 | 1 156 | 28.8 | 6.8 | 47.8 |
| Sullivan | 166 | 1 188 | 374 | D | 287 | 26 | 22 | 30 | 25 375 | 165 | 26.7 | 6.1 | 38.2 |
| Susquehanna | 891 | 6 703 | 1 000 | 627 | 1 277 | 178 | 272 | 195 | 29 025 | 1 008 | 30.8 | 5.0 | 42.2 |
| Tioga | 901 | 10 863 | 1 804 | 2 295 | 1 981 | 354 | 320 | 366 | 33 683 | 1 011 | 23.0 | 7.2 | 44.8 |
| Union | 899 | 14 932 | 3 709 | 1 269 | 1 622 | 382 | 309 | 463 | 30 986 | 575 | 36.2 | 2.8 | 57.2 |
| Venango | 1 194 | 16 788 | 3 507 | 4 332 | 2 480 | D | 294 | 542 | 32 313 | 487 | 36.6 | 4.3 | 38.2 |
| Warren | 874 | 13 531 | 3 075 | 2 774 | 2 415 | D | 245 | 444 | 32 794 | 831 | 33.0 | 3.2 | 33.2 |
| Washington | 5 035 | 80 983 | 13 028 | 9 443 | 8 607 | 1 668 | 3 460 | 3 669 | 45 305 | 2 023 | 39.1 | 2.1 | 37.7 |
| Wayne | 1 335 | 12 531 | 2 435 | 597 | 2 614 | 507 | 310 | 371 | 29 583 | 603 | 24.2 | 4.1 | 52.1 |
| Westmoreland | 8 663 | 120 783 | 20 299 | 18 283 | 17 881 | 2 844 | 5 029 | 4 466 | 36 972 | 1 415 | 39.6 | 3.9 | 41.7 |
| Wyoming | 643 | 8 213 | 926 | D | 1 186 | 199 | 285 | 322 | 39 262 | 649 | 36.4 | 2.8 | 30.0 |
| York | 8 519 | 155 366 | 22 789 | 32 027 | 21 341 | 3 824 | 5 770 | 6 062 | 39 018 | 2 370 | 58.9 | 5.2 | 45.2 |
| RHODE ISLAND | 28 181 | 406 222 | 84 176 | 39 802 | 48 083 | 24 441 | 23 555 | 17 275 | 42 525 | 1 219 | 68.7 | 0.6 | 50.9 |
| Bristol | 1 208 | 13 446 | 2 947 | 1 826 | 1 200 | 277 | 389 | 390 | 29 024 | 51 | 76.5 | 0.0 | 47.1 |
| Kent | 4 734 | 66 624 | 11 693 | 7 073 | 10 982 | 5 277 | 3 410 | 2 741 | 41 137 | 143 | 68.5 | 0.7 | 60.8 |
| Newport | 2 713 | 28 967 | 4 838 | 1 991 | 4 000 | 756 | 3 299 | 1 125 | 38 824 | 187 | 66.3 | 0.0 | 58.8 |
| Providence | 15 561 | 254 281 | 56 333 | 23 032 | 25 272 | 16 845 | 14 398 | 11 179 | 43 964 | 469 | 69.9 | 0.2 | 46.7 |
| Washington | 3 754 | 40 263 | 8 252 | 5 879 | 6 536 | 1 042 | 1 371 | 1 685 | 41 844 | 369 | 67.2 | 1.4 | 49.1 |
| SOUTH CAROLINA | 100 481 | 1 521 123 | 217 275 | 204 309 | 219 433 | 65 516 | 81 397 | 54 433 | 35 785 | 25 867 | 42.3 | 7.4 | 37.7 |
| Abbeville | 334 | 4 119 | 469 | 1 784 | 384 | 113 | D | 119 | 28 867 | 566 | 34.8 | 5.7 | 33.6 |
| Aiken | 2 693 | 48 010 | 5 837 | 6 859 | 6 709 | 1 151 | 3 330 | 2 232 | 46 480 | 1 206 | 46.7 | 4.1 | 38.9 |
| Allendale | 127 | 1 487 | 261 | 727 | 129 | D | D | 55 | 37 105 | 185 | 22.7 | 23.2 | 28.1 |
| Anderson | 3 622 | 51 091 | 7 930 | 10 566 | 8 256 | 1 085 | 1 723 | 1 682 | 32 917 | 1 650 | 43.0 | 3.2 | 32.9 |
| Bamberg | 281 | 3 341 | 700 | 839 | 521 | D | 63 | 95 | 28 558 | 390 | 18.2 | 15.9 | 25.6 |
| Barnwell | 341 | 4 870 | D | 1 832 | 796 | 129 | D | 146 | 29 990 | 412 | 29.1 | 11.2 | 35.9 |
| Beaufort | 4 673 | 46 242 | 6 865 | 461 | 8 735 | 1 407 | 2 692 | 1 460 | 31 569 | 125 | 62.4 | 14.4 | 43.2 |
| Berkeley | 2 607 | 37 558 | 2 007 | 4 717 | 6 022 | 1 009 | 2 588 | 1 524 | 40 587 | 314 | 55.1 | 7.3 | 40.8 |
| Calhoun | 245 | 3 073 | D | 1 132 | 250 | 44 | 38 | 110 | 35 911 | 341 | 26.4 | 16.4 | 41.6 |
| Charleston | 11 657 | 174 422 | 29 515 | 11 596 | 25 836 | 6 196 | 14 365 | 6 838 | 39 205 | 332 | 62.0 | 5.7 | 45.8 |
| Cherokee | 972 | 16 746 | 1 271 | 5 264 | 2 865 | 314 | 191 | 479 | 28 632 | 416 | 37.3 | 3.6 | 37.7 |
| Chester | 517 | 6 116 | D | 2 046 | 801 | 151 | 127 | 214 | 34 989 | 544 | 31.8 | 8.5 | 36.8 |
| Chesterfield | 693 | 11 342 | 1 508 | 4 279 | 1 374 | 206 | 92 | 377 | 33 211 | 848 | 33.5 | 5.9 | 32.0 |
| Clarendon | 498 | 5 387 | 1 613 | 356 | 1 314 | 223 | D | 132 | 24 535 | 491 | 33.0 | 14.7 | 46.6 |
| Colleton | 760 | 7 284 | 1 198 | 711 | 1 651 | 297 | 214 | 209 | 28 717 | 525 | 40.4 | 10.5 | 34.9 |
| Darlington | 1 123 | 17 645 | 2 537 | 3 190 | 2 330 | 437 | 263 | 702 | 39 763 | 369 | 35.0 | 21.1 | 43.1 |
| Dillon | 490 | 8 512 | 1 126 | 2 201 | 1 265 | 192 | 94 | 200 | 23 450 | 222 | 20.3 | 21.2 | 52.7 |
| Dorchester | 2 112 | 23 563 | 2 836 | 4 025 | 3 623 | 900 | 706 | 722 | 30 641 | 377 | 50.1 | 7.2 | 44.3 |
| Edgefield | 328 | 4 293 | 537 | 1 139 | 458 | 63 | 45 | 131 | 30 439 | 407 | 39.8 | 7.4 | 36.9 |
| Fairfield | 318 | 5 641 | 672 | 744 | 631 | 66 | 56 | 292 | 51 786 | 187 | 26.7 | 12.3 | 47.6 |
| Florence | 3 105 | 54 280 | 13 713 | 5 471 | 8 597 | 4 374 | 2 349 | 1 809 | 33 326 | 675 | 38.5 | 12.0 | 40.9 |
| Georgetown | 1 716 | 17 585 | 2 139 | 1 846 | 2 645 | 632 | 732 | 555 | 31 559 | 252 | 37.7 | 9.5 | 35.7 |
| Greenville | 11 978 | 208 518 | 25 886 | 27 009 | 24 304 | 7 545 | 16 963 | 8 082 | 38 757 | 1 100 | 65.5 | 0.8 | 30.5 |
| Greenwood | 1 386 | 23 293 | 4 832 | 5 684 | 3 149 | 609 | 1 668 | 805 | 34 579 | 493 | 44.0 | 4.3 | 30.6 |
| Hampton | 370 | 3 559 | 501 | 628 | 626 | 121 | 106 | 121 | 33 867 | 295 | 25.8 | 18.0 | 37.6 |
| Horry | 8 048 | 93 009 | 10 255 | 2 868 | 20 232 | 3 516 | 2 910 | 2 511 | 26 999 | 914 | 37.1 | 7.5 | 46.2 |
| Jasper | 526 | 5 473 | 879 | 330 | 1 361 | 109 | 89 | 160 | 29 170 | 109 | 35.8 | 16.5 | 38.5 |
| Kershaw | 1 122 | 15 236 | 2 355 | 3 341 | 2 069 | 509 | 449 | 492 | 32 273 | 499 | 46.5 | 6.8 | 42.3 |
| Lancaster | 1 176 | 14 069 | 2 369 | 1 638 | 2 675 | 712 | 451 | 491 | 34 895 | 573 | 42.9 | 3.0 | 38.2 |
| Laurens | 938 | 15 866 | 1 982 | 5 566 | 1 664 | 449 | D | 522 | 32 878 | 830 | 37.2 | 6.6 | 35.1 |
| Lee | 215 | 2 061 | 372 | 267 | 419 | 82 | 46 | 55 | 26 915 | 476 | 28.2 | 12.4 | 40.8 |
| Lexington | 6 014 | 86 980 | 12 602 | 8 857 | 15 935 | 3 096 | 3 160 | 2 908 | 33 428 | 948 | 55.8 | 2.5 | 34.2 |
| McCormick | 89 | 927 | D | 312 | 131 | D | D | 26 | 27 781 | 79 | 26.6 | 17.7 | 34.2 |
| Marion | 500 | 6 148 | 661 | 918 | 1 093 | 236 | 64 | 184 | 29 869 | 308 | 43.2 | 11.0 | 39.0 |
| Marlboro | 346 | 4 618 | 808 | 1 962 | 728 | 129 | 53 | 132 | 28 497 | 233 | 25.8 | 25.8 | 47.6 |
| Newberry | 709 | 11 457 | 1 199 | 4 963 | 1 364 | 217 | 132 | 347 | 30 322 | 614 | 32.4 | 5.4 | 40.6 |
| Oconee | 1 443 | 19 174 | 2 872 | 4 747 | 2 973 | 432 | 453 | 745 | 38 862 | 804 | 53.6 | 2.4 | 35.3 |
| Orangeburg | 1 693 | 25 845 | 3 953 | 6 240 | 4 200 | 763 | 381 | 800 | 30 960 | 1 002 | 29.8 | 13.4 | 31.5 |
| Pickens | 2 034 | 25 403 | 3 697 | 4 575 | 4 373 | 759 | 811 | 714 | 28 123 | 829 | 66.5 | 1.0 | 31.5 |
| Richland | 8 728 | 152 564 | 26 683 | 10 112 | 17 536 | 16 889 | 10 827 | 5 941 | 38 944 | 364 | 55.5 | 3.6 | 43.4 |
| Saluda | 254 | 3 732 | 450 | D | 410 | 61 | 35 | 97 | 26 020 | 606 | 29.9 | 7.4 | 41.6 |
| Spartanburg | 6 142 | 110 969 | 14 011 | 22 512 | 13 535 | 2 224 | 3 731 | 4 183 | 37 697 | 1 242 | 53.8 | 2.4 | 39.7 |

| STATE County | Land in farms | | Acres | | | Value of land and buildings (dollars) | | Value of machinery and equipment, average per farm (dollars) | Value of products sold | | Percent from: | | Percent of farms with sales of: | | Government payments | |
|---|---|---|---|---|---|---|---|---|---|---|---|---|---|---|---|---|
| | Acreage (1,000) | Percent change, 2002–2007 | Average size of farm | Total irrigated (1,000) | Total cropland (1,000) | Average per farm | Average per acre | | Total (mil dol) | Average per farm (dollars) | Crops | Live-stock and poultry products | $10,000 or more | $100,000 or more | Total ($1,000) | Percent of farms |
| | 117 | 118 | 119 | 120 | 121 | 122 | 123 | 124 | 125 | 126 | 127 | 128 | 129 | 130 | 131 | 132 |
| PENNSYLVANIA—Cont'd | | | | | | | | | | | | | | | | |
| Potter | 88 | -6.4 | 234 | D | 40.4 | 607 773 | 2 597 | 77 189 | 31.4 | 83 008 | 20.2 | 79.8 | 31.0 | 13.2 | 790 | 33.6 |
| Schuylkill | 119 | 7.2 | 123 | 1.9 | 81.3 | 614 809 | 5 012 | 80 239 | 124.8 | 129 143 | 45.1 | 54.9 | 34.3 | 15.0 | 1 917 | 48.3 |
| Snyder | 100 | 0.0 | 100 | 1.0 | 65.4 | 500 022 | 4 981 | 62 844 | 109.0 | 109 259 | 13.6 | 86.4 | 47.0 | 20.7 | 1 189 | 28.7 |
| Somerset | 207 | -7.2 | 179 | 0.2 | 120.5 | 511 174 | 2 859 | 84 012 | 83.2 | 71 931 | 14.0 | 86.0 | 43.1 | 18.5 | 1 575 | 37.5 |
| Sullivan | 28 | -9.7 | 169 | 0.0 | 14.5 | 418 154 | 2 480 | 64 418 | 7.2 | 43 878 | 12.3 | 87.7 | 27.9 | 10.3 | 221 | 37.0 |
| Susquehanna | 158 | -16.4 | 157 | 0.1 | 75.9 | 514 686 | 3 279 | 61 132 | 49.3 | 48 896 | 9.7 | 90.3 | 29.1 | 11.8 | 1 447 | 27.4 |
| Tioga | 184 | -8.0 | 182 | 0.1 | 96.9 | 538 400 | 2 957 | 69 355 | 53.8 | 53 243 | 11.7 | 88.3 | 33.5 | 14.2 | 2 735 | 38.8 |
| Union | 64 | -7.2 | 111 | 0.2 | 50.2 | 655 528 | 5 908 | 81 201 | 90.5 | 157 386 | 10.4 | 89.6 | 58.1 | 36.5 | 706 | 34.6 |
| Venango | 65 | 0.0 | 133 | 0.0 | 31.0 | 365 006 | 2 743 | 55 316 | 11.8 | 24 221 | 46.4 | 53.6 | 23.0 | 6.0 | 472 | 20.3 |
| Warren | 100 | 28.2 | 120 | 0.1 | 43.5 | 315 242 | 2 631 | 42 759 | 18.6 | 22 387 | 14.9 | 85.1 | 17.9 | 5.2 | 440 | 13.4 |
| Washington | 211 | -19.2 | 104 | 0.4 | 101.0 | 460 864 | 4 418 | 54 163 | 28.6 | 14 161 | 44.8 | 55.2 | 21.7 | 2.8 | 836 | 12.0 |
| Wayne | 93 | -17.7 | 154 | 0.1 | 42.4 | 637 576 | 4 137 | 70 329 | 29.4 | 48 803 | 10.9 | 89.1 | 38.8 | 14.1 | 384 | 21.7 |
| Westmoreland | 167 | 10.6 | 118 | 0.4 | 107.3 | 533 173 | 4 504 | 73 537 | 58.4 | 41 298 | 37.4 | 62.6 | 32.2 | 7.7 | 1 346 | 24.5 |
| Wyoming | 78 | 25.8 | 120 | 0.1 | 41.4 | 417 786 | 3 478 | 47 025 | 13.5 | 20 796 | 31.0 | 69.0 | 19.3 | 6.2 | 557 | 23.3 |
| York | 293 | 2.8 | 123 | 1.0 | 225.4 | 701 059 | 5 680 | 81 789 | 212.6 | 89 719 | 47.1 | 52.9 | 38.4 | 13.9 | 2 722 | 22.7 |
| RHODE ISLAND | 68 | 11.5 | 56 | 4.3 | 24.5 | 936 229 | 16 828 | 65 343 | 65.9 | 54 067 | 84.4 | 15.6 | 36.5 | 9.6 | 743 | 8.3 |
| Bristol | 2 | 100.0 | 33 | 0.1 | 1.1 | 833 282 | 25 524 | 42 030 | 2.8 | 55 510 | 88.6 | 11.4 | 41.2 | 11.8 | 1 | 5.9 |
| Kent | 10 | 25.0 | 68 | 0.2 | 2.5 | 904 942 | 13 378 | 55 522 | 3.8 | 26 320 | 91.7 | 8.3 | 29.4 | 7.7 | 37 | 6.3 |
| Newport | 10 | -9.1 | 54 | 0.6 | 5.7 | 1 233 570 | 22 734 | 70 050 | 18.3 | 97 857 | 88.2 | 11.8 | 51.3 | 17.1 | 279 | 10.7 |
| Providence | 22 | 29.4 | 46 | 0.8 | 5.8 | 807 987 | 17 477 | 56 116 | 15.1 | 32 137 | 76.5 | 23.5 | 32.0 | 6.0 | 162 | 8.3 |
| Washington | 25 | 0.0 | 67 | 2.6 | 9.4 | 974 894 | 14 593 | 81 846 | 25.9 | 70 301 | 84.7 | 15.3 | 36.9 | 10.8 | 264 | 8.1 |
| SOUTH CAROLINA | 4 889 | 0.9 | 189 | 132.4 | 2 151.2 | 540 200 | 2 858 | 64 977 | 2 352.7 | 90 953 | 33.9 | 66.1 | 23.4 | 7.0 | 67 253 | 29.8 |
| Abbeville | 91 | -4.2 | 161 | 1.5 | 26.4 | 434 890 | 2 699 | 47 588 | 10.2 | 18 102 | 29.2 | 70.8 | 25.8 | 1.6 | 532 | 26.0 |
| Aiken | 159 | 10.4 | 132 | 3.2 | 62.2 | 473 766 | 3 586 | 52 149 | 102.8 | 85 237 | 10.1 | 89.9 | 22.6 | 6.7 | 1 497 | 21.8 |
| Allendale | 125 | 15.7 | 677 | 6.6 | 49.1 | 1 233 183 | 1 822 | 71 668 | 15.2 | 82 427 | 77.8 | 22.2 | 21.6 | 12.4 | 1 745 | 68.6 |
| Anderson | 173 | -2.3 | 105 | 0.7 | 63.8 | 413 318 | 3 939 | 48 678 | 50.2 | 30 443 | 11.0 | 89.0 | 19.2 | 2.2 | 941 | 18.6 |
| Bamberg | 125 | 19.0 | 320 | 5.5 | 53.9 | 687 030 | 2 145 | 81 584 | 23.5 | 60 136 | 69.8 | 30.2 | 25.1 | 9.5 | 2 168 | 70.8 |
| Barnwell | 93 | 9.4 | 225 | 3.9 | 46.8 | 584 928 | 2 600 | 62 223 | 21.0 | 51 078 | 43.9 | 56.1 | 22.1 | 9.0 | 1 689 | 52.9 |
| Beaufort | 49 | 11.4 | 395 | 2.4 | 7.4 | 871 559 | 2 205 | 72 402 | 28.3 | 226 066 | 97.1 | 2.9 | 37.6 | 7.2 | 52 | 12.8 |
| Berkeley | 53 | -7.0 | 168 | 0.6 | 11.3 | 577 404 | 3 439 | 52 482 | D | D | D | D | 14.3 | 2.5 | 203 | 19.1 |
| Calhoun | 111 | 16.8 | 324 | 10.0 | 60.9 | 793 325 | 2 448 | 108 715 | 46.4 | 136 080 | 64.7 | 35.3 | 29.3 | 12.3 | 3 540 | 47.8 |
| Charleston | 42 | -12.5 | 126 | 1.3 | 11.3 | 870 286 | 6 929 | 66 426 | 24.0 | 72 413 | 72.9 | 27.1 | 24.4 | 6.9 | 45 | 6.6 |
| Cherokee | 63 | -1.6 | 151 | 0.1 | 18.7 | 424 703 | 2 817 | 55 171 | 40.4 | 97 065 | 3.8 | 96.2 | 20.4 | 3.1 | 562 | 19.5 |
| Chester | 112 | 15.5 | 206 | D | 29.7 | 643 186 | 3 129 | 56 788 | 30.1 | 55 359 | 6.0 | 94.0 | 24.6 | 5.0 | 377 | 11.0 |
| Chesterfield | 141 | 9.3 | 166 | 1.1 | 47.2 | 392 060 | 2 364 | 52 307 | 80.2 | 94 563 | 11.4 | 88.6 | 19.2 | 6.5 | 1 068 | 41.0 |
| Clarendon | 155 | 4.7 | 315 | 2.8 | 104.5 | 623 510 | 1 978 | 92 095 | 82.0 | 167 021 | 46.1 | 53.9 | 33.0 | 15.3 | 2 383 | 62.1 |
| Colleton | 175 | 27.7 | 333 | 2.6 | 37.5 | 661 892 | 1 988 | 61 236 | 22.4 | 42 617 | 85.1 | 14.9 | 19.0 | 2.9 | 908 | 35.2 |
| Darlington | 173 | 7.5 | 468 | 4.1 | 115.4 | 825 008 | 1 764 | 158 230 | 75.1 | 203 499 | 41.7 | 58.3 | 41.7 | 20.3 | 4 481 | 56.6 |
| Dillon | 105 | -6.3 | 473 | 1.1 | 84.5 | 953 258 | 2 017 | 140 889 | 77.1 | 347 198 | 33.6 | 66.4 | 47.3 | 24.3 | 3 882 | 66.7 |
| Dorchester | 65 | 12.1 | 172 | 1.8 | 37.4 | 575 269 | 3 336 | 82 312 | 32.2 | 85 322 | 45.0 | 55.0 | 26.8 | 10.3 | 1 506 | 31.0 |
| Edgefield | 77 | 4.1 | 188 | 5.0 | 25.8 | 573 544 | 3 047 | 68 039 | 46.7 | 114 691 | 82.8 | 17.2 | 23.6 | 5.9 | 744 | 27.5 |
| Fairfield | 52 | -7.1 | 277 | 0.2 | 10.6 | 777 047 | 2 802 | 58 076 | 26.8 | 143 516 | 5.6 | 94.4 | 25.1 | 8.0 | 37 | 5.9 |
| Florence | 159 | -7.0 | 235 | 2.5 | 111.6 | 606 692 | 2 580 | 77 178 | 33.8 | 50 043 | 89.6 | 10.4 | 31.4 | 8.7 | 3 189 | 53.3 |
| Georgetown | 58 | 5.5 | 229 | 0.7 | 17.6 | 624 429 | 2 730 | 53 717 | 23.5 | 93 135 | 88.8 | 11.2 | 17.9 | 8.7 | 518 | 54.0 |
| Greenville | 73 | -16.1 | 66 | 1.8 | 26.7 | 373 917 | 5 662 | 40 844 | 19.3 | 17 520 | 85.4 | 14.6 | 14.3 | 2.0 | 132 | 4.9 |
| Greenwood | 71 | -12.3 | 143 | 0.1 | 18.0 | 401 827 | 2 802 | 51 596 | 14.1 | 28 535 | 43.1 | 56.9 | 19.1 | 1.4 | 245 | 14.2 |
| Hampton | 127 | -0.8 | 430 | 2.8 | 50.2 | 948 327 | 2 207 | 99 976 | 12.3 | 41 789 | 95.8 | 4.2 | 32.5 | 10.2 | 2 996 | 64.4 |
| Horry | 164 | -12.8 | 179 | 1.3 | 97.3 | 619 386 | 3 460 | 77 868 | 65.9 | 72 046 | 65.9 | 34.1 | 29.3 | 10.7 | 2 240 | 47.4 |
| Jasper | 52 | -34.2 | 478 | D | 8.6 | 974 585 | 2 038 | 76 466 | D | D | D | D | 22.0 | 2.8 | 100 | 33.0 |
| Kershaw | 86 | 22.9 | 171 | 1.4 | 23.3 | 522 010 | 3 046 | 62 870 | 169.5 | 339 629 | 2.8 | 97.2 | 22.4 | 10.6 | 681 | 28.1 |
| Lancaster | 65 | -19.8 | 114 | 0.3 | 17.8 | 418 802 | 3 680 | 57 206 | 67.7 | 118 174 | 3.0 | 97.0 | 22.3 | 5.6 | 284 | 15.0 |
| Laurens | 130 | -9.1 | 157 | 0.4 | 38.8 | 484 696 | 3 093 | 46 674 | 38.1 | 45 880 | 6.1 | 93.9 | 22.0 | 3.5 | 804 | 17.7 |
| Lee | 141 | 14.6 | 296 | 4.3 | 92.8 | 626 887 | 2 116 | 130 715 | 69.9 | 146 807 | 39.2 | 60.8 | 24.4 | 11.6 | 5 117 | 67.9 |
| Lexington | 90 | -12.6 | 95 | 11.1 | 45.9 | 419 804 | 4 406 | 68 639 | 166.5 | 175 586 | 28.9 | 71.1 | 24.6 | 11.6 | 1 003 | 13.6 |
| McCormick | 25 | 8.7 | 316 | D | 7.1 | 800 706 | 2 537 | 51 638 | D | D | D | 0.0 | 17.7 | 3.8 | 175 | 25.3 |
| Marion | 70 | -24.7 | 226 | 0.9 | 42.4 | 541 397 | 2 398 | 93 475 | 21.7 | 70 544 | 51.0 | 49.0 | 23.4 | 8.4 | 1 240 | 59.7 |
| Marlboro | 123 | 7.0 | 526 | 1.6 | 76.1 | 961 123 | 1 828 | 100 243 | 37.8 | 162 233 | 35.2 | 64.8 | 41.6 | 18.5 | 3 063 | 66.1 |
| Newberry | 101 | -2.9 | 164 | 1.4 | 33.0 | 479 798 | 2 923 | 65 468 | 99.5 | 161 999 | 3.7 | 96.3 | 26.4 | 8.3 | 607 | 21.5 |
| Oconee | 71 | -9.0 | 88 | 0.3 | 21.6 | 478 112 | 5 436 | 52 165 | 128.8 | 160 243 | 2.4 | 97.6 | 23.8 | 8.1 | 403 | 11.3 |
| Orangeburg | 288 | 5.1 | 287 | 23.6 | 157.2 | 647 310 | 2 256 | 88 391 | 149.7 | 149 446 | 42.2 | 57.8 | 28.9 | 11.5 | 5 880 | 51.1 |
| Pickens | 51 | 8.5 | 62 | 0.8 | 17.9 | 354 880 | 5 739 | 44 376 | 8.2 | 9 948 | D | D | 11.0 | 1.0 | 152 | 5.4 |
| Richland | 59 | -6.3 | 162 | 1.4 | 23.5 | 514 598 | 3 185 | 63 279 | 10.2 | 27 924 | 66.3 | 33.7 | 21.7 | 5.5 | 483 | 10.7 |
| Saluda | 110 | 2.8 | 181 | 4.2 | 35.0 | 503 974 | 2 782 | 61 531 | 86.0 | 141 945 | 7.5 | 92.5 | 34.0 | 10.7 | 587 | 25.2 |
| Spartanburg | 110 | -12.7 | 89 | 2.1 | 41.5 | 432 985 | 4 892 | 41 123 | 26.3 | 21 172 | 57.4 | 42.6 | 18.0 | 2.7 | 499 | 10.6 |

| STATE County | Water use, 2005 | | Wholesale trade,[1] 2007 | | | | Retail trade,[2] 2007 | | | | Real estate and rental and leasing,[2] 2007 | | | |
|---|---|---|---|---|---|---|---|---|---|---|---|---|---|---|
| | Total water withdrawn (mil gal/day) | Gallons withdrawn per person | Number of establishments | Number of employees | Sales (mil dol) | Annual payroll (mil dol) | Number of establishments | Number of employees | Sales (mil dol) | Annual payroll (mil dol) | Number of establishments | Number of employees | Receipts (mil dol) | Annual payroll (mil dol) |
| | 133 | 134 | 135 | 136 | 137 | 138 | 139 | 140 | 141 | 142 | 143 | 144 | 145 | 146 |
| PENNSYLVANIA—Cont'd | | | | | | | | | | | | | | |
| Potter | 20.1 | 1 125 | 8 | 44 | 19.0 | 0.9 | 77 | 611 | 138.4 | 13.3 | 9 | D | D | D |
| Schuylkill | 58.0 | 394 | 111 | 1 946 | 1 070.2 | 69.4 | 542 | 6 085 | 1 317.9 | 116.0 | 69 | 349 | 52.4 | 7.6 |
| Snyder | 218.1 | 5 708 | 33 | 462 | 191.2 | 17.9 | 197 | 2 774 | 566.3 | 51.9 | 16 | 72 | 8.6 | 1.8 |
| Somerset | 33.8 | 428 | 76 | D | D | D | 288 | 3 146 | 764.7 | 63.1 | 50 | 186 | 21.4 | 4.7 |
| Sullivan | 0.6 | 94 | 3 | D | D | D | 27 | 234 | 45.0 | 3.9 | 4 | D | D | D |
| Susquehanna | 4.2 | 99 | 40 | 385 | 215.8 | 11.1 | 153 | 1 399 | 403.6 | 27.2 | 17 | D | D | D |
| Tioga | 6.3 | 152 | 22 | 362 | 201.8 | 11.7 | 166 | 1 867 | 413.5 | 33.9 | 22 | 64 | 8.6 | 1.6 |
| Union | 6.2 | 143 | 29 | D | D | D | 136 | 1 658 | 372.1 | 32.7 | 26 | 158 | 23.1 | 4.2 |
| Venango | 8.5 | 151 | 48 | D | D | D | 219 | 2 754 | 594.2 | 51.7 | 27 | 111 | 9.8 | 2.0 |
| Warren | 14.5 | 346 | 23 | D | D | D | 156 | 2 468 | 485.3 | 70.4 | 17 | 67 | 8.5 | 1.5 |
| Washington | 806.6 | 3 908 | 226 | 3 427 | 2 454.7 | 182.4 | 688 | 9 027 | 2 283.2 | 192.3 | 150 | 1 109 | 214.6 | 42.2 |
| Wayne | 13.1 | 261 | 34 | 333 | 112.0 | 11.7 | 251 | 2 925 | 692.3 | 64.6 | 37 | 132 | 19.1 | 3.4 |
| Westmoreland | 39.8 | 108 | 353 | 7 050 | 5 390.5 | 288.0 | 1 350 | 18 320 | 4 154.7 | 368.1 | 255 | 1 118 | 178.8 | 29.9 |
| Wyoming | 11.5 | 407 | 16 | 397 | 95.2 | 17.2 | 113 | 1 156 | 288.6 | 22.9 | 9 | 28 | 1.9 | 0.3 |
| York | 2 596.5 | 6 352 | 371 | 6 539 | 3 822.9 | 299.4 | 1 344 | 21 762 | 4 942.7 | 455.6 | 285 | 2 158 | 294.5 | 75.5 |
| RHODE ISLAND | 405.2 | 376 | 1 277 | 18 128 | 9 182.8 | 914.9 | 4 080 | 50 865 | 12 286.5 | 1 215.4 | 1 233 | 6 493 | 1 462.8 | 227.2 |
| Bristol | 0.7 | 14 | 52 | 399 | 227.4 | 18.9 | 154 | 1 362 | 295.7 | 31.8 | 45 | 124 | 24.8 | 4.2 |
| Kent | 3.0 | 18 | 251 | 2 688 | 1 381.3 | 132.7 | 756 | 12 020 | 3 242.9 | 302.7 | 219 | 1 573 | 272.6 | 57.0 |
| Newport | 8.2 | 98 | 75 | 407 | 264.0 | 18.4 | 471 | 4 251 | 1 096.2 | 111.0 | 126 | 702 | 102.1 | 24.1 |
| Providence | 369.6 | 578 | 771 | 12 496 | 5 856.9 | 563.2 | 2 117 | 25 827 | 5 924.9 | 582.2 | 674 | 3 676 | 982.7 | 130.0 |
| Washington | 23.6 | 184 | 128 | 2 138 | 1 453.2 | 181.7 | 582 | 7 405 | 1 726.7 | 187.7 | 169 | 418 | 80.6 | 11.9 |
| SOUTH CAROLINA | 7 845.2 | 1 844 | 4 323 | 58 524 | 40 498.0 | 2 599.4 | 18 886 | 231 685 | 54 298.4 | 4 878.1 | 5 473 | 30 417 | 5 194.1 | 989.8 |
| Abbeville | 4.8 | 182 | 9 | D | D | D | 59 | 385 | 71.9 | 6.1 | 6 | D | D | D |
| Aiken | 209.5 | 1 395 | 75 | D | D | D | 548 | 7 076 | 1 599.8 | 133.8 | 141 | 529 | 92.9 | 11.6 |
| Allendale | 11.6 | 1 060 | 6 | D | D | D | 33 | 231 | 32.6 | 3.3 | 1 | D | D | D |
| Anderson | 163.6 | 932 | 183 | D | D | D | 755 | 8 901 | 2 004.7 | 178.1 | 140 | 502 | 97.1 | 14.2 |
| Bamberg | 5.5 | 348 | 7 | D | D | D | 57 | 506 | 102.8 | 10.6 | 3 | D | D | D |
| Barnwell | 4.1 | 173 | 3 | D | D | D | 85 | 859 | 169.1 | 15.5 | 13 | D | D | D |
| Beaufort | 30.9 | 224 | 113 | 607 | 298.2 | 30.7 | 831 | 9 776 | 2 255.1 | 219.3 | 458 | 3 902 | 452.0 | 146.7 |
| Berkeley | 589.3 | 3 885 | 127 | 2 367 | 1 766.5 | 109.9 | 417 | 6 328 | 1 552.3 | 136.7 | 145 | 913 | 147.3 | 27.9 |
| Calhoun | 75.8 | 5 022 | 9 | 146 | 144.5 | 4.9 | 44 | 292 | 66.8 | 4.1 | 8 | 35 | 7.6 | 1.0 |
| Charleston | 114.7 | 347 | 456 | 6 015 | 3 267.4 | 282.6 | 2 079 | 27 439 | 6 321.0 | 628.8 | 781 | 3 982 | 734.2 | 133.9 |
| Cherokee | 11.7 | 217 | 23 | D | D | D | 249 | 2 817 | 718.1 | 50.5 | 38 | 134 | 19.3 | 2.5 |
| Chester | 5.8 | 173 | 13 | D | D | D | 103 | 902 | 210.9 | 16.0 | 19 | D | D | D |
| Chesterfield | 8.8 | 202 | 30 | 377 | 150.3 | 11.9 | 163 | 1 354 | 298.1 | 26.0 | 22 | 70 | 8.4 | 1.7 |
| Clarendon | 4.7 | 140 | 17 | 191 | 54.8 | 5.8 | 130 | 1 399 | 296.4 | 24.0 | 14 | 41 | 5.9 | 1.2 |
| Colleton | 11.2 | 284 | 26 | D | D | D | 181 | 1 858 | 419.7 | 35.6 | 55 | 184 | 32.6 | 4.5 |
| Darlington | 792.1 | 11 762 | 59 | 426 | 226.1 | 15.7 | 251 | 2 548 | 527.5 | 45.6 | 31 | 129 | 78.6 | 3.4 |
| Dillon | 5.5 | 179 | 18 | 511 | 300.1 | 17.6 | 136 | 1 331 | 381.7 | 22.1 | 20 | 55 | 7.1 | 1.0 |
| Dorchester | 9.8 | 87 | 66 | 467 | 170.2 | 19.3 | 303 | 4 078 | 879.5 | 75.8 | 118 | 317 | 54.4 | 8.0 |
| Edgefield | 6.0 | 235 | 10 | D | D | D | 65 | 444 | 120.3 | 8.7 | 8 | 33 | 2.2 | 0.6 |
| Fairfield | 1 539.2 | 64 010 | 10 | D | D | D | 65 | 652 | 216.2 | 12.6 | 15 | 32 | 4.7 | 0.8 |
| Florence | 43.6 | 332 | 162 | 2 645 | 1 358.7 | 102.6 | 776 | 9 415 | 2 237.9 | 187.5 | 139 | 686 | 104.0 | 17.8 |
| Georgetown | 68.4 | 1 122 | 34 | D | D | D | 331 | 3 181 | 702.2 | 67.4 | 124 | 424 | 60.0 | 13.1 |
| Greenville | 70.3 | 173 | 735 | 10 557 | 11 581.9 | 554.2 | 1 836 | 25 425 | 6 036.6 | 561.9 | 618 | 3 268 | 752.1 | 121.6 |
| Greenwood | 14.6 | 214 | 46 | 476 | 271.2 | 17.7 | 301 | 3 710 | 774.3 | 74.2 | 64 | 189 | 26.3 | 5.0 |
| Hampton | 7.7 | 362 | 9 | 144 | 92.0 | 7.4 | 105 | 759 | 150.7 | 12.7 | 10 | 123 | 8.5 | 3.1 |
| Horry | 171.2 | 754 | 256 | 2 237 | 907.6 | 82.2 | 1 810 | 21 072 | 4 967.2 | 459.4 | 708 | 5 839 | 829.9 | 187.4 |
| Jasper | 22.8 | 1 067 | 30 | 342 | 145.1 | 13.4 | 104 | 1 489 | 400.8 | 38.0 | 23 | 73 | 14.1 | 3.4 |
| Kershaw | 11.7 | 206 | 22 | D | D | D | 199 | 2 472 | 577.7 | 45.4 | 42 | 96 | 13.2 | 2.5 |
| Lancaster | 28.6 | 453 | 40 | D | D | D | 236 | 2 447 | 587.9 | 48.7 | 39 | D | D | D |
| Laurens | 9.7 | 138 | 33 | 225 | 67.0 | 9.4 | 191 | 1 585 | 370.1 | 29.2 | 31 | 75 | 9.4 | 1.7 |
| Lee | 3.6 | 175 | 14 | 98 | 49.6 | 3.2 | 49 | 416 | 154.6 | 6.9 | 7 | 18 | 3.7 | 0.5 |
| Lexington | 220.9 | 939 | 289 | 6 123 | 3 588.4 | 280.6 | 1 057 | 15 882 | 3 666.1 | 330.3 | 249 | 1 180 | 218.4 | 33.2 |
| McCormick | 1.9 | 192 | 1 | D | D | D | 30 | 144 | 34.8 | 2.3 | 6 | D | D | D |
| Marion | 4.7 | 134 | 21 | 144 | 104.4 | 4.7 | 143 | 1 316 | 269.9 | 25.6 | 15 | 69 | 6.4 | 1.5 |
| Marlboro | 25.2 | 899 | 14 | D | D | D | 99 | 824 | 159.0 | 13.1 | 16 | 42 | 3.9 | 0.6 |
| Newberry | 8.9 | 240 | 28 | D | D | D | 155 | 1 543 | 369.9 | 30.4 | 24 | 82 | 20.6 | 2.2 |
| Oconee | 2 607.0 | 37 470 | 43 | D | D | D | 281 | 3 107 | 743.5 | 67.0 | 86 | 253 | 40.0 | 7.7 |
| Orangeburg | 30.8 | 335 | 68 | 801 | 405.7 | 25.0 | 419 | 4 494 | 1 007.0 | 85.1 | 55 | 226 | 24.6 | 5.4 |
| Pickens | 26.3 | 231 | 69 | 588 | 253.2 | 23.4 | 359 | 4 451 | 1 153.5 | 99.3 | 86 | 337 | 60.5 | 9.1 |
| Richland | 543.4 | 1 598 | 372 | 6 129 | 3 150.7 | 274.8 | 1 376 | 19 518 | 4 367.7 | 420.7 | 467 | 3 828 | 845.8 | 134.4 |
| Saluda | 3.6 | 189 | 8 | D | D | D | 49 | 323 | 73.4 | 6.1 | 5 | 8 | 0.6 | 0.1 |
| Spartanburg | 100.7 | 377 | 440 | 6 437 | 5 482.0 | 278.5 | 1 089 | 13 937 | 3 638.4 | 309.0 | 279 | 1 279 | 220.8 | 45.1 |

1. Merchant wholesalers, except manufacturers' sales branches and offices.  2. Employer establishments.

| STATE County | Professional, scientific, and technical services,[1] 2007 | | | | Manufacturing, 2007 | | | | Accommodation and food services, 2007 | | | |
|---|---|---|---|---|---|---|---|---|---|---|---|---|
| | Number of establishments | Number of employees | Receipts (mil dol) | Annual payroll (mil dol) | Number of establishments | Number of employees | Receipts (mil dol) | Annual payroll (mil dol) | Number of establishments | Number of employees | Sales (mil dol) | Annual payroll (mil dol) |
| | 147 | 148 | 149 | 150 | 151 | 152 | 153 | 154 | 155 | 156 | 157 | 158 |
| PENNSYLVANIA—Cont'd | | | | | | | | | | | | |
| Potter | 27 | 139 | 19.5 | 9.9 | 24 | 847 | 205.9 | 27.4 | 44 | 237 | 10.6 | 2.3 |
| Schuylkill | 156 | D | D | D | 199 | 10 211 | 3 043.4 | 397.8 | 283 | 2 971 | 135.8 | 34.2 |
| Snyder | 46 | 232 | 20.6 | 8.3 | 70 | 5 014 | D | 175.0 | 85 | 1 423 | 54.0 | 15.6 |
| Somerset | 99 | D | D | D | 131 | 3 933 | 955.5 | 146.0 | 167 | 2 204 | 81.4 | 22.4 |
| Sullivan | 9 | D | D | D | NA | NA | NA | NA | 25 | 120 | 6.8 | 1.4 |
| Susquehanna | 51 | 243 | 17.2 | 5.0 | 68 | 785 | 115.7 | 24.8 | 84 | 691 | 32.1 | 7.8 |
| Tioga | 52 | 251 | 20.1 | 8.4 | 43 | 2 220 | 463.1 | 75.2 | 99 | 1 048 | 40.0 | 9.8 |
| Union | 78 | 334 | 27.5 | 9.6 | 37 | 2 086 | D | 78.8 | 95 | 2 094 | 80.2 | 23.4 |
| Venango | 63 | D | D | D | 88 | 4 097 | 1 113.0 | 187.8 | 105 | 1 407 | 44.3 | 12.6 |
| Warren | 52 | D | D | D | 67 | 2 932 | D | 129.5 | 85 | 870 | 35.0 | 8.8 |
| Washington | 401 | D | D | D | 263 | 9 565 | 3 672.9 | 430.6 | 384 | 6 106 | 233.7 | 64.3 |
| Wayne | 105 | D | D | D | 66 | 727 | 115.0 | 24.7 | 172 | 2 482 | 187.8 | 54.9 |
| Westmoreland | 751 | D | D | D | 603 | 21 064 | 7 077.0 | 907.1 | 762 | 12 797 | 454.3 | 129.6 |
| Wyoming | 41 | D | D | D | 30 | 2 737 | D | 71.9 | 60 | 571 | 22.3 | 6.1 |
| York | 726 | 5 437 | 620.4 | 240.9 | 600 | 38 016 | 11 957.4 | 1 669.8 | 736 | 13 112 | 527.9 | 146.4 |
| RHODE ISLAND | 3 096 | 22 732 | 2 777.8 | 1 173.9 | 1 831 | 53 718 | 12 061.5 | 2 374.8 | 2 926 | 44 426 | 2 148.7 | 622.1 |
| Bristol | 119 | D | D | D | 105 | 2 573 | 496.5 | 106.2 | 126 | 1 694 | 68.3 | 19.2 |
| Kent | 521 | 2 701 | 336.1 | 123.1 | 284 | 11 531 | 3 039.1 | 562.5 | 459 | 8 862 | 398.6 | 116.0 |
| Newport | 321 | D | D | D | 86 | 2 796 | 346.1 | 181.9 | 366 | 5 148 | 343.0 | 103.6 |
| Providence | 1 780 | D | D | D | 1 195 | 29 601 | 6 422.9 | 1 177.0 | 1 527 | 23 350 | 1 065.9 | 303.8 |
| Washington | 355 | 1 442 | 208.5 | 75.4 | 161 | 7 217 | 1 757.0 | 347.3 | 448 | 5 372 | 272.8 | 79.5 |
| SOUTH CAROLINA | 9 459 | 74 372 | 9 343.3 | 3 622.6 | 4 335 | 242 153 | 93 977.5 | 10 061.5 | 9 291 | 182 899 | 8 383.5 | 2 311.0 |
| Abbeville | 14 | D | D | D | 31 | 2 098 | 657.5 | 67.3 | 32 | 329 | 11.0 | 2.9 |
| Aiken | 236 | D | D | D | 96 | 7 853 | 3 959.3 | 375.4 | 238 | 4 608 | 172.9 | 46.1 |
| Allendale | 10 | 39 | 4.7 | 1.6 | 7 | 920 | 385.4 | 33.0 | 8 | 86 | 2.9 | 0.6 |
| Anderson | 288 | D | D | D | 222 | 12 655 | 4 886.3 | 495.2 | 350 | 6 420 | 235.8 | 64.5 |
| Bamberg | 19 | 45 | 4.7 | 1.1 | 22 | 913 | D | 28.0 | 21 | 286 | 9.4 | 2.5 |
| Barnwell | 24 | 157 | 16.0 | 4.8 | 21 | 2 635 | 681.3 | 85.3 | 28 | 471 | 14.7 | 3.8 |
| Beaufort | 563 | D | D | D | 90 | 1 092 | 223.4 | 35.8 | 458 | 9 686 | 530.5 | 174.2 |
| Berkeley | 206 | D | D | D | 98 | 5 794 | 5 527.3 | 322.0 | 208 | 3 935 | 161.2 | 42.2 |
| Calhoun | 12 | 52 | 4.8 | 1.3 | 17 | 1 057 | D | D | 9 | 113 | 4.1 | 1.0 |
| Charleston | 1 449 | D | D | D | 302 | 10 706 | 5 338.1 | 479.6 | 1 045 | 24 504 | 1 382.7 | 377.1 |
| Cherokee | 51 | D | D | D | 62 | 6 205 | 2 484.9 | 208.7 | 97 | 1 833 | 68.2 | 18.2 |
| Chester | 28 | D | D | D | 51 | 3 002 | 1 407.5 | 132.6 | 42 | 616 | 25.2 | 6.5 |
| Chesterfield | 25 | 77 | 7.3 | 1.8 | 54 | 4 663 | 1 361.0 | 166.1 | 76 | 803 | 30.5 | 7.5 |
| Clarendon | 22 | 122 | 15.9 | 8.2 | 18 | 1 147 | 291.4 | 37.0 | 66 | 778 | 29.8 | 7.2 |
| Colleton | 53 | 250 | 26.4 | 7.4 | 32 | 1 583 | 245.2 | 48.8 | 71 | 1 146 | 56.0 | 12.1 |
| Darlington | 67 | D | D | D | 66 | 4 742 | 2 433.4 | 212.9 | 88 | 1 230 | 53.9 | 13.7 |
| Dillon | 21 | 76 | 5.5 | 1.5 | 24 | 2 687 | 432.6 | 65.3 | 58 | 867 | 31.6 | 8.3 |
| Dorchester | 166 | D | D | D | 93 | 5 543 | 2 361.4 | 240.2 | 153 | 2 811 | 104.0 | 29.3 |
| Edgefield | 15 | D | D | D | 20 | 1 112 | 343.9 | 37.7 | 25 | 262 | 7.9 | 2.3 |
| Fairfield | 25 | 70 | 5.3 | 2.1 | 16 | D | 263.2 | 42.4 | 22 | 261 | 8.9 | 2.4 |
| Florence | 220 | D | D | D | 116 | 7 150 | 2 885.4 | 333.4 | 286 | 5 943 | 250.0 | 68.0 |
| Georgetown | 189 | D | D | D | 47 | 2 206 | 1 046.2 | 116.7 | 169 | 2 982 | 136.6 | 40.5 |
| Greenville | 1 441 | 13 561 | 2 034.0 | 790.8 | 605 | 29 758 | 10 821.4 | 1 244.5 | 1 005 | 19 205 | 817.8 | 232.7 |
| Greenwood | 118 | D | D | D | 71 | 7 950 | 2 821.1 | 342.0 | 124 | 2 484 | 86.1 | 24.2 |
| Hampton | 21 | D | D | D | 15 | 878 | 280.3 | 36.9 | 43 | 459 | 17.6 | 4.3 |
| Horry | 660 | D | D | D | 168 | 4 103 | 894.8 | 166.8 | 1 178 | 25 931 | 1 483.8 | 396.2 |
| Jasper | 26 | D | D | D | 23 | 515 | 76.4 | 16.2 | 56 | 679 | 32.4 | 8.1 |
| Kershaw | 90 | 472 | 41.7 | 14.1 | 68 | 3 696 | 1 419.1 | 161.8 | 95 | 1 386 | 52.2 | 13.6 |
| Lancaster | 73 | 457 | 58.8 | 20.2 | 68 | 2 473 | 1 247.6 | 103.7 | 93 | 1 331 | 56.3 | 12.9 |
| Laurens | 35 | 181 | 11.1 | 6.4 | 95 | 5 523 | 1 562.3 | 201.4 | 80 | 1 512 | 53.7 | 13.2 |
| Lee | 9 | 52 | 3.4 | 1.7 | NA | NA | NA | NA | 19 | 284 | 10.7 | 2.5 |
| Lexington | 551 | D | D | D | 219 | 9 772 | 3 465.7 | 404.4 | 489 | 10 726 | 434.5 | 123.1 |
| McCormick | 6 | D | D | D | NA | NA | NA | NA | 13 | 73 | 2.0 | 0.6 |
| Marion | 28 | 73 | 5.9 | 2.1 | 29 | 1 846 | 367.7 | 58.0 | 46 | 859 | 31.2 | 7.8 |
| Marlboro | 14 | D | D | D | 24 | 2 808 | 989.8 | 95.9 | 31 | 336 | 13.4 | 3.2 |
| Newberry | 41 | 138 | 11.2 | 4.7 | 46 | 4 931 | 1 277.5 | 159.0 | 61 | 827 | 30.4 | 7.3 |
| Oconee | 129 | D | D | D | 79 | 4 971 | 1 546.4 | 219.7 | 113 | 1 581 | 62.8 | 15.8 |
| Orangeburg | 95 | D | D | D | 83 | 6 962 | 2 597.9 | 284.9 | 177 | 3 686 | 152.2 | 36.8 |
| Pickens | 135 | 791 | 102.7 | 28.7 | 125 | 5 999 | 1 460.0 | 226.2 | 219 | 3 727 | 142.9 | 36.5 |
| Richland | 1 207 | D | D | D | 248 | 13 434 | 6 109.8 | 625.7 | 779 | 16 632 | 733.6 | 210.8 |
| Saluda | 12 | 43 | 2.1 | 1.0 | NA | NA | NA | NA | 17 | 95 | 4.3 | 1.1 |
| Spartanburg | 467 | D | D | D | 462 | 26 108 | 11 731.8 | 1 204.9 | 528 | 10 002 | 411.5 | 113.6 |

1. Establishment subject to federal tax.

# Table B. States and Counties — Health Care and Social Assistance, Other Services, and Federal Funds

| STATE County | Health care and social assistance, 2007 | | | | Other services, 2007 | | | | Federal funds and grants, 2009–2010 Expenditures (mil dol) | | | |
|---|---|---|---|---|---|---|---|---|---|---|---|---|
| | | | | | | | | | | Direct payments for individuals[1] | | |
| | Number of establishments | Number of employees | Receipts (mil dol) | Annual payroll (mil dol) | Number of establishments | Number of employees | Receipts (mil dol) | Annual payroll (mil dol) | Total | Social Security and government retirement | Medicare | Food Stamps and Supplemental Security Income |
| | 159 | 160 | 161 | 162 | 163 | 164 | 165 | 166 | 167 | 168 | 169 | 170 |
| PENNSYLVANIA—Cont'd | | | | | | | | | | | | |
| Potter | 42 | 959 | 78.9 | 36.6 | 25 | 112 | 7.9 | 1.8 | 156.0 | 65.8 | 38.0 | 7.2 |
| Schuylkill | 329 | 8 127 | 582.5 | 249.2 | 257 | 1 183 | 88.5 | 22.8 | 1 338.9 | 561.7 | 446.3 | 39.0 |
| Snyder | 71 | 873 | 91.6 | 31.2 | 68 | 299 | 24.2 | 5.7 | 234.0 | 114.8 | 63.6 | 6.6 |
| Somerset | 190 | 3 365 | 255.4 | 98.5 | 154 | 653 | 44.4 | 10.6 | 747.8 | 282.4 | 222.0 | 27.2 |
| Sullivan | 16 | D | D | D | 14 | 36 | 2.8 | 0.5 | 70.9 | 28.2 | 15.5 | 1.3 |
| Susquehanna | 58 | 1 150 | 66.1 | 30.2 | 71 | 276 | 20.3 | 4.6 | 303.7 | 144.9 | 80.7 | 12.7 |
| Tioga | 102 | 1 718 | 120.4 | 48.4 | 61 | 237 | 17.5 | 3.5 | 356.3 | 153.1 | 87.0 | 13.9 |
| Union | 127 | 3 445 | 295.0 | 119.2 | 61 | 263 | 20.9 | 4.1 | 376.8 | 124.0 | 58.4 | 5.8 |
| Venango | 175 | 3 506 | 275.1 | 106.9 | 118 | 568 | 47.7 | 11.9 | 504.0 | 210.9 | 153.4 | 26.4 |
| Warren | 111 | 2 982 | 206.3 | 94.5 | 83 | 528 | 24.5 | 6.4 | 388.3 | 155.4 | 99.1 | 13.9 |
| Washington | 667 | 11 459 | 1 051.3 | 428.0 | 408 | 2 500 | 208.2 | 64.5 | 1 986.3 | 814.7 | 665.6 | 74.6 |
| Wayne | 121 | 2 206 | 164.1 | 62.8 | 115 | 734 | 49.3 | 15.0 | 467.8 | 249.7 | 108.4 | 13.4 |
| Westmoreland | 1 208 | 18 721 | 1 494.6 | 612.9 | 838 | 4 651 | 586.3 | 92.4 | 3 355.8 | 1 380.8 | 1 135.4 | 110.8 |
| Wyoming | 70 | 1 134 | 74.3 | 31.2 | 52 | 207 | 17.3 | 4.3 | 206.9 | 102.2 | 55.5 | 9.1 |
| York | 925 | 20 265 | 1 931.3 | 790.7 | 746 | 5 098 | 582.7 | 115.6 | 3 882.1 | 1 330.7 | 554.7 | 77.2 |
| RHODE ISLAND | 3 274 | 81 947 | 7 161.4 | 3 091.6 | 2 382 | 14 379 | 1 449.0 | 373.1 | 11 759.4 | 3 139.9 | 1 988.8 | 430.8 |
| Bristol | 125 | 2 477 | 122.6 | 61.2 | 109 | 508 | 38.2 | 10.9 | 410.0 | 161.1 | 91.9 | 14.6 |
| Kent | 560 | 11 848 | 1 044.5 | 404.2 | 404 | 2 163 | 261.2 | 52.9 | 1 424.9 | 587.1 | 333.1 | 56.5 |
| Newport | 248 | 4 372 | 328.4 | 140.2 | 205 | 1 192 | 111.3 | 33.0 | 1 694.4 | 332.7 | 138.5 | 27.0 |
| Providence | 1 929 | 55 833 | 5 104.0 | 2 241.1 | 1 377 | 9 041 | 908.3 | 243.3 | 6 553.7 | 1 648.0 | 1 246.2 | 298.6 |
| Washington | 412 | 7 417 | 562.0 | 244.9 | 287 | 1 475 | 130.0 | 32.9 | 986.9 | 410.8 | 179.0 | 34.0 |
| SOUTH CAROLINA | 9 291 | 200 216 | 20 408.6 | 7 761.4 | 7 088 | 45 520 | 3 901.6 | 1 127.5 | 46 578.1 | 15 285.1 | 5 203.7 | 1 896.8 |
| Abbeville | 31 | 662 | 51.4 | 20.1 | 26 | 67 | 5.4 | 1.1 | 168.9 | 79.0 | 27.5 | 11.7 |
| Aiken | 294 | 5 266 | 409.6 | 149.4 | 199 | 1 171 | 94.2 | 22.0 | 3 494.6 | 597.9 | 199.1 | 60.8 |
| Allendale | 14 | D | D | D | 12 | D | D | D | 118.3 | 27.1 | 19.2 | 15.1 |
| Anderson | 362 | 8 112 | 786.0 | 301.2 | 244 | 1 871 | 154.5 | 55.0 | 1 233.9 | 629.3 | 227.6 | 51.1 |
| Bamberg | 38 | 731 | 60.2 | 24.8 | 24 | D | D | D | 178.7 | 48.4 | 29.8 | 14.9 |
| Barnwell | 45 | 588 | 41.2 | 17.5 | 26 | 100 | 10.4 | 2.4 | 218.5 | 73.6 | 41.3 | 20.3 |
| Beaufort | 386 | 6 365 | 642.3 | 230.6 | 308 | 3 068 | 238.0 | 84.7 | 1 968.8 | 700.8 | 146.8 | 38.9 |
| Berkeley | 189 | 1 837 | 109.4 | 42.3 | 168 | 880 | 63.2 | 18.6 | 1 787.3 | 464.3 | 96.8 | 56.0 |
| Calhoun | 25 | D | D | D | 14 | 59 | 4.4 | 1.0 | 98.5 | 38.7 | 14.2 | 8.6 |
| Charleston | 1 172 | 27 107 | 3 473.9 | 1 178.0 | 808 | 5 844 | 526.7 | 158.5 | 5 819.0 | 1 300.4 | 469.9 | 163.2 |
| Cherokee | 81 | 1 272 | 123.5 | 43.5 | 76 | 324 | 31.3 | 6.5 | 338.5 | 163.9 | 65.7 | 21.3 |
| Chester | 47 | D | D | D | 37 | 112 | 8.0 | 2.2 | 257.1 | 113.1 | 57.0 | 21.9 |
| Chesterfield | 71 | 1 480 | 110.1 | 45.2 | 51 | 169 | 12.7 | 3.6 | 366.3 | 131.7 | 60.5 | 27.6 |
| Clarendon | 48 | D | D | D | 36 | 163 | 11.2 | 3.4 | 334.5 | 120.7 | 50.0 | 30.7 |
| Colleton | 69 | 1 254 | 116.6 | 43.1 | 45 | 155 | 12.7 | 3.1 | 373.8 | 146.5 | 75.1 | 30.0 |
| Darlington | 91 | 2 494 | 206.3 | 84.5 | 85 | 353 | 28.5 | 7.1 | 548.4 | 209.4 | 96.0 | 46.8 |
| Dillon | 40 | 1 072 | 90.3 | 34.8 | 40 | 94 | 8.1 | 1.8 | 292.7 | 86.3 | 57.6 | 29.9 |
| Dorchester | 197 | 2 586 | 233.9 | 88.1 | 183 | 831 | 62.9 | 19.0 | 735.5 | 439.5 | 94.0 | 37.1 |
| Edgefield | 23 | 513 | 24.6 | 10.7 | 23 | 88 | 10.8 | 2.4 | 180.6 | 55.5 | 23.8 | 11.3 |
| Fairfield | 38 | 748 | 44.5 | 20.1 | 13 | 47 | 4.2 | 1.0 | 191.1 | 77.9 | 36.7 | 17.5 |
| Florence | 346 | 11 564 | 1 326.6 | 490.1 | 206 | 1 439 | 126.8 | 33.5 | 1 192.9 | 452.3 | 203.5 | 91.0 |
| Georgetown | 203 | 2 044 | 196.3 | 80.6 | 118 | 628 | 41.3 | 12.4 | 595.2 | 306.0 | 116.7 | 32.6 |
| Greenville | 1 015 | 23 581 | 2 447.5 | 997.9 | 750 | 5 475 | 472.2 | 148.4 | 2 980.6 | 1 307.3 | 474.3 | 126.3 |
| Greenwood | 146 | 4 589 | 530.7 | 197.4 | 88 | 619 | 39.9 | 10.0 | 522.9 | 251.9 | 84.5 | 28.4 |
| Hampton | 33 | 486 | 35.2 | 14.8 | 28 | 134 | 8.6 | 2.1 | 237.4 | 71.6 | 36.8 | 16.9 |
| Horry | 611 | 9 079 | 976.0 | 358.7 | 512 | 3 110 | 265.6 | 65.3 | 1 722.0 | 1 023.9 | 245.0 | 78.9 |
| Jasper | 40 | 679 | 58.0 | 22.5 | 36 | 139 | 10.6 | 3.0 | 154.8 | 52.9 | 24.0 | 12.3 |
| Kershaw | 93 | 1 990 | 179.3 | 74.3 | 92 | 374 | 26.1 | 7.0 | 418.8 | 229.6 | 71.7 | 19.4 |
| Lancaster | 114 | D | D | D | 104 | 434 | 55.0 | 13.9 | 436.4 | 212.5 | 86.5 | 28.2 |
| Laurens | 88 | 2 025 | 149.6 | 58.9 | 58 | 416 | 22.2 | 9.5 | 478.7 | 220.3 | 81.3 | 32.4 |
| Lee | 32 | 406 | 17.5 | 7.9 | 17 | 87 | 6.0 | 1.3 | 171.2 | 53.8 | 27.9 | 21.0 |
| Lexington | 498 | 10 985 | 869.5 | 379.9 | 487 | 2 989 | 252.0 | 79.3 | 1 540.0 | 781.4 | 202.0 | 54.8 |
| McCormick | 7 | D | D | D | 6 | D | D | D | 117.7 | 55.6 | 12.4 | 5.1 |
| Marion | 72 | D | D | D | 37 | 139 | 9.5 | 2.5 | 462.6 | 111.5 | 75.6 | 32.3 |
| Marlboro | 51 | 942 | 68.5 | 28.0 | 20 | 67 | 4.1 | 1.1 | 311.8 | 93.4 | 55.9 | 22.6 |
| Newberry | 55 | 1 125 | 84.0 | 32.3 | 60 | 281 | 21.9 | 6.3 | 305.9 | 137.5 | 53.9 | 18.0 |
| Oconee | 144 | 2 853 | 264.3 | 105.4 | 99 | 613 | 40.1 | 11.7 | 526.8 | 300.9 | 97.7 | 19.6 |
| Orangeburg | 225 | 3 525 | 326.0 | 128.6 | 134 | 606 | 44.5 | 13.3 | 932.4 | 308.8 | 140.0 | 78.0 |
| Pickens | 195 | 3 134 | 291.7 | 105.9 | 144 | 767 | 108.9 | 18.6 | 830.3 | 389.4 | 120.1 | 29.9 |
| Richland | 919 | 24 686 | 2 939.7 | 1 122.2 | 701 | 5 188 | 511.3 | 144.2 | 6 622.7 | 1 142.5 | 354.1 | 147.5 |
| Saluda | 23 | D | D | D | 20 | 54 | 5.3 | 0.9 | 122.9 | 47.6 | 18.1 | 10.3 |
| Spartanburg | 510 | 13 349 | 1 287.4 | 520.8 | 433 | 2 920 | 283.9 | 69.8 | 1 826.7 | 951.9 | 320.5 | 93.8 |

1. State totals may include programs not allocated by county.

# Table B. States and Counties — Federal Funds, Residential Construction, and Local Government Finances

| STATE County | Salaries and wages | Defense | Other | Medicaid and other health-related | Nutrition and family welfare | Education | Other | New construction ($1,000) | Number of housing units | Total (mil dol) | Inter-govern-mental (mil dol) | Total (mil dol) | Total (per capita) | Property (per capita) |
|---|---|---|---|---|---|---|---|---|---|---|---|---|---|---|
| | 171 | 172 | 173 | 174 | 175 | 176 | 177 | 178 | 179 | 180 | 181 | 182 | 183 | 184 |
| **PENNSYLVANIA—Cont'd** | | | | | | | | | | | | | | |
| Potter | 4.1 | 0.6 | 1.0 | 25.6 | 3.8 | 0.7 | 7.7 | 2 700 | 16 | 59.2 | 28.4 | 21.1 | 1 243 | 1 045 |
| Schuylkill | 68.6 | 1.5 | 11.3 | 146.9 | 26.2 | 3.3 | 9.4 | 17 924 | 101 | 487.1 | 237.9 | 148.6 | 1 009 | 738 |
| Snyder | 8.4 | 0.5 | 2.2 | 24.6 | 5.1 | 1.0 | 1.8 | 9 786 | 61 | 92.5 | 35.1 | 41.8 | 1 096 | 749 |
| Somerset | 25.0 | 33.0 | 26.5 | 102.3 | 16.7 | 2.2 | 5.0 | 8 731 | 46 | 210.7 | 109.0 | 69.2 | 889 | 710 |
| Sullivan | 2.1 | 0.0 | 14.4 | 7.2 | 1.2 | 0.2 | 0.3 | 1 008 | 10 | 25.5 | 10.9 | 10.5 | 1 691 | 1 501 |
| Susquehanna | 13.7 | 0.2 | 2.7 | 34.8 | 8.1 | 1.2 | 2.0 | 9 737 | 56 | 132.7 | 70.7 | 49.3 | 1 200 | 1 091 |
| Tioga | 18.4 | 0.7 | 3.8 | 50.8 | 11.2 | 1.9 | 4.4 | 12 530 | 80 | 128.5 | 69.6 | 45.1 | 1 109 | 897 |
| Union | 123.8 | 0.9 | 20.5 | 21.6 | 10.8 | 0.8 | 5.4 | 7 000 | 37 | 130.0 | 65.4 | 39.8 | 910 | 633 |
| Venango | 12.8 | 0.6 | 2.7 | 74.1 | 12.5 | 2.0 | 4.9 | 4 553 | 33 | 192.2 | 105.2 | 56.3 | 1 028 | 831 |
| Warren | 14.2 | 46.3 | 10.4 | 35.2 | 8.2 | 1.4 | 1.4 | 5 285 | 26 | 118.4 | 61.9 | 43.1 | 1 052 | 821 |
| Washington | 63.6 | 16.9 | 15.9 | 233.6 | 38.9 | 5.9 | 18.9 | 82 571 | 391 | 726.5 | 346.0 | 248.0 | 1 206 | 952 |
| Wayne | 36.9 | 0.2 | 9.7 | 32.1 | 8.9 | 1.3 | 5.6 | 18 263 | 98 | 169.3 | 51.0 | 97.7 | 1 890 | 1 783 |
| Westmoreland | 102.1 | 46.5 | 27.6 | 343.9 | 73.3 | 8.5 | 84.3 | 65 302 | 337 | 1 224.2 | 534.1 | 467.5 | 1 290 | 1 050 |
| Wyoming | 6.2 | 1.8 | 1.4 | 21.2 | 5.5 | 0.6 | 1.8 | 11 774 | 72 | 90.1 | 44.9 | 38.0 | 1 364 | 1 152 |
| York | 216.5 | 1 323.7 | 41.4 | 211.8 | 48.0 | 7.3 | 31.6 | 103 376 | 638 | 1 629.2 | 579.2 | 662.4 | 1 573 | 1 241 |
| **RHODE ISLAND** | 996.8 | 776.9 | 224.5 | 1 752.5 | 292.4 | 269.5 | 837.6 | 129 276 | 700 | X | X | X | X | X |
| Bristol | 31.3 | 2.6 | 2.5 | 41.1 | 7.8 | 3.5 | 45.4 | 4 615 | 22 | 185.5 | 43.7 | 124.1 | 2 479 | 2 435 |
| Kent | 145.5 | 10.5 | 22.7 | 133.7 | 27.8 | 16.4 | 37.5 | 8 886 | 64 | 568.3 | 142.9 | 357.9 | 2 122 | 2 051 |
| Newport | 359.5 | 682.4 | 23.2 | 80.2 | 17.6 | 8.0 | 10.4 | 22 439 | 86 | 326.7 | 90.6 | 190.3 | 2 299 | 2 138 |
| Providence | 375.3 | 53.4 | 148.4 | 1 405.3 | 198.7 | 234.7 | 664.1 | 43 628 | 277 | 2 177.8 | 878.6 | 1 009.4 | 1 604 | 1 566 |
| Washington | 85.1 | 28.0 | 27.6 | 91.7 | 19.1 | 6.9 | 72.6 | 49 707 | 251 | 515.3 | 119.5 | 338.2 | 2 665 | 2 615 |
| **SOUTH CAROLINA** | 4 617.9 | 4 496.7 | 3 674.6 | 4 833.3 | 853.8 | 667.4 | 1 855.9 | 2 760 219 | 15 542 | X | X | X | X | X |
| Abbeville | 6.1 | 0.0 | 1.1 | 34.6 | 4.0 | 2.0 | 0.8 | 4 588 | 32 | 53.0 | 25.7 | 20.2 | 795 | 713 |
| Aiken | 82.5 | 6.5 | 2 325.8 | 145.8 | 21.1 | 10.3 | 12.1 | 123 538 | 771 | 380.4 | 163.8 | 139.7 | 917 | 767 |
| Allendale | 4.0 | 0.0 | 0.5 | 42.2 | 3.5 | 1.4 | 1.6 | 120 | 1 | 43.7 | 16.8 | 12.1 | 1 153 | 958 |
| Anderson | 86.7 | 14.6 | 6.6 | 132.5 | 19.3 | 15.9 | 25.4 | 49 797 | 280 | 424.3 | 186.7 | 168.4 | 936 | 819 |
| Bamberg | 6.0 | 0.0 | 9.4 | 40.1 | 4.7 | 8.6 | 4.5 | 740 | 4 | 39.2 | 22.2 | 13.2 | 857 | 741 |
| Barnwell | 6.4 | 0.0 | 0.9 | 52.2 | 4.9 | 2.6 | 7.9 | 2 662 | 15 | 75.6 | 46.3 | 20.8 | 906 | 715 |
| Beaufort | 200.3 | 742.3 | 5.6 | 69.7 | 19.2 | 8.3 | 12.3 | 120 685 | 455 | 661.2 | 72.8 | 303.2 | 2 058 | 1 726 |
| Berkeley | 95.4 | 895.7 | 6.7 | 79.4 | 20.3 | 15.7 | 11.3 | 187 359 | 1 007 | 362.8 | 163.8 | 133.8 | 818 | 731 |
| Calhoun | 1.9 | 0.0 | 0.4 | 23.7 | 3.0 | 1.2 | 1.8 | 3 036 | 17 | 31.9 | 14.2 | 13.8 | 937 | 897 |
| Charleston | 797.7 | 1 578.6 | 713.8 | 545.4 | 49.3 | 24.2 | 110.2 | 360 947 | 2 346 | 1 355.3 | 335.2 | 644.7 | 1 880 | 1 389 |
| Cherokee | 14.7 | 0.0 | 2.2 | 49.1 | 7.5 | 4.6 | 1.0 | 6 989 | 71 | 145.4 | 61.9 | 47.9 | 887 | 717 |
| Chester | 9.2 | 0.0 | 1.2 | 40.9 | 6.5 | 3.5 | 2.3 | 4 858 | 32 | 123.5 | 39.8 | 32.3 | 992 | 842 |
| Chesterfield | 10.6 | 0.1 | 1.6 | 99.5 | 11.1 | 3.7 | 12.1 | 2 637 | 20 | 121.2 | 54.2 | 33.1 | 773 | 549 |
| Clarendon | 12.5 | 1.2 | 4.6 | 90.9 | 8.0 | 3.0 | 1.3 | 4 828 | 44 | 138.9 | 44.1 | 26.3 | 802 | 701 |
| Colleton | 15.3 | 0.5 | 3.3 | 78.2 | 10.7 | 3.5 | 5.2 | 10 221 | 46 | 98.5 | 42.3 | 40.7 | 1 047 | 968 |
| Darlington | 23.2 | 0.1 | 1.7 | 126.8 | 14.5 | 7.1 | 7.0 | 13 000 | 75 | 162.8 | 76.3 | 58.9 | 881 | 723 |
| Dillon | 7.4 | 0.1 | 1.0 | 84.9 | 8.0 | 3.6 | 4.1 | 1 463 | 14 | 71.5 | 44.0 | 18.4 | 598 | 396 |
| Dorchester | 27.8 | 17.9 | 4.3 | 82.6 | 12.3 | 5.4 | 1.0 | 115 550 | 469 | 289.3 | 125.9 | 115.9 | 938 | 794 |
| Edgefield | 35.7 | 0.0 | 6.8 | 33.2 | 3.9 | 2.0 | 1.3 | 8 269 | 47 | 50.9 | 27.1 | 19.6 | 773 | 721 |
| Fairfield | 5.4 | 0.0 | 1.1 | 39.8 | 4.9 | 3.0 | 1.9 | 3 429 | 30 | 77.5 | 27.6 | 42.7 | 1 832 | 1 720 |
| Florence | 68.1 | 5.1 | 15.0 | 241.7 | 28.9 | 14.0 | 21.1 | 34 921 | 314 | 379.9 | 174.4 | 126.8 | 961 | 742 |
| Georgetown | 31.2 | 12.7 | 2.1 | 67.2 | 11.1 | 4.6 | 4.6 | 35 484 | 149 | 206.5 | 57.5 | 110.3 | 1 823 | 1 565 |
| Greenville | 193.0 | 303.4 | 30.1 | 258.8 | 53.2 | 30.0 | 58.9 | 358 700 | 1 425 | 2 045.9 | 401.8 | 436.9 | 1 020 | 860 |
| Greenwood | 22.8 | 0.0 | 2.4 | 67.2 | 23.9 | 7.7 | 6.7 | 6 623 | 47 | 412.2 | 79.0 | 67.3 | 985 | 904 |
| Hampton | 39.1 | 0.4 | 7.0 | 52.8 | 5.4 | 2.1 | 0.6 | 1 617 | 10 | 59.4 | 31.6 | 22.6 | 1 064 | 849 |
| Horry | 64.1 | 6.7 | 8.1 | 151.2 | 30.3 | 14.0 | 29.6 | 265 401 | 1 776 | 984.4 | 221.7 | 404.4 | 1 618 | 1 288 |
| Jasper | 3.6 | 11.8 | 2.0 | 40.5 | 4.2 | 1.9 | 0.6 | 34 279 | 182 | 66.3 | 23.8 | 30.3 | 1 378 | 1 095 |
| Kershaw | 15.4 | 0.6 | 2.1 | 61.1 | 7.6 | 5.6 | 1.1 | 23 058 | 179 | 207.0 | 94.4 | 47.8 | 821 | 676 |
| Lancaster | 17.7 | 0.4 | 6.5 | 59.3 | 9.5 | 6.7 | 4.1 | 14 927 | 105 | 175.3 | 75.3 | 56.8 | 774 | 635 |
| Laurens | 36.3 | 0.0 | 2.0 | 69.4 | 8.9 | 4.6 | 15.5 | 9 593 | 58 | 180.1 | 61.5 | 44.6 | 640 | 548 |
| Lee | 2.3 | 0.0 | 0.4 | 50.9 | 5.3 | 2.1 | 0.5 | 332 | 4 | 44.5 | 24.3 | 15.1 | 758 | 634 |
| Lexington | 75.2 | 33.3 | 14.6 | 93.2 | 22.5 | 180.2 | 55.3 | 238 494 | 1 378 | 1 143.7 | 299.0 | 308.1 | 1 267 | 1 118 |
| McCormick | 5.7 | 14.0 | 0.7 | 21.0 | 1.8 | 0.7 | 0.3 | 3 605 | 22 | 20.5 | 7.3 | 9.8 | 973 | 906 |
| Marion | 35.8 | 89.6 | 1.3 | 87.7 | 8.5 | 3.5 | 7.4 | 2 303 | 18 | 88.5 | 48.6 | 24.2 | 714 | 592 |
| Marlboro | 26.4 | 5.8 | 4.9 | 84.7 | 7.7 | 2.9 | 0.8 | 1 517 | 11 | 67.3 | 41.4 | 16.0 | 554 | 482 |
| Newberry | 26.6 | 0.2 | 2.6 | 49.8 | 5.3 | 2.9 | 2.6 | 7 475 | 57 | 105.5 | 43.9 | 39.1 | 1 039 | 946 |
| Oconee | 17.6 | 0.4 | 3.7 | 57.8 | 7.6 | 5.1 | 10.6 | 49 514 | 169 | 189.5 | 66.8 | 95.4 | 1 348 | 1 274 |
| Orangeburg | 38.0 | 6.3 | 3.6 | 196.7 | 26.6 | 27.4 | 50.1 | 11 942 | 80 | 389.8 | 104.1 | 96.8 | 1 076 | 873 |
| Pickens | 40.8 | 34.9 | 4.6 | 69.3 | 11.3 | 7.3 | 104.2 | 63 648 | 266 | 235.2 | 98.6 | 87.6 | 755 | 669 |
| Richland | 1 907.3 | 523.7 | 359.6 | 480.8 | 193.6 | 109.0 | 1 166.4 | 144 703 | 1 270 | 984.0 | 339.5 | 464.6 | 1 299 | 1 124 |
| Saluda | 7.3 | 0.0 | 0.5 | 27.0 | 2.9 | 2.2 | 0.4 | 3 637 | 23 | 34.3 | 16.1 | 13.1 | 701 | 638 |
| Spartanburg | 85.6 | 4.8 | 10.7 | 239.6 | 37.1 | 19.4 | 22.2 | 61 288 | 532 | 1 277.3 | 308.7 | 290.4 | 1 054 | 930 |

1. State totals may include programs not allocated by county.    2. Based on the resident population estimated as of July 1 of the year shown.

| STATE County | Total (mil dol) | Per capita[1] (dollars) | Education | Health and hospitals | Police protection | Public welfare | Highways | Total (mil dol) | Per capita[1] (dollars) | Federal civilian | Federal military | State and local | Demo-cratic | Republi-can | All other |
|---|---|---|---|---|---|---|---|---|---|---|---|---|---|---|---|
| | 185 | 186 | 187 | 188 | 189 | 190 | 191 | 192 | 193 | 194 | 195 | 196 | 197 | 198 | 199 |
| **PENNSYLVANIA—Cont'd** | | | | | | | | | | | | | | | |
| Potter | 56.0 | 3 295 | 58.4 | 0.1 | 1.4 | 0.6 | 9.3 | 90.4 | 5 321 | 48 | 44 | 1 066 | 30.6 | 68.1 | 1.3 |
| Schuylkill | 504.0 | 3 422 | 50.6 | 4.7 | 2.0 | 6.5 | 4.9 | 441.8 | 3 000 | 642 | 376 | 7 327 | 44.9 | 53.5 | 1.6 |
| Snyder | 87.6 | 2 299 | 58.7 | 0.0 | 5.1 | 2.9 | 5.8 | 140.5 | 3 688 | 107 | 102 | 2 281 | 34.8 | 64.0 | 1.3 |
| Somerset | 208.2 | 2 673 | 61.1 | 0.4 | 1.8 | 5.5 | 5.4 | 345.2 | 4 434 | 200 | 197 | 4 442 | 36.6 | 61.7 | 1.7 |
| Sullivan | 24.5 | 3 956 | 45.9 | 0.4 | 0.7 | 3.3 | 9.3 | 27.1 | 4 370 | 22 | 16 | 371 | 39.5 | 59.0 | 1.5 |
| Susquehanna | 125.1 | 3 043 | 74.0 | 0.6 | 0.4 | 1.9 | 6.6 | 80.7 | 1 962 | 111 | 110 | 1 919 | 43.5 | 55.1 | 1.4 |
| Tioga | 119.2 | 2 931 | 58.9 | 0.0 | 1.0 | 13.3 | 5.5 | 178.1 | 4 378 | 151 | 109 | 3 018 | 35.5 | 63.0 | 1.5 |
| Union | 148.5 | 3 397 | 69.8 | 0.5 | 1.4 | 3.2 | 3.9 | 126.2 | 2 887 | 1 563 | 116 | 1 533 | 42.1 | 56.7 | 1.2 |
| Venango | 202.6 | 3 700 | 57.6 | 0.0 | 2.2 | 10.6 | 3.5 | 237.8 | 4 342 | 102 | 139 | 3 483 | 39.6 | 58.9 | 1.5 |
| Warren | 102.1 | 2 492 | 58.6 | 0.4 | 2.3 | 2.2 | 9.8 | 75.0 | 1 830 | 174 | 106 | 1 925 | 46.1 | 52.3 | 1.6 |
| Washington | 719.2 | 3 499 | 51.8 | 4.4 | 2.5 | 10.9 | 4.8 | 822.2 | 4 000 | 504 | 556 | 10 005 | 47.0 | 51.8 | 1.2 |
| Wayne | 157.7 | 3 049 | 74.2 | 0.0 | 0.9 | 0.0 | 4.6 | 257.6 | 4 982 | 503 | 135 | 2 596 | 43.3 | 55.6 | 1.1 |
| Westmoreland | 1 207.4 | 3 332 | 54.9 | 0.1 | 2.5 | 9.8 | 3.4 | 1 763.3 | 4 867 | 923 | 932 | 15 460 | 41.1 | 57.8 | 1.1 |
| Wyoming | 85.6 | 3 077 | 58.2 | 0.1 | 4.6 | 6.7 | 8.8 | 51.6 | 1 855 | 65 | 72 | 1 203 | 45.6 | 53.2 | 1.3 |
| York | 1 595.0 | 3 788 | 45.1 | 4.3 | 2.9 | 10.1 | 2.6 | 2 349.1 | 5 579 | 4 584 | 1 407 | 16 679 | 42.7 | 56.3 | 1.1 |
| **RHODE ISLAND** | X | X | X | X | X | X | X | X | X | 10 261 | 7 376 | 54 474 | 63.3 | 35.0 | 1.7 |
| Bristol | 182.9 | 3 653 | 65.9 | 0.1 | 4.4 | 0.1 | 4.2 | 146.5 | 2 926 | 89 | 237 | 1 856 | 62.6 | 35.9 | 1.5 |
| Kent | 570.6 | 3 383 | 57.1 | 0.3 | 8.1 | 0.5 | 2.3 | 416.9 | 2 472 | 785 | 761 | 7 258 | 57.7 | 40.5 | 1.8 |
| Newport | 312.6 | 3 776 | 54.5 | 0.1 | 8.7 | 0.5 | 2.8 | 164.3 | 1 985 | 4 535 | 2 783 | 3 150 | 60.9 | 37.6 | 1.6 |
| Providence | 2 190.3 | 3 480 | 51.8 | 0.2 | 7.2 | 0.1 | 2.1 | 1 393.9 | 2 215 | 4 272 | 2 982 | 30 280 | 66.9 | 31.5 | 1.6 |
| Washington | 505.4 | 3 983 | 67.5 | 0.4 | 5.6 | 0.4 | 4.6 | 218.7 | 1 723 | 580 | 613 | 11 930 | 59.0 | 39.2 | 1.8 |
| **SOUTH CAROLINA** | X | X | X | X | X | X | X | X | X | 32 828 | 54 069 | 306 039 | 44.9 | 53.9 | 1.2 |
| Abbeville | 48.5 | 1 904 | 64.6 | 2.1 | 5.0 | 0.0 | 2.9 | 23.8 | 935 | 40 | 107 | 1 406 | 41.8 | 56.9 | 1.3 |
| Aiken | 372.9 | 2 448 | 55.3 | 1.4 | 5.8 | 0.1 | 2.5 | 188.9 | 1 240 | 787 | 686 | 7 268 | 37.4 | 61.4 | 1.2 |
| Allendale | 43.2 | 4 126 | 47.0 | 28.8 | 4.0 | 0.0 | 1.0 | 27.2 | 2 596 | 22 | 43 | 1 187 | 75.3 | 23.5 | 1.2 |
| Anderson | 416.3 | 2 313 | 65.6 | 1.5 | 6.3 | 0.0 | 2.4 | 418.4 | 2 325 | 336 | 805 | 11 187 | 32.7 | 66.0 | 1.3 |
| Bamberg | 39.8 | 2 574 | 65.6 | 1.3 | 4.9 | 0.0 | 1.6 | 14.3 | 929 | 32 | 68 | 1 115 | 65.0 | 33.9 | 1.2 |
| Barnwell | 70.1 | 3 050 | 58.9 | 1.1 | 5.0 | 0.1 | 1.1 | 51.3 | 2 234 | 48 | 95 | 1 501 | 50.3 | 48.7 | 1.0 |
| Beaufort | 610.6 | 4 145 | 36.1 | 17.6 | 5.4 | 0.2 | 3.5 | 1 360.5 | 9 235 | 2 346 | 10 211 | 7 452 | 44.1 | 54.9 | 0.9 |
| Berkeley | 432.0 | 2 640 | 66.9 | 0.4 | 4.4 | 0.2 | 1.3 | 1 187.6 | 7 258 | 1 025 | 782 | 7 492 | 42.8 | 55.9 | 1.3 |
| Calhoun | 32.5 | 2 201 | 63.0 | 3.3 | 6.2 | 1.7 | 0.9 | 86.8 | 5 873 | 23 | 65 | 802 | 51.3 | 47.8 | 0.9 |
| Charleston | 1 276.1 | 3 721 | 36.1 | 1.3 | 8.0 | 0.4 | 4.0 | 3 078.9 | 8 977 | 8 723 | 11 854 | 36 192 | 53.5 | 45.2 | 1.2 |
| Cherokee | 131.6 | 2 437 | 69.3 | 1.6 | 4.4 | 0.3 | 1.6 | 1 309.2 | 24 238 | 95 | 237 | 2 095 | 34.7 | 64.1 | 1.2 |
| Chester | 115.1 | 3 538 | 49.3 | 29.3 | 3.6 | 0.0 | 0.6 | 72.1 | 2 216 | 66 | 140 | 1 569 | 53.5 | 45.2 | 1.3 |
| Chesterfield | 111.3 | 2 603 | 68.9 | 0.0 | 7.3 | 0.0 | 2.4 | 127.2 | 2 975 | 85 | 198 | 1 994 | 47.9 | 50.9 | 1.2 |
| Clarendon | 134.5 | 4 098 | 36.9 | 40.4 | 4.2 | 0.0 | 3.7 | 83.2 | 2 534 | 61 | 148 | 2 292 | 55.8 | 43.5 | 0.8 |
| Colleton | 105.3 | 2 705 | 59.2 | 1.0 | 8.7 | 0.0 | 3.6 | 241.5 | 6 209 | 100 | 166 | 2 041 | 49.7 | 49.2 | 1.0 |
| Darlington | 163.1 | 2 441 | 68.1 | 1.9 | 5.3 | 0.2 | 2.0 | 115.7 | 1 731 | 136 | 291 | 2 944 | 49.4 | 49.6 | 1.0 |
| Dillon | 77.6 | 2 527 | 64.3 | 1.5 | 5.9 | 0.2 | 3.6 | 55.6 | 1 811 | 80 | 135 | 1 492 | 55.2 | 43.8 | 1.0 |
| Dorchester | 309.3 | 2 504 | 72.0 | 0.1 | 4.8 | 0.0 | 1.3 | 499.8 | 4 047 | 192 | 597 | 5 622 | 41.6 | 57.1 | 1.3 |
| Edgefield | 48.8 | 1 919 | 71.5 | 2.5 | 7.6 | 0.0 | 1.2 | 10.2 | 402 | 409 | 114 | 1 309 | 44.1 | 55.0 | 1.0 |
| Fairfield | 75.0 | 3 213 | 59.5 | 4.8 | 5.9 | 0.1 | 1.5 | 18.6 | 797 | 35 | 100 | 1 587 | 65.3 | 33.7 | 1.0 |
| Florence | 357.4 | 2 710 | 58.3 | 9.3 | 6.0 | 0.2 | 2.3 | 265.6 | 2 014 | 672 | 594 | 12 271 | 48.0 | 51.2 | 0.9 |
| Georgetown | 192.7 | 3 185 | 53.2 | 1.9 | 4.7 | 0.1 | 1.9 | 349.9 | 5 783 | 129 | 295 | 4 609 | 46.9 | 52.1 | 1.0 |
| Greenville | 2 189.8 | 5 113 | 32.9 | 38.4 | 2.9 | 0.0 | 2.3 | 3 759.6 | 8 779 | 1 830 | 2 041 | 26 753 | 37.2 | 61.0 | 1.8 |
| Greenwood | 378.3 | 5 542 | 33.1 | 47.4 | 2.2 | 0.0 | 1.0 | 448.0 | 6 564 | 142 | 298 | 7 270 | 41.6 | 57.3 | 1.1 |
| Hampton | 58.0 | 2 736 | 66.8 | 3.0 | 6.4 | 0.0 | 1.8 | 14.7 | 695 | 345 | 89 | 1 230 | 62.2 | 36.8 | 1.0 |
| Horry | 982.5 | 3 931 | 45.9 | 11.4 | 5.3 | 0.3 | 2.6 | 1 240.3 | 4 963 | 605 | 1 180 | 14 513 | 37.1 | 61.7 | 1.3 |
| Jasper | 82.1 | 3 741 | 64.8 | 0.0 | 6.1 | 1.2 | 3.0 | 91.2 | 4 155 | 58 | 107 | 1 396 | 60.9 | 38.0 | 1.1 |
| Kershaw | 207.4 | 3 566 | 43.0 | 38.3 | 2.5 | 0.0 | 0.2 | 257.4 | 4 424 | 107 | 265 | 3 327 | 40.1 | 58.8 | 1.0 |
| Lancaster | 168.5 | 2 295 | 66.4 | 2.2 | 4.2 | 0.0 | 2.7 | 206.5 | 2 814 | 99 | 332 | 3 354 | 42.0 | 56.8 | 1.2 |
| Laurens | 191.2 | 2 748 | 47.4 | 26.7 | 3.7 | 0.1 | 1.7 | 159.1 | 2 286 | 98 | 287 | 3 685 | 40.2 | 58.3 | 1.4 |
| Lee | 45.1 | 2 257 | 60.7 | 0.0 | 5.0 | 0.0 | 2.7 | 47.5 | 2 374 | 29 | 81 | 1 204 | 65.1 | 33.6 | 1.3 |
| Lexington | 1 179.7 | 4 850 | 46.8 | 35.4 | 3.1 | 0.0 | 0.9 | 975.3 | 4 009 | 613 | 1 139 | 17 896 | 30.4 | 68.4 | 1.1 |
| McCormick | 19.6 | 1 944 | 58.0 | 4.7 | 6.4 | 0.3 | 2.4 | 25.8 | 2 553 | 77 | 43 | 764 | 52.7 | 46.6 | 0.8 |
| Marion | 86.9 | 2 563 | 62.9 | 1.4 | 7.9 | 0.6 | 2.6 | 25.6 | 755 | 81 | 144 | 1 609 | 63.3 | 35.7 | 1.0 |
| Marlboro | 73.4 | 2 547 | 63.4 | 1.7 | 6.2 | 2.1 | 1.0 | 43.0 | 1 491 | 364 | 121 | 1 551 | 62.5 | 36.7 | 0.8 |
| Newberry | 113.0 | 3 002 | 65.4 | 0.9 | 3.9 | 0.1 | 2.3 | 94.9 | 2 522 | 96 | 161 | 2 318 | 40.6 | 58.2 | 1.2 |
| Oconee | 187.6 | 2 652 | 65.0 | 1.5 | 5.1 | 0.3 | 3.9 | 165.9 | 2 344 | 132 | 317 | 4 268 | 30.5 | 68.0 | 1.6 |
| Orangeburg | 394.9 | 4 390 | 38.0 | 39.8 | 3.9 | 0.1 | 2.9 | 387.6 | 4 309 | 200 | 398 | 7 058 | 68.6 | 30.5 | 0.9 |
| Pickens | 224.7 | 1 937 | 58.9 | 0.3 | 8.6 | 0.1 | 3.9 | 876.5 | 7 556 | 197 | 526 | 8 809 | 25.9 | 72.1 | 2.0 |
| Richland | 1 071.2 | 2 994 | 61.3 | 1.3 | 5.5 | 0.1 | 1.1 | 1 515.5 | 4 236 | 9 634 | 10 906 | 42 968 | 64.0 | 35.1 | 0.9 |
| Saluda | 32.1 | 1 710 | 55.5 | 1.8 | 7.1 | 0.1 | 2.8 | 20.3 | 1 083 | 36 | 85 | 903 | 38.6 | 60.3 | 1.0 |
| Spartanburg | 1 311.4 | 4 760 | 35.2 | 42.2 | 3.2 | 0.4 | 1.5 | 2 196.7 | 7 973 | 466 | 1 227 | 18 854 | 38.4 | 60.0 | 1.5 |

1. Based on the resident population estimated as of July 1 of the year shown.    2. © 2013 Election Data Services, Inc. All rights reserved.

# Table B. States and Counties — Land Area and Population

| STATE/County code | CBSA code[1] | County type[2] | STATE County | Land area[3] (sq km) 2010 | Total persons | Rank | Per square kilometer | White | Black | American Indian, Alaska Native | Asian and Pacific Islander | Percent Hispanic or Latino[4] | Under 5 years | 5 to 17 years | 18 to 24 years | 25 to 34 years | 35 to 44 years | 45 to 54 years |
|---|---|---|---|---|---|---|---|---|---|---|---|---|---|---|---|---|---|---|
| | | | | 1 | 2 | 3 | 4 | 5 | 6 | 7 | 8 | 9 | 10 | 11 | 12 | 13 | 14 | 15 |
| | | | **SOUTH CAROLINA—Cont'd** | | | | | | | | | | | | | | | |
| 45 085 | 44940 | 3 | Sumter | 1 723 | 108 052 | 548 | 62.7 | 48.2 | 47.4 | 0.8 | 1.8 | 3.5 | 7.3 | 17.9 | 11.0 | 13.2 | 11.7 | 13.8 |
| 45 087 | 46420 | 6 | Union | 1 332 | 28 252 | 1 480 | 21.2 | 67.1 | 32.0 | 0.5 | 0.6 | 1.1 | 6.0 | 16.7 | 8.2 | 10.4 | 12.4 | 15.3 |
| 45 089 | ... | 6 | Williamsburg | 2 419 | 33 620 | 1 336 | 13.9 | 32.1 | 65.3 | 0.5 | 0.6 | 2.2 | 6.1 | 17.0 | 8.8 | 11.8 | 12.2 | 14.1 |
| 45 091 | 16740 | 1 | York | 1 763 | 234 635 | 276 | 133.1 | 73.9 | 19.8 | 1.3 | 1.9 | 4.7 | 6.7 | 18.5 | 9.2 | 12.2 | 14.5 | 15.0 |
| 46 000 | ... | X | **SOUTH DAKOTA** | 196 350 | 833 354 | X | 4.2 | 86.1 | 1.9 | 9.6 | 1.4 | 2.9 | 7.2 | 17.4 | 10.1 | 13.1 | 11.3 | 13.9 |
| 46 003 | ... | 9 | Aurora | 1 835 | 2 742 | 2 994 | 1.5 | 93.4 | 0.5 | 2.0 | 0.9 | 3.9 | 6.8 | 19.7 | 5.7 | 10.4 | 10.2 | 14.5 |
| 46 005 | 26700 | 7 | Beadle | 3 260 | 17 753 | 1 930 | 5.4 | 85.6 | 1.4 | 1.7 | 4.6 | 8.0 | 7.7 | 16.8 | 7.8 | 11.8 | 10.3 | 15.3 |
| 46 007 | ... | 9 | Bennett | 3 068 | 3 436 | 2 945 | 1.1 | 37.3 | 0.7 | 62.1 | 1.0 | 2.8 | 10.4 | 23.9 | 10.2 | 11.9 | 9.9 | 11.9 |
| 46 009 | ... | 9 | Bon Homme | 1 460 | 7 029 | 2 680 | 4.8 | 89.6 | 1.2 | 8.1 | 0.4 | 1.9 | 4.7 | 14.7 | 7.6 | 12.9 | 12.6 | 15.9 |
| 46 011 | 15100 | 7 | Brookings | 2 052 | 32 629 | 1 367 | 15.9 | 93.2 | 1.1 | 1.7 | 3.3 | 2.0 | 5.9 | 12.8 | 29.2 | 13.6 | 9.1 | 10.0 |
| 46 013 | 10100 | 5 | Brown | 4 437 | 37 331 | 1 237 | 8.4 | 93.8 | 1.0 | 3.9 | 1.4 | 1.5 | 6.9 | 16.2 | 10.3 | 12.8 | 11.1 | 14.0 |
| 46 015 | ... | 9 | Brule | 2 117 | 5 293 | 2 819 | 2.5 | 89.5 | 0.7 | 10.0 | 0.5 | 1.8 | 6.9 | 18.5 | 6.6 | 11.4 | 11.0 | 15.0 |
| 46 017 | ... | 9 | Buffalo | 1 221 | 2 020 | 3 051 | 1.7 | 18.0 | 0.4 | 80.0 | 0.3 | 2.5 | 12.5 | 28.1 | 10.4 | 13.4 | 10.4 | 10.8 |
| 46 019 | ... | 6 | Butte | 5 827 | 10 228 | 2 423 | 1.8 | 94.2 | 0.7 | 3.6 | 0.6 | 3.3 | 7.1 | 17.8 | 7.6 | 11.6 | 10.3 | 15.0 |
| 46 021 | ... | 9 | Campbell | 1 900 | 1 396 | 3 089 | 0.7 | 98.0 | 0.2 | 0.6 | 0.4 | 1.3 | 3.9 | 13.4 | 5.3 | 6.7 | 7.2 | 21.3 |
| 46 023 | ... | 9 | Charles Mix | 2 842 | 9 216 | 2 499 | 3.2 | 66.8 | 0.6 | 32.6 | 0.6 | 2.1 | 8.6 | 21.1 | 7.5 | 10.3 | 9.8 | 13.7 |
| 46 025 | ... | 9 | Clark | 2 480 | 3 585 | 2 938 | 1.4 | 97.5 | 0.5 | 0.5 | 0.2 | 2.1 | 7.4 | 16.2 | 5.6 | 10.1 | 9.6 | 14.0 |
| 46 027 | 46820 | 6 | Clay | 1 068 | 14 131 | 2 167 | 13.2 | 91.4 | 2.0 | 4.3 | 2.3 | 2.2 | 5.4 | 11.8 | 34.0 | 12.0 | 8.3 | 9.2 |
| 46 029 | 47980 | 7 | Codington | 1 783 | 27 606 | 1 509 | 15.5 | 95.4 | 0.7 | 2.7 | 0.7 | 1.6 | 7.5 | 17.1 | 9.4 | 12.8 | 11.5 | 14.5 |
| 46 031 | ... | 9 | Corson | 6 396 | 4 077 | 2 899 | 0.6 | 32.8 | 0.6 | 65.5 | 0.7 | 3.2 | 9.2 | 25.4 | 9.7 | 12.3 | 10.2 | 13.1 |
| 46 033 | ... | 8 | Custer | 4 033 | 8 339 | 2 578 | 2.1 | 93.6 | 0.8 | 4.4 | 0.6 | 2.5 | 4.5 | 14.7 | 4.7 | 8.5 | 9.0 | 15.8 |
| 46 035 | 33580 | 7 | Davison | 1 128 | 19 769 | 1 846 | 17.5 | 94.6 | 1.1 | 3.3 | 0.9 | 1.7 | 7.0 | 16.1 | 10.9 | 12.7 | 10.2 | 13.6 |
| 46 037 | ... | 9 | Day | 2 662 | 5 613 | 2 795 | 2.1 | 88.9 | 0.6 | 10.5 | 0.5 | 1.3 | 6.0 | 15.7 | 6.1 | 9.6 | 9.0 | 15.0 |
| 46 039 | ... | 9 | Deuel | 1 613 | 4 380 | 2 875 | 2.7 | 96.7 | 0.6 | 0.8 | 0.3 | 2.3 | 6.2 | 17.0 | 6.2 | 10.5 | 11.1 | 15.7 |
| 46 041 | ... | 9 | Dewey | 5 963 | 5 538 | 2 801 | 0.9 | 25.5 | 0.6 | 74.3 | 0.7 | 2.5 | 9.7 | 24.2 | 10.5 | 11.9 | 11.3 | 13.6 |
| 46 043 | ... | 9 | Douglas | 1 118 | 2 970 | 2 982 | 2.7 | 96.5 | 0.7 | 2.2 | 0.2 | 1.0 | 5.3 | 17.1 | 6.0 | 8.4 | 9.4 | 15.3 |
| 46 045 | 10100 | 9 | Edmunds | 2 916 | 4 026 | 2 902 | 1.4 | 97.6 | 0.5 | 1.1 | 0.5 | 1.5 | 5.6 | 18.2 | 6.3 | 8.9 | 9.7 | 15.8 |
| 46 047 | ... | 7 | Fall River | 4 506 | 6 971 | 2 688 | 1.5 | 89.4 | 1.3 | 8.5 | 0.9 | 2.6 | 3.8 | 13.4 | 5.9 | 8.2 | 9.6 | 15.2 |
| 46 049 | ... | 9 | Faulk | 2 543 | 2 377 | 3 018 | 0.9 | 98.7 | 0.4 | 0.8 | 0.2 | 0.8 | 6.0 | 17.3 | 6.5 | 9.0 | 8.8 | 15.7 |
| 46 051 | ... | 7 | Grant | 1 765 | 7 259 | 2 656 | 4.1 | 96.5 | 0.3 | 1.0 | 0.4 | 2.4 | 5.9 | 16.8 | 6.4 | 9.8 | 10.3 | 17.2 |
| 46 053 | ... | 9 | Gregory | 2 629 | 4 265 | 2 885 | 1.6 | 91.4 | 0.6 | 8.5 | 0.6 | 1.0 | 5.9 | 16.5 | 5.6 | 8.2 | 9.9 | 14.2 |
| 46 055 | ... | 8 | Haakon | 4 689 | 1 939 | 3 062 | 0.4 | 96.3 | 1.0 | 3.7 | 0.9 | 0.9 | 7.1 | 16.4 | 4.5 | 10.7 | 9.0 | 15.8 |
| 46 057 | 47980 | 9 | Hamlin | 1 314 | 5 918 | 2 768 | 4.5 | 96.5 | 0.5 | 0.7 | 0.3 | 2.6 | 9.0 | 21.1 | 7.2 | 10.5 | 10.6 | 13.3 |
| 46 059 | ... | 9 | Hand | 3 721 | 3 388 | 2 948 | 0.9 | 98.7 | 0.4 | 0.6 | 0.6 | 0.6 | 5.3 | 15.3 | 5.8 | 10.1 | 9.1 | 15.8 |
| 46 061 | 33580 | 8 | Hanson | 1 125 | 3 377 | 2 949 | 3.0 | 98.2 | 0.2 | 0.7 | 0.5 | 0.9 | 8.8 | 23.2 | 6.0 | 10.9 | 12.6 | 13.0 |
| 46 063 | ... | 9 | Harding | 6 919 | 1 316 | 3 093 | 0.2 | 96.8 | 0.4 | 2.5 | 0.3 | 1.6 | 5.6 | 17.3 | 7.4 | 10.6 | 11.3 | 15.9 |
| 46 065 | 38180 | 7 | Hughes | 1 921 | 17 450 | 1 956 | 9.1 | 85.9 | 1.2 | 11.8 | 0.9 | 2.3 | 6.9 | 16.9 | 7.2 | 13.6 | 12.5 | 15.5 |
| 46 067 | ... | 8 | Hutchinson | 2 105 | 7 187 | 2 660 | 3.4 | 96.9 | 0.8 | 1.1 | 0.3 | 1.7 | 6.0 | 17.7 | 5.3 | 8.8 | 10.0 | 13.9 |
| 46 069 | ... | 9 | Hyde | 2 229 | 1 437 | 3 086 | 0.6 | 91.2 | 0.9 | 8.1 | 0.6 | 1.1 | 5.9 | 16.3 | 7.2 | 10.2 | 9.1 | 14.0 |
| 46 071 | ... | 8 | Jackson | 4 828 | 3 191 | 2 961 | 0.7 | 47.2 | 1.3 | 54.1 | 0.5 | 1.9 | 9.2 | 23.4 | 9.5 | 11.6 | 10.0 | 12.6 |
| 46 073 | ... | 9 | Jerauld | 1 363 | 2 047 | 3 047 | 1.5 | 94.4 | 0.5 | 0.6 | 0.5 | 4.7 | 7.1 | 14.5 | 4.1 | 11.4 | 8.7 | 13.3 |
| 46 075 | ... | 9 | Jones | 2 511 | 1 013 | 3 108 | 0.4 | 95.4 | 0.7 | 4.4 | 0.4 | 1.6 | 6.3 | 16.3 | 6.9 | 8.6 | 11.0 | 16.0 |
| 46 077 | ... | 9 | Kingsbury | 2 155 | 5 220 | 2 825 | 2.4 | 97.0 | 0.5 | 1.2 | 0.5 | 1.8 | 6.2 | 15.9 | 5.6 | 10.7 | 9.4 | 15.6 |
| 46 079 | ... | 6 | Lake | 1 459 | 11 771 | 2 312 | 8.1 | 96.3 | 1.0 | 1.3 | 0.9 | 1.6 | 5.5 | 15.2 | 12.4 | 10.9 | 9.7 | 14.6 |
| 46 081 | 43940 | 6 | Lawrence | 2 072 | 24 397 | 1 630 | 11.8 | 93.7 | 0.9 | 3.3 | 1.1 | 2.7 | 5.5 | 13.6 | 14.1 | 11.6 | 9.7 | 13.7 |
| 46 083 | 43620 | 3 | Lincoln | 1 495 | 48 296 | 1 006 | 32.3 | 96.0 | 1.3 | 1.2 | 1.5 | 1.4 | 9.4 | 19.8 | 6.8 | 17.4 | 14.5 | 12.7 |
| 46 085 | ... | 9 | Lyman | 4 253 | 3 789 | 2 921 | 0.9 | 61.2 | 0.7 | 39.1 | 0.5 | 1.2 | 6.9 | 21.5 | 8.8 | 11.3 | 10.5 | 13.6 |
| 46 087 | 43620 | 3 | McCook | 1 487 | 5 610 | 2 797 | 3.8 | 96.9 | 0.5 | 0.9 | 0.3 | 2.0 | 7.3 | 18.2 | 5.6 | 10.6 | 10.7 | 15.0 |
| 46 089 | ... | 9 | McPherson | 2 944 | 2 439 | 3 011 | 0.8 | 98.2 | 0.2 | 0.7 | 0.5 | 1.2 | 5.3 | 16.5 | 5.1 | 7.1 | 9.4 | 13.1 |
| 46 091 | ... | 9 | Marshall | 2 171 | 4 671 | 2 859 | 2.2 | 85.3 | 0.5 | 8.0 | 0.4 | 6.9 | 6.2 | 15.8 | 7.5 | 12.5 | 9.5 | 14.1 |
| 46 093 | 39660 | 3 | Meade | 8 990 | 26 052 | 1 559 | 2.9 | 91.8 | 2.2 | 3.8 | 1.4 | 3.5 | 7.3 | 17.0 | 11.0 | 13.5 | 10.9 | 14.5 |
| 46 095 | ... | 9 | Mellette | 3 386 | 2 101 | 3 043 | 0.6 | 44.8 | 1.1 | 57.9 | 0.6 | 1.8 | 9.3 | 22.9 | 8.7 | 10.8 | 10.4 | 12.8 |
| 46 097 | ... | 8 | Miner | 1 477 | 2 326 | 3 023 | 1.6 | 97.9 | 0.8 | 0.5 | 0.4 | 1.4 | 6.4 | 17.0 | 6.0 | 8.9 | 9.1 | 16.3 |
| 46 099 | 43620 | 3 | Minnehaha | 2 091 | 175 037 | 357 | 83.7 | 87.9 | 4.6 | 3.2 | 2.0 | 4.3 | 7.5 | 17.3 | 9.8 | 15.7 | 12.6 | 14.2 |
| 46 101 | ... | 8 | Moody | 1 345 | 6 446 | 2 729 | 4.8 | 82.8 | 1.1 | 15.3 | 1.3 | 1.9 | 7.3 | 18.5 | 7.3 | 11.4 | 10.9 | 14.9 |
| 46 103 | 39660 | 3 | Pennington | 7 191 | 104 347 | 565 | 14.5 | 84.4 | 2.0 | 11.1 | 1.8 | 4.0 | 7.3 | 17.1 | 9.4 | 14.0 | 11.5 | 14.1 |
| 46 105 | ... | 9 | Perkins | 7 435 | 3 037 | 2 976 | 0.4 | 97.1 | 0.5 | 2.4 | 0.4 | 0.8 | 5.3 | 15.9 | 5.3 | 10.1 | 9.3 | 15.5 |
| 46 107 | ... | 9 | Potter | 2 230 | 2 359 | 3 021 | 1.1 | 97.5 | 0.4 | 1.6 | 0.8 | 0.8 | 5.6 | 14.6 | 5.3 | 8.4 | 8.8 | 14.8 |
| 46 109 | ... | 9 | Roberts | 2 852 | 10 303 | 2 414 | 3.6 | 63.8 | 0.6 | 36.3 | 0.6 | 1.7 | 8.3 | 20.3 | 7.6 | 10.0 | 10.4 | 12.9 |
| 46 111 | ... | 9 | Sanborn | 1 475 | 2 324 | 3 024 | 1.6 | 97.9 | 0.3 | 1.1 | 0.7 | 1.3 | 5.6 | 15.3 | 6.4 | 10.1 | 9.0 | 15.5 |
| 46 113 | ... | 7 | Shannon | 5 423 | 14 059 | 2 172 | 2.6 | 5.9 | 0.5 | 91.4 | 0.6 | 3.0 | 11.4 | 27.7 | 13.3 | 13.0 | 10.9 | 10.4 |
| 46 115 | ... | 7 | Spink | 3 895 | 6 611 | 2 714 | 1.7 | 96.9 | 0.5 | 1.9 | 0.3 | 1.3 | 5.9 | 18.8 | 6.7 | 10.1 | 9.6 | 14.5 |
| 46 117 | 38180 | 9 | Stanley | 3 741 | 2 969 | 2 983 | 0.8 | 91.8 | 0.8 | 8.6 | 0.7 | 0.9 | 6.1 | 17.0 | 6.9 | 11.5 | 12.0 | 14.3 |
| 46 119 | ... | 9 | Sully | 2 608 | 1 427 | 3 087 | 0.5 | 97.4 | 0.9 | 2.1 | 0.1 | 1.0 | 6.3 | 15.4 | 5.3 | 11.1 | 9.7 | 17.5 |
| 46 121 | ... | 9 | Todd | 3 596 | 9 942 | 2 448 | 2.8 | 12.1 | 0.5 | 85.7 | 0.5 | 2.9 | 13.3 | 27.7 | 11.2 | 13.3 | 10.1 | 9.9 |

1. CBSA = Core Based Statistical Area. See Appendix A for explanation. See Appendix B for list of metropolitan areas with component counties.  2. County type code from the Economic Research Service of USDA Rural-Urban Continuum Codes. See Appendix A for definition.  3. Dry land or land partially or temporarily covered by water.  4. May be of any race.

| STATE County | 55 to 64 years | 65 to 74 years | 75 years and over | Percent female | 2000 | 2010 | 2000–2010 | 2010–2012 | Births | Deaths | Net migration | Number | Percent change, 2000–2010 | Persons per household | Female family householder[1] | One person |
|---|---|---|---|---|---|---|---|---|---|---|---|---|---|---|---|---|
| | 16 | 17 | 18 | 19 | 20 | 21 | 22 | 23 | 24 | 25 | 26 | 27 | 28 | 29 | 30 | 31 |
| **SOUTH CAROLINA—Cont'd** | | | | | | | | | | | | | | | | |
| Sumter | 11.8 | 7.5 | 5.8 | 51.8 | 104 646 | 107 456 | 2.7 | 0.6 | 3 392 | 2 231 | -547 | 40 398 | 7.1 | 2.59 | 20.2 | 25.8 |
| Union | 14.3 | 9.3 | 7.6 | 52.4 | 29 881 | 28 961 | -3.1 | -2.4 | 694 | 867 | -536 | 11 974 | -0.9 | 2.38 | 19.1 | 29.0 |
| Williamsburg | 15.2 | 8.6 | 6.4 | 51.4 | 37 217 | 34 423 | -7.5 | -2.3 | 818 | 894 | -751 | 13 007 | -5.2 | 2.53 | 23.0 | 29.0 |
| York | 12.1 | 7.0 | 4.7 | 51.7 | 164 614 | 226 073 | 37.3 | 3.8 | 6 421 | 3 846 | 5 873 | 85 864 | 40.6 | 2.59 | 13.9 | 23.5 |
| **SOUTH DAKOTA** | 12.5 | 7.2 | 7.2 | 49.9 | 754 844 | 814 180 | 7.9 | 2.4 | 26 110 | 15 876 | 8 822 | 322 282 | 11.0 | 2.42 | 9.7 | 29.4 |
| Aurora | 13.3 | 9.7 | 9.9 | 48.8 | 3 058 | 2 710 | -11.4 | 1.2 | 73 | 54 | 17 | 1 102 | -5.4 | 2.37 | 5.4 | 29.9 |
| Beadle | 13.5 | 7.6 | 9.2 | 49.6 | 17 023 | 17 398 | 2.2 | 2.0 | 616 | 460 | 211 | 7 276 | 0.9 | 2.31 | 8.3 | 33.0 |
| Bennett | 10.8 | 5.3 | 5.8 | 50.3 | 3 574 | 3 431 | -4.0 | 0.1 | 150 | 44 | -102 | 1 090 | -2.9 | 3.11 | 20.1 | 24.3 |
| Bon Homme | 12.6 | 8.2 | 10.8 | 41.8 | 7 260 | 7 070 | -2.6 | -0.6 | 128 | 179 | 10 | 2 457 | -6.8 | 2.24 | 5.5 | 32.8 |
| Brookings | 9.4 | 5.1 | 4.9 | 48.8 | 28 220 | 31 965 | 13.3 | 2.1 | 843 | 451 | 277 | 12 029 | 12.8 | 2.36 | 6.1 | 29.6 |
| Brown | 12.8 | 7.2 | 8.7 | 51.2 | 35 460 | 36 531 | 3.0 | 2.2 | 1 058 | 825 | 577 | 15 489 | 5.8 | 2.27 | 8.1 | 33.0 |
| Brule | 13.8 | 7.7 | 9.2 | 51.3 | 5 364 | 5 255 | -2.0 | -0.7 | 150 | 124 | 10 | 2 136 | 6.9 | 2.40 | 8.6 | 30.5 |
| Buffalo | 7.5 | 4.8 | 2.1 | 50.9 | 2 032 | 1 912 | -5.9 | 5.6 | 116 | 28 | 19 | 532 | 1.1 | 3.59 | 33.1 | 19.0 |
| Butte | 14.9 | 8.5 | 7.3 | 49.7 | 9 094 | 10 110 | 11.2 | 1.2 | 288 | 239 | 50 | 4 160 | 18.3 | 2.40 | 9.8 | 28.5 |
| Campbell | 15.8 | 12.6 | 13.7 | 49.0 | 1 782 | 1 466 | -17.7 | -4.8 | 27 | 25 | -77 | 694 | -4.3 | 2.11 | 3.0 | 35.6 |
| Charles Mix | 11.7 | 8.3 | 9.1 | 50.4 | 9 350 | 9 129 | -2.4 | 1.0 | 356 | 254 | -18 | 3 249 | -2.8 | 2.63 | 12.9 | 29.0 |
| Clark | 15.0 | 10.0 | 12.0 | 49.5 | 4 143 | 3 691 | -10.9 | -2.9 | 103 | 120 | -92 | 1 445 | -9.6 | 2.22 | 4.8 | 32.5 |
| Clay | 9.2 | 5.2 | 4.9 | 51.3 | 13 537 | 13 864 | 2.4 | 1.9 | 342 | 213 | 132 | 5 110 | 4.8 | 2.28 | 7.3 | 32.4 |
| Codington | 12.3 | 7.2 | 7.6 | 49.9 | 25 897 | 27 227 | 5.1 | 1.4 | 845 | 541 | 91 | 11 432 | 10.4 | 2.35 | 9.0 | 30.6 |
| Corson | 9.7 | 6.1 | 4.3 | 49.8 | 4 181 | 4 050 | -3.1 | 0.7 | 171 | 63 | -87 | 1 260 | -0.9 | 3.21 | 21.9 | 22.7 |
| Custer | 20.8 | 13.7 | 8.4 | 49.8 | 7 275 | 8 216 | 12.9 | 1.5 | 163 | 181 | 133 | 3 636 | 22.4 | 2.19 | 5.5 | 28.4 |
| Davison | 12.4 | 7.4 | 9.7 | 50.4 | 18 741 | 19 504 | 4.1 | 1.4 | 588 | 412 | 105 | 8 296 | 9.4 | 2.26 | 8.5 | 34.3 |
| Day | 15.7 | 10.5 | 12.5 | 49.6 | 6 267 | 5 710 | -8.9 | -1.7 | 144 | 201 | -43 | 2 504 | -3.2 | 2.22 | 7.9 | 34.0 |
| Deuel | 13.8 | 9.4 | 10.1 | 48.6 | 4 498 | 4 364 | -3.0 | 0.4 | 105 | 90 | 2 | 1 819 | -1.3 | 2.37 | 5.0 | 29.1 |
| Dewey | 9.4 | 5.3 | 4.1 | 50.6 | 5 972 | 5 301 | -11.2 | 4.5 | 275 | 91 | 55 | 1 730 | -7.1 | 3.05 | 24.2 | 24.6 |
| Douglas | 14.5 | 9.9 | 14.1 | 50.3 | 3 458 | 3 002 | -13.2 | -1.1 | 77 | 96 | -14 | 1 210 | -8.4 | 2.33 | 4.2 | 29.1 |
| Edmunds | 14.1 | 9.9 | 11.5 | 49.4 | 4 367 | 4 071 | -6.8 | -1.1 | 92 | 113 | -24 | 1 607 | -4.4 | 2.27 | 4.0 | 31.0 |
| Fall River | 20.1 | 12.7 | 11.2 | 49.1 | 7 453 | 7 094 | -4.8 | -1.7 | 109 | 250 | 11 | 3 272 | 4.6 | 2.10 | 8.9 | 37.6 |
| Faulk | 13.3 | 9.7 | 13.8 | 50.1 | 2 640 | 2 364 | -10.5 | 0.5 | 60 | 47 | 1 | 869 | -14.3 | 2.15 | 4.1 | 36.1 |
| Grant | 14.8 | 9.0 | 9.9 | 49.2 | 7 847 | 7 356 | -6.3 | -1.3 | 159 | 185 | -70 | 3 089 | -0.9 | 2.35 | 6.1 | 29.6 |
| Gregory | 15.9 | 10.6 | 13.2 | 49.6 | 4 792 | 4 271 | -10.9 | -0.1 | 99 | 140 | 39 | 1 936 | -4.3 | 2.18 | 7.4 | 36.6 |
| Haakon | 15.6 | 10.3 | 11.0 | 49.4 | 2 196 | 1 937 | -11.8 | 0.1 | 54 | 29 | -27 | 850 | -2.3 | 2.24 | 4.2 | 33.2 |
| Hamlin | 11.0 | 8.5 | 9.0 | 49.7 | 5 540 | 5 903 | 6.6 | 0.3 | 228 | 173 | -39 | 2 108 | 2.9 | 2.68 | 5.6 | 25.6 |
| Hand | 13.8 | 9.8 | 15.0 | 50.2 | 3 741 | 3 431 | -8.3 | -1.3 | 85 | 71 | -56 | 1 494 | -3.2 | 2.26 | 5.3 | 32.2 |
| Hanson | 11.6 | 8.7 | 5.1 | 49.6 | 3 139 | 3 331 | 6.1 | 1.4 | 98 | 35 | -20 | 1 045 | -6.3 | 2.69 | 3.5 | 21.7 |
| Harding | 17.4 | 7.8 | 6.6 | 47.5 | 1 353 | 1 255 | -7.2 | 4.9 | 26 | 16 | 45 | 539 | 2.7 | 2.27 | 4.8 | 32.1 |
| Hughes | 14.0 | 6.8 | 6.5 | 51.1 | 16 481 | 17 022 | 3.3 | 2.5 | 536 | 362 | 259 | 7 066 | 8.5 | 2.30 | 9.4 | 32.3 |
| Hutchinson | 13.5 | 9.3 | 15.5 | 51.1 | 8 075 | 7 343 | -9.1 | -2.1 | 167 | 247 | -91 | 2 930 | -8.2 | 2.22 | 5.0 | 33.4 |
| Hyde | 15.3 | 9.5 | 12.6 | 48.5 | 1 671 | 1 420 | -15.0 | 1.2 | 31 | 36 | 21 | 600 | -11.6 | 2.30 | 5.5 | 33.0 |
| Jackson | 10.4 | 7.0 | 6.3 | 49.7 | 2 930 | 3 031 | 3.4 | 5.3 | 158 | 53 | 48 | 996 | 5.4 | 3.00 | 16.2 | 26.2 |
| Jerauld | 16.0 | 10.5 | 14.4 | 50.9 | 2 295 | 2 071 | -9.8 | -1.2 | 62 | 53 | -36 | 870 | -11.9 | 2.18 | 6.2 | 30.9 |
| Jones | 14.9 | 9.2 | 11.1 | 50.4 | 1 193 | 1 006 | -15.7 | 0.7 | 33 | 11 | -21 | 458 | -10.0 | 2.20 | 5.2 | 35.8 |
| Kingsbury | 15.0 | 9.5 | 12.0 | 49.1 | 5 815 | 5 148 | -11.5 | 1.4 | 142 | 161 | 81 | 2 222 | -7.6 | 2.23 | 5.0 | 32.2 |
| Lake | 14.7 | 8.8 | 8.3 | 48.9 | 11 276 | 11 200 | -0.7 | 5.1 | 295 | 265 | 511 | 4 483 | 2.5 | 2.30 | 6.8 | 30.9 |
| Lawrence | 15.1 | 8.5 | 8.2 | 50.3 | 21 802 | 24 097 | 10.5 | 1.2 | 534 | 467 | 232 | 10 536 | 18.6 | 2.19 | 8.1 | 33.2 |
| Lincoln | 10.2 | 4.9 | 4.3 | 50.4 | 24 131 | 44 828 | 85.8 | 7.7 | 1 797 | 439 | 2 074 | 16 649 | 89.6 | 2.68 | 7.3 | 20.2 |
| Lyman | 12.6 | 8.7 | 6.1 | 47.4 | 3 895 | 3 755 | -3.6 | 0.9 | 147 | 55 | -54 | 1 392 | -0.6 | 2.67 | 15.2 | 27.2 |
| McCook | 13.5 | 9.1 | 9.9 | 50.0 | 5 832 | 5 618 | -3.7 | -0.1 | 165 | 182 | -3 | 2 168 | -1.6 | 2.45 | 6.0 | 26.2 |
| McPherson | 13.6 | 12.4 | 17.6 | 51.1 | 2 904 | 2 459 | -15.3 | -0.8 | 50 | 61 | -11 | 1 025 | -16.5 | 2.06 | 4.3 | 36.3 |
| Marshall | 15.2 | 9.6 | 9.5 | 45.9 | 4 576 | 4 656 | 1.7 | 0.3 | 127 | 150 | 27 | 1 815 | -1.6 | 2.36 | 6.0 | 31.4 |
| Meade | 13.4 | 6.9 | 5.6 | 48.7 | 24 253 | 25 434 | 4.9 | 2.4 | 700 | 402 | 323 | 9 903 | 12.5 | 2.49 | 8.8 | 23.6 |
| Mellette | 12.2 | 6.2 | 6.7 | 49.4 | 2 083 | 2 048 | -1.7 | 2.6 | 72 | 23 | -4 | 693 | -0.1 | 2.88 | 19.0 | 24.7 |
| Miner | 13.9 | 9.4 | 12.9 | 49.6 | 2 884 | 2 389 | -17.2 | -2.6 | 52 | 70 | -45 | 1 032 | -14.9 | 2.24 | 5.6 | 37.6 |
| Minnehaha | 11.4 | 5.8 | 5.5 | 50.1 | 148 281 | 169 468 | 14.3 | 3.3 | 6 058 | 2 872 | 2 396 | 67 028 | 15.6 | 2.43 | 10.5 | 29.3 |
| Moody | 14.4 | 8.2 | 7.1 | 50.0 | 6 595 | 6 486 | -1.7 | -0.6 | 192 | 122 | -115 | 2 554 | 1.1 | 2.48 | 8.8 | 27.4 |
| Pennington | 12.9 | 7.3 | 6.6 | 50.0 | 88 565 | 100 948 | 14.0 | 3.4 | 3 388 | 1 648 | 1 684 | 41 251 | 19.1 | 2.38 | 11.7 | 29.0 |
| Perkins | 16.3 | 10.0 | 12.4 | 49.2 | 3 363 | 2 982 | -11.3 | 1.8 | 65 | 77 | 67 | 1 291 | -9.7 | 2.26 | 4.9 | 32.0 |
| Potter | 16.6 | 10.8 | 15.1 | 51.0 | 2 693 | 2 329 | -13.5 | 1.3 | 55 | 79 | 54 | 1 062 | -7.2 | 2.13 | 4.2 | 35.5 |
| Roberts | 13.3 | 8.7 | 8.5 | 49.8 | 10 016 | 10 149 | 1.3 | 1.5 | 388 | 234 | -2 | 3 823 | 3.8 | 2.58 | 13.4 | 27.3 |
| Sanborn | 15.8 | 9.4 | 11.5 | 47.7 | 2 675 | 2 355 | -12.0 | -1.3 | 53 | 41 | -43 | 975 | -6.5 | 2.24 | 6.3 | 31.1 |
| Shannon | 7.0 | 4.0 | 2.2 | 51.0 | 12 466 | 13 586 | 9.0 | 3.5 | 778 | 274 | -35 | 3 144 | 12.9 | 4.29 | 38.0 | 14.8 |
| Spink | 14.6 | 9.0 | 10.7 | 49.8 | 7 454 | 6 415 | -13.9 | 3.1 | 158 | 194 | 227 | 2 608 | -8.4 | 2.30 | 6.4 | 31.8 |
| Stanley | 15.6 | 11.1 | 5.5 | 49.6 | 2 772 | 2 966 | 7.0 | 0.1 | 94 | 26 | -65 | 1 228 | 10.5 | 2.42 | 8.5 | 26.2 |
| Sully | 16.2 | 9.5 | 9.0 | 46.3 | 1 556 | 1 373 | -11.8 | 3.9 | 37 | 21 | 39 | 610 | -3.2 | 2.25 | 4.6 | 31.6 |
| Todd | 8.3 | 3.6 | 2.5 | 50.6 | 9 050 | 9 612 | 6.2 | 3.4 | 608 | 175 | -112 | 2 780 | 12.9 | 3.45 | 34.7 | 21.1 |

1. No spouse present.

| STATE County | Persons in group quarters, 2010 | Daytime population, 2007–2011 | | Births, 2011 | | Deaths, 2011 | | Persons under 65 with no health insurance, 2010 | | Medicare, 2012 | | | Serious crimes known to police,[2] 2011 Total | |
|---|---|---|---|---|---|---|---|---|---|---|---|---|---|---|
| | | Number | Employ-ment/resi-dence ratio | Total | Rate[1] | Number | Rate[1] | Number | Percent | Eligible for Medicare | Enrolled in Medicare Advantage | Enrolled in a Medicare prescription drug plan | Number | Rate[3] |
| | 32 | 33 | 34 | 35 | 36 | 37 | 38 | 39 | 40 | 41 | 42 | 43 | 44 | 45 |
| SOUTH CAROLINA—Cont'd | | | | | | | | | | | | | | |
| Sumter | 2 774 | 106 588 | 0.99 | 1 571 | 14.6 | 966 | 9.0 | 17 636 | 19.4 | 18 568 | 2 328 | 7 434 | 4 886 | 4 495 |
| Union | 503 | 26 444 | 0.77 | 344 | 12.0 | 377 | 13.1 | 4 320 | 18.2 | 7 021 | 1 831 | 2 801 | 1 179 | 4 024 |
| Williamsburg | 1 476 | 33 527 | 0.89 | 391 | 11.5 | 368 | 10.8 | 6 414 | 22.9 | 6 952 | 1 170 | 3 381 | 1 361 | 3 908 |
| York | 3 905 | 204 738 | 0.84 | 2 944 | 12.8 | 1 641 | 7.1 | 36 870 | 18.7 | 34 687 | 6 150 | 14 207 | 7 681 | 3 358 |
| SOUTH DAKOTA | 34 050 | 811 417 | 1.01 | 11 763 | 14.3 | 6 772 | 8.2 | 94 404 | 13.9 | 144 369 | 0 | 82 874 | 17 073 | 2 072 |
| Aurora | 96 | 2 482 | 0.83 | 30 | 11.1 | 25 | 9.3 | 430 | 20.6 | 584 | 65 | 415 | 4 | 146 |
| Beadle | 620 | 17 329 | 1.02 | 271 | 15.4 | 203 | 11.6 | 2 026 | 14.3 | 3 401 | 475 | 2 101 | NA | NA |
| Bennett | 37 | 3 310 | 0.88 | 63 | 18.3 | 18 | 5.2 | 642 | 21.2 | 452 | 18 | 283 | 24 | 691 |
| Bon Homme | 1 556 | 6 535 | 0.83 | 51 | 7.3 | 77 | 11.0 | 676 | 15.3 | 1 457 | 133 | 950 | 0 | 0 |
| Brookings | 3 588 | 32 600 | 1.06 | 382 | 11.9 | 202 | 6.3 | 3 338 | 13.1 | 3 642 | 482 | 2 176 | 177 | 547 |
| Brown | 1 365 | 37 553 | 1.07 | 470 | 12.8 | 346 | 9.4 | 3 296 | 11.0 | 6 590 | 367 | 4 361 | 574 | 1 617 |
| Brule | 132 | 5 369 | 1.07 | 66 | 12.5 | 57 | 10.8 | 712 | 16.7 | 886 | 84 | 570 | NA | NA |
| Buffalo | 3 | 1 945 | 1.01 | 51 | 25.7 | 12 | 6.0 | 337 | 19.1 | 206 | D | 121 | NA | NA |
| Butte | 111 | 8 679 | 0.71 | 139 | 13.5 | 106 | 10.3 | 1 406 | 16.7 | 1 867 | 370 | 933 | 137 | 1 339 |
| Campbell | 0 | 1 295 | 0.85 | 16 | 11.2 | 8 | 5.6 | 182 | 16.6 | 384 | 49 | 264 | 5 | 337 |
| Charles Mix | 589 | 9 285 | 1.05 | 162 | 17.6 | 111 | 12.1 | 1 375 | 18.9 | 1 787 | 96 | 1 273 | 69 | 863 |
| Clark | 489 | 3 419 | 0.85 | 55 | 15.2 | 50 | 13.8 | 517 | 18.0 | 805 | 149 | 590 | 10 | 268 |
| Clay | 2 237 | 13 037 | 0.88 | 169 | 12.0 | 94 | 6.7 | 1 623 | 15.7 | 1 686 | 192 | 1 135 | 92 | 656 |
| Codington | 381 | 28 244 | 1.07 | 389 | 14.2 | 242 | 8.8 | 2 804 | 12.2 | 4 801 | 1 120 | 3 178 | 670 | 2 431 |
| Corson | 1 | 3 922 | 0.90 | 70 | 17.4 | 31 | 7.7 | 772 | 21.6 | 528 | 18 | 333 | 18 | 525 |
| Custer | 255 | 7 401 | 0.80 | 60 | 7.2 | 77 | 9.2 | 898 | 14.3 | 1 973 | 289 | 824 | 35 | 421 |
| Davison | 769 | 20 817 | 1.13 | 290 | 14.8 | 164 | 8.3 | 2 186 | 14.0 | 3 785 | 316 | 2 706 | 472 | 2 391 |
| Day | 139 | 5 422 | 0.90 | 63 | 11.0 | 98 | 17.1 | 866 | 19.9 | 1 420 | 142 | 951 | NA | NA |
| Deuel | 50 | 4 043 | 0.86 | 43 | 9.9 | 36 | 8.3 | 596 | 17.1 | 995 | 209 | 636 | 22 | 498 |
| Dewey | 19 | 5 712 | 1.21 | 112 | 20.7 | 32 | 5.9 | 1 110 | 23.2 | 752 | 28 | 425 | 8 | 149 |
| Douglas | 178 | 2 977 | 0.98 | 30 | 10.1 | 37 | 12.4 | 398 | 17.8 | 736 | 93 | 516 | 5 | 165 |
| Edmunds | 420 | 3 634 | 0.79 | 45 | 11.1 | 52 | 12.8 | 475 | 15.0 | 880 | 54 | 638 | 0 | 0 |
| Fall River | 235 | 7 202 | 1.05 | 44 | 6.3 | 104 | 14.9 | 841 | 15.9 | 2 139 | 225 | 815 | NA | NA |
| Faulk | 497 | 2 248 | 0.88 | 29 | 12.3 | 16 | 6.8 | 313 | 17.5 | 537 | 49 | 381 | 12 | 501 |
| Grant | 104 | 7 698 | 1.09 | 80 | 11.0 | 87 | 12.0 | 843 | 14.2 | 1 674 | 310 | 1 051 | NA | NA |
| Gregory | 44 | 4 121 | 0.93 | 43 | 10.2 | 61 | 14.5 | 656 | 20.6 | 1 106 | 138 | 716 | NA | NA |
| Haakon | 36 | 1 724 | 0.99 | 24 | 12.6 | 11 | 5.8 | 316 | 21.4 | 416 | 46 | 276 | NA | NA |
| Hamlin | 245 | 4 969 | 0.68 | 103 | 17.2 | 77 | 12.9 | 747 | 15.5 | 1 012 | 178 | 668 | 41 | 686 |
| Hand | 61 | 3 330 | 0.96 | 29 | 8.5 | 24 | 7.0 | 416 | 16.4 | 856 | 52 | 635 | 14 | 403 |
| Hanson | 520 | 2 592 | 0.48 | 43 | 12.7 | 13 | 3.9 | 444 | 15.6 | 1 355 | 126 | 640 | 12 | 356 |
| Harding | 29 | 1 394 | 1.10 | 10 | 7.9 | 4 | 3.2 | 273 | 26.3 | 210 | 22 | 116 | 1 | 79 |
| Hughes | 772 | 17 929 | 1.10 | 258 | 14.9 | 161 | 9.3 | 1 732 | 12.1 | 2 779 | 165 | 1 739 | 586 | 3 401 |
| Hutchinson | 832 | 7 085 | 0.93 | 81 | 11.2 | 109 | 15.0 | 832 | 15.4 | 1 919 | 321 | 1 389 | 11 | 148 |
| Hyde | 38 | 1 505 | 1.12 | 15 | 10.8 | 16 | 11.5 | 203 | 18.7 | 316 | 18 | 206 | NA | NA |
| Jackson | 42 | 3 001 | 0.97 | 73 | 23.0 | 20 | 6.3 | 607 | 23.4 | 449 | 47 | 251 | NA | NA |
| Jerauld | 176 | 2 162 | 1.12 | 34 | 16.3 | 24 | 11.5 | 261 | 16.9 | 631 | 58 | 402 | 7 | 334 |
| Jones | 0 | 1 149 | 0.90 | 16 | 16.0 | 5 | 5.0 | 191 | 24.1 | 229 | 18 | 141 | NA | NA |
| Kingsbury | 203 | 4 769 | 0.85 | 63 | 12.2 | 66 | 12.7 | 561 | 14.1 | 1 222 | 141 | 813 | NA | NA |
| Lake | 874 | 10 662 | 0.91 | 127 | 11.0 | 113 | 9.8 | 1 075 | 12.2 | 2 790 | 303 | 1 584 | NA | NA |
| Lawrence | 1 071 | 23 830 | 0.99 | 252 | 10.4 | 201 | 8.3 | 2 837 | 14.6 | 4 722 | 747 | 2 261 | 696 | 2 854 |
| Lincoln | 284 | 32 334 | 0.54 | 831 | 17.8 | 178 | 3.8 | 3 504 | 8.4 | 4 767 | 805 | 2 685 | 1 052 | 2 337 |
| Lyman | 37 | 3 591 | 0.91 | 54 | 14.2 | 25 | 6.6 | 727 | 23.0 | 638 | 51 | 383 | NA | NA |
| McCook | 312 | 4 733 | 0.69 | 82 | 14.8 | 80 | 14.4 | 621 | 13.8 | 1 105 | 122 | 735 | 48 | 844 |
| McPherson | 347 | 2 397 | 0.92 | 20 | 8.2 | 24 | 9.8 | 362 | 21.1 | 743 | 50 | 550 | 3 | 121 |
| Marshall | 373 | 4 339 | 0.87 | 62 | 13.5 | 64 | 13.9 | 712 | 19.0 | 980 | 69 | 645 | 40 | 849 |
| Meade | 797 | 21 239 | 0.70 | 304 | 11.9 | 179 | 7.0 | 3 028 | 14.0 | 4 382 | 695 | 1 820 | 284 | 1 103 |
| Mellette | 49 | 1 874 | 0.76 | 34 | 16.4 | 9 | 4.4 | 353 | 20.3 | 312 | 12 | 203 | 18 | 868 |
| Miner | 80 | 2 165 | 0.82 | 29 | 12.3 | 27 | 11.4 | 264 | 14.3 | 562 | 34 | 386 | 19 | 786 |
| Minnehaha | 6 291 | 185 533 | 1.19 | 2 696 | 15.7 | 1 214 | 7.1 | 17 987 | 12.2 | 27 240 | 4 074 | 14 837 | 4 904 | 2 859 |
| Moody | 164 | 5 776 | 0.79 | 85 | 13.1 | 55 | 8.5 | 851 | 15.4 | 1 179 | 135 | 705 | 85 | 1 295 |
| Pennington | 2 575 | 103 660 | 1.08 | 1 548 | 15.1 | 681 | 6.6 | 12 562 | 14.6 | 19 059 | 3 019 | 8 287 | 3 976 | 3 891 |
| Perkins | 65 | 2 944 | 1.03 | 28 | 9.3 | 32 | 10.7 | 581 | 25.6 | 756 | 69 | 495 | 16 | 530 |
| Potter | 63 | 2 367 | 0.99 | 21 | 8.9 | 40 | 16.9 | 246 | 14.4 | 645 | 21 | 416 | 4 | 170 |
| Roberts | 281 | 9 678 | 0.91 | 168 | 16.3 | 100 | 9.7 | 1 568 | 18.8 | 1 970 | 241 | 1 164 | 150 | 1 460 |
| Sanborn | 174 | 2 065 | 0.73 | 24 | 10.0 | 19 | 7.9 | 390 | 20.9 | 482 | 38 | 327 | NA | NA |
| Shannon | 91 | 14 370 | 1.25 | 336 | 24.1 | 114 | 8.2 | 2 168 | 17.2 | 1 131 | 14 | 548 | 0 | 0 |
| Spink | 404 | 6 423 | 0.98 | 60 | 9.3 | 90 | 13.9 | 608 | 12.3 | 1 485 | 90 | 1 067 | 59 | 909 |
| Stanley | 0 | 2 375 | 0.68 | 40 | 13.3 | 8 | 2.7 | 403 | 15.9 | 548 | 52 | 300 | 36 | 1 199 |
| Sully | 0 | 1 296 | 0.89 | 18 | 13.1 | 7 | 5.1 | 171 | 15.1 | 299 | 30 | 174 | 9 | 647 |
| Todd | 28 | 9 906 | 1.09 | 268 | 27.3 | 93 | 9.5 | 1 362 | 15.4 | 795 | 13 | 466 | NA | NA |

1. Per 1,000 estimated resident population.   2. Data for serious crimes have not been adjusted for underreporting; this may affect comparability between geographic areas and over time.   3. Per 100,000 population estimated by the FBI.

# Table B. States and Counties — Crime, Education, Money Income, and Poverty

| STATE County | Serious crimes known to police, 2011 (cont.)[1] Rate[2] | | Education School enrollment and attainment, 2007–2011 | | | | Local government expenditures,[5] 2009–2010 | | Money income, 2007–2011 | Households | | | Income and poverty, 2011 Percent below poverty level | | |
|---|---|---|---|---|---|---|---|---|---|---|---|---|---|---|---|
| | | | Enrollment[3] | | Attainment[4] (percent) | | | | | | Median income | | | | |
| | Violent | Property | Total | Percent private | High school graduate or less | Bachelor's degree or more | Total current expenditures (mil dol) | Current expenditures per student (dollars) | Per capita income[6] (dollars) | Dollars | Percent change, 2000 to 2007–2011 (constant 2011 dollars) | Percent with income of $200,000 or more | Median household income (dollars) | All persons | Children under 18 years | Children 5 to 17 years in families |
| | 46 | 47 | 48 | 49 | 50 | 51 | 52 | 53 | 54 | 55 | 56 | 57 | 58 | 59 | 60 | 61 |
| **SOUTH CAROLINA—Cont'd** | | | | | | | | | | | | | | | | |
| Sumter | 1 135 | 3 359 | 28 078 | 15.1 | 50.6 | 17.8 | 147.2 | 8 478 | 19 686 | 40 542 | -9.8 | 1.2 | 40 858 | 17.6 | 27.9 | 27.1 |
| Union | 471 | 3 553 | 6 600 | 8.5 | 59.9 | 12.7 | 38.0 | 8 332 | 19 165 | 33 679 | -20.7 | 0.7 | 33 981 | 20.3 | 31.2 | 30.6 |
| Williamsburg | 669 | 3 239 | 8 843 | 10.6 | 66.3 | 11.3 | 57.2 | 10 857 | 13 895 | 24 530 | -25.0 | 0.3 | 27 750 | 30.9 | 42.1 | 38.7 |
| York | 488 | 2 871 | 59 274 | 11.7 | 42.3 | 28.2 | 353.4 | 8 954 | 26 751 | 53 536 | -11.0 | 3.3 | 51 017 | 15.1 | 21.1 | 19.5 |
| **SOUTH DAKOTA** | 254 | 1 818 | 210 655 | 12.5 | 42.3 | 25.8 | 1 094.4 | 8 846 | 24 925 | 48 010 | 0.8 | 2.4 | 48 188 | 14.1 | 19.2 | 16.6 |
| Aurora | 0 | 146 | 636 | 19.4 | 54.7 | 13.9 | 6.3 | 11 263 | 21 974 | 46 205 | 14.9 | 1.7 | 45 615 | 12.2 | 18.3 | 15.6 |
| Beadle | NA | NA | 3 661 | 19.4 | 51.5 | 19.4 | 20.2 | 8 498 | 24 567 | 40 455 | -1.8 | 1.8 | 43 803 | 14.4 | 20.7 | 18.8 |
| Bennett | 288 | 403 | 994 | 12.4 | 44.9 | 15.6 | 5.8 | 9 950 | 17 285 | 34 500 | 0.9 | 1.9 | 31 712 | 37.0 | 49.2 | 43.5 |
| Bon Homme | 0 | 0 | 1 320 | 7.2 | 53.3 | 17.5 | 9.8 | 9 064 | 20 975 | 43 456 | 5.0 | 2.4 | 41 711 | 16.6 | 19.8 | 16.7 |
| Brookings | 25 | 522 | 13 366 | 4.0 | 35.8 | 38.2 | 34.6 | 8 484 | 22 036 | 46 101 | -3.7 | 1.8 | 48 233 | 15.1 | 12.6 | 10.8 |
| Brown | 208 | 1 408 | 9 372 | 13.4 | 41.9 | 25.0 | 39.0 | 7 796 | 24 671 | 47 327 | 0.1 | 1.9 | 50 115 | 10.0 | 12.9 | 10.5 |
| Brule | NA | NA | 1 136 | 17.3 | 53.6 | 21.8 | 12.7 | 11 252 | 21 726 | 48 170 | 10.2 | 1.4 | 45 265 | 13.0 | 17.8 | 14.9 |
| Buffalo | NA | NA | 591 | 24.0 | 61.9 | 9.5 | NA | NA | 11 162 | 28 493 | 66.3 | 0.0 | 21 269 | 39.3 | 48.6 | 43.5 |
| Butte | 156 | 1 182 | 2 383 | 13.6 | 49.0 | 16.9 | 13.2 | 7 770 | 20 921 | 41 145 | 4.9 | 2.0 | 39 615 | 15.8 | 24.3 | 20.5 |
| Campbell | 0 | 337 | 275 | 16.0 | 54.3 | 16.0 | 1.5 | 11 075 | 22 679 | 40 385 | 3.9 | 0.8 | 40 855 | 11.0 | 12.2 | 9.9 |
| Charles Mix | 100 | 763 | 2 312 | 17.5 | 53.8 | 15.4 | 17.9 | 11 137 | 18 150 | 36 757 | 4.5 | 2.3 | 37 448 | 24.5 | 36.0 | 30.1 |
| Clark | 27 | 241 | 757 | 3.6 | 54.1 | 17.5 | 5.8 | 9 877 | 26 644 | 45 844 | 12.4 | 2.5 | 43 496 | 14.2 | 23.9 | 20.8 |
| Clay | 50 | 606 | 7 047 | 4.7 | 33.5 | 41.7 | 10.4 | 8 030 | 20 326 | 39 118 | 5.2 | 1.1 | 39 870 | 23.5 | 21.3 | 18.2 |
| Codington | 272 | 2 159 | 6 806 | 12.2 | 46.0 | 24.2 | 33.7 | 7 708 | 25 215 | 44 672 | -8.7 | 2.5 | 47 282 | 12.2 | 14.9 | 12.2 |
| Corson | 0 | 525 | 1 266 | 2.2 | 50.3 | 13.2 | 12.8 | 15 115 | 13 323 | 28 506 | 2.2 | 1.3 | 28 770 | 38.0 | 49.0 | 42.9 |
| Custer | 48 | 373 | 1 458 | 9.9 | 35.1 | 30.4 | 9.6 | 9 035 | 25 525 | 48 115 | -1.8 | 0.9 | 49 649 | 10.9 | 20.5 | 17.4 |
| Davison | 268 | 2 122 | 4 800 | 20.2 | 42.1 | 23.1 | 25.2 | 8 648 | 23 510 | 44 597 | -1.3 | 0.9 | 47 100 | 13.0 | 16.1 | 14.2 |
| Day | NA | NA | 1 163 | 12.8 | 53.5 | 16.9 | 7.4 | 9 909 | 20 870 | 40 335 | -1.2 | 0.9 | 39 223 | 17.4 | 23.0 | 19.9 |
| Deuel | 23 | 475 | 926 | 9.1 | 55.3 | 17.5 | 4.1 | 7 581 | 24 518 | 46 186 | 7.6 | 2.5 | 45 700 | 9.7 | 14.2 | 11.9 |
| Dewey | 19 | 130 | 1 650 | 2.9 | 57.1 | 14.2 | 11.0 | 18 352 | 16 410 | 30 645 | -2.5 | 1.9 | 33 902 | 30.3 | 39.9 | 34.9 |
| Douglas | 0 | 165 | 585 | 27.0 | 60.1 | 13.7 | 3.3 | 9 431 | 24 814 | 45 957 | 19.5 | 4.1 | 46 224 | 11.6 | 15.0 | 12.1 |
| Edmunds | 0 | 0 | 739 | 13.5 | 48.5 | 23.5 | 6.1 | 9 326 | 24 600 | 48 032 | 10.5 | 3.0 | 49 467 | 12.3 | 17.1 | 14.1 |
| Fall River | NA | NA | 1 139 | 15.6 | 43.7 | 20.9 | 11.0 | 9 602 | 24 494 | 34 948 | -12.6 | 1.0 | 39 444 | 15.3 | 24.1 | 19.2 |
| Faulk | 0 | 501 | 467 | 27.4 | 52.4 | 15.7 | 3.2 | 9 947 | 22 537 | 40 125 | -1.7 | 2.9 | 43 030 | 13.9 | 20.1 | 17.5 |
| Grant | NA | NA | 1 604 | 11.0 | 55.6 | 18.4 | 9.9 | 8 734 | 24 344 | 44 444 | -0.5 | 1.4 | 47 131 | 11.0 | 14.2 | 11.8 |
| Gregory | NA | NA | 816 | 4.9 | 51.2 | 15.1 | 7.9 | 11 151 | 22 550 | 35 975 | 17.2 | 1.6 | 33 991 | 20.1 | 30.1 | 25.7 |
| Haakon | NA | NA | 243 | 8.2 | 46.6 | 17.2 | 2.6 | 8 841 | 29 162 | 49 432 | 22.5 | 1.9 | 44 653 | 12.8 | 16.7 | 14.3 |
| Hamlin | 117 | 569 | 1 443 | 8.5 | 51.3 | 18.2 | 10.1 | 8 023 | 23 244 | 47 771 | 4.5 | 3.1 | 50 864 | 11.9 | 17.3 | 14.9 |
| Hand | 0 | 403 | 651 | 12.0 | 51.7 | 17.9 | 4.3 | 9 360 | 23 595 | 44 375 | 1.5 | 0.6 | 41 975 | 10.7 | 14.6 | 11.9 |
| Hanson | 0 | 356 | 889 | 23.5 | 54.2 | 21.0 | 5.0 | 9 014 | 20 085 | 47 700 | 6.9 | 1.6 | 57 519 | 8.6 | 12.2 | 10.5 |
| Harding | 0 | 79 | 330 | 5.8 | 39.8 | 31.2 | 2.9 | 13 755 | 22 717 | 46 797 | 38.6 | 2.1 | 42 575 | 14.7 | 24.4 | 20.6 |
| Hughes | 296 | 3 105 | 3 669 | 9.6 | 32.8 | 34.9 | 19.2 | 7 590 | 29 628 | 58 082 | 0.1 | 2.5 | 60 677 | 9.7 | 14.0 | 12.0 |
| Hutchinson | 27 | 121 | 1 594 | 10.1 | 49.0 | 26.1 | 14.7 | 9 707 | 23 305 | 42 386 | 4.6 | 2.3 | 46 309 | 13.1 | 18.3 | 15.0 |
| Hyde | NA | NA | 263 | 4.6 | 58.8 | 17.5 | 2.6 | 8 915 | 25 301 | 43 906 | 4.6 | 0.8 | 44 997 | 12.4 | 16.2 | 13.7 |
| Jackson | NA | NA | 1 037 | 0.6 | 43.2 | 16.7 | 4.4 | 12 577 | 15 721 | 38 581 | 19.3 | 2.2 | 31 854 | 33.1 | 45.4 | 39.9 |
| Jerauld | 0 | 334 | 398 | 0.8 | 56.1 | 14.6 | 3.0 | 10 168 | 26 786 | 43 705 | 5.5 | 4.0 | 47 433 | 15.3 | 25.8 | 23.9 |
| Jones | NA | NA | 292 | 15.4 | 46.1 | 16.5 | 1.9 | 11 440 | 25 407 | 50 795 | 24.2 | 2.6 | 40 171 | 13.3 | 23.0 | 19.8 |
| Kingsbury | NA | NA | 1 039 | 5.7 | 51.6 | 20.8 | 9.2 | 9 001 | 24 954 | 47 152 | 11.7 | 0.5 | 46 244 | 10.9 | 15.7 | 13.6 |
| Lake | NA | NA | 3 302 | 7.5 | 44.5 | 26.6 | 16.1 | 7 928 | 24 503 | 46 412 | 0.8 | 1.1 | 49 893 | 11.1 | 14.1 | 11.5 |
| Lawrence | 123 | 2 731 | 6 237 | 6.3 | 39.7 | 31.2 | 24.0 | 8 462 | 26 994 | 45 137 | 5.3 | 2.0 | 42 495 | 15.4 | 17.4 | 14.4 |
| Lincoln | 178 | 2 160 | 11 639 | 17.6 | 30.7 | 36.4 | 40.1 | 7 681 | 33 958 | 70 043 | 7.3 | 4.9 | 76 907 | 4.9 | 5.9 | 5.1 |
| Lyman | NA | NA | 927 | 8.2 | 53.3 | 19.2 | 5.1 | 12 891 | 19 322 | 41 389 | 7.5 | 1.0 | 37 914 | 22.3 | 31.6 | 26.2 |
| McCook | 35 | 809 | 1 315 | 14.1 | 47.6 | 19.6 | 9.9 | 10 406 | 27 141 | 46 964 | -1.7 | 2.5 | 51 365 | 10.6 | 14.6 | 13.0 |
| McPherson | 80 | 40 | 492 | 5.3 | 56.5 | 17.3 | 4.3 | 9 880 | 19 879 | 35 065 | 16.0 | 1.2 | 35 473 | 17.8 | 27.1 | 22.2 |
| Marshall | 127 | 721 | 1 147 | 9.7 | 50.8 | 16.2 | 6.0 | 8 350 | 21 367 | 41 731 | 1.1 | 1.2 | 44 849 | 14.6 | 22.0 | 19.5 |
| Meade | 105 | 998 | 6 149 | 12.5 | 41.4 | 21.5 | 21.5 | 7 946 | 24 133 | 47 504 | -4.9 | 1.7 | 50 985 | 12.2 | 17.6 | 14.6 |
| Mellette | 338 | 531 | 693 | 1.6 | 48.5 | 15.4 | 5.6 | 13 587 | 15 429 | 34 013 | 8.5 | 0.6 | 30 170 | 36.6 | 49.8 | 45.0 |
| Miner | 0 | 786 | 459 | 7.2 | 50.8 | 20.0 | 3.5 | 9 388 | 28 097 | 42 361 | 6.3 | 1.9 | 44 316 | 12.5 | 17.3 | 14.5 |
| Minnehaha | 242 | 2 617 | 42 758 | 18.4 | 38.5 | 29.2 | 226.7 | 8 084 | 26 714 | 52 758 | -8.2 | 2.7 | 50 307 | 11.3 | 14.5 | 12.0 |
| Moody | 259 | 1 036 | 1 507 | 8.6 | 45.0 | 21.7 | 8.2 | 9 367 | 24 596 | 49 016 | 2.4 | 2.2 | 50 307 | 11.4 | 16.3 | 14.1 |
| Pennington | 486 | 3 405 | 25 958 | 12.4 | 36.6 | 27.7 | 140.1 | 8 346 | 26 451 | 48 378 | -4.4 | 3.2 | 48 083 | 13.3 | 19.6 | 17.3 |
| Perkins | 66 | 464 | 540 | 14.1 | 48.1 | 18.3 | 5.0 | 12 891 | 23 325 | 36 042 | -3.8 | 2.1 | 37 919 | 15.3 | 22.3 | 18.2 |
| Potter | 85 | 85 | 445 | 9.9 | 49.2 | 19.1 | 3.8 | 10 291 | 24 833 | 45 682 | 12.5 | 1.4 | 45 851 | 11.2 | 15.9 | 13.2 |
| Roberts | 165 | 1 295 | 2 501 | 5.6 | 51.4 | 16.1 | 16.1 | 10 523 | 20 357 | 41 483 | 8.5 | 1.9 | 41 407 | 18.9 | 27.6 | 24.6 |
| Sanborn | NA | NA | 479 | 14.2 | 57.1 | 16.7 | 3.8 | 10 031 | 22 268 | 46 736 | 3.7 | 1.0 | 47 141 | 14.1 | 20.8 | 17.8 |
| Shannon | 0 | 0 | 4 816 | 3.1 | 52.6 | 13.0 | 21.5 | 18 147 | 7 887 | 25 228 | -10.7 | 0.0 | 27 200 | 48.1 | 51.5 | 48.1 |
| Spink | 169 | 739 | 1 453 | 10.7 | 51.1 | 19.5 | 12.3 | 9 196 | 26 524 | 47 983 | 12.0 | 3.5 | 44 455 | 12.0 | 16.2 | 12.5 |
| Stanley | 167 | 1 033 | 590 | 11.2 | 45.1 | 28.2 | 4.6 | 9 520 | 27 732 | 55 679 | 0.2 | 2.6 | 53 986 | 9.8 | 16.6 | 14.0 |
| Sully | 144 | 504 | 300 | 10.7 | 45.5 | 28.5 | 2.7 | 9 755 | 28 347 | 51 429 | 17.2 | 2.6 | 55 194 | 8.8 | 9.7 | 8.5 |
| Todd | NA | NA | 3 670 | 2.6 | 48.9 | 14.9 | 28.1 | 14 301 | 11 446 | 27 431 | 1.4 | 1.3 | 26 639 | 44.2 | 52.2 | 47.7 |

1. Data for serious crimes have not been adjusted for underreporting; this may affect comparability between geographic areas and over time.   2. Per 100,000 population estimated by the FBI.   3. All persons 3 years old and over enrolled in nursery school through college.   4. Persons 25 years old and over.   5. Elementary and secondary education expenditures.   6. Based on population estimated by the American Community Survey, 2007–2011.

# Table B. States and Counties — Personal Income

| | Personal income, 2011 | | | | | | | | | | | | |
| | | | Per capita[1] | | | | | | Transfer payments (mil dol) | | | | |
| | | | | | | | | | | Government payments to individuals | | | |
| STATE County | Total (mil dol) | Percent change, 2010–2011 | Dollars | Rank | Wages and salaries[2] (mil dol) | Proprietors' income (mil dol) | Dividends, interest, and rent (mil dol) | Total | Total | Social Security | Medical payments | Income mainte-nance | Unemploy-ment insurance |
| | 62 | 63 | 64 | 65 | 66 | 67 | 68 | 69 | 70 | 71 | 72 | 73 | 74 |
| SOUTH CAROLINA—Cont'd | | | | | | | | | | | | | |
| Sumter | 3 215 | 3.6 | 29 915 | 2 305 | 2 196 | 135 | 401 | 900 | 878 | 253 | 318 | 158 | 32 |
| Union | 770 | 3.3 | 26 859 | 2 782 | 299 | 30 | 76 | 279 | 273 | 103 | 104 | 37 | 12 |
| Williamsburg | 929 | 4.2 | 27 263 | 2 724 | 454 | 43 | 96 | 346 | 339 | 91 | 138 | 71 | 16 |
| York | 7 850 | 5.6 | 34 053 | 1 503 | 4 059 | 402 | 880 | 1 465 | 1 414 | 544 | 526 | 171 | 47 |
| SOUTH DAKOTA | 36 439 | 12.8 | 44 217 | X | 19 011 | 7 301 | 7 209 | 5 369 | 5 187 | 1 935 | 2 129 | 563 | 61 |
| Aurora | 159 | 34.5 | 59 097 | 78 | 36 | 78 | 22 | 18 | 17 | 7 | 8 | 1 | 0 |
| Beadle | 843 | 19.8 | 48 057 | 268 | 380 | 210 | 167 | 124 | 121 | 43 | 57 | 12 | 1 |
| Bennett | 116 | 22.8 | 33 701 | 1 563 | 35 | 30 | 15 | 27 | 26 | 5 | 11 | 7 | 0 |
| Bon Homme | 276 | 17.0 | 39 568 | 797 | 71 | 100 | 50 | 46 | 44 | 18 | 20 | 3 | 0 |
| Brookings | 1 313 | 12.3 | 40 730 | 684 | 845 | 201 | 269 | 141 | 134 | 51 | 46 | 10 | 2 |
| Brown | 1 851 | 14.9 | 50 274 | 200 | 960 | 448 | 376 | 232 | 224 | 88 | 96 | 18 | 2 |
| Brule | 268 | 26.0 | 50 823 | 191 | 76 | 113 | 44 | 36 | 35 | 12 | 18 | 3 | 0 |
| Buffalo | 61 | 31.6 | 30 829 | 2 136 | 28 | 25 | 5 | 18 | 17 | 2 | 7 | 5 | 0 |
| Butte | 319 | 11.9 | 31 109 | 2 077 | 109 | 68 | 58 | 63 | 60 | 25 | 22 | 8 | 1 |
| Campbell | 90 | 44.4 | 62 956 | 47 | 15 | 48 | 13 | 12 | 12 | 4 | 6 | 1 | 0 |
| Charles Mix | 369 | 15.3 | 40 120 | 732 | 135 | 126 | 57 | 76 | 74 | 21 | 35 | 12 | 1 |
| Clark | 196 | 55.4 | 54 145 | 128 | 39 | 98 | 31 | 24 | 23 | 10 | 10 | 2 | 0 |
| Clay | 606 | 9.1 | 43 106 | 502 | 270 | 175 | 89 | 79 | 75 | 24 | 29 | 7 | 1 |
| Codington | 1 134 | 11.5 | 41 322 | 633 | 703 | 132 | 268 | 162 | 155 | 65 | 61 | 15 | 2 |
| Corson | 158 | 27.0 | 39 189 | 833 | 42 | 60 | 14 | 35 | 34 | 5 | 15 | 9 | 0 |
| Custer | 300 | 7.1 | 35 985 | 1 212 | 106 | 40 | 71 | 59 | 57 | 27 | 19 | 4 | 1 |
| Davison | 868 | 8.2 | 44 148 | 433 | 506 | 146 | 195 | 143 | 139 | 50 | 64 | 12 | 1 |
| Day | 263 | 21.7 | 45 836 | 344 | 77 | 86 | 56 | 47 | 45 | 18 | 20 | 4 | 1 |
| Deuel | 208 | 21.0 | 47 677 | 275 | 80 | 62 | 33 | 29 | 28 | 12 | 11 | 2 | 0 |
| Dewey | 216 | 14.8 | 39 922 | 754 | 103 | 61 | 23 | 50 | 49 | 8 | 19 | 14 | 1 |
| Douglas | 176 | 25.3 | 59 215 | 76 | 47 | 85 | 25 | 22 | 22 | 9 | 11 | 1 | 0 |
| Edmunds | 261 | 49.5 | 64 239 | 41 | 54 | 117 | 45 | 26 | 25 | 10 | 12 | 2 | 0 |
| Fall River | 273 | 12.5 | 39 056 | 850 | 143 | 35 | 55 | 68 | 66 | 25 | 23 | 5 | 1 |
| Faulk | 146 | 62.0 | 61 877 | 52 | 27 | 79 | 24 | 17 | 16 | 6 | 8 | 1 | 0 |
| Grant | 329 | 7.1 | 45 356 | 377 | 163 | 72 | 71 | 52 | 51 | 22 | 22 | 4 | 1 |
| Gregory | 204 | 26.9 | 48 358 | 258 | 53 | 85 | 36 | 36 | 35 | 13 | 16 | 4 | 0 |
| Haakon | 125 | 34.7 | 65 465 | 35 | 32 | 57 | 26 | 12 | 11 | 5 | 5 | 1 | 0 |
| Hamlin | 248 | 27.3 | 41 566 | 609 | 67 | 78 | 41 | 33 | 31 | 14 | 14 | 2 | 0 |
| Hand | 201 | 58.0 | 58 614 | 80 | 50 | 92 | 38 | 23 | 22 | 10 | 9 | 1 | 0 |
| Hanson | 202 | 19.3 | 59 943 | 69 | 25 | 68 | 54 | 35 | 34 | 20 | 11 | 1 | 0 |
| Harding | 62 | 34.2 | 48 673 | 247 | 23 | 25 | 10 | 6 | 5 | 3 | 2 | 1 | 0 |
| Hughes | 803 | 8.1 | 46 451 | 321 | 500 | 150 | 154 | 101 | 97 | 38 | 41 | 10 | 1 |
| Hutchinson | 384 | 18.8 | 52 872 | 143 | 102 | 161 | 67 | 56 | 54 | 23 | 25 | 3 | 0 |
| Hyde | 92 | 42.0 | 65 902 | 34 | 27 | 42 | 18 | 10 | 9 | 4 | 4 | 1 | 0 |
| Jackson | 100 | 28.6 | 31 408 | 2 014 | 30 | 36 | 13 | 24 | 23 | 5 | 9 | 6 | 0 |
| Jerauld | 136 | 30.6 | 65 209 | 37 | 61 | 65 | 17 | 17 | 17 | 7 | 8 | 1 | 0 |
| Jones | 60 | 46.8 | 60 021 | 68 | 17 | 31 | 7 | 7 | 7 | 3 | 3 | 1 | 0 |
| Kingsbury | 296 | 33.9 | 57 149 | 93 | 72 | 129 | 45 | 38 | 37 | 16 | 17 | 2 | 0 |
| Lake | 537 | 14.6 | 46 426 | 322 | 202 | 134 | 113 | 89 | 86 | 40 | 33 | 5 | 1 |
| Lawrence | 846 | 4.3 | 34 799 | 1 403 | 449 | 69 | 233 | 164 | 159 | 66 | 59 | 13 | 2 |
| Lincoln | 2 600 | 13.0 | 55 556 | 108 | 775 | 252 | 431 | 142 | 131 | 69 | 39 | 10 | 3 |
| Lyman | 197 | 30.5 | 51 747 | 169 | 58 | 88 | 24 | 28 | 27 | 9 | 11 | 5 | 0 |
| McCook | 277 | 19.0 | 49 806 | 208 | 57 | 119 | 40 | 36 | 35 | 14 | 16 | 2 | 0 |
| McPherson | 109 | 28.5 | 44 401 | 427 | 23 | 41 | 25 | 17 | 17 | 8 | 6 | 1 | 0 |
| Marshall | 219 | 24.8 | 47 600 | 277 | 66 | 80 | 54 | 29 | 28 | 12 | 12 | 2 | 0 |
| Meade | 1 017 | 8.2 | 39 801 | 769 | 348 | 252 | 157 | 152 | 146 | 58 | 52 | 15 | 2 |
| Mellette | 81 | 21.6 | 39 117 | 843 | 14 | 35 | 7 | 17 | 17 | 3 | 8 | 4 | 0 |
| Miner | 121 | 23.0 | 51 271 | 179 | 28 | 51 | 20 | 17 | 17 | 7 | 8 | 1 | 0 |
| Minnehaha | 7 166 | 5.2 | 41 724 | 600 | 5 927 | 865 | 1 476 | 1 042 | 1 004 | 393 | 418 | 107 | 13 |
| Moody | 342 | 20.4 | 52 743 | 148 | 105 | 118 | 47 | 38 | 36 | 15 | 14 | 3 | 1 |
| Pennington | 4 283 | 7.0 | 41 655 | 604 | 2 767 | 186 | 1 095 | 750 | 727 | 264 | 273 | 78 | 8 |
| Perkins | 114 | 10.5 | 37 915 | 983 | 42 | 30 | 28 | 23 | 22 | 9 | 10 | 2 | 0 |
| Potter | 167 | 25.6 | 70 706 | 23 | 34 | 79 | 39 | 19 | 19 | 8 | 9 | 1 | 0 |
| Roberts | 390 | 15.5 | 37 921 | 982 | 143 | 108 | 58 | 77 | 74 | 25 | 30 | 10 | 1 |
| Sanborn | 118 | 21.9 | 49 527 | 219 | 26 | 39 | 23 | 16 | 15 | 6 | 7 | 1 | 0 |
| Shannon | 299 | 6.3 | 21 451 | 3 090 | 206 | 15 | 15 | 135 | 132 | 12 | 56 | 38 | 2 |
| Spink | 461 | 42.8 | 71 305 | 22 | 106 | 224 | 70 | 70 | 69 | 18 | 45 | 3 | 0 |
| Stanley | 147 | 17.3 | 49 052 | 231 | 52 | 33 | 25 | 17 | 16 | 8 | 6 | 2 | 0 |
| Sully | 160 | 39.8 | 116 067 | 2 | 25 | 101 | 22 | 8 | 8 | 4 | 3 | 0 | 0 |
| Todd | 240 | 8.1 | 24 401 | 3 010 | 142 | 31 | 16 | 88 | 86 | 9 | 36 | 25 | 1 |

1. Based on the resident population estimated as of July 1 of the year shown.    2. Includes supplements to wages and salaries.

# Table B. States and Counties — Earnings, Social Security, and Housing

| STATE County | Earnings, 2011 | | | | | | | | | Social Security beneficiaries, December 2011 | | | Housing units, 2010 | |
|---|---|---|---|---|---|---|---|---|---|---|---|---|---|---|
| | | | Percent by selected industries | | | | | | | | | | | |
| | | | Goods-related[1] | | Service-related and health | | | | | | | | | |
| | Total (mil dol) | Farm | Total | Manu-facturing | Infor-mation and profes-sional and technical services | Retail trade | Finance, insur-ance, and real estate | Health care and social services | Govern-ment | Number | Rate[2] | Supple-mental Security Income recipients, December 2011 | Total | Percent change, 2000–2010 |
| | 75 | 76 | 77 | 78 | 79 | 80 | 81 | 82 | 83 | 84 | 85 | 86 | 87 | 88 |
| SOUTH CAROLINA—Cont'd | | | | | | | | | | | | | | |
| Sumter | 2 330 | 0.1 | 19.9 | 13.8 | 4.1 | 5.6 | 2.7 | 10.7 | 39.6 | 21 455 | 200 | 4 144 | 46 011 | 10.2 |
| Union | 329 | 2.2 | D | 24.7 | D | 7.5 | 4.2 | D | 30.9 | 8 300 | 289 | 1 042 | 14 153 | 6.0 |
| Williamsburg | 497 | 3.3 | 32.8 | 28.9 | D | 5.0 | 3.5 | D | 25.4 | 8 190 | 240 | 2 088 | 15 359 | -1.2 |
| York | 4 461 | 0.5 | 20.0 | 15.8 | 8.8 | 9.7 | 9.6 | 9.5 | 14.8 | 39 390 | 171 | 3 529 | 94 196 | 42.6 |
| SOUTH DAKOTA | 26 312 | 18.4 | 14.1 | 8.4 | 4.8 | 6.4 | 7.0 | 12.7 | 16.8 | 156 102 | 189 | 14 151 | 363 438 | 12.4 |
| Aurora | 114 | 61.2 | D | D | D | 2.5 | D | 10.1 | 7.4 | 615 | 228 | 27 | 1 324 | 2.0 |
| Beadle | 590 | 26.0 | D | 14.5 | 2.2 | 6.3 | 4.2 | D | 13.0 | 3 625 | 207 | 381 | 8 304 | 1.2 |
| Bennett | 65 | 43.0 | D | D | D | 4.8 | D | D | 27.7 | 495 | 144 | 150 | 1 263 | -1.2 |
| Bon Homme | 171 | 46.1 | D | 3.5 | 1.9 | 3.9 | 2.4 | D | 15.9 | 1 540 | 221 | 79 | 2 931 | -2.5 |
| Brookings | 1 045 | 13.6 | D | 25.1 | 3.1 | 4.9 | 3.0 | 3.7 | 25.2 | 3 895 | 121 | 215 | 13 137 | 13.5 |
| Brown | 1 408 | 16.6 | D | 13.1 | 3.8 | 7.0 | 5.5 | 14.4 | 12.3 | 7 075 | 192 | 476 | 16 706 | 5.3 |
| Brule | 189 | 49.0 | D | 0.4 | 2.6 | 6.1 | 2.2 | 7.6 | 9.9 | 1 025 | 194 | 90 | 2 433 | 7.2 |
| Buffalo | 54 | 48.6 | D | 0.0 | D | D | D | D | 46.3 | 235 | 118 | 115 | 609 | 1.2 |
| Butte | 178 | 20.6 | D | 2.5 | 3.8 | 9.1 | 2.5 | 6.4 | 15.6 | 2 075 | 202 | 184 | 4 621 | 13.8 |
| Campbell | 64 | 73.0 | D | D | D | 2.4 | D | 1.0 | 5.6 | 410 | 287 | 19 | 980 | 1.9 |
| Charles Mix | 261 | 37.8 | 5.1 | 1.4 | 2.0 | 4.5 | D | D | 23.7 | 1 935 | 210 | 247 | 3 849 | -0.1 |
| Clark | 136 | 65.3 | 7.8 | 2.6 | D | 2.3 | D | 3.0 | 7.1 | 845 | 233 | 67 | 1 710 | -9.0 |
| Clay | 445 | 21.6 | 8.1 | 4.2 | 2.9 | 5.2 | 2.2 | D | 33.0 | 1 845 | 131 | 143 | 5 639 | 3.7 |
| Codington | 836 | 6.1 | 29.9 | 23.4 | 3.1 | 8.6 | 5.9 | 14.0 | 13.3 | 5 275 | 192 | 356 | 12 397 | 9.5 |
| Corson | 102 | 59.3 | 0.6 | 0.0 | D | 1.0 | D | D | 30.1 | 570 | 142 | 235 | 1 540 | 0.4 |
| Custer | 146 | 6.8 | 13.3 | 0.2 | D | 6.5 | 3.1 | D | 31.1 | 2 115 | 254 | 109 | 4 628 | 27.7 |
| Davison | 652 | 9.6 | 23.9 | 16.4 | D | 9.9 | 4.2 | D | 10.5 | 4 175 | 212 | 349 | 8 852 | 9.4 |
| Day | 162 | 47.1 | 11.1 | 5.5 | D | 4.4 | 2.8 | 5.9 | 12.1 | 1 575 | 274 | 95 | 3 630 | 0.3 |
| Deuel | 142 | 32.8 | 24.5 | 12.5 | D | 3.3 | 1.6 | D | 7.4 | 1 095 | 251 | 47 | 2 204 | 1.5 |
| Dewey | 164 | 30.3 | D | 0.2 | D | 4.4 | D | D | 47.2 | 850 | 157 | 384 | 2 002 | -6.1 |
| Douglas | 132 | 60.2 | 6.2 | 2.8 | D | 1.9 | D | D | 5.8 | 755 | 254 | 39 | 1 439 | -0.9 |
| Edmunds | 171 | 60.6 | 4.9 | 2.0 | 1.3 | 4.2 | 2.0 | D | 8.5 | 915 | 226 | 39 | 1 966 | -2.8 |
| Fall River | 178 | 18.4 | 3.7 | 0.9 | 1.9 | 3.6 | 1.5 | D | 38.1 | 2 215 | 317 | 178 | 4 191 | 9.9 |
| Faulk | 105 | 73.2 | D | D | 1.3 | D | 1.4 | D | 6.3 | 550 | 232 | 50 | 1 136 | -8.0 |
| Grant | 235 | 24.5 | 22.4 | 15.5 | 1.7 | 5.5 | 5.7 | D | 7.1 | 1 805 | 249 | 88 | 3 526 | 2.0 |
| Gregory | 138 | 53.2 | D | 0.5 | 1.6 | 5.9 | 3.3 | 8.4 | 9.3 | 1 185 | 281 | 103 | 2 503 | 4.1 |
| Haakon | 89 | 56.5 | D | D | D | 3.6 | 4.2 | D | 6.4 | 420 | 220 | 0 | 1 013 | 1.1 |
| Hamlin | 146 | 53.0 | D | D | D | 4.0 | D | 2.8 | 13.6 | 1 125 | 188 | 47 | 2 760 | 5.1 |
| Hand | 142 | 61.9 | 3.4 | 0.9 | D | 2.9 | D | D | 7.3 | 885 | 259 | 50 | 1 815 | -1.4 |
| Hanson | 92 | 67.2 | D | 3.1 | D | 1.5 | D | 0.4 | 8.6 | 1 515 | 449 | 63 | 1 177 | -3.4 |
| Harding | 49 | 50.8 | D | 0.0 | D | 2.2 | D | D | 12.2 | 230 | 181 | 0 | 731 | -9.1 |
| Hughes | 650 | 13.1 | 3.6 | 0.6 | 5.5 | 7.3 | 6.5 | 10.6 | 36.5 | 3 015 | 174 | 276 | 7 623 | 8.1 |
| Hutchinson | 262 | 53.6 | 6.8 | 3.5 | 0.9 | 4.1 | 2.7 | D | 7.6 | 2 020 | 278 | 125 | 3 351 | -4.7 |
| Hyde | 69 | 62.9 | D | D | D | 2.6 | D | D | 13.2 | 335 | 240 | 18 | 708 | -7.9 |
| Jackson | 66 | 50.7 | D | D | D | 3.4 | D | D | 29.6 | 515 | 163 | 130 | 1 193 | 1.7 |
| Jerauld | 126 | 46.4 | D | D | D | 2.1 | D | D | 4.5 | 630 | 302 | 41 | 1 070 | -8.3 |
| Jones | 48 | 60.9 | D | 0.0 | D | 4.3 | 1.6 | 0.9 | 12.4 | 255 | 254 | 11 | 589 | -4.1 |
| Kingsbury | 201 | 58.3 | 10.6 | 7.0 | D | 2.6 | D | 4.1 | 6.7 | 1 305 | 252 | 60 | 2 720 | -0.1 |
| Lake | 336 | 28.9 | D | 12.0 | 3.8 | 6.5 | 2.1 | 7.5 | 16.0 | 2 990 | 258 | 148 | 5 559 | 5.3 |
| Lawrence | 518 | 1.0 | D | 4.9 | 4.0 | 10.5 | 6.2 | 13.9 | 18.8 | 5 095 | 210 | 323 | 12 756 | 22.3 |
| Lincoln | 1 027 | 13.3 | D | 9.8 | 5.7 | 7.2 | 14.2 | 12.0 | 6.3 | 5 055 | 108 | 178 | 17 875 | 95.8 |
| Lyman | 146 | 59.6 | D | D | D | 5.0 | 0.7 | 0.2 | 23.7 | 745 | 196 | 86 | 1 704 | 4.2 |
| McCook | 176 | 58.0 | D | D | 2.6 | 3.1 | 2.6 | 5.1 | 7.6 | 1 190 | 214 | 55 | 2 491 | 4.5 |
| McPherson | 64 | 65.6 | 3.9 | 2.9 | D | D | 3.8 | 5.0 | 10.7 | 760 | 310 | 64 | 1 418 | -3.2 |
| Marshall | 146 | 48.5 | D | 11.6 | D | 3.3 | D | D | 10.3 | 1 035 | 225 | 75 | 2 534 | -1.1 |
| Meade | 600 | 9.9 | D | 1.6 | 6.1 | 5.4 | 5.1 | 7.0 | 31.8 | 4 790 | 188 | 348 | 11 000 | 8.4 |
| Mellette | 49 | 71.2 | D | 0.0 | D | D | D | 0.6 | 19.3 | 345 | 167 | 112 | 838 | 1.7 |
| Miner | 79 | 63.1 | D | 2.0 | D | 2.7 | D | 6.2 | 9.6 | 590 | 250 | 27 | 1 308 | -7.0 |
| Minnehaha | 6 793 | 1.8 | D | 8.3 | 7.8 | 7.7 | 14.0 | 20.2 | 10.7 | 29 470 | 172 | 2 568 | 71 557 | 18.8 |
| Moody | 223 | 49.4 | 13.3 | 5.5 | D | 2.5 | D | D | 16.3 | 1 260 | 195 | 48 | 2 824 | 2.9 |
| Pennington | 2 952 | 1.0 | 11.4 | 4.1 | 6.0 | 8.5 | 5.9 | 18.8 | 27.0 | 20 615 | 201 | 1 887 | 44 949 | 20.7 |
| Perkins | 71 | 33.1 | D | D | 1.6 | 6.7 | D | 6.1 | 16.1 | 810 | 270 | 52 | 1 739 | -6.3 |
| Potter | 114 | 48.0 | 5.1 | 1.9 | 1.1 | 23.8 | 2.7 | D | 6.4 | 660 | 279 | 22 | 1 500 | -14.8 |
| Roberts | 251 | 38.1 | D | 4.1 | 1.5 | 3.8 | D | 6.1 | 29.7 | 2 230 | 217 | 254 | 4 905 | 3.7 |
| Sanborn | 65 | 59.5 | D | D | D | 1.2 | D | D | 10.6 | 540 | 226 | 22 | 1 172 | -3.9 |
| Shannon | 221 | 5.5 | D | D | 1.6 | 2.1 | D | 1.6 | 79.2 | 1 360 | 98 | 1 098 | 3 593 | 15.0 |
| Spink | 330 | 64.8 | 5.2 | 1.8 | D | 1.7 | 2.2 | D | 13.5 | 1 570 | 243 | 187 | 3 139 | -6.4 |
| Stanley | 85 | 32.3 | D | D | D | 5.2 | 2.6 | D | 11.7 | 585 | 195 | 27 | 1 387 | 8.6 |
| Sully | 126 | 79.5 | D | D | D | 1.9 | D | D | 4.1 | 325 | 236 | 0 | 845 | 0.1 |
| Todd | 173 | 17.6 | D | D | D | 2.8 | D | D | 67.3 | 940 | 96 | 557 | 3 142 | 13.6 |

1. Includes mining, construction, and manufacturing.  2. Per 1,000 resident population enumerated in the 2010 census.

# Table B. States and Counties — Housing, Labor Force, and Employment

| | Housing units, 2007–2011 | | | | | | | | Civilian labor force, 2012 | | | | Civilian employment,[6] 2007–2011 | | |
| --- | --- | --- | --- | --- | --- | --- | --- | --- | --- | --- | --- | --- | --- | --- | --- |
| | Occupied units | | | | | | | | | | Unemployment | | | Percent | |
| | Owner-occupied | | | | | Renter-occupied | | | | | | | | | |
| | | | | Median owner cost as a percent of income | | | | | | | | | | | Con-struction, produc-tion, and mainte-nance occu-pations |
| STATE County | Total | Percent | Median value[1] | With a mort-gage | Without a mort-gage[2] | Median rent[3] | Median rent as a per-cent of income | Sub-stand-ard units[4] (percent) | Total | Percent change, 2011–2012 | Total | Rate[5] | Total | Manage-ment, business, science and arts | |
| | 89 | 90 | 91 | 92 | 93 | 94 | 95 | 96 | 97 | 98 | 99 | 100 | 101 | 102 | 103 |
| SOUTH CAROLINA—Cont'd | | | | | | | | | | | | | | | |
| Sumter | 39 273 | 66.5 | 100 900 | 21.9 | 11.9 | 671 | 27.2 | 2.4 | 44 701 | -0.9 | 4 608 | 10.3 | 40 200 | 27.5 | 29.9 |
| Union | 12 052 | 73.7 | 73 100 | 21.8 | 12.9 | 586 | 30.3 | 2.0 | 11 412 | -1.4 | 1 599 | 14.0 | 11 373 | 23.0 | 37.1 |
| Williamsburg | 11 185 | 68.1 | 64 700 | 26.2 | 13.5 | 527 | 29.5 | 3.5 | 14 802 | -6.2 | 1 936 | 13.1 | 11 155 | 21.3 | 33.3 |
| York | 84 262 | 72.2 | 161 200 | 22.5 | 9.9 | 763 | 28.4 | 1.9 | 113 336 | -1.1 | 12 324 | 10.9 | 106 346 | 36.3 | 22.0 |
| SOUTH DAKOTA | 318 466 | 68.7 | 127 000 | 22.0 | 11.2 | 595 | 26.1 | 2.4 | 445 728 | 0.4 | 19 628 | 4.4 | 413 552 | 34.5 | 23.8 |
| Aurora | 1 060 | 79.2 | 65 500 | 15.9 | 10.8 | 568 | 22.3 | 1.2 | 1 632 | 3.8 | 52 | 3.2 | 1 414 | 33.9 | 24.0 |
| Beadle | 7 298 | 65.7 | 84 000 | 18.9 | 10.9 | 444 | 24.4 | 2.8 | 9 975 | 1.3 | 345 | 3.5 | 8 960 | 29.4 | 32.6 |
| Bennett | 1 138 | 59.1 | 47 600 | 18.5 | 9.9 | 405 | 24.7 | 7.6 | 1 459 | 3.3 | 82 | 5.6 | 1 039 | 33.3 | 24.4 |
| Bon Homme | 2 547 | 80.8 | 70 300 | 19.4 | 12.4 | 401 | 23.5 | 1.2 | 3 007 | -0.8 | 145 | 4.8 | 3 024 | 40.8 | 20.1 |
| Brookings | 11 597 | 59.6 | 138 500 | 21.6 | 11.3 | 616 | 29.2 | 1.0 | 18 776 | -0.7 | 712 | 3.8 | 17 568 | 34.4 | 27.5 |
| Brown | 15 201 | 69.8 | 123 100 | 21.5 | 12.4 | 498 | 22.5 | 1.0 | 21 268 | 0.8 | 771 | 3.6 | 19 761 | 31.6 | 23.8 |
| Brule | 2 025 | 71.2 | 92 100 | 22.1 | 11.1 | 462 | 23.2 | 1.7 | 2 833 | -1.6 | 99 | 3.5 | 2 776 | 37.5 | 26.8 |
| Buffalo | 551 | 30.7 | 67 000 | 13.8 | 17.3 | 501 | 18.8 | 16.7 | 551 | 2.4 | 79 | 14.3 | 607 | 28.2 | 21.6 |
| Butte | 3 989 | 74.8 | 117 600 | 24.4 | 12.3 | 506 | 32.2 | 3.8 | 5 283 | -0.3 | 245 | 4.6 | 4 830 | 26.6 | 30.4 |
| Campbell | 622 | 85.7 | 41 300 | 24.4 | 13.0 | 432 | 19.5 | 0.6 | 835 | 0.5 | 33 | 4.0 | 734 | 44.8 | 22.9 |
| Charles Mix | 3 238 | 70.7 | 69 700 | 21.7 | 12.2 | 438 | 21.3 | 5.9 | 4 136 | -0.8 | 208 | 5.0 | 3 998 | 34.6 | 23.5 |
| Clark | 1 375 | 78.8 | 62 800 | 21.2 | 11.0 | 431 | 20.2 | 3.3 | 1 908 | 0.8 | 87 | 4.6 | 1 779 | 37.2 | 31.4 |
| Clay | 5 012 | 56.3 | 126 000 | 20.5 | 13.0 | 602 | 32.1 | 1.7 | 7 509 | 0.3 | 297 | 4.0 | 7 474 | 37.1 | 16.8 |
| Codington | 11 434 | 72.1 | 130 100 | 21.3 | 12.4 | 580 | 27.2 | 0.9 | 16 258 | 1.2 | 620 | 3.8 | 14 789 | 33.3 | 26.6 |
| Corson | 1 143 | 57.3 | 45 200 | 19.5 | 11.5 | 415 | 21.1 | 12.7 | 1 414 | -0.4 | 118 | 8.3 | 1 228 | 46.0 | 21.3 |
| Custer | 3 737 | 78.2 | 164 300 | 26.1 | 12.4 | 534 | 20.5 | 1.4 | 4 746 | -0.6 | 217 | 4.6 | 3 804 | 47.2 | 21.1 |
| Davison | 8 224 | 62.3 | 115 500 | 22.0 | 10.4 | 572 | 27.4 | 1.6 | 11 529 | 1.4 | 386 | 3.3 | 10 366 | 30.9 | 23.5 |
| Day | 2 460 | 71.1 | 66 500 | 21.5 | 12.5 | 455 | 18.9 | 3.7 | 2 833 | -0.5 | 178 | 6.3 | 2 757 | 31.3 | 27.5 |
| Deuel | 1 800 | 82.7 | 87 100 | 21.0 | 11.3 | 418 | 21.7 | 1.7 | 2 685 | 0.3 | 148 | 5.5 | 2 289 | 31.8 | 36.0 |
| Dewey | 1 720 | 57.9 | 58 400 | 21.0 | 9.9 | 402 | 26.8 | 7.5 | 2 670 | 0.5 | 353 | 13.2 | 1 882 | 47.4 | 20.0 |
| Douglas | 1 230 | 77.9 | 64 800 | 19.2 | 10.3 | 514 | 23.8 | 1.7 | 1 805 | -0.6 | 61 | 3.4 | 1 473 | 40.5 | 27.0 |
| Edmunds | 1 616 | 78.9 | 78 000 | 21.1 | 9.9 | 555 | 22.9 | 0.9 | 1 987 | 0.7 | 72 | 3.6 | 2 035 | 35.9 | 28.0 |
| Fall River | 3 200 | 68.5 | 91 000 | 21.8 | 11.2 | 430 | 27.7 | 2.4 | 3 662 | -2.1 | 188 | 5.1 | 3 113 | 33.4 | 19.1 |
| Faulk | 931 | 77.6 | 55 200 | 19.1 | 11.1 | 433 | 33.6 | 4.8 | 1 157 | -0.6 | 48 | 4.1 | 1 096 | 40.0 | 23.9 |
| Grant | 3 180 | 74.1 | 105 600 | 24.3 | 10.4 | 446 | 23.8 | 0.8 | 4 051 | -1.3 | 199 | 4.9 | 4 043 | 31.2 | 24.8 |
| Gregory | 1 983 | 76.3 | 57 300 | 18.7 | 12.8 | 441 | 25.9 | 2.0 | 2 364 | 0.5 | 96 | 4.1 | 2 038 | 45.0 | 19.4 |
| Haakon | 750 | 83.5 | 80 000 | 17.3 | 9.9 | 525 | 20.2 | 1.5 | 1 149 | 0.2 | 36 | 3.1 | 957 | 38.9 | 25.5 |
| Hamlin | 2 008 | 80.7 | 95 200 | 20.5 | 11.2 | 468 | 24.9 | 5.9 | 2 982 | 1.6 | 128 | 4.3 | 2 746 | 31.9 | 34.2 |
| Hand | 1 555 | 71.3 | 82 200 | 21.5 | 10.9 | 427 | 26.1 | 1.1 | 1 907 | 1.8 | 60 | 3.1 | 1 851 | 34.3 | 30.8 |
| Hanson | 1 132 | 83.0 | 88 400 | 23.8 | 13.1 | 525 | 19.8 | 1.7 | 1 840 | 1.5 | 87 | 4.7 | 1 528 | 35.9 | 31.9 |
| Harding | 515 | 74.2 | 66 200 | 18.6 | 10.5 | 429 | 21.5 | 1.7 | 841 | -0.1 | 30 | 3.6 | 692 | 46.8 | 27.5 |
| Hughes | 7 102 | 69.6 | 145 900 | 22.1 | 9.9 | 519 | 24.4 | 2.6 | 10 220 | -0.2 | 350 | 3.4 | 9 541 | 44.2 | 13.8 |
| Hutchinson | 2 946 | 78.8 | 73 300 | 18.8 | 11.9 | 488 | 26.2 | 0.7 | 3 825 | -0.6 | 138 | 3.6 | 3 482 | 40.8 | 28.3 |
| Hyde | 605 | 77.4 | 62 100 | 16.6 | 10.2 | 441 | 23.7 | 1.3 | 754 | -1.2 | 28 | 3.7 | 713 | 41.8 | 24.1 |
| Jackson | 960 | 62.9 | 55 700 | 20.0 | 13.4 | 457 | 23.4 | 14.7 | 1 234 | -1.0 | 91 | 7.4 | 1 079 | 39.3 | 22.8 |
| Jerauld | 868 | 69.6 | 65 100 | 21.8 | 9.9 | 488 | 19.2 | 1.4 | 1 565 | 3.2 | 40 | 2.6 | 1 010 | 32.5 | 31.4 |
| Jones | 460 | 73.0 | 77 500 | 14.2 | 10.8 | 463 | 19.8 | 1.5 | 678 | -5.3 | 24 | 3.5 | 576 | 39.4 | 18.8 |
| Kingsbury | 2 314 | 76.1 | 73 600 | 18.7 | 10.9 | 396 | 16.1 | 0.6 | 3 118 | 3.8 | 110 | 3.5 | 2 659 | 32.3 | 32.8 |
| Lake | 4 509 | 71.3 | 114 900 | 21.1 | 12.0 | 489 | 25.6 | 0.4 | 6 602 | 1.0 | 273 | 4.1 | 5 916 | 31.0 | 31.1 |
| Lawrence | 10 715 | 65.5 | 163 700 | 23.5 | 12.1 | 543 | 28.2 | 2.1 | 12 875 | -1.6 | 590 | 4.6 | 12 763 | 31.2 | 22.6 |
| Lincoln | 16 466 | 76.5 | 177 100 | 22.3 | 9.9 | 809 | 25.2 | 0.9 | 26 378 | 1.4 | 925 | 3.5 | 24 241 | 42.2 | 20.0 |
| Lyman | 1 440 | 63.2 | 65 900 | 20.4 | 9.9 | 419 | 14.9 | 6.2 | 1 994 | -0.2 | 115 | 5.8 | 1 730 | 41.3 | 23.4 |
| McCook | 2 192 | 79.1 | 92 500 | 19.6 | 11.1 | 560 | 26.3 | 2.9 | 2 719 | 1.5 | 121 | 4.5 | 2 927 | 33.4 | 26.1 |
| McPherson | 1 029 | 80.9 | 48 600 | 17.3 | 13.5 | 310 | 25.8 | 2.4 | 1 121 | -0.4 | 55 | 4.9 | 1 025 | 42.7 | 26.2 |
| Marshall | 1 704 | 73.1 | 88 000 | 20.7 | 12.1 | 501 | 22.8 | 3.1 | 2 165 | 0.7 | 123 | 5.7 | 2 150 | 30.6 | 32.4 |
| Meade | 9 933 | 71.4 | 153 400 | 26.4 | 12.9 | 615 | 27.1 | 1.7 | 12 524 | -0.5 | 591 | 4.7 | 12 284 | 29.3 | 25.0 |
| Mellette | 633 | 64.3 | 53 600 | 24.0 | 11.4 | 443 | 25.2 | 11.2 | 881 | 1.4 | 67 | 7.6 | 703 | 43.8 | 19.2 |
| Miner | 1 094 | 77.8 | 58 300 | 19.0 | 12.2 | 434 | 20.9 | 0.2 | 1 158 | -0.8 | 48 | 4.1 | 1 255 | 44.1 | 27.3 |
| Minnehaha | 66 238 | 65.4 | 147 600 | 22.0 | 10.1 | 669 | 27.0 | 1.7 | 98 325 | 1.3 | 4 171 | 4.2 | 94 009 | 32.3 | 22.7 |
| Moody | 2 614 | 74.7 | 109 600 | 22.7 | 11.3 | 500 | 19.2 | 1.6 | 3 852 | -2.4 | 219 | 5.7 | 3 523 | 33.3 | 32.0 |
| Pennington | 40 306 | 66.1 | 153 700 | 24.0 | 12.1 | 708 | 28.2 | 2.0 | 54 689 | -0.3 | 2 442 | 4.5 | 49 657 | 34.8 | 20.8 |
| Perkins | 1 307 | 72.6 | 55 000 | 20.6 | 10.4 | 370 | 20.4 | 1.1 | 1 544 | -1.6 | 62 | 4.0 | 1 464 | 43.8 | 23.3 |
| Potter | 1 028 | 83.9 | 57 500 | 17.2 | 12.3 | 547 | 30.7 | 0.6 | 1 252 | -0.9 | 52 | 4.2 | 1 232 | 30.0 | 30.0 |
| Roberts | 3 657 | 70.3 | 81 900 | 21.6 | 11.0 | 430 | 21.7 | 4.1 | 4 824 | -1.2 | 289 | 6.0 | 4 463 | 32.4 | 26.0 |
| Sanborn | 1 008 | 71.6 | 69 000 | 18.7 | 9.9 | 550 | 17.6 | 3.6 | 1 370 | -0.8 | 48 | 3.5 | 1 190 | 31.5 | 30.8 |
| Shannon | 2 753 | 51.9 | 16 800 | 25.6 | 13.3 | 383 | 16.0 | 33.2 | 4 022 | 3.0 | 553 | 13.7 | 3 346 | 39.3 | 14.8 |
| Spink | 2 603 | 75.8 | 62 900 | 16.9 | 9.9 | 452 | 23.8 | 1.2 | 3 367 | -1.8 | 142 | 4.2 | 3 062 | 36.8 | 23.6 |
| Stanley | 1 159 | 79.9 | 115 400 | 18.4 | 11.6 | 814 | 23.8 | 0.9 | 2 014 | -0.7 | 58 | 2.9 | 1 784 | 36.8 | 24.8 |
| Sully | 606 | 74.3 | 72 500 | 20.3 | 9.9 | 567 | 14.7 | 2.8 | 1 042 | 0.8 | 27 | 2.6 | 832 | 35.7 | 26.6 |
| Todd | 2 566 | 42.9 | 47 900 | 26.4 | 9.9 | 437 | 17.4 | 18.1 | 3 496 | -3.4 | 316 | 9.0 | 2 904 | 36.0 | 21.2 |

1. Specified owner-occupied units. 2. A value of 9.9 represents 9.9 percent or less. 3. Specified renter-occupied units. A value of 10.0 represents 10 percent or less. 4. Overcrowded or lacking complete plumbing facilities. 5. Percent of civilian labor force. 6. Persons 16 years old and over.

| | Private nonfarm establishments, employment and payroll, 2011 | | | | | | | | Agriculture, 2007 | | | |
|---|---|---|---|---|---|---|---|---|---|---|---|---|
| | | Employment | | | | | Annual payroll | | Farms | | | |
| | | | | | | | | | | Percent with: | | |
| STATE County | Number of establishments | Total | Health care and social assistance | Manufacturing | Retail trade | Finance and insurance | Professional, scientific, and technical services | Total (mil dol) | Average per employee (dollars) | Number | Fewer than 50 acres | 500 acres or more | Farm operators whose principal occupation is farming (percent) |
| | 104 | 105 | 106 | 107 | 108 | 109 | 110 | 111 | 112 | 113 | 114 | 115 | 116 |
| SOUTH CAROLINA—Cont'd | | | | | | | | | | | | | |
| Sumter | 1 784 | 28 937 | 5 321 | 5 671 | 4 458 | 851 | 743 | 845 | 29 197 | 554 | 43.0 | 12.8 | 49.6 |
| Union | 484 | 6 740 | 882 | 1 606 | 913 | 235 | 156 | 190 | 28 196 | 262 | 30.2 | 5.0 | 30.5 |
| Williamsburg | 515 | 6 693 | 820 | D | 854 | 213 | 467 | 232 | 34 651 | 861 | 33.0 | 12.1 | 34.7 |
| York | 4 399 | 65 807 | 8 708 | 8 232 | 9 116 | 5 357 | 2 612 | 2 433 | 36 973 | 1 038 | 47.4 | 3.8 | 33.5 |
| SOUTH DAKOTA | 25 494 | 326 749 | 62 373 | 40 284 | 50 247 | 24 743 | 10 269 | 11 189 | 34 242 | 31 169 | 15.5 | 46.7 | 60.2 |
| Aurora | 89 | 572 | D | D | D | D | D | 15 | 26 374 | 379 | 14.5 | 43.8 | 61.7 |
| Beadle | 572 | 6 970 | 1 438 | 1 588 | 1 247 | 336 | 125 | 202 | 28 975 | 750 | 19.2 | 47.6 | 61.2 |
| Bennett | 67 | 657 | 170 | D | 128 | D | D | 17 | 25 513 | 265 | 6.8 | 69.1 | 70.9 |
| Bon Homme | 174 | 1 353 | 417 | 311 | 192 | 58 | 19 | 35 | 25 704 | 563 | 12.4 | 40.3 | 70.0 |
| Brookings | 854 | 12 939 | 1 329 | 4 494 | 1 711 | 381 | 355 | 414 | 32 013 | 986 | 25.5 | 26.6 | 48.8 |
| Brown | 1 320 | 17 971 | 3 145 | 2 564 | 2 902 | 993 | 472 | 610 | 33 932 | 1 036 | 16.5 | 46.1 | 56.9 |
| Brule | 209 | 1 783 | 469 | 24 | 285 | 71 | 44 | 44 | 24 955 | 370 | 11.6 | 64.3 | 66.5 |
| Buffalo | 10 | 153 | D | D | D | NA | D | 3 | 22 235 | 86 | 16.3 | 66.3 | 70.9 |
| Butte | 298 | 2 180 | 278 | 165 | 414 | 92 | 82 | 61 | 27 899 | 584 | 20.0 | 40.4 | 50.7 |
| Campbell | 52 | 255 | 23 | D | D | D | 7 | 7 | 27 604 | 318 | 8.8 | 56.9 | 53.1 |
| Charles Mix | 280 | 2 336 | 527 | 85 | 414 | 105 | 46 | 58 | 24 792 | 693 | 13.1 | 47.6 | 68.3 |
| Clark | 108 | 566 | D | D | 81 | D | D | 17 | 30 357 | 577 | 10.6 | 44.2 | 62.9 |
| Clay | 314 | 3 564 | 770 | 43 | 877 | 105 | 40 | 72 | 20 242 | 484 | 21.5 | 42.1 | 61.0 |
| Codington | 1 092 | 13 751 | 1 733 | 3 324 | 2 522 | 760 | 275 | 428 | 31 110 | 663 | 24.7 | 29.6 | 45.6 |
| Corson | 37 | 179 | 23 | NA | 62 | D | NA | 5 | 26 346 | 392 | 5.1 | 71.7 | 70.7 |
| Custer | 269 | 1 276 | D | 14 | 255 | D | D | 43 | 33 507 | 359 | 20.9 | 35.7 | 48.5 |
| Davison | 737 | 11 269 | 2 227 | 1 573 | 2 052 | 330 | 373 | 346 | 30 726 | 406 | 24.4 | 35.7 | 51.7 |
| Day | 173 | 1 520 | 310 | 212 | 317 | D | D | 39 | 25 878 | 675 | 8.0 | 43.6 | 58.2 |
| Deuel | 132 | 1 494 | 172 | 648 | D | D | D | 58 | 38 834 | 583 | 15.4 | 34.8 | 55.4 |
| Dewey | 105 | 789 | 188 | D | 160 | 89 | D | 22 | 28 294 | 410 | 5.4 | 72.9 | 65.1 |
| Douglas | 104 | 869 | D | 111 | 101 | D | 62 | 24 | 27 932 | 363 | 15.4 | 44.1 | 67.5 |
| Edmunds | 124 | 857 | 197 | 58 | 154 | 62 | D | 26 | 30 387 | 425 | 6.4 | 56.7 | 60.7 |
| Fall River | 224 | 2 188 | D | D | 283 | 59 | D | 94 | 42 863 | 330 | 13.0 | 49.7 | 53.9 |
| Faulk | 68 | 418 | D | D | 78 | D | D | 12 | 28 952 | 294 | 6.8 | 72.8 | 74.8 |
| Grant | 285 | 3 186 | 375 | 575 | 463 | D | 45 | 104 | 32 653 | 555 | 12.4 | 39.6 | 62.5 |
| Gregory | 178 | 1 072 | 291 | 43 | 253 | D | D | 26 | 23 842 | 511 | 10.0 | 54.6 | 64.4 |
| Haakon | 85 | 597 | D | D | 91 | D | D | 17 | 28 454 | 284 | 2.5 | 79.6 | 71.8 |
| Hamlin | 157 | 966 | 180 | D | 136 | 53 | D | 28 | 29 181 | 449 | 24.5 | 36.7 | 50.1 |
| Hand | 120 | 958 | 210 | 45 | D | D | 28 | 26 | 27 125 | 484 | 7.2 | 61.6 | 75.0 |
| Hanson | 59 | 241 | D | D | D | 32 | D | 8 | 31 270 | 308 | 17.2 | 40.9 | 61.4 |
| Harding | 38 | 339 | D | NA | 28 | D | D | 13 | 39 404 | 252 | 2.0 | 82.1 | 75.4 |
| Hughes | 675 | 6 313 | 1 187 | D | 1 397 | 427 | 269 | 184 | 29 117 | 305 | 18.0 | 43.9 | 53.8 |
| Hutchinson | 238 | 2 069 | 645 | 204 | 382 | 108 | 28 | 57 | 27 443 | 723 | 13.1 | 46.5 | 67.5 |
| Hyde | 41 | 522 | D | NA | 71 | D | D | 16 | 30 933 | 181 | 7.2 | 68.5 | 68.0 |
| Jackson | 43 | 265 | D | D | 131 | D | D | 6 | 20 819 | 297 | 6.7 | 76.1 | 77.1 |
| Jerauld | 77 | D | D | D | D | 24 | D | D | D | 239 | 6.7 | 49.4 | 57.3 |
| Jones | 55 | 320 | D | NA | 115 | D | D | 8 | 23 906 | 163 | 4.9 | 73.0 | 68.1 |
| Kingsbury | 167 | 1 291 | 201 | 349 | 147 | 112 | 20 | 42 | 32 435 | 551 | 14.9 | 43.2 | 58.6 |
| Lake | 348 | 3 451 | 669 | 759 | 503 | 109 | 141 | 107 | 31 034 | 514 | 24.5 | 37.7 | 54.7 |
| Lawrence | 992 | 9 533 | D | 447 | 1 411 | 663 | 279 | 264 | 27 645 | 301 | 26.9 | 19.3 | 42.9 |
| Lincoln | 1 124 | 11 271 | 2 022 | 1 952 | 1 352 | 657 | 384 | 413 | 36 646 | 855 | 29.2 | 24.0 | 54.6 |
| Lyman | 72 | 766 | D | NA | 281 | D | D | 14 | 17 636 | 443 | 6.5 | 59.8 | 54.4 |
| McCook | 180 | 871 | 233 | D | 152 | 40 | 47 | 23 | 26 246 | 545 | 20.2 | 39.8 | 63.7 |
| McPherson | 77 | 343 | D | 45 | D | 53 | D | 8 | 21 950 | 398 | 6.3 | 50.8 | 55.3 |
| Marshall | 146 | 1 046 | D | 276 | 184 | 60 | D | 32 | 30 700 | 523 | 11.3 | 49.9 | 59.3 |
| Meade | 674 | 4 757 | D | 261 | 609 | 185 | 195 | 195 | 40 929 | 879 | 17.3 | 55.9 | 58.7 |
| Mellette | 25 | D | D | NA | D | D | D | D | D | 216 | 2.3 | 83.8 | 75.5 |
| Miner | 78 | 483 | 126 | D | D | D | D | 15 | 31 569 | 356 | 11.5 | 46.9 | 61.0 |
| Minnehaha | 5 366 | 108 609 | 22 724 | 10 894 | 14 855 | 12 710 | 3 743 | 4 170 | 38 391 | 1 194 | 34.5 | 24.5 | 51.3 |
| Moody | 158 | 1 710 | D | 298 | 199 | 40 | 55 | 55 | 31 913 | 556 | 22.3 | 28.2 | 53.4 |
| Pennington | 3 577 | 43 610 | 8 353 | 2 175 | 7 961 | 2 650 | 1 869 | 1 474 | 33 806 | 655 | 20.8 | 40.0 | 51.5 |
| Perkins | 135 | 749 | 150 | D | D | 52 | D | 20 | 27 200 | 432 | 4.2 | 78.2 | 74.3 |
| Potter | 109 | 747 | D | D | 153 | D | 8 | 23 | 31 419 | 238 | 7.1 | 60.1 | 65.5 |
| Roberts | 228 | 2 173 | 510 | D | 373 | 104 | D | 54 | 24 736 | 887 | 13.5 | 39.1 | 63.7 |
| Sanborn | 64 | D | D | D | 41 | D | 23 | 12 | D | 354 | 8.8 | 45.8 | 61.6 |
| Shannon | 62 | 1 796 | 295 | D | 151 | D | D | 52 | 28 735 | 250 | 6.8 | 60.0 | 61.6 |
| Spink | 184 | 1 252 | 303 | 102 | D | 78 | D | 40 | 31 727 | 624 | 6.9 | 62.7 | 69.7 |
| Stanley | 104 | 1 010 | 15 | NA | 106 | D | 23 | 29 | 28 984 | 165 | 10.9 | 74.5 | 52.1 |
| Sully | 64 | 330 | 8 | D | 85 | D | D | 10 | 30 621 | 195 | 4.1 | 71.8 | 76.9 |
| Todd | 52 | 1 704 | D | D | 234 | D | D | 37 | 21 771 | 258 | 6.6 | 55.8 | 64.7 |

| STATE County | Land in farms | | | | | Value of land and buildings (dollars) | | Value of machinery and equipment, average per farm (dollars) | Value of products sold | | | | Percent of farms with sales of: | | Government payments | |
|---|---|---|---|---|---|---|---|---|---|---|---|---|---|---|---|---|
| | | | Acres | | | | | | | | Percent from: | | | | | |
| | Acreage (1,000) | Percent change, 2002–2007 | Average size of farm | Total irrigated (1,000) | Total cropland (1,000) | Average per farm | Average per acre | | Total (mil dol) | Average per farm (dollars) | Crops | Livestock and poultry products | $10,000 or more | $100,000 or more | Total ($1,000) | Percent of farms |
| | 117 | 118 | 119 | 120 | 121 | 122 | 123 | 124 | 125 | 126 | 127 | 128 | 129 | 130 | 131 | 132 |
| SOUTH CAROLINA—Cont'd | | | | | | | | | | | | | | | | |
| Sumter | 153 | 12.5 | 277 | 9.5 | 88.8 | 552 862 | 1 996 | 91 687 | 88.8 | 160 337 | 37.3 | 62.7 | 25.6 | 11.0 | 4 016 | 54.0 |
| Union | 46 | -9.8 | 174 | 0.1 | 9.5 | 446 475 | 2 570 | 48 427 | D | D | D | 0.0 | 16.0 | 0.8 | 133 | 10.3 |
| Williamsburg | 209 | 1.5 | 243 | 0.9 | 105.6 | 592 524 | 2 436 | 66 117 | 42.4 | 49 302 | 70.8 | 29.2 | 23.9 | 7.8 | 3 738 | 58.5 |
| York | 124 | 4.2 | 120 | 1.0 | 39.3 | 477 437 | 3 991 | 47 917 | 92.5 | 89 082 | D | D | 17.2 | 2.7 | 609 | 13.9 |
| SOUTH DAKOTA | 43 666 | -0.3 | 1 401 | 373.8 | 19 094.3 | 1 255 332 | 896 | 155 652 | 6 570.5 | 210 801 | 51.5 | 48.5 | 65.4 | 38.3 | 270 748 | 73.5 |
| Aurora | 365 | 4.0 | 962 | 0.0 | 228.8 | 1 316 163 | 1 368 | 144 420 | 102.7 | 271 018 | 46.0 | 54.0 | 68.6 | 38.5 | 3 133 | 84.7 |
| Beadle | 770 | -4.9 | 1 026 | 20.0 | 492.4 | 1 338 462 | 1 304 | 185 877 | 195.4 | 260 566 | 50.9 | 49.1 | 66.7 | 43.5 | 7 087 | 73.5 |
| Bennett | 753 | 3.6 | 2 843 | 6.7 | 257.2 | 1 053 384 | 371 | 162 231 | 38.1 | 143 879 | 46.6 | 53.4 | 76.2 | 41.1 | 2 561 | 73.6 |
| Bon Homme | 309 | -10.4 | 548 | 8.2 | 219.8 | 804 317 | 1 467 | 126 226 | 109.2 | 193 914 | 40.0 | 60.0 | 79.0 | 42.3 | 2 953 | 88.6 |
| Brookings | 463 | 10.8 | 469 | 15.9 | 351.3 | 1 001 355 | 2 134 | 134 499 | 186.7 | 189 376 | 46.7 | 53.3 | 54.0 | 30.1 | 6 565 | 71.0 |
| Brown | 1 085 | -6.1 | 1 047 | 7.5 | 827.6 | 1 656 624 | 1 582 | 213 411 | 248.8 | 240 121 | 74.5 | 25.5 | 59.6 | 38.0 | 12 461 | 72.8 |
| Brule | 518 | 15.9 | 1 401 | 5.5 | 287.6 | 1 471 816 | 1 050 | 218 093 | 99.7 | 269 491 | 45.2 | 54.8 | 76.8 | 49.7 | 3 704 | 77.8 |
| Buffalo | 312 | 9.5 | 3 629 | 1.5 | 73.8 | 1 990 955 | 549 | 219 024 | 25.0 | 291 226 | 43.2 | 56.8 | 68.6 | 47.7 | 1 525 | 73.3 |
| Butte | 1 140 | -9.7 | 1 953 | 47.7 | 163.4 | 956 959 | 490 | 84 311 | 55.4 | 94 936 | 16.1 | 83.9 | 56.2 | 20.5 | 2 310 | 42.3 |
| Campbell | 401 | 2.6 | 1 261 | 1.1 | 205.6 | 924 190 | 733 | 152 437 | 49.4 | 155 318 | 59.9 | 40.1 | 52.5 | 31.8 | 3 362 | 87.4 |
| Charles Mix | 661 | -10.2 | 953 | 9.8 | 403.4 | 1 196 875 | 1 256 | 172 826 | 176.2 | 254 293 | 43.8 | 56.2 | 72.4 | 45.3 | 4 812 | 84.1 |
| Clark | 509 | -3.2 | 882 | 6.6 | 335.7 | 1 285 162 | 1 458 | 164 048 | 146.5 | 253 893 | 43.8 | 56.2 | 67.1 | 41.8 | 5 639 | 87.2 |
| Clay | 267 | -28.4 | 551 | 12.5 | 237.3 | 1 281 632 | 2 326 | 184 260 | 80.8 | 166 986 | 80.2 | 19.8 | 70.9 | 45.5 | 3 874 | 83.5 |
| Codington | 367 | -5.2 | 554 | 4.6 | 247.7 | 867 278 | 1 566 | 125 614 | 107.8 | 162 581 | 49.9 | 50.1 | 54.4 | 28.5 | 4 054 | 70.9 |
| Corson | 1 283 | -7.6 | 3 273 | 1.2 | 372.9 | 1 231 837 | 376 | 139 259 | 65.5 | 167 027 | 45.5 | 54.5 | 74.2 | 41.6 | 3 734 | 76.5 |
| Custer | 601 | 2.0 | 1 674 | 3.6 | 87.2 | 962 135 | 575 | 67 814 | 14.4 | 40 048 | 4.0 | 96.0 | 39.8 | 11.4 | 1 075 | 25.9 |
| Davison | 280 | 0.4 | 688 | 1.6 | 214.9 | 1 174 521 | 1 706 | 133 167 | 78.1 | 192 467 | 59.4 | 40.6 | 62.8 | 35.0 | 2 368 | 65.5 |
| Day | 567 | 6.8 | 840 | 0.3 | 387.0 | 1 035 545 | 1 232 | 137 370 | 97.8 | 144 910 | 70.7 | 29.3 | 54.5 | 32.0 | 8 133 | 84.1 |
| Deuel | 317 | -3.4 | 544 | 0.6 | 199.6 | 855 693 | 1 573 | 124 117 | 105.1 | 180 261 | 40.4 | 59.6 | 59.3 | 30.4 | 4 440 | 82.0 |
| Dewey | 1 450 | 6.0 | 3 536 | D | 250.0 | 1 239 985 | 351 | 125 059 | 49.1 | 119 731 | 34.8 | 65.2 | 72.4 | 37.3 | 3 573 | 60.0 |
| Douglas | 225 | -5.1 | 620 | 2.5 | 157.3 | 910 819 | 1 468 | 130 148 | 107.1 | 294 948 | 34.1 | 65.9 | 81.3 | 54.0 | 1 933 | 80.7 |
| Edmunds | 657 | 12.3 | 1 545 | 1.1 | 454.3 | 1 586 042 | 1 026 | 222 248 | 162.5 | 382 407 | 56.5 | 43.5 | 65.4 | 45.9 | 4 594 | 81.6 |
| Fall River | 950 | -3.3 | 2 878 | 8.1 | 97.1 | 1 162 239 | 404 | 83 397 | 96.9 | 293 719 | 1.4 | 98.6 | 45.8 | 19.1 | 1 527 | 40.9 |
| Faulk | 615 | 15.0 | 2 091 | D | 373.4 | 2 027 335 | 970 | 273 805 | 109.7 | 372 986 | 63.2 | 36.8 | 78.2 | 57.5 | 5 840 | 88.1 |
| Grant | 364 | 4.0 | 655 | 4.0 | 263.7 | 1 042 232 | 1 590 | 168 499 | 133.5 | 240 587 | 50.3 | 49.7 | 70.1 | 41.1 | 3 704 | 80.7 |
| Gregory | 654 | 0.5 | 1 281 | 1.7 | 256.3 | 932 875 | 728 | 124 613 | 73.4 | 143 689 | 42.2 | 57.8 | 76.3 | 34.8 | 1 932 | 73.0 |
| Haakon | 1 151 | -5.8 | 4 053 | 0.0 | 324.7 | 1 722 236 | 425 | 154 974 | 53.0 | 186 751 | 38.6 | 61.4 | 77.5 | 50.4 | 4 459 | 79.9 |
| Hamlin | 310 | 1.0 | 690 | 8.7 | 244.8 | 1 289 702 | 1 870 | 183 276 | 111.0 | 247 164 | 56.3 | 43.7 | 63.3 | 39.9 | 3 877 | 79.1 |
| Hand | 899 | 3.6 | 1 857 | 2.4 | 506.2 | 1 724 861 | 929 | 207 910 | 163.9 | 338 738 | 59.7 | 40.3 | 71.1 | 48.8 | 6 471 | 81.8 |
| Hanson | 219 | -12.0 | 711 | 2.7 | 174.4 | 1 390 310 | 1 955 | 196 282 | 67.3 | 218 569 | 54.9 | 45.1 | 67.9 | 42.2 | 2 319 | 76.0 |
| Harding | 1 596 | -4.7 | 6 334 | 1.0 | 207.6 | 2 304 456 | 364 | 155 526 | 41.3 | 163 695 | 18.5 | 81.5 | 79.0 | 48.8 | 2 661 | 72.6 |
| Hughes | 411 | 11.7 | 1 348 | 9.2 | 235.1 | 1 124 194 | 834 | 169 567 | 60.8 | 199 253 | 65.7 | 34.3 | 62.6 | 34.8 | 3 091 | 69.2 |
| Hutchinson | 510 | 0.8 | 705 | 3.3 | 394.7 | 1 291 838 | 1 832 | 169 124 | 192.4 | 266 048 | 53.9 | 46.1 | 71.9 | 49.5 | 5 499 | 86.4 |
| Hyde | 481 | 2.6 | 2 657 | D | 207.2 | 1 694 362 | 638 | 191 459 | 47.2 | 260 600 | 59.4 | 40.6 | 71.8 | 45.9 | 2 813 | 76.8 |
| Jackson | 1 184 | -0.6 | 3 987 | 1.3 | 229.0 | 1 426 638 | 358 | 127 970 | 36.9 | 124 182 | 31.5 | 68.5 | 75.1 | 42.4 | 2 881 | 65.3 |
| Jerauld | 329 | -2.1 | 1 375 | 1.3 | 185.6 | 1 259 237 | 916 | 179 222 | 68.7 | 287 599 | 49.3 | 50.7 | 68.2 | 40.2 | 1 932 | 79.5 |
| Jones | 519 | 0.6 | 3 186 | 0.7 | 190.5 | 1 244 663 | 391 | 143 369 | 28.8 | 176 753 | 50.5 | 49.5 | 74.8 | 46.6 | 2 514 | 84.0 |
| Kingsbury | 477 | -8.1 | 867 | 1.8 | 356.9 | 1 314 692 | 1 517 | 176 214 | 172.5 | 313 044 | 52.8 | 47.2 | 69.9 | 44.1 | 5 771 | 79.5 |
| Lake | 315 | -3.1 | 613 | 2.8 | 260.0 | 1 478 016 | 2 412 | 181 240 | 131.8 | 256 512 | 62.1 | 37.9 | 63.2 | 42.6 | 3 953 | 75.3 |
| Lawrence | 134 | -5.0 | 444 | 3.8 | 30.5 | 640 919 | 1 445 | 55 318 | 11.6 | 38 605 | 21.5 | 78.5 | 39.9 | 8.3 | 115 | 10.3 |
| Lincoln | 333 | 7.4 | 389 | 2.1 | 303.4 | 1 194 710 | 3 070 | 130 819 | 158.1 | 184 923 | 64.2 | 35.8 | 69.5 | 34.3 | 4 690 | 73.9 |
| Lyman | 976 | 10.3 | 2 204 | 9.8 | 467.7 | 1 379 745 | 626 | 157 717 | 84.4 | 190 620 | 60.6 | 39.4 | 58.9 | 37.7 | 6 744 | 80.4 |
| McCook | 363 | 5.2 | 667 | 0.0 | 289.2 | 1 396 692 | 2 095 | 157 585 | 129.2 | 237 076 | 62.1 | 37.9 | 67.2 | 45.9 | 4 422 | 81.5 |
| McPherson | 518 | -3.5 | 1 302 | 0.5 | 250.3 | 975 939 | 750 | 131 359 | 84.9 | 213 210 | 33.3 | 66.7 | 55.5 | 33.4 | 3 206 | 84.7 |
| Marshall | 534 | 1.7 | 1 021 | 0.6 | 328.2 | 1 190 237 | 1 165 | 186 355 | 161.3 | 308 394 | 34.6 | 65.4 | 62.9 | 38.2 | 7 791 | 83.7 |
| Meade | 2 209 | -0.9 | 2 513 | 6.6 | 520.4 | 1 264 860 | 503 | 107 585 | 78.4 | 89 201 | 25.9 | 74.1 | 57.2 | 25.9 | 5 967 | 48.7 |
| Mellette | 730 | 10.6 | 3 379 | 1.0 | 127.3 | 1 221 424 | 362 | 123 889 | 53.3 | 246 611 | 12.6 | 87.4 | 87.5 | 48.1 | 1 447 | 68.5 |
| Miner | 300 | 3.1 | 843 | 0.0 | 201.7 | 1 271 442 | 1 508 | 163 285 | 75.0 | 210 594 | 54.7 | 45.3 | 62.4 | 42.1 | 3 065 | 80.3 |
| Minnehaha | 421 | -0.2 | 353 | 2.7 | 326.4 | 973 600 | 2 759 | 135 251 | 190.3 | 159 415 | 57.5 | 42.5 | 60.7 | 33.8 | 5 630 | 67.2 |
| Moody | 293 | 3.5 | 528 | 2.4 | 235.5 | 1 322 921 | 2 507 | 158 890 | 158.1 | 284 378 | 49.4 | 50.6 | 61.5 | 37.2 | 4 864 | 83.1 |
| Pennington | 1 185 | -2.1 | 1 809 | 7.9 | 280.3 | 1 240 492 | 686 | 100 796 | 56.0 | 85 554 | 33.0 | 67.0 | 46.7 | 18.2 | 3 274 | 37.3 |
| Perkins | 1 829 | 2.6 | 4 234 | 0.6 | 427.3 | 1 735 967 | 410 | 135 386 | 59.5 | 137 696 | 23.1 | 76.9 | 71.8 | 43.8 | 5 362 | 79.4 |
| Potter | 517 | 14.1 | 2 171 | D | 355.9 | 2 022 031 | 931 | 253 542 | 90.4 | 379 730 | 84.2 | 15.8 | 68.1 | 51.3 | 3 916 | 81.5 |
| Roberts | 593 | 0.0 | 668 | 1.3 | 412.4 | 982 539 | 1 470 | 156 315 | 135.3 | 152 589 | 67.3 | 32.7 | 61.7 | 35.2 | 7 806 | 82.1 |
| Sanborn | 318 | -16.3 | 899 | D | 175.1 | 1 105 508 | 1 230 | 144 063 | 63.6 | 179 623 | 43.0 | 57.0 | 66.7 | 39.0 | 3 005 | 83.9 |
| Shannon | 1 334 | 5.3 | 5 335 | D | 104.9 | 1 138 819 | 213 | 86 381 | 19.8 | 79 214 | 20.3 | 79.7 | 56.8 | 24.8 | 1 229 | 40.8 |
| Spink | 908 | -0.3 | 1 455 | 19.1 | 686.9 | 1 997 548 | 1 373 | 274 523 | 229.1 | 367 210 | 65.6 | 34.4 | 75.2 | 53.0 | 10 508 | 89.3 |
| Stanley | 921 | 6.4 | 5 582 | 0.0 | 233.6 | 2 211 090 | 396 | 165 522 | 35.2 | 213 384 | 66.0 | 34.0 | 65.5 | 38.2 | 2 890 | 62.4 |
| Sully | 609 | 6.3 | 3 123 | 15.4 | 488.9 | 2 819 856 | 903 | 310 864 | 116.5 | 597 224 | 80.0 | 20.0 | 77.4 | 60.0 | 5 482 | 87.7 |
| Todd | 869 | -5.2 | 3 370 | 8.5 | 139.6 | 983 601 | 292 | 125 329 | 35.8 | 138 783 | 26.8 | 73.2 | 68.2 | 30.6 | 488 | 33.7 |

| STATE County | Water use, 2005 | | Wholesale trade,[1] 2007 | | | | Retail trade,[2] 2007 | | | | Real estate and rental and leasing,[2] 2007 | | | |
|---|---|---|---|---|---|---|---|---|---|---|---|---|---|---|
| | Total water withdrawn (mil gal/day) | Gallons withdrawn per person | Number of establishments | Number of employees | Sales (mil dol) | Annual payroll (mil dol) | Number of establishments | Number of employees | Sales (mil dol) | Annual payroll (mil dol) | Number of establishments | Number of employees | Receipts (mil dol) | Annual payroll (mil dol) |
| | 133 | 134 | 135 | 136 | 137 | 138 | 139 | 140 | 141 | 142 | 143 | 144 | 145 | 146 |
| SOUTH CAROLINA—Cont'd | | | | | | | | | | | | | | |
| Sumter | 24.9 | 236 | 73 | D | D | D | 417 | 4 919 | 1 021.5 | 91.8 | 87 | 308 | 36.7 | 6.8 |
| Union | 6.5 | 227 | 15 | D | D | D | 107 | 885 | 192.2 | 16.9 | 14 | 37 | 3.7 | 0.7 |
| Williamsburg | 6.2 | 174 | 19 | 237 | 102.5 | 7.5 | 124 | 995 | 224.6 | 16.9 | 14 | 46 | 3.9 | 0.9 |
| York | 177.7 | 935 | 222 | 2 949 | 2 150.1 | 141.9 | 689 | 8 200 | 2 172.7 | 179.1 | 229 | 825 | 113.7 | 21.4 |
| SOUTH DAKOTA | 500.4 | 645 | 1 248 | 13 402 | 11 400.5 | 550.8 | 4 172 | 50 842 | 12 266.2 | 1 045.3 | 888 | 3 844 | 523.9 | 90.3 |
| Aurora | 0.8 | 283 | 5 | 22 | 19.2 | 0.6 | 15 | 86 | 38.1 | 1.3 | 2 | D | D | D |
| Beadle | 12.0 | 757 | 25 | D | D | D | 97 | 1 262 | 245.8 | 23.2 | 31 | 108 | 12.4 | 1.3 |
| Bennett | 9.8 | 2 728 | 1 | D | D | D | 15 | 118 | 24.0 | 1.9 | NA | NA | NA | NA |
| Bon Homme | 6.4 | 897 | 11 | 87 | 43.2 | 2.0 | 38 | 231 | 40.7 | 3.4 | 3 | 6 | 0.2 | 0.0 |
| Brookings | 15.1 | 535 | 30 | D | D | D | 118 | 1 729 | 338.2 | 30.7 | 38 | 151 | 14.4 | 3.4 |
| Brown | 7.9 | 227 | 78 | 863 | 1 471.6 | 34.6 | 209 | 2 980 | 692.2 | 65.4 | 55 | 264 | 39.3 | 5.8 |
| Brule | 2.7 | 526 | 11 | 70 | 46.8 | 2.7 | 42 | 320 | 78.5 | 5.0 | 2 | D | D | D |
| Buffalo | 5.3 | 2 529 | NA | NA | NA | NA | 2 | D | D | D | 1 | D | D | D |
| Butte | 51.3 | 5 501 | 9 | 67 | 29.1 | 2.2 | 46 | 386 | 108.9 | 8.9 | 11 | D | D | D |
| Campbell | 2.5 | 1 610 | 5 | D | D | D | 5 | 21 | 3.9 | 0.2 | 1 | D | D | D |
| Charles Mix | 14.2 | 1 543 | 15 | 113 | 73.1 | 3.2 | 60 | 428 | 82.1 | 6.2 | 3 | 5 | 1.0 | 0.1 |
| Clark | 6.3 | 1 648 | 8 | 50 | 64.3 | 2.0 | 16 | 82 | 21.0 | 1.6 | 1 | D | D | D |
| Clay | 7.0 | 536 | 10 | D | D | D | 45 | 772 | 140.1 | 12.2 | 14 | 75 | 5.3 | 0.6 |
| Codington | 8.5 | 328 | 62 | 536 | 344.0 | 22.7 | 201 | 2 602 | 560.7 | 51.7 | 40 | D | D | D |
| Corson | 1.6 | 355 | 4 | D | D | D | 7 | 59 | 10.6 | 0.9 | NA | NA | NA | NA |
| Custer | 7.8 | 988 | 4 | D | D | D | 30 | 228 | 51.5 | 5.1 | 9 | 17 | 2.8 | 0.3 |
| Davison | 1.6 | 84 | 33 | 393 | 407.0 | 17.7 | 135 | 2 055 | 436.2 | 38.6 | 27 | D | D | D |
| Day | 4.0 | 693 | 11 | 128 | 97.1 | 4.4 | 35 | 245 | 51.0 | 3.9 | 5 | D | D | D |
| Deuel | 1.8 | 412 | 3 | D | D | D | 24 | 142 | 36.4 | 2.6 | 1 | D | D | D |
| Dewey | 1.2 | 192 | 7 | 39 | 12.5 | 1.1 | 20 | 132 | 23.8 | 1.5 | 2 | D | D | D |
| Douglas | 3.2 | 961 | 6 | D | D | D | 16 | 113 | 22.5 | 1.9 | 2 | D | D | D |
| Edmunds | 1.3 | 323 | 12 | 119 | 196.3 | 4.5 | 24 | 159 | 39.7 | 2.7 | 3 | 10 | 0.1 | 0.0 |
| Fall River | 26.5 | 3 608 | 3 | 20 | 3.6 | 0.4 | 40 | 338 | 68.7 | 5.4 | 6 | 32 | 3.0 | 0.2 |
| Faulk | 0.8 | 339 | 8 | 49 | 72.7 | 1.2 | 13 | 75 | 20.3 | 1.7 | 1 | D | D | D |
| Grant | 9.0 | 1 216 | 11 | 114 | 122.8 | 5.2 | 48 | 500 | 99.8 | 9.3 | 10 | 29 | 2.7 | 0.3 |
| Gregory | 2.5 | 576 | 10 | 41 | 27.3 | 0.8 | 38 | 277 | 53.0 | 4.5 | 1 | D | D | D |
| Haakon | 1.9 | 1 004 | 6 | 31 | 54.6 | 1.0 | 15 | 106 | 23.9 | 1.7 | 1 | D | D | D |
| Hamlin | 6.2 | 1 085 | 8 | 90 | 80.7 | 4.5 | 24 | 147 | 49.1 | 3.1 | 1 | D | D | D |
| Hand | 2.2 | 665 | 11 | 107 | 76.5 | 3.7 | 24 | 150 | 30.3 | 2.7 | NA | NA | NA | NA |
| Hanson | 1.4 | 382 | 6 | D | D | D | 5 | 45 | 6.0 | 0.5 | 2 | D | D | D |
| Harding | 1.7 | 1 388 | NA | NA | NA | NA | 6 | 36 | 8.7 | 0.5 | NA | NA | NA | NA |
| Hughes | 25.3 | 1 499 | 22 | 227 | 250.1 | 6.9 | 120 | 1 409 | 262.3 | 27.8 | 31 | 134 | 6.8 | 1.1 |
| Hutchinson | 2.8 | 369 | 24 | 237 | 321.5 | 7.2 | 48 | 338 | 74.0 | 5.7 | 3 | 4 | 0.4 | 0.1 |
| Hyde | 0.8 | 489 | NA | NA | NA | NA | 10 | 116 | 37.5 | 2.0 | 2 | D | D | D |
| Jackson | 3.2 | 1 106 | 2 | D | D | D | 15 | 114 | 29.1 | 2.0 | NA | NA | NA | NA |
| Jerauld | 2.1 | 988 | 8 | D | D | D | 11 | 79 | 20.5 | 1.5 | 2 | D | D | D |
| Jones | 0.8 | 726 | 2 | D | D | D | 13 | 99 | 23.0 | 1.9 | NA | NA | NA | NA |
| Kingsbury | 4.5 | 813 | 6 | 82 | 103.3 | 3.6 | 30 | 155 | 34.1 | 2.6 | 2 | D | D | D |
| Lake | 1.8 | 160 | 12 | 215 | 225.0 | 8.6 | 54 | 516 | 134.7 | 10.4 | 15 | 44 | 2.3 | 0.5 |
| Lawrence | 12.9 | 575 | 23 | D | D | D | 148 | 1 532 | 435.1 | 35.0 | 61 | 197 | 19.8 | 4.4 |
| Lincoln | 4.3 | 129 | 47 | 355 | 337.8 | 14.4 | 115 | 1 241 | 444.4 | 33.9 | 34 | D | D | D |
| Lyman | 2.5 | 630 | 5 | D | D | D | 19 | 278 | 69.0 | 4.3 | 1 | D | D | D |
| McCook | 1.5 | 256 | 10 | 59 | 41.4 | 1.7 | 26 | 152 | 43.5 | 3.0 | 5 | D | D | D |
| McPherson | 3.2 | 1 207 | 3 | D | D | D | 16 | 60 | 15.7 | 1.0 | 3 | 3 | 0.2 | 0.0 |
| Marshall | 2.3 | 518 | 11 | 75 | 38.1 | 2.1 | 27 | 177 | 48.2 | 3.1 | 1 | D | D | D |
| Meade | 9.3 | 379 | 21 | 88 | 39.2 | 3.6 | 86 | 702 | 194.3 | 15.1 | 29 | 94 | 15.6 | 1.5 |
| Mellette | 2.5 | 1 193 | 2 | D | D | D | 6 | 47 | 9.3 | 0.7 | NA | NA | NA | NA |
| Miner | 0.7 | 263 | 5 | D | D | D | 13 | 64 | 10.7 | 0.9 | NA | NA | NA | NA |
| Minnehaha | 32.2 | 201 | 322 | 4 798 | 3 023.5 | 224.1 | 851 | 14 984 | 3 823.8 | 329.4 | 205 | 1 263 | 204.2 | 36.8 |
| Moody | 3.1 | 467 | 7 | 32 | 16.5 | 1.0 | 20 | 180 | 38.3 | 3.2 | 2 | D | D | D |
| Pennington | 35.3 | 378 | 155 | 1 934 | 1 007.2 | 75.1 | 600 | 7 902 | 1 967.8 | 178.9 | 158 | 677 | 112.7 | 16.5 |
| Perkins | 1.5 | 490 | 4 | D | D | D | 26 | 144 | 28.2 | 2.7 | 1 | D | D | D |
| Potter | 1.4 | 608 | 7 | 59 | 52.0 | 2.3 | 21 | 169 | 26.8 | 2.0 | 2 | D | D | D |
| Roberts | 3.2 | 322 | 16 | 108 | 211.1 | 3.4 | 51 | 384 | 81.0 | 6.0 | 1 | D | D | D |
| Sanborn | 0.8 | 299 | 7 | 75 | 51.0 | 3.4 | 7 | 65 | 6.7 | 0.5 | NA | NA | NA | NA |
| Shannon | 1.4 | 104 | NA | NA | NA | NA | 15 | 194 | 39.2 | 2.4 | 1 | D | D | D |
| Spink | 21.9 | 3 173 | 10 | 127 | 248.3 | 5.6 | 30 | 199 | 41.1 | 3.6 | 3 | 7 | 0.4 | 0.0 |
| Stanley | 0.9 | 325 | 4 | D | D | D | 19 | 114 | 30.7 | 2.3 | 3 | 3 | 0.3 | 0.1 |
| Sully | 10.0 | 7 000 | 2 | D | D | D | 13 | 86 | 31.3 | 1.7 | 1 | D | D | D |
| Todd | 11.4 | 1 158 | 1 | D | D | D | 21 | 241 | 39.5 | 2.9 | NA | NA | NA | NA |

1. Merchant wholesalers, except manufacturers' sales branches and offices.    2. Employer establishments.

# Table B. States and Counties — Professional Services, Manufacturing, and Accommodation and Food Services

| STATE County | Professional, scientific, and technical services,[1] 2007 | | | | Manufacturing, 2007 | | | | Accommodation and food services, 2007 | | | |
|---|---|---|---|---|---|---|---|---|---|---|---|---|
| | Number of establishments | Number of employees | Receipts (mil dol) | Annual payroll (mil dol) | Number of establishments | Number of employees | Receipts (mil dol) | Annual payroll (mil dol) | Number of establishments | Number of employees | Sales (mil dol) | Annual payroll (mil dol) |
| | 147 | 148 | 149 | 150 | 151 | 152 | 153 | 154 | 155 | 156 | 157 | 158 |
| SOUTH CAROLINA—Cont'd | | | | | | | | | | | | |
| Sumter | 139 | D | D | D | 82 | 7 707 | 1 922.0 | 253.3 | 149 | 3 173 | 109.4 | 29.8 |
| Union | 25 | 192 | 6.9 | 2.2 | 31 | 2 062 | 488.4 | 72.4 | 32 | 554 | 18.5 | 4.9 |
| Williamsburg | 31 | 117 | 10.1 | 3.9 | 35 | 2 811 | 1 398.1 | 93.0 | 29 | 404 | 12.8 | 3.1 |
| York | 403 | D | D | D | 233 | 10 096 | 3 621.2 | 457.8 | 365 | 6 983 | 285.8 | 78.0 |
| SOUTH DAKOTA | 1 735 | 10 073 | 1 093.4 | 385.9 | 1 052 | 40 961 | 13 051.1 | 1 539.3 | 2 426 | 36 710 | 1 622.8 | 436.2 |
| Aurora | 5 | 25 | 2.2 | 0.4 | NA | NA | NA | NA | 11 | D | D | D |
| Beadle | 24 | D | D | D | 32 | 1 140 | 298.6 | 32.3 | 54 | 609 | 20.8 | 5.4 |
| Bennett | 4 | 9 | 0.3 | 0.1 | NA | NA | NA | NA | 8 | 57 | 1.8 | 0.4 |
| Bon Homme | 8 | 13 | 1.5 | 0.3 | NA | NA | NA | NA | 15 | 80 | 2.3 | 0.5 |
| Brookings | 64 | 350 | 33.7 | 12.4 | 42 | 5 104 | 2 265.7 | 210.4 | 76 | 1 636 | 53.2 | 14.1 |
| Brown | 85 | 419 | 41.1 | 15.3 | 37 | D | D | D | 116 | 1 989 | 74.1 | 19.8 |
| Brule | 13 | 33 | 2.3 | 0.8 | NA | NA | NA | NA | 26 | 252 | 9.9 | 2.4 |
| Buffalo | NA | NA | NA | NA | NA | NA | NA | NA | 1 | D | D | D |
| Butte | 23 | 67 | 5.7 | 1.9 | NA | NA | NA | NA | 32 | 261 | 8.5 | 2.2 |
| Campbell | 3 | 7 | 0.2 | 0.1 | NA | NA | NA | NA | 7 | D | D | D |
| Charles Mix | 13 | 47 | 4.3 | 1.0 | NA | NA | NA | NA | 26 | 453 | 18.2 | 6.7 |
| Clark | 6 | 19 | 1.6 | 0.3 | NA | NA | NA | NA | 7 | 47 | 1.6 | 0.4 |
| Clay | 18 | D | D | D | NA | NA | NA | NA | 44 | 703 | 19.3 | 5.2 |
| Codington | 64 | D | D | D | 73 | D | D | D | 88 | 1 873 | 75.6 | 22.1 |
| Corson | NA | NA | NA | NA | NA | NA | NA | NA | 3 | 5 | 0.1 | 0.0 |
| Custer | 15 | 40 | 2.4 | 0.9 | NA | NA | NA | NA | 58 | 281 | 27.8 | 7.3 |
| Davison | 44 | D | D | D | 45 | 1 717 | D | 68.7 | 69 | 1 211 | 45.6 | 13.5 |
| Day | 8 | 31 | 1.9 | 0.7 | NA | NA | NA | NA | 21 | 146 | 4.3 | 1.2 |
| Deuel | 4 | D | D | D | NA | NA | NA | NA | 15 | 60 | 2.5 | 0.5 |
| Dewey | 4 | D | D | D | NA | NA | NA | NA | 7 | D | D | D |
| Douglas | 6 | 13 | 0.9 | 0.2 | NA | NA | NA | NA | 10 | D | D | D |
| Edmunds | 6 | 19 | 2.2 | 0.7 | NA | NA | NA | NA | 15 | 81 | 1.9 | 0.4 |
| Fall River | 19 | 72 | 3.7 | 1.2 | NA | NA | NA | NA | 41 | 248 | 10.0 | 2.6 |
| Faulk | 2 | D | D | D | NA | NA | NA | NA | 9 | D | D | D |
| Grant | 18 | 64 | 4.5 | 1.4 | 13 | 531 | 634.2 | 20.6 | 30 | 297 | 9.1 | 2.4 |
| Gregory | 8 | 25 | 2.3 | 0.5 | NA | NA | NA | NA | 19 | 102 | 2.8 | 0.7 |
| Haakon | 7 | 12 | 1.2 | 0.4 | NA | NA | NA | NA | 9 | D | D | D |
| Hamlin | 2 | D | D | D | NA | NA | NA | NA | 15 | 77 | 2.3 | 0.5 |
| Hand | 11 | 23 | 2.3 | 0.8 | NA | NA | NA | NA | 14 | 56 | 2.7 | 0.5 |
| Hanson | 3 | D | D | D | NA | NA | NA | NA | 3 | 23 | 0.4 | 0.1 |
| Harding | 1 | D | D | D | NA | NA | NA | NA | 3 | 15 | 0.9 | 0.1 |
| Hughes | 61 | 248 | 29.9 | 9.5 | NA | NA | NA | NA | 55 | 935 | 35.1 | 9.4 |
| Hutchinson | 10 | 28 | 1.8 | 0.7 | NA | NA | NA | NA | 17 | 135 | 3.9 | 0.8 |
| Hyde | 3 | D | D | D | NA | NA | NA | NA | 1 | D | D | D |
| Jackson | 1 | D | D | D | NA | NA | NA | NA | 13 | 30 | 1.9 | 0.5 |
| Jerauld | 6 | 10 | 1.2 | 0.2 | 1 | D | D | D | 7 | D | D | D |
| Jones | 3 | D | D | D | NA | NA | NA | NA | 13 | 70 | 3.7 | 1.1 |
| Kingsbury | 9 | 21 | 2.7 | 0.5 | NA | NA | NA | NA | 17 | 106 | 3.7 | 0.9 |
| Lake | 30 | 143 | 22.1 | 4.4 | 26 | 935 | 342.9 | 35.0 | 45 | 471 | 14.3 | 3.7 |
| Lawrence | 62 | 250 | 21.7 | 7.4 | 44 | D | D | 17.3 | 140 | 2 623 | 221.7 | 42.6 |
| Lincoln | 64 | D | D | D | 67 | 1 630 | D | 59.2 | 45 | 840 | 27.6 | 8.0 |
| Lyman | 2 | D | D | D | NA | NA | NA | NA | 19 | 249 | 15.9 | 3.4 |
| McCook | 12 | D | D | D | NA | NA | NA | NA | 21 | 91 | 3.4 | 0.6 |
| McPherson | 4 | 7 | 0.4 | 0.1 | NA | NA | NA | NA | 7 | D | D | D |
| Marshall | 13 | 28 | 2.1 | 0.6 | NA | NA | NA | NA | 17 | 90 | 4.4 | 1.1 |
| Meade | 38 | D | D | D | NA | NA | NA | NA | 71 | 557 | 33.4 | 8.2 |
| Mellette | 2 | D | D | D | NA | NA | NA | NA | 4 | D | D | D |
| Miner | 3 | 19 | 0.9 | 0.4 | NA | NA | NA | NA | 8 | D | D | D |
| Minnehaha | 469 | D | D | D | 184 | 11 483 | 3 518.8 | 475.0 | 426 | 9 651 | 389.9 | 118.4 |
| Moody | 10 | 21 | 1.1 | 0.4 | NA | NA | NA | NA | 17 | D | D | D |
| Pennington | 288 | D | D | D | 119 | 2 893 | 678.3 | D | 341 | 5 981 | 286.5 | 80.6 |
| Perkins | 4 | 12 | 0.6 | 0.1 | NA | NA | NA | NA | 7 | D | D | D |
| Potter | 3 | 9 | 0.5 | 0.1 | NA | NA | NA | NA | 12 | 81 | 4.2 | 0.8 |
| Roberts | 12 | D | D | D | NA | NA | NA | NA | 28 | 221 | 7.2 | 1.7 |
| Sanborn | 5 | 13 | 1.6 | 0.4 | NA | NA | NA | NA | 7 | 28 | 1.1 | 0.2 |
| Shannon | 2 | D | D | D | NA | NA | NA | NA | 8 | 343 | 18.1 | 6.1 |
| Spink | 4 | 21 | 2.0 | 0.6 | NA | NA | NA | NA | 16 | 143 | 4.6 | 1.4 |
| Stanley | 4 | 36 | 2.2 | 0.7 | NA | NA | NA | NA | 12 | 166 | 5.4 | 1.3 |
| Sully | 2 | D | D | D | NA | NA | NA | NA | 9 | 54 | 2.0 | 0.5 |
| Todd | NA | NA | NA | NA | NA | NA | NA | NA | 4 | 24 | 1.7 | 0.4 |

1. Establishment subject to federal tax.

# Table B. States and Counties — Health Care and Social Assistance, Other Services, and Federal Funds

| STATE County | Health care and social assistance, 2007 | | | | Other services, 2007 | | | | Federal funds and grants, 2009–2010 Expenditures (mil dol) | | | |
| | Number of establishments | Number of employees | Receipts (mil dol) | Annual payroll (mil dol) | Number of establishments | Number of employees | Receipts (mil dol) | Annual payroll (mil dol) | Total | Direct payments for individuals[1] Social Security and government retirement | Medicare | Food Stamps and Supplemental Security Income |
|---|---|---|---|---|---|---|---|---|---|---|---|---|
| | 159 | 160 | 161 | 162 | 163 | 164 | 165 | 166 | 167 | 168 | 169 | 170 |
| SOUTH CAROLINA—Cont'd | | | | | | | | | | | | |
| Sumter | 180 | 4 812 | 469.3 | 172.7 | 152 | 1 141 | 69.7 | 21.7 | 1 422.2 | 401.7 | 121.4 | 78.0 |
| Union | 38 | 843 | 67.2 | 27.3 | 36 | 130 | 7.0 | 2.4 | 245.3 | 110.4 | 51.1 | 14.4 |
| Williamsburg | 51 | 827 | 49.6 | 20.3 | 47 | 216 | 9.9 | 3.1 | 388.3 | 103.5 | 57.4 | 37.7 |
| York | 341 | 7 680 | 718.6 | 271.7 | 285 | 1 897 | 155.7 | 47.3 | 1 138.6 | 661.8 | 182.8 | 52.8 |
| SOUTH DAKOTA | 2 241 | 56 480 | 4 767.2 | 2 038.8 | 1 815 | 8 518 | 749.6 | 181.9 | 9 506.6 | 2 544.7 | 994.9 | 232.9 |
| Aurora | 9 | D | D | D | 5 | D | D | D | 29.1 | 8.3 | 5.9 | 0.3 |
| Beadle | 55 | 1 392 | 77.8 | 34.6 | 54 | 230 | 14.4 | 3.9 | 208.0 | 63.6 | 32.2 | 3.3 |
| Bennett | 5 | D | D | D | 4 | D | D | D | 34.6 | 7.6 | 3.8 | 4.2 |
| Bon Homme | 22 | 454 | 20.9 | 9.1 | 11 | 27 | 1.9 | 0.4 | 56.3 | 22.7 | 15.0 | 0.9 |
| Brookings | 67 | 1 209 | 62.3 | 28.9 | 69 | 307 | 49.5 | 7.2 | 214.7 | 62.3 | 26.8 | 4.3 |
| Brown | 153 | 3 178 | 275.0 | 99.1 | 89 | 467 | 31.6 | 8.1 | 439.8 | 123.4 | 59.9 | 7.4 |
| Brule | 21 | 378 | 21.3 | 9.1 | 17 | 61 | 6.6 | 1.3 | 62.2 | 16.7 | 10.1 | 2.8 |
| Buffalo | 3 | D | D | D | NA | NA | NA | NA | 39.8 | 2.8 | 2.4 | 0.5 |
| Butte | 21 | 137 | 9.2 | 3.9 | 25 | 79 | 6.2 | 1.6 | 67.5 | 34.2 | 10.0 | 3.1 |
| Campbell | 4 | D | D | D | 2 | D | D | D | 25.5 | 9.3 | 5.2 | 0.2 |
| Charles Mix | 25 | 495 | 22.8 | 10.2 | 26 | 81 | 7.8 | 1.7 | 125.2 | 26.2 | 16.7 | 4.4 |
| Clark | 8 | 114 | 5.0 | 2.1 | 7 | D | D | D | 48.9 | 13.0 | 7.6 | 0.8 |
| Clay | 30 | D | D | D | 24 | 155 | 31.3 | 2.6 | 112.4 | 27.6 | 13.3 | 3.7 |
| Codington | 85 | 1 592 | 157.0 | 49.1 | 86 | 386 | 29.0 | 6.7 | 178.5 | 79.0 | 26.8 | 5.4 |
| Corson | 5 | 16 | 0.8 | 0.3 | NA | NA | NA | NA | 56.1 | 13.4 | 8.4 | 4.0 |
| Custer | 15 | 52 | 3.1 | 1.4 | 13 | 75 | 5.6 | 1.7 | 76.8 | 40.8 | 7.8 | 1.6 |
| Davison | 92 | D | D | D | 55 | D | D | D | 162.7 | 57.7 | 34.0 | 5.4 |
| Day | 21 | 327 | 13.6 | 5.6 | 13 | 37 | 2.7 | 0.6 | 92.4 | 28.7 | 14.6 | 2.3 |
| Deuel | 7 | 210 | 8.8 | 4.1 | 5 | 22 | 1.2 | 0.3 | 39.2 | 14.1 | 7.7 | 0.8 |
| Dewey | 14 | 176 | 21.1 | 7.7 | 6 | 12 | 1.0 | 0.4 | 109.6 | 13.5 | 5.0 | 6.1 |
| Douglas | 8 | 231 | 10.8 | 5.1 | 8 | D | D | D | 30.3 | 11.1 | 7.0 | 0.6 |
| Edmunds | 12 | 199 | 9.7 | 4.0 | 7 | 19 | 1.9 | 0.3 | 52.0 | 13.2 | 9.3 | 0.4 |
| Fall River | 21 | 593 | 65.4 | 34.0 | 20 | 62 | 4.5 | 1.0 | 114.0 | 50.1 | 12.0 | 2.4 |
| Faulk | 5 | D | D | D | 8 | D | D | D | 34.1 | 7.9 | 6.0 | 0.3 |
| Grant | 21 | 260 | 13.5 | 4.9 | 21 | 75 | 6.2 | 1.4 | 67.7 | 28.1 | 14.1 | 1.4 |
| Gregory | 17 | 266 | 17.2 | 7.6 | 12 | D | D | D | 46.2 | 16.6 | 11.1 | 1.7 |
| Haakon | 6 | D | D | D | 3 | D | D | D | 21.2 | 8.0 | 3.5 | 0.2 |
| Hamlin | 11 | 182 | 5.6 | 2.4 | 7 | 17 | 1.0 | 0.3 | 42.2 | 15.2 | 7.3 | 0.8 |
| Hand | 8 | 208 | 8.5 | 4.2 | 10 | D | D | D | 48.5 | 10.7 | 6.8 | 0.6 |
| Hanson | 2 | D | D | D | 3 | D | D | D | 38.5 | 24.8 | 2.9 | 0.5 |
| Harding | 5 | D | D | D | 2 | D | D | D | 12.2 | 5.6 | 1.6 | 0.2 |
| Hughes | 52 | D | D | D | 92 | 382 | 55.6 | 11.0 | 846.1 | 47.0 | 18.1 | 3.6 |
| Hutchinson | 19 | 684 | 33.3 | 15.0 | 14 | 40 | 3.7 | 0.7 | 85.3 | 30.2 | 16.9 | 1.3 |
| Hyde | 4 | D | D | D | 2 | D | D | D | 57.2 | 4.7 | 2.9 | 0.3 |
| Jackson | 1 | D | D | D | 1 | D | D | D | 27.7 | 6.6 | 1.8 | 2.2 |
| Jerauld | 6 | D | D | D | 6 | D | D | D | 22.6 | 6.9 | 6.3 | 0.3 |
| Jones | 3 | D | D | D | 1 | D | D | D | 14.5 | 3.4 | 2.1 | 0.1 |
| Kingsbury | 16 | 274 | 12.2 | 6.0 | 10 | 33 | 3.4 | 0.7 | 61.4 | 22.0 | 13.4 | 0.9 |
| Lake | 34 | 623 | 34.1 | 15.3 | 23 | 126 | 5.5 | 3.2 | 109.4 | 47.3 | 18.6 | 2.1 |
| Lawrence | 68 | 1 002 | 71.9 | 30.2 | 67 | 233 | 17.2 | 4.5 | 170.2 | 86.0 | 27.0 | 4.6 |
| Lincoln | 95 | 1 906 | 189.0 | 75.1 | 53 | 223 | 21.5 | 5.9 | 92.6 | 48.2 | 15.4 | 1.7 |
| Lyman | 3 | D | D | D | 1 | D | D | D | 55.4 | 10.5 | 4.7 | 1.7 |
| McCook | 22 | 240 | 11.9 | 5.1 | 9 | D | D | D | 68.6 | 19.0 | 10.3 | 0.9 |
| McPherson | 8 | 58 | 3.0 | 1.0 | 7 | 33 | 1.5 | 0.3 | 31.8 | 9.2 | 5.2 | 0.4 |
| Marshall | 13 | 177 | 9.4 | 3.8 | 8 | 28 | 2.5 | 0.5 | 67.5 | 18.4 | 9.2 | 0.9 |
| Meade | 37 | D | D | D | 45 | 128 | 18.0 | 3.2 | 260.5 | 87.8 | 24.3 | 4.2 |
| Mellette | 3 | D | D | D | 1 | D | D | D | 21.4 | 4.2 | 3.1 | 2.5 |
| Miner | 8 | D | D | D | 5 | D | D | D | 33.3 | 10.1 | 7.3 | 0.8 |
| Minnehaha | 459 | 19 818 | 1 859.2 | 861.9 | 380 | 2 417 | 200.5 | 55.5 | 1 667.9 | 512.0 | 150.7 | 34.5 |
| Moody | 15 | 184 | 9.5 | 4.2 | 6 | 40 | 4.4 | 1.5 | 72.7 | 17.4 | 10.1 | 0.8 |
| Pennington | 328 | D | D | D | 259 | 1 546 | 127.6 | 34.5 | 1 134.0 | 384.3 | 91.1 | 36.3 |
| Perkins | 13 | D | D | D | 18 | 42 | 3.0 | 0.9 | 46.3 | 14.7 | 7.7 | 0.6 |
| Potter | 13 | 168 | 8.1 | 3.5 | 10 | 27 | 1.7 | 0.3 | 34.5 | 9.7 | 7.3 | 0.4 |
| Roberts | 21 | 472 | 24.2 | 10.8 | 18 | 53 | 2.7 | 0.8 | 118.7 | 29.9 | 15.2 | 5.3 |
| Sanborn | 5 | D | D | D | 4 | D | D | D | 28.0 | 8.3 | 6.1 | 0.5 |
| Shannon | 12 | 320 | 27.4 | 10.6 | 7 | D | D | D | 315.0 | 21.6 | 10.1 | 22.4 |
| Spink | 16 | 274 | 14.9 | 7.1 | 9 | 16 | 1.2 | 0.3 | 102.2 | 24.9 | 17.6 | 1.3 |
| Stanley | 3 | D | D | D | 7 | 21 | 1.0 | 0.2 | 22.7 | 9.8 | 2.7 | 0.4 |
| Sully | 2 | D | D | D | 3 | 0 | 0.2 | 0.1 | 24.1 | 4.1 | 2.1 | 0.1 |
| Todd | 8 | D | D | D | NA | NA | NA | NA | 165.0 | 13.2 | 7.3 | 15.1 |

1. State totals may include programs not allocated by county.

Items 159–170

| STATE County | Salaries and wages | Defense | Other | Medicaid and other health-related | Nutrition and family welfare | Education | Other | New construction ($1,000) | Number of housing units | Total (mil dol) | Inter-govern-mental (mil dol) | Total (mil dol) | Total | Property |
|---|---|---|---|---|---|---|---|---|---|---|---|---|---|---|
| | 171 | 172 | 173 | 174 | 175 | 176 | 177 | 178 | 179 | 180 | 181 | 182 | 183 | 184 |
| SOUTH CAROLINA—Cont'd | | | | | | | | | | | | | | |
| Sumter | 294.5 | 176.0 | 76.3 | 180.0 | 28.4 | 13.9 | 15.1 | 36 527 | 345 | 256.0 | 124.9 | 98.3 | 946 | 684 |
| Union | 19.7 | 0.0 | 1.2 | 37.0 | 5.1 | 2.3 | 2.0 | 2 075 | 17 | 111.2 | 43.0 | 19.3 | 695 | 649 |
| Williamsburg | 33.4 | 1.6 | 3.5 | 108.7 | 9.9 | 4.9 | 11.8 | 566 | 24 | 81.6 | 47.5 | 24.0 | 678 | 642 |
| York | 61.5 | 7.2 | 10.6 | 88.5 | 24.4 | 13.0 | 14.9 | 323 277 | 1 305 | 564.7 | 201.0 | 252.5 | 1 209 | 1 112 |
| SOUTH DAKOTA | 1 030.6 | 560.7 | 352.2 | 761.9 | 216.0 | 251.0 | 1 021.2 | 391 886 | 2 813 | X | X | X | X | X |
| Aurora | 1.5 | 0.0 | 0.3 | 1.6 | 0.6 | 0.1 | 0.1 | 1 653 | 10 | 8.8 | 2.8 | 5.0 | 1 738 | 1 457 |
| Beadle | 30.4 | 12.3 | 7.4 | 24.9 | 2.3 | 0.4 | 1.6 | 9 170 | 76 | 47.9 | 13.9 | 22.9 | 1 460 | 1 068 |
| Bennett | 1.2 | 0.0 | 0.2 | 5.3 | 0.5 | 2.8 | 1.5 | 0 | 0 | 9.4 | 5.2 | 2.8 | 816 | 677 |
| Bon Homme | 2.3 | 0.0 | 0.5 | 6.4 | 1.2 | 0.3 | 0.0 | 1 734 | 12 | 17.9 | 7.4 | 8.5 | 1 200 | 985 |
| Brookings | 20.7 | 6.5 | 3.2 | 15.9 | 2.7 | 1.1 | 45.6 | 17 285 | 134 | 137.4 | 18.8 | 38.7 | 1 324 | 935 |
| Brown | 42.3 | 57.4 | 10.6 | 33.1 | 6.8 | 1.2 | 3.6 | 18 840 | 201 | 102.4 | 31.6 | 52.2 | 1 487 | 1 021 |
| Brule | 3.9 | 3.4 | 0.5 | 6.9 | 0.9 | 1.2 | 6.7 | 1 256 | 6 | 19.3 | 7.6 | 8.1 | 1 565 | 1 191 |
| Buffalo | 6.4 | 1.0 | 10.8 | 3.3 | 1.0 | 0.2 | 2.9 | NA | NA | 0.6 | 0.2 | 0.3 | 157 | 151 |
| Butte | 5.7 | 0.0 | 1.1 | 5.8 | 3.1 | 0.3 | 0.5 | 2 027 | 19 | 27.7 | 10.7 | 9.9 | 1 050 | 762 |
| Campbell | 0.8 | 0.0 | 0.2 | 3.7 | 0.3 | 0.0 | 0.1 | 0 | 0 | 5.1 | 1.8 | 2.4 | 1 728 | 1 561 |
| Charles Mix | 12.4 | 4.8 | 6.1 | 16.0 | 5.0 | 10.6 | 6.1 | 570 | 3 | 35.1 | 16.8 | 14.3 | 1 598 | 1 358 |
| Clark | 2.1 | 0.0 | 0.5 | 5.8 | 0.8 | 0.1 | 0.2 | 2 814 | 25 | 11.0 | 3.3 | 5.8 | 1 664 | 1 496 |
| Clay | 8.8 | 0.0 | 0.8 | 20.1 | 3.9 | 2.3 | 13.2 | 4 345 | 48 | 31.5 | 11.0 | 14.6 | 1 093 | 862 |
| Codington | 20.4 | 1.0 | 3.3 | 19.2 | 3.1 | 1.0 | 3.4 | 11 981 | 101 | 85.9 | 28.0 | 36.7 | 1 394 | 908 |
| Corson | 3.6 | 0.0 | 0.7 | 7.9 | 1.2 | 9.6 | 0.6 | 0 | 0 | 15.9 | 11.8 | 2.1 | 492 | 427 |
| Custer | 16.6 | 0.0 | 2.6 | 4.8 | 0.9 | 0.4 | 0.4 | 3 933 | 52 | 22.7 | 7.0 | 11.9 | 1 522 | 1 249 |
| Davison | 27.9 | 0.3 | 1.3 | 18.6 | 2.6 | 0.6 | 1.2 | 5 426 | 32 | 64.0 | 19.5 | 28.9 | 1 520 | 961 |
| Day | 5.2 | 0.0 | 2.4 | 11.7 | 1.5 | 0.4 | 0.6 | 3 253 | 22 | 14.6 | 5.1 | 7.6 | 1 336 | 1 086 |
| Deuel | 2.1 | 2.2 | 0.5 | 4.8 | 0.7 | 0.1 | 0.1 | 1 305 | 7 | 9.6 | 2.7 | 5.4 | 1 261 | 1 088 |
| Dewey | 18.1 | 2.8 | 8.3 | 10.9 | 3.7 | 10.6 | 17.8 | 0 | 0 | 13.5 | 10.2 | 2.5 | 418 | 326 |
| Douglas | 1.9 | 0.0 | 0.5 | 2.1 | 0.6 | 0.1 | 0.7 | 730 | 5 | 8.0 | 2.7 | 4.0 | 1 325 | 1 126 |
| Edmunds | 1.6 | 0.0 | 0.5 | 3.7 | 0.6 | 0.1 | 0.0 | 4 180 | 22 | 15.3 | 3.3 | 6.8 | 1 705 | 1 530 |
| Fall River | 17.4 | 3.5 | 13.4 | 8.5 | 1.2 | 1.5 | 2.4 | 304 | 2 | 22.1 | 7.6 | 9.8 | 1 358 | 1 079 |
| Faulk | 1.5 | 0.0 | 0.4 | 2.1 | 0.4 | 0.1 | 0.0 | 1 000 | 3 | 10.3 | 2.5 | 3.8 | 1 667 | 1 468 |
| Grant | 6.3 | 0.0 | 0.6 | 7.9 | 1.2 | 0.1 | 0.4 | 3 069 | 12 | 22.3 | 6.5 | 11.2 | 1 560 | 1 260 |
| Gregory | 2.8 | 0.0 | 0.6 | 5.8 | 1.0 | 1.2 | 0.6 | 1 505 | 9 | 15.4 | 6.8 | 6.0 | 1 463 | 1 224 |
| Haakon | 1.0 | 0.1 | 0.4 | 0.0 | 0.4 | 0.1 | 0.3 | 0 | 0 | 10.1 | 2.7 | 3.2 | 1 750 | 1 443 |
| Hamlin | 2.3 | 0.0 | 1.8 | 3.2 | 1.1 | 0.2 | 1.2 | 2 682 | 21 | 19.9 | 6.6 | 8.4 | 1 499 | 1 348 |
| Hand | 1.9 | 0.0 | 0.5 | 3.2 | 0.5 | 0.0 | 0.3 | 826 | 4 | 9.2 | 2.5 | 5.5 | 1 687 | 1 489 |
| Hanson | 0.8 | 0.0 | 0.2 | 1.1 | 0.5 | 0.1 | 0.0 | 0 | 0 | 7.5 | 3.0 | 3.8 | 1 059 | 973 |
| Harding | 1.4 | 0.0 | 0.5 | 0.0 | 0.2 | 0.0 | 0.0 | 0 | 0 | 6.0 | 2.8 | 2.5 | 2 141 | 1 925 |
| Hughes | 25.0 | 9.3 | 14.6 | 46.0 | 34.1 | 83.3 | 541.3 | 8 644 | 56 | 47.3 | 13.6 | 22.1 | 1 309 | 903 |
| Hutchinson | 5.3 | 0.0 | 1.1 | 8.6 | 1.3 | 0.3 | 0.2 | 1 845 | 8 | 25.8 | 9.2 | 12.7 | 1 731 | 1 536 |
| Hyde | 0.2 | 0.0 | 37.0 | 1.1 | 0.3 | 0.2 | 2.7 | 0 | 0 | 8.8 | 1.5 | 3.4 | 2 322 | 2 070 |
| Jackson | 4.3 | 0.0 | 2.2 | 1.1 | 0.3 | 0.7 | 0.6 | 0 | 0 | 6.4 | 3.7 | 2.1 | 755 | 606 |
| Jerauld | 1.0 | 0.0 | 0.2 | 1.6 | 0.4 | 0.1 | 0.5 | 1 015 | 4 | 6.2 | 1.6 | 3.3 | 1 649 | 1 387 |
| Jones | 0.6 | 0.0 | 0.1 | 1.1 | 0.1 | 0.0 | 2.0 | 222 | 7 | 4.2 | 1.4 | 2.2 | 2 054 | 1 868 |
| Kingsbury | 4.2 | 0.0 | 1.1 | 3.2 | 0.9 | 0.1 | 3.6 | 1 596 | 11 | 16.7 | 5.8 | 8.5 | 1 573 | 1 406 |
| Lake | 14.0 | 0.1 | 0.7 | 8.0 | 4.6 | 0.2 | 3.2 | 3 111 | 16 | 31.6 | 8.8 | 15.4 | 1 350 | 1 068 |
| Lawrence | 14.3 | 0.1 | 2.6 | 16.0 | 2.4 | 1.0 | 8.3 | 18 395 | 108 | 72.9 | 18.4 | 37.7 | 1 616 | 1 115 |
| Lincoln | 4.1 | 0.0 | 1.0 | 6.9 | 1.8 | 0.4 | 3.1 | 21 775 | 143 | 56.4 | 15.4 | 31.9 | 844 | 751 |
| Lyman | 4.5 | 0.0 | 1.1 | 5.1 | 1.0 | 1.5 | 7.0 | 285 | 3 | 8.7 | 2.9 | 4.4 | 1 132 | 861 |
| McCook | 14.1 | 0.0 | 0.6 | 4.2 | 0.9 | 0.1 | 8.7 | 1 641 | 8 | 17.0 | 5.8 | 9.2 | 1 598 | 1 403 |
| McPherson | 0.6 | 0.0 | 0.1 | 4.2 | 0.5 | 0.1 | 0.1 | 80 | 1 | 8.5 | 2.8 | 4.7 | 1 881 | 1 685 |
| Marshall | 2.2 | 0.0 | 0.5 | 5.3 | 0.9 | 0.1 | 3.1 | 3 020 | 23 | 12.4 | 4.0 | 6.1 | 1 420 | 1 202 |
| Meade | 37.6 | 58.1 | 18.4 | 9.6 | 2.8 | 2.9 | 6.1 | 8 225 | 63 | 66.4 | 21.8 | 26.9 | 1 120 | 925 |
| Mellette | 0.8 | 0.0 | 0.2 | 5.3 | 0.7 | 1.6 | 0.0 | 254 | 2 | 7.5 | 4.8 | 1.8 | 871 | 777 |
| Miner | 1.5 | 0.0 | 0.3 | 5.4 | 0.5 | 0.0 | 0.5 | 2 172 | 17 | 8.4 | 2.4 | 4.8 | 1 939 | 1 708 |
| Minnehaha | 198.3 | 43.2 | 103.6 | 117.9 | 17.3 | 3.7 | 121.7 | 121 609 | 960 | 524.1 | 143.6 | 281.6 | 1 607 | 1 007 |
| Moody | 7.6 | 0.0 | 19.1 | 3.5 | 1.0 | 0.6 | 5.1 | 2 554 | 12 | 15.8 | 4.8 | 8.3 | 1 280 | 1 039 |
| Pennington | 312.8 | 76.7 | 22.2 | 71.7 | 18.8 | 13.5 | 57.8 | 51 577 | 349 | 314.3 | 95.0 | 159.0 | 1 651 | 1 140 |
| Perkins | 2.1 | 0.0 | 0.7 | 6.4 | 0.6 | 0.2 | 6.6 | 0 | 0 | 11.7 | 5.6 | 4.6 | 1 568 | 1 308 |
| Potter | 1.3 | 0.0 | 0.2 | 2.6 | 0.5 | 0.1 | 1.2 | 0 | 0 | 11.8 | 2.7 | 7.9 | 3 632 | 3 375 |
| Roberts | 11.2 | 0.1 | 4.6 | 19.0 | 4.6 | 4.1 | 7.6 | 3 028 | 20 | 29.7 | 11.6 | 10.0 | 1 016 | 815 |
| Sanborn | 1.2 | 0.0 | 0.3 | 2.6 | 0.5 | 0.1 | 0.0 | 1 050 | 7 | 7.8 | 2.5 | 4.0 | 1 653 | 1 486 |
| Shannon | 30.0 | 0.1 | 18.3 | 44.7 | 13.9 | 22.7 | 83.7 | NA | NA | 20.8 | 19.1 | 0.7 | 55 | 30 |
| Spink | 6.1 | 0.0 | 1.0 | 8.5 | 0.9 | 0.1 | 0.9 | 5 471 | 20 | 28.0 | 6.8 | 11.5 | 1 712 | 1 419 |
| Stanley | 0.8 | 0.1 | 0.2 | 0.5 | 0.5 | 0.3 | 0.2 | 1 810 | 11 | 10.3 | 4.4 | 4.6 | 1 667 | 1 358 |
| Sully | 0.5 | 0.0 | 0.1 | 0.0 | 0.2 | 0.0 | 0.1 | 1 265 | 6 | 10.9 | 1.8 | 4.3 | 3 039 | 2 763 |
| Todd | 15.9 | 0.0 | 9.0 | 28.9 | 6.8 | 16.4 | 17.6 | 0 | 0 | 31.5 | 27.0 | 2.4 | 231 | 156 |

1. State totals may include programs not allocated by county.    2. Based on the resident population estimated as of July 1 of the year shown.

## Table B. States and Counties — Local Government Finances, Government Employment, and Voting

| | Local government finances, 2007 (cont.) | | | | | | | | | Government employment, 2011 | | | Presidential election,[2] 2012 | | |
| | Direct general expenditure | | | | | | | Debt outstanding | | | | | Percent of vote cast: | | |
| | | | | Percent of total for: | | | | | | | | | | | |
| STATE County | Total (mil dol) | Per capita[1] (dollars) | Educa-tion | Health and hospitals | Police protec-tion | Public welfare | High-ways | Total (mil dol) | Per capita[1] (dollars) | Federal civilian | Federal military | State and local | Demo-cratic | Republi-can | All other |
| | 185 | 186 | 187 | 188 | 189 | 190 | 191 | 192 | 193 | 194 | 195 | 196 | 197 | 198 | 199 |
| **SOUTH CAROLINA—Cont'd** | | | | | | | | | | | | | | | |
| Sumter | 251.4 | 2 418 | 60.8 | 1.6 | 6.9 | 0.0 | 2.4 | 433.8 | 4 174 | 1 311 | 5 341 | 5 832 | 57.3 | 41.9 | 0.8 |
| Union | 114.7 | 4 129 | 36.8 | 33.1 | 3.6 | 0.0 | 1.1 | 122.2 | 4 399 | 72 | 122 | 1 907 | 43.8 | 55.0 | 1.2 |
| Williamsburg | 82.7 | 2 333 | 65.1 | 3.4 | 6.5 | 0.2 | 1.7 | 78.6 | 2 218 | 370 | 145 | 1 893 | 68.6 | 30.4 | 1.0 |
| York | 583.0 | 2 792 | 66.0 | 0.5 | 5.1 | 0.0 | 2.5 | 875.1 | 4 191 | 424 | 983 | 11 250 | 40.5 | 58.2 | 1.4 |
| **SOUTH DAKOTA** | X | X | X | X | X | X | X | X | X | 11 560 | 8 801 | 64 761 | 44.7 | 53.2 | 2.1 |
| Aurora | 8.5 | 2 973 | 60.4 | 0.5 | 2.6 | 0.2 | 16.8 | 2.0 | 709 | 22 | 17 | 191 | 43.8 | 53.1 | 3.1 |
| Beadle | 43.2 | 2 756 | 44.3 | 0.3 | 3.8 | 0.7 | 8.0 | 24.6 | 1 570 | 316 | 111 | 931 | 45.3 | 52.6 | 2.2 |
| Bennett | 8.7 | 2 516 | 58.1 | 0.2 | 8.0 | 0.0 | 5.6 | 1.6 | 456 | 28 | 22 | 359 | 46.1 | 50.8 | 3.1 |
| Bon Homme | 16.2 | 2 294 | 60.8 | 1.5 | 3.1 | 0.0 | 15.5 | 27.3 | 3 855 | 32 | 44 | 585 | 43.1 | 53.9 | 3.0 |
| Brookings | 123.8 | 4 232 | 24.7 | 19.3 | 2.5 | 0.2 | 5.8 | 71.2 | 2 435 | 157 | 210 | 5 816 | 51.7 | 46.1 | 2.2 |
| Brown | 112.2 | 3 196 | 35.3 | 0.9 | 4.6 | 0.8 | 10.9 | 104.1 | 2 965 | 535 | 234 | 2 680 | 51.9 | 46.3 | 1.8 |
| Brule | 20.2 | 3 894 | 66.5 | 2.4 | 2.7 | 0.3 | 8.3 | 8.8 | 1 691 | 38 | 34 | 361 | 39.6 | 57.7 | 2.7 |
| Buffalo | 0.6 | 261 | 0.0 | 2.5 | 13.1 | 0.0 | 31.9 | 0.0 | 0 | 146 | 13 | 294 | 73.3 | 25.2 | 1.5 |
| Butte | 26.3 | 2 776 | 48.3 | 0.5 | 3.8 | 0.3 | 7.1 | 18.5 | 1 953 | 55 | 65 | 587 | 30.7 | 66.3 | 3.0 |
| Campbell | 5.4 | 3 886 | 43.5 | 0.6 | 3.0 | 0.1 | 19.5 | 0.3 | 188 | 12 | 0 | 82 | 28.5 | 69.2 | 2.3 |
| Charles Mix | 29.8 | 3 333 | 63.7 | 2.0 | 2.6 | 0.1 | 6.4 | 9.1 | 1 018 | 179 | 58 | 1 162 | 45.4 | 53.0 | 1.6 |
| Clark | 10.9 | 3 138 | 47.7 | 8.7 | 2.5 | 0.1 | 19.6 | 4.4 | 1 274 | 26 | 23 | 234 | 42.8 | 54.9 | 2.3 |
| Clay | 29.2 | 2 183 | 42.8 | 0.4 | 6.4 | 0.2 | 13.7 | 27.1 | 2 025 | 38 | 93 | 3 333 | 61.0 | 36.8 | 2.2 |
| Codington | 81.5 | 3 092 | 58.1 | 0.2 | 4.3 | 0.3 | 8.6 | 40.5 | 1 537 | 184 | 174 | 1 914 | 45.9 | 52.3 | 1.8 |
| Corson | 14.2 | 3 369 | 82.1 | 0.1 | 2.3 | 0.0 | 6.2 | 0.0 | 7 | 75 | 26 | 600 | 59.5 | 38.1 | 2.4 |
| Custer | 20.9 | 2 675 | 46.2 | 4.0 | 4.6 | 1.9 | 9.8 | 17.4 | 2 219 | 217 | 53 | 561 | 32.7 | 64.5 | 2.7 |
| Davison | 59.3 | 3 116 | 51.1 | 0.5 | 5.6 | 1.0 | 9.7 | 40.8 | 2 144 | 110 | 125 | 1 253 | 42.0 | 56.0 | 2.0 |
| Day | 13.7 | 2 409 | 49.1 | 0.8 | 4.0 | 0.2 | 19.5 | 4.4 | 769 | 68 | 36 | 383 | 55.7 | 42.8 | 1.5 |
| Deuel | 10.5 | 2 465 | 39.3 | 2.8 | 4.5 | 0.6 | 19.6 | 6.0 | 1 403 | 31 | 28 | 235 | 47.5 | 49.1 | 3.4 |
| Dewey | 12.9 | 2 144 | 81.5 | 0.5 | 2.5 | 0.0 | 7.3 | 2.1 | 344 | 364 | 34 | 1 178 | 65.8 | 32.6 | 1.6 |
| Douglas | 7.7 | 2 536 | 43.8 | 0.8 | 2.6 | 0.1 | 19.3 | 1.5 | 505 | 26 | 19 | 164 | 24.1 | 73.6 | 2.2 |
| Edmunds | 14.7 | 3 667 | 40.1 | 17.5 | 2.1 | 7.7 | 14.4 | 2.1 | 517 | 24 | 26 | 362 | 39.5 | 58.4 | 2.1 |
| Fall River | 23.6 | 3 277 | 42.8 | 7.6 | 4.4 | 0.1 | 13.6 | 5.0 | 691 | 514 | 44 | 564 | 35.1 | 61.6 | 3.2 |
| Faulk | 13.0 | 5 726 | 23.2 | 53.1 | 2.5 | 0.1 | 10.0 | 7.7 | 3 386 | 22 | 15 | 133 | 35.7 | 62.0 | 2.3 |
| Grant | 21.4 | 2 988 | 49.8 | 1.0 | 3.3 | 0.2 | 13.6 | 51.5 | 7 194 | 33 | 46 | 335 | 46.6 | 50.9 | 2.4 |
| Gregory | 16.2 | 3 935 | 60.1 | 0.8 | 2.4 | 0.2 | 14.6 | 4.4 | 1 069 | 35 | 27 | 267 | 34.3 | 63.3 | 2.4 |
| Haakon | 10.5 | 5 694 | 26.3 | 0.4 | 2.1 | 0.2 | 17.5 | 2.6 | 1 389 | 15 | 12 | 103 | 16.2 | 81.4 | 2.3 |
| Hamlin | 19.1 | 3 402 | 50.9 | 1.0 | 1.8 | 12.9 | 15.0 | 10.7 | 1 901 | 29 | 38 | 465 | 37.4 | 59.6 | 3.0 |
| Hand | 8.6 | 2 627 | 46.9 | 0.5 | 4.5 | 0.2 | 22.0 | 2.9 | 875 | 20 | 22 | 214 | 35.7 | 62.0 | 2.3 |
| Hanson | 7.1 | 1 973 | 65.6 | 0.4 | 2.7 | 2.4 | 12.6 | 1.9 | 520 | 0 | 21 | 193 | 39.5 | 58.7 | 1.8 |
| Harding | 5.8 | 4 873 | 49.5 | 0.7 | 3.3 | 0.0 | 26.2 | 0.0 | 0 | 28 | 0 | 104 | 18.4 | 78.3 | 3.3 |
| Hughes | 43.9 | 2 600 | 44.9 | 0.7 | 6.7 | 0.2 | 7.0 | 58.2 | 3 446 | 300 | 110 | 3 698 | 35.9 | 62.6 | 1.6 |
| Hutchinson | 23.3 | 3 177 | 58.0 | 3.6 | 2.6 | 0.2 | 17.5 | 8.4 | 1 142 | 44 | 46 | 443 | 34.4 | 63.3 | 2.2 |
| Hyde | 8.2 | 5 592 | 26.2 | 0.1 | 1.7 | 0.1 | 11.8 | 2.7 | 1 821 | 0 | 0 | 209 | 28.8 | 69.7 | 1.5 |
| Jackson | 5.8 | 2 078 | 65.4 | 0.9 | 3.2 | 0.1 | 11.2 | 0.2 | 74 | 119 | 20 | 243 | 38.4 | 59.0 | 2.6 |
| Jerauld | 6.4 | 3 209 | 47.9 | 3.4 | 3.9 | 0.1 | 15.1 | 10.0 | 5 012 | 16 | 13 | 124 | 49.0 | 49.4 | 1.5 |
| Jones | 3.9 | 3 668 | 54.2 | 0.3 | 4.1 | 0.1 | 15.9 | 0.0 | 29 | 10 | 0 | 141 | 23.4 | 73.8 | 2.7 |
| Kingsbury | 15.9 | 2 946 | 57.6 | 0.5 | 2.9 | 0.0 | 15.0 | 10.1 | 1 869 | 41 | 33 | 268 | 45.9 | 51.5 | 2.6 |
| Lake | 29.4 | 2 587 | 55.3 | 0.6 | 4.5 | 0.4 | 14.4 | 80.4 | 7 068 | 61 | 73 | 1 111 | 49.3 | 48.6 | 2.1 |
| Lawrence | 63.7 | 2 730 | 37.7 | 0.5 | 6.2 | 0.1 | 9.3 | 111.2 | 4 764 | 186 | 154 | 1 859 | 40.9 | 56.3 | 2.8 |
| Lincoln | 57.9 | 1 534 | 60.6 | 0.6 | 3.8 | 0.2 | 9.9 | 195.7 | 5 183 | 49 | 297 | 1 234 | 41.6 | 56.8 | 1.6 |
| Lyman | 7.6 | 1 936 | 53.5 | 1.8 | 4.0 | 0.0 | 13.7 | 0.9 | 219 | 95 | 24 | 634 | 43.3 | 54.5 | 2.3 |
| McCook | 17.4 | 3 016 | 56.5 | 1.4 | 3.3 | 0.5 | 14.2 | 10.5 | 1 828 | 33 | 35 | 275 | 41.4 | 55.9 | 2.7 |
| McPherson | 8.8 | 3 514 | 53.0 | 0.6 | 1.7 | 0.6 | 20.8 | 0.6 | 238 | 12 | 16 | 163 | 32.1 | 66.5 | 1.4 |
| Marshall | 13.2 | 3 053 | 51.3 | 1.2 | 4.3 | 0.2 | 17.0 | 4.4 | 1 027 | 29 | 29 | 338 | 57.6 | 41.1 | 1.4 |
| Meade | 60.5 | 2 522 | 54.5 | 2.6 | 5.0 | 0.0 | 10.5 | 22.0 | 916 | 1 402 | 157 | 1 428 | 32.3 | 64.8 | 2.9 |
| Mellette | 7.7 | 3 833 | 64.6 | 5.1 | 4.0 | 0.0 | 5.9 | 0.4 | 218 | 17 | 13 | 228 | 44.2 | 52.8 | 3.0 |
| Miner | 8.9 | 3 594 | 46.1 | 1.3 | 3.9 | 0.2 | 27.6 | 0.1 | 46 | 22 | 15 | 147 | 49.7 | 47.4 | 3.0 |
| Minnehaha | 538.1 | 3 070 | 45.1 | 2.0 | 5.5 | 0.7 | 6.3 | 446.1 | 2 545 | 2 447 | 1 160 | 8 116 | 49.5 | 48.7 | 1.8 |
| Moody | 15.2 | 2 331 | 51.5 | 1.9 | 6.8 | 0.1 | 13.7 | 15.5 | 2 381 | 131 | 41 | 659 | 51.1 | 46.3 | 2.6 |
| Pennington | 307.9 | 3 198 | 44.6 | 2.1 | 6.6 | 0.3 | 6.8 | 217.5 | 2 259 | 1 561 | 4 152 | 6 168 | 38.5 | 59.6 | 1.9 |
| Perkins | 12.3 | 4 228 | 37.8 | 1.6 | 3.3 | 1.6 | 12.0 | 1.5 | 500 | 28 | 19 | 251 | 29.6 | 65.4 | 5.0 |
| Potter | 10.3 | 4 703 | 38.2 | 0.5 | 2.6 | 0.0 | 17.0 | 1.3 | 616 | 20 | 15 | 149 | 33.5 | 65.1 | 1.5 |
| Roberts | 33.3 | 3 371 | 57.7 | 0.7 | 2.2 | 0.3 | 10.8 | 16.9 | 1 714 | 195 | 65 | 1 317 | 58.9 | 39.3 | 1.8 |
| Sanborn | 8.3 | 3 377 | 61.9 | 0.9 | 3.2 | 0.4 | 14.1 | 3.5 | 1 428 | 18 | 15 | 158 | 41.4 | 55.4 | 3.1 |
| Shannon | 19.1 | 1 406 | 96.9 | 0.1 | 0.6 | 0.0 | 1.0 | 0.0 | 1 | 606 | 88 | 2 497 | 88.7 | 9.9 | 1.4 |
| Spink | 28.1 | 4 163 | 44.6 | 27.0 | 3.8 | 0.4 | 11.8 | 2.3 | 338 | 50 | 41 | 965 | 47.4 | 50.8 | 1.8 |
| Stanley | 9.9 | 3 565 | 42.4 | 1.1 | 2.1 | 0.2 | 21.1 | 6.9 | 2 464 | 10 | 19 | 213 | 32.8 | 65.5 | 1.7 |
| Sully | 10.1 | 7 172 | 29.8 | 0.2 | 1.9 | 0.0 | 13.4 | 0.1 | 57 | 12 | 0 | 112 | 28.0 | 69.7 | 2.3 |
| Todd | 30.7 | 3 020 | 90.3 | 0.1 | 0.5 | 0.0 | 2.9 | 0.1 | 12 | 281 | 62 | 2 188 | 78.1 | 20.2 | 1.7 |

1. Based on the resident population estimated as of July 1 of the year shown.   2. © 2013 Election Data Services, Inc. All rights reserved.

# Table B. States and Counties — Land Area and Population

| STATE/County code | CBSA code[1] | County type[2] | STATE County | Land area[3] (sq km) 2010 | Population 2012 | | | Race alone or in combination, not Hispanic or Latino (percent) | | | | Percent Hispanic or Latino[4] | Age (percent) | | | | | |
| | | | | | Total persons | Rank | Per square kilometer | White | Black | American Indian, Alaska Native | Asian and Pacific Islander | | Under 5 years | 5 to 17 years | 18 to 24 years | 25 to 34 years | 35 to 44 years | 45 to 54 years |
| | | | | 1 | 2 | 3 | 4 | 5 | 6 | 7 | 8 | 9 | 10 | 11 | 12 | 13 | 14 | 15 |
| | | | **SOUTH DAKOTA—Cont'd** | | | | | | | | | | | | | | | |
| 46 123 | ... | 7 | Tripp | 4 176 | 5 485 | 2 807 | 1.3 | 85.0 | 0.5 | 15.1 | 0.4 | 1.2 | 5.9 | 17.2 | 7.3 | 9.4 | 9.7 | 15.9 |
| 46 125 | 43620 | 3 | Turner | 1 598 | 8 308 | 2 582 | 5.2 | 97.0 | 0.5 | 1.4 | 0.4 | 1.5 | 6.1 | 17.5 | 6.2 | 10.8 | 11.4 | 14.9 |
| 46 127 | 43580 | 3 | Union | 1 193 | 14 855 | 2 118 | 12.5 | 95.2 | 1.1 | 1.4 | 1.3 | 2.3 | 6.5 | 19.0 | 6.5 | 11.2 | 13.1 | 14.7 |
| 46 129 | ... | 7 | Walworth | 1 835 | 5 459 | 2 808 | 3.0 | 84.7 | 0.5 | 16.0 | 0.6 | 0.9 | 6.3 | 15.8 | 6.6 | 9.9 | 9.6 | 13.7 |
| 46 135 | 49460 | 7 | Yankton | 1 350 | 22 603 | 1 705 | 16.7 | 92.2 | 2.0 | 3.2 | 0.9 | 3.0 | 5.7 | 15.8 | 8.3 | 12.7 | 12.4 | 15.6 |
| 46 137 | ... | 9 | Ziebach | 5 080 | 2 869 | 2 988 | 0.6 | 25.5 | 0.7 | 72.3 | 0.6 | 3.5 | 11.1 | 27.7 | 9.4 | 12.8 | 10.5 | 13.5 |
| | | | | | | | | | | | | | | | | | | |
| 47 000 | ... | X | **TENNESSEE** | 106 798 | 6 456 243 | X | 60.5 | 76.7 | 17.4 | 0.8 | 1.9 | 4.7 | 6.3 | 17.0 | 9.6 | 13.0 | 13.2 | 14.4 |
| | | | | | | | | | | | | | | | | | | |
| 47 001 | 28940 | 2 | Anderson | 873 | 75 416 | 727 | 86.4 | 92.2 | 4.8 | 1.0 | 1.5 | 2.3 | 5.4 | 16.0 | 7.9 | 11.1 | 12.2 | 15.2 |
| 47 003 | 43180 | 6 | Bedford | 1 227 | 45 573 | 1 056 | 37.1 | 79.6 | 8.6 | 0.6 | 1.0 | 11.6 | 7.4 | 19.1 | 8.4 | 12.9 | 13.3 | 13.8 |
| 47 005 | ... | 7 | Benton | 1 021 | 16 361 | 2 021 | 16.0 | 94.9 | 2.6 | 0.9 | 0.7 | 2.0 | 5.3 | 14.9 | 6.8 | 9.6 | 12.3 | 14.9 |
| 47 007 | ... | 8 | Bledsoe | 1 053 | 12 792 | 2 251 | 12.1 | 93.4 | 4.4 | 1.0 | 0.3 | 2.1 | 4.9 | 16.3 | 7.8 | 11.1 | 13.8 | 16.0 |
| 47 009 | 28940 | 2 | Blount | 1 447 | 124 177 | 493 | 85.8 | 93.0 | 3.5 | 0.9 | 1.0 | 2.9 | 5.4 | 16.4 | 8.1 | 11.1 | 13.2 | 15.1 |
| 47 011 | 17420 | 3 | Bradley | 851 | 101 134 | 580 | 118.8 | 89.4 | 5.0 | 0.9 | 1.3 | 4.9 | 5.9 | 16.9 | 10.4 | 12.4 | 13.3 | 14.3 |
| 47 013 | 29220 | 6 | Campbell | 1 244 | 40 420 | 1 168 | 32.5 | 97.7 | 0.7 | 1.0 | 0.4 | 1.3 | 5.5 | 16.2 | 7.7 | 11.0 | 13.5 | 14.1 |
| 47 015 | 34980 | 1 | Cannon | 688 | 13 811 | 2 186 | 20.1 | 96.4 | 1.9 | 1.0 | 0.5 | 1.6 | 5.4 | 16.2 | 8.1 | 11.1 | 13.1 | 16.0 |
| | | | | | | | | | | | | | | | | | | |
| 47 017 | ... | 6 | Carroll | 1 552 | 28 390 | 1 475 | 18.3 | 86.8 | 11.1 | 0.9 | 0.5 | 2.1 | 5.9 | 16.0 | 9.4 | 10.3 | 12.1 | 14.1 |
| 47 019 | 27740 | 3 | Carter | 884 | 57 355 | 888 | 64.9 | 96.3 | 2.0 | 0.7 | 0.5 | 1.6 | 5.2 | 14.7 | 9.3 | 11.2 | 12.9 | 14.8 |
| 47 021 | 34980 | 1 | Cheatham | 783 | 39 271 | 1 191 | 50.2 | 95.1 | 2.2 | 0.9 | 0.6 | 2.4 | 6.1 | 18.5 | 7.7 | 11.2 | 14.6 | 17.1 |
| 47 023 | 27180 | 3 | Chester | 740 | 17 171 | 1 967 | 23.2 | 87.6 | 10.0 | 1.0 | 0.8 | 2.2 | 5.5 | 17.2 | 14.5 | 11.1 | 12.1 | 13.0 |
| 47 025 | ... | 6 | Claiborne | 1 126 | 31 736 | 1 395 | 28.2 | 97.2 | 1.3 | 0.8 | 1.0 | 0.9 | 5.0 | 15.7 | 9.7 | 11.3 | 13.0 | 14.2 |
| 47 027 | ... | 8 | Clay | 613 | 7 840 | 2 611 | 12.8 | 96.5 | 1.9 | 0.8 | 0.2 | 1.6 | 6.0 | 14.7 | 7.1 | 9.8 | 11.9 | 15.4 |
| 47 029 | 35460 | 6 | Cocke | 1 126 | 35 571 | 1 286 | 31.6 | 95.2 | 2.7 | 1.1 | 0.5 | 1.9 | 5.5 | 15.6 | 7.5 | 10.3 | 12.9 | 15.4 |
| 47 031 | 46100 | 4 | Coffee | 1 111 | 53 222 | 935 | 47.9 | 91.1 | 4.6 | 0.7 | 1.2 | 3.9 | 6.4 | 17.6 | 8.2 | 11.8 | 12.5 | 14.7 |
| 47 033 | ... | 8 | Crockett | 688 | 14 623 | 2 130 | 21.3 | 77.9 | 13.5 | 0.5 | 0.4 | 8.9 | 6.4 | 18.0 | 8.1 | 11.8 | 12.1 | 14.7 |
| | | | | | | | | | | | | | | | | | | |
| 47 035 | 18900 | 7 | Cumberland | 1 764 | 57 029 | 890 | 32.3 | 96.1 | 0.7 | 0.8 | 0.6 | 2.5 | 4.9 | 13.9 | 6.7 | 9.1 | 10.5 | 13.2 |
| 47 037 | 34980 | 1 | Davidson | 1 305 | 648 295 | 95 | 496.8 | 59.2 | 28.3 | 0.7 | 3.8 | 9.9 | 7.1 | 14.7 | 11.2 | 18.4 | 13.6 | 13.3 |
| 47 039 | ... | 9 | Decatur | 865 | 11 673 | 2 319 | 13.5 | 93.5 | 3.4 | 0.7 | 0.5 | 2.9 | 5.7 | 15.7 | 7.0 | 10.5 | 11.7 | 13.9 |
| 47 041 | ... | 6 | DeKalb | 788 | 18 901 | 1 879 | 24.0 | 91.0 | 1.9 | 0.7 | 0.4 | 6.9 | 5.8 | 16.9 | 7.9 | 11.7 | 12.7 | 14.8 |
| 47 043 | 34980 | 1 | Dickson | 1 269 | 50 381 | 973 | 39.7 | 91.6 | 5.2 | 0.8 | 0.7 | 3.2 | 6.4 | 18.2 | 8.0 | 12.3 | 13.4 | 15.5 |
| 47 045 | 20540 | 5 | Dyer | 1 327 | 38 255 | 1 210 | 28.8 | 82.3 | 15.2 | 0.7 | 0.7 | 2.7 | 6.5 | 18.1 | 8.2 | 11.6 | 12.9 | 14.7 |
| 47 047 | 32820 | 1 | Fayette | 1 825 | 38 659 | 1 206 | 21.2 | 69.0 | 28.0 | 0.7 | 0.7 | 2.4 | 6.3 | 16.3 | 7.0 | 11.4 | 12.1 | 15.5 |
| 47 049 | ... | 9 | Fentress | 1 291 | 17 940 | 1 923 | 13.9 | 98.0 | 0.5 | 0.8 | 0.4 | 1.1 | 5.4 | 17.4 | 7.1 | 9.9 | 12.8 | 14.6 |
| 47 051 | 46100 | 6 | Franklin | 1 436 | 40 772 | 1 160 | 28.4 | 90.9 | 6.0 | 1.1 | 1.1 | 2.6 | 5.0 | 16.4 | 10.3 | 10.2 | 12.0 | 14.3 |
| | | | | | | | | | | | | | | | | | | |
| 47 053 | 26480 | 4 | Gibson | 1 561 | 49 626 | 990 | 31.8 | 78.6 | 19.3 | 0.6 | 0.5 | 2.1 | 6.4 | 18.3 | 7.6 | 11.7 | 12.3 | 14.4 |
| 47 055 | ... | 6 | Giles | 1 582 | 29 072 | 1 448 | 18.4 | 87.0 | 11.3 | 1.0 | 0.7 | 1.7 | 5.8 | 16.0 | 8.9 | 10.6 | 11.9 | 15.3 |
| 47 057 | 34100 | 3 | Grainger | 727 | 22 706 | 1 700 | 31.2 | 96.6 | 0.9 | 0.8 | 0.3 | 2.4 | 5.8 | 16.2 | 7.8 | 10.2 | 13.7 | 15.2 |
| 47 059 | 24620 | 6 | Greene | 1 611 | 68 819 | 771 | 42.7 | 94.5 | 2.6 | 0.7 | 0.5 | 2.6 | 5.3 | 15.8 | 8.3 | 10.5 | 12.9 | 14.9 |
| 47 061 | ... | 8 | Grundy | 934 | 13 650 | 2 202 | 14.6 | 97.8 | 0.8 | 1.2 | 0.4 | 1.0 | 5.7 | 17.1 | 7.8 | 11.1 | 12.3 | 14.2 |
| 47 063 | 34100 | 3 | Hamblen | 417 | 62 746 | 833 | 150.5 | 83.9 | 4.0 | 0.6 | 1.1 | 11.0 | 6.3 | 17.2 | 8.1 | 12.1 | 13.3 | 14.1 |
| 47 065 | 16860 | 2 | Hamilton | 1 405 | 345 545 | 191 | 245.9 | 73.3 | 20.7 | 0.7 | 2.2 | 4.6 | 6.1 | 15.4 | 10.1 | 13.0 | 12.7 | 14.3 |
| 47 067 | ... | 8 | Hancock | 576 | 6 720 | 2 705 | 11.7 | 90.8 | 0.8 | 0.9 | 0.4 | 0.3 | 5.7 | 15.6 | 7.5 | 11.5 | 11.9 | 14.8 |
| 47 069 | ... | 6 | Hardeman | 1 730 | 26 533 | 1 545 | 15.3 | 56.5 | 41.6 | 0.6 | 0.8 | 1.5 | 5.3 | 15.3 | 9.1 | 14.5 | 13.0 | 15.2 |
| | | | | | | | | | | | | | | | | | | |
| 47 071 | ... | 6 | Hardin | 1 495 | 25 950 | 1 566 | 17.4 | 93.5 | 4.3 | 1.0 | 0.6 | 2.0 | 5.3 | 15.8 | 7.8 | 10.1 | 12.3 | 14.7 |
| 47 073 | 28700 | 3 | Hawkins | 1 261 | 56 587 | 896 | 44.9 | 96.4 | 1.9 | 0.7 | 0.7 | 1.3 | 5.3 | 16.5 | 7.1 | 10.6 | 13.7 | 15.0 |
| 47 075 | 15140 | 6 | Haywood | 1 381 | 18 240 | 1 909 | 13.2 | 45.9 | 50.1 | 0.4 | 0.3 | 4.0 | 6.5 | 18.5 | 8.4 | 11.7 | 11.6 | 15.2 |
| 47 077 | ... | 6 | Henderson | 1 347 | 28 023 | 1 493 | 20.8 | 89.4 | 9.0 | 0.6 | 0.5 | 2.1 | 6.4 | 17.7 | 8.0 | 12.0 | 13.1 | 14.6 |
| 47 079 | 37540 | 7 | Henry | 1 456 | 32 341 | 1 382 | 22.2 | 89.3 | 8.9 | 0.8 | 0.8 | 1.9 | 5.6 | 15.9 | 7.0 | 10.2 | 11.7 | 14.7 |
| 47 081 | 34980 | 1 | Hickman | 1 586 | 24 170 | 1 635 | 15.2 | 92.5 | 5.2 | 1.1 | 0.5 | 1.9 | 5.4 | 16.5 | 8.6 | 12.1 | 13.9 | 15.7 |
| 47 083 | ... | 8 | Houston | 519 | 8 413 | 2 571 | 16.2 | 95.0 | 3.3 | 0.8 | 0.6 | 1.8 | 5.8 | 17.4 | 7.4 | 10.5 | 12.2 | 13.8 |
| 47 085 | ... | 6 | Humphreys | 1 375 | 18 275 | 1 908 | 13.3 | 95.0 | 3.1 | 0.7 | 0.4 | 1.7 | 5.6 | 17.5 | 7.3 | 10.6 | 12.2 | 14.5 |
| 47 087 | 18260 | 8 | Jackson | 799 | 11 441 | 2 329 | 14.3 | 97.4 | 0.9 | 1.0 | 0.3 | 1.5 | 4.8 | 15.0 | 7.4 | 9.5 | 12.8 | 16.4 |
| | | | | | | | | | | | | | | | | | | |
| 47 089 | 34100 | 3 | Jefferson | 710 | 52 191 | 952 | 73.5 | 93.5 | 2.8 | 0.8 | 0.7 | 3.3 | 5.6 | 16.2 | 9.7 | 10.6 | 12.9 | 14.7 |
| 47 091 | ... | 6 | Johnson | 773 | 18 095 | 1 916 | 23.4 | 95.8 | 2.4 | 0.7 | 0.4 | 1.6 | 4.7 | 13.4 | 7.7 | 12.1 | 14.0 | 15.3 |
| 47 093 | 28940 | 2 | Knox | 1 316 | 441 311 | 152 | 335.3 | 86.3 | 9.8 | 0.8 | 2.4 | 3.6 | 5.9 | 15.6 | 12.2 | 13.5 | 13.0 | 14.1 |
| 47 095 | ... | 9 | Lake | 429 | 7 690 | 2 628 | 17.9 | 69.5 | 28.6 | 0.7 | 0.5 | 2.0 | 4.5 | 12.4 | 10.6 | 17.8 | 15.1 | 13.9 |
| 47 097 | ... | 6 | Lauderdale | 1 222 | 27 718 | 1 503 | 22.7 | 62.4 | 35.2 | 0.9 | 0.4 | 2.1 | 6.4 | 17.4 | 9.4 | 14.6 | 13.5 | 14.4 |
| 47 099 | 29980 | 6 | Lawrence | 1 598 | 42 086 | 1 127 | 26.3 | 95.8 | 2.4 | 1.0 | 0.5 | 1.7 | 6.7 | 18.2 | 8.2 | 11.0 | 12.6 | 14.2 |
| 47 101 | ... | 6 | Lewis | 731 | 11 896 | 2 303 | 16.3 | 95.3 | 2.6 | 0.8 | 0.6 | 2.0 | 5.9 | 17.8 | 7.6 | 10.9 | 12.2 | 14.6 |
| 47 103 | ... | 6 | Lincoln | 1 477 | 33 503 | 1 338 | 22.7 | 89.3 | 7.9 | 1.2 | 0.6 | 2.7 | 6.4 | 16.7 | 8.0 | 10.7 | 12.2 | 15.4 |
| 47 105 | 28940 | 2 | Loudon | 594 | 49 793 | 985 | 83.8 | 90.7 | 1.7 | 0.7 | 0.8 | 7.1 | 5.2 | 14.7 | 6.7 | 9.5 | 11.7 | 13.8 |
| | | | | | | | | | | | | | | | | | | |
| 47 107 | 11940 | 4 | McMinn | 1 114 | 52 416 | 948 | 47.1 | 91.7 | 5.1 | 1.1 | 1.0 | 2.9 | 5.6 | 16.5 | 8.4 | 10.7 | 12.7 | 14.8 |
| 47 109 | ... | 6 | McNairy | 1 458 | 26 180 | 1 556 | 18.0 | 91.9 | 6.7 | 0.7 | 0.4 | 1.6 | 5.8 | 17.2 | 7.7 | 11.0 | 12.2 | 14.2 |
| 47 111 | 34980 | 1 | Macon | 795 | 22 498 | 1 711 | 28.3 | 94.1 | 1.0 | 0.7 | 0.5 | 4.6 | 7.0 | 18.0 | 8.5 | 11.7 | 13.6 | 14.0 |
| 47 113 | 27180 | 3 | Madison | 1 443 | 98 656 | 594 | 68.4 | 59.1 | 36.9 | 0.5 | 1.3 | 3.5 | 6.8 | 16.9 | 11.5 | 12.5 | 12.0 | 14.2 |
| 47 115 | 16860 | 2 | Marion | 1 290 | 28 291 | 1 478 | 21.9 | 93.8 | 4.3 | 0.9 | 0.7 | 1.4 | 5.4 | 16.1 | 7.8 | 10.9 | 12.7 | 15.1 |

1. CBSA = Core Based Statistical Area. See Appendix A for explanation. See Appendix B for list of metropolitan areas with component counties. 2. County type code from the Economic Research Service of USDA Rural-Urban Continuum Codes. See Appendix A for definition. 3. Dry land or land partially or temporarily covered by water. 4. May be of any race.

| STATE County | Population, 2011 (cont.) Age (percent) (cont.) 55 to 64 years | 65 to 74 years | 75 years and over | Percent female | Population change and components of change, 2000-2012 Total persons 2000 | 2010 | Percent change 2000-2010 | 2010-2012 | Components of change, 2010-2012 Births | Deaths | Net migration | Households, 2010 Number | Percent change, 2000-2010 | Persons per house-hold | Percent Female family house-holder[1] | One per-son |
|---|---|---|---|---|---|---|---|---|---|---|---|---|---|---|---|---|
| | 16 | 17 | 18 | 19 | 20 | 21 | 22 | 23 | 24 | 25 | 26 | 27 | 28 | 29 | 30 | 31 |
| **SOUTH DAKOTA—Cont'd** | | | | | | | | | | | | | | | | |
| Tripp | 13.6 | 9.5 | 11.5 | 50.6 | 6 430 | 5 644 | -12.2 | -2.8 | 147 | 165 | -141 | 2 419 | -5.1 | 2.28 | 8.4 | 34.6 |
| Turner | 14.3 | 8.5 | 10.3 | 49.5 | 8 849 | 8 347 | -5.7 | -0.5 | 201 | 219 | -20 | 3 452 | -1.7 | 2.37 | 5.9 | 27.4 |
| Union | 14.6 | 7.5 | 7.0 | 49.6 | 12 584 | 14 399 | 14.4 | 3.2 | 383 | 271 | 347 | 5 756 | 16.8 | 2.49 | 7.5 | 25.1 |
| Walworth | 14.6 | 10.6 | 12.9 | 51.0 | 5 974 | 5 438 | -9.0 | 0.4 | 146 | 159 | 35 | 2 392 | -4.5 | 2.21 | 8.9 | 32.8 |
| Yankton | 13.2 | 7.9 | 8.5 | 48.3 | 21 652 | 22 438 | 3.6 | 0.7 | 562 | 479 | 79 | 8 770 | 7.1 | 2.30 | 8.8 | 32.0 |
| Ziebach | 8.2 | 4.1 | 2.8 | 50.9 | 2 519 | 2 801 | 11.2 | 2.4 | 101 | 33 | 0 | 836 | 12.8 | 3.35 | 29.3 | 20.9 |
| TENNESSEE | 12.8 | 7.9 | 5.9 | 51.3 | 5 689 283 | 6 346 105 | 11.5 | 1.7 | 179 801 | 135 379 | 65 779 | 2 493 552 | 11.7 | 2.48 | 13.9 | 26.9 |
| Anderson | 14.6 | 9.0 | 8.5 | 51.6 | 71 330 | 75 129 | 5.3 | 0.4 | 1 774 | 2 002 | 552 | 31 253 | 4.9 | 2.37 | 12.5 | 29.0 |
| Bedford | 11.7 | 7.9 | 5.4 | 50.5 | 37 586 | 45 058 | 19.9 | 1.1 | 1 464 | 943 | -14 | 16 530 | 18.9 | 2.69 | 13.1 | 23.0 |
| Benton | 15.9 | 12.0 | 8.4 | 50.9 | 16 537 | 16 489 | -0.3 | -0.8 | 374 | 573 | 69 | 7 063 | 2.9 | 2.31 | 11.3 | 29.1 |
| Bledsoe | 14.1 | 10.1 | 6.0 | 46.0 | 12 367 | 12 876 | 4.1 | -0.7 | 275 | 308 | -50 | 4 697 | 6.0 | 2.51 | 9.1 | 24.0 |
| Blount | 14.1 | 9.6 | 7.0 | 51.7 | 105 823 | 123 010 | 16.2 | 0.9 | 2 805 | 2 706 | 1 071 | 49 265 | 15.5 | 2.46 | 11.2 | 24.9 |
| Bradley | 12.4 | 8.5 | 6.0 | 51.3 | 87 965 | 98 963 | 12.5 | 2.2 | 2 564 | 2 065 | 1 661 | 37 947 | 10.7 | 2.54 | 12.4 | 23.8 |
| Campbell | 14.4 | 10.4 | 7.1 | 51.2 | 39 854 | 40 716 | 2.2 | -0.7 | 953 | 1 222 | -19 | 16 354 | 1.4 | 2.46 | 13.0 | 26.0 |
| Cannon | 13.2 | 9.7 | 7.2 | 50.6 | 12 826 | 13 801 | 7.6 | 0.1 | 288 | 321 | 42 | 5 472 | 9.5 | 2.49 | 10.6 | 26.0 |
| Carroll | 14.0 | 10.0 | 8.2 | 51.8 | 29 475 | 28 522 | -3.2 | -0.5 | 732 | 865 | 20 | 11 507 | -2.3 | 2.39 | 12.6 | 27.7 |
| Carter | 14.5 | 10.1 | 7.3 | 51.1 | 56 742 | 57 424 | 1.2 | -0.1 | 1 262 | 1 506 | 148 | 24 197 | 3.0 | 2.31 | 11.9 | 28.6 |
| Cheatham | 13.3 | 7.2 | 4.2 | 50.1 | 35 912 | 39 105 | 8.9 | 0.4 | 965 | 793 | -3 | 14 520 | 12.8 | 2.67 | 10.8 | 20.1 |
| Chester | 12.0 | 8.1 | 6.7 | 51.9 | 15 540 | 17 131 | 10.2 | 0.2 | 408 | 372 | -17 | 6 208 | 9.7 | 2.56 | 12.7 | 23.6 |
| Claiborne | 14.5 | 10.1 | 6.6 | 51.1 | 29 862 | 32 213 | 7.9 | -1.5 | 754 | 908 | -317 | 12 853 | 8.9 | 2.41 | 11.4 | 26.4 |
| Clay | 14.8 | 12.6 | 7.8 | 50.6 | 7 976 | 7 861 | -1.4 | -0.3 | 209 | 239 | -6 | 3 358 | -0.6 | 2.31 | 10.6 | 29.7 |
| Cocke | 15.2 | 10.6 | 6.8 | 51.5 | 33 565 | 35 662 | 6.2 | -0.3 | 837 | 993 | 76 | 14 788 | 7.5 | 2.39 | 14.0 | 27.5 |
| Coffee | 12.8 | 8.9 | 7.1 | 51.4 | 48 014 | 52 796 | 10.0 | 0.8 | 1 469 | 1 392 | 375 | 20 926 | 10.8 | 2.50 | 12.6 | 25.9 |
| Crockett | 12.5 | 8.9 | 7.6 | 52.1 | 14 532 | 14 586 | 0.4 | 0.3 | 412 | 412 | 35 | 5 709 | 1.4 | 2.52 | 14.8 | 25.8 |
| Cumberland | 15.2 | 15.7 | 11.0 | 51.2 | 46 802 | 56 053 | 19.8 | 1.7 | 1 285 | 1 615 | 1 272 | 23 791 | 22.0 | 2.33 | 9.7 | 24.4 |
| Davidson | 11.2 | 5.6 | 4.9 | 51.6 | 569 891 | 626 681 | 10.0 | 3.4 | 21 556 | 11 285 | 11 474 | 259 499 | 9.3 | 2.32 | 14.7 | 34.5 |
| Decatur | 14.5 | 11.5 | 9.4 | 50.9 | 11 731 | 11 757 | 0.2 | -0.7 | 271 | 402 | 48 | 4 927 | 0.4 | 2.34 | 10.9 | 29.7 |
| DeKalb | 14.2 | 9.3 | 6.8 | 50.4 | 17 423 | 18 723 | 7.5 | 1.0 | 463 | 522 | 235 | 7 420 | 6.2 | 2.48 | 12.1 | 26.0 |
| Dickson | 12.5 | 7.9 | 5.7 | 51.0 | 43 156 | 49 666 | 15.1 | 1.4 | 1 368 | 1 012 | 378 | 19 107 | 16.0 | 2.57 | 13.1 | 23.9 |
| Dyer | 13.3 | 8.5 | 6.3 | 51.8 | 37 279 | 38 335 | 2.8 | -0.2 | 1 079 | 944 | -217 | 15 183 | 2.9 | 2.49 | 15.7 | 26.1 |
| Fayette | 15.8 | 9.6 | 6.0 | 50.3 | 28 806 | 38 413 | 33.4 | 0.6 | 1 079 | 832 | -24 | 14 505 | 38.6 | 2.62 | 13.2 | 20.8 |
| Fentress | 15.0 | 11.2 | 6.6 | 50.8 | 16 625 | 17 959 | 8.0 | -0.1 | 428 | 521 | 59 | 7 250 | 8.3 | 2.46 | 12.1 | 26.6 |
| Franklin | 14.2 | 10.0 | 7.6 | 51.2 | 39 270 | 41 052 | 4.5 | -0.7 | 839 | 989 | -111 | 16 011 | 6.7 | 2.45 | 11.6 | 24.6 |
| Gibson | 12.6 | 8.6 | 8.0 | 52.4 | 48 152 | 49 683 | 3.2 | -0.1 | 1 348 | 1 507 | 121 | 19 690 | 0.9 | 2.47 | 15.7 | 27.1 |
| Giles | 14.2 | 10.1 | 7.2 | 51.3 | 29 447 | 29 485 | 0.1 | -1.4 | 725 | 762 | -374 | 11 875 | 1.4 | 2.43 | 12.6 | 27.4 |
| Grainger | 14.7 | 10.5 | 5.9 | 50.0 | 20 659 | 22 657 | 9.7 | 0.2 | 549 | 578 | 87 | 9 029 | 9.2 | 2.49 | 9.9 | 23.3 |
| Greene | 14.4 | 10.6 | 7.4 | 51.0 | 62 909 | 68 831 | 9.4 | 0.0 | 1 526 | 1 849 | 320 | 28 018 | 8.8 | 2.39 | 11.6 | 26.8 |
| Grundy | 13.8 | 11.0 | 7.1 | 50.6 | 14 332 | 13 703 | -4.4 | -0.4 | 350 | 409 | -15 | 5 405 | -2.8 | 2.50 | 12.4 | 26.4 |
| Hamblen | 12.7 | 9.3 | 6.9 | 51.2 | 58 128 | 62 544 | 7.6 | 0.3 | 1 734 | 1 515 | 23 | 24 560 | 5.8 | 2.51 | 13.1 | 25.7 |
| Hamilton | 13.6 | 7.9 | 6.9 | 51.9 | 307 896 | 336 463 | 9.3 | 2.7 | 9 363 | 7 274 | 7 035 | 136 682 | 9.8 | 2.39 | 13.9 | 29.3 |
| Hancock | 15.5 | 10.6 | 7.0 | 50.6 | 6 786 | 6 819 | 0.5 | -1.5 | 164 | 227 | -35 | 2 825 | 2.0 | 2.36 | 12.7 | 29.0 |
| Hardeman | 13.0 | 8.4 | 6.1 | 45.5 | 28 105 | 27 253 | -3.0 | -2.6 | 629 | 635 | -714 | 9 301 | -1.2 | 2.52 | 18.7 | 27.1 |
| Hardin | 15.1 | 11.0 | 8.0 | 51.4 | 25 578 | 26 026 | 1.8 | -0.3 | 607 | 760 | 88 | 10 643 | 2.1 | 2.41 | 12.0 | 26.7 |
| Hawkins | 14.6 | 10.4 | 6.7 | 51.0 | 53 563 | 56 833 | 6.1 | -0.4 | 1 232 | 1 467 | -32 | 23 343 | 6.4 | 2.42 | 11.3 | 25.8 |
| Haywood | 13.9 | 7.8 | 6.3 | 53.1 | 19 797 | 18 787 | -5.1 | -2.9 | 514 | 494 | -597 | 7 459 | -1.3 | 2.50 | 23.0 | 27.6 |
| Henderson | 13.3 | 8.7 | 6.3 | 51.8 | 25 522 | 27 769 | 8.8 | 0.9 | 744 | 667 | 163 | 11 224 | 8.9 | 2.45 | 13.1 | 27.1 |
| Henry | 14.9 | 11.6 | 8.4 | 51.6 | 31 115 | 32 330 | 3.9 | 0.0 | 762 | 1 037 | 302 | 13 604 | 4.5 | 2.34 | 12.0 | 28.4 |
| Hickman | 13.4 | 8.6 | 5.9 | 47.6 | 22 295 | 24 690 | 10.7 | -2.1 | 541 | 571 | -492 | 8 976 | 11.1 | 2.58 | 12.1 | 24.5 |
| Houston | 14.4 | 10.7 | 7.7 | 50.6 | 8 088 | 8 426 | 4.2 | -0.2 | 209 | 228 | 8 | 3 349 | 4.1 | 2.46 | 11.0 | 28.1 |
| Humphreys | 14.4 | 10.4 | 7.4 | 50.8 | 17 929 | 18 538 | 3.4 | -1.4 | 457 | 503 | -213 | 7 454 | 3.0 | 2.46 | 11.5 | 26.4 |
| Jackson | 16.1 | 11.1 | 6.8 | 50.1 | 10 984 | 11 638 | 6.0 | -1.7 | 213 | 335 | -72 | 4 789 | 7.2 | 2.39 | 10.5 | 27.3 |
| Jefferson | 13.6 | 10.5 | 6.2 | 50.9 | 44 294 | 51 407 | 16.1 | 1.5 | 1 186 | 1 273 | 815 | 19 864 | 15.8 | 2.51 | 11.0 | 23.1 |
| Johnson | 14.3 | 11.2 | 7.4 | 46.3 | 17 499 | 18 244 | 4.3 | -0.8 | 344 | 484 | -10 | 7 195 | 5.4 | 2.28 | 11.0 | 29.7 |
| Knox | 12.4 | 7.3 | 6.0 | 51.3 | 382 032 | 432 226 | 13.1 | 2.1 | 11 618 | 8 814 | 6 394 | 177 249 | 12.3 | 2.37 | 11.5 | 29.7 |
| Lake | 11.7 | 7.8 | 6.1 | 36.4 | 7 954 | 7 832 | -1.5 | -1.8 | 146 | 221 | -70 | 2 270 | -5.8 | 2.35 | 17.8 | 32.0 |
| Lauderdale | 11.7 | 7.5 | 5.2 | 47.5 | 27 101 | 27 815 | 2.6 | -0.3 | 775 | 604 | -258 | 9 795 | 2.4 | 2.56 | 20.5 | 25.6 |
| Lawrence | 12.7 | 9.2 | 7.2 | 51.1 | 39 926 | 41 869 | 4.9 | 0.5 | 1 228 | 1 085 | 100 | 16 275 | 5.1 | 2.55 | 11.5 | 25.6 |
| Lewis | 14.6 | 9.5 | 7.0 | 50.9 | 11 367 | 12 161 | 7.0 | -2.2 | 288 | 300 | -251 | 4 781 | 9.1 | 2.50 | 12.9 | 25.6 |
| Lincoln | 13.8 | 9.7 | 7.2 | 51.2 | 31 340 | 33 361 | 6.4 | 0.4 | 840 | 854 | 178 | 13 382 | 7.0 | 2.47 | 12.0 | 25.7 |
| Loudon | 15.9 | 13.8 | 8.6 | 51.0 | 39 086 | 48 556 | 24.2 | 2.5 | 1 171 | 1 165 | 1 231 | 19 826 | 24.3 | 2.42 | 8.8 | 23.2 |
| McMinn | 14.0 | 9.9 | 7.3 | 51.4 | 49 015 | 52 266 | 6.6 | 0.3 | 1 237 | 1 383 | 323 | 20 865 | 5.8 | 2.46 | 11.4 | 26.0 |
| McNairy | 14.2 | 10.5 | 7.2 | 50.9 | 24 653 | 26 075 | 5.8 | 0.4 | 650 | 783 | 242 | 10 326 | 3.5 | 2.49 | 12.1 | 26.1 |
| Macon | 12.9 | 8.5 | 5.8 | 50.8 | 20 386 | 22 248 | 9.1 | 1.1 | 711 | 597 | 134 | 8 561 | 8.1 | 2.57 | 11.3 | 24.3 |
| Madison | 12.6 | 7.4 | 6.1 | 52.5 | 91 837 | 98 294 | 7.0 | 0.4 | 2 907 | 2 016 | -486 | 38 073 | 7.1 | 2.47 | 17.9 | 27.7 |
| Marion | 15.4 | 9.9 | 6.6 | 50.8 | 27 776 | 28 237 | 1.7 | 0.2 | 719 | 734 | 89 | 11 403 | 3.3 | 2.45 | 12.3 | 25.5 |

1. No spouse present.

# Table B. States and Counties — Population, Vital Statistics, Medicare, and Crime

| STATE County | Persons in group quarters, 2010 | Daytime population, 2007–2011 Number | Employment/ residence ratio | Births, 2011 Total | Rate[1] | Deaths, 2011 Number | Rate[1] | Persons under 65 with no health insurance, 2010 Number | Percent | Medicare, 2012 Eligible for Medicare | Enrolled in Medicare Advantage | Enrolled in a Medicare prescription drug plan | Serious crimes known to police,[2] 2011 Total Number | Rate[3] |
|---|---|---|---|---|---|---|---|---|---|---|---|---|---|---|
| | 32 | 33 | 34 | 35 | 36 | 37 | 38 | 39 | 40 | 41 | 42 | 43 | 44 | 45 |
| SOUTH DAKOTA—Cont'd | | | | | | | | | | | | | | |
| Tripp | 131 | 5 687 | 1.00 | 66 | 11.8 | 71 | 12.6 | 884 | 20.2 | 1 271 | 57 | 887 | 31 | 543 |
| Turner | 153 | 6 725 | 0.63 | 84 | 10.1 | 95 | 11.4 | 904 | 13.5 | 1 674 | 276 | 1 126 | 42 | 497 |
| Union | 89 | 15 802 | 1.22 | 180 | 12.3 | 109 | 7.4 | 1 001 | 8.0 | 2 532 | 409 | 1 470 | NA | NA |
| Walworth | 152 | 5 317 | 0.96 | 68 | 12.2 | 68 | 12.2 | 648 | 15.7 | 1 425 | 92 | 916 | 94 | 1 708 |
| Yankton | 2 296 | 23 909 | 1.14 | 252 | 11.1 | 193 | 8.5 | 2 145 | 12.6 | 4 258 | 547 | 2 728 | 481 | 2 118 |
| Ziebach | 0 | 2 532 | 0.71 | 54 | 18.9 | 7 | 2.5 | 540 | 21.0 | 152 | D | 91 | 5 | 176 |
| TENNESSEE | 153 472 | 6 338 695 | 1.01 | 80 536 | 12.6 | 58 883 | 9.2 | 888 747 | 16.6 | 1 141 887 | 319 301 | 462 580 | 269 205 | 4 204 |
| Anderson | 1 183 | 88 537 | 1.45 | 772 | 10.3 | 860 | 11.4 | 8 602 | 14.0 | 16 481 | 5 273 | 4 462 | 3 074 | 4 055 |
| Bedford | 545 | 42 316 | 0.87 | 659 | 14.5 | 408 | 9.0 | 8 542 | 22.0 | 7 814 | 1 629 | 3 459 | 1 177 | 2 589 |
| Benton | 162 | 15 056 | 0.77 | 172 | 10.5 | 265 | 16.1 | 2 333 | 17.8 | 4 433 | 464 | 2 660 | 469 | 2 819 |
| Bledsoe | 1 101 | 11 658 | 0.68 | 112 | 8.7 | 136 | 10.6 | 1 846 | 18.8 | 2 408 | 448 | 1 237 | 153 | 1 178 |
| Blount | 2 027 | 114 658 | 0.86 | 1 273 | 10.3 | 1 122 | 9.1 | 15 189 | 15.0 | 25 756 | 9 269 | 7 455 | 3 705 | 2 985 |
| Bradley | 2 744 | 96 670 | 0.96 | 1 156 | 11.6 | 879 | 8.8 | 13 911 | 16.9 | 19 688 | 5 975 | 7 862 | 3 800 | 3 805 |
| Campbell | 519 | 37 385 | 0.76 | 436 | 10.8 | 549 | 13.6 | 5 493 | 16.5 | 9 990 | 4 061 | 3 557 | 2 085 | 5 075 |
| Cannon | 164 | 10 717 | 0.44 | 125 | 9.1 | 133 | 9.7 | 2 038 | 17.8 | 2 889 | 779 | 1 255 | 222 | 1 594 |
| Carroll | 974 | 25 166 | 0.70 | 329 | 11.6 | 385 | 13.5 | 3 656 | 16.2 | 6 960 | 816 | 4 115 | 809 | 2 811 |
| Carter | 1 491 | 47 728 | 0.58 | 559 | 9.8 | 675 | 11.8 | 8 272 | 17.8 | 13 378 | 5 299 | 4 492 | 1 738 | 3 000 |
| Cheatham | 283 | 29 592 | 0.49 | 442 | 11.3 | 346 | 8.9 | 5 523 | 16.0 | 6 182 | 2 325 | 1 882 | 1 208 | 3 061 |
| Chester | 1 262 | 14 400 | 0.63 | 179 | 10.4 | 148 | 8.6 | 2 187 | 16.3 | 3 346 | 351 | 1 995 | 341 | 1 973 |
| Claiborne | 1 257 | 29 880 | 0.82 | 341 | 10.6 | 410 | 12.7 | 4 122 | 15.9 | 7 806 | 2 910 | 3 038 | 1 015 | 3 123 |
| Clay | 96 | 6 793 | 0.66 | 100 | 12.9 | 105 | 13.5 | 1 167 | 18.7 | 1 916 | 229 | 1 153 | 112 | 1 412 |
| Cocke | 294 | 32 356 | 0.75 | 384 | 10.8 | 448 | 12.6 | 5 285 | 18.0 | 8 888 | 3 448 | 3 251 | 2 071 | 5 755 |
| Coffee | 557 | 56 284 | 1.17 | 643 | 12.1 | 622 | 11.7 | 7 384 | 16.8 | 11 123 | 1 996 | 5 311 | 2 042 | 3 833 |
| Crockett | 194 | 12 579 | 0.68 | 192 | 13.2 | 182 | 12.5 | 2 371 | 19.6 | 3 065 | 225 | 2 035 | 272 | 1 848 |
| Cumberland | 636 | 54 690 | 0.95 | 558 | 9.9 | 711 | 12.6 | 7 963 | 19.3 | 18 513 | 2 287 | 9 102 | 2 470 | 4 367 |
| Davidson | 25 870 | 730 763 | 1.36 | 9 669 | 15.2 | 4 973 | 7.8 | 106 801 | 19.8 | 84 625 | 31 775 | 24 450 | 38 897 | 6 151 |
| Decatur | 213 | 10 943 | 0.82 | 125 | 10.7 | 183 | 15.7 | 1 660 | 18.0 | 3 287 | 343 | 1 970 | 261 | 2 200 |
| DeKalb | 298 | 18 147 | 0.93 | 195 | 10.3 | 221 | 11.7 | 3 234 | 20.8 | 3 931 | 1 530 | 1 385 | 644 | 3 409 |
| Dickson | 617 | 44 784 | 0.79 | 580 | 11.6 | 425 | 8.5 | 6 621 | 15.5 | 8 727 | 2 615 | 3 328 | 1 697 | 3 386 |
| Dyer | 516 | 39 105 | 1.06 | 490 | 12.8 | 417 | 10.9 | 4 811 | 14.8 | 7 855 | 649 | 4 928 | 1 915 | 4 951 |
| Fayette | 421 | 30 123 | 0.52 | 502 | 13.0 | 359 | 9.3 | 4 736 | 14.7 | 7 740 | 1 472 | 3 545 | 807 | 2 082 |
| Fentress | 132 | 16 495 | 0.78 | 197 | 10.9 | 234 | 13.0 | 2 679 | 18.1 | 4 734 | 543 | 2 929 | 633 | 3 493 |
| Franklin | 1 776 | 37 556 | 0.79 | 379 | 9.3 | 433 | 10.6 | 4 990 | 15.5 | 9 223 | 1 649 | 4 313 | 1 067 | 2 576 |
| Gibson | 991 | 46 611 | 0.86 | 595 | 11.9 | 650 | 13.0 | 6 441 | 15.7 | 10 807 | 975 | 6 712 | 1 706 | 3 403 |
| Giles | 678 | 28 154 | 0.88 | 340 | 11.6 | 340 | 11.6 | 3 960 | 16.5 | 6 461 | 746 | 3 231 | 739 | 2 484 |
| Grainger | 151 | 17 935 | 0.47 | 249 | 10.9 | 253 | 11.1 | 3 502 | 18.5 | 5 185 | 2 336 | 1 671 | 524 | 2 292 |
| Greene | 1 752 | 67 680 | 0.97 | 699 | 10.1 | 799 | 11.5 | 9 689 | 17.4 | 16 996 | 6 079 | 6 229 | 2 499 | 3 598 |
| Grundy | 180 | 12 442 | 0.71 | 156 | 11.5 | 173 | 12.8 | 1 904 | 17.0 | 3 470 | 657 | 1 839 | 413 | 2 987 |
| Hamblen | 918 | 67 668 | 1.21 | 734 | 12.4 | 640 | 10.1 | 10 214 | 19.6 | 13 499 | 4 595 | 5 222 | 3 032 | 4 804 |
| Hamilton | 9 778 | 372 268 | 1.25 | 4 174 | 12.2 | 3 208 | 9.4 | 45 813 | 16.4 | 62 165 | 17 153 | 26 914 | 16 888 | 4 974 |
| Hancock | 149 | 5 926 | 0.61 | 82 | 12.2 | 100 | 14.8 | 971 | 17.5 | 1 275 | 452 | 555 | 302 | 4 389 |
| Hardeman | 3 825 | 26 153 | 0.85 | 304 | 11.3 | 281 | 10.5 | 3 200 | 16.2 | 5 396 | 503 | 3 292 | 959 | 3 487 |
| Hardin | 371 | 25 269 | 0.92 | 271 | 10.5 | 328 | 12.7 | 3 763 | 17.8 | 6 677 | 623 | 4 163 | 1 158 | 4 410 |
| Hawkins | 456 | 47 770 | 0.60 | 569 | 10.0 | 650 | 11.5 | 7 247 | 15.4 | 13 819 | 7 197 | 3 759 | 1 896 | 3 306 |
| Haywood | 174 | 18 018 | 0.89 | 235 | 12.7 | 222 | 12.0 | 2 818 | 17.6 | 3 578 | 445 | 2 154 | 1 022 | 5 391 |
| Henderson | 218 | 25 487 | 0.81 | 322 | 11.5 | 287 | 10.3 | 3 730 | 15.9 | 5 324 | 565 | 3 215 | 1 050 | 3 747 |
| Henry | 491 | 31 854 | 0.97 | 360 | 11.1 | 469 | 14.5 | 4 332 | 16.9 | 8 159 | 874 | 4 560 | 1 075 | 3 295 |
| Hickman | 1 513 | 19 653 | 0.50 | 249 | 10.2 | 250 | 10.2 | 3 405 | 17.2 | 4 544 | 1 449 | 1 879 | 394 | 1 582 |
| Houston | 177 | 7 193 | 0.61 | 97 | 11.6 | 102 | 12.2 | 1 217 | 17.7 | 1 730 | 259 | 965 | 210 | 2 470 |
| Humphreys | 205 | 18 285 | 0.97 | 210 | 11.4 | 223 | 12.1 | 2 445 | 16.2 | 4 089 | 502 | 2 333 | 322 | 1 721 |
| Jackson | 177 | 9 426 | 0.49 | 96 | 8.4 | 162 | 14.2 | 1 720 | 18.1 | 2 824 | 371 | 1 603 | 272 | 2 316 |
| Jefferson | 1 594 | 44 049 | 0.67 | 535 | 10.4 | 569 | 11.0 | 7 237 | 17.4 | 11 511 | 4 266 | 3 970 | 1 768 | 3 408 |
| Johnson | 1 827 | 16 672 | 0.76 | 156 | 8.6 | 206 | 11.3 | 2 252 | 17.0 | 4 650 | 1 476 | 1 795 | 387 | 2 102 |
| Knox | 12 348 | 458 687 | 1.14 | 5 222 | 12.0 | 3 846 | 8.8 | 53 027 | 14.5 | 73 571 | 27 168 | 24 536 | 21 514 | 4 933 |
| Lake | 2 506 | 7 979 | 1.09 | 66 | 8.5 | 100 | 12.9 | 681 | 15.4 | 1 218 | 80 | 893 | 165 | 2 088 |
| Lauderdale | 2 734 | 25 950 | 0.81 | 369 | 13.3 | 274 | 9.9 | 3 519 | 16.3 | 4 856 | 619 | 2 876 | 1 153 | 4 108 |
| Lawrence | 407 | 38 195 | 0.79 | 538 | 12.8 | 476 | 11.3 | 6 176 | 17.7 | 9 284 | 1 121 | 5 439 | 1 538 | 3 640 |
| Lewis | 217 | 10 698 | 0.67 | 137 | 11.3 | 129 | 10.6 | 1 888 | 18.7 | 2 462 | 420 | 1 259 | 377 | 3 072 |
| Lincoln | 283 | 29 688 | 0.76 | 386 | 11.5 | 377 | 11.3 | 4 167 | 15.1 | 7 175 | 1 185 | 3 274 | 1 144 | 3 398 |
| Loudon | 480 | 45 035 | 0.85 | 537 | 10.9 | 501 | 10.2 | 6 372 | 16.8 | 13 156 | 4 887 | 3 924 | 1 248 | 2 547 |
| McMinn | 942 | 51 169 | 0.95 | 554 | 10.6 | 597 | 11.4 | 6 979 | 16.3 | 11 755 | 2 891 | 5 322 | 2 145 | 4 067 |
| McNairy | 313 | 24 188 | 0.82 | 288 | 11.0 | 337 | 12.9 | 3 604 | 16.8 | 6 483 | 567 | 4 030 | 719 | 2 733 |
| Macon | 269 | 19 446 | 0.69 | 310 | 13.8 | 267 | 11.9 | 3 883 | 20.5 | 4 437 | 1 184 | 2 165 | 369 | 1 644 |
| Madison | 4 418 | 111 794 | 1.34 | 1 343 | 13.7 | 869 | 8.8 | 12 945 | 15.9 | 17 206 | 1 939 | 9 659 | 5 256 | 5 299 |
| Marion | 250 | 24 949 | 0.72 | 337 | 11.9 | 310 | 11.0 | 3 963 | 16.8 | 6 304 | 1 613 | 3 182 | 705 | 2 474 |

1. Per 1,000 estimated resident population.   2. Data for serious crimes have not been adjusted for underreporting; this may affect comparability between geographic areas and over time.   3. Per 100,000 population estimated by the FBI.

# Table B. States and Counties — Crime, Education, Money Income, and Poverty

Serious crimes known to police, 2011 (cont.)[1] — Rate[2] (columns 46–47). Education (columns 48–53). Money income, 2007–2011 (columns 54–56). Income and poverty, 2011 (columns 57–61).

| STATE County | Violent | Property | Enrollment[3] Total | Enrollment Percent private | Attainment[4] High school grad. or less | Attainment Bachelor's degree or more | Local govt. expenditures[5] 2009–2010 Total current expenditures (mil dol) | Current expenditures per student (dollars) | Per capita income[6] (dollars) | Median income Dollars | Median income Percent change, 2000 to 2007–2011 (constant 2011 dollars) | Percent with income of $200,000 or more | Median household income (dollars) | Percent below poverty level — All persons | Children under 18 years | Children 5 to 17 years in families |
|---|---|---|---|---|---|---|---|---|---|---|---|---|---|---|---|---|
| | 46 | 47 | 48 | 49 | 50 | 51 | 52 | 53 | 54 | 55 | 56 | 57 | 58 | 59 | 60 | 61 |
| **SOUTH DAKOTA—Cont'd** | | | | | | | | | | | | | | | | |
| Tripp | 105 | 438 | 1 192 | 5.3 | 48.3 | 18.7 | 7.7 | 7 899 | 20 950 | 40 609 | 6.2 | 1.0 | 38 360 | 20.1 | 28.4 | 23.0 |
| Turner | 47 | 450 | 1 944 | 10.1 | 49.0 | 21.5 | 14.3 | 9 570 | 23 660 | 50 143 | 3.0 | 1.2 | 50 469 | 9.1 | 11.7 | 10.1 |
| Union | NA | NA | 3 612 | 15.0 | 40.3 | 29.6 | 23.8 | 8 650 | 34 310 | 63 773 | 5.5 | 5.4 | 66 242 | 6.5 | 9.2 | 7.5 |
| Walworth | 127 | 1 581 | 1 167 | 8.4 | 48.5 | 23.5 | 7.7 | 8 755 | 24 587 | 40 879 | 8.8 | 3.0 | 39 920 | 16.3 | 24.1 | 20.8 |
| Yankton | 181 | 1 937 | 5 306 | 21.1 | 44.9 | 25.9 | 25.3 | 8 338 | 26 227 | 51 680 | 8.2 | 3.2 | 48 147 | 13.3 | 16.4 | 13.4 |
| Ziebach | 35 | 141 | 940 | 4.3 | 52.8 | 13.8 | 4.4 | 12 319 | 11 677 | 27 917 | 14.5 | 0.0 | 28 350 | 49.9 | 52.0 | 43.8 |
| **TENNESSEE** | 608 | 3 596 | 1 568 926 | 17.1 | 50.1 | 23.0 | 7 834.2 | 8 055 | 24 197 | 43 989 | -10.4 | 2.8 | 41 691 | 18.4 | 26.5 | 24.4 |
| Anderson | 419 | 3 636 | 15 965 | 12.0 | 52.0 | 21.4 | 117.8 | 9 587 | 24 618 | 44 872 | -6.3 | 2.1 | 41 694 | 16.7 | 25.1 | 22.5 |
| Bedford | 312 | 2 277 | 10 436 | 11.1 | 67.0 | 12.7 | 52.3 | 6 595 | 18 813 | 39 480 | -20.4 | 0.8 | 39 552 | 18.6 | 27.6 | 26.6 |
| Benton | 198 | 2 621 | 3 189 | 7.1 | 66.9 | 11.4 | 19.5 | 7 918 | 18 421 | 34 152 | -11.8 | 0.4 | 32 527 | 21.1 | 34.5 | 31.9 |
| Bledsoe | 139 | 1 039 | 2 791 | 7.1 | 68.3 | 9.0 | 16.3 | 8 515 | 14 234 | 35 137 | -10.2 | 0.2 | 33 500 | 23.8 | 34.0 | 30.8 |
| Blount | 354 | 2 631 | 27 711 | 14.8 | 50.5 | 20.5 | 151.2 | 8 166 | 24 096 | 47 298 | -7.5 | 2.0 | 45 539 | 14.6 | 21.1 | 18.8 |
| Bradley | 681 | 3 124 | 25 151 | 24.4 | 52.3 | 18.4 | 113.1 | 7 333 | 21 689 | 40 541 | -14.3 | 2.0 | 38 667 | 20.7 | 27.8 | 25.5 |
| Campbell | 341 | 4 734 | 8 331 | 14.1 | 71.7 | 9.1 | 40.9 | 6 809 | 16 769 | 31 337 | -8.2 | 0.6 | 29 044 | 28.8 | 39.0 | 35.5 |
| Cannon | 208 | 1 386 | 2 870 | 9.4 | 70.6 | 12.3 | 16.6 | 7 351 | 18 567 | 36 742 | -17.1 | 0.7 | 36 959 | 21.8 | 32.1 | 29.1 |
| Carroll | 327 | 2 484 | 6 543 | 14.0 | 61.8 | 16.0 | 35.6 | 7 418 | 19 254 | 36 455 | -11.4 | 1.4 | 34 979 | 22.0 | 32.0 | 30.0 |
| Carter | 228 | 2 772 | 12 589 | 13.0 | 60.0 | 15.7 | 66.2 | 8 239 | 18 269 | 32 148 | -13.0 | 0.8 | 33 772 | 20.6 | 31.4 | 29.8 |
| Cheatham | 337 | 2 724 | 9 598 | 15.0 | 54.7 | 18.8 | 48.2 | 6 923 | 24 733 | 53 337 | -13.8 | 1.8 | 50 225 | 14.3 | 20.8 | 18.5 |
| Chester | 318 | 1 655 | 4 720 | 28.9 | 60.0 | 13.8 | 19.0 | 6 876 | 18 779 | 39 776 | -14.2 | 1.4 | 38 749 | 22.0 | 26.7 | 23.8 |
| Claiborne | 348 | 2 775 | 7 106 | 16.2 | 68.3 | 12.3 | 37.1 | 7 663 | 18 012 | 33 178 | -4.7 | 0.8 | 34 454 | 26.5 | 37.0 | 36.1 |
| Clay | 88 | 1 324 | 1 290 | 5.3 | 70.5 | 10.8 | 9.2 | 8 236 | 18 025 | 28 682 | -11.3 | 1.0 | 27 978 | 24.1 | 35.3 | 36.2 |
| Cocke | 770 | 4 986 | 6 488 | 4.5 | 71.9 | 8.1 | 43.7 | 7 703 | 17 014 | 28 563 | -17.2 | 0.9 | 30 092 | 26.9 | 41.1 | 37.6 |
| Coffee | 449 | 3 385 | 12 494 | 10.6 | 56.8 | 19.1 | 77.0 | 8 264 | 20 627 | 39 268 | -16.7 | 1.4 | 35 571 | 21.1 | 28.6 | 26.7 |
| Crockett | 340 | 1 508 | 3 264 | 7.3 | 66.5 | 11.8 | 20.8 | 7 182 | 19 386 | 36 743 | -9.3 | 1.2 | 34 474 | 20.0 | 29.0 | 27.4 |
| Cumberland | 474 | 3 893 | 9 934 | 9.5 | 58.1 | 16.0 | 52.9 | 7 166 | 20 513 | 36 955 | -11.4 | 1.4 | 35 873 | 18.7 | 34.0 | 30.4 |
| Davidson | 1 176 | 4 975 | 156 130 | 31.8 | 39.6 | 34.4 | 741.4 | 8 526 | 28 526 | 46 737 | -13.0 | 4.1 | 43 893 | 19.4 | 29.4 | 28.2 |
| Decatur | 135 | 2 065 | 2 463 | 10.2 | 63.0 | 12.8 | 11.4 | 6 722 | 22 648 | 30 311 | -21.9 | 3.0 | 34 400 | 22.4 | 32.5 | 31.6 |
| DeKalb | 344 | 3 065 | 4 068 | 8.4 | 67.3 | 13.1 | 20.7 | 7 097 | 19 254 | 36 870 | -10.1 | 1.8 | 37 136 | 19.4 | 31.9 | 30.0 |
| Dickson | 413 | 2 973 | 11 676 | 11.3 | 59.9 | 15.5 | 61.4 | 7 234 | 21 306 | 44 201 | -16.2 | 1.1 | 43 019 | 15.5 | 22.4 | 20.6 |
| Dyer | 595 | 4 356 | 9 201 | 8.0 | 61.6 | 15.8 | 54.7 | 7 875 | 20 367 | 38 909 | -12.1 | 1.4 | 37 766 | 19.4 | 30.3 | 28.9 |
| Fayette | 369 | 1 713 | 8 818 | 37.5 | 52.0 | 20.4 | 30.8 | 8 263 | 28 606 | 57 437 | 5.6 | 5.3 | 49 760 | 14.2 | 21.4 | 19.6 |
| Fentress | 226 | 3 267 | 3 289 | 3.6 | 73.1 | 10.0 | 18.4 | 5 855 | 17 404 | 29 245 | -6.8 | 0.3 | 28 666 | 27.1 | 38.5 | 35.7 |
| Franklin | 345 | 2 231 | 10 314 | 21.5 | 57.6 | 17.8 | 45.0 | 7 425 | 21 716 | 41 726 | -14.3 | 1.7 | 39 935 | 18.3 | 25.8 | 24.1 |
| Gibson | 571 | 2 833 | 11 852 | 10.3 | 58.5 | 15.2 | 66.8 | 7 270 | 20 415 | 37 577 | -10.5 | 1.1 | 36 365 | 18.8 | 26.5 | 24.1 |
| Giles | 279 | 2 205 | 6 773 | 14.5 | 64.1 | 13.2 | 35.6 | 8 341 | 20 105 | 37 981 | -19.2 | 1.4 | 39 916 | 18.0 | 26.3 | 23.9 |
| Grainger | 140 | 2 152 | 4 641 | 8.8 | 73.5 | 7.9 | 25.0 | 6 828 | 17 381 | 31 711 | -16.1 | 1.0 | 34 077 | 22.0 | 32.3 | 31.2 |
| Greene | 382 | 3 217 | 14 022 | 9.0 | 62.9 | 14.8 | 77.5 | 7 557 | 19 036 | 36 310 | -11.5 | 1.1 | 32 880 | 24.4 | 37.8 | 34.9 |
| Grundy | 586 | 2 401 | 2 909 | 4.7 | 76.4 | 7.8 | 18.3 | 8 216 | 14 819 | 25 890 | -16.5 | 0.3 | 27 428 | 31.2 | 44.7 | 42.1 |
| Hamblen | 532 | 4 272 | 14 141 | 9.5 | 58.6 | 15.7 | 72.8 | 7 250 | 21 331 | 39 604 | -9.3 | 1.8 | 35 630 | 19.7 | 29.0 | 25.7 |
| Hamilton | 606 | 4 368 | 81 712 | 22.1 | 42.1 | 27.4 | 357.1 | 8 537 | 26 924 | 45 826 | -12.8 | 3.7 | 42 609 | 19.2 | 28.3 | 27.2 |
| Hancock | 610 | 3 779 | 1 325 | 7.5 | 78.0 | 7.6 | 9.6 | 8 591 | 13 417 | 22 052 | -17.3 | 0.0 | 25 297 | 33.8 | 45.3 | 43.0 |
| Hardeman | 425 | 3 062 | 5 805 | 17.4 | 67.5 | 10.6 | 34.8 | 8 158 | 15 785 | 32 601 | -17.1 | 0.8 | 31 437 | 27.9 | 31.2 | 29.0 |
| Hardin | 430 | 3 979 | 5 380 | 11.6 | 69.6 | 9.8 | 30.4 | 7 969 | 18 653 | 32 131 | -14.5 | 2.5 | 31 281 | 26.0 | 39.8 | 36.8 |
| Hawkins | 232 | 3 074 | 12 240 | 8.8 | 62.9 | 12.4 | 62.9 | 7 469 | 20 293 | 36 795 | -12.9 | 0.9 | 37 095 | 17.9 | 28.5 | 26.5 |
| Haywood | 1 055 | 4 336 | 4 752 | 6.2 | 65.4 | 12.6 | 27.5 | 8 053 | 17 828 | 33 504 | -10.3 | 0.9 | 32 422 | 24.4 | 34.7 | 31.3 |
| Henderson | 507 | 3 241 | 6 478 | 10.2 | 61.9 | 12.2 | 36.6 | 7 581 | 20 331 | 37 627 | -13.1 | 1.4 | 36 392 | 18.5 | 25.6 | 24.1 |
| Henry | 270 | 3 026 | 6 546 | 9.3 | 62.2 | 15.1 | 37.3 | 7 692 | 20 274 | 36 463 | -10.5 | 1.1 | 35 270 | 18.7 | 30.0 | 27.9 |
| Hickman | 217 | 1 365 | 5 559 | 12.5 | 66.5 | 10.9 | 29.6 | 7 564 | 18 914 | 43 935 | 4.9 | 0.6 | 35 094 | 20.7 | 30.5 | 28.0 |
| Houston | 306 | 2 164 | 1 845 | 4.8 | 66.7 | 9.6 | 10.8 | 7 101 | 18 973 | 34 942 | -13.6 | 0.9 | 36 858 | 20.5 | 30.4 | 27.3 |
| Humphreys | 150 | 1 572 | 4 289 | 5.1 | 60.4 | 13.5 | 23.5 | 7 257 | 21 203 | 41 810 | -13.5 | 0.9 | 43 987 | 16.5 | 26.6 | 24.0 |
| Jackson | 179 | 2 137 | 2 052 | 5.8 | 73.6 | 9.3 | 12.7 | 7 763 | 17 811 | 32 846 | -8.2 | 1.1 | 31 903 | 24.9 | 37.3 | 32.7 |
| Jefferson | 214 | 3 194 | 11 861 | 19.7 | 58.9 | 13.4 | 53.6 | 7 136 | 19 839 | 38 015 | -14.2 | 1.4 | 38 174 | 19.5 | 28.5 | 26.8 |
| Johnson | 532 | 1 570 | 3 063 | 6.4 | 69.3 | 10.7 | 19.6 | 8 312 | 16 957 | 32 159 | 3.3 | 0.8 | 30 897 | 26.1 | 37.0 | 35.1 |
| Knox | 535 | 4 398 | 112 164 | 16.8 | 37.7 | 34.0 | 447.2 | 7 858 | 28 042 | 47 277 | -6.5 | 3.8 | 45 149 | 14.7 | 20.0 | 18.2 |
| Lake | 405 | 1 683 | 1 303 | 9.5 | 74.3 | 6.2 | 7.8 | 8 834 | 12 941 | 26 797 | -9.8 | 1.1 | 26 587 | 43.7 | 47.5 | 41.8 |
| Lauderdale | 602 | 3 506 | 6 527 | 6.7 | 70.6 | 10.2 | 35.6 | 7 586 | 18 059 | 34 078 | -15.2 | 1.0 | 31 770 | 30.7 | 39.1 | 34.0 |
| Lawrence | 542 | 3 098 | 10 179 | 10.1 | 64.9 | 11.2 | 52.7 | 7 675 | 18 059 | 35 737 | -13.2 | 0.8 | 33 963 | 18.9 | 27.1 | 25.6 |
| Lewis | 391 | 2 681 | 2 518 | 6.7 | 65.1 | 10.4 | 13.3 | 6 668 | 17 209 | 32 337 | -21.3 | 0.7 | 31 877 | 21.5 | 32.7 | 30.5 |
| Lincoln | 428 | 2 971 | 7 569 | 18.3 | 64.9 | 14.9 | 37.7 | 7 202 | 21 986 | 41 454 | -8.2 | 1.7 | 39 246 | 16.9 | 25.1 | 22.2 |
| Loudon | 229 | 2 319 | 9 095 | 11.8 | 48.2 | 23.6 | 54.3 | 7 337 | 28 220 | 50 458 | -7.5 | 3.0 | 50 375 | 13.1 | 24.1 | 23.1 |
| McMinn | 531 | 3 536 | 11 767 | 13.5 | 61.9 | 14.6 | 60.6 | 7 302 | 19 977 | 38 604 | -10.4 | 1.0 | 37 319 | 20.1 | 27.5 | 24.9 |
| McNairy | 448 | 2 284 | 5 958 | 16.7 | 67.0 | 11.8 | 32.3 | 7 175 | 18 891 | 34 953 | -14.1 | 1.3 | 33 738 | 22.4 | 32.0 | 29.0 |
| Macon | 383 | 1 261 | 5 062 | 6.0 | 70.8 | 8.3 | 24.5 | 6 445 | 17 409 | 34 747 | -13.8 | 0.9 | 34 262 | 22.4 | 33.4 | 30.8 |
| Madison | 812 | 4 488 | 27 070 | 27.3 | 48.8 | 24.0 | 111.2 | 8 355 | 23 186 | 40 667 | -18.6 | 3.0 | 39 510 | 19.9 | 31.9 | 32.2 |
| Marion | 347 | 2 127 | 6 123 | 17.2 | 61.1 | 14.7 | 34.9 | 7 513 | 21 083 | 39 857 | -6.0 | 0.9 | 40 136 | 17.9 | 28.8 | 26.5 |

1. Data for serious crimes have not been adjusted for underreporting; this may affect comparability between geographic areas and over time.   2. Per 100,000 population estimated by the FBI.   3. All persons 3 years old and over enrolled in nursery school through college.   4. Persons 25 years old and over.   5. Elementary and secondary education expenditures.   6. Based on population estimated by the American Community Survey, 2007–2011.

# Table B. States and Counties — Personal Income

| STATE County | Total (mil dol) | Percent change, 2010–2011 | Per capita Dollars | Per capita Rank | Wages and salaries[2] (mil dol) | Proprietors' income (mil dol) | Dividends, interest, and rent (mil dol) | Transfer payments Total | Gov. payments to individuals Total | Social Security | Medical payments | Income mainte-nance | Unemploy-ment insurance |
|---|---|---|---|---|---|---|---|---|---|---|---|---|---|
| | 62 | 63 | 64 | 65 | 66 | 67 | 68 | 69 | 70 | 71 | 72 | 73 | 74 |
| SOUTH DAKOTA—Cont'd | | | | | | | | | | | | | |
| Tripp | 282 | 32.0 | 50 169 | 202 | 83 | 121 | 42 | 45 | 44 | 15 | 20 | 5 | 0 |
| Turner | 437 | 18.3 | 52 458 | 153 | 86 | 153 | 62 | 51 | 49 | 21 | 21 | 4 | 1 |
| Union | 946 | 12.2 | 64 557 | 40 | 498 | 174 | 234 | 85 | 82 | 38 | 33 | 5 | 1 |
| Walworth | 223 | 14.7 | 40 035 | 743 | 84 | 48 | 58 | 44 | 43 | 18 | 17 | 5 | 1 |
| Yankton | 870 | 9.5 | 38 458 | 915 | 543 | 106 | 186 | 152 | 147 | 57 | 67 | 13 | 2 |
| Ziebach | 80 | 27.3 | 27 912 | 2 626 | 16 | 33 | 7 | 16 | 16 | 2 | 6 | 5 | 0 |
| TENNESSEE | 234 154 | 4.9 | 36 567 | X | 144 048 | 27 717 | 28 652 | 50 835 | 49 421 | 16 520 | 21 027 | 6 805 | 1 633 |
| Anderson | 2 730 | 3.2 | 36 289 | 1 171 | 2 571 | 410 | 364 | 645 | 628 | 245 | 260 | 74 | 19 |
| Bedford | 1 403 | 3.8 | 30 832 | 2 134 | 763 | 131 | 176 | 333 | 323 | 114 | 127 | 51 | 13 |
| Benton | 463 | 3.8 | 28 199 | 2 589 | 147 | 33 | 74 | 179 | 175 | 64 | 77 | 19 | 5 |
| Bledsoe | 310 | 2.7 | 24 087 | 3 025 | 74 | 17 | 32 | 106 | 103 | 32 | 48 | 15 | 3 |
| Blount | 3 964 | 3.6 | 31 995 | 1 892 | 2 213 | 371 | 545 | 945 | 917 | 383 | 356 | 98 | 28 |
| Bradley | 3 170 | 5.6 | 31 687 | 1 958 | 1 813 | 403 | 355 | 821 | 799 | 287 | 335 | 97 | 21 |
| Campbell | 1 133 | 3.1 | 27 965 | 2 619 | 368 | 79 | 123 | 449 | 440 | 132 | 203 | 65 | 11 |
| Cannon | 416 | 2.5 | 30 217 | 2 251 | 77 | 43 | 50 | 133 | 130 | 40 | 65 | 15 | 4 |
| Carroll | 884 | 5.2 | 31 057 | 2 084 | 316 | 77 | 98 | 340 | 334 | 96 | 143 | 34 | 11 |
| Carter | 1 599 | 3.6 | 27 962 | 2 620 | 422 | 142 | 198 | 523 | 510 | 181 | 214 | 64 | 12 |
| Cheatham | 1 300 | 3.9 | 33 268 | 1 662 | 377 | 163 | 113 | 260 | 251 | 95 | 99 | 31 | 12 |
| Chester | 481 | 5.5 | 28 057 | 2 609 | 142 | 51 | 48 | 136 | 132 | 46 | 53 | 18 | 4 |
| Claiborne | 893 | 3.2 | 27 764 | 2 646 | 349 | 45 | 114 | 336 | 329 | 104 | 149 | 46 | 8 |
| Clay | 212 | 3.8 | 27 358 | 2 709 | 63 | 32 | 24 | 81 | 79 | 25 | 38 | 11 | 2 |
| Cocke | 913 | 3.0 | 25 696 | 2 910 | 322 | 51 | 96 | 368 | 360 | 116 | 154 | 57 | 14 |
| Coffee | 1 802 | 3.8 | 33 998 | 1 508 | 1 160 | 258 | 230 | 486 | 475 | 164 | 209 | 56 | 14 |
| Crockett | 470 | 6.8 | 32 309 | 1 821 | 159 | 91 | 49 | 145 | 142 | 42 | 71 | 18 | 5 |
| Cumberland | 1 692 | 4.2 | 29 871 | 2 313 | 650 | 164 | 318 | 612 | 599 | 266 | 235 | 58 | 12 |
| Davidson | 30 069 | 4.6 | 47 318 | 289 | 26 165 | 7 931 | 3 681 | 4 414 | 4 274 | 1 262 | 1 902 | 646 | 161 |
| Decatur | 394 | 5.8 | 33 739 | 1 554 | 171 | 38 | 45 | 147 | 144 | 44 | 76 | 15 | 4 |
| DeKalb | 579 | 3.0 | 30 692 | 2 157 | 218 | 84 | 76 | 173 | 169 | 55 | 78 | 23 | 5 |
| Dickson | 1 547 | 4.2 | 30 887 | 2 127 | 640 | 132 | 163 | 383 | 372 | 129 | 159 | 47 | 15 |
| Dyer | 1 235 | 4.1 | 32 333 | 1 816 | 675 | 163 | 140 | 369 | 361 | 113 | 155 | 52 | 14 |
| Fayette | 1 678 | 8.9 | 43 579 | 462 | 371 | 268 | 168 | 282 | 274 | 111 | 99 | 40 | 12 |
| Fentress | 507 | 4.1 | 28 142 | 2 596 | 169 | 64 | 51 | 212 | 208 | 60 | 107 | 28 | 4 |
| Franklin | 1 210 | 4.2 | 29 579 | 2 367 | 397 | 91 | 169 | 364 | 355 | 132 | 155 | 37 | 10 |
| Gibson | 1 520 | 4.2 | 30 436 | 2 216 | 604 | 194 | 176 | 529 | 518 | 154 | 267 | 59 | 20 |
| Giles | 880 | 3.6 | 29 929 | 2 302 | 389 | 66 | 118 | 275 | 268 | 93 | 121 | 31 | 7 |
| Grainger | 650 | 4.2 | 28 567 | 2 529 | 136 | 37 | 66 | 211 | 206 | 70 | 93 | 27 | 8 |
| Greene | 2 242 | 4.8 | 32 331 | 1 817 | 1 129 | 104 | 259 | 895 | 880 | 232 | 518 | 72 | 20 |
| Grundy | 349 | 2.5 | 25 788 | 2 902 | 78 | 36 | 33 | 155 | 152 | 46 | 72 | 25 | 4 |
| Hamblen | 1 894 | 3.9 | 30 034 | 2 285 | 1 400 | 137 | 224 | 549 | 535 | 194 | 209 | 66 | 20 |
| Hamilton | 13 637 | 4.8 | 40 007 | 744 | 10 440 | 1 584 | 1 842 | 2 813 | 2 738 | 931 | 1 194 | 332 | 75 |
| Hancock | 135 | 1.8 | 20 079 | 3 103 | 34 | 3 | 15 | 65 | 64 | 15 | 33 | 12 | 2 |
| Hardeman | 711 | 2.8 | 26 505 | 2 822 | 311 | 63 | 71 | 249 | 243 | 73 | 112 | 41 | 8 |
| Hardin | 855 | 4.6 | 33 038 | 1 702 | 379 | 97 | 112 | 288 | 282 | 90 | 137 | 36 | 7 |
| Hawkins | 1 621 | 4.6 | 28 610 | 2 522 | 607 | 58 | 178 | 528 | 515 | 202 | 207 | 65 | 14 |
| Haywood | 586 | 1.3 | 31 710 | 1 953 | 243 | 90 | 56 | 175 | 171 | 47 | 77 | 34 | 7 |
| Henderson | 767 | 5.4 | 27 496 | 2 688 | 367 | 48 | 99 | 244 | 238 | 76 | 113 | 30 | 9 |
| Henry | 991 | 4.4 | 30 629 | 2 167 | 429 | 122 | 155 | 327 | 320 | 118 | 137 | 37 | 9 |
| Hickman | 587 | 2.7 | 24 065 | 3 027 | 140 | 34 | 60 | 199 | 193 | 63 | 87 | 28 | 6 |
| Houston | 247 | 4.4 | 29 690 | 2 343 | 59 | 15 | 28 | 87 | 85 | 24 | 44 | 9 | 2 |
| Humphreys | 583 | 4.2 | 31 566 | 1 984 | 329 | 29 | 79 | 174 | 169 | 62 | 76 | 19 | 5 |
| Jackson | 348 | 3.3 | 30 621 | 2 169 | 63 | 82 | 33 | 120 | 118 | 37 | 58 | 15 | 4 |
| Jefferson | 1 485 | 3.7 | 28 742 | 2 495 | 518 | 116 | 184 | 472 | 461 | 165 | 199 | 53 | 16 |
| Johnson | 452 | 5.7 | 24 806 | 2 982 | 169 | 30 | 61 | 179 | 175 | 59 | 81 | 23 | 3 |
| Knox | 16 994 | 5.6 | 38 894 | 862 | 12 079 | 1 818 | 2 254 | 3 052 | 2 956 | 1 078 | 1 195 | 356 | 91 |
| Lake | 158 | 6.6 | 20 253 | 3 102 | 62 | 4 | 18 | 79 | 77 | 16 | 46 | 11 | 2 |
| Lauderdale | 639 | 5.7 | 23 033 | 3 056 | 271 | 55 | 67 | 234 | 228 | 66 | 105 | 41 | 7 |
| Lawrence | 1 099 | 4.5 | 26 093 | 2 872 | 419 | 116 | 131 | 387 | 377 | 130 | 177 | 44 | 11 |
| Lewis | 296 | 3.0 | 24 344 | 3 013 | 89 | 25 | 30 | 117 | 115 | 34 | 56 | 14 | 4 |
| Lincoln | 1 070 | 4.7 | 32 021 | 1 883 | 389 | 82 | 133 | 279 | 271 | 98 | 122 | 33 | 5 |
| Loudon | 1 856 | 5.2 | 37 698 | 1 002 | 681 | 78 | 355 | 479 | 468 | 201 | 198 | 37 | 12 |
| McMinn | 1 502 | 4.2 | 28 598 | 2 524 | 768 | 113 | 184 | 485 | 473 | 164 | 202 | 56 | 15 |
| McNairy | 699 | 3.8 | 26 771 | 2 795 | 245 | 43 | 72 | 273 | 267 | 87 | 125 | 36 | 6 |
| Macon | 638 | 5.3 | 28 353 | 2 564 | 169 | 76 | 72 | 193 | 188 | 60 | 88 | 28 | 6 |
| Madison | 3 470 | 4.6 | 35 315 | 1 322 | 2 651 | 345 | 440 | 829 | 807 | 249 | 334 | 122 | 27 |
| Marion | 906 | 3.8 | 32 107 | 1 861 | 310 | 48 | 102 | 278 | 272 | 90 | 124 | 34 | 8 |

1. Based on the resident population estimated as of July 1 of the year shown.  2. Includes supplements to wages and salaries.

# Table B. States and Counties — Earnings, Social Security, and Housing

| | Earnings, 2011 | | | | | | | | | Social Security beneficiaries, December 2011 | | | Housing units, 2010 | |
| | | | | Percent by selected industries | | | | | | | | | | |
| | | | Goods-related[1] | | Service-related and health | | | | | | | | | |
| STATE County | Total (mil dol) | Farm | Total | Manu-facturing | Infor-mation and profes-sional and technical services | Retail trade | Finance, insur-ance, and real estate | Health care and social services | Govern-ment | Number | Rate[2] | Supple-mental Security Income recipients, December 2011 | Total | Percent change, 2000–2010 |
| | 75 | 76 | 77 | 78 | 79 | 80 | 81 | 82 | 83 | 84 | 85 | 86 | 87 | 88 |

| | | | | | | | | | | | | | | |
|---|---|---|---|---|---|---|---|---|---|---|---|---|---|---|
| **SOUTH DAKOTA—Cont'd** | | | | | | | | | | | | | | |
| Tripp | 204 | 52.7 | D | 1.9 | 2.7 | 6.8 | D | D | 8.9 | 1 370 | 244 | 140 | 3 072 | 1.2 |
| Turner | 239 | 54.2 | D | 6.8 | 2.3 | 2.1 | D | D | 7.7 | 1 750 | 210 | 78 | 3 939 | 2.3 |
| Union | 673 | 16.0 | 15.4 | 13.2 | 7.0 | 2.7 | 6.7 | 12.6 | 5.5 | 2 780 | 190 | 87 | 6 280 | 17.5 |
| Walworth | 132 | 24.9 | D | 0.6 | D | 9.5 | 3.4 | D | 13.9 | 1 510 | 271 | 128 | 3 003 | -4.5 |
| Yankton | 649 | 14.9 | D | 21.9 | D | 6.0 | 4.8 | 14.8 | 16.2 | 4 610 | 204 | 383 | 9 652 | 9.2 |
| Ziebach | 49 | 70.0 | D | D | D | D | D | D | 17.6 | 175 | 61 | 87 | 987 | 12.3 |
| | | | | | | | | | | | | | | |
| TENNESSEE | 171 765 | 0.2 | 18.5 | 12.4 | 8.8 | 7.3 | 7.4 | 14.8 | 14.9 | 1 287 683 | 201 | 179 325 | 2 812 133 | 15.3 |
| | | | | | | | | | | | | | | |
| Anderson | 2 981 | -0.1 | 35.0 | 27.4 | 22.7 | 4.2 | 3.3 | 8.2 | 12.1 | 18 680 | 248 | 2 363 | 34 717 | 7.0 |
| Bedford | 894 | -0.7 | D | 33.4 | D | 6.3 | 5.1 | D | 11.4 | 9 130 | 201 | 1 051 | 18 360 | 22.5 |
| Benton | 180 | -0.6 | D | 13.0 | D | 11.3 | D | D | 24.6 | 5 160 | 314 | 563 | 8 975 | 4.4 |
| Bledsoe | 91 | -3.9 | D | 1.9 | D | 5.6 | 4.7 | 6.8 | 48.4 | 2 745 | 213 | 428 | 5 718 | 11.2 |
| Blount | 2 584 | -0.2 | D | 17.5 | 3.9 | 9.1 | 5.8 | 8.4 | 15.1 | 28 825 | 233 | 2 772 | 55 266 | 17.4 |
| Bradley | 2 216 | -0.1 | D | 24.1 | 3.8 | 7.4 | 5.0 | D | 11.6 | 22 630 | 226 | 2 647 | 41 395 | 12.4 |
| Campbell | 447 | -0.6 | D | 12.7 | 3.1 | 10.7 | 6.2 | D | 21.2 | 11 515 | 284 | 2 827 | 19 966 | 7.9 |
| Cannon | 120 | 0.0 | D | 6.4 | D | 8.0 | D | 14.0 | 21.0 | 3 300 | 240 | 399 | 6 037 | 11.4 |
| | | | | | | | | | | | | | | |
| Carroll | 393 | 6.7 | 16.2 | 12.4 | D | 6.8 | 5.0 | D | 17.9 | 7 820 | 275 | 919 | 13 184 | 0.9 |
| Carter | 564 | -0.5 | D | 8.9 | 4.2 | 11.9 | 5.3 | D | 20.9 | 15 420 | 270 | 2 278 | 27 746 | 7.0 |
| Cheatham | 541 | 3.2 | D | 23.6 | D | 6.5 | 2.8 | D | 13.9 | 7 175 | 184 | 649 | 15 663 | 16.0 |
| Chester | 193 | 3.5 | D | 10.1 | D | 9.1 | 4.1 | D | 22.6 | 3 865 | 225 | 471 | 6 980 | 13.0 |
| Claiborne | 394 | -1.4 | 28.5 | 18.6 | D | 6.8 | 6.2 | D | 22.0 | 9 145 | 284 | 2 041 | 14 859 | 11.8 |
| Clay | 95 | -2.4 | D | 7.2 | D | 10.2 | 3.1 | D | 20.8 | 2 265 | 292 | 388 | 4 282 | 8.2 |
| Cocke | 372 | 0.4 | D | 24.6 | 1.7 | 10.6 | 3.4 | D | 22.9 | 10 240 | 288 | 2 021 | 17 459 | 10.2 |
| Coffee | 1 418 | 0.5 | 20.9 | 16.4 | 26.3 | 6.8 | 3.4 | 10.5 | 14.4 | 12 905 | 243 | 1 524 | 23 434 | 13.0 |
| Crockett | 251 | 11.5 | 30.1 | 24.9 | 2.5 | 10.8 | 3.3 | D | 14.1 | 3 535 | 243 | 455 | 6 425 | 4.7 |
| | | | | | | | | | | | | | | |
| Cumberland | 814 | -2.2 | 22.7 | 13.8 | 5.2 | 11.2 | 4.4 | 16.1 | 14.2 | 20 230 | 357 | 1 711 | 28 151 | 25.4 |
| Davidson | 34 097 | 0.0 | 9.1 | 3.9 | 13.1 | 5.9 | 8.4 | 25.1 | 10.0 | 91 910 | 145 | 14 641 | 283 978 | 12.3 |
| Decatur | 209 | 0.7 | D | 11.0 | 3.1 | 6.3 | 7.7 | 26.5 | 15.2 | 3 695 | 316 | 443 | 6 873 | 6.6 |
| DeKalb | 302 | 4.2 | D | 23.1 | D | 6.3 | 2.6 | D | 13.0 | 4 590 | 243 | 670 | 9 405 | 11.9 |
| Dickson | 772 | -1.5 | D | 19.9 | D | 10.4 | 4.3 | 14.3 | 16.4 | 10 070 | 201 | 1 119 | 20 820 | 18.2 |
| Dyer | 837 | 3.9 | 33.7 | 24.4 | D | 8.1 | 4.8 | 13.1 | 15.1 | 9 140 | 239 | 1 547 | 16 703 | 3.6 |
| Fayette | 639 | 4.9 | 28.6 | 23.4 | D | 10.0 | 9.8 | D | 12.2 | 8 475 | 220 | 1 347 | 15 669 | 39.8 |
| Fentress | 233 | 0.1 | D | 5.6 | 2.9 | 12.3 | 6.2 | 15.3 | 17.7 | 5 495 | 305 | 1 169 | 8 961 | 17.9 |
| Franklin | 488 | 2.8 | 21.3 | 16.2 | 3.7 | 9.9 | 3.7 | D | 17.5 | 10 385 | 254 | 1 038 | 18 697 | 11.2 |
| | | | | | | | | | | | | | | |
| Gibson | 798 | 6.9 | 27.5 | 20.6 | 3.6 | 9.6 | 5.4 | D | 17.7 | 12 415 | 249 | 1 517 | 21 999 | 4.5 |
| Giles | 455 | -2.0 | D | 29.0 | D | 8.7 | 4.6 | D | 15.0 | 7 395 | 252 | 821 | 13 844 | 5.6 |
| Grainger | 173 | -2.0 | D | 22.3 | D | 8.6 | 3.0 | 4.5 | 24.1 | 5 985 | 263 | 1 044 | 10 894 | 11.9 |
| Greene | 1 233 | -1.3 | D | 27.1 | 2.3 | 9.8 | 8.5 | D | 16.2 | 19 425 | 280 | 2 495 | 32 025 | 13.9 |
| Grundy | 114 | 0.0 | D | 5.6 | D | 11.2 | 4.5 | 12.1 | 26.3 | 4 030 | 298 | 837 | 6 397 | 1.8 |
| Hamblen | 1 537 | 0.6 | D | 28.9 | 2.8 | 8.3 | 3.0 | 13.2 | 12.4 | 15 440 | 245 | 1 943 | 26 963 | 9.2 |
| Hamilton | 12 024 | -0.1 | D | 13.2 | 8.1 | 7.5 | 11.8 | 12.1 | 16.8 | 68 325 | 200 | 8 422 | 151 107 | 12.2 |
| Hancock | 37 | 0.5 | D | D | D | 9.5 | D | 16.3 | 49.5 | 1 450 | 215 | 516 | 3 624 | 10.6 |
| Hardeman | 373 | 4.7 | D | 23.7 | 1.6 | 5.1 | 2.4 | D | 24.8 | 6 210 | 231 | 1 396 | 10 851 | 1.5 |
| | | | | | | | | | | | | | | |
| Hardin | 476 | 0.8 | D | 27.7 | 9.5 | 9.2 | 5.0 | D | 18.0 | 7 605 | 294 | 1 249 | 13 946 | 8.9 |
| Hawkins | 665 | -0.7 | D | 33.4 | D | 5.9 | 2.3 | D | 19.4 | 16 170 | 285 | 2 197 | 26 870 | 10.1 |
| Haywood | 333 | 17.2 | 28.2 | 24.5 | D | 5.2 | 5.3 | 5.9 | 18.3 | 4 105 | 222 | 1 033 | 8 315 | 2.8 |
| Henderson | 416 | 0.6 | D | 28.3 | 2.0 | 8.5 | 7.4 | 7.4 | 16.2 | 6 330 | 227 | 867 | 12 776 | 11.6 |
| Henry | 551 | 5.1 | D | 15.3 | 3.3 | 10.0 | 5.5 | D | 22.7 | 9 315 | 288 | 964 | 17 054 | 8.1 |
| Hickman | 173 | -1.0 | D | 15.1 | D | 6.1 | 2.8 | 7.4 | 32.4 | 5 260 | 216 | 706 | 10 311 | 15.8 |
| Houston | 74 | -3.1 | D | D | D | 8.1 | D | D | 26.8 | 1 950 | 234 | 266 | 4 188 | 7.4 |
| Humphreys | 358 | -2.3 | D | 33.9 | 4.1 | 5.7 | 2.2 | D | 24.6 | 4 785 | 259 | 510 | 8 865 | 4.5 |
| Jackson | 145 | -0.8 | 18.2 | 8.9 | D | 7.9 | D | 8.2 | 14.9 | 3 230 | 284 | 536 | 5 843 | 13.2 |
| | | | | | | | | | | | | | | |
| Jefferson | 635 | 0.0 | D | 23.5 | 3.2 | 8.7 | 3.8 | D | 17.8 | 13 265 | 257 | 1 401 | 23 499 | 21.6 |
| Johnson | 200 | -0.6 | D | 20.8 | D | 8.3 | 3.6 | 9.8 | 20.7 | 5 280 | 290 | 896 | 8 956 | 13.7 |
| Knox | 13 896 | -0.1 | 11.7 | 5.4 | 12.3 | 8.0 | 6.9 | 16.3 | 15.6 | 79 920 | 183 | 9 699 | 194 949 | 13.7 |
| Lake | 65 | 5.4 | D | D | D | 6.1 | 1.6 | 12.1 | 50.4 | 1 415 | 182 | 364 | 2 598 | -4.3 |
| Lauderdale | 327 | 10.3 | 21.7 | 19.9 | D | 6.2 | 4.4 | 7.6 | 27.9 | 5 655 | 204 | 1 245 | 11 256 | 6.5 |
| Lawrence | 535 | 3.0 | D | 18.5 | 3.6 | 10.3 | 3.5 | D | 18.5 | 10 795 | 256 | 1 270 | 18 177 | 8.1 |
| Lewis | 114 | -1.8 | 14.3 | 8.3 | 2.9 | 14.9 | 2.1 | D | 25.1 | 2 925 | 241 | 364 | 5 470 | 13.5 |
| Lincoln | 470 | 0.0 | D | 26.1 | D | 9.6 | 3.8 | 4.8 | 23.2 | 8 030 | 240 | 864 | 15 241 | 8.9 |
| Loudon | 759 | 2.2 | D | 22.9 | 5.9 | 7.9 | 4.0 | 7.5 | 14.9 | 14 325 | 291 | 898 | 21 725 | 25.7 |
| | | | | | | | | | | | | | | |
| McMinn | 881 | -0.9 | D | 35.2 | D | 8.3 | 4.5 | D | 12.7 | 13 315 | 254 | 1 759 | 23 341 | 7.9 |
| McNairy | 288 | 0.2 | D | 26.4 | 1.7 | 7.5 | 2.3 | D | 19.4 | 7 415 | 284 | 1 110 | 11 933 | 6.4 |
| Macon | 245 | 4.6 | 16.4 | 8.5 | 7.2 | 12.5 | 7.0 | D | 19.4 | 5 220 | 232 | 805 | 9 861 | 10.9 |
| Madison | 2 996 | 0.9 | D | 17.0 | D | 7.7 | 3.8 | 13.5 | 22.0 | 19 475 | 198 | 3 146 | 41 877 | 9.6 |
| Marion | 358 | -0.2 | D | 23.5 | D | 10.6 | 4.2 | D | 16.5 | 7 290 | 258 | 1 082 | 12 954 | 6.7 |

1. Includes mining, construction, and manufacturing.   2. Per 1,000 resident population enumerated in the 2010 census.

# Table B. States and Counties — Housing, Labor Force, and Employment

| STATE County | Housing units, 2007–2011 | | | | | | | | Civilian labor force, 2012 | | | | Civilian employment,[6] 2007–2011 | | |
|---|---|---|---|---|---|---|---|---|---|---|---|---|---|---|---|
| | Occupied units | | | | | | | | | | Unemployment | | | Percent | |
| | | | Owner-occupied | | | Renter-occupied | | | | | | | | | |
| | | | | Median owner cost as a percent of income | | | | | | | | | | | Con-struction, produc-tion, and mainte-nance occu-pations |
| | Total | Percent | Median value[1] | With a mort-gage | Without a mort-gage[2] | Median rent[3] | Median rent as a per-cent of income | Sub-stand-ard units[4] (percent) | Total | Percent change, 2011–2012 | Total | Rate[5] | Total | Manage-ment, business, science and arts | |
| | 89 | 90 | 91 | 92 | 93 | 94 | 95 | 96 | 97 | 98 | 99 | 100 | 101 | 102 | 103 |
| SOUTH DAKOTA—Cont'd | | | | | | | | | | | | | | | |
| Tripp | 2 482 | 72.5 | 66 800 | 20.7 | 9.9 | 486 | 29.9 | 5.0 | 2 906 | -0.5 | 123 | 4.2 | 2 906 | 45.9 | 24.7 |
| Turner | 3 411 | 80.8 | 86 000 | 22.9 | 11.9 | 511 | 20.6 | 1.4 | 4 283 | 1.3 | 164 | 3.8 | 4 542 | 29.8 | 30.7 |
| Union | 5 833 | 74.2 | 139 000 | 19.0 | 11.3 | 724 | 20.9 | 0.7 | 8 320 | 0.3 | 392 | 4.7 | 7 420 | 38.1 | 23.9 |
| Walworth | 2 201 | 72.5 | 71 100 | 22.4 | 9.9 | 450 | 24.7 | 2.4 | 2 671 | -0.3 | 152 | 5.7 | 2 502 | 36.4 | 22.0 |
| Yankton | 8 654 | 70.4 | 123 000 | 20.8 | 9.9 | 523 | 27.7 | 1.7 | 11 827 | 1.3 | 472 | 4.0 | 11 144 | 30.5 | 26.6 |
| Ziebach | 799 | 55.3 | 76 400 | 19.3 | 13.8 | 431 | 34.0 | 13.4 | 1 071 | 0.5 | 79 | 7.4 | 867 | 50.6 | 21.8 |
| TENNESSEE | 2 457 997 | 69.0 | 137 200 | 23.4 | 11.1 | 707 | 30.2 | 2.3 | 3 113 562 | -0.1 | 249 400 | 8.0 | 2 818 005 | 32.5 | 25.0 |
| Anderson | 31 086 | 71.3 | 121 300 | 21.4 | 10.5 | 637 | 28.1 | 1.8 | 36 368 | -1.0 | 2 850 | 7.8 | 31 774 | 33.5 | 24.5 |
| Bedford | 16 053 | 70.9 | 114 200 | 23.2 | 11.8 | 643 | 30.8 | 4.5 | 22 681 | -1.5 | 2 018 | 8.9 | 18 529 | 22.5 | 40.8 |
| Benton | 7 023 | 80.5 | 73 800 | 22.5 | 12.4 | 495 | 28.6 | 3.0 | 6 954 | -1.4 | 712 | 10.2 | 6 231 | 25.7 | 37.0 |
| Bledsoe | 4 505 | 78.8 | 109 500 | 27.5 | 9.9 | 507 | 28.7 | 3.9 | 4 877 | -1.5 | 485 | 9.9 | 4 211 | 20.3 | 38.1 |
| Blount | 48 464 | 74.8 | 162 300 | 23.2 | 10.4 | 676 | 28.4 | 1.6 | 63 856 | -1.3 | 4 358 | 6.8 | 56 448 | 30.9 | 25.0 |
| Bradley | 37 258 | 67.3 | 137 000 | 23.5 | 10.5 | 655 | 31.4 | 2.8 | 50 082 | 3.1 | 3 716 | 7.4 | 43 376 | 28.4 | 30.5 |
| Campbell | 16 027 | 72.2 | 87 900 | 22.4 | 12.2 | 480 | 30.1 | 1.9 | 16 980 | 1.3 | 1 789 | 10.5 | 13 832 | 24.1 | 36.1 |
| Cannon | 5 364 | 76.2 | 114 700 | 26.1 | 13.0 | 540 | 23.9 | 2.7 | 6 606 | 1.1 | 483 | 7.3 | 5 522 | 22.1 | 39.2 |
| Carroll | 10 932 | 78.0 | 79 100 | 22.2 | 11.9 | 497 | 25.7 | 2.5 | 13 799 | -1.0 | 1 503 | 10.9 | 11 535 | 28.7 | 33.4 |
| Carter | 24 190 | 72.9 | 96 900 | 22.8 | 11.6 | 512 | 29.4 | 2.1 | 28 013 | -1.6 | 2 250 | 8.0 | 23 946 | 27.5 | 29.8 |
| Cheatham | 14 355 | 81.0 | 157 200 | 23.8 | 9.9 | 790 | 35.5 | 2.3 | 20 733 | 1.4 | 1 500 | 7.2 | 18 927 | 32.0 | 26.1 |
| Chester | 5 962 | 74.5 | 109 400 | 23.3 | 12.3 | 630 | 25.8 | 2.2 | 8 379 | 0.0 | 713 | 8.5 | 6 929 | 28.2 | 32.4 |
| Claiborne | 12 766 | 77.0 | 92 700 | 24.0 | 9.9 | 499 | 33.4 | 1.7 | 13 223 | -0.7 | 1 371 | 10.4 | 12 049 | 25.4 | 36.1 |
| Clay | 3 610 | 76.0 | 93 500 | 20.6 | 13.8 | 455 | 27.6 | 3.1 | 3 459 | -0.3 | 344 | 9.9 | 3 154 | 21.5 | 37.8 |
| Cocke | 14 955 | 71.4 | 98 000 | 25.5 | 11.3 | 507 | 29.7 | 4.4 | 16 441 | -0.6 | 1 824 | 11.1 | 13 672 | 19.3 | 34.4 |
| Coffee | 21 042 | 70.0 | 118 600 | 24.0 | 11.7 | 618 | 29.7 | 3.0 | 26 830 | 1.0 | 2 008 | 7.5 | 21 582 | 30.1 | 30.6 |
| Crockett | 5 529 | 70.0 | 86 200 | 22.9 | 12.7 | 612 | 24.6 | 2.5 | 6 825 | 0.9 | 697 | 10.2 | 6 353 | 24.4 | 33.8 |
| Cumberland | 23 231 | 79.2 | 142 600 | 25.1 | 10.7 | 593 | 29.4 | 2.0 | 24 473 | 1.2 | 2 214 | 9.0 | 21 104 | 27.9 | 29.3 |
| Davidson | 254 111 | 56.8 | 166 300 | 25.1 | 11.2 | 798 | 30.5 | 2.6 | 335 020 | 1.3 | 22 259 | 6.6 | 315 217 | 37.7 | 17.8 |
| Decatur | 5 133 | 77.3 | 68 800 | 22.4 | 11.5 | 491 | 33.4 | 2.2 | 5 753 | -0.8 | 553 | 9.6 | 4 540 | 31.1 | 30.7 |
| DeKalb | 7 074 | 74.0 | 101 300 | 21.9 | 12.3 | 536 | 24.1 | 1.2 | 9 927 | -1.5 | 768 | 7.7 | 7 728 | 27.3 | 37.3 |
| Dickson | 18 809 | 73.3 | 132 000 | 23.9 | 10.7 | 685 | 30.1 | 1.9 | 25 126 | 1.2 | 2 035 | 8.1 | 22 136 | 28.8 | 31.2 |
| Dyer | 15 283 | 64.7 | 93 700 | 22.4 | 13.8 | 602 | 29.7 | 2.6 | 17 215 | -0.8 | 1 995 | 11.6 | 16 295 | 26.1 | 35.2 |
| Fayette | 13 825 | 82.6 | 176 600 | 23.6 | 9.9 | 660 | 24.6 | 1.9 | 17 646 | -0.6 | 1 742 | 9.9 | 16 954 | 31.1 | 26.7 |
| Fentress | 7 448 | 78.2 | 95 300 | 25.9 | 12.9 | 479 | 30.6 | 2.3 | 8 280 | 1.1 | 745 | 9.0 | 6 481 | 30.7 | 39.6 |
| Franklin | 15 885 | 77.0 | 113 700 | 21.9 | 11.8 | 597 | 25.9 | 1.5 | 20 266 | 1.2 | 1 577 | 7.8 | 17 172 | 30.7 | 33.9 |
| Gibson | 19 452 | 71.1 | 86 900 | 22.6 | 12.1 | 545 | 29.5 | 2.2 | 21 257 | -3.4 | 2 457 | 11.6 | 19 981 | 28.4 | 31.9 |
| Giles | 11 602 | 75.3 | 98 500 | 21.1 | 12.0 | 565 | 37.0 | 1.6 | 13 617 | -1.1 | 1 248 | 9.2 | 12 117 | 27.7 | 34.3 |
| Grainger | 8 940 | 82.8 | 91 200 | 23.3 | 11.7 | 523 | 28.4 | 2.8 | 9 808 | -1.8 | 1 016 | 10.4 | 8 989 | 22.0 | 42.5 |
| Greene | 28 431 | 74.2 | 108 000 | 23.4 | 10.1 | 547 | 29.0 | 1.8 | 29 052 | -2.6 | 3 165 | 10.9 | 28 679 | 27.1 | 33.9 |
| Grundy | 5 259 | 79.9 | 79 800 | 28.0 | 12.6 | 510 | 28.4 | 3.6 | 6 094 | 1.2 | 571 | 9.4 | 4 863 | 20.4 | 39.9 |
| Hamblen | 24 645 | 70.5 | 120 200 | 23.0 | 10.6 | 617 | 28.7 | 1.5 | 29 194 | -1.7 | 2 628 | 9.0 | 26 365 | 23.8 | 36.7 |
| Hamilton | 134 030 | 65.7 | 151 000 | 22.7 | 10.6 | 695 | 29.9 | 2.2 | 166 532 | -0.3 | 12 446 | 7.5 | 157 956 | 36.6 | 20.1 |
| Hancock | 2 938 | 70.7 | 76 500 | 27.0 | 12.2 | 376 | 27.5 | 7.0 | 2 327 | -5.3 | 273 | 11.7 | 2 214 | 23.5 | 39.2 |
| Hardeman | 8 798 | 72.8 | 86 900 | 25.7 | 11.9 | 528 | 34.5 | 2.9 | 10 907 | -0.4 | 1 203 | 11.0 | 9 212 | 26.2 | 32.8 |
| Hardin | 10 538 | 77.5 | 89 700 | 24.3 | 12.0 | 536 | 29.7 | 2.3 | 12 156 | -1.0 | 1 154 | 9.5 | 9 905 | 23.9 | 35.7 |
| Hawkins | 23 707 | 77.3 | 108 000 | 22.9 | 10.8 | 522 | 28.7 | 1.9 | 26 044 | -1.7 | 2 066 | 7.9 | 23 235 | 29.6 | 34.3 |
| Haywood | 7 199 | 63.2 | 90 300 | 23.7 | 13.0 | 627 | 34.5 | 6.1 | 8 771 | -1.8 | 984 | 11.2 | 7 646 | 21.0 | 36.5 |
| Henderson | 10 733 | 78.9 | 95 600 | 23.7 | 11.1 | 580 | 28.5 | 2.0 | 12 505 | -1.0 | 1 320 | 10.6 | 11 558 | 26.1 | 34.5 |
| Henry | 13 231 | 76.1 | 87 700 | 21.9 | 10.4 | 563 | 27.5 | 1.5 | 13 724 | -1.1 | 1 401 | 10.2 | 12 502 | 24.0 | 33.1 |
| Hickman | 8 948 | 80.6 | 102 900 | 22.9 | 9.9 | 596 | 27.7 | 3.7 | 10 534 | 1.2 | 968 | 9.2 | 10 438 | 22.9 | 35.8 |
| Houston | 3 451 | 71.7 | 88 200 | 20.9 | 13.7 | 559 | 26.4 | 3.6 | 4 125 | 0.5 | 397 | 9.6 | 3 038 | 22.9 | 42.1 |
| Humphreys | 7 665 | 75.8 | 107 400 | 23.4 | 10.5 | 524 | 21.4 | 1.4 | 9 189 | -0.6 | 853 | 9.3 | 7 604 | 22.9 | 35.5 |
| Jackson | 4 710 | 75.1 | 96 900 | 24.5 | 13.8 | 505 | 29.1 | 2.0 | 5 080 | -2.0 | 475 | 9.4 | 4 146 | 25.0 | 39.0 |
| Jefferson | 19 338 | 75.3 | 122 400 | 22.9 | 11.9 | 650 | 30.5 | 1.7 | 23 925 | -1.1 | 2 407 | 10.1 | 22 252 | 25.2 | 30.6 |
| Johnson | 7 285 | 77.4 | 97 700 | 25.5 | 10.8 | 510 | 26.7 | 3.1 | 7 371 | -2.2 | 724 | 9.8 | 6 462 | 26.0 | 39.1 |
| Knox | 179 705 | 66.6 | 154 900 | 22.5 | 10.3 | 722 | 29.9 | 1.7 | 232 486 | -1.2 | 14 573 | 6.3 | 211 055 | 39.4 | 16.9 |
| Lake | 2 352 | 59.6 | 65 200 | 22.0 | 11.9 | 429 | 32.0 | 2.2 | 2 796 | 0.3 | 286 | 10.2 | 2 014 | 16.6 | 33.4 |
| Lauderdale | 9 577 | 65.8 | 78 100 | 23.6 | 12.5 | 580 | 27.3 | 3.6 | 9 916 | -0.3 | 1 233 | 12.4 | 10 067 | 24.0 | 35.4 |
| Lawrence | 15 958 | 76.2 | 95 300 | 23.4 | 11.9 | 505 | 31.1 | 2.4 | 16 537 | -1.7 | 1 870 | 11.3 | 16 874 | 23.6 | 36.5 |
| Lewis | 4 655 | 76.4 | 93 200 | 23.7 | 12.4 | 601 | 28.5 | 0.7 | 5 293 | -1.1 | 567 | 10.7 | 4 484 | 25.8 | 30.9 |
| Lincoln | 13 298 | 75.4 | 112 300 | 22.6 | 11.7 | 538 | 27.2 | 0.8 | 17 593 | 0.1 | 968 | 5.5 | 14 330 | 26.7 | 33.9 |
| Loudon | 19 773 | 77.0 | 173 300 | 22.7 | 9.9 | 691 | 25.2 | 2.2 | 24 775 | -1.4 | 1 668 | 6.7 | 20 085 | 28.8 | 28.9 |
| McMinn | 20 802 | 75.6 | 110 100 | 22.3 | 10.4 | 573 | 30.3 | 1.3 | 24 414 | 3.1 | 2 235 | 9.2 | 21 131 | 25.7 | 39.4 |
| McNairy | 10 057 | 76.0 | 85 100 | 22.9 | 11.6 | 541 | 31.3 | 2.9 | 10 729 | -3.3 | 1 037 | 9.7 | 9 482 | 25.1 | 40.1 |
| Macon | 8 186 | 74.6 | 92 300 | 23.7 | 11.9 | 545 | 29.0 | 2.6 | 10 986 | 0.9 | 886 | 8.1 | 8 866 | 24.4 | 40.9 |
| Madison | 36 188 | 66.7 | 112 400 | 23.5 | 11.4 | 717 | 36.5 | 2.2 | 49 727 | -0.2 | 4 075 | 8.2 | 42 697 | 32.0 | 24.6 |
| Marion | 11 344 | 76.0 | 114 300 | 24.0 | 11.5 | 574 | 28.2 | 2.5 | 12 547 | -1.0 | 1 117 | 8.9 | 11 680 | 22.9 | 35.7 |

1. Specified owner-occupied units.  2. A value of 9.9 represents 9.9 percent or less.  3. Specified renter-occupied units. A value of 10.0 represents 10 percent or less.  4. Overcrowded or lacking complete plumbing facilities.  5. Percent of civilian labor force.  6. Persons 16 years old and over.

# Table B. States and Counties — Nonfarm Employment and Agriculture

| STATE County | Number of establishments | Employment Total | Health care and social assistance | Manufacturing | Retail trade | Finance and insurance | Professional, scientific, and technical services | Annual payroll Total (mil dol) | Average per employee (dollars) | Farms Number | Percent with: Fewer than 50 acres | 500 acres or more | Farm operators whose principal occupation is farming (percent) |
|---|---|---|---|---|---|---|---|---|---|---|---|---|---|
| | 104 | 105 | 106 | 107 | 108 | 109 | 110 | 111 | 112 | 113 | 114 | 115 | 116 |
| **SOUTH DAKOTA—Cont'd** | | | | | | | | | | | | | |
| Tripp | 218 | 1 621 | 500 | D | 386 | D | 53 | 43 | 26 616 | 624 | 8.8 | 61.9 | 62.8 |
| Turner | 251 | 1 544 | 450 | 193 | 250 | 88 | 43 | 44 | 28 496 | 722 | 22.2 | 34.1 | 60.9 |
| Union | 482 | 7 940 | 901 | 1 451 | 467 | 872 | 248 | 372 | 46 817 | 521 | 21.9 | 36.5 | 62.4 |
| Walworth | 206 | 1 786 | 369 | D | 382 | D | 92 | 48 | 26 966 | 279 | 19.0 | 48.4 | 56.3 |
| Yankton | 730 | 10 376 | 2 059 | 2 685 | 1 588 | 667 | 212 | 338 | 32 580 | 658 | 18.8 | 34.2 | 58.7 |
| Ziebach | 17 | 63 | D | D | D | D | NA | 2 | 32 603 | 234 | 7.3 | 77.4 | 71.8 |
| **TENNESSEE** | 129 489 | 2 300 542 | 377 420 | 289 477 | 305 578 | 109 092 | 99 809 | 91 783 | 39 896 | 79 280 | 44.4 | 4.6 | 38.9 |
| Anderson | 1 571 | 43 143 | 3 556 | 9 412 | 3 633 | 1 170 | 9 669 | 2 320 | 53 766 | 538 | 54.8 | 0.4 | 29.7 |
| Bedford | 751 | 11 921 | 1 076 | 3 779 | 1 535 | 434 | 219 | 379 | 31 758 | 1 554 | 43.4 | 5.8 | 43.6 |
| Benton | 294 | 3 226 | 692 | 673 | 626 | 123 | 55 | 82 | 25 566 | 500 | 32.2 | 3.6 | 35.8 |
| Bledsoe | 94 | 476 | 112 | 50 | D | 43 | 10 | 13 | 27 305 | 580 | 29.0 | 4.8 | 37.9 |
| Blount | 2 239 | 38 247 | 5 962 | D | 5 623 | 2 222 | 2 588 | 1 404 | 36 709 | 1 154 | 54.5 | 1.9 | 42.5 |
| Bradley | 1 842 | 35 729 | 4 891 | 7 302 | 4 673 | 1 575 | 797 | 1 223 | 34 218 | 959 | 55.3 | 3.2 | 40.9 |
| Campbell | 558 | 6 794 | 1 852 | 1 172 | 1 417 | 301 | 101 | 190 | 27 987 | 404 | 43.8 | 2.2 | 37.6 |
| Cannon | 154 | 1 389 | 405 | D | 217 | 49 | D | 38 | 27 660 | 880 | 37.4 | 4.4 | 40.0 |
| Carroll | 439 | 6 166 | 1 691 | 963 | 862 | 174 | 120 | 171 | 27 706 | 971 | 39.1 | 6.0 | 36.5 |
| Carter | 710 | 8 719 | 1 902 | 971 | 1 689 | 349 | 161 | 232 | 26 575 | 516 | 59.1 | 1.9 | 36.8 |
| Cheatham | 517 | 5 837 | 522 | 1 933 | 876 | 143 | 209 | 194 | 33 196 | 554 | 43.3 | 3.1 | 43.3 |
| Chester | 248 | 3 098 | 436 | 534 | 396 | 120 | 35 | 78 | 25 064 | 484 | 30.2 | 4.5 | 36.6 |
| Claiborne | 415 | 6 867 | 1 263 | 1 931 | 826 | 280 | 72 | 205 | 29 896 | 1 090 | 41.3 | 3.0 | 40.9 |
| Clay | 102 | 1 024 | D | D | 138 | D | 9 | 25 | 24 838 | 462 | 26.2 | 7.8 | 40.9 |
| Cocke | 482 | 5 942 | 808 | 1 538 | 1 390 | 224 | 89 | 178 | 29 951 | 705 | 46.1 | 1.3 | 38.4 |
| Coffee | 1 192 | 18 749 | 2 832 | 3 873 | 2 725 | 722 | 642 | 712 | 37 952 | 1 008 | 48.6 | 6.3 | 41.0 |
| Crockett | 215 | 1 949 | D | 285 | 230 | 83 | 31 | 63 | 32 183 | 470 | 40.6 | 15.5 | 35.1 |
| Cumberland | 1 045 | 13 710 | 2 880 | 2 148 | 2 528 | 384 | 264 | 397 | 28 972 | 842 | 46.4 | 5.5 | 37.3 |
| Davidson | 17 809 | 377 254 | 71 654 | 17 857 | 37 534 | 17 914 | 21 803 | 17 973 | 47 642 | 515 | 57.3 | 1.6 | 25.2 |
| Decatur | 243 | 3 059 | 1 014 | 468 | 354 | D | D | 106 | 34 713 | 455 | 26.6 | 6.4 | 37.1 |
| DeKalb | 300 | 5 621 | 533 | 2 311 | 552 | 95 | 66 | 153 | 27 264 | 722 | 39.6 | 4.3 | 39.9 |
| Dickson | 897 | 12 072 | 2 038 | 3 143 | 2 252 | 422 | 244 | 374 | 30 962 | 1 285 | 45.1 | 2.3 | 30.0 |
| Dyer | 781 | 12 837 | 2 160 | 3 788 | 1 918 | 461 | 183 | 439 | 34 230 | 584 | 37.5 | 20.7 | 39.6 |
| Fayette | 548 | 6 314 | 588 | 2 027 | 898 | 239 | 110 | 234 | 37 004 | 952 | 38.3 | 9.7 | 36.0 |
| Fentress | 242 | 3 349 | 1 351 | 354 | 640 | 165 | 39 | 85 | 25 519 | 623 | 46.7 | 5.6 | 40.1 |
| Franklin | 665 | 9 370 | 1 444 | 2 830 | 1 418 | 234 | 147 | 323 | 34 450 | 1 104 | 50.9 | 5.3 | 40.9 |
| Gibson | 934 | 11 846 | 2 000 | 2 723 | 2 175 | 334 | 220 | 334 | 28 196 | 1 049 | 36.7 | 10.5 | 40.2 |
| Giles | 543 | 7 337 | 881 | 2 358 | 1 322 | 268 | D | 232 | 31 671 | 1 789 | 34.3 | 4.4 | 40.6 |
| Grainger | 218 | 1 971 | D | 794 | 322 | D | D | 53 | 26 794 | 1 008 | 45.6 | 0.8 | 41.5 |
| Greene | 1 096 | 20 894 | 4 042 | 5 223 | 2 710 | D | 284 | 626 | 29 960 | 3 061 | 56.8 | 1.1 | 42.5 |
| Grundy | 163 | 1 358 | 336 | 212 | 265 | D | D | 33 | 23 957 | 328 | 47.0 | 6.4 | 39.9 |
| Hamblen | 1 303 | 26 216 | 4 192 | 8 618 | 4 071 | 549 | 309 | 873 | 33 293 | 715 | 48.3 | 2.2 | 40.1 |
| Hamilton | 8 506 | 172 601 | 26 370 | 24 478 | 20 043 | 12 173 | 7 559 | 6 486 | 37 576 | 669 | 57.1 | 2.2 | 39.3 |
| Hancock | 57 | 459 | 159 | D | 161 | D | D | 13 | 28 370 | 462 | 31.6 | 2.6 | 43.1 |
| Hardeman | 358 | 5 261 | 1 352 | D | 577 | 153 | D | 155 | 29 367 | 624 | 23.7 | 9.6 | 30.4 |
| Hardin | 493 | 6 382 | 1 131 | 1 556 | 1 291 | 192 | 92 | 229 | 35 902 | 623 | 37.6 | 8.2 | 31.8 |
| Hawkins | 591 | 8 673 | 1 390 | 3 265 | 1 293 | 217 | 111 | 277 | 31 964 | 1 683 | 48.1 | 1.5 | 43.7 |
| Haywood | 319 | 4 598 | 418 | D | 613 | D | D | 156 | 33 838 | 491 | 33.4 | 18.9 | 43.2 |
| Henderson | 488 | 6 425 | 829 | 1 466 | 1 192 | D | 120 | 183 | 28 407 | 1 017 | 28.9 | 4.8 | 29.0 |
| Henry | 700 | 8 524 | 1 567 | 1 486 | 1 548 | 298 | 242 | 221 | 25 983 | 958 | 30.7 | 7.4 | 40.9 |
| Hickman | 253 | 2 296 | 510 | 560 | 328 | D | D | 64 | 27 692 | 651 | 30.1 | 7.4 | 39.9 |
| Houston | 102 | 1 109 | D | 198 | 159 | D | D | 30 | 27 305 | 382 | 37.2 | 3.4 | 42.1 |
| Humphreys | 337 | 4 118 | 613 | 1 224 | 584 | D | 212 | 168 | 40 903 | 638 | 35.1 | 9.2 | 31.2 |
| Jackson | 82 | 721 | D | D | 110 | 27 | D | 21 | 29 226 | 587 | 38.8 | 4.4 | 37.0 |
| Jefferson | 652 | 9 944 | 1 107 | 1 820 | 1 819 | 244 | 160 | 304 | 30 564 | 1 211 | 53.6 | 1.6 | 40.7 |
| Johnson | 228 | 2 639 | 576 | 458 | 395 | 98 | 57 | 88 | 33 298 | 513 | 49.3 | 1.2 | 37.0 |
| Knox | 10 980 | 199 285 | 34 463 | 11 493 | 29 933 | 9 788 | 9 878 | 7 665 | 38 461 | 1 224 | 61.0 | 1.1 | 40.8 |
| Lake | 77 | 530 | D | NA | 87 | D | D | 12 | 22 389 | 59 | 6.8 | 59.3 | 67.8 |
| Lauderdale | 305 | 4 821 | 594 | 1 093 | 732 | 175 | D | 134 | 27 807 | 602 | 42.2 | 12.3 | 34.2 |
| Lawrence | 706 | 8 214 | 1 314 | 1 634 | 1 510 | D | 200 | 227 | 27 639 | 1 842 | 40.6 | 4.2 | 40.4 |
| Lewis | 196 | 1 688 | 434 | 228 | 405 | D | 41 | 41 | 24 492 | 260 | 39.2 | 5.4 | 36.9 |
| Lincoln | 572 | 6 798 | 908 | 2 262 | 1 256 | 214 | 160 | 216 | 31 707 | 1 782 | 40.8 | 4.7 | 39.2 |
| Loudon | 857 | 12 156 | 1 497 | 3 377 | 1 760 | 363 | 339 | 419 | 34 435 | 768 | 56.4 | 4.3 | 41.3 |
| McMinn | 865 | 15 347 | 2 195 | 4 098 | 2 161 | 559 | 275 | 485 | 31 623 | 1 204 | 50.9 | 2.3 | 41.3 |
| McNairy | 429 | 4 553 | 819 | 1 329 | 716 | 128 | 71 | 136 | 29 927 | 763 | 29.0 | 5.9 | 28.4 |
| Macon | 328 | 3 297 | 618 | 798 | 725 | D | 44 | 94 | 28 558 | 1 066 | 40.8 | 3.4 | 39.6 |
| Madison | 2 547 | 49 652 | 11 475 | 7 688 | 6 912 | 1 186 | 1 150 | 1 714 | 34 518 | 706 | 35.3 | 11.2 | 37.3 |
| Marion | 429 | 5 250 | 826 | 1 252 | 1 074 | 164 | 84 | 161 | 30 621 | 392 | 42.1 | 3.6 | 42.3 |

# Table B. States and Counties — **Agriculture**

| STATE County | Land in farms Acreage (1,000) [117] | Percent change, 2002–2007 [118] | Average size of farm [119] | Total irrigated (1,000) [120] | Total cropland (1,000) [121] | Value of land and buildings Average per farm [122] | Average per acre [123] | Value of machinery and equipment, average per farm (dollars) [124] | Value of products sold Total (mil dol) [125] | Average per farm (dollars) [126] | Percent from: Crops [127] | Livestock and poultry products [128] | Percent of farms with sales of: $10,000 or more [129] | $100,000 or more [130] | Government payments Total ($1,000) [131] | Percent of farms [132] |
|---|---|---|---|---|---|---|---|---|---|---|---|---|---|---|---|---|
| **SOUTH DAKOTA—Cont'd** | | | | | | | | | | | | | | | | |
| Tripp | 1 014 | -3.8 | 1 626 | 3.5 | 440.9 | 1 183 311 | 728 | 150 856 | 136.7 | 219 033 | 32.3 | 67.7 | 76.6 | 42.6 | 3 930 | 77.9 |
| Turner | 371 | 6.6 | 514 | 25.6 | 308.3 | 1 154 468 | 2 244 | 153 032 | 173.4 | 240 225 | 51.3 | 48.7 | 70.6 | 42.8 | 5 054 | 78.4 |
| Union | 279 | 0.7 | 535 | 39.9 | 251.4 | 1 382 073 | 2 582 | 182 970 | 128.2 | 246 075 | 61.7 | 38.3 | 71.8 | 46.4 | 4 762 | 83.7 |
| Walworth | 444 | 4.0 | 1 592 | 2.5 | 238.3 | 1 154 542 | 725 | 163 187 | 54.6 | 195 742 | 65.0 | 35.0 | 55.6 | 38.7 | 3 485 | 68.1 |
| Yankton | 322 | -5.8 | 490 | 10.7 | 249.3 | 965 996 | 1 973 | 140 192 | 123.6 | 187 828 | 55.4 | 44.6 | 68.7 | 40.9 | 3 961 | 79.2 |
| Ziebach | 1 058 | -9.8 | 4 523 | 0.0 | 258.6 | 1 351 815 | 299 | 132 937 | 37.5 | 160 176 | 46.3 | 53.7 | 73.5 | 41.9 | 2 524 | 61.5 |
| **TENNESSEE** | 10 970 | -6.1 | 138 | 81.4 | 6 047.3 | 467 420 | 3 378 | 58 882 | 2 617.4 | 33 015 | 43.9 | 56.1 | 25.2 | 4.8 | 95 744 | 21.8 |
| Anderson | 40 | -16.7 | 75 | 0.1 | 17.0 | 398 508 | 5 342 | 58 265 | 4.4 | 8 224 | 26.1 | 73.9 | 15.8 | 1.1 | 20 | 4.8 |
| Bedford | 231 | 5.5 | 149 | 0.3 | 106.9 | 550 239 | 3 698 | 55 372 | 113.6 | 73 078 | 4.2 | 95.8 | 33.3 | 10.0 | 563 | 16.7 |
| Benton | 73 | -6.4 | 145 | 0.0 | 37.6 | 324 173 | 2 235 | 47 759 | 4.6 | 9 207 | 45.4 | 54.6 | 18.2 | 1.2 | 572 | 40.4 |
| Bledsoe | 92 | -1.1 | 159 | 0.7 | 43.0 | 505 425 | 3 185 | 77 922 | 27.7 | 47 692 | 19.7 | 80.3 | 40.0 | 7.6 | 161 | 18.1 |
| Blount | 98 | -6.7 | 85 | 0.5 | 51.5 | 474 105 | 5 560 | 49 673 | 17.4 | 15 052 | D | D | 20.5 | 2.3 | 103 | 9.9 |
| Bradley | 96 | 1.1 | 100 | 0.1 | 40.5 | 478 879 | 4 804 | 54 985 | 98.5 | 102 671 | 4.2 | 95.8 | 28.5 | 12.2 | 140 | 7.4 |
| Campbell | 34 | 0.0 | 85 | D | 14.9 | 293 806 | 3 473 | 53 708 | 2.9 | 7 121 | 23.8 | 76.2 | 15.6 | 0.5 | 10 | 5.9 |
| Cannon | 117 | -4.1 | 133 | 0.1 | 48.6 | 428 757 | 3 233 | 50 431 | 13.5 | 15 391 | 36.3 | 63.7 | 24.8 | 3.3 | 361 | 18.8 |
| Carroll | 180 | -1.6 | 185 | 0.7 | 122.0 | 470 286 | 2 541 | 56 702 | 27.9 | 28 749 | 86.9 | 13.1 | 19.5 | 4.8 | 3 200 | 56.7 |
| Carter | 39 | 5.4 | 76 | 0.1 | 18.3 | 308 364 | 4 041 | 47 616 | 6.0 | 11 632 | 25.3 | 74.7 | 21.9 | 1.4 | 34 | 8.7 |
| Cheatham | 63 | -12.5 | 114 | 0.3 | 30.3 | 467 056 | 4 099 | 54 389 | 8.4 | 15 211 | 64.3 | 35.7 | 24.9 | 3.4 | 43 | 7.9 |
| Chester | 72 | -8.9 | 148 | 0.1 | 36.4 | 361 531 | 2 441 | 50 367 | 5.0 | 10 262 | 58.6 | 41.4 | 18.6 | 2.5 | 834 | 58.9 |
| Claiborne | 125 | -7.4 | 114 | 0.0 | 44.0 | 355 675 | 3 108 | 45 003 | 13.1 | 11 981 | 12.2 | 87.8 | 21.1 | 1.3 | 81 | 13.7 |
| Clay | 78 | 11.4 | 168 | D | 31.5 | 415 764 | 2 470 | 59 611 | 34.7 | 75 080 | 2.9 | 97.1 | 33.8 | 7.6 | 267 | 23.4 |
| Cocke | 64 | -12.3 | 91 | 0.5 | 27.6 | 343 441 | 3 774 | 54 145 | 22.2 | 31 541 | 29.5 | 70.5 | 22.4 | 3.3 | 154 | 8.1 |
| Coffee | 140 | -3.4 | 139 | D | 83.8 | 486 522 | 3 504 | 64 689 | 37.4 | 37 092 | 39.2 | 60.8 | 27.0 | 6.1 | 712 | 17.4 |
| Crockett | 149 | 2.8 | 318 | 3.3 | 134.0 | 742 358 | 2 338 | 113 304 | 31.1 | 66 064 | 93.8 | 6.2 | 32.8 | 14.9 | 6 749 | 79.6 |
| Cumberland | 123 | 11.8 | 146 | 0.4 | 54.3 | 510 586 | 3 508 | 72 559 | 42.0 | 49 916 | 22.2 | 77.8 | 26.5 | 3.0 | 165 | 11.9 |
| Davidson | 41 | -19.6 | 80 | 0.5 | 17.4 | 499 368 | 6 219 | 46 450 | 11.6 | 22 464 | 84.2 | 15.8 | 12.4 | 1.6 | 18 | 3.1 |
| Decatur | 76 | -13.6 | 168 | 0.4 | 33.1 | 353 247 | 2 104 | 46 646 | 5.9 | 13 017 | 22.2 | 77.8 | 25.3 | 2.0 | 223 | 31.0 |
| DeKalb | 95 | -5.0 | 132 | 1.1 | 38.7 | 419 666 | 3 179 | 51 939 | 72.0 | 99 752 | 91.7 | 8.3 | 28.9 | 4.4 | 147 | 19.3 |
| Dickson | 139 | -12.0 | 108 | 0.3 | 55.3 | 367 318 | 3 391 | 47 953 | 13.5 | 10 470 | 25.3 | 74.7 | 20.2 | 1.2 | 112 | 10.4 |
| Dyer | 239 | 12.2 | 409 | 10.6 | 218.9 | 1 124 138 | 2 751 | 119 717 | 61.8 | 105 847 | 95.4 | 4.6 | 42.6 | 18.5 | 5 688 | 67.6 |
| Fayette | 227 | -17.2 | 239 | 2.2 | 154.6 | 771 945 | 3 231 | 78 232 | 35.2 | 36 975 | 77.1 | 22.9 | 22.9 | 7.4 | 5 812 | 48.9 |
| Fentress | 84 | 5.0 | 135 | 0.0 | 34.3 | 473 001 | 3 493 | 65 409 | 49.8 | 79 914 | 6.0 | 94.0 | 33.1 | 10.1 | 214 | 23.6 |
| Franklin | 144 | -5.9 | 131 | 1.7 | 93.1 | 487 683 | 3 732 | 73 098 | 78.7 | 71 312 | 24.4 | 75.6 | 34.1 | 10.8 | 1 422 | 26.4 |
| Gibson | 287 | -7.7 | 273 | 2.2 | 250.3 | 699 824 | 2 560 | 87 456 | 71.7 | 68 329 | 88.8 | 11.2 | 31.8 | 11.2 | 7 852 | 68.8 |
| Giles | 261 | -3.7 | 146 | 1.3 | 104.0 | 462 339 | 3 164 | 52 670 | 32.1 | 17 917 | 20.0 | 80.0 | 27.7 | 2.7 | 1 165 | 27.6 |
| Grainger | 92 | -10.7 | 91 | 0.4 | 39.8 | 345 012 | 3 964 | 45 819 | 17.3 | 17 175 | 43.9 | 56.2 | 25.3 | 2.2 | 64 | 7.6 |
| Greene | 229 | -7.3 | 75 | 0.4 | 118.6 | 319 705 | 4 270 | 52 619 | 76.7 | 25 065 | 10.1 | 89.9 | 20.8 | 3.5 | 557 | 12.6 |
| Grundy | 43 | 2.4 | 130 | 0.7 | 22.1 | 421 717 | 3 242 | 65 141 | 34.4 | 104 769 | 26.7 | 73.3 | 35.7 | 17.7 | 75 | 5.5 |
| Hamblen | 69 | 19.0 | 97 | D | 38.9 | 370 033 | 3 813 | 51 491 | 29.4 | 41 173 | D | D | 20.6 | 3.6 | 61 | 7.6 |
| Hamilton | 55 | -12.7 | 82 | 0.1 | 22.5 | 443 871 | 5 439 | 53 761 | 9.2 | 13 825 | 24.6 | 75.4 | 15.2 | 1.9 | 32 | 3.6 |
| Hancock | 61 | -4.7 | 131 | 0.0 | 23.1 | 387 894 | 2 955 | 42 371 | 7.0 | 15 110 | 10.3 | 89.7 | 27.1 | 1.9 | 42 | 13.2 |
| Hardeman | 148 | -3.9 | 237 | D | 78.7 | 587 967 | 2 480 | 49 151 | 14.0 | 22 471 | 68.4 | 31.6 | 19.7 | 5.0 | 3 145 | 61.5 |
| Hardin | 110 | -1.8 | 176 | 1.0 | 63.5 | 449 058 | 2 549 | 50 904 | 11.2 | 17 898 | 67.2 | 32.8 | 21.7 | 4.5 | 1 156 | 42.4 |
| Hawkins | 151 | -10.1 | 90 | 0.2 | 56.3 | 326 463 | 3 638 | 45 112 | 18.7 | 11 084 | 22.5 | 77.5 | 20.0 | 1.2 | 194 | 13.3 |
| Haywood | 214 | 1.4 | 437 | 5.2 | 196.3 | 1 056 476 | 2 420 | 143 687 | 46.0 | 93 765 | 96.6 | 3.4 | 33.0 | 17.7 | 8 558 | 77.6 |
| Henderson | 165 | -4.6 | 163 | 0.2 | 86.2 | 380 482 | 2 339 | 50 442 | 19.5 | 19 160 | 43.8 | 56.2 | 24.9 | 3.4 | 1 762 | 55.2 |
| Henry | 193 | -0.5 | 202 | 1.7 | 126.5 | 547 644 | 2 713 | 70 034 | 54.7 | 57 113 | 48.6 | 51.4 | 29.6 | 8.9 | 1 885 | 52.9 |
| Hickman | 112 | -13.2 | 172 | 0.1 | 43.7 | 471 801 | 2 738 | 48 760 | 9.8 | 15 105 | 24.6 | 75.4 | 28.1 | 2.0 | 173 | 17.2 |
| Houston | 47 | -4.1 | 124 | D | 18.4 | 298 207 | 2 414 | 40 494 | 4.4 | 11 557 | 7.8 | 92.2 | 18.1 | 1.6 | 24 | 11.3 |
| Humphreys | 118 | -12.6 | 186 | 0.0 | 52.7 | 477 999 | 2 575 | 69 275 | 9.6 | 15 034 | 39.2 | 60.8 | 27.4 | 3.0 | 243 | 12.5 |
| Jackson | 76 | -3.8 | 129 | 0.1 | 27.9 | 350 839 | 2 723 | 45 516 | 5.1 | 8 664 | 25.9 | 74.1 | 21.1 | 0.5 | 64 | 12.3 |
| Jefferson | 102 | -5.6 | 84 | D | 49.2 | 392 469 | 4 679 | 50 058 | 29.3 | 24 214 | 19.9 | 80.1 | 21.2 | 2.3 | 123 | 8.5 |
| Johnson | 44 | -10.2 | 85 | 0.0 | 18.1 | 370 818 | 4 369 | 51 716 | 5.6 | 10 997 | 34.1 | 65.9 | 18.7 | 1.6 | 32 | 6.6 |
| Knox | 83 | -11.7 | 68 | 0.5 | 35.1 | 438 547 | 6 472 | 49 922 | 19.4 | 15 832 | 61.8 | 38.2 | 13.2 | 1.1 | 102 | 4.2 |
| Lake | 84 | -6.7 | 1 425 | 5.5 | 81.1 | 3 936 558 | 2 762 | 355 817 | 25.8 | 437 818 | 99.8 | 0.2 | 96.6 | 61.0 | 2 169 | 91.5 |
| Lauderdale | 192 | -10.7 | 319 | 4.9 | 162.7 | 696 984 | 2 183 | 85 066 | 44.0 | 73 126 | 94.7 | 5.3 | 24.4 | 10.6 | 5 356 | 68.4 |
| Lawrence | 238 | 0.8 | 129 | 0.5 | 120.9 | 401 150 | 3 101 | 51 422 | 45.5 | 24 726 | 25.8 | 74.2 | 29.6 | 4.5 | 2 059 | 35.0 |
| Lewis | 36 | -2.7 | 137 | D | 14.0 | 391 603 | 2 863 | 42 361 | 2.6 | 10 031 | 12.3 | 87.7 | 22.3 | 1.2 | 27 | 16.5 |
| Lincoln | 261 | -8.1 | 146 | 3.1 | 117.9 | 503 358 | 3 438 | 60 944 | 57.8 | 32 439 | 29.1 | 70.9 | 30.8 | 4.3 | 1 400 | 17.5 |
| Loudon | 77 | -7.2 | 100 | 0.2 | 39.3 | 495 878 | 4 943 | 86 645 | 60.2 | 78 427 | D | D | 21.9 | 3.0 | 159 | 15.2 |
| McMinn | 123 | -3.9 | 102 | 0.3 | 56.4 | 409 461 | 4 024 | 54 646 | 48.4 | 40 237 | 4.8 | 95.2 | 24.5 | 5.8 | 177 | 8.7 |
| McNairy | 123 | -8.2 | 161 | 0.7 | 68.3 | 355 340 | 2 209 | 51 034 | 12.0 | 15 771 | 73.6 | 26.4 | 18.2 | 3.5 | 1 587 | 62.8 |
| Macon | 128 | -11.7 | 120 | 0.1 | 55.4 | 391 972 | 3 269 | 47 359 | 22.8 | 21 374 | 45.7 | 54.3 | 25.9 | 4.1 | 228 | 18.0 |
| Madison | 177 | 9.3 | 251 | 1.5 | 134.4 | 702 495 | 2 801 | 80 584 | 28.2 | 39 885 | 81.2 | 18.8 | 21.7 | 7.9 | 5 548 | 65.3 |
| Marion | 51 | 0.0 | 129 | 0.1 | 24.7 | 468 342 | 3 629 | 61 859 | 20.3 | 51 762 | 11.4 | 88.6 | 23.0 | 7.1 | 115 | 10.2 |

# Table B. States and Counties — Water Use, Wholesale Trade, Retail Trade, and Real Estate

| STATE County | Water use, 2005 | | Wholesale trade,[1] 2007 | | | | Retail trade,[2] 2007 | | | | Real estate and rental and leasing,[2] 2007 | | | |
|---|---|---|---|---|---|---|---|---|---|---|---|---|---|---|
| | Total water withdrawn (mil gal/day) | Gallons withdrawn per person | Number of establishments | Number of employees | Sales (mil dol) | Annual payroll (mil dol) | Number of establishments | Number of employees | Sales (mil dol) | Annual payroll (mil dol) | Number of establishments | Number of employees | Receipts (mil dol) | Annual payroll (mil dol) |
| | 133 | 134 | 135 | 136 | 137 | 138 | 139 | 140 | 141 | 142 | 143 | 144 | 145 | 146 |
| **SOUTH DAKOTA—Cont'd** | | | | | | | | | | | | | | |
| Tripp | 6.1 | 999 | 12 | 142 | 70.4 | 4.2 | 48 | 411 | 88.4 | 7.3 | 5 | 4 | 0.7 | 0.1 |
| Turner | 20.7 | 2 434 | 17 | 119 | 166.6 | 4.1 | 43 | 302 | 52.4 | 4.4 | 1 | D | D | D |
| Union | 18.6 | 1 383 | 24 | D | D | D | 46 | 541 | 304.2 | 12.4 | 17 | 36 | 8.0 | 1.6 |
| Walworth | 7.3 | 1 321 | 9 | 69 | 107.0 | 2.6 | 49 | 411 | 74.8 | 6.0 | 4 | 13 | 0.8 | 0.1 |
| Yankton | 19.4 | 891 | 32 | D | D | D | 138 | 1 559 | 293.0 | 29.5 | 22 | 87 | 8.3 | 1.5 |
| Ziebach | 0.5 | 182 | 3 | D | D | D | 4 | D | D | D | NA | NA | NA | NA |
| **TENNESSEE** | 10 838.3 | 1 818 | 6 282 | 99 238 | 80 116.5 | 4 593.4 | 24 234 | 320 739 | 77 547.3 | 7 244.6 | 6 087 | 37 737 | 6 950.4 | 1 243.0 |
| Anderson | 570.2 | 7 873 | 37 | 269 | 208.3 | 11.8 | 268 | 3 457 | 907.8 | 78.4 | 64 | 309 | 42.3 | 7.3 |
| Bedford | 26.3 | 623 | 25 | D | D | D | 156 | 1 508 | 340.6 | 31.6 | 29 | 156 | 23.1 | 4.7 |
| Benton | 2.5 | 152 | 10 | 82 | 35.2 | 2.5 | 69 | 644 | 136.8 | 12.0 | 9 | 25 | 2.4 | 0.4 |
| Bledsoe | 1.9 | 145 | 3 | 9 | 3.4 | 0.2 | 21 | 134 | 30.5 | 2.0 | 2 | D | D | D |
| Blount | 14.6 | 127 | 80 | 1 069 | 898.0 | 49.1 | 407 | 6 236 | 1 551.1 | 152.4 | 93 | 354 | 70.0 | 9.9 |
| Bradley | 18.2 | 197 | 60 | D | D | D | 396 | 4 673 | 1 164.6 | 107.3 | 82 | 461 | 88.0 | 12.4 |
| Campbell | 4.6 | 114 | 20 | 329 | 134.4 | 8.7 | 147 | 1 562 | 361.8 | 31.5 | 18 | 123 | 11.1 | 2.2 |
| Cannon | 1.8 | 138 | 4 | D | D | D | 33 | 268 | 53.6 | 5.6 | 7 | 22 | 2.6 | 0.2 |
| Carroll | 5.4 | 187 | 15 | 280 | 71.8 | 7.0 | 104 | 950 | 188.9 | 16.7 | 16 | 44 | 7.1 | 0.9 |
| Carter | 21.7 | 369 | 13 | 76 | 35.0 | 3.3 | 154 | 1 806 | 461.3 | 37.4 | 29 | 100 | 12.5 | 1.9 |
| Cheatham | 3.4 | 88 | 17 | 59 | 33.8 | 2.0 | 80 | 1 010 | 238.8 | 20.1 | 19 | 49 | 8.7 | 1.1 |
| Chester | 2.0 | 127 | 12 | 66 | 24.4 | 1.7 | 55 | 450 | 117.7 | 9.9 | 7 | 22 | 1.6 | 0.3 |
| Claiborne | 4.4 | 140 | 11 | 77 | 26.0 | 2.0 | 93 | 820 | 155.9 | 14.4 | 24 | 75 | 16.5 | 1.6 |
| Clay | 13.7 | 1 709 | 3 | D | D | D | 25 | 149 | 37.3 | 2.9 | 7 | 28 | 2.3 | 0.9 |
| Cocke | 5.4 | 154 | 9 | D | D | D | 122 | 1 430 | 326.9 | 28.0 | 24 | 119 | 8.5 | 2.0 |
| Coffee | 32.1 | 632 | 41 | 425 | 196.6 | 17.4 | 272 | 3 148 | 790.8 | 68.5 | 45 | 184 | 21.3 | 3.8 |
| Crockett | 3.5 | 242 | 11 | 158 | 112.1 | 5.9 | 48 | 262 | 65.0 | 4.2 | 3 | 6 | 1.0 | 0.1 |
| Cumberland | 6.5 | 126 | 37 | D | D | D | 252 | 2 531 | 597.0 | 51.9 | 56 | 279 | 32.5 | 6.2 |
| Davidson | 160.7 | 279 | 1 009 | 20 028 | 11 942.6 | 983.6 | 2 795 | 42 241 | 10 581.8 | 1 046.2 | 934 | 6 617 | 1 588.0 | 252.2 |
| Decatur | 2.2 | 189 | 3 | D | D | D | 56 | 433 | 98.9 | 9.8 | 5 | 6 | 0.4 | 0.1 |
| DeKalb | 2.2 | 123 | 7 | 47 | 8.5 | 1.5 | 63 | 551 | 119.4 | 10.8 | 10 | 22 | 2.5 | 0.4 |
| Dickson | 5.7 | 125 | 26 | 413 | 327.9 | 17.1 | 198 | 2 394 | 605.9 | 51.8 | 36 | 130 | 18.7 | 2.3 |
| Dyer | 15.8 | 417 | 41 | 315 | 252.5 | 11.1 | 191 | 2 187 | 514.1 | 47.7 | 36 | 89 | 15.1 | 3.2 |
| Fayette | 5.6 | 162 | 27 | 161 | 74.4 | 6.3 | 82 | 580 | 126.6 | 11.8 | 23 | 49 | 5.8 | 0.8 |
| Fentress | 2.2 | 126 | 3 | D | D | D | 68 | 687 | 140.5 | 13.0 | 6 | 101 | 15.2 | 3.1 |
| Franklin | 7.3 | 178 | 18 | D | D | D | 156 | 1 471 | 343.6 | 31.4 | 21 | 98 | 11.4 | 2.0 |
| Gibson | 10.4 | 215 | 39 | D | D | D | 207 | 2 054 | 439.0 | 38.8 | 32 | 101 | 11.5 | 2.5 |
| Giles | 4.7 | 160 | 22 | 311 | 112.9 | 13.4 | 126 | 1 300 | 313.3 | 27.1 | 15 | 73 | 6.4 | 1.4 |
| Grainger | 4.6 | 204 | 5 | 37 | 8.6 | 0.5 | 53 | 371 | 79.5 | 5.9 | 6 | 13 | 1.1 | 0.2 |
| Greene | 12.5 | 191 | 42 | D | D | D | 217 | 2 900 | 682.0 | 61.1 | 41 | 156 | 23.6 | 3.4 |
| Grundy | 2.3 | 154 | 3 | D | D | D | 49 | 324 | 67.5 | 5.5 | 3 | 17 | 1.0 | 0.1 |
| Hamblen | 9.9 | 165 | 59 | 1 370 | 591.7 | 57.0 | 307 | 4 199 | 1 055.0 | 91.8 | 57 | 268 | 41.6 | 6.3 |
| Hamilton | 1 648.6 | 5 302 | 497 | 5 989 | 2 958.5 | 268.0 | 1 500 | 20 722 | 4 865.7 | 467.7 | 403 | 2 354 | 367.5 | 100.3 |
| Hancock | 0.8 | 112 | 1 | D | D | D | 18 | 182 | 24.4 | 2.9 | 2 | D | D | D |
| Hardeman | 3.9 | 137 | 19 | 148 | 42.1 | 3.6 | 80 | 723 | 158.8 | 13.7 | 6 | 32 | 2.7 | 0.6 |
| Hardin | 27.7 | 1 067 | 22 | 124 | 79.7 | 4.7 | 130 | 1 129 | 313.7 | 25.9 | 24 | 59 | 8.4 | 1.7 |
| Hawkins | 700.7 | 12 469 | 14 | D | D | D | 124 | 1 356 | 286.9 | 24.7 | 26 | 75 | 6.8 | 1.5 |
| Haywood | 3.9 | 198 | 18 | 91 | 74.2 | 2.7 | 61 | 676 | 180.6 | 12.6 | 10 | 29 | 2.4 | 0.7 |
| Henderson | 3.8 | 143 | 19 | 135 | 31.8 | 3.6 | 116 | 1 082 | 279.6 | 21.7 | 11 | 24 | 3.6 | 0.5 |
| Henry | 5.8 | 182 | 32 | D | D | D | 163 | 1 658 | 404.2 | 35.9 | 26 | 83 | 10.0 | 1.7 |
| Hickman | 3.2 | 136 | 10 | D | D | D | 52 | 296 | 76.9 | 6.1 | 10 | D | D | D |
| Houston | 1.3 | 166 | NA | NA | NA | NA | 26 | 156 | 33.4 | 2.7 | 3 | 8 | 0.9 | 0.2 |
| Humphreys | 1 292.7 | 70 979 | 12 | 138 | 57.2 | 4.4 | 69 | 635 | 181.9 | 12.6 | 10 | 37 | 2.0 | 0.6 |
| Jackson | 1.0 | 90 | 5 | 37 | 7.2 | 0.9 | 26 | 116 | 27.8 | 1.7 | 1 | D | D | D |
| Jefferson | 6.9 | 142 | 17 | 101 | 35.3 | 3.9 | 145 | 1 650 | 554.3 | 35.6 | 34 | 106 | 11.2 | 1.5 |
| Johnson | 2.8 | 152 | 3 | D | D | D | 56 | 453 | 93.2 | 7.9 | 17 | 39 | 3.9 | 0.4 |
| Knox | 68.6 | 169 | 699 | 10 084 | 7 402.5 | 474.4 | 1 904 | 33 315 | 8 209.4 | 794.3 | 542 | 3 195 | 624.4 | 103.4 |
| Lake | 5.2 | 688 | 4 | D | D | D | 23 | 103 | 19.5 | 1.9 | 3 | 9 | 0.8 | 0.1 |
| Lauderdale | 6.6 | 247 | 19 | 520 | 829.7 | 23.5 | 82 | 809 | 151.8 | 14.3 | 16 | 34 | 4.5 | 1.0 |
| Lawrence | 7.5 | 183 | 39 | D | D | D | 181 | 1 587 | 381.0 | 33.5 | 26 | 95 | 9.3 | 1.7 |
| Lewis | 1.8 | 158 | 5 | D | D | D | 49 | 460 | 132.8 | 9.2 | 7 | 21 | 2.1 | 0.4 |
| Lincoln | 7.9 | 245 | 22 | 244 | 147.5 | 8.7 | 148 | 1 396 | 366.5 | 31.8 | 22 | 110 | 10.6 | 2.6 |
| Loudon | 16.9 | 390 | 44 | 610 | 360.6 | 17.1 | 141 | 1 714 | 435.6 | 35.3 | 36 | 104 | 15.8 | 2.4 |
| McMinn | 71.5 | 1 393 | 33 | D | D | D | 201 | 2 334 | 561.3 | 49.6 | 30 | 106 | 15.9 | 2.2 |
| McNairy | 4.3 | 170 | 13 | 99 | 45.7 | 5.2 | 107 | 788 | 194.7 | 14.0 | 11 | 54 | 10.3 | 1.4 |
| Macon | 3.2 | 149 | 10 | 111 | 30.4 | 2.5 | 72 | 738 | 167.3 | 15.0 | 20 | 39 | 4.4 | 0.5 |
| Madison | 20.0 | 211 | 154 | 2 008 | 1 160.4 | 84.0 | 509 | 7 057 | 1 696.5 | 153.0 | 108 | 765 | 101.1 | 19.3 |
| Marion | 5.3 | 190 | 23 | D | D | D | 109 | 1 194 | 286.6 | 24.1 | 14 | 32 | 2.8 | 0.5 |

1. Merchant wholesalers, except manufacturers' sales branches and offices.  2. Employer establishments.

# Table B. States and Counties — Professional Services, Manufacturing, and Accommodation and Food Services

| STATE County | Professional, scientific, and technical services,[1] 2007 | | | | Manufacturing, 2007 | | | | Accommodation and food services, 2007 | | | |
|---|---|---|---|---|---|---|---|---|---|---|---|---|
| | Number of establishments | Number of employees | Receipts (mil dol) | Annual payroll (mil dol) | Number of establishments | Number of employees | Receipts (mil dol) | Annual payroll (mil dol) | Number of establishments | Number of employees | Sales (mil dol) | Annual payroll (mil dol) |
| | 147 | 148 | 149 | 150 | 151 | 152 | 153 | 154 | 155 | 156 | 157 | 158 |
| **SOUTH DAKOTA—Cont'd** | | | | | | | | | | | | |
| Tripp | 16 | 53 | 6.1 | 1.5 | NA | NA | NA | NA | 25 | 208 | 8.1 | 2.0 |
| Turner | 11 | D | D | D | NA | NA | NA | NA | 18 | 90 | 2.2 | 0.5 |
| Union | 36 | D | D | D | 26 | D | D | 55.7 | 40 | 459 | 19.7 | 4.2 |
| Walworth | 16 | 101 | 7.1 | 2.2 | NA | NA | NA | NA | 31 | 370 | 19.8 | 5.3 |
| Yankton | 42 | 205 | 23.2 | 7.8 | 30 | 2 710 | 635.2 | 91.7 | 71 | 1 068 | 34.5 | 9.2 |
| Ziebach | NA | NA | NA | NA | NA | NA | NA | NA | 2 | D | D | D |
| **TENNESSEE** | 11 278 | D | D | D | 6 752 | 369 165 | 140 447.8 | 15 165.6 | 11 592 | 239 379 | 10 626.8 | 3 009.2 |
| Anderson | 219 | D | D | D | 114 | 9 827 | 1 911.2 | 543.9 | 126 | 3 030 | 126.6 | 35.9 |
| Bedford | 49 | 252 | 21.3 | 6.7 | 54 | 4 805 | 1 047.3 | 177.0 | 58 | 863 | 35.3 | 9.5 |
| Benton | 20 | 55 | 4.2 | 1.2 | 21 | 629 | 82.3 | 17.3 | 30 | 395 | 13.3 | 3.0 |
| Bledsoe | 5 | D | D | D | NA | NA | NA | NA | 10 | 107 | 3.5 | 0.8 |
| Blount | 186 | D | D | D | 125 | 7 527 | 5 312.3 | 375.7 | 209 | 4 739 | 208.5 | 63.7 |
| Bradley | 151 | D | D | D | 131 | 9 540 | D | D | 164 | 3 211 | 130.5 | 35.7 |
| Campbell | 28 | 120 | 10.9 | 4.0 | 39 | 1 737 | 333.9 | 64.2 | 54 | 901 | 35.4 | 9.3 |
| Cannon | 11 | D | D | D | NA | NA | NA | NA | 10 | 190 | 7.1 | 1.6 |
| Carroll | 28 | D | D | D | 37 | 1 640 | 767.0 | 58.6 | 39 | 448 | 15.4 | 3.6 |
| Carter | 41 | D | D | D | 42 | 1 880 | 296.7 | D | 67 | 1 151 | 41.9 | 12.1 |
| Cheatham | 47 | 161 | 18.8 | 5.3 | 37 | 2 198 | 754.9 | 86.3 | 44 | 580 | 23.3 | 5.6 |
| Chester | 16 | D | D | D | NA | NA | NA | NA | 21 | 293 | 11.6 | 3.3 |
| Claiborne | 22 | 83 | 6.0 | 2.1 | 35 | 2 880 | 436.2 | 79.4 | 27 | 576 | 21.6 | 5.9 |
| Clay | 5 | D | D | D | NA | NA | NA | NA | 11 | 73 | 4.0 | 1.0 |
| Cocke | 28 | D | D | D | 38 | 1 542 | 601.3 | 64.8 | 67 | 998 | 44.3 | 12.4 |
| Coffee | 87 | D | D | D | 77 | 5 036 | D | 201.5 | 102 | 2 204 | 79.3 | 23.3 |
| Crockett | 10 | 35 | 6.6 | 1.3 | NA | NA | NA | NA | 10 | 122 | 7.0 | 1.2 |
| Cumberland | 74 | 307 | 26.5 | 8.8 | 56 | 2 163 | 468.9 | 80.9 | 91 | 1 297 | 61.7 | 16.0 |
| Davidson | 1 912 | 23 798 | 2 943.3 | 1 285.4 | 633 | 23 715 | 7 347.2 | 999.0 | 1 605 | 38 979 | 2 203.0 | 626.4 |
| Decatur | 18 | 84 | 9.2 | 1.5 | 27 | 765 | D | 24.0 | 21 | 176 | 6.0 | 1.5 |
| DeKalb | 26 | 97 | 6.8 | 2.7 | 29 | 2 873 | 743.8 | 97.4 | 28 | 307 | 12.1 | 3.1 |
| Dickson | 59 | 244 | 23.9 | 8.7 | 56 | 3 805 | 876.6 | 141.8 | 95 | 1 527 | 60.5 | 17.7 |
| Dyer | 48 | D | D | D | 45 | 5 251 | 1 647.0 | 189.0 | 70 | 1 107 | 42.8 | 11.4 |
| Fayette | 40 | 261 | 17.2 | 8.0 | 49 | 2 337 | 889.8 | 92.7 | 39 | 355 | 12.6 | 3.3 |
| Fentress | 17 | 75 | 4.8 | 1.0 | NA | NA | NA | NA | 23 | 272 | 8.2 | 2.2 |
| Franklin | 43 | D | D | D | 46 | D | 3 187.1 | D | 51 | 971 | 28.0 | 8.7 |
| Gibson | 53 | 247 | 17.7 | 5.6 | 68 | 3 910 | 977.4 | 147.6 | 71 | 879 | 30.8 | 7.8 |
| Giles | 32 | 130 | 10.7 | 3.6 | 48 | 2 710 | 1 004.2 | 99.5 | 49 | 632 | 24.9 | 5.8 |
| Grainger | 10 | D | D | D | 29 | 912 | 171.3 | 28.5 | 13 | 150 | 6.1 | 1.1 |
| Greene | 83 | D | D | D | 109 | 6 613 | 1 814.0 | 225.1 | 100 | 1 681 | 62.0 | 18.0 |
| Grundy | 10 | D | D | D | NA | NA | NA | NA | 15 | 262 | 9.8 | 2.4 |
| Hamblen | 80 | D | D | D | 117 | 12 923 | 3 214.0 | 453.8 | 107 | 2 342 | 91.3 | 26.3 |
| Hamilton | 783 | D | D | D | 478 | 26 947 | 8 040.6 | 1 125.0 | 763 | 15 719 | 663.3 | 196.0 |
| Hancock | 3 | D | D | D | NA | NA | NA | NA | 3 | 42 | 1.4 | 0.3 |
| Hardeman | 11 | 42 | 4.2 | 0.8 | 27 | 1 913 | 423.7 | 54.8 | 32 | 370 | 15.6 | 3.7 |
| Hardin | 33 | 96 | 7.0 | 2.4 | 43 | 1 678 | 691.8 | 80.9 | 52 | 626 | 28.7 | 7.6 |
| Hawkins | 35 | 103 | 9.6 | 2.5 | 49 | 4 154 | 1 148.7 | 144.2 | 62 | 852 | 31.7 | 8.9 |
| Haywood | 19 | D | D | D | 21 | 2 761 | 631.5 | 89.4 | 35 | 414 | 13.9 | 3.6 |
| Henderson | 31 | 222 | 8.7 | 2.8 | 42 | 1 588 | 566.7 | 59.5 | 38 | 579 | 20.9 | 5.6 |
| Henry | 42 | 239 | 16.0 | 7.0 | 46 | 1 695 | D | D | 64 | 1 054 | 29.4 | 8.4 |
| Hickman | 10 | 37 | 3.3 | 1.0 | 35 | 666 | D | 21.0 | 27 | 219 | 7.1 | 1.8 |
| Houston | 5 | D | D | D | NA | NA | NA | NA | 13 | 93 | 2.7 | 0.7 |
| Humphreys | 18 | 73 | 6.7 | 3.0 | 23 | 1 301 | 1 052.9 | 81.1 | 40 | 441 | 17.8 | 4.1 |
| Jackson | 6 | D | D | D | NA | NA | NA | NA | 11 | 78 | 2.6 | 0.7 |
| Jefferson | 40 | 264 | 14.6 | 6.1 | 48 | 2 682 | 862.9 | 84.0 | 72 | 1 329 | 48.3 | 13.6 |
| Johnson | 15 | 36 | 3.9 | 1.1 | 18 | 603 | 118.2 | 22.4 | 25 | 210 | 6.6 | 1.9 |
| Knox | 1 265 | D | D | D | 452 | 14 456 | 4 470.9 | 601.7 | 890 | 21 308 | 919.2 | 273.6 |
| Lake | 4 | D | D | D | NA | NA | NA | NA | 13 | 174 | 5.9 | 1.6 |
| Lauderdale | 18 | 30 | 3.4 | 0.9 | 16 | 2 281 | 372.9 | 70.0 | 20 | 318 | 9.7 | 3.0 |
| Lawrence | 45 | 231 | 18.3 | 6.1 | 55 | 2 015 | D | 67.9 | 51 | 1 007 | 37.4 | 9.1 |
| Lewis | 16 | D | D | D | NA | NA | NA | NA | 18 | 232 | 8.0 | 2.2 |
| Lincoln | 41 | 148 | 15.9 | 4.1 | 42 | 2 680 | D | 87.5 | 45 | 649 | 26.2 | 5.6 |
| Loudon | 57 | D | D | D | 57 | 3 361 | 1 502.3 | 144.5 | 71 | 1 325 | 50.8 | 16.1 |
| McMinn | 53 | D | D | D | 73 | 6 792 | 2 381.0 | 317.2 | 83 | 1 499 | 57.5 | 16.4 |
| McNairy | 19 | D | D | D | 44 | 1 903 | 420.9 | 68.5 | 37 | 472 | 13.1 | 3.9 |
| Macon | 23 | 67 | 5.6 | 1.7 | 34 | 917 | D | 29.6 | 23 | 282 | 11.9 | 2.7 |
| Madison | 190 | D | D | D | 116 | 9 613 | D | D | 214 | 5 487 | 204.9 | 55.2 |
| Marion | 27 | D | D | D | 26 | 1 089 | D | 37.0 | 57 | 786 | 32.7 | 9.1 |

1. Establishment subject to federal tax.

# Table B. States and Counties — Health Care and Social Assistance, Other Services, and Federal Funds

| STATE County | Health care and social assistance, 2007 | | | | Other services, 2007 | | | | Federal funds and grants, 2009–2010 Expenditures (mil dol) | | | |
|---|---|---|---|---|---|---|---|---|---|---|---|---|
| | | | | | | | | | | Direct payments for individuals[1] | | |
| | Number of establishments | Number of employees | Receipts (mil dol) | Annual payroll (mil dol) | Number of establishments | Number of employees | Receipts (mil dol) | Annual payroll (mil dol) | Total | Social Security and government retirement | Medicare | Food Stamps and Supplemental Security Income |
| | 159 | 160 | 161 | 162 | 163 | 164 | 165 | 166 | 167 | 168 | 169 | 170 |
| SOUTH DAKOTA—Cont'd | | | | | | | | | | | | |
| Tripp | 24 | 416 | 23.8 | 10.0 | 14 | 35 | 3.0 | 0.7 | 54.1 | 18.6 | 10.1 | 2.9 |
| Turner | 23 | 456 | 19.7 | 10.0 | 14 | D | D | D | 65.1 | 28.8 | 14.1 | 1.4 |
| Union | 49 | D | D | D | 32 | 147 | 8.4 | 2.8 | 362.9 | 42.4 | 20.2 | 1.9 |
| Walworth | 11 | 363 | 21.1 | 9.1 | 19 | 82 | 4.9 | 1.4 | 53.5 | 17.2 | 7.8 | 2.6 |
| Yankton | 67 | 1 777 | 158.2 | 65.2 | 57 | 231 | 16.6 | 3.9 | 171.0 | 67.1 | 31.9 | 4.5 |
| Ziebach | 2 | D | D | D | 1 | D | D | D | 20.8 | 3.0 | 1.3 | 2.8 |
| TENNESSEE | 14 267 | 337 741 | 33 799.9 | 13 093.2 | 8 811 | 62 425 | 6 338.7 | 1 681.0 | 68 865.5 | 20 061.6 | 13 284.1 | 3 020.5 |
| Anderson | 189 | 4 039 | 374.3 | 150.2 | 130 | 683 | 158.7 | 17.7 | 4 611.2 | 334.0 | 191.0 | 40.0 |
| Bedford | 86 | 1 078 | 72.8 | 28.3 | 46 | 196 | 17.7 | 4.6 | 276.0 | 127.0 | 71.7 | 11.9 |
| Benton | 40 | 784 | 38.6 | 14.9 | 21 | 80 | 6.0 | 2.0 | 176.0 | 78.0 | 52.2 | 8.5 |
| Bledsoe | 11 | 126 | 6.5 | 2.8 | 2 | D | D | D | 109.3 | 34.0 | 32.2 | 8.2 |
| Blount | 219 | 5 817 | 466.8 | 199.2 | 182 | 962 | 84.2 | 27.1 | 894.6 | 453.6 | 202.8 | 41.0 |
| Bradley | 229 | 4 355 | 364.9 | 139.7 | 112 | D | D | D | 676.0 | 315.0 | 174.0 | 36.0 |
| Campbell | 55 | 1 720 | 121.5 | 49.7 | 36 | 159 | 13.6 | 3.1 | 465.6 | 168.4 | 137.1 | 38.6 |
| Cannon | 15 | D | D | D | 14 | D | D | D | 117.1 | 47.6 | 41.0 | 5.3 |
| Carroll | 63 | 1 482 | 92.8 | 36.8 | 32 | 106 | 9.0 | 2.6 | 363.2 | 118.7 | 105.6 | 14.4 |
| Carter | 83 | 1 825 | 125.0 | 48.0 | 51 | D | D | D | 465.4 | 191.7 | 126.5 | 32.2 |
| Cheatham | 44 | D | D | D | 27 | 70 | 5.6 | 1.5 | 218.9 | 103.2 | 46.7 | 9.6 |
| Chester | 24 | 377 | 24.3 | 12.7 | 17 | 45 | 4.5 | 0.9 | 133.6 | 44.2 | 36.1 | 5.4 |
| Claiborne | 39 | 1 367 | 72.7 | 34.4 | 31 | 138 | 13.2 | 4.3 | 355.2 | 122.8 | 101.2 | 29.2 |
| Clay | 11 | D | D | D | 7 | 13 | 1.3 | 0.3 | 99.8 | 22.3 | 33.2 | 3.8 |
| Cocke | 37 | 655 | 54.5 | 24.5 | 20 | D | D | D | 385.7 | 135.0 | 108.8 | 27.6 |
| Coffee | 202 | 2 650 | 246.7 | 85.2 | 82 | 600 | 60.4 | 18.3 | 956.7 | 212.8 | 120.6 | 21.1 |
| Crockett | 28 | 462 | 28.4 | 11.9 | 17 | 37 | 3.4 | 0.6 | 169.3 | 46.7 | 51.6 | 6.0 |
| Cumberland | 128 | 2 705 | 202.3 | 82.7 | 58 | 614 | 37.3 | 10.2 | 426.4 | 283.7 | 116.1 | 21.2 |
| Davidson | 1 805 | 55 649 | 7 038.6 | 2 486.9 | 1 351 | 13 834 | 1 315.2 | 434.2 | 9 471.1 | 1 524.1 | 1 217.1 | 307.8 |
| Decatur | 22 | 945 | 64.5 | 29.9 | 19 | 68 | 7.8 | 1.9 | 127.9 | 41.2 | 50.1 | 5.7 |
| DeKalb | 34 | 560 | 43.4 | 15.6 | 23 | 124 | 10.7 | 3.3 | 169.7 | 60.8 | 56.6 | 9.9 |
| Dickson | 118 | 1 857 | 190.8 | 69.2 | 54 | 291 | 27.0 | 7.9 | 335.7 | 151.8 | 88.0 | 18.4 |
| Dyer | 116 | 1 698 | 162.5 | 56.8 | 52 | 209 | 15.3 | 4.3 | 402.3 | 131.8 | 113.7 | 25.5 |
| Fayette | 51 | 649 | 48.4 | 18.8 | 43 | 150 | 11.8 | 3.4 | 291.2 | 93.7 | 82.7 | 17.6 |
| Fentress | 31 | 839 | 60.7 | 24.8 | 18 | 47 | 5.3 | 0.9 | 223.4 | 66.4 | 74.8 | 15.3 |
| Franklin | 90 | D | D | D | 38 | D | D | D | 355.2 | 146.2 | 104.6 | 14.8 |
| Gibson | 109 | 1 808 | 115.3 | 43.3 | 54 | 262 | 19.6 | 5.7 | 574.5 | 176.9 | 173.0 | 24.5 |
| Giles | 70 | 862 | 69.5 | 25.0 | 31 | 129 | 10.5 | 2.3 | 280.3 | 106.4 | 85.9 | 11.4 |
| Grainger | 12 | D | D | D | 16 | 72 | 5.9 | 1.4 | 216.5 | 81.9 | 64.2 | 14.3 |
| Greene | 142 | 3 580 | 255.9 | 100.8 | 75 | 451 | 32.0 | 8.8 | 664.5 | 263.5 | 150.6 | 34.9 |
| Grundy | 15 | 288 | 15.9 | 7.7 | 11 | 18 | 2.2 | 0.4 | 152.6 | 52.1 | 46.5 | 14.0 |
| Hamblen | 177 | 4 036 | 343.4 | 131.7 | 82 | 406 | 28.0 | 7.5 | 568.2 | 221.4 | 140.4 | 30.3 |
| Hamilton | 1 040 | 24 700 | 2 639.2 | 1 019.6 | 624 | 5 007 | 487.4 | 130.9 | 3 591.5 | 1 224.3 | 800.6 | 173.8 |
| Hancock | 6 | 154 | 9.1 | 3.7 | 5 | D | D | D | 99.7 | 17.7 | 35.2 | 8.3 |
| Hardeman | 41 | 1 453 | 77.6 | 38.1 | 25 | 50 | 5.0 | 1.2 | 465.2 | 84.1 | 99.4 | 22.1 |
| Hardin | 52 | 961 | 62.3 | 25.5 | 21 | 80 | 6.6 | 1.8 | 285.4 | 92.9 | 89.6 | 18.1 |
| Hawkins | 50 | 1 350 | 87.7 | 35.9 | 41 | D | D | D | 502.8 | 227.1 | 123.4 | 30.0 |
| Haywood | 29 | D | D | D | 27 | D | D | D | 248.8 | 46.4 | 83.9 | 17.6 |
| Henderson | 45 | 651 | 50.1 | 18.2 | 39 | 139 | 11.2 | 3.0 | 248.2 | 90.9 | 82.3 | 12.3 |
| Henry | 78 | 1 536 | 123.0 | 47.8 | 52 | 257 | 12.4 | 3.9 | 349.1 | 144.6 | 93.0 | 14.5 |
| Hickman | 35 | 580 | 41.6 | 16.2 | 22 | D | D | D | 193.7 | 76.3 | 46.2 | 9.8 |
| Houston | 15 | 361 | 22.4 | 9.2 | 7 | D | D | D | 90.9 | 37.9 | 24.7 | 4.0 |
| Humphreys | 31 | 560 | 34.4 | 13.0 | 27 | 118 | 8.0 | 2.9 | 398.8 | 74.5 | 48.8 | 6.6 |
| Jackson | 7 | D | D | D | 3 | D | D | D | 127.8 | 32.6 | 38.9 | 6.2 |
| Jefferson | 56 | D | D | D | 50 | 173 | 13.6 | 4.3 | 416.8 | 220.1 | 99.4 | 21.4 |
| Johnson | 20 | 371 | 22.5 | 10.1 | 16 | 34 | 2.6 | 0.6 | 197.5 | 71.3 | 59.8 | 11.4 |
| Knox | 1 200 | 30 846 | 3 184.9 | 1 259.7 | 760 | 5 638 | 513.6 | 159.1 | 3 928.4 | 1 363.2 | 814.7 | 171.3 |
| Lake | 9 | D | D | D | 7 | D | D | D | 95.8 | 19.8 | 30.3 | 5.9 |
| Lauderdale | 31 | 845 | 36.7 | 15.2 | 16 | 82 | 6.1 | 1.9 | 312.0 | 76.6 | 94.7 | 20.9 |
| Lawrence | 78 | 1 133 | 90.6 | 31.6 | 41 | 129 | 8.8 | 2.5 | 403.5 | 174.6 | 114.1 | 18.9 |
| Lewis | 27 | 445 | 22.0 | 8.7 | 15 | 57 | 3.5 | 1.0 | 110.3 | 37.4 | 33.5 | 5.6 |
| Lincoln | 69 | 933 | 63.6 | 25.0 | 47 | 155 | 12.3 | 3.4 | 287.4 | 121.9 | 75.7 | 12.8 |
| Loudon | 85 | D | D | D | 54 | D | D | D | 385.0 | 248.0 | 99.3 | 15.2 |
| McMinn | 100 | 1 932 | 158.2 | 56.3 | 52 | 258 | 16.0 | 4.6 | 490.1 | 198.4 | 119.7 | 24.3 |
| McNairy | 43 | 758 | 52.9 | 21.8 | 27 | 76 | 8.0 | 1.9 | 360.0 | 113.6 | 103.9 | 19.2 |
| Macon | 36 | 521 | 33.0 | 12.7 | 23 | 89 | 7.4 | 2.2 | 207.9 | 58.3 | 55.5 | 8.9 |
| Madison | 304 | 10 656 | 1 030.8 | 435.5 | 143 | 948 | 71.3 | 26.0 | 878.2 | 291.6 | 232.4 | 49.0 |
| Marion | 48 | D | D | D | 31 | D | D | D | 258.1 | 105.2 | 85.0 | 16.6 |

1. State totals may include programs not allocated by county.

# Table B. States and Counties — Federal Funds, Residential Construction, and Local Government Finances

| | Federal funds and grants, 2009–2010 (cont.) | | | | | | | Value of residential construction authorized by building permits, 2011 | | Local government finances, 2007 | | | | |
|---|---|---|---|---|---|---|---|---|---|---|---|---|---|---|
| | Expenditures (mil dol) (cont.) | | | | | | | | | General revenue | | | | |
| | Procurement contract awards | | | Grants[1] | | | | | | | | Taxes | | |
| | | | | | | | | | | | | | Per capita[2] (dollars) | |
| STATE County | Salaries and wages | Defense | Other | Medicaid and other health-related | Nutrition and family welfare | Education | Other | New construction ($1,000) | Number of housing units | Total (mil dol) | Inter-govern-mental (mil dol) | Total (mil dol) | Total | Property |
| | 171 | 172 | 173 | 174 | 175 | 176 | 177 | 178 | 179 | 180 | 181 | 182 | 183 | 184 |
| SOUTH DAKOTA—Cont'd | | | | | | | | | | | | | | |
| Tripp | 3.3 | 0.0 | 0.7 | 7.4 | 1.1 | 0.8 | 0.1 | 230 | 2 | 20.4 | 8.1 | 8.3 | 1 428 | 1 102 |
| Turner | 2.6 | 0.0 | 0.7 | 7.4 | 1.1 | 0.2 | 0.1 | 3 162 | 18 | 24.2 | 8.0 | 11.3 | 1 348 | 1 123 |
| Union | 3.8 | 272.3 | 5.0 | 8.4 | 1.8 | 0.1 | 0.4 | 18 949 | 69 | 52.4 | 10.1 | 25.2 | 1 805 | 1 494 |
| Walworth | 4.2 | 0.0 | 0.8 | 6.9 | 1.1 | 4.8 | 1.2 | 250 | 1 | 16.1 | 7.0 | 6.4 | 1 217 | 836 |
| Yankton | 22.6 | 5.3 | 3.1 | 19.9 | 2.6 | 0.4 | 1.3 | 8 761 | 42 | 60.4 | 16.9 | 31.8 | 1 467 | 1 106 |
| Ziebach | 0.3 | 0.0 | 0.0 | 3.7 | 0.4 | 1.5 | 0.4 | NA | NA | 5.3 | 3.7 | 1.1 | 420 | 353 |
| TENNESSEE | 3 837.3 | 3 100.9 | 7 039.8 | 8 035.9 | 1 360.7 | 1 441.1 | 3 256.8 | 2 353 489 | 14 977 | X | X | X | X | X |
| Anderson | 74.0 | 107.4 | 3 681.9 | 130.3 | 13.0 | 7.3 | 15.3 | 12 582 | 64 | 209.6 | 76.5 | 99.2 | 1 350 | 809 |
| Bedford | 10.4 | 0.2 | 1.3 | 35.8 | 5.1 | 4.4 | 1.7 | 9 986 | 58 | 117.8 | 44.4 | 49.2 | 1 117 | 505 |
| Benton | 5.6 | 1.4 | 1.0 | 23.6 | 2.9 | 1.8 | 0.0 | 4 848 | 50 | 41.6 | 21.8 | 10.5 | 646 | 352 |
| Bledsoe | 1.3 | 0.0 | 0.3 | 20.0 | 4.9 | 2.6 | 4.2 | NA | NA | 25.6 | 18.1 | 4.3 | 331 | 246 |
| Blount | 52.6 | 11.7 | 12.4 | 84.0 | 12.6 | 8.0 | 6.2 | 27 091 | 188 | 602.9 | 125.8 | 136.8 | 1 142 | 821 |
| Bradley | 16.6 | 0.1 | 4.9 | 69.3 | 22.7 | 10.1 | 2.3 | 31 440 | 274 | 205.5 | 83.8 | 71.6 | 750 | 475 |
| Campbell | 12.3 | 3.3 | 2.8 | 80.0 | 7.8 | 4.2 | 3.7 | 13 537 | 132 | 80.7 | 45.7 | 22.3 | 548 | 337 |
| Cannon | 2.3 | 0.0 | 0.5 | 16.4 | 1.8 | 1.1 | 0.2 | 1 196 | 9 | 26.2 | 15.8 | 6.3 | 469 | 342 |
| Carroll | 15.0 | 3.4 | 1.6 | 57.4 | 4.9 | 4.5 | 3.8 | 684 | 6 | 55.7 | 35.0 | 9.2 | 318 | 162 |
| Carter | 13.5 | 0.0 | 2.1 | 76.0 | 8.9 | 4.7 | 3.0 | 10 843 | 80 | 104.0 | 55.0 | 30.6 | 516 | 282 |
| Cheatham | 10.6 | 2.5 | 1.7 | 16.9 | 4.1 | 2.4 | 0.2 | 8 658 | 45 | 86.2 | 42.9 | 29.5 | 753 | 445 |
| Chester | 13.0 | 0.0 | 0.4 | 22.7 | 6.0 | 1.1 | 0.3 | 1 250 | 11 | 28.0 | 15.8 | 8.6 | 535 | 263 |
| Claiborne | 9.1 | 0.8 | 2.2 | 67.1 | 9.9 | 3.9 | 0.9 | 7 458 | 89 | 137.9 | 35.6 | 15.6 | 498 | 342 |
| Clay | 2.4 | 3.2 | 2.3 | 26.2 | 1.6 | 0.9 | 2.0 | NA | NA | 17.1 | 11.0 | 4.2 | 539 | 319 |
| Cocke | 11.0 | 0.0 | 3.8 | 85.0 | 6.7 | 3.3 | 1.2 | 316 | 4 | 66.9 | 36.3 | 23.7 | 670 | 379 |
| Coffee | 51.1 | 471.9 | 4.7 | 48.4 | 6.7 | 4.3 | 2.3 | 11 236 | 62 | 119.7 | 48.1 | 50.9 | 983 | 487 |
| Crockett | 4.7 | 11.0 | 0.8 | 32.5 | 2.7 | 1.3 | 0.0 | 0 | 0 | 33.7 | 19.7 | 9.2 | 647 | 367 |
| Cumberland | 9.1 | 3.1 | -71.3 | 46.4 | 6.7 | 3.2 | 3.6 | 27 539 | 176 | 94.8 | 39.4 | 38.5 | 727 | 328 |
| Davidson | 786.7 | 83.2 | 560.2 | 1 385.5 | 348.3 | 971.9 | 1 955.4 | 322 532 | 1 966 | 2 386.1 | 563.2 | 1 174.7 | 1 896 | 1 237 |
| Decatur | 5.7 | 0.0 | 0.7 | 20.4 | 1.9 | 1.1 | 0.3 | 0 | 0 | 33.7 | 12.7 | 6.7 | 589 | 248 |
| DeKalb | 3.2 | 4.8 | 0.8 | 27.4 | 2.6 | 1.6 | 0.4 | 656 | 5 | 36.7 | 20.9 | 9.5 | 517 | 384 |
| Dickson | 19.0 | 0.3 | 1.8 | 37.8 | 6.3 | 3.2 | 3.7 | 13 107 | 88 | 120.6 | 44.2 | 56.6 | 1 194 | 604 |
| Dyer | 20.8 | 0.0 | 2.3 | 71.2 | 5.4 | 4.5 | 1.5 | 4 625 | 48 | 103.4 | 42.6 | 40.1 | 1 064 | 535 |
| Fayette | 5.3 | 0.0 | 1.2 | 74.6 | 6.3 | 2.1 | 0.1 | 29 848 | 125 | 44.1 | 26.6 | 11.0 | 296 | 148 |
| Fentress | 13.9 | 0.2 | 0.7 | 46.0 | 3.5 | 1.3 | 0.7 | 0 | 0 | 32.3 | 18.6 | 8.4 | 485 | 219 |
| Franklin | 18.1 | 5.3 | 2.7 | 44.6 | 5.3 | 3.3 | 2.1 | 16 284 | 125 | 78.2 | 39.3 | 26.1 | 633 | 478 |
| Gibson | 45.2 | 27.7 | 5.7 | 86.8 | 8.3 | 4.4 | 3.0 | 18 439 | 161 | 126.1 | 65.7 | 33.8 | 697 | 392 |
| Giles | 6.7 | 1.9 | 3.4 | 49.2 | 4.1 | 2.1 | 0.9 | 683 | 4 | 62.9 | 27.8 | 24.4 | 840 | 561 |
| Grainger | 3.6 | 0.0 | 0.8 | 44.5 | 3.4 | 1.8 | 0.3 | 0 | 0 | 38.2 | 25.4 | 8.0 | 355 | 257 |
| Greene | 24.2 | 12.3 | 38.9 | 89.4 | 8.9 | 25.3 | 5.8 | 14 520 | 107 | 140.5 | 60.4 | 55.6 | 843 | 563 |
| Grundy | 9.8 | 0.0 | 0.5 | 24.3 | 2.8 | 1.7 | 0.3 | 0 | 0 | 27.2 | 19.3 | 5.9 | 412 | 294 |
| Hamblen | 17.4 | 25.4 | 7.2 | 75.3 | 15.9 | 6.3 | 5.5 | 6 008 | 58 | 127.1 | 47.7 | 53.2 | 861 | 375 |
| Hamilton | 182.9 | 41.7 | 507.5 | 338.3 | 48.4 | 28.9 | 164.3 | 137 932 | 1 095 | 1 549.8 | 288.0 | 418.6 | 1 268 | 886 |
| Hancock | 0.8 | 0.0 | 0.4 | 33.2 | 1.9 | 0.9 | 0.5 | 0 | 0 | 16.8 | 11.8 | 2.4 | 357 | 246 |
| Hardeman | 8.5 | 160.8 | 2.2 | 74.9 | 6.0 | 2.9 | 0.5 | 4 305 | 24 | 55.2 | 30.8 | 16.1 | 578 | 319 |
| Hardin | 9.7 | 0.0 | 2.1 | 60.1 | 4.2 | 2.4 | 2.0 | 714 | 11 | 83.0 | 27.7 | 19.3 | 739 | 336 |
| Hawkins | 8.0 | 0.0 | 13.0 | 83.0 | 7.6 | 4.4 | 0.8 | 2 094 | 15 | 102.5 | 51.8 | 35.7 | 625 | 385 |
| Haywood | 9.7 | 0.0 | 1.6 | 68.6 | 5.5 | 1.6 | 1.3 | 1 086 | 12 | 50.2 | 25.5 | 15.1 | 787 | 526 |
| Henderson | 7.6 | 0.0 | 0.9 | 45.3 | 3.7 | 2.1 | 0.4 | 1 133 | 9 | 57.7 | 27.4 | 20.4 | 763 | 363 |
| Henry | 14.7 | 0.0 | 13.4 | 45.2 | 4.9 | 4.0 | 8.0 | 959 | 11 | 141.6 | 40.8 | 23.1 | 732 | 376 |
| Hickman | 14.7 | 13.0 | 1.1 | 24.2 | 2.9 | 1.6 | 1.4 | 150 | 2 | 48.7 | 26.9 | 13.8 | 582 | 352 |
| Houston | 4.2 | 0.0 | 0.7 | 13.7 | 3.3 | 0.7 | 0.3 | 52 | 1 | 19.7 | 11.4 | 5.3 | 657 | 402 |
| Humphreys | 4.2 | 0.2 | 232.4 | 24.9 | 2.6 | 1.4 | 0.3 | 216 | 1 | 44.2 | 19.9 | 13.8 | 758 | 432 |
| Jackson | 2.0 | 0.0 | 0.5 | 26.0 | 1.8 | 0.9 | 16.8 | NA | NA | 21.2 | 14.5 | 4.6 | 430 | 335 |
| Jefferson | 12.2 | 0.0 | 2.4 | 45.1 | 5.5 | 3.3 | 1.0 | 17 397 | 76 | 91.0 | 42.6 | 34.3 | 683 | 379 |
| Johnson | 3.2 | 4.2 | 0.9 | 39.7 | 3.0 | 1.5 | 0.6 | 110 | 2 | 34.5 | 21.4 | 7.2 | 400 | 280 |
| Knox | 277.9 | 71.7 | 399.6 | 400.3 | 53.8 | 34.2 | 167.2 | 133 365 | 741 | 1 168.8 | 322.6 | 585.6 | 1 382 | 753 |
| Lake | 8.8 | 2.1 | 0.3 | 21.3 | 1.7 | 0.7 | 0.1 | 753 | 9 | 19.5 | 10.3 | 3.5 | 476 | 294 |
| Lauderdale | 7.2 | 8.2 | 7.8 | 70.3 | 6.2 | 2.9 | 4.9 | 2 438 | 29 | 61.5 | 33.9 | 16.6 | 622 | 371 |
| Lawrence | 16.7 | 0.0 | 2.0 | 59.2 | 6.2 | 3.4 | 1.6 | 392 | 4 | 95.5 | 40.3 | 34.3 | 839 | 430 |
| Lewis | 6.1 | 0.0 | 3.5 | 16.7 | 1.8 | 1.0 | 2.3 | 420 | 6 | 26.0 | 14.4 | 6.5 | 564 | 270 |
| Lincoln | 5.9 | 0.3 | 1.5 | 46.3 | 11.1 | 2.6 | 2.8 | 15 643 | 138 | 102.9 | 31.3 | 16.6 | 507 | 315 |
| Loudon | 15.0 | 4.2 | -50.2 | 39.6 | 5.4 | 2.8 | 1.7 | 47 738 | 142 | 98.1 | 40.1 | 35.0 | 771 | 504 |
| McMinn | 27.3 | 39.8 | 2.2 | 56.5 | 6.7 | 4.2 | 3.5 | 677 | 13 | 124.2 | 50.2 | 33.3 | 638 | 489 |
| McNairy | 10.7 | 0.6 | 1.8 | 73.0 | 3.9 | 2.6 | 27.9 | 264 | 8 | 51.4 | 28.2 | 13.7 | 536 | 362 |
| Macon | 8.8 | 0.0 | 0.6 | 30.1 | 2.8 | 1.9 | 25.2 | 4 279 | 67 | 43.6 | 24.0 | 13.6 | 629 | 357 |
| Madison | 72.2 | 0.1 | 8.5 | 138.3 | 14.2 | 10.9 | 13.2 | 30 654 | 163 | 842.2 | 102.3 | 134.7 | 1 396 | 706 |
| Marion | 4.1 | 0.0 | 1.0 | 36.2 | 4.3 | 2.7 | 1.1 | 9 706 | 50 | 55.5 | 28.1 | 17.9 | 636 | 346 |

1. State totals may include programs not allocated by county.  2. Based on the resident population estimated as of July 1 of the year shown.

# Table B. States and Counties — Local Government Finances, Government Employment, and Voting

| STATE County | Local government finances, 2007 (cont.) | | | | | | | | | Government employment, 2011 | | | Presidential election,[2] 2012 | | |
|---|---|---|---|---|---|---|---|---|---|---|---|---|---|---|---|
| | Direct general expenditure | | | | | | | Debt outstanding | | | | | Percent of vote cast: | | |
| | | | Percent of total for: | | | | | | | | | | | | |
| | Total (mil dol) | Per capita[1] (dollars) | Education | Health and hospitals | Police protection | Public welfare | Highways | Total (mil dol) | Per capita[1] (dollars) | Federal civilian | Federal military | State and local | Democratic | Republican | All other |
| | 185 | 186 | 187 | 188 | 189 | 190 | 191 | 192 | 193 | 194 | 195 | 196 | 197 | 198 | 199 |
| **SOUTH DAKOTA—Cont'd** | | | | | | | | | | | | | | | |
| Tripp | 18.0 | 3 094 | 51.1 | 0.9 | 4.2 | 0.0 | 17.2 | 17.3 | 2 986 | 33 | 36 | 376 | 32.2 | 65.5 | 2.3 |
| Turner | 19.9 | 2 378 | 53.4 | 0.7 | 4.4 | 0.2 | 15.8 | 25.1 | 2 996 | 33 | 53 | 414 | 38.6 | 58.3 | 3.1 |
| Union | 46.3 | 3 317 | 49.9 | 0.3 | 5.8 | 0.1 | 10.6 | 39.4 | 2 826 | 45 | 93 | 718 | 42.1 | 56.0 | 1.9 |
| Walworth | 15.8 | 3 001 | 42.9 | 0.6 | 5.3 | 0.3 | 16.4 | 2.3 | 446 | 30 | 35 | 399 | 34.8 | 62.9 | 2.2 |
| Yankton | 58.3 | 2 692 | 46.1 | 1.3 | 5.1 | 0.3 | 9.4 | 45.2 | 2 087 | 220 | 143 | 1 711 | 47.7 | 49.7 | 2.5 |
| Ziebach | 5.6 | 2 102 | 71.6 | 0.4 | 2.4 | 0.1 | 15.9 | 0.4 | 132 | 0 | 18 | 164 | 62.2 | 35.0 | 2.8 |
| **TENNESSEE** | X | X | X | X | X | X | X | X | X | 51 033 | 23 350 | 380 193 | 41.8 | 56.9 | 1.3 |
| Anderson | 227.2 | 3 092 | 49.6 | 2.5 | 4.8 | 0.0 | 3.2 | 272.6 | 3 711 | 1 011 | 254 | 4 083 | 36.1 | 62.3 | 1.6 |
| Bedford | 119.0 | 2 700 | 59.2 | 2.7 | 4.4 | 5.9 | 5.1 | 165.1 | 3 747 | 64 | 152 | 2 215 | 32.4 | 65.9 | 1.7 |
| Benton | 38.5 | 2 364 | 50.4 | 1.4 | 5.6 | 0.0 | 5.6 | 32.3 | 1 983 | 50 | 55 | 938 | 40.8 | 57.0 | 2.1 |
| Bledsoe | 26.4 | 2 017 | 55.7 | 3.2 | 2.7 | 0.0 | 6.0 | 16.7 | 1 273 | 19 | 43 | 1 079 | 31.7 | 66.2 | 2.1 |
| Blount | 580.7 | 4 845 | 24.7 | 27.5 | 3.1 | 0.1 | 2.3 | 2 169.5 | 18 101 | 272 | 435 | 7 186 | 29.5 | 68.9 | 1.6 |
| Bradley | 222.2 | 2 328 | 48.7 | 12.7 | 8.3 | 0.2 | 5.2 | 227.3 | 2 381 | 212 | 335 | 4 695 | 24.5 | 74.2 | 1.3 |
| Campbell | 78.8 | 1 934 | 52.4 | 1.7 | 5.9 | 0.4 | 5.8 | 89.8 | 2 202 | 83 | 135 | 2 044 | 30.6 | 67.6 | 1.8 |
| Cannon | 24.9 | 1 855 | 62.1 | 3.6 | 5.9 | 0.8 | 8.4 | 17.2 | 1 283 | 33 | 46 | 539 | 36.9 | 60.9 | 2.3 |
| Carroll | 60.6 | 2 095 | 59.0 | 0.3 | 5.3 | 0.2 | 7.2 | 32.8 | 1 133 | 87 | 95 | 1 435 | 34.2 | 64.0 | 1.8 |
| Carter | 101.4 | 1 714 | 65.5 | 0.6 | 4.7 | 0.0 | 5.1 | 45.7 | 772 | 76 | 191 | 2 395 | 25.7 | 72.8 | 1.5 |
| Cheatham | 75.8 | 1 937 | 66.0 | 2.9 | 4.8 | 0.1 | 5.3 | 66.3 | 1 695 | 72 | 130 | 1 473 | 33.5 | 65.1 | 1.4 |
| Chester | 26.2 | 1 621 | 61.5 | 0.9 | 9.6 | 0.6 | 7.5 | 17.6 | 1 093 | 29 | 57 | 1 036 | 27.8 | 71.0 | 1.2 |
| Claiborne | 88.7 | 2 837 | 41.6 | 38.4 | 2.7 | 0.0 | 5.1 | 78.4 | 2 506 | 66 | 107 | 1 955 | 29.5 | 68.9 | 1.6 |
| Clay | 17.4 | 2 208 | 56.6 | 1.4 | 5.8 | 0.2 | 9.7 | 15.4 | 1 954 | 44 | 26 | 413 | 41.7 | 56.0 | 2.3 |
| Cocke | 64.2 | 1 816 | 64.0 | 0.5 | 6.5 | 0.0 | 6.6 | 37.2 | 1 053 | 63 | 119 | 1 816 | 26.8 | 71.7 | 1.6 |
| Coffee | 111.6 | 2 156 | 64.8 | 2.6 | 8.4 | 0.1 | 2.9 | 82.1 | 1 588 | 502 | 236 | 3 229 | 34.3 | 63.7 | 2.0 |
| Crockett | 32.0 | 2 249 | 60.2 | 2.9 | 3.6 | 0.6 | 7.3 | 32.2 | 2 262 | 36 | 49 | 782 | 32.6 | 66.2 | 1.3 |
| Cumberland | 93.1 | 1 754 | 56.3 | 3.3 | 6.2 | 0.3 | 3.6 | 97.0 | 1 828 | 101 | 189 | 2 278 | 30.7 | 67.8 | 1.5 |
| Davidson | 2 353.5 | 3 798 | 29.1 | 7.7 | 7.6 | 1.3 | 2.3 | 4 619.2 | 7 455 | 8 562 | 2 647 | 40 876 | 59.9 | 38.9 | 1.2 |
| Decatur | 34.1 | 3 004 | 35.9 | 31.1 | 5.6 | 0.0 | 5.2 | 37.4 | 3 298 | 28 | 39 | 751 | 32.9 | 65.1 | 2.0 |
| DeKalb | 30.4 | 1 649 | 61.6 | 1.6 | 5.3 | 0.2 | 7.2 | 43.5 | 2 358 | 39 | 63 | 799 | 40.1 | 57.8 | 2.1 |
| Dickson | 106.4 | 2 246 | 55.4 | 3.0 | 8.1 | 0.0 | 5.2 | 158.1 | 3 337 | 85 | 168 | 2 562 | 38.5 | 59.8 | 1.7 |
| Dyer | 101.3 | 2 689 | 54.6 | 2.1 | 6.5 | 0.6 | 7.4 | 76.2 | 2 021 | 105 | 127 | 2 606 | 30.5 | 68.2 | 1.2 |
| Fayette | 64.3 | 1 729 | 47.3 | 2.6 | 6.7 | 0.0 | 7.4 | 56.8 | 1 527 | 59 | 128 | 1 735 | 35.8 | 63.2 | 1.0 |
| Fentress | 30.4 | 1 746 | 57.5 | 3.9 | 4.4 | 0.0 | 9.3 | 20.0 | 1 149 | 40 | 60 | 882 | 27.2 | 71.1 | 1.8 |
| Franklin | 79.9 | 1 939 | 57.8 | 0.4 | 6.8 | 0.1 | 7.7 | 108.7 | 2 638 | 135 | 136 | 1 630 | 37.9 | 60.5 | 1.6 |
| Gibson | 149.0 | 3 069 | 52.1 | 1.7 | 6.4 | 0.0 | 4.8 | 183.4 | 3 776 | 160 | 168 | 2 819 | 34.8 | 63.6 | 1.6 |
| Giles | 60.5 | 2 085 | 55.7 | 2.8 | 6.5 | 0.1 | 7.9 | 21.4 | 736 | 69 | 98 | 1 468 | 39.5 | 59.0 | 1.5 |
| Grainger | 47.7 | 2 114 | 72.7 | 2.3 | 3.2 | 0.1 | 4.1 | 52.0 | 2 305 | 54 | 76 | 906 | 27.5 | 70.6 | 1.9 |
| Greene | 131.0 | 1 985 | 57.8 | 4.7 | 4.9 | 0.0 | 5.7 | 125.8 | 1 907 | 238 | 231 | 3 750 | 28.8 | 69.5 | 1.7 |
| Grundy | 25.8 | 1 805 | 71.4 | 0.7 | 3.6 | 0.0 | 7.5 | 15.5 | 1 086 | 20 | 45 | 745 | 42.6 | 55.3 | 2.1 |
| Hamblen | 117.4 | 1 899 | 60.2 | 1.4 | 5.4 | 0.1 | 1.8 | 90.9 | 1 469 | 178 | 211 | 3 718 | 30.0 | 68.4 | 1.6 |
| Hamilton | 1 378.8 | 4 176 | 24.7 | 33.5 | 5.7 | 1.5 | 2.8 | 1 502.7 | 4 551 | 5 999 | 1 184 | 22 132 | 43.6 | 55.4 | 1.1 |
| Hancock | 16.5 | 2 449 | 53.3 | 9.2 | 2.8 | 0.0 | 10.3 | 20.1 | 2 988 | 0 | 22 | 473 | 27.0 | 70.9 | 2.2 |
| Hardeman | 49.9 | 1 793 | 63.2 | 3.3 | 7.7 | 0.1 | 6.5 | 16.8 | 605 | 56 | 90 | 2 014 | 52.7 | 46.5 | 0.8 |
| Hardin | 81.5 | 3 127 | 38.0 | 32.9 | 2.6 | 3.2 | 4.6 | 37.0 | 1 418 | 123 | 86 | 1 671 | 27.8 | 70.5 | 1.6 |
| Hawkins | 91.8 | 1 609 | 65.5 | 0.7 | 5.4 | 0.2 | 5.7 | 80.3 | 1 407 | 248 | 189 | 2 213 | 28.2 | 70.1 | 1.7 |
| Haywood | 51.5 | 2 693 | 54.0 | 3.2 | 7.6 | 0.0 | 6.7 | 12.8 | 671 | 94 | 62 | 1 156 | 60.3 | 39.0 | 0.8 |
| Henderson | 51.7 | 1 932 | 62.8 | 0.4 | 6.2 | 0.4 | 6.7 | 39.6 | 1 479 | 58 | 93 | 1 298 | 27.9 | 70.8 | 1.3 |
| Henry | 127.6 | 4 033 | 28.3 | 48.0 | 3.3 | 0.0 | 4.6 | 59.1 | 1 868 | 123 | 141 | 2 386 | 38.0 | 60.4 | 1.6 |
| Hickman | 50.6 | 2 128 | 59.6 | 2.9 | 4.5 | 0.2 | 4.2 | 64.1 | 2 698 | 53 | 81 | 1 170 | 41.9 | 56.3 | 1.8 |
| Houston | 19.3 | 2 385 | 53.4 | 3.2 | 6.8 | 0.0 | 8.0 | 16.7 | 2 072 | 18 | 28 | 531 | 50.0 | 47.9 | 2.0 |
| Humphreys | 43.6 | 2 402 | 49.6 | 0.8 | 4.2 | 0.0 | 10.3 | 84.4 | 4 646 | 358 | 62 | 1 005 | 47.5 | 50.4 | 2.1 |
| Jackson | 20.7 | 1 918 | 62.3 | 3.0 | 4.8 | 0.3 | 10.5 | 19.0 | 1 757 | 27 | 38 | 481 | 49.4 | 48.5 | 2.0 |
| Jefferson | 93.7 | 1 866 | 56.8 | 4.6 | 6.1 | 0.2 | 5.7 | 56.4 | 1 122 | 110 | 173 | 2 329 | 27.9 | 70.6 | 1.4 |
| Johnson | 35.3 | 1 947 | 60.8 | 0.8 | 4.0 | 0.2 | 6.8 | 20.8 | 1 147 | 39 | 61 | 998 | 27.9 | 70.1 | 2.0 |
| Knox | 1 118.5 | 2 639 | 39.4 | 2.5 | 7.1 | 0.4 | 2.1 | 1 826.1 | 4 308 | 3 709 | 1 550 | 32 848 | 37.7 | 60.7 | 1.5 |
| Lake | 18.5 | 2 496 | 39.6 | 3.5 | 5.6 | 0.5 | 10.1 | 23.7 | 3 200 | 15 | 26 | 810 | 45.8 | 52.5 | 1.7 |
| Lauderdale | 57.3 | 2 145 | 58.5 | 2.5 | 7.3 | 0.3 | 4.9 | 43.8 | 1 639 | 55 | 93 | 2 051 | 46.3 | 52.8 | 0.9 |
| Lawrence | 83.9 | 2 051 | 55.5 | 1.7 | 5.9 | 0.2 | 8.0 | 443.8 | 10 854 | 120 | 140 | 1 936 | 32.2 | 66.0 | 1.8 |
| Lewis | 24.6 | 2 119 | 53.8 | 0.6 | 5.6 | 0.0 | 6.7 | 12.3 | 1 059 | 29 | 41 | 666 | 37.3 | 61.0 | 1.6 |
| Lincoln | 80.7 | 2 464 | 45.0 | 28.1 | 3.7 | 0.1 | 4.9 | 63.2 | 1 931 | 58 | 112 | 2 439 | 28.1 | 70.3 | 1.6 |
| Loudon | 103.2 | 2 271 | 53.7 | 0.6 | 7.1 | 0.3 | 3.4 | 1 504.0 | 33 094 | 144 | 164 | 1 859 | 27.3 | 71.3 | 1.4 |
| McMinn | 124.9 | 2 396 | 47.2 | 21.1 | 3.9 | 0.0 | 4.2 | 41.2 | 791 | 104 | 175 | 2 072 | 29.5 | 69.1 | 1.4 |
| McNairy | 48.7 | 1 904 | 61.2 | 1.1 | 5.4 | 0.0 | 4.8 | 36.5 | 1 426 | 81 | 87 | 1 246 | 30.0 | 68.5 | 1.5 |
| Macon | 40.6 | 1 882 | 61.9 | 3.9 | 7.1 | 0.6 | 4.0 | 21.4 | 991 | 35 | 75 | 1 117 | 28.0 | 69.9 | 2.1 |
| Madison | 944.7 | 9 788 | 12.8 | 70.7 | 2.0 | 0.0 | 0.8 | 1 397.2 | 14 476 | 469 | 331 | 11 368 | 46.1 | 53.1 | 0.8 |
| Marion | 57.5 | 2 043 | 59.4 | 0.8 | 4.9 | 0.0 | 4.7 | 76.2 | 2 708 | 66 | 94 | 1 211 | 39.4 | 59.0 | 1.6 |

1. Based on the resident population estimated as of July 1 of the year shown.   2. © 2013 Election Data Services, Inc. All rights reserved.

Items 185—199

# Table B. States and Counties — **Land Area and Population**

| | | | | Population 2012 | | | | Population characteristics[6], 2011 | | | | | | | | | | |
|---|---|---|---|---|---|---|---|---|---|---|---|---|---|---|---|---|---|---|
| | | | | | | | | Race alone or in combination, not Hispanic or Latino (percent) | | | | | Age (percent) | | | | | |
| STATE/ County code | CBSA code[1] | County type[2] | STATE County | Land area,[3] (sq km) 2010 | Total persons | Rank | Per square kilometer | White | Black | American Indian, Alaska Native | Asian and Pacific Islander | Percent Hispanic or Latino[4] | Under 5 years | 5 to 17 years | 18 to 24 years | 25 to 34 years | 35 to 44 years | 45 to 54 years |
| | | | | 1 | 2 | 3 | 4 | 5 | 6 | 7 | 8 | 9 | 10 | 11 | 12 | 13 | 14 | 15 |
| | | | TENNESSEE—Cont'd | | | | | | | | | | | | | | | |
| 47 117 | 30280 | 6 | Marshall | 972 | 30 883 | 1 413 | 31.8 | 87.7 | 7.4 | 0.8 | 0.7 | 4.8 | 6.2 | 17.9 | 7.9 | 12.3 | 13.5 | 14.9 |
| 47 119 | 17940 | 4 | Maury | 1 588 | 81 990 | 675 | 51.6 | 81.5 | 13.4 | 0.7 | 0.9 | 5.0 | 7.1 | 17.0 | 8.0 | 13.5 | 12.5 | 15.0 |
| 47 121 | ... | 8 | Meigs | 505 | 11 698 | 2 317 | 23.2 | 96.3 | 1.8 | 1.1 | 0.4 | 1.5 | 4.9 | 16.0 | 7.1 | 10.5 | 13.4 | 14.8 |
| 47 123 | ... | 6 | Monroe | 1 646 | 45 133 | 1 064 | 27.4 | 93.4 | 2.6 | 1.3 | 0.6 | 3.5 | 5.9 | 16.8 | 7.6 | 11.0 | 12.8 | 14.2 |
| 47 125 | 17300 | 3 | Montgomery | 1 396 | 184 468 | 343 | 132.1 | 69.9 | 20.7 | 1.1 | 3.7 | 8.1 | 8.6 | 19.1 | 12.0 | 17.8 | 13.4 | 12.3 |
| 47 127 | 46100 | 9 | Moore | 335 | 6 339 | 2 737 | 18.9 | 95.6 | 3.0 | 0.7 | 0.5 | 1.3 | 4.5 | 17.3 | 7.1 | 9.6 | 13.1 | 15.3 |
| 47 129 | ... | 6 | Morgan | 1 352 | 21 931 | 1 734 | 16.2 | 94.6 | 4.1 | 1.1 | 0.5 | 0.9 | 4.9 | 15.7 | 8.4 | 13.5 | 14.8 | 15.5 |
| 47 131 | 46460 | 7 | Obion | 1 411 | 31 340 | 1 407 | 22.2 | 85.7 | 11.2 | 0.4 | 0.4 | 3.2 | 5.5 | 16.9 | 7.8 | 11.2 | 13.0 | 14.4 |
| 47 133 | 18260 | 7 | Overton | 1 123 | 22 190 | 1 724 | 19.8 | 97.7 | 0.9 | 1.0 | 0.4 | 1.1 | 5.7 | 17.3 | 7.4 | 10.6 | 13.0 | 14.1 |
| 47 135 | ... | 8 | Perry | 1 074 | 7 860 | 2 610 | 7.3 | 95.5 | 2.3 | 1.2 | 0.5 | 1.9 | 6.0 | 16.3 | 7.5 | 10.5 | 11.5 | 13.9 |
| 47 137 | ... | 9 | Pickett | 422 | 5 100 | 2 832 | 12.1 | 97.7 | 0.5 | 0.5 | 0.3 | 1.6 | 4.4 | 14.5 | 6.5 | 9.6 | 11.1 | 14.4 |
| 47 139 | 17420 | 3 | Polk | 1 126 | 16 686 | 1 998 | 14.8 | 97.2 | 0.9 | 1.2 | 0.4 | 1.5 | 5.2 | 16.8 | 7.4 | 10.2 | 13.6 | 15.0 |
| 47 141 | 18260 | 4 | Putnam | 1 039 | 73 229 | 742 | 70.5 | 90.8 | 2.7 | 0.8 | 1.5 | 5.4 | 5.9 | 15.3 | 15.4 | 12.2 | 11.7 | 12.6 |
| 47 143 | ... | 6 | Rhea | 817 | 32 247 | 1 383 | 39.5 | 93.0 | 2.8 | 1.0 | 0.7 | 3.8 | 6.0 | 17.1 | 9.4 | 11.1 | 12.5 | 14.1 |
| 47 145 | 25340 | 4 | Roane | 934 | 53 469 | 930 | 57.2 | 94.7 | 3.4 | 1.1 | 0.8 | 1.4 | 4.8 | 15.7 | 7.2 | 9.6 | 12.3 | 15.4 |
| 47 147 | 34980 | 1 | Robertson | 1 234 | 66 931 | 788 | 54.2 | 85.4 | 8.1 | 0.8 | 0.8 | 6.1 | 6.9 | 18.8 | 7.7 | 13.0 | 13.5 | 15.6 |
| 47 149 | 34980 | 1 | Rutherford | 1 604 | 274 454 | 242 | 171.1 | 77.0 | 13.7 | 0.7 | 3.7 | 6.9 | 7.1 | 18.7 | 12.1 | 15.6 | 14.6 | 13.6 |
| 47 151 | ... | 6 | Scott | 1 379 | 22 173 | 1 725 | 16.1 | 98.7 | 0.3 | 0.8 | 0.4 | 0.6 | 6.4 | 18.6 | 8.3 | 12.3 | 13.4 | 14.1 |
| 47 153 | 16860 | 3 | Sequatchie | 689 | 14 423 | 2 143 | 20.9 | 95.4 | 0.8 | 1.0 | 0.5 | 3.3 | 5.9 | 16.9 | 7.8 | 10.8 | 13.3 | 14.5 |
| 47 155 | 42940 | 4 | Sevier | 1 535 | 92 512 | 626 | 60.3 | 92.3 | 1.4 | 1.0 | 1.1 | 5.3 | 5.8 | 16.1 | 8.2 | 11.5 | 13.3 | 15.0 |
| 47 157 | 32820 | 1 | Shelby | 1 977 | 940 764 | 50 | 475.9 | 39.6 | 52.5 | 0.6 | 2.8 | 5.8 | 7.2 | 18.8 | 10.4 | 14.1 | 13.2 | 14.0 |
| 47 159 | 34980 | 1 | Smith | 814 | 19 102 | 1 869 | 23.5 | 94.7 | 2.8 | 1.0 | 0.4 | 2.3 | 5.8 | 18.1 | 8.0 | 11.7 | 13.1 | 16.1 |
| 47 161 | 17300 | 3 | Stewart | 1 190 | 13 297 | 2 224 | 11.2 | 94.3 | 2.2 | 1.6 | 1.4 | 2.1 | 4.9 | 17.3 | 7.6 | 9.9 | 12.7 | 15.6 |
| 47 163 | 28700 | 3 | Sullivan | 1 071 | 156 786 | 401 | 146.4 | 95.2 | 2.9 | 0.7 | 0.8 | 1.6 | 5.1 | 15.2 | 7.7 | 10.3 | 13.0 | 15.0 |
| 47 165 | 34980 | 1 | Sumner | 1 371 | 166 123 | 377 | 121.2 | 87.9 | 7.2 | 0.7 | 1.5 | 4.0 | 6.4 | 18.5 | 7.7 | 12.2 | 14.2 | 15.4 |
| 47 167 | 32820 | 1 | Tipton | 1 187 | 61 705 | 843 | 52.0 | 77.9 | 19.3 | 1.0 | 1.2 | 2.3 | 6.4 | 20.4 | 8.7 | 12.1 | 13.7 | 15.4 |
| 47 169 | 34980 | 1 | Trousdale | 296 | 7 795 | 2 617 | 26.3 | 86.9 | 10.6 | 0.9 | 0.4 | 2.7 | 6.0 | 18.0 | 8.4 | 11.9 | 12.8 | 15.0 |
| 47 171 | 27740 | 3 | Unicoi | 482 | 18 235 | 1 910 | 37.8 | 95.1 | 0.7 | 0.8 | 0.4 | 4.1 | 4.8 | 15.2 | 6.8 | 10.7 | 12.4 | 15.0 |
| 47 173 | 28940 | 2 | Union | 579 | 19 127 | 1 868 | 33.0 | 97.7 | 0.7 | 1.1 | 0.3 | 1.5 | 6.3 | 17.3 | 8.3 | 11.5 | 13.0 | 15.6 |
| 47 175 | ... | 9 | Van Buren | 708 | 5 628 | 2 793 | 7.9 | 98.0 | 0.9 | 0.8 | 0.2 | 0.9 | 4.4 | 15.8 | 6.9 | 10.1 | 12.6 | 15.2 |
| 47 177 | 32660 | 6 | Warren | 1 121 | 39 839 | 1 174 | 35.5 | 88.0 | 3.5 | 0.7 | 0.8 | 8.2 | 6.4 | 17.8 | 7.8 | 12.1 | 13.3 | 14.4 |
| 47 179 | 27740 | 3 | Washington | 846 | 125 094 | 490 | 147.9 | 91.3 | 4.8 | 0.7 | 1.5 | 3.0 | 5.4 | 14.6 | 11.2 | 12.7 | 13.0 | 14.2 |
| 47 181 | ... | 8 | Wayne | 1 901 | 16 996 | 1 982 | 8.9 | 91.8 | 6.3 | 0.7 | 0.3 | 1.7 | 4.4 | 14.7 | 8.4 | 13.8 | 14.1 | 15.1 |
| 47 183 | 32280 | 7 | Weakley | 1 503 | 34 793 | 1 305 | 23.1 | 88.5 | 8.4 | 0.7 | 1.5 | 2.1 | 5.4 | 14.3 | 17.9 | 10.6 | 11.0 | 12.9 |
| 47 185 | ... | 7 | White | 976 | 26 082 | 1 558 | 26.7 | 95.4 | 2.6 | 0.8 | 0.7 | 1.8 | 5.8 | 16.5 | 7.6 | 11.2 | 12.4 | 14.3 |
| 47 187 | 34980 | 1 | Williamson | 1 509 | 192 911 | 330 | 127.8 | 87.5 | 5.1 | 0.6 | 3.6 | 4.6 | 6.4 | 22.3 | 6.2 | 9.8 | 15.7 | 17.0 |
| 47 189 | 34980 | 1 | Wilson | 1 478 | 118 961 | 511 | 80.5 | 88.5 | 7.3 | 0.8 | 1.4 | 3.4 | 6.1 | 18.4 | 7.5 | 11.4 | 14.7 | 16.1 |
| 48 000 | ... | X | TEXAS | 676 587 | 26 059 203 | X | 38.5 | 45.9 | 12.1 | 0.7 | 4.5 | 38.1 | 7.6 | 19.5 | 10.2 | 14.4 | 13.6 | 13.5 |
| 48 001 | 37300 | 5 | Anderson | 2 752 | 58 190 | 880 | 21.1 | 61.6 | 21.5 | 0.7 | 0.8 | 16.4 | 5.4 | 14.3 | 8.1 | 15.7 | 16.1 | 15.8 |
| 48 003 | 11380 | 6 | Andrews | 3 887 | 16 117 | 2 038 | 4.1 | 47.0 | 1.9 | 1.0 | 0.7 | 50.2 | 8.4 | 21.3 | 9.7 | 13.6 | 12.4 | 13.7 |
| 48 005 | 31260 | 5 | Angelina | 2 066 | 87 597 | 650 | 42.4 | 63.4 | 15.3 | 0.7 | 1.1 | 20.5 | 7.4 | 19.2 | 9.3 | 12.5 | 12.5 | 13.3 |
| 48 007 | 18580 | 2 | Aransas | 653 | 23 818 | 1 652 | 36.5 | 70.4 | 1.8 | 1.2 | 2.3 | 25.5 | 5.1 | 14.2 | 7.0 | 8.9 | 9.6 | 13.9 |
| 48 009 | 48660 | 3 | Archer | 2 339 | 8 735 | 2 540 | 3.7 | 90.5 | 1.0 | 1.2 | 0.5 | 8.0 | 4.6 | 18.7 | 7.8 | 8.5 | 12.0 | 17.6 |
| 48 011 | 11100 | 3 | Armstrong | 2 355 | 1 944 | 3 061 | 0.8 | 91.9 | 1.6 | 1.0 | 0.3 | 6.2 | 5.4 | 16.7 | 5.8 | 9.8 | 11.5 | 14.3 |
| 48 013 | 41700 | 1 | Atascosa | 3 159 | 46 446 | 1 041 | 14.7 | 36.2 | 1.0 | 0.7 | 0.5 | 62.3 | 7.4 | 21.0 | 8.6 | 11.7 | 12.3 | 13.6 |
| 48 015 | 26420 | 1 | Austin | 1 674 | 28 618 | 1 462 | 17.1 | 65.4 | 9.6 | 0.7 | 0.7 | 24.6 | 6.4 | 18.4 | 7.6 | 10.8 | 11.7 | 15.0 |
| 48 017 | ... | 7 | Bailey | 2 141 | 7 130 | 2 670 | 3.3 | 37.7 | 1.4 | 0.5 | 0.5 | 60.4 | 10.0 | 21.4 | 9.1 | 12.9 | 10.8 | 11.7 |
| 48 019 | 41700 | 1 | Bandera | 2 049 | 20 537 | 1 811 | 10.0 | 81.3 | 0.9 | 1.3 | 0.6 | 17.0 | 4.3 | 14.5 | 6.0 | 7.5 | 10.2 | 17.5 |
| 48 021 | 12420 | 1 | Bastrop | 2 300 | 74 763 | 731 | 32.5 | 58.0 | 8.0 | 1.0 | 1.1 | 33.2 | 6.6 | 19.3 | 7.8 | 11.6 | 13.2 | 15.7 |
| 48 023 | ... | 6 | Baylor | 2 247 | 3 623 | 2 933 | 1.6 | 84.5 | 2.5 | 0.7 | 0.6 | 12.7 | 5.8 | 14.9 | 6.7 | 9.7 | 10.1 | 14.0 |
| 48 025 | 13300 | 4 | Bee | 2 280 | 32 527 | 1 376 | 14.3 | 34.7 | 8.3 | 0.5 | 0.8 | 56.4 | 5.9 | 16.0 | 11.4 | 16.6 | 14.5 | 14.4 |
| 48 027 | 28660 | 2 | Bell | 2 722 | 323 037 | 202 | 118.7 | 52.9 | 22.1 | 1.1 | 5.0 | 22.2 | 9.0 | 19.3 | 12.2 | 17.2 | 12.5 | 12.0 |
| 48 029 | 41700 | 1 | Bexar | 3 211 | 1 785 704 | 19 | 556.1 | 31.3 | 7.5 | 0.6 | 3.1 | 58.9 | 7.5 | 19.4 | 11.0 | 14.9 | 13.3 | 13.1 |
| 48 031 | ... | 8 | Blanco | 1 837 | 10 655 | 2 383 | 5.8 | 79.2 | 1.2 | 1.0 | 0.7 | 18.9 | 4.9 | 16.4 | 6.0 | 8.7 | 11.2 | 15.8 |
| 48 033 | ... | 9 | Borden | 2 324 | 616 | 3 134 | 0.3 | 84.7 | 0.6 | 0.8 | 0.2 | 14.5 | 5.0 | 15.5 | 7.5 | 7.7 | 12.1 | 16.1 |
| 48 035 | ... | 6 | Bosque | 2 546 | 18 125 | 1 914 | 7.1 | 80.8 | 2.2 | 1.0 | 0.6 | 16.5 | 5.4 | 17.0 | 6.9 | 9.1 | 11.0 | 14.1 |
| 48 037 | 45500 | 3 | Bowie | 2 292 | 93 148 | 619 | 40.6 | 67.2 | 24.8 | 1.4 | 1.2 | 7.1 | 6.4 | 17.8 | 8.8 | 13.4 | 12.9 | 14.1 |
| 48 039 | 26420 | 1 | Brazoria | 3 516 | 324 769 | 199 | 92.4 | 53.7 | 12.6 | 0.8 | 6.0 | 28.3 | 7.8 | 19.7 | 8.3 | 13.8 | 14.9 | 14.6 |
| 48 041 | 17780 | 3 | Brazos | 1 516 | 200 665 | 314 | 132.4 | 60.0 | 11.1 | 0.7 | 5.9 | 23.9 | 6.4 | 13.7 | 32.0 | 14.6 | 9.6 | 9.1 |
| 48 043 | ... | 7 | Brewster | 16 016 | 9 316 | 2 491 | 0.6 | 54.5 | 1.9 | 1.1 | 1.0 | 42.8 | 5.6 | 13.7 | 13.4 | 12.4 | 10.6 | 12.4 |
| 48 045 | ... | 9 | Briscoe | 2 331 | 1 561 | 3 080 | 0.7 | 70.4 | 3.2 | 1.0 | 0.7 | 26.3 | 6.8 | 16.7 | 5.9 | 10.8 | 11.1 | 13.7 |
| 48 047 | ... | 6 | Brooks | 2 443 | 7 161 | 2 663 | 2.9 | 8.4 | 0.5 | 0.2 | 0.4 | 90.7 | 9.0 | 19.0 | 10.0 | 10.4 | 9.4 | 12.5 |
| 48 049 | 15220 | 5 | Brown | 2 446 | 37 825 | 1 226 | 15.5 | 75.1 | 4.2 | 1.1 | 0.7 | 20.1 | 6.1 | 17.6 | 9.1 | 11.2 | 11.4 | 13.7 |
| 48 051 | 17780 | 3 | Burleson | 1 707 | 17 291 | 1 962 | 10.1 | 68.1 | 12.6 | 0.8 | 0.5 | 19.1 | 6.2 | 17.3 | 7.4 | 10.1 | 11.4 | 15.2 |
| 48 053 | 31920 | 6 | Burnet | 2 575 | 43 448 | 1 100 | 16.9 | 76.5 | 2.3 | 1.0 | 0.8 | 20.6 | 5.7 | 17.2 | 7.3 | 10.3 | 11.1 | 14.5 |

1. CBSA = Core Based Statistical Area. See Appendix A for explanation. See Appendix B for list of metropolitan areas with component counties.   2. County type code from the Economic Research Service of USDA Rural-Urban Continuum Codes. See Appendix A for definition.   3. Dry land or land partially or temporarily covered by water.   4. May be of any race.

# Table B. States and Counties — Population and Households

| STATE County | 55 to 64 years | 65 to 74 years | 75 years and over | Percent female | Total persons 2000 | Total persons 2010 | Percent change 2000–2010 | Percent change 2010–2012 | Births | Deaths | Net migration | Number | Percent change 2000–2010 | Persons per household | Female family householder[1] | One person |
|---|---|---|---|---|---|---|---|---|---|---|---|---|---|---|---|---|
| | 16 | 17 | 18 | 19 | 20 | 21 | 22 | 23 | 24 | 25 | 26 | 27 | 28 | 29 | 30 | 31 |
| **TENNESSEE—Cont'd** | | | | | | | | | | | | | | | | |
| Marshall | 13.6 | 8.0 | 5.5 | 50.9 | 26 767 | 30 617 | 14.4 | 0.9 | 797 | 696 | 150 | 11 850 | 15.0 | 2.55 | 13.0 | 24.4 |
| Maury | 13.6 | 7.6 | 5.9 | 51.7 | 69 498 | 80 956 | 16.5 | 1.3 | 2 514 | 1 805 | 355 | 31 663 | 19.7 | 2.52 | 14.1 | 24.3 |
| Meigs | 15.9 | 11.4 | 6.0 | 50.5 | 11 086 | 11 753 | 6.0 | -0.5 | 264 | 348 | 31 | 4 686 | 8.9 | 2.48 | 10.8 | 23.2 |
| Monroe | 14.7 | 10.7 | 6.3 | 50.4 | 38 961 | 44 519 | 14.3 | 1.4 | 1 104 | 1 085 | 590 | 17 711 | 15.5 | 2.49 | 11.3 | 24.9 |
| Montgomery | 8.8 | 4.7 | 3.3 | 50.9 | 134 768 | 172 331 | 27.9 | 7.0 | 6 957 | 2 437 | 7 497 | 63 673 | 31.7 | 2.65 | 15.0 | 22.5 |
| Moore | 14.1 | 11.4 | 7.7 | 50.6 | 5 740 | 6 362 | 10.8 | -0.4 | 97 | 130 | 10 | 2 492 | 12.7 | 2.51 | 8.1 | 22.6 |
| Morgan | 13.4 | 8.3 | 5.6 | 45.0 | 19 757 | 21 987 | 11.3 | -0.3 | 419 | 521 | 40 | 7 692 | 10.0 | 2.53 | 11.5 | 24.3 |
| Obion | 13.9 | 9.8 | 7.5 | 51.8 | 32 450 | 31 807 | -2.0 | -1.5 | 794 | 903 | -352 | 13 077 | -0.8 | 2.40 | 12.9 | 27.3 |
| Overton | 14.3 | 10.5 | 6.9 | 50.8 | 20 118 | 22 083 | 9.8 | 0.5 | 525 | 660 | 242 | 8 820 | 8.8 | 2.47 | 11.0 | 25.7 |
| Perry | 15.1 | 11.2 | 8.0 | 49.8 | 7 631 | 7 915 | 3.7 | -0.7 | 220 | 219 | -70 | 3 160 | 4.5 | 2.47 | 10.1 | 26.6 |
| Pickett | 16.6 | 13.3 | 9.6 | 50.1 | 4 945 | 5 077 | 2.7 | 0.5 | 93 | 121 | 45 | 2 177 | 4.1 | 2.30 | 8.2 | 29.0 |
| Polk | 14.4 | 10.7 | 6.8 | 50.5 | 16 050 | 16 825 | 4.8 | -0.8 | 400 | 457 | -76 | 6 653 | 3.2 | 2.49 | 10.3 | 25.0 |
| Putnam | 11.8 | 8.4 | 6.6 | 50.6 | 62 315 | 72 321 | 16.1 | 1.3 | 2 086 | 1 547 | 398 | 28 930 | 16.3 | 2.41 | 10.9 | 28.0 |
| Rhea | 13.7 | 9.7 | 6.5 | 50.8 | 28 400 | 31 809 | 12.0 | 1.4 | 836 | 786 | 397 | 12 276 | 9.8 | 2.52 | 12.9 | 24.6 |
| Roane | 15.9 | 11.0 | 8.2 | 50.9 | 51 910 | 54 181 | 4.4 | -1.3 | 1 080 | 1 517 | -261 | 22 376 | 5.5 | 2.39 | 10.9 | 26.9 |
| Robertson | 12.4 | 7.2 | 4.9 | 50.8 | 54 433 | 66 283 | 21.8 | 1.0 | 2 093 | 1 262 | -162 | 24 197 | 21.6 | 2.71 | 11.9 | 19.9 |
| Rutherford | 9.8 | 5.1 | 3.4 | 50.6 | 182 023 | 262 604 | 44.3 | 4.5 | 8 302 | 3 461 | 6 795 | 96 232 | 44.8 | 2.68 | 12.8 | 22.1 |
| Scott | 12.6 | 8.6 | 5.6 | 50.8 | 21 127 | 22 228 | 5.2 | -0.2 | 574 | 566 | -55 | 8 671 | 5.7 | 2.53 | 13.2 | 25.6 |
| Sequatchie | 14.0 | 10.7 | 6.0 | 50.8 | 11 370 | 14 112 | 24.1 | 2.2 | 340 | 368 | 315 | 5 519 | 23.7 | 2.52 | 11.8 | 23.4 |
| Sevier | 14.2 | 9.8 | 6.1 | 50.8 | 71 170 | 89 889 | 26.3 | 2.9 | 2 439 | 1 991 | 2 164 | 35 343 | 24.2 | 2.52 | 11.4 | 23.4 |
| Shelby | 11.9 | 5.8 | 4.7 | 52.3 | 897 472 | 927 644 | 3.4 | 1.4 | 31 656 | 17 332 | -943 | 350 971 | 3.7 | 2.59 | 21.7 | 28.3 |
| Smith | 13.3 | 8.4 | 5.5 | 50.6 | 17 712 | 19 166 | 8.2 | -0.3 | 432 | 472 | -25 | 7 410 | 7.7 | 2.57 | 11.0 | 24.5 |
| Stewart | 14.9 | 10.1 | 6.9 | 50.2 | 12 370 | 13 324 | 7.7 | -0.2 | 281 | 377 | 70 | 5 386 | 9.2 | 2.46 | 9.6 | 25.5 |
| Sullivan | 14.6 | 10.5 | 8.5 | 51.6 | 153 048 | 156 823 | 2.5 | 0.0 | 3 512 | 4 098 | 664 | 66 298 | 4.3 | 2.33 | 11.4 | 28.8 |
| Sumner | 12.7 | 7.8 | 5.2 | 51.2 | 130 449 | 160 645 | 23.1 | 3.4 | 4 401 | 3 016 | 3 884 | 60 975 | 24.6 | 2.61 | 11.7 | 22.1 |
| Tipton | 11.8 | 7.0 | 4.5 | 51.0 | 51 271 | 61 081 | 19.1 | 1.0 | 1 737 | 1 206 | 76 | 21 617 | 19.4 | 2.78 | 15.7 | 19.7 |
| Trousdale | 14.2 | 8.2 | 5.6 | 50.5 | 7 259 | 7 870 | 8.4 | -1.0 | 195 | 194 | -76 | 2 976 | 7.1 | 2.60 | 12.6 | 23.5 |
| Unicoi | 15.2 | 11.1 | 8.8 | 51.1 | 17 667 | 18 313 | 3.7 | -0.4 | 361 | 589 | 161 | 7 726 | 2.8 | 2.32 | 10.7 | 28.5 |
| Union | 13.8 | 9.0 | 5.2 | 50.1 | 17 808 | 19 109 | 7.3 | 0.1 | 468 | 418 | -42 | 7 391 | 9.6 | 2.56 | 10.9 | 23.1 |
| Van Buren | 17.3 | 11.4 | 6.4 | 50.2 | 5 508 | 5 548 | 0.7 | 1.4 | 112 | 105 | 72 | 2 246 | 3.0 | 2.43 | 11.7 | 24.3 |
| Warren | 13.0 | 8.7 | 6.6 | 50.6 | 38 276 | 39 839 | 4.1 | 0.0 | 1 083 | 1 010 | -49 | 15 850 | 4.4 | 2.48 | 12.6 | 27.0 |
| Washington | 13.2 | 8.9 | 6.8 | 51.1 | 107 198 | 122 979 | 14.7 | 1.7 | 2 992 | 2 733 | 1 906 | 51 322 | 16.1 | 2.31 | 10.7 | 29.9 |
| Wayne | 13.3 | 9.2 | 7.0 | 44.9 | 16 842 | 17 021 | 1.1 | -0.1 | 313 | 449 | 87 | 6 136 | 3.4 | 2.43 | 10.4 | 26.5 |
| Weakley | 12.4 | 8.3 | 7.2 | 51.1 | 34 895 | 35 021 | 0.4 | -0.7 | 869 | 817 | -286 | 13 898 | 2.2 | 2.36 | 11.4 | 28.2 |
| White | 14.1 | 10.2 | 7.8 | 51.0 | 23 102 | 25 841 | 11.9 | 0.9 | 604 | 729 | 369 | 10 272 | 11.3 | 2.48 | 12.1 | 24.9 |
| Williamson | 12.6 | 5.9 | 4.2 | 51.2 | 126 638 | 183 182 | 44.7 | 5.3 | 4 484 | 2 092 | 7 234 | 64 886 | 45.1 | 2.81 | 8.2 | 17.7 |
| Wilson | 13.2 | 7.9 | 4.8 | 51.0 | 88 809 | 113 993 | 28.4 | 4.4 | 2 967 | 1 989 | 3 853 | 42 563 | 29.8 | 2.65 | 11.2 | 19.9 |
| **TEXAS** | 10.7 | 6.0 | 4.5 | 50.4 | 20 851 820 | 25 145 561 | 20.6 | 3.6 | 856 583 | 381 060 | 432 773 | 8 922 933 | 20.7 | 2.75 | 14.1 | 24.2 |
| Anderson | 11.8 | 7.3 | 5.5 | 39.2 | 55 109 | 58 458 | 6.1 | -0.5 | 1 307 | 1 423 | -136 | 17 218 | 9.8 | 2.57 | 13.8 | 25.7 |
| Andrews | 10.2 | 5.5 | 5.2 | 50.1 | 13 004 | 14 786 | 13.7 | 9.0 | 587 | 270 | 999 | 5 259 | 14.3 | 2.80 | 11.6 | 21.3 |
| Angelina | 11.8 | 7.5 | 6.3 | 51.0 | 80 130 | 86 771 | 8.3 | 1.0 | 2 761 | 1 971 | 84 | 31 090 | 8.4 | 2.70 | 15.4 | 23.9 |
| Aransas | 16.4 | 14.9 | 10.0 | 50.5 | 22 497 | 23 158 | 2.9 | 2.8 | 566 | 713 | 747 | 9 795 | 7.3 | 2.32 | 9.8 | 27.8 |
| Archer | 14.0 | 9.5 | 7.2 | 49.7 | 8 854 | 9 054 | 2.3 | -3.5 | 157 | 145 | -335 | 3 538 | 5.3 | 2.54 | 8.1 | 23.4 |
| Armstrong | 16.1 | 10.7 | 9.7 | 51.6 | 2 148 | 1 901 | -11.5 | 2.3 | 44 | 53 | 52 | 751 | -6.4 | 2.46 | 6.1 | 23.4 |
| Atascosa | 12.1 | 7.7 | 5.6 | 50.6 | 38 628 | 44 911 | 16.3 | 3.4 | 1 435 | 865 | 969 | 15 246 | 19.0 | 2.92 | 14.2 | 20.7 |
| Austin | 14.2 | 9.1 | 6.7 | 50.3 | 23 590 | 28 417 | 20.5 | 0.7 | 786 | 602 | 12 | 10 837 | 23.9 | 2.60 | 10.5 | 23.4 |
| Bailey | 10.1 | 7.1 | 6.9 | 48.8 | 6 594 | 7 165 | 8.7 | -0.5 | 291 | 121 | -214 | 2 468 | 5.1 | 2.86 | 10.7 | 22.9 |
| Bandera | 18.9 | 12.9 | 8.1 | 50.3 | 17 645 | 20 485 | 16.1 | 0.3 | 363 | 424 | 119 | 8 564 | 22.2 | 2.35 | 8.1 | 26.1 |
| Bastrop | 13.7 | 7.2 | 4.8 | 48.8 | 57 733 | 74 171 | 28.5 | 0.8 | 1 883 | 1 295 | -2 | 25 840 | 28.6 | 2.78 | 11.8 | 22.4 |
| Baylor | 13.3 | 13.3 | 12.2 | 52.2 | 4 093 | 3 726 | -9.0 | -2.8 | 85 | 132 | -51 | 1 669 | -6.8 | 2.19 | 8.3 | 34.3 |
| Bee | 10.5 | 5.9 | 4.8 | 40.3 | 32 359 | 31 861 | -1.5 | 2.1 | 798 | 539 | 403 | 9 042 | -0.2 | 2.69 | 16.1 | 25.4 |
| Bell | 9.0 | 5.0 | 3.9 | 50.5 | 237 974 | 310 235 | 30.4 | 4.1 | 13 895 | 4 226 | 3 082 | 114 035 | 33.4 | 2.65 | 14.9 | 24.0 |
| Bexar | 10.4 | 5.7 | 4.7 | 50.9 | 1 392 931 | 1 714 773 | 23.1 | 4.1 | 58 420 | 25 392 | 37 547 | 608 931 | 24.5 | 2.75 | 16.6 | 25.3 |
| Blanco | 18.1 | 11.5 | 7.3 | 49.2 | 8 418 | 10 497 | 24.7 | 1.5 | 206 | 263 | 220 | 4 309 | 30.5 | 2.41 | 7.6 | 26.2 |
| Borden | 16.3 | 10.5 | 9.3 | 47.9 | 729 | 641 | -12.1 | -3.9 | 11 | 11 | -27 | 264 | -9.6 | 2.43 | 4.9 | 22.0 |
| Bosque | 14.9 | 12.5 | 9.2 | 50.6 | 17 204 | 18 212 | 5.9 | -0.5 | 407 | 536 | 49 | 7 254 | 7.9 | 2.47 | 9.1 | 26.5 |
| Bowie | 12.3 | 7.8 | 6.5 | 49.5 | 89 306 | 92 565 | 3.6 | 0.6 | 2 635 | 2 202 | 189 | 34 669 | 4.9 | 2.49 | 16.7 | 27.7 |
| Brazoria | 11.0 | 5.8 | 4.0 | 49.3 | 241 767 | 313 166 | 29.5 | 3.7 | 10 490 | 4 556 | 5 675 | 106 589 | 30.1 | 2.84 | 12.1 | 19.9 |
| Brazos | 7.2 | 4.1 | 3.3 | 49.3 | 152 415 | 194 851 | 27.8 | 3.0 | 5 862 | 2 046 | 1 964 | 71 739 | 30.0 | 2.53 | 10.7 | 26.6 |
| Brewster | 14.9 | 10.2 | 6.8 | 49.9 | 8 866 | 9 232 | 4.1 | 0.9 | 268 | 171 | -17 | 4 207 | 14.7 | 2.18 | 9.3 | 37.0 |
| Briscoe | 13.7 | 10.9 | 10.5 | 50.3 | 1 790 | 1 637 | -8.5 | -4.6 | 48 | 26 | -110 | 692 | -4.4 | 2.37 | 6.5 | 28.3 |
| Brooks | 12.3 | 9.3 | 8.0 | 50.5 | 7 976 | 7 223 | -9.4 | -0.9 | 310 | 189 | -183 | 2 642 | -2.5 | 2.71 | 20.6 | 26.1 |
| Brown | 13.2 | 9.9 | 7.8 | 50.7 | 37 674 | 38 106 | 1.1 | -0.7 | 957 | 1 019 | -198 | 14 778 | 3.3 | 2.47 | 11.8 | 26.9 |
| Burleson | 14.7 | 9.1 | 8.5 | 50.4 | 16 470 | 17 187 | 4.4 | 0.6 | 422 | 427 | 102 | 6 822 | 7.2 | 2.50 | 11.2 | 26.5 |
| Burnet | 15.0 | 10.7 | 8.1 | 50.8 | 34 147 | 42 750 | 25.2 | 1.6 | 1 042 | 934 | 527 | 16 511 | 25.7 | 2.53 | 9.7 | 23.7 |

1. No spouse present.

# Table B. States and Counties — Population, Vital Statistics, Medicare, and Crime

| STATE County | Persons in group quarters, 2010 | Daytime population, 2007–2011 Number | Employment/residence ratio | Births, 2011 Total | Rate[1] | Deaths, 2011 Number | Rate[1] | Persons under 65 with no health insurance, 2010 Number | Percent | Medicare, 2012 Eligible for Medicare | Enrolled in Medicare Advantage | Enrolled in a Medicare prescription drug plan | Serious crimes known to police,[2] 2011 Total Number | Rate[3] |
|---|---|---|---|---|---|---|---|---|---|---|---|---|---|---|
| | 32 | 33 | 34 | 35 | 36 | 37 | 38 | 39 | 40 | 41 | 42 | 43 | 44 | 45 |

## TENNESSEE—Cont'd

| STATE County | 32 | 33 | 34 | 35 | 36 | 37 | 38 | 39 | 40 | 41 | 42 | 43 | 44 | 45 |
|---|---|---|---|---|---|---|---|---|---|---|---|---|---|---|
| Marshall | 359 | 28 068 | 0.83 | 346 | 11.2 | 303 | 9.8 | 4 836 | 18.3 | 5 605 | 1 320 | 2 227 | 602 | 1 949 |
| Maury | 1 009 | 75 136 | 0.86 | 1 114 | 13.7 | 805 | 9.9 | 11 035 | 15.8 | 14 758 | 3 165 | 6 240 | 2 816 | 3 447 |
| Meigs | 128 | 9 614 | 0.50 | 120 | 10.2 | 131 | 11.2 | 1 607 | 16.5 | 2 685 | 774 | 1 162 | 384 | 3 238 |
| Monroe | 500 | 41 927 | 0.85 | 491 | 10.9 | 465 | 10.4 | 6 657 | 18.1 | 10 476 | 3 684 | 3 810 | 1 557 | 3 466 |
| Montgomery | 3 416 | 148 196 | 0.73 | 3 019 | 17.1 | 1 068 | 6.0 | 21 403 | 13.7 | 18 908 | 3 185 | 6 505 | 6 204 | 3 568 |
| Moore | 104 | 5 258 | 0.63 | 45 | 7.0 | 54 | 8.4 | 785 | 15.3 | 1 237 | 121 | 510 | 108 | 1 683 |
| Morgan | 2 527 | 18 396 | 0.55 | 182 | 8.3 | 216 | 9.9 | 2 697 | 16.3 | 4 758 | 1 917 | 1 547 | 622 | 2 804 |
| Obion | 461 | 33 646 | 1.13 | 347 | 10.9 | 407 | 12.8 | 4 264 | 16.3 | 7 169 | 505 | 3 714 | 1 120 | 3 490 |
| Overton | 286 | 19 038 | 0.67 | 231 | 10.4 | 289 | 13.0 | 3 072 | 16.9 | 5 136 | 593 | 2 925 | 409 | 1 836 |
| Perry | 123 | 7 614 | 0.92 | 104 | 13.2 | 96 | 12.2 | 1 278 | 20.0 | 1 876 | 418 | 957 | 140 | 1 753 |
| Pickett | 74 | 4 555 | 0.77 | 37 | 7.2 | 50 | 9.8 | 835 | 21.4 | 1 435 | 138 | 859 | 67 | 1 308 |
| Polk | 244 | 13 616 | 0.51 | 173 | 10.3 | 210 | 12.5 | 2 398 | 17.4 | 3 811 | 737 | 1 945 | 443 | 2 609 |
| Putnam | 2 715 | 79 047 | 1.26 | 943 | 12.9 | 674 | 9.2 | 11 109 | 18.7 | 14 382 | 1 905 | 7 540 | 3 371 | 4 620 |
| Rhea | 924 | 32 655 | 1.09 | 378 | 11.8 | 348 | 10.8 | 4 460 | 17.2 | 6 751 | 1 159 | 3 679 | 744 | 2 318 |
| Roane | 646 | 48 250 | 0.73 | 466 | 8.7 | 668 | 12.4 | 6 117 | 14.0 | 13 146 | 4 296 | 4 116 | 1 517 | 2 775 |
| Robertson | 703 | 55 605 | 0.67 | 988 | 14.7 | 549 | 8.2 | 9 792 | 16.9 | 10 685 | 3 740 | 3 852 | 1 829 | 2 735 |
| Rutherford | 5 109 | 238 752 | 0.85 | 3 628 | 13.5 | 1 452 | 5.4 | 36 554 | 15.5 | 30 566 | 10 023 | 9 615 | 9 362 | 3 533 |
| Scott | 264 | 21 290 | 0.88 | 262 | 11.8 | 269 | 12.1 | 3 325 | 17.5 | 4 787 | 1 219 | 2 522 | 785 | 3 500 |
| Sequatchie | 188 | 12 013 | 0.63 | 150 | 10.5 | 152 | 10.6 | 2 026 | 17.3 | 3 336 | 667 | 1 770 | 479 | 3 364 |
| Sevier | 982 | 88 579 | 0.99 | 1 092 | 11.9 | 850 | 9.3 | 16 161 | 21.5 | 18 919 | 7 612 | 5 799 | 4 173 | 4 601 |
| Shelby | 18 329 | 1 000 128 | 1.18 | 14 217 | 15.2 | 7 535 | 8.1 | 143 767 | 17.7 | 125 903 | 24 969 | 57 525 | 59 898 | 6 399 |
| Smith | 159 | 17 072 | 0.74 | 194 | 10.1 | 210 | 11.0 | 2 762 | 16.8 | 3 482 | 872 | 1 583 | 467 | 2 415 |
| Stewart | 92 | 11 729 | 0.70 | 126 | 9.6 | 169 | 12.8 | 1 838 | 16.7 | 2 907 | 397 | 1 336 | 208 | 1 547 |
| Sullivan | 2 631 | 163 864 | 1.11 | 1 558 | 9.9 | 1 731 | 11.0 | 19 222 | 15.3 | 38 529 | 20 275 | 9 761 | 6 773 | 4 280 |
| Sumner | 1 252 | 134 903 | 0.68 | 1 964 | 12.0 | 1 314 | 8.0 | 21 472 | 15.4 | 26 819 | 10 335 | 8 732 | 3 430 | 2 116 |
| Tipton | 962 | 46 678 | 0.47 | 775 | 12.6 | 531 | 8.7 | 7 541 | 14.2 | 9 276 | 1 580 | 4 152 | 1 763 | 2 861 |
| Trousdale | 130 | 6 170 | 0.49 | 88 | 11.3 | 80 | 10.2 | 1 180 | 17.5 | 1 548 | 474 | 668 | 329 | 4 143 |
| Unicoi | 405 | 16 877 | 0.81 | 157 | 8.6 | 265 | 14.5 | 2 352 | 16.2 | 4 784 | 1 666 | 1 819 | 386 | 2 089 |
| Union | 152 | 15 674 | 0.50 | 205 | 10.7 | 188 | 9.8 | 2 980 | 18.3 | 4 065 | 1 926 | 1 291 | 718 | 3 724 |
| Van Buren | 94 | 4 632 | 0.61 | 49 | 8.9 | 33 | 6.0 | 827 | 18.3 | 1 414 | 170 | 817 | 116 | 2 072 |
| Warren | 580 | 38 780 | 0.94 | 483 | 12.1 | 427 | 10.7 | 7 325 | 21.9 | 8 348 | 1 644 | 4 334 | 1 202 | 2 990 |
| Washington | 4 649 | 130 866 | 1.17 | 1 340 | 10.8 | 1 169 | 9.4 | 15 135 | 15.0 | 25 038 | 9 122 | 8 167 | 4 624 | 3 726 |
| Wayne | 2 140 | 16 031 | 0.83 | 143 | 8.4 | 199 | 11.7 | 2 232 | 18.2 | 3 640 | 434 | 2 124 | 157 | 914 |
| Weakley | 2 244 | 31 229 | 0.77 | 400 | 11.4 | 357 | 10.2 | 5 064 | 18.3 | 6 699 | 555 | 3 943 | 832 | 2 354 |
| White | 382 | 23 651 | 0.80 | 264 | 10.1 | 306 | 11.7 | 3 745 | 17.8 | 6 060 | 928 | 3 246 | 902 | 3 459 |
| Williamson | 1 153 | 191 382 | 1.14 | 2 019 | 10.7 | 848 | 4.5 | 13 859 | 8.5 | 22 904 | 7 051 | 7 320 | 2 487 | 1 346 |
| Wilson | 1 232 | 97 102 | 0.72 | 1 299 | 11.1 | 841 | 7.2 | 12 556 | 12.7 | 19 221 | 6 168 | 6 679 | 3 113 | 2 706 |
| **TEXAS** | 581 139 | 24 759 314 | 1.00 | 396 133 | 15.4 | 165 335 | 6.4 | 5 820 793 | 26.3 | 3 293 001 | 127 300 | 426 236 | 996 372 | 3 881 |
| Anderson | 14 217 | 57 096 | 0.95 | 611 | 10.5 | 647 | 11.1 | 9 722 | 25.6 | 9 072 | 1 470 | 4 145 | 1 683 | 2 820 |
| Andrews | 82 | 14 183 | 0.95 | 258 | 16.7 | 101 | 6.5 | 3 579 | 27.3 | 1 909 | 207 | 963 | 393 | 2 603 |
| Angelina | 2 953 | 85 979 | 1.00 | 1 287 | 14.7 | 863 | 9.8 | 18 818 | 25.9 | 15 387 | 2 761 | 7 281 | 3 118 | 3 519 |
| Aransas | 459 | 21 615 | 0.82 | 266 | 11.4 | 327 | 14.0 | 4 615 | 26.8 | 6 449 | 2 043 | 2 070 | 790 | 3 341 |
| Archer | 56 | 7 268 | 0.58 | 92 | 10.4 | 58 | 6.6 | 1 959 | 25.9 | 1 683 | 101 | 847 | 71 | 768 |
| Armstrong | 54 | 1 512 | 0.51 | 22 | 11.4 | 25 | 13.0 | 324 | 21.8 | 407 | 37 | 202 | 15 | 773 |
| Atascosa | 384 | 37 393 | 0.60 | 654 | 14.3 | 382 | 8.4 | 10 415 | 26.7 | 7 290 | 2 381 | 2 374 | 1 107 | 2 414 |
| Austin | 212 | 26 996 | 0.91 | 372 | 13.0 | 273 | 9.5 | 5 809 | 24.4 | 5 168 | 658 | 2 352 | 517 | 1 782 |
| Bailey | 106 | 6 906 | 0.94 | 168 | 23.2 | 47 | 6.5 | 2 039 | 33.6 | 1 072 | 61 | 727 | 172 | 2 351 |
| Bandera | 320 | 16 346 | 0.53 | 153 | 7.4 | 178 | 8.7 | 4 230 | 26.2 | 4 761 | 734 | 1 489 | 200 | 956 |
| Bastrop | 2 337 | 58 251 | 0.53 | 887 | 11.8 | 580 | 7.7 | 16 948 | 26.6 | 11 149 | 1 697 | 4 100 | 1 733 | 2 288 |
| Baylor | 65 | 3 780 | 1.01 | 43 | 11.5 | 51 | 13.6 | 784 | 28.3 | 1 022 | 75 | 547 | 62 | 1 630 |
| Bee | 7 499 | 32 085 | 1.02 | 332 | 10.3 | 215 | 6.7 | 4 753 | 22.7 | 4 116 | 953 | 1 727 | 528 | 1 623 |
| Bell | 8 079 | 316 609 | 1.10 | 6 055 | 19.2 | 1 817 | 5.8 | 57 592 | 20.7 | 36 393 | 9 206 | 8 861 | 11 235 | 3 560 |
| Bexar | 42 001 | 1 735 175 | 1.06 | 26 726 | 15.2 | 11 060 | 6.3 | 348 909 | 23.1 | 235 088 | 85 108 | 53 119 | 101 326 | 5 787 |
| Blanco | 106 | 9 399 | 0.82 | 84 | 7.9 | 110 | 10.4 | 2 329 | 27.2 | 2 177 | 252 | 800 | 147 | 1 372 |
| Borden | 0 | 546 | 0.78 | 9 | 14.4 | 7 | 11.2 | 101 | 20.0 | 130 | D | 58 | 7 | 1 070 |
| Bosque | 329 | 15 585 | 0.64 | 184 | 10.1 | 233 | 12.7 | 4 019 | 28.2 | 4 306 | 1 019 | 1 652 | 250 | 1 408 |
| Bowie | 6 206 | 98 625 | 1.18 | 1 160 | 12.5 | 951 | 10.2 | 16 326 | 22.1 | 17 178 | 2 244 | 6 991 | 4 530 | 4 793 |
| Brazoria | 10 559 | 263 626 | 0.69 | 4 946 | 15.5 | 1 958 | 6.1 | 58 652 | 21.4 | 38 000 | 7 504 | 12 868 | 6 887 | 2 154 |
| Brazos | 13 512 | 193 425 | 1.04 | 2 682 | 13.6 | 879 | 4.4 | 37 110 | 22.2 | 17 869 | 1 879 | 6 334 | 7 693 | 3 867 |
| Brewster | 75 | 9 089 | 1.00 | 113 | 12.0 | 66 | 7.0 | 2 169 | 28.2 | 1 720 | 274 | 643 | 189 | 2 005 |
| Briscoe | 0 | 1 501 | 0.70 | 27 | 16.4 | 11 | 6.7 | 515 | 40.5 | 414 | 42 | 220 | 0 | 0 |
| Brooks | 67 | 7 897 | 1.25 | 147 | 20.4 | 80 | 11.1 | 1 512 | 25.6 | 1 590 | 342 | 909 | 172 | 2 332 |
| Brown | 1 668 | 39 675 | 1.10 | 460 | 12.0 | 435 | 11.4 | 8 099 | 26.7 | 8 178 | 871 | 4 030 | 1 130 | 2 904 |
| Burleson | 163 | 14 639 | 0.66 | 191 | 11.1 | 187 | 10.8 | 3 868 | 27.4 | 3 606 | 632 | 1 436 | 229 | 1 305 |
| Burnet | 1 059 | 40 902 | 0.91 | 477 | 11.1 | 401 | 9.3 | 10 015 | 29.6 | 9 849 | 1 430 | 4 034 | 908 | 2 080 |

1. Per 1,000 estimated resident population.　2. Data for serious crimes have not been adjusted for underreporting; this may affect comparability between geographic areas and over time.　3. Per 100,000 population estimated by the FBI.

# Table B. States and Counties — Crime, Education, Money Income, and Poverty

| STATE County | Serious crimes known to police, 2011 (cont.)[1] Rate[2] | | Education School enrollment and attainment, 2007–2011 | | | | Local government expenditures,[5] 2009–2010 | | Money income, 2007–2011 | | | | Income and poverty, 2011 | | | |
|---|---|---|---|---|---|---|---|---|---|---|---|---|---|---|---|---|
| | | | Enrollment[3] | | Attainment[4] (percent) | | | | Per capita income[6] (dollars) | Households Median income | | Percent with income of $200,000 or more | Percent below poverty level | | | |
| | Violent | Property | Total | Percent private | High school graduate or less | Bachelor's degree or more | Total current expenditures (mil dol) | Current expenditures per student (dollars) | | Dollars | Percent change, 2000 to 2007–2011 (constant 2011 dollars) | | Median household income (dollars) | All persons | Children under 18 years | Children 5 to 17 years in families |
| | 46 | 47 | 48 | 49 | 50 | 51 | 52 | 53 | 54 | 55 | 56 | 57 | 58 | 59 | 60 | 61 |
| **TENNESSEE—Cont'd** | | | | | | | | | | | | | | | | |
| Marshall | 317 | 1 631 | 6 683 | 8.9 | 64.1 | 11.2 | 38.3 | 7 152 | 20 569 | 41 620 | -19.8 | 1.3 | 40 214 | 16.4 | 24.2 | 22.5 |
| Maury | 594 | 2 854 | 18 482 | 16.6 | 53.6 | 16.6 | 90.0 | 7 670 | 23 098 | 46 552 | -17.1 | 1.7 | 42 569 | 16.6 | 25.2 | 25.0 |
| Meigs | 405 | 2 833 | 2 292 | 5.8 | 66.8 | 7.9 | 14.0 | 7 338 | 19 118 | 34 942 | -11.8 | 0.4 | 37 129 | 23.3 | 33.2 | 29.7 |
| Monroe | 381 | 3 085 | 9 293 | 11.1 | 66.6 | 9.6 | 50.7 | 7 101 | 18 702 | 35 096 | -14.3 | 1.4 | 32 720 | 22.7 | 34.0 | 30.5 |
| Montgomery | 572 | 2 996 | 48 558 | 12.0 | 41.8 | 22.7 | 221.0 | 7 584 | 22 589 | 49 695 | -5.6 | 1.4 | 47 684 | 16.5 | 23.8 | 23.4 |
| Moore | 31 | 1 651 | 1 514 | 7.1 | 62.9 | 14.0 | 8.2 | 8 288 | 24 113 | 45 950 | -7.0 | 2.4 | 48 229 | 12.4 | 22.6 | 19.7 |
| Morgan | 176 | 2 628 | 3 958 | 9.7 | 72.9 | 5.9 | 25.6 | 7 727 | 17 373 | 37 130 | -0.8 | 0.9 | 35 266 | 22.1 | 30.2 | 27.0 |
| Obion | 312 | 3 178 | 7 229 | 6.9 | 64.4 | 12.4 | 41.7 | 7 693 | 21 274 | 39 671 | -10.3 | 1.6 | 38 429 | 18.3 | 28.4 | 26.0 |
| Overton | 296 | 1 539 | 4 720 | 4.3 | 66.9 | 10.9 | 24.6 | 6 939 | 18 489 | 34 108 | -6.1 | 1.5 | 32 308 | 25.1 | 33.7 | 30.1 |
| Perry | 250 | 1 503 | 1 736 | 7.8 | 68.5 | 10.7 | 9.7 | 8 445 | 17 083 | 31 857 | -15.9 | 0.5 | 31 505 | 19.7 | 31.1 | 29.8 |
| Pickett | 59 | 1 249 | 857 | 0.6 | 67.2 | 11.9 | 5.8 | 8 259 | 19 856 | 31 157 | -6.5 | 1.0 | 31 518 | 19.2 | 30.5 | 27.1 |
| Polk | 236 | 2 374 | 3 612 | 10.3 | 64.6 | 11.3 | 20.6 | 7 568 | 18 199 | 36 204 | -9.5 | 0.5 | 35 628 | 17.7 | 27.3 | 25.1 |
| Putnam | 408 | 4 211 | 19 069 | 6.2 | 55.7 | 21.9 | 79.4 | 7 384 | 19 292 | 34 305 | -17.8 | 1.6 | 35 053 | 23.5 | 29.4 | 27.8 |
| Rhea | 284 | 2 035 | 7 401 | 12.6 | 62.2 | 10.8 | 36.3 | 7 119 | 17 860 | 36 934 | -10.1 | 0.9 | 34 920 | 23.1 | 30.7 | 29.6 |
| Roane | 218 | 2 557 | 10 651 | 8.9 | 53.9 | 17.3 | 59.7 | 8 016 | 24 059 | 43 129 | -3.9 | 1.8 | 42 542 | 17.8 | 28.5 | 23.1 |
| Robertson | 405 | 2 330 | 15 898 | 15.5 | 57.8 | 15.2 | 77.1 | 6 874 | 22 937 | 50 759 | -12.9 | 1.7 | 48 179 | 15.1 | 22.4 | 20.7 |
| Rutherford | 420 | 3 113 | 77 589 | 12.1 | 41.3 | 27.0 | 331.8 | 7 413 | 24 879 | 54 433 | -12.9 | 2.2 | 52 586 | 12.1 | 15.9 | 14.7 |
| Scott | 263 | 3 237 | 5 232 | 3.4 | 68.5 | 9.5 | 32.1 | 7 802 | 15 212 | 29 454 | -9.5 | 0.2 | 29 882 | 24.8 | 33.5 | 31.3 |
| Sequatchie | 386 | 2 978 | 3 239 | 7.3 | 63.8 | 15.7 | 15.7 | 6 825 | 19 318 | 33 536 | -19.8 | 1.7 | 38 008 | 19.2 | 32.0 | 30.1 |
| Sevier | 343 | 4 258 | 18 679 | 10.8 | 56.9 | 15.0 | 118.6 | 8 267 | 22 600 | 42 569 | -9.2 | 1.6 | 40 353 | 16.8 | 28.6 | 27.6 |
| Shelby | 1 188 | 5 211 | 264 021 | 19.0 | 42.1 | 28.3 | 1 405.3 | 8 922 | 25 470 | 46 102 | -13.8 | 4.1 | 44 051 | 21.5 | 31.0 | 27.3 |
| Smith | 398 | 2 017 | 4 445 | 8.8 | 66.6 | 12.3 | 23.2 | 6 890 | 21 294 | 43 580 | -9.4 | 1.3 | 42 182 | 16.8 | 26.7 | 24.8 |
| Stewart | 283 | 1 265 | 3 237 | 9.7 | 58.0 | 12.9 | 17.6 | 7 693 | 21 723 | 42 771 | -2.0 | 0.6 | 40 508 | 17.6 | 25.7 | 22.8 |
| Sullivan | 518 | 3 762 | 34 422 | 14.1 | 51.4 | 20.4 | 191.9 | 8 636 | 23 536 | 40 572 | -10.4 | 2.3 | 39 564 | 18.2 | 26.9 | 25.0 |
| Sumner | 234 | 1 882 | 39 789 | 14.5 | 46.7 | 23.0 | 206.4 | 7 602 | 27 212 | 55 211 | -11.2 | 3.3 | 52 704 | 10.9 | 16.7 | 15.3 |
| Tipton | 479 | 2 382 | 16 419 | 14.4 | 54.7 | 13.5 | 85.7 | 7 112 | 22 062 | 50 869 | -10.0 | 1.0 | 50 401 | 15.2 | 22.9 | 20.3 |
| Trousdale | 529 | 3 614 | 1 943 | 11.2 | 67.7 | 12.9 | 9.0 | 6 730 | 20 973 | 44 163 | 1.5 | 2.9 | 38 541 | 19.5 | 27.9 | 24.3 |
| Unicoi | 189 | 1 900 | 3 816 | 7.8 | 63.3 | 11.7 | 19.0 | 7 101 | 20 753 | 35 265 | -12.5 | 1.4 | 33 522 | 20.4 | 29.0 | 26.5 |
| Union | 301 | 3 423 | 4 063 | 11.0 | 74.8 | 6.6 | 25.1 | 8 530 | 16 423 | 31 535 | -14.6 | 0.8 | 35 740 | 21.0 | 33.6 | 31.9 |
| Van Buren | 304 | 1 768 | 1 111 | 16.7 | 80.4 | 8.5 | 6.5 | 8 515 | 17 872 | 31 155 | -18.1 | 1.5 | 32 896 | 19.6 | 30.8 | 27.3 |
| Warren | 303 | 2 687 | 8 885 | 12.6 | 66.5 | 11.8 | 48.6 | 7 547 | 19 035 | 35 575 | -14.8 | 1.5 | 32 823 | 22.6 | 31.6 | 29.7 |
| Washington | 394 | 3 332 | 31 996 | 10.1 | 44.1 | 28.2 | 126.1 | 7 623 | 24 742 | 42 104 | -5.8 | 3.2 | 41 358 | 18.3 | 23.5 | 23.5 |
| Wayne | 122 | 792 | 3 285 | 2.5 | 72.4 | 7.0 | 20.9 | 8 144 | 15 466 | 33 630 | -6.3 | 0.5 | 29 883 | 28.3 | 32.0 | 28.2 |
| Weakley | 294 | 2 060 | 10 329 | 5.2 | 58.1 | 17.8 | 34.8 | 7 159 | 19 647 | 33 932 | -16.3 | 2.0 | 34 457 | 20.4 | 25.3 | 23.4 |
| White | 272 | 3 187 | 5 488 | 7.6 | 69.8 | 11.3 | 27.7 | 6 754 | 18 196 | 34 642 | -12.7 | 1.3 | 33 094 | 19.9 | 29.7 | 28.6 |
| Williamson | 110 | 1 235 | 52 124 | 26.6 | 23.5 | 51.5 | 275.6 | 8 027 | 41 558 | 89 063 | -4.5 | 12.7 | 90 207 | 6.2 | 7.3 | 6.5 |
| Wilson | 369 | 2 337 | 27 852 | 20.6 | 46.6 | 24.7 | 134.4 | 7 258 | 28 110 | 61 400 | -9.3 | 3.3 | 59 769 | 11.8 | 16.6 | 14.9 |
| **TEXAS** | 408 | 3 472 | 6 986 128 | 11.1 | 45.2 | 26.1 | 42 380.6 | 8 738 | 25 548 | 50 920 | -5.5 | 4.4 | 49 390 | 18.5 | 26.6 | 24.9 |
| Anderson | 283 | 2 537 | 12 747 | 5.2 | 59.7 | 11.5 | 74.0 | 8 735 | 18 487 | 40 577 | -6.0 | 2.0 | 38 558 | 23.3 | 27.0 | 25.2 |
| Andrews | 596 | 2 007 | 3 960 | 6.3 | 55.1 | 13.9 | 32.2 | 10 246 | 29 126 | 51 598 | 12.3 | 4.6 | 52 865 | 13.3 | 18.4 | 16.9 |
| Angelina | 357 | 3 163 | 22 863 | 6.3 | 51.7 | 15.6 | 143.6 | 8 305 | 20 779 | 39 325 | -13.8 | 1.7 | 39 169 | 19.1 | 28.7 | 26.3 |
| Aransas | 182 | 3 159 | 4 441 | 11.8 | 47.2 | 23.0 | 31.9 | 10 098 | 26 288 | 44 129 | 6.5 | 3.1 | 38 887 | 21.3 | 37.7 | 35.4 |
| Archer | 97 | 671 | 2 199 | 5.2 | 54.0 | 18.8 | 16.4 | 8 896 | 25 895 | 53 113 | 2.1 | 2.6 | 52 318 | 11.8 | 16.6 | 14.0 |
| Armstrong | 0 | 773 | 446 | 1.3 | 34.7 | 25.2 | 4.0 | 12 327 | 24 510 | 56 538 | 9.6 | 1.8 | 49 501 | 10.6 | 15.9 | 14.3 |
| Atascosa | 150 | 2 264 | 12 021 | 6.1 | 61.8 | 12.1 | 81.5 | 9 308 | 19 216 | 43 261 | -3.1 | 1.7 | 41 236 | 21.8 | 32.2 | 30.3 |
| Austin | 200 | 1 582 | 6 980 | 16.2 | 50.6 | 19.4 | 52.7 | 9 410 | 27 055 | 52 510 | 0.7 | 4.0 | 48 209 | 13.0 | 20.2 | 18.9 |
| Bailey | 342 | 2 009 | 1 993 | 6.7 | 57.0 | 19.1 | 13.9 | 9 638 | 17 505 | 41 106 | 9.1 | 0.7 | 35 816 | 17.9 | 28.3 | 28.4 |
| Bandera | 96 | 861 | 3 935 | 9.0 | 40.6 | 21.7 | 27.6 | 9 651 | 23 666 | 45 595 | -13.4 | 2.2 | 46 652 | 12.3 | 24.4 | 21.7 |
| Bastrop | 259 | 2 030 | 17 463 | 11.4 | 52.1 | 16.8 | 124.7 | 8 395 | 23 584 | 52 882 | -10.1 | 2.1 | 51 947 | 14.6 | 22.6 | 20.7 |
| Baylor | 342 | 1 288 | 712 | 3.9 | 46.9 | 23.5 | 6.1 | 10 524 | 23 968 | 37 159 | 11.8 | 3.2 | 32 208 | 19.6 | 32.0 | 29.6 |
| Bee | 203 | 1 420 | 7 235 | 11.0 | 60.1 | 8.7 | 45.2 | 8 632 | 13 681 | 39 247 | 2.4 | 2.2 | 36 048 | 29.6 | 36.3 | 34.5 |
| Bell | 379 | 3 181 | 86 602 | 11.1 | 40.8 | 20.9 | 528.5 | 8 373 | 22 945 | 49 466 | -0.6 | 2.1 | 45 797 | 15.8 | 23.3 | 22.2 |
| Bexar | 450 | 5 337 | 496 694 | 13.8 | 43.5 | 25.6 | 2 813.7 | 8 695 | 23 866 | 48 083 | -7.1 | 3.3 | 46 589 | 17.9 | 25.6 | 24.2 |
| Blanco | 140 | 1 232 | 2 166 | 7.6 | 41.5 | 26.8 | 18.4 | 11 104 | 27 698 | 46 457 | -12.6 | 4.0 | 54 000 | 11.5 | 21.1 | 18.7 |
| Borden | 0 | 1 070 | 174 | 1.1 | 56.5 | 23.5 | 4.4 | 19 986 | 40 060 | 59 643 | 51.3 | 11.3 | 51 426 | 11.8 | 16.4 | 15.5 |
| Bosque | 152 | 1 256 | 4 068 | 3.5 | 55.0 | 14.5 | 24.6 | 9 429 | 22 383 | 44 744 | -3.0 | 1.8 | 41 361 | 16.8 | 26.1 | 24.5 |
| Bowie | 691 | 4 102 | 23 300 | 6.9 | 48.7 | 18.5 | 161.4 | 8 998 | 22 718 | 43 210 | -3.0 | 2.6 | 43 364 | 19.1 | 28.0 | 25.3 |
| Brazoria | 170 | 1 984 | 84 753 | 11.4 | 40.5 | 26.5 | 471.5 | 7 826 | 28 533 | 67 018 | 2.1 | 5.0 | 62 180 | 12.1 | 16.9 | 17.1 |
| Brazos | 386 | 3 481 | 84 668 | 5.4 | 37.6 | 39.0 | 220.1 | 8 325 | 21 292 | 37 161 | -5.4 | 3.5 | 37 623 | 29.0 | 24.2 | 24.2 |
| Brewster | 106 | 1 899 | 2 286 | 8.4 | 39.5 | 32.4 | 15.8 | 12 533 | 26 265 | 39 615 | 7.1 | 1.9 | 43 896 | 16.6 | 23.5 | 22.3 |
| Briscoe | 0 | 0 | 342 | 4.1 | 52.0 | 14.2 | 4.5 | 12 151 | 17 828 | 34 130 | -15.5 | 0.3 | 38 372 | 16.3 | 27.4 | 25.9 |
| Brooks | 325 | 2 007 | 1 589 | 2.9 | 73.4 | 10.5 | 18.9 | 11 421 | 14 193 | 19 936 | -20.7 | 0.0 | 24 567 | 35.4 | 48.1 | 48.1 |
| Brown | 301 | 2 604 | 9 399 | 13.8 | 57.1 | 15.2 | 63.8 | 9 060 | 20 892 | 39 965 | -4.4 | 2.1 | 38 466 | 20.4 | 30.7 | 27.3 |
| Burleson | 177 | 1 128 | 3 975 | 8.2 | 62.5 | 11.3 | 28.4 | 9 920 | 21 922 | 42 679 | -4.3 | 1.1 | 42 025 | 18.3 | 26.2 | 23.7 |
| Burnet | 176 | 1 904 | 9 285 | 9.9 | 62.5 | 22.3 | 69.5 | 9 426 | 25 011 | 48 291 | -5.7 | 2.8 | 44 636 | 16.6 | 26.7 | 24.2 |

1. Data for serious crimes have not been adjusted for underreporting; this may affect comparability between geographic areas and over time.    2.  Per 100,000 population estimated by the FBI.    3.  All persons 3 years old and over enrolled in nursery school through college.    4.  Persons 25 years old and over.    5.  Elementary and secondary education expenditures.    6.  Based on population estimated by the American Community Survey, 2007–2011.

Items 46—61

# Table B. States and Counties — **Personal Income**

| | Personal income, 2011 | | | | | | | | | | | | |
|---|---|---|---|---|---|---|---|---|---|---|---|---|---|
| | | | Per capita[1] | | | | | Transfer payments (mil dol) | | | | | |
| | | | | | | | | | Government payments to individuals | | | | |
| STATE County | Total (mil dol) | Percent change, 2010–2011 | Dollars | Rank | Wages and salaries[2] (mil dol) | Proprietors' income (mil dol) | Dividends, interest, and rent (mil dol) | Total | Total | Social Security | Medical payments | Income mainte-nance | Unemploy-ment insurance |
| | 62 | 63 | 64 | 65 | 66 | 67 | 68 | 69 | 70 | 71 | 72 | 73 | 74 |
| TENNESSEE—Cont'd | | | | | | | | | | | | | |
| Marshall | 792 | 3.9 | 25 647 | 2 916 | 328 | 70 | 113 | 234 | 227 | 83 | 97 | 29 | 9 |
| Maury | 2 567 | 4.9 | 31 498 | 2 002 | 1 432 | 282 | 317 | 662 | 644 | 222 | 277 | 79 | 25 |
| Meigs | 342 | 4.8 | 29 118 | 2 434 | 82 | 45 | 39 | 112 | 110 | 39 | 46 | 16 | 4 |
| Monroe | 1 186 | 5.8 | 26 428 | 2 833 | 553 | 98 | 144 | 407 | 397 | 146 | 164 | 53 | 13 |
| Montgomery | 7 680 | 12.1 | 43 485 | 468 | 2 128 | 466 | 683 | 1 058 | 1 023 | 268 | 343 | 154 | 34 |
| Moore | 219 | 5.6 | 34 213 | 1 484 | 90 | 2 | 25 | 46 | 45 | 18 | 19 | 4 | 1 |
| Morgan | 542 | 3.2 | 24 803 | 2 983 | 136 | 52 | 49 | 182 | 177 | 66 | 69 | 25 | 6 |
| Obion | 1 029 | 6.0 | 32 372 | 1 809 | 591 | 105 | 140 | 302 | 295 | 106 | 122 | 35 | 18 |
| Overton | 566 | 3.3 | 25 514 | 2 928 | 193 | 43 | 67 | 208 | 203 | 69 | 93 | 25 | 6 |
| Perry | 215 | 2.0 | 27 268 | 2 721 | 61 | 20 | 28 | 90 | 89 | 26 | 48 | 8 | 2 |
| Pickett | 135 | 3.6 | 26 376 | 2 842 | 34 | 8 | 22 | 57 | 56 | 19 | 27 | 6 | 1 |
| Polk | 460 | 3.0 | 27 412 | 2 700 | 100 | 15 | 48 | 162 | 159 | 54 | 75 | 19 | 4 |
| Putnam | 2 288 | 3.9 | 31 362 | 2 029 | 1 423 | 206 | 385 | 626 | 609 | 205 | 266 | 75 | 16 |
| Rhea | 867 | 5.2 | 27 027 | 2 760 | 560 | 44 | 90 | 305 | 298 | 95 | 137 | 40 | 10 |
| Roane | 1 892 | 3.1 | 35 142 | 1 351 | 1 239 | 54 | 235 | 549 | 537 | 193 | 235 | 52 | 14 |
| Robertson | 2 261 | 6.5 | 33 699 | 1 564 | 788 | 201 | 205 | 463 | 448 | 161 | 188 | 57 | 17 |
| Rutherford | 8 714 | 5.9 | 32 404 | 1 802 | 5 456 | 938 | 869 | 1 407 | 1 347 | 468 | 478 | 190 | 68 |
| Scott | 521 | 2.1 | 23 516 | 3 046 | 199 | 32 | 51 | 233 | 228 | 60 | 105 | 38 | 10 |
| Sequatchie | 456 | 6.6 | 31 791 | 1 934 | 85 | 24 | 46 | 138 | 134 | 45 | 61 | 17 | 3 |
| Sevier | 2 933 | 5.2 | 32 065 | 1 866 | 1 347 | 263 | 378 | 697 | 676 | 271 | 250 | 86 | 33 |
| Shelby | 38 117 | 3.5 | 40 763 | 680 | 30 668 | 4 482 | 4 378 | 6 894 | 6 688 | 1 808 | 2 680 | 1 484 | 254 |
| Smith | 610 | 7.1 | 31 878 | 1 911 | 222 | 48 | 80 | 162 | 158 | 50 | 76 | 19 | 6 |
| Stewart | 441 | 6.3 | 33 477 | 1 604 | 177 | 18 | 53 | 122 | 119 | 41 | 48 | 13 | 4 |
| Sullivan | 5 510 | 5.1 | 35 000 | 1 373 | 3 921 | 336 | 797 | 1 470 | 1 435 | 569 | 586 | 146 | 29 |
| Sumner | 6 007 | 5.8 | 36 698 | 1 111 | 2 042 | 359 | 721 | 1 120 | 1 084 | 415 | 439 | 117 | 40 |
| Tipton | 2 143 | 6.0 | 34 959 | 1 380 | 454 | 118 | 162 | 436 | 422 | 133 | 175 | 68 | 17 |
| Trousdale | 294 | 4.8 | 37 583 | 1 017 | 61 | 94 | 25 | 73 | 71 | 21 | 35 | 8 | 2 |
| Unicoi | 565 | 3.9 | 30 910 | 2 121 | 292 | 22 | 62 | 207 | 203 | 59 | 100 | 18 | 4 |
| Union | 493 | 3.5 | 25 662 | 2 914 | 125 | 17 | 49 | 159 | 155 | 55 | 61 | 26 | 5 |
| Van Buren | 151 | 4.2 | 27 573 | 2 673 | 35 | 11 | 15 | 61 | 59 | 20 | 29 | 7 | 1 |
| Warren | 1 094 | 3.2 | 27 396 | 2 702 | 545 | 77 | 156 | 387 | 378 | 116 | 189 | 48 | 11 |
| Washington | 4 379 | 6.2 | 35 215 | 1 337 | 2 938 | 248 | 584 | 1 018 | 990 | 359 | 408 | 101 | 25 |
| Wayne | 376 | 2.8 | 22 178 | 3 081 | 143 | 15 | 47 | 155 | 151 | 50 | 74 | 17 | 4 |
| Weakley | 1 038 | 6.3 | 29 679 | 2 346 | 470 | 112 | 134 | 314 | 307 | 97 | 132 | 34 | 14 |
| White | 661 | 3.2 | 25 274 | 2 945 | 276 | 51 | 78 | 248 | 242 | 84 | 111 | 30 | 7 |
| Williamson | 11 200 | 7.0 | 59 399 | 72 | 6 319 | 1 322 | 1 663 | 827 | 785 | 369 | 290 | 50 | 28 |
| Wilson | 4 485 | 5.6 | 38 461 | 914 | 1 789 | 336 | 507 | 783 | 757 | 297 | 318 | 72 | 27 |
| TEXAS | 1 030 750 | 6.8 | 40 147 | X | 659 450 | 138 170 | 142 470 | 160 440 | 154 756 | 44 990 | 69 084 | 22 904 | 5 671 |
| Anderson | 1 689 | 7.8 | 28 966 | 2 452 | 1 001 | 184 | 218 | 438 | 425 | 123 | 212 | 45 | 12 |
| Andrews | 609 | 14.3 | 39 435 | 811 | 395 | 62 | 63 | 93 | 90 | 28 | 46 | 11 | 2 |
| Angelina | 2 930 | 5.0 | 33 423 | 1 621 | 1 658 | 309 | 435 | 777 | 757 | 217 | 375 | 97 | 18 |
| Aransas | 994 | 6.2 | 42 512 | 540 | 238 | 66 | 248 | 246 | 241 | 93 | 106 | 24 | 5 |
| Archer | 404 | 6.7 | 45 689 | 353 | 88 | 75 | 56 | 56 | 54 | 23 | 20 | 4 | 2 |
| Armstrong | 83 | 3.6 | 43 129 | 501 | 17 | 8 | 16 | 17 | 17 | 6 | 9 | 1 | 0 |
| Atascosa | 1 378 | 5.6 | 30 238 | 2 247 | 465 | 132 | 136 | 347 | 337 | 90 | 160 | 55 | 9 |
| Austin | 1 129 | 4.0 | 39 374 | 817 | 607 | 101 | 228 | 213 | 207 | 75 | 98 | 19 | 7 |
| Bailey | 254 | 13.0 | 35 115 | 1 354 | 112 | 63 | 37 | 53 | 51 | 13 | 28 | 7 | 1 |
| Bandera | 747 | 4.7 | 36 390 | 1 150 | 119 | 70 | 148 | 158 | 154 | 66 | 55 | 13 | 4 |
| Bastrop | 2 139 | 4.4 | 28 473 | 2 545 | 652 | 158 | 274 | 456 | 440 | 156 | 179 | 56 | 16 |
| Baylor | 136 | 12.3 | 36 307 | 1 168 | 51 | 24 | 19 | 41 | 41 | 14 | 22 | 3 | 1 |
| Bee | 857 | 8.0 | 26 697 | 2 803 | 407 | 87 | 105 | 235 | 228 | 51 | 118 | 32 | 6 |
| Bell | 12 678 | 7.4 | 40 222 | 721 | 11 296 | 663 | 1 420 | 2 013 | 1 950 | 478 | 668 | 273 | 90 |
| Bexar | 63 533 | 6.0 | 36 177 | 1 191 | 45 300 | 7 408 | 8 876 | 12 078 | 11 696 | 2 952 | 5 150 | 1 785 | 358 |
| Blanco | 499 | 6.1 | 47 043 | 297 | 129 | 122 | 104 | 81 | 79 | 30 | 38 | 5 | 2 |
| Borden | 25 | -13.6 | 40 693 | 687 | 7 | 4 | 5 | 3 | 3 | 2 | 1 | 0 | 0 |
| Bosque | 594 | 4.1 | 32 431 | 1 792 | 160 | 53 | 111 | 161 | 157 | 59 | 71 | 13 | 4 |
| Bowie | 3 281 | 3.7 | 35 360 | 1 315 | 2 154 | 238 | 540 | 794 | 774 | 215 | 366 | 104 | 23 |
| Brazoria | 12 376 | 6.1 | 38 677 | 883 | 5 519 | 731 | 1 311 | 1 740 | 1 669 | 579 | 731 | 185 | 74 |
| Brazos | 5 740 | 4.7 | 29 045 | 2 444 | 4 007 | 374 | 1 100 | 847 | 803 | 247 | 293 | 131 | 36 |
| Brewster | 367 | 6.2 | 39 139 | 841 | 205 | 32 | 80 | 66 | 64 | 22 | 22 | 6 | 2 |
| Briscoe | 46 | -18.0 | 27 769 | 2 645 | 14 | 1 | 10 | 15 | 15 | 5 | 8 | 1 | 0 |
| Brooks | 220 | 10.3 | 30 423 | 2 217 | 132 | 10 | 22 | 91 | 90 | 17 | 53 | 16 | 2 |
| Brown | 1 227 | 4.5 | 32 136 | 1 852 | 634 | 105 | 183 | 392 | 384 | 111 | 204 | 36 | 8 |
| Burleson | 592 | 3.0 | 34 291 | 1 472 | 215 | 61 | 81 | 140 | 136 | 48 | 60 | 14 | 3 |
| Burnet | 1 756 | 5.6 | 40 734 | 682 | 592 | 261 | 462 | 341 | 331 | 144 | 133 | 28 | 8 |

1. Based on the resident population estimated as of July 1 of the year shown.   2. Includes supplements to wages and salaries.

# Table B. States and Counties — **Earnings, Social Security, and Housing**

| STATE County | Earnings, 2011 Total (mil dol) | Farm | Goods-related[1] Total | Manu-facturing | Service-related and health: Information and professional and technical services | Retail trade | Finance, insurance, and real estate | Health care and social services | Govern-ment | Social Security beneficiaries, December 2011 Number | Rate[2] | Supplemental Security Income recipients, December 2011 | Housing units, 2010 Total | Percent change, 2000–2010 |
|---|---|---|---|---|---|---|---|---|---|---|---|---|---|---|
| | 75 | 76 | 77 | 78 | 79 | 80 | 81 | 82 | 83 | 84 | 85 | 86 | 87 | 88 |
| **TENNESSEE—Cont'd** | | | | | | | | | | | | | | |
| Marshall | 398 | -1.0 | D | 31.3 | D | 8.6 | 4.7 | 4.2 | 20.1 | 6 405 | 207 | 629 | 13 119 | 17.3 |
| Maury | 1 714 | -0.7 | D | 15.3 | 7.4 | 8.7 | 8.6 | 13.6 | 20.4 | 16 705 | 205 | 1 725 | 35 254 | 22.9 |
| Meigs | 127 | -2.4 | 37.6 | 27.8 | D | 5.2 | D | 4.2 | 17.6 | 3 175 | 271 | 468 | 5 628 | 8.5 |
| Monroe | 652 | -0.7 | D | 39.8 | 1.9 | 8.4 | 2.6 | D | 13.4 | 12 060 | 269 | 1 770 | 20 787 | 20.2 |
| Montgomery | 2 594 | 0.3 | D | 14.4 | 6.6 | 9.7 | 4.8 | 11.1 | 21.3 | 22 335 | 126 | 3 131 | 70 098 | 34.4 |
| Moore | 92 | -4.2 | D | 50.1 | D | 1.8 | 1.5 | 5.5 | 33.8 | 1 400 | 218 | 90 | 2 915 | 15.9 |
| Morgan | 188 | -1.9 | D | 8.8 | D | 6.1 | D | D | 31.2 | 5 620 | 257 | 920 | 8 920 | 15.6 |
| Obion | 696 | 4.4 | 40.1 | 36.1 | D | 8.7 | 5.1 | 7.7 | 12.2 | 8 215 | 258 | 1 010 | 14 659 | 1.2 |
| Overton | 237 | -2.2 | D | 18.1 | 3.1 | 8.7 | 6.3 | 13.9 | 23.0 | 6 055 | 273 | 842 | 10 295 | 12.3 |
| Perry | 80 | -2.0 | D | 15.3 | D | 8.4 | D | 23.0 | 23.1 | 2 180 | 276 | 236 | 4 599 | 11.8 |
| Pickett | 41 | -3.8 | D | 6.1 | D | 14.2 | D | 17.1 | 27.7 | 1 635 | 319 | 206 | 3 462 | 17.1 |
| Polk | 115 | 0.7 | D | 7.4 | D | 10.3 | D | D | 36.4 | 4 445 | 265 | 621 | 7 991 | 8.4 |
| Putnam | 1 629 | -0.5 | 23.1 | 16.7 | 5.0 | 9.0 | 5.0 | 10.1 | 26.0 | 16 395 | 225 | 1 947 | 31 882 | 18.5 |
| Rhea | 604 | -0.1 | 29.5 | 25.7 | D | 5.4 | 2.0 | D | 41.9 | 7 665 | 239 | 1 190 | 14 365 | 14.3 |
| Roane | 1 293 | -0.4 | D | 5.0 | 44.7 | 5.9 | 1.3 | D | 16.1 | 14 780 | 275 | 1 781 | 25 716 | 10.0 |
| Robertson | 989 | 3.4 | D | 26.0 | D | 9.1 | 3.3 | 5.2 | 17.9 | 12 300 | 183 | 1 308 | 26 086 | 24.2 |
| Rutherford | 6 394 | -0.1 | D | 24.7 | 6.4 | 6.6 | 5.7 | 11.6 | 16.0 | 34 770 | 129 | 3 543 | 102 968 | 45.8 |
| Scott | 231 | -1.3 | 27.6 | 17.3 | 2.5 | 9.9 | 3.2 | D | 25.6 | 5 570 | 251 | 1 512 | 9 910 | 11.2 |
| Sequatchie | 109 | 0.5 | 11.8 | 3.1 | D | 11.5 | 9.3 | 8.2 | 26.4 | 3 775 | 263 | 549 | 6 368 | 29.5 |
| Sevier | 1 610 | -0.2 | D | 3.4 | 3.7 | 13.6 | 8.1 | 5.5 | 15.8 | 21 550 | 236 | 1 895 | 55 918 | 50.1 |
| Shelby | 35 150 | 0.0 | 14.1 | 9.6 | 6.0 | 6.2 | 8.1 | 11.7 | 15.2 | 141 075 | 151 | 32 795 | 398 274 | 9.7 |
| Smith | 270 | 0.4 | D | 22.7 | 1.9 | 7.2 | 5.5 | D | 18.2 | 4 125 | 215 | 528 | 8 529 | 11.3 |
| Stewart | 195 | -0.2 | 27.8 | 12.7 | D | 4.5 | 3.2 | 5.0 | 49.5 | 3 395 | 257 | 416 | 6 778 | 13.4 |
| Sullivan | 4 256 | -0.2 | 36.8 | 28.6 | 5.4 | 7.0 | 3.8 | 17.8 | 9.4 | 43 685 | 278 | 4 782 | 73 760 | 6.8 |
| Sumner | 2 401 | -0.1 | D | 13.9 | 6.8 | 7.8 | 5.8 | 12.1 | 16.8 | 30 250 | 185 | 2 567 | 65 968 | 27.7 |
| Tipton | 572 | 5.0 | D | 13.5 | D | 9.3 | 3.2 | D | 23.4 | 10 765 | 176 | 1 623 | 23 199 | 21.7 |
| Trousdale | 155 | 0.4 | D | 7.4 | 13.1 | 11.1 | D | 13.2 | 15.5 | 1 795 | 230 | 259 | 3 368 | 8.8 |
| Unicoi | 313 | 0.0 | D | 38.3 | D | 4.7 | 1.7 | 5.6 | 17.3 | 5 050 | 276 | 649 | 8 830 | 7.5 |
| Union | 141 | -2.2 | D | 32.5 | D | 7.8 | D | 6.4 | 26.3 | 4 720 | 246 | 895 | 8 958 | 13.2 |
| Van Buren | 46 | -4.5 | 27.9 | 19.8 | 1.1 | 4.5 | D | D | 34.8 | 1 645 | 300 | 239 | 2 663 | 8.6 |
| Warren | 623 | 1.9 | 34.5 | 28.8 | 3.6 | 8.1 | 3.4 | 11.6 | 15.8 | 9 640 | 241 | 1 526 | 17 821 | 6.8 |
| Washington | 3 186 | 0.0 | 14.1 | 10.0 | 6.9 | 7.6 | 5.4 | 22.2 | 23.6 | 28 080 | 226 | 3 060 | 57 254 | 19.8 |
| Wayne | 158 | -0.2 | D | 12.2 | D | 7.5 | 5.5 | 8.5 | 34.3 | 4 240 | 250 | 493 | 7 287 | 8.7 |
| Weakley | 583 | 7.0 | D | 6.5 | D | 6.0 | 11.1 | D | 28.4 | 7 770 | 222 | 913 | 15 495 | 3.8 |
| White | 327 | -2.0 | D | 28.6 | 3.0 | 9.9 | 3.0 | 10.7 | 17.3 | 7 040 | 269 | 899 | 11 511 | 12.9 |
| Williamson | 7 641 | 0.0 | D | 2.7 | 17.2 | 7.9 | 15.7 | 15.0 | 6.8 | 24 080 | 128 | 1 026 | 68 498 | 45.7 |
| Wilson | 2 125 | -0.7 | D | 14.5 | D | 14.4 | 4.9 | 8.8 | 11.4 | 21 200 | 182 | 1 579 | 45 568 | 30.5 |
| **TEXAS** | 797 621 | 0.5 | 22.9 | 9.6 | 11.4 | 5.9 | 8.3 | 9.4 | 15.7 | 3 551 961 | 138 | 640 422 | 9 977 436 | 22.3 |
| Anderson | 1 185 | 0.8 | 10.4 | 2.0 | 5.3 | 6.0 | 5.1 | 12.7 | 23.7 | 9 875 | 169 | 1 367 | 20 116 | 9.1 |
| Andrews | 457 | 0.9 | 47.9 | 2.3 | 2.9 | 3.4 | 7.2 | D | 15.0 | 2 130 | 138 | 311 | 5 814 | 7.7 |
| Angelina | 1 967 | 0.0 | 24.3 | 18.4 | 5.4 | 9.0 | 4.6 | 16.0 | 17.3 | 17 435 | 199 | 3 155 | 35 589 | 9.7 |
| Aransas | 304 | -0.2 | D | 0.9 | 6.4 | 13.7 | 9.0 | D | 17.5 | 7 065 | 302 | 728 | 15 355 | 19.5 |
| Archer | 163 | 7.8 | 30.0 | 2.1 | D | 6.1 | 2.2 | 1.4 | 15.4 | 1 800 | 204 | 158 | 4 107 | 6.1 |
| Armstrong | 25 | 21.1 | D | 0.0 | 4.4 | 1.9 | D | D | 23.4 | 440 | 228 | 23 | 904 | -1.7 |
| Atascosa | 597 | 0.5 | 22.3 | 3.1 | 3.5 | 10.1 | 6.5 | D | 19.3 | 8 260 | 181 | 1 729 | 17 631 | 18.5 |
| Austin | 708 | 1.0 | 34.1 | 23.5 | 8.3 | 10.0 | 4.9 | 6.0 | 13.2 | 5 540 | 193 | 509 | 12 926 | 26.7 |
| Bailey | 175 | 32.8 | D | D | D | 3.8 | 3.4 | 3.2 | 15.3 | 1 170 | 161 | 157 | 2 784 | 1.7 |
| Bandera | 189 | 3.5 | D | 0.7 | 6.4 | 6.7 | 9.6 | D | 20.8 | 5 185 | 252 | 369 | 11 561 | 21.7 |
| Bastrop | 810 | 1.4 | 21.8 | 7.3 | 4.6 | 10.2 | 4.6 | 6.5 | 29.4 | 12 325 | 164 | 1 629 | 29 316 | 31.8 |
| Baylor | 75 | 18.8 | 6.8 | 0.8 | D | 5.3 | D | 19.6 | 15.8 | 1 120 | 299 | 124 | 2 665 | -5.5 |
| Bee | 494 | 3.0 | 20.3 | 2.2 | 4.6 | 8.5 | 3.7 | D | 33.3 | 4 605 | 143 | 1 134 | 10 649 | -2.7 |
| Bell | 11 959 | 0.0 | D | 2.8 | 4.0 | 4.0 | 2.0 | 8.9 | 63.7 | 40 905 | 130 | 6 852 | 125 470 | 35.2 |
| Bexar | 52 708 | 0.0 | 12.4 | 4.5 | 10.3 | 6.5 | 11.2 | 11.1 | 25.4 | 256 680 | 146 | 54 558 | 662 872 | 27.1 |
| Blanco | 251 | 3.2 | D | 3.1 | D | 4.5 | 14.7 | D | 12.2 | 2 255 | 213 | 133 | 5 532 | 37.2 |
| Borden | 12 | 39.9 | D | D | 2.3 | D | 0.0 | 0.0 | 37.4 | 130 | 208 | 0 | 385 | -11.5 |
| Bosque | 212 | 3.8 | 28.0 | 13.4 | 3.0 | 7.0 | 6.6 | D | 23.6 | 4 540 | 248 | 392 | 9 623 | 11.3 |
| Bowie | 2 392 | 0.3 | 7.5 | 3.7 | 3.7 | 8.5 | 7.0 | 18.8 | 34.1 | 18 650 | 201 | 4 046 | 38 493 | 5.6 |
| Brazoria | 6 250 | 0.3 | 43.6 | 23.8 | 5.5 | 6.9 | 4.2 | 5.9 | 14.8 | 41 660 | 130 | 5 074 | 118 336 | 30.6 |
| Brazos | 4 381 | 0.2 | 14.9 | 5.9 | D | 7.4 | 4.3 | 11.4 | 38.2 | 18 805 | 95 | 3 218 | 77 700 | 31.7 |
| Brewster | 237 | 3.0 | 7.8 | 2.0 | 7.3 | 9.9 | 5.7 | 7.1 | 35.6 | 1 840 | 196 | 204 | 5 383 | 16.7 |
| Briscoe | 15 | -1.1 | D | D | D | 9.4 | D | D | 31.9 | 435 | 263 | 42 | 953 | -5.3 |
| Brooks | 142 | 1.6 | D | D | D | 6.2 | 2.7 | D | 44.1 | 1 760 | 244 | 620 | 3 239 | 1.1 |
| Brown | 739 | 1.2 | 28.6 | 23.0 | 3.0 | 10.2 | 4.6 | D | 19.1 | 9 120 | 239 | 1 253 | 18 287 | 2.2 |
| Burleson | 276 | 1.9 | 36.1 | 5.5 | D | 13.0 | 4.1 | D | 14.6 | 3 925 | 228 | 479 | 8 832 | 7.7 |
| Burnet | 853 | 0.4 | 22.0 | 7.3 | 7.4 | 10.0 | 8.6 | 11.4 | 15.1 | 10 595 | 246 | 676 | 20 870 | 30.8 |

1. Includes mining, construction, and manufacturing.  2. Per 1,000 resident population enumerated in the 2010 census.

# Table B. States and Counties — Housing, Labor Force, and Employment

| STATE County | Housing units, 2007–2011 Occupied units — Owner-occupied | | | | | Renter-occupied | | | Civilian labor force, 2012 | | Unemployment | | Civilian employment,[6] 2007–2011 | Percent | |
|---|---|---|---|---|---|---|---|---|---|---|---|---|---|---|---|
| | Total | Percent | Median value[1] | With a mortgage | Without a mortgage[2] | Median rent[3] | Median rent as a percent of income | Sub-standard units[4] (percent) | Total | Percent change, 2011–2012 | Total | Rate[5] | Total | Management, business, science and arts | Construction, production, and maintenance occupations |
| | 89 | 90 | 91 | 92 | 93 | 94 | 95 | 96 | 97 | 98 | 99 | 100 | 101 | 102 | 103 |
| TENNESSEE—Cont'd | | | | | | | | | | | | | | | |
| Marshall | 11 533 | 74.8 | 106 000 | 23.4 | 11.7 | 632 | 29.1 | 2.6 | 12 427 | -0.4 | 1 389 | 11.2 | 13 307 | 23.0 | 36.8 |
| Maury | 31 811 | 72.4 | 138 200 | 23.1 | 11.2 | 652 | 29.2 | 2.2 | 36 185 | -0.5 | 3 383 | 9.3 | 37 701 | 28.8 | 26.8 |
| Meigs | 4 646 | 78.7 | 102 100 | 23.4 | 11.1 | 605 | 26.0 | 6.8 | 5 397 | 3.3 | 537 | 9.9 | 4 394 | 22.6 | 43.9 |
| Monroe | 17 565 | 72.8 | 108 700 | 23.7 | 11.7 | 575 | 28.2 | 2.1 | 18 887 | 0.5 | 2 000 | 10.6 | 17 101 | 20.5 | 39.4 |
| Montgomery | 61 902 | 64.1 | 135 300 | 22.4 | 10.1 | 765 | 28.4 | 2.1 | 77 909 | 0.9 | 6 102 | 7.8 | 67 659 | 30.5 | 24.7 |
| Moore | 2 423 | 81.7 | 134 500 | 21.2 | 11.2 | 613 | 24.1 | 3.4 | 3 382 | 2.1 | 250 | 7.4 | 2 951 | 29.8 | 35.9 |
| Morgan | 7 930 | 81.9 | 84 600 | 22.3 | 11.9 | 582 | 24.0 | 3.5 | 8 872 | -0.5 | 923 | 10.4 | 7 848 | 24.2 | 36.1 |
| Obion | 12 669 | 70.3 | 88 600 | 21.3 | 11.6 | 543 | 28.0 | 1.4 | 14 480 | -4.6 | 1 930 | 13.3 | 13 652 | 23.5 | 34.1 |
| Overton | 9 004 | 80.2 | 88 800 | 22.6 | 12.2 | 490 | 30.1 | 2.2 | 10 282 | -2.2 | 891 | 8.7 | 8 916 | 25.9 | 38.0 |
| Perry | 3 240 | 72.2 | 79 900 | 24.8 | 10.7 | 534 | 31.6 | 5.0 | 2 674 | 2.5 | 315 | 11.8 | 2 707 | 27.4 | 31.4 |
| Pickett | 2 288 | 76.2 | 93 000 | 23.4 | 10.5 | 429 | 27.2 | 1.0 | 1 948 | 1.1 | 243 | 12.5 | 2 336 | 33.9 | 37.8 |
| Polk | 6 486 | 81.9 | 101 600 | 24.7 | 10.9 | 570 | 31.5 | 3.2 | 7 705 | 2.4 | 743 | 9.6 | 6 561 | 23.7 | 39.4 |
| Putnam | 27 856 | 64.4 | 131 600 | 24.0 | 11.5 | 581 | 32.3 | 1.9 | 36 137 | -1.7 | 2 749 | 7.6 | 29 785 | 33.3 | 23.1 |
| Rhea | 11 949 | 72.0 | 103 800 | 25.4 | 10.9 | 536 | 31.2 | 2.4 | 13 583 | -1.6 | 1 432 | 10.5 | 12 340 | 22.1 | 41.1 |
| Roane | 22 457 | 76.2 | 121 300 | 22.4 | 10.8 | 601 | 28.5 | 1.7 | 27 490 | -2.0 | 2 097 | 7.6 | 22 581 | 29.5 | 30.2 |
| Robertson | 24 028 | 77.0 | 153 900 | 24.6 | 11.1 | 741 | 27.9 | 2.3 | 35 168 | 1.5 | 2 482 | 7.1 | 30 548 | 28.2 | 32.6 |
| Rutherford | 94 173 | 69.0 | 159 600 | 23.0 | 9.9 | 830 | 29.7 | 2.6 | 145 966 | 1.3 | 9 440 | 6.5 | 127 978 | 33.8 | 24.2 |
| Scott | 8 555 | 76.3 | 78 500 | 23.3 | 12.1 | 463 | 34.6 | 2.2 | 8 077 | -2.6 | 1 406 | 17.4 | 8 055 | 23.5 | 37.1 |
| Sequatchie | 5 323 | 77.7 | 115 400 | 24.7 | 9.9 | 576 | 29.3 | 4.4 | 6 306 | -0.7 | 491 | 7.8 | 5 642 | 30.0 | 32.6 |
| Sevier | 37 218 | 68.5 | 158 700 | 23.7 | 9.9 | 691 | 27.3 | 2.7 | 50 709 | 0.7 | 4 434 | 8.7 | 43 901 | 23.3 | 21.8 |
| Shelby | 340 394 | 60.8 | 136 200 | 24.8 | 13.2 | 812 | 33.8 | 3.4 | 435 210 | -0.7 | 39 416 | 9.1 | 417 811 | 34.2 | 21.0 |
| Smith | 7 013 | 76.8 | 117 100 | 21.7 | 9.9 | 541 | 30.3 | 2.8 | 9 274 | 0.8 | 699 | 7.5 | 8 036 | 26.4 | 34.0 |
| Stewart | 5 215 | 82.1 | 108 500 | 20.7 | 9.9 | 569 | 35.5 | 3.0 | 5 937 | 0.4 | 600 | 10.1 | 4 836 | 28.0 | 35.1 |
| Sullivan | 66 554 | 74.8 | 115 700 | 21.7 | 10.2 | 569 | 27.9 | 1.3 | 75 061 | -1.4 | 5 219 | 7.0 | 67 543 | 30.9 | 25.7 |
| Sumner | 60 112 | 73.2 | 171 800 | 23.8 | 10.6 | 787 | 28.0 | 1.8 | 85 354 | 1.4 | 5 698 | 6.7 | 75 580 | 34.3 | 21.8 |
| Tipton | 21 578 | 73.5 | 137 400 | 22.6 | 11.4 | 677 | 31.2 | 2.0 | 28 417 | -0.9 | 2 519 | 8.9 | 26 423 | 28.9 | 30.9 |
| Trousdale | 2 805 | 79.4 | 112 500 | 22.6 | 9.9 | 619 | 28.6 | 0.7 | 3 732 | 0.1 | 304 | 8.1 | 3 362 | 23.1 | 38.1 |
| Unicoi | 7 437 | 72.9 | 115 200 | 21.8 | 9.9 | 542 | 27.0 | 0.9 | 8 565 | -1.0 | 785 | 9.2 | 7 375 | 28.3 | 33.6 |
| Union | 7 334 | 79.6 | 92 200 | 24.6 | 11.1 | 527 | 32.4 | 2.5 | 8 893 | -1.6 | 721 | 8.1 | 7 276 | 19.8 | 37.6 |
| Van Buren | 2 066 | 85.3 | 75 800 | 23.2 | 12.2 | 416 | 32.4 | 3.8 | 2 292 | -1.3 | 265 | 11.6 | 2 376 | 23.5 | 38.2 |
| Warren | 15 292 | 72.7 | 90 500 | 24.4 | 10.4 | 557 | 25.9 | 2.2 | 17 393 | -1.3 | 1 599 | 9.2 | 16 006 | 24.6 | 37.9 |
| Washington | 50 523 | 66.4 | 142 900 | 23.2 | 10.3 | 636 | 29.3 | 1.0 | 63 721 | -1.5 | 4 295 | 6.7 | 55 668 | 35.9 | 18.8 |
| Wayne | 5 927 | 84.4 | 70 300 | 22.8 | 11.5 | 424 | 28.1 | 1.7 | 6 495 | -1.0 | 699 | 10.8 | 5 705 | 22.3 | 37.0 |
| Weakley | 13 958 | 65.4 | 84 400 | 20.7 | 11.7 | 539 | 31.7 | 1.6 | 16 374 | 1.9 | 1 936 | 11.8 | 14 875 | 29.6 | 28.7 |
| White | 9 824 | 76.4 | 100 400 | 23.5 | 11.4 | 578 | 29.4 | 2.9 | 11 124 | -0.9 | 1 255 | 11.3 | 10 462 | 23.0 | 39.9 |
| Williamson | 64 011 | 82.2 | 336 900 | 22.7 | 9.9 | 1 067 | 27.7 | 1.0 | 99 322 | 2.0 | 5 322 | 5.4 | 86 775 | 52.7 | 10.2 |
| Wilson | 42 183 | 81.0 | 190 900 | 22.8 | 10.2 | 795 | 29.9 | 2.2 | 63 002 | 1.6 | 4 053 | 6.4 | 54 309 | 34.9 | 23.7 |
| TEXAS | 8 667 807 | 64.5 | 126 400 | 23.1 | 12.4 | 814 | 29.6 | 5.4 | 12 597 465 | 0.9 | 854 865 | 6.8 | 11 288 597 | 34.2 | 23.3 |
| Anderson | 15 992 | 71.6 | 82 900 | 20.7 | 13.7 | 663 | 30.9 | 3.5 | 22 201 | 1.4 | 1 703 | 7.7 | 20 576 | 23.7 | 27.5 |
| Andrews | 5 193 | 81.4 | 87 500 | 18.0 | 11.7 | 603 | 24.1 | 7.3 | 8 839 | 10.9 | 331 | 3.7 | 6 750 | 21.5 | 38.6 |
| Angelina | 31 048 | 68.6 | 82 900 | 21.8 | 12.3 | 715 | 29.9 | 3.7 | 40 059 | -0.9 | 2 664 | 6.7 | 36 323 | 27.6 | 29.3 |
| Aransas | 10 134 | 76.8 | 125 100 | 27.9 | 14.7 | 814 | 37.2 | 4.9 | 10 936 | 1.0 | 666 | 6.1 | 9 318 | 30.6 | 26.0 |
| Archer | 3 262 | 81.6 | 101 200 | 19.2 | 11.6 | 606 | 28.6 | 2.7 | 4 879 | -1.4 | 240 | 4.9 | 4 245 | 26.6 | 33.4 |
| Armstrong | 676 | 79.9 | 96 700 | 18.9 | 9.9 | 646 | 21.5 | 2.8 | 987 | -0.6 | 47 | 4.8 | 852 | 36.4 | 21.7 |
| Atascosa | 14 940 | 76.4 | 81 600 | 21.4 | 12.5 | 646 | 25.4 | 7.6 | 19 767 | 0.2 | 1 310 | 6.6 | 18 309 | 24.9 | 33.4 |
| Austin | 10 502 | 76.6 | 152 600 | 23.6 | 11.6 | 707 | 24.4 | 3.7 | 14 248 | 0.8 | 854 | 6.0 | 13 257 | 31.0 | 29.6 |
| Bailey | 2 414 | 72.0 | 70 700 | 19.8 | 13.0 | 561 | 25.6 | 7.6 | 3 249 | -2.9 | 215 | 6.6 | 3 028 | 30.2 | 25.2 |
| Bandera | 8 377 | 79.3 | 139 200 | 23.3 | 12.0 | 749 | 30.1 | 1.3 | 9 799 | 0.6 | 584 | 6.0 | 8 862 | 36.3 | 23.6 |
| Bastrop | 25 522 | 78.5 | 119 800 | 23.2 | 13.0 | 858 | 30.5 | 5.2 | 35 558 | 1.3 | 2 266 | 6.4 | 33 042 | 31.5 | 30.6 |
| Baylor | 1 723 | 78.4 | 62 800 | 17.2 | 13.1 | 439 | 26.8 | 3.1 | 2 263 | 9.3 | 97 | 4.3 | 1 469 | 32.5 | 30.1 |
| Bee | 8 507 | 66.0 | 67 700 | 21.1 | 14.3 | 713 | 27.0 | 5.6 | 12 912 | 2.7 | 904 | 7.0 | 9 133 | 21.2 | 21.9 |
| Bell | 102 547 | 57.6 | 117 500 | 22.8 | 11.5 | 843 | 28.6 | 3.0 | 135 700 | -0.2 | 9 942 | 7.3 | 117 652 | 31.8 | 21.9 |
| Bexar | 590 364 | 61.6 | 121 200 | 23.0 | 11.7 | 791 | 29.8 | 4.7 | 815 285 | 0.6 | 53 673 | 6.6 | 751 152 | 34.2 | 19.7 |
| Blanco | 4 009 | 80.4 | 165 500 | 21.5 | 13.5 | 727 | 27.2 | 7.2 | 5 163 | 0.2 | 285 | 5.5 | 4 989 | 33.1 | 22.9 |
| Borden | 266 | 59.0 | 78 300 | 10.0 | 9.9 | 496 | 11.2 | 1.1 | 592 | 13.2 | 18 | 3.0 | 339 | 43.1 | 24.8 |
| Bosque | 6 833 | 77.3 | 87 200 | 22.0 | 12.2 | 612 | 24.7 | 4.2 | 8 127 | -2.9 | 598 | 7.4 | 7 359 | 29.3 | 29.1 |
| Bowie | 33 324 | 67.3 | 91 600 | 19.9 | 10.7 | 659 | 29.7 | 2.6 | 44 652 | -1.9 | 3 031 | 6.8 | 38 681 | 30.3 | 26.2 |
| Brazoria | 103 919 | 75.3 | 143 900 | 21.6 | 11.3 | 842 | 27.1 | 4.2 | 155 381 | 1.4 | 10 878 | 7.0 | 142 798 | 39.4 | 23.8 |
| Brazos | 67 612 | 46.3 | 145 900 | 22.3 | 11.4 | 793 | 42.2 | 4.1 | 99 208 | -1.4 | 5 473 | 5.5 | 89 597 | 39.9 | 17.7 |
| Brewster | 4 066 | 59.8 | 106 700 | 21.2 | 9.9 | 573 | 23.3 | 5.7 | 5 124 | -1.0 | 240 | 4.7 | 4 607 | 33.6 | 21.6 |
| Briscoe | 656 | 80.3 | 43 300 | 22.9 | 11.8 | 538 | 36.3 | 2.1 | 572 | -13.6 | 36 | 6.3 | 726 | 36.1 | 26.7 |
| Brooks | 2 671 | 63.9 | 45 200 | 18.2 | 12.6 | 452 | 31.8 | 6.4 | 3 379 | 0.1 | 241 | 7.1 | 2 378 | 20.1 | 16.6 |
| Brown | 13 412 | 72.1 | 83 300 | 21.4 | 13.3 | 590 | 30.5 | 1.9 | 18 435 | -2.0 | 1 109 | 6.0 | 15 415 | 26.8 | 30.0 |
| Burleson | 6 490 | 80.8 | 88 000 | 20.5 | 10.0 | 591 | 27.0 | 4.7 | 7 852 | -1.4 | 475 | 6.0 | 7 375 | 26.8 | 35.1 |
| Burnet | 16 477 | 73.4 | 141 500 | 25.3 | 12.0 | 721 | 29.3 | 4.5 | 22 465 | -2.2 | 1 221 | 5.4 | 18 844 | 27.3 | 25.1 |

1. Specified owner-occupied units. 2. A value of 9.9 represents 9.9 percent or less. 3. Specified renter-occupied units. 4. Overcrowded or lacking complete plumbing facilities. 5. Percent of civilian labor force. 6. Persons 16 years old and over.

# Table B. States and Counties — **Nonfarm Employment and Agriculture**

| | Private nonfarm establishments, employment and payroll, 2011 | | | | | | | | Agriculture, 2007 | | | |
|---|---|---|---|---|---|---|---|---|---|---|---|---|
| | | Employment | | | | | Annual payroll | | Farms | | | |
| | | | | | | | | | | Percent with: | | |
| STATE County | Number of establishments | Total | Health care and social assistance | Manufacturing | Retail trade | Finance and insurance | Professional, scientific, and technical services | Total (mil dol) | Average per employee (dollars) | Number | Fewer than 50 acres | 500 acres or more | Farm operators whose principal occupation is farming (percent) |
| | 104 | 105 | 106 | 107 | 108 | 109 | 110 | 111 | 112 | 113 | 114 | 115 | 116 |
| **TENNESSEE—Cont'd** | | | | | | | | | | | | | |
| Marshall | 473 | 6 507 | 672 | 2 535 | 1 044 | 182 | 93 | 218 | 33 495 | 1 078 | 38.0 | 5.0 | 42.4 |
| Maury | 1 620 | 22 564 | 5 092 | 3 068 | 3 879 | 1 671 | 577 | 811 | 35 949 | 1 696 | 42.5 | 4.4 | 37.9 |
| Meigs | 105 | 1 559 | 148 | 909 | 224 | 32 | D | 52 | 33 338 | 367 | 43.3 | 4.1 | 46.0 |
| Monroe | 696 | 9 923 | 1 274 | 3 957 | 1 543 | 366 | 200 | 312 | 31 402 | 935 | 49.5 | 2.4 | 39.8 |
| Montgomery | 2 547 | 40 417 | 7 163 | 4 498 | 7 852 | 1 222 | 1 590 | 1 266 | 31 316 | 862 | 38.1 | 7.8 | 45.0 |
| Moore | 70 | D | 158 | D | D | D | D | D | D | 346 | 31.5 | 4.6 | 43.4 |
| Morgan | 165 | 1 497 | 345 | D | 223 | D | D | 46 | 30 764 | 407 | 37.3 | 2.5 | 42.5 |
| Obion | 695 | 11 364 | 1 289 | 4 215 | 1 659 | 379 | 133 | 366 | 32 248 | 693 | 39.4 | 15.2 | 41.0 |
| Overton | 280 | 3 528 | 783 | 824 | 468 | D | 96 | 106 | 30 118 | 1 009 | 44.1 | 3.2 | 33.0 |
| Perry | 116 | 1 256 | 383 | 461 | 150 | D | D | 35 | 27 781 | 257 | 21.4 | 7.8 | 39.7 |
| Pickett | 81 | 542 | D | 91 | 106 | D | D | 15 | 27 188 | 365 | 41.1 | 1.6 | 31.5 |
| Polk | 223 | 1 427 | 343 | D | 306 | 71 | 21 | 40 | 27 905 | 305 | 50.2 | 2.0 | 51.5 |
| Putnam | 1 706 | 27 666 | 5 574 | 4 891 | 4 563 | 935 | 608 | 838 | 30 298 | 1 069 | 48.4 | 2.6 | 33.1 |
| Rhea | 488 | 8 190 | 1 039 | 3 171 | 1 123 | 190 | D | 242 | 29 515 | 449 | 40.1 | 4.7 | 36.1 |
| Roane | 725 | 8 744 | 1 910 | 1 056 | 1 749 | 257 | 233 | 237 | 27 127 | 580 | 45.2 | 1.2 | 37.2 |
| Robertson | 1 051 | 15 886 | 1 881 | 4 962 | 2 424 | 375 | D | 491 | 30 918 | 1 408 | 46.0 | 6.6 | 41.4 |
| Rutherford | 4 476 | 82 596 | 10 244 | 14 140 | 12 197 | 5 050 | 2 269 | 3 202 | 38 769 | 1 525 | 52.7 | 3.7 | 35.3 |
| Scott | 315 | 3 380 | 792 | 709 | 686 | 139 | 41 | 88 | 25 917 | 261 | 41.0 | 3.1 | 26.4 |
| Sequatchie | 178 | 1 762 | 488 | 150 | D | D | 40 | 42 | 24 087 | 232 | 50.0 | 4.7 | 31.9 |
| Sevier | 2 493 | 31 603 | 2 029 | 957 | 7 671 | 1 009 | 745 | 780 | 24 697 | 707 | 50.5 | 0.7 | 38.0 |
| Shelby | 19 487 | 418 711 | 65 113 | 25 486 | 45 590 | 18 380 | 15 809 | 18 812 | 44 928 | 600 | 58.2 | 5.2 | 41.5 |
| Smith | 272 | 3 592 | 511 | 989 | 601 | 142 | D | 120 | 33 272 | 981 | 39.2 | 2.8 | 36.6 |
| Stewart | 159 | 1 307 | 169 | D | 251 | D | 32 | 35 | 26 796 | 353 | 28.9 | 5.9 | 39.4 |
| Sullivan | 3 339 | 64 241 | 12 412 | D | 8 272 | 1 867 | 1 724 | 2 797 | 43 532 | 1 280 | 66.6 | 1.6 | 33.5 |
| Sumner | 2 833 | 36 154 | 5 097 | 5 465 | 5 698 | 1 444 | 1 650 | 1 190 | 32 919 | 1 673 | 51.8 | 3.2 | 34.7 |
| Tipton | 717 | 8 241 | 1 217 | 1 287 | 1 769 | 275 | 133 | 231 | 27 973 | 610 | 44.6 | 9.7 | 47.4 |
| Trousdale | 123 | 1 065 | 240 | D | 210 | 59 | 28 | 26 | 23 975 | 338 | 39.1 | 3.6 | 36.7 |
| Unicoi | 248 | 3 990 | 745 | 1 642 | 477 | 74 | D | 146 | 36 598 | 86 | 55.8 | 1.2 | 38.4 |
| Union | 196 | 1 582 | 172 | 514 | 354 | D | D | 42 | 26 647 | 494 | 45.1 | 1.2 | 38.5 |
| Van Buren | 44 | 527 | D | D | D | D | NA | 14 | 25 638 | 213 | 34.3 | 8.5 | 39.9 |
| Warren | 715 | 9 114 | 1 536 | 2 948 | 1 653 | 320 | D | 280 | 30 701 | 1 331 | 48.3 | 4.3 | 47.0 |
| Washington | 2 814 | 49 087 | 12 492 | 4 592 | 8 302 | 2 671 | 2 243 | 1 609 | 32 775 | 1 650 | 60.2 | 1.8 | 39.9 |
| Wayne | 205 | 2 458 | 356 | 700 | 335 | 160 | D | 63 | 25 729 | 646 | 25.5 | 6.8 | 37.6 |
| Weakley | 564 | 7 010 | 1 787 | 1 118 | 1 180 | 226 | 90 | 179 | 25 539 | 1 214 | 39.5 | 8.6 | 38.3 |
| White | 388 | 5 278 | 760 | 2 144 | 829 | 103 | D | 160 | 30 362 | 1 035 | 41.4 | 4.2 | 44.2 |
| Williamson | 6 060 | 94 792 | 11 774 | 2 392 | 13 079 | 11 187 | 7 724 | 5 208 | 54 937 | 1 442 | 50.2 | 3.1 | 36.9 |
| Wilson | 2 329 | 29 635 | 3 820 | 2 788 | 5 242 | 960 | 952 | 1 027 | 34 652 | 1 745 | 45.1 | 2.8 | 39.7 |
| **TEXAS** | 525 420 | 8 987 663 | 1 314 698 | 733 679 | 1 152 579 | 464 679 | 578 855 | 414 113 | 46 076 | 247 437 | 37.9 | 16.2 | 39.9 |
| Anderson | 938 | 11 415 | 2 072 | D | 2 019 | 299 | 214 | 408 | 35 727 | 1 771 | 36.3 | 7.1 | 36.9 |
| Andrews | 345 | 4 577 | D | D | 312 | D | 83 | 230 | 50 174 | 175 | 36.0 | 36.0 | 36.0 |
| Angelina | 1 862 | 29 843 | 8 035 | 4 548 | 4 870 | 843 | 670 | 918 | 30 754 | 1 109 | 55.9 | 2.2 | 38.9 |
| Aransas | 475 | 3 977 | 616 | D | 1 044 | 157 | 131 | 103 | 25 813 | 94 | 61.7 | 11.7 | 23.4 |
| Archer | 195 | 1 444 | 267 | D | 123 | 24 | D | 50 | 34 467 | 513 | 17.3 | 38.8 | 46.4 |
| Armstrong | 29 | 184 | D | NA | D | D | D | 4 | 19 663 | 291 | 4.1 | 54.6 | 44.7 |
| Atascosa | 626 | 6 788 | 1 331 | 161 | 1 508 | D | 224 | 250 | 36 805 | 1 810 | 33.3 | 16.1 | 38.6 |
| Austin | 572 | 8 536 | 647 | 2 750 | 896 | 322 | 209 | 351 | 41 139 | 2 112 | 39.3 | 5.9 | 34.5 |
| Bailey | 159 | 1 416 | 219 | D | 233 | 67 | D | 35 | 24 685 | 564 | 9.4 | 41.8 | 45.4 |
| Bandera | 359 | 2 089 | 327 | D | 364 | 84 | 96 | 57 | 27 339 | 972 | 36.8 | 15.7 | 42.2 |
| Bastrop | 1 038 | 11 436 | 2 005 | 972 | 2 337 | 366 | 414 | 344 | 30 091 | 2 207 | 44.4 | 7.1 | 38.0 |
| Baylor | 114 | 952 | 491 | 52 | 96 | D | D | 19 | 20 011 | 268 | 13.8 | 44.0 | 47.8 |
| Bee | 449 | 5 106 | 1 452 | D | 1 038 | 186 | 165 | 145 | 28 407 | 952 | 31.3 | 20.0 | 39.8 |
| Bell | 4 772 | 82 286 | 20 935 | 5 527 | 13 232 | 2 702 | 3 471 | 2 926 | 35 554 | 2 384 | 50.8 | 8.1 | 36.2 |
| Bexar | 32 612 | 640 651 | 104 963 | 31 664 | 82 620 | 56 646 | 38 483 | 25 738 | 40 176 | 2 496 | 61.4 | 5.3 | 43.5 |
| Blanco | 235 | 1 718 | 150 | 116 | 221 | D | D | 62 | 35 808 | 888 | 31.6 | 22.0 | 42.0 |
| Borden | 3 | D | NA | NA | D | NA | D | D | 0 | 116 | 8.6 | 64.7 | 44.8 |
| Bosque | 289 | 2 713 | 651 | 599 | 404 | 134 | D | 79 | 29 033 | 1 399 | 25.9 | 16.7 | 39.0 |
| Bowie | 2 146 | 30 875 | 6 793 | 1 802 | 6 474 | 1 188 | 1 182 | 965 | 31 244 | 1 610 | 48.8 | 7.9 | 38.4 |
| Brazoria | 4 848 | 72 007 | 7 966 | 12 000 | 13 287 | 1 974 | 2 686 | 3 094 | 42 969 | 2 580 | 61.9 | 7.1 | 33.7 |
| Brazos | 3 747 | 54 027 | 8 149 | 4 601 | 10 038 | 1 362 | 2 981 | 1 649 | 30 525 | 1 350 | 44.9 | 8.1 | 35.0 |
| Brewster | 295 | 2 807 | 593 | 87 | 394 | 184 | 61 | 66 | 23 671 | 158 | 20.9 | 60.1 | 47.5 |
| Briscoe | 39 | 166 | D | D | D | D | NA | 3 | 20 867 | 333 | 7.5 | 49.2 | 47.4 |
| Brooks | 128 | 1 648 | D | NA | 339 | 81 | D | 46 | 27 666 | 494 | 22.3 | 17.2 | 45.3 |
| Brown | 918 | 12 540 | 3 100 | 2 487 | 1 842 | 388 | 214 | 363 | 28 914 | 1 726 | 32.5 | 16.4 | 37.4 |
| Burleson | 302 | 2 621 | D | 365 | 585 | 116 | 123 | 93 | 35 341 | 1 582 | 30.8 | 9.8 | 38.7 |
| Burnet | 1 079 | 10 118 | 1 351 | 785 | 2 022 | 407 | 296 | 329 | 32 484 | 1 531 | 37.4 | 13.1 | 36.4 |

# Table B. States and Counties — Agriculture

| | Agriculture, 2007 (cont.) | | | | | | | | | | | | | | |
| STATE County | Land in farms | | | | Value of land and buildings (dollars) | | Value of machinery and equipment, average per farm (dollars) | Value of products sold | | | | Percent of farms with sales of: | | Government payments | |
| | | | Acres | | | | | | | Percent from: | | | | | |
| | Acreage (1,000) | Percent change, 2002–2007 | Average size of farm | Total irrigated (1,000) | Total cropland (1,000) | Average per farm | Average per acre | | Total (mil dol) | Average per farm (dollars) | Crops | Live-stock and poultry products | $10,000 or more | $100,000 or more | Total ($1,000) | Percent of farms |
| | 117 | 118 | 119 | 120 | 121 | 122 | 123 | 124 | 125 | 126 | 127 | 128 | 129 | 130 | 131 | 132 |
| **TENNESSEE—Cont'd** | | | | | | | | | | | | | | | | |
| Marshall | 152 | -13.1 | 141 | 0.1 | 63.1 | 459 053 | 3 265 | 48 755 | 25.8 | 23 941 | 6.7 | 93.3 | 31.2 | 4.0 | 213 | 15.2 |
| Maury | 226 | -6.2 | 133 | 0.4 | 107.3 | 505 101 | 3 784 | 51 885 | 28.5 | 16 808 | 19.3 | 80.7 | 24.4 | 2.6 | 470 | 15.6 |
| Meigs | 49 | 0.0 | 134 | 0.2 | 21.3 | 479 098 | 3 580 | 56 582 | 6.4 | 17 396 | 3.9 | 96.1 | 29.4 | 2.7 | 145 | 12.8 |
| Monroe | 93 | -6.1 | 99 | 0.0 | 43.6 | 404 826 | 4 089 | 51 427 | 23.5 | 25 139 | 6.8 | 93.2 | 23.4 | 3.6 | 133 | 11.1 |
| Montgomery | 151 | -9.6 | 176 | 0.8 | 87.8 | 568 924 | 3 238 | 72 512 | 27.8 | 32 277 | 66.1 | 33.9 | 32.7 | 6.5 | 690 | 20.8 |
| Moore | 52 | -17.5 | 150 | 0.0 | 21.2 | 491 455 | 3 282 | 79 392 | 18.3 | 52 795 | 3.2 | 96.8 | 35.5 | 7.5 | 34 | 5.2 |
| Morgan | 53 | -7.0 | 131 | 0.0 | 20.6 | 378 576 | 2 889 | 58 942 | 12.8 | 31 352 | 3.8 | 96.2 | 20.9 | 4.4 | 23 | 7.1 |
| Obion | 252 | -4.5 | 363 | 0.8 | 211.7 | 926 419 | 2 549 | 115 722 | 85.6 | 123 497 | 68.3 | 31.7 | 38.2 | 17.5 | 4 467 | 66.5 |
| Overton | 115 | -7.3 | 114 | 0.2 | 49.7 | 369 485 | 3 247 | 53 260 | 15.1 | 14 921 | 10.8 | 89.2 | 25.4 | 2.1 | 67 | 8.2 |
| Perry | 51 | 2.0 | 198 | 0.1 | 19.4 | 419 021 | 2 116 | 47 295 | 2.9 | 11 283 | 28.5 | 71.5 | 27.6 | 2.3 | 138 | 30.7 |
| Pickett | 38 | -9.5 | 104 | D | 17.6 | 361 120 | 3 476 | 44 107 | 11.7 | 32 027 | 4.7 | 95.3 | 31.0 | 3.8 | 19 | 10.4 |
| Polk | 32 | 0.0 | 106 | 0.1 | 17.8 | 495 514 | 4 665 | 67 210 | 25.1 | 82 213 | 7.0 | 93.0 | 26.9 | 10.2 | 148 | 17.0 |
| Putnam | 104 | -12.6 | 97 | 0.1 | 41.2 | 403 524 | 4 161 | 49 621 | 11.5 | 10 804 | 20.2 | 79.8 | 19.9 | 1.9 | 98 | 9.6 |
| Rhea | 56 | -8.2 | 125 | 0.4 | 26.5 | 449 752 | 3 594 | 53 202 | 11.9 | 26 600 | 41.5 | 58.5 | 24.3 | 4.2 | 160 | 14.9 |
| Roane | 53 | -15.9 | 91 | 0.0 | 18.8 | 385 280 | 4 250 | 43 203 | 5.1 | 8 858 | 28.0 | 71.9 | 21.7 | 0.9 | 21 | 6.2 |
| Robertson | 227 | -2.6 | 161 | 2.1 | 160.1 | 620 415 | 3 843 | 76 736 | 82.0 | 58 259 | 71.8 | 28.2 | 35.2 | 10.9 | 1 771 | 34.4 |
| Rutherford | 164 | -22.3 | 108 | 1.4 | 77.9 | 493 027 | 4 573 | 47 070 | 24.5 | 16 039 | 42.5 | 57.5 | 20.6 | 2.3 | 660 | 11.1 |
| Scott | 31 | -11.4 | 119 | D | 12.0 | 373 615 | 3 137 | 50 265 | 5.0 | 19 077 | 4.2 | 95.8 | 10.7 | 2.3 | D | 8.8 |
| Sequatchie | 29 | 3.6 | 124 | 0.0 | 12.6 | 418 376 | 3 385 | 50 649 | 4.9 | 21 307 | 10.0 | 90.0 | 18.5 | 3.4 | 75 | 16.8 |
| Sevier | 56 | -25.3 | 80 | 0.1 | 22.3 | 441 378 | 5 528 | 48 410 | 6.8 | 9 593 | 15.2 | 84.8 | 19.0 | 1.4 | 16 | 4.4 |
| Shelby | 92 | -20.7 | 154 | 1.7 | 68.7 | 716 648 | 4 659 | 64 056 | 23.5 | 39 232 | 89.4 | 10.6 | 17.8 | 5.3 | 2 279 | 21.5 |
| Smith | 127 | -9.9 | 130 | 0.2 | 49.3 | 408 529 | 3 153 | 52 143 | 14.1 | 14 399 | 34.1 | 65.9 | 23.9 | 1.9 | 197 | 16.0 |
| Stewart | 55 | 0.0 | 157 | 0.3 | 19.4 | 425 012 | 2 710 | 51 950 | 6.0 | 17 071 | D | D | 26.3 | 4.0 | 82 | 11.0 |
| Sullivan | 82 | -18.8 | 64 | 0.1 | 36.8 | 326 716 | 5 094 | 56 038 | 17.1 | 13 394 | 17.3 | 82.7 | 17.6 | 2.3 | 47 | 7.9 |
| Sumner | 183 | -5.2 | 110 | 0.3 | 89.5 | 443 513 | 4 045 | 60 727 | 32.4 | 19 342 | 42.1 | 57.9 | 22.5 | 2.8 | 283 | 13.0 |
| Tipton | 170 | 0.6 | 279 | 2.6 | 145.0 | 655 800 | 2 351 | 90 326 | 37.0 | 60 699 | 92.8 | 7.2 | 28.9 | 9.3 | 4 502 | 47.0 |
| Trousdale | 44 | -6.4 | 130 | 0.1 | 19.8 | 421 195 | 3 235 | 45 920 | 4.3 | 12 647 | 25.4 | 74.6 | 26.9 | 2.1 | 22 | 6.2 |
| Unicoi | 5 | -44.4 | 55 | 0.1 | 1.8 | 398 631 | 7 230 | 38 391 | 1.3 | 15 073 | 5.9 | 94.1 | 10.5 | 3.5 | D | 1.2 |
| Union | 46 | -4.2 | 93 | 0.0 | 19.8 | 340 540 | 3 664 | 50 606 | 4.1 | 8 293 | 11.6 | 88.4 | 18.2 | 0.6 | 10 | 6.3 |
| Van Buren | 35 | 9.4 | 164 | D | 14.3 | 465 800 | 2 847 | 63 970 | 4.2 | 19 709 | 6.9 | 93.1 | 35.7 | 2.8 | D | 1.9 |
| Warren | 161 | -6.9 | 121 | 6.8 | 91.4 | 426 095 | 3 532 | 70 573 | 108.6 | 81 569 | 81.8 | 18.2 | 42.8 | 12.4 | 410 | 13.9 |
| Washington | 119 | -11.2 | 72 | 0.9 | 62.6 | 396 345 | 5 514 | 56 808 | 38.9 | 23 601 | 24.7 | 75.3 | 22.8 | 3.5 | 195 | 15.5 |
| Wayne | 115 | -8.0 | 178 | 0.2 | 41.3 | 393 113 | 2 202 | 51 363 | 12.6 | 19 429 | 10.7 | 89.3 | 27.1 | 2.8 | 235 | 26.0 |
| Weakley | 256 | 6.7 | 211 | 0.5 | 204.7 | 532 829 | 2 531 | 74 806 | 75.0 | 61 797 | 61.5 | 38.5 | 27.3 | 11.0 | 3 614 | 58.7 |
| White | 132 | -3.6 | 127 | 0.1 | 56.8 | 417 998 | 3 286 | 55 475 | 23.2 | 22 412 | 7.5 | 92.5 | 33.5 | 4.2 | 116 | 10.7 |
| Williamson | 162 | -19.8 | 112 | 0.9 | 69.8 | 602 384 | 5 367 | 52 188 | 26.9 | 18 621 | 29.9 | 70.1 | 21.6 | 2.5 | 180 | 8.9 |
| Wilson | 193 | -17.9 | 111 | 0.1 | 69.1 | 452 626 | 4 094 | 52 680 | 21.3 | 12 230 | 9.2 | 90.8 | 23.6 | 1.5 | 241 | 11.8 |
| **TEXAS** | 130 399 | 0.4 | 527 | 5 010.4 | 33 667.2 | 669 154 | 1 270 | 64 350 | 21 001.1 | 84 874 | 31.3 | 68.7 | 29.0 | 7.1 | 720 903 | 19.4 |
| Anderson | 346 | -5.2 | 195 | 2.3 | 74.9 | 436 160 | 2 232 | 51 164 | 39.4 | 22 225 | 32.7 | 67.3 | 24.8 | 2.0 | 172 | 2.9 |
| Andrews | 808 | 0.5 | 4 620 | 12.2 | 62.2 | 1 572 018 | 340 | 90 734 | 15.9 | 90 965 | 71.4 | 28.6 | 24.6 | 14.9 | 1 634 | 36.6 |
| Angelina | 115 | -1.7 | 104 | 0.5 | 43.3 | 290 792 | 2 798 | 44 485 | 29.4 | 26 545 | 6.9 | 93.1 | 18.2 | 2.1 | 145 | 2.2 |
| Aransas | 51 | 2.0 | 542 | 0.0 | D | 747 807 | 1 380 | 36 197 | 1.7 | 17 757 | 2.7 | 97.3 | 10.6 | 2.1 | D | 2.1 |
| Archer | 508 | -5.2 | 989 | 1.0 | 110.4 | 963 189 | 973 | 89 155 | 61.0 | 118 877 | 8.6 | 91.4 | 53.8 | 21.6 | 1 229 | 42.7 |
| Armstrong | 516 | 2.0 | 1 774 | 5.9 | 159.4 | 1 533 026 | 864 | 94 828 | 37.4 | 128 435 | 42.0 | 58.0 | 48.5 | 20.6 | 3 041 | 75.9 |
| Atascosa | 644 | -3.9 | 356 | 22.6 | 139.1 | 584 079 | 1 643 | 52 911 | 50.3 | 27 764 | 33.0 | 67.0 | 22.6 | 3.3 | 1 855 | 12.8 |
| Austin | 334 | -9.0 | 158 | 1.6 | 96.6 | 539 487 | 3 412 | 48 817 | 30.9 | 14 649 | 31.6 | 68.4 | 28.2 | 2.3 | 688 | 6.9 |
| Bailey | 476 | 20.8 | 844 | 69.7 | 326.0 | 766 537 | 908 | 102 476 | 234.0 | 414 872 | 16.8 | 83.2 | 42.6 | 23.8 | 8 612 | 77.0 |
| Bandera | 329 | -10.4 | 339 | 0.6 | 21.4 | 776 642 | 2 292 | 42 876 | 7.0 | 7 175 | 13.6 | 86.4 | 11.9 | 0.6 | 260 | 3.8 |
| Bastrop | 402 | -5.0 | 182 | 2.5 | 76.1 | 499 654 | 2 743 | 46 194 | 38.2 | 17 303 | 28.5 | 71.5 | 23.7 | 1.7 | 428 | 6.3 |
| Baylor | 547 | 66.8 | 2 041 | 3.3 | 141.7 | 1 198 087 | 587 | 107 654 | 42.9 | 160 238 | 21.6 | 78.4 | 56.7 | 22.0 | 2 121 | 67.5 |
| Bee | 548 | 7.5 | 576 | 5.7 | 104.9 | 820 945 | 1 425 | 57 604 | 39.2 | 41 180 | 48.7 | 51.3 | 25.4 | 5.9 | 1 571 | 15.4 |
| Bell | 432 | -4.2 | 181 | 2.7 | 183.8 | 427 359 | 2 359 | 50 594 | 61.7 | 25 901 | 51.8 | 48.2 | 24.4 | 3.6 | 2 176 | 17.8 |
| Bexar | 426 | -3.4 | 171 | 14.1 | 125.0 | 467 393 | 2 739 | 42 868 | 84.2 | 33 743 | 76.5 | 23.5 | 15.3 | 2.2 | 573 | 7.7 |
| Blanco | 396 | 1.8 | 446 | 1.0 | 43.6 | 1 116 042 | 2 505 | 43 459 | 18.2 | 20 459 | 51.7 | 48.3 | 20.6 | 1.7 | 286 | 5.5 |
| Borden | 435 | -9.4 | 3 751 | 2.2 | 93.8 | 2 171 362 | 579 | 126 920 | 13.2 | 114 081 | 60.7 | 39.3 | 49.1 | 30.2 | 1 987 | 62.9 |
| Bosque | 551 | -2.1 | 394 | 1.0 | 96.2 | 849 731 | 2 158 | 50 349 | 42.8 | 30 591 | 29.0 | 71.0 | 26.2 | 3.0 | 552 | 12.9 |
| Bowie | 292 | -5.2 | 181 | 3.4 | 96.2 | 335 490 | 1 852 | 52 632 | 48.4 | 30 062 | 19.5 | 80.5 | 26.5 | 3.8 | 1 270 | 10.5 |
| Brazoria | 529 | -13.8 | 205 | 12.0 | 186.2 | 448 494 | 2 188 | 48 795 | 55.1 | 21 365 | 54.7 | 45.3 | 19.2 | 3.0 | 2 697 | 6.1 |
| Brazos | 276 | -10.7 | 204 | 9.0 | 62.7 | 563 474 | 2 759 | 62 995 | 54.5 | 40 378 | 23.0 | 77.0 | 28.2 | 4.1 | 1 356 | 5.0 |
| Brewster | 1 747 | 4.2 | 11 058 | 0.5 | 50.1 | 3 797 111 | 343 | 81 828 | 9.6 | 60 517 | 12.8 | 87.2 | 42.4 | 13.9 | 202 | 13.9 |
| Briscoe | 547 | 28.4 | 1 642 | 31.7 | 166.7 | 1 016 703 | 619 | 99 624 | 27.9 | 83 905 | 71.4 | 28.6 | 39.9 | 19.8 | 6 290 | 85.3 |
| Brooks | 549 | 24.8 | 1 111 | 1.5 | 58.4 | 1 153 983 | 1 039 | 44 947 | 19.1 | 38 686 | 4.8 | 95.2 | 20.2 | 2.6 | 524 | 16.2 |
| Brown | 560 | 16.2 | 324 | 3.7 | 95.3 | 585 658 | 1 805 | 39 183 | 35.9 | 20 791 | 16.4 | 83.6 | 25.3 | 2.8 | 917 | 16.2 |
| Burleson | 361 | -7.2 | 228 | 14.5 | 92.3 | 515 165 | 2 257 | 56 109 | 56.4 | 35 651 | 33.6 | 66.4 | 34.1 | 4.7 | 1 559 | 6.3 |
| Burnet | 482 | -14.7 | 315 | 1.3 | 57.6 | 712 764 | 2 263 | 40 614 | 12.3 | 8 030 | 18.3 | 81.7 | 18.2 | 1.1 | 111 | 3.6 |

| STATE / County | Water use, 2005 | | Wholesale trade,[1] 2007 | | | | Retail trade,[2] 2007 | | | | Real estate and rental and leasing,[2] 2007 | | | |
|---|---|---|---|---|---|---|---|---|---|---|---|---|---|---|
| | Total water withdrawn (mil gal/day) | Gallons withdrawn per person | Number of establishments | Number of employees | Sales (mil dol) | Annual payroll (mil dol) | Number of establishments | Number of employees | Sales (mil dol) | Annual payroll (mil dol) | Number of establishments | Number of employees | Receipts (mil dol) | Annual payroll (mil dol) |
| | 133 | 134 | 135 | 136 | 137 | 138 | 139 | 140 | 141 | 142 | 143 | 144 | 145 | 146 |
| **TENNESSEE—Cont'd** | | | | | | | | | | | | | | |
| Marshall | 4.0 | 141 | 10 | D | D | D | 122 | 1 176 | 269.7 | 24.3 | 19 | 53 | 5.9 | 0.7 |
| Maury | 14.3 | 187 | 58 | 649 | 245.1 | 29.4 | 333 | 3 824 | 898.3 | 81.1 | 89 | 355 | 56.8 | 9.8 |
| Meigs | 1.5 | 125 | 2 | D | D | D | 22 | 149 | 29.8 | 2.7 | 2 | D | D | D |
| Monroe | 9.6 | 222 | 28 | 315 | 173.4 | 8.6 | 150 | 1 695 | 453.0 | 37.9 | 28 | 88 | 9.6 | 1.5 |
| Montgomery | 24.3 | 165 | 72 | 629 | 345.5 | 26.3 | 522 | 8 016 | 1 877.6 | 180.3 | 145 | 577 | 110.7 | 15.3 |
| Moore | 1.7 | 281 | 1 | D | D | D | 11 | 85 | 16.3 | 1.2 | NA | NA | NA | NA |
| Morgan | 2.2 | 109 | 6 | D | D | D | 40 | 300 | 58.5 | 4.6 | 3 | D | D | D |
| Obion | 12.8 | 399 | 39 | D | D | D | 158 | 1 767 | 403.5 | 37.0 | 24 | 76 | 8.2 | 1.5 |
| Overton | 3.3 | 158 | 9 | 70 | 46.7 | 2.6 | 66 | 457 | 110.7 | 8.0 | 7 | D | D | D |
| Perry | 1.5 | 194 | 2 | D | D | D | 24 | 144 | 24.3 | 1.9 | 5 | D | D | D |
| Pickett | 0.9 | 185 | 2 | D | D | D | 24 | 115 | 23.6 | 2.1 | 1 | D | D | D |
| Polk | 6.0 | 375 | 3 | D | D | D | 48 | 297 | 67.7 | 6.1 | 8 | 17 | 1.7 | 0.4 |
| Putnam | 14.7 | 220 | 70 | 745 | 465.7 | 30.8 | 379 | 4 766 | 1 193.0 | 106.6 | 72 | 241 | 40.3 | 5.5 |
| Rhea | 192.8 | 6 446 | 10 | 73 | 17.9 | 2.0 | 108 | 1 097 | 250.8 | 21.0 | 20 | 89 | 8.2 | 1.3 |
| Roane | 1 291.6 | 24 422 | 20 | D | D | D | 157 | 1 852 | 436.4 | 39.2 | 33 | 487 | 36.0 | 11.4 |
| Robertson | 8.0 | 133 | 52 | 742 | 779.4 | 20.7 | 183 | 2 433 | 627.8 | 53.8 | 52 | 148 | 19.9 | 2.9 |
| Rutherford | 35.2 | 161 | 232 | 5 472 | 6 226.3 | 256.0 | 758 | 11 262 | 2 804.3 | 250.1 | 212 | 1 110 | 381.8 | 29.8 |
| Scott | 2.9 | 131 | 8 | 54 | 28.4 | 1.1 | 83 | 771 | 159.6 | 14.5 | 8 | 24 | 3.9 | 0.5 |
| Sequatchie | 1.3 | 101 | 11 | D | D | D | 47 | 441 | 105.3 | 8.1 | 15 | 59 | 5.9 | 0.8 |
| Sevier | 12.3 | 155 | 40 | D | D | D | 750 | 8 050 | 1 641.1 | 170.8 | 198 | 2 343 | 462.4 | 77.6 |
| Shelby | 626.5 | 689 | 1 271 | 26 595 | 29 636.0 | 1 384.8 | 3 300 | 49 554 | 11 932.9 | 1 177.7 | 1 044 | 8 375 | 1 532.0 | 329.3 |
| Smith | 2.5 | 132 | 12 | 66 | 52.5 | 1.6 | 66 | 598 | 117.8 | 13.9 | 11 | 34 | 3.6 | 0.6 |
| Stewart | 2 082.9 | 160 605 | 4 | D | D | D | 34 | 233 | 63.7 | 5.6 | 4 | 33 | 1.8 | 0.2 |
| Sullivan | 534.4 | 3 500 | 183 | 2 207 | 1 055.3 | 99.4 | 622 | 8 148 | 2 026.3 | 183.8 | 132 | 649 | 108.4 | 17.1 |
| Sumner | 966.5 | 6 665 | 134 | 2 007 | 1 634.9 | 81.8 | 428 | 5 565 | 1 300.1 | 121.9 | 152 | 801 | 182.0 | 30.0 |
| Tipton | 5.5 | 98 | 24 | 253 | 241.9 | 7.3 | 164 | 1 690 | 404.2 | 33.0 | 27 | 115 | 11.8 | 2.1 |
| Trousdale | 1.2 | 155 | 2 | D | D | D | 27 | 203 | 41.7 | 3.4 | 1 | D | D | D |
| Unicoi | 6.2 | 355 | 8 | D | D | D | 44 | 514 | 119.5 | 10.1 | 6 | 22 | 2.2 | 0.7 |
| Union | 2.0 | 103 | 11 | 40 | 6.6 | 0.8 | 37 | 297 | 60.5 | 5.0 | 9 | 54 | 3.6 | 0.9 |
| Van Buren | 1.1 | 192 | NA | NA | NA | NA | 7 | 35 | 9.2 | 0.4 | 6 | 26 | 1.2 | 0.5 |
| Warren | 7.8 | 196 | 36 | D | D | D | 179 | 1 834 | 373.7 | 38.8 | 22 | 59 | 8.3 | 1.3 |
| Washington | 22.4 | 199 | 135 | 2 000 | 1 090.8 | 70.6 | 551 | 8 257 | 1 869.1 | 169.3 | 127 | 957 | 114.1 | 17.8 |
| Wayne | 2.2 | 132 | 7 | 52 | 38.0 | 1.3 | 50 | 347 | 66.6 | 5.4 | 5 | D | D | D |
| Weakley | 5.5 | 162 | 32 | D | D | D | 120 | 1 256 | 265.4 | 22.5 | 20 | 68 | 7.8 | 1.4 |
| White | 4.1 | 168 | 11 | 88 | 28.9 | 2.8 | 81 | 793 | 195.4 | 17.7 | 11 | 52 | 3.5 | 0.9 |
| Williamson | 5.6 | 36 | 211 | 2 340 | 2 756.0 | 151.2 | 783 | 13 038 | 3 307.0 | 306.4 | 277 | 2 658 | 406.2 | 84.2 |
| Wilson | 15.5 | 154 | 80 | 1 298 | 967.9 | 62.5 | 394 | 4 621 | 1 165.0 | 103.4 | 115 | 541 | 85.9 | 16.1 |
| **TEXAS** | 26 747.0 | 1 170 | 27 066 | 386 370 | 424 238.2 | 20 260.6 | 78 795 | 1 138 440 | 311 334.8 | 26 395.2 | 26 593 | 173 745 | 36 399.2 | 7 067.2 |
| Anderson | 16.0 | 284 | 33 | 409 | 365.3 | 16.8 | 183 | 1 958 | 495.5 | 42.5 | 36 | 149 | 53.3 | 6.1 |
| Andrews | 53.4 | 4 185 | 12 | D | D | D | 36 | 314 | 98.3 | 7.5 | 12 | 70 | 12.9 | 4.7 |
| Angelina | 22.8 | 280 | 63 | D | D | D | 356 | 5 086 | 1 174.1 | 106.3 | 75 | 359 | 49.1 | 9.6 |
| Aransas | 3.5 | 142 | 10 | 32 | 13.5 | 1.0 | 95 | 1 125 | 241.5 | 23.5 | 37 | 152 | 14.3 | 2.7 |
| Archer | 56.8 | 6 240 | 13 | 52 | 43.4 | 2.3 | 23 | 91 | 39.4 | 2.0 | 4 | D | D | D |
| Armstrong | 7.7 | 3 520 | 1 | D | D | D | 4 | 24 | 2.4 | 0.2 | NA | NA | NA | NA |
| Atascosa | 35.8 | 827 | 22 | 187 | 69.4 | 6.3 | 124 | 1 499 | 362.9 | 30.4 | 25 | 86 | 11.9 | 1.6 |
| Austin | 12.9 | 495 | 18 | D | D | D | 95 | 878 | 234.2 | 19.8 | 22 | 54 | 9.1 | 1.7 |
| Bailey | 147.2 | 21 882 | 20 | 137 | 69.9 | 4.4 | 27 | 229 | 41.7 | 3.6 | 1 | D | D | D |
| Bandera | 3.2 | 159 | 5 | 18 | 1.4 | 0.5 | 56 | 359 | 76.5 | 6.4 | 14 | 38 | 5.8 | 0.8 |
| Bastrop | 250.9 | 3 588 | 33 | 198 | 51.6 | 8.0 | 167 | 2 069 | 684.7 | 48.1 | 52 | 173 | 18.6 | 4.1 |
| Baylor | 6.6 | 1 717 | 8 | 48 | 33.8 | 1.7 | 16 | 107 | 27.1 | 1.3 | 3 | D | D | D |
| Bee | 10.1 | 306 | 7 | D | D | D | 82 | 1 071 | 247.1 | 23.4 | 25 | 87 | 10.8 | 2.6 |
| Bell | 105.7 | 413 | 125 | 2 933 | 4 202.7 | 125.3 | 924 | 12 506 | 3 350.0 | 283.0 | 308 | 1 501 | 209.4 | 40.3 |
| Bexar | 784.8 | 517 | 1 427 | 22 636 | 12 232.1 | 1 042.4 | 4 737 | 81 409 | 22 815.3 | 1 891.9 | 1 793 | 12 057 | 2 215.6 | 425.7 |
| Blanco | 2.2 | 238 | 10 | D | D | D | 30 | 213 | 50.6 | 3.6 | 7 | D | D | D |
| Borden | 8.2 | 12 623 | NA | NA | NA | NA | 1 | D | D | D | NA | NA | NA | NA |
| Bosque | 7.9 | 438 | 12 | 70 | 28.4 | 2.7 | 55 | 457 | 106.5 | 9.2 | 10 | 13 | 2.0 | 0.3 |
| Bowie | 121.5 | 1 341 | 104 | D | D | D | 487 | 6 447 | 1 535.4 | 141.3 | 102 | 483 | 67.3 | 11.5 |
| Brazoria | 970.1 | 3 483 | 181 | 1 572 | 841.9 | 74.6 | 743 | 11 791 | 2 958.8 | 265.3 | 252 | 1 604 | 366.6 | 61.3 |
| Brazos | 39.8 | 255 | 111 | 1 498 | 779.6 | 56.5 | 646 | 9 149 | 2 119.1 | 189.9 | 226 | 1 192 | 196.3 | 32.4 |
| Brewster | 8.6 | 948 | 9 | 58 | 20.3 | 1.4 | 60 | 470 | 86.8 | 8.9 | 23 | 61 | 5.6 | 1.1 |
| Briscoe | 29.5 | 17 920 | 3 | 20 | 5.4 | 0.3 | 8 | 27 | 6.7 | 0.4 | NA | NA | NA | NA |
| Brooks | 2.9 | 377 | 2 | D | D | D | 25 | 345 | 81.6 | 6.9 | 1 | D | D | D |
| Brown | 14.8 | 383 | 40 | 392 | 171.0 | 13.0 | 196 | 1 973 | 512.5 | 41.0 | 40 | 116 | 16.1 | 2.8 |
| Burleson | 29.0 | 1 684 | 17 | D | D | D | 49 | 501 | 183.8 | 12.0 | 5 | 16 | 2.2 | 0.5 |
| Burnet | 10.8 | 258 | 31 | 163 | 81.9 | 7.4 | 195 | 2 139 | 639.5 | 51.6 | 57 | 295 | 26.6 | 6.9 |

1. Merchant wholesalers, except manufacturers' sales branches and offices.  2. Employer establishments.

# Table B. States and Counties — Professional Services, Manufacturing, and Accommodation and Food Services

| STATE County | Professional, scientific, and technical services,[1] 2007 | | | | Manufacturing, 2007 | | | | Accommodation and food services, 2007 | | | |
|---|---|---|---|---|---|---|---|---|---|---|---|---|
| | Number of establish- ments | Number of employees | Receipts (mil dol) | Annual payroll (mil dol) | Number of establish- ments | Number of employees | Receipts (mil dol) | Annual payroll (mil dol) | Number of establish- ments | Number of employees | Sales (mil dol) | Annual payroll (mil dol) |
| | 147 | 148 | 149 | 150 | 151 | 152 | 153 | 154 | 155 | 156 | 157 | 158 |
| TENNESSEE—Cont'd | | | | | | | | | | | | |
| Marshall | 28 | 93 | 6.8 | 1.9 | 52 | 3 821 | 1 490.1 | 145.0 | 37 | 518 | 21.1 | 5.2 |
| Maury | 108 | D | D | D | 82 | 4 575 | D | 312.3 | 144 | 2 835 | 97.3 | 28.3 |
| Meigs | 3 | D | D | D | 14 | 770 | 253.0 | 28.8 | 6 | 46 | 2.0 | 0.6 |
| Monroe | 48 | 160 | 12.2 | 5.7 | 72 | 5 246 | 1 386.2 | 189.2 | 81 | 1 224 | 41.0 | 11.3 |
| Montgomery | 160 | D | D | D | 70 | 6 052 | D | D | 300 | 6 151 | 245.2 | 64.7 |
| Moore | 2 | D | D | D | NA | NA | NA | NA | 8 | 48 | 1.4 | 0.5 |
| Morgan | 10 | D | D | D | NA | NA | NA | NA | 8 | 105 | 3.5 | 1.1 |
| Obion | 34 | D | D | D | 43 | 5 506 | D | D | 65 | D | D | D |
| Overton | 22 | D | D | D | 35 | 1 101 | D | 32.3 | 25 | 317 | 13.3 | 3.3 |
| Perry | 3 | D | D | D | 12 | 1 042 | 170.0 | 30.1 | 6 | D | D | D |
| Pickett | 5 | D | D | D | NA | NA | NA | NA | 9 | 67 | 3.1 | 0.5 |
| Polk | 11 | D | D | D | NA | NA | NA | NA | 23 | 175 | 8.8 | 2.4 |
| Putnam | 139 | D | D | D | 112 | 6 106 | 1 384.0 | 203.1 | 154 | 3 387 | 138.0 | 38.5 |
| Rhea | 38 | 97 | 8.6 | 3.1 | 33 | 4 705 | 894.7 | 149.7 | 45 | 761 | 26.9 | 6.9 |
| Roane | 60 | 182 | 19.6 | 6.9 | 23 | 1 440 | 369.7 | 54.9 | 66 | 1 304 | 46.0 | 12.7 |
| Robertson | 56 | D | D | D | 84 | 6 281 | 1 667.5 | 211.8 | 83 | 1 669 | 60.7 | 17.3 |
| Rutherford | 325 | D | D | D | 203 | 18 166 | 11 304.8 | 901.6 | 417 | 9 745 | 387.0 | 111.2 |
| Scott | 16 | 68 | 6.4 | 4.3 | 44 | 1 499 | 401.7 | 46.8 | 29 | 410 | 14.6 | 3.9 |
| Sequatchie | 12 | D | D | D | 13 | 749 | D | 19.2 | 23 | 244 | 9.4 | 2.5 |
| Sevier | 162 | 703 | 65.8 | 24.1 | 82 | 1 448 | 341.5 | 50.4 | 517 | 10 254 | 611.9 | 169.6 |
| Shelby | 1 913 | 16 716 | 2 230.2 | 920.2 | 704 | 31 108 | 17 969.7 | 1 490.7 | 1 724 | 39 318 | 1 788.0 | 501.5 |
| Smith | 16 | 47 | 5.2 | 1.5 | 27 | 1 387 | D | 49.2 | 20 | 347 | 12.4 | 3.2 |
| Stewart | 7 | D | D | D | NA | NA | NA | NA | 19 | 164 | 6.1 | 1.6 |
| Sullivan | 252 | 1 726 | 214.8 | 68.6 | 157 | 15 632 | 5 463.6 | 742.7 | 312 | 6 590 | 255.1 | 70.1 |
| Sumner | 219 | D | D | D | 213 | 7 023 | 1 741.4 | 273.0 | 217 | 4 053 | 155.5 | 45.0 |
| Tipton | 39 | D | D | D | 36 | 2 080 | 774.2 | 81.5 | 61 | 846 | 29.8 | 7.5 |
| Trousdale | 8 | 44 | 2.7 | 1.1 | NA | NA | NA | NA | 10 | 114 | 4.6 | 1.3 |
| Unicoi | 13 | D | D | D | 25 | 2 100 | 348.6 | D | 27 | 361 | 13.0 | 3.3 |
| Union | 9 | D | D | D | 23 | 615 | 125.6 | 20.5 | 12 | 198 | 5.7 | 1.2 |
| Van Buren | 2 | D | D | D | NA | NA | NA | NA | 1 | D | D | D |
| Warren | 38 | 121 | 12.7 | 3.1 | 67 | 3 140 | 852.3 | 144.5 | 52 | 803 | 28.8 | 7.8 |
| Washington | 231 | D | D | D | 145 | 6 166 | 1 577.7 | 214.1 | 254 | 6 361 | 247.1 | 74.9 |
| Wayne | 8 | D | D | D | 27 | 736 | 109.9 | 20.5 | 20 | 193 | 8.5 | 2.1 |
| Weakley | 25 | D | D | D | 36 | 1 680 | D | D | 58 | D | D | D |
| White | 22 | 64 | 4.9 | 1.5 | 45 | 2 118 | 552.2 | 66.4 | 28 | 398 | 16.8 | 5.2 |
| Williamson | 782 | D | D | D | 126 | 3 524 | 1 106.8 | 129.5 | 366 | 8 329 | 383.5 | 109.9 |
| Wilson | 185 | D | D | D | 111 | 6 274 | D | 273.8 | 179 | 3 640 | 147.3 | 43.5 |
| TEXAS | 57 373 | 534 386 | 90 668.7 | 35 376.4 | 21 115 | 893 842 | 593 541.5 | 42 835.7 | 43 509 | 866 189 | 42 054.6 | 11 502.3 |
| Anderson | 79 | 258 | 25.1 | 7.2 | NA | NA | NA | NA | 69 | 1 046 | 48.6 | 11.9 |
| Andrews | 19 | 62 | 9.1 | 2.5 | NA | NA | NA | NA | 23 | 340 | 14.9 | 3.3 |
| Angelina | 155 | 688 | 81.9 | 28.9 | 75 | 6 343 | 1 291.4 | 217.7 | 133 | 2 748 | 112.6 | 31.5 |
| Aransas | 39 | D | D | D | NA | NA | NA | NA | 84 | 1 089 | 48.8 | 13.4 |
| Archer | 6 | D | D | D | NA | NA | NA | NA | 7 | 38 | 1.4 | 0.4 |
| Armstrong | 1 | D | D | D | NA | NA | NA | NA | 6 | 16 | 0.6 | 0.2 |
| Atascosa | 34 | 264 | 25.9 | 5.5 | NA | NA | NA | NA | 66 | 904 | 32.2 | 8.5 |
| Austin | 57 | D | D | D | 39 | 2 222 | D | D | 46 | 568 | 25.0 | 6.2 |
| Bailey | 12 | 45 | 4.5 | 1.4 | NA | NA | NA | NA | 10 | 185 | 7.0 | 1.9 |
| Bandera | 32 | D | D | D | NA | NA | NA | NA | 55 | 499 | 23.2 | 5.8 |
| Bastrop | 84 | 340 | 33.8 | 11.9 | 64 | 1 068 | 238.6 | 37.7 | 97 | 2 015 | 115.1 | 33.1 |
| Baylor | 6 | 26 | 1.2 | 0.5 | NA | NA | NA | NA | 7 | 95 | 3.2 | 0.9 |
| Bee | 40 | D | D | D | NA | NA | NA | NA | 52 | 711 | 25.5 | 7.0 |
| Bell | 342 | D | D | D | 136 | 7 028 | 1 925.0 | 246.6 | 500 | 9 329 | 401.4 | 104.9 |
| Bexar | 3 625 | D | D | D | 986 | 35 502 | 12 305.1 | 1 366.0 | 3 207 | 75 006 | 3 829.0 | 1 073.1 |
| Blanco | 27 | 103 | 9.3 | 3.6 | NA | NA | NA | NA | 32 | 225 | 9.4 | 2.9 |
| Borden | 1 | D | D | D | NA | NA | NA | NA | NA | NA | NA | NA |
| Bosque | 22 | 84 | 7.7 | 2.5 | NA | NA | NA | NA | 20 | 104 | 5.3 | 1.2 |
| Bowie | 169 | D | D | D | 65 | 2 579 | 1 729.2 | 103.9 | 166 | 3 668 | 166.5 | 49.4 |
| Brazoria | 411 | D | D | D | 225 | 13 787 | 31 048.1 | 1 020.4 | 383 | 7 330 | 313.5 | 85.2 |
| Brazos | 388 | D | D | D | 111 | 4 881 | 979.4 | 167.5 | 368 | 8 497 | 340.3 | 91.4 |
| Brewster | 22 | 59 | 5.8 | 1.3 | NA | NA | NA | NA | 48 | 630 | 25.4 | 7.1 |
| Briscoe | NA | NA | NA | NA | NA | NA | NA | NA | 4 | 17 | 0.3 | 0.1 |
| Brooks | 12 | 23 | 2.0 | 0.5 | NA | NA | NA | NA | 28 | 326 | 14.2 | 4.1 |
| Brown | 54 | 184 | 16.8 | 4.9 | 41 | 3 100 | 1 249.4 | 125.4 | 87 | 1 374 | 49.9 | 13.7 |
| Burleson | 19 | D | D | D | NA | NA | NA | NA | 36 | 338 | 12.8 | 3.2 |
| Burnet | 82 | 335 | 31.5 | 12.5 | 57 | 924 | D | 49.7 | 102 | 1 386 | 74.4 | 21.6 |

1. Establishment subject to federal tax.

| STATE County | Health care and social assistance, 2007 | | | | Other services, 2007 | | | | Federal funds and grants, 2009–2010 Expenditures (mil dol) | | | |
|---|---|---|---|---|---|---|---|---|---|---|---|---|
| | | | | | | | | | | Direct payments for individuals[1] | | |
| | Number of establishments | Number of employees | Receipts (mil dol) | Annual payroll (mil dol) | Number of establishments | Number of employees | Receipts (mil dol) | Annual payroll (mil dol) | Total | Social Security and government retirement | Medicare | Food Stamps and Supplemental Security Income |
| | 159 | 160 | 161 | 162 | 163 | 164 | 165 | 166 | 167 | 168 | 169 | 170 |
| **TENNESSEE—Cont'd** | | | | | | | | | | | | |
| Marshall | 61 | 725 | 48.0 | 17.6 | 29 | D | D | D | 216.8 | 88.7 | 65.9 | 9.5 |
| Maury | 205 | 5 346 | 450.4 | 191.8 | 105 | 631 | 55.6 | 15.6 | 593.2 | 268.3 | 152.2 | 31.0 |
| Meigs | 7 | D | D | D | 5 | 8 | 0.7 | 0.2 | 110.4 | 48.7 | 24.3 | 7.1 |
| Monroe | 61 | 1 200 | 82.6 | 31.9 | 39 | 147 | 10.0 | 2.9 | 382.0 | 165.6 | 91.2 | 22.4 |
| Montgomery | 270 | D | D | D | 189 | 1 066 | 72.9 | 20.9 | 1 075.2 | 555.2 | 152.8 | 51.3 |
| Moore | 11 | D | D | D | 4 | D | D | D | 29.7 | 15.1 | 9.0 | 1.3 |
| Morgan | 17 | 399 | 21.9 | 9.4 | 10 | 21 | 4.3 | 1.0 | 224.2 | 66.1 | 47.8 | 12.9 |
| Obion | 89 | D | D | D | 47 | D | D | D | 319.1 | 127.5 | 93.3 | 15.8 |
| Overton | 34 | D | D | D | 15 | D | D | D | 224.7 | 70.9 | 77.8 | 10.6 |
| Perry | 17 | 367 | 20.0 | 8.1 | 6 | 46 | 1.0 | 0.3 | 84.6 | 29.9 | 30.6 | 3.5 |
| Pickett | 5 | D | D | D | 5 | D | D | D | 59.7 | 17.0 | 21.5 | 2.5 |
| Polk | 20 | 395 | 28.7 | 11.6 | 9 | D | D | D | 174.7 | 69.7 | 54.3 | 8.5 |
| Putnam | 214 | 4 527 | 428.2 | 151.4 | 117 | 591 | 47.0 | 13.3 | 690.5 | 277.4 | 157.2 | 26.5 |
| Rhea | 65 | 831 | 49.5 | 22.4 | 24 | 90 | 6.5 | 1.8 | 298.4 | 127.5 | 81.0 | 19.3 |
| Roane | 88 | 1 812 | 118.1 | 51.2 | 43 | 172 | 14.9 | 4.0 | 608.3 | 244.2 | 154.5 | 27.9 |
| Robertson | 107 | 1 606 | 145.3 | 52.0 | 79 | 297 | 24.3 | 6.1 | 398.7 | 188.4 | 101.3 | 18.3 |
| Rutherford | 447 | 9 041 | 1 019.4 | 424.6 | 285 | 2 300 | 227.1 | 69.6 | 1 642.8 | 563.8 | 199.2 | 44.4 |
| Scott | 42 | 719 | 52.3 | 22.0 | 21 | 107 | 8.3 | 2.5 | 286.3 | 71.0 | 84.3 | 22.3 |
| Sequatchie | 22 | D | D | D | 12 | D | D | D | 116.5 | 40.1 | 25.7 | 7.4 |
| Sevier | 134 | 1 672 | 136.2 | 46.3 | 152 | 884 | 72.3 | 19.5 | 620.2 | 309.3 | 109.9 | 26.6 |
| Shelby | 2 166 | 62 091 | 6 542.5 | 2 623.9 | 1 349 | 12 280 | 1 807.9 | 356.1 | 10 393.2 | 2 345.3 | 1 990.9 | 697.4 |
| Smith | 33 | 632 | 55.0 | 21.1 | 22 | 69 | 5.0 | 1.6 | 207.4 | 54.8 | 58.7 | 6.4 |
| Stewart | 15 | D | D | D | 8 | 22 | 2.0 | 0.5 | 145.4 | 66.3 | 30.7 | 5.7 |
| Sullivan | 446 | 12 705 | 1 354.3 | 507.3 | 253 | D | D | D | 1 642.8 | 669.5 | 374.0 | 77.7 |
| Sumner | 313 | 5 031 | 518.5 | 196.1 | 202 | 1 110 | 96.1 | 22.8 | 971.9 | 446.2 | 220.2 | 40.3 |
| Tipton | 85 | 1 224 | 96.6 | 35.4 | 45 | 198 | 14.0 | 3.8 | 437.8 | 184.3 | 105.0 | 25.5 |
| Trousdale | 21 | 254 | 19.7 | 6.7 | 7 | D | D | D | 63.6 | 21.5 | 23.7 | 3.5 |
| Unicoi | 27 | 681 | 41.5 | 17.4 | 21 | D | D | D | 224.2 | 84.9 | 56.2 | 9.8 |
| Union | 12 | D | D | D | 17 | D | D | D | 126.3 | 51.6 | 32.7 | 9.3 |
| Van Buren | 4 | D | D | D | 2 | D | D | D | 49.7 | 14.5 | 14.3 | 2.6 |
| Warren | 92 | 1 571 | 137.2 | 44.4 | 52 | 194 | 14.0 | 4.5 | 367.8 | 138.0 | 126.6 | 18.9 |
| Washington | 319 | 10 712 | 1 168.4 | 459.6 | 195 | 1 042 | 73.8 | 22.8 | 1 173.2 | 488.0 | 245.0 | 50.1 |
| Wayne | 29 | 236 | 12.8 | 5.1 | 10 | 28 | 4.6 | 0.7 | 150.4 | 49.9 | 46.2 | 9.7 |
| Weakley | 74 | 1 527 | 111.8 | 46.0 | 38 | D | D | D | 307.0 | 100.2 | 87.1 | 13.0 |
| White | 39 | 740 | 61.0 | 22.1 | 24 | 71 | 6.9 | 1.9 | 228.0 | 95.1 | 69.2 | 11.6 |
| Williamson | 616 | 10 109 | 1 089.7 | 493.9 | 312 | 2 111 | 177.7 | 52.9 | 734.6 | 398.3 | 128.3 | 16.6 |
| Wilson | 230 | 3 596 | 306.6 | 114.5 | 131 | 616 | 48.4 | 13.2 | 645.7 | 301.8 | 160.9 | 24.2 |
| **TEXAS** | 54 991 | 1 166 613 | 113 830.2 | 43 118.2 | 34 462 | 253 503 | 25 778.5 | 6 993.6 | 225 724.9 | 56 814.1 | 27 711.9 | 9 056.0 |
| Anderson | 135 | 2 083 | 188.4 | 67.2 | 53 | 319 | 17.2 | 7.4 | 433.7 | 169.4 | 107.5 | 19.5 |
| Andrews | 20 | 433 | 35.3 | 14.6 | 22 | 277 | 40.5 | 10.7 | 77.5 | 31.6 | 21.1 | 5.7 |
| Angelina | 270 | 7 552 | 517.1 | 207.1 | 129 | 732 | 120.8 | 17.8 | 693.4 | 276.8 | 159.8 | 36.6 |
| Aransas | 42 | 522 | 42.3 | 12.7 | 49 | 153 | 11.9 | 3.1 | 174.9 | 102.2 | 38.6 | 11.0 |
| Archer | 12 | D | D | D | 10 | 22 | 1.4 | 0.4 | 88.9 | 23.7 | 11.3 | 22.0 |
| Armstrong | 4 | D | D | D | 2 | D | D | D | 18.1 | 8.5 | 4.3 | 0.1 |
| Atascosa | 85 | 1 000 | 93.5 | 32.8 | 44 | 222 | 18.3 | 4.9 | 283.3 | 117.8 | 51.6 | 22.8 |
| Austin | 32 | 590 | 31.3 | 14.6 | 33 | 110 | 9.8 | 2.4 | 830.6 | 86.8 | 47.6 | 6.2 |
| Bailey | 16 | 199 | 13.5 | 5.0 | 19 | 62 | 3.8 | 0.9 | 63.0 | 16.5 | 14.6 | 3.0 |
| Bandera | 20 | 247 | 17.7 | 5.9 | 30 | 92 | 8.1 | 1.8 | 139.8 | 91.4 | 19.8 | 4.1 |
| Bastrop | 89 | 1 648 | 97.1 | 43.5 | 81 | 332 | 30.4 | 7.6 | 419.4 | 205.3 | 66.6 | 17.9 |
| Baylor | 14 | 535 | 13.2 | 6.7 | 17 | 39 | 4.3 | 0.6 | 50.0 | 17.8 | 14.2 | 1.2 |
| Bee | 49 | 868 | 63.7 | 28.0 | 41 | 178 | 13.6 | 3.2 | 241.5 | 70.4 | 56.0 | 16.4 |
| Bell | 476 | 18 504 | 1 979.2 | 802.1 | 401 | 2 418 | 173.8 | 50.9 | 11 820.3 | 1 045.2 | 220.7 | 89.4 |
| Bexar | 4 094 | 99 461 | 9 820.8 | 3 564.2 | 2 505 | 18 260 | 1 516.2 | 428.4 | 20 014.5 | 5 248.5 | 2 064.1 | 758.3 |
| Blanco | 18 | 128 | 6.6 | 2.9 | 19 | 58 | 5.1 | 1.1 | 94.5 | 50.6 | 27.0 | 1.1 |
| Borden | NA | NA | NA | NA | NA | NA | NA | NA | 7.5 | 1.3 | 0.8 | 0.0 |
| Bosque | 19 | 588 | 43.2 | 18.1 | 26 | 97 | 9.6 | 1.7 | 163.1 | 71.0 | 37.8 | 4.6 |
| Bowie | 304 | 6 810 | 654.9 | 261.4 | 153 | 940 | 72.8 | 20.8 | 1 123.7 | 370.9 | 186.6 | 46.5 |
| Brazoria | 501 | 7 074 | 500.6 | 206.8 | 341 | 2 203 | 207.4 | 65.3 | 1 269.0 | 673.7 | 261.9 | 70.4 |
| Brazos | 389 | 7 161 | 872.8 | 287.0 | 260 | 1 859 | 359.3 | 42.4 | 1 175.4 | 313.8 | 104.6 | 43.0 |
| Brewster | 20 | 434 | 33.5 | 14.0 | 20 | 83 | 5.4 | 1.4 | 104.5 | 27.2 | 11.8 | 2.8 |
| Briscoe | 1 | D | D | D | 2 | D | D | D | 26.0 | 6.1 | 6.5 | 0.5 |
| Brooks | 18 | 707 | 15.2 | 8.1 | 12 | D | D | D | 125.3 | 20.1 | 19.9 | 10.3 |
| Brown | 124 | 3 034 | 194.7 | 73.1 | 72 | 417 | 25.9 | 7.4 | 337.5 | 137.2 | 94.8 | 17.3 |
| Burleson | 18 | 258 | 21.6 | 9.0 | 24 | 100 | 8.3 | 1.8 | 154.9 | 57.6 | 29.7 | 7.0 |
| Burnet | 113 | 1 250 | 102.6 | 37.7 | 72 | 286 | 21.1 | 6.0 | 294.8 | 185.5 | 48.1 | 9.4 |

1. State totals may include programs not allocated by county.

# Table B. States and Counties — Federal Funds, Residential Construction, and Local Government Finances

| STATE County | Federal funds and grants, 2009–2010 (cont.) | | | | | | | Value of residential construction authorized by building permits, 2011 | | Local government finances, 2007 | | | | |
| | Expenditures (mil dol) (cont.) | | | | | | | | | General revenue | | | | |
| | Procurement contract awards | | | Grants[1] | | | | | | | | Taxes | | |
| | | | | | | | | | | | | | Per capita[2] (dollars) | |
| | Salaries and wages | Defense | Other | Medicaid and other health-related | Nutrition and family welfare | Education | Other | New construction ($1,000) | Number of housing units | Total (mil dol) | Inter-governmental (mil dol) | Total (mil dol) | Total | Property |
| | 171 | 172 | 173 | 174 | 175 | 176 | 177 | 178 | 179 | 180 | 181 | 182 | 183 | 184 |
| **TENNESSEE—Cont'd** | | | | | | | | | | | | | | |
| Marshall | 11.5 | 1.8 | 1.2 | 29.5 | 3.4 | 2.9 | 0.4 | 7 666 | 48 | 62.8 | 24.8 | 24.6 | 844 | 525 |
| Maury | 23.2 | 0.5 | 17.0 | 69.8 | 9.0 | 5.5 | 1.1 | 62 512 | 402 | 375.7 | 67.0 | 68.2 | 853 | 533 |
| Meigs | 12.9 | 0.0 | 0.4 | 13.5 | 1.8 | 0.9 | 0.1 | 4 943 | 28 | 22.4 | 14.9 | 4.9 | 419 | 312 |
| Monroe | 13.5 | 10.6 | 2.9 | 59.5 | 6.0 | 3.6 | 3.9 | 3 126 | 53 | 82.7 | 44.1 | 26.0 | 579 | 297 |
| Montgomery | 104.7 | 20.4 | 7.3 | 74.7 | 20.9 | 11.8 | 9.7 | 192 175 | 1 850 | 387.2 | 154.6 | 148.2 | 959 | 614 |
| Moore | 0.6 | 0.0 | 0.1 | 2.2 | 0.7 | 0.4 | 0.0 | 2 861 | 16 | 13.5 | 7.3 | 4.0 | 659 | 537 |
| Morgan | 2.9 | 0.3 | 0.8 | 30.3 | 5.3 | 1.4 | 52.8 | 203 | 2 | 37.0 | 23.2 | 9.0 | 440 | 348 |
| Obion | 14.5 | 0.0 | 2.3 | 46.3 | 5.2 | 3.2 | 0.6 | 1 529 | 15 | 72.2 | 33.4 | 26.2 | 828 | 386 |
| Overton | 7.7 | 0.0 | 0.9 | 48.2 | 3.2 | 1.8 | 1.6 | 264 | 3 | 39.0 | 23.7 | 10.8 | 514 | 281 |
| Perry | 1.6 | 0.0 | 0.3 | 15.3 | 1.2 | 0.7 | 0.4 | 0 | 0 | 20.8 | 11.4 | 6.0 | 781 | 590 |
| Pickett | 1.0 | 0.0 | 0.2 | 15.1 | 1.0 | 0.4 | 0.2 | NA | NA | 12.0 | 7.1 | 3.0 | 637 | 316 |
| Polk | 4.6 | 0.0 | 4.9 | 28.1 | 2.4 | 1.4 | 0.2 | 18 062 | 102 | 30.8 | 18.8 | 8.4 | 535 | 353 |
| Putnam | 33.7 | 2.3 | 60.5 | 74.7 | 17.0 | 5.3 | 14.1 | 38 196 | 299 | 321.0 | 56.7 | 70.2 | 1 004 | 502 |
| Rhea | 7.9 | 0.0 | 4.4 | 43.9 | 4.4 | 2.7 | 3.2 | 4 056 | 44 | 83.5 | 33.2 | 19.1 | 629 | 339 |
| Roane | 18.0 | 0.0 | 45.2 | 75.1 | 9.5 | 4.5 | 2.0 | 1 348 | 12 | 137.2 | 45.1 | 42.7 | 799 | 479 |
| Robertson | 13.9 | 0.4 | 7.2 | 43.9 | 6.8 | 3.6 | 0.7 | 19 425 | 142 | 142.1 | 55.2 | 60.7 | 959 | 531 |
| Rutherford | 192.5 | 6.5 | 443.1 | 82.7 | 18.5 | 14.9 | 15.8 | 158 430 | 866 | 635.2 | 190.0 | 319.2 | 1 322 | 582 |
| Scott | 9.3 | 1.0 | 27.6 | 61.1 | 5.2 | 2.2 | 0.8 | 366 | 6 | 42.0 | 26.0 | 8.2 | 372 | 203 |
| Sequatchie | 3.8 | 0.0 | 19.9 | 12.9 | 2.0 | 1.7 | 2.4 | 1 185 | 15 | 26.4 | 13.0 | 10.5 | 787 | 350 |
| Sevier | 27.2 | 0.3 | 77.6 | 49.4 | 9.0 | 4.4 | 3.3 | 13 255 | 198 | 307.7 | 65.3 | 178.1 | 2 133 | 558 |
| Shelby | 909.3 | 1 627.9 | 593.9 | 1 431.4 | 243.5 | 81.7 | 265.2 | 227 880 | 1 400 | 3 929.4 | 1 243.7 | 1 718.7 | 1 888 | 1 323 |
| Smith | 9.2 | 42.4 | 0.9 | 23.6 | 2.5 | 1.0 | 0.1 | 4 527 | 25 | 39.0 | 19.8 | 13.0 | 691 | 378 |
| Stewart | 4.7 | 0.1 | 14.6 | 17.8 | 1.8 | 1.3 | 0.1 | 260 | 1 | 28.6 | 17.4 | 7.8 | 593 | 395 |
| Sullivan | 50.8 | 205.4 | 10.3 | 173.1 | 28.4 | 12.2 | 17.2 | 31 176 | 194 | 378.1 | 124.5 | 176.4 | 1 149 | 738 |
| Sumner | 30.7 | 3.3 | 98.2 | 79.2 | 13.2 | 6.7 | 2.2 | 72 508 | 422 | 360.7 | 138.1 | 134.3 | 879 | 642 |
| Tipton | 15.3 | 7.0 | 2.1 | 67.9 | 8.6 | 3.1 | 2.7 | 8 860 | 61 | 138.8 | 76.0 | 41.3 | 716 | 464 |
| Trousdale | 0.9 | 0.0 | 0.3 | 9.4 | 1.1 | 0.4 | 0.2 | 2 320 | 24 | 16.1 | 9.8 | 3.9 | 502 | 310 |
| Unicoi | 7.8 | 1.1 | 27.9 | 29.8 | 2.8 | 1.5 | 1.6 | 373 | 2 | 61.1 | 19.6 | 8.3 | 472 | 347 |
| Union | 2.1 | 0.3 | 0.5 | 24.0 | 3.0 | 1.4 | 0.4 | 5 200 | 45 | 35.1 | 23.4 | 6.1 | 325 | 202 |
| Van Buren | 0.5 | 0.0 | 8.4 | 7.7 | 0.9 | 0.5 | 0.4 | NA | NA | 15.1 | 10.4 | 2.8 | 523 | 333 |
| Warren | 16.1 | 0.8 | 2.7 | 49.7 | 5.4 | 3.5 | 1.3 | 5 633 | 42 | 88.3 | 38.6 | 31.8 | 802 | 420 |
| Washington | 116.8 | 10.9 | 65.6 | 119.3 | 13.7 | 12.4 | 13.8 | 47 582 | 317 | 286.5 | 93.0 | 132.8 | 1 138 | 551 |
| Wayne | 7.5 | 0.0 | 0.6 | 30.7 | 2.7 | 1.2 | 0.4 | 50 | 1 | 44.2 | 24.3 | 8.3 | 498 | 279 |
| Weakley | 27.4 | 0.1 | 2.0 | 35.4 | 15.6 | 2.3 | 1.9 | 4 945 | 35 | 69.3 | 33.9 | 18.6 | 559 | 310 |
| White | 4.8 | 0.0 | 1.0 | 38.7 | 3.5 | 2.0 | 0.6 | 390 | 5 | 44.4 | 25.7 | 11.3 | 456 | 283 |
| Williamson | 35.5 | 28.1 | 37.7 | 42.7 | 9.6 | 5.3 | 1.5 | 281 982 | 1 061 | 605.4 | 133.8 | 279.1 | 1 680 | 837 |
| Wilson | 55.8 | 1.5 | 11.0 | 54.2 | 15.3 | 4.9 | 2.1 | 122 360 | 677 | 235.8 | 78.6 | 109.6 | 1 030 | 512 |
| **TEXAS** | 29 926.4 | 30 331.5 | 10 263.0 | 23 603.8 | 5 505.0 | 3 710.8 | 11 804.5 | 14 736 206 | 97 450 | X | X | X | X | X |
| Anderson | 18.7 | 0.0 | 2.4 | 102.5 | 5.8 | 1.5 | 3.7 | 2 322 | 13 | 112.0 | 41.0 | 54.0 | 951 | 766 |
| Andrews | 1.4 | -0.2 | 2.9 | 9.4 | 2.3 | 0.3 | 0.0 | 8 562 | 60 | 102.4 | 7.9 | 65.3 | 4 972 | 4 694 |
| Angelina | 39.2 | 10.9 | 9.3 | 124.6 | 12.2 | 3.5 | 0.9 | 25 912 | 408 | 279.1 | 113.9 | 86.3 | 1 042 | 772 |
| Aransas | 2.2 | 0.1 | 0.7 | 13.8 | 3.8 | 0.8 | 0.3 | 8 183 | 70 | 66.2 | 11.3 | 43.8 | 1 771 | 1 534 |
| Archer | 20.8 | 0.0 | 0.3 | 7.4 | 0.8 | 0.2 | 0.0 | 495 | 9 | 25.1 | 10.5 | 10.9 | 1 216 | 1 043 |
| Armstrong | 0.3 | 0.0 | 0.1 | 2.0 | 0.2 | 0.1 | 0.0 | 0 | 0 | 5.8 | 2.8 | 2.0 | 981 | 864 |
| Atascosa | 4.2 | 0.0 | 1.0 | 65.7 | 8.1 | 4.1 | 2.9 | 8 601 | 68 | 120.4 | 64.8 | 35.6 | 816 | 677 |
| Austin | 8.5 | 640.6 | 1.7 | 33.3 | 2.5 | 0.4 | 0.3 | 2 276 | 17 | 86.6 | 23.5 | 44.0 | 1 654 | 1 475 |
| Bailey | 1.7 | 0.0 | 0.3 | 9.6 | 1.7 | 0.2 | 2.5 | 320 | 4 | 28.9 | 10.7 | 7.4 | 1 170 | 1 033 |
| Bandera | 12.1 | 0.0 | 0.6 | 8.3 | 1.6 | 0.5 | 0.3 | 90 | 1 | 42.3 | 11.6 | 24.7 | 1 222 | 1 092 |
| Bastrop | 32.5 | 2.0 | 8.0 | 71.1 | 9.0 | 1.8 | 1.7 | 8 011 | 80 | 206.2 | 64.3 | 90.4 | 1 251 | 1 113 |
| Baylor | 1.4 | 0.0 | 0.2 | 9.9 | 1.0 | 0.1 | 0.3 | 0 | 0 | 18.3 | 5.3 | 4.1 | 1 078 | 927 |
| Bee | 3.7 | 1.7 | 0.7 | 58.4 | 10.8 | 3.3 | 4.0 | 1 039 | 9 | 103.8 | 57.0 | 24.9 | 760 | 618 |
| Bell | 8 698.5 | 1 281.2 | 91.4 | 153.7 | 32.7 | 67.0 | 36.0 | 277 814 | 2 025 | 1 034.5 | 481.0 | 303.9 | 1 097 | 838 |
| Bexar | 4 388.8 | 3 693.9 | 582.7 | 2 025.9 | 319.3 | 117.0 | 331.7 | 609 080 | 4 961 | 6 200.6 | 2 179.4 | 2 329.0 | 1 461 | 1 212 |
| Blanco | 8.1 | 0.0 | 1.1 | 5.1 | 0.6 | 0.2 | 0.2 | 325 | 2 | 26.5 | 6.4 | 17.4 | 1 924 | 1 748 |
| Borden | 0.2 | 0.0 | 0.0 | 0.0 | 0.2 | 1.8 | 0.0 | NA | NA | 11.3 | 0.8 | 9.6 | 16 426 | 16 357 |
| Bosque | 4.8 | 18.3 | 1.2 | 21.7 | 2.0 | 0.5 | 0.1 | 335 | 3 | 47.6 | 19.2 | 20.2 | 1 126 | 997 |
| Bowie | 161.6 | 131.5 | 9.8 | 157.1 | 15.7 | 3.8 | 16.5 | 18 858 | 316 | 287.0 | 133.2 | 99.2 | 1 084 | 844 |
| Brazoria | 53.5 | 11.4 | 22.3 | 115.2 | 22.2 | 5.8 | 8.5 | 291 977 | 1 941 | 973.1 | 219.1 | 530.2 | 1 802 | 1 569 |
| Brazos | 123.3 | 47.9 | 30.8 | 190.7 | 23.2 | 10.5 | 229.2 | 147 672 | 1 426 | 454.6 | 109.1 | 248.8 | 1 455 | 1 132 |
| Brewster | 17.3 | 0.7 | 16.1 | 11.6 | 1.6 | 4.4 | 2.1 | 2 841 | 17 | 28.9 | 11.8 | 11.3 | 1 222 | 978 |
| Briscoe | 0.6 | 0.0 | 0.1 | 6.6 | 0.1 | 0.1 | 0.0 | NA | NA | 4.4 | 1.6 | 2.2 | 1 510 | 1 371 |
| Brooks | 17.6 | 0.1 | 1.3 | 49.5 | 2.9 | 0.6 | 1.3 | 0 | 0 | 38.8 | 10.7 | 21.0 | 2 767 | 2 565 |
| Brown | 10.8 | 1.0 | 2.0 | 58.3 | 6.4 | 1.3 | 2.6 | 3 995 | 28 | 117.2 | 48.2 | 45.7 | 1 185 | 903 |
| Burleson | 3.4 | 10.9 | 0.8 | 37.4 | 2.7 | 0.5 | 0.6 | 1 030 | 11 | 43.5 | 15.0 | 22.2 | 1 336 | 1 183 |
| Burnet | 7.4 | 0.5 | 2.8 | 26.8 | 1.9 | 0.9 | 3.1 | 31 733 | 136 | 118.5 | 20.6 | 78.0 | 1 785 | 1 545 |

1. State totals may include programs not allocated by county.    2. Based on the resident population estimated as of July 1 of the year shown.

# Table B. States and Counties — Local Government Finances, Government Employment, and Voting

| STATE County | Local government finances, 2007 (cont.) | | | | | | | | | Government employment, 2011 | | | Presidential election,[2] 2012 | | |
|---|---|---|---|---|---|---|---|---|---|---|---|---|---|---|---|
| | Direct general expenditure | | | | | | | Debt outstanding | | | | | Percent of vote cast: | | |
| | | | Percent of total for: | | | | | | | | | | | | |
| | Total (mil dol) | Per capita[1] (dollars) | Educa-tion | Health and hospitals | Police protec-tion | Public welfare | High-ways | Total (mil dol) | Per capita[1] (dollars) | Federal civilian | Federal military | State and local | Demo-cratic | Republi-can | All other |
| | 185 | 186 | 187 | 188 | 189 | 190 | 191 | 192 | 193 | 194 | 195 | 196 | 197 | 198 | 199 |
| **TENNESSEE—Cont'd** | | | | | | | | | | | | | | | |
| Marshall | 56.1 | 1 923 | 63.4 | 4.6 | 6.0 | 0.2 | 6.5 | 60.0 | 2 056 | 62 | 103 | 1 543 | 38.3 | 59.8 | 1.9 |
| Maury | 378.8 | 4 736 | 22.7 | 51.9 | 4.1 | 0.0 | 2.7 | 277.9 | 3 475 | 173 | 273 | 6 442 | 38.7 | 60.1 | 1.2 |
| Meigs | 20.7 | 1 774 | 63.5 | 2.1 | 3.5 | 0.0 | 9.8 | 7.4 | 636 | 28 | 39 | 438 | 32.4 | 66.0 | 1.6 |
| Monroe | 84.7 | 1 888 | 56.7 | 4.0 | 5.6 | 0.1 | 4.9 | 59.9 | 1 336 | 87 | 150 | 1 716 | 30.1 | 68.5 | 1.4 |
| Montgomery | 381.6 | 2 471 | 50.9 | 1.9 | 6.6 | 0.1 | 4.3 | 7 887.6 | 51 066 | 1 094 | 578 | 8 554 | 45.5 | 53.4 | 1.1 |
| Moore | 13.8 | 2 257 | 54.3 | 2.1 | 5.0 | 0.0 | 9.0 | 0.8 | 136 | 0 | 21 | 798 | 29.8 | 68.1 | 2.1 |
| Morgan | 39.5 | 1 939 | 64.0 | 2.9 | 2.8 | 0.2 | 7.8 | 21.6 | 1 061 | 39 | 73 | 1 336 | 28.9 | 69.1 | 2.0 |
| Obion | 71.7 | 2 266 | 58.5 | 0.2 | 6.1 | 2.8 | 5.8 | 33.4 | 1 055 | 113 | 106 | 1 645 | 32.2 | 66.3 | 1.6 |
| Overton | 38.1 | 1 814 | 60.8 | 3.0 | 2.6 | 0.2 | 6.8 | 27.5 | 1 311 | 44 | 74 | 1 325 | 42.3 | 55.6 | 2.2 |
| Perry | 18.8 | 2 457 | 45.8 | 3.8 | 7.6 | 0.0 | 13.0 | 10.3 | 1 341 | 17 | 26 | 389 | 44.3 | 53.2 | 2.5 |
| Pickett | 12.1 | 2 533 | 47.3 | 4.8 | 3.8 | 0.0 | 10.2 | 12.1 | 2 541 | 0 | 17 | 284 | 32.0 | 66.9 | 1.2 |
| Polk | 34.0 | 2 168 | 56.9 | 2.9 | 3.5 | 0.3 | 6.9 | 23.1 | 1 475 | 80 | 56 | 766 | 32.7 | 65.6 | 1.7 |
| Putnam | 302.0 | 4 320 | 24.9 | 54.1 | 3.8 | 0.0 | 1.6 | 257.6 | 3 684 | 251 | 248 | 7 911 | 35.7 | 62.6 | 1.7 |
| Rhea | 75.0 | 2 475 | 46.5 | 23.0 | 3.9 | 0.0 | 4.2 | 30.4 | 1 004 | 1 235 | 107 | 1 578 | 26.2 | 72.4 | 1.4 |
| Roane | 141.4 | 2 648 | 39.8 | 26.7 | 3.6 | 0.1 | 4.2 | 102.1 | 1 912 | 468 | 180 | 3 260 | 31.0 | 67.3 | 1.7 |
| Robertson | 130.7 | 2 064 | 52.4 | 2.7 | 8.5 | 0.0 | 3.9 | 230.8 | 3 644 | 92 | 224 | 3 482 | 33.7 | 64.8 | 1.4 |
| Rutherford | 622.8 | 2 579 | 50.7 | 2.2 | 8.8 | 1.4 | 7.7 | 887.7 | 3 676 | 2 636 | 904 | 14 524 | 39.8 | 58.9 | 1.4 |
| Scott | 45.6 | 2 073 | 66.4 | 0.8 | 4.7 | 1.8 | 6.2 | 62.6 | 2 849 | 89 | 74 | 1 357 | 25.4 | 72.7 | 1.9 |
| Sequatchie | 27.9 | 2 090 | 66.7 | 2.8 | 3.3 | 0.0 | 4.5 | 17.7 | 1 326 | 12 | 48 | 635 | 31.6 | 66.4 | 2.0 |
| Sevier | 321.2 | 3 846 | 34.9 | 1.2 | 5.3 | 0.2 | 5.1 | 507.7 | 6 078 | 349 | 305 | 4 322 | 25.3 | 73.4 | 1.2 |
| Shelby | 4 041.0 | 4 440 | 47.3 | 9.7 | 8.2 | 1.0 | 2.3 | 6 595.8 | 7 247 | 14 096 | 4 265 | 58 925 | 63.4 | 36.0 | 0.6 |
| Smith | 38.3 | 2 035 | 56.7 | 2.4 | 7.1 | 0.1 | 7.1 | 27.3 | 1 448 | 119 | 64 | 950 | 38.7 | 58.9 | 2.4 |
| Stewart | 30.7 | 2 347 | 53.4 | 3.7 | 5.4 | 0.2 | 6.7 | 44.4 | 3 394 | 518 | 44 | 600 | 44.9 | 53.7 | 1.5 |
| Sullivan | 358.0 | 2 332 | 51.8 | 1.7 | 7.0 | 0.0 | 5.1 | 328.2 | 2 138 | 532 | 526 | 7 208 | 28.7 | 70.0 | 1.3 |
| Sumner | 333.5 | 2 184 | 54.0 | 2.0 | 5.9 | 0.1 | 3.7 | 439.4 | 2 877 | 475 | 546 | 7 301 | 32.0 | 66.9 | 1.2 |
| Tipton | 122.0 | 2 114 | 70.1 | 0.5 | 3.9 | 0.2 | 4.7 | 72.5 | 1 257 | 99 | 204 | 2 563 | 31.3 | 67.8 | 0.9 |
| Trousdale | 16.3 | 2 107 | 56.6 | 0.4 | 7.3 | 0.3 | 10.3 | 10.4 | 1 346 | 42 | 26 | 447 | 45.5 | 52.1 | 2.3 |
| Unicoi | 63.6 | 3 591 | 30.2 | 43.1 | 3.2 | 0.3 | 5.1 | 25.0 | 1 411 | 76 | 61 | 1 060 | 29.2 | 69.4 | 1.5 |
| Union | 37.8 | 2 003 | 65.8 | 4.0 | 2.9 | 0.0 | 5.6 | 19.9 | 1 053 | 22 | 64 | 771 | 28.6 | 69.8 | 1.6 |
| Van Buren | 10.6 | 1 948 | 60.2 | 3.1 | 4.9 | 0.0 | 10.1 | 10.4 | 1 904 | 0 | 18 | 366 | 38.5 | 58.7 | 2.9 |
| Warren | 84.5 | 2 129 | 51.7 | 2.2 | 4.6 | 0.8 | 3.6 | 55.4 | 1 395 | 99 | 133 | 1 856 | 38.3 | 59.5 | 2.2 |
| Washington | 242.4 | 2 078 | 49.2 | 1.3 | 6.5 | 0.7 | 5.8 | 927.7 | 7 952 | 2 502 | 460 | 11 556 | 32.5 | 66.0 | 1.4 |
| Wayne | 46.2 | 2 774 | 50.9 | 0.7 | 2.9 | 14.5 | 8.2 | 38.0 | 2 282 | 24 | 57 | 1 412 | 24.5 | 73.7 | 1.7 |
| Weakley | 63.5 | 1 911 | 51.5 | 2.1 | 5.7 | 10.4 | 8.8 | 59.5 | 1 791 | 128 | 121 | 3 582 | 33.6 | 64.7 | 1.7 |
| White | 43.2 | 1 737 | 67.8 | 1.7 | 2.7 | 0.0 | 6.5 | 17.9 | 718 | 53 | 87 | 1 428 | 35.0 | 63.3 | 1.8 |
| Williamson | 636.4 | 3 831 | 46.4 | 20.7 | 4.2 | 0.2 | 4.7 | 772.2 | 4 648 | 381 | 629 | 9 158 | 29.8 | 69.3 | 1.0 |
| Wilson | 245.8 | 2 311 | 58.7 | 0.5 | 10.0 | 0.0 | 4.5 | 313.6 | 2 948 | 186 | 390 | 4 387 | 31.1 | 67.6 | 1.3 |
| **TEXAS** | X | X | X | X | X | X | X | X | X | 202 169 | 185 308 | 1 597 210 | 43.7 | 55.5 | 0.9 |
| Anderson | 108.4 | 1 910 | 62.1 | 0.2 | 4.2 | 0.1 | 4.2 | 54.6 | 961 | 133 | 129 | 5 654 | 27.8 | 71.4 | 0.8 |
| Andrews | 106.2 | 8 081 | 56.3 | 24.5 | 3.2 | 0.0 | 2.1 | 45.4 | 3 458 | 15 | 34 | 1 205 | 17.1 | 82.4 | 0.5 |
| Angelina | 260.0 | 3 140 | 60.2 | 10.2 | 4.7 | 0.3 | 3.1 | 196.3 | 2 370 | 365 | 195 | 6 793 | 32.2 | 67.1 | 0.7 |
| Aransas | 60.3 | 2 438 | 56.2 | 1.5 | 7.0 | 1.0 | 6.0 | 41.4 | 1 673 | 20 | 52 | 1 041 | 30.7 | 68.4 | 0.8 |
| Archer | 22.8 | 2 528 | 66.0 | 1.7 | 4.7 | 0.0 | 8.0 | 15.0 | 1 661 | 20 | 39 | 507 | 17.0 | 82.4 | 0.7 |
| Armstrong | 5.4 | 2 615 | 61.4 | 0.0 | 3.7 | 0.0 | 11.4 | 2.6 | 1 274 | 0 | 0 | 129 | 12.9 | 86.5 | 0.6 |
| Atascosa | 123.7 | 2 839 | 59.5 | 13.4 | 3.4 | 1.1 | 3.6 | 95.3 | 2 187 | 50 | 101 | 2 364 | 44.4 | 55.0 | 0.6 |
| Austin | 88.1 | 3 310 | 59.8 | 10.8 | 4.0 | 0.2 | 4.7 | 98.0 | 3 682 | 85 | 64 | 1 777 | 24.1 | 75.0 | 1.0 |
| Bailey | 26.2 | 4 125 | 49.5 | 28.0 | 5.2 | 0.0 | 4.2 | 48.5 | 7 625 | 27 | 16 | 605 | 29.4 | 69.9 | 0.7 |
| Bandera | 37.2 | 1 843 | 66.6 | 1.2 | 4.4 | 4.9 | 5.0 | 37.6 | 1 861 | 13 | 46 | 769 | 24.2 | 74.6 | 1.2 |
| Bastrop | 218.9 | 3 030 | 57.6 | 11.8 | 5.4 | 0.8 | 3.6 | 455.6 | 6 307 | 385 | 166 | 3 894 | 45.1 | 53.3 | 1.6 |
| Baylor | 17.7 | 4 611 | 31.7 | 40.5 | 4.1 | 0.3 | 3.7 | 2.7 | 711 | 18 | 0 | 255 | 22.3 | 76.8 | 0.9 |
| Bee | 102.0 | 3 119 | 70.4 | 1.0 | 3.0 | 1.0 | 3.1 | 53.5 | 1 637 | 38 | 71 | 3 571 | 44.7 | 54.8 | 0.5 |
| Bell | 996.8 | 3 599 | 60.1 | 2.3 | 3.9 | 0.4 | 2.4 | 1 580.9 | 5 708 | 11 537 | 48 613 | 19 692 | 44.7 | 54.5 | 0.8 |
| Bexar | 6 277.8 | 3 937 | 50.4 | 12.3 | 5.0 | 1.1 | 2.4 | 14 684.7 | 9 210 | 34 921 | 34 972 | 104 017 | 52.4 | 46.8 | 0.7 |
| Blanco | 21.5 | 2 374 | 68.9 | 0.0 | 4.2 | 0.6 | 3.1 | 29.0 | 3 198 | 66 | 23 | 537 | 29.7 | 69.2 | 1.1 |
| Borden | 10.5 | 18 022 | 88.4 | 0.0 | 0.7 | 0.0 | 5.9 | 0.0 | 0 | 0 | 0 | 88 | 11.1 | 87.5 | 1.4 |
| Bosque | 45.8 | 2 550 | 65.6 | 0.1 | 3.7 | 6.4 | 3.4 | 51.4 | 2 865 | 73 | 41 | 1 005 | 23.5 | 75.4 | 1.1 |
| Bowie | 266.1 | 2 907 | 67.3 | 0.7 | 4.5 | 0.3 | 3.6 | 320.2 | 3 498 | 4 868 | 220 | 6 499 | 30.7 | 68.7 | 0.6 |
| Brazoria | 1 101.8 | 3 745 | 55.7 | 5.0 | 3.8 | 0.2 | 6.7 | 2 869.0 | 9 751 | 473 | 777 | 17 367 | 34.8 | 64.3 | 0.9 |
| Brazos | 480.7 | 2 812 | 49.0 | 2.2 | 5.6 | 0.3 | 4.3 | 778.8 | 4 556 | 823 | 526 | 31 041 | 34.9 | 63.9 | 1.2 |
| Brewster | 26.2 | 2 835 | 59.5 | 3.4 | 5.0 | 0.4 | 5.0 | 11.2 | 1 216 | 311 | 21 | 1 053 | 50.5 | 47.6 | 1.9 |
| Briscoe | 3.2 | 2 185 | 64.5 | 0.1 | 3.9 | 0.0 | 8.3 | 6.6 | 4 450 | 13 | 0 | 108 | 24.7 | 74.3 | 1.0 |
| Brooks | 37.5 | 4 939 | 52.3 | 2.1 | 9.1 | 0.2 | 4.7 | 10.4 | 1 366 | 288 | 16 | 514 | 75.7 | 24.1 | 0.3 |
| Brown | 132.1 | 3 424 | 56.9 | 6.2 | 4.0 | 0.4 | 4.0 | 142.9 | 3 703 | 125 | 85 | 2 690 | 18.8 | 80.3 | 0.9 |
| Burleson | 43.4 | 2 615 | 64.9 | 1.0 | 4.7 | 0.0 | 8.6 | 31.5 | 1 899 | 45 | 38 | 821 | 30.8 | 68.2 | 1.0 |
| Burnet | 118.7 | 2 716 | 54.7 | 1.6 | 7.0 | 0.4 | 3.7 | 184.0 | 4 213 | 82 | 96 | 2 373 | 27.3 | 71.4 | 1.3 |

1. Based on the resident population estimated as of July 1 of the year shown.    2. © 2013 Election Data Services, Inc. All rights reserved.

# Table B. States and Counties — Land Area and Population

| STATE/ County code | CBSA code[1] | County type[2] | STATE County | Land area,[3] (sq km) 2010 | Population 2012 Total persons | Rank | Per square kilometer | Race alone or in combination, not Hispanic or Latino (percent) — White | Black | American Indian, Alaska Native | Asian and Pacific Islander | Percent Hispanic or Latino[4] | Age (percent) Under 5 years | 5 to 17 years | 18 to 24 years | 25 to 34 years | 35 to 44 years | 45 to 54 years |
|---|---|---|---|---|---|---|---|---|---|---|---|---|---|---|---|---|---|---|
| | | | | 1 | 2 | 3 | 4 | 5 | 6 | 7 | 8 | 9 | 10 | 11 | 12 | 13 | 14 | 15 |
| | | | **TEXAS—Cont'd** | | | | | | | | | | | | | | | |
| 48 055 | 12420 | 1 | Caldwell | 1 412 | 38 734 | 1 202 | 27.4 | 44.3 | 7.0 | 0.6 | 1.1 | 47.9 | 6.7 | 19.6 | 11.9 | 12.2 | 12.5 | 13.5 |
| 48 057 | 47020 | 3 | Calhoun | 1 313 | 21 609 | 1 748 | 16.5 | 45.5 | 3.0 | 0.5 | 4.6 | 47.1 | 7.0 | 19.1 | 8.8 | 11.7 | 11.4 | 14.1 |
| 48 059 | 10180 | 6 | Callahan | 2 329 | 13 517 | 2 213 | 5.8 | 88.9 | 1.9 | 1.2 | 0.9 | 8.5 | 5.8 | 17.6 | 7.0 | 10.5 | 11.1 | 14.9 |
| 48 061 | 15180 | 2 | Cameron | 2 307 | 415 557 | 164 | 180.1 | 10.8 | 0.4 | 0.2 | 0.7 | 88.1 | 8.8 | 23.8 | 10.2 | 12.6 | 12.8 | 11.2 |
| 48 063 | ... | 6 | Camp | 507 | 12 449 | 2 275 | 24.6 | 59.9 | 17.7 | 1.0 | 1.0 | 22.1 | 6.9 | 19.5 | 8.4 | 11.5 | 10.6 | 13.2 |
| 48 065 | 11100 | 3 | Carson | 2 383 | 6 157 | 2 747 | 2.6 | 88.8 | 1.4 | 1.7 | 0.6 | 9.0 | 5.8 | 19.5 | 6.3 | 10.6 | 11.0 | 15.1 |
| 48 067 | ... | 6 | Cass | 2 427 | 30 166 | 1 426 | 12.4 | 77.6 | 18.0 | 1.0 | 0.6 | 3.9 | 5.8 | 17.3 | 7.1 | 10.5 | 11.4 | 14.3 |
| 48 069 | ... | 6 | Castro | 2 317 | 8 164 | 2 593 | 3.5 | 36.4 | 2.1 | 0.5 | 0.5 | 60.8 | 9.0 | 22.7 | 8.1 | 11.7 | 11.0 | 12.6 |
| 48 071 | 26420 | 1 | Chambers | 1 547 | 36 196 | 1 271 | 23.4 | 70.1 | 8.8 | 0.8 | 1.4 | 20.0 | 7.0 | 21.2 | 8.0 | 12.3 | 14.7 | 14.8 |
| 48 073 | 27380 | 6 | Cherokee | 2 727 | 51 206 | 967 | 18.8 | 63.2 | 15.1 | 0.8 | 0.7 | 21.5 | 7.1 | 18.9 | 9.6 | 11.6 | 12.0 | 13.3 |
| 48 075 | ... | 7 | Childress | 1 804 | 7 029 | 2 680 | 3.9 | 61.3 | 10.5 | 0.9 | 0.9 | 27.4 | 5.9 | 14.9 | 11.8 | 18.9 | 11.3 | 11.8 |
| 48 077 | 48660 | 6 | Clay | 2 820 | 10 535 | 2 394 | 3.7 | 92.5 | 1.3 | 1.9 | 0.5 | 5.1 | 5.6 | 17.3 | 6.4 | 9.5 | 11.4 | 15.7 |
| 48 079 | ... | 9 | Cochran | 2 008 | 3 046 | 2 974 | 1.5 | 40.7 | 4.0 | 0.6 | 0.3 | 54.8 | 8.7 | 20.8 | 9.8 | 11.2 | 9.9 | 13.0 |
| 48 081 | ... | 8 | Coke | 2 361 | 3 231 | 2 958 | 1.4 | 79.2 | 0.8 | 1.3 | 0.5 | 19.4 | 5.4 | 14.8 | 6.3 | 9.0 | 8.9 | 14.8 |
| 48 083 | ... | 6 | Coleman | 3 268 | 8 675 | 2 553 | 2.7 | 79.8 | 2.9 | 1.0 | 0.7 | 16.7 | 6.0 | 15.8 | 6.4 | 8.7 | 11.2 | 13.9 |
| 48 085 | 19100 | 1 | Collin | 2 179 | 834 642 | 65 | 383.0 | 64.1 | 9.3 | 0.9 | 12.5 | 15.2 | 7.2 | 21.1 | 7.4 | 13.7 | 17.2 | 15.2 |
| 48 087 | ... | 9 | Collingsworth | 2 379 | 3 036 | 2 977 | 1.3 | 63.0 | 4.7 | 1.9 | 0.4 | 31.1 | 8.2 | 19.5 | 7.2 | 11.8 | 10.6 | 12.9 |
| 48 089 | ... | 6 | Colorado | 2 487 | 20 696 | 1 798 | 8.3 | 59.8 | 12.8 | 0.5 | 0.7 | 27.0 | 6.3 | 17.3 | 7.5 | 10.0 | 12.4 | 14.4 |
| 48 091 | 41700 | 1 | Comal | 1 449 | 114 384 | 528 | 78.9 | 71.3 | 2.1 | 0.8 | 1.2 | 25.6 | 5.6 | 17.6 | 7.1 | 10.1 | 12.4 | 15.8 |
| 48 093 | ... | 7 | Comanche | 2 429 | 13 765 | 2 192 | 5.7 | 72.0 | 0.6 | 0.9 | 0.5 | 26.9 | 6.7 | 17.0 | 7.5 | 9.5 | 11.3 | 13.4 |
| 48 095 | ... | 8 | Concho | 2 548 | 4 010 | 2 903 | 1.6 | 43.2 | 1.7 | 0.6 | 0.7 | 54.2 | 4.2 | 10.1 | 7.0 | 16.7 | 19.5 | 15.9 |
| 48 097 | 23620 | 6 | Cooke | 2 266 | 38 688 | 1 204 | 17.1 | 79.0 | 3.5 | 1.4 | 1.2 | 16.4 | 6.8 | 18.7 | 8.8 | 11.0 | 11.1 | 13.9 |
| 48 099 | 28660 | 3 | Coryell | 2 725 | 77 231 | 707 | 28.3 | 64.0 | 17.5 | 1.2 | 4.2 | 16.6 | 8.3 | 19.2 | 12.1 | 19.0 | 14.2 | 11.7 |
| 48 101 | ... | 9 | Cottle | 2 332 | 1 486 | 3 083 | 0.6 | 69.0 | 9.6 | 0.6 | 0.3 | 21.0 | 4.3 | 18.1 | 6.5 | 8.5 | 9.7 | 14.7 |
| 48 103 | ... | 6 | Crane | 2 033 | 4 562 | 2 865 | 2.2 | 39.9 | 3.4 | 1.1 | 0.5 | 55.5 | 7.7 | 21.1 | 9.0 | 11.9 | 12.4 | 15.3 |
| 48 105 | ... | 7 | Crockett | 7 271 | 3 743 | 2 927 | 0.5 | 35.7 | 0.8 | 0.5 | 0.5 | 63.1 | 7.6 | 18.7 | 6.8 | 11.8 | 11.5 | 14.5 |
| 48 107 | 31180 | 3 | Crosby | 2 332 | 6 126 | 2 750 | 2.6 | 43.3 | 4.2 | 0.6 | 0.3 | 52.3 | 8.2 | 20.3 | 8.2 | 10.7 | 10.8 | 12.7 |
| 48 109 | ... | 9 | Culberson | 9 875 | 2 290 | 3 029 | 0.2 | 23.0 | 1.0 | 1.0 | 1.2 | 74.7 | 7.5 | 20.1 | 8.4 | 11.4 | 11.3 | 13.4 |
| 48 111 | ... | 7 | Dallam | 3 893 | 6 996 | 2 685 | 1.8 | 56.3 | 2.1 | 1.0 | 0.9 | 41.0 | 8.8 | 21.3 | 9.2 | 14.1 | 13.6 | 12.9 |
| 48 113 | 19100 | 1 | Dallas | 2 257 | 2 453 843 | 9 | 1 087.2 | 33.8 | 22.3 | 0.7 | 5.6 | 38.9 | 8.2 | 19.4 | 9.9 | 16.2 | 14.3 | 13.3 |
| 48 115 | 29500 | 7 | Dawson | 2 332 | 13 640 | 2 203 | 5.8 | 38.7 | 6.8 | 0.6 | 0.5 | 54.2 | 7.5 | 16.9 | 10.6 | 17.4 | 11.6 | 12.2 |
| 48 117 | 25820 | 6 | Deaf Smith | 3 877 | 19 360 | 1 862 | 5.0 | 30.0 | 1.1 | 0.5 | 0.5 | 68.4 | 9.8 | 22.5 | 9.8 | 13.1 | 11.7 | 11.8 |
| 48 119 | 19100 | 1 | Delta | 665 | 5 329 | 2 815 | 8.0 | 84.0 | 9.0 | 2.3 | 1.1 | 6.1 | 5.6 | 16.7 | 7.7 | 9.5 | 10.9 | 14.5 |
| 48 121 | 19100 | 1 | Denton | 2 275 | 707 304 | 85 | 310.9 | 65.4 | 9.2 | 1.1 | 7.6 | 18.7 | 7.3 | 20.0 | 10.2 | 15.0 | 16.1 | 14.5 |
| 48 123 | ... | 6 | DeWitt | 2 354 | 20 465 | 1 818 | 8.7 | 57.5 | 9.3 | 0.5 | 0.5 | 32.9 | 6.3 | 16.0 | 7.1 | 11.3 | 12.2 | 15.2 |
| 48 125 | ... | 8 | Dickens | 2 335 | 2 323 | 3 025 | 1.0 | 63.8 | 4.8 | 1.1 | 1.0 | 30.1 | 5.8 | 14.2 | 8.1 | 14.3 | 11.6 | 13.2 |
| 48 127 | ... | 6 | Dimmit | 3 442 | 10 461 | 2 398 | 3.0 | 12.5 | 1.1 | 0.1 | 0.7 | 85.7 | 7.7 | 21.6 | 9.3 | 10.4 | 11.4 | 12.5 |
| 48 129 | ... | 7 | Donley | 2 401 | 3 598 | 2 936 | 1.5 | 84.8 | 5.5 | 0.9 | 0.6 | 9.5 | 6.0 | 14.5 | 12.8 | 10.2 | 8.9 | 12.7 |
| 48 131 | ... | 7 | Duval | 4 645 | 11 717 | 2 316 | 2.5 | 10.6 | 1.0 | 0.2 | 0.2 | 88.1 | 7.2 | 18.9 | 10.1 | 11.6 | 11.5 | 13.8 |
| 48 133 | ... | 6 | Eastland | 2 400 | 18 421 | 1 899 | 7.7 | 81.8 | 2.5 | 1.0 | 0.6 | 15.1 | 5.9 | 16.7 | 10.1 | 10.2 | 9.5 | 14.0 |
| 48 135 | 36220 | 3 | Ector | 2 325 | 144 325 | 439 | 62.1 | 40.6 | 4.5 | 0.8 | 1.1 | 53.9 | 9.0 | 20.0 | 11.2 | 14.8 | 11.9 | 12.8 |
| 48 137 | ... | 9 | Edwards | 5 485 | 1 968 | 3 057 | 0.4 | 46.9 | 0.7 | 0.8 | 0.3 | 51.5 | 5.3 | 15.1 | 7.2 | 9.5 | 9.7 | 13.6 |
| 48 139 | 19100 | 1 | Ellis | 2 423 | 153 969 | 409 | 63.5 | 65.7 | 9.4 | 0.9 | 1.0 | 24.3 | 7.2 | 21.4 | 9.0 | 12.2 | 13.7 | 14.4 |
| 48 141 | 21340 | 2 | El Paso | 2 623 | 827 398 | 66 | 315.4 | 14.3 | 3.2 | 0.5 | 1.5 | 81.4 | 8.1 | 21.6 | 11.5 | 13.7 | 12.9 | 12.4 |
| 48 143 | 44500 | 6 | Erath | 2 805 | 39 231 | 1 190 | 14.0 | 77.6 | 1.7 | 1.0 | 0.9 | 19.8 | 6.3 | 15.7 | 20.2 | 12.0 | 10.6 | 12.0 |
| 48 145 | ... | 6 | Falls | 1 983 | 17 610 | 1 941 | 8.9 | 53.0 | 25.1 | 0.7 | 0.5 | 21.5 | 6.0 | 15.7 | 9.5 | 13.2 | 12.3 | 14.6 |
| 48 147 | 14300 | 6 | Fannin | 2 307 | 33 831 | 1 332 | 14.7 | 81.4 | 7.4 | 1.9 | 0.7 | 10.2 | 5.7 | 16.4 | 8.3 | 12.2 | 12.3 | 14.9 |
| 48 149 | ... | 6 | Fayette | 2 461 | 24 695 | 1 616 | 10.0 | 73.5 | 6.8 | 0.6 | 0.5 | 19.3 | 5.6 | 16.1 | 6.5 | 9.4 | 9.9 | 15.0 |
| 48 151 | ... | 8 | Fisher | 2 328 | 3 844 | 2 918 | 1.7 | 69.5 | 3.8 | 0.8 | 0.4 | 26.3 | 5.2 | 16.4 | 7.3 | 9.1 | 11.8 | 13.8 |
| 48 153 | ... | 6 | Floyd | 2 570 | 6 367 | 2 734 | 2.5 | 42.2 | 3.5 | 0.4 | 0.3 | 53.9 | 7.9 | 21.0 | 7.5 | 10.8 | 11.3 | 12.4 |
| 48 155 | ... | 9 | Foard | 1 824 | 1 307 | 3 095 | 0.7 | 79.7 | 4.3 | 0.3 | 0.4 | 15.6 | 4.0 | 16.6 | 7.1 | 8.2 | 11.3 | 15.3 |
| 48 157 | 26420 | 1 | Fort Bend | 2 231 | 627 293 | 102 | 281.2 | 37.4 | 21.3 | 0.6 | 18.3 | 24.2 | 7.3 | 21.8 | 8.0 | 12.5 | 15.7 | 15.5 |
| 48 159 | ... | 8 | Franklin | 737 | 10 640 | 2 385 | 14.4 | 80.6 | 4.9 | 1.4 | 0.7 | 13.7 | 6.6 | 17.8 | 7.7 | 10.3 | 11.0 | 13.9 |
| 48 161 | ... | 7 | Freestone | 2 273 | 19 515 | 1 856 | 8.6 | 68.8 | 16.3 | 0.8 | 0.5 | 14.5 | 6.2 | 17.0 | 6.9 | 11.9 | 13.0 | 14.4 |
| 48 163 | ... | 6 | Frio | 2 936 | 17 702 | 1 934 | 6.0 | 16.6 | 3.3 | 0.4 | 2.3 | 77.9 | 6.9 | 17.4 | 12.7 | 17.4 | 12.5 | 11.8 |
| 48 165 | ... | 7 | Gaines | 3 891 | 18 413 | 1 901 | 4.7 | 59.5 | 1.8 | 0.6 | 0.4 | 38.2 | 10.2 | 24.6 | 10.0 | 13.9 | 11.3 | 12.5 |
| 48 167 | 26420 | 1 | Galveston | 980 | 300 484 | 217 | 306.6 | 60.1 | 14.0 | 0.8 | 3.6 | 22.9 | 6.9 | 18.4 | 8.8 | 13.0 | 13.2 | 15.5 |
| 48 169 | ... | 8 | Garza | 2 314 | 6 412 | 2 731 | 2.8 | 45.8 | 6.5 | 0.5 | 0.3 | 47.4 | 5.9 | 14.2 | 13.6 | 18.9 | 11.5 | 14.3 |
| 48 171 | 23240 | 7 | Gillespie | 2 741 | 25 153 | 1 602 | 9.2 | 78.3 | 0.6 | 0.7 | 0.5 | 20.6 | 5.1 | 14.8 | 6.1 | 8.4 | 9.5 | 13.5 |
| 48 173 | ... | 8 | Glasscock | 2 332 | 1 259 | 3 099 | 0.5 | 66.1 | 1.6 | 0.3 | 0.3 | 31.9 | 6.6 | 20.7 | 7.0 | 10.8 | 12.9 | 15.5 |
| 48 175 | 47020 | 3 | Goliad | 2 207 | 7 351 | 2 650 | 3.3 | 59.7 | 4.8 | 0.8 | 0.4 | 35.1 | 5.3 | 17.1 | 6.4 | 8.6 | 10.9 | 15.8 |
| 48 177 | ... | 6 | Gonzales | 2 763 | 20 045 | 1 838 | 7.3 | 44.3 | 7.0 | 0.4 | 0.6 | 48.4 | 7.8 | 19.6 | 8.7 | 11.6 | 11.5 | 13.7 |
| 48 179 | 37420 | 6 | Gray | 2 398 | 22 978 | 1 690 | 9.6 | 68.9 | 5.4 | 1.5 | 0.7 | 24.9 | 7.2 | 17.8 | 7.9 | 13.2 | 12.9 | 13.6 |
| 48 181 | 43300 | 3 | Grayson | 2 416 | 121 935 | 503 | 50.5 | 79.9 | 6.7 | 2.3 | 1.4 | 11.8 | 6.4 | 17.4 | 9.3 | 11.4 | 11.8 | 14.7 |
| 48 183 | 30980 | 3 | Gregg | 708 | 122 658 | 498 | 173.2 | 61.5 | 20.4 | 0.9 | 1.5 | 17.2 | 7.6 | 17.9 | 10.4 | 13.8 | 11.9 | 13.3 |
| 48 185 | ... | 6 | Grimes | 2 040 | 26 783 | 1 536 | 13.1 | 60.9 | 16.6 | 0.8 | 0.7 | 22.2 | 5.8 | 16.5 | 8.4 | 12.3 | 12.8 | 15.7 |

1. CBSA = Core Based Statistical Area. See Appendix A for explanation. See Appendix B for list of metropolitan areas with component counties.  2. County type code from the Economic Research Service of USDA Rural-Urban Continuum Codes. See Appendix A for definition.  3. Dry land or land partially or temporarily covered by water.  4. May be of any race.

| STATE County | 55 to 64 years | 65 to 74 years | 75 years and over | Percent female | Total persons 2000 | Total persons 2010 | Percent change 2000–2010 | Percent change 2010–2012 | Births | Deaths | Net migration | Households 2010 Number | Percent change, 2000–2010 | Persons per house-hold | Female family house-holder[1] | One per-son |
|---|---|---|---|---|---|---|---|---|---|---|---|---|---|---|---|---|
| | 16 | 17 | 18 | 19 | 20 | 21 | 22 | 23 | 24 | 25 | 26 | 27 | 28 | 29 | 30 | 31 |
| **TEXAS—Cont'd** | | | | | | | | | | | | | | | | |
| Caldwell | 11.7 | 6.5 | 5.4 | 49.7 | 32 194 | 38 066 | 18.2 | 1.8 | 1 082 | 695 | 291 | 12 301 | 13.7 | 2.82 | 14.5 | 23.1 |
| Calhoun | 12.4 | 8.7 | 6.7 | 49.2 | 20 647 | 21 381 | 3.6 | 1.1 | 636 | 463 | 55 | 7 766 | 4.4 | 2.72 | 11.7 | 23.2 |
| Callahan | 14.8 | 10.3 | 8.0 | 51.1 | 12 905 | 13 544 | 5.0 | -0.2 | 273 | 413 | 98 | 5 447 | 7.6 | 2.47 | 10.0 | 24.7 |
| Cameron | 9.4 | 6.2 | 5.1 | 51.8 | 335 227 | 406 220 | 21.2 | 2.3 | 17 135 | 5 393 | -2 283 | 119 631 | 23.0 | 3.36 | 20.0 | 16.4 |
| Camp | 13.6 | 9.3 | 7.1 | 50.9 | 11 549 | 12 401 | 7.4 | 0.4 | 371 | 302 | -14 | 4 678 | 7.9 | 2.64 | 14.5 | 24.9 |
| Carson | 14.7 | 8.6 | 8.4 | 50.9 | 6 516 | 6 182 | -5.1 | -0.4 | 133 | 165 | 2 | 2 452 | -0.7 | 2.49 | 7.9 | 23.7 |
| Cass | 14.1 | 11.0 | 8.4 | 51.4 | 30 438 | 30 464 | 0.1 | -1.0 | 742 | 932 | -209 | 12 429 | 2.0 | 2.42 | 13.8 | 27.3 |
| Castro | 11.2 | 7.0 | 6.6 | 49.1 | 8 285 | 8 062 | -2.7 | 1.3 | 311 | 119 | -100 | 2 744 | -0.6 | 2.91 | 10.5 | 21.5 |
| Chambers | 12.3 | 6.0 | 3.7 | 49.6 | 26 031 | 35 096 | 34.8 | 3.1 | 1 035 | 511 | 574 | 11 952 | 30.8 | 2.92 | 9.9 | 16.7 |
| Cherokee | 12.4 | 8.5 | 6.6 | 49.1 | 46 659 | 50 845 | 9.0 | 0.7 | 1 661 | 1 163 | -121 | 17 894 | 7.5 | 2.68 | 14.1 | 24.1 |
| Childress | 10.5 | 7.6 | 7.4 | 41.6 | 7 688 | 7 041 | -8.4 | -0.2 | 181 | 158 | -36 | 2 326 | -6.0 | 2.42 | 11.0 | 30.8 |
| Clay | 15.8 | 10.8 | 7.6 | 50.5 | 11 006 | 10 752 | -2.3 | -2.0 | 204 | 284 | -132 | 4 319 | -0.1 | 2.47 | 8.3 | 23.9 |
| Cochran | 11.8 | 7.8 | 7.1 | 51.2 | 3 730 | 3 127 | -16.2 | -2.6 | 126 | 53 | -157 | 1 113 | -15.0 | 2.74 | 13.7 | 24.0 |
| Coke | 14.9 | 14.1 | 11.9 | 51.2 | 3 864 | 3 320 | -14.1 | -2.7 | 68 | 133 | -27 | 1 466 | -5.1 | 2.24 | 8.0 | 31.2 |
| Coleman | 15.6 | 12.3 | 10.1 | 50.3 | 9 235 | 8 895 | -3.7 | -2.5 | 207 | 282 | -138 | 3 857 | -0.8 | 2.30 | 10.9 | 31.0 |
| Collin | 10.1 | 5.2 | 2.9 | 50.8 | 491 675 | 782 341 | 59.1 | 6.7 | 23 275 | 7 312 | 35 233 | 283 759 | 55.9 | 2.74 | 9.6 | 22.0 |
| Collingsworth | 12.6 | 8.3 | 8.9 | 50.6 | 3 206 | 3 057 | -4.6 | -0.7 | 116 | 80 | -59 | 1 179 | -8.9 | 2.55 | 10.9 | 26.5 |
| Colorado | 14.6 | 10.2 | 9.2 | 50.4 | 20 390 | 20 874 | 2.4 | -0.9 | 578 | 593 | -152 | 8 182 | 7.1 | 2.51 | 10.9 | 27.1 |
| Comal | 15.2 | 9.4 | 6.7 | 50.9 | 78 021 | 108 472 | 39.0 | 5.5 | 2 812 | 2 094 | 5 085 | 41 363 | 42.3 | 2.60 | 9.5 | 21.4 |
| Comanche | 13.5 | 12.0 | 9.1 | 50.5 | 14 026 | 13 974 | -0.4 | -1.5 | 379 | 405 | -200 | 5 580 | 1.1 | 2.48 | 9.2 | 27.8 |
| Concho | 12.5 | 8.2 | 5.8 | 31.5 | 3 966 | 4 087 | 3.1 | -1.9 | 71 | 71 | -82 | 1 041 | -1.6 | 2.40 | 10.2 | 26.5 |
| Cooke | 13.5 | 9.0 | 7.2 | 50.6 | 36 363 | 38 437 | 5.7 | 0.7 | 1 106 | 894 | 31 | 14 513 | 6.4 | 2.60 | 11.1 | 24.1 |
| Coryell | 7.8 | 4.7 | 3.0 | 51.0 | 74 978 | 75 388 | 0.5 | 2.4 | 2 253 | 872 | 439 | 22 545 | 13.0 | 2.84 | 13.8 | 20.4 |
| Cottle | 13.9 | 13.4 | 10.8 | 53.4 | 1 904 | 1 505 | -21.0 | -1.3 | 33 | 25 | -23 | 677 | -17.4 | 2.22 | 11.5 | 33.1 |
| Crane | 11.0 | 6.5 | 5.2 | 50.8 | 3 996 | 4 375 | 9.5 | 4.3 | 143 | 62 | 106 | 1 471 | 8.2 | 2.92 | 10.7 | 19.2 |
| Crockett | 14.1 | 8.4 | 6.6 | 50.9 | 4 099 | 3 719 | -9.3 | 0.6 | 139 | 75 | -41 | 1 422 | -6.7 | 2.58 | 9.6 | 24.4 |
| Crosby | 12.0 | 9.6 | 7.6 | 51.8 | 7 072 | 6 059 | -14.3 | 1.1 | 200 | 160 | 24 | 2 237 | -10.9 | 2.68 | 12.4 | 25.0 |
| Culberson | 12.9 | 8.5 | 6.6 | 51.3 | 2 975 | 2 398 | -19.4 | -4.5 | 54 | 31 | -140 | 908 | -13.7 | 2.63 | 17.0 | 27.0 |
| Dallam | 10.7 | 5.8 | 3.6 | 47.9 | 6 222 | 6 703 | 7.7 | 4.4 | 302 | 77 | 48 | 2 448 | 5.7 | 2.72 | 11.3 | 24.4 |
| Dallas | 9.8 | 5.0 | 3.9 | 50.5 | 2 218 899 | 2 368 139 | 6.7 | 3.6 | 88 336 | 32 505 | 30 397 | 855 960 | 6.0 | 2.73 | 16.0 | 28.0 |
| Dawson | 9.9 | 6.9 | 7.0 | 43.3 | 14 985 | 13 833 | -7.7 | -1.4 | 426 | 326 | -300 | 4 385 | -7.2 | 2.67 | 13.3 | 26.1 |
| Deaf Smith | 9.9 | 5.9 | 5.4 | 50.2 | 18 561 | 19 372 | 4.4 | -0.1 | 791 | 386 | -421 | 6 365 | 3.0 | 2.99 | 14.2 | 20.2 |
| Delta | 14.4 | 12.3 | 8.3 | 50.9 | 5 327 | 5 231 | -1.8 | 1.9 | 130 | 160 | 110 | 2 088 | -0.3 | 2.47 | 11.7 | 25.8 |
| Denton | 9.5 | 4.7 | 2.7 | 50.8 | 432 976 | 662 614 | 53.0 | 6.7 | 20 373 | 6 428 | 30 158 | 240 289 | 51.2 | 2.71 | 10.2 | 22.7 |
| DeWitt | 13.6 | 9.2 | 9.1 | 47.8 | 20 013 | 20 097 | 0.4 | 1.8 | 513 | 532 | 359 | 7 407 | 2.8 | 2.47 | 12.5 | 28.3 |
| Dickens | 13.7 | 10.9 | 8.3 | 42.9 | 2 762 | 2 444 | -11.5 | -5.0 | 47 | 44 | -133 | 930 | -5.1 | 2.29 | 7.5 | 30.3 |
| Dimmit | 12.5 | 7.8 | 6.8 | 51.6 | 10 248 | 9 996 | -2.5 | 4.7 | 336 | 181 | 299 | 3 421 | 3.4 | 2.89 | 19.8 | 22.0 |
| Donley | 13.4 | 11.5 | 10.1 | 50.6 | 3 828 | 3 677 | -3.9 | -2.1 | 64 | 115 | -29 | 1 517 | -3.9 | 2.27 | 9.7 | 31.3 |
| Duval | 10.7 | 9.0 | 7.3 | 48.4 | 13 120 | 11 782 | -10.2 | -0.6 | 388 | 306 | -145 | 4 090 | -6.0 | 2.74 | 17.6 | 25.0 |
| Eastland | 13.5 | 10.9 | 9.2 | 51.0 | 18 297 | 18 583 | 1.6 | -0.9 | 483 | 603 | -37 | 7 465 | 2.0 | 2.37 | 11.2 | 29.9 |
| Ector | 10.2 | 5.5 | 4.5 | 50.4 | 121 123 | 137 130 | 13.2 | 5.2 | 5 597 | 2 588 | 4 100 | 48 688 | 11.0 | 2.77 | 15.4 | 24.5 |
| Edwards | 16.9 | 13.6 | 9.0 | 49.5 | 2 162 | 2 002 | -7.4 | -1.7 | 53 | 30 | -61 | 839 | 4.7 | 2.38 | 8.6 | 28.0 |
| Ellis | 11.5 | 6.3 | 4.1 | 50.6 | 111 360 | 149 610 | 34.3 | 2.9 | 4 559 | 2 336 | 2 094 | 50 503 | 36.4 | 2.93 | 12.4 | 17.5 |
| El Paso | 9.5 | 5.5 | 4.8 | 51.4 | 679 622 | 800 647 | 17.8 | 3.3 | 31 019 | 10 553 | 6 485 | 256 557 | 22.2 | 3.06 | 20.3 | 19.8 |
| Erath | 10.5 | 6.9 | 5.9 | 50.7 | 33 001 | 37 890 | 14.8 | 3.8 | 1 063 | 711 | 1 024 | 14 569 | 15.9 | 2.47 | 8.4 | 27.0 |
| Falls | 12.4 | 8.6 | 7.7 | 52.4 | 18 576 | 17 866 | -3.8 | -1.4 | 448 | 429 | -275 | 6 302 | -3.0 | 2.51 | 15.1 | 28.9 |
| Fannin | 13.0 | 9.6 | 7.6 | 47.0 | 31 242 | 33 915 | 8.6 | -0.2 | 782 | 955 | 88 | 12 149 | 9.4 | 2.53 | 10.9 | 25.1 |
| Fayette | 15.7 | 11.5 | 10.3 | 50.8 | 21 804 | 24 554 | 12.6 | 0.6 | 536 | 671 | 246 | 10 078 | 15.5 | 2.39 | 8.9 | 27.3 |
| Fisher | 14.6 | 11.3 | 10.7 | 50.5 | 4 344 | 3 974 | -8.5 | -3.3 | 81 | 120 | -93 | 1 668 | -6.6 | 2.37 | 9.5 | 29.0 |
| Floyd | 11.6 | 8.7 | 8.9 | 50.5 | 7 771 | 6 446 | -17.1 | -1.2 | 202 | 159 | -119 | 2 402 | -12.0 | 2.67 | 12.0 | 23.5 |
| Foard | 13.6 | 12.2 | 11.9 | 51.9 | 1 622 | 1 336 | -17.6 | -2.2 | 28 | 31 | -25 | 573 | -13.7 | 2.28 | 8.9 | 30.0 |
| Fort Bend | 11.5 | 4.9 | 2.9 | 50.8 | 354 452 | 585 375 | 65.1 | 7.2 | 17 434 | 5 472 | 29 093 | 187 384 | 68.9 | 3.09 | 12.9 | 14.9 |
| Franklin | 14.0 | 10.7 | 8.1 | 51.1 | 9 458 | 10 605 | 12.1 | 0.3 | 249 | 304 | 88 | 4 159 | 10.8 | 2.52 | 11.5 | 24.8 |
| Freestone | 13.6 | 9.6 | 7.4 | 47.6 | 17 867 | 19 816 | 10.9 | -1.5 | 490 | 430 | -359 | 7 259 | 10.2 | 2.51 | 10.5 | 27.0 |
| Frio | 9.8 | 6.4 | 5.1 | 41.7 | 16 252 | 17 217 | 5.9 | 2.8 | 550 | 290 | 217 | 4 854 | 2.3 | 2.87 | 18.4 | 23.5 |
| Gaines | 8.5 | 4.9 | 4.0 | 49.6 | 14 467 | 17 526 | 21.1 | 5.1 | 798 | 240 | 286 | 5 606 | 19.8 | 3.11 | 9.5 | 18.2 |
| Galveston | 12.7 | 6.7 | 4.8 | 50.5 | 250 158 | 291 309 | 16.5 | 3.1 | 8 845 | 5 200 | 5 554 | 108 969 | 15.0 | 2.60 | 13.5 | 24.7 |
| Garza | 10.7 | 5.9 | 4.9 | 37.0 | 4 872 | 6 461 | 32.6 | -0.8 | 168 | 90 | -128 | 1 671 | 0.5 | 2.60 | 12.7 | 25.5 |
| Gillespie | 15.7 | 13.6 | 13.4 | 51.7 | 20 814 | 24 837 | 19.3 | 1.3 | 556 | 806 | 551 | 10 572 | 24.1 | 2.31 | 8.0 | 28.4 |
| Glasscock | 13.1 | 8.3 | 5.0 | 47.2 | 1 406 | 1 226 | -12.8 | 2.7 | 29 | 15 | 18 | 441 | -8.7 | 2.78 | 3.9 | 18.8 |
| Goliad | 16.3 | 10.9 | 8.6 | 50.1 | 6 928 | 7 210 | 4.1 | 2.0 | 141 | 146 | 147 | 2 868 | 8.5 | 2.48 | 11.0 | 24.8 |
| Gonzales | 12.2 | 8.0 | 7.0 | 49.6 | 18 628 | 19 807 | 6.3 | 1.2 | 641 | 470 | 77 | 7 120 | 5.0 | 2.74 | 13.8 | 24.9 |
| Gray | 11.7 | 7.9 | 7.8 | 48.1 | 22 744 | 22 535 | -0.9 | 2.0 | 717 | 580 | 285 | 8 443 | -4.0 | 2.48 | 10.1 | 27.5 |
| Grayson | 13.2 | 8.8 | 7.1 | 51.3 | 110 595 | 120 877 | 9.3 | 0.9 | 3 352 | 2 848 | 625 | 46 905 | 9.5 | 2.53 | 12.2 | 25.5 |
| Gregg | 11.5 | 7.0 | 6.7 | 51.1 | 111 379 | 121 730 | 9.3 | 0.8 | 4 243 | 2 879 | -433 | 45 798 | 7.3 | 2.65 | 14.8 | 27.0 |
| Grimes | 14.0 | 8.6 | 5.9 | 45.6 | 23 552 | 26 604 | 13.0 | 0.7 | 668 | 536 | 81 | 8 902 | 14.8 | 2.65 | 12.5 | 24.1 |

1. No spouse present.

# Table B. States and Counties — Population, Vital Statistics, Medicare, and Crime

| STATE County | Persons in group quarters, 2010 | Daytime population, 2007–2011 Number | Employ-ment/resi-dence ratio | Births, 2011 Total | Rate[1] | Deaths, 2011 Number | Rate[1] | Persons under 65 with no health insurance, 2010 Number | Percent | Medicare, 2012 Eligible for Medicare | Enrolled in Medicare Advantage | Enrolled in a Medicare prescription drug plan | Serious crimes known to police,[2] 2011 Total Number | Rate[3] |
|---|---|---|---|---|---|---|---|---|---|---|---|---|---|---|
| | 32 | 33 | 34 | 35 | 36 | 37 | 38 | 39 | 40 | 41 | 42 | 43 | 44 | 45 |
| **TEXAS—Cont'd** | | | | | | | | | | | | | | |
| Caldwell | 3 376 | 31 149 | 0.56 | 487 | 12.7 | 291 | 7.6 | 8 810 | 27.5 | 5 767 | 773 | 2 557 | 799 | 2 056 |
| Calhoun | 249 | 24 851 | 1.42 | 284 | 13.2 | 210 | 9.8 | 4 406 | 24.5 | 3 758 | 260 | 1 568 | 757 | 3 704 |
| Callahan | 75 | 10 465 | 0.46 | 141 | 10.4 | 175 | 12.9 | 2 629 | 23.9 | 2 953 | 396 | 1 291 | 140 | 1 012 |
| Cameron | 3 730 | 397 909 | 0.98 | 7 924 | 19.1 | 2 296 | 5.5 | 134 358 | 37.6 | 51 310 | 13 223 | 24 101 | 18 272 | 4 405 |
| Camp | 67 | 11 786 | 0.88 | 159 | 12.8 | 133 | 10.7 | 2 991 | 28.9 | 2 473 | 388 | 1 179 | 384 | 3 033 |
| Carson | 71 | 5 223 | 0.62 | 48 | 7.7 | 81 | 12.9 | 902 | 17.7 | 1 133 | 141 | 503 | 79 | 1 252 |
| Cass | 354 | 27 418 | 0.75 | 333 | 11.0 | 415 | 13.7 | 5 370 | 22.0 | 7 095 | 1 108 | 3 193 | 879 | 2 826 |
| Castro | 64 | 7 305 | 0.81 | 154 | 19.0 | 59 | 7.3 | 2 523 | 36.3 | 1 148 | 51 | 683 | 203 | 2 466 |
| Chambers | 229 | 29 336 | 0.72 | 499 | 14.0 | 216 | 6.1 | 6 427 | 20.3 | 4 762 | 852 | 1 751 | 988 | 2 757 |
| Cherokee | 2 851 | 47 931 | 0.87 | 784 | 15.3 | 498 | 9.7 | 12 400 | 30.5 | 9 336 | 1 691 | 4 246 | 1 822 | 3 519 |
| Childress | 1 418 | 7 322 | 1.09 | 87 | 12.5 | 81 | 11.6 | 1 193 | 26.0 | 1 269 | 162 | 619 | 112 | 1 558 |
| Clay | 70 | 7 920 | 0.41 | 117 | 10.9 | 122 | 11.4 | 2 056 | 23.5 | 2 266 | 178 | 1 070 | 144 | 1 312 |
| Cochran | 78 | 3 036 | 0.92 | 65 | 20.9 | 21 | 6.8 | 893 | 34.1 | 551 | 52 | 317 | 87 | 2 725 |
| Coke | 35 | 3 061 | 0.74 | 35 | 10.6 | 62 | 18.8 | 800 | 32.6 | 826 | 76 | 384 | 9 | 265 |
| Coleman | 40 | 8 336 | 0.84 | 94 | 10.7 | 118 | 13.5 | 2 096 | 30.3 | 2 267 | 208 | 1 170 | 273 | 3 006 |
| Collin | 3 914 | 715 973 | 0.88 | 10 433 | 12.8 | 3 056 | 3.8 | 120 888 | 16.7 | 78 839 | 14 782 | 31 249 | 19 430 | 2 432 |
| Collingsworth | 52 | 2 924 | 0.91 | 46 | 14.9 | 34 | 11.0 | 942 | 38.0 | 605 | 66 | 343 | 1 | 32 |
| Colorado | 328 | 19 758 | 0.88 | 277 | 13.3 | 252 | 12.1 | 4 764 | 28.5 | 4 503 | 207 | 2 470 | 444 | 2 083 |
| Comal | 1 060 | 100 720 | 0.89 | 1 264 | 11.3 | 854 | 7.6 | 18 812 | 20.5 | 22 263 | 4 884 | 6 742 | 2 897 | 2 616 |
| Comanche | 161 | 12 832 | 0.80 | 176 | 12.7 | 179 | 12.9 | 3 792 | 34.6 | 3 290 | 304 | 1 617 | 381 | 2 670 |
| Concho | 1 588 | 4 140 | 1.05 | 31 | 7.6 | 35 | 8.6 | 537 | 27.5 | 613 | 56 | 302 | NA | NA |
| Cooke | 686 | 36 340 | 0.89 | 510 | 13.3 | 408 | 10.6 | 9 096 | 28.6 | 7 032 | 858 | 3 313 | NA | NA |
| Coryell | 11 444 | 63 376 | 0.63 | 978 | 12.8 | 383 | 5.0 | 12 277 | 20.9 | 7 704 | 1 480 | 1 672 | 1 402 | 1 821 |
| Cottle | 0 | 1 583 | 0.84 | 12 | 8.0 | 14 | 9.3 | 429 | 37.5 | 459 | 48 | 262 | 3 | 195 |
| Crane | 86 | 4 145 | 0.94 | 69 | 15.7 | 30 | 6.8 | 1 020 | 26.5 | 602 | 62 | 262 | 47 | 1 052 |
| Crockett | 49 | 3 950 | 1.12 | 61 | 16.4 | 24 | 6.4 | 993 | 31.5 | 608 | 40 | 346 | NA | NA |
| Crosby | 62 | 5 538 | 0.76 | 110 | 18.1 | 77 | 12.6 | 1 336 | 26.9 | 1 207 | 171 | 665 | 83 | 1 342 |
| Culberson | 12 | 2 559 | 1.12 | 26 | 10.9 | 11 | 4.6 | 730 | 36.0 | 441 | 48 | 286 | 10 | 408 |
| Dallam | 39 | 6 801 | 1.06 | 128 | 18.6 | 44 | 6.4 | 2 054 | 34.1 | 895 | 78 | 465 | 146 | 2 133 |
| Dallas | 30 398 | 2 683 140 | 1.31 | 41 569 | 17.2 | 14 149 | 5.9 | 663 878 | 31.0 | 266 833 | 58 514 | 112 435 | 114 049 | 4 717 |
| Dawson | 2 146 | 14 190 | 1.08 | 208 | 15.1 | 139 | 10.1 | 2 676 | 27.3 | 2 291 | 217 | 1 340 | 333 | 2 358 |
| Deaf Smith | 371 | 19 409 | 1.02 | 392 | 20.0 | 187 | 9.5 | 5 620 | 33.1 | 2 587 | 282 | 1 399 | 578 | 2 922 |
| Delta | 69 | 4 104 | 0.47 | 60 | 11.5 | 62 | 11.9 | 1 149 | 27.4 | 1 237 | 100 | 582 | 149 | 2 790 |
| Denton | 10 344 | 519 961 | 0.61 | 9 121 | 13.3 | 2 724 | 4.0 | 109 698 | 17.9 | 62 672 | 13 091 | 23 162 | 16 340 | 2 415 |
| DeWitt | 1 790 | 19 379 | 0.92 | 250 | 12.3 | 221 | 10.9 | 3 720 | 25.0 | 4 136 | 255 | 2 314 | 328 | 1 598 |
| Dickens | 315 | 2 477 | 1.06 | 26 | 10.8 | 26 | 10.8 | 528 | 32.0 | 497 | 47 | 291 | 13 | 521 |
| Dimmit | 104 | 10 960 | 1.28 | 145 | 14.3 | 84 | 8.3 | 2 357 | 27.7 | 1 747 | 336 | 952 | 263 | 2 577 |
| Donley | 240 | 3 353 | 0.82 | 33 | 9.0 | 48 | 13.1 | 909 | 34.2 | 826 | 83 | 423 | 30 | 799 |
| Duval | 578 | 11 386 | 0.89 | 178 | 15.3 | 145 | 12.4 | 2 248 | 24.2 | 2 269 | 504 | 1 198 | 367 | 3 051 |
| Eastland | 885 | 18 202 | 0.95 | 230 | 12.3 | 258 | 13.8 | 4 101 | 28.9 | 4 232 | 618 | 1 949 | 421 | 2 219 |
| Ector | 2 175 | 133 797 | 0.97 | 2 677 | 19.1 | 1 154 | 8.2 | 35 639 | 29.5 | 17 409 | 2 240 | 8 799 | 5 189 | 3 706 |
| Edwards | 5 | 2 039 | 1.02 | 16 | 8.1 | 13 | 6.6 | 549 | 35.2 | 478 | 41 | 214 | 44 | 2 153 |
| Ellis | 1 610 | 124 293 | 0.67 | 2 127 | 13.9 | 1 014 | 6.6 | 30 926 | 23.1 | 20 252 | 2 865 | 8 496 | 3 771 | 2 469 |
| El Paso | 15 792 | 786 162 | 1.00 | 13 862 | 16.9 | 4 572 | 5.6 | 230 924 | 32.8 | 105 997 | 40 752 | 32 888 | 22 653 | 2 771 |
| Erath | 1 888 | 37 509 | 1.00 | 496 | 13.0 | 326 | 8.5 | 9 840 | 31.3 | 5 561 | 705 | 2 341 | 927 | 2 396 |
| Falls | 2 068 | 15 828 | 0.69 | 212 | 11.8 | 175 | 9.8 | 3 602 | 27.7 | 3 217 | 709 | 1 304 | 200 | 1 096 |
| Fannin | 3 145 | 29 251 | 0.65 | 375 | 11.0 | 444 | 13.1 | 6 607 | 25.8 | 6 807 | 681 | 3 047 | 623 | 1 799 |
| Fayette | 455 | 23 475 | 0.92 | 241 | 9.7 | 297 | 12.0 | 4 817 | 25.2 | 5 821 | 467 | 2 856 | 400 | 1 595 |
| Fisher | 22 | 3 538 | 0.70 | 35 | 8.9 | 65 | 16.6 | 849 | 27.7 | 946 | 91 | 494 | 53 | 1 306 |
| Floyd | 35 | 5 962 | 0.81 | 101 | 15.8 | 69 | 10.8 | 1 481 | 28.2 | 1 216 | 173 | 652 | 143 | 2 173 |
| Foard | 30 | 1 196 | 0.84 | 11 | 8.2 | 14 | 10.4 | 337 | 32.9 | 353 | 25 | 183 | 5 | 367 |
| Fort Bend | 5 936 | 439 075 | 0.53 | 7 952 | 13.1 | 2 269 | 3.7 | 106 182 | 19.6 | 55 811 | 13 996 | 19 717 | 12 632 | 2 115 |
| Franklin | 114 | 10 558 | 0.98 | 111 | 10.5 | 137 | 13.0 | 2 198 | 25.7 | 2 208 | 304 | 1 074 | 135 | 1 247 |
| Freestone | 1 581 | 19 324 | 0.97 | 207 | 10.5 | 185 | 9.4 | 3 674 | 24.4 | 3 514 | 388 | 1 585 | 416 | 2 056 |
| Frio | 3 271 | 17 273 | 1.03 | 247 | 14.2 | 134 | 7.7 | 3 030 | 25.2 | 2 278 | 466 | 1 378 | 350 | 1 991 |
| Gaines | 87 | 16 446 | 0.91 | 373 | 20.7 | 117 | 6.5 | 5 790 | 36.4 | 1 817 | 121 | 1 050 | 149 | 833 |
| Galveston | 4 297 | 259 527 | 0.78 | 4 137 | 14.0 | 2 299 | 7.8 | 55 473 | 21.7 | 42 304 | 7 398 | 14 948 | 9 520 | 3 201 |
| Garza | 2 109 | 6 544 | 1.13 | 82 | 12.5 | 45 | 6.9 | 988 | 26.9 | 802 | 162 | 382 | 40 | 606 |
| Gillespie | 390 | 24 737 | 1.02 | 258 | 10.3 | 347 | 13.8 | 5 099 | 28.0 | 7 013 | 678 | 3 083 | 358 | 1 412 |
| Glasscock | 0 | 1 308 | 1.25 | 14 | 11.2 | 6 | 4.8 | 283 | 26.5 | 184 | D | 100 | 6 | 479 |
| Goliad | 93 | 5 955 | 0.60 | 72 | 9.9 | 64 | 8.8 | 1 290 | 22.3 | 1 477 | 150 | 735 | 83 | 1 127 |
| Gonzales | 311 | 19 299 | 0.95 | 298 | 15.0 | 196 | 9.8 | 5 256 | 31.6 | 3 538 | 324 | 1 919 | 587 | 2 902 |
| Gray | 1 610 | 22 704 | 1.01 | 309 | 13.6 | 268 | 11.8 | 4 716 | 27.2 | 4 078 | 380 | 1 964 | 1 022 | 4 442 |
| Grayson | 2 214 | 115 432 | 0.91 | 1 542 | 12.7 | 1 224 | 10.1 | 27 565 | 27.4 | 23 719 | 2 559 | 10 189 | 4 244 | 3 439 |
| Gregg | 4 414 | 139 875 | 1.35 | 1 943 | 15.8 | 1 240 | 10.1 | 26 251 | 25.7 | 21 020 | 3 287 | 9 784 | 5 558 | 4 472 |
| Grimes | 3 012 | 24 646 | 0.82 | 291 | 10.8 | 195 | 7.3 | 5 568 | 27.4 | 4 448 | 629 | 1 934 | 674 | 2 481 |

1. Per 1,000 estimated resident population.    2. Data for serious crimes have not been adjusted for underreporting; this may affect comparability between geographic areas and over time.    3. Per 100,000 population estimated by the FBI.

# Table B. States and Counties — Crime, Education, Money Income, and Poverty

| STATE County | Serious crimes known to police, 2011 (cont.)[1] Rate[2] | | Education School enrollment and attainment, 2007–2011 | | | | Local government expenditures,[5] 2009–2010 | | Money income, 2007–2011 | Households Median income | | | Income and poverty, 2011 Percent below poverty level | | |
|---|---|---|---|---|---|---|---|---|---|---|---|---|---|---|---|
| | | | Enrollment[3] | | Attainment[4] (percent) | | | | | | | | | | |
| | Violent | Property | Total | Percent private | High school graduate or less | Bachelor's degree or more | Total current expenditures (mil dol) | Current expenditures per student (dollars) | Per capita income[6] (dollars) | Dollars | Percent change, 2000 to 2007–2011 (constant 2011 dollars) | Percent with income of $200,000 or more | Median household income (dollars) | All persons | Children under 18 years | Children 5 to 17 years in families |
| | 46 | 47 | 48 | 49 | 50 | 51 | 52 | 53 | 54 | 55 | 56 | 57 | 58 | 59 | 60 | 61 |
| **TEXAS—Cont'd** | | | | | | | | | | | | | | | | |
| Caldwell | 244 | 1 811 | 9 575 | 7.7 | 61.8 | 14.8 | 54.2 | 8 535 | 19 227 | 43 136 | -12.6 | 2.3 | 40 721 | 19.6 | 26.8 | 24.9 |
| Calhoun | 450 | 3 254 | 5 306 | 9.9 | 53.8 | 15.0 | 39.4 | 9 223 | 21 751 | 44 433 | -8.2 | 2.0 | 43 339 | 18.7 | 26.9 | 23.9 |
| Callahan | 72 | 940 | 3 225 | 10.4 | 50.1 | 16.6 | 23.8 | 9 390 | 21 680 | 45 933 | 4.8 | 0.6 | 43 074 | 15.8 | 25.5 | 23.3 |
| Cameron | 293 | 4 112 | 125 727 | 5.0 | 61.4 | 14.6 | 919.3 | 9 197 | 14 183 | 32 156 | -8.9 | 1.6 | 31 902 | 33.7 | 46.7 | 45.5 |
| Camp | 237 | 2 796 | 3 106 | 4.2 | 55.2 | 17.0 | 22.2 | 9 098 | 19 331 | 36 998 | -12.1 | 1.4 | 36 393 | 21.8 | 35.7 | 36.0 |
| Carson | 253 | 998 | 1 602 | 4.2 | 44.7 | 23.5 | 13.8 | 10 477 | 26 287 | 60 028 | 10.4 | 2.1 | 55 250 | 8.8 | 12.5 | 10.8 |
| Cass | 257 | 2 569 | 6 949 | 6.9 | 56.9 | 12.5 | 52.2 | 9 248 | 20 580 | 35 592 | -7.3 | 1.6 | 36 061 | 17.3 | 26.0 | 24.2 |
| Castro | 85 | 2 381 | 2 240 | 4.1 | 63.0 | 16.0 | 16.0 | 9 247 | 16 684 | 36 893 | -10.8 | 1.3 | 38 175 | 20.5 | 31.1 | 29.0 |
| Chambers | 218 | 2 539 | 9 419 | 5.7 | 44.6 | 16.6 | 65.5 | 9 768 | 29 237 | 72 850 | 12.5 | 3.1 | 69 378 | 9.6 | 13.7 | 12.2 |
| Cherokee | 516 | 3 004 | 12 602 | 8.0 | 62.1 | 11.9 | 89.1 | 8 451 | 18 049 | 37 758 | -4.6 | 1.3 | 35 119 | 21.5 | 32.2 | 29.1 |
| Childress | 306 | 1 252 | 1 614 | 8.3 | 56.6 | 15.9 | 11.7 | 10 393 | 17 567 | 47 605 | 28.4 | 2.9 | 33 780 | 24.5 | 32.4 | 30.4 |
| Clay | 36 | 1 275 | 2 303 | 7.5 | 48.4 | 18.8 | 18.6 | 10 532 | 25 242 | 52 868 | 9.6 | 2.4 | 48 358 | 10.7 | 17.6 | 15.6 |
| Cochran | 63 | 2 662 | 812 | 4.6 | 63.7 | 12.4 | 19.1 | 14 700 | 17 012 | 40 513 | 9.0 | 0.6 | 38 276 | 21.0 | 33.3 | 32.1 |
| Coke | 29 | 236 | 753 | 5.4 | 50.3 | 14.0 | 6.8 | 11 927 | 20 028 | 40 000 | 1.9 | 1.7 | 37 441 | 13.1 | 20.6 | 18.8 |
| Coleman | 165 | 2 841 | 1 626 | 4.1 | 59.0 | 14.1 | 14.9 | 10 700 | 17 503 | 27 910 | -19.4 | 1.1 | 31 865 | 22.9 | 38.6 | 36.5 |
| Collin | 174 | 2 258 | 222 560 | 14.7 | 22.8 | 48.7 | 1 336.1 | 8 232 | 37 825 | 82 758 | -13.5 | 9.6 | 82 765 | 8.2 | 9.9 | 8.7 |
| Collingsworth | 32 | 0 | 677 | 2.2 | 58.5 | 18.3 | 6.8 | 10 488 | 21 100 | 38 750 | 12.8 | 3.6 | 34 634 | 21.7 | 36.8 | 35.1 |
| Colorado | 160 | 1 924 | 4 415 | 16.7 | 57.6 | 16.4 | 33.1 | 9 564 | 23 789 | 43 252 | -1.2 | 3.5 | 42 451 | 16.8 | 25.8 | 23.6 |
| Comal | 256 | 2 360 | 25 022 | 15.4 | 36.0 | 32.6 | 197.2 | 7 986 | 33 181 | 65 521 | 5.2 | 6.7 | 59 754 | 9.4 | 15.6 | 13.9 |
| Comanche | 217 | 2 453 | 2 966 | 6.1 | 57.6 | 18.5 | 22.6 | 9 959 | 18 868 | 36 326 | -5.3 | 1.0 | 35 296 | 23.2 | 35.9 | 33.6 |
| Concho | NA | NA | 614 | 6.2 | 64.5 | 12.2 | 4.7 | 11 509 | 18 119 | 46 528 | 10.1 | 0.9 | 35 514 | 29.2 | 31.3 | 30.2 |
| Cooke | NA | NA | 9 181 | 10.8 | 49.8 | 19.0 | 56.7 | 8 893 | 23 520 | 50 176 | -1.3 | 2.5 | 49 127 | 14.3 | 23.8 | 21.7 |
| Coryell | 213 | 1 608 | 20 994 | 7.6 | 46.0 | 14.9 | 94.1 | 8 271 | 19 218 | 48 920 | 0.6 | 1.0 | 47 864 | 16.1 | 22.3 | 21.7 |
| Cottle | 0 | 195 | 414 | 1.4 | 59.7 | 14.0 | 3.2 | 13 468 | 18 700 | 39 038 | 13.6 | 1.6 | 32 656 | 20.9 | 32.8 | 27.2 |
| Crane | 67 | 985 | 1 236 | 2.3 | 59.2 | 13.5 | 13.7 | 13 661 | 18 978 | 48 648 | 11.9 | 0.2 | 49 831 | 11.2 | 15.3 | 13.9 |
| Crockett | NA | NA | 737 | 5.7 | 62.0 | 6.8 | 11.7 | 15 663 | 20 406 | 51 522 | 30.0 | 0.5 | 44 331 | 16.0 | 25.7 | 23.8 |
| Crosby | 194 | 1 148 | 1 526 | 5.2 | 63.4 | 11.7 | 16.7 | 12 982 | 16 953 | 35 655 | 2.5 | 1.4 | 32 661 | 27.8 | 39.8 | 37.8 |
| Culberson | 123 | 286 | 482 | 0.0 | 71.6 | 18.0 | 6.4 | 13 175 | 15 760 | 37 500 | 7.3 | 0.8 | 31 186 | 26.0 | 38.2 | 34.0 |
| Dallam | 248 | 1 885 | 1 783 | 17.9 | 63.9 | 8.6 | 17.0 | 9 201 | 19 836 | 47 500 | 25.9 | 2.2 | 43 454 | 14.0 | 22.3 | 21.2 |
| Dallas | 453 | 4 264 | 633 804 | 13.4 | 46.4 | 28.1 | 3 931.4 | 8 589 | 26 617 | 48 942 | -16.3 | 5.0 | 47 335 | 20.0 | 30.0 | 28.3 |
| Dawson | 524 | 1 834 | 3 402 | 5.2 | 66.8 | 8.5 | 26.3 | 10 368 | 15 746 | 39 454 | 3.6 | 1.5 | 37 492 | 23.3 | 32.1 | 31.8 |
| Deaf Smith | 359 | 2 563 | 5 309 | 8.2 | 64.4 | 13.9 | 38.5 | 8 714 | 17 372 | 41 134 | 2.9 | 0.8 | 36 073 | 22.1 | 30.5 | 28.5 |
| Delta | 75 | 2 715 | 1 288 | 4.5 | 55.3 | 12.1 | 7.9 | 9 300 | 20 177 | 34 710 | -11.6 | 1.4 | 34 968 | 21.7 | 32.4 | 30.0 |
| Denton | 184 | 2 231 | 202 879 | 12.7 | 27.8 | 40.0 | 979.9 | 8 566 | 33 252 | 72 305 | -8.0 | 7.1 | 70 243 | 9.4 | 11.6 | 10.0 |
| DeWitt | 190 | 1 408 | 4 302 | 6.3 | 60.9 | 12.3 | 43.2 | 10 132 | 22 689 | 43 380 | 11.9 | 3.3 | 38 620 | 18.1 | 28.4 | 26.4 |
| Dickens | 160 | 361 | 404 | 4.5 | 60.3 | 14.6 | 6.6 | 16 402 | 18 017 | 35 333 | 1.0 | 3.1 | 32 925 | 23.8 | 35.1 | 33.3 |
| Dimmit | 441 | 2 136 | 2 602 | 6.0 | 72.7 | 11.2 | 22.6 | 9 453 | 14 260 | 26 730 | -9.7 | 0.0 | 30 503 | 26.8 | 40.2 | 38.4 |
| Donley | 80 | 719 | 1 055 | 15.3 | 49.4 | 18.5 | 7.4 | 11 099 | 21 545 | 44 300 | 13.1 | 1.7 | 34 606 | 19.9 | 31.9 | 31.5 |
| Duval | 831 | 2 219 | 2 865 | 4.8 | 68.5 | 8.2 | 29.7 | 11 151 | 16 172 | 35 144 | 16.1 | 1.5 | 31 294 | 27.1 | 39.0 | 36.4 |
| Eastland | 232 | 1 987 | 4 475 | 7.5 | 55.0 | 15.4 | 33.6 | 10 968 | 20 078 | 34 531 | -4.7 | 1.8 | 36 761 | 20.4 | 30.2 | 27.8 |
| Ector | 679 | 3 027 | 37 244 | 8.0 | 56.7 | 13.3 | 217.0 | 7 773 | 24 010 | 50 056 | 19.0 | 3.2 | 47 930 | 15.8 | 21.2 | 20.6 |
| Edwards | 294 | 1 859 | 397 | 2.8 | 57.5 | 23.3 | 8.4 | 14 475 | 28 820 | 43 095 | 26.2 | 3.2 | 33 102 | 23.6 | 38.1 | 34.2 |
| Ellis | 189 | 2 279 | 42 715 | 12.3 | 46.7 | 20.8 | 252.3 | 8 045 | 26 059 | 62 639 | -7.9 | 3.9 | 60 931 | 12.6 | 17.7 | 16.0 |
| El Paso | 396 | 2 375 | 258 970 | 7.0 | 52.4 | 19.8 | 1 583.7 | 8 890 | 17 618 | 38 259 | -8.7 | 1.9 | 39 116 | 24.6 | 34.1 | 33.7 |
| Erath | 119 | 2 277 | 12 537 | 2.2 | 46.2 | 24.5 | 49.6 | 8 413 | 21 825 | 40 096 | -3.3 | 2.8 | 38 860 | 20.0 | 26.2 | 27.1 |
| Falls | 110 | 987 | 4 514 | 6.7 | 62.1 | 11.7 | 28.4 | 11 094 | 15 364 | 31 543 | -12.1 | 0.4 | 33 125 | 26.3 | 34.4 | 33.2 |
| Fannin | 165 | 1 634 | 7 544 | 10.5 | 57.6 | 14.6 | 52.3 | 9 421 | 20 153 | 44 136 | -5.3 | 1.6 | 39 985 | 19.4 | 26.8 | 24.6 |
| Fayette | 176 | 1 420 | 5 056 | 9.7 | 57.1 | 17.6 | 34.7 | 9 445 | 27 499 | 47 285 | 1.4 | 3.1 | 44 862 | 14.7 | 22.1 | 19.3 |
| Fisher | 99 | 1 207 | 975 | 4.1 | 58.1 | 15.9 | 6.9 | 10 825 | 24 713 | 43 724 | 17.1 | 1.9 | 38 717 | 14.0 | 21.8 | 19.2 |
| Floyd | 334 | 1 838 | 1 763 | 3.6 | 55.5 | 17.3 | 15.7 | 10 975 | 18 397 | 35 967 | -0.8 | 0.5 | 35 399 | 20.2 | 31.9 | 29.5 |
| Foard | 0 | 367 | 209 | 0.0 | 56.5 | 21.1 | 2.8 | 12 724 | 18 840 | 31 006 | -11.0 | 0.0 | 30 488 | 17.9 | 25.6 | 21.8 |
| Fort Bend | 281 | 1 834 | 173 510 | 14.5 | 30.8 | 40.7 | 1 255.0 | 7 904 | 32 924 | 82 571 | -4.2 | 10.3 | 82 147 | 8.9 | 12.2 | 11.0 |
| Franklin | 194 | 1 053 | 2 687 | 6.5 | 48.2 | 22.9 | 13.8 | 8 980 | 25 657 | 47 500 | 10.1 | 4.0 | 40 936 | 17.1 | 29.0 | 27.1 |
| Freestone | 292 | 1 764 | 4 755 | 2.7 | 56.3 | 13.5 | 39.5 | 10 721 | 22 823 | 45 816 | 8.5 | 3.6 | 44 564 | 15.5 | 21.8 | 20.5 |
| Frio | 210 | 1 781 | 4 660 | 6.9 | 68.5 | 8.3 | 32.9 | 10 315 | 15 413 | 37 769 | 14.2 | 0.9 | 31 996 | 34.6 | 41.0 | 38.8 |
| Gaines | 78 | 754 | 4 307 | 18.6 | 67.0 | 13.3 | 40.8 | 13 057 | 21 869 | 47 157 | 14.8 | 4.2 | 43 703 | 17.4 | 24.5 | 23.5 |
| Galveston | 269 | 2 932 | 79 439 | 9.4 | 40.0 | 27.3 | 657.6 | 8 695 | 29 936 | 59 645 | 4.1 | 5.2 | 58 106 | 14.9 | 21.5 | 19.5 |
| Garza | 30 | 576 | 1 419 | 9.8 | 63.7 | 9.9 | 12.0 | 12 025 | 13 442 | 42 883 | 16.7 | 1.2 | 39 004 | 28.6 | 30.0 | 28.9 |
| Gillespie | 75 | 1 337 | 4 591 | 17.4 | 44.2 | 25.9 | 33.2 | 9 245 | 28 506 | 54 843 | 6.6 | 3.2 | 51 981 | 12.5 | 20.5 | 18.8 |
| Glasscock | 160 | 319 | 331 | 10.0 | 39.9 | 20.0 | 4.3 | 15 749 | 32 692 | 72 188 | 50.0 | 3.2 | 59 309 | 11.0 | 17.6 | 15.6 |
| Goliad | 190 | 937 | 1 556 | 15.5 | 49.1 | 16.4 | 15.6 | 11 592 | 27 310 | 51 389 | 11.3 | 3.3 | 43 737 | 16.0 | 24.7 | 22.0 |
| Gonzales | 485 | 2 418 | 4 669 | 10.9 | 64.3 | 12.8 | 36.2 | 9 399 | 19 098 | 38 623 | 0.8 | 2.1 | 36 408 | 23.4 | 37.1 | 38.4 |
| Gray | 526 | 3 916 | 4 910 | 8.7 | 55.5 | 12.9 | 34.0 | 8 766 | 21 746 | 42 845 | 1.2 | 2.1 | 41 488 | 14.6 | 19.4 | 19.0 |
| Grayson | 272 | 3 166 | 29 281 | 13.2 | 47.7 | 19.8 | 188.2 | 8 947 | 23 818 | 46 993 | -6.4 | 2.5 | 44 080 | 16.5 | 23.7 | 22.3 |
| Gregg | 427 | 4 045 | 31 192 | 13.0 | 46.3 | 20.5 | 220.3 | 9 305 | 23 734 | 44 608 | -5.6 | 2.9 | 43 356 | 17.7 | 25.9 | 22.9 |
| Grimes | 335 | 2 146 | 5 771 | 6.4 | 63.3 | 11.0 | 40.3 | 9 556 | 19 238 | 40 509 | -7.1 | 1.7 | 41 981 | 19.1 | 25.7 | 23.7 |

1. Data for serious crimes have not been adjusted for underreporting; this may affect comparability between geographic areas and over time.   2. Per 100,000 population estimated by the FBI.   3. All persons 3 years old and over enrolled in nursery school through college.   4. Persons 25 years old and over.   5. Elementary and secondary education expenditures.   6. Based on population estimated by the American Community Survey, 2007–2011.

# Table B. States and Counties — Personal Income

| STATE County | Personal income, 2011 | | | | | | | | Transfer payments (mil dol) | | | | | |
|---|---|---|---|---|---|---|---|---|---|---|---|---|---|---|
| | | | Per capita[1] | | | | | | | Government payments to individuals | | | | |
| | Total (mil dol) | Percent change, 2010–2011 | Dollars | Rank | Wages and salaries[2] (mil dol) | Proprietors' income (mil dol) | Dividends, interest, and rent (mil dol) | Total | Total | Social Security | Medical payments | Income mainte-nance | Unemploy-ment insurance |
| | 62 | 63 | 64 | 65 | 66 | 67 | 68 | 69 | 70 | 71 | 72 | 73 | 74 |

| STATE County | 62 | 63 | 64 | 65 | 66 | 67 | 68 | 69 | 70 | 71 | 72 | 73 | 74 |
|---|---|---|---|---|---|---|---|---|---|---|---|---|---|
| TEXAS—Cont'd | | | | | | | | | | | | | |
| Caldwell | 983 | 2.7 | 25 577 | 2 923 | 325 | 71 | 132 | 267 | 259 | 75 | 126 | 34 | 8 |
| Calhoun | 695 | 5.1 | 32 413 | 1 800 | 748 | 70 | 92 | 169 | 164 | 54 | 76 | 20 | 5 |
| Callahan | 452 | 5.1 | 33 412 | 1 624 | 92 | 32 | 66 | 114 | 111 | 39 | 51 | 11 | 2 |
| Cameron | 9 623 | 4.6 | 23 236 | 3 049 | 5 112 | 790 | 1 027 | 3 180 | 3 086 | 545 | 1 482 | 765 | 109 |
| Camp | 420 | 3.9 | 33 828 | 1 544 | 163 | 48 | 65 | 115 | 112 | 36 | 54 | 15 | 3 |
| Carson | 243 | -2.0 | 38 854 | 872 | 444 | 25 | 28 | 41 | 39 | 16 | 18 | 2 | 1 |
| Cass | 995 | 3.7 | 32 899 | 1 725 | 349 | 106 | 145 | 321 | 315 | 97 | 158 | 33 | 9 |
| Castro | 392 | 22.9 | 48 285 | 260 | 106 | 193 | 28 | 57 | 55 | 15 | 29 | 8 | 1 |
| Chambers | 1 741 | 7.9 | 48 969 | 233 | 667 | 48 | 179 | 212 | 204 | 76 | 85 | 19 | 9 |
| Cherokee | 1 479 | 4.8 | 28 923 | 2 463 | 632 | 143 | 205 | 447 | 436 | 127 | 220 | 52 | 11 |
| Childress | 159 | -5.9 | 22 754 | 3 065 | 95 | 9 | 25 | 55 | 53 | 16 | 27 | 6 | 1 |
| Clay | 470 | 6.1 | 43 795 | 452 | 69 | 93 | 57 | 81 | 79 | 32 | 32 | 6 | 2 |
| Cochran | 104 | -19.4 | 33 329 | 1 647 | 37 | 17 | 18 | 29 | 28 | 7 | 15 | 4 | 1 |
| Coke | 107 | 7.7 | 32 525 | 1 789 | 28 | 11 | 19 | 33 | 32 | 12 | 17 | 2 | 1 |
| Coleman | 289 | 4.4 | 33 007 | 1 707 | 84 | 35 | 50 | 106 | 105 | 30 | 59 | 9 | 2 |
| Collin | 42 576 | 8.8 | 52 419 | 155 | 20 911 | 4 956 | 5 512 | 3 013 | 2 833 | 1 181 | 1 010 | 267 | 170 |
| Collingsworth | 98 | -1.1 | 31 836 | 1 921 | 38 | 6 | 21 | 28 | 28 | 8 | 16 | 3 | 0 |
| Colorado | 812 | 6.4 | 39 030 | 854 | 315 | 90 | 160 | 185 | 181 | 63 | 88 | 18 | 4 |
| Comal | 4 984 | 8.5 | 44 519 | 419 | 1 902 | 405 | 942 | 804 | 779 | 321 | 309 | 57 | 22 |
| Comanche | 507 | 7.0 | 36 476 | 1 140 | 152 | 96 | 98 | 139 | 136 | 43 | 70 | 13 | 3 |
| Concho | 92 | 1.8 | 22 631 | 3 069 | 40 | 6 | 15 | 29 | 28 | 8 | 16 | 2 | 1 |
| Cooke | 1 757 | 10.4 | 45 765 | 349 | 882 | 266 | 289 | 297 | 288 | 101 | 123 | 27 | 7 |
| Coryell | 2 826 | 6.8 | 36 932 | 1 082 | 723 | 106 | 267 | 419 | 406 | 101 | 147 | 54 | 18 |
| Cottle | 54 | -0.1 | 35 709 | 1 261 | 20 | 4 | 11 | 17 | 17 | 6 | 9 | 2 | 0 |
| Crane | 159 | 15.5 | 36 362 | 1 156 | 114 | 12 | 12 | 27 | 26 | 9 | 13 | 3 | 1 |
| Crockett | 134 | 15.6 | 35 950 | 1 218 | 64 | 14 | 25 | 25 | 24 | 8 | 12 | 3 | 1 |
| Crosby | 191 | -18.0 | 31 281 | 2 052 | 70 | -2 | 27 | 70 | 69 | 15 | 42 | 8 | 2 |
| Culberson | 73 | 4.1 | 30 522 | 2 194 | 45 | 6 | 8 | 21 | 21 | 5 | 11 | 4 | 0 |
| Dallam | 299 | 8.2 | 43 556 | 464 | 190 | 135 | 26 | 49 | 47 | 11 | 26 | 5 | 1 |
| Dallas | 109 692 | 4.9 | 45 402 | 372 | 107 035 | 23 507 | 15 882 | 13 764 | 13 229 | 3 766 | 5 801 | 2 316 | 555 |
| Dawson | 366 | -13.6 | 26 625 | 2 808 | 193 | 13 | 66 | 126 | 123 | 29 | 73 | 14 | 3 |
| Deaf Smith | 703 | 12.8 | 35 880 | 1 229 | 326 | 198 | 85 | 140 | 135 | 33 | 74 | 22 | 3 |
| Delta | 163 | 10.6 | 31 187 | 2 067 | 47 | 13 | 20 | 52 | 51 | 16 | 26 | 5 | 1 |
| Denton | 29 084 | 7.6 | 42 371 | 554 | 9 780 | 1 587 | 3 420 | 2 746 | 2 594 | 951 | 958 | 250 | 145 |
| DeWitt | 703 | 8.3 | 34 727 | 1 414 | 314 | 77 | 132 | 193 | 189 | 54 | 104 | 20 | 4 |
| Dickens | 65 | -4.5 | 27 118 | 2 751 | 25 | 3 | 9 | 27 | 26 | 7 | 16 | 2 | 1 |
| Dimmit | 348 | 25.5 | 34 379 | 1 455 | 230 | 24 | 32 | 97 | 95 | 18 | 52 | 19 | 2 |
| Donley | 134 | 8.3 | 36 670 | 1 115 | 37 | 26 | 17 | 35 | 34 | 11 | 15 | 3 | 1 |
| Duval | 411 | 12.9 | 35 227 | 1 335 | 172 | 27 | 33 | 144 | 141 | 25 | 90 | 18 | 3 |
| Eastland | 960 | 14.3 | 51 520 | 175 | 346 | 303 | 149 | 199 | 195 | 56 | 98 | 17 | 4 |
| Ector | 5 378 | 14.8 | 38 385 | 926 | 4 014 | 439 | 547 | 922 | 891 | 244 | 433 | 139 | 26 |
| Edwards | 66 | 19.7 | 33 662 | 1 574 | 20 | 14 | 14 | 18 | 18 | 6 | 8 | 2 | 0 |
| Ellis | 5 329 | 6.1 | 34 885 | 1 388 | 1 926 | 295 | 574 | 895 | 861 | 299 | 368 | 107 | 34 |
| El Paso | 24 696 | 7.2 | 30 088 | 2 273 | 15 584 | 2 931 | 2 650 | 5 695 | 5 519 | 1 130 | 2 392 | 1 164 | 210 |
| Erath | 1 207 | 6.9 | 31 532 | 1 995 | 598 | 137 | 182 | 274 | 265 | 74 | 127 | 24 | 7 |
| Falls | 504 | 4.7 | 28 073 | 2 607 | 160 | 54 | 61 | 158 | 154 | 40 | 81 | 19 | 4 |
| Fannin | 1 009 | 4.7 | 29 708 | 2 336 | 314 | 92 | 142 | 299 | 292 | 95 | 141 | 26 | 8 |
| Fayette | 989 | 7.2 | 39 970 | 748 | 405 | 71 | 263 | 221 | 216 | 80 | 107 | 14 | 4 |
| Fisher | 133 | -3.7 | 34 088 | 1 498 | 40 | 15 | 21 | 39 | 38 | 12 | 20 | 3 | 1 |
| Floyd | 228 | -4.6 | 35 673 | 1 270 | 77 | 48 | 34 | 61 | 59 | 16 | 32 | 8 | 1 |
| Foard | 45 | 16.2 | 33 685 | 1 566 | 12 | 6 | 8 | 17 | 16 | 5 | 10 | 1 | 0 |
| Fort Bend | 29 465 | 8.2 | 48 545 | 252 | 8 626 | 2 521 | 3 425 | 2 278 | 2 144 | 787 | 776 | 318 | 123 |
| Franklin | 350 | 2.0 | 33 141 | 1 684 | 130 | 58 | 60 | 86 | 83 | 32 | 37 | 8 | 2 |
| Freestone | 621 | 4.6 | 31 573 | 1 982 | 316 | 72 | 108 | 143 | 139 | 48 | 61 | 14 | 4 |
| Frio | 450 | 9.7 | 25 836 | 2 895 | 225 | 25 | 45 | 133 | 130 | 25 | 73 | 23 | 3 |
| Gaines | 521 | 0.1 | 28 934 | 2 462 | 296 | 66 | 63 | 98 | 94 | 23 | 54 | 12 | 2 |
| Galveston | 12 849 | 4.8 | 43 444 | 475 | 5 702 | 771 | 1 867 | 2 011 | 1 943 | 633 | 901 | 217 | 77 |
| Garza | 192 | -1.5 | 29 245 | 2 419 | 85 | 55 | 28 | 44 | 42 | 10 | 25 | 4 | 1 |
| Gillespie | 1 194 | 6.4 | 47 550 | 280 | 387 | 115 | 473 | 235 | 230 | 98 | 105 | 13 | 4 |
| Glasscock | 40 | -27.7 | 32 256 | 1 834 | 18 | -4 | 13 | 6 | 6 | 3 | 2 | 1 | 0 |
| Goliad | 215 | 3.9 | 29 735 | 2 332 | 67 | 8 | 46 | 63 | 62 | 20 | 31 | 6 | 1 |
| Gonzales | 622 | 1.8 | 31 270 | 2 058 | 272 | 73 | 99 | 160 | 156 | 45 | 79 | 22 | 3 |
| Gray | 885 | 6.9 | 38 903 | 861 | 494 | 150 | 112 | 185 | 180 | 59 | 94 | 15 | 5 |
| Grayson | 4 056 | 5.3 | 33 404 | 1 626 | 2 112 | 251 | 641 | 1 028 | 1 001 | 337 | 458 | 95 | 28 |
| Gregg | 5 320 | 7.1 | 43 222 | 493 | 4 255 | 950 | 796 | 1 043 | 1 015 | 300 | 510 | 113 | 26 |
| Grimes | 845 | 8.7 | 31 418 | 2 012 | 436 | 74 | 134 | 186 | 180 | 62 | 80 | 23 | 5 |

1. Based on the resident population estimated as of July 1 of the year shown.   2. Includes supplements to wages and salaries.

| STATE County | Earnings, 2011 Total (mil dol) | Farm | Goods-related[1] Total | Manu-facturing | Service-related and health — Information and professional and technical services | Retail trade | Finance, insurance, and real estate | Health care and social services | Government | Social Security beneficiaries, December 2011 Number | Rate[2] | Supplemental Security Income recipients, December 2011 | Housing units, 2010 Total | Percent change, 2000–2010 |
|---|---|---|---|---|---|---|---|---|---|---|---|---|---|---|
| | 75 | 76 | 77 | 78 | 79 | 80 | 81 | 82 | 83 | 84 | 85 | 86 | 87 | 88 |
| TEXAS—Cont'd | | | | | | | | | | | | | | |
| Caldwell | 396 | 1.0 | 19.5 | 6.1 | 3.1 | 9.3 | 5.2 | 13.3 | 22.1 | 6 320 | 164 | 985 | 13 759 | 15.6 |
| Calhoun | 818 | 1.9 | 67.4 | 45.0 | D | 4.6 | 2.2 | 2.1 | 9.1 | 4 180 | 195 | 531 | 11 410 | 11.4 |
| Callahan | 125 | 3.6 | 27.5 | 5.5 | D | 9.7 | 5.9 | D | 26.7 | 3 185 | 236 | 338 | 6 549 | 10.5 |
| Cameron | 5 902 | 1.0 | 8.9 | 5.2 | 4.2 | 8.8 | 4.4 | 20.7 | 29.6 | 56 485 | 136 | 22 317 | 141 924 | 18.6 |
| Camp | 211 | 4.8 | 11.1 | 3.0 | D | 9.0 | 7.3 | D | 14.1 | 2 810 | 226 | 452 | 5 656 | 8.2 |
| Carson | 469 | 2.1 | D | D | D | 1.5 | 0.6 | D | 11.7 | 1 215 | 194 | 64 | 2 784 | -1.1 |
| Cass | 455 | 3.3 | 30.5 | 22.5 | 2.5 | 8.1 | 5.7 | D | 19.8 | 7 990 | 264 | 1 118 | 14 379 | 3.5 |
| Castro | 298 | 68.3 | D | 0.9 | 1.2 | 2.1 | 1.3 | 3.5 | 8.7 | 1 270 | 156 | 155 | 3 166 | -1.0 |
| Chambers | 716 | 1.3 | 41.6 | 26.6 | D | 4.1 | 6.5 | D | 14.5 | 5 450 | 153 | 550 | 13 291 | 28.6 |
| Cherokee | 775 | 5.7 | 21.6 | 13.0 | 3.8 | 7.0 | 5.4 | 9.0 | 25.3 | 10 320 | 202 | 1 601 | 20 859 | 8.8 |
| Childress | 104 | -0.7 | D | 0.5 | 3.6 | 10.0 | 4.7 | 6.5 | 51.8 | 1 345 | 193 | 180 | 2 883 | -5.8 |
| Clay | 162 | 7.2 | 27.5 | 4.5 | D | 7.4 | 6.4 | D | 15.8 | 2 495 | 233 | 192 | 5 150 | 3.2 |
| Cochran | 54 | 26.4 | D | 0.0 | D | 4.5 | D | 4.9 | 30.9 | 640 | 206 | 122 | 1 360 | -14.3 |
| Coke | 40 | 12.1 | 17.6 | 2.6 | D | 5.6 | D | 2.4 | 35.4 | 935 | 283 | 65 | 2 667 | -6.2 |
| Coleman | 119 | 4.7 | 15.5 | 2.1 | D | 9.1 | 7.5 | D | 28.2 | 2 510 | 286 | 294 | 5 543 | 5.6 |
| Collin | 25 867 | 0.1 | 16.1 | 8.6 | 20.7 | 6.9 | 11.6 | 9.8 | 9.2 | 79 370 | 98 | 6 920 | 300 960 | 54.4 |
| Collingsworth | 44 | 7.8 | D | D | D | 3.9 | 5.7 | D | 25.1 | 655 | 212 | 88 | 1 616 | -6.2 |
| Colorado | 405 | 3.7 | 32.0 | 17.7 | 3.0 | 7.1 | 7.2 | D | 12.7 | 4 835 | 232 | 519 | 10 527 | 11.7 |
| Comal | 2 306 | 0.2 | 21.1 | 7.8 | 5.9 | 10.2 | 5.5 | 10.2 | 13.4 | 23 500 | 210 | 1 364 | 47 108 | 44.0 |
| Comanche | 248 | 19.0 | D | 2.8 | 7.9 | 8.3 | 4.5 | 5.3 | 18.2 | 3 610 | 260 | 398 | 7 223 | 1.7 |
| Concho | 46 | 4.4 | D | D | D | 3.5 | D | 9.3 | 25.0 | 680 | 167 | 71 | 1 637 | 10.0 |
| Cooke | 1 147 | 1.2 | 49.1 | 16.1 | D | 5.9 | 4.3 | 3.5 | 12.7 | 7 595 | 198 | 677 | 16 606 | 10.3 |
| Coryell | 828 | 0.4 | D | 1.6 | 13.7 | 6.4 | 5.3 | D | 37.1 | 8 985 | 117 | 1 122 | 25 178 | 15.6 |
| Cottle | 24 | 15.0 | D | D | D | 8.4 | D | 4.2 | 26.6 | 485 | 324 | 57 | 968 | -11.0 |
| Crane | 126 | 0.6 | D | D | D | 3.5 | D | 3.9 | 15.0 | 680 | 155 | 105 | 1 632 | 2.3 |
| Crockett | 78 | 9.8 | D | D | D | 5.5 | 3.7 | 0.9 | 24.1 | 675 | 181 | 59 | 1 866 | -8.9 |
| Crosby | 68 | -7.6 | 6.6 | 1.5 | D | 25.8 | D | D | 31.7 | 1 310 | 215 | 205 | 2 902 | -9.4 |
| Culberson | 51 | 11.3 | D | 0.3 | D | 10.7 | D | D | 39.3 | 495 | 208 | 123 | 1 137 | -13.9 |
| Dallam | 325 | 21.2 | D | 8.6 | 4.4 | 4.0 | 11.0 | 1.8 | 8.2 | 965 | 141 | 107 | 2 827 | 4.8 |
| Dallas | 130 542 | 0.0 | 17.5 | 8.6 | 16.8 | 4.7 | 14.0 | 9.5 | 9.2 | 283 560 | 117 | 59 614 | 943 257 | 10.4 |
| Dawson | 206 | -4.5 | 18.2 | 2.2 | 2.6 | 13.7 | 3.8 | D | 35.1 | 2 465 | 179 | 474 | 5 220 | -5.1 |
| Deaf Smith | 525 | 32.2 | D | 12.8 | 3.2 | 5.8 | 2.8 | 2.0 | 12.3 | 2 800 | 143 | 465 | 7 077 | 2.4 |
| Delta | 60 | 11.5 | D | D | D | 2.0 | 2.8 | 18.5 | 23.6 | 1 370 | 263 | 191 | 2 458 | 2.0 |
| Denton | 11 366 | 0.3 | 17.1 | 9.0 | 11.8 | 8.1 | 7.5 | 10.2 | 17.8 | 65 810 | 96 | 5 798 | 256 139 | 52.4 |
| DeWitt | 391 | 1.6 | 27.6 | 13.8 | 4.5 | 7.1 | 10.5 | D | 25.4 | 4 535 | 224 | 647 | 9 176 | 4.8 |
| Dickens | 29 | 8.6 | D | D | D | 5.8 | D | 1.8 | 27.6 | 600 | 250 | 56 | 1 282 | -6.3 |
| Dimmit | 254 | 3.7 | 36.8 | 0.5 | D | 4.7 | 1.6 | D | 29.5 | 1 925 | 190 | 709 | 4 350 | 5.8 |
| Donley | 63 | 30.7 | 7.3 | 4.2 | D | 6.4 | 3.7 | 6.1 | 27.2 | 905 | 248 | 75 | 2 142 | -9.9 |
| Duval | 199 | 3.2 | D | D | D | 3.0 | 2.8 | 3.9 | 32.3 | 2 550 | 219 | 728 | 5 523 | -0.4 |
| Eastland | 649 | 0.0 | 55.0 | 5.3 | 2.0 | 4.2 | D | D | 11.5 | 4 655 | 250 | 600 | 10 258 | 7.4 |
| Ector | 4 452 | 0.0 | 38.7 | 8.2 | 4.9 | 6.1 | 4.6 | 6.6 | 11.8 | 19 435 | 139 | 3 809 | 53 027 | 7.1 |
| Edwards | 35 | 25.9 | D | 0.0 | D | 10.3 | D | 2.8 | 29.7 | 505 | 257 | 88 | 1 606 | 32.0 |
| Ellis | 2 220 | 0.2 | 34.0 | 25.5 | 3.8 | 8.1 | 4.0 | 7.2 | 16.3 | 22 165 | 145 | 2 539 | 54 365 | 39.1 |
| El Paso | 18 515 | 0.2 | 13.3 | 6.5 | 4.8 | 6.9 | 6.0 | 9.6 | 38.7 | 112 490 | 137 | 29 302 | 270 307 | 20.4 |
| Erath | 735 | 9.6 | 18.5 | 11.1 | D | 7.6 | 4.7 | 9.9 | 20.7 | 5 945 | 155 | 623 | 16 987 | 17.8 |
| Falls | 215 | 6.3 | D | 3.6 | D | 8.9 | 2.8 | 9.0 | 38.1 | 3 515 | 196 | 809 | 7 724 | 0.9 |
| Fannin | 406 | 2.5 | 14.0 | 5.6 | 3.0 | 9.1 | 4.3 | D | 35.6 | 7 550 | 222 | 878 | 14 191 | 10.1 |
| Fayette | 476 | 1.0 | 19.5 | 8.1 | 5.3 | 9.6 | 8.3 | 9.8 | 20.4 | 6 135 | 248 | 439 | 13 868 | 24.8 |
| Fisher | 56 | 22.1 | D | D | D | 3.4 | D | 3.6 | 27.3 | 1 000 | 255 | 105 | 2 212 | -2.9 |
| Floyd | 125 | 34.0 | D | 2.7 | D | 4.6 | D | 3.5 | 22.0 | 1 350 | 211 | 175 | 3 004 | -6.7 |
| Foard | 18 | 26.2 | D | D | D | 5.1 | D | D | 24.2 | 400 | 298 | 38 | 789 | -7.2 |
| Fort Bend | 11 148 | 0.3 | 31.5 | 12.7 | 8.9 | 7.0 | 6.8 | 8.7 | 11.8 | 56 675 | 93 | 9 678 | 197 030 | 69.9 |
| Franklin | 188 | 3.8 | D | D | D | 5.5 | 6.2 | 21.5 | 11.2 | 2 450 | 232 | 237 | 5 770 | 12.4 |
| Freestone | 388 | -0.6 | 31.6 | 2.2 | 3.8 | 8.5 | 4.5 | D | 18.8 | 3 800 | 193 | 410 | 9 265 | 13.9 |
| Frio | 249 | 5.2 | 11.5 | 0.7 | 3.3 | 6.5 | 3.4 | D | 28.1 | 2 590 | 149 | 777 | 5 846 | 3.3 |
| Gaines | 362 | 0.8 | 34.1 | 1.3 | 1.7 | 8.3 | 3.0 | 1.0 | 17.7 | 1 970 | 109 | 339 | 6 301 | 16.5 |
| Galveston | 6 474 | 0.0 | 26.0 | 16.5 | 6.4 | 6.7 | 7.3 | 7.1 | 27.2 | 45 780 | 155 | 6 292 | 132 492 | 18.6 |
| Garza | 140 | -3.4 | 42.8 | 3.6 | D | 3.8 | D | 1.9 | 14.6 | 875 | 133 | 109 | 2 237 | 16.0 |
| Gillespie | 502 | 2.7 | 21.8 | 7.4 | D | 10.9 | 7.0 | 18.7 | 12.1 | 7 350 | 293 | 276 | 12 778 | 29.0 |
| Glasscock | 14 | -34.8 | D | 0.0 | D | D | D | D | 34.8 | 200 | 160 | 0 | 580 | -12.1 |
| Goliad | 75 | -0.3 | D | D | D | 6.9 | D | D | 29.4 | 1 665 | 230 | 209 | 3 710 | 8.3 |
| Gonzales | 345 | 14.8 | 21.5 | 13.0 | 3.4 | 7.0 | 3.2 | D | 19.7 | 3 900 | 196 | 597 | 8 794 | 7.3 |
| Gray | 644 | 4.9 | 48.5 | 21.3 | 2.9 | 6.0 | 2.8 | 5.5 | 11.7 | 4 540 | 200 | 413 | 10 158 | -3.9 |
| Grayson | 2 363 | 0.7 | 27.9 | 19.8 | 4.2 | 8.7 | 6.7 | 17.8 | 14.2 | 25 705 | 212 | 2 910 | 53 727 | 11.2 |
| Gregg | 5 204 | 0.0 | 37.3 | 14.3 | 7.4 | 8.0 | 4.2 | 12.1 | 7.5 | 23 140 | 188 | 4 005 | 49 514 | 6.8 |
| Grimes | 510 | 1.6 | 37.6 | 30.7 | 2.6 | 5.1 | 4.4 | D | 20.5 | 4 960 | 184 | 743 | 10 917 | 15.0 |

1. Includes mining, construction, and manufacturing.  2. Per 1,000 resident population enumerated in the 2010 census.

# Table B. States and Counties — Housing, Labor Force, and Employment

| STATE County | Housing units, 2007–2011 | | | | | | | | Civilian labor force, 2012 | | Unemployment | | Civilian employment,[6] 2007–2011 | | |
|---|---|---|---|---|---|---|---|---|---|---|---|---|---|---|---|
| | Occupied units | | | | | | | | | | | | Percent | | |
| | Owner-occupied | | | | Renter-occupied | | | | | | | | | | |
| | | | | Median owner cost as a percent of income | | | | | | | | | | | Construction, production, and maintenance occupations |
| | Total | Percent | Median value[1] | With a mortgage | Without a mortgage[2] | Median rent[3] | Median rent as a percent of income | Substandard units[4] (percent) | Total | Percent change, 2011–2012 | Total | Rate[5] | Total | Management, business, science and arts | |
| | 89 | 90 | 91 | 92 | 93 | 94 | 95 | 96 | 97 | 98 | 99 | 100 | 101 | 102 | 103 |
| TEXAS—Cont'd | | | | | | | | | | | | | | | |
| Caldwell | 11 464 | 66.4 | 103 400 | 23.6 | 12.9 | 716 | 28.7 | 5.9 | 16 604 | 1.2 | 1 167 | 7.0 | 15 199 | 27.4 | 26.5 |
| Calhoun | 7 936 | 73.2 | 90 800 | 22.9 | 11.8 | 670 | 25.5 | 5.8 | 10 284 | -0.5 | 721 | 7.0 | 8 847 | 26.5 | 34.6 |
| Callahan | 5 133 | 83.7 | 75 900 | 20.4 | 12.3 | 680 | 23.3 | 4.2 | 6 976 | -0.6 | 353 | 5.1 | 5 825 | 27.9 | 29.9 |
| Cameron | 114 881 | 68.3 | 76 000 | 26.3 | 13.7 | 614 | 32.2 | 11.8 | 162 955 | -0.2 | 17 070 | 10.5 | 140 754 | 26.9 | 22.8 |
| Camp | 4 490 | 67.8 | 101 100 | 25.6 | 10.5 | 585 | 25.4 | 9.8 | 5 703 | -3.2 | 440 | 7.7 | 4 985 | 28.6 | 36.6 |
| Carson | 2 347 | 88.0 | 87 000 | 18.1 | 10.8 | 580 | 14.3 | 2.6 | 3 275 | -0.8 | 147 | 4.5 | 2 789 | 33.0 | 35.5 |
| Cass | 12 086 | 70.0 | 71 600 | 21.6 | 10.9 | 491 | 27.3 | 4.2 | 13 017 | -3.3 | 1 183 | 9.1 | 11 880 | 23.8 | 33.2 |
| Castro | 2 609 | 75.2 | 68 400 | 23.8 | 12.8 | 567 | 25.0 | 6.5 | 3 508 | -2.8 | 178 | 5.1 | 3 427 | 28.1 | 36.7 |
| Chambers | 11 482 | 86.5 | 148 200 | 20.8 | 11.8 | 774 | 22.0 | 3.6 | 17 777 | 1.8 | 1 369 | 7.7 | 15 076 | 33.7 | 32.8 |
| Cherokee | 16 989 | 73.0 | 71 000 | 22.2 | 12.9 | 593 | 29.7 | 5.1 | 21 328 | -1.2 | 1 650 | 7.7 | 19 731 | 23.2 | 34.0 |
| Childress | 2 088 | 74.3 | 56 000 | 15.7 | 12.5 | 588 | 29.8 | 1.1 | 3 056 | -4.1 | 161 | 5.3 | 2 837 | 28.8 | 18.9 |
| Clay | 4 344 | 85.4 | 79 900 | 21.1 | 11.6 | 618 | 21.4 | 3.8 | 5 829 | -1.3 | 297 | 5.1 | 5 033 | 34.1 | 26.6 |
| Cochran | 1 090 | 78.8 | 37 100 | 18.3 | 9.9 | 558 | 20.4 | 7.2 | 1 361 | -2.5 | 105 | 7.7 | 1 219 | 23.3 | 46.1 |
| Coke | 1 378 | 71.6 | 63 800 | 21.7 | 10.4 | 535 | 26.3 | 3.6 | 1 242 | -3.3 | 77 | 6.2 | 1 400 | 35.6 | 25.1 |
| Coleman | 3 568 | 67.2 | 63 400 | 25.8 | 14.9 | 540 | 27.9 | 0.7 | 4 189 | -2.1 | 246 | 5.9 | 3 115 | 30.4 | 32.8 |
| Collin | 276 234 | 70.3 | 202 000 | 22.8 | 11.7 | 996 | 27.3 | 2.4 | 447 064 | 1.3 | 27 150 | 6.1 | 394 850 | 50.9 | 11.2 |
| Collingsworth | 1 207 | 73.7 | 57 200 | 20.7 | 11.2 | 449 | 19.0 | 4.6 | 1 364 | -4.1 | 64 | 4.7 | 1 255 | 33.7 | 30.8 |
| Colorado | 8 069 | 78.9 | 98 200 | 22.0 | 13.0 | 576 | 22.7 | 3.6 | 11 524 | 1.4 | 653 | 5.7 | 9 008 | 28.9 | 34.4 |
| Comal | 40 119 | 75.6 | 196 300 | 22.2 | 11.0 | 888 | 28.3 | 4.1 | 56 249 | 0.8 | 3 415 | 6.1 | 49 467 | 37.5 | 21.6 |
| Comanche | 5 233 | 78.4 | 84 000 | 24.0 | 13.0 | 526 | 25.3 | 6.2 | 6 450 | -3.8 | 372 | 5.8 | 5 251 | 29.1 | 33.6 |
| Concho | 965 | 80.6 | 66 900 | 15.9 | 12.9 | 394 | 21.2 | 6.1 | 1 316 | -2.9 | 93 | 7.1 | 1 320 | 29.5 | 29.2 |
| Cooke | 14 442 | 69.2 | 111 300 | 21.7 | 13.0 | 751 | 28.0 | 5.4 | 23 852 | 2.2 | 1 047 | 4.4 | 18 204 | 26.9 | 32.9 |
| Coryell | 20 134 | 58.9 | 96 600 | 22.1 | 10.8 | 845 | 26.7 | 3.1 | 24 773 | -0.1 | 2 140 | 8.6 | 23 964 | 29.6 | 23.8 |
| Cottle | 638 | 82.1 | 40 900 | 22.3 | 11.5 | 277 | 23.8 | 2.8 | 791 | 2.7 | 48 | 6.1 | 702 | 23.5 | 26.5 |
| Crane | 1 442 | 77.6 | 56 600 | 17.6 | 9.9 | 583 | 35.0 | 5.8 | 1 933 | 7.2 | 102 | 5.3 | 1 713 | 22.7 | 37.5 |
| Crockett | 1 301 | 55.8 | 53 900 | 20.1 | 9.9 | 566 | 13.2 | 7.1 | 2 236 | 2.8 | 89 | 4.0 | 1 733 | 12.5 | 48.8 |
| Crosby | 2 115 | 70.0 | 51 700 | 21.1 | 13.1 | 545 | 28.7 | 6.6 | 2 484 | -2.4 | 170 | 6.8 | 2 478 | 26.5 | 30.4 |
| Culberson | 852 | 71.2 | 43 700 | 22.7 | 17.2 | 657 | 31.7 | 4.6 | 1 686 | -0.8 | 59 | 3.5 | 1 026 | 28.4 | 15.4 |
| Dallam | 2 172 | 64.0 | 69 800 | 21.9 | 9.9 | 698 | 22.6 | 5.6 | 3 799 | -1.6 | 148 | 3.9 | 3 445 | 22.0 | 40.6 |
| Dallas | 840 663 | 54.2 | 129 300 | 25.3 | 13.3 | 855 | 29.6 | 6.6 | 1 184 434 | 1.0 | 85 157 | 7.2 | 1 114 379 | 32.4 | 24.9 |
| Dawson | 4 373 | 74.2 | 48 100 | 21.0 | 12.1 | 472 | 20.5 | 3.7 | 5 334 | -3.4 | 370 | 6.9 | 4 700 | 24.7 | 29.7 |
| Deaf Smith | 6 196 | 65.0 | 78 100 | 22.3 | 12.2 | 660 | 24.8 | 7.8 | 9 066 | -3.2 | 440 | 4.9 | 8 045 | 23.9 | 39.6 |
| Delta | 2 023 | 81.5 | 61 400 | 22.1 | 11.9 | 668 | 42.6 | 1.1 | 2 284 | 0.8 | 174 | 7.6 | 2 130 | 22.6 | 35.3 |
| Denton | 231 355 | 66.2 | 180 400 | 22.9 | 12.1 | 904 | 28.3 | 2.1 | 383 908 | 1.3 | 22 958 | 6.0 | 343 098 | 42.5 | 15.6 |
| DeWitt | 7 069 | 76.2 | 73 100 | 20.1 | 10.3 | 573 | 24.2 | 4.8 | 10 022 | 2.2 | 499 | 5.0 | 8 286 | 24.5 | 37.2 |
| Dickens | 838 | 81.0 | 46 900 | 17.5 | 13.8 | 447 | 19.5 | 1.9 | 974 | -6.8 | 93 | 9.5 | 829 | 30.6 | 26.5 |
| Dimmit | 3 451 | 70.6 | 47 700 | 21.6 | 14.3 | 522 | 25.7 | 5.6 | 6 552 | 16.4 | 333 | 5.1 | 3 740 | 22.4 | 31.5 |
| Donley | 1 318 | 70.0 | 58 600 | 19.0 | 11.7 | 542 | 22.9 | 4.6 | 1 802 | -8.1 | 100 | 5.5 | 1 512 | 38.8 | 25.1 |
| Duval | 3 928 | 72.6 | 54 900 | 23.1 | 13.7 | 572 | 19.5 | 7.2 | 5 903 | 4.8 | 393 | 6.7 | 4 665 | 19.3 | 35.2 |
| Eastland | 7 105 | 74.3 | 66 900 | 20.4 | 13.2 | 520 | 24.1 | 6.4 | 9 074 | -2.0 | 553 | 6.1 | 7 207 | 28.3 | 30.1 |
| Ector | 48 318 | 66.9 | 83 100 | 19.0 | 10.7 | 686 | 25.0 | 6.3 | 83 462 | 6.2 | 3 515 | 4.2 | 62 748 | 22.4 | 33.8 |
| Edwards | 842 | 83.5 | 62 800 | 18.5 | 11.0 | 554 | 22.9 | 5.3 | 878 | -9.0 | 60 | 6.8 | 969 | 33.7 | 29.0 |
| Ellis | 49 233 | 76.2 | 136 600 | 22.5 | 12.2 | 876 | 30.4 | 4.6 | 75 030 | 0.9 | 5 127 | 6.8 | 70 555 | 31.8 | 26.1 |
| El Paso | 247 305 | 63.6 | 108 000 | 24.1 | 11.7 | 660 | 31.0 | 7.6 | 324 613 | -0.5 | 30 309 | 9.3 | 308 988 | 28.9 | 23.4 |
| Erath | 14 075 | 60.0 | 116 300 | 21.2 | 12.2 | 639 | 32.6 | 3.9 | 18 960 | -2.5 | 1 051 | 5.5 | 18 517 | 30.0 | 30.4 |
| Falls | 5 647 | 70.2 | 61 200 | 23.2 | 13.8 | 601 | 29.1 | 4.9 | 6 643 | -2.6 | 561 | 8.4 | 6 539 | 25.6 | 27.8 |
| Fannin | 11 817 | 73.9 | 84 800 | 22.2 | 13.3 | 672 | 29.6 | 4.1 | 13 490 | -2.2 | 1 155 | 8.6 | 13 648 | 28.2 | 32.7 |
| Fayette | 10 517 | 77.1 | 133 400 | 23.0 | 11.5 | 639 | 23.9 | 3.5 | 12 773 | 0.1 | 610 | 4.8 | 11 804 | 27.4 | 33.4 |
| Fisher | 1 676 | 74.8 | 54 500 | 19.5 | 12.7 | 479 | 24.4 | 3.9 | 1 997 | -1.6 | 103 | 5.2 | 1 766 | 31.1 | 34.3 |
| Floyd | 2 571 | 69.3 | 61 800 | 19.9 | 11.1 | 498 | 32.3 | 8.4 | 2 964 | -3.5 | 202 | 6.8 | 2 945 | 30.6 | 31.9 |
| Foard | 557 | 65.2 | 35 300 | 23.6 | 14.0 | 376 | 26.2 | 1.6 | 667 | -7.1 | 38 | 5.7 | 565 | 33.1 | 28.0 |
| Fort Bend | 177 980 | 80.0 | 175 100 | 23.4 | 12.0 | 1 097 | 27.4 | 3.5 | 310 188 | 1.9 | 18 912 | 6.1 | 271 123 | 46.6 | 14.8 |
| Franklin | 3 804 | 80.9 | 103 100 | 22.3 | 12.5 | 711 | 28.9 | 5.2 | 5 211 | -2.8 | 338 | 6.5 | 4 376 | 29.6 | 25.3 |
| Freestone | 6 972 | 77.3 | 85 000 | 20.1 | 12.3 | 704 | 33.4 | 3.1 | 10 353 | -0.2 | 556 | 5.4 | 7 351 | 33.8 | 30.4 |
| Frio | 4 745 | 65.9 | 50 200 | 23.3 | 12.4 | 646 | 22.7 | 13.5 | 8 923 | 6.9 | 499 | 5.6 | 6 167 | 19.7 | 30.0 |
| Gaines | 5 367 | 74.3 | 78 100 | 17.0 | 9.9 | 507 | 23.5 | 8.9 | 8 026 | 3.3 | 367 | 4.6 | 7 494 | 26.7 | 42.8 |
| Galveston | 107 996 | 68.8 | 144 700 | 22.6 | 12.8 | 873 | 31.5 | 4.2 | 149 740 | 1.6 | 11 510 | 7.7 | 137 643 | 39.1 | 21.9 |
| Garza | 1 631 | 68.2 | 58 600 | 16.2 | 12.2 | 438 | 24.9 | 2.4 | 2 615 | -1.1 | 160 | 6.1 | 1 745 | 28.4 | 28.4 |
| Gillespie | 10 610 | 75.2 | 195 700 | 24.4 | 12.8 | 798 | 27.8 | 2.4 | 13 931 | -1.1 | 585 | 4.2 | 11 804 | 33.4 | 23.9 |
| Glasscock | 406 | 78.6 | 103 700 | 15.9 | 9.9 | 1 040 | 10.0 | 3.4 | 694 | 3.0 | 30 | 4.3 | 531 | 37.9 | 36.2 |
| Goliad | 2 942 | 80.6 | 102 000 | 15.8 | 9.9 | 629 | 31.6 | 4.2 | 3 636 | 0.9 | 193 | 5.3 | 3 080 | 28.3 | 28.9 |
| Gonzales | 7 075 | 68.5 | 74 300 | 20.3 | 12.7 | 518 | 24.3 | 11.1 | 10 337 | 0.0 | 477 | 4.6 | 8 344 | 25.6 | 38.2 |
| Gray | 8 180 | 76.5 | 71 400 | 19.7 | 11.7 | 593 | 25.0 | 2.4 | 11 781 | 0.8 | 568 | 4.8 | 9 355 | 23.7 | 36.8 |
| Grayson | 45 878 | 69.0 | 102 300 | 23.3 | 13.2 | 736 | 27.9 | 3.4 | 57 766 | -0.9 | 4 147 | 7.2 | 53 936 | 30.7 | 26.2 |
| Gregg | 45 290 | 63.2 | 114 600 | 21.2 | 11.1 | 716 | 27.2 | 4.4 | 68 222 | 1.2 | 3 873 | 5.7 | 55 560 | 29.0 | 28.4 |
| Grimes | 8 433 | 75.1 | 86 000 | 21.4 | 12.5 | 660 | 26.3 | 5.5 | 12 611 | 2.5 | 814 | 6.5 | 10 182 | 23.7 | 32.7 |

1. Specified owner-occupied units.   2. A value of 9.9 represents 9.9 percent or less.   3. Specified renter-occupied units. A value of 10.0 represents 10 percent or less.   4. Overcrowded or lacking complete plumbing facilities.   5. Percent of civilian labor force.   6. Persons 16 years old and over.

# Table B. States and Counties — Nonfarm Employment and Agriculture

| STATE County | Private nonfarm establishments, employment and payroll, 2011 | | | | | | | | | Agriculture, 2007 | | | |
| | Number of establish-ments | Employment | | | | | | Annual payroll | | Farms | | | Farm operators whose principal occu-pation is farming (percent) |
| | | Total | Health care and social assistance | Manufac-turing | Retail trade | Finance and insurance | Professional, scientific, and technical services | Total (mil dol) | Average per employee (dollars) | Number | Percent with: Fewer than 50 acres | 500 acres or more | |
| | 104 | 105 | 106 | 107 | 108 | 109 | 110 | 111 | 112 | 113 | 114 | 115 | 116 |
|---|---|---|---|---|---|---|---|---|---|---|---|---|---|
| TEXAS—Cont'd | | | | | | | | | | | | | |
| Caldwell | 517 | 5 409 | 1 207 | 683 | 979 | 171 | 124 | 150 | 27 639 | 1 421 | 41.3 | 9.3 | 39.8 |
| Calhoun | 412 | 7 801 | 615 | 2 950 | 889 | 181 | 287 | 452 | 57 946 | 291 | 31.6 | 36.4 | 46.4 |
| Callahan | 219 | 1 535 | 140 | 100 | 349 | 79 | 29 | 46 | 29 868 | 1 058 | 31.9 | 19.3 | 38.3 |
| Cameron | 6 285 | 99 119 | 30 705 | 5 569 | 17 069 | 3 353 | 2 346 | 2 477 | 24 990 | 1 241 | 63.1 | 13.7 | 43.3 |
| Camp | 207 | 2 592 | D | D | 372 | 114 | 28 | 105 | 40 418 | 482 | 40.7 | 3.7 | 44.2 |
| Carson | 113 | 4 179 | D | 37 | 163 | D | 13 | 312 | 74 756 | 422 | 13.0 | 57.1 | 53.8 |
| Cass | 499 | 5 567 | 1 108 | 1 267 | 839 | 263 | 123 | 179 | 32 108 | 1 067 | 36.0 | 7.0 | 37.8 |
| Castro | 168 | 985 | D | 50 | 199 | D | 98 | 28 | 28 087 | 485 | 7.8 | 59.4 | 67.0 |
| Chambers | 498 | 8 691 | 407 | D | 619 | 110 | 365 | 484 | 55 700 | 650 | 47.7 | 17.5 | 37.7 |
| Cherokee | 774 | 11 628 | 2 712 | 2 721 | 1 448 | 333 | 274 | 346 | 29 773 | 1 625 | 39.6 | 5.7 | 35.2 |
| Childress | 164 | 1 610 | 494 | D | 404 | 65 | D | 38 | 23 541 | 374 | 11.2 | 32.6 | 39.0 |
| Clay | 119 | 967 | 179 | D | 233 | D | D | 26 | 26 480 | 931 | 18.3 | 28.5 | 44.9 |
| Cochran | 60 | 302 | 90 | D | 68 | D | D | 10 | 32 649 | 341 | 1.8 | 56.9 | 46.0 |
| Coke | 64 | 270 | D | D | 71 | D | D | 7 | 26 233 | 430 | 7.9 | 45.1 | 45.1 |
| Coleman | 208 | 1 479 | D | D | 227 | 84 | D | 37 | 25 057 | 1 003 | 9.7 | 35.1 | 40.9 |
| Collin | 18 207 | 304 938 | 31 790 | 18 067 | 43 590 | 32 401 | 24 675 | 16 770 | 54 995 | 2 235 | 66.0 | 4.6 | 32.8 |
| Collingsworth | 59 | 544 | D | D | 113 | D | 11 | 13 | 24 217 | 442 | 6.3 | 41.6 | 43.9 |
| Colorado | 556 | 5 936 | 925 | 1 413 | 870 | 165 | 134 | 187 | 31 529 | 1 790 | 29.9 | 13.5 | 41.8 |
| Comal | 2 836 | 35 698 | 5 435 | 2 928 | 5 564 | 845 | 1 099 | 1 216 | 34 072 | 939 | 43.5 | 9.2 | 34.8 |
| Comanche | 264 | 2 530 | 770 | D | 442 | 163 | 100 | 74 | 29 391 | 1 451 | 25.6 | 19.9 | 48.0 |
| Concho | 49 | 720 | 150 | D | D | D | D | 21 | 29 604 | 418 | 4.8 | 50.0 | 50.7 |
| Cooke | 837 | 12 690 | 1 084 | 3 297 | 1 825 | 316 | 274 | 501 | 39 499 | 1 956 | 44.1 | 10.2 | 34.2 |
| Coryell | 762 | 10 178 | 1 341 | 221 | 1 797 | 355 | 1 031 | 259 | 25 430 | 1 339 | 31.2 | 18.6 | 39.7 |
| Cottle | 33 | 163 | D | NA | 51 | 24 | NA | 3 | 19 472 | 299 | 5.7 | 42.1 | 41.1 |
| Crane | 85 | 939 | D | D | 109 | D | 7 | 44 | 46 870 | 37 | 21.6 | 59.5 | 32.4 |
| Crockett | 133 | 1 062 | D | D | 248 | D | 12 | 44 | 41 713 | 183 | 3.8 | 73.2 | 57.4 |
| Crosby | 104 | 703 | 185 | D | 134 | D | D | 29 | 41 279 | 371 | 4.9 | 49.9 | 52.6 |
| Culberson | 49 | 532 | D | D | 183 | NA | D | 12 | 22 188 | 55 | 5.5 | 85.5 | 63.6 |
| Dallam | 218 | 1 962 | 62 | D | 209 | D | 165 | 59 | 29 981 | 452 | 2.9 | 64.4 | 50.7 |
| Dallas | 61 034 | 1 239 445 | 150 563 | 92 934 | 114 404 | 95 577 | 115 598 | 68 003 | 54 866 | 755 | 64.9 | 4.4 | 38.0 |
| Dawson | 281 | 2 626 | 420 | 146 | 503 | D | 64 | 84 | 31 905 | 555 | 9.7 | 45.0 | 51.0 |
| Deaf Smith | 424 | 5 470 | 506 | 1 567 | 776 | 193 | 155 | 186 | 34 078 | 637 | 14.6 | 52.6 | 54.0 |
| Delta | 55 | 616 | D | D | D | D | D | 9 | 14 459 | 538 | 37.2 | 10.4 | 38.3 |
| Denton | 11 449 | 166 739 | 20 467 | 10 458 | 25 056 | 12 517 | 8 195 | 6 621 | 39 706 | 2 575 | 69.8 | 4.5 | 32.7 |
| DeWitt | 437 | 4 622 | 1 094 | 596 | 659 | 256 | 107 | 139 | 30 081 | 1 811 | 24.3 | 15.1 | 43.1 |
| Dickens | 41 | 217 | 28 | NA | 56 | D | D | 7 | 33 382 | 446 | 5.8 | 32.1 | 37.4 |
| Dimmit | 187 | 3 229 | 470 | D | 434 | D | D | 161 | 50 005 | 388 | 25.0 | 32.7 | 35.3 |
| Donley | 78 | 471 | 68 | D | 116 | D | 23 | 8 | 16 310 | 392 | 7.1 | 29.8 | 40.8 |
| Duval | 154 | 2 109 | D | D | 211 | 56 | D | 71 | 33 569 | 1 507 | 11.3 | 22.6 | 36.6 |
| Eastland | 461 | 5 270 | 986 | 582 | 876 | D | 103 | 269 | 51 120 | 1 324 | 18.0 | 19.0 | 38.1 |
| Ector | 3 313 | 53 018 | 7 851 | 3 803 | 7 340 | 1 283 | 2 008 | 2 448 | 46 172 | 301 | 74.4 | 13.0 | 29.2 |
| Edwards | 35 | 201 | D | NA | 50 | D | D | 5 | 23 891 | 480 | 11.0 | 41.9 | 38.8 |
| Ellis | 2 455 | 32 677 | 3 445 | 8 442 | 5 192 | 789 | 715 | 1 111 | 33 986 | 2 415 | 53.4 | 7.0 | 35.3 |
| El Paso | 13 494 | 210 200 | 36 929 | 14 083 | 35 069 | 6 567 | 9 644 | 6 254 | 29 755 | 590 | 78.3 | 7.5 | 47.6 |
| Erath | 909 | 12 033 | 1 892 | 2 393 | 1 905 | 332 | 345 | 347 | 28 800 | 2 189 | 31.1 | 13.9 | 39.2 |
| Falls | 235 | 1 873 | 455 | D | 454 | 102 | D | 50 | 26 507 | 1 295 | 27.2 | 15.5 | 47.7 |
| Fannin | 466 | 4 646 | 1 266 | 569 | 908 | 166 | 130 | 143 | 30 792 | 2 110 | 36.9 | 9.1 | 39.7 |
| Fayette | 727 | 6 647 | 1 273 | 871 | 1 134 | 233 | 294 | 202 | 30 417 | 2 991 | 32.2 | 7.3 | 38.4 |
| Fisher | 68 | 509 | 120 | D | D | 45 | D | 18 | 35 397 | 661 | 10.1 | 37.5 | 44.3 |
| Floyd | 165 | 966 | 267 | D | 137 | 59 | 22 | 27 | 27 442 | 650 | 8.0 | 40.2 | 43.8 |
| Foard | 28 | 170 | 52 | D | D | D | D | 3 | 19 576 | 212 | 9.0 | 43.4 | 47.2 |
| Fort Bend | 9 705 | 119 383 | 16 450 | 10 339 | 22 732 | 3 695 | 7 785 | 5 217 | 43 698 | 1 404 | 51.6 | 10.8 | 38.2 |
| Franklin | 174 | 6 042 | D | D | 288 | 64 | D | 107 | 17 784 | 564 | 30.3 | 14.2 | 47.5 |
| Freestone | 344 | 3 786 | 649 | D | 486 | D | D | 141 | 37 241 | 1 473 | 35.5 | 12.0 | 40.9 |
| Frio | 273 | 3 521 | 1 052 | 42 | 601 | 106 | D | 118 | 33 537 | 724 | 18.9 | 33.0 | 41.9 |
| Gaines | 358 | 3 420 | D | 139 | 568 | 95 | 62 | 146 | 42 768 | 825 | 7.2 | 49.8 | 57.9 |
| Galveston | 5 197 | 78 831 | 14 546 | 5 919 | 10 973 | 3 927 | 6 183 | 3 017 | 38 276 | 692 | 74.9 | 7.2 | 32.4 |
| Garza | 122 | 1 221 | D | D | 152 | D | D | 42 | 34 235 | 300 | 15.3 | 49.0 | 44.3 |
| Gillespie | 888 | 7 736 | 1 497 | 652 | 1 545 | 278 | 250 | 224 | 28 911 | 1 853 | 32.3 | 16.7 | 40.7 |
| Glasscock | 20 | D | NA | D | D | D | D | 6 | D | 185 | 7.0 | 67.6 | 60.5 |
| Goliad | 121 | 794 | 121 | D | 153 | D | 23 | 27 | 33 569 | 1 083 | 23.7 | 17.4 | 41.2 |
| Gonzales | 387 | 4 740 | 713 | 1 540 | 729 | 163 | 123 | 146 | 30 881 | 1 861 | 24.7 | 17.4 | 43.4 |
| Gray | 633 | 6 460 | 884 | D | 1 101 | 212 | D | 275 | 42 615 | 391 | 12.5 | 43.7 | 39.9 |
| Grayson | 2 464 | 38 460 | 8 781 | 6 571 | 6 097 | 2 206 | 816 | 1 239 | 32 217 | 2 723 | 55.3 | 4.9 | 35.1 |
| Gregg | 4 055 | 64 681 | 11 155 | 7 902 | 9 387 | 2 056 | 2 203 | 2 515 | 38 884 | 486 | 63.0 | 3.5 | 31.3 |
| Grimes | 365 | 5 208 | 391 | 1 918 | 585 | 181 | 160 | 204 | 39 221 | 1 853 | 40.0 | 9.9 | 40.2 |

Items 104—116

# Table B. States and Counties — **Agriculture**

| STATE County | Land in farms — Acreage (1,000) [117] | Percent change, 2002–2007 [118] | Acres — Average size of farm [119] | Acres — Total irrigated (1,000) [120] | Acres — Total cropland (1,000) [121] | Value of land and buildings (dollars) — Average per farm [122] | Value of land and buildings (dollars) — Average per acre [123] | Value of machinery and equipment, average per farm (dollars) [124] | Value of products sold — Total (mil dol) [125] | Value of products sold — Average per farm (dollars) [126] | Percent from: Crops [127] | Percent from: Livestock and poultry products [128] | Percent of farms with sales of: $10,000 or more [129] | Percent of farms with sales of: $100,000 or more [130] | Government payments — Total ($1,000) [131] | Government payments — Percent of farms [132] |
|---|---|---|---|---|---|---|---|---|---|---|---|---|---|---|---|---|
| TEXAS—Cont'd | | | | | | | | | | | | | | | | |
| Caldwell | 305 | 0.0 | 214 | 0.9 | 71.5 | 496 921 | 2 317 | 47 346 | 47.0 | 33 098 | 15.9 | 84.1 | 23.6 | 3.0 | 791 | 6.5 |
| Calhoun | 230 | -7.3 | 792 | 3.6 | 88.9 | 1 261 479 | 1 593 | 123 615 | 29.0 | 99 525 | 69.3 | 30.7 | 48.1 | 21.6 | 2 770 | 39.2 |
| Callahan | 533 | 3.5 | 503 | 0.6 | 104.3 | 640 488 | 1 272 | 48 345 | 25.4 | 24 012 | 16.0 | 84.0 | 29.0 | 4.8 | 876 | 22.0 |
| Cameron | 349 | -0.3 | 282 | 101.1 | 226.1 | 544 393 | 1 933 | 73 172 | 112.4 | 90 532 | 93.5 | 6.5 | 33.1 | 11.9 | 7 614 | 41.6 |
| Camp | 69 | 0.0 | 142 | 2.1 | 23.4 | 387 269 | 2 723 | 61 878 | 143.1 | 296 803 | 2.1 | 97.9 | 35.7 | 8.3 | 140 | 6.8 |
| Carson | 537 | 18.8 | 1 274 | 41.5 | 331.0 | 1 039 725 | 816 | 146 348 | 93.7 | 221 930 | 56.2 | 43.8 | 49.8 | 30.6 | 6 625 | 73.7 |
| Cass | 177 | -8.3 | 166 | 0.3 | 51.6 | 356 841 | 2 155 | 46 284 | 68.8 | 64 518 | 8.2 | 91.8 | 27.9 | 5.4 | 152 | 3.3 |
| Castro | 567 | 0.5 | 1 170 | 213.3 | 434.6 | 1 209 915 | 1 034 | 276 986 | 973.4 | 2 006 911 | 15.1 | 84.9 | 66.0 | 52.2 | 11 405 | 77.9 |
| Chambers | 267 | -2.9 | 411 | 11.5 | 115.6 | 596 789 | 1 451 | 68 100 | 17.6 | 27 088 | 50.1 | 49.9 | 23.2 | 6.0 | 2 338 | 17.1 |
| Cherokee | 294 | 2.8 | 181 | 1.1 | 76.6 | 421 476 | 2 327 | 61 321 | 140.3 | 86 312 | 63.5 | 36.5 | 31.9 | 5.2 | 269 | 4.0 |
| Childress | 399 | 8.1 | 1 068 | 14.0 | 143.2 | 761 909 | 713 | 82 171 | 25.9 | 69 248 | 72.7 | 27.3 | 35.6 | 16.0 | 4 360 | 76.2 |
| Clay | 662 | 1.2 | 711 | 1.0 | 117.0 | 939 178 | 1 322 | 69 857 | 56.9 | 61 098 | 9.3 | 90.7 | 44.3 | 10.6 | 988 | 27.4 |
| Cochran | 489 | 11.4 | 1 434 | 82.5 | 305.3 | 1 251 971 | 873 | 157 465 | 91.7 | 268 802 | D | D | 41.6 | 30.2 | 8 875 | 85.9 |
| Coke | 491 | 1.2 | 1 142 | D | 45.9 | 894 646 | 783 | 43 258 | 13.6 | 31 719 | 4.4 | 95.6 | 28.6 | 5.6 | 486 | 28.8 |
| Coleman | 699 | 8.9 | 697 | 1.2 | 188.4 | 897 473 | 1 287 | 60 942 | 20.0 | 19 975 | 27.2 | 72.8 | 35.2 | 4.0 | 1 648 | 38.7 |
| Collin | 291 | -6.1 | 130 | 0.7 | 150.2 | 450 519 | 3 462 | 46 504 | 61.2 | 27 366 | 57.1 | 42.9 | 17.0 | 2.9 | 1 492 | 8.5 |
| Collingsworth | 513 | 1.2 | 1 160 | 29.7 | 193.5 | 999 653 | 862 | 106 334 | 50.3 | 113 822 | 71.9 | 28.1 | 42.8 | 18.3 | 6 775 | 76.0 |
| Colorado | 527 | -2.2 | 295 | 31.5 | 169.0 | 695 995 | 2 362 | 57 933 | 72.0 | 40 221 | 49.2 | 50.8 | 33.7 | 6.3 | 4 503 | 11.8 |
| Comal | 192 | -5.4 | 205 | 0.5 | 37.5 | 616 173 | 3 006 | 34 985 | 6.6 | 6 982 | 44.5 | 55.5 | 14.4 | 1.0 | 219 | 6.2 |
| Comanche | 579 | 6.6 | 399 | 12.6 | 170.3 | 785 609 | 1 969 | 71 389 | 144.9 | 99 881 | 14.9 | 85.1 | 45.8 | 7.2 | 1 482 | 20.6 |
| Concho | 551 | 1.3 | 1 319 | 4.5 | 106.0 | 1 346 320 | 1 021 | 85 095 | 21.2 | 50 699 | 48.2 | 51.8 | 51.9 | 12.2 | 2 874 | 68.4 |
| Cooke | 455 | -0.9 | 233 | 0.5 | 136.6 | 579 478 | 2 489 | 55 791 | 58.3 | 29 802 | 19.6 | 80.4 | 30.2 | 5.1 | 815 | 14.4 |
| Coryell | 488 | -1.0 | 365 | 0.8 | 120.9 | 730 994 | 2 004 | 59 922 | 40.1 | 29 984 | 16.8 | 83.2 | 28.2 | 4.8 | 759 | 18.1 |
| Cottle | 535 | -6.8 | 1 788 | 1.6 | 153.1 | 1 151 133 | 644 | 68 300 | 17.5 | 58 665 | 45.2 | 54.8 | 30.1 | 11.0 | 3 995 | 79.9 |
| Crane | 375 | NA | 10 140 | 0.0 | 15.3 | 3 877 193 | 382 | 31 050 | 1.7 | 45 237 | 0.4 | 99.6 | 48.6 | 18.9 | 117 | 24.3 |
| Crockett | 1 602 | -7.7 | 8 757 | 0.5 | 18.6 | 3 560 877 | 407 | 68 139 | 13.6 | 74 515 | D | D | 53.6 | 18.6 | 614 | 28.4 |
| Crosby | 553 | 12.9 | 1 490 | 110.0 | 289.0 | 1 027 919 | 690 | 192 112 | 92.7 | 249 975 | 94.5 | 5.5 | 48.5 | 39.4 | 11 537 | 85.4 |
| Culberson | 1 374 | -18.9 | 24 982 | 32.8 | 47.2 | 7 549 126 | 302 | 221 613 | 15.1 | 274 175 | 46.7 | 53.3 | 63.6 | 40.0 | 611 | 30.9 |
| Dallam | 937 | 6.0 | 2 073 | 230.9 | 534.2 | 1 751 802 | 845 | 254 557 | 552.9 | 1 223 139 | 27.6 | 72.4 | 56.6 | 44.2 | 7 856 | 71.5 |
| Dallas | 88 | -1.1 | 117 | 0.9 | 43.5 | 385 282 | 3 305 | 46 240 | 35.2 | 46 588 | 88.5 | 11.5 | 18.9 | 3.7 | 220 | 5.6 |
| Dawson | 568 | -0.7 | 1 023 | 77.7 | 462.4 | 871 403 | 851 | 160 721 | 112.3 | 202 418 | 96.7 | 3.3 | 49.2 | 38.2 | 18 924 | 85.2 |
| Deaf Smith | 946 | -1.9 | 1 485 | 131.6 | 524.2 | 1 356 340 | 913 | 190 751 | 1 148.4 | 1 802 762 | 7.7 | 92.3 | 54.6 | 38.9 | 12 593 | 69.7 |
| Delta | 133 | -6.3 | 247 | D | 67.4 | 398 611 | 1 614 | 60 070 | 17.2 | 32 031 | 51.8 | 48.2 | 30.1 | 6.3 | 735 | 29.2 |
| Denton | 350 | 0.3 | 136 | 1.3 | 140.9 | 486 155 | 3 574 | 50 899 | 79.2 | 30 772 | 23.4 | 76.6 | 19.6 | 3.0 | 848 | 8.8 |
| DeWitt | 549 | -4.9 | 303 | 1.2 | 78.6 | 563 032 | 1 856 | 45 578 | 41.0 | 22 630 | 16.2 | 83.8 | 35.3 | 3.5 | 396 | 6.5 |
| Dickens | 574 | 1.2 | 1 288 | 4.6 | 143.3 | 1 061 647 | 825 | 65 532 | 21.1 | 47 351 | 52.3 | 47.7 | 30.7 | 10.3 | 4 035 | 77.8 |
| Dimmit | 708 | 24.0 | 1 825 | 5.5 | 29.1 | 1 838 263 | 1 007 | 64 983 | 21.7 | 55 905 | 12.1 | 87.9 | 21.4 | 5.9 | 304 | 5.9 |
| Donley | 589 | 0.9 | 1 502 | 16.9 | 83.7 | 964 711 | 642 | 80 416 | 85.8 | 218 916 | 15.3 | 84.7 | 35.2 | 12.0 | 3 802 | 66.3 |
| Duval | 1 021 | 20.1 | 678 | 4.6 | 120.3 | 690 308 | 1 019 | 38 885 | 14.8 | 9 802 | 26.7 | 73.3 | 13.5 | 1.3 | 1 931 | 27.3 |
| Eastland | 520 | 4.4 | 393 | 5.1 | 118.4 | 679 600 | 1 730 | 53 202 | 28.0 | 21 168 | 25.7 | 74.3 | 33.5 | 4.3 | 1 533 | 21.4 |
| Ector | 424 | -15.9 | 1 408 | 1.1 | 7.0 | 560 521 | 398 | 43 889 | 3.6 | 11 824 | 27.5 | 72.5 | 15.3 | 3.3 | 109 | 4.3 |
| Edwards | 996 | 2.3 | 2 076 | 0.9 | 24.9 | 1 663 356 | 801 | 54 390 | 8.8 | 18 354 | 6.1 | 93.8 | 28.1 | 5.6 | 1 169 | 18.5 |
| Ellis | 443 | -4.5 | 183 | 0.8 | 204.6 | 448 222 | 2 445 | 50 017 | 49.4 | 20 448 | 67.6 | 32.4 | 20.4 | 3.1 | 3 435 | 21.0 |
| El Paso | 169 | 48.2 | 286 | 37.8 | 54.1 | 418 167 | 1 464 | 78 916 | 47.5 | 80 447 | 86.2 | 13.8 | 26.1 | 11.4 | 894 | 10.3 |
| Erath | 623 | 7.2 | 285 | 12.1 | 165.0 | 683 811 | 2 403 | 69 014 | 250.2 | 114 295 | 5.1 | 94.9 | 32.3 | 7.1 | 1 087 | 8.9 |
| Falls | 445 | 8.8 | 344 | 4.4 | 218.6 | 546 113 | 1 588 | 73 854 | 126.8 | 97 928 | 24.6 | 75.4 | 45.5 | 12.6 | 2 117 | 24.7 |
| Fannin | 474 | -1.9 | 225 | 5.3 | 207.5 | 435 434 | 1 939 | 53 890 | 48.7 | 23 090 | 49.2 | 50.8 | 25.3 | 3.3 | 2 086 | 21.3 |
| Fayette | 566 | 2.5 | 189 | 1.3 | 122.5 | 521 538 | 2 757 | 45 517 | 52.8 | 17 652 | 20.0 | 80.0 | 29.3 | 2.3 | 557 | 10.4 |
| Fisher | 545 | 13.8 | 824 | 4.6 | 239.4 | 746 880 | 906 | 76 973 | 50.5 | 76 392 | 57.2 | 42.8 | 38.3 | 13.0 | 7 961 | 81.7 |
| Floyd | 628 | 9.4 | 966 | 129.8 | 420.7 | 974 761 | 1 009 | 142 624 | 263.0 | 404 673 | D | D | 38.3 | 27.7 | 16 505 | 84.2 |
| Foard | 376 | 31.5 | 1 773 | 2.4 | 120.5 | 1 241 100 | 700 | 96 036 | 17.6 | 83 141 | 64.2 | 35.8 | 49.5 | 17.0 | 1 825 | 77.8 |
| Fort Bend | 383 | -7.7 | 273 | 8.3 | 152.1 | 630 401 | 2 312 | 72 989 | 94.5 | 67 304 | 85.0 | 15.0 | 29.8 | 7.8 | 4 237 | 23.4 |
| Franklin | 134 | 1.5 | 237 | 2.1 | 34.7 | 534 117 | 2 256 | 66 542 | 85.8 | 152 198 | 4.4 | 95.6 | 44.5 | 14.9 | 229 | 12.4 |
| Freestone | 400 | -6.8 | 271 | 0.3 | 80.1 | 473 115 | 1 744 | 53 438 | 33.9 | 23 031 | 9.5 | 90.5 | 31.1 | 3.1 | 188 | 4.3 |
| Frio | 645 | 7.0 | 891 | 42.9 | 151.3 | 1 203 065 | 1 350 | 76 282 | 70.3 | 97 069 | 56.4 | 43.6 | 28.5 | 9.8 | 2 541 | 17.1 |
| Gaines | 948 | 24.9 | 1 149 | 242.6 | 641.7 | 1 092 377 | 951 | 236 962 | 193.2 | 234 175 | 96.8 | 3.2 | 53.0 | 41.9 | 28 297 | 78.3 |
| Galveston | 103 | -18.9 | 149 | 0.6 | 21.8 | 365 699 | 2 448 | 40 300 | 8.3 | 11 923 | 60.4 | 39.6 | 14.2 | 1.3 | 353 | 2.6 |
| Garza | 512 | 2.4 | 1 708 | 17.1 | 99.8 | 1 049 034 | 614 | 72 113 | 27.4 | 91 479 | 82.2 | 17.8 | 38.3 | 19.7 | 4 024 | 68.0 |
| Gillespie | 653 | 1.2 | 352 | 1.9 | 90.4 | 916 819 | 2 602 | 41 962 | 28.6 | 15 427 | 26.1 | 73.9 | 26.0 | 2.2 | 684 | 15.1 |
| Glasscock | 480 | -2.6 | 2 593 | 29.5 | 126.7 | 1 910 119 | 737 | 243 043 | 46.3 | 250 041 | 95.3 | 4.7 | 64.9 | 45.4 | 5 262 | 70.8 |
| Goliad | 470 | -7.1 | 434 | 0.9 | 58.9 | 705 897 | 1 628 | 52 833 | 20.0 | 18 477 | 23.5 | 76.5 | 30.6 | 2.8 | 356 | 6.6 |
| Gonzales | 654 | -6.0 | 351 | 5.3 | 99.0 | 745 355 | 2 121 | 61 318 | 404.0 | 217 098 | 3.8 | 96.2 | 38.1 | 9.0 | 441 | 5.8 |
| Gray | 509 | 12.4 | 1 303 | 23.9 | 180.6 | 950 279 | 729 | 88 232 | 191.5 | 489 715 | 10.8 | 89.2 | 34.5 | 14.8 | 3 237 | 59.3 |
| Grayson | 400 | -9.3 | 147 | 3.1 | 166.5 | 446 159 | 3 033 | 48 025 | 52.8 | 19 405 | 56.5 | 43.5 | 21.0 | 3.0 | 1 251 | 11.1 |
| Gregg | 45 | -4.3 | 93 | 0.3 | 11.6 | 318 554 | 3 426 | 40 183 | 3.8 | 7 731 | 41.9 | 58.1 | 16.3 | 1.4 | 17 | 1.9 |
| Grimes | 437 | 5.3 | 236 | 2.0 | 87.0 | 575 760 | 2 441 | 61 013 | 49.9 | 26 938 | 15.0 | 85.0 | 30.3 | 3.1 | 80 | 1.1 |

| STATE County | Water use, 2005 | | Wholesale trade,[1] 2007 | | | | Retail trade,[2] 2007 | | | | Real estate and rental and leasing,[2] 2007 | | | |
|---|---|---|---|---|---|---|---|---|---|---|---|---|---|---|
| | Total water withdrawn (mil gal/day) | Gallons withdrawn per person | Number of establishments | Number of employees | Sales (mil dol) | Annual payroll (mil dol) | Number of establishments | Number of employees | Sales (mil dol) | Annual payroll (mil dol) | Number of establishments | Number of employees | Receipts (mil dol) | Annual payroll (mil dol) |
| | 133 | 134 | 135 | 136 | 137 | 138 | 139 | 140 | 141 | 142 | 143 | 144 | 145 | 146 |
| TEXAS—Cont'd | | | | | | | | | | | | | | |
| Caldwell | 18.6 | 508 | 18 | 89 | 26.4 | 2.8 | 84 | 997 | 298.3 | 21.3 | 26 | 135 | 15.4 | 2.9 |
| Calhoun | 41.2 | 1 997 | 16 | D | D | D | 69 | 972 | 322.2 | 26.1 | 14 | D | D | D |
| Callahan | 2.6 | 190 | 16 | 61 | 20.5 | 1.5 | 39 | 340 | 118.9 | 6.6 | 10 | 33 | 3.1 | 0.7 |
| Cameron | 210.1 | 555 | 341 | 3 704 | 1 516.6 | 96.3 | 1 230 | 17 667 | 3 911.7 | 340.0 | 341 | 1 593 | 169.4 | 30.0 |
| Camp | 4.1 | 331 | 8 | 62 | 33.5 | 2.3 | 46 | 389 | 96.9 | 7.4 | 8 | D | D | D |
| Carson | 54.0 | 8 198 | 5 | D | D | D | 23 | 130 | 49.7 | 2.9 | 1 | D | D | D |
| Cass | 3.1 | 103 | 20 | 184 | 155.0 | 7.2 | 98 | 888 | 216.8 | 17.7 | 20 | 51 | 6.6 | 0.9 |
| Castro | 360.6 | 47 200 | 14 | 109 | 154.6 | 3.7 | 36 | 196 | 40.0 | 2.9 | 3 | D | D | D |
| Chambers | 533.3 | 18 770 | 30 | 308 | 137.2 | 11.8 | 81 | 757 | 274.9 | 15.0 | 16 | 102 | 44.4 | 4.1 |
| Cherokee | 209.4 | 4 321 | 31 | D | D | D | 143 | 1 468 | 363.2 | 28.7 | 36 | 141 | 10.5 | 2.0 |
| Childress | 10.1 | 1 318 | 7 | 68 | 31.4 | 2.2 | 28 | 361 | 75.5 | 6.6 | 8 | 18 | 1.8 | 0.3 |
| Clay | 16.8 | 1 488 | 8 | 26 | 5.4 | 0.6 | 29 | 226 | 77.6 | 6.0 | 6 | D | D | D |
| Cochran | 126.4 | 38 440 | 4 | 17 | 12.0 | 0.6 | 13 | 68 | 26.9 | 1.4 | NA | NA | NA | NA |
| Coke | 60.3 | 16 705 | 1 | D | D | D | 12 | 71 | 24.5 | 1.3 | NA | NA | NA | NA |
| Coleman | 48.0 | 5 535 | 7 | 38 | 16.2 | 1.2 | 34 | 230 | 47.9 | 4.1 | 11 | 21 | 3.4 | 0.4 |
| Collin | 593.8 | 900 | 735 | 10 505 | 9 374.9 | 733.2 | 2 287 | 41 634 | 12 350.8 | 1 038.1 | 886 | 5 430 | 1 054.0 | 228.6 |
| Collingsworth | 51.8 | 17 463 | 3 | D | D | D | 13 | 77 | 17.2 | 1.7 | 1 | D | D | D |
| Colorado | 125.8 | 6 068 | 32 | 254 | 136.8 | 7.7 | 108 | 942 | 226.8 | 19.0 | 21 | D | D | D |
| Comal | 30.4 | 317 | 103 | 1 045 | 960.6 | 48.9 | 379 | 5 003 | 1 539.7 | 123.8 | 143 | 643 | 89.4 | 15.5 |
| Comanche | 28.0 | 2 039 | 24 | 157 | 83.1 | 4.6 | 54 | 457 | 117.8 | 8.7 | 8 | 27 | 2.3 | 0.4 |
| Concho | 4.3 | 1 138 | 2 | D | D | D | 13 | 100 | 17.7 | 1.2 | 2 | D | D | D |
| Cooke | 9.8 | 252 | 38 | 365 | 99.8 | 12.2 | 181 | 1 935 | 499.7 | 42.9 | 31 | 99 | 24.1 | 2.3 |
| Coryell | 8.8 | 116 | 17 | 80 | 34.3 | 3.5 | 140 | 1 752 | 442.6 | 36.7 | 51 | 153 | 16.9 | 2.7 |
| Cottle | 4.7 | 2 703 | NA | NA | NA | NA | 14 | 50 | 12.7 | 0.9 | NA | NA | NA | NA |
| Crane | 21.2 | 5 533 | 4 | 17 | 23.2 | 0.8 | 14 | 109 | 47.8 | 2.5 | NA | NA | NA | NA |
| Crockett | 9.5 | 2 410 | 4 | D | D | D | 27 | 262 | 58.9 | 4.2 | 3 | D | D | D |
| Crosby | 126.1 | 18 860 | 11 | 149 | 119.4 | 8.4 | 21 | 126 | 23.8 | 2.2 | 3 | D | D | D |
| Culberson | 18.8 | 7 164 | 2 | D | D | D | 19 | 221 | 106.2 | 3.6 | 2 | D | D | D |
| Dallam | 368.1 | 59 624 | 18 | 281 | 311.1 | 9.8 | 33 | 178 | 85.4 | 4.6 | 9 | 21 | 3.0 | 0.3 |
| Dallas | 979.4 | 425 | 3 935 | 72 986 | 58 165.1 | 4 220.6 | 7 719 | 118 275 | 33 177.2 | 3 063.0 | 3 505 | 36 320 | 8 668.8 | 1 992.1 |
| Dawson | 108.2 | 7 588 | 19 | 110 | 91.3 | 3.1 | 48 | 583 | 148.4 | 11.4 | 8 | 19 | 1.4 | 0.2 |
| Deaf Smith | 218.1 | 11 764 | 34 | D | D | D | 66 | 744 | 224.2 | 15.9 | 18 | 71 | 5.4 | 1.0 |
| Delta | 1.9 | 338 | 2 | D | D | D | 14 | 57 | 26.4 | 1.4 | 3 | 14 | 2.2 | 0.6 |
| Denton | 87.1 | 157 | 472 | 9 066 | 12 359.0 | 466.0 | 1 519 | 25 683 | 7 668.3 | 600.8 | 564 | 2 757 | 519.2 | 93.1 |
| DeWitt | 4.7 | 228 | 15 | 83 | 30.5 | 2.7 | 71 | 692 | 159.9 | 14.0 | 12 | 87 | 10.6 | 2.9 |
| Dickens | 9.4 | 3 556 | NA | NA | NA | NA | 11 | 73 | 11.3 | 0.9 | 1 | D | D | D |
| Dimmit | 6.3 | 605 | 4 | D | D | D | 26 | 330 | 74.8 | 6.6 | 6 | D | D | D |
| Donley | 34.2 | 8 791 | 2 | D | D | D | 23 | 123 | 29.2 | 2.2 | 3 | D | D | D |
| Duval | 14.1 | 1 119 | 8 | 64 | 17.5 | 2.6 | 27 | 188 | 49.6 | 2.8 | 4 | D | D | D |
| Eastland | 13.0 | 706 | 12 | 153 | 180.8 | 8.8 | 99 | 895 | 259.7 | 18.1 | 17 | 39 | 6.1 | 1.0 |
| Ector | 64.0 | 511 | 286 | 4 048 | 2 004.3 | 219.0 | 476 | 6 660 | 2 090.6 | 167.6 | 157 | 1 383 | 338.4 | 74.3 |
| Edwards | 1.0 | 513 | 1 | D | D | D | 6 | 53 | 11.7 | 0.6 | 1 | D | D | D |
| Ellis | 23.5 | 176 | 100 | 716 | 279.2 | 30.4 | 376 | 4 725 | 1 323.1 | 107.3 | 114 | 374 | 58.7 | 9.4 |
| El Paso | 267.3 | 370 | 911 | 8 442 | 5 002.5 | 303.1 | 2 334 | 33 948 | 8 460.9 | 683.1 | 672 | 3 599 | 629.2 | 106.8 |
| Erath | 17.1 | 501 | 38 | D | D | D | 156 | 1 912 | 445.0 | 39.7 | 43 | 124 | 17.7 | 3.3 |
| Falls | 15.8 | 893 | 13 | 79 | 53.1 | 2.3 | 44 | 330 | 71.6 | 6.0 | 12 | 32 | 5.3 | 0.5 |
| Fannin | 9.3 | 281 | 11 | D | D | D | 85 | 874 | 297.3 | 25.3 | 16 | 97 | 7.7 | 2.6 |
| Fayette | 767.4 | 34 048 | 29 | 376 | 158.7 | 15.8 | 133 | 1 041 | 262.0 | 23.8 | 33 | 94 | 20.3 | 2.4 |
| Fisher | 6.1 | 1 497 | 1 | D | D | D | 14 | 64 | 12.0 | 1.0 | 1 | D | D | D |
| Floyd | 156.8 | 21 855 | 15 | 113 | 65.6 | 4.1 | 24 | 137 | 40.0 | 2.6 | 3 | D | D | D |
| Foard | 4.7 | 3 109 | 5 | D | D | D | 6 | 25 | 7.0 | 0.5 | NA | NA | NA | NA |
| Fort Bend | 1 396.8 | 3 013 | 526 | 5 754 | 6 615.3 | 275.2 | 1 213 | 19 344 | 5 306.2 | 442.9 | 392 | 1 546 | 337.8 | 56.0 |
| Franklin | 6.0 | 584 | 4 | 21 | 4.8 | 0.8 | 32 | 304 | 87.9 | 5.7 | 9 | 24 | 4.3 | 1.1 |
| Freestone | 513.1 | 27 291 | 11 | 71 | 41.6 | 3.1 | 66 | 605 | 254.3 | 14.3 | 16 | 122 | 23.9 | 4.5 |
| Frio | 84.8 | 5 177 | 11 | 66 | 31.5 | 3.2 | 50 | 472 | 107.6 | 9.2 | 9 | 65 | 6.0 | 2.0 |
| Gaines | 23.9 | 1 621 | 18 | 290 | 169.3 | 12.8 | 46 | 393 | 82.6 | 7.7 | 9 | 28 | 4.8 | 1.0 |
| Galveston | 129.7 | 467 | 191 | 1 715 | 1 761.6 | 69.2 | 860 | 10 790 | 2 750.3 | 246.1 | 265 | 1 197 | 221.1 | 33.8 |
| Garza | 18.2 | 3 635 | 5 | 23 | 10.0 | 1.3 | 20 | 152 | 35.0 | 2.0 | 4 | D | D | D |
| Gillespie | 4.5 | 196 | 35 | 224 | 100.4 | 6.1 | 170 | 1 592 | 311.1 | 33.5 | 35 | 109 | 14.0 | 2.3 |
| Glasscock | 43.1 | 32 509 | 2 | D | D | D | 2 | D | D | D | NA | NA | NA | NA |
| Goliad | 9.0 | 1 267 | 3 | D | D | D | 24 | 149 | 37.3 | 2.2 | 4 | D | D | D |
| Gonzales | 12.9 | 657 | 21 | 188 | 90.2 | 7.3 | 83 | 682 | 179.2 | 13.4 | 16 | 33 | 3.4 | 0.5 |
| Gray | 39.4 | 1 833 | 31 | D | D | D | 104 | D | D | D | 29 | 192 | 29.1 | 7.8 |
| Grayson | 23.6 | 202 | 103 | 1 004 | 651.7 | 33.1 | 497 | 6 333 | 1 594.7 | 140.4 | 114 | 456 | 69.9 | 11.1 |
| Gregg | 257.5 | 2 226 | 239 | 3 138 | 1 401.5 | 129.5 | 701 | 9 168 | 2 405.2 | 220.9 | 182 | 1 333 | 290.8 | 56.4 |
| Grimes | 33.5 | 1 330 | 20 | 216 | 142.5 | 9.1 | 60 | 597 | 157.3 | 11.3 | 14 | 41 | 9.8 | 1.3 |

1. Merchant wholesalers, except manufacturers' sales branches and offices.    2. Employer establishments.

# Table B. States and Counties — Professional Services, Manufacturing, and Accommodation and Food Services

| STATE County | Professional, scientific, and technical services,[1] 2007 | | | | Manufacturing, 2007 | | | | Accommodation and food services, 2007 | | | |
|---|---|---|---|---|---|---|---|---|---|---|---|---|
| | Number of establish-ments | Number of employees | Receipts (mil dol) | Annual payroll (mil dol) | Number of establish-ments | Number of employees | Receipts (mil dol) | Annual payroll (mil dol) | Number of establish-ments | Number of employees | Sales (mil dol) | Annual payroll (mil dol) |
| | 147 | 148 | 149 | 150 | 151 | 152 | 153 | 154 | 155 | 156 | 157 | 158 |
| **TEXAS—Cont'd** | | | | | | | | | | | | |
| Caldwell | 27 | D | D | D | 18 | 615 | 89.8 | 13.9 | 54 | 672 | 28.2 | 7.2 |
| Calhoun | 31 | D | D | D | 17 | D | D | D | 60 | 514 | 21.1 | 5.3 |
| Callahan | 13 | D | D | D | NA | NA | NA | NA | 16 | 220 | 7.6 | 2.1 |
| Cameron | 474 | D | D | D | 221 | D | D | D | 643 | 12 287 | 503.1 | 131.4 |
| Camp | 16 | 39 | 4.9 | 1.6 | NA | NA | NA | NA | 15 | 202 | 7.5 | 1.9 |
| Carson | 6 | D | D | D | NA | NA | NA | NA | 12 | 65 | 1.8 | 0.5 |
| Cass | 26 | 97 | 8.8 | 2.8 | 30 | 1 339 | 644.7 | 68.9 | 37 | 432 | 17.5 | 4.2 |
| Castro | 10 | 29 | 3.5 | 1.0 | NA | NA | NA | NA | 11 | 76 | 2.4 | 0.6 |
| Chambers | 37 | 349 | 30.1 | 14.6 | 23 | D | D | 131.2 | 50 | 804 | 31.4 | 8.4 |
| Cherokee | 45 | 170 | 14.8 | 4.0 | 75 | 3 431 | 552.5 | 90.1 | 66 | 959 | 36.5 | 9.9 |
| Childress | 9 | 32 | 4.9 | 1.3 | NA | NA | NA | NA | 24 | 358 | 11.7 | 3.2 |
| Clay | 9 | D | D | D | NA | NA | NA | NA | 9 | 111 | 2.6 | 0.9 |
| Cochran | 3 | 4 | 0.2 | 0.1 | NA | NA | NA | NA | 4 | 15 | 0.3 | 0.1 |
| Coke | 3 | D | D | D | NA | NA | NA | NA | 6 | D | D | D |
| Coleman | 14 | 39 | 3.0 | 0.7 | NA | NA | NA | NA | 21 | 166 | 5.1 | 1.3 |
| Collin | 2 581 | D | D | D | 420 | 20 823 | 7 433.8 | 1 175.1 | 1 290 | 27 578 | 1 380.4 | 392.5 |
| Collingsworth | 6 | D | D | D | NA | NA | NA | NA | 8 | 41 | 1.4 | 0.4 |
| Colorado | 46 | 144 | 13.4 | 4.4 | 28 | 1 155 | 307.3 | 38.3 | 43 | 570 | 21.7 | 5.9 |
| Comal | 251 | 1 268 | 112.1 | 38.3 | 106 | 3 475 | 1 093.7 | 128.6 | 255 | 4 362 | 184.4 | 48.5 |
| Comanche | 22 | 67 | 6.1 | 1.3 | NA | NA | NA | NA | 17 | D | D | D |
| Concho | 2 | D | D | D | NA | NA | NA | NA | 6 | 50 | 4.3 | 0.9 |
| Cooke | 65 | 290 | 37.4 | 14.7 | 75 | 3 439 | 579.7 | 128.9 | 84 | 1 322 | 52.6 | 13.9 |
| Coryell | 56 | D | D | D | 19 | 504 | D | D | 74 | 1 231 | 45.4 | 11.3 |
| Cottle | 1 | D | D | D | NA | NA | NA | NA | 4 | D | D | D |
| Crane | 2 | D | D | D | NA | NA | NA | NA | 5 | 33 | 1.0 | 0.2 |
| Crockett | 6 | 13 | 1.0 | 0.3 | NA | NA | NA | NA | 18 | 153 | 8.3 | 1.7 |
| Crosby | 4 | 8 | 0.5 | 0.2 | NA | NA | NA | NA | 5 | D | D | D |
| Culberson | 1 | D | D | D | NA | NA | NA | NA | 19 | 239 | 10.3 | 2.4 |
| Dallam | 14 | 56 | 6.7 | 1.8 | NA | NA | NA | NA | 26 | 295 | 12.5 | 2.7 |
| Dallas | 8 664 | 110 830 | 21 051.4 | 8 025.1 | 2 706 | 133 063 | 39 047.0 | 6 512.8 | 4 753 | 102 354 | 5 705.1 | 1 600.9 |
| Dawson | 19 | 58 | 7.0 | 2.3 | NA | NA | NA | NA | 26 | 279 | 12.5 | 3.2 |
| Deaf Smith | 22 | 93 | 11.4 | 2.5 | 31 | 1 104 | 470.8 | 35.7 | 33 | 377 | 17.3 | 3.8 |
| Delta | 2 | D | D | D | NA | NA | NA | NA | 3 | D | D | D |
| Denton | 1 372 | 6 160 | 1 012.6 | 306.7 | 363 | 11 406 | 4 008.3 | 476.3 | 909 | 17 865 | 797.9 | 219.5 |
| DeWitt | 29 | 113 | 8.4 | 3.1 | 28 | 835 | 110.4 | 25.5 | 43 | 464 | 14.9 | 3.9 |
| Dickens | 2 | D | D | D | NA | NA | NA | NA | 6 | 27 | 0.9 | 0.3 |
| Dimmit | 7 | 20 | 1.6 | 0.3 | NA | NA | NA | NA | 19 | 253 | 8.3 | 2.9 |
| Donley | 6 | 20 | 2.3 | 0.4 | NA | NA | NA | NA | 12 | 105 | 3.7 | 0.8 |
| Duval | 6 | 10 | 1.0 | 0.3 | NA | NA | NA | NA | 13 | 55 | 3.7 | 0.7 |
| Eastland | 29 | 109 | 9.1 | 3.3 | 22 | 608 | 135.5 | 22.6 | 44 | 427 | 17.7 | 4.3 |
| Ector | 224 | D | D | D | 240 | 4 814 | 2 049.7 | 222.0 | 245 | 5 213 | 228.6 | 59.4 |
| Edwards | 2 | D | D | D | NA | NA | NA | NA | 5 | D | D | D |
| Ellis | 164 | D | D | D | 178 | 9 369 | 4 080.6 | 416.0 | 185 | 2 828 | 126.6 | 34.4 |
| El Paso | 1 151 | D | D | D | 588 | 16 091 | 14 423.5 | 617.6 | 1 269 | 24 563 | 1 031.3 | 268.5 |
| Erath | 68 | 355 | 31.3 | 11.9 | 40 | 2 577 | 849.3 | 108.1 | 81 | 1 489 | 55.4 | 15.9 |
| Falls | 8 | 26 | 4.1 | 0.7 | NA | NA | NA | NA | 20 | D | D | D |
| Fannin | 30 | 120 | 8.6 | 2.9 | 37 | 531 | 135.9 | 17.2 | 37 | 464 | 18.5 | 5.3 |
| Fayette | 60 | 205 | 17.1 | 5.6 | 40 | 1 024 | 277.8 | 36.3 | 67 | 782 | 32.0 | 8.4 |
| Fisher | 4 | D | D | D | NA | NA | NA | NA | 2 | D | D | D |
| Floyd | 10 | 19 | 1.3 | 0.4 | NA | NA | NA | NA | 11 | 42 | 1.8 | 0.4 |
| Foard | 2 | D | D | D | NA | NA | NA | NA | 3 | D | D | D |
| Fort Bend | 1 154 | D | D | D | 344 | 15 306 | 4 986.6 | 771.0 | 657 | 12 354 | 583.4 | 158.9 |
| Franklin | 13 | 28 | 2.8 | 1.0 | NA | NA | NA | NA | 18 | 180 | 6.5 | 2.2 |
| Freestone | 30 | 118 | 9.7 | 3.4 | NA | NA | NA | NA | 25 | 480 | 22.5 | 5.8 |
| Frio | 11 | 46 | 2.4 | 1.1 | NA | NA | NA | NA | 24 | 232 | 7.4 | 2.1 |
| Gaines | 10 | 53 | 4.1 | 2.0 | NA | NA | NA | NA | 27 | 249 | 9.5 | 2.1 |
| Galveston | 502 | 2 262 | 319.0 | 122.0 | 158 | 6 061 | 23 480.8 | 519.4 | 589 | 12 643 | 591.0 | 160.0 |
| Garza | 4 | 7 | 0.5 | 0.2 | NA | NA | NA | NA | 15 | 157 | 6.2 | 1.7 |
| Gillespie | 79 | 253 | 25.6 | 7.9 | 50 | 620 | 88.3 | 20.7 | 88 | 1 220 | 52.2 | 15.9 |
| Glasscock | 2 | D | D | D | NA | NA | NA | NA | NA | NA | NA | NA |
| Goliad | 12 | D | D | D | NA | NA | NA | NA | 12 | 97 | 3.9 | 1.1 |
| Gonzales | 38 | 109 | 10.4 | 2.9 | 22 | 1 416 | 444.7 | 48.1 | 38 | 399 | 17.4 | 4.5 |
| Gray | 46 | D | D | D | 22 | D | 683.7 | 74.3 | 41 | D | D | D |
| Grayson | 220 | 1 086 | 92.5 | 34.5 | 132 | 6 148 | 2 542.8 | 293.7 | 226 | 4 001 | 167.7 | 48.6 |
| Gregg | 340 | D | D | D | 184 | 10 510 | 4 234.0 | 456.9 | 294 | 6 063 | 246.7 | 71.9 |
| Grimes | 24 | 134 | 13.2 | 3.4 | 28 | 2 194 | 892.6 | 93.9 | 31 | 259 | 12.5 | 3.0 |

1. Establishment subject to federal tax.

# Table B. States and Counties — Health Care and Social Assistance, Other Services, and Federal Funds

| | Health care and social assistance, 2007 | | | | Other services, 2007 | | | | Federal funds and grants, 2009–2010 | | | |
|---|---|---|---|---|---|---|---|---|---|---|---|---|
| | | | | | | | | | Expenditures (mil dol) | | | |
| | | | | | | | | | Total | Direct payments for individuals[1] | | |
| STATE County | Number of establishments | Number of employees | Receipts (mil dol) | Annual payroll (mil dol) | Number of establishments | Number of employees | Receipts (mil dol) | Annual payroll (mil dol) | Total | Social Security and government retirement | Medicare | Food Stamps and Supplemental Security Income |
| | 159 | 160 | 161 | 162 | 163 | 164 | 165 | 166 | 167 | 168 | 169 | 170 |
| **TEXAS—Cont'd** | | | | | | | | | | | | |
| Caldwell | 60 | 1 137 | 75.1 | 31.8 | 33 | 104 | 7.4 | 1.8 | 244.8 | 96.7 | 54.1 | 13.2 |
| Calhoun | 30 | 634 | 42.4 | 16.8 | 38 | 192 | 20.2 | 5.4 | 159.6 | 61.6 | 29.4 | 8.4 |
| Callahan | 10 | 115 | 4.0 | 1.8 | 12 | 45 | 3.5 | 0.9 | 117.5 | 48.2 | 23.8 | 4.1 |
| Cameron | 925 | 27 384 | 1 711.7 | 686.6 | 424 | 2 214 | 140.9 | 36.3 | 2 895.6 | 668.7 | 441.3 | 326.4 |
| Camp | 31 | 401 | 31.8 | 10.7 | 12 | 37 | 5.4 | 0.9 | 121.5 | 46.5 | 31.0 | 5.6 |
| Carson | 3 | D | D | D | 9 | D | D | D | 49.1 | 22.8 | 12.9 | 0.7 |
| Cass | 49 | 1 305 | 70.8 | 29.2 | 38 | 303 | 31.2 | 5.6 | 315.8 | 129.8 | 74.9 | 16.5 |
| Castro | 8 | D | D | D | 16 | 50 | 5.5 | 1.1 | 62.4 | 17.5 | 12.4 | 3.9 |
| Chambers | 34 | 638 | 36.5 | 15.8 | 30 | 182 | 16.3 | 5.6 | 220.0 | 52.5 | 37.3 | 5.8 |
| Cherokee | 88 | 2 576 | 163.2 | 77.3 | 53 | 188 | 13.4 | 3.9 | 355.9 | 130.1 | 97.3 | 18.7 |
| Childress | 20 | 363 | 28.5 | 10.8 | 9 | 25 | 2.2 | 0.5 | 58.5 | 19.9 | 14.9 | 3.0 |
| Clay | 13 | D | D | D | 10 | 36 | 1.6 | 0.4 | 66.7 | 32.8 | 17.9 | 1.9 |
| Cochran | 7 | D | D | D | 3 | D | D | D | 44.5 | 10.3 | 7.4 | 2.5 |
| Coke | NA | NA | NA | NA | 6 | D | D | D | 27.5 | 13.5 | 7.7 | 0.7 |
| Coleman | 20 | 357 | 17.6 | 8.7 | 14 | 43 | 3.2 | 0.7 | 112.2 | 36.4 | 37.0 | 4.1 |
| Collin | 2 014 | 24 679 | 3 179.0 | 1 127.8 | 878 | 6 502 | 493.2 | 154.1 | 3 155.0 | 1 274.4 | 242.2 | 59.0 |
| Collingsworth | 8 | 177 | 8.2 | 3.7 | 6 | 17 | 1.0 | 0.1 | 49.8 | 9.7 | 10.0 | 1.8 |
| Colorado | 34 | 837 | 60.1 | 24.0 | 33 | 151 | 10.5 | 2.9 | 186.7 | 66.5 | 44.1 | 7.2 |
| Comal | 271 | 3 624 | 323.2 | 130.3 | 197 | 1 392 | 78.5 | 44.0 | 1 068.3 | 444.6 | 104.2 | 15.1 |
| Comanche | 24 | 555 | 33.9 | 13.9 | 17 | 57 | 4.0 | 0.9 | 138.8 | 48.2 | 41.4 | 4.2 |
| Concho | 6 | 107 | 5.8 | 2.6 | 1 | D | D | D | 33.7 | 9.5 | 8.5 | 0.6 |
| Cooke | 85 | 1 158 | 90.7 | 35.2 | 62 | 417 | 29.3 | 8.7 | 238.7 | 110.2 | 62.0 | 11.0 |
| Coryell | 56 | D | D | D | 76 | 516 | 52.9 | 13.2 | 418.8 | 236.3 | 46.8 | 13.4 |
| Cottle | 4 | 44 | 1.6 | 0.7 | 2 | D | D | D | 23.0 | 6.7 | 5.6 | 1.1 |
| Crane | 8 | 159 | 9.5 | 4.5 | 2 | D | D | D | 21.4 | 8.8 | 8.0 | 1.3 |
| Crockett | 4 | 24 | 0.9 | 0.5 | 8 | 20 | 1.0 | 0.2 | 25.4 | 9.7 | 5.0 | 1.2 |
| Crosby | 11 | D | D | D | 8 | D | D | D | 75.5 | 16.8 | 23.4 | 4.7 |
| Culberson | 4 | D | D | D | 1 | D | D | D | 24.4 | 6.0 | 5.3 | 2.0 |
| Dallam | 12 | D | D | D | 21 | 47 | 9.2 | 1.2 | 65.0 | 23.8 | 14.1 | 2.2 |
| Dallas | 6 140 | 127 611 | 15 499.3 | 6 007.4 | 3 633 | 32 949 | 4 299.4 | 1 068.5 | 18 044.2 | 4 578.2 | 2 656.6 | 853.9 |
| Dawson | 20 | 352 | 35.8 | 9.6 | 19 | 77 | 5.2 | 1.5 | 157.8 | 40.4 | 46.3 | 8.7 |
| Deaf Smith | 24 | 492 | 31.4 | 11.6 | 37 | 168 | 14.2 | 3.3 | 136.3 | 43.3 | 28.3 | 9.7 |
| Delta | 6 | 289 | 6.4 | 3.1 | 5 | D | D | D | 61.7 | 19.3 | 14.9 | 2.3 |
| Denton | 1 199 | 16 986 | 1 795.5 | 641.2 | 674 | 4 360 | 369.5 | 112.8 | 1 841.9 | 907.3 | 235.7 | 50.6 |
| DeWitt | 41 | 1 007 | 62.3 | 25.3 | 39 | 159 | 12.5 | 3.2 | 185.6 | 55.9 | 48.4 | 9.0 |
| Dickens | 6 | 28 | 0.7 | 0.4 | 2 | D | D | D | 33.6 | 8.6 | 13.7 | 1.0 |
| Dimmit | 29 | 403 | 23.4 | 11.1 | 11 | D | D | D | 130.4 | 21.2 | 20.7 | 11.7 |
| Donley | 7 | 37 | 4.7 | 1.4 | 5 | 14 | 1.4 | 0.3 | 36.8 | 13.1 | 9.8 | 1.3 |
| Duval | 10 | 520 | 16.5 | 9.3 | 6 | 45 | 7.2 | 1.7 | 179.0 | 32.9 | 41.5 | 11.1 |
| Eastland | 38 | 1 038 | 42.7 | 22.7 | 34 | 156 | 10.9 | 3.1 | 187.5 | 68.3 | 54.4 | 7.0 |
| Ector | 300 | 6 988 | 644.3 | 248.5 | 246 | 2 115 | 283.6 | 64.3 | 749.5 | 287.9 | 194.9 | 70.3 |
| Edwards | 3 | D | D | D | 4 | D | D | D | 30.4 | 8.6 | 11.5 | 1.7 |
| Ellis | 214 | 3 320 | 254.6 | 99.6 | 157 | 863 | 55.1 | 16.6 | 703.8 | 368.6 | 149.4 | 32.4 |
| El Paso | 1 345 | 34 489 | 3 057.1 | 1 096.2 | 916 | 6 163 | 402.6 | 125.2 | 9 449.6 | 1 712.4 | 810.7 | 497.2 |
| Erath | 75 | 1 916 | 150.0 | 53.5 | 70 | 405 | 33.5 | 8.2 | 227.3 | 89.4 | 55.9 | 7.7 |
| Falls | 24 | 484 | 31.1 | 12.4 | 18 | 48 | 2.8 | 0.8 | 189.8 | 52.4 | 40.1 | 11.3 |
| Fannin | 55 | 1 291 | 117.6 | 48.0 | 36 | D | D | D | 542.8 | 118.5 | 68.0 | 10.4 |
| Fayette | 62 | 1 053 | 78.5 | 30.5 | 56 | 237 | 15.7 | 4.0 | 220.7 | 92.0 | 56.7 | 5.7 |
| Fisher | 6 | 151 | 10.0 | 4.0 | 7 | 17 | 1.1 | 0.2 | 52.6 | 14.2 | 12.9 | 1.2 |
| Floyd | 22 | 273 | 16.8 | 6.7 | 15 | 47 | 2.4 | 0.6 | 84.4 | 18.6 | 17.8 | 4.1 |
| Foard | 5 | 49 | 2.0 | 0.8 | 4 | D | D | D | 25.7 | 5.9 | 5.1 | 0.7 |
| Fort Bend | 993 | 12 302 | 1 197.4 | 443.3 | 518 | 3 251 | 318.1 | 89.4 | 1 338.5 | 719.9 | 163.0 | 70.4 |
| Franklin | 21 | 4 888 | 83.1 | 46.0 | 19 | 75 | 6.2 | 1.5 | 66.3 | 30.2 | 18.6 | 2.4 |
| Freestone | 31 | 550 | 37.6 | 13.2 | 29 | 117 | 9.8 | 1.7 | 136.2 | 57.8 | 28.5 | 6.4 |
| Frio | 29 | 474 | 27.9 | 10.6 | 15 | 45 | 2.9 | 0.7 | 183.5 | 32.1 | 23.6 | 11.9 |
| Gaines | 13 | D | D | D | 34 | 186 | 36.3 | 4.9 | 115.8 | 27.7 | 24.2 | 5.2 |
| Galveston | 526 | 14 414 | 1 219.8 | 484.8 | 422 | 2 658 | 336.9 | 70.9 | 2 443.9 | 755.1 | 424.3 | 106.5 |
| Garza | 13 | D | D | D | 5 | D | D | D | 43.7 | 12.5 | 13.9 | 2.4 |
| Gillespie | 86 | 1 533 | 119.2 | 51.8 | 54 | 249 | 25.6 | 5.9 | 195.0 | 116.7 | 44.5 | 2.7 |
| Glasscock | NA | NA | NA | NA | NA | NA | NA | NA | 20.2 | 6.1 | 1.1 | 0.1 |
| Goliad | 12 | 129 | 6.3 | 3.0 | 8 | 23 | 1.8 | 0.3 | 62.0 | 22.6 | 14.7 | 2.9 |
| Gonzales | 24 | 648 | 37.8 | 16.9 | 25 | 106 | 8.5 | 2.2 | 360.1 | 55.7 | 37.8 | 9.5 |
| Gray | 59 | 929 | 73.7 | 27.2 | 48 | 198 | 17.6 | 4.5 | 183.1 | 72.4 | 68.3 | 7.6 |
| Grayson | 382 | 8 254 | 706.2 | 279.6 | 165 | 820 | 59.1 | 16.6 | 868.6 | 401.2 | 214.3 | 37.4 |
| Gregg | 426 | 9 705 | 943.9 | 336.1 | 261 | 1 827 | 189.8 | 52.1 | 948.9 | 410.1 | 223.3 | 53.3 |
| Grimes | 22 | 266 | 19.3 | 9.9 | 23 | 80 | 7.0 | 1.9 | 185.2 | 69.6 | 38.7 | 10.0 |

1. State totals may include programs not allocated by county.

| | Federal funds and grants, 2009–2010 (cont.) | | | | | | | Value of residential construction authorized by building permits, 2011 | | Local government finances, 2007 | | | | |
| | Expenditures (mil dol) (cont.) | | | | | | | | | General revenue | | | | |
| | | Procurement contract awards | | Grants[1] | | | | | | | | Taxes | | |
| | | | | | | | | | | | | | Per capita[2] (dollars) | |
| STATE County | Salaries and wages | Defense | Other | Medicaid and other health-related | Nutrition and family welfare | Education | Other | New construction ($1,000) | Number of housing units | Total (mil dol) | Inter-govern-mental (mil dol) | Total (mil dol) | Total | Property |
| | 171 | 172 | 173 | 174 | 175 | 176 | 177 | 178 | 179 | 180 | 181 | 182 | 183 | 184 |
| TEXAS—Cont'd | | | | | | | | | | | | | | |
| Caldwell | 5.0 | 0.0 | 2.3 | 63.9 | 2.4 | 1.1 | 1.2 | 1 225 | 12 | 86.7 | 37.9 | 31.8 | 867 | 743 |
| Calhoun | 5.8 | 16.7 | 1.1 | 23.5 | 4.0 | 0.6 | 0.6 | 9 139 | 65 | 123.8 | 10.3 | 72.3 | 3 553 | 3 347 |
| Callahan | 2.1 | 3.5 | 0.5 | 14.5 | 1.2 | 0.9 | 0.9 | 511 | 4 | 32.2 | 16.8 | 10.4 | 773 | 644 |
| Cameron | 234.8 | 17.6 | 103.1 | 761.1 | 155.1 | 35.2 | 63.4 | 109 449 | 1 136 | 1 402.5 | 780.0 | 367.1 | 948 | 734 |
| Camp | 2.7 | 0.0 | 0.6 | 33.1 | 0.7 | 0.5 | 0.2 | 0 | 0 | 29.8 | 12.8 | 13.2 | 1 050 | 894 |
| Carson | 1.0 | 0.0 | 0.2 | 3.3 | 0.6 | 0.2 | 0.0 | 0 | 0 | 21.9 | 4.3 | 14.9 | 2 336 | 2 272 |
| Cass | 5.7 | 0.0 | 1.4 | 73.8 | 10.0 | 1.0 | 0.5 | 162 | 2 | 92.2 | 38.7 | 27.6 | 941 | 850 |
| Castro | 1.2 | 0.0 | 0.2 | 8.6 | 3.5 | 0.4 | 0.1 | 2 670 | 32 | 35.8 | 13.0 | 8.9 | 1 228 | 1 076 |
| Chambers | 4.1 | 53.4 | 32.5 | 16.8 | 2.6 | 1.1 | 0.4 | 36 857 | 216 | 137.8 | 25.8 | 91.7 | 3 187 | 2 996 |
| Cherokee | 7.0 | 0.1 | 1.6 | 82.9 | 7.7 | 1.8 | 2.3 | 32 024 | 74 | 110.2 | 60.5 | 36.9 | 766 | 637 |
| Childress | 1.9 | 0.0 | 0.6 | 11.6 | 1.5 | 0.2 | 0.1 | 0 | 0 | 39.2 | 10.0 | 5.1 | 671 | 505 |
| Clay | 2.1 | 0.0 | 0.5 | 7.8 | 1.1 | 0.3 | 0.1 | 179 | 1 | 43.4 | 11.9 | 13.2 | 1 185 | 1 062 |
| Cochran | 0.6 | 0.0 | 0.1 | 6.1 | 0.6 | 0.3 | 0.0 | 0 | 0 | 21.5 | 6.6 | 12.6 | 4 093 | 4 001 |
| Coke | 1.3 | 0.0 | 0.2 | 2.6 | 0.4 | 0.1 | 0.1 | 93 | 2 | 19.4 | 8.1 | 5.7 | 1 590 | 1 468 |
| Coleman | 3.3 | 0.6 | 0.7 | 22.2 | 5.1 | 0.4 | 0.3 | 12 | 1 | 32.4 | 14.8 | 8.5 | 992 | 762 |
| Collin | 134.5 | 1 046.7 | 184.4 | 95.8 | 35.8 | 6.6 | 19.0 | 1 306 631 | 5 450 | 2 925.7 | 413.4 | 1 736.2 | 2 376 | 2 008 |
| Collingsworth | 13.5 | 0.0 | 0.3 | 8.6 | 0.7 | 0.1 | 0.1 | 0 | 0 | 11.4 | 5.3 | 4.0 | 1 333 | 1 174 |
| Colorado | 4.2 | 0.0 | 5.7 | 45.2 | 3.5 | 0.6 | 0.6 | 688 | 8 | 62.9 | 15.1 | 30.9 | 1 494 | 1 317 |
| Comal | 175.0 | 254.3 | 4.1 | 37.9 | 9.2 | 3.3 | 3.0 | 193 096 | 1 016 | 325.8 | 52.2 | 212.2 | 2 017 | 1 685 |
| Comanche | 3.8 | 7.2 | 0.8 | 28.1 | 1.8 | 0.4 | 0.2 | 0 | 0 | 51.7 | 17.2 | 11.4 | 842 | 751 |
| Concho | 2.1 | 0.0 | 1.0 | 7.0 | 0.7 | 0.1 | 0.1 | NA | NA | 42.3 | 33.1 | 5.1 | 1 430 | 1 288 |
| Cooke | 5.6 | 0.8 | 1.5 | 22.6 | 4.1 | 1.5 | 6.4 | 2 585 | 15 | 175.9 | 48.1 | 57.8 | 1 503 | 1 250 |
| Coryell | 28.6 | 24.5 | 2.1 | 31.4 | 8.1 | 16.1 | 0.4 | 24 275 | 178 | 156.0 | 71.8 | 43.3 | 600 | 487 |
| Cottle | 0.6 | 0.0 | 0.1 | 5.1 | 0.2 | 0.1 | 0.1 | 0 | 0 | 7.1 | 3.4 | 2.9 | 1 829 | 1 678 |
| Crane | 0.5 | 0.0 | 0.1 | 2.0 | 0.3 | 0.1 | 0.0 | 0 | 0 | 42.0 | 4.6 | 31.6 | 8 195 | 7 934 |
| Crockett | 0.4 | 0.0 | 0.2 | 6.1 | 1.0 | 0.1 | 0.0 | NA | NA | 48.1 | 4.1 | 38.4 | 10 130 | 10 033 |
| Crosby | 1.3 | 0.0 | 0.3 | 11.5 | 1.7 | 0.4 | 0.3 | 402 | 6 | 31.4 | 17.9 | 5.7 | 905 | 809 |
| Culberson | 4.9 | 0.0 | 1.2 | 3.4 | 0.2 | 0.2 | 0.2 | 150 | 1 | 19.6 | 3.7 | 7.6 | 3 061 | 2 687 |
| Dallam | 1.0 | 0.0 | 0.2 | 4.0 | 1.2 | 0.2 | 5.2 | 2 497 | 16 | 22.7 | 7.2 | 11.6 | 1 897 | 1 564 |
| Dallas | 2 323.5 | 3 142.1 | 1 165.9 | 1 874.2 | 339.8 | 105.8 | 663.4 | 1 220 526 | 8 552 | 11 121.0 | 2 421.7 | 5 443.7 | 2 300 | 1 772 |
| Dawson | 3.9 | 0.0 | 0.6 | 27.3 | 7.8 | 0.7 | 0.5 | 270 | 1 | 76.8 | 33.2 | 23.6 | 1 700 | 1 502 |
| Deaf Smith | 2.7 | 0.0 | 1.8 | 24.8 | 5.2 | 0.8 | 0.0 | 300 | 4 | 176.4 | 65.8 | 18.9 | 1 026 | 869 |
| Delta | 1.7 | 0.0 | 0.4 | 16.4 | 1.7 | 0.2 | 0.1 | 358 | 2 | 16.3 | 5.6 | 5.2 | 958 | 850 |
| Denton | 153.1 | 130.1 | 55.6 | 74.6 | 29.7 | 13.0 | 60.6 | 618 752 | 3 343 | 1 636.7 | 270.9 | 1 070.2 | 1 748 | 1 513 |
| DeWitt | 6.1 | 0.0 | 0.7 | 54.6 | 6.1 | 1.7 | 0.7 | 613 | 4 | 92.1 | 46.7 | 21.9 | 1 109 | 994 |
| Dickens | 1.0 | 0.0 | 0.2 | 6.6 | 0.7 | 0.1 | 0.1 | NA | NA | 9.2 | 2.6 | 4.8 | 1 919 | 1 572 |
| Dimmit | 16.9 | 0.0 | 0.4 | 44.8 | 10.6 | 0.8 | 1.9 | 1 301 | 5 | 44.1 | 27.2 | 11.3 | 1 149 | 929 |
| Donley | 1.0 | 0.0 | 0.1 | 5.6 | 0.8 | 0.1 | 0.1 | 0 | 0 | 21.4 | 8.2 | 4.3 | 1 103 | 941 |
| Duval | 9.6 | 0.8 | 0.2 | 76.3 | 3.8 | 0.7 | 0.8 | NA | NA | 66.9 | 21.4 | 22.7 | 1 862 | 1 698 |
| Eastland | 4.8 | 0.1 | 2.2 | 35.4 | 2.6 | 0.8 | 0.6 | 228 | 2 | 76.2 | 29.3 | 17.3 | 946 | 784 |
| Ector | 28.1 | 0.0 | 3.8 | 92.7 | 28.4 | 8.5 | 16.4 | 90 369 | 740 | 609.9 | 162.7 | 189.3 | 1 461 | 1 149 |
| Edwards | 1.6 | 0.0 | 0.2 | 4.0 | 0.6 | 0.1 | 1.4 | NA | NA | 12.4 | 2.9 | 8.0 | 4 150 | 4 014 |
| Ellis | 23.9 | 4.0 | 9.0 | 85.7 | 10.0 | 2.7 | 0.7 | 87 724 | 731 | 413.0 | 112.4 | 231.8 | 1 616 | 1 377 |
| El Paso | 3 576.5 | 958.0 | 360.1 | 892.5 | 190.6 | 57.3 | 171.8 | 576 503 | 4 153 | 2 916.2 | 1 424.5 | 895.6 | 1 219 | 955 |
| Erath | 13.8 | 0.4 | 1.2 | 32.3 | 3.8 | 2.3 | 1.8 | 5 371 | 48 | 84.1 | 29.5 | 41.6 | 1 166 | 931 |
| Falls | 3.5 | 0.0 | 0.7 | 67.8 | 2.7 | 0.8 | 0.9 | 123 | 2 | 44.6 | 24.5 | 10.9 | 636 | 531 |
| Fannin | 254.5 | 1.0 | 3.3 | 67.8 | 5.4 | 0.8 | 2.5 | 588 | 6 | 73.4 | 35.1 | 25.8 | 782 | 672 |
| Fayette | 6.1 | 0.0 | 2.4 | 51.8 | 2.8 | 0.4 | 0.7 | 1 676 | 7 | 62.3 | 12.1 | 37.2 | 1 651 | 1 437 |
| Fisher | 1.6 | 0.0 | 0.3 | 10.1 | 0.6 | 0.1 | 0.2 | 0 | 0 | 24.5 | 11.1 | 6.2 | 1 570 | 1 476 |
| Floyd | 2.0 | 0.0 | 0.4 | 16.4 | 2.8 | 0.4 | 0.7 | 0 | 0 | 28.4 | 13.5 | 6.1 | 915 | 806 |
| Foard | 0.4 | 3.6 | 0.1 | 4.5 | 2.0 | 0.1 | 0.1 | NA | NA | 5.6 | 2.6 | 2.4 | 1 724 | 1 575 |
| Fort Bend | 90.5 | 67.7 | 50.8 | 78.8 | 31.0 | 7.1 | 22.4 | 1 041 711 | 5 598 | 1 337.9 | 321.4 | 798.6 | 1 566 | 1 390 |
| Franklin | 1.8 | 0.0 | 0.4 | 9.6 | 1.8 | 0.3 | 0.7 | 226 | 2 | 23.7 | 4.4 | 14.3 | 1 291 | 1 213 |
| Freestone | 3.2 | 0.1 | 0.7 | 34.9 | 2.5 | 0.5 | 0.2 | 982 | 10 | 98.4 | 11.3 | 73.9 | 3 934 | 3 836 |
| Frio | 7.3 | 0.1 | 49.2 | 44.3 | 5.9 | 0.9 | 4.1 | 275 | 11 | 59.3 | 31.4 | 13.6 | 846 | 695 |
| Gaines | 1.4 | 0.0 | 0.3 | 12.1 | 3.3 | 0.7 | 0.1 | 2 901 | 23 | 98.2 | 12.6 | 57.4 | 3 844 | 3 729 |
| Galveston | 115.6 | 432.3 | 51.6 | 400.5 | 38.5 | 17.5 | 51.2 | 350 096 | 1 853 | 1 247.5 | 280.4 | 735.9 | 2 591 | 2 267 |
| Garza | 1.0 | 0.0 | 2.2 | 7.1 | 1.4 | 0.2 | 0.1 | 0 | 0 | 17.8 | 5.0 | 10.4 | 2 220 | 2 146 |
| Gillespie | 14.3 | 1.1 | 1.3 | 8.6 | 2.9 | 0.4 | 0.4 | 6 548 | 33 | 62.5 | 9.5 | 42.0 | 1 785 | 1 472 |
| Glasscock | 0.3 | 0.0 | 0.1 | 1.5 | 0.3 | 0.0 | 0.0 | NA | NA | 13.4 | 1.2 | 10.5 | 8 920 | 8 861 |
| Goliad | 1.7 | 0.0 | 0.3 | 16.2 | 1.2 | 0.2 | 0.1 | NA | NA | 27.1 | 5.3 | 19.8 | 2 772 | 2 612 |
| Gonzales | 191.2 | 0.0 | 1.3 | 55.3 | 4.2 | 1.2 | 0.7 | 150 | 1 | 67.5 | 24.1 | 18.4 | 957 | 774 |
| Gray | 4.5 | 0.0 | 1.0 | 24.1 | 1.6 | 0.5 | 0.0 | 482 | 3 | 57.0 | 15.1 | 32.2 | 1 461 | 1 224 |
| Grayson | 25.3 | 6.5 | 10.0 | 123.9 | 16.0 | 2.7 | 7.8 | 10 054 | 76 | 363.4 | 126.4 | 155.6 | 1 311 | 1 087 |
| Gregg | 40.0 | 0.7 | 7.0 | 145.3 | 28.2 | 3.9 | 12.2 | 45 928 | 430 | 474.8 | 179.5 | 207.5 | 1 771 | 1 273 |
| Grimes | 4.4 | 0.5 | 2.0 | 53.6 | 3.5 | 1.1 | 0.6 | 1 571 | 13 | 58.0 | 18.1 | 32.2 | 1 258 | 1 120 |

1. State totals may include programs not allocated by county.   2. Based on the resident population estimated as of July 1 of the year shown.

| STATE County | Local government finances, 2007 (cont.) | | | | | | | | | Government employment, 2011 | | | Presidential election,[2] 2012 | | |
|---|---|---|---|---|---|---|---|---|---|---|---|---|---|---|---|
| | Direct general expenditure | | | | | | | Debt outstanding | | | | | Percent of vote cast: | | |
| | | | Percent of total for: | | | | | | | | | | | | |
| | Total (mil dol) | Per capita[1] (dollars) | Education | Health and hospitals | Police protection | Public welfare | Highways | Total (mil dol) | Per capita[1] (dollars) | Federal civilian | Federal military | State and local | Democratic | Republican | All other |
| | 185 | 186 | 187 | 188 | 189 | 190 | 191 | 192 | 193 | 194 | 195 | 196 | 197 | 198 | 199 |
| **TEXAS—Cont'd** | | | | | | | | | | | | | | | |
| Caldwell | 82.6 | 2 251 | 59.8 | 2.1 | 5.2 | 0.4 | 4.4 | 76.0 | 2 072 | 59 | 85 | 1 692 | 46.4 | 52.4 | 1.2 |
| Calhoun | 127.2 | 6 252 | 46.9 | 18.7 | 2.7 | 1.4 | 3.7 | 75.9 | 3 731 | 37 | 103 | 1 389 | 39.7 | 59.7 | 0.6 |
| Callahan | 31.9 | 2 361 | 72.5 | 0.1 | 3.5 | 0.3 | 1.7 | 16.6 | 1 226 | 46 | 30 | 667 | 18.6 | 80.3 | 1.1 |
| Cameron | 1 380.8 | 3 566 | 64.6 | 1.2 | 4.1 | 0.4 | 2.2 | 2 023.2 | 5 225 | 3 032 | 1 028 | 27 579 | 64.1 | 35.3 | 0.7 |
| Camp | 26.1 | 2 080 | 73.3 | 0.3 | 5.3 | 0.1 | 4.4 | 25.6 | 2 039 | 31 | 27 | 617 | 38.0 | 61.3 | 0.8 |
| Carson | 21.0 | 3 300 | 69.9 | 1.9 | 2.6 | 0.1 | 3.8 | 3.3 | 524 | 241 | 14 | 441 | 13.6 | 85.5 | 0.9 |
| Cass | 84.8 | 2 888 | 58.3 | 18.9 | 5.1 | 0.2 | 2.7 | 46.3 | 1 578 | 63 | 67 | 1 877 | 29.5 | 69.9 | 0.7 |
| Castro | 28.6 | 3 972 | 55.7 | 26.6 | 4.2 | 0.0 | 4.0 | 40.0 | 5 550 | 20 | 18 | 601 | 31.4 | 68.2 | 0.4 |
| Chambers | 136.5 | 4 745 | 61.7 | 5.7 | 3.8 | 0.3 | 3.7 | 201.2 | 6 992 | 57 | 79 | 1 877 | 24.0 | 75.1 | 0.9 |
| Cherokee | 99.8 | 2 071 | 63.7 | 8.3 | 6.6 | 0.3 | 3.9 | 49.7 | 1 031 | 71 | 113 | 4 158 | 28.1 | 71.2 | 0.7 |
| Childress | 41.7 | 5 516 | 34.8 | 50.0 | 1.9 | 0.0 | 1.2 | 8.0 | 1 064 | 23 | 15 | 1 109 | 21.6 | 77.6 | 0.7 |
| Clay | 42.0 | 3 774 | 46.6 | 15.8 | 2.6 | 0.1 | 4.9 | 306.9 | 27 605 | 27 | 24 | 540 | 20.3 | 78.9 | 0.8 |
| Cochran | 21.3 | 6 909 | 68.5 | 13.2 | 3.0 | 0.0 | 3.9 | 0.2 | 66 | 13 | 0 | 331 | 26.9 | 71.7 | 1.4 |
| Coke | 17.1 | 4 799 | 50.1 | 0.0 | 2.6 | 24.0 | 3.0 | 0.1 | 31 | 13 | 0 | 366 | 19.1 | 79.8 | 1.1 |
| Coleman | 29.5 | 3 452 | 53.7 | 18.9 | 3.1 | 0.0 | 3.6 | 16.1 | 1 885 | 42 | 19 | 709 | 17.4 | 81.3 | 1.3 |
| Collin | 3 278.1 | 4 486 | 51.8 | 0.5 | 3.7 | 0.0 | 4.1 | 8 428.6 | 11 535 | 1 229 | 1 824 | 40 006 | 36.8 | 62.3 | 0.9 |
| Collingsworth | 11.4 | 3 849 | 57.2 | 9.4 | 4.6 | 0.0 | 4.6 | 4.7 | 1 585 | 19 | 0 | 233 | 19.6 | 78.9 | 1.5 |
| Colorado | 59.4 | 2 873 | 52.7 | 13.9 | 4.6 | 0.1 | 6.3 | 94.3 | 4 564 | 56 | 46 | 943 | 30.0 | 69.4 | 0.6 |
| Comal | 354.7 | 3 372 | 64.4 | 0.4 | 5.2 | 0.5 | 4.0 | 693.7 | 6 595 | 166 | 248 | 5 402 | 25.7 | 73.2 | 1.1 |
| Comanche | 47.7 | 3 521 | 41.2 | 34.6 | 2.6 | 0.0 | 4.1 | 33.9 | 2 504 | 48 | 31 | 1 028 | 25.6 | 73.1 | 1.3 |
| Concho | 40.8 | 11 339 | 11.9 | 7.0 | 1.5 | 0.0 | 1.0 | 8.2 | 2 275 | 29 | 0 | 214 | 23.9 | 74.9 | 1.2 |
| Cooke | 170.0 | 4 418 | 52.4 | 20.7 | 4.7 | 0.1 | 2.9 | 166.4 | 4 324 | 61 | 85 | 2 825 | 20.3 | 79.0 | 0.7 |
| Coryell | 153.5 | 2 127 | 63.3 | 12.4 | 4.2 | 0.0 | 2.8 | 125.4 | 1 738 | 196 | 231 | 5 759 | 36.1 | 63.0 | 0.9 |
| Cottle | 5.9 | 3 648 | 43.1 | 1.7 | 1.9 | 0.1 | 5.3 | 0.7 | 457 | 12 | 0 | 137 | 26.5 | 72.2 | 1.3 |
| Crane | 36.0 | 9 332 | 70.4 | 9.7 | 2.4 | 0.1 | 1.4 | 4.1 | 1 067 | 0 | 10 | 366 | 21.9 | 77.0 | 1.1 |
| Crockett | 43.5 | 11 467 | 65.8 | 2.0 | 2.0 | 7.1 | 4.5 | 2.9 | 772 | 0 | 0 | 424 | 33.1 | 66.4 | 0.5 |
| Crosby | 27.4 | 4 340 | 60.2 | 0.1 | 2.6 | 0.8 | 2.9 | 0.7 | 108 | 21 | 13 | 490 | 35.7 | 63.8 | 0.5 |
| Culberson | 17.6 | 7 069 | 46.4 | 26.4 | 3.3 | 0.0 | 2.1 | 3.6 | 1 443 | 90 | 0 | 234 | 64.8 | 33.9 | 1.3 |
| Dallam | 24.6 | 4 010 | 64.6 | 0.0 | 4.7 | 0.0 | 4.7 | 26.0 | 4 239 | 15 | 15 | 541 | 19.0 | 79.9 | 1.1 |
| Dallas | 10 545.4 | 4 456 | 40.0 | 12.2 | 5.9 | 0.2 | 5.1 | 20 793.0 | 8 786 | 27 125 | 6 311 | 139 302 | 57.3 | 42.0 | 0.7 |
| Dawson | 54.8 | 3 953 | 58.8 | 16.6 | 4.1 | 0.9 | 2.6 | 154.1 | 11 112 | 55 | 30 | 1 483 | 28.1 | 70.9 | 0.9 |
| Deaf Smith | 160.0 | 8 672 | 21.0 | 7.8 | 1.7 | 0.0 | 1.7 | 1 888.1 | 102 327 | 44 | 43 | 1 305 | 26.3 | 73.1 | 0.7 |
| Delta | 13.0 | 2 419 | 68.3 | 0.0 | 6.4 | 0.3 | 4.7 | 12.8 | 2 382 | 22 | 12 | 316 | 26.9 | 72.2 | 0.8 |
| Denton | 1 666.0 | 2 721 | 58.0 | 1.4 | 4.9 | 0.1 | 5.1 | 4 761.3 | 7 775 | 1 717 | 1 547 | 31 596 | 37.5 | 61.6 | 0.9 |
| DeWitt | 86.0 | 4 359 | 47.5 | 30.7 | 2.7 | 0.2 | 2.7 | 63.9 | 3 240 | 37 | 45 | 2 141 | 25.9 | 73.8 | 0.3 |
| Dickens | 10.1 | 4 006 | 73.6 | 0.1 | 1.0 | 0.4 | 3.3 | 8.0 | 3 198 | 13 | 0 | 162 | 24.1 | 75.1 | 0.8 |
| Dimmit | 40.0 | 4 064 | 52.3 | 25.6 | 2.5 | 0.0 | 2.8 | 15.1 | 1 538 | 268 | 22 | 900 | 75.0 | 24.4 | 0.6 |
| Donley | 21.0 | 5 380 | 72.9 | 0.2 | 2.4 | 9.6 | 3.5 | 18.4 | 4 714 | 15 | 0 | 407 | 17.2 | 81.3 | 1.5 |
| Duval | 70.0 | 5 741 | 45.6 | 31.6 | 3.7 | 0.5 | 3.0 | 102.2 | 8 390 | 150 | 26 | 1 071 | 74.8 | 24.4 | 0.8 |
| Eastland | 76.2 | 4 158 | 69.2 | 14.9 | 1.7 | 0.1 | 2.0 | 46.7 | 2 546 | 54 | 110 | 1 464 | 19.5 | 79.4 | 1.1 |
| Ector | 554.0 | 4 275 | 41.9 | 34.4 | 3.8 | 0.0 | 2.2 | 306.9 | 2 369 | 165 | 311 | 9 386 | 25.6 | 73.6 | 0.8 |
| Edwards | 10.6 | 5 489 | 75.6 | 1.5 | 2.4 | 0.1 | 4.4 | 0.4 | 231 | 22 | 0 | 166 | 33.4 | 65.0 | 1.5 |
| Ellis | 450.0 | 3 136 | 66.4 | 0.3 | 4.6 | 0.6 | 3.9 | 1 154.7 | 8 049 | 221 | 338 | 6 730 | 28.5 | 70.7 | 0.8 |
| El Paso | 2 885.0 | 3 927 | 57.2 | 12.5 | 4.4 | 0.3 | 2.0 | 3 658.4 | 4 980 | 12 869 | 27 488 | 54 284 | 65.9 | 33.4 | 0.8 |
| Erath | 83.2 | 2 336 | 51.6 | 12.1 | 8.2 | 0.3 | 5.3 | 73.8 | 2 070 | 77 | 86 | 3 585 | 22.3 | 76.8 | 0.9 |
| Falls | 41.4 | 2 411 | 68.0 | 0.9 | 3.9 | 0.6 | 4.9 | 36.2 | 2 111 | 406 | 40 | 1 320 | 39.7 | 59.4 | 0.8 |
| Fannin | 74.7 | 2 259 | 65.8 | 2.2 | 6.0 | 0.5 | 5.1 | 87.8 | 2 656 | 610 | 75 | 1 937 | 29.6 | 69.2 | 1.2 |
| Fayette | 58.0 | 2 573 | 58.6 | 2.6 | 5.2 | 0.1 | 9.8 | 21.9 | 972 | 69 | 55 | 1 606 | 28.1 | 70.8 | 1.1 |
| Fisher | 20.8 | 5 266 | 32.0 | 23.3 | 2.8 | 0.1 | 4.6 | 53.2 | 13 443 | 23 | 0 | 325 | 38.5 | 60.7 | 0.8 |
| Floyd | 29.2 | 4 389 | 59.6 | 24.5 | 3.7 | 0.0 | 1.0 | 19.6 | 2 942 | 30 | 14 | 529 | 29.0 | 70.8 | 0.3 |
| Foard | 4.6 | 3 228 | 63.0 | 3.8 | 5.0 | 0.0 | 8.9 | 1.6 | 1 094 | 0 | 0 | 103 | 36.8 | 60.8 | 2.4 |
| Fort Bend | 1 343.3 | 2 635 | 58.9 | 0.7 | 4.6 | 0.5 | 3.8 | 3 071.3 | 6 024 | 770 | 1 355 | 21 767 | 48.5 | 50.9 | 0.6 |
| Franklin | 22.1 | 1 988 | 61.1 | 0.0 | 4.7 | 0.1 | 9.0 | 12.2 | 1 099 | 18 | 23 | 401 | 23.1 | 75.5 | 1.4 |
| Freestone | 92.7 | 4 930 | 79.5 | 7.5 | 3.7 | 0.0 | 0.8 | 101.9 | 5 422 | 34 | 44 | 1 561 | 27.9 | 71.4 | 0.7 |
| Frio | 55.0 | 3 412 | 58.0 | 2.0 | 4.3 | 0.0 | 2.9 | 259.6 | 16 093 | 108 | 39 | 1 302 | 59.2 | 40.5 | 0.3 |
| Gaines | 99.6 | 6 674 | 56.1 | 27.6 | 2.5 | 0.1 | 4.6 | 226.5 | 15 174 | 26 | 40 | 1 311 | 16.0 | 83.2 | 0.8 |
| Galveston | 1 237.2 | 4 357 | 58.4 | 5.5 | 4.8 | 0.6 | 3.0 | 2 036.6 | 7 172 | 935 | 1 049 | 25 946 | 39.8 | 59.3 | 0.9 |
| Garza | 16.6 | 3 541 | 68.6 | 1.9 | 5.9 | 0.0 | 4.1 | 9.7 | 2 073 | 15 | 15 | 369 | 21.4 | 77.5 | 1.1 |
| Gillespie | 59.5 | 2 533 | 60.4 | 3.6 | 8.1 | 0.0 | 6.3 | 38.3 | 1 630 | 60 | 56 | 1 106 | 20.9 | 77.5 | 1.6 |
| Glasscock | 14.5 | 12 371 | 86.1 | 8.0 | 0.4 | 0.0 | 0.8 | 8.1 | 6 897 | 0 | 0 | 115 | 9.3 | 90.1 | 0.5 |
| Goliad | 26.4 | 3 690 | 74.9 | 3.1 | 5.3 | 0.6 | 5.0 | 14.9 | 2 085 | 19 | 16 | 462 | 36.4 | 62.9 | 0.8 |
| Gonzales | 70.1 | 3 648 | 48.7 | 26.7 | 3.9 | 0.0 | 5.6 | 29.3 | 1 528 | 70 | 44 | 1 372 | 34.5 | 64.8 | 0.7 |
| Gray | 54.7 | 2 482 | 59.7 | 0.7 | 5.8 | 0.2 | 5.7 | 137.3 | 6 230 | 49 | 50 | 1 517 | 14.2 | 85.1 | 0.7 |
| Grayson | 365.4 | 3 079 | 62.8 | 2.5 | 4.5 | 0.1 | 3.3 | 392.7 | 3 309 | 335 | 270 | 6 122 | 30.6 | 68.5 | 1.0 |
| Gregg | 419.7 | 3 584 | 59.9 | 5.8 | 5.1 | 0.0 | 2.4 | 428.1 | 3 655 | 327 | 274 | 7 156 | 30.9 | 68.5 | 0.6 |
| Grimes | 67.4 | 2 634 | 71.6 | 0.1 | 4.2 | 0.1 | 6.4 | 53.5 | 2 089 | 43 | 60 | 1 957 | 32.5 | 66.8 | 0.7 |

1. Based on the resident population estimated as of July 1 of the year shown.  2. © 2013 Election Data Services, Inc. All rights reserved.

# Table B. States and Counties — Land Area and Population

| STATE/ County code | CBSA code[1] | County type[2] | STATE County | Population 2012 | | | | Population characteristics[6], 2011 | | | | | | | | | | |
|---|---|---|---|---|---|---|---|---|---|---|---|---|---|---|---|---|---|---|
| | | | | | | | | Race alone or in combination, not Hispanic or Latino (percent) | | | | | Age (percent) | | | | | |
| | | | | Land area,[3] (sq km) 2010 | Total persons | Rank | Per square kilometer | White | Black | American Indian, Alaska Native | Asian and Pacific Islander | Percent Hispanic or Latino[4] | Under 5 years | 5 to 17 years | 18 to 24 years | 25 to 34 years | 35 to 44 years | 45 to 54 years |
| | | | | 1 | 2 | 3 | 4 | 5 | 6 | 7 | 8 | 9 | 10 | 11 | 12 | 13 | 14 | 15 |
| | | | TEXAS—Cont'd | | | | | | | | | | | | | | | |
| 48 187 | 41700 | 1 | Guadalupe | 1 842 | 139 841 | 448 | 75.9 | 55.6 | 7.1 | 0.8 | 2.2 | 36.0 | 6.8 | 20.4 | 8.7 | 12.1 | 14.2 | 14.7 |
| 48 189 | 38380 | 4 | Hale | 2 602 | 36 385 | 1 266 | 14.0 | 37.3 | 5.3 | 0.7 | 0.6 | 56.9 | 8.4 | 20.5 | 11.4 | 13.2 | 12.0 | 12.5 |
| 48 191 | ... | 9 | Hall | 2 288 | 3 293 | 2 954 | 1.4 | 58.5 | 7.1 | 0.7 | 0.4 | 34.1 | 6.5 | 19.3 | 7.5 | 8.5 | 9.5 | 12.6 |
| 48 193 | ... | 6 | Hamilton | 2 165 | 8 307 | 2 583 | 3.8 | 87.3 | 1.1 | 0.8 | 0.6 | 10.9 | 5.5 | 15.8 | 7.0 | 9.1 | 10.5 | 13.6 |
| 48 195 | ... | 7 | Hansford | 2 382 | 5 521 | 2 803 | 2.3 | 54.6 | 1.2 | 0.6 | 0.5 | 44.0 | 8.0 | 21.9 | 8.1 | 11.0 | 12.1 | 13.8 |
| 48 197 | ... | 7 | Hardeman | 1 800 | 4 082 | 2 896 | 2.3 | 72.1 | 6.1 | 1.0 | 0.6 | 21.8 | 6.8 | 17.6 | 6.4 | 10.4 | 10.9 | 13.8 |
| 48 199 | 13140 | 2 | Hardin | 2 307 | 55 190 | 910 | 23.9 | 88.0 | 6.3 | 0.9 | 0.7 | 4.9 | 6.8 | 18.9 | 8.2 | 12.4 | 12.6 | 14.6 |
| 48 201 | 26420 | 1 | Harris | 4 412 | 4 253 700 | 3 | 964.1 | 33.6 | 18.8 | 0.5 | 6.8 | 41.4 | 8.2 | 19.6 | 10.0 | 16.1 | 14.3 | 13.2 |
| 48 203 | 32220 | 4 | Harrison | 2 331 | 67 450 | 785 | 28.9 | 65.1 | 22.3 | 1.0 | 0.9 | 11.9 | 7.1 | 18.9 | 9.2 | 12.3 | 12.0 | 14.4 |
| 48 205 | ... | 9 | Hartley | 3 787 | 6 144 | 2 749 | 1.6 | 68.0 | 7.3 | 0.6 | 0.7 | 24.0 | 5.6 | 16.4 | 5.0 | 15.1 | 18.6 | 16.5 |
| 48 207 | ... | 6 | Haskell | 2 339 | 5 901 | 2 774 | 2.5 | 71.0 | 4.3 | 0.7 | 1.0 | 24.2 | 5.3 | 15.6 | 7.7 | 11.4 | 11.1 | 13.9 |
| 48 209 | 12420 | 1 | Hays | 1 756 | 168 990 | 366 | 96.2 | 59.0 | 4.0 | 0.8 | 1.8 | 35.8 | 6.6 | 17.7 | 18.2 | 13.4 | 12.6 | 12.3 |
| 48 211 | ... | 9 | Hemphill | 2 347 | 4 080 | 2 898 | 1.7 | 68.8 | 0.8 | 0.8 | 1.0 | 29.2 | 8.5 | 20.6 | 7.2 | 13.5 | 12.6 | 13.0 |
| 48 213 | 11980 | 4 | Henderson | 2 263 | 79 094 | 695 | 35.0 | 81.0 | 6.8 | 1.1 | 0.7 | 11.5 | 5.8 | 16.7 | 8.0 | 10.3 | 11.4 | 14.1 |
| 48 215 | 32580 | 2 | Hidalgo | 4 069 | 806 552 | 72 | 198.2 | 7.9 | 0.5 | 0.1 | 1.0 | 90.7 | 9.7 | 24.7 | 10.8 | 13.8 | 13.2 | 10.4 |
| 48 217 | ... | 6 | Hill | 2 483 | 35 115 | 1 298 | 14.1 | 73.7 | 7.1 | 0.9 | 0.6 | 18.9 | 6.5 | 17.7 | 8.4 | 10.8 | 11.0 | 13.3 |
| 48 219 | 30220 | 6 | Hockley | 2 353 | 23 072 | 1 686 | 9.8 | 50.8 | 4.0 | 0.7 | 0.4 | 44.8 | 7.4 | 19.5 | 12.3 | 12.5 | 10.5 | 13.4 |
| 48 221 | 24180 | 4 | Hood | 1 089 | 52 044 | 954 | 47.8 | 87.1 | 1.0 | 1.2 | 0.9 | 10.8 | 5.5 | 15.4 | 6.7 | 10.1 | 10.5 | 14.2 |
| 48 223 | 44860 | 6 | Hopkins | 1 987 | 35 469 | 1 289 | 17.9 | 75.8 | 7.8 | 1.1 | 0.8 | 15.9 | 6.7 | 18.6 | 8.3 | 11.5 | 12.3 | 13.9 |
| 48 225 | ... | 7 | Houston | 3 188 | 23 161 | 1 682 | 7.3 | 62.7 | 26.5 | 0.7 | 0.7 | 10.5 | 5.5 | 14.9 | 7.2 | 11.6 | 12.5 | 15.3 |
| 48 227 | 13700 | 5 | Howard | 2 333 | 35 408 | 1 291 | 15.2 | 53.8 | 6.4 | 1.0 | 1.1 | 38.5 | 6.5 | 15.9 | 10.7 | 13.2 | 11.9 | 17.0 |
| 48 229 | ... | 8 | Hudspeth | 11 839 | 3 337 | 2 953 | 0.3 | 19.4 | 1.3 | 0.8 | 0.7 | 78.6 | 6.8 | 22.0 | 8.4 | 10.3 | 11.1 | 13.8 |
| 48 231 | 19100 | 1 | Hunt | 2 176 | 87 079 | 652 | 40.0 | 75.1 | 9.0 | 1.4 | 1.5 | 14.5 | 6.5 | 18.4 | 9.8 | 11.9 | 12.3 | 14.6 |
| 48 233 | 14420 | 6 | Hutchinson | 2 298 | 21 922 | 1 735 | 9.5 | 74.6 | 3.0 | 2.4 | 0.8 | 20.9 | 7.4 | 18.9 | 7.9 | 12.4 | 11.7 | 13.8 |
| 48 235 | 41660 | 3 | Irion | 2 724 | 1 573 | 3 079 | 0.6 | 72.4 | 1.9 | 1.1 | 0.4 | 25.5 | 4.3 | 18.1 | 7.9 | 8.4 | 11.5 | 18.0 |
| 48 237 | ... | 6 | Jack | 2 359 | 8 983 | 2 523 | 3.8 | 80.0 | 4.3 | 0.8 | 0.6 | 15.0 | 5.6 | 16.4 | 9.4 | 12.8 | 13.3 | 15.4 |
| 48 239 | ... | 6 | Jackson | 2 148 | 14 255 | 2 158 | 6.6 | 62.5 | 7.3 | 0.5 | 0.6 | 29.8 | 7.4 | 18.0 | 7.8 | 12.0 | 10.7 | 14.2 |
| 48 241 | ... | 6 | Jasper | 2 432 | 35 923 | 1 278 | 14.8 | 75.4 | 17.6 | 1.0 | 1.0 | 6.3 | 6.9 | 18.1 | 7.8 | 11.3 | 11.5 | 14.4 |
| 48 243 | ... | 9 | Jeff Davis | 5 865 | 2 307 | 3 028 | 0.4 | 64.5 | 1.4 | 1.0 | 0.7 | 34.2 | 3.5 | 15.3 | 5.0 | 6.3 | 8.0 | 15.2 |
| 48 245 | 13140 | 2 | Jefferson | 2 270 | 251 813 | 262 | 110.9 | 45.0 | 33.9 | 0.7 | 3.9 | 17.7 | 6.9 | 17.0 | 10.6 | 14.3 | 12.3 | 12.4 |
| 48 247 | ... | 6 | Jim Hogg | 2 943 | 5 249 | 2 823 | 1.8 | 6.9 | 0.6 | 0.4 | 0.4 | 92.1 | 8.5 | 20.2 | 8.8 | 12.5 | 11.1 | 12.5 |
| 48 249 | 10860 | 4 | Jim Wells | 2 240 | 41 754 | 1 134 | 18.6 | 19.9 | 0.8 | 0.4 | 0.5 | 78.8 | 8.3 | 20.3 | 9.5 | 12.4 | 11.5 | 13.3 |
| 48 251 | 19100 | 1 | Johnson | 1 877 | 153 441 | 412 | 81.7 | 76.6 | 3.3 | 1.1 | 1.4 | 18.9 | 7.0 | 19.9 | 8.6 | 12.6 | 13.4 | 14.7 |
| 48 253 | 10180 | 3 | Jones | 2 405 | 19 973 | 1 842 | 8.3 | 62.1 | 12.0 | 0.7 | 0.7 | 25.5 | 4.6 | 13.6 | 9.7 | 15.9 | 15.1 | 15.5 |
| 48 255 | ... | 6 | Karnes | 1 936 | 15 233 | 2 090 | 7.9 | 39.5 | 9.4 | 0.4 | 0.4 | 50.6 | 5.5 | 14.5 | 10.5 | 17.0 | 13.4 | 14.0 |
| 48 257 | 19100 | 1 | Kaufman | 2 022 | 106 753 | 558 | 52.8 | 70.0 | 11.0 | 1.1 | 1.2 | 18.0 | 7.4 | 21.3 | 7.8 | 12.9 | 14.3 | 14.5 |
| 48 259 | 41700 | 1 | Kendall | 1 716 | 35 956 | 1 277 | 21.0 | 76.9 | 1.1 | 1.0 | 0.9 | 21.2 | 5.1 | 18.6 | 6.9 | 8.6 | 11.7 | 16.4 |
| 48 261 | 28780 | 9 | Kenedy | 3 777 | 431 | 3 140 | 0.1 | 19.5 | 0.9 | 1.8 | 0.7 | 77.3 | 7.3 | 18.8 | 9.6 | 11.2 | 11.2 | 13.7 |
| 48 263 | ... | 9 | Kent | 2 337 | 839 | 3 116 | 0.4 | 83.3 | 1.5 | 1.6 | 0.1 | 15.2 | 5.0 | 18.4 | 3.8 | 7.6 | 10.2 | 15.2 |
| 48 265 | 28500 | 4 | Kerr | 2 858 | 49 786 | 986 | 17.4 | 72.4 | 2.0 | 1.0 | 1.1 | 24.6 | 5.3 | 14.6 | 8.1 | 9.2 | 9.6 | 13.3 |
| 48 267 | ... | 7 | Kimble | 3 240 | 4 560 | 2 866 | 1.4 | 74.5 | 0.6 | 0.7 | 0.7 | 23.9 | 5.2 | 14.9 | 5.8 | 9.6 | 9.8 | 13.9 |
| 48 269 | ... | 9 | King | 2 359 | 276 | 3 141 | 0.1 | 85.9 | 1.6 | 0.8 | 0.4 | 12.9 | 4.7 | 18.0 | 6.3 | 8.2 | 14.9 | 16.9 |
| 48 271 | ... | 9 | Kinney | 3 523 | 3 603 | 2 935 | 1.0 | 42.0 | 1.7 | 0.8 | 0.4 | 55.7 | 5.2 | 15.0 | 7.7 | 10.3 | 12.0 | 11.8 |
| 48 273 | 28780 | 4 | Kleberg | 2 283 | 32 025 | 1 390 | 14.0 | 23.3 | 4.1 | 0.4 | 2.7 | 70.3 | 7.7 | 16.9 | 20.5 | 13.0 | 10.1 | 10.5 |
| 48 275 | ... | 9 | Knox | 2 203 | 3 789 | 2 921 | 1.7 | 65.2 | 6.2 | 0.7 | 0.5 | 31.2 | 7.8 | 17.0 | 6.8 | 11.5 | 10.5 | 13.6 |
| 48 277 | 37580 | 4 | Lamar | 2 350 | 49 811 | 983 | 21.2 | 77.5 | 14.4 | 2.2 | 1.0 | 7.0 | 6.5 | 17.6 | 9.2 | 11.1 | 12.4 | 13.6 |
| 48 279 | ... | 6 | Lamb | 2 632 | 14 008 | 2 176 | 5.3 | 42.4 | 4.6 | 0.5 | 0.3 | 52.8 | 8.4 | 21.3 | 8.2 | 11.5 | 11.0 | 13.0 |
| 48 281 | 28660 | 2 | Lampasas | 1 846 | 20 107 | 1 834 | 10.9 | 76.5 | 4.1 | 1.6 | 1.9 | 18.2 | 6.0 | 18.3 | 7.6 | 10.4 | 12.7 | 15.2 |
| 48 283 | ... | 6 | La Salle | 3 851 | 7 109 | 2 671 | 1.8 | 13.3 | 0.5 | 0.5 | 0.3 | 85.7 | 6.6 | 15.4 | 18.0 | 16.6 | 11.0 | 10.3 |
| 48 285 | ... | 6 | Lavaca | 2 512 | 19 468 | 1 858 | 7.8 | 75.8 | 7.0 | 0.4 | 0.6 | 16.9 | 6.4 | 16.6 | 6.6 | 9.5 | 10.7 | 14.0 |
| 48 287 | ... | 6 | Lee | 1 629 | 16 601 | 2 002 | 10.2 | 65.5 | 11.4 | 0.7 | 0.7 | 23.0 | 6.4 | 19.3 | 8.3 | 10.4 | 11.4 | 15.1 |
| 48 289 | ... | 8 | Leon | 2 779 | 16 803 | 1 995 | 6.0 | 77.5 | 7.9 | 0.9 | 0.9 | 13.9 | 6.3 | 16.2 | 6.8 | 10.0 | 9.8 | 14.7 |
| 48 291 | 26420 | 1 | Liberty | 3 000 | 76 571 | 716 | 25.5 | 69.1 | 11.4 | 0.9 | 0.8 | 19.1 | 7.1 | 18.4 | 9.3 | 13.4 | 13.4 | 14.7 |
| 48 293 | ... | 6 | Limestone | 2 345 | 23 585 | 1 660 | 10.1 | 61.9 | 18.0 | 0.7 | 0.6 | 19.9 | 6.8 | 17.1 | 8.9 | 12.5 | 11.5 | 13.7 |
| 48 295 | ... | 9 | Lipscomb | 2 414 | 3 480 | 2 942 | 1.4 | 66.5 | 1.4 | 1.4 | 0.5 | 31.6 | 7.5 | 20.1 | 7.7 | 13.4 | 10.3 | 14.3 |
| 48 297 | ... | 6 | Live Oak | 2 693 | 11 664 | 2 320 | 4.3 | 58.5 | 4.4 | 0.9 | 0.7 | 36.2 | 4.7 | 15.1 | 7.7 | 12.2 | 12.1 | 14.9 |
| 48 299 | ... | 7 | Llano | 2 419 | 19 085 | 1 870 | 7.9 | 89.3 | 1.2 | 1.1 | 0.7 | 8.7 | 4.2 | 11.4 | 4.5 | 7.2 | 8.0 | 13.0 |
| 48 301 | ... | 9 | Loving | 1 733 | 71 | 3 143 | 0.0 | 74.5 | 2.1 | 4.3 | 0.0 | 19.1 | 5.3 | 7.4 | 9.6 | 5.3 | 10.6 | 16.0 |
| 48 303 | 31180 | 3 | Lubbock | 2 320 | 285 760 | 230 | 123.2 | 57.6 | 7.6 | 0.7 | 2.6 | 32.6 | 7.3 | 16.9 | 17.6 | 14.3 | 10.8 | 12.0 |
| 48 305 | ... | 6 | Lynn | 2 310 | 5 783 | 2 781 | 2.5 | 50.4 | 2.6 | 0.6 | 0.4 | 46.6 | 7.8 | 19.4 | 7.7 | 11.0 | 11.2 | 15.2 |
| 48 307 | ... | 7 | McCulloch | 2 760 | 8 313 | 2 581 | 3.0 | 66.4 | 2.4 | 0.5 | 0.6 | 30.8 | 6.7 | 17.9 | 6.8 | 10.0 | 10.7 | 13.3 |
| 48 309 | 47380 | 3 | McLennan | 2 686 | 238 707 | 272 | 88.9 | 59.4 | 15.1 | 0.7 | 2.0 | 24.2 | 7.0 | 18.1 | 15.0 | 12.8 | 11.2 | 12.5 |
| 48 311 | ... | 8 | McMullen | 2 951 | 726 | 3 127 | 0.2 | 61.2 | 2.0 | 0.1 | 0.9 | 36.2 | 3.6 | 13.3 | 6.2 | 9.4 | 10.1 | 14.6 |
| 48 313 | ... | 6 | Madison | 1 207 | 13 677 | 2 199 | 11.3 | 58.7 | 20.4 | 0.6 | 0.8 | 20.6 | 5.8 | 15.8 | 11.8 | 17.1 | 13.0 | 11.5 |
| 48 315 | ... | 8 | Marion | 986 | 10 324 | 2 413 | 10.5 | 72.9 | 22.7 | 1.6 | 1.0 | 3.8 | 4.9 | 13.9 | 6.5 | 8.7 | 10.4 | 16.5 |
| 48 317 | ... | 6 | Martin | 2 370 | 5 017 | 2 837 | 2.1 | 53.1 | 2.2 | 0.6 | 0.5 | 44.4 | 8.8 | 21.3 | 9.2 | 11.8 | 12.0 | 13.7 |

1. CBSA = Core Based Statistical Area. See Appendix A for explanation. See Appendix B for list of metropolitan areas with component counties.   2. County type code from the Economic Research Service of USDA Rural-Urban Continuum Codes. See Appendix A for definition.   3. Dry land or land partially or temporarily covered by water.   4. May be of any race.

# Table B. States and Counties — **Population and Households**

| | Population, 2011 (cont.) | | | | Population change and components of change, 2000–2012 | | | | | | | Households, 2010 | | | | |
|---|---|---|---|---|---|---|---|---|---|---|---|---|---|---|---|---|
| | Age (percent) (cont.) | | | | Total persons | | Percent change | | Components of change, 2010–2012 | | | | | | Percent | |
| STATE County | 55 to 64 years | 65 to 74 years | 75 years and over | Percent female | 2000 | 2010 | 2000–2010 | 2010–2012 | Births | Deaths | Net migration | Number | Percent change, 2000–2010 | Persons per household | Female family householder[1] | One person |
| | 16 | 17 | 18 | 19 | 20 | 21 | 22 | 23 | 24 | 25 | 26 | 27 | 28 | 29 | 30 | 31 |
| **TEXAS—Cont'd** | | | | | | | | | | | | | | | | |
| Guadalupe | 11.3 | 6.9 | 4.9 | 50.8 | 89 023 | 131 533 | 47.8 | 6.3 | 3 711 | 1 943 | 6 357 | 45 762 | 48.1 | 2.83 | 12.3 | 19.3 |
| Hale | 9.8 | 6.3 | 5.9 | 48.5 | 36 602 | 36 273 | -0.9 | 0.3 | 1 335 | 736 | -508 | 11 846 | -1.1 | 2.83 | 14.3 | 22.2 |
| Hall | 13.2 | 12.4 | 10.4 | 50.1 | 3 782 | 3 353 | -11.3 | -1.8 | 89 | 100 | -48 | 1 372 | -11.4 | 2.41 | 9.7 | 31.6 |
| Hamilton | 13.5 | 12.5 | 12.6 | 50.6 | 8 229 | 8 517 | 3.5 | -2.5 | 200 | 285 | -121 | 3 442 | 2.0 | 2.40 | 9.0 | 27.6 |
| Hansford | 11.6 | 7.0 | 6.4 | 49.8 | 5 369 | 5 613 | 4.5 | -1.6 | 173 | 100 | -166 | 2 006 | 0.0 | 2.77 | 6.8 | 22.1 |
| Hardeman | 14.2 | 11.1 | 8.7 | 50.3 | 4 724 | 4 139 | -12.4 | -1.4 | 106 | 98 | -78 | 1 722 | -11.4 | 2.39 | 12.6 | 29.3 |
| Hardin | 12.8 | 8.0 | 5.9 | 50.6 | 48 073 | 54 635 | 13.7 | 1.0 | 1 523 | 1 143 | 205 | 20 462 | 14.9 | 2.65 | 11.6 | 21.3 |
| Harris | 10.1 | 4.9 | 3.4 | 50.2 | 3 400 578 | 4 092 459 | 20.3 | 3.9 | 151 278 | 51 053 | 62 197 | 1 435 155 | 19.0 | 2.82 | 15.3 | 25.2 |
| Harrison | 12.9 | 7.6 | 5.7 | 50.9 | 62 110 | 65 631 | 5.7 | 2.8 | 1 958 | 1 284 | 1 154 | 24 523 | 6.2 | 2.62 | 14.8 | 24.3 |
| Hartley | 10.5 | 6.5 | 5.7 | 38.7 | 5 537 | 6 062 | 9.5 | 1.4 | 122 | 69 | 2 | 1 771 | 10.4 | 2.63 | 5.3 | 22.8 |
| Haskell | 13.7 | 10.1 | 11.3 | 47.5 | 6 093 | 5 899 | -3.2 | 0.0 | 114 | 174 | 50 | 2 297 | -10.6 | 2.33 | 10.0 | 30.3 |
| Hays | 10.4 | 5.4 | 3.4 | 50.2 | 97 589 | 157 107 | 61.0 | 7.6 | 4 686 | 1 811 | 8 829 | 55 245 | 65.4 | 2.72 | 9.8 | 21.7 |
| Hemphill | 11.8 | 6.8 | 6.0 | 49.4 | 3 351 | 3 807 | 13.6 | 7.2 | 149 | 67 | 183 | 1 382 | 8.0 | 2.73 | 7.2 | 22.1 |
| Henderson | 14.1 | 11.2 | 8.3 | 51.1 | 73 277 | 78 532 | 7.2 | 0.7 | 2 051 | 2 188 | 720 | 31 020 | 7.7 | 2.49 | 11.8 | 25.6 |
| Hidalgo | 7.9 | 5.2 | 4.3 | 51.2 | 569 463 | 774 769 | 36.1 | 4.1 | 36 410 | 8 534 | 3 827 | 216 471 | 38.0 | 3.55 | 18.8 | 14.0 |
| Hill | 13.7 | 10.5 | 8.2 | 51.1 | 32 321 | 35 089 | 8.6 | 0.1 | 981 | 868 | -64 | 13 238 | 8.5 | 2.59 | 11.6 | 24.1 |
| Hockley | 11.5 | 7.3 | 5.7 | 50.7 | 22 716 | 22 935 | 1.0 | 0.6 | 724 | 495 | -100 | 8 242 | 3.1 | 2.70 | 12.9 | 22.7 |
| Hood | 15.5 | 12.8 | 9.3 | 50.7 | 41 100 | 51 182 | 24.5 | 1.7 | 1 211 | 1 235 | 895 | 20 795 | 28.6 | 2.43 | 8.6 | 24.0 |
| Hopkins | 12.8 | 8.8 | 7.0 | 50.4 | 31 960 | 35 161 | 10.0 | 0.9 | 1 069 | 832 | 57 | 13 308 | 8.3 | 2.61 | 11.5 | 24.2 |
| Houston | 13.5 | 10.5 | 9.0 | 46.3 | 23 185 | 23 732 | 2.4 | -2.4 | 525 | 659 | -444 | 8 656 | 4.8 | 2.41 | 14.1 | 28.9 |
| Howard | 11.6 | 6.9 | 6.3 | 43.6 | 33 627 | 35 012 | 4.1 | 1.1 | 958 | 790 | 214 | 11 333 | -0.5 | 2.55 | 14.4 | 27.1 |
| Hudspeth | 13.2 | 8.5 | 5.7 | 49.1 | 3 344 | 3 476 | 3.9 | -4.0 | 113 | 32 | -222 | 1 174 | 7.5 | 2.89 | 12.9 | 23.8 |
| Hunt | 12.5 | 8.3 | 5.8 | 50.4 | 76 596 | 86 129 | 12.4 | 1.1 | 2 379 | 1 909 | 489 | 32 076 | 11.6 | 2.63 | 12.2 | 24.0 |
| Hutchinson | 13.1 | 7.7 | 7.2 | 50.1 | 23 857 | 22 150 | -7.2 | -1.0 | 683 | 533 | -406 | 8 812 | -5.1 | 2.50 | 10.5 | 26.6 |
| Irion | 13.4 | 10.2 | 8.2 | 50.9 | 1 771 | 1 599 | -9.7 | -1.6 | 33 | 30 | -33 | 653 | -5.9 | 2.45 | 8.6 | 25.0 |
| Jack | 12.0 | 8.6 | 6.5 | 44.4 | 8 763 | 9 044 | 3.2 | -0.7 | 227 | 186 | -97 | 3 136 | 2.9 | 2.52 | 9.1 | 25.7 |
| Jackson | 13.2 | 8.9 | 7.8 | 50.5 | 14 391 | 14 075 | -2.2 | 1.3 | 412 | 286 | 43 | 5 284 | -1.0 | 2.62 | 11.0 | 24.6 |
| Jasper | 13.4 | 9.5 | 7.2 | 50.7 | 35 604 | 35 710 | 0.3 | 0.6 | 1 065 | 904 | 49 | 13 770 | 2.4 | 2.52 | 13.8 | 24.9 |
| Jeff Davis | 22.1 | 15.6 | 9.0 | 49.7 | 2 207 | 2 342 | 6.1 | -1.5 | 42 | 47 | -36 | 1 034 | 15.4 | 2.18 | 5.8 | 30.2 |
| Jefferson | 11.7 | 6.4 | 6.2 | 48.9 | 252 051 | 252 273 | 0.1 | -0.2 | 7 693 | 5 468 | -2 666 | 93 441 | 0.6 | 2.53 | 16.9 | 28.6 |
| Jim Hogg | 11.7 | 8.9 | 5.9 | 50.5 | 5 281 | 5 300 | 0.4 | -1.0 | 199 | 110 | -143 | 1 902 | 4.8 | 2.78 | 15.8 | 25.4 |
| Jim Wells | 11.5 | 7.4 | 5.9 | 50.5 | 39 326 | 40 838 | 3.8 | 2.2 | 1 471 | 865 | 321 | 13 961 | 7.7 | 2.90 | 16.9 | 21.1 |
| Johnson | 11.9 | 7.2 | 4.7 | 50.0 | 126 811 | 150 934 | 19.0 | 1.7 | 4 418 | 2 635 | 768 | 52 193 | 19.6 | 2.84 | 11.5 | 18.6 |
| Jones | 11.9 | 7.5 | 6.1 | 38.5 | 20 785 | 20 202 | -2.8 | -1.1 | 376 | 431 | -192 | 6 034 | -1.7 | 2.52 | 10.5 | 25.4 |
| Karnes | 11.2 | 6.8 | 7.2 | 40.2 | 15 446 | 14 824 | -4.0 | 2.8 | 334 | 354 | 404 | 4 463 | 0.2 | 2.57 | 14.3 | 27.1 |
| Kaufman | 11.3 | 6.5 | 4.0 | 50.8 | 71 313 | 103 350 | 44.9 | 3.3 | 3 170 | 1 829 | 1 999 | 34 964 | 43.5 | 2.92 | 12.4 | 17.5 |
| Kendall | 15.2 | 9.9 | 7.4 | 51.2 | 23 743 | 33 410 | 40.7 | 7.6 | 769 | 713 | 2 429 | 12 617 | 46.5 | 2.61 | 8.2 | 21.7 |
| Kenedy | 14.9 | 6.4 | 6.9 | 47.1 | 414 | 416 | 0.5 | 3.6 | 8 | 3 | 9 | 147 | 6.5 | 2.83 | 11.6 | 25.2 |
| Kent | 14.2 | 11.3 | 14.4 | 51.5 | 859 | 808 | -5.9 | 3.8 | 10 | 28 | 47 | 350 | -0.8 | 2.16 | 9.4 | 37.1 |
| Kerr | 14.6 | 12.8 | 12.3 | 51.6 | 43 653 | 49 625 | 13.7 | 0.3 | 1 153 | 1 510 | 533 | 20 550 | 15.4 | 2.32 | 10.2 | 29.1 |
| Kimble | 17.5 | 13.7 | 9.6 | 50.4 | 4 468 | 4 607 | 3.1 | -1.0 | 99 | 135 | -9 | 2 016 | 8.0 | 2.26 | 8.6 | 31.4 |
| King | 15.7 | 8.6 | 6.7 | 51.8 | 356 | 286 | -19.7 | -3.5 | 6 | 0 | -16 | 113 | 4.6 | 2.53 | 4.4 | 20.4 |
| Kinney | 14.0 | 12.5 | 11.5 | 45.4 | 3 379 | 3 598 | 6.5 | 0.1 | 77 | 77 | 1 | 1 350 | 2.7 | 2.42 | 6.8 | 28.3 |
| Kleberg | 9.5 | 6.7 | 5.1 | 49.4 | 31 549 | 32 061 | 1.6 | -0.1 | 1 113 | 600 | -551 | 11 097 | 1.8 | 2.71 | 16.1 | 23.7 |
| Knox | 12.0 | 9.8 | 11.0 | 50.9 | 4 253 | 3 719 | -12.6 | 1.9 | 109 | 118 | 74 | 1 506 | -10.9 | 2.40 | 11.0 | 30.6 |
| Lamar | 12.5 | 9.8 | 7.3 | 51.8 | 48 499 | 49 793 | 2.7 | 0.0 | 1 450 | 1 387 | -71 | 19 829 | 3.9 | 2.48 | 14.5 | 27.3 |
| Lamb | 10.9 | 7.9 | 7.7 | 50.0 | 14 709 | 13 977 | -5.0 | 0.2 | 503 | 346 | -121 | 5 081 | -5.2 | 2.71 | 12.4 | 24.1 |
| Lampasas | 13.6 | 9.3 | 6.8 | 50.7 | 17 762 | 19 677 | 10.8 | 2.2 | 514 | 419 | 340 | 7 539 | 15.0 | 2.58 | 10.0 | 23.0 |
| La Salle | 9.5 | 7.5 | 5.2 | 40.7 | 5 866 | 6 886 | 17.4 | 3.2 | 210 | 86 | 102 | 1 931 | 6.2 | 2.75 | 16.4 | 26.6 |
| Lavaca | 14.8 | 10.7 | 10.7 | 51.1 | 19 210 | 19 263 | 0.3 | 1.1 | 473 | 552 | 281 | 7 808 | 1.8 | 2.41 | 9.5 | 27.8 |
| Lee | 13.1 | 8.6 | 7.4 | 49.4 | 15 657 | 16 612 | 6.1 | -0.1 | 417 | 334 | -97 | 6 151 | 8.6 | 2.62 | 9.6 | 23.9 |
| Leon | 14.4 | 12.8 | 8.9 | 50.3 | 15 335 | 16 801 | 9.6 | 0.0 | 459 | 472 | 19 | 6 896 | 11.4 | 2.42 | 9.9 | 25.8 |
| Liberty | 12.1 | 6.9 | 4.6 | 50.9 | 70 154 | 75 643 | 7.8 | 1.2 | 2 344 | 1 586 | 187 | 25 073 | 7.9 | 2.81 | 12.8 | 21.8 |
| Limestone | 13.2 | 9.1 | 7.1 | 48.2 | 22 051 | 23 384 | 6.0 | 0.9 | 695 | 620 | 136 | 8 499 | 7.5 | 2.56 | 13.7 | 26.3 |
| Lipscomb | 12.4 | 7.5 | 6.7 | 49.6 | 3 057 | 3 302 | 8.0 | 5.4 | 113 | 61 | 119 | 1 263 | 4.8 | 2.59 | 8.2 | 26.7 |
| Live Oak | 13.8 | 10.8 | 8.7 | 45.9 | 12 309 | 11 531 | -6.3 | 1.2 | 238 | 251 | 149 | 4 257 | 0.6 | 2.44 | 9.5 | 26.9 |
| Llano | 19.0 | 18.3 | 14.4 | 51.7 | 17 044 | 19 301 | 13.2 | -1.1 | 321 | 658 | 85 | 9 008 | 14.3 | 2.12 | 6.9 | 31.5 |
| Loving | 31.9 | 8.5 | 5.3 | 48.9 | 67 | 82 | 22.4 | -13.4 | 0 | 1 | -10 | 39 | 25.8 | 2.10 | 10.3 | 30.8 |
| Lubbock | 10.0 | 5.9 | 5.2 | 50.6 | 242 628 | 278 831 | 14.9 | 2.5 | 9 054 | 5 158 | 2 991 | 105 781 | 14.3 | 2.53 | 13.5 | 27.5 |
| Lynn | 11.9 | 8.8 | 7.1 | 50.4 | 6 550 | 5 915 | -9.7 | -2.2 | 159 | 106 | -184 | 2 246 | -4.6 | 2.61 | 11.2 | 24.7 |
| McCulloch | 14.9 | 10.4 | 9.4 | 50.7 | 8 205 | 8 283 | 1.0 | 0.4 | 246 | 275 | 54 | 3 338 | 1.9 | 2.45 | 10.4 | 28.4 |
| McLennan | 10.9 | 6.5 | 6.0 | 51.3 | 213 517 | 234 906 | 10.0 | 1.6 | 7 606 | 4 448 | 701 | 86 892 | 10.2 | 2.60 | 14.7 | 26.2 |
| McMullen | 15.5 | 15.4 | 11.7 | 49.1 | 851 | 707 | -16.9 | 2.7 | 14 | 17 | 20 | 310 | -12.7 | 2.28 | 7.1 | 28.1 |
| Madison | 10.9 | 8.1 | 6.1 | 42.4 | 12 940 | 13 664 | 5.6 | 0.1 | 342 | 277 | -57 | 4 187 | 7.0 | 2.65 | 13.6 | 24.6 |
| Marion | 17.2 | 12.8 | 9.0 | 51.0 | 10 941 | 10 546 | -3.6 | -2.1 | 199 | 345 | -77 | 4 595 | -0.3 | 2.26 | 12.5 | 31.3 |
| Martin | 10.6 | 7.1 | 5.4 | 49.5 | 4 746 | 4 799 | 1.1 | 4.5 | 178 | 86 | 119 | 1 649 | 1.5 | 2.88 | 12.4 | 21.2 |

1. No spouse present.

# Table B. States and Counties — Population, Vital Statistics, Medicare, and Crime

| STATE County | Persons in group quarters, 2010 | Daytime population, 2007–2011 Number | Employ-ment/resi-dence ratio | Births, 2011 Total | Rate[1] | Deaths, 2011 Number | Rate[1] | Persons under 65 with no health insurance, 2010 Number | Percent | Medicare, 2012 Eligible for Medicare | Enrolled in Medicare Advantage | Enrolled in a Medicare prescription drug plan | Serious crimes known to police,[2] 2011 Total Number | Rate[3] |
|---|---|---|---|---|---|---|---|---|---|---|---|---|---|---|
| | 32 | 33 | 34 | 35 | 36 | 37 | 38 | 39 | 40 | 41 | 42 | 43 | 44 | 45 |
| **TEXAS—Cont'd** | | | | | | | | | | | | | | |
| Guadalupe | 1 888 | 104 341 | 0.61 | 1 688 | 12.4 | 837 | 6.2 | 25 616 | 22.2 | 19 324 | 4 062 | 5 783 | 3 396 | 2 529 |
| Hale | 2 802 | 36 881 | 1.06 | 636 | 17.4 | 342 | 9.4 | 7 635 | 26.2 | 5 138 | 572 | 2 681 | 1 169 | 3 156 |
| Hall | 44 | 3 208 | 0.86 | 49 | 14.5 | 39 | 11.5 | 1 004 | 39.1 | 786 | 79 | 429 | 21 | 613 |
| Hamilton | 254 | 8 367 | 0.96 | 87 | 10.3 | 129 | 15.2 | 1 890 | 29.8 | 2 121 | 514 | 869 | 151 | 2 072 |
| Hansford | 60 | 5 114 | 0.84 | 80 | 14.3 | 45 | 8.1 | 1 475 | 30.6 | 872 | 39 | 505 | 96 | 1 675 |
| Hardeman | 21 | 3 891 | 0.81 | 63 | 15.1 | 45 | 10.8 | 912 | 27.4 | 911 | 68 | 455 | 100 | 2 366 |
| Hardin | 380 | 43 644 | 0.55 | 723 | 13.1 | 485 | 8.8 | 9 524 | 20.2 | 9 479 | 2 525 | 3 391 | 1 017 | 1 823 |
| Harris | 44 524 | 4 313 976 | 1.15 | 71 460 | 17.1 | 22 304 | 5.3 | 1 117 424 | 29.9 | 423 039 | 132 421 | 142 334 | 206 027 | 4 931 |
| | | | | | | | | | | | | | | |
| Harrison | 1 363 | 61 236 | 0.87 | 896 | 13.5 | 605 | 9.1 | 14 299 | 25.7 | 11 175 | 1 746 | 4 818 | 2 090 | 3 119 |
| Hartley | 1 406 | 6 235 | 1.12 | 59 | 9.9 | 25 | 4.2 | 959 | 24.2 | 641 | 47 | 364 | 95 | 1 535 |
| Haskell | 544 | 5 645 | 0.90 | 57 | 9.5 | 73 | 12.2 | 1 275 | 31.1 | 1 368 | 126 | 768 | 77 | 1 278 |
| Hays | 7 017 | 134 334 | 0.74 | 2 079 | 12.7 | 749 | 4.6 | 30 683 | 22.3 | 18 389 | 3 194 | 6 647 | 3 545 | 2 210 |
| Hemphill | 40 | 4 114 | 1.19 | 56 | 14.1 | 34 | 8.6 | 813 | 24.8 | 530 | 25 | 288 | 88 | 2 264 |
| Henderson | 1 242 | 69 667 | 0.72 | 897 | 11.4 | 977 | 12.4 | 18 035 | 28.8 | 18 163 | 2 852 | 7 943 | 2 570 | 3 214 |
| Hidalgo | 6 982 | 746 649 | 0.96 | 16 884 | 21.2 | 3 641 | 4.6 | 265 156 | 38.1 | 83 728 | 16 274 | 47 002 | 33 632 | 4 251 |
| Hill | 829 | 31 046 | 0.72 | 454 | 12.8 | 374 | 10.6 | 7 625 | 27.1 | 7 608 | 1 007 | 3 429 | 714 | 1 993 |
| Hockley | 641 | 21 625 | 0.87 | 319 | 13.9 | 212 | 9.3 | 5 103 | 26.5 | 3 610 | 503 | 1 613 | 609 | 2 601 |
| | | | | | | | | | | | | | | |
| Hood | 701 | 44 743 | 0.73 | 560 | 10.8 | 539 | 10.4 | 9 560 | 24.0 | 12 835 | 2 182 | 5 063 | 1 111 | 2 126 |
| Hopkins | 431 | 34 141 | 0.95 | 468 | 13.2 | 354 | 10.0 | 9 045 | 30.7 | 6 614 | 384 | 3 490 | 472 | 1 315 |
| Houston | 2 908 | 23 400 | 0.97 | 258 | 11.0 | 312 | 13.3 | 4 865 | 29.6 | 4 823 | 575 | 2 339 | 446 | 1 841 |
| Howard | 6 080 | 35 004 | 1.03 | 470 | 13.4 | 336 | 9.6 | 5 863 | 23.9 | 5 221 | 569 | 2 194 | 1 356 | 3 793 |
| Hudspeth | 86 | 3 465 | 1.03 | 48 | 14.0 | 4 | 1.2 | 1 205 | 41.4 | 536 | 107 | 269 | 23 | 648 |
| Hunt | 1 869 | 80 776 | 0.87 | 1 084 | 12.5 | 844 | 9.8 | 18 701 | 25.8 | 15 311 | 1 390 | 7 347 | 3 132 | 3 620 |
| Hutchinson | 161 | 22 435 | 1.04 | 330 | 14.9 | 229 | 10.3 | 4 816 | 25.8 | 3 772 | 333 | 1 994 | 760 | 3 672 |
| Irion | 0 | 1 336 | 0.78 | 10 | 6.2 | 14 | 8.6 | 354 | 26.9 | 317 | 22 | 141 | 22 | 1 347 |
| Jack | 1 140 | 9 417 | 1.11 | 93 | 10.3 | 76 | 8.4 | 1 755 | 26.8 | 1 576 | 174 | 757 | 115 | 1 245 |
| | | | | | | | | | | | | | | |
| Jackson | 217 | 13 755 | 0.96 | 194 | 13.8 | 122 | 8.7 | 2 788 | 24.0 | 2 643 | 284 | 1 202 | 211 | 1 468 |
| Jasper | 941 | 34 585 | 0.93 | 492 | 13.6 | 388 | 10.7 | 7 223 | 24.9 | 7 337 | 1 216 | 3 431 | 684 | 1 876 |
| Jeff Davis | 88 | 2 531 | 1.18 | 16 | 7.0 | 18 | 7.9 | 526 | 30.6 | 583 | 75 | 214 | 17 | 711 |
| Jefferson | 15 983 | 277 931 | 1.27 | 3 554 | 14.1 | 2 470 | 9.8 | 56 409 | 27.5 | 39 900 | 10 072 | 16 758 | 13 348 | 5 182 |
| Jim Hogg | 16 | 5 310 | 1.04 | 86 | 16.3 | 63 | 12.0 | 1 345 | 30.0 | 933 | 160 | 512 | 33 | 610 |
| Jim Wells | 357 | 40 903 | 1.00 | 697 | 16.9 | 363 | 8.8 | 8 425 | 23.9 | 6 994 | 2 182 | 2 928 | 1 889 | 4 530 |
| Johnson | 2 644 | 127 028 | 0.66 | 2 151 | 14.1 | 1 124 | 7.4 | 32 777 | 24.9 | 23 435 | 8 085 | 7 203 | 4 075 | 2 644 |
| Jones | 5 007 | 19 665 | 0.92 | 172 | 8.5 | 180 | 8.9 | 3 232 | 25.6 | 3 141 | 360 | 1 581 | 535 | 2 594 |
| Karnes | 3 336 | 15 254 | 1.08 | 162 | 10.8 | 161 | 10.8 | 2 215 | 23.2 | 2 584 | 243 | 1 454 | 343 | 2 266 |
| | | | | | | | | | | | | | | |
| Kaufman | 1 336 | 83 571 | 0.61 | 1 488 | 14.1 | 813 | 7.7 | 21 788 | 23.7 | 14 944 | 3 016 | 6 070 | 2 816 | 2 669 |
| Kendall | 519 | 31 106 | 0.90 | 357 | 10.3 | 308 | 8.9 | 5 326 | 19.1 | 7 141 | 1 336 | 2 306 | 547 | 1 603 |
| Kenedy | 0 | 590 | 3.25 | 7 | 16.0 | 0 | 0.0 | 91 | 25.6 | 53 | D | 29 | 9 | 2 118 |
| Kent | 52 | 918 | 1.14 | 6 | 7.3 | 14 | 17.0 | 144 | 24.5 | 183 | 18 | 91 | 33 | 4 000 |
| Kerr | 1 910 | 49 554 | 1.02 | 573 | 11.5 | 684 | 13.7 | 10 009 | 27.8 | 13 793 | 1 286 | 5 381 | 1 063 | 2 098 |
| Kimble | 43 | 4 284 | 0.87 | 52 | 11.2 | 53 | 11.4 | 1 186 | 33.6 | 1 122 | 95 | 532 | 104 | 2 211 |
| King | 0 | 297 | 1.28 | 2 | 7.8 | 0 | 0.0 | 46 | 18.5 | 28 | D | 13 | 1 | 342 |
| Kinney | 332 | 3 542 | 0.89 | 46 | 12.7 | 35 | 9.6 | 674 | 28.1 | 882 | 153 | 325 | 2 | 54 |
| Kleberg | 1 974 | 31 224 | 0.95 | 539 | 16.7 | 254 | 7.9 | 6 815 | 25.7 | 4 506 | 1 289 | 1 349 | 1 605 | 4 903 |
| | | | | | | | | | | | | | | |
| Knox | 104 | 3 851 | 1.10 | 57 | 15.2 | 51 | 13.6 | 925 | 32.0 | 842 | 54 | 478 | 40 | 1 053 |
| Lamar | 713 | 50 408 | 1.04 | 633 | 12.6 | 622 | 12.4 | 10 269 | 25.0 | 10 427 | 523 | 5 355 | 2 034 | 4 001 |
| Lamb | 184 | 13 733 | 0.94 | 246 | 17.4 | 150 | 10.6 | 3 588 | 30.8 | 2 545 | 325 | 1 429 | 441 | 3 318 |
| Lampasas | 222 | 16 281 | 0.59 | 217 | 10.9 | 175 | 8.8 | 4 635 | 28.1 | 4 088 | 770 | 1 171 | 359 | 1 892 |
| La Salle | 1 583 | 7 049 | 1.11 | 101 | 14.4 | 33 | 4.7 | 1 282 | 28.8 | 1 063 | 268 | 550 | 41 | 583 |
| Lavaca | 409 | 17 708 | 0.82 | 226 | 11.7 | 246 | 12.7 | 3 750 | 24.9 | 4 622 | 333 | 2 477 | 300 | 1 525 |
| Lee | 525 | 15 265 | 0.82 | 194 | 11.6 | 136 | 8.2 | 4 037 | 29.7 | 3 017 | 441 | 1 196 | 307 | 1 810 |
| Leon | 104 | 17 069 | 1.05 | 215 | 12.7 | 213 | 12.6 | 3 617 | 27.6 | 4 541 | 601 | 1 948 | 201 | 1 172 |
| Liberty | 5 144 | 64 872 | 0.64 | 1 126 | 14.8 | 710 | 9.3 | 16 385 | 26.3 | 11 241 | 3 177 | 4 122 | 2 785 | 3 606 |
| | | | | | | | | | | | | | | |
| Limestone | 1 592 | 23 470 | 1.02 | 351 | 14.9 | 260 | 11.0 | 4 757 | 26.0 | 4 656 | 759 | 2 081 | 911 | 3 816 |
| Lipscomb | 37 | 3 160 | 0.94 | 50 | 15.0 | 39 | 11.7 | 862 | 30.9 | 540 | 16 | 287 | 18 | 534 |
| Live Oak | 1 164 | 11 338 | 0.96 | 92 | 8.0 | 111 | 9.7 | 2 007 | 24.2 | 1 783 | 320 | 799 | 162 | 1 376 |
| Llano | 184 | 18 433 | 0.91 | 153 | 8.0 | 278 | 14.5 | 3 198 | 24.1 | 5 900 | 825 | 2 384 | 438 | 2 223 |
| Loving | 0 | 290 | 5.07 | 0 | 0.0 | 0 | 0.0 | 18 | 26.7 | 14 | D | D | 0 | 0 |
| Lubbock | 11 037 | 277 490 | 1.02 | 4 232 | 14.9 | 2 258 | 8.0 | 54 095 | 22.6 | 38 516 | 7 885 | 16 543 | 15 536 | 5 457 |
| Lynn | 42 | 5 149 | 0.70 | 63 | 10.7 | 46 | 7.8 | 1 419 | 28.8 | 1 045 | 122 | 619 | 100 | 1 656 |
| McCulloch | 109 | 8 236 | 1.00 | 122 | 14.7 | 118 | 14.2 | 1 888 | 28.8 | 1 932 | 82 | 1 006 | 152 | 1 797 |
| McLennan | 9 085 | 238 229 | 1.06 | 3 362 | 14.1 | 1 930 | 8.1 | 47 444 | 23.9 | 36 846 | 7 576 | 15 078 | 10 675 | 4 451 |
| | | | | | | | | | | | | | | |
| McMullen | 0 | 1 011 | 1.71 | 4 | 5.8 | 9 | 13.0 | 114 | 21.5 | 173 | 34 | 63 | 10 | 1 385 |
| Madison | 2 554 | 13 837 | 1.07 | 163 | 11.9 | 130 | 9.5 | 3 003 | 31.9 | 2 219 | 295 | 991 | 280 | 2 007 |
| Marion | 167 | 9 603 | 0.73 | 92 | 8.8 | 149 | 14.2 | 2 229 | 27.4 | 2 667 | 448 | 1 246 | 318 | 2 953 |
| Martin | 48 | 4 635 | 0.97 | 91 | 18.4 | 39 | 7.9 | 1 069 | 25.5 | 709 | 47 | 376 | 80 | 1 633 |

1. Per 1,000 estimated resident population.   2. Data for serious crimes have not been adjusted for underreporting; this may affect comparability between geographic areas and over time.   3. Per 100,000 population estimated by the FBI.

# Table B. States and Counties — Crime, Education, Money Income, and Poverty

| | Serious crimes known to police, 2011 (cont.)[1] | | Education | | | | | | Money income, 2007–2011 | | | | Income and poverty, 2011 | | | |
|---|---|---|---|---|---|---|---|---|---|---|---|---|---|---|---|---|
| | Rate[2] | | School enrollment and attainment, 2007–2011 | | | | Local government expenditures,[5] 2009–2010 | | | Households | | | Percent below poverty level | | | |
| | | | Enrollment[3] | | Attainment[4] (percent) | | | | | | Median income | | | | | |
| STATE County | Violent | Property | Total | Percent private | High school graduate or less | Bachelor's degree or more | Total current expenditures (mil dol) | Current expenditures per student (dollars) | Per capita income[6] (dollars) | Dollars | Percent change, 2000 to 2007–2011 (constant 2011 dollars) | Percent with income of $200,000 or more | Median household income (dollars) | All persons | Children under 18 years | Children 5 to 17 years in families |
| | 46 | 47 | 48 | 49 | 50 | 51 | 52 | 53 | 54 | 55 | 56 | 57 | 58 | 59 | 60 | 61 |
| **TEXAS—Cont'd** | | | | | | | | | | | | | | | | |
| Guadalupe | 212 | 2 316 | 36 554 | 12.9 | 44.2 | 24.1 | 174.1 | 7 843 | 25 627 | 61 608 | 3.8 | 2.3 | 57 576 | 10.8 | 16.2 | 14.8 |
| Hale | 227 | 2 930 | 10 414 | 15.0 | 60.5 | 13.9 | 64.4 | 8 367 | 17 255 | 39 335 | -6.9 | 1.8 | 36 142 | 25.8 | 36.5 | 34.3 |
| Hall | 117 | 496 | 813 | 2.6 | 60.4 | 14.3 | 6.1 | 10 933 | 19 999 | 32 059 | 3.2 | 1.7 | 30 376 | 24.5 | 40.5 | 36.7 |
| Hamilton | 220 | 1 852 | 1 766 | 3.6 | 51.2 | 22.2 | 17.1 | 9 743 | 22 134 | 40 757 | -3.1 | 1.8 | 37 936 | 16.9 | 28.5 | 26.1 |
| Hansford | 140 | 1 536 | 1 539 | 4.4 | 55.4 | 21.4 | 15.8 | 11 778 | 21 512 | 52 610 | 10.0 | 2.3 | 50 505 | 13.7 | 20.3 | 17.9 |
| Hardeman | 118 | 2 248 | 848 | 9.2 | 60.1 | 17.5 | 9.7 | 13 105 | 18 749 | 36 568 | -4.3 | 0.9 | 34 294 | 19.0 | 31.8 | 30.3 |
| Hardin | 161 | 1 662 | 13 321 | 9.6 | 54.0 | 14.9 | 94.4 | 8 674 | 25 110 | 54 588 | 7.5 | 2.2 | 52 514 | 13.0 | 19.0 | 17.8 |
| Harris | 690 | 4 241 | 1 131 217 | 10.8 | 45.9 | 27.9 | 6 529.3 | 8 711 | 27 570 | 52 675 | -8.4 | 5.7 | 50 924 | 19.4 | 29.1 | 27.5 |
| Harrison | 451 | 2 668 | 17 235 | 14.7 | 50.4 | 17.9 | 120.0 | 9 394 | 22 519 | 45 357 | 0.2 | 2.1 | 44 427 | 16.4 | 25.2 | 22.8 |
| Hartley | 162 | 1 373 | 1 389 | 20.1 | 56.9 | 22.0 | 4.1 | 11 832 | 25 413 | 69 414 | 11.0 | 6.5 | 60 548 | 11.4 | 12.4 | 11.2 |
| Haskell | 116 | 1 162 | 1 059 | 3.5 | 60.1 | 12.9 | 10.6 | 11 205 | 23 748 | 39 578 | 23.7 | 2.9 | 32 493 | 23.6 | 36.7 | 33.6 |
| Hays | 205 | 2 005 | 52 282 | 7.4 | 33.4 | 35.5 | 243.3 | 8 491 | 26 388 | 58 247 | -4.1 | 4.0 | 56 557 | 14.9 | 17.5 | 16.1 |
| Hemphill | 437 | 1 827 | 874 | 12.9 | 46.5 | 17.9 | 9.7 | 12 285 | 30 937 | 54 360 | 13.6 | 3.7 | 58 502 | 8.9 | 12.3 | 11.5 |
| Henderson | 411 | 2 803 | 18 027 | 6.4 | 54.7 | 14.5 | 106.5 | 8 900 | 22 325 | 41 242 | -6.1 | 2.0 | 38 191 | 16.3 | 26.7 | 24.0 |
| Hidalgo | 295 | 3 956 | 249 749 | 4.3 | 63.9 | 15.3 | 1 906.6 | 9 180 | 13 821 | 32 479 | -3.2 | 1.6 | 31 021 | 37.3 | 47.9 | 46.2 |
| Hill | 109 | 1 884 | 8 311 | 9.2 | 51.8 | 15.0 | 63.7 | 9 801 | 20 689 | 39 944 | -6.4 | 1.3 | 39 184 | 19.0 | 28.4 | 26.3 |
| Hockley | 414 | 2 186 | 6 709 | 6.1 | 51.4 | 18.2 | 51.8 | 10 820 | 21 560 | 48 201 | 14.8 | 2.4 | 42 710 | 17.5 | 25.6 | 24.4 |
| Hood | 170 | 1 956 | 9 821 | 8.7 | 42.3 | 23.6 | 72.9 | 9 488 | 30 554 | 54 002 | -8.4 | 4.1 | 48 622 | 11.4 | 20.1 | 18.8 |
| Hopkins | 198 | 1 117 | 8 317 | 7.2 | 54.4 | 16.6 | 58.1 | 8 793 | 21 501 | 42 844 | -1.3 | 1.9 | 40 441 | 18.9 | 31.9 | 30.2 |
| Houston | 157 | 1 684 | 4 792 | 6.3 | 61.8 | 14.0 | 34.2 | 9 848 | 19 413 | 32 437 | -14.6 | 1.7 | 31 892 | 24.1 | 34.2 | 33.2 |
| Howard | 571 | 3 222 | 7 865 | 5.5 | 56.2 | 10.8 | 47.8 | 8 936 | 17 997 | 41 887 | 0.7 | 1.3 | 41 125 | 23.3 | 32.3 | 29.6 |
| Hudspeth | 28 | 620 | 1 047 | 3.1 | 72.1 | 10.7 | 9.4 | 11 987 | 12 347 | 22 634 | -20.3 | 1.3 | 28 624 | 31.4 | 46.6 | 41.8 |
| Hunt | 355 | 3 265 | 22 724 | 10.0 | 53.3 | 17.3 | 130.1 | 8 890 | 22 356 | 45 253 | -8.8 | 2.0 | 47 394 | 16.4 | 24.4 | 22.7 |
| Hutchinson | 614 | 3 059 | 5 759 | 6.5 | 51.7 | 12.2 | 39.8 | 9 279 | 22 411 | 44 120 | -10.7 | 0.8 | 49 038 | 13.4 | 20.1 | 18.6 |
| Irion | 0 | 1 347 | 324 | 4.9 | 60.3 | 10.8 | 4.4 | 13 281 | 30 611 | 45 250 | -10.6 | 2.8 | 54 628 | 10.5 | 17.2 | 14.6 |
| Jack | 108 | 1 137 | 1 960 | 13.6 | 55.9 | 12.2 | 18.1 | 11 623 | 21 314 | 46 136 | 5.1 | 2.6 | 45 069 | 15.0 | 20.1 | 18.0 |
| Jackson | 174 | 1 294 | 3 189 | 10.2 | 53.6 | 17.8 | 29.7 | 9 191 | 24 476 | 50 010 | 5.1 | 3.3 | 43 740 | 16.0 | 23.0 | 20.8 |
| Jasper | 244 | 1 632 | 8 360 | 12.1 | 58.1 | 12.8 | 56.5 | 9 062 | 19 859 | 40 099 | -3.9 | 0.9 | 38 260 | 19.1 | 28.4 | 26.7 |
| Jeff Davis | 125 | 586 | 382 | 13.6 | 40.4 | 31.7 | 6.2 | 16 341 | 24 260 | 49 149 | 13.0 | 0.8 | 48 161 | 14.1 | 28.2 | 24.5 |
| Jefferson | 663 | 4 519 | 64 543 | 9.6 | 50.4 | 18.0 | 421.1 | 10 040 | 22 643 | 42 883 | -8.5 | 2.6 | 41 363 | 20.0 | 28.7 | 26.3 |
| Jim Hogg | 222 | 388 | 1 149 | 0.1 | 76.1 | 8.9 | 11.6 | 10 170 | 16 902 | 36 752 | 5.4 | 1.6 | 32 179 | 25.0 | 35.8 | 34.0 |
| Jim Wells | 664 | 3 866 | 11 447 | 5.9 | 63.8 | 10.8 | 74.1 | 8 857 | 18 268 | 37 413 | -3.9 | 1.5 | 39 120 | 25.5 | 38.1 | 34.9 |
| Johnson | 241 | 2 403 | 38 333 | 11.5 | 52.0 | 16.3 | 265.7 | 8 829 | 24 381 | 55 970 | -7.1 | 2.8 | 54 412 | 13.1 | 20.1 | 18.8 |
| Jones | 233 | 2 361 | 3 970 | 7.2 | 65.4 | 9.4 | 28.0 | 10 243 | 14 197 | 37 872 | -5.1 | 0.8 | 35 709 | 25.8 | 30.5 | 28.0 |
| Karnes | 172 | 2 094 | 2 916 | 7.8 | 65.7 | 10.1 | 23.4 | 10 228 | 17 622 | 39 297 | 9.7 | 2.0 | 35 904 | 26.7 | 32.1 | 29.3 |
| Kaufman | 245 | 2 423 | 27 827 | 11.0 | 50.0 | 17.6 | 188.4 | 8 291 | 24 390 | 60 575 | 0.2 | 3.1 | 59 986 | 12.4 | 17.5 | 16.1 |
| Kendall | 97 | 1 507 | 8 063 | 18.9 | 28.6 | 36.6 | 69.6 | 9 138 | 36 426 | 72 092 | 7.8 | 9.5 | 71 388 | 10.1 | 15.0 | 12.6 |
| Kenedy | 1 176 | 941 | 58 | 0.0 | 58.4 | 15.9 | 1.6 | 19 482 | 14 754 | 45 625 | 35.2 | 0.0 | 34 851 | 16.6 | 27.3 | 24.7 |
| Kent | 727 | 3 273 | 175 | 1.7 | 51.7 | 19.0 | 3.1 | 21 299 | 23 726 | 43 750 | 6.5 | 0.0 | 42 829 | 11.3 | 19.2 | 16.5 |
| Kerr | 170 | 1 928 | 10 364 | 20.5 | 40.7 | 28.0 | 61.5 | 8 965 | 25 942 | 44 529 | -3.8 | 3.2 | 45 621 | 14.6 | 27.4 | 24.4 |
| Kimble | 255 | 1 956 | 884 | 2.7 | 54.8 | 20.6 | 6.2 | 9 344 | 24 520 | 43 653 | 10.0 | 0.4 | 35 867 | 20.0 | 35.4 | 32.7 |
| King | 0 | 342 | 34 | 0.0 | 35.1 | 29.3 | 3.1 | 24 825 | 36 564 | 61 250 | 27.3 | 11.0 | 51 237 | 11.0 | 10.3 | 8.7 |
| Kinney | 0 | 54 | 660 | 0.9 | 54.9 | 16.1 | 6.4 | 10 692 | 15 522 | 25 703 | -32.8 | 0.6 | 37 917 | 22.9 | 32.7 | 30.6 |
| Kleberg | 767 | 4 136 | 11 573 | 5.3 | 49.4 | 21.7 | 53.2 | 9 718 | 19 156 | 37 222 | -6.0 | 2.6 | 36 198 | 27.5 | 34.9 | 33.8 |
| Knox | 158 | 895 | 790 | 3.7 | 64.0 | 13.1 | 9.1 | 11 921 | 19 424 | 32 646 | -5.0 | 0.8 | 33 395 | 23.1 | 34.6 | 32.3 |
| Lamar | 403 | 3 597 | 12 307 | 6.9 | 52.1 | 16.7 | 76.4 | 8 610 | 20 972 | 40 050 | -6.2 | 1.5 | 38 685 | 20.0 | 30.3 | 28.6 |
| Lamb | 339 | 2 979 | 3 748 | 6.3 | 61.0 | 13.0 | 31.0 | 9 695 | 17 356 | 35 589 | -5.5 | 1.4 | 34 524 | 24.5 | 36.2 | 32.8 |
| Lampasas | 95 | 1 797 | 4 511 | 5.7 | 46.0 | 18.9 | 32.3 | 8 752 | 24 216 | 48 760 | -0.2 | 2.7 | 47 135 | 17.2 | 27.7 | 24.0 |
| La Salle | 185 | 398 | 1 610 | 4.4 | 73.8 | 6.0 | 13.5 | 11 491 | 14 014 | 25 313 | -14.2 | 2.1 | 29 938 | 36.3 | 42.2 | 41.3 |
| Lavaca | 71 | 1 454 | 3 984 | 17.3 | 61.2 | 14.5 | 19.2 | 9 558 | 23 597 | 43 570 | 10.8 | 2.0 | 44 186 | 12.7 | 19.0 | 17.3 |
| Lee | 295 | 1 515 | 3 905 | 13.0 | 55.4 | 13.7 | 29.8 | 8 955 | 23 719 | 45 754 | -6.6 | 1.9 | 44 411 | 14.0 | 20.7 | 18.0 |
| Leon | 134 | 1 038 | 3 198 | 4.0 | 57.3 | 12.6 | 32.5 | 10 414 | 22 813 | 42 150 | 0.8 | 2.3 | 43 545 | 17.6 | 28.3 | 26.8 |
| Liberty | 407 | 3 199 | 18 768 | 7.7 | 61.7 | 8.5 | 127.8 | 8 615 | 19 628 | 47 460 | -8.4 | 1.3 | 45 712 | 19.3 | 26.5 | 24.8 |
| Limestone | 641 | 3 175 | 4 908 | 3.7 | 57.4 | 11.9 | 41.9 | 10 262 | 19 236 | 42 851 | 8.1 | 0.7 | 36 887 | 22.4 | 33.5 | 32.7 |
| Lipscomb | 0 | 534 | 783 | 2.9 | 52.2 | 19.9 | 11.1 | 14 057 | 25 676 | 55 457 | 28.5 | 3.1 | 52 256 | 12.8 | 18.3 | 17.0 |
| Live Oak | 161 | 1 215 | 2 413 | 7.0 | 57.6 | 13.6 | 18.1 | 10 223 | 21 843 | 45 276 | 4.6 | 2.5 | 41 601 | 20.2 | 28.2 | 25.3 |
| Llano | 66 | 2 157 | 2 904 | 10.1 | 42.0 | 26.7 | 18.9 | 9 684 | 32 277 | 41 837 | -11.0 | 5.0 | 42 282 | 15.6 | 28.9 | 27.4 |
| Loving | 0 | 0 | 0 | 0.0 | 85.7 | 5.4 | NA | NA | 31 502 | 78 125 | 44.7 | 0.0 | 46 204 | 17.0 | 41.7 | 42.9 |
| Lubbock | 686 | 4 771 | 91 903 | 9.8 | 42.5 | 27.4 | 403.5 | 8 749 | 23 353 | 43 983 | 1.2 | 3.1 | 42 978 | 20.4 | 26.3 | 23.8 |
| Lynn | 149 | 1 507 | 1 422 | 9.3 | 60.4 | 16.0 | 14.8 | 11 242 | 19 932 | 46 456 | 28.9 | 0.7 | 36 530 | 19.6 | 30.3 | 28.7 |
| McCulloch | 201 | 1 596 | 1 668 | 7.2 | 57.2 | 18.4 | 17.4 | 10 975 | 21 464 | 37 861 | 9.1 | 3.4 | 35 775 | 22.7 | 37.4 | 34.3 |
| McLennan | 469 | 3 981 | 71 628 | 24.8 | 47.2 | 21.6 | 385.4 | 9 010 | 21 630 | 41 656 | -8.1 | 2.4 | 40 563 | 23.7 | 33.9 | 31.5 |
| McMullen | 139 | 1 247 | 159 | 7.5 | 68.6 | 8.6 | 3.1 | 18 176 | 21 743 | 29 500 | -32.8 | 1.9 | 46 528 | 10.4 | 18.2 | 14.9 |
| Madison | 158 | 1 849 | 3 441 | 9.8 | 64.1 | 10.4 | 21.4 | 7 993 | 14 915 | 37 437 | -5.7 | 1.6 | 35 218 | 23.7 | 31.0 | 28.5 |
| Marion | 436 | 2 517 | 1 808 | 9.2 | 57.4 | 12.1 | 13.0 | 10 480 | 20 075 | 31 903 | -6.8 | 1.9 | 31 922 | 22.1 | 33.3 | 30.0 |
| Martin | 204 | 1 429 | 1 222 | 3.7 | 63.8 | 12.2 | 12.7 | 12 840 | 21 633 | 42 050 | -2.2 | 1.9 | 46 680 | 16.4 | 25.6 | 24.5 |

1. Data for serious crimes have not been adjusted for underreporting; this may affect comparability between geographic areas and over time.   2. Per 100,000 population estimated by the FBI.   3. All persons 3 years old and over enrolled in nursery school through college.   4. Persons 25 years old and over.   5. Elementary and secondary education expenditures.   6. Based on population estimated by the American Community Survey, 2007–2011.

Items 46—61

# Table B. States and Counties — **Personal Income**

| STATE County | Personal income, 2011 | | | | | | | Transfer payments (mil dol) | | | | | |
|---|---|---|---|---|---|---|---|---|---|---|---|---|---|
| | | | Per capita[1] | | | | | | Government payments to individuals | | | | |
| | Total (mil dol) | Percent change, 2010–2011 | Dollars | Rank | Wages and salaries[2] (mil dol) | Proprietors' income (mil dol) | Dividends, interest, and rent (mil dol) | Total | Total | Social Security | Medical payments | Income mainte-nance | Unemploy-ment insurance |
| | 62 | 63 | 64 | 65 | 66 | 67 | 68 | 69 | 70 | 71 | 72 | 73 | 74 |
| TEXAS—Cont'd | | | | | | | | | | | | | |
| Guadalupe | 5 044 | 8.8 | 37 157 | 1 065 | 1 454 | 166 | 592 | 812 | 782 | 263 | 303 | 85 | 25 |
| Hale | 1 026 | -0.7 | 28 120 | 2 603 | 600 | 115 | 139 | 275 | 267 | 66 | 138 | 42 | 7 |
| Hall | 80 | -19.6 | 23 662 | 3 040 | 35 | 5 | 14 | 35 | 34 | 10 | 18 | 4 | 1 |
| Hamilton | 300 | 5.2 | 35 367 | 1 314 | 110 | 28 | 67 | 84 | 82 | 28 | 42 | 6 | 1 |
| Hansford | 287 | 27.6 | 51 525 | 174 | 105 | 123 | 40 | 33 | 32 | 12 | 15 | 3 | 1 |
| Hardeman | 131 | 2.9 | 31 356 | 2 032 | 50 | 8 | 22 | 40 | 39 | 12 | 21 | 4 | 1 |
| Hardin | 2 148 | 6.3 | 38 882 | 866 | 592 | 178 | 255 | 458 | 446 | 145 | 221 | 40 | 15 |
| Harris | 204 593 | 8.3 | 48 935 | 236 | 162 104 | 41 272 | 27 370 | 23 121 | 22 181 | 5 958 | 10 153 | 3 651 | 948 |
| Harrison | 2 743 | 9.1 | 41 371 | 626 | 1 324 | 265 | 338 | 503 | 488 | 155 | 209 | 67 | 16 |
| Hartley | 292 | 29.4 | 48 920 | 237 | 85 | 98 | 34 | 16 | 15 | 8 | 3 | 2 | 1 |
| Haskell | 170 | -8.9 | 28 444 | 2 551 | 84 | 10 | 28 | 59 | 57 | 18 | 30 | 6 | 1 |
| Hays | 5 364 | 8.8 | 32 700 | 1 757 | 2 182 | 496 | 860 | 788 | 751 | 262 | 266 | 87 | 31 |
| Hemphill | 231 | 23.7 | 58 261 | 83 | 136 | 49 | 44 | 20 | 19 | 7 | 10 | 1 | 0 |
| Henderson | 2 514 | 3.4 | 31 891 | 1 909 | 673 | 208 | 400 | 710 | 692 | 262 | 295 | 72 | 17 |
| Hidalgo | 17 248 | 4.5 | 21 620 | 3 088 | 9 093 | 2 119 | 1 588 | 5 478 | 5 302 | 830 | 2 383 | 1 523 | 216 |
| Hill | 1 142 | 4.2 | 32 266 | 1 831 | 377 | 100 | 195 | 326 | 318 | 107 | 145 | 31 | 8 |
| Hockley | 860 | 3.1 | 37 566 | 1 019 | 507 | 61 | 95 | 199 | 194 | 48 | 96 | 21 | 4 |
| Hood | 2 105 | 5.0 | 40 740 | 681 | 596 | 120 | 467 | 441 | 430 | 188 | 177 | 30 | 11 |
| Hopkins | 1 159 | 4.5 | 32 766 | 1 747 | 543 | 118 | 193 | 282 | 274 | 92 | 134 | 30 | 7 |
| Houston | 710 | 5.8 | 30 225 | 2 250 | 345 | 36 | 135 | 227 | 222 | 66 | 116 | 25 | 5 |
| Howard | 1 116 | 4.1 | 31 781 | 1 936 | 676 | 99 | 142 | 280 | 272 | 69 | 138 | 31 | 6 |
| Hudspeth | 102 | 6.8 | 29 923 | 2 304 | 82 | 11 | 12 | 23 | 23 | 5 | 9 | 6 | 1 |
| Hunt | 2 746 | 4.1 | 31 736 | 1 947 | 1 572 | 181 | 304 | 668 | 649 | 221 | 281 | 76 | 19 |
| Hutchinson | 825 | 4.5 | 37 298 | 1 048 | 580 | 58 | 109 | 161 | 156 | 58 | 69 | 15 | 5 |
| Irion | 89 | 11.3 | 54 975 | 113 | 34 | 11 | 15 | 11 | 11 | 4 | 4 | 1 | 0 |
| Jack | 342 | 9.1 | 37 903 | 986 | 160 | 42 | 51 | 63 | 61 | 22 | 30 | 5 | 2 |
| Jackson | 476 | 8.5 | 33 937 | 1 523 | 257 | 32 | 74 | 123 | 120 | 36 | 63 | 13 | 3 |
| Jasper | 1 190 | 5.8 | 32 797 | 1 742 | 473 | 125 | 133 | 364 | 356 | 107 | 186 | 39 | 11 |
| Jeff Davis | 81 | 6.8 | 35 273 | 1 328 | 32 | 8 | 20 | 16 | 16 | 7 | 6 | 1 | 0 |
| Jefferson | 9 786 | 5.5 | 38 712 | 879 | 7 933 | 790 | 1 605 | 2 256 | 2 198 | 589 | 1 155 | 260 | 78 |
| Jim Hogg | 197 | 12.4 | 37 442 | 1 033 | 100 | 11 | 29 | 51 | 50 | 10 | 28 | 8 | 1 |
| Jim Wells | 1 645 | 14.7 | 39 800 | 770 | 1 057 | 150 | 149 | 422 | 413 | 90 | 242 | 58 | 9 |
| Johnson | 5 081 | 4.3 | 33 269 | 1 661 | 2 033 | 432 | 570 | 1 025 | 992 | 333 | 446 | 107 | 32 |
| Jones | 539 | 2.5 | 26 734 | 2 798 | 166 | 46 | 57 | 156 | 151 | 42 | 83 | 15 | 4 |
| Karnes | 409 | 6.8 | 27 377 | 2 703 | 174 | 44 | 61 | 127 | 124 | 31 | 69 | 15 | 3 |
| Kaufman | 3 572 | 6.4 | 33 901 | 1 533 | 1 251 | 261 | 311 | 690 | 667 | 222 | 311 | 78 | 23 |
| Kendall | 2 007 | 10.2 | 57 707 | 86 | 570 | 121 | 469 | 238 | 230 | 103 | 91 | 13 | 6 |
| Kenedy | 22 | 23.9 | 51 037 | 184 | 32 | 5 | 3 | 2 | 2 | 1 | 1 | 1 | 0 |
| Kent | 26 | 5.6 | 31 367 | 2 026 | 12 | 1 | 7 | 8 | 8 | 3 | 4 | 1 | 0 |
| Kerr | 2 119 | 4.8 | 42 572 | 531 | 795 | 244 | 732 | 451 | 440 | 193 | 166 | 36 | 8 |
| Kimble | 171 | 24.5 | 37 017 | 1 075 | 68 | 23 | 42 | 42 | 41 | 15 | 19 | 4 | 1 |
| King | 16 | 62.2 | 62 071 | 50 | 11 | 3 | 2 | 1 | 1 | 0 | 0 | 0 | 0 |
| Kinney | 111 | 7.7 | 30 579 | 2 184 | 46 | 5 | 25 | 30 | 30 | 11 | 12 | 3 | 1 |
| Kleberg | 1 086 | 7.5 | 33 734 | 1 557 | 663 | 51 | 117 | 264 | 257 | 55 | 121 | 38 | 8 |
| Knox | 123 | 3.1 | 32 652 | 1 769 | 61 | 11 | 15 | 41 | 40 | 11 | 24 | 4 | 1 |
| Lamar | 1 657 | 4.5 | 33 092 | 1 692 | 896 | 209 | 239 | 476 | 465 | 143 | 217 | 55 | 13 |
| Lamb | 423 | -1.3 | 29 840 | 2 317 | 187 | 59 | 51 | 127 | 124 | 32 | 69 | 16 | 3 |
| Lampasas | 973 | 8.1 | 48 898 | 238 | 187 | 53 | 123 | 198 | 194 | 52 | 89 | 16 | 4 |
| La Salle | 191 | 21.9 | 27 326 | 2 714 | 148 | 14 | 20 | 50 | 49 | 11 | 25 | 9 | 1 |
| Lavaca | 731 | 6.7 | 37 793 | 998 | 257 | 65 | 154 | 192 | 187 | 63 | 100 | 13 | 3 |
| Lee | 636 | 10.7 | 38 172 | 946 | 342 | 33 | 92 | 120 | 116 | 42 | 55 | 10 | 3 |
| Leon | 594 | 6.7 | 35 114 | 1 355 | 298 | 39 | 108 | 169 | 166 | 66 | 74 | 13 | 3 |
| Liberty | 2 618 | 4.3 | 34 353 | 1 464 | 816 | 247 | 237 | 624 | 607 | 169 | 323 | 70 | 19 |
| Limestone | 719 | 2.5 | 30 421 | 2 218 | 358 | 60 | 83 | 228 | 223 | 62 | 118 | 23 | 5 |
| Lipscomb | 141 | 22.1 | 42 451 | 547 | 66 | 26 | 29 | 19 | 18 | 7 | 8 | 2 | 0 |
| Live Oak | 412 | 18.2 | 36 016 | 1 206 | 201 | 42 | 62 | 82 | 80 | 24 | 42 | 9 | 2 |
| Llano | 714 | 4.9 | 37 212 | 1 057 | 178 | 38 | 212 | 192 | 188 | 82 | 79 | 12 | 4 |
| Loving | 5 | 13.9 | 51 309 | 178 | 2 | 0 | 2 | 0 | 0 | 0 | 0 | 0 | 0 |
| Lubbock | 9 836 | 3.8 | 34 644 | 1 426 | 5 816 | 1 050 | 1 620 | 2 043 | 1 980 | 532 | 1 010 | 254 | 51 |
| Lynn | 150 | -28.8 | 25 406 | 2 937 | 60 | -6 | 28 | 52 | 51 | 14 | 27 | 7 | 1 |
| McCulloch | 324 | 16.6 | 39 026 | 855 | 167 | 46 | 49 | 85 | 83 | 24 | 46 | 9 | 1 |
| McLennan | 8 098 | 3.8 | 33 943 | 1 520 | 5 153 | 732 | 1 171 | 1 691 | 1 638 | 501 | 640 | 231 | 50 |
| McMullen | 36 | 31.1 | 52 810 | 145 | 22 | 5 | 9 | 6 | 5 | 2 | 2 | 0 | 0 |
| Madison | 352 | 6.5 | 25 625 | 2 919 | 170 | 36 | 47 | 101 | 98 | 31 | 48 | 13 | 3 |
| Marion | 323 | 5.5 | 30 771 | 2 143 | 71 | 26 | 47 | 108 | 105 | 36 | 47 | 13 | 3 |
| Martin | 158 | -12.7 | 32 061 | 1 868 | 78 | 0 | 27 | 36 | 35 | 9 | 20 | 5 | 1 |

1. Based on the resident population estimated as of July 1 of the year shown.   2. Includes supplements to wages and salaries.

# Table B. States and Counties — Earnings, Social Security, and Housing

| STATE County | Earnings, 2011 | | | | | | | | | Social Security beneficiaries, December 2011 | | | Housing units, 2010 | |
| | | | | Percent by selected industries | | | | | | | | | | |
| | | | Goods-related[1] | | Service-related and health | | | | | | | | | |
| | Total (mil dol) | Farm | Total | Manufacturing | Information and professional and technical services | Retail trade | Finance, insurance, and real estate | Health care and social services | Government | Number | Rate[2] | Supplemental Security Income recipients, December 2011 | Total | Percent change, 2000–2010 |
| | 75 | 76 | 77 | 78 | 79 | 80 | 81 | 82 | 83 | 84 | 85 | 86 | 87 | 88 |
| TEXAS—Cont'd | | | | | | | | | | | | | | |
| Guadalupe | 1 620 | 0.4 | 30.0 | 21.5 | D | 8.4 | 4.2 | 6.9 | 20.1 | 21 210 | 156 | 2 096 | 50 015 | 48.9 |
| Hale | 714 | 6.6 | 20.4 | 16.5 | 2.7 | 8.9 | 4.2 | D | 17.4 | 5 615 | 154 | 937 | 13 541 | 0.1 |
| Hall | 40 | -1.4 | 6.2 | 4.2 | D | 6.4 | 9.7 | 7.1 | 29.6 | 845 | 250 | 89 | 1 943 | -2.3 |
| Hamilton | 138 | 10.1 | D | 5.8 | 3.2 | 10.7 | 3.0 | 8.3 | 22.9 | 2 255 | 266 | 180 | 4 566 | 2.5 |
| Hansford | 228 | 53.7 | 14.2 | 1.8 | D | 2.3 | D | 1.1 | 11.9 | 915 | 164 | 65 | 2 338 | 0.4 |
| Hardeman | 59 | 4.5 | D | D | D | 7.0 | 6.2 | D | 39.6 | 990 | 237 | 125 | 2 417 | 2.5 |
| Hardin | 770 | -0.3 | 28.2 | 7.4 | 5.5 | 9.6 | 4.7 | 14.8 | 14.7 | 10 720 | 194 | 1 250 | 22 597 | 13.9 |
| Harris | 203 376 | 0.0 | 29.2 | 9.9 | 13.7 | 4.3 | 7.5 | 7.1 | 8.8 | 447 610 | 107 | 99 053 | 1 598 698 | 23.2 |
| Harrison | 1 588 | 0.2 | 43.1 | 14.1 | D | 5.6 | 7.3 | D | 11.2 | 12 405 | 187 | 2 213 | 27 704 | 5.5 |
| Hartley | 182 | 59.4 | D | D | D | 2.1 | D | D | 16.0 | 585 | 98 | 31 | 1 946 | 10.6 |
| Haskell | 94 | -2.0 | 30.6 | 0.5 | D | 11.6 | D | 11.1 | 21.1 | 1 520 | 254 | 201 | 3 443 | -3.2 |
| Hays | 2 679 | 0.2 | 19.2 | 8.8 | 7.8 | 11.5 | 5.3 | 10.1 | 23.8 | 19 520 | 119 | 1 708 | 59 417 | 66.7 |
| Hemphill | 185 | 14.2 | 29.4 | 0.9 | 2.2 | D | 9.5 | 1.7 | 10.8 | 525 | 132 | 25 | 1 629 | 5.2 |
| Henderson | 882 | 0.9 | 21.9 | 9.8 | 5.8 | 11.1 | 4.8 | D | 18.8 | 20 095 | 255 | 2 346 | 39 595 | 10.2 |
| Hidalgo | 11 212 | 0.4 | 9.1 | 2.4 | 4.3 | 10.3 | 4.4 | 20.6 | 26.4 | 93 105 | 117 | 41 579 | 248 287 | 28.9 |
| Hill | 477 | 2.4 | 25.4 | 8.2 | 4.2 | 11.1 | 3.8 | D | 22.1 | 8 415 | 238 | 966 | 16 118 | 10.2 |
| Hockley | 568 | -1.0 | 43.1 | 4.1 | 2.2 | 4.5 | 2.8 | D | 17.0 | 3 885 | 170 | 546 | 9 293 | 1.6 |
| Hood | 716 | 0.7 | 24.6 | 5.4 | 6.8 | 10.7 | 7.7 | 9.4 | 15.1 | 13 395 | 259 | 680 | 24 951 | 30.6 |
| Hopkins | 661 | 4.8 | 23.6 | 11.5 | 4.7 | 9.3 | 4.8 | D | 16.7 | 7 405 | 209 | 933 | 15 029 | 7.2 |
| Houston | 382 | 1.6 | 19.7 | 8.9 | 9.1 | 5.9 | 6.0 | 7.9 | 25.3 | 5 355 | 228 | 939 | 11 532 | 7.5 |
| Howard | 774 | -0.6 | 31.6 | 11.1 | 2.5 | 5.5 | 3.3 | D | 29.2 | 5 795 | 165 | 956 | 13 124 | -3.4 |
| Hudspeth | 93 | 13.6 | D | D | D | 2.0 | D | D | 70.4 | 570 | 167 | 169 | 1 527 | 3.8 |
| Hunt | 1 753 | 0.1 | D | 37.3 | 4.1 | 7.5 | 3.3 | 7.7 | 20.0 | 17 140 | 198 | 2 498 | 36 704 | 13.0 |
| Hutchinson | 638 | 1.3 | 62.6 | 22.1 | D | 4.4 | D | 3.2 | 11.7 | 4 270 | 193 | 433 | 10 629 | -2.2 |
| Irion | 45 | 10.8 | D | D | D | 1.6 | D | 2.3 | 12.5 | 345 | 213 | 22 | 856 | -6.3 |
| Jack | 202 | 0.1 | 47.5 | 2.0 | D | 2.6 | 6.1 | 4.5 | 14.4 | 1 735 | 192 | 154 | 4 095 | 11.6 |
| Jackson | 289 | 3.4 | D | D | 5.7 | 4.9 | 2.4 | 3.0 | 16.7 | 2 850 | 203 | 321 | 6 590 | 0.7 |
| Jasper | 598 | 0.2 | 31.2 | 19.5 | D | 8.9 | 5.3 | 11.1 | 17.1 | 8 455 | 233 | 1 383 | 16 798 | 1.3 |
| Jeff Davis | 39 | 12.0 | D | D | D | 2.3 | D | D | 39.0 | 625 | 273 | 39 | 1 613 | 13.6 |
| Jefferson | 8 723 | 0.2 | 39.3 | 23.0 | 8.0 | 6.4 | 3.5 | 10.8 | 13.2 | 44 995 | 178 | 9 032 | 104 424 | 2.3 |
| Jim Hogg | 111 | 3.3 | 10.8 | 2.3 | D | 6.9 | D | D | 49.6 | 1 020 | 194 | 319 | 2 441 | 5.8 |
| Jim Wells | 1 207 | 1.9 | 42.5 | 3.9 | 2.6 | 4.9 | 6.1 | D | 9.3 | 8 015 | 194 | 2 026 | 16 147 | 9.0 |
| Johnson | 2 465 | 0.8 | 31.0 | 14.0 | 4.9 | 7.7 | 4.6 | 8.1 | 15.3 | 25 155 | 165 | 2 850 | 56 719 | 22.6 |
| Jones | 212 | 2.5 | 25.6 | 5.9 | D | 6.3 | 6.7 | D | 28.2 | 3 480 | 173 | 451 | 7 422 | 2.6 |
| Karnes | 218 | 3.3 | 20.0 | 7.4 | D | 5.7 | 4.1 | 4.6 | 33.2 | 2 795 | 187 | 512 | 5 650 | 3.1 |
| Kaufman | 1 512 | 0.4 | 28.2 | 13.9 | 4.3 | 8.2 | 4.7 | 7.2 | 21.3 | 16 870 | 160 | 2 065 | 38 322 | 46.7 |
| Kendall | 691 | 1.6 | 18.3 | 6.5 | 11.5 | 13.2 | 8.3 | 10.5 | 14.6 | 7 325 | 211 | 289 | 14 055 | 46.2 |
| Kenedy | 37 | 22.4 | D | 0.0 | D | D | 0.0 | D | 9.9 | 60 | 137 | 0 | 233 | -17.1 |
| Kent | 13 | 12.3 | D | 0.0 | D | D | D | 13.0 | 50.8 | 210 | 255 | 15 | 552 | 0.2 |
| Kerr | 1 039 | 2.1 | 15.6 | 4.6 | 7.2 | 11.4 | 6.6 | 16.1 | 19.1 | 14 640 | 294 | 934 | 23 831 | 17.8 |
| Kimble | 91 | 12.8 | D | 3.2 | D | 7.8 | 23.4 | 2.8 | 18.3 | 1 235 | 267 | 124 | 3 371 | 12.5 |
| King | 14 | 34.0 | 0.0 | 0.0 | D | D | 0.0 | 0.0 | 25.3 | 25 | 98 | 0 | 186 | 6.9 |
| Kinney | 51 | 9.0 | D | D | 0.4 | D | D | 1.5 | 64.1 | 960 | 264 | 132 | 1 940 | 1.7 |
| Kleberg | 714 | 1.8 | 9.9 | 1.8 | D | 7.4 | 4.2 | D | 44.4 | 4 915 | 153 | 1 212 | 12 787 | 0.3 |
| Knox | 72 | 8.5 | D | D | D | 6.1 | 3.5 | 4.2 | 25.0 | 890 | 237 | 141 | 2 044 | -4.0 |
| Lamar | 1 105 | 0.5 | D | 25.1 | 2.4 | 8.2 | 4.6 | 15.2 | 13.9 | 11 660 | 233 | 2 034 | 22 481 | 6.5 |
| Lamb | 246 | 23.4 | D | 10.4 | D | 6.5 | D | 4.7 | 19.0 | 2 805 | 198 | 445 | 6 128 | -2.6 |
| Lampasas | 241 | 1.3 | 26.3 | 11.0 | 3.2 | 16.2 | 5.6 | 10.3 | 20.8 | 4 320 | 217 | 434 | 8 718 | 14.7 |
| La Salle | 162 | 3.9 | D | 0.0 | D | 3.3 | 1.0 | D | 25.5 | 1 185 | 169 | 349 | 2 746 | 12.7 |
| Lavaca | 322 | 1.4 | 34.1 | 21.2 | 2.9 | 8.1 | 5.6 | D | 13.9 | 5 075 | 262 | 440 | 10 344 | 7.1 |
| Lee | 375 | 0.2 | 46.3 | 6.9 | 4.3 | 4.8 | 5.5 | D | 17.4 | 3 270 | 196 | 322 | 7 499 | 9.5 |
| Leon | 337 | 2.5 | 53.7 | 17.0 | 2.2 | 4.7 | 5.2 | 1.4 | 12.8 | 4 875 | 288 | 438 | 9 509 | 14.6 |
| Liberty | 1 063 | 0.5 | 25.5 | 12.2 | D | 10.3 | 4.6 | D | 20.3 | 13 015 | 171 | 2 148 | 28 759 | 9.1 |
| Limestone | 418 | 1.1 | 21.7 | 9.3 | 1.9 | 7.1 | 3.5 | 12.3 | 33.2 | 5 190 | 220 | 885 | 10 536 | 8.3 |
| Lipscomb | 92 | 25.7 | D | D | D | 2.0 | D | 0.2 | 18.7 | 550 | 165 | 33 | 1 512 | -1.9 |
| Live Oak | 243 | 1.4 | D | D | D | 4.4 | 4.1 | 2.4 | 23.3 | 1 955 | 171 | 266 | 6 065 | -2.1 |
| Llano | 216 | 1.7 | 13.1 | 2.7 | 3.8 | 6.1 | 8.8 | D | 20.7 | 6 180 | 322 | 370 | 14 280 | 20.9 |
| Loving | 1 | 4.8 | D | D | D | 0.0 | 0.0 | 0.0 | 53.1 | 15 | 160 | 0 | 50 | -28.6 |
| Lubbock | 6 866 | 0.1 | 11.0 | 3.8 | 7.7 | 8.9 | 8.1 | 16.7 | 23.3 | 41 630 | 147 | 6 450 | 115 064 | 14.4 |
| Lynn | 54 | -7.7 | 4.4 | 2.6 | 8.1 | 4.4 | 7.5 | 3.0 | 42.2 | 1 165 | 198 | 164 | 2 676 | 0.2 |
| McCulloch | 213 | 3.3 | 24.3 | 17.9 | 1.7 | 8.1 | 2.8 | 6.5 | 14.3 | 2 070 | 250 | 324 | 4 302 | 2.8 |
| McLennan | 5 886 | 0.2 | 25.0 | 17.9 | 5.4 | 6.0 | 10.8 | 11.1 | 17.0 | 40 475 | 170 | 7 048 | 95 124 | 12.2 |
| McMullen | 27 | 18.5 | D | D | D | D | D | D | 20.1 | 190 | 275 | 14 | 485 | -18.1 |
| Madison | 206 | 17.8 | D | 2.3 | 3.0 | 12.4 | 3.4 | 7.0 | 28.3 | 2 465 | 179 | 317 | 5 096 | 6.2 |
| Marion | 97 | 0.8 | D | 10.9 | D | 9.7 | D | D | 21.6 | 2 995 | 285 | 504 | 6 218 | -2.6 |
| Martin | 78 | -9.2 | D | D | D | 8.4 | D | D | 28.1 | 770 | 156 | 108 | 1 852 | -2.4 |

1. Includes mining, construction, and manufacturing.    2. Per 1,000 resident population enumerated in the 2010 census.

| STATE County | Housing units, 2007–2011 Occupied units Owner-occupied Total | Percent | Median value[1] | Median owner cost as a percent of income With a mortgage | Without a mortgage[2] | Renter-occupied Median rent[3] | Median rent as a percent of income | Substandard units[4] (percent) | Civilian labor force, 2012 Total | Percent change, 2011–2012 | Unemployment Total | Rate[5] | Civilian employment[6] 2007–2011 Total | Percent Management, business, science and arts | Construction, production, and maintenance occupations |
|---|---|---|---|---|---|---|---|---|---|---|---|---|---|---|---|
| | 89 | 90 | 91 | 92 | 93 | 94 | 95 | 96 | 97 | 98 | 99 | 100 | 101 | 102 | 103 |
| **TEXAS—Cont'd** | | | | | | | | | | | | | | | |
| Guadalupe | 44 554 | 78.3 | 150 700 | 21.7 | 10.9 | 799 | 28.3 | 4.7 | 67 059 | 0.8 | 3 917 | 5.8 | 59 931 | 34.6 | 22.2 |
| Hale | 11 707 | 63.6 | 73 500 | 20.4 | 10.8 | 569 | 26.5 | 6.5 | 17 246 | -1.9 | 1 122 | 6.5 | 14 392 | 25.0 | 33.3 |
| Hall | 1 402 | 68.7 | 37 800 | 18.5 | 12.9 | 542 | 30.9 | 5.4 | 1 318 | -5.9 | 106 | 8.0 | 1 310 | 29.5 | 33.4 |
| Hamilton | 3 024 | 81.2 | 82 600 | 23.2 | 15.1 | 611 | 22.1 | 2.6 | 4 252 | -3.3 | 228 | 5.4 | 3 371 | 28.1 | 28.4 |
| Hansford | 1 895 | 78.4 | 69 400 | 17.5 | 10.1 | 601 | 22.2 | 7.2 | 2 764 | -0.5 | 108 | 3.9 | 2 658 | 29.7 | 35.6 |
| Hardeman | 1 692 | 77.4 | 46 800 | 22.7 | 10.2 | 615 | 34.1 | 5.3 | 2 007 | -8.4 | 102 | 5.1 | 1 547 | 34.5 | 26.2 |
| Hardin | 20 204 | 78.7 | 99 200 | 18.9 | 10.6 | 726 | 23.4 | 2.8 | 27 796 | -1.5 | 2 201 | 7.9 | 23 431 | 29.8 | 31.1 |
| Harris | 1 391 103 | 57.6 | 132 300 | 23.6 | 12.3 | 849 | 29.8 | 6.8 | 2 088 269 | 1.8 | 142 655 | 6.8 | 1 917 791 | 33.7 | 25.1 |
| Harrison | 23 423 | 73.8 | 104 600 | 20.4 | 10.8 | 637 | 25.8 | 3.6 | 33 966 | -0.2 | 2 337 | 6.9 | 28 462 | 27.7 | 30.8 |
| Hartley | 1 727 | 73.4 | 138 200 | 19.9 | 9.9 | 644 | 26.4 | 3.0 | 2 767 | -1.6 | 123 | 4.4 | 2 275 | 43.8 | 21.2 |
| Haskell | 2 544 | 73.5 | 40 700 | 17.1 | 11.9 | 344 | 14.6 | 3.3 | 2 805 | -11.7 | 156 | 5.6 | 2 408 | 30.7 | 29.2 |
| Hays | 52 717 | 67.3 | 174 800 | 24.1 | 12.2 | 872 | 37.3 | 3.9 | 86 786 | 1.9 | 4 929 | 5.7 | 73 042 | 37.9 | 18.0 |
| Hemphill | 1 573 | 75.3 | 104 900 | 16.5 | 9.9 | 646 | 21.9 | 4.6 | 3 213 | 9.1 | 75 | 2.3 | 1 950 | 28.3 | 38.8 |
| Henderson | 30 552 | 77.3 | 87 000 | 23.9 | 14.1 | 661 | 29.0 | 4.0 | 35 824 | -1.9 | 2 618 | 7.3 | 31 630 | 26.0 | 29.8 |
| Hidalgo | 209 796 | 70.1 | 75 500 | 25.6 | 13.7 | 620 | 34.3 | 14.8 | 316 032 | -0.3 | 34 702 | 11.0 | 275 737 | 25.4 | 24.0 |
| Hill | 13 231 | 75.1 | 85 400 | 23.8 | 13.4 | 664 | 29.3 | 4.4 | 16 141 | -1.2 | 1 106 | 6.9 | 14 578 | 25.6 | 34.1 |
| Hockley | 8 147 | 73.0 | 77 000 | 17.7 | 9.9 | 620 | 23.2 | 4.8 | 13 157 | 3.7 | 623 | 4.7 | 10 422 | 27.1 | 30.3 |
| Hood | 20 916 | 77.3 | 150 400 | 23.3 | 12.2 | 854 | 28.3 | 2.7 | 27 462 | 1.7 | 1 548 | 5.6 | 22 395 | 36.3 | 25.2 |
| Hopkins | 13 200 | 72.6 | 93 700 | 23.3 | 12.7 | 675 | 28.0 | 4.6 | 18 424 | 0.8 | 1 102 | 6.0 | 15 134 | 29.9 | 32.7 |
| Houston | 7 880 | 71.8 | 67 900 | 22.1 | 13.9 | 584 | 31.8 | 4.5 | 8 569 | -3.0 | 814 | 9.5 | 8 907 | 24.9 | 28.3 |
| Howard | 11 016 | 67.7 | 61 800 | 19.5 | 10.9 | 628 | 29.1 | 3.7 | 14 447 | 0.3 | 877 | 6.1 | 12 157 | 24.7 | 28.1 |
| Hudspeth | 951 | 80.4 | 42 200 | 35.0 | 16.6 | 529 | 30.0 | 8.8 | 1 699 | -5.7 | 96 | 5.7 | 1 078 | 19.1 | 37.5 |
| Hunt | 30 624 | 71.5 | 92 900 | 22.7 | 13.2 | 733 | 32.9 | 5.6 | 40 278 | 1.5 | 3 130 | 7.8 | 36 625 | 30.6 | 28.2 |
| Hutchinson | 8 372 | 81.0 | 64 600 | 16.4 | 11.0 | 671 | 27.1 | 3.1 | 11 592 | -1.3 | 640 | 5.5 | 9 218 | 25.1 | 33.0 |
| Irion | 607 | 81.2 | 71 800 | 15.4 | 11.1 | 718 | 28.3 | 0.5 | 869 | 0.3 | 37 | 4.3 | 864 | 30.0 | 33.8 |
| Jack | 2 972 | 73.4 | 69 700 | 20.5 | 11.6 | 630 | 19.0 | 3.9 | 5 438 | 1.6 | 242 | 4.5 | 3 479 | 23.9 | 38.3 |
| Jackson | 5 173 | 75.3 | 85 900 | 18.5 | 11.3 | 666 | 21.7 | 4.3 | 7 289 | 0.9 | 380 | 5.2 | 6 273 | 32.4 | 31.5 |
| Jasper | 13 684 | 78.1 | 78 600 | 20.3 | 10.9 | 620 | 29.1 | 4.6 | 16 077 | -0.5 | 1 593 | 9.9 | 13 591 | 24.5 | 32.8 |
| Jeff Davis | 991 | 83.4 | 99 000 | 18.7 | 9.9 | 470 | 21.1 | 3.5 | 1 136 | 0.9 | 63 | 5.5 | 1 168 | 35.0 | 23.7 |
| Jefferson | 91 432 | 64.4 | 93 100 | 20.9 | 12.7 | 720 | 29.0 | 3.6 | 120 782 | -0.6 | 12 896 | 10.7 | 102 898 | 29.9 | 27.0 |
| Jim Hogg | 1 708 | 70.0 | 49 800 | 31.0 | 10.8 | 598 | 27.8 | 6.1 | 3 149 | 1.6 | 150 | 4.8 | 2 143 | 14.3 | 41.7 |
| Jim Wells | 13 541 | 73.8 | 68 300 | 22.5 | 12.9 | 682 | 30.5 | 7.6 | 25 341 | 6.6 | 1 253 | 4.9 | 17 006 | 24.4 | 30.3 |
| Johnson | 51 220 | 75.5 | 113 500 | 22.1 | 12.3 | 831 | 27.4 | 4.3 | 74 645 | 1.3 | 4 904 | 6.6 | 67 558 | 28.5 | 31.4 |
| Jones | 5 910 | 77.7 | 57 100 | 22.7 | 12.8 | 500 | 22.5 | 3.8 | 8 007 | -0.7 | 501 | 6.3 | 5 790 | 26.7 | 30.3 |
| Karnes | 4 630 | 70.2 | 70 100 | 18.5 | 11.6 | 584 | 29.6 | 5.8 | 5 728 | 2.8 | 392 | 6.8 | 4 573 | 31.1 | 26.5 |
| Kaufman | 34 014 | 77.9 | 129 300 | 23.5 | 13.4 | 851 | 31.3 | 4.6 | 50 330 | 1.0 | 3 574 | 7.1 | 46 963 | 34.2 | 24.4 |
| Kendall | 12 469 | 75.0 | 264 500 | 23.9 | 10.9 | 983 | 30.7 | 4.3 | 17 131 | 0.9 | 942 | 5.5 | 15 662 | 46.4 | 17.0 |
| Kenedy | 82 | 46.3 | 54 400 | 0.0 | 9.9 | 680 | 30.6 | 4.9 | 271 | 0.4 | 9 | 3.3 | 118 | 28.0 | 54.2 |
| Kent | 410 | 75.9 | 57 700 | 18.5 | 10.5 | 430 | 41.4 | 0.0 | 438 | -2.2 | 22 | 5.0 | 452 | 34.1 | 32.3 |
| Kerr | 20 278 | 72.9 | 136 700 | 24.2 | 12.8 | 749 | 27.8 | 3.7 | 22 991 | -1.2 | 1 273 | 5.5 | 20 893 | 32.4 | 19.3 |
| Kimble | 1 839 | 69.9 | 85 300 | 21.4 | 11.4 | 613 | 25.8 | 3.7 | 1 976 | -2.1 | 108 | 5.5 | 2 273 | 28.7 | 27.7 |
| King | 100 | 45.0 | 275 000 | 20.0 | 13.1 | 531 | 10.0 | 4.0 | 174 | -15.9 | 11 | 6.3 | 176 | 56.3 | 18.8 |
| Kinney | 1 156 | 82.5 | 49 100 | 18.1 | 16.1 | 523 | 34.9 | 4.1 | 1 482 | -2.2 | 111 | 7.5 | 1 092 | 15.3 | 32.2 |
| Kleberg | 11 119 | 57.1 | 72 000 | 24.5 | 9.9 | 651 | 29.4 | 7.0 | 17 800 | 0.5 | 1 052 | 5.9 | 12 647 | 33.0 | 24.1 |
| Knox | 1 613 | 64.9 | 40 000 | 20.1 | 12.5 | 451 | 26.0 | 3.8 | 1 684 | -7.1 | 95 | 5.6 | 1 519 | 30.6 | 29.8 |
| Lamar | 19 045 | 68.4 | 84 300 | 19.3 | 13.5 | 618 | 29.0 | 3.7 | 23 298 | -3.0 | 2 089 | 9.0 | 21 319 | 28.6 | 28.4 |
| Lamb | 4 767 | 73.0 | 54 000 | 21.9 | 11.4 | 629 | 26.9 | 4.1 | 6 595 | -4.5 | 510 | 7.7 | 6 002 | 23.2 | 36.7 |
| Lampasas | 7 067 | 75.8 | 124 100 | 20.8 | 12.9 | 736 | 27.1 | 4.7 | 9 715 | 0.1 | 666 | 6.9 | 8 309 | 28.4 | 28.3 |
| La Salle | 1 957 | 64.2 | 42 500 | 21.9 | 15.4 | 515 | 26.7 | 8.2 | 4 486 | 18.5 | 192 | 4.3 | 2 349 | 17.8 | 40.4 |
| Lavaca | 7 928 | 78.9 | 85 000 | 21.7 | 10.2 | 566 | 20.3 | 5.7 | 10 240 | -0.3 | 465 | 4.5 | 8 907 | 28.7 | 35.7 |
| Lee | 6 063 | 76.5 | 111 800 | 21.4 | 13.3 | 624 | 22.9 | 4.4 | 10 318 | 1.7 | 509 | 4.9 | 7 506 | 28.1 | 31.2 |
| Leon | 6 478 | 84.8 | 83 000 | 23.8 | 13.6 | 629 | 22.7 | 4.4 | 7 674 | -4.6 | 512 | 6.7 | 6 483 | 24.2 | 36.9 |
| Liberty | 24 217 | 78.4 | 83 500 | 20.6 | 11.4 | 715 | 28.0 | 7.3 | 32 416 | 1.2 | 2 867 | 8.8 | 29 595 | 21.5 | 37.4 |
| Limestone | 7 913 | 78.9 | 81 600 | 19.2 | 13.7 | 660 | 24.4 | 4.2 | 11 313 | -1.0 | 686 | 6.1 | 9 148 | 32.1 | 29.8 |
| Lipscomb | 1 169 | 70.5 | 77 100 | 17.1 | 9.9 | 555 | 14.9 | 5.0 | 1 809 | 0.5 | 64 | 3.5 | 1 641 | 30.8 | 40.1 |
| Live Oak | 3 848 | 83.3 | 88 200 | 19.2 | 11.9 | 678 | 25.9 | 4.3 | 6 833 | 10.7 | 286 | 4.2 | 3 981 | 29.9 | 26.5 |
| Llano | 8 221 | 79.5 | 159 800 | 24.9 | 13.6 | 628 | 30.4 | 1.6 | 8 524 | -0.1 | 551 | 6.5 | 7 691 | 33.6 | 19.3 |
| Loving | 27 | 44.4 | 66 700 | 0.0 | 9.9 | 1 375 | 20.0 | 0.0 | 43 | 2.4 | 4 | 9.3 | 56 | 19.6 | 33.9 |
| Lubbock | 102 910 | 59.5 | 105 400 | 21.7 | 11.6 | 749 | 32.7 | 4.3 | 143 988 | -0.4 | 7 900 | 5.5 | 133 777 | 32.3 | 19.9 |
| Lynn | 2 136 | 74.5 | 67 000 | 20.0 | 11.0 | 531 | 24.9 | 2.4 | 2 672 | -5.1 | 183 | 6.8 | 2 647 | 25.7 | 31.6 |
| McCulloch | 3 160 | 75.1 | 68 900 | 20.5 | 12.3 | 515 | 26.9 | 6.2 | 4 432 | 1.5 | 234 | 5.3 | 3 670 | 28.7 | 28.1 |
| McLennan | 83 851 | 60.0 | 104 800 | 22.4 | 12.7 | 757 | 33.5 | 3.8 | 116 314 | -0.4 | 7 593 | 6.5 | 104 761 | 31.8 | 24.3 |
| McMullen | 270 | 83.7 | 82 100 | 16.5 | 11.8 | 469 | 38.1 | 5.9 | 647 | 12.5 | 17 | 2.6 | 400 | 22.0 | 38.0 |
| Madison | 3 604 | 77.4 | 82 700 | 20.5 | 13.3 | 564 | 27.5 | 3.6 | 5 520 | -1.4 | 382 | 6.9 | 4 410 | 22.8 | 27.1 |
| Marion | 4 667 | 77.4 | 63 300 | 23.6 | 11.3 | 548 | 29.7 | 2.8 | 5 012 | -2.4 | 398 | 7.9 | 4 185 | 22.8 | 35.6 |
| Martin | 1 545 | 69.8 | 71 600 | 18.7 | 11.9 | 450 | 20.4 | 3.0 | 2 541 | 2.8 | 108 | 4.3 | 2 094 | 31.1 | 34.4 |

1. Specified owner-occupied units. 2. A value of 9.9 represents 9.9 percent or less. 3. Specified renter-occupied units. A value of 10.0 represents 10 percent or less. 4. Overcrowded or lacking complete plumbing facilities. 5. Percent of civilian labor force. 6. Persons 16 years old and over.

| | Private nonfarm establishments, employment and payroll, 2011 | | | | | | | | | Agriculture, 2007 | | | |
| | Employment | | | | | | | Annual payroll | | Farms | | | |
| | | | | | | | | | | | Percent with: | | |
| STATE County | Number of establishments | Total | Health care and social assistance | Manufacturing | Retail trade | Finance and insurance | Professional, scientific, and technical services | Total (mil dol) | Average per employee (dollars) | Number | Fewer than 50 acres | 500 acres or more | Farm operators whose principal occupation is farming (percent) |
|---|---|---|---|---|---|---|---|---|---|---|---|---|---|
| | 104 | 105 | 106 | 107 | 108 | 109 | 110 | 111 | 112 | 113 | 114 | 115 | 116 |
| **TEXAS—Cont'd** | | | | | | | | | | | | | |
| Guadalupe | 1 811 | 25 647 | 3 257 | 5 477 | 3 934 | D | 487 | 865 | 33 715 | 2 462 | 50.5 | 5.2 | 39.9 |
| Hale | 712 | 11 275 | 979 | 2 519 | 1 540 | 336 | 219 | 352 | 31 187 | 957 | 12.2 | 36.4 | 46.4 |
| Hall | 72 | 529 | 97 | 43 | 96 | 49 | D | 13 | 24 076 | 382 | 3.7 | 44.2 | 44.5 |
| Hamilton | 207 | 2 021 | 578 | 153 | 337 | 56 | D | 60 | 29 514 | 1 045 | 14.7 | 20.9 | 42.3 |
| Hansford | 151 | 1 198 | D | D | D | 100 | 45 | 43 | 36 189 | 242 | 6.6 | 69.0 | 63.6 |
| Hardeman | 81 | 805 | 241 | D | 151 | 45 | D | 24 | 29 519 | 332 | 6.3 | 46.4 | 44.9 |
| Hardin | 782 | 8 514 | 1 321 | 665 | 2 087 | 223 | 200 | 289 | 33 922 | 699 | 67.2 | 2.7 | 33.2 |
| Harris | 91 945 | 1 780 376 | 223 613 | 150 760 | 186 415 | 76 489 | 153 796 | 105 534 | 59 276 | 2 210 | 69.8 | 4.3 | 38.4 |
| Harrison | 1 316 | 19 287 | 1 789 | 3 991 | 2 182 | 957 | 778 | 780 | 40 441 | 1 205 | 45.8 | 7.5 | 38.3 |
| Hartley | 104 | 1 008 | 278 | D | D | D | D | 32 | 31 714 | 282 | 3.9 | 65.2 | 62.4 |
| Haskell | 139 | 1 019 | 137 | D | 289 | 59 | 27 | 27 | 26 647 | 553 | 9.2 | 40.3 | 49.4 |
| Hays | 3 224 | 40 584 | 5 762 | 3 421 | 10 049 | 1 265 | 1 597 | 1 189 | 29 301 | 1 136 | 46.8 | 8.0 | 34.1 |
| Hemphill | 163 | 1 491 | 160 | D | 168 | 66 | D | 70 | 47 189 | 233 | 8.2 | 54.9 | 46.4 |
| Henderson | 1 246 | 13 073 | 2 686 | 1 754 | 2 629 | 453 | 340 | 379 | 28 991 | 2 109 | 48.5 | 5.5 | 38.1 |
| Hidalgo | 11 206 | 169 833 | 54 623 | 5 039 | 34 056 | 6 345 | 6 273 | 4 425 | 26 053 | 2 151 | 61.6 | 14.9 | 44.1 |
| Hill | 647 | 6 773 | 1 322 | 828 | 1 490 | 197 | 110 | 195 | 28 767 | 2 113 | 37.2 | 10.3 | 38.7 |
| Hockley | 504 | 5 952 | 1 038 | D | 941 | 210 | 107 | 245 | 41 126 | 842 | 15.4 | 33.5 | 39.0 |
| Hood | 1 206 | 12 115 | 2 299 | 501 | 2 427 | 449 | 352 | 399 | 32 957 | 1 076 | 58.6 | 7.5 | 34.8 |
| Hopkins | 726 | 9 605 | 1 304 | D | 1 583 | 440 | 236 | 313 | 32 562 | 1 955 | 35.4 | 9.7 | 44.1 |
| Houston | 357 | 3 533 | 761 | 672 | 659 | 150 | D | 105 | 29 667 | 1 562 | 27.4 | 12.5 | 46.7 |
| Howard | 703 | 9 592 | 2 384 | 527 | 1 359 | 327 | 200 | 350 | 36 532 | 519 | 26.6 | 32.8 | 37.4 |
| Hudspeth | 38 | 281 | D | D | 30 | D | D | 9 | 31 167 | 169 | 21.9 | 49.7 | 53.3 |
| Hunt | 1 371 | 21 323 | 3 156 | 7 103 | 3 536 | 479 | 961 | 888 | 41 637 | 3 139 | 52.9 | 3.9 | 37.1 |
| Hutchinson | 478 | 6 372 | 479 | 1 594 | 857 | 162 | 212 | 319 | 50 136 | 259 | 29.3 | 35.5 | 42.1 |
| Irion | 44 | 356 | D | D | D | D | D | D | 42 056 | 156 | 28.8 | 49.4 | 42.9 |
| Jack | 206 | 2 356 | D | D | 174 | 24 | 46 | 96 | 40 759 | 902 | 18.1 | 22.4 | 34.3 |
| Jackson | 282 | 3 871 | 270 | D | 456 | D | 76 | 156 | 40 346 | 847 | 28.1 | 26.9 | 46.6 |
| Jasper | 612 | 8 213 | 2 398 | D | 1 719 | 278 | 141 | 249 | 30 329 | 920 | 66.8 | 2.3 | 29.1 |
| Jeff Davis | 57 | 333 | 76 | NA | 43 | D | 6 | 8 | 24 988 | 105 | 12.4 | 61.9 | 41.0 |
| Jefferson | 5 725 | 100 093 | 17 163 | 13 108 | 13 857 | 2 699 | 5 964 | 4 430 | 44 259 | 793 | 52.1 | 16.6 | 47.2 |
| Jim Hogg | 98 | 1 348 | D | 60 | 216 | 86 | 6 | 32 | 23 622 | 240 | 10.8 | 48.8 | 36.3 |
| Jim Wells | 904 | 14 759 | 4 584 | 476 | 1 676 | 358 | 346 | 574 | 38 897 | 1 109 | 31.4 | 15.6 | 44.0 |
| Johnson | 2 510 | 32 937 | 3 601 | 4 649 | 4 929 | 786 | 727 | 1 221 | 37 073 | 2 746 | 62.3 | 4.4 | 33.5 |
| Jones | 299 | 2 438 | 687 | 288 | 238 | 112 | 30 | 70 | 28 906 | 1 053 | 21.6 | 22.3 | 40.6 |
| Karnes | 260 | 2 601 | 545 | 241 | 464 | 95 | 67 | 98 | 37 752 | 1 208 | 16.0 | 17.5 | 44.0 |
| Kaufman | 1 635 | 19 594 | 3 049 | 3 460 | 3 612 | 601 | 498 | 646 | 32 958 | 2 563 | 59.1 | 5.0 | 36.9 |
| Kendall | 1 093 | 10 338 | 1 765 | 1 116 | 2 040 | D | 455 | 398 | 38 517 | 1 164 | 43.0 | 13.9 | 34.4 |
| Kenedy | 13 | 132 | NA | NA | NA | NA | D | 6 | 43 394 | 25 | 4.0 | 76.0 | 72.0 |
| Kent | 14 | 119 | NA | NA | NA | D | NA | 6 | 50 218 | 212 | 3.8 | 44.8 | 36.3 |
| Kerr | 1 374 | 15 035 | 3 759 | 426 | 2 975 | D | 648 | 477 | 31 724 | 1 226 | 33.0 | 16.6 | 36.0 |
| Kimble | 137 | 860 | D | D | 266 | D | D | 22 | 25 944 | 639 | 16.6 | 40.2 | 42.9 |
| King | NA | NA | NA | NA | NA | NA | NA | NA | NA | 64 | 3.1 | 56.3 | 34.4 |
| Kinney | 30 | 367 | D | NA | 75 | NA | NA | 9 | 24 403 | 220 | 5.5 | 55.0 | 40.5 |
| Kleberg | 563 | 6 824 | 1 449 | D | 1 525 | 300 | 166 | 196 | 28 675 | 349 | 52.4 | 12.3 | 45.8 |
| Knox | 104 | 788 | 207 | NA | 151 | D | D | 24 | 30 768 | 219 | 11.0 | 52.1 | 56.6 |
| Lamar | 1 161 | 16 691 | 3 593 | 3 640 | 2 457 | 507 | 333 | 541 | 32 442 | 1 817 | 29.4 | 12.5 | 38.5 |
| Lamb | 260 | 2 620 | 379 | D | 372 | D | 47 | 87 | 33 035 | 987 | 6.3 | 37.9 | 47.1 |
| Lampasas | 373 | 3 669 | 533 | 569 | 668 | 107 | D | 97 | 26 454 | 966 | 32.1 | 21.7 | 37.9 |
| La Salle | 89 | 978 | 99 | NA | 208 | D | NA | 30 | 30 613 | 399 | 10.3 | 45.1 | 46.6 |
| Lavaca | 451 | 5 220 | 1 145 | 1 347 | 740 | 292 | 64 | 164 | 31 507 | 2 747 | 32.0 | 7.1 | 38.4 |
| Lee | 400 | 3 912 | 419 | 367 | 659 | 226 | 79 | 140 | 35 808 | 1 844 | 33.7 | 7.5 | 36.0 |
| Leon | 348 | 4 227 | 229 | 567 | 502 | D | 97 | 184 | 43 511 | 2 066 | 34.8 | 11.9 | 45.8 |
| Liberty | 1 035 | 11 730 | 1 939 | 1 443 | 2 435 | 327 | 320 | 402 | 34 276 | 1 589 | 56.4 | 8.3 | 36.2 |
| Limestone | 395 | 5 140 | 1 124 | 758 | 1 026 | 243 | 74 | 161 | 31 236 | 1 494 | 25.2 | 16.2 | 47.1 |
| Lipscomb | 96 | 790 | D | D | 106 | D | D | 27 | 33 699 | 294 | 2.7 | 60.2 | 49.3 |
| Live Oak | 257 | 2 403 | D | D | 380 | D | 57 | 118 | 48 911 | 896 | 19.0 | 25.6 | 39.8 |
| Llano | 436 | 3 328 | 604 | 75 | 481 | 171 | 114 | 87 | 26 077 | 791 | 26.8 | 32.0 | 38.8 |
| Loving | NA | NA | NA | NA | NA | NA | NA | NA | NA | 9 | 11.1 | 77.8 | 66.7 |
| Lubbock | 6 839 | 105 271 | 23 012 | 5 308 | 16 672 | 4 876 | 3 967 | 3 312 | 31 465 | 1 205 | 40.1 | 23.2 | 41.2 |
| Lynn | 87 | 677 | 157 | D | 102 | 66 | D | 21 | 31 062 | 506 | 12.6 | 48.0 | 61.1 |
| McCulloch | 211 | 2 134 | 293 | D | 457 | 107 | D | 75 | 35 213 | 694 | 13.4 | 32.6 | 42.8 |
| McLennan | 4 938 | 95 918 | 17 706 | 13 785 | 11 675 | 4 692 | 2 478 | 3 099 | 32 314 | 2 798 | 52.9 | 7.0 | 34.8 |
| McMullen | 17 | 232 | NA | NA | D | D | D | 12 | 52 358 | 225 | 6.2 | 64.0 | 37.3 |
| Madison | 216 | 2 120 | D | D | 618 | 80 | D | 62 | 29 057 | 1 057 | 33.9 | 10.8 | 40.2 |
| Marion | 151 | 1 394 | 352 | 220 | 225 | 40 | 36 | 34 | 24 726 | 258 | 32.2 | 7.0 | 35.3 |
| Martin | 98 | 834 | 154 | NA | 141 | D | D | 34 | 41 342 | 464 | 15.1 | 42.2 | 53.0 |

| STATE County | Land in farms Acreage (1,000) | Percent change, 2002–2007 | Average size of farm | Total irrigated (1,000) | Total cropland (1,000) | Value of land and buildings (dollars) Average per farm | Average per acre | Value of machinery and equipment, average per farm (dollars) | Value of products sold Total (mil dol) | Average per farm (dollars) | Percent from: Crops | Live-stock and poultry products | Percent of farms with sales of: $10,000 or more | $100,000 or more | Government payments Total ($1,000) | Percent of farms |
|---|---|---|---|---|---|---|---|---|---|---|---|---|---|---|---|---|
| | 117 | 118 | 119 | 120 | 121 | 122 | 123 | 124 | 125 | 126 | 127 | 128 | 129 | 130 | 131 | 132 |
| **TEXAS—Cont'd** | | | | | | | | | | | | | | | | |
| Guadalupe | 385 | 0.0 | 156 | 1.1 | 126.0 | 406 933 | 2 602 | 43 017 | 41.2 | 16 725 | 45.7 | 54.3 | 22.0 | 2.6 | 1 263 | 11.8 |
| Hale | 589 | -2.6 | 615 | 243.5 | 462.3 | 712 744 | 1 159 | 170 015 | 364.4 | 380 811 | 43.8 | 56.2 | 44.4 | 30.3 | 21 470 | 81.4 |
| Hall | 534 | 23.6 | 1 398 | 27.9 | 219.0 | 1 165 765 | 834 | 104 525 | 43.5 | 113 802 | 85.3 | 14.7 | 44.2 | 22.8 | 7 509 | 85.6 |
| Hamilton | 471 | 4.7 | 451 | 0.8 | 97.6 | 770 944 | 1 711 | 56 406 | 51.4 | 49 163 | 8.5 | 91.5 | 37.0 | 5.3 | 458 | 17.7 |
| Hansford | 585 | -1.3 | 2 419 | 100.7 | 331.5 | 1 949 295 | 806 | 293 887 | 589.8 | 2 437 187 | 14.7 | 85.3 | 69.8 | 57.0 | 4 932 | 75.2 |
| Hardeman | 370 | 6.9 | 1 115 | 11.5 | 162.4 | 904 259 | 811 | 86 255 | 24.0 | 72 195 | 41.9 | 58.1 | 49.4 | 15.7 | 2 685 | 75.6 |
| Hardin | 91 | 31.9 | 130 | 1.0 | 22.1 | 296 543 | 2 273 | 49 252 | 6.3 | 9 033 | 54.3 | 45.7 | 14.6 | 2.3 | 231 | 2.3 |
| Harris | 259 | -15.1 | 117 | 7.0 | 91.4 | 395 227 | 3 372 | 50 849 | 62.5 | 28 295 | 62.8 | 37.2 | 17.5 | 3.1 | 723 | 2.9 |
| Harrison | 201 | -12.2 | 167 | 0.8 | 52.3 | 367 952 | 2 207 | 50 846 | 14.1 | 11 708 | 20.3 | 79.7 | 20.6 | 1.4 | 200 | 4.1 |
| Hartley | 911 | 15.5 | 3 230 | 171.7 | 345.2 | 2 184 140 | 676 | 361 687 | 724.5 | 2 569 176 | 20.3 | 79.7 | 63.8 | 56.4 | 5 096 | 74.8 |
| Haskell | 495 | 0.6 | 895 | 35.1 | 290.9 | 794 365 | 888 | 112 606 | 67.7 | 122 430 | 65.1 | 34.9 | 51.0 | 18.8 | 9 853 | 80.8 |
| Hays | 236 | -15.1 | 207 | 0.9 | 39.3 | 585 716 | 2 825 | 33 253 | 11.5 | 10 081 | 41.8 | 58.2 | 13.2 | 1.6 | 248 | 3.6 |
| Hemphill | 549 | 0.5 | 2 355 | 5.3 | 75.6 | 1 715 338 | 728 | 105 978 | 117.7 | 505 163 | 1.6 | 98.4 | 50.2 | 25.8 | 1 156 | 48.1 |
| Henderson | 318 | -6.7 | 151 | 1.3 | 86.5 | 369 324 | 2 446 | 48 910 | 44.5 | 21 106 | 43.0 | 57.0 | 27.4 | 2.3 | 124 | 3.9 |
| Hidalgo | 723 | 21.9 | 336 | 169.3 | 404.3 | 732 730 | 2 181 | 88 682 | 314.3 | 146 098 | 91.8 | 8.2 | 35.1 | 11.0 | 10 723 | 19.6 |
| Hill | 525 | 4.2 | 248 | 1.2 | 253.9 | 457 258 | 1 841 | 61 171 | 74.2 | 35 095 | 58.4 | 41.6 | 29.1 | 4.9 | 3 662 | 25.0 |
| Hockley | 484 | -1.4 | 575 | 132.3 | 411.4 | 614 787 | 1 069 | 129 960 | 107.7 | 127 921 | 94.1 | 5.9 | 37.4 | 25.4 | 14 237 | 76.4 |
| Hood | 206 | 2.0 | 191 | 4.3 | 80.8 | 521 853 | 2 730 | 52 883 | 18.9 | 17 590 | 38.1 | 61.9 | 24.0 | 3.1 | 290 | 10.9 |
| Hopkins | 390 | -9.5 | 200 | 11.6 | 143.0 | 456 522 | 2 286 | 67 748 | 208.3 | 106 522 | 7.9 | 92.1 | 40.4 | 9.8 | 636 | 8.8 |
| Houston | 440 | -5.4 | 282 | 4.6 | 109.2 | 578 277 | 2 051 | 61 623 | 40.7 | 26 027 | 22.3 | 77.7 | 36.6 | 3.6 | 410 | 4.4 |
| Howard | 523 | 1.0 | 1 007 | 8.4 | 228.0 | 773 530 | 768 | 81 064 | 40.9 | 78 714 | 81.4 | 18.5 | 30.6 | 15.4 | 7 075 | 61.8 |
| Hudspeth | 2 258 | 6.4 | 13 358 | 27.3 | 106.5 | 3 776 355 | 283 | 157 771 | 31.1 | 183 861 | 64.9 | 35.1 | 52.1 | 23.7 | 766 | 24.9 |
| Hunt | 388 | -3.0 | 124 | 2.1 | 171.5 | 305 177 | 2 466 | 45 239 | 40.5 | 12 905 | 55.7 | 44.3 | 17.3 | 1.6 | 1 144 | 10.4 |
| Hutchinson | 557 | 0.7 | 2 152 | 33.0 | 144.1 | 1 436 458 | 668 | 116 890 | 49.6 | 191 338 | 53.3 | 46.7 | 35.1 | 22.8 | 2 154 | 33.2 |
| Irion | 625 | 16.6 | 4 004 | 1.3 | 7.5 | 2 492 999 | 623 | 54 142 | 6.1 | 38 959 | 11.6 | 88.4 | 42.3 | 10.3 | 509 | 22.4 |
| Jack | 576 | -3.4 | 639 | 0.7 | 72.0 | 950 445 | 1 488 | 51 512 | 18.3 | 20 259 | 10.3 | 89.7 | 30.2 | 4.3 | 233 | 11.0 |
| Jackson | 493 | 4.7 | 582 | 8.9 | 198.8 | 793 028 | 1 364 | 106 143 | 64.6 | 76 294 | 72.8 | 27.2 | 42.3 | 14.6 | 6 455 | 30.8 |
| Jasper | 96 | 0.0 | 104 | 0.3 | 20.2 | 292 057 | 2 801 | 44 807 | 6.7 | 7 243 | 43.7 | 56.3 | 16.8 | 1.0 | 644 | 10.8 |
| Jeff Davis | 1 391 | -6.6 | 13 247 | 0.3 | 44.0 | 3 697 058 | 279 | 90 527 | 10.4 | 99 458 | 1.4 | 98.6 | 44.8 | 20.0 | 179 | 9.5 |
| Jefferson | 333 | -14.2 | 420 | 16.9 | 153.6 | 584 497 | 1 391 | 61 295 | 26.8 | 33 755 | 49.2 | 50.8 | 27.1 | 6.7 | 3 061 | 17.4 |
| Jim Hogg | 640 | 6.0 | 2 668 | D | 9.8 | 1 722 887 | 646 | 58 337 | 7.4 | 31 035 | D | D | 37.1 | 4.2 | 314 | 12.9 |
| Jim Wells | 463 | -7.0 | 417 | 1.8 | 150.9 | 609 575 | 1 461 | 54 010 | 61.0 | 55 035 | 40.7 | 59.3 | 20.5 | 4.1 | 2 862 | 20.6 |
| Johnson | 331 | -8.6 | 121 | 1.9 | 116.7 | 411 185 | 3 408 | 48 534 | 62.0 | 22 562 | 21.3 | 78.7 | 20.3 | 2.0 | 977 | 7.0 |
| Jones | 573 | 10.8 | 544 | 3.9 | 334.8 | 597 255 | 1 097 | 72 611 | 59.2 | 56 265 | 68.8 | 31.2 | 29.3 | 11.5 | 10 566 | 58.3 |
| Karnes | 417 | -12.2 | 346 | 1.4 | 104.5 | 596 572 | 1 726 | 49 042 | 24.6 | 20 334 | 43.3 | 56.7 | 33.9 | 3.5 | 1 180 | 21.8 |
| Kaufman | 422 | 0.5 | 165 | 1.6 | 155.1 | 430 143 | 2 614 | 46 495 | 43.7 | 17 031 | 32.1 | 67.9 | 17.6 | 2.2 | 480 | 3.4 |
| Kendall | 343 | 4.9 | 294 | 0.7 | 34.1 | 799 738 | 2 718 | 35 979 | 7.6 | 6 557 | 12.9 | 87.1 | 15.8 | 0.6 | 280 | 7.1 |
| Kenedy | 909 | 91.8 | 36 362 | 0.4 | 2.8 | 21 107 929 | 580 | 327 043 | 19.0 | 758 441 | D | D | 64.0 | 28.0 | 34 | 20.0 |
| Kent | 568 | 1.2 | 2 677 | 0.8 | 53.6 | 1 612 444 | 602 | 54 334 | 6.8 | 31 928 | 22.2 | 77.8 | 34.9 | 9.9 | 1 672 | 63.2 |
| Kerr | 614 | 8.9 | 500 | 2.3 | 40.2 | 892 896 | 1 784 | 44 264 | 13.4 | 10 948 | 8.9 | 91.1 | 15.1 | 1.3 | 344 | 5.5 |
| Kimble | 620 | 0.6 | 970 | 2.5 | 35.9 | 1 447 847 | 1 492 | 43 088 | 8.4 | 13 196 | 16.0 | 84.0 | 23.0 | 2.3 | 523 | 11.7 |
| King | 542 | -0.9 | 8 471 | D | 29.4 | 3 211 985 | 379 | 132 974 | 17.9 | 279 617 | 8.7 | 91.3 | 40.6 | 15.6 | 750 | 82.8 |
| Kinney | 601 | -2.1 | 2 733 | 2.6 | 11.6 | 2 473 089 | 905 | 60 734 | 6.4 | 29 276 | 12.1 | 87.9 | 30.5 | 7.3 | 515 | 14.5 |
| Kleberg | 498 | NA | 1 428 | 0.0 | 82.6 | 1 689 955 | 1 183 | 61 633 | 65.0 | 186 222 | 38.6 | 61.4 | 28.4 | 6.0 | 1 755 | 27.5 |
| Knox | 493 | -12.6 | 2 253 | 21.9 | 212.7 | 1 924 591 | 854 | 188 199 | 38.4 | 175 549 | 61.8 | 38.2 | 61.2 | 36.5 | 5 030 | 81.7 |
| Lamar | 521 | 10.9 | 287 | 4.0 | 218.6 | 472 031 | 1 646 | 62 669 | 60.4 | 33 234 | 44.0 | 56.0 | 33.1 | 4.8 | 3 768 | 27.4 |
| Lamb | 635 | 1.0 | 643 | 234.8 | 515.0 | 667 082 | 1 037 | 159 305 | 406.3 | 411 642 | 35.2 | 64.8 | 42.1 | 30.8 | 17 326 | 83.7 |
| Lampasas | 416 | 1.0 | 431 | 0.4 | 70.6 | 800 073 | 1 858 | 55 974 | 14.0 | 14 464 | 15.2 | 84.8 | 26.9 | 2.4 | 208 | 8.5 |
| La Salle | 649 | 16.1 | 1 627 | 8.8 | 76.3 | 1 814 392 | 1 115 | 62 863 | 31.0 | 77 818 | 25.1 | 74.9 | 29.3 | 8.0 | 981 | 16.3 |
| Lavaca | 567 | -5.8 | 206 | 3.2 | 113.1 | 438 979 | 2 128 | 44 220 | 58.9 | 21 454 | 12.7 | 87.3 | 32.6 | 2.4 | 714 | 9.9 |
| Lee | 326 | -10.9 | 177 | 1.4 | 68.3 | 458 300 | 2 595 | 49 848 | 40.9 | 22 191 | 20.1 | 79.9 | 32.5 | 2.1 | 267 | 8.6 |
| Leon | 569 | 1.1 | 275 | 2.8 | 121.1 | 556 154 | 2 019 | 53 192 | 85.8 | 41 530 | 9.9 | 90.1 | 29.2 | 3.6 | 197 | 2.5 |
| Liberty | 298 | -2.3 | 187 | 5.3 | 127.7 | 374 776 | 1 999 | 52 280 | 25.1 | 15 781 | 40.4 | 59.6 | 19.1 | 2.8 | 1 603 | 5.8 |
| Limestone | 506 | -4.5 | 339 | 0.8 | 141.9 | 530 153 | 1 566 | 51 422 | 45.7 | 30 591 | 20.1 | 79.9 | 35.1 | 4.1 | 1 190 | 12.0 |
| Lipscomb | 571 | -1.2 | 1 942 | 19.4 | 127.0 | 1 411 816 | 727 | 133 035 | 80.5 | 273 900 | 14.7 | 85.3 | 50.7 | 24.5 | 2 436 | 76.9 |
| Live Oak | 501 | -4.6 | 559 | 2.1 | 90.6 | 834 010 | 1 491 | 56 075 | 21.0 | 23 402 | 25.5 | 74.5 | 29.6 | 4.8 | 1 222 | 17.5 |
| Llano | 539 | 1.1 | 681 | 0.3 | 27.3 | 1 283 993 | 1 885 | 43 574 | 11.8 | 14 904 | 2.2 | 97.8 | 29.6 | 2.4 | 240 | 8.0 |
| Loving | 427 | -17.1 | 47 421 | 0.0 | D | 6 220 443 | 131 | 66 219 | 0.5 | 55 217 | 0.0 | 100.0 | 66.7 | 33.3 | 47 | 44.4 |
| Lubbock | 516 | -7.4 | 428 | 159.5 | 415.8 | 513 145 | 1 199 | 128 861 | 209.0 | 173 453 | D | D | 37.4 | 21.9 | 17 900 | 57.8 |
| Lynn | 494 | -6.8 | 976 | 73.7 | 408.8 | 863 702 | 885 | 210 645 | 98.9 | 195 388 | 97.9 | 2.1 | 54.5 | 36.8 | 17 028 | 86.0 |
| McCulloch | 613 | 12.3 | 883 | 0.9 | 108.5 | 1 172 811 | 1 329 | 63 892 | 18.1 | 26 081 | 30.6 | 69.4 | 35.4 | 6.2 | 1 629 | 37.8 |
| McLennan | 530 | -1.5 | 189 | 2.9 | 241.6 | 390 384 | 2 062 | 49 514 | 104.7 | 37 431 | 39.8 | 60.2 | 21.9 | 3.7 | 2 612 | 16.0 |
| McMullen | 506 | -15.2 | 2 251 | D | 38.5 | 2 366 821 | 1 051 | 81 980 | 8.8 | 39 012 | 3.4 | 96.6 | 37.8 | 5.8 | 177 | 12.4 |
| Madison | 273 | 11.4 | 258 | 0.5 | 39.6 | 542 272 | 2 099 | 61 512 | 83.3 | 78 813 | D | D | 34.3 | 3.4 | 88 | 2.4 |
| Marion | 42 | -30.0 | 164 | 0.2 | 11.0 | 332 071 | 2 027 | 51 191 | 4.2 | 16 085 | 26.5 | 73.5 | 19.8 | 1.9 | 31 | 3.1 |
| Martin | 458 | -12.9 | 987 | 16.9 | 276.0 | 637 030 | 645 | 124 129 | 52.9 | 114 009 | 96.8 | 3.2 | 41.8 | 28.4 | 10 662 | 82.3 |

| STATE County | Water use, 2005 | | Wholesale trade,[1] 2007 | | | | Retail trade,[2] 2007 | | | | Real estate and rental and leasing,[2] 2007 | | | |
|---|---|---|---|---|---|---|---|---|---|---|---|---|---|---|
| | Total water withdrawn (mil gal/day) | Gallons withdrawn per person | Number of establishments | Number of employees | Sales (mil dol) | Annual payroll (mil dol) | Number of establishments | Number of employees | Sales (mil dol) | Annual payroll (mil dol) | Number of establishments | Number of employees | Receipts (mil dol) | Annual payroll (mil dol) |
| | 133 | 134 | 135 | 136 | 137 | 138 | 139 | 140 | 141 | 142 | 143 | 144 | 145 | 146 |
| **TEXAS—Cont'd** | | | | | | | | | | | | | | |
| Guadalupe | 34.3 | 333 | 85 | 1 519 | 822.1 | 66.5 | 281 | 3 718 | 1 026.1 | 83.1 | 88 | 401 | 53.9 | 10.2 |
| Hale | 325.3 | 8 978 | 55 | D | D | D | 129 | 1 490 | 325.1 | 26.8 | 29 | 77 | 10.7 | 1.8 |
| Hall | 25.6 | 6 905 | 3 | D | D | D | 17 | 88 | 23.2 | 1.3 | 1 | D | D | D |
| Hamilton | 2.7 | 328 | 8 | 85 | 44.8 | 3.3 | 59 | 365 | 78.6 | 7.0 | 3 | D | D | D |
| Hansford | 211.4 | 40 428 | 18 | 101 | 89.3 | 3.5 | 23 | 188 | 60.1 | 3.5 | 2 | D | D | D |
| Hardeman | 5.8 | 1 342 | 4 | 16 | 18.6 | 0.6 | 16 | 116 | 22.2 | 1.7 | 1 | D | D | D |
| Hardin | 19.9 | 390 | 17 | 115 | 35.9 | 3.9 | 147 | 2 170 | 612.4 | 51.5 | 26 | 70 | 5.5 | 0.9 |
| Harris | 764.3 | 207 | 6 086 | 98 893 | 205 478.8 | 5 991.8 | 12 342 | 183 618 | 51 899.1 | 4 543.5 | 5 047 | 40 175 | 9 714.3 | 1 786.5 |
| Harrison | 39.8 | 627 | 56 | 469 | 303.6 | 22.7 | 207 | 2 144 | 603.9 | 48.9 | 46 | 170 | 24.3 | 4.7 |
| Hartley | 365.4 | 67 048 | 5 | 39 | 41.9 | 2.0 | 9 | 176 | 34.1 | 2.6 | 5 | 20 | 1.8 | 0.5 |
| Haskell | 35.3 | 128 | 2 | D | D | D | 29 | 212 | 59.2 | 3.8 | 3 | D | D | D |
| Hays | 15.9 | 128 | 110 | 925 | 451.2 | 37.4 | 556 | 8 797 | 1 954.7 | 171.3 | 178 | 666 | 124.9 | 20.0 |
| Hemphill | 3.9 | 1 151 | 16 | 88 | 63.5 | 4.1 | 21 | 119 | 39.2 | 2.9 | 4 | 28 | 4.2 | 0.9 |
| Henderson | 117.0 | 1 463 | 38 | D | D | D | 245 | 2 819 | 657.4 | 59.7 | 55 | 206 | 28.4 | 4.5 |
| Hidalgo | 394.4 | 581 | 670 | 7 808 | 4 301.1 | 257.5 | 2 132 | 32 803 | 7 898.8 | 635.3 | 491 | 2 289 | 366.9 | 53.2 |
| Hill | 11.7 | 330 | 17 | 82 | 41.6 | 2.3 | 197 | 1 742 | 400.3 | 31.4 | 29 | 110 | 17.3 | 1.9 |
| Hockley | 175.6 | 7 707 | 28 | D | D | D | 73 | 971 | 201.7 | 16.3 | 13 | 41 | 2.9 | 0.9 |
| Hood | 66.7 | 1 391 | 40 | 278 | 95.5 | 11.5 | 214 | 2 513 | 730.0 | 60.2 | 64 | D | D | D |
| Hopkins | 13.9 | 416 | 37 | D | D | D | 155 | 1 702 | 447.7 | 35.3 | 30 | 86 | 12.6 | 1.8 |
| Houston | 8.3 | 357 | 13 | 119 | 39.1 | 3.4 | 67 | 707 | 159.3 | 13.2 | 9 | 39 | 4.9 | 0.8 |
| Howard | 23.5 | 722 | 23 | 173 | 88.5 | 6.9 | 121 | 1 297 | 341.2 | 27.6 | 39 | 183 | 36.5 | 3.5 |
| Hudspeth | 149.5 | 45 363 | 1 | D | D | D | 13 | 53 | 12.5 | 0.5 | 2 | D | D | D |
| Hunt | 123.2 | 1 492 | 45 | 463 | 263.4 | 15.0 | 262 | 3 554 | 931.3 | 85.6 | 82 | 328 | 40.0 | 6.5 |
| Hutchinson | 110.2 | 4 902 | 22 | D | D | D | 78 | 835 | 210.8 | 16.0 | 13 | 83 | 32.3 | 3.5 |
| Irion | 2.8 | 1 617 | 1 | D | D | D | 4 | D | D | D | NA | NA | NA | NA |
| Jack | 2.8 | 306 | 8 | 80 | 112.3 | 4.1 | 32 | 200 | 34.1 | 3.2 | 10 | 21 | 2.9 | 0.6 |
| Jackson | 69.6 | 4 853 | 16 | 113 | 67.0 | 4.0 | 52 | 508 | 133.5 | 9.7 | 10 | D | D | D |
| Jasper | 51.2 | 1 439 | 31 | 215 | 123.3 | 7.0 | 153 | 1 563 | 371.0 | 32.2 | 20 | 59 | 6.5 | 1.0 |
| Jeff Davis | 3.9 | 1 709 | 1 | D | D | D | 6 | 39 | 7.1 | 0.8 | 2 | D | D | D |
| Jefferson | 263.4 | 1 064 | 267 | 4 147 | 2 852.5 | 196.1 | 1 050 | 14 764 | 3 973.1 | 339.4 | 289 | 1 562 | 333.1 | 54.7 |
| Jim Hogg | 2.0 | 396 | 3 | D | D | D | 30 | 262 | 61.6 | 3.8 | 2 | D | D | D |
| Jim Wells | 8.8 | 216 | 36 | 422 | 193.4 | 20.3 | 148 | 1 645 | 462.4 | 34.7 | 42 | 389 | 85.1 | 21.3 |
| Johnson | 18.7 | 127 | 117 | 1 210 | 536.2 | 50.2 | 355 | 4 679 | 1 269.6 | 108.0 | 109 | 369 | 70.7 | 12.4 |
| Jones | 4.5 | 228 | 19 | 111 | 379.0 | 4.0 | 51 | 446 | 163.3 | 9.8 | 9 | 21 | 1.4 | 0.2 |
| Karnes | 4.7 | 307 | 7 | 57 | 40.7 | 2.3 | 50 | 443 | 101.8 | 8.8 | 6 | 13 | 3.9 | 0.2 |
| Kaufman | 7.0 | 78 | 69 | 690 | 443.1 | 25.8 | 305 | 3 493 | 943.8 | 79.6 | 57 | 199 | 26.0 | 4.3 |
| Kendall | 4.2 | 148 | 46 | 284 | 285.3 | 12.3 | 152 | 1 977 | 808.1 | 55.7 | 60 | 222 | 46.4 | 8.6 |
| Kenedy | 1.0 | 2 326 | NA | NA | NA | NA | NA | NA | NA | NA | NA | NA | NA | NA |
| Kent | 15.9 | 20 307 | NA | NA | NA | NA | 4 | D | D | D | NA | NA | NA | NA |
| Kerr | 10.1 | 217 | 39 | D | D | D | 227 | 2 888 | 719.9 | 68.4 | 89 | 279 | 39.5 | 6.4 |
| Kimble | 3.2 | 690 | 3 | 14 | 0.1 | 0.0 | 37 | 267 | 78.7 | 4.6 | 5 | D | D | D |
| King | 3.2 | 10 358 | NA | NA | NA | NA | NA | NA | 8.1 | 0.7 | 1 | D | D | D |
| Kinney | 5.3 | 1 578 | 2 | D | D | D | 8 | 59 | D | D | NA | NA | NA | NA |
| Kleberg | 16.0 | 520 | 3 | D | D | D | 116 | 1 985 | 657.1 | 47.9 | 32 | 111 | 10.7 | 1.8 |
| Knox | 37.3 | 9 873 | 15 | 89 | 41.6 | 2.5 | 18 | 193 | 34.3 | 1.9 | 1 | D | D | D |
| Lamar | 25.9 | 521 | 42 | D | D | D | 230 | 2 627 | 637.6 | 55.5 | 44 | 148 | 20.8 | 3.3 |
| Lamb | 351.9 | 24 322 | 18 | 152 | 84.2 | 6.2 | 51 | 350 | 95.8 | 6.5 | 4 | D | D | D |
| Lampasas | 1.2 | 61 | 5 | 25 | 11.5 | 0.9 | 61 | 644 | 207.1 | 14.4 | 18 | 50 | 5.7 | 2.0 |
| La Salle | 5.7 | 949 | NA | NA | NA | NA | 19 | 162 | 79.9 | 2.5 | 5 | D | D | D |
| Lavaca | 10.6 | 562 | 21 | 627 | 221.2 | 16.5 | 89 | 789 | 172.0 | 15.7 | 12 | D | D | D |
| Lee | 5.4 | 326 | 21 | 210 | 58.2 | 6.7 | 77 | 760 | 162.6 | 14.4 | 17 | 90 | 21.0 | 3.6 |
| Leon | 7.7 | 468 | 15 | 244 | 92.3 | 8.3 | 76 | 593 | 159.9 | 10.1 | 18 | 54 | 12.4 | 1.8 |
| Liberty | 379.9 | 5 055 | 36 | 293 | 151.5 | 9.6 | 207 | 2 602 | 653.0 | 58.1 | 40 | 279 | 50.5 | 9.2 |
| Limestone | 23.8 | 1 043 | 12 | 66 | 27.4 | 2.4 | 90 | 1 043 | 268.3 | 21.4 | 10 | 42 | 2.6 | 0.6 |
| Lipscomb | 23.0 | 7 401 | 5 | 66 | 47.2 | 2.1 | 18 | 65 | 24.5 | 0.9 | 1 | D | D | D |
| Live Oak | 12.1 | 1 034 | 9 | 52 | 25.3 | 1.6 | 41 | 378 | 112.7 | 6.9 | 7 | D | D | D |
| Llano | 165.4 | 9 070 | 12 | 235 | 94.9 | 8.9 | 81 | 459 | 113.0 | 9.1 | 28 | 82 | 42.2 | 7.2 |
| Loving | 1.5 | 23 710 | NA | NA | NA | NA | NA | NA | NA | NA | NA | NA | NA | NA |
| Lubbock | 204.0 | 809 | 376 | 4 888 | 3 707.4 | 212.8 | 1 043 | 16 793 | 3 924.9 | 346.3 | 380 | D | D | D |
| Lynn | 83.0 | 13 314 | 6 | D | D | D | 14 | 88 | 19.7 | 1.7 | 4 | 6 | 0.4 | 0.1 |
| McCulloch | 6.6 | 835 | 8 | 53 | 31.1 | 1.4 | 40 | 391 | 104.3 | 7.7 | 7 | D | D | D |
| McLennan | 198.4 | 883 | 243 | 3 197 | 4 606.2 | 123.3 | 872 | 11 703 | 2 942.6 | 248.7 | 211 | 1 408 | 281.7 | 54.3 |
| McMullen | 2.0 | 2 276 | NA | NA | NA | NA | 4 | D | D | D | NA | NA | NA | NA |
| Madison | 13.6 | 1 034 | 7 | 32 | 31.9 | 0.9 | 35 | 477 | 178.9 | 11.2 | 13 | 35 | 14.2 | 0.9 |
| Marion | 16.4 | 1 499 | 4 | 9 | 5.5 | 0.3 | 38 | 221 | 66.3 | 5.0 | 5 | D | D | D |
| Martin | 18.0 | 4 092 | 4 | 28 | 24.4 | 1.2 | 18 | 135 | 45.4 | 2.9 | NA | NA | NA | NA |

1. Merchant wholesalers, except manufacturers' sales branches and offices.  2. Employer establishments.

# Table B. States and Counties — Professional Services, Manufacturing, and Accommodation and Food Services

| STATE County | Professional, scientific, and technical services,[1] 2007 | | | | Manufacturing, 2007 | | | | Accommodation and food services, 2007 | | | |
|---|---|---|---|---|---|---|---|---|---|---|---|---|
| | Number of establishments | Number of employees | Receipts (mil dol) | Annual payroll (mil dol) | Number of establishments | Number of employees | Receipts (mil dol) | Annual payroll (mil dol) | Number of establishments | Number of employees | Sales (mil dol) | Annual payroll (mil dol) |
| | 147 | 148 | 149 | 150 | 151 | 152 | 153 | 154 | 155 | 156 | 157 | 158 |
| **TEXAS—Cont'd** | | | | | | | | | | | | |
| Guadalupe | 126 | 411 | 33.7 | 13.0 | 119 | 7 311 | 2 154.1 | 312.4 | 158 | 2 690 | 116.5 | 33.1 |
| Hale | 49 | D | D | D | 25 | 2 720 | D | 83.0 | 71 | 1 050 | 40.3 | 10.9 |
| Hall | 3 | D | D | D | NA | NA | NA | NA | 8 | 79 | 1.8 | 0.5 |
| Hamilton | 16 | 45 | 4.2 | 0.8 | NA | NA | NA | NA | 18 | 160 | 6.0 | 1.8 |
| Hansford | 8 | 36 | 6.0 | 1.7 | NA | NA | NA | NA | 13 | 95 | 3.1 | 0.6 |
| Hardeman | 3 | 6 | 0.4 | 0.1 | NA | NA | NA | NA | 14 | 128 | 3.4 | 1.1 |
| Hardin | 53 | D | D | D | 34 | 795 | D | 32.4 | 63 | 1 023 | 37.2 | 10.3 |
| Harris | 12 246 | D | D | D | 4 215 | 168 354 | 169 275.1 | 8 937.2 | 7 132 | 147 118 | 7 874.7 | 2 104.9 |
| Harrison | 113 | 671 | 90.9 | 34.0 | 85 | 4 505 | 1 564.3 | 150.9 | 91 | 1 579 | 64.0 | 16.7 |
| Hartley | 5 | D | D | D | NA | NA | NA | NA | 4 | 32 | 1.0 | 0.2 |
| Haskell | 7 | 25 | 0.8 | 0.2 | NA | NA | NA | NA | 14 | 115 | 4.7 | 1.1 |
| Hays | 310 | 1 899 | 141.7 | 53.4 | 135 | 3 692 | 1 081.8 | 154.0 | 286 | 5 739 | 235.3 | 66.8 |
| Hemphill | 10 | 19 | 4.0 | 1.0 | NA | NA | NA | NA | 10 | 98 | 4.1 | 1.1 |
| Henderson | 101 | 343 | 42.2 | 12.1 | 55 | 1 411 | 201.9 | 48.1 | 124 | 1 632 | 63.1 | 18.0 |
| Hidalgo | 793 | D | D | D | 276 | 6 007 | 1 503.2 | 183.5 | 896 | 17 219 | 758.0 | 186.5 |
| Hill | 39 | 142 | 14.4 | 4.4 | 42 | 832 | 153.6 | 25.9 | 67 | 1 053 | 44.3 | 12.1 |
| Hockley | 24 | 185 | 8.4 | 9.2 | NA | NA | NA | NA | 40 | 559 | 19.8 | 5.6 |
| Hood | 113 | 383 | 43.0 | 15.1 | 40 | D | D | D | 91 | 1 564 | 61.9 | 17.5 |
| Hopkins | 53 | 258 | 28.0 | 9.9 | 39 | 1 564 | 923.1 | 60.2 | 53 | 865 | 29.2 | 8.6 |
| Houston | 29 | 103 | 8.9 | 2.5 | 19 | 840 | 265.4 | 32.0 | 35 | 413 | 18.7 | 4.8 |
| Howard | 48 | 193 | 15.1 | 5.4 | 22 | 890 | 2 449.6 | 44.9 | 70 | 1 022 | 42.5 | 10.8 |
| Hudspeth | 1 | D | D | D | NA | NA | NA | NA | 5 | 34 | 2.0 | 0.4 |
| Hunt | 91 | D | D | D | 85 | 14 100 | 3 134.4 | D | 115 | D | D | D |
| Hutchinson | 29 | 117 | 14.6 | 4.5 | 23 | 1 832 | D | 145.2 | 46 | 539 | 21.1 | 5.4 |
| Irion | 3 | D | D | D | NA | NA | NA | NA | 1 | D | D | D |
| Jack | 13 | 48 | 5.3 | 2.2 | NA | NA | NA | NA | 16 | 144 | 6.5 | 1.9 |
| Jackson | 23 | 64 | 5.9 | 1.9 | 10 | D | D | D | 21 | 219 | 9.9 | 2.3 |
| Jasper | 45 | 170 | 18.7 | 4.2 | 21 | 1 708 | 725.6 | 104.7 | 54 | 794 | 32.6 | 7.7 |
| Jeff Davis | 1 | D | D | D | NA | NA | NA | NA | 10 | 148 | 7.1 | 1.9 |
| Jefferson | 527 | D | D | D | 215 | 15 460 | D | 997.3 | 419 | 9 143 | 387.5 | 110.1 |
| Jim Hogg | 3 | 11 | 0.3 | 0.2 | NA | NA | NA | NA | 9 | 102 | 3.6 | 1.1 |
| Jim Wells | 40 | 155 | 18.2 | 5.6 | NA | NA | NA | NA | 76 | 1 177 | 46.1 | 12.0 |
| Johnson | 190 | 749 | 78.9 | 25.0 | 173 | 5 314 | 1 441.4 | 230.2 | 189 | 3 086 | 126.4 | 33.3 |
| Jones | 10 | D | D | D | NA | NA | NA | NA | 15 | 137 | 4.6 | 1.3 |
| Karnes | 16 | 63 | 4.4 | 1.1 | NA | NA | NA | NA | 25 | 235 | 8.6 | 2.3 |
| Kaufman | 122 | D | D | D | 108 | D | 1 172.6 | 148.1 | 142 | 2 240 | 93.7 | 26.5 |
| Kendall | 121 | 551 | 59.7 | 24.7 | 32 | 814 | 180.9 | 27.3 | 83 | 1 229 | 55.8 | 17.1 |
| Kenedy | 1 | D | D | D | NA | NA | NA | NA | NA | NA | NA | NA |
| Kent | NA | NA | NA | NA | NA | NA | NA | NA | 2 | D | D | D |
| Kerr | 150 | 685 | 58.2 | 24.1 | 44 | 784 | 161.8 | 31.8 | 122 | 1 958 | 97.6 | 28.3 |
| Kimble | 10 | 16 | 1.0 | 0.3 | NA | NA | NA | NA | 22 | 184 | 8.2 | 2.2 |
| King | NA | NA | NA | NA | NA | NA | NA | NA | NA | NA | NA | NA |
| Kinney | NA | NA | NA | NA | NA | NA | NA | NA | 4 | 19 | 1.1 | 0.2 |
| Kleberg | 35 | D | D | D | NA | NA | NA | NA | 70 | 1 160 | 43.2 | 11.9 |
| Knox | 4 | D | D | D | NA | NA | NA | NA | 6 | 33 | 1.4 | 0.3 |
| Lamar | 62 | D | D | D | 59 | 4 501 | 2 411.6 | 192.5 | 87 | 1 413 | 61.1 | 16.8 |
| Lamb | 18 | 41 | 3.1 | 1.0 | 10 | D | D | D | 25 | 188 | 7.0 | 1.8 |
| Lampasas | 29 | D | D | D | NA | NA | NA | NA | 36 | 380 | 16.1 | 4.0 |
| La Salle | NA | NA | NA | NA | NA | NA | NA | NA | 11 | 127 | 5.3 | 1.3 |
| Lavaca | 32 | 74 | 6.5 | 1.6 | 35 | 1 701 | 238.2 | 45.2 | 25 | 249 | 9.1 | 2.4 |
| Lee | 23 | 102 | 7.8 | 2.9 | 19 | 503 | 128.5 | 17.8 | 28 | 283 | 13.2 | 3.0 |
| Leon | 29 | 76 | 7.7 | 1.8 | 20 | 501 | D | 34.8 | 25 | 263 | 13.1 | 2.8 |
| Liberty | 83 | D | D | D | 33 | D | D | D | 88 | 1 294 | 48.9 | 13.1 |
| Limestone | 33 | 147 | 11.0 | 5.2 | 18 | 1 073 | 210.8 | 35.3 | 40 | 395 | 18.2 | 4.1 |
| Lipscomb | 5 | 21 | 2.1 | 0.7 | NA | NA | NA | NA | 5 | D | D | D |
| Live Oak | 24 | 59 | 6.4 | 2.4 | NA | NA | NA | NA | 24 | 345 | 11.7 | 2.8 |
| Llano | 40 | 148 | 14.6 | 5.1 | NA | NA | NA | NA | 50 | 1 017 | 61.1 | 21.3 |
| Loving | NA | NA | NA | NA | NA | NA | NA | NA | 1 | D | D | D |
| Lubbock | 581 | 3 402 | 374.1 | 128.5 | 255 | D | D | D | 582 | D | D | D |
| Lynn | 6 | 17 | 0.8 | 0.3 | NA | NA | NA | NA | 5 | 27 | 0.8 | 0.2 |
| McCulloch | 18 | 76 | 5.6 | 2.2 | NA | NA | NA | NA | 22 | 243 | 8.8 | 2.1 |
| McLennan | 352 | D | D | D | 255 | 13 971 | 5 888.9 | 550.4 | 468 | 9 123 | 375.3 | 100.9 |
| McMullen | 1 | D | D | D | NA | NA | NA | NA | 1 | D | D | D |
| Madison | 16 | 242 | 12.5 | 3.3 | NA | NA | NA | NA | 26 | 326 | 13.1 | 3.2 |
| Marion | 8 | 18 | 1.3 | 0.7 | NA | NA | NA | NA | 22 | 154 | 5.8 | 1.5 |
| Martin | 6 | 12 | 0.9 | 0.4 | NA | NA | NA | NA | 3 | D | D | D |

1. Establishment subject to federal tax.

# Table B. States and Counties — Health Care and Social Assistance, Other Services, and Federal Funds

| STATE County | Health care and social assistance, 2007 | | | | Other services, 2007 | | | | Federal funds and grants, 2009–2010 Expenditures (mil dol) | | | |
|---|---|---|---|---|---|---|---|---|---|---|---|---|
| | | | | | | | | | Total | Direct payments for individuals[1] | | |
| | Number of establishments | Number of employees | Receipts (mil dol) | Annual payroll (mil dol) | Number of establishments | Number of employees | Receipts (mil dol) | Annual payroll (mil dol) | | Social Security and government retirement | Medicare | Food Stamps and Supplemental Security Income |
| | 159 | 160 | 161 | 162 | 163 | 164 | 165 | 166 | 167 | 168 | 169 | 170 |
| TEXAS—Cont'd | | | | | | | | | | | | |
| Guadalupe | 169 | 2 773 | 207.8 | 83.7 | 135 | 739 | 55.0 | 15.6 | 783.2 | 483.7 | 94.4 | 25.3 |
| Hale | 78 | 1 101 | 81.5 | 28.9 | 56 | 329 | 19.2 | 6.7 | 295.7 | 82.0 | 73.8 | 17.5 |
| Hall | 7 | 31 | 1.6 | 0.7 | 6 | 11 | 3.3 | 0.5 | 44.9 | 11.5 | 12.2 | 1.8 |
| Hamilton | 23 | 447 | 28.3 | 12.7 | 18 | 42 | 3.7 | 0.9 | 76.1 | 29.5 | 26.4 | 2.1 |
| Hansford | 5 | D | D | D | 16 | 75 | 5.8 | 1.8 | 47.4 | 22.2 | 8.5 | 0.8 |
| Hardeman | 14 | 231 | 14.9 | 6.0 | 11 | 39 | 3.1 | 0.7 | 47.7 | 14.7 | 13.7 | 1.9 |
| Hardin | 76 | 1 426 | 62.9 | 32.3 | 47 | 291 | 27.0 | 7.7 | 338.0 | 163.0 | 93.1 | 16.5 |
| Harris | 9 464 | 205 171 | 23 069.3 | 8 823.8 | 5 961 | 54 568 | 6 434.3 | 1 777.1 | 27 347.6 | 6 861.6 | 3 878.8 | 1 583.2 |
| Harrison | 107 | 1 714 | 133.0 | 46.3 | 91 | 754 | 71.9 | 27.3 | 497.3 | 163.6 | 101.5 | 27.9 |
| Hartley | 5 | D | D | D | 8 | 32 | 3.8 | 0.7 | 16.8 | 4.1 | 1.6 | 0.1 |
| Haskell | 15 | 224 | 11.5 | 4.5 | 12 | 28 | 2.2 | 0.5 | 72.9 | 21.9 | 18.7 | 3.0 |
| Hays | 267 | 4 674 | 354.5 | 138.2 | 183 | 973 | 95.1 | 25.5 | 696.2 | 322.8 | 76.0 | 21.4 |
| Hemphill | 8 | 177 | 10.4 | 4.1 | 12 | D | D | D | 17.2 | 7.4 | 6.6 | 0.3 |
| Henderson | 134 | 2 665 | 222.5 | 80.9 | 81 | 360 | 26.5 | 7.1 | 485.2 | 216.7 | 120.4 | 24.8 |
| Hidalgo | 1 655 | 44 931 | 2 877.2 | 1 137.1 | 573 | 3 257 | 238.5 | 61.9 | 4 297.2 | 973.0 | 654.8 | 575.5 |
| Hill | 48 | 951 | 66.8 | 24.6 | 43 | 155 | 21.0 | 4.0 | 312.9 | 130.8 | 69.0 | 13.5 |
| Hockley | 37 | 839 | 73.4 | 20.1 | 24 | 133 | 15.7 | 3.2 | 197.4 | 54.3 | 43.2 | 9.7 |
| Hood | 116 | 1 591 | 141.6 | 54.4 | 85 | 503 | 26.3 | 8.8 | 331.8 | 227.6 | 65.8 | 8.6 |
| Hopkins | 64 | 1 136 | 82.6 | 31.8 | 46 | 177 | 14.9 | 3.8 | 244.2 | 98.7 | 65.8 | 7.0 |
| Houston | 37 | 613 | 44.6 | 15.9 | 28 | 139 | 13.8 | 3.8 | 245.5 | 79.9 | 58.6 | 11.9 |
| Howard | 80 | 2 276 | 215.7 | 93.4 | 50 | 266 | 18.8 | 5.5 | 350.5 | 112.2 | 81.4 | 14.6 |
| Hudspeth | 1 | D | D | D | 2 | D | D | D | 62.3 | 6.5 | 3.9 | 1.5 |
| Hunt | 161 | 2 871 | 245.4 | 102.5 | 97 | D | D | D | 2 001.6 | 250.9 | 138.0 | 32.2 |
| Hutchinson | 45 | 481 | 32.0 | 14.6 | 38 | 240 | 25.4 | 6.6 | 154.7 | 68.9 | 44.8 | 7.1 |
| Irion | 1 | D | D | D | 2 | D | D | D | 12.1 | 5.7 | 2.7 | 0.3 |
| Jack | 11 | 184 | 10.4 | 4.4 | 8 | 15 | 2.9 | 0.4 | 51.4 | 23.2 | 15.3 | 2.5 |
| Jackson | 18 | 309 | 18.1 | 7.8 | 25 | 90 | 6.2 | 1.3 | 132.2 | 44.1 | 33.7 | 4.9 |
| Jasper | 76 | 3 505 | 149.9 | 51.2 | 45 | 158 | 12.5 | 3.1 | 336.6 | 114.0 | 88.5 | 16.6 |
| Jeff Davis | 5 | D | D | D | 7 | D | D | D | 18.0 | 8.8 | 3.2 | 0.4 |
| Jefferson | 849 | 17 840 | 1 618.2 | 580.6 | 404 | 3 012 | 265.8 | 73.0 | 2 284.4 | 711.0 | 624.6 | 141.3 |
| Jim Hogg | 8 | 488 | 8.4 | 4.6 | 4 | D | D | D | 80.1 | 12.2 | 15.3 | 3.7 |
| Jim Wells | 105 | 3 981 | 170.6 | 84.9 | 74 | 480 | 41.5 | 12.9 | 410.1 | 118.7 | 93.3 | 24.6 |
| Johnson | 190 | 3 530 | 234.8 | 93.3 | 173 | 1 046 | 82.0 | 29.2 | 780.5 | 442.5 | 168.2 | 30.7 |
| Jones | 27 | 675 | 29.9 | 14.3 | 21 | 65 | 4.1 | 1.2 | 157.8 | 49.7 | 39.7 | 9.0 |
| Karnes | 32 | 386 | 24.5 | 10.7 | 15 | 53 | 2.6 | 0.6 | 157.2 | 40.3 | 34.7 | 7.9 |
| Kaufman | 139 | 3 213 | 198.6 | 86.8 | 113 | 747 | 50.3 | 23.5 | 630.6 | 308.1 | 156.2 | 25.4 |
| Kendall | 101 | 975 | 72.6 | 29.4 | 65 | 358 | 27.6 | 9.0 | 274.7 | 172.6 | 33.8 | 3.2 |
| Kenedy | NA | NA | NA | NA | 1 | D | D | D | 3.0 | 0.8 | 0.6 | 0.1 |
| Kent | 1 | D | D | D | NA | NA | NA | NA | 9.5 | 3.0 | 2.2 | 0.1 |
| Kerr | 173 | 3 825 | 305.3 | 143.8 | 106 | 654 | 53.8 | 14.3 | 446.1 | 259.2 | 96.0 | 13.6 |
| Kimble | 10 | 144 | 8.4 | 3.8 | 6 | 32 | 1.5 | 0.5 | 36.0 | 17.4 | 9.1 | 1.6 |
| King | NA | NA | NA | NA | NA | NA | NA | NA | 2.9 | 0.4 | 0.3 | 0.0 |
| Kinney | 2 | D | D | D | 4 | D | D | D | 46.3 | 17.4 | 7.3 | 1.8 |
| Kleberg | 69 | 1 466 | 78.0 | 37.6 | 51 | D | D | D | 436.4 | 77.8 | 48.3 | 22.4 |
| Knox | 8 | 147 | 7.8 | 3.2 | 13 | D | D | D | 51.7 | 12.3 | 14.1 | 2.2 |
| Lamar | 180 | 3 332 | 297.7 | 102.7 | 84 | 390 | 27.3 | 7.3 | 481.8 | 168.5 | 97.9 | 25.1 |
| Lamb | 26 | 383 | 22.5 | 10.6 | 14 | 42 | 2.9 | 0.6 | 140.3 | 36.6 | 37.8 | 7.8 |
| Lampasas | 26 | D | D | D | 27 | 149 | 13.0 | 2.9 | 174.5 | 102.6 | 36.4 | 6.0 |
| La Salle | 11 | 99 | 6.1 | 2.5 | 6 | D | D | D | 73.5 | 13.4 | 11.7 | 5.0 |
| Lavaca | 50 | 900 | 57.6 | 21.7 | 44 | 162 | 11.5 | 2.2 | 218.1 | 80.6 | 58.9 | 5.1 |
| Lee | 29 | 309 | 17.4 | 7.7 | 29 | 99 | 8.9 | 2.4 | 96.6 | 44.7 | 21.9 | 3.4 |
| Leon | 18 | 146 | 8.0 | 3.3 | 22 | 127 | 8.8 | 2.3 | 185.7 | 78.0 | 41.8 | 6.6 |
| Liberty | 101 | 1 881 | 154.1 | 52.9 | 69 | 293 | 27.5 | 5.9 | 524.4 | 216.4 | 152.4 | 34.2 |
| Limestone | 45 | 893 | 66.9 | 25.1 | 18 | 87 | 7.1 | 1.5 | 209.6 | 74.9 | 46.3 | 10.9 |
| Lipscomb | 1 | D | D | D | 4 | D | D | D | 20.4 | 8.2 | 6.0 | 0.3 |
| Live Oak | 12 | D | D | D | 21 | 66 | 5.6 | 1.1 | 90.1 | 26.7 | 19.8 | 3.8 |
| Llano | 34 | 791 | 49.5 | 23.8 | 31 | 79 | 8.2 | 1.7 | 152.8 | 91.2 | 41.6 | 3.1 |
| Loving | NA | NA | NA | NA | NA | NA | NA | NA | 0.9 | 0.3 | 0.0 | 0.0 |
| Lubbock | 813 | D | D | D | 473 | D | D | D | 1 892.2 | 644.2 | 457.1 | 105.1 |
| Lynn | 7 | 124 | 5.7 | 2.7 | 4 | 19 | 1.0 | 0.2 | 72.3 | 17.5 | 15.7 | 3.2 |
| McCulloch | 22 | 290 | 19.5 | 7.7 | 17 | 58 | 4.0 | 0.9 | 86.4 | 28.5 | 24.0 | 4.0 |
| McLennan | 525 | 15 510 | 1 219.3 | 504.2 | 394 | 2 615 | 244.7 | 64.2 | 2 019.0 | 701.0 | 261.8 | 104.5 |
| McMullen | 1 | D | D | D | NA | NA | NA | NA | 6.4 | 2.8 | 1.0 | 0.2 |
| Madison | 17 | 265 | 20.5 | 7.6 | 16 | 71 | 6.2 | 1.6 | 81.7 | 32.3 | 18.1 | 5.3 |
| Marion | 15 | D | D | D | 14 | 30 | 2.3 | 0.5 | 114.9 | 36.1 | 20.6 | 6.7 |
| Martin | 10 | 168 | 9.5 | 5.1 | 7 | 17 | 2.0 | 0.4 | 81.5 | 16.2 | 9.0 | 2.2 |

1. State totals may include programs not allocated by county.

# Federal Funds, Residential Construction, and Local Government Finances

| | Federal funds and grants, 2009–2010 (cont.) | | | | | | | Value of residential construction authorized by building permits, 2011 | | Local government finances, 2007 | | | | |
|---|---|---|---|---|---|---|---|---|---|---|---|---|---|---|
| | Expenditures (mil dol) (cont.) | | | | | | | | | General revenue | | | | |
| | Procurement contract awards | | | Grants[1] | | | | | | | | Taxes | | |
| | | | | | | | | | | | | | Per capita[2] (dollars) | |
| STATE County | Salaries and wages | Defense | Other | Medicaid and other health-related | Nutrition and family welfare | Education | Other | New construction ($1,000) | Number of housing units | Total (mil dol) | Inter-govern-mental (mil dol) | Total (mil dol) | Total | Property |
| | 171 | 172 | 173 | 174 | 175 | 176 | 177 | 178 | 179 | 180 | 181 | 182 | 183 | 184 |
| TEXAS—Cont'd | | | | | | | | | | | | | | |
| Guadalupe | 24.7 | 25.5 | 3.6 | 81.9 | 11.1 | 2.9 | 3.1 | 144 672 | 823 | 264.6 | 85.6 | 131.0 | 1 162 | 988 |
| Hale | 9.2 | 0.1 | -0.3 | 60.4 | 9.7 | 1.3 | 1.4 | 335 | 5 | 102.5 | 48.9 | 38.4 | 1 075 | 875 |
| Hall | 1.3 | 0.0 | 0.2 | 11.2 | 0.7 | 0.2 | 0.1 | 0 | 0 | 13.4 | 6.9 | 4.5 | 1 290 | 1 059 |
| Hamilton | 2.3 | 0.0 | 0.5 | 12.6 | 0.7 | 0.2 | 0.2 | 200 | 1 | 58.2 | 12.1 | 10.0 | 1 231 | 1 017 |
| Hansford | 1.0 | 0.0 | 0.2 | 2.5 | 0.6 | 0.2 | 0.0 | 0 | 0 | 25.9 | 4.2 | 18.8 | 3 587 | 3 392 |
| Hardeman | 1.2 | 0.0 | 0.2 | 11.1 | 1.0 | 0.1 | 0.5 | 0 | 0 | 30.4 | 5.4 | 9.8 | 2 374 | 2 136 |
| Hardin | 6.3 | 0.0 | 1.5 | 49.3 | 5.2 | 1.2 | 0.0 | 10 599 | 73 | 143.4 | 71.1 | 54.1 | 1 049 | 905 |
| Harris | 2 397.3 | 2 658.4 | 4 427.2 | 3 288.1 | 512.6 | 196.3 | 944.0 | 2 419 283 | 17 338 | 16 357.1 | 4 096.2 | 7 980.7 | 2 028 | 1 652 |
| Harrison | 15.5 | 9.5 | 2.2 | 143.4 | 10.9 | 4.8 | 3.6 | 12 236 | 127 | 169.9 | 43.8 | 101.7 | 1 602 | 1 421 |
| Hartley | 0.3 | 0.0 | 0.0 | 0.5 | 0.4 | 0.1 | 0.0 | NA | NA | 6.2 | 1.1 | 4.5 | 869 | 810 |
| Haskell | 2.1 | 0.0 | 0.4 | 12.6 | 1.0 | 0.3 | 0.2 | 75 | 2 | 20.4 | 8.6 | 6.3 | 1 208 | 1 057 |
| Hays | 39.8 | 7.3 | 62.2 | 77.7 | 17.0 | 6.1 | 11.2 | 243 744 | 2 474 | 440.1 | 109.5 | 236.3 | 1 670 | 1 325 |
| Hemphill | 0.6 | 0.0 | 0.1 | 1.0 | 0.5 | 0.1 | 0.0 | 0 | 0 | 30.3 | 1.5 | 23.2 | 6 903 | 6 568 |
| Henderson | 9.6 | 0.0 | 2.5 | 86.3 | 7.3 | 2.1 | 1.2 | 8 004 | 56 | 186.4 | 63.6 | 90.2 | 1 143 | 986 |
| Hidalgo | 296.2 | -35.5 | 207.6 | 1 025.4 | 205.3 | 97.6 | 84.4 | 408 214 | 3 105 | 2 583.5 | 1 512.6 | 687.4 | 968 | 774 |
| Hill | 8.0 | 0.6 | 2.9 | 59.7 | 3.8 | 1.6 | 0.4 | 396 | 6 | 105.2 | 47.5 | 39.2 | 1 108 | 885 |
| Hockley | 3.9 | 0.1 | 0.9 | 25.6 | 16.5 | 2.0 | 3.4 | 1 325 | 8 | 140.2 | 48.3 | 58.0 | 2 608 | 2 458 |
| Hood | 9.2 | 0.9 | -2.6 | 14.3 | 4.1 | 0.9 | 0.1 | 21 603 | 110 | 113.7 | 22.1 | 72.7 | 1 479 | 1 232 |
| Hopkins | 7.2 | 1.1 | 1.6 | 53.1 | 6.3 | 1.2 | 0.3 | 1 682 | 14 | 125.1 | 38.5 | 38.5 | 1 141 | 899 |
| Houston | 6.8 | 0.0 | 1.2 | 77.0 | 2.0 | 1.8 | 3.5 | 311 | 6 | 51.8 | 22.0 | 21.3 | 936 | 768 |
| Howard | 41.8 | 0.6 | 14.0 | 56.1 | 5.8 | 1.6 | 3.5 | 541 | 5 | 182.9 | 106.9 | 42.1 | 1 304 | 1 011 |
| Hudspeth | 23.1 | 4.5 | 18.5 | 1.0 | 0.9 | 0.3 | 0.5 | NA | NA | 17.7 | 9.6 | 5.5 | 1 656 | 1 587 |
| Hunt | 34.4 | 1 391.0 | 3.7 | 107.3 | 9.3 | 3.8 | 8.3 | 5 438 | 41 | 309.9 | 91.5 | 93.3 | 1 125 | 932 |
| Hutchinson | 4.8 | 0.0 | 1.9 | 16.7 | 2.0 | 0.7 | 0.4 | 50 | 1 | 103.2 | 29.6 | 41.6 | 1 905 | 1 673 |
| Irion | 0.4 | 0.0 | 0.1 | 1.5 | 0.1 | 0.1 | 0.0 | NA | NA | 9.3 | 1.2 | 7.2 | 4 145 | 4 004 |
| Jack | 1.8 | 0.0 | 0.4 | 6.6 | 0.9 | 0.2 | 0.0 | 210 | 6 | 28.1 | 6.4 | 17.3 | 1 960 | 1 741 |
| Jackson | 2.3 | 0.0 | 0.5 | 22.3 | 2.6 | 0.7 | 1.2 | 814 | 8 | 61.7 | 15.6 | 29.8 | 2 113 | 1 921 |
| Jasper | 6.3 | 15.7 | 1.3 | 73.4 | 6.4 | 1.2 | 11.4 | 499 | 2 | 97.1 | 49.4 | 36.1 | 1 045 | 889 |
| Jeff Davis | 1.3 | 0.1 | 0.8 | 3.0 | 0.2 | 0.1 | 0.0 | NA | NA | 8.5 | 4.8 | 3.0 | 1 345 | 1 170 |
| Jefferson | 197.1 | 49.8 | 38.6 | 359.9 | 47.2 | 12.0 | 43.0 | 81 941 | 743 | 977.4 | 265.4 | 471.5 | 1 948 | 1 561 |
| Jim Hogg | 18.0 | 0.4 | 0.2 | 26.4 | 1.7 | 0.2 | 0.4 | NA | NA | 18.9 | 5.4 | 12.1 | 2 438 | 2 305 |
| Jim Wells | 7.5 | 5.3 | 1.4 | 125.6 | 22.0 | 1.9 | 1.5 | 1 411 | 23 | 192.1 | 67.0 | 65.9 | 1 603 | 1 309 |
| Johnson | 22.9 | 0.1 | 16.9 | 73.6 | 11.7 | 2.5 | 3.2 | 64 047 | 415 | 394.2 | 134.7 | 187.7 | 1 253 | 1 059 |
| Jones | 13.5 | 0.0 | 0.7 | 28.3 | 3.5 | 0.6 | 0.4 | 0 | 0 | 47.0 | 22.4 | 12.4 | 644 | 526 |
| Karnes | 2.8 | 0.0 | 1.9 | 58.2 | 6.1 | 1.0 | 0.6 | 3 139 | 24 | 38.5 | 21.7 | 11.5 | 761 | 636 |
| Kaufman | 46.5 | 0.1 | 4.0 | 65.2 | 11.4 | 3.3 | 3.4 | 28 737 | 156 | 310.3 | 113.3 | 154.7 | 1 605 | 1 382 |
| Kendall | 4.9 | 41.0 | 7.6 | 6.6 | 1.6 | 0.8 | 0.7 | 44 153 | 204 | 107.3 | 15.4 | 77.8 | 2 482 | 2 196 |
| Kenedy | 0.2 | 0.0 | 0.1 | 0.5 | 0.0 | 0.0 | 0.2 | NA | NA | 7.9 | 0.2 | 7.3 | 18 434 | 18 348 |
| Kent | 0.8 | 0.0 | 0.1 | 1.7 | 0.2 | 0.0 | 0.1 | NA | NA | 9.2 | 0.9 | 7.4 | 10 116 | 10 023 |
| Kerr | 23.7 | 0.5 | 6.5 | 23.3 | 4.8 | 1.4 | 12.1 | 8 672 | 41 | 114.0 | 26.6 | 70.9 | 1 481 | 1 174 |
| Kimble | 0.9 | 0.0 | 0.2 | 4.6 | 0.9 | 0.1 | 0.2 | 175 | 1 | 16.6 | 3.4 | 5.7 | 1 273 | 967 |
| King | 0.3 | 0.0 | 0.0 | 0.5 | 0.0 | 0.1 | 0.0 | NA | NA | 10.8 | 5.3 | 3.4 | 1 024 | 922 |
| Kinney | 10.2 | 0.0 | 0.1 | 6.6 | 0.8 | 0.1 | 0.3 | 0 | 0 | 7.0 | 0.4 | 6.1 | 20 873 | 20 869 |
| Kleberg | 110.0 | 76.5 | 1.1 | 57.6 | 7.2 | 4.6 | 6.8 | 5 882 | 41 | 87.0 | 37.2 | 35.8 | 1 177 | 919 |
| Knox | 1.6 | 0.0 | 0.3 | 12.1 | 1.2 | 0.2 | 0.2 | NA | NA | 17.7 | 6.9 | 4.8 | 1 362 | 1 159 |
| Lamar | 14.8 | 1.3 | 2.9 | 133.5 | 7.1 | 2.4 | 4.4 | 3 882 | 41 | 156.5 | 64.4 | 60.9 | 1 235 | 953 |
| Lamb | 2.7 | 0.0 | 0.6 | 28.8 | 2.5 | 0.6 | 0.3 | 539 | 7 | 68.0 | 26.4 | 19.9 | 1 433 | 1 308 |
| Lampasas | 4.0 | 0.9 | 0.8 | 17.2 | 3.1 | 0.8 | 0.2 | 575 | 5 | 45.0 | 19.0 | 17.8 | 851 | 727 |
| La Salle | 9.2 | 0.0 | 1.0 | 28.5 | 2.1 | 0.3 | 0.9 | 283 | 6 | 20.6 | 9.8 | 9.0 | 1 506 | 1 332 |
| Lavaca | 4.6 | 0.0 | 1.2 | 62.7 | 2.4 | 0.5 | 0.4 | 1 323 | 18 | 55.2 | 8.5 | 21.9 | 1 169 | 1 066 |
| Lee | 2.7 | 0.0 | 0.8 | 19.7 | 2.1 | 0.4 | 0.4 | 1 031 | 7 | 41.8 | 13.7 | 21.6 | 1 323 | 1 138 |
| Leon | 4.0 | 0.0 | 0.9 | 51.2 | 1.8 | 0.5 | 0.2 | NA | NA | 49.1 | 13.9 | 29.7 | 1 806 | 1 665 |
| Liberty | 11.2 | 3.5 | 2.5 | 83.1 | 10.2 | 2.2 | 1.7 | 23 041 | 260 | 201.0 | 79.7 | 94.7 | 1 256 | 1 112 |
| Limestone | 4.6 | 0.0 | 1.0 | 60.7 | 3.8 | 0.7 | 0.6 | 5 602 | 26 | 81.6 | 28.3 | 38.2 | 1 705 | 1 506 |
| Lipscomb | 1.5 | 0.0 | 0.3 | 2.0 | 0.5 | 0.2 | 0.0 | 44 | 1 | 19.5 | 3.2 | 14.5 | 4 795 | 4 628 |
| Live Oak | 20.0 | 0.0 | 0.9 | 14.7 | 1.2 | 0.3 | 0.2 | 450 | 2 | 28.8 | 6.6 | 18.5 | 1 626 | 1 450 |
| Llano | 2.5 | 0.0 | 0.5 | 11.1 | 0.9 | 0.4 | 0.2 | 33 487 | 150 | 48.9 | 4.9 | 36.6 | 1 990 | 1 910 |
| Loving | 0.1 | 0.0 | 0.0 | 0.0 | 0.0 | 0.0 | 0.0 | NA | NA | 2.8 | 0.0 | 2.4 | 44 055 | 43 800 |
| Lubbock | 155.5 | 13.8 | 17.3 | 246.8 | 42.4 | 9.9 | 111.4 | 175 724 | 1 501 | 991.2 | 278.9 | 342.3 | 1 312 | 991 |
| Lynn | 1.3 | 0.0 | 0.2 | 13.1 | 1.8 | 0.3 | 0.1 | 469 | 3 | 34.5 | 14.0 | 10.1 | 1 719 | 1 632 |
| McCulloch | 2.2 | 0.0 | 0.4 | 21.7 | 1.9 | 0.4 | 0.6 | 0 | 0 | 36.4 | 13.7 | 8.8 | 1 118 | 859 |
| McLennan | 190.6 | 256.7 | 34.8 | 300.0 | 33.5 | 11.5 | 35.7 | 99 673 | 523 | 1 359.6 | 479.5 | 300.6 | 1 318 | 1 012 |
| McMullen | 0.4 | 0.5 | 0.1 | 0.5 | 0.3 | 0.0 | 0.1 | NA | NA | 10.5 | 0.8 | 8.8 | 10 059 | 9 875 |
| Madison | 1.9 | 0.0 | 0.4 | 21.2 | 1.7 | 0.4 | 0.2 | 866 | 16 | 36.6 | 17.3 | 13.3 | 997 | 814 |
| Marion | 2.3 | 7.2 | 0.4 | 37.9 | 2.4 | 0.4 | 0.1 | 290 | 2 | 19.9 | 6.0 | 11.6 | 1 083 | 955 |
| Martin | 0.8 | 0.0 | 0.2 | 9.6 | 2.6 | 0.2 | 29.6 | 150 | 2 | 25.9 | 4.8 | 13.9 | 3 115 | 2 982 |

1. State totals may include programs not allocated by county.   2. Based on the resident population estimated as of July 1 of the year shown.

# Table B. States and Counties — Local Government Finances, Government Employment, and Voting

| STATE County | Local government finances, 2007 (cont.) Direct general expenditure — Total (mil dol) | Per capita[1] (dollars) | Percent of total for: Education | Health and hospitals | Police protection | Public welfare | Highways | Debt outstanding Total (mil dol) | Per capita[1] (dollars) | Government employment, 2011 Federal civilian | Federal military | State and local | Presidential election,[2] 2012 Percent of vote cast: Democratic | Republican | All other |
|---|---|---|---|---|---|---|---|---|---|---|---|---|---|---|---|
| | 185 | 186 | 187 | 188 | 189 | 190 | 191 | 192 | 193 | 194 | 195 | 196 | 197 | 198 | 199 |
| **TEXAS—Cont'd** | | | | | | | | | | | | | | | |
| Guadalupe | 287.3 | 2 548 | 63.7 | 1.2 | 5.7 | 0.8 | 4.6 | 529.0 | 4 691 | 197 | 301 | 5 718 | 34.0 | 65.0 | 0.9 |
| Hale | 94.9 | 2 657 | 63.7 | 7.5 | 6.7 | 0.9 | 2.5 | 38.4 | 1 075 | 120 | 81 | 2 411 | 27.2 | 72.1 | 0.6 |
| Hall | 12.6 | 3 605 | 64.9 | 2.9 | 3.1 | 0.1 | 3.7 | 0.8 | 222 | 18 | 0 | 278 | 25.6 | 73.6 | 0.8 |
| Hamilton | 48.4 | 5 943 | 27.3 | 25.4 | 1.8 | 28.7 | 1.5 | 26.0 | 3 190 | 26 | 19 | 664 | 22.8 | 76.1 | 1.0 |
| Hansford | 25.7 | 4 915 | 78.5 | 1.3 | 2.5 | 0.0 | 2.5 | 27.9 | 5 327 | 16 | 12 | 560 | 11.4 | 87.9 | 0.7 |
| Hardeman | 28.4 | 6 891 | 31.4 | 44.9 | 2.4 | 0.0 | 4.2 | 4.9 | 1 191 | 18 | 0 | 498 | 23.4 | 75.2 | 1.4 |
| Hardin | 143.0 | 2 771 | 65.0 | 0.5 | 3.8 | 0.3 | 3.3 | 118.2 | 2 291 | 73 | 122 | 2 380 | 19.0 | 80.2 | 0.8 |
| Harris | 16 565.0 | 4 209 | 43.9 | 9.5 | 6.2 | 0.3 | 3.2 | 44 270.4 | 11 248 | 24 631 | 10 285 | 233 860 | 50.4 | 48.8 | 0.7 |
| Harrison | 160.2 | 2 522 | 66.7 | 0.6 | 5.5 | 1.1 | 2.1 | 208.6 | 3 285 | 133 | 147 | 3 454 | 34.0 | 65.4 | 0.6 |
| Hartley | 5.9 | 1 137 | 67.5 | 0.2 | 6.8 | 0.0 | 7.6 | 0.5 | 97 | 0 | 13 | 661 | 12.6 | 86.2 | 1.2 |
| Haskell | 20.1 | 3 836 | 50.4 | 23.3 | 3.3 | 0.0 | 6.3 | 10.9 | 2 068 | 31 | 13 | 424 | 33.0 | 65.6 | 1.4 |
| Hays | 515.2 | 3 642 | 58.2 | 5.4 | 4.4 | 0.2 | 2.1 | 1 136.7 | 8 034 | 188 | 384 | 11 496 | 48.1 | 50.2 | 1.7 |
| Hemphill | 27.6 | 8 211 | 69.7 | 17.2 | 0.7 | 0.0 | 2.6 | 20.5 | 6 091 | 11 | 0 | 401 | 13.8 | 85.7 | 0.6 |
| Henderson | 199.4 | 2 527 | 73.0 | 0.3 | 5.8 | 0.0 | 3.5 | 122.2 | 1 548 | 97 | 176 | 3 294 | 27.3 | 71.9 | 0.8 |
| Hidalgo | 2 724.7 | 3 835 | 70.2 | 1.7 | 3.5 | 0.8 | 2.3 | 2 783.8 | 3 918 | 3 478 | 1 814 | 49 745 | 69.0 | 30.3 | 0.7 |
| Hill | 100.2 | 2 835 | 73.3 | 0.4 | 3.4 | 0.0 | 3.2 | 140.1 | 3 962 | 91 | 78 | 2 204 | 28.9 | 70.2 | 0.9 |
| Hockley | 139.9 | 6 294 | 80.6 | 0.3 | 1.9 | 0.3 | 2.5 | 150.7 | 6 780 | 48 | 51 | 1 918 | 23.5 | 75.8 | 0.7 |
| Hood | 102.2 | 2 079 | 63.4 | 0.2 | 5.3 | 0.2 | 4.6 | 162.9 | 3 314 | 98 | 114 | 1 922 | 22.5 | 76.6 | 0.9 |
| Hopkins | 129.2 | 3 825 | 45.8 | 29.7 | 4.1 | 0.1 | 4.6 | 63.1 | 1 870 | 80 | 78 | 2 271 | 27.3 | 72.0 | 0.7 |
| Houston | 60.2 | 2 643 | 72.3 | 0.3 | 4.1 | 0.0 | 4.3 | 35.3 | 1 549 | 80 | 52 | 1 953 | 30.8 | 68.1 | 1.1 |
| Howard | 173.8 | 5 383 | 40.1 | 10.4 | 3.0 | 0.2 | 2.0 | 292.8 | 9 065 | 930 | 78 | 2 780 | 26.3 | 72.5 | 1.2 |
| Hudspeth | 17.1 | 5 200 | 55.4 | 0.2 | 6.5 | 0.1 | 6.7 | 3.4 | 1 034 | 379 | 0 | 318 | 47.9 | 51.0 | 1.1 |
| Hunt | 298.2 | 3 595 | 38.8 | 26.0 | 5.3 | 0.2 | 2.8 | 436.5 | 5 262 | 249 | 265 | 6 649 | 29.1 | 69.7 | 1.2 |
| Hutchinson | 100.3 | 4 592 | 61.1 | 14.7 | 3.3 | 0.1 | 2.0 | 120.9 | 5 534 | 77 | 49 | 1 490 | 15.1 | 84.0 | 0.9 |
| Irion | 8.3 | 4 782 | 69.7 | 0.2 | 4.2 | 0.0 | 5.2 | 19.4 | 11 155 | 0 | 0 | 116 | 20.1 | 78.8 | 1.1 |
| Jack | 27.4 | 3 100 | 69.6 | 0.0 | 4.9 | 0.0 | 3.4 | 45.0 | 5 090 | 18 | 20 | 590 | 15.5 | 83.6 | 0.8 |
| Jackson | 57.8 | 4 103 | 57.5 | 17.5 | 3.2 | 0.0 | 4.7 | 128.1 | 9 089 | 31 | 31 | 993 | 25.7 | 73.6 | 0.7 |
| Jasper | 87.5 | 2 533 | 65.5 | 2.3 | 5.1 | 0.6 | 4.6 | 123.8 | 3 583 | 81 | 80 | 2 064 | 28.6 | 70.6 | 0.8 |
| Jeff Davis | 7.3 | 3 204 | 83.9 | 1.7 | 2.9 | 0.3 | 0.4 | 1.3 | 559 | 28 | 0 | 267 | 37.9 | 60.6 | 1.5 |
| Jefferson | 895.5 | 3 701 | 44.2 | 5.1 | 6.5 | 0.6 | 3.3 | 1 676.5 | 6 928 | 2 010 | 798 | 16 326 | 50.8 | 48.6 | 0.6 |
| Jim Hogg | 17.8 | 3 570 | 64.4 | 0.8 | 8.3 | 0.9 | 10.7 | 3.9 | 783 | 277 | 12 | 379 | 73.6 | 26.0 | 0.4 |
| Jim Wells | 195.3 | 4 750 | 37.9 | 31.7 | 1.5 | 0.0 | 11.1 | 118.5 | 2 883 | 81 | 116 | 2 189 | 57.8 | 41.7 | 0.6 |
| Johnson | 409.6 | 2 735 | 63.1 | 0.4 | 4.7 | 0.2 | 5.5 | 843.1 | 5 628 | 240 | 339 | 6 962 | 25.8 | 73.3 | 0.9 |
| Jones | 46.3 | 2 398 | 58.5 | 21.7 | 4.0 | 0.0 | 4.2 | 52.4 | 2 715 | 79 | 49 | 1 306 | 26.3 | 72.4 | 1.3 |
| Karnes | 35.4 | 2 347 | 66.3 | 1.1 | 4.1 | 0.0 | 4.7 | 16.2 | 1 073 | 35 | 33 | 1 541 | 38.9 | 60.4 | 0.7 |
| Kaufman | 335.8 | 3 484 | 63.0 | 5.5 | 3.9 | 0.3 | 3.2 | 646.8 | 6 711 | 176 | 234 | 6 344 | 31.8 | 67.5 | 0.7 |
| Kendall | 123.5 | 3 939 | 76.4 | 1.1 | 5.1 | 0.0 | 2.4 | 180.4 | 5 756 | 53 | 77 | 1 732 | 21.5 | 77.5 | 1.1 |
| Kenedy | 8.6 | 21 766 | 92.3 | 0.0 | 0.7 | 0.1 | 1.2 | 3.3 | 8 368 | 0 | 0 | 86 | 53.5 | 46.5 | 0.0 |
| Kent | 7.8 | 10 601 | 93.4 | 0.3 | 0.9 | 0.0 | 0.6 | 0.9 | 1 165 | 0 | 0 | 183 | 22.1 | 76.3 | 1.6 |
| Kerr | 104.4 | 2 181 | 56.6 | 0.6 | 8.6 | 0.8 | 4.6 | 90.3 | 1 887 | 547 | 111 | 2 791 | 24.7 | 74.3 | 1.0 |
| Kimble | 14.4 | 3 232 | 43.0 | 33.0 | 2.3 | 0.0 | 2.5 | 29.4 | 6 583 | 14 | 10 | 353 | 18.6 | 80.7 | 0.8 |
| King | 4.5 | 15 351 | 74.9 | 0.0 | 1.5 | 0.0 | 9.9 | 0.0 | 0 | 0 | 0 | 70 | 4.9 | 92.6 | 2.5 |
| Kinney | 9.2 | 2 762 | 63.7 | 1.2 | 9.3 | 0.9 | 2.8 | 0.5 | 141 | 154 | 0 | 302 | 40.8 | 58.5 | 0.7 |
| Kleberg | 79.8 | 2 624 | 64.2 | 0.3 | 9.0 | 0.3 | 3.4 | 104.9 | 3 451 | 958 | 429 | 3 852 | 53.2 | 46.0 | 0.8 |
| Knox | 18.0 | 5 106 | 58.9 | 21.9 | 2.8 | 0.2 | 3.2 | 4.1 | 1 165 | 26 | 0 | 380 | 26.8 | 72.1 | 1.1 |
| Lamar | 146.9 | 2 983 | 65.3 | 1.9 | 7.4 | 1.3 | 4.6 | 187.6 | 3 808 | 153 | 112 | 3 016 | 28.6 | 70.5 | 0.9 |
| Lamb | 62.2 | 4 474 | 50.5 | 17.6 | 5.1 | 0.0 | 3.7 | 229.1 | 16 480 | 38 | 31 | 989 | 25.5 | 73.9 | 0.6 |
| Lampasas | 44.1 | 2 113 | 64.7 | 2.1 | 6.9 | 0.2 | 5.8 | 114.0 | 5 459 | 47 | 44 | 992 | 24.9 | 74.0 | 1.0 |
| La Salle | 20.4 | 3 393 | 67.6 | 0.2 | 1.4 | 0.0 | 2.8 | 43.2 | 7 183 | 124 | 16 | 556 | 59.2 | 40.2 | 0.6 |
| Lavaca | 55.4 | 2 952 | 49.9 | 19.3 | 4.2 | 0.1 | 6.3 | 25.1 | 1 338 | 52 | 43 | 911 | 22.7 | 76.5 | 0.7 |
| Lee | 39.4 | 2 408 | 66.0 | 1.0 | 5.7 | 0.1 | 7.5 | 102.8 | 6 282 | 30 | 37 | 1 282 | 31.4 | 67.6 | 1.0 |
| Leon | 43.2 | 2 621 | 74.4 | 0.1 | 2.4 | 0.4 | 5.8 | 39.8 | 2 419 | 44 | 37 | 870 | 20.1 | 79.1 | 0.8 |
| Liberty | 194.5 | 2 579 | 63.0 | 0.5 | 4.2 | 0.5 | 5.2 | 185.1 | 2 454 | 116 | 169 | 4 388 | 27.7 | 71.4 | 0.9 |
| Limestone | 74.4 | 3 317 | 61.4 | 11.9 | 3.9 | 0.0 | 2.9 | 29.6 | 1 318 | 48 | 52 | 3 091 | 32.9 | 66.4 | 0.7 |
| Lipscomb | 18.2 | 5 985 | 74.4 | 0.7 | 2.4 | 0.1 | 5.0 | 5.1 | 1 671 | 21 | 0 | 391 | 12.3 | 87.0 | 0.6 |
| Live Oak | 26.1 | 2 297 | 65.4 | 0.1 | 6.2 | 0.6 | 5.7 | 23.2 | 2 040 | 283 | 25 | 600 | 25.1 | 74.1 | 0.8 |
| Llano | 45.7 | 2 484 | 62.3 | 0.0 | 7.2 | 0.1 | 4.9 | 63.5 | 3 454 | 25 | 43 | 844 | 23.4 | 75.6 | 1.0 |
| Loving | 1.5 | 26 600 | 0.0 | 0.0 | 13.7 | 0.0 | 18.6 | 0.0 | 0 | 0 | 0 | 16 | 15.2 | 84.8 | 0.0 |
| Lubbock | 1 034.7 | 3 966 | 39.5 | 30.6 | 4.8 | 0.1 | 3.0 | 1 365.1 | 5 232 | 1 326 | 692 | 25 156 | 31.3 | 68.0 | 0.8 |
| Lynn | 30.3 | 5 159 | 50.2 | 24.5 | 2.7 | 0.0 | 3.7 | 7.5 | 1 271 | 24 | 13 | 519 | 29.6 | 69.6 | 0.8 |
| McCulloch | 33.2 | 4 225 | 48.3 | 23.3 | 2.8 | 0.0 | 2.1 | 51.3 | 6 521 | 30 | 18 | 628 | 24.2 | 75.2 | 0.6 |
| McLennan | 1 351.0 | 5 922 | 29.1 | 1.9 | 3.4 | 0.3 | 1.4 | 15 878.1 | 69 603 | 3 068 | 603 | 14 314 | 37.7 | 61.6 | 0.8 |
| McMullen | 8.5 | 9 737 | 76.7 | 0.7 | 4.3 | 0.3 | 6.6 | 1.7 | 1 951 | 0 | 0 | 117 | 24.6 | 74.5 | 0.9 |
| Madison | 30.9 | 2 311 | 71.0 | 0.2 | 4.4 | 0.2 | 3.5 | 35.2 | 2 632 | 19 | 30 | 1 250 | 28.1 | 71.0 | 0.9 |
| Marion | 19.6 | 1 826 | 67.4 | 1.0 | 7.4 | 0.0 | 4.4 | 9.3 | 867 | 35 | 23 | 407 | 38.7 | 60.4 | 1.0 |
| Martin | 25.5 | 5 712 | 53.5 | 28.8 | 2.1 | 0.1 | 3.1 | 2.4 | 536 | 16 | 11 | 392 | 18.3 | 81.0 | 0.7 |

1. Based on the resident population estimated as of July 1 of the year shown.   2. © 2013 Election Data Services, Inc. All rights reserved.

# Table B. States and Counties — **Land Area and Population**

| STATE/ County code | CBSA code[1] | County type[2] | STATE County | Land area,[3] (sq km) 2010 | Total persons | Rank | Per square kilometer | White | Black | American Indian, Alaska Native | Asian and Pacific Islander | Percent Hispanic or Latino[4] | Under 5 years | 5 to 17 years | 18 to 24 years | 25 to 34 years | 35 to 44 years | 45 to 54 years |
|---|---|---|---|---|---|---|---|---|---|---|---|---|---|---|---|---|---|---|
| | | | | 1 | 2 | 3 | 4 | 5 | 6 | 7 | 8 | 9 | 10 | 11 | 12 | 13 | 14 | 15 |
| | | | TEXAS—Cont'd | | | | | | | | | | | | | | | |
| 48 319 | ... | 9 | Mason | 2 406 | 4 003 | 2 904 | 1.7 | 77.0 | 0.6 | 0.5 | 0.4 | 22.0 | 4.7 | 15.8 | 5.6 | 7.4 | 10.4 | 14.2 |
| 48 321 | 13060 | 4 | Matagorda | 2 850 | 36 547 | 1 260 | 12.8 | 47.5 | 11.4 | 0.6 | 2.2 | 39.2 | 7.2 | 18.8 | 8.9 | 11.7 | 10.9 | 14.9 |
| 48 323 | 20580 | 5 | Maverick | 3 313 | 55 365 | 908 | 16.7 | 3.3 | 0.3 | 0.9 | 0.4 | 95.2 | 8.6 | 24.4 | 10.7 | 11.9 | 12.7 | 11.3 |
| 48 325 | 41700 | 1 | Medina | 3 433 | 46 765 | 1 033 | 13.6 | 46.6 | 2.5 | 0.7 | 0.9 | 50.1 | 6.1 | 19.1 | 9.6 | 11.1 | 12.1 | 15.1 |
| 48 327 | ... | 8 | Menard | 2 336 | 2 240 | 3 033 | 1.0 | 63.2 | 0.8 | 0.5 | 0.4 | 35.4 | 5.3 | 13.5 | 5.9 | 8.7 | 8.3 | 14.3 |
| 48 329 | 33260 | 3 | Midland | 2 332 | 146 645 | 432 | 62.9 | 53.1 | 6.8 | 0.8 | 1.6 | 38.8 | 8.2 | 19.2 | 9.9 | 15.0 | 11.7 | 13.8 |
| 48 331 | ... | 6 | Milam | 2 634 | 24 157 | 1 636 | 9.2 | 65.3 | 10.1 | 0.7 | 0.6 | 24.3 | 7.0 | 19.5 | 7.5 | 9.9 | 11.1 | 14.0 |
| 48 333 | ... | 9 | Mills | 1 938 | 4 828 | 2 849 | 2.5 | 81.5 | 1.1 | 0.7 | 0.4 | 17.1 | 5.6 | 17.8 | 6.5 | 7.8 | 10.4 | 12.8 |
| 48 335 | ... | 7 | Mitchell | 2 360 | 9 336 | 2 488 | 4.0 | 50.4 | 11.8 | 0.7 | 0.5 | 37.2 | 5.3 | 14.1 | 12.5 | 17.8 | 13.5 | 12.7 |
| 48 337 | ... | 6 | Montague | 2 411 | 19 565 | 1 855 | 8.1 | 87.9 | 0.9 | 1.4 | 0.6 | 10.3 | 6.4 | 16.6 | 7.3 | 10.3 | 11.4 | 14.3 |
| 48 339 | 26420 | 1 | Montgomery | 2 698 | 485 047 | 138 | 179.8 | 71.5 | 4.8 | 0.9 | 2.7 | 21.4 | 7.2 | 20.1 | 8.1 | 12.9 | 14.2 | 14.8 |
| 48 341 | 20300 | 6 | Moore | 2 330 | 22 313 | 1 718 | 9.6 | 38.2 | 2.0 | 1.0 | 6.7 | 53.0 | 9.3 | 22.8 | 9.7 | 14.0 | 12.4 | 12.4 |
| 48 343 | ... | 6 | Morris | 653 | 12 787 | 2 252 | 19.6 | 67.7 | 23.3 | 1.2 | 0.7 | 8.6 | 6.5 | 16.5 | 7.7 | 10.9 | 10.8 | 13.9 |
| 48 345 | ... | 8 | Motley | 2 563 | 1 202 | 3 100 | 0.5 | 82.1 | 2.6 | 0.8 | 0.1 | 15.0 | 4.1 | 16.6 | 5.9 | 9.2 | 8.8 | 12.7 |
| 48 347 | 34860 | 5 | Nacogdoches | 2 452 | 66 034 | 798 | 26.9 | 62.3 | 18.3 | 0.9 | 1.6 | 18.2 | 7.0 | 16.3 | 21.3 | 11.9 | 10.0 | 11.3 |
| 48 349 | 18620 | 4 | Navarro | 2 615 | 47 979 | 1 013 | 18.3 | 60.1 | 14.1 | 0.7 | 1.6 | 24.5 | 7.4 | 19.7 | 9.0 | 11.5 | 12.1 | 13.5 |
| 48 351 | ... | 8 | Newton | 2 418 | 14 200 | 2 162 | 5.9 | 74.8 | 20.9 | 1.2 | 0.9 | 3.6 | 5.8 | 17.1 | 8.8 | 11.0 | 12.4 | 14.6 |
| 48 353 | 45020 | 6 | Nolan | 2 362 | 14 924 | 2 114 | 6.3 | 60.0 | 5.3 | 0.7 | 0.6 | 34.4 | 7.3 | 18.6 | 8.8 | 11.5 | 11.3 | 12.4 |
| 48 355 | 18580 | 2 | Nueces | 2 172 | 347 691 | 190 | 160.1 | 33.2 | 4.0 | 0.6 | 2.1 | 61.0 | 6.9 | 18.7 | 10.4 | 13.8 | 12.1 | 13.8 |
| 48 357 | ... | 7 | Ochiltree | 2 377 | 10 728 | 2 379 | 4.5 | 48.8 | 0.5 | 1.1 | 0.5 | 49.7 | 9.3 | 22.7 | 8.9 | 13.9 | 12.6 | 12.9 |
| 48 359 | ... | 8 | Oldham | 3 886 | 2 060 | 3 045 | 0.5 | 83.0 | 4.0 | 1.4 | 1.1 | 12.1 | 4.6 | 30.0 | 5.4 | 10.8 | 11.1 | 14.0 |
| 48 361 | 13140 | 2 | Orange | 864 | 82 977 | 671 | 96.0 | 83.3 | 9.1 | 1.0 | 1.4 | 6.4 | 6.6 | 18.3 | 8.8 | 12.2 | 12.3 | 15.0 |
| 48 363 | 33420 | 6 | Palo Pinto | 2 465 | 27 856 | 1 501 | 11.3 | 78.0 | 2.7 | 1.0 | 0.8 | 18.6 | 6.8 | 17.9 | 8.2 | 11.0 | 11.6 | 14.4 |
| 48 365 | ... | 6 | Panola | 2 077 | 24 020 | 1 643 | 11.6 | 74.0 | 16.8 | 0.9 | 0.7 | 8.8 | 6.3 | 18.1 | 8.8 | 12.3 | 11.4 | 13.6 |
| 48 367 | 19100 | 1 | Parker | 2 340 | 119 712 | 509 | 51.2 | 85.5 | 2.3 | 1.4 | 0.9 | 11.2 | 6.1 | 18.9 | 8.5 | 11.2 | 13.3 | 16.3 |
| 48 369 | ... | 7 | Parmer | 2 281 | 10 183 | 2 425 | 4.5 | 37.8 | 1.2 | 0.4 | 0.5 | 60.6 | 8.5 | 22.0 | 10.2 | 12.9 | 11.5 | 13.1 |
| 48 371 | ... | 7 | Pecos | 12 338 | 15 619 | 2 072 | 1.3 | 28.0 | 3.6 | 0.6 | 0.8 | 67.5 | 7.8 | 17.0 | 8.8 | 14.3 | 14.0 | 14.7 |
| 48 373 | ... | 6 | Polk | 2 738 | 45 656 | 1 055 | 16.7 | 72.8 | 11.8 | 2.3 | 0.7 | 13.5 | 5.8 | 15.3 | 7.7 | 11.3 | 12.0 | 14.4 |
| 48 375 | 11100 | 3 | Potter | 2 353 | 122 335 | 500 | 52.0 | 49.7 | 10.5 | 1.0 | 4.2 | 36.0 | 8.6 | 19.4 | 9.9 | 14.9 | 12.6 | 13.2 |
| 48 377 | ... | 7 | Presidio | 9 985 | 7 525 | 2 639 | 0.8 | 14.3 | 0.9 | 0.5 | 1.1 | 83.7 | 7.4 | 21.0 | 8.1 | 9.5 | 11.7 | 11.8 |
| 48 379 | ... | 8 | Rains | 594 | 10 943 | 2 363 | 18.4 | 87.4 | 3.1 | 1.6 | 0.8 | 8.4 | 5.3 | 16.1 | 6.5 | 9.2 | 11.3 | 14.5 |
| 48 381 | 11100 | 3 | Randall | 2 361 | 125 082 | 491 | 53.0 | 77.7 | 3.1 | 1.1 | 1.9 | 17.6 | 6.7 | 17.9 | 11.8 | 13.7 | 12.0 | 13.4 |
| 48 383 | ... | 6 | Reagan | 3 044 | 3 475 | 2 943 | 1.1 | 35.3 | 2.2 | 0.6 | 0.3 | 62.4 | 8.0 | 22.4 | 8.7 | 13.1 | 11.9 | 14.5 |
| 48 385 | ... | 9 | Real | 1 811 | 3 369 | 2 950 | 1.9 | 71.5 | 1.2 | 1.4 | 0.6 | 26.5 | 5.0 | 14.9 | 6.4 | 7.5 | 9.4 | 13.5 |
| 48 387 | ... | 6 | Red River | 2 685 | 12 694 | 2 262 | 4.7 | 74.7 | 17.7 | 1.5 | 0.5 | 7.0 | 5.4 | 15.6 | 7.1 | 9.9 | 11.3 | 14.3 |
| 48 389 | 37780 | 7 | Reeves | 6 826 | 13 798 | 2 188 | 2.0 | 19.9 | 5.1 | 0.3 | 1.0 | 74.0 | 6.7 | 15.7 | 11.9 | 15.3 | 14.8 | 13.6 |
| 48 391 | ... | 6 | Refugio | 1 995 | 7 259 | 2 656 | 3.6 | 45.1 | 6.2 | 0.7 | 0.7 | 48.1 | 6.3 | 17.1 | 8.8 | 9.0 | 11.3 | 14.1 |
| 48 393 | 37420 | 9 | Roberts | 2 393 | 854 | 3 115 | 0.4 | 86.9 | 1.3 | 1.3 | 0.9 | 11.0 | 7.2 | 18.5 | 6.3 | 12.6 | 9.9 | 14.7 |
| 48 395 | 17780 | 3 | Robertson | 2 216 | 16 545 | 2 009 | 7.5 | 58.4 | 21.6 | 0.8 | 0.9 | 19.4 | 7.0 | 18.5 | 8.1 | 11.1 | 11.4 | 13.8 |
| 48 397 | 19100 | 1 | Rockwall | 329 | 83 021 | 670 | 252.3 | 74.5 | 6.4 | 0.9 | 3.1 | 16.6 | 7.0 | 22.1 | 6.9 | 12.1 | 15.6 | 15.4 |
| 48 399 | ... | 6 | Runnels | 2 722 | 10 449 | 2 399 | 3.8 | 64.2 | 2.0 | 0.6 | 0.4 | 33.3 | 6.3 | 18.5 | 7.1 | 10.2 | 10.8 | 13.5 |
| 48 401 | 30980 | 3 | Rusk | 2 393 | 54 026 | 923 | 22.6 | 66.4 | 18.2 | 0.9 | 0.7 | 15.2 | 6.6 | 16.7 | 9.1 | 13.5 | 12.7 | 14.6 |
| 48 403 | ... | 9 | Sabine | 1 273 | 10 433 | 2 401 | 8.2 | 88.3 | 7.8 | 1.1 | 0.5 | 3.5 | 4.8 | 14.5 | 6.4 | 7.5 | 9.0 | 13.8 |
| 48 405 | ... | 9 | San Augustine | 1 374 | 8 818 | 2 531 | 6.4 | 64.4 | 23.5 | 0.7 | 0.6 | 6.6 | 5.6 | 15.4 | 7.1 | 9.1 | 9.9 | 14.9 |
| 48 407 | 26420 | 1 | San Jacinto | 1 474 | 27 126 | 1 525 | 18.4 | 77.1 | 10.7 | 1.3 | 0.4 | 11.8 | 6.2 | 17.7 | 7.7 | 9.9 | 11.0 | 14.9 |
| 48 409 | 18580 | 2 | San Patricio | 1 796 | 65 600 | 805 | 36.5 | 42.2 | 2.0 | 0.6 | 1.2 | 54.9 | 7.4 | 20.5 | 8.9 | 12.1 | 12.0 | 13.8 |
| 48 411 | ... | 7 | San Saba | 2 940 | 6 002 | 2 759 | 2.0 | 67.4 | 3.8 | 0.9 | 0.3 | 28.4 | 5.9 | 15.0 | 9.6 | 14.0 | 9.6 | 12.1 |
| 48 413 | ... | 8 | Schleicher | 3 395 | 3 264 | 2 957 | 1.0 | 50.0 | 1.5 | 0.2 | 0.4 | 48.4 | 8.4 | 20.8 | 7.9 | 12.0 | 11.6 | 12.1 |
| 48 415 | 43660 | 7 | Scurry | 2 345 | 17 126 | 1 968 | 7.3 | 54.7 | 5.1 | 0.5 | 0.5 | 37.0 | 7.2 | 17.5 | 9.9 | 13.5 | 11.8 | 14.0 |
| 48 417 | ... | 8 | Shackelford | 2 368 | 3 356 | 2 952 | 1.4 | 88.1 | 1.5 | 0.9 | 0.4 | 10.5 | 6.0 | 18.3 | 7.2 | 8.9 | 12.1 | 16.2 |
| 48 419 | ... | 6 | Shelby | 2 061 | 26 019 | 1 563 | 12.6 | 65.0 | 17.6 | 0.6 | 0.5 | 17.1 | 7.7 | 19.2 | 8.8 | 11.5 | 12.3 | 13.1 |
| 48 421 | ... | 9 | Sherman | 2 391 | 3 073 | 2 972 | 1.3 | 58.2 | 0.9 | 0.7 | 0.5 | 40.6 | 6.6 | 22.3 | 8.0 | 13.4 | 13.8 | 14.6 |
| 48 423 | 46340 | 3 | Smith | 2 387 | 214 821 | 293 | 90.0 | 62.7 | 18.3 | 0.8 | 1.6 | 17.9 | 7.1 | 18.4 | 10.6 | 13.0 | 12.0 | 12.8 |
| 48 425 | 24180 | 8 | Somervell | 483 | 8 598 | 2 556 | 17.8 | 78.3 | 1.8 | 1.3 | 0.8 | 19.3 | 5.5 | 19.8 | 7.9 | 10.3 | 12.1 | 15.2 |
| 48 427 | 40100 | 4 | Starr | 3 168 | 61 615 | 844 | 19.4 | 4.1 | 0.1 | 0.1 | 0.3 | 95.6 | 9.4 | 24.5 | 11.1 | 12.6 | 12.9 | 10.7 |
| 48 429 | ... | 7 | Stephens | 2 322 | 9 464 | 2 475 | 4.1 | 75.5 | 2.7 | 0.8 | 0.5 | 21.3 | 6.1 | 17.3 | 8.9 | 12.3 | 10.9 | 13.0 |
| 48 431 | ... | 8 | Sterling | 2 392 | 1 191 | 3 101 | 0.5 | 64.3 | 2.2 | 1.7 | 0.3 | 32.9 | 7.0 | 16.9 | 8.4 | 12.9 | 10.4 | 15.9 |
| 48 433 | ... | 8 | Stonewall | 2 373 | 1 475 | 3 084 | 0.6 | 80.2 | 3.5 | 0.7 | 1.2 | 15.6 | 5.2 | 16.8 | 5.5 | 9.2 | 9.7 | 14.7 |
| 48 435 | ... | 7 | Sutton | 3 766 | 3 950 | 2 911 | 1.0 | 39.3 | 0.4 | 0.2 | 0.1 | 60.1 | 7.9 | 18.1 | 8.6 | 10.9 | 12.1 | 14.4 |
| 48 437 | ... | 6 | Swisher | 2 306 | 7 891 | 2 606 | 3.4 | 50.9 | 7.7 | 0.8 | 0.4 | 41.2 | 7.6 | 18.2 | 9.2 | 13.2 | 10.6 | 13.1 |
| 48 439 | 19100 | 1 | Tarrant | 2 237 | 1 880 153 | 15 | 840.5 | 52.7 | 15.3 | 0.9 | 5.5 | 27.3 | 7.8 | 20.0 | 9.5 | 14.7 | 14.3 | 14.1 |
| 48 441 | 10180 | 3 | Taylor | 2 371 | 133 473 | 470 | 56.3 | 68.0 | 8.0 | 0.9 | 2.3 | 22.6 | 7.5 | 16.9 | 14.0 | 14.2 | 10.8 | 12.7 |
| 48 443 | ... | 9 | Terrell | 6 107 | 917 | 3 112 | 0.2 | 51.1 | 1.1 | 1.0 | 0.7 | 46.8 | 6.7 | 13.4 | 4.8 | 11.9 | 10.6 | 12.0 |
| 48 445 | ... | 6 | Terry | 2 302 | 12 613 | 2 265 | 5.5 | 44.9 | 4.8 | 0.5 | 0.4 | 50.1 | 8.1 | 18.0 | 10.5 | 13.9 | 10.9 | 13.5 |
| 48 447 | ... | 9 | Throckmorton | 2 363 | 1 601 | 3 078 | 0.7 | 88.1 | 1.1 | 1.2 | 0.5 | 9.8 | 5.2 | 17.0 | 7.0 | 8.6 | 10.2 | 15.2 |
| 48 449 | 34420 | 7 | Titus | 1 052 | 32 663 | 1 366 | 31.0 | 48.9 | 9.7 | 0.7 | 0.9 | 40.6 | 9.1 | 21.5 | 10.0 | 12.5 | 12.7 | 12.2 |

1. CBSA = Core Based Statistical Area. See Appendix A for explanation. See Appendix B for list of metropolitan areas with component counties. 2. County type code from the Economic Research Service of USDA Rural-Urban Continuum Codes. See Appendix A for definition. 3. Dry land or land partially or temporarily covered by water. 4. May be of any race.

| | Population, 2011 (cont.) Age (percent) (cont.) | | | | Population change and components of change, 2000–2012 Total persons | | Percent change | | Components of change, 2010–2012 | | | Households, 2010 | | | Percent | |
|---|---|---|---|---|---|---|---|---|---|---|---|---|---|---|---|---|
| STATE County | 55 to 64 years | 65 to 74 years | 75 years and over | Percent female | 2000 | 2010 | 2000– 2010 | 2010– 2012 | Births | Deaths | Net migration | Number | Percent change, 2000– 2010 | Persons per house-hold | Female family house-holder[1] | One per-son |
| | 16 | 17 | 18 | 19 | 20 | 21 | 22 | 23 | 24 | 25 | 26 | 27 | 28 | 29 | 30 | 31 |

TEXAS—Cont'd

| | | | | | | | | | | | | | | | | |
|---|---|---|---|---|---|---|---|---|---|---|---|---|---|---|---|---|
| Mason | 16.6 | 14.5 | 10.8 | 50.6 | 3 738 | 4 012 | 7.3 | -0.2 | 71 | 103 | 21 | 1 754 | 9.1 | 2.29 | 8.6 | 29.2 |
| Matagorda | 13.1 | 8.3 | 6.3 | 50.0 | 37 957 | 36 702 | -3.3 | -0.4 | 1 169 | 808 | -512 | 13 894 | -0.1 | 2.61 | 13.4 | 26.4 |
| Maverick | 9.6 | 6.1 | 4.7 | 51.0 | 47 297 | 54 258 | 14.7 | 2.0 | 2 288 | 755 | -404 | 15 563 | 18.9 | 3.42 | 18.4 | 15.5 |
| Medina | 13.1 | 7.8 | 6.0 | 48.6 | 39 304 | 46 006 | 17.1 | 1.6 | 1 165 | 848 | 440 | 15 530 | 20.6 | 2.81 | 12.6 | 20.0 |
| Menard | 16.6 | 14.8 | 12.5 | 50.1 | 2 360 | 2 242 | -5.0 | -0.1 | 32 | 53 | 23 | 994 | 0.4 | 2.22 | 8.4 | 32.3 |
| Midland | 11.3 | 5.5 | 5.4 | 50.7 | 116 009 | 136 872 | 18.0 | 7.1 | 5 112 | 2 260 | 6 735 | 50 845 | 18.9 | 2.66 | 12.8 | 24.8 |
| Milam | 13.6 | 9.2 | 8.3 | 50.7 | 24 238 | 24 757 | 2.1 | -2.4 | 695 | 601 | -710 | 9 408 | 2.3 | 2.59 | 12.7 | 26.5 |
| Mills | 15.1 | 13.0 | 11.0 | 50.9 | 5 151 | 4 936 | -4.2 | -2.2 | 90 | 162 | -34 | 1 975 | -1.3 | 2.42 | 9.4 | 26.7 |
| Mitchell | 11.0 | 6.9 | 6.2 | 38.9 | 9 698 | 9 403 | -3.0 | -0.7 | 230 | 200 | -93 | 2 809 | -1.0 | 2.49 | 12.0 | 28.2 |
| Montague | 13.8 | 11.0 | 8.8 | 50.9 | 19 117 | 19 719 | 3.1 | -0.8 | 537 | 589 | -109 | 7 989 | 2.8 | 2.43 | 9.3 | 26.9 |
| Montgomery | 12.0 | 6.7 | 4.1 | 50.5 | 293 768 | 455 746 | 55.1 | 6.4 | 14 229 | 6 763 | 21 256 | 162 530 | 57.3 | 2.78 | 10.6 | 20.6 |
| Moore | 9.8 | 5.2 | 4.5 | 48.5 | 20 121 | 21 904 | 8.9 | 1.9 | 884 | 330 | -148 | 7 197 | 6.2 | 3.02 | 11.3 | 19.3 |
| Morris | 14.1 | 10.7 | 8.9 | 51.9 | 13 048 | 12 934 | -0.9 | -1.1 | 355 | 345 | -154 | 5 226 | 0.2 | 2.45 | 15.0 | 27.5 |
| Motley | 14.4 | 16.3 | 12.1 | 48.6 | 1 426 | 1 210 | -15.1 | -0.7 | 22 | 41 | 8 | 542 | -10.6 | 2.23 | 7.4 | 32.3 |
| Nacogdoches | 10.5 | 6.4 | 5.3 | 52.2 | 59 203 | 64 524 | 9.0 | 2.3 | 2 063 | 1 238 | 702 | 23 861 | 8.4 | 2.49 | 13.6 | 28.7 |
| Navarro | 12.3 | 8.3 | 6.2 | 50.5 | 45 124 | 47 735 | 5.8 | 0.5 | 1 517 | 1 122 | -143 | 17 380 | 5.4 | 2.70 | 13.8 | 23.8 |
| Newton | 13.8 | 9.8 | 6.7 | 48.7 | 15 072 | 14 445 | -4.2 | -1.7 | 328 | 405 | -181 | 5 476 | -1.9 | 2.51 | 13.4 | 26.2 |
| Nolan | 13.4 | 9.1 | 7.8 | 50.2 | 15 802 | 15 216 | -3.7 | -1.9 | 441 | 405 | -340 | 5 999 | -2.8 | 2.47 | 13.4 | 28.8 |
| Nueces | 12.0 | 6.7 | 5.6 | 50.9 | 313 645 | 340 223 | 8.5 | 2.2 | 10 400 | 5 926 | 3 004 | 124 587 | 12.9 | 2.68 | 16.6 | 25.1 |
| Ochiltree | 9.5 | 5.4 | 4.9 | 49.0 | 9 006 | 10 223 | 13.5 | 4.9 | 410 | 188 | 280 | 3 617 | 10.9 | 2.81 | 10.2 | 21.8 |
| Oldham | 11.8 | 7.4 | 4.9 | 49.5 | 2 185 | 2 052 | -6.1 | 0.4 | 38 | 18 | -12 | 691 | -6.0 | 2.56 | 8.7 | 21.6 |
| Orange | 12.7 | 7.9 | 6.3 | 50.4 | 84 966 | 81 837 | -3.7 | 1.4 | 2 317 | 1 972 | 826 | 31 031 | -1.9 | 2.62 | 13.5 | 23.0 |
| Palo Pinto | 13.6 | 9.8 | 6.7 | 51.0 | 27 026 | 28 111 | 4.0 | -0.9 | 831 | 722 | -386 | 10 871 | 2.6 | 2.56 | 11.5 | 25.4 |
| Panola | 13.7 | 9.0 | 6.8 | 50.4 | 22 756 | 23 796 | 4.6 | 0.9 | 655 | 567 | 146 | 9 271 | 5.1 | 2.53 | 12.3 | 25.4 |
| Parker | 13.2 | 7.7 | 5.0 | 49.4 | 88 495 | 116 927 | 32.1 | 2.4 | 2 914 | 2 039 | 1 831 | 42 069 | 35.1 | 2.71 | 9.4 | 19.7 |
| Parmer | 9.8 | 6.4 | 5.6 | 48.7 | 10 016 | 10 269 | 2.5 | -0.8 | 338 | 113 | -317 | 3 413 | 2.7 | 2.99 | 9.4 | 19.3 |
| Pecos | 11.3 | 7.0 | 5.1 | 43.7 | 16 809 | 15 507 | -7.7 | 0.7 | 512 | 213 | -193 | 4 894 | -5.0 | 2.75 | 13.2 | 22.8 |
| Polk | 14.5 | 11.7 | 7.3 | 46.6 | 41 133 | 45 413 | 10.4 | 0.5 | 1 107 | 1 375 | 493 | 16 503 | 9.2 | 2.49 | 12.4 | 26.3 |
| Potter | 10.5 | 5.7 | 5.2 | 48.8 | 113 546 | 121 073 | 6.6 | 1.0 | 4 653 | 2 528 | -854 | 42 933 | 5.3 | 2.66 | 16.3 | 27.8 |
| Presidio | 12.1 | 9.7 | 8.6 | 50.7 | 7 304 | 7 818 | 7.0 | -3.7 | 268 | 109 | -459 | 2 906 | 14.9 | 2.69 | 14.3 | 27.3 |
| Rains | 15.8 | 13.3 | 8.1 | 49.9 | 9 139 | 10 914 | 19.4 | 0.3 | 228 | 263 | 62 | 4 377 | 21.0 | 2.48 | 10.3 | 23.3 |
| Randall | 12.0 | 6.8 | 5.6 | 51.3 | 104 312 | 120 725 | 15.7 | 3.6 | 3 597 | 2 093 | 2 819 | 47 975 | 16.3 | 2.47 | 10.2 | 26.0 |
| Reagan | 11.1 | 5.6 | 4.7 | 48.2 | 3 326 | 3 367 | 1.2 | 3.2 | 106 | 46 | 46 | 1 156 | 4.4 | 2.89 | 9.3 | 20.7 |
| Real | 18.0 | 14.9 | 10.4 | 50.4 | 3 047 | 3 309 | 8.6 | 1.8 | 78 | 107 | 88 | 1 374 | 10.4 | 2.36 | 8.8 | 26.3 |
| Red River | 14.7 | 12.0 | 9.7 | 51.4 | 14 314 | 12 860 | -10.2 | -1.3 | 291 | 424 | -39 | 5 469 | -6.1 | 2.32 | 13.7 | 30.2 |
| Reeves | 9.8 | 6.5 | 5.6 | 39.9 | 13 137 | 13 783 | 4.9 | 0.1 | 366 | 241 | -117 | 3 839 | -6.2 | 2.78 | 15.6 | 24.9 |
| Refugio | 13.6 | 11.2 | 8.7 | 50.2 | 7 828 | 7 383 | -5.7 | -1.7 | 201 | 162 | -164 | 2 841 | -4.8 | 2.55 | 13.3 | 25.7 |
| Roberts | 13.4 | 11.2 | 6.3 | 51.8 | 887 | 929 | 4.7 | -8.1 | 24 | 14 | -91 | 359 | -0.8 | 2.59 | 4.5 | 17.5 |
| Robertson | 13.5 | 9.4 | 7.4 | 50.6 | 16 000 | 16 622 | 3.9 | -0.5 | 466 | 400 | -137 | 6 541 | 5.9 | 2.51 | 15.2 | 27.2 |
| Rockwall | 11.0 | 6.1 | 3.9 | 50.8 | 43 080 | 78 337 | 81.8 | 6.0 | 2 170 | 958 | 3 354 | 26 448 | 82.0 | 2.94 | 9.3 | 16.0 |
| Runnels | 13.9 | 10.3 | 9.3 | 50.5 | 11 495 | 10 501 | -8.6 | -0.5 | 279 | 298 | -62 | 4 165 | -5.9 | 2.47 | 11.8 | 27.3 |
| Rusk | 12.7 | 7.7 | 6.4 | 47.2 | 47 372 | 53 330 | 12.6 | 1.3 | 1 525 | 1 257 | 448 | 18 476 | 6.4 | 2.60 | 12.6 | 24.6 |
| Sabine | 16.5 | 16.3 | 11.2 | 51.1 | 10 469 | 10 834 | 3.5 | -3.7 | 203 | 342 | -297 | 4 738 | 5.6 | 2.27 | 10.7 | 28.2 |
| San Augustine | 14.9 | 12.2 | 10.7 | 51.1 | 8 946 | 8 865 | -0.9 | -0.5 | 225 | 335 | 63 | 3 625 | 1.4 | 2.38 | 13.1 | 28.7 |
| San Jacinto | 15.2 | 10.9 | 6.5 | 50.0 | 22 246 | 26 384 | 18.6 | 2.8 | 634 | 603 | 680 | 10 096 | 16.7 | 2.60 | 11.4 | 24.2 |
| San Patricio | 11.9 | 7.6 | 5.9 | 50.5 | 67 138 | 64 804 | -3.5 | 1.2 | 2 087 | 1 285 | -15 | 22 637 | 2.5 | 2.83 | 14.6 | 21.0 |
| San Saba | 14.5 | 10.1 | 9.2 | 45.0 | 6 186 | 6 131 | -0.9 | -2.1 | 137 | 156 | -112 | 2 257 | -1.4 | 2.41 | 9.4 | 27.4 |
| Schleicher | 13.6 | 7.8 | 5.7 | 49.8 | 2 935 | 3 461 | 17.9 | -5.7 | 85 | 38 | -249 | 1 182 | 6.0 | 2.93 | 9.1 | 22.8 |
| Scurry | 12.0 | 7.1 | 6.9 | 46.6 | 16 361 | 16 921 | 3.4 | 1.2 | 564 | 354 | -8 | 5 838 | 1.4 | 2.60 | 11.8 | 25.5 |
| Shackelford | 14.3 | 8.6 | 8.5 | 51.4 | 3 302 | 3 378 | 2.3 | -0.7 | 61 | 76 | -7 | 1 367 | 5.2 | 2.44 | 9.4 | 28.3 |
| Shelby | 12.0 | 8.8 | 6.6 | 50.4 | 25 224 | 25 448 | 0.9 | 2.2 | 831 | 639 | 387 | 9 648 | 0.6 | 2.62 | 13.0 | 25.9 |
| Sherman | 10.6 | 7.0 | 6.6 | 48.8 | 3 186 | 3 034 | -4.8 | 1.3 | 79 | 42 | 3 | 1 081 | -3.8 | 2.78 | 6.3 | 21.6 |
| Smith | 11.6 | 7.7 | 6.7 | 51.6 | 174 706 | 209 714 | 20.0 | 2.4 | 6 711 | 4 215 | 2 637 | 79 055 | 20.3 | 2.60 | 13.3 | 25.3 |
| Somervell | 13.5 | 9.1 | 6.6 | 51.1 | 6 809 | 8 490 | 24.7 | 1.3 | 182 | 201 | 107 | 3 078 | 26.3 | 2.67 | 8.8 | 21.8 |
| Starr | 8.4 | 6.0 | 4.5 | 51.6 | 53 597 | 60 968 | 13.8 | 1.1 | 3 082 | 832 | -1 622 | 17 001 | 18.0 | 3.54 | 19.2 | 13.6 |
| Stephens | 13.3 | 9.7 | 8.4 | 48.3 | 9 674 | 9 630 | -0.5 | -1.7 | 224 | 265 | -121 | 3 665 | 0.1 | 2.47 | 10.8 | 28.3 |
| Sterling | 13.0 | 7.4 | 8.1 | 49.3 | 1 393 | 1 143 | -17.9 | 4.2 | 28 | 36 | 55 | 440 | -14.2 | 2.52 | 7.5 | 24.1 |
| Stonewall | 14.0 | 11.5 | 13.4 | 51.9 | 1 693 | 1 490 | -12.0 | -1.0 | 20 | 37 | -7 | 642 | -10.0 | 2.28 | 10.1 | 31.2 |
| Sutton | 13.5 | 7.5 | 7.1 | 50.6 | 4 077 | 4 128 | 1.3 | -4.3 | 116 | 54 | -244 | 1 550 | 2.3 | 2.65 | 10.7 | 24.6 |
| Swisher | 11.2 | 8.5 | 8.4 | 46.9 | 8 378 | 7 854 | -6.3 | 0.5 | 268 | 173 | -57 | 2 762 | -5.6 | 2.61 | 11.9 | 24.9 |
| Tarrant | 10.3 | 5.2 | 3.9 | 50.9 | 1 446 219 | 1 809 034 | 25.1 | 3.9 | 62 107 | 24 761 | 33 290 | 657 134 | 23.1 | 2.72 | 13.8 | 24.9 |
| Taylor | 10.7 | 6.7 | 6.4 | 51.4 | 126 555 | 131 506 | 3.9 | 1.5 | 4 549 | 2 882 | 285 | 50 725 | 7.3 | 2.49 | 12.9 | 27.4 |
| Terrell | 17.3 | 12.7 | 10.6 | 48.2 | 1 081 | 984 | -9.0 | -6.8 | 25 | 17 | -84 | 430 | -2.9 | 2.29 | 6.3 | 37.2 |
| Terry | 10.7 | 7.7 | 6.6 | 46.9 | 12 761 | 12 651 | -0.9 | -0.3 | 427 | 296 | -161 | 4 200 | -1.8 | 2.73 | 13.3 | 23.5 |
| Throckmorton | 13.1 | 12.7 | 11.0 | 51.2 | 1 850 | 1 641 | -11.3 | -2.4 | 27 | 43 | -24 | 721 | -5.8 | 2.26 | 6.9 | 31.8 |
| Titus | 10.4 | 6.5 | 5.2 | 50.6 | 28 118 | 32 334 | 15.0 | 1.0 | 1 166 | 567 | -268 | 10 813 | 13.2 | 2.96 | 13.5 | 21.6 |

1. No spouse present.

# Table B. States and Counties — Population, Vital Statistics, Medicare, and Crime

| STATE County | Persons in group quarters, 2010 | Daytime population, 2007–2011 Number | Daytime population Employment/residence ratio | Births, 2011 Total | Births Rate[1] | Deaths, 2011 Number | Deaths Rate[1] | Persons under 65 with no health insurance, 2010 Number | Percent | Medicare, 2012 Eligible for Medicare | Enrolled in Medicare Advantage | Enrolled in a Medicare prescription drug plan | Serious crimes known to police,[2] 2011 Total Number | Rate[3] |
|---|---|---|---|---|---|---|---|---|---|---|---|---|---|---|
| | 32 | 33 | 34 | 35 | 36 | 37 | 38 | 39 | 40 | 41 | 42 | 43 | 44 | 45 |
| **TEXAS—Cont'd** | | | | | | | | | | | | | | |
| Mason | 3 | 3 833 | 0.93 | 26 | 6.5 | 46 | 11.5 | 940 | 31.0 | 1 106 | 83 | 539 | 33 | 806 |
| Matagorda | 400 | 35 903 | 0.95 | 515 | 14.0 | 363 | 9.9 | 8 882 | 28.5 | 6 171 | 879 | 2 708 | 1 271 | 3 392 |
| Maverick | 969 | 51 592 | 0.90 | 1 058 | 19.1 | 328 | 5.9 | 16 075 | 33.9 | 8 440 | 2 074 | 4 629 | 1 646 | 2 971 |
| Medina | 2 309 | 38 100 | 0.59 | 531 | 11.5 | 378 | 8.2 | 9 557 | 25.3 | 7 565 | 1 804 | 2 392 | 668 | 1 458 |
| Menard | 38 | 2 203 | 0.98 | 16 | 7.1 | 21 | 9.3 | 627 | 38.5 | 600 | 42 | 288 | 8 | 349 |
| Midland | 1 678 | 139 452 | 1.07 | 2 216 | 15.8 | 990 | 7.1 | 29 402 | 24.4 | 17 266 | 1 894 | 8 463 | 4 215 | 3 016 |
| Milam | 405 | 22 981 | 0.81 | 341 | 13.8 | 262 | 10.6 | 5 283 | 26.3 | 5 138 | 1 652 | 1 516 | 656 | 2 595 |
| Mills | 151 | 4 710 | 0.91 | 37 | 7.6 | 76 | 15.7 | 1 226 | 33.0 | 1 209 | 301 | 481 | 79 | 1 567 |
| Mitchell | 2 406 | 9 161 | 0.92 | 104 | 11.0 | 85 | 9.0 | 1 358 | 23.2 | 1 425 | 121 | 732 | 202 | 2 104 |
| Montague | 266 | 17 941 | 0.78 | 244 | 12.4 | 280 | 14.2 | 4 206 | 26.8 | 4 674 | 341 | 2 367 | 534 | 2 800 |
| Montgomery | 3 224 | 393 924 | 0.76 | 6 385 | 13.5 | 2 901 | 6.1 | 88 220 | 21.7 | 62 067 | 17 657 | 20 730 | 10 500 | 2 256 |
| Moore | 154 | 22 145 | 1.08 | 409 | 18.6 | 146 | 6.7 | 5 962 | 30.2 | 2 302 | 155 | 1 179 | 505 | 2 258 |
| Morris | 145 | 13 041 | 1.00 | 173 | 13.5 | 154 | 12.0 | 2 428 | 23.5 | 3 322 | 647 | 1 467 | 426 | 3 226 |
| Motley | 0 | 1 071 | 1.11 | 11 | 8.9 | 11 | 8.9 | 264 | 29.8 | 331 | 25 | 162 | 15 | 1 215 |
| Nacogdoches | 5 144 | 64 052 | 1.01 | 938 | 14.3 | 553 | 8.4 | 14 748 | 28.3 | 9 716 | 1 153 | 4 567 | 2 096 | 3 181 |
| Navarro | 736 | 45 586 | 0.90 | 698 | 14.5 | 513 | 10.7 | 11 942 | 29.6 | 8 971 | 991 | 4 355 | 2 055 | 4 216 |
| Newton | 724 | 11 784 | 0.51 | 143 | 9.9 | 174 | 12.0 | 2 668 | 23.5 | 2 436 | 413 | 1 187 | 99 | 671 |
| Nolan | 410 | 15 618 | 1.08 | 215 | 14.1 | 185 | 12.1 | 3 081 | 24.9 | 2 945 | 301 | 1 586 | 568 | 3 656 |
| Nueces | 5 792 | 348 148 | 1.07 | 4 741 | 13.8 | 2 597 | 7.6 | 70 283 | 23.9 | 50 666 | 21 318 | 12 678 | 18 174 | 5 232 |
| Ochiltree | 54 | 10 814 | 1.15 | 198 | 18.8 | 85 | 8.1 | 2 863 | 31.5 | 1 206 | 53 | 629 | 164 | 1 571 |
| Oldham | 282 | 2 203 | 1.18 | 15 | 7.2 | 6 | 2.9 | 369 | 23.9 | 356 | 22 | 155 | 27 | 1 289 |
| Orange | 639 | 74 615 | 0.77 | 1 067 | 12.9 | 850 | 10.3 | 15 157 | 21.7 | 15 361 | 3 741 | 6 526 | 3 175 | 3 800 |
| Palo Pinto | 263 | 26 267 | 0.85 | 384 | 13.7 | 326 | 11.6 | 6 489 | 27.8 | 5 389 | 464 | 2 530 | 991 | 3 453 |
| Panola | 358 | 23 837 | 1.02 | 286 | 11.9 | 251 | 10.4 | 4 463 | 22.5 | 4 405 | 544 | 1 986 | 610 | 2 511 |
| Parker | 3 121 | 95 847 | 0.63 | 1 340 | 11.3 | 876 | 7.4 | 21 663 | 21.7 | 18 460 | 2 524 | 6 921 | 2 322 | 1 945 |
| Parmer | 73 | 11 156 | 1.22 | 142 | 13.7 | 45 | 4.4 | 2 970 | 33.0 | 1 358 | 40 | 820 | 150 | 1 431 |
| Pecos | 2 025 | 16 329 | 1.15 | 246 | 15.7 | 91 | 5.8 | 3 379 | 28.8 | 2 112 | 231 | 1 101 | 484 | 3 057 |
| Polk | 4 241 | 44 268 | 0.91 | 536 | 11.7 | 627 | 13.7 | 9 609 | 29.3 | 16 801 | 2 983 | 6 119 | 1 043 | 2 249 |
| Potter | 6 919 | 143 932 | 1.43 | 2 248 | 18.4 | 1 112 | 9.1 | 30 269 | 29.7 | 16 627 | 2 238 | 8 374 | 6 203 | 5 018 |
| Presidio | 0 | 7 557 | 0.94 | 140 | 18.0 | 49 | 6.3 | 2 447 | 37.9 | 1 741 | 206 | 1 053 | 29 | 363 |
| Rains | 66 | 8 594 | 0.50 | 104 | 9.4 | 111 | 10.0 | 2 522 | 29.2 | 2 546 | 305 | 1 202 | 204 | 1 831 |
| Randall | 2 000 | 95 400 | 0.61 | 1 566 | 12.7 | 913 | 7.4 | 21 886 | 21.0 | 18 101 | 2 284 | 7 907 | 5 339 | 4 331 |
| Reagan | 27 | 3 588 | 1.15 | 48 | 14.2 | 13 | 3.8 | 1 004 | 33.3 | 425 | 28 | 238 | 5 | 145 |
| Real | 70 | 3 280 | 0.97 | 36 | 10.5 | 57 | 16.6 | 830 | 34.3 | 1 040 | 99 | 437 | 13 | 385 |
| Red River | 189 | 11 007 | 0.62 | 137 | 10.8 | 182 | 14.3 | 2 385 | 23.7 | 3 258 | 215 | 1 761 | 293 | 2 231 |
| Reeves | 3 110 | 13 459 | 1.00 | 184 | 13.4 | 106 | 7.7 | 2 577 | 28.4 | 2 028 | 154 | 1 282 | 276 | 1 961 |
| Refugio | 129 | 6 882 | 0.82 | 86 | 11.8 | 60 | 8.2 | 1 406 | 23.9 | 1 705 | 168 | 850 | 116 | 1 539 |
| Roberts | 0 | 823 | 0.86 | 8 | 9.8 | 9 | 11.0 | 156 | 19.9 | 162 | 25 | 76 | 18 | 1 897 |
| Robertson | 193 | 16 397 | 0.97 | 205 | 12.2 | 161 | 9.6 | 3 693 | 27.0 | 3 247 | 471 | 1 332 | 378 | 2 227 |
| Rockwall | 659 | 65 162 | 0.69 | 980 | 12.1 | 384 | 4.7 | 12 996 | 18.3 | 9 899 | 1 689 | 4 002 | 1 698 | 2 123 |
| Runnels | 194 | 9 787 | 0.85 | 124 | 11.8 | 132 | 12.5 | 2 253 | 26.9 | 2 356 | 139 | 1 315 | 167 | 1 558 |
| Rusk | 5 210 | 47 220 | 0.74 | 708 | 13.2 | 536 | 10.0 | 10 419 | 25.4 | 8 787 | 1 240 | 3 936 | 1 598 | 2 935 |
| Sabine | 79 | 10 325 | 0.88 | 98 | 9.1 | 142 | 13.2 | 2 000 | 25.2 | 3 278 | 393 | 1 509 | 154 | 1 511 |
| San Augustine | 223 | 8 653 | 0.89 | 95 | 10.7 | 137 | 15.4 | 1 849 | 27.5 | 2 283 | 337 | 1 123 | 143 | 1 580 |
| San Jacinto | 128 | 20 577 | 0.40 | 289 | 10.8 | 232 | 8.7 | 6 235 | 28.7 | 5 257 | 1 383 | 2 064 | 855 | 3 174 |
| San Patricio | 680 | 58 967 | 0.75 | 1 009 | 15.6 | 526 | 8.1 | 12 577 | 22.6 | 11 228 | 4 550 | 3 084 | 2 043 | 3 088 |
| San Saba | 684 | 5 783 | 0.90 | 66 | 11.0 | 73 | 12.1 | 1 380 | 31.8 | 1 317 | 182 | 539 | 71 | 1 134 |
| Schleicher | 0 | 3 014 | 0.80 | 48 | 14.5 | 24 | 7.3 | 998 | 33.0 | 515 | 40 | 250 | 13 | 368 |
| Scurry | 1 724 | 17 170 | 1.06 | 239 | 14.1 | 174 | 10.3 | 3 272 | 25.3 | 2 746 | 253 | 1 519 | 437 | 2 529 |
| Shackelford | 36 | 3 105 | 0.91 | 34 | 10.2 | 37 | 11.7 | 801 | 28.9 | 639 | 64 | 351 | 50 | 1 450 |
| Shelby | 172 | 25 228 | 0.97 | 441 | 17.1 | 302 | 11.7 | 6 525 | 30.6 | 4 945 | 650 | 2 473 | 551 | 2 121 |
| Sherman | 31 | 2 882 | 0.89 | 30 | 9.9 | 18 | 5.9 | 936 | 35.7 | 354 | 19 | 205 | 34 | 1 097 |
| Smith | 4 127 | 215 600 | 1.10 | 3 086 | 14.5 | 1 824 | 8.5 | 48 073 | 27.2 | 37 397 | 5 395 | 16 742 | 7 765 | 3 626 |
| Somervell | 287 | 9 232 | 1.27 | 85 | 10.1 | 95 | 11.2 | 1 737 | 24.1 | 1 399 | 251 | 562 | 93 | 1 073 |
| Starr | 810 | 58 716 | 0.91 | 1 406 | 22.8 | 341 | 5.5 | 19 259 | 35.8 | 8 312 | 655 | 6 016 | 1 219 | 1 958 |
| Stephens | 591 | 9 650 | 1.02 | 107 | 11.2 | 111 | 11.6 | 2 189 | 29.8 | 1 896 | 214 | 1 002 | 104 | 1 058 |
| Sterling | 35 | 1 299 | 1.17 | 12 | 10.4 | 31 | 26.8 | 261 | 27.6 | 209 | 16 | 123 | 5 | 428 |
| Stonewall | 27 | 1 430 | 1.05 | 6 | 4.1 | 12 | 8.2 | 325 | 28.5 | 361 | D | 209 | 26 | 1 709 |
| Sutton | 13 | 4 850 | 1.35 | 55 | 13.7 | 28 | 7.0 | 1 035 | 29.3 | 645 | 20 | 400 | 31 | 735 |
| Swisher | 645 | 7 123 | 0.76 | 130 | 16.7 | 75 | 9.6 | 1 639 | 27.7 | 1 497 | 78 | 933 | 150 | 1 871 |
| Tarrant | 20 634 | 1 759 697 | 0.98 | 28 624 | 15.5 | 10 693 | 5.8 | 386 174 | 23.6 | 208 811 | 68 655 | 60 945 | 82 657 | 4 479 |
| Taylor | 5 287 | 134 855 | 1.07 | 2 111 | 15.9 | 1 303 | 9.8 | 26 199 | 23.7 | 21 406 | 2 552 | 9 277 | 4 938 | 3 678 |
| Terrell | 0 | 1 008 | 1.15 | 8 | 8.3 | 9 | 9.4 | 244 | 31.0 | 232 | 33 | 106 | 13 | 1 294 |
| Terry | 1 166 | 11 983 | 0.88 | 204 | 16.1 | 141 | 11.1 | 2 901 | 29.8 | 2 057 | 372 | 977 | 278 | 2 152 |
| Throckmorton | 13 | 1 528 | 0.69 | 10 | 6.2 | 20 | 12.4 | 430 | 34.8 | 385 | 27 | 220 | 1 | 60 |
| Titus | 357 | 34 174 | 1.20 | 599 | 18.4 | 225 | 6.9 | 9 049 | 31.9 | 4 466 | 532 | 2 033 | 903 | 2 735 |

1. Per 1,000 estimated resident population.  2. Data for serious crimes have not been adjusted for underreporting; this may affect comparability between geographic areas and over time.  3. Per 100,000 population estimated by the FBI.

# Table B. States and Counties — Crime, Education, Money Income, and Poverty

| STATE County | Serious crimes known to police, 2011 (cont.)[1] Rate[2] | | Education School enrollment and attainment, 2007–2011 Enrollment[3] | | Attainment[4] (percent) | | Local government expenditures,[5] 2009–2010 | | Money income, 2007–2011 | Households Median income | | Percent with income of $200,000 or more | Income and poverty, 2011 Median house-hold income (dollars) | Percent below poverty level | | |
|---|---|---|---|---|---|---|---|---|---|---|---|---|---|---|---|---|
| | Violent | Property | Total | Percent private | High school graduate or less | Bachelor's degree or more | Total current expenditures (mil dol) | Current expenditures per student (dollars) | Per capita income[6] (dollars) | Dollars | Percent change, 2000 to 2007–2011 (constant 2011 dollars) | | | All persons | Children under 18 years | Children 5 to 17 years in families |
| | 46 | 47 | 48 | 49 | 50 | 51 | 52 | 53 | 54 | 55 | 56 | 57 | 58 | 59 | 60 | 61 |
| **TEXAS—Cont'd** | | | | | | | | | | | | | | | | |
| Mason | 73 | 732 | 901 | 6.2 | 50.8 | 27.6 | 7.3 | 10 711 | 25 229 | 41 462 | -0.7 | 5.3 | 39 080 | 15.0 | 30.1 | 26.6 |
| Matagorda | 267 | 3 125 | 8 907 | 6.7 | 57.8 | 15.6 | 74.6 | 10 392 | 23 312 | 43 962 | 1.2 | 2.2 | 40 778 | 20.4 | 29.5 | 25.9 |
| Maverick | 336 | 2 635 | 18 277 | 2.8 | 67.4 | 12.5 | 129.9 | 8 982 | 13 176 | 29 504 | 2.9 | 1.6 | 28 502 | 31.2 | 42.8 | 38.1 |
| Medina | 172 | 1 285 | 12 196 | 10.7 | 49.3 | 19.3 | 78.7 | 8 756 | 21 381 | 50 101 | 2.9 | 2.1 | 47 191 | 17.6 | 25.8 | 23.4 |
| Menard | 262 | 87 | 484 | 0.6 | 55.0 | 13.3 | 5.1 | 15 213 | 22 033 | 41 923 | 25.4 | 3.8 | 30 349 | 23.4 | 39.4 | 37.5 |
| Midland | 286 | 2 731 | 36 604 | 14.3 | 43.5 | 23.7 | 198.7 | 8 436 | 31 986 | 57 807 | 9.6 | 7.3 | 54 996 | 12.8 | 18.8 | 18.4 |
| Milam | 166 | 2 429 | 6 156 | 8.8 | 59.8 | 14.3 | 40.9 | 8 792 | 21 678 | 39 751 | -11.3 | 2.4 | 38 244 | 20.0 | 31.8 | 30.0 |
| Mills | 278 | 1 290 | 910 | 5.1 | 55.9 | 17.7 | 11.3 | 12 984 | 20 737 | 38 138 | -7.6 | 3.1 | 39 185 | 17.9 | 29.0 | 26.5 |
| Mitchell | 323 | 1 781 | 2 320 | 1.6 | 56.6 | 8.4 | 15.7 | 10 710 | 15 237 | 41 281 | 20.4 | 1.1 | 36 724 | 23.1 | 27.9 | 26.0 |
| Montague | 173 | 2 627 | 4 240 | 11.3 | 52.6 | 15.9 | 32.4 | 9 699 | 23 338 | 43 509 | 3.8 | 2.8 | 44 768 | 15.6 | 25.0 | 22.7 |
| Montgomery | 204 | 2 052 | 118 292 | 13.4 | 39.0 | 30.1 | 666.8 | 7 638 | 32 543 | 66 657 | -2.9 | 8.4 | 61 996 | 13.7 | 20.0 | 18.2 |
| Moore | 317 | 1 941 | 6 489 | 2.9 | 58.3 | 13.8 | 43.8 | 8 749 | 18 566 | 48 394 | 2.8 | 0.6 | 45 795 | 15.9 | 24.1 | 22.7 |
| Morris | 341 | 2 885 | 2 842 | 5.8 | 53.6 | 15.5 | 23.3 | 9 987 | 20 568 | 39 698 | 1.3 | 1.1 | 35 972 | 20.7 | 30.7 | 29.5 |
| Motley | 81 | 1 134 | 199 | 10.1 | 58.1 | 17.5 | 2.9 | 15 668 | 18 572 | 33 281 | -13.0 | 0.0 | 34 852 | 17.6 | 27.2 | 22.8 |
| Nacogdoches | 291 | 2 890 | 21 518 | 4.9 | 48.6 | 24.1 | 89.4 | 8 458 | 19 004 | 35 378 | -7.4 | 1.7 | 38 046 | 24.2 | 32.6 | 30.7 |
| Navarro | 620 | 3 597 | 13 208 | 6.2 | 54.5 | 14.9 | 83.1 | 8 613 | 20 641 | 41 074 | -2.7 | 2.5 | 38 057 | 19.7 | 28.8 | 26.8 |
| Newton | 54 | 617 | 3 128 | 6.7 | 66.9 | 7.7 | 23.2 | 10 690 | 19 113 | 38 409 | -0.2 | 2.1 | 36 492 | 20.4 | 29.8 | 26.8 |
| Nolan | 676 | 2 980 | 3 753 | 4.6 | 56.4 | 15.0 | 32.2 | 10 484 | 19 532 | 37 177 | 5.1 | 1.6 | 34 920 | 21.6 | 32.2 | 30.1 |
| Nueces | 603 | 4 629 | 92 220 | 8.4 | 47.5 | 20.6 | 537.7 | 8 765 | 23 525 | 44 815 | -7.7 | 2.6 | 43 470 | 20.0 | 32.1 | 29.9 |
| Ochiltree | 77 | 1 495 | 2 650 | 6.5 | 62.1 | 16.8 | 18.5 | 8 207 | 21 935 | 49 794 | -3.0 | 2.4 | 52 866 | 14.3 | 19.4 | 17.5 |
| Oldham | 48 | 1 241 | 548 | 7.3 | 40.7 | 28.8 | 13.4 | 16 642 | 24 112 | 57 054 | 25.3 | 3.3 | 46 597 | 14.6 | 26.4 | 19.3 |
| Orange | 442 | 3 358 | 20 056 | 7.6 | 57.2 | 11.9 | 137.5 | 8 933 | 23 451 | 48 833 | -3.8 | 1.5 | 44 758 | 16.1 | 22.5 | 20.6 |
| Palo Pinto | 324 | 3 129 | 6 320 | 5.3 | 57.4 | 14.8 | 46.1 | 9 448 | 21 727 | 40 385 | -4.1 | 2.1 | 34 574 | 20.8 | 28.7 | 28.3 |
| Panola | 226 | 2 284 | 5 558 | 7.0 | 56.1 | 10.9 | 39.1 | 9 869 | 24 105 | 40 088 | 11.6 | 1.5 | 45 212 | 15.9 | 22.4 | 20.7 |
| Parker | 162 | 1 783 | 29 019 | 12.7 | 42.0 | 23.1 | 160.8 | 8 369 | 29 972 | 63 725 | 3.7 | 5.0 | 63 584 | 10.7 | 16.1 | 14.7 |
| Parmer | 210 | 1 221 | 2 834 | 6.5 | 60.8 | 14.3 | 24.2 | 9 892 | 17 646 | 40 926 | -1.6 | 1.3 | 39 195 | 16.9 | 22.5 | 21.1 |
| Pecos | 373 | 2 684 | 3 377 | 1.6 | 67.8 | 11.9 | 35.4 | 11 703 | 17 867 | 40 925 | 8.1 | 2.0 | 42 984 | 19.8 | 24.3 | 23.8 |
| Polk | 205 | 2 044 | 9 230 | 10.2 | 59.8 | 11.1 | 65.6 | 9 457 | 18 470 | 36 073 | -12.4 | 1.2 | 37 665 | 20.0 | 32.6 | 29.4 |
| Potter | 570 | 4 447 | 32 591 | 7.1 | 51.8 | 15.1 | 293.4 | 8 256 | 19 304 | 37 766 | -5.2 | 1.6 | 35 690 | 22.8 | 32.2 | 31.0 |
| Presidio | 63 | 301 | 1 923 | 1.5 | 68.7 | 17.3 | 21.0 | 11 313 | 16 510 | 28 724 | 7.1 | 1.2 | 31 297 | 23.7 | 36.1 | 33.0 |
| Rains | 153 | 1 678 | 2 241 | 7.4 | 57.1 | 13.3 | 14.8 | 9 399 | 21 513 | 45 168 | -0.8 | 0.3 | 40 595 | 17.0 | 29.2 | 25.1 |
| Randall | 486 | 3 845 | 34 479 | 9.3 | 32.0 | 30.4 | 84.8 | 9 437 | 29 197 | 57 121 | -0.9 | 4.0 | 57 402 | 9.9 | 13.5 | 12.4 |
| Reagan | 29 | 116 | 845 | 1.2 | 70.5 | 9.8 | 9.8 | 12 586 | 23 871 | 58 491 | 30.4 | 0.8 | 47 493 | 9.9 | 13.1 | 12.1 |
| Real | 0 | 385 | 639 | 6.4 | 51.0 | 16.7 | 6.6 | 18 413 | 15 557 | 25 870 | -23.7 | 0.4 | 30 499 | 20.7 | 39.3 | 39.9 |
| Red River | 168 | 2 064 | 2 837 | 5.4 | 64.0 | 9.7 | 27.4 | 11 442 | 18 917 | 36 969 | -0.6 | 0.4 | 32 615 | 21.4 | 34.1 | 30.3 |
| Reeves | 256 | 1 705 | 2 790 | 0.6 | 74.9 | 6.7 | 25.1 | 10 629 | 14 556 | 35 552 | 13.0 | 0.5 | 32 839 | 33.0 | 38.4 | 37.0 |
| Refugio | 212 | 1 327 | 1 766 | 2.5 | 57.5 | 9.7 | 19.8 | 13 562 | 20 626 | 42 470 | 4.9 | 1.6 | 38 407 | 17.2 | 28.1 | 25.6 |
| Roberts | 0 | 1 897 | 161 | 3.1 | 33.8 | 36.8 | 2.6 | 15 034 | 34 085 | 61 042 | 0.9 | 6.4 | 59 699 | 8.5 | 15.1 | 14.3 |
| Robertson | 224 | 2 003 | 4 096 | 9.4 | 60.6 | 15.1 | 37.6 | 11 442 | 21 301 | 38 397 | -1.5 | 3.5 | 38 073 | 21.3 | 31.9 | 29.6 |
| Rockwall | 143 | 1 980 | 22 328 | 13.7 | 31.5 | 35.8 | 157.6 | 8 615 | 33 869 | 82 146 | -6.6 | 6.9 | 84 763 | 6.0 | 9.1 | 8.4 |
| Runnels | 298 | 1 259 | 2 323 | 2.0 | 60.6 | 15.8 | 21.4 | 10 027 | 20 935 | 38 556 | 2.7 | 1.7 | 34 515 | 20.8 | 31.6 | 29.3 |
| Rusk | 323 | 2 611 | 12 286 | 10.4 | 55.2 | 13.6 | 72.8 | 9 395 | 21 854 | 46 438 | 4.5 | 2.7 | 41 840 | 17.1 | 23.4 | 21.4 |
| Sabine | 186 | 1 324 | 1 992 | 2.0 | 58.5 | 12.8 | 19.5 | 9 530 | 18 968 | 33 109 | -9.8 | 0.2 | 34 605 | 22.0 | 34.0 | 31.3 |
| San Augustine | 365 | 1 215 | 1 964 | 7.3 | 67.0 | 12.2 | 12.8 | 9 590 | 17 510 | 26 841 | -26.4 | 0.9 | 32 543 | 24.2 | 37.9 | 34.3 |
| San Jacinto | 434 | 2 740 | 5 539 | 8.6 | 62.6 | 12.2 | 32.8 | 9 192 | 22 551 | 48 750 | 12.1 | 2.8 | 41 650 | 21.8 | 31.7 | 29.4 |
| San Patricio | 336 | 2 752 | 17 832 | 5.8 | 53.9 | 15.2 | 128.8 | 8 958 | 21 492 | 48 389 | 2.9 | 2.1 | 45 965 | 19.8 | 30.1 | 25.3 |
| San Saba | 96 | 1 038 | 1 387 | 3.5 | 50.4 | 17.7 | 10.8 | 11 297 | 20 812 | 38 675 | -4.8 | 3.3 | 35 978 | 20.4 | 33.1 | 31.4 |
| Schleicher | 0 | 368 | 963 | 6.4 | 57.6 | 16.1 | 6.2 | 9 749 | 21 181 | 46 058 | 14.7 | 3.5 | 41 533 | 16.7 | 24.1 | 22.1 |
| Scurry | 440 | 2 089 | 4 266 | 3.4 | 53.0 | 15.8 | 31.1 | 9 724 | 22 398 | 46 380 | 8.5 | 2.7 | 45 907 | 17.6 | 23.2 | 22.1 |
| Shackelford | 29 | 1 421 | 772 | 9.7 | 48.5 | 22.7 | 7.5 | 10 693 | 22 831 | 44 647 | 8.5 | 1.7 | 42 976 | 14.0 | 20.9 | 17.9 |
| Shelby | 308 | 1 813 | 5 819 | 7.5 | 62.0 | 12.4 | 50.5 | 9 569 | 21 059 | 34 164 | -13.1 | 2.9 | 36 677 | 21.0 | 31.5 | 27.2 |
| Sherman | 355 | 742 | 815 | 9.9 | 53.3 | 20.7 | 8.2 | 8 437 | 20 811 | 49 135 | 9.7 | 1.7 | 44 699 | 12.8 | 16.8 | 14.3 |
| Smith | 365 | 3 261 | 56 751 | 12.1 | 42.1 | 24.5 | 287.4 | 8 653 | 25 787 | 46 615 | -7.1 | 3.9 | 44 261 | 17.1 | 23.6 | 20.5 |
| Somervell | 58 | 1 015 | 2 096 | 9.1 | 40.0 | 29.9 | 22.0 | 12 155 | 25 795 | 48 401 | -9.0 | 4.1 | 52 134 | 10.2 | 17.9 | 16.0 |
| Starr | 243 | 1 716 | 19 900 | 3.7 | 73.3 | 9.6 | 162.0 | 9 515 | 12 125 | 25 598 | 14.9 | 1.3 | 24 537 | 39.3 | 46.4 | 44.7 |
| Stephens | 81 | 976 | 1 973 | 5.8 | 53.8 | 11.4 | 14.6 | 9 244 | 19 354 | 37 400 | -6.4 | 1.1 | 37 167 | 19.4 | 29.8 | 27.6 |
| Sterling | 86 | 343 | 237 | 2.5 | 60.8 | 18.0 | 3.1 | 15 675 | 18 500 | 41 944 | -11.6 | 0.7 | 50 943 | 11.4 | 18.9 | 17.4 |
| Stonewall | 0 | 1 709 | 272 | 7.0 | 46.5 | 23.7 | 3.1 | 13 004 | 26 287 | 47 083 | 24.8 | 2.8 | 37 513 | 17.5 | 26.1 | 23.0 |
| Sutton | 71 | 664 | 1 085 | 2.0 | 62.6 | 12.7 | 11.9 | 12 780 | 25 066 | 55 122 | 18.7 | 3.4 | 53 501 | 12.6 | 20.2 | 19.5 |
| Swisher | 137 | 1 733 | 1 854 | 4.7 | 58.2 | 16.1 | 15.2 | 10 169 | 17 146 | 38 988 | -3.2 | 1.5 | 35 736 | 21.8 | 31.1 | 28.1 |
| Tarrant | 442 | 4 037 | 503 161 | 14.6 | 40.3 | 28.9 | 2 691.1 | 8 018 | 27 920 | 56 178 | -9.9 | 4.6 | 52 882 | 16.8 | 23.8 | 22.1 |
| Taylor | 331 | 3 347 | 36 676 | 27.0 | 43.5 | 24.0 | 204.2 | 9 021 | 22 759 | 43 065 | -6.3 | 2.1 | 40 718 | 16.8 | 21.2 | 19.4 |
| Terrell | 398 | 896 | 128 | 0.0 | 57.8 | 18.8 | 3.6 | 21 299 | 22 595 | 41 417 | 26.7 | 0.0 | 39 260 | 16.8 | 26.6 | 26.0 |
| Terry | 225 | 1 928 | 3 184 | 3.1 | 64.8 | 14.9 | 24.1 | 10 678 | 20 585 | 35 485 | -6.4 | 2.9 | 31 984 | 23.3 | 32.8 | 30.2 |
| Throckmorton | 60 | 0 | 337 | 10.7 | 54.4 | 18.4 | 4.2 | 13 180 | 22 860 | 40 380 | 5.8 | 1.3 | 39 860 | 15.3 | 24.8 | 21.5 |
| Titus | 185 | 2 550 | 8 795 | 6.6 | 57.4 | 13.4 | 73.2 | 10 610 | 18 223 | 39 886 | -9.0 | 1.9 | 38 221 | 18.3 | 26.1 | 25.7 |

1. Data for serious crimes have not been adjusted for underreporting; this may affect comparability between geographic areas and over time.　2. Per 100,000 population estimated by the FBI.　3. All persons 3 years old and over enrolled in nursery school through college.　4. Persons 25 years old and over.　5. Elementary and secondary education expenditures.　6. Based on population estimated by the American Community Survey, 2007–2011.

# Table B. States and Counties — **Personal Income**

| STATE County | Total (mil dol) 62 | Percent change, 2010-2011 63 | Per capita[1] Dollars 64 | Per capita[1] Rank 65 | Wages and salaries[2] (mil dol) 66 | Proprietors' income (mil dol) 67 | Dividends, interest, and rent (mil dol) 68 | Transfer payments Total 69 | Gov't payments to individuals Total 70 | Social Security 71 | Medical payments 72 | Income mainte-nance 73 | Unemploy-ment insurance 74 |
|---|---|---|---|---|---|---|---|---|---|---|---|---|---|
| **TEXAS—Cont'd** | | | | | | | | | | | | | |
| Mason | 142 | 11.1 | 35 561 | 1 280 | 40 | 25 | 39 | 35 | 35 | 14 | 16 | 3 | 1 |
| Matagorda | 1 225 | 5.6 | 33 287 | 1 657 | 662 | 118 | 158 | 297 | 288 | 87 | 134 | 41 | 12 |
| Maverick | 1 229 | 7.3 | 22 188 | 3 080 | 667 | 114 | 71 | 462 | 450 | 72 | 236 | 108 | 20 |
| Medina | 1 513 | 5.9 | 32 638 | 1 772 | 340 | 105 | 197 | 345 | 335 | 94 | 163 | 40 | 9 |
| Menard | 68 | 11.4 | 30 157 | 2 258 | 16 | 8 | 15 | 22 | 22 | 7 | 11 | 2 | 0 |
| Midland | 9 144 | 14.6 | 65 173 | 38 | 5 160 | 2 393 | 1 302 | 827 | 796 | 250 | 350 | 132 | 21 |
| Milam | 790 | 3.1 | 32 003 | 1 890 | 301 | 76 | 115 | 220 | 215 | 70 | 100 | 25 | 6 |
| Mills | 173 | 2.5 | 35 690 | 1 264 | 53 | 19 | 41 | 51 | 50 | 15 | 28 | 4 | 1 |
| Mitchell | 236 | 5.0 | 25 002 | 2 964 | 124 | 21 | 34 | 68 | 66 | 19 | 35 | 6 | 2 |
| Montague | 792 | 7.9 | 40 161 | 728 | 221 | 95 | 147 | 190 | 185 | 65 | 95 | 14 | 4 |
| Montgomery | 22 883 | 7.4 | 48 508 | 253 | 7 941 | 1 512 | 3 379 | 2 621 | 2 515 | 944 | 1 083 | 260 | 93 |
| Moore | 748 | 10.9 | 34 060 | 1 502 | 509 | 113 | 75 | 113 | 108 | 33 | 50 | 18 | 3 |
| Morris | 448 | 4.3 | 34 904 | 1 385 | 291 | 39 | 60 | 146 | 143 | 46 | 70 | 16 | 4 |
| Motley | 44 | 7.6 | 35 515 | 1 288 | 15 | 8 | 7 | 11 | 11 | 4 | 5 | 1 | 0 |
| Nacogdoches | 1 927 | 3.3 | 29 441 | 2 388 | 983 | 176 | 336 | 506 | 491 | 137 | 231 | 63 | 12 |
| Navarro | 1 591 | 5.5 | 33 112 | 1 689 | 695 | 144 | 264 | 434 | 423 | 123 | 192 | 53 | 11 |
| Newton | 405 | 6.5 | 28 040 | 2 612 | 71 | 12 | 39 | 121 | 118 | 33 | 59 | 15 | 5 |
| Nolan | 503 | 4.9 | 32 914 | 1 722 | 280 | 38 | 78 | 151 | 148 | 39 | 76 | 17 | 3 |
| Nueces | 13 196 | 6.1 | 38 441 | 919 | 8 677 | 1 809 | 1 740 | 2 716 | 2 640 | 654 | 1 315 | 395 | 81 |
| Ochiltree | 453 | 14.5 | 43 016 | 511 | 276 | 98 | 61 | 49 | 47 | 17 | 21 | 6 | 1 |
| Oldham | 95 | 19.4 | 45 718 | 351 | 44 | 32 | 11 | 12 | 12 | 5 | 5 | 1 | 0 |
| Orange | 3 148 | 5.7 | 38 163 | 948 | 1 271 | 141 | 344 | 813 | 794 | 240 | 404 | 75 | 27 |
| Palo Pinto | 942 | 3.7 | 33 497 | 1 602 | 433 | 88 | 146 | 231 | 225 | 75 | 107 | 25 | 6 |
| Panola | 954 | 8.0 | 39 654 | 784 | 497 | 116 | 145 | 196 | 191 | 61 | 91 | 20 | 6 |
| Parker | 4 962 | 13.2 | 41 914 | 579 | 1 423 | 472 | 619 | 690 | 664 | 271 | 249 | 63 | 23 |
| Parmer | 414 | 26.2 | 40 057 | 739 | 223 | 139 | 53 | 59 | 56 | 18 | 28 | 8 | 1 |
| Pecos | 470 | 4.6 | 29 912 | 2 307 | 344 | 32 | 47 | 100 | 96 | 25 | 53 | 13 | 3 |
| Polk | 1 735 | 4.4 | 37 950 | 979 | 486 | 108 | 426 | 641 | 631 | 256 | 284 | 49 | 10 |
| Potter | 4 123 | 4.0 | 33 714 | 1 561 | 3 965 | 1 004 | 502 | 1 025 | 998 | 224 | 516 | 142 | 21 |
| Presidio | 219 | 8.3 | 28 209 | 2 584 | 132 | 18 | 29 | 61 | 59 | 14 | 24 | 14 | 4 |
| Rains | 333 | 4.2 | 30 131 | 2 264 | 64 | 35 | 48 | 97 | 95 | 38 | 40 | 8 | 2 |
| Randall | 4 934 | 6.7 | 40 001 | 745 | 1 284 | 264 | 813 | 543 | 516 | 258 | 125 | 59 | 19 |
| Reagan | 126 | 9.4 | 37 180 | 1 062 | 135 | 12 | 13 | 19 | 18 | 6 | 9 | 2 | 0 |
| Real | 104 | 8.1 | 30 296 | 2 242 | 24 | 11 | 27 | 37 | 36 | 13 | 17 | 3 | 1 |
| Red River | 402 | 3.6 | 31 664 | 1 964 | 104 | 22 | 69 | 150 | 147 | 40 | 82 | 15 | 4 |
| Reeves | 323 | 6.2 | 23 505 | 3 047 | 186 | 17 | 32 | 100 | 97 | 24 | 52 | 15 | 3 |
| Refugio | 291 | 10.9 | 39 958 | 749 | 123 | 22 | 53 | 74 | 72 | 23 | 37 | 7 | 1 |
| Roberts | 41 | 19.2 | 50 759 | 193 | 10 | 4 | 8 | 5 | 5 | 2 | 2 | 0 | 0 |
| Robertson | 600 | 5.4 | 35 859 | 1 237 | 207 | 73 | 107 | 148 | 144 | 43 | 70 | 19 | 4 |
| Rockwall | 4 155 | 9.2 | 51 116 | 183 | 994 | 294 | 520 | 383 | 365 | 153 | 144 | 30 | 16 |
| Runnels | 309 | 4.1 | 29 355 | 2 400 | 121 | 31 | 54 | 100 | 98 | 31 | 51 | 10 | 2 |
| Rusk | 1 657 | 6.9 | 30 821 | 2 139 | 749 | 110 | 230 | 379 | 367 | 124 | 173 | 41 | 10 |
| Sabine | 337 | 3.2 | 31 382 | 2 020 | 116 | 23 | 64 | 139 | 137 | 49 | 68 | 10 | 3 |
| San Augustine | 255 | 1.3 | 28 703 | 2 505 | 68 | 21 | 32 | 110 | 108 | 31 | 59 | 11 | 3 |
| San Jacinto | 847 | 5.7 | 31 607 | 1 976 | 96 | 39 | 110 | 220 | 214 | 77 | 91 | 29 | 6 |
| San Patricio | 2 465 | 6.3 | 38 087 | 958 | 1 109 | 129 | 285 | 567 | 553 | 152 | 278 | 74 | 16 |
| San Saba | 189 | 8.0 | 31 384 | 2 019 | 67 | 25 | 37 | 55 | 54 | 17 | 29 | 5 | 1 |
| Schleicher | 110 | 27.6 | 33 136 | 1 685 | 51 | 15 | 14 | 21 | 20 | 6 | 10 | 2 | 1 |
| Scurry | 642 | 10.5 | 37 970 | 976 | 408 | 62 | 101 | 125 | 121 | 38 | 63 | 12 | 3 |
| Shackelford | 171 | 19.4 | 51 496 | 176 | 72 | 46 | 28 | 27 | 26 | 9 | 13 | 2 | 1 |
| Shelby | 818 | 1.7 | 31 737 | 1 946 | 349 | 102 | 111 | 247 | 242 | 66 | 131 | 29 | 6 |
| Sherman | 175 | 35.7 | 57 622 | 87 | 38 | 93 | 16 | 15 | 15 | 5 | 7 | 1 | 0 |
| Smith | 8 218 | 5.2 | 38 515 | 907 | 4 829 | 1 118 | 1 536 | 1 628 | 1 578 | 536 | 703 | 173 | 46 |
| Somervell | 311 | 4.3 | 36 809 | 1 100 | 284 | 30 | 38 | 60 | 58 | 20 | 28 | 5 | 2 |
| Starr | 1 187 | 5.0 | 19 235 | 3 106 | 535 | 90 | 75 | 528 | 514 | 66 | 265 | 147 | 24 |
| Stephens | 386 | 10.6 | 40 449 | 705 | 154 | 100 | 56 | 89 | 87 | 27 | 46 | 9 | 2 |
| Sterling | 42 | 11.7 | 35 840 | 1 242 | 26 | 3 | 9 | 9 | 8 | 3 | 5 | 1 | 0 |
| Stonewall | 59 | 10.4 | 40 298 | 716 | 24 | 4 | 16 | 16 | 15 | 5 | 9 | 1 | 0 |
| Sutton | 317 | 54.4 | 79 103 | 7 | 294 | 20 | 36 | 29 | 28 | 8 | 15 | 3 | 1 |
| Swisher | 284 | 10.2 | 36 463 | 1 144 | 87 | 95 | 38 | 59 | 57 | 19 | 27 | 7 | 1 |
| Tarrant | 75 777 | 5.9 | 40 965 | 661 | 47 620 | 9 150 | 9 825 | 9 823 | 9 414 | 3 022 | 3 907 | 1 366 | 424 |
| Taylor | 4 929 | 5.6 | 37 132 | 1 067 | 3 101 | 503 | 877 | 1 027 | 999 | 288 | 480 | 118 | 25 |
| Terrell | 45 | 15.4 | 46 475 | 320 | 23 | 3 | 8 | 9 | 9 | 2 | 4 | 1 | 0 |
| Terry | 384 | -8.9 | 30 313 | 2 236 | 191 | 19 | 53 | 115 | 112 | 27 | 66 | 14 | 3 |
| Throckmorton | 77 | 16.6 | 48 144 | 266 | 19 | 24 | 11 | 15 | 15 | 5 | 8 | 1 | 0 |
| Titus | 930 | 1.6 | 28 542 | 2 535 | 672 | 80 | 124 | 237 | 230 | 63 | 113 | 31 | 6 |

1. Based on the resident population estimated as of July 1 of the year shown.   2. Includes supplements to wages and salaries.

# Table B. States and Counties — Earnings, Social Security, and Housing

| STATE County | Earnings, 2011 Total (mil dol) | Farm | Goods-related[1] Total | Manu-facturing | Service-related and health Information and professional and technical services | Retail trade | Finance, insur-ance, and real estate | Health care and social services | Govern-ment | Social Security beneficiaries, December 2011 Number | Rate[2] | Supplemental Security Income recipients, December 2011 | Housing units, 2010 Total | Percent change, 2000–2010 |
|---|---|---|---|---|---|---|---|---|---|---|---|---|---|---|
| | 75 | 76 | 77 | 78 | 79 | 80 | 81 | 82 | 83 | 84 | 85 | 86 | 87 | 88 |
| **TEXAS—Cont'd** | | | | | | | | | | | | | | |
| Mason | 65 | 16.6 | D | 0.6 | D | 5.3 | 11.3 | 4.6 | 19.0 | 1 145 | 287 | 81 | 2 733 | 15.2 |
| Matagorda | 780 | 7.0 | 12.8 | 6.9 | 4.9 | 5.1 | 3.8 | D | 15.8 | 6 885 | 187 | 1 127 | 18 801 | 1.0 |
| Maverick | 781 | 1.0 | 6.6 | 3.1 | 2.6 | 9.3 | 3.2 | 14.7 | 43.0 | 9 310 | 168 | 4 115 | 17 462 | 17.3 |
| Medina | 445 | 3.0 | 13.1 | 1.6 | 4.7 | 9.5 | 6.1 | D | 31.5 | 8 290 | 179 | 1 212 | 17 991 | 21.4 |
| Menard | 24 | 12.0 | D | 0.0 | D | 8.6 | 7.2 | 3.5 | 34.1 | 665 | 294 | 68 | 1 702 | 5.9 |
| Midland | 7 553 | 0.0 | 52.8 | 3.6 | 6.2 | 4.3 | 4.5 | 4.8 | 6.8 | 18 855 | 134 | 2 335 | 54 351 | 13.1 |
| Milam | 378 | 2.2 | 31.0 | 15.8 | D | 6.2 | 6.3 | D | 15.9 | 5 660 | 229 | 846 | 11 305 | 4.0 |
| Mills | 72 | 6.2 | D | 3.5 | D | 13.9 | D | 13.6 | 21.4 | 1 280 | 264 | 127 | 2 846 | 5.8 |
| Mitchell | 145 | 3.8 | 14.5 | 1.6 | D | 5.9 | D | 4.9 | 46.4 | 1 570 | 167 | 218 | 4 064 | -2.5 |
| Montague | 316 | 1.4 | 32.5 | 4.6 | 6.3 | 7.9 | 5.8 | D | 19.7 | 5 130 | 260 | 441 | 10 131 | 2.7 |
| Montgomery | 9 454 | 0.1 | 26.8 | 9.0 | 10.2 | 8.1 | 6.5 | 9.2 | 13.4 | 66 570 | 141 | 7 146 | 177 647 | 57.5 |
| Moore | 621 | 9.1 | D | D | D | 6.2 | 2.7 | D | 14.0 | 2 535 | 115 | 314 | 7 881 | 5.4 |
| Morris | 330 | 1.1 | D | 52.0 | D | 2.7 | 2.3 | 2.9 | 9.6 | 3 680 | 286 | 583 | 6 024 | 0.1 |
| Motley | 24 | 28.9 | D | 6.0 | D | 5.6 | D | D | 20.4 | 350 | 285 | 35 | 779 | -7.2 |
| Nacogdoches | 1 159 | 2.0 | 24.2 | 12.2 | 3.6 | 8.7 | 5.2 | 13.4 | 25.0 | 10 860 | 166 | 2 017 | 27 406 | 9.4 |
| Navarro | 839 | 1.0 | 25.8 | 16.5 | 2.8 | 7.7 | 5.5 | 11.2 | 20.7 | 10 100 | 210 | 1 739 | 20 234 | 9.7 |
| Newton | 83 | -4.1 | 16.3 | 7.8 | D | 5.7 | D | 11.9 | 34.7 | 2 805 | 194 | 580 | 7 142 | -2.6 |
| Nolan | 318 | -0.5 | 27.2 | 14.3 | 3.9 | 9.6 | 3.9 | 5.5 | 25.9 | 3 235 | 212 | 552 | 7 152 | 0.6 |
| Nueces | 10 486 | 0.7 | 27.1 | 7.9 | 6.2 | 5.9 | 4.3 | 13.5 | 20.7 | 55 720 | 162 | 12 965 | 141 033 | 14.7 |
| Ochiltree | 374 | 13.6 | 46.6 | 0.7 | 2.5 | 5.0 | 2.6 | 1.6 | 9.6 | 1 320 | 125 | 115 | 4 062 | 7.8 |
| Oldham | 76 | 47.7 | D | D | D | 1.3 | D | D | 18.9 | 395 | 190 | 28 | 841 | 3.2 |
| Orange | 1 411 | 0.8 | 43.8 | 33.8 | 3.5 | 7.2 | 4.1 | 5.9 | 15.7 | 17 685 | 214 | 2 495 | 35 313 | 1.5 |
| Palo Pinto | 521 | 1.0 | 42.0 | 21.7 | 2.8 | 7.3 | 3.8 | 3.7 | 17.7 | 6 005 | 214 | 746 | 15 214 | 7.9 |
| Panola | 613 | 1.5 | 45.3 | 6.3 | 4.0 | 4.8 | 3.0 | D | 11.6 | 4 825 | 201 | 679 | 10 920 | 3.8 |
| Parker | 1 895 | 1.4 | 30.6 | 7.0 | 6.2 | 9.6 | 5.2 | 8.5 | 13.9 | 19 850 | 168 | 1 454 | 46 628 | 36.8 |
| Parmer | 362 | 43.6 | D | D | D | 2.1 | 1.3 | 1.7 | 10.8 | 1 445 | 140 | 143 | 3 799 | 1.8 |
| Pecos | 376 | 3.1 | 40.1 | 0.3 | 0.9 | 6.2 | 3.6 | 2.6 | 25.4 | 2 280 | 145 | 412 | 5 585 | -11.9 |
| Polk | 594 | 0.0 | 20.9 | 11.9 | 5.3 | 11.5 | 4.2 | 9.0 | 24.5 | 18 845 | 412 | 1 722 | 22 683 | 7.1 |
| Potter | 4 970 | 0.2 | 17.0 | 8.9 | 9.2 | 7.1 | 7.3 | 16.4 | 16.3 | 18 320 | 150 | 3 307 | 47 271 | 6.0 |
| Presidio | 150 | 23.6 | D | D | D | 5.1 | 1.8 | 1.3 | 51.1 | 1 720 | 222 | 743 | 3 825 | 15.9 |
| Rains | 98 | 3.4 | D | 4.0 | D | 12.1 | 4.6 | D | 21.7 | 2 870 | 260 | 265 | 5 269 | 16.5 |
| Randall | 1 548 | 6.6 | 15.1 | 6.1 | 6.5 | 10.5 | 7.5 | 8.6 | 16.4 | 18 615 | 151 | 1 170 | 51 587 | 19.2 |
| Reagan | 147 | 2.7 | 29.9 | 0.0 | D | 1.2 | 0.7 | 0.3 | 11.5 | 445 | 131 | 47 | 1 372 | -5.5 |
| Real | 35 | 14.5 | D | D | D | 6.1 | D | 10.4 | 26.5 | 1 125 | 328 | 133 | 2 599 | 29.4 |
| Red River | 126 | 6.6 | 19.7 | 8.7 | 1.9 | 5.5 | 7.5 | 16.4 | 26.8 | 3 575 | 281 | 544 | 6 826 | -1.3 |
| Reeves | 202 | 2.7 | 15.6 | 1.3 | 1.6 | 7.9 | 2.7 | 3.9 | 41.7 | 2 240 | 163 | 557 | 4 640 | -8.0 |
| Refugio | 145 | 8.1 | D | D | D | 4.8 | 6.7 | 4.1 | 23.2 | 1 840 | 252 | 245 | 3 726 | 1.6 |
| Roberts | 14 | 29.1 | D | 0.0 | D | D | D | 0.0 | 28.6 | 170 | 208 | 0 | 439 | -2.2 |
| Robertson | 280 | 4.8 | 33.6 | 7.0 | 2.3 | 6.1 | 5.6 | 4.7 | 18.0 | 3 530 | 211 | 678 | 8 484 | 7.7 |
| Rockwall | 1 289 | 0.0 | D | 6.2 | 9.9 | 9.5 | 8.2 | 16.5 | 15.1 | 10 600 | 130 | 685 | 27 939 | 82.0 |
| Runnels | 152 | 3.8 | 31.8 | 21.8 | D | 6.7 | D | 6.8 | 24.5 | 2 630 | 250 | 319 | 5 298 | -1.9 |
| Rusk | 859 | 1.4 | 38.3 | 7.4 | D | 5.9 | 4.6 | 6.4 | 14.0 | 9 770 | 182 | 1 357 | 21 191 | 6.7 |
| Sabine | 139 | 1.8 | D | D | D | 6.1 | D | D | 17.1 | 3 710 | 345 | 388 | 7 988 | 4.3 |
| San Augustine | 89 | 5.8 | D | 3.3 | D | 8.3 | D | 16.8 | 22.2 | 2 555 | 288 | 468 | 5 342 | -0.3 |
| San Jacinto | 134 | -0.2 | D | 4.3 | 6.3 | 6.4 | 5.0 | 4.4 | 32.1 | 5 895 | 220 | 944 | 13 187 | 14.5 |
| San Patricio | 1 238 | 4.5 | 39.8 | 12.8 | 3.6 | 5.5 | 2.4 | 4.3 | 26.3 | 12 630 | 195 | 2 416 | 26 521 | 6.4 |
| San Saba | 92 | 7.3 | D | 2.0 | D | 8.3 | 3.8 | 6.3 | 25.9 | 1 410 | 234 | 157 | 3 177 | 7.7 |
| Schleicher | 66 | 14.3 | D | D | D | 1.9 | 2.4 | 4.4 | 17.6 | 540 | 163 | 77 | 1 489 | 8.6 |
| Scurry | 470 | -1.1 | 44.9 | 1.6 | 2.8 | 5.1 | 3.3 | D | 17.6 | 3 035 | 179 | 373 | 6 963 | -2.1 |
| Shackelford | 117 | 6.0 | D | D | D | 2.7 | D | D | 9.4 | 710 | 214 | 55 | 1 754 | 8.7 |
| Shelby | 451 | 5.5 | 35.1 | 18.6 | 3.5 | 8.8 | 4.4 | D | 14.8 | 5 580 | 217 | 1 035 | 11 873 | -0.7 |
| Sherman | 131 | 71.0 | D | D | D | 1.7 | D | D | 10.3 | 365 | 120 | 17 | 1 252 | -1.8 |
| Smith | 5 947 | 0.3 | 21.5 | 7.5 | 8.7 | 8.6 | 5.8 | 22.7 | 12.2 | 40 205 | 188 | 5 222 | 87 309 | 21.8 |
| Somervell | 314 | 0.6 | D | 0.7 | D | 2.6 | D | D | 13.2 | 1 520 | 180 | 124 | 3 674 | 33.6 |
| Starr | 624 | 1.2 | 7.1 | 0.4 | 1.4 | 8.8 | 2.3 | 17.5 | 47.5 | 9 325 | 151 | 5 092 | 19 526 | 11.0 |
| Stephens | 254 | 1.7 | 54.9 | 5.6 | 2.3 | 4.1 | 5.8 | 6.3 | 20.0 | 2 120 | 222 | 242 | 4 938 | 0.9 |
| Sterling | 29 | 8.0 | D | D | 2.7 | D | D | D | 20.0 | 230 | 199 | 24 | 615 | -2.8 |
| Stonewall | 28 | 2.8 | D | D | D | 5.1 | D | 0.5 | 36.1 | 405 | 275 | 31 | 928 | -0.9 |
| Sutton | 314 | 1.5 | 27.6 | 2.1 | D | 1.4 | 1.7 | 0.5 | 6.9 | 685 | 171 | 76 | 2 031 | 1.7 |
| Swisher | 182 | 48.2 | 4.0 | 2.3 | D | 3.6 | D | D | 19.2 | 1 605 | 206 | 158 | 3 221 | -2.8 |
| Tarrant | 56 770 | 0.1 | 23.4 | 13.0 | 9.2 | 6.5 | 8.3 | 10.1 | 12.8 | 222 290 | 120 | 33 132 | 714 803 | 26.3 |
| Taylor | 3 604 | 0.0 | 14.6 | 3.3 | 5.8 | 7.2 | 6.5 | 15.1 | 28.9 | 23 230 | 175 | 3 669 | 55 750 | 7.1 |
| Terrell | 26 | 12.3 | D | 0.0 | D | 2.3 | D | D | 52.8 | 225 | 234 | 29 | 700 | -29.4 |
| Terry | 210 | -2.6 | 30.4 | 4.4 | D | 14.7 | 3.3 | D | 25.2 | 2 260 | 178 | 392 | 4 828 | -5.1 |
| Throckmorton | 43 | 43.4 | D | D | D | 1.0 | D | 3.7 | 18.4 | 415 | 258 | 22 | 1 079 | 1.2 |
| Titus | 752 | 0.7 | 38.3 | 30.9 | 2.3 | 9.5 | 4.0 | 7.3 | 20.2 | 5 020 | 154 | 767 | 12 054 | 12.9 |

1. Includes mining, construction, and manufacturing.   2. Per 1,000 resident population enumerated in the 2010 census.

Items 75—88

| STATE County | Total | Percent | Median value[1] | With a mortgage | Without a mortgage[2] | Median rent[3] | Median rent as a percent of income | Substandard units[4] (percent) | Total | Percent change, 2011–2012 | Total | Rate[5] | Total | Management, business, science and arts | Construction, production, and maintenance occupations |
|---|---|---|---|---|---|---|---|---|---|---|---|---|---|---|---|
| | 89 | 90 | 91 | 92 | 93 | 94 | 95 | 96 | 97 | 98 | 99 | 100 | 101 | 102 | 103 |
| **TEXAS—Cont'd** | | | | | | | | | | | | | | | |
| Mason | 1 631 | 82.6 | 152 700 | 14.7 | 12.9 | 580 | 28.1 | 4.1 | 2 342 | -0.8 | 100 | 4.3 | 1 725 | 39.7 | 17.7 |
| Matagorda | 13 461 | 73.6 | 87 500 | 18.7 | 12.7 | 660 | 31.1 | 4.6 | 17 401 | -3.6 | 1 729 | 9.9 | 15 690 | 27.8 | 34.3 |
| Maverick | 14 749 | 69.7 | 81 900 | 28.8 | 14.9 | 532 | 30.4 | 13.9 | 23 475 | -2.4 | 2 950 | 12.6 | 19 316 | 21.9 | 28.0 |
| Medina | 15 350 | 76.5 | 107 200 | 19.9 | 11.8 | 683 | 26.8 | 4.9 | 20 667 | 0.6 | 1 332 | 6.4 | 18 606 | 32.0 | 26.6 |
| Menard | 838 | 76.1 | 63 400 | 23.3 | 11.6 | 507 | 22.3 | 2.5 | 997 | 0.8 | 61 | 6.1 | 1 078 | 26.7 | 23.7 |
| Midland | 49 534 | 70.2 | 133 100 | 20.0 | 11.1 | 855 | 28.0 | 3.9 | 90 130 | 7.2 | 3 125 | 3.5 | 67 256 | 31.0 | 26.1 |
| Milam | 9 323 | 70.8 | 85 100 | 22.5 | 12.7 | 665 | 28.0 | 4.6 | 11 157 | -0.8 | 886 | 7.9 | 10 316 | 26.2 | 31.3 |
| Mills | 1 841 | 78.9 | 90 600 | 24.0 | 12.0 | 467 | 27.0 | 2.7 | 2 277 | -3.5 | 116 | 5.1 | 1 942 | 34.8 | 27.1 |
| Mitchell | 2 711 | 75.6 | 58 800 | 24.9 | 10.9 | 524 | 19.0 | 1.6 | 3 483 | -2.5 | 224 | 6.4 | 2 847 | 23.4 | 34.4 |
| Montague | 7 890 | 77.1 | 85 800 | 21.2 | 13.0 | 688 | 30.9 | 4.4 | 10 822 | 0.8 | 534 | 4.9 | 8 487 | 29.4 | 35.3 |
| Montgomery | 155 712 | 74.3 | 161 700 | 22.5 | 11.8 | 912 | 27.6 | 4.4 | 238 848 | 2.0 | 14 279 | 6.0 | 208 587 | 37.2 | 22.9 |
| Moore | 6 669 | 71.6 | 83 400 | 18.4 | 10.2 | 615 | 21.3 | 11.3 | 11 862 | -1.7 | 491 | 4.1 | 10 063 | 23.2 | 39.6 |
| Morris | 5 095 | 74.0 | 72 100 | 18.9 | 10.4 | 530 | 27.0 | 4.1 | 6 244 | -0.1 | 574 | 9.2 | 5 121 | 29.2 | 32.5 |
| Motley | 415 | 78.8 | 54 100 | 20.8 | 16.3 | 381 | 35.5 | 1.2 | 553 | -15.8 | 30 | 5.4 | 392 | 41.8 | 21.2 |
| Nacogdoches | 23 006 | 59.0 | 90 800 | 21.1 | 11.3 | 667 | 34.5 | 5.6 | 31 217 | -2.9 | 1 976 | 6.3 | 27 505 | 32.0 | 27.3 |
| Navarro | 17 299 | 70.8 | 78 900 | 23.7 | 13.4 | 661 | 29.0 | 5.6 | 22 265 | 0.4 | 1 724 | 7.7 | 20 694 | 25.4 | 33.9 |
| Newton | 5 048 | 84.4 | 73 200 | 21.6 | 11.6 | 446 | 23.1 | 3.6 | 5 685 | -3.4 | 668 | 11.8 | 5 578 | 25.1 | 35.8 |
| Nolan | 5 693 | 68.4 | 52 400 | 18.5 | 11.2 | 520 | 25.1 | 3.8 | 7 622 | -4.0 | 427 | 5.6 | 6 883 | 28.0 | 27.6 |
| Nueces | 121 969 | 60.7 | 107 900 | 23.7 | 13.5 | 819 | 32.2 | 5.4 | 177 140 | 1.6 | 11 015 | 6.2 | 150 998 | 31.0 | 24.1 |
| Ochiltree | 3 735 | 71.1 | 79 600 | 16.6 | 13.1 | 627 | 21.4 | 5.8 | 6 133 | 3.8 | 205 | 3.3 | 4 478 | 28.2 | 40.4 |
| Oldham | 697 | 71.0 | 89 600 | 19.1 | 11.8 | 846 | 30.4 | 3.2 | 1 072 | 11.2 | 47 | 4.4 | 977 | 36.9 | 18.8 |
| Orange | 31 161 | 77.1 | 84 000 | 19.7 | 10.8 | 700 | 26.8 | 3.5 | 41 461 | -1.5 | 4 053 | 9.8 | 34 026 | 26.2 | 35.3 |
| Palo Pinto | 10 737 | 69.9 | 81 600 | 22.1 | 12.7 | 715 | 30.7 | 4.1 | 14 456 | -0.8 | 900 | 6.2 | 11 760 | 26.0 | 33.1 |
| Panola | 8 640 | 82.7 | 80 900 | 20.2 | 10.3 | 583 | 24.6 | 2.8 | 14 823 | 2.0 | 835 | 5.6 | 9 712 | 26.0 | 39.8 |
| Parker | 41 579 | 79.4 | 150 000 | 22.9 | 12.8 | 849 | 27.2 | 3.3 | 57 682 | 1.4 | 3 512 | 6.1 | 51 933 | 34.5 | 26.9 |
| Parmer | 3 359 | 71.6 | 90 500 | 22.6 | 11.6 | 588 | 27.3 | 7.6 | 4 385 | -5.7 | 210 | 4.8 | 4 595 | 24.4 | 46.3 |
| Pecos | 4 774 | 68.7 | 54 700 | 17.5 | 10.2 | 570 | 24.0 | 2.3 | 8 911 | -0.8 | 403 | 4.5 | 6 101 | 20.3 | 33.6 |
| Polk | 16 842 | 79.1 | 73 700 | 23.4 | 12.7 | 658 | 32.4 | 5.3 | 18 225 | -1.3 | 1 513 | 8.3 | 16 171 | 24.6 | 32.1 |
| Potter | 41 768 | 59.2 | 82 800 | 23.0 | 11.2 | 668 | 31.2 | 5.3 | 57 302 | -0.9 | 3 227 | 5.6 | 54 795 | 24.4 | 29.3 |
| Presidio | 2 735 | 70.3 | 58 200 | 34.2 | 10.8 | 355 | 22.4 | 9.0 | 4 151 | 2.5 | 514 | 12.4 | 3 090 | 29.9 | 20.4 |
| Rains | 4 079 | 83.7 | 90 300 | 21.8 | 14.1 | 582 | 24.5 | 4.4 | 5 127 | 0.2 | 373 | 7.3 | 4 793 | 25.8 | 33.9 |
| Randall | 46 735 | 69.6 | 135 800 | 20.3 | 10.6 | 722 | 29.4 | 2.6 | 72 535 | -0.8 | 3 046 | 4.2 | 61 777 | 36.9 | 19.5 |
| Reagan | 1 144 | 71.8 | 60 500 | 13.4 | 10.6 | 629 | 14.3 | 8.5 | 2 932 | 6.0 | 69 | 2.4 | 1 636 | 22.7 | 45.8 |
| Real | 1 334 | 74.8 | 79 600 | 20.9 | 16.4 | 544 | 33.4 | 4.5 | 1 367 | -8.7 | 98 | 7.2 | 1 047 | 35.0 | 27.5 |
| Red River | 5 180 | 69.8 | 67 000 | 19.3 | 12.6 | 525 | 28.4 | 3.4 | 5 584 | -5.4 | 578 | 10.4 | 5 084 | 26.3 | 38.8 |
| Reeves | 3 557 | 76.8 | 35 300 | 15.2 | 12.5 | 445 | 30.4 | 7.4 | 4 485 | -5.2 | 431 | 9.6 | 5 111 | 21.0 | 29.5 |
| Refugio | 2 729 | 78.8 | 67 500 | 19.1 | 11.6 | 579 | 27.6 | 5.1 | 4 513 | 3.0 | 208 | 4.6 | 2 811 | 24.5 | 26.3 |
| Roberts | 330 | 77.9 | 116 800 | 17.0 | 11.5 | 684 | 10.0 | 0.9 | 564 | 2.0 | 22 | 3.9 | 437 | 39.1 | 17.2 |
| Robertson | 5 971 | 67.8 | 77 200 | 22.8 | 11.8 | 545 | 31.9 | 6.9 | 7 178 | -1.8 | 550 | 7.7 | 6 549 | 27.1 | 29.1 |
| Rockwall | 25 717 | 82.6 | 193 000 | 24.2 | 13.9 | 1 142 | 26.7 | 3.2 | 41 337 | 1.2 | 2 561 | 6.2 | 36 913 | 43.7 | 16.6 |
| Runnels | 3 886 | 72.2 | 59 800 | 19.5 | 12.9 | 494 | 22.7 | 1.4 | 4 569 | -0.9 | 281 | 6.2 | 4 580 | 25.5 | 30.1 |
| Rusk | 17 994 | 78.1 | 89 500 | 18.7 | 10.5 | 637 | 25.2 | 3.7 | 27 016 | 1.5 | 1 675 | 6.2 | 21 596 | 24.2 | 34.8 |
| Sabine | 4 491 | 87.8 | 72 900 | 19.8 | 12.9 | 440 | 24.3 | 5.7 | 3 271 | -4.7 | 501 | 15.3 | 3 160 | 26.6 | 34.6 |
| San Augustine | 3 581 | 76.4 | 73 300 | 19.9 | 13.1 | 419 | 33.1 | 2.4 | 3 522 | -4.7 | 371 | 10.5 | 2 874 | 24.1 | 36.1 |
| San Jacinto | 8 980 | 82.7 | 81 000 | 22.6 | 11.5 | 676 | 21.7 | 3.1 | 11 192 | 1.4 | 900 | 8.0 | 9 822 | 26.3 | 33.4 |
| San Patricio | 22 453 | 65.4 | 91 800 | 21.3 | 13.1 | 747 | 29.1 | 7.3 | 29 100 | 0.9 | 2 202 | 7.6 | 27 323 | 29.0 | 27.9 |
| San Saba | 2 133 | 81.5 | 72 100 | 20.8 | 12.3 | 479 | 31.2 | 2.6 | 2 028 | -12.1 | 159 | 7.8 | 2 436 | 27.5 | 39.1 |
| Schleicher | 1 000 | 76.3 | 71 700 | 18.8 | 9.9 | 565 | 20.2 | 3.4 | 1 675 | 5.2 | 73 | 4.4 | 1 465 | 37.1 | 34.1 |
| Scurry | 6 039 | 71.2 | 78 200 | 16.7 | 11.3 | 620 | 28.2 | 6.8 | 9 104 | 7.9 | 392 | 4.3 | 7 112 | 27.9 | 35.8 |
| Shackelford | 1 265 | 74.1 | 68 100 | 21.4 | 12.1 | 491 | 20.4 | 2.5 | 2 724 | 13.9 | 78 | 2.9 | 1 527 | 30.6 | 30.6 |
| Shelby | 9 778 | 75.4 | 66 800 | 19.6 | 11.5 | 518 | 30.8 | 5.7 | 13 394 | 1.9 | 873 | 6.5 | 10 372 | 25.8 | 40.5 |
| Sherman | 1 015 | 77.0 | 82 800 | 20.9 | 11.2 | 630 | 23.1 | 6.2 | 1 374 | -6.3 | 63 | 4.6 | 1 358 | 32.8 | 37.0 |
| Smith | 77 934 | 68.9 | 119 800 | 22.2 | 12.5 | 783 | 31.9 | 4.6 | 102 902 | -0.8 | 7 189 | 7.0 | 93 762 | 31.9 | 23.5 |
| Somervell | 3 146 | 72.4 | 139 000 | 21.7 | 15.1 | 637 | 23.9 | 5.7 | 4 655 | 1.5 | 277 | 6.0 | 3 659 | 47.2 | 19.7 |
| Starr | 15 571 | 80.7 | 59 900 | 25.2 | 13.9 | 468 | 35.0 | 11.8 | 25 322 | -1.4 | 3 809 | 15.0 | 20 566 | 23.9 | 26.1 |
| Stephens | 3 598 | 76.3 | 70 100 | 25.0 | 12.9 | 633 | 27.0 | 1.6 | 4 786 | -1.3 | 271 | 5.7 | 3 952 | 24.0 | 33.8 |
| Sterling | 424 | 75.7 | 63 500 | 19.0 | 11.9 | 614 | 38.8 | 7.1 | 842 | 8.5 | 25 | 3.0 | 515 | 35.0 | 38.1 |
| Stonewall | 600 | 79.2 | 51 200 | 19.2 | 10.6 | 413 | 31.9 | 3.2 | 847 | 1.0 | 33 | 3.9 | 689 | 38.3 | 21.0 |
| Sutton | 1 382 | 75.5 | 76 400 | 15.9 | 9.9 | 586 | 13.7 | 5.1 | 3 016 | 1.9 | 96 | 3.2 | 1 889 | 27.8 | 42.4 |
| Swisher | 2 612 | 71.4 | 59 400 | 20.7 | 12.9 | 554 | 30.7 | 5.6 | 3 419 | -4.2 | 195 | 5.7 | 2 969 | 28.7 | 31.3 |
| Tarrant | 643 917 | 63.0 | 136 100 | 23.3 | 13.2 | 855 | 29.7 | 4.3 | 953 692 | 1.1 | 62 667 | 6.6 | 863 487 | 35.4 | 22.5 |
| Taylor | 49 439 | 62.3 | 90 900 | 21.2 | 12.4 | 730 | 30.5 | 3.0 | 69 243 | -0.3 | 3 660 | 5.3 | 59 184 | 31.8 | 20.7 |
| Terrell | 421 | 73.4 | 58 200 | 17.5 | 9.9 | 575 | 14.8 | 0.7 | 430 | 5.1 | 27 | 6.3 | 413 | 26.4 | 30.5 |
| Terry | 3 940 | 71.3 | 60 000 | 18.5 | 11.4 | 523 | 33.1 | 5.5 | 5 856 | -2.6 | 389 | 6.6 | 4 920 | 27.5 | 31.7 |
| Throckmorton | 795 | 80.9 | 50 500 | 19.4 | 14.1 | 430 | 23.0 | 3.6 | 948 | -5.8 | 43 | 4.5 | 741 | 23.5 | 34.4 |
| Titus | 10 717 | 72.0 | 88 300 | 22.5 | 12.3 | 606 | 27.7 | 9.5 | 13 810 | -3.5 | 980 | 7.1 | 13 363 | 21.6 | 42.3 |

1. Specified owner-occupied units, lacking complete plumbing facilities.  2. A value of 9.9 represents 9.9 percent or less.  3. Specified renter-occupied units. A value of 10.0 represents 10 percent or less.  4. Overcrowded or  5. Percent of civilian labor force.  6. Persons 16 years old and over.

# Table B. States and Counties — Nonfarm Employment and Agriculture

| | Private nonfarm establishments, employment and payroll, 2011 | | | | | | | | | Agriculture, 2007 | | | |
| STATE County | Number of establishments | Employment | | | | | | Annual payroll | | Farms | | | |
| | | Total | Health care and social assistance | Manufac- turing | Retail trade | Finance and insurance | Professional, scientific, and technical services | Total (mil dol) | Average per employee (dollars) | Number | Percent with: | | Farm operators whose principal occu- pation is farming (percent) |
| | | | | | | | | | | | Fewer than 50 acres | 500 acres or more | |
| | 104 | 105 | 106 | 107 | 108 | 109 | 110 | 111 | 112 | 113 | 114 | 115 | 116 |

## TEXAS—Cont'd

| | | | | | | | | | | | | | |
|---|---|---|---|---|---|---|---|---|---|---|---|---|---|
| Mason | 131 | 755 | 142 | 51 | 143 | 44 | D | 15 | 20 317 | 647 | 14.4 | 40.6 | 48.5 |
| Matagorda | 746 | 8 504 | 1 349 | 518 | 1 280 | 225 | 179 | 400 | 46 988 | 903 | 29.1 | 25.2 | 50.1 |
| Maverick | 762 | 11 246 | 4 033 | 386 | 2 477 | 377 | 177 | 252 | 22 432 | 312 | 49.0 | 19.2 | 42.0 |
| Medina | 659 | 5 594 | 904 | D | 1 158 | 239 | 332 | 152 | 27 247 | 2 139 | 35.9 | 15.2 | 39.5 |
| Menard | 41 | 184 | D | D | 51 | 25 | D | 4 | 19 614 | 356 | 14.0 | 41.3 | 51.4 |
| Midland | 4 655 | 65 689 | 7 619 | 2 382 | 8 054 | 1 888 | 3 672 | 3 588 | 54 621 | 601 | 51.1 | 16.5 | 28.6 |
| Milam | 424 | 4 132 | 853 | 323 | 651 | D | 110 | 131 | 31 791 | 2 045 | 32.2 | 11.9 | 42.5 |
| Mills | 115 | 898 | 249 | 67 | 218 | 51 | 27 | 21 | 22 958 | 921 | 19.0 | 23.9 | 41.3 |
| Mitchell | 132 | 1 345 | D | D | 266 | 45 | D | 45 | 33 113 | 519 | 14.5 | 26.0 | 29.5 |
| Montague | 430 | 3 981 | 715 | 250 | 715 | 177 | 107 | 151 | 37 944 | 1 545 | 24.7 | 15.0 | 38.1 |
| Montgomery | 9 137 | 128 218 | 15 896 | 9 702 | 20 903 | 4 221 | 8 001 | 6 373 | 49 702 | 1 886 | 69.1 | 3.2 | 31.8 |
| Moore | 468 | 8 744 | D | 4 246 | 959 | 162 | 86 | 298 | 34 050 | 283 | 8.8 | 67.1 | 60.1 |
| Morris | 232 | 3 959 | 240 | D | 340 | 131 | 91 | 188 | 47 547 | 457 | 41.1 | 7.9 | 36.8 |
| Motley | 31 | D | D | D | D | D | D | 4 | D | 229 | 1.7 | 59.8 | 42.8 |
| Nacogdoches | 1 276 | 17 924 | 3 638 | 3 616 | 2 772 | 551 | 369 | 521 | 29 075 | 1 277 | 34.5 | 8.0 | 43.6 |
| Navarro | 912 | 12 350 | 2 208 | 2 429 | 2 085 | 419 | 311 | 367 | 29 755 | 2 078 | 37.4 | 12.0 | 42.2 |
| Newton | 129 | 1 178 | 332 | D | 166 | 33 | 68 | 32 | 26 814 | 403 | 61.8 | 1.2 | 38.7 |
| Nolan | 336 | 4 121 | 566 | 852 | 775 | D | 88 | 133 | 32 377 | 580 | 15.5 | 32.1 | 30.3 |
| Nueces | 7 770 | 127 227 | 26 701 | 7 610 | 16 796 | 3 637 | 5 439 | 4 781 | 37 578 | 712 | 42.7 | 22.9 | 42.1 |
| Ochiltree | 354 | 3 558 | D | 48 | 442 | 137 | D | 172 | 48 417 | 382 | 5.2 | 53.7 | 61.3 |
| Oldham | 36 | D | D | D | D | D | D | D | D | 150 | 4.7 | 68.7 | 58.0 |
| Orange | 1 338 | 19 026 | 1 649 | 4 754 | 3 062 | 542 | 426 | 834 | 43 819 | 675 | 77.2 | 3.3 | 33.5 |
| Palo Pinto | 599 | 6 132 | 794 | 1 285 | 1 058 | 170 | 134 | 197 | 32 089 | 1 194 | 39.4 | 16.0 | 34.2 |
| Panola | 491 | 8 187 | 699 | 880 | 819 | 176 | 221 | 367 | 44 766 | 1 042 | 35.4 | 10.7 | 41.7 |
| Parker | 2 217 | 24 484 | 2 942 | 2 195 | 4 597 | 645 | 811 | 896 | 36 582 | 3 677 | 66.9 | 3.8 | 34.0 |
| Parmer | 200 | 3 119 | D | D | 166 | 84 | 33 | 101 | 32 539 | 555 | 10.8 | 53.3 | 61.8 |
| Pecos | 335 | 4 477 | 425 | D | 781 | 161 | 91 | 210 | 46 851 | 287 | 11.5 | 63.8 | 42.5 |
| Polk | 700 | 8 262 | 1 361 | D | 1 595 | 309 | 215 | 253 | 30 667 | 812 | 48.4 | 5.8 | 38.9 |
| Potter | 3 579 | 58 953 | 12 308 | D | 8 640 | 4 001 | 2 029 | 2 136 | 36 226 | 279 | 40.5 | 26.5 | 29.4 |
| Presidio | 121 | 745 | D | D | 227 | 75 | D | 19 | 25 379 | 148 | 14.2 | 60.8 | 37.8 |
| Rains | 154 | 1 165 | 118 | D | 380 | D | 138 | 28 | 23 736 | 657 | 48.6 | 6.4 | 37.1 |
| Randall | 2 297 | 27 366 | 4 196 | 1 368 | 5 131 | 1 368 | 761 | 836 | 30 537 | 887 | 36.1 | 27.3 | 34.0 |
| Reagan | 111 | 930 | D | D | 73 | 17 | D | 43 | 45 937 | 137 | 5.8 | 71.5 | 51.1 |
| Real | 81 | 487 | 186 | D | 49 | D | D | 11 | 23 427 | 301 | 19.9 | 37.5 | 40.5 |
| Red River | 168 | 1 475 | 407 | 287 | 206 | 111 | D | 39 | 26 576 | 1 206 | 23.7 | 17.1 | 44.9 |
| Reeves | 187 | 2 063 | D | 6 | 491 | 34 | 46 | 75 | 36 131 | 221 | 19.5 | 43.9 | 32.6 |
| Refugio | 143 | 1 514 | 242 | D | 225 | 97 | 18 | 70 | 46 392 | 295 | 26.1 | 30.5 | 55.3 |
| Roberts | 13 | D | NA | D | D | NA | D | 4 | D | 108 | 4.6 | 69.4 | 46.3 |
| Robertson | 267 | 2 476 | 363 | D | 335 | 98 | 45 | 109 | 44 206 | 1 562 | 30.3 | 12.7 | 45.6 |
| Rockwall | 1 721 | 19 861 | 3 449 | 1 151 | 3 778 | 592 | 1 130 | 628 | 31 607 | 347 | 65.1 | 4.6 | 32.0 |
| Runnels | 231 | 2 156 | D | 547 | 496 | 107 | D | 64 | 29 718 | 953 | 12.3 | 27.7 | 42.4 |
| Rusk | 812 | 11 045 | 1 589 | 1 370 | 1 280 | D | 777 | 433 | 39 215 | 1 521 | 32.8 | 8.0 | 35.8 |
| Sabine | 159 | 1 358 | 261 | D | 291 | 64 | D | 43 | 31 385 | 223 | 39.9 | 4.9 | 29.1 |
| San Augustine | 141 | 1 259 | 510 | D | 215 | 50 | 16 | 33 | 26 324 | 346 | 32.4 | 10.4 | 43.6 |
| San Jacinto | 180 | 953 | D | 79 | 212 | D | 30 | 28 | 29 637 | 688 | 52.5 | 3.5 | 33.1 |
| San Patricio | 1 012 | 12 783 | 1 642 | D | 2 249 | 376 | 268 | 509 | 39 803 | 652 | 45.7 | 22.9 | 44.3 |
| San Saba | 152 | 891 | 74 | D | 235 | D | 31 | 26 | 28 769 | 725 | 15.7 | 33.9 | 40.3 |
| Schleicher | 51 | 433 | D | D | 60 | 13 | 12 | 16 | 37 393 | 332 | 10.5 | 59.9 | 55.1 |
| Scurry | 424 | 5 428 | 555 | 100 | 672 | 160 | D | 247 | 45 515 | 681 | 18.9 | 31.1 | 36.0 |
| Shackelford | 127 | 981 | 93 | 127 | 89 | D | D | 47 | 48 175 | 254 | 12.2 | 48.0 | 53.5 |
| Shelby | 490 | 6 612 | 753 | 1 713 | 1 106 | 379 | 134 | 211 | 31 897 | 1 123 | 29.3 | 7.2 | 47.8 |
| Sherman | 54 | 272 | D | D | 38 | 4 | D | 8 | 29 051 | 362 | 6.4 | 61.3 | 54.7 |
| Smith | 5 504 | 86 101 | 21 611 | 7 513 | 11 864 | 3 114 | 3 916 | 3 315 | 38 504 | 2 514 | 53.1 | 4.5 | 35.0 |
| Somervell | 197 | 3 354 | D | D | 240 | D | 56 | 191 | 57 041 | 366 | 43.7 | 9.3 | 37.2 |
| Starr | 511 | 9 394 | 5 554 | 40 | 1 704 | 323 | 83 | 180 | 19 145 | 1 104 | 13.2 | 26.0 | 44.5 |
| Stephens | 252 | 2 360 | 313 | D | 366 | 112 | 163 | 84 | 35 714 | 487 | 9.7 | 36.1 | 34.3 |
| Sterling | 33 | 287 | D | D | D | D | D | 17 | 60 523 | 74 | 10.8 | 64.9 | 59.5 |
| Stonewall | 47 | 359 | D | NA | 36 | D | D | 12 | 32 462 | 376 | 4.8 | 40.7 | 39.4 |
| Sutton | 144 | 1 209 | D | D | 182 | D | D | 51 | 42 231 | 234 | 8.5 | 72.2 | 47.9 |
| Swisher | 152 | 1 084 | 208 | 106 | 156 | 46 | D | 26 | 24 292 | 527 | 8.3 | 46.3 | 52.6 |
| Tarrant | 37 210 | 687 510 | 86 255 | 72 451 | 90 441 | 39 130 | 37 176 | 30 349 | 44 143 | 1 248 | 73.2 | 4.8 | 34.9 |
| Taylor | 3 326 | 51 220 | 11 310 | 1 907 | 7 948 | 2 771 | 1 756 | 1 612 | 31 473 | 1 292 | 30.0 | 19.3 | 29.7 |
| Terrell | 16 | D | D | NA | D | D | D | 3 | D | 107 | 4.7 | 70.1 | 44.9 |
| Terry | 250 | 2 276 | 394 | D | 434 | 95 | 48 | 77 | 33 981 | 624 | 13.8 | 44.7 | 54.2 |
| Throckmorton | 47 | 247 | 68 | D | 22 | D | D | 6 | 25 955 | 264 | 4.5 | 43.9 | 48.9 |
| Titus | 643 | 12 419 | 2 149 | 4 555 | 1 893 | D | 164 | 385 | 31 003 | 810 | 37.0 | 6.5 | 35.1 |

# Table B. States and Counties — **Agriculture**

| STATE County | Land in farms — Acreage (1,000) [117] | Land in farms — Percent change, 2002–2007 [118] | Acres — Average size of farm [119] | Acres — Total irrigated (1,000) [120] | Acres — Total cropland (1,000) [121] | Value of land and buildings — Average per farm (dollars) [122] | Value of land and buildings — Average per acre [123] | Value of machinery and equipment, average per farm (dollars) [124] | Value of products sold — Total (mil dol) [125] | Value of products sold — Average per farm (dollars) [126] | Percent from: Crops [127] | Percent from: Livestock and poultry products [128] | Percent of farms with sales of: $10,000 or more [129] | Percent of farms with sales of: $100,000 or more [130] | Government payments — Total ($1,000) [131] | Government payments — Percent of farms [132] |
|---|---|---|---|---|---|---|---|---|---|---|---|---|---|---|---|---|
| **TEXAS—Cont'd** | | | | | | | | | | | | | | | | |
| Mason | 536 | -3.6 | 829 | 4.2 | 57.1 | 1 518 909 | 1 832 | 50 104 | 48.0 | 74 256 | 3.8 | 96.2 | 44.8 | 7.0 | 720 | 22.7 |
| Matagorda | 578 | -6.6 | 640 | 35.8 | 234.7 | 882 948 | 1 380 | 105 674 | 106.8 | 118 224 | 57.0 | 43.0 | 46.7 | 17.4 | 5 890 | 30.6 |
| Maverick | 474 | -0.4 | 1 518 | 13.0 | 30.8 | 1 371 322 | 903 | 45 793 | 26.1 | 83 629 | 7.4 | 92.6 | 23.7 | 5.1 | 392 | 5.8 |
| Medina | 748 | -7.1 | 350 | 41.2 | 173.5 | 689 884 | 1 972 | 52 028 | 80.9 | 37 798 | 53.5 | 46.5 | 22.3 | 4.0 | 2 526 | 15.3 |
| Menard | 491 | -10.6 | 1 380 | 2.1 | 22.7 | 1 502 957 | 1 089 | 50 239 | 7.9 | 22 275 | 7.7 | 92.3 | 36.8 | 6.2 | 592 | 28.1 |
| Midland | 457 | 26.2 | 760 | 8.3 | 90.0 | 660 020 | 869 | 59 919 | 15.4 | 25 621 | 77.7 | 22.3 | 18.5 | 5.5 | 2 750 | 29.8 |
| Milam | 539 | -6.6 | 263 | 2.8 | 205.1 | 504 079 | 1 914 | 61 152 | 105.3 | 51 509 | 27.5 | 72.5 | 35.0 | 6.9 | 2 675 | 15.6 |
| Mills | 474 | 11.0 | 515 | 4.9 | 74.6 | 867 829 | 1 685 | 53 750 | 37.6 | 40 873 | 14.1 | 85.9 | 37.5 | 4.8 | 349 | 16.7 |
| Mitchell | 575 | 17.8 | 1 108 | 4.1 | 163.8 | 910 923 | 822 | 77 643 | 27.3 | 52 571 | 63.8 | 36.2 | 23.5 | 10.0 | 5 546 | 73.6 |
| Montague | 508 | 0.8 | 329 | 0.6 | 120.1 | 676 962 | 2 060 | 51 734 | 36.6 | 23 716 | 19.5 | 80.5 | 31.5 | 4.1 | 599 | 13.2 |
| Montgomery | 170 | -14.1 | 90 | 2.3 | 33.8 | 341 332 | 3 789 | 45 703 | 42.6 | 22 607 | 58.9 | 41.1 | 15.5 | 1.5 | 47 | 1.0 |
| Moore | 553 | 0.5 | 1 955 | 105.1 | 297.7 | 1 677 878 | 858 | 230 886 | 463.2 | 1 636 750 | 17.0 | 83.0 | 63.6 | 47.3 | 5 402 | 66.1 |
| Morris | 86 | -14.0 | 187 | 0.1 | 19.8 | 424 709 | 2 266 | 52 656 | 38.6 | 84 570 | 3.1 | 96.9 | 32.2 | 8.5 | 148 | 8.1 |
| Motley | 575 | 18.1 | 2 510 | 3.3 | 105.3 | 1 493 116 | 595 | 73 206 | 16.4 | 71 724 | 44.1 | 55.9 | 48.9 | 17.9 | 3 172 | 75.1 |
| Nacogdoches | 265 | -3.3 | 208 | 0.5 | 59.4 | 502 706 | 2 421 | 65 918 | 317.3 | 248 463 | 1.7 | 98.3 | 40.3 | 15.3 | 135 | 2.7 |
| Navarro | 587 | 9.3 | 282 | 1.1 | 164.2 | 455 317 | 1 612 | 58 640 | 52.4 | 25 220 | 41.6 | 58.4 | 27.9 | 3.8 | 2 578 | 18.7 |
| Newton | 59 | -14.5 | 147 | 0.1 | 8.1 | 275 975 | 1 878 | 55 735 | 2.1 | 5 200 | 29.5 | 70.5 | 12.7 | 0.7 | 150 | 6.2 |
| Nolan | 540 | 12.3 | 931 | 5.2 | 132.6 | 956 626 | 1 027 | 71 333 | 37.1 | 64 008 | 56.0 | 44.0 | 23.6 | 8.1 | 5 288 | 54.7 |
| Nueces | 509 | -2.9 | 715 | 4.3 | 369.4 | 922 672 | 1 290 | 118 802 | 110.9 | 155 766 | 97.4 | 2.6 | 35.3 | 18.7 | 9 869 | 37.5 |
| Ochiltree | 579 | 3.6 | 1 517 | 66.1 | 355.4 | 1 232 313 | 812 | 209 240 | 395.1 | 1 034 196 | D | D | 65.7 | 39.3 | 5 450 | 75.7 |
| Oldham | 880 | -6.0 | 5 870 | 2.3 | 105.3 | 1 915 816 | 326 | 119 270 | 119.4 | 795 699 | 7.1 | 92.9 | 62.7 | 42.0 | 2 206 | 85.3 |
| Orange | 64 | -12.3 | 94 | 0.6 | 15.2 | 239 279 | 2 534 | 39 998 | D | D | D | 0.0 | 12.3 | 1.2 | 460 | 4.1 |
| Palo Pinto | 551 | 13.6 | 462 | 0.6 | 84.9 | 895 335 | 1 938 | 47 812 | 23.5 | 19 669 | 16.0 | 84.0 | 22.9 | 3.8 | 209 | 6.4 |
| Panola | 218 | -2.2 | 209 | 0.4 | 50.7 | 415 045 | 1 986 | 58 408 | 63.4 | 60 886 | 4.3 | 95.7 | 29.8 | 6.0 | 202 | 4.1 |
| Parker | 442 | -9.2 | 120 | 1.5 | 103.8 | 438 074 | 3 648 | 44 533 | 60.0 | 16 327 | 24.7 | 75.3 | 17.8 | 2.0 | 232 | 3.1 |
| Parmer | 561 | -2.6 | 1 010 | 175.0 | 437.2 | 1 029 842 | 1 019 | 237 005 | 937.7 | 1 689 485 | 13.3 | 86.7 | 65.8 | 49.7 | 12 236 | 76.9 |
| Pecos | 2 908 | -0.3 | 10 132 | 17.3 | 101.4 | 2 747 518 | 271 | 114 819 | 27.5 | 95 974 | 42.7 | 57.3 | 40.1 | 16.0 | 1 543 | 25.4 |
| Polk | 132 | 1.5 | 162 | 1.4 | 23.7 | 372 410 | 2 297 | 53 217 | 9.9 | 12 236 | 39.5 | 60.5 | 22.0 | 1.7 | 162 | 2.7 |
| Potter | 573 | 9.8 | 2 054 | 7.0 | 74.4 | 1 359 920 | 662 | 56 973 | 29.9 | 107 002 | 17.5 | 82.5 | 31.9 | 12.5 | 1 191 | 27.6 |
| Presidio | 1 560 | 3.7 | 10 539 | 2.0 | 28.1 | 4 379 252 | 416 | 75 093 | D | D | D | D | 39.2 | 14.9 | 389 | 13.5 |
| Rains | 98 | 4.3 | 149 | 0.6 | 32.7 | 359 804 | 2 422 | 41 527 | 13.9 | 21 180 | 33.5 | 66.5 | 27.7 | 4.3 | 121 | 5.6 |
| Randall | 575 | 12.3 | 648 | 19.8 | 270.1 | 742 860 | 1 146 | 71 915 | 393.4 | 443 484 | 6.1 | 93.9 | 31.9 | 12.6 | 6 386 | 45.7 |
| Reagan | 684 | 27.1 | 4 991 | 8.5 | 57.9 | 2 507 427 | 502 | 188 481 | 16.5 | 120 227 | 75.2 | 24.8 | 54.7 | 28.5 | 1 940 | 54.0 |
| Real | 372 | -7.0 | 1 237 | 0.5 | 26.1 | 1 336 437 | 1 080 | 43 939 | 2.8 | 9 149 | 14.0 | 86.0 | 13.3 | 2.3 | 110 | 5.6 |
| Red River | 450 | 6.4 | 373 | 2.8 | 104.5 | 495 457 | 1 329 | 53 657 | 35.9 | 29 743 | 20.6 | 79.4 | 34.7 | 5.7 | 1 816 | 18.5 |
| Reeves | 1 040 | 3.0 | 4 707 | 8.0 | 136.7 | 1 482 120 | 315 | 58 257 | 17.2 | 77 733 | 24.9 | 75.1 | 28.5 | 10.4 | 2 835 | 54.3 |
| Refugio | 491 | -3.0 | 1 663 | D | 94.3 | 1 217 943 | 732 | 81 772 | 29.4 | 99 582 | 68.2 | 31.8 | 39.3 | 16.6 | 2 739 | 28.1 |
| Roberts | 485 | -2.0 | 4 493 | 8.5 | 61.4 | 3 024 216 | 673 | 123 863 | 16.7 | 154 816 | 40.3 | 59.7 | 55.6 | 31.5 | 1 271 | 57.4 |
| Robertson | 455 | -11.7 | 291 | 21.5 | 117.4 | 587 284 | 2 015 | 65 850 | 116.0 | 74 295 | 16.2 | 83.8 | 36.6 | 6.2 | 2 137 | 10.2 |
| Rockwall | 37 | -19.6 | 108 | 0.1 | 14.5 | 486 897 | 4 513 | 49 077 | 3.9 | 11 129 | 47.6 | 52.4 | 15.9 | 1.2 | 97 | 5.2 |
| Runnels | 656 | 12.1 | 689 | 3.5 | 264.8 | 775 878 | 1 127 | 82 243 | 53.8 | 56 495 | 57.2 | 42.8 | 39.9 | 12.1 | 5 788 | 65.4 |
| Rusk | 301 | 10.7 | 198 | 0.8 | 67.3 | 405 054 | 2 047 | 56 959 | 56.1 | 36 897 | 31.1 | 68.9 | 26.8 | 3.1 | 94 | 1.8 |
| Sabine | 32 | 3.2 | 142 | 0.0 | 7.8 | 364 379 | 2 561 | 50 738 | 8.5 | 37 918 | 3.5 | 96.5 | 21.1 | 2.2 | 97 | 3.6 |
| San Augustine | 73 | 23.7 | 210 | 0.1 | 12.8 | 417 017 | 1 986 | 63 482 | 55.6 | 160 807 | 2.5 | 97.5 | 37.3 | 10.1 | 191 | 6.4 |
| San Jacinto | 95 | 2.2 | 139 | 0.9 | 21.0 | 364 629 | 2 627 | 47 812 | 6.9 | 10 002 | 33.9 | 66.1 | 17.9 | 1.2 | 73 | 2.3 |
| San Patricio | 370 | 7.2 | 567 | 14.2 | 258.7 | 702 535 | 1 239 | 126 104 | 109.2 | 167 486 | 82.1 | 17.9 | 35.3 | 20.6 | 8 744 | 35.4 |
| San Saba | 718 | 1.3 | 399 | 3.8 | 80.2 | 1 609 135 | 1 625 | 68 399 | 28.6 | 39 422 | 23.6 | 76.4 | 45.2 | 9.5 | 523 | 16.8 |
| Schleicher | 801 | 3.0 | 2 411 | 0.6 | 49.9 | 2 180 436 | 904 | 68 855 | 13.6 | 40 982 | 24.0 | 76.0 | 46.7 | 10.5 | 1 719 | 40.7 |
| Scurry | 520 | -8.0 | 763 | 2.9 | 214.3 | 684 653 | 897 | 75 845 | 43.4 | 63 780 | 65.0 | 35.0 | 28.3 | 11.0 | 6 440 | 67.1 |
| Shackelford | 552 | -0.9 | 2 175 | D | 71.5 | 1 823 967 | 839 | 66 055 | 16.1 | 63 327 | 12.9 | 87.1 | 45.3 | 15.4 | 1 049 | 44.1 |
| Shelby | 198 | 3.1 | 176 | 0.6 | 45.5 | 494 931 | 2 810 | 77 590 | 403.1 | 358 963 | 1.0 | 99.0 | 47.6 | 23.1 | 163 | 2.7 |
| Sherman | 584 | 7.0 | 1 614 | 157.6 | 392.7 | 1 313 201 | 814 | 231 515 | 448.9 | 1 239 944 | 23.2 | 76.8 | 50.0 | 39.0 | 8 146 | 82.9 |
| Smith | 302 | 5.2 | 120 | 2.7 | 91.8 | 377 217 | 3 136 | 53 392 | 68.0 | 27 049 | 62.5 | 37.5 | 23.3 | 2.8 | 68 | 1.7 |
| Somervell | 83 | -1.2 | 226 | 0.5 | 20.0 | 715 789 | 3 171 | 46 090 | D | D | 0.0 | D | 19.9 | 1.4 | 57 | 7.1 |
| Starr | 653 | 14.6 | 591 | 6.5 | 173.2 | 731 696 | 1 237 | 45 665 | 64.4 | 58 290 | 19.5 | 80.5 | 20.2 | 4.1 | 2 409 | 19.5 |
| Stephens | 429 | 0.2 | 881 | 0.2 | 67.1 | 1 086 812 | 1 233 | 49 688 | 12.4 | 25 468 | 8.3 | 91.7 | 33.7 | 3.1 | 374 | 25.3 |
| Sterling | 578 | -8.7 | 7 815 | 0.3 | 9.5 | 2 869 436 | 367 | 91 979 | D | D | D | D | 51.4 | 23.0 | 549 | 37.8 |
| Stonewall | 486 | -7.3 | 1 292 | 2.4 | 101.7 | 864 088 | 669 | 47 892 | 13.7 | 36 546 | 29.4 | 70.6 | 36.2 | 9.6 | 2 550 | 26.1 |
| Sutton | 895 | 1.7 | 3 823 | 0.9 | 21.6 | 3 044 106 | 796 | 75 347 | 9.6 | 41 082 | 3.5 | 96.5 | 47.4 | 15.0 | 641 | 26.1 |
| Swisher | 563 | -0.5 | 1 068 | 83.8 | 380.1 | 775 406 | 726 | 142 939 | 453.7 | 860 821 | 14.6 | 85.4 | 46.7 | 28.8 | 10 979 | 80.6 |
| Tarrant | 154 | -11.0 | 124 | 1.4 | 46.1 | 448 616 | 3 627 | 43 657 | 61.4 | 49 173 | 87.4 | 12.6 | 16.9 | 3.5 | 145 | 4.2 |
| Taylor | 579 | 8.4 | 449 | 5.1 | 204.3 | 554 558 | 1 236 | 52 849 | 50.6 | 39 178 | 31.0 | 69.0 | 20.4 | 4.4 | 4 438 | 44.0 |
| Terrell | 1 302 | -7.9 | 12 170 | D | 15.1 | 2 734 256 | 225 | 62 635 | 4.0 | 37 669 | D | D | 30.8 | 7.5 | 313 | 16.8 |
| Terry | 497 | 11.7 | 796 | 142.0 | 419.3 | 704 407 | 885 | 198 671 | 124.8 | 199 992 | 90.1 | 9.9 | 49.4 | 33.7 | 17 287 | 83.2 |
| Throckmorton | 574 | 2.3 | 2 174 | 1.4 | 94.5 | 1 894 914 | 872 | 71 772 | 21.9 | 82 946 | 21.7 | 78.2 | 50.4 | 11.7 | 1 383 | 48.9 |
| Titus | 166 | -6.7 | 205 | 0.5 | 42.1 | 421 723 | 2 053 | 50 812 | 79.5 | 98 170 | 4.0 | 96.0 | 34.1 | 5.8 | 140 | 8.8 |

# Table B. States and Counties — **Water Use, Wholesale Trade, Retail Trade, and Real Estate**

| STATE<br>County | Water use, 2005 | | Wholesale trade,[1] 2007 | | | | Retail trade,[2] 2007 | | | | Real estate and rental and leasing,[2] 2007 | | | |
|---|---|---|---|---|---|---|---|---|---|---|---|---|---|---|
| | Total water withdrawn (mil gal/day) | Gallons withdrawn per person | Number of establishments | Number of employees | Sales (mil dol) | Annual payroll (mil dol) | Number of establishments | Number of employees | Sales (mil dol) | Annual payroll (mil dol) | Number of establishments | Number of employees | Receipts (mil dol) | Annual payroll (mil dol) |
| | 133 | 134 | 135 | 136 | 137 | 138 | 139 | 140 | 141 | 142 | 143 | 144 | 145 | 146 |
| **TEXAS—Cont'd** | | | | | | | | | | | | | | |
| Mason | 10.2 | 2 621 | 9 | 65 | 41.3 | 1.6 | 27 | 137 | 29.0 | 2.1 | 5 | 6 | 2.7 | 0.2 |
| Matagorda | 223.0 | 5 892 | 31 | D | D | D | 157 | 1 428 | 313.9 | 26.8 | 36 | 286 | 30.2 | 10.8 |
| Maverick | 52.0 | 1 017 | 32 | D | D | D | 184 | 2 327 | 504.8 | 41.7 | 34 | 84 | 15.1 | 1.9 |
| Medina | 55.1 | 1 280 | 19 | 170 | 189.9 | 5.1 | 110 | 1 179 | 360.1 | 25.6 | 28 | 66 | 6.6 | 1.0 |
| Menard | 1.9 | 845 | 4 | 40 | 6.7 | 0.6 | 11 | 56 | 16.3 | 0.8 | 1 | D | D | D |
| Midland | 31.1 | 256 | 259 | 3 334 | 2 411.7 | 162.2 | 551 | 7 744 | 2 276.7 | 183.9 | 227 | 1 418 | 270.7 | 56.8 |
| Milam | 55.6 | 2 192 | 25 | 171 | 87.3 | 6.6 | 72 | 705 | 181.4 | 14.3 | 16 | 66 | 9.3 | 2.1 |
| Mills | 2.7 | 517 | 5 | D | D | D | 29 | 235 | 70.4 | 4.7 | 2 | D | D | D |
| Mitchell | 11.9 | 1 266 | 4 | 14 | 3.4 | 0.4 | 31 | 266 | 55.8 | 4.6 | 2 | D | D | D |
| Montague | 8.3 | 421 | 26 | 91 | 38.6 | 3.5 | 73 | 782 | 213.7 | 15.9 | 14 | 32 | 2.9 | 0.4 |
| Montgomery | 67.9 | 180 | 426 | 4 234 | 6 399.3 | 198.6 | 1 263 | 19 489 | 5 260.1 | 433.1 | 390 | 2 045 | 340.9 | 63.9 |
| Moore | 276.2 | 13 573 | 22 | D | D | D | 72 | 889 | 217.9 | 17.5 | 13 | 49 | 5.9 | 0.9 |
| Morris | 50.9 | 3 936 | 11 | 332 | 138.9 | 13.6 | 41 | 339 | 70.3 | 5.8 | 7 | 22 | 2.9 | 0.5 |
| Motley | 9.7 | 7 452 | 3 | D | D | D | 6 | 28 | 5.2 | 0.5 | NA | NA | NA | NA |
| Nacogdoches | 24.6 | 407 | 44 | D | D | D | 244 | 2 819 | 691.2 | 61.4 | 44 | 142 | 19.4 | 3.2 |
| Navarro | 7.9 | 161 | 26 | 415 | 285.7 | 13.8 | 184 | 2 168 | 471.8 | 41.1 | 45 | 139 | 19.8 | 3.3 |
| Newton | 3.9 | 274 | 6 | 46 | 10.0 | 1.1 | 23 | 174 | 50.9 | 2.5 | 2 | D | D | D |
| Nolan | 7.0 | 468 | 17 | D | D | D | 64 | 804 | 179.7 | 13.7 | 10 | 34 | 4.7 | 0.6 |
| Nueces | 349.5 | 1 093 | 399 | 4 448 | 2 978.5 | 207.0 | 1 174 | 16 877 | 4 314.5 | 365.5 | 432 | 2 613 | 415.5 | 79.1 |
| Ochiltree | 69.8 | 7 440 | 27 | 295 | 139.2 | 14.9 | 49 | 442 | 97.4 | 7.5 | 14 | 105 | 28.6 | 5.2 |
| Oldham | 6.2 | 2 946 | 1 | D | D | D | 9 | 50 | 16.8 | 0.9 | NA | NA | NA | NA |
| Orange | 1 181.8 | 13 906 | 39 | 235 | 114.4 | 12.1 | 270 | 3 207 | 852.0 | 62.9 | 58 | 179 | 36.3 | 4.4 |
| Palo Pinto | 118.1 | 4 298 | 18 | D | D | D | 124 | 1 135 | 272.7 | 23.0 | 29 | 102 | 14.0 | 2.4 |
| Panola | 12.6 | 547 | 22 | 152 | 80.0 | 4.0 | 89 | 825 | 222.0 | 15.3 | 27 | 122 | 21.3 | 3.0 |
| Parker | 10.9 | 106 | 95 | 692 | 524.2 | 25.3 | 309 | 4 566 | 1 517.8 | 113.9 | 95 | 312 | 55.9 | 8.3 |
| Parmer | 424.7 | 43 542 | 30 | 181 | 224.9 | 5.3 | 29 | 167 | 39.5 | 3.0 | 6 | D | D | D |
| Pecos | 60.1 | 3 789 | 9 | 108 | 117.0 | 4.2 | 68 | 702 | 154.0 | 11.8 | 9 | 24 | 3.8 | 0.6 |
| Polk | 18.9 | 405 | 22 | 101 | 51.1 | 3.7 | 120 | 1 721 | 445.4 | 37.0 | 32 | 100 | 9.2 | 2.3 |
| Potter | 14.6 | 122 | 179 | 2 786 | 2 064.1 | 117.3 | 579 | 8 653 | 2 490.0 | 183.4 | 159 | D | D | D |
| Presidio | 8.0 | 1 040 | 3 | 9 | 3.2 | 0.2 | 34 | 229 | 42.5 | 3.1 | 3 | D | D | D |
| Rains | 3.2 | 287 | 4 | D | D | D | 33 | 289 | 93.9 | 6.5 | 5 | 88 | 1.7 | 0.6 |
| Randall | 53.7 | 488 | 76 | D | D | D | 346 | 5 080 | 1 465.5 | 122.4 | 133 | D | D | D |
| Reagan | 16.6 | 5 549 | 3 | 25 | 4.4 | 1.0 | 18 | 98 | 23.7 | 1.8 | 1 | D | D | D |
| Real | 0.8 | 247 | 4 | D | D | D | 15 | 38 | 9.4 | 0.7 | 4 | 10 | 1.0 | 0.1 |
| Red River | 8.6 | 636 | 7 | 32 | 15.1 | 0.9 | 43 | 297 | 61.2 | 5.3 | 8 | 10 | 2.3 | 0.2 |
| Reeves | 83.8 | 7 201 | 8 | D | D | D | 34 | 446 | 113.2 | 7.8 | 6 | 17 | 1.4 | 0.3 |
| Refugio | 11.6 | 1 515 | 5 | 32 | 18.0 | 1.3 | 24 | 231 | 62.0 | 3.8 | 9 | 51 | 5.6 | 1.4 |
| Roberts | 13.6 | 16 610 | NA | NA | NA | NA | 2 | D | D | D | NA | NA | NA | NA |
| Robertson | 35.0 | 2 163 | 2 | D | D | D | 53 | 420 | 115.2 | 7.8 | 10 | 32 | 9.7 | 1.6 |
| Rockwall | 1.9 | 29 | 63 | D | D | D | 222 | 3 272 | 946.3 | 73.8 | 61 | 218 | 38.9 | 6.6 |
| Runnels | 5.3 | 483 | 8 | 41 | 24.6 | 1.2 | 51 | 480 | 128.4 | 11.5 | 3 | D | D | D |
| Rusk | 2 248.1 | 46 863 | 21 | 205 | 99.8 | 7.8 | 141 | 1 423 | 354.3 | 28.4 | 24 | 81 | 10.1 | 1.8 |
| Sabine | 3.5 | 334 | NA | NA | NA | NA | 35 | 237 | 51.9 | 4.0 | 4 | D | D | D |
| San Augustine | 3.2 | 354 | 5 | 36 | 6.4 | 0.9 | 28 | 247 | 70.1 | 4.1 | 3 | D | D | D |
| San Jacinto | 5.4 | 216 | 3 | D | D | D | 31 | 230 | 54.7 | 4.4 | 8 | 29 | 5.1 | 0.5 |
| San Patricio | 35.8 | 517 | 32 | 232 | 135.2 | 8.8 | 180 | 2 265 | 621.6 | 51.6 | 72 | 247 | 31.5 | 4.8 |
| San Saba | 11.5 | 1 896 | 12 | 96 | 18.1 | 2.9 | 38 | 232 | 60.5 | 4.3 | 4 | D | D | D |
| Schleicher | 1.9 | 682 | 6 | 30 | 13.1 | 0.9 | 10 | 71 | 10.4 | 1.0 | NA | NA | NA | NA |
| Scurry | 34.4 | 2 118 | 28 | D | D | D | 59 | 674 | 199.6 | 13.7 | 21 | 139 | 19.4 | 4.2 |
| Shackelford | 2.0 | 628 | 5 | 16 | 4.1 | 0.3 | 18 | 103 | 14.8 | 1.5 | 3 | 14 | 0.5 | 0.2 |
| Shelby | 12.2 | 462 | 12 | 81 | 97.6 | 4.8 | 95 | 1 106 | 246.5 | 21.2 | 13 | 38 | 4.0 | 0.6 |
| Sherman | 352.1 | 117 288 | 8 | D | D | D | 10 | 49 | 10.1 | 0.8 | NA | NA | NA | NA |
| Smith | 45.5 | 239 | 242 | 2 216 | 922.1 | 97.5 | 855 | 12 347 | 3 110.1 | 287.8 | 229 | 1 447 | 204.5 | 41.3 |
| Somervell | 63.2 | 8 333 | 7 | 32 | 14.8 | 1.3 | 37 | 259 | 55.2 | 4.7 | 8 | D | D | D |
| Starr | 17.2 | 282 | 14 | D | D | D | 134 | 1 878 | 445.3 | 31.2 | 10 | 32 | 3.2 | 0.7 |
| Stephens | 30.2 | 3 154 | 9 | 28 | 21.4 | 0.9 | 36 | 369 | 78.8 | 7.9 | 6 | 26 | 3.5 | 0.5 |
| Sterling | 1.8 | 1 389 | 2 | D | D | D | 5 | D | D | D | NA | NA | NA | NA |
| Stonewall | 3.3 | 2 434 | 2 | D | D | D | 10 | 42 | 8.6 | 0.6 | 2 | D | D | D |
| Sutton | 2.1 | 491 | 6 | 53 | 29.3 | 3.3 | 25 | 147 | 41.9 | 2.6 | 6 | 47 | 7.1 | 1.5 |
| Swisher | 154.1 | 19 686 | 14 | 130 | 42.4 | 3.1 | 22 | 164 | 35.2 | 2.6 | 6 | D | D | D |
| Tarrant | 522.3 | 322 | 1 932 | 32 231 | 25 801.5 | 1 571.5 | 5 539 | 89 503 | 24 931.4 | 2 192.6 | 1 827 | 11 203 | 2 770.6 | 432.7 |
| Taylor | 25.0 | 200 | 135 | 1 540 | 1 079.7 | 58.0 | 579 | 8 333 | 2 063.3 | 181.8 | 160 | 637 | 133.6 | 19.4 |
| Terrell | 1.1 | 1 054 | 1 | D | D | D | 4 | 12 | 3.9 | 0.3 | NA | NA | NA | NA |
| Terry | 108.5 | 8 736 | 18 | 187 | 87.3 | 7.7 | 42 | 478 | 133.7 | 9.3 | 12 | 73 | 7.6 | 3.1 |
| Throckmorton | 2.2 | 1 384 | 4 | 11 | 3.4 | 0.4 | 6 | 22 | 6.8 | 0.4 | NA | NA | NA | NA |
| Titus | 1 427.7 | 48 488 | 29 | D | D | D | 148 | 1 782 | 425.1 | 39.1 | 29 | 84 | 11.6 | 1.8 |

1. Merchant wholesalers, except manufacturers' sales branches and offices.　　2. Employer establishments.

— **Professional Services, Manufacturing, and Accommodation and Food Services**

| STATE County | Professional, scientific, and technical services,[1] 2007 | | | | Manufacturing, 2007 | | | | Accommodation and food services, 2007 | | | |
|---|---|---|---|---|---|---|---|---|---|---|---|---|
| | Number of establishments | Number of employees | Receipts (mil dol) | Annual payroll (mil dol) | Number of establishments | Number of employees | Receipts (mil dol) | Annual payroll (mil dol) | Number of establishments | Number of employees | Sales (mil dol) | Annual payroll (mil dol) |
| | 147 | 148 | 149 | 150 | 151 | 152 | 153 | 154 | 155 | 156 | 157 | 158 |
| **TEXAS—Cont'd** | | | | | | | | | | | | |
| Mason | 12 | 43 | 3.2 | 0.9 | NA | NA | NA | NA | 11 | 147 | 3.7 | 1.4 |
| Matagorda | 51 | 177 | 15.6 | 4.8 | 27 | 604 | D | 43.6 | 77 | 1 023 | 38.8 | 10.0 |
| Maverick | 39 | D | D | D | NA | NA | NA | NA | 64 | 1 126 | 48.5 | 11.3 |
| Medina | 58 | 320 | 20.0 | 7.3 | 30 | 554 | 75.3 | 12.2 | 73 | 771 | 29.8 | 8.4 |
| Menard | 3 | 4 | 0.6 | 0.1 | NA | NA | NA | NA | 5 | D | D | D |
| Midland | 436 | D | D | D | 140 | 2 366 | 533.8 | 95.2 | 254 | 5 324 | 259.2 | 69.3 |
| Milam | 32 | 200 | 14.8 | 6.8 | 15 | 1 521 | D | D | 38 | 481 | 17.7 | 4.4 |
| Mills | 8 | 20 | 2.1 | 0.4 | NA | NA | NA | NA | 10 | 64 | 2.1 | 0.6 |
| Mitchell | 7 | 25 | 4.3 | 0.7 | NA | NA | NA | NA | 13 | 140 | 3.7 | 0.9 |
| Montague | 44 | 131 | 12.5 | 4.0 | NA | NA | NA | NA | 24 | 323 | 10.9 | 3.0 |
| Montgomery | 1 101 | D | D | D | 373 | 11 265 | 3 667.0 | 522.7 | 621 | 14 471 | 728.6 | 196.7 |
| Moore | 24 | 90 | 10.1 | 3.3 | 17 | D | D | D | 43 | 548 | 23.0 | 5.1 |
| Morris | 11 | 95 | 9.3 | 3.9 | 18 | 2 675 | 1 140.4 | 125.1 | 21 | 229 | 8.8 | 2.2 |
| Motley | NA | NA | NA | NA | NA | NA | NA | NA | 3 | 9 | 0.3 | 0.0 |
| Nacogdoches | 92 | D | D | D | 64 | 4 034 | 1 418.9 | 126.1 | 108 | 2 253 | 87.8 | 23.2 |
| Navarro | 60 | 370 | 19.1 | 7.0 | 57 | 3 149 | 758.5 | 103.4 | 64 | 932 | 42.7 | 11.2 |
| Newton | 4 | 7 | 1.4 | 0.4 | NA | NA | NA | NA | 6 | 40 | 1.9 | 0.4 |
| Nolan | 27 | 97 | 10.6 | 3.0 | 13 | 866 | 224.9 | 35.0 | 39 | 537 | 16.8 | 4.3 |
| Nueces | 785 | D | D | D | 215 | 8 284 | D | 508.2 | 811 | 15 167 | 662.0 | 186.1 |
| Ochiltree | 21 | 169 | 18.6 | 9.2 | NA | NA | NA | NA | 19 | 217 | 9.2 | 2.1 |
| Oldham | 2 | D | D | D | NA | NA | NA | NA | 11 | 39 | 2.9 | 0.8 |
| Orange | 89 | D | D | D | 85 | 5 308 | D | 339.7 | 128 | 2 060 | 85.3 | 21.6 |
| Palo Pinto | 44 | 178 | 16.7 | 4.6 | 36 | 1 283 | 307.2 | 44.0 | 70 | 891 | 44.9 | 11.5 |
| Panola | 39 | 211 | 21.2 | 5.9 | 19 | 947 | 264.0 | 29.0 | 31 | 461 | 18.3 | 4.8 |
| Parker | 173 | D | D | D | 135 | 2 814 | 550.4 | 104.1 | 156 | 2 502 | 110.4 | 29.7 |
| Parmer | 14 | 37 | 3.1 | 0.7 | 4 | D | D | D | 9 | 56 | 1.8 | 0.4 |
| Pecos | 17 | 123 | 3.7 | 4.6 | NA | NA | NA | NA | 34 | 529 | 24.3 | 5.3 |
| Polk | 56 | 268 | 30.2 | 8.2 | 23 | D | 98.5 | 17.2 | 54 | 833 | 33.4 | 8.1 |
| Potter | 291 | D | D | D | 134 | D | D | D | 338 | 6 829 | 326.0 | 85.8 |
| Presidio | 4 | 10 | 0.7 | 0.2 | NA | NA | NA | NA | 27 | 153 | 5.0 | 1.3 |
| Rains | 8 | 180 | 4.5 | 2.3 | NA | NA | NA | NA | 15 | 163 | 6.2 | 1.7 |
| Randall | 187 | D | D | D | 73 | D | D | D | 171 | 3 442 | 131.9 | 35.3 |
| Reagan | 6 | 7 | 0.6 | 0.1 | NA | NA | NA | NA | 8 | 58 | 2.2 | 0.4 |
| Real | 7 | 21 | 2.0 | 0.7 | NA | NA | NA | NA | 13 | 41 | 3.7 | 0.7 |
| Red River | 7 | 20 | 2.2 | 0.7 | 16 | 634 | 101.8 | 18.3 | 14 | D | D | D |
| Reeves | 15 | D | D | D | NA | NA | NA | NA | 26 | 297 | 12.4 | 3.4 |
| Refugio | 7 | 11 | 1.2 | 0.3 | NA | NA | NA | NA | 16 | D | D | D |
| Roberts | 2 | D | D | D | NA | NA | NA | NA | 2 | D | D | D |
| Robertson | 11 | D | D | D | NA | NA | NA | NA | 23 | 303 | 15.2 | 3.4 |
| Rockwall | 185 | D | D | D | 68 | D | 301.3 | D | 124 | 2 500 | 105.9 | 30.4 |
| Runnels | 12 | 72 | 10.6 | 3.4 | 17 | 959 | 207.0 | 35.9 | 21 | 168 | 5.6 | 1.4 |
| Rusk | 58 | D | D | D | 35 | 1 484 | D | 46.9 | 55 | 666 | 29.7 | 7.8 |
| Sabine | 8 | 20 | 1.7 | 0.4 | NA | NA | NA | NA | 12 | 89 | 3.3 | 0.8 |
| San Augustine | 10 | 23 | 1.6 | 0.5 | NA | NA | NA | NA | 6 | 41 | 1.4 | 0.3 |
| San Jacinto | 17 | D | D | D | NA | NA | NA | NA | 9 | 115 | 4.0 | 1.4 |
| San Patricio | 83 | D | D | D | 33 | 1 586 | D | D | 135 | 2 042 | 77.6 | 19.2 |
| San Saba | 15 | 33 | 2.4 | 0.6 | NA | NA | NA | NA | 17 | 94 | 4.1 | 0.9 |
| Schleicher | 3 | 8 | 0.8 | 0.1 | NA | NA | NA | NA | 3 | 21 | 0.3 | 0.1 |
| Scurry | 25 | 137 | 13.6 | 4.9 | NA | NA | NA | NA | 47 | 517 | 20.6 | 5.9 |
| Shackelford | 6 | 10 | 1.5 | 0.3 | NA | NA | NA | NA | 7 | 61 | 1.9 | 0.6 |
| Shelby | 29 | 102 | 15.8 | 2.9 | 25 | 2 242 | 552.0 | 69.2 | 24 | 304 | 14.9 | 3.4 |
| Sherman | 2 | D | D | D | NA | NA | NA | NA | 3 | D | D | D |
| Smith | 548 | D | D | D | 224 | 10 737 | 5 423.5 | 474.5 | 339 | 7 563 | 337.3 | 93.6 |
| Somervell | 15 | 26 | 4.2 | 1.2 | NA | NA | NA | NA | 27 | 437 | 23.1 | 7.1 |
| Starr | 20 | 75 | 5.1 | 1.6 | NA | NA | NA | NA | 44 | 578 | 26.2 | 6.0 |
| Stephens | 22 | 101 | 20.7 | 3.0 | NA | NA | NA | NA | 20 | 193 | 6.2 | 1.8 |
| Sterling | 2 | D | D | D | NA | NA | NA | NA | 3 | D | D | D |
| Stonewall | 2 | D | D | D | NA | NA | NA | NA | 2 | D | D | D |
| Sutton | 10 | 24 | 2.1 | 0.6 | NA | NA | NA | NA | 18 | 229 | 9.7 | 2.5 |
| Swisher | 7 | 24 | 1.3 | 0.6 | NA | NA | NA | NA | 13 | 142 | 4.0 | 1.1 |
| Tarrant | 4 064 | D | D | D | 1 789 | 100 996 | 43 337.5 | 5 192.3 | 3 141 | 73 070 | 3 763.5 | 1 035.3 |
| Taylor | 276 | D | D | D | 99 | 2 341 | D | D | 286 | 6 524 | 246.2 | 69.0 |
| Terrell | 2 | D | D | D | NA | NA | NA | NA | 2 | D | D | D |
| Terry | 14 | 60 | 4.1 | 1.1 | NA | NA | NA | NA | 25 | 237 | 9.9 | 2.6 |
| Throckmorton | 2 | D | D | D | NA | NA | NA | NA | 4 | D | D | D |
| Titus | 33 | 135 | 11.8 | 3.8 | 41 | 5 696 | 1 291.5 | 164.4 | 56 | 1 030 | 40.7 | 11.6 |

1. Establishment subject to federal tax.

| STATE County | Health care and social assistance, 2007 | | | | Other services, 2007 | | | | Federal funds and grants, 2009–2010 Expenditures (mil dol) | | | |
|---|---|---|---|---|---|---|---|---|---|---|---|---|
| | | | | | | | | | | Direct payments for individuals[1] | | |
| | Number of establishments | Number of employees | Receipts (mil dol) | Annual payroll (mil dol) | Number of establishments | Number of employees | Receipts (mil dol) | Annual payroll (mil dol) | Total | Social Security and government retirement | Medicare | Food Stamps and Supplemental Security Income |
| | 159 | 160 | 161 | 162 | 163 | 164 | 165 | 166 | 167 | 168 | 169 | 170 |
| TEXAS—Cont'd | | | | | | | | | | | | |
| Mason | 10 | 119 | 5.4 | 2.7 | 9 | 24 | 1.2 | 0.2 | 36.5 | 16.4 | 9.3 | 1.1 |
| Matagorda | 65 | 1 248 | 111.1 | 37.0 | 69 | 331 | 35.5 | 12.4 | 255.8 | 103.2 | 58.3 | 18.4 |
| Maverick | 85 | D | D | D | 31 | 116 | 8.7 | 1.8 | 445.3 | 86.8 | 70.5 | 58.5 |
| Medina | 58 | 655 | 45.5 | 17.9 | 45 | 187 | 15.3 | 4.2 | 309.5 | 136.7 | 51.8 | 12.6 |
| Menard | 1 | D | D | D | 3 | D | D | D | 24.8 | 9.0 | 7.1 | 1.1 |
| Midland | 359 | 5 999 | 697.2 | 241.4 | 255 | 2 469 | 287.0 | 65.5 | 638.5 | 281.9 | 156.8 | 40.0 |
| Milam | 43 | 901 | 46.0 | 22.8 | 35 | 145 | 12.5 | 2.6 | 219.5 | 85.0 | 41.8 | 11.8 |
| Mills | 13 | 238 | 9.4 | 5.0 | 10 | D | D | D | 47.2 | 18.4 | 14.4 | 1.8 |
| Mitchell | 7 | D | D | D | 11 | 31 | 2.0 | 0.4 | 72.5 | 23.4 | 20.4 | 2.9 |
| Montague | 35 | 747 | 45.4 | 19.6 | 34 | 102 | 8.0 | 1.9 | 171.4 | 79.4 | 47.9 | 6.2 |
| Montgomery | 771 | 12 641 | 1 617.6 | 531.2 | 515 | 4 034 | 322.1 | 102.0 | 1 780.5 | 1 040.1 | 342.8 | 84.3 |
| Moore | 43 | 592 | 40.8 | 17.6 | 40 | 127 | 9.1 | 2.1 | 86.3 | 38.2 | 19.8 | 4.0 |
| Morris | 21 | D | D | D | 22 | 76 | 10.5 | 2.6 | 135.0 | 54.6 | 34.6 | 7.0 |
| Motley | 3 | D | D | D | 5 | D | D | D | 16.8 | 5.5 | 4.8 | 0.5 |
| Nacogdoches | 196 | 3 849 | 361.3 | 125.5 | 95 | 469 | 31.8 | 8.4 | 495.9 | 161.2 | 107.6 | 23.5 |
| Navarro | 87 | 1 687 | 111.9 | 46.7 | 60 | 220 | 18.5 | 4.3 | 415.3 | 145.5 | 82.7 | 22.2 |
| Newton | 10 | 301 | 11.6 | 5.7 | 5 | D | D | D | 117.0 | 40.0 | 28.2 | 8.5 |
| Nolan | 38 | 645 | 40.2 | 17.7 | 21 | 93 | 9.3 | 2.3 | 153.6 | 48.7 | 37.8 | 7.8 |
| Nueces | 1 014 | 24 413 | 2 103.8 | 808.8 | 571 | 4 159 | 454.4 | 120.5 | 3 257.7 | 939.8 | 518.2 | 195.1 |
| Ochiltree | 19 | 287 | 22.3 | 6.7 | 21 | 100 | 7.4 | 1.9 | 48.0 | 21.4 | 10.7 | 2.0 |
| Oldham | 2 | D | D | D | 3 | D | D | D | 18.9 | 8.9 | 3.6 | 0.2 |
| Orange | 142 | 1 666 | 146.0 | 54.4 | 95 | 755 | 115.9 | 20.8 | 636.6 | 276.6 | 186.3 | 38.0 |
| Palo Pinto | 52 | D | D | D | 40 | D | D | D | 202.3 | 85.9 | 55.6 | 12.7 |
| Panola | 47 | 710 | 52.6 | 17.5 | 32 | 164 | 17.7 | 3.3 | 182.0 | 67.7 | 47.0 | 8.0 |
| Parker | 171 | D | D | D | 137 | 773 | 59.9 | 15.7 | 518.5 | 310.9 | 93.1 | 15.3 |
| Parmer | 9 | 94 | 7.8 | 3.2 | 16 | 45 | 4.0 | 0.9 | 79.0 | 26.7 | 13.6 | 2.6 |
| Pecos | 17 | 464 | 35.1 | 13.7 | 25 | 171 | 9.2 | 2.4 | 85.6 | 28.0 | 18.0 | 7.7 |
| Polk | 59 | 1 013 | 81.4 | 29.3 | 55 | 338 | 21.9 | 5.7 | 515.5 | 297.0 | 113.0 | 21.9 |
| Potter | 469 | 12 106 | 1 391.8 | 482.7 | 258 | 1 942 | 218.0 | 44.0 | 4 241.0 | 515.7 | 229.2 | 65.4 |
| Presidio | 2 | D | D | D | 7 | D | D | D | 113.6 | 17.0 | 9.8 | 8.9 |
| Rains | 6 | 22 | 1.2 | 0.4 | 10 | D | D | D | 71.4 | 41.5 | 14.4 | 1.8 |
| Randall | 220 | 2 528 | 233.1 | 73.0 | 161 | 913 | 75.5 | 18.9 | 224.7 | 94.5 | 59.1 | 8.1 |
| Reagan | 4 | D | D | D | 6 | D | D | D | 18.6 | 7.5 | 3.9 | 0.8 |
| Real | 11 | 146 | 6.3 | 3.2 | 1 | D | D | D | 33.7 | 16.4 | 6.8 | 1.9 |
| Red River | 21 | 437 | 34.5 | 12.0 | 15 | 44 | 2.6 | 0.7 | 188.7 | 50.6 | 42.6 | 6.2 |
| Reeves | 15 | 271 | 21.0 | 8.4 | 12 | D | D | D | 106.6 | 26.3 | 22.6 | 8.5 |
| Refugio | 9 | 235 | 17.8 | 6.2 | 8 | 31 | 1.6 | 0.4 | 80.2 | 27.4 | 19.7 | 3.7 |
| Roberts | NA | NA | NA | NA | NA | NA | NA | NA | 5.7 | 2.1 | 1.7 | 0.0 |
| Robertson | 23 | 331 | 14.9 | 6.9 | 27 | 74 | 6.4 | 1.4 | 174.9 | 49.5 | 33.5 | 11.2 |
| Rockwall | 175 | 2 455 | 238.8 | 100.4 | 83 | 607 | 44.0 | 14.7 | 332.2 | 163.4 | 34.3 | 6.6 |
| Runnels | 18 | 327 | 17.7 | 7.2 | 14 | 31 | 2.7 | 0.7 | 113.0 | 38.0 | 28.0 | 4.8 |
| Rusk | 65 | 1 145 | 95.5 | 34.2 | 46 | 266 | 19.7 | 6.0 | 320.1 | 122.0 | 82.2 | 16.1 |
| Sabine | 13 | 171 | 11.8 | 5.1 | 13 | 40 | 2.8 | 0.9 | 144.3 | 66.2 | 38.7 | 5.3 |
| San Augustine | 19 | 472 | 21.1 | 9.1 | 9 | 23 | 1.3 | 0.3 | 103.9 | 33.9 | 25.3 | 4.2 |
| San Jacinto | 12 | 111 | 6.0 | 2.6 | 15 | 40 | 3.4 | 0.7 | 151.2 | 65.6 | 37.4 | 10.0 |
| San Patricio | 96 | 1 415 | 95.9 | 38.1 | 78 | 391 | 25.7 | 7.1 | 557.6 | 206.9 | 113.4 | 40.0 |
| San Saba | 13 | 227 | 8.9 | 4.6 | 9 | 30 | 2.2 | 0.5 | 76.3 | 19.6 | 17.4 | 2.4 |
| Schleicher | 4 | D | D | D | 5 | D | D | D | 22.5 | 8.4 | 5.7 | 1.0 |
| Scurry | 23 | 503 | 38.7 | 14.3 | 34 | 226 | 25.8 | 6.2 | 126.4 | 42.5 | 34.4 | 6.4 |
| Shackelford | 5 | 71 | 3.8 | 1.8 | 5 | D | D | D | 28.1 | 11.0 | 6.9 | 0.8 |
| Shelby | 36 | 637 | 39.4 | 16.5 | 31 | D | D | D | 264.5 | 77.6 | 65.5 | 12.4 |
| Sherman | 1 | D | D | D | 4 | D | D | D | 26.8 | 9.1 | 4.8 | 0.2 |
| Smith | 636 | 19 044 | 2 002.7 | 784.8 | 334 | 2 556 | 192.7 | 71.9 | 1 498.6 | 640.5 | 307.9 | 66.0 |
| Somervell | 21 | 449 | 31.2 | 13.2 | 11 | 28 | 2.6 | 0.7 | 43.3 | 21.9 | 10.1 | 2.1 |
| Starr | 67 | 4 455 | 134.6 | 68.3 | 26 | 90 | 4.0 | 0.9 | 442.6 | 76.7 | 59.7 | 76.8 |
| Stephens | 24 | 358 | 18.1 | 8.4 | 15 | 57 | 3.6 | 1.2 | 78.5 | 28.4 | 24.4 | 3.2 |
| Sterling | 3 | D | D | D | 1 | D | D | D | 8.0 | 3.1 | 2.2 | 0.2 |
| Stonewall | 4 | 130 | 6.4 | 2.9 | 5 | D | D | D | 17.1 | 5.8 | 4.7 | 0.6 |
| Sutton | 4 | 82 | 8.6 | 2.3 | 10 | 35 | 3.6 | 0.6 | 22.2 | 10.0 | 5.6 | 1.0 |
| Swisher | 13 | 249 | 12.2 | 5.5 | 10 | 30 | 1.7 | 0.5 | 84.8 | 25.9 | 17.1 | 2.9 |
| Tarrant | 3 999 | 75 845 | 8 750.6 | 3 062.5 | 2 408 | 19 973 | 1 777.8 | 505.0 | 18 312.5 | 3 714.9 | 1 585.2 | 422.3 |
| Taylor | 377 | 11 521 | 833.6 | 333.5 | 249 | 1 554 | 147.9 | 31.0 | 1 246.9 | 420.0 | 195.8 | 49.2 |
| Terrell | 1 | D | D | D | 2 | D | D | D | 16.4 | 4.3 | 2.2 | 0.5 |
| Terry | 20 | 601 | 28.0 | 11.0 | 19 | 79 | 4.5 | 1.4 | 130.4 | 33.6 | 32.4 | 7.1 |
| Throckmorton | 4 | 69 | 3.2 | 1.6 | 3 | D | D | D | 19.6 | 6.3 | 4.9 | 0.4 |
| Titus | 86 | 1 907 | 144.5 | 62.0 | 39 | 227 | 16.5 | 6.7 | 208.8 | 75.2 | 54.3 | 9.6 |

1. State totals may include programs not allocated by county.

# Table B. States and Counties — Federal Funds, Residential Construction, and Local Government Finances

| | Federal funds and grants, 2009–2010 (cont.) | | | | | | | Value of residential construction authorized by building permits, 2011 | | Local government finances, 2007 | | | | |
| | Expenditures (mil dol) (cont.) | | | | | | | | | General revenue | | | | |
| | Procurement contract awards | | Grants[1] | | | | | | | | | Taxes | | |
| | | | | | | | | | | | | | Per capita[2] (dollars) | |
| STATE County | Salaries and wages | Defense | Other | Medicaid and other health-related | Nutrition and family welfare | Education | Other | New construction ($1,000) | Number of housing units | Total (mil dol) | Intergovern-mental (mil dol) | Total (mil dol) | Total | Property |
|---|---|---|---|---|---|---|---|---|---|---|---|---|---|---|
| | 171 | 172 | 173 | 174 | 175 | 176 | 177 | 178 | 179 | 180 | 181 | 182 | 183 | 184 |
| TEXAS—Cont'd | | | | | | | | | | | | | | |
| Mason | 1.4 | 0.0 | 0.4 | 6.6 | 0.5 | 0.1 | 0.2 | 556 | 6 | 12.4 | 6.1 | 4.5 | 1 161 | 1 032 |
| Matagorda | 6.5 | -16.8 | 2.4 | 48.5 | 18.3 | 1.3 | 2.4 | 7 182 | 63 | 194.4 | 33.8 | 71.7 | 1 937 | 1 770 |
| Maverick | 64.0 | 2.7 | 4.0 | 131.1 | 13.7 | 5.0 | 4.7 | 7 726 | 136 | 177.0 | 115.8 | 35.4 | 685 | 515 |
| Medina | 32.0 | 0.1 | 8.0 | 51.6 | 6.4 | 1.5 | 0.8 | 3 428 | 22 | 115.9 | 52.2 | 37.0 | 843 | 751 |
| Menard | 0.5 | 0.0 | 0.1 | 6.1 | 0.2 | 0.1 | 0.1 | NA | NA | 12.2 | 6.1 | 3.2 | 1 512 | 1 299 |
| Midland | 57.0 | 0.2 | 10.5 | 53.0 | 9.0 | 4.2 | 10.7 | 96 880 | 539 | 587.8 | 144.8 | 231.6 | 1 832 | 1 400 |
| Milam | 4.6 | 0.0 | 1.1 | 62.2 | 3.2 | 0.9 | 1.2 | 40 | 1 | 81.2 | 27.4 | 29.6 | 1 189 | 1 025 |
| Mills | 1.4 | 0.0 | 0.3 | 9.1 | 0.6 | 0.4 | 0.1 | NA | NA | 15.5 | 9.6 | 4.6 | 913 | 773 |
| Mitchell | 1.8 | 0.0 | 0.4 | 17.2 | 0.8 | 0.3 | 0.2 | 0 | 0 | 41.5 | 9.9 | 14.7 | 1 583 | 1 416 |
| Montague | 4.7 | 0.0 | 1.1 | 27.8 | 2.6 | 0.5 | 0.2 | 120 | 1 | 86.6 | 42.9 | 21.6 | 1 101 | 969 |
| Montgomery | 102.6 | 2.7 | 17.8 | 116.5 | 24.7 | 6.2 | 22.2 | 664 576 | 4 009 | 1 080.2 | 277.7 | 641.4 | 1 554 | 1 378 |
| Moore | 4.0 | 0.0 | 0.3 | 6.6 | 1.0 | 0.6 | 0.1 | 2 785 | 34 | 85.0 | 13.0 | 41.5 | 2 065 | 1 920 |
| Morris | 2.4 | 0.0 | 0.6 | 31.9 | 2.5 | 0.4 | 0.4 | 0 | 0 | 30.7 | 9.6 | 16.9 | 1 292 | 1 155 |
| Motley | 0.6 | 0.0 | 0.1 | 3.5 | 0.1 | 0.0 | 0.0 | NA | NA | 4.0 | 1.7 | 1.8 | 1 364 | 1 226 |
| Nacogdoches | 26.3 | 0.0 | 2.6 | 110.9 | 13.5 | 4.2 | 9.1 | 9 600 | 64 | 235.6 | 68.3 | 63.1 | 1 010 | 865 |
| Navarro | 22.1 | 2.4 | 3.5 | 97.2 | 7.5 | 2.1 | 1.4 | 2 182 | 28 | 177.9 | 75.0 | 57.4 | 1 163 | 935 |
| Newton | 2.5 | 0.0 | 0.7 | 32.9 | 2.7 | 0.5 | 0.2 | 0 | 0 | 34.4 | 14.9 | 15.9 | 1 149 | 1 079 |
| Nolan | 3.5 | 0.8 | 0.4 | 26.4 | 3.0 | 0.7 | 12.8 | 0 | 0 | 73.5 | 19.0 | 24.8 | 1 695 | 1 392 |
| Nueces | 326.5 | 477.9 | 75.8 | 486.9 | 83.4 | 16.5 | 46.9 | 132 948 | 959 | 1 198.6 | 393.8 | 537.4 | 1 673 | 1 295 |
| Ochiltree | 1.7 | 0.0 | 0.3 | 2.5 | 0.5 | 0.2 | 0.1 | 392 | 2 | 38.6 | 7.9 | 18.5 | 1 930 | 1 619 |
| Oldham | 0.6 | 0.0 | 0.1 | 1.0 | 0.3 | 0.3 | 0.0 | 320 | 1 | 15.0 | 6.6 | 3.5 | 1 668 | 1 465 |
| Orange | 11.1 | 0.0 | 2.7 | 85.5 | 12.6 | 2.2 | 7.8 | 39 346 | 363 | 262.4 | 87.2 | 109.0 | 1 318 | 1 094 |
| Palo Pinto | 4.7 | 1.1 | 1.1 | 33.9 | 3.9 | 0.9 | 1.0 | 598 | 8 | 116.9 | 33.5 | 45.3 | 1 660 | 1 365 |
| Panola | 5.7 | 0.0 | 1.1 | 45.0 | 1.9 | 0.6 | 1.0 | 1 450 | 19 | 113.3 | 17.0 | 78.0 | 3 389 | 3 277 |
| Parker | 20.2 | 3.1 | 10.0 | 33.8 | 13.8 | 2.9 | 2.9 | 36 919 | 282 | 330.3 | 83.4 | 153.2 | 1 409 | 1 211 |
| Parmer | 3.8 | 0.0 | 0.3 | 8.1 | 1.5 | 0.4 | 0.0 | 0 | 0 | 32.4 | 16.5 | 10.9 | 1 160 | 963 |
| Pecos | 3.8 | 0.0 | 0.4 | 17.2 | 5.2 | 0.6 | 0.7 | 645 | 6 | 104.4 | 13.9 | 67.0 | 4 195 | 4 061 |
| Polk | 8.9 | 0.0 | 1.4 | 60.8 | 6.6 | 1.9 | 2.5 | 42 126 | 238 | 100.1 | 37.7 | 44.8 | 968 | 809 |
| Potter | 138.1 | 2 428.4 | 637.6 | 103.3 | 30.2 | 8.5 | 50.7 | 146 067 | 648 | 641.0 | 244.4 | 260.4 | 2 156 | 1 553 |
| Presidio | 24.1 | 1.5 | 21.2 | 27.6 | 1.9 | 0.9 | 0.3 | 341 | 2 | 31.3 | 22.9 | 5.2 | 686 | 575 |
| Rains | 1.5 | 0.0 | 0.4 | 10.1 | 1.0 | 0.3 | 0.0 | 445 | 2 | 22.3 | 7.3 | 10.7 | 956 | 754 |
| Randall | 4.2 | 0.5 | 1.0 | 14.7 | 5.1 | 3.6 | 0.1 | 10 519 | 55 | 103.7 | 27.1 | 60.4 | 535 | 491 |
| Reagan | 0.5 | 0.0 | 0.1 | 1.0 | 1.0 | 0.1 | 0.0 | 575 | 4 | 30.9 | 3.3 | 22.1 | 7 223 | 6 821 |
| Real | 0.4 | 0.0 | 0.4 | 7.1 | 0.4 | 0.2 | 0.0 | 0 | 0 | 8.0 | 1.2 | 6.3 | 2 112 | 2 043 |
| Red River | 3.4 | 0.0 | 0.8 | 76.3 | 3.1 | 0.5 | 0.3 | 471 | 6 | 39.3 | 23.2 | 10.5 | 802 | 686 |
| Reeves | 4.9 | 0.0 | 3.2 | 33.9 | 4.4 | 0.7 | 0.5 | 180 | 1 | 113.5 | 12.0 | 18.7 | 1 670 | 1 427 |
| Refugio | 2.9 | 0.0 | 1.0 | 14.7 | 1.2 | 0.3 | 0.3 | 221 | 2 | 34.9 | 6.7 | 22.7 | 3 083 | 2 914 |
| Roberts | 0.4 | 0.0 | 0.1 | 0.5 | 0.1 | 0.0 | 0.0 | NA | NA | 10.9 | 0.6 | 9.7 | 11 650 | 11 496 |
| Robertson | 3.4 | 0.0 | 0.8 | 67.2 | 1.4 | 0.7 | 1.4 | 1 105 | 7 | 76.1 | 20.2 | 45.8 | 2 895 | 2 709 |
| Rockwall | 9.1 | 100.1 | 2.9 | 8.1 | 2.4 | 0.6 | 0.4 | 96 112 | 411 | 217.4 | 46.3 | 140.5 | 1 903 | 1 676 |
| Runnels | 3.2 | 0.0 | 0.7 | 25.3 | 1.8 | 0.4 | 0.2 | 230 | 2 | 43.4 | 18.9 | 13.5 | 1 301 | 1 063 |
| Rusk | 7.7 | 0.2 | 3.8 | 79.9 | 4.7 | 1.3 | 0.6 | 1 164 | 7 | 125.5 | 33.2 | 75.8 | 1 560 | 1 405 |
| Sabine | 3.9 | 0.0 | 0.7 | 26.8 | 1.2 | 1.1 | 0.2 | 0 | 0 | 28.1 | 12.6 | 7.9 | 782 | 651 |
| San Augustine | 1.5 | 0.0 | 0.4 | 36.9 | 0.6 | 0.5 | 0.3 | 0 | 0 | 19.6 | 11.4 | 5.5 | 631 | 518 |
| San Jacinto | 2.9 | 0.0 | 0.7 | 31.9 | 1.2 | 0.8 | 0.0 | 125 | 2 | 44.0 | 18.6 | 21.2 | 853 | 797 |
| San Patricio | 19.7 | 9.7 | 1.9 | 117.8 | 15.7 | 2.5 | 5.0 | 18 416 | 113 | 223.6 | 100.2 | 89.9 | 1 312 | 1 146 |
| San Saba | 1.5 | 0.0 | 0.3 | 19.2 | 9.2 | 0.3 | 4.9 | 0 | 0 | 20.5 | 12.9 | 5.4 | 909 | 760 |
| Schleicher | 0.5 | 0.0 | 0.1 | 4.0 | 0.7 | 0.1 | 0.1 | 280 | 2 | 14.6 | 2.3 | 7.8 | 2 769 | 2 549 |
| Scurry | 3.0 | 0.0 | 0.6 | 21.7 | 4.3 | 2.5 | 0.0 | 7 802 | 89 | 103.7 | 19.3 | 48.3 | 3 018 | 2 603 |
| Shackelford | 1.0 | 0.2 | 0.2 | 3.8 | 0.7 | 0.1 | 2.4 | NA | NA | 11.9 | 4.5 | 5.7 | 1 807 | 1 576 |
| Shelby | 5.6 | 0.9 | 1.0 | 91.0 | 7.4 | 1.2 | 0.4 | 1 149 | 5 | 67.6 | 35.0 | 23.9 | 903 | 750 |
| Sherman | 0.3 | 0.0 | 0.0 | 0.5 | 0.4 | 0.1 | 0.0 | 751 | 8 | 16.3 | 2.4 | 11.2 | 3 846 | 3 677 |
| Smith | 80.8 | 56.3 | 30.8 | 223.4 | 25.1 | 8.5 | 17.5 | 33 578 | 262 | 557.5 | 164.4 | 281.6 | 1 417 | 1 075 |
| Somervell | 1.5 | 0.0 | 0.3 | 6.6 | 0.3 | 0.1 | 0.1 | 1 404 | 8 | 43.2 | 5.1 | 32.0 | 4 122 | 4 047 |
| Starr | 41.6 | 3.7 | 3.5 | 139.1 | 24.7 | 5.7 | 5.8 | NA | NA | 234.2 | 147.0 | 46.0 | 744 | 664 |
| Stephens | 1.5 | 0.1 | 0.4 | 12.6 | 1.5 | 0.3 | 5.4 | 211 | 2 | 32.6 | 6.6 | 15.3 | 1 608 | 1 366 |
| Sterling | 0.1 | 0.0 | 0.0 | 1.0 | 0.2 | 0.0 | 0.0 | NA | NA | 13.3 | 1.1 | 10.1 | 8 145 | 7 994 |
| Stonewall | 0.8 | 0.0 | 0.2 | 2.0 | 0.4 | 0.1 | 0.0 | NA | NA | 9.4 | 2.0 | 4.2 | 2 958 | 2 843 |
| Sutton | 0.3 | 0.0 | 0.0 | 4.0 | 0.3 | 0.1 | 0.3 | 0 | 0 | 33.9 | 3.3 | 25.7 | 5 979 | 5 668 |
| Swisher | 1.9 | 0.0 | 0.3 | 10.2 | 2.9 | 0.3 | 1.7 | 0 | 0 | 34.8 | 12.4 | 7.0 | 913 | 794 |
| Tarrant | 1 257.2 | 9 369.9 | 531.6 | 805.9 | 168.8 | 62.4 | 205.1 | 879 403 | 5 421 | 6 450.0 | 1 550.5 | 3 416.9 | 1 990 | 1 600 |
| Taylor | 303.6 | 71.2 | 8.5 | 125.6 | 24.0 | 5.4 | 16.2 | 27 518 | 155 | 391.1 | 163.7 | 163.1 | 1 289 | 927 |
| Terrell | 4.6 | 0.1 | 0.1 | 2.9 | 0.3 | 0.1 | 0.1 | NA | NA | 15.1 | 0.6 | 13.3 | 14 267 | 13 931 |
| Terry | 2.3 | 0.0 | 0.5 | 25.8 | 3.1 | 0.6 | 0.0 | 0 | 0 | 54.3 | 16.1 | 20.1 | 1 646 | 1 457 |
| Throckmorton | 0.7 | 0.8 | 0.9 | 3.0 | 0.1 | 0.1 | 0.0 | NA | NA | 8.2 | 2.3 | 3.5 | 2 116 | 1 992 |
| Titus | 8.7 | 0.1 | 2.9 | 43.0 | 5.7 | 1.9 | 0.2 | 1 300 | 7 | 183.7 | 44.7 | 52.0 | 1 769 | 1 480 |

1. State totals may include programs not allocated by county.    2. Based on the resident population estimated as of July 1 of the year shown.

Items 171—184

# Table B. States and Counties — Local Government Finances, Government Employment, and Voting

| | Local government finances, 2007 (cont.) | | | | | | | | | Government employment, 2011 | | | Presidential election,[2] 2012 | | |
| | Direct general expenditure | | | | | | | Debt outstanding | | | | | Percent of vote cast: | | |
| | | | Percent of total for: | | | | | | | | | | | | |
| STATE County | Total (mil dol) | Per capita[1] (dollars) | Education | Health and hospitals | Police protection | Public welfare | Highways | Total (mil dol) | Per capita[1] (dollars) | Federal civilian | Federal military | State and local | Democratic | Republican | All other |
| | 185 | 186 | 187 | 188 | 189 | 190 | 191 | 192 | 193 | 194 | 195 | 196 | 197 | 198 | 199 |
| TEXAS—Cont'd | | | | | | | | | | | | | | | |
| Mason | 9.6 | 2 465 | 61.0 | 1.9 | 6.6 | 0.4 | 6.7 | 2.8 | 720 | 19 | 0 | 268 | 25.7 | 72.8 | 1.5 |
| Matagorda | 189.8 | 5 126 | 38.8 | 39.4 | 3.2 | 0.1 | 3.6 | 119.2 | 3 219 | 84 | 82 | 2 430 | 35.9 | 63.3 | 0.8 |
| Maverick | 171.7 | 3 323 | 65.0 | 1.7 | 4.3 | 0.0 | 2.7 | 123.3 | 2 388 | 918 | 123 | 4 923 | 78.2 | 21.2 | 0.6 |
| Medina | 116.2 | 2 650 | 61.1 | 10.4 | 4.0 | 0.2 | 4.5 | 178.7 | 4 078 | 61 | 103 | 2 892 | 32.7 | 66.6 | 0.7 |
| Menard | 12.1 | 5 672 | 40.2 | 0.0 | 2.5 | 15.1 | 2.2 | 2.3 | 1 074 | 0 | 0 | 194 | 29.0 | 69.9 | 1.1 |
| Midland | 564.0 | 4 462 | 39.4 | 32.9 | 4.4 | 0.0 | 1.9 | 394.8 | 3 123 | 565 | 312 | 8 058 | 21.0 | 78.2 | 0.8 |
| Milam | 81.6 | 3 282 | 51.5 | 19.7 | 3.0 | 0.5 | 4.6 | 114.7 | 4 613 | 55 | 55 | 1 187 | 36.4 | 62.4 | 1.1 |
| Mills | 15.4 | 3 066 | 73.7 | 2.0 | 2.5 | 0.4 | 3.8 | 4.1 | 806 | 19 | 11 | 346 | 18.3 | 80.5 | 1.2 |
| Mitchell | 36.6 | 3 950 | 42.8 | 34.8 | 3.1 | 0.2 | 5.4 | 17.2 | 1 855 | 22 | 21 | 1 208 | 24.1 | 74.7 | 1.2 |
| Montague | 86.1 | 4 381 | 34.3 | 45.6 | 3.3 | 0.3 | 3.6 | 39.2 | 1 995 | 52 | 44 | 1 392 | 20.1 | 78.6 | 1.4 |
| Montgomery | 1 143.6 | 2 772 | 60.9 | 4.3 | 4.7 | 0.1 | 5.5 | 2 844.3 | 6 893 | 771 | 1 047 | 23 152 | 23.3 | 75.9 | 0.8 |
| Moore | 79.3 | 3 948 | 49.0 | 27.9 | 6.1 | 0.1 | 3.4 | 19.5 | 972 | 68 | 49 | 1 644 | 20.7 | 78.8 | 0.6 |
| Morris | 28.6 | 2 193 | 70.8 | 0.1 | 4.8 | 0.5 | 3.0 | 19.3 | 1 477 | 26 | 28 | 660 | 39.2 | 60.2 | 0.7 |
| Motley | 3.6 | 2 789 | 71.1 | 3.3 | 4.4 | 0.1 | 5.4 | 0.9 | 667 | 11 | 0 | 101 | 11.3 | 87.9 | 0.8 |
| Nacogdoches | 226.8 | 3 633 | 35.4 | 36.3 | 3.6 | 0.2 | 2.0 | 208.2 | 3 335 | 153 | 150 | 5 277 | 35.9 | 63.4 | 0.7 |
| Navarro | 169.3 | 3 428 | 65.8 | 3.5 | 5.5 | 0.3 | 3.6 | 220.4 | 4 461 | 102 | 106 | 3 598 | 33.1 | 66.2 | 0.7 |
| Newton | 30.8 | 2 231 | 76.9 | 0.0 | 3.9 | 0.6 | 3.8 | 27.7 | 2 005 | 26 | 32 | 640 | 33.3 | 65.5 | 1.2 |
| Nolan | 68.8 | 4 708 | 44.9 | 29.4 | 4.6 | 0.0 | 2.9 | 59.2 | 4 051 | 45 | 34 | 1 680 | 30.0 | 68.8 | 1.1 |
| Nueces | 1 247.9 | 3 886 | 50.5 | 5.3 | 5.8 | 0.1 | 4.0 | 1 480.1 | 4 609 | 6 662 | 3 167 | 22 067 | 47.3 | 51.8 | 0.9 |
| Ochiltree | 39.9 | 4 163 | 46.5 | 25.7 | 4.5 | 0.0 | 5.4 | 8.0 | 832 | 23 | 23 | 767 | 7.8 | 91.7 | 0.5 |
| Oldham | 14.5 | 7 004 | 80.5 | 0.0 | 3.6 | 0.0 | 2.2 | 1.4 | 664 | 0 | 0 | 299 | 11.1 | 88.4 | 0.5 |
| Orange | 240.6 | 2 911 | 53.9 | 0.8 | 6.3 | 0.2 | 2.9 | 611.0 | 7 390 | 104 | 183 | 4 191 | 26.0 | 73.1 | 0.9 |
| Palo Pinto | 118.3 | 4 331 | 49.1 | 27.0 | 2.2 | 0.0 | 3.3 | 96.2 | 3 520 | 56 | 62 | 1 759 | 25.3 | 73.4 | 1.3 |
| Panola | 106.3 | 4 620 | 77.2 | 0.0 | 2.5 | 0.2 | 4.8 | 57.8 | 2 513 | 72 | 53 | 1 407 | 25.3 | 74.2 | 0.5 |
| Parker | 322.4 | 2 966 | 56.1 | 16.2 | 3.7 | 0.1 | 4.3 | 662.6 | 6 096 | 160 | 263 | 4 835 | 21.9 | 77.1 | 1.0 |
| Parmer | 29.4 | 3 118 | 71.6 | 2.4 | 3.4 | 5.4 | 4.4 | 10.7 | 1 132 | 67 | 23 | 837 | 19.4 | 80.0 | 0.7 |
| Pecos | 92.6 | 5 797 | 56.5 | 18.9 | 2.6 | 0.2 | 2.7 | 38.1 | 2 386 | 56 | 35 | 1 838 | 36.8 | 61.8 | 1.3 |
| Polk | 93.5 | 2 017 | 65.0 | 0.1 | 5.9 | 0.4 | 7.2 | 221.3 | 4 776 | 106 | 101 | 3 011 | 30.9 | 68.1 | 0.9 |
| Potter | 664.3 | 5 501 | 56.2 | 6.0 | 5.1 | 0.1 | 3.2 | 459.6 | 3 805 | 1 847 | 341 | 11 876 | 29.8 | 69.2 | 1.0 |
| Presidio | 24.1 | 3 182 | 65.9 | 1.0 | 2.7 | 0.0 | 2.0 | 33.4 | 4 413 | 370 | 17 | 701 | 71.3 | 27.8 | 0.9 |
| Rains | 20.3 | 1 810 | 64.1 | 0.0 | 2.1 | 0.2 | 5.0 | 10.2 | 910 | 21 | 25 | 448 | 24.7 | 74.3 | 1.0 |
| Randall | 99.7 | 882 | 51.1 | 1.2 | 6.7 | 0.0 | 2.8 | 251.5 | 2 225 | 72 | 273 | 5 365 | 18.3 | 80.9 | 0.8 |
| Reagan | 34.0 | 11 137 | 60.0 | 11.1 | 1.6 | 0.0 | 3.3 | 49.6 | 16 247 | 12 | 0 | 359 | 19.8 | 80.0 | 0.2 |
| Real | 5.4 | 1 809 | 61.4 | 0.6 | 4.2 | 1.9 | 3.3 | 16.9 | 5 712 | 0 | 0 | 233 | 23.0 | 76.0 | 0.9 |
| Red River | 36.1 | 2 757 | 77.4 | 0.0 | 4.5 | 0.5 | 6.0 | 18.4 | 1 404 | 39 | 28 | 747 | 30.5 | 68.5 | 1.0 |
| Reeves | 108.1 | 9 671 | 22.7 | 11.9 | 4.1 | 0.1 | 1.2 | 82.0 | 7 332 | 78 | 30 | 1 625 | 52.2 | 47.0 | 0.8 |
| Refugio | 39.7 | 5 389 | 73.8 | 1.8 | 3.5 | 0.0 | 4.0 | 18.9 | 2 573 | 43 | 16 | 676 | 42.4 | 56.9 | 0.7 |
| Roberts | 10.6 | 12 699 | 87.7 | 0.5 | 0.9 | 2.5 | 2.0 | 3.0 | 3 564 | 0 | 0 | 91 | 7.9 | 92.1 | 0.0 |
| Robertson | 87.1 | 5 508 | 74.8 | 0.5 | 3.8 | 1.0 | 3.8 | 61.9 | 3 911 | 42 | 37 | 1 031 | 39.9 | 59.3 | 0.8 |
| Rockwall | 281.2 | 3 810 | 63.2 | 0.4 | 4.6 | 0.1 | 6.0 | 680.7 | 9 222 | 93 | 180 | 3 456 | 26.5 | 72.7 | 0.9 |
| Runnels | 35.9 | 3 469 | 53.9 | 18.0 | 3.5 | 1.0 | 2.8 | 57.9 | 5 592 | 40 | 23 | 794 | 18.6 | 80.6 | 0.7 |
| Rusk | 120.9 | 2 490 | 71.1 | 0.1 | 4.9 | 0.4 | 5.2 | 117.0 | 2 410 | 76 | 119 | 2 410 | 26.6 | 72.9 | 0.5 |
| Sabine | 27.3 | 2 695 | 58.1 | 18.4 | 4.5 | 0.0 | 5.6 | 23.8 | 2 344 | 49 | 24 | 468 | 22.1 | 76.9 | 1.0 |
| San Augustine | 17.8 | 2 059 | 71.3 | 2.7 | 3.7 | 0.1 | 4.7 | 22.0 | 2 542 | 18 | 20 | 402 | 35.7 | 63.0 | 1.2 |
| San Jacinto | 41.1 | 1 658 | 72.7 | 0.0 | 3.7 | 0.8 | 8.2 | 44.5 | 1 792 | 25 | 59 | 931 | 30.4 | 68.7 | 1.0 |
| San Patricio | 223.6 | 3 263 | 61.7 | 6.4 | 4.8 | 0.5 | 3.2 | 222.1 | 3 241 | 103 | 1 328 | 3 929 | 41.4 | 58.0 | 0.6 |
| San Saba | 16.8 | 2 817 | 60.1 | 1.4 | 3.6 | 1.0 | 6.0 | 6.1 | 1 023 | 21 | 13 | 499 | 19.8 | 79.0 | 1.2 |
| Schleicher | 12.2 | 4 355 | 46.6 | 22.3 | 4.6 | 0.7 | 7.2 | 0.9 | 323 | 11 | 0 | 261 | 24.8 | 74.4 | 0.8 |
| Scurry | 101.3 | 6 327 | 62.3 | 18.3 | 1.8 | 0.2 | 2.8 | 39.4 | 2 462 | 40 | 37 | 1 663 | 19.5 | 79.3 | 1.2 |
| Shackelford | 10.5 | 3 336 | 65.8 | 4.5 | 5.6 | 0.0 | 4.9 | 2.3 | 724 | 14 | 0 | 227 | 13.8 | 85.3 | 0.9 |
| Shelby | 60.7 | 2 288 | 73.1 | 0.6 | 5.1 | 0.0 | 6.3 | 50.3 | 1 897 | 73 | 57 | 1 298 | 27.6 | 71.9 | 0.5 |
| Sherman | 15.5 | 5 352 | 64.2 | 2.2 | 3.7 | 13.5 | 6.6 | 4.1 | 1 425 | 10 | 0 | 303 | 12.5 | 86.7 | 0.9 |
| Smith | 599.0 | 3 015 | 63.3 | 5.0 | 4.6 | 0.4 | 3.7 | 786.9 | 3 960 | 861 | 484 | 12 094 | 29.8 | 69.4 | 0.8 |
| Somervell | 38.8 | 4 997 | 69.4 | 1.7 | 6.6 | 0.0 | 1.3 | 11.7 | 1 514 | 14 | 19 | 851 | 22.6 | 75.8 | 1.6 |
| Starr | 236.2 | 3 820 | 71.4 | 9.5 | 2.4 | 0.0 | 2.8 | 244.4 | 3 952 | 604 | 137 | 4 846 | 84.5 | 15.2 | 0.3 |
| Stephens | 36.8 | 3 861 | 48.8 | 24.3 | 2.9 | 0.0 | 3.8 | 25.5 | 2 674 | 19 | 21 | 777 | 17.8 | 81.4 | 0.9 |
| Sterling | 13.0 | 10 439 | 64.7 | 2.0 | 2.2 | 16.4 | 2.5 | 24.3 | 19 556 | 0 | 0 | 149 | 15.7 | 84.0 | 0.3 |
| Stonewall | 8.8 | 6 238 | 31.4 | 48.9 | 2.1 | 0.0 | 5.3 | 1.1 | 811 | 11 | 0 | 231 | 28.0 | 71.3 | 0.7 |
| Sutton | 27.8 | 6 458 | 73.2 | 10.2 | 2.3 | 0.0 | 2.8 | 6.5 | 1 506 | 0 | 0 | 439 | 24.1 | 75.3 | 0.5 |
| Swisher | 29.4 | 3 823 | 46.9 | 27.3 | 4.5 | 0.1 | 3.7 | 10.4 | 1 349 | 30 | 17 | 735 | 32.1 | 66.4 | 1.5 |
| Tarrant | 6 134.2 | 3 572 | 46.0 | 10.5 | 6.4 | 0.1 | 4.1 | 14 177.4 | 8 255 | 14 796 | 5 165 | 91 808 | 43.7 | 55.4 | 0.8 |
| Taylor | 405.0 | 3 200 | 56.5 | 4.2 | 6.7 | 0.4 | 2.6 | 256.2 | 2 025 | 1 212 | 4 977 | 9 800 | 26.8 | 72.3 | 0.9 |
| Terrell | 13.6 | 14 604 | 82.1 | 1.5 | 1.3 | 0.0 | 3.0 | 1.1 | 1 151 | 65 | 0 | 130 | 35.8 | 62.2 | 1.9 |
| Terry | 49.9 | 4 094 | 44.3 | 24.0 | 4.0 | 0.1 | 4.0 | 13.5 | 1 104 | 31 | 28 | 1 116 | 32.2 | 67.3 | 0.5 |
| Throckmorton | 8.4 | 5 067 | 44.8 | 30.0 | 0.5 | 0.0 | 11.3 | 1.6 | 990 | 11 | 0 | 202 | 19.8 | 80.1 | 0.1 |
| Titus | 180.2 | 6 131 | 53.5 | 30.7 | 1.9 | 0.0 | 2.0 | 169.8 | 5 778 | 93 | 72 | 2 976 | 34.0 | 65.2 | 0.8 |

1. Based on the resident population estimated as of July 1 of the year shown.    2. © 2013 Election Data Services, Inc. All rights reserved.

# Table B. States and Counties — Land Area and Population

| | | | | | Population 2012 | | | Population characteristics[6], 2011 | | | | | | | | | | |
| | | | | | | | | Race alone or in combination, not Hispanic or Latino (percent) | | | | | Age (percent) | | | | | |
| STATE/ County code | CBSA code[1] | County type[2] | STATE County | Land area,[3] (sq km) 2010 | Total persons | Rank | Per square kilometer | White | Black | American Indian, Alaska Native | Asian and Pacific Islander | Percent Hispanic or Latino[4] | Under 5 years | 5 to 17 years | 18 to 24 years | 25 to 34 years | 35 to 44 years | 45 to 54 years |
| | | | | 1 | 2 | 3 | 4 | 5 | 6 | 7 | 8 | 9 | 10 | 11 | 12 | 13 | 14 | 15 |
|---|---|---|---|---|---|---|---|---|---|---|---|---|---|---|---|---|---|---|
| | | | TEXAS—Cont'd | | | | | | | | | | | | | | | |
| 48 451 | 41660 | 3 | Tom Green | 3 942 | 113 281 | 529 | 28.7 | 58.1 | 4.5 | 0.8 | 1.6 | 36.3 | 7.1 | 16.4 | 13.5 | 13.9 | 10.8 | 12.8 |
| 48 453 | 12420 | 1 | Travis | 2 565 | 1 095 584 | 37 | 427.1 | 51.8 | 8.8 | 0.7 | 6.6 | 33.9 | 7.4 | 16.5 | 12.0 | 19.0 | 15.2 | 12.8 |
| 48 455 | ... | 8 | Trinity | 1 796 | 14 309 | 2 152 | 8.0 | 80.5 | 10.1 | 1.0 | 0.6 | 9.1 | 5.5 | 15.7 | 6.7 | 9.3 | 10.1 | 13.9 |
| 48 457 | ... | 6 | Tyler | 2 394 | 21 458 | 1 756 | 9.0 | 80.8 | 11.4 | 1.0 | 0.4 | 7.4 | 5.2 | 14.9 | 8.5 | 13.1 | 11.9 | 13.4 |
| 48 459 | 30980 | 3 | Upshur | 1 510 | 39 995 | 1 173 | 26.5 | 82.5 | 9.8 | 1.3 | 0.8 | 7.4 | 6.5 | 18.3 | 7.8 | 11.1 | 11.7 | 14.9 |
| 48 461 | ... | 8 | Upton | 3 215 | 3 283 | 2 955 | 1.0 | 46.8 | 1.9 | 1.3 | 0.4 | 50.4 | 8.0 | 18.9 | 7.3 | 13.8 | 10.2 | 13.7 |
| 48 463 | 46620 | 7 | Uvalde | 4 020 | 26 752 | 1 538 | 6.7 | 29.0 | 0.7 | 0.4 | 0.6 | 69.7 | 7.8 | 20.7 | 10.2 | 11.2 | 11.6 | 12.2 |
| 48 465 | 19620 | 5 | Val Verde | 8 145 | 48 705 | 1 002 | 6.0 | 17.8 | 1.5 | 0.4 | 0.8 | 80.1 | 8.2 | 21.3 | 10.8 | 13.2 | 12.6 | 11.4 |
| 48 467 | ... | 6 | Van Zandt | 2 182 | 52 427 | 947 | 24.0 | 85.8 | 3.4 | 1.5 | 0.6 | 10.0 | 6.0 | 17.9 | 7.4 | 10.1 | 11.7 | 14.5 |
| 48 469 | 47020 | 3 | Victoria | 2 285 | 89 269 | 640 | 39.1 | 48.1 | 6.5 | 0.5 | 1.3 | 44.5 | 7.5 | 19.0 | 9.1 | 13.1 | 11.5 | 13.9 |
| 48 471 | 26660 | 4 | Walker | 2 031 | 68 408 | 776 | 33.7 | 59.0 | 22.8 | 0.7 | 1.3 | 17.5 | 4.8 | 11.6 | 20.4 | 14.1 | 13.4 | 14.4 |
| 48 473 | 26420 | 1 | Waller | 1 330 | 44 357 | 1 079 | 33.4 | 45.1 | 23.9 | 0.8 | 0.8 | 30.4 | 7.3 | 17.6 | 17.3 | 11.0 | 11.3 | 13.5 |
| 48 475 | ... | 6 | Ward | 2 164 | 10 879 | 2 369 | 5.0 | 45.4 | 4.8 | 1.0 | 0.6 | 49.1 | 7.8 | 19.7 | 8.7 | 12.7 | 10.8 | 13.7 |
| 48 477 | 14780 | 6 | Washington | 1 564 | 34 093 | 1 326 | 21.8 | 66.9 | 17.8 | 0.6 | 1.5 | 14.2 | 5.9 | 16.0 | 10.7 | 10.2 | 10.5 | 14.1 |
| 48 479 | 29700 | 3 | Webb | 8 706 | 259 172 | 255 | 29.8 | 3.7 | 0.3 | 0.1 | 0.6 | 95.4 | 9.8 | 25.0 | 11.0 | 13.8 | 13.7 | 10.9 |
| 48 481 | 20900 | 4 | Wharton | 2 813 | 41 285 | 1 145 | 14.7 | 47.5 | 13.9 | 0.4 | 0.6 | 38.3 | 7.3 | 19.2 | 8.9 | 12.2 | 11.3 | 13.9 |
| 48 483 | ... | 9 | Wheeler | 2 369 | 5 626 | 2 794 | 2.4 | 71.0 | 2.7 | 1.1 | 0.8 | 25.7 | 6.9 | 18.2 | 7.1 | 11.8 | 11.7 | 13.0 |
| 48 485 | 48660 | 3 | Wichita | 1 626 | 131 559 | 477 | 80.9 | 69.5 | 11.0 | 1.4 | 2.8 | 17.2 | 6.8 | 16.1 | 13.8 | 14.3 | 11.2 | 13.4 |
| 48 487 | 46900 | 6 | Wilbarger | 2 514 | 13 258 | 2 226 | 5.3 | 63.0 | 8.7 | 1.3 | 1.1 | 27.1 | 7.1 | 18.5 | 9.5 | 12.1 | 10.8 | 13.8 |
| 48 489 | 39700 | 6 | Willacy | 1 530 | 22 058 | 1 728 | 14.4 | 10.2 | 1.9 | 0.2 | 0.8 | 87.2 | 7.1 | 19.2 | 12.6 | 15.1 | 12.9 | 11.3 |
| 48 491 | 12420 | 1 | Williamson | 2 896 | 456 232 | 146 | 157.5 | 64.8 | 6.9 | 0.8 | 5.9 | 23.6 | 7.7 | 20.7 | 7.6 | 14.9 | 16.5 | 13.7 |
| 48 493 | 41700 | 1 | Wilson | 2 082 | 44 370 | 1 078 | 21.3 | 59.0 | 2.0 | 0.7 | 0.7 | 38.5 | 5.9 | 19.9 | 7.5 | 10.2 | 13.2 | 16.4 |
| 48 495 | ... | 6 | Winkler | 2 178 | 7 330 | 2 652 | 3.4 | 43.1 | 2.4 | 0.8 | 0.5 | 54.0 | 8.7 | 20.7 | 8.5 | 12.4 | 11.8 | 14.6 |
| 48 497 | 19100 | 1 | Wise | 2 342 | 60 432 | 858 | 25.8 | 79.6 | 1.7 | 1.3 | 0.7 | 17.9 | 6.7 | 19.1 | 8.4 | 11.7 | 13.0 | 15.9 |
| 48 499 | ... | 6 | Wood | 1 671 | 42 022 | 1 130 | 25.1 | 85.0 | 5.4 | 1.1 | 0.7 | 8.9 | 5.2 | 14.8 | 7.3 | 9.0 | 9.9 | 13.4 |
| 48 501 | ... | 7 | Yoakum | 2 071 | 8 075 | 2 596 | 3.9 | 38.8 | 1.2 | 0.9 | 0.4 | 59.4 | 9.5 | 22.2 | 9.3 | 12.0 | 12.1 | 13.4 |
| 48 503 | ... | 6 | Young | 2 368 | 18 339 | 1 906 | 7.7 | 80.6 | 1.8 | 1.1 | 0.6 | 17.0 | 6.7 | 17.3 | 7.5 | 11.0 | 10.9 | 14.2 |
| 48 505 | ... | 6 | Zapata | 2 586 | 14 290 | 2 153 | 5.5 | 6.5 | 0.4 | 0.2 | 0.2 | 92.8 | 11.1 | 23.1 | 10.9 | 13.4 | 11.8 | 10.7 |
| 48 507 | ... | 7 | Zavala | 3 360 | 11 961 | 2 300 | 3.6 | 6.2 | 0.5 | 0.2 | 0.1 | 93.2 | 8.8 | 22.5 | 11.8 | 11.5 | 11.5 | 11.1 |
| 49 000 | ... | X | UTAH | 212 818 | 2 855 287 | X | 13.4 | 81.7 | 1.4 | 1.5 | 4.1 | 13.2 | 9.3 | 21.9 | 11.6 | 15.9 | 12.2 | 10.9 |
| 49 001 | 14940 | 9 | Beaver | 6 708 | 6 501 | 2 724 | 1.0 | 86.6 | 0.5 | 1.3 | 1.6 | 11.0 | 9.1 | 24.2 | 7.6 | 12.9 | 11.1 | 11.4 |
| 49 003 | 14940 | 4 | Box Elder | 14 881 | 50 171 | 975 | 3.4 | 89.4 | 0.6 | 1.3 | 1.8 | 8.5 | 9.6 | 24.0 | 8.4 | 13.7 | 11.4 | 12.0 |
| 49 005 | 30860 | 3 | Cache | 3 017 | 115 520 | 523 | 38.3 | 86.3 | 1.0 | 0.9 | 3.3 | 10.0 | 9.8 | 21.2 | 19.1 | 15.6 | 10.2 | 8.9 |
| 49 007 | 39220 | 7 | Carbon | 3 829 | 21 246 | 1 772 | 5.5 | 85.3 | 0.9 | 1.6 | 1.4 | 12.4 | 7.9 | 18.8 | 10.2 | 13.8 | 10.4 | 12.5 |
| 49 009 | ... | 8 | Daggett | 1 805 | 1 090 | 3 105 | 0.6 | 94.7 | 0.8 | 1.1 | 0.7 | 3.5 | 6.9 | 17.2 | 4.7 | 14.1 | 10.6 | 12.3 |
| 49 011 | 36260 | 2 | Davis | 774 | 315 809 | 207 | 408.0 | 87.4 | 1.7 | 0.8 | 3.7 | 8.6 | 9.9 | 24.2 | 9.3 | 15.4 | 12.7 | 11.3 |
| 49 013 | ... | 6 | Duchesne | 8 394 | 19 244 | 1 864 | 2.3 | 88.5 | 0.5 | 5.6 | 1.1 | 6.4 | 10.6 | 23.1 | 9.0 | 15.0 | 10.5 | 11.5 |
| 49 015 | ... | 9 | Emery | 11 557 | 10 933 | 2 364 | 0.9 | 92.3 | 0.5 | 1.0 | 0.7 | 6.2 | 8.8 | 22.7 | 7.8 | 13.2 | 10.5 | 12.2 |
| 49 017 | ... | 9 | Garfield | 13 404 | 5 095 | 2 834 | 0.4 | 91.8 | 0.6 | 1.8 | 1.7 | 4.9 | 6.9 | 19.8 | 7.2 | 11.4 | 10.1 | 12.9 |
| 49 019 | ... | 7 | Grand | 9 509 | 9 328 | 2 489 | 1.0 | 85.3 | 0.8 | 4.6 | 1.5 | 9.4 | 6.8 | 16.2 | 6.8 | 13.5 | 12.6 | 14.7 |
| 49 021 | 16260 | 4 | Iron | 8 538 | 46 750 | 1 034 | 5.5 | 87.9 | 0.9 | 2.7 | 2.2 | 8.1 | 8.9 | 20.4 | 18.1 | 13.7 | 9.9 | 9.7 |
| 49 023 | 39340 | 2 | Juab | 8 786 | 10 341 | 2 409 | 1.2 | 94.3 | 0.6 | 1.3 | 0.9 | 4.0 | 9.9 | 26.8 | 7.9 | 13.0 | 11.7 | 10.7 |
| 49 025 | ... | 6 | Kane | 10 335 | 7 221 | 2 658 | 0.7 | 93.9 | 0.5 | 2.0 | 0.8 | 3.8 | 6.2 | 17.1 | 6.6 | 10.8 | 9.3 | 12.9 |
| 49 027 | ... | 7 | Millard | 17 023 | 12 569 | 2 269 | 0.7 | 85.2 | 0.3 | 1.2 | 1.1 | 13.0 | 8.7 | 23.4 | 7.4 | 11.6 | 10.0 | 12.6 |
| 49 029 | 36260 | 2 | Morgan | 1 578 | 9 821 | 2 454 | 6.2 | 96.4 | 0.5 | 0.5 | 0.8 | 2.6 | 9.3 | 25.6 | 7.7 | 10.8 | 12.5 | 12.7 |
| 49 031 | ... | 9 | Piute | 1 963 | 1 524 | 3 081 | 0.8 | 90.7 | 0.8 | 0.9 | 0.8 | 7.7 | 6.6 | 22.4 | 4.9 | 8.3 | 9.3 | 12.3 |
| 49 033 | ... | 8 | Rich | 2 665 | 2 267 | 3 030 | 0.9 | 94.4 | 0.4 | 1.1 | 0.3 | 4.6 | 8.2 | 23.2 | 6.7 | 12.0 | 10.9 | 11.1 |
| 49 035 | 41620 | 2 | Salt Lake | 1 923 | 1 063 842 | 39 | 553.2 | 75.5 | 1.9 | 1.1 | 6.1 | 17.4 | 8.6 | 20.3 | 10.3 | 17.2 | 13.3 | 11.8 |
| 49 037 | ... | 7 | San Juan | 20 254 | 14 965 | 2 110 | 0.7 | 45.9 | 0.8 | 48.7 | 1.3 | 5.3 | 9.0 | 24.2 | 10.5 | 11.7 | 11.1 | 12.1 |
| 49 039 | ... | 6 | Sanpete | 4 118 | 27 906 | 1 499 | 6.8 | 87.7 | 1.0 | 1.5 | 1.8 | 9.4 | 7.5 | 22.2 | 15.8 | 12.3 | 10.8 | 9.9 |
| 49 041 | ... | 7 | Sevier | 4 948 | 20 784 | 1 790 | 4.2 | 93.6 | 0.5 | 1.7 | 0.8 | 4.6 | 8.4 | 23.2 | 7.9 | 13.4 | 10.5 | 11.4 |
| 49 043 | 41620 | 2 | Summit | 4 848 | 38 003 | 1 222 | 7.8 | 85.9 | 0.8 | 0.6 | 2.1 | 11.8 | 6.7 | 20.8 | 7.4 | 12.3 | 14.7 | 16.9 |
| 49 045 | 41620 | 2 | Tooele | 17 978 | 59 870 | 866 | 3.3 | 85.4 | 1.2 | 1.4 | 1.9 | 11.7 | 9.8 | 26.0 | 7.7 | 14.6 | 14.4 | 11.2 |
| 49 047 | 46860 | 7 | Uintah | 11 602 | 34 524 | 1 311 | 3.0 | 84.1 | 0.6 | 8.4 | 1.2 | 7.5 | 10.4 | 22.8 | 9.5 | 16.3 | 11.6 | 11.1 |
| 49 049 | 39340 | 2 | Utah | 5 189 | 540 504 | 120 | 104.2 | 85.6 | 0.9 | 0.9 | 3.8 | 11.0 | 10.9 | 23.8 | 16.8 | 16.1 | 11.1 | 8.3 |
| 49 051 | 25720 | 6 | Wasatch | 3 045 | 25 273 | 1 600 | 8.3 | 84.9 | 0.5 | 0.8 | 1.4 | 13.5 | 9.4 | 24.1 | 7.6 | 13.6 | 14.3 | 12.5 |
| 49 053 | 41100 | 3 | Washington | 6 284 | 144 809 | 437 | 23.0 | 86.8 | 0.9 | 1.7 | 2.4 | 10.0 | 8.7 | 21.4 | 9.2 | 13.1 | 10.1 | 9.5 |
| 49 055 | ... | 9 | Wayne | 6 373 | 2 737 | 2 997 | 0.4 | 90.4 | 0.6 | 1.0 | 1.4 | 4.4 | 6.7 | 22.4 | 6.0 | 10.6 | 11.1 | 12.9 |
| 49 057 | 36260 | 2 | Weber | 1 492 | 236 640 | 274 | 158.6 | 79.5 | 1.8 | 1.1 | 2.5 | 17.1 | 8.8 | 21.0 | 10.2 | 15.9 | 12.0 | 12.0 |
| 50 000 | ... | X | VERMONT | 23 871 | 626 011 | X | 26.2 | 95.7 | 1.5 | 1.1 | 1.8 | 1.6 | 5.0 | 15.1 | 10.6 | 11.3 | 12.1 | 16.0 |
| 50 001 | ... | 6 | Addison | 1 985 | 36 745 | 1 254 | 18.5 | 95.6 | 1.2 | 0.9 | 2.1 | 1.9 | 4.5 | 15.2 | 13.3 | 9.2 | 12.1 | 16.0 |
| 50 003 | 13540 | 6 | Bennington | 1 748 | 36 697 | 1 256 | 21.0 | 96.7 | 1.2 | 0.7 | 1.1 | 1.5 | 5.0 | 15.0 | 8.9 | 9.4 | 10.9 | 16.0 |
| 50 005 | ... | 7 | Caledonia | 1 681 | 31 121 | 1 409 | 18.5 | 96.9 | 1.0 | 1.3 | 1.1 | 1.2 | 5.4 | 16.1 | 9.7 | 10.5 | 11.5 | 15.3 |

1. CBSA = Core Based Statistical Area. See Appendix A for explanation. See Appendix B for list of metropolitan areas with component counties.  2. County type code from the Economic Research Service of USDA Rural-Urban Continuum Codes. See Appendix A for definition.  3. Dry land or land partially or temporarily covered by water.  4. May be of any race.

# Table B. States and Counties — Population and Households

| | Population, 2011 (cont.) | | | | Population change and components of change, 2000–2012 | | | | | | | Households, 2010 | | | | |
| | Age (percent) (cont.) | | | | Total persons | | Percent change | | Components of change, 2010–2012 | | | | | | Percent | |
| STATE County | 55 to 64 years | 65 to 74 years | 75 years and over | Percent female | 2000 | 2010 | 2000–2010 | 2010–2012 | Births | Deaths | Net migration | Number | Percent change, 2000–2010 | Persons per house-hold | Female family house-holder[1] | One per-son |
|---|---|---|---|---|---|---|---|---|---|---|---|---|---|---|---|---|
| | 16 | 17 | 18 | 19 | 20 | 21 | 22 | 23 | 24 | 25 | 26 | 27 | 28 | 29 | 30 | 31 |
| **TEXAS—Cont'd** | | | | | | | | | | | | | | | | |
| Tom Green | 11.6 | 7.2 | 6.7 | 50.9 | 104 010 | 110 224 | 6.0 | 2.8 | 3 432 | 2 200 | 1 841 | 42 331 | 7.2 | 2.48 | 13.3 | 28.1 |
| Travis | 9.6 | 4.3 | 3.2 | 49.5 | 812 280 | 1 024 266 | 26.1 | 7.0 | 35 369 | 10 543 | 45 581 | 404 467 | 26.1 | 2.48 | 11.0 | 30.8 |
| Trinity | 16.2 | 13.1 | 9.6 | 51.3 | 13 779 | 14 585 | 5.8 | -1.9 | 355 | 478 | -169 | 6 142 | 7.3 | 2.37 | 12.2 | 28.7 |
| Tyler | 13.8 | 10.9 | 8.3 | 46.2 | 20 871 | 21 766 | 4.3 | -1.4 | 491 | 550 | -230 | 8 007 | 3.0 | 2.41 | 10.4 | 27.1 |
| Upshur | 13.9 | 9.2 | 6.7 | 50.5 | 35 291 | 39 309 | 11.4 | 1.7 | 1 091 | 911 | 513 | 14 925 | 12.3 | 2.60 | 11.7 | 23.4 |
| Upton | 13.1 | 8.0 | 7.0 | 49.6 | 3 404 | 3 355 | -1.4 | -2.1 | 106 | 45 | -135 | 1 256 | 0.0 | 2.62 | 9.9 | 25.4 |
| Uvalde | 11.4 | 8.0 | 7.1 | 50.9 | 25 926 | 26 405 | 1.8 | 1.3 | 923 | 575 | 4 | 9 025 | 5.4 | 2.86 | 15.9 | 21.7 |
| Val Verde | 9.8 | 7.1 | 5.7 | 49.7 | 44 856 | 48 879 | 9.0 | -0.4 | 1 941 | 814 | -1 325 | 15 654 | 10.6 | 3.00 | 16.3 | 20.2 |
| Van Zandt | 14.1 | 10.4 | 7.8 | 50.9 | 48 140 | 52 579 | 9.2 | -0.3 | 1 265 | 1 431 | 27 | 20 047 | 10.2 | 2.59 | 10.3 | 23.6 |
| Victoria | 12.3 | 7.3 | 6.3 | 51.2 | 84 088 | 86 793 | 3.2 | 2.9 | 2 864 | 1 661 | 1 297 | 32 187 | 7.0 | 2.65 | 14.5 | 24.5 |
| Walker | 10.8 | 6.3 | 4.3 | 41.2 | 61 758 | 67 861 | 9.9 | 0.8 | 1 391 | 1 192 | 356 | 20 969 | 14.6 | 2.44 | 12.6 | 27.9 |
| Waller | 11.5 | 6.4 | 4.0 | 50.4 | 32 663 | 43 205 | 32.3 | 2.7 | 1 284 | 665 | 498 | 14 040 | 33.0 | 2.81 | 13.1 | 21.1 |
| Ward | 11.9 | 7.4 | 7.3 | 51.5 | 10 909 | 10 658 | -2.3 | 2.1 | 330 | 218 | 110 | 3 995 | 0.8 | 2.64 | 13.6 | 25.4 |
| Washington | 13.9 | 9.5 | 9.3 | 51.0 | 30 373 | 33 718 | 11.0 | 1.1 | 926 | 820 | 280 | 13 037 | 15.1 | 2.45 | 11.7 | 27.6 |
| Webb | 7.7 | 4.5 | 3.5 | 51.4 | 193 117 | 250 304 | 29.6 | 3.5 | 12 204 | 2 676 | -582 | 67 106 | 32.3 | 3.68 | 20.9 | 13.4 |
| Wharton | 12.5 | 7.7 | 7.1 | 50.9 | 41 188 | 41 280 | 0.2 | 0.0 | 1 260 | 894 | -359 | 15 132 | 2.3 | 2.70 | 14.4 | 24.6 |
| Wheeler | 13.3 | 9.9 | 8.0 | 50.5 | 5 284 | 5 410 | 2.4 | 4.0 | 151 | 140 | 200 | 2 181 | 1.3 | 2.46 | 9.0 | 26.8 |
| Wichita | 11.1 | 6.7 | 6.5 | 48.7 | 131 664 | 131 500 | -0.1 | 0.0 | 3 972 | 2 885 | -1 040 | 49 016 | 1.2 | 2.44 | 13.6 | 29.3 |
| Wilbarger | 12.7 | 8.1 | 7.5 | 50.1 | 14 676 | 13 535 | -7.8 | -2.0 | 387 | 339 | -323 | 5 289 | -4.5 | 2.44 | 13.1 | 29.9 |
| Willacy | 9.9 | 6.5 | 5.4 | 45.6 | 20 082 | 22 134 | 10.2 | -0.3 | 723 | 390 | -414 | 5 764 | 3.2 | 3.28 | 19.3 | 18.0 |
| Williamson | 9.8 | 5.6 | 3.7 | 50.8 | 249 967 | 422 679 | 69.1 | 7.9 | 13 792 | 4 344 | 23 382 | 152 606 | 75.9 | 2.74 | 10.8 | 21.2 |
| Wilson | 13.7 | 7.6 | 5.5 | 50.3 | 32 408 | 42 918 | 32.4 | 3.4 | 1 006 | 788 | 1 236 | 15 009 | 36.0 | 2.82 | 10.0 | 17.4 |
| Winkler | 11.2 | 6.7 | 5.3 | 49.5 | 7 173 | 7 110 | -0.9 | 3.1 | 243 | 121 | 82 | 2 578 | -0.2 | 2.72 | 13.2 | 23.2 |
| Wise | 12.4 | 8.0 | 4.8 | 49.6 | 48 793 | 59 127 | 21.2 | 2.2 | 1 686 | 1 096 | 700 | 21 015 | 22.3 | 2.77 | 9.5 | 19.4 |
| Wood | 15.5 | 14.8 | 10.1 | 50.9 | 36 752 | 41 964 | 14.2 | 0.1 | 911 | 1 319 | 470 | 17 118 | 17.4 | 2.39 | 8.9 | 25.2 |
| Yoakum | 10.2 | 6.0 | 5.2 | 50.3 | 7 322 | 7 879 | 7.6 | 2.5 | 300 | 118 | 7 | 2 643 | 7.0 | 2.96 | 9.5 | 18.2 |
| Young | 13.6 | 9.4 | 9.3 | 50.7 | 17 943 | 18 550 | 3.4 | -1.1 | 508 | 531 | -185 | 7 343 | 2.5 | 2.49 | 11.1 | 25.3 |
| Zapata | 8.7 | 6.1 | 4.3 | 49.7 | 12 182 | 14 018 | 15.1 | 1.9 | 701 | 222 | -213 | 4 297 | 9.6 | 3.26 | 15.9 | 18.1 |
| Zavala | 10.7 | 6.5 | 5.5 | 50.4 | 11 600 | 11 677 | 0.7 | 2.4 | 466 | 189 | 2 | 3 573 | 4.2 | 3.15 | 24.0 | 19.8 |
| **UTAH** | 9.0 | 5.1 | 4.1 | 49.8 | 2 233 169 | 2 763 885 | 23.8 | 3.3 | 115 478 | 33 363 | 9 173 | 877 692 | 25.2 | 3.10 | 9.7 | 18.7 |
| Beaver | 10.9 | 7.2 | 5.6 | 48.3 | 6 005 | 6 629 | 10.4 | -1.9 | 270 | 134 | -276 | 2 265 | 14.3 | 2.92 | 7.2 | 22.1 |
| Box Elder | 9.6 | 6.1 | 5.3 | 49.5 | 42 745 | 49 975 | 16.9 | 0.4 | 1 952 | 736 | -1 048 | 16 058 | 22.2 | 3.09 | 8.7 | 17.2 |
| Cache | 7.4 | 4.3 | 3.6 | 50.4 | 91 391 | 112 656 | 23.3 | 2.5 | 5 423 | 1 084 | -1 510 | 34 722 | 26.1 | 3.14 | 7.7 | 16.3 |
| Carbon | 12.8 | 7.2 | 6.4 | 50.4 | 20 422 | 21 403 | 4.8 | -0.7 | 718 | 449 | -438 | 7 978 | 7.6 | 2.61 | 10.7 | 25.5 |
| Daggett | 15.6 | 11.7 | 7.0 | 44.5 | 921 | 1 059 | 15.0 | 2.9 | 30 | 9 | 5 | 426 | 25.3 | 2.34 | 4.9 | 29.1 |
| Davis | 8.8 | 4.6 | 3.7 | 49.8 | 238 994 | 306 479 | 28.2 | 3.0 | 12 853 | 3 144 | -414 | 93 545 | 31.4 | 3.24 | 9.6 | 15.2 |
| Duchesne | 9.3 | 6.5 | 4.6 | 49.2 | 14 371 | 18 607 | 29.5 | 3.4 | 914 | 266 | -18 | 6 003 | 31.7 | 3.05 | 8.6 | 17.7 |
| Emery | 12.4 | 7.6 | 4.8 | 49.2 | 10 860 | 10 976 | 1.1 | -0.4 | 393 | 196 | -237 | 3 732 | 7.6 | 2.93 | 7.4 | 18.4 |
| Garfield | 15.5 | 8.8 | 7.3 | 48.1 | 4 735 | 5 172 | 9.2 | -1.5 | 131 | 78 | -125 | 1 930 | 22.5 | 2.59 | 6.2 | 26.2 |
| Grand | 15.5 | 7.7 | 6.2 | 49.9 | 8 485 | 9 225 | 8.7 | 1.1 | 301 | 174 | -40 | 3 889 | 13.2 | 2.34 | 10.2 | 30.7 |
| Iron | 9.0 | 6.1 | 4.1 | 50.3 | 33 779 | 46 163 | 36.7 | 1.3 | 1 953 | 591 | -808 | 15 022 | 41.4 | 3.00 | 8.9 | 18.3 |
| Juab | 9.7 | 5.7 | 4.5 | 48.9 | 8 238 | 10 246 | 24.4 | 0.9 | 424 | 198 | -145 | 3 093 | 25.9 | 3.27 | 8.8 | 17.3 |
| Kane | 17.0 | 12.3 | 7.8 | 50.7 | 6 046 | 7 125 | 17.8 | 1.3 | 193 | 155 | 59 | 2 900 | 29.6 | 2.42 | 6.2 | 29.6 |
| Millard | 11.6 | 7.9 | 6.6 | 49.0 | 12 405 | 12 503 | 0.8 | 0.5 | 430 | 215 | -171 | 4 201 | 9.4 | 2.95 | 6.3 | 19.8 |
| Morgan | 10.6 | 6.5 | 4.4 | 49.8 | 7 129 | 9 469 | 32.8 | 3.7 | 346 | 86 | 92 | 2 820 | 37.8 | 3.36 | 5.2 | 12.1 |
| Piute | 14.2 | 13.4 | 8.8 | 49.2 | 1 435 | 1 556 | 8.4 | -2.1 | 32 | 31 | -43 | 576 | 13.2 | 2.64 | 5.6 | 24.8 |
| Rich | 13.0 | 8.6 | 6.3 | 48.5 | 1 961 | 2 264 | 15.5 | 0.1 | 89 | 40 | -51 | 805 | 24.8 | 2.81 | 5.2 | 18.4 |
| Salt Lake | 9.7 | 5.0 | 3.9 | 49.7 | 898 387 | 1 029 655 | 14.6 | 3.3 | 40 318 | 12 824 | 6 972 | 342 622 | 16.1 | 2.96 | 10.9 | 21.9 |
| San Juan | 10.2 | 6.6 | 4.5 | 49.4 | 14 413 | 14 746 | 2.3 | 1.5 | 534 | 199 | -111 | 4 505 | 10.2 | 3.21 | 14.7 | 20.7 |
| Sanpete | 9.7 | 6.9 | 4.9 | 47.7 | 22 763 | 27 822 | 22.2 | 0.3 | 875 | 399 | -411 | 7 952 | 21.5 | 3.19 | 8.1 | 17.4 |
| Sevier | 10.6 | 8.1 | 6.6 | 49.4 | 18 842 | 20 802 | 10.4 | -0.1 | 748 | 445 | -317 | 7 094 | 16.7 | 2.89 | 8.0 | 20.1 |
| Summit | 13.1 | 5.7 | 2.3 | 48.5 | 29 736 | 36 324 | 22.2 | 4.6 | 1 114 | 310 | 857 | 12 990 | 25.7 | 2.79 | 6.6 | 20.1 |
| Tooele | 8.7 | 4.5 | 3.1 | 49.6 | 40 735 | 58 218 | 42.9 | 2.8 | 2 269 | 681 | 75 | 17 971 | 41.8 | 3.22 | 10.0 | 16.8 |
| Uintah | 9.2 | 5.0 | 4.1 | 49.8 | 25 224 | 32 588 | 29.2 | 5.9 | 1 460 | 486 | 940 | 10 563 | 29.0 | 3.07 | 10.2 | 18.1 |
| Utah | 6.3 | 3.7 | 2.9 | 49.8 | 368 536 | 516 564 | 40.2 | 4.6 | 26 540 | 4 416 | 1 831 | 140 602 | 40.7 | 3.57 | 8.0 | 11.6 |
| Wasatch | 9.8 | 5.5 | 3.2 | 49.2 | 15 215 | 23 530 | 54.7 | 7.4 | 838 | 263 | 1 146 | 7 287 | 53.6 | 3.19 | 7.4 | 15.5 |
| Washington | 10.4 | 9.4 | 8.2 | 50.5 | 90 354 | 138 115 | 52.9 | 4.8 | 5 236 | 2 359 | 3 649 | 46 334 | 54.8 | 2.94 | 8.4 | 18.8 |
| Wayne | 14.4 | 9.4 | 6.6 | 49.8 | 2 509 | 2 778 | 10.7 | -1.5 | 66 | 50 | -69 | 1 059 | 19.0 | 2.61 | 5.9 | 26.3 |
| Weber | 9.8 | 5.4 | 4.8 | 49.8 | 196 533 | 231 236 | 17.7 | 2.3 | 9 028 | 3 345 | -221 | 78 748 | 19.9 | 2.90 | 11.5 | 21.4 |
| **VERMONT** | 14.9 | 8.3 | 6.7 | 50.7 | 608 827 | 625 741 | 2.8 | 0.0 | 13 415 | 11 827 | -1 134 | 256 442 | 6.6 | 2.34 | 9.6 | 28.2 |
| Addison | 15.4 | 8.0 | 6.3 | 50.1 | 35 974 | 36 821 | 2.4 | -0.2 | 684 | 709 | -55 | 14 084 | 7.8 | 2.41 | 8.6 | 25.5 |
| Bennington | 15.4 | 10.0 | 9.4 | 51.5 | 36 994 | 37 125 | 0.4 | -1.2 | 764 | 984 | -185 | 15 470 | 4.2 | 2.30 | 10.6 | 29.9 |
| Caledonia | 15.8 | 8.5 | 7.2 | 50.3 | 29 702 | 31 227 | 5.1 | -0.3 | 681 | 616 | -151 | 12 553 | 7.6 | 2.38 | 10.1 | 27.5 |

1. No spouse present.

# Table B. States and Counties — **Population, Vital Statistics, Medicare, and Crime**

| STATE County | Persons in group quarters, 2010 | Daytime population, 2007–2011 Number | Daytime population, 2007–2011 Employment/residence ratio | Births, 2011 Total | Births, 2011 Rate[1] | Deaths, 2011 Number | Deaths, 2011 Rate[1] | Persons under 65 with no health insurance, 2010 Number | Persons under 65 with no health insurance, 2010 Percent | Medicare, 2012 Eligible for Medicare | Medicare, 2012 Enrolled in Medicare Advantage | Medicare, 2012 Enrolled in a Medicare prescription drug plan | Serious crimes known to police,[2] 2011 Total Number | Serious crimes known to police,[2] 2011 Total Rate[3] |
|---|---|---|---|---|---|---|---|---|---|---|---|---|---|---|
| | 32 | 33 | 34 | 35 | 36 | 37 | 38 | 39 | 40 | 41 | 42 | 43 | 44 | 45 |
| **TEXAS—Cont'd** | | | | | | | | | | | | | | |
| Tom Green | 5 165 | 109 276 | 1.00 | 1 563 | 14.0 | 938 | 8.4 | 22 092 | 24.3 | 19 101 | 2 146 | 7 928 | 4 275 | 3 799 |
| Travis | 23 046 | 1 113 849 | 1.20 | 16 240 | 15.3 | 4 455 | 4.2 | 212 259 | 22.7 | 101 226 | 18 775 | 37 325 | 50 745 | 4 852 |
| Trinity | 48 | 13 086 | 0.70 | 156 | 10.6 | 198 | 13.5 | 3 071 | 27.2 | 3 937 | 601 | 1 803 | 347 | 2 330 |
| Tyler | 2 448 | 19 870 | 0.74 | 240 | 11.1 | 227 | 10.5 | 3 833 | 24.4 | 4 540 | 691 | 2 035 | 487 | 2 191 |
| Upshur | 516 | 31 543 | 0.54 | 485 | 12.2 | 367 | 9.2 | 8 360 | 25.5 | 7 525 | 1 245 | 3 358 | 1 031 | 2 646 |
| Upton | 61 | 3 283 | 1.00 | 56 | 16.7 | 21 | 6.3 | 889 | 31.5 | 543 | 64 | 267 | 26 | 759 |
| Uvalde | 564 | 26 534 | 1.02 | 439 | 16.5 | 268 | 10.1 | 6 422 | 29.1 | 4 767 | 832 | 2 246 | 721 | 2 674 |
| Val Verde | 1 945 | 47 724 | 0.96 | 886 | 18.0 | 361 | 7.4 | 12 708 | 30.9 | 7 476 | 1 058 | 3 541 | 1 069 | 2 142 |
| Van Zandt | 667 | 44 121 | 0.60 | 636 | 12.1 | 620 | 11.7 | 11 882 | 27.8 | 10 986 | 1 630 | 5 107 | 1 257 | 2 341 |
| Victoria | 1 508 | 86 500 | 1.00 | 1 350 | 15.4 | 722 | 8.2 | 18 199 | 24.6 | 14 908 | 1 691 | 7 364 | 4 244 | 4 789 |
| Walker | 16 708 | 68 965 | 1.10 | 704 | 10.3 | 524 | 7.7 | 11 663 | 26.0 | 8 065 | 1 544 | 2 882 | 1 743 | 2 516 |
| Waller | 3 703 | 37 084 | 0.74 | 629 | 14.3 | 270 | 6.1 | 10 859 | 30.6 | 5 151 | 1 064 | 1 900 | 934 | 2 117 |
| Ward | 125 | 10 324 | 0.94 | 144 | 13.4 | 95 | 8.9 | 2 469 | 27.6 | 1 871 | 224 | 940 | 221 | 2 031 |
| Washington | 1 816 | 34 076 | 1.06 | 401 | 11.9 | 350 | 10.4 | 6 236 | 23.8 | 7 066 | 709 | 3 413 | 821 | 2 385 |
| Webb | 3 479 | 246 569 | 1.01 | 5 698 | 22.2 | 1 112 | 4.3 | 83 761 | 36.8 | 26 319 | 2 066 | 14 962 | 12 078 | 4 726 |
| Wharton | 449 | 38 385 | 0.86 | 613 | 14.8 | 384 | 9.3 | 9 859 | 28.2 | 7 080 | 799 | 3 567 | 1 511 | 3 585 |
| Wheeler | 46 | 5 930 | 1.26 | 66 | 12.1 | 71 | 13.0 | 1 378 | 31.5 | 1 054 | 56 | 563 | 88 | 1 593 |
| Wichita | 12 017 | 135 867 | 1.08 | 1 804 | 13.8 | 1 264 | 10.0 | 24 742 | 24.0 | 21 528 | 1 575 | 9 688 | 6 017 | 4 481 |
| Wilbarger | 615 | 13 854 | 1.06 | 179 | 13.4 | 149 | 11.1 | 2 762 | 24.8 | 2 581 | 331 | 1 182 | 485 | 3 509 |
| Willacy | 3 254 | 21 177 | 0.87 | 352 | 15.9 | 174 | 7.9 | 4 779 | 29.4 | 3 215 | 705 | 1 716 | 979 | 4 332 |
| Williamson | 5 097 | 352 434 | 0.71 | 6 280 | 14.2 | 1 813 | 4.1 | 68 383 | 17.8 | 50 018 | 10 966 | 16 843 | 8 654 | 2 005 |
| Wilson | 551 | 31 190 | 0.44 | 439 | 10.0 | 329 | 7.5 | 8 519 | 22.8 | 6 592 | 1 761 | 1 839 | 633 | 1 445 |
| Winkler | 97 | 6 717 | 0.88 | 118 | 16.4 | 48 | 6.7 | 1 669 | 27.2 | 1 044 | 116 | 504 | 94 | 1 295 |
| Wise | 980 | 53 535 | 0.80 | 756 | 12.6 | 490 | 8.2 | 13 368 | 26.3 | 9 138 | 1 591 | 3 687 | 601 | 996 |
| Wood | 1 103 | 38 954 | 0.81 | 418 | 9.9 | 575 | 13.6 | 8 463 | 27.3 | 12 110 | 1 889 | 5 519 | 897 | 2 093 |
| Yoakum | 53 | 8 476 | 1.20 | 149 | 18.6 | 46 | 5.7 | 2 096 | 30.3 | 1 106 | 63 | 629 | 86 | 1 069 |
| Young | 279 | 18 159 | 0.98 | 247 | 13.4 | 246 | 13.3 | 3 996 | 26.8 | 4 051 | 223 | 2 293 | 375 | 1 980 |
| Zapata | 30 | 14 045 | 1.04 | 336 | 23.5 | 108 | 7.6 | 4 573 | 36.6 | 1 739 | 114 | 978 | 285 | 1 991 |
| Zavala | 409 | 11 310 | 0.90 | 237 | 20.0 | 82 | 6.9 | 2 705 | 27.6 | 1 881 | 502 | 995 | 189 | 1 585 |
| **UTAH** | 46 152 | 2 714 429 | 1.00 | 52 003 | 18.5 | 14 314 | 5.1 | 414 476 | 16.7 | 309 985 | 109 892 | 92 191 | 89 252 | 3 168 |
| Beaver | 24 | 6 444 | 0.98 | 130 | 19.7 | 68 | 10.3 | 1 190 | 20.7 | 1 027 | 232 | 524 | 40 | 686 |
| Box Elder | 339 | 48 048 | 0.95 | 907 | 18.0 | 310 | 6.2 | 6 626 | 15.0 | 6 784 | 2 374 | 2 120 | 1 169 | 2 446 |
| Cache | 3 594 | 108 374 | 0.97 | 2 434 | 21.2 | 466 | 4.1 | 15 995 | 15.9 | 10 632 | 4 646 | 2 914 | 1 318 | 1 148 |
| Carbon | 544 | 21 160 | 1.02 | 310 | 14.5 | 189 | 8.9 | 2 504 | 13.9 | 3 770 | 333 | 2 168 | 621 | 3 031 |
| Daggett | 63 | 886 | 0.99 | 14 | 12.1 | 3 | 2.6 | 148 | 18.0 | 202 | 47 | 57 | 18 | 1 668 |
| Davis | 3 293 | 272 120 | 0.79 | 5 812 | 18.6 | 1 379 | 4.4 | 32 387 | 11.5 | 31 626 | 11 086 | 6 663 | 6 669 | 2 135 |
| Duchesne | 297 | 18 419 | 1.05 | 407 | 21.5 | 109 | 5.8 | 3 059 | 18.7 | 2 595 | 510 | 1 146 | 461 | 2 431 |
| Emery | 43 | 10 736 | 0.98 | 173 | 15.8 | 85 | 7.8 | 1 500 | 15.7 | 1 705 | 308 | 732 | 116 | 1 037 |
| Garfield | 171 | 5 141 | 1.04 | 59 | 11.5 | 28 | 5.4 | 786 | 18.8 | 931 | 208 | 327 | NA | NA |
| Grand | 143 | 9 709 | 1.14 | 136 | 14.6 | 80 | 8.6 | 1 847 | 23.2 | 1 612 | 227 | 700 | 341 | 3 627 |
| Iron | 1 050 | 44 729 | 0.96 | 882 | 18.9 | 260 | 5.6 | 9 251 | 22.5 | 5 892 | 1 741 | 2 019 | 1 345 | 3 042 |
| Juab | 122 | 9 243 | 0.80 | 191 | 18.5 | 82 | 7.9 | 1 546 | 17.0 | 1 307 | 57 | 725 | 252 | 2 413 |
| Kane | 100 | 6 979 | 0.99 | 80 | 11.0 | 68 | 9.4 | 1 000 | 17.7 | 1 570 | 43 | 797 | NA | NA |
| Millard | 122 | 12 261 | 0.99 | 203 | 16.1 | 88 | 7.0 | 2 509 | 23.6 | 2 019 | 448 | 754 | 254 | 1 993 |
| Morgan | 0 | 7 357 | 0.53 | 160 | 16.5 | 35 | 3.6 | 1 082 | 12.7 | 1 216 | 390 | 242 | 65 | 673 |
| Piute | 37 | 1 606 | 0.91 | 16 | 10.7 | 12 | 8.0 | 294 | 25.0 | 377 | 108 | 118 | NA | NA |
| Rich | 1 | 2 229 | 0.99 | 37 | 16.1 | 11 | 4.8 | 396 | 20.8 | 338 | 64 | 136 | 43 | 1 863 |
| Salt Lake | 14 006 | 1 086 508 | 1.14 | 18 109 | 17.3 | 5 548 | 5.3 | 166 372 | 17.9 | 113 127 | 45 638 | 33 132 | 48 402 | 4 614 |
| San Juan | 289 | 14 360 | 0.97 | 241 | 16.3 | 83 | 5.6 | 2 950 | 22.5 | 1 749 | 236 | 990 | 177 | 1 178 |
| Sanpete | 2 417 | 25 718 | 0.85 | 397 | 14.2 | 166 | 5.9 | 5 143 | 23.0 | 3 838 | 968 | 1 529 | NA | NA |
| Sevier | 301 | 20 949 | 1.03 | 345 | 16.5 | 187 | 8.9 | 2 985 | 17.0 | 3 544 | 929 | 1 550 | 529 | 2 495 |
| Summit | 116 | 40 097 | 1.22 | 500 | 13.3 | 128 | 3.4 | 5 378 | 16.0 | 3 802 | 1 157 | 1 213 | 948 | 2 560 |
| Tooele | 355 | 49 250 | 0.69 | 1 022 | 17.2 | 281 | 4.7 | 7 194 | 13.4 | 5 747 | 1 235 | 1 505 | 1 681 | 2 833 |
| Uintah | 192 | 32 388 | 1.04 | 630 | 19.0 | 200 | 6.0 | 5 968 | 20.4 | 3 438 | 787 | 1 365 | 749 | 2 255 |
| Utah | 13 912 | 482 925 | 0.91 | 11 909 | 22.4 | 1 881 | 3.5 | 71 578 | 15.1 | 42 167 | 17 514 | 12 546 | 12 064 | 2 291 |
| Wasatch | 250 | 19 483 | 0.68 | 379 | 15.5 | 105 | 4.3 | 4 554 | 21.4 | 2 506 | 910 | 787 | 254 | 1 059 |
| Washington | 1 853 | 137 118 | 1.00 | 2 408 | 17.0 | 980 | 6.9 | 23 224 | 20.7 | 26 296 | 8 105 | 8 425 | 2 422 | 1 720 |
| Wayne | 9 | 2 814 | 1.06 | 29 | 10.6 | 29 | 10.6 | 517 | 22.2 | 510 | 14 | 274 | 33 | 1 165 |
| Weber | 2 509 | 217 378 | 0.90 | 4 083 | 17.4 | 1 453 | 6.2 | 36 492 | 17.7 | 29 658 | 9 577 | 6 733 | 8 516 | 3 613 |
| **VERMONT** | 25 329 | 622 257 | 0.99 | 5 955 | 9.5 | 5 102 | 8.1 | 49 750 | 9.7 | 121 073 | 8 078 | 65 678 | 15 311 | 2 444 |
| Addison | 2 852 | 33 675 | 0.83 | 305 | 8.3 | 302 | 8.2 | 3 022 | 10.4 | 6 445 | 500 | 3 435 | 646 | 1 752 |
| Bennington | 1 475 | 39 215 | 1.12 | 361 | 9.8 | 436 | 11.8 | 2 855 | 9.8 | 8 565 | 546 | 5 069 | 1 011 | 2 720 |
| Caledonia | 1 345 | 29 363 | 0.88 | 308 | 9.9 | 273 | 8.8 | 2 811 | 11.1 | 6 282 | 420 | 3 491 | 553 | 1 769 |

1. Per 1,000 estimated resident population.　　2. Data for serious crimes have not been adjusted for underreporting; this may affect comparability between geographic areas and over time.　　3. Per 100,000 population estimated by the FBI.

| STATE County | Serious crimes known to police, 2011 (cont.)[1] Rate[2] | | Education School enrollment and attainment, 2007–2011 Enrollment[3] | | Attainment[4] (percent) | | Local government expenditures,[5] 2009–2010 | | Money income, 2007–2011 | Households Median income | | | Income and poverty, 2011 Percent below poverty level | | |
|---|---|---|---|---|---|---|---|---|---|---|---|---|---|---|---|
| | Violent | Property | Total | Per-cent private | High school graduate or less | Bach-elor's degree or more | Total current expendi-tures (mil dol) | Current expendi-tures per student (dollars) | Per capita income[6] (dollars) | Dollars | Percent change, 2000 to 2007–2011 (constant 2011 dollars) | Percent with income of $200,000 or more | Median house-hold income (dollars) | All per-sons | Children under 18 years | Children 5 to 17 years in families |
| | 46 | 47 | 48 | 49 | 50 | 51 | 52 | 53 | 54 | 55 | 56 | 57 | 58 | 59 | 60 | 61 |
| **TEXAS—Cont'd** | | | | | | | | | | | | | | | | |
| Tom Green | 256 | 3 543 | 28 339 | 8.8 | 48.2 | 22.3 | 164.7 | 9 005 | 22 870 | 43 465 | -2.9 | 2.2 | 41 626 | 17.7 | 25.4 | 24.6 |
| Travis | 367 | 4 485 | 285 823 | 12.8 | 30.3 | 44.0 | 1 367.4 | 9 380 | 32 619 | 55 452 | -12.2 | 6.7 | 53 303 | 18.1 | 24.1 | 22.8 |
| Trinity | 383 | 1 947 | 2 813 | 3.1 | 66.0 | 10.6 | 23.5 | 10 397 | 20 002 | 38 138 | 4.3 | 1.5 | 32 745 | 21.2 | 33.9 | 31.0 |
| Tyler | 346 | 1 845 | 4 176 | 4.2 | 57.7 | 12.0 | 35.8 | 10 039 | 19 443 | 35 847 | -10.9 | 1.3 | 36 384 | 21.0 | 28.7 | 26.8 |
| Upshur | 311 | 2 335 | 9 128 | 11.7 | 51.1 | 14.9 | 65.8 | 9 372 | 22 919 | 46 734 | 3.8 | 2.4 | 44 434 | 15.9 | 24.5 | 22.9 |
| Upton | 29 | 730 | 842 | 4.3 | 58.6 | 16.6 | 12.4 | 17 276 | 22 985 | 52 455 | 34.1 | 1.4 | 47 854 | 16.4 | 23.1 | 22.0 |
| Uvalde | 226 | 2 448 | 8 169 | 7.3 | 54.9 | 15.8 | 59.3 | 9 617 | 16 906 | 34 456 | -6.1 | 1.9 | 32 749 | 25.8 | 38.9 | 36.4 |
| Val Verde | 202 | 1 940 | 13 185 | 7.8 | 61.0 | 16.4 | 84.7 | 8 043 | 17 180 | 38 747 | 1.1 | 0.8 | 38 574 | 21.5 | 32.3 | 30.4 |
| Van Zandt | 175 | 2 166 | 11 868 | 10.4 | 58.0 | 12.2 | 86.8 | 8 649 | 20 969 | 42 359 | -10.4 | 1.5 | 41 452 | 17.5 | 26.7 | 24.1 |
| Victoria | 529 | 4 260 | 21 825 | 12.3 | 49.8 | 16.5 | 132.7 | 8 898 | 24 571 | 49 676 | -5.0 | 2.9 | 45 687 | 18.5 | 29.3 | 27.4 |
| Walker | 404 | 2 111 | 20 458 | 5.7 | 52.3 | 18.1 | 66.0 | 9 175 | 15 240 | 36 885 | -13.2 | 1.4 | 38 138 | 25.5 | 28.2 | 26.3 |
| Waller | 211 | 1 906 | 12 881 | 21.5 | 57.7 | 19.7 | 78.8 | 8 777 | 22 859 | 50 609 | -1.7 | 4.4 | 47 180 | 18.3 | 26.0 | 25.1 |
| Ward | 202 | 1 829 | 2 555 | 2.3 | 60.9 | 11.3 | 20.6 | 9 802 | 20 923 | 41 939 | 5.7 | 2.4 | 43 871 | 15.2 | 23.7 | 22.3 |
| Washington | 212 | 2 173 | 7 920 | 14.0 | 49.7 | 25.5 | 45.6 | 8 639 | 25 515 | 45 320 | -8.7 | 3.2 | 44 897 | 14.6 | 21.8 | 20.2 |
| Webb | 480 | 4 245 | 86 000 | 4.8 | 57.7 | 17.1 | 592.3 | 8 834 | 14 465 | 37 868 | -0.2 | 1.5 | 35 295 | 32.1 | 43.9 | 42.1 |
| Wharton | 463 | 3 122 | 10 691 | 8.8 | 57.8 | 17.1 | 77.5 | 9 498 | 22 070 | 43 689 | 0.5 | 2.2 | 41 911 | 18.5 | 27.1 | 26.2 |
| Wheeler | 217 | 1 376 | 1 117 | 4.2 | 53.8 | 17.1 | 14.0 | 13 732 | 28 013 | 48 000 | 14.6 | 3.7 | 45 848 | 12.8 | 21.3 | 19.7 |
| Wichita | 401 | 4 080 | 33 251 | 8.2 | 50.0 | 19.8 | 191.8 | 8 881 | 23 292 | 44 786 | -1.8 | 2.5 | 42 738 | 16.2 | 24.9 | 23.5 |
| Wilbarger | 449 | 3 061 | 3 337 | 7.0 | 57.1 | 17.9 | 22.4 | 8 453 | 20 714 | 40 050 | 0.6 | 1.6 | 35 785 | 18.8 | 27.2 | 25.7 |
| Willacy | 956 | 3 376 | 5 988 | 2.8 | 71.8 | 9.2 | 48.5 | 10 760 | 11 231 | 22 894 | -23.3 | 1.1 | 28 487 | 38.9 | 43.3 | 40.7 |
| Williamson | 133 | 1 873 | 116 277 | 13.5 | 29.0 | 37.6 | 807.6 | 8 232 | 30 688 | 71 346 | -12.9 | 4.0 | 70 276 | 7.4 | 10.5 | 9.8 |
| Wilson | 110 | 1 335 | 10 952 | 11.5 | 49.9 | 18.8 | 69.5 | 8 271 | 26 989 | 62 689 | 16.1 | 2.9 | 56 873 | 12.4 | 17.9 | 15.7 |
| Winkler | 207 | 1 088 | 1 860 | 5.1 | 61.0 | 9.8 | 21.1 | 13 519 | 20 202 | 44 573 | 7.9 | 1.2 | 47 674 | 15.2 | 21.9 | 20.7 |
| Wise | 80 | 916 | 14 679 | 6.5 | 53.3 | 15.6 | 85.8 | 9 658 | 25 180 | 57 511 | 1.6 | 3.4 | 55 118 | 12.0 | 16.8 | 14.9 |
| Wood | 166 | 1 928 | 8 355 | 9.3 | 53.9 | 16.5 | 57.6 | 9 421 | 22 606 | 41 260 | -7.1 | 2.0 | 39 514 | 17.6 | 27.5 | 25.5 |
| Yoakum | 149 | 920 | 2 110 | 7.9 | 62.0 | 13.1 | 22.6 | 11 455 | 20 411 | 48 173 | 9.2 | 2.9 | 48 521 | 13.1 | 18.3 | 17.6 |
| Young | 169 | 1 811 | 4 133 | 6.8 | 57.3 | 14.9 | 30.7 | 8 709 | 25 757 | 39 898 | -3.1 | 3.4 | 40 133 | 16.9 | 26.0 | 23.6 |
| Zapata | 147 | 1 844 | 3 942 | 1.9 | 73.0 | 9.7 | 35.8 | 9 527 | 14 897 | 26 009 | -21.8 | 1.8 | 30 104 | 33.6 | 46.3 | 44.3 |
| Zavala | 294 | 1 292 | 3 243 | 2.1 | 62.8 | 9.6 | 28.0 | 11 305 | 11 754 | 23 952 | 5.3 | 1.6 | 22 982 | 36.3 | 46.4 | 44.3 |
| **UTAH** | 195 | 2 973 | 881 819 | 14.7 | 33.9 | 29.6 | 3 505.0 | 6 117 | 23 650 | 57 783 | -6.4 | 3.3 | 55 802 | 13.6 | 16.2 | 14.9 |
| Beaver | 69 | 617 | 1 792 | 3.2 | 51.3 | 10.5 | 10.5 | 6 413 | 17 951 | 43 225 | -7.3 | 1.6 | 44 126 | 10.8 | 15.1 | 13.5 |
| Box Elder | 113 | 2 333 | 15 316 | 10.0 | 42.2 | 22.5 | 64.9 | 5 660 | 21 031 | 55 588 | -7.8 | 1.3 | 51 558 | 10.1 | 12.6 | 11.5 |
| Cache | 50 | 1 098 | 42 922 | 7.1 | 29.9 | 35.6 | 140.4 | 6 119 | 20 152 | 48 083 | -9.9 | 2.1 | 47 589 | 16.7 | 16.7 | 14.8 |
| Carbon | 176 | 2 855 | 5 963 | 6.9 | 43.2 | 12.8 | 30.9 | 7 619 | 20 587 | 43 659 | -5.0 | 0.9 | 47 585 | 14.8 | 18.7 | 17.3 |
| Daggett | 0 | 1 668 | 121 | 9.9 | 52.4 | 18.5 | 2.6 | 14 829 | 23 789 | 44 750 | 7.5 | 1.3 | 48 751 | 7.8 | 8.2 | 7.5 |
| Davis | 98 | 2 037 | 99 275 | 9.0 | 27.2 | 34.1 | 417.1 | 5 843 | 25 935 | 69 147 | -4.7 | 4.0 | 68 974 | 8.3 | 10.2 | 9.5 |
| Duchesne | 316 | 2 114 | 4 988 | 5.1 | 50.3 | 16.8 | 30.2 | 6 753 | 23 431 | 55 790 | 32.0 | 2.7 | 54 973 | 12.0 | 15.1 | 13.5 |
| Emery | 9 | 1 028 | 2 864 | 6.6 | 47.7 | 13.1 | 19.9 | 8 422 | 20 257 | 50 800 | -5.6 | 0.8 | 48 745 | 12.6 | 16.9 | 15.2 |
| Garfield | NA | NA | 1 126 | 5.9 | 40.8 | 20.9 | 10.4 | 10 822 | 23 161 | 46 029 | -3.1 | 2.0 | 40 762 | 14.6 | 19.5 | 17.5 |
| Grand | 170 | 3 456 | 1 796 | 11.5 | 38.8 | 27.0 | 11.8 | 7 174 | 22 135 | 42 004 | -3.9 | 1.5 | 41 410 | 15.5 | 24.3 | 22.7 |
| Iron | 217 | 2 825 | 16 100 | 10.0 | 35.1 | 27.1 | 55.9 | 5 942 | 17 356 | 42 226 | -5.6 | 1.2 | 41 094 | 21.1 | 25.2 | 23.7 |
| Juab | 96 | 2 317 | 3 235 | 7.2 | 45.8 | 14.1 | 16.5 | 6 563 | 18 348 | 54 000 | 4.9 | 1.6 | 51 762 | 13.2 | 17.7 | 16.3 |
| Kane | NA | NA | 1 442 | 4.9 | 31.9 | 26.8 | 11.0 | 8 112 | 26 699 | 45 439 | -1.7 | 2.1 | 42 515 | 11.9 | 18.8 | 17.4 |
| Millard | 141 | 1 852 | 3 357 | 3.3 | 43.7 | 19.5 | 23.2 | 8 811 | 19 452 | 47 062 | -3.7 | 1.8 | 47 316 | 17.2 | 24.2 | 20.5 |
| Morgan | 31 | 642 | 3 024 | 7.1 | 33.7 | 27.4 | 13.3 | 5 678 | 25 138 | 76 472 | 12.7 | 3.3 | 74 509 | 5.9 | 7.1 | 6.3 |
| Piute | NA | NA | 433 | 4.2 | 51.3 | 16.7 | 3.9 | 11 957 | 16 969 | 36 667 | -8.3 | 0.3 | 34 079 | 21.1 | 36.7 | 32.1 |
| Rich | 130 | 1 733 | 611 | 8.5 | 38.4 | 20.0 | 5.5 | 11 657 | 24 168 | 53 924 | 0.4 | 2.0 | 50 980 | 11.5 | 16.6 | 14.8 |
| Salt Lake | 324 | 4 289 | 305 771 | 13.5 | 35.4 | 30.2 | 1 191.6 | 6 110 | 25 555 | 59 168 | -9.4 | 3.8 | 56 166 | 14.5 | 18.8 | 17.5 |
| San Juan | 86 | 1 091 | 4 710 | 7.2 | 52.4 | 18.3 | 32.2 | 10 546 | 14 853 | 37 611 | -1.0 | 1.0 | 37 444 | 29.9 | 32.5 | 27.8 |
| Sanpete | NA | NA | 9 629 | 13.1 | 42.3 | 18.3 | 37.7 | 6 833 | 16 587 | 44 799 | 0.4 | 2.0 | 45 231 | 17.8 | 21.3 | 19.6 |
| Sevier | 141 | 2 353 | 5 965 | 4.3 | 43.9 | 16.2 | 29.1 | 6 206 | 18 863 | 44 731 | -7.5 | 1.2 | 43 190 | 15.2 | 21.2 | 18.9 |
| Summit | 95 | 2 466 | 9 314 | 11.2 | 24.4 | 49.8 | 62.1 | 8 811 | 41 532 | 84 752 | -3.4 | 13.0 | 85 221 | 7.7 | 12.1 | 10.5 |
| Tooele | 169 | 2 664 | 18 436 | 9.7 | 39.6 | 19.5 | 82.8 | 5 834 | 22 620 | 63 228 | 2.3 | 2.2 | 61 719 | 9.6 | 12.2 | 11.0 |
| Uintah | 211 | 2 044 | 8 791 | 7.4 | 52.8 | 15.0 | 42.9 | 6 286 | 24 396 | 62 450 | 34.0 | 2.8 | 58 936 | 11.7 | 14.3 | 13.4 |
| Utah | 75 | 2 216 | 199 668 | 27.1 | 24.3 | 35.9 | 660.4 | 5 650 | 20 794 | 59 338 | -4.1 | 3.3 | 58 077 | 14.3 | 12.8 | 11.9 |
| Wasatch | 83 | 976 | 6 959 | 11.8 | 31.5 | 30.5 | 34.9 | 6 380 | 25 978 | 64 651 | -3.5 | 6.3 | 56 379 | 8.8 | 13.1 | 12.1 |
| Washington | 146 | 1 574 | 39 884 | 11.2 | 36.1 | 24.9 | 169.8 | 6 262 | 21 467 | 50 307 | 0.1 | 2.2 | 46 001 | 15.7 | 23.8 | 22.1 |
| Wayne | 0 | 1 165 | 788 | 5.6 | 39.6 | 21.9 | 4.8 | 8 075 | 17 931 | 49 847 | 15.4 | 0.7 | 39 593 | 16.4 | 25.9 | 22.5 |
| Weber | 224 | 3 389 | 67 539 | 9.3 | 40.9 | 22.2 | 288.7 | 6 224 | 23 297 | 54 666 | -8.0 | 2.2 | 52 183 | 13.2 | 16.9 | 14.5 |
| **VERMONT** | 135 | 2 309 | 156 289 | 19.8 | 40.7 | 33.8 | 1 400.2 | 15 711 | 28 376 | 53 422 | -3.2 | 3.1 | 52 033 | 11.9 | 15.8 | 13.0 |
| Addison | 87 | 1 666 | 10 137 | 33.7 | 42.5 | 34.6 | 81.3 | 17 074 | 27 683 | 57 203 | -1.8 | 2.8 | 54 542 | 11.1 | 13.7 | 10.9 |
| Bennington | 129 | 2 591 | 8 735 | 25.3 | 42.0 | 31.8 | 72.5 | 15 340 | 27 989 | 48 083 | -10.8 | 3.0 | 44 701 | 14.5 | 20.4 | 17.4 |
| Caledonia | 134 | 1 635 | 7 593 | 23.5 | 45.9 | 28.2 | 53.8 | 12 626 | 23 246 | 44 433 | -5.4 | 1.5 | 42 452 | 14.0 | 21.0 | 17.9 |

1. Data for serious crimes have not been adjusted for underreporting; this may affect comparability between geographic areas and over time. 2. Per 100,000 population estimated by the FBI. 3. All persons 3 years old and over enrolled in nursery school through college. 4. Persons 25 years old and over. 5. Elementary and secondary education expenditures. 6. Based on population estimated by the American Community Survey, 2007–2011.

# Table B. States and Counties — Personal Income

| | Personal income, 2011 | | | | | | | | | | | | |
| STATE County | Total (mil dol) | Percent change, 2010–2011 | Per capita[1] Dollars | Per capita[1] Rank | Wages and salaries[2] (mil dol) | Proprietors' income (mil dol) | Dividends, interest, and rent (mil dol) | Total | Transfer payments (mil dol) Government payments to individuals Total | Social Security | Medical payments | Income mainte-nance | Unemploy-ment insurance |
|---|---|---|---|---|---|---|---|---|---|---|---|---|---|
| | 62 | 63 | 64 | 65 | 66 | 67 | 68 | 69 | 70 | 71 | 72 | 73 | 74 |
| **TEXAS—Cont'd** | | | | | | | | | | | | | |
| Tom Green | 4 169 | 6.5 | 37 279 | 1 050 | 2 374 | 343 | 841 | 846 | 822 | 255 | 385 | 94 | 20 |
| Travis | 45 925 | 6.2 | 43 198 | 495 | 39 364 | 5 907 | 8 136 | 4 732 | 4 496 | 1 435 | 1 727 | 646 | 217 |
| Trinity | 416 | 4.5 | 28 395 | 2 557 | 87 | 25 | 58 | 155 | 152 | 57 | 67 | 17 | 3 |
| Tyler | 641 | 5.3 | 29 607 | 2 361 | 165 | 37 | 75 | 198 | 194 | 65 | 95 | 19 | 6 |
| Upshur | 1 420 | 8.7 | 35 663 | 1 272 | 315 | 86 | 150 | 331 | 323 | 108 | 154 | 35 | 8 |
| Upton | 151 | 11.2 | 45 030 | 393 | 96 | 12 | 15 | 25 | 24 | 8 | 12 | 3 | 0 |
| Uvalde | 860 | 6.6 | 32 404 | 1 802 | 388 | 89 | 161 | 257 | 251 | 55 | 118 | 44 | 6 |
| Val Verde | 1 508 | 3.9 | 30 702 | 2 154 | 965 | 111 | 161 | 354 | 343 | 72 | 160 | 72 | 12 |
| Van Zandt | 1 791 | 3.8 | 33 942 | 1 521 | 414 | 100 | 224 | 465 | 453 | 157 | 223 | 39 | 11 |
| Victoria | 3 716 | 8.4 | 42 452 | 546 | 1 924 | 569 | 542 | 710 | 691 | 212 | 334 | 88 | 17 |
| Walker | 1 737 | 3.9 | 25 508 | 2 929 | 1 041 | 100 | 279 | 386 | 371 | 115 | 152 | 46 | 12 |
| Waller | 1 290 | 4.7 | 29 320 | 2 404 | 786 | 88 | 166 | 271 | 262 | 74 | 108 | 33 | 9 |
| Ward | 415 | 13.4 | 38 699 | 881 | 246 | 48 | 50 | 83 | 80 | 26 | 39 | 9 | 2 |
| Washington | 1 495 | 6.0 | 44 229 | 430 | 673 | 214 | 348 | 307 | 300 | 99 | 138 | 27 | 6 |
| Webb | 6 409 | 7.5 | 24 985 | 2 965 | 3 864 | 792 | 584 | 1 665 | 1 608 | 266 | 712 | 470 | 46 |
| Wharton | 1 469 | 7.8 | 35 556 | 1 282 | 628 | 158 | 219 | 342 | 333 | 98 | 163 | 41 | 10 |
| Wheeler | 243 | 18.7 | 44 463 | 425 | 109 | 49 | 41 | 51 | 49 | 14 | 30 | 3 | 1 |
| Wichita | 4 637 | 3.6 | 35 477 | 1 298 | 2 920 | 588 | 775 | 998 | 970 | 294 | 449 | 110 | 27 |
| Wilbarger | 463 | 1.5 | 34 571 | 1 432 | 283 | 33 | 70 | 129 | 126 | 34 | 64 | 14 | 2 |
| Willacy | 585 | 5.9 | 26 462 | 2 827 | 203 | 58 | 37 | 200 | 195 | 33 | 106 | 42 | 8 |
| Williamson | 17 741 | 10.0 | 40 067 | 737 | 8 345 | 979 | 2 233 | 1 864 | 1 766 | 738 | 630 | 171 | 86 |
| Wilson | 1 524 | 8.9 | 34 810 | 1 401 | 271 | 64 | 163 | 283 | 274 | 87 | 123 | 29 | 8 |
| Winkler | 255 | 13.5 | 35 493 | 1 295 | 158 | 17 | 22 | 55 | 54 | 15 | 30 | 6 | 1 |
| Wise | 2 124 | 4.5 | 35 494 | 1 294 | 1 136 | 253 | 263 | 348 | 335 | 134 | 134 | 32 | 12 |
| Wood | 1 331 | 4.0 | 31 575 | 1 980 | 392 | 84 | 253 | 449 | 440 | 175 | 201 | 30 | 8 |
| Yoakum | 329 | -0.1 | 41 060 | 654 | 256 | 33 | 50 | 50 | 49 | 15 | 25 | 5 | 1 |
| Young | 739 | 7.0 | 39 998 | 747 | 331 | 148 | 120 | 173 | 169 | 56 | 89 | 15 | 4 |
| Zapata | 359 | 15.1 | 25 162 | 2 953 | 263 | 27 | 40 | 103 | 100 | 18 | 51 | 24 | 3 |
| Zavala | 248 | 10.7 | 20 926 | 3 093 | 103 | 27 | 20 | 110 | 107 | 18 | 55 | 27 | 4 |
| **UTAH** | 94 401 | 5.9 | 33 509 | X | 65 634 | 8 073 | 14 739 | 13 437 | 12 815 | 4 387 | 4 711 | 1 762 | 522 |
| Beaver | 198 | 8.9 | 29 994 | 2 293 | 125 | 24 | 27 | 42 | 40 | 13 | 17 | 4 | 1 |
| Box Elder | 1 516 | 6.0 | 30 148 | 2 260 | 831 | 110 | 210 | 251 | 239 | 95 | 90 | 29 | 10 |
| Cache | 3 169 | 4.2 | 27 631 | 2 666 | 2 140 | 205 | 537 | 496 | 471 | 151 | 163 | 71 | 17 |
| Carbon | 701 | 4.6 | 32 886 | 1 726 | 486 | 34 | 82 | 169 | 165 | 56 | 68 | 19 | 4 |
| Daggett | 33 | 5.7 | 28 746 | 2 494 | 19 | 9 | 6 | 7 | 6 | 3 | 2 | 0 | 0 |
| Davis | 10 837 | 5.8 | 34 755 | 1 411 | 6 148 | 784 | 1 454 | 1 245 | 1 176 | 429 | 418 | 143 | 52 |
| Duchesne | 694 | 9.7 | 36 725 | 1 109 | 459 | 38 | 83 | 105 | 101 | 37 | 42 | 12 | 3 |
| Emery | 354 | 17.4 | 32 391 | 1 807 | 285 | 7 | 39 | 66 | 63 | 27 | 24 | 7 | 2 |
| Garfield | 140 | 1.2 | 27 206 | 2 738 | 89 | 3 | 21 | 32 | 31 | 12 | 11 | 3 | 2 |
| Grand | 321 | 6.7 | 34 402 | 1 451 | 184 | 28 | 85 | 59 | 57 | 22 | 20 | 9 | 3 |
| Iron | 1 100 | 4.9 | 23 541 | 3 045 | 629 | 82 | 179 | 264 | 254 | 85 | 88 | 39 | 9 |
| Juab | 252 | 4.0 | 24 351 | 3 012 | 130 | 17 | 27 | 58 | 56 | 18 | 25 | 7 | 2 |
| Kane | 231 | 4.3 | 31 779 | 1 937 | 119 | 13 | 41 | 52 | 50 | 23 | 19 | 4 | 2 |
| Millard | 375 | 7.7 | 29 669 | 2 349 | 221 | 51 | 52 | 74 | 71 | 28 | 28 | 9 | 2 |
| Morgan | 322 | 7.0 | 33 278 | 1 658 | 97 | 15 | 55 | 37 | 35 | 16 | 12 | 2 | 1 |
| Piute | 37 | 3.1 | 24 904 | 2 971 | 12 | 3 | 6 | 13 | 13 | 5 | 5 | 1 | 0 |
| Rich | 72 | 5.6 | 31 286 | 2 047 | 23 | 8 | 16 | 11 | 11 | 5 | 3 | 1 | 0 |
| Salt Lake | 40 995 | 5.7 | 39 081 | 845 | 34 501 | 3 937 | 6 610 | 5 148 | 4 916 | 1 658 | 1 860 | 683 | 203 |
| San Juan | 331 | 2.5 | 22 325 | 3 076 | 194 | 10 | 48 | 97 | 93 | 21 | 33 | 32 | 3 |
| Sanpete | 614 | 4.6 | 21 956 | 3 086 | 277 | 58 | 82 | 163 | 156 | 55 | 61 | 21 | 5 |
| Sevier | 560 | 3.4 | 26 716 | 2 800 | 342 | 33 | 83 | 139 | 134 | 50 | 56 | 17 | 4 |
| Summit | 2 731 | 7.5 | 72 643 | 18 | 1 049 | 291 | 707 | 135 | 126 | 61 | 37 | 10 | 7 |
| Tooele | 1 646 | 5.8 | 27 748 | 2 650 | 960 | 49 | 163 | 236 | 223 | 71 | 84 | 34 | 11 |
| Uintah | 1 037 | 10.2 | 31 278 | 2 055 | 840 | 57 | 121 | 142 | 135 | 49 | 53 | 19 | 5 |
| Utah | 13 724 | 6.6 | 25 870 | 2 893 | 8 752 | 1 465 | 1 780 | 2 108 | 1 990 | 620 | 728 | 298 | 81 |
| Wasatch | 670 | 6.2 | 27 442 | 2 691 | 267 | 43 | 150 | 91 | 86 | 38 | 27 | 9 | 4 |
| Washington | 3 848 | 4.9 | 27 159 | 2 744 | 1 955 | 298 | 916 | 911 | 880 | 379 | 305 | 97 | 28 |
| Wayne | 75 | 2.0 | 27 334 | 2 712 | 40 | 4 | 17 | 16 | 16 | 7 | 5 | 2 | 1 |
| Weber | 7 817 | 5.6 | 33 344 | 1 643 | 4 461 | 398 | 1 143 | 1 271 | 1 219 | 355 | 427 | 177 | 57 |
| **VERMONT** | 26 042 | 4.7 | 41 572 | X | 15 598 | 2 176 | 4 416 | 5 371 | 5 233 | 1 711 | 2 412 | 602 | 165 |
| Addison | 1 419 | 5.8 | 38 624 | 893 | 700 | 173 | 251 | 246 | 238 | 90 | 98 | 27 | 9 |
| Bennington | 1 534 | 3.8 | 41 502 | 617 | 833 | 126 | 344 | 348 | 340 | 125 | 145 | 40 | 11 |
| Caledonia | 1 059 | 4.6 | 33 973 | 1 517 | 526 | 121 | 154 | 257 | 250 | 85 | 102 | 37 | 9 |

1. Based on the resident population estimated as of July 1 of the year shown.　2. Includes supplements to wages and salaries.

# Table B. States and Counties — Earnings, Social Security, and Housing

| STATE County | Total (mil dol) | Farm | Goods-related¹ Total | Manu-facturing | Infor-mation and profes-sional and technical services | Retail trade | Finance, insur-ance, and real estate | Health care and social services | Govern-ment | Number | Rate² | Supple-mental Security Income recipients, December 2011 | Total | Percent change, 2000–2010 |
|---|---|---|---|---|---|---|---|---|---|---|---|---|---|---|
| | 75 | 76 | 77 | 78 | 79 | 80 | 81 | 82 | 83 | 84 | 85 | 86 | 87 | 88 |
| **TEXAS—Cont'd** | | | | | | | | | | | | | | |
| Tom Green | 2 717 | 0.5 | 19.2 | 9.6 | 5.9 | 7.0 | 5.2 | 14.9 | 28.8 | 20 725 | 185 | 2 899 | 46 571 | 6.0 |
| Travis | 45 271 | 0.0 | 16.9 | 9.7 | 19.9 | 5.4 | 8.7 | 9.2 | 17.9 | 105 125 | 99 | 16 988 | 441 240 | 31.4 |
| Trinity | 113 | 1.2 | D | 7.2 | D | 7.3 | 3.9 | D | 25.5 | 4 405 | 300 | 648 | 8 713 | 7.0 |
| Tyler | 203 | 5.0 | 7.6 | 2.4 | D | 7.2 | D | 6.9 | 40.8 | 5 015 | 231 | 663 | 10 579 | 1.5 |
| Upshur | 401 | 0.7 | 19.6 | 4.3 | 12.3 | 7.4 | 4.9 | 8.5 | 21.1 | 8 530 | 214 | 1 163 | 16 613 | 11.3 |
| Upton | 108 | 3.6 | D | D | D | 1.2 | 1.2 | 0.6 | 20.7 | 625 | 187 | 85 | 1 548 | -3.8 |
| Uvalde | 477 | 5.6 | 9.8 | 3.7 | D | 10.1 | 3.9 | D | 32.0 | 5 290 | 199 | 1 242 | 10 811 | 6.3 |
| Val Verde | 1 076 | 0.8 | D | 6.2 | 1.8 | 8.4 | 3.3 | 8.2 | 49.8 | 7 900 | 161 | 2 433 | 18 651 | 14.5 |
| Van Zandt | 514 | 6.4 | 20.9 | 7.1 | 4.1 | 8.4 | 4.8 | 9.3 | 22.0 | 12 195 | 231 | 1 225 | 22 817 | 9.2 |
| Victoria | 2 493 | 0.6 | 27.3 | 9.0 | 3.9 | 11.8 | 5.3 | 15.1 | 13.5 | 16 600 | 190 | 2 670 | 35 417 | 7.5 |
| Walker | 1 141 | 0.9 | 9.1 | 4.9 | 3.7 | 7.2 | 3.6 | 8.2 | 55.3 | 8 750 | 129 | 1 254 | 24 058 | 14.0 |
| Waller | 873 | 2.7 | 35.2 | 25.3 | 6.6 | 6.7 | 2.5 | 2.7 | 22.5 | 5 555 | 126 | 820 | 15 839 | 32.5 |
| Ward | 293 | -0.2 | 49.2 | 3.0 | 5.2 | 4.5 | 8.2 | 2.3 | 13.6 | 2 130 | 199 | 341 | 4 694 | -2.9 |
| Washington | 888 | 1.0 | 39.6 | 28.6 | 4.2 | 7.8 | 7.7 | 7.1 | 16.8 | 7 485 | 222 | 903 | 15 514 | 17.2 |
| Webb | 4 656 | 0.6 | 9.9 | 0.7 | 4.0 | 8.7 | 4.5 | 10.7 | 29.2 | 28 850 | 112 | 12 046 | 73 496 | 33.1 |
| Wharton | 787 | 9.0 | 22.8 | 8.9 | 2.9 | 9.3 | 7.1 | 7.5 | 18.3 | 7 815 | 189 | 1 128 | 17 127 | 3.1 |
| Wheeler | 158 | 21.6 | D | D | 4.9 | 4.7 | 2.7 | 2.9 | 16.1 | 1 170 | 214 | 84 | 2 730 | 1.6 |
| Wichita | 3 508 | 0.1 | 23.2 | 10.0 | D | 6.8 | 4.9 | 13.4 | 29.5 | 23 795 | 182 | 3 827 | 55 566 | 4.2 |
| Wilbarger | 316 | 1.3 | 21.3 | 17.4 | 2.7 | 7.9 | 3.8 | 3.5 | 42.7 | 2 855 | 213 | 428 | 6 318 | -0.8 |
| Willacy | 261 | 13.2 | D | 0.6 | D | 5.9 | 3.1 | D | 24.8 | 3 540 | 160 | 1 411 | 7 040 | 4.7 |
| Williamson | 9 324 | 0.2 | 18.1 | 10.1 | 6.7 | 7.5 | 7.2 | 7.9 | 13.2 | 52 725 | 119 | 3 862 | 162 773 | 80.2 |
| Wilson | 335 | 0.8 | 17.3 | 4.6 | 7.5 | 13.7 | 4.3 | D | 30.7 | 7 240 | 165 | 808 | 16 766 | 38.4 |
| Winkler | 175 | 0.4 | D | D | D | 3.2 | 10.0 | 0.9 | 17.5 | 1 225 | 171 | 258 | 3 027 | -5.8 |
| Wise | 1 389 | 0.5 | 36.6 | 7.9 | 2.9 | 7.4 | 3.3 | 6.8 | 13.3 | 9 940 | 166 | 742 | 23 781 | 23.6 |
| Wood | 477 | 3.3 | 21.5 | 8.9 | 5.8 | 11.6 | 5.9 | D | 19.1 | 12 995 | 308 | 965 | 20 861 | 16.3 |
| Yoakum | 289 | -0.4 | 54.3 | 6.5 | 0.8 | 2.6 | 3.1 | 1.0 | 14.0 | 1 205 | 151 | 148 | 2 978 | 0.1 |
| Young | 479 | 0.8 | 45.8 | 15.2 | 4.4 | 5.9 | 5.3 | 6.1 | 14.1 | 4 365 | 236 | 533 | 8 622 | 1.4 |
| Zapata | 290 | 1.6 | 45.9 | 1.2 | 1.1 | 4.7 | 1.9 | 3.3 | 23.5 | 1 890 | 132 | 641 | 6 203 | 0.6 |
| Zavala | 129 | 15.5 | D | D | D | 4.5 | D | D | 26.8 | 2 210 | 187 | 915 | 4 283 | 5.1 |
| **UTAH** | 73 707 | 0.4 | 18.9 | 10.6 | 11.2 | 7.4 | 8.3 | 8.8 | 19.0 | 335 444 | 119 | 29 447 | 979 709 | 27.5 |
| Beaver | 148 | 25.9 | 12.8 | 2.2 | D | 5.4 | D | D | 22.1 | 1 070 | 162 | 60 | 2 908 | 9.3 |
| Box Elder | 940 | 4.7 | 44.5 | 38.9 | D | 6.9 | 2.1 | 5.8 | 12.8 | 7 500 | 149 | 450 | 17 326 | 21.9 |
| Cache | 2 345 | 1.1 | 30.0 | 24.5 | 7.3 | 7.0 | 3.6 | 9.5 | 23.6 | 11 570 | 101 | 778 | 37 024 | 27.5 |
| Carbon | 520 | -0.1 | 30.1 | 4.3 | D | 7.7 | 2.3 | D | 19.6 | 4 215 | 198 | 462 | 9 551 | 9.3 |
| Daggett | 28 | -1.3 | D | D | D | D | D | 2.8 | 44.0 | 230 | 199 | 0 | 1 141 | 5.3 |
| Davis | 6 932 | 0.1 | D | 10.2 | 9.9 | 6.3 | 4.5 | 7.4 | 35.0 | 33 275 | 107 | 2 238 | 97 570 | 31.6 |
| Duchesne | 497 | -1.0 | 42.7 | 1.9 | 3.4 | 4.8 | 1.9 | 4.7 | 17.7 | 3 020 | 160 | 325 | 9 493 | 35.8 |
| Emery | 292 | -0.8 | D | 0.5 | D | 3.6 | D | D | 13.7 | 1 995 | 182 | 140 | 4 489 | 8.4 |
| Garfield | 93 | -2.8 | D | 1.5 | D | 5.2 | 1.5 | D | 35.3 | 1 010 | 196 | 46 | 3 726 | 34.7 |
| Grand | 211 | -0.9 | D | 0.6 | 4.7 | 11.6 | 3.9 | 6.9 | 24.3 | 1 750 | 188 | 151 | 4 816 | 20.0 |
| Iron | 711 | 2.6 | 14.4 | 10.2 | 4.1 | 8.6 | 7.1 | 8.7 | 31.0 | 6 655 | 142 | 568 | 19 667 | 44.4 |
| Juab | 147 | 4.0 | 35.5 | 22.3 | D | 4.1 | 2.4 | D | 20.4 | 1 490 | 144 | 109 | 3 502 | 24.6 |
| Kane | 132 | -0.5 | D | D | D | 6.3 | 5.0 | D | 27.7 | 1 745 | 240 | 64 | 5 815 | 54.4 |
| Millard | 272 | 18.1 | 10.2 | 4.5 | D | 5.4 | 1.5 | D | 18.7 | 2 250 | 178 | 124 | 4 939 | 9.2 |
| Morgan | 113 | 0.3 | D | 12.1 | D | 5.8 | 3.6 | D | 16.8 | 1 220 | 126 | 39 | 3 006 | 39.3 |
| Piute | 15 | 15.8 | D | 0.0 | D | D | D | D | 40.9 | 430 | 287 | 0 | 898 | 20.5 |
| Rich | 30 | 14.0 | D | D | D | 4.5 | D | D | 30.1 | 370 | 161 | 14 | 2 834 | 17.7 |
| Salt Lake | 38 438 | 0.0 | 17.3 | 9.8 | 12.2 | 7.3 | 11.2 | 8.2 | 16.1 | 121 905 | 116 | 12 644 | 364 031 | 17.1 |
| San Juan | 204 | 0.5 | 21.8 | 1.7 | D | 3.5 | D | D | 39.4 | 1 940 | 131 | 612 | 5 734 | 5.2 |
| Sanpete | 335 | 6.5 | 16.3 | 8.4 | D | 6.6 | 4.3 | 7.2 | 35.1 | 4 435 | 158 | 325 | 10 379 | 31.7 |
| Sevier | 376 | 0.8 | 19.5 | 5.5 | 3.8 | 10.4 | 2.6 | D | 22.3 | 3 970 | 189 | 279 | 8 449 | 20.4 |
| Summit | 1 340 | 0.5 | 12.6 | 4.7 | 8.8 | 9.0 | 14.3 | 6.2 | 10.6 | 4 000 | 106 | 104 | 26 545 | 51.8 |
| Tooele | 1 009 | 0.4 | 18.2 | 11.0 | D | 4.6 | 1.7 | 5.7 | 33.4 | 6 185 | 104 | 604 | 19 455 | 40.9 |
| Uintah | 897 | 0.2 | 38.9 | 1.0 | 4.2 | 5.9 | 4.6 | 4.6 | 16.9 | 3 880 | 117 | 320 | 11 972 | 32.4 |
| Utah | 10 216 | 0.4 | 17.4 | 10.3 | 18.4 | 8.0 | 5.4 | 10.1 | 13.6 | 47 475 | 89 | 4 266 | 148 350 | 42.2 |
| Wasatch | 309 | -0.5 | 20.4 | 3.7 | D | 8.8 | 5.9 | 7.5 | 22.7 | 2 800 | 115 | 96 | 10 577 | 61.1 |
| Washington | 2 253 | -0.2 | 14.4 | 4.9 | 6.3 | 10.6 | 6.4 | 18.1 | 16.8 | 28 455 | 201 | 1 193 | 57 734 | 58.3 |
| Wayne | 44 | 7.5 | D | 1.2 | D | 3.7 | D | D | 34.0 | 565 | 206 | 22 | 1 591 | 19.7 |
| Weber | 4 859 | 0.0 | D | 16.1 | 5.0 | 8.3 | 5.7 | 12.5 | 25.2 | 30 040 | 128 | 3 388 | 86 187 | 22.3 |
| **VERMONT** | 17 775 | 1.3 | 19.2 | 12.0 | 9.5 | 8.0 | 5.9 | 14.3 | 18.8 | 132 268 | 211 | 15 652 | 322 539 | 9.6 |
| Addison | 873 | 6.4 | 23.8 | 15.6 | 7.0 | 9.0 | 3.3 | 13.1 | 12.2 | 6 925 | 188 | 621 | 16 760 | 9.4 |
| Bennington | 959 | 0.2 | D | 14.6 | D | 11.5 | 4.8 | 17.2 | 12.9 | 9 465 | 256 | 1 180 | 20 922 | 7.8 |
| Caledonia | 647 | 1.5 | D | 12.6 | 8.7 | 10.2 | 3.8 | 14.0 | 17.1 | 6 875 | 221 | 974 | 15 942 | 9.9 |

1. Includes mining, construction, and manufacturing.　　2. Per 1,000 resident population enumerated in the 2010 census.

# Table B. States and Counties — **Housing, Labor Force, and Employment**

| STATE County | Housing units, 2007–2011 Occupied units Total | Percent | Owner-occupied Median value[1] | Median owner cost as a percent of income With a mortgage | Without a mortgage[2] | Renter-occupied Median rent[3] | Median rent as a percent of income | Substandard units[4] (percent) | Civilian labor force, 2012 Total | Percent change, 2011–2012 | Unemployment Total | Rate[5] | Civilian employment,[6] 2007–2011 Total | Percent Management, business, science and arts | Construction, production, and maintenance occupations |
|---|---|---|---|---|---|---|---|---|---|---|---|---|---|---|---|
| | 89 | 90 | 91 | 92 | 93 | 94 | 95 | 96 | 97 | 98 | 99 | 100 | 101 | 102 | 103 |
| **TEXAS—Cont'd** | | | | | | | | | | | | | | | |
| Tom Green | 41 468 | 67.1 | 91 100 | 21.2 | 12.1 | 686 | 29.7 | 3.3 | 55 218 | 0.6 | 2 926 | 5.3 | 49 266 | 29.4 | 22.0 |
| Travis | 399 679 | 52.3 | 210 500 | 23.9 | 12.6 | 930 | 30.8 | 4.5 | 590 462 | 2.0 | 33 528 | 5.7 | 535 250 | 44.4 | 15.8 |
| Trinity | 4 893 | 82.7 | 79 500 | 20.9 | 12.9 | 571 | 29.8 | 2.7 | 5 749 | -2.3 | 453 | 7.9 | 4 794 | 22.9 | 30.9 |
| Tyler | 8 238 | 82.9 | 74 000 | 21.0 | 12.3 | 595 | 28.2 | 4.9 | 8 276 | -3.0 | 828 | 10.0 | 6 863 | 28.3 | 33.0 |
| Upshur | 14 793 | 78.6 | 88 300 | 20.4 | 10.4 | 628 | 23.6 | 5.8 | 20 902 | 0.8 | 1 211 | 5.8 | 16 732 | 26.5 | 32.2 |
| Upton | 1 203 | 80.5 | 39 800 | 18.1 | 9.9 | 543 | 12.0 | 3.4 | 1 994 | 2.8 | 68 | 3.4 | 1 479 | 25.5 | 34.6 |
| Uvalde | 8 689 | 73.7 | 67 500 | 22.1 | 14.1 | 633 | 31.2 | 11.9 | 11 871 | -2.1 | 945 | 8.0 | 10 048 | 25.6 | 30.6 |
| Val Verde | 14 909 | 68.1 | 85 100 | 22.5 | 13.9 | 585 | 28.6 | 6.3 | 20 582 | -2.4 | 1 567 | 7.6 | 19 051 | 26.3 | 26.0 |
| Van Zandt | 19 292 | 77.7 | 97 600 | 22.4 | 13.6 | 692 | 29.4 | 4.9 | 25 862 | -0.9 | 1 650 | 6.4 | 21 588 | 26.8 | 31.0 |
| Victoria | 32 004 | 67.2 | 103 700 | 21.3 | 12.1 | 704 | 29.3 | 4.5 | 47 262 | 0.8 | 2 546 | 5.4 | 39 897 | 29.6 | 27.2 |
| Walker | 20 077 | 58.6 | 108 100 | 22.0 | 13.4 | 695 | 35.2 | 2.0 | 28 051 | 0.0 | 1 892 | 6.7 | 21 945 | 31.9 | 18.5 |
| Waller | 13 653 | 68.3 | 128 500 | 26.5 | 12.4 | 784 | 27.6 | 5.2 | 20 310 | 1.8 | 1 414 | 7.0 | 19 259 | 28.6 | 29.6 |
| Ward | 3 808 | 75.1 | 49 100 | 16.8 | 10.9 | 543 | 21.2 | 3.9 | 5 763 | 6.7 | 259 | 4.5 | 4 359 | 23.3 | 33.1 |
| Washington | 12 613 | 68.1 | 137 700 | 24.3 | 11.9 | 766 | 28.9 | 2.7 | 17 411 | -0.2 | 883 | 5.1 | 14 502 | 31.1 | 26.3 |
| Webb | 65 796 | 63.9 | 106 500 | 28.3 | 15.0 | 722 | 33.9 | 17.7 | 100 354 | 0.7 | 7 086 | 7.1 | 97 544 | 25.3 | 22.6 |
| Wharton | 14 600 | 69.2 | 87 100 | 18.9 | 14.0 | 625 | 28.9 | 5.2 | 21 385 | -1.1 | 1 453 | 6.8 | 19 706 | 27.5 | 34.7 |
| Wheeler | 2 124 | 77.1 | 68 100 | 19.3 | 9.9 | 583 | 29.6 | 2.3 | 3 445 | 0.4 | 125 | 3.6 | 2 436 | 32.6 | 33.5 |
| Wichita | 48 001 | 65.2 | 88 800 | 21.8 | 12.8 | 705 | 28.2 | 2.6 | 61 676 | -1.3 | 3 897 | 6.3 | 55 818 | 29.3 | 25.1 |
| Wilbarger | 5 069 | 66.0 | 60 700 | 18.9 | 13.5 | 590 | 28.0 | 3.6 | 7 675 | -2.2 | 353 | 4.6 | 5 601 | 28.9 | 28.5 |
| Willacy | 5 309 | 73.5 | 51 400 | 24.4 | 16.1 | 590 | 26.8 | 8.7 | 8 794 | -4.9 | 1 233 | 14.0 | 5 410 | 24.0 | 19.9 |
| Williamson | 147 912 | 69.4 | 175 400 | 23.3 | 12.2 | 1 013 | 27.7 | 2.6 | 234 473 | 1.9 | 13 739 | 5.9 | 203 793 | 45.3 | 15.3 |
| Wilson | 15 076 | 84.7 | 133 500 | 20.6 | 11.3 | 684 | 25.1 | 4.6 | 20 286 | 0.4 | 1 194 | 5.9 | 20 303 | 34.8 | 27.9 |
| Winkler | 2 526 | 83.0 | 41 600 | 15.1 | 9.9 | 536 | 17.7 | 3.6 | 3 748 | 4.2 | 175 | 4.7 | 2 815 | 21.0 | 45.7 |
| Wise | 19 995 | 81.4 | 120 700 | 21.7 | 12.9 | 844 | 24.3 | 3.1 | 28 899 | 1.5 | 1 835 | 6.3 | 27 063 | 28.3 | 32.2 |
| Wood | 15 983 | 80.4 | 99 100 | 22.3 | 12.8 | 665 | 25.5 | 2.9 | 18 213 | -1.9 | 1 314 | 7.2 | 15 716 | 27.4 | 28.4 |
| Yoakum | 2 629 | 80.1 | 58 900 | 14.6 | 9.9 | 559 | 19.5 | 6.9 | 4 917 | 5.9 | 173 | 3.5 | 3 431 | 22.8 | 50.8 |
| Young | 7 432 | 69.3 | 72 800 | 18.5 | 12.5 | 653 | 27.6 | 3.4 | 9 695 | -0.3 | 488 | 5.0 | 8 122 | 23.4 | 35.8 |
| Zapata | 4 282 | 75.6 | 52 600 | 18.2 | 13.8 | 505 | 33.9 | 16.9 | 6 724 | 5.0 | 440 | 6.5 | 4 827 | 22.1 | 35.2 |
| Zavala | 3 635 | 70.5 | 39 500 | 22.8 | 16.0 | 377 | 33.2 | 8.8 | 4 215 | -1.0 | 593 | 14.1 | 3 912 | 21.0 | 28.7 |
| **UTAH** | 871 358 | 70.7 | 221 300 | 24.6 | 9.9 | 813 | 28.7 | 3.9 | 1 353 597 | 0.5 | 77 348 | 5.7 | 1 251 302 | 35.3 | 22.3 |
| Beaver | 2 061 | 76.6 | 152 000 | 21.5 | 10.9 | 682 | 37.0 | 4.3 | 3 173 | -5.6 | 188 | 5.9 | 2 600 | 26.8 | 30.2 |
| Box Elder | 15 891 | 81.0 | 167 400 | 22.6 | 9.9 | 617 | 24.1 | 2.5 | 20 261 | -4.0 | 1 389 | 6.9 | 21 340 | 32.9 | 30.6 |
| Cache | 34 599 | 63.8 | 185 000 | 24.2 | 9.9 | 661 | 28.2 | 4.3 | 60 614 | -0.7 | 2 681 | 4.4 | 52 651 | 35.0 | 23.8 |
| Carbon | 7 897 | 70.2 | 117 200 | 21.2 | 10.7 | 558 | 27.1 | 2.3 | 9 540 | -4.0 | 682 | 7.1 | 8 795 | 27.7 | 32.8 |
| Daggett | 373 | 64.6 | 162 500 | 21.2 | 9.9 | 878 | 24.5 | 1.9 | 440 | -6.6 | 26 | 5.9 | 366 | 26.0 | 18.9 |
| Davis | 92 652 | 78.6 | 228 200 | 23.6 | 9.9 | 854 | 27.1 | 2.4 | 145 169 | 0.0 | 7 752 | 5.3 | 136 700 | 39.9 | 19.4 |
| Duchesne | 6 691 | 74.5 | 169 700 | 21.5 | 9.9 | 733 | 26.3 | 5.0 | 10 795 | 7.4 | 442 | 4.1 | 7 401 | 30.0 | 34.8 |
| Emery | 3 716 | 79.7 | 116 200 | 17.8 | 9.9 | 633 | 20.9 | 5.3 | 4 658 | -7.8 | 358 | 7.7 | 4 571 | 25.1 | 40.8 |
| Garfield | 2 144 | 79.3 | 149 500 | 22.4 | 9.9 | 473 | 18.3 | 3.2 | 2 741 | -4.6 | 287 | 10.5 | 2 548 | 31.9 | 23.3 |
| Grand | 3 653 | 67.8 | 222 100 | 25.2 | 9.9 | 802 | 29.0 | 5.1 | 5 425 | 1.0 | 475 | 8.8 | 4 381 | 30.8 | 20.9 |
| Iron | 15 313 | 61.2 | 196 400 | 28.2 | 10.3 | 641 | 28.7 | 6.5 | 19 195 | -2.7 | 1 423 | 7.4 | 18 823 | 31.9 | 24.0 |
| Juab | 3 092 | 81.6 | 169 500 | 21.8 | 9.9 | 732 | 24.3 | 4.9 | 4 110 | 0.9 | 282 | 6.9 | 4 317 | 23.9 | 36.1 |
| Kane | 3 213 | 82.0 | 171 600 | 21.6 | 9.9 | 750 | 24.4 | 4.4 | 3 339 | -2.3 | 241 | 7.2 | 3 407 | 34.8 | 20.2 |
| Millard | 4 094 | 74.6 | 128 600 | 20.9 | 9.9 | 553 | 26.8 | 5.3 | 5 991 | -5.3 | 293 | 4.9 | 5 167 | 25.7 | 35.6 |
| Morgan | 2 757 | 87.4 | 259 100 | 24.6 | 9.9 | 627 | 19.1 | 0.5 | 4 288 | 0.6 | 229 | 5.3 | 4 088 | 37.8 | 22.9 |
| Piute | 584 | 86.1 | 161 600 | 21.4 | 11.3 | 638 | 29.4 | 3.8 | 685 | -9.4 | 41 | 6.0 | 613 | 37.0 | 26.9 |
| Rich | 739 | 85.4 | 140 300 | 22.9 | 9.9 | 607 | 24.4 | 2.8 | 1 208 | -3.7 | 54 | 4.5 | 998 | 38.2 | 34.6 |
| Salt Lake | 339 035 | 67.7 | 240 900 | 25.0 | 9.9 | 851 | 29.5 | 4.1 | 551 992 | 0.7 | 30 222 | 5.5 | 502 667 | 35.2 | 21.6 |
| San Juan | 4 241 | 83.2 | 116 000 | 22.2 | 9.9 | 494 | 26.5 | 18.1 | 4 983 | -4.9 | 534 | 10.7 | 4 839 | 28.6 | 28.8 |
| Sanpete | 7 716 | 76.8 | 156 200 | 24.1 | 9.9 | 552 | 23.3 | 4.6 | 10 716 | 0.4 | 804 | 7.5 | 10 366 | 29.6 | 31.1 |
| Sevier | 6 989 | 80.9 | 150 100 | 22.4 | 9.9 | 627 | 25.3 | 3.9 | 9 487 | -1.5 | 606 | 6.4 | 8 502 | 29.2 | 28.7 |
| Summit | 13 342 | 76.9 | 497 200 | 24.6 | 9.9 | 1 027 | 27.5 | 2.5 | 22 195 | 1.1 | 1 182 | 5.3 | 19 056 | 42.8 | 18.2 |
| Tooele | 18 019 | 75.0 | 188 400 | 22.9 | 9.9 | 764 | 26.3 | 2.5 | 28 188 | 1.1 | 1 764 | 6.3 | 24 714 | 31.5 | 26.6 |
| Uintah | 10 762 | 77.0 | 188 700 | 22.4 | 9.9 | 923 | 24.0 | 3.4 | 18 153 | 2.9 | 715 | 3.9 | 13 955 | 25.4 | 36.4 |
| Utah | 138 804 | 69.1 | 234 800 | 25.5 | 9.9 | 809 | 29.6 | 4.7 | 225 703 | 2.2 | 12 452 | 5.5 | 218 980 | 38.9 | 18.5 |
| Wasatch | 7 265 | 77.5 | 315 100 | 27.3 | 9.9 | 923 | 29.0 | 4.0 | 9 998 | 0.8 | 688 | 6.9 | 10 699 | 35.1 | 21.9 |
| Washington | 46 088 | 70.1 | 235 300 | 29.0 | 9.9 | 918 | 30.3 | 4.3 | 57 958 | 1.1 | 4 071 | 7.0 | 54 003 | 30.7 | 22.7 |
| Wayne | 814 | 78.5 | 166 600 | 21.9 | 9.9 | 706 | 17.6 | 5.2 | 1 252 | -6.9 | 150 | 12.0 | 1 271 | 32.9 | 22.0 |
| Weber | 78 814 | 71.9 | 171 900 | 23.8 | 9.9 | 736 | 27.0 | 2.6 | 111 337 | -0.4 | 7 316 | 6.6 | 103 484 | 31.0 | 26.4 |
| **VERMONT** | 256 711 | 71.4 | 213 000 | 25.7 | 16.5 | 843 | 30.9 | 2.1 | 356 329 | -0.6 | 17 777 | 5.0 | 328 365 | 39.7 | 21.1 |
| Addison | 14 159 | 74.8 | 228 600 | 25.5 | 16.6 | 856 | 29.5 | 2.2 | 20 496 | -2.8 | 953 | 4.6 | 19 357 | 42.4 | 25.0 |
| Bennington | 15 512 | 72.3 | 204 800 | 26.0 | 16.0 | 760 | 31.4 | 3.0 | 20 024 | -0.1 | 1 186 | 5.9 | 18 862 | 36.2 | 22.2 |
| Caledonia | 12 615 | 72.0 | 157 400 | 24.0 | 16.2 | 643 | 31.1 | 2.8 | 16 108 | -2.5 | 1 024 | 6.4 | 15 841 | 35.8 | 23.6 |

1. Specified owner-occupied units. lacking complete plumbing facilities.   2. A value of 9.9 represents 9.9 percent or less.   3. Specified renter-occupied units. A value of 10.0 represents 10 percent or less.   4. Overcrowded or 5. Percent of civilian labor force.   6. Persons 16 years old and over.

| STATE County | Private nonfarm establishments, employment and payroll, 2011 | | | | | | Annual payroll | | Agriculture, 2007 | | | |
|---|---|---|---|---|---|---|---|---|---|---|---|---|
| | | Employment | | | | | | | Farms | | | |
| | | | | | | | | | | Percent with: | | |
| | Number of establishments | Total | Health care and social assistance | Manufacturing | Retail trade | Finance and insurance | Professional, scientific, and technical services | Total (mil dol) | Average per employee (dollars) | Number | Fewer than 50 acres | 500 acres or more | Farm operators whose principal occupation is farming (percent) |
| | 104 | 105 | 106 | 107 | 108 | 109 | 110 | 111 | 112 | 113 | 114 | 115 | 116 |

| | 104 | 105 | 106 | 107 | 108 | 109 | 110 | 111 | 112 | 113 | 114 | 115 | 116 |
|---|---|---|---|---|---|---|---|---|---|---|---|---|---|
| TEXAS—Cont'd | | | | | | | | | | | | | |
| Tom Green | 2 592 | 36 211 | 7 229 | 3 137 | 6 173 | 1 300 | 1 292 | 1 170 | 32 308 | 1 180 | 45.2 | 24.7 | 37.5 |
| Travis | 28 910 | 478 110 | 58 280 | 24 962 | 54 826 | 23 750 | 56 863 | 24 438 | 51 113 | 1 214 | 51.4 | 8.9 | 36.0 |
| Trinity | 192 | 1 744 | 368 | 164 | D | D | 45 | 44 | 25 243 | 576 | 35.4 | 8.7 | 43.8 |
| Tyler | 262 | 2 166 | 571 | 47 | 553 | D | 67 | 53 | 24 473 | 792 | 55.6 | 4.4 | 37.1 |
| Upshur | 470 | 4 188 | 640 | 358 | 795 | 208 | 193 | 125 | 29 842 | 1 507 | 48.6 | 4.8 | 38.0 |
| Upton | 90 | 932 | D | D | 73 | D | 7 | 54 | 57 705 | 110 | 19.1 | 49.1 | 43.6 |
| Uvalde | 586 | 6 560 | 1 574 | 616 | 1 227 | 249 | 171 | 168 | 25 557 | 690 | 22.9 | 34.8 | 48.4 |
| Val Verde | 783 | 10 292 | 3 181 | 352 | 2 177 | 505 | 191 | 232 | 22 512 | 402 | 46.8 | 34.1 | 40.5 |
| Van Zandt | 791 | 7 548 | 1 153 | 775 | 1 373 | 249 | 207 | 224 | 29 716 | 3 253 | 51.6 | 5.1 | 40.3 |
| Victoria | 2 286 | 31 026 | 6 561 | 2 048 | 5 546 | 1 066 | 905 | 1 190 | 38 368 | 1 351 | 41.7 | 14.4 | 38.3 |
| Walker | 909 | 11 066 | 2 161 | 823 | 2 224 | 381 | 428 | 309 | 27 884 | 1 188 | 51.7 | 7.3 | 42.1 |
| Waller | 667 | 9 538 | 1 047 | 2 494 | 1 110 | D | D | 397 | 41 661 | 1 640 | 58.4 | 7.4 | 38.7 |
| Ward | 277 | 2 644 | 231 | D | 276 | 77 | 45 | 131 | 49 415 | 119 | 37.8 | 29.4 | 31.1 |
| Washington | 894 | 12 766 | 2 063 | 2 934 | 2 099 | D | 282 | 404 | 31 684 | 2 399 | 42.8 | 4.8 | 39.2 |
| Webb | 4 779 | 66 417 | 13 988 | 700 | 12 550 | 2 432 | 1 619 | 1 772 | 26 682 | 663 | 15.7 | 41.3 | 34.1 |
| Wharton | 937 | 11 195 | 1 977 | 1 361 | 2 126 | 389 | 364 | 358 | 31 961 | 1 506 | 39.0 | 21.0 | 47.3 |
| Wheeler | 189 | 1 676 | 298 | D | 277 | D | D | 60 | 35 888 | 507 | 8.5 | 41.4 | 39.6 |
| Wichita | 3 155 | 45 954 | 10 664 | 4 594 | 7 627 | 1 741 | 1 252 | 1 445 | 31 439 | 658 | 42.6 | 13.8 | 36.8 |
| Wilbarger | 301 | 3 675 | 512 | D | 680 | 129 | D | 104 | 28 375 | 461 | 13.4 | 35.4 | 51.0 |
| Willacy | 201 | 2 789 | 1 248 | D | D | 88 | 33 | 77 | 27 540 | 352 | 39.5 | 27.3 | 51.7 |
| Williamson | 8 235 | 118 078 | 14 581 | 6 414 | 21 097 | 6 674 | 5 491 | 5 462 | 46 258 | 2 728 | 51.4 | 8.5 | 37.0 |
| Wilson | 520 | 4 860 | 1 295 | 335 | 1 018 | D | 171 | 131 | 26 968 | 2 570 | 38.5 | 7.4 | 39.6 |
| Winkler | 174 | 1 305 | D | NA | 178 | D | D | 64 | 48 775 | 53 | 35.8 | 39.6 | 49.1 |
| Wise | 1 205 | 16 345 | 2 433 | 1 396 | 2 217 | 368 | 263 | 706 | 43 202 | 3 164 | 58.0 | 5.0 | 35.0 |
| Wood | 797 | 7 367 | 1 108 | 843 | 1 360 | 379 | 189 | 224 | 30 390 | 1 718 | 46.7 | 5.4 | 40.7 |
| Yoakum | 169 | 2 112 | D | 75 | 190 | 66 | 15 | 115 | 54 464 | 348 | 6.6 | 54.0 | 53.7 |
| Young | 584 | 5 563 | 1 022 | 784 | 832 | 236 | 165 | 199 | 35 850 | 806 | 17.7 | 25.3 | 35.7 |
| Zapata | 161 | 2 279 | 264 | D | 273 | 87 | D | 87 | 38 086 | 459 | 8.9 | 46.8 | 41.0 |
| Zavala | 110 | 1 726 | D | D | 201 | 44 | D | 36 | 20 993 | 311 | 11.6 | 48.2 | 41.2 |
| UTAH | 68 747 | 1 029 103 | 120 650 | 106 865 | 134 892 | 58 316 | 68 950 | 39 923 | 38 794 | 16 700 | 55.8 | 13.2 | 38.0 |
| Beaver | 161 | 1 371 | 235 | 75 | 357 | D | D | 37 | 26 973 | 229 | 37.6 | 22.3 | 52.0 |
| Box Elder | 987 | 15 277 | 1 266 | D | 1 657 | 289 | 207 | 710 | 46 469 | 1 113 | 45.6 | 22.4 | 42.6 |
| Cache | 3 032 | 36 414 | 5 090 | 10 569 | 5 400 | 976 | 2 365 | 1 106 | 30 379 | 1 195 | 50.5 | 8.4 | 36.1 |
| Carbon | 495 | 7 051 | 894 | 559 | 1 159 | 231 | 104 | 260 | 36 911 | 294 | 58.5 | 16.7 | 35.4 |
| Daggett | 23 | D | NA | NA | D | NA | D | 3 | D | 48 | 33.3 | 22.9 | 37.5 |
| Davis | 6 173 | 71 354 | 8 916 | 8 378 | 12 504 | 2 684 | 7 010 | 2 448 | 34 301 | 496 | 83.1 | 1.4 | 38.5 |
| Duchesne | 651 | 6 183 | D | 189 | 772 | 112 | D | 290 | 46 879 | 879 | 38.5 | 13.4 | 37.8 |
| Emery | 196 | 2 744 | D | 27 | 537 | 53 | 122 | 135 | 49 358 | 545 | 42.9 | 17.1 | 32.8 |
| Garfield | 133 | 1 132 | D | D | 116 | 20 | D | 34 | 30 439 | 275 | 43.3 | 13.5 | 45.8 |
| Grand | 435 | 3 548 | D | D | 650 | 70 | 106 | 101 | 28 374 | 90 | 55.6 | 17.8 | 54.4 |
| Iron | 1 182 | 11 029 | 1 627 | 1 382 | 2 010 | 387 | 459 | 276 | 25 070 | 487 | 40.9 | 22.8 | 41.7 |
| Juab | 185 | 1 933 | D | 320 | 323 | 40 | D | 57 | 29 661 | 335 | 27.2 | 27.2 | 30.4 |
| Kane | 266 | 2 103 | 196 | D | 359 | D | D | 66 | 31 587 | 145 | 33.1 | 30.3 | 37.2 |
| Millard | 246 | 2 719 | 241 | 390 | 568 | 74 | D | 104 | 38 366 | 703 | 26.2 | 31.7 | 47.8 |
| Morgan | 219 | 1 265 | D | D | 166 | D | 57 | 47 | 37 437 | 316 | 53.5 | 15.2 | 30.7 |
| Piute | 21 | 75 | D | NA | D | D | NA | 2 | 21 413 | 113 | 21.2 | 26.5 | 59.3 |
| Rich | 77 | 265 | D | D | D | D | 7 | 11 | 40 053 | 167 | 28.1 | 45.5 | 53.9 |
| Salt Lake | 28 649 | 495 829 | 57 633 | 45 628 | 57 168 | 34 609 | 33 974 | 21 429 | 43 218 | 587 | 79.6 | 6.0 | 32.7 |
| San Juan | 247 | 2 522 | 560 | D | 467 | 89 | 25 | 79 | 31 514 | 758 | 70.3 | 14.8 | 60.9 |
| Sanpete | 401 | 3 974 | 897 | D | 867 | 136 | 62 | 100 | 25 150 | 879 | 45.4 | 14.3 | 43.1 |
| Sevier | 497 | 5 745 | 714 | D | 1 309 | 130 | 157 | 182 | 31 675 | 655 | 57.9 | 9.2 | 34.5 |
| Summit | 2 005 | 23 899 | 1 067 | 517 | 4 041 | 709 | 898 | 662 | 27 712 | 629 | 57.7 | 11.0 | 29.9 |
| Tooele | 736 | 10 536 | 1 196 | 1 623 | 1 650 | 181 | 1 780 | 435 | 41 257 | 379 | 59.4 | 17.2 | 34.3 |
| Uintah | 1 136 | 10 160 | 713 | 198 | 1 557 | 175 | 420 | 480 | 47 272 | 981 | 51.6 | 12.0 | 30.5 |
| Utah | 10 722 | 157 312 | 19 593 | 15 113 | 22 210 | 4 263 | 12 404 | 5 638 | 35 838 | 2 175 | 75.9 | 5.3 | 34.0 |
| Wasatch | 730 | 4 268 | 533 | 186 | 802 | 139 | 293 | 122 | 28 634 | 432 | 71.8 | 4.9 | 28.2 |
| Washington | 3 844 | 36 114 | 6 809 | 1 896 | 7 194 | 1 194 | 1 619 | 1 052 | 29 117 | 593 | 60.4 | 13.2 | 31.0 |
| Wayne | 84 | 569 | D | 8 | 114 | D | 16 | 16 | 27 369 | 201 | 23.4 | 11.9 | 53.7 |
| Weber | 4 881 | 67 602 | 10 332 | 11 556 | 10 842 | 3 352 | 4 017 | 2 312 | 34 204 | 1 001 | 78.3 | 2.3 | 33.8 |
| VERMONT | 21 190 | 264 208 | 50 353 | 30 675 | 39 135 | 12 105 | 21 524 | 9 590 | 36 297 | 6 984 | 35.8 | 7.6 | 49.6 |
| Addison | 1 152 | 12 307 | 2 100 | 1 683 | 1 903 | 321 | 424 | 417 | 33 853 | 773 | 35.3 | 12.8 | 52.8 |
| Bennington | 1 439 | 14 433 | 2 939 | 2 156 | 3 161 | 313 | 374 | 502 | 34 758 | 226 | 42.9 | 6.6 | 44.2 |
| Caledonia | 930 | 9 182 | 1 798 | 1 491 | 1 666 | 327 | 466 | 318 | 34 666 | 531 | 35.0 | 5.5 | 48.4 |

# Table B. States and Counties — **Agriculture**

| STATE County | Agriculture, 2007 (cont.) | | | | | | | | | | | | | | | |
|---|---|---|---|---|---|---|---|---|---|---|---|---|---|---|---|---|
| | Land in farms | | | | | Value of land and buildings (dollars) | | | Value of products sold | | | | Percent of farms with sales of: | | Government payments | |
| | | | Acres | | | | | Value of machinery and equipment, average per farm (dollars) | | | | Percent from: | | | | | |
| | Acreage (1,000) | Percent change, 2002–2007 | Average size of farm | Total irrigated (1,000) | Total cropland (1,000) | Average per farm | Average per acre | | Total (mil dol) | Average per farm (dollars) | Crops | Live-stock and poultry products | $10,000 or more | $100,000 or more | Total ($1,000) | Percent of farms |
| | 117 | 118 | 119 | 120 | 121 | 122 | 123 | 124 | 125 | 126 | 127 | 128 | 129 | 130 | 131 | 132 |
| TEXAS—Cont'd | | | | | | | | | | | | | | | | |
| Tom Green | 924 | 9.3 | 783 | 33.7 | 228.0 | 844 202 | 1 079 | 79 066 | 133.0 | 112 704 | 37.6 | 62.4 | 26.9 | 12.5 | 5 800 | 25.8 |
| Travis | 262 | -12.1 | 216 | 1.6 | 76.0 | 612 252 | 2 832 | 46 601 | 22.8 | 18 808 | 67.5 | 32.5 | 20.7 | 4.0 | 1 036 | 14.3 |
| Trinity | 109 | 3.8 | 189 | 0.3 | 27.3 | 363 908 | 1 923 | 58 355 | 9.2 | 16 026 | 13.7 | 86.3 | 34.4 | 2.1 | D | 0.7 |
| Tyler | 84 | 5.0 | 106 | 0.4 | 19.7 | 298 244 | 2 804 | 49 342 | 21.8 | 27 479 | D | D | 14.9 | 0.5 | 217 | 5.3 |
| Upshur | 198 | 1.0 | 131 | 1.5 | 60.2 | 339 710 | 2 584 | 44 425 | 48.9 | 32 481 | 9.9 | 90.1 | 20.0 | 3.6 | 182 | 2.3 |
| Upton | 635 | -12.2 | 5 768 | 7.3 | 32.0 | 2 956 855 | 513 | 103 983 | 8.6 | 77 940 | 72.7 | 27.3 | 38.2 | 19.1 | 1 325 | 34.5 |
| Uvalde | 990 | 2.2 | 1 435 | 45.3 | 131.4 | 1 558 967 | 1 087 | 100 482 | 77.7 | 112 588 | 40.9 | 59.1 | 28.1 | 10.9 | 2 749 | 22.0 |
| Val Verde | 1 494 | -10.1 | 3 716 | 2.3 | 24.8 | 1 697 190 | 457 | 54 411 | 12.0 | 29 791 | 3.4 | 96.6 | 19.9 | 5.5 | 737 | 10.9 |
| Van Zandt | 416 | -1.4 | 128 | 5.5 | 141.8 | 389 067 | 3 043 | 49 569 | 95.2 | 29 253 | 51.3 | 48.7 | 27.5 | 2.7 | 219 | 3.2 |
| Victoria | 494 | -3.9 | 366 | 2.8 | 134.1 | 566 841 | 1 551 | 63 405 | 43.4 | 32 142 | 54.1 | 45.9 | 29.2 | 5.6 | 2 645 | 17.7 |
| Walker | 224 | 8.7 | 189 | 0.9 | 37.1 | 462 208 | 2 451 | 57 851 | 26.9 | 22 651 | 52.5 | 47.5 | 20.8 | 1.7 | 32 | 0.7 |
| Waller | 271 | -2.2 | 165 | 9.9 | 103.5 | 545 765 | 3 303 | 59 849 | 55.1 | 33 611 | 66.3 | 33.7 | 24.4 | 4.5 | 1 696 | 9.1 |
| Ward | 433 | -7.1 | 3 638 | 1.6 | 22.9 | 1 347 150 | 370 | 46 873 | 1.5 | 12 852 | 31.3 | 68.7 | 28.6 | 2.5 | 243 | 12.6 |
| Washington | 338 | -4.8 | 141 | 1.4 | 90.4 | 523 071 | 3 708 | 51 773 | 44.8 | 18 679 | 23.0 | 77.0 | 28.8 | 2.3 | 110 | 4.1 |
| Webb | 1 856 | -9.2 | 2 799 | 5.1 | 58.8 | 2 090 515 | 747 | 57 689 | 24.7 | 37 298 | 1.2 | 98.8 | 26.4 | 5.4 | 298 | 5.0 |
| Wharton | 616 | -3.4 | 409 | 61.7 | 376.0 | 721 807 | 1 765 | 108 858 | 240.2 | 159 493 | 60.8 | 39.2 | 44.2 | 18.9 | 12 968 | 44.1 |
| Wheeler | 584 | 9.4 | 1 151 | 14.1 | 151.1 | 782 659 | 680 | 65 934 | 129.5 | 255 380 | 6.1 | 93.9 | 39.6 | 10.1 | 3 608 | 60.9 |
| Wichita | 331 | 9.6 | 503 | 6.7 | 129.5 | 487 974 | 971 | 59 809 | 27.2 | 41 407 | 57.9 | 42.1 | 30.9 | 7.9 | 1 853 | 29.3 |
| Wilbarger | 614 | -29.6 | 1 332 | 15.5 | 237.3 | 982 831 | 738 | 95 736 | 42.9 | 93 102 | 66.6 | 33.4 | 54.4 | 23.2 | 5 072 | 69.0 |
| Willacy | 338 | -8.6 | 960 | 18.5 | 196.4 | 1 146 610 | 1 194 | 144 559 | 51.2 | 145 453 | 90.2 | 9.8 | 44.9 | 25.6 | 6 422 | 58.8 |
| Williamson | 542 | -7.0 | 199 | 1.0 | 229.7 | 559 150 | 2 816 | 48 657 | 190.4 | 69 792 | 28.6 | 71.4 | 23.6 | 5.1 | 5 108 | 25.7 |
| Wilson | 467 | 4.7 | 182 | 13.5 | 153.9 | 429 236 | 2 361 | 45 025 | 52.9 | 20 590 | 29.4 | 70.6 | 22.6 | 2.4 | 1 699 | 16.6 |
| Winkler | 533 | 8.3 | 10 054 | 0.2 | D | 2 637 615 | 262 | 64 310 | 3.3 | 61 545 | D | D | 37.7 | 13.2 | 67 | 9.4 |
| Wise | 443 | -10.1 | 140 | 2.5 | 134.0 | 441 108 | 3 152 | 43 677 | 41.1 | 12 983 | 33.1 | 66.9 | 21.7 | 2.1 | 344 | 5.9 |
| Wood | 234 | 2.6 | 136 | 1.9 | 71.7 | 394 364 | 2 898 | 51 757 | 104.0 | 60 550 | 13.3 | 86.7 | 29.1 | 5.2 | 171 | 5.0 |
| Yoakum | 444 | -2.4 | 1 275 | 101.1 | 281.9 | 1 077 712 | 846 | 198 120 | 90.1 | 258 995 | 90.1 | 9.9 | 46.6 | 36.8 | 11 394 | 78.7 |
| Young | 527 | 3.3 | 654 | D | 127.8 | 822 775 | 1 258 | 59 948 | 21.2 | 26 321 | 26.4 | 73.6 | 33.0 | 5.6 | 1 367 | 25.7 |
| Zapata | 459 | 15.3 | 1 001 | 2.0 | 45.8 | 920 368 | 919 | 63 172 | 13.1 | 28 541 | D | D | 27.0 | 2.2 | 149 | 4.8 |
| Zavala | 752 | 6.4 | 2 418 | 26.1 | 101.5 | 2 544 549 | 1 052 | 84 687 | 59.8 | 192 187 | 30.9 | 69.1 | 36.0 | 16.4 | 1 206 | 19.6 |
| UTAH | 11 095 | -5.4 | 664 | 1 134.1 | 1 837.9 | 829 816 | 1 249 | 75 365 | 1 415.7 | 84 771 | 26.3 | 73.7 | 34.9 | 9.7 | 22 759 | 17.7 |
| Beaver | 158 | 13.7 | 691 | 29.9 | 35.4 | 1 608 052 | 2 326 | 137 667 | 210.6 | 919 807 | 4.0 | 96.0 | 60.3 | 31.9 | 233 | 26.2 |
| Box Elder | 1 320 | -5.8 | 1 186 | 112.1 | 327.7 | 1 087 702 | 917 | 106 044 | 141.2 | 126 903 | 35.8 | 64.2 | 49.6 | 19.3 | 6 343 | 42.1 |
| Cache | 252 | 2.0 | 211 | 80.2 | 143.7 | 661 074 | 3 140 | 92 952 | 136.1 | 113 861 | 17.9 | 82.1 | 44.5 | 14.3 | 2 537 | 36.2 |
| Carbon | 216 | 8.5 | 733 | 14.8 | 22.8 | 784 277 | 1 070 | 52 777 | 5.1 | 17 364 | 16.5 | 83.5 | 24.8 | 5.4 | 242 | 7.8 |
| Daggett | D | D | D | 9.2 | 8.6 | 690 141 | 1 578 | 95 709 | 1.7 | 35 530 | 27.0 | 73.1 | 45.8 | 6.3 | 12 | 8.3 |
| Davis | 49 | -25.8 | 99 | 12.2 | 12.4 | 533 777 | 5 373 | 65 164 | 37.2 | 75 093 | 84.0 | 16.0 | 27.2 | 8.1 | 78 | 10.1 |
| Duchesne | 1 076 | -17.5 | 1 225 | 102.0 | 93.4 | 809 965 | 661 | 78 236 | 34.4 | 39 166 | 18.7 | 81.3 | 43.1 | 8.2 | 469 | 10.2 |
| Emery | 205 | NA | 376 | 41.8 | 58.6 | 484 195 | 1 289 | 63 677 | 11.3 | 20 778 | 19.4 | 80.6 | 37.4 | 3.9 | 376 | 18.7 |
| Garfield | 82 | 2.5 | 298 | 22.3 | 17.4 | 782 863 | 2 630 | 77 121 | 6.1 | 22 310 | 18.3 | 81.7 | 31.3 | 5.5 | 111 | 5.8 |
| Grand | D | D | D | 4.7 | 8.0 | 1 022 079 | 419 | 69 638 | 2.6 | 28 362 | 37.0 | 63.0 | 36.7 | 7.8 | 57 | 7.8 |
| Iron | 492 | 2.7 | 1 011 | 59.1 | 87.6 | 1 622 977 | 1 606 | 105 129 | 70.5 | 144 831 | 59.9 | 40.1 | 41.9 | 14.6 | 460 | 15.0 |
| Juab | 260 | -3.7 | 777 | 27.1 | 65.7 | 913 824 | 1 175 | 92 017 | 19.8 | 59 152 | 42.5 | 57.5 | 35.8 | 8.4 | 1 098 | 47.8 |
| Kane | 113 | -27.6 | 782 | 4.3 | 8.7 | 1 167 784 | 1 493 | 51 145 | 9.4 | 65 080 | 3.0 | 97.0 | 33.8 | 4.8 | 193 | 11.0 |
| Millard | 567 | 27.4 | 806 | 103.3 | 153.7 | 952 187 | 1 181 | 116 556 | 137.8 | 196 024 | 30.5 | 69.5 | 58.9 | 20.8 | 2 114 | 40.7 |
| Morgan | 301 | NA | 953 | 13.8 | 23.4 | 1 305 632 | 1 097 | 57 621 | 11.9 | 37 573 | 11.9 | 88.1 | 30.4 | 7.3 | 285 | 7.3 |
| Piute | 42 | NA | 375 | 16.9 | 19.5 | 1 055 538 | 2 814 | 159 699 | 12.3 | 108 566 | 2.5 | 97.5 | 61.9 | 15.9 | 153 | 26.5 |
| Rich | 364 | -28.5 | 2 177 | 51.8 | 76.5 | 1 761 002 | 809 | 115 904 | 17.0 | 101 628 | 4.6 | 95.4 | 63.5 | 31.1 | 403 | 16.2 |
| Salt Lake | 107 | 30.5 | 183 | 9.9 | 29.1 | 594 651 | 3 248 | 48 495 | 21.4 | 36 423 | 83.6 | 16.4 | 18.6 | 3.7 | 81 | 1.9 |
| San Juan | 1 547 | -0.8 | 2 041 | 5.2 | 143.2 | 736 197 | 361 | 35 193 | 10.3 | 13 588 | 42.6 | 57.4 | 12.4 | 3.8 | 2 033 | 26.6 |
| Sanpete | 312 | -12.6 | 354 | 70.8 | 98.2 | 778 418 | 2 196 | 95 990 | 129.3 | 147 047 | 8.6 | 91.4 | 42.5 | 14.4 | 1 728 | 20.1 |
| Sevier | 186 | 12.7 | 284 | 52.5 | 42.6 | 562 086 | 1 983 | 74 184 | 50.7 | 77 439 | 24.8 | 75.2 | 35.1 | 10.8 | 367 | 14.0 |
| Summit | 415 | 10.4 | 660 | 24.0 | 30.7 | 948 930 | 1 439 | 53 954 | 25.4 | 40 415 | 6.2 | 93.8 | 31.2 | 8.7 | 207 | 6.2 |
| Tooele | 253 | -39.0 | 667 | 24.5 | 23.4 | 1 093 601 | 1 639 | 68 992 | 32.7 | 86 156 | 23.3 | 76.7 | 27.7 | 7.1 | 106 | 6.9 |
| Uintah | 1 800 | NA | 1 835 | 84.5 | 83.2 | 977 970 | 533 | 67 209 | 33.1 | 33 789 | 25.3 | 74.7 | 32.4 | 6.1 | 620 | 8.4 |
| Utah | 346 | 0.9 | 159 | 77.5 | 117.8 | 679 389 | 4 275 | 62 282 | 181.7 | 83 554 | 37.9 | 62.1 | 27.8 | 6.0 | 1 452 | 9.3 |
| Wasatch | 66 | -5.7 | 153 | 17.4 | 13.5 | 731 866 | 4 795 | 59 413 | 8.0 | 18 578 | 16.9 | 83.1 | 19.9 | 4.2 | 61 | 3.0 |
| Washington | 174 | -19.8 | 294 | 13.8 | 42.8 | 915 375 | 3 116 | 56 838 | 9.8 | 16 587 | 39.0 | 61.0 | 26.1 | 3.4 | 268 | 10.3 |
| Wayne | 45 | 7.1 | 225 | 18.9 | 19.2 | 614 413 | 2 731 | 98 590 | 15.4 | 76 551 | 6.7 | 93.3 | 63.2 | 13.4 | 254 | 49.8 |
| Weber | 106 | 21.8 | 106 | 29.6 | 31.3 | 525 416 | 4 950 | 58 846 | 32.7 | 32 648 | 36.4 | 63.6 | 22.2 | 5.2 | 418 | 8.5 |
| VERMONT | 1 233 | -1.0 | 177 | 2.3 | 516.9 | 512 684 | 2 903 | 74 500 | 673.7 | 96 465 | 14.7 | 85.3 | 41.1 | 15.4 | 6 773 | 19.3 |
| Addison | 187 | -3.1 | 243 | 0.4 | 116.1 | 636 913 | 2 626 | 111 549 | 161.4 | 208 819 | 9.1 | 90.9 | 51.4 | 24.7 | 1 059 | 33.1 |
| Bennington | 37 | -9.8 | 162 | 0.2 | 13.2 | 596 966 | 3 688 | 70 462 | 10.5 | 46 542 | 30.2 | 69.8 | 35.4 | 6.6 | 63 | 8.4 |
| Caledonia | 82 | -2.4 | 154 | 0.0 | 30.8 | 407 288 | 2 639 | 66 406 | 31.5 | 59 401 | 11.8 | 88.2 | 36.7 | 13.0 | 328 | 16.2 |

# Table B. States and Counties — Water Use, Wholesale Trade, Retail Trade, and Real Estate

| STATE County | Water use, 2005 | | Wholesale trade,[1] 2007 | | | | Retail trade,[2] 2007 | | | | Real estate and rental and leasing,[2] 2007 | | | |
|---|---|---|---|---|---|---|---|---|---|---|---|---|---|---|
| | Total water withdrawn (mil gal/day) | Gallons withdrawn per person | Number of establishments | Number of employees | Sales (mil dol) | Annual payroll (mil dol) | Number of establishments | Number of employees | Sales (mil dol) | Annual payroll (mil dol) | Number of establishments | Number of employees | Receipts (mil dol) | Annual payroll (mil dol) |
| | 133 | 134 | 135 | 136 | 137 | 138 | 139 | 140 | 141 | 142 | 143 | 144 | 145 | 146 |
| TEXAS—Cont'd | | | | | | | | | | | | | | |
| Tom Green | 42.0 | 406 | 119 | D | D | D | 448 | D | D | D | 135 | 631 | 76.0 | 15.8 |
| Travis | 563.1 | 634 | 1 129 | 19 691 | 14 119.8 | 1 362.7 | 3 352 | 52 883 | 13 879.5 | 1 341.0 | 1 776 | 12 622 | 2 423.6 | 501.6 |
| Trinity | 3.5 | 244 | 4 | 93 | 34.0 | 3.8 | 44 | 316 | 57.0 | 4.4 | 6 | 29 | 1.4 | 0.3 |
| Tyler | 5.3 | 256 | 7 | 55 | 70.5 | 4.5 | 56 | 596 | 115.0 | 10.2 | 3 | D | D | D |
| Upshur | 21.5 | 567 | 12 | 171 | 58.4 | 3.5 | 100 | 835 | 216.7 | 15.5 | 11 | 23 | 1.9 | 0.2 |
| Upton | 16.8 | 5 504 | 5 | 29 | 21.8 | 1.4 | 10 | 69 | 16.7 | 0.9 | 2 | D | D | D |
| Uvalde | 65.0 | 2 411 | 27 | 214 | 120.7 | 7.3 | 109 | 1 350 | 322.2 | 27.1 | 32 | 88 | 10.6 | 1.8 |
| Val Verde | 17.4 | 365 | 23 | 127 | 39.3 | 3.7 | 169 | 2 172 | 524.4 | 41.4 | 26 | 92 | 11.3 | 2.1 |
| Van Zandt | 15.5 | 296 | 29 | 209 | 50.1 | 7.4 | 150 | 1 543 | 410.5 | 30.7 | 35 | 101 | 26.9 | 1.6 |
| Victoria | 27.1 | 316 | 104 | 1 284 | 651.1 | 54.6 | 403 | 5 951 | 1 434.3 | 129.2 | 124 | 869 | 162.2 | 36.1 |
| Walker | 7.5 | 119 | 32 | D | D | D | 155 | 2 300 | 626.3 | 47.2 | 51 | 261 | 68.1 | 8.6 |
| Waller | 27.3 | 784 | 43 | 788 | 451.6 | 30.6 | 103 | 1 589 | 593.1 | 46.2 | 23 | 70 | 8.5 | 1.6 |
| Ward | 24.3 | 2 373 | 9 | 305 | 52.0 | 8.3 | 37 | 291 | 94.6 | 6.1 | 11 | 79 | 20.9 | 4.2 |
| Washington | 8.1 | 255 | 28 | D | D | D | 148 | 1 964 | 509.9 | 44.2 | 46 | 202 | 35.2 | 5.8 |
| Webb | 88.8 | 395 | 351 | 2 519 | 1 472.1 | 79.2 | 819 | 12 864 | 2 913.5 | 235.4 | 205 | 724 | 119.6 | 18.9 |
| Wharton | 291.7 | 7 020 | 53 | 808 | 541.1 | 32.6 | 179 | 1 961 | 466.7 | 43.6 | 40 | 169 | 37.9 | 6.8 |
| Wheeler | 11.9 | 2 482 | 8 | 55 | 25.8 | 1.4 | 30 | 200 | 46.1 | 3.2 | 5 | 12 | 0.7 | 0.1 |
| Wichita | 42.2 | 335 | 155 | 1 396 | 548.0 | 52.3 | 537 | 7 577 | 1 715.9 | 156.9 | 179 | 832 | 99.2 | 19.2 |
| Wilbarger | 32.1 | 2 309 | 15 | D | D | D | 55 | 674 | 170.2 | 12.8 | 9 | 28 | 2.6 | 0.5 |
| Willacy | 35.0 | 1 718 | 6 | D | D | D | 38 | 468 | 122.9 | 9.2 | 12 | 32 | 2.4 | 0.5 |
| Williamson | 54.1 | 162 | 307 | 2 913 | 1 525.2 | 153.3 | 1 188 | 21 116 | 9 918.0 | 525.2 | 399 | 1 732 | 363.2 | 60.2 |
| Wilson | 21.6 | 575 | 18 | 98 | 49.0 | 2.5 | 74 | 820 | 180.5 | 16.9 | 13 | 43 | 4.2 | 0.6 |
| Winkler | 15.1 | 2 253 | 7 | 42 | 29.1 | 2.0 | 25 | 167 | 40.3 | 3.0 | 5 | 50 | 7.6 | 1.7 |
| Wise | 12.8 | 225 | 55 | 506 | 418.4 | 23.8 | 162 | 2 002 | 565.3 | 49.6 | 39 | 365 | 63.5 | 17.4 |
| Wood | 20.6 | 504 | 38 | 268 | 137.0 | 7.4 | 142 | 1 448 | 383.5 | 30.7 | 36 | 154 | 21.6 | 3.2 |
| Yoakum | 131.2 | 17 713 | 17 | 160 | 51.2 | 6.8 | 27 | 169 | 37.0 | 3.3 | 5 | D | D | D |
| Young | 161.9 | 8 996 | 25 | 198 | 86.2 | 9.1 | 74 | 834 | 185.2 | 17.0 | 22 | 60 | 45.4 | 1.9 |
| Zapata | 5.6 | 421 | 3 | D | D | D | 37 | 318 | 62.1 | 4.3 | 7 | 18 | 2.8 | 0.5 |
| Zavala | 53.2 | 4 507 | 2 | D | D | D | 19 | 202 | 33.3 | 3.1 | NA | NA | NA | NA |
| UTAH | 5 115.2 | 2 008 | 3 043 | 43 900 | 25 417.4 | 2 012.0 | 8 984 | 142 266 | 36 574.2 | 3 240.7 | 4 886 | 20 413 | 3 390.8 | 617.4 |
| Beaver | 91.4 | 14 411 | NA | NA | NA | NA | 32 | 312 | 89.7 | 4.7 | 3 | 3 | 0.3 | 0.1 |
| Box Elder | 435.9 | 9 621 | 30 | D | D | D | 135 | 1 790 | 447.4 | 34.5 | 48 | 88 | 12.0 | 1.7 |
| Cache | 280.4 | 2 708 | 110 | 796 | 361.6 | 29.3 | 398 | 5 347 | 1 095.1 | 96.9 | 191 | D | D | D |
| Carbon | 54.4 | 2 811 | 29 | D | D | D | 98 | 1 271 | 298.9 | 25.4 | 17 | 63 | 13.1 | 1.5 |
| Daggett | 34.7 | 36 064 | NA | NA | NA | NA | 5 | D | D | D | NA | NA | NA | NA |
| Davis | 123.9 | 445 | 218 | D | D | D | 780 | 13 393 | 3 217.7 | 286.7 | 404 | 1 120 | 174.1 | 27.5 |
| Duchesne | 334.5 | 21 954 | 18 | 138 | 54.7 | 4.7 | 69 | 795 | 216.0 | 16.7 | 25 | 87 | 27.8 | 3.4 |
| Emery | 224.7 | 21 421 | 3 | 3 | 1.0 | 0.1 | 44 | 503 | 128.6 | 8.0 | 3 | D | D | D |
| Garfield | 87.7 | 18 648 | 2 | D | D | D | 22 | 134 | 22.9 | 1.8 | 10 | 13 | 1.9 | 0.4 |
| Grand | 22.5 | 2 550 | 12 | 84 | 19.7 | 3.2 | 76 | 661 | 159.9 | 14.7 | 36 | 106 | 16.2 | 2.6 |
| Iron | 275.2 | 6 648 | 40 | D | D | D | 191 | 2 274 | 652.2 | 48.4 | 96 | 203 | 35.0 | 4.5 |
| Juab | 74.0 | 8 240 | 5 | 43 | 19.3 | 1.3 | 34 | 318 | 112.2 | 4.8 | 2 | D | D | D |
| Kane | 31.7 | 5 109 | 5 | 10 | 3.8 | 0.3 | 49 | 351 | 72.1 | 6.2 | 22 | 53 | 6.8 | 1.0 |
| Millard | 425.5 | 32 304 | 11 | 62 | 23.2 | 1.9 | 65 | 566 | 125.1 | 9.1 | 3 | 5 | 0.5 | 0.1 |
| Morgan | 40.2 | 4 716 | 6 | D | D | D | 23 | 184 | 42.7 | 3.4 | 9 | D | D | D |
| Piute | 59.2 | 43 253 | 1 | D | D | D | 7 | D | D | D | NA | NA | NA | NA |
| Rich | 184.6 | 89 544 | NA | NA | NA | NA | 9 | 56 | 11.5 | 0.9 | 11 | 67 | 6.8 | 1.8 |
| Salt Lake | 344.4 | 352 | 1 649 | 28 039 | 16 956.4 | 1 350.3 | 3 424 | 60 133 | 16 758.7 | 1 510.5 | 2 085 | 11 470 | 2 022.2 | 384.1 |
| San Juan | 29.3 | 2 011 | 4 | D | D | D | 37 | 378 | 44.6 | 4.4 | 2 | D | D | D |
| Sanpete | 273.0 | 10 723 | 12 | 58 | 31.2 | 1.4 | 88 | 956 | 196.9 | 16.9 | 22 | 274 | 14.3 | 5.5 |
| Sevier | 189.9 | 9 666 | 14 | 126 | 112.0 | 4.2 | 108 | 1 312 | 324.6 | 27.4 | 10 | 65 | 5.2 | 1.4 |
| Summit | 94.8 | 2 613 | 57 | 322 | 165.8 | 11.7 | 294 | 3 224 | 659.9 | 64.7 | 270 | 1 214 | 221.5 | 41.6 |
| Tooele | 212.5 | 4 076 | 14 | 71 | 73.6 | 5.1 | 100 | 1 773 | 503.6 | 37.1 | 35 | 91 | 13.5 | 1.8 |
| Uintah | 287.8 | 10 704 | 44 | D | D | D | 135 | 1 703 | 461.4 | 37.0 | 75 | 364 | 138.5 | 19.2 |
| Utah | 402.3 | 882 | 406 | 6 033 | 2 425.0 | 275.6 | 1 357 | 23 988 | 5 772.2 | 518.3 | 753 | D | D | D |
| Wasatch | 60.6 | 3 029 | 12 | D | D | D | 80 | 1 253 | 228.4 | 27.1 | 46 | 134 | 12.3 | 2.5 |
| Washington | 98.9 | 778 | 146 | 1 260 | 510.8 | 48.3 | 593 | 8 035 | 2 087.8 | 185.9 | 367 | 856 | 122.0 | 20.0 |
| Wayne | 68.1 | 27 177 | NA | NA | NA | NA | 17 | 101 | 27.8 | 1.5 | 2 | D | D | D |
| Weber | 273.4 | 1 279 | 195 | 2 790 | 2 218.2 | 111.3 | 714 | 11 422 | 2 810.6 | 247.5 | 339 | D | D | D |
| VERMONT | 522.5 | 839 | 762 | 9 852 | 5 121.7 | 424.8 | 3 852 | 40 416 | 9 310.1 | 938.7 | 797 | 3 395 | 497.3 | 95.9 |
| Addison | 13.6 | 367 | 32 | 216 | 101.4 | 8.0 | 212 | 2 139 | 464.8 | 53.2 | 38 | D | D | D |
| Bennington | 6.7 | 180 | 31 | D | D | D | 338 | 3 415 | 833.0 | 82.6 | 64 | 230 | 35.2 | 6.8 |
| Caledonia | 4.9 | 162 | 26 | 212 | 66.2 | 10.1 | 188 | 1 743 | 412.7 | 39.7 | 26 | 81 | 14.2 | 2.6 |

1. Merchant wholesalers, except manufacturers' sales branches and offices.    2. Employer establishments.

Items 133—146

# Table B. States and Counties — Professional Services, Manufacturing, and Accommodation and Food Services

| STATE County | Professional, scientific, and technical services,[1] 2007 | | | | Manufacturing, 2007 | | | | Accommodation and food services, 2007 | | | |
|---|---|---|---|---|---|---|---|---|---|---|---|---|
| | Number of establishments | Number of employees | Receipts (mil dol) | Annual payroll (mil dol) | Number of establishments | Number of employees | Receipts (mil dol) | Annual payroll (mil dol) | Number of establishments | Number of employees | Sales (mil dol) | Annual payroll (mil dol) |
| | 147 | 148 | 149 | 150 | 151 | 152 | 153 | 154 | 155 | 156 | 157 | 158 |
| TEXAS—Cont'd | | | | | | | | | | | | |
| Tom Green | 185 | D | D | D | 120 | D | D | D | 209 | D | D | D |
| Travis | 4 745 | D | D | D | 768 | 35 731 | 28 294.7 | 1 827.7 | 2 277 | 52 877 | 2 833.7 | 797.8 |
| Trinity | 11 | 42 | 2.8 | 0.9 | NA | NA | NA | NA | 16 | 195 | 11.9 | 2.0 |
| Tyler | 16 | 60 | 5.0 | 1.4 | NA | NA | NA | NA | 21 | 225 | 9.8 | 2.1 |
| Upshur | 38 | D | D | D | 31 | 512 | D | 18.5 | 31 | 587 | 20.2 | 6.6 |
| Upton | 3 | D | D | D | NA | NA | NA | NA | 9 | D | D | D |
| Uvalde | 43 | 149 | 13.1 | 4.3 | 23 | 630 | 203.7 | 23.2 | 75 | 1 014 | 39.9 | 10.9 |
| Val Verde | 44 | D | D | D | NA | NA | NA | NA | 88 | 1 436 | 59.0 | 15.5 |
| Van Zandt | 52 | 212 | 25.6 | 8.0 | 35 | 645 | 119.9 | 24.8 | 64 | 839 | 32.9 | 9.4 |
| Victoria | 155 | D | D | D | 78 | D | D | D | 170 | 3 166 | 130.8 | 35.4 |
| Walker | 84 | 499 | 35.3 | 10.8 | 39 | 1 043 | D | 40.5 | 95 | 1 960 | 73.8 | 19.9 |
| Waller | 54 | 285 | 52.7 | 17.7 | 65 | 2 352 | D | 111.0 | 41 | 642 | 24.7 | 5.9 |
| Ward | 13 | 40 | 3.1 | 1.2 | NA | NA | NA | NA | 20 | 218 | 8.9 | 1.8 |
| Washington | 59 | 265 | 32.5 | 9.2 | 46 | 2 782 | 762.8 | 108.0 | 76 | 1 024 | 41.3 | 11.9 |
| Webb | 309 | D | D | D | 89 | 914 | 242.4 | 30.7 | 360 | 7 489 | 317.3 | 86.5 |
| Wharton | 59 | 304 | 34.8 | 13.6 | 47 | 3 941 | 464.0 | 56.6 | 76 | 1 160 | 45.9 | 12.1 |
| Wheeler | 10 | 30 | 2.7 | 0.9 | NA | NA | NA | NA | 19 | 197 | 9.3 | 2.3 |
| Wichita | 237 | D | D | D | 142 | 6 047 | 1 492.5 | 262.7 | 290 | 6 626 | 254.8 | 79.7 |
| Wilbarger | 22 | 85 | 5.4 | 1.5 | 9 | D | D | 31.9 | 33 | 368 | 16.1 | 4.2 |
| Willacy | 9 | D | D | D | NA | NA | NA | NA | 26 | 287 | 13.2 | 2.6 |
| Williamson | 886 | D | D | D | 269 | 6 524 | 1 647.6 | 312.5 | 636 | 12 187 | 583.6 | 156.5 |
| Wilson | 37 | D | D | D | NA | NA | NA | NA | 47 | 553 | 20.8 | 5.6 |
| Winkler | 9 | 15 | 4.0 | 0.5 | NA | NA | NA | NA | 9 | 85 | 4.7 | 1.0 |
| Wise | 78 | D | D | D | 76 | 1 728 | 376.5 | 72.3 | 93 | 1 356 | 59.3 | 16.6 |
| Wood | 66 | 221 | 20.2 | 6.2 | 44 | 1 026 | 708.0 | 41.2 | 66 | 761 | 30.4 | 8.3 |
| Yoakum | 6 | 14 | 1.5 | 0.4 | NA | NA | NA | NA | 18 | 147 | 6.0 | 1.4 |
| Young | 34 | 117 | 11.4 | 4.1 | 23 | 973 | 301.4 | 41.1 | 40 | 481 | 17.7 | 5.0 |
| Zapata | 6 | 19 | 1.4 | 0.3 | NA | NA | NA | NA | 22 | 212 | 9.4 | 2.0 |
| Zavala | 5 | 19 | 1.4 | 0.3 | NA | NA | NA | NA | 16 | 108 | 4.6 | 1.1 |
| UTAH | 8 203 | 67 426 | 8 197.7 | 3 157.3 | 3 368 | 123 249 | 42 431.7 | 5 508.5 | 4 541 | 91 808 | 3 980.6 | 1 148.6 |
| Beaver | 5 | 11 | 1.3 | 0.3 | NA | NA | NA | NA | 25 | 310 | 12.8 | 3.2 |
| Box Elder | 63 | D | D | D | 78 | 10 869 | 3 150.9 | D | 70 | 1 171 | 36.8 | 11.9 |
| Cache | 351 | D | D | D | 214 | 10 326 | D | 405.8 | 135 | 2 727 | 95.2 | 29.5 |
| Carbon | 39 | D | D | D | NA | NA | NA | NA | 40 | 763 | 26.2 | 6.8 |
| Daggett | 3 | D | D | D | NA | NA | NA | NA | 8 | 67 | 6.4 | 1.8 |
| Davis | 791 | D | D | D | 273 | 9 914 | 4 985.2 | D | 368 | 7 425 | 274.3 | 76.9 |
| Duchesne | 37 | 88 | 11.4 | 3.5 | NA | NA | NA | NA | 30 | 374 | 13.6 | 3.8 |
| Emery | 11 | 71 | 5.0 | 1.8 | NA | NA | NA | NA | 25 | 245 | 10.8 | 2.7 |
| Garfield | 5 | D | D | D | NA | NA | NA | NA | 43 | 460 | 49.3 | 12.1 |
| Grand | 33 | 157 | 14.3 | 5.3 | NA | NA | NA | NA | 80 | 1 369 | 68.2 | 19.9 |
| Iron | 116 | D | D | D | 72 | 1 665 | 736.0 | 59.4 | 101 | 1 618 | 59.6 | 16.9 |
| Juab | 14 | 277 | 25.2 | 9.7 | NA | NA | NA | NA | 21 | 223 | 7.2 | 1.8 |
| Kane | 18 | 27 | 2.9 | 0.9 | NA | NA | NA | NA | 42 | 404 | 20.9 | 6.1 |
| Millard | 5 | D | D | D | NA | NA | NA | NA | 26 | 342 | 11.6 | 3.2 |
| Morgan | 25 | D | D | D | NA | NA | NA | NA | 11 | 142 | 5.7 | 1.3 |
| Piute | 1 | D | D | D | NA | NA | NA | NA | 7 | D | D | D |
| Rich | 3 | D | D | D | NA | NA | NA | NA | 12 | 65 | 3.7 | 0.9 |
| Salt Lake | 3 763 | D | D | D | 1 483 | 51 595 | 18 860.5 | 2 351.7 | 1 826 | 40 212 | 1 874.6 | 556.6 |
| San Juan | 10 | D | D | D | NA | NA | NA | NA | 61 | D | D | D |
| Sanpete | 20 | 224 | 8.7 | 3.1 | NA | NA | NA | NA | 32 | 363 | 8.3 | 2.4 |
| Sevier | 37 | 134 | 14.3 | 5.8 | NA | NA | NA | NA | 45 | 828 | 24.7 | 7.2 |
| Summit | 293 | 896 | 130.5 | 44.8 | NA | NA | NA | NA | 167 | 4 907 | 228.9 | 70.4 |
| Tooele | 55 | D | D | D | 39 | D | D | D | 55 | 931 | 35.2 | 8.8 |
| Uintah | 104 | 324 | 44.6 | 14.3 | NA | NA | NA | NA | 64 | 1 005 | 46.5 | 11.1 |
| Utah | 1 428 | 16 469 | 1 328.9 | 499.4 | 522 | D | D | D | 543 | 11 712 | 451.7 | 128.4 |
| Wasatch | 76 | 346 | 37.0 | 12.8 | NA | NA | NA | NA | 43 | 722 | 38.8 | 9.1 |
| Washington | 432 | D | D | D | 154 | 3 225 | 609.6 | 117.4 | 279 | 5 631 | 254.5 | 74.5 |
| Wayne | 3 | D | D | D | NA | NA | NA | NA | 24 | 117 | 7.7 | 1.8 |
| Weber | 462 | D | D | D | 244 | 12 066 | D | 494.1 | 358 | 7 107 | 261.2 | 70.9 |
| VERMONT | 2 100 | 16 346 | 1 615.6 | 649.5 | 1 108 | 35 571 | 10 751.5 | 1 650.1 | 1 942 | 31 176 | 1 367.6 | 427.9 |
| Addison | 115 | 390 | 42.5 | 17.3 | 57 | 1 948 | 539.0 | 93.0 | 83 | 971 | 48.2 | 16.2 |
| Bennington | 125 | 407 | 53.7 | 16.5 | 75 | 2 443 | 571.6 | 97.4 | 152 | 2 316 | 106.7 | 33.0 |
| Caledonia | 66 | D | D | D | 60 | 2 120 | 339.1 | 70.8 | 73 | 712 | 29.9 | 8.4 |

1. Establishment subject to federal tax.

# Table B. States and Counties — Health Care and Social Assistance, Other Services, and Federal Funds

| STATE County | Health care and social assistance, 2007 | | | | Other services, 2007 | | | | Federal funds and grants, 2009–2010 Expenditures (mil dol) | | | |
|---|---|---|---|---|---|---|---|---|---|---|---|---|
| | | | | | | | | | Total | Direct payments for individuals[1] | | |
| | Number of establishments | Number of employees | Receipts (mil dol) | Annual payroll (mil dol) | Number of establishments | Number of employees | Receipts (mil dol) | Annual payroll (mil dol) | | Social Security and government retirement | Medicare | Food Stamps and Supplemental Security Income |
| | 159 | 160 | 161 | 162 | 163 | 164 | 165 | 166 | 167 | 168 | 169 | 170 |
| **TEXAS—Cont'd** | | | | | | | | | | | | |
| Tom Green | 259 | D | D | D | 212 | D | D | D | 1 004.2 | 349.5 | 150.3 | 39.6 |
| Travis | 2 549 | 48 334 | 5 562.7 | 2 156.3 | 1 930 | 18 213 | 2 025.4 | 609.7 | 16 359.5 | 1 800.2 | 625.1 | 235.7 |
| Trinity | 22 | 314 | 20.8 | 8.4 | 20 | 85 | 5.2 | 1.1 | 155.9 | 64.4 | 42.9 | 7.7 |
| Tyler | 22 | 479 | 27.0 | 11.8 | 11 | 42 | 3.6 | 0.9 | 175.3 | 74.7 | 50.3 | 9.3 |
| Upshur | 43 | 602 | 41.1 | 16.9 | 31 | 96 | 11.6 | 2.4 | 268.8 | 119.4 | 70.3 | 12.7 |
| Upton | 7 | D | D | D | 1 | D | D | D | 26.8 | 9.6 | 7.3 | 1.9 |
| Uvalde | 58 | 1 392 | 90.5 | 40.0 | 35 | 208 | 14.2 | 4.1 | 232.1 | 66.6 | 38.3 | 19.6 |
| Val Verde | 83 | 2 891 | 127.5 | 53.8 | 49 | 257 | 16.5 | 3.4 | 567.1 | 119.3 | 45.0 | 34.7 |
| Van Zandt | 82 | 1 209 | 67.2 | 29.5 | 57 | 255 | 22.6 | 6.0 | 359.7 | 173.4 | 103.3 | 14.4 |
| Victoria | 322 | 6 266 | 586.9 | 233.1 | 166 | 1 202 | 112.2 | 33.1 | 625.0 | 256.1 | 134.2 | 37.9 |
| Walker | 101 | 2 028 | 133.5 | 56.2 | 64 | 384 | 23.1 | 6.3 | 359.4 | 130.1 | 65.3 | 18.1 |
| Waller | 43 | 678 | 38.4 | 17.4 | 50 | 185 | 16.9 | 4.3 | 239.9 | 70.1 | 37.7 | 13.4 |
| Ward | 13 | 242 | 14.8 | 7.2 | 17 | 74 | 8.9 | 2.1 | 78.8 | 30.1 | 20.2 | 5.7 |
| Washington | 81 | 1 825 | 104.7 | 42.6 | 52 | 281 | 17.9 | 5.1 | 287.5 | 116.5 | 50.9 | 10.6 |
| Webb | 441 | 12 142 | 723.4 | 284.3 | 257 | 1 465 | 124.3 | 28.6 | 1 613.9 | 325.1 | 210.5 | 164.0 |
| Wharton | 63 | 2 282 | 165.5 | 56.7 | 74 | 291 | 20.7 | 5.3 | 382.7 | 112.8 | 84.1 | 17.0 |
| Wheeler | 14 | 227 | 13.3 | 6.2 | 8 | 19 | 1.8 | 0.4 | 52.6 | 16.7 | 20.0 | 1.8 |
| Wichita | 374 | 10 412 | 823.4 | 329.8 | 264 | 1 486 | 141.7 | 34.9 | 1 486.8 | 488.6 | 210.5 | 33.0 |
| Wilbarger | 35 | D | D | D | 23 | 126 | 6.1 | 1.8 | 128.3 | 40.6 | 38.4 | 5.4 |
| Willacy | 32 | 1 199 | 53.1 | 27.9 | 17 | D | D | D | 249.6 | 39.1 | 34.0 | 20.3 |
| Williamson | 748 | 9 836 | 926.3 | 368.7 | 518 | 3 892 | 305.6 | 101.9 | 2 047.8 | 847.6 | 145.0 | 32.0 |
| Wilson | 51 | 1 206 | 65.5 | 28.8 | 42 | 112 | 13.3 | 1.9 | 237.5 | 126.5 | 35.2 | 9.1 |
| Winkler | 11 | 139 | 9.2 | 3.7 | 11 | D | D | D | 49.0 | 17.0 | 17.9 | 3.4 |
| Wise | 104 | D | D | D | 70 | 383 | 30.9 | 8.5 | 261.5 | 146.5 | 51.2 | 9.2 |
| Wood | 73 | 1 004 | 76.3 | 27.4 | 53 | 245 | 16.4 | 4.4 | 398.5 | 199.1 | 84.5 | 11.8 |
| Yoakum | 5 | D | D | D | 9 | 48 | 4.5 | 1.0 | 53.8 | 17.9 | 11.8 | 2.3 |
| Young | 59 | 950 | 65.9 | 26.9 | 39 | 126 | 9.4 | 2.7 | 155.3 | 64.2 | 45.5 | 7.0 |
| Zapata | 14 | 325 | 8.6 | 3.8 | 6 | D | D | D | 103.8 | 21.8 | 25.1 | 10.2 |
| Zavala | 12 | 542 | 14.4 | 6.9 | 3 | D | D | D | 112.3 | 20.9 | 21.0 | 15.3 |
| **UTAH** | 6 392 | 112 646 | 10 860.4 | 4 156.2 | 4 141 | 26 236 | 2 356.1 | 653.1 | 23 545.2 | 5 855.1 | 3 539.1 | 538.1 |
| Beaver | 16 | 232 | 17.8 | 5.8 | 8 | D | D | D | 65.8 | 18.1 | 25.0 | 1.1 |
| Box Elder | 109 | 1 128 | 93.0 | 31.2 | 59 | D | D | D | 948.9 | 132.6 | 61.5 | 8.0 |
| Cache | 299 | D | D | D | 161 | D | D | D | 687.3 | 177.6 | 99.0 | 14.0 |
| Carbon | 76 | 933 | 82.1 | 24.3 | 52 | D | NA | NA | 181.0 | 69.9 | 59.7 | 11.7 |
| Daggett | 1 | D | D | D | NA | NA | NA | NA | 21.1 | 4.6 | 2.3 | 0.1 |
| Davis | 584 | 8 030 | 679.7 | 262.5 | 363 | 2 225 | 161.9 | 47.1 | 2 964.4 | 745.0 | 212.4 | 39.4 |
| Duchesne | 46 | 1 048 | 87.8 | 31.9 | 34 | 137 | 13.5 | 3.3 | 129.3 | 43.2 | 31.6 | 11.1 |
| Emery | 14 | D | D | D | 10 | D | D | D | 79.3 | 29.6 | 20.3 | 3.7 |
| Garfield | 7 | 170 | 13.1 | 4.8 | 2 | D | D | D | 60.6 | 17.2 | 12.0 | 1.3 |
| Grand | 22 | 249 | 21.4 | 8.5 | 21 | 55 | 4.5 | 1.2 | 112.1 | 28.2 | 14.3 | 3.9 |
| Iron | 108 | 1 434 | 123.3 | 42.3 | 69 | 394 | 25.3 | 6.8 | 244.3 | 107.6 | 37.6 | 10.2 |
| Juab | 21 | D | D | D | 8 | D | D | D | 49.6 | 22.1 | 15.9 | 1.7 |
| Kane | 15 | 166 | 15.5 | 3.9 | 14 | D | D | D | 56.8 | 27.4 | 9.9 | 1.9 |
| Millard | 24 | D | D | D | 14 | 46 | 9.6 | 1.2 | 91.5 | 32.3 | 23.9 | 4.1 |
| Morgan | 10 | 49 | 3.0 | 0.8 | 9 | 61 | 3.4 | 1.2 | 42.1 | 28.9 | 7.0 | 0.4 |
| Piute | 1 | D | D | D | 1 | D | D | D | 23.2 | 6.2 | 8.9 | 0.6 |
| Rich | 2 | D | D | D | 8 | D | D | D | 12.8 | 6.0 | 2.7 | 0.3 |
| Salt Lake | 2 644 | 53 465 | 5 733.1 | 2 203.6 | 1 907 | 13 222 | 1 262.1 | 355.0 | 8 889.3 | 1 975.0 | 1 518.8 | 218.8 |
| San Juan | 27 | D | D | D | 8 | D | D | D | 248.8 | 25.2 | 95.6 | 14.8 |
| Sanpete | 47 | 830 | 54.2 | 22.9 | 27 | D | D | D | 176.0 | 61.3 | 48.9 | 6.6 |
| Sevier | 48 | 694 | 51.0 | 19.5 | 25 | 133 | 13.4 | 4.9 | 161.0 | 60.1 | 46.2 | 7.3 |
| Summit | 108 | D | D | D | 95 | 868 | 98.8 | 22.3 | 127.8 | 66.7 | 11.9 | 1.8 |
| Tooele | 92 | D | D | D | 57 | 269 | 20.7 | 6.0 | 679.6 | 145.5 | 48.6 | 9.9 |
| Uintah | 57 | 598 | 62.7 | 18.5 | 64 | 297 | 39.7 | 9.0 | 174.8 | 58.2 | 40.3 | 8.3 |
| Utah | 1 014 | D | D | D | 539 | D | D | D | 2 526.1 | 727.1 | 480.6 | 65.9 |
| Wasatch | 43 | 464 | 39.7 | 13.6 | 42 | D | D | D | 78.0 | 41.3 | 17.8 | 1.9 |
| Washington | 393 | 6 648 | 628.5 | 250.2 | 198 | 1 116 | 95.0 | 27.4 | 1 063.0 | 435.9 | 120.4 | 18.5 |
| Wayne | 4 | D | D | D | 3 | D | D | D | 25.3 | 7.8 | 5.4 | 0.3 |
| Weber | 560 | 10 314 | 914.5 | 357.4 | 343 | 2 171 | 160.9 | 48.8 | 2 115.7 | 750.9 | 460.4 | 70.6 |
| **VERMONT** | 2 176 | 41 917 | 3 537.1 | 1 495.3 | 1 629 | 7 269 | 798.6 | 182.9 | 7 404.8 | 1 929.1 | 756.7 | 205.9 |
| Addison | 125 | 1 840 | 126.7 | 55.6 | 88 | 344 | 55.3 | 8.5 | 366.4 | 94.5 | 37.0 | 9.4 |
| Bennington | 166 | 2 867 | 238.3 | 103.6 | 97 | 441 | 29.7 | 8.0 | 303.4 | 130.2 | 57.2 | 13.4 |
| Caledonia | 105 | 1 763 | 124.0 | 55.5 | 72 | 252 | 20.3 | 5.1 | 248.5 | 95.6 | 40.4 | 13.5 |

1. State totals may include programs not allocated by county.

# Federal Funds, Residential Construction, and Local Government Finances

| STATE County | Federal funds and grants, 2009–2010 (cont.) | | | | | | | Value of residential construction authorized by building permits, 2011 | | Local government finances, 2007 | | | | |
|---|---|---|---|---|---|---|---|---|---|---|---|---|---|---|
| | Expenditures (mil dol) (cont.) | | | | | | | | | General revenue | | | | |
| | | Procurement contract awards | | Grants[1] | | | | | | | | Taxes | | |
| | | | | | | | | | | | | | Per capita[2] (dollars) | |
| | Salaries and wages | Defense | Other | Medicaid and other health-related | Nutrition and family welfare | Education | Other | New construction ($1,000) | Number of housing units | Total (mil dol) | Inter-govern-mental (mil dol) | Total (mil dol) | Total | Property |
| | 171 | 172 | 173 | 174 | 175 | 176 | 177 | 178 | 179 | 180 | 181 | 182 | 183 | 184 |
| TEXAS—Cont'd | | | | | | | | | | | | | | |
| Tom Green | 205.1 | 64.0 | 5.4 | 111.2 | 22.7 | 3.7 | 16.8 | 24 414 | 145 | 289.4 | 126.4 | 115.4 | 1 085 | 797 |
| Travis | 914.4 | 473.2 | 697.7 | 1 200.0 | 1 079.3 | 1 315.3 | 7 734.6 | 749 526 | 5 761 | 3 808.7 | 655.4 | 2 194.7 | 2 252 | 1 820 |
| Trinity | 2.5 | 0.0 | 0.6 | 34.5 | 1.0 | 0.5 | 1.1 | 78 | 6 | 30.3 | 16.5 | 10.2 | 719 | 614 |
| Tyler | 3.6 | 0.3 | 0.7 | 30.8 | 3.0 | 0.8 | 0.2 | 0 | 0 | 67.1 | 26.7 | 23.4 | 1 149 | 1 066 |
| Upshur | 5.7 | 0.5 | 1.2 | 53.1 | 3.2 | 1.1 | 0.3 | 5 529 | 40 | 84.2 | 34.6 | 39.9 | 1 051 | 960 |
| Upton | 0.6 | 0.0 | 0.2 | 3.5 | 0.7 | 0.1 | 0.0 | 20 | 1 | 48.5 | 2.0 | 39.8 | 13 028 | 12 849 |
| Uvalde | 17.5 | 0.3 | 1.5 | 51.8 | 7.2 | 2.9 | 5.0 | 12 904 | 146 | 141.3 | 54.3 | 28.8 | 1 083 | 850 |
| Val Verde | 190.0 | 51.9 | 12.9 | 83.9 | 17.5 | 2.7 | 3.9 | 802 | 53 | 156.5 | 95.3 | 39.0 | 811 | 597 |
| Van Zandt | 7.5 | 0.1 | 2.9 | 47.5 | 5.6 | 1.4 | 1.3 | 2 500 | 9 | 117.7 | 54.4 | 44.5 | 855 | 737 |
| Victoria | 34.1 | 0.2 | 4.6 | 98.8 | 17.5 | 3.9 | 5.7 | 14 783 | 83 | 401.0 | 96.8 | 116.6 | 1 351 | 1 031 |
| Walker | 29.4 | 10.4 | 2.3 | 60.9 | 7.2 | 3.9 | 5.1 | 7 938 | 46 | 258.5 | 58.0 | 54.7 | 855 | 668 |
| Waller | 7.1 | 17.0 | 8.0 | 27.7 | 3.9 | 8.5 | 17.0 | 1 209 | 37 | 113.2 | 42.3 | 57.9 | 1 611 | 1 369 |
| Ward | 1.6 | 0.0 | 0.4 | 18.7 | 1.0 | 0.3 | 0.3 | 1 358 | 12 | 48.9 | 6.0 | 30.9 | 3 011 | 2 840 |
| Washington | 7.6 | 3.7 | 1.3 | 74.3 | 1.9 | 0.7 | 1.7 | 6 705 | 56 | 149.2 | 42.3 | 53.3 | 1 665 | 1 346 |
| Webb | 205.4 | 2.8 | 40.7 | 421.4 | 132.8 | 21.3 | 39.6 | 115 842 | 956 | 1 057.5 | 514.3 | 342.7 | 1 470 | 1 182 |
| Wharton | 27.2 | 0.1 | 1.8 | 85.7 | 7.1 | 2.0 | 0.8 | 981 | 10 | 167.0 | 52.1 | 67.9 | 1 660 | 1 428 |
| Wheeler | 2.2 | 0.0 | 1.2 | 8.1 | 0.7 | 0.2 | 0.0 | 0 | 0 | 40.4 | 5.0 | 26.7 | 5 574 | 5 337 |
| Wichita | 357.2 | 181.1 | 8.9 | 129.8 | 26.2 | 5.5 | 16.7 | 31 091 | 160 | 352.8 | 118.3 | 165.0 | 1 289 | 967 |
| Wilbarger | 2.9 | 0.1 | 0.5 | 22.8 | 2.9 | 0.5 | 0.3 | 0 | 0 | 69.8 | 19.9 | 24.0 | 1 707 | 1 506 |
| Willacy | 9.7 | 0.0 | 0.7 | 68.8 | 5.5 | 1.5 | 54.7 | 2 218 | 19 | 73.7 | 43.3 | 20.1 | 979 | 797 |
| Williamson | 70.7 | 442.1 | 226.7 | 87.8 | 21.9 | 13.7 | 118.6 | 365 190 | 1 912 | 1 329.7 | 229.3 | 866.0 | 2 319 | 1 958 |
| Wilson | 5.7 | 0.0 | 1.5 | 41.5 | 2.7 | 0.8 | 10.5 | 2 466 | 32 | 102.7 | 42.9 | 33.1 | 843 | 776 |
| Winkler | 0.9 | 0.0 | 0.2 | 8.1 | 0.6 | 0.2 | 0.2 | 156 | 1 | 48.6 | 6.9 | 32.1 | 4 904 | 4 553 |
| Wise | 22.8 | 0.4 | 1.9 | 22.8 | 3.7 | 0.8 | 0.2 | 4 054 | 23 | 148.3 | 29.8 | 99.2 | 1 722 | 1 529 |
| Wood | 11.8 | 0.1 | 1.9 | 48.5 | 4.8 | 3.0 | 29.0 | 165 | 2 | 85.9 | 27.3 | 46.4 | 1 105 | 992 |
| Yoakum | 0.8 | 0.0 | 0.2 | 5.6 | 2.1 | 0.2 | 0.0 | 739 | 5 | 84.9 | 6.2 | 59.8 | 8 028 | 7 870 |
| Young | 4.1 | 0.0 | 3.0 | 25.8 | 2.4 | 0.5 | 0.3 | 530 | 5 | 78.1 | 23.2 | 22.6 | 1 278 | 976 |
| Zapata | 10.8 | 0.1 | 0.3 | 30.3 | 1.1 | 0.9 | 2.3 | NA | NA | 66.6 | 10.8 | 52.0 | 3 823 | 3 781 |
| Zavala | 1.0 | 0.0 | 0.2 | 46.6 | 1.7 | 1.1 | 1.2 | 271 | 6 | 36.8 | 25.8 | 7.1 | 608 | 531 |
| UTAH | 3 194.8 | 2 521.6 | 1 236.8 | 2 083.8 | 491.2 | 447.5 | 1 964.2 | 1 759 629 | 9 983 | X | X | X | X | X |
| Beaver | 3.3 | 0.0 | 0.6 | 14.6 | 1.1 | 0.1 | 1.2 | 2 231 | 13 | 39.6 | 12.9 | 9.1 | 1 490 | 1 110 |
| Box Elder | 19.1 | 105.2 | 572.9 | 23.9 | 6.7 | 0.5 | 8.7 | 33 524 | 233 | 140.9 | 71.5 | 43.8 | 916 | 660 |
| Cache | 37.4 | 52.6 | 24.2 | 48.1 | 18.7 | 23.8 | 150.4 | 62 294 | 508 | 263.3 | 116.5 | 85.0 | 780 | 461 |
| Carbon | 13.4 | 0.0 | -14.2 | 24.3 | 8.3 | 0.9 | 1.8 | 9 259 | 34 | 89.4 | 40.7 | 30.0 | 1 526 | 1 139 |
| Daggett | 2.9 | 0.0 | 1.0 | 1.1 | 0.1 | 0.0 | 8.7 | 1 103 | 11 | 10.1 | 4.1 | 2.1 | 2 303 | 1 916 |
| Davis | 815.2 | 854.0 | 146.9 | 76.1 | 34.8 | 3.7 | 20.9 | 234 401 | 1 348 | 780.0 | 331.1 | 247.1 | 857 | 564 |
| Duchesne | 5.2 | 0.0 | 12.8 | 14.7 | 3.7 | 0.5 | 3.5 | 18 823 | 89 | 62.4 | 30.0 | 20.9 | 1 290 | 968 |
| Emery | 3.4 | 0.0 | 1.1 | 9.4 | 2.5 | 0.2 | 5.8 | 4 461 | 22 | 61.5 | 21.6 | 23.1 | 2 222 | 1 883 |
| Garfield | 7.5 | 0.0 | 4.4 | 5.7 | 1.2 | 0.1 | 11.3 | 4 692 | 27 | 36.3 | 13.4 | 7.7 | 1 698 | 1 017 |
| Grand | 11.5 | 0.5 | 42.1 | 6.8 | 1.6 | 0.4 | 1.8 | 29 772 | 184 | 56.4 | 14.9 | 15.5 | 1 716 | 901 |
| Iron | 25.2 | 3.1 | 13.9 | 13.4 | 8.7 | 2.3 | 5.6 | 11 300 | 68 | 134.3 | 45.5 | 49.7 | 1 141 | 810 |
| Juab | 1.9 | -1.7 | 1.6 | 5.7 | 1.3 | 0.2 | 0.1 | 2 407 | 12 | 34.6 | 18.6 | 10.3 | 1 069 | 843 |
| Kane | 4.6 | 0.0 | 8.5 | 1.2 | 1.2 | 0.1 | 1.3 | 5 544 | 30 | 43.9 | 12.1 | 14.3 | 2 190 | 1 403 |
| Millard | 6.6 | 0.0 | 9.4 | 9.1 | 3.5 | 0.3 | 0.6 | 2 520 | 13 | 54.9 | 22.3 | 22.8 | 1 909 | 1 703 |
| Morgan | 1.0 | 0.2 | 0.8 | 2.3 | 0.9 | 0.0 | 0.0 | 11 846 | 39 | 22.7 | 9.7 | 8.2 | 985 | 773 |
| Piute | 0.6 | 0.0 | 0.2 | 5.6 | 0.5 | 0.1 | 0.2 | 218 | 3 | 7.7 | 5.9 | 1.1 | 839 | 630 |
| Rich | 0.7 | 0.0 | 0.2 | 2.0 | 0.4 | 0.1 | 0.1 | 5 424 | 24 | 11.0 | 5.1 | 4.0 | 1 911 | 1 578 |
| Salt Lake | 1 212.6 | 564.2 | 304.1 | 1 124.2 | 227.6 | 228.6 | 1 316.5 | 500 163 | 3 137 | 3 181.0 | 979.6 | 1 290.8 | 1 279 | 869 |
| San Juan | 8.5 | 0.0 | 2.2 | 80.3 | 3.9 | 9.5 | 4.8 | 10 117 | 61 | 73.3 | 41.7 | 12.1 | 837 | 615 |
| Sanpete | 14.0 | 0.1 | 1.2 | 25.0 | 5.6 | 1.9 | 4.4 | 2 709 | 22 | 81.0 | 37.4 | 17.3 | 701 | 467 |
| Sevier | 15.1 | 1.0 | 2.9 | 18.2 | 4.3 | 0.4 | 3.5 | 6 199 | 33 | 74.0 | 40.9 | 19.2 | 972 | 639 |
| Summit | 6.3 | 8.4 | 1.1 | 2.6 | 2.7 | 0.3 | 23.3 | 47 169 | 108 | 220.6 | 26.3 | 143.3 | 4 032 | 2 784 |
| Tooele | 61.1 | 372.4 | 2.9 | 19.5 | 5.9 | 1.8 | 10.1 | 29 791 | 212 | 173.2 | 75.6 | 45.5 | 828 | 602 |
| Uintah | 24.6 | 0.0 | 5.4 | 17.7 | 8.8 | 1.6 | 7.4 | 28 678 | 261 | 157.7 | 76.7 | 50.2 | 1 728 | 1 092 |
| Utah | 165.0 | 498.8 | 26.1 | 239.0 | 55.1 | 13.5 | 130.9 | 380 925 | 1 920 | 1 294.5 | 535.9 | 423.4 | 875 | 571 |
| Wasatch | 3.7 | 0.4 | 1.3 | 8.0 | 2.0 | 0.2 | 0.5 | 60 640 | 205 | 96.8 | 25.4 | 36.8 | 1 792 | 1 280 |
| Washington | 377.3 | 0.4 | 27.3 | 27.9 | 11.5 | 4.2 | 17.9 | 166 770 | 893 | 442.8 | 162.8 | 155.0 | 1 158 | 767 |
| Wayne | 4.8 | 0.0 | 2.4 | 2.7 | 0.7 | 0.1 | 0.5 | 1 709 | 11 | 11.1 | 7.9 | 2.1 | 841 | 622 |
| Weber | 342.5 | 61.8 | 33.5 | 254.6 | 36.1 | 9.7 | 15.0 | 84 940 | 462 | 629.8 | 249.9 | 227.5 | 1 026 | 678 |
| VERMONT | 724.0 | 711.3 | 220.4 | 1 088.4 | 192.4 | 140.1 | 959.0 | 221 336 | 1 299 | X | X | X | X | X |
| Addison | 12.7 | 138.4 | 10.1 | 42.7 | 7.0 | 0.8 | 4.6 | 12 258 | 76 | 114.3 | 86.0 | 16.9 | 460 | 453 |
| Bennington | 16.6 | 9.3 | 2.0 | 48.7 | 7.7 | 2.4 | 7.6 | 12 917 | 52 | 120.4 | 85.3 | 23.1 | 633 | 583 |
| Caledonia | 16.1 | 5.1 | 2.0 | 54.2 | 7.1 | 2.8 | 6.8 | 6 512 | 40 | 87.7 | 64.0 | 17.1 | 556 | 550 |

1. State totals may include programs not allocated by county.    2. Based on the resident population estimated as of July 1 of the year shown.

| STATE County | Local government finances, 2007 (cont.) | | | | | | | Debt outstanding | | Government employment, 2011 | | | Presidential election,[2] 2012 | | |
|---|---|---|---|---|---|---|---|---|---|---|---|---|---|---|---|
| | Direct general expenditure | | | | | | | | | | | | Percent of vote cast: | | |
| | | | Percent of total for: | | | | | | | | | | | | |
| | Total (mil dol) | Per capita[1] (dollars) | Educa-tion | Health and hospitals | Police protec-tion | Public welfare | High-ways | Total (mil dol) | Per capita[1] (dollars) | Federal civilian | Federal military | State and local | Demo-cratic | Republi-can | All other |
| | 185 | 186 | 187 | 188 | 189 | 190 | 191 | 192 | 193 | 194 | 195 | 196 | 197 | 198 | 199 |
| TEXAS—Cont'd | | | | | | | | | | | | | | | |
| Tom Green | 278.9 | 2 623 | 53.3 | 4.0 | 6.3 | 0.3 | 2.9 | 198.6 | 1 868 | 1 436 | 3 695 | 7 496 | 28.7 | 70.4 | 0.9 |
| Travis | 3 653.4 | 3 749 | 46.1 | 4.9 | 6.8 | 0.5 | 2.9 | 11 856.4 | 12 168 | 9 697 | 2 630 | 118 146 | 63.9 | 34.4 | 1.7 |
| Trinity | 29.2 | 2 058 | 71.4 | 1.9 | 4.2 | 0.3 | 5.3 | 12.6 | 888 | 24 | 32 | 612 | 31.7 | 67.4 | 0.9 |
| Tyler | 61.6 | 3 017 | 55.8 | 17.0 | 3.4 | 0.0 | 3.2 | 26.3 | 1 290 | 49 | 48 | 1 719 | 27.4 | 71.4 | 1.3 |
| Upshur | 78.0 | 2 056 | 75.2 | 0.0 | 3.3 | 0.1 | 3.8 | 66.6 | 1 756 | 58 | 88 | 1 714 | 25.0 | 74.0 | 1.0 |
| Upton | 44.0 | 14 424 | 77.7 | 17.4 | 0.2 | 0.0 | 0.8 | 6.0 | 1 956 | 0 | 0 | 473 | 24.1 | 75.0 | 0.9 |
| Uvalde | 136.8 | 5 145 | 61.1 | 24.7 | 3.1 | 0.2 | 1.5 | 65.8 | 2 475 | 247 | 59 | 2 483 | 47.1 | 52.4 | 0.6 |
| Val Verde | 138.6 | 2 885 | 56.0 | 0.6 | 5.1 | 0.4 | 4.5 | 147.5 | 3 072 | 2 357 | 1 547 | 2 739 | 54.5 | 44.9 | 0.7 |
| Van Zandt | 119.2 | 2 289 | 72.9 | 0.4 | 3.2 | 0.2 | 3.0 | 191.9 | 3 687 | 84 | 117 | 2 397 | 22.1 | 77.1 | 0.8 |
| Victoria | 362.6 | 4 202 | 41.8 | 30.5 | 5.4 | 0.0 | 2.6 | 485.6 | 5 628 | 220 | 200 | 6 319 | 32.8 | 66.4 | 0.7 |
| Walker | 273.4 | 4 278 | 24.0 | 2.1 | 2.4 | 0.0 | 2.0 | 976.6 | 15 283 | 145 | 185 | 12 283 | 38.3 | 60.7 | 1.0 |
| Waller | 99.9 | 2 779 | 70.4 | 0.1 | 4.0 | 0.4 | 4.2 | 134.0 | 3 728 | 56 | 106 | 3 987 | 46.1 | 53.3 | 0.6 |
| Ward | 49.9 | 4 857 | 56.1 | 10.8 | 3.5 | 0.0 | 4.7 | 34.3 | 3 337 | 17 | 24 | 785 | 25.0 | 74.0 | 1.0 |
| Washington | 141.6 | 4 420 | 72.8 | 1.3 | 3.5 | 0.7 | 3.5 | 118.5 | 3 698 | 81 | 75 | 3 050 | 28.1 | 70.8 | 1.2 |
| Webb | 1 026.5 | 4 402 | 63.3 | 1.1 | 5.2 | 0.5 | 0.9 | 1 283.2 | 5 504 | 3 347 | 569 | 18 226 | 71.4 | 28.0 | 0.5 |
| Wharton | 169.4 | 4 141 | 64.3 | 9.7 | 4.0 | 0.3 | 5.7 | 97.8 | 2 392 | 92 | 92 | 2 956 | 34.2 | 65.4 | 0.3 |
| Wheeler | 36.9 | 7 703 | 63.4 | 24.6 | 2.5 | 0.0 | 1.9 | 7.3 | 1 519 | 26 | 12 | 548 | 14.0 | 85.4 | 0.6 |
| Wichita | 328.5 | 2 564 | 54.1 | 4.1 | 7.1 | 0.7 | 4.4 | 381.0 | 2 976 | 2 173 | 5 577 | 9 441 | 30.2 | 69.0 | 0.8 |
| Wilbarger | 67.8 | 4 831 | 62.2 | 15.3 | 2.7 | 0.1 | 3.3 | 29.3 | 2 086 | 40 | 30 | 3 138 | 26.5 | 72.8 | 0.7 |
| Willacy | 67.3 | 3 281 | 69.5 | 1.1 | 3.4 | 0.3 | 4.6 | 90.3 | 4 402 | 98 | 49 | 1 197 | 69.5 | 29.7 | 0.8 |
| Williamson | 1 392.3 | 3 729 | 61.6 | 3.3 | 3.7 | 0.1 | 6.7 | 3 211.8 | 8 602 | 1 475 | 983 | 20 429 | 42.7 | 55.8 | 1.5 |
| Wilson | 102.6 | 2 613 | 62.6 | 18.7 | 2.7 | 0.0 | 3.3 | 237.8 | 6 055 | 65 | 97 | 2 147 | 32.8 | 66.6 | 0.6 |
| Winkler | 47.5 | 7 260 | 64.7 | 10.5 | 1.8 | 0.3 | 2.0 | 74.4 | 11 370 | 0 | 16 | 610 | 23.5 | 75.2 | 1.3 |
| Wise | 132.0 | 2 292 | 61.8 | 1.6 | 4.7 | 1.0 | 9.8 | 162.0 | 2 813 | 108 | 133 | 3 392 | 21.7 | 77.4 | 0.9 |
| Wood | 90.8 | 2 161 | 70.4 | 0.4 | 5.0 | 0.2 | 5.6 | 89.4 | 2 127 | 86 | 93 | 1 796 | 22.5 | 76.8 | 0.7 |
| Yoakum | 72.2 | 9 692 | 63.1 | 20.0 | 2.4 | 0.0 | 2.9 | 16.4 | 2 198 | 15 | 18 | 821 | 18.3 | 80.9 | 0.8 |
| Young | 77.8 | 4 402 | 40.2 | 31.0 | 3.7 | 0.1 | 3.2 | 163.3 | 9 237 | 48 | 41 | 1 382 | 17.8 | 81.3 | 0.8 |
| Zapata | 54.8 | 4 031 | 89.3 | 0.1 | 1.5 | 0.1 | 2.3 | 25.6 | 1 879 | 169 | 32 | 1 016 | 67.7 | 32.1 | 0.3 |
| Zavala | 39.3 | 3 371 | 73.7 | 0.7 | 3.9 | 0.0 | 0.8 | 44.7 | 3 835 | 11 | 26 | 890 | 84.2 | 15.4 | 0.4 |
| UTAH | X | X | X | X | X | X | X | X | X | 36 676 | 16 943 | 183 962 | 34.4 | 62.6 | 3.0 |
| Beaver | 35.4 | 5 810 | 29.7 | 29.4 | 5.2 | 0.0 | 5.5 | 46.2 | 7 585 | 47 | 30 | 654 | 21.6 | 75.8 | 2.6 |
| Box Elder | 129.8 | 2 714 | 50.3 | 1.5 | 5.6 | 0.1 | 5.0 | 121.8 | 2 545 | 213 | 229 | 2 238 | 17.4 | 79.9 | 2.7 |
| Cache | 249.4 | 2 290 | 50.8 | 4.0 | 5.2 | 0.2 | 5.1 | 220.9 | 2 028 | 355 | 525 | 10 265 | 24.9 | 70.5 | 4.6 |
| Carbon | 78.1 | 3 978 | 43.0 | 6.0 | 6.7 | 0.0 | 10.8 | 100.7 | 5 131 | 169 | 97 | 1 857 | 29.8 | 67.7 | 2.5 |
| Daggett | 8.4 | 9 026 | 33.6 | 0.8 | 13.5 | 0.0 | 5.1 | 6.0 | 6 472 | 57 | 0 | 171 | 29.8 | 67.7 | 2.5 |
| Davis | 820.0 | 2 846 | 53.4 | 3.5 | 5.4 | 0.3 | 4.6 | 606.1 | 2 103 | 13 045 | 5 164 | 13 741 | 15.9 | 81.6 | 2.5 |
| Duchesne | 64.8 | 3 995 | 54.9 | 1.5 | 3.7 | 0.0 | 10.8 | 49.4 | 3 048 | 84 | 86 | 1 889 | 21.9 | 75.5 | 2.6 |
| Emery | 61.1 | 5 878 | 37.6 | 4.5 | 5.5 | 0.0 | 5.7 | 249.1 | 23 950 | 57 | 50 | 826 | | | |
| Garfield | 29.2 | 6 441 | 34.7 | 26.2 | 2.9 | 0.1 | 7.8 | 19.7 | 4 359 | 188 | 23 | 399 | 18.8 | 79.2 | 2.0 |
| Grand | 52.5 | 5 816 | 21.5 | 32.9 | 5.3 | 0.3 | 6.0 | 91.2 | 10 102 | 250 | 42 | 696 | 50.7 | 45.9 | 3.4 |
| Iron | 127.9 | 2 939 | 45.2 | 0.4 | 6.4 | 0.0 | 7.5 | 133.3 | 3 063 | 343 | 212 | 3 895 | 19.8 | 76.1 | 4.1 |
| Juab | 34.0 | 3 540 | 54.0 | 1.2 | 7.3 | 0.0 | 8.9 | 39.8 | 4 144 | 28 | 47 | 720 | 20.5 | 74.2 | 5.3 |
| Kane | 37.0 | 5 676 | 35.6 | 26.8 | 12.1 | 0.0 | 6.1 | 27.6 | 4 225 | 99 | 33 | 619 | 27.1 | 70.1 | 2.7 |
| Millard | 51.5 | 4 306 | 50.4 | 3.4 | 6.8 | 0.0 | 8.8 | 7.6 | 639 | 93 | 57 | 931 | 16.0 | 77.1 | 6.9 |
| Morgan | 24.4 | 2 917 | 68.7 | 0.6 | 5.6 | 0.0 | 4.3 | 56.4 | 6 750 | 10 | 44 | 412 | 16.6 | 79.6 | 3.9 |
| Piute | 6.6 | 4 942 | 62.4 | 1.0 | 7.1 | 0.0 | 8.9 | 2.5 | 1 886 | 0 | 0 | 130 | 17.7 | 79.6 | 2.8 |
| Rich | 9.6 | 4 570 | 54.6 | 0.8 | 5.7 | 3.0 | 7.5 | 7.5 | 3 587 | 11 | 10 | 185 | 15.3 | 82.6 | 2.1 |
| Salt Lake | 2 909.0 | 2 882 | 39.8 | 6.6 | 6.6 | 1.7 | 4.4 | 6 051.5 | 5 994 | 10 682 | 4 970 | 82 632 | 48.7 | 48.6 | 2.8 |
| San Juan | 69.1 | 4 769 | 50.1 | 15.2 | 2.9 | 0.0 | 14.1 | 21.3 | 1 473 | 162 | 67 | 1 472 | 46.9 | 51.4 | 1.7 |
| Sanpete | 80.8 | 3 280 | 49.3 | 22.2 | 4.3 | 0.0 | 4.5 | 63.7 | 2 587 | 82 | 127 | 2 458 | 18.6 | 76.0 | 5.4 |
| Sevier | 70.3 | 3 567 | 46.0 | 6.2 | 5.5 | 0.0 | 16.9 | 61.1 | 3 100 | 204 | 95 | 1 470 | 17.0 | 79.9 | 3.2 |
| Summit | 200.7 | 5 646 | 35.3 | 1.6 | 6.8 | 0.0 | 10.4 | 137.4 | 3 867 | 63 | 242 | 2 441 | 56.7 | 41.4 | 1.9 |
| Tooele | 172.0 | 3 132 | 48.3 | 1.8 | 6.7 | 2.0 | 3.5 | 163.9 | 2 985 | 1 815 | 346 | 2 707 | 33.6 | 63.4 | 2.9 |
| Uintah | 140.3 | 4 832 | 47.5 | 6.5 | 5.2 | 3.3 | 16.3 | 75.2 | 2 591 | 400 | 150 | 2 445 | 14.4 | 83.2 | 2.4 |
| Utah | 1 203.3 | 2 488 | 51.4 | 3.6 | 5.9 | 0.3 | 4.2 | 1 998.2 | 4 131 | 972 | 2 422 | 26 712 | 18.8 | 77.7 | 3.5 |
| Wasatch | 81.5 | 3 971 | 47.7 | 3.0 | 5.2 | 0.0 | 4.9 | 149.3 | 7 270 | 49 | 111 | 1 193 | 33.9 | 63.7 | 2.4 |
| Washington | 406.0 | 3 035 | 48.1 | 2.7 | 6.5 | 0.0 | 5.3 | 645.9 | 4 828 | 553 | 643 | 6 660 | 21.9 | 75.3 | 2.8 |
| Wayne | 10.7 | 4 229 | 53.7 | 0.3 | 8.8 | 0.0 | 14.4 | 1.9 | 736 | 102 | 12 | 183 | 25.5 | 71.5 | 3.0 |
| Weber | 626.3 | 2 823 | 47.0 | 1.4 | 6.7 | 4.3 | 2.9 | 545.6 | 2 459 | 6 536 | 1 097 | 13 961 | 35.0 | 62.5 | 2.5 |
| VERMONT | X | X | X | X | X | X | X | X | X | 6 472 | 4 330 | 46 131 | 67.5 | 30.4 | 2.1 |
| Addison | 151.9 | 4 134 | 80.3 | 0.3 | 1.6 | 0.1 | 6.6 | 48.1 | 1 308 | 119 | 247 | 1 772 | 68.6 | 29.5 | 1.9 |
| Bennington | 149.5 | 4 101 | 74.3 | 0.1 | 2.6 | 0.0 | 6.0 | 43.2 | 1 186 | 173 | 249 | 1 983 | 65.5 | 32.1 | 2.5 |
| Caledonia | 91.1 | 2 971 | 73.2 | 0.2 | 1.7 | 0.0 | 10.2 | 30.2 | 987 | 103 | 210 | 1 969 | 60.4 | 37.2 | 2.4 |

1. Based on the resident population estimated as of July 1 of the year shown.   2. © 2013 Election Data Services, Inc. All rights reserved.

# Table B. States and Counties — Land Area and Population

| STATE/ County code | CBSA code[1] | County type[2] | STATE County | Land area,[3] (sq km) 2010 | Total persons | Rank | Per square kilometer | White | Black | American Indian, Alaska Native | Asian and Pacific Islander | Percent Hispanic or Latino[4] | Under 5 years | 5 to 17 years | 18 to 24 years | 25 to 34 years | 35 to 44 years | 45 to 54 years |
|---|---|---|---|---|---|---|---|---|---|---|---|---|---|---|---|---|---|---|
| | | | | 1 | 2 | 3 | 4 | 5 | 6 | 7 | 8 | 9 | 10 | 11 | 12 | 13 | 14 | 15 |
| | | | **VERMONT—Cont'd** | | | | | | | | | | | | | | | |
| 50 007 | 15540 | 3 | Chittenden | 1 390 | 158 504 | 398 | 114.0 | 92.7 | 2.7 | 0.9 | 3.7 | 1.9 | 4.9 | 14.5 | 16.0 | 13.2 | 12.3 | 15.1 |
| 50 009 | 13620 | 9 | Essex | 1 719 | 6 226 | 2 742 | 3.6 | 97.7 | 0.7 | 1.5 | 0.4 | 1.1 | 4.5 | 14.0 | 6.4 | 8.4 | 12.0 | 17.2 |
| 50 011 | 15540 | 3 | Franklin | 1 641 | 48 214 | 1 007 | 29.4 | 96.7 | 0.9 | 2.4 | 0.8 | 1.3 | 6.0 | 18.1 | 7.4 | 11.9 | 14.0 | 16.7 |
| 50 013 | 15540 | 3 | Grand Isle | 212 | 6 983 | 2 687 | 32.9 | 96.9 | 1.0 | 2.6 | 0.9 | 1.3 | 4.5 | 15.0 | 6.8 | 9.8 | 12.1 | 18.3 |
| 50 015 | ... | 8 | Lamoille | 1 188 | 24 958 | 1 609 | 21.0 | 96.9 | 1.2 | 1.1 | 0.9 | 1.4 | 5.9 | 15.9 | 9.6 | 11.9 | 13.4 | 15.8 |
| 50 017 | 30100 | 9 | Orange | 1 779 | 28 924 | 1 453 | 16.3 | 97.5 | 0.8 | 1.0 | 1.0 | 1.1 | 4.9 | 15.5 | 8.1 | 10.6 | 11.8 | 17.1 |
| 50 019 | ... | 7 | Orleans | 1 796 | 27 109 | 1 526 | 15.1 | 97.3 | 0.9 | 1.4 | 0.6 | 1.2 | 5.1 | 15.6 | 7.3 | 10.8 | 12.1 | 14.9 |
| 50 021 | 40860 | 5 | Rutland | 2 408 | 60 869 | 849 | 25.3 | 97.4 | 0.9 | 0.8 | 0.9 | 1.2 | 4.5 | 14.3 | 9.7 | 10.1 | 11.4 | 16.5 |
| 50 023 | 12740 | 4 | Washington | 1 780 | 59 465 | 869 | 33.4 | 96.4 | 1.2 | 1.1 | 1.3 | 1.7 | 5.1 | 15.1 | 9.3 | 11.0 | 12.8 | 16.2 |
| 50 025 | ... | 6 | Windham | 2 034 | 43 985 | 1 086 | 21.6 | 95.7 | 1.5 | 1.0 | 1.6 | 1.9 | 4.7 | 14.7 | 8.1 | 10.7 | 11.2 | 16.6 |
| 50 027 | 30100 | 7 | Windsor | 2 511 | 56 211 | 901 | 22.4 | 96.8 | 1.0 | 1.0 | 1.4 | 1.3 | 4.7 | 14.6 | 6.4 | 11.0 | 11.3 | 16.7 |
| 51 000 | ... | X | **VIRGINIA** | 102 279 | 8 185 867 | X | 80.0 | 66.5 | 20.2 | 0.8 | 6.8 | 8.2 | 6.3 | 16.6 | 10.1 | 13.8 | 13.5 | 14.9 |
| 51 001 | ... | 7 | Accomack | 1 164 | 33 341 | 1 346 | 28.6 | 61.9 | 28.6 | 0.9 | 0.9 | 9.1 | 6.0 | 15.1 | 7.5 | 10.7 | 10.9 | 14.9 |
| 51 003 | 16820 | 3 | Albemarle | 1 867 | 102 251 | 572 | 54.8 | 79.5 | 10.8 | 0.6 | 5.7 | 5.6 | 5.6 | 15.7 | 12.1 | 13.0 | 11.7 | 14.3 |
| 51 005 | ... | 6 | Alleghany | 1 154 | 16 230 | 2 027 | 14.1 | 93.3 | 5.6 | 0.6 | 0.6 | 1.2 | 4.7 | 16.2 | 6.5 | 9.0 | 12.0 | 15.3 |
| 51 007 | 40060 | 1 | Amelia | 920 | 12 759 | 2 256 | 13.9 | 73.4 | 24.0 | 0.8 | 0.5 | 2.5 | 5.7 | 16.1 | 7.4 | 10.7 | 12.2 | 16.8 |
| 51 009 | 31340 | 3 | Amherst | 1 227 | 32 384 | 1 380 | 26.4 | 77.5 | 20.0 | 1.6 | 1.0 | 2.0 | 5.2 | 15.6 | 10.2 | 10.3 | 11.9 | 15.5 |
| 51 011 | 31340 | 3 | Appomattox | 864 | 15 128 | 2 097 | 17.5 | 78.1 | 21.1 | 0.5 | 0.5 | 1.3 | 5.4 | 16.5 | 7.6 | 11.1 | 12.0 | 15.6 |
| 51 013 | 47900 | 1 | Arlington | 67 | 221 045 | 287 | 3 299.2 | 66.2 | 9.4 | 0.7 | 11.2 | 15.2 | 5.8 | 10.2 | 8.7 | 28.4 | 15.9 | 12.3 |
| 51 015 | 44420 | 4 | Augusta | 2 505 | 73 658 | 739 | 29.4 | 92.8 | 4.6 | 0.7 | 0.8 | 2.2 | 4.9 | 15.9 | 7.6 | 10.8 | 13.0 | 16.4 |
| 51 017 | ... | 9 | Bath | 1 371 | 4 652 | 2 863 | 3.4 | 92.7 | 5.1 | 0.5 | 0.4 | 2.2 | 3.3 | 13.5 | 7.4 | 8.1 | 12.6 | 16.1 |
| 51 019 | 31340 | 3 | Bedford | 1 950 | 69 590 | 764 | 35.7 | 90.8 | 6.4 | 0.7 | 1.4 | 1.8 | 4.7 | 17.0 | 6.9 | 8.7 | 12.9 | 17.1 |
| 51 021 | ... | 8 | Bland | 927 | 6 738 | 2 704 | 7.3 | 95.2 | 3.8 | 0.4 | 0.5 | 0.7 | 4.0 | 13.7 | 6.6 | 11.8 | 15.5 | 15.1 |
| 51 023 | 40220 | 2 | Botetourt | 1 402 | 33 154 | 1 350 | 23.6 | 94.7 | 3.7 | 0.6 | 0.8 | 1.2 | 4.5 | 17.3 | 6.3 | 8.1 | 12.7 | 17.3 |
| 51 025 | ... | 6 | Brunswick | 1 466 | 17 010 | 1 980 | 11.6 | 40.8 | 57.1 | 0.6 | 0.5 | 1.8 | 4.5 | 14.0 | 10.5 | 12.8 | 12.0 | 14.7 |
| 51 027 | ... | 9 | Buchanan | 1 302 | 23 859 | 1 650 | 18.3 | 96.4 | 2.9 | 0.3 | 0.4 | 0.4 | 4.4 | 13.9 | 7.7 | 12.0 | 13.2 | 16.7 |
| 51 029 | ... | 8 | Buckingham | 1 501 | 17 088 | 1 973 | 11.4 | 62.8 | 35.5 | 0.8 | 0.7 | 1.7 | 5.5 | 13.5 | 8.6 | 13.2 | 14.0 | 16.3 |
| 51 031 | 31340 | 3 | Campbell | 1 305 | 55 163 | 912 | 42.3 | 82.2 | 15.3 | 0.7 | 1.5 | 1.9 | 5.2 | 16.1 | 9.3 | 11.4 | 12.8 | 15.2 |
| 51 033 | 40060 | 1 | Caroline | 1 366 | 28 972 | 1 451 | 21.2 | 65.6 | 30.6 | 1.5 | 1.5 | 3.5 | 6.8 | 16.8 | 7.6 | 13.6 | 13.2 | 15.4 |
| 51 035 | ... | 6 | Carroll | 1 229 | 29 851 | 1 430 | 24.3 | 96.0 | 1.0 | 0.5 | 0.4 | 2.8 | 5.1 | 15.2 | 6.8 | 9.7 | 13.0 | 15.0 |
| 51 036 | 40060 | 1 | Charles City | 473 | 7 157 | 2 664 | 15.1 | 43.1 | 48.9 | 7.9 | 1.3 | 1.5 | 3.6 | 13.7 | 7.2 | 9.8 | 11.6 | 19.0 |
| 51 037 | ... | 8 | Charlotte | 1 231 | 12 404 | 2 278 | 10.1 | 67.5 | 30.3 | 0.7 | 0.6 | 2.2 | 5.2 | 17.0 | 8.1 | 9.6 | 11.2 | 15.6 |
| 51 041 | 40060 | 1 | Chesterfield | 1 096 | 323 856 | 201 | 295.5 | 66.8 | 23.1 | 0.8 | 4.2 | 7.4 | 6.1 | 19.4 | 8.7 | 12.0 | 14.2 | 15.7 |
| 51 043 | 47900 | 1 | Clarke | 456 | 14 323 | 2 140 | 31.4 | 89.5 | 6.3 | 0.9 | 1.6 | 3.6 | 5.1 | 17.1 | 6.5 | 8.8 | 12.0 | 18.4 |
| 51 045 | 40220 | 2 | Craig | 853 | 5 213 | 2 827 | 6.1 | 98.4 | 0.7 | 0.5 | 0.4 | 0.9 | 4.9 | 16.6 | 6.9 | 9.4 | 12.5 | 17.3 |
| 51 047 | 19020 | 6 | Culpeper | 982 | 47 911 | 1 016 | 48.8 | 73.7 | 17.0 | 0.7 | 1.9 | 8.9 | 6.9 | 18.5 | 8.0 | 12.7 | 13.6 | 15.6 |
| 51 049 | 40060 | 1 | Cumberland | 770 | 9 849 | 2 453 | 12.8 | 65.1 | 32.9 | 1.0 | 0.8 | 2.1 | 6.1 | 16.3 | 8.8 | 10.9 | 14.8 | |
| 51 051 | ... | 9 | Dickenson | 856 | 15 690 | 2 065 | 18.3 | 98.6 | 0.7 | 0.4 | 0.3 | 0.6 | 5.3 | 15.2 | 7.4 | 11.7 | 12.7 | 15.4 |
| 51 053 | 40060 | 1 | Dinwiddie | 1 305 | 27 994 | 1 494 | 21.5 | 63.8 | 33.1 | 0.8 | 1.0 | 2.7 | 5.2 | 16.7 | 8.9 | 11.3 | 13.2 | 17.2 |
| 51 057 | ... | 8 | Essex | 666 | 11 233 | 2 343 | 16.9 | 57.5 | 39.0 | 0.9 | 1.2 | 3.2 | 5.7 | 15.9 | 8.6 | 10.5 | 11.4 | 15.0 |
| 51 059 | 47900 | 1 | Fairfax | 1 013 | 1 118 602 | 36 | 1 104.2 | 56.6 | 10.1 | 0.6 | 19.8 | 15.8 | 6.7 | 17.4 | 7.7 | 14.7 | 15.0 | 15.9 |
| 51 061 | 47900 | 1 | Fauquier | 1 677 | 66 542 | 791 | 39.7 | 83.3 | 9.4 | 0.8 | 2.0 | 6.5 | 5.7 | 18.9 | 7.5 | 9.8 | 13.3 | 17.9 |
| 51 063 | ... | 8 | Floyd | 985 | 15 390 | 2 080 | 15.6 | 94.8 | 2.4 | 0.5 | 0.5 | 2.7 | 5.4 | 16.0 | 6.5 | 10.2 | 12.7 | 15.2 |
| 51 065 | 16820 | 3 | Fluvanna | 741 | 25 967 | 1 564 | 35.0 | 80.6 | 16.6 | 0.7 | 1.0 | 3.0 | 5.9 | 16.6 | 6.5 | 11.8 | 14.6 | 15.6 |
| 51 067 | 40220 | 2 | Franklin | 1 788 | 56 411 | 899 | 31.5 | 88.2 | 9.0 | 0.5 | 0.8 | 2.7 | 5.4 | 15.0 | 8.8 | 9.5 | 11.9 | 15.5 |
| 51 069 | 49020 | 3 | Frederick | 1 071 | 80 317 | 687 | 75.0 | 87.2 | 5.1 | 0.7 | 1.8 | 6.9 | 6.2 | 18.5 | 8.0 | 11.9 | 13.8 | 16.1 |
| 51 071 | 13980 | 3 | Giles | 921 | 16 928 | 1 987 | 18.4 | 96.6 | 2.2 | 0.5 | 0.6 | 1.2 | 5.2 | 15.8 | 7.4 | 10.3 | 12.9 | 14.6 |
| 51 073 | 47260 | 1 | Gloucester | 564 | 36 886 | 1 250 | 65.4 | 87.3 | 9.5 | 1.1 | 1.5 | 2.7 | 4.9 | 16.4 | 7.9 | 10.8 | 12.5 | 17.6 |
| 51 075 | 40060 | 1 | Goochland | 729 | 21 347 | 1 764 | 29.3 | 77.1 | 19.7 | 0.7 | 1.5 | 2.1 | 4.4 | 15.1 | 5.9 | 9.0 | 14.1 | 18.8 |
| 51 077 | ... | 9 | Grayson | 1 145 | 15 183 | 2 093 | 13.3 | 94.5 | 2.6 | 0.6 | 0.3 | 2.8 | 4.3 | 14.3 | 6.9 | 9.0 | 12.4 | 15.2 |
| 51 079 | 16820 | 3 | Greene | 405 | 18 771 | 1 885 | 46.3 | 87.0 | 7.9 | 0.7 | 1.7 | 4.5 | 7.0 | 17.8 | 7.0 | 12.1 | 13.5 | 16.3 |
| 51 081 | ... | 6 | Greensville | 765 | 11 851 | 2 307 | 15.5 | 38.1 | 59.9 | 0.5 | 0.7 | 1.5 | 4.2 | 12.1 | 8.9 | 15.4 | 16.3 | 17.2 |
| 51 083 | ... | 6 | Halifax | 2 118 | 35 849 | 1 279 | 16.9 | 61.0 | 37.1 | 0.6 | 0.7 | 1.7 | 5.3 | 16.4 | 7.1 | 9.7 | 11.5 | 14.5 |
| 51 085 | 40060 | 1 | Hanover | 1 214 | 100 668 | 582 | 82.9 | 86.2 | 10.2 | 0.8 | 1.9 | 2.3 | 5.2 | 19.1 | 8.2 | 9.1 | 13.7 | 17.4 |
| 51 087 | 40060 | 1 | Henrico | 605 | 314 932 | 208 | 520.5 | 58.4 | 30.3 | 0.8 | 7.5 | 5.1 | 6.5 | 17.3 | 8.1 | 14.5 | 14.0 | 14.8 |
| 51 089 | 32300 | 4 | Henry | 990 | 52 969 | 939 | 53.5 | 72.4 | 22.7 | 0.5 | 0.8 | 5.0 | 5.4 | 14.8 | 7.2 | 9.9 | 12.2 | 15.6 |
| 51 091 | ... | 9 | Highland | 1 075 | 2 245 | 3 032 | 2.1 | 98.2 | 0.5 | 0.4 | 0.2 | 0.9 | 2.9 | 11.2 | 5.7 | 7.4 | 8.9 | 16.9 |
| 51 093 | 47260 | 1 | Isle of Wight | 817 | 35 399 | 1 292 | 43.3 | 72.2 | 25.3 | 0.9 | 1.3 | 2.0 | 5.2 | 16.9 | 7.2 | 9.4 | 12.4 | 18.3 |
| 51 095 | 47260 | 1 | James City | 369 | 68 967 | 770 | 186.9 | 79.1 | 14.2 | 0.9 | 3.3 | 4.8 | 5.0 | 16.0 | 7.1 | 9.6 | 11.7 | 14.5 |
| 51 097 | 40060 | 1 | King and Queen | 816 | 7 046 | 2 677 | 8.6 | 67.4 | 28.6 | 2.3 | 0.6 | 2.9 | 4.7 | 15.0 | 7.2 | 10.4 | 11.5 | 16.1 |
| 51 099 | ... | 8 | King George | 465 | 24 500 | 1 620 | 52.7 | 76.5 | 19.3 | 1.2 | 2.1 | 3.6 | 7.3 | 19.7 | 8.3 | 12.3 | 14.2 | 16.5 |
| 51 101 | 40060 | 1 | King William | 710 | 15 981 | 2 049 | 22.5 | 77.5 | 19.0 | 2.3 | 1.3 | 2.2 | 6.4 | 17.9 | 7.6 | 12.2 | 13.8 | 16.3 |
| 51 103 | ... | 9 | Lancaster | 345 | 11 236 | 2 342 | 32.6 | 70.0 | 28.2 | 0.5 | 0.9 | 1.2 | 3.8 | 12.0 | 5.8 | 7.4 | 8.1 | 13.5 |
| 51 105 | ... | 8 | Lee | 1 128 | 25 474 | 1 588 | 22.6 | 93.7 | 4.1 | 0.8 | 0.4 | 1.7 | 5.2 | 15.1 | 7.9 | 12.9 | 14.3 | 14.9 |
| 51 107 | 47900 | 1 | Loudoun | 1 335 | 336 898 | 193 | 252.4 | 64.4 | 8.8 | 0.7 | 16.8 | 12.6 | 8.4 | 21.8 | 6.0 | 13.6 | 18.6 | 15.8 |

1. CBSA = Core Based Statistical Area. See Appendix A for explanation. See Appendix B for list of metropolitan areas with component counties.  2. County type code from the Economic Research Service of USDA Rural-Urban Continuum Codes. See Appendix A for definition.  3. Dry land or land partially or temporarily covered by water.  4. May be of any race.

# Table B. States and Counties — **Population and Households**

| STATE County | 55 to 64 years (16) | 65 to 74 years (17) | 75 years and over (18) | Percent female (19) | Total persons 2000 (20) | 2010 (21) | Percent change 2000–2010 (22) | 2010–2012 (23) | Births (24) | Deaths (25) | Net migration (26) | Number (27) | Percent change, 2000–2010 (28) | Persons per household (29) | Female family householder[1] (30) | One person (31) |
|---|---|---|---|---|---|---|---|---|---|---|---|---|---|---|---|---|
| **VERMONT—Cont'd** | | | | | | | | | | | | | | | | |
| Chittenden | 12.4 | 6.3 | 5.4 | 51.2 | 146 571 | 156 545 | 6.8 | 1.3 | 3 322 | 2 223 | 862 | 61 827 | 9.5 | 2.37 | 9.1 | 27.7 |
| Essex | 17.8 | 11.8 | 8.0 | 49.3 | 6 459 | 6 306 | -2.4 | -1.3 | 136 | 149 | -76 | 2 818 | 8.3 | 2.23 | 8.7 | 29.3 |
| Franklin | 13.4 | 7.0 | 5.4 | 50.4 | 45 417 | 47 746 | 5.1 | 1.0 | 1 218 | 762 | 32 | 18 513 | 10.4 | 2.55 | 10.7 | 22.7 |
| Grand Isle | 19.1 | 9.4 | 5.0 | 49.9 | 6 901 | 6 970 | 1.0 | 0.2 | 134 | 119 | 0 | 2 902 | 5.1 | 2.40 | 8.6 | 22.5 |
| Lamoille | 13.6 | 8.0 | 5.7 | 50.1 | 23 233 | 24 475 | 5.3 | 2.0 | 627 | 421 | 282 | 10 014 | 8.6 | 2.37 | 9.4 | 27.3 |
| Orange | 16.6 | 8.9 | 6.5 | 50.1 | 28 226 | 28 936 | 2.5 | 0.0 | 588 | 548 | -48 | 11 887 | 8.7 | 2.37 | 9.3 | 25.9 |
| Orleans | 15.8 | 10.2 | 8.2 | 49.8 | 26 277 | 27 231 | 3.6 | -0.4 | 607 | 626 | -86 | 11 320 | 8.4 | 2.33 | 9.6 | 27.8 |
| Rutland | 16.2 | 9.5 | 7.7 | 50.6 | 63 400 | 61 642 | -2.8 | -1.3 | 1 222 | 1 400 | -580 | 25 984 | 1.2 | 2.28 | 9.9 | 30.2 |
| Washington | 15.8 | 8.0 | 6.9 | 50.6 | 58 039 | 59 534 | 2.6 | -0.1 | 1 380 | 1 131 | -288 | 25 027 | 5.8 | 2.28 | 10.0 | 29.7 |
| Windham | 17.2 | 9.5 | 7.4 | 50.8 | 44 216 | 44 513 | 0.7 | -1.2 | 933 | 958 | -484 | 19 290 | 5.0 | 2.23 | 10.1 | 31.8 |
| Windsor | 16.7 | 10.2 | 8.2 | 51.1 | 57 418 | 56 670 | -1.3 | -0.8 | 1 119 | 1 181 | -357 | 24 753 | 2.4 | 2.25 | 9.0 | 30.0 |
| **VIRGINIA** | 12.3 | 7.1 | 5.4 | 50.9 | 7 078 515 | 8 001 024 | 13.0 | 2.3 | 228 798 | 134 908 | 88 259 | 3 056 058 | 13.2 | 2.54 | 12.4 | 26.0 |
| Accomack | 15.5 | 11.0 | 8.4 | 51.2 | 38 305 | 33 164 | -13.4 | 0.5 | 986 | 1 019 | 208 | 13 798 | -9.8 | 2.37 | 13.5 | 28.8 |
| Albemarle | 13.0 | 7.5 | 7.0 | 52.0 | 79 236 | 98 970 | 24.9 | 3.3 | 2 401 | 1 641 | 2 365 | 38 157 | 19.7 | 2.41 | 9.6 | 28.0 |
| Alleghany | 15.6 | 11.8 | 8.8 | 51.1 | 17 215 | 16 250 | 25.7 | -0.1 | 321 | 543 | 134 | 6 891 | 33.8 | 2.32 | 9.6 | 28.9 |
| Amelia | 15.0 | 9.9 | 6.3 | 51.0 | 11 400 | 12 690 | 11.3 | 0.5 | 317 | 265 | 19 | 4 821 | 13.7 | 2.61 | 11.3 | 21.2 |
| Amherst | 14.1 | 9.7 | 7.5 | 52.3 | 31 894 | 32 353 | 1.4 | 0.1 | 717 | 780 | 91 | 12 560 | 5.2 | 2.45 | 13.4 | 25.4 |
| Appomattox | 13.9 | 10.5 | 7.4 | 51.3 | 13 705 | 14 973 | 9.3 | 1.0 | 375 | 362 | 122 | 6 033 | 13.4 | 2.47 | 12.6 | 24.3 |
| Arlington | 10.1 | 5.0 | 3.7 | 49.9 | 189 453 | 207 627 | 9.6 | 6.5 | 6 887 | 2 098 | 8 498 | 98 050 | 13.5 | 2.09 | 5.9 | 41.3 |
| Augusta | 14.7 | 9.6 | 6.9 | 49.3 | 65 615 | 73 750 | 12.4 | -0.1 | 1 366 | 1 462 | -105 | 28 516 | 14.9 | 2.49 | 9.2 | 22.5 |
| Bath | 16.0 | 13.4 | 9.6 | 49.6 | 5 048 | 4 731 | -6.3 | -1.7 | 80 | 126 | -32 | 2 162 | 5.3 | 2.16 | 6.8 | 32.9 |
| Bedford | 15.8 | 10.3 | 6.4 | 50.4 | 60 371 | 68 676 | 13.8 | 1.3 | 1 364 | 1 404 | 915 | 27 465 | 15.2 | 2.49 | 8.1 | 21.9 |
| Bland | 15.4 | 10.9 | 7.0 | 44.8 | 6 871 | 6 824 | -0.7 | -1.3 | 105 | 189 | 0 | 2 566 | -0.1 | 2.39 | 8.7 | 24.7 |
| Botetourt | 16.7 | 10.0 | 7.0 | 50.5 | 30 496 | 33 148 | 8.7 | 0.0 | 518 | 694 | 140 | 13 126 | 12.2 | 2.50 | 7.7 | 21.6 |
| Brunswick | 14.2 | 9.6 | 7.6 | 47.6 | 18 419 | 17 434 | -5.3 | -2.4 | 331 | 508 | -258 | 6 366 | 1.4 | 2.40 | 19.2 | 29.2 |
| Buchanan | 15.7 | 10.4 | 6.1 | 48.8 | 26 978 | 24 098 | -10.7 | -1.0 | 452 | 649 | -99 | 9 968 | -4.7 | 2.30 | 10.6 | 27.9 |
| Buckingham | 14.2 | 8.7 | 6.0 | 44.8 | 15 623 | 17 146 | 9.7 | -0.3 | 376 | 340 | -105 | 5 965 | 12.0 | 2.48 | 15.3 | 26.1 |
| Campbell | 13.8 | 9.1 | 7.0 | 51.3 | 51 078 | 54 842 | 7.4 | 0.6 | 1 145 | 1 105 | 255 | 22 441 | 8.7 | 2.42 | 12.4 | 26.2 |
| Caroline | 13.0 | 8.2 | 5.5 | 50.9 | 22 121 | 28 545 | 29.0 | 1.5 | 846 | 546 | 131 | 10 456 | 30.4 | 2.68 | 14.0 | 22.0 |
| Carroll | 15.5 | 11.2 | 8.5 | 50.6 | 29 245 | 30 042 | 2.7 | -0.6 | 554 | 821 | 79 | 12 831 | 5.3 | 2.32 | 9.6 | 28.1 |
| Charles City | 17.6 | 10.6 | 7.0 | 50.6 | 6 926 | 7 256 | 4.8 | -1.4 | 106 | 199 | -22 | 2 955 | 10.7 | 2.46 | 15.5 | 23.6 |
| Charlotte | 14.5 | 10.1 | 8.7 | 50.9 | 12 472 | 12 586 | 0.9 | -1.4 | 288 | 350 | -123 | 5 109 | 3.2 | 2.43 | 14.2 | 28.5 |
| Chesterfield | 13.1 | 6.6 | 4.4 | 51.9 | 259 903 | 316 236 | 21.7 | 2.4 | 8 130 | 4 331 | 3 795 | 115 680 | 23.4 | 2.69 | 13.2 | 20.7 |
| Clarke | 15.4 | 9.0 | 7.6 | 50.1 | 12 652 | 14 034 | 10.9 | 2.1 | 285 | 336 | 342 | 5 509 | 11.5 | 2.50 | 8.9 | 24.9 |
| Craig | 15.8 | 10.1 | 6.6 | 50.4 | 5 091 | 5 190 | 1.9 | 0.4 | 89 | 125 | 34 | 2 183 | 6.0 | 2.37 | 8.2 | 26.6 |
| Culpeper | 12.2 | 7.6 | 5.1 | 49.3 | 34 262 | 46 689 | 36.3 | 2.6 | 1 399 | 793 | 626 | 16 231 | 33.7 | 2.77 | 11.9 | 21.1 |
| Cumberland | 14.6 | 9.9 | 6.9 | 51.6 | 9 017 | 10 052 | 11.5 | -2.0 | 243 | 204 | -250 | 3 980 | 12.8 | 2.52 | 14.6 | 26.1 |
| Dickenson | 15.2 | 10.2 | 6.9 | 49.9 | 16 395 | 15 903 | -3.0 | -1.3 | 376 | 462 | -134 | 6 590 | -2.1 | 2.36 | 10.1 | 27.2 |
| Dinwiddie | 13.5 | 8.6 | 5.5 | 50.8 | 24 533 | 28 001 | 14.1 | 0.0 | 518 | 587 | 33 | 10 504 | 15.3 | 2.58 | 15.3 | 23.0 |
| Essex | 15.2 | 9.9 | 7.9 | 52.9 | 9 989 | 11 151 | 11.6 | 0.7 | 312 | 247 | 4 | 4 517 | 13.1 | 2.43 | 15.5 | 27.3 |
| Fairfax | 12.5 | 6.1 | 4.1 | 50.5 | 969 749 | 1 081 726 | 11.5 | 3.4 | 33 471 | 10 528 | 14 163 | 391 627 | 11.7 | 2.74 | 9.2 | 22.7 |
| Fauquier | 13.6 | 7.9 | 5.3 | 50.7 | 55 139 | 65 203 | 18.3 | 2.1 | 1 660 | 1 147 | 801 | 23 658 | 19.2 | 2.74 | 9.2 | 20.4 |
| Floyd | 15.7 | 10.8 | 7.4 | 49.9 | 13 874 | 15 279 | 10.1 | 0.7 | 333 | 341 | 120 | 6 415 | 10.8 | 2.37 | 7.9 | 27.2 |
| Fluvanna | 13.0 | 9.4 | 6.6 | 54.2 | 20 047 | 25 691 | 28.2 | 1.1 | 631 | 416 | 56 | 9 449 | 27.9 | 2.58 | 10.4 | 20.2 |
| Franklin | 15.6 | 11.1 | 7.2 | 50.7 | 47 286 | 56 159 | 18.8 | 0.4 | 1 193 | 1 229 | 282 | 22 780 | 20.1 | 2.40 | 10.5 | 24.7 |
| Frederick | 12.4 | 7.7 | 5.4 | 50.3 | 59 209 | 78 305 | 32.3 | 2.6 | 2 046 | 1 244 | 1 213 | 28 864 | 30.6 | 2.68 | 10.0 | 20.5 |
| Giles | 15.2 | 10.5 | 8.0 | 51.0 | 16 657 | 17 286 | 3.8 | -2.1 | 391 | 463 | -294 | 7 215 | 3.2 | 2.38 | 10.5 | 27.9 |
| Gloucester | 14.6 | 9.2 | 6.1 | 50.6 | 34 780 | 36 858 | 6.0 | 0.1 | 781 | 833 | 85 | 14 293 | 8.9 | 2.55 | 10.3 | 21.3 |
| Goochland | 17.0 | 9.9 | 6.0 | 50.4 | 16 863 | 21 717 | 28.8 | -1.7 | 357 | 342 | -416 | 7 998 | 29.9 | 2.54 | 8.1 | 18.7 |
| Grayson | 16.6 | 11.6 | 9.7 | 51.0 | 17 917 | 15 533 | -13.3 | -2.3 | 274 | 448 | -177 | 6 846 | -5.7 | 2.24 | 9.5 | 29.3 |
| Greene | 13.0 | 8.3 | 5.0 | 50.6 | 15 244 | 18 403 | 20.7 | 2.0 | 506 | 307 | 156 | 6 780 | 21.6 | 2.69 | 10.9 | 20.1 |
| Greensville | 13.1 | 7.7 | 5.2 | 37.4 | 11 560 | 12 243 | 5.9 | -3.2 | 293 | 270 | -438 | 3 566 | 5.7 | 2.44 | 19.5 | 26.7 |
| Halifax | 15.7 | 10.9 | 8.9 | 52.3 | 37 355 | 36 241 | -3.0 | -1.1 | 777 | 1 077 | -101 | 15 085 | 0.4 | 2.35 | 15.6 | 30.1 |
| Hanover | 13.7 | 7.8 | 5.9 | 50.9 | 86 320 | 99 863 | 15.7 | 0.8 | 2 026 | 1 616 | 386 | 36 589 | 17.6 | 2.68 | 10.4 | 19.2 |
| Henrico | 12.1 | 6.4 | 6.2 | 52.9 | 262 300 | 306 935 | 17.0 | 2.6 | 8 738 | 5 435 | 4 833 | 124 601 | 15.2 | 2.44 | 14.8 | 28.9 |
| Henry | 14.5 | 11.5 | 8.9 | 51.8 | 57 930 | 54 151 | -6.5 | -2.2 | 1 109 | 1 536 | -810 | 23 151 | -3.2 | 2.31 | 13.9 | 29.2 |
| Highland | 20.3 | 16.3 | 10.2 | 50.5 | 2 536 | 2 321 | -8.5 | -3.3 | 31 | 53 | -57 | 1 081 | -4.4 | 2.15 | 6.1 | 29.0 |
| Isle of Wight | 15.2 | 9.2 | 6.2 | 51.3 | 29 728 | 35 270 | 18.6 | 0.4 | 750 | 748 | 139 | 13 718 | 21.2 | 2.55 | 12.6 | 21.4 |
| James City | 14.6 | 11.9 | 9.6 | 51.7 | 48 102 | 67 009 | 39.3 | 2.9 | 1 547 | 1 272 | 1 730 | 26 860 | 41.3 | 2.45 | 9.5 | 21.9 |
| King and Queen | 16.8 | 10.5 | 7.8 | 50.3 | 6 630 | 6 945 | 4.8 | 1.5 | 139 | 168 | 106 | 2 882 | 7.8 | 2.41 | 13.1 | 26.5 |
| King George | 11.2 | 6.6 | 3.8 | 49.6 | 16 803 | 23 584 | 40.4 | 3.9 | 672 | 318 | 541 | 8 376 | 37.5 | 2.78 | 10.7 | 19.8 |
| King William | 13.2 | 7.4 | 5.2 | 51.2 | 13 146 | 15 935 | 21.2 | 0.3 | 434 | 304 | -88 | 5 979 | 23.4 | 2.65 | 11.3 | 19.8 |
| Lancaster | 18.0 | 15.8 | 15.6 | 52.9 | 11 567 | 11 391 | -1.5 | -1.4 | 187 | 446 | 79 | 5 265 | 5.2 | 2.13 | 11.0 | 31.6 |
| Lee | 14.4 | 9.4 | 6.1 | 47.8 | 23 589 | 25 587 | 8.5 | -0.4 | 569 | 649 | -76 | 10 159 | 4.7 | 2.35 | 12.0 | 29.1 |
| Loudoun | 8.9 | 4.1 | 2.7 | 50.5 | 169 599 | 312 311 | 84.1 | 7.9 | 11 063 | 2 333 | 15 467 | 104 583 | 74.6 | 2.98 | 8.3 | 17.8 |

1. No spouse present.

# Table B. States and Counties — Population, Vital Statistics, Medicare, and Crime

| STATE County | Persons in group quarters, 2010 | Daytime population, 2007–2011 Number | Daytime population, 2007–2011 Employment/residence ratio | Births, 2011 Total | Births, 2011 Rate[1] | Deaths, 2011 Number | Deaths, 2011 Rate[1] | Persons under 65 with no health insurance, 2010 Number | Persons under 65 with no health insurance, 2010 Percent | Medicare, 2012 Eligible for Medicare | Medicare, 2012 Enrolled in Medicare Advantage | Medicare, 2012 Enrolled in a Medicare prescription drug plan | Serious crimes known to police,[2] 2011 Total Number | Serious crimes known to police,[2] 2011 Total Rate[3] |
|---|---|---|---|---|---|---|---|---|---|---|---|---|---|---|
| | 32 | 33 | 34 | 35 | 36 | 37 | 38 | 39 | 40 | 41 | 42 | 43 | 44 | 45 |
| **VERMONT—Cont'd** | | | | | | | | | | | | | | |
| Chittenden | 9 795 | 170 413 | 1.17 | 1 463 | 9.3 | 940 | 6.0 | 10 967 | 8.5 | 24 333 | 1 715 | 11 800 | 5 020 | 3 203 |
| Essex | 16 | 5 095 | 0.56 | 57 | 9.1 | 60 | 9.5 | 653 | 12.8 | 1 747 | 113 | 980 | 16 | 253 |
| Franklin | 529 | 41 198 | 0.74 | 535 | 11.1 | 326 | 6.8 | 3 988 | 9.6 | 7 321 | 481 | 4 148 | 1 049 | 2 195 |
| Grand Isle | 0 | 5 003 | 0.44 | 55 | 7.9 | 55 | 7.9 | 623 | 10.5 | 1 551 | 142 | 725 | 57 | 817 |
| Lamoille | 694 | 23 542 | 0.95 | 274 | 11.1 | 181 | 7.3 | 2 377 | 11.5 | 4 333 | 260 | 2 502 | 429 | 1 751 |
| Orange | 715 | 23 637 | 0.64 | 247 | 8.5 | 241 | 8.3 | 2 523 | 10.5 | 5 635 | 306 | 2 964 | 361 | 1 246 |
| Orleans | 818 | 26 392 | 0.93 | 286 | 10.5 | 268 | 9.9 | 2 636 | 12.1 | 6 488 | 468 | 3 843 | 654 | 2 399 |
| Rutland | 2 318 | 61 200 | 0.98 | 546 | 8.9 | 607 | 9.9 | 5 011 | 10.2 | 14 208 | 864 | 8 658 | 2 250 | 3 661 |
| Washington | 2 410 | 63 254 | 1.12 | 615 | 10.3 | 490 | 8.2 | 4 463 | 9.1 | 11 484 | 807 | 5 937 | 1 482 | 2 487 |
| Windham | 1 464 | 46 624 | 1.10 | 411 | 9.3 | 411 | 9.3 | 3 692 | 10.2 | 9 446 | 540 | 5 352 | 1 262 | 2 832 |
| Windsor | 898 | 53 646 | 0.89 | 492 | 8.7 | 512 | 9.0 | 4 128 | 9.0 | 13 235 | 916 | 6 774 | 982 | 1 820 |
| **VIRGINIA** | 239 834 | 7 839 929 | 0.98 | 101 935 | 12.6 | 58 943 | 7.3 | 1 009 466 | 14.8 | 1 240 224 | 188 368 | 517 968 | 198 064 | 2 446 |
| Accomack | 428 | 32 285 | 0.90 | 420 | 12.6 | 455 | 13.6 | 6 046 | 22.6 | 7 888 | 869 | 3 920 | 752 | 2 241 |
| Albemarle | 6 864 | 105 453 | 1.16 | 1 065 | 10.6 | 709 | 7.1 | 10 277 | 13.1 | 15 861 | 1 350 | 8 227 | 2 069 | 2 066 |
| Alleghany | 281 | 16 860 | 1.08 | 163 | 10.1 | 248 | 15.3 | 1 981 | 15.4 | 4 299 | 558 | 2 732 | 285 | 1 733 |
| Amelia | 128 | 10 148 | 0.54 | 152 | 11.9 | 106 | 8.3 | 2 262 | 21.1 | 2 562 | 456 | 1 220 | 149 | 1 160 |
| Amherst | 1 538 | 26 289 | 0.59 | 317 | 9.9 | 343 | 10.7 | 4 481 | 17.2 | 6 893 | 1 178 | 3 716 | 586 | 1 790 |
| Appomattox | 56 | 11 818 | 0.54 | 162 | 10.8 | 146 | 9.7 | 2 103 | 16.9 | 3 424 | 514 | 1 950 | 140 | 924 |
| Arlington | 2 892 | 256 005 | 1.40 | 2 988 | 13.8 | 967 | 4.5 | 22 549 | 12.0 | 20 479 | 2 000 | 6 389 | 4 418 | 2 103 |
| Augusta | 2 708 | 66 474 | 0.79 | 614 | 8.3 | 642 | 8.7 | 9 379 | 15.8 | 15 211 | 2 061 | 8 450 | 906 | 1 214 |
| Bath | 53 | 4 552 | 0.91 | 31 | 6.7 | 57 | 12.2 | 666 | 18.1 | 1 220 | 89 | 778 | 41 | 856 |
| Bedford | 287 | 51 018 | 0.47 | 607 | 8.8 | 603 | 8.7 | 8 652 | 15.1 | 14 870 | 2 200 | 7 357 | 912 | 1 312 |
| Bland | 686 | 6 322 | 0.80 | 41 | 6.0 | 84 | 12.3 | 830 | 16.6 | 1 637 | 271 | 850 | 59 | 854 |
| Botetourt | 275 | 26 594 | 0.61 | 242 | 7.3 | 301 | 9.1 | 3 638 | 13.3 | 7 191 | 1 372 | 3 242 | 312 | 930 |
| Brunswick | 2 184 | 15 159 | 0.61 | 157 | 9.1 | 222 | 12.9 | 2 199 | 17.5 | 3 642 | 525 | 2 067 | 222 | 1 258 |
| Buchanan | 1 173 | 25 120 | 1.13 | 205 | 8.7 | 290 | 12.3 | 3 105 | 16.1 | 7 432 | 2 096 | 3 608 | 573 | 2 350 |
| Buckingham | 2 326 | 15 475 | 0.69 | 170 | 9.8 | 147 | 8.5 | 2 565 | 20.4 | 3 115 | 340 | 1 626 | 264 | 1 522 |
| Campbell | 468 | 48 906 | 0.77 | 488 | 8.9 | 474 | 8.6 | 7 695 | 16.8 | 11 390 | 2 136 | 5 968 | 1 006 | 1 813 |
| Caroline | 513 | 21 240 | 0.46 | 372 | 13.0 | 251 | 8.8 | 4 006 | 16.4 | 4 798 | 611 | 2 074 | 540 | 1 869 |
| Carroll | 337 | 27 057 | 0.76 | 250 | 8.3 | 372 | 12.4 | 4 939 | 20.3 | 7 360 | 896 | 4 504 | 706 | 2 322 |
| Charles City | 0 | 5 637 | 0.53 | 49 | 6.8 | 91 | 12.6 | 1 293 | 21.2 | 1 562 | 394 | 645 | 22 | 300 |
| Charlotte | 175 | 10 600 | 0.59 | 114 | 9.1 | 154 | 12.3 | 2 112 | 20.7 | 3 149 | 388 | 1 825 | 144 | 1 131 |
| Chesterfield | 4 651 | 272 054 | 0.74 | 3 629 | 11.3 | 1 885 | 5.9 | 37 668 | 13.5 | 45 258 | 8 458 | 17 485 | 7 155 | 2 236 |
| Clarke | 255 | 11 529 | 0.63 | 126 | 8.8 | 145 | 10.2 | 1 594 | 13.8 | 2 602 | 259 | 1 117 | 202 | 1 422 |
| Craig | 9 | 3 348 | 0.30 | 41 | 8.0 | 67 | 13.1 | 772 | 17.9 | 1 220 | 216 | 577 | 18 | 343 |
| Culpeper | 1 761 | 41 936 | 0.79 | 626 | 13.2 | 345 | 7.3 | 6 478 | 16.4 | 7 504 | 840 | 3 309 | 839 | 1 776 |
| Cumberland | 37 | 7 393 | 0.38 | 106 | 10.6 | 93 | 9.3 | 1 704 | 20.1 | 1 998 | 313 | 1 016 | 62 | 610 |
| Dickenson | 335 | 15 280 | 0.86 | 162 | 10.3 | 199 | 12.6 | 2 092 | 16.0 | 4 600 | 1 372 | 1 856 | 262 | 1 628 |
| Dinwiddie | 919 | 22 712 | 0.59 | 226 | 8.1 | 251 | 9.0 | 4 013 | 17.0 | 5 067 | 855 | 2 240 | 477 | 1 683 |
| Essex | 190 | 10 230 | 0.84 | 141 | 12.6 | 107 | 9.5 | 1 511 | 16.3 | 2 528 | 305 | 1 296 | 231 | 2 047 |
| Fairfax | 9 290 | 1 065 362 | 1.00 | 14 966 | 13.6 | 4 631 | 4.2 | 124 784 | 12.9 | 121 685 | 12 676 | 33 049 | 16 852 | 1 539 |
| Fauquier | 389 | 55 721 | 0.72 | 729 | 11.0 | 503 | 7.6 | 7 551 | 13.4 | 9 914 | 888 | 3 724 | 989 | 1 499 |
| Floyd | 85 | 12 241 | 0.59 | 155 | 10.1 | 142 | 9.2 | 2 565 | 20.3 | 3 453 | 532 | 1 823 | 197 | 1 274 |
| Fluvanna | 1 272 | 18 683 | 0.42 | 288 | 11.1 | 171 | 6.6 | 2 963 | 14.5 | 4 839 | 485 | 2 168 | 227 | 873 |
| Franklin | 1 472 | 47 411 | 0.66 | 543 | 9.6 | 538 | 9.5 | 8 346 | 18.5 | 12 719 | 2 806 | 6 078 | 940 | 1 654 |
| Frederick | 967 | 68 909 | 0.78 | 909 | 11.4 | 527 | 6.6 | 10 558 | 15.7 | 12 521 | 1 287 | 5 522 | 1 698 | 2 143 |
| Giles | 136 | 15 858 | 0.81 | 178 | 10.4 | 205 | 12.0 | 2 346 | 16.5 | 4 259 | 835 | 1 947 | 363 | 2 075 |
| Gloucester | 368 | 28 816 | 0.56 | 349 | 9.5 | 367 | 9.9 | 4 866 | 15.5 | 6 981 | 978 | 2 459 | 569 | 1 526 |
| Goochland | 1 405 | 22 861 | 1.15 | 166 | 7.6 | 144 | 6.6 | 1 751 | 10.3 | 4 357 | 806 | 1 905 | 260 | 1 183 |
| Grayson | 178 | 12 588 | 0.52 | 125 | 8.2 | 185 | 12.1 | 2 413 | 19.6 | 4 346 | 402 | 2 590 | 200 | 1 272 |
| Greene | 137 | 12 830 | 0.40 | 234 | 12.5 | 128 | 6.9 | 2 771 | 17.3 | 3 025 | 285 | 1 528 | 284 | 1 525 |
| Greensville | 3 527 | 12 159 | 0.99 | 122 | 10.1 | 107 | 8.8 | 1 121 | 15.4 | 2 198 | 691 | 1 466 | 186 | 1 501 |
| Halifax | 738 | 35 588 | 0.95 | 368 | 10.2 | 482 | 13.4 | 4 848 | 16.8 | 9 019 | 1 650 | 5 330 | 982 | 2 678 |
| Hanover | 1 980 | 91 537 | 0.84 | 918 | 9.1 | 686 | 6.8 | 8 094 | 9.6 | 16 383 | 3 207 | 6 783 | 1 418 | 1 403 |
| Henrico | 2 494 | 313 869 | 1.07 | 3 895 | 12.5 | 2 375 | 7.7 | 38 937 | 14.6 | 46 104 | 9 247 | 19 187 | 8 214 | 2 645 |
| Henry | 561 | 50 636 | 0.82 | 515 | 9.6 | 666 | 12.4 | 9 350 | 21.6 | 14 638 | 4 077 | 8 149 | 1 717 | 3 133 |
| Highland | 0 | 2 262 | 0.91 | 14 | 6.2 | 24 | 10.6 | 436 | 24.8 | 682 | 67 | 380 | 11 | 468 |
| Isle of Wight | 310 | 28 535 | 0.62 | 347 | 9.8 | 318 | 9.0 | 3 622 | 12.1 | 6 665 | 1 137 | 2 582 | 679 | 1 902 |
| James City | 1 100 | 61 416 | 0.86 | 666 | 9.8 | 533 | 7.8 | 6 143 | 11.8 | 16 043 | 1 607 | 5 673 | 1 064 | 1 569 |
| King and Queen | 0 | 4 977 | 0.37 | 55 | 7.9 | 71 | 10.1 | 1 087 | 18.8 | 1 498 | 213 | 788 | 74 | 1 053 |
| King George | 301 | 23 828 | 1.04 | 285 | 11.8 | 126 | 5.2 | 2 246 | 10.7 | 2 977 | 192 | 966 | 364 | 1 525 |
| King William | 72 | 12 380 | 0.56 | 203 | 12.7 | 129 | 8.1 | 1 984 | 14.2 | 2 709 | 348 | 1 438 | 171 | 1 060 |
| Lancaster | 183 | 12 249 | 1.16 | 86 | 7.8 | 196 | 17.4 | 1 413 | 18.1 | 3 968 | 401 | 1 905 | 195 | 1 692 |
| Lee | 1 706 | 22 584 | 0.68 | 251 | 10.0 | 309 | 12.3 | 3 279 | 16.4 | 6 141 | 1 758 | 2 764 | 265 | 1 023 |
| Loudoun | 1 172 | 278 168 | 0.84 | 4 943 | 15.2 | 971 | 3.0 | 25 479 | 8.7 | 25 291 | 3 187 | 8 025 | 4 012 | 1 269 |

1. Per 1,000 estimated resident population.    2. Data for serious crimes have not been adjusted for underreporting; this may affect comparability between geographic areas and over time.    3. Per 100,000 population estimated by the FBI.

# Table B. States and Counties — Crime, Education, Money Income, and Poverty

| STATE County | Serious crimes known to police, 2011 (cont.)[1] Rate[2] Violent | Property | Education — School enrollment and attainment, 2007–2011 Enrollment[3] Total | Per cent private | Attainment[4] (percent) High school graduate or less | Bachelor's degree or more | Local government expenditures,[5] 2009–2010 Total current expenditures (mil dol) | Current expenditures per student (dollars) | Money income, 2007–2011 Per capita income[6] (dollars) | Households Median income Dollars | Percent change, 2000 to 2007–2011 (constant 2011 dollars) | Percent with income of $200,000 or more | Income and poverty, 2011 Median household income (dollars) | Percent below poverty level All persons | Children under 18 years | Children 5 to 17 years in families |
|---|---|---|---|---|---|---|---|---|---|---|---|---|---|---|---|---|
| | 46 | 47 | 48 | 49 | 50 | 51 | 52 | 53 | 54 | 55 | 56 | 57 | 58 | 59 | 60 | 61 |
| **VERMONT—Cont'd** | | | | | | | | | | | | | | | | |
| Chittenden | 186 | 3 018 | 46 477 | 18.1 | 28.9 | 45.8 | 334.2 | 15 434 | 32 533 | 62 260 | -3.3 | 5.2 | 60 865 | 10.5 | 10.7 | 8.5 |
| Essex | 63 | 190 | 1 227 | 13.7 | 61.2 | 15.2 | 11.6 | 15 101 | 20 641 | 37 679 | -8.5 | 1.2 | 34 535 | 16.7 | 27.0 | 23.6 |
| Franklin | 188 | 2 006 | 11 436 | 8.9 | 51.7 | 21.1 | 117.6 | 13 938 | 25 811 | 55 181 | -1.9 | 1.6 | 53 412 | 11.5 | 16.4 | 13.5 |
| Grand Isle | 57 | 760 | 1 520 | 15.5 | 42.4 | 28.9 | 11.8 | 12 791 | 33 491 | 59 566 | 2.5 | 5.2 | 56 241 | 10.5 | 15.9 | 13.1 |
| Lamoille | 78 | 1 673 | 5 772 | 9.9 | 40.2 | 34.6 | 53.8 | 14 862 | 27 457 | 53 368 | 0.4 | 3.5 | 46 549 | 13.6 | 18.7 | 15.8 |
| Orange | 79 | 1 167 | 6 702 | 18.2 | 46.1 | 27.8 | 73.1 | 15 812 | 26 269 | 52 407 | -2.6 | 1.9 | 50 192 | 11.5 | 17.5 | 15.3 |
| Orleans | 139 | 2 260 | 5 378 | 9.1 | 56.3 | 19.7 | 67.6 | 17 196 | 21 000 | 40 929 | -2.5 | 1.1 | 39 598 | 18.4 | 26.9 | 22.4 |
| Rutland | 151 | 3 510 | 14 566 | 13.7 | 47.6 | 26.4 | 141.8 | 16 518 | 25 814 | 48 190 | -2.9 | 2.1 | 46 542 | 12.9 | 18.0 | 14.8 |
| Washington | 104 | 2 383 | 14 467 | 25.8 | 36.4 | 38.2 | 129.7 | 15 150 | 28 992 | 57 163 | 3.3 | 3.0 | 54 840 | 8.7 | 12.5 | 10.4 |
| Windham | 213 | 2 619 | 10 073 | 30.3 | 39.9 | 35.0 | 106.6 | 17 689 | 28 131 | 48 953 | -5.1 | 2.2 | 46 566 | 10.8 | 16.9 | 14.4 |
| Windsor | 135 | 1 685 | 12 206 | 22.2 | 41.0 | 33.4 | 144.9 | 17 561 | 30 236 | 53 129 | -3.3 | 3.5 | 49 295 | 12.4 | 15.5 | 12.2 |
| **VIRGINIA** | 197 | 2 250 | 2 099 526 | 17.2 | 39.0 | 34.4 | 13 189.4 | 10 591 | 33 040 | 63 302 | 0.4 | 7.0 | 61 877 | 11.6 | 15.6 | 14.3 |
| Accomack | 191 | 2 050 | 6 631 | 14.5 | 59.6 | 17.4 | 50.2 | 9 758 | 23 556 | 41 595 | 1.8 | 2.1 | 37 714 | 19.3 | 30.5 | 27.3 |
| Albemarle | 112 | 1 954 | 29 835 | 21.4 | 27.8 | 51.8 | [7]213.5 | [7]12 521 | 37 256 | 65 934 | -3.8 | 8.8 | 63 972 | 9.7 | 10.6 | 9.6 |
| Alleghany | 134 | 1 599 | 3 597 | 9.3 | 55.6 | 15.3 | 29.0 | 10 199 | 22 444 | 44 329 | 0.0 | 0.5 | 45 108 | 13.5 | 20.4 | 17.6 |
| Amelia | 132 | 1 028 | 2 499 | 11.4 | 59.5 | 13.7 | 16.8 | 9 134 | 24 664 | 51 540 | -5.2 | 2.5 | 49 399 | 11.9 | 18.4 | 17.0 |
| Amherst | 95 | 1 695 | 7 680 | 27.1 | 55.0 | 16.2 | 43.8 | 9 444 | 22 128 | 44 383 | -12.1 | 0.6 | 44 494 | 13.4 | 20.2 | 18.3 |
| Appomattox | 86 | 838 | 3 379 | 17.9 | 58.3 | 13.9 | 19.7 | 8 449 | 22 721 | 47 992 | -2.6 | 0.7 | 44 097 | 14.8 | 22.3 | 20.5 |
| Arlington | 155 | 1 948 | 42 733 | 29.8 | 16.5 | 70.7 | 355.1 | 17 519 | 60 223 | 99 651 | 17.2 | 16.9 | 98 060 | 7.4 | 10.1 | 10.6 |
| Augusta | 117 | 1 097 | 15 714 | 17.0 | 58.1 | 19.1 | 100.0 | 9 251 | 23 861 | 51 719 | -11.0 | 1.5 | 51 036 | 10.0 | 14.1 | 12.9 |
| Bath | 42 | 815 | 804 | 17.4 | 64.3 | 13.3 | 8.9 | 12 675 | 24 878 | 52 500 | 11.1 | 0.7 | 42 423 | 10.8 | 15.9 | 13.4 |
| Bedford | 68 | 1 245 | 16 073 | 22.0 | 46.8 | 24.8 | [8]92.0 | [8]8 490 | 27 845 | 56 021 | -3.8 | 3.1 | 58 264 | 9.2 | 13.7 | 11.8 |
| Bland | 72 | 782 | 1 306 | 7.9 | 61.1 | 10.8 | 8.4 | 9 150 | 20 291 | 42 864 | 4.4 | 0.8 | 41 654 | 14.4 | 18.7 | 16.1 |
| Botetourt | 75 | 856 | 7 562 | 19.9 | 45.2 | 22.9 | 47.4 | 9 329 | 30 293 | 65 633 | -0.2 | 4.7 | 62 204 | 7.5 | 10.1 | 8.8 |
| Brunswick | 85 | 1 173 | 3 949 | 23.2 | 62.3 | 13.5 | 22.9 | 10 457 | 16 991 | 34 170 | -19.1 | 0.6 | 35 207 | 25.6 | 31.0 | 25.0 |
| Buchanan | 135 | 2 214 | 4 643 | 10.8 | 64.8 | 9.4 | 37.6 | 11 119 | 17 592 | 30 606 | 2.0 | 0.7 | 32 722 | 24.3 | 30.8 | 27.1 |
| Buckingham | 138 | 1 383 | 2 362 | 25.4 | 68.8 | 13.5 | 21.1 | 10 325 | 16 938 | 36 378 | -9.8 | 0.4 | 47 450 | 15.2 | 23.0 | 21.0 |
| Campbell | 105 | 1 708 | 13 442 | 24.0 | 54.0 | 16.1 | 77.6 | 8 987 | 22 588 | 45 992 | -8.6 | 1.0 | 52 496 | 12.2 | 18.9 | 18.2 |
| Caroline | 132 | 1 738 | 6 109 | 9.2 | 55.0 | 17.6 | 36.1 | 8 446 | 26 030 | 58 707 | 9.1 | 1.5 | 34 891 | 19.9 | 29.4 | 25.6 |
| Carroll | 135 | 2 187 | 6 196 | 8.4 | 60.8 | 12.6 | 39.4 | 9 568 | 19 187 | 35 841 | -13.2 | 0.2 | 45 960 | 11.7 | 18.1 | 15.1 |
| Charles City | 68 | 232 | 1 463 | 11.6 | 65.7 | 12.4 | 11.3 | 12 990 | 25 241 | 47 093 | -18.4 | 2.4 | 35 677 | 20.9 | 30.5 | 26.9 |
| Charlotte | 165 | 966 | 2 969 | 7.3 | 58.6 | 15.2 | 21.5 | 9 791 | 18 210 | 37 173 | -4.8 | 0.3 | 71 074 | 7.2 | 10.4 | 9.4 |
| Chesterfield | 121 | 2 115 | 89 360 | 14.5 | 34.8 | 36.0 | 533.9 | 8 971 | 32 546 | 72 886 | -7.8 | 5.7 | 74 472 | 8.2 | 10.3 | 8.9 |
| Clarke | 84 | 1 338 | 3 166 | 26.2 | 40.8 | 30.7 | 19.6 | 8 972 | 37 551 | 77 048 | 10.6 | 8.7 | 45 789 | 12.2 | 19.9 | 17.7 |
| Craig | 95 | 248 | 1 055 | 17.8 | 52.5 | 15.0 | 7.4 | 10 125 | 25 046 | 54 120 | 7.4 | 0.9 | 58 596 | 11.7 | 16.4 | 15.3 |
| Culpeper | 210 | 1 566 | 11 253 | 17.7 | 51.3 | 21.8 | 70.6 | 9 237 | 27 075 | 66 458 | 8.7 | 2.8 | 40 080 | 17.9 | 27.1 | 25.4 |
| Cumberland | 98 | 511 | 2 208 | 8.1 | 62.5 | 14.1 | 16.7 | 10 907 | 21 250 | 45 184 | 5.2 | 2.2 | 33 494 | 21.8 | 26.9 | 23.9 |
| Dickenson | 124 | 1 504 | 3 106 | 2.1 | 70.2 | 8.9 | 26.5 | 10 295 | 17 089 | 30 556 | -3.4 | 0.9 | 50 152 | 13.3 | 18.9 | 17.1 |
| Dinwiddie | 152 | 1 532 | 6 225 | 9.3 | 62.6 | 13.0 | 42.4 | 8 986 | 23 246 | 50 583 | -9.9 | 1.4 | 42 550 | 14.9 | 24.7 | 24.7 |
| Essex | 213 | 1 834 | 2 236 | 14.0 | 58.7 | 16.2 | 16.7 | 10 183 | 22 495 | 44 581 | -11.7 | 0.3 | 105 409 | 6.8 | 9.0 | 7.9 |
| Fairfax | 90 | 1 449 | 292 083 | 21.3 | 21.7 | 58.2 | [9]2 159.5 | [9]12 554 | 50 145 | 108 439 | -0.9 | 18.8 | 85 096 | 6.3 | 8.8 | 7.4 |
| Fauquier | 88 | 1 411 | 17 802 | 20.6 | 37.3 | 32.3 | 123.9 | 10 968 | 40 569 | 87 958 | 5.1 | 10.5 | 39 997 | 13.5 | 20.9 | 19.2 |
| Floyd | 71 | 1 203 | 3 083 | 23.1 | 54.6 | 19.3 | 19.0 | 9 140 | 21 298 | 40 761 | -4.4 | 0.9 | 62 086 | 7.6 | 10.2 | 9.1 |
| Fluvanna | 38 | 835 | 5 469 | 13.8 | 44.7 | 28.1 | 37.1 | 9 802 | 28 864 | 68 615 | 9.6 | 2.8 | 49 003 | 13.1 | 21.7 | 20.6 |
| Franklin | 111 | 1 543 | 12 172 | 18.0 | 54.4 | 17.6 | 71.6 | 9 494 | 24 677 | 47 606 | -7.3 | 2.1 | 64 501 | 8.9 | 12.4 | 10.7 |
| Frederick | 101 | 2 042 | 19 723 | 15.4 | 48.0 | 24.2 | [10]174.4 | [10]10 288 | 29 409 | 66 440 | 4.8 | 3.8 | 43 139 | 12.6 | 19.1 | 17.4 |
| Giles | 172 | 1 904 | 3 913 | 12.3 | 56.3 | 16.7 | 23.3 | 9 099 | 21 891 | 43 012 | -8.8 | 1.6 | 58 282 | 10.2 | 15.1 | 13.8 |
| Gloucester | 86 | 1 440 | 8 757 | 10.9 | 46.3 | 20.0 | 56.9 | 9 372 | 28 623 | 62 067 | 1.2 | 2.9 | 76 804 | 8.1 | 10.4 | 9.2 |
| Goochland | 146 | 1 037 | 4 236 | 29.6 | 40.1 | 37.1 | 27.1 | 11 058 | 46 697 | 81 288 | 6.9 | 13.1 | 31 286 | 18.6 | 29.0 | 26.2 |
| Grayson | 127 | 1 145 | 2 790 | 3.0 | 63.0 | 11.9 | 20.7 | 10 444 | 21 013 | 31 599 | -18.4 | 1.2 | 60 170 | 9.2 | 13.9 | 13.3 |
| Greene | 145 | 1 380 | 3 856 | 13.0 | 54.2 | 21.6 | 28.2 | 9 963 | 26 711 | 58 550 | -5.6 | 1.6 | 37 861 | 24.7 | 26.1 | 24.6 |
| Greensville | 129 | 1 372 | 1 915 | 9.5 | 72.8 | 7.8 | [11]25.7 | [11]9 630 | 18 004 | 42 000 | -2.8 | 1.9 | 35 170 | 19.3 | 26.2 | 24.2 |
| Halifax | 188 | 2 490 | 8 256 | 10.1 | 60.8 | 14.1 | 58.8 | 9 804 | 20 744 | 34 889 | -13.7 | 2.2 | 71 714 | 6.1 | 7.3 | 6.1 |
| Hanover | 72 | 1 331 | 27 218 | 18.2 | 36.6 | 33.7 | 170.2 | 9 026 | 34 505 | 77 506 | -3.1 | 6.7 | 58 110 | 10.8 | 14.9 | 13.3 |
| Henrico | 141 | 2 504 | 79 352 | 17.1 | 33.6 | 39.2 | 438.7 | 8 879 | 33 364 | 61 206 | -7.8 | 5.4 | 32 590 | 20.5 | 33.8 | 30.4 |
| Henry | 312 | 2 821 | 11 502 | 9.4 | 60.8 | 11.3 | 67.6 | 9 001 | 19 511 | 33 695 | -21.6 | 1.1 | 37 286 | 13.8 | 22.9 | 19.3 |
| Highland | 43 | 426 | 306 | 15.4 | 61.2 | 22.1 | 3.6 | 13 996 | 24 922 | 43 045 | 7.2 | 0.9 | 60 922 | 11.2 | 15.6 | 12.5 |
| Isle of Wight | 146 | 1 757 | 8 828 | 21.5 | 44.0 | 25.2 | 52.4 | 9 479 | 30 500 | 64 925 | 5.9 | 4.0 | 73 575 | 7.4 | 11.2 | 10.3 |
| James City | 124 | 1 445 | 15 531 | 14.6 | 28.1 | 45.6 | [12]116.7 | [12]10 807 | 39 311 | 75 938 | 1.2 | 8.0 | 45 087 | 13.2 | 20.3 | 18.7 |
| King and Queen | 128 | 925 | 1 148 | 20.7 | 63.7 | 11.3 | 10.2 | 13 172 | 25 012 | 48 170 | -0.7 | 2.3 | 75 935 | 6.9 | 9.7 | 8.9 |
| King George | 96 | 1 429 | 6 035 | 15.5 | 40.6 | 29.5 | 33.8 | 8 197 | 34 024 | 82 173 | 22.0 | 7.0 | 43 470 | 15.7 | 27.4 | 25.4 |
| King William | 68 | 992 | 3 790 | 12.6 | 53.3 | 18.8 | 29.1 | 9 605 | 27 796 | 64 982 | -3.5 | 1.7 | 57 779 | 8.7 | 12.9 | 11.7 |
| Lancaster | 113 | 1 579 | 1 655 | 12.6 | 47.3 | 25.6 | 15.0 | 10 812 | 29 845 | 46 625 | 3.9 | 2.7 | 30 341 | 27.6 | 35.6 | 33.0 |
| Lee | 131 | 892 | 5 140 | 9.5 | 59.8 | 11.8 | 40.4 | 11 063 | 16 669 | 32 588 | 5.1 | 0.7 | 30 341 | 15.7 | — | — |
| Loudoun | 97 | 1 173 | 92 065 | 19.6 | 20.5 | 57.6 | 721.9 | 12 031 | 46 493 | 120 096 | 10.3 | 19.1 | 119 525 | 4.0 | 4.5 | 4.1 |

1. Data for serious crimes have not been adjusted for underreporting; this may affect comparability between geographic areas and over time.   2. Per 100,000 population estimated by the FBI.   3. All persons 3 years old and over enrolled in nursery school through college.   4. Persons 25 years old and over.   5. Elementary and secondary education expenditures.   6. Based on population estimated by the American Community Survey, 2007–2011.   7. Charlottesville city is included with Albemarle county.   8. Bedford city is included with Bedford county.   9. Fairfax city is included with Fairfax county.   10. Winchester city is included with Frederick county.   11. Emporia city is included with Greensville county.   12. Williamsburg city is included with James City county.

# Table B. States and Counties — **Personal Income**

| STATE County | Personal income, 2011 Total (mil dol) | Percent change, 2010–2011 | Per capita[1] Dollars | Per capita[1] Rank | Wages and salaries[2] (mil dol) | Proprietors' income (mil dol) | Dividends, interest, and rent (mil dol) | Transfer payments (mil dol) Total | Government payments to individuals Total | Social Security | Medical payments | Income maintenance | Unemployment insurance |
|---|---|---|---|---|---|---|---|---|---|---|---|---|---|
| | 62 | 63 | 64 | 65 | 66 | 67 | 68 | 69 | 70 | 71 | 72 | 73 | 74 |
| **VERMONT—Cont'd** | | | | | | | | | | | | | |
| Chittenden | 7 042 | 4.7 | 44 715 | 404 | 5 857 | 544 | 1 174 | 1 114 | 1 079 | 357 | 495 | 121 | 33 |
| Essex | 166 | 3.8 | 26 433 | 2 832 | 50 | 16 | 23 | 56 | 55 | 24 | 16 | 8 | 2 |
| Franklin | 1 977 | 7.0 | 41 088 | 652 | 866 | 187 | 194 | 341 | 330 | 98 | 143 | 54 | 12 |
| Grand Isle | 301 | 0.7 | 43 433 | 477 | 50 | 23 | 59 | 51 | 50 | 23 | 15 | 7 | 2 |
| Lamoille | 1 019 | 5.4 | 41 237 | 640 | 490 | 110 | 198 | 193 | 188 | 60 | 87 | 23 | 9 |
| Orange | 1 053 | 4.2 | 36 309 | 1 167 | 349 | 95 | 168 | 218 | 211 | 77 | 85 | 26 | 7 |
| Orleans | 973 | 5.9 | 35 812 | 1 249 | 446 | 113 | 154 | 291 | 285 | 83 | 135 | 40 | 10 |
| Rutland | 2 527 | 4.2 | 41 233 | 641 | 1 368 | 120 | 376 | 782 | 768 | 202 | 441 | 74 | 19 |
| Washington | 2 635 | 4.5 | 44 190 | 432 | 1 780 | 192 | 413 | 567 | 554 | 165 | 279 | 50 | 15 |
| Windham | 1 792 | 3.8 | 40 487 | 704 | 1 111 | 150 | 343 | 418 | 409 | 135 | 179 | 45 | 12 |
| Windsor | 2 544 | 4.4 | 44 894 | 396 | 1 171 | 206 | 564 | 487 | 475 | 188 | 193 | 48 | 14 |
| **VIRGINIA** | 373 312 | 5.4 | 46 107 | X | 257 102 | 23 144 | 57 609 | 50 329 | 48 566 | 17 408 | 19 272 | 5 601 | 1 259 |
| Accomack | 1 112 | 1.9 | 33 368 | 1 637 | 577 | 74 | 218 | 302 | 295 | 107 | 125 | 42 | 6 |
| Albemarle | [3]6 779 | [3]5.6 | [3]47 052 | [3]296 | [3]5 342 | [3]691 | [3]1 681 | [3]833 | [3]802 | [3]316 | [3]335 | [3]78 | [3]19 |
| Alleghany | [4]741 | [4]5.2 | [4]33 513 | [4]1 600 | [4]458 | [4]25 | [4]108 | [4]231 | [4]226 | [4]81 | [4]95 | [4]21 | [4]4 |
| Amelia | 447 | 5.1 | 34 892 | 1 386 | 106 | 37 | 58 | 97 | 94 | 39 | 37 | 11 | 2 |
| Amherst | 969 | 2.9 | 30 120 | 2 266 | 418 | 32 | 136 | 250 | 243 | 100 | 97 | 27 | 5 |
| Appomattox | 466 | 3.8 | 30 992 | 2 105 | 133 | 24 | 60 | 126 | 123 | 48 | 49 | 15 | 2 |
| Arlington | 17 818 | 7.0 | 82 491 | 5 | 20 467 | 1 196 | 2 662 | 885 | 838 | 249 | 299 | 62 | 27 |
| Augusta | [5]4 086 | [5]4.9 | [5]34 442 | [5]1 445 | [5]2 179 | [5]327 | [5]749 | [5]914 | [5]887 | [5]373 | [5]356 | [5]86 | [5]18 |
| Bath | 179 | 6.7 | 38 375 | 927 | 99 | 3 | 47 | 43 | 42 | 17 | 19 | 3 | 1 |
| Bedford | [6]2 911 | [6]4.4 | [6]38 595 | [6]900 | [6]845 | [6]155 | [6]501 | [6]547 | [6]530 | [6]242 | [6]180 | [6]44 | [6]11 |
| Bland | 208 | 5.0 | 30 495 | 2 200 | 106 | 6 | 28 | 58 | 56 | 23 | 23 | 4 | 1 |
| Botetourt | 1 401 | 4.8 | 42 560 | 534 | 465 | 63 | 212 | 235 | 228 | 103 | 79 | 14 | 5 |
| Brunswick | 468 | 3.0 | 27 208 | 2 736 | 174 | 21 | 58 | 169 | 166 | 48 | 70 | 23 | 3 |
| Buchanan | 770 | 6.9 | 32 662 | 1 766 | 514 | 60 | 77 | 288 | 282 | 111 | 116 | 34 | 3 |
| Buckingham | 427 | 3.9 | 24 722 | 2 985 | 152 | 35 | 58 | 125 | 121 | 41 | 52 | 18 | 3 |
| Campbell | [7]4 210 | [7]4.4 | [7]32 008 | [7]1 887 | [7]3 589 | [7]183 | [7]719 | [7]1 168 | [7]1 139 | [7]360 | [7]495 | [7]128 | [7]22 |
| Caroline | 1 037 | 6.8 | 36 160 | 1 192 | 275 | 65 | 106 | 190 | 184 | 68 | 73 | 24 | 5 |
| Carroll | [8]1 098 | [8]4.6 | [8]29 698 | [8]2 338 | [8]482 | [8]62 | [8]147 | [8]382 | [8]374 | [8]125 | [8]186 | [8]39 | [8]8 |
| Charles City | 237 | 3.0 | 32 755 | 1 749 | 74 | 18 | 36 | 60 | 58 | 23 | 25 | 6 | 1 |
| Charlotte | 346 | 3.2 | 27 678 | 2 656 | 109 | 28 | 55 | 117 | 114 | 42 | 48 | 16 | 2 |
| Chesterfield | 14 156 | 6.2 | 44 198 | 431 | 6 784 | 827 | 1 960 | 1 724 | 1 653 | 710 | 578 | 172 | 49 |
| Clarke | 590 | 3.8 | 41 366 | 628 | 204 | 28 | 130 | 86 | 83 | 37 | 34 | 5 | 2 |
| Craig | 161 | 3.8 | 31 500 | 2 000 | 29 | 8 | 25 | 41 | 40 | 17 | 13 | 4 | 1 |
| Culpeper | 1 702 | 6.3 | 35 850 | 1 241 | 747 | 113 | 240 | 287 | 276 | 106 | 116 | 32 | 7 |
| Cumberland | 304 | 4.0 | 30 459 | 2 208 | 53 | 13 | 37 | 79 | 77 | 28 | 33 | 11 | 2 |
| Dickenson | 477 | 4.1 | 30 306 | 2 239 | 206 | 17 | 55 | 187 | 184 | 67 | 75 | 21 | 2 |
| Dinwiddie | [9]2 952 | [9]6.4 | [9]37 994 | [9]971 | [9]1 554 | [9]64 | [9]380 | [9]845 | [9]828 | [9]221 | [9]420 | [9]103 | [9]16 |
| Essex | 378 | 5.4 | 33 734 | 1 557 | 155 | 27 | 66 | 105 | 102 | 37 | 46 | 13 | 2 |
| Fairfax | [10]78 392 | [10]4.3 | [10]69 008 | [10]26 | [10]62 936 | [10]7 362 | [10]12 457 | [10]4 584 | [10]4 335 | [10]1 634 | [10]1 636 | [10]378 | [10]138 |
| Fauquier | 3 594 | 4.9 | 54 400 | 123 | 1 237 | 229 | 696 | 345 | 330 | 145 | 131 | 25 | 8 |
| Floyd | 435 | 6.0 | 28 260 | 2 575 | 115 | 32 | 69 | 122 | 118 | 46 | 48 | 12 | 2 |
| Fluvanna | 951 | 6.4 | 36 507 | 1 137 | 209 | 23 | 134 | 165 | 160 | 71 | 64 | 12 | 3 |
| Franklin | 1 841 | 5.3 | 32 626 | 1 774 | 546 | 67 | 338 | 447 | 434 | 182 | 166 | 44 | 9 |
| Frederick | [11]3 972 | [11]5.9 | [11]37 382 | [11]1 039 | [11]2 756 | [11]216 | [11]663 | [11]622 | [11]598 | [11]245 | [11]224 | [11]66 | [11]18 |
| Giles | 516 | 4.6 | 30 123 | 2 265 | 254 | 12 | 76 | 158 | 154 | 60 | 65 | 15 | 3 |
| Gloucester | 1 435 | 4.8 | 38 886 | 864 | 394 | 48 | 209 | 257 | 249 | 98 | 95 | 25 | 6 |
| Goochland | 1 390 | 6.2 | 63 540 | 44 | 1 002 | 104 | 382 | 153 | 148 | 67 | 46 | 8 | 3 |
| Grayson | 378 | 2.2 | 24 651 | 2 993 | 94 | 9 | 67 | 149 | 146 | 56 | 62 | 16 | 3 |
| Greene | 710 | 6.7 | 38 073 | 960 | 163 | 30 | 81 | 111 | 107 | 43 | 43 | 11 | 3 |
| Greensville | [12]434 | [12]4.9 | [12]24 158 | [12]3 023 | [12]344 | [12]17 | [12]57 | [12]153 | [12]149 | [12]47 | [12]47 | [12]25 | [12]3 |
| Halifax | 1 071 | 2.8 | 29 698 | 2 338 | 542 | 59 | 172 | 337 | 329 | 121 | 138 | 46 | 8 |
| Hanover | 4 599 | 4.9 | 45 832 | 345 | 2 312 | 307 | 695 | 573 | 551 | 261 | 206 | 35 | 15 |
| Henrico | 13 824 | 5.2 | 44 529 | 418 | 11 434 | 786 | 2 516 | 1 801 | 1 733 | 717 | 656 | 207 | 49 |
| Henry | [13]2 026 | [13]2.2 | [13]30 097 | [13]2 271 | [13]1 021 | [13]88 | [13]381 | [13]692 | [13]677 | [13]266 | [13]268 | [13]90 | [13]17 |
| Highland | 82 | 5.4 | 36 272 | 1 177 | 20 | 4 | 27 | 23 | 23 | 9 | 10 | 1 | 0 |
| Isle of Wight | 1 516 | 5.7 | 42 883 | 515 | 511 | 71 | 188 | 263 | 255 | 98 | 106 | 25 | 6 |
| James City | [14]4 316 | [14]7.4 | [14]52 228 | [14]160 | [14]1 907 | [14]269 | [14]1 130 | [14]653 | [14]635 | [14]275 | [14]262 | [14]37 | [14]12 |
| King and Queen | 231 | 6.8 | 33 018 | 1 705 | 60 | 27 | 30 | 56 | 55 | 21 | 23 | 6 | 1 |
| King George | 981 | 7.1 | 40 586 | 697 | 1 095 | 63 | 139 | 113 | 108 | 36 | 43 | 13 | 4 |
| King William | 621 | 6.8 | 38 882 | 866 | 172 | 22 | 82 | 103 | 99 | 42 | 39 | 10 | 3 |
| Lancaster | 548 | 5.7 | 48 607 | 250 | 203 | 30 | 212 | 130 | 127 | 58 | 52 | 11 | 2 |
| Lee | 718 | 4.5 | 28 553 | 2 532 | 254 | 44 | 80 | 266 | 260 | 81 | 120 | 40 | 4 |
| Loudoun | 18 627 | 9.8 | 57 242 | 92 | 10 559 | 752 | 2 116 | 927 | 855 | 349 | 304 | 71 | 36 |

1. Based on the resident population estimated as of July 1 of the year shown.    2. Includes supplements to wages and salaries.    3. Charlottesville city is included with Albemarle county.    4. Covington city is included with Alleghany county.    5. Staunton and Waynesboro cities are included with Augusta county.    6. Bedford city is included with Bedford county.    7. Lynchburg city is included with Campbell county.    8. Galax city is included with Carroll county.    9. Petersburg and Colonial Heights cities are included with Dinwiddie county.    10. Fairfax city and Falls Church city are included with Fairfax county.    11. Winchester city is included with Frederick county.    12. Emporia city is included with Greensville county.    13. Martinsville city is included with Henry county.    14. Williamsburg city is included with James City county.

| STATE County | Total (mil dol) | Farm | Total | Manufacturing | Information and professional and technical services | Retail trade | Finance, insurance, and real estate | Health care and social services | Government | Number | Rate[2] | Supplemental Security Income recipients, December 2011 | Total | Percent change, 2000–2010 |
|---|---|---|---|---|---|---|---|---|---|---|---|---|---|---|
| | 75 | 76 | 77 | 78 | 79 | 80 | 81 | 82 | 83 | 84 | 85 | 86 | 87 | 88 |
| **VERMONT—Cont'd** | | | | | | | | | | | | | | |
| Chittenden | 6 401 | 0.2 | 20.5 | 14.1 | 13.7 | 7.3 | 6.9 | 14.9 | 17.7 | 26 065 | 166 | 2 885 | 65 722 | 11.6 |
| Essex | 66 | 5.3 | D | D | D | 4.9 | D | D | 36.4 | 1 995 | 317 | 249 | 5 019 | 5.4 |
| Franklin | 1 053 | 5.6 | D | 17.0 | D | 9.6 | 2.3 | 11.9 | 26.7 | 8 170 | 170 | 1 288 | 21 588 | 12.5 |
| Grand Isle | 72 | 5.3 | D | D | D | 8.6 | D | D | 21.4 | 1 710 | 247 | 147 | 5 048 | 8.3 |
| Lamoille | 600 | 1.5 | D | 4.4 | 10.2 | 7.9 | 5.3 | 13.7 | 15.1 | 4 765 | 193 | 507 | 12 969 | 17.8 |
| Orange | 444 | 3.0 | 18.2 | 6.0 | 7.0 | 6.8 | 3.4 | 16.1 | 22.5 | 6 165 | 213 | 700 | 14 845 | 10.9 |
| Orleans | 559 | 5.2 | D | 10.5 | D | 9.0 | 4.3 | 17.0 | 20.8 | 7 185 | 264 | 1 100 | 16 162 | 10.1 |
| Rutland | 1 487 | 0.8 | 22.1 | 14.2 | 5.1 | 8.9 | 3.4 | 17.3 | 17.2 | 15 775 | 257 | 2 066 | 33 768 | 4.5 |
| Washington | 1 973 | 0.4 | 12.6 | 7.1 | 7.4 | 7.8 | 12.3 | 11.2 | 24.7 | 12 745 | 214 | 1 502 | 29 941 | 8.3 |
| Windham | 1 261 | 0.5 | D | 10.3 | 6.2 | 7.2 | 4.9 | 12.7 | 12.7 | 10 300 | 233 | 1 208 | 29 735 | 10.0 |
| Windsor | 1 378 | 0.4 | 15.4 | 7.2 | 10.9 | 6.5 | 3.7 | 14.5 | 24.9 | 14 130 | 249 | 1 225 | 34 118 | 7.9 |
| **VIRGINIA** | 280 246 | 0.2 | 11.3 | 5.8 | 20.7 | 5.0 | 6.5 | 8.5 | 25.5 | 1 318 580 | 163 | 151 013 | 3 364 939 | 15.9 |
| Accomack | 651 | 5.5 | 23.0 | 18.5 | 8.1 | 5.8 | 2.8 | D | 29.8 | 8 710 | 261 | 1 104 | 21 002 | 7.4 |
| Albemarle | [3]6 032 | [3]-0.1 | [3]9.5 | [3]3.7 | [3]14.1 | [3]5.2 | [3]6.4 | [3]10.7 | [3]35.2 | 16 280 | 162 | 849 | 42 122 | 24.8 |
| Alleghany | [4]483 | [4]-0.3 | [4]D | [4]D | [4]D | [4]6.3 | [4]D | [4]D | [4]17.3 | 4 480 | 277 | 489 | 8 074 | 2.4 |
| Amelia | 143 | 3.2 | D | 7.2 | D | 7.8 | D | D | 18.5 | 3 000 | 234 | 323 | 5 359 | 16.3 |
| Amherst | 450 | -0.6 | 26.5 | 19.8 | D | 6.9 | 2.1 | D | 30.0 | 7 775 | 242 | 816 | 13 976 | 7.9 |
| Appomattox | 157 | -1.7 | D | 5.6 | 4.2 | 11.9 | 3.4 | D | 28.2 | 3 860 | 257 | 533 | 6 921 | 18.8 |
| Arlington | 21 663 | 0.0 | D | 0.4 | 28.0 | 1.8 | 5.3 | 2.9 | 38.7 | 17 455 | 81 | 2 014 | 105 404 | 16.6 |
| Augusta | [5]2 506 | [5]0.9 | [5]D | [5]19.0 | [5]7.4 | [5]7.2 | [5]3.6 | [5]D | [5]18.1 | 16 955 | 231 | 975 | 31 194 | 16.7 |
| Bath | 101 | -0.5 | 8.9 | 1.4 | D | 2.3 | 3.2 | 9.9 | 17.1 | 1 325 | 285 | 91 | 3 270 | 13.0 |
| Bedford | [6]1 000 | [6]-0.8 | [6]23.3 | [6]13.6 | [6]9.1 | [6]7.1 | [6]5.8 | [6]10.3 | [6]15.2 | 16 360 | 236 | 1 052 | 31 937 | 19.0 |
| Bland | 112 | -0.3 | D | 35.8 | D | D | D | 11.2 | 26.2 | 1 855 | 272 | 132 | 3 265 | 3.3 |
| Botetourt | 528 | -0.4 | 33.4 | 22.6 | 5.0 | D | 3.0 | 5.9 | 14.1 | 7 575 | 230 | 462 | 14 562 | 15.8 |
| Brunswick | 195 | 3.3 | D | 7.2 | D | 4.4 | 2.7 | D | 27.0 | 4 110 | 239 | 702 | 8 166 | 8.3 |
| Buchanan | 575 | -0.2 | 55.8 | 4.3 | 2.8 | 3.7 | 1.8 | 5.1 | 13.7 | 8 915 | 378 | 1 842 | 11 576 | -2.6 |
| Buckingham | 187 | 0.3 | D | 3.0 | 4.0 | 6.1 | 2.2 | 11.1 | 36.1 | 3 445 | 199 | 502 | 7 244 | 15.2 |
| Campbell | [7]3 773 | [7]0.0 | [7]D | [7]21.7 | [7]12.0 | [7]6.8 | [7]6.6 | [7]15.0 | [7]10.8 | 12 915 | 235 | 1 309 | 24 769 | 12.1 |
| Caroline | 341 | 2.8 | D | 4.2 | D | 4.1 | 2.4 | D | 31.6 | 5 360 | 187 | 457 | 11 729 | 31.9 |
| Carroll | [8]544 | [8]-0.2 | [8]D | [8]17.6 | [8]D | [8]11.6 | [8]2.8 | [8]D | [8]21.9 | 8 350 | 279 | 788 | 16 569 | 12.9 |
| Charles City | 93 | 5.8 | D | 13.4 | D | 3.3 | D | 1.9 | 18.0 | 1 710 | 236 | 157 | 3 229 | 11.5 |
| Charlotte | 137 | 5.3 | D | 12.3 | D | 5.9 | D | D | 31.6 | 3 615 | 289 | 611 | 6 273 | 9.4 |
| Chesterfield | 7 611 | 0.0 | D | 10.6 | 10.7 | 7.6 | 9.3 | 10.3 | 17.4 | 49 335 | 154 | 3 926 | 122 555 | 25.5 |
| Clarke | 232 | -1.7 | D | 14.3 | 13.1 | 4.6 | 4.3 | 6.4 | 16.9 | 2 705 | 190 | 143 | 6 235 | 15.7 |
| Craig | 37 | -0.7 | D | D | D | 8.0 | 7.7 | 8.5 | 31.7 | 1 380 | 271 | 120 | 2 809 | 10.0 |
| Culpeper | 860 | 0.4 | 18.0 | 8.3 | 10.7 | 8.9 | 3.5 | 14.3 | 22.3 | 8 185 | 172 | 775 | 17 657 | 37.2 |
| Cumberland | 66 | 14.3 | 16.5 | 8.1 | D | 6.6 | D | D | 33.7 | 2 320 | 233 | 299 | 4 626 | 13.2 |
| Dickenson | 223 | -0.9 | 48.6 | 1.4 | D | 5.8 | D | D | 20.9 | 5 500 | 349 | 1 082 | 7 579 | -1.4 |
| Dinwiddie | [9]1 618 | [9]0.4 | [9]D | [9]12.8 | [9]D | [9]9.8 | [9]D | [9]D | [9]25.9 | 5 780 | 207 | 793 | 11 422 | 17.7 |
| Essex | 182 | 5.7 | 14.1 | 9.9 | 3.5 | 13.5 | 8.5 | D | 15.8 | 2 865 | 256 | 297 | 5 757 | 16.9 |
| Fairfax | [10]70 297 | [10]0.0 | [10]5.3 | [10]1.1 | [10]41.5 | [10]3.7 | [10]7.2 | [10]5.9 | [10]15.6 | 108 550 | 99 | 10 492 | 407 998 | 13.5 |
| Fauquier | 1 467 | -0.3 | D | 3.3 | 16.3 | 7.6 | 6.4 | 10.5 | 21.5 | 10 210 | 155 | 541 | 25 600 | 21.5 |
| Floyd | 147 | 2.4 | D | 11.3 | 6.7 | 7.3 | 5.2 | D | 21.4 | 3 745 | 244 | 317 | 7 790 | 15.2 |
| Fluvanna | 232 | -0.1 | D | 1.8 | 4.5 | 4.0 | 2.3 | D | 32.0 | 5 170 | 198 | 260 | 10 383 | 29.5 |
| Franklin | 614 | 1.9 | 27.8 | 17.9 | 3.6 | 9.7 | 3.6 | D | 18.6 | 14 040 | 249 | 1 177 | 29 315 | 29.1 |
| Frederick | [11]2 972 | [11]0.0 | [11]D | [11]15.5 | [11]D | [11]9.2 | [11]4.3 | [11]18.8 | [11]18.7 | 13 415 | 168 | 895 | 31 346 | 34.4 |
| Giles | 267 | -0.7 | 41.8 | 31.9 | 8.2 | 7.7 | 2.1 | D | 14.8 | 4 795 | 280 | 562 | 8 319 | 7.6 |
| Gloucester | 442 | 1.3 | D | 2.3 | 4.9 | 12.6 | 4.6 | 13.7 | 28.5 | 7 610 | 206 | 618 | 15 852 | 9.4 |
| Goochland | 1 106 | -0.1 | D | 2.5 | 5.0 | 2.1 | 2.8 | D | 6.5 | 4 525 | 207 | 212 | 8 618 | 31.5 |
| Grayson | 104 | 0.0 | D | 16.9 | 1.4 | 5.4 | 10.3 | D | 31.0 | 4 890 | 319 | 491 | 9 156 | 0.4 |
| Greene | 192 | 0.8 | D | 2.7 | 18.4 | 11.0 | 2.0 | D | 23.2 | 3 280 | 176 | 246 | 7 509 | 25.4 |
| Greensville | [12]361 | [12]2.0 | [12]D | [12]24.1 | [12]D | [12]6.6 | [12]D | [12]15.5 | [12]26.5 | 2 595 | 214 | 409 | 4 090 | 8.6 |
| Halifax | 601 | 3.2 | D | 17.5 | 2.3 | 6.6 | 2.6 | D | 19.0 | 10 340 | 287 | 1 695 | 18 004 | 6.2 |
| Hanover | 2 619 | 0.4 | 19.0 | 7.0 | 6.9 | 9.0 | 4.3 | 13.1 | 11.4 | 17 735 | 177 | 773 | 38 360 | 19.1 |
| Henrico | 12 221 | 0.0 | D | 3.8 | 15.1 | 6.1 | 19.2 | 13.3 | 9.6 | 49 905 | 161 | 4 776 | 132 778 | 18.0 |
| Henry | [13]1 108 | [13]0.2 | [13]D | [13]20.6 | [13]D | [13]9.8 | [13]3.6 | [13]13.3 | [13]17.7 | 16 700 | 311 | 1 491 | 26 268 | 1.3 |
| Highland | 24 | -2.1 | 15.2 | 3.7 | D | 4.5 | D | 6.5 | 29.9 | 765 | 337 | 24 | 1 837 | 0.8 |
| Isle of Wight | 581 | 2.1 | D | 6.8 | D | 5.4 | 3.4 | D | 15.0 | 7 345 | 208 | 601 | 14 633 | 21.3 |
| James City | [14]2 176 | [14]0.0 | [14]D | [14]D | [14]D | [14]6.7 | [14]D | [14]D | [14]25.0 | 16 430 | 241 | 496 | 29 797 | 43.4 |
| King and Queen | 87 | 9.0 | D | 8.3 | D | 4.1 | D | D | 27.0 | 1 675 | 239 | 148 | 3 414 | 13.6 |
| King George | 1 158 | 0.0 | 3.0 | 0.2 | 21.8 | 1.4 | 1.2 | D | 63.1 | 3 015 | 125 | 234 | 9 477 | 39.0 |
| King William | 194 | 5.5 | D | 33.3 | D | 5.6 | 3.5 | D | 20.6 | 3 080 | 193 | 222 | 6 522 | 25.7 |
| Lancaster | 232 | 0.4 | D | 2.0 | 9.5 | 10.2 | 9.7 | 22.4 | 11.9 | 4 250 | 377 | 274 | 7 402 | 13.9 |
| Lee | 298 | -0.4 | 19.3 | 1.5 | 1.8 | 8.5 | 2.7 | D | 33.2 | 7 095 | 282 | 1 868 | 11 745 | 5.9 |
| Loudoun | 11 311 | 0.0 | D | 4.2 | 30.9 | 5.4 | 4.4 | 5.8 | 14.8 | 24 080 | 74 | 1 685 | 109 442 | 76.1 |

1. Includes mining, construction, and manufacturing. 2. Per 1,000 resident population enumerated in the 2010 census. 3. Charlottesville city is included with Albemarle county. 4. Covington city is included with Alleghany county. 5. Staunton and Waynesboro cities are included with Augusta county. 6. Bedford city is included with Bedford county. 7. Lynchburg city is included with Campbell county. 8. Galax city is included with Carroll county. 9. Petersburg and Colonial Heights cities are included with Dinwiddie county. 10. Fairfax city and Falls Church city are included with Fairfax county. 11. Winchester city is included with Frederick county. 12. Emporia city is included with Greensville county. 13. Martinsville city is included with Henry county. 14. Williamsburg city is included with James City county.

# Table B. States and Counties — Housing, Labor Force, and Employment

| STATE County | Housing units, 2007–2011 | | | | | | | | Civilian labor force, 2012 | | Unemployment | | Civilian employment,[6] 2007–2011 | | |
|---|---|---|---|---|---|---|---|---|---|---|---|---|---|---|---|
| | Occupied units | | | | | | | | | | | | Percent | | |
| | | | Owner-occupied | | | Renter-occupied | | | | | | | | | |
| | | | | Median owner cost as a percent of income | | | | | | | | | | | Con-struction, produc-tion, and mainte-nance occu-pations |
| | Total | Percent | Median value[1] | With a mort-gage | Without a mort-gage[2] | Median rent[3] | Median rent as a per-cent of income | Sub-stand-ard units[4] (percent) | Total | Percent change, 2011–2012 | Total | Rate[5] | Total | Manage-ment, business, science and arts | |
| | 89 | 90 | 91 | 92 | 93 | 94 | 95 | 96 | 97 | 98 | 99 | 100 | 101 | 102 | 103 |
| **VERMONT—Cont'd** | | | | | | | | | | | | | | | |
| Chittenden | 61 989 | 65.9 | 263 200 | 25.5 | 15.0 | 1 005 | 33.1 | 1.5 | 92 944 | 0.0 | 3 681 | 4.0 | 86 706 | 45.0 | 14.2 |
| Essex | 2 808 | 83.2 | 126 000 | 26.7 | 16.8 | 629 | 37.0 | 1.5 | 3 045 | -3.1 | 220 | 7.2 | 2 931 | 27.6 | 34.7 |
| Franklin | 18 561 | 75.0 | 205 700 | 26.1 | 15.7 | 866 | 31.6 | 1.7 | 26 387 | -0.4 | 1 240 | 4.7 | 24 977 | 32.5 | 28.6 |
| Grand Isle | 3 194 | 79.6 | 249 600 | 27.0 | 17.3 | 831 | 29.7 | 0.8 | 3 861 | -0.6 | 227 | 5.9 | 3 852 | 35.9 | 22.8 |
| Lamoille | 10 097 | 69.2 | 214 600 | 26.9 | 16.7 | 930 | 31.8 | 2.3 | 15 971 | 0.4 | 896 | 5.6 | 12 960 | 38.0 | 21.2 |
| Orange | 11 805 | 81.7 | 182 600 | 24.8 | 15.8 | 778 | 31.4 | 2.8 | 16 068 | -1.3 | 786 | 4.9 | 15 344 | 37.7 | 23.7 |
| Orleans | 10 745 | 76.1 | 153 000 | 26.0 | 18.3 | 671 | 33.2 | 2.0 | 15 187 | 1.9 | 1 108 | 7.3 | 12 326 | 30.4 | 30.5 |
| Rutland | 26 108 | 70.4 | 175 200 | 25.1 | 17.5 | 767 | 29.6 | 1.6 | 34 511 | -1.4 | 2 086 | 6.0 | 30 968 | 34.8 | 25.0 |
| Washington | 24 728 | 72.8 | 203 100 | 25.1 | 16.7 | 802 | 27.8 | 2.2 | 34 511 | -0.4 | 1 658 | 4.8 | 31 918 | 45.3 | 17.4 |
| Windham | 19 527 | 70.2 | 206 400 | 27.3 | 17.0 | 749 | 28.3 | 2.1 | 25 415 | 0.0 | 1 279 | 5.0 | 23 244 | 38.6 | 23.4 |
| Windsor | 24 863 | 71.6 | 213 500 | 26.0 | 17.7 | 842 | 30.0 | 2.7 | 31 805 | -2.0 | 1 435 | 4.5 | 29 079 | 40.2 | 21.4 |
| **VIRGINIA** | 2 991 025 | 68.4 | 254 600 | 24.5 | 11.0 | 1 024 | 29.6 | 2.3 | 4 209 532 | 0.3 | 247 036 | 5.9 | 3 843 773 | 41.6 | 19.1 |
| Accomack | 13 757 | 74.1 | 153 400 | 24.3 | 11.4 | 722 | 26.0 | 5.2 | 18 215 | -2.1 | 1 257 | 6.9 | 14 878 | 30.4 | 31.9 |
| Albemarle | 37 398 | 66.1 | 350 400 | 23.1 | 10.5 | 1 071 | 29.6 | 1.4 | 54 473 | -0.1 | 2 601 | 4.8 | 47 759 | 52.4 | 13.0 |
| Alleghany | 6 935 | 81.2 | 112 700 | 19.5 | 11.0 | 512 | 28.4 | 1.5 | 7 011 | 0.0 | 520 | 7.4 | 7 199 | 28.6 | 32.4 |
| Amelia | 5 001 | 81.0 | 198 600 | 25.1 | 12.1 | 828 | 24.6 | 1.1 | 6 553 | 0.2 | 375 | 5.7 | 5 490 | 29.5 | 31.9 |
| Amherst | 12 693 | 75.9 | 149 200 | 22.9 | 9.9 | 606 | 23.9 | 0.7 | 14 838 | -0.6 | 1 020 | 6.9 | 15 259 | 29.2 | 27.8 |
| Appomattox | 5 857 | 75.4 | 140 000 | 22.6 | 9.9 | 526 | 26.6 | 0.5 | 7 094 | -0.4 | 512 | 7.2 | 6 672 | 26.1 | 34.5 |
| Arlington | 92 436 | 46.6 | 575 600 | 23.2 | 11.1 | 1 604 | 25.8 | 2.6 | 135 845 | 0.9 | 4 921 | 3.6 | 130 305 | 67.2 | 6.6 |
| Augusta | 28 021 | 81.4 | 194 100 | 23.5 | 10.3 | 683 | 26.8 | 1.7 | 37 823 | -0.4 | 2 089 | 5.5 | 34 343 | 28.6 | 31.1 |
| Bath | 1 926 | 84.8 | 137 100 | 20.4 | 10.3 | 937 | 24.1 | 2.1 | 2 788 | 2.3 | 144 | 5.2 | 2 334 | 16.5 | 37.4 |
| Bedford | 26 979 | 84.2 | 193 200 | 22.9 | 9.9 | 688 | 28.7 | 1.3 | 34 705 | -0.5 | 2 028 | 5.8 | 33 073 | 34.5 | 26.3 |
| Bland | 2 663 | 83.9 | 90 600 | 21.9 | 9.9 | 485 | 19.0 | 2.3 | 3 418 | 0.5 | 200 | 5.9 | 2 788 | 26.5 | 32.0 |
| Botetourt | 12 789 | 87.8 | 208 800 | 22.2 | 9.9 | 746 | 23.1 | 2.4 | 17 520 | 0.7 | 943 | 5.4 | 16 652 | 35.3 | 23.3 |
| Brunswick | 6 126 | 70.4 | 101 400 | 23.8 | 11.6 | 602 | 33.8 | 1.7 | 6 605 | -1.8 | 697 | 10.6 | 6 220 | 22.4 | 30.7 |
| Buchanan | 9 135 | 78.7 | 70 300 | 19.5 | 9.9 | 569 | 39.8 | 1.7 | 9 575 | 2.6 | 748 | 7.8 | 7 438 | 24.3 | 37.0 |
| Buckingham | 5 699 | 73.3 | 119 000 | 25.9 | 9.9 | 658 | 24.1 | 2.4 | 7 366 | -0.1 | 574 | 7.8 | 5 042 | 27.8 | 24.0 |
| Campbell | 21 610 | 75.5 | 144 200 | 21.8 | 9.9 | 598 | 28.2 | 1.9 | 26 956 | -0.9 | 1 630 | 6.0 | 25 523 | 30.9 | 29.6 |
| Caroline | 10 476 | 82.7 | 212 200 | 26.2 | 10.8 | 946 | 31.1 | 2.7 | 14 534 | 0.5 | 1 030 | 7.1 | 13 001 | 33.2 | 25.8 |
| Carroll | 12 556 | 77.5 | 98 300 | 23.4 | 9.9 | 526 | 29.6 | 1.6 | 13 696 | -2.4 | 1 145 | 8.4 | 12 888 | 21.0 | 38.3 |
| Charles City | 2 747 | 85.1 | 151 200 | 25.5 | 9.9 | 807 | 28.7 | 2.1 | 3 843 | 0.8 | 297 | 7.7 | 3 429 | 22.2 | 38.5 |
| Charlotte | 4 534 | 77.5 | 107 600 | 24.8 | 11.7 | 513 | 27.8 | 4.0 | 5 256 | -1.4 | 445 | 8.5 | 5 096 | 23.5 | 40.4 |
| Chesterfield | 112 895 | 78.1 | 237 600 | 23.7 | 9.9 | 1 036 | 29.1 | 1.4 | 175 379 | 1.0 | 9 950 | 5.7 | 158 358 | 41.7 | 17.4 |
| Clarke | 5 564 | 76.7 | 356 700 | 23.5 | 9.9 | 1 038 | 27.1 | 1.6 | 7 842 | 1.0 | 399 | 5.1 | 7 019 | 42.5 | 22.4 |
| Craig | 1 976 | 88.9 | 144 500 | 19.8 | 9.9 | 579 | 20.7 | 0.5 | 2 491 | 0.0 | 170 | 6.8 | 2 647 | 28.7 | 26.8 |
| Culpeper | 15 750 | 72.9 | 285 000 | 27.2 | 11.3 | 987 | 32.5 | 2.0 | 21 103 | 0.4 | 1 345 | 6.4 | 22 368 | 34.5 | 23.0 |
| Cumberland | 3 976 | 76.0 | 150 300 | 26.1 | 10.3 | 815 | 29.7 | 5.1 | 4 738 | 1.1 | 323 | 6.8 | 4 259 | 26.5 | 27.8 |
| Dickenson | 6 183 | 78.2 | 71 800 | 21.5 | 11.3 | 460 | 35.5 | 2.7 | 6 111 | -4.1 | 562 | 9.2 | 4 755 | 22.8 | 35.1 |
| Dinwiddie | 9 598 | 77.5 | 167 500 | 24.6 | 10.6 | 918 | 27.5 | 1.4 | 13 827 | 1.2 | 895 | 6.5 | 12 234 | 25.7 | 32.3 |
| Essex | 4 420 | 76.4 | 176 900 | 26.1 | 13.6 | 800 | 29.4 | 1.7 | 5 628 | -0.8 | 432 | 7.7 | 5 198 | 26.4 | 23.3 |
| Fairfax | 385 570 | 71.0 | 493 100 | 23.6 | 9.9 | 1 572 | 27.9 | 2.8 | 622 666 | 0.9 | 26 171 | 4.2 | 575 807 | 56.2 | 10.5 |
| Fauquier | 22 888 | 78.6 | 376 100 | 24.3 | 10.6 | 1 148 | 29.6 | 1.9 | 36 190 | 0.9 | 1 719 | 4.7 | 33 513 | 43.5 | 18.6 |
| Floyd | 6 148 | 77.4 | 147 900 | 23.8 | 9.9 | 554 | 21.6 | 2.8 | 7 427 | 0.2 | 460 | 6.2 | 7 237 | 31.4 | 29.0 |
| Fluvanna | 9 315 | 87.1 | 235 900 | 23.4 | 11.5 | 893 | 25.1 | 1.4 | 13 926 | -0.5 | 656 | 4.7 | 11 922 | 38.4 | 18.2 |
| Franklin | 23 581 | 79.3 | 163 800 | 24.1 | 9.9 | 632 | 23.8 | 2.3 | 28 432 | 0.2 | 1 687 | 5.9 | 25 163 | 29.8 | 30.2 |
| Frederick | 28 655 | 78.5 | 244 700 | 24.7 | 11.9 | 1 058 | 29.8 | 2.2 | 43 393 | 0.6 | 2 309 | 5.3 | 38 759 | 35.6 | 25.7 |
| Giles | 7 054 | 77.9 | 98 800 | 21.6 | 9.9 | 553 | 25.1 | 1.2 | 8 244 | 1.5 | 565 | 6.9 | 7 313 | 31.0 | 32.0 |
| Gloucester | 13 892 | 84.1 | 229 300 | 24.6 | 10.4 | 779 | 25.5 | 1.5 | 19 706 | -0.1 | 1 064 | 5.4 | 17 923 | 32.5 | 27.7 |
| Goochland | 7 822 | 92.8 | 354 700 | 24.0 | 9.9 | 1 027 | 26.2 | 0.6 | 11 664 | 1.0 | 569 | 4.9 | 9 338 | 45.8 | 14.1 |
| Grayson | 6 760 | 80.1 | 96 200 | 22.7 | 9.9 | 453 | 25.2 | 0.7 | 6 572 | -2.8 | 606 | 9.2 | 6 678 | 25.6 | 38.0 |
| Greene | 6 802 | 80.0 | 226 300 | 24.6 | 9.9 | 1 061 | 31.2 | 1.1 | 10 719 | -0.2 | 529 | 4.9 | 9 111 | 32.0 | 19.3 |
| Greensville | 3 264 | 72.3 | 104 300 | 20.1 | 13.8 | 717 | 28.9 | 3.7 | 4 210 | -1.6 | 391 | 9.3 | 3 920 | 22.0 | 34.6 |
| Halifax | 14 533 | 76.2 | 102 300 | 22.1 | 12.9 | 549 | 32.1 | 1.9 | 15 713 | -1.8 | 1 483 | 9.4 | 13 987 | 29.1 | 31.8 |
| Hanover | 36 489 | 83.8 | 280 000 | 23.1 | 10.8 | 1 016 | 27.9 | 0.8 | 54 951 | 1.2 | 3 029 | 5.5 | 51 526 | 44.3 | 17.4 |
| Henrico | 122 919 | 66.3 | 229 500 | 24.3 | 10.7 | 971 | 29.4 | 1.6 | 172 220 | 1.0 | 9 668 | 5.6 | 156 461 | 42.0 | 15.6 |
| Henry | 22 871 | 74.5 | 93 600 | 23.0 | 11.0 | 543 | 28.7 | 3.3 | 23 305 | -2.2 | 2 317 | 9.9 | 22 341 | 24.5 | 34.8 |
| Highland | 1 110 | 80.2 | 181 900 | 31.0 | 9.9 | 561 | 28.1 | 0.3 | 1 139 | 1.3 | 70 | 6.1 | 1 087 | 33.5 | 33.7 |
| Isle of Wight | 13 528 | 81.2 | 257 000 | 24.2 | 10.8 | 758 | 28.7 | 2.6 | 18 746 | -0.3 | 1 119 | 6.0 | 17 136 | 36.9 | 26.3 |
| James City | 26 356 | 75.9 | 347 600 | 24.2 | 9.9 | 1 128 | 29.2 | 0.7 | 34 794 | 0.2 | 1 765 | 5.1 | 30 811 | 46.9 | 12.1 |
| King and Queen | 2 891 | 80.4 | 159 900 | 26.0 | 9.9 | 824 | 21.1 | 0.7 | 3 361 | 0.7 | 228 | 6.8 | 3 257 | 19.2 | 41.4 |
| King George | 8 200 | 74.8 | 289 800 | 23.1 | 9.9 | 1 002 | 26.1 | 2.5 | 10 452 | -1.1 | 736 | 7.0 | 10 979 | 44.3 | 19.2 |
| King William | 5 985 | 83.2 | 207 300 | 24.0 | 9.9 | 852 | 27.7 | 0.8 | 8 580 | 1.2 | 539 | 6.3 | 7 875 | 25.3 | 34.9 |
| Lancaster | 5 570 | 77.2 | 254 300 | 27.3 | 11.5 | 817 | 27.6 | 2.9 | 5 353 | -1.7 | 438 | 8.2 | 5 231 | 30.0 | 24.2 |
| Lee | 10 001 | 75.0 | 77 900 | 23.0 | 9.9 | 453 | 32.5 | 3.8 | 9 732 | -2.0 | 811 | 8.3 | 9 038 | 26.7 | 29.8 |
| Loudoun | 99 761 | 79.2 | 472 000 | 26.1 | 10.6 | 1 603 | 29.1 | 2.1 | 188 048 | 1.0 | 7 852 | 4.2 | 161 452 | 56.0 | 10.2 |

1. Specified owner-occupied units. 2. A value of 9.9 represents 9.9 percent or less. 3. Specified renter-occupied units. A value of 10.0 represents 10 percent or less. 4. Overcrowded or lacking complete plumbing facilities. 5. Percent of civilian labor force. 6. Persons 16 years old and over.

# Table B. States and Counties — Nonfarm Employment and Agriculture

| | Private nonfarm establishments, employment and payroll, 2011 | | | | | | | | Agriculture, 2007 | | | |
| | Employment | | | | | | Annual payroll | | Farms | | | |
| | | | | | | | | | | Percent with: | | |
| STATE County | Number of establishments | Total | Health care and social assistance | Manufacturing | Retail trade | Finance and insurance | Professional, scientific, and technical services | Total (mil dol) | Average per employee (dollars) | Number | Fewer than 50 acres | 500 acres or more | Farm operators whose principal occupation is farming (percent) |
|---|---|---|---|---|---|---|---|---|---|---|---|---|---|
| | 104 | 105 | 106 | 107 | 108 | 109 | 110 | 111 | 112 | 113 | 114 | 115 | 116 |
| **VERMONT—Cont'd** | | | | | | | | | | | | | |
| Chittenden | 5 431 | 84 605 | 14 603 | 10 368 | 12 464 | 3 329 | 9 207 | 3 822 | 45 178 | 591 | 43.8 | 6.1 | 45.9 |
| Essex | 122 | 503 | D | D | D | D | D | 14 | 27 742 | 94 | 13.8 | 25.5 | 55.3 |
| Franklin | 984 | 11 983 | 2 715 | 2 628 | 2 163 | 299 | 497 | 412 | 34 357 | 740 | 27.0 | 12.0 | 52.4 |
| Grand Isle | 180 | 636 | 53 | 48 | 156 | 16 | D | 21 | 33 046 | 114 | 34.2 | 6.1 | 52.6 |
| Lamoille | 969 | 10 183 | 1 475 | 430 | 1 599 | D | 357 | 293 | 28 799 | 300 | 31.3 | 7.3 | 43.3 |
| Orange | 776 | 5 991 | 1 348 | D | 1 037 | D | 342 | 210 | 35 004 | 683 | 30.9 | 5.1 | 45.7 |
| Orleans | 813 | 7 744 | 1 668 | D | 1 334 | 233 | 151 | 242 | 31 276 | 635 | 30.6 | 9.8 | 55.0 |
| Rutland | 2 215 | 24 452 | 4 766 | 2 935 | 4 397 | 600 | 787 | 815 | 33 326 | 658 | 34.3 | 9.0 | 51.7 |
| Washington | 2 211 | 25 932 | 4 331 | 3 294 | 3 800 | 2 139 | 988 | 1 002 | 38 625 | 444 | 39.6 | 3.2 | 49.5 |
| Windham | 1 769 | 21 387 | 3 190 | 1 920 | 2 550 | 540 | 633 | 709 | 33 149 | 428 | 46.5 | 3.7 | 48.6 |
| Windsor | 2 077 | 28 136 | D | 1 868 | 2 824 | D | 1 004 | 713 | 25 359 | 767 | 43.0 | 3.5 | 47.7 |
| **VIRGINIA** | 191 063 | 3 029 030 | 392 532 | 230 162 | 407 160 | 148 964 | 420 887 | 145 346 | 47 984 | 47 383 | 39.5 | 7.0 | 42.8 |
| Accomack | 786 | 9 030 | 1 212 | D | 1 330 | 243 | 460 | 253 | 28 034 | 248 | 46.0 | 18.1 | 54.8 |
| Albemarle | 2 446 | 36 528 | 6 289 | 2 591 | 5 812 | D | 2 979 | 1 633 | 44 697 | 895 | 33.8 | 7.7 | 41.6 |
| Alleghany | 231 | 2 284 | 807 | 302 | 266 | 53 | 26 | 70 | 30 779 | 209 | 32.5 | 3.8 | 39.2 |
| Amelia | 271 | 1 868 | D | 263 | 226 | D | 39 | 54 | 28 943 | 455 | 29.7 | 10.8 | 37.4 |
| Amherst | 591 | 6 632 | 689 | 1 271 | 1 123 | 128 | D | 199 | 29 941 | 424 | 31.4 | 9.4 | 42.2 |
| Appomattox | 282 | 2 355 | 436 | 118 | 651 | 87 | D | 54 | 22 827 | 323 | 18.3 | 9.3 | 44.9 |
| Arlington | 6 101 | 134 091 | 9 164 | 222 | 8 947 | 3 154 | 40 342 | 9 781 | 72 944 | 6 | 100.0 | 0.0 | 16.7 |
| Augusta | 1 373 | 18 789 | 3 661 | 4 549 | 2 148 | 313 | 381 | 721 | 38 380 | 1 729 | 44.9 | 6.9 | 49.4 |
| Bath | 128 | 1 827 | 152 | 42 | 78 | D | D | 54 | 29 435 | 120 | 30.8 | 20.0 | 49.2 |
| Bedford | 1 366 | 12 049 | 1 102 | 2 167 | 2 180 | 312 | 657 | 415 | 34 445 | 1 428 | 35.7 | 4.9 | 38.7 |
| Bland | 79 | 1 192 | D | 514 | 64 | D | D | 51 | 43 139 | 387 | 21.7 | 7.8 | 46.5 |
| Botetourt | 727 | 9 198 | 755 | 1 906 | 832 | 192 | 220 | 344 | 37 376 | 638 | 40.0 | 5.3 | 35.9 |
| Brunswick | 267 | 2 753 | 200 | 316 | 277 | 47 | D | 71 | 25 863 | 367 | 21.3 | 11.2 | 36.0 |
| Buchanan | 453 | 6 483 | 620 | 303 | 626 | D | 510 | 311 | 47 965 | 107 | 27.5 | 0.9 | 21.5 |
| Buckingham | 250 | 1 725 | D | 113 | 290 | D | D | 59 | 34 166 | 411 | 27.5 | 7.5 | 41.6 |
| Campbell | 1 130 | 13 668 | 940 | 3 124 | 1 708 | 411 | 789 | 520 | 38 067 | 722 | 25.1 | 8.4 | 35.6 |
| Caroline | 377 | 3 747 | D | 256 | 644 | 58 | 204 | 137 | 36 535 | 225 | 43.6 | 12.0 | 34.2 |
| Carroll | 399 | 4 374 | 651 | 966 | 803 | D | 161 | 109 | 25 031 | 1 001 | 39.1 | 3.9 | 41.4 |
| Charles City | 134 | 1 274 | D | D | 57 | D | 37 | 44 | 34 461 | 80 | 43.8 | 16.3 | 51.3 |
| Charlotte | 237 | 1 671 | 270 | 359 | 217 | D | 46 | 43 | 25 936 | 489 | 21.9 | 10.8 | 44.2 |
| Chesterfield | 6 658 | 95 418 | 10 888 | 8 799 | 16 225 | 6 208 | 6 426 | 3 920 | 41 087 | 220 | 57.3 | 3.2 | 44.5 |
| Clarke | 370 | 3 117 | 275 | D | 263 | D | 205 | 129 | 41 406 | 496 | 51.2 | 6.0 | 47.4 |
| Craig | 55 | 372 | D | 17 | 106 | 29 | 12 | 10 | 26 567 | 193 | 29.5 | 9.8 | 46.6 |
| Culpeper | 944 | 11 196 | 1 968 | 1 231 | 2 171 | 337 | 599 | 422 | 37 674 | 667 | 43.6 | 6.7 | 47.8 |
| Cumberland | 146 | 868 | 81 | D | 201 | D | D | 23 | 26 786 | 285 | 23.9 | 7.4 | 46.0 |
| Dickenson | 223 | 2 781 | 384 | D | 478 | 72 | 192 | 128 | 45 985 | 170 | 45.9 | 1.8 | 38.8 |
| Dinwiddie | 364 | 4 213 | 280 | 709 | 528 | 126 | 53 | 171 | 40 515 | 374 | 35.6 | 8.8 | 42.8 |
| Essex | 301 | 3 308 | 559 | 476 | 889 | 140 | 91 | 90 | 27 301 | 102 | 40.2 | 28.4 | 51.0 |
| Fairfax | 28 871 | 569 388 | 51 734 | 7 876 | 49 424 | 27 653 | 189 282 | 40 130 | 70 480 | 166 | 75.3 | 0.0 | 34.3 |
| Fauquier | 1 766 | 15 891 | 2 595 | 653 | 2 655 | 700 | 1 403 | 639 | 40 186 | 1 222 | 44.5 | 7.1 | 46.5 |
| Floyd | 302 | 1 973 | 234 | D | 356 | D | 52 | 48 | 24 158 | 864 | 33.6 | 5.1 | 46.9 |
| Fluvanna | 370 | 2 381 | 257 | D | 309 | 38 | D | 70 | 29 442 | 327 | 36.7 | 5.2 | 45.0 |
| Franklin | 1 121 | 10 865 | 1 221 | 2 167 | 1 930 | 314 | 281 | 320 | 29 447 | 1 043 | 31.4 | 7.0 | 46.4 |
| Frederick | 1 399 | 20 843 | 1 586 | 4 457 | 3 293 | D | 778 | 774 | 37 149 | 676 | 43.3 | 5.6 | 35.9 |
| Giles | 290 | 3 622 | 538 | 975 | 690 | 81 | D | 133 | 36 701 | 344 | 26.5 | 6.1 | 43.0 |
| Gloucester | 880 | 7 128 | 1 177 | 209 | 1 941 | 294 | 271 | 186 | 26 109 | 159 | 70.4 | 8.8 | 57.9 |
| Goochland | 594 | 11 469 | 576 | D | 505 | 4 785 | 312 | 789 | 68 795 | 379 | 55.7 | 6.1 | 36.9 |
| Grayson | 174 | 1 183 | 76 | 249 | 164 | D | 23 | 30 | 25 697 | 852 | 37.6 | 7.5 | 40.0 |
| Greene | 314 | 2 541 | D | D | 756 | D | 80 | 71 | 31 299 | 222 | 33.8 | 5.0 | 38.3 |
| Greensville | 107 | 2 291 | D | 823 | D | D | D | 71 | 30 904 | 143 | 27.3 | 18.2 | 37.1 |
| Halifax | 746 | 10 547 | 1 772 | 1 826 | 1 419 | 196 | 163 | 324 | 30 743 | 908 | 22.9 | 7.8 | 45.2 |
| Hanover | 2 994 | 39 163 | 4 715 | 3 048 | 5 887 | 634 | 1 289 | 1 394 | 35 591 | 625 | 51.8 | 6.7 | 41.9 |
| Henrico | 8 608 | 158 151 | 23 037 | 5 525 | 22 796 | 20 473 | 12 130 | 7 722 | 48 825 | 178 | 61.2 | 2.2 | 43.3 |
| Henry | 836 | 11 473 | 825 | 3 022 | 1 524 | 303 | 262 | 316 | 27 512 | 340 | 34.7 | 3.8 | 46.2 |
| Highland | 83 | 365 | D | D | 43 | D | D | 8 | 21 852 | 239 | 15.1 | 18.4 | 50.2 |
| Isle of Wight | 640 | 7 844 | 575 | D | 928 | 184 | 288 | 277 | 35 298 | 195 | 44.6 | 22.1 | 49.2 |
| James City | 1 626 | 22 857 | 2 459 | 1 722 | 3 647 | 605 | 1 377 | 761 | 33 315 | 74 | 67.6 | 1.4 | 51.4 |
| King and Queen | 99 | 1 009 | D | 46 | D | D | D | 47 | 46 358 | 153 | 24.2 | 19.0 | 42.5 |
| King George | 439 | 5 943 | 270 | D | 437 | D | 3 224 | 334 | 56 173 | 180 | 31.7 | 8.9 | 44.4 |
| King William | 317 | 2 750 | 316 | D | 443 | 92 | 144 | 109 | 39 771 | 136 | 40.4 | 14.0 | 41.9 |
| Lancaster | 500 | 4 145 | 1 063 | 57 | 779 | 318 | 302 | 132 | 31 897 | 64 | 56.3 | 14.1 | 53.1 |
| Lee | 279 | 3 383 | 743 | 131 | 889 | 197 | 50 | 92 | 27 211 | 1 044 | 34.8 | 2.1 | 39.8 |
| Loudoun | 8 191 | 122 154 | 9 048 | D | 17 377 | 3 771 | 16 789 | 6 828 | 55 894 | 1 427 | 68.9 | 3.9 | 44.0 |

# Table B. States and Counties — **Agriculture**

| STATE County | Land in farms — Acreage (1,000) | Percent change, 2002–2007 | Acres — Average size of farm | Total irrigated (1,000) | Total cropland (1,000) | Value of land and buildings (dollars) Average per farm | Average per acre | Value of machinery and equipment, average per farm (dollars) | Value of products sold Total (mil dol) | Average per farm (dollars) | Percent from: Crops | Livestock and poultry products | Percent of farms with sales of: $10,000 or more | $100,000 or more | Government payments Total ($1,000) | Percent of farms |
|---|---|---|---|---|---|---|---|---|---|---|---|---|---|---|---|---|
| | 117 | 118 | 119 | 120 | 121 | 122 | 123 | 124 | 125 | 126 | 127 | 128 | 129 | 130 | 131 | 132 |
| **VERMONT—Cont'd** | | | | | | | | | | | | | | | | |
| Chittenden | 83 | 7.8 | 141 | 0.4 | 31.2 | 535 965 | 3 799 | 59 871 | 33.7 | 56 958 | 41.0 | 59.0 | 37.9 | 9.8 | 200 | 10.5 |
| Essex | 27 | 35.0 | 284 | 0.0 | 11.6 | 443 431 | 1 559 | 98 230 | 12.1 | 129 222 | 8.3 | 91.7 | 40.4 | 25.5 | 111 | 28.7 |
| Franklin | 180 | -5.3 | 243 | 0.2 | 85.1 | 605 808 | 2 490 | 111 550 | 160.6 | 217 052 | 6.2 | 93.8 | 54.6 | 30.4 | 2 143 | 33.1 |
| Grand Isle | 17 | 6.3 | 150 | 0.0 | 11.3 | 541 859 | 3 604 | 78 410 | 13.4 | 117 463 | 10.2 | 89.8 | 46.5 | 13.2 | 220 | 30.7 |
| Lamoille | 50 | -7.4 | 166 | 0.1 | 17.3 | 517 751 | 3 122 | 72 059 | 21.6 | 71 980 | 34.0 | 66.0 | 39.3 | 15.0 | 326 | 21.7 |
| Orange | 102 | -7.3 | 149 | 0.2 | 35.6 | 440 724 | 2 961 | 59 124 | 43.3 | 63 385 | 21.4 | 78.6 | 37.5 | 13.0 | 516 | 17.7 |
| Orleans | 130 | -1.5 | 205 | 0.1 | 55.2 | 474 493 | 2 312 | 74 048 | 82.3 | 129 682 | 5.6 | 94.4 | 49.1 | 19.7 | 603 | 22.4 |
| Rutland | 131 | 8.3 | 198 | 0.3 | 46.3 | 495 992 | 2 499 | 69 361 | 35.3 | 53 626 | 24.7 | 75.3 | 40.1 | 14.6 | 571 | 20.5 |
| Washington | 61 | 13.0 | 137 | 0.2 | 20.7 | 475 291 | 3 458 | 63 371 | 21.5 | 48 448 | 24.0 | 76.0 | 36.3 | 7.2 | 302 | 10.4 |
| Windham | 51 | -17.7 | 119 | 0.3 | 15.0 | 439 951 | 3 709 | 50 866 | 21.4 | 50 018 | 39.7 | 60.3 | 29.2 | 9.1 | 157 | 8.6 |
| Windsor | 96 | 6.7 | 125 | 0.1 | 27.6 | 502 248 | 4 014 | 55 055 | 25.0 | 32 566 | 31.6 | 68.4 | 31.3 | 7.2 | 173 | 9.8 |
| **VIRGINIA** | 8 104 | -6.0 | 171 | 82.2 | 3 274.1 | 720 538 | 4 213 | 65 870 | 2 906.2 | 61 334 | 29.5 | 70.5 | 32.9 | 7.9 | 54 940 | 20.8 |
| Accomack | 94 | 3.3 | 378 | 6.5 | 76.6 | 1 143 944 | 3 026 | 138 683 | 153.0 | 617 096 | 34.7 | 65.3 | 66.5 | 43.5 | 1 618 | 42.3 |
| Albemarle | 158 | -10.7 | 177 | 1.0 | 46.2 | 1 029 626 | 5 821 | 59 279 | 24.2 | 27 010 | 40.1 | 59.9 | 29.1 | 3.8 | 225 | 7.9 |
| Alleghany | 29 | -12.1 | 138 | D | 8.0 | 392 728 | 2 842 | 46 550 | 2.1 | 10 092 | 13.4 | 86.6 | 17.2 | 0.5 | 34 | 12.4 |
| Amelia | 91 | 0.0 | 201 | 0.6 | 33.5 | 720 230 | 3 583 | 106 026 | 68.7 | 151 086 | 11.3 | 88.7 | 33.0 | 11.6 | 458 | 35.4 |
| Amherst | 88 | -12.0 | 209 | 0.1 | 21.0 | 638 897 | 3 063 | 53 647 | 7.6 | 18 030 | 17.8 | 82.2 | 32.3 | 3.1 | 89 | 14.9 |
| Appomattox | 76 | -10.6 | 235 | 0.0 | 26.9 | 655 944 | 2 792 | 64 148 | 7.5 | 23 099 | 16.3 | 83.7 | 39.6 | 4.6 | 209 | 27.9 |
| Arlington | 0 | NA | 6 | 0.0 | 0.0 | 355 896 | 59 316 | 16 833 | 0.0 | 3 431 | D | D | 16.7 | 0.0 | 0 | 0.0 |
| Augusta | 286 | -6.5 | 166 | 3.8 | 107.8 | 810 635 | 4 897 | 72 873 | 194.8 | 112 675 | 10.3 | 89.7 | 44.2 | 14.4 | 1 364 | 20.1 |
| Bath | 38 | -26.9 | 320 | 0.0 | 11.8 | 1 191 441 | 3 722 | 63 386 | 3.9 | 32 242 | 28.7 | 71.3 | 37.5 | 5.8 | 42 | 15.8 |
| Bedford | 212 | 6.5 | 149 | 0.6 | 68.9 | 702 581 | 4 727 | 60 495 | 23.6 | 16 560 | 16.5 | 83.5 | 28.7 | 3.2 | 342 | 11.9 |
| Bland | 81 | -13.8 | 209 | 0.0 | 19.6 | 614 260 | 2 943 | 63 023 | 8.6 | 22 186 | 4.9 | 95.1 | 38.0 | 2.8 | 68 | 21.7 |
| Botetourt | 88 | -9.3 | 138 | 0.1 | 27.7 | 584 921 | 4 245 | 56 887 | 13.5 | 21 234 | 18.4 | 81.6 | 24.5 | 3.4 | 241 | 12.2 |
| Brunswick | 87 | 10.1 | 236 | 1.3 | 26.8 | 589 501 | 2 495 | 54 693 | 12.1 | 33 023 | 57.9 | 42.1 | 24.3 | 5.4 | 1 300 | 47.4 |
| Buchanan | 9 | 0.0 | 87 | D | 2.0 | 234 924 | 2 694 | 29 908 | 0.4 | 3 392 | 28.9 | 71.1 | 9.3 | 0.0 | 4 | 3.7 |
| Buckingham | 77 | -4.9 | 188 | 0.0 | 28.7 | 579 314 | 3 080 | 62 002 | 32.6 | 79 359 | 4.3 | 95.7 | 34.8 | 9.7 | 311 | 24.1 |
| Campbell | 140 | 0.7 | 194 | 0.8 | 49.9 | 652 029 | 3 354 | 66 627 | 25.3 | 35 104 | 12.7 | 87.3 | 28.7 | 3.6 | 751 | 32.5 |
| Caroline | 56 | -5.1 | 247 | 2.1 | 36.0 | 1 150 906 | 4 662 | 109 969 | 10.8 | 47 822 | 76.4 | 23.6 | 28.0 | 10.7 | 627 | 27.6 |
| Carroll | 124 | 1.6 | 124 | 0.6 | 41.7 | 507 488 | 4 107 | 47 358 | 34.4 | 34 413 | 25.0 | 75.0 | 39.0 | 5.3 | 380 | 12.8 |
| Charles City | 27 | -6.9 | 344 | 0.7 | 18.4 | 1 238 678 | 3 605 | 104 058 | 10.5 | 131 610 | D | D | 37.5 | 13.8 | 458 | 17.5 |
| Charlotte | 126 | -6.0 | 257 | 0.7 | 40.7 | 684 892 | 2 668 | 62 044 | 19.4 | 39 645 | 34.4 | 65.6 | 34.6 | 7.6 | 578 | 31.3 |
| Chesterfield | 22 | -4.3 | 98 | 0.2 | 6.6 | 551 410 | 5 635 | 68 307 | 4.5 | 20 397 | 48.3 | 51.7 | 18.6 | 2.7 | 65 | 12.3 |
| Clarke | 68 | -8.1 | 137 | 0.5 | 32.5 | 934 785 | 6 827 | 66 704 | 21.9 | 44 156 | 23.9 | 76.1 | 27.8 | 7.1 | 350 | 12.5 |
| Craig | 42 | -12.5 | 216 | 0.0 | 11.1 | 765 895 | 3 551 | 68 201 | 5.5 | 28 530 | 8.7 | 91.3 | 39.4 | 4.1 | 82 | 16.6 |
| Culpeper | 111 | -11.2 | 167 | 1.3 | 56.1 | 990 792 | 5 934 | 73 158 | 27.1 | 40 685 | 47.2 | 52.8 | 31.9 | 6.1 | 376 | 17.4 |
| Cumberland | 57 | -9.5 | 199 | D | 17.1 | 778 053 | 3 903 | 61 355 | 42.0 | 147 222 | 4.6 | 95.4 | 33.3 | 11.9 | 216 | 30.9 |
| Dickenson | 14 | 16.7 | 84 | D | 3.1 | 269 312 | 3 192 | 34 795 | 0.6 | 3 645 | 23.9 | 76.1 | 12.4 | 0.0 | 2 | 3.5 |
| Dinwiddie | 79 | -14.1 | 211 | 1.9 | 35.3 | 670 930 | 3 183 | 66 683 | 12.6 | 33 663 | 65.6 | 34.4 | 25.9 | 6.1 | 1 688 | 42.2 |
| Essex | 53 | -8.6 | 523 | D | 38.3 | 1 696 251 | 3 243 | 148 984 | 9.9 | 96 717 | 93.6 | 6.4 | 40.2 | 23.5 | 808 | 53.9 |
| Fairfax | 7 | -30.0 | 42 | 0.0 | 2.9 | 543 876 | 12 841 | 27 898 | 2.0 | 12 006 | 85.9 | 14.1 | 22.9 | 0.6 | 12 | 9.0 |
| Fauquier | 222 | -6.7 | 182 | 0.9 | 85.1 | 1 052 419 | 5 780 | 73 883 | 48.0 | 39 264 | 21.3 | 78.7 | 30.6 | 5.0 | 628 | 11.5 |
| Floyd | 129 | -4.4 | 149 | 0.1 | 45.0 | 619 915 | 4 156 | 58 108 | 43.4 | 50 186 | 43.2 | 56.8 | 37.4 | 5.2 | 182 | 11.1 |
| Fluvanna | 49 | -18.3 | 149 | 0.3 | 18.1 | 743 771 | 4 975 | 64 086 | 5.6 | 17 110 | 47.5 | 52.5 | 23.9 | 1.8 | 79 | 11.6 |
| Franklin | 167 | -3.5 | 160 | 0.9 | 66.8 | 665 563 | 4 167 | 82 567 | 54.0 | 51 743 | 13.0 | 87.0 | 33.1 | 8.2 | 684 | 20.1 |
| Frederick | 98 | -13.3 | 145 | 0.3 | 37.9 | 849 880 | 5 846 | 65 281 | 28.0 | 41 356 | 71.1 | 28.9 | 25.1 | 5.0 | 228 | 7.2 |
| Giles | 65 | -4.4 | 190 | 0.0 | 16.0 | 595 734 | 3 129 | 53 207 | 5.0 | 14 626 | 15.6 | 84.4 | 33.4 | 2.3 | 78 | 11.6 |
| Gloucester | 23 | -11.5 | 144 | 0.1 | 16.4 | 811 941 | 5 623 | 77 321 | 9.0 | 56 298 | D | D | 31.4 | 13.2 | 318 | 19.5 |
| Goochland | 59 | 13.5 | 156 | 0.0 | 22.8 | 827 846 | 5 292 | 63 826 | 11.2 | 29 647 | 32.5 | 67.6 | 19.3 | 5.5 | 122 | 11.9 |
| Grayson | 137 | -9.3 | 161 | 0.1 | 40.3 | 740 517 | 4 614 | 59 445 | 23.4 | 27 452 | 15.3 | 84.7 | 36.0 | 4.2 | 274 | 17.0 |
| Greene | 31 | -6.1 | 140 | 0.2 | 12.6 | 915 588 | 6 554 | 69 142 | 7.7 | 34 669 | 22.4 | 77.6 | 38.7 | 4.1 | 61 | 25.7 |
| Greensville | 49 | 16.7 | 341 | D | 29.6 | 944 097 | 2 770 | 81 771 | 7.2 | 50 028 | 93.6 | 6.4 | 33.6 | 12.6 | 2 511 | 74.8 |
| Halifax | 194 | -12.6 | 213 | 1.5 | 70.6 | 590 848 | 2 770 | 49 469 | 29.3 | 32 227 | 45.9 | 54.1 | 27.9 | 5.3 | 1 039 | 43.0 |
| Hanover | 92 | -8.9 | 147 | 3.2 | 56.0 | 832 305 | 5 667 | 81 120 | 43.9 | 70 247 | 81.1 | 18.9 | 31.2 | 8.2 | 859 | 13.6 |
| Henrico | 20 | -28.6 | 113 | D | 12.2 | 612 368 | 5 424 | 47 849 | 8.5 | 47 653 | 96.5 | 3.5 | 26.4 | 5.1 | 85 | 10.7 |
| Henry | 51 | -3.8 | 149 | 0.5 | 15.3 | 466 656 | 3 125 | 42 383 | 11.0 | 32 228 | 11.0 | 89.0 | 17.4 | 2.1 | 125 | 10.3 |
| Highland | 77 | -19.8 | 321 | 0.0 | 12.6 | 974 901 | 3 035 | 55 259 | 13.1 | 54 921 | 1.8 | 98.2 | 55.6 | 8.8 | 48 | 25.9 |
| Isle of Wight | 73 | -16.1 | 377 | 0.7 | 50.6 | 1 191 659 | 3 163 | 141 306 | 23.0 | 118 020 | 60.0 | 40.0 | 49.2 | 22.6 | 2 808 | 53.8 |
| James City | 6 | -33.3 | 79 | 0.0 | 3.0 | 661 643 | 8 397 | 69 119 | 2.9 | 38 735 | 51.3 | 48.8 | 31.1 | 12.2 | 62 | 23.0 |
| King and Queen | 53 | -10.2 | 347 | D | 32.3 | 1 255 077 | 3 615 | 100 445 | 11.9 | 77 761 | 61.0 | 39.0 | 47.1 | 14.4 | 709 | 40.4 |
| King George | 37 | 15.6 | 204 | 0.7 | 15.4 | 856 220 | 4 197 | 69 653 | 4.5 | 24 781 | 84.6 | 15.4 | 36.7 | 3.3 | 389 | 39.4 |
| King William | 46 | -24.6 | 339 | 2.7 | 25.6 | 1 302 697 | 3 846 | 122 914 | 16.3 | 119 749 | 86.4 | 13.6 | 36.8 | 15.4 | 543 | 20.6 |
| Lancaster | 14 | 16.7 | 220 | D | 10.4 | 934 311 | 4 242 | 76 187 | 2.9 | 44 629 | 95.9 | 4.1 | 29.7 | 12.5 | 322 | 48.4 |
| Lee | 118 | -7.8 | 113 | 0.3 | 37.7 | 309 252 | 2 741 | 40 225 | 14.3 | 13 659 | 29.6 | 70.4 | 26.3 | 1.8 | 408 | 30.7 |
| Loudoun | 142 | -13.9 | 100 | 3.5 | 73.6 | 737 428 | 7 387 | 53 042 | 33.8 | 23 691 | 57.7 | 42.3 | 22.9 | 4.1 | 277 | 6.9 |

# Table B. States and Counties — Water Use, Wholesale Trade, Retail Trade, and Real Estate

| STATE County | Water use, 2005 | | Wholesale trade,[1] 2007 | | | | Retail trade,[2] 2007 | | | | Real estate and rental and leasing,[2] 2007 | | | |
|---|---|---|---|---|---|---|---|---|---|---|---|---|---|---|
| | Total water withdrawn (mil gal/day) | Gallons withdrawn per person | Number of establishments | Number of employees | Sales (mil dol) | Annual payroll (mil dol) | Number of establishments | Number of employees | Sales (mil dol) | Annual payroll (mil dol) | Number of establishments | Number of employees | Receipts (mil dol) | Annual payroll (mil dol) |
| | 133 | 134 | 135 | 136 | 137 | 138 | 139 | 140 | 141 | 142 | 143 | 144 | 145 | 146 |
| VERMONT—Cont'd | | | | | | | | | | | | | | |
| Chittenden | 19.0 | 127 | 260 | 3 812 | 2 392.5 | 192.8 | 907 | 12 646 | 2 740.9 | 292.5 | 244 | 1 548 | 256.4 | 46.4 |
| Essex | 2.3 | 352 | 2 | D | D | D | 19 | 86 | 15.0 | 1.0 | 1 | D | D | D |
| Franklin | 8.0 | 168 | 42 | 667 | 413.3 | 23.2 | 222 | 2 022 | 545.3 | 42.6 | 30 | 111 | 10.1 | 2.0 |
| Grand Isle | 5.1 | 668 | 6 | 15 | 9.1 | 0.3 | 32 | 176 | 39.5 | 3.4 | 6 | 15 | 2.0 | 0.4 |
| Lamoille | 2.9 | 118 | 28 | D | D | D | 185 | 1 532 | 313.5 | 32.2 | 35 | 106 | 24.4 | 4.2 |
| Orange | 4.5 | 155 | 25 | D | D | D | 115 | 1 019 | 237.2 | 22.3 | 23 | D | D | D |
| Orleans | 4.5 | 161 | 31 | 299 | 73.4 | 9.4 | 157 | 1 351 | 324.1 | 31.3 | 23 | 89 | 12.7 | 2.3 |
| Rutland | 10.8 | 169 | 79 | 800 | 267.6 | 29.2 | 450 | 4 556 | 1 084.9 | 103.3 | 80 | 303 | 33.4 | 6.9 |
| Washington | 7.2 | 121 | 88 | D | D | D | 390 | 3 974 | 946.6 | 95.2 | 68 | 242 | 27.4 | 6.4 |
| Windham | 426.8 | 9 669 | 52 | 1 541 | 867.1 | 63.9 | 300 | 2 896 | 660.7 | 69.0 | 71 | 246 | 28.4 | 5.7 |
| Windsor | 6.2 | 106 | 60 | 749 | 327.7 | 31.0 | 337 | 2 861 | 691.7 | 70.3 | 88 | D | D | D |
| VIRGINIA | 10 618.8 | 1 403 | 6 502 | 98 304 | 60 513.4 | 4 787.4 | 29 633 | 431 634 | 105 663.3 | 9 991.9 | 9 475 | 60 502 | 12 636.8 | 2 408.7 |
| Accomack | 11.6 | 293 | 30 | 135 | 59.4 | 4.4 | 184 | 1 288 | 298.0 | 25.6 | 37 | 126 | 15.6 | 2.8 |
| Albemarle | 15.5 | 170 | 72 | 1 329 | 530.6 | 68.3 | 367 | 6 496 | 1 689.3 | 168.6 | 163 | 1 023 | 136.3 | 29.6 |
| Alleghany | 47.2 | 2 825 | 4 | 26 | 2.2 | 0.6 | 50 | 597 | 123.1 | 11.5 | 6 | 17 | 1.7 | 0.3 |
| Amelia | 1.4 | 117 | 5 | 150 | 55.4 | 6.2 | 30 | 236 | 68.0 | 4.8 | 10 | 17 | 1.6 | 0.3 |
| Amherst | 19.1 | 595 | 14 | 306 | 161.9 | 10.1 | 104 | 1 319 | 311.8 | 26.7 | 21 | 52 | 5.2 | 0.9 |
| Appomattox | 2.3 | 168 | 8 | 70 | 16.8 | 2.7 | 61 | 529 | 107.2 | 9.7 | 11 | 35 | 5.7 | 0.7 |
| Arlington | 0.1 | 1 | 89 | 1 289 | 453.2 | 94.4 | 641 | 10 702 | 2 482.9 | 275.4 | 326 | 3 620 | 1 333.9 | 243.0 |
| Augusta | 44.1 | 633 | 45 | 899 | 306.3 | 32.9 | 205 | 2 310 | 636.3 | 51.5 | 58 | 178 | 26.9 | 4.1 |
| Bath | 259.2 | 52 508 | 3 | 6 | 1.5 | 0.1 | 25 | 123 | 21.0 | 1.6 | 10 | 43 | 8.0 | 1.8 |
| Bedford | 18.5 | 283 | 48 | 393 | 369.0 | 13.3 | 182 | 2 048 | 466.5 | 44.9 | 77 | 160 | 20.8 | 5.1 |
| Bland | 1.0 | 141 | 5 | D | D | D | 20 | 114 | 38.4 | 1.8 | 1 | D | D | D |
| Botetourt | 19.0 | 594 | 34 | D | D | D | 87 | 833 | 247.8 | 16.2 | 23 | D | D | D |
| Brunswick | 27.6 | 1 542 | 7 | 46 | 42.0 | 1.9 | 51 | 377 | 74.6 | 6.3 | 4 | 11 | 0.9 | 0.1 |
| Buchanan | 8.0 | 322 | 23 | 229 | 189.8 | 9.3 | 93 | 750 | 143.9 | 12.6 | 10 | 30 | 4.4 | 0.8 |
| Buckingham | 2.5 | 154 | 11 | 76 | 21.5 | 2.1 | 41 | 284 | 68.7 | 5.5 | 5 | 10 | 1.0 | 0.1 |
| Campbell | 10.7 | 203 | 40 | 584 | 249.4 | 23.3 | 217 | 2 060 | 511.8 | 43.0 | 58 | 151 | 19.2 | 2.9 |
| Caroline | 5.6 | 220 | 10 | 59 | 21.2 | 1.9 | 61 | 760 | 365.9 | 13.7 | 15 | 43 | 5.5 | 0.6 |
| Carroll | 3.1 | 105 | 19 | 113 | 33.6 | 2.4 | 97 | 775 | 203.0 | 13.7 | 18 | 43 | 3.7 | 1.0 |
| Charles City | 1.1 | 152 | 7 | D | D | D | 10 | 58 | 10.9 | 2.0 | 4 | 31 | 5.3 | 1.1 |
| Charlotte | 1.7 | 135 | 6 | 29 | 10.1 | 1.0 | 36 | 261 | 62.1 | 4.8 | 6 | 16 | 0.5 | 0.2 |
| Chesterfield | 1 016.6 | 3 519 | 297 | 3 719 | 1 561.2 | 189.2 | 987 | 19 112 | 4 615.9 | 423.1 | 327 | 1 563 | 307.5 | 58.4 |
| Clarke | 1.8 | 126 | 14 | D | D | D | 41 | 299 | 91.6 | 5.5 | 15 | 38 | 3.6 | 0.6 |
| Craig | 0.5 | 101 | 1 | D | D | D | 10 | 116 | 15.8 | 1.7 | 2 | D | D | D |
| Culpeper | 4.7 | 111 | 32 | D | D | D | 170 | 2 282 | 547.4 | 50.9 | 38 | D | D | D |
| Cumberland | 2.1 | 225 | 5 | D | D | D | 31 | 260 | 46.1 | 5.2 | 3 | 8 | 0.5 | 0.1 |
| Dickenson | 5.5 | 340 | 6 | 18 | 8.3 | 0.5 | 61 | 519 | 122.8 | 9.0 | 4 | 6 | 0.7 | 0.2 |
| Dinwiddie | 2.0 | 79 | 14 | 335 | 267.0 | 15.4 | 63 | 529 | 114.9 | 9.7 | 6 | 18 | 1.9 | 0.5 |
| Essex | 1.1 | 101 | 5 | 33 | 8.5 | 1.1 | 65 | 1 007 | 224.6 | 23.0 | 10 | 37 | 4.9 | 1.2 |
| Fairfax | 313.8 | 312 | 837 | 14 481 | 13 299.5 | 1 136.9 | 2 976 | 53 158 | 14 002.4 | 1 444.8 | 1 461 | 11 691 | 3 549.6 | 644.9 |
| Fauquier | 26.4 | 407 | 39 | D | D | D | 248 | 2 989 | 853.1 | 78.8 | 84 | 270 | 36.8 | 9.5 |
| Floyd | 1.9 | 126 | 9 | 29 | 25.9 | 1.0 | 46 | 355 | 72.4 | 6.3 | 5 | 15 | 2.9 | 0.2 |
| Fluvanna | 223.5 | 9 031 | 9 | 61 | 10.4 | 2.3 | 37 | 326 | 79.4 | 6.8 | 25 | 39 | 7.0 | 1.3 |
| Franklin | 5.2 | 103 | 42 | 558 | 473.6 | 29.6 | 204 | 2 047 | 444.5 | 43.4 | 75 | 215 | 27.2 | 5.7 |
| Frederick | 7.3 | 106 | 85 | 1 746 | 632.2 | 78.3 | 193 | 3 291 | 1 120.7 | 83.0 | 53 | D | D | D |
| Giles | 333.6 | 19 512 | 7 | 37 | 18.9 | 1.9 | 74 | 742 | 172.4 | 14.4 | 8 | 22 | 4.5 | 0.6 |
| Gloucester | 3.6 | 94 | 23 | D | D | D | 145 | 2 107 | 500.1 | 45.9 | 51 | 162 | 15.9 | 2.8 |
| Goochland | 2.8 | 143 | 31 | 215 | 97.4 | 9.3 | 64 | 593 | 184.0 | 15.3 | 22 | 117 | 14.5 | 4.2 |
| Grayson | 2.2 | 134 | 5 | D | D | D | 34 | 230 | 47.5 | 3.6 | 7 | 11 | 1.0 | 0.2 |
| Greene | 0.8 | 48 | 9 | 79 | 24.6 | 4.2 | 48 | 371 | 96.0 | 9.6 | 8 | 30 | 2.5 | 0.6 |
| Greensville | 4.6 | 410 | 4 | D | D | D | 27 | 187 | 101.9 | 3.1 | 2 | D | D | D |
| Halifax | 15.6 | 430 | 21 | 260 | 133.7 | 8.7 | 141 | 1 474 | 324.1 | 29.4 | 31 | 143 | 11.8 | 2.1 |
| Hanover | 155.3 | 1 594 | 232 | 4 834 | 3 405.9 | 219.4 | 373 | 5 829 | 1 706.4 | 150.8 | 137 | 579 | 114.8 | 20.2 |
| Henrico | 45.7 | 163 | 377 | 7 248 | 6 197.3 | 368.7 | 1 321 | 23 829 | 6 737.2 | 565.7 | 449 | 3 800 | 724.7 | 135.6 |
| Henry | 13.6 | 240 | 40 | 714 | 527.7 | 19.9 | 199 | 1 623 | 437.0 | 33.7 | 26 | 116 | 13.3 | 2.5 |
| Highland | 15.5 | 6 263 | 1 | D | D | D | 24 | 54 | 8.9 | 0.7 | 1 | D | D | D |
| Isle of Wight | 97.7 | 2 925 | 20 | 192 | 148.2 | 9.6 | 109 | 1 034 | 212.7 | 19.0 | 37 | 118 | 16.5 | 3.1 |
| James City | 13.1 | 227 | 40 | 422 | 140.1 | 17.4 | 297 | 3 636 | 658.8 | 77.2 | 94 | 554 | 101.2 | 19.1 |
| King and Queen | 0.8 | 110 | 4 | 32 | 22.0 | 1.3 | 11 | 36 | 16.2 | 0.8 | 3 | 3 | 0.4 | 0.1 |
| King George | 5.9 | 285 | 9 | 43 | 8.2 | 1.3 | 50 | 464 | 155.0 | 10.4 | 19 | 69 | 11.2 | 1.5 |
| King William | 65.6 | 4 450 | 12 | 57 | 30.7 | 2.0 | 51 | 497 | 126.0 | 10.0 | 15 | 50 | 4.9 | 0.9 |
| Lancaster | 1.1 | 91 | 17 | 116 | 49.3 | 3.1 | 97 | 782 | 166.6 | 16.7 | 27 | 52 | 8.2 | 2.3 |
| Lee | 3.8 | 160 | 13 | 60 | 27.5 | 1.4 | 82 | 905 | 171.6 | 15.2 | 12 | 19 | 2.2 | 0.4 |
| Loudoun | 10.7 | 42 | 227 | 2 901 | 1 492.0 | 175.2 | 954 | 16 811 | 4 469.5 | 432.0 | 328 | 1 621 | 401.1 | 67.2 |

1. Merchant wholesalers, except manufacturers' sales branches and offices.  2. Employer establishments.

| STATE County | Professional, scientific, and technical services,[1] 2007 | | | | Manufacturing, 2007 | | | | Accommodation and food services, 2007 | | | |
|---|---|---|---|---|---|---|---|---|---|---|---|---|
| | Number of establishments | Number of employees | Receipts (mil dol) | Annual payroll (mil dol) | Number of establishments | Number of employees | Receipts (mil dol) | Annual payroll (mil dol) | Number of establishments | Number of employees | Sales (mil dol) | Annual payroll (mil dol) |
| | 147 | 148 | 149 | 150 | 151 | 152 | 153 | 154 | 155 | 156 | 157 | 158 |
| VERMONT—Cont'd | | | | | | | | | | | | |
| Chittenden | 713 | 5 579 | 920.1 | 347.2 | 207 | 12 224 | 4 823.5 | 713.8 | 421 | 7 330 | 360.8 | 104.9 |
| Essex | 5 | D | D | D | 12 | 574 | 62.8 | 17.7 | 18 | 128 | 3.1 | 1.0 |
| Franklin | 60 | 637 | 39.6 | 15.7 | 54 | D | D | 111.2 | 104 | 903 | 39.6 | 11.4 |
| Grand Isle | 23 | 38 | 4.0 | 1.4 | NA | NA | NA | NA | 23 | 52 | 6.5 | 1.8 |
| Lamoille | 96 | 367 | 42.8 | 16.8 | NA | NA | NA | NA | 113 | 3 837 | 174.2 | 59.5 |
| Orange | 79 | D | D | D | 56 | 846 | 161.9 | 29.2 | 54 | 556 | 26.2 | 8.1 |
| Orleans | 50 | D | D | D | 36 | 1 199 | D | D | 68 | 1 002 | 36.3 | 11.3 |
| Rutland | 185 | D | D | D | 111 | 3 885 | 640.8 | 178.5 | 235 | 3 190 | 124.4 | 37.1 |
| Washington | 244 | D | D | D | 131 | 2 690 | 1 011.9 | 103.5 | 172 | 2 907 | 119.0 | 38.2 |
| Windham | 140 | 667 | 65.4 | 25.1 | 111 | 2 163 | 375.1 | 89.2 | 232 | 3 861 | 138.4 | 47.5 |
| Windsor | 199 | D | D | D | 138 | 2 306 | 406.5 | 89.2 | 194 | 3 411 | 154.4 | 49.4 |
| VIRGINIA | 27 078 | 376 172 | 66 543.7 | 26 936.8 | 5 777 | 277 456 | 92 417.8 | 12 169.6 | 15 765 | 302 446 | 15 340.5 | 4 273.0 |
| Accomack | 71 | 955 | 187.0 | 50.7 | 28 | D | 526.2 | 67.4 | 105 | 1 005 | 48.1 | 13.0 |
| Albemarle | 288 | D | D | D | 64 | 1 487 | 307.1 | 60.2 | 148 | 2 454 | 120.2 | 36.1 |
| Alleghany | 12 | 26 | 3.4 | 0.4 | 10 | 642 | D | 21.5 | 22 | 302 | 11.0 | 3.5 |
| Amelia | 14 | 47 | 3.2 | 1.0 | NA | NA | NA | NA | 9 | 122 | 3.8 | 0.8 |
| Amherst | 37 | 153 | 11.1 | 3.8 | 41 | 1 573 | 554.2 | 68.2 | 40 | 583 | 23.8 | 6.6 |
| Appomattox | 15 | D | D | D | 15 | 572 | D | 16.0 | 15 | 195 | 7.3 | 1.9 |
| Arlington | 1 585 | 34 964 | 7 990.5 | 2 819.1 | NA | NA | NA | NA | 596 | 14 421 | 1 164.0 | 304.7 |
| Augusta | 71 | D | D | D | 68 | 4 655 | 1 582.6 | 195.5 | 80 | 1 271 | 57.1 | 14.5 |
| Bath | 11 | D | D | D | NA | NA | NA | NA | 17 | D | D | D |
| Bedford | 152 | 810 | 82.7 | 28.1 | 60 | 2 098 | 785.4 | 102.7 | 59 | 585 | 27.9 | 8.6 |
| Bland | 3 | D | D | D | 9 | 589 | 192.1 | 23.5 | 4 | D | D | D |
| Botetourt | 62 | 284 | 27.3 | 10.9 | 33 | 2 444 | 883.9 | D | 47 | D | D | D |
| Brunswick | 20 | 60 | 3.9 | 1.5 | 19 | 578 | 96.5 | 16.3 | 16 | 258 | 8.8 | 2.8 |
| Buchanan | 30 | 250 | 12.4 | 4.8 | NA | NA | NA | NA | 21 | 337 | 12.1 | 3.3 |
| Buckingham | 12 | 72 | 11.4 | 3.4 | NA | NA | NA | NA | 7 | D | D | D |
| Campbell | 80 | 713 | 79.1 | 39.0 | 67 | 3 798 | 1 527.6 | 170.8 | 57 | 901 | 32.7 | 9.0 |
| Caroline | 34 | 175 | 10.9 | 5.0 | NA | NA | NA | NA | 24 | 271 | 14.7 | 3.5 |
| Carroll | 27 | D | D | D | 22 | 1 190 | 236.8 | 27.7 | 37 | 532 | 23.3 | 5.2 |
| Charles City | 5 | 23 | 4.4 | 1.0 | NA | NA | NA | NA | 5 | D | D | D |
| Charlotte | 12 | D | D | D | 16 | 615 | 91.9 | 19.8 | 7 | 81 | 2.7 | 0.9 |
| Chesterfield | 758 | 7 220 | 726.3 | 357.6 | 189 | 10 511 | 3 850.0 | 574.4 | 510 | 10 924 | 491.5 | 133.5 |
| Clarke | 50 | D | D | D | 20 | 1 223 | 228.3 | 47.0 | 20 | 160 | 9.0 | 2.4 |
| Craig | 4 | D | D | D | NA | NA | NA | NA | 4 | D | D | D |
| Culpeper | 94 | D | D | D | 40 | D | D | D | 65 | 942 | 45.3 | 12.3 |
| Cumberland | 4 | D | D | D | NA | NA | NA | NA | 5 | 50 | 1.2 | 0.4 |
| Dickenson | 13 | D | D | D | NA | NA | NA | NA | 18 | 181 | 5.2 | 1.4 |
| Dinwiddie | 15 | 47 | 3.0 | 1.2 | 16 | 934 | 645.7 | 52.6 | 17 | 315 | 13.8 | 3.1 |
| Essex | 23 | D | D | D | 15 | 530 | 56.9 | 12.7 | 31 | 522 | 19.4 | 5.9 |
| Fairfax | 7 447 | 169 544 | 32 423.1 | 13 770.6 | 440 | 9 872 | 2 052.7 | 454.7 | 2 035 | 38 874 | 2 705.7 | 718.7 |
| Fauquier | 269 | D | D | D | 50 | 854 | 159.6 | 36.8 | 117 | 2 144 | 104.4 | 33.6 |
| Floyd | 22 | D | D | D | NA | NA | NA | NA | 23 | 209 | 6.6 | 2.0 |
| Fluvanna | 42 | 99 | 9.7 | 3.9 | NA | NA | NA | NA | 17 | 349 | 11.9 | 3.9 |
| Franklin | 93 | 286 | 21.4 | 8.0 | 59 | 3 462 | D | 118.9 | 68 | 961 | 40.3 | 10.8 |
| Frederick | 103 | D | D | D | 86 | 5 423 | 2 578.7 | 214.0 | 103 | 2 074 | 86.7 | 25.0 |
| Giles | 9 | D | D | D | 15 | 959 | D | 47.8 | 24 | 289 | 12.5 | 3.7 |
| Gloucester | 70 | D | D | D | NA | NA | NA | NA | 63 | 1 070 | 40.1 | 11.9 |
| Goochland | 68 | 233 | 26.8 | 11.5 | NA | NA | NA | NA | 36 | 280 | 15.8 | 4.8 |
| Grayson | 5 | D | D | D | 17 | 557 | 93.4 | 18.2 | 14 | D | D | D |
| Greene | 23 | D | D | D | NA | NA | NA | NA | 18 | 209 | 10.0 | 2.9 |
| Greensville | 1 | D | D | D | 7 | D | 248.7 | 29.9 | 15 | 243 | 14.1 | 3.3 |
| Halifax | 44 | D | D | D | 40 | 1 985 | 620.1 | 79.1 | 62 | 839 | 31.2 | 8.4 |
| Hanover | 284 | 1 672 | 216.1 | 84.1 | 143 | 3 702 | 926.3 | 149.8 | 170 | 2 915 | 137.0 | 39.1 |
| Henrico | 1 060 | D | D | D | 209 | 9 569 | 3 265.0 | 458.3 | 656 | 14 769 | 685.8 | 192.0 |
| Henry | 36 | D | D | D | 79 | 5 479 | 1 097.9 | 169.8 | 70 | 984 | 38.4 | 10.0 |
| Highland | 5 | D | D | D | NA | NA | NA | NA | 6 | D | D | D |
| Isle of Wight | 47 | 248 | 19.7 | 7.5 | 21 | D | D | D | 48 | 795 | 33.0 | 9.3 |
| James City | 226 | D | D | D | 34 | 2 364 | 1 567.2 | 117.0 | 118 | 3 273 | 164.4 | 47.8 |
| King and Queen | 6 | 19 | 1.4 | 0.5 | NA | NA | NA | NA | 2 | D | D | D |
| King George | 93 | D | D | D | NA | NA | NA | NA | 36 | 339 | 14.7 | 3.7 |
| King William | 27 | 155 | 11.2 | 4.5 | NA | NA | NA | NA | 15 | 216 | 7.5 | 1.9 |
| Lancaster | 59 | 242 | 23.7 | 9.5 | NA | NA | NA | NA | 43 | 461 | 16.0 | 4.9 |
| Lee | 19 | D | D | D | NA | NA | NA | NA | 19 | 336 | 8.6 | 2.3 |
| Loudoun | 1 765 | D | D | D | 157 | 5 266 | 1 400.2 | 322.6 | 526 | 10 275 | 610.2 | 173.3 |

1. Establishment subject to federal tax.

| STATE County | Health care and social assistance, 2007 | | | | Other services, 2007 | | | | Federal funds and grants, 2009–2010 Expenditures (mil dol) | | | |
|---|---|---|---|---|---|---|---|---|---|---|---|---|
| | | | | | | | | | | Direct payments for individuals[1] | | |
| | Number of establishments | Number of employees | Receipts (mil dol) | Annual payroll (mil dol) | Number of establishments | Number of employees | Receipts (mil dol) | Annual payroll (mil dol) | Total | Social Security and government retirement | Medicare | Food Stamps and Supplemental Security Income |
| | 159 | 160 | 161 | 162 | 163 | 164 | 165 | 166 | 167 | 168 | 169 | 170 |
| VERMONT—Cont'd | | | | | | | | | | | | |
| Chittenden | 558 | 13 272 | 1 316.5 | 514.9 | 402 | 2 035 | 174.5 | 54.8 | 1 877.5 | 365.3 | 135.3 | 36.7 |
| Essex | 10 | D | D | D | 8 | 39 | 6.0 | 0.5 | 66.0 | 28.4 | 10.3 | 3.1 |
| Franklin | 113 | 2 413 | 169.5 | 74.0 | 71 | 289 | 19.0 | 5.2 | 490.8 | 124.4 | 51.4 | 15.4 |
| Grand Isle | 12 | 69 | 2.9 | 1.2 | 12 | 15 | 2.2 | 0.5 | 46.5 | 24.3 | 7.9 | 2.3 |
| Lamoille | 81 | D | D | D | 75 | 317 | 125.7 | 7.8 | 194.2 | 97.6 | 26.4 | 8.1 |
| Orange | 76 | 1 188 | 89.8 | 41.5 | 56 | 219 | 23.4 | 5.7 | 221.2 | 89.9 | 32.8 | 10.1 |
| Orleans | 73 | 1 705 | 129.5 | 51.4 | 70 | 230 | 21.0 | 4.4 | 253.8 | 98.0 | 36.7 | 14.1 |
| Rutland | 226 | 4 434 | 370.4 | 155.8 | 176 | 773 | 60.8 | 16.3 | 688.9 | 234.2 | 100.4 | 27.0 |
| Washington | 236 | 4 379 | 318.6 | 143.2 | 226 | 1 030 | 120.0 | 32.5 | 1 251.8 | 192.5 | 73.3 | 19.7 |
| Windham | 197 | 2 850 | 214.3 | 93.1 | 129 | 576 | 55.2 | 14.0 | 365.5 | 140.4 | 61.8 | 15.9 |
| Windsor | 198 | 3 736 | 327.4 | 158.4 | 147 | 709 | 85.5 | 19.8 | 654.7 | 212.5 | 85.7 | 17.2 |
| VIRGINIA | 17 540 | 371 067 | 37 522.0 | 14 962.4 | 15 072 | 111 129 | 16 498.2 | 3 915.1 | 136 082.9 | 27 413.1 | 8 408.4 | 2 104.8 |
| Accomack | 60 | 1 229 | 63.6 | 26.3 | 60 | 368 | 25.8 | 8.0 | 495.5 | 140.2 | 64.8 | 17.1 |
| Albemarle | 262 | 4 140 | 493.7 | 194.5 | 144 | 1 431 | 299.4 | 59.9 | 658.3 | 196.0 | 90.9 | 10.2 |
| Alleghany | 45 | 864 | 82.1 | 28.9 | 19 | 89 | 7.3 | 1.6 | 100.4 | 41.3 | 23.2 | 5.2 |
| Amelia | 22 | 314 | 17.3 | 8.1 | 22 | 62 | 4.5 | 1.5 | 80.8 | 44.5 | 11.6 | 2.9 |
| Amherst | 42 | D | D | D | 63 | 166 | 12.4 | 3.3 | 204.7 | 109.7 | 34.8 | 9.1 |
| Appomattox | 22 | D | D | D | 17 | 56 | 4.2 | 1.1 | 92.4 | 47.1 | 14.9 | 5.0 |
| Arlington | 451 | 6 844 | 1 089.9 | 314.5 | 612 | 10 109 | 2 803.2 | 629.2 | 15 854.6 | 594.2 | 214.1 | 29.5 |
| Augusta | 103 | 3 817 | 394.1 | 139.2 | 85 | 479 | 39.7 | 12.1 | 315.4 | 170.4 | 60.5 | 8.4 |
| Bath | 7 | D | D | D | 7 | D | D | D | 46.3 | 22.4 | 12.9 | 0.9 |
| Bedford | 87 | D | D | D | 83 | 378 | 22.9 | 7.3 | 403.0 | 271.8 | 55.2 | 10.8 |
| Bland | 7 | 57 | 8.0 | 2.2 | 7 | 20 | 3.3 | 0.5 | 104.4 | 26.8 | 12.9 | 1.1 |
| Botetourt | 43 | D | D | D | 52 | D | D | D | 252.3 | 123.6 | 32.5 | 3.7 |
| Brunswick | 13 | 190 | 8.7 | 4.4 | 20 | D | D | D | 168.7 | 59.2 | 30.5 | 9.3 |
| Buchanan | 45 | 762 | 57.7 | 22.2 | 29 | 139 | 10.6 | 2.9 | 266.8 | 117.6 | 61.3 | 21.0 |
| Buckingham | 16 | 354 | 12.1 | 8.9 | 12 | 59 | 8.8 | 1.9 | 108.7 | 39.6 | 21.5 | 5.9 |
| Campbell | 76 | 913 | 40.8 | 18.5 | 84 | 428 | 34.3 | 9.7 | 378.9 | 160.1 | 43.6 | 19.0 |
| Caroline | 20 | 271 | 19.5 | 9.5 | 31 | 193 | 15.1 | 4.3 | 246.1 | 101.4 | 30.1 | 7.0 |
| Carroll | 35 | 586 | 30.9 | 13.7 | 26 | 76 | 8.1 | 2.2 | 190.8 | 86.9 | 40.3 | 7.9 |
| Charles City | 4 | D | D | D | 12 | 34 | 3.1 | 0.7 | 58.0 | 32.6 | 9.0 | 3.0 |
| Charlotte | 22 | 232 | 13.9 | 6.1 | 15 | 29 | 3.2 | 0.5 | 129.7 | 61.1 | 24.5 | 9.0 |
| Chesterfield | 668 | 9 348 | 867.4 | 385.7 | 471 | 3 356 | 329.6 | 81.4 | 1 303.1 | 660.8 | 141.6 | 47.4 |
| Clarke | 20 | D | D | D | 31 | 98 | 11.2 | 2.6 | 127.4 | 48.4 | 15.0 | 1.5 |
| Craig | 4 | D | D | D | 2 | D | D | D | 31.3 | 18.2 | 5.7 | 1.0 |
| Culpeper | 63 | 1 703 | 163.2 | 68.6 | 77 | 558 | 50.3 | 16.8 | 260.5 | 147.8 | 46.3 | 8.9 |
| Cumberland | 14 | D | D | D | 6 | 24 | 1.3 | 0.4 | 56.8 | 22.6 | 9.3 | 3.7 |
| Dickenson | 25 | 387 | 23.9 | 9.8 | 17 | D | D | D | 168.5 | 78.1 | 37.0 | 13.8 |
| Dinwiddie | 21 | 314 | 14.3 | 6.2 | 36 | 177 | 13.7 | 7.3 | 159.6 | 82.2 | 30.1 | 7.0 |
| Essex | 33 | 621 | 54.1 | 18.3 | 22 | D | D | D | 89.4 | 43.4 | 24.3 | 4.2 |
| Fairfax | 2 599 | 41 062 | 4 494.5 | 1 837.0 | 1 879 | 17 014 | 2 856.0 | 738.2 | 31 238.1 | 3 049.1 | 448.3 | 118.5 |
| Fauquier | 135 | 2 365 | 241.9 | 98.8 | 128 | 858 | 70.5 | 24.1 | 465.1 | 226.2 | 54.2 | 9.0 |
| Floyd | 18 | D | D | D | 21 | 65 | 6.3 | 1.5 | 102.2 | 49.0 | 19.4 | 4.0 |
| Fluvanna | 21 | D | D | D | 24 | D | D | D | 142.0 | 89.7 | 24.7 | 2.7 |
| Franklin | 62 | D | D | D | 94 | 282 | 22.8 | 5.7 | 302.4 | 169.8 | 53.8 | 12.1 |
| Frederick | 76 | 1 364 | 100.9 | 45.9 | 90 | 518 | 53.5 | 15.2 | 264.5 | 167.9 | 36.0 | 10.4 |
| Giles | 30 | 542 | 48.4 | 17.5 | 27 | D | D | D | 144.0 | 72.9 | 34.0 | 6.6 |
| Gloucester | 64 | 1 201 | 82.8 | 33.1 | 75 | 320 | 24.0 | 6.6 | 258.2 | 163.2 | 41.9 | 9.4 |
| Goochland | 33 | D | D | D | 38 | 378 | 38.0 | 17.6 | 113.7 | 60.2 | 16.1 | 2.9 |
| Grayson | 12 | D | D | D | 13 | D | D | D | 120.5 | 50.4 | 26.7 | 4.0 |
| Greene | 10 | D | D | D | 27 | D | D | D | 85.1 | 50.3 | 15.1 | 2.6 |
| Greensville | 3 | D | D | D | 6 | D | D | D | 41.6 | 13.7 | 6.2 | 3.2 |
| Halifax | 83 | 1 562 | 140.4 | 57.7 | 69 | 284 | 24.8 | 4.8 | 378.9 | 142.5 | 65.9 | 15.3 |
| Hanover | 218 | 4 557 | 531.6 | 184.8 | 253 | 1 493 | 138.0 | 43.1 | 897.8 | 333.5 | 93.6 | 12.8 |
| Henrico | 904 | 21 906 | 2 351.1 | 905.8 | 657 | 4 832 | 750.1 | 151.6 | 1 256.7 | 464.5 | 271.6 | 39.4 |
| Henry | 46 | 798 | 41.8 | 17.7 | 66 | 316 | 24.0 | 6.7 | 322.2 | 173.2 | 71.8 | 16.4 |
| Highland | 6 | D | D | D | 9 | D | D | D | 23.4 | 11.1 | 6.4 | 0.5 |
| Isle of Wight | 44 | 463 | 34.4 | 14.6 | 53 | 212 | 14.6 | 4.9 | 265.8 | 152.6 | 40.2 | 8.2 |
| James City | 151 | 2 000 | 194.7 | 75.0 | 98 | 475 | 33.2 | 10.5 | 222.0 | 161.5 | 22.4 | 6.5 |
| King and Queen | 5 | D | D | D | 8 | 13 | 1.5 | 0.3 | 51.5 | 25.7 | 10.4 | 2.1 |
| King George | 20 | 242 | 17.6 | 7.0 | 33 | 123 | 9.2 | 2.7 | 939.2 | 89.9 | 16.2 | 3.7 |
| King William | 23 | 307 | 16.4 | 7.9 | 37 | 110 | 11.0 | 2.6 | 94.3 | 48.6 | 18.9 | 2.4 |
| Lancaster | 41 | 1 063 | 84.9 | 37.9 | 44 | 169 | 12.6 | 4.1 | 170.6 | 82.8 | 33.5 | 4.1 |
| Lee | 33 | 640 | 53.1 | 21.8 | 21 | 78 | 5.8 | 1.5 | 505.4 | 93.7 | 58.5 | 23.5 |
| Loudoun | 596 | 7 622 | 813.8 | 330.8 | 480 | 3 824 | 485.0 | 126.6 | 4 776.5 | 600.3 | 73.9 | 14.6 |

1. State totals may include programs not allocated by county.

# Table B. States and Counties — Federal Funds, Residential Construction, and Local Government Finances

| STATE County | Federal funds and grants, 2009–2010 (cont.) Expenditures (mil dol) (cont.) | | | | | | | Value of residential construction authorized by building permits, 2011 | | Local government finances, 2007 General revenue | | | | |
| | Procurement contract awards | | | Grants[1] | | | | | | | | Taxes | | |
| | | | | | | | | | | | | | Per capita[2] (dollars) | |
| | Salaries and wages | Defense | Other | Medicaid and other health-related | Nutrition and family welfare | Education | Other | New construction ($1,000) | Number of housing units | Total (mil dol) | Inter-govern-mental (mil dol) | Total (mil dol) | Total | Property |
| | 171 | 172 | 173 | 174 | 175 | 176 | 177 | 178 | 179 | 180 | 181 | 182 | 183 | 184 |
| VERMONT—Cont'd | | | | | | | | | | | | | | |
| Chittenden | 310.7 | 475.0 | 61.6 | 276.6 | 26.5 | 13.7 | 114.7 | 81 519 | 558 | 530.7 | 336.2 | 97.2 | 640 | 528 |
| Essex | 7.0 | 0.0 | 0.6 | 12.1 | 1.7 | 0.3 | 1.4 | 707 | 6 | 18.5 | 14.5 | 3.0 | 468 | 462 |
| Franklin | 107.2 | 28.0 | 53.9 | 86.7 | 10.3 | 1.7 | 5.9 | 17 760 | 107 | 146.9 | 114.8 | 17.5 | 365 | 351 |
| Grand Isle | 1.8 | 0.0 | 0.5 | 7.6 | 1.3 | 0.2 | 0.0 | 2 192 | 16 | 21.4 | 16.0 | 3.9 | 511 | 501 |
| Lamoille | 11.5 | 0.4 | 1.4 | 38.6 | 4.8 | 0.7 | 1.5 | 19 679 | 43 | 86.9 | 58.1 | 17.4 | 705 | 702 |
| Orange | 13.6 | 11.2 | 2.8 | 46.1 | 6.3 | 1.2 | 2.2 | 4 066 | 23 | 97.5 | 76.2 | 14.6 | 503 | 501 |
| Orleans | 23.0 | 0.1 | 3.4 | 58.7 | 10.3 | 1.2 | 3.9 | 10 187 | 105 | 87.1 | 67.2 | 13.3 | 487 | 477 |
| Rutland | 40.6 | 29.2 | 12.0 | 140.0 | 14.3 | 2.3 | 77.1 | 6 077 | 36 | 203.9 | 139.3 | 38.2 | 603 | 580 |
| Washington | 63.3 | 8.4 | 6.0 | 138.1 | 54.7 | 69.3 | 583.6 | 19 946 | 111 | 183.6 | 124.2 | 32.8 | 556 | 553 |
| Windham | 22.9 | 0.7 | 3.8 | 54.2 | 11.9 | 2.4 | 35.1 | 11 956 | 66 | 170.6 | 118.8 | 34.2 | 786 | 772 |
| Windsor | 77.0 | 5.3 | 60.5 | 78.6 | 10.5 | 1.2 | 101.0 | 15 560 | 60 | 197.8 | 130.6 | 42.2 | 742 | 733 |
| VIRGINIA | 21 112.2 | 40 377.7 | 17 960.0 | 5 483.9 | 1 142.6 | 1 214.5 | 4 386.5 | 3 390 840 | 23 297 | X | X | X | X | X |
| Accomack | 58.7 | 16.7 | 114.0 | 54.6 | 9.0 | 2.4 | 7.4 | 11 047 | 67 | 101.0 | 56.8 | 32.3 | 838 | 579 |
| Albemarle | 94.5 | 150.2 | 22.3 | 73.2 | 4.7 | 4.6 | 5.3 | 111 699 | 672 | 326.1 | 125.7 | 165.6 | 1 778 | 1 268 |
| Alleghany | 2.4 | 0.0 | 0.5 | 17.8 | 3.3 | 2.1 | 0.1 | 1 499 | 10 | 58.8 | 32.6 | 18.3 | 1 119 | 892 |
| Amelia | 2.3 | 0.4 | 0.8 | 13.4 | 1.5 | 0.9 | 0.0 | 3 367 | 22 | 28.1 | 18.3 | 7.6 | 601 | 420 |
| Amherst | 6.8 | 0.1 | 10.8 | 25.9 | 2.9 | 2.0 | 0.9 | 7 049 | 43 | 72.4 | 42.6 | 23.5 | 731 | 490 |
| Appomattox | 3.7 | 0.0 | 0.8 | 16.8 | 1.5 | 1.0 | 0.8 | 9 111 | 62 | 33.4 | 20.6 | 10.6 | 747 | 542 |
| Arlington | 4 304.0 | 4 901.8 | 4 849.9 | 69.3 | 22.5 | 55.7 | 637.8 | 128 217 | 1 945 | 1 827.6 | 380.0 | 705.0 | 3 446 | 2 575 |
| Augusta | 11.5 | 3.6 | 6.1 | 34.0 | 7.3 | 3.7 | 0.2 | 28 516 | 219 | 162.5 | 88.1 | 59.9 | 844 | 577 |
| Bath | 2.4 | 0.0 | 0.5 | 5.6 | 0.7 | 0.4 | 0.3 | 2 419 | 11 | 16.4 | 4.4 | 10.9 | 2 361 | 2 169 |
| Bedford | 9.1 | 17.3 | 2.3 | 25.0 | 5.3 | 3.0 | 0.7 | 43 124 | 267 | 181.4 | 87.9 | 67.5 | 1 011 | 830 |
| Bland | 53.4 | 0.0 | 0.4 | 8.1 | 0.9 | 0.6 | 0.0 | 1 507 | 10 | 21.4 | 9.8 | 3.8 | 552 | 413 |
| Botetourt | 4.5 | 67.9 | 2.8 | 12.5 | 2.2 | 1.5 | 0.0 | 11 637 | 55 | 83.5 | 38.3 | 34.2 | 1 069 | 830 |
| Brunswick | 4.5 | 7.1 | 1.0 | 31.2 | 3.9 | 3.8 | 0.2 | 6 517 | 43 | 43.6 | 28.5 | 10.5 | 592 | 454 |
| Buchanan | 5.6 | 0.1 | 1.1 | 48.4 | 8.6 | 2.8 | 0.1 | 1 120 | 12 | 77.6 | 44.1 | 28.7 | 1 202 | 607 |
| Buckingham | 2.0 | 0.5 | 0.6 | 27.9 | 2.8 | 1.1 | 6.3 | 3 387 | 30 | 41.8 | 30.9 | 9.2 | 576 | 450 |
| Campbell | 27.5 | 74.9 | 1.4 | 37.7 | 5.5 | 3.9 | 0.9 | 16 596 | 95 | 127.7 | 74.3 | 39.8 | 754 | 543 |
| Caroline | 32.4 | 48.1 | 2.7 | 16.2 | 2.8 | 1.6 | 0.0 | 10 005 | 62 | 53.5 | 32.6 | 17.9 | 658 | 418 |
| Carroll | 4.3 | 0.5 | 1.2 | 39.3 | 4.0 | 2.8 | 1.5 | 6 296 | 51 | 67.5 | 36.1 | 19.9 | 684 | 501 |
| Charles City | 1.5 | 0.7 | 0.3 | 8.1 | 1.1 | 0.5 | 0.1 | 3 936 | 27 | 19.4 | 8.4 | 7.0 | 973 | 878 |
| Charlotte | 4.3 | 0.0 | 0.9 | 22.5 | 2.5 | 1.0 | 0.1 | 3 452 | 34 | 34.3 | 23.5 | 8.6 | 696 | 545 |
| Chesterfield | 156.3 | 184.9 | 18.6 | 27.1 | 16.5 | 15.6 | 8.4 | 117 979 | 684 | 1 060.4 | 422.7 | 441.0 | 1 472 | 1 118 |
| Clarke | 4.7 | 0.7 | 42.7 | 8.1 | 0.8 | 0.6 | 3.7 | 5 769 | 17 | 58.2 | 24.9 | 19.7 | 1 373 | 1 128 |
| Craig | 1.3 | 0.0 | 0.2 | 3.1 | 0.6 | 0.4 | 0.0 | 909 | 64 | 11.2 | 6.3 | 3.1 | 601 | 480 |
| Culpeper | 12.3 | 0.2 | 6.7 | 28.7 | 4.3 | 2.1 | 0.8 | 30 349 | 139 | 163.4 | 61.1 | 63.8 | 1 396 | 1 027 |
| Cumberland | 1.2 | 0.0 | 0.3 | 14.4 | 4.1 | 0.7 | 0.0 | 2 256 | 19 | 27.2 | 18.9 | 7.9 | 823 | 687 |
| Dickenson | 2.8 | 0.4 | 0.6 | 28.2 | 3.0 | 1.5 | 1.7 | 2 126 | 23 | 51.5 | 28.0 | 19.5 | 1 205 | 491 |
| Dinwiddie | 3.4 | 0.0 | 0.8 | 27.8 | 2.6 | 1.6 | 0.0 | 10 581 | 62 | 74.3 | 40.1 | 27.1 | 1 052 | 827 |
| Essex | 1.8 | 0.0 | 0.3 | 11.0 | 1.1 | 0.9 | 0.2 | 3 931 | 24 | 29.6 | 14.5 | 13.2 | 1 216 | 774 |
| Fairfax | 2 789.1 | 16 145.7 | 8 126.3 | 163.6 | 64.4 | 50.8 | 91.2 | 141 258 | 785 | 4 579.8 | 1 059.6 | 2 848.4 | 2 820 | 2 253 |
| Fauquier | 47.3 | 2.1 | 89.4 | 19.9 | 4.7 | 2.7 | 6.2 | 39 905 | 169 | 227.3 | 72.8 | 126.5 | 1 908 | 1 541 |
| Floyd | 3.7 | 0.0 | 0.9 | 12.2 | 1.5 | 0.9 | 9.3 | 10 194 | 42 | 26.0 | 15.5 | 9.6 | 659 | 506 |
| Fluvanna | 4.1 | 0.0 | 1.0 | 14.4 | 1.6 | 1.0 | 1.5 | 11 370 | 61 | 43.7 | 21.5 | 20.3 | 803 | 694 |
| Franklin | 10.1 | 0.4 | 2.0 | 36.3 | 5.6 | 3.3 | 0.8 | 30 198 | 114 | 126.9 | 66.1 | 51.3 | 1 003 | 647 |
| Frederick | 4.8 | 5.7 | 3.6 | 18.7 | 4.3 | 3.3 | 0.3 | 94 707 | 382 | 215.9 | 88.9 | 105.6 | 1 450 | 1 051 |
| Giles | 3.6 | 0.5 | 1.0 | 20.6 | 2.1 | 1.3 | 0.6 | 4 601 | 26 | 44.2 | 24.1 | 15.6 | 903 | 710 |
| Gloucester | 9.2 | 1.6 | 2.2 | 12.8 | 3.3 | 1.8 | 7.5 | 15 088 | 93 | 94.1 | 46.8 | 40.5 | 1 057 | 759 |
| Goochland | 2.8 | 0.4 | 1.3 | 9.4 | 1.3 | 1.0 | 0.1 | 13 406 | 47 | 60.9 | 16.9 | 39.1 | 1 895 | 1 624 |
| Grayson | 2.6 | 0.0 | 0.7 | 29.3 | 2.4 | 1.3 | 2.0 | 5 550 | 32 | 32.4 | 21.2 | 8.8 | 545 | 396 |
| Greene | 2.7 | 0.5 | 0.6 | 10.3 | 1.3 | 1.0 | 0.0 | 14 366 | 84 | 50.6 | 24.1 | 17.1 | 957 | 739 |
| Greensville | 0.2 | 1.7 | 0.2 | 10.3 | 2.8 | 1.2 | 0.0 | 3 119 | 27 | 39.8 | 26.0 | 7.0 | 587 | 401 |
| Halifax | 10.4 | 0.0 | 1.8 | 85.2 | 7.9 | 3.0 | 36.9 | 10 397 | 124 | 109.9 | 65.5 | 30.4 | 856 | 567 |
| Hanover | 16.6 | 401.0 | 4.7 | 19.3 | 4.6 | 3.4 | 1.1 | 55 536 | 314 | 317.8 | 132.7 | 149.9 | 1 515 | 1 191 |
| Henrico | 74.0 | 33.0 | 121.7 | 81.7 | 120.6 | 12.0 | 20.3 | 113 382 | 640 | 1 039.7 | 380.5 | 480.9 | 1 659 | 1 195 |
| Henry | 5.7 | 4.0 | 2.5 | 34.0 | 6.5 | 5.0 | 1.3 | 7 705 | 53 | 124.9 | 70.5 | 42.2 | 760 | 393 |
| Highland | 1.0 | 0.0 | 0.2 | 3.5 | 0.3 | 0.3 | 0.0 | 1 556 | 13 | 9.3 | 4.1 | 4.5 | 1 840 | 1 595 |
| Isle of Wight | 8.3 | 19.8 | 1.3 | 24.0 | 3.9 | 1.3 | 0.2 | 23 331 | 94 | 92.8 | 43.4 | 43.2 | 1 234 | 997 |
| James City | 1.8 | 3.7 | 4.7 | 11.2 | 4.0 | 0.5 | 0.1 | 77 354 | 360 | 224.3 | 50.8 | 128.7 | 2 103 | 1 586 |
| King and Queen | 1.3 | 1.2 | 2.1 | 5.3 | 1.0 | 0.5 | 0.4 | 3 520 | 20 | 25.6 | 13.8 | 6.3 | 913 | 759 |
| King George | 269.1 | 545.7 | 2.3 | 7.2 | 1.5 | 1.0 | 0.0 | 12 253 | 68 | 63.0 | 27.0 | 21.2 | 938 | 671 |
| King William | 10.7 | 0.0 | 0.8 | 6.9 | 2.8 | 0.8 | 0.0 | 5 399 | 45 | 43.1 | 19.9 | 20.2 | 1 290 | 1 108 |
| Lancaster | 3.6 | 31.9 | 1.0 | 10.0 | 1.6 | 0.6 | 0.3 | 11 219 | 65 | 23.1 | 8.0 | 13.2 | 1 145 | 913 |
| Lee | 27.1 | 0.3 | 212.2 | 73.3 | 8.1 | 2.6 | 3.2 | 1 998 | 24 | 59.5 | 43.9 | 11.1 | 475 | 317 |
| Loudoun | 415.7 | 2 972.3 | 491.3 | 138.1 | 8.7 | 7.0 | 39.1 | 473 704 | 3 070 | 1 240.1 | 276.2 | 831.9 | 2 984 | 2 406 |

1. State totals may include programs not allocated by county.    2. Based on the resident population estimated as of July 1 of the year shown.

# Table B. States and Counties — Local Government Finances, Government Employment, and Voting

| | Local government finances, 2007 (cont.) | | | | | | | | | Government employment, 2011 | | | Presidential election,[2] 2012 | | |
| | Direct general expenditure | | | | | | | Debt outstanding | | | | | Percent of vote cast: | | |
| | | | Percent of total for: | | | | | | | | | | | | |
| STATE County | Total (mil dol) | Per capita[1] (dollars) | Education | Health and hospitals | Police protection | Public welfare | Highways | Total (mil dol) | Per capita[1] (dollars) | Federal civilian | Federal military | State and local | Democratic | Republican | All other |
| | 185 | 186 | 187 | 188 | 189 | 190 | 191 | 192 | 193 | 194 | 195 | 196 | 197 | 198 | 199 |
| VERMONT—Cont'd | | | | | | | | | | | | | | | |
| Chittenden | 605.4 | 3 988 | 62.5 | 0.3 | 4.7 | 0.0 | 4.5 | 428.9 | 2 825 | 2 319 | 1 123 | 13 500 | 71.4 | 26.7 | 1.9 |
| Essex | 20.1 | 3 099 | 79.6 | 0.2 | 0.5 | 0.0 | 8.6 | 1.9 | 300 | 94 | 42 | 304 | 55.9 | 41.4 | 2.7 |
| Franklin | 159.6 | 3 330 | 78.0 | 0.5 | 1.7 | 0.0 | 6.4 | 57.4 | 1 198 | 1 112 | 324 | 2 921 | 61.4 | 36.6 | 2.0 |
| Grand Isle | 20.3 | 2 673 | 76.7 | 0.0 | 0.9 | 0.0 | 8.8 | 13.5 | 1 774 | 18 | 47 | 298 | 63.1 | 34.9 | 2.0 |
| Lamoille | 102.0 | 4 135 | 71.1 | 1.3 | 3.4 | 0.0 | 8.2 | 78.0 | 3 159 | 64 | 166 | 1 565 | 70.4 | 27.7 | 1.9 |
| Orange | 124.9 | 4 305 | 81.3 | 0.4 | 1.4 | 0.1 | 6.1 | 46.0 | 1 587 | 90 | 195 | 1 888 | 64.6 | 33.2 | 2.2 |
| Orleans | 108.9 | 3 987 | 79.3 | 0.1 | 1.3 | 0.0 | 7.6 | 36.0 | 1 318 | 252 | 183 | 1 810 | 62.6 | 35.1 | 2.3 |
| Rutland | 242.7 | 3 836 | 74.9 | 0.1 | 2.5 | 0.1 | 6.5 | 76.5 | 1 209 | 309 | 414 | 4 227 | 61.2 | 36.6 | 2.1 |
| Washington | 218.7 | 3 711 | 71.2 | 0.9 | 2.8 | 0.0 | 6.7 | 90.9 | 1 543 | 275 | 443 | 7 447 | 69.3 | 28.4 | 2.3 |
| Windham | 213.6 | 4 912 | 74.6 | 0.2 | 2.2 | 0.2 | 7.1 | 57.9 | 1 333 | 154 | 298 | 2 862 | 73.0 | 24.9 | 2.1 |
| Windsor | 233.8 | 4 110 | 68.6 | 0.5 | 3.5 | 0.0 | 9.4 | 84.2 | 1 480 | 1 390 | 389 | 3 585 | 68.8 | 29.1 | 2.0 |
| VIRGINIA | X | X | X | X | X | X | X | X | X | 191 928 | 146 801 | 533 049 | 52.6 | 46.3 | 1.0 |
| Accomack | 116.0 | 3 015 | 59.9 | 0.9 | 4.5 | 6.3 | 0.8 | 68.1 | 1 770 | 656 | 277 | 2 181 | 48.7 | 50.1 | 1.2 |
| Albemarle | 304.5 | 3 270 | 54.3 | 2.4 | 4.8 | 4.3 | 0.3 | 317.7 | 3 412 | [3]1 253 | [3]828 | [3]28 260 | 58.4 | 40.4 | 1.2 |
| Alleghany | 55.7 | 3 398 | 57.1 | 0.3 | 4.4 | 7.2 | 1.2 | 45.0 | 2 748 | [4]75 | [4]69 | [4]1 633 | 48.2 | 50.4 | 1.4 |
| Amelia | 29.0 | 2 283 | 57.5 | 0.6 | 6.8 | 4.6 | 0.0 | 6.6 | 518 | 29 | 40 | 497 | 38.1 | 60.8 | 1.1 |
| Amherst | 73.1 | 2 270 | 63.4 | 1.5 | 7.1 | 3.7 | 0.1 | 34.1 | 1 057 | 44 | 100 | 2 676 | 41.5 | 57.6 | 0.9 |
| Appomattox | 33.0 | 2 322 | 60.6 | 2.4 | 5.9 | 5.7 | 0.0 | 25.3 | 1 782 | 53 | 47 | 837 | 34.6 | 64.3 | 1.1 |
| Arlington | 2 264.3 | 11 069 | 20.3 | 1.5 | 2.4 | 2.7 | 2.5 | 6 059.5 | 29 621 | 33 586 | 11 272 | 11 386 | 71.7 | 27.1 | 1.2 |
| Augusta | 198.4 | 2 798 | 68.5 | 7.5 | 3.5 | 6.0 | 0.1 | 132.5 | 1 869 | [5]278 | [5]371 | [5]8 471 | 29.5 | 69.4 | 1.2 |
| Bath | 15.1 | 3 258 | 66.6 | 0.5 | 6.0 | 4.6 | 0.1 | 0.0 | 0 | 32 | 15 | 341 | 42.9 | 55.5 | 1.6 |
| Bedford | 196.5 | 2 943 | 58.4 | 0.3 | 3.2 | 9.5 | 0.5 | 130.1 | 1 949 | [6]136 | [6]235 | [6]2 999 | 30.7 | 68.2 | 1.1 |
| Bland | 14.3 | 2 078 | 59.5 | 1.6 | 5.1 | 7.7 | 0.0 | 24.2 | 3 511 | 14 | 21 | 586 | 29.2 | 68.6 | 2.2 |
| Botetourt | 108.9 | 3 401 | 58.0 | 0.3 | 4.5 | 2.5 | 0.1 | 88.2 | 2 755 | 51 | 103 | 1 340 | 32.7 | 65.9 | 1.4 |
| Brunswick | 42.4 | 2 381 | 59.3 | 0.7 | 6.5 | 6.6 | 0.1 | 26.5 | 1 487 | 52 | 54 | 1 141 | 62.8 | 36.4 | 0.8 |
| Buchanan | 77.2 | 3 232 | 47.4 | 0.9 | 4.0 | 10.5 | 4.3 | 12.5 | 525 | 67 | 74 | 1 567 | 46.5 | 52.0 | 1.5 |
| Buckingham | 43.0 | 2 696 | 54.3 | 1.4 | 3.9 | 3.2 | 0.0 | 21.5 | 1 352 | 31 | 54 | 1 293 | 49.9 | 49.0 | 1.1 |
| Campbell | 125.0 | 2 366 | 64.8 | 1.3 | 3.9 | 8.3 | 1.4 | 107.0 | 2 024 | [7]497 | [7]431 | [7]7 153 | 31.3 | 67.6 | 1.1 |
| Caroline | 53.3 | 1 952 | 68.4 | 0.0 | 3.1 | 8.7 | 0.6 | 58.2 | 2 134 | 489 | 96 | 1 186 | 55.4 | 43.5 | 1.1 |
| Carroll | 62.3 | 2 138 | 62.3 | 7.3 | 4.6 | 6.5 | 0.4 | 101.2 | 3 474 | [8]98 | [8]116 | [8]2 487 | 32.7 | 65.1 | 2.2 |
| Charles City | 24.0 | 3 351 | 57.4 | 1.2 | 5.4 | 11.4 | 0.0 | 2.8 | 387 | 18 | 23 | 329 | 68.3 | 31.0 | 0.7 |
| Charlotte | 31.7 | 2 574 | 65.0 | 0.8 | 5.1 | 4.1 | 0.1 | 31.8 | 2 575 | 47 | 39 | 909 | 43.9 | 54.8 | 1.3 |
| Chesterfield | 977.9 | 3 263 | 57.6 | 4.7 | 6.0 | 3.7 | 2.3 | 781.7 | 2 608 | 3 014 | 1 009 | 17 725 | 45.8 | 53.3 | 0.8 |
| Clarke | 47.8 | 3 327 | 47.7 | 0.7 | 5.0 | 4.9 | 0.3 | 161.5 | 11 248 | 40 | 44 | 707 | 46.5 | 51.7 | 1.8 |
| Craig | 11.6 | 2 263 | 57.9 | 0.5 | 6.1 | 7.5 | 0.3 | 5.0 | 978 | 15 | 16 | 236 | 33.5 | 64.7 | 1.9 |
| Culpeper | 180.4 | 3 945 | 52.9 | 10.7 | 6.0 | 6.7 | 1.4 | 134.7 | 2 945 | 209 | 148 | 3 153 | 44.6 | 54.3 | 1.2 |
| Cumberland | 30.8 | 3 199 | 75.1 | 0.3 | 4.7 | 3.1 | 0.0 | 27.6 | 2 864 | 12 | 31 | 450 | 47.7 | 51.2 | 1.1 |
| Dickenson | 51.1 | 3 161 | 51.2 | 4.4 | 6.2 | 5.8 | 5.7 | 13.0 | 804 | 36 | 49 | 995 | 48.5 | 49.2 | 2.2 |
| Dinwiddie | 95.5 | 3 708 | 73.9 | 1.9 | 4.8 | 3.1 | 0.0 | 99.4 | 3 860 | [9]241 | [9]246 | [9]7 503 | 48.4 | 50.6 | 0.9 |
| Essex | 33.8 | 3 116 | 53.8 | 0.1 | 4.4 | 4.2 | 1.0 | 37.2 | 3 422 | 22 | 35 | 530 | 54.7 | 44.4 | 1.0 |
| Fairfax | 4 458.6 | 4 413 | 52.1 | 4.3 | 5.0 | 5.2 | 1.1 | 4 786.8 | 4 738 | [10]42 995 | [10]7 872 | [10]59 999 | 60.1 | 38.9 | 0.9 |
| Fauquier | 217.7 | 3 283 | 55.8 | 1.4 | 5.5 | 3.8 | 0.9 | 144.1 | 2 172 | 565 | 206 | 3 878 | 42.7 | 56.2 | 1.1 |
| Floyd | 28.4 | 1 943 | 63.7 | 2.2 | 4.5 | 2.0 | 0.0 | 34.1 | 2 328 | 54 | 48 | 600 | 39.1 | 59.1 | 1.8 |
| Fluvanna | 46.7 | 1 845 | 73.2 | 0.2 | 4.7 | 9.4 | 0.0 | 2.8 | 111 | 29 | 81 | 1 297 | 48.6 | 50.4 | 1.0 |
| Franklin | 120.1 | 2 348 | 60.1 | 0.4 | 5.0 | 7.8 | 1.1 | 57.9 | 1 132 | 103 | 176 | 2 111 | 37.9 | 60.7 | 1.5 |
| Frederick | 202.3 | 2 776 | 71.3 | 1.2 | 4.8 | 2.5 | 0.2 | 156.6 | 2 149 | [11]1 671 | [11]345 | [11]5 842 | 38.6 | 59.9 | 1.5 |
| Giles | 41.8 | 2 428 | 58.7 | 1.7 | 6.4 | 4.7 | 2.8 | 29.9 | 1 736 | 37 | 53 | 874 | 40.9 | 57.2 | 1.8 |
| Gloucester | 89.4 | 2 331 | 67.6 | 0.9 | 5.2 | 3.8 | 0.0 | 81.8 | 2 134 | 87 | 115 | 2 430 | 36.0 | 62.9 | 1.1 |
| Goochland | 58.3 | 2 827 | 54.9 | 10.2 | 2.9 | 3.3 | 1.4 | 34.5 | 1 674 | 34 | 68 | 1 327 | 38.3 | 60.8 | 0.8 |
| Grayson | 33.2 | 2 069 | 68.3 | 0.8 | 5.3 | 6.5 | 0.3 | 4.8 | 297 | 30 | 48 | 708 | 34.3 | 62.9 | 2.8 |
| Greene | 50.8 | 2 843 | 58.1 | 1.3 | 5.3 | 5.9 | 1.3 | 51.8 | 2 898 | 35 | 58 | 839 | 38.4 | 60.3 | 1.3 |
| Greensville | 42.9 | 3 606 | 54.1 | 0.2 | 8.4 | 7.4 | 0.4 | 29.1 | 2 447 | [12]32 | [12]56 | [12]1 963 | 63.9 | 35.4 | 0.7 |
| Halifax | 111.2 | 3 129 | 57.8 | 8.9 | 4.8 | 5.4 | 1.0 | 29.6 | 832 | 87 | 113 | 2 346 | 48.2 | 51.0 | 0.7 |
| Hanover | 299.2 | 3 024 | 59.7 | 0.0 | 8.2 | 2.3 | 3.0 | 233.9 | 2 364 | 160 | 314 | 5 076 | 32.8 | 66.4 | 0.8 |
| Henrico | 1 035.5 | 3 573 | 45.5 | 2.8 | 6.0 | 2.8 | 4.5 | 1 005.1 | 3 468 | 2 192 | 969 | 16 585 | 55.7 | 43.5 | 0.8 |
| Henry | 124.6 | 2 243 | 64.0 | 0.4 | 4.7 | 5.7 | 0.0 | 68.2 | 1 228 | [13]129 | [13]210 | [13]3 603 | 44.1 | 54.6 | 1.3 |
| Highland | 7.9 | 3 244 | 50.0 | 4.5 | 7.2 | 3.7 | 1.3 | 2.1 | 847 | 11 | 0 | 149 | 38.0 | 59.8 | 2.2 |
| Isle of Wight | 82.1 | 2 344 | 62.8 | 5.8 | 5.0 | 0.0 | 1.9 | 86.1 | 2 457 | 98 | 110 | 1 479 | 42.9 | 56.3 | 0.8 |
| James City | 229.5 | 3 751 | 48.9 | 6.3 | 4.2 | 2.3 | 0.0 | 379.8 | 6 206 | [14]239 | [14]635 | [14]8 773 | 44.9 | 54.2 | 0.9 |
| King and Queen | 26.5 | 3 844 | 46.6 | 2.0 | 3.1 | 3.5 | 0.0 | 12.7 | 1 842 | 14 | 85 | 247 | 51.8 | 47.6 | 0.6 |
| King George | 52.6 | 2 325 | 58.3 | 0.6 | 7.2 | 6.1 | 0.3 | 157.5 | 6 958 | 4 018 | 758 | 980 | 42.7 | 56.2 | 1.1 |
| King William | 42.1 | 2 680 | 66.8 | 0.9 | 5.9 | 3.8 | 0.6 | 54.5 | 3 473 | 21 | 50 | 763 | 39.9 | 59.2 | 0.9 |
| Lancaster | 27.5 | 2 381 | 58.1 | 3.0 | 5.2 | 4.5 | 3.1 | 9.2 | 801 | 37 | 35 | 525 | 46.6 | 52.6 | 0.8 |
| Lee | 61.8 | 2 635 | 64.9 | 0.7 | 4.3 | 11.7 | 0.5 | 13.4 | 571 | 425 | 78 | 1 241 | 34.9 | 63.1 | 2.0 |
| Loudoun | 1 242.7 | 4 457 | 58.3 | 2.7 | 4.6 | 3.5 | 1.8 | 2 076.3 | 7 447 | 4 401 | 1 015 | 17 415 | 53.7 | 45.4 | 0.9 |

1. Based on the resident population estimated as of July 1 of the year shown.   2. © 2013 Election Data Services, Inc. All rights reserved.   3. Charlottesville city is included with Albemarle county.   4. Covington city is included with Alleghany county.   5. Staunton and Waynesboro cities are included with Augusta county.   6. Bedford city is included with Bedford county.   7. Lynchburg city is included with Campbell county.   8. Galax city is included with Carroll county.   9. Petersburg and Colonial Heights cities are included with Dinwiddie county.   10. Fairfax city and Falls Church city are included with Fairfax county.   11. Winchester city is included with Frederick county.   12. Emporia city is included with Greensville county.   13. Martinsville city is included with Henry county.   14. Williamsburg city is included with James City county.

| STATE/County code | CBSA code[1] | County type[2] | STATE County | Land area[3] (sq km) 2010 | Total persons | Rank | Per square kilometer | White | Black | American Indian, Alaska Native | Asian and Pacific Islander | Percent Hispanic or Latino[4] | Under 5 years | 5 to 17 years | 18 to 24 years | 25 to 34 years | 35 to 44 years | 45 to 54 years |
|---|---|---|---|---|---|---|---|---|---|---|---|---|---|---|---|---|---|---|
| | | | | 1 | 2 | 3 | 4 | 5 | 6 | 7 | 8 | 9 | 10 | 11 | 12 | 13 | 14 | 15 |
| | | | VIRGINIA—Cont'd | | | | | | | | | | | | | | | |
| 51 109 | 40060 | 1 | Louisa | 1 285 | 33 430 | 1 341 | 26.0 | 79.0 | 18.9 | 0.9 | 1.0 | 2.4 | 5.9 | 15.8 | 6.9 | 11.5 | 12.6 | 16.9 |
| 51 111 | ... | 9 | Lunenburg | 1 118 | 12 588 | 2 268 | 11.3 | 61.1 | 35.1 | 0.8 | 0.7 | 3.9 | 5.1 | 14.1 | 8.2 | 11.3 | 12.9 | 15.5 |
| 51 113 | ... | 8 | Madison | 831 | 13 200 | 2 231 | 15.9 | 87.4 | 11.2 | 0.7 | 1.1 | 1.8 | 5.3 | 16.2 | 7.3 | 9.8 | 11.5 | 16.0 |
| 51 115 | 47260 | 1 | Mathews | 223 | 8 884 | 2 528 | 39.8 | 88.4 | 10.0 | 1.0 | 1.0 | 1.5 | 3.9 | 14.0 | 5.8 | 7.4 | 10.4 | 15.3 |
| 51 117 | ... | 7 | Mecklenburg | 1 620 | 31 749 | 1 394 | 19.6 | 59.9 | 37.0 | 0.7 | 1.2 | 2.7 | 4.6 | 14.6 | 7.4 | 10.4 | 11.3 | 14.9 |
| 51 119 | ... | 8 | Middlesex | 337 | 10 822 | 2 371 | 32.1 | 79.6 | 18.8 | 0.8 | 0.6 | 1.6 | 4.0 | 11.5 | 6.5 | 8.5 | 9.5 | 15.7 |
| 51 121 | 13980 | 3 | Montgomery | 1 002 | 95 194 | 609 | 95.0 | 87.0 | 4.8 | 0.6 | 6.8 | 2.9 | 4.4 | 10.9 | 32.8 | 12.6 | 10.1 | 10.0 |
| 51 125 | 16820 | 3 | Nelson | 1 220 | 14 827 | 2 123 | 12.2 | 82.4 | 13.9 | 0.8 | 0.9 | 3.4 | 4.8 | 14.3 | 6.2 | 9.5 | 10.7 | 15.4 |
| 51 127 | 40060 | 1 | New Kent | 543 | 19 169 | 1 866 | 35.3 | 81.9 | 14.5 | 1.8 | 1.7 | 2.2 | 5.1 | 16.6 | 6.9 | 10.2 | 14.1 | 17.9 |
| 51 131 | ... | 9 | Northampton | 548 | 12 226 | 2 289 | 22.3 | 55.3 | 37.1 | 0.5 | 1.1 | 7.4 | 5.5 | 14.1 | 7.5 | 10.2 | 9.4 | 14.8 |
| 51 133 | ... | 9 | Northumberland | 495 | 12 346 | 2 284 | 24.9 | 71.4 | 25.5 | 0.5 | 0.5 | 3.2 | 4.0 | 12.1 | 6.0 | 7.3 | 7.9 | 14.0 |
| 51 135 | ... | 6 | Nottoway | 814 | 15 830 | 2 055 | 19.4 | 56.1 | 39.6 | 0.6 | 0.6 | 4.1 | 5.7 | 14.9 | 8.5 | 13.6 | 12.2 | 15.2 |
| 51 137 | ... | 6 | Orange | 883 | 34 246 | 1 321 | 38.8 | 82.3 | 14.0 | 0.9 | 1.3 | 3.5 | 5.7 | 16.7 | 6.9 | 10.8 | 12.6 | 15.2 |
| 51 139 | ... | 6 | Page | 805 | 23 895 | 1 649 | 29.7 | 95.6 | 2.6 | 0.5 | 0.7 | 1.6 | 5.2 | 15.8 | 7.4 | 10.9 | 12.8 | 15.5 |
| 51 141 | ... | 8 | Patrick | 1 251 | 18 451 | 1 898 | 14.7 | 90.6 | 6.8 | 0.6 | 0.5 | 2.5 | 4.5 | 14.3 | 6.0 | 8.9 | 12.7 | 15.5 |
| 51 143 | 19260 | 3 | Pittsylvania | 2 510 | 62 807 | 830 | 25.0 | 75.1 | 22.5 | 0.5 | 0.6 | 2.2 | 5.0 | 15.8 | 7.2 | 10.0 | 12.3 | 16.5 |
| 51 145 | 40060 | 1 | Powhatan | 674 | 28 123 | 1 489 | 41.7 | 83.6 | 14.1 | 0.6 | 0.8 | 1.9 | 4.5 | 17.4 | 7.9 | 9.8 | 15.1 | 17.8 |
| 51 147 | ... | 6 | Prince Edward | 906 | 23 238 | 1 679 | 25.6 | 63.6 | 33.4 | 0.6 | 1.5 | 2.3 | 4.4 | 12.7 | 25.8 | 10.1 | 9.9 | 11.9 |
| 51 149 | 40060 | 1 | Prince George | 687 | 36 941 | 1 248 | 53.8 | 59.6 | 32.3 | 1.1 | 2.7 | 6.5 | 5.5 | 16.9 | 9.2 | 14.6 | 15.4 | 15.5 |
| 51 153 | 47900 | 1 | Prince William | 871 | 430 289 | 159 | 494.0 | 51.2 | 21.7 | 0.9 | 9.4 | 20.5 | 8.1 | 20.4 | 8.6 | 14.9 | 15.9 | 15.1 |
| 51 155 | 13980 | 3 | Pulaski | 828 | 34 736 | 1 307 | 42.0 | 92.6 | 6.0 | 0.7 | 0.8 | 1.4 | 4.9 | 14.3 | 7.3 | 10.5 | 13.8 | 14.9 |
| 51 157 | ... | 8 | Rappahannock | 690 | 7 456 | 2 645 | 10.8 | 91.1 | 5.7 | 0.7 | 0.9 | 3.3 | 4.6 | 14.8 | 6.9 | 8.2 | 11.1 | 16.7 |
| 51 159 | ... | 9 | Richmond | 496 | 9 059 | 2 514 | 18.3 | 62.8 | 31.3 | 0.8 | 0.8 | 5.8 | 4.2 | 12.6 | 7.6 | 13.4 | 14.1 | 16.9 |
| 51 161 | 40220 | 2 | Roanoke | 649 | 92 901 | 622 | 143.1 | 89.3 | 6.0 | 0.5 | 3.3 | 2.3 | 4.9 | 16.4 | 7.5 | 10.0 | 13.2 | 15.5 |
| 51 163 | ... | 6 | Rockbridge | 1 548 | 22 394 | 1 715 | 14.5 | 94.5 | 3.6 | 1.0 | 0.8 | 1.5 | 4.5 | 14.3 | 7.8 | 9.5 | 11.5 | 15.2 |
| 51 165 | 25500 | 3 | Rockingham | 2 199 | 77 391 | 706 | 35.2 | 91.8 | 2.3 | 0.4 | 1.0 | 5.5 | 5.8 | 17.5 | 8.9 | 10.9 | 12.5 | 15.2 |
| 51 167 | ... | 6 | Russell | 1 227 | 28 445 | 1 471 | 23.2 | 97.6 | 1.2 | 0.4 | 0.3 | 1.0 | 5.2 | 14.8 | 7.8 | 11.2 | 13.0 | 16.0 |
| 51 169 | 28700 | 3 | Scott | 1 387 | 22 781 | 1 696 | 16.4 | 97.7 | 1.0 | 0.5 | 0.3 | 1.1 | 4.9 | 14.1 | 7.0 | 10.7 | 12.8 | 14.8 |
| 51 171 | ... | 6 | Shenandoah | 1 318 | 42 583 | 1 120 | 32.3 | 90.9 | 2.6 | 0.7 | 0.8 | 6.3 | 5.7 | 16.1 | 7.3 | 10.6 | 12.4 | 14.9 |
| 51 173 | ... | 6 | Smyth | 1 168 | 31 718 | 1 397 | 27.2 | 95.6 | 2.6 | 0.5 | 0.5 | 1.7 | 5.2 | 14.9 | 8.2 | 10.5 | 13.1 | 14.7 |
| 51 175 | ... | 6 | Southampton | 1 552 | 18 409 | 1 902 | 11.9 | 60.7 | 38.0 | 0.7 | 0.7 | 1.2 | 5.1 | 15.6 | 7.7 | 10.0 | 12.2 | 19.0 |
| 51 177 | 47900 | 1 | Spotsylvania | 1 040 | 125 684 | 489 | 120.9 | 74.1 | 16.6 | 1.0 | 3.4 | 7.8 | 6.5 | 20.4 | 8.6 | 12.4 | 14.3 | 16.0 |
| 51 179 | 47900 | 1 | Stafford | 697 | 134 352 | 467 | 192.8 | 70.0 | 18.3 | 1.1 | 4.3 | 9.5 | 6.6 | 21.5 | 9.7 | 12.6 | 14.7 | 17.0 |
| 51 181 | 47260 | 1 | Surry | 722 | 6 844 | 2 695 | 9.5 | 52.6 | 46.0 | 0.8 | 0.7 | 1.4 | 4.8 | 15.3 | 8.2 | 9.3 | 11.2 | 19.3 |
| 51 183 | 40060 | 1 | Sussex | 1 270 | 11 972 | 2 299 | 9.4 | 39.5 | 57.8 | 0.6 | 0.6 | 2.4 | 4.7 | 12.1 | 10.0 | 16.2 | 13.6 | 15.4 |
| 51 185 | 14140 | 7 | Tazewell | 1 344 | 44 268 | 1 082 | 32.9 | 95.3 | 3.5 | 0.5 | 0.9 | 0.7 | 5.0 | 14.9 | 7.7 | 11.6 | 12.6 | 14.8 |
| 51 187 | 47900 | 1 | Warren | 553 | 38 070 | 1 219 | 68.8 | 89.9 | 5.8 | 0.9 | 1.6 | 3.7 | 6.1 | 17.5 | 8.8 | 11.1 | 13.3 | 16.9 |
| 51 191 | 28700 | 3 | Washington | 1 453 | 55 190 | 910 | 38.0 | 96.3 | 1.8 | 0.5 | 0.6 | 1.4 | 4.8 | 14.5 | 8.1 | 10.8 | 12.9 | 15.4 |
| 51 193 | ... | 7 | Westmoreland | 594 | 17 524 | 1 949 | 29.5 | 65.0 | 28.8 | 1.0 | 1.1 | 6.1 | 5.6 | 14.2 | 7.8 | 9.9 | 10.3 | 15.0 |
| 51 195 | ... | 7 | Wise | 1 044 | 40 918 | 1 155 | 39.2 | 92.9 | 5.7 | 0.4 | 0.5 | 1.3 | 5.6 | 15.1 | 10.7 | 13.1 | 13.5 | 13.8 |
| 51 197 | ... | 6 | Wythe | 1 196 | 29 251 | 1 442 | 24.5 | 95.1 | 3.7 | 0.5 | 0.7 | 1.0 | 5.1 | 15.4 | 6.9 | 11.1 | 13.3 | 15.1 |
| 51 199 | 47260 | 1 | York | 271 | 66 146 | 796 | 244.1 | 75.6 | 14.8 | 1.0 | 6.8 | 4.8 | 5.4 | 19.9 | 8.8 | 10.8 | 12.9 | 17.2 |
| | ... | | Independent cities | | | | | | | | | | | | | | | |
| 51 510 | 47900 | 1 | Alexandria city | 39 | 146 294 | 434 | 3 751.1 | 55.4 | 22.3 | 0.7 | 7.7 | 16.4 | 7.4 | 10.1 | 6.7 | 24.7 | 17.6 | 13.1 |
| 51 515 | 31340 | 3 | Bedford city | 18 | 5 964 | 2 762 | 331.3 | 76.7 | 21.3 | 0.5 | 1.0 | 2.3 | 5.7 | 14.1 | 9.3 | 11.2 | 10.7 | 13.6 |
| 51 520 | 28700 | 3 | Bristol city | 34 | 17 662 | 1 936 | 519.5 | 91.5 | 6.9 | 0.8 | 1.1 | 1.5 | 5.5 | 14.7 | 9.4 | 12.6 | 12.0 | 13.8 |
| 51 530 | ... | 6 | Buena Vista city | 17 | 6 707 | 2 707 | 394.5 | 90.7 | 6.3 | 1.6 | 1.2 | 1.9 | 5.9 | 15.1 | 14.5 | 12.0 | 11.1 | 12.4 |
| 51 540 | 16820 | 3 | Charlottesville city | 27 | 43 956 | 1 087 | 1 628.0 | 68.8 | 20.2 | 0.7 | 8.0 | 5.1 | 5.3 | 9.4 | 29.6 | 18.0 | 9.9 | 9.6 |
| 51 550 | 47260 | 1 | Chesapeake city | 883 | 228 417 | 281 | 258.7 | 62.3 | 30.7 | 1.0 | 4.2 | 4.6 | 6.4 | 19.0 | 9.2 | 13.0 | 13.4 | 16.4 |
| 51 570 | 40060 | 1 | Colonial Heights city | 19 | 17 479 | 1 953 | 919.9 | 80.1 | 11.6 | 0.8 | 4.2 | 4.4 | 5.8 | 16.5 | 8.3 | 11.5 | 11.6 | 13.7 |
| 51 580 | ... | 6 | Covington city | 14 | 5 771 | 2 783 | 412.2 | 84.5 | 14.0 | 0.9 | 0.9 | 1.6 | 5.2 | 15.5 | 8.2 | 11.2 | 12.4 | 15.1 |
| 51 590 | 19260 | 3 | Danville city | 111 | 42 996 | 1 112 | 387.4 | 47.4 | 49.0 | 0.5 | 1.3 | 3.0 | 6.5 | 15.2 | 9.7 | 11.0 | 10.5 | 13.8 |
| 51 595 | ... | 6 | Emporia city | 18 | 5 740 | 2 790 | 318.9 | 31.9 | 62.3 | 0.5 | 1.3 | 5.1 | 6.1 | 18.7 | 9.4 | 11.6 | 11.7 | 12.8 |
| 51 600 | 47900 | 1 | Fairfax city | 16 | 23 461 | 1 664 | 1 466.3 | 62.2 | 6.5 | 0.9 | 17.3 | 16.2 | 6.1 | 14.2 | 11.7 | 14.0 | 14.3 | 14.8 |
| 51 610 | 47900 | 1 | Falls Church city | 5 | 13 229 | 2 228 | 2 645.8 | 76.4 | 5.8 | 0.9 | 11.4 | 9.1 | 6.4 | 18.5 | 6.8 | 13.0 | 14.8 | 16.2 |
| 51 620 | ... | 6 | Franklin city | 21 | 8 528 | 2 562 | 406.1 | 41.4 | 56.6 | 0.8 | 1.3 | 1.9 | 7.5 | 16.3 | 9.2 | 10.9 | 11.0 | 14.1 |
| 51 630 | 47900 | 1 | Fredericksburg city | 27 | 27 307 | 1 520 | 1 011.4 | 63.1 | 24.0 | 0.8 | 4.0 | 11.0 | 7.1 | 13.6 | 21.6 | 16.0 | 11.7 | 11.4 |
| 51 640 | ... | 6 | Galax city | 21 | 6 908 | 2 693 | 329.0 | 79.7 | 7.0 | 0.5 | 0.8 | 13.5 | 6.2 | 15.8 | 7.9 | 10.3 | 12.1 | 13.5 |
| 51 650 | 47260 | 1 | Hampton city | 133 | 136 836 | 455 | 1 028.8 | 43.3 | 50.3 | 1.3 | 3.6 | 4.7 | 6.4 | 16.2 | 12.7 | 14.2 | 11.2 | 14.8 |
| 51 660 | 25500 | 3 | Harrisonburg city | 45 | 50 981 | 969 | 1 132.9 | 73.1 | 7.2 | 0.4 | 5.0 | 16.2 | 5.0 | 9.9 | 41.7 | 12.7 | 8.1 | 7.7 |
| 51 670 | 40060 | 1 | Hopewell city | 27 | 22 348 | 1 717 | 827.7 | 55.3 | 37.6 | 1.1 | 2.0 | 6.7 | 7.9 | 16.9 | 9.5 | 14.1 | 11.7 | 13.6 |
| 51 678 | ... | 6 | Lexington city | 6 | 6 998 | 2 684 | 1 166.3 | 84.4 | 9.6 | 0.7 | 3.6 | 3.8 | 2.3 | 6.4 | 48.1 | 7.0 | 5.3 | 6.3 |
| 51 680 | 31340 | 3 | Lynchburg city | 127 | 77 113 | 708 | 607.2 | 64.9 | 30.2 | 0.8 | 3.1 | 3.2 | 6.1 | 13.4 | 22.2 | 13.2 | 9.5 | 11.0 |
| 51 683 | 47900 | 1 | Manassas city | 26 | 40 605 | 1 164 | 1 561.7 | 49.0 | 15.2 | 0.7 | 6.0 | 31.5 | 8.2 | 19.9 | 9.6 | 16.7 | 14.4 | 14.2 |

1. CBSA = Core Based Statistical Area. See Appendix A for explanation. See Appendix B for list of metropolitan areas with component counties.   2. County type code from the Economic Research Service of USDA Rural-Urban Continuum Codes. See Appendix A for definition.   3. Dry land or land partially or temporarily covered by water.   4. May be of any race.

| STATE County | \<Population, 2011 (cont.)\> Age (percent) (cont.) 55 to 64 years | 65 to 74 years | 75 years and over | Percent female | \<Population change and components of change, 2000–2012\> Total persons 2000 | 2010 | Percent change 2000–2010 | 2010–2012 | Components of change, 2010–2012 Births | Deaths | Net migration | \<Households, 2010\> Number | Percent change, 2000–2010 | Persons per house-hold | Percent Female family house-holder[1] | One per-son |
|---|---|---|---|---|---|---|---|---|---|---|---|---|---|---|---|---|
| | 16 | 17 | 18 | 19 | 20 | 21 | 22 | 23 | 24 | 25 | 26 | 27 | 28 | 29 | 30 | 31 |
| VIRGINIA—Cont'd | | | | | | | | | | | | | | | | |
| Louisa | 15.4 | 9.5 | 5.5 | 50.7 | 25 627 | 33 153 | 29.4 | 0.8 | 835 | 651 | 97 | 12 944 | 30.2 | 2.54 | 10.5 | 21.9 |
| Lunenburg | 15.5 | 9.9 | 7.5 | 46.8 | 13 146 | 12 914 | -1.8 | -2.5 | 260 | 357 | -229 | 4 957 | -0.8 | 2.36 | 14.2 | 29.9 |
| Madison | 15.5 | 10.6 | 7.8 | 51.3 | 12 520 | 13 308 | 6.3 | -0.8 | 296 | 268 | -136 | 5 083 | 7.3 | 2.58 | 9.7 | 21.2 |
| Mathews | 17.0 | 15.1 | 11.0 | 51.3 | 9 207 | 8 978 | -2.5 | -1.0 | 131 | 259 | 40 | 3 858 | -1.9 | 2.30 | 8.7 | 26.5 |
| Mecklenburg | 15.6 | 11.9 | 9.4 | 50.5 | 32 380 | 32 727 | 1.1 | -3.0 | 656 | 1 009 | -624 | 13 495 | 4.2 | 2.30 | 14.9 | 30.4 |
| Middlesex | 17.9 | 15.4 | 11.0 | 50.5 | 9 932 | 10 959 | 10.3 | -1.3 | 194 | 311 | -14 | 4 708 | 10.7 | 2.24 | 9.3 | 27.6 |
| Montgomery | 9.2 | 5.6 | 4.5 | 48.2 | 83 629 | 94 392 | 12.9 | 0.8 | 1 883 | 1 271 | 211 | 35 767 | 15.4 | 2.38 | 7.9 | 26.4 |
| Nelson | 18.6 | 12.3 | 8.2 | 51.2 | 14 445 | 15 020 | 4.0 | -1.3 | 296 | 365 | -117 | 6 396 | 8.6 | 2.33 | 11.1 | 27.4 |
| New Kent | 16.2 | 8.8 | 4.1 | 49.2 | 13 462 | 18 429 | 36.9 | 4.0 | 403 | 284 | 619 | 6 813 | 38.3 | 2.62 | 8.7 | 17.0 |
| Northampton | 16.3 | 11.5 | 10.7 | 52.3 | 13 093 | 12 389 | -5.4 | -1.3 | 326 | 444 | -71 | 5 323 | 0.0 | 2.27 | 14.8 | 32.0 |
| Northumberland | 17.8 | 18.0 | 13.0 | 51.3 | 12 259 | 12 330 | 0.6 | 0.1 | 225 | 383 | 185 | 5 540 | 1.3 | 2.23 | 9.9 | 27.4 |
| Nottoway | 12.9 | 9.0 | 7.9 | 47.1 | 15 725 | 15 853 | 0.8 | -0.1 | 371 | 467 | 68 | 5 706 | 0.7 | 2.46 | 16.2 | 29.7 |
| Orange | 13.7 | 10.5 | 7.8 | 51.0 | 25 881 | 33 481 | 29.4 | 2.3 | 856 | 685 | 597 | 12 895 | 27.0 | 2.55 | 10.9 | 22.5 |
| Page | 14.4 | 10.1 | 7.9 | 50.8 | 23 177 | 24 042 | 3.7 | -0.6 | 506 | 653 | -26 | 9 746 | 4.7 | 2.45 | 11.1 | 25.7 |
| Patrick | 15.8 | 12.8 | 9.4 | 51.0 | 19 407 | 18 490 | -4.7 | -0.2 | 320 | 530 | 172 | 8 081 | -0.7 | 2.26 | 9.3 | 29.4 |
| Pittsylvania | 15.5 | 10.4 | 7.3 | 51.0 | 61 745 | 63 506 | 2.9 | -1.1 | 1 112 | 1 491 | -379 | 26 183 | 6.1 | 2.39 | 13.2 | 26.5 |
| Powhatan | 14.5 | 8.6 | 4.5 | 46.1 | 22 377 | 28 046 | 25.3 | 0.3 | 510 | 443 | -4 | 9 494 | 30.8 | 2.70 | 8.4 | 16.4 |
| Prince Edward | 11.1 | 7.3 | 6.9 | 50.3 | 19 720 | 23 368 | 18.5 | -0.6 | 452 | 490 | -120 | 7 916 | 20.7 | 2.41 | 15.0 | 29.4 |
| Prince George | 12.2 | 6.7 | 3.9 | 45.3 | 33 047 | 35 725 | 8.1 | 3.4 | 808 | 477 | 854 | 11 451 | 12.7 | 2.70 | 13.3 | 18.9 |
| Prince William | 9.8 | 4.6 | 2.5 | 50.2 | 280 813 | 402 002 | 43.2 | 7.0 | 14 996 | 3 416 | 16 450 | 130 785 | 38.3 | 3.05 | 12.1 | 17.7 |
| Pulaski | 15.9 | 10.8 | 7.6 | 50.5 | 35 127 | 34 872 | -0.7 | -0.4 | 635 | 918 | 149 | 14 821 | 1.2 | 2.29 | 11.7 | 29.3 |
| Rappahannock | 18.1 | 12.1 | 7.4 | 50.0 | 6 983 | 7 373 | 5.6 | 1.1 | 137 | 160 | -38 | 3 072 | 10.2 | 2.39 | 8.6 | 26.3 |
| Richmond | 12.6 | 9.6 | 9.0 | 43.6 | 8 809 | 9 254 | 5.1 | -2.1 | 156 | 222 | -128 | 3 159 | 7.6 | 2.36 | 12.9 | 31.2 |
| Roanoke | 14.9 | 9.2 | 8.4 | 52.2 | 85 778 | 92 376 | 7.7 | 0.6 | 1 867 | 2 004 | 547 | 37 608 | 8.4 | 2.39 | 9.9 | 26.7 |
| Rockbridge | 16.2 | 11.7 | 9.5 | 50.7 | 20 808 | 22 307 | 7.2 | 0.4 | 410 | 493 | 126 | 9 555 | 12.6 | 2.32 | 9.8 | 27.3 |
| Rockingham | 13.3 | 8.4 | 7.4 | 50.9 | 67 725 | 76 314 | 12.7 | 1.4 | 1 904 | 1 447 | 505 | 29 177 | 15.1 | 2.57 | 9.2 | 22.8 |
| Russell | 15.3 | 9.8 | 7.0 | 51.1 | 30 308 | 28 897 | -4.7 | -1.6 | 619 | 786 | -280 | 11 943 | 1.3 | 2.38 | 10.1 | 26.3 |
| Scott | 14.9 | 11.8 | 9.0 | 50.2 | 23 403 | 23 177 | -1.0 | -1.7 | 457 | 687 | -185 | 9 775 | -0.2 | 2.30 | 9.8 | 28.7 |
| Shenandoah | 14.0 | 10.7 | 8.4 | 51.2 | 35 075 | 41 993 | 19.7 | 1.4 | 1 027 | 969 | 554 | 17 076 | 19.4 | 2.43 | 10.5 | 25.8 |
| Smyth | 14.7 | 10.2 | 8.3 | 51.2 | 33 081 | 32 208 | -2.6 | -1.5 | 706 | 996 | -184 | 13 319 | -1.3 | 2.36 | 12.3 | 27.7 |
| Southampton | 14.7 | 9.2 | 6.6 | 48.3 | 17 482 | 18 570 | 6.2 | -0.9 | 327 | 456 | -70 | 6 719 | 7.0 | 2.53 | 14.5 | 23.9 |
| Spotsylvania | 11.6 | 6.1 | 4.1 | 51.1 | 90 395 | 122 397 | 35.4 | 2.7 | 3 493 | 1 698 | 1 405 | 41 942 | 34.0 | 2.91 | 11.7 | 17.5 |
| Stafford | 10.2 | 4.8 | 2.8 | 49.8 | 92 446 | 128 961 | 39.5 | 4.2 | 3 778 | 1 305 | 2 866 | 41 769 | 38.4 | 3.00 | 11.3 | 15.7 |
| Surry | 15.7 | 9.6 | 6.6 | 50.7 | 6 829 | 7 058 | 3.4 | -3.0 | 140 | 137 | -218 | 2 826 | 7.9 | 2.50 | 13.9 | 25.7 |
| Sussex | 13.4 | 8.1 | 6.4 | 41.1 | 12 504 | 12 087 | -3.3 | -1.0 | 247 | 314 | -61 | 3 994 | -3.2 | 2.38 | 18.3 | 29.5 |
| Tazewell | 15.6 | 9.9 | 7.8 | 50.5 | 44 598 | 45 078 | 1.1 | -1.8 | 986 | 1 434 | -377 | 18 449 | 0.9 | 2.35 | 10.7 | 27.3 |
| Warren | 13.1 | 7.8 | 5.4 | 50.2 | 31 584 | 37 575 | 19.0 | 1.3 | 972 | 769 | 422 | 14 085 | 16.5 | 2.62 | 11.2 | 24.1 |
| Washington | 15.3 | 10.5 | 7.6 | 50.8 | 51 103 | 54 876 | 7.4 | 0.6 | 1 218 | 1 323 | 400 | 22 843 | 8.5 | 2.33 | 9.1 | 27.6 |
| Westmoreland | 16.2 | 12.6 | 8.5 | 51.1 | 16 718 | 17 454 | 4.4 | 0.4 | 412 | 442 | 105 | 7 310 | 6.8 | 2.38 | 13.4 | 28.5 |
| Wise | 13.8 | 8.2 | 6.3 | 48.2 | 40 123 | 41 452 | 3.3 | -1.3 | 995 | 1 066 | -482 | 15 968 | -0.3 | 2.40 | 12.6 | 27.4 |
| Wythe | 14.9 | 10.4 | 7.8 | 51.2 | 27 599 | 29 235 | 5.9 | 0.1 | 629 | 790 | 187 | 12 472 | 8.3 | 2.32 | 10.7 | 28.7 |
| York | 12.4 | 7.4 | 5.0 | 51.2 | 56 297 | 65 464 | 16.3 | 1.0 | 1 363 | 920 | 469 | 24 006 | 20.0 | 2.70 | 10.6 | 18.4 |
| Independent cities | | | | | | | | | | | | | | | | |
| Alexandria city | 11.1 | 5.4 | 3.9 | 51.7 | 128 283 | 139 966 | 9.1 | 4.5 | 5 936 | 1 607 | 1 968 | 68 082 | 10.0 | 2.03 | 8.6 | 43.4 |
| Bedford city | 13.5 | 8.5 | 13.4 | 53.9 | 6 299 | 6 222 | -1.2 | -4.1 | 110 | 216 | -176 | 2 627 | 4.3 | 2.23 | 17.2 | 33.0 |
| Bristol city | 13.2 | 9.5 | 9.3 | 53.0 | 17 367 | 17 835 | 2.7 | -1.0 | 320 | 567 | 90 | 7 879 | 2.6 | 2.21 | 14.5 | 34.6 |
| Buena Vista city | 12.6 | 9.4 | 6.9 | 53.2 | 6 349 | 6 650 | 4.7 | 0.9 | 157 | 188 | 89 | 2 603 | 2.2 | 2.40 | 14.4 | 28.9 |
| Charlottesville city | 8.9 | 5.0 | 4.4 | 52.1 | 45 049 | 43 475 | -3.5 | 1.1 | 1 174 | 612 | -140 | 17 778 | 5.5 | 2.31 | 11.3 | 34.1 |
| Chesapeake city | 11.8 | 6.2 | 4.5 | 51.4 | 199 184 | 222 209 | 11.6 | 2.8 | 6 196 | 3 480 | 3 521 | 79 574 | 13.8 | 2.75 | 15.6 | 19.8 |
| Colonial Heights city | 12.5 | 9.4 | 10.6 | 53.8 | 16 897 | 17 411 | 3.0 | 0.4 | 544 | 462 | -6 | 7 275 | 3.5 | 2.37 | 14.5 | 30.4 |
| Covington city | 13.4 | 9.7 | 9.3 | 51.1 | 6 303 | 5 961 | -5.4 | -3.2 | 166 | 166 | -237 | 2 632 | -7.2 | 2.23 | 13.7 | 36.1 |
| Danville city | 14.2 | 9.2 | 10.0 | 54.2 | 48 411 | 43 055 | -11.1 | -0.1 | 1 293 | 1 522 | 125 | 18 831 | -8.6 | 2.21 | 21.4 | 36.5 |
| Emporia city | 12.2 | 8.4 | 9.0 | 53.1 | 5 665 | 5 927 | 4.6 | -3.2 | 81 | 190 | -89 | 2 316 | 4.0 | 2.45 | 24.9 | 32.6 |
| Fairfax city | 12.2 | 7.1 | 6.4 | 51.0 | 21 498 | 22 565 | 5.0 | 4.0 | 967 | 464 | 288 | 8 347 | 3.9 | 2.64 | 9.6 | 24.0 |
| Falls Church city | 14.1 | 5.9 | 4.4 | 50.8 | 10 377 | 12 332 | 18.8 | 7.3 | 376 | 156 | 668 | 5 101 | 14.1 | 2.41 | 8.3 | 31.0 |
| Franklin city | 13.4 | 8.9 | 8.7 | 55.1 | 8 346 | 8 582 | 2.8 | -0.6 | 326 | 239 | -165 | 3 530 | 4.3 | 2.39 | 24.0 | 30.1 |
| Fredericksburg city | 9.0 | 4.8 | 4.8 | 54.2 | 19 279 | 24 286 | 26.0 | 12.4 | 929 | 447 | 2 481 | 9 505 | 17.3 | 2.28 | 14.6 | 36.0 |
| Galax city | 13.1 | 9.6 | 11.4 | 53.4 | 6 837 | 7 042 | 3.0 | -1.9 | 258 | 231 | -182 | 2 922 | -0.9 | 2.28 | 15.2 | 33.7 |
| Hampton city | 12.0 | 7.0 | 5.6 | 52.1 | 146 437 | 137 436 | -6.1 | -0.4 | 3 944 | 2 595 | -2 053 | 55 031 | 2.1 | 2.42 | 18.1 | 29.2 |
| Harrisonburg city | 6.4 | 3.9 | 4.6 | 53.0 | 40 468 | 48 914 | 20.9 | 4.2 | 1 194 | 585 | 1 347 | 15 988 | 21.7 | 2.59 | 10.1 | 27.3 |
| Hopewell city | 11.5 | 7.6 | 7.2 | 53.4 | 22 354 | 22 591 | 1.1 | -1.1 | 814 | 633 | -421 | 9 129 | 0.8 | 2.45 | 23.1 | 30.1 |
| Lexington city | 8.1 | 7.2 | 9.2 | 44.6 | 6 867 | 7 042 | 2.5 | -0.6 | 120 | 135 | -59 | 2 237 | 0.2 | 2.00 | 8.4 | 43.0 |
| Lynchburg city | 10.5 | 6.6 | 7.5 | 53.0 | 65 269 | 75 568 | 15.8 | 2.0 | 2 384 | 1 610 | 724 | 28 476 | 11.8 | 2.30 | 16.3 | 33.3 |
| Manassas city | 10.2 | 4.1 | 2.9 | 49.6 | 35 135 | 37 821 | 7.6 | 7.4 | 1 511 | 375 | 1 639 | 12 527 | 6.5 | 3.02 | 13.8 | 22.1 |

1. No spouse present.

# Table B. States and Counties — Population, Vital Statistics, Medicare, and Crime

| STATE County | Persons in group quarters, 2010 | Daytime population, 2007–2011 Number | Employ-ment/resi-dence ratio | Births, 2011 Total | Rate[1] | Deaths, 2011 Number | Rate[1] | Persons under 65 with no health insurance, 2010 Number | Percent | Medicare, 2012 Eligible for Medicare | Enrolled in Medicare Advantage | Enrolled in a Medicare prescription drug plan | Serious crimes known to police,[2] 2011 Total Number | Rate[3] |
|---|---|---|---|---|---|---|---|---|---|---|---|---|---|---|
| | 32 | 33 | 34 | 35 | 36 | 37 | 38 | 39 | 40 | 41 | 42 | 43 | 44 | 45 |
| VIRGINIA—Cont'd | | | | | | | | | | | | | | |
| Louisa | 211 | 26 281 | 0.59 | 373 | 11.2 | 281 | 8.4 | 4 620 | 16.3 | 6 255 | 884 | 2 819 | 393 | 1 171 |
| Lunenburg | 1 203 | 11 327 | 0.66 | 116 | 9.0 | 163 | 12.7 | 1 918 | 20.1 | 2 737 | 266 | 1 541 | 162 | 1 240 |
| Madison | 193 | 10 763 | 0.61 | 137 | 10.4 | 113 | 8.6 | 2 161 | 19.7 | 2 588 | 267 | 1 330 | 135 | 1 002 |
| Mathews | 94 | 7 202 | 0.53 | 63 | 7.0 | 115 | 12.8 | 1 128 | 16.9 | 2 542 | 305 | 1 007 | 126 | 1 387 |
| Mecklenburg | 1 740 | 34 180 | 1.12 | 298 | 9.1 | 448 | 13.7 | 4 891 | 19.8 | 8 505 | 1 433 | 4 526 | 742 | 2 240 |
| Middlesex | 393 | 9 931 | 0.80 | 81 | 7.5 | 138 | 12.7 | 1 422 | 17.9 | 3 204 | 467 | 1 537 | 170 | 1 533 |
| Montgomery | 9 237 | 98 499 | 1.12 | 845 | 9.0 | 542 | 5.7 | 13 108 | 17.2 | 11 940 | 1 582 | 6 636 | 2 131 | 2 231 |
| Nelson | 102 | 12 603 | 0.65 | 138 | 9.1 | 139 | 9.2 | 2 241 | 18.6 | 3 832 | 322 | 1 994 | 208 | 1 369 |
| New Kent | 551 | 13 120 | 0.44 | 178 | 9.5 | 100 | 5.3 | 2 108 | 13.4 | 3 214 | 533 | 1 268 | 288 | 1 544 |
| Northampton | 326 | 12 888 | 1.08 | 138 | 11.1 | 215 | 17.4 | 1 912 | 20.2 | 3 263 | 371 | 1 890 | 271 | 2 162 |
| Northumberland | 0 | 10 989 | 0.72 | 104 | 8.3 | 158 | 12.7 | 1 699 | 19.7 | 4 341 | 394 | 1 824 | 158 | 1 266 |
| Nottoway | 1 836 | 15 673 | 0.97 | 166 | 10.5 | 216 | 13.6 | 2 297 | 19.8 | 3 411 | 415 | 2 048 | 292 | 1 820 |
| Orange | 601 | 27 429 | 0.59 | 358 | 10.5 | 273 | 8.0 | 4 435 | 16.4 | 7 592 | 670 | 3 162 | 439 | 1 296 |
| Page | 194 | 20 392 | 0.65 | 228 | 9.5 | 277 | 11.6 | 3 651 | 18.5 | 5 485 | 654 | 2 769 | 488 | 2 006 |
| Patrick | 203 | 17 095 | 0.79 | 151 | 8.2 | 230 | 12.5 | 2 802 | 19.3 | 4 825 | 994 | 2 642 | 383 | 2 047 |
| Pittsylvania | 839 | 51 365 | 0.56 | 535 | 8.5 | 659 | 10.5 | 9 537 | 18.3 | 14 426 | 3 140 | 7 634 | 788 | 1 226 |
| Powhatan | 2 395 | 22 374 | 0.54 | 224 | 8.0 | 191 | 6.8 | 3 047 | 13.8 | 4 606 | 851 | 1 929 | 259 | 913 |
| Prince Edward | 4 318 | 25 038 | 1.23 | 209 | 9.0 | 221 | 9.5 | 2 936 | 18.2 | 4 164 | 532 | 2 320 | 404 | 1 708 |
| Prince George | 4 772 | 38 945 | 1.23 | 364 | 10.0 | 216 | 5.9 | 3 426 | 12.6 | 4 872 | 534 | 1 803 | 492 | 1 361 |
| Prince William | 2 520 | 311 681 | 0.61 | 6 554 | 15.6 | 1 424 | 3.4 | 57 972 | 15.5 | 35 256 | 4 275 | 10 455 | 7 650 | 1 881 |
| Pulaski | 960 | 33 935 | 0.93 | 291 | 8.4 | 393 | 11.4 | 4 446 | 15.9 | 8 287 | 1 211 | 4 440 | 1 307 | 3 704 |
| Rappahannock | 35 | 6 447 | 0.74 | 63 | 8.5 | 70 | 9.4 | 1 075 | 18.2 | 1 718 | 111 | 795 | 58 | 777 |
| Richmond | 1 792 | 8 951 | 0.90 | 71 | 7.7 | 98 | 10.6 | 1 148 | 19.4 | 1 761 | 274 | 819 | 58 | 619 |
| Roanoke | 2 328 | 81 761 | 0.78 | 828 | 8.9 | 860 | 9.3 | 8 641 | 11.6 | 20 171 | 3 431 | 9 337 | 1 582 | 1 692 |
| Rockbridge | 175 | 20 530 | 0.82 | 189 | 8.4 | 203 | 9.1 | 3 055 | 17.4 | 5 285 | 990 | 2 718 | 331 | 1 466 |
| Rockingham | 1 471 | 70 048 | 0.85 | 856 | 11.2 | 640 | 8.4 | 11 822 | 18.7 | 14 609 | 2 371 | 7 933 | 650 | 842 |
| Russell | 434 | 26 462 | 0.77 | 285 | 9.9 | 347 | 12.1 | 4 177 | 17.3 | 7 477 | 1 779 | 3 518 | 549 | 1 877 |
| Scott | 652 | 20 243 | 0.66 | 212 | 9.2 | 305 | 13.2 | 2 883 | 15.8 | 6 300 | 2 871 | 2 147 | 586 | 2 499 |
| Shenandoah | 427 | 37 176 | 0.76 | 457 | 10.8 | 436 | 10.3 | 6 258 | 18.4 | 9 201 | 1 017 | 4 398 | 727 | 1 711 |
| Smyth | 774 | 31 965 | 0.98 | 308 | 9.6 | 436 | 13.6 | 4 295 | 16.4 | 8 355 | 1 440 | 4 653 | 734 | 2 252 |
| Southampton | 1 567 | 14 524 | 0.51 | 150 | 8.1 | 207 | 11.2 | 2 158 | 15.0 | 3 604 | 369 | 2 111 | 318 | 1 692 |
| Spotsylvania | 524 | 95 618 | 0.56 | 1 542 | 12.4 | 729 | 5.9 | 14 845 | 13.5 | 15 627 | 1 468 | 5 704 | 2 850 | 2 301 |
| Stafford | 3 593 | 101 574 | 0.60 | 1 654 | 12.5 | 564 | 4.3 | 12 372 | 10.7 | 12 439 | 824 | 3 903 | 2 122 | 1 626 |
| Surry | 0 | 6 282 | 0.76 | 66 | 9.5 | 56 | 8.1 | 912 | 15.4 | 1 407 | 293 | 537 | 69 | 966 |
| Sussex | 2 593 | 12 146 | 1.00 | 102 | 8.4 | 144 | 11.9 | 1 440 | 18.2 | 2 192 | 336 | 1 134 | 220 | 1 799 |
| Tazewell | 1 645 | 44 539 | 0.98 | 470 | 10.5 | 635 | 14.2 | 6 188 | 17.1 | 11 257 | 2 268 | 5 908 | 1 210 | 2 653 |
| Warren | 725 | 32 834 | 0.76 | 430 | 11.4 | 330 | 8.7 | 5 388 | 16.7 | 6 153 | 533 | 2 857 | 844 | 2 220 |
| Washington | 1 627 | 54 735 | 1.00 | 555 | 10.1 | 583 | 10.6 | 7 365 | 16.8 | 13 481 | 3 717 | 5 690 | 1 377 | 2 480 |
| Westmoreland | 70 | 14 730 | 0.65 | 185 | 10.5 | 191 | 10.9 | 2 635 | 19.1 | 4 310 | 361 | 1 855 | 213 | 1 206 |
| Wise | 3 131 | 42 780 | 1.09 | 479 | 11.5 | 473 | 11.4 | 5 514 | 16.7 | 9 944 | 2 995 | 4 037 | 1 067 | 2 544 |
| Wythe | 260 | 28 825 | 0.98 | 272 | 9.3 | 353 | 12.1 | 4 481 | 18.6 | 7 015 | 1 214 | 3 793 | 465 | 1 572 |
| York | 648 | 56 997 | 0.75 | 590 | 8.9 | 392 | 5.9 | 6 044 | 10.7 | 9 653 | 924 | 2 602 | 1 305 | 1 970 |
| Independent cities | | | | | | | | | | | | | | |
| Alexandria city | 1 827 | 147 113 | 1.12 | 2 630 | 18.2 | 700 | 4.9 | 18 912 | 15.0 | 14 636 | 1 239 | 4 625 | 3 453 | 2 438 |
| Bedford city | 368 | 8 996 | 2.10 | 49 | 7.9 | 84 | 13.6 | 784 | 16.3 | 1 610 | 206 | 914 | 98 983 | 3 978 |
| Bristol city | 431 | 22 218 | 1.65 | 152 | 8.6 | 260 | 14.6 | 2 280 | 16.1 | 4 457 | 1 568 | 1 766 | 713 | 3 951 |
| Buena Vista city | 400 | 5 829 | 0.72 | 67 | 10.1 | 86 | 13.0 | 919 | 17.5 | 1 344 | 269 | 769 | 56 | 832 |
| Charlottesville city | 2 438 | 59 379 | 1.81 | 554 | 12.7 | 270 | 6.2 | 6 633 | 17.6 | 5 491 | 391 | 3 288 | 1 653 | 3 757 |
| Chesapeake city | 3 721 | 204 604 | 0.85 | 2 757 | 12.3 | 1 544 | 6.9 | 24 048 | 12.3 | 30 300 | 4 719 | 9 325 | 8 110 | 3 607 |
| Colonial Heights city | 171 | 18 848 | 1.17 | 239 | 13.7 | 201 | 11.5 | 2 188 | 15.7 | 3 915 | 398 | 1 489 | 959 | 5 443 |
| Covington city | 87 | 5 342 | 0.73 | 48 | 8.1 | 76 | 12.8 | 768 | 16.0 | 1 659 | 161 | 1 003 | 160 | 2 653 |
| Danville city | 1 483 | 51 976 | 1.51 | 568 | 13.3 | 677 | 15.8 | 5 955 | 17.4 | 10 857 | 1 674 | 6 212 | 2 260 | 5 187 |
| Emporia city | 246 | 6 830 | 1.44 | 37 | 6.3 | 83 | 14.1 | 897 | 18.2 | 1 210 | 117 | 354 | 430 | 7 169 |
| Fairfax city | 521 | 45 684 | 2.98 | 396 | 17.6 | 194 | 8.6 | 2 638 | 13.7 | 3 321 | 368 | 855 | 581 | 2 544 |
| Falls Church city | 42 | 14 893 | 1.48 | 175 | 13.7 | 76 | 6.0 | 906 | 8.2 | 1 575 | 159 | 445 | 233 | 1 867 |
| Franklin city | 129 | 9 982 | 1.46 | 138 | 16.1 | 93 | 10.8 | 1 168 | 16.4 | 1 799 | 147 | 1 120 | 509 | 5 861 |
| Fredericksburg city | 2 596 | 37 294 | 2.23 | 396 | 15.4 | 202 | 7.9 | 3 561 | 18.1 | 3 362 | 231 | 1 605 | 1 166 | 4 744 |
| Galax city | 377 | 8 489 | 1.52 | 118 | 16.9 | 108 | 15.5 | 1 151 | 20.4 | 1 974 | 104 | 1 322 | 388 | 5 445 |
| Hampton city | 4 454 | 140 468 | 1.04 | 1 826 | 13.4 | 1 149 | 8.4 | 18 007 | 15.4 | 21 887 | 3 541 | 6 610 | 5 620 | 4 041 |
| Harrisonburg city | 7 583 | 59 619 | 1.56 | 517 | 10.3 | 241 | 4.8 | 8 494 | 22.4 | 4 604 | 487 | 2 664 | 1 164 | 2 352 |
| Hopewell city | 237 | 21 870 | 0.92 | 391 | 17.3 | 273 | 12.1 | 3 522 | 18.2 | 4 150 | 491 | 1 862 | 1 099 | 4 807 |
| Lexington city | 2 567 | 9 458 | 2.19 | 43 | 6.1 | 50 | 7.1 | 640 | 18.7 | 1 540 | 218 | 840 | 79 | 1 109 |
| Lynchburg city | 10 198 | 98 255 | 1.73 | 1 056 | 13.8 | 693 | 9.1 | 9 733 | 17.4 | 13 710 | 2 186 | 7 704 | 2 763 | 3 613 |
| Manassas city | 46 | 40 306 | 1.19 | 638 | 16.2 | 155 | 3.9 | 7 451 | 21.1 | 3 518 | 408 | 1 393 | 963 | 2 516 |

1. Per 1,000 estimated resident population. 2. Data for serious crimes have not been adjusted for underreporting; this may affect comparability between geographic areas and over time. 3. Per 100,000 population estimated by the FBI.

# Table B. States and Counties — Crime, Education, Money Income, and Poverty

| | Serious crimes known to police, 2011 (cont.)[1] | | Education | | | | | | | Money income, 2007–2011 | | | | Income and poverty, 2011 | | |
| | Rate[2] | | School enrollment and attainment, 2007–2011 | | | | Local government expenditures,[5] 2009–2010 | | | Households | | | | Percent below poverty level | | |
| | | | Enrollment[3] | | Attainment[4] (percent) | | | | | Median income | | | | | | |
| STATE County | Violent | Property | Total | Percent private | High school graduate or less | Bachelor's degree or more | Total current expenditures (mil dol) | Current expenditures per student (dollars) | Per capita income[6] (dollars) | Dollars | Percent change, 2000 to 2007–2011 (constant 2011 dollars) | Percent with income of $200,000 or more | Median household income (dollars) | All persons | Children under 18 years | Children 5 to 17 years in families |
| | 46 | 47 | 48 | 49 | 50 | 51 | 52 | 53 | 54 | 55 | 56 | 57 | 58 | 59 | 60 | 61 |
| **VIRGINIA—Cont'd** | | | | | | | | | | | | | | | | |
| Louisa | 92 | 1 079 | 6 712 | 12.7 | 56.6 | 18.1 | 46.4 | 9 853 | 28 030 | 56 502 | 6.2 | 3.8 | 53 267 | 10.8 | 17.0 | 15.7 |
| Lunenburg | 115 | 1 125 | 2 721 | 13.8 | 69.6 | 9.6 | 16.6 | 10 051 | 17 187 | 35 210 | -6.5 | 0.9 | 34 488 | 22.6 | 29.4 | 26.7 |
| Madison | 111 | 891 | 2 856 | 9.0 | 53.4 | 21.4 | 17.2 | 9 204 | 27 359 | 59 734 | 11.0 | 1.7 | 52 116 | 11.9 | 17.7 | 15.7 |
| Mathews | 66 | 1 321 | 1 582 | 6.6 | 51.9 | 22.7 | 12.2 | 9 881 | 29 479 | 54 118 | -7.3 | 2.8 | 54 113 | 10.0 | 18.1 | 16.2 |
| Mecklenburg | 172 | 2 068 | 6 599 | 10.3 | 60.0 | 12.7 | 44.2 | 9 164 | 19 843 | 36 069 | -14.9 | 1.3 | 36 372 | 19.0 | 28.7 | 26.3 |
| Middlesex | 99 | 1 434 | 1 886 | 18.1 | 48.5 | 25.3 | 12.1 | 9 712 | 30 654 | 53 615 | 7.7 | 4.3 | 46 171 | 12.8 | 23.9 | 21.6 |
| Montgomery | 103 | 2 128 | 41 868 | 6.4 | 34.5 | 40.7 | 96.4 | 9 866 | 22 861 | 44 231 | 1.3 | 3.2 | 44 066 | 22.5 | 17.0 | 16.1 |
| Nelson | 39 | 1 329 | 2 937 | 12.3 | 54.2 | 24.6 | 22.2 | 11 211 | 26 060 | 47 426 | -4.5 | 1.8 | 46 055 | 13.6 | 21.0 | 19.8 |
| New Kent | 166 | 1 378 | 4 202 | 9.3 | 47.5 | 22.9 | 24.3 | 8 500 | 32 155 | 71 198 | -1.6 | 3.8 | 69 885 | 6.9 | 10.8 | 9.4 |
| Northampton | 152 | 2 010 | 2 003 | 20.7 | 57.9 | 21.0 | 19.4 | 10 778 | 22 824 | 36 965 | -3.2 | 3.6 | 35 594 | 22.7 | 35.1 | 31.8 |
| Northumberland | 80 | 1 186 | 1 874 | 10.6 | 48.2 | 22.2 | 14.0 | 9 706 | 28 538 | 51 256 | -0.4 | 2.8 | 45 908 | 13.8 | 28.3 | 25.9 |
| Nottoway | 162 | 1 658 | 3 611 | 13.6 | 65.5 | 11.9 | 21.9 | 9 250 | 20 695 | 37 507 | -10.0 | 1.8 | 36 712 | 22.1 | 29.1 | 27.3 |
| Orange | 71 | 1 225 | 7 211 | 15.6 | 50.9 | 21.9 | 45.2 | 8 558 | 26 820 | 56 837 | -1.8 | 2.6 | 56 967 | 11.9 | 17.2 | 16.0 |
| Page | 66 | 1 940 | 4 857 | 8.0 | 69.1 | 12.1 | 35.6 | 9 777 | 22 722 | 43 435 | -3.6 | 1.9 | 40 118 | 17.1 | 23.5 | 21.4 |
| Patrick | 118 | 1 929 | 3 877 | 6.5 | 62.1 | 10.6 | 23.8 | 9 237 | 18 589 | 36 057 | -7.0 | 1.0 | 34 486 | 18.0 | 27.0 | 24.6 |
| Pittsylvania | 90 | 1 136 | 14 197 | 15.4 | 57.8 | 12.7 | 81.2 | 8 740 | 21 219 | 40 333 | -15.0 | 0.8 | 40 664 | 14.7 | 20.8 | 19.1 |
| Powhatan | 60 | 853 | 6 015 | 16.5 | 47.1 | 24.3 | 43.8 | 9 782 | 29 987 | 76 235 | 4.6 | 5.2 | 71 507 | 7.4 | 9.7 | 8.2 |
| Prince Edward | 140 | 1 569 | 8 906 | 19.8 | 60.8 | 19.7 | 26.3 | 10 075 | 17 534 | 36 789 | -12.9 | 1.4 | 36 503 | 25.0 | 27.3 | 25.2 |
| Prince George | 108 | 1 253 | 8 784 | 9.9 | 53.5 | 16.8 | 57.5 | 9 122 | 25 620 | 62 924 | -6.6 | 2.4 | 56 374 | 10.7 | 13.6 | 12.5 |
| Prince William | 134 | 1 747 | 115 676 | 15.8 | 33.3 | 37.7 | 783.1 | 10 188 | 36 842 | 95 531 | 7.3 | 11.2 | 93 101 | 6.9 | 9.7 | 9.3 |
| Pulaski | 159 | 3 545 | 6 924 | 5.6 | 52.7 | 14.7 | 46.4 | 9 818 | 21 623 | 40 987 | -10.4 | 0.5 | 39 054 | 16.5 | 23.9 | 21.2 |
| Rappahannock | 67 | 710 | 1 547 | 23.5 | 41.8 | 37.2 | 10.8 | 11 626 | 39 735 | 64 113 | 3.4 | 7.9 | 59 277 | 10.0 | 16.2 | 14.6 |
| Richmond | 107 | 513 | 1 588 | 8.9 | 65.3 | 9.7 | 13.0 | 10 643 | 20 812 | 46 456 | 4.2 | 1.3 | 39 624 | 20.4 | 25.9 | 23.5 |
| Roanoke | 144 | 1 548 | 21 964 | 16.1 | 36.0 | 32.8 | 130.4 | 8 817 | 31 617 | 62 895 | -2.3 | 3.4 | 60 382 | 8.0 | 10.3 | 8.9 |
| Rockbridge | 102 | 1 364 | 4 789 | 19.6 | 52.6 | 22.0 | 28.7 | 10 225 | 23 022 | 45 489 | -6.5 | 1.6 | 42 567 | 12.9 | 18.6 | 16.6 |
| Rockingham | 65 | 777 | 17 954 | 19.2 | 57.1 | 22.6 | (7)164.6 | (7)9 950 | 26 226 | 51 775 | -5.9 | 2.8 | 51 826 | 9.6 | 13.2 | 12.1 |
| Russell | 89 | 1 789 | 5 945 | 8.2 | 65.0 | 10.5 | 38.5 | 8 920 | 18 331 | 32 555 | -10.1 | 0.6 | 30 562 | 23.5 | 27.2 | 24.9 |
| Scott | 115 | 2 383 | 4 287 | 6.9 | 63.1 | 11.6 | 36.1 | 9 041 | 20 501 | 35 846 | -2.9 | 0.9 | 35 342 | 18.7 | 24.9 | 23.0 |
| Shenandoah | 101 | 1 610 | 8 493 | 13.2 | 58.8 | 18.0 | 63.4 | 10 173 | 24 913 | 50 535 | -4.5 | 1.5 | 47 669 | 13.4 | 20.3 | 19.2 |
| Smyth | 239 | 2 013 | 6 717 | 8.1 | 61.2 | 14.3 | 46.2 | 9 251 | 20 626 | 34 533 | -15.0 | 1.4 | 34 916 | 19.4 | 27.9 | 25.1 |
| Southampton | 112 | 1 580 | 4 007 | 13.0 | 56.8 | 12.7 | 28.9 | 9 866 | 21 212 | 46 733 | 1.8 | 1.3 | 43 374 | 16.0 | 22.1 | 19.6 |
| Spotsylvania | 218 | 2 083 | 35 095 | 12.2 | 41.1 | 29.7 | 226.4 | 9 408 | 31 352 | 78 299 | 0.8 | 4.8 | 75 627 | 7.6 | 11.6 | 10.7 |
| Stafford | 131 | 1 495 | 38 853 | 13.3 | 34.4 | 35.9 | 249.3 | 9 214 | 35 568 | 94 658 | 4.9 | 9.3 | 90 748 | 6.3 | 7.9 | 7.0 |
| Surry | 196 | 770 | 1 697 | 29.1 | 57.4 | 11.5 | 15.1 | 14 890 | 23 986 | 53 505 | 5.5 | 0.4 | 46 486 | 12.8 | 20.3 | 18.4 |
| Sussex | 139 | 1 660 | 2 565 | 13.8 | 73.6 | 10.1 | 18.8 | 15 184 | 16 974 | 40 088 | -4.2 | 0.4 | 37 329 | 20.7 | 23.2 | 22.0 |
| Tazewell | 118 | 2 534 | 9 558 | 9.6 | 57.0 | 13.9 | 58.2 | 8 580 | 19 276 | 36 436 | -1.2 | 0.7 | 36 521 | 17.6 | 23.1 | 20.9 |
| Warren | 97 | 2 122 | 9 137 | 20.1 | 52.3 | 21.7 | 47.0 | 8 635 | 30 069 | 61 379 | 7.2 | 3.9 | 56 450 | 10.4 | 15.8 | 14.3 |
| Washington | 86 | 2 393 | 11 564 | 22.0 | 50.6 | 21.0 | 68.2 | 9 104 | 25 043 | 41 526 | -6.1 | 2.2 | 40 513 | 12.8 | 19.8 | 17.7 |
| Westmoreland | 125 | 1 081 | 3 457 | 6.2 | 60.1 | 14.9 | 24.2 | 10 096 | 26 936 | 52 258 | 8.1 | 2.2 | 43 175 | 17.3 | 28.5 | 25.2 |
| Wise | 160 | 2 384 | 9 003 | 6.7 | 62.0 | 12.7 | 65.4 | 9 646 | 18 458 | 34 717 | -1.7 | 1.3 | 36 286 | 22.8 | 27.8 | 26.0 |
| Wythe | 125 | 1 447 | 6 297 | 6.9 | 54.2 | 14.9 | 39.5 | 9 118 | 23 561 | 40 920 | -6.0 | 2.2 | 39 879 | 14.3 | 22.2 | 20.6 |
| York | 112 | 1 858 | 19 312 | 11.0 | 25.9 | 41.6 | 118.4 | 9 308 | 36 755 | 83 747 | 7.0 | 6.7 | 80 178 | 5.4 | 7.5 | 6.3 |
| **Independent cities** | | | | | | | | | | | | | | | | |
| Alexandria city | 179 | 2 259 | 27 796 | 29.4 | 21.7 | 60.1 | 204.9 | 17 574 | 54 892 | 82 899 | 9.5 | 12.5 | 82 070 | 8.1 | 14.7 | 17.2 |
| Bedford city | 378 | 3 600 | 1 500 | 9.2 | 49.3 | 20.8 | (8) | (8) | 21 533 | 34 647 | -10.9 | 0.0 | 36 552 | 19.7 | 29.4 | 27.8 |
| Bristol city | 316 | 3 635 | 4 030 | 14.6 | 49.4 | 20.5 | 23.5 | 9 980 | 19 273 | 32 122 | -13.1 | 0.3 | 29 612 | 25.8 | 35.2 | 34.0 |
| Buena Vista city | 30 | 802 | 1 942 | 23.2 | 63.8 | 15.5 | 9.6 | 8 412 | 18 268 | 35 426 | -19.0 | 0.0 | 32 855 | 15.1 | 22.1 | 20.6 |
| Charlottesville city | 416 | 3 341 | 17 803 | 8.1 | 33.6 | 48.5 | (9) | (9) | 25 464 | 43 980 | 5.1 | 3.5 | 41 826 | 23.0 | 22.2 | 23.5 |
| Chesapeake city | 398 | 3 208 | 62 976 | 15.7 | 37.5 | 28.1 | 409.9 | 10 278 | 29 985 | 70 115 | 2.3 | 4.2 | 65 699 | 9.3 | 13.5 | 12.0 |
| Colonial Heights city | 182 | 5 261 | 3 878 | 8.8 | 49.1 | 21.2 | 31.9 | 11 146 | 27 633 | 51 396 | -11.9 | 1.0 | 48 299 | 9.7 | 16.1 | 15.4 |
| Covington city | 365 | 2 288 | 1 337 | 0.5 | 57.8 | 10.7 | 10.3 | 11 336 | 21 474 | 36 242 | -11.5 | 1.3 | 35 921 | 16.3 | 25.6 | 22.6 |
| Danville city | 381 | 4 806 | 10 949 | 17.8 | 52.5 | 16.9 | 69.4 | 10 692 | 18 816 | 31 011 | -14.6 | 1.2 | 31 545 | 26.5 | 41.3 | 40.1 |
| Emporia city | 667 | 6 502 | 1 211 | 15.5 | 63.8 | 16.0 | (10) | (10) | 19 492 | 30 481 | -25.6 | 1.4 | 32 807 | 22.8 | 33.5 | 30.3 |
| Fairfax city | 158 | 2 387 | 5 778 | 20.2 | 20.1 | 52.7 | (11) | (11) | 44 980 | 99 300 | 8.7 | 14.6 | 87 307 | 7.3 | 8.6 | 8.5 |
| Falls Church city | 80 | 1 787 | 3 384 | 22.1 | 15.3 | 72.0 | 36.8 | 18 209 | 57 246 | 120 332 | 19.0 | 23.2 | 117 481 | 2.9 | 2.9 | 2.3 |
| Franklin city | 438 | 5 423 | 2 113 | 11.9 | 55.0 | 20.1 | 15.8 | 12 090 | 18 920 | 33 956 | -20.6 | 1.4 | 30 725 | 21.8 | 33.7 | 34.3 |
| Fredericksburg city | 411 | 4 333 | 7 864 | 13.4 | 42.0 | 31.6 | 36.2 | 12 074 | 27 806 | 44 498 | -4.7 | 4.4 | 50 522 | 15.9 | 22.9 | 23.8 |
| Galax city | 449 | 4 996 | 1 263 | 7.4 | 57.2 | 13.0 | 12.6 | 9 206 | 20 232 | 24 711 | -35.2 | 1.4 | 31 740 | 22.9 | 37.3 | 35.5 |
| Hampton city | 247 | 3 794 | 39 688 | 20.9 | 40.5 | 22.5 | 229.4 | 10 637 | 24 715 | 51 083 | -4.3 | 1.2 | 48 656 | 15.3 | 23.7 | 23.0 |
| Harrisonburg city | 200 | 2 152 | 23 305 | 7.2 | 45.4 | 35.1 | (7) | (7) | 16 992 | 37 850 | -6.4 | 1.7 | 36 370 | 27.0 | 23.7 | 23.6 |
| Hopewell city | 612 | 4 195 | 4 830 | 6.8 | 63.6 | 10.6 | 41.3 | 9 922 | 19 463 | 36 477 | -18.6 | 0.7 | 36 792 | 18.3 | 30.2 | 28.9 |
| Lexington city | 56 | 1 052 | 4 266 | 21.4 | 40.6 | 43.6 | 4.5 | 9 086 | 15 088 | 33 670 | -14.0 | 3.4 | 40 105 | 22.8 | 14.1 | 11.7 |
| Lynchburg city | 366 | 3 247 | 26 365 | 53.1 | 42.9 | 30.1 | 90.6 | 10 538 | 22 107 | 37 733 | -13.3 | 3.0 | 36 657 | 22.1 | 25.2 | 25.6 |
| Manassas city | 342 | 2 174 | 10 386 | 14.9 | 45.0 | 27.6 | 80.9 | 11 777 | 28 781 | 73 091 | -10.4 | 5.1 | 65 590 | 10.3 | 16.7 | 15.8 |

1. Data for serious crimes have not been adjusted for underreporting; this may affect comparability between geographic areas and over time.   2. Per 100,000 population estimated by the FBI.   3. All persons 3 years old and over enrolled in nursery school through college.   4. Persons 25 years old and over.   5. Elementary and secondary education expenditures.   6. Based on population estimated by the American Community Survey, 2007–2011.   7. Harrisonburg city is included with Rockingham county.   8. Bedford city is included with Bedford county.   9. Charlottesville city is included with Albemarle county.   10. Emporia city is included with Greensville county.   11. Fairfax city is included with Fairfax county.

# Table B. States and Counties — Personal Income

| STATE County | Personal income, 2011 Total (mil dol) | Per capita Percent change, 2010–2011 | Per capita Dollars | Per capita Rank | Wages and salaries[2] (mil dol) | Proprietors' income (mil dol) | Dividends, interest, and rent (mil dol) | Transfer payments (mil dol) Total | Government payments to individuals Total | Social Security | Medical payments | Income maintenance | Unemployment insurance |
|---|---|---|---|---|---|---|---|---|---|---|---|---|---|
| | 62 | 63 | 64 | 65 | 66 | 67 | 68 | 69 | 70 | 71 | 72 | 73 | 74 |
| **VIRGINIA—Cont'd** | | | | | | | | | | | | | |
| Louisa | 1 372 | 6.1 | 41 096 | 651 | 510 | 199 | 150 | 238 | 231 | 91 | 97 | 24 | 5 |
| Lunenburg | 343 | 3.1 | 26 630 | 2 806 | 111 | 16 | 55 | 108 | 105 | 36 | 44 | 15 | 2 |
| Madison | 479 | 4.8 | 36 389 | 1 151 | 133 | 41 | 91 | 90 | 87 | 35 | 38 | 8 | 2 |
| Mathews | 473 | 4.5 | 52 738 | 149 | 60 | 36 | 110 | 89 | 87 | 36 | 33 | 5 | 1 |
| Mecklenburg | 1 008 | 3.4 | 30 911 | 2 120 | 509 | 56 | 175 | 312 | 305 | 117 | 129 | 38 | 7 |
| Middlesex | 445 | 4.7 | 41 036 | 657 | 137 | 21 | 126 | 111 | 109 | 48 | 42 | 9 | 1 |
| Montgomery | (3)3 175 | (3)5.5 | (3)28 668 | (3)2 513 | (3)2 424 | (3)130 | (3)604 | (3)580 | (3)555 | (3)204 | (3)204 | (3)65 | (3)17 |
| Nelson | 602 | 5.5 | 39 862 | 760 | 145 | 20 | 126 | 136 | 132 | 54 | 56 | 12 | 2 |
| New Kent | 691 | 6.6 | 36 705 | 1 110 | 176 | 20 | 100 | 112 | 108 | 50 | 39 | 8 | 3 |
| Northampton | 446 | 3.0 | 36 011 | 1 209 | 208 | 50 | 93 | 125 | 122 | 43 | 53 | 19 | 2 |
| Northumberland | 523 | 6.5 | 41 936 | 576 | 113 | 32 | 178 | 137 | 134 | 62 | 54 | 11 | 2 |
| Nottoway | 486 | 4.1 | 30 664 | 2 160 | 251 | 18 | 69 | 156 | 153 | 42 | 76 | 19 | 2 |
| Orange | 1 184 | 4.3 | 34 884 | 1 389 | 420 | 39 | 220 | 263 | 255 | 106 | 102 | 21 | 5 |
| Page | 706 | 3.7 | 29 479 | 2 380 | 229 | 43 | 116 | 195 | 189 | 74 | 78 | 21 | 6 |
| Patrick | 481 | 3.1 | 26 156 | 2 864 | 184 | 27 | 74 | 170 | 166 | 66 | 71 | 19 | 4 |
| Pittsylvania | (4)3 308 | (4)4.1 | (4)31 297 | (4)2 044 | (4)1 693 | (4)172 | (4)514 | (4)989 | (4)966 | (4)358 | (4)387 | (4)141 | (4)23 |
| Powhatan | 1 233 | 6.1 | 43 860 | 450 | 358 | 55 | 168 | 153 | 147 | 73 | 51 | 10 | 4 |
| Prince Edward | 524 | 3.4 | 22 457 | 3 074 | 377 | 8 | 91 | 166 | 161 | 55 | 63 | 24 | 4 |
| Prince George | (5)2 302 | (5)8.5 | (5)38 924 | (5)859 | (5)2 449 | (5)63 | (5)280 | (5)411 | (5)399 | (5)135 | (5)153 | (5)57 | (5)10 |
| Prince William | (6)21 307 | (6)7.4 | (6)44 986 | (6)394 | (6)9 108 | (6)795 | (6)2 230 | (6)1 773 | (6)1 669 | (6)552 | (6)608 | (6)225 | (6)62 |
| Pulaski | 1 140 | 5.4 | 32 947 | 1 717 | 591 | 35 | 150 | 329 | 321 | 122 | 138 | 31 | 6 |
| Rappahannock | 321 | 6.0 | 43 172 | 497 | 86 | 25 | 91 | 54 | 52 | 24 | 21 | 3 | 1 |
| Richmond | 248 | 6.1 | 26 941 | 2 770 | 129 | 19 | 47 | 69 | 67 | 24 | 30 | 8 | 1 |
| Roanoke | (7)4 789 | (7)4.3 | (7)40 688 | (7)688 | (7)3 369 | (7)312 | (7)932 | (7)869 | (7)843 | (7)364 | (7)307 | (7)56 | (7)17 |
| Rockbridge | (8)1 153 | (8)4.6 | (8)32 028 | (8)1 879 | (8)590 | (8)52 | (8)270 | (8)280 | (8)272 | (8)115 | (8)107 | (8)25 | (8)6 |
| Rockingham | (9)3 964 | (9)4.9 | (9)31 324 | (9)2 037 | (9)2 890 | (9)293 | (9)720 | (9)690 | (9)662 | (9)273 | (9)245 | (9)78 | (9)19 |
| Russell | 828 | 3.2 | 28 811 | 2 485 | 336 | 24 | 97 | 311 | 305 | 105 | 142 | 35 | 5 |
| Scott | 646 | 4.5 | 27 942 | 2 624 | 213 | 13 | 79 | 236 | 231 | 85 | 105 | 26 | 4 |
| Shenandoah | 1 381 | 5.1 | 32 652 | 1 769 | 570 | 87 | 270 | 302 | 293 | 129 | 111 | 28 | 7 |
| Smyth | 918 | 4.3 | 28 669 | 2 512 | 523 | 32 | 121 | 307 | 300 | 114 | 126 | 38 | 7 |
| Southampton | (10)845 | (10)2.6 | (10)31 313 | (10)2 039 | (10)364 | (10)38 | (10)136 | (10)242 | (10)236 | (10)78 | (10)103 | (10)33 | (10)5 |
| Spotsylvania | (11)6 135 | (11)6.0 | (11)40 893 | (11)667 | (11)2 792 | (11)294 | (11)802 | (11)785 | (11)752 | (11)266 | (11)295 | (11)89 | (11)23 |
| Stafford | 5 539 | 5.4 | 41 917 | 578 | 2 876 | 126 | 623 | 553 | 525 | 171 | 191 | 52 | 17 |
| Surry | 242 | 4.6 | 34 860 | 1 393 | 243 | 11 | 27 | 53 | 52 | 20 | 21 | 6 | 1 |
| Sussex | 359 | 6.5 | 29 736 | 2 331 | 161 | 10 | 43 | 98 | 96 | 31 | 46 | 13 | 2 |
| Tazewell | 1 485 | 5.1 | 33 203 | 1 673 | 755 | 53 | 219 | 463 | 453 | 162 | 185 | 47 | 7 |
| Warren | 1 483 | 5.0 | 39 289 | 824 | 545 | 49 | 179 | 232 | 224 | 91 | 85 | 26 | 7 |
| Washington | (12)2 457 | (12)6.1 | (12)33 851 | (12)1 539 | (12)1 512 | (12)135 | (12)415 | (12)652 | (12)636 | (12)254 | (12)249 | (12)71 | (12)14 |
| Westmoreland | 643 | 6.2 | 36 557 | 1 130 | 142 | 29 | 114 | 156 | 152 | 56 | 67 | 17 | 3 |
| Wise | (13)1 497 | (13)3.4 | (13)32 805 | (13)1 741 | (13)1 077 | (13)84 | (13)153 | (13)485 | (13)475 | (13)158 | (13)206 | (13)60 | (13)7 |
| Wythe | 848 | 5.6 | 29 035 | 2 446 | 487 | 26 | 121 | 256 | 249 | 97 | 101 | 27 | 6 |
| York | (14)3 716 | (14)6.0 | (14)47 564 | (14)279 | (14)1 221 | (14)156 | (14)593 | (14)421 | (14)404 | (14)167 | (14)142 | (14)26 | (14)10 |
| **Independent cities** | | | | | | | | | | | | | |
| Alexandria city | 11 311 | 6.2 | 78 383 | 10 | 9 070 | 498 | 1 744 | 616 | 584 | 186 | 237 | 68 | 22 |
| Bedford city | (15) | (15) | (15) | (15) | (15) | (15) | (15) | (15) | (15) | (15) | (15) | (15) | (15) |
| Bristol city | (12) | (12) | (12) | (12) | (12) | (12) | (12) | (12) | (12) | (12) | (12) | (12) | (12) |
| Buena Vista city | (8) | (8) | (8) | (8) | (8) | (8) | (8) | (8) | (8) | (8) | (8) | (8) | (8) |
| Charlottesville city | (16) | (16) | (16) | (16) | (16) | (16) | (16) | (16) | (16) | (16) | (16) | (16) | (16) |
| Chesapeake city | 9 566 | 4.9 | 42 504 | 541 | 5 013 | 360 | 1 080 | 1 313 | 1 264 | 420 | 490 | 149 | 37 |
| Colonial Heights city | (17) | (17) | (17) | (17) | (17) | (17) | (17) | (17) | (17) | (17) | (17) | (17) | (17) |
| Covington city | (18) | (18) | (18) | (18) | (18) | (18) | (18) | (18) | (18) | (18) | (18) | (18) | (18) |
| Danville city | (4) | (4) | (4) | (4) | (4) | (4) | (4) | (4) | (4) | (4) | (4) | (4) | (4) |
| Emporia city | (19) | (19) | (19) | (19) | (19) | (19) | (19) | (19) | (19) | (19) | (19) | (19) | (19) |
| Fairfax city | (20) | (20) | (20) | (20) | (20) | (20) | (20) | (20) | (20) | (20) | (20) | (20) | (20) |
| Falls Church city | (20) | (20) | (20) | (20) | (20) | (20) | (20) | (20) | (20) | (20) | (20) | (20) | (20) |
| Franklin city | (10) | (10) | (10) | (10) | (10) | (10) | (10) | (10) | (10) | (10) | (10) | (10) | (10) |
| Fredericksburg city | (11) | (11) | (11) | (11) | (11) | (11) | (11) | (11) | (11) | (11) | (11) | (11) | (11) |
| Galax city | (21) | (21) | (21) | (21) | (21) | (21) | (21) | (21) | (21) | (21) | (21) | (21) | (21) |
| Hampton city | 5 456 | 3.7 | 40 001 | 745 | 4 288 | 141 | 680 | 1 043 | 1 014 | 299 | 382 | 142 | 27 |
| Harrisonburg city | (9) | (9) | (9) | (9) | (9) | (9) | (9) | (9) | (9) | (9) | (9) | (9) | (9) |
| Hopewell city | (5) | (5) | (5) | (5) | (5) | (5) | (5) | (5) | (5) | (5) | (5) | (5) | (5) |
| Lexington city | (8) | (8) | (8) | (8) | (8) | (8) | (8) | (8) | (8) | (8) | (8) | (8) | (8) |
| Lynchburg city | (22) | (22) | (22) | (22) | (22) | (22) | (22) | (22) | (22) | (22) | (22) | (22) | (22) |
| Manassas city | (6) | (6) | (6) | (6) | (6) | (6) | (6) | (6) | (6) | (6) | (6) | (6) | (6) |

1. Based on the resident population estimated as of July 1 of the year shown.   2. Includes supplements to wages and salaries.   3. Radford city is included with Montgomery county.   4. Danville city is included with Pittsylvania county.   5. Hopewell city is included with Prince George county.   6. Manassas and Manassas Park cities are included with Prince William county.   7. Salem city is included with Roanoke county.   8. Buena Vista and Lexington cities are included with Rockbridge county.   9. Harrisonburg city is included with Rockingham county.   10. Franklin city is included with Southhampton county.   11. Fredericksburg city is included with Spotsylvania county.   12. Bristol city included with Washington county.   13. Norton city is included with Wise county.   14. Poquoson city is included with York county.   15. Bedford city is included with Bedford county.   16. Charlottesville city is included with Albemarle county.   17. Petersburg and Colonial Heights cities are included with Dinwiddie county.   18. Covington city is included with Alleghany county.   19. Emporia city is included with Greensville county.   20. Fairfax city and Falls Church city are included with Fairfax county.   21. Galax city is included with Carroll county.   22. Lynchburg city is included with Campbell county.

| STATE County | Earnings, 2011 | | | | | | | | | Social Security beneficiaries, December 2011 | | | Housing units, 2010 | |
|---|---|---|---|---|---|---|---|---|---|---|---|---|---|---|
| | | | | Percent by selected industries | | | | | | | | | | |
| | | | Goods-related[1] | | Service-related and health | | | | | | | | | |
| | Total (mil dol) | Farm | Total | Manu-facturing | Information and profes-sional and technical services | Retail trade | Finance, insur-ance, and real estate | Health care and social services | Govern-ment | Number | Rate[2] | Supple-mental Security Income recipients, December 2011 | Total | Percent change, 2000–2010 |
| | 75 | 76 | 77 | 78 | 79 | 80 | 81 | 82 | 83 | 84 | 85 | 86 | 87 | 88 |

| STATE County | 75 | 76 | 77 | 78 | 79 | 80 | 81 | 82 | 83 | 84 | 85 | 86 | 87 | 88 |
|---|---|---|---|---|---|---|---|---|---|---|---|---|---|---|
| **VIRGINIA—Cont'd** | | | | | | | | | | | | | | |
| Louisa | 709 | -0.4 | D | 14.3 | D | 5.3 | 3.7 | 3.0 | 11.4 | 6 955 | 208 | 641 | 16 319 | 37.7 |
| Lunenburg | 127 | 4.9 | 16.1 | 8.8 | D | 6.2 | D | 7.8 | 30.9 | 3 040 | 236 | 485 | 5 935 | 3.5 |
| Madison | 174 | -0.1 | 16.7 | 6.9 | D | 20.5 | D | 5.4 | 17.6 | 2 795 | 212 | 204 | 5 932 | 13.2 |
| Mathews | 97 | 1.8 | 13.6 | 3.3 | D | 8.3 | D | D | 22.0 | 2 710 | 302 | 128 | 5 669 | 6.3 |
| Mecklenburg | 566 | 2.6 | D | 9.6 | D | 7.9 | 3.4 | 15.2 | 20.4 | 9 595 | 294 | 1 306 | 18 591 | 6.8 |
| Middlesex | 157 | 2.4 | 15.6 | 5.9 | D | 7.9 | 3.7 | D | 30.9 | 3 475 | 320 | 227 | 7 133 | 12.0 |
| Montgomery | [3]2 553 | [3]0.1 | [3]D | [3]15.8 | [3]D | [3]6.0 | [3]3.2 | [3]D | [3]38.2 | 13 035 | 138 | 1 253 | 38 569 | 18.6 |
| Nelson | 166 | 1.0 | D | 6.4 | 9.3 | 4.9 | 3.8 | 7.7 | 21.6 | 4 185 | 277 | 364 | 9 931 | 16.1 |
| New Kent | 196 | 0.9 | 26.1 | 3.6 | 3.8 | 6.7 | 2.0 | D | 26.0 | 3 530 | 188 | 172 | 7 295 | 40.2 |
| Northampton | 258 | 17.8 | 11.5 | 8.2 | 2.8 | 5.4 | 3.2 | 21.2 | 19.7 | 3 555 | 287 | 673 | 7 301 | 11.5 |
| Northumberland | 145 | 6.3 | D | 22.9 | D | 6.4 | 3.6 | D | 17.2 | 4 520 | 363 | 245 | 8 995 | 11.5 |
| Nottoway | 270 | 1.8 | D | 5.9 | 2.4 | 6.4 | 2.8 | D | 46.1 | 3 635 | 229 | 580 | 6 650 | 4.3 |
| Orange | 459 | 4.2 | D | 10.5 | 5.0 | 6.4 | 5.6 | 3.4 | 22.6 | 8 060 | 237 | 533 | 14 616 | 28.7 |
| Page | 272 | 6.9 | 18.9 | 12.4 | D | 8.1 | 2.3 | D | 27.9 | 6 135 | 256 | 561 | 11 600 | 9.9 |
| Patrick | 210 | 1.3 | 30.4 | 26.8 | 6.3 | 7.8 | 2.0 | 11.8 | 18.7 | 5 465 | 297 | 531 | 10 083 | 2.6 |
| Pittsylvania | [4]1 865 | [4]0.9 | [4]D | [4]23.4 | [4]3.1 | [4]8.3 | [4]3.2 | [4]13.8 | [4]18.6 | 16 820 | 268 | 2 017 | 31 307 | 11.8 |
| Powhatan | 413 | 0.8 | D | 2.2 | 7.6 | 3.5 | 14.7 | 3.6 | 31.7 | 5 020 | 179 | 249 | 10 043 | 33.7 |
| Prince Edward | 385 | 0.9 | 4.7 | 1.4 | 2.5 | 10.8 | 3.1 | D | 32.1 | 4 575 | 196 | 918 | 9 149 | 21.5 |
| Prince George | [5]2 513 | [5]0.0 | [5]D | [5]10.4 | [5]D | [5]2.0 | [5]1.0 | [5]D | [5]66.3 | 5 500 | 150 | 476 | 12 056 | 12.4 |
| Prince William | [6]9 903 | [6]0.0 | [6]D | [6]4.0 | [6]D | [6]D | [6]D | [6]D | [6]31.3 | 35 465 | 85 | 3 576 | 137 115 | 39.8 |
| Pulaski | 626 | 0.2 | D | 39.0 | 2.7 | 7.8 | 1.8 | D | 18.4 | 9 565 | 276 | 940 | 17 235 | 5.6 |
| Rappahannock | 111 | -5.1 | 15.4 | 2.1 | 35.8 | 6.0 | 3.5 | 2.7 | 16.0 | 1 790 | 240 | 85 | 3 839 | 14.4 |
| Richmond | 147 | 5.8 | 11.3 | 4.3 | 8.3 | 4.9 | 3.2 | D | 34.4 | 1 990 | 216 | 213 | 3 850 | 9.8 |
| Roanoke | [7]3 681 | [7]0.0 | [7]D | [7]19.9 | [7]7.8 | [7]6.3 | [7]7.0 | [7]D | [7]15.8 | 20 465 | 221 | 1 128 | 40 016 | 10.8 |
| Rockbridge | [8]641 | [8]0.0 | [8]D | [8]D | [8]D | [8]7.3 | [8]D | [8]D | [8]22.8 | 5 735 | 256 | 485 | 11 152 | 16.8 |
| Rockingham | [9]3 183 | [9]2.5 | [9]D | [9]19.7 | [9]7.7 | [9]7.9 | [9]3.8 | [9]11.8 | [9]17.5 | 16 010 | 209 | 945 | 33 660 | 23.2 |
| Russell | 360 | -0.2 | 22.3 | 4.1 | 8.2 | 8.3 | 3.8 | D | 21.8 | 8 660 | 301 | 1 521 | 13 484 | 2.2 |
| Scott | 226 | -1.8 | D | 21.9 | D | 9.6 | D | 14.4 | 27.0 | 7 195 | 311 | 1 300 | 11 916 | 4.9 |
| Shenandoah | 657 | 0.7 | D | 25.0 | 6.9 | 7.3 | 3.4 | D | 17.0 | 10 015 | 237 | 646 | 20 876 | 24.9 |
| Smyth | 555 | 0.1 | D | 32.5 | D | 6.6 | 2.3 | D | 24.8 | 9 700 | 303 | 1 343 | 15 427 | 2.1 |
| Southampton | [10]402 | [10]6.1 | [10]9.9 | [10]7.7 | [10]7.8 | [10]4.2 | [10]D | [10]D | [10]31.2 | 4 135 | 225 | 488 | 7 473 | 5.9 |
| Spotsylvania | [11]3 086 | [11]-0.1 | [11]D | [11]D | [11]10.5 | [11]11.9 | [11]5.0 | [11]22.0 | [11]17.5 | 16 790 | 135 | 1 215 | 45 185 | 35.6 |
| Stafford | 3 001 | -0.1 | D | 1.5 | 12.5 | 4.9 | D | 4.3 | 40.7 | 12 925 | 98 | 871 | 43 978 | 40.0 |
| Surry | 253 | 1.5 | 5.8 | 1.8 | 1.8 | 0.5 | 0.6 | 0.2 | 10.0 | 1 600 | 231 | 173 | 3 444 | 4.6 |
| Sussex | 171 | 6.1 | D | D | D | 8.2 | 1.7 | D | 44.4 | 2 510 | 208 | 434 | 4 696 | 0.9 |
| Tazewell | 808 | 0.1 | 24.8 | 13.0 | 4.8 | 11.2 | 3.5 | D | 19.8 | 12 935 | 289 | 2 000 | 20 826 | 2.1 |
| Warren | 594 | -0.8 | D | 11.2 | 4.5 | 8.5 | 3.6 | 11.1 | 18.4 | 6 870 | 182 | 587 | 16 034 | 21.2 |
| Washington | [12]1 647 | [12]0.0 | [12]D | [12]18.0 | [12]4.1 | [12]8.9 | [12]3.6 | [12]D | [12]15.9 | 15 250 | 278 | 1 601 | 25 601 | 11.4 |
| Westmoreland | 171 | 7.4 | 21.8 | 15.0 | D | 6.6 | 4.0 | 5.0 | 24.8 | 4 485 | 255 | 418 | 10 618 | 14.3 |
| Wise | [13]1 161 | [13]-0.1 | [13]36.4 | [13]1.8 | [13]5.5 | [13]7.3 | [13]1.7 | [13]D | [13]20.1 | 11 710 | 282 | 2 517 | 17 940 | 0.8 |
| Wythe | 513 | -0.2 | 29.5 | 24.8 | 3.1 | 10.8 | 3.2 | 11.9 | 22.8 | 7 970 | 273 | 774 | 14 079 | 10.5 |
| York | [14]1 376 | [14]0.1 | [14]12.0 | [14]1.8 | [14]D | [14]8.1 | [14]D | [14]5.6 | [14]33.6 | 9 940 | 150 | 419 | 26 849 | 29.7 |
| **Independent cities** | | | | | | | | | | | | | | |
| Alexandria city | 9 568 | 0.0 | D | D | 26.7 | 3.7 | 5.5 | 4.5 | 31.4 | 12 830 | 89 | 1 629 | 72 376 | 12.6 |
| Bedford city | (15) | (15) | (15) | (15) | (15) | (15) | (15) | (15) | (15) | 1 760 | 285 | 244 | 2 920 | 8.1 |
| Bristol city | (12) | (12) | (12) | (12) | (12) | (12) | (12) | (12) | (12) | 5 055 | 285 | 881 | 8 831 | 4.3 |
| Buena Vista city | (8) | (8) | (8) | (8) | (8) | (8) | (8) | (8) | (8) | 1 540 | 232 | 186 | 2 936 | 8.1 |
| Charlottesville city | (16) | (16) | (16) | (16) | (16) | (16) | (16) | (16) | (16) | 5 790 | 133 | 909 | 19 189 | 9.2 |
| Chesapeake city | 5 373 | 0.2 | 16.3 | 5.8 | 13.9 | 8.9 | 4.9 | 6.9 | 19.8 | 32 645 | 145 | 3 310 | 83 196 | 14.5 |
| Colonial Heights city | (17) | (17) | (17) | (17) | (17) | (17) | (17) | (17) | (17) | 4 275 | 245 | 293 | 7 831 | 6.7 |
| Covington city | (18) | (18) | (18) | (18) | (18) | (18) | (18) | (18) | (18) | 1 840 | 310 | 323 | 3 067 | -4.0 |
| Danville city | (4) | (4) | (4) | (4) | (4) | (4) | (4) | (4) | (4) | 12 210 | 285 | 2 565 | 22 438 | -2.9 |
| Emporia city | (19) | (19) | (19) | (19) | (19) | (19) | (19) | (19) | (19) | 1 295 | 221 | 389 | 2 565 | 6.3 |
| Fairfax city | (20) | (20) | (20) | (20) | (20) | (20) | (20) | (20) | (20) | 3 135 | 139 | 229 | 8 680 | 5.8 |
| Falls Church city | (20) | (20) | (20) | (20) | (20) | (20) | (20) | (20) | (20) | 1 345 | 105 | 93 | 5 489 | 16.2 |
| Franklin city | (10) | (10) | (10) | (10) | (10) | (10) | (10) | (10) | (10) | 2 060 | 240 | 512 | 3 901 | 3.6 |
| Fredericksburg city | (11) | (11) | (11) | (11) | (11) | (11) | (11) | (11) | (11) | 3 485 | 136 | 473 | 10 467 | 17.8 |
| Galax city | (21) | (21) | (21) | (21) | (21) | (21) | (21) | (21) | (21) | 2 200 | 315 | 357 | 3 252 | 1.1 |
| Hampton city | 4 430 | 0.0 | 6.7 | 3.5 | 12.5 | 4.7 | 2.0 | 7.8 | 52.9 | 24 015 | 176 | 3 197 | 59 566 | 3.9 |
| Harrisonburg city | (9) | (9) | (9) | (9) | (9) | (9) | (9) | (9) | (9) | 5 020 | 100 | 706 | 17 444 | 27.5 |
| Hopewell city | (5) | (5) | (5) | (5) | (5) | (5) | (5) | (5) | (5) | 4 800 | 213 | 950 | 10 121 | 3.8 |
| Lexington city | (8) | (8) | (8) | (8) | (8) | (8) | (8) | (8) | (8) | 1 625 | 232 | 128 | 2 546 | 7.2 |
| Lynchburg city | (22) | (22) | (22) | (22) | (22) | (22) | (22) | (22) | (22) | 15 005 | 196 | 2 429 | 31 992 | 15.7 |
| Manassas city | (6) | (6) | (6) | (6) | (6) | (6) | (6) | (6) | (6) | 3 670 | 93 | 389 | 13 123 | 8.3 |

1. Includes mining, construction, and manufacturing.   2. Per 1,000 resident population enumerated in the 2010 census.   3. Radford city is included with Montgomery county.   4. Danville city is included with Pittsylvania county.   5. Hopewell city is included with Prince George county.   6. Manassas and Manassas Park cities are included with Prince William county.   7. Salem city is included with Roanoke county.   8. Buena Vista and Lexington cities are included with Rockbridge county.   9. Harrisonburg city is included with Rockingham county.   10. Franklin city is included with Southampton county.   11. Fredericksburg city is included with Spotsylvania county.   12. Bristol city included with Washington county.   13. Norton city is included with Wise county.   14. Poquoson city is included with York county.   15. Bedford city is included with Bedford county.   16. Charlottesville city is included with Albemarle county.   17. Petersburg and Colonial Heights cities are included with Dinwiddie county.   18. Covington city is included with Alleghany county.   19. Emporia city is included with Greensville county.   20. Fairfax city and Falls Church city are included with Fairfax county.   21. Galax city is included with Carroll county.   22. Lynchburg city is included with Campbell county.

# Table B. States and Counties — Housing, Labor Force, and Employment

| | Housing units, 2007–2011 | | | | | | | | Civilian labor force, 2012 | | | | Civilian employment,[6] 2007–2011 | | |
|---|---|---|---|---|---|---|---|---|---|---|---|---|---|---|---|
| | Occupied units | | | | | | | | | | Unemployment | | Percent | | |
| | | Owner-occupied | | | | Renter-occupied | | | | | | | | | |
| | | | | Median owner cost as a percent of income | | | | | | | | | | | |
| STATE County | Total | Percent | Median value[1] | With a mortgage | Without a mortgage[2] | Median rent[3] | Median rent as a percent of income | Sub-standard units[4] (percent) | Total | Percent change, 2011–2012 | Total | Rate[5] | Total | Management, business, science and arts | Construction, production, and maintenance occupations |
| | 89 | 90 | 91 | 92 | 93 | 94 | 95 | 96 | 97 | 98 | 99 | 100 | 101 | 102 | 103 |

**VIRGINIA—Cont'd**

| | | | | | | | | | | | | | | | |
|---|---|---|---|---|---|---|---|---|---|---|---|---|---|---|---|
| Louisa | 13 213 | 77.9 | 211 200 | 23.5 | 10.4 | 820 | 26.9 | 1.7 | 16 797 | 0.8 | 1 081 | 6.4 | 16 027 | 29.4 | 30.2 |
| Lunenburg | 4 471 | 73.1 | 104 800 | 25.4 | 13.2 | 658 | 36.1 | 3.1 | 5 170 | -2.1 | 436 | 8.4 | 4 828 | 20.8 | 29.5 |
| Madison | 5 185 | 79.3 | 254 100 | 24.7 | 10.8 | 867 | 26.7 | 2.2 | 7 189 | 0.5 | 340 | 4.7 | 6 758 | 30.9 | 29.2 |
| Mathews | 3 788 | 83.1 | 219 300 | 20.0 | 9.9 | 884 | 30.5 | 1.4 | 4 370 | -0.4 | 234 | 5.4 | 3 779 | 29.2 | 33.6 |
| Mecklenburg | 12 547 | 74.5 | 124 000 | 26.3 | 13.9 | 603 | 30.9 | 3.0 | 13 151 | -2.4 | 1 285 | 9.8 | 12 364 | 27.2 | 29.7 |
| Middlesex | 4 339 | 81.6 | 254 700 | 23.5 | 10.3 | 749 | 28.6 | 0.4 | 5 010 | -0.1 | 314 | 6.3 | 4 611 | 32.6 | 30.8 |
| Montgomery | 34 591 | 55.0 | 196 300 | 22.0 | 9.9 | 771 | 37.5 | 1.1 | 48 007 | 2.0 | 2 936 | 6.1 | 44 961 | 45.4 | 16.0 |
| Nelson | 6 539 | 75.0 | 187 900 | 24.1 | 9.9 | 705 | 24.5 | 3.6 | 7 698 | -0.1 | 415 | 5.4 | 7 119 | 36.1 | 23.3 |
| New Kent | 6 552 | 90.9 | 255 100 | 24.2 | 12.2 | 1 060 | 28.6 | 0.9 | 10 260 | 0.7 | 574 | 5.6 | 9 118 | 35.9 | 25.2 |
| Northampton | 5 195 | 69.4 | 206 600 | 24.1 | 13.2 | 654 | 28.1 | 4.2 | 6 297 | -1.1 | 552 | 8.8 | 5 322 | 36.7 | 26.1 |
| Northumberland | 5 569 | 83.1 | 246 000 | 29.5 | 10.4 | 743 | 33.2 | 1.5 | 5 650 | -2.9 | 478 | 8.5 | 5 367 | 29.1 | 27.0 |
| Nottoway | 5 571 | 67.7 | 130 900 | 25.1 | 13.3 | 800 | 36.2 | 2.0 | 6 348 | -1.6 | 455 | 7.2 | 6 657 | 22.8 | 29.2 |
| Orange | 12 614 | 76.3 | 238 500 | 26.2 | 9.9 | 952 | 26.2 | 1.9 | 15 322 | 0.6 | 1 011 | 6.6 | 14 371 | 32.5 | 27.9 |
| Page | 9 538 | 75.3 | 177 300 | 23.8 | 12.6 | 695 | 30.1 | 2.9 | 11 627 | -3.1 | 1 177 | 10.1 | 10 835 | 22.8 | 35.8 |
| Patrick | 7 191 | 79.8 | 106 500 | 22.0 | 9.9 | 438 | 28.1 | 1.2 | 8 706 | -1.7 | 695 | 8.0 | 7 314 | 25.8 | 34.0 |
| Pittsylvania | 26 325 | 79.6 | 105 100 | 23.6 | 12.4 | 583 | 27.6 | 2.5 | 31 965 | -1.1 | 2 330 | 7.3 | 27 611 | 24.8 | 34.6 |
| Powhatan | 9 468 | 88.8 | 283 300 | 23.5 | 10.8 | 1 008 | 28.5 | 0.3 | 14 304 | 1.1 | 773 | 5.4 | 12 248 | 39.0 | 20.6 |
| Prince Edward | 7 334 | 65.7 | 147 400 | 23.5 | 10.6 | 718 | 31.0 | 2.9 | 9 876 | -0.7 | 864 | 8.7 | 9 047 | 29.5 | 22.4 |
| Prince George | 10 725 | 75.9 | 206 900 | 22.8 | 10.2 | 1 097 | 30.4 | 0.6 | 14 908 | 1.2 | 967 | 6.5 | 13 081 | 32.7 | 27.1 |
| Prince William | 127 170 | 74.2 | 353 300 | 25.9 | 9.9 | 1 402 | 29.8 | 2.8 | 230 271 | 0.8 | 11 212 | 4.9 | 200 941 | 43.4 | 17.6 |
| Pulaski | 14 884 | 72.5 | 127 600 | 22.1 | 10.5 | 570 | 28.6 | 1.3 | 17 546 | 1.7 | 1 147 | 6.5 | 15 338 | 26.0 | 31.4 |
| Rappahannock | 3 310 | 75.1 | 415 400 | 24.8 | 14.3 | 975 | 28.1 | 3.1 | 4 266 | 1.6 | 214 | 5.0 | 3 829 | 43.2 | 23.3 |
| Richmond | 2 909 | 79.0 | 155 200 | 21.9 | 12.1 | 717 | 25.2 | 1.6 | 3 525 | -11.7 | 307 | 8.7 | 3 728 | 21.2 | 32.8 |
| Roanoke | 37 975 | 77.1 | 196 500 | 22.1 | 9.9 | 793 | 24.9 | 1.1 | 49 085 | 0.6 | 2 569 | 5.2 | 47 118 | 42.5 | 19.4 |
| Rockbridge | 9 291 | 73.5 | 179 100 | 26.8 | 11.2 | 644 | 28.6 | 2.2 | 10 878 | -2.0 | 647 | 5.9 | 10 108 | 28.5 | 32.5 |
| Rockingham | 29 711 | 76.4 | 196 700 | 24.4 | 9.9 | 764 | 25.8 | 3.0 | 41 737 | -0.3 | 2 217 | 5.3 | 37 523 | 30.5 | 31.4 |
| Russell | 11 302 | 76.7 | 89 000 | 22.3 | 10.5 | 503 | 33.5 | 1.6 | 11 513 | -1.8 | 1 018 | 8.8 | 10 992 | 25.5 | 35.2 |
| Scott | 9 701 | 78.0 | 90 400 | 19.3 | 9.9 | 442 | 26.1 | 3.1 | 10 070 | 0.2 | 847 | 8.4 | 9 089 | 23.9 | 33.7 |
| Shenandoah | 17 152 | 70.3 | 215 100 | 24.8 | 9.9 | 748 | 30.2 | 2.3 | 19 752 | -1.6 | 1 297 | 6.6 | 19 651 | 26.5 | 32.8 |
| Smyth | 12 681 | 71.4 | 87 400 | 20.9 | 10.0 | 514 | 25.9 | 2.0 | 14 442 | -1.5 | 1 264 | 8.8 | 12 979 | 30.9 | 33.1 |
| Southampton | 6 618 | 73.8 | 150 900 | 24.1 | 12.2 | 724 | 29.5 | 3.0 | 8 155 | 2.0 | 580 | 7.1 | 8 312 | 24.8 | 34.4 |
| Spotsylvania | 41 282 | 78.0 | 286 800 | 24.9 | 10.3 | 1 213 | 30.3 | 1.4 | 66 541 | 0.6 | 3 330 | 5.0 | 58 538 | 38.9 | 18.5 |
| Stafford | 40 691 | 78.9 | 334 800 | 24.7 | 9.9 | 1 329 | 29.1 | 1.8 | 69 672 | 0.7 | 3 397 | 4.9 | 60 000 | 44.7 | 16.1 |
| Surry | 2 547 | 74.1 | 174 500 | 23.8 | 11.9 | 575 | 20.5 | 5.9 | 3 677 | -0.3 | 270 | 7.3 | 3 239 | 20.2 | 38.8 |
| Sussex | 3 600 | 64.3 | 122 400 | 22.8 | 13.1 | 671 | 27.4 | 1.7 | 4 399 | 0.5 | 366 | 8.3 | 4 738 | 21.4 | 31.3 |
| Tazewell | 18 019 | 72.7 | 84 900 | 20.7 | 9.9 | 535 | 28.4 | 1.3 | 20 605 | -0.7 | 1 447 | 7.0 | 17 152 | 28.1 | 28.6 |
| Warren | 14 203 | 74.3 | 244 000 | 24.0 | 11.5 | 884 | 30.0 | 1.9 | 20 029 | 0.4 | 1 184 | 5.9 | 19 271 | 30.1 | 26.4 |
| Washington | 23 064 | 74.9 | 128 900 | 22.4 | 9.9 | 610 | 26.4 | 1.8 | 27 760 | -1.0 | 1 964 | 7.1 | 24 627 | 31.9 | 27.2 |
| Westmoreland | 7 077 | 75.0 | 190 000 | 24.7 | 11.6 | 851 | 24.1 | 4.0 | 8 765 | -3.8 | 656 | 7.5 | 7 767 | 28.0 | 28.2 |
| Wise | 15 477 | 70.0 | 79 800 | 20.1 | 10.5 | 524 | 25.7 | 3.5 | 18 841 | -4.1 | 1 451 | 7.7 | 15 047 | 26.9 | 30.2 |
| Wythe | 11 610 | 73.8 | 112 400 | 21.4 | 9.9 | 554 | 24.6 | 2.3 | 15 638 | -1.0 | 1 045 | 6.7 | 13 193 | 28.4 | 33.1 |
| York | 24 259 | 77.2 | 323 900 | 22.8 | 10.1 | 1 257 | 28.2 | 1.4 | 33 416 | 0.0 | 1 706 | 5.1 | 29 389 | 49.7 | 15.3 |
| Independent cities | | | | | | | | | | | | | | | |
| Alexandria city | 64 217 | 45.0 | 480 300 | 23.7 | 11.6 | 1 395 | 27.1 | 2.4 | 90 927 | 0.9 | 4 214 | 4.6 | 84 559 | 58.3 | 9.6 |
| Bedford city | 2 776 | 62.5 | 148 000 | 23.5 | 16.3 | 707 | 31.1 | 0.0 | 2 472 | -0.3 | 212 | 8.6 | 2 678 | 29.9 | 30.2 |
| Bristol city | 7 873 | 60.6 | 97 400 | 24.1 | 12.2 | 564 | 28.2 | 1.9 | 8 053 | -1.5 | 643 | 8.0 | 7 018 | 28.4 | 23.7 |
| Buena Vista city | 2 681 | 63.9 | 122 800 | 20.1 | 12.7 | 640 | 36.8 | 2.1 | 3 237 | -2.2 | 235 | 7.3 | 2 982 | 26.6 | 32.6 |
| Charlottesville city | 17 387 | 41.3 | 283 800 | 24.7 | 13.6 | 967 | 33.8 | 1.9 | 22 105 | -0.4 | 1 310 | 5.9 | 21 066 | 48.9 | 11.2 |
| Chesapeake city | 78 898 | 74.3 | 271 700 | 27.2 | 12.4 | 1 090 | 31.8 | 2.2 | 117 375 | -0.1 | 7 097 | 6.0 | 106 084 | 39.4 | 19.9 |
| Colonial Heights city | 7 136 | 65.3 | 189 000 | 24.4 | 11.8 | 881 | 26.7 | 0.8 | 8 975 | 0.5 | 608 | 6.8 | 8 166 | 30.9 | 22.7 |
| Covington city | 2 546 | 70.3 | 64 900 | 23.5 | 12.2 | 638 | 24.8 | 0.3 | 2 669 | 1.4 | 253 | 9.5 | 2 525 | 22.1 | 29.3 |
| Danville city | 18 938 | 55.1 | 88 900 | 24.7 | 13.4 | 589 | 34.6 | 2.3 | 19 100 | -1.5 | 2 024 | 10.6 | 17 197 | 27.4 | 27.7 |
| Emporia city | 2 525 | 48.2 | 94 500 | 27.0 | 18.3 | 587 | 29.1 | 3.9 | 2 487 | -3.3 | 288 | 11.6 | 2 256 | 33.9 | 21.9 |
| Fairfax city | 8 470 | 69.4 | 472 600 | 24.6 | 9.9 | 1 653 | 31.1 | 1.4 | 13 393 | 0.5 | 826 | 6.2 | 11 869 | 53.2 | 10.8 |
| Falls Church city | 4 807 | 61.7 | 658 500 | 22.4 | 12.5 | 1 484 | 28.0 | 1.5 | 7 769 | 0.5 | 532 | 6.8 | 6 336 | 67.6 | 4.3 |
| Franklin city | 3 472 | 42.5 | 196 100 | 27.0 | 14.4 | 765 | 36.9 | 2.5 | 3 927 | 2.3 | 401 | 10.2 | 3 123 | 29.9 | 24.2 |
| Fredericksburg city | 9 341 | 38.7 | 333 000 | 23.8 | 12.8 | 1 050 | 34.3 | 1.4 | 14 309 | 0.0 | 1 213 | 8.5 | 10 782 | 39.5 | 16.6 |
| Galax city | 3 525 | 63.2 | 91 700 | 23.8 | 14.8 | 452 | 28.9 | 1.8 | 3 072 | -3.0 | 267 | 8.7 | 2 974 | 24.7 | 31.7 |
| Hampton city | 52 667 | 61.1 | 197 500 | 26.1 | 14.2 | 963 | 32.1 | 6.3 | 63 959 | -0.5 | 4 988 | 7.8 | 61 625 | 31.8 | 24.2 |
| Harrisonburg city | 15 179 | 37.3 | 218 400 | 22.6 | 9.9 | 815 | 32.9 | 4.9 | 25 277 | -0.5 | 1 726 | 6.8 | 20 396 | 31.1 | 26.4 |
| Hopewell city | 8 859 | 50.1 | 140 000 | 26.7 | 11.7 | 769 | 28.7 | 3.0 | 10 244 | -0.8 | 891 | 8.7 | 8 321 | 23.2 | 28.7 |
| Lexington city | 1 727 | 51.0 | 253 700 | 23.2 | 11.5 | 695 | 28.6 | 3.5 | 2 284 | -1.8 | 261 | 11.4 | 2 036 | 38.3 | 6.7 |
| Lynchburg city | 28 513 | 55.4 | 146 100 | 23.6 | 11.9 | 697 | 32.0 | 2.0 | 34 770 | -0.8 | 2 650 | 7.6 | 32 891 | 34.1 | 18.0 |
| Manassas city | 11 872 | 66.4 | 278 900 | 24.6 | 14.6 | 1 226 | 35.5 | 7.7 | 21 906 | 0.8 | 1 374 | 6.3 | 18 994 | 33.0 | 23.1 |

1. Specified owner-occupied units. 2. A value of 9.9 represents 9.9 percent or less. 3. Specified renter-occupied units. A value of 10.0 represents 10 percent or less. 4. Overcrowded or lacking complete plumbing facilities. 5. Percent of civilian labor force. 6. Persons 16 years old and over.

**Nonfarm Employment and Agriculture**

| STATE County | \| Private nonfarm establishments, employment and payroll, 2011 | | | | | | | | \| Agriculture, 2007 | | | |
|---|---|---|---|---|---|---|---|---|---|---|---|---|
| | Number of establishments | Employment | | | | | | Annual payroll | | Farms | | | |
| | | Total | Health care and social assistance | Manufacturing | Retail trade | Finance and insurance | Professional, scientific, and technical services | Total (mil dol) | Average per employee (dollars) | Number | Percent with: | | Farm operators whose principal occupation is farming (percent) |
| | | | | | | | | | | | Fewer than 50 acres | 500 acres or more | |
| | 104 | 105 | 106 | 107 | 108 | 109 | 110 | 111 | 112 | 113 | 114 | 115 | 116 |

VIRGINIA—Cont'd

| | | | | | | | | | | | | | |
|---|---|---|---|---|---|---|---|---|---|---|---|---|---|
| Louisa | 535 | 6 663 | 336 | 1 102 | 1 082 | 114 | 154 | 292 | 43 794 | 534 | 39.0 | 5.8 | 40.3 |
| Lunenburg | 178 | 1 514 | 233 | D | 233 | D | 39 | 41 | 27 118 | 371 | 21.0 | 10.5 | 39.4 |
| Madison | 264 | 2 566 | D | 196 | 944 | 26 | 51 | 74 | 28 851 | 564 | 43.6 | 8.0 | 44.9 |
| Mathews | 177 | 964 | 130 | D | 217 | 21 | D | 22 | 22 327 | 50 | 72.0 | 4.0 | 34.0 |
| Mecklenburg | 802 | 9 674 | 1 774 | 1 419 | 1 774 | 293 | 304 | 270 | 27 915 | 580 | 20.2 | 13.4 | 48.3 |
| Middlesex | 338 | 2 139 | 433 | 153 | 441 | D | 124 | 57 | 26 642 | 76 | 44.7 | 9.2 | 43.4 |
| Montgomery | 1 948 | 26 204 | 3 801 | 3 470 | 4 858 | 920 | 1 978 | 839 | 32 013 | 628 | 42.2 | 5.7 | 43.6 |
| Nelson | 391 | 2 997 | D | D | 328 | 41 | 150 | 70 | 23 476 | 462 | 35.3 | 5.0 | 32.7 |
| New Kent | 336 | 2 491 | 521 | 109 | 425 | D | 61 | 76 | 30 440 | 121 | 52.1 | 8.3 | 40.5 |
| Northampton | 319 | 3 038 | D | D | 554 | D | D | 91 | 30 013 | 151 | 41.7 | 22.5 | 62.3 |
| Northumberland | 359 | 1 813 | D | 433 | 357 | 69 | 83 | 57 | 31 456 | 129 | 42.6 | 21.7 | 54.3 |
| Nottoway | 310 | 3 583 | D | 380 | 646 | 132 | 120 | 94 | 26 345 | 394 | 29.7 | 5.1 | 43.9 |
| Orange | 662 | 5 443 | 401 | 760 | 941 | 140 | 288 | 183 | 33 543 | 518 | 35.9 | 9.5 | 38.8 |
| Page | 402 | 4 092 | 537 | 645 | 763 | D | 169 | 108 | 26 413 | 530 | 49.2 | 4.2 | 49.2 |
| Patrick | 304 | 3 661 | 570 | 1 525 | 516 | 78 | D | 94 | 25 627 | 613 | 35.9 | 3.6 | 38.5 |
| Pittsylvania | 843 | 8 192 | 1 168 | 1 957 | 979 | 135 | 136 | 231 | 28 160 | 1 356 | 22.4 | 8.8 | 44.8 |
| Powhatan | 628 | 3 859 | 205 | 154 | 537 | D | 213 | 122 | 31 700 | 228 | 49.6 | 5.7 | 38.6 |
| Prince Edward | 536 | 6 906 | 2 004 | 121 | 1 572 | 198 | D | 187 | 27 150 | 446 | 23.1 | 6.7 | 39.9 |
| Prince George | 440 | 6 486 | 307 | 687 | 797 | 146 | 545 | 231 | 35 576 | 186 | 37.6 | 10.8 | 39.8 |
| Prince William | 7 037 | 86 289 | 8 285 | 1 920 | 19 921 | 1 907 | 10 811 | 3 318 | 38 457 | 345 | 60.9 | 2.0 | 34.5 |
| Pulaski | 625 | 9 402 | 1 073 | 3 128 | 1 621 | 147 | D | 354 | 37 690 | 415 | 39.3 | 7.2 | 34.9 |
| Rappahannock | 182 | 961 | 41 | D | 134 | D | 80 | 29 | 30 566 | 416 | 46.6 | 5.8 | 44.7 |
| Richmond | 188 | 2 084 | D | 120 | 290 | 64 | D | 52 | 24 974 | 124 | 28.2 | 18.5 | 53.2 |
| Roanoke | 2 061 | 29 965 | 4 768 | 3 558 | 3 635 | 4 272 | 1 775 | 1 099 | 36 663 | 345 | 55.1 | 2.6 | 40.9 |
| Rockbridge | 428 | 4 337 | 213 | D | 1 173 | D | D | 113 | 26 111 | 805 | 36.8 | 7.1 | 41.1 |
| Rockingham | 1 382 | 22 532 | 1 686 | 6 785 | 1 850 | 420 | 353 | 818 | 36 298 | 1 970 | 43.3 | 3.3 | 51.3 |
| Russell | 476 | 5 540 | 874 | 576 | 1 006 | D | 226 | 168 | 30 399 | 1 019 | 38.2 | 4.7 | 35.9 |
| Scott | 299 | 3 365 | 571 | D | 729 | 100 | 200 | 111 | 32 848 | 1 396 | 36.4 | 2.5 | 38.0 |
| Shenandoah | 889 | 11 322 | 1 123 | 3 419 | 1 752 | 305 | 308 | 330 | 29 159 | 1 043 | 46.9 | 5.1 | 43.6 |
| Smyth | 536 | 8 997 | 1 793 | 3 109 | 1 289 | 154 | D | 280 | 31 102 | 761 | 45.6 | 7.4 | 40.7 |
| Southampton | 227 | 1 932 | 154 | 486 | 300 | D | D | 53 | 27 668 | 342 | 23.1 | 25.4 | 50.0 |
| Spotsylvania | 2 256 | 26 692 | 2 503 | 1 581 | 7 050 | 806 | 2 060 | 901 | 33 771 | 359 | 50.4 | 6.7 | 42.6 |
| Stafford | 2 054 | 28 221 | 3 152 | 691 | 4 392 | D | 4 029 | 1 107 | 39 215 | 233 | 55.4 | 2.6 | 48.1 |
| Surry | 78 | D | D | D | 54 | D | D | D | D | 121 | 38.8 | 20.7 | 52.1 |
| Sussex | 181 | 1 982 | 440 | 99 | 300 | 40 | D | 57 | 28 948 | 151 | 24.5 | 23.8 | 55.6 |
| Tazewell | 1 107 | 13 452 | 2 396 | 1 476 | 3 118 | 561 | 377 | 427 | 31 777 | 576 | 30.6 | 14.1 | 42.2 |
| Warren | 792 | 9 418 | 1 216 | 991 | 1 702 | 242 | 412 | 283 | 29 996 | 387 | 48.3 | 4.9 | 33.6 |
| Washington | 1 174 | 16 814 | 2 485 | 3 903 | 3 097 | 487 | 729 | 580 | 34 474 | 1 791 | 49.7 | 3.5 | 37.9 |
| Westmoreland | 329 | 2 738 | 240 | 641 | 426 | D | 125 | 66 | 23 985 | 171 | 28.1 | 22.2 | 50.3 |
| Wise | 815 | 11 355 | 1 677 | 154 | 2 080 | 248 | 442 | 469 | 41 300 | 178 | 55.1 | 5.1 | 28.7 |
| Wythe | 685 | 8 898 | 1 229 | 1 978 | 1 926 | D | 173 | 269 | 30 204 | 946 | 30.9 | 6.1 | 41.2 |
| York | 1 425 | 16 986 | 1 898 | 307 | 4 057 | 420 | 1 023 | 499 | 29 378 | 45 | 84.4 | 0.0 | 60.0 |
| Independent cities | | | | | | | | | | | | | |
| Alexandria city | 4 525 | 80 378 | 7 150 | 1 333 | 7 355 | 2 753 | 17 943 | 4 567 | 56 822 | NA | NA | NA | NA |
| Bedford city | 298 | 3 645 | 920 | 814 | 383 | 136 | 118 | 103 | 28 261 | NA | NA | NA | NA |
| Bristol city | 628 | 11 960 | 631 | 1 715 | 1 675 | 354 | 236 | 457 | 38 198 | NA | NA | NA | NA |
| Buena Vista city | 116 | 1 912 | 262 | 963 | 123 | 32 | D | 68 | 35 540 | NA | NA | NA | NA |
| Charlottesville city | 2 016 | 30 253 | 9 218 | 524 | 3 594 | 800 | 2 243 | 1 257 | 41 562 | NA | NA | NA | NA |
| Chesapeake city | 5 272 | 84 312 | 9 394 | 3 831 | 15 036 | 3 540 | 7 570 | 3 090 | 36 648 | 291 | 70.4 | 7.9 | 54.3 |
| Colonial Heights city | 693 | 9 626 | 1 581 | D | 3 763 | 243 | 529 | 235 | 24 447 | NA | NA | NA | NA |
| Covington city | 237 | 3 525 | 177 | D | D | D | 96 | 59 | 44 182 | NA | NA | NA | NA |
| Danville city | 1 338 | 23 173 | 4 785 | 4 568 | 4 240 | 899 | 421 | 714 | 30 808 | NA | NA | NA | NA |
| Emporia city | 231 | 3 931 | 1 172 | D | 770 | 74 | 72 | 114 | 28 946 | NA | NA | NA | NA |
| Fairfax city | 2 289 | 27 013 | 3 176 | 203 | 5 627 | 1 296 | 6 103 | 1 315 | 48 664 | NA | NA | NA | NA |
| Falls Church city | 804 | 9 813 | 1 775 | D | 1 166 | 190 | 1 800 | 444 | 45 250 | NA | NA | NA | NA |
| Franklin city | 287 | 3 492 | 1 210 | D | 971 | 204 | D | 95 | 27 333 | NA | NA | NA | NA |
| Fredericksburg city | 1 316 | 20 522 | 6 117 | 283 | 3 988 | 664 | 1 135 | 796 | 38 766 | NA | NA | NA | NA |
| Galax city | 316 | 5 125 | 1 509 | 1 045 | 1 137 | 126 | 147 | 142 | 27 771 | NA | NA | NA | NA |
| Hampton city | 2 373 | 41 368 | 6 970 | 2 088 | 6 642 | 1 027 | 4 258 | 1 489 | 35 995 | NA | NA | NA | NA |
| Harrisonburg city | 1 576 | 25 867 | 5 235 | 2 104 | 5 744 | 878 | 900 | 810 | 31 302 | NA | NA | NA | NA |
| Hopewell city | 459 | 6 990 | 1 343 | D | 772 | 127 | 562 | 311 | 44 487 | NA | NA | NA | NA |
| Lexington city | 306 | 3 784 | 657 | D | 427 | 108 | 106 | 130 | 34 286 | NA | NA | NA | NA |
| Lynchburg city | 2 162 | 55 867 | 9 678 | 9 044 | 7 470 | 2 956 | 3 554 | 2 211 | 39 568 | NA | NA | NA | NA |
| Manassas city | 1 384 | 21 146 | 4 223 | 3 934 | 2 489 | 447 | 3 374 | 1 238 | 58 543 | NA | NA | NA | NA |

# Table B. States and Counties — **Agriculture**

| | Agriculture, 2007 (cont.) | | | | | | | | | | | | | | |
|---|---|---|---|---|---|---|---|---|---|---|---|---|---|---|---|
| | Land in farms | | | | | Value of land and buildings (dollars) | | | Value of products sold | | | | Percent of farms with sales of: | | Government payments | |
| | | | Acres | | | | | | | | Percent from: | | | | | |
| STATE County | Acreage (1,000) | Percent change, 2002–2007 | Average size of farm | Total irrigated (1,000) | Total cropland (1,000) | Average per farm | Average per acre | Value of machinery and equipment, average per farm (dollars) | Total (mil dol) | Average per farm (dollars) | Crops | Live-stock and poultry products | $10,000 or more | $100,000 or more | Total ($1,000) | Percent of farms |
| | 117 | 118 | 119 | 120 | 121 | 122 | 123 | 124 | 125 | 126 | 127 | 128 | 129 | 130 | 131 | 132 |
| VIRGINIA—Cont'd | | | | | | | | | | | | | | | | |
| Louisa | 79 | -9.2 | 147 | 0.3 | 30.1 | 720 509 | 4 901 | 51 235 | 12.2 | 22 816 | 29.3 | 70.7 | 25.7 | 4.1 | 258 | 21.5 |
| Lunenburg | 83 | -9.8 | 224 | 0.8 | 31.6 | 660 098 | 2 942 | 58 144 | 9.7 | 26 064 | 45.8 | 54.2 | 31.0 | 3.8 | 439 | 34.8 |
| Madison | 103 | 0.0 | 182 | 0.1 | 42.0 | 1 052 790 | 5 778 | 68 641 | 20.2 | 35 857 | 28.3 | 71.7 | 34.9 | 7.1 | 310 | 19.1 |
| Mathews | 4 | NA | 88 | 0.1 | 3.2 | 503 398 | 5 705 | 41 862 | 3.0 | 60 390 | 86.1 | 13.9 | 38.0 | 12.0 | 54 | 18.0 |
| Mecklenburg | 157 | -6.5 | 271 | 3.2 | 66.1 | 858 108 | 3 164 | 74 587 | 32.3 | 55 628 | 65.8 | 34.2 | 34.3 | 9.8 | 587 | 24.8 |
| Middlesex | 18 | -14.3 | 233 | 0.5 | 13.7 | 1 172 720 | 5 033 | 108 046 | 6.2 | 82 077 | 89.9 | 10.1 | 48.7 | 10.5 | 373 | 42.1 |
| Montgomery | 89 | -11.0 | 142 | 0.4 | 30.2 | 587 681 | 4 128 | 57 023 | 19.0 | 30 219 | 27.6 | 72.4 | 34.9 | 4.8 | 327 | 12.9 |
| Nelson | 73 | -14.1 | 158 | 0.8 | 22.9 | 741 745 | 4 685 | 49 064 | 12.4 | 26 937 | 69.2 | 30.8 | 34.4 | 3.2 | 76 | 10.2 |
| New Kent | 20 | 5.3 | 168 | 0.5 | 14.1 | 898 236 | 5 338 | 59 461 | 4.6 | 38 132 | 93.5 | 6.5 | 27.3 | 9.1 | 214 | 19.8 |
| Northampton | 64 | 23.1 | 422 | 9.3 | 58.2 | 1 662 991 | 3 938 | 222 557 | 90.1 | 596 486 | 65.9 | 34.1 | 74.8 | 51.0 | 1 181 | 43.7 |
| Northumberland | 44 | 10.0 | 344 | 0.1 | 36.9 | 1 305 871 | 3 796 | 161 323 | 11.9 | 92 047 | 95.4 | 4.6 | 47.3 | 19.4 | 971 | 47.3 |
| Nottoway | 65 | -8.5 | 166 | 0.4 | 24.9 | 579 671 | 3 496 | 59 078 | 37.3 | 94 656 | 6.5 | 93.5 | 34.3 | 6.1 | 125 | 20.3 |
| Orange | 105 | 0.0 | 202 | 0.6 | 45.2 | 1 119 940 | 5 546 | 84 145 | 76.1 | 146 877 | 66.6 | 33.4 | 33.4 | 10.0 | 341 | 19.3 |
| Page | 64 | 0.0 | 121 | 0.3 | 27.7 | 747 898 | 6 156 | 59 891 | 148.3 | 279 895 | 1.4 | 98.6 | 46.8 | 25.7 | 239 | 15.1 |
| Patrick | 80 | -12.1 | 131 | 0.4 | 25.4 | 453 225 | 3 472 | 49 869 | 15.9 | 25 959 | 47.3 | 52.7 | 28.1 | 3.4 | 358 | 22.2 |
| Pittsylvania | 274 | -5.2 | 202 | 4.2 | 103.6 | 638 676 | 3 157 | 73 087 | 62.6 | 46 198 | 37.4 | 62.6 | 32.1 | 7.9 | 1 494 | 34.1 |
| Powhatan | 30 | -45.5 | 131 | 0.0 | 11.6 | 839 981 | 6 428 | 57 175 | 8.7 | 38 305 | 30.8 | 69.2 | 22.8 | 4.4 | 77 | 11.8 |
| Prince Edward | 82 | 3.8 | 185 | 0.1 | 25.0 | 568 244 | 3 078 | 55 372 | 15.5 | 34 750 | 12.7 | 87.3 | 27.6 | 5.2 | 239 | 32.7 |
| Prince George | 45 | -18.2 | 241 | D | 22.3 | 906 129 | 3 762 | 80 713 | 5.5 | 29 504 | 91.1 | 8.9 | 27.4 | 6.5 | 625 | 39.2 |
| Prince William | 33 | 0.0 | 95 | 0.7 | 18.2 | 697 825 | 7 336 | 68 245 | 9.4 | 27 330 | 51.6 | 48.4 | 21.4 | 1.7 | 107 | 6.1 |
| Pulaski | 75 | -7.4 | 182 | 0.2 | 21.1 | 663 148 | 3 647 | 66 549 | 13.3 | 32 142 | 4.6 | 95.4 | 32.3 | 4.8 | 185 | 12.5 |
| Rappahannock | 65 | -16.7 | 156 | 0.1 | 20.9 | 972 016 | 6 213 | 46 567 | 7.5 | 18 122 | 32.7 | 67.3 | 30.3 | 3.8 | 110 | 11.1 |
| Richmond | 37 | -17.8 | 301 | 0.2 | 24.2 | 1 108 946 | 3 681 | 104 507 | 10.6 | 85 176 | 90.9 | 9.1 | 43.5 | 13.7 | 704 | 56.5 |
| Roanoke | 29 | -6.5 | 85 | 0.1 | 8.8 | 428 456 | 5 060 | 40 485 | 4.9 | 14 195 | 70.2 | 29.8 | 26.1 | 2.0 | 12 | 7.5 |
| Rockbridge | 138 | -12.1 | 172 | 0.1 | 40.5 | 747 890 | 4 353 | 56 686 | 19.7 | 24 447 | 19.2 | 80.8 | 36.4 | 3.6 | 292 | 13.9 |
| Rockingham | 233 | -6.4 | 118 | 4.8 | 114.5 | 727 644 | 6 150 | 84 927 | 534.1 | 271 138 | 3.8 | 96.2 | 54.7 | 31.6 | 1 356 | 16.1 |
| Russell | 152 | -10.1 | 149 | 0.1 | 35.4 | 421 070 | 2 831 | 46 379 | 20.7 | 20 321 | 7.4 | 92.6 | 30.5 | 2.8 | 255 | 15.8 |
| Scott | 154 | -2.5 | 110 | 0.2 | 41.9 | 325 065 | 2 949 | 46 321 | 13.1 | 9 413 | 36.5 | 63.5 | 21.7 | 1.1 | 243 | 18.6 |
| Shenandoah | 141 | 6.0 | 135 | 0.8 | 60.2 | 730 823 | 5 395 | 67 444 | 101.6 | 97 389 | 11.1 | 88.9 | 36.5 | 11.0 | 907 | 16.5 |
| Smyth | 127 | 1.6 | 167 | 0.2 | 30.3 | 553 385 | 3 308 | 52 255 | 26.1 | 34 307 | 8.1 | 91.9 | 35.6 | 6.6 | 279 | 20.8 |
| Southampton | 162 | -4.1 | 473 | 3.5 | 91.3 | 1 224 543 | 2 591 | 121 365 | 35.7 | 104 335 | 77.1 | 22.9 | 42.1 | 21.9 | 6 288 | 74.6 |
| Spotsylvania | 52 | -7.1 | 145 | 0.1 | 23.8 | 738 592 | 5 077 | 61 026 | 8.2 | 22 893 | 29.4 | 70.6 | 25.1 | 4.2 | 350 | 21.7 |
| Stafford | 20 | -23.1 | 85 | 0.2 | 10.6 | 750 722 | 8 827 | 57 439 | 2.8 | 12 011 | 61.5 | 38.5 | 17.6 | 3.0 | 158 | 17.2 |
| Surry | 41 | -14.6 | 340 | 1.0 | 29.3 | 1 122 105 | 3 303 | 104 126 | 13.9 | 114 603 | 59.4 | 40.6 | 47.1 | 16.5 | 1 375 | 43.8 |
| Sussex | 74 | 0.0 | 492 | 1.6 | 38.3 | 1 554 000 | 3 161 | 154 396 | 16.9 | 112 235 | D | D | 40.4 | 13.9 | 1 942 | 55.6 |
| Tazewell | 154 | 10.8 | 267 | 0.3 | 31.5 | 609 596 | 2 285 | 56 491 | 21.5 | 37 308 | 4.7 | 95.3 | 34.2 | 7.6 | 137 | 14.1 |
| Warren | 48 | -2.0 | 123 | 0.1 | 13.4 | 781 852 | 6 352 | 51 288 | 5.6 | 14 365 | 21.7 | 78.3 | 24.5 | 2.1 | 11 | 3.9 |
| Washington | 199 | 1.0 | 111 | 0.4 | 64.2 | 487 860 | 4 394 | 45 394 | 44.0 | 24 546 | 11.1 | 88.9 | 27.1 | 3.7 | 960 | 23.8 |
| Westmoreland | 64 | -5.9 | 374 | 1.7 | 44.7 | 1 346 860 | 3 600 | 196 964 | 25.4 | 148 442 | 95.6 | 4.4 | 53.2 | 25.7 | 888 | 55.6 |
| Wise | 22 | 15.8 | 125 | 0.1 | 3.8 | 347 538 | 2 790 | 39 902 | 1.2 | 6 680 | 17.7 | 82.3 | 15.2 | 1.1 | 50 | 3.9 |
| Wythe | 159 | 5.3 | 168 | 0.2 | 52.0 | 660 726 | 3 928 | 66 160 | 38.2 | 40 350 | 6.5 | 93.5 | 42.6 | 7.1 | 485 | 21.7 |
| York | 1 | 0.0 | 29 | 0.0 | 0.3 | 510 872 | 17 684 | 44 240 | 4.0 | 88 372 | D | D | 35.6 | 13.3 | 3 | 8.9 |
| Independent cities | | | | | | | | | | | | | | | | |
| Alexandria city | NA | NA | NA | NA | NA | NA | NA | NA | NA | NA | NA | NA | NA | NA | NA | NA |
| Bedford city | NA | NA | NA | NA | NA | NA | NA | NA | NA | NA | NA | NA | NA | NA | NA | NA |
| Bristol city | NA | NA | NA | NA | NA | NA | NA | NA | NA | NA | NA | NA | NA | NA | NA | NA |
| Buena Vista city | NA | NA | NA | NA | NA | NA | NA | NA | NA | NA | NA | NA | NA | NA | NA | NA |
| Charlottesville city | NA | NA | NA | NA | NA | NA | NA | NA | NA | NA | NA | NA | NA | NA | NA | NA |
| Chesapeake city | 51 | -16.4 | 176 | 0.2 | 43.2 | 945 593 | 5 382 | 104 082 | 35.6 | 122 430 | 86.9 | 13.1 | 28.2 | 12.7 | 750 | 23.7 |
| Colonial Heights city | NA | NA | NA | NA | NA | NA | NA | NA | NA | NA | NA | NA | NA | NA | NA | NA |
| Covington city | NA | NA | NA | NA | NA | NA | NA | NA | NA | NA | NA | NA | NA | NA | NA | NA |
| Danville city | NA | NA | NA | NA | NA | NA | NA | NA | NA | NA | NA | NA | NA | NA | NA | NA |
| Emporia city | NA | NA | NA | NA | NA | NA | NA | NA | NA | NA | NA | NA | NA | NA | NA | NA |
| Fairfax city | NA | NA | NA | NA | NA | NA | NA | NA | NA | NA | NA | NA | NA | NA | NA | NA |
| Falls Church city | NA | NA | NA | NA | NA | NA | NA | NA | NA | NA | NA | NA | NA | NA | NA | NA |
| Franklin city | NA | NA | NA | NA | NA | NA | NA | NA | NA | NA | NA | NA | NA | NA | NA | NA |
| Fredericksburg city | NA | NA | NA | NA | NA | NA | NA | NA | NA | NA | NA | NA | NA | NA | NA | NA |
| Galax city | NA | NA | NA | NA | NA | NA | NA | NA | NA | NA | NA | NA | NA | NA | NA | NA |
| Hampton city | NA | NA | NA | NA | NA | NA | NA | NA | NA | NA | NA | NA | NA | NA | NA | NA |
| Harrisonburg city | NA | NA | NA | NA | NA | NA | NA | NA | NA | NA | NA | NA | NA | NA | NA | NA |
| Hopewell city | NA | NA | NA | NA | NA | NA | NA | NA | NA | NA | NA | NA | NA | NA | NA | NA |
| Lexington city | NA | NA | NA | NA | NA | NA | NA | NA | NA | NA | NA | NA | NA | NA | NA | NA |
| Lynchburg city | NA | NA | NA | NA | NA | NA | NA | NA | NA | NA | NA | NA | NA | NA | NA | NA |
| Manassas city | NA | NA | NA | NA | NA | NA | NA | NA | NA | NA | NA | NA | NA | NA | NA | NA |

**Water Use, Wholesale Trade, Retail Trade, and Real Estate**

| STATE County | Water use, 2005 | | Wholesale trade,[1] 2007 | | | | Retail trade,[2] 2007 | | | | Real estate and rental and leasing,[2] 2007 | | | |
|---|---|---|---|---|---|---|---|---|---|---|---|---|---|---|
| | Total water withdrawn (mil gal/day) | Gallons withdrawn per person | Number of establish-ments | Number of employees | Sales (mil dol) | Annual payroll (mil dol) | Number of establish-ments | Number of employees | Sales (mil dol) | Annual payroll (mil dol) | Number of establish-ments | Number of employees | Receipts (mil dol) | Annual payroll (mil dol) |
| | 133 | 134 | 135 | 136 | 137 | 138 | 139 | 140 | 141 | 142 | 143 | 144 | 145 | 146 |
| VIRGINIA—Cont'd | | | | | | | | | | | | | | |
| Louisa | 2 281.4 | 75 997 | 13 | 216 | 102.9 | 10.4 | 71 | 601 | 153.8 | 11.4 | 22 | 106 | 25.1 | 4.8 |
| Lunenburg | 2.0 | 151 | 5 | 144 | 45.7 | 3.1 | 43 | 300 | 54.7 | 5.4 | 4 | 6 | 1.2 | 0.1 |
| Madison | 3.2 | 237 | 9 | 32 | 8.7 | 0.9 | 52 | 504 | 112.9 | 11.3 | 6 | 21 | 1.9 | 0.2 |
| Mathews | 0.7 | 74 | 6 | D | D | D | 35 | 268 | 59.4 | 5.3 | 16 | D | D | D |
| Mecklenburg | 61.1 | 1 879 | 36 | 256 | 74.7 | 6.0 | 180 | 1 822 | 406.3 | 34.1 | 39 | 155 | 15.9 | 3.7 |
| Middlesex | 1.0 | 96 | 19 | 162 | 31.5 | 5.7 | 65 | 460 | 94.5 | 9.9 | 23 | 50 | 5.4 | 1.0 |
| Montgomery | 35.3 | 419 | 49 | 368 | 97.3 | 14.2 | 357 | 5 195 | 1 102.6 | 109.8 | 96 | 499 | 83.4 | 13.8 |
| Nelson | 4.8 | 317 | 5 | 7 | 6.7 | 0.2 | 58 | 345 | 75.6 | 6.1 | 17 | 51 | 6.6 | 1.6 |
| New Kent | 31.3 | 1 943 | 6 | D | D | D | 37 | 395 | 135.2 | 7.9 | 20 | 36 | 4.5 | 0.9 |
| Northampton | 4.7 | 350 | 16 | 149 | 59.3 | 3.4 | 80 | 681 | 135.1 | 11.7 | 16 | 41 | 5.9 | 0.8 |
| Northumberland | 3.7 | 289 | 13 | 76 | 29.7 | 2.1 | 52 | 421 | 90.2 | 7.9 | 18 | 44 | 6.0 | 0.6 |
| Nottoway | 1.7 | 107 | 12 | 125 | 80.2 | 3.2 | 65 | 754 | 137.3 | 14.5 | 8 | 25 | 2.1 | 0.5 |
| Orange | 3.3 | 109 | 12 | 219 | 212.2 | 12.1 | 112 | 1 031 | 280.3 | 23.4 | 29 | 59 | 6.7 | 1.7 |
| Page | 3.7 | 154 | 8 | 60 | 9.6 | 1.6 | 78 | 773 | 167.4 | 15.0 | 14 | 53 | 9.4 | 1.6 |
| Patrick | 2.6 | 137 | 6 | 46 | 19.0 | 1.7 | 49 | 559 | 148.6 | 11.5 | 11 | 18 | 2.2 | 0.2 |
| Pittsylvania | 60.1 | 971 | 33 | 648 | 247.6 | 15.6 | 157 | 1 083 | 269.3 | 19.5 | 20 | 84 | 5.7 | 1.2 |
| Powhatan | 2.9 | 109 | 28 | 158 | 46.6 | 6.1 | 75 | 604 | 159.3 | 15.5 | 26 | 76 | 11.2 | 2.3 |
| Prince Edward | 1.5 | 71 | 20 | 148 | 43.1 | 4.6 | 121 | 1 473 | 350.6 | 30.3 | 21 | 88 | 9.7 | 1.6 |
| Prince George | 58.1 | 1 583 | 20 | 718 | 502.6 | 24.1 | 61 | 559 | 197.8 | 13.5 | 19 | 58 | 5.3 | 1.2 |
| Prince William | 254.9 | 731 | 159 | 2 119 | 1 750.6 | 112.7 | 1 119 | 19 373 | 4 948.9 | 465.4 | 334 | 1 417 | 284.8 | 46.3 |
| Pulaski | 6.8 | 192 | 15 | 136 | 39.2 | 4.5 | 122 | 1 498 | 317.3 | 30.7 | 25 | 81 | 8.8 | 1.4 |
| Rappahannock | 1.0 | 138 | 2 | D | D | D | 30 | 142 | 21.9 | 3.0 | 10 | 10 | 1.2 | 0.2 |
| Richmond | 1.1 | 123 | 12 | D | D | D | 43 | 301 | 75.6 | 6.3 | 10 | 40 | 1.5 | 0.4 |
| Roanoke | 20.1 | 228 | 99 | 1 023 | 504.7 | 43.5 | 293 | 3 973 | 835.7 | 86.9 | 110 | 491 | 70.0 | 13.9 |
| Rockbridge | 37.1 | 1 746 | 11 | 92 | 32.7 | 3.0 | 82 | 1 253 | 338.4 | 25.3 | 15 | 33 | 2.8 | 0.5 |
| Rockingham | 44.2 | 620 | 61 | 990 | 539.9 | 41.6 | 225 | 1 985 | 455.5 | 42.0 | 47 | 939 | 104.3 | 28.7 |
| Russell | 22.0 | 761 | 21 | 82 | 36.5 | 2.0 | 94 | 966 | 255.6 | 20.6 | 10 | 39 | 3.5 | 0.7 |
| Scott | 2.5 | 108 | 8 | D | D | D | 90 | 837 | 197.2 | 14.4 | 9 | D | D | D |
| Shenandoah | 18.8 | 479 | 22 | 312 | 347.2 | 11.6 | 164 | 1 875 | 494.2 | 37.6 | 32 | 169 | 15.3 | 2.6 |
| Smyth | 25.8 | 791 | 14 | 130 | 52.7 | 4.2 | 127 | 1 337 | 300.3 | 28.4 | 18 | 88 | 7.9 | 2.4 |
| Southampton | 39.9 | 2 271 | 14 | 117 | 70.5 | 4.2 | 37 | 267 | 57.9 | 4.8 | 8 | 21 | 2.3 | 0.5 |
| Spotsylvania | 9.6 | 82 | 66 | 845 | 430.4 | 38.0 | 416 | 7 219 | 2 148.5 | 177.8 | 106 | 645 | 73.8 | 19.6 |
| Stafford | 20.2 | 172 | 60 | 1 370 | 1 249.9 | 60.4 | 267 | 3 737 | 930.3 | 84.8 | 95 | 376 | 69.5 | 11.0 |
| Surry | 2 062.9 | 294 151 | 1 | D | D | D | 14 | 56 | 12.6 | 1.0 | 3 | D | D | D |
| Sussex | 2.2 | 182 | 10 | D | D | D | 50 | 314 | 68.9 | 6.0 | 6 | 13 | 1.7 | 0.3 |
| Tazewell | 8.4 | 188 | 63 | D | D | D | 240 | 3 396 | 811.8 | 67.0 | 57 | 265 | 23.2 | 5.4 |
| Warren | 11.2 | 315 | 13 | 88 | 18.7 | 2.5 | 134 | 1 311 | 369.6 | 30.2 | 31 | 135 | 12.5 | 2.7 |
| Washington | 82.5 | 1 584 | 43 | 417 | 279.6 | 20.7 | 230 | 2 940 | 701.6 | 59.0 | 48 | 131 | 15.4 | 3.1 |
| Westmoreland | 1.8 | 103 | 13 | 79 | 38.9 | 2.8 | 47 | 479 | 100.4 | 9.3 | 21 | 57 | 4.7 | 1.2 |
| Wise | 7.4 | 177 | 35 | 512 | 496.1 | 22.6 | 205 | 2 077 | 438.6 | 38.0 | 26 | 80 | 23.0 | 2.6 |
| Wythe | 12.5 | 440 | 19 | 318 | 105.5 | 10.8 | 160 | 2 130 | 908.1 | 45.4 | 32 | 235 | 21.4 | 4.8 |
| York | 1 011.0 | 16 371 | 49 | 262 | 149.7 | 8.9 | 243 | 3 759 | 852.2 | 84.2 | 71 | 267 | 36.0 | 7.1 |
| Independent cities | | | | | | | | | | | | | | |
| Alexandria city | 249.9 | 1 846 | 91 | 1 262 | 525.7 | 65.2 | 528 | 8 052 | 2 353.8 | 232.5 | 229 | 2 484 | 811.8 | 127.1 |
| Bedford city | 0.0 | 0 | 4 | 85 | 28.9 | 2.7 | 56 | 553 | 124.9 | 10.7 | 14 | 44 | 5.1 | 1.0 |
| Bristol city | 0.1 | 3 | 34 | 883 | 318.8 | 28.8 | 172 | 1 884 | 343.5 | 34.2 | 27 | D | D | D |
| Buena Vista city | 1.4 | 217 | 1 | D | D | D | 25 | 162 | 30.6 | 3.1 | 6 | 18 | 0.7 | 0.2 |
| Charlottesville city | 0.0 | 0 | 55 | 473 | 203.4 | 20.4 | 349 | 3 880 | 699.4 | 78.1 | 98 | 557 | 86.5 | 19.7 |
| Chesapeake city | 553.3 | 2 527 | 239 | 3 428 | 2 123.3 | 156.1 | 869 | 16 523 | 3 977.8 | 345.5 | 273 | 1 355 | 274.7 | 49.0 |
| Colonial Heights city | 0.0 | 0 | 8 | 86 | 28.4 | 2.6 | 204 | 4 064 | 761.1 | 71.4 | 26 | 134 | 22.6 | 4.5 |
| Covington city | 39.8 | 6 421 | 5 | 38 | 13.0 | 1.1 | 70 | 491 | 104.6 | 9.5 | 10 | 21 | 1.8 | 0.4 |
| Danville city | 3.7 | 81 | 55 | 462 | 204.1 | 18.8 | 330 | 4 395 | 892.2 | 81.8 | 66 | 332 | 41.4 | 8.8 |
| Emporia city | 1.0 | 184 | 4 | D | D | D | 64 | 705 | 131.6 | 13.2 | 15 | 50 | 5.0 | 0.9 |
| Fairfax city | 0.1 | 4 | 48 | 265 | 192.3 | 13.0 | 289 | 6 460 | 1 884.0 | 178.4 | 80 | 241 | 36.0 | 9.8 |
| Falls Church city | 0.0 | 0 | 16 | D | D | D | 104 | 1 129 | 288.0 | 35.4 | 30 | 195 | 58.1 | 6.3 |
| Franklin city | 1.2 | 135 | 6 | 50 | 25.5 | 1.4 | 63 | 900 | 186.3 | 19.5 | 17 | 65 | 8.0 | 1.6 |
| Fredericksburg city | 0.0 | 0 | 32 | D | D | D | 280 | 4 436 | 1 052.1 | 94.6 | 77 | 403 | 70.0 | 15.4 |
| Galax city | 1.7 | 261 | 5 | 48 | 36.9 | 1.6 | 78 | 1 085 | 227.5 | 22.5 | 13 | 62 | 10.3 | 1.5 |
| Hampton city | 0.3 | 2 | 60 | 800 | 288.9 | 33.5 | 436 | 7 295 | 1 805.7 | 162.3 | 115 | 873 | 113.9 | 24.2 |
| Harrisonburg city | 0.1 | 2 | 55 | 1 033 | 378.5 | 42.7 | 376 | 6 265 | 1 465.3 | 158.1 | 80 | 346 | 68.3 | 8.8 |
| Hopewell city | 186.1 | 8 203 | 12 | 130 | 58.1 | 8.8 | 84 | 696 | 173.9 | 15.1 | 22 | 98 | 19.3 | 3.2 |
| Lexington city | 0.0 | 0 | 3 | 6 | 1.9 | 0.2 | 48 | 447 | 86.8 | 9.8 | 21 | 50 | 6.1 | 1.2 |
| Lynchburg city | 0.1 | 2 | 82 | 1 125 | 541.5 | 43.2 | 419 | 7 266 | 1 665.1 | 151.2 | 107 | 466 | 72.4 | 15.3 |
| Manassas city | 0.1 | 3 | 44 | D | D | D | 187 | 2 635 | 921.2 | 85.3 | 59 | 230 | 41.7 | 8.3 |

1.  Merchant wholesalers, except manufacturers' sales branches and offices.   2.  Employer establishments.

# Table B. States and Counties — Professional Services, Manufacturing, and Accommodation and Food Services

| STATE County | Professional, scientific, and technical services,¹ 2007 | | | | Manufacturing, 2007 | | | | Accommodation and food services, 2007 | | | |
|---|---|---|---|---|---|---|---|---|---|---|---|---|
| | Number of establishments | Number of employees | Receipts (mil dol) | Annual payroll (mil dol) | Number of establishments | Number of employees | Receipts (mil dol) | Annual payroll (mil dol) | Number of establishments | Number of employees | Sales (mil dol) | Annual payroll (mil dol) |
| | 147 | 148 | 149 | 150 | 151 | 152 | 153 | 154 | 155 | 156 | 157 | 158 |
| VIRGINIA—Cont'd | | | | | | | | | | | | |
| Louisa | 55 | 188 | 19.2 | 7.0 | 34 | 1 377 | 435.9 | 62.1 | 22 | 357 | 13.9 | 3.8 |
| Lunenburg | 10 | D | D | D | 8 | 778 | D | 21.6 | 10 | D | D | D |
| Madison | 31 | D | D | D | NA | NA | NA | NA | 16 | 210 | 10.1 | 3.0 |
| Mathews | 22 | 54 | 3.7 | 1.6 | NA | NA | NA | NA | 15 | D | D | D |
| Mecklenburg | 48 | 295 | 21.7 | 8.1 | 31 | 1 847 | 281.0 | 47.7 | 76 | 1 111 | 43.5 | 12.5 |
| Middlesex | 30 | 130 | 7.8 | 3.8 | NA | NA | NA | NA | 23 | 255 | 8.7 | 2.6 |
| Montgomery | 234 | D | D | D | 55 | 3 097 | 838.1 | 141.9 | 187 | 4 037 | 148.3 | 44.8 |
| Nelson | 39 | D | D | D | NA | NA | NA | NA | 20 | 152 | 6.2 | 1.6 |
| New Kent | 20 | 52 | 3.0 | 1.1 | NA | NA | NA | NA | 23 | 211 | 9.7 | 2.2 |
| Northampton | 22 | D | D | D | 9 | D | D | D | 37 | 494 | 23.6 | 7.3 |
| Northumberland | 29 | D | D | D | 23 | 595 | D | 17.5 | 20 | 116 | 5.2 | 1.4 |
| Nottoway | 23 | 125 | 7.5 | 2.7 | NA | NA | NA | NA | 27 | 379 | 11.1 | 3.0 |
| Orange | 70 | 311 | 34.0 | 13.0 | 21 | 947 | 222.2 | 36.0 | 51 | 668 | 26.0 | 7.1 |
| Page | 27 | 194 | 11.4 | 4.9 | 15 | 868 | 204.1 | 23.2 | 57 | 679 | 35.4 | 9.2 |
| Patrick | 17 | D | D | D | 42 | 1 823 | 248.5 | 51.1 | 22 | 152 | 6.6 | 1.5 |
| Pittsylvania | 49 | D | D | D | 53 | 2 441 | 752.1 | 81.3 | 43 | 449 | 15.3 | 4.3 |
| Powhatan | 56 | 185 | 20.1 | 8.9 | NA | NA | NA | NA | 29 | 384 | 17.6 | 4.0 |
| Prince Edward | 30 | D | D | D | NA | NA | NA | NA | 51 | 994 | 40.0 | 11.1 |
| Prince George | 36 | 144 | 18.4 | 7.2 | 22 | 1 330 | 783.8 | 61.0 | 28 | 426 | 23.1 | 4.9 |
| Prince William | 918 | D | D | D | 120 | 2 548 | 563.6 | 121.6 | 568 | 10 617 | 537.9 | 148.4 |
| Pulaski | 47 | D | D | D | 49 | 6 611 | 2 797.1 | 305.5 | 70 | 917 | 40.7 | 10.0 |
| Rappahannock | 31 | D | D | D | NA | NA | NA | NA | 16 | 253 | 20.0 | 5.5 |
| Richmond | 13 | D | D | D | NA | NA | NA | NA | 11 | D | D | D |
| Roanoke | 190 | D | D | D | 67 | 3 769 | 896.1 | 155.4 | 128 | 2 668 | 112.7 | 32.7 |
| Rockbridge | 26 | 93 | 8.2 | 2.9 | 27 | 1 221 | 326.0 | 39.0 | 59 | 875 | 49.2 | 13.7 |
| Rockingham | 83 | D | D | D | 87 | 7 288 | 5 437.5 | 296.8 | 82 | 2 042 | 62.1 | 27.0 |
| Russell | 34 | D | D | D | 15 | 1 219 | 192.9 | 28.0 | 34 | 420 | 15.6 | 4.2 |
| Scott | 23 | 94 | 5.6 | 1.7 | 8 | 768 | 451.5 | 30.0 | 21 | 315 | 11.6 | 3.4 |
| Shenandoah | 77 | D | D | D | 39 | 5 034 | 1 058.1 | 160.9 | 71 | 1 157 | 50.1 | 15.0 |
| Smyth | 34 | D | D | D | 47 | 3 870 | 777.2 | 138.7 | 53 | 679 | 24.1 | 6.6 |
| Southampton | 11 | D | D | D | 14 | 1 917 | 831.4 | 112.2 | 9 | D | D | D |
| Spotsylvania | 217 | 1 387 | 228.3 | 78.2 | 64 | 2 164 | 496.4 | 88.8 | 190 | 3 542 | 169.8 | 47.9 |
| Stafford | 284 | D | D | D | 46 | 727 | 140.8 | 25.3 | 179 | 3 324 | 140.3 | 38.8 |
| Surry | 5 | 20 | 1.9 | 0.5 | NA | NA | NA | NA | 2 | D | D | D |
| Sussex | 8 | D | D | D | NA | NA | NA | NA | 14 | 284 | 15.7 | 4.0 |
| Tazewell | 71 | D | D | D | 61 | 1 485 | 354.5 | D | 59 | 1 368 | 52.2 | 15.0 |
| Warren | 77 | 477 | 36.6 | 17.4 | 24 | 1 002 | D | 41.2 | 67 | 837 | 41.3 | 11.4 |
| Washington | 110 | 742 | 49.6 | 24.7 | 74 | 4 862 | 1 359.5 | 171.4 | 91 | 1 505 | 59.2 | 16.7 |
| Westmoreland | 28 | 130 | 13.7 | 7.1 | 14 | 573 | 199.6 | 19.1 | 35 | 426 | 14.2 | 4.1 |
| Wise | 50 | 383 | 39.3 | 13.7 | NA | NA | NA | NA | 58 | 1 040 | 40.1 | 10.4 |
| Wythe | 42 | 149 | 16.8 | 6.2 | 44 | 2 009 | 567.4 | 73.2 | 76 | 1 385 | 63.2 | 17.5 |
| York | 153 | 1 461 | 184.8 | 74.2 | 39 | 592 | D | 31.7 | 134 | 3 614 | 187.4 | 50.9 |
| Independent cities | | | | | | | | | | | | |
| Alexandria city | 1 166 | D | D | D | 88 | 1 483 | 284.5 | 56.3 | 355 | 6 961 | 471.7 | 135.1 |
| Bedford city | 31 | D | D | D | 23 | 1 204 | D | 40.3 | 26 | 442 | 15.4 | 4.7 |
| Bristol city | 43 | 276 | 21.2 | 11.6 | 32 | 1 673 | 659.8 | 62.1 | 82 | 2 053 | 76.6 | 23.1 |
| Buena Vista city | 8 | D | D | D | 15 | 988 | 202.8 | 37.4 | 13 | D | D | D |
| Charlottesville city | 290 | D | D | D | 51 | 1 589 | 677.1 | 79.1 | 261 | 5 617 | 303.6 | 85.8 |
| Chesapeake city | 485 | D | D | D | 139 | 4 487 | 1 437.1 | 200.1 | 431 | 8 991 | 369.8 | 105.5 |
| Colonial Heights city | 56 | 466 | 31.4 | 12.6 | NA | NA | NA | NA | 81 | 1 768 | 76.1 | 19.5 |
| Covington city | 21 | D | D | D | 8 | D | D | D | 21 | D | D | D |
| Danville city | 76 | D | D | D | 43 | 4 485 | 1 275.9 | 212.7 | 140 | 2 741 | 110.3 | 30.0 |
| Emporia city | 17 | D | D | D | 11 | 1 074 | 311.5 | 34.5 | 25 | 566 | 24.2 | 7.0 |
| Fairfax city | 655 | D | D | D | NA | NA | NA | NA | 150 | 2 521 | 140.3 | 36.8 |
| Falls Church city | 158 | D | D | D | 14 | D | D | D | 101 | 872 | 56.3 | 14.6 |
| Franklin city | 16 | D | D | D | NA | NA | NA | NA | 27 | 802 | 22.6 | 6.7 |
| Fredericksburg city | 166 | D | D | D | NA | NA | NA | NA | 178 | 4 003 | 171.6 | 53.4 |
| Galax city | 23 | 157 | 12.2 | 4.7 | 17 | 1 935 | 204.1 | 40.4 | 38 | 632 | 22.5 | 6.9 |
| Hampton city | 280 | D | D | D | 77 | 2 790 | 522.4 | 122.0 | 233 | 5 888 | 233.6 | 69.2 |
| Harrisonburg city | 150 | D | D | D | 47 | 2 824 | 746.3 | 103.1 | 175 | 4 284 | 168.6 | 46.7 |
| Hopewell city | 34 | 328 | 27.8 | 15.8 | 14 | 1 297 | 1 496.0 | 98.0 | 56 | 923 | 47.8 | 11.9 |
| Lexington city | 28 | D | D | D | NA | NA | NA | NA | 52 | 655 | 31.3 | 7.8 |
| Lynchburg city | 203 | D | D | D | 96 | 9 486 | 2 801.6 | 500.1 | 234 | 5 226 | 190.0 | 58.3 |
| Manassas city | 218 | D | D | D | 41 | 4 038 | 1 408.7 | 340.5 | 101 | 1 307 | 75.6 | 19.0 |

1. Establishment subject to federal tax.

# Table B. States and Counties — Health Care and Social Assistance, Other Services, and Federal Funds

| STATE County | Health care and social assistance, 2007 | | | | Other services, 2007 | | | | Federal funds and grants, 2009–2010 Expenditures (mil dol) | | | |
|---|---|---|---|---|---|---|---|---|---|---|---|---|
| | | | | | | | | | Total | Direct payments for individuals[1] | | |
| | Number of establishments | Number of employees | Receipts (mil dol) | Annual payroll (mil dol) | Number of establishments | Number of employees | Receipts (mil dol) | Annual payroll (mil dol) | | Social Security and government retirement | Medicare | Food Stamps and Supplemental Security Income |
| | 159 | 160 | 161 | 162 | 163 | 164 | 165 | 166 | 167 | 168 | 169 | 170 |
| VIRGINIA—Cont'd | | | | | | | | | | | | |
| Louisa | 23 | D | D | D | 45 | 232 | 16.8 | 4.8 | 210.4 | 120.7 | 36.7 | 6.4 |
| Lunenburg | 17 | 237 | 9.3 | 4.2 | 16 | D | D | D | 93.4 | 39.4 | 19.9 | 7.4 |
| Madison | 23 | 318 | 13.8 | 6.0 | 19 | 64 | 7.6 | 2.6 | 86.6 | 41.1 | 18.9 | 2.7 |
| Mathews | 11 | D | D | D | 12 | D | D | D | 94.7 | 53.5 | 22.2 | 2.1 |
| Mecklenburg | 75 | 1 807 | 149.4 | 58.5 | 71 | 328 | 21.1 | 5.8 | 433.3 | 138.4 | 63.4 | 9.6 |
| Middlesex | 20 | D | D | D | 36 | 108 | 7.5 | 2.2 | 101.1 | 61.1 | 20.7 | 3.0 |
| Montgomery | 213 | 4 007 | 427.0 | 162.2 | 159 | 816 | 249.3 | 18.0 | 660.2 | 206.1 | 71.8 | 17.4 |
| Nelson | 19 | 230 | 13.3 | 6.2 | 24 | 135 | 10.0 | 3.8 | 147.9 | 76.8 | 26.5 | 5.8 |
| New Kent | 18 | D | D | D | 28 | 103 | 8.9 | 3.3 | 96.9 | 63.7 | 17.4 | 1.9 |
| Northampton | 42 | 1 041 | 83.2 | 34.6 | 24 | 60 | 5.1 | 1.1 | 147.1 | 53.0 | 25.7 | 9.5 |
| Northumberland | 10 | 47 | 2.3 | 0.8 | 29 | 94 | 5.9 | 1.5 | 134.6 | 79.5 | 28.2 | 3.5 |
| Nottoway | 24 | 826 | 39.6 | 22.0 | 39 | 131 | 10.9 | 3.3 | 281.5 | 65.1 | 30.2 | 7.2 |
| Orange | 42 | 283 | 17.9 | 6.9 | 54 | 332 | 35.2 | 10.4 | 267.7 | 166.0 | 46.9 | 6.4 |
| Page | 34 | 522 | 36.3 | 15.9 | 38 | 118 | 8.4 | 2.4 | 200.6 | 92.2 | 37.6 | 6.1 |
| Patrick | 25 | 602 | 29.2 | 13.4 | 17 | 49 | 4.1 | 1.2 | 147.0 | 72.1 | 27.8 | 6.9 |
| Pittsylvania | 57 | 655 | 30.7 | 13.9 | 67 | 300 | 19.0 | 5.0 | 395.7 | 171.2 | 71.5 | 17.2 |
| Powhatan | 28 | 250 | 15.3 | 6.9 | 44 | 153 | 17.7 | 6.0 | 139.7 | 81.3 | 17.0 | 2.6 |
| Prince Edward | 78 | 1 677 | 106.9 | 48.8 | 38 | 157 | 18.5 | 3.3 | 170.4 | 78.9 | 30.1 | 9.5 |
| Prince George | 15 | D | D | D | 33 | 125 | 9.1 | 3.4 | 1 648.2 | 102.9 | 17.4 | 4.7 |
| Prince William | 530 | 7 037 | 690.9 | 267.2 | 500 | 3 204 | 512.8 | 96.7 | 4 426.5 | 998.8 | 87.8 | 44.8 |
| Pulaski | 67 | 1 356 | 89.9 | 40.0 | 50 | 210 | 17.7 | 5.1 | 275.8 | 126.3 | 68.9 | 12.0 |
| Rappahannock | 8 | D | D | D | 11 | 37 | 3.0 | 0.9 | 66.3 | 40.7 | 12.5 | 1.2 |
| Richmond | 19 | 797 | 27.3 | 13.6 | 12 | 66 | 6.6 | 2.1 | 70.4 | 33.6 | 19.0 | 2.4 |
| Roanoke | 238 | 4 618 | 340.9 | 163.7 | 163 | 824 | 68.4 | 21.3 | 290.3 | 167.0 | 48.8 | 9.9 |
| Rockbridge | 32 | 197 | 15.0 | 5.4 | 29 | 93 | 8.5 | 2.0 | 114.3 | 54.9 | 19.3 | 3.9 |
| Rockingham | 85 | 1 625 | 86.1 | 36.1 | 104 | 508 | 39.3 | 12.2 | 343.9 | 189.5 | 70.7 | 10.2 |
| Russell | 50 | 865 | 61.3 | 25.5 | 30 | 91 | 6.7 | 2.1 | 272.1 | 119.8 | 64.3 | 19.5 |
| Scott | 40 | D | D | D | 18 | D | D | D | 305.1 | 98.3 | 51.7 | 12.0 |
| Shenandoah | 69 | D | D | D | 90 | 363 | 31.5 | 7.6 | 284.7 | 166.6 | 51.1 | 7.0 |
| Smyth | 62 | 2 205 | 141.3 | 70.6 | 44 | 183 | 17.0 | 4.3 | 295.2 | 126.2 | 58.6 | 14.6 |
| Southampton | 9 | D | D | D | 18 | D | D | D | 128.4 | 49.0 | 28.2 | 6.3 |
| Spotsylvania | 176 | 2 198 | 135.5 | 58.7 | 177 | 1 020 | 91.7 | 27.7 | 566.3 | 270.4 | 31.1 | 12.9 |
| Stafford | 146 | 1 939 | 129.0 | 59.4 | 193 | 1 203 | 99.5 | 32.9 | 837.1 | 406.1 | 36.1 | 10.4 |
| Surry | 3 | D | D | D | 1 | D | D | D | 52.4 | 26.8 | 10.6 | 2.6 |
| Sussex | 14 | D | D | D | 16 | 94 | 6.0 | 1.8 | 111.5 | 44.1 | 27.1 | 6.7 |
| Tazewell | 149 | 2 424 | 187.5 | 77.1 | 92 | 595 | 55.8 | 15.6 | 438.7 | 219.0 | 105.3 | 26.7 |
| Warren | 55 | D | D | D | 77 | 525 | 36.1 | 11.9 | 211.1 | 120.3 | 35.4 | 8.8 |
| Washington | 143 | 2 092 | 197.7 | 76.1 | 73 | 357 | 22.1 | 7.6 | 390.9 | 185.5 | 64.5 | 14.7 |
| Westmoreland | 18 | 287 | 10.5 | 5.4 | 32 | 109 | 6.2 | 1.5 | 189.7 | 112.0 | 39.3 | 7.2 |
| Wise | 82 | 1 601 | 101.3 | 38.9 | 70 | D | D | D | 508.1 | 186.8 | 90.4 | 35.6 |
| Wythe | 70 | 1 283 | 92.5 | 37.2 | 51 | 275 | 21.2 | 5.3 | 263.0 | 126.4 | 52.4 | 11.0 |
| York | 94 | 1 620 | 176.7 | 67.1 | 138 | 702 | 47.5 | 16.3 | 682.6 | 391.8 | 40.6 | 6.1 |
| Independent cities | | | | | | | | | | | | |
| Alexandria city | 397 | 6 347 | 909.3 | 332.6 | 591 | 9 336 | 2 436.1 | 524.5 | 5 465.0 | 659.2 | 230.2 | 31.7 |
| Bedford city | 44 | D | D | D | 36 | 268 | 21.3 | 7.3 | 105.4 | 65.8 | 16.8 | 4.9 |
| Bristol city | 47 | D | D | D | 48 | D | D | D | 268.4 | 111.7 | 50.7 | 10.9 |
| Buena Vista city | 15 | 318 | 15.9 | 8.6 | 7 | D | D | D | 61.1 | 28.5 | 12.4 | 3.6 |
| Charlottesville city | 190 | 10 090 | 1 339.7 | 449.4 | 165 | 1 389 | 295.9 | 42.8 | 842.8 | 195.7 | 73.1 | 18.0 |
| Chesapeake city | 469 | 7 730 | 746.9 | 298.9 | 404 | 3 023 | 333.8 | 91.6 | 1 748.9 | 847.9 | 194.7 | 52.2 |
| Colonial Heights city | 84 | 1 275 | 94.0 | 46.2 | 55 | 361 | 26.9 | 8.8 | 163.8 | 102.4 | 33.3 | 3.7 |
| Covington city | 20 | 232 | 8.0 | 3.6 | 19 | D | D | D | 120.9 | 67.3 | 30.5 | 5.0 |
| Danville city | 208 | 4 620 | 407.1 | 161.8 | 126 | 620 | 53.0 | 13.4 | 503.8 | 225.6 | 108.7 | 31.9 |
| Emporia city | 35 | 923 | 70.3 | 27.7 | 21 | 78 | 6.7 | 1.7 | 92.9 | 36.4 | 24.8 | 7.2 |
| Fairfax city | 221 | 3 303 | 269.8 | 121.2 | 181 | 1 155 | 132.0 | 39.9 | 1 031.5 | 388.9 | 69.6 | 7.8 |
| Falls Church city | 101 | D | D | D | 86 | 536 | 68.2 | 19.7 | 1 196.5 | 80.6 | 66.7 | 1.8 |
| Franklin city | 53 | 933 | 76.1 | 29.4 | 32 | 205 | 14.5 | 3.8 | 118.6 | 46.5 | 25.0 | 8.0 |
| Fredericksburg city | 212 | 5 813 | 824.6 | 293.8 | 106 | 947 | 60.1 | 21.3 | 440.1 | 252.0 | 74.5 | 7.9 |
| Galax city | 49 | 1 451 | 115.3 | 49.9 | 22 | 84 | 7.0 | 2.0 | 109.5 | 54.6 | 26.1 | 5.3 |
| Hampton city | 243 | 6 619 | 660.4 | 300.7 | 191 | 1 177 | 96.6 | 29.1 | 3 200.3 | 615.3 | 171.6 | 55.2 |
| Harrisonburg city | 160 | 4 724 | 463.1 | 193.2 | 133 | 725 | 79.2 | 18.1 | 232.7 | 84.2 | 40.7 | 7.6 |
| Hopewell city | 61 | D | D | D | 42 | 303 | 42.2 | 6.9 | 214.2 | 101.0 | 43.5 | 16.8 |
| Lexington city | 47 | 759 | 69.7 | 24.1 | 30 | 228 | 29.2 | 6.5 | 121.6 | 55.7 | 15.3 | 1.3 |
| Lynchburg city | 261 | 8 776 | 828.1 | 355.5 | 175 | 1 058 | 80.3 | 24.4 | 979.1 | 278.1 | 124.2 | 28.2 |
| Manassas city | 179 | 3 373 | 357.5 | 175.1 | 132 | 803 | 75.2 | 22.1 | 1 231.8 | 261.8 | 44.9 | 9.5 |

1. State totals may include programs not allocated by county.

# Table B. States and Counties — Federal Funds, Residential Construction, and Local Government Finances

| | Federal funds and grants, 2009–2010 (cont.) | | | | | | | Value of residential construction authorized by building permits, 2011 | | Local government finances, 2007 | | | | |
| | Expenditures (mil dol) (cont.) | | | | | | | | | General revenue | | | | |
| | | Procurement contract awards | | Grants[1] | | | | | | | | Taxes | | |
| | | | | | | | | | | | | | Per capita[2] (dollars) | |
| STATE County | Salaries and wages | Defense | Other | Medicaid and other health-related | Nutrition and family welfare | Education | Other | New construction ($1,000) | Number of housing units | Total (mil dol) | Inter-govern-mental (mil dol) | Total (mil dol) | Total | Property |
| | 171 | 172 | 173 | 174 | 175 | 176 | 177 | 178 | 179 | 180 | 181 | 182 | 183 | 184 |
| VIRGINIA—Cont'd | | | | | | | | | | | | | | |
| Louisa | 5.0 | 7.1 | 1.8 | 26.2 | 2.9 | 1.5 | 0.7 | 21 675 | 108 | 91.2 | 29.2 | 50.3 | 1 573 | 1 373 |
| Lunenburg | 1.9 | 0.0 | 0.5 | 18.0 | 2.5 | 0.8 | 0.1 | 3 483 | 22 | 32.0 | 21.7 | 7.5 | 572 | 401 |
| Madison | 3.7 | 0.9 | 1.0 | 14.4 | 2.4 | 0.8 | 0.1 | 508 | 31 | 30.9 | 14.5 | 13.3 | 966 | 723 |
| Mathews | 4.4 | 1.1 | 1.6 | 5.3 | 0.9 | 0.5 | 0.0 | 6 313 | 22 | 22.9 | 10.4 | 11.0 | 1 220 | 1 047 |
| Mecklenburg | 9.3 | 21.8 | 97.9 | 59.7 | 4.7 | 2.1 | 19.2 | 14 288 | 92 | 84.6 | 46.6 | 31.1 | 970 | 664 |
| Middlesex | 3.6 | 0.4 | 0.5 | 5.6 | 1.3 | 1.3 | 0.1 | 6 775 | 39 | 25.9 | 11.1 | 13.3 | 1 250 | 988 |
| Montgomery | 33.7 | 46.0 | 31.1 | 80.0 | 6.9 | 5.3 | 135.7 | 30 983 | 216 | 214.6 | 95.2 | 84.7 | 949 | 621 |
| Nelson | 5.5 | 0.0 | 1.4 | 21.4 | 1.8 | 0.8 | 7.4 | 11 513 | 45 | 39.7 | 18.8 | 18.6 | 1 221 | 926 |
| New Kent | 3.9 | 0.1 | 0.9 | 5.9 | 1.0 | 0.9 | 0.2 | 27 934 | 156 | 40.1 | 20.1 | 16.9 | 990 | 810 |
| Northampton | 4.5 | 9.9 | 2.3 | 32.7 | 3.6 | 1.1 | 0.1 | 7 644 | 44 | 102.0 | 24.9 | 17.6 | 1 315 | 960 |
| Northumberland | 2.7 | 7.0 | 0.7 | 8.1 | 1.6 | 0.8 | 0.2 | 13 800 | 47 | 30.4 | 12.2 | 16.5 | 1 276 | 1 081 |
| Nottoway | 116.2 | 5.0 | 1.2 | 20.3 | 3.0 | 1.6 | 30.1 | 2 391 | 22 | 38.9 | 24.6 | 9.6 | 607 | 398 |
| Orange | 5.5 | 0.0 | 4.7 | 25.0 | 3.7 | 1.5 | 0.5 | 13 714 | 71 | 82.0 | 38.8 | 34.5 | 1 061 | 817 |
| Page | 10.2 | 0.0 | 27.4 | 20.6 | 2.5 | 1.9 | 1.7 | 5 418 | 37 | 60.9 | 39.7 | 14.1 | 585 | 431 |
| Patrick | 3.7 | 8.5 | 1.5 | 20.0 | 2.3 | 1.4 | 0.7 | 8 378 | 33 | 37.1 | 23.3 | 10.6 | 561 | 409 |
| Pittsylvania | 8.2 | 0.5 | 2.5 | 95.1 | 9.1 | 4.5 | 0.4 | 11 070 | 118 | 141.5 | 91.2 | 44.8 | 737 | 627 |
| Powhatan | 28.4 | 0.0 | 1.1 | 5.9 | 1.3 | 0.9 | 0.0 | 16 727 | 68 | 66.6 | 33.3 | 25.3 | 908 | 724 |
| Prince Edward | 9.0 | 3.4 | 1.3 | 25.6 | 2.9 | 1.9 | 1.2 | 6 642 | 72 | 67.2 | 34.4 | 17.9 | 838 | 452 |
| Prince George | 1 131.5 | 353.8 | 18.4 | 7.8 | 2.4 | 4.8 | 0.0 | 6 656 | 37 | 107.0 | 65.3 | 30.2 | 842 | 658 |
| Prince William | 762.7 | 2 205.3 | 168.3 | 30.0 | 16.5 | 13.4 | 56.6 | 229 527 | 1 545 | 1 505.3 | 562.4 | 700.8 | 1 944 | 1 490 |
| Pulaski | 10.5 | 1.7 | 1.8 | 32.4 | 4.5 | 2.9 | 5.5 | 5 833 | 45 | 100.2 | 46.9 | 28.2 | 804 | 606 |
| Rappahannock | 1.8 | 0.1 | 0.9 | 7.2 | 0.6 | 0.4 | 0.5 | 6 000 | 14 | 18.5 | 6.8 | 10.6 | 1 474 | 1 251 |
| Richmond | 2.9 | 0.0 | 0.9 | 8.7 | 1.1 | 0.5 | 0.1 | 1 624 | 13 | 29.1 | 14.6 | 10.0 | 1 085 | 794 |
| Roanoke | 4.9 | 27.0 | 2.6 | 18.1 | 5.3 | 4.2 | 0.0 | 39 791 | 208 | 291.4 | 125.3 | 145.1 | 1 605 | 1 170 |
| Rockbridge | 3.9 | 3.7 | 3.3 | 16.2 | 2.5 | 1.3 | 3.4 | 11 726 | 53 | 65.0 | 27.2 | 26.0 | 1 208 | 807 |
| Rockingham | 13.3 | 0.4 | 8.8 | 35.6 | 4.8 | 3.7 | 0.0 | 35 956 | 219 | 202.3 | 106.5 | 69.1 | 939 | 752 |
| Russell | 5.0 | 0.0 | 1.5 | 49.6 | 5.4 | 2.6 | 0.9 | 3 820 | 29 | 64.9 | 42.1 | 20.2 | 700 | 403 |
| Scott | 15.2 | 0.3 | 1.1 | 58.8 | 5.7 | 2.1 | 57.2 | 2 304 | 24 | 69.4 | 48.3 | 15.8 | 693 | 463 |
| Shenandoah | 20.8 | 0.6 | 8.8 | 20.7 | 2.9 | 2.5 | 1.3 | 12 255 | 97 | 112.6 | 50.4 | 44.2 | 1 095 | 808 |
| Smyth | 10.1 | 8.2 | 6.5 | 53.6 | 8.1 | 2.2 | 3.1 | 4 485 | 25 | 90.1 | 56.9 | 24.3 | 759 | 493 |
| Southampton | 4.0 | 0.0 | 0.8 | 29.8 | 2.8 | 1.4 | 0.1 | 8 137 | 47 | 51.6 | 27.3 | 17.8 | 1 010 | 760 |
| Spotsylvania | 5.5 | 202.8 | 9.3 | 13.7 | 6.6 | 3.9 | 0.1 | 57 513 | 248 | 361.3 | 163.4 | 154.3 | 1 295 | 923 |
| Stafford | 59.5 | 124.6 | 155.9 | 11.5 | 6.9 | 4.9 | 0.7 | 85 606 | 471 | 401.5 | 172.6 | 179.9 | 1 490 | 1 127 |
| Surry | 1.6 | 0.1 | 0.3 | 6.6 | 1.1 | 0.4 | 0.0 | 2 143 | 18 | 31.3 | 7.7 | 21.6 | 3 052 | 2 961 |
| Sussex | 5.9 | 0.0 | 0.7 | 21.2 | 2.3 | 0.8 | 0.0 | 1 804 | 15 | 44.4 | 17.7 | 19.6 | 1 605 | 704 |
| Tazewell | 8.6 | 0.0 | 1.5 | 51.7 | 8.0 | 5.7 | 0.6 | 6 511 | 39 | 122.4 | 69.8 | 34.8 | 793 | 574 |
| Warren | 16.8 | 1.0 | 7.7 | 14.9 | 2.6 | 2.0 | 0.4 | 10 199 | 57 | 97.0 | 41.3 | 45.0 | 1 240 | 920 |
| Washington | 14.0 | 0.1 | 4.2 | 72.1 | 9.8 | 4.1 | 7.0 | 18 084 | 118 | 190.0 | 121.9 | 41.5 | 787 | 564 |
| Westmoreland | 4.5 | 6.0 | 1.1 | 12.5 | 3.3 | 1.3 | 0.1 | 12 302 | 72 | 46.8 | 21.3 | 21.2 | 1 228 | 832 |
| Wise | 12.8 | 1.4 | 65.3 | 65.5 | 8.1 | 4.8 | 26.1 | 4 127 | 29 | 136.2 | 80.0 | 44.8 | 1 075 | 501 |
| Wythe | 8.8 | 0.0 | 1.7 | 36.2 | 3.9 | 4.8 | 9.5 | 6 854 | 67 | 86.0 | 45.8 | 22.7 | 797 | 452 |
| York | 110.9 | 57.0 | 24.4 | 9.7 | 5.4 | 10.5 | 0.2 | 18 208 | 89 | 224.8 | 95.1 | 99.5 | 1 624 | 1 137 |
| Independent cities | | | | | | | | | | | | | | |
| Alexandria city | 1 997.9 | 922.9 | 1 128.3 | 86.0 | 13.7 | 12.5 | 348.9 | 124 862 | 759 | 559.1 | 66.4 | 429.0 | 3 064 | 2 220 |
| Bedford city | 9.8 | 0.9 | 2.3 | 4.1 | 0.2 | 0.2 | 0.3 | 49 | 1 | 16.8 | 7.3 | 6.6 | 1 057 | 612 |
| Bristol city | 20.5 | 0.1 | 4.8 | 35.3 | 2.7 | 1.7 | 26.0 | 2 566 | 34 | 98.2 | 32.0 | 28.3 | 1 609 | 940 |
| Buena Vista city | 1.7 | 0.4 | 1.6 | 9.7 | 0.7 | 0.5 | 0.0 | 183 | 2 | 19.6 | 10.2 | 6.0 | 922 | 664 |
| Charlottesville city | 71.4 | 48.5 | 31.1 | 276.5 | 5.3 | 15.4 | 88.8 | 14 801 | 146 | 183.3 | 68.7 | 86.6 | 2 100 | 1 259 |
| Chesapeake city | 102.3 | 299.2 | 73.7 | 77.7 | 16.7 | 12.2 | 17.3 | 184 508 | 1 044 | 1 117.3 | 369.5 | 418.2 | 1 908 | 1 343 |
| Colonial Heights city | 5.9 | 8.3 | 0.8 | 5.6 | 1.0 | 1.3 | 0.1 | 603 | 6 | 57.2 | 16.5 | 35.6 | 1 999 | 1 045 |
| Covington city | 5.7 | 0.6 | 0.8 | 9.4 | 0.7 | 0.7 | 0.2 | 131 | 2 | 25.6 | 10.8 | 11.5 | 1 864 | 1 214 |
| Danville city | 15.2 | 0.5 | 6.1 | 76.2 | 9.3 | 4.4 | 11.4 | 2 716 | 24 | 165.3 | 85.6 | 47.9 | 1 066 | 577 |
| Emporia city | 4.1 | 0.0 | 0.5 | 18.4 | 0.2 | 0.6 | 0.4 | 1 189 | 19 | 16.0 | 3.4 | 9.2 | 1 641 | 739 |
| Fairfax city | 107.7 | 124.6 | 104.3 | 34.6 | 8.0 | 36.5 | 120.4 | 8 781 | 52 | 106.6 | 9.9 | 82.6 | 3 537 | 2 149 |
| Falls Church city | 402.3 | 561.6 | 30.7 | 32.6 | 0.6 | 2.0 | 2.4 | 3 468 | 10 | 71.7 | 9.7 | 46.9 | 4 284 | 3 252 |
| Franklin city | 3.2 | -0.1 | 0.5 | 23.7 | 3.5 | 1.4 | 2.4 | 134 | 2 | 48.1 | 26.3 | 13.8 | 1 551 | 793 |
| Fredericksburg city | 28.6 | 17.3 | 14.6 | 15.3 | 2.3 | 1.3 | 19.6 | 27 125 | 412 | 150.3 | 48.2 | 59.2 | 2 639 | 1 232 |
| Galax city | 6.4 | 0.4 | 0.6 | 11.6 | 2.8 | 0.7 | 0.6 | 375 | 3 | 27.6 | 12.1 | 10.1 | 1 480 | 746 |
| Hampton city | 1 087.7 | 483.9 | 498.1 | 61.1 | 15.3 | 19.2 | 120.4 | 34 204 | 442 | 550.7 | 234.8 | 218.3 | 1 491 | 1 014 |
| Harrisonburg city | 21.9 | 22.8 | 5.8 | 13.1 | 3.3 | 2.3 | 15.8 | 4 360 | 29 | 119.7 | 38.5 | 56.9 | 1 293 | 539 |
| Hopewell city | 3.2 | 8.7 | 5.2 | 20.8 | 4.2 | 2.8 | 4.7 | 1 774 | 24 | 88.4 | 40.7 | 28.1 | 1 222 | 967 |
| Lexington city | 22.9 | 4.1 | 0.8 | 10.4 | 0.6 | 0.2 | 7.7 | 710 | 5 | 21.2 | 6.3 | 6.9 | 987 | 546 |
| Lynchburg city | 36.9 | 22.2 | 296.0 | 68.6 | 10.9 | 6.4 | 15.7 | 12 931 | 61 | 262.8 | 103.6 | 103.9 | 1 457 | 803 |
| Manassas city | 56.1 | 756.4 | 57.4 | 22.3 | 4.1 | 3.4 | 11.2 | 4 776 | 44 | 164.4 | 50.2 | 80.4 | 2 271 | 1 676 |

1. State totals may include programs not allocated by county.    2. Based on the resident population estimated as of July 1 of the year shown.

| STATE County | Total (mil dol) 185 | Per capita[1] (dollars) 186 | Education 187 | Health and hospitals 188 | Police protection 189 | Public welfare 190 | Highways 191 | Total (mil dol) 192 | Per capita[1] (dollars) 193 | Federal civilian 194 | Federal military 195 | State and local 196 | Democratic 197 | Republican 198 | All other 199 |
|---|---|---|---|---|---|---|---|---|---|---|---|---|---|---|---|
| **VIRGINIA—Cont'd** | | | | | | | | | | | | | | | |
| Louisa | 79.8 | 2 497 | 60.6 | 2.8 | 5.4 | 6.4 | 0.2 | 38.6 | 1 206 | 57 | 104 | 1 499 | 45.5 | 53.3 | 1.3 |
| Lunenburg | 37.2 | 2 860 | 52.8 | 1.2 | 8.0 | 5.6 | 1.4 | 27.9 | 2 142 | 21 | 40 | 784 | 47.8 | 51.3 | 0.8 |
| Madison | 27.8 | 2 024 | 66.1 | 3.3 | 5.8 | 5.7 | 0.0 | 85.3 | 6 221 | 69 | 41 | 521 | 42.7 | 56.1 | 1.2 |
| Mathews | 20.6 | 2 276 | 58.7 | 0.8 | 6.5 | 8.7 | 0.1 | 15.5 | 1 715 | 22 | 69 | 361 | 35.6 | 63.5 | 0.9 |
| Mecklenburg | 88.3 | 2 750 | 60.3 | 0.9 | 7.6 | 2.4 | 2.2 | 97.7 | 3 043 | 130 | 102 | 2 180 | 47.3 | 51.8 | 0.9 |
| Middlesex | 36.1 | 3 389 | 61.6 | 0.8 | 3.7 | 4.5 | 1.0 | 39.7 | 3 730 | 18 | 34 | 1 024 | 39.8 | 59.0 | 1.2 |
| Montgomery | 201.9 | 2 264 | 45.3 | 2.1 | 6.7 | 3.0 | 6.4 | 294.7 | 3 304 | (3)379 | (3)404 | (3)16 217 | 51.7 | 46.8 | 1.5 |
| Nelson | 42.9 | 2 817 | 75.4 | 1.0 | 1.7 | 4.2 | 0.0 | 0.0 | 0 | 52 | 47 | 641 | 54.0 | 44.8 | 1.2 |
| New Kent | 36.9 | 2 158 | 58.6 | 1.2 | 6.1 | 4.4 | 0.0 | 31.2 | 1 822 | 42 | 59 | 899 | 35.0 | 63.9 | 1.1 |
| Northampton | 79.7 | 5 950 | 27.6 | 1.2 | 2.7 | 4.2 | 0.1 | 244.1 | 18 218 | 36 | 67 | 920 | 57.7 | 41.2 | 1.1 |
| Northumberland | 25.8 | 2 001 | 60.9 | 1.0 | 3.4 | 6.0 | 0.2 | 2.1 | 163 | 27 | 39 | 446 | 44.7 | 54.6 | 0.7 |
| Nottoway | 39.6 | 2 511 | 65.2 | 0.3 | 6.5 | 6.1 | 2.9 | 17.3 | 1 100 | 344 | 53 | 2 031 | 48.8 | 50.1 | 1.1 |
| Orange | 78.3 | 2 410 | 55.5 | 1.3 | 5.7 | 3.0 | 0.7 | 74.1 | 2 281 | 60 | 106 | 2 118 | 45.0 | 53.8 | 1.2 |
| Page | 63.8 | 2 641 | 65.3 | 0.0 | 5.9 | 4.3 | 1.7 | 27.0 | 1 119 | 198 | 75 | 1 270 | 40.8 | 58.1 | 1.1 |
| Patrick | 39.8 | 2 110 | 73.2 | 0.9 | 4.1 | 4.8 | 0.0 | 5.6 | 298 | 44 | 57 | 824 | 33.7 | 64.4 | 1.9 |
| Pittsylvania | 135.9 | 2 235 | 59.5 | 0.5 | 5.1 | 13.0 | 1.3 | 65.6 | 1 079 | (4)223 | (4)331 | (4)6 622 | 37.5 | 61.5 | 0.9 |
| Powhatan | 62.8 | 2 259 | 67.5 | 0.3 | 3.9 | 5.9 | 0.0 | 105.0 | 3 775 | 44 | 88 | 2 375 | 29.3 | 69.8 | 0.9 |
| Prince Edward | 64.4 | 3 013 | 45.7 | 5.9 | 5.9 | 5.3 | 5.7 | 47.3 | 2 213 | 89 | 73 | 2 230 | 54.3 | 44.5 | 1.2 |
| Prince George | 126.4 | 3 524 | 44.8 | 0.4 | 4.2 | 1.8 | 0.2 | 146.8 | 4 091 | (5)5 222 | (5)8 055 | (5)3 158 | 44.5 | 54.7 | 0.8 |
| Prince William | 1 469.9 | 4 078 | 56.0 | 3.7 | 6.2 | 2.9 | 1.5 | 1 542.2 | 4 279 | (6)7 687 | (6)6 791 | (6)22 190 | 57.5 | 41.6 | 0.9 |
| Pulaski | 95.8 | 2 732 | 46.1 | 2.7 | 5.3 | 8.5 | 1.4 | 65.1 | 1 856 | 44 | 108 | 2 460 | 39.3 | 58.9 | 1.8 |
| Rappahannock | 17.7 | 2 464 | 64.5 | 1.2 | 3.2 | 3.0 | 1.1 | 17.6 | 2 442 | 20 | 23 | 307 | 47.8 | 50.6 | 1.7 |
| Richmond | 26.2 | 2 857 | 51.6 | 0.7 | 1.1 | 4.3 | 0.2 | 21.1 | 2 305 | 37 | 29 | 900 | 43.2 | 55.9 | 0.9 |
| Roanoke | 267.0 | 2 952 | 53.5 | 0.3 | 8.0 | 6.0 | 0.7 | 370.9 | 4 102 | (7)2 140 | (7)368 | (7)6 686 | 38.9 | 60.0 | 1.2 |
| Rockbridge | 68.4 | 3 180 | 41.8 | 0.7 | 3.1 | 7.1 | 0.1 | 72.7 | 3 384 | (8)102 | (8)145 | (8)2 567 | 42.6 | 56.2 | 1.1 |
| Rockingham | 231.4 | 3 147 | 55.3 | 3.7 | 4.7 | 8.9 | 2.1 | 151.0 | 2 054 | (9)356 | (9)399 | (9)9 986 | 31.4 | 67.4 | 1.2 |
| Russell | 56.7 | 1 967 | 66.7 | 0.0 | 3.0 | 8.8 | 0.6 | 67.6 | 2 346 | 60 | 90 | 1 450 | 42.9 | 55.6 | 1.5 |
| Scott | 80.1 | 3 515 | 54.2 | 1.1 | 6.3 | 9.8 | 1.2 | 16.7 | 734 | 62 | 72 | 1 207 | 27.6 | 70.7 | 1.7 |
| Shenandoah | 110.0 | 2 724 | 55.9 | 0.3 | 7.8 | 5.8 | 2.6 | 100.7 | 2 493 | 139 | 132 | 2 211 | 36.0 | 62.5 | 1.6 |
| Smyth | 84.8 | 2 646 | 60.1 | 1.3 | 6.1 | 6.4 | 2.5 | 110.6 | 3 452 | 71 | 100 | 2 819 | 34.5 | 63.5 | 2.0 |
| Southampton | 53.0 | 3 000 | 56.0 | 0.7 | 0.5 | 4.2 | 0.3 | 73.3 | 4 151 | (10)74 | (10)84 | (10)2 518 | 48.5 | 50.5 | 0.9 |
| Spotsylvania | 386.4 | 3 242 | 60.2 | 0.5 | 3.8 | 3.7 | 2.7 | 501.9 | 4 210 | (11)367 | (11)469 | (11)9 062 | 46.0 | 52.9 | 1.0 |
| Stafford | 416.4 | 3 449 | 68.9 | 0.4 | 7.7 | 2.8 | 0.1 | 398.5 | 3 301 | 3 457 | 2 676 | 6 263 | 46.4 | 52.7 | 0.9 |
| Surry | 27.1 | 3 819 | 63.4 | 1.8 | 4.1 | 8.2 | 0.0 | 31.9 | 4 501 | 15 | 22 | 470 | 60.7 | 38.5 | 0.8 |
| Sussex | 36.2 | 2 964 | 58.1 | 0.6 | 7.1 | 6.0 | 0.2 | 17.5 | 1 433 | 49 | 38 | 1 338 | 61.6 | 37.8 | 0.7 |
| Tazewell | 114.1 | 2 602 | 52.6 | 13.7 | 4.8 | 4.8 | 2.7 | 40.9 | 932 | 82 | 140 | 3 496 | 32.8 | 65.7 | 1.5 |
| Warren | 93.8 | 2 585 | 48.0 | 0.9 | 8.2 | 7.2 | 2.3 | 120.8 | 3 327 | 191 | 118 | 1 694 | 43.4 | 55.1 | 1.6 |
| Washington | 150.4 | 2 853 | 45.0 | 9.2 | 4.2 | 3.9 | 1.6 | 108.0 | 2 048 | (12)231 | (12)256 | (12)4 610 | 32.9 | 65.6 | 1.5 |
| Westmoreland | 40.7 | 2 362 | 62.8 | 1.3 | 6.6 | 4.1 | 0.5 | 9.0 | 523 | 64 | 55 | 811 | 54.6 | 44.4 | 1.0 |
| Wise | 130.2 | 3 124 | 56.5 | 3.7 | 4.7 | 6.7 | 2.0 | 72.6 | 1 742 | (13)238 | (13)143 | (13)4 304 | 35.3 | 63.0 | 1.6 |
| Wythe | 93.0 | 3 258 | 42.7 | 0.1 | 5.2 | 5.4 | 2.7 | 97.7 | 3 424 | 110 | 91 | 2 437 | 32.9 | 65.7 | 1.4 |
| York | 219.1 | 3 576 | 59.7 | 1.1 | 3.5 | 2.5 | 0.1 | 162.2 | 2 647 | (14)1 084 | (14)1 707 | (14)3 644 | 40.4 | 58.5 | 1.1 |
| **Independent cities** | | | | | | | | | | | | | | | |
| Alexandria city | 593.3 | 4 237 | 33.9 | 6.3 | 8.9 | 8.0 | 3.5 | 435.5 | 3 110 | 13 381 | 1 713 | 8 271 | 71.7 | 27.3 | 1.0 |
| Bedford city | 19.9 | 3 171 | 33.3 | 2.0 | 13.3 | 1.0 | 11.1 | 18.8 | 2 998 | (15) | (15) | (15) | 44.2 | 54.8 | 1.1 |
| Bristol city | 90.9 | 5 167 | 25.6 | 0.7 | 6.8 | 5.0 | 4.3 | 121.3 | 6 897 | (12) | (12) | (12) | 36.2 | 62.2 | 1.6 |
| Buena Vista city | 21.6 | 3 326 | 48.4 | 0.0 | 7.4 | 4.4 | 4.6 | 25.9 | 3 998 | (8) | (8) | (8) | 45.7 | 52.9 | 1.4 |
| Charlottesville city | 181.0 | 4 391 | 35.6 | 6.2 | 6.7 | 10.5 | 3.1 | 103.9 | 2 520 | (16) | (16) | (16) | 78.4 | 20.3 | 1.3 |
| Chesapeake city | 993.3 | 4 532 | 45.2 | 21.2 | 4.1 | 2.3 | 4.4 | 821.8 | 3 750 | 1 082 | 1 516 | 15 308 | 50.2 | 48.9 | 0.8 |
| Colonial Heights city | 58.2 | 3 272 | 53.6 | 0.3 | 4.9 | 1.0 | 6.0 | 23.4 | 1 315 | (17) | (17) | (17) | 29.0 | 69.6 | 1.4 |
| Covington city | 27.2 | 4 411 | 41.9 | 1.2 | 5.5 | 7.0 | 5.7 | 29.7 | 4 810 | (18) | (18) | (18) | 55.4 | 43.3 | 1.3 |
| Danville city | 157.1 | 3 495 | 44.9 | 0.4 | 5.8 | 5.3 | 4.7 | 193.3 | 4 301 | (4) | (4) | (4) | 59.1 | 40.0 | 0.8 |
| Emporia city | 15.9 | 2 833 | 24.5 | 1.3 | 19.5 | 3.4 | 5.2 | 17.9 | 3 180 | (19) | (19) | (19) | 65.0 | 34.3 | 0.7 |
| Fairfax city | 137.4 | 5 883 | 55.5 | 0.6 | 7.6 | 0.0 | 3.9 | 206.2 | 8 830 | (20) | (20) | (20) | 57.7 | 41.2 | 1.2 |
| Falls Church city | 100.1 | 9 143 | 35.1 | 0.0 | 5.3 | 1.6 | 2.0 | 66.8 | 6 104 | (20) | (20) | (20) | 69.6 | 29.2 | 1.3 |
| Franklin city | 48.1 | 5 400 | 35.4 | 0.4 | 6.5 | 3.6 | 3.3 | 29.2 | 3 280 | (10) | (10) | (10) | 63.7 | 35.6 | 0.7 |
| Fredericksburg city | 162.4 | 7 246 | 22.0 | 13.3 | 10.4 | 0.4 | 4.2 | 646.0 | 28 826 | (11) | (11) | (11) | 63.6 | 35.3 | 1.1 |
| Galax city | 26.4 | 3 867 | 44.7 | 0.9 | 7.1 | 6.9 | 7.1 | 17.6 | 2 585 | (21) | (21) | (21) | 43.8 | 54.8 | 1.4 |
| Hampton city | 519.1 | 3 545 | 45.1 | 0.7 | 5.4 | 5.5 | 0.9 | 336.2 | 2 296 | 8 464 | 8 096 | 8 233 | 69.1 | 30.1 | 0.8 |
| Harrisonburg city | 143.3 | 3 255 | 54.2 | 0.7 | 4.8 | 1.8 | 7.1 | 404.6 | 9 186 | (9) | (9) | (9) | 57.5 | 41.2 | 1.2 |
| Hopewell city | 95.8 | 4 158 | 41.3 | 0.2 | 5.7 | 4.2 | 6.4 | 45.6 | 1 981 | (5) | (5) | (5) | 55.5 | 43.6 | 0.9 |
| Lexington city | 26.4 | 3 763 | 20.4 | 2.2 | 10.1 | 0.0 | 12.5 | 27.7 | 3 944 | (8) | (8) | (8) | 62.2 | 36.9 | 0.9 |
| Lynchburg city | 246.4 | 3 457 | 38.5 | 6.1 | 7.6 | 3.2 | 4.7 | 67.6 | 949 | (22) | (22) | (22) | 47.4 | 51.4 | 1.3 |
| Manassas city | 163.6 | 4 621 | 58.1 | 3.4 | 8.1 | 0.2 | 8.0 | 152.7 | 4 312 | (6) | (6) | (6) | 55.2 | 43.8 | 1.0 |

1. Based on the resident population estimated as of July 1 of the year shown.   2. © 2013 Election Data Services, Inc. All rights reserved.   3. Radford city is included with Montgomery county.   4. Danville city is included with Pittsylvania county.   5. Hopewell city is included with Prince George county.   6. Manassas and Manassas Park cities are included with Prince William county.   7. Salem city is included with Roanoke county.   8. Buena Vista and Lexington cities are included with Rockbridge county.   9. Harrisonburg city is included with Rockingham county.   10. Franklin city is included with Southhampton county.   11. Fredericksburg city is included with Spotsylvania county.   12. Bristol city included with Washington county.   13. Norton city is included with Wise county.   14. Poquoson city is included with York county.   15. Bedford city is included with Bedford county.   16. Charlottesville city is included with Albemarle county.   17. Petersburg and Colonial Heights cities are included with Dinwiddie county.   18. Covington city is included with Alleghany county.   19. Emporia city is included with Greensville county.   20. Fairfax city and Falls Church city are included with Fairfax county.   21. Galax city is included with Carroll county.   22. Lynchburg city is included with Campbell county.

# Table B. States and Counties — Land Area and Population

| STATE/ County code | CBSA code[1] | County type[2] | STATE County | Land area,[3] (sq km) 2010 | Population 2012 | | | Population characteristics[6], 2011 | | | | | | | | | | |
|---|---|---|---|---|---|---|---|---|---|---|---|---|---|---|---|---|---|---|
| | | | | | | | | Race alone or in combination, not Hispanic or Latino (percent) | | | | | Age (percent) | | | | | |
| | | | | | Total persons | Rank | Per square kilometer | White | Black | American Indian, Alaska Native | Asian and Pacific Islander | Percent Hispanic or Latino[4] | Under 5 years | 5 to 17 years | 18 to 24 years | 25 to 34 years | 35 to 44 years | 45 to 54 years |
| | | | | 1 | 2 | 3 | 4 | 5 | 6 | 7 | 8 | 9 | 10 | 11 | 12 | 13 | 14 | 15 |
| | | | **VIRGINIA—Cont'd** | | | | | | | | | | | | | | | |
| 51 685 | 47900 | 1 | Manassas Park city | 7 | 15 798 | 2 058 | 2 256.9 | 44.1 | 14.3 | 0.8 | 10.1 | 33.5 | 9.0 | 19.9 | 9.4 | 19.6 | 16.4 | 13.1 |
| 51 690 | 32300 | 4 | Martinsville city | 28 | 13 733 | 2 196 | 490.5 | 50.1 | 45.7 | 0.6 | 1.4 | 3.9 | 6.5 | 15.2 | 7.9 | 11.1 | 11.7 | 15.6 |
| 51 700 | 47260 | 1 | Newport News city | 178 | 180 726 | 350 | 1 015.3 | 49.0 | 41.5 | 1.2 | 4.3 | 7.6 | 7.6 | 16.7 | 13.2 | 16.0 | 11.7 | 13.7 |
| 51 710 | 47260 | 1 | Norfolk city | 140 | 245 782 | 267 | 1 755.6 | 47.0 | 43.4 | 1.2 | 4.8 | 6.9 | 6.9 | 14.0 | 19.6 | 17.5 | 11.1 | 11.9 |
| 51 720 | ... | 7 | Norton city | 19 | 4 068 | 2 900 | 214.1 | 89.0 | 8.3 | 0.8 | 1.9 | 2.2 | 6.2 | 15.8 | 10.3 | 12.9 | 12.3 | 14.3 |
| 51 730 | 40060 | 1 | Petersburg city | 59 | 31 973 | 1 391 | 541.9 | 17.6 | 77.8 | 0.8 | 1.6 | 4.1 | 7.4 | 14.0 | 11.3 | 13.0 | 10.6 | 15.0 |
| 51 735 | 47260 | 1 | Poquoson city | 40 | 12 097 | 2 292 | 302.4 | 94.4 | 1.5 | 0.8 | 2.7 | 1.9 | 4.0 | 18.9 | 7.7 | 8.4 | 12.6 | 17.8 |
| 51 740 | 47260 | 1 | Portsmouth city | 87 | 96 470 | 605 | 1 108.9 | 42.5 | 53.6 | 1.2 | 2.0 | 3.3 | 7.4 | 16.3 | 10.6 | 15.4 | 11.6 | 13.7 |
| 51 750 | 13980 | 3 | Radford city | 26 | 16 685 | 1 999 | 641.7 | 86.7 | 9.4 | 0.7 | 3.2 | 2.4 | 3.6 | 8.9 | 48.9 | 8.9 | 7.3 | 7.0 |
| 51 760 | 40060 | 1 | Richmond city | 155 | 210 309 | 298 | 1 356.8 | 41.2 | 50.6 | 0.9 | 3.0 | 6.3 | 6.6 | 12.5 | 16.6 | 18.1 | 11.4 | 12.4 |
| 51 770 | 40220 | 2 | Roanoke city | 110 | 97 469 | 601 | 886.1 | 64.0 | 29.7 | 0.8 | 2.3 | 5.6 | 7.3 | 14.5 | 8.7 | 15.1 | 12.7 | 14.1 |
| 51 775 | 40220 | 2 | Salem city | 37 | 24 970 | 1 608 | 674.9 | 88.1 | 7.9 | 0.6 | 2.1 | 2.6 | 4.8 | 14.8 | 13.6 | 10.1 | 11.5 | 14.1 |
| 51 790 | 44420 | 4 | Staunton city | 52 | 23 921 | 1 647 | 460.0 | 84.0 | 13.7 | 0.8 | 1.4 | 2.4 | 5.7 | 13.5 | 9.6 | 12.9 | 11.2 | 13.3 |
| 51 800 | 47260 | 1 | Suffolk city | 1 036 | 85 181 | 662 | 82.2 | 52.4 | 43.1 | 1.0 | 2.4 | 3.2 | 6.8 | 18.9 | 8.2 | 12.2 | 14.2 | 16.0 |
| 51 810 | 47260 | 1 | Virginia Beach city | 645 | 447 021 | 149 | 693.1 | 67.0 | 20.7 | 1.0 | 8.0 | 7.0 | 6.6 | 17.0 | 10.7 | 15.9 | 13.1 | 14.5 |
| 51 820 | 44420 | 4 | Waynesboro city | 39 | 21 107 | 1 777 | 541.2 | 81.3 | 12.4 | 0.9 | 1.4 | 6.7 | 7.2 | 16.3 | 8.1 | 14.0 | 11.7 | 13.6 |
| 51 830 | 47260 | 1 | Williamsburg city | 23 | 15 167 | 2 095 | 659.4 | 72.8 | 15.3 | 0.9 | 7.2 | 6.9 | 3.5 | 7.0 | 41.5 | 12.4 | 6.8 | 7.3 |
| 51 840 | 49020 | 3 | Winchester city | 24 | 26 881 | 1 534 | 1 120.0 | 70.8 | 12.2 | 0.7 | 2.7 | 15.8 | 7.0 | 15.6 | 12.3 | 14.9 | 11.6 | 13.3 |
| 53 000 | ... | X | **WASHINGTON** | 172 119 | 6 897 012 | X | 40.1 | 75.4 | 4.6 | 2.5 | 9.9 | 11.6 | 6.5 | 16.7 | 9.7 | 14.1 | 13.3 | 14.3 |
| 53 001 | ... | 6 | Adams | 4 986 | 19 005 | 1 875 | 3.8 | 38.7 | 0.5 | 0.8 | 0.8 | 59.9 | 11.2 | 23.9 | 9.9 | 13.1 | 11.9 | 10.4 |
| 53 003 | 30300 | 3 | Asotin | 1 648 | 21 888 | 1 738 | 13.3 | 94.1 | 1.0 | 2.6 | 1.4 | 3.1 | 5.8 | 15.6 | 8.0 | 11.7 | 10.6 | 14.3 |
| 53 005 | 28420 | 3 | Benton | 4 404 | 182 398 | 346 | 41.4 | 76.2 | 1.9 | 1.6 | 3.8 | 18.8 | 7.4 | 19.3 | 9.0 | 13.5 | 12.3 | 14.0 |
| 53 007 | 48300 | 3 | Chelan | 7 564 | 73 687 | 738 | 9.7 | 71.4 | 0.6 | 1.6 | 1.6 | 26.5 | 7.0 | 17.9 | 8.6 | 11.9 | 11.2 | 14.0 |
| 53 009 | 38820 | 5 | Clallam | 4 502 | 71 863 | 749 | 16.0 | 87.3 | 1.5 | 6.4 | 2.9 | 5.3 | 4.6 | 13.2 | 7.4 | 10.1 | 9.6 | 13.2 |
| 53 011 | 38900 | 1 | Clark | 1 629 | 438 287 | 153 | 269.1 | 84.5 | 2.9 | 1.8 | 6.6 | 7.8 | 6.7 | 19.3 | 8.4 | 12.9 | 13.8 | 14.3 |
| 53 013 | ... | 6 | Columbia | 2 250 | 3 995 | 2 905 | 1.8 | 91.3 | 0.9 | 2.0 | 1.4 | 6.2 | 4.8 | 14.2 | 5.6 | 8.4 | 10.0 | 15.4 |
| 53 015 | 31020 | 3 | Cowlitz | 2 953 | 101 996 | 573 | 34.5 | 88.0 | 1.2 | 3.1 | 2.6 | 8.1 | 6.2 | 17.7 | 8.2 | 11.3 | 12.0 | 14.4 |
| 53 017 | 48300 | 3 | Douglas | 4 712 | 39 350 | 1 189 | 8.4 | 68.9 | 0.7 | 1.6 | 1.5 | 28.9 | 7.2 | 19.5 | 8.4 | 12.2 | 12.0 | 13.3 |
| 53 019 | ... | 9 | Ferry | 5 706 | 7 705 | 2 627 | 1.4 | 78.9 | 1.1 | 18.8 | 2.0 | 3.7 | 5.0 | 14.6 | 8.6 | 9.0 | 9.7 | 14.5 |
| 53 021 | 28420 | 3 | Franklin | 3 217 | 85 845 | 657 | 26.7 | 44.9 | 2.4 | 1.1 | 2.6 | 50.5 | 10.6 | 23.5 | 10.2 | 16.4 | 12.9 | 10.6 |
| 53 023 | ... | 8 | Garfield | 1 841 | 2 228 | 3 034 | 1.2 | 93.4 | 0.4 | 1.1 | 2.0 | 4.4 | 3.9 | 15.8 | 5.6 | 8.4 | 10.0 | 14.5 |
| 53 025 | 34180 | 4 | Grant | 6 940 | 91 723 | 629 | 13.2 | 58.4 | 1.3 | 1.7 | 1.7 | 38.7 | 9.0 | 21.7 | 10.0 | 13.1 | 11.8 | 11.9 |
| 53 027 | 10140 | 4 | Grays Harbor | 4 926 | 71 692 | 750 | 14.6 | 84.0 | 1.7 | 6.0 | 2.6 | 8.9 | 5.8 | 15.5 | 8.4 | 11.9 | 11.4 | 14.5 |
| 53 029 | 36020 | 4 | Island | 540 | 79 177 | 693 | 146.6 | 85.7 | 3.1 | 1.9 | 7.3 | 5.9 | 5.7 | 14.4 | 8.9 | 12.0 | 10.3 | 13.4 |
| 53 031 | ... | 6 | Jefferson | 4 672 | 29 854 | 1 428 | 6.4 | 91.9 | 1.4 | 3.8 | 2.9 | 3.0 | 3.4 | 10.8 | 5.4 | 8.0 | 8.8 | 14.0 |
| 53 033 | 42660 | 1 | King | 5 479 | 2 007 440 | 13 | 366.4 | 68.0 | 7.4 | 1.7 | 18.2 | 9.2 | 6.2 | 14.9 | 9.1 | 16.5 | 15.2 | 14.7 |
| 53 035 | 14740 | 3 | Kitsap | 1 023 | 254 991 | 259 | 249.3 | 83.0 | 4.0 | 2.9 | 8.8 | 6.6 | 5.8 | 16.0 | 10.6 | 13.0 | 11.7 | 14.8 |
| 53 037 | 21260 | 6 | Kittitas | 5 950 | 41 672 | 1 135 | 7.0 | 87.5 | 1.6 | 2.0 | 3.5 | 8.0 | 5.0 | 12.8 | 24.1 | 11.5 | 9.7 | 11.9 |
| 53 039 | ... | 6 | Klickitat | 4 847 | 20 699 | 1 797 | 4.3 | 85.4 | 0.8 | 3.7 | 1.5 | 11.1 | 5.4 | 16.3 | 6.3 | 9.9 | 11.5 | 14.6 |
| 53 041 | 16500 | 4 | Lewis | 6 223 | 75 621 | 723 | 12.2 | 88.0 | 1.1 | 2.8 | 1.8 | 8.9 | 6.1 | 16.6 | 8.5 | 11.4 | 11.2 | 14.1 |
| 53 043 | ... | 8 | Lincoln | 5 984 | 10 437 | 2 400 | 1.7 | 94.9 | 0.9 | 2.9 | 0.9 | 2.5 | 4.9 | 17.2 | 6.0 | 8.1 | 10.1 | 15.0 |
| 53 045 | 43220 | 6 | Mason | 2 485 | 60 832 | 850 | 24.5 | 85.7 | 1.7 | 5.0 | 2.9 | 8.2 | 5.3 | 14.7 | 7.5 | 11.5 | 11.3 | 14.4 |
| 53 047 | ... | 6 | Okanogan | 13 644 | 41 275 | 1 146 | 3.0 | 70.2 | 0.7 | 12.2 | 1.3 | 18.1 | 6.9 | 16.5 | 7.3 | 10.4 | 10.8 | 14.1 |
| 53 049 | ... | 7 | Pacific | 2 416 | 20 575 | 1 808 | 8.5 | 86.8 | 0.9 | 4.1 | 2.9 | 8.3 | 4.7 | 13.3 | 6.2 | 8.9 | 9.1 | 13.6 |
| 53 051 | ... | 8 | Pend Oreille | 3 626 | 12 980 | 2 242 | 3.6 | 91.6 | 1.1 | 5.0 | 1.5 | 3.2 | 5.3 | 15.8 | 5.9 | 8.1 | 10.0 | 15.9 |
| 53 053 | 42660 | 1 | Pierce | 4 324 | 811 681 | 70 | 187.7 | 75.0 | 8.8 | 2.6 | 10.4 | 9.4 | 6.9 | 17.4 | 10.4 | 14.5 | 13.2 | 14.4 |
| 53 055 | ... | 9 | San Juan | 450 | 15 824 | 2 057 | 35.2 | 91.7 | 0.9 | 1.6 | 2.2 | 5.7 | 3.2 | 11.9 | 5.1 | 8.0 | 9.5 | 15.2 |
| 53 057 | 34580 | 3 | Skagit | 4 484 | 118 222 | 514 | 26.4 | 78.2 | 1.1 | 2.7 | 2.9 | 17.3 | 6.4 | 17.0 | 8.4 | 12.1 | 11.7 | 13.6 |
| 53 059 | 38900 | 1 | Skamania | 4 288 | 11 187 | 2 347 | 2.6 | 91.3 | 1.1 | 2.9 | 1.8 | 5.6 | 5.1 | 16.4 | 6.5 | 10.2 | 12.2 | 17.0 |
| 53 061 | 42660 | 1 | Snohomish | 5 406 | 733 036 | 83 | 135.6 | 77.4 | 3.5 | 2.3 | 11.7 | 9.2 | 6.5 | 17.4 | 8.7 | 14.0 | 14.4 | 15.7 |
| 53 063 | 44060 | 2 | Spokane | 4 568 | 475 735 | 139 | 104.1 | 89.5 | 2.8 | 2.6 | 4.0 | 4.7 | 6.3 | 16.6 | 11.2 | 13.5 | 12.0 | 14.1 |
| 53 065 | ... | 6 | Stevens | 6 417 | 43 538 | 1 098 | 6.8 | 90.5 | 0.9 | 7.0 | 1.6 | 3.0 | 5.2 | 18.0 | 6.5 | 8.5 | 10.9 | 15.4 |
| 53 067 | 36500 | 3 | Thurston | 1 870 | 258 332 | 256 | 138.1 | 82.3 | 4.0 | 2.6 | 8.4 | 7.4 | 6.1 | 16.5 | 9.3 | 13.8 | 12.8 | 14.2 |
| 53 069 | ... | 8 | Wahkiakum | 682 | 3 993 | 2 906 | 5.9 | 94.4 | 1.0 | 2.9 | 1.5 | 3.1 | 3.7 | 14.7 | 4.4 | 8.0 | 9.4 | 13.7 |
| 53 071 | 47460 | 4 | Walla Walla | 3 290 | 59 404 | 871 | 18.1 | 75.3 | 2.3 | 1.6 | 2.6 | 20.3 | 5.9 | 16.5 | 13.1 | 12.7 | 11.4 | 12.9 |
| 53 073 | 13380 | 3 | Whatcom | 5 457 | 205 262 | 306 | 37.6 | 84.1 | 1.7 | 3.7 | 5.7 | 8.2 | 5.5 | 14.9 | 15.1 | 12.8 | 11.6 | 13.1 |
| 53 075 | 39420 | 4 | Whitman | 5 592 | 46 606 | 1 038 | 8.3 | 84.3 | 2.6 | 1.5 | 10.3 | 4.9 | 4.4 | 10.0 | 38.5 | 12.5 | 7.9 | 8.8 |
| 53 077 | 49420 | 3 | Yakima | 11 125 | 246 977 | 266 | 22.2 | 48.6 | 1.2 | 4.6 | 1.8 | 45.8 | 8.9 | 21.5 | 10.1 | 13.2 | 11.9 | 12.1 |
| 54 000 | ... | X | **WEST VIRGINIA** | 62 259 | 1 855 413 | X | 29.8 | 94.3 | 4.2 | 0.7 | 1.0 | 1.3 | 5.6 | 15.2 | 9.2 | 11.9 | 12.6 | 14.6 |
| 54 001 | ... | 7 | Barbour | 883 | 16 493 | 2 012 | 18.7 | 97.6 | 1.4 | 1.3 | 0.4 | 0.7 | 5.4 | 16.0 | 9.5 | 10.7 | 12.8 | 14.7 |
| 54 003 | 25180 | 3 | Berkeley | 832 | 107 098 | 554 | 128.7 | 87.9 | 8.5 | 0.8 | 1.4 | 3.8 | 6.7 | 18.1 | 7.8 | 13.5 | 14.3 | 15.1 |
| 54 005 | 16620 | 2 | Boone | 1 299 | 24 478 | 1 623 | 18.8 | 98.7 | 0.8 | 0.4 | 0.2 | 0.4 | 6.1 | 16.6 | 7.3 | 11.5 | 13.8 | 14.2 |
| 54 007 | ... | 8 | Braxton | 1 323 | 14 468 | 2 141 | 10.9 | 98.5 | 0.8 | 0.7 | 0.3 | 0.5 | 5.5 | 15.1 | 7.4 | 10.8 | 12.2 | 15.2 |

1. CBSA = Core Based Statistical Area. See Appendix A for explanation. See Appendix B for list of metropolitan areas with component counties. 2. County type code from the Economic Research Service of USDA Rural-Urban Continuum Codes. See Appendix A for definition. 3. Dry land or land partially or temporarily covered by water. 4. May be of any race.

# Table B. States and Counties — **Population and Households**

| STATE County | 55 to 64 years | 65 to 74 years | 75 years and over | Percent female | Total persons 2000 | Total persons 2010 | Percent change 2000–2010 | Percent change 2010–2012 | Births | Deaths | Net migration | Number | Percent change, 2000–2010 | Persons per household | Female family householder[1] | One person |
|---|---|---|---|---|---|---|---|---|---|---|---|---|---|---|---|---|
| | 16 | 17 | 18 | 19 | 20 | 21 | 22 | 23 | 24 | 25 | 26 | 27 | 28 | 29 | 30 | 31 |
| VIRGINIA—Cont'd | | | | | | | | | | | | | | | | |
| Manassas Park city | 7.5 | 3.1 | 2.0 | 49.3 | 10 290 | 14 273 | 38.7 | 10.7 | 536 | 87 | 1 028 | 4 507 | 38.5 | 3.17 | 13.1 | 21.3 |
| Martinsville city | 13.4 | 9.1 | 9.7 | 54.6 | 15 416 | 13 821 | -10.3 | -0.6 | 511 | 487 | -156 | 6 084 | -6.4 | 2.21 | 21.5 | 37.5 |
| Newport News city | 10.3 | 5.9 | 5.0 | 51.7 | 180 150 | 180 719 | 0.3 | 0.0 | 6 723 | 3 102 | -3 875 | 70 664 | 1.4 | 2.45 | 18.9 | 29.1 |
| Norfolk city | 9.6 | 4.8 | 4.6 | 48.3 | 234 403 | 242 803 | 3.6 | 1.2 | 8 430 | 4 317 | -1 136 | 86 485 | 0.3 | 2.43 | 19.3 | 31.1 |
| Norton city | 14.2 | 7.5 | 6.6 | 53.6 | 3 904 | 3 958 | 1.4 | 2.8 | 136 | 77 | 38 | 1 750 | 1.2 | 2.22 | 15.4 | 37.4 |
| Petersburg city | 13.2 | 8.2 | 7.3 | 53.7 | 33 740 | 32 420 | -3.9 | -1.4 | 1 452 | 995 | -963 | 13 634 | -1.2 | 2.30 | 25.9 | 36.0 |
| Poquoson city | 14.5 | 9.6 | 6.6 | 50.6 | 11 566 | 12 150 | 5.0 | -0.4 | 180 | 229 | -16 | 4 525 | 8.6 | 2.67 | 8.7 | 17.5 |
| Portsmouth city | 11.8 | 6.7 | 6.4 | 51.9 | 100 565 | 95 535 | -5.0 | 1.0 | 3 514 | 2 293 | -236 | 37 324 | -2.2 | 2.47 | 21.7 | 29.4 |
| Radford city | 6.6 | 4.6 | 4.1 | 53.0 | 15 859 | 16 408 | 3.5 | 1.7 | 303 | 177 | 123 | 5 990 | 3.1 | 2.30 | 9.3 | 31.4 |
| Richmond city | 11.4 | 5.6 | 5.4 | 52.3 | 197 790 | 204 214 | 3.2 | 3.0 | 6 682 | 4 219 | 3 621 | 87 151 | 3.1 | 2.20 | 18.9 | 37.9 |
| Roanoke city | 13.2 | 7.0 | 7.3 | 52.2 | 94 911 | 97 032 | 2.2 | 0.5 | 3 237 | 2 616 | -70 | 42 712 | 1.7 | 2.22 | 17.3 | 37.1 |
| Salem city | 13.4 | 8.9 | 8.7 | 52.4 | 24 747 | 24 802 | 0.2 | 0.7 | 597 | 700 | 214 | 10 045 | 0.9 | 2.30 | 13.1 | 30.9 |
| Staunton city | 13.8 | 9.9 | 10.1 | 54.6 | 23 853 | 23 746 | -0.4 | 0.7 | 689 | 694 | 186 | 10 480 | 8.3 | 2.15 | 13.1 | 36.3 |
| Suffolk city | 11.9 | 6.9 | 4.9 | 51.9 | 63 677 | 84 585 | 32.8 | 0.7 | 2 484 | 1 562 | -318 | 30 868 | 32.6 | 2.70 | 16.2 | 20.9 |
| Virginia Beach city | 11.2 | 6.1 | 4.8 | 51.0 | 425 257 | 437 994 | 3.0 | 2.1 | 13 872 | 6 220 | 1 530 | 165 089 | 6.9 | 2.60 | 13.9 | 23.3 |
| Waynesboro city | 12.1 | 8.8 | 8.3 | 52.5 | 19 520 | 21 006 | 7.6 | 0.5 | 743 | 540 | -136 | 8 903 | 6.9 | 2.34 | 15.3 | 30.8 |
| Williamsburg city | 8.5 | 7.2 | 5.7 | 53.2 | 11 998 | 14 068 | 17.3 | 7.8 | 238 | 219 | 976 | 4 571 | 26.3 | 2.17 | 9.4 | 31.4 |
| Winchester city | 11.3 | 6.9 | 7.2 | 50.5 | 23 585 | 26 203 | 11.1 | 2.6 | 892 | 595 | 389 | 10 607 | 6.1 | 2.38 | 13.0 | 34.3 |
| WASHINGTON | 12.8 | 7.1 | 5.6 | 50.1 | 5 894 121 | 6 724 540 | 14.1 | 2.6 | 194 307 | 109 513 | 88 104 | 2 620 076 | 15.4 | 2.51 | 10.5 | 27.2 |
| Adams | 9.3 | 5.7 | 4.6 | 49.0 | 16 428 | 18 728 | 14.0 | 1.5 | 967 | 279 | -442 | 5 720 | 9.4 | 3.25 | 11.8 | 18.8 |
| Asotin | 14.8 | 10.6 | 8.8 | 52.0 | 20 551 | 21 623 | 5.2 | 1.2 | 526 | 517 | 264 | 9 236 | 10.4 | 2.32 | 12.1 | 29.4 |
| Benton | 12.6 | 6.7 | 5.1 | 49.9 | 142 475 | 175 177 | 23.0 | 4.1 | 5 702 | 2 743 | 4 205 | 65 304 | 23.5 | 2.66 | 11.1 | 24.3 |
| Chelan | 13.6 | 8.3 | 7.4 | 50.1 | 66 616 | 72 453 | 8.8 | 1.7 | 2 221 | 1 374 | 379 | 27 827 | 11.2 | 2.57 | 9.7 | 26.3 |
| Clallam | 17.3 | 13.2 | 11.4 | 50.3 | 64 525 | 71 404 | 10.7 | 0.6 | 1 482 | 2 022 | 1 032 | 31 329 | 15.3 | 2.22 | 9.2 | 30.4 |
| Clark | 12.6 | 7.0 | 4.9 | 50.6 | 345 238 | 425 363 | 23.2 | 3.0 | 12 203 | 6 550 | 7 197 | 158 099 | 24.3 | 2.67 | 11.3 | 23.1 |
| Columbia | 17.4 | 13.8 | 10.5 | 50.3 | 4 064 | 4 078 | 0.3 | -2.0 | 72 | 92 | -69 | 1 762 | 4.4 | 2.27 | 9.2 | 29.3 |
| Cowlitz | 14.2 | 9.0 | 7.0 | 50.5 | 92 948 | 102 410 | 10.2 | -0.4 | 2 772 | 2 189 | -998 | 40 244 | 12.3 | 2.51 | 11.8 | 25.8 |
| Douglas | 12.8 | 8.0 | 6.5 | 49.8 | 32 603 | 38 431 | 17.9 | 2.4 | 1 168 | 696 | 448 | 13 894 | 18.5 | 2.75 | 10.7 | 20.8 |
| Ferry | 19.4 | 12.1 | 7.1 | 48.2 | 7 260 | 7 551 | 4.0 | 2.0 | 142 | 170 | 186 | 3 190 | 13.0 | 2.29 | 9.2 | 28.5 |
| Franklin | 8.5 | 4.3 | 3.0 | 47.7 | 49 347 | 78 163 | 58.4 | 9.8 | 3 892 | 872 | 4 552 | 23 245 | 56.6 | 3.28 | 13.4 | 16.4 |
| Garfield | 18.7 | 10.8 | 12.3 | 51.2 | 2 397 | 2 266 | -5.5 | -1.7 | 37 | 49 | -23 | 989 | 0.2 | 2.25 | 6.1 | 30.2 |
| Grant | 10.6 | 6.7 | 5.2 | 49.1 | 74 698 | 89 120 | 19.3 | 2.9 | 3 620 | 1 398 | 410 | 30 041 | 19.2 | 2.93 | 11.5 | 22.0 |
| Grays Harbor | 15.5 | 9.0 | 7.0 | 48.5 | 67 194 | 72 797 | 8.3 | -1.5 | 1 781 | 1 697 | -1 198 | 28 579 | 6.6 | 2.45 | 11.9 | 27.6 |
| Island | 15.9 | 11.5 | 7.9 | 50.5 | 71 558 | 78 506 | 9.7 | 0.9 | 2 040 | 1 356 | 16 | 32 746 | 17.9 | 2.35 | 7.9 | 25.9 |
| Jefferson | 21.8 | 16.7 | 10.9 | 50.4 | 25 953 | 29 872 | 15.1 | -0.1 | 439 | 756 | 326 | 14 049 | 20.6 | 2.08 | 7.3 | 32.2 |
| King | 12.2 | 6.1 | 5.1 | 50.1 | 1 737 034 | 1 931 249 | 11.2 | 3.9 | 54 922 | 26 775 | 48 286 | 789 232 | 11.0 | 2.40 | 9.1 | 31.0 |
| Kitsap | 14.3 | 8.0 | 5.7 | 49.1 | 231 969 | 251 133 | 8.3 | 1.5 | 6 559 | 4 387 | 1 699 | 97 220 | 12.5 | 2.49 | 10.2 | 25.2 |
| Kittitas | 12.1 | 7.8 | 5.3 | 49.5 | 33 362 | 40 915 | 22.6 | 1.9 | 934 | 602 | 415 | 16 595 | 24.0 | 2.32 | 7.3 | 28.7 |
| Klickitat | 17.7 | 11.2 | 7.0 | 49.6 | 19 161 | 20 318 | 6.0 | 1.9 | 504 | 379 | 267 | 8 327 | 11.4 | 2.42 | 8.5 | 26.4 |
| Lewis | 14.4 | 10.0 | 7.7 | 50.0 | 68 600 | 75 455 | 10.0 | 0.2 | 2 059 | 1 784 | -76 | 29 743 | 13.1 | 2.51 | 10.9 | 25.7 |
| Lincoln | 17.4 | 12.1 | 9.1 | 50.0 | 10 184 | 10 570 | 3.8 | -1.3 | 210 | 292 | -43 | 4 422 | 6.5 | 2.37 | 7.7 | 27.1 |
| Mason | 16.3 | 11.2 | 7.7 | 48.3 | 49 405 | 60 699 | 22.9 | 0.2 | 1 431 | 1 291 | 25 | 23 832 | 26.0 | 2.45 | 9.5 | 25.3 |
| Okanogan | 16.2 | 10.5 | 7.2 | 49.5 | 39 564 | 41 120 | 3.9 | 0.4 | 1 262 | 897 | -202 | 16 519 | 9.9 | 2.45 | 10.7 | 28.0 |
| Pacific | 19.0 | 14.8 | 10.5 | 49.8 | 20 984 | 20 920 | -0.3 | -1.6 | 426 | 696 | -62 | 9 499 | 4.4 | 2.17 | 8.1 | 33.0 |
| Pend Oreille | 19.0 | 12.6 | 7.5 | 49.3 | 11 732 | 13 001 | 10.8 | -0.2 | 258 | 332 | 61 | 5 479 | 18.1 | 2.35 | 9.1 | 28.2 |
| Pierce | 11.9 | 6.3 | 4.9 | 50.3 | 700 820 | 795 225 | 13.5 | 2.1 | 24 911 | 13 120 | 4 759 | 299 918 | 15.0 | 2.59 | 13.0 | 25.1 |
| San Juan | 22.3 | 15.5 | 9.2 | 51.5 | 14 077 | 15 769 | 12.0 | 0.3 | 193 | 252 | 122 | 7 613 | 17.7 | 2.05 | 6.6 | 34.0 |
| Skagit | 14.2 | 9.2 | 7.4 | 50.4 | 102 979 | 116 901 | 13.5 | 1.1 | 3 282 | 2 458 | 487 | 45 557 | 17.3 | 2.53 | 10.1 | 25.6 |
| Skamania | 17.3 | 9.3 | 6.0 | 49.7 | 9 872 | 11 066 | 12.1 | 1.1 | 238 | 203 | 89 | 4 522 | 20.4 | 2.44 | 8.9 | 25.6 |
| Snohomish | 12.4 | 6.1 | 4.7 | 49.9 | 606 024 | 713 335 | 17.7 | 2.8 | 19 896 | 10 308 | 9 992 | 268 325 | 19.3 | 2.62 | 10.4 | 24.3 |
| Spokane | 13.0 | 7.1 | 6.2 | 50.5 | 417 939 | 471 221 | 12.7 | 1.0 | 13 068 | 8 907 | 457 | 187 167 | 14.4 | 2.44 | 11.2 | 28.6 |
| Stevens | 17.5 | 11.4 | 6.6 | 49.8 | 40 066 | 43 531 | 8.6 | 0.0 | 939 | 873 | -34 | 17 316 | 15.3 | 2.50 | 9.0 | 24.6 |
| Thurston | 13.9 | 7.6 | 5.3 | 51.1 | 207 355 | 252 264 | 21.7 | 2.4 | 6 897 | 4 052 | 3 266 | 100 650 | 23.3 | 2.46 | 11.4 | 25.9 |
| Wahkiakum | 20.0 | 16.4 | 9.7 | 49.6 | 3 824 | 3 978 | 4.0 | 0.4 | 58 | 100 | 49 | 1 737 | 11.8 | 2.26 | 6.2 | 26.8 |
| Walla Walla | 12.5 | 7.3 | 7.8 | 49.2 | 55 180 | 58 781 | 6.5 | 1.1 | 1 489 | 1 263 | 377 | 21 719 | 10.5 | 2.50 | 10.5 | 28.2 |
| Whatcom | 13.2 | 7.7 | 6.1 | 50.4 | 166 814 | 201 140 | 20.6 | 2.0 | 5 058 | 3 122 | 2 257 | 80 370 | 24.7 | 2.43 | 8.8 | 27.8 |
| Whitman | 8.2 | 5.2 | 4.5 | 49.0 | 40 740 | 44 776 | 9.9 | 4.1 | 938 | 531 | 1 417 | 17 468 | 14.5 | 2.22 | 5.4 | 32.7 |
| Yakima | 10.6 | 6.4 | 5.3 | 49.9 | 222 581 | 243 231 | 9.3 | 1.5 | 9 711 | 4 129 | -1 789 | 80 592 | 8.9 | 2.97 | 14.7 | 21.6 |
| WEST VIRGINIA | 14.7 | 9.0 | 7.2 | 50.7 | 1 808 344 | 1 852 994 | 2.5 | 0.1 | 45 849 | 49 008 | 5 665 | 763 831 | 3.7 | 2.36 | 11.2 | 28.4 |
| Barbour | 14.3 | 9.5 | 7.3 | 50.6 | 15 557 | 16 589 | 6.6 | -0.6 | 358 | 450 | 0 | 6 548 | 6.9 | 2.46 | 10.9 | 24.2 |
| Berkeley | 12.8 | 7.2 | 4.6 | 50.5 | 75 905 | 104 169 | 37.2 | 2.8 | 2 917 | 1 884 | 1 848 | 39 855 | 34.8 | 2.59 | 12.0 | 23.4 |
| Boone | 16.1 | 8.3 | 6.1 | 50.3 | 25 535 | 24 629 | -3.5 | -0.6 | 691 | 702 | -136 | 9 928 | -3.5 | 2.47 | 11.3 | 25.7 |
| Braxton | 16.0 | 10.1 | 7.6 | 49.8 | 14 702 | 14 523 | -1.2 | -0.4 | 350 | 378 | -38 | 6 000 | 4.0 | 2.36 | 9.5 | 27.9 |

1. No spouse present.

# Table B. States and Counties — Population, Vital Statistics, Medicare, and Crime

| STATE County | Persons in group quarters, 2010 | Daytime population, 2007–2011 | | Births, 2011 | | Deaths, 2011 | | Persons under 65 with no health insurance, 2010 | | Medicare, 2012 | | | Serious crimes known to police,[2] 2011 Total | |
|---|---|---|---|---|---|---|---|---|---|---|---|---|---|---|
| | | Number | Employ-ment/resi-dence ratio | Total | Rate[1] | Number | Rate[1] | Number | Percent | Eligible for Medicare | Enrolled in Medicare Advantage | Enrolled in a Medicare prescription drug plan | Number | Rate[3] |
| | 32 | 33 | 34 | 35 | 36 | 37 | 38 | 39 | 40 | 41 | 42 | 43 | 44 | 45 |
| VIRGINIA—Cont'd | | | | | | | | | | | | | | |
| Manassas Park city | 6 | 9 547 | 0.41 | 233 | 15.2 | 34 | 2.2 | 3 204 | 23.6 | 961 | 149 | 370 | 184 | 1 274 |
| Martinsville city | 377 | 17 338 | 1.66 | 203 | 15.0 | 212 | 15.6 | 1 978 | 17.9 | 3 735 | 783 | 2 455 | 545 | 3 897 |
| Newport News city | 7 499 | 198 868 | 1.20 | 3 033 | 16.9 | 1 379 | 7.7 | 24 063 | 15.5 | 24 578 | 4 153 | 8 269 | 6 910 | 3 778 |
| Norfolk city | 32 780 | 307 045 | 1.53 | 3 793 | 15.6 | 1 977 | 8.1 | 33 158 | 17.5 | 29 071 | 5 060 | 10 906 | 13 733 | 5 589 |
| Norton city | 68 | 6 240 | 2.37 | 59 | 14.6 | 37 | 9.1 | 439 | 12.9 | 1 142 | 256 | 555 | 239 | 5 968 |
| Petersburg city | 1 058 | 34 628 | 1.18 | 664 | 20.5 | 453 | 14.0 | 5 159 | 18.7 | 6 813 | 892 | 3 394 | 1 630 | 4 968 |
| Poquoson city | 51 | 8 894 | 0.45 | 78 | 6.5 | 94 | 7.8 | 1 104 | 10.9 | 2 260 | 189 | 568 | 155 | 1 261 |
| Portsmouth city | 3 416 | 107 774 | 1.26 | 1 568 | 16.4 | 1 048 | 11.0 | 11 957 | 14.9 | 16 510 | 2 944 | 5 716 | 5 820 | 6 020 |
| Radford city | 2 652 | 16 820 | 1.07 | 135 | 8.2 | 76 | 4.6 | 2 314 | 18.6 | 1 938 | 273 | 1 120 | 534 | 3 216 |
| Richmond city | 12 725 | 272 539 | 1.74 | 3 034 | 14.8 | 1 880 | 9.1 | 34 020 | 19.8 | 29 859 | 6 671 | 13 896 | 10 105 | 4 890 |
| Roanoke city | 2 126 | 124 819 | 1.65 | 1 454 | 15.0 | 1 137 | 11.8 | 15 299 | 18.5 | 18 760 | 3 647 | 9 185 | 5 245 | 5 342 |
| Salem city | 1 718 | 34 945 | 1.88 | 262 | 10.5 | 298 | 11.9 | 2 646 | 13.9 | 5 538 | 791 | 2 750 | 673 | 2 681 |
| Staunton city | 1 185 | 25 164 | 1.12 | 297 | 12.5 | 298 | 12.5 | 2 999 | 16.3 | 5 762 | 527 | 3 222 | 569 | 2 368 |
| Suffolk city | 1 128 | 72 984 | 0.73 | 1 114 | 13.1 | 686 | 8.1 | 9 550 | 12.9 | 13 111 | 2 195 | 5 198 | 2 669 | 3 118 |
| Virginia Beach city | 9 253 | 402 900 | 0.85 | 6 101 | 13.8 | 2 710 | 6.1 | 51 730 | 13.5 | 57 358 | 7 277 | 17 958 | 12 997 | 2 932 |
| Waynesboro city | 192 | 21 373 | 1.04 | 309 | 14.5 | 225 | 10.6 | 3 014 | 17.2 | 4 482 | 458 | 2 677 | 847 | 3 985 |
| Williamsburg city | 4 171 | 22 716 | 2.58 | 112 | 7.8 | 93 | 6.4 | 1 505 | 18.4 | 2 255 | 258 | 935 | 259 | 1 819 |
| Winchester city | 976 | 38 043 | 1.95 | 402 | 15.1 | 239 | 9.0 | 4 653 | 21.4 | 4 693 | 393 | 2 333 | 1 188 | 4 480 |
| WASHINGTON | 139 375 | 6 603 452 | 0.98 | 86 767 | 12.7 | 48 434 | 7.1 | 936 767 | 16.1 | 1 065 750 | 305 156 | 369 296 | 264 267 | 3 869 |
| Adams | 162 | 18 262 | 1.00 | 458 | 24.1 | 128 | 6.7 | 4 067 | 24.3 | 2 233 | 315 | 1 128 | 867 | 4 558 |
| Asotin | 174 | 18 980 | 0.72 | 236 | 10.8 | 235 | 10.7 | 2 607 | 15.0 | 5 344 | 747 | 2 532 | 693 | 3 155 |
| Benton | 1 426 | 171 301 | 1.00 | 2 504 | 13.9 | 1 199 | 6.6 | 23 958 | 15.5 | 26 604 | 3 617 | 12 444 | 5 438 | 3 056 |
| Chelan | 928 | 77 201 | 1.17 | 1 017 | 13.8 | 624 | 8.5 | 12 337 | 20.3 | 14 043 | 2 435 | 6 099 | 2 107 | 2 863 |
| Clallam | 1 899 | 70 577 | 0.98 | 657 | 9.1 | 900 | 12.5 | 9 742 | 18.4 | 21 188 | 1 769 | 9 899 | 2 409 | 3 322 |
| Clark | 3 210 | 376 230 | 0.76 | 5 454 | 12.6 | 2 864 | 6.6 | 57 210 | 15.2 | 65 381 | 32 688 | 14 248 | 12 366 | 2 863 |
| Columbia | 75 | 3 913 | 0.95 | 33 | 8.1 | 45 | 11.1 | 550 | 17.4 | 1 112 | 35 | 600 | 186 | 4 491 |
| Cowlitz | 1 207 | 98 937 | 0.93 | 1 234 | 12.0 | 971 | 9.5 | 13 984 | 16.3 | 21 545 | 9 208 | 6 564 | 3 773 | 3 627 |
| Douglas | 190 | 31 359 | 0.62 | 529 | 13.6 | 294 | 7.5 | 7 418 | 22.5 | 6 434 | 1 052 | 2 871 | 1 004 | 2 572 |
| Ferry | 252 | 7 535 | 1.00 | 61 | 7.9 | 71 | 9.2 | 1 325 | 21.6 | 1 833 | 258 | 751 | 42 | 548 |
| Franklin | 1 846 | 74 548 | 0.98 | 1 690 | 20.3 | 383 | 4.6 | 15 910 | 22.3 | 7 815 | 1 064 | 3 813 | 2 041 | 2 571 |
| Garfield | 36 | 2 153 | 0.90 | 17 | 7.5 | 25 | 11.1 | 328 | 18.5 | 549 | 59 | 317 | 66 | 2 867 |
| Grant | 1 245 | 88 458 | 1.04 | 1 628 | 17.8 | 623 | 6.8 | 18 579 | 23.8 | 13 223 | 1 800 | 6 513 | 4 020 | 4 705 |
| Grays Harbor | 2 731 | 70 370 | 0.93 | 823 | 11.3 | 743 | 10.2 | 11 725 | 20.0 | 15 694 | 804 | 8 673 | 2 527 | 3 418 |
| Island | 1 466 | 70 977 | 0.78 | 895 | 11.3 | 588 | 7.4 | 9 325 | 14.8 | 17 353 | 5 123 | 4 741 | 1 535 | 1 925 |
| Jefferson | 631 | 28 282 | 0.88 | 197 | 6.6 | 321 | 10.7 | 3 920 | 18.1 | 9 731 | 708 | 4 547 | 674 | 2 221 |
| King | 37 131 | 2 070 978 | 1.16 | 24 464 | 12.4 | 11 781 | 6.0 | 242 037 | 14.2 | 261 493 | 81 175 | 93 107 | 83 729 | 4 269 |
| Kitsap | 8 722 | 239 902 | 0.92 | 2 886 | 11.3 | 1 952 | 7.7 | 29 481 | 13.9 | 42 588 | 8 011 | 12 406 | 8 132 | 3 188 |
| Kittitas | 2 417 | 39 008 | 0.92 | 426 | 10.2 | 258 | 6.2 | 6 223 | 18.6 | 6 604 | 318 | 3 141 | 1 636 | 3 937 |
| Klickitat | 198 | 19 235 | 0.87 | 227 | 11.0 | 190 | 9.2 | 3 166 | 19.0 | 4 849 | 215 | 2 585 | 272 | 1 318 |
| Lewis | 941 | 72 966 | 0.92 | 945 | 12.5 | 786 | 10.4 | 11 055 | 17.9 | 16 927 | 4 547 | 6 606 | 2 140 | 2 815 |
| Lincoln | 94 | 9 982 | 0.88 | 90 | 8.6 | 127 | 12.1 | 1 319 | 15.8 | 2 588 | 293 | 1 368 | 182 | 1 695 |
| Mason | 2 332 | 54 062 | 0.72 | 657 | 10.8 | 569 | 9.3 | 8 720 | 18.4 | 14 057 | 2 878 | 5 618 | 2 686 | 4 357 |
| Okanogan | 640 | 41 053 | 1.02 | 572 | 13.8 | 397 | 9.6 | 8 782 | 25.9 | 9 111 | 1 053 | 4 169 | 804 | 1 936 |
| Pacific | 292 | 20 167 | 0.88 | 182 | 8.7 | 333 | 15.9 | 3 194 | 20.5 | 6 489 | 545 | 3 565 | 539 | 2 537 |
| Pend Oreille | 98 | 12 271 | 0.84 | 134 | 10.4 | 146 | 11.3 | 1 697 | 16.2 | 3 273 | 519 | 1 400 | 428 | 3 241 |
| Pierce | 17 945 | 746 172 | 0.88 | 10 957 | 13.6 | 5 836 | 7.2 | 106 253 | 15.3 | 117 948 | 31 525 | 36 465 | 34 898 | 4 321 |
| San Juan | 187 | 15 533 | 0.98 | 97 | 6.1 | 117 | 7.4 | 2 314 | 19.3 | 4 318 | 909 | 1 763 | 196 | 1 224 |
| Skagit | 1 624 | 116 436 | 1.00 | 1 479 | 12.5 | 1 085 | 9.2 | 17 902 | 18.4 | 23 701 | 7 741 | 7 673 | 5 302 | 4 465 |
| Skamania | 25 | 9 365 | 0.66 | 102 | 9.2 | 86 | 7.7 | 1 482 | 15.7 | 1 933 | 257 | 838 | 224 | 2 181 |
| Snohomish | 10 391 | 633 786 | 0.80 | 8 995 | 12.5 | 4 519 | 6.3 | 98 129 | 15.5 | 96 399 | 40 541 | 25 310 | 21 450 | 2 961 |
| Spokane | 14 692 | 475 343 | 1.04 | 5 873 | 12.4 | 3 964 | 8.4 | 64 130 | 16.1 | 81 479 | 26 081 | 26 857 | 26 235 | 5 481 |
| Stevens | 266 | 38 706 | 0.71 | 417 | 9.6 | 398 | 9.2 | 6 564 | 18.3 | 9 945 | 1 466 | 4 197 | 898 | 2 044 |
| Thurston | 4 222 | 234 842 | 0.88 | 3 015 | 11.8 | 1 815 | 7.1 | 30 150 | 13.9 | 43 614 | 13 840 | 11 137 | 7 694 | 3 003 |
| Wahkiakum | 48 | 3 647 | 0.75 | 29 | 7.3 | 43 | 10.8 | 513 | 17.3 | 1 180 | 246 | 462 | 18 | 446 |
| Walla Walla | 4 489 | 60 147 | 1.08 | 662 | 11.1 | 580 | 9.7 | 9 090 | 19.7 | 10 827 | 1 247 | 4 710 | 2 105 | 3 526 |
| Whatcom | 5 704 | 194 290 | 0.95 | 2 270 | 11.1 | 1 366 | 6.7 | 28 264 | 16.6 | 34 937 | 12 233 | 11 469 | 6 436 | 3 150 |
| Whitman | 5 948 | 46 512 | 1.12 | 428 | 9.5 | 224 | 5.0 | 5 605 | 16.1 | 5 045 | 320 | 2 253 | 817 | 1 808 |
| Yakima | 3 485 | 239 966 | 1.00 | 4 427 | 17.9 | 1 848 | 7.5 | 57 694 | 27.0 | 36 363 | 7 514 | 16 457 | 11 237 | 4 549 |
| WEST VIRGINIA | 49 382 | 1 825 158 | 0.97 | 20 642 | 11.1 | 21 640 | 11.7 | 262 794 | 17.4 | 398 829 | 93 034 | 175 767 | 48 050 | 2 590 |
| Barbour | 469 | 13 919 | 0.61 | 170 | 10.3 | 197 | 11.9 | 2 710 | 20.3 | 3 581 | 683 | 1 661 | 149 | 897 |
| Berkeley | 910 | 86 498 | 0.66 | 1 300 | 12.3 | 844 | 8.0 | 15 115 | 16.5 | 16 917 | 2 702 | 5 996 | 2 734 | 2 621 |
| Boone | 131 | 26 134 | 1.17 | 313 | 12.8 | 300 | 12.3 | 3 203 | 15.3 | 5 493 | 1 200 | 3 005 | 414 | 2 048 |
| Braxton | 335 | 13 895 | 0.87 | 156 | 10.8 | 177 | 12.2 | 2 194 | 18.9 | 3 249 | 904 | 1 401 | 162 | 1 336 |

1. Per 1,000 estimated resident population.   2. Data for serious crimes have not been adjusted for underreporting; this may affect comparability between geographic areas and over time.   3. Per 100,000 population estimated by the FBI.

| STATE County | Serious crimes known to police, 2011 (cont.)[1] Rate[2] | | Education School enrollment and attainment, 2007-2011 Enrollment[3] | | Attainment[4] (percent) | | Local government expenditures,[5] 2009-2010 | | Money income, 2007-2011 | Households Median income | | | Income and poverty, 2011 | Percent below poverty level | | |
|---|---|---|---|---|---|---|---|---|---|---|---|---|---|---|---|---|
| | Violent | Property | Total | Percent private | High school graduate or less | Bachelor's degree or more | Total current expenditures (mil dol) | Current expenditures per student (dollars) | Per capita income[6] (dollars) | Dollars | Percent change, 2000 to 2007-2011 (constant 2011 dollars) | Percent with income of $200,000 or more | Median household income (dollars) | All persons | Children under 18 years | Children 5 to 17 years in families |
| | 46 | 47 | 48 | 49 | 50 | 51 | 52 | 53 | 54 | 55 | 56 | 57 | 58 | 59 | 60 | 61 |
| VIRGINIA—Cont'd | | | | | | | | | | | | | | | | |
| Manassas Park city | 83 | 1 191 | 3 875 | 9.0 | 48.3 | 22.5 | 29.3 | 10 841 | 26 979 | 70 137 | -14.6 | 4.3 | 71 976 | 8.0 | 14.2 | 14.0 |
| Martinsville city | 322 | 3 575 | 3 241 | 12.8 | 50.2 | 18.7 | 25.8 | 10 413 | 19 689 | 32 440 | -12.4 | 2.0 | 30 227 | 24.5 | 36.6 | 35.2 |
| Newport News city | 464 | 3 314 | 52 667 | 15.3 | 39.9 | 23.5 | 312.2 | 10 115 | 25 196 | 50 942 | 3.1 | 2.3 | 47 969 | 15.5 | 22.7 | 20.9 |
| Norfolk city | 581 | 5 008 | 66 559 | 13.3 | 44.0 | 24.7 | 359.7 | 10 576 | 24 357 | 43 914 | 2.2 | 2.4 | 42 201 | 20.3 | 28.0 | 28.3 |
| Norton city | 50 | 5 918 | 998 | 2.8 | 40.3 | 23.0 | 7.3 | 8 554 | 23 881 | 36 944 | 20.1 | 1.7 | 32 624 | 20.5 | 32.1 | 30.0 |
| Petersburg city | 479 | 4 490 | 6 649 | 4.5 | 62.6 | 13.9 | 48.8 | 10 536 | 19 005 | 36 289 | -6.8 | 0.9 | 32 615 | 24.3 | 37.7 | 39.8 |
| Poquoson city | 65 | 1 196 | 3 305 | 10.5 | 32.1 | 36.7 | 20.6 | 8 525 | 37 988 | 86 611 | 5.3 | 8.1 | 81 040 | 5.2 | 6.8 | 5.4 |
| Portsmouth city | 577 | 5 443 | 25 003 | 16.1 | 47.4 | 19.1 | 149.9 | 9 802 | 23 108 | 46 340 | 1.7 | 1.4 | 41 910 | 18.0 | 28.1 | 26.3 |
| Radford city | 337 | 2 879 | 9 045 | 3.8 | 35.0 | 36.0 | 14.5 | 9 388 | 16 723 | 29 101 | -12.6 | 0.6 | 33 848 | 26.8 | 19.4 | 18.4 |
| Richmond city | 692 | 4 197 | 56 263 | 19.2 | 43.5 | 32.9 | 309.6 | 13 154 | 26 584 | 39 201 | -6.7 | 3.9 | 38 368 | 26.4 | 36.2 | 33.9 |
| Roanoke city | 604 | 4 738 | 22 084 | 13.1 | 48.7 | 22.4 | 143.8 | 11 106 | 23 023 | 37 753 | -9.0 | 1.3 | 38 482 | 19.5 | 29.6 | 28.7 |
| Salem city | 112 | 2 570 | 6 921 | 32.9 | 41.8 | 30.1 | 39.2 | 9 949 | 27 143 | 48 050 | -8.7 | 4.4 | 44 499 | 11.1 | 14.9 | 13.3 |
| Staunton city | 196 | 2 172 | 5 370 | 28.2 | 49.5 | 27.9 | 30.1 | 10 561 | 24 595 | 42 757 | -3.9 | 1.4 | 41 006 | 16.0 | 23.4 | 22.8 |
| Suffolk city | 307 | 2 811 | 23 101 | 18.9 | 44.1 | 25.3 | 135.7 | 9 419 | 28 990 | 65 351 | 17.7 | 3.4 | 61 335 | 12.2 | 18.1 | 16.9 |
| Virginia Beach city | 177 | 2 755 | 120 450 | 17.8 | 31.0 | 32.3 | 730.8 | 10 267 | 31 589 | 65 910 | 0.2 | 4.2 | 64 107 | 8.9 | 12.6 | 11.8 |
| Waynesboro city | 339 | 3 646 | 4 671 | 11.7 | 56.2 | 21.1 | 31.5 | 9 927 | 24 695 | 43 605 | -1.2 | 2.6 | 40 342 | 18.0 | 28.0 | 26.4 |
| Williamsburg city | 190 | 1 630 | 7 149 | 4.1 | 27.4 | 47.3 | (7) | (7) | 22 383 | 50 742 | 1.3 | 5.4 | 46 358 | 19.1 | 23.4 | 22.9 |
| Winchester city | 238 | 4 243 | 6 204 | 19.1 | 47.4 | 29.2 | (8) | (8) | 26 343 | 46 065 | -0.6 | 3.7 | 42 539 | 17.8 | 23.6 | 22.7 |
| WASHINGTON | 295 | 3 575 | 1 678 674 | 15.0 | 34.1 | 31.4 | 9 781.5 | 9 449 | 30 481 | 58 890 | -4.7 | 4.5 | 56 811 | 13.9 | 18.5 | 16.9 |
| Adams | 279 | 4 279 | 4 635 | 6.3 | 61.0 | 12.5 | 41.1 | 9 548 | 16 452 | 41 219 | -9.9 | 1.0 | 40 675 | 20.0 | 28.6 | 27.9 |
| Asotin | 164 | 2 992 | 4 735 | 11.7 | 48.0 | 15.9 | 32.7 | 9 641 | 23 875 | 41 993 | -7.2 | 1.9 | 41 864 | 17.2 | 26.3 | 23.6 |
| Benton | 235 | 2 821 | 45 344 | 9.7 | 36.6 | 27.7 | 285.3 | 8 804 | 27 673 | 59 974 | -5.6 | 3.6 | 61 539 | 11.7 | 17.2 | 16.4 |
| Chelan | 169 | 2 695 | 16 888 | 10.1 | 45.9 | 23.0 | 124.3 | 9 691 | 24 944 | 49 509 | -1.7 | 3.1 | 48 458 | 15.9 | 24.1 | 21.9 |
| Clallam | 265 | 3 057 | 13 873 | 12.5 | 36.9 | 24.3 | 95.4 | 8 313 | 25 672 | 46 212 | -6.1 | 1.7 | 47 903 | 13.2 | 20.3 | 18.8 |
| Clark | 222 | 2 640 | 111 707 | 12.3 | 35.0 | 25.8 | 709.9 | 9 273 | 27 916 | 59 051 | -9.6 | 3.4 | 56 750 | 13.7 | 18.1 | 16.1 |
| Columbia | 169 | 4 322 | 634 | 6.6 | 41.5 | 18.0 | 6.0 | 11 050 | 26 120 | 44 038 | -2.6 | 1.8 | 42 463 | 14.9 | 23.0 | 20.7 |
| Cowlitz | 309 | 3 319 | 24 438 | 12.0 | 43.7 | 15.0 | 152.1 | 8 753 | 23 575 | 46 461 | -13.5 | 1.7 | 43 611 | 19.5 | 27.4 | 25.7 |
| Douglas | 138 | 2 434 | 9 814 | 6.5 | 47.0 | 17.6 | 63.5 | 9 181 | 22 751 | 49 707 | -4.3 | 1.9 | 47 958 | 17.4 | 27.3 | 25.7 |
| Ferry | 65 | 482 | 1 587 | 1.4 | 49.1 | 15.5 | 13.0 | 12 144 | 18 937 | 35 684 | -13.0 | 1.4 | 34 543 | 21.6 | 29.0 | 25.3 |
| Franklin | 302 | 2 269 | 21 912 | 10.6 | 56.9 | 15.1 | 154.2 | 9 255 | 18 878 | 50 731 | -3.6 | 2.1 | 48 904 | 24.2 | 35.6 | 33.4 |
| Garfield | 174 | 2 693 | 442 | 2.0 | 36.8 | 20.6 | 3.9 | 11 609 | 25 181 | 47 379 | 5.1 | 0.8 | 46 302 | 13.2 | 17.6 | 14.1 |
| Grant | 294 | 4 411 | 23 271 | 7.0 | 54.1 | 15.2 | 175.1 | 9 459 | 20 427 | 44 237 | -7.1 | 2.6 | 43 149 | 20.3 | 28.1 | 26.1 |
| Grays Harbor | 185 | 3 232 | 16 202 | 7.3 | 47.1 | 14.2 | 111.4 | 10 026 | 21 389 | 42 729 | -7.4 | 1.0 | 40 886 | 21.1 | 29.4 | 24.3 |
| Island | 125 | 1 800 | 17 210 | 14.1 | 29.4 | 30.4 | 75.4 | 8 861 | 30 352 | 59 328 | -3.5 | 2.6 | 58 179 | 10.1 | 15.4 | 14.2 |
| Jefferson | 152 | 2 070 | 4 816 | 10.9 | 29.2 | 36.1 | 30.4 | 10 703 | 29 333 | 46 887 | -8.3 | 3.1 | 47 045 | 13.6 | 23.9 | 19.8 |
| King | 343 | 3 925 | 466 423 | 19.6 | 25.5 | 45.7 | 2 320.0 | 9 699 | 39 313 | 70 567 | -1.7 | 8.3 | 68 596 | 12.1 | 14.5 | 12.9 |
| Kitsap | 307 | 2 881 | 59 704 | 14.4 | 31.0 | 28.7 | 365.0 | 9 864 | 30 913 | 61 112 | -3.4 | 3.9 | 60 294 | 11.0 | 14.4 | 12.0 |
| Kittitas | 147 | 3 790 | 14 219 | 6.7 | 37.9 | 32.5 | 46.7 | 9 491 | 23 931 | 42 769 | -2.7 | 1.4 | 41 823 | 25.5 | 21.8 | 19.6 |
| Klickitat | 63 | 1 255 | 4 261 | 11.5 | 46.9 | 18.5 | 34.1 | 10 633 | 21 481 | 38 774 | -16.2 | 1.6 | 43 340 | 15.9 | 26.6 | 24.1 |
| Lewis | 228 | 2 588 | 17 097 | 10.9 | 46.6 | 15.0 | 111.6 | 9 576 | 22 297 | 44 373 | -7.5 | 1.3 | 42 072 | 14.9 | 23.5 | 21.7 |
| Lincoln | 102 | 1 593 | 2 194 | 13.4 | 39.3 | 19.2 | 27.5 | 12 794 | 25 317 | 46 765 | -1.8 | 2.3 | 47 602 | 12.5 | 19.0 | 15.8 |
| Mason | 284 | 4 073 | 13 023 | 10.8 | 42.9 | 18.1 | 77.8 | 9 531 | 23 082 | 48 912 | -8.5 | 1.3 | 44 331 | 14.8 | 22.1 | 20.3 |
| Okanogan | 217 | 1 720 | 8 382 | 9.0 | 49.6 | 18.3 | 65.4 | 10 383 | 20 518 | 40 537 | 1.0 | 1.4 | 38 680 | 21.7 | 34.5 | 32.3 |
| Pacific | 113 | 2 424 | 3 788 | 9.2 | 46.0 | 16.6 | 32.9 | 11 242 | 23 193 | 40 599 | -3.7 | 1.3 | 37 632 | 18.2 | 28.1 | 25.6 |
| Pend Oreille | 129 | 3 112 | 2 538 | 8.6 | 45.6 | 17.6 | 18.7 | 11 057 | 22 458 | 38 922 | -9.0 | 1.3 | 37 457 | 19.8 | 32.5 | 29.9 |
| Pierce | 420 | 3 901 | 202 813 | 15.9 | 39.2 | 23.6 | 1 213.9 | 9 362 | 28 179 | 58 824 | -3.6 | 3.1 | 55 215 | 12.7 | 16.6 | 15.2 |
| San Juan | 119 | 1 105 | 2 255 | 16.3 | 24.7 | 44.9 | 18.6 | 11 252 | 36 453 | 51 395 | -12.5 | 5.2 | 52 371 | 11.9 | 19.6 | 17.0 |
| Skagit | 201 | 4 264 | 26 396 | 10.8 | 37.1 | 23.7 | 192.3 | 10 128 | 27 447 | 55 555 | -2.9 | 2.5 | 52 013 | 15.0 | 22.6 | 20.5 |
| Skamania | 97 | 2 084 | 2 378 | 5.6 | 41.4 | 22.4 | 14.2 | 8 803 | 26 624 | 52 884 | -0.4 | 2.7 | 51 548 | 14.9 | 21.2 | 17.8 |
| Snohomish | 166 | 2 795 | 175 417 | 14.5 | 34.2 | 28.4 | 1 135.8 | 8 942 | 31 276 | 67 777 | -5.4 | 4.0 | 63 766 | 11.0 | 15.3 | 13.8 |
| Spokane | 343 | 5 138 | 124 927 | 17.9 | 32.8 | 28.6 | 709.4 | 9 525 | 25 752 | 49 257 | -2.2 | 2.9 | 48 693 | 15.2 | 18.4 | 17.2 |
| Stevens | 84 | 1 960 | 10 031 | 13.9 | 41.6 | 19.2 | 74.9 | 9 413 | 22 232 | 44 354 | -5.3 | 1.7 | 41 166 | 20.3 | 29.3 | 24.7 |
| Thurston | 229 | 2 774 | 62 524 | 12.2 | 30.7 | 32.5 | 375.5 | 9 274 | 30 331 | 63 129 | -0.5 | 3.0 | 59 694 | 12.8 | 17.3 | 16.1 |
| Wahkiakum | 149 | 297 | 873 | 6.2 | 41.6 | 14.8 | 4.1 | 8 822 | 21 455 | 41 149 | -22.7 | 1.9 | 41 286 | 14.3 | 25.7 | 22.7 |
| Walla Walla | 281 | 3 244 | 16 873 | 23.8 | 36.2 | 24.2 | 87.1 | 9 847 | 23 547 | 46 793 | -3.5 | 2.2 | 47 570 | 17.3 | 23.4 | 21.4 |
| Whatcom | 196 | 2 954 | 56 875 | 13.3 | 31.7 | 31.8 | 244.7 | 9 146 | 26 273 | 51 389 | -4.9 | 2.6 | 51 315 | 15.6 | 17.8 | 15.8 |
| Whitman | 111 | 1 698 | 22 764 | 3.6 | 23.7 | 48.1 | 51.0 | 11 388 | 20 226 | 35 409 | -8.3 | 2.4 | 35 860 | 31.8 | 18.7 | 15.3 |
| Yakima | 327 | 4 222 | 65 411 | 8.6 | 55.7 | 16.0 | 486.6 | 9 591 | 19 730 | 44 419 | -5.5 | 1.8 | 41 666 | 23.0 | 31.2 | 29.6 |
| WEST VIRGINIA | 316 | 2 274 | 421 431 | 11.1 | 58.4 | 17.6 | 3 248.7 | 11 493 | 22 010 | 39 550 | -1.4 | 1.7 | 38 587 | 18.7 | 26.1 | 24.0 |
| Barbour | 325 | 572 | 3 870 | 19.3 | 70.8 | 12.7 | 26.9 | 10 839 | 17 897 | 33 158 | -0.7 | 0.9 | 33 004 | 22.8 | 33.9 | 29.8 |
| Berkeley | 236 | 2 385 | 25 324 | 13.6 | 54.2 | 19.4 | 195.7 | 11 216 | 26 183 | 52 504 | 0.3 | 1.7 | 51 029 | 14.8 | 21.4 | 19.5 |
| Boone | 262 | 1 786 | 4 868 | 3.1 | 72.2 | 8.0 | 59.7 | 12 774 | 21 355 | 41 359 | 19.3 | 1.1 | 38 357 | 19.6 | 26.8 | 24.7 |
| Braxton | 206 | 1 130 | 2 681 | 6.3 | 71.0 | 10.1 | 27.5 | 12 314 | 18 141 | 31 686 | -3.9 | 0.7 | 32 369 | 22.2 | 30.1 | 28.9 |

1. Data for serious crimes have not been adjusted for underreporting; this may affect comparability between geographic areas and over time. 2. Per 100,000 population estimated by the FBI. 3. All persons 3 years old and over enrolled in nursery school through college. 4. Persons 25 years old and over. 5. Elementary and secondary education expenditures. 6. Based on population estimated by the American Community Survey, 2007–2011. 7. Williamsburg city is included with James City county. 8. Winchester city is included with Frederick county.

# Table B. States and Counties — **Personal Income**

| | Personal income, 2011 | | Per capita[1] | | | | | Transfer payments (mil dol) | | | | | |
|---|---|---|---|---|---|---|---|---|---|---|---|---|---|
| | | | | | | | | | Government payments to individuals | | | | |
| STATE County | Total (mil dol) | Percent change, 2010–2011 | Dollars | Rank | Wages and salaries[2] (mil dol) | Proprietors' income (mil dol) | Dividends, interest, and rent (mil dol) | Total | Total | Social Security | Medical payments | Income mainte- nance | Unemploy- ment insurance |
| | 62 | 63 | 64 | 65 | 66 | 67 | 68 | 69 | 70 | 71 | 72 | 73 | 74 |
| VIRGINIA—Cont'd | | | | | | | | | | | | | |
| Manassas Park city | (3) | (3) | (3) | (3) | (3) | (3) | (3) | (3) | (3) | (3) | (3) | (3) | (3) |
| Martinsville city | (4) | (4) | (4) | (4) | (4) | (4) | (4) | (4) | (4) | (4) | (4) | (4) | (4) |
| Newport News city | 6 242 | 4.1 | 34 752 | 1 412 | 6 635 | 191 | 901 | 1 260 | 1 222 | 340 | 467 | 212 | 34 |
| Norfolk city | 8 947 | 4.4 | 36 873 | 1 089 | 14 301 | 594 | 1 347 | 1 709 | 1 663 | 380 | 708 | 302 | 46 |
| Norton city | (5) | (5) | (5) | (5) | (5) | (5) | (5) | (5) | (5) | (5) | (5) | (5) | (5) |
| Petersburg city | (6) | (6) | (6) | (6) | (6) | (6) | (6) | (6) | (6) | (6) | (6) | (6) | (6) |
| Poquoson city | (7) | (7) | (7) | (7) | (7) | (7) | (7) | (7) | (7) | (7) | (7) | (7) | (7) |
| Portsmouth city | 3 596 | 5.4 | 37 583 | 1 017 | 3 651 | 177 | 450 | 845 | 825 | 201 | 348 | 139 | 20 |
| Radford city | (8) | (8) | (8) | (8) | (8) | (8) | (8) | (8) | (8) | (8) | (8) | (8) | (8) |
| Richmond city | 8 887 | 5.3 | 43 239 | 491 | 10 793 | 959 | 1 697 | 1 755 | 1 710 | 416 | 819 | 300 | 45 |
| Roanoke city | 3 889 | 5.4 | 40 215 | 724 | 3 711 | 241 | 695 | 900 | 879 | 245 | 360 | 130 | 19 |
| Salem city | (9) | (9) | (9) | (9) | (9) | (9) | (9) | (9) | (9) | (9) | (9) | (9) | (9) |
| Staunton city | (10) | (10) | (10) | (10) | (10) | (10) | (10) | (10) | (10) | (10) | (10) | (10) | (10) |
| Suffolk city | 3 336 | 5.3 | 39 279 | 825 | 1 431 | 114 | 443 | 594 | 576 | 181 | 237 | 81 | 14 |
| Virginia Beach city | 20 718 | 4.9 | 46 799 | 310 | 10 708 | 1 253 | 3 198 | 2 561 | 2 470 | 828 | 873 | 248 | 66 |
| Waynesboro city | (10) | (10) | (10) | (10) | (10) | (10) | (10) | (10) | (10) | (10) | (10) | (10) | (10) |
| Williamsburg city | (11) | (11) | (11) | (11) | (11) | (11) | (11) | (11) | (11) | (11) | (11) | (11) | (11) |
| Winchester city | (12) | (12) | (12) | (12) | (12) | (12) | (12) | (12) | (12) | (12) | (12) | (12) | (12) |
| **WASHINGTON** | 299 685 | 5.8 | 43 878 | X | 195 845 | 24 281 | 51 035 | 49 152 | 47 655 | 15 324 | 17 420 | 5 853 | 3 225 |
| Adams | 603 | 8.9 | 31 704 | 1 955 | 299 | 102 | 112 | 135 | 131 | 30 | 63 | 23 | 5 |
| Asotin | 773 | 3.6 | 35 230 | 1 334 | 231 | 69 | 153 | 219 | 214 | 77 | 89 | 29 | 3 |
| Benton | 7 173 | 5.0 | 39 700 | 779 | 5 334 | 496 | 1 041 | 1 210 | 1 170 | 402 | 424 | 150 | 67 |
| Chelan | 2 764 | 4.8 | 37 619 | 1 013 | 1 749 | 266 | 566 | 595 | 579 | 199 | 219 | 74 | 30 |
| Clallam | 2 596 | 3.6 | 36 138 | 1 195 | 1 086 | 199 | 683 | 754 | 738 | 302 | 277 | 70 | 28 |
| Clark | 16 338 | 6.8 | 37 695 | 1 004 | 7 372 | 982 | 2 987 | 2 937 | 2 841 | 965 | 1 005 | 390 | 149 |
| Columbia | 159 | 6.3 | 39 259 | 827 | 62 | 19 | 30 | 41 | 40 | 15 | 17 | 4 | 1 |
| Cowlitz | 3 341 | 3.1 | 32 607 | 1 778 | 1 913 | 223 | 540 | 969 | 947 | 333 | 351 | 138 | 45 |
| Douglas | 1 189 | 5.5 | 30 500 | 2 196 | 435 | 47 | 234 | 290 | 282 | 93 | 122 | 31 | 16 |
| Ferry | 203 | 3.9 | 26 353 | 2 845 | 81 | 8 | 36 | 78 | 76 | 26 | 30 | 11 | 3 |
| Franklin | 2 479 | 9.1 | 29 711 | 2 334 | 1 364 | 296 | 282 | 506 | 487 | 106 | 207 | 93 | 27 |
| Garfield | 81 | 3.7 | 35 999 | 1 210 | 42 | 5 | 18 | 21 | 20 | 8 | 8 | 2 | 0 |
| Grant | 2 829 | 7.0 | 30 999 | 2 102 | 1 567 | 423 | 408 | 681 | 660 | 184 | 270 | 112 | 41 |
| Grays Harbor | 2 202 | 4.4 | 30 355 | 2 227 | 1 090 | 123 | 357 | 737 | 721 | 234 | 287 | 98 | 46 |
| Island | 3 022 | 4.9 | 38 268 | 937 | 1 441 | 163 | 755 | 623 | 607 | 260 | 196 | 44 | 29 |
| Jefferson | 1 254 | 3.7 | 41 920 | 577 | 362 | 63 | 392 | 320 | 314 | 139 | 115 | 24 | 12 |
| King | 113 922 | 7.1 | 57 837 | 84 | 93 947 | 12 113 | 20 048 | 12 313 | 11 878 | 3 778 | 4 219 | 1 297 | 971 |
| Kitsap | 10 842 | 4.7 | 42 580 | 530 | 6 213 | 494 | 2 090 | 1 808 | 1 754 | 552 | 647 | 175 | 105 |
| Kittitas | 1 375 | 4.7 | 33 031 | 1 703 | 625 | 137 | 296 | 288 | 279 | 98 | 91 | 30 | 16 |
| Klickitat | 797 | 5.5 | 38 529 | 905 | 373 | 68 | 165 | 199 | 195 | 69 | 76 | 26 | 7 |
| Lewis | 2 368 | 3.9 | 31 192 | 2 065 | 1 120 | 131 | 417 | 758 | 741 | 248 | 296 | 93 | 42 |
| Lincoln | 372 | 6.4 | 35 466 | 1 300 | 131 | 45 | 85 | 95 | 93 | 37 | 35 | 9 | 3 |
| Mason | 1 852 | 3.3 | 30 345 | 2 229 | 627 | 85 | 349 | 564 | 550 | 204 | 208 | 59 | 29 |
| Okanogan | 1 466 | 5.1 | 35 409 | 1 309 | 606 | 264 | 248 | 397 | 388 | 124 | 160 | 55 | 20 |
| Pacific | 683 | 3.6 | 32 648 | 1 771 | 257 | 34 | 156 | 242 | 238 | 95 | 93 | 26 | 9 |
| Pend Oreille | 395 | 4.4 | 30 561 | 2 185 | 158 | 11 | 68 | 139 | 136 | 46 | 55 | 19 | 5 |
| Pierce | 33 118 | 4.7 | 40 992 | 660 | 19 344 | 2 089 | 4 490 | 5 966 | 5 794 | 1 701 | 2 048 | 743 | 469 |
| San Juan | 831 | 4.9 | 52 439 | 154 | 230 | 58 | 395 | 132 | 128 | 63 | 44 | 7 | 5 |
| Skagit | 4 552 | 4.4 | 38 543 | 903 | 2 396 | 294 | 985 | 1 017 | 991 | 347 | 379 | 111 | 64 |
| Skamania | 377 | 5.5 | 33 877 | 1 536 | 97 | 9 | 67 | 77 | 75 | 29 | 25 | 10 | 4 |
| Snohomish | 31 266 | 4.7 | 43 281 | 487 | 17 171 | 1 253 | 4 011 | 4 493 | 4 334 | 1 419 | 1 467 | 472 | 412 |
| Spokane | 17 027 | 4.3 | 35 940 | 1 220 | 11 127 | 1 001 | 3 033 | 3 880 | 3 776 | 1 133 | 1 456 | 514 | 206 |
| Stevens | 1 242 | 4.1 | 28 559 | 2 531 | 448 | 67 | 226 | 407 | 397 | 138 | 153 | 51 | 19 |
| Thurston | 10 585 | 4.8 | 41 251 | 637 | 5 554 | 598 | 1 643 | 1 940 | 1 884 | 649 | 631 | 193 | 120 |
| Wahkiakum | 129 | 4.1 | 32 301 | 1 824 | 35 | 7 | 32 | 40 | 39 | 18 | 15 | 3 | 1 |
| Walla Walla | 2 102 | 5.2 | 35 276 | 1 327 | 1 299 | 209 | 394 | 463 | 450 | 149 | 171 | 61 | 14 |
| Whatcom | 7 759 | 5.4 | 38 098 | 957 | 4 345 | 662 | 1 698 | 1 458 | 1 413 | 492 | 500 | 173 | 88 |
| Whitman | 1 369 | 7.2 | 30 379 | 2 225 | 946 | 140 | 258 | 252 | 242 | 74 | 76 | 30 | 5 |
| Yakima | 8 247 | 5.3 | 33 371 | 1 636 | 4 366 | 1 029 | 1 287 | 2 107 | 2 053 | 489 | 896 | 406 | 106 |
| **WEST VIRGINIA** | 61 976 | 5.1 | 33 403 | X | 36 879 | 4 068 | 7 278 | 17 034 | 16 624 | 5 870 | 6 918 | 1 850 | 411 |
| Barbour | 431 | 4.5 | 26 109 | 2 869 | 153 | 26 | 48 | 148 | 145 | 49 | 61 | 18 | 4 |
| Berkeley | 3 352 | 5.5 | 31 696 | 1 956 | 1 625 | 194 | 328 | 650 | 626 | 247 | 194 | 87 | 22 |
| Boone | 707 | 3.6 | 28 912 | 2 466 | 668 | 34 | 56 | 238 | 233 | 90 | 88 | 30 | 4 |
| Braxton | 380 | 3.7 | 26 224 | 2 861 | 165 | 23 | 37 | 128 | 125 | 44 | 50 | 17 | 4 |

1.  Based on the resident population estimated as of July 1 of the year shown.    2.  Includes supplements to wages and salaries.    3.  Manassas and Manassas Park cities are included with Prince William county.    4.  Martinsville city is included with Henry county.    5.  Norton city is included with Wise county.    6.  Petersburg and Colonial Heights cities are included with Dinwiddie county.    7.  Poquoson city is included with York county.    8.  Radford city is included with Montgomery county.    9.  Salem city is included with Roanoke county.    10.  Staunton and Waynesboro cities are included with Augusta county.    11.  Williamsburg city is included with James City county.    12.  Winchester city is included with Frederick county.

# Table B. States and Counties — Earnings, Social Security, and Housing

| STATE County | Earnings, 2011 | | | | | | | | | Social Security beneficiaries, December 2011 | | Supplemental Security Income recipients, December 2011 | Housing units, 2010 | |
|---|---|---|---|---|---|---|---|---|---|---|---|---|---|---|
| | | | Goods-related[1] | | Service-related and health | | | | | | | | | |
| | Total (mil dol) | Farm | Total | Manu-facturing | Infor-mation and profes-sional and technical services | Retail trade | Finance, insur-ance, and real estate | Health care and social services | Govern-ment | Number | Rate[2] | | Total | Percent change, 2000–2010 |
| | 75 | 76 | 77 | 78 | 79 | 80 | 81 | 82 | 83 | 84 | 85 | 86 | 87 | 88 |
| VIRGINIA—Cont'd | | | | | | | | | | | | | | |
| Manassas Park city | (3) | (3) | (3) | (3) | (3) | (3) | (3) | (3) | (3) | 1 060 | 69 | 132 | 4 904 | 45.7 |
| Martinsville city | (4) | (4) | (4) | (4) | (4) | (4) | (4) | (4) | (4) | 4 530 | 334 | 695 | 7 205 | -0.6 |
| Newport News city | 6 826 | 0.0 | D | 28.8 | 7.6 | 4.3 | 3.5 | 8.7 | 29.4 | 27 085 | 151 | 4 490 | 76 198 | 2.5 |
| Norfolk city | 14 896 | 0.0 | 5.0 | 2.8 | D | 2.7 | 4.3 | 9.0 | 55.4 | 32 115 | 132 | 7 346 | 95 018 | 0.6 |
| Norton city | (5) | (5) | (5) | (5) | (5) | (5) | (5) | (5) | (5) | 1 395 | 344 | 330 | 1 945 | -0.1 |
| Petersburg city | (6) | (6) | (6) | (6) | (6) | (6) | (6) | (6) | (6) | 7 600 | 235 | 2 246 | 16 326 | 2.3 |
| Poquoson city | (7) | (7) | (7) | (7) | (7) | (7) | (7) | (7) | (7) | 2 295 | 191 | 59 | 4 726 | 9.9 |
| Portsmouth city | 3 828 | 0.0 | 7.4 | 3.7 | 3.7 | 2.3 | 1.3 | 8.0 | 62.0 | 17 730 | 185 | 3 783 | 40 806 | -1.9 |
| Radford city | (8) | (8) | (8) | (8) | (8) | (8) | (8) | (8) | (8) | 2 180 | 133 | 249 | 6 427 | 4.7 |
| Richmond city | 11 751 | 0.0 | D | 4.8 | D | 2.4 | 7.7 | 11.3 | 25.7 | 32 815 | 160 | 9 196 | 98 349 | 6.5 |
| Roanoke city | 3 953 | 0.0 | D | 6.4 | 7.9 | 6.7 | 7.1 | 22.2 | 13.9 | 20 050 | 207 | 4 185 | 47 453 | 4.8 |
| Salem city | (9) | (9) | (9) | (9) | (9) | (9) | (9) | (9) | (9) | 5 920 | 237 | 419 | 10 832 | 4.1 |
| Staunton city | (10) | (10) | (10) | (10) | (10) | (10) | (10) | (10) | (10) | 6 335 | 267 | 567 | 11 738 | 12.6 |
| Suffolk city | 1 544 | 0.9 | D | 10.2 | 7.5 | 6.9 | 3.5 | 13.9 | 28.2 | 14 600 | 172 | 2 293 | 33 035 | 33.7 |
| Virginia Beach city | 11 961 | 0.1 | 9.9 | 2.8 | 11.2 | 6.1 | 10.6 | 9.7 | 32.6 | 61 290 | 138 | 5 109 | 177 879 | 9.6 |
| Waynesboro city | (10) | (10) | (10) | (10) | (10) | (10) | (10) | (10) | (10) | 5 020 | 236 | 554 | 9 717 | 9.6 |
| Williamsburg city | (11) | (11) | (11) | (11) | (11) | (11) | (11) | (11) | (11) | 2 275 | 158 | 159 | 5 176 | 33.4 |
| Winchester city | (12) | (12) | (12) | (12) | (12) | (12) | (12) | (12) | (12) | 5 010 | 188 | 617 | 11 872 | 12.1 |
| WASHINGTON | 220 126 | 1.4 | 16.7 | 10.9 | 16.4 | 6.4 | 6.0 | 10.2 | 20.4 | 1 127 126 | 165 | 142 932 | 2 885 677 | 17.7 |
| Adams | 401 | 22.9 | 16.8 | 15.0 | 1.5 | 5.0 | 1.8 | D | 19.1 | 2 455 | 129 | 332 | 6 242 | 8.1 |
| Asotin | 299 | 2.4 | D | 4.5 | 4.4 | 13.8 | 5.1 | 16.6 | 19.6 | 5 955 | 272 | 705 | 9 872 | 8.4 |
| Benton | 5 830 | 3.4 | D | 4.7 | 22.0 | 5.5 | 3.1 | 8.8 | 15.9 | 28 485 | 158 | 3 341 | 68 618 | 22.6 |
| Chelan | 2 015 | 7.5 | D | 6.1 | 4.9 | 7.9 | 4.1 | 18.0 | 20.6 | 15 130 | 206 | 1 472 | 35 465 | 16.6 |
| Clallam | 1 285 | 0.1 | 13.3 | 7.1 | 5.1 | 9.8 | 3.5 | 8.7 | 36.5 | 22 610 | 315 | 1 853 | 35 582 | 16.0 |
| Clark | 8 354 | 0.1 | 17.6 | 9.7 | 11.2 | 7.0 | 5.9 | 15.0 | 19.0 | 70 305 | 162 | 8 025 | 167 413 | 24.9 |
| Columbia | 81 | 22.8 | D | 4.0 | 2.2 | 4.2 | 1.6 | D | 33.0 | 1 200 | 296 | 144 | 2 136 | 5.8 |
| Cowlitz | 2 136 | 0.1 | 34.4 | 21.4 | 3.7 | 7.2 | 3.0 | 13.7 | 15.4 | 24 305 | 237 | 3 433 | 43 450 | 12.5 |
| Douglas | 482 | 15.4 | 9.6 | 4.8 | 6.1 | 10.0 | 2.2 | 6.7 | 29.5 | 7 040 | 181 | 557 | 16 004 | 23.6 |
| Ferry | 89 | -1.9 | D | D | D | 7.2 | 2.6 | D | 59.2 | 2 140 | 278 | 303 | 4 403 | 16.6 |
| Franklin | 1 660 | 16.0 | D | 8.5 | 2.9 | 6.9 | 2.4 | 6.8 | 21.0 | 8 390 | 101 | 1 644 | 24 423 | 51.8 |
| Garfield | 47 | 10.4 | D | D | D | 4.7 | 1.5 | 1.0 | 63.8 | 620 | 274 | 35 | 1 233 | -4.3 |
| Grant | 1 990 | 23.6 | D | 14.1 | 2.0 | 5.9 | 2.8 | 5.0 | 24.8 | 14 705 | 161 | 2 114 | 35 083 | 20.6 |
| Grays Harbor | 1 214 | 1.5 | 21.2 | 15.3 | 4.1 | 8.1 | 3.5 | 10.2 | 28.8 | 17 815 | 246 | 2 744 | 35 166 | 8.2 |
| Island | 1 604 | 0.4 | D | 2.5 | D | 5.7 | 2.4 | 4.3 | 63.4 | 18 790 | 238 | 972 | 40 234 | 24.3 |
| Jefferson | 425 | 0.1 | 17.7 | 10.3 | 7.4 | 8.3 | 6.3 | 8.4 | 31.6 | 10 220 | 342 | 584 | 17 767 | 25.6 |
| King | 106 060 | 0.0 | 14.8 | 9.8 | 26.3 | 5.9 | 7.5 | 8.4 | 12.2 | 259 810 | 132 | 36 613 | 851 261 | 14.7 |
| Kitsap | 6 708 | 0.2 | 6.0 | 1.6 | 7.1 | 6.0 | 3.0 | 9.9 | 56.2 | 44 170 | 173 | 5 014 | 107 367 | 15.9 |
| Kittitas | 761 | 7.0 | D | 3.5 | 4.9 | 8.4 | 3.6 | 5.5 | 35.5 | 7 125 | 171 | 502 | 21 900 | 32.9 |
| Klickitat | 441 | 7.5 | D | 5.6 | 22.2 | 3.5 | 2.2 | 3.8 | 22.5 | 5 360 | 259 | 591 | 9 786 | 13.4 |
| Lewis | 1 250 | 2.9 | 19.6 | 13.7 | 3.4 | 10.0 | 2.5 | 13.2 | 21.8 | 19 070 | 251 | 2 423 | 34 050 | 15.1 |
| Lincoln | 176 | 22.6 | 6.3 | 0.7 | 4.8 | 5.2 | 2.5 | D | 36.0 | 2 885 | 275 | 227 | 5 776 | 9.0 |
| Mason | 711 | 0.6 | D | 10.9 | D | 7.6 | 3.6 | 5.5 | 42.9 | 15 530 | 255 | 1 532 | 32 518 | 27.4 |
| Okanogan | 871 | 20.0 | 8.3 | 1.5 | 4.5 | 9.0 | 4.0 | 6.1 | 30.0 | 10 145 | 245 | 1 325 | 22 245 | 16.6 |
| Pacific | 291 | 2.5 | D | 10.7 | 3.2 | 7.3 | 4.1 | D | 40.1 | 7 130 | 341 | 670 | 15 547 | 11.1 |
| Pend Oreille | 170 | 1.1 | 20.9 | 13.6 | 3.0 | 4.1 | 3.3 | D | 53.2 | 3 710 | 287 | 506 | 7 936 | 20.1 |
| Pierce | 21 434 | 0.1 | 12.5 | 6.1 | 5.0 | 5.9 | 4.2 | 13.7 | 39.1 | 127 255 | 158 | 18 463 | 325 375 | 17.4 |
| San Juan | 288 | -0.3 | D | 3.3 | D | 9.7 | 6.0 | 5.8 | 19.4 | 4 460 | 281 | 137 | 13 313 | 36.5 |
| Skagit | 2 690 | 2.7 | 24.9 | 16.3 | 4.8 | 10.1 | 5.3 | 8.5 | 24.2 | 25 415 | 215 | 2 308 | 51 473 | 20.6 |
| Skamania | 107 | -1.2 | D | 10.5 | D | 6.4 | D | D | 41.9 | 2 165 | 194 | 209 | 5 628 | 23.0 |
| Snohomish | 18 423 | 0.2 | 40.0 | 33.5 | 7.6 | 6.6 | 5.4 | 8.5 | 16.5 | 101 425 | 140 | 11 553 | 286 659 | 21.4 |
| Spokane | 12 128 | 0.2 | 14.2 | 8.0 | 7.8 | 8.0 | 7.9 | 17.4 | 20.6 | 86 990 | 184 | 13 051 | 201 434 | 15.1 |
| Stevens | 514 | 1.9 | 17.2 | 11.8 | D | 8.3 | 2.1 | 14.4 | 32.0 | 11 110 | 255 | 1 279 | 21 156 | 20.2 |
| Thurston | 6 152 | 0.4 | 8.0 | 3.2 | 6.1 | 7.2 | 4.5 | 13.2 | 40.0 | 47 985 | 187 | 4 924 | 108 182 | 24.8 |
| Wahkiakum | 41 | 1.4 | 11.6 | 3.7 | D | 4.7 | D | D | 30.3 | 1 285 | 322 | 88 | 2 067 | 15.3 |
| Walla Walla | 1 508 | 10.4 | D | 14.8 | 4.1 | 6.1 | 4.1 | 14.5 | 25.6 | 11 400 | 191 | 1 309 | 23 451 | 10.9 |
| Whatcom | 5 007 | 2.9 | 22.7 | 13.7 | 9.6 | 8.4 | 4.7 | 11.5 | 19.0 | 37 155 | 182 | 4 221 | 90 665 | 22.7 |
| Whitman | 1 086 | 7.7 | D | 14.3 | 2.4 | 4.5 | 2.0 | 6.5 | 47.2 | 5 450 | 121 | 418 | 19 323 | 15.9 |
| Yakima | 5 395 | 16.1 | 11.9 | 7.7 | 3.5 | 7.0 | 3.3 | 14.2 | 19.1 | 39 930 | 162 | 7 311 | 85 474 | 8.0 |
| WEST VIRGINIA | 40 946 | -0.1 | 23.3 | 8.7 | 7.2 | 7.0 | 4.3 | 14.2 | 22.7 | 451 039 | 243 | 80 796 | 881 917 | 4.4 |
| Barbour | 178 | -0.8 | 27.7 | 1.6 | 3.6 | 5.8 | 2.7 | D | 23.7 | 4 135 | 250 | 872 | 7 849 | 6.8 |
| Berkeley | 1 819 | 0.2 | D | 4.8 | 10.4 | 6.3 | 3.6 | 11.7 | 40.2 | 18 785 | 178 | 2 048 | 44 762 | 36.0 |
| Boone | 702 | 0.0 | 54.8 | 0.3 | D | 3.5 | 1.0 | 2.8 | 13.3 | 6 600 | 270 | 1 498 | 11 070 | -4.4 |
| Braxton | 188 | -0.4 | 16.7 | 8.9 | 3.4 | 14.7 | 3.0 | D | 25.4 | 3 610 | 249 | 813 | 7 415 | 0.6 |

1. Includes mining, construction, and manufacturing.   2. Per 1,000 resident population enumerated in the 2010 census.   3. Manassas and Manassas Park cities are included with Prince William county.   4. Martinsville city is included with Henry county.   5. Norton city is included with Wise county.   6. Petersburg and Colonial Heights cities are included with Dinwiddie county.   7. Poquoson city is included with York county.   8. Radford city is included with Montgomery county.   9. Salem city is included with Roanoke county.   10. Staunton and Waynesboro cities are included with Augusta county.   11. Williamsburg city is included with James City county.   12. Winchester city is included with Frederick county.

# Table B. States and Counties — **Housing, Labor Force, and Employment**

| STATE County | Housing units, 2007–2011 | | | | | | | | Civilian labor force, 2012 | | | | Civilian employment,[6] 2007–2011 | | |
|---|---|---|---|---|---|---|---|---|---|---|---|---|---|---|---|
| | Occupied units | | | | | Renter-occupied | | | | | Unemployment | | | Percent | |
| | | | Owner-occupied | | | | | | | | | | | | Construction, production, and maintenance occupations |
| | | | | Median owner cost as a percent of income | | | | | | | | | | Management, business, science and arts | |
| | Total | Percent | Median value[1] | With a mortgage | Without a mortgage[2] | Median rent[3] | Median rent as a percent of income | Substandard units[4] (percent) | Total | Percent change, 2011–2012 | Total | Rate[5] | Total | | |
| | 89 | 90 | 91 | 92 | 93 | 94 | 95 | 96 | 97 | 98 | 99 | 100 | 101 | 102 | 103 |
| VIRGINIA—Cont'd | | | | | | | | | | | | | | | |
| Manassas Park city | 4 238 | 67.6 | 261 500 | 31.9 | 13.4 | 1 404 | 30.7 | 2.0 | 8 689 | 1.0 | 436 | 5.0 | 7 224 | 32.6 | 23.8 |
| Martinsville city | 5 958 | 57.8 | 90 500 | 23.8 | 13.8 | 560 | 35.2 | 3.3 | 5 344 | -3.7 | 854 | 16.0 | 5 327 | 26.4 | 26.2 |
| Newport News city | 69 977 | 51.8 | 204 100 | 25.1 | 13.2 | 928 | 30.3 | 2.1 | 88 287 | -0.4 | 6 398 | 7.2 | 83 374 | 31.9 | 23.2 |
| Norfolk city | 85 076 | 46.4 | 211 600 | 28.1 | 14.0 | 888 | 32.5 | 3.3 | 103 838 | -0.2 | 8 216 | 7.9 | 102 040 | 31.4 | 23.0 |
| Norton city | 1 750 | 54.8 | 82 800 | 19.0 | 9.9 | 563 | 25.8 | 1.3 | 1 824 | -4.7 | 123 | 6.7 | 1 807 | 31.5 | 23.3 |
| Petersburg city | 12 179 | 47.9 | 119 600 | 24.9 | 12.6 | 819 | 32.1 | 2.4 | 14 023 | 0.3 | 1 582 | 11.3 | 12 874 | 25.4 | 25.0 |
| Poquoson city | 4 525 | 83.6 | 332 800 | 23.3 | 11.7 | 1 236 | 30.1 | 0.6 | 6 401 | 0.3 | 346 | 5.4 | 5 749 | 47.3 | 16.8 |
| Portsmouth city | 36 899 | 61.0 | 184 700 | 28.5 | 14.5 | 919 | 33.0 | 2.5 | 43 818 | -0.1 | 3 616 | 8.3 | 41 248 | 30.6 | 22.9 |
| Radford city | 5 644 | 48.6 | 152 200 | 19.7 | 9.9 | 638 | 43.9 | 0.1 | 8 152 | 1.7 | 629 | 7.7 | 6 883 | 34.0 | 16.2 |
| Richmond city | 83 615 | 44.9 | 204 500 | 27.1 | 14.9 | 838 | 33.9 | 3.2 | 101 841 | 0.6 | 8 686 | 8.5 | 96 802 | 37.5 | 17.1 |
| Roanoke city | 42 892 | 56.4 | 131 800 | 26.1 | 13.3 | 659 | 29.9 | 2.1 | 47 693 | -0.1 | 3 476 | 7.3 | 45 222 | 29.0 | 24.3 |
| Salem city | 9 944 | 69.0 | 166 200 | 24.1 | 12.3 | 771 | 28.1 | 1.1 | 12 951 | 0.6 | 767 | 5.9 | 11 783 | 35.4 | 14.4 |
| Staunton city | 10 517 | 60.6 | 167 600 | 23.5 | 11.8 | 663 | 33.5 | 2.5 | 11 399 | -0.4 | 732 | 6.4 | 10 928 | 33.0 | 21.3 |
| Suffolk city | 30 305 | 75.1 | 254 800 | 27.1 | 12.7 | 940 | 34.3 | 2.1 | 41 739 | -0.1 | 2 818 | 6.8 | 37 497 | 37.0 | 24.9 |
| Virginia Beach city | 164 041 | 65.9 | 276 500 | 27.2 | 12.8 | 1 191 | 30.6 | 1.2 | 226 690 | 0.0 | 12 770 | 5.6 | 209 472 | 38.6 | 17.1 |
| Waynesboro city | 8 750 | 58.6 | 172 100 | 22.8 | 12.7 | 696 | 33.1 | 2.7 | 9 789 | -1.0 | 676 | 6.9 | 9 088 | 29.3 | 25.2 |
| Williamsburg city | 4 206 | 43.5 | 331 200 | 24.4 | 10.8 | 1 043 | 32.2 | 0.2 | 6 274 | -0.3 | 841 | 13.4 | 5 703 | 40.6 | 8.4 |
| Winchester city | 10 147 | 49.8 | 255 000 | 26.8 | 13.4 | 906 | 29.1 | 2.5 | 14 468 | 0.3 | 981 | 6.8 | 12 795 | 36.5 | 21.7 |
| WASHINGTON | 2 602 568 | 64.4 | 283 200 | 26.6 | 12.1 | 923 | 29.8 | 3.1 | 3 481 463 | 0.0 | 284 170 | 8.2 | 3 135 962 | 38.3 | 21.1 |
| Adams | 5 666 | 62.9 | 133 400 | 25.1 | 11.5 | 563 | 24.0 | 11.4 | 8 581 | 3.0 | 754 | 8.8 | 7 081 | 24.6 | 42.6 |
| Asotin | 8 880 | 71.3 | 170 100 | 25.1 | 9.9 | 665 | 28.9 | 1.7 | 10 084 | -1.2 | 887 | 8.8 | 9 199 | 30.9 | 24.6 |
| Benton | 63 240 | 69.6 | 173 500 | 20.4 | 9.9 | 766 | 28.4 | 2.6 | 94 895 | -0.9 | 8 220 | 8.7 | 79 060 | 37.4 | 24.1 |
| Chelan | 26 862 | 66.5 | 256 200 | 25.4 | 10.5 | 712 | 26.8 | 3.1 | 40 751 | 1.7 | 3 153 | 7.7 | 32 187 | 30.2 | 29.1 |
| Clallam | 31 056 | 71.1 | 239 800 | 27.6 | 11.0 | 800 | 31.2 | 2.4 | 28 607 | -1.1 | 2 818 | 9.9 | 27 580 | 31.4 | 23.0 |
| Clark | 157 179 | 67.1 | 254 200 | 27.1 | 12.0 | 895 | 30.1 | 2.7 | 211 442 | -1.0 | 22 021 | 10.4 | 190 779 | 35.0 | 23.7 |
| Columbia | 1 790 | 73.7 | 145 900 | 21.2 | 10.9 | 554 | 33.4 | 2.5 | 1 514 | 1.3 | 155 | 10.2 | 1 626 | 34.8 | 23.3 |
| Cowlitz | 39 793 | 67.3 | 193 800 | 25.5 | 11.8 | 705 | 34.2 | 3.1 | 43 067 | 0.0 | 4 687 | 10.9 | 41 229 | 28.2 | 31.1 |
| Douglas | 13 937 | 71.9 | 216 700 | 24.5 | 11.3 | 724 | 27.5 | 7.0 | 21 879 | 1.9 | 1 643 | 7.5 | 17 431 | 24.4 | 34.1 |
| Ferry | 2 825 | 75.0 | 144 700 | 27.4 | 9.9 | 528 | 29.0 | 4.2 | 2 818 | -2.9 | 365 | 13.0 | 2 239 | 30.3 | 31.0 |
| Franklin | 22 004 | 67.2 | 152 300 | 23.3 | 9.9 | 687 | 30.2 | 8.6 | 37 587 | -1.3 | 3 533 | 9.4 | 31 205 | 23.7 | 37.3 |
| Garfield | 959 | 74.5 | 131 600 | 22.2 | 9.9 | 557 | 19.5 | 3.0 | 1 015 | 0.8 | 79 | 7.8 | 947 | 36.2 | 26.1 |
| Grant | 29 922 | 60.5 | 152 300 | 22.6 | 9.9 | 626 | 24.6 | 7.0 | 42 369 | 3.0 | 3 993 | 9.4 | 36 619 | 26.6 | 37.3 |
| Grays Harbor | 27 570 | 69.8 | 160 000 | 25.8 | 11.4 | 691 | 28.7 | 3.8 | 29 101 | -2.8 | 3 633 | 12.5 | 27 983 | 24.9 | 30.7 |
| Island | 33 196 | 71.9 | 312 000 | 29.1 | 12.0 | 987 | 28.5 | 1.3 | 31 479 | -0.2 | 2 583 | 8.2 | 31 747 | 33.9 | 22.6 |
| Jefferson | 14 440 | 72.3 | 308 900 | 27.9 | 12.3 | 801 | 34.7 | 3.8 | 12 041 | -1.9 | 1 134 | 9.4 | 11 855 | 37.4 | 20.6 |
| King | 790 070 | 59.6 | 402 300 | 26.8 | 13.1 | 1 060 | 28.9 | 3.0 | 1 118 933 | 0.4 | 76 390 | 6.8 | 1 014 031 | 47.7 | 15.1 |
| Kitsap | 96 683 | 67.7 | 284 300 | 26.1 | 12.1 | 958 | 30.4 | 2.3 | 120 076 | -1.5 | 8 907 | 7.4 | 107 386 | 37.5 | 21.0 |
| Kittitas | 16 658 | 57.1 | 265 000 | 27.9 | 11.9 | 772 | 42.7 | 2.5 | 20 819 | -0.4 | 1 722 | 8.3 | 18 715 | 34.5 | 21.4 |
| Klickitat | 8 228 | 69.4 | 200 600 | 25.1 | 11.4 | 691 | 33.4 | 3.9 | 10 699 | 0.3 | 1 032 | 9.6 | 7 930 | 30.5 | 33.5 |
| Lewis | 29 586 | 70.8 | 192 700 | 25.0 | 12.1 | 713 | 30.6 | 3.8 | 29 898 | -0.8 | 3 716 | 12.4 | 30 112 | 27.0 | 32.7 |
| Lincoln | 4 661 | 79.0 | 156 900 | 22.7 | 10.6 | 590 | 26.2 | 3.3 | 4 725 | -0.9 | 365 | 7.7 | 4 639 | 37.3 | 23.1 |
| Mason | 22 914 | 79.4 | 223 800 | 28.7 | 10.9 | 817 | 32.3 | 3.1 | 24 055 | -1.6 | 2 501 | 10.4 | 22 091 | 28.4 | 28.3 |
| Okanogan | 15 648 | 68.2 | 164 300 | 25.0 | 10.0 | 587 | 28.6 | 5.2 | 21 080 | 0.5 | 1 933 | 9.2 | 16 562 | 31.0 | 29.1 |
| Pacific | 9 390 | 74.4 | 166 800 | 23.6 | 12.5 | 647 | 31.1 | 4.4 | 8 729 | 0.7 | 989 | 11.3 | 8 012 | 28.7 | 31.5 |
| Pend Oreille | 5 450 | 78.3 | 192 500 | 25.5 | 9.9 | 599 | 34.6 | 3.4 | 5 198 | -0.5 | 603 | 11.6 | 4 326 | 28.9 | 32.9 |
| Pierce | 297 839 | 63.1 | 265 200 | 27.9 | 13.3 | 948 | 30.9 | 2.8 | 385 463 | -0.3 | 34 345 | 8.9 | 352 720 | 32.4 | 23.7 |
| San Juan | 8 051 | 69.2 | 494 500 | 32.7 | 11.8 | 932 | 29.8 | 5.5 | 8 172 | 3.1 | 503 | 6.2 | 7 811 | 37.1 | 22.3 |
| Skagit | 45 475 | 68.9 | 280 800 | 28.8 | 12.8 | 911 | 30.5 | 3.9 | 56 435 | -0.5 | 5 214 | 9.2 | 51 185 | 30.9 | 27.6 |
| Skamania | 4 435 | 74.9 | 257 600 | 27.8 | 9.9 | 684 | 26.5 | 4.1 | 5 060 | -0.8 | 545 | 10.8 | 4 789 | 34.3 | 28.0 |
| Snohomish | 266 331 | 67.8 | 332 000 | 28.5 | 13.4 | 1 052 | 30.1 | 2.6 | 386 288 | 0.1 | 30 039 | 7.8 | 349 680 | 36.2 | 22.0 |
| Spokane | 185 983 | 64.7 | 192 800 | 24.7 | 11.1 | 733 | 31.2 | 1.9 | 229 965 | -0.3 | 19 882 | 8.6 | 212 594 | 35.2 | 18.7 |
| Stevens | 17 652 | 80.9 | 179 300 | 26.7 | 10.3 | 584 | 27.8 | 3.9 | 17 622 | -1.8 | 2 032 | 11.5 | 16 866 | 33.3 | 25.3 |
| Thurston | 100 147 | 67.4 | 259 500 | 26.1 | 11.7 | 974 | 29.0 | 2.8 | 126 669 | -0.8 | 9 871 | 7.8 | 115 691 | 41.0 | 17.3 |
| Wahkiakum | 1 648 | 77.4 | 207 200 | 24.7 | 10.7 | 605 | 34.6 | 4.4 | 1 473 | -2.1 | 179 | 12.2 | 1 382 | 26.8 | 38.8 |
| Walla Walla | 21 645 | 62.3 | 201 600 | 24.3 | 12.1 | 666 | 28.5 | 3.9 | 30 599 | -0.5 | 2 198 | 7.2 | 25 377 | 34.2 | 21.2 |
| Whatcom | 79 003 | 62.9 | 290 400 | 27.9 | 12.4 | 842 | 32.4 | 2.7 | 105 360 | 0.2 | 7 948 | 7.5 | 96 968 | 34.3 | 21.6 |
| Whitman | 16 187 | 47.4 | 187 600 | 21.4 | 9.9 | 668 | 47.4 | 0.8 | 21 657 | 0.5 | 1 355 | 6.3 | 20 406 | 46.3 | 12.3 |
| Yakima | 79 565 | 63.5 | 154 800 | 24.4 | 11.3 | 693 | 30.3 | 7.2 | 125 257 | 1.9 | 12 243 | 9.8 | 97 922 | 26.3 | 33.9 |
| WEST VIRGINIA | 740 080 | 74.3 | 96 500 | 19.9 | 9.9 | 574 | 29.1 | 1.8 | 804 917 | 0.2 | 59 075 | 7.3 | 762 595 | 30.7 | 26.2 |
| Barbour | 6 210 | 76.3 | 84 900 | 22.6 | 9.9 | 500 | 29.9 | 1.0 | 6 763 | -1.3 | 525 | 7.8 | 6 335 | 22.1 | 35.7 |
| Berkeley | 39 303 | 75.5 | 183 000 | 24.3 | 10.1 | 746 | 31.5 | 2.4 | 47 002 | 1.5 | 3 290 | 7.0 | 48 349 | 31.2 | 27.3 |
| Boone | 9 755 | 77.4 | 75 500 | 17.0 | 9.9 | 488 | 26.3 | 1.7 | 9 306 | 4.2 | 1 010 | 10.9 | 8 605 | 29.7 | 34.8 |
| Braxton | 6 087 | 77.5 | 78 600 | 19.3 | 9.9 | 508 | 29.0 | 5.0 | 5 698 | -1.2 | 543 | 9.5 | 5 282 | 21.2 | 34.7 |

1. Specified owner-occupied units. lacking complete plumbing facilities.   2. A value of 9.9 represents 9.9 percent or less.   3. Specified renter-occupied units. A value of 10.0 represents 10 percent or less.   4. Overcrowded or
5. Percent of civilian labor force.   6. Persons 16 years old and over.

# Table B. States and Counties — **Nonfarm Employment and Agriculture**

| STATE County | Number of establishments | Total | Health care and social assistance | Manufacturing | Retail trade | Finance and insurance | Professional, scientific, and technical services | Total (mil dol) | Average per employee (dollars) | Number | Fewer than 50 acres | 500 acres or more | Farm operators whose principal occupation is farming (percent) |
|---|---|---|---|---|---|---|---|---|---|---|---|---|---|
| | 104 | 105 | 106 | 107 | 108 | 109 | 110 | 111 | 112 | 113 | 114 | 115 | 116 |
| VIRGINIA—Cont'd | | | | | | | | | | | | | |
| Manassas Park city | 294 | 3 203 | D | D | 252 | D | 100 | 138 | 43 209 | NA | NA | NA | NA |
| Martinsville city | 599 | 9 433 | 2 224 | D | 1 634 | 266 | 233 | 257 | 27 294 | NA | NA | NA | NA |
| Newport News city | 3 702 | 85 658 | 12 654 | D | 9 933 | 1 593 | 5 697 | 3 677 | 42 925 | NA | NA | NA | NA |
| Norfolk city | 5 558 | 109 275 | 18 856 | 7 016 | 12 399 | 4 850 | 10 970 | 4 536 | 41 511 | NA | NA | NA | NA |
| Norton city | 252 | 4 632 | 1 139 | D | 907 | D | 145 | 173 | 37 393 | NA | NA | NA | NA |
| Petersburg city | 724 | 12 221 | 4 622 | D | 1 457 | 201 | 223 | 429 | 35 095 | NA | NA | NA | NA |
| Poquoson city | 205 | 1 332 | 166 | D | 281 | D | 109 | 34 | 25 586 | NA | NA | NA | NA |
| Portsmouth city | 1 735 | 27 602 | 7 051 | 2 136 | 3 145 | 602 | 1 761 | 966 | 35 003 | NA | NA | NA | NA |
| Radford city | 330 | 5 539 | 464 | 2 603 | 622 | 184 | 199 | 257 | 46 413 | NA | NA | NA | NA |
| Richmond city | 5 981 | 109 283 | 18 103 | 7 131 | 8 376 | 9 232 | 12 173 | 5 806 | 53 132 | NA | NA | NA | NA |
| Roanoke city | 3 133 | 63 068 | 12 415 | 3 927 | 9 458 | 3 643 | 3 315 | 2 534 | 40 176 | NA | NA | NA | NA |
| Salem city | 965 | 18 412 | 4 512 | 3 453 | 2 039 | 658 | 567 | 788 | 42 793 | NA | NA | NA | NA |
| Staunton city | 755 | 9 265 | 1 828 | 350 | 1 885 | 466 | 313 | 273 | 29 485 | NA | NA | NA | NA |
| Suffolk city | 1 450 | 20 009 | 3 861 | 1 583 | 3 357 | 703 | 1 440 | 725 | 36 214 | 311 | 54.3 | 11.9 | 53.4 |
| Virginia Beach city | 10 658 | 143 023 | 16 943 | 5 921 | 22 281 | 11 286 | 13 501 | 5 161 | 36 087 | 174 | 70.1 | 5.7 | 43.1 |
| Waynesboro city | 604 | 9 596 | 762 | 1 867 | 1 981 | 330 | 265 | 304 | 31 689 | NA | NA | NA | NA |
| Williamsburg city | 477 | 9 956 | 1 530 | D | 1 712 | 155 | 194 | 279 | 27 983 | NA | NA | NA | NA |
| Winchester city | 1 294 | 22 194 | 6 139 | 2 036 | 3 869 | 626 | 1 094 | 880 | 39 665 | NA | NA | NA | NA |
| WASHINGTON | 173 511 | 2 355 123 | 370 319 | 226 738 | 305 352 | 94 607 | 166 080 | 118 648 | 50 379 | 39 284 | 61.1 | 11.4 | 45.9 |
| Adams | 359 | 4 340 | D | D | 598 | 79 | D | 149 | 34 294 | 782 | 17.6 | 44.6 | 57.8 |
| Asotin | 432 | 4 374 | 974 | 296 | 1 130 | 156 | 208 | 133 | 30 479 | 192 | 41.1 | 41.7 | 53.1 |
| Benton | 3 919 | 59 670 | 9 780 | 3 375 | 8 912 | 1 647 | 9 939 | 2 940 | 49 273 | 1 630 | 73.5 | 8.9 | 40.1 |
| Chelan | 2 372 | 25 619 | 5 259 | 1 767 | 4 077 | 863 | 1 242 | 932 | 36 396 | 979 | 70.8 | 2.8 | 55.4 |
| Clallam | 2 118 | 17 230 | 3 955 | 1 558 | 3 348 | 531 | 796 | 556 | 32 254 | 512 | 80.1 | 0.8 | 41.2 |
| Clark | 9 303 | 107 452 | 18 946 | 11 195 | 15 238 | 4 633 | 6 535 | 4 633 | 43 121 | 2 101 | 83.4 | 0.6 | 38.8 |
| Columbia | 129 | 757 | 172 | 68 | 123 | D | D | 24 | 32 339 | 283 | 27.9 | 36.0 | 51.9 |
| Cowlitz | 2 149 | 30 312 | 5 634 | 5 974 | 4 678 | 877 | 838 | 1 272 | 41 954 | 481 | 67.8 | 1.9 | 44.3 |
| Douglas | 672 | 6 196 | 844 | D | 1 497 | 193 | 176 | 180 | 29 058 | 955 | 45.4 | 26.3 | 55.9 |
| Ferry | 132 | 838 | D | 88 | 160 | 20 | D | 37 | 43 753 | 232 | 21.6 | 16.4 | 44.8 |
| Franklin | 1 358 | 17 098 | 1 846 | 2 393 | 3 151 | 379 | 545 | 602 | 35 193 | 891 | 35.8 | 28.7 | 62.0 |
| Garfield | 45 | 334 | D | D | 74 | D | 5 | 9 | 28 246 | 239 | 17.2 | 45.6 | 48.1 |
| Grant | 1 717 | 19 089 | 2 957 | 4 006 | 3 007 | 569 | 402 | 673 | 35 254 | 1 858 | 34.1 | 26.0 | 55.9 |
| Grays Harbor | 1 709 | 15 169 | 2 834 | 2 204 | 2 854 | 660 | 425 | 515 | 33 950 | 628 | 62.4 | 3.0 | 43.9 |
| Island | 1 696 | 11 702 | 2 547 | 655 | 2 102 | 480 | 836 | 358 | 30 603 | 458 | 81.7 | 0.4 | 46.5 |
| Jefferson | 999 | 6 187 | 1 217 | 727 | 1 023 | 161 | 249 | 195 | 31 585 | 211 | 70.6 | 0.9 | 48.8 |
| King | 62 569 | 1 030 931 | 131 768 | 70 955 | 98 592 | 41 290 | 95 085 | 65 843 | 63 867 | 1 790 | 89.8 | 0.4 | 42.1 |
| Kitsap | 5 541 | 55 525 | 12 827 | 1 750 | 10 425 | 1 956 | 4 049 | 2 009 | 36 177 | 664 | 91.3 | 0.3 | 45.5 |
| Kittitas | 1 114 | 9 731 | 1 539 | 475 | 1 572 | 195 | 333 | 265 | 27 223 | 1 038 | 59.5 | 8.1 | 42.5 |
| Klickitat | 528 | 3 423 | 611 | D | 289 | 85 | 304 | 126 | 36 955 | 893 | 47.4 | 18.8 | 42.6 |
| Lewis | 1 798 | 18 256 | 3 306 | 2 967 | 3 414 | 409 | 481 | 612 | 33 527 | 1 717 | 63.5 | 1.4 | 41.4 |
| Lincoln | 247 | 1 582 | 406 | 20 | 275 | 73 | 109 | 54 | 34 079 | 798 | 14.4 | 54.4 | 62.3 |
| Mason | 970 | 9 276 | 1 693 | 1 162 | 1 656 | 397 | 234 | 293 | 31 564 | 471 | 79.8 | 1.3 | 35.0 |
| Okanogan | 1 133 | 7 920 | 1 868 | D | 1 804 | 252 | 237 | 219 | 27 663 | 1 662 | 48.3 | 14.1 | 44.7 |
| Pacific | 593 | 3 867 | 618 | 694 | 592 | 172 | 104 | 109 | 28 061 | 390 | 54.1 | 6.4 | 49.7 |
| Pend Oreille | 218 | 1 566 | 410 | D | 235 | 53 | 62 | 60 | 38 443 | 316 | 43.4 | 6.6 | 35.4 |
| Pierce | 16 370 | 220 454 | 43 202 | 15 167 | 32 395 | 9 507 | 8 231 | 8 615 | 39 079 | 1 448 | 84.6 | 0.4 | 41.9 |
| San Juan | 938 | 3 862 | 436 | 148 | 597 | 140 | 269 | 131 | 33 953 | 291 | 67.7 | 1.7 | 38.8 |
| Skagit | 3 358 | 36 338 | 7 060 | 5 036 | 6 882 | 1 523 | 1 315 | 1 365 | 37 575 | 1 215 | 74.7 | 4.4 | 39.4 |
| Skamania | 177 | 1 185 | 85 | D | 142 | D | D | 36 | 29 986 | 123 | 76.4 | 1.6 | 43.9 |
| Snohomish | 16 674 | 216 021 | 28 689 | 52 865 | 32 448 | 8 396 | 9 529 | 10 264 | 47 515 | 1 670 | 81.6 | 1.7 | 39.5 |
| Spokane | 12 151 | 169 532 | 34 231 | 13 925 | 24 570 | 10 416 | 8 312 | 6 569 | 38 750 | 2 502 | 54.8 | 10.6 | 36.3 |
| Stevens | 883 | 6 830 | 1 708 | 970 | 1 266 | 191 | 187 | 210 | 30 777 | 1 258 | 40.4 | 10.5 | 47.6 |
| Thurston | 5 733 | 63 511 | 11 842 | 2 520 | 11 917 | 2 444 | 5 930 | 2 300 | 36 222 | 1 288 | 76.9 | 2.0 | 40.5 |
| Wahkiakum | 91 | 609 | D | D | 58 | D | D | 17 | 28 174 | 119 | 45.4 | 1.7 | 52.9 |
| Walla Walla | 1 370 | 19 298 | 4 123 | D | 2 428 | D | 505 | 650 | 33 707 | 929 | 50.5 | 26.0 | 48.4 |
| Whatcom | 6 117 | 66 595 | 10 024 | 8 400 | 10 506 | 2 127 | 3 123 | 2 489 | 37 373 | 1 483 | 71.2 | 2.2 | 45.2 |
| Whitman | 814 | 9 183 | 1 846 | 1 732 | 1 406 | 243 | 247 | 301 | 32 802 | 1 247 | 19.6 | 47.8 | 56.2 |
| Yakima | 4 583 | 61 150 | 12 954 | 7 576 | 9 876 | 1 558 | 1 815 | 2 086 | 34 108 | 3 540 | 69.8 | 6.0 | 51.6 |
| WEST VIRGINIA | 38 150 | 568 344 | 126 591 | 52 104 | 85 982 | 18 058 | 24 522 | 20 682 | 36 390 | 23 618 | 29.5 | 5.3 | 41.5 |
| Barbour | 239 | 2 768 | 757 | 121 | 325 | 66 | D | 73 | 26 199 | 539 | 21.5 | 6.7 | 42.5 |
| Berkeley | 1 562 | 20 968 | 5 106 | 2 283 | 3 825 | 613 | 1 240 | 724 | 34 526 | 833 | 57.0 | 2.5 | 35.1 |
| Boone | 318 | 6 857 | 785 | 43 | 783 | 141 | 117 | 395 | 57 669 | 22 | 54.5 | 4.5 | 45.5 |
| Braxton | 269 | 2 991 | 854 | 363 | 612 | D | D | 81 | 27 031 | 381 | 19.4 | 9.2 | 42.8 |

# Table B. States and Counties — Agriculture

| | Agriculture, 2007 (cont.) | | | | | | | | | | | | | | | |
| STATE County | Land in farms | | Acres | | | Value of land and buildings (dollars) | | Value of machinery and equipment, average per farm (dollars) | Value of products sold | | Percent from: | | Percent of farms with sales of: | | Government payments | |
| | Acreage (1,000) | Percent change, 2002–2007 | Average size of farm | Total irrigated (1,000) | Total cropland (1,000) | Average per farm | Average per acre | | Total (mil dol) | Average per farm (dollars) | Crops | Live-stock and poultry products | $10,000 or more | $100,000 or more | Total ($1,000) | Percent of farms |
| | 117 | 118 | 119 | 120 | 121 | 122 | 123 | 124 | 125 | 126 | 127 | 128 | 129 | 130 | 131 | 132 |
| VIRGINIA—Cont'd | | | | | | | | | | | | | | | | |
| Manassas Park city | NA | NA | NA | NA | NA | NA | NA | NA | NA | NA | NA | NA | NA | NA | NA | NA |
| Martinsville city | NA | NA | NA | NA | NA | NA | NA | NA | NA | NA | NA | NA | NA | NA | NA | NA |
| Newport News city | NA | NA | NA | NA | NA | NA | NA | NA | NA | NA | NA | NA | NA | NA | NA | NA |
| Norfolk city | NA | NA | NA | NA | NA | NA | NA | NA | NA | NA | NA | NA | NA | NA | NA | NA |
| Norton city | NA | NA | NA | NA | NA | NA | NA | NA | NA | NA | NA | NA | NA | NA | NA | NA |
| Petersburg city | NA | NA | NA | NA | NA | NA | NA | NA | NA | NA | NA | NA | NA | NA | NA | NA |
| Poquoson city | NA | NA | NA | NA | NA | NA | NA | NA | NA | NA | NA | NA | NA | NA | NA | NA |
| Portsmouth city | NA | NA | NA | NA | NA | NA | NA | NA | NA | NA | NA | NA | NA | NA | NA | NA |
| Radford city | NA | NA | NA | NA | NA | NA | NA | NA | NA | NA | NA | NA | NA | NA | NA | NA |
| Richmond city | NA | NA | NA | NA | NA | NA | NA | NA | NA | NA | NA | NA | NA | NA | NA | NA |
| Roanoke city | NA | NA | NA | NA | NA | NA | NA | NA | NA | NA | NA | NA | NA | NA | NA | NA |
| Salem city | NA | NA | NA | NA | NA | NA | NA | NA | NA | NA | NA | NA | NA | NA | NA | NA |
| Staunton city | NA | NA | NA | NA | NA | NA | NA | NA | NA | NA | NA | NA | NA | NA | NA | NA |
| Suffolk city | 71 | 0.0 | 230 | 0.6 | 53.8 | 1 045 364 | 4 554 | 117 887 | 51.3 | 164 859 | 82.4 | 17.6 | 41.5 | 20.6 | 2 913 | 45.7 |
| Virginia Beach city | 27 | -3.6 | 153 | 0.2 | 21.5 | 954 463 | 6 227 | 93 578 | 12.6 | 72 240 | D | D | 31.6 | 13.2 | 354 | 25.9 |
| Waynesboro city | NA | NA | NA | NA | NA | NA | NA | NA | NA | NA | NA | NA | NA | NA | NA | NA |
| Williamsburg city | NA | NA | NA | NA | NA | NA | NA | NA | NA | NA | NA | NA | NA | NA | NA | NA |
| Winchester city | NA | NA | NA | NA | NA | NA | NA | NA | NA | NA | NA | NA | NA | NA | NA | NA |
| WASHINGTON | 14 973 | -2.3 | 381 | 1 735.9 | 7 609.2 | 759 146 | 1 992 | 83 468 | 6 792.9 | 172 917 | 70.0 | 30.0 | 33.9 | 15.2 | 138 272 | 17.6 |
| Adams | 1 098 | 2.9 | 1 405 | 124.5 | 825.9 | 1 438 309 | 1 024 | 191 192 | 344.1 | 440 064 | 71.7 | 28.3 | 46.3 | 32.9 | 14 454 | 69.7 |
| Asotin | 274 | -2.1 | 1 426 | 0.3 | 80.4 | 1 185 136 | 831 | 99 164 | 13.4 | 69 668 | D | D | 37.5 | 18.2 | 2 339 | 43.2 |
| Benton | 633 | 4.1 | 388 | 181.6 | 476.5 | 901 747 | 2 323 | 104 430 | 525.9 | 322 649 | 89.4 | 10.6 | 33.0 | 14.5 | 6 064 | 9.6 |
| Chelan | 94 | -16.1 | 96 | 28.2 | 43.5 | 698 166 | 7 280 | 63 054 | 208.8 | 213 278 | 98.2 | 1.8 | 69.5 | 33.3 | 292 | 3.4 |
| Clallam | 23 | 4.5 | 45 | 4.5 | 8.8 | 467 520 | 10 489 | 45 634 | 10.8 | 21 030 | D | D | 23.8 | 3.7 | 59 | 3.1 |
| Clark | 78 | 9.9 | 37 | 4.4 | 34.3 | 493 410 | 13 230 | 36 479 | 52.7 | 25 079 | 42.4 | 57.6 | 14.7 | 2.5 | 115 | 1.6 |
| Columbia | 313 | 6.1 | 1 107 | 4.2 | 184.1 | 1 104 813 | 998 | 119 009 | 39.8 | 140 702 | 91.0 | 9.0 | 38.2 | 22.3 | 5 257 | 73.5 |
| Cowlitz | 31 | -22.5 | 64 | 3.0 | 10.9 | 485 875 | 7 612 | 51 689 | 26.5 | 55 007 | 40.2 | 59.8 | 18.3 | 5.6 | 29 | 1.9 |
| Douglas | 883 | 0.5 | 925 | 19.4 | 539.5 | 1 020 277 | 1 103 | 100 225 | 193.4 | 202 479 | 96.7 | 3.3 | 53.2 | 29.0 | 11 647 | 39.7 |
| Ferry | 749 | -6.3 | 3 230 | 3.4 | 14.8 | 1 423 137 | 441 | 42 795 | 2.9 | 12 555 | 22.3 | 77.7 | 24.1 | 3.9 | 73 | 9.5 |
| Franklin | 609 | -8.4 | 684 | 217.2 | 467.9 | 1 477 309 | 2 161 | 202 364 | 467.0 | 524 145 | 82.1 | 17.9 | 62.3 | 47.4 | 7 238 | 33.4 |
| Garfield | 308 | -1.3 | 1 290 | 0.5 | 174.6 | 1 043 703 | 809 | 111 192 | 26.4 | 110 629 | 87.8 | 12.2 | 38.1 | 25.9 | 5 086 | 72.8 |
| Grant | 1 088 | 1.3 | 586 | 469.8 | 771.8 | 1 460 726 | 2 495 | 204 775 | 1 190.2 | 640 576 | 71.2 | 28.8 | 58.2 | 41.5 | 11 192 | 34.1 |
| Grays Harbor | 119 | 120.4 | 190 | 4.9 | 24.1 | 508 492 | 2 677 | 42 517 | 32.8 | 52 263 | 53.4 | 46.6 | 22.9 | 5.1 | 326 | 6.8 |
| Island | 18 | 20.0 | 39 | 1.8 | 8.6 | 475 138 | 12 295 | 35 920 | 14.3 | 31 319 | 25.5 | 74.5 | 18.3 | 2.8 | 161 | 3.9 |
| Jefferson | 13 | 8.3 | 60 | 0.6 | 3.8 | 439 708 | 7 296 | 50 482 | 8.7 | 41 179 | 12.9 | 87.1 | 27.0 | 4.7 | 59 | 5.2 |
| King | 49 | 16.7 | 28 | 3.3 | 18.0 | 489 767 | 17 788 | 43 236 | 127.3 | 71 100 | 35.9 | 64.1 | 25.1 | 5.5 | 316 | 2.9 |
| Kitsap | 15 | -6.3 | 23 | 0.9 | 3.7 | 429 990 | 18 668 | 31 903 | 7.0 | 10 520 | 75.5 | 24.6 | 17.2 | 1.2 | 88 | 2.6 |
| Kittitas | 191 | -17.3 | 184 | 82.1 | 69.7 | 719 491 | 3 908 | 72 666 | 60.9 | 58 717 | 63.6 | 36.4 | 34.9 | 11.3 | 435 | 7.7 |
| Klickitat | 601 | -1.0 | 673 | 21.3 | 191.4 | 839 128 | 1 246 | 67 202 | 57.3 | 64 163 | 76.6 | 23.4 | 28.4 | 9.1 | 4 400 | 34.2 |
| Lewis | 132 | 0.8 | 77 | 7.3 | 54.4 | 453 053 | 5 913 | 48 925 | 110.0 | 64 063 | 26.2 | 73.8 | 20.3 | 5.4 | 255 | 5.1 |
| Lincoln | 1 090 | -11.6 | 1 366 | 32.1 | 743.2 | 1 360 226 | 996 | 142 374 | 126.2 | 158 165 | 93.3 | 6.7 | 49.2 | 34.8 | 15 371 | 74.6 |
| Mason | 25 | 13.6 | 53 | 1.2 | 6.1 | 439 720 | 8 223 | 52 101 | 37.0 | 78 478 | 4.3 | 95.7 | 24.8 | 7.4 | 39 | 2.3 |
| Okanogan | 1 205 | -2.9 | 725 | 51.6 | 127.1 | 879 713 | 1 213 | 58 180 | 208.8 | 125 606 | 88.2 | 11.8 | 38.0 | 15.3 | 1 065 | 4.5 |
| Pacific | 62 | 19.2 | 158 | 2.3 | 15.0 | 525 009 | 3 316 | 78 009 | 35.0 | 89 734 | 20.6 | 79.4 | 37.9 | 14.4 | 173 | 6.9 |
| Pend Oreille | 55 | -9.8 | 174 | 1.1 | 19.0 | 526 951 | 3 022 | 50 271 | 2.8 | 8 917 | 44.9 | 55.1 | 12.3 | 1.3 | 50 | 2.8 |
| Pierce | 48 | -15.8 | 33 | 4.5 | 17.3 | 485 594 | 14 748 | 42 222 | 83.4 | 57 598 | 38.8 | 61.2 | 16.1 | 4.5 | 68 | 1.2 |
| San Juan | 21 | 23.5 | 74 | 0.4 | 9.0 | 641 253 | 8 691 | 30 459 | 3.6 | 12 431 | 46.7 | 53.3 | 26.8 | 0.7 | 165 | 4.1 |
| Skagit | 109 | -4.4 | 89 | 16.3 | 69.8 | 602 607 | 6 746 | 80 332 | 256.2 | 210 904 | 68.0 | 32.0 | 26.5 | 10.8 | 630 | 8.9 |
| Skamania | 5 | -16.7 | 44 | 0.3 | 1.6 | 392 013 | 8 812 | 41 944 | 2.7 | 21 635 | 38.1 | 61.9 | 23.6 | 4.9 | 15 | 2.4 |
| Snohomish | 77 | 11.6 | 46 | 5.5 | 37.0 | 497 509 | 10 813 | 44 159 | 125.6 | 75 221 | 46.9 | 53.1 | 22.6 | 6.6 | 630 | 4.0 |
| Spokane | 626 | -2.6 | 250 | 13.5 | 394.9 | 588 545 | 2 351 | 65 660 | 117.1 | 46 789 | 84.2 | 15.8 | 23.6 | 8.3 | 5 929 | 24.5 |
| Stevens | 531 | 0.6 | 422 | 15.0 | 88.3 | 588 494 | 1 394 | 55 880 | 24.5 | 19 499 | 47.6 | 52.4 | 26.6 | 3.7 | 846 | 14.2 |
| Thurston | 81 | 9.5 | 63 | 6.9 | 26.3 | 535 414 | 8 554 | 56 688 | 117.9 | 91 525 | 36.5 | 63.5 | 18.9 | 4.7 | 297 | 2.8 |
| Wahkiakum | 12 | 0.0 | 101 | 0.2 | 4.7 | 402 743 | 3 986 | 49 220 | 3.1 | 25 773 | 7.2 | 92.8 | 26.9 | 4.2 | 142 | 17.6 |
| Walla Walla | 682 | -2.7 | 734 | 92.4 | 567.2 | 1 266 236 | 1 724 | 145 553 | 344.5 | 370 818 | D | D | 36.0 | 22.9 | 11 909 | 43.3 |
| Whatcom | 103 | -30.4 | 69 | 35.0 | 73.7 | 773 740 | 11 186 | 95 287 | 326.5 | 220 128 | 30.6 | 69.4 | 36.2 | 16.8 | 1 050 | 19.7 |
| Whitman | 1 271 | -4.3 | 1 019 | 6.9 | 1 057.6 | 1 137 925 | 1 116 | 153 010 | 254.0 | 203 714 | 95.9 | 4.1 | 49.9 | 37.0 | 25 305 | 72.4 |
| Yakima | 1 649 | -1.8 | 466 | 267.6 | 344.5 | 712 970 | 1 530 | 97 908 | 1 203.8 | 340 058 | 65.4 | 34.6 | 52.6 | 21.8 | 4 705 | 9.2 |
| WEST VIRGINIA | 3 698 | 3.2 | 157 | 2.2 | 942.1 | 373 435 | 2 385 | 38 871 | 591.7 | 25 051 | 13.2 | 86.8 | 20.1 | 3.2 | 2 929 | 9.2 |
| Barbour | 91 | 15.2 | 169 | 0.0 | 23.1 | 277 451 | 1 643 | 36 250 | 7.2 | 13 275 | 19.1 | 80.9 | 26.3 | 2.6 | 15 | 5.6 |
| Berkeley | 75 | -1.3 | 90 | 0.2 | 38.3 | 603 895 | 6 698 | 39 635 | 21.7 | 26 069 | 64.6 | 35.4 | 20.0 | 3.8 | 176 | 16.7 |
| Boone | 2 | -33.3 | 105 | 0.0 | 0.2 | 161 392 | 1 544 | 9 033 | 0.1 | 2 545 | 12.5 | 87.5 | 0.0 | 0.0 | 0 | 0.0 |
| Braxton | 79 | 19.7 | 208 | D | 12.9 | 336 083 | 1 612 | 35 120 | 3.1 | 8 040 | 10.1 | 89.9 | 23.4 | 0.3 | 14 | 4.7 |

| STATE County | Water use, 2005 | | Wholesale trade,[1] 2007 | | | | Retail trade,[2] 2007 | | | | Real estate and rental and leasing,[2] 2007 | | | |
|---|---|---|---|---|---|---|---|---|---|---|---|---|---|---|
| | Total water withdrawn (mil gal/day) | Gallons withdrawn per person | Number of establish-ments | Number of employees | Sales (mil dol) | Annual payroll (mil dol) | Number of establish-ments | Number of employees | Sales (mil dol) | Annual payroll (mil dol) | Number of establish-ments | Number of employees | Receipts (mil dol) | Annual payroll (mil dol) |
| | 133 | 134 | 135 | 136 | 137 | 138 | 139 | 140 | 141 | 142 | 143 | 144 | 145 | 146 |
| VIRGINIA—Cont'd | | | | | | | | | | | | | | |
| Manassas Park city | 0.4 | 35 | 17 | D | D | D | 33 | 403 | 158.0 | 12.2 | 5 | 63 | 8.9 | 1.7 |
| Martinsville city | 0.0 | 0 | 22 | D | D | D | 117 | 1 748 | 316.9 | 34.0 | 36 | 141 | 22.5 | 3.3 |
| Newport News city | 38.0 | 211 | 116 | 1 470 | 902.0 | 68.5 | 727 | 10 894 | 2 431.3 | 233.8 | 273 | 2 884 | 374.2 | 84.2 |
| Norfolk city | 2.4 | 10 | 250 | 8 577 | 3 280.4 | 247.2 | 975 | 13 764 | 2 724.1 | 293.5 | 324 | 2 898 | 385.8 | 98.3 |
| Norton city | 0.9 | 242 | 8 | 54 | 94.2 | 2.5 | 61 | 886 | 283.8 | 20.0 | 9 | 15 | 3.8 | 0.6 |
| Petersburg city | 0.0 | 0 | 29 | 647 | 356.1 | 19.0 | 155 | 1 569 | 324.2 | 37.5 | 36 | 192 | 21.4 | 4.6 |
| Poquoson city | 0.0 | 0 | 4 | D | D | D | 23 | 331 | 54.7 | 5.5 | 14 | 34 | 4.6 | 0.7 |
| Portsmouth city | 19.2 | 191 | 48 | 611 | 173.6 | 27.4 | 296 | 3 428 | 682.1 | 75.7 | 93 | 383 | 48.6 | 8.5 |
| Radford city | 2.3 | 156 | 9 | 57 | 30.3 | 2.3 | 47 | 575 | 109.7 | 11.7 | 24 | 90 | 10.6 | 2.3 |
| Richmond city | 225.0 | 1 161 | 289 | 4 408 | 2 843.3 | 231.1 | 883 | 9 029 | 1 922.8 | 211.6 | 302 | 2 361 | 636.4 | 126.2 |
| Roanoke city | 5.6 | 60 | 198 | 3 098 | 2 233.6 | 130.4 | 588 | 9 765 | 2 039.8 | 215.4 | 161 | 1 274 | 188.6 | 33.5 |
| Salem city | 3.9 | 158 | 65 | 1 074 | 621.2 | 54.0 | 156 | 2 163 | 537.8 | 50.3 | 40 | 210 | 31.9 | 5.2 |
| Staunton city | 0.1 | 6 | 20 | 238 | 68.3 | 7.3 | 165 | 2 026 | 447.5 | 43.9 | 45 | 222 | 23.9 | 8.0 |
| Suffolk city | 98.7 | 1 249 | 50 | 1 105 | 715.8 | 55.7 | 228 | 3 174 | 820.3 | 70.4 | 74 | 287 | 44.5 | 10.6 |
| Virginia Beach city | 4.1 | 9 | 374 | 5 069 | 2 835.1 | 207.4 | 1 625 | 25 639 | 5 579.9 | 568.5 | 717 | 6 190 | 830.7 | 197.8 |
| Waynesboro city | 7.1 | 334 | 17 | 327 | 113.2 | 15.8 | 127 | 1 842 | 386.6 | 38.7 | 36 | 111 | 11.4 | 2.3 |
| Williamsburg city | 1.7 | 144 | 4 | D | D | D | 114 | 1 913 | 323.0 | 39.5 | 28 | 150 | 49.1 | 5.4 |
| Winchester city | 0.2 | 6 | 30 | D | D | D | 307 | 4 695 | 998.7 | 101.1 | 76 | 329 | 63.3 | 12.0 |
| WASHINGTON | 5 637.1 | 897 | 8 181 | 111 294 | 76 791.0 | 5 557.6 | 23 075 | 328 053 | 92 968.5 | 8 585.3 | 10 480 | 51 196 | 10 467.3 | 1 818.7 |
| Adams | 158.3 | 9 420 | 32 | 530 | 574.2 | 19.1 | 60 | 587 | 144.8 | 12.0 | 12 | D | D | D |
| Asotin | 5.2 | 245 | 12 | D | D | D | 57 | 764 | 208.9 | 20.6 | 24 | 81 | 6.7 | 1.2 |
| Benton | 842.6 | 5 334 | 103 | 1 062 | 755.4 | 42.6 | 579 | 8 702 | 2 122.0 | 205.5 | 211 | 1 020 | 197.8 | 30.5 |
| Chelan | 91.1 | 1 306 | 98 | 2 025 | 788.3 | 71.4 | 399 | 4 401 | 1 022.0 | 107.1 | 122 | 535 | 71.6 | 13.5 |
| Clallam | 20.2 | 290 | 53 | D | D | D | 306 | 3 678 | 838.3 | 92.9 | 118 | 356 | 39.9 | 8.4 |
| Clark | 165.5 | 410 | 398 | 3 778 | 4 238.1 | 213.4 | 1 036 | 16 868 | 4 170.0 | 401.5 | 509 | 2 600 | 386.6 | 88.1 |
| Columbia | 4.7 | 1 129 | 20 | 48 | 30.8 | 1.4 | 23 | 136 | 28.9 | 2.3 | 5 | 5 | 0.8 | 0.1 |
| Cowlitz | 147.8 | 1 518 | 78 | 1 136 | 1 415.8 | 51.8 | 360 | 5 018 | 1 219.7 | 117.1 | 117 | 442 | 54.3 | 9.7 |
| Douglas | 39.0 | 1 114 | 39 | 469 | 127.4 | 13.6 | 106 | 1 583 | 413.6 | 38.3 | 24 | 93 | 14.8 | 2.1 |
| Ferry | 6.0 | 794 | 1 | D | D | D | 25 | 213 | 35.0 | 3.7 | 3 | D | D | D |
| Franklin | 551.9 | 8 759 | 100 | 1 291 | 1 028.0 | 51.2 | 183 | 2 775 | 788.5 | 74.8 | 59 | 256 | 46.9 | 6.7 |
| Garfield | 1.2 | 520 | 8 | 120 | 70.5 | 3.7 | 12 | 56 | 11.7 | 1.0 | NA | NA | NA | NA |
| Grant | 1 161.2 | 14 296 | 107 | 1 415 | 599.6 | 49.9 | 306 | 3 137 | 777.5 | 73.9 | 88 | 180 | 29.6 | 3.9 |
| Grays Harbor | 67.7 | 955 | 54 | D | D | D | 293 | 3 214 | 768.6 | 79.2 | 93 | 332 | 35.6 | 7.1 |
| Island | 9.5 | 120 | 42 | D | D | D | 246 | 2 411 | 519.9 | 58.4 | 123 | 349 | 51.4 | 8.4 |
| Jefferson | 22.6 | 790 | 22 | 119 | 51.1 | 4.9 | 159 | 1 201 | 210.9 | 24.7 | 55 | 159 | 21.5 | 3.2 |
| King | 227.9 | 127 | 3 444 | 53 288 | 41 042.7 | 3 092.0 | 6 976 | 106 600 | 37 153.9 | 2 985.0 | 4 090 | 24 282 | 5 961.1 | 1 049.6 |
| Kitsap | 28.0 | 116 | 150 | 1 011 | 553.1 | 41.7 | 840 | 11 918 | 2 936.2 | 301.3 | 392 | 1 332 | 224.2 | 37.3 |
| Kittitas | 280.8 | 7 622 | 37 | D | D | D | 168 | 1 817 | 472.7 | 41.0 | 63 | 240 | 26.7 | 5.2 |
| Klickitat | 40.6 | 2 044 | 14 | 91 | 25.8 | 2.8 | 55 | 370 | 65.7 | 6.6 | 21 | 37 | 5.4 | 0.7 |
| Lewis | 47.1 | 651 | 71 | D | D | D | 355 | 3 853 | 910.6 | 92.6 | 86 | 380 | 40.6 | 8.8 |
| Lincoln | 36.8 | 3 547 | 40 | 160 | 133.2 | 6.7 | 48 | 292 | 91.6 | 8.0 | 9 | 11 | 1.8 | 0.2 |
| Mason | 19.5 | 359 | 33 | D | D | D | 153 | 1 846 | 420.2 | 44.5 | 58 | 299 | 32.0 | 6.7 |
| Okanogan | 92.6 | 2 328 | 40 | 590 | 224.4 | 15.7 | 205 | 1 780 | 417.2 | 39.9 | 59 | 143 | 15.9 | 2.6 |
| Pacific | 7.6 | 351 | 7 | D | D | D | 116 | 620 | 114.5 | 14.8 | 27 | 82 | 7.2 | 1.4 |
| Pend Oreille | 4.3 | 340 | 5 | 6 | 1.7 | 0.2 | 38 | 296 | 66.6 | 5.3 | 13 | D | D | D |
| Pierce | 198.5 | 263 | 704 | 11 348 | 6 090.5 | 468.5 | 2 306 | 35 815 | 9 741.6 | 952.3 | 1 094 | 5 695 | 970.6 | 161.2 |
| San Juan | 1.9 | 127 | 19 | D | D | D | 119 | 777 | 155.3 | 21.6 | 71 | 148 | 20.8 | 3.2 |
| Skagit | 44.2 | 390 | 124 | 1 557 | 698.0 | 61.2 | 616 | 7 788 | 2 134.8 | 200.4 | 181 | 653 | 105.5 | 18.3 |
| Skamania | 9.7 | 905 | 4 | 7 | 2.4 | 0.3 | 22 | 161 | 26.0 | 2.6 | 8 | 8 | 1.3 | 0.2 |
| Snohomish | 127.7 | 195 | 783 | 7 873 | 6 708.4 | 400.3 | 2 267 | 34 313 | 9 057.1 | 930.4 | 1 003 | 3 977 | 766.8 | 134.1 |
| Spokane | 191.7 | 435 | 655 | 9 341 | 5 354.3 | 394.8 | 1 712 | 26 853 | 6 741.2 | 697.7 | 662 | 3 426 | 630.3 | 105.1 |
| Stevens | 29.6 | 705 | 25 | 205 | 47.2 | 5.6 | 137 | 1 230 | 281.6 | 27.9 | 36 | 125 | 16.6 | 2.3 |
| Thurston | 46.2 | 202 | 177 | 1 766 | 1 003.4 | 78.8 | 822 | 12 136 | 3 103.0 | 313.2 | 323 | 1 234 | 238.8 | 31.6 |
| Wahkiakum | 1.3 | 333 | NA | NA | NA | NA | 14 | 50 | 11.7 | 0.9 | 5 | D | D | D |
| Walla Walla | 156.4 | 2 717 | 55 | 555 | 257.5 | 18.8 | 212 | 2 551 | 534.1 | 59.7 | 64 | 215 | 26.3 | 5.3 |
| Whatcom | 81.3 | 443 | 306 | 3 294 | 1 373.6 | 144.5 | 851 | 11 100 | 2 556.0 | 263.5 | 352 | 1 254 | 240.2 | 33.3 |
| Whitman | 10.8 | 269 | 70 | 520 | 388.9 | 21.4 | 113 | 1 243 | 271.1 | 23.6 | 45 | 205 | 19.6 | 3.4 |
| Yakima | 658.3 | 2 843 | 251 | D | D | D | 780 | 9 900 | 2 425.6 | 239.5 | 255 | 977 | 151.6 | 23.7 |
| WEST VIRGINIA | 4 811.8 | 2 648 | 1 372 | 16 790 | 11 036.5 | 656.0 | 7 047 | 92 227 | 20 538.8 | 1 776.5 | 1 586 | 7 055 | 1 171.0 | 175.3 |
| Barbour | 1.9 | 118 | 7 | D | D | D | 43 | 340 | 75.0 | 5.8 | 4 | 8 | 1.2 | 0.2 |
| Berkeley | 19.7 | 211 | 42 | 878 | 573.5 | 42.7 | 278 | 3 536 | 886.4 | 74.2 | 93 | 339 | 40.3 | 6.8 |
| Boone | 5.1 | 200 | 10 | D | D | D | 81 | 959 | 190.6 | 16.3 | 8 | 16 | 1.8 | 0.4 |
| Braxton | 8.6 | 580 | 10 | 120 | 57.4 | 4.9 | 83 | 687 | 219.6 | 14.2 | 6 | 29 | 3.2 | 0.7 |

1. Merchant wholesalers, except manufacturers' sales branches and offices.  2. Employer establishments.

# Table B. States and Counties — Professional Services, Manufacturing, and Accommodation and Food Services

| STATE County | Professional, scientific, and technical services,[1] 2007 | | | | Manufacturing, 2007 | | | | Accommodation and food services, 2007 | | | |
|---|---|---|---|---|---|---|---|---|---|---|---|---|
| | Number of establish-ments | Number of employees | Receipts (mil dol) | Annual payroll (mil dol) | Number of establish-ments | Number of employees | Receipts (mil dol) | Annual payroll (mil dol) | Number of establish-ments | Number of employees | Sales (mil dol) | Annual payroll (mil dol) |
| | 147 | 148 | 149 | 150 | 151 | 152 | 153 | 154 | 155 | 156 | 157 | 158 |
| VIRGINIA—Cont'd | | | | | | | | | | | | |
| Manassas Park city | 19 | D | D | D | NA | NA | NA | NA | 14 | 91 | 5.3 | 1.6 |
| Martinsville city | 45 | 200 | 16.5 | 8.0 | 24 | 1 157 | 201.4 | 36.7 | 51 | 875 | 28.7 | 7.9 |
| Newport News city | 345 | D | D | D | 107 | 24 155 | 4 702.7 | 1 216.0 | 384 | 7 660 | 329.1 | 89.9 |
| Norfolk city | 653 | D | D | D | 166 | 7 448 | 1 280.8 | 300.0 | 551 | 11 667 | 505.0 | 140.2 |
| Norton city | 22 | D | D | D | 9 | D | D | D | 25 | 464 | 17.3 | 4.9 |
| Petersburg city | 35 | D | D | D | 42 | 2 114 | 595.9 | 102.1 | 70 | 864 | 36.6 | 9.7 |
| Poquoson city | 21 | 95 | 6.7 | 2.2 | NA | NA | NA | NA | 19 | 290 | 9.2 | 2.6 |
| Portsmouth city | 144 | D | D | D | 63 | 2 360 | 652.9 | 105.2 | 169 | 2 513 | 106.2 | 28.8 |
| Radford city | 28 | D | D | D | 25 | 1 610 | D | 68.6 | 39 | 923 | 36.2 | 8.8 |
| Richmond city | 826 | 10 582 | 1 682.7 | 785.0 | 224 | 9 341 | 10 192.1 | 545.8 | 547 | 10 136 | 476.8 | 143.5 |
| Roanoke city | 321 | D | D | D | 115 | 4 544 | 1 582.4 | 182.7 | 294 | 6 162 | 267.2 | 83.3 |
| Salem city | 74 | D | D | D | 69 | 3 736 | 984.0 | 170.7 | 87 | 1 897 | 67.9 | 20.7 |
| Staunton city | 60 | 342 | 33.5 | 14.2 | 27 | 546 | 101.4 | 20.7 | 85 | 1 706 | 65.5 | 20.7 |
| Suffolk city | 122 | D | D | D | 48 | 2 362 | 1 307.8 | 109.7 | 121 | 1 981 | 72.8 | 20.2 |
| Virginia Beach city | 1 310 | D | D | D | 243 | 6 544 | 1 806.5 | 236.9 | 1 134 | 21 694 | 1 074.2 | 294.9 |
| Waynesboro city | 43 | D | D | D | 35 | 2 218 | 759.9 | 86.0 | 64 | 1 148 | 48.9 | 13.5 |
| Williamsburg city | 34 | 168 | 13.7 | 6.8 | NA | NA | NA | NA | 134 | 3 984 | 239.6 | 72.7 |
| Winchester city | 147 | D | D | D | 30 | D | D | D | 123 | 2 343 | 104.6 | 29.5 |
| WASHINGTON | 19 242 | 150 367 | 23 394.7 | 9 778.0 | 7 650 | 269 851 | 112 053.3 | 13 274.5 | 15 893 | 233 235 | 12 389.4 | 3 618.1 |
| Adams | 15 | D | D | D | 13 | 1 042 | 442.2 | D | 29 | 322 | 14.8 | 4.1 |
| Asotin | 31 | D | D | D | NA | NA | NA | NA | 39 | 591 | 23.0 | 7.4 |
| Benton | 397 | D | D | D | 139 | 3 740 | D | 166.4 | 338 | 5 248 | 238.0 | 69.6 |
| Chelan | 190 | D | D | D | 103 | 1 870 | D | D | 271 | 3 245 | 171.2 | 51.0 |
| Clallam | 163 | D | D | D | 76 | 1 491 | 470.4 | 72.7 | 227 | 2 376 | 105.7 | 31.6 |
| Clark | 1 066 | D | D | D | 457 | 14 492 | D | D | 701 | 10 681 | 493.3 | 143.2 |
| Columbia | 8 | D | D | D | NA | NA | NA | NA | 13 | 67 | 2.7 | 0.5 |
| Cowlitz | 150 | D | D | D | 128 | 7 001 | 2 914.7 | 356.7 | 215 | 2 782 | 124.0 | 36.2 |
| Douglas | 36 | D | D | D | NA | NA | NA | NA | 56 | 835 | 30.4 | 9.4 |
| Ferry | 11 | D | D | D | NA | NA | NA | NA | 13 | 67 | 2.1 | 0.5 |
| Franklin | 73 | D | D | D | 51 | 2 235 | D | 75.3 | 109 | 1 386 | 67.7 | 19.5 |
| Garfield | 3 | D | D | D | NA | NA | NA | NA | 3 | 19 | 0.5 | 0.1 |
| Grant | 113 | 460 | 43.7 | 14.7 | 68 | 3 528 | 993.0 | 139.9 | 187 | 1 942 | 95.8 | 27.4 |
| Grays Harbor | 94 | D | D | D | 84 | 3 158 | 1 056.9 | 132.5 | 238 | 2 234 | 111.0 | 31.7 |
| Island | 191 | D | D | D | 51 | 710 | D | 27.9 | 176 | 1 980 | 77.6 | 22.8 |
| Jefferson | 95 | D | D | D | 82 | 770 | 209.5 | 33.6 | 114 | 1 110 | 48.7 | 15.1 |
| King | 9 050 | D | D | D | 2 485 | 95 136 | 37 390.8 | 5 067.7 | 5 516 | 90 130 | 5 478.9 | 1 611.9 |
| Kitsap | 716 | D | D | D | 163 | 2 154 | D | 78.3 | 505 | 7 483 | 392.8 | 117.4 |
| Kittitas | 73 | D | D | D | 26 | 892 | 81.1 | 21.8 | 160 | 2 165 | 84.4 | 28.0 |
| Klickitat | 55 | D | D | D | 31 | 740 | D | 37.2 | 51 | 332 | 16.1 | 4.8 |
| Lewis | 123 | D | D | D | 132 | 3 757 | 1 109.1 | 153.6 | 192 | 2 040 | 96.2 | 26.6 |
| Lincoln | 13 | 86 | 7.6 | 4.3 | NA | NA | NA | NA | 24 | 88 | 4.0 | 1.0 |
| Mason | 76 | D | D | D | 57 | 1 695 | D | 59.0 | 111 | 1 684 | 115.4 | 33.9 |
| Okanogan | 74 | D | D | D | NA | NA | NA | NA | 128 | 1 122 | 49.0 | 14.5 |
| Pacific | 37 | 131 | 11.2 | 4.0 | 35 | 941 | 138.7 | 24.5 | 114 | 737 | 37.2 | 8.8 |
| Pend Oreille | 16 | 72 | 6.7 | 2.5 | 14 | 606 | D | D | 32 | 192 | 9.2 | 2.5 |
| Pierce | 1 386 | D | D | D | 668 | 20 326 | 4 958.6 | 894.2 | 1 578 | 24 076 | 1 172.5 | 332.7 |
| San Juan | 112 | D | D | D | NA | NA | NA | NA | 97 | 735 | 63.3 | 17.9 |
| Skagit | 305 | D | D | D | 205 | 6 387 | 8 918.2 | 294.5 | 347 | 4 734 | 251.0 | 74.1 |
| Skamania | 25 | D | D | D | NA | NA | NA | NA | 24 | 644 | 28.5 | 12.5 |
| Snohomish | 1 503 | D | D | D | 871 | 50 214 | 22 552.3 | 2 847.5 | 1 521 | 19 961 | 1 049.8 | 294.9 |
| Spokane | 1 231 | 8 631 | 1 157.2 | 432.4 | 589 | 17 412 | 3 895.4 | 730.7 | 993 | 17 046 | 780.2 | 232.2 |
| Stevens | 57 | 180 | 17.0 | 6.4 | 46 | 1 374 | 383.6 | 52.6 | 89 | 689 | 27.7 | 7.6 |
| Thurston | 598 | D | D | D | 189 | 3 118 | 870.1 | 120.7 | 497 | 7 612 | 346.7 | 102.7 |
| Wahkiakum | 6 | D | D | D | NA | NA | NA | NA | 12 | 60 | 1.8 | 0.7 |
| Walla Walla | 105 | D | D | D | 114 | 3 094 | 2 155.5 | 138.4 | 120 | 1 723 | 75.8 | 22.9 |
| Whatcom | 670 | 3 562 | 419.2 | 163.4 | 334 | 10 165 | 11 809.7 | 467.2 | 505 | 8 461 | 407.9 | 116.2 |
| Whitman | 55 | 246 | 20.9 | 7.6 | 27 | 1 248 | D | D | 121 | 1 349 | 49.0 | 13.5 |
| Yakima | 320 | D | D | D | 255 | 8 696 | 2 686.1 | 304.4 | 427 | 5 287 | 245.6 | 70.8 |
| WEST VIRGINIA | 2 906 | 20 766 | 2 341.1 | 857.5 | 1 413 | 59 981 | 25 080.6 | 2 645.8 | 3 650 | 61 711 | 2 553.3 | 712.8 |
| Barbour | 19 | 85 | 7.0 | 2.5 | NA | NA | NA | NA | 25 | 289 | 9.9 | 2.8 |
| Berkeley | 131 | D | D | D | 45 | D | D | D | 179 | 2 777 | 156.4 | 35.9 |
| Boone | 19 | D | D | D | NA | NA | NA | NA | 24 | 349 | 13.2 | 3.8 |
| Braxton | 12 | 39 | 2.6 | 0.9 | NA | NA | NA | NA | 37 | 495 | 16.8 | 4.8 |

1. Establishment subject to federal tax.

# Table B. States and Counties — Health Care and Social Assistance, Other Services, and Federal Funds

| STATE County | Health care and social assistance, 2007 | | | | Other services, 2007 | | | | Federal funds and grants, 2009–2010 Expenditures (mil dol) | | | |
|---|---|---|---|---|---|---|---|---|---|---|---|---|
| | | | | | | | | | | Direct payments for individuals[1] | | |
| | Number of establishments | Number of employees | Receipts (mil dol) | Annual payroll (mil dol) | Number of establishments | Number of employees | Receipts (mil dol) | Annual payroll (mil dol) | Total | Social Security and government retirement | Medicare | Food Stamps and Supplemental Security Income |
| | 159 | 160 | 161 | 162 | 163 | 164 | 165 | 166 | 167 | 168 | 169 | 170 |
| VIRGINIA—Cont'd | | | | | | | | | | | | |
| Manassas Park city | 3 | D | D | D | 45 | 223 | 25.0 | 7.7 | 36.4 | 5.8 | 0.3 | 2.0 |
| Martinsville city | 120 | 1 182 | 115.8 | 42.8 | 50 | 190 | 16.9 | 3.4 | 230.9 | 121.8 | 47.9 | 10.5 |
| Newport News city | 384 | 12 477 | 1 114.9 | 486.6 | 316 | 2 165 | 161.4 | 52.0 | 5 698.8 | 638.8 | 215.2 | 93.0 |
| Norfolk city | 543 | 19 046 | 2 097.9 | 833.8 | 448 | 3 670 | 470.1 | 117.0 | 6 285.5 | 706.2 | 351.9 | 157.6 |
| Norton city | 41 | 1 305 | 129.3 | 51.7 | 21 | 108 | 5.2 | 3.5 | 70.9 | 25.3 | 13.8 | 4.2 |
| Petersburg city | 121 | 3 782 | 324.7 | 136.8 | 85 | 562 | 46.0 | 13.3 | 449.9 | 164.7 | 105.0 | 24.8 |
| Poquoson city | 13 | D | D | D | 26 | D | D | D | 62.0 | 36.7 | 7.8 | 0.7 |
| Portsmouth city | 218 | 7 247 | 635.9 | 271.9 | 175 | 1 535 | 122.3 | 41.0 | 2 334.9 | 389.4 | 202.1 | 66.8 |
| Radford city | 42 | 520 | 36.8 | 16.3 | 25 | D | D | D | 212.3 | 48.3 | 22.9 | 4.7 |
| Richmond city | 641 | 24 371 | 2 530.9 | 1 052.8 | 577 | 4 024 | 535.3 | 122.0 | 6 277.3 | 1 306.2 | 542.8 | 187.8 |
| Roanoke city | 318 | 11 059 | 1 301.2 | 448.7 | 271 | 2 009 | 155.7 | 45.9 | 1 295.2 | 518.6 | 236.7 | 53.8 |
| Salem city | 98 | 5 127 | 596.1 | 259.9 | 103 | 657 | 37.9 | 15.0 | 381.7 | 136.2 | 50.7 | 3.2 |
| Staunton city | 97 | 2 054 | 140.2 | 69.9 | 68 | 387 | 26.9 | 8.9 | 279.5 | 137.1 | 60.4 | 7.6 |
| Suffolk city | 142 | 3 165 | 347.0 | 128.6 | 97 | 586 | 116.2 | 11.4 | 943.0 | 329.4 | 91.9 | 31.4 |
| Virginia Beach city | 933 | 15 592 | 1 547.4 | 617.9 | 897 | 5 832 | 633.2 | 125.9 | 5 534.8 | 1 712.0 | 327.6 | 96.1 |
| Waynesboro city | 52 | 715 | 44.0 | 16.4 | 60 | 397 | 38.4 | 11.5 | 193.9 | 108.1 | 40.5 | 9.2 |
| Williamsburg city | 46 | 1 580 | 118.5 | 77.4 | 26 | 335 | 65.0 | 11.7 | 347.1 | 193.8 | 60.4 | 1.4 |
| Winchester city | 236 | 5 527 | 637.1 | 278.1 | 86 | 576 | 43.9 | 14.6 | 386.6 | 158.4 | 51.1 | 6.9 |
| WASHINGTON | 18 474 | 345 161 | 35 886.4 | 14 349.6 | 12 324 | 71 213 | 8 920.8 | 2 030.0 | 70 437.5 | 19 564.4 | 6 975.9 | 2 305.3 |
| Adams | 26 | 636 | 59.9 | 25.3 | 25 | 85 | 6.3 | 1.3 | 161.7 | 33.8 | 15.9 | 9.8 |
| Asotin | 50 | 835 | 84.3 | 26.7 | 30 | 123 | 8.2 | 2.1 | 179.2 | 90.7 | 34.1 | 13.6 |
| Benton | 498 | 8 313 | 812.5 | 315.2 | 238 | 1 300 | 103.9 | 30.9 | 4 220.9 | 525.1 | 137.5 | 65.7 |
| Chelan | 208 | D | D | D | 165 | 663 | 60.2 | 14.1 | 564.2 | 243.0 | 79.6 | 26.9 |
| Clallam | 258 | 3 757 | 291.6 | 122.1 | 155 | 672 | 50.2 | 15.5 | 783.1 | 385.4 | 127.0 | 24.3 |
| Clark | 933 | D | D | D | 635 | 3 111 | 362.0 | 80.8 | 2 433.2 | 1 205.0 | 317.1 | 128.6 |
| Columbia | 12 | 183 | 11.9 | 5.6 | 14 | 56 | 7.1 | 2.0 | 58.5 | 19.7 | 7.6 | 2.0 |
| Cowlitz | 249 | 5 122 | 487.3 | 198.6 | 146 | 894 | 75.9 | 22.8 | 779.0 | 356.7 | 134.8 | 53.8 |
| Douglas | 53 | D | D | D | 39 | 143 | 9.6 | 2.5 | 236.3 | 98.4 | 49.1 | 7.6 |
| Ferry | 15 | D | D | D | 7 | D | D | D | 64.9 | 29.9 | 7.7 | 4.6 |
| Franklin | 115 | 1 477 | 140.0 | 59.3 | 87 | 508 | 47.4 | 13.6 | 393.2 | 135.5 | 48.6 | 29.5 |
| Garfield | 6 | D | D | D | 1 | D | D | D | 42.4 | 13.5 | 4.9 | 1.5 |
| Grant | 133 | 2 721 | 236.8 | 99.9 | 128 | 526 | 36.1 | 9.4 | 580.7 | 225.6 | 77.4 | 31.3 |
| Grays Harbor | 205 | 2 691 | 236.1 | 90.8 | 121 | 575 | 38.2 | 10.5 | 639.6 | 279.2 | 133.5 | 46.3 |
| Island | 188 | 2 273 | 176.6 | 76.6 | 99 | 432 | 33.2 | 10.7 | 821.9 | 393.9 | 69.8 | 14.4 |
| Jefferson | 104 | 1 284 | 103.5 | 44.2 | 93 | 342 | 27.7 | 8.7 | 286.8 | 168.4 | 48.3 | 9.6 |
| King | 6 535 | 122 486 | 14 324.2 | 5 614.7 | 4 508 | 28 932 | 5 137.7 | 935.6 | 18 153.0 | 4 438.3 | 2 112.0 | 576.6 |
| Kitsap | 659 | 12 424 | 1 169.6 | 482.9 | 392 | 2 004 | 157.5 | 48.0 | 4 004.4 | 1 088.8 | 231.7 | 79.6 |
| Kittitas | 98 | 1 407 | 99.1 | 41.4 | 77 | 327 | 26.7 | 7.3 | 239.4 | 105.7 | 38.4 | 9.4 |
| Klickitat | 35 | 575 | 45.3 | 20.5 | 33 | 116 | 8.8 | 2.2 | 237.9 | 86.2 | 24.4 | 10.9 |
| Lewis | 178 | 3 000 | 271.4 | 115.9 | 126 | 521 | 44.5 | 11.5 | 649.1 | 302.5 | 124.8 | 37.1 |
| Lincoln | 17 | 443 | 31.8 | 14.3 | 19 | 50 | 5.5 | 1.2 | 158.3 | 54.3 | 19.1 | 3.3 |
| Mason | 101 | 1 611 | 141.5 | 51.2 | 85 | 353 | 23.5 | 7.0 | 465.0 | 275.2 | 82.3 | 26.2 |
| Okanogan | 122 | 1 971 | 133.9 | 59.4 | 77 | 246 | 26.7 | 4.7 | 412.1 | 154.5 | 50.6 | 22.6 |
| Pacific | 50 | 748 | 51.5 | 21.8 | 46 | 149 | 10.8 | 2.7 | 223.2 | 108.0 | 47.2 | 11.4 |
| Pend Oreille | 22 | D | D | D | 14 | 34 | 3.3 | 0.6 | 140.1 | 57.8 | 14.7 | 9.4 |
| Pierce | 1 880 | 42 047 | 4 395.2 | 1 781.3 | 1 301 | 8 493 | 803.1 | 251.2 | 11 944.2 | 2 496.4 | 737.4 | 314.3 |
| San Juan | 62 | 410 | 26.2 | 10.2 | 56 | 172 | 27.7 | 4.6 | 101.5 | 65.2 | 18.3 | 2.0 |
| Skagit | 342 | 6 346 | 614.5 | 241.6 | 237 | 1 158 | 94.1 | 27.6 | 846.6 | 417.2 | 158.3 | 40.4 |
| Skamania | 15 | D | D | D | 10 | 18 | 1.6 | 0.4 | 64.1 | 29.2 | 6.7 | 4.1 |
| Snohomish | 1 656 | 24 552 | 2 423.9 | 980.0 | 1 144 | 6 150 | 523.3 | 170.6 | 3 752.7 | 1 585.6 | 562.4 | 171.4 |
| Spokane | 1 424 | 33 424 | 3 273.7 | 1 325.9 | 863 | 5 436 | 479.1 | 132.2 | 4 074.6 | 1 547.5 | 616.2 | 199.1 |
| Stevens | 84 | 1 452 | 109.5 | 47.3 | 60 | 176 | 15.7 | 4.1 | 346.8 | 162.8 | 46.4 | 17.8 |
| Thurston | 710 | 11 596 | 1 238.4 | 447.6 | 464 | 2 812 | 273.7 | 88.2 | 4 306.4 | 924.1 | 232.8 | 71.1 |
| Wahkiakum | 8 | D | D | D | 4 | D | D | D | 34.0 | 19.2 | 7.8 | 1.1 |
| Walla Walla | 164 | 3 939 | 387.3 | 160.0 | 79 | 454 | 34.6 | 7.9 | 562.1 | 198.9 | 77.2 | 22.3 |
| Whatcom | 636 | 9 730 | 862.9 | 348.7 | 390 | 2 155 | 207.5 | 59.0 | 1 279.8 | 567.6 | 165.5 | 57.7 |
| Whitman | 86 | 1 633 | 127.4 | 53.4 | 59 | 221 | 13.7 | 3.9 | 445.6 | 97.5 | 39.7 | 7.7 |
| Yakima | 537 | 11 636 | 1 119.8 | 441.2 | 297 | 1 767 | 132.9 | 33.9 | 1 822.9 | 574.3 | 269.3 | 140.3 |
| WEST VIRGINIA | 4 860 | 114 663 | 9 874.7 | 3 828.9 | 2 927 | 16 527 | 1 550.2 | 388.3 | 21 510.6 | 7 227.8 | 3 417.0 | 1 000.0 |
| Barbour | 29 | 736 | 36.3 | 14.3 | 14 | 34 | 2.7 | 0.5 | 149.3 | 56.4 | 30.5 | 9.8 |
| Berkeley | 194 | D | D | D | 133 | 643 | 51.0 | 15.1 | 1 012.8 | 347.9 | 86.2 | 23.0 |
| Boone | 41 | 693 | 35.4 | 14.5 | 22 | 145 | 10.4 | 4.2 | 216.3 | 101.2 | 44.6 | 19.0 |
| Braxton | 20 | 918 | 36.1 | 14.3 | 17 | 74 | 8.3 | 2.2 | 138.9 | 49.9 | 22.4 | 10.0 |

1. State totals may include programs not allocated by county.

# Table B. States and Counties — Federal Funds, Residential Construction, and Local Government Finances

| STATE County | Salaries and wages | Defense | Other | Medicaid and other health-related | Nutrition and family welfare | Education | Other | New construction ($1,000) | Number of housing units | Total (mil dol) | Inter-govern-mental (mil dol) | Total (mil dol) | Per capita² (dollars) Total | Property |
|---|---|---|---|---|---|---|---|---|---|---|---|---|---|---|
| | 171 | 172 | 173 | 174 | 175 | 176 | 177 | 178 | 179 | 180 | 181 | 182 | 183 | 184 |
| VIRGINIA—Cont'd | | | | | | | | | | | | | | |
| Manassas Park city............... | 7.5 | 3.2 | 0.5 | 15.0 | 0.6 | 0.8 | 0.0 | 600 | 3 | 54.7 | 20.4 | 29.1 | 2 550 | 2 043 |
| Martinsville city.................... | 8.1 | 0.1 | 1.2 | 24.9 | 1.9 | 2.6 | 3.7 | 884 | 5 | 53.1 | 28.7 | 17.1 | 1 171 | 602 |
| Newport News city................. | 1 284.3 | 3 013.8 | 198.7 | 116.7 | 25.3 | 16.9 | 39.7 | 37 107 | 785 | 777.0 | 333.3 | 301.9 | 1 685 | 1 162 |
| Norfolk city......................... | 2 195.3 | 2 126.5 | 79.0 | 301.4 | 53.1 | 38.9 | 77.8 | 46 348 | 519 | 1 361.6 | 550.3 | 396.5 | 1 682 | 1 005 |
| Norton city.......................... | 8.8 | 0.0 | 0.3 | 7.8 | 4.3 | 0.5 | 5.0 | 371 | 9 | 16.8 | 8.1 | 7.0 | 1 876 | 637 |
| Petersburg city..................... | 11.6 | 0.9 | 5.6 | 75.9 | 7.0 | 9.9 | 20.5 | 1 179 | 10 | 125.8 | 73.7 | 40.3 | 1 227 | 806 |
| Poquoson city...................... | 11.7 | 1.7 | 0.1 | 0.9 | 0.5 | 0.8 | 0.0 | 4 796 | 17 | 42.0 | 18.7 | 18.3 | 1 547 | 1 312 |
| Portsmouth city.................... | 691.9 | 664.0 | 93.6 | 149.4 | 17.1 | 13.6 | 22.9 | 26 995 | 153 | 447.3 | 230.3 | 143.6 | 1 408 | 977 |
| Radford city......................... | 8.8 | 100.7 | 1.6 | 8.3 | 4.0 | 0.7 | 3.0 | 3 497 | 43 | 32.5 | 14.4 | 10.8 | 666 | 393 |
| Richmond city...................... | 586.2 | 48.1 | 139.5 | 677.9 | 167.0 | 545.1 | 1 948.0 | 40 144 | 343 | 1 013.8 | 400.9 | 395.9 | 1 978 | 1 311 |
| Roanoke city........................ | 129.4 | 30.1 | 84.1 | 137.3 | 22.1 | 8.9 | 34.0 | 7 947 | 52 | 425.3 | 194.0 | 166.5 | 1 798 | 1 008 |
| Salem city........................... | 78.3 | 3.9 | 51.3 | 17.2 | 2.1 | 1.6 | 0.1 | 2 525 | 17 | 81.6 | 24.6 | 46.3 | 1 835 | 1 097 |
| Staunton city....................... | 27.7 | 0.1 | 3.9 | 27.1 | 2.2 | 1.5 | 3.1 | 3 282 | 25 | 79.9 | 36.2 | 30.4 | 1 276 | 754 |
| Suffolk city.......................... | 93.7 | 252.5 | 17.0 | 86.1 | 10.0 | 4.4 | 8.9 | 48 746 | 278 | 306.9 | 134.4 | 141.0 | 1 733 | 1 324 |
| Virginia Beach city ............... | 760.4 | 2 086.2 | 150.1 | 73.6 | 32.2 | 31.9 | 59.8 | 153 303 | 1 479 | 1 817.7 | 634.2 | 844.0 | 1 941 | 1 349 |
| Waynesboro city................... | 3.7 | 0.3 | 1.8 | 11.4 | 2.3 | 1.2 | 14.3 | 3 355 | 34 | 56.7 | 24.3 | 26.3 | 1 214 | 675 |
| Williamsburg city.................. | 35.3 | 4.8 | 11.3 | 7.1 | 1.5 | 3.3 | 23.0 | 6 060 | 29 | 48.0 | 11.3 | 30.8 | 2 476 | 841 |
| Winchester city.................... | 117.2 | 3.5 | 14.6 | 22.9 | 1.9 | 2.7 | 4.1 | 7 220 | 32 | 122.6 | 34.6 | 60.7 | 2 360 | 1 154 |
| WASHINGTON................. | 11 538.6 | 5 150.5 | 4 890.3 | 7 161.4 | 1 608.2 | 1 188.1 | 4 767.7 | 4 036 365 | 20 864 | X | X | X | X | X |
| Adams ............................... | 2.4 | 0.0 | 4.0 | 45.0 | 5.7 | 1.0 | 0.5 | 4 178 | 24 | 108.4 | 57.5 | 17.6 | 1 039 | 765 |
| Asotin ............................... | 3.4 | 1.7 | 1.2 | 21.0 | 4.0 | 1.7 | 1.8 | 2 803 | 16 | 62.4 | 36.7 | 14.6 | 692 | 529 |
| Benton .............................. | 74.3 | 15.3 | 3 127.6 | 93.0 | 25.6 | 7.5 | 116.8 | 238 531 | 1 127 | 767.4 | 352.2 | 190.3 | 1 194 | 672 |
| Chelan .............................. | 44.2 | 0.1 | 13.7 | 66.8 | 16.4 | 4.7 | 43.6 | 28 464 | 154 | 323.2 | 121.0 | 99.6 | 1 402 | 840 |
| Clallam.............................. | 50.2 | 20.9 | 61.0 | 52.3 | 13.8 | 6.1 | 19.6 | 27 781 | 154 | 346.1 | 98.8 | 76.9 | 1 091 | 650 |
| Clark................................. | 288.6 | 30.7 | 77.8 | 209.1 | 56.1 | 22.6 | 43.3 | 225 228 | 961 | 1 400.6 | 617.9 | 511.7 | 1 224 | 787 |
| Columbia ........................... | 2.9 | 2.7 | 0.6 | 7.7 | 1.2 | 0.1 | 0.1 | 547 | 4 | 25.6 | 11.0 | 4.2 | 1 065 | 770 |
| Cowlitz.............................. | 46.3 | 17.2 | 6.0 | 92.5 | 19.4 | 18.2 | 16.7 | 22 148 | 113 | 372.1 | 160.5 | 105.3 | 1 048 | 664 |
| Douglas............................. | 8.8 | 15.2 | 0.4 | 18.4 | 6.3 | 1.0 | 1.8 | 17 720 | 92 | 130.6 | 75.7 | 29.8 | 823 | 615 |
| Ferry ................................ | 10.4 | 0.0 | 2.7 | 4.7 | 2.5 | 1.6 | 0.2 | 1 032 | 13 | 35.5 | 24.4 | 4.6 | 620 | 496 |
| Franklin............................. | 48.7 | 20.8 | 12.1 | 37.5 | 17.1 | 5.9 | 6.1 | 127 901 | 570 | 238.2 | 124.3 | 63.4 | 911 | 542 |
| Garfield............................. | 5.2 | 4.5 | 1.1 | 1.2 | 0.6 | 0.1 | 0.0 | 313 | 2 | 11.5 | 7.9 | 2.2 | 1 085 | 847 |
| Grant ................................ | 63.8 | 5.0 | 31.3 | 59.4 | 19.5 | 8.6 | 4.1 | 36 047 | 187 | 453.5 | 194.1 | 84.9 | 1 023 | 700 |
| Grays Harbor....................... | 23.2 | 5.6 | 6.3 | 86.8 | 18.0 | 6.7 | 11.2 | 20 841 | 114 | 296.9 | 142.4 | 87.0 | 1 219 | 714 |
| Island............................... | 199.0 | 95.5 | 2.8 | 19.1 | 9.3 | 6.4 | 3.4 | 33 262 | 164 | 250.9 | 85.7 | 74.3 | 1 370 | 886 |
| Jefferson............................ | 12.9 | 13.7 | 3.1 | 18.5 | 6.6 | 2.2 | 2.3 | 20 367 | 86 | 134.0 | 32.5 | 40.0 | 1 370 | 557 |
| King.................................. | 1 927.4 | 2 723.5 | 828.5 | 3 419.0 | 300.1 | 100.8 | 1 398.9 | 1 217 540 | 6 143 | 10 357.4 | 2 943.2 | 4 126.9 | 2 220 | 1 144 |
| Kitsap............................... | 969.1 | 598.8 | 59.3 | 132.3 | 45.2 | 26.1 | 709.1 | 105 792 | 540 | 945.8 | 465.9 | 310.5 | 1 312 | 828 |
| Kittitas.............................. | 13.4 | 0.2 | 3.1 | 26.7 | 7.4 | 4.4 | 10.1 | 36 699 | 174 | 152.8 | 55.6 | 43.8 | 1 137 | 642 |
| Klickitat............................. | 6.6 | 73.0 | 5.0 | 17.4 | 4.5 | 0.8 | 0.4 | 8 203 | 58 | 114.5 | 43.4 | 20.4 | 1 017 | 682 |
| Lewis................................ | 34.7 | 3.2 | 9.4 | 86.0 | 16.1 | 10.1 | 16.7 | 12 466 | 93 | 249.3 | 118.1 | 74.0 | 1 005 | 609 |
| Lincoln.............................. | 4.6 | 0.0 | 1.8 | 4.2 | 2.1 | 0.4 | 1.0 | 5 880 | 32 | 73.5 | 43.5 | 11.3 | 1 103 | 929 |
| Mason............................... | 6.4 | 1.6 | 3.4 | 32.1 | 11.0 | 4.1 | 14.6 | 26 809 | 134 | 216.0 | 73.1 | 64.2 | 1 138 | 719 |
| Okanogan........................... | 28.4 | 14.8 | 21.4 | 43.3 | 14.5 | 5.8 | 21.7 | 18 277 | 130 | 187.5 | 84.2 | 32.4 | 816 | 550 |
| Pacific.............................. | 11.2 | 0.0 | 2.7 | 22.8 | 5.0 | 1.1 | 11.6 | 6 540 | 111 | 109.0 | 37.8 | 29.6 | 1 377 | 980 |
| Pend Oreille ....................... | 7.2 | 0.2 | 1.4 | 13.9 | 3.2 | 0.6 | 30.4 | 10 602 | 48 | 67.6 | 25.4 | 12.9 | 1 007 | 777 |
| Pierce ............................... | 6 284.9 | 644.9 | 143.8 | 724.3 | 134.3 | 56.9 | 277.0 | 480 753 | 2 566 | 2 957.3 | 1 201.4 | 1 093.9 | 1 415 | 896 |
| San Juan ........................... | 5.0 | 0.4 | 3.5 | 2.1 | 2.0 | 0.2 | 2.0 | 30 259 | 105 | 72.5 | 22.0 | 33.3 | 2 189 | 1 353 |
| Skagit............................... | 29.4 | 19.2 | 34.2 | 69.5 | 23.5 | 15.8 | 19.7 | 35 595 | 179 | 655.4 | 196.6 | 178.4 | 1 533 | 973 |
| Skamania ........................... | 9.0 | 3.7 | 4.2 | 4.6 | 1.9 | 0.2 | 0.1 | 7 219 | 34 | 35.4 | 16.7 | 8.4 | 787 | 556 |
| Snohomish ......................... | 291.6 | 344.3 | 108.3 | 355.8 | 87.9 | 27.3 | 154.9 | 516 204 | 2 521 | 2 605.7 | 907.9 | 921.4 | 1 361 | 841 |
| Spokane ............................ | 486.6 | 237.7 | 134.2 | 482.5 | 91.6 | 32.6 | 129.8 | 257 698 | 1 785 | 1 575.8 | 697.5 | 548.2 | 1 202 | 709 |
| Stevens ............................. | 22.1 | 12.5 | 24.2 | 33.6 | 10.7 | 4.9 | 4.4 | 10 672 | 54 | 129.4 | 80.5 | 31.3 | 749 | 537 |
| Thurston............................ | 122.2 | 119.1 | 24.2 | 287.1 | 340.4 | 673.5 | 1 437.6 | 215 611 | 1 028 | 882.4 | 347.7 | 334.2 | 1 401 | 841 |
| Wahkiakum.......................... | 1.2 | 0.1 | 0.8 | 2.8 | 0.5 | 0.1 | 0.4 | 1 848 | 10 | 30.0 | 18.4 | 3.7 | 914 | 611 |
| Walla Walla ........................ | 80.8 | 16.7 | 39.7 | 48.6 | 13.2 | 5.8 | 6.6 | 25 391 | 202 | 207.3 | 95.1 | 68.6 | 1 189 | 802 |
| Whatcom............................ | 120.9 | 22.1 | 48.4 | 128.8 | 33.0 | 12.1 | 69.1 | 108 013 | 605 | 612.9 | 225.3 | 248.7 | 1 288 | 756 |
| Whitman............................ | 25.8 | 3.2 | 6.4 | 57.8 | 8.5 | 10.8 | 75.8 | 14 811 | 93 | 164.7 | 52.8 | 41.2 | 1 000 | 705 |
| Yakima.............................. | 134.0 | 62.6 | 30.9 | 333.3 | 103.9 | 48.1 | 58.2 | 76 321 | 438 | 808.0 | 483.0 | 196.6 | 844 | 524 |
| WEST VIRGINIA................ | 1 936.4 | 344.6 | 1 437.9 | 2 463.2 | 510.8 | 338.2 | 1 658.0 | 306 401 | 2 220 | X | X | X | X | X |
| Barbour.............................. | 3.5 | 0.1 | 0.8 | 32.5 | 2.8 | 1.4 | 8.5 | 564 | 8 | 36.6 | 20.2 | 6.9 | 445 | 242 |
| Berkeley............................. | 217.2 | 17.7 | 246.7 | 39.4 | 12.0 | 3.7 | 3.8 | 58 990 | 324 | 205.4 | 94.6 | 79.1 | 794 | 638 |
| Boone................................ | 7.3 | 0.0 | 1.3 | 32.1 | 4.4 | 2.1 | 2.2 | 2 211 | 15 | 104.1 | 33.0 | 32.5 | 1 291 | 1 247 |
| Braxton.............................. | 12.0 | 1.6 | 0.8 | 35.5 | 3.5 | 1.6 | 0.9 | 0 | 0 | 31.3 | 18.4 | 5.1 | 347 | 303 |

1. State totals may include programs not allocated by county.   2. Based on the resident population estimated as of July 1 of the year shown.

# Table B. States and Counties — Local Government Finances, Government Employment, and Voting

| | Local government finances, 2007 (cont.) | | | | | | | | | Government employment, 2011 | | | Presidential election,[2] 2012 | | |
| | Direct general expenditure | | | | | | | Debt outstanding | | | | | Percent of vote cast: | | |
| | | | Percent of total for: | | | | | | | | | | | | |
| STATE County | Total (mil dol) | Per capita[1] (dollars) | Education | Health and hospitals | Police protection | Public welfare | Highways | Total (mil dol) | Per capita[1] (dollars) | Federal civilian | Federal military | State and local | Democratic | Republican | All other |
| | 185 | 186 | 187 | 188 | 189 | 190 | 191 | 192 | 193 | 194 | 195 | 196 | 197 | 198 | 199 |
| VIRGINIA—Cont'd | | | | | | | | | | | | | | | |
| Manassas Park city | 60.3 | 5 280 | 65.0 | 0.0 | 6.4 | 6.2 | 1.1 | 151.2 | 13 237 | (3) | (3) | (3) | 59.5 | 39.5 | 1.0 |
| Martinsville city | 56.2 | 3 857 | 47.6 | 0.0 | 6.8 | 3.6 | 5.2 | 25.1 | 1 722 | (4) | (4) | (4) | 63.5 | 35.4 | 1.1 |
| Newport News city | 742.7 | 4 146 | 44.2 | 10.3 | 5.8 | 6.5 | 4.1 | 1 027.6 | 5 736 | 5 351 | 6 985 | 12 718 | 63.9 | 35.3 | 0.8 |
| Norfolk city | 1 408.2 | 5 973 | 38.4 | 4.4 | 4.4 | 5.7 | 3.3 | 1 971.4 | 8 362 | 16 479 | 47 104 | 20 468 | 71.0 | 28.1 | 0.9 |
| Norton city | 17.5 | 4 712 | 43.4 | 0.4 | 8.9 | 8.4 | 9.2 | 10.1 | 2 706 | (5) | (5) | (5) | 49.1 | 49.2 | 1.7 |
| Petersburg city | 124.4 | 3 782 | 45.7 | 0.9 | 12.1 | 6.5 | 3.5 | 86.6 | 2 634 | (6) | (6) | (6) | 88.6 | 10.2 | 1.2 |
| Poquoson city | 38.7 | 3 261 | 56.6 | 0.8 | 6.0 | 1.3 | 4.5 | 51.7 | 4 361 | (7) | (7) | (7) | 24.7 | 74.0 | 1.2 |
| Portsmouth city | 423.3 | 4 151 | 40.6 | 2.6 | 6.6 | 6.5 | 1.4 | 473.9 | 4 647 | 12 384 | 5 988 | 6 237 | 69.3 | 30.0 | 0.8 |
| Radford city | 32.4 | 2 009 | 44.6 | 0.7 | 10.3 | 1.5 | 6.6 | 11.2 | 697 | (8) | (8) | (8) | 54.0 | 44.5 | 1.5 |
| Richmond city | 1 028.4 | 5 139 | 31.1 | 5.0 | 10.9 | 7.3 | 3.8 | 1 724.5 | 8 617 | 4 868 | 1 273 | 37 946 | 79.1 | 20.0 | 0.9 |
| Roanoke city | 423.6 | 4 574 | 39.1 | 0.5 | 4.8 | 9.0 | 3.3 | 394.7 | 4 263 | 1 566 | 325 | 7 020 | 61.2 | 37.8 | 1.1 |
| Salem city | 99.9 | 3 960 | 40.8 | 1.2 | 8.6 | 0.0 | 9.8 | 100.1 | 3 965 | (9) | (9) | (9) | 41.6 | 57.1 | 1.2 |
| Staunton city | 88.5 | 3 711 | 37.0 | 8.4 | 5.9 | 6.7 | 3.5 | 67.4 | 2 827 | (10) | (10) | (10) | 50.6 | 48.4 | 1.1 |
| Suffolk city | 298.4 | 3 669 | 48.6 | 0.4 | 4.5 | 3.5 | 4.9 | 531.1 | 6 531 | 643 | 466 | 4 822 | 56.2 | 43.0 | 0.7 |
| Virginia Beach city | 1 719.3 | 3 955 | 48.5 | 3.5 | 5.0 | 2.4 | 3.5 | 1 697.0 | 3 903 | 5 354 | 20 087 | 22 855 | 49.1 | 49.8 | 1.0 |
| Waynesboro city | 70.2 | 3 242 | 62.2 | 0.9 | 5.4 | 0.0 | 5.8 | 60.0 | 2 771 | (10) | (10) | (10) | 44.1 | 54.3 | 1.6 |
| Williamsburg city | 59.7 | 4 803 | 19.4 | 0.8 | 6.8 | 2.8 | 11.6 | 32.6 | 2 620 | (11) | (11) | (11) | 63.8 | 34.7 | 1.6 |
| Winchester city | 142.5 | 5 536 | 46.2 | 0.4 | 4.6 | 5.2 | 3.4 | 231.0 | 8 978 | (12) | (12) | (12) | 52.0 | 46.7 | 1.3 |
| WASHINGTON | X | X | X | X | X | X | X | X | X | 74 077 | 81 182 | 470 095 | 57.7 | 40.5 | 1.9 |
| Adams | 98.4 | 5 793 | 37.0 | 21.9 | 3.2 | 0.0 | 8.9 | 107.7 | 6 344 | 43 | 56 | 1 516 | 31.9 | 66.3 | 1.7 |
| Asotin | 59.7 | 2 829 | 49.9 | 5.8 | 4.0 | 0.0 | 10.0 | 37.9 | 1 795 | 53 | 65 | 1 140 | 42.3 | 55.7 | 1.9 |
| Benton | 696.0 | 4 366 | 43.8 | 24.4 | 3.7 | 0.0 | 4.7 | 7 452.6 | 46 750 | 820 | 545 | 11 530 | 36.1 | 62.2 | 1.8 |
| Chelan | 275.9 | 3 886 | 44.2 | 12.8 | 4.4 | 0.0 | 5.5 | 1 441.3 | 20 303 | 664 | 217 | 5 928 | 43.1 | 55.1 | 1.8 |
| Clallam | 372.2 | 5 281 | 23.1 | 40.1 | 2.7 | 0.0 | 3.3 | 168.1 | 2 386 | 475 | 553 | 6 726 | 50.5 | 47.2 | 2.2 |
| Clark | 1 361.4 | 3 256 | 49.4 | 3.4 | 4.1 | 0.4 | 6.1 | 2 008.5 | 4 804 | 3 097 | 1 317 | 21 010 | 52.2 | 46.1 | 1.7 |
| Columbia | 27.0 | 6 770 | 21.2 | 43.5 | 4.6 | 0.0 | 9.8 | 31.0 | 7 765 | 65 | 12 | 393 | 30.8 | 67.3 | 1.9 |
| Cowlitz | 352.0 | 3 503 | 42.9 | 4.2 | 5.1 | 0.0 | 6.6 | 638.1 | 6 351 | 233 | 303 | 5 466 | 54.4 | 43.2 | 2.4 |
| Douglas | 108.7 | 3 004 | 57.3 | 6.3 | 4.4 | 0.0 | 12.9 | 301.5 | 8 335 | 233 | 115 | 1 910 | 38.5 | 59.8 | 1.7 |
| Ferry | 37.2 | 5 043 | 32.7 | 34.6 | 2.4 | 0.3 | 10.3 | 6.3 | 859 | 168 | 23 | 793 | 41.9 | 54.7 | 3.4 |
| Franklin | 230.6 | 3 314 | 55.6 | 1.0 | 3.8 | 0.0 | 6.7 | 243.2 | 3 496 | 491 | 246 | 5 418 | 37.4 | 61.1 | 1.5 |
| Garfield | 11.1 | 5 398 | 36.5 | 5.2 | 6.8 | 0.0 | 16.2 | 5.2 | 2 546 | 123 | 0 | 362 | 28.0 | 70.5 | 1.5 |
| Grant | 406.4 | 4 894 | 38.1 | 25.7 | 3.2 | 0.6 | 5.3 | 1 439.4 | 17 332 | 680 | 270 | 7 185 | 35.0 | 62.5 | 2.5 |
| Grays Harbor | 284.7 | 3 992 | 48.4 | 6.6 | 5.1 | 0.0 | 6.0 | 341.5 | 4 787 | 219 | 252 | 6 029 | 56.0 | 41.5 | 2.5 |
| Island | 233.4 | 2 870 | 43.4 | 23.2 | 3.8 | 0.0 | 5.2 | 411.2 | 5 056 | 1 409 | 6 270 | 3 234 | 52.3 | 46.1 | 1.6 |
| Jefferson | 129.5 | 4 433 | 22.4 | 37.1 | 3.2 | 0.0 | 4.4 | 142.2 | 4 871 | 182 | 100 | 1 965 | 66.3 | 31.7 | 2.0 |
| King | 9 655.6 | 5 193 | 27.8 | 11.0 | 5.0 | 0.8 | 4.4 | 18 860.4 | 10 144 | 21 221 | 7 188 | 147 224 | 70.3 | 28.2 | 1.5 |
| Kitsap | 934.1 | 3 946 | 41.1 | 3.4 | 4.0 | 0.0 | 4.0 | 820.7 | 3 467 | 16 373 | 10 904 | 13 072 | 55.2 | 42.9 | 1.9 |
| Kittitas | 145.4 | 3 772 | 30.8 | 27.5 | 4.5 | 0.0 | 8.0 | 110.5 | 2 867 | 156 | 133 | 4 645 | 44.9 | 53.0 | 2.1 |
| Klickitat | 106.2 | 5 286 | 33.8 | 30.7 | 3.8 | 0.0 | 8.9 | 254.9 | 12 683 | 109 | 61 | 1 666 | 48.8 | 48.6 | 2.5 |
| Lewis | 265.1 | 3 600 | 42.6 | 7.1 | 4.3 | 0.0 | 6.6 | 322.2 | 4 375 | 230 | 223 | 4 699 | 39.3 | 58.4 | 2.3 |
| Lincoln | 69.4 | 6 769 | 37.1 | 33.2 | 3.2 | 0.0 | 9.0 | 19.9 | 1 939 | 72 | 31 | 1 270 | 34.0 | 63.6 | 2.4 |
| Mason | 201.1 | 3 566 | 41.5 | 24.1 | 3.5 | 0.0 | 7.3 | 117.9 | 2 090 | 72 | 180 | 5 248 | 53.2 | 44.5 | 2.3 |
| Okanogan | 189.8 | 4 787 | 44.0 | 24.8 | 3.7 | 0.2 | 4.8 | 92.0 | 2 320 | 490 | 122 | 4 217 | 45.1 | 52.2 | 2.7 |
| Pacific | 105.5 | 4 911 | 35.9 | 29.1 | 3.7 | 0.0 | 5.7 | 88.5 | 4 116 | 64 | 169 | 1 767 | 55.7 | 41.6 | 2.6 |
| Pend Oreille | 61.5 | 4 821 | 28.5 | 32.2 | 3.6 | 0.0 | 9.5 | 42.7 | 3 350 | 118 | 38 | 1 380 | 39.1 | 56.7 | 4.2 |
| Pierce | 3 026.4 | 3 914 | 45.2 | 3.8 | 5.1 | 0.4 | 5.5 | 4 196.0 | 5 427 | 13 228 | 37 565 | 45 270 | 55.2 | 43.0 | 1.8 |
| San Juan | 74.4 | 4 891 | 23.8 | 6.9 | 3.1 | 0.2 | 6.5 | 62.7 | 4 121 | 64 | 47 | 956 | 70.0 | 28.1 | 1.9 |
| Skagit | 668.9 | 5 747 | 25.6 | 41.8 | 3.1 | 0.0 | 3.7 | 488.5 | 4 197 | 408 | 348 | 10 563 | 53.8 | 44.2 | 2.1 |
| Skamania | 35.3 | 3 294 | 36.4 | 5.6 | 5.6 | 0.1 | 7.6 | 99.1 | 9 244 | 134 | 33 | 604 | 51.3 | 46.0 | 2.7 |
| Snohomish | 2 481.6 | 3 666 | 45.4 | 9.9 | 4.4 | 0.5 | 4.8 | 3 324.1 | 4 911 | 2 281 | 6 721 | 34 960 | 58.5 | 39.6 | 2.0 |
| Spokane | 1 516.3 | 3 324 | 49.0 | 4.6 | 5.4 | 0.1 | 5.0 | 957.6 | 2 099 | 4 603 | 4 272 | 30 670 | 48.2 | 49.3 | 2.5 |
| Stevens | 130.5 | 3 120 | 51.2 | 5.7 | 3.5 | 0.0 | 6.5 | 53.7 | 1 283 | 327 | 128 | 2 723 | 38.0 | 58.8 | 3.2 |
| Thurston | 845.2 | 3 543 | 48.3 | 5.0 | 3.8 | 0.0 | 5.0 | 708.9 | 2 972 | 904 | 826 | 34 763 | 59.9 | 38.2 | 1.9 |
| Wahkiakum | 27.5 | 6 813 | 16.1 | 41.3 | 3.3 | 0.1 | 9.5 | 4.3 | 1 061 | 15 | 12 | 248 | 48.9 | 48.2 | 3.0 |
| Walla Walla | 188.3 | 3 263 | 43.6 | 5.8 | 7.1 | 0.0 | 10.0 | 204.0 | 3 536 | 1 262 | 179 | 4 412 | 40.8 | 57.4 | 1.9 |
| Whatcom | 575.8 | 2 984 | 41.1 | 3.0 | 5.3 | 0.0 | 6.1 | 473.4 | 2 453 | 1 404 | 667 | 14 010 | 58.0 | 40.1 | 1.9 |
| Whitman | 158.6 | 3 847 | 31.1 | 32.9 | 3.8 | 1.3 | 5.2 | 86.9 | 2 109 | 272 | 147 | 9 201 | 51.6 | 46.1 | 2.4 |
| Yakima | 822.6 | 3 529 | 56.3 | 1.4 | 4.6 | 1.2 | 5.4 | 518.4 | 2 224 | 1 315 | 837 | 15 922 | 43.9 | 54.4 | 1.7 |
| WEST VIRGINIA | X | X | X | X | X | X | X | X | X | 23 548 | 9 662 | 128 169 | 42.6 | 55.7 | 1.7 |
| Barbour | 33.7 | 2 172 | 59.6 | 0.1 | 4.5 | 0.0 | 3.2 | 32.6 | 2 102 | 39 | 81 | 764 | 38.8 | 59.1 | 2.1 |
| Berkeley | 229.5 | 2 302 | 65.4 | 0.2 | 3.9 | 0.0 | 0.8 | 280.6 | 2 814 | 3 849 | 582 | 4 965 | 42.9 | 55.9 | 1.2 |
| Boone | 102.2 | 4 054 | 43.2 | 33.2 | 3.7 | 0.0 | 0.4 | 11.6 | 461 | 80 | 121 | 1 642 | 54.1 | 43.4 | 2.5 |
| Braxton | 29.1 | 1 987 | 73.0 | 0.1 | 2.0 | 0.5 | 0.1 | 88.7 | 6 059 | 54 | 71 | 980 | 50.0 | 48.6 | 1.4 |

1. Based on the resident population estimated as of July 1 of the year shown.   2. © 2013 Election Data Services, Inc. All rights reserved.   3. Manassas and Manassas Park cities are included with Prince William county.   4. Martinsville city is included with Henry county.   5. Norton city is included with Wise county.   6. Petersburg and Colonial Heights cities are included with Dinwiddie county.   7. Poquoson city is included with York county.   8. Radford city is included with Montgomery county.   9. Salem city is included with Roanoke county.   10. Staunton and Waynesboro cities are included with Augusta county.   11. Williamsburg city is included with James City county.   12. Winchester city is included with Frederick county.

# Table B. States and Counties — **Land Area and Population**

| STATE/ County code | CBSA code[1] | County type[2] | STATE County | Land area[3] (sq km) 2010 | Total persons | Rank | Per square kilometer | White | Black | American Indian, Alaska Native | Asian and Pacific Islander | Percent Hispanic or Latino[4] | Under 5 years | 5 to 17 years | 18 to 24 years | 25 to 34 years | 35 to 44 years | 45 to 54 years |
|---|---|---|---|---|---|---|---|---|---|---|---|---|---|---|---|---|---|---|
| | | | | 1 | 2 | 3 | 4 | 5 | 6 | 7 | 8 | 9 | 10 | 11 | 12 | 13 | 14 | 15 |
| | | | **WEST VIRGINIA—Cont'd** | | | | | | | | | | | | | | | |
| 54 009 | 44600 | 3 | Brooke | 231 | 23 853 | 1 651 | 103.3 | 97.5 | 1.8 | 0.5 | 0.6 | 0.7 | 4.4 | 14.4 | 9.6 | 9.6 | 11.8 | 14.8 |
| 54 011 | 26580 | 2 | Cabell | 728 | 96 974 | 603 | 133.2 | 92.4 | 6.1 | 0.8 | 1.5 | 1.2 | 5.9 | 13.7 | 13.2 | 13.2 | 11.9 | 13.0 |
| 54 013 | ... | 8 | Calhoun | 723 | 7 607 | 2 633 | 10.5 | 98.5 | 0.4 | 0.9 | 0.3 | 0.8 | 5.4 | 14.4 | 6.7 | 11.0 | 11.5 | 15.6 |
| 54 015 | 16620 | 2 | Clay | 886 | 9 297 | 2 494 | 10.5 | 99.0 | 0.4 | 0.7 | 0.2 | 0.4 | 6.3 | 17.7 | 6.9 | 10.8 | 12.9 | 14.6 |
| 54 017 | 17220 | 9 | Doddridge | 828 | 8 178 | 2 592 | 9.9 | 97.4 | 1.9 | 0.9 | 0.3 | 0.5 | 4.6 | 15.2 | 8.9 | 11.8 | 12.6 | 15.6 |
| 54 019 | 36060 | 6 | Fayette | 1 713 | 45 869 | 1 050 | 26.8 | 93.9 | 5.2 | 0.7 | 0.4 | 1.0 | 5.8 | 14.8 | 7.8 | 11.7 | 12.6 | 14.5 |
| 54 021 | ... | 9 | Gilmer | 877 | 8 732 | 2 542 | 10.0 | 80.7 | 12.6 | 1.1 | 1.0 | 5.9 | 4.1 | 10.4 | 14.6 | 16.5 | 14.6 | 14.1 |
| 54 023 | ... | 6 | Grant | 1 236 | 11 816 | 2 309 | 9.6 | 97.8 | 1.1 | 0.4 | 0.3 | 1.2 | 5.4 | 15.6 | 6.8 | 10.1 | 12.6 | 14.9 |
| 54 025 | ... | 7 | Greenbrier | 2 641 | 35 820 | 1 281 | 13.6 | 95.2 | 3.4 | 0.9 | 0.6 | 1.3 | 5.3 | 14.7 | 7.5 | 11.0 | 11.6 | 14.7 |
| 54 027 | 49020 | 3 | Hampshire | 1 658 | 23 709 | 1 656 | 14.3 | 97.3 | 1.5 | 0.7 | 0.4 | 1.1 | 5.1 | 16.9 | 6.9 | 10.5 | 13.0 | 15.4 |
| 54 029 | 44600 | 3 | Hancock | 214 | 30 305 | 1 423 | 141.6 | 96.0 | 3.0 | 0.5 | 0.5 | 1.1 | 4.8 | 15.1 | 6.3 | 10.4 | 12.7 | 15.6 |
| 54 031 | ... | 8 | Hardy | 1 508 | 13 866 | 2 181 | 9.2 | 93.0 | 2.6 | 0.5 | 1.1 | 3.6 | 5.5 | 15.5 | 7.4 | 10.8 | 13.2 | 15.6 |
| 54 033 | 17220 | 5 | Harrison | 1 077 | 69 141 | 769 | 64.2 | 96.2 | 2.4 | 0.8 | 0.8 | 1.3 | 5.8 | 16.0 | 7.3 | 11.9 | 12.7 | 15.1 |
| 54 035 | ... | 6 | Jackson | 1 203 | 29 234 | 1 445 | 24.3 | 98.4 | 0.8 | 0.6 | 0.5 | 0.7 | 5.7 | 16.5 | 7.5 | 11.1 | 12.5 | 15.0 |
| 54 037 | 47900 | 1 | Jefferson | 543 | 54 504 | 917 | 100.4 | 86.9 | 7.8 | 0.9 | 1.9 | 4.8 | 6.0 | 17.4 | 9.7 | 11.2 | 14.4 | 15.8 |
| 54 039 | 16620 | 2 | Kanawha | 2 335 | 192 179 | 331 | 82.3 | 90.2 | 8.5 | 0.8 | 1.4 | 1.1 | 5.7 | 14.8 | 7.8 | 12.6 | 12.2 | 14.9 |
| 54 041 | ... | 7 | Lewis | 997 | 16 371 | 2 019 | 16.4 | 98.0 | 0.9 | 0.7 | 0.5 | 0.8 | 5.7 | 14.7 | 7.3 | 11.5 | 12.7 | 14.9 |
| 54 043 | 16620 | 2 | Lincoln | 1 132 | 21 627 | 1 747 | 19.1 | 99.1 | 0.4 | 0.4 | 0.2 | 0.5 | 5.9 | 16.6 | 7.2 | 11.4 | 13.5 | 15.4 |
| 54 045 | ... | 6 | Logan | 1 175 | 36 168 | 1 272 | 30.8 | 96.5 | 2.6 | 0.4 | 0.4 | 0.8 | 5.2 | 15.2 | 7.2 | 12.2 | 13.6 | 14.7 |
| 54 047 | ... | 7 | McDowell | 1 382 | 21 326 | 1 767 | 15.4 | 90.0 | 9.9 | 0.6 | 0.2 | 0.5 | 5.7 | 14.4 | 7.7 | 11.4 | 12.3 | 15.7 |
| 54 049 | 21900 | 4 | Marion | 800 | 56 678 | 895 | 70.8 | 94.8 | 4.2 | 0.7 | 0.8 | 1.0 | 5.5 | 14.1 | 10.9 | 12.1 | 12.5 | 13.6 |
| 54 051 | 48540 | 3 | Marshall | 791 | 32 674 | 1 365 | 41.3 | 97.9 | 1.0 | 0.5 | 0.5 | 0.9 | 5.2 | 15.4 | 7.5 | 10.4 | 12.3 | 15.0 |
| 54 053 | 38580 | 6 | Mason | 1 116 | 27 179 | 1 524 | 24.4 | 98.2 | 1.3 | 0.6 | 0.5 | 0.5 | 5.5 | 16.0 | 7.1 | 11.7 | 12.4 | 15.3 |
| 54 055 | 14140 | 5 | Mercer | 1 085 | 62 523 | 836 | 57.6 | 92.2 | 6.8 | 0.8 | 0.7 | 0.9 | 6.1 | 14.7 | 9.0 | 11.4 | 12.0 | 13.4 |
| 54 057 | 19060 | 3 | Mineral | 849 | 27 956 | 1 496 | 32.9 | 95.7 | 3.7 | 0.5 | 0.6 | 0.8 | 5.4 | 15.0 | 9.7 | 10.4 | 12.4 | 14.4 |
| 54 059 | ... | 6 | Mingo | 1 096 | 26 103 | 1 557 | 23.8 | 97.2 | 2.5 | 0.4 | 0.4 | 0.5 | 6.0 | 15.9 | 7.7 | 12.3 | 13.2 | 15.2 |
| 54 061 | 34060 | 3 | Monongalia | 933 | 100 332 | 587 | 107.5 | 91.0 | 4.5 | 0.6 | 3.7 | 2.0 | 4.6 | 11.1 | 26.7 | 15.3 | 10.6 | 11.0 |
| 54 063 | ... | 8 | Monroe | 1 224 | 13 463 | 2 215 | 11.0 | 98.0 | 1.4 | 0.8 | 0.4 | 0.7 | 5.3 | 15.3 | 6.9 | 9.9 | 12.1 | 14.7 |
| 54 065 | 25180 | 3 | Morgan | 593 | 17 471 | 1 954 | 29.5 | 97.2 | 1.4 | 0.8 | 0.6 | 1.2 | 4.6 | 15.5 | 6.5 | 9.4 | 13.0 | 15.9 |
| 54 067 | ... | 6 | Nicholas | 1 675 | 26 229 | 1 552 | 15.7 | 98.6 | 0.6 | 0.7 | 0.5 | 0.6 | 5.7 | 15.2 | 7.3 | 10.7 | 12.7 | 15.0 |
| 54 069 | 48540 | 3 | Ohio | 274 | 44 075 | 1 084 | 160.9 | 94.4 | 5.0 | 0.5 | 1.2 | 0.9 | 5.1 | 13.9 | 10.9 | 10.8 | 10.9 | 14.5 |
| 54 071 | ... | 8 | Pendleton | 1 803 | 7 566 | 2 637 | 4.2 | 96.3 | 2.6 | 0.7 | 0.5 | 1.1 | 5.0 | 13.6 | 7.4 | 9.7 | 10.4 | 15.2 |
| 54 073 | 37620 | 3 | Pleasants | 337 | 7 595 | 2 634 | 22.5 | 97.4 | 1.8 | 0.6 | 0.3 | 0.8 | 4.8 | 15.5 | 7.4 | 11.4 | 14.2 | 16.0 |
| 54 075 | ... | 9 | Pocahontas | 2 435 | 8 692 | 2 549 | 3.6 | 97.8 | 1.1 | 0.9 | 0.3 | 1.0 | 4.9 | 12.9 | 6.8 | 10.9 | 11.4 | 16.5 |
| 54 077 | 34060 | 3 | Preston | 1 680 | 33 832 | 1 331 | 20.1 | 97.6 | 1.4 | 0.6 | 0.3 | 0.8 | 5.2 | 14.1 | 7.3 | 13.6 | 13.5 | 15.2 |
| 54 079 | 16620 | 2 | Putnam | 895 | 56 435 | 898 | 63.1 | 97.0 | 1.5 | 0.6 | 1.1 | 0.9 | 5.7 | 17.6 | 6.5 | 11.5 | 14.1 | 15.4 |
| 54 081 | 13220 | 4 | Raleigh | 1 568 | 79 021 | 697 | 50.4 | 89.2 | 9.0 | 0.8 | 1.3 | 1.3 | 6.0 | 14.9 | 7.9 | 12.8 | 13.2 | 13.7 |
| 54 083 | ... | 7 | Randolph | 2 693 | 29 384 | 1 437 | 10.9 | 97.4 | 1.6 | 0.6 | 0.5 | 0.7 | 5.1 | 14.0 | 8.5 | 11.7 | 12.4 | 15.0 |
| 54 085 | ... | 8 | Ritchie | 1 171 | 10 236 | 2 422 | 8.7 | 98.8 | 0.6 | 0.6 | 0.3 | 0.6 | 5.1 | 15.7 | 6.8 | 10.3 | 12.1 | 16.4 |
| 54 087 | ... | 6 | Roane | 1 252 | 14 684 | 2 017 | 11.7 | 98.3 | 0.6 | 0.6 | 0.5 | 0.8 | 5.4 | 16.0 | 6.8 | 10.4 | 12.6 | 15.2 |
| 54 089 | ... | 7 | Summers | 934 | 13 737 | 2 194 | 14.7 | 93.1 | 5.5 | 0.9 | 0.5 | 1.4 | 4.6 | 13.3 | 6.1 | 11.9 | 12.7 | 15.4 |
| 54 091 | 17220 | 6 | Taylor | 447 | 16 991 | 1 983 | 38.0 | 97.5 | 1.4 | 0.6 | 0.5 | 0.9 | 5.7 | 15.0 | 7.2 | 12.3 | 13.3 | 15.4 |
| 54 093 | ... | 9 | Tucker | 1 085 | 6 995 | 2 686 | 6.4 | 98.5 | 0.6 | 0.5 | 0.3 | 0.7 | 4.8 | 14.3 | 6.6 | 9.9 | 11.7 | 15.5 |
| 54 095 | ... | 6 | Tyler | 664 | 9 037 | 2 518 | 13.6 | 98.6 | 0.5 | 0.5 | 0.3 | 0.7 | 5.0 | 15.5 | 6.7 | 9.1 | 12.9 | 15.7 |
| 54 097 | ... | 7 | Upshur | 919 | 24 477 | 1 624 | 26.6 | 97.5 | 1.3 | 0.6 | 0.5 | 1.0 | 5.7 | 14.8 | 11.6 | 10.8 | 11.8 | 14.0 |
| 54 099 | 26580 | 2 | Wayne | 1 310 | 41 649 | 1 136 | 31.8 | 98.7 | 0.5 | 0.7 | 0.3 | 0.6 | 5.4 | 16.5 | 7.9 | 11.3 | 13.3 | 14.3 |
| 54 101 | ... | 9 | Webster | 1 433 | 9 043 | 2 517 | 6.3 | 99.1 | 0.5 | 0.8 | 0.2 | 0.5 | 6.1 | 15.1 | 7.3 | 9.9 | 12.5 | 14.9 |
| 54 103 | ... | 6 | Wetzel | 927 | 16 422 | 2 017 | 17.7 | 98.9 | 0.5 | 0.4 | 0.4 | 0.5 | 5.0 | 15.4 | 7.6 | 9.6 | 12.1 | 15.4 |
| 54 105 | 37620 | 3 | Wirt | 602 | 5 847 | 2 778 | 9.7 | 98.8 | 0.6 | 0.7 | 0.3 | 0.5 | 5.1 | 15.6 | 6.9 | 10.5 | 12.2 | 18.0 |
| 54 107 | 37620 | 3 | Wood | 949 | 86 701 | 654 | 91.4 | 97.1 | 1.9 | 0.6 | 0.8 | 0.9 | 5.7 | 16.0 | 7.6 | 11.5 | 12.6 | 15.2 |
| 54 109 | ... | 7 | Wyoming | 1 294 | 23 273 | 1 677 | 18.0 | 98.6 | 1.1 | 0.6 | 0.3 | 0.5 | 5.6 | 16.0 | 7.5 | 10.8 | 13.1 | 14.8 |
| 55 000 | ... | X | **WISCONSIN** | 140 268 | 5 726 398 | X | 40.8 | 84.4 | 6.9 | 1.3 | 2.8 | 6.1 | 6.2 | 17.0 | 9.7 | 12.8 | 12.4 | 15.1 |
| 55 001 | ... | 8 | Adams | 1 672 | 20 679 | 1 799 | 12.4 | 91.7 | 3.4 | 1.4 | 0.7 | 3.8 | 4.0 | 12.2 | 5.7 | 10.1 | 11.0 | 15.9 |
| 55 003 | ... | 7 | Ashland | 2 707 | 15 992 | 2 048 | 5.9 | 86.5 | 0.9 | 12.8 | 0.9 | 2.0 | 6.3 | 16.7 | 9.9 | 11.4 | 10.8 | 15.0 |
| 55 005 | ... | 6 | Barron | 2 234 | 45 733 | 1 053 | 20.5 | 95.6 | 1.3 | 1.3 | 0.8 | 2.0 | 5.9 | 16.0 | 7.4 | 11.3 | 11.3 | 15.1 |
| 55 007 | ... | 8 | Bayfield | 3 828 | 15 099 | 2 101 | 3.9 | 88.4 | 0.9 | 11.4 | 0.9 | 1.2 | 4.5 | 14.3 | 5.3 | 8.5 | 10.0 | 16.8 |
| 55 009 | 24580 | 2 | Brown | 1 372 | 253 032 | 261 | 184.4 | 84.9 | 3.1 | 3.0 | 3.3 | 7.5 | 6.9 | 17.8 | 9.9 | 13.9 | 12.8 | 15.0 |
| 55 011 | ... | 8 | Buffalo | 1 740 | 13 333 | 2 221 | 7.7 | 97.1 | 0.5 | 0.6 | 0.4 | 2.0 | 5.5 | 16.2 | 7.1 | 10.2 | 11.5 | 16.1 |
| 55 013 | ... | 8 | Burnett | 2 129 | 15 382 | 2 082 | 7.2 | 93.0 | 1.0 | 6.1 | 0.8 | 1.4 | 4.9 | 14.4 | 5.8 | 8.3 | 9.9 | 15.6 |
| 55 015 | 11540 | 3 | Calumet | 824 | 49 634 | 989 | 60.2 | 93.2 | 1.0 | 0.7 | 2.4 | 3.6 | 6.7 | 19.8 | 6.8 | 11.9 | 14.4 | 16.5 |
| 55 017 | 20740 | 3 | Chippewa | 2 612 | 62 922 | 828 | 24.1 | 95.3 | 1.9 | 0.9 | 1.6 | 1.3 | 6.4 | 16.9 | 7.4 | 13.0 | 12.6 | 15.8 |
| 55 019 | ... | 8 | Clark | 3 133 | 34 435 | 1 314 | 11.0 | 94.9 | 0.5 | 0.8 | 0.5 | 3.8 | 8.2 | 20.8 | 7.5 | 10.9 | 11.0 | 14.0 |
| 55 021 | 31540 | 2 | Columbia | 1 983 | 56 539 | 897 | 28.5 | 95.0 | 1.6 | 0.8 | 0.8 | 2.6 | 5.8 | 17.1 | 6.8 | 11.9 | 13.3 | 16.2 |
| 55 023 | ... | 7 | Crawford | 1 478 | 16 560 | 2 007 | 11.2 | 96.5 | 2.1 | 0.5 | 0.6 | 1.0 | 5.5 | 16.5 | 6.6 | 10.6 | 10.7 | 15.9 |
| 55 025 | 31540 | 2 | Dane | 3 101 | 503 523 | 130 | 162.4 | 83.4 | 6.3 | 0.8 | 5.6 | 6.1 | 6.1 | 15.3 | 13.6 | 16.0 | 12.9 | 13.7 |

1. CBSA = Core Based Statistical Area. See Appendix A for explanation. See Appendix B for list of metropolitan areas with component counties.   2. County type code from the Economic Research Service of USDA Rural-Urban Continuum Codes. See Appendix A for definition.   3. Dry land or land partially or temporarily covered by water.   4. May be of any race.

# Table B. States and Counties — **Population and Households**

| STATE County | 55 to 64 years | 65 to 74 years | 75 years and over | Percent female | 2000 | 2010 | 2000– 2010 | 2010– 2012 | Births | Deaths | Net migration | Number | Percent change, 2000– 2010 | Persons per house-hold | Female family house-holder[1] | One per-son |
|---|---|---|---|---|---|---|---|---|---|---|---|---|---|---|---|---|
| | 16 | 17 | 18 | 19 | 20 | 21 | 22 | 23 | 24 | 25 | 26 | 27 | 28 | 29 | 30 | 31 |
| **WEST VIRGINIA—Cont'd** | | | | | | | | | | | | | | | | |
| Brooke | 16.4 | 9.4 | 9.6 | 51.3 | 25 447 | 24 069 | -5.4 | -0.9 | 430 | 738 | 89 | 10 020 | -3.6 | 2.32 | 10.7 | 29.2 |
| Cabell | 13.2 | 8.3 | 7.6 | 51.3 | 96 784 | 96 319 | -0.5 | 0.7 | 2 692 | 2 484 | 517 | 41 223 | 0.1 | 2.24 | 12.3 | 33.5 |
| Calhoun | 16.7 | 10.1 | 8.4 | 50.0 | 7 582 | 7 627 | 0.6 | -0.3 | 202 | 211 | -9 | 3 268 | 6.4 | 2.33 | 9.7 | 28.5 |
| Clay | 14.7 | 9.1 | 7.0 | 50.4 | 10 330 | 9 386 | -9.1 | -0.9 | 284 | 245 | -144 | 3 728 | -7.3 | 2.50 | 9.7 | 26.2 |
| Doddridge | 15.6 | 9.6 | 6.2 | 46.3 | 7 403 | 8 202 | 10.8 | -0.3 | 159 | 175 | -23 | 3 099 | 8.9 | 2.41 | 9.1 | 26.1 |
| Fayette | 15.9 | 9.0 | 7.8 | 49.8 | 47 579 | 46 039 | -3.2 | -0.4 | 1 270 | 1 494 | 54 | 18 813 | -0.7 | 2.35 | 12.5 | 29.1 |
| Gilmer | 11.8 | 7.6 | 6.4 | 39.6 | 7 160 | 8 693 | 21.4 | 0.4 | 168 | 176 | 39 | 2 753 | -0.5 | 2.34 | 10.1 | 27.6 |
| Grant | 15.6 | 11.0 | 8.0 | 50.3 | 11 299 | 11 937 | 5.6 | -1.0 | 269 | 261 | -134 | 4 941 | 7.6 | 2.39 | 8.3 | 25.7 |
| Greenbrier | 15.9 | 10.8 | 8.6 | 51.0 | 34 453 | 35 480 | 3.0 | 1.0 | 841 | 1 071 | 586 | 15 443 | 6.0 | 2.26 | 10.8 | 30.6 |
| Hampshire | 15.2 | 10.3 | 6.6 | 49.3 | 20 203 | 23 964 | 18.6 | -1.1 | 485 | 555 | -170 | 9 595 | 20.6 | 2.44 | 9.1 | 25.8 |
| Hancock | 16.2 | 9.3 | 9.6 | 51.8 | 32 667 | 30 676 | -6.1 | -1.2 | 634 | 964 | -24 | 13 297 | -2.8 | 2.29 | 12.2 | 29.5 |
| Hardy | 14.8 | 10.4 | 6.8 | 49.7 | 12 669 | 14 025 | 10.7 | -1.1 | 347 | 347 | -184 | 5 818 | 11.8 | 2.40 | 10.0 | 27.0 |
| Harrison | 14.3 | 8.8 | 7.9 | 51.3 | 68 652 | 69 099 | 0.7 | 0.1 | 1 788 | 1 968 | 257 | 28 533 | 2.4 | 2.39 | 11.9 | 28.3 |
| Jackson | 13.9 | 9.7 | 8.1 | 50.7 | 28 000 | 29 211 | 4.3 | 0.1 | 709 | 761 | 90 | 11 931 | 7.9 | 2.43 | 10.3 | 25.0 |
| Jefferson | 13.3 | 7.5 | 4.7 | 50.4 | 42 190 | 53 498 | 26.8 | 1.9 | 1 338 | 936 | 595 | 19 931 | 23.3 | 2.61 | 10.1 | 22.7 |
| Kanawha | 15.3 | 8.9 | 8.0 | 51.9 | 200 073 | 193 063 | -3.5 | -0.5 | 4 968 | 5 509 | -312 | 84 201 | -2.3 | 2.26 | 13.1 | 32.5 |
| Lewis | 14.8 | 10.5 | 7.8 | 50.6 | 16 919 | 16 372 | -3.2 | 0.0 | 412 | 499 | 83 | 6 863 | -1.2 | 2.35 | 10.9 | 28.5 |
| Lincoln | 14.7 | 9.2 | 6.1 | 50.2 | 22 108 | 21 720 | -1.8 | -0.4 | 548 | 626 | -14 | 8 783 | 1.4 | 2.47 | 10.7 | 25.6 |
| Logan | 16.5 | 8.6 | 6.9 | 50.6 | 37 710 | 36 743 | -2.6 | -1.6 | 931 | 1 133 | -366 | 14 907 | 0.2 | 2.43 | 12.5 | 26.1 |
| McDowell | 16.3 | 9.2 | 7.4 | 50.6 | 27 329 | 22 113 | -19.1 | -3.6 | 608 | 815 | -604 | 9 176 | -17.8 | 2.36 | 13.9 | 28.8 |
| Marion | 14.3 | 9.1 | 7.9 | 51.1 | 56 598 | 56 418 | -0.3 | 0.5 | 1 429 | 1 517 | 381 | 23 786 | 0.6 | 2.32 | 11.1 | 29.3 |
| Marshall | 16.8 | 9.4 | 8.1 | 51.3 | 35 519 | 33 107 | -6.8 | -1.3 | 707 | 869 | -267 | 13 869 | -2.4 | 2.35 | 11.5 | 28.0 |
| Mason | 14.7 | 9.7 | 7.6 | 51.8 | 25 957 | 27 324 | 5.3 | -0.5 | 625 | 780 | 15 | 11 149 | 5.3 | 2.39 | 11.6 | 27.4 |
| Mercer | 15.3 | 9.7 | 8.3 | 52.2 | 62 980 | 62 264 | -1.1 | 0.4 | 1 799 | 2 005 | 468 | 26 603 | 0.4 | 2.30 | 12.9 | 30.1 |
| Mineral | 14.9 | 10.5 | 7.2 | 50.4 | 27 078 | 28 212 | 4.2 | -0.9 | 677 | 739 | -177 | 11 550 | 7.1 | 2.39 | 10.0 | 27.0 |
| Mingo | 15.9 | 8.1 | 5.7 | 51.0 | 28 253 | 26 839 | -5.0 | -2.7 | 802 | 825 | -719 | 11 125 | -1.6 | 2.40 | 11.8 | 27.7 |
| Monongalia | 10.4 | 5.6 | 4.6 | 48.5 | 81 866 | 96 189 | 17.5 | 4.3 | 2 197 | 1 414 | 3 332 | 39 777 | 18.9 | 2.24 | 8.2 | 31.7 |
| Monroe | 15.7 | 11.6 | 8.5 | 50.6 | 14 583 | 13 502 | -7.4 | -0.3 | 278 | 378 | 64 | 5 655 | 3.8 | 2.38 | 9.3 | 26.9 |
| Morgan | 16.2 | 11.1 | 7.9 | 50.3 | 14 943 | 17 541 | 17.4 | -0.4 | 334 | 486 | 98 | 7 303 | 18.8 | 2.39 | 8.9 | 25.7 |
| Nicholas | 15.9 | 10.1 | 7.3 | 50.7 | 26 562 | 26 233 | -1.2 | 0.0 | 693 | 778 | 79 | 10 938 | 2.0 | 2.38 | 10.7 | 26.5 |
| Ohio | 15.5 | 8.8 | 9.6 | 52.4 | 47 427 | 44 443 | -6.3 | -0.8 | 1 104 | 1 340 | -102 | 18 914 | -4.2 | 2.21 | 11.7 | 35.3 |
| Pendleton | 16.1 | 11.6 | 10.9 | 49.3 | 8 196 | 7 695 | -6.1 | -1.7 | 192 | 176 | -144 | 3 285 | -1.9 | 2.28 | 7.1 | 29.0 |
| Pleasants | 14.2 | 9.4 | 7.0 | 46.4 | 7 514 | 7 605 | 1.2 | -0.1 | 128 | 200 | 58 | 2 861 | -0.9 | 2.44 | 9.8 | 24.9 |
| Pocahontas | 17.0 | 11.3 | 8.3 | 48.5 | 9 131 | 8 719 | -4.5 | -0.3 | 207 | 276 | 25 | 3 758 | -2.0 | 2.24 | 9.1 | 31.3 |
| Preston | 14.9 | 9.2 | 7.0 | 48.5 | 29 334 | 33 520 | 14.3 | 0.9 | 729 | 773 | 351 | 12 895 | 11.7 | 2.42 | 9.1 | 24.6 |
| Putnam | 14.5 | 8.7 | 6.1 | 50.8 | 51 589 | 55 486 | 7.6 | 1.7 | 1 306 | 1 209 | 818 | 21 981 | 9.8 | 2.51 | 9.5 | 22.3 |
| Raleigh | 15.4 | 8.6 | 7.5 | 50.0 | 79 220 | 78 859 | -0.5 | 0.2 | 2 122 | 2 255 | 340 | 31 831 | 0.1 | 2.36 | 12.2 | 28.6 |
| Randolph | 15.0 | 10.6 | 7.7 | 48.4 | 28 262 | 29 405 | 4.0 | -0.1 | 628 | 807 | 169 | 11 695 | 5.6 | 2.32 | 10.5 | 28.4 |
| Ritchie | 15.7 | 10.7 | 7.3 | 49.9 | 10 343 | 10 449 | 1.0 | -2.0 | 196 | 319 | -111 | 4 367 | 4.4 | 2.37 | 9.8 | 28.2 |
| Roane | 15.8 | 10.3 | 7.4 | 50.3 | 15 446 | 14 926 | -3.4 | -1.6 | 316 | 404 | -147 | 6 195 | 0.6 | 2.39 | 9.9 | 27.2 |
| Summers | 16.6 | 10.6 | 9.0 | 55.2 | 12 999 | 13 927 | 7.1 | -1.4 | 256 | 404 | -30 | 5 572 | 0.8 | 2.26 | 10.9 | 30.8 |
| Taylor | 15.0 | 8.8 | 7.3 | 49.4 | 16 089 | 16 895 | 5.0 | 0.6 | 415 | 441 | 131 | 6 778 | 7.2 | 2.42 | 10.6 | 26.1 |
| Tucker | 16.4 | 11.8 | 9.1 | 49.9 | 7 321 | 7 141 | -2.5 | -2.0 | 150 | 227 | -56 | 3 057 | 0.2 | 2.29 | 7.5 | 28.3 |
| Tyler | 16.4 | 10.3 | 8.4 | 50.8 | 9 592 | 9 208 | -4.0 | -1.9 | 188 | 274 | -80 | 3 858 | 0.6 | 2.37 | 8.7 | 27.2 |
| Upshur | 14.4 | 9.7 | 7.2 | 50.8 | 23 404 | 24 254 | 3.6 | 0.9 | 590 | 624 | 255 | 9 619 | 7.2 | 2.40 | 9.6 | 26.9 |
| Wayne | 14.2 | 9.6 | 7.4 | 51.2 | 42 903 | 42 481 | -1.0 | -2.0 | 849 | 1 112 | -639 | 17 347 | 0.6 | 2.43 | 11.7 | 26.4 |
| Webster | 16.3 | 10.3 | 7.5 | 50.4 | 9 719 | 9 154 | -5.8 | -1.2 | 267 | 268 | -124 | 3 792 | -5.4 | 2.40 | 11.2 | 26.5 |
| Wetzel | 15.0 | 11.1 | 8.8 | 50.9 | 17 693 | 16 583 | -6.3 | -1.0 | 386 | 522 | -28 | 6 968 | -2.7 | 2.36 | 10.4 | 27.4 |
| Wirt | 15.8 | 10.1 | 5.8 | 49.9 | 5 873 | 5 717 | -2.7 | 2.3 | 107 | 115 | 131 | 2 391 | 4.7 | 2.39 | 9.5 | 25.2 |
| Wood | 14.3 | 9.6 | 7.5 | 51.8 | 87 986 | 86 956 | -1.2 | -0.3 | 2 210 | 2 321 | -118 | 36 571 | 0.8 | 2.35 | 11.6 | 28.4 |
| Wyoming | 16.9 | 8.9 | 6.4 | 50.2 | 25 708 | 23 796 | -7.4 | -2.2 | 563 | 768 | -308 | 9 687 | -7.3 | 2.45 | 10.3 | 25.1 |
| **WISCONSIN** | 12.8 | 7.2 | 6.7 | 50.3 | 5 363 675 | 5 686 986 | 6.0 | 0.7 | 153 926 | 106 193 | -8 256 | 2 279 768 | 9.4 | 2.43 | 10.3 | 28.2 |
| Adams | 17.3 | 14.6 | 9.1 | 46.1 | 18 643 | 20 875 | 12.0 | -0.9 | 339 | 558 | 17 | 8 666 | 9.7 | 2.24 | 8.1 | 27.7 |
| Ashland | 13.9 | 8.4 | 7.7 | 50.1 | 16 866 | 16 157 | -4.2 | -1.0 | 432 | 408 | -201 | 6 736 | 0.3 | 2.31 | 11.6 | 32.4 |
| Barron | 14.5 | 9.7 | 8.9 | 50.2 | 44 963 | 45 870 | 2.0 | -0.3 | 1 137 | 1 069 | -172 | 19 173 | 7.4 | 2.36 | 8.7 | 27.7 |
| Bayfield | 19.4 | 12.9 | 8.3 | 48.8 | 15 013 | 15 014 | 0.0 | 0.6 | 278 | 398 | 193 | 6 686 | 7.7 | 2.23 | 7.1 | 29.2 |
| Brown | 11.9 | 6.2 | 5.6 | 50.5 | 226 778 | 248 007 | 9.4 | 2.0 | 7 594 | 3 617 | 1 164 | 98 383 | 12.7 | 2.45 | 10.2 | 27.7 |
| Buffalo | 14.8 | 9.8 | 8.7 | 49.2 | 13 804 | 13 587 | -1.6 | -1.9 | 304 | 317 | -234 | 5 708 | 3.6 | 2.36 | 7.1 | 27.5 |
| Burnett | 17.3 | 14.1 | 9.7 | 49.3 | 15 674 | 15 457 | -1.4 | -0.5 | 317 | 337 | -43 | 6 807 | 2.9 | 2.25 | 7.9 | 28.4 |
| Calumet | 12.2 | 6.1 | 5.5 | 49.9 | 40 631 | 48 971 | 20.5 | 1.4 | 1 285 | 718 | 49 | 18 575 | 24.6 | 2.63 | 6.8 | 21.1 |
| Chippewa | 13.4 | 7.6 | 6.9 | 48.1 | 55 195 | 62 415 | 13.1 | 0.8 | 1 673 | 1 169 | 28 | 24 410 | 14.3 | 2.45 | 8.9 | 25.8 |
| Clark | 12.0 | 7.4 | 8.1 | 49.3 | 33 557 | 34 690 | 3.4 | -0.7 | 1 259 | 776 | -725 | 12 679 | 5.2 | 2.69 | 6.9 | 25.3 |
| Columbia | 13.8 | 7.9 | 7.1 | 49.2 | 52 468 | 56 833 | 8.3 | -0.5 | 1 403 | 1 152 | -543 | 22 735 | 11.2 | 2.43 | 8.4 | 26.0 |
| Crawford | 15.5 | 10.4 | 8.3 | 48.6 | 17 243 | 16 644 | -3.5 | -0.5 | 374 | 382 | -75 | 6 812 | 2.0 | 2.33 | 9.1 | 29.3 |
| Dane | 11.8 | 5.7 | 4.9 | 50.5 | 426 526 | 488 073 | 14.4 | 3.2 | 13 605 | 6 355 | 8 096 | 203 750 | 17.4 | 2.33 | 8.6 | 30.5 |

1. No spouse present.

| STATE County | Persons in group quarters, 2010 | Daytime population, 2007-2011 | | Births, 2011 | | Deaths, 2011 | | Persons under 65 with no health insurance, 2010 | | Medicare, 2012 | | | Serious crimes known to police,[2] 2011 Total | |
|---|---|---|---|---|---|---|---|---|---|---|---|---|---|---|
| | | Number | Employment/residence ratio | Total | Rate[1] | Number | Rate[1] | Number | Percent | Eligible for Medicare | Enrolled in Medicare Advantage | Enrolled in a Medicare prescription drug plan | Number | Rate[3] |
| | 32 | 33 | 34 | 35 | 36 | 37 | 38 | 39 | 40 | 41 | 42 | 43 | 44 | 45 |
| **WEST VIRGINIA—Cont'd** | | | | | | | | | | | | | | |
| Brooke | 872 | 22 131 | 0.81 | 196 | 8.2 | 314 | 13.2 | 3 040 | 16.4 | 5 337 | 1 858 | 2 265 | 211 | 915 |
| Cabell | 3 936 | 109 056 | 1.33 | 1 239 | 12.8 | 1 075 | 11.1 | 13 336 | 17.2 | 20 474 | 5 697 | 8 309 | 3 525 | 3 655 |
| Calhoun | 22 | 6 811 | 0.67 | 90 | 11.8 | 89 | 11.6 | 1 279 | 20.6 | 1 942 | 305 | 977 | 71 | 1 004 |
| Clay | 74 | 8 622 | 0.71 | 127 | 13.6 | 111 | 11.9 | 1 473 | 18.8 | 2 343 | 699 | 1 022 | NA | NA |
| Doddridge | 722 | 6 381 | 0.45 | 73 | 8.9 | 77 | 9.4 | 1 247 | 20.4 | 1 391 | 340 | 500 | NA | NA |
| Fayette | 1 840 | 43 039 | 0.81 | 581 | 12.7 | 672 | 14.7 | 7 037 | 19.2 | 10 312 | 2 463 | 4 593 | NA | NA |
| Gilmer | 2 239 | 8 675 | 1.05 | 73 | 8.4 | 84 | 9.6 | 1 108 | 20.9 | 1 385 | 341 | 610 | NA | NA |
| Grant | 126 | 11 277 | 0.88 | 120 | 10.1 | 117 | 9.8 | 1 855 | 19.3 | 2 780 | 466 | 1 290 | 90 | 979 |
| Greenbrier | 616 | 36 398 | 1.07 | 388 | 10.8 | 477 | 13.3 | 5 848 | 20.8 | 8 874 | 1 714 | 4 260 | 396 | 1 115 |
| Hampshire | 508 | 19 218 | 0.52 | 222 | 9.3 | 232 | 9.7 | 4 029 | 20.7 | 4 908 | 726 | 2 321 | 349 | 1 454 |
| Hancock | 226 | 28 779 | 0.85 | 281 | 9.2 | 435 | 14.2 | 3 977 | 16.1 | 7 152 | 1 706 | 3 570 | 208 | 740 |
| Hardy | 58 | 14 623 | 1.12 | 155 | 11.1 | 158 | 11.4 | 2 218 | 19.1 | 3 024 | 587 | 1 343 | 233 | 1 659 |
| Harrison | 885 | 73 893 | 1.18 | 804 | 11.6 | 879 | 12.7 | 10 115 | 17.7 | 15 005 | 2 909 | 6 661 | 1 515 | 2 353 |
| Jackson | 180 | 26 432 | 0.76 | 316 | 10.8 | 343 | 11.7 | 4 188 | 17.6 | 6 660 | 1 281 | 2 549 | 275 | 940 |
| Jefferson | 1 391 | 45 160 | 0.70 | 598 | 11.0 | 408 | 7.5 | 6 688 | 14.6 | 8 459 | 1 414 | 2 876 | 714 | 1 333 |
| Kanawha | 3 163 | 213 646 | 1.25 | 2 271 | 11.8 | 2 440 | 12.7 | 24 979 | 15.8 | 42 874 | 12 395 | 16 304 | 7 361 | 3 930 |
| Lewis | 248 | 16 887 | 1.07 | 185 | 11.3 | 238 | 14.5 | 2 577 | 19.5 | 4 048 | 1 143 | 1 547 | 119 | 726 |
| Lincoln | 65 | 17 916 | 0.41 | 246 | 11.4 | 278 | 12.9 | 3 466 | 19.0 | 4 896 | 1 386 | 2 243 | NA | NA |
| Logan | 464 | 37 637 | 1.09 | 408 | 11.2 | 509 | 14.0 | 6 025 | 19.6 | 8 702 | 2 242 | 4 228 | 878 | 2 459 |
| McDowell | 471 | 22 886 | 1.13 | 285 | 13.1 | 358 | 16.5 | 3 622 | 20.1 | 5 908 | 1 364 | 3 336 | 332 | 1 833 |
| Marion | 1 340 | 53 367 | 0.88 | 633 | 11.2 | 673 | 11.9 | 8 231 | 18.0 | 12 293 | 2 260 | 6 473 | 668 | 1 315 |
| Marshall | 447 | 31 264 | 0.85 | 314 | 9.6 | 397 | 12.1 | 4 256 | 15.9 | 6 536 | 2 339 | 2 366 | 768 | 2 537 |
| Mason | 635 | 25 270 | 0.81 | 270 | 9.9 | 331 | 12.1 | 3 240 | 14.8 | 6 156 | 1 077 | 2 569 | 449 | 1 802 |
| Mercer | 1 188 | 61 660 | 0.98 | 805 | 12.9 | 890 | 14.2 | 9 351 | 18.7 | 15 449 | 3 053 | 7 904 | 1 442 | 2 367 |
| Mineral | 646 | 24 720 | 0.71 | 308 | 10.9 | 340 | 12.1 | 3 800 | 16.9 | 6 109 | 753 | 3 073 | 531 | 1 989 |
| Mingo | 85 | 25 653 | 0.84 | 348 | 13.1 | 364 | 13.7 | 4 010 | 17.4 | 6 759 | 1 804 | 3 371 | 333 | 1 335 |
| Monongalia | 7 262 | 106 820 | 1.28 | 938 | 9.5 | 607 | 6.2 | 13 384 | 16.8 | 11 855 | 2 739 | 5 055 | 2 143 | 2 368 |
| Monroe | 57 | 10 823 | 0.50 | 121 | 8.9 | 155 | 11.5 | 2 280 | 21.2 | 3 406 | 616 | 1 525 | 137 | 1 013 |
| Morgan | 123 | 14 042 | 0.51 | 156 | 8.9 | 202 | 11.5 | 2 749 | 19.4 | 3 897 | 516 | 1 561 | 257 | 1 564 |
| Nicholas | 162 | 25 905 | 0.97 | 326 | 12.4 | 342 | 13.0 | 3 857 | 17.9 | 6 535 | 1 834 | 2 678 | 612 | 2 528 |
| Ohio | 2 618 | 54 317 | 1.48 | 502 | 11.3 | 598 | 13.5 | 5 290 | 15.6 | 10 418 | 4 208 | 3 484 | 1 258 | 2 929 |
| Pendleton | 196 | 6 774 | 0.74 | 93 | 12.1 | 74 | 9.6 | 1 246 | 21.2 | 1 960 | 380 | 934 | NA | NA |
| Pleasants | 623 | 7 702 | 1.02 | 61 | 8.0 | 79 | 10.4 | 881 | 15.2 | 1 588 | 403 | 747 | 22 | 382 |
| Pocahontas | 318 | 8 869 | 1.03 | 100 | 11.4 | 119 | 13.5 | 1 427 | 21.2 | 2 127 | 431 | 917 | 98 | 1 277 |
| Preston | 2 378 | 27 854 | 0.60 | 322 | 9.5 | 325 | 9.6 | 5 042 | 19.5 | 6 685 | 1 245 | 3 200 | 508 | 1 581 |
| Putnam | 225 | 50 629 | 0.81 | 583 | 10.4 | 519 | 9.3 | 6 822 | 14.5 | 10 638 | 3 123 | 3 662 | 713 | 1 306 |
| Raleigh | 3 857 | 80 495 | 1.06 | 943 | 11.9 | 1 003 | 12.7 | 10 657 | 17.0 | 18 489 | 3 921 | 8 527 | 2 636 | 3 407 |
| Randolph | 2 273 | 29 936 | 1.05 | 277 | 9.4 | 367 | 12.5 | 4 106 | 18.6 | 6 679 | 1 220 | 3 281 | 481 | 1 634 |
| Ritchie | 106 | 10 289 | 0.96 | 98 | 9.5 | 146 | 14.2 | 1 686 | 19.7 | 2 559 | 510 | 1 279 | 161 | 1 539 |
| Roane | 98 | 13 558 | 0.71 | 139 | 9.4 | 187 | 12.6 | 2 422 | 19.8 | 3 785 | 1 029 | 1 612 | 150 | 1 004 |
| Summers | 1 329 | 12 382 | 0.67 | 121 | 8.7 | 157 | 11.3 | 1 951 | 19.4 | 3 292 | 717 | 1 689 | 254 | 1 821 |
| Taylor | 511 | 13 194 | 0.46 | 190 | 11.2 | 189 | 11.2 | 2 513 | 18.4 | 3 477 | 600 | 1 731 | 39 | 231 |
| Tucker | 142 | 6 917 | 0.94 | 68 | 9.7 | 119 | 16.9 | 1 146 | 20.7 | 1 644 | 380 | 784 | 31 | 547 |
| Tyler | 67 | 8 309 | 0.71 | 90 | 9.9 | 116 | 12.7 | 1 294 | 17.4 | 2 160 | 677 | 896 | 126 | 1 367 |
| Upshur | 1 215 | 24 108 | 1.00 | 263 | 10.8 | 270 | 11.1 | 3 654 | 19.3 | 5 161 | 1 417 | 1 966 | 365 | 1 503 |
| Wayne | 246 | 37 700 | 0.70 | 386 | 9.2 | 485 | 11.5 | 6 372 | 18.2 | 9 470 | 2 307 | 3 911 | 979 | 2 340 |
| Webster | 58 | 8 312 | 0.72 | 129 | 14.1 | 128 | 14.0 | 1 419 | 18.9 | 2 448 | 604 | 1 259 | NA | NA |
| Wetzel | 124 | 16 697 | 1.02 | 167 | 10.2 | 241 | 14.7 | 2 310 | 17.5 | 3 951 | 1 444 | 1 426 | 109 | 669 |
| Wirt | 0 | 4 515 | 0.41 | 39 | 6.8 | 46 | 8.0 | 964 | 20.1 | 1 426 | 289 | 766 | 100 | 1 747 |
| Wood | 1 046 | 90 701 | 1.11 | 1 001 | 11.5 | 1 011 | 11.6 | 11 579 | 16.3 | 20 221 | 3 251 | 10 875 | 2 156 | 2 476 |
| Wyoming | 56 | 22 393 | 0.80 | 254 | 10.8 | 348 | 14.9 | 3 527 | 17.6 | 5 942 | 1 362 | 3 379 | 442 | 2 047 |
| **WISCONSIN** | 150 214 | 5 612 471 | 0.98 | 69 346 | 12.1 | 46 070 | 8.1 | 518 026 | 10.8 | 973 320 | 316 932 | 353 208 | 152 481 | 2 670 |
| Adams | 1 432 | 17 913 | 0.62 | 166 | 8.0 | 232 | 11.2 | 1 722 | 11.8 | 5 875 | 1 132 | 2 393 | 623 | 2 970 |
| Ashland | 623 | 17 590 | 1.20 | 202 | 12.5 | 176 | 10.9 | 1 610 | 12.2 | 3 509 | 897 | 1 376 | 620 | 3 821 |
| Barron | 681 | 45 640 | 0.99 | 490 | 10.7 | 468 | 10.2 | 4 704 | 12.6 | 10 224 | 3 262 | 3 801 | 641 | 1 504 |
| Bayfield | 126 | 12 938 | 0.68 | 127 | 8.4 | 185 | 12.3 | 1 709 | 14.4 | 3 948 | 1 142 | 1 364 | 265 | 1 757 |
| Brown | 6 629 | 265 513 | 1.15 | 3 376 | 13.4 | 1 567 | 6.2 | 22 681 | 10.6 | 37 337 | 16 198 | 10 699 | 4 954 | 1 989 |
| Buffalo | 107 | 11 394 | 0.67 | 141 | 10.4 | 126 | 9.3 | 1 260 | 11.4 | 2 925 | 562 | 1 233 | 33 | 304 |
| Burnett | 139 | 14 462 | 0.81 | 140 | 9.0 | 152 | 9.8 | 1 677 | 14.2 | 4 571 | 1 312 | 1 696 | 307 | 1 978 |
| Calumet | 198 | 36 764 | 0.54 | 566 | 11.4 | 317 | 6.4 | 3 488 | 8.1 | 6 639 | 3 897 | 1 423 | 686 | 1 395 |
| Chippewa | 2 542 | 58 517 | 0.89 | 738 | 11.8 | 522 | 8.3 | 5 191 | 10.1 | 11 398 | 3 261 | 4 167 | 1 099 | 1 753 |
| Clark | 536 | 31 925 | 0.83 | 565 | 16.3 | 333 | 9.6 | 5 364 | 18.4 | 6 108 | 2 817 | 1 524 | 400 | 1 148 |
| Columbia | 1 526 | 49 008 | 0.74 | 642 | 11.3 | 491 | 8.6 | 4 396 | 9.3 | 10 345 | 2 426 | 4 882 | 871 | 1 526 |
| Crawford | 785 | 17 463 | 1.09 | 175 | 10.5 | 175 | 10.5 | 1 558 | 12.0 | 3 774 | 1 124 | 1 526 | 236 | 1 412 |
| Dane | 12 775 | 520 443 | 1.14 | 6 032 | 12.2 | 2 747 | 5.5 | 37 720 | 8.8 | 65 519 | 12 936 | 35 662 | 14 751 | 3 017 |

1. Per 1,000 estimated resident population.  2. Data for serious crimes have not been adjusted for underreporting; this may affect comparability between geographic areas and over time.  3. Per 100,000 population estimated by the FBI.

# Table B. States and Counties — Crime, Education, Money Income, and Poverty

| | Serious crimes known to police, 2011 (cont.)[1] Rate[2] | | Education — School enrollment and attainment, 2007–2011 | | | | Education — Local government expenditures,[5] 2009–2010 | | Money income, 2007–2011 | Money income — Households | | | Income and poverty, 2011 — Percent below poverty level | | | |
|---|---|---|---|---|---|---|---|---|---|---|---|---|---|---|---|---|
| | | | Enrollment[3] | | Attainment[4] (percent) | | | | | Median income | | | | | | |
| STATE County | Violent | Property | Total | Percent private | High school graduate or less | Bachelor's degree or more | Total current expenditures (mil dol) | Current expenditures per student (dollars) | Per capita income[6] (dollars) | Dollars | Percent change, 2000 to 2007–2011 (constant 2011 dollars) | Percent with income of $200,000 or more | Median household income (dollars) | All persons | Children under 18 years | Children 5 to 17 years in families |
| | 46 | 47 | 48 | 49 | 50 | 51 | 52 | 53 | 54 | 55 | 56 | 57 | 58 | 59 | 60 | 61 |
| **WEST VIRGINIA—Cont'd** | | | | | | | | | | | | | | | | |
| Brooke | 95 | 819 | 5 375 | 14.4 | 58.0 | 15.6 | 40.3 | 11 834 | 22 793 | 41 441 | -6.9 | 0.9 | 41 034 | 15.0 | 23.0 | 19.8 |
| Cabell | 280 | 3 375 | 25 022 | 12.0 | 48.8 | 23.6 | 146.5 | 11 669 | 22 302 | 35 691 | -7.2 | 1.9 | 36 864 | 22.3 | 28.4 | 26.0 |
| Calhoun | 254 | 749 | 1 526 | 1.6 | 75.0 | 7.7 | 12.5 | 11 313 | 18 128 | 26 099 | -10.4 | 0.6 | 28 581 | 25.8 | 33.5 | 31.9 |
| Clay | NA | NA | 2 199 | 0.5 | 74.4 | 7.6 | 21.5 | 10 543 | 16 127 | 29 105 | -2.5 | 1.2 | 29 802 | 29.2 | 41.6 | 35.1 |
| Doddridge | NA | NA | 1 658 | 6.8 | 67.0 | 10.0 | 14.8 | 12 672 | 16 042 | 32 063 | -11.2 | 1.2 | 35 261 | 19.5 | 25.6 | 23.0 |
| Fayette | NA | NA | 9 931 | 12.2 | 66.8 | 10.8 | 81.3 | 12 026 | 18 152 | 32 940 | -1.6 | 0.6 | 32 316 | 21.8 | 30.0 | 29.5 |
| Gilmer | NA | NA | 2 389 | 22.0 | 64.1 | 12.5 | 12.5 | 13 265 | 15 686 | 33 309 | 7.9 | 2.3 | 33 196 | 28.2 | 27.5 | 26.7 |
| Grant | 196 | 783 | 2 502 | 5.4 | 72.1 | 12.5 | 19.6 | 10 137 | 20 405 | 40 008 | 2.5 | 0.4 | 37 953 | 17.6 | 28.7 | 26.9 |
| Greenbrier | 65 | 1 050 | 7 391 | 11.9 | 60.7 | 17.0 | 62.6 | 11 847 | 21 025 | 35 180 | -3.2 | 1.2 | 35 924 | 17.9 | 25.4 | 23.9 |
| Hampshire | 463 | 992 | 5 283 | 12.6 | 75.8 | 8.8 | 38.6 | 10 124 | 17 388 | 29 001 | -32.2 | 0.5 | 36 588 | 21.3 | 28.8 | 26.3 |
| Hancock | 46 | 693 | 6 215 | 11.6 | 55.3 | 15.5 | 46.1 | 10 689 | 23 381 | 38 369 | -15.8 | 1.8 | 38 013 | 16.6 | 25.6 | 23.8 |
| Hardy | 385 | 1 275 | 2 834 | 6.1 | 68.8 | 9.3 | 23.2 | 10 043 | 19 193 | 33 060 | -23.1 | 0.8 | 38 013 | 16.2 | 24.3 | 22.4 |
| Harrison | 189 | 2 163 | 14 795 | 9.7 | 56.1 | 18.0 | 131.9 | 11 784 | 21 846 | 40 556 | -1.7 | 1.4 | 39 899 | 17.4 | 26.2 | 23.2 |
| Jackson | 51 | 889 | 6 796 | 5.8 | 56.9 | 15.5 | 56.7 | 11 248 | 21 855 | 43 191 | -1.4 | 1.1 | 41 066 | 17.8 | 26.5 | 23.9 |
| Jefferson | 90 | 1 243 | 14 335 | 15.8 | 45.7 | 28.7 | 102.4 | 11 909 | 29 602 | 65 285 | 9.0 | 4.2 | 59 280 | 11.4 | 14.5 | 12.9 |
| Kanawha | 496 | 3 433 | 41 544 | 15.2 | 51.2 | 24.1 | 321.9 | 11 042 | 26 790 | 44 265 | -2.9 | 3.1 | 40 409 | 17.2 | 27.4 | 25.4 |
| Lewis | 116 | 610 | 2 990 | 10.7 | 66.9 | 13.1 | 31.1 | 11 722 | 20 112 | 34 617 | -5.3 | 2.4 | 37 270 | 19.8 | 28.8 | 25.9 |
| Lincoln | NA | NA | 4 096 | 5.0 | 73.1 | 8.0 | 44.5 | 12 261 | 17 183 | 31 880 | 4.2 | 1.1 | 32 517 | 27.1 | 34.5 | 32.1 |
| Logan | 499 | 1 960 | 7 209 | 3.2 | 69.3 | 9.1 | 72.2 | 11 232 | 19 019 | 36 562 | 10.1 | 0.6 | 34 001 | 21.4 | 28.4 | 27.7 |
| McDowell | 348 | 1 485 | 3 869 | 8.6 | 77.8 | 6.3 | 48.7 | 13 257 | 13 345 | 21 967 | -3.9 | 0.3 | 23 751 | 34.2 | 45.8 | 44.3 |
| Marion | 152 | 1 164 | 12 966 | 11.3 | 56.0 | 19.3 | 94.9 | 11 688 | 22 024 | 39 870 | 3.2 | 1.2 | 39 774 | 16.3 | 23.4 | 20.8 |
| Marshall | 201 | 2 335 | 7 501 | 9.8 | 58.9 | 13.2 | 63.8 | 13 224 | 22 545 | 37 313 | -10.8 | 0.9 | 41 974 | 15.6 | 22.3 | 19.9 |
| Mason | 149 | 1 654 | 5 828 | 7.7 | 64.6 | 11.0 | 51.4 | 11 938 | 20 040 | 36 468 | -0.5 | 1.4 | 35 132 | 19.5 | 28.6 | 26.6 |
| Mercer | 276 | 2 091 | 13 635 | 12.0 | 60.5 | 16.8 | 108.0 | 11 305 | 19 527 | 33 704 | -6.3 | 1.4 | 33 500 | 21.5 | 33.6 | 31.8 |
| Mineral | 307 | 1 682 | 6 330 | 5.4 | 64.7 | 12.5 | 52.9 | 11 865 | 20 540 | 34 691 | -17.5 | 1.2 | 38 073 | 17.2 | 24.8 | 22.4 |
| Mingo | 293 | 1 043 | 5 553 | 5.4 | 70.0 | 8.8 | 57.7 | 12 592 | 18 610 | 32 794 | 13.8 | 0.7 | 31 681 | 26.0 | 32.1 | 28.2 |
| Monongalia | 333 | 2 035 | 35 503 | 5.8 | 42.6 | 36.8 | 118.7 | 11 347 | 23 610 | 41 325 | 6.9 | 3.1 | 43 447 | 19.0 | 16.8 | 16.3 |
| Monroe | 111 | 902 | 2 599 | 15.4 | 64.7 | 13.6 | 21.7 | 11 132 | 19 166 | 39 047 | 4.9 | 0.0 | 37 066 | 17.6 | 27.5 | 24.9 |
| Morgan | 103 | 1 461 | 3 596 | 8.7 | 64.5 | 14.9 | 30.1 | 11 346 | 21 801 | 36 703 | -22.4 | 0.8 | 40 762 | 14.1 | 21.7 | 19.3 |
| Nicholas | 838 | 1 689 | 5 287 | 4.0 | 67.0 | 12.7 | 43.5 | 10 761 | 20 455 | 39 636 | 8.8 | 1.4 | 36 080 | 21.3 | 29.3 | 27.3 |
| Ohio | 629 | 2 300 | 11 222 | 27.9 | 45.8 | 26.8 | 64.5 | 12 205 | 24 901 | 41 188 | -1.1 | 2.5 | 36 836 | 16.6 | 21.6 | 20.3 |
| Pendleton | NA | NA | 1 215 | 4.0 | 65.2 | 11.9 | 13.5 | 12 444 | 19 328 | 32 989 | -19.7 | 0.0 | 37 042 | 18.1 | 26.5 | 24.5 |
| Pleasants | 52 | 330 | 1 769 | 3.4 | 57.9 | 10.7 | 17.8 | 13 725 | 19 035 | 39 052 | -11.6 | 0.0 | 41 596 | 15.7 | 21.3 | 18.5 |
| Pocahontas | 104 | 1 173 | 1 460 | 7.3 | 62.3 | 16.4 | 15.1 | 12 571 | 17 861 | 33 816 | -5.1 | 0.3 | 34 928 | 18.7 | 28.7 | 27.2 |
| Preston | 246 | 1 335 | 6 097 | 7.7 | 66.2 | 12.1 | 50.7 | 10 955 | 20 438 | 43 434 | 15.2 | 1.4 | 40 375 | 16.8 | 23.9 | 22.8 |
| Putnam | 163 | 1 143 | 11 957 | 9.5 | 48.3 | 23.7 | 106.4 | 11 182 | 27 220 | 53 640 | -5.2 | 3.4 | 53 964 | 11.5 | 14.9 | 13.0 |
| Raleigh | 331 | 3 076 | 16 429 | 17.0 | 60.2 | 16.3 | 138.6 | 11 234 | 21 230 | 38 596 | 1.4 | 1.4 | 38 154 | 17.0 | 23.4 | 21.3 |
| Randolph | 333 | 1 301 | 5 936 | 13.3 | 64.3 | 18.1 | 48.3 | 11 093 | 18 974 | 35 560 | -3.5 | 1.2 | 33 529 | 20.1 | 30.6 | 28.6 |
| Ritchie | 124 | 1 415 | 2 185 | 4.1 | 60.2 | 11.6 | 19.9 | 12 222 | 18 337 | 34 204 | -7.3 | 0.9 | 35 421 | 19.5 | 27.7 | 25.0 |
| Roane | 134 | 870 | 2 953 | 4.9 | 74.7 | 9.5 | 27.1 | 10 600 | 15 448 | 27 772 | -16.1 | 0.2 | 28 131 | 23.6 | 33.1 | 29.5 |
| Summers | 143 | 1 678 | 2 719 | 9.1 | 64.6 | 12.0 | 17.1 | 11 054 | 16 664 | 32 194 | 12.8 | 0.7 | 30 751 | 24.4 | 35.7 | 33.7 |
| Taylor | 18 | 213 | 3 583 | 5.6 | 63.1 | 14.2 | 23.7 | 9 680 | 20 092 | 39 142 | 6.9 | 1.0 | 39 055 | 17.6 | 24.7 | 24.1 |
| Tucker | 177 | 371 | 1 300 | 11.5 | 64.3 | 15.8 | 12.4 | 11 307 | 19 579 | 36 502 | 3.0 | 0.3 | 35 019 | 17.2 | 25.4 | 23.0 |
| Tyler | 228 | 1 139 | 1 745 | 1.0 | 67.7 | 8.8 | 19.1 | 12 864 | 19 097 | 36 563 | -7.5 | 1.0 | 36 952 | 20.3 | 28.0 | 23.6 |
| Upshur | 58 | 1 445 | 6 083 | 24.8 | 67.6 | 14.7 | 43.9 | 11 479 | 18 831 | 37 689 | 3.5 | 1.3 | 36 719 | 20.0 | 28.3 | 26.4 |
| Wayne | 131 | 2 209 | 10 248 | 6.6 | 62.5 | 12.1 | 85.5 | 11 316 | 18 680 | 36 029 | -2.4 | 0.8 | 35 418 | 20.8 | 28.1 | 27.1 |
| Webster | NA | NA | 1 553 | 3.9 | 75.9 | 8.6 | 18.3 | 11 598 | 16 899 | 25 990 | -8.6 | 0.7 | 28 697 | 26.8 | 38.0 | 36.8 |
| Wetzel | 43 | 626 | 3 469 | 5.0 | 63.5 | 13.0 | 36.0 | 12 570 | 21 281 | 37 673 | -9.8 | 0.8 | 38 457 | 17.9 | 26.5 | 23.9 |
| Wirt | 437 | 1 310 | 1 249 | 8.2 | 63.0 | 10.8 | 11.4 | 11 770 | 18 731 | 37 482 | -9.7 | 0.4 | 36 084 | 19.9 | 30.2 | 27.3 |
| Wood | 402 | 2 074 | 19 951 | 11.5 | 47.5 | 18.7 | 150.0 | 11 125 | 23 413 | 42 257 | -6.0 | 1.9 | 38 005 | 18.0 | 27.7 | 24.6 |
| Wyoming | 315 | 1 732 | 4 808 | 5.3 | 72.0 | 9.9 | 48.2 | 11 595 | 17 947 | 36 641 | 13.4 | 0.3 | 32 851 | 25.6 | 34.1 | 32.0 |
| **WISCONSIN** | 237 | 2 433 | 1 487 947 | 16.9 | 43.8 | 26.0 | 9 829.0 | 11 266 | 27 192 | 52 374 | -11.4 | 2.8 | 50 401 | 13.1 | 18.4 | 16.5 |
| Adams | 91 | 2 881 | 3 577 | 8.0 | 57.4 | 11.2 | 20.9 | 11 538 | 22 296 | 41 152 | -8.8 | 1.0 | 40 339 | 16.7 | 28.6 | 26.7 |
| Ashland | 216 | 3 605 | 4 036 | 23.0 | 44.3 | 22.6 | 31.4 | 11 582 | 20 367 | 37 900 | -11.2 | 1.3 | 36 683 | 16.9 | 26.0 | 23.1 |
| Barron | 68 | 1 436 | 9 938 | 10.3 | 52.6 | 17.4 | 86.8 | 11 007 | 23 267 | 44 806 | -11.0 | 1.6 | 44 666 | 12.7 | 20.1 | 17.5 |
| Bayfield | 153 | 1 605 | 2 964 | 13.0 | 40.1 | 26.7 | 22.8 | 14 679 | 24 502 | 44 190 | -2.0 | 1.0 | 42 558 | 12.8 | 20.8 | 16.9 |
| Brown | 196 | 1 793 | 66 895 | 16.5 | 43.6 | 25.9 | 454.0 | 10 698 | 27 344 | 53 353 | -14.9 | 2.9 | 52 744 | 10.9 | 15.2 | 13.7 |
| Buffalo | 28 | 276 | 2 977 | 8.3 | 55.3 | 16.2 | 23.8 | 10 644 | 23 240 | 46 073 | -8.3 | 1.3 | 44 425 | 12.2 | 17.6 | 15.3 |
| Burnett | 167 | 1 810 | 2 932 | 10.0 | 51.5 | 16.4 | 28.0 | 9 599 | 22 872 | 40 686 | -11.9 | 1.4 | 40 295 | 15.3 | 26.6 | 23.1 |
| Calumet | 116 | 1 279 | 12 452 | 15.0 | 46.1 | 26.1 | 39.0 | 9 811 | 28 182 | 63 395 | -10.7 | 2.6 | 66 543 | 6.2 | 8.4 | 7.6 |
| Chippewa | 110 | 1 643 | 13 944 | 12.7 | 50.1 | 18.1 | 94.9 | 10 613 | 24 346 | 50 239 | -6.0 | 1.4 | 50 120 | 10.9 | 16.0 | 15.1 |
| Clark | 224 | 924 | 8 063 | 20.1 | 62.3 | 11.6 | 54.5 | 10 692 | 20 202 | 42 756 | -8.4 | 1.6 | 40 056 | 18.1 | 27.2 | 25.0 |
| Columbia | 152 | 1 373 | 13 423 | 13.7 | 46.0 | 20.5 | 97.0 | 10 888 | 28 160 | 57 805 | -5.0 | 2.4 | 57 457 | 9.2 | 14.2 | 12.1 |
| Crawford | 36 | 1 376 | 3 979 | 13.9 | 56.3 | 15.5 | 26.9 | 11 945 | 22 049 | 40 933 | -11.2 | 1.4 | 41 181 | 13.4 | 19.8 | 17.9 |
| Dane | 230 | 2 787 | 144 908 | 12.5 | 26.7 | 45.4 | 796.1 | 11 583 | 33 118 | 61 913 | -6.8 | 4.4 | 60 489 | 12.8 | 14.5 | 12.9 |

1. Data for serious crimes have not been adjusted for underreporting; this may affect comparability between geographic areas and over time.   2. Per 100,000 population estimated by the FBI.   3. All persons 3 years old and over enrolled in nursery school through college.   4. Persons 25 years old and over.   5. Elementary and secondary education expenditures.   6. Based on population estimated by the American Community Survey, 2007–2011.

| STATE County | Personal income, 2011 | | | | | | | | | | | | |
|---|---|---|---|---|---|---|---|---|---|---|---|---|---|
| | | | Per capita[1] | | | | | Transfer payments (mil dol) | | | | | |
| | | | | | | | | | Government payments to individuals | | | | |
| | Total (mil dol) | Percent change, 2010–2011 | Dollars | Rank | Wages and salaries[2] (mil dol) | Proprietors' income (mil dol) | Dividends, interest, and rent (mil dol) | Total | Total | Social Security | Medical payments | Income mainte-nance | Unemploy-ment insurance |
| | 62 | 63 | 64 | 65 | 66 | 67 | 68 | 69 | 70 | 71 | 72 | 73 | 74 |
| WEST VIRGINIA—Cont'd | | | | | | | | | | | | | |
| Brooke | 740 | 3.7 | 31 037 | 2 090 | 399 | 61 | 94 | 219 | 213 | 87 | 89 | 18 | 7 |
| Cabell | 3 294 | 3.7 | 34 079 | 1 500 | 2 722 | 187 | 457 | 944 | 923 | 289 | 392 | 105 | 20 |
| Calhoun | 176 | 6.5 | 23 003 | 3 058 | 69 | 11 | 19 | 75 | 73 | 25 | 31 | 10 | 2 |
| Clay | 222 | 4.1 | 23 708 | 3 038 | 106 | 9 | 19 | 87 | 85 | 32 | 30 | 14 | 3 |
| Doddridge | 167 | 3.0 | 20 412 | 3 100 | 47 | 13 | 19 | 43 | 41 | 17 | 12 | 6 | 2 |
| Fayette | 1 338 | 5.3 | 29 277 | 2 412 | 605 | 65 | 118 | 482 | 471 | 151 | 215 | 53 | 10 |
| Gilmer | 196 | 7.3 | 22 482 | 3 073 | 116 | 7 | 22 | 66 | 64 | 19 | 28 | 7 | 2 |
| Grant | 359 | 5.9 | 30 162 | 2 257 | 214 | 30 | 45 | 111 | 108 | 38 | 49 | 11 | 3 |
| Greenbrier | 1 150 | 5.8 | 32 130 | 1 855 | 602 | 88 | 153 | 380 | 372 | 124 | 171 | 33 | 8 |
| Hampshire | 587 | 3.9 | 24 634 | 2 994 | 170 | 37 | 76 | 176 | 171 | 70 | 61 | 23 | 5 |
| Hancock | 938 | 4.1 | 30 670 | 2 159 | 498 | 21 | 117 | 315 | 308 | 117 | 139 | 27 | 12 |
| Hardy | 367 | 3.2 | 26 356 | 2 844 | 225 | 15 | 49 | 96 | 93 | 41 | 27 | 13 | 3 |
| Harrison | 2 687 | 5.3 | 38 703 | 880 | 1 946 | 299 | 327 | 631 | 616 | 218 | 260 | 67 | 13 |
| Jackson | 779 | 3.4 | 26 624 | 2 809 | 346 | 51 | 83 | 259 | 253 | 99 | 98 | 30 | 12 |
| Jefferson | 2 067 | 5.1 | 38 127 | 954 | 733 | 97 | 237 | 337 | 325 | 123 | 99 | 34 | 9 |
| Kanawha | 8 213 | 4.8 | 42 704 | 525 | 6 092 | 866 | 1 046 | 1 987 | 1 945 | 659 | 897 | 190 | 40 |
| Lewis | 576 | 8.8 | 35 075 | 1 361 | 395 | 29 | 74 | 154 | 151 | 57 | 60 | 20 | 3 |
| Lincoln | 533 | 2.6 | 24 722 | 2 985 | 177 | 14 | 45 | 186 | 181 | 70 | 58 | 32 | 5 |
| Logan | 1 227 | 8.5 | 33 665 | 1 571 | 688 | 24 | 101 | 465 | 457 | 136 | 204 | 48 | 7 |
| McDowell | 595 | 6.9 | 27 360 | 2 708 | 408 | 12 | 52 | 260 | 256 | 84 | 99 | 47 | 5 |
| Marion | 2 056 | 5.6 | 36 338 | 1 161 | 1 134 | 140 | 230 | 510 | 497 | 186 | 193 | 48 | 11 |
| Marshall | 1 190 | 6.2 | 36 275 | 1 174 | 664 | 210 | 115 | 275 | 268 | 101 | 113 | 29 | 9 |
| Mason | 714 | 2.4 | 26 167 | 2 862 | 354 | 25 | 74 | 259 | 253 | 91 | 108 | 29 | 9 |
| Mercer | 2 040 | 4.5 | 32 656 | 1 768 | 1 011 | 109 | 272 | 733 | 719 | 216 | 330 | 84 | 12 |
| Mineral | 895 | 3.6 | 31 733 | 1 948 | 385 | 40 | 91 | 255 | 249 | 86 | 107 | 23 | 7 |
| Mingo | 820 | 7.0 | 30 862 | 2 130 | 601 | 21 | 66 | 308 | 302 | 104 | 122 | 45 | 5 |
| Monongalia | 3 708 | 5.3 | 37 632 | 1 011 | 3 138 | 318 | 445 | 644 | 622 | 181 | 290 | 49 | 16 |
| Monroe | 368 | 6.6 | 27 200 | 2 739 | 103 | 19 | 40 | 118 | 115 | 48 | 43 | 11 | 3 |
| Morgan | 558 | 4.2 | 31 830 | 1 925 | 118 | 25 | 69 | 148 | 144 | 57 | 58 | 14 | 4 |
| Nicholas | 817 | 5.9 | 31 088 | 2 078 | 429 | 51 | 84 | 266 | 260 | 97 | 106 | 31 | 6 |
| Ohio | 1 680 | 4.2 | 37 969 | 977 | 1 318 | 43 | 362 | 462 | 452 | 158 | 207 | 38 | 10 |
| Pendleton | 238 | 4.2 | 31 013 | 2 096 | 90 | 17 | 38 | 69 | 67 | 26 | 30 | 6 | 1 |
| Pleasants | 241 | 6.1 | 31 718 | 1 952 | 159 | 20 | 26 | 81 | 79 | 25 | 44 | 6 | 2 |
| Pocahontas | 268 | 4.0 | 30 446 | 2 212 | 119 | 23 | 38 | 104 | 102 | 30 | 56 | 8 | 3 |
| Preston | 951 | 4.3 | 28 197 | 2 591 | 362 | 60 | 100 | 259 | 251 | 94 | 101 | 27 | 7 |
| Putnam | 2 275 | 6.9 | 40 617 | 695 | 1 213 | 113 | 214 | 393 | 380 | 170 | 132 | 35 | 12 |
| Raleigh | 2 916 | 6.8 | 36 852 | 1 095 | 1 811 | 190 | 315 | 819 | 801 | 281 | 333 | 82 | 15 |
| Randolph | 902 | 5.0 | 30 623 | 2 168 | 485 | 70 | 106 | 305 | 298 | 89 | 148 | 29 | 7 |
| Ritchie | 300 | 5.3 | 29 152 | 2 427 | 147 | 20 | 33 | 98 | 95 | 37 | 37 | 11 | 2 |
| Roane | 374 | 4.7 | 25 142 | 2 955 | 133 | 15 | 43 | 146 | 143 | 52 | 58 | 19 | 5 |
| Summers | 342 | 4.4 | 24 629 | 2 995 | 104 | 11 | 38 | 149 | 146 | 39 | 71 | 16 | 3 |
| Taylor | 457 | 3.9 | 27 030 | 2 758 | 131 | 15 | 52 | 137 | 133 | 45 | 53 | 16 | 3 |
| Tucker | 202 | 4.5 | 28 837 | 2 480 | 88 | 10 | 26 | 70 | 69 | 24 | 34 | 5 | 2 |
| Tyler | 241 | 6.1 | 26 470 | 2 825 | 127 | 8 | 33 | 78 | 76 | 34 | 27 | 9 | 2 |
| Upshur | 712 | 6.7 | 29 288 | 2 410 | 408 | 56 | 85 | 196 | 191 | 72 | 71 | 24 | 5 |
| Wayne | 1 237 | 3.8 | 29 361 | 2 399 | 558 | 34 | 109 | 316 | 306 | 129 | 80 | 51 | 9 |
| Webster | 228 | 4.0 | 24 896 | 2 973 | 114 | 8 | 24 | 95 | 93 | 33 | 35 | 15 | 2 |
| Wetzel | 510 | 3.3 | 31 194 | 2 064 | 177 | 14 | 70 | 171 | 168 | 61 | 75 | 18 | 5 |
| Wirt | 131 | 5.7 | 22 699 | 3 067 | 28 | 6 | 13 | 50 | 49 | 20 | 17 | 7 | 2 |
| Wood | 2 846 | 4.4 | 32 666 | 1 765 | 1 908 | 151 | 393 | 845 | 826 | 302 | 346 | 92 | 21 |
| Wyoming | 682 | 6.2 | 29 106 | 2 438 | 294 | 12 | 52 | 239 | 233 | 96 | 81 | 31 | 5 |
| WISCONSIN | 226 042 | 4.5 | 39 575 | X | 147 053 | 17 137 | 35 513 | 39 852 | 38 588 | 14 664 | 15 507 | 4 079 | 2 079 |
| Adams | 691 | 3.9 | 33 340 | 1 645 | 200 | 113 | 97 | 189 | 185 | 87 | 65 | 16 | 5 |
| Ashland | 521 | 2.0 | 32 283 | 1 827 | 373 | 43 | 72 | 149 | 146 | 49 | 67 | 14 | 7 |
| Barron | 1 518 | 3.2 | 33 083 | 1 694 | 871 | 148 | 230 | 368 | 357 | 143 | 148 | 33 | 16 |
| Bayfield | 504 | 3.9 | 33 364 | 1 639 | 149 | 38 | 103 | 137 | 133 | 56 | 53 | 10 | 6 |
| Brown | 9 929 | 4.1 | 39 493 | 805 | 8 289 | 793 | 1 646 | 1 467 | 1 412 | 565 | 505 | 145 | 91 |
| Buffalo | 547 | 4.0 | 40 436 | 707 | 200 | 100 | 85 | 100 | 97 | 40 | 41 | 7 | 3 |
| Burnett | 533 | 4.0 | 34 372 | 1 459 | 192 | 55 | 92 | 151 | 148 | 67 | 56 | 11 | 5 |
| Calumet | 2 152 | 8.0 | 43 473 | 469 | 554 | 187 | 240 | 227 | 216 | 103 | 71 | 15 | 16 |
| Chippewa | 2 158 | 3.9 | 34 375 | 1 458 | 1 029 | 264 | 329 | 439 | 425 | 161 | 180 | 39 | 23 |
| Clark | 1 061 | 6.3 | 30 541 | 2 190 | 442 | 162 | 161 | 237 | 230 | 81 | 107 | 17 | 12 |
| Columbia | 2 309 | 3.6 | 40 580 | 698 | 999 | 205 | 349 | 389 | 376 | 155 | 152 | 24 | 25 |
| Crawford | 542 | 4.4 | 32 425 | 1 796 | 310 | 52 | 86 | 130 | 127 | 51 | 52 | 11 | 6 |
| Dane | 23 269 | 6.2 | 46 916 | 302 | 18 505 | 1 618 | 4 042 | 2 693 | 2 584 | 1 020 | 976 | 261 | 125 |

1. Based on the resident population estimated as of July 1 of the year shown.    2. Includes supplements to wages and salaries.

| STATE County | Earnings, 2011 | | | | | | | | | Social Security beneficiaries, December 2011 | | | Housing units, 2010 | |
|---|---|---|---|---|---|---|---|---|---|---|---|---|---|---|
| | | | Percent by selected industries | | | | | | | | | Supplemental Security Income recipients, December 2011 | | |
| | | | Goods-related[1] | | Service-related and health | | | | | | | | | |
| | Total (mil dol) | Farm | Total | Manufacturing | Information and professional and technical services | Retail trade | Finance, insurance, and real estate | Health care and social services | Government | Number | Rate[2] | | Total | Percent change, 2000–2010 |
| | 75 | 76 | 77 | 78 | 79 | 80 | 81 | 82 | 83 | 84 | 85 | 86 | 87 | 88 |
| WEST VIRGINIA—Cont'd | | | | | | | | | | | | | | |
| Brooke | 461 | -0.1 | D | 34.4 | 1.9 | 5.0 | 3.6 | D | 11.2 | 6 265 | 263 | 621 | 10 967 | -2.0 |
| Cabell | 2 909 | -0.1 | D | 12.1 | 6.7 | 8.1 | 4.2 | 24.6 | 18.2 | 21 910 | 227 | 4 389 | 46 169 | 1.2 |
| Calhoun | 80 | -1.9 | D | 0.8 | D | 5.8 | D | D | 21.9 | 2 215 | 289 | 673 | 3 963 | 3.0 |
| Clay | 116 | -0.6 | 45.7 | 2.9 | D | 4.2 | D | 7.8 | 24.2 | 2 715 | 290 | 756 | 4 572 | -5.5 |
| Doddridge | 60 | -2.2 | D | D | D | 9.8 | D | 7.6 | 43.4 | 1 415 | 173 | 245 | 3 946 | 7.8 |
| Fayette | 670 | -0.1 | 23.3 | 6.1 | 3.8 | 8.9 | 3.2 | D | 27.5 | 12 115 | 265 | 2 684 | 21 618 | 0.0 |
| Gilmer | 123 | -2.0 | D | 7.5 | D | 3.8 | D | D | 53.5 | 1 625 | 187 | 346 | 3 448 | -4.8 |
| Grant | 244 | 0.0 | 32.9 | 6.2 | D | 4.6 | 2.6 | 7.3 | 19.4 | 3 160 | 266 | 426 | 6 366 | 4.3 |
| Greenbrier | 690 | 0.8 | 12.1 | 5.5 | 4.4 | 9.7 | 2.8 | D | 19.6 | 9 945 | 278 | 1 461 | 18 980 | 7.6 |
| Hampshire | 206 | -0.8 | D | 4.1 | D | 7.6 | 5.3 | D | 33.9 | 5 665 | 238 | 769 | 13 688 | 22.4 |
| Hancock | 519 | -0.1 | D | 37.2 | 4.1 | 7.0 | 3.4 | 7.1 | 14.8 | 8 250 | 270 | 830 | 14 541 | -1.0 |
| Hardy | 239 | -1.5 | D | D | D | 7.0 | 3.1 | D | 17.0 | 3 375 | 243 | 431 | 8 078 | 13.5 |
| Harrison | 2 246 | -0.2 | 17.2 | 5.8 | 10.1 | 6.9 | 3.5 | 12.2 | 29.3 | 17 015 | 245 | 3 052 | 31 431 | 1.0 |
| Jackson | 397 | -1.5 | D | 23.6 | 5.6 | 9.5 | 4.3 | 11.4 | 20.0 | 7 620 | 261 | 1 320 | 13 305 | 8.7 |
| Jefferson | 830 | 0.4 | D | 5.5 | 6.1 | 6.4 | 4.0 | 7.9 | 30.8 | 9 090 | 168 | 805 | 22 037 | 25.0 |
| Kanawha | 6 958 | 0.0 | 16.9 | 4.5 | 12.1 | 6.0 | 7.2 | 17.1 | 19.4 | 48 360 | 251 | 7 585 | 92 618 | -1.2 |
| Lewis | 424 | -0.6 | 40.3 | 1.9 | D | 6.1 | 4.2 | D | 18.4 | 4 600 | 280 | 958 | 7 958 | 0.2 |
| Lincoln | 191 | -0.3 | D | 0.3 | 4.0 | 4.6 | 1.2 | D | 27.1 | 5 735 | 266 | 1 839 | 9 887 | 0.4 |
| Logan | 712 | 0.0 | D | 5.5 | 3.9 | 8.6 | 1.9 | D | 16.7 | 10 325 | 283 | 2 480 | 16 743 | -0.4 |
| McDowell | 420 | 0.0 | 48.5 | 0.3 | 2.3 | 4.7 | 1.8 | D | 27.1 | 7 015 | 323 | 3 066 | 11 322 | -16.6 |
| Marion | 1 273 | 0.0 | D | 5.2 | 11.4 | 7.9 | 4.4 | 8.5 | 18.9 | 13 815 | 244 | 2 030 | 26 463 | -0.7 |
| Marshall | 873 | -0.4 | 52.0 | 26.3 | D | 5.0 | 1.9 | D | 11.7 | 7 485 | 228 | 961 | 15 918 | 0.7 |
| Mason | 379 | 0.9 | D | 13.8 | 2.4 | 5.1 | 2.6 | D | 22.0 | 7 120 | 261 | 1 329 | 13 006 | 7.9 |
| Mercer | 1 120 | -0.2 | 13.9 | 6.4 | 4.9 | 10.0 | 3.6 | 16.1 | 25.2 | 17 185 | 275 | 3 736 | 30 115 | -0.1 |
| Mineral | 425 | -0.2 | 39.7 | 33.6 | 7.7 | 7.6 | 4.0 | D | 20.7 | 6 435 | 228 | 768 | 13 039 | 7.8 |
| Mingo | 622 | 0.0 | 55.6 | 3.2 | 2.8 | 2.7 | 1.5 | 6.1 | 12.4 | 7 990 | 301 | 2 849 | 12 699 | -1.5 |
| Monongalia | 3 457 | -0.1 | 17.6 | 9.2 | 8.3 | 5.1 | 4.9 | 18.6 | 29.5 | 13 060 | 133 | 1 775 | 43 238 | 17.8 |
| Monroe | 122 | -2.9 | 31.1 | 20.5 | D | 5.0 | D | 7.0 | 41.0 | 3 855 | 285 | 509 | 7 601 | 4.6 |
| Morgan | 143 | -1.0 | D | 10.5 | 3.6 | 8.7 | 4.9 | D | 27.3 | 4 290 | 245 | 352 | 9 753 | 20.8 |
| Nicholas | 479 | -0.2 | 36.4 | 8.6 | 2.6 | 11.3 | 2.0 | D | 21.6 | 7 565 | 288 | 1 394 | 13 064 | 5.3 |
| Ohio | 1 362 | 0.0 | D | 5.1 | 10.4 | 8.1 | 5.7 | 22.5 | 16.4 | 11 550 | 261 | 1 418 | 21 172 | -4.5 |
| Pendleton | 107 | 3.6 | D | D | 4.0 | 5.6 | D | D | 45.1 | 2 220 | 289 | 229 | 5 132 | 0.6 |
| Pleasants | 179 | -0.4 | D | D | 3.2 | 4.0 | D | 6.1 | 18.4 | 1 865 | 245 | 279 | 3 390 | 5.5 |
| Pocahontas | 142 | 0.1 | D | D | 8.8 | 7.4 | 3.5 | D | 27.9 | 2 440 | 278 | 329 | 8 847 | 16.5 |
| Preston | 421 | -0.3 | 26.3 | 6.7 | 3.5 | 7.4 | 2.9 | 6.9 | 35.2 | 7 470 | 222 | 1 253 | 15 097 | 12.3 |
| Putnam | 1 327 | 0.1 | 25.1 | 11.5 | 7.7 | 6.0 | 5.2 | 7.9 | 10.9 | 12 190 | 218 | 1 311 | 23 438 | 8.4 |
| Raleigh | 2 002 | 0.0 | 24.2 | 3.6 | 6.6 | 8.3 | 3.1 | 15.6 | 20.6 | 21 325 | 270 | 3 700 | 35 931 | 0.7 |
| Randolph | 554 | 0.0 | 20.3 | 8.9 | D | 9.6 | 4.1 | D | 22.1 | 7 435 | 252 | 1 371 | 14 189 | 5.3 |
| Ritchie | 167 | -1.1 | 46.4 | 22.3 | D | 5.4 | 2.9 | D | 16.1 | 3 090 | 300 | 589 | 5 843 | 6.0 |
| Roane | 148 | -2.8 | D | 5.6 | 3.2 | 11.9 | 5.2 | 18.8 | 23.9 | 4 400 | 296 | 1 107 | 7 351 | -0.1 |
| Summers | 115 | 0.3 | 4.9 | 0.8 | D | 7.2 | 3.3 | 13.2 | 30.3 | 3 375 | 243 | 896 | 7 680 | 4.8 |
| Taylor | 146 | 0.1 | D | D | D | 11.8 | D | D | 39.7 | 3 670 | 217 | 737 | 7 541 | 5.8 |
| Tucker | 99 | -0.3 | D | 14.4 | D | 6.3 | 5.0 | 9.8 | 31.6 | 1 845 | 263 | 223 | 5 346 | 15.4 |
| Tyler | 135 | -0.2 | 48.7 | 42.2 | D | 3.9 | D | 9.6 | 22.6 | 2 530 | 277 | 354 | 5 000 | 4.6 |
| Upshur | 464 | -0.1 | 32.2 | 8.6 | 4.6 | 9.6 | 4.7 | D | 15.4 | 5 825 | 239 | 1 124 | 11 099 | 3.2 |
| Wayne | 592 | 0.0 | D | 6.5 | 2.2 | 4.9 | 1.1 | D | 39.6 | 10 450 | 248 | 2 578 | 19 227 | 0.6 |
| Webster | 122 | -0.2 | D | 3.9 | 2.4 | 3.9 | D | 5.6 | 26.0 | 2 825 | 309 | 802 | 5 428 | 2.9 |
| Wetzel | 191 | -0.1 | 15.2 | 2.7 | 3.6 | 14.5 | 3.5 | D | 32.4 | 4 520 | 276 | 840 | 8 173 | -1.7 |
| Wirt | 34 | -1.4 | D | D | D | 7.2 | D | 9.8 | 40.5 | 1 695 | 294 | 387 | 3 231 | -1.1 |
| Wood | 2 059 | -0.2 | 20.1 | 13.0 | 5.0 | 9.7 | 5.9 | 16.4 | 22.8 | 22 805 | 262 | 3 779 | 40 215 | 1.1 |
| Wyoming | 305 | 0.0 | 45.9 | 1.8 | 2.2 | 6.0 | 1.5 | D | 21.3 | 7 170 | 306 | 1 820 | 10 958 | -6.3 |
| WISCONSIN | 164 189 | 1.8 | 24.6 | 19.3 | 7.7 | 6.1 | 7.6 | 12.7 | 14.8 | 1 085 632 | 190 | 110 959 | 2 624 358 | 13.1 |
| Adams | 313 | 5.7 | D | D | D | 6.0 | D | 5.4 | 22.7 | 6 610 | 319 | 507 | 17 436 | 23.5 |
| Ashland | 416 | 1.3 | 21.5 | 14.5 | 3.5 | 7.6 | 2.8 | D | 24.2 | 4 005 | 248 | 409 | 9 656 | 8.7 |
| Barron | 1 019 | 4.7 | D | 24.8 | D | 9.1 | 3.4 | 11.9 | 18.6 | 11 500 | 251 | 898 | 23 614 | 12.6 |
| Bayfield | 187 | 2.8 | 11.9 | 3.2 | D | 8.4 | 3.4 | D | 36.2 | 4 335 | 287 | 284 | 12 999 | 11.7 |
| Brown | 9 082 | 1.0 | 22.8 | 17.7 | D | 5.5 | 8.7 | 13.6 | 11.3 | 41 920 | 167 | 4 499 | 104 371 | 15.7 |
| Buffalo | 300 | 11.8 | 10.5 | 5.2 | D | 9.6 | 3.3 | 4.2 | 16.0 | 3 285 | 243 | 196 | 6 664 | 9.3 |
| Burnett | 247 | 3.8 | D | 21.5 | D | 7.0 | 2.4 | D | 27.9 | 5 105 | 329 | 279 | 15 278 | 21.4 |
| Calumet | 741 | 7.2 | D | 29.8 | 5.9 | 5.2 | 5.8 | D | 10.1 | 7 535 | 152 | 420 | 19 695 | 25.0 |
| Chippewa | 1 293 | 5.4 | 34.7 | 26.4 | 3.0 | 9.9 | 2.9 | 9.5 | 14.5 | 12 760 | 203 | 1 127 | 27 185 | 19.1 |
| Clark | 605 | 13.2 | D | 22.8 | 2.0 | 6.0 | 2.5 | 6.5 | 15.6 | 6 765 | 195 | 483 | 15 076 | 11.4 |
| Columbia | 1 204 | 5.1 | D | 26.1 | 2.9 | 6.9 | 3.9 | 10.5 | 16.7 | 11 565 | 203 | 562 | 26 137 | 15.2 |
| Crawford | 362 | 5.9 | D | 21.6 | 1.7 | 16.8 | 3.1 | D | 13.8 | 4 290 | 257 | 332 | 8 802 | 3.8 |
| Dane | 20 123 | 0.8 | 13.9 | 8.9 | 14.3 | 5.3 | 10.9 | 9.6 | 24.6 | 71 010 | 143 | 7 186 | 216 022 | 19.7 |

1. Includes mining, construction, and manufacturing.    2. Per 1,000 resident population enumerated in the 2010 census.

| | Housing units, 2007–2011 | | | | | | | | Civilian labor force, 2012 | | | | Civilian employment,[6] 2007–2011 | | |
|---|---|---|---|---|---|---|---|---|---|---|---|---|---|---|---|
| | Occupied units | | | | | | | | | | Unemployment | | | Percent | |
| | | | Owner-occupied | | | Renter-occupied | | | | | | | | | | |
| | | | | Median owner cost as a percent of income | | | | | | | | | | | Con-struction, produc-tion, and mainte-nance occu-pations |
| STATE County | Total | Percent | Median value[1] | With a mort-gage | Without a mort-gage[2] | Median rent[3] | Median rent as a per-cent of income | Sub-stand-ard units[4] (percent) | Total | Percent change, 2011–2012 | Total | Rate[5] | Total | Manage-ment, business, science and arts | |
| | 89 | 90 | 91 | 92 | 93 | 94 | 95 | 96 | 97 | 98 | 99 | 100 | 101 | 102 | 103 |
| **WEST VIRGINIA—Cont'd** | | | | | | | | | | | | | | | |
| Brooke | 9 756 | 79.0 | 85 000 | 18.4 | 10.2 | 524 | 24.9 | 0.8 | 10 400 | -0.9 | 996 | 9.6 | 10 478 | 26.2 | 27.0 |
| Cabell | 40 397 | 62.4 | 99 500 | 19.6 | 9.9 | 601 | 31.9 | 1.1 | 43 441 | -0.6 | 2 946 | 6.8 | 40 792 | 34.7 | 18.0 |
| Calhoun | 3 146 | 77.1 | 72 900 | 17.8 | 9.9 | 378 | 30.7 | 2.2 | 2 773 | -0.8 | 303 | 10.9 | 2 622 | 20.3 | 39.9 |
| Clay | 3 512 | 80.2 | 76 400 | 17.9 | 11.0 | 414 | 30.8 | 2.0 | 3 257 | 0.7 | 399 | 12.3 | 3 127 | 25.1 | 37.4 |
| Doddridge | 2 823 | 82.5 | 78 100 | 21.5 | 9.9 | 514 | 23.3 | 4.8 | 3 191 | 0.1 | 226 | 7.1 | 3 093 | 19.5 | 35.2 |
| Fayette | 17 801 | 77.7 | 70 700 | 19.1 | 11.2 | 502 | 28.4 | 2.0 | 18 076 | 0.1 | 1 477 | 8.2 | 16 083 | 25.7 | 28.5 |
| Gilmer | 2 420 | 76.0 | 72 300 | 19.3 | 9.9 | 564 | 36.0 | 2.1 | 3 293 | -0.6 | 231 | 7.0 | 2 857 | 21.1 | 27.7 |
| Grant | 4 915 | 78.6 | 109 100 | 20.2 | 10.5 | 517 | 27.0 | 0.7 | 5 073 | 0.8 | 548 | 10.8 | 5 848 | 25.5 | 39.9 |
| Greenbrier | 15 412 | 74.6 | 99 600 | 21.7 | 9.9 | 593 | 28.5 | 2.3 | 15 236 | 0.2 | 1 187 | 7.8 | 14 296 | 28.3 | 28.9 |
| Hampshire | 10 331 | 60.8 | 138 600 | 23.3 | 11.0 | 499 | 29.7 | 1.9 | 9 537 | 1.3 | 713 | 7.5 | 9 659 | 18.7 | 42.9 |
| Hancock | 13 149 | 76.0 | 87 400 | 20.4 | 11.2 | 542 | 28.1 | 1.3 | 13 765 | -1.6 | 1 296 | 9.4 | 13 198 | 27.9 | 26.9 |
| Hardy | 4 829 | 76.2 | 134 100 | 22.2 | 9.9 | 530 | 26.3 | 0.7 | 6 552 | -0.5 | 537 | 8.2 | 5 979 | 20.7 | 50.0 |
| Harrison | 27 696 | 73.4 | 94 700 | 19.4 | 10.7 | 574 | 30.4 | 2.3 | 31 361 | 0.7 | 1 983 | 6.3 | 29 047 | 31.0 | 24.1 |
| Jackson | 11 483 | 79.6 | 104 200 | 18.3 | 9.9 | 533 | 28.1 | 3.0 | 11 076 | 0.5 | 1 003 | 9.1 | 11 730 | 32.7 | 27.2 |
| Jefferson | 19 415 | 77.2 | 237 100 | 26.2 | 10.3 | 852 | 26.1 | 3.0 | 25 226 | 1.4 | 1 278 | 5.1 | 25 835 | 39.2 | 18.5 |
| Kanawha | 82 337 | 71.3 | 99 900 | 18.9 | 9.9 | 628 | 25.8 | 1.2 | 90 086 | -0.4 | 5 739 | 6.4 | 88 334 | 36.1 | 17.7 |
| Lewis | 6 587 | 72.4 | 91 600 | 19.0 | 9.9 | 520 | 24.5 | 2.8 | 8 353 | 3.0 | 503 | 6.0 | 6 846 | 24.8 | 30.3 |
| Lincoln | 8 711 | 78.5 | 69 500 | 21.1 | 9.9 | 517 | 32.5 | 3.6 | 7 711 | 0.4 | 761 | 9.9 | 6 857 | 20.0 | 37.3 |
| Logan | 14 660 | 72.8 | 78 300 | 19.0 | 9.9 | 501 | 22.1 | 2.3 | 13 434 | 0.2 | 1 219 | 9.1 | 11 992 | 27.0 | 30.8 |
| McDowell | 8 292 | 76.1 | 33 300 | 21.8 | 10.3 | 424 | 35.8 | 2.9 | 7 761 | -0.1 | 753 | 9.7 | 4 980 | 28.7 | 34.3 |
| Marion | 22 794 | 75.2 | 87 900 | 18.2 | 11.7 | 598 | 29.9 | 2.0 | 26 763 | 0.8 | 1 691 | 6.3 | 24 941 | 29.0 | 26.0 |
| Marshall | 13 915 | 79.2 | 81 200 | 19.4 | 10.2 | 494 | 28.1 | 1.0 | 14 253 | -0.7 | 1 186 | 8.3 | 13 088 | 26.6 | 29.8 |
| Mason | 10 715 | 79.3 | 83 200 | 18.9 | 9.9 | 524 | 29.1 | 2.8 | 9 822 | -1.2 | 1 077 | 11.0 | 10 188 | 22.5 | 35.0 |
| Mercer | 25 611 | 73.3 | 74 400 | 19.8 | 9.9 | 528 | 31.7 | 2.2 | 24 099 | -1.1 | 1 789 | 7.4 | 23 095 | 36.1 | 25.5 |
| Mineral | 11 276 | 73.3 | 114 300 | 20.8 | 10.4 | 505 | 30.3 | 1.2 | 13 636 | 0.1 | 1 009 | 7.4 | 11 611 | 25.9 | 31.8 |
| Mingo | 10 776 | 76.9 | 63 500 | 19.5 | 9.9 | 453 | 24.8 | 3.1 | 8 810 | -1.5 | 868 | 9.9 | 8 210 | 26.4 | 35.1 |
| Monongalia | 35 266 | 57.2 | 154 900 | 19.0 | 9.9 | 666 | 35.0 | 1.0 | 51 120 | 1.7 | 2 502 | 4.9 | 44 992 | 41.0 | 18.0 |
| Monroe | 5 615 | 86.4 | 97 300 | 20.0 | 9.9 | 474 | 23.2 | 2.9 | 5 688 | 0.0 | 362 | 6.4 | 5 582 | 30.3 | 34.7 |
| Morgan | 7 171 | 67.0 | 165 900 | 22.0 | 11.3 | 651 | 28.5 | 1.6 | 7 297 | 1.4 | 530 | 7.3 | 7 216 | 24.1 | 32.9 |
| Nicholas | 10 149 | 81.9 | 75 800 | 18.9 | 9.9 | 511 | 29.1 | 2.0 | 10 602 | -0.9 | 967 | 9.1 | 10 391 | 26.6 | 33.4 |
| Ohio | 18 624 | 70.7 | 95 800 | 18.7 | 9.9 | 515 | 28.8 | 0.9 | 20 272 | -0.8 | 1 392 | 6.9 | 21 046 | 33.4 | 19.0 |
| Pendleton | 3 305 | 77.2 | 93 900 | 21.7 | 9.9 | 539 | 29.9 | 1.8 | 3 542 | 1.5 | 219 | 6.2 | 3 545 | 19.6 | 37.4 |
| Pleasants | 2 630 | 80.3 | 92 400 | 19.3 | 9.9 | 512 | 28.5 | 2.5 | 3 121 | -1.0 | 262 | 8.4 | 2 664 | 28.9 | 30.5 |
| Pocahontas | 3 819 | 81.8 | 98 700 | 24.7 | 9.9 | 469 | 28.3 | 0.8 | 3 410 | -1.2 | 367 | 10.8 | 3 579 | 29.6 | 28.8 |
| Preston | 12 908 | 82.7 | 100 200 | 19.4 | 9.9 | 549 | 25.3 | 2.8 | 15 926 | 1.6 | 1 026 | 6.4 | 14 084 | 23.9 | 34.8 |
| Putnam | 20 999 | 86.1 | 140 800 | 19.0 | 9.9 | 668 | 25.1 | 0.6 | 27 151 | -0.9 | 1 579 | 5.8 | 25 088 | 38.2 | 22.1 |
| Raleigh | 31 211 | 75.9 | 89 100 | 19.2 | 10.1 | 548 | 27.1 | 0.5 | 33 969 | 1.3 | 2 351 | 6.9 | 30 289 | 30.9 | 25.6 |
| Randolph | 11 276 | 77.4 | 94 500 | 21.8 | 9.9 | 540 | 35.5 | 1.9 | 12 310 | 0.6 | 1 055 | 8.6 | 11 631 | 29.5 | 26.1 |
| Ritchie | 4 127 | 78.9 | 76 100 | 20.7 | 9.9 | 497 | 26.9 | 0.3 | 4 478 | 2.2 | 317 | 7.1 | 4 079 | 27.5 | 33.7 |
| Roane | 5 970 | 76.6 | 75 900 | 20.8 | 9.9 | 447 | 28.2 | 3.0 | 5 364 | -0.9 | 587 | 10.9 | 5 162 | 21.7 | 34.2 |
| Summers | 5 108 | 79.9 | 79 400 | 19.9 | 10.1 | 464 | 28.5 | 1.8 | 4 610 | -0.5 | 413 | 9.0 | 4 617 | 27.8 | 30.5 |
| Taylor | 6 592 | 78.2 | 80 600 | 18.9 | 9.9 | 464 | 27.0 | 1.0 | 7 321 | 0.7 | 515 | 7.0 | 6 931 | 29.3 | 31.1 |
| Tucker | 3 215 | 80.2 | 97 600 | 20.6 | 10.1 | 473 | 28.8 | 0.9 | 2 726 | -0.5 | 255 | 9.4 | 3 146 | 31.3 | 31.2 |
| Tyler | 3 752 | 84.9 | 76 300 | 17.8 | 9.9 | 485 | 30.1 | 1.6 | 3 735 | 1.5 | 328 | 8.8 | 3 345 | 22.7 | 35.0 |
| Upshur | 9 139 | 78.4 | 95 500 | 19.9 | 9.9 | 511 | 25.0 | 1.5 | 10 611 | -0.8 | 749 | 7.1 | 9 553 | 26.8 | 30.1 |
| Wayne | 16 833 | 77.1 | 84 300 | 19.8 | 9.9 | 549 | 33.9 | 2.1 | 16 936 | -0.3 | 1 317 | 7.8 | 16 106 | 26.9 | 26.4 |
| Webster | 4 020 | 79.4 | 62 300 | 26.4 | 9.9 | 454 | 28.7 | 3.3 | 3 088 | 0.4 | 384 | 12.4 | 3 313 | 16.9 | 40.4 |
| Wetzel | 6 957 | 79.4 | 81 500 | 18.0 | 9.9 | 498 | 31.3 | 2.4 | 6 539 | 3.1 | 677 | 10.4 | 6 219 | 26.2 | 34.9 |
| Wirt | 2 325 | 83.4 | 73 100 | 16.9 | 9.9 | 459 | 26.4 | 6.6 | 2 348 | -0.3 | 246 | 10.5 | 2 115 | 29.6 | 34.8 |
| Wood | 35 990 | 74.1 | 104 600 | 20.0 | 9.9 | 580 | 31.0 | 1.5 | 38 772 | -1.0 | 2 848 | 7.3 | 37 115 | 31.7 | 24.5 |
| Wyoming | 8 965 | 81.8 | 57 600 | 17.9 | 9.9 | 492 | 26.3 | 2.3 | 8 230 | 1.0 | 741 | 9.0 | 7 430 | 26.6 | 39.9 |
| **WISCONSIN** | 2 279 738 | 69.1 | 169 700 | 24.4 | 13.9 | 735 | 28.9 | 2.1 | 3 051 732 | -0.4 | 211 444 | 6.9 | 2 859 925 | 33.3 | 26.1 |
| Adams | 9 168 | 81.7 | 135 000 | 26.6 | 17.1 | 630 | 28.1 | 1.6 | 9 811 | -1.0 | 975 | 9.9 | 8 178 | 19.0 | 33.4 |
| Ashland | 6 952 | 70.2 | 113 700 | 24.1 | 14.2 | 514 | 26.5 | 3.5 | 8 570 | -0.8 | 748 | 8.7 | 7 534 | 29.4 | 27.4 |
| Barron | 19 265 | 75.0 | 135 000 | 24.9 | 15.2 | 616 | 29.7 | 1.8 | 24 177 | -0.4 | 1 840 | 7.6 | 22 574 | 28.3 | 33.7 |
| Bayfield | 6 852 | 82.3 | 157 900 | 24.6 | 15.1 | 538 | 25.6 | 3.4 | 7 918 | 0.3 | 815 | 10.3 | 6 898 | 34.2 | 26.2 |
| Brown | 97 485 | 67.0 | 159 900 | 23.3 | 12.9 | 668 | 27.4 | 2.4 | 141 247 | 0.0 | 8 921 | 6.3 | 126 676 | 32.0 | 25.3 |
| Buffalo | 5 754 | 77.3 | 134 100 | 25.3 | 14.3 | 683 | 28.7 | 1.8 | 7 088 | -4.7 | 402 | 5.7 | 6 980 | 28.8 | 34.7 |
| Burnett | 7 372 | 80.2 | 155 400 | 29.6 | 15.3 | 693 | 35.7 | 2.7 | 8 169 | 0.3 | 657 | 8.0 | 6 572 | 26.3 | 31.4 |
| Calumet | 18 248 | 82.9 | 161 300 | 23.1 | 13.1 | 658 | 24.6 | 1.5 | 27 193 | -0.3 | 1 460 | 5.4 | 25 522 | 33.5 | 32.1 |
| Chippewa | 24 239 | 73.3 | 147 900 | 24.0 | 13.1 | 661 | 27.7 | 1.3 | 34 037 | 0.3 | 2 205 | 6.5 | 30 996 | 28.1 | 32.6 |
| Clark | 13 132 | 78.6 | 111 900 | 24.9 | 14.1 | 566 | 24.9 | 5.2 | 17 410 | 0.1 | 1 240 | 7.1 | 16 051 | 27.0 | 38.8 |
| Columbia | 22 888 | 75.9 | 177 000 | 25.1 | 13.4 | 713 | 26.8 | 1.4 | 31 734 | -0.6 | 2 127 | 6.7 | 29 592 | 29.0 | 30.0 |
| Crawford | 6 785 | 76.2 | 116 100 | 23.9 | 14.0 | 560 | 27.5 | 2.1 | 9 047 | -1.8 | 685 | 7.6 | 7 934 | 25.5 | 35.2 |
| Dane | 199 767 | 61.2 | 231 400 | 25.0 | 12.4 | 866 | 29.8 | 2.0 | 300 069 | -0.2 | 14 240 | 4.7 | 273 518 | 47.1 | 14.4 |

1. Specified owner-occupied units. 2. A value of 9.9 represents 9.9 percent or less. 3. Specified renter-occupied units. A value of 10.0 represents 10 percent or less. 4. Overcrowded or lacking complete plumbing facilities. 5. Percent of civilian labor force. 6. Persons 16 years old and over.

# Table B. States and Counties — Nonfarm Employment and Agriculture

| STATE County | Number of establish-ments | Total | Health care and social assistance | Manufac-turing | Retail trade | Finance and insurance | Professional, scientific, and technical services | Total (mil dol) | Average per employee (dollars) | Number | Fewer than 50 acres | 500 acres or more | Farm operators whose principal occu-pation is farming (percent) |
|---|---|---|---|---|---|---|---|---|---|---|---|---|---|
| | 104 | 105 | 106 | 107 | 108 | 109 | 110 | 111 | 112 | 113 | 114 | 115 | 116 |
| WEST VIRGINIA—Cont'd | | | | | | | | | | | | | |
| Brooke | 400 | 6 843 | 1 902 | 1 820 | 968 | 161 | D | 240 | 35 113 | 104 | 28.8 | 3.8 | 56.7 |
| Cabell | 2 531 | 46 099 | 12 861 | 5 017 | 6 743 | 1 251 | 2 121 | 1 641 | 35 595 | 462 | 27.9 | 1.3 | 33.3 |
| Calhoun | 113 | 949 | D | D | 143 | D | D | 36 | 37 606 | 287 | 22.0 | 7.7 | 35.5 |
| Clay | 104 | 1 304 | 346 | D | 132 | D | D | 56 | 42 717 | 145 | 20.7 | 1.4 | 40.7 |
| Doddridge | 74 | 534 | D | D | 98 | 29 | D | 13 | 25 135 | 490 | 23.5 | 4.9 | 38.6 |
| Fayette | 795 | 8 691 | 2 075 | 694 | 1 793 | D | 170 | 275 | 31 685 | 265 | 33.2 | 2.3 | 41.9 |
| Gilmer | 134 | 1 257 | 233 | D | 159 | D | 54 | 35 | 27 599 | 263 | 13.3 | 12.9 | 40.7 |
| Grant | 232 | 2 490 | 695 | 302 | 371 | 97 | D | 93 | 37 194 | 471 | 24.0 | 11.9 | 45.0 |
| Greenbrier | 958 | 11 740 | 2 824 | 1 484 | 2 022 | D | 278 | 335 | 28 563 | 881 | 29.6 | 9.1 | 43.7 |
| Hampshire | 333 | 2 631 | 845 | 165 | 434 | 189 | 77 | 69 | 26 288 | 677 | 38.8 | 9.0 | 41.9 |
| Hancock | 602 | 9 559 | 1 222 | D | 996 | 308 | 411 | 320 | 33 513 | 109 | 40.4 | 0.9 | 56.9 |
| Hardy | 245 | 4 964 | 476 | 2 812 | 606 | 203 | D | 130 | 26 125 | 514 | 33.7 | 11.1 | 49.8 |
| Harrison | 1 812 | 27 041 | 6 125 | 1 845 | 4 900 | 521 | 1 087 | 1 004 | 37 138 | 774 | 28.0 | 4.3 | 42.1 |
| Jackson | 514 | 6 242 | 1 127 | D | 1 114 | D | 162 | 207 | 33 200 | 950 | 24.3 | 2.6 | 37.4 |
| Jefferson | 873 | 12 768 | 1 294 | 820 | 1 826 | 324 | 429 | 392 | 30 717 | 546 | 54.4 | 6.6 | 51.3 |
| Kanawha | 5 291 | 87 645 | 18 658 | 3 509 | 11 545 | 4 908 | 6 326 | 3 493 | 39 850 | 256 | 46.9 | 0.4 | 41.4 |
| Lewis | 406 | 5 131 | D | 164 | 809 | 107 | 61 | 180 | 35 149 | 507 | 23.5 | 6.1 | 34.5 |
| Lincoln | 213 | 2 103 | D | D | 297 | 61 | 70 | 85 | 40 280 | 215 | 17.7 | 2.8 | 31.6 |
| Logan | 695 | 10 445 | 1 821 | 686 | 1 954 | 206 | 227 | 454 | 43 509 | 34 | 76.5 | 0.0 | 55.9 |
| McDowell | 280 | 3 239 | 851 | D | 605 | D | 80 | 128 | 39 580 | 15 | 53.3 | 6.7 | 40.0 |
| Marion | 1 263 | 17 556 | 2 719 | 1 124 | 2 295 | 502 | 1 289 | 666 | 37 936 | 550 | 31.6 | 0.9 | 40.0 |
| Marshall | 486 | 8 447 | 1 667 | 473 | 1 187 | D | 137 | 339 | 40 145 | 752 | 21.0 | 1.7 | 36.6 |
| Mason | 344 | 4 512 | 1 045 | D | 670 | 117 | 84 | 183 | 40 558 | 946 | 30.1 | 4.7 | 41.2 |
| Mercer | 1 324 | 18 849 | 4 866 | 1 262 | 3 340 | 518 | 503 | 578 | 30 641 | 445 | 32.6 | 3.1 | 44.3 |
| Mineral | 452 | 6 445 | 1 232 | D | 962 | 132 | 103 | 206 | 31 945 | 493 | 33.9 | 4.9 | 39.8 |
| Mingo | 440 | 5 629 | D | 157 | 403 | 185 | 255 | 243 | 43 108 | 37 | 64.9 | 8.1 | 27.0 |
| Monongalia | 2 206 | 41 271 | 12 274 | 3 548 | 5 961 | 726 | 2 485 | 1 586 | 38 419 | 457 | 28.4 | 2.6 | 36.3 |
| Monroe | 189 | 1 334 | 319 | D | 180 | 47 | D | 37 | 27 771 | 707 | 22.8 | 7.9 | 46.1 |
| Morgan | 242 | 2 154 | 553 | D | 418 | 104 | 58 | 67 | 30 960 | 212 | 43.9 | 2.8 | 51.4 |
| Nicholas | 571 | 7 956 | 1 455 | 744 | 1 510 | D | 225 | 298 | 37 418 | 434 | 35.7 | 3.0 | 40.3 |
| Ohio | 1 449 | 27 806 | 6 584 | 1 458 | 3 365 | 1 153 | 1 610 | 868 | 31 210 | 241 | 27.8 | 2.9 | 38.6 |
| Pendleton | 134 | 1 183 | 310 | 122 | 228 | 63 | D | 31 | 25 931 | 600 | 20.0 | 15.5 | 47.3 |
| Pleasants | 120 | 2 298 | D | 535 | 174 | 65 | 40 | 106 | 46 221 | 246 | 28.9 | 1.2 | 32.1 |
| Pocahontas | 214 | 2 921 | 387 | 295 | 314 | 54 | D | 60 | 20 601 | 390 | 19.2 | 16.2 | 47.4 |
| Preston | 537 | 4 594 | 1 142 | 470 | 919 | D | 190 | 135 | 29 392 | 1 048 | 27.6 | 4.3 | 45.8 |
| Putnam | 1 160 | 15 754 | 1 741 | 1 964 | 2 206 | 464 | 763 | 619 | 39 323 | 625 | 35.0 | 1.1 | 39.4 |
| Raleigh | 1 861 | 29 751 | 7 239 | 1 117 | 5 047 | 573 | 874 | 1 159 | 38 959 | 351 | 42.5 | 4.0 | 37.0 |
| Randolph | 714 | 9 406 | 2 674 | 1 206 | 1 457 | 268 | 180 | 258 | 27 432 | 484 | 30.0 | 10.1 | 43.8 |
| Ritchie | 210 | 2 239 | D | 673 | 288 | 91 | D | 85 | 38 084 | 441 | 14.3 | 7.5 | 38.3 |
| Roane | 255 | 2 493 | D | 239 | 563 | 123 | 48 | 72 | 28 946 | 674 | 16.6 | 6.4 | 45.4 |
| Summers | 171 | 1 440 | 402 | 41 | 222 | D | 112 | 40 | 27 778 | 383 | 23.5 | 4.4 | 47.0 |
| Taylor | 221 | 1 971 | 565 | D | 443 | 50 | D | 56 | 28 370 | 471 | 41.8 | 2.8 | 34.2 |
| Tucker | 176 | 1 954 | 266 | D | 217 | 52 | 30 | 52 | 26 511 | 197 | 24.9 | 7.1 | 46.2 |
| Tyler | 112 | 1 417 | 450 | D | 148 | 65 | D | 67 | 47 566 | 277 | 17.3 | 4.7 | 45.8 |
| Upshur | 574 | 6 923 | 1 580 | 813 | 1 150 | 126 | 221 | 233 | 33 639 | 503 | 27.4 | 3.2 | 36.8 |
| Wayne | 545 | 6 975 | D | 608 | 1 087 | D | 156 | 294 | 42 080 | 261 | 23.8 | 5.0 | 49.8 |
| Webster | 131 | 1 280 | 395 | 113 | 163 | D | D | 42 | 32 666 | 123 | 39.0 | 0.0 | 52.8 |
| Wetzel | 351 | 4 373 | 689 | D | 905 | 122 | 65 | 161 | 36 781 | 353 | 19.0 | 2.8 | 41.1 |
| Wirt | 67 | 456 | D | D | 72 | 17 | D | 9 | 20 441 | 238 | 17.2 | 5.5 | 37.4 |
| Wood | 2 098 | 34 076 | 7 989 | 2 962 | 6 333 | 975 | 1 136 | 1 109 | 32 541 | 902 | 35.6 | 0.6 | 38.7 |
| Wyoming | 325 | 3 998 | 848 | 77 | 693 | 84 | 65 | 142 | 35 544 | 37 | 43.2 | 5.4 | 54.1 |
| WISCONSIN | 138 045 | 2 354 284 | 383 665 | 424 211 | 295 401 | 140 381 | 106 554 | 95 532 | 40 578 | 78 463 | 31.6 | 7.8 | 47.2 |
| Adams | 329 | 3 274 | 505 | 411 | 466 | D | 64 | 83 | 25 405 | 408 | 26.7 | 11.8 | 43.1 |
| Ashland | 542 | 6 506 | 1 538 | 1 035 | 929 | 205 | 149 | 221 | 34 024 | 203 | 22.7 | 13.8 | 40.4 |
| Barron | 1 288 | 15 979 | 2 876 | 4 519 | 3 103 | 696 | 325 | 528 | 33 045 | 1 484 | 26.5 | 9.4 | 48.1 |
| Bayfield | 429 | 2 190 | D | 173 | 412 | 78 | D | 53 | 24 177 | 383 | 19.8 | 10.4 | 44.6 |
| Brown | 6 287 | 133 575 | 18 448 | 24 218 | 14 483 | D | 5 196 | 5 623 | 42 096 | 1 053 | 44.0 | 6.8 | 54.7 |
| Buffalo | 330 | 3 378 | 369 | 408 | 277 | D | 52 | 111 | 32 976 | 1 229 | 20.5 | 11.5 | 46.3 |
| Burnett | 408 | 3 251 | 590 | 724 | 549 | 97 | 93 | 102 | 31 387 | 531 | 27.9 | 7.7 | 39.4 |
| Calumet | 861 | 11 934 | 1 067 | 3 438 | 1 645 | 634 | 190 | 439 | 36 783 | 732 | 29.9 | 9.6 | 55.7 |
| Chippewa | 1 521 | 19 617 | 3 186 | 5 493 | 3 408 | 502 | 655 | 679 | 34 588 | 1 575 | 19.8 | 8.7 | 53.6 |
| Clark | 733 | 7 898 | 1 331 | 2 836 | 941 | D | 152 | 248 | 31 366 | 2 170 | 19.7 | 6.3 | 65.5 |
| Columbia | 1 388 | 19 119 | 2 443 | 4 797 | 2 985 | 395 | 390 | 598 | 31 265 | 1 585 | 35.5 | 9.4 | 48.7 |
| Crawford | 415 | 6 106 | 1 150 | 1 429 | 948 | D | 179 | 175 | 28 654 | 1 347 | 26.5 | 5.8 | 40.5 |
| Dane | 13 179 | 249 351 | 42 465 | 22 515 | 29 184 | 22 163 | 19 239 | 11 094 | 44 491 | 3 331 | 46.2 | 6.9 | 44.3 |

# Table B. States and Counties — Agriculture

| STATE County | Acreage (1,000) 117 | Percent change, 2002–2007 118 | Average size of farm 119 | Total irrigated (1,000) 120 | Total cropland (1,000) 121 | Average per farm 122 | Average per acre 123 | Value of machinery and equipment, average per farm (dollars) 124 | Total (mil dol) 125 | Average per farm (dollars) 126 | Crops 127 | Live-stock and poultry products 128 | $10,000 or more 129 | $100,000 or more 130 | Total ($1,000) 131 | Percent of farms 132 |
|---|---|---|---|---|---|---|---|---|---|---|---|---|---|---|---|---|
| WEST VIRGINIA—Cont'd | | | | | | | | | | | | | | | | |
| Brooke | 15 | 7.1 | 148 | D | 5.1 | 243 010 | 1 640 | 37 970 | 1.0 | 9 475 | 23.1 | 76.9 | 21.2 | 1.0 | 4 | 5.8 |
| Cabell | 48 | 14.3 | 103 | 0.0 | 9.2 | 260 208 | 2 524 | 32 911 | 1.5 | 3 340 | 45.4 | 54.6 | 5.4 | 0.4 | 10 | 5.8 |
| Calhoun | 56 | 12.0 | 195 | D | 9.3 | 302 156 | 1 548 | 28 348 | 1.6 | 5 409 | 8.2 | 91.8 | 9.8 | 0.3 | 3 | 1.0 |
| Clay | 20 | 5.3 | 138 | 0.0 | 4.2 | 228 220 | 1 659 | 23 174 | 0.7 | 4 537 | 12.5 | 87.4 | 11.0 | 0.0 | 14 | 10.3 |
| Doddridge | 81 | -14.7 | 166 | 0.1 | 16.4 | 244 177 | 1 471 | 25 662 | 1.7 | 3 550 | 29.7 | 70.3 | 7.8 | 0.0 | 2 | 1.0 |
| Fayette | 27 | 12.5 | 101 | D | 7.9 | 206 292 | 2 049 | 32 691 | 1.7 | 6 507 | 20.6 | 79.5 | 14.3 | 0.0 | 7 | 6.4 |
| Gilmer | 64 | -3.0 | 243 | D | 12.1 | 355 692 | 1 461 | 38 203 | 2.2 | 8 478 | 9.8 | 90.2 | 22.8 | 0.4 | 14 | 4.6 |
| Grant | 109 | 0.9 | 231 | 0.1 | 20.6 | 537 679 | 2 327 | 45 431 | 42.1 | 89 434 | 1.5 | 98.5 | 34.4 | 13.0 | 212 | 17.0 |
| Greenbrier | 177 | -8.3 | 201 | 0.1 | 38.5 | 484 704 | 2 413 | 50 458 | 43.0 | 48 781 | 4.0 | 96.0 | 35.9 | 6.8 | 130 | 14.2 |
| Hampshire | 129 | -7.2 | 191 | 0.0 | 33.5 | 911 704 | 4 778 | 55 484 | 32.5 | 48 078 | 10.4 | 89.6 | 31.2 | 7.1 | 365 | 20.7 |
| Hancock | 10 | 42.9 | 89 | D | 3.1 | 241 981 | 2 734 | 28 811 | 0.4 | 3 358 | 50.5 | 49.5 | 5.5 | 0.0 | 0 | 9.2 |
| Hardy | 134 | 4.7 | 261 | 0.0 | 28.3 | 797 092 | 3 049 | 66 109 | 148.0 | 287 994 | 1.3 | 98.7 | 44.4 | 28.0 | 218 | 15.4 |
| Harrison | 112 | -6.7 | 144 | 0.0 | 26.8 | 300 421 | 2 082 | 34 693 | 6.9 | 8 889 | 22.3 | 77.7 | 15.8 | 0.8 | 38 | 3.7 |
| Jackson | 129 | 0.0 | 136 | 0.1 | 36.8 | 269 258 | 1 976 | 33 387 | 6.1 | 6 389 | 20.8 | 79.2 | 13.7 | 0.9 | 65 | 6.4 |
| Jefferson | 72 | 0.0 | 132 | 0.2 | 43.0 | 896 621 | 6 791 | 64 102 | 19.5 | 35 639 | 41.2 | 58.8 | 27.8 | 7.9 | 476 | 22.7 |
| Kanawha | 24 | 20.0 | 93 | 0.0 | 4.0 | 253 222 | 2 729 | 24 408 | 0.9 | 3 558 | 33.2 | 66.8 | 6.6 | 0.4 | 9 | 5.9 |
| Lewis | 92 | 16.5 | 182 | D | 22.1 | 308 072 | 1 695 | 41 362 | 7.2 | 14 248 | 5.2 | 94.8 | 24.3 | 0.8 | 5 | 3.4 |
| Lincoln | 32 | -8.6 | 151 | 0.0 | 6.7 | 223 448 | 1 483 | 38 793 | 0.7 | 3 205 | 19.7 | 80.3 | 9.3 | 0.0 | 8 | 7.9 |
| Logan | 1 | -50.0 | 41 | D | 0.3 | 116 296 | 2 839 | 42 212 | D | D | 0.0 | D | 5.9 | 2.9 | D | 2.9 |
| McDowell | 1 | 0.0 | 99 | D | 0.5 | 219 419 | 2 222 | 42 871 | 0.1 | 5 514 | 9.6 | 90.4 | 6.7 | 0.0 | 0 | 0.0 |
| Marion | 58 | 16.0 | 105 | 0.0 | 16.0 | 223 716 | 2 121 | 28 220 | 2.7 | 4 870 | 41.1 | 58.8 | 10.0 | 0.9 | 8 | 3.6 |
| Marshall | 96 | 5.5 | 127 | 0.1 | 30.3 | 237 948 | 1 868 | 33 433 | 3.0 | 4 036 | 25.5 | 74.5 | 9.6 | 0.3 | 25 | 5.1 |
| Mason | 132 | -7.0 | 140 | 0.4 | 40.4 | 311 226 | 2 227 | 38 471 | 18.8 | 19 837 | 61.5 | 38.5 | 18.7 | 3.0 | 243 | 14.5 |
| Mercer | 54 | -3.6 | 121 | 0.0 | 11.6 | 267 233 | 2 203 | 30 255 | 3.7 | 8 354 | 25.8 | 74.2 | 17.8 | 1.3 | 13 | 3.1 |
| Mineral | 78 | -3.7 | 158 | 0.2 | 19.6 | 438 363 | 2 772 | 36 194 | 15.5 | 31 379 | 8.2 | 91.8 | 18.1 | 4.7 | 63 | 13.0 |
| Mingo | 4 | 100.0 | 108 | 0.0 | 0.3 | 106 359 | 986 | 10 762 | 0.1 | 2 778 | 1.9 | 97.1 | 8.1 | 0.0 | 0 | 0.0 |
| Monongalia | 59 | -1.7 | 130 | 0.0 | 16.7 | 357 613 | 2 758 | 41 183 | 3.1 | 6 734 | 22.5 | 77.5 | 17.3 | 0.4 | 20 | 5.3 |
| Monroe | 133 | -8.3 | 188 | 0.0 | 31.4 | 431 149 | 2 294 | 50 221 | 16.4 | 23 204 | 7.0 | 93.0 | 34.8 | 4.5 | 140 | 19.9 |
| Morgan | 22 | -4.3 | 106 | 0.0 | 7.8 | 458 846 | 4 335 | 33 576 | 1.9 | 8 733 | 55.8 | 44.2 | 19.8 | 1.4 | 32 | 17.9 |
| Nicholas | 51 | 15.9 | 118 | D | 15.3 | 239 319 | 2 023 | 36 259 | 2.7 | 6 252 | 15.5 | 84.5 | 16.6 | 0.7 | 18 | 8.5 |
| Ohio | 31 | 40.9 | 128 | 0.0 | 10.7 | 270 831 | 2 119 | 31 697 | 2.5 | 10 179 | 22.8 | 77.2 | 14.5 | 2.9 | 46 | 17.4 |
| Pendleton | 170 | -0.6 | 283 | 0.0 | 29.6 | 602 289 | 2 127 | 60 443 | 91.8 | 152 980 | 1.5 | 98.5 | 52.5 | 18.5 | 131 | 21.3 |
| Pleasants | 26 | 13.0 | 105 | D | 7.6 | 218 584 | 2 086 | 25 439 | D | D | 0.0 | D | 8.5 | 0.4 | D | 0.4 |
| Pocahontas | 122 | -0.8 | 313 | 0.0 | 23.7 | 633 940 | 2 029 | 60 712 | 8.2 | 20 935 | 6.1 | 93.9 | 33.1 | 3.8 | 88 | 28.5 |
| Preston | 152 | 7.0 | 145 | 0.0 | 46.3 | 347 363 | 2 391 | 44 699 | 13.6 | 13 019 | 18.2 | 81.8 | 26.4 | 1.4 | 72 | 6.6 |
| Putnam | 66 | 15.8 | 106 | 0.2 | 15.0 | 253 355 | 2 384 | 33 068 | 7.4 | 11 892 | 76.8 | 23.2 | 8.6 | 0.5 | 23 | 6.7 |
| Raleigh | 43 | 30.3 | 124 | 0.0 | 14.1 | 284 192 | 2 298 | 35 459 | 2.5 | 6 985 | 27.6 | 72.4 | 17.1 | 1.4 | 16 | 6.6 |
| Randolph | 104 | 3.0 | 216 | 0.0 | 25.6 | 431 626 | 2 000 | 41 657 | 8.2 | 16 938 | 11.1 | 88.9 | 26.0 | 2.3 | 62 | 14.7 |
| Ritchie | 91 | 12.3 | 206 | 0.0 | 21.8 | 344 698 | 1 673 | 37 744 | 4.1 | 9 250 | 18.2 | 81.8 | 15.6 | 1.1 | 3 | 1.4 |
| Roane | 118 | 19.2 | 174 | 0.0 | 29.5 | 302 235 | 1 733 | 34 460 | 5.0 | 7 459 | 19.8 | 80.3 | 19.7 | 0.6 | 27 | 5.0 |
| Summers | 60 | 9.1 | 156 | 0.0 | 13.6 | 312 136 | 2 005 | 43 382 | 5.3 | 13 965 | 30.9 | 69.1 | 19.8 | 1.8 | 21 | 5.7 |
| Taylor | 54 | 25.6 | 114 | 0.0 | 14.0 | 250 911 | 2 196 | 32 974 | 6.3 | 13 293 | 31.4 | 68.6 | 15.3 | 2.8 | 11 | 2.1 |
| Tucker | 35 | 0.0 | 177 | 0.0 | 8.6 | 341 698 | 1 930 | 35 345 | 1.7 | 8 834 | 22.8 | 77.2 | 25.9 | 0.0 | 11 | 13.7 |
| Tyler | 48 | -9.4 | 172 | 0.0 | 12.0 | 322 560 | 1 880 | 36 274 | 1.9 | 6 801 | 22.9 | 77.0 | 11.9 | 0.7 | 22 | 9.7 |
| Upshur | 71 | 2.9 | 141 | 0.0 | 19.5 | 299 677 | 2 127 | 35 035 | 4.1 | 8 217 | 18.5 | 81.5 | 19.3 | 1.0 | 15 | 3.6 |
| Wayne | 40 | 11.1 | 153 | 0.0 | 7.2 | 276 589 | 1 812 | 25 133 | 1.6 | 5 954 | 31.0 | 69.0 | 12.6 | 0.8 | 7 | 3.1 |
| Webster | 12 | 9.1 | 94 | 0.0 | 2.8 | 184 900 | 1 972 | 17 239 | 0.2 | 1 969 | 22.3 | 77.7 | 2.4 | 0.0 | 6 | 6.5 |
| Wetzel | 52 | 6.1 | 147 | 0.0 | 10.0 | 226 386 | 1 541 | 25 293 | 1.0 | 2 755 | 31.4 | 68.6 | 2.8 | 0.3 | 4 | 3.4 |
| Wirt | 41 | 2.5 | 173 | D | 9.9 | 280 691 | 1 621 | 40 644 | 3.5 | 14 776 | 8.9 | 91.1 | 16.8 | 0.3 | 2 | 2.5 |
| Wood | 89 | 15.6 | 99 | 0.0 | 27.4 | 225 326 | 2 284 | 26 009 | 3.5 | 3 920 | 32.1 | 67.9 | 8.4 | 0.3 | 13 | 2.0 |
| Wyoming | 4 | 0.0 | 109 | D | 0.8 | 148 664 | 1 361 | 25 604 | 0.1 | 3 572 | 34.8 | 65.2 | 5.4 | 0.0 | 0 | 8.1 |
| WISCONSIN | 15 191 | -3.5 | 194 | 377.3 | 10 116.3 | 624 428 | 3 225 | 96 278 | 8 967.4 | 114 288 | 29.8 | 70.2 | 45.2 | 21.2 | 195 787 | 60.5 |
| Adams | 115 | -7.3 | 283 | 37.6 | 79.6 | 895 606 | 3 168 | 119 690 | 74.8 | 183 276 | 89.6 | 10.4 | 38.2 | 15.9 | 781 | 61.8 |
| Ashland | 55 | -6.8 | 273 | 0.0 | 26.5 | 584 484 | 2 143 | 63 121 | 11.9 | 58 855 | 10.7 | 89.3 | 36.0 | 7.9 | 179 | 23.2 |
| Barron | 324 | -8.0 | 218 | 10.3 | 207.2 | 541 130 | 2 477 | 106 042 | 206.4 | 139 109 | 19.7 | 80.3 | 48.0 | 24.2 | 3 388 | 62.3 |
| Bayfield | 89 | -20.5 | 233 | 0.2 | 47.6 | 505 901 | 2 170 | 63 949 | 16.2 | 42 310 | 27.5 | 72.5 | 38.6 | 9.4 | 213 | 22.5 |
| Brown | 187 | -5.1 | 178 | 0.5 | 160.6 | 697 205 | 3 922 | 131 817 | 253.8 | 240 985 | 12.2 | 87.8 | 54.0 | 31.2 | 2 774 | 59.6 |
| Buffalo | 307 | -2.8 | 250 | 3.2 | 159.1 | 641 667 | 2 568 | 104 653 | 159.1 | 129 487 | 16.6 | 83.4 | 48.0 | 21.7 | 3 169 | 69.5 |
| Burnett | 96 | -2.0 | 181 | 0.2 | 48.5 | 463 610 | 2 560 | 52 790 | 22.8 | 42 891 | 24.1 | 75.9 | 31.8 | 8.7 | 546 | 45.8 |
| Calumet | 152 | 1.3 | 207 | 0.1 | 128.5 | 791 675 | 3 821 | 130 933 | 167.0 | 228 080 | 17.3 | 82.7 | 68.3 | 32.5 | 1 978 | 72.5 |
| Chippewa | 353 | -5.6 | 224 | 3.0 | 226.3 | 558 659 | 2 489 | 98 921 | 165.6 | 105 150 | 15.5 | 84.5 | 52.1 | 26.9 | 4 181 | 63.3 |
| Clark | 440 | -4.6 | 203 | 0.2 | 291.6 | 507 601 | 2 501 | 101 342 | 278.9 | 128 516 | 9.5 | 90.5 | 62.9 | 37.2 | 3 880 | 50.6 |
| Columbia | 316 | -9.2 | 199 | 1.4 | 241.9 | 747 274 | 3 746 | 101 916 | 166.7 | 105 156 | 45.8 | 54.2 | 50.1 | 19.9 | 5 505 | 64.2 |
| Crawford | 238 | -6.7 | 177 | 0.1 | 105.4 | 459 109 | 2 596 | 56 927 | 61.1 | 45 369 | 34.2 | 65.8 | 33.5 | 12.3 | 2 286 | 62.5 |
| Dane | 536 | 4.1 | 161 | 6.0 | 417.2 | 696 424 | 4 330 | 106 389 | 470.6 | 141 277 | 28.6 | 71.4 | 42.3 | 19.1 | 10 441 | 57.5 |

# Table B. States and Counties — Water Use, Wholesale Trade, Retail Trade, and Real Estate

| STATE County | Water use, 2005 | | Wholesale trade,[1] 2007 | | | | Retail trade,[2] 2007 | | | | Real estate and rental and leasing,[2] 2007 | | | |
|---|---|---|---|---|---|---|---|---|---|---|---|---|---|---|
| | Total water withdrawn (mil gal/day) | Gallons withdrawn per person | Number of establishments | Number of employees | Sales (mil dol) | Annual payroll (mil dol) | Number of establishments | Number of employees | Sales (mil dol) | Annual payroll (mil dol) | Number of establishments | Number of employees | Receipts (mil dol) | Annual payroll (mil dol) |
| | 133 | 134 | 135 | 136 | 137 | 138 | 139 | 140 | 141 | 142 | 143 | 144 | 145 | 146 |
| WEST VIRGINIA—Cont'd | | | | | | | | | | | | | | |
| Brooke | 81.3 | 3 314 | 11 | D | D | D | 63 | 651 | 158.1 | 14.4 | 6 | 21 | 4.8 | 0.5 |
| Cabell | 58.8 | 625 | 112 | 1 698 | 778.9 | 66.7 | 486 | 7 531 | 1 496.1 | 142.7 | 113 | 413 | 68.4 | 10.8 |
| Calhoun | 0.8 | 104 | 1 | D | D | D | 25 | 147 | 34.1 | 2.2 | 5 | 11 | 0.6 | 0.2 |
| Clay | 1.5 | 147 | NA | NA | NA | NA | 24 | 148 | 41.3 | 2.5 | 1 | D | D | D |
| Doddridge | 0.8 | 104 | 2 | D | D | D | 16 | 105 | 19.3 | 1.2 | 2 | D | D | D |
| Fayette | 40.3 | 860 | 27 | D | D | D | 165 | 1 860 | 345.7 | 34.4 | 24 | 58 | 7.5 | 0.8 |
| Gilmer | 1.5 | 216 | 3 | D | D | D | 24 | 153 | 34.3 | 2.9 | 3 | 4 | 0.3 | 0.0 |
| Grant | 1 165.9 | 99 877 | 2 | D | D | D | 44 | 394 | 118.3 | 7.8 | 8 | 18 | 1.4 | 0.1 |
| Greenbrier | 9.3 | 266 | 30 | 256 | 59.1 | 7.3 | 198 | 2 133 | 490.2 | 43.1 | 43 | 150 | 21.4 | 3.5 |
| Hampshire | 3.5 | 161 | 7 | D | D | D | 57 | 442 | 112.2 | 8.3 | 14 | D | D | D |
| Hancock | 185.3 | 5 911 | 10 | 157 | 118.0 | 4.7 | 109 | 1 247 | 238.5 | 22.6 | 29 | 93 | 10.0 | 1.9 |
| Hardy | 23.4 | 1 763 | 3 | 31 | 7.2 | 0.9 | 54 | 660 | 132.1 | 12.5 | 8 | 23 | 2.2 | 0.5 |
| Harrison | 56.4 | 826 | 72 | 858 | 322.8 | 30.5 | 334 | 4 909 | 1 148.5 | 96.0 | 61 | 337 | 107.7 | 8.5 |
| Jackson | 31.8 | 1 119 | 15 | 171 | 77.4 | 5.5 | 110 | 1 467 | 325.2 | 28.2 | 16 | 43 | 5.3 | 1.0 |
| Jefferson | 16.4 | 332 | 20 | D | D | D | 138 | 2 356 | 455.7 | 49.9 | 52 | 172 | 23.3 | 4.1 |
| Kanawha | 502.2 | 2 595 | 270 | 3 829 | 1 727.0 | 163.6 | 853 | 13 517 | 2 947.3 | 259.8 | 277 | 1 799 | 367.7 | 54.8 |
| Lewis | 4.1 | 239 | 15 | 93 | 54.8 | 3.4 | 78 | 843 | 212.9 | 14.5 | 12 | 33 | 4.6 | 0.8 |
| Lincoln | 1.8 | 81 | 3 | D | D | D | 47 | 359 | 73.4 | 5.9 | 7 | D | D | D |
| Logan | 6.6 | 181 | 36 | 354 | 155.7 | 15.7 | 151 | 2 006 | 494.7 | 41.2 | 30 | 109 | 13.0 | 3.1 |
| McDowell | 5.6 | 229 | 6 | 20 | 20.0 | 0.6 | 66 | 711 | 129.4 | 11.7 | 10 | 35 | 4.3 | 0.9 |
| Marion | 46.3 | 820 | 43 | D | D | D | 189 | 2 277 | 614.9 | 48.1 | 43 | 197 | 25.3 | 4.0 |
| Marshall | 723.2 | 21 062 | 14 | D | D | D | 96 | 1 341 | 272.4 | 25.4 | 12 | 41 | 3.2 | 0.9 |
| Mason | 1 094.0 | 42 468 | 5 | D | D | D | 62 | 675 | 135.4 | 11.2 | 18 | 58 | 5.7 | 1.0 |
| Mercer | 12.4 | 201 | 48 | D | D | D | 281 | 3 612 | 765.6 | 74.5 | 45 | 183 | 58.1 | 4.6 |
| Mineral | 4.4 | 164 | 13 | D | D | D | 87 | 1 009 | 223.6 | 18.5 | 12 | D | D | D |
| Mingo | 7.0 | 256 | 13 | 165 | 50.5 | 6.0 | 68 | 481 | 108.2 | 10.1 | 17 | 45 | 12.1 | 0.8 |
| Monongalia | 168.8 | 2 000 | 47 | 413 | 370.3 | 16.8 | 383 | 6 453 | 1 289.7 | 112.7 | 130 | 589 | 78.5 | 14.7 |
| Monroe | 5.0 | 372 | 7 | 29 | 3.7 | 0.5 | 35 | 190 | 31.6 | 3.2 | 5 | 10 | 0.5 | 0.1 |
| Morgan | 4.8 | 298 | 5 | 26 | 5.7 | 0.6 | 48 | 458 | 94.8 | 8.8 | 15 | 45 | 2.9 | 0.7 |
| Nicholas | 5.1 | 192 | 20 | 173 | 136.7 | 6.1 | 111 | 1 460 | 345.9 | 28.6 | 19 | 42 | 5.8 | 1.1 |
| Ohio | 18.4 | 408 | 74 | 1 578 | 3 117.0 | 54.3 | 213 | 3 045 | 649.9 | 62.4 | 66 | 368 | 37.0 | 8.2 |
| Pendleton | 11.8 | 1 504 | 4 | 12 | 4.2 | 0.1 | 28 | 215 | 39.4 | 3.5 | 2 | D | D | D |
| Pleasants | 100.7 | 13 646 | 2 | D | D | D | 18 | 152 | 40.4 | 3.0 | 3 | D | D | D |
| Pocahontas | 6.1 | 688 | 2 | D | D | D | 39 | 332 | 60.2 | 5.2 | 7 | 49 | 9.8 | 0.7 |
| Preston | 111.2 | 3 691 | 16 | D | D | D | 104 | 912 | 221.1 | 15.3 | 21 | 36 | 4.2 | 0.8 |
| Putnam | 57.0 | 1 046 | 67 | 904 | 541.7 | 41.2 | 185 | 2 366 | 589.8 | 42.8 | 48 | 225 | 42.0 | 6.6 |
| Raleigh | 15.4 | 195 | 94 | D | D | D | 376 | 5 507 | 1 260.8 | 114.0 | 76 | 328 | 43.8 | 8.5 |
| Randolph | 18.4 | 643 | 24 | 309 | 366.9 | 10.5 | 135 | 1 513 | 319.2 | 28.2 | 24 | 81 | 12.7 | 1.8 |
| Ritchie | 2.6 | 245 | 6 | 54 | 23.3 | 1.6 | 35 | 259 | 60.4 | 4.0 | 5 | 12 | 1.1 | 0.2 |
| Roane | 2.3 | 149 | 9 | 57 | 40.7 | 1.8 | 56 | 613 | 142.0 | 11.7 | 10 | 21 | 2.0 | 0.4 |
| Summers | 3.8 | 276 | 6 | D | D | D | 28 | 274 | 53.7 | 5.1 | 4 | 6 | 0.6 | 0.2 |
| Taylor | 11.1 | 680 | 5 | D | D | D | 30 | 435 | 91.7 | 8.7 | 2 | D | D | D |
| Tucker | 17.6 | 2 533 | 2 | D | D | D | 32 | 239 | 53.4 | 4.3 | 11 | 78 | 4.3 | 1.0 |
| Tyler | 20.1 | 2 148 | 1 | D | D | D | 29 | 248 | 45.5 | 3.5 | 1 | D | D | D |
| Upshur | 6.5 | 275 | 12 | 216 | 179.3 | 7.4 | 90 | 1 202 | 297.1 | 24.4 | 21 | 104 | 6.4 | 1.4 |
| Wayne | 20.0 | 475 | 18 | 288 | 77.4 | 10.1 | 123 | 1 112 | 232.8 | 19.1 | 21 | 83 | 5.7 | 1.0 |
| Webster | 1.6 | 167 | 3 | D | D | D | 31 | 176 | 40.1 | 3.5 | 5 | D | D | D |
| Wetzel | 25.6 | 1 497 | 8 | 43 | 14.4 | 1.2 | 80 | 967 | 206.4 | 19.6 | 15 | 76 | 9.1 | 1.4 |
| Wirt | 0.8 | 131 | 1 | D | D | D | 15 | 76 | 14.4 | 0.9 | 2 | D | D | D |
| Wood | 51.6 | 593 | 84 | 760 | 330.7 | 26.1 | 422 | 6 796 | 1 712.2 | 131.8 | 85 | D | D | D |
| Wyoming | 5.9 | 242 | 5 | 31 | 5.9 | 0.6 | 91 | 671 | 147.0 | 12.3 | 9 | 41 | 5.7 | 0.8 |
| WISCONSIN | 8 597.4 | 1 553 | 6 215 | 99 773 | 59 996.2 | 4 639.0 | 21 205 | 320 140 | 72 283.3 | 6 778.3 | 5 119 | 27 226 | 4 043.5 | 788.9 |
| Adams | 45.8 | 2 200 | 6 | 27 | 12.6 | 0.8 | 50 | 440 | 130.4 | 9.0 | 13 | 38 | 3.9 | 0.9 |
| Ashland | 55.2 | 3 317 | 13 | 105 | 30.2 | 3.6 | 90 | 846 | 193.6 | 19.4 | 20 | 74 | 7.6 | 1.4 |
| Barron | 19.6 | 427 | 51 | 433 | 126.6 | 14.8 | 256 | 3 268 | 670.8 | 65.2 | 41 | 100 | 15.8 | 2.1 |
| Bayfield | 13.8 | 912 | 9 | 62 | 29.6 | 1.7 | 78 | 520 | 107.6 | 9.0 | 12 | 38 | 2.9 | 0.5 |
| Brown | 519.7 | 2 174 | 349 | 5 907 | 3 388.3 | 270.8 | 984 | 15 914 | 3 538.4 | 327.1 | 236 | 1 594 | 229.9 | 45.4 |
| Buffalo | 538.2 | 38 533 | 7 | 75 | 24.2 | 2.7 | 51 | 311 | 74.0 | 5.5 | 7 | 19 | 0.9 | 0.1 |
| Burnett | 2.5 | 154 | 9 | 24 | 5.5 | 0.7 | 78 | 622 | 118.7 | 10.8 | 19 | 38 | 3.6 | 0.7 |
| Calumet | 7.3 | 166 | 33 | 401 | 149.0 | 14.6 | 116 | 1 801 | 390.1 | 36.6 | 23 | 89 | 8.7 | 1.2 |
| Chippewa | 16.0 | 266 | 43 | 464 | 206.0 | 16.7 | 246 | 3 712 | 1 059.6 | 83.8 | 28 | 107 | 13.9 | 2.9 |
| Clark | 6.5 | 191 | 34 | 252 | 107.2 | 9.7 | 119 | 1 014 | 263.9 | 20.3 | 10 | 24 | 1.3 | 0.2 |
| Columbia | 28.3 | 510 | 45 | 435 | 203.4 | 17.9 | 217 | 2 819 | 631.3 | 54.9 | 48 | D | D | D |
| Crawford | 3.7 | 215 | 15 | 368 | 101.0 | 8.4 | 88 | 1 159 | 218.3 | 22.7 | 12 | 23 | 2.5 | 0.3 |
| Dane | 298.1 | 651 | 600 | 11 205 | 6 043.0 | 529.6 | 1 788 | 32 582 | 7 132.4 | 715.1 | 683 | 4 691 | 638.1 | 144.2 |

1. Merchant wholesalers, except manufacturers' sales branches and offices.  2. Employer establishments.

Items 133—146

# Table B. States and Counties — Professional Services, Manufacturing, and Accommodation and Food Services

| STATE County | Professional, scientific, and technical services,[1] 2007 | | | | Manufacturing, 2007 | | | | Accommodation and food services, 2007 | | | |
|---|---|---|---|---|---|---|---|---|---|---|---|---|
| | Number of establishments | Number of employees | Receipts (mil dol) | Annual payroll (mil dol) | Number of establishments | Number of employees | Receipts (mil dol) | Annual payroll (mil dol) | Number of establishments | Number of employees | Sales (mil dol) | Annual payroll (mil dol) |
| | 147 | 148 | 149 | 150 | 151 | 152 | 153 | 154 | 155 | 156 | 157 | 158 |
| WEST VIRGINIA—Cont'd | | | | | | | | | | | | |
| Brooke | 17 | D | D | D | 24 | 3 217 | 2 645.1 | 181.0 | 58 | 711 | 31.3 | 8.0 |
| Cabell | 195 | D | D | D | 97 | 5 623 | D | D | 279 | 5 340 | 205.2 | 57.9 |
| Calhoun | 6 | D | D | D | NA | NA | NA | NA | 7 | 42 | 1.3 | 0.4 |
| Clay | 1 | D | D | D | NA | NA | NA | NA | 7 | 39 | 1.3 | 0.3 |
| Doddridge | 3 | D | D | D | NA | NA | NA | NA | 2 | D | D | D |
| Fayette | 57 | D | D | D | 31 | 694 | D | 30.0 | 69 | 803 | 35.7 | 9.3 |
| Gilmer | 9 | 43 | 4.7 | 0.9 | NA | NA | NA | NA | 13 | 190 | 5.2 | 1.3 |
| Grant | 14 | 66 | 4.5 | 1.4 | NA | NA | NA | NA | 20 | 176 | 6.1 | 1.5 |
| Greenbrier | 65 | D | D | D | 33 | 886 | 148.3 | 31.9 | 85 | 2 595 | 139.5 | 47.9 |
| Hampshire | 24 | D | D | D | NA | NA | NA | NA | 41 | 373 | 17.4 | 4.6 |
| Hancock | 54 | D | D | D | 22 | 2 278 | D | 79.4 | 93 | 851 | 34.0 | 8.1 |
| Hardy | 17 | 40 | 4.5 | 0.8 | 13 | D | D | D | 27 | 447 | 10.8 | 3.7 |
| Harrison | 115 | D | D | D | 58 | D | D | D | 162 | 2 911 | 117.6 | 32.3 |
| Jackson | 33 | 135 | 12.0 | 3.6 | 21 | 2 211 | 1 296.6 | 124.8 | 49 | 815 | 31.8 | 8.3 |
| Jefferson | 81 | D | D | D | 22 | D | D | D | 112 | 1 463 | 71.9 | 20.7 |
| Kanawha | 587 | D | D | D | 133 | 3 450 | D | 193.4 | 480 | 9 058 | 414.9 | 115.0 |
| Lewis | 19 | D | D | D | NA | NA | NA | NA | 34 | 559 | 27.3 | 9.3 |
| Lincoln | 18 | 104 | 8.4 | 3.0 | NA | NA | NA | NA | 13 | 84 | 2.8 | 0.7 |
| Logan | 35 | D | D | D | 38 | 706 | 124.9 | 26.4 | 67 | 1 134 | 39.6 | 10.3 |
| McDowell | 16 | D | D | D | NA | NA | NA | NA | 19 | 166 | 6.9 | 1.7 |
| Marion | 112 | D | D | D | 53 | 1 285 | 546.4 | 49.3 | 111 | 1 692 | 67.2 | 17.2 |
| Marshall | 27 | D | D | D | NA | NA | NA | NA | 57 | 793 | 26.3 | 7.0 |
| Mason | 23 | 67 | 6.0 | 1.6 | 21 | 707 | D | D | 29 | 319 | 12.1 | 3.6 |
| Mercer | 80 | D | D | D | 63 | 1 741 | 252.5 | D | 108 | 2 299 | 88.4 | 24.1 |
| Mineral | 32 | D | D | D | 14 | 1 620 | D | 86.7 | 53 | 538 | 21.4 | 5.3 |
| Mingo | 55 | D | D | D | NA | NA | NA | NA | 38 | 281 | 10.0 | 2.9 |
| Monongalia | 195 | D | D | D | 66 | 3 099 | D | 151.7 | 229 | 5 085 | 192.8 | 53.3 |
| Monroe | 11 | 31 | 2.2 | 0.6 | NA | NA | NA | NA | 14 | 87 | 2.8 | 0.8 |
| Morgan | 16 | D | D | D | NA | NA | NA | NA | 25 | 309 | 11.5 | 4.1 |
| Nicholas | 42 | D | D | D | 32 | 800 | 192.6 | 27.8 | 51 | 756 | 30.5 | 8.2 |
| Ohio | 141 | D | D | D | 59 | 1 329 | D | D | 131 | 2 403 | 98.3 | 27.5 |
| Pendleton | 8 | D | D | D | NA | NA | NA | NA | 12 | 83 | 3.1 | 0.7 |
| Pleasants | 7 | D | D | D | 10 | D | D | D | 11 | 191 | 6.6 | 1.8 |
| Pocahontas | 10 | D | D | D | NA | NA | NA | NA | 23 | 1 760 | 60.4 | 22.2 |
| Preston | 36 | D | D | D | 32 | 819 | D | 22.1 | 37 | 316 | 12.2 | 3.0 |
| Putnam | 92 | 652 | 67.2 | 24.8 | 37 | 2 156 | D | 119.9 | 87 | 1 441 | 61.6 | 15.2 |
| Raleigh | 125 | D | D | D | 65 | 1 284 | D | 49.9 | 151 | 3 402 | 144.3 | 40.8 |
| Randolph | 42 | D | D | D | 29 | 1 873 | 321.3 | 55.4 | 61 | 965 | 30.7 | 8.6 |
| Ritchie | 10 | 40 | 2.4 | 0.8 | 17 | 1 116 | D | 33.5 | 17 | 94 | 3.6 | 0.7 |
| Roane | 15 | 52 | 4.5 | 1.3 | NA | NA | NA | NA | 9 | 201 | 7.3 | 1.7 |
| Summers | 11 | 94 | 13.5 | 5.3 | NA | NA | NA | NA | 20 | 243 | 9.1 | 2.5 |
| Taylor | 8 | D | D | D | NA | NA | NA | NA | 18 | D | D | D |
| Tucker | 9 | 25 | 1.3 | 0.4 | NA | NA | NA | NA | 30 | 358 | 12.1 | 3.0 |
| Tyler | 5 | D | D | D | 7 | D | 218.6 | 35.3 | 8 | 39 | 1.8 | 0.3 |
| Upshur | 37 | 162 | 9.5 | 3.4 | 23 | 1 314 | 264.8 | 55.7 | 50 | 609 | 24.5 | 6.1 |
| Wayne | 23 | D | D | D | 29 | 791 | D | D | 50 | 457 | 18.4 | 5.0 |
| Webster | 7 | 28 | 1.6 | 0.5 | NA | NA | NA | NA | 12 | 74 | 2.0 | 0.6 |
| Wetzel | 20 | 95 | 5.0 | 1.7 | 16 | 1 394 | D | 92.1 | 46 | 522 | 21.0 | 5.4 |
| Wirt | 5 | D | D | D | NA | NA | NA | NA | 5 | 34 | 0.9 | 0.3 |
| Wood | 138 | D | D | D | 69 | D | D | D | 228 | 4 173 | 157.9 | 47.7 |
| Wyoming | 17 | 79 | 3.8 | 1.4 | NA | NA | NA | NA | 27 | 286 | 9.9 | 2.8 |
| WISCONSIN | 11 255 | 97 445 | 12 797.3 | 4 999.0 | 9 659 | 487 573 | 163 563.2 | 21 850.3 | 14 439 | 227 475 | 9 247.3 | 2 535.2 |
| Adams | 19 | 71 | 5.0 | 2.2 | NA | NA | NA | NA | 60 | 928 | 42.0 | 12.3 |
| Ashland | 26 | 155 | 11.7 | 5.0 | 35 | 1 411 | 222.4 | 50.6 | 78 | 730 | 29.5 | 8.2 |
| Barron | 71 | 316 | 38.3 | 11.9 | 95 | 5 176 | 1 207.4 | 182.5 | 139 | 1 425 | 50.4 | 13.8 |
| Bayfield | 16 | 42 | 2.7 | 1.0 | NA | NA | NA | NA | 111 | 700 | 34.2 | 9.0 |
| Brown | 511 | D | D | D | 446 | 25 490 | 9 321.9 | 1 099.3 | 613 | 12 801 | 464.6 | 135.1 |
| Buffalo | 22 | 76 | 4.5 | 1.4 | NA | NA | NA | NA | 44 | D | D | D |
| Burnett | 25 | 85 | 9.2 | 2.7 | 28 | 856 | 227.0 | 34.0 | 69 | D | D | D |
| Calumet | 55 | 210 | 16.4 | 7.1 | 66 | 3 946 | 1 355.2 | 169.0 | 86 | 1 515 | 40.1 | 11.1 |
| Chippewa | 86 | 555 | 71.1 | 30.9 | 131 | 5 184 | 1 575.0 | 202.3 | 158 | 1 512 | 56.3 | 13.6 |
| Clark | 32 | 150 | 22.2 | 5.8 | 75 | 3 001 | 1 475.2 | 106.3 | 64 | D | D | D |
| Columbia | 83 | D | D | D | 100 | 4 853 | 1 744.1 | D | 194 | 4 000 | 164.2 | 45.8 |
| Crawford | 19 | 75 | 5.9 | 2.3 | 24 | 2 048 | 820.8 | 69.8 | 49 | 629 | 22.6 | 6.1 |
| Dane | 1 584 | D | D | D | 590 | 27 640 | 6 968.1 | 1 295.0 | 1 204 | 23 413 | 916.7 | 268.9 |

1. Establishment subject to federal tax.

# Table B. States and Counties — Health Care and Social Assistance, Other Services, and Federal Funds

| STATE County | Health care and social assistance, 2007 | | | | Other services, 2007 | | | | Federal funds and grants, 2009–2010 Expenditures (mil dol) | | | |
|---|---|---|---|---|---|---|---|---|---|---|---|---|
| | | | | | | | | | | Direct payments for individuals[1] | | |
| | Number of establish-ments | Number of employees | Receipts (mil dol) | Annual payroll (mil dol) | Number of establish-ments | Number of employees | Receipts (mil dol) | Annual payroll (mil dol) | Total | Social Security and government retirement | Medicare | Food Stamps and Supplemental Security Income |
| | 159 | 160 | 161 | 162 | 163 | 164 | 165 | 166 | 167 | 168 | 169 | 170 |
| WEST VIRGINIA—Cont'd | | | | | | | | | | | | |
| Brooke | 62 | 1 774 | 153.3 | 62.5 | 36 | 155 | 8.8 | 2.4 | 206.6 | 106.7 | 54.0 | 10.8 |
| Cabell | 370 | D | D | D | 193 | 1 104 | 96.4 | 23.8 | 1 021.2 | 419.8 | 185.4 | 58.7 |
| Calhoun | 9 | D | D | D | 8 | D | D | D | 81.5 | 26.6 | 15.9 | 7.6 |
| Clay | 20 | 344 | 14.4 | 7.0 | 5 | D | D | D | 100.8 | 38.7 | 18.2 | 10.2 |
| Doddridge | 10 | D | D | D | 4 | D | D | D | 47.4 | 19.5 | 8.8 | 3.9 |
| Fayette | 93 | 1 811 | 135.4 | 49.3 | 59 | 288 | 34.7 | 6.9 | 534.9 | 202.0 | 123.2 | 34.6 |
| Gilmer | 16 | 209 | 9.9 | 4.4 | 7 | 19 | 1.1 | 0.3 | 94.6 | 22.4 | 12.8 | 5.9 |
| Grant | 24 | 627 | 36.1 | 15.3 | 19 | 64 | 5.3 | 1.3 | 113.9 | 55.1 | 16.2 | 7.3 |
| Greenbrier | 141 | 2 482 | 208.1 | 80.7 | 68 | 212 | 18.9 | 3.8 | 337.2 | 147.5 | 72.1 | 14.9 |
| Hampshire | 40 | 789 | 37.7 | 17.1 | 26 | 87 | 6.9 | 1.7 | 154.6 | 80.4 | 28.1 | 8.0 |
| Hancock | 83 | 1 193 | 60.1 | 23.8 | 52 | 234 | 15.2 | 3.8 | 317.8 | 172.4 | 98.5 | 8.8 |
| Hardy | 35 | 420 | 19.4 | 7.8 | 19 | 61 | 4.7 | 1.0 | 128.4 | 46.7 | 15.5 | 3.8 |
| Harrison | 222 | D | D | D | 136 | 643 | 57.4 | 12.2 | 1 152.8 | 280.9 | 144.3 | 41.0 |
| Jackson | 60 | 946 | 60.2 | 23.7 | 33 | 139 | 12.8 | 3.1 | 227.5 | 113.7 | 43.5 | 14.1 |
| Jefferson | 73 | 1 041 | 87.0 | 34.9 | 71 | 411 | 47.8 | 10.2 | 542.4 | 191.2 | 47.0 | 9.3 |
| Kanawha | 739 | 16 612 | 1 720.2 | 627.3 | 419 | 3 169 | 299.7 | 77.6 | 3 516.9 | 775.2 | 428.7 | 99.6 |
| Lewis | 32 | 1 112 | 86.2 | 33.9 | 37 | 117 | 8.8 | 1.8 | 170.0 | 68.0 | 35.7 | 12.2 |
| Lincoln | 26 | 461 | 20.9 | 9.5 | 17 | D | D | D | 214.8 | 83.9 | 35.3 | 21.4 |
| Logan | 90 | 1 753 | 151.6 | 48.5 | 58 | 458 | 77.8 | 16.3 | 443.3 | 173.5 | 94.7 | 32.8 |
| McDowell | 41 | 812 | 55.8 | 19.7 | 22 | 106 | 12.3 | 5.1 | 371.0 | 112.9 | 79.2 | 40.6 |
| Marion | 158 | 2 944 | 233.3 | 89.6 | 107 | 747 | 51.5 | 19.4 | 636.1 | 229.7 | 116.9 | 29.8 |
| Marshall | 69 | 1 475 | 89.7 | 36.2 | 45 | 216 | 14.3 | 4.0 | 236.4 | 109.2 | 62.5 | 13.7 |
| Mason | 35 | 1 052 | 91.3 | 38.3 | 33 | 98 | 5.9 | 1.4 | 218.4 | 100.2 | 45.0 | 14.8 |
| Mercer | 225 | 4 790 | 399.6 | 147.9 | 102 | 805 | 71.5 | 22.0 | 679.6 | 286.0 | 155.8 | 45.4 |
| Mineral | 62 | 1 083 | 54.1 | 22.5 | 42 | 221 | 13.4 | 3.3 | 301.5 | 101.4 | 59.8 | 8.1 |
| Mingo | 46 | 727 | 65.4 | 23.8 | 25 | D | D | D | 343.6 | 129.4 | 59.5 | 33.6 |
| Monongalia | 221 | D | D | D | 143 | 990 | 163.0 | 23.8 | 1 075.0 | 214.8 | 104.3 | 24.1 |
| Monroe | 18 | D | D | D | 13 | 38 | 2.5 | 0.6 | 146.9 | 61.2 | 28.9 | 5.5 |
| Morgan | 16 | D | D | D | 30 | 178 | 19.5 | 7.2 | 112.4 | 71.6 | 20.6 | 4.1 |
| Nicholas | 53 | 1 339 | 86.8 | 35.8 | 41 | 189 | 18.0 | 4.9 | 234.1 | 113.7 | 48.2 | 16.8 |
| Ohio | 236 | 6 249 | 553.5 | 210.2 | 131 | 923 | 75.3 | 20.8 | 498.3 | 184.3 | 114.9 | 21.1 |
| Pendleton | 17 | 271 | 13.7 | 5.6 | 13 | 61 | 6.5 | 1.5 | 95.4 | 31.4 | 14.5 | 2.1 |
| Pleasants | 15 | D | D | D | 11 | D | D | D | 51.8 | 25.5 | 13.1 | 3.1 |
| Pocahontas | 23 | 369 | 21.0 | 8.6 | 25 | 171 | 7.2 | 2.1 | 85.3 | 34.8 | 20.5 | 3.0 |
| Preston | 51 | D | D | D | 43 | 200 | 14.2 | 3.5 | 343.0 | 113.3 | 48.9 | 16.0 |
| Putnam | 125 | 1 624 | 138.6 | 45.7 | 61 | 380 | 37.6 | 10.8 | 325.6 | 172.2 | 54.8 | 13.7 |
| Raleigh | 274 | 6 168 | 560.5 | 224.8 | 138 | 820 | 70.6 | 19.7 | 850.8 | 351.3 | 161.8 | 45.3 |
| Randolph | 110 | 2 418 | 164.4 | 65.5 | 43 | 156 | 15.5 | 3.4 | 282.4 | 115.8 | 55.1 | 14.4 |
| Ritchie | 16 | 179 | 8.7 | 3.8 | 12 | 42 | 3.8 | 0.7 | 86.8 | 39.7 | 17.7 | 5.8 |
| Roane | 29 | 671 | 37.2 | 17.8 | 12 | D | D | D | 132.8 | 53.0 | 27.0 | 9.8 |
| Summers | 26 | 485 | 30.1 | 12.2 | 17 | 49 | 2.7 | 0.8 | 198.0 | 54.6 | 26.9 | 10.7 |
| Taylor | 28 | D | D | D | 20 | D | D | D | 126.4 | 53.5 | 24.4 | 9.2 |
| Tucker | 12 | 259 | 11.7 | 5.3 | 15 | 123 | 12.7 | 3.0 | 69.5 | 28.1 | 11.8 | 2.6 |
| Tyler | 14 | 467 | 21.0 | 10.3 | 11 | 30 | 2.4 | 0.5 | 65.6 | 32.5 | 14.5 | 4.5 |
| Upshur | 75 | 1 593 | 75.8 | 35.8 | 32 | 134 | 9.7 | 3.3 | 184.5 | 84.5 | 31.9 | 14.4 |
| Wayne | 61 | D | D | D | 46 | 187 | 18.6 | 5.6 | 442.6 | 127.1 | 53.8 | 26.1 |
| Webster | 12 | 401 | 20.3 | 8.7 | 9 | D | D | D | 111.5 | 38.1 | 20.5 | 10.2 |
| Wetzel | 42 | 609 | 46.3 | 17.4 | 41 | 121 | 7.0 | 1.8 | 158.1 | 76.1 | 32.9 | 11.4 |
| Wirt | 4 | D | D | D | 4 | D | D | D | 52.0 | 22.6 | 8.8 | 3.9 |
| Wood | 286 | D | D | D | 170 | 943 | 81.1 | 17.2 | 911.1 | 360.3 | 168.0 | 45.7 |
| Wyoming | 31 | 793 | 34.2 | 16.1 | 17 | 69 | 5.6 | 1.5 | 253.2 | 111.5 | 52.8 | 23.5 |
| WISCONSIN | 14 417 | 369 289 | 33 841.3 | 14 082.9 | 10 724 | 66 392 | 6 359.6 | 1 678.7 | 54 866.1 | 16 179.8 | 7 536.0 | 1 653.2 |
| Adams | 29 | 519 | 35.1 | 14.0 | 25 | 124 | 11.0 | 3.2 | 159.6 | 63.1 | 28.6 | 6.1 |
| Ashland | 66 | 1 484 | 112.1 | 52.3 | 36 | D | D | D | 177.2 | 60.0 | 34.5 | 6.0 |
| Barron | 128 | 2 608 | 234.9 | 96.3 | 101 | 345 | 25.7 | 7.1 | 367.3 | 163.6 | 66.0 | 11.9 |
| Bayfield | 17 | 207 | 9.2 | 4.7 | 25 | 57 | 6.4 | 1.7 | 151.8 | 55.3 | 24.2 | 3.3 |
| Brown | 586 | 19 287 | 2 001.9 | 777.2 | 480 | 3 089 | 233.0 | 66.2 | 1 443.2 | 635.1 | 221.0 | 55.7 |
| Buffalo | 26 | 401 | 17.1 | 8.2 | 22 | D | D | D | 109.6 | 48.0 | 20.1 | 3.6 |
| Burnett | 31 | 587 | 30.1 | 15.3 | 22 | 75 | 6.6 | 1.6 | 141.7 | 67.7 | 24.4 | 4.2 |
| Calumet | 66 | 920 | 62.5 | 26.3 | 70 | 250 | 15.8 | 4.0 | 175.4 | 76.8 | 32.6 | 3.0 |
| Chippewa | 126 | 3 053 | 236.3 | 97.9 | 102 | 566 | 56.6 | 15.8 | 431.5 | 176.3 | 81.5 | 14.2 |
| Clark | 60 | 1 295 | 53.3 | 27.1 | 63 | 179 | 14.3 | 3.3 | 242.6 | 96.1 | 60.7 | 5.5 |
| Columbia | 113 | 2 602 | 189.6 | 80.0 | 99 | 395 | 35.9 | 8.9 | 446.1 | 197.6 | 86.2 | 7.4 |
| Crawford | 51 | 1 212 | 69.5 | 31.9 | 31 | 109 | 7.3 | 1.8 | 135.5 | 52.6 | 25.6 | 3.7 |
| Dane | 1 188 | 39 141 | 4 098.2 | 1 670.0 | 1 054 | 8 466 | 1 352.9 | 263.8 | 6 407.9 | 1 095.7 | 406.8 | 82.1 |

1. State totals may include programs not allocated by county.

# Table B. States and Counties — Federal Funds, Residential Construction, and Local Government Finances

| STATE County | Federal funds and grants, 2009–2010 (cont.) | | | | | | | Value of residential construction authorized by building permits, 2011 | | Local government finances, 2007 | | | | |
| | Expenditures (mil dol) (cont.) | | | | | | | | | General revenue | | | | |
| | Procurement contract awards | | | Grants[1] | | | | | | | | Taxes | | |
| | | | | | | | | | | | | | Per capita[2] (dollars) | |
| | Salaries and wages | Defense | Other | Medicaid and other health-related | Nutrition and family welfare | Education | Other | New construction ($1,000) | Number of housing units | Total (mil dol) | Inter-governmental (mil dol) | Total (mil dol) | Total | Property |
| | 171 | 172 | 173 | 174 | 175 | 176 | 177 | 178 | 179 | 180 | 181 | 182 | 183 | 184 |
| **WEST VIRGINIA—Cont'd** | | | | | | | | | | | | | | |
| Brooke | 6.3 | 0.0 | 0.8 | 14.9 | 3.2 | 1.7 | 4.9 | 985 | 7 | 46.1 | 23.1 | 18.0 | 761 | 707 |
| Cabell | 71.0 | 2.8 | 33.2 | 137.5 | 19.7 | 8.4 | 46.7 | 17 375 | 171 | 258.8 | 104.5 | 94.6 | 1 001 | 772 |
| Calhoun | 2.3 | 0.1 | 0.4 | 25.9 | 1.5 | 0.9 | 0.0 | NA | NA | 13.1 | 10.1 | 2.4 | 328 | 308 |
| Clay | 2.3 | 0.0 | 0.6 | 27.1 | 2.4 | 0.9 | 0.2 | 938 | 18 | 30.8 | 25.3 | 4.1 | 403 | 391 |
| Doddridge | 1.2 | 0.0 | 0.3 | 11.6 | 1.3 | 0.6 | 0.0 | NA | NA | 19.6 | 11.9 | 6.6 | 909 | 902 |
| Fayette | 47.8 | 0.0 | 10.0 | 82.6 | 9.4 | 3.4 | 17.3 | 5 426 | 37 | 145.6 | 61.0 | 53.3 | 1 150 | 557 |
| Gilmer | 21.7 | 0.0 | 6.2 | 17.8 | 1.5 | 0.9 | 1.3 | 200 | 3 | 19.9 | 6.3 | 4.2 | 615 | 591 |
| Grant | 5.0 | 0.0 | 2.1 | 19.7 | 3.5 | 0.7 | 1.4 | 2 736 | 36 | 56.1 | 16.2 | 8.1 | 678 | 626 |
| Greenbrier | 17.2 | 1.7 | 2.9 | 53.9 | 6.6 | 2.2 | 6.8 | 16 626 | 99 | 86.7 | 39.2 | 28.6 | 826 | 566 |
| Hampshire | 6.5 | 0.0 | 0.8 | 24.5 | 3.1 | 1.3 | 0.3 | 4 955 | 38 | 45.8 | 25.7 | 14.4 | 640 | 585 |
| Hancock | 5.6 | 2.5 | 2.2 | 17.4 | 3.9 | 1.7 | 2.8 | 1 065 | 9 | 90.9 | 29.9 | 25.6 | 848 | 696 |
| Hardy | 5.6 | 0.3 | 1.3 | 24.6 | 1.8 | 0.9 | 25.4 | 5 532 | 34 | 25.1 | 14.5 | 7.3 | 532 | 482 |
| Harrison | 281.9 | 42.8 | 248.1 | 72.7 | 13.2 | 7.0 | 8.7 | 13 529 | 112 | 181.2 | 82.5 | 70.1 | 1 026 | 726 |
| Jackson | 10.2 | 0.1 | 3.0 | 29.4 | 4.2 | 1.9 | 6.3 | 81 | 2 | 70.9 | 38.4 | 22.5 | 796 | 726 |
| Jefferson | 62.1 | 17.7 | 156.2 | 21.1 | 5.1 | 1.9 | 4.2 | 30 592 | 135 | 122.3 | 40.9 | 56.3 | 1 107 | 835 |
| Kanawha | 251.1 | 17.9 | 54.6 | 247.5 | 140.4 | 172.3 | 1 237.6 | 24 008 | 134 | 528.1 | 217.8 | 219.7 | 1 149 | 781 |
| Lewis | 11.8 | 0.9 | 1.1 | 35.2 | 2.9 | 1.3 | 0.5 | 0 | 0 | 34.2 | 17.7 | 14.4 | 838 | 656 |
| Lincoln | 3.4 | 0.0 | 0.8 | 62.1 | 4.2 | 2.7 | 0.1 | 490 | 4 | 44.3 | 32.8 | 8.7 | 389 | 364 |
| Logan | 13.0 | 5.8 | 7.6 | 65.5 | 8.7 | 3.8 | 11.2 | 315 | 13 | 76.6 | 44.0 | 23.6 | 663 | 628 |
| McDowell | 8.9 | 0.3 | 11.5 | 99.1 | 6.5 | 3.6 | 7.9 | 0 | 0 | 58.8 | 32.9 | 15.8 | 689 | 612 |
| Marion | 29.7 | 22.5 | 91.8 | 56.0 | 14.1 | 8.7 | 18.0 | 409 | 5 | 143.1 | 66.4 | 44.3 | 781 | 581 |
| Marshall | 11.0 | 0.1 | 1.2 | 26.3 | 5.0 | 2.6 | 2.8 | 0 | 0 | 100.7 | 38.4 | 30.5 | 921 | 789 |
| Mason | 7.2 | 7.4 | 1.3 | 33.3 | 3.8 | 2.0 | 1.5 | 290 | 1 | 60.5 | 31.0 | 19.2 | 751 | 684 |
| Mercer | 43.8 | 1.5 | 6.4 | 100.4 | 12.2 | 9.4 | 4.7 | 784 | 8 | 213.9 | 123.4 | 31.8 | 518 | 396 |
| Mineral | 4.8 | 65.6 | 23.9 | 23.1 | 5.0 | 2.6 | 4.8 | 8 000 | 48 | 56.7 | 36.4 | 13.6 | 508 | 457 |
| Mingo | 7.7 | 0.5 | 4.4 | 74.7 | 9.9 | 2.8 | 19.8 | 0 | 0 | 67.7 | 40.7 | 20.8 | 779 | 720 |
| Monongalia | 119.6 | 19.7 | 326.4 | 124.6 | 11.4 | 7.5 | 80.0 | 31 096 | 398 | 201.5 | 73.5 | 75.4 | 862 | 642 |
| Monroe | 14.4 | 0.0 | 4.3 | 28.4 | 2.6 | 1.1 | 0.0 | 0 | 0 | 26.2 | 20.6 | 3.8 | 283 | 269 |
| Morgan | 2.8 | 0.1 | 1.3 | 8.3 | 1.9 | 1.0 | 0.0 | 6 313 | 37 | 45.2 | 14.1 | 12.0 | 737 | 679 |
| Nicholas | 8.9 | 3.2 | 1.4 | 32.7 | 5.6 | 2.1 | 0.9 | 0 | 0 | 95.2 | 33.9 | 15.4 | 590 | 449 |
| Ohio | 46.8 | 9.3 | 13.3 | 48.0 | 11.1 | 2.9 | 27.5 | 3 380 | 20 | 173.1 | 69.3 | 50.1 | 1 129 | 648 |
| Pendleton | 10.8 | 7.5 | 0.7 | 16.8 | 1.2 | 0.9 | 8.8 | 2 869 | 22 | 13.7 | 9.4 | 3.1 | 410 | 371 |
| Pleasants | 1.0 | 0.0 | 0.3 | 7.0 | 1.1 | 0.4 | 0.0 | 1 253 | 7 | 38.4 | 9.2 | 11.2 | 1 558 | 1 471 |
| Pocahontas | 4.0 | 0.2 | 3.3 | 15.5 | 1.6 | 0.6 | 0.4 | 0 | 0 | 25.6 | 9.0 | 7.1 | 829 | 678 |
| Preston | 85.8 | 3.7 | 25.8 | 37.8 | 5.0 | 2.6 | 1.9 | 76 | 1 | 53.0 | 33.1 | 8.5 | 279 | 261 |
| Putnam | 34.7 | 6.9 | 2.6 | 29.8 | 6.5 | 2.2 | 0.5 | 19 547 | 124 | 116.0 | 49.4 | 42.5 | 773 | 705 |
| Raleigh | 107.3 | 0.2 | 45.9 | 88.7 | 15.0 | 5.2 | 9.2 | 19 409 | 119 | 193.2 | 100.3 | 61.6 | 778 | 602 |
| Randolph | 19.1 | 0.0 | 6.4 | 50.7 | 5.0 | 3.7 | 7.3 | 870 | 10 | 59.1 | 39.3 | 10.8 | 381 | 302 |
| Ritchie | 2.5 | 0.0 | 0.5 | 16.6 | 1.8 | 0.9 | 0.7 | 179 | 1 | 22.3 | 11.9 | 7.0 | 679 | 635 |
| Roane | 7.4 | 0.0 | 0.6 | 27.7 | 3.0 | 1.5 | 2.1 | 2 197 | 33 | 25.7 | 19.1 | 4.6 | 299 | 215 |
| Summers | 3.1 | 61.1 | 0.5 | 36.9 | 2.2 | 1.1 | 0.3 | 2 880 | 27 | 18.4 | 11.8 | 4.7 | 353 | 242 |
| Taylor | 10.7 | 0.4 | 2.7 | 20.2 | 2.6 | 1.4 | 0.3 | 200 | 2 | 30.0 | 17.3 | 8.9 | 554 | 484 |
| Tucker | 4.0 | 0.0 | 1.2 | 13.0 | 1.3 | 0.6 | 6.8 | 688 | 6 | 19.9 | 8.8 | 4.8 | 704 | 625 |
| Tyler | 1.7 | 0.0 | 0.4 | 9.3 | 1.5 | 0.8 | 0.2 | 0 | 0 | 28.8 | 11.7 | 5.7 | 639 | 619 |
| Upshur | 9.5 | 1.8 | 1.8 | 27.0 | 5.2 | 1.8 | 1.9 | 4 575 | 34 | 50.3 | 28.7 | 12.7 | 542 | 450 |
| Wayne | 87.5 | 5.9 | 39.7 | 79.3 | 6.1 | 2.7 | 11.2 | 2 103 | 23 | 83.4 | 55.1 | 22.3 | 540 | 495 |
| Webster | 1.3 | 0.0 | 0.3 | 31.7 | 1.9 | 1.3 | 5.2 | 0 | 0 | 18.6 | 12.6 | 3.7 | 395 | 310 |
| Wetzel | 4.6 | 0.1 | 0.8 | 28.2 | 2.7 | 1.4 | 0.0 | 600 | 14 | 65.6 | 23.8 | 12.2 | 741 | 584 |
| Wirt | 1.2 | 3.5 | 0.3 | 10.1 | 1.0 | 0.5 | 0.0 | 369 | 5 | 10.1 | 7.3 | 1.9 | 321 | 306 |
| Wood | 161.6 | 10.8 | 33.5 | 78.4 | 12.2 | 6.4 | 14.1 | 11 697 | 76 | 205.4 | 90.2 | 69.4 | 807 | 626 |
| Wyoming | 6.8 | 0.0 | 1.8 | 44.5 | 7.5 | 2.5 | 1.1 | 0 | 0 | 55.7 | 32.2 | 17.7 | 748 | 640 |
| **WISCONSIN** | 2 926.4 | 8 469.0 | 1 336.1 | 6 592.2 | 1 312.1 | 860.1 | 3 227.7 | 1 605 963 | 9 939 | X | X | X | X | X |
| Adams | 21.6 | 0.0 | 1.5 | 29.8 | 3.6 | 0.9 | 1.0 | 8 068 | 50 | 68.5 | 28.2 | 29.2 | 1 412 | 1 312 |
| Ashland | 11.2 | 0.1 | 5.3 | 34.0 | 5.1 | 4.2 | 5.3 | 3 684 | 28 | 82.0 | 50.2 | 19.8 | 1 216 | 1 107 |
| Barron | 13.1 | 0.0 | 2.4 | 80.0 | 15.4 | 3.1 | 1.5 | 9 949 | 70 | 182.1 | 86.8 | 66.3 | 1 454 | 1 317 |
| Bayfield | 10.6 | 1.9 | 5.8 | 24.7 | 5.4 | 2.3 | 17.5 | 11 435 | 67 | 69.4 | 28.9 | 30.4 | 2 023 | 1 887 |
| Brown | 109.4 | 49.8 | 58.2 | 174.4 | 37.8 | 16.7 | 35.5 | 89 037 | 709 | 1 061.0 | 468.5 | 389.7 | 1 603 | 1 467 |
| Buffalo | 6.6 | 1.4 | 3.2 | 19.3 | 3.0 | 0.8 | 0.0 | 3 164 | 18 | 52.4 | 31.0 | 15.6 | 1 133 | 1 073 |
| Burnett | 2.5 | 4.7 | 0.6 | 25.3 | 4.0 | 1.2 | 3.8 | 16 170 | 97 | 58.2 | 22.9 | 28.2 | 1 728 | 1 651 |
| Calumet | 34.8 | 2.3 | 1.2 | 13.9 | 4.5 | 1.9 | 0.1 | 13 444 | 63 | 109.4 | 49.9 | 36.5 | 824 | 806 |
| Chippewa | 53.1 | 5.8 | 3.1 | 66.3 | 10.7 | 4.1 | 5.4 | 19 502 | 135 | 210.1 | 108.4 | 62.3 | 1 032 | 946 |
| Clark | 12.1 | 0.0 | 3.0 | 47.0 | 6.3 | 2.5 | 0.2 | 4 249 | 39 | 137.6 | 78.4 | 30.4 | 909 | 897 |
| Columbia | 25.0 | 0.0 | 55.0 | 46.8 | 12.1 | 3.1 | 3.3 | 9 877 | 40 | 240.1 | 102.6 | 99.0 | 1 792 | 1 670 |
| Crawford | 7.6 | 0.3 | 1.2 | 31.9 | 3.5 | 1.1 | 5.7 | 4 282 | 34 | 66.8 | 38.3 | 20.5 | 1 208 | 1 099 |
| Dane | 438.3 | 166.7 | 182.8 | 965.7 | 283.4 | 450.2 | 2 189.6 | 236 783 | 1 371 | 2 063.7 | 709.8 | 953.7 | 2 000 | 1 842 |

1. State totals may include programs not allocated by county.   2. Based on the resident population estimated as of July 1 of the year shown.

# Table B. States and Counties — Local Government Finances, Government Employment, and Voting

| | Local government finances, 2007 (cont.) | | | | | | | | | Government employment, 2011 | | | Presidential election,[2] 2012 | | |
| | Direct general expenditure | | | | | | | Debt outstanding | | | | | Percent of vote cast: | | |
| | | | Percent of total for: | | | | | | | | | | | | |
| STATE County | Total (mil dol) | Per capita[1] (dollars) | Education | Health and hospitals | Police protection | Public welfare | Highways | Total (mil dol) | Per capita[1] (dollars) | Federal civilian | Federal military | State and local | Democratic | Republican | All other |
| | 185 | 186 | 187 | 188 | 189 | 190 | 191 | 192 | 193 | 194 | 195 | 196 | 197 | 198 | 199 |
| WEST VIRGINIA—Cont'd | | | | | | | | | | | | | | | |
| Brooke | 41.8 | 1 765 | 72.5 | 0.3 | 7.4 | 0.1 | 1.1 | 18.6 | 787 | 32 | 118 | 965 | 47.9 | 50.3 | 1.8 |
| Cabell | 241.6 | 2 558 | 48.5 | 2.4 | 6.0 | 0.4 | 0.9 | 161.8 | 1 714 | 1 076 | 581 | 7 230 | 44.2 | 54.3 | 1.5 |
| Calhoun | 13.9 | 1 932 | 86.0 | 0.2 | 1.1 | 0.0 | 0.3 | 2.9 | 399 | 21 | 38 | 318 | 40.9 | 56.2 | 2.9 |
| Clay | 30.1 | 2 974 | 84.5 | 7.5 | 2.0 | 0.0 | 0.1 | 1.4 | 134 | 21 | 46 | 549 | 43.5 | 53.8 | 2.7 |
| Doddridge | 23.5 | 3 242 | 83.8 | 2.0 | 2.8 | 0.0 | 0.1 | 7.6 | 1 048 | 12 | 40 | 509 | 24.4 | 73.5 | 2.2 |
| Fayette | 128.7 | 2 777 | 48.6 | 0.7 | 4.1 | 0.2 | 6.6 | 75.1 | 1 621 | 290 | 226 | 3 110 | 47.7 | 50.4 | 1.9 |
| Gilmer | 15.9 | 2 308 | 56.7 | 0.2 | 2.3 | 0.0 | 0.6 | 5.3 | 766 | 322 | 43 | 668 | 39.8 | 57.3 | 2.9 |
| Grant | 55.1 | 4 617 | 32.5 | 49.5 | 2.3 | 0.0 | 0.6 | 13.6 | 1 138 | 44 | 59 | 942 | 23.6 | 75.1 | 1.3 |
| Greenbrier | 76.4 | 2 209 | 61.8 | 1.7 | 3.5 | 0.1 | 1.4 | 60.6 | 1 753 | 111 | 177 | 2 367 | 42.8 | 55.1 | 2.1 |
| Hampshire | 46.6 | 2 064 | 72.2 | 2.3 | 1.6 | 0.0 | 0.5 | 20.0 | 886 | 45 | 117 | 1 378 | 35.7 | 62.6 | 1.7 |
| Hancock | 87.1 | 2 886 | 43.8 | 11.9 | 5.6 | 0.0 | 4.3 | 65.1 | 2 155 | 57 | 151 | 1 382 | 41.6 | 56.9 | 1.5 |
| Hardy | 25.7 | 1 883 | 70.0 | 2.0 | 5.5 | 0.0 | 1.3 | 6.9 | 508 | 47 | 69 | 827 | 35.2 | 62.4 | 2.4 |
| Harrison | 171.2 | 2 506 | 61.4 | 0.9 | 5.6 | 0.0 | 3.6 | 137.4 | 2 012 | 4 118 | 344 | 4 139 | 42.6 | 55.9 | 1.5 |
| Jackson | 68.1 | 2 412 | 67.6 | 3.7 | 5.2 | 0.0 | 0.7 | 29.5 | 1 046 | 86 | 144 | 1 370 | 39.7 | 58.4 | 1.9 |
| Jefferson | 135.5 | 2 666 | 66.9 | 1.5 | 5.0 | 0.1 | 1.3 | 58.9 | 1 158 | 873 | 267 | 3 064 | 51.8 | 47.0 | 1.1 |
| Kanawha | 547.1 | 2 860 | 51.1 | 0.4 | 5.7 | 0.0 | 3.4 | 304.1 | 1 590 | 2 006 | 1 010 | 19 911 | 49.2 | 49.6 | 1.1 |
| Lewis | 32.0 | 1 865 | 77.8 | 2.2 | 2.9 | 0.3 | 1.5 | 0.6 | 34 | 59 | 81 | 1 451 | 31.9 | 65.6 | 2.5 |
| Lincoln | 44.4 | 1 990 | 88.9 | 0.6 | 0.5 | 0.0 | 0.0 | 6.0 | 270 | 35 | 106 | 902 | 44.3 | 53.2 | 2.5 |
| Logan | 84.3 | 2 365 | 77.7 | 1.4 | 1.2 | 0.1 | 0.5 | 24.5 | 688 | 112 | 180 | 2 057 | 43.6 | 54.4 | 2.0 |
| McDowell | 52.3 | 2 276 | 75.7 | 0.1 | 2.5 | 0.0 | 0.7 | 7.7 | 334 | 371 | 107 | 1 735 | 53.3 | 44.8 | 1.8 |
| Marion | 151.7 | 2 675 | 61.1 | 0.2 | 3.6 | 0.2 | 0.9 | 282.1 | 4 974 | 199 | 280 | 4 287 | 49.2 | 48.7 | 2.1 |
| Marshall | 94.9 | 2 863 | 53.9 | 3.9 | 4.9 | 0.2 | 1.3 | 212.4 | 6 407 | 57 | 162 | 1 867 | 42.8 | 55.4 | 1.8 |
| Mason | 76.0 | 2 974 | 73.7 | 0.2 | 2.3 | 0.0 | 3.0 | 59.0 | 2 309 | 111 | 135 | 1 538 | 42.3 | 55.2 | 2.5 |
| Mercer | 208.1 | 3 393 | 40.4 | 39.1 | 2.6 | 0.0 | 1.7 | 147.3 | 2 401 | 208 | 308 | 4 974 | 35.4 | 63.0 | 1.6 |
| Mineral | 54.4 | 2 036 | 74.4 | 1.9 | 2.9 | 0.1 | 1.0 | 25.2 | 945 | 61 | 139 | 1 641 | 32.5 | 66.0 | 1.6 |
| Mingo | 67.7 | 2 530 | 64.5 | 2.1 | 2.4 | 0.0 | 0.7 | 27.6 | 1 033 | 71 | 131 | 1 383 | 43.0 | 55.0 | 2.0 |
| Monongalia | 209.8 | 2 397 | 55.7 | 3.4 | 5.6 | 0.3 | 1.8 | 226.6 | 2 589 | 1 265 | 497 | 15 366 | 51.1 | 47.3 | 1.6 |
| Monroe | 24.8 | 1 830 | 76.4 | 0.0 | 3.9 | 0.0 | 0.2 | 64.5 | 4 765 | 210 | 67 | 543 | 36.1 | 60.9 | 2.9 |
| Morgan | 47.4 | 2 898 | 50.4 | 23.5 | 4.1 | 0.0 | 0.0 | 12.3 | 751 | 27 | 87 | 807 | 37.4 | 60.9 | 1.7 |
| Nicholas | 97.3 | 3 719 | 42.3 | 37.8 | 4.4 | 0.0 | 0.8 | 22.4 | 858 | 98 | 130 | 1 812 | 46.5 | 51.3 | 2.1 |
| Ohio | 164.5 | 3 704 | 33.3 | 0.8 | 8.9 | 0.1 | 3.6 | 139.1 | 3 132 | 434 | 218 | 3 843 | 44.0 | 54.7 | 1.3 |
| Pendleton | 13.5 | 1 770 | 76.8 | 2.7 | 0.9 | 0.0 | 0.2 | 3.3 | 436 | 128 | 234 | 344 | 38.6 | 59.9 | 1.5 |
| Pleasants | 37.8 | 5 265 | 44.5 | 0.3 | 2.7 | 0.7 | 0.5 | 171.4 | 23 860 | 11 | 38 | 655 | 38.4 | 59.6 | 2.1 |
| Pocahontas | 26.5 | 3 094 | 47.1 | 27.6 | 2.2 | 0.1 | 0.2 | 5.4 | 626 | 61 | 43 | 783 | 42.5 | 55.2 | 2.3 |
| Preston | 51.7 | 1 708 | 73.2 | 0.9 | 2.2 | 0.0 | 0.8 | 35.8 | 1 184 | 602 | 166 | 1 692 | 35.6 | 62.1 | 2.3 |
| Putnam | 123.4 | 2 243 | 68.6 | 3.2 | 4.0 | 0.0 | 0.6 | 218.1 | 3 966 | 184 | 277 | 2 330 | 37.7 | 61.2 | 1.1 |
| Raleigh | 196.1 | 2 477 | 58.3 | 1.3 | 7.0 | 0.6 | 1.4 | 128.6 | 1 624 | 1 842 | 452 | 3 845 | 36.2 | 62.1 | 1.7 |
| Randolph | 56.9 | 2 012 | 65.1 | 3.4 | 2.9 | 0.2 | 1.7 | 29.2 | 1 031 | 188 | 145 | 2 104 | 41.9 | 55.9 | 2.2 |
| Ritchie | 21.2 | 2 049 | 69.3 | 4.7 | 3.8 | 0.0 | 0.5 | 1.9 | 183 | 26 | 51 | 542 | 25.9 | 72.3 | 1.7 |
| Roane | 25.1 | 1 644 | 85.6 | 0.1 | 1.1 | 0.0 | 1.7 | 8.8 | 576 | 31 | 73 | 640 | 45.1 | 52.9 | 2.0 |
| Summers | 18.7 | 1 419 | 77.5 | 1.5 | 4.4 | 0.0 | 1.7 | 3.1 | 238 | 44 | 68 | 737 | 43.1 | 54.4 | 2.5 |
| Taylor | 27.7 | 1 717 | 73.3 | 0.0 | 2.1 | 0.0 | 2.2 | 15.9 | 989 | 48 | 83 | 1 103 | 39.7 | 58.1 | 2.2 |
| Tucker | 21.4 | 3 119 | 50.0 | 3.9 | 3.3 | 0.0 | 1.3 | 23.3 | 3 388 | 52 | 35 | 653 | 36.7 | 60.5 | 2.7 |
| Tyler | 25.5 | 2 851 | 60.0 | 24.0 | 1.8 | 0.1 | 0.7 | 18.3 | 2 043 | 19 | 45 | 580 | 33.2 | 64.6 | 2.3 |
| Upshur | 51.4 | 2 186 | 66.8 | 0.6 | 3.6 | 0.3 | 1.4 | 17.7 | 752 | 120 | 120 | 1 229 | 32.6 | 65.9 | 1.5 |
| Wayne | 83.6 | 2 028 | 81.1 | 1.0 | 3.5 | 0.4 | 0.7 | 25.3 | 615 | 1 338 | 217 | 1 950 | 39.8 | 58.0 | 2.2 |
| Webster | 18.5 | 1 963 | 78.7 | 1.1 | 1.1 | 0.0 | 0.1 | 2.7 | 288 | 14 | 45 | 597 | 50.8 | 45.3 | 3.9 |
| Wetzel | 63.3 | 3 854 | 45.3 | 38.6 | 3.1 | 0.0 | 0.9 | 29.0 | 1 765 | 38 | 81 | 1 193 | 45.6 | 51.8 | 2.6 |
| Wirt | 10.5 | 1 804 | 85.8 | 0.0 | 0.1 | 0.0 | 0.2 | 1.1 | 188 | 11 | 28 | 275 | 33.6 | 64.3 | 2.1 |
| Wood | 219.0 | 2 544 | 65.9 | 1.0 | 5.3 | 0.1 | 2.8 | 217.5 | 2 526 | 2 209 | 432 | 4 507 | 34.9 | 63.6 | 1.5 |
| Wyoming | 53.9 | 2 276 | 76.4 | 0.7 | 4.6 | 0.0 | 0.5 | 30.2 | 1 275 | 81 | 116 | 1 124 | 36.3 | 61.4 | 2.3 |
| WISCONSIN | X | X | X | X | X | X | X | X | X | 29 496 | 16 750 | 385 310 | 56.2 | 42.3 | 1.5 |
| Adams | 72.5 | 3 505 | 30.8 | 6.7 | 6.6 | 4.7 | 19.6 | 69.8 | 3 377 | 307 | 58 | 846 | 58.1 | 39.8 | 2.1 |
| Ashland | 83.0 | 5 096 | 41.7 | 2.8 | 5.2 | 10.3 | 13.9 | 40.5 | 2 484 | 177 | 45 | 1 946 | 67.9 | 30.7 | 1.4 |
| Barron | 192.4 | 4 219 | 46.4 | 0.8 | 4.1 | 11.5 | 14.1 | 137.7 | 3 018 | 136 | 129 | 3 919 | 52.8 | 45.7 | 1.5 |
| Bayfield | 74.1 | 4 930 | 31.7 | 11.6 | 3.9 | 3.1 | 20.8 | 48.4 | 3 221 | 127 | 56 | 1 309 | 63.1 | 35.5 | 1.4 |
| Brown | 1 085.3 | 4 464 | 50.3 | 3.8 | 5.1 | 6.0 | 7.5 | 1 603.5 | 6 595 | 1 027 | 742 | 16 872 | 53.9 | 44.8 | 1.3 |
| Buffalo | 59.3 | 4 296 | 43.7 | 0.9 | 2.3 | 8.2 | 22.8 | 39.7 | 2 871 | 159 | 38 | 686 | 56.4 | 41.8 | 1.8 |
| Burnett | 60.3 | 3 692 | 40.8 | 6.4 | 3.9 | 5.3 | 19.9 | 45.0 | 2 756 | 27 | 43 | 1 672 | 49.9 | 48.3 | 1.7 |
| Calumet | 110.0 | 2 482 | 39.4 | 5.9 | 5.0 | 6.4 | 13.7 | 117.0 | 2 639 | 123 | 138 | 1 227 | 50.2 | 48.1 | 1.7 |
| Chippewa | 205.1 | 3 395 | 47.6 | 3.2 | 4.0 | 8.5 | 14.5 | 674.3 | 11 163 | 200 | 176 | 3 255 | 53.7 | 44.6 | 1.7 |
| Clark | 140.1 | 4 184 | 43.2 | 7.8 | 3.3 | 15.9 | 10.5 | 57.2 | 1 709 | 116 | 97 | 1 880 | 52.5 | 45.0 | 2.5 |
| Columbia | 248.1 | 4 488 | 47.8 | 1.2 | 4.4 | 10.1 | 9.6 | 218.9 | 3 960 | 202 | 161 | 3 557 | 56.9 | 41.7 | 1.4 |
| Crawford | 64.4 | 3 790 | 41.2 | 2.7 | 4.7 | 10.7 | 15.0 | 46.8 | 2 754 | 69 | 47 | 938 | 62.5 | 35.5 | 2.1 |
| Dane | 2 082.0 | 4 367 | 45.1 | 2.2 | 5.8 | 8.6 | 5.9 | 2 406.9 | 5 048 | 5 079 | 1 479 | 76 326 | 72.8 | 25.8 | 1.4 |

1. Based on the resident population estimated as of July 1 of the year shown.   2. © 2013 Election Data Services, Inc. All rights reserved.

# Table B. States and Counties — Land Area and Population

| STATE/ County code | CBSA code[1] | County type[2] | STATE County | Population 2012 | | | | Population characteristics[6], 2011 | | | | | | | | | | |
|---|---|---|---|---|---|---|---|---|---|---|---|---|---|---|---|---|---|---|
| | | | | | | | | Race alone or in combination, not Hispanic or Latino (percent) | | | | | Age (percent) | | | | | |
| | | | | Land area,[3] (sq km) 2010 | Total persons | Rank | Per square kilometer | White | Black | Amer- ican Indian, Alaska Native | Asian and Pacific Islander | Percent Hispanic or Latino[4] | Under 5 years | 5 to 17 years | 18 to 24 years | 25 to 34 years | 35 to 44 years | 45 to 54 years |
| | | | | 1 | 2 | 3 | 4 | 5 | 6 | 7 | 8 | 9 | 10 | 11 | 12 | 13 | 14 | 15 |
| | | | WISCONSIN—Cont'd | | | | | | | | | | | | | | | |
| 55 027 | 13180 | 4 | Dodge | 2 268 | 88 415 | 644 | 39.0 | 92.2 | 3.0 | 0.7 | 0.9 | 4.0 | 5.5 | 16.2 | 7.6 | 12.9 | 13.3 | 16.6 |
| 55 029 | ... | 6 | Door | 1 248 | 27 817 | 1 502 | 22.3 | 95.8 | 0.8 | 1.0 | 0.7 | 2.6 | 4.5 | 13.4 | 5.9 | 9.0 | 10.1 | 15.9 |
| 55 031 | 20260 | 2 | Douglas | 3 378 | 43 785 | 1 092 | 13.0 | 94.8 | 1.9 | 3.2 | 1.4 | 1.2 | 5.9 | 15.4 | 10.0 | 12.6 | 11.9 | 15.4 |
| 55 033 | 32860 | 6 | Dunn | 2 202 | 44 072 | 1 085 | 20.0 | 94.7 | 1.0 | 0.9 | 3.2 | 1.5 | 5.2 | 14.9 | 20.4 | 11.3 | 11.0 | 13.1 |
| 55 035 | 20740 | 3 | Eau Claire | 1 652 | 100 677 | 581 | 60.9 | 93.1 | 1.5 | 0.9 | 4.0 | 2.0 | 5.7 | 14.9 | 17.9 | 13.3 | 10.8 | 12.7 |
| 55 037 | 27020 | 9 | Florence | 1 264 | 4 482 | 2 870 | 3.5 | 97.4 | 0.9 | 1.2 | 0.5 | 1.1 | 4.0 | 13.1 | 5.7 | 8.3 | 10.3 | 19.1 |
| 55 039 | 22540 | 3 | Fond du Lac | 1 864 | 101 843 | 574 | 54.6 | 92.6 | 1.7 | 0.8 | 1.4 | 4.5 | 5.9 | 16.6 | 8.9 | 12.3 | 12.3 | 15.5 |
| 55 041 | ... | 9 | Forest | 2 626 | 9 206 | 2 502 | 3.5 | 83.9 | 1.7 | 14.5 | 0.7 | 1.7 | 5.3 | 16.5 | 8.9 | 9.4 | 10.8 | 14.5 |
| 55 043 | 38420 | 6 | Grant | 2 970 | 51 087 | 968 | 17.2 | 96.5 | 1.4 | 0.4 | 1.0 | 1.4 | 5.7 | 15.2 | 17.5 | 10.6 | 10.0 | 13.4 |
| 55 045 | 33820 | 6 | Green | 1 512 | 36 909 | 1 249 | 24.4 | 95.8 | 0.8 | 0.4 | 0.8 | 2.9 | 6.1 | 17.7 | 6.6 | 11.1 | 12.9 | 16.4 |
| 55 047 | ... | 6 | Green Lake | 905 | 19 039 | 1 872 | 21.0 | 94.3 | 0.7 | 0.5 | 0.7 | 4.3 | 5.7 | 17.0 | 6.4 | 9.8 | 11.1 | 15.4 |
| 55 049 | 31540 | 2 | Iowa | 1 975 | 23 807 | 1 654 | 12.1 | 97.4 | 0.7 | 0.5 | 0.8 | 1.4 | 6.6 | 17.7 | 6.5 | 11.2 | 12.6 | 16.8 |
| 55 051 | ... | 9 | Iron | 1 964 | 5 934 | 2 767 | 3.0 | 98.0 | 0.5 | 1.1 | 0.7 | 0.7 | 3.7 | 12.8 | 5.2 | 7.9 | 10.3 | 17.2 |
| 55 053 | ... | 6 | Jackson | 2 558 | 20 485 | 1 815 | 8.0 | 88.9 | 2.3 | 6.6 | 0.7 | 2.8 | 6.2 | 16.3 | 7.6 | 12.1 | 12.3 | 15.6 |
| 55 055 | 48020 | 4 | Jefferson | 1 441 | 84 498 | 666 | 58.6 | 91.3 | 1.1 | 0.7 | 1.0 | 6.9 | 6.1 | 17.4 | 10.1 | 12.1 | 13.0 | 15.0 |
| 55 057 | ... | 7 | Juneau | 1 986 | 26 631 | 1 543 | 13.4 | 93.3 | 2.4 | 1.9 | 0.7 | 2.6 | 5.5 | 15.6 | 6.7 | 11.4 | 12.4 | 16.6 |
| 55 059 | 16980 | 1 | Kenosha | 704 | 167 936 | 372 | 238.5 | 79.6 | 7.5 | 0.8 | 2.0 | 12.0 | 6.5 | 18.9 | 10.0 | 12.6 | 13.5 | 15.8 |
| 55 061 | 24580 | 2 | Kewaunee | 887 | 20 624 | 1 804 | 23.3 | 96.3 | 0.7 | 0.9 | 0.6 | 2.4 | 5.5 | 17.5 | 6.6 | 11.1 | 12.4 | 16.0 |
| 55 063 | 29100 | 3 | La Crosse | 1 170 | 116 461 | 521 | 99.5 | 92.3 | 2.1 | 0.8 | 4.8 | 1.6 | 5.9 | 15.1 | 16.0 | 12.8 | 11.2 | 13.4 |
| 55 065 | ... | 8 | Lafayette | 1 641 | 16 853 | 1 991 | 10.3 | 95.6 | 0.6 | 0.4 | 0.5 | 3.3 | 6.6 | 18.7 | 7.8 | 11.3 | 11.0 | 15.9 |
| 55 067 | ... | 6 | Langlade | 2 255 | 19 646 | 1 851 | 8.7 | 96.4 | 0.8 | 1.6 | 0.7 | 1.8 | 5.1 | 15.5 | 6.7 | 9.9 | 11.0 | 16.5 |
| 55 069 | 32980 | 6 | Lincoln | 2 277 | 28 392 | 1 474 | 12.5 | 97.2 | 0.9 | 0.8 | 0.8 | 1.3 | 5.1 | 16.5 | 6.4 | 9.5 | 12.1 | 17.4 |
| 55 071 | 31820 | 4 | Manitowoc | 1 526 | 80 671 | 684 | 52.9 | 93.1 | 0.9 | 0.9 | 2.8 | 3.3 | 5.4 | 16.5 | 7.3 | 10.9 | 11.9 | 16.5 |
| 55 073 | 48140 | 3 | Marathon | 4 001 | 134 735 | 466 | 33.7 | 91.0 | 1.1 | 0.8 | 5.9 | 2.3 | 6.4 | 17.7 | 7.8 | 12.4 | 12.7 | 15.5 |
| 55 075 | 31940 | 6 | Marinette | 3 624 | 41 563 | 1 140 | 11.5 | 97.0 | 0.6 | 1.1 | 0.8 | 1.4 | 4.7 | 15.1 | 7.6 | 10.0 | 10.4 | 16.4 |
| 55 077 | ... | 8 | Marquette | 1 180 | 15 205 | 2 092 | 12.9 | 95.7 | 0.8 | 0.8 | 0.6 | 2.6 | 4.9 | 15.0 | 6.1 | 9.1 | 10.7 | 16.9 |
| 55 078 | ... | 8 | Menominee | 926 | 4 340 | 2 880 | 4.7 | 13.5 | 1.4 | 81.0 | 0.4 | 5.3 | 10.7 | 22.5 | 10.8 | 10.6 | 10.4 | 13.8 |
| 55 079 | 33340 | 1 | Milwaukee | 625 | 955 205 | 47 | 1 528.3 | 56.0 | 27.5 | 1.2 | 4.0 | 13.6 | 7.4 | 17.5 | 11.1 | 15.8 | 12.4 | 13.2 |
| 55 081 | ... | 6 | Monroe | 2 333 | 45 100 | 1 066 | 19.3 | 93.1 | 1.6 | 1.4 | 1.1 | 3.9 | 7.1 | 18.6 | 7.3 | 12.3 | 11.7 | 15.4 |
| 55 083 | 24580 | 2 | Oconto | 2 585 | 37 442 | 1 235 | 14.5 | 96.7 | 0.5 | 1.8 | 0.5 | 1.5 | 5.5 | 16.5 | 6.7 | 10.0 | 12.7 | 17.7 |
| 55 085 | ... | 7 | Oneida | 2 883 | 35 714 | 1 283 | 12.4 | 96.9 | 0.8 | 1.4 | 0.8 | 1.2 | 4.6 | 13.4 | 6.3 | 9.4 | 10.6 | 17.0 |
| 55 087 | 11540 | 3 | Outagamie | 1 651 | 178 816 | 353 | 108.3 | 90.5 | 1.5 | 2.0 | 3.4 | 3.8 | 6.5 | 18.2 | 8.7 | 13.7 | 13.3 | 15.8 |
| 55 089 | 33340 | 1 | Ozaukee | 604 | 86 823 | 653 | 143.7 | 94.1 | 1.8 | 0.5 | 2.4 | 2.4 | 5.1 | 17.8 | 7.7 | 9.5 | 12.2 | 17.3 |
| 55 091 | ... | 8 | Pepin | 601 | 7 390 | 2 648 | 12.3 | 98.0 | 0.5 | 0.6 | 0.4 | 1.1 | 6.2 | 16.6 | 6.5 | 10.2 | 11.3 | 15.7 |
| 55 093 | 33460 | 1 | Pierce | 1 486 | 40 814 | 1 159 | 27.5 | 96.6 | 1.0 | 0.8 | 1.3 | 1.5 | 5.7 | 16.1 | 17.0 | 11.2 | 11.9 | 15.0 |
| 55 095 | ... | 6 | Polk | 2 367 | 43 610 | 1 097 | 18.4 | 96.7 | 0.6 | 1.4 | 0.6 | 1.6 | 5.9 | 17.3 | 6.5 | 10.6 | 12.2 | 16.4 |
| 55 097 | 44620 | 4 | Portage | 2 074 | 70 433 | 759 | 34.0 | 93.4 | 1.0 | 0.7 | 3.2 | 2.8 | 5.5 | 14.9 | 17.0 | 12.0 | 10.9 | 14.2 |
| 55 099 | ... | 9 | Price | 3 249 | 13 869 | 2 180 | 4.3 | 97.2 | 0.6 | 1.0 | 1.1 | 1.2 | 4.1 | 14.5 | 5.3 | 8.5 | 10.9 | 17.6 |
| 55 101 | 39540 | 3 | Racine | 861 | 194 797 | 325 | 226.2 | 75.9 | 11.9 | 0.8 | 1.5 | 11.7 | 6.5 | 18.1 | 8.1 | 12.2 | 12.8 | 16.0 |
| 55 103 | ... | 6 | Richland | 1 518 | 17 818 | 1 928 | 11.7 | 96.2 | 0.9 | 0.5 | 0.8 | 2.4 | 6.3 | 16.7 | 7.8 | 10.2 | 10.9 | 14.6 |
| 55 105 | 27500 | 3 | Rock | 1 860 | 160 418 | 392 | 86.2 | 86.0 | 5.9 | 0.7 | 1.5 | 7.8 | 6.4 | 18.2 | 8.6 | 12.7 | 13.0 | 14.9 |
| 55 107 | ... | 6 | Rusk | 2 366 | 14 316 | 2 150 | 6.1 | 97.4 | 0.8 | 1.0 | 0.5 | 1.3 | 5.5 | 16.5 | 6.3 | 9.0 | 10.8 | 16.0 |
| 55 109 | 33460 | 1 | St. Croix | 1 871 | 85 242 | 660 | 45.6 | 95.7 | 1.1 | 0.8 | 1.5 | 2.1 | 7.0 | 19.8 | 6.7 | 13.4 | 14.8 | 16.0 |
| 55 111 | 12660 | 4 | Sauk | 2 152 | 62 597 | 834 | 29.1 | 93.2 | 1.1 | 1.5 | 0.8 | 4.4 | 6.3 | 17.4 | 7.4 | 12.6 | 12.6 | 15.2 |
| 55 113 | ... | 9 | Sawyer | 3 256 | 16 581 | 2 004 | 5.1 | 81.2 | 1.2 | 18.4 | 0.7 | 1.7 | 5.8 | 14.8 | 6.5 | 8.8 | 10.4 | 15.6 |
| 55 115 | ... | 6 | Shawano | 2 313 | 41 607 | 1 139 | 18.0 | 89.7 | 0.8 | 8.4 | 0.6 | 2.3 | 5.5 | 16.7 | 7.1 | 10.5 | 12.2 | 15.8 |
| 55 117 | 43100 | 3 | Sheboygan | 1 324 | 115 009 | 525 | 86.9 | 87.8 | 1.9 | 0.8 | 5.1 | 5.6 | 6.1 | 17.5 | 7.7 | 12.0 | 12.6 | 16.0 |
| 55 119 | ... | 6 | Taylor | 2 525 | 20 486 | 1 814 | 8.1 | 97.3 | 0.6 | 0.5 | 0.6 | 1.7 | 6.5 | 17.7 | 6.8 | 10.8 | 11.9 | 16.8 |
| 55 121 | ... | 8 | Trempealeau | 1 898 | 29 297 | 1 439 | 15.4 | 93.0 | 0.5 | 0.5 | 0.7 | 5.9 | 6.6 | 17.4 | 6.8 | 11.9 | 12.5 | 15.3 |
| 55 123 | ... | 6 | Vernon | 2 050 | 30 260 | 1 425 | 14.8 | 97.5 | 0.8 | 0.6 | 0.6 | 1.4 | 7.0 | 19.1 | 6.7 | 10.0 | 10.9 | 15.4 |
| 55 125 | ... | 9 | Vilas | 2 219 | 21 338 | 1 765 | 9.6 | 87.3 | 0.5 | 11.3 | 0.6 | 1.4 | 4.4 | 12.9 | 5.6 | 7.6 | 9.7 | 15.9 |
| 55 127 | 48580 | 4 | Walworth | 1 438 | 102 851 | 569 | 71.5 | 87.3 | 1.4 | 0.5 | 1.2 | 10.5 | 5.8 | 17.1 | 12.5 | 11.2 | 12.1 | 14.8 |
| 55 129 | ... | 6 | Washburn | 2 065 | 15 826 | 2 056 | 7.7 | 96.7 | 0.6 | 2.0 | 0.7 | 1.4 | 5.2 | 14.6 | 5.7 | 9.3 | 10.4 | 15.9 |
| 55 131 | 33340 | 1 | Washington | 1 116 | 132 661 | 471 | 118.9 | 94.9 | 1.3 | 0.6 | 1.5 | 2.7 | 5.9 | 18.1 | 6.7 | 11.2 | 13.6 | 17.2 |
| 55 133 | 33340 | 1 | Waukesha | 1 423 | 392 292 | 171 | 275.7 | 91.3 | 1.7 | 0.5 | 3.3 | 4.3 | 5.3 | 18.2 | 7.0 | 10.4 | 12.8 | 17.3 |
| 55 135 | ... | 6 | Waupaca | 1 937 | 52 131 | 953 | 26.9 | 96.2 | 0.6 | 0.8 | 0.6 | 2.6 | 5.6 | 16.6 | 6.8 | 10.6 | 11.9 | 16.2 |
| 55 137 | ... | 8 | Waushara | 1 622 | 24 461 | 1 626 | 15.1 | 91.2 | 2.2 | 1.0 | 0.6 | 5.9 | 4.8 | 14.8 | 6.4 | 10.2 | 11.5 | 16.4 |
| 55 139 | 36780 | 3 | Winnebago | 1 125 | 168 794 | 369 | 150.0 | 91.6 | 2.3 | 1.0 | 2.8 | 3.6 | 5.9 | 15.5 | 11.5 | 13.5 | 12.5 | 15.2 |
| 55 141 | 32270 | 4 | Wood | 2 054 | 74 424 | 735 | 36.2 | 94.5 | 0.9 | 1.1 | 2.1 | 2.3 | 6.0 | 16.4 | 7.4 | 11.4 | 11.5 | 16.2 |
| 56 000 | ... | X | WYOMING | 251 470 | 576 412 | X | 2.3 | 86.9 | 1.3 | 2.9 | 1.4 | 9.1 | 7.0 | 16.8 | 10.1 | 13.9 | 11.7 | 14.2 |
| 56 001 | 29660 | 4 | Albany | 11 069 | 37 276 | 1 240 | 3.4 | 86.0 | 1.8 | 1.5 | 3.7 | 8.9 | 5.3 | 10.7 | 30.8 | 15.7 | 9.0 | 9.5 |
| 56 003 | ... | 9 | Big Horn | 8 125 | 11 794 | 2 311 | 1.5 | 89.5 | 0.5 | 1.6 | 0.6 | 8.9 | 6.4 | 19.0 | 7.3 | 10.1 | 10.6 | 13.5 |
| 56 005 | 23940 | 5 | Campbell | 12 439 | 47 874 | 1 017 | 3.8 | 90.3 | 0.8 | 1.9 | 1.0 | 7.7 | 8.7 | 19.4 | 9.4 | 16.8 | 12.8 | 15.6 |
| 56 007 | ... | 7 | Carbon | 20 455 | 15 666 | 2 067 | 0.8 | 80.6 | 1.3 | 1.6 | 1.1 | 16.7 | 7.0 | 16.4 | 8.0 | 14.2 | 12.2 | 14.9 |
| 56 009 | ... | 6 | Converse | 11 020 | 14 008 | 2 176 | 1.3 | 91.8 | 0.7 | 1.4 | 0.7 | 6.6 | 7.0 | 17.8 | 7.8 | 12.2 | 12.4 | 15.3 |

1. CBSA = Core Based Statistical Area. See Appendix A for explanation. See Appendix B for list of metropolitan areas with component counties.   2. County type code from the Economic Research Service of USDA Rural-Urban Continuum Codes. See Appendix A for definition.   3. Dry land or land partially or temporarily covered by water.   4. May be of any race.

| STATE County | 55 to 64 years | 65 to 74 years | 75 years and over | Percent female | 2000 | 2010 | 2000–2010 | 2010–2012 | Births | Deaths | Net migration | Number | Percent change, 2000–2010 | Persons per house-hold | Female family house-holder[1] | One per-son |
|---|---|---|---|---|---|---|---|---|---|---|---|---|---|---|---|---|
| | 16 | 17 | 18 | 19 | 20 | 21 | 22 | 23 | 24 | 25 | 26 | 27 | 28 | 29 | 30 | 31 |
| WISCONSIN—Cont'd | | | | | | | | | | | | | | | | |
| Dodge | 12.7 | 7.5 | 7.6 | 47.3 | 85 897 | 88 759 | 3.3 | -0.4 | 1 893 | 1 992 | -352 | 33 840 | 7.7 | 2.44 | 8.4 | 26.5 |
| Door | 18.2 | 12.5 | 10.5 | 50.7 | 27 961 | 27 785 | -0.6 | 0.1 | 563 | 747 | 171 | 12 548 | 6.1 | 2.19 | 6.5 | 29.9 |
| Douglas | 14.3 | 7.8 | 6.8 | 50.0 | 43 287 | 44 159 | 2.0 | -0.8 | 1 063 | 910 | -533 | 18 555 | 4.2 | 2.31 | 10.9 | 30.2 |
| Dunn | 11.8 | 6.4 | 6.0 | 49.6 | 39 858 | 43 857 | 10.0 | 0.5 | 1 012 | 662 | -165 | 16 373 | 14.2 | 2.47 | 7.1 | 25.7 |
| Eau Claire | 11.9 | 6.5 | 6.3 | 51.0 | 93 142 | 98 736 | 6.0 | 2.0 | 2 584 | 1 625 | 1 002 | 39 493 | 10.2 | 2.38 | 8.9 | 28.4 |
| Florence | 17.7 | 13.1 | 8.7 | 48.6 | 5 088 | 4 423 | -13.1 | 1.3 | 80 | 124 | 68 | 1 987 | -6.8 | 2.20 | 5.0 | 28.1 |
| Fond du Lac | 13.3 | 7.7 | 7.7 | 50.8 | 97 296 | 101 633 | 4.5 | 0.2 | 2 504 | 2 008 | -210 | 40 697 | 10.2 | 2.41 | 8.7 | 27.6 |
| Forest | 14.3 | 10.7 | 9.6 | 49.3 | 10 024 | 9 304 | -7.2 | -1.1 | 243 | 245 | -94 | 3 836 | -5.1 | 2.33 | 11.3 | 28.5 |
| Grant | 12.2 | 7.6 | 7.9 | 47.9 | 49 597 | 51 208 | 3.2 | -0.2 | 1 233 | 1 090 | -240 | 19 396 | 5.0 | 2.44 | 7.7 | 27.1 |
| Green | 13.9 | 7.9 | 7.4 | 50.5 | 33 647 | 36 842 | 9.5 | 0.2 | 924 | 770 | -139 | 14 866 | 12.5 | 2.45 | 8.1 | 25.7 |
| Green Lake | 15.1 | 9.8 | 9.7 | 50.0 | 19 105 | 19 051 | -0.3 | -0.1 | 453 | 521 | 53 | 7 919 | 2.8 | 2.38 | 7.9 | 29.0 |
| Iowa | 14.6 | 7.5 | 6.7 | 49.9 | 22 780 | 23 687 | 4.0 | 0.5 | 648 | 428 | -172 | 9 547 | 8.9 | 2.46 | 7.8 | 26.0 |
| Iron | 17.5 | 12.5 | 13.0 | 49.9 | 6 861 | 5 916 | -13.8 | 0.3 | 79 | 218 | 123 | 2 822 | -8.5 | 2.06 | 7.2 | 34.3 |
| Jackson | 13.5 | 9.2 | 7.2 | 46.8 | 19 100 | 20 449 | 7.1 | 0.2 | 549 | 408 | -91 | 7 843 | 10.9 | 2.44 | 9.4 | 26.9 |
| Jefferson | 12.9 | 7.5 | 5.9 | 50.2 | 74 021 | 83 686 | 13.1 | 1.0 | 2 152 | 1 437 | 135 | 32 117 | 13.9 | 2.49 | 8.7 | 25.2 |
| Juneau | 14.2 | 9.9 | 7.8 | 47.3 | 24 316 | 26 664 | 9.7 | -0.1 | 597 | 602 | -25 | 10 527 | 8.6 | 2.38 | 9.4 | 28.5 |
| Kenosha | 11.5 | 6.0 | 5.4 | 50.5 | 149 577 | 166 426 | 11.3 | 0.9 | 4 699 | 2 773 | -373 | 62 650 | 11.8 | 2.58 | 13.0 | 26.2 |
| Kewaunee | 13.8 | 8.7 | 8.3 | 49.2 | 20 187 | 20 574 | 1.9 | 0.2 | 483 | 406 | -35 | 8 239 | 8.1 | 2.48 | 6.8 | 25.8 |
| La Crosse | 12.2 | 6.7 | 6.8 | 51.1 | 107 120 | 114 638 | 7.0 | 1.6 | 2 990 | 2 109 | 959 | 46 137 | 10.9 | 2.37 | 8.7 | 29.6 |
| Lafayette | 13.2 | 7.8 | 7.7 | 49.0 | 16 137 | 16 836 | 4.3 | 0.1 | 462 | 325 | -136 | 6 609 | 6.4 | 2.53 | 7.6 | 25.7 |
| Langlade | 15.1 | 10.8 | 9.6 | 49.8 | 20 740 | 19 977 | -3.7 | -1.7 | 400 | 524 | -227 | 8 587 | 1.6 | 2.29 | 8.7 | 29.0 |
| Lincoln | 14.3 | 9.8 | 8.9 | 49.8 | 29 641 | 28 743 | -3.0 | -1.2 | 654 | 687 | -315 | 12 094 | 3.2 | 2.33 | 8.3 | 27.3 |
| Manitowoc | 14.3 | 8.5 | 8.6 | 50.2 | 82 887 | 81 442 | -1.7 | -0.9 | 1 757 | 1 802 | -743 | 34 013 | 3.9 | 2.36 | 7.7 | 29.1 |
| Marathon | 13.1 | 7.4 | 7.0 | 49.8 | 125 834 | 134 063 | 6.5 | 0.5 | 3 644 | 2 407 | -605 | 53 176 | 11.5 | 2.49 | 8.5 | 25.8 |
| Marinette | 15.3 | 11.0 | 9.5 | 50.4 | 43 384 | 41 749 | -3.8 | -0.4 | 843 | 1 075 | 73 | 17 974 | 2.2 | 2.26 | 8.4 | 29.9 |
| Marquette | 15.9 | 12.3 | 9.0 | 49.1 | 15 832 | 15 404 | -2.7 | -1.3 | 342 | 398 | -161 | 6 571 | 9.8 | 2.32 | 7.1 | 27.3 |
| Menominee | 9.9 | 7.4 | 3.9 | 50.0 | 4 562 | 4 232 | -7.2 | 2.6 | 222 | 68 | -48 | 1 318 | -2.0 | 3.17 | 26.6 | 18.3 |
| Milwaukee | 11.1 | 5.5 | 5.9 | 51.6 | 940 164 | 947 735 | 0.8 | 0.8 | 33 034 | 17 910 | -7 531 | 383 591 | 1.6 | 2.41 | 17.4 | 33.7 |
| Monroe | 13.5 | 7.6 | 6.5 | 49.2 | 40 899 | 44 673 | 9.2 | 1.0 | 1 407 | 920 | -88 | 17 376 | 12.8 | 2.52 | 9.7 | 26.8 |
| Oconto | 14.9 | 9.3 | 6.8 | 49.1 | 35 634 | 37 660 | 5.7 | -0.6 | 871 | 823 | -252 | 15 415 | 10.3 | 2.42 | 7.0 | 24.5 |
| Oneida | 16.7 | 12.1 | 9.9 | 50.0 | 36 776 | 35 998 | -2.1 | -0.8 | 671 | 990 | 42 | 16 003 | 4.4 | 2.21 | 7.5 | 28.9 |
| Outagamie | 11.8 | 6.3 | 5.7 | 50.1 | 160 971 | 176 695 | 9.8 | 1.2 | 4 953 | 2 661 | -113 | 69 648 | 15.1 | 2.49 | 8.8 | 25.8 |
| Ozaukee | 14.7 | 8.3 | 7.4 | 51.0 | 82 317 | 86 395 | 5.0 | 0.5 | 1 708 | 1 645 | 409 | 34 228 | 10.9 | 2.47 | 6.9 | 24.8 |
| Pepin | 15.4 | 9.4 | 8.6 | 49.5 | 7 213 | 7 469 | 3.5 | -1.1 | 189 | 198 | -87 | 3 051 | 10.6 | 2.40 | 6.7 | 26.8 |
| Pierce | 12.1 | 6.1 | 4.8 | 50.3 | 36 804 | 41 019 | 11.5 | -0.5 | 908 | 583 | -543 | 15 002 | 15.3 | 2.55 | 7.7 | 22.1 |
| Polk | 14.5 | 9.1 | 7.4 | 49.7 | 41 319 | 44 205 | 7.0 | -1.3 | 1 053 | 954 | -677 | 18 004 | 10.8 | 2.43 | 8.3 | 26.3 |
| Portage | 12.6 | 6.9 | 6.1 | 50.0 | 67 182 | 70 019 | 4.2 | 0.6 | 1 731 | 1 075 | -234 | 27 814 | 11.1 | 2.39 | 7.5 | 27.2 |
| Price | 17.6 | 11.1 | 10.3 | 49.3 | 15 822 | 14 159 | -10.5 | -2.0 | 235 | 376 | -155 | 6 329 | -3.6 | 2.20 | 6.7 | 31.0 |
| Racine | 12.9 | 7.1 | 6.3 | 50.4 | 188 831 | 195 408 | 3.5 | -0.3 | 5 589 | 3 557 | -2 608 | 75 651 | 6.8 | 2.52 | 13.0 | 26.4 |
| Richland | 15.2 | 9.1 | 9.1 | 49.7 | 17 924 | 18 021 | 0.5 | -1.1 | 476 | 413 | -267 | 7 349 | 3.2 | 2.41 | 8.1 | 28.3 |
| Rock | 12.5 | 7.3 | 6.5 | 50.9 | 152 307 | 160 331 | 5.3 | 0.1 | 4 347 | 3 023 | -1 236 | 62 905 | 7.3 | 2.50 | 12.3 | 26.3 |
| Rusk | 15.4 | 10.6 | 9.8 | 50.1 | 15 347 | 14 755 | -3.9 | -3.0 | 344 | 381 | -399 | 6 232 | 2.2 | 2.34 | 8.0 | 30.2 |
| St. Croix | 11.9 | 5.8 | 4.6 | 50.0 | 63 155 | 84 345 | 33.6 | 1.1 | 2 431 | 1 218 | -346 | 31 799 | 35.8 | 2.63 | 8.1 | 21.4 |
| Sauk | 13.2 | 8.0 | 7.3 | 50.1 | 55 225 | 61 976 | 12.2 | 1.0 | 1 713 | 1 309 | 179 | 25 192 | 16.4 | 2.43 | 9.2 | 27.3 |
| Sawyer | 16.8 | 12.8 | 8.5 | 49.1 | 16 196 | 16 557 | 2.2 | 0.1 | 404 | 417 | 36 | 7 038 | 6.0 | 2.31 | 10.7 | 27.9 |
| Shawano | 13.6 | 10.0 | 8.7 | 50.0 | 40 664 | 41 949 | 3.2 | -0.8 | 946 | 890 | -386 | 17 019 | 7.6 | 2.42 | 8.8 | 26.6 |
| Sheboygan | 13.4 | 7.4 | 7.3 | 49.7 | 112 646 | 115 507 | 2.5 | -0.4 | 2 883 | 2 286 | -1 118 | 46 390 | 6.5 | 2.42 | 8.6 | 27.9 |
| Taylor | 13.2 | 8.1 | 8.2 | 48.9 | 19 680 | 20 689 | 5.1 | -1.0 | 525 | 439 | -343 | 8 388 | 11.4 | 2.44 | 6.8 | 26.8 |
| Trempealeau | 13.4 | 8.4 | 7.7 | 49.3 | 27 010 | 28 816 | 6.7 | 1.7 | 835 | 622 | 251 | 11 524 | 7.2 | 2.46 | 7.9 | 26.7 |
| Vernon | 14.1 | 8.6 | 8.1 | 50.0 | 28 056 | 29 773 | 6.1 | 1.6 | 929 | 669 | 176 | 11 616 | 7.3 | 2.53 | 7.2 | 27.3 |
| Vilas | 17.3 | 14.8 | 11.7 | 49.2 | 21 033 | 21 430 | 1.9 | -0.4 | 434 | 637 | 131 | 9 658 | 6.5 | 2.20 | 8.0 | 28.7 |
| Walworth | 12.9 | 7.3 | 6.3 | 49.9 | 93 759 | 102 228 | 9.0 | 0.6 | 2 462 | 1 935 | 85 | 39 699 | 15.0 | 2.51 | 9.1 | 26.6 |
| Washburn | 16.7 | 12.6 | 9.6 | 50.3 | 16 036 | 15 911 | -0.8 | -0.5 | 344 | 479 | 43 | 6 916 | 4.7 | 2.27 | 7.5 | 28.3 |
| Washington | 13.4 | 7.4 | 6.5 | 50.4 | 117 493 | 131 887 | 12.3 | 0.6 | 3 034 | 2 274 | 46 | 51 605 | 17.7 | 2.53 | 7.4 | 22.9 |
| Waukesha | 14.3 | 7.6 | 7.1 | 50.9 | 360 767 | 389 891 | 8.1 | 0.6 | 8 312 | 6 919 | 1 118 | 152 663 | 12.9 | 2.52 | 7.1 | 23.8 |
| Waupaca | 13.9 | 8.9 | 9.4 | 49.6 | 51 731 | 52 410 | 1.3 | -0.5 | 1 229 | 1 628 | 138 | 21 387 | 7.7 | 2.37 | 8.1 | 28.0 |
| Waushara | 15.8 | 11.1 | 9.1 | 47.4 | 23 154 | 24 496 | 5.8 | -0.1 | 523 | 554 | 15 | 9 949 | 6.6 | 2.34 | 6.9 | 27.5 |
| Winnebago | 12.4 | 6.8 | 6.8 | 49.7 | 156 763 | 166 994 | 6.5 | 1.1 | 4 273 | 3 130 | 673 | 67 875 | 11.0 | 2.34 | 9.1 | 29.9 |
| Wood | 13.8 | 8.5 | 8.8 | 50.8 | 75 555 | 74 749 | -1.1 | -0.4 | 2 060 | 1 661 | -689 | 31 598 | 4.9 | 2.34 | 8.9 | 29.5 |
| WYOMING | 13.6 | 7.2 | 5.5 | 49.0 | 493 782 | 563 626 | 14.1 | 2.3 | 16 657 | 9 937 | 5 881 | 226 879 | 17.2 | 2.42 | 8.9 | 28.0 |
| Albany | 10.0 | 5.2 | 3.8 | 48.0 | 32 014 | 36 299 | 13.4 | 2.7 | 943 | 422 | 451 | 15 691 | 18.3 | 2.17 | 6.7 | 34.9 |
| Big Horn | 14.9 | 10.2 | 8.0 | 49.9 | 11 461 | 11 668 | 1.8 | 1.1 | 311 | 286 | 103 | 4 561 | 5.8 | 2.52 | 7.6 | 26.2 |
| Campbell | 11.5 | 3.7 | 2.2 | 47.7 | 33 698 | 46 133 | 36.9 | 3.8 | 1 719 | 611 | 610 | 17 172 | 40.7 | 2.66 | 8.6 | 22.4 |
| Carbon | 14.3 | 7.8 | 5.2 | 45.6 | 15 639 | 15 885 | 1.6 | -1.4 | 442 | 310 | -358 | 6 388 | 4.2 | 2.36 | 7.8 | 29.6 |
| Converse | 14.2 | 7.6 | 5.7 | 49.3 | 12 052 | 13 833 | 14.8 | 1.3 | 400 | 241 | 3 | 5 673 | 20.9 | 2.42 | 8.2 | 26.5 |

1. No spouse present.

# Table B. States and Counties — Population, Vital Statistics, Medicare, and Crime

| STATE County | Daytime population, 2007–2011 | | Births, 2011 | | Deaths, 2011 | | Persons under 65 with no health insurance, 2010 | | Medicare, 2012 | | | Serious crimes known to police,[2] 2011 Total | |
|---|---|---|---|---|---|---|---|---|---|---|---|---|---|
| | Persons in group quarters, 2010 | Number / Employment/residence ratio | Total | Rate[1] | Number | Rate[1] | Number | Percent | Eligible for Medicare | Enrolled in Medicare Advantage | Enrolled in a Medicare prescription drug plan | Number | Rate[3] |
| | 32 | 33 / 34 | 35 | 36 | 37 | 38 | 39 | 40 | 41 | 42 | 43 | 44 | 45 |

WISCONSIN—Cont'd

| County | 32 | 33 | 34 | 35 | 36 | 37 | 38 | 39 | 40 | 41 | 42 | 43 | 44 | 45 |
|---|---|---|---|---|---|---|---|---|---|---|---|---|---|---|
| Dodge | 6 192 | 80 235 | 0.80 | 865 | 9.8 | 852 | 9.6 | 6 185 | 8.8 | 15 092 | 4 201 | 5 719 | 1 318 | 1 494 |
| Door | 348 | 27 752 | 0.99 | 266 | 9.6 | 329 | 11.8 | 2 400 | 11.3 | 7 771 | 1 690 | 3 330 | 279 | 1 000 |
| Douglas | 1 372 | 40 310 | 0.83 | 474 | 10.7 | 396 | 9.0 | 4 223 | 11.5 | 8 432 | 2 851 | 3 440 | 1 890 | 4 261 |
| Dunn | 3 415 | 39 940 | 0.83 | 449 | 10.2 | 288 | 6.5 | 3 710 | 10.5 | 7 553 | 2 041 | 3 465 | 712 | 1 616 |
| Eau Claire | 4 796 | 104 661 | 1.13 | 1 145 | 11.5 | 704 | 7.0 | 7 891 | 9.6 | 16 611 | 4 663 | 6 551 | 2 559 | 2 581 |
| Florence | 59 | 3 795 | 0.65 | 35 | 7.9 | 52 | 11.7 | 483 | 13.9 | 1 229 | 250 | 440 | 95 | 2 139 |
| Fond du Lac | 3 589 | 96 618 | 0.91 | 1 154 | 11.3 | 860 | 8.4 | 8 507 | 10.2 | 18 345 | 7 638 | 5 918 | 1 808 | 1 771 |
| Forest | 379 | 9 400 | 0.99 | 103 | 11.2 | 105 | 11.4 | 1 043 | 14.2 | 2 403 | 616 | 842 | 264 | 2 825 |
| Grant | 3 897 | 46 768 | 0.83 | 559 | 10.9 | 470 | 9.2 | 4 734 | 11.8 | 9 433 | 3 248 | 4 723 | 1 225 | 2 576 |
| Green | 405 | 33 597 | 0.84 | 422 | 11.4 | 348 | 9.4 | 3 135 | 10.1 | 6 608 | 913 | 2 753 | 722 | 1 951 |
| Green Lake | 212 | 17 634 | 0.85 | 201 | 10.5 | 235 | 12.3 | 1 742 | 11.4 | 4 324 | 1 998 | 1 174 | 289 | 1 613 |
| Iowa | 214 | 22 486 | 0.91 | 300 | 12.7 | 173 | 7.3 | 2 070 | 10.2 | 4 166 | 1 109 | 2 063 | 348 | 1 463 |
| Iron | 96 | 5 655 | 0.86 | 35 | 5.9 | 94 | 15.9 | 599 | 13.6 | 1 832 | 705 | 568 | 147 | 2 474 |
| Jackson | 1 333 | 19 627 | 0.92 | 254 | 12.4 | 172 | 8.4 | 2 091 | 13.1 | 3 951 | 1 477 | 1 174 | 348 | 1 694 |
| Jefferson | 3 678 | 73 607 | 0.77 | 985 | 11.7 | 630 | 7.5 | 7 296 | 10.5 | 13 826 | 2 988 | 6 544 | 1 488 | 1 809 |
| Juneau | 1 651 | 24 859 | 0.85 | 271 | 10.1 | 253 | 9.5 | 2 772 | 13.3 | 5 743 | 1 037 | 2 171 | 536 | 2 116 |
| Kenosha | 4 601 | 145 501 | 0.74 | 2 126 | 12.7 | 1 189 | 7.1 | 16 805 | 11.7 | 24 289 | 5 081 | 10 197 | 4 648 | 2 781 |
| Kewaunee | 178 | 18 286 | 0.78 | 221 | 10.7 | 186 | 9.0 | 1 798 | 10.6 | 3 875 | 1 491 | 1 222 | 248 | 1 200 |
| La Crosse | 5 195 | 122 211 | 1.14 | 1 353 | 11.7 | 914 | 7.9 | 9 260 | 9.7 | 18 886 | 8 207 | 6 247 | 3 109 | 2 700 |
| Lafayette | 120 | 13 563 | 0.63 | 201 | 12.0 | 147 | 8.7 | 2 027 | 14.4 | 3 040 | 762 | 1 429 | 224 | 1 325 |
| Langlade | 281 | 19 531 | 0.94 | 173 | 8.7 | 230 | 11.6 | 1 943 | 12.3 | 4 922 | 1 725 | 1 579 | 751 | 3 743 |
| Lincoln | 560 | 26 409 | 0.82 | 306 | 10.7 | 294 | 10.3 | 2 266 | 9.8 | 6 513 | 2 322 | 1 981 | 635 | 2 200 |
| Manitowoc | 1 100 | 76 898 | 0.89 | 791 | 9.8 | 794 | 9.8 | 6 656 | 9.9 | 16 661 | 6 059 | 5 212 | 1 340 | 1 638 |
| Marathon | 1 655 | 135 968 | 1.04 | 1 618 | 12.0 | 1 032 | 7.7 | 11 640 | 10.2 | 22 880 | 9 317 | 6 342 | 2 615 | 1 942 |
| Marinette | 1 073 | 43 213 | 1.07 | 374 | 9.0 | 472 | 11.3 | 3 612 | 11.0 | 10 383 | 3 070 | 3 739 | 923 | 2 201 |
| Marquette | 153 | 13 224 | 0.68 | 151 | 9.8 | 167 | 10.8 | 1 402 | 11.6 | 3 992 | 1 033 | 1 456 | 250 | 1 616 |
| Menominee | 59 | 4 906 | 1.46 | 96 | 22.1 | 36 | 8.3 | 504 | 13.1 | 724 | 165 | 286 | 42 | 988 |
| Milwaukee | 24 490 | 984 032 | 1.10 | 15 010 | 15.8 | 7 852 | 8.2 | 117 397 | 14.3 | 139 539 | 43 768 | 49 709 | 50 120 | 5 265 |
| Monroe | 859 | 46 068 | 1.08 | 620 | 13.8 | 411 | 9.1 | 5 173 | 13.6 | 7 551 | 2 535 | 2 046 | 898 | 2 023 |
| Oconto | 281 | 29 459 | 0.56 | 399 | 10.6 | 361 | 9.6 | 3 571 | 11.4 | 7 829 | 3 374 | 2 139 | 693 | 1 832 |
| Oneida | 610 | 36 580 | 1.02 | 305 | 8.5 | 431 | 12.0 | 3 046 | 11.0 | 9 954 | 2 909 | 3 540 | 523 | 1 447 |
| Outagamie | 3 039 | 182 209 | 1.07 | 2 184 | 12.3 | 1 147 | 6.4 | 14 914 | 9.7 | 26 533 | 14 396 | 6 166 | 3 535 | 1 992 |
| Ozaukee | 1 804 | 80 931 | 0.88 | 765 | 8.8 | 706 | 8.2 | 4 554 | 6.4 | 15 837 | 4 709 | 5 701 | 959 | 1 105 |
| Pepin | 136 | 6 401 | 0.70 | 96 | 13.0 | 88 | 11.9 | 778 | 12.8 | 1 861 | 372 | 855 | 63 | 840 |
| Pierce | 2 766 | 29 363 | 0.49 | 413 | 10.1 | 253 | 6.2 | 3 237 | 9.5 | 5 755 | 1 917 | 2 306 | 896 | 2 175 |
| Polk | 461 | 39 386 | 0.77 | 491 | 11.1 | 421 | 9.6 | 4 120 | 11.2 | 8 863 | 2 864 | 3 194 | 744 | 1 676 |
| Portage | 3 509 | 69 547 | 0.99 | 789 | 11.3 | 458 | 6.5 | 5 730 | 9.9 | 11 309 | 4 044 | 3 807 | 1 319 | 1 876 |
| Price | 204 | 14 331 | 1.01 | 105 | 7.5 | 159 | 11.4 | 1 144 | 10.3 | 3 696 | 1 295 | 1 199 | 205 | 1 442 |
| Racine | 4 995 | 182 113 | 0.86 | 2 535 | 13.0 | 1 537 | 7.9 | 16 950 | 10.3 | 33 781 | 10 056 | 11 415 | 6 095 | 3 106 |
| Richland | 336 | 16 905 | 0.86 | 217 | 12.1 | 183 | 10.2 | 1 825 | 12.5 | 3 526 | 522 | 1 543 | 126 | 696 |
| Rock | 2 934 | 149 230 | 0.85 | 1 937 | 12.1 | 1 308 | 8.2 | 16 472 | 12.1 | 28 071 | 6 525 | 12 558 | 5 270 | 3 273 |
| Rusk | 174 | 14 480 | 0.95 | 167 | 11.4 | 159 | 10.9 | 1 497 | 12.8 | 3 571 | 1 296 | 1 101 | 167 | 1 127 |
| St. Croix | 850 | 71 712 | 0.73 | 1 097 | 12.9 | 522 | 6.1 | 6 321 | 8.4 | 10 926 | 3 757 | 3 915 | 1 345 | 1 588 |
| Sauk | 858 | 63 277 | 1.05 | 777 | 12.5 | 573 | 9.2 | 6 110 | 11.7 | 11 475 | 3 603 | 5 215 | 1 953 | 3 222 |
| Sawyer | 325 | 17 232 | 1.09 | 193 | 11.6 | 184 | 11.1 | 2 091 | 16.1 | 4 590 | 1 147 | 1 739 | 580 | 3 488 |
| Shawano | 794 | 37 214 | 0.76 | 426 | 10.2 | 373 | 8.9 | 4 735 | 14.0 | 8 853 | 4 384 | 2 096 | 778 | 1 848 |
| Sheboygan | 3 023 | 115 371 | 1.00 | 1 316 | 11.4 | 1 014 | 8.8 | 9 552 | 9.9 | 20 523 | 7 332 | 6 158 | 2 551 | 2 199 |
| Taylor | 231 | 20 156 | 0.95 | 240 | 11.6 | 193 | 9.3 | 2 083 | 12.1 | 3 637 | 1 549 | 992 | 306 | 1 473 |
| Trempealeau | 512 | 28 467 | 0.99 | 381 | 13.1 | 277 | 9.6 | 2 818 | 11.7 | 5 462 | 2 114 | 1 730 | 277 | 1 004 |
| Vernon | 390 | 26 749 | 0.79 | 431 | 14.4 | 307 | 10.2 | 3 691 | 15.0 | 6 087 | 2 954 | 1 528 | 327 | 1 198 |
| Vilas | 190 | 21 454 | 0.98 | 199 | 9.3 | 286 | 13.3 | 2 364 | 15.0 | 7 382 | 1 824 | 2 841 | 329 | 1 529 |
| Walworth | 2 709 | 96 174 | 0.88 | 1 111 | 10.8 | 850 | 8.3 | 11 232 | 13.1 | 16 783 | 2 487 | 7 703 | 2 123 | 2 068 |
| Washburn | 205 | 15 589 | 0.95 | 155 | 9.7 | 203 | 12.8 | 1 532 | 12.3 | 4 493 | 1 395 | 1 663 | 300 | 1 877 |
| Washington | 1 143 | 114 169 | 0.76 | 1 399 | 10.6 | 970 | 7.3 | 9 262 | 8.2 | 21 761 | 6 780 | 7 543 | 2 295 | 1 733 |
| Waukesha | 5 650 | 412 548 | 1.12 | 3 665 | 9.4 | 2 927 | 7.5 | 20 442 | 6.2 | 68 283 | 20 810 | 23 869 | 5 048 | 1 443 |
| Waupaca | 1 635 | 49 586 | 0.88 | 568 | 10.8 | 708 | 13.4 | 4 330 | 10.2 | 11 265 | 5 238 | 3 317 | 1 211 | 2 356 |
| Waushara | 1 261 | 21 323 | 0.69 | 228 | 9.3 | 229 | 9.3 | 2 551 | 13.8 | 5 811 | 2 596 | 1 520 | 401 | 1 630 |
| Winnebago | 8 239 | 175 043 | 1.11 | 1 911 | 11.4 | 1 364 | 8.1 | 13 679 | 10.0 | 27 364 | 13 406 | 7 547 | 3 516 | 2 096 |
| Wood | 891 | 79 148 | 1.13 | 928 | 12.4 | 703 | 9.4 | 5 169 | 8.4 | 15 293 | 7 351 | 4 242 | 1 560 | 2 078 |
| WYOMING | 13 712 | 562 346 | 1.03 | 7 555 | 13.3 | 4 433 | 7.8 | 83 761 | 17.3 | 86 764 | 1 459 | 45 008 | 14 123 | 2 486 |
| Albany | 2 248 | 35 082 | 0.98 | 424 | 11.5 | 176 | 4.8 | 5 325 | 17.2 | 3 890 | 232 | 1 827 | 979 | 2 676 |
| Big Horn | 183 | 11 055 | 0.90 | 133 | 11.3 | 121 | 10.3 | 2 042 | 21.7 | 2 341 | 45 | 1 386 | 58 | 618 |
| Campbell | 422 | 48 968 | 1.18 | 776 | 16.6 | 283 | 6.1 | 6 198 | 14.2 | 3 668 | 193 | 2 009 | 1 128 | 2 426 |
| Carbon | 780 | 15 724 | 1.00 | 206 | 13.0 | 153 | 9.7 | 2 297 | 17.6 | 2 430 | 95 | 1 426 | 437 | 2 807 |
| Converse | 103 | 13 008 | 0.92 | 178 | 12.9 | 117 | 8.5 | 1 781 | 14.9 | 2 159 | 64 | 1 325 | 351 | 2 517 |

1. Per 1,000 estimated resident population.  2. Data for serious crimes have not been adjusted for underreporting; this may affect comparability between geographic areas and over time.  3. Per 100,000 population estimated by the FBI.

# Table B. States and Counties — Crime, Education, Money Income, and Poverty

| STATE County | Serious crimes known to police, 2011 (cont.)[1] — Rate[2] Violent | Property | Education — Enrollment[3] Total | Percent private | Attainment[4] (percent) High school graduate or less | Bachelor's degree or more | Local government expenditures,[5] 2009-2010 Total current expenditures (mil dol) | Current expenditures per student (dollars) | Money income, 2007-2011 Per capita income[6] (dollars) | Households Median income Dollars | Percent change, 2000 to 2007-2011 (constant 2011 dollars) | Percent with income of $200,000 or more | Income and poverty, 2011 Median household income (dollars) | Percent below poverty level All persons | Children under 18 years | Children 5 to 17 years in families |
|---|---|---|---|---|---|---|---|---|---|---|---|---|---|---|---|---|
| | 46 | 47 | 48 | 49 | 50 | 51 | 52 | 53 | 54 | 55 | 56 | 57 | 58 | 59 | 60 | 61 |
| WISCONSIN—Cont'd | | | | | | | | | | | | | | | | |
| Dodge | 67 | 1 427 | 19 729 | 19.4 | 53.0 | 15.2 | 120.1 | 11 035 | 24 691 | 53 589 | -12.2 | 1.3 | 52 130 | 10.8 | 13.7 | 11.8 |
| Door | 47 | 953 | 4 705 | 12.0 | 43.5 | 27.9 | 45.5 | 12 564 | 29 437 | 48 680 | -7.1 | 2.2 | 46 441 | 11.1 | 16.1 | 14.2 |
| Douglas | 149 | 4 113 | 10 869 | 9.9 | 41.3 | 21.8 | 73.4 | 10 962 | 24 741 | 44 140 | -7.2 | 1.2 | 45 935 | 14.1 | 19.9 | 18.4 |
| Dunn | 104 | 1 512 | 14 956 | 8.4 | 44.8 | 24.9 | 63.7 | 10 570 | 22 156 | 48 342 | -7.6 | 1.1 | 45 878 | 14.5 | 16.6 | 15.2 |
| Eau Claire | 176 | 2 404 | 30 610 | 10.7 | 37.2 | 31.0 | 150.0 | 10 866 | 25 413 | 46 826 | -11.6 | 2.4 | 47 660 | 14.5 | 15.8 | 14.2 |
| Florence | 158 | 1 981 | 942 | 9.1 | 55.1 | 14.5 | 6.8 | 14 232 | 22 030 | 43 000 | -8.4 | 0.7 | 46 041 | 13.0 | 20.4 | 17.5 |
| Fond du Lac | 180 | 1 591 | 25 298 | 20.3 | 50.8 | 18.7 | 144.4 | 10 750 | 25 934 | 52 717 | -14.3 | 2.1 | 53 305 | 9.9 | 13.9 | 11.7 |
| Forest | 75 | 2 750 | 2 093 | 6.3 | 55.5 | 12.8 | 20.5 | 12 138 | 20 992 | 38 176 | -11.7 | 1.2 | 39 282 | 15.6 | 23.4 | 21.3 |
| Grant | 177 | 2 400 | 15 101 | 11.0 | 51.0 | 19.0 | 83.5 | 11 695 | 20 955 | 45 022 | -8.1 | 1.1 | 45 748 | 16.3 | 19.6 | 17.7 |
| Green | 114 | 1 838 | 8 860 | 8.0 | 49.0 | 19.1 | 65.2 | 10 858 | 26 852 | 53 933 | -7.6 | 2.2 | 53 051 | 9.7 | 12.3 | 10.7 |
| Green Lake | 17 | 1 596 | 4 058 | 15.5 | 55.2 | 15.7 | 34.4 | 11 155 | 25 762 | 48 937 | -8.2 | 2.1 | 47 094 | 12.0 | 21.3 | 19.3 |
| Iowa | 156 | 1 307 | 5 358 | 11.8 | 44.5 | 21.7 | 42.1 | 11 580 | 26 025 | 55 625 | -3.1 | 1.7 | 51 740 | 10.4 | 13.5 | 12.6 |
| Iron | 438 | 2 036 | 980 | 2.2 | 47.2 | 19.0 | 10.0 | 13 071 | 22 154 | 37 413 | -6.3 | 0.8 | 38 355 | 13.9 | 22.1 | 19.5 |
| Jackson | 58 | 1 636 | 4 156 | 9.1 | 56.1 | 15.8 | 35.0 | 10 954 | 21 255 | 44 106 | -11.7 | 1.2 | 41 337 | 14.8 | 22.3 | 20.9 |
| Jefferson | 164 | 1 645 | 22 938 | 17.8 | 46.4 | 22.5 | 148.9 | 10 910 | 25 445 | 55 615 | -12.2 | 1.9 | 53 710 | 10.1 | 14.1 | 12.7 |
| Juneau | 166 | 1 950 | 5 895 | 8.6 | 57.4 | 12.5 | 45.2 | 11 771 | 23 695 | 45 507 | -4.6 | 1.5 | 41 226 | 17.2 | 25.0 | 23.5 |
| Kenosha | 191 | 2 590 | 48 086 | 14.9 | 45.4 | 23.7 | 347.5 | 11 542 | 26 936 | 54 846 | -13.5 | 3.0 | 51 966 | 14.3 | 19.4 | 17.9 |
| Kewaunee | 48 | 1 152 | 4 858 | 17.3 | 55.3 | 13.6 | 36.9 | 10 353 | 24 936 | 54 783 | -7.4 | 1.2 | 54 727 | 8.9 | 12.9 | 11.3 |
| La Crosse | 179 | 2 521 | 34 201 | 15.0 | 36.9 | 28.8 | 191.1 | 11 925 | 25 680 | 50 510 | -5.2 | 2.3 | 49 698 | 14.7 | 15.4 | 13.7 |
| Lafayette | 30 | 1 295 | 3 967 | 9.7 | 55.2 | 16.5 | 34.7 | 12 022 | 22 645 | 49 850 | -0.8 | 1.3 | 48 231 | 12.1 | 20.4 | 19.2 |
| Langlade | 164 | 3 579 | 4 183 | 20.0 | 59.4 | 12.2 | 38.0 | 12 344 | 22 295 | 42 045 | -6.1 | 1.2 | 41 994 | 14.2 | 22.5 | 18.9 |
| Lincoln | 132 | 2 068 | 6 068 | 15.4 | 54.5 | 14.7 | 49.2 | 11 096 | 23 987 | 47 426 | -10.2 | 0.9 | 45 927 | 10.8 | 15.9 | 14.1 |
| Manitowoc | 130 | 1 509 | 19 303 | 18.9 | 52.2 | 17.7 | 123.4 | 10 687 | 25 831 | 50 181 | -14.1 | 1.8 | 48 804 | 8.6 | 13.4 | 11.8 |
| Marathon | 149 | 1 794 | 33 548 | 12.9 | 49.4 | 21.2 | 221.7 | 11 175 | 26 763 | 54 316 | -10.9 | 2.4 | 51 908 | 11.2 | 15.9 | 13.7 |
| Marinette | 69 | 2 132 | 8 984 | 14.1 | 54.9 | 14.3 | 66.4 | 10 587 | 23 827 | 41 574 | -12.7 | 1.1 | 39 705 | 13.4 | 18.3 | 16.3 |
| Marquette | 45 | 1 571 | 2 838 | 9.6 | 60.1 | 12.4 | 23.0 | 11 949 | 23 139 | 45 046 | -6.7 | 0.6 | 41 814 | 16.0 | 26.2 | 23.3 |
| Menominee | 24 | 965 | 1 180 | 8.6 | 50.2 | 14.1 | 16.1 | 18 893 | 15 346 | 32 017 | -19.5 | 0.0 | 30 156 | 32.6 | 47.7 | 46.4 |
| Milwaukee | 757 | 4 508 | 268 101 | 24.5 | 44.7 | 27.1 | 1 727.4 | 12 317 | 24 051 | 43 397 | -15.6 | 2.1 | 40 780 | 21.8 | 31.9 | 30.0 |
| Monroe | 101 | 1 921 | 10 213 | 17.2 | 52.8 | 16.3 | 76.3 | 10 909 | 23 320 | 48 306 | -3.7 | 1.3 | 45 841 | 15.7 | 25.4 | 21.6 |
| Oconto | 24 | 1 808 | 8 282 | 7.8 | 55.7 | 13.3 | 49.7 | 10 591 | 25 852 | 49 396 | -11.2 | 1.4 | 53 280 | 10.1 | 14.7 | 13.2 |
| Oneida | 75 | 1 372 | 7 260 | 10.9 | 42.2 | 21.8 | 60.9 | 13 266 | 27 181 | 45 184 | -11.0 | 2.1 | 39 418 | 13.0 | 19.5 | 18.0 |
| Outagamie | 150 | 1 842 | 46 122 | 15.9 | 43.0 | 25.8 | 344.5 | 10 292 | 27 573 | 57 190 | -14.6 | 2.4 | 56 901 | 8.1 | 10.5 | 9.7 |
| Ozaukee | 55 | 1 050 | 23 446 | 29.4 | 26.8 | 43.1 | 147.2 | 11 034 | 41 272 | 75 634 | -10.7 | 9.6 | 74 631 | 5.3 | 6.0 | 5.2 |
| Pepin | 53 | 786 | 1 652 | 20.2 | 53.1 | 17.6 | 15.6 | 12 371 | 24 066 | 48 717 | -4.1 | 1.8 | 45 193 | 12.2 | 21.6 | 19.9 |
| Pierce | 194 | 1 981 | 12 859 | 10.5 | 38.1 | 26.6 | 79.3 | 10 805 | 27 132 | 61 443 | -8.2 | 2.3 | 57 866 | 9.7 | 9.3 | 8.4 |
| Polk | 239 | 1 437 | 10 285 | 9.2 | 48.8 | 18.9 | 85.7 | 10 820 | 25 139 | 49 527 | -10.9 | 1.6 | 46 872 | 11.1 | 16.3 | 15.1 |
| Portage | 108 | 1 768 | 21 468 | 11.3 | 45.2 | 26.8 | 104.5 | 11 008 | 25 207 | 51 887 | -11.6 | 2.1 | 50 712 | 14.8 | 15.0 | 12.9 |
| Price | 127 | 1 315 | 2 801 | 13.0 | 55.8 | 15.5 | 25.8 | 11 987 | 23 590 | 41 458 | -12.9 | 1.2 | 41 576 | 13.6 | 22.0 | 17.9 |
| Racine | 231 | 2 874 | 50 372 | 18.2 | 46.7 | 22.5 | 347.1 | 11 155 | 26 953 | 54 356 | -16.2 | 3.0 | 52 900 | 13.2 | 21.0 | 18.9 |
| Richland | 44 | 652 | 4 005 | 18.1 | 55.4 | 15.1 | 20.1 | 11 496 | 21 913 | 44 326 | -3.4 | 1.1 | 43 222 | 15.3 | 23.0 | 22.0 |
| Rock | 244 | 3 029 | 41 547 | 13.4 | 49.9 | 19.5 | 309.3 | 10 993 | 24 119 | 50 532 | -17.8 | 1.5 | 47 857 | 14.6 | 21.1 | 17.8 |
| Rusk | 162 | 965 | 3 096 | 11.0 | 58.3 | 15.5 | 28.4 | 12 368 | 20 994 | 38 821 | -8.3 | 0.8 | 36 810 | 16.6 | 29.1 | 25.7 |
| St. Croix | 54 | 1 533 | 22 434 | 13.6 | 34.0 | 32.0 | 135.5 | 9 915 | 31 895 | 68 513 | -7.6 | 4.2 | 64 490 | 7.6 | 9.1 | 8.4 |
| Sauk | 162 | 3 061 | 13 971 | 10.1 | 50.1 | 20.2 | 128.1 | 10 897 | 25 734 | 51 121 | -9.7 | 1.6 | 48 874 | 12.2 | 18.0 | 15.8 |
| Sawyer | 289 | 3 199 | 3 157 | 13.8 | 47.3 | 21.2 | 26.7 | 11 885 | 24 001 | 39 228 | -10.0 | 1.8 | 40 002 | 17.3 | 28.4 | 26.9 |
| Shawano | 109 | 1 738 | 9 239 | 13.0 | 58.8 | 14.5 | 63.8 | 11 205 | 22 828 | 45 587 | -11.3 | 1.3 | 42 795 | 11.8 | 18.2 | 16.8 |
| Sheboygan | 136 | 2 063 | 29 252 | 17.3 | 47.9 | 21.6 | 212.1 | 10 824 | 25 830 | 52 993 | -15.1 | 1.8 | 51 541 | 8.8 | 13.1 | 11.4 |
| Taylor | 39 | 1 434 | 4 654 | 12.5 | 60.2 | 13.5 | 33.1 | 10 750 | 22 920 | 45 054 | -13.3 | 1.3 | 42 460 | 12.2 | 18.6 | 17.2 |
| Trempealeau | 14 | 989 | 6 505 | 8.8 | 55.3 | 17.1 | 65.2 | 10 992 | 24 065 | 47 437 | -7.3 | 1.4 | 46 203 | 11.8 | 17.9 | 16.7 |
| Vernon | 55 | 1 143 | 6 766 | 23.6 | 50.9 | 18.4 | 47.6 | 11 499 | 22 066 | 44 058 | -1.6 | 1.2 | 42 670 | 16.3 | 25.9 | 23.0 |
| Vilas | 65 | 1 464 | 3 821 | 10.4 | 43.3 | 23.5 | 41.0 | 14 815 | 26 863 | 41 195 | -9.6 | 2.4 | 40 901 | 12.9 | 23.2 | 21.3 |
| Walworth | 108 | 1 960 | 27 910 | 11.6 | 45.0 | 25.6 | 184.9 | 11 315 | 27 410 | 55 237 | -11.6 | 3.2 | 52 300 | 13.3 | 17.7 | 16.5 |
| Washburn | 75 | 1 802 | 3 032 | 10.6 | 51.0 | 18.7 | 31.4 | 12 253 | 23 989 | 41 135 | -9.6 | 1.3 | 39 777 | 14.9 | 25.3 | 23.0 |
| Washington | 107 | 1 625 | 32 383 | 22.1 | 40.0 | 26.7 | 211.7 | 10 545 | 31 521 | 66 476 | -13.7 | 3.6 | 67 760 | 6.3 | 8.1 | 7.1 |
| Waukesha | 62 | 1 381 | 100 952 | 23.7 | 30.6 | 39.4 | 691.5 | 10 896 | 37 310 | 75 845 | -10.6 | 7.0 | 73 025 | 5.5 | 6.6 | 5.8 |
| Waupaca | 121 | 2 235 | 12 057 | 11.5 | 56.6 | 16.3 | 100.5 | 10 806 | 24 215 | 48 604 | -12.0 | 1.0 | 47 601 | 11.7 | 17.4 | 15.0 |
| Waushara | 122 | 1 508 | 4 911 | 15.7 | 57.7 | 13.4 | 31.6 | 10 889 | 22 363 | 43 544 | -12.8 | 1.0 | 39 836 | 12.8 | 21.6 | 19.7 |
| Winnebago | 191 | 1 905 | 44 595 | 12.0 | 45.3 | 24.3 | 242.3 | 10 477 | 26 880 | 51 596 | -14.0 | 2.6 | 49 279 | 12.4 | 16.1 | 14.0 |
| Wood | 29 | 2 049 | 16 947 | 11.6 | 49.0 | 18.3 | 147.0 | 11 288 | 25 456 | 47 182 | -16.0 | 2.1 | 46 558 | 12.3 | 17.8 | 15.6 |
| WYOMING | 219 | 2 266 | 140 099 | 9.2 | 38.6 | 24.2 | 1 333.6 | 15 220 | 28 952 | 56 380 | 10.2 | 2.9 | 56 044 | 11.3 | 15.5 | 13.4 |
| Albany | 118 | 2 558 | 15 146 | 7.8 | 21.1 | 48.0 | 52.0 | 14 438 | 25 928 | 45 760 | 17.7 | 2.5 | 45 651 | 21.6 | 18.9 | 16.7 |
| Big Horn | 171 | 448 | 2 763 | 6.8 | 42.2 | 19.0 | 36.8 | 17 800 | 25 452 | 52 597 | 19.2 | 1.5 | 49 929 | 11.5 | 15.4 | 12.5 |
| Campbell | 140 | 2 286 | 10 837 | 4.3 | 45.0 | 17.5 | 118.9 | 14 480 | 33 092 | 78 356 | 17.2 | 3.7 | 70 438 | 7.0 | 9.7 | 8.1 |
| Carbon | 360 | 2 447 | 3 253 | 8.1 | 46.7 | 17.2 | 40.3 | 16 443 | 27 962 | 58 655 | 20.5 | 2.1 | 52 855 | 13.8 | 16.3 | 13.9 |
| Converse | 179 | 2 338 | 3 186 | 13.0 | 46.9 | 18.1 | 36.3 | 15 352 | 28 517 | 56 673 | 6.0 | 2.5 | 59 507 | 10.3 | 14.8 | 12.5 |

1. Data for serious crimes have not been adjusted for underreporting; this may affect comparability between geographic areas and over time.   2. Per 100,000 population estimated by the FBI.   3. All persons 3 years old and over enrolled in nursery school through college.   4. Persons 25 years old and over.   5. Elementary and secondary education expenditures.   6. Based on population estimated by the American Community Survey, 2007-2011.

# Table B. States and Counties — Personal Income

| | Personal income, 2011 | | | | | | | | | | | | |
|---|---|---|---|---|---|---|---|---|---|---|---|---|---|
| | | | Per capita[1] | | | | | Transfer payments (mil dol) | | | | | |
| | | | | | | | | | Government payments to individuals | | | | |
| STATE County | Total (mil dol) | Percent change, 2010–2011[2] | Dollars | Rank | Wages and salaries[2] (mil dol) | Proprietors' income (mil dol) | Dividends, interest, and rent (mil dol) | Total | Total | Social Security | Medical payments | Income mainte-nance | Unemploy-ment insurance |
| | 62 | 63 | 64 | 65 | 66 | 67 | 68 | 69 | 70 | 71 | 72 | 73 | 74 |
| WISCONSIN—Cont'd | | | | | | | | | | | | | |
| Dodge | 3 111 | 5.1 | 35 086 | 1 360 | 1 729 | 366 | 426 | 531 | 511 | 229 | 192 | 37 | 33 |
| Door | 1 178 | 3.9 | 42 359 | 555 | 506 | 92 | 333 | 261 | 255 | 118 | 99 | 12 | 17 |
| Douglas | 1 388 | 2.1 | 31 478 | 2 007 | 833 | 58 | 194 | 372 | 363 | 115 | 151 | 39 | 10 |
| Dunn | 1 426 | 5.6 | 32 426 | 1 795 | 790 | 134 | 198 | 278 | 268 | 102 | 102 | 26 | 13 |
| Eau Claire | 3 716 | 3.7 | 37 203 | 1 058 | 2 728 | 318 | 632 | 668 | 646 | 240 | 260 | 58 | 32 |
| Florence | 159 | 5.0 | 35 870 | 1 233 | 32 | 3 | 30 | 40 | 39 | 18 | 14 | 3 | 1 |
| Fond du Lac | 3 766 | 4.5 | 36 897 | 1 084 | 2 255 | 288 | 571 | 717 | 695 | 272 | 293 | 47 | 35 |
| Forest | 290 | 2.1 | 31 394 | 2 017 | 134 | 32 | 43 | 88 | 85 | 33 | 34 | 8 | 4 |
| Grant | 1 719 | 5.8 | 33 569 | 1 588 | 779 | 230 | 286 | 358 | 346 | 130 | 152 | 24 | 13 |
| Green | 1 414 | 6.6 | 38 324 | 933 | 679 | 170 | 252 | 238 | 230 | 97 | 92 | 20 | 12 |
| Green Lake | 725 | 6.7 | 37 961 | 978 | 316 | 83 | 154 | 151 | 146 | 64 | 60 | 10 | 7 |
| Iowa | 919 | 4.6 | 38 940 | 858 | 496 | 92 | 140 | 141 | 136 | 58 | 52 | 12 | 9 |
| Iron | 217 | 2.6 | 36 856 | 1 094 | 63 | 45 | 39 | 64 | 63 | 26 | 27 | 4 | 2 |
| Jackson | 707 | 6.8 | 34 383 | 1 453 | 412 | 85 | 94 | 143 | 139 | 55 | 55 | 13 | 6 |
| Jefferson | 2 939 | 3.7 | 35 016 | 1 371 | 1 572 | 257 | 420 | 547 | 528 | 214 | 226 | 35 | 31 |
| Juneau | 790 | 4.6 | 29 559 | 2 371 | 380 | 73 | 109 | 213 | 207 | 81 | 85 | 18 | 11 |
| Kenosha | 5 983 | 4.4 | 35 766 | 1 255 | 2 765 | 336 | 713 | 1 121 | 1 084 | 383 | 429 | 128 | 63 |
| Kewaunee | 787 | 6.4 | 38 207 | 941 | 404 | 55 | 119 | 136 | 131 | 56 | 52 | 8 | 7 |
| La Crosse | 4 368 | 3.8 | 37 796 | 997 | 3 401 | 260 | 726 | 769 | 744 | 270 | 307 | 61 | 29 |
| Lafayette | 587 | 11.2 | 34 927 | 1 383 | 162 | 120 | 105 | 102 | 99 | 41 | 40 | 9 | 5 |
| Langlade | 677 | 2.9 | 34 223 | 1 482 | 316 | 85 | 105 | 181 | 177 | 69 | 74 | 17 | 8 |
| Lincoln | 957 | 2.6 | 33 463 | 1 613 | 496 | 62 | 145 | 243 | 237 | 96 | 97 | 16 | 15 |
| Manitowoc | 3 119 | 5.4 | 38 519 | 906 | 1 800 | 222 | 489 | 605 | 587 | 248 | 236 | 38 | 34 |
| Marathon | 5 002 | 3.2 | 37 214 | 1 056 | 3 361 | 420 | 752 | 858 | 828 | 337 | 313 | 76 | 56 |
| Marinette | 1 453 | 4.4 | 34 881 | 1 390 | 900 | 114 | 208 | 385 | 376 | 153 | 155 | 27 | 17 |
| Marquette | 465 | 4.2 | 30 105 | 2 268 | 149 | 31 | 74 | 135 | 132 | 58 | 50 | 9 | 7 |
| Menominee | 113 | 2.6 | 26 087 | 2 873 | 95 | 1 | 10 | 44 | 43 | 10 | 16 | 10 | 2 |
| Milwaukee | 37 035 | 2.9 | 38 881 | 868 | 30 388 | 3 483 | 4 934 | 8 194 | 7 984 | 2 064 | 3 566 | 1 561 | 414 |
| Monroe | 1 505 | 4.8 | 33 402 | 1 628 | 1 020 | 116 | 226 | 289 | 279 | 98 | 104 | 28 | 15 |
| Oconto | 1 368 | 4.3 | 36 508 | 1 136 | 350 | 110 | 181 | 268 | 260 | 114 | 94 | 20 | 17 |
| Oneida | 1 376 | 3.0 | 38 440 | 920 | 732 | 140 | 269 | 357 | 349 | 150 | 143 | 21 | 15 |
| Outagamie | 6 832 | 5.4 | 38 400 | 925 | 5 494 | 452 | 1 002 | 1 008 | 968 | 416 | 348 | 77 | 65 |
| Ozaukee | 5 247 | 5.2 | 60 615 | 65 | 2 188 | 328 | 1 127 | 544 | 525 | 266 | 188 | 19 | 26 |
| Pepin | 269 | 7.7 | 36 229 | 1 184 | 97 | 30 | 46 | 60 | 58 | 24 | 26 | 3 | 2 |
| Pierce | 1 389 | 4.7 | 33 989 | 1 509 | 478 | 101 | 200 | 216 | 207 | 86 | 79 | 14 | 6 |
| Polk | 1 460 | 4.7 | 33 145 | 1 683 | 692 | 83 | 216 | 322 | 312 | 131 | 125 | 26 | 13 |
| Portage | 2 494 | 3.1 | 35 585 | 1 278 | 1 646 | 137 | 375 | 453 | 437 | 167 | 170 | 33 | 24 |
| Price | 477 | 2.3 | 34 115 | 1 493 | 252 | 25 | 90 | 137 | 133 | 54 | 59 | 9 | 5 |
| Racine | 7 508 | 3.7 | 38 425 | 922 | 4 247 | 319 | 1 222 | 1 399 | 1 356 | 535 | 533 | 152 | 84 |
| Richland | 574 | 4.3 | 31 902 | 1 906 | 267 | 57 | 89 | 132 | 128 | 48 | 57 | 12 | 6 |
| Rock | 5 332 | 4.3 | 33 305 | 1 655 | 3 090 | 260 | 841 | 1 180 | 1 145 | 440 | 436 | 129 | 86 |
| Rusk | 399 | 2.2 | 27 299 | 2 717 | 198 | 34 | 65 | 127 | 124 | 48 | 50 | 12 | 6 |
| St. Croix | 3 374 | 6.5 | 39 734 | 775 | 1 358 | 182 | 449 | 400 | 382 | 172 | 143 | 28 | 14 |
| Sauk | 2 291 | 5.0 | 36 782 | 1 104 | 1 608 | 215 | 343 | 416 | 402 | 168 | 159 | 33 | 23 |
| Sawyer | 570 | 2.8 | 34 331 | 1 467 | 281 | 45 | 112 | 170 | 166 | 67 | 65 | 16 | 7 |
| Shawano | 1 374 | 3.6 | 32 911 | 1 723 | 521 | 149 | 200 | 309 | 300 | 126 | 117 | 24 | 17 |
| Sheboygan | 4 596 | 3.3 | 39 910 | 756 | 3 036 | 452 | 751 | 750 | 724 | 320 | 266 | 59 | 50 |
| Taylor | 611 | 4.2 | 29 588 | 2 363 | 349 | 76 | 88 | 137 | 132 | 51 | 55 | 12 | 9 |
| Trempealeau | 1 008 | 5.5 | 34 761 | 1 410 | 634 | 72 | 138 | 210 | 204 | 76 | 94 | 16 | 9 |
| Vernon | 901 | 4.8 | 30 094 | 2 272 | 359 | 103 | 138 | 206 | 200 | 81 | 81 | 17 | 8 |
| Vilas | 751 | 4.1 | 35 018 | 1 370 | 283 | 31 | 218 | 230 | 225 | 109 | 84 | 12 | 9 |
| Walworth | 3 585 | 5.0 | 34 830 | 1 397 | 1 820 | 257 | 619 | 644 | 621 | 264 | 230 | 53 | 33 |
| Washburn | 530 | 3.8 | 33 312 | 1 653 | 232 | 35 | 92 | 173 | 169 | 63 | 67 | 13 | 6 |
| Washington | 5 978 | 7.2 | 45 159 | 390 | 2 665 | 260 | 911 | 771 | 742 | 352 | 270 | 41 | 49 |
| Waukesha | 21 430 | 5.2 | 54 847 | 115 | 14 207 | 1 178 | 3 757 | 2 391 | 2 305 | 1 120 | 852 | 100 | 129 |
| Waupaca | 1 942 | 3.8 | 36 867 | 1 091 | 931 | 83 | 300 | 445 | 433 | 164 | 192 | 27 | 20 |
| Waushara | 749 | 5.7 | 30 457 | 2 210 | 236 | 51 | 135 | 193 | 187 | 85 | 69 | 14 | 9 |
| Winnebago | 6 447 | 4.0 | 38 444 | 917 | 5 296 | 352 | 1 058 | 1 047 | 1 010 | 422 | 394 | 78 | 55 |
| Wood | 2 929 | 4.2 | 39 172 | 838 | 2 431 | 112 | 421 | 609 | 593 | 231 | 253 | 49 | 28 |
| WYOMING | 27 214 | 6.3 | 47 898 | X | 16 433 | 2 680 | 6 563 | 3 606 | 3 481 | 1 241 | 1 335 | 270 | 144 |
| Albany | 1 360 | 6.3 | 36 864 | 1 093 | 821 | 53 | 355 | 206 | 197 | 55 | 67 | 13 | 5 |
| Big Horn | 396 | 8.2 | 33 682 | 1 568 | 223 | 42 | 77 | 84 | 81 | 32 | 32 | 5 | 3 |
| Campbell | 2 218 | 2.0 | 47 584 | 278 | 2 028 | 87 | 368 | 185 | 175 | 58 | 62 | 14 | 10 |
| Carbon | 650 | 5.6 | 41 165 | 646 | 405 | 56 | 142 | 100 | 96 | 34 | 37 | 8 | 4 |
| Converse | 627 | 5.5 | 45 582 | 360 | 351 | 49 | 113 | 85 | 82 | 31 | 32 | 7 | 3 |

1. Based on the resident population estimated as of July 1 of the year shown.   2. Includes supplements to wages and salaries.

# Table B. States and Counties — Earnings, Social Security, and Housing

| STATE County | Earnings, 2011 Total (mil dol) | Farm | Goods-related[1] Total | Manu-facturing | Service-related and health — Information and profes-sional and technical services | Retail trade | Finance, insur-ance, and real estate | Health care and social services | Govern-ment | Social Security beneficiaries, December 2011 — Number | Rate[2] | Supple-mental Security Income recipients, December 2011 | Housing units, 2010 — Total | Percent change, 2000–2010 |
|---|---|---|---|---|---|---|---|---|---|---|---|---|---|---|
| | 75 | 76 | 77 | 78 | 79 | 80 | 81 | 82 | 83 | 84 | 85 | 86 | 87 | 88 |
| **WISCONSIN—Cont'd** | | | | | | | | | | | | | | |
| Dodge | 2 095 | 5.2 | D | 29.5 | 2.6 | 5.2 | 2.4 | 10.3 | 13.3 | 16 830 | 190 | 798 | 37 005 | 9.9 |
| Door | 597 | 2.8 | D | 16.3 | D | 9.9 | 5.4 | 13.0 | 16.1 | 8 460 | 304 | 256 | 23 966 | 22.4 |
| Douglas | 891 | 0.3 | D | 12.9 | 2.9 | 7.0 | 2.9 | 8.1 | 20.0 | 9 025 | 205 | 1 221 | 22 825 | 12.1 |
| Dunn | 924 | 7.6 | D | 20.9 | 3.8 | 6.1 | 3.2 | D | 22.3 | 8 455 | 192 | 719 | 17 964 | 17.6 |
| Eau Claire | 3 046 | 0.8 | D | 10.2 | 5.9 | 7.5 | 7.4 | 20.7 | 14.5 | 18 435 | 185 | 1 941 | 42 151 | 12.5 |
| Florence | 35 | 1.6 | 22.6 | 17.8 | D | D | 5.6 | 7.1 | 37.6 | 1 420 | 320 | 99 | 4 780 | 12.8 |
| Fond du Lac | 2 542 | 3.8 | 33.3 | 25.0 | 4.2 | 6.7 | 4.6 | 13.2 | 12.8 | 20 080 | 197 | 1 366 | 43 910 | 11.8 |
| Forest | 166 | 0.4 | D | 8.0 | D | 4.7 | D | D | 50.4 | 2 670 | 289 | 230 | 8 970 | 7.8 |
| Grant | 1 009 | 12.3 | D | 12.4 | D | 7.0 | 5.0 | 8.8 | 23.6 | 10 510 | 205 | 779 | 21 581 | 8.2 |
| Green | 848 | 8.8 | D | 22.5 | D | 13.5 | 2.7 | 13.1 | 12.4 | 7 365 | 200 | 430 | 15 856 | 14.3 |
| Green Lake | 400 | 7.0 | 29.0 | 19.5 | D | 6.0 | 5.3 | 14.3 | 14.2 | 4 835 | 253 | 280 | 10 616 | 8.0 |
| Iowa | 588 | 9.0 | D | 8.4 | 2.2 | 35.1 | 2.6 | D | 12.3 | 4 635 | 196 | 311 | 10 719 | 11.9 |
| Iron | 108 | 0.7 | D | 26.0 | D | 9.1 | 3.9 | 10.1 | 16.6 | 2 085 | 354 | 134 | 5 999 | 5.1 |
| Jackson | 497 | 7.6 | D | 11.9 | 1.1 | 4.6 | 2.3 | 9.2 | 22.1 | 4 485 | 218 | 411 | 9 727 | 21.1 |
| Jefferson | 1 829 | 3.3 | D | 31.2 | 4.5 | 6.5 | 3.6 | 9.7 | 12.0 | 15 515 | 185 | 930 | 35 147 | 16.7 |
| Juneau | 453 | 6.5 | 31.5 | 26.9 | 1.4 | 6.1 | 3.1 | D | 20.1 | 6 555 | 245 | 575 | 14 669 | 18.6 |
| Kenosha | 3 101 | 0.6 | D | 15.0 | 4.4 | 7.3 | 3.1 | 14.4 | 18.9 | 27 885 | 167 | 3 510 | 69 288 | 15.5 |
| Kewaunee | 459 | 12.3 | D | 21.0 | 3.4 | 3.6 | 2.5 | 3.0 | 14.2 | 4 295 | 209 | 194 | 9 304 | 13.2 |
| La Crosse | 3 662 | 0.5 | D | 14.0 | 5.3 | 6.6 | 6.7 | 22.4 | 14.4 | 20 560 | 178 | 2 184 | 48 402 | 11.3 |
| Lafayette | 282 | 31.9 | D | 14.4 | D | 3.8 | 3.5 | 2.4 | 17.5 | 3 415 | 203 | 216 | 7 230 | 8.3 |
| Langlade | 401 | 5.0 | D | 19.5 | 2.4 | 13.1 | 3.5 | D | 13.5 | 5 535 | 280 | 456 | 12 360 | 10.5 |
| Lincoln | 558 | 1.4 | D | 27.5 | D | 7.2 | 10.9 | 7.4 | 18.2 | 7 330 | 256 | 430 | 16 784 | 14.3 |
| Manitowoc | 2 023 | 4.7 | 37.9 | 31.9 | 3.7 | 5.0 | 2.4 | 11.7 | 11.6 | 18 610 | 230 | 1 246 | 37 189 | 7.3 |
| Marathon | 3 781 | 2.2 | 28.1 | 23.1 | 6.1 | 7.1 | 10.2 | 13.4 | 11.4 | 25 455 | 189 | 2 081 | 57 734 | 14.6 |
| Marinette | 1 014 | 2.7 | D | 35.3 | 2.5 | 7.8 | 2.9 | D | 11.1 | 11 880 | 285 | 780 | 30 379 | 15.7 |
| Marquette | 180 | 10.8 | D | 33.4 | 2.4 | 5.1 | 3.4 | D | 20.4 | 4 455 | 289 | 249 | 9 896 | 14.2 |
| Menominee | 97 | 0.0 | D | D | 0.1 | D | D | 0.0 | 96.2 | 870 | 200 | 253 | 2 253 | 7.4 |
| Milwaukee | 33 890 | 0.0 | D | 14.5 | 10.5 | 4.2 | 10.9 | 14.5 | 13.1 | 156 575 | 164 | 40 306 | 418 053 | 4.5 |
| Monroe | 1 135 | 3.7 | D | 17.4 | 3.0 | 5.5 | 2.6 | 6.4 | 32.1 | 8 425 | 187 | 800 | 19 204 | 15.2 |
| Oconto | 460 | 9.5 | 26.5 | 20.5 | 2.5 | 7.4 | 2.7 | D | 20.2 | 8 920 | 238 | 571 | 23 537 | 18.8 |
| Oneida | 872 | 0.5 | 20.2 | 10.5 | 4.5 | 14.2 | 4.6 | 18.4 | 16.6 | 11 230 | 314 | 585 | 30 125 | 13.1 |
| Outagamie | 5 947 | 1.2 | D | 20.9 | 7.0 | 6.9 | 8.4 | 11.5 | 11.3 | 30 275 | 170 | 2 103 | 73 149 | 16.8 |
| Ozaukee | 2 516 | 0.8 | D | 24.9 | 9.5 | 5.9 | 10.4 | 13.1 | 9.3 | 17 065 | 197 | 464 | 36 267 | 13.2 |
| Pepin | 127 | 19.5 | 12.4 | 5.0 | D | 7.9 | D | 10.1 | 17.7 | 2 025 | 273 | 100 | 3 579 | 17.8 |
| Pierce | 580 | 7.5 | D | 12.0 | D | 4.4 | 3.7 | 8.1 | 32.0 | 6 350 | 155 | 304 | 16 132 | 19.6 |
| Polk | 774 | 3.8 | 30.4 | 25.2 | D | 7.1 | 3.7 | D | 17.4 | 10 135 | 230 | 590 | 24 248 | 14.8 |
| Portage | 1 783 | 2.5 | D | 13.4 | 4.6 | 7.2 | 18.6 | 9.6 | 16.3 | 12 635 | 180 | 955 | 30 054 | 13.0 |
| Price | 277 | 2.2 | D | 41.9 | 5.1 | 5.7 | 2.5 | 9.0 | 16.5 | 4 205 | 300 | 298 | 11 120 | 16.2 |
| Racine | 4 566 | 0.6 | 39.5 | 34.9 | 5.4 | 5.6 | 4.3 | 12.5 | 13.2 | 38 435 | 197 | 4 860 | 82 164 | 10.0 |
| Richland | 324 | 6.9 | D | 28.9 | D | 8.1 | 2.7 | 12.2 | 17.4 | 3 930 | 219 | 406 | 8 868 | 8.6 |
| Rock | 3 350 | 2.4 | 23.2 | 17.5 | 4.3 | 9.2 | 3.4 | 16.5 | 15.5 | 32 180 | 201 | 3 582 | 68 422 | 10.0 |
| Rusk | 232 | 7.8 | 29.0 | 26.4 | D | 7.1 | 2.8 | D | 23.2 | 3 995 | 273 | 355 | 8 883 | 16.7 |
| St. Croix | 1 540 | 3.8 | 29.2 | 22.9 | 6.0 | 8.2 | 4.8 | 12.1 | 14.4 | 12 240 | 144 | 601 | 33 983 | 40.0 |
| Sauk | 1 823 | 3.1 | D | 19.2 | 4.1 | 8.7 | 5.1 | 10.4 | 14.9 | 12 810 | 206 | 818 | 29 708 | 22.3 |
| Sawyer | 326 | 1.8 | D | 10.5 | 4.1 | 9.3 | 5.0 | 11.2 | 28.9 | 5 160 | 311 | 385 | 15 975 | 16.4 |
| Shawano | 670 | 10.0 | D | 19.2 | D | 7.2 | 3.3 | 8.7 | 19.5 | 9 805 | 235 | 634 | 20 720 | 13.1 |
| Sheboygan | 3 488 | 1.5 | D | 39.9 | 3.0 | 5.6 | 5.8 | 12.4 | 9.7 | 23 110 | 201 | 1 659 | 50 766 | 10.5 |
| Taylor | 425 | 10.1 | D | 21.8 | 3.0 | 6.4 | 3.4 | D | 11.6 | 4 145 | 201 | 282 | 10 582 | 23.1 |
| Trempealeau | 706 | 7.2 | D | 43.1 | 2.2 | 4.0 | 2.8 | D | 14.8 | 6 135 | 212 | 421 | 12 619 | 9.9 |
| Vernon | 462 | 14.0 | 12.2 | 7.3 | D | 7.0 | 4.8 | D | 18.1 | 6 820 | 228 | 599 | 13 720 | 10.5 |
| Vilas | 314 | 0.8 | D | 4.0 | D | 9.9 | 4.2 | 6.8 | 32.9 | 8 060 | 376 | 327 | 25 116 | 12.1 |
| Walworth | 2 076 | 2.5 | D | 25.3 | 3.7 | 6.4 | 3.7 | 8.2 | 19.4 | 18 730 | 182 | 1 123 | 51 531 | 17.8 |
| Washburn | 267 | 4.0 | 19.8 | 17.2 | 5.7 | 10.7 | 2.5 | D | 24.3 | 4 985 | 313 | 391 | 12 979 | 20.0 |
| Washington | 2 926 | 1.2 | 34.4 | 29.0 | 4.3 | 7.5 | 6.6 | 11.3 | 10.9 | 24 065 | 182 | 836 | 54 695 | 19.4 |
| Waukesha | 15 385 | 0.1 | 28.6 | 21.5 | 10.9 | 6.4 | 9.0 | 10.2 | 7.2 | 73 570 | 188 | 2 614 | 160 864 | 14.7 |
| Waupaca | 1 014 | 3.8 | 36.4 | 32.6 | 3.8 | 5.7 | 3.2 | 9.9 | 17.8 | 12 570 | 239 | 726 | 25 396 | 12.8 |
| Waushara | 287 | 11.5 | D | 15.9 | 2.9 | 6.7 | 2.8 | D | 20.0 | 6 620 | 269 | 390 | 14 843 | 8.6 |
| Winnebago | 5 648 | 0.6 | D | 34.6 | 6.0 | 4.4 | 4.5 | 10.7 | 11.8 | 30 920 | 184 | 2 313 | 73 329 | 13.3 |
| Wood | 2 543 | 1.7 | D | 15.3 | 4.1 | 5.2 | 2.3 | 39.1 | 10.9 | 17 170 | 230 | 1 300 | 34 088 | 7.6 |
| **WYOMING** | 19 112 | 1.3 | 29.5 | 3.9 | 5.4 | 6.0 | 5.2 | 7.4 | 23.9 | 93 748 | 165 | 6 531 | 261 868 | 17.0 |
| Albany | 874 | 0.2 | D | 2.2 | 8.1 | 6.2 | 4.5 | 9.4 | 48.5 | 4 015 | 109 | 281 | 17 939 | 17.9 |
| Big Horn | 265 | 7.8 | 30.3 | 4.9 | D | D | 3.0 | 2.3 | 29.6 | 2 510 | 213 | 150 | 5 379 | 5.4 |
| Campbell | 2 114 | 0.2 | 49.7 | 2.2 | 3.5 | 4.3 | 2.1 | 3.2 | 13.8 | 4 155 | 89 | 268 | 18 955 | 42.6 |
| Carbon | 461 | 2.1 | D | D | 3.1 | 5.9 | 2.7 | D | 27.8 | 2 565 | 162 | 134 | 8 576 | 3.2 |
| Converse | 400 | 1.3 | 39.9 | 2.2 | 3.2 | 3.9 | 2.8 | D | 21.2 | 2 335 | 170 | 143 | 6 403 | 12.9 |

1. Includes mining, construction, and manufacturing.  2. Per 1,000 resident population enumerated in the 2010 census.

| STATE County | Total | Percent | Median value[1] | With a mortgage | Without a mortgage[2] | Median rent[3] | Median rent as a percent of income | Substandard units[4] (percent) | Total | Percent change, 2011–2012 | Total | Rate[5] | Total | Management, business, science and arts | Construction, production, and maintenance occupations |
|---|---|---|---|---|---|---|---|---|---|---|---|---|---|---|---|
| | 89 | 90 | 91 | 92 | 93 | 94 | 95 | 96 | 97 | 98 | 99 | 100 | 101 | 102 | 103 |
| **WISCONSIN—Cont'd** | | | | | | | | | | | | | | | |
| Dodge | 33 964 | 73.9 | 157 400 | 25.3 | 14.4 | 724 | 25.8 | 1.5 | 46 425 | 0.0 | 3 406 | 7.3 | 44 428 | 27.1 | 35.9 |
| Door | 13 550 | 75.7 | 189 400 | 25.9 | 14.8 | 679 | 26.8 | 1.2 | 16 764 | 0.2 | 1 551 | 9.3 | 14 427 | 30.6 | 27.2 |
| Douglas | 19 171 | 68.4 | 133 600 | 23.2 | 13.2 | 625 | 29.2 | 1.4 | 22 879 | -0.9 | 1 462 | 6.4 | 22 008 | 30.7 | 25.6 |
| Dunn | 16 257 | 68.9 | 158 300 | 24.8 | 13.9 | 684 | 29.0 | 1.7 | 25 418 | -0.4 | 1 507 | 5.9 | 22 086 | 29.5 | 29.0 |
| Eau Claire | 39 272 | 64.3 | 148 600 | 22.9 | 13.3 | 679 | 30.2 | 2.2 | 57 256 | 0.8 | 3 369 | 5.9 | 52 597 | 32.7 | 22.0 |
| Florence | 1 988 | 86.0 | 129 600 | 25.9 | 14.4 | 537 | 29.5 | 2.2 | 2 315 | -1.7 | 170 | 7.3 | 2 115 | 28.7 | 29.9 |
| Fond du Lac | 40 832 | 71.7 | 145 200 | 23.6 | 13.5 | 650 | 27.6 | 1.8 | 54 769 | -0.5 | 3 596 | 6.6 | 52 953 | 26.7 | 33.4 |
| Forest | 4 021 | 76.6 | 120 100 | 23.5 | 14.2 | 482 | 23.1 | 2.0 | 4 589 | -1.9 | 436 | 9.5 | 3 860 | 25.3 | 30.4 |
| Grant | 19 230 | 74.1 | 121 500 | 23.2 | 13.7 | 602 | 28.3 | 2.4 | 28 045 | -1.1 | 1 620 | 5.8 | 25 538 | 28.4 | 30.9 |
| Green | 14 527 | 76.5 | 154 000 | 25.7 | 14.2 | 638 | 26.6 | 1.1 | 19 857 | 0.2 | 1 280 | 6.4 | 19 514 | 31.2 | 30.0 |
| Green Lake | 7 980 | 76.6 | 140 000 | 24.2 | 13.0 | 579 | 23.8 | 2.1 | 9 968 | -0.5 | 761 | 7.6 | 9 638 | 25.0 | 36.2 |
| Iowa | 9 695 | 77.5 | 159 200 | 25.0 | 14.4 | 670 | 25.8 | 1.3 | 13 917 | -0.2 | 858 | 6.2 | 12 758 | 31.3 | 28.1 |
| Iron | 2 989 | 79.3 | 109 100 | 24.0 | 15.0 | 481 | 27.3 | 4.2 | 2 770 | -0.6 | 321 | 11.6 | 2 628 | 26.8 | 29.9 |
| Jackson | 8 145 | 75.7 | 124 000 | 25.2 | 14.4 | 571 | 28.2 | 3.8 | 9 867 | 1.2 | 758 | 7.7 | 9 394 | 29.2 | 32.1 |
| Jefferson | 31 936 | 72.2 | 183 100 | 25.8 | 14.7 | 751 | 27.7 | 1.5 | 41 604 | -0.7 | 3 038 | 7.3 | 43 609 | 28.9 | 30.4 |
| Juneau | 10 934 | 76.7 | 116 500 | 25.3 | 14.6 | 654 | 26.3 | 2.6 | 13 099 | -1.3 | 1 137 | 8.7 | 12 422 | 23.2 | 32.3 |
| Kenosha | 62 215 | 68.5 | 180 000 | 26.2 | 14.9 | 813 | 30.6 | 2.2 | 86 622 | 0.2 | 7 100 | 8.2 | 79 647 | 32.1 | 25.1 |
| Kewaunee | 8 203 | 81.3 | 147 200 | 24.0 | 14.0 | 626 | 26.4 | 1.7 | 11 517 | -0.4 | 707 | 6.1 | 10 572 | 26.1 | 38.3 |
| La Crosse | 45 704 | 65.2 | 151 900 | 22.8 | 13.4 | 690 | 29.6 | 1.6 | 66 191 | 0.5 | 3 528 | 5.3 | 61 265 | 33.7 | 23.3 |
| Lafayette | 6 513 | 79.3 | 119 700 | 25.2 | 14.4 | 567 | 23.5 | 1.7 | 9 186 | -1.1 | 510 | 5.6 | 8 799 | 28.6 | 34.8 |
| Langlade | 8 850 | 78.2 | 107 100 | 23.8 | 13.4 | 506 | 31.1 | 5.2 | 10 253 | -1.6 | 896 | 8.7 | 9 609 | 22.9 | 37.4 |
| Lincoln | 12 881 | 76.5 | 131 000 | 22.6 | 12.8 | 564 | 27.4 | 2.3 | 14 517 | -1.3 | 1 374 | 9.5 | 14 275 | 25.0 | 36.3 |
| Manitowoc | 34 266 | 76.6 | 125 600 | 22.7 | 13.6 | 572 | 24.6 | 1.2 | 43 677 | -1.5 | 3 331 | 7.6 | 41 484 | 25.9 | 36.3 |
| Marathon | 52 865 | 74.5 | 141 700 | 22.4 | 12.5 | 663 | 25.8 | 2.5 | 71 412 | -1.7 | 5 136 | 7.2 | 69 504 | 31.3 | 30.7 |
| Marinette | 19 092 | 78.2 | 109 100 | 23.2 | 14.7 | 570 | 25.0 | 2.3 | 21 621 | -0.3 | 1 739 | 8.0 | 19 316 | 24.7 | 39.3 |
| Marquette | 6 654 | 79.8 | 143 000 | 26.0 | 16.1 | 686 | 26.4 | 1.4 | 7 483 | -2.0 | 649 | 8.7 | 7 048 | 23.4 | 37.2 |
| Menominee | 1 441 | 67.4 | 96 000 | 26.2 | 14.5 | 462 | 19.5 | 3.3 | 1 554 | -1.7 | 237 | 15.3 | 1 443 | 17.7 | 27.4 |
| Milwaukee | 378 527 | 52.8 | 165 300 | 26.0 | 16.4 | 771 | 31.8 | 3.0 | 460 067 | -0.4 | 38 742 | 8.4 | 441 390 | 33.9 | 22.1 |
| Monroe | 17 302 | 71.0 | 131 900 | 23.6 | 13.6 | 706 | 26.1 | 4.3 | 24 042 | -2.2 | 1 614 | 6.7 | 21 451 | 28.6 | 32.9 |
| Oconto | 16 322 | 81.9 | 147 300 | 25.2 | 14.6 | 574 | 27.3 | 1.3 | 19 979 | -0.5 | 1 569 | 7.9 | 19 062 | 27.6 | 36.0 |
| Oneida | 16 985 | 79.6 | 170 700 | 26.0 | 14.1 | 658 | 29.8 | 1.0 | 18 537 | 0.5 | 1 645 | 8.9 | 17 548 | 27.3 | 28.2 |
| Outagamie | 69 070 | 72.6 | 155 300 | 23.0 | 12.9 | 687 | 25.0 | 1.7 | 96 145 | -0.5 | 6 285 | 6.5 | 93 400 | 31.2 | 27.9 |
| Ozaukee | 34 067 | 77.7 | 256 800 | 23.5 | 12.6 | 793 | 26.6 | 0.6 | 46 917 | -0.1 | 2 668 | 5.7 | 45 218 | 43.8 | 17.9 |
| Pepin | 3 069 | 76.1 | 139 200 | 24.1 | 16.1 | 543 | 24.9 | 2.9 | 4 011 | 0.0 | 225 | 5.6 | 3 765 | 28.5 | 34.7 |
| Pierce | 14 960 | 76.2 | 197 400 | 25.7 | 14.4 | 762 | 31.0 | 1.9 | 23 706 | 0.7 | 1 249 | 5.3 | 22 762 | 31.1 | 30.3 |
| Polk | 18 323 | 80.4 | 167 100 | 27.7 | 15.1 | 687 | 29.7 | 2.0 | 23 774 | 0.0 | 1 897 | 8.0 | 21 594 | 27.3 | 34.1 |
| Portage | 27 840 | 68.9 | 144 400 | 22.1 | 12.2 | 644 | 28.2 | 1.6 | 41 818 | -1.3 | 2 755 | 6.6 | 36 540 | 30.0 | 26.1 |
| Price | 6 789 | 79.3 | 114 000 | 24.6 | 14.4 | 562 | 25.3 | 4.5 | 7 459 | -2.2 | 512 | 6.9 | 7 039 | 26.4 | 40.8 |
| Racine | 75 599 | 69.8 | 177 300 | 25.0 | 14.3 | 731 | 30.0 | 1.8 | 97 131 | -0.2 | 8 279 | 8.5 | 92 504 | 31.3 | 28.1 |
| Richland | 7 510 | 75.3 | 123 600 | 25.7 | 14.0 | 577 | 27.9 | 3.6 | 9 883 | 0.6 | 594 | 6.0 | 8 975 | 25.6 | 39.0 |
| Rock | 62 745 | 72.8 | 139 000 | 24.1 | 13.9 | 727 | 31.3 | 1.4 | 78 820 | 0.1 | 6 644 | 8.4 | 76 424 | 28.6 | 30.8 |
| Rusk | 6 639 | 76.9 | 108 100 | 24.6 | 14.9 | 575 | 28.4 | 3.6 | 6 619 | -2.4 | 605 | 9.1 | 6 635 | 27.2 | 41.1 |
| St. Croix | 31 986 | 78.5 | 220 300 | 25.0 | 12.8 | 835 | 28.3 | 1.6 | 47 524 | 0.7 | 2 522 | 5.3 | 44 526 | 38.5 | 24.4 |
| Sauk | 25 504 | 72.2 | 167 200 | 25.5 | 14.1 | 726 | 27.9 | 1.6 | 34 847 | -1.0 | 2 412 | 6.9 | 32 845 | 28.0 | 29.3 |
| Sawyer | 7 680 | 74.2 | 167 900 | 25.7 | 14.0 | 546 | 29.0 | 3.8 | 8 762 | -0.1 | 859 | 9.8 | 7 377 | 28.1 | 28.5 |
| Shawano | 17 203 | 76.0 | 124 800 | 23.7 | 14.2 | 593 | 26.8 | 1.7 | 21 880 | -1.3 | 1 680 | 7.7 | 19 852 | 28.1 | 31.9 |
| Sheboygan | 46 318 | 72.4 | 154 300 | 23.0 | 14.0 | 647 | 26.6 | 1.8 | 61 249 | -1.3 | 4 038 | 6.6 | 58 977 | 28.1 | 32.5 |
| Taylor | 8 851 | 79.0 | 122 400 | 24.9 | 14.1 | 531 | 26.2 | 2.5 | 10 121 | -2.7 | 786 | 7.8 | 10 106 | 26.5 | 44.7 |
| Trempealeau | 11 513 | 75.1 | 132 100 | 24.4 | 14.4 | 575 | 25.3 | 2.9 | 16 647 | 1.1 | 902 | 5.4 | 14 584 | 29.0 | 37.8 |
| Vernon | 11 831 | 78.9 | 133 300 | 24.8 | 13.8 | 581 | 25.3 | 4.7 | 14 767 | -1.5 | 929 | 6.3 | 13 763 | 30.7 | 32.9 |
| Vilas | 10 612 | 78.9 | 195 000 | 27.6 | 14.8 | 676 | 28.7 | 1.4 | 10 397 | -0.5 | 986 | 9.5 | 9 524 | 34.0 | 22.0 |
| Walworth | 39 083 | 70.8 | 198 700 | 25.9 | 13.8 | 784 | 31.2 | 2.8 | 54 903 | -0.5 | 3 991 | 7.3 | 51 800 | 30.7 | 27.1 |
| Washburn | 7 550 | 83.0 | 146 400 | 26.5 | 15.9 | 614 | 32.9 | 3.3 | 7 911 | 1.6 | 630 | 8.0 | 7 110 | 31.0 | 30.7 |
| Washington | 51 864 | 78.1 | 231 200 | 24.7 | 13.9 | 788 | 27.4 | 1.1 | 74 126 | -0.3 | 4 747 | 6.4 | 70 892 | 35.1 | 26.2 |
| Waukesha | 152 181 | 77.1 | 261 100 | 23.8 | 13.3 | 894 | 27.6 | 1.1 | 214 241 | -0.3 | 12 909 | 6.0 | 204 914 | 42.9 | 18.0 |
| Waupaca | 21 603 | 75.2 | 138 300 | 24.4 | 14.4 | 629 | 26.9 | 1.9 | 27 646 | -1.0 | 2 039 | 7.4 | 25 360 | 24.3 | 38.8 |
| Waushara | 10 143 | 81.3 | 138 500 | 26.0 | 14.8 | 613 | 28.4 | 2.6 | 12 572 | -0.8 | 1 017 | 8.1 | 10 790 | 24.4 | 37.6 |
| Winnebago | 66 861 | 68.2 | 140 800 | 22.8 | 13.7 | 635 | 26.4 | 1.1 | 94 345 | -0.5 | 6 002 | 6.4 | 84 627 | 30.0 | 26.5 |
| Wood | 32 126 | 74.6 | 117 900 | 21.7 | 12.4 | 576 | 28.5 | 1.3 | 40 850 | -0.4 | 2 921 | 7.2 | 36 609 | 28.3 | 30.5 |
| **WYOMING** | 219 628 | 70.5 | 181 900 | 21.6 | 9.9 | 708 | 24.5 | 2.6 | 306 064 | 0.9 | 16 443 | 5.4 | 287 634 | 31.7 | 29.0 |
| Albany | 14 683 | 53.7 | 194 900 | 22.6 | 9.9 | 689 | 33.7 | 1.3 | 20 334 | 1.0 | 903 | 4.4 | 19 864 | 44.0 | 15.7 |
| Big Horn | 4 612 | 76.0 | 120 400 | 19.2 | 9.9 | 549 | 19.4 | 3.1 | 5 228 | 0.3 | 323 | 6.2 | 5 359 | 32.1 | 34.6 |
| Campbell | 16 472 | 76.4 | 199 800 | 19.7 | 9.9 | 858 | 22.4 | 4.3 | 28 007 | 1.0 | 1 203 | 4.3 | 25 265 | 23.5 | 42.7 |
| Carbon | 6 217 | 74.3 | 139 200 | 19.2 | 9.9 | 694 | 19.9 | 2.9 | 7 998 | 2.7 | 443 | 5.5 | 8 014 | 25.2 | 33.9 |
| Converse | 5 635 | 70.7 | 180 500 | 20.6 | 9.9 | 664 | 23.0 | 2.8 | 8 160 | 4.5 | 341 | 4.2 | 7 109 | 26.8 | 42.7 |

1. Specified owner-occupied units.    2. A value of 9.9 represents 9.9 percent or less.    3. Specified renter-occupied units. A value of 10.0 represents 10 percent or less.    4. Overcrowded or lacking complete plumbing facilities.    5. Percent of civilian labor force.    6. Persons 16 years old and over.

# Table B. States and Counties — Nonfarm Employment and Agriculture

| | Private nonfarm establishments, employment and payroll, 2011 | | | | | | | | | Agriculture, 2007 | | | |
| | | Employment | | | | | | Annual payroll | | Farms | | | |
| | | | | | | | | | | | Percent with: | | |
| STATE County | Number of establishments | Total | Health care and social assistance | Manufacturing | Retail trade | Finance and insurance | Professional, scientific, and technical services | Total (mil dol) | Average per employee (dollars) | Number | Fewer than 50 acres | 500 acres or more | Farm operators whose principal occupation is farming (percent) |
| | 104 | 105 | 106 | 107 | 108 | 109 | 110 | 111 | 112 | 113 | 114 | 115 | 116 |
| **WISCONSIN—Cont'd** | | | | | | | | | | | | | |
| Dodge | 1 781 | 27 750 | 4 630 | 9 683 | 3 321 | 714 | 481 | 1 026 | 36 983 | 1 979 | 30.8 | 9.7 | 53.9 |
| Door | 1 266 | 9 829 | 1 506 | 2 002 | 1 530 | 323 | 233 | 302 | 30 763 | 854 | 37.4 | 4.8 | 41.1 |
| Douglas | 1 044 | 13 713 | 1 972 | 1 492 | 2 058 | 344 | 304 | 473 | 34 510 | 333 | 21.3 | 9.9 | 44.7 |
| Dunn | 878 | 12 389 | 2 491 | 2 385 | 1 699 | D | 371 | 417 | 33 625 | 1 690 | 26.9 | 9.8 | 39.9 |
| Eau Claire | 2 679 | 49 287 | 10 357 | 4 896 | 7 094 | 3 090 | 1 725 | 1 651 | 33 493 | 1 223 | 28.6 | 4.4 | 41.3 |
| Florence | 106 | 463 | D | 70 | D | D | D | 11 | 22 721 | 115 | 27.0 | 5.2 | 44.3 |
| Fond du Lac | 2 393 | 38 783 | 5 881 | 7 846 | 5 297 | 1 752 | 1 089 | 1 356 | 34 965 | 1 643 | 30.3 | 8.9 | 51.6 |
| Forest | 247 | 1 646 | 272 | 226 | 266 | D | D | 43 | 26 143 | 173 | 28.9 | 4.6 | 37.0 |
| Grant | 1 236 | 13 471 | 2 359 | 2 281 | 2 406 | 736 | 509 | 395 | 29 357 | 2 866 | 27.2 | 8.6 | 49.3 |
| Green | 946 | 11 871 | 1 994 | 2 805 | 2 350 | 367 | 274 | 412 | 34 725 | 1 534 | 33.9 | 8.0 | 48.8 |
| Green Lake | 493 | 5 795 | 1 212 | 1 213 | 984 | 285 | 96 | 204 | 35 144 | 723 | 30.7 | 7.9 | 46.6 |
| Iowa | 538 | 8 557 | 1 053 | D | D | 183 | 131 | 308 | 35 960 | 1 813 | 25.9 | 8.9 | 41.5 |
| Iron | 216 | 1 441 | 301 | 200 | 254 | D | D | 35 | 24 128 | 54 | 20.4 | 11.1 | 42.6 |
| Jackson | 413 | 5 945 | 1 025 | 752 | 816 | 192 | 109 | 239 | 40 182 | 945 | 21.6 | 11.1 | 48.9 |
| Jefferson | 1 915 | 29 338 | 3 930 | 8 537 | 3 928 | 708 | 648 | 988 | 33 685 | 1 434 | 39.6 | 6.3 | 44.3 |
| Juneau | 553 | 6 092 | 981 | 1 627 | 978 | D | 64 | 200 | 32 904 | 797 | 26.5 | 8.7 | 42.8 |
| Kenosha | 2 988 | 46 682 | 8 954 | 5 327 | 8 740 | 960 | 1 516 | 1 610 | 34 485 | 460 | 52.0 | 7.4 | 47.0 |
| Kewaunee | 482 | 5 370 | 528 | 1 867 | 545 | D | D | 219 | 40 858 | 893 | 29.5 | 6.5 | 51.6 |
| La Crosse | 2 959 | 57 747 | 10 743 | 6 831 | 8 153 | 2 900 | 1 677 | 2 027 | 35 107 | 845 | 23.3 | 7.7 | 49.5 |
| Lafayette | 352 | 2 607 | 244 | 609 | 418 | 150 | D | 68 | 26 007 | 1 342 | 31.1 | 10.8 | 55.8 |
| Langlade | 573 | 6 465 | 965 | 1 585 | 1 279 | 248 | 101 | 202 | 31 252 | 487 | 24.6 | 12.1 | 49.3 |
| Lincoln | 685 | 8 278 | 946 | 2 356 | 1 266 | 885 | 105 | 279 | 33 686 | 575 | 31.1 | 5.4 | 42.6 |
| Manitowoc | 1 790 | 30 104 | 4 800 | 10 177 | 3 516 | 815 | 667 | 1 127 | 37 428 | 1 444 | 38.8 | 7.5 | 45.5 |
| Marathon | 3 371 | 59 017 | 9 463 | 15 384 | 7 872 | 4 737 | 2 035 | 2 210 | 37 454 | 2 545 | 25.3 | 6.4 | 53.8 |
| Marinette | 1 119 | 16 289 | 2 747 | 5 369 | 2 290 | 474 | 213 | 579 | 35 515 | 746 | 34.5 | 7.4 | 40.8 |
| Marquette | 287 | 3 274 | 243 | 1 272 | 351 | D | D | 102 | 31 278 | 626 | 32.3 | 8.9 | 42.0 |
| Menominee | 20 | D | D | D | 38 | NA | D | D | D | 4 | 75.0 | 0.0 | 0.0 |
| Milwaukee | 19 534 | 445 979 | 87 024 | 49 662 | 41 815 | 39 066 | 29 971 | 21 196 | 47 527 | 96 | 71.9 | 1.0 | 68.8 |
| Monroe | 943 | 14 359 | 2 185 | 3 229 | 1 959 | 426 | 529 | 492 | 34 268 | 2 115 | 27.7 | 5.2 | 44.4 |
| Oconto | 754 | 6 678 | 1 580 | D | 942 | 167 | 162 | 187 | 27 991 | 1 244 | 36.7 | 6.8 | 44.1 |
| Oneida | 1 320 | 13 455 | D | 1 336 | 3 253 | 351 | 349 | 484 | 35 949 | 179 | 33.5 | 8.4 | 36.3 |
| Outagamie | 4 977 | 92 844 | 11 532 | 17 084 | 12 620 | 5 684 | 3 867 | 3 689 | 39 738 | 1 362 | 40.9 | 8.6 | 51.6 |
| Ozaukee | 2 701 | 35 528 | 4 854 | 7 741 | 4 558 | 1 816 | 2 134 | 1 412 | 39 738 | 513 | 45.6 | 5.8 | 45.0 |
| Pepin | 222 | 1 690 | 335 | D | 309 | D | 45 | 55 | 32 292 | 503 | 24.1 | 9.1 | 49.5 |
| Pierce | 789 | 5 990 | 931 | 1 034 | 939 | 293 | 223 | 179 | 29 935 | 1 531 | 33.8 | 7.4 | 41.9 |
| Polk | 1 097 | 11 626 | 2 449 | 3 448 | 1 868 | D | 331 | 366 | 31 451 | 1 582 | 30.6 | 7.1 | 42.9 |
| Portage | 1 607 | 27 682 | 3 771 | 4 186 | 3 855 | 4 001 | 675 | 971 | 35 064 | 1 066 | 26.1 | 9.8 | 49.3 |
| Price | 431 | 4 648 | 939 | 1 745 | 553 | 169 | 83 | 150 | 32 333 | 545 | 21.7 | 7.2 | 37.2 |
| Racine | 4 037 | 66 884 | 10 739 | 14 394 | 8 481 | 1 852 | 2 333 | 2 776 | 41 506 | 652 | 53.7 | 7.5 | 44.6 |
| Richland | 382 | 4 744 | D | 1 508 | 948 | D | 146 | 146 | 30 673 | 1 545 | 27.4 | 5.9 | 36.7 |
| Rock | 3 236 | 49 944 | 8 625 | 7 886 | 8 638 | 1 675 | 1 095 | 1 847 | 36 989 | 1 556 | 45.5 | 9.6 | 47.6 |
| Rusk | 301 | 4 073 | 898 | 1 407 | 625 | 123 | 47 | 118 | 28 896 | 651 | 16.5 | 10.4 | 55.6 |
| St. Croix | 2 053 | 24 636 | 4 687 | 5 110 | 3 785 | 843 | 1 108 | 834 | 33 839 | 1 808 | 35.7 | 6.2 | 41.3 |
| Sauk | 1 755 | 29 368 | 3 933 | 5 170 | 3 970 | 866 | 920 | 952 | 32 405 | 1 923 | 31.4 | 7.4 | 41.3 |
| Sawyer | 666 | 4 859 | 759 | 561 | 938 | 203 | 150 | 146 | 30 098 | 231 | 34.2 | 10.0 | 51.5 |
| Shawano | 892 | 10 031 | 1 627 | 1 870 | 1 522 | 278 | 198 | 302 | 30 107 | 1 450 | 26.5 | 7.3 | 54.6 |
| Sheboygan | 2 674 | 49 695 | 6 975 | 15 547 | 6 082 | 1 948 | 1 270 | 1 889 | 38 021 | 1 059 | 42.0 | 9.4 | 53.7 |
| Taylor | 476 | 7 105 | 968 | 2 549 | 876 | 269 | D | 234 | 32 867 | 1 208 | 28.4 | 7.8 | 47.6 |
| Trempealeau | 650 | 11 456 | 1 348 | 5 806 | 1 059 | 367 | 193 | 428 | 37 388 | 1 721 | 21.2 | 7.4 | 41.6 |
| Vernon | 610 | 6 872 | 1 779 | D | 1 180 | 254 | 168 | 201 | 29 298 | 2 492 | 36.3 | 3.6 | 46.7 |
| Vilas | 929 | 5 614 | 718 | D | 1 087 | 222 | 106 | 144 | 25 726 | 71 | 52.1 | 7.0 | 40.8 |
| Walworth | 2 621 | 32 700 | 3 831 | 8 062 | 4 516 | 834 | 935 | 1 084 | 33 161 | 1 000 | 41.4 | 10.7 | 49.1 |
| Washburn | 514 | 4 485 | 998 | 1 133 | 741 | 124 | 153 | 124 | 27 559 | 558 | 28.1 | 6.8 | 37.3 |
| Washington | 3 116 | 46 192 | 5 427 | 12 369 | 6 766 | 2 188 | 1 489 | 1 756 | 38 023 | 831 | 43.3 | 7.0 | 52.6 |
| Waukesha | 12 354 | 217 963 | 25 864 | 42 639 | 25 608 | 12 905 | 12 246 | 10 343 | 47 454 | 675 | 59.7 | 5.5 | 47.3 |
| Waupaca | 1 219 | 16 319 | 2 800 | 5 771 | 2 270 | 578 | 272 | 536 | 32 844 | 1 330 | 30.5 | 8.2 | 47.4 |
| Waushara | 464 | 4 356 | 836 | D | 670 | 130 | D | 115 | 26 506 | 677 | 27.8 | 9.7 | 42.7 |
| Winnebago | 3 525 | 85 684 | 14 136 | 24 047 | 7 633 | 3 137 | 2 756 | 3 717 | 43 378 | 1 001 | 39.6 | 8.1 | 44.5 |
| Wood | 1 787 | 35 505 | 10 003 | 5 563 | 4 103 | 1 293 | 527 | 1 461 | 41 160 | 1 114 | 26.7 | 8.3 | 54.3 |
| **WYOMING** | 20 329 | 208 385 | 31 600 | 9 644 | 30 100 | 6 824 | 8 837 | 9 110 | 43 716 | 11 069 | 24.0 | 38.3 | 49.2 |
| Albany | 1 001 | 9 890 | 2 121 | 323 | 1 791 | 480 | 876 | 305 | 30 869 | 448 | 18.5 | 41.1 | 36.4 |
| Big Horn | 299 | 2 594 | D | D | 397 | 77 | 66 | 100 | 38 704 | 621 | 28.2 | 23.5 | 52.3 |
| Campbell | 1 484 | 23 572 | D | 533 | 2 421 | D | 830 | 1 338 | 56 757 | 633 | 24.3 | 49.3 | 38.7 |
| Carbon | 526 | 4 829 | 663 | D | 677 | D | 94 | 212 | 43 918 | 287 | 16.4 | 54.0 | 54.4 |
| Converse | 465 | 3 860 | 608 | D | 426 | D | 79 | 188 | 48 660 | 435 | 17.0 | 48.0 | 48.0 |

| STATE County | Acreage (1,000) 117 | Percent change, 2002–2007 118 | Average size of farm 119 | Total irrigated (1,000) 120 | Total cropland (1,000) 121 | Average per farm 122 | Average per acre 123 | Value of machinery and equipment, average per farm (dollars) 124 | Total (mil dol) 125 | Average per farm (dollars) 126 | Crops 127 | Live-stock and poultry products 128 | $10,000 or more 129 | $100,000 or more 130 | Total ($1,000) 131 | Percent of farms 132 |
|---|---|---|---|---|---|---|---|---|---|---|---|---|---|---|---|---|
| **WISCONSIN—Cont'd** | | | | | | | | | | | | | | | | |
| Dodge | 413 | 2.2 | 209 | 0.6 | 342.9 | 765 236 | 3 667 | 130 875 | 294.8 | 148 980 | 34.4 | 65.6 | 59.0 | 29.9 | 7 462 | 71.4 |
| Door | 134 | -0.7 | 157 | 0.8 | 99.0 | 530 569 | 3 370 | 89 005 | 60.5 | 70 849 | 40.9 | 59.1 | 43.6 | 16.7 | 1 960 | 59.5 |
| Douglas | 73 | -14.1 | 218 | 0.1 | 29.8 | 448 195 | 2 053 | 48 152 | 6.1 | 18 321 | 29.4 | 70.6 | 29.4 | 5.1 | 43 | 9.9 |
| Dunn | 383 | -4.0 | 226 | 29.3 | 250.8 | 633 800 | 2 800 | 90 324 | 173.6 | 102 723 | 29.6 | 70.4 | 36.6 | 18.2 | 4 699 | 66.6 |
| Eau Claire | 205 | 0.5 | 168 | 3.7 | 131.6 | 469 888 | 2 798 | 70 746 | 84.0 | 68 653 | 33.6 | 66.4 | 39.6 | 15.5 | 3 036 | 69.1 |
| Florence | 20 | -4.8 | 176 | D | 9.4 | 416 398 | 2 363 | 62 220 | 2.5 | 21 610 | 17.5 | 82.5 | 22.6 | 6.1 | 34 | 28.7 |
| Fond du Lac | 336 | -2.3 | 204 | 0.9 | 279.9 | 721 664 | 3 532 | 127 243 | 290.4 | 176 760 | 24.0 | 76.0 | 56.1 | 30.6 | 5 413 | 77.6 |
| Forest | 34 | 0.0 | 195 | D | 11.0 | 376 172 | 1 925 | 42 069 | 2.5 | 14 282 | 35.8 | 64.2 | 27.7 | 2.9 | 41 | 29.5 |
| Grant | 611 | 0.8 | 213 | 0.5 | 354.6 | 671 204 | 3 149 | 106 736 | 329.7 | 115 041 | 23.8 | 76.2 | 51.8 | 26.6 | 10 445 | 69.7 |
| Green | 307 | 0.0 | 200 | 2.6 | 240.0 | 714 250 | 3 571 | 111 791 | 188.1 | 122 610 | 29.4 | 70.6 | 49.4 | 29.1 | 5 726 | 74.4 |
| Green Lake | 143 | -3.4 | 197 | 3.4 | 108.5 | 686 818 | 3 478 | 95 370 | 74.1 | 102 436 | 47.2 | 52.8 | 46.3 | 21.0 | 2 023 | 62.5 |
| Iowa | 365 | -0.5 | 201 | 6.7 | 201.8 | 662 634 | 3 292 | 86 696 | 157.9 | 87 119 | 24.9 | 75.1 | 39.3 | 20.2 | 6 966 | 80.5 |
| Iron | 10 | -23.1 | 187 | 0.2 | 4.1 | 355 729 | 1 900 | 55 451 | D | D | D | D | 24.1 | 11.1 | D | 11.1 |
| Jackson | 239 | -7.4 | 253 | 4.2 | 127.1 | 654 119 | 2 587 | 99 927 | 121.0 | 128 055 | 45.6 | 54.4 | 45.6 | 24.2 | 2 273 | 63.4 |
| Jefferson | 244 | -1.6 | 170 | 7.5 | 190.2 | 688 346 | 4 042 | 98 958 | 209.3 | 145 951 | 41.3 | 58.7 | 48.1 | 19.0 | 4 095 | 72.3 |
| Juneau | 181 | 0.6 | 227 | 8.8 | 111.6 | 649 950 | 2 861 | 92 326 | 90.3 | 113 260 | 54.5 | 45.5 | 40.9 | 18.2 | 2 279 | 66.8 |
| Kenosha | 84 | -5.6 | 183 | 0.2 | 71.7 | 933 034 | 5 089 | 105 704 | 59.7 | 129 839 | 70.9 | 29.1 | 42.8 | 21.5 | 1 245 | 44.1 |
| Kewaunee | 175 | 0.6 | 196 | 0.1 | 142.2 | 686 411 | 3 494 | 139 521 | 194.9 | 218 270 | 18.5 | 81.5 | 51.4 | 28.7 | 2 654 | 76.0 |
| La Crosse | 165 | -5.2 | 196 | 0.9 | 87.7 | 566 874 | 2 897 | 90 238 | 60.8 | 71 947 | 29.4 | 70.6 | 43.4 | 18.2 | 1 725 | 64.9 |
| Lafayette | 343 | 0.0 | 255 | 0.1 | 249.9 | 898 536 | 3 519 | 131 055 | 219.3 | 163 391 | 32.4 | 67.6 | 56.8 | 34.9 | 7 134 | 76.6 |
| Langlade | 123 | -12.8 | 252 | 17.5 | 78.3 | 644 726 | 2 555 | 115 616 | 74.0 | 152 051 | 55.9 | 44.1 | 45.8 | 23.4 | 767 | 47.8 |
| Lincoln | 87 | -11.2 | 151 | 0.3 | 42.6 | 385 627 | 2 555 | 70 177 | 30.1 | 52 294 | 37.5 | 62.5 | 31.1 | 11.8 | 397 | 29.0 |
| Manitowoc | 248 | -3.5 | 172 | 0.7 | 199.7 | 600 456 | 3 493 | 105 670 | 257.2 | 178 096 | 14.7 | 85.3 | 46.2 | 24.9 | 3 662 | 65.4 |
| Marathon | 491 | -7.5 | 193 | 7.1 | 323.6 | 526 977 | 2 734 | 100 135 | 307.4 | 120 800 | 14.8 | 85.2 | 54.9 | 29.0 | 4 727 | 50.3 |
| Marinette | 144 | -3.4 | 193 | 2.1 | 86.6 | 520 600 | 2 691 | 81 884 | 66.9 | 89 684 | 19.6 | 80.4 | 32.0 | 14.1 | 1 249 | 39.3 |
| Marquette | 136 | -6.8 | 217 | 6.5 | 90.3 | 666 068 | 3 068 | 80 159 | 55.7 | 88 955 | 43.2 | 56.8 | 33.4 | 12.6 | 1 506 | 54.2 |
| Menominee | 0 | NA | 80 | 0.0 | 0.3 | 93 333 | 1 174 | 13 283 | D | D | D | D | 25.0 | 0.0 | D | 50.0 |
| Milwaukee | 5 | -16.7 | 57 | 0.1 | 4.6 | 410 021 | 7 212 | 47 954 | 9.9 | 103 411 | 97.5 | 2.5 | 60.4 | 16.7 | 78 | 21.9 |
| Monroe | 351 | -0.3 | 166 | 4.0 | 167.2 | 492 944 | 2 968 | 77 892 | 165.1 | 78 058 | 36.4 | 63.6 | 40.3 | 15.8 | 3 188 | 54.4 |
| Oconto | 206 | -5.9 | 166 | 1.3 | 146.8 | 492 990 | 2 978 | 78 199 | 115.8 | 93 111 | 20.0 | 80.0 | 39.9 | 19.0 | 2 388 | 50.0 |
| Oneida | 39 | -23.5 | 219 | 2.7 | 13.9 | 622 980 | 2 847 | 58 245 | 17.5 | 97 892 | 83.0 | 17.0 | 21.8 | 11.7 | 15 | 11.2 |
| Outagamie | 247 | -6.1 | 182 | 0.2 | 207.5 | 671 959 | 3 698 | 128 126 | 236.7 | 173 791 | 22.8 | 77.2 | 54.3 | 28.5 | 4 370 | 66.4 |
| Ozaukee | 71 | -5.3 | 138 | 0.4 | 57.7 | 659 419 | 4 785 | 87 055 | 59.1 | 115 120 | 35.4 | 64.6 | 43.9 | 19.3 | 1 058 | 63.4 |
| Pepin | 108 | -2.7 | 216 | 1.5 | 67.5 | 589 201 | 2 733 | 92 461 | 53.2 | 105 795 | 25.1 | 74.9 | 49.9 | 21.3 | 1 539 | 82.3 |
| Pierce | 271 | 1.5 | 177 | 0.3 | 178.0 | 591 718 | 3 341 | 86 651 | 115.2 | 75 241 | 33.5 | 66.5 | 39.8 | 16.7 | 4 235 | 67.1 |
| Polk | 289 | -1.4 | 183 | 1.0 | 172.2 | 527 048 | 2 885 | 71 601 | 103.7 | 65 524 | 19.7 | 80.3 | 33.9 | 13.1 | 2 875 | 61.7 |
| Portage | 282 | -3.4 | 264 | 91.7 | 206.8 | 908 590 | 3 440 | 128 456 | 196.1 | 183 914 | 68.2 | 31.8 | 47.7 | 21.7 | 1 860 | 53.6 |
| Price | 102 | -1.9 | 188 | D | 40.4 | 366 093 | 1 948 | 51 180 | 22.3 | 40 900 | 31.2 | 68.8 | 28.6 | 7.7 | 293 | 20.9 |
| Racine | 120 | -3.2 | 185 | 3.5 | 105.0 | 883 553 | 4 782 | 131 796 | 101.9 | 156 324 | 61.3 | 38.7 | 45.1 | 18.3 | 2 081 | 52.8 |
| Richland | 254 | -1.6 | 164 | 1.5 | 118.4 | 462 704 | 2 817 | 62 546 | 84.0 | 54 348 | 17.2 | 82.8 | 30.2 | 12.1 | 2 710 | 63.7 |
| Rock | 344 | 0.0 | 221 | 15.6 | 298.2 | 891 333 | 4 028 | 113 908 | 195.6 | 125 720 | 62.2 | 37.8 | 46.9 | 21.7 | 7 095 | 71.7 |
| Rusk | 161 | -6.9 | 247 | 0.1 | 81.6 | 572 272 | 2 321 | 85 830 | 53.0 | 81 348 | 11.9 | 88.1 | 45.3 | 20.9 | 1 000 | 49.5 |
| St. Croix | 308 | -0.6 | 171 | 4.8 | 222.4 | 650 052 | 3 812 | 80 560 | 142.5 | 78 828 | 22.6 | 77.4 | 33.6 | 13.4 | 4 957 | 66.7 |
| Sauk | 359 | 1.7 | 187 | 15.6 | 209.6 | 633 243 | 3 393 | 92 570 | 179.8 | 93 510 | 23.0 | 77.0 | 42.2 | 17.6 | 4 034 | 60.5 |
| Sawyer | 47 | -13.0 | 204 | 0.6 | 22.5 | 606 685 | 2 976 | 64 633 | 17.4 | 75 148 | 40.6 | 59.4 | 37.2 | 12.1 | 330 | 22.9 |
| Shawano | 272 | 0.4 | 187 | 0.3 | 189.1 | 577 079 | 3 080 | 106 084 | 199.1 | 137 314 | 11.0 | 89.0 | 52.5 | 26.6 | 3 097 | 64.8 |
| Sheboygan | 192 | -1.5 | 181 | 0.1 | 157.6 | 700 484 | 3 869 | 124 039 | 166.9 | 157 569 | 20.3 | 79.7 | 54.3 | 26.3 | 2 134 | 59.2 |
| Taylor | 243 | -5.4 | 201 | 0.1 | 129.8 | 467 348 | 2 324 | 80 630 | 92.4 | 76 489 | 14.6 | 85.4 | 42.7 | 20.9 | 1 561 | 42.9 |
| Trempealeau | 341 | -7.3 | 198 | 5.8 | 192.3 | 518 480 | 2 614 | 82 079 | 192.4 | 111 818 | 16.5 | 83.5 | 39.7 | 18.4 | 4 715 | 75.2 |
| Vernon | 357 | -6.5 | 143 | 0.2 | 187.9 | 425 193 | 2 967 | 59 654 | 167.5 | 67 211 | 18.1 | 81.9 | 40.9 | 13.6 | 3 162 | 47.2 |
| Vilas | 10 | 0.0 | 140 | 1.0 | 3.6 | 696 398 | 4 973 | 87 651 | 8.6 | 120 532 | D | D | 38.0 | 12.7 | 1 | 8.5 |
| Walworth | 218 | -0.9 | 218 | 2.5 | 182.3 | 942 876 | 4 333 | 105 261 | 145.5 | 145 520 | 45.1 | 54.9 | 51.0 | 24.2 | 4 258 | 65.9 |
| Washburn | 102 | -2.9 | 183 | 1.1 | 45.6 | 498 360 | 2 730 | 51 420 | 19.8 | 35 412 | 25.6 | 74.4 | 22.8 | 8.4 | 483 | 30.1 |
| Washington | 130 | 0.0 | 156 | 0.5 | 104.3 | 795 218 | 5 092 | 117 770 | 107.8 | 129 684 | 37.1 | 62.9 | 50.4 | 24.1 | 1 740 | 51.5 |
| Waukesha | 87 | -11.2 | 128 | 1.4 | 69.4 | 703 625 | 5 484 | 83 027 | 45.2 | 67 027 | 67.2 | 32.8 | 36.6 | 14.7 | 1 568 | 36.6 |
| Waupaca | 234 | -5.3 | 176 | 8.6 | 159.8 | 569 244 | 3 230 | 89 366 | 137.0 | 102 973 | 23.1 | 76.9 | 43.2 | 20.0 | 2 580 | 59.3 |
| Waushara | 149 | -22.8 | 220 | 35.6 | 108.9 | 777 250 | 3 532 | 119 149 | 97.5 | 143 982 | 74.4 | 25.6 | 41.4 | 16.1 | 1 071 | 50.4 |
| Winnebago | 164 | -3.5 | 164 | 0.3 | 133.3 | 563 264 | 3 438 | 93 394 | 107.8 | 107 655 | 28.6 | 71.4 | 45.2 | 19.2 | 2 690 | 69.9 |
| Wood | 222 | -2.6 | 199 | 6.9 | 127.0 | 599 051 | 3 007 | 101 330 | 143.9 | 129 201 | 45.6 | 54.4 | 52.3 | 26.6 | 1 727 | 52.8 |
| **WYOMING** | 30 170 | -12.3 | 2 726 | 1 550.7 | 2 576.0 | 1 397 691 | 513 | 97 356 | 1 157.5 | 104 575 | 18.5 | 81.5 | 47.7 | 19.2 | 28 157 | 25.2 |
| Albany | 1 856 | -22.1 | 4 143 | 148.8 | 104.9 | 1 950 763 | 471 | 71 595 | 35.9 | 80 232 | 10.2 | 89.8 | 41.1 | 19.4 | 487 | 7.1 |
| Big Horn | 438 | 6.3 | 705 | 111.0 | 116.5 | 618 696 | 877 | 103 028 | 51.8 | 83 377 | 47.5 | 52.5 | 45.1 | 17.4 | 1 365 | 32.2 |
| Campbell | 2 346 | -21.4 | 3 706 | 4.0 | 170.4 | 1 446 525 | 390 | 96 333 | 41.1 | 64 994 | 8.2 | 91.8 | 42.3 | 17.4 | 1 643 | 23.5 |
| Carbon | 2 173 | -6.7 | 7 570 | 146.5 | 123.5 | 2 377 318 | 314 | 138 927 | 59.8 | 208 509 | 3.3 | 96.7 | 55.4 | 30.3 | 478 | 9.8 |
| Converse | 2 366 | -6.0 | 5 439 | 37.8 | 60.9 | 1 868 944 | 344 | 94 379 | 34.8 | 79 891 | 8.6 | 91.4 | 44.1 | 18.9 | 1 001 | 14.7 |

| STATE County | Water use, 2005 | | Wholesale trade,[1] 2007 | | | | Retail trade,[2] 2007 | | | | Real estate and rental and leasing,[2] 2007 | | | |
|---|---|---|---|---|---|---|---|---|---|---|---|---|---|---|
| | Total water withdrawn (mil gal/day) | Gallons withdrawn per person | Number of establishments | Number of employees | Sales (mil dol) | Annual payroll (mil dol) | Number of establishments | Number of employees | Sales (mil dol) | Annual payroll (mil dol) | Number of establishments | Number of employees | Receipts (mil dol) | Annual payroll (mil dol) |
| | 133 | 134 | 135 | 136 | 137 | 138 | 139 | 140 | 141 | 142 | 143 | 144 | 145 | 146 |
| WISCONSIN—Cont'd | | | | | | | | | | | | | | |
| Dodge | 15.6 | 177 | 68 | 1 064 | 557.8 | 35.5 | 238 | 3 387 | 735.7 | 68.5 | 50 | 136 | 14.0 | 2.6 |
| Door | 6.7 | 237 | 27 | 112 | 40.5 | 4.5 | 284 | 1 771 | 406.3 | 38.7 | 53 | 201 | 19.2 | 3.9 |
| Douglas | 9.2 | 208 | 48 | D | D | D | 163 | 2 174 | 504.5 | 48.9 | 34 | 96 | 10.8 | 1.8 |
| Dunn | 31.9 | 764 | 39 | D | D | D | 125 | 1 640 | 381.8 | 33.0 | 25 | 75 | 6.6 | 1.3 |
| Eau Claire | 18.9 | 200 | 104 | 1 899 | 909.8 | 72.6 | 442 | 7 608 | 1 512.5 | 144.2 | 109 | 683 | 76.8 | 14.4 |
| Florence | 0.4 | 72 | 6 | D | D | D | 17 | 77 | 21.4 | 1.3 | 2 | D | D | D |
| Fond du Lac | 13.5 | 136 | 104 | 1 330 | 993.6 | 59.5 | 407 | 5 999 | 1 277.7 | 118.3 | 77 | 305 | 34.3 | 5.3 |
| Forest | 1.8 | 181 | 7 | 40 | 10.4 | 1.3 | 35 | 301 | 56.6 | 4.5 | 6 | 29 | 3.4 | 0.3 |
| Grant | 264.4 | 5 322 | 62 | 481 | 210.6 | 16.3 | 204 | 2 190 | 480.1 | 41.5 | 50 | 148 | 9.6 | 2.3 |
| Green | 11.0 | 313 | 48 | D | D | D | 155 | 2 338 | 766.6 | 72.2 | 18 | 63 | 7.2 | 1.3 |
| Green Lake | 9.4 | 492 | 16 | 95 | 30.6 | 2.8 | 91 | 1 180 | 252.9 | 23.0 | 13 | 51 | 4.7 | 0.6 |
| Iowa | 10.5 | 446 | 28 | 252 | 150.6 | 12.5 | 108 | 4 385 | 1 707.9 | 164.1 | 13 | D | D | D |
| Iron | 1.0 | 152 | 7 | 90 | 16.3 | 1.9 | 34 | 318 | 74.6 | 6.5 | 9 | 26 | 3.8 | 0.4 |
| Jackson | 7.5 | 378 | 12 | 133 | 31.2 | 3.5 | 74 | 966 | 251.0 | 17.4 | 16 | 30 | 5.7 | 0.5 |
| Jefferson | 30.8 | 388 | 74 | D | D | D | 296 | 4 179 | 857.2 | 76.4 | 74 | 292 | 33.2 | 5.8 |
| Juneau | 12.4 | 465 | 21 | 154 | 51.9 | 3.8 | 95 | 983 | 284.5 | 19.9 | 15 | 66 | 3.8 | 0.8 |
| Kenosha | 30.6 | 191 | 108 | 1 805 | 1 547.8 | 89.0 | 526 | 7 504 | 1 800.6 | 165.7 | 148 | 629 | 87.3 | 12.9 |
| Kewaunee | 828.7 | 39 765 | 10 | 73 | 15.1 | 2.0 | 80 | 640 | 152.9 | 12.1 | 7 | 9 | 0.6 | 0.1 |
| La Crosse | 69.9 | 642 | 129 | D | D | D | 449 | 8 676 | 1 799.7 | 166.7 | 125 | 604 | 82.5 | 14.9 |
| Lafayette | 3.7 | 226 | 16 | 209 | 88.8 | 7.9 | 51 | 452 | 96.8 | 8.8 | 7 | 11 | 0.8 | 0.1 |
| Langlade | 34.8 | 1 679 | 28 | 310 | 438.8 | 14.0 | 109 | 1 350 | 309.2 | 30.6 | 18 | 56 | 6.6 | 1.6 |
| Lincoln | 12.5 | 413 | 19 | D | D | D | 133 | 1 395 | 289.5 | 25.9 | 19 | 73 | 7.1 | 2.4 |
| Manitowoc | 2 142.7 | 26 147 | 65 | D | D | D | 302 | 3 808 | 815.5 | 74.5 | 49 | 346 | 21.6 | 5.4 |
| Marathon | 232.9 | 1 806 | 184 | 2 965 | 1 146.4 | 122.1 | 505 | 10 000 | 2 139.1 | 196.5 | 99 | 473 | 75.4 | 11.9 |
| Marinette | 48.5 | 1 116 | 32 | D | D | D | 214 | 2 616 | 526.9 | 47.4 | 19 | 44 | 8.9 | 0.7 |
| Marquette | 10.4 | 681 | 9 | 47 | 12.2 | 1.3 | 45 | 352 | 79.7 | 6.4 | 13 | 27 | 2.2 | 0.3 |
| Menominee | 1.2 | 251 | NA | NA | NA | NA | 3 | 33 | 5.2 | 0.4 | 1 | D | D | D |
| Milwaukee | 1 224.2 | 1 328 | 904 | 17 503 | 10 955.3 | 871.9 | 2 889 | 46 927 | 10 207.3 | 1 006.5 | 808 | 5 418 | 1 080.4 | 205.4 |
| Monroe | 10.3 | 240 | 38 | 432 | 306.1 | 18.2 | 161 | 1 985 | 502.2 | 41.5 | 29 | 141 | 16.9 | 2.8 |
| Oconto | 8.4 | 224 | 25 | 98 | 28.4 | 2.6 | 123 | 969 | 257.5 | 18.8 | 30 | 94 | 7.6 | 1.6 |
| Oneida | 33.6 | 909 | 34 | 465 | 186.7 | 20.5 | 254 | 3 527 | 921.2 | 81.3 | 56 | 256 | 45.9 | 5.2 |
| Outagamie | 100.7 | 589 | 272 | 4 467 | 3 528.1 | 223.3 | 794 | 13 406 | 2 903.0 | 272.2 | 147 | 793 | 152.3 | 24.0 |
| Ozaukee | 301.7 | 3 506 | 160 | 1 751 | 707.5 | 84.4 | 331 | 4 584 | 976.5 | 99.3 | 111 | 362 | 57.4 | 9.1 |
| Pepin | 3.0 | 412 | 9 | 250 | 134.7 | 7.8 | 40 | 320 | 90.0 | 6.9 | 4 | 4 | 1.3 | 0.2 |
| Pierce | 4.9 | 125 | 21 | D | D | D | 99 | 959 | 208.5 | 18.2 | 35 | 51 | 5.1 | 1.3 |
| Polk | 11.6 | 261 | 26 | 355 | 134.3 | 12.9 | 197 | 2 069 | 423.2 | 39.7 | 40 | 82 | 7.7 | 1.1 |
| Portage | 139.1 | 2 059 | 71 | D | D | D | 257 | 4 518 | 937.9 | 86.4 | 56 | 268 | 31.6 | 6.9 |
| Price | 13.0 | 856 | 16 | 100 | 31.0 | 3.8 | 86 | 622 | 121.1 | 12.8 | 10 | 43 | 3.2 | 0.6 |
| Racine | 42.3 | 216 | 186 | D | D | D | 654 | 10 082 | 2 230.0 | 198.7 | 140 | 596 | 64.5 | 13.4 |
| Richland | 5.5 | 297 | 12 | 55 | 73.6 | 1.5 | 80 | 1 037 | 223.3 | 22.0 | 11 | 36 | 3.1 | 0.6 |
| Rock | 96.0 | 609 | 132 | 3 075 | 2 700.1 | 151.1 | 579 | 9 269 | 2 439.8 | 216.8 | 126 | 432 | 92.6 | 10.3 |
| Rusk | 3.9 | 259 | 7 | 108 | 12.5 | 2.6 | 59 | 889 | 198.4 | 15.5 | 11 | 33 | 1.4 | 0.3 |
| St. Croix | 17.7 | 229 | 83 | 919 | 1 987.0 | 44.7 | 258 | 3 919 | 933.4 | 87.8 | 87 | 244 | 27.2 | 4.5 |
| Sauk | 25.7 | 445 | 61 | D | D | D | 343 | 4 506 | 1 050.9 | 95.8 | 68 | 429 | 80.5 | 16.1 |
| Sawyer | 2.8 | 162 | 16 | 155 | 50.2 | 7.2 | 117 | 1 040 | 224.1 | 21.7 | 37 | 108 | 9.7 | 1.9 |
| Shawano | 8.5 | 206 | 40 | 467 | 256.4 | 18.1 | 144 | 1 636 | 414.0 | 34.6 | 19 | 83 | 6.3 | 1.6 |
| Sheboygan | 402.3 | 3 510 | 88 | 1 206 | 503.5 | 58.1 | 427 | 6 386 | 1 398.7 | 131.5 | 80 | 372 | 73.8 | 12.1 |
| Taylor | 3.3 | 164 | 12 | 83 | 26.0 | 2.7 | 82 | 827 | 189.1 | 14.7 | 11 | 31 | 2.2 | 0.4 |
| Trempealeau | 11.3 | 405 | 31 | 237 | 114.7 | 9.0 | 106 | 1 025 | 251.8 | 21.6 | 8 | 23 | 2.4 | 0.4 |
| Vernon | 215.2 | 7 406 | 21 | 273 | 153.8 | 15.3 | 111 | 1 194 | 250.5 | 24.2 | 17 | 34 | 3.1 | 0.7 |
| Vilas | 8.3 | 372 | 13 | 102 | 29.4 | 3.2 | 198 | 1 381 | 312.2 | 28.5 | 39 | 79 | 15.9 | 3.1 |
| Walworth | 17.4 | 174 | 104 | 1 678 | 1 124.6 | 86.8 | 396 | 4 746 | 1 091.2 | 103.5 | 104 | 405 | 50.8 | 8.5 |
| Washburn | 4.6 | 276 | 13 | 146 | 27.9 | 3.6 | 98 | 762 | 178.1 | 15.5 | 21 | 65 | 10.7 | 1.8 |
| Washington | 13.8 | 110 | 156 | 2 852 | 2 800.5 | 144.1 | 389 | 7 320 | 1 760.0 | 151.4 | 90 | 323 | 56.1 | 8.5 |
| Waukesha | 36.4 | 96 | 913 | 14 527 | 6 882.1 | 788.2 | 1 403 | 27 197 | 5 955.0 | 596.1 | 465 | 3 554 | 480.0 | 114.7 |
| Waupaca | 19.3 | 368 | 33 | 289 | 86.2 | 10.9 | 221 | 2 371 | 516.6 | 49.2 | 33 | 111 | 12.3 | 1.9 |
| Waushara | 52.0 | 2 098 | 16 | 150 | 49.8 | 5.9 | 86 | 768 | 203.0 | 15.2 | 15 | 36 | 3.1 | 0.7 |
| Winnebago | 76.6 | 480 | 160 | 2 536 | 1 109.2 | 102.8 | 540 | 8 027 | 1 796.5 | 162.1 | 125 | 756 | 97.5 | 19.6 |
| Wood | 268.8 | 3 573 | 57 | 1 591 | 893.2 | 90.5 | 337 | 4 542 | 1 002.9 | 95.7 | 65 | 238 | 39.5 | 5.3 |
| WYOMING | 4 591.9 | 9 016 | 705 | 6 347 | 6 352.9 | 306.6 | 2 951 | 32 033 | 8 957.6 | 758.1 | 1 121 | 4 651 | 991.6 | 159.7 |
| Albany | 275.1 | 8 906 | 21 | 149 | 113.5 | 4.7 | 170 | 1 927 | 468.8 | 38.6 | 56 | 158 | 23.8 | 3.4 |
| Big Horn | 385.4 | 34 004 | 7 | D | D | D | 53 | 377 | 71.0 | 6.3 | 13 | 27 | 2.0 | 0.3 |
| Campbell | 109.1 | 2 917 | 93 | 1 219 | 917.3 | 68.7 | 191 | 2 490 | 775.1 | 63.3 | 71 | 375 | 90.1 | 11.7 |
| Carbon | 366.9 | 23 932 | 9 | 47 | 51.5 | 1.5 | 96 | 819 | 295.3 | 18.5 | 28 | 92 | 28.2 | 1.6 |
| Converse | 305.5 | 23 928 | 10 | D | D | D | 65 | 511 | 134.3 | 10.0 | 22 | 53 | 5.0 | 0.8 |

1. Merchant wholesalers, except manufacturers' sales branches and offices.  2. Employer establishments.

# Table B. States and Counties — Professional Services, Manufacturing, and Accommodation and Food Services

| STATE County | Professional, scientific, and technical services,[1] 2007 | | | | Manufacturing, 2007 | | | | Accommodation and food services, 2007 | | | |
|---|---|---|---|---|---|---|---|---|---|---|---|---|
| | Number of establishments | Number of employees | Receipts (mil dol) | Annual payroll (mil dol) | Number of establishments | Number of employees | Receipts (mil dol) | Annual payroll (mil dol) | Number of establishments | Number of employees | Sales (mil dol) | Annual payroll (mil dol) |
| | 147 | 148 | 149 | 150 | 151 | 152 | 153 | 154 | 155 | 156 | 157 | 158 |
| WISCONSIN—Cont'd | | | | | | | | | | | | |
| Dodge | 79 | 558 | 63.1 | 25.1 | 155 | 9 924 | 3 094.4 | 429.8 | 179 | 2 148 | 66.1 | 18.1 |
| Door | 78 | 324 | 30.5 | 12.0 | 59 | 2 204 | 432.8 | 85.8 | 250 | 2 120 | 130.1 | 35.4 |
| Douglas | 65 | D | D | D | 49 | 1 246 | 1 311.6 | 57.9 | 167 | 2 126 | 76.6 | 20.5 |
| Dunn | 56 | 349 | 32.7 | 13.4 | 56 | 2 768 | 1 613.5 | 117.1 | 98 | 1 425 | 42.6 | 11.9 |
| Eau Claire | 179 | 1 205 | 124.3 | 54.4 | 97 | 5 578 | 1 534.0 | 221.9 | 260 | 4 893 | 170.3 | 49.5 |
| Florence | 7 | D | D | D | NA | NA | NA | NA | 27 | 165 | 4.6 | 1.1 |
| Fond du Lac | 157 | 1 320 | 101.9 | 65.4 | 151 | 9 745 | 2 903.2 | 392.3 | 242 | 4 001 | 131.5 | 37.5 |
| Forest | 9 | 81 | 8.9 | 2.8 | NA | NA | NA | NA | 39 | D | D | D |
| Grant | 75 | 458 | 43.5 | 18.2 | 73 | 2 390 | D | 82.0 | 139 | 1 297 | 40.9 | 10.3 |
| Green | 64 | D | D | D | 80 | 2 722 | 925.8 | 95.9 | 89 | 956 | 33.5 | 8.8 |
| Green Lake | 29 | 112 | 9.1 | 3.1 | 41 | 1 636 | 321.5 | 58.2 | 58 | 655 | 22.4 | 7.3 |
| Iowa | 48 | D | D | D | 37 | 874 | 395.5 | D | 61 | 609 | 25.9 | 7.1 |
| Iron | 9 | D | D | D | NA | NA | NA | NA | 57 | D | D | D |
| Jackson | 28 | 119 | 8.0 | 3.4 | 27 | 947 | 229.1 | 28.6 | 59 | 659 | 23.2 | 6.1 |
| Jefferson | 123 | 645 | 82.7 | 23.7 | 154 | 9 430 | 3 674.3 | 387.6 | 204 | 2 475 | 86.4 | 22.8 |
| Juneau | 21 | 85 | 6.5 | 3.3 | 46 | 1 720 | 374.9 | 63.7 | 81 | 666 | 28.3 | 7.5 |
| Kenosha | 208 | D | D | D | 197 | 7 716 | 3 093.7 | 353.0 | 362 | 5 419 | 214.0 | 59.3 |
| Kewaunee | 27 | D | D | D | 44 | 1 923 | 408.1 | 79.1 | 51 | 513 | 14.4 | 3.9 |
| La Crosse | 225 | D | D | D | 166 | 7 109 | D | 254.6 | 313 | 6 067 | 214.4 | 63.0 |
| Lafayette | 15 | 52 | 5.5 | 1.5 | 21 | 525 | 209.7 | 17.4 | 37 | D | D | D |
| Langlade | 21 | 126 | 7.4 | 3.8 | 54 | 1 684 | 372.3 | 60.5 | 69 | 625 | 25.3 | 6.5 |
| Lincoln | 29 | 124 | 9.1 | 3.8 | 53 | 3 135 | D | 121.1 | 97 | 780 | 27.2 | 6.9 |
| Manitowoc | 98 | 596 | 66.4 | 21.4 | 197 | 11 319 | 3 018.8 | 459.1 | 177 | 2 699 | 82.4 | 23.4 |
| Marathon | 235 | D | D | D | 250 | 18 678 | D | 765.6 | 321 | 4 813 | 173.7 | 48.8 |
| Marinette | 49 | 217 | 19.3 | 8.2 | 90 | 6 520 | 1 784.2 | 276.9 | 153 | 1 466 | 54.4 | 14.4 |
| Marquette | 16 | 50 | 4.3 | 1.3 | 25 | 1 260 | 254.8 | 49.1 | 48 | D | D | D |
| Menominee | 2 | D | D | D | NA | NA | NA | NA | 1 | D | D | D |
| Milwaukee | 2 024 | 24 421 | 3 245.0 | 1 426.3 | 1 164 | 60 678 | 19 065.4 | 3 148.4 | 1 913 | 35 759 | 1 570.6 | 442.9 |
| Monroe | 53 | 278 | 23.4 | 8.8 | 65 | 3 644 | 1 055.8 | 124.8 | 116 | 1 791 | 71.4 | 20.3 |
| Oconto | 50 | D | D | D | 62 | 2 069 | 400.5 | 66.5 | 105 | 793 | 28.2 | 7.5 |
| Oneida | 89 | 351 | 33.5 | 12.9 | 55 | 1 439 | 494.2 | 64.9 | 200 | 1 796 | 84.1 | 21.3 |
| Outagamie | 357 | 4 411 | 478.4 | 188.3 | 349 | 18 954 | 6 802.6 | 875.2 | 438 | 8 070 | 296.1 | 82.4 |
| Ozaukee | 357 | D | D | D | 222 | 10 712 | 3 161.9 | 540.1 | 203 | 3 558 | 124.9 | 38.4 |
| Pepin | 11 | 38 | 2.9 | 1.1 | NA | NA | NA | NA | 29 | D | D | D |
| Pierce | 71 | D | D | D | 54 | 1 217 | 529.0 | 53.4 | 92 | 972 | 32.9 | 8.4 |
| Polk | 73 | D | D | D | 116 | 4 143 | 958.5 | 149.4 | 129 | 1 158 | 41.8 | 11.2 |
| Portage | 107 | D | D | D | 86 | 4 636 | 1 449.5 | 185.3 | 187 | 2 908 | 97.0 | 27.1 |
| Price | 26 | 101 | 7.9 | 2.9 | 49 | 2 317 | 529.4 | 82.5 | 45 | D | D | D |
| Racine | 346 | D | D | D | 345 | 17 183 | 7 863.3 | 890.8 | 388 | 6 239 | 242.7 | 66.1 |
| Richland | 23 | 66 | 4.9 | 1.6 | 32 | 1 827 | 613.1 | 73.6 | 38 | D | D | D |
| Rock | 199 | D | D | D | 236 | 13 527 | 12 381.6 | 720.3 | 383 | 5 673 | 211.7 | 58.6 |
| Rusk | 14 | 48 | 3.2 | 1.0 | 24 | 1 735 | 301.2 | 54.2 | 26 | D | D | D |
| St. Croix | 206 | D | D | D | 169 | 5 973 | 1 347.3 | 245.7 | 198 | 3 239 | 110.9 | 32.4 |
| Sauk | 123 | D | D | D | 92 | 5 942 | 1 638.3 | 224.0 | 258 | 7 494 | 462.1 | 122.5 |
| Sawyer | 37 | 148 | 13.6 | 5.3 | 46 | 621 | 180.9 | 28.6 | 128 | 1 222 | 74.7 | 20.6 |
| Shawano | 37 | 236 | 15.5 | 6.0 | 74 | 2 252 | 582.0 | 87.3 | 120 | 1 290 | 42.7 | 11.0 |
| Sheboygan | 176 | 1 743 | 209.1 | 70.5 | 246 | 18 774 | 6 126.1 | 816.0 | 271 | 4 869 | 193.0 | 54.8 |
| Taylor | 16 | 89 | 8.9 | 3.6 | 44 | 3 142 | 630.7 | 106.0 | 44 | D | D | D |
| Trempealeau | 37 | 199 | 13.8 | 5.9 | 66 | 6 224 | 1 438.9 | 234.4 | 80 | D | D | D |
| Vernon | 44 | 161 | 12.4 | 4.1 | 36 | 778 | 178.4 | 28.0 | 60 | D | D | D |
| Vilas | 44 | 138 | 18.0 | 5.7 | NA | NA | NA | NA | 231 | 2 691 | 161.6 | 47.3 |
| Walworth | 187 | 924 | 85.4 | 34.9 | 212 | 8 944 | 2 247.4 | 381.9 | 293 | 5 925 | 267.2 | 76.4 |
| Washburn | 34 | 157 | 14.5 | 5.6 | 33 | 1 005 | D | 40.1 | 88 | 681 | 25.3 | 6.7 |
| Washington | 225 | D | D | D | 331 | 14 138 | 3 393.4 | 615.3 | 259 | 4 495 | 152.9 | 42.5 |
| Waukesha | 1 361 | D | D | D | 1 023 | 45 147 | 15 663.5 | 2 286.8 | 819 | 15 832 | 616.6 | 177.5 |
| Waupaca | 61 | 337 | 25.5 | 9.6 | 97 | 6 303 | 2 133.6 | 275.0 | 145 | 1 645 | 55.6 | 14.9 |
| Waushara | 19 | 103 | 6.1 | 2.6 | 35 | 772 | 111.3 | 25.3 | 75 | 787 | 25.1 | 7.3 |
| Winnebago | 250 | D | D | D | 319 | 23 777 | 9 198.9 | 1 149.8 | 377 | 6 071 | 212.1 | 58.4 |
| Wood | 97 | D | D | D | 126 | 6 990 | 2 562.6 | 311.7 | 193 | 2 373 | 84.3 | 24.2 |
| WYOMING | 1 890 | 8 711 | 1 079.3 | 387.5 | 596 | 11 904 | 8 834.8 | 573.7 | 1 768 | 26 992 | 1 469.0 | 411.9 |
| Albany | 114 | D | D | D | NA | NA | NA | NA | 105 | 1 608 | 65.8 | 18.1 |
| Big Horn | 20 | 83 | 4.5 | 1.9 | NA | NA | NA | NA | 28 | 202 | 5.6 | 1.5 |
| Campbell | 116 | 711 | 70.9 | 28.9 | 36 | 716 | 262.5 | 36.6 | 79 | 1 713 | 89.2 | 23.3 |
| Carbon | 34 | 92 | 10.9 | 4.3 | NA | NA | NA | NA | 80 | 791 | 42.9 | 11.2 |
| Converse | 23 | 74 | 10.8 | 2.1 | NA | NA | NA | NA | 36 | 490 | 20.9 | 5.2 |

1. Establishment subject to federal tax.

| STATE County | Health care and social assistance, 2007 | | | | Other services, 2007 | | | | Federal funds and grants, 2009–2010 Expenditures (mil dol) | | | |
|---|---|---|---|---|---|---|---|---|---|---|---|---|
| | | | | | | | | | | Direct payments for individuals[1] | | |
| | Number of establishments | Number of employees | Receipts (mil dol) | Annual payroll (mil dol) | Number of establishments | Number of employees | Receipts (mil dol) | Annual payroll (mil dol) | Total | Social Security and government retirement | Medicare | Food Stamps and Supplemental Security Income |
| | 159 | 160 | 161 | 162 | 163 | 164 | 165 | 166 | 167 | 168 | 169 | 170 |
| WISCONSIN—Cont'd | | | | | | | | | | | | |
| Dodge | 207 | 4 080 | 318.3 | 138.0 | 146 | 1 209 | 39.1 | 32.6 | 406.6 | 188.6 | 88.9 | 9.1 |
| Door | 68 | 1 360 | 99.9 | 44.0 | 91 | 736 | 42.9 | 11.1 | 309.4 | 117.8 | 53.5 | 4.0 |
| Douglas | 114 | 2 153 | 143.6 | 57.9 | 81 | 518 | 28.1 | 8.8 | 395.4 | 166.7 | 74.7 | 18.9 |
| Dunn | 93 | 2 327 | 143.8 | 64.6 | 72 | 330 | 19.7 | 7.7 | 257.2 | 107.7 | 38.6 | 11.0 |
| Eau Claire | 315 | 9 957 | 981.7 | 441.6 | 211 | 1 181 | 94.2 | 27.0 | 669.7 | 285.7 | 120.5 | 28.6 |
| Florence | 3 | D | D | D | 5 | D | D | D | 36.1 | 16.3 | 8.0 | 1.0 |
| Fond du Lac | 266 | 6 180 | 607.2 | 223.9 | 193 | 1 206 | 88.4 | 24.4 | 626.2 | 314.9 | 134.3 | 14.8 |
| Forest | 18 | 310 | 10.6 | 5.7 | 14 | 45 | 3.4 | 0.7 | 107.8 | 39.4 | 16.9 | 2.9 |
| Grant | 103 | 2 299 | 130.7 | 58.4 | 117 | 409 | 38.7 | 7.7 | 371.0 | 154.9 | 80.2 | 7.4 |
| Green | 70 | 1 988 | 166.1 | 71.1 | 78 | D | D | D | 210.8 | 103.6 | 48.4 | 5.3 |
| Green Lake | 50 | 1 086 | 84.4 | 36.9 | 39 | 147 | 9.0 | 2.7 | 157.7 | 69.2 | 34.9 | 3.1 |
| Iowa | 56 | 1 043 | 67.5 | 27.5 | 36 | 130 | 9.6 | 2.5 | 137.6 | 58.8 | 24.3 | 3.3 |
| Iron | 12 | 279 | 10.9 | 6.7 | 13 | D | D | D | 62.5 | 26.6 | 15.0 | 1.5 |
| Jackson | 37 | 918 | 61.4 | 28.4 | 29 | 127 | 7.3 | 2.0 | 150.6 | 63.4 | 26.1 | 5.6 |
| Jefferson | 208 | 3 809 | 268.8 | 118.9 | 145 | 774 | 45.7 | 13.8 | 519.1 | 247.0 | 112.2 | 8.8 |
| Juneau | 48 | 1 115 | 86.5 | 37.3 | 48 | 199 | 18.8 | 4.7 | 254.0 | 99.7 | 41.8 | 7.7 |
| Kenosha | 401 | 8 243 | 692.6 | 291.2 | 252 | 1 578 | 92.5 | 29.7 | 1 009.8 | 420.4 | 207.9 | 48.7 |
| Kewaunee | 37 | 486 | 18.0 | 8.7 | 33 | 65 | 7.5 | 1.5 | 129.0 | 63.3 | 29.0 | 2.1 |
| La Crosse | 271 | D | D | D | 233 | D | D | D | 781.3 | 321.0 | 123.6 | 31.7 |
| Lafayette | 21 | 283 | 18.4 | 5.7 | 22 | 146 | 15.7 | 4.1 | 117.0 | 42.9 | 24.3 | 2.2 |
| Langlade | 53 | 943 | 95.3 | 34.4 | 55 | 216 | 12.2 | 3.6 | 180.9 | 76.2 | 39.5 | 4.7 |
| Lincoln | 64 | D | D | D | 54 | D | D | D | 263.0 | 114.7 | 51.6 | 6.1 |
| Manitowoc | 191 | 4 811 | 358.8 | 171.3 | 140 | 621 | 46.6 | 12.5 | 551.1 | 263.9 | 128.8 | 14.0 |
| Marathon | 345 | 9 438 | 926.4 | 379.0 | 253 | 1 591 | 139.1 | 36.2 | 828.7 | 350.2 | 152.5 | 30.7 |
| Marinette | 115 | 2 700 | 208.5 | 93.3 | 82 | D | D | D | 536.7 | 182.1 | 74.8 | 10.2 |
| Marquette | 29 | 311 | 13.3 | 6.4 | 32 | 384 | 32.9 | 11.3 | 147.9 | 73.6 | 29.7 | 3.4 |
| Menominee | NA | NA | NA | NA | 2 | D | D | D | 68.4 | 10.5 | 5.2 | 4.5 |
| Milwaukee | 3 129 | 84 815 | 8 090.0 | 3 381.2 | 1 613 | 12 259 | 1 464.3 | 359.9 | 9 118.4 | 2 362.8 | 1 859.7 | 763.1 |
| Monroe | 77 | 2 387 | 181.4 | 95.4 | 66 | 371 | 25.7 | 7.5 | 774.6 | 168.8 | 48.9 | 9.5 |
| Oconto | 72 | 1 279 | 84.6 | 35.5 | 41 | 114 | 10.4 | 2.2 | 233.5 | 113.8 | 46.6 | 6.6 |
| Oneida | 118 | 2 972 | 298.8 | 119.9 | 99 | 388 | 31.2 | 8.8 | 332.8 | 172.8 | 68.9 | 8.9 |
| Outagamie | 467 | 11 774 | 1 169.2 | 491.3 | 358 | 2 530 | 217.6 | 59.7 | 937.9 | 480.1 | 148.3 | 21.8 |
| Ozaukee | 278 | 4 369 | 395.2 | 165.7 | 202 | 1 285 | 78.0 | 25.1 | 436.9 | 270.7 | 94.6 | 4.1 |
| Pepin | 16 | 230 | 19.8 | 7.5 | 16 | D | D | D | 57.9 | 24.7 | 13.4 | 1.0 |
| Pierce | 64 | 738 | 41.6 | 18.6 | 66 | D | D | D | 248.9 | 104.4 | 38.5 | 4.2 |
| Polk | 102 | 2 090 | 163.3 | 69.8 | 77 | 261 | 20.4 | 4.7 | 285.6 | 136.4 | 58.6 | 8.3 |
| Portage | 151 | 3 874 | 299.9 | 126.6 | 131 | 817 | 63.1 | 17.5 | 403.9 | 176.0 | 67.9 | 14.4 |
| Price | 46 | 978 | 47.3 | 22.8 | 34 | 94 | 6.6 | 1.8 | 139.2 | 61.3 | 29.4 | 4.2 |
| Racine | 417 | 11 897 | 946.4 | 478.0 | 343 | 2 167 | 162.7 | 49.1 | 1 319.4 | 599.0 | 262.3 | 65.9 |
| Richland | 43 | 810 | 61.3 | 24.3 | 26 | 113 | 7.8 | 2.0 | 129.1 | 50.8 | 26.8 | 4.3 |
| Rock | 330 | 9 276 | 878.5 | 337.0 | 285 | 1 578 | 108.7 | 30.6 | 1 258.0 | 478.3 | 210.7 | 48.9 |
| Rusk | 28 | 899 | 66.8 | 24.5 | 20 | D | D | D | 138.2 | 52.3 | 24.9 | 6.3 |
| St. Croix | 157 | 3 042 | 282.0 | 108.2 | 145 | D | D | D | 321.2 | 177.5 | 52.4 | 7.0 |
| Sauk | 143 | 3 776 | 286.8 | 124.6 | 144 | 492 | 42.9 | 13.4 | 420.6 | 178.4 | 80.2 | 8.6 |
| Sawyer | 38 | 642 | 50.0 | 21.8 | 46 | 190 | 12.9 | 3.6 | 173.2 | 67.4 | 28.8 | 7.1 |
| Shawano | 79 | 1 482 | 115.5 | 42.6 | 71 | 247 | 16.3 | 4.8 | 297.1 | 134.1 | 59.5 | 7.3 |
| Sheboygan | 292 | 6 709 | 501.4 | 242.7 | 217 | 1 093 | 76.8 | 20.2 | 765.1 | 334.6 | 141.0 | 18.9 |
| Taylor | 40 | 1 005 | 64.3 | 28.6 | 36 | 122 | 9.4 | 2.2 | 134.3 | 51.3 | 27.7 | 3.8 |
| Trempealeau | 53 | 1 344 | 80.2 | 33.5 | 42 | 133 | 12.0 | 3.1 | 229.4 | 90.3 | 44.2 | 6.4 |
| Vernon | 58 | 1 540 | 106.9 | 44.4 | 47 | 113 | 7.7 | 1.7 | 224.9 | 91.5 | 39.9 | 5.7 |
| Vilas | 45 | 685 | 40.7 | 16.0 | 64 | 329 | 26.5 | 13.8 | 205.1 | 105.0 | 43.5 | 3.1 |
| Walworth | 216 | 4 082 | 284.3 | 120.9 | 209 | 1 025 | 68.6 | 20.2 | 524.1 | 269.3 | 113.6 | 11.8 |
| Washburn | 40 | 862 | 45.8 | 20.5 | 32 | 122 | 9.2 | 2.7 | 191.4 | 89.9 | 28.8 | 4.4 |
| Washington | 253 | 5 876 | 470.4 | 203.1 | 263 | 1 421 | 102.1 | 31.4 | 618.1 | 366.1 | 119.7 | 9.8 |
| Waukesha | 1 219 | 23 720 | 2 271.3 | 960.5 | 848 | 6 424 | 610.5 | 199.0 | 2 157.8 | 1 185.3 | 399.3 | 28.6 |
| Waupaca | 112 | 2 526 | 151.6 | 67.5 | 102 | 339 | 28.3 | 7.0 | 430.8 | 202.6 | 85.5 | 8.6 |
| Waushara | 40 | 803 | 42.3 | 18.0 | 39 | 93 | 7.6 | 1.7 | 176.9 | 85.4 | 36.9 | 6.4 |
| Winnebago | 430 | 12 589 | 1 344.9 | 476.6 | 290 | 2 355 | 199.8 | 61.9 | 8 060.3 | 447.7 | 214.4 | 25.8 |
| Wood | 182 | 9 246 | 1 105.4 | 432.7 | 146 | 731 | 84.9 | 16.6 | 635.7 | 283.5 | 123.7 | 20.9 |
| WYOMING | 1 710 | 29 242 | 2 576.3 | 1 072.8 | 1 385 | 6 526 | 766.2 | 179.3 | 6 210.6 | 1 607.9 | 567.4 | 87.8 |
| Albany | 112 | 1 936 | 157.5 | 64.9 | 89 | 453 | 93.0 | 9.9 | 281.2 | 69.5 | 32.3 | 4.7 |
| Big Horn | 21 | 305 | 18.6 | 8.7 | 22 | 45 | 3.4 | 0.7 | 103.5 | 40.7 | 19.3 | 1.4 |
| Campbell | 85 | 1 583 | 154.8 | 71.9 | 135 | 873 | 118.0 | 32.7 | 132.9 | 61.9 | 17.9 | 3.5 |
| Carbon | 56 | 619 | 55.0 | 19.5 | 39 | 143 | 15.3 | 3.6 | 234.8 | 43.1 | 21.3 | 2.1 |
| Converse | 25 | 538 | 45.3 | 18.7 | 33 | 102 | 9.0 | 2.1 | 67.6 | 36.7 | 11.3 | 2.1 |

1. State totals may include programs not allocated by county.

# Table B. States and Counties — Federal Funds, Residential Construction, and Local Government Finances

| | Federal funds and grants, 2009–2010 (cont.) | | | | | | | Value of residential construction authorized by building permits, 2011 | | Local government finances, 2007 | | | | |
| | Expenditures (mil dol) (cont.) | | | | | | | | | General revenue | | | | |
| | Procurement contract awards | | | Grants[1] | | | | | | | | Taxes | | |
| | | | | | | | | | | | | | Per capita[2] (dollars) | |
| STATE County | Salaries and wages | Defense | Other | Medicaid and other health-related | Nutrition and family welfare | Education | Other | New construction ($1,000) | Number of housing units | Total (mil dol) | Inter-govern-mental (mil dol) | Total (mil dol) | Total | Property |
|---|---|---|---|---|---|---|---|---|---|---|---|---|---|---|
| | 171 | 172 | 173 | 174 | 175 | 176 | 177 | 178 | 179 | 180 | 181 | 182 | 183 | 184 |
| **WISCONSIN—Cont'd** | | | | | | | | | | | | | | |
| Dodge | 36.5 | 0.2 | 5.3 | 44.5 | 9.9 | 5.9 | 5.4 | 18 621 | 113 | 258.5 | 130.8 | 89.0 | 1 014 | 930 |
| Door | 87.0 | 3.4 | 4.3 | 25.6 | 4.0 | 1.4 | 2.5 | 21 814 | 132 | 127.8 | 42.0 | 67.0 | 2 409 | 2 246 |
| Douglas | 18.0 | 0.5 | 3.3 | 75.1 | 13.2 | 4.1 | 10.2 | 11 335 | 77 | 228.6 | 106.8 | 84.5 | 1 933 | 1 795 |
| Dunn | 17.8 | 0.5 | 3.5 | 46.4 | 7.3 | 3.9 | 1.9 | 11 207 | 76 | 154.6 | 76.0 | 49.2 | 1 163 | 1 084 |
| Eau Claire | 32.0 | 16.1 | 8.3 | 115.7 | 15.2 | 6.7 | 10.0 | 29 694 | 229 | 385.1 | 174.6 | 149.6 | 1 536 | 1 409 |
| Florence | 1.4 | 0.0 | 1.7 | 5.9 | 1.3 | 0.2 | 0.1 | 3 365 | 22 | 20.5 | 8.9 | 9.2 | 1 936 | 1 890 |
| Fond du Lac | 23.2 | 7.1 | 5.1 | 78.8 | 14.5 | 6.4 | 4.9 | 29 161 | 237 | 412.3 | 176.1 | 143.4 | 1 447 | 1 409 |
| Forest | 6.4 | 0.0 | 2.6 | 24.7 | 3.4 | 1.7 | 7.8 | 4 299 | 34 | 43.0 | 20.7 | 18.7 | 1 906 | 1 849 |
| Grant | 16.0 | 0.1 | 3.2 | 65.6 | 8.1 | 4.3 | 3.2 | 11 833 | 96 | 199.8 | 103.5 | 57.5 | 1 179 | 1 118 |
| Green | 8.9 | 0.0 | 2.4 | 25.6 | 4.8 | 2.6 | 0.2 | 3 110 | 17 | 139.6 | 67.5 | 45.4 | 1 271 | 1 180 |
| Green Lake | 8.3 | 3.9 | 9.3 | 21.4 | 3.0 | 1.0 | 0.1 | 8 278 | 38 | 78.2 | 32.4 | 35.5 | 1 897 | 1 790 |
| Iowa | 12.2 | 0.1 | 1.6 | 21.4 | 5.2 | 1.2 | 2.7 | 5 587 | 32 | 85.6 | 40.1 | 32.0 | 1 359 | 1 272 |
| Iron | 2.4 | 0.0 | 0.4 | 14.2 | 1.7 | 0.4 | 0.1 | 4 448 | 25 | 32.4 | 16.3 | 12.1 | 1 922 | 1 790 |
| Jackson | 4.3 | 0.0 | 1.0 | 37.8 | 5.0 | 1.6 | 0.8 | 5 473 | 52 | 78.6 | 44.8 | 20.8 | 1 045 | 962 |
| Jefferson | 29.6 | 21.8 | 5.8 | 68.4 | 9.7 | 4.5 | 0.6 | 16 488 | 85 | 297.9 | 129.3 | 110.8 | 1 381 | 1 275 |
| Juneau | 43.3 | 8.4 | 2.5 | 37.7 | 5.0 | 1.9 | 1.8 | 16 860 | 95 | 99.4 | 53.1 | 34.5 | 1 298 | 1 211 |
| Kenosha | 39.6 | 65.7 | 14.4 | 121.4 | 24.9 | 10.1 | 22.9 | 35 767 | 227 | 753.1 | 346.2 | 295.4 | 1 813 | 1 702 |
| Kewaunee | 4.6 | 1.4 | 1.0 | 15.1 | 2.9 | 1.1 | 2.7 | 6 162 | 34 | 79.3 | 40.9 | 24.6 | 1 196 | 1 176 |
| La Crosse | 52.8 | 39.0 | 31.3 | 110.9 | 19.9 | 7.4 | 13.2 | 37 875 | 278 | 517.1 | 238.8 | 175.8 | 1 578 | 1 447 |
| Lafayette | 4.8 | 0.0 | 1.1 | 19.7 | 2.9 | 1.2 | 1.8 | 2 508 | 18 | 83.9 | 41.2 | 18.8 | 1 189 | 1 137 |
| Langlade | 6.4 | 2.4 | 1.2 | 39.4 | 5.1 | 1.7 | 1.0 | 2 805 | 33 | 81.7 | 40.8 | 28.0 | 1 381 | 1 289 |
| Lincoln | 20.7 | 16.0 | 1.4 | 38.9 | 5.8 | 1.7 | 4.3 | 7 275 | 57 | 117.5 | 54.4 | 38.2 | 1 287 | 1 211 |
| Manitowoc | 23.1 | 0.3 | 10.7 | 79.0 | 10.9 | 4.6 | 2.1 | 17 035 | 94 | 293.9 | 151.0 | 86.5 | 1 069 | 1 040 |
| Marathon | 72.1 | 2.2 | 42.5 | 122.5 | 19.4 | 6.0 | 6.0 | 46 349 | 276 | 538.7 | 241.1 | 193.6 | 1 489 | 1 374 |
| Marinette | 18.3 | 2.7 | 163.0 | 65.5 | 8.1 | 2.3 | 1.3 | 12 484 | 80 | 160.9 | 75.3 | 57.3 | 1 345 | 1 250 |
| Marquette | 4.4 | 0.1 | 1.8 | 14.4 | 2.7 | 0.7 | 13.9 | 3 359 | 22 | 49.3 | 22.0 | 22.5 | 1 502 | 1 428 |
| Menominee | 0.7 | 0.0 | 0.4 | 11.7 | 4.9 | 8.7 | 7.1 | 332 | 3 | 26.6 | 20.4 | 5.3 | 1 139 | 1 133 |
| Milwaukee | 637.2 | 142.9 | 377.9 | 1 845.2 | 278.2 | 104.3 | 552.7 | 91 560 | 802 | 4 546.0 | 2 114.9 | 1 522.4 | 1 600 | 1 476 |
| Monroe | 241.8 | 204.5 | 21.8 | 57.4 | 7.2 | 2.8 | 5.8 | 16 699 | 157 | 162.4 | 90.1 | 46.7 | 1 084 | 989 |
| Oconto | 8.2 | 0.0 | 2.0 | 38.7 | 6.3 | 2.0 | 1.1 | 15 287 | 137 | 122.9 | 62.4 | 43.9 | 1 172 | 1 107 |
| Oneida | 16.2 | 0.6 | 5.4 | 41.5 | 10.4 | 2.8 | 1.3 | 26 984 | 142 | 168.5 | 44.4 | 102.9 | 2 839 | 2 683 |
| Outagamie | 37.3 | 48.2 | 21.6 | 101.5 | 18.2 | 8.6 | 22.9 | 73 624 | 585 | 781.1 | 360.3 | 279.2 | 1 607 | 1 568 |
| Ozaukee | 13.6 | 2.4 | 4.3 | 20.9 | 7.8 | 3.3 | 4.9 | 41 234 | 132 | 314.2 | 89.2 | 167.3 | 1 954 | 1 818 |
| Pepin | 2.0 | 0.0 | 0.5 | 11.7 | 1.6 | 0.5 | 0.5 | 2 821 | 15 | 33.6 | 18.9 | 11.1 | 1 500 | 1 431 |
| Pierce | 20.6 | 19.9 | 2.2 | 34.8 | 5.9 | 3.6 | 0.4 | 10 603 | 66 | 160.3 | 76.1 | 59.2 | 1 495 | 1 413 |
| Polk | 10.7 | 4.6 | 3.7 | 45.2 | 8.2 | 2.0 | 0.5 | 7 304 | 46 | 178.6 | 78.9 | 71.2 | 1 609 | 1 515 |
| Portage | 33.1 | 0.6 | 3.4 | 53.5 | 13.0 | 4.2 | 7.8 | 18 079 | 131 | 250.3 | 126.0 | 81.8 | 1 199 | 1 091 |
| Price | 7.3 | 0.0 | 2.0 | 29.3 | 3.6 | 0.7 | 0.2 | 6 607 | 46 | 61.5 | 32.1 | 22.2 | 1 533 | 1 460 |
| Racine | 53.3 | 54.5 | 10.7 | 196.2 | 34.6 | 13.0 | 18.6 | 28 343 | 107 | 724.8 | 359.2 | 255.6 | 1 310 | 1 266 |
| Richland | 6.0 | 0.1 | 1.0 | 31.9 | 3.1 | 1.0 | 1.3 | 2 796 | 22 | 73.4 | 31.3 | 17.7 | 976 | 905 |
| Rock | 40.5 | 204.1 | 16.2 | 176.1 | 29.3 | 13.4 | 15.9 | 18 301 | 99 | 656.4 | 360.8 | 202.7 | 1 270 | 1 232 |
| Rusk | 6.9 | 0.1 | 2.1 | 32.8 | 6.5 | 1.2 | 2.2 | 7 676 | 45 | 89.4 | 40.5 | 17.0 | 1 163 | 1 079 |
| St. Croix | 23.3 | 0.7 | 4.8 | 30.3 | 7.7 | 2.1 | 5.9 | 26 226 | 159 | 266.1 | 115.8 | 109.1 | 1 345 | 1 229 |
| Sauk | 32.1 | 28.1 | 11.0 | 53.7 | 8.1 | 2.8 | 11.0 | 17 510 | 118 | 246.4 | 104.9 | 105.8 | 1 809 | 1 491 |
| Sawyer | 11.5 | 0.1 | 1.0 | 29.4 | 5.3 | 4.2 | 6.3 | 12 160 | 80 | 67.4 | 24.9 | 34.8 | 2 038 | 1 891 |
| Shawano | 10.6 | 0.0 | 2.3 | 60.2 | 6.9 | 3.2 | 3.0 | 7 202 | 54 | 140.7 | 74.1 | 42.4 | 1 033 | 962 |
| Sheboygan | 28.1 | 38.1 | 90.0 | 78.4 | 16.4 | 5.6 | 4.7 | 15 459 | 73 | 493.2 | 225.5 | 180.9 | 1 580 | 1 523 |
| Taylor | 13.6 | 2.2 | 1.1 | 20.5 | 3.8 | 1.1 | 2.6 | 3 391 | 37 | 70.5 | 41.6 | 21.1 | 1 090 | 1 029 |
| Trempealeau | 17.0 | 0.3 | 1.9 | 51.7 | 9.2 | 1.7 | 0.9 | 8 610 | 64 | 142.6 | 75.2 | 36.6 | 1 314 | 1 235 |
| Vernon | 9.5 | 3.7 | 2.0 | 55.4 | 5.4 | 2.4 | 3.1 | 5 971 | 45 | 106.6 | 55.5 | 30.1 | 1 039 | 975 |
| Vilas | 5.4 | 0.1 | 2.9 | 26.4 | 5.3 | 3.9 | 6.5 | 24 162 | 123 | 84.7 | 20.2 | 54.4 | 2 463 | 2 309 |
| Walworth | 24.6 | 0.7 | 4.6 | 56.2 | 11.6 | 5.3 | 5.9 | 39 081 | 122 | 387.8 | 128.2 | 198.0 | 1 964 | 1 812 |
| Washburn | 9.9 | 9.7 | 2.2 | 31.3 | 3.8 | 1.2 | 1.1 | 6 766 | 51 | 72.9 | 25.2 | 36.3 | 2 174 | 2 035 |
| Washington | 34.6 | 1.2 | 8.1 | 50.7 | 13.6 | 4.9 | 4.1 | 40 239 | 202 | 432.5 | 161.7 | 201.1 | 1 569 | 1 448 |
| Waukesha | 97.2 | 146.4 | 54.5 | 120.9 | 37.8 | 15.3 | 42.7 | 141 293 | 457 | 1 415.4 | 404.5 | 788.3 | 2 078 | 2 010 |
| Waupaca | 22.8 | 29.3 | 2.8 | 54.1 | 8.5 | 2.8 | 8.3 | 17 176 | 96 | 212.4 | 109.5 | 73.1 | 1 404 | 1 329 |
| Waushara | 5.0 | 0.0 | 1.2 | 31.9 | 4.4 | 1.0 | 0.0 | 6 108 | 47 | 79.7 | 37.2 | 33.2 | 1 340 | 1 269 |
| Winnebago | 82.1 | 7 100.1 | 11.7 | 112.5 | 23.6 | 7.7 | 10.5 | 49 954 | 385 | 566.0 | 263.6 | 202.6 | 1 249 | 1 209 |
| Wood | 24.0 | 0.4 | 6.7 | 100.0 | 13.2 | 4.7 | 44.9 | 13 570 | 91 | 323.0 | 161.2 | 112.3 | 1 519 | 1 426 |
| **WYOMING** | 709.3 | 155.4 | 414.0 | 441.9 | 114.6 | 134.2 | 1 563.4 | 425 156 | 2 114 | X | X | X | X | X |
| Albany | 24.7 | 7.7 | 5.4 | 41.2 | 5.6 | 10.5 | 50.2 | 41 320 | 463 | 169.4 | 60.7 | 32.2 | 1 001 | 544 |
| Big Horn | 7.9 | 9.1 | 2.3 | 15.1 | 1.9 | 0.7 | -0.2 | 1 719 | 12 | 98.1 | 59.8 | 15.3 | 1 361 | 1 145 |
| Campbell | 15.8 | 0.0 | 15.2 | 5.9 | 4.7 | 2.6 | 3.1 | 75 429 | 201 | 453.7 | 82.5 | 217.4 | 5 378 | 4 185 |
| Carbon | 13.1 | 0.0 | 131.0 | 17.4 | 3.4 | 0.8 | 1.0 | 6 208 | 28 | 126.7 | 39.3 | 55.2 | 3 562 | 2 496 |
| Converse | 5.7 | 0.0 | 0.5 | 7.0 | 1.7 | 0.5 | 0.3 | 4 911 | 47 | 88.4 | 36.0 | 26.6 | 2 064 | 1 706 |

1. State totals may include programs not allocated by county.    2. Based on the resident population estimated as of July 1 of the year shown.

# Table B. States and Counties — Local Government Finances, Government Employment, and Voting

| STATE County | Direct general expenditure — Total (mil dol) 185 | Per capita[1] (dollars) 186 | Education 187 | Health and hospitals 188 | Police protection 189 | Public welfare 190 | Highways 191 | Debt outstanding — Total (mil dol) 192 | Per capita[1] (dollars) 193 | Federal civilian 194 | Federal military 195 | State and local 196 | Democratic 197 | Republican 198 | All other 199 |
|---|---|---|---|---|---|---|---|---|---|---|---|---|---|---|---|
| WISCONSIN—Cont'd | | | | | | | | | | | | | | | |
| Dodge | 256.8 | 2 925 | 33.9 | 6.1 | 6.0 | 12.6 | 12.8 | 205.8 | 2 344 | 187 | 248 | 4 751 | 44.8 | 53.7 | 1.5 |
| Door | 135.0 | 4 855 | 34.1 | 7.1 | 5.2 | 3.3 | 13.1 | 143.8 | 5 169 | 80 | 149 | 1 683 | 58.0 | 40.7 | 1.3 |
| Douglas | 227.4 | 5 202 | 53.5 | 5.9 | 4.8 | 4.6 | 8.5 | 263.5 | 6 027 | 150 | 124 | 3 151 | 65.8 | 32.6 | 1.7 |
| Dunn | 158.9 | 3 754 | 38.9 | 1.9 | 5.2 | 16.9 | 12.8 | 108.2 | 2 557 | 92 | 123 | 4 306 | 56.6 | 41.6 | 1.8 |
| Eau Claire | 398.1 | 4 087 | 53.9 | 6.0 | 5.3 | 4.5 | 8.1 | 218.8 | 2 246 | 372 | 280 | 7 847 | 60.3 | 38.1 | 1.6 |
| Florence | 18.7 | 3 925 | 37.9 | 9.7 | 5.4 | 0.5 | 16.9 | 11.1 | 2 320 | 21 | 12 | 259 | 42.2 | 56.3 | 1.5 |
| Fond du Lac | 425.1 | 4 289 | 50.7 | 12.4 | 4.9 | 4.6 | 6.8 | 370.8 | 3 740 | 213 | 285 | 5 527 | 44.8 | 53.8 | 1.3 |
| Forest | 41.4 | 4 222 | 52.4 | 3.2 | 4.6 | 4.5 | 15.2 | 12.5 | 1 270 | 105 | 26 | 1 623 | 57.1 | 41.9 | 1.0 |
| Grant | 204.7 | 4 195 | 52.0 | 6.5 | 3.8 | 8.3 | 11.4 | 104.5 | 2 142 | 157 | 143 | 5 001 | 61.2 | 37.3 | 1.6 |
| Green | 144.0 | 4 030 | 43.5 | 3.6 | 5.8 | 12.1 | 13.3 | 102.1 | 2 858 | 84 | 103 | 2 015 | 62.1 | 36.3 | 1.6 |
| Green Lake | 78.6 | 4 198 | 45.7 | 6.6 | 5.6 | 4.7 | 11.2 | 53.6 | 2 860 | 56 | 53 | 1 132 | 41.9 | 56.6 | 1.5 |
| Iowa | 85.7 | 3 637 | 51.0 | 1.0 | 5.0 | 9.3 | 14.3 | 50.7 | 2 151 | 85 | 66 | 1 303 | 66.7 | 32.0 | 1.3 |
| Iron | 33.6 | 5 320 | 31.4 | 9.3 | 6.5 | 0.4 | 18.3 | 27.9 | 4 427 | 15 | 16 | 332 | 55.8 | 42.7 | 1.6 |
| Jackson | 79.7 | 4 013 | 42.9 | 10.1 | 3.7 | 10.9 | 13.0 | 36.4 | 1 836 | 50 | 57 | 2 371 | 60.2 | 38.4 | 1.4 |
| Jefferson | 296.9 | 3 701 | 45.4 | 11.2 | 6.0 | 4.8 | 8.8 | 297.7 | 3 712 | 184 | 234 | 3 823 | 49.7 | 48.9 | 1.4 |
| Juneau | 101.2 | 3 811 | 46.3 | 5.7 | 4.7 | 4.7 | 10.8 | 121.1 | 4 562 | 268 | 76 | 1 444 | 53.7 | 44.6 | 1.7 |
| Kenosha | 762.0 | 4 677 | 54.6 | 4.9 | 5.6 | 6.2 | 3.5 | 712.6 | 4 374 | 260 | 491 | 9 416 | 58.2 | 40.1 | 1.7 |
| Kewaunee | 85.2 | 4 151 | 43.1 | 7.0 | 3.9 | 7.1 | 18.3 | 41.2 | 2 008 | 69 | 58 | 1 174 | 54.7 | 43.7 | 1.6 |
| La Crosse | 520.5 | 4 672 | 47.9 | 2.7 | 4.4 | 15.5 | 5.7 | 400.1 | 3 591 | 473 | 328 | 9 344 | 60.9 | 37.5 | 1.6 |
| Lafayette | 82.3 | 5 200 | 42.6 | 13.0 | 2.6 | 13.9 | 11.6 | 48.1 | 3 043 | 60 | 47 | 1 007 | 60.4 | 38.1 | 1.5 |
| Langlade | 81.5 | 4 012 | 47.8 | 4.3 | 4.5 | 5.2 | 15.0 | 69.6 | 3 428 | 45 | 55 | 1 012 | 49.8 | 48.8 | 1.3 |
| Lincoln | 119.6 | 4 033 | 41.3 | 7.6 | 5.5 | 11.0 | 13.0 | 67.6 | 2 280 | 66 | 81 | 1 802 | 55.2 | 42.7 | 2.1 |
| Manitowoc | 313.6 | 3 875 | 39.4 | 1.1 | 5.2 | 13.4 | 10.9 | 352.8 | 4 359 | 199 | 252 | 3 869 | 52.9 | 45.3 | 1.8 |
| Marathon | 586.2 | 4 511 | 46.6 | 14.1 | 4.0 | 3.7 | 9.8 | 477.0 | 3 670 | 499 | 377 | 7 104 | 53.5 | 44.7 | 1.8 |
| Marinette | 159.2 | 3 739 | 44.0 | 5.2 | 5.4 | 6.6 | 13.5 | 153.8 | 3 613 | 125 | 118 | 2 059 | 52.7 | 45.8 | 1.6 |
| Marquette | 53.1 | 3 546 | 44.9 | 7.3 | 6.6 | 4.9 | 16.9 | 35.7 | 2 385 | 55 | 43 | 693 | 51.8 | 46.6 | 1.6 |
| Menominee | 27.7 | 6 010 | 62.5 | 0.0 | 4.8 | 15.2 | 6.8 | 7.9 | 1 702 | 0 | 12 | 2 111 | 86.8 | 12.8 | 0.4 |
| Milwaukee | 4 664.5 | 4 904 | 40.9 | 8.6 | 7.7 | 4.9 | 4.4 | 5 285.0 | 5 556 | 9 392 | 3 025 | 53 082 | 67.3 | 31.4 | 1.2 |
| Monroe | 159.0 | 3 687 | 45.3 | 1.3 | 4.4 | 13.9 | 13.8 | 148.7 | 3 449 | 2 724 | 223 | 2 443 | 53.2 | 45.2 | 1.5 |
| Oconto | 130.7 | 3 489 | 39.1 | 8.6 | 6.5 | 5.1 | 18.8 | 95.8 | 2 557 | 110 | 105 | 1 788 | 52.3 | 46.2 | 1.5 |
| Oneida | 162.7 | 4 488 | 55.3 | 2.4 | 6.0 | 3.9 | 10.2 | 81.3 | 2 243 | 197 | 101 | 2 247 | 54.3 | 43.9 | 1.8 |
| Outagamie | 841.8 | 4 846 | 55.6 | 4.0 | 4.4 | 4.8 | 8.2 | 817.0 | 4 704 | 569 | 507 | 10 226 | 54.9 | 43.3 | 1.7 |
| Ozaukee | 326.3 | 3 812 | 43.1 | 4.9 | 6.8 | 6.8 | 12.1 | 306.4 | 3 580 | 149 | 242 | 3 655 | 38.6 | 60.3 | 1.2 |
| Pepin | 35.7 | 4 838 | 46.5 | 7.2 | 3.7 | 6.5 | 17.1 | 16.1 | 2 178 | 25 | 21 | 484 | 55.7 | 42.9 | 1.4 |
| Pierce | 161.0 | 4 069 | 48.4 | 8.2 | 4.4 | 2.9 | 14.7 | 137.0 | 3 461 | 102 | 117 | 3 842 | 53.4 | 44.4 | 2.2 |
| Polk | 190.0 | 4 293 | 48.2 | 5.7 | 3.6 | 6.5 | 12.5 | 180.7 | 4 081 | 145 | 123 | 2 509 | 48.0 | 49.8 | 2.1 |
| Portage | 244.4 | 3 579 | 39.8 | 14.0 | 5.1 | 5.7 | 12.5 | 141.5 | 2 073 | 186 | 203 | 5 678 | 63.0 | 35.0 | 2.0 |
| Price | 62.8 | 4 344 | 40.4 | 2.1 | 4.5 | 11.7 | 15.8 | 26.5 | 1 830 | 89 | 39 | 865 | 55.6 | 42.2 | 2.1 |
| Racine | 733.5 | 3 760 | 46.9 | 4.9 | 8.3 | 6.0 | 7.2 | 719.6 | 3 688 | 366 | 546 | 8 789 | 53.1 | 45.7 | 1.3 |
| Richland | 69.8 | 3 845 | 29.6 | 14.7 | 4.2 | 17.9 | 11.9 | 26.5 | 1 460 | 57 | 50 | 1 144 | 59.7 | 39.0 | 1.3 |
| Rock | 655.8 | 4 109 | 49.7 | 6.8 | 6.1 | 7.0 | 6.4 | 520.8 | 3 262 | 292 | 448 | 8 539 | 63.8 | 34.6 | 1.6 |
| Rusk | 87.9 | 5 999 | 35.2 | 21.7 | 3.2 | 10.6 | 12.1 | 44.1 | 3 012 | 50 | 41 | 1 118 | 53.0 | 44.7 | 2.3 |
| St. Croix | 270.2 | 3 330 | 47.6 | 3.0 | 5.3 | 10.8 | 13.6 | 339.8 | 4 189 | 162 | 237 | 4 099 | 47.2 | 51.0 | 1.8 |
| Sauk | 260.6 | 4 456 | 40.4 | 8.9 | 5.9 | 4.4 | 9.1 | 235.3 | 4 024 | 159 | 175 | 5 324 | 60.8 | 37.8 | 1.5 |
| Sawyer | 70.8 | 4 145 | 38.6 | 6.5 | 4.3 | 6.7 | 20.0 | 29.8 | 1 744 | 82 | 46 | 1 985 | 52.4 | 46.2 | 1.3 |
| Shawano | 147.3 | 3 586 | 43.5 | 5.7 | 5.0 | 7.3 | 14.4 | 89.3 | 2 175 | 119 | 117 | 2 766 | 51.1 | 47.5 | 1.5 |
| Sheboygan | 509.8 | 4 452 | 52.0 | 6.2 | 5.0 | 8.7 | 7.4 | 481.1 | 4 202 | 207 | 338 | 5 552 | 48.9 | 49.6 | 1.5 |
| Taylor | 70.1 | 3 629 | 47.2 | 3.3 | 4.2 | 8.7 | 15.1 | 43.7 | 2 262 | 63 | 58 | 942 | 48.8 | 49.1 | 2.1 |
| Trempealeau | 148.6 | 5 342 | 42.8 | 2.0 | 3.5 | 19.1 | 11.4 | 102.0 | 3 668 | 123 | 81 | 2 031 | 62.5 | 36.1 | 1.4 |
| Vernon | 107.4 | 3 702 | 45.4 | 1.5 | 3.6 | 16.0 | 13.4 | 86.9 | 2 997 | 109 | 84 | 1 737 | 60.1 | 38.1 | 1.7 |
| Vilas | 88.6 | 4 011 | 45.5 | 1.7 | 6.8 | 5.6 | 13.2 | 91.0 | 4 122 | 66 | 60 | 2 070 | 47.2 | 51.3 | 1.5 |
| Walworth | 391.6 | 3 885 | 45.8 | 6.6 | 7.7 | 5.6 | 7.8 | 504.9 | 5 009 | 197 | 287 | 7 466 | 47.9 | 50.5 | 1.5 |
| Washburn | 78.3 | 4 693 | 41.7 | 1.6 | 3.4 | 10.4 | 20.0 | 40.3 | 2 417 | 106 | 44 | 1 152 | 51.5 | 47.2 | 1.3 |
| Washington | 452.8 | 3 532 | 45.8 | 5.5 | 6.0 | 5.8 | 10.5 | 440.9 | 3 439 | 257 | 372 | 5 155 | 34.6 | 64.1 | 1.3 |
| Waukesha | 1 411.4 | 3 721 | 54.9 | 3.0 | 6.2 | 3.5 | 6.3 | 1 455.4 | 3 837 | 815 | 1 091 | 16 847 | 36.6 | 62.3 | 1.0 |
| Waupaca | 217.4 | 4 178 | 47.0 | 2.6 | 4.6 | 10.5 | 11.8 | 218.9 | 4 205 | 135 | 147 | 3 548 | 50.8 | 47.9 | 1.3 |
| Waushara | 79.7 | 3 218 | 42.7 | 2.9 | 4.8 | 12.4 | 13.9 | 29.6 | 1 196 | 50 | 69 | 1 142 | 49.5 | 48.7 | 1.8 |
| Winnebago | 592.7 | 3 655 | 40.8 | 2.6 | 5.6 | 11.6 | 8.2 | 694.9 | 4 285 | 467 | 478 | 11 758 | 54.9 | 43.3 | 1.8 |
| Wood | 345.7 | 4 675 | 54.8 | 7.9 | 5.0 | 6.1 | 8.2 | 289.7 | 3 917 | 199 | 209 | 4 735 | 55.6 | 42.5 | 1.9 |
| WYOMING | X | X | X | X | X | X | X | X | X | 7 707 | 6 329 | 60 924 | 32.5 | 64.8 | 2.7 |
| Albany | 164.6 | 5 107 | 29.1 | 39.0 | 5.3 | 0.3 | 3.2 | 41.8 | 1 297 | 183 | 225 | 7 617 | 50.5 | 46.4 | 3.1 |
| Big Horn | 88.5 | 7 858 | 52.9 | 18.2 | 3.8 | 0.2 | 2.6 | 25.0 | 2 222 | 109 | 67 | 1 406 | 20.9 | 76.2 | 3.0 |
| Campbell | 392.0 | 9 694 | 35.0 | 24.5 | 3.6 | 0.5 | 6.7 | 123.7 | 3 059 | 90 | 266 | 4 378 | 18.3 | 79.7 | 2.0 |
| Carbon | 122.4 | 7 902 | 36.4 | 19.3 | 4.4 | 0.0 | 7.4 | 8.2 | 528 | 226 | 90 | 1 909 | 34.1 | 63.2 | 2.7 |
| Converse | 88.0 | 6 836 | 48.7 | 24.1 | 3.9 | 0.1 | 4.4 | 22.2 | 1 724 | 69 | 78 | 1 385 | 21.4 | 76.3 | 2.3 |

1. Based on the resident population estimated as of July 1 of the year shown.  2. © 2013 Election Data Services, Inc. All rights reserved.

# Table B. States and Counties — Land Area and Population

| STATE/ County code | CBSA code[1] | County type[2] | STATE County | Population 2012 | | | | Population characteristics[6], 2011 | | | | | | | | | | |
|---|---|---|---|---|---|---|---|---|---|---|---|---|---|---|---|---|---|---|
| | | | | | | | | Race alone or in combination, not Hispanic or Latino (percent) | | | | | Age (percent) | | | | | |
| | | | | Land area,[3] (sq km) 2010 | Total persons | Rank | Per square kilometer | White | Black | American Indian, Alaska Native | Asian and Pacific Islander | Percent Hispanic or Latino[4] | Under 5 years | 5 to 17 years | 18 to 24 years | 25 to 34 years | 35 to 44 years | 45 to 54 years |
| | | | | 1 | 2 | 3 | 4 | 5 | 6 | 7 | 8 | 9 | 10 | 11 | 12 | 13 | 14 | 15 |
| | | | WYOMING—Cont'd | | | | | | | | | | | | | | | |
| 56 011 | ... | 9 | Crook | 7 393 | 7 155 | 2 665 | 1.0 | 96.6 | 0.7 | 1.4 | 0.4 | 2.1 | 7.0 | 16.2 | 6.9 | 10.9 | 10.4 | 15.9 |
| 56 013 | 40180 | 7 | Fremont | 23 786 | 41 110 | 1 151 | 1.7 | 74.0 | 0.6 | 20.8 | 0.9 | 5.9 | 7.6 | 17.7 | 8.7 | 12.4 | 10.9 | 13.7 |
| 56 015 | ... | 7 | Goshen | 5 764 | 13 636 | 2 204 | 2.4 | 88.2 | 0.9 | 1.3 | 0.5 | 10.0 | 5.5 | 14.7 | 10.4 | 10.9 | 10.7 | 14.6 |
| 56 017 | ... | 7 | Hot Springs | 5 191 | 4 822 | 2 850 | 0.9 | 95.0 | 0.6 | 2.4 | 0.8 | 2.5 | 5.4 | 14.1 | 6.6 | 10.0 | 8.6 | 16.4 |
| 56 019 | ... | 7 | Johnson | 10 759 | 8 615 | 2 555 | 0.8 | 94.6 | 0.6 | 1.5 | 0.8 | 3.6 | 6.5 | 15.5 | 5.9 | 11.6 | 11.0 | 14.2 |
| 56 021 | 16940 | 3 | Laramie | 6 956 | 94 483 | 614 | 13.6 | 82.3 | 3.1 | 1.4 | 2.0 | 13.3 | 7.1 | 16.9 | 9.6 | 13.7 | 12.2 | 14.4 |
| 56 023 | ... | 7 | Lincoln | 10 557 | 17 961 | 1 922 | 1.7 | 94.4 | 0.6 | 1.3 | 0.6 | 4.1 | 7.5 | 19.9 | 6.4 | 12.4 | 12.0 | 14.3 |
| 56 025 | 16220 | 3 | Natrona | 13 831 | 78 621 | 698 | 5.7 | 90.3 | 1.6 | 1.6 | 1.1 | 7.1 | 7.0 | 16.7 | 9.5 | 14.7 | 12.0 | 14.3 |
| 56 027 | ... | 9 | Niobrara | 6 801 | 2 456 | 3 010 | 0.4 | 95.5 | 1.0 | 1.8 | 0.6 | 2.7 | 3.8 | 13.8 | 6.7 | 11.9 | 12.4 | 14.3 |
| 56 029 | ... | 7 | Park | 17 980 | 28 702 | 1 459 | 1.6 | 93.2 | 0.6 | 1.3 | 1.1 | 5.1 | 5.6 | 15.0 | 8.8 | 11.4 | 10.7 | 14.3 |
| 56 031 | ... | 7 | Platte | 5 398 | 8 756 | 2 538 | 1.6 | 91.7 | 0.6 | 1.2 | 0.6 | 7.0 | 4.6 | 14.9 | 6.4 | 9.4 | 10.4 | 15.7 |
| 56 033 | 43260 | 7 | Sheridan | 6 537 | 29 596 | 1 435 | 4.5 | 94.0 | 0.7 | 1.8 | 1.2 | 3.6 | 6.1 | 15.8 | 8.1 | 11.7 | 11.4 | 14.8 |
| 56 035 | ... | 9 | Sublette | 12 656 | 10 368 | 2 408 | 0.8 | 90.5 | 0.9 | 1.5 | 0.9 | 7.3 | 6.8 | 16.9 | 7.2 | 14.0 | 13.5 | 16.4 |
| 56 037 | 40540 | 5 | Sweetwater | 27 005 | 45 267 | 1 061 | 1.7 | 81.7 | 1.4 | 1.4 | 1.4 | 15.5 | 8.2 | 18.9 | 9.7 | 16.2 | 12.1 | 14.2 |
| 56 039 | 27220 | 7 | Teton | 10 348 | 21 675 | 1 745 | 2.1 | 82.6 | 0.5 | 0.9 | 1.8 | 15.4 | 6.2 | 13.1 | 7.2 | 19.6 | 15.5 | 14.2 |
| 56 041 | 21740 | 7 | Uinta | 5 390 | 21 025 | 1 779 | 3.9 | 89.4 | 0.7 | 1.5 | 1.1 | 9.1 | 8.2 | 21.8 | 7.6 | 13.4 | 12.3 | 14.5 |
| 56 043 | ... | 7 | Washakie | 5 798 | 8 464 | 2 567 | 1.5 | 84.7 | 0.6 | 1.4 | 0.8 | 13.7 | 6.4 | 18.7 | 6.1 | 11.2 | 10.5 | 14.3 |
| 56 045 | ... | 7 | Weston | 6 211 | 7 082 | 2 676 | 1.1 | 94.5 | 0.7 | 2.4 | 0.7 | 3.2 | 5.8 | 16.4 | 7.3 | 12.9 | 11.4 | 15.3 |

1. CBSA = Core Based Statistical Area. See Appendix A for explanation. See Appendix B for list of metropolitan areas with component counties. Service of USDA Rural-Urban Continuum Codes. See Appendix A for definition. 3. Dry land or land partially or temporarily covered by water. 2. County type code from the Economic Research 4. May be of any race.

| | Population, 2011 (cont.) | | | | Population change and components of change, 2000–2012 | | | | | | | Households, 2010 | | | | |
|---|---|---|---|---|---|---|---|---|---|---|---|---|---|---|---|---|
| | Age (percent) (cont.) | | | | Total persons | | Percent change | | Components of change, 2010–2012 | | | | | | Percent | |
| STATE County | 55 to 64 years | 65 to 74 years | 75 years and over | Percent female | 2000 | 2010 | 2000–2010 | 2010–2012 | Births | Deaths | Net migration | Number | Percent change, 2000–2010 | Persons per house-hold | Female family house-holder[1] | One per-son |
| | 16 | 17 | 18 | 19 | 20 | 21 | 22 | 23 | 24 | 25 | 26 | 27 | 28 | 29 | 30 | 31 |
| WYOMING—Cont'd | | | | | | | | | | | | | | | | |
| Crook | 16.4 | 10.2 | 6.2 | 48.8 | 5 887 | 7 083 | 20.3 | 1.0 | 207 | 142 | 8 | 2 921 | 26.6 | 2.41 | 6.5 | 25.0 |
| Fremont | 14.4 | 8.2 | 6.4 | 50.2 | 35 804 | 40 123 | 12.1 | 2.5 | 1 351 | 866 | 483 | 15 455 | 14.1 | 2.54 | 12.2 | 27.0 |
| Goshen | 14.6 | 10.2 | 8.4 | 47.8 | 12 538 | 13 249 | 5.7 | 2.9 | 296 | 310 | 389 | 5 311 | 4.9 | 2.29 | 7.9 | 30.0 |
| Hot Springs | 16.1 | 12.6 | 10.1 | 50.4 | 4 882 | 4 812 | -1.4 | 0.2 | 106 | 162 | 65 | 2 185 | 3.7 | 2.16 | 8.3 | 32.6 |
| Johnson | 16.5 | 10.6 | 8.3 | 49.2 | 7 075 | 8 569 | 21.1 | 0.5 | 221 | 200 | 29 | 3 782 | 27.8 | 2.25 | 6.7 | 31.8 |
| Laramie | 13.2 | 7.2 | 5.7 | 49.8 | 81 607 | 91 738 | 12.4 | 3.0 | 2 791 | 1 640 | 1 610 | 37 576 | 17.7 | 2.40 | 10.7 | 29.1 |
| Lincoln | 14.4 | 7.9 | 5.0 | 48.9 | 14 573 | 18 106 | 24.2 | -0.8 | 563 | 273 | -429 | 6 861 | 30.3 | 2.63 | 5.3 | 22.8 |
| Natrona | 13.3 | 6.5 | 6.0 | 49.6 | 66 533 | 75 450 | 13.4 | 4.2 | 2 272 | 1 470 | 2 325 | 30 616 | 14.2 | 2.41 | 10.9 | 28.5 |
| Niobrara | 16.0 | 11.4 | 9.7 | 53.3 | 2 407 | 2 484 | 3.2 | -1.1 | 38 | 51 | -13 | 1 069 | 5.7 | 2.12 | 7.4 | 34.5 |
| Park | 16.2 | 10.2 | 7.7 | 50.4 | 25 786 | 28 205 | 9.4 | 1.8 | 677 | 553 | 375 | 11 885 | 15.3 | 2.29 | 7.2 | 28.5 |
| Platte | 16.9 | 12.4 | 9.2 | 49.8 | 8 807 | 8 667 | -1.6 | 1.0 | 163 | 201 | 119 | 3 838 | 5.9 | 2.23 | 6.9 | 30.6 |
| Sheridan | 16.1 | 8.9 | 7.1 | 50.0 | 26 560 | 29 116 | 9.6 | 1.6 | 774 | 679 | 367 | 12 360 | 10.7 | 2.27 | 8.4 | 30.9 |
| Sublette | 14.4 | 7.0 | 3.8 | 45.7 | 5 920 | 10 247 | 73.1 | 1.2 | 275 | 116 | -68 | 3 906 | 64.7 | 2.48 | 5.1 | 25.6 |
| Sweetwater | 12.1 | 5.1 | 3.5 | 47.8 | 37 613 | 43 806 | 16.5 | 3.3 | 1 466 | 552 | 514 | 16 475 | 16.8 | 2.62 | 9.0 | 24.0 |
| Teton | 13.7 | 6.7 | 3.8 | 47.5 | 18 251 | 21 294 | 16.7 | 1.8 | 552 | 187 | 20 | 8 973 | 16.7 | 2.34 | 5.6 | 29.2 |
| Uinta | 12.8 | 5.8 | 3.5 | 49.5 | 19 742 | 21 118 | 7.0 | -0.4 | 705 | 296 | -509 | 7 668 | 12.4 | 2.72 | 9.7 | 22.6 |
| Washakie | 14.4 | 10.0 | 8.4 | 49.6 | 8 289 | 8 533 | 2.9 | -0.8 | 210 | 210 | -70 | 3 492 | 6.5 | 2.40 | 7.9 | 27.7 |
| Weston | 15.3 | 8.2 | 7.5 | 47.4 | 6 644 | 7 208 | 8.5 | -1.7 | 175 | 159 | -143 | 3 021 | 15.1 | 2.28 | 6.9 | 29.9 |

1. No spouse present.

# Table B. States and Counties — **Population, Vital Statistics, Medicare, and Crime**

| STATE County | Persons in group quarters, 2010 | Daytime population, 2007–2011 Number | Daytime population, 2007–2011 Employment/residence ratio | Births, 2011 Total | Births, 2011 Rate[1] | Deaths, 2011 Number | Deaths, 2011 Rate[1] | Persons under 65 with no health insurance, 2010 Number | Persons under 65 with no health insurance, 2010 Percent | Medicare, 2012 Eligible for Medicare | Medicare, 2012 Enrolled in Medicare Advantage | Medicare, 2012 Enrolled in a Medicare prescription drug plan | Serious crimes known to police,[2] 2011 Total Number | Serious crimes known to police,[2] 2011 Total Rate[3] |
|---|---|---|---|---|---|---|---|---|---|---|---|---|---|---|
| | 32 | 33 | 34 | 35 | 36 | 37 | 38 | 39 | 40 | 41 | 42 | 43 | 44 | 45 |
| WYOMING—Cont'd | | | | | | | | | | | | | | |
| Crook ........................... | 34 | 6 407 | 0.84 | 95 | 13.4 | 63 | 8.9 | 1 149 | 19.4 | 1 288 | 83 | 637 | 74 | 1 036 |
| Fremont ....................... | 864 | 39 137 | 0.98 | 609 | 15.0 | 391 | 9.6 | 7 217 | 21.5 | 7 166 | 502 | 3 756 | 962 | 2 378 |
| Goshen ........................ | 1 070 | 12 377 | 0.89 | 134 | 9.9 | 139 | 10.3 | 1 853 | 18.9 | 2 744 | 29 | 1 693 | 230 | 1 722 |
| Hot Springs ................ | 86 | 4 632 | 0.94 | 45 | 9.4 | 76 | 15.8 | 739 | 20.1 | 1 300 | 13 | 768 | 74 | 1 525 |
| Johnson ...................... | 71 | 8 170 | 0.93 | 102 | 11.8 | 86 | 10.0 | 1 399 | 20.2 | 1 768 | 189 | 899 | 152 | 1 760 |
| Laramie ....................... | 1 644 | 92 493 | 1.05 | 1 264 | 13.6 | 720 | 7.8 | 13 281 | 16.8 | 15 100 | 1 134 | 6 764 | 2 785 | 3 012 |
| Lincoln ........................ | 71 | 16 609 | 0.86 | 262 | 14.5 | 115 | 6.4 | 3 039 | 19.3 | 2 762 | 62 | 1 435 | 208 | 1 212 |
| Natrona ....................... | 1 645 | 74 993 | 1.01 | 1 033 | 13.5 | 667 | 8.7 | 10 302 | 15.9 | 11 731 | 545 | 6 591 | 2 626 | 3 453 |
| Niobrara ...................... | 214 | 2 436 | 0.97 | 18 | 7.2 | 21 | 8.4 | 430 | 24.6 | 550 | D | 346 | 15 | 599 |
| Park ............................. | 942 | 28 398 | 1.03 | 290 | 10.1 | 239 | 8.4 | 3 881 | 17.2 | 6 117 | 85 | 3 282 | 602 | 2 117 |
| Platte ........................... | 103 | 8 865 | 1.05 | 64 | 7.3 | 89 | 10.1 | 1 286 | 19.0 | 2 045 | 24 | 1 163 | 191 | 2 186 |
| Sheridan ..................... | 1 009 | 27 601 | 0.92 | 349 | 11.9 | 299 | 10.2 | 4 251 | 17.8 | 5 724 | 266 | 2 787 | 567 | 1 932 |
| Sublette ...................... | 550 | 11 439 | 1.32 | 129 | 12.7 | 52 | 5.1 | 1 457 | 15.8 | 1 164 | 61 | 562 | 161 | 1 559 |
| Sweetwater ................ | 679 | 45 636 | 1.11 | 664 | 15.0 | 249 | 5.6 | 6 370 | 16.1 | 4 795 | 559 | 2 067 | 1 233 | 2 792 |
| Teton .......................... | 271 | 24 460 | 1.26 | 266 | 12.3 | 78 | 3.6 | 4 084 | 21.3 | 2 526 | 107 | 1 364 | 404 | 1 882 |
| Uinta ........................... | 270 | 19 844 | 0.91 | 332 | 15.8 | 140 | 6.7 | 3 115 | 16.4 | 2 451 | 237 | 1 210 | 377 | 1 968 |
| Washakie .................... | 140 | 8 585 | 1.05 | 98 | 11.5 | 88 | 10.4 | 1 287 | 18.6 | 1 723 | 15 | 996 | 37 | 430 |
| Weston......................... | 313 | 6 427 | 0.80 | 84 | 11.8 | 71 | 10.0 | 978 | 17.0 | 1 322 | 105 | 715 | 99 | 1 608 |

1. Per 1,000 estimated resident population.  2. Data for serious crimes have not been adjusted for underreporting; this may affect comparability between geographic areas and over time.  3. Per 100,000 population estimated by the FBI.

# Table B. States and Counties — Crime, Education, Money Income, and Poverty

| STATE County | Serious crimes known to police, 2011 (cont.)[1] Rate[2] | | Education | | | | | | Money income, 2007–2011 | | | | Income and poverty, 2011 | | | |
|---|---|---|---|---|---|---|---|---|---|---|---|---|---|---|---|---|
| | | | School enrollment and attainment, 2007–2011 | | | | Local government expenditures,[5] 2009–2010 | | | Households | | | | Percent below poverty level | | |
| | | | Enrollment[3] | | Attainment[4] (percent) | | | | | Median income | | | | | | |
| | Violent | Property | Total | Percent private | High school graduate or less | Bachelor's degree or more | Total current expenditures (mil dol) | Current expenditures per student (dollars) | Per capita income[6] (dollars) | Dollars | Percent change, 2000 to 2007–2011 (constant 2011 dollars) | Percent with income of $200,000 or more | Median household income (dollars) | All persons | Children under 18 years | Children 5 to 17 years in families |
| | 46 | 47 | 48 | 49 | 50 | 51 | 52 | 53 | 54 | 55 | 56 | 57 | 58 | 59 | 60 | 61 |
| **WYOMING—Cont'd** | | | | | | | | | | | | | | | | |
| Crook | 56 | 980 | 1 528 | 15.0 | 44.1 | 23.0 | 18.4 | 16 700 | 25 653 | 49 757 | 3.5 | 1.2 | 55 294 | 8.3 | 12.0 | 11.0 |
| Fremont | 161 | 2 218 | 9 578 | 8.8 | 37.7 | 21.4 | 121.1 | 19 142 | 24 206 | 48 788 | 11.2 | 1.6 | 45 731 | 15.6 | 22.3 | 19.6 |
| Goshen | 135 | 1 587 | 3 098 | 11.5 | 42.8 | 21.5 | 28.3 | 15 288 | 23 845 | 42 126 | -3.2 | 1.4 | 41 014 | 17.0 | 22.8 | 18.3 |
| Hot Springs | 21 | 1 505 | 728 | 8.9 | 45.4 | 19.8 | 11.0 | 16 916 | 24 025 | 43 063 | 6.7 | 0.5 | 41 845 | 13.1 | 18.9 | 15.5 |
| Johnson | 243 | 1 517 | 1 648 | 8.5 | 40.8 | 25.8 | 20.5 | 16 614 | 29 901 | 55 094 | 20.0 | 4.5 | 53 577 | 9.1 | 12.9 | 11.2 |
| Laramie | 244 | 2 767 | 23 348 | 11.1 | 35.6 | 24.4 | 199.1 | 14 036 | 28 648 | 54 156 | 1.3 | 2.7 | 53 839 | 9.9 | 15.6 | 13.6 |
| Lincoln | 175 | 1 037 | 4 416 | 7.8 | 43.8 | 20.9 | 47.5 | 14 656 | 25 451 | 60 543 | 9.9 | 2.4 | 60 062 | 9.2 | 13.1 | 11.3 |
| Natrona | 247 | 3 205 | 19 223 | 10.8 | 38.4 | 21.6 | 173.5 | 14 792 | 29 620 | 53 519 | 8.2 | 3.5 | 52 904 | 11.5 | 16.0 | 13.7 |
| Niobrara | 80 | 519 | 493 | 12.2 | 43.9 | 15.7 | 7.7 | 12 543 | 25 277 | 44 875 | 11.9 | 1.7 | 41 712 | 14.6 | 18.1 | 14.3 |
| Park | 243 | 1 875 | 6 269 | 7.9 | 35.8 | 28.2 | 58.4 | 14 721 | 28 103 | 50 105 | 3.6 | 1.7 | 50 141 | 11.4 | 17.5 | 14.8 |
| Platte | 149 | 2 037 | 1 933 | 12.9 | 43.3 | 18.9 | 22.9 | 18 225 | 25 280 | 46 171 | 1.0 | 1.1 | 47 916 | 12.0 | 18.5 | 14.7 |
| Sheridan | 109 | 1 823 | 6 381 | 10.9 | 37.4 | 24.6 | 61.0 | 14 435 | 27 805 | 51 667 | 10.8 | 2.8 | 53 217 | 9.9 | 14.4 | 12.5 |
| Sublette | 97 | 1 462 | 2 211 | 9.8 | 32.8 | 25.6 | 29.5 | 17 833 | 35 049 | 79 250 | 50.3 | 3.7 | 75 242 | 6.3 | 8.5 | 7.3 |
| Sweetwater | 378 | 2 414 | 11 360 | 9.8 | 45.0 | 17.0 | 107.8 | 14 116 | 31 125 | 72 096 | 14.7 | 3.5 | 69 756 | 10.0 | 14.9 | 13.5 |
| Teton | 331 | 1 551 | 3 582 | 10.5 | 23.7 | 52.7 | 39.5 | 17 018 | 43 877 | 73 627 | -0.2 | 8.4 | 69 095 | 8.3 | 14.9 | 13.3 |
| Uinta | 63 | 1 905 | 5 730 | 6.3 | 44.5 | 18.4 | 61.9 | 14 091 | 25 660 | 59 851 | -0.5 | 2.3 | 61 266 | 9.7 | 13.7 | 11.6 |
| Washakie | 35 | 395 | 1 918 | 7.3 | 41.7 | 22.6 | 23.6 | 16 439 | 30 193 | 50 177 | 6.4 | 3.3 | 49 747 | 11.3 | 15.4 | 12.8 |
| Weston | 114 | 1 494 | 1 470 | 2.7 | 49.5 | 18.4 | 17.5 | 15 995 | 29 558 | 55 156 | 26.3 | 3.1 | 53 313 | 11.5 | 15.6 | 12.9 |

1. Data for serious crimes have not been adjusted for underreporting; this may affect comparability between geographic areas and over time. 2. Per 100,000 population estimated by the FBI. 3. All persons 3 years old and over enrolled in nursery school through college. 4. Persons 25 years old and over. 5. Elementary and secondary education expenditures. 6. Based on population estimated by the American Community Survey, 2007–2011.

| STATE County | Personal income, 2011 | | | | | | | | | | | | |
|---|---|---|---|---|---|---|---|---|---|---|---|---|---|
| | | | Per capita[1] | | | | | | Transfer payments (mil dol) | | | | |
| | | | | | | | | | | Government payments to individuals | | | |
| | Total (mil dol) | Percent change, 2010– 2011 | Dollars | Rank | Wages and salaries[2] (mil dol) | Proprietors' income (mil dol) | Dividends, interest, and rent (mil dol) | Total | Total | Social Security | Medical payments | Income maintenance | Unemploy- ment insurance |
| | 62 | 63 | 64 | 65 | 66 | 67 | 68 | 69 | 70 | 71 | 72 | 73 | 74 |
| WYOMING—Cont'd | | | | | | | | | | | | | |
| Crook.................................. | 312 | 3.4 | 43 877 | 448 | 116 | 28 | 76 | 43 | 41 | 19 | 14 | 2 | 1 |
| Fremont............................... | 1 598 | 6.4 | 39 389 | 815 | 877 | 101 | 372 | 331 | 322 | 101 | 151 | 30 | 12 |
| Goshen................................ | 469 | 7.5 | 34 648 | 1 425 | 210 | 38 | 107 | 103 | 100 | 37 | 41 | 9 | 2 |
| Hot Springs ........................ | 209 | 5.7 | 43 615 | 460 | 97 | 28 | 45 | 48 | 47 | 18 | 21 | 3 | 1 |
| Johnson............................... | 352 | 5.1 | 40 786 | 678 | 150 | 35 | 120 | 55 | 54 | 25 | 18 | 3 | 2 |
| Laramie................................ | 4 345 | 6.5 | 46 882 | 305 | 2 801 | 319 | 933 | 660 | 640 | 201 | 247 | 55 | 23 |
| Lincoln................................. | 682 | 7.5 | 37 739 | 1 000 | 364 | 64 | 162 | 100 | 96 | 41 | 35 | 6 | 6 |
| Natrona................................ | 4 132 | 7.7 | 54 108 | 129 | 2 410 | 574 | 963 | 501 | 485 | 173 | 190 | 46 | 22 |
| Niobrara............................... | 106 | 9.7 | 42 410 | 552 | 46 | 15 | 25 | 20 | 19 | 7 | 9 | 2 | 0 |
| Park..................................... | 1 309 | 6.0 | 45 799 | 347 | 687 | 135 | 378 | 217 | 211 | 89 | 80 | 14 | 7 |
| Platte................................... | 387 | 8.5 | 44 020 | 439 | 208 | 46 | 90 | 72 | 70 | 28 | 28 | 4 | 2 |
| Sheridan.............................. | 1 485 | 4.8 | 50 803 | 192 | 684 | 120 | 505 | 208 | 201 | 77 | 69 | 13 | 10 |
| Sublette............................... | 635 | 10.9 | 62 557 | 48 | 461 | 76 | 125 | 40 | 38 | 17 | 11 | 2 | 2 |
| Sweetwater.......................... | 2 291 | 9.5 | 51 860 | 165 | 1 776 | 324 | 345 | 221 | 212 | 78 | 73 | 14 | 10 |
| Teton................................... | 2 066 | 6.3 | 95 861 | 3 | 890 | 307 | 996 | 100 | 95 | 39 | 30 | 3 | 12 |
| Uinta.................................... | 878 | 0.9 | 41 833 | 591 | 503 | 60 | 118 | 118 | 113 | 37 | 46 | 10 | 5 |
| Washakie.............................. | 355 | 7.1 | 41 837 | 589 | 205 | 35 | 81 | 62 | 60 | 24 | 25 | 4 | 2 |
| Weston ................................ | 351 | 5.3 | 49 320 | 225 | 120 | 87 | 68 | 47 | 46 | 19 | 18 | 3 | 1 |

1. Based on the resident population estimated as of July 1 of the year shown.   2. Includes supplements to wages and salaries.

| STATE County | Earnings, 2011 | | | | | | | | | Social Security beneficiaries, December 2011 | | | Housing units, 2010 | |
|---|---|---|---|---|---|---|---|---|---|---|---|---|---|---|
| | | | Percent by selected industries | | | | | | | | | Supplemental Security Income recipients, December 2011 | | |
| | | | Goods-related[1] | | Service-related and health | | | | | | | | | |
| | Total (mil dol) | Farm | Total | Manufacturing | Information and professional and technical services | Retail trade | Finance, insurance, and real estate | Health care and social services | Government | Number | Rate[2] | | Total | Percent change, 2000–2010 |
| | 75 | 76 | 77 | 78 | 79 | 80 | 81 | 82 | 83 | 84 | 85 | 86 | 87 | 88 |
| WYOMING—Cont'd | | | | | | | | | | | | | | |
| Crook | 145 | 3.0 | 31.0 | 7.3 | D | 7.3 | D | D | 26.5 | 1 435 | 202 | 39 | 3 595 | 22.5 |
| Fremont | 978 | 2.0 | 18.7 | 1.1 | 5.4 | 7.5 | 4.7 | D | 34.3 | 8 040 | 198 | 877 | 17 796 | 14.5 |
| Goshen | 248 | 7.2 | D | 5.6 | 4.5 | 6.1 | 4.7 | 15.3 | 32.9 | 2 985 | 221 | 220 | 5 972 | 1.5 |
| Hot Springs | 124 | 2.3 | D | 2.5 | D | 4.0 | 2.3 | 9.8 | 24.1 | 1 415 | 295 | 86 | 2 582 | 1.8 |
| Johnson | 185 | 1.0 | 24.5 | 0.9 | 4.4 | 6.1 | 7.2 | D | 31.3 | 1 925 | 223 | 40 | 4 553 | 30.0 |
| Laramie | 3 120 | 2.0 | D | 4.4 | 6.5 | 6.8 | 5.6 | 8.3 | 41.2 | 15 655 | 169 | 1 411 | 40 462 | 18.3 |
| Lincoln | 428 | 1.8 | 38.9 | 1.6 | 4.6 | 5.4 | 3.4 | 3.1 | 23.9 | 3 050 | 169 | 129 | 8 946 | 31.0 |
| Natrona | 2 984 | 0.2 | 31.6 | 4.4 | 5.5 | 6.4 | 5.7 | 13.1 | 13.1 | 12 935 | 169 | 1 168 | 33 807 | 13.1 |
| Niobrara | 61 | 14.7 | D | D | D | D | D | D | 38.4 | 590 | 237 | 35 | 1 338 | 0.0 |
| Park | 822 | 2.3 | 23.5 | 3.0 | 5.3 | 8.2 | 4.1 | 10.4 | 26.0 | 6 695 | 234 | 269 | 13 562 | 14.3 |
| Platte | 254 | 10.4 | 10.9 | 0.8 | 2.3 | 6.4 | 3.8 | D | 20.3 | 2 185 | 248 | 98 | 4 667 | 3.1 |
| Sheridan | 804 | -0.2 | 16.5 | 2.2 | 7.5 | 7.6 | 6.0 | 10.5 | 28.3 | 5 940 | 203 | 298 | 13 939 | 10.8 |
| Sublette | 537 | 1.5 | 57.1 | 0.7 | D | 3.8 | 3.4 | D | 13.2 | 1 250 | 123 | 40 | 5 770 | 62.4 |
| Sweetwater | 2 101 | 0.2 | 55.9 | 7.3 | 2.8 | 4.2 | 3.3 | 2.6 | 13.2 | 5 500 | 125 | 343 | 18 735 | 17.7 |
| Teton | 1 197 | 0.5 | D | 0.7 | 10.6 | 6.8 | 17.1 | 5.2 | 13.1 | 2 520 | 117 | 63 | 12 813 | 24.8 |
| Uinta | 562 | 0.4 | 31.6 | 3.7 | 7.4 | 6.7 | 4.0 | D | 20.8 | 2 755 | 131 | 273 | 8 713 | 8.8 |
| Washakie | 241 | 6.1 | 27.4 | 11.8 | 5.1 | 5.0 | 5.5 | 10.6 | 21.4 | 1 870 | 220 | 103 | 3 833 | 4.9 |
| Weston | 207 | 0.3 | 38.9 | 8.5 | 4.2 | 8.6 | 5.9 | D | 20.9 | 1 425 | 200 | 63 | 3 533 | 9.3 |

1. Includes mining, construction, and manufacturing.    2. Per 1,000 resident population enumerated in the 2010 census.

# Table B. States and Counties — Housing, Labor Force, and Employment

| STATE County | Housing units, 2007–2011 Occupied units | | Owner-occupied Median value[1] | Median owner cost as a percent of income With a mortgage | Without a mortgage[2] | Renter-occupied Median rent[3] | Median rent as a percent of income | Sub-standard units[4] (percent) | Civilian labor force, 2012 Total | Percent change, 2011–2012 | Unemployment Total | Rate[5] | Civilian employment,[6] 2007–2011 Total | Percent Management, business, science and arts | Con-struction, produc-tion, and mainte-nance occu-pations |
|---|---|---|---|---|---|---|---|---|---|---|---|---|---|---|---|
| | Total | Percent | | | | | | | | | | | | | |
| | 89 | 90 | 91 | 92 | 93 | 94 | 95 | 96 | 97 | 98 | 99 | 100 | 101 | 102 | 103 |
| WYOMING—Cont'd | | | | | | | | | | | | | | | |
| Crook | 2 894 | 74.8 | 156 300 | 21.2 | 9.9 | 640 | 17.2 | 4.0 | 3 628 | 1.4 | 186 | 5.1 | 3 447 | 34.8 | 35.1 |
| Fremont | 15 598 | 71.7 | 166 500 | 21.4 | 11.3 | 623 | 23.6 | 5.0 | 19 812 | 0.6 | 1 309 | 6.6 | 18 969 | 34.1 | 25.2 |
| Goshen | 5 286 | 69.1 | 132 400 | 22.7 | 10.6 | 582 | 26.4 | 3.4 | 6 623 | 0.9 | 362 | 5.5 | 6 666 | 32.5 | 31.7 |
| Hot Springs | 2 098 | 66.0 | 136 000 | 20.2 | 10.4 | 503 | 25.2 | 0.6 | 2 605 | -0.5 | 122 | 4.7 | 2 188 | 29.9 | 23.1 |
| Johnson | 3 748 | 77.5 | 215 500 | 23.5 | 9.9 | 642 | 23.2 | 5.0 | 4 037 | 0.6 | 241 | 6.0 | 4 437 | 35.6 | 27.2 |
| Laramie | 36 566 | 68.7 | 174 100 | 23.2 | 9.9 | 698 | 24.8 | 1.5 | 45 331 | 1.1 | 2 769 | 6.1 | 44 510 | 34.4 | 22.2 |
| Lincoln | 6 238 | 80.0 | 205 800 | 22.6 | 9.9 | 773 | 20.5 | 2.1 | 7 857 | -5.9 | 604 | 7.7 | 8 542 | 28.2 | 33.0 |
| Natrona | 29 850 | 69.8 | 177 700 | 21.2 | 9.9 | 731 | 26.7 | 1.2 | 43 900 | 2.7 | 2 137 | 4.9 | 38 731 | 30.2 | 27.5 |
| Niobrara | 1 041 | 67.2 | 105 400 | 18.3 | 9.9 | 526 | 25.7 | 0.5 | 1 357 | 2.8 | 56 | 4.1 | 1 179 | 40.6 | 28.0 |
| Park | 11 874 | 71.0 | 203 000 | 24.7 | 12.1 | 669 | 22.1 | 1.8 | 15 757 | 2.6 | 909 | 5.8 | 14 675 | 31.6 | 26.1 |
| Platte | 3 647 | 78.1 | 136 100 | 21.0 | 9.9 | 547 | 24.1 | 1.9 | 4 189 | -2.0 | 238 | 5.7 | 4 171 | 31.0 | 29.9 |
| Sheridan | 12 268 | 69.6 | 224 900 | 23.4 | 11.0 | 728 | 25.7 | 2.9 | 16 236 | -0.3 | 996 | 6.1 | 14 964 | 32.4 | 27.2 |
| Sublette | 3 564 | 73.3 | 287 100 | 21.2 | 9.9 | 1 017 | 22.7 | 4.9 | 7 339 | -5.0 | 270 | 3.7 | 5 419 | 37.4 | 35.8 |
| Sweetwater | 16 418 | 73.3 | 180 300 | 19.2 | 9.9 | 851 | 20.3 | 3.8 | 25 142 | 0.4 | 1 145 | 4.6 | 22 370 | 23.8 | 38.4 |
| Teton | 7 246 | 62.3 | 715 300 | 26.0 | 9.9 | 902 | 23.8 | 3.6 | 13 658 | 1.1 | 908 | 6.6 | 13 491 | 41.2 | 16.9 |
| Uinta | 7 265 | 76.4 | 178 300 | 19.2 | 9.9 | 601 | 26.9 | 3.3 | 11 147 | 0.7 | 573 | 5.1 | 10 435 | 27.3 | 34.2 |
| Washakie | 3 464 | 72.1 | 148 400 | 22.3 | 9.9 | 522 | 18.1 | 2.6 | 4 394 | -0.9 | 237 | 5.4 | 4 154 | 29.5 | 33.8 |
| Weston | 2 944 | 78.3 | 139 800 | 18.5 | 9.9 | 599 | 17.5 | 1.9 | 3 322 | 0.8 | 168 | 5.1 | 3 675 | 27.3 | 44.0 |

1. Specified owner-occupied units. lacking complete plumbing facilities.　2. A value of 9.9 represents 9.9 percent or less.　3. Specified renter-occupied units. A value of 10.0 represents 10 percent or less.　4. Overcrowded or
5. Percent of civilian labor force.　6. Persons 16 years old and over.

# Table B. States and Counties — Nonfarm Employment and Agriculture

| STATE County | Private nonfarm establishments, employment and payroll, 2011 | | | | | | | | | Agriculture, 2007 | | | |
| | Number of establish-ments | Employment | | | | | | Annual payroll | | Farms | | | |
| | | Total | Health care and social assistance | Manufac-turing | Retail trade | Finance and insurance | Professional, scientific, and technical services | Total (mil dol) | Average per employee (dollars) | Number | Percent with: | | Farm operators whose principal occu-pation is farming (percent) |
| | | | | | | | | | | | Fewer than 50 acres | 500 acres or more | |
| | 104 | 105 | 106 | 107 | 108 | 109 | 110 | 111 | 112 | 113 | 114 | 115 | 116 |
| WYOMING—Cont'd | | | | | | | | | | | | | |
| Crook | 230 | 1 485 | 240 | D | 192 | D | D | 57 | 38 058 | 457 | 7.0 | 64.8 | 65.2 |
| Fremont | 1 344 | 11 520 | 2 106 | 248 | 2 227 | 316 | 442 | 408 | 35 388 | 1 394 | 32.6 | 21.4 | 48.8 |
| Goshen | 349 | 3 019 | 812 | D | 396 | D | 151 | 83 | 27 654 | 815 | 14.6 | 41.2 | 54.0 |
| Hot Springs | 194 | 1 672 | 440 | D | 197 | D | 48 | 54 | 32 254 | 180 | 29.4 | 33.9 | 51.1 |
| Johnson | 407 | 2 461 | 439 | 73 | 357 | 133 | 140 | 81 | 32 716 | 319 | 8.5 | 58.3 | 59.6 |
| Laramie | 2 780 | 30 566 | 6 413 | 1 361 | 5 242 | 1 654 | 1 481 | 1 110 | 36 320 | 844 | 20.9 | 39.7 | 39.6 |
| Lincoln | 592 | 4 159 | 711 | D | 570 | 119 | D | 179 | 42 981 | 535 | 37.0 | 21.1 | 51.0 |
| Natrona | 2 902 | 32 295 | 5 015 | 1 925 | 4 806 | 1 159 | 1 613 | 1 425 | 44 125 | 413 | 28.8 | 41.4 | 46.2 |
| Niobrara | 96 | 444 | 69 | D | 123 | 30 | D | 11 | 24 234 | 235 | 3.8 | 80.0 | 73.6 |
| Park | 1 210 | 9 648 | D | 534 | 1 625 | 317 | 383 | 352 | 36 456 | 782 | 35.9 | 22.0 | 49.4 |
| Platte | 270 | 2 155 | 344 | D | 402 | 110 | D | 78 | 36 226 | 487 | 16.2 | 49.9 | 58.3 |
| Sheridan | 1 146 | 9 983 | 2 578 | 293 | 1 663 | 361 | 627 | 369 | 37 010 | 599 | 25.9 | 39.7 | 46.4 |
| Sublette | 474 | 3 366 | 201 | D | 336 | D | 117 | 215 | 63 909 | 366 | 31.4 | 34.4 | 40.4 |
| Sweetwater | 1 339 | 16 739 | 1 177 | 1 756 | 2 497 | 310 | 503 | 935 | 55 885 | 244 | 14.8 | 33.2 | 38.9 |
| Teton | 1 870 | 14 762 | 1 073 | D | 1 883 | 408 | 746 | 530 | 35 881 | 180 | 43.9 | 12.8 | 39.4 |
| Uinta | 605 | 7 831 | 1 333 | D | 1 203 | D | 238 | 364 | 46 453 | 344 | 36.0 | 33.4 | 50.9 |
| Washakie | 378 | 3 262 | 851 | 403 | 341 | D | 110 | 100 | 30 675 | 214 | 26.2 | 43.0 | 62.6 |
| Weston | 217 | 1 717 | 421 | D | 326 | D | 39 | 54 | 31 222 | 237 | 4.2 | 67.1 | 44.3 |

# Table B. States and Counties — **Agriculture**

| STATE County | Acreage (1,000) | Percent change, 2002–2007 | Average size of farm | Total irrigated (1,000) | Total cropland (1,000) | Average per farm | Average per acre | Value of machinery and equipment, average per farm (dollars) | Total (mil dol) | Average per farm (dollars) | Crops | Live-stock and poultry products | $10,000 or more | $100,000 or more | Total ($1,000) | Percent of farms |
|---|---|---|---|---|---|---|---|---|---|---|---|---|---|---|---|---|
| | 117 | 118 | 119 | 120 | 121 | 122 | 123 | 124 | 125 | 126 | 127 | 128 | 129 | 130 | 131 | 132 |
| WYOMING—Cont'd | | | | | | | | | | | | | | | | |
| Crook | 1 570 | 3.1 | 3 435 | 4.6 | 166.6 | 2 054 086 | 598 | 122 506 | 44.0 | 96 243 | 10.0 | 90.0 | 56.5 | 23.6 | 972 | 45.5 |
| Fremont | 1 801 | -28.1 | 1 292 | 164.3 | 170.1 | 1 182 494 | 916 | 83 180 | 86.7 | 62 196 | 25.8 | 74.2 | 42.8 | 14.5 | 2 330 | 13.0 |
| Goshen | 1 368 | 8.7 | 1 679 | 111.5 | 286.2 | 1 002 457 | 597 | 105 641 | 157.5 | 193 266 | 20.3 | 79.7 | 58.2 | 24.5 | 4 291 | 56.3 |
| Hot Springs | 547 | -37.6 | 3 039 | 21.4 | 40.5 | 2 230 236 | 734 | 74 689 | 13.4 | 74 526 | 11.3 | 88.7 | 52.8 | 19.4 | 181 | 17.8 |
| Johnson | 1 946 | -9.7 | 6 101 | 40.3 | 45.0 | 2 357 058 | 386 | 109 274 | 28.0 | 87 734 | 7.3 | 92.7 | 58.6 | 26.3 | 837 | 24.5 |
| Laramie | 1 692 | -3.6 | 2 004 | 53.0 | 345.6 | 971 638 | 485 | 88 824 | 124.1 | 147 031 | 17.5 | 82.5 | 37.3 | 14.5 | 4 352 | 38.7 |
| Lincoln | 343 | -6.0 | 640 | 65.3 | 93.9 | 734 860 | 1 147 | 96 088 | 30.1 | 56 197 | 22.7 | 77.3 | 43.6 | 14.6 | 570 | 32.5 |
| Natrona | 2 181 | -24.0 | 5 282 | 40.3 | 49.6 | 1 762 052 | 334 | 92 949 | 32.7 | 79 187 | 16.5 | 83.5 | 47.0 | 17.4 | 1 623 | 19.4 |
| Niobrara | 1 449 | -9.4 | 6 166 | 12.3 | 52.8 | 2 326 340 | 377 | 120 272 | 37.1 | 157 690 | 8.1 | 91.9 | 74.5 | 38.7 | 743 | 36.2 |
| Park | 882 | 8.9 | 1 128 | 111.9 | 113.5 | 935 351 | 830 | 102 491 | 81.8 | 104 571 | 41.1 | 58.9 | 44.4 | 18.8 | 996 | 24.7 |
| Platte | 1 308 | -2.7 | 2 686 | 75.7 | 196.2 | 1 643 815 | 612 | 109 962 | 97.1 | 199 324 | 11.8 | 88.2 | 52.4 | 21.6 | 3 037 | 40.9 |
| Sheridan | 1 225 | -25.2 | 2 044 | 56.3 | 91.4 | 1 606 503 | 786 | 86 611 | 48.7 | 81 239 | 12.0 | 88.0 | 48.6 | 15.2 | 621 | 14.4 |
| Sublette | 599 | 2.2 | 1 637 | 141.4 | 117.9 | 1 657 964 | 1 013 | 91 670 | 36.3 | 99 085 | 8.6 | 91.4 | 39.3 | 20.5 | 157 | 3.6 |
| Sweetwater | 1 486 | 0.4 | 6 092 | 30.3 | 46.1 | 1 087 499 | 179 | 75 900 | 14.5 | 59 451 | 29.9 | 70.1 | 54.5 | 14.3 | 281 | 14.3 |
| Teton | 53 | -7.0 | 294 | 18.2 | 18.5 | 536 771 | 1 825 | 71 552 | 9.2 | 50 929 | 25.1 | 74.9 | 26.7 | 11.1 | 60 | 5.0 |
| Uinta | 743 | -19.1 | 2 159 | 104.8 | 70.2 | 1 270 517 | 588 | 95 624 | 27.1 | 78 667 | 3.3 | 96.7 | 52.9 | 16.0 | 80 | 7.0 |
| Washakie | 470 | 10.1 | 2 195 | 44.4 | 46.6 | 1 252 034 | 570 | 154 625 | 39.6 | 184 819 | 39.6 | 60.4 | 65.0 | 36.0 | 994 | 25.7 |
| Weston | 1 328 | -17.3 | 5 605 | 6.6 | 49.3 | 2 484 428 | 443 | 100 407 | 26.5 | 111 818 | 2.8 | 97.2 | 56.5 | 23.2 | 1 058 | 33.3 |

| STATE County | Water use, 2005 | | Wholesale trade,[1] 2007 | | | | Retail trade,[2] 2007 | | | | Real estate and rental and leasing,[2] 2007 | | | |
|---|---|---|---|---|---|---|---|---|---|---|---|---|---|---|
| | Total water withdrawn (mil gal/day) | Gallons withdrawn per person | Number of establish-ments | Number of employees | Sales (mil dol) | Annual payroll (mil dol) | Number of establish-ments | Number of employees | Sales (mil dol) | Annual payroll (mil dol) | Number of establish-ments | Number of employees | Receipts (mil dol) | Annual payroll (mil dol) |
| | 133 | 134 | 135 | 136 | 137 | 138 | 139 | 140 | 141 | 142 | 143 | 144 | 145 | 146 |
| WYOMING—Cont'd | | | | | | | | | | | | | | |
| Crook | 42.6 | 6 897 | 6 | 29 | 14.1 | 1.4 | 29 | 177 | 56.4 | 3.6 | 5 | 6 | 0.6 | 0.2 |
| Fremont | 413.6 | 11 335 | 36 | 254 | 76.2 | 8.0 | 203 | 2 145 | 558.4 | 53.8 | 78 | 439 | 116.1 | 19.0 |
| Goshen | 312.3 | 25 507 | 20 | 131 | 52.4 | 4.7 | 61 | 517 | 116.1 | 9.1 | 22 | 35 | 4.4 | 0.7 |
| Hot Springs | 90.7 | 19 987 | 3 | D | D | D | 34 | 228 | 38.3 | 3.4 | 7 | 9 | 0.9 | 0.1 |
| Johnson | 121.4 | 15 725 | 5 | D | D | D | 55 | 407 | 71.8 | 7.3 | 27 | 56 | 9.4 | 2.1 |
| Laramie | 272.5 | 3 200 | 98 | 800 | 628.1 | 35.2 | 360 | 5 603 | 1 720.5 | 133.4 | 134 | 519 | 94.2 | 14.3 |
| Lincoln | 201.9 | 12 616 | 9 | 103 | 26.8 | 2.7 | 92 | 699 | 221.7 | 14.7 | 24 | 62 | 4.5 | 0.8 |
| Natrona | 119.5 | 1 712 | 158 | 1 765 | 2 889.4 | 90.0 | 406 | 5 138 | 1 377.0 | 130.4 | 164 | 1 076 | 263.3 | 45.7 |
| Niobrara | 84.5 | 36 942 | 3 | D | D | D | 12 | 86 | 19.6 | 1.5 | 5 | 5 | 1.2 | 0.0 |
| Park | 340.5 | 12 769 | 37 | 200 | 155.5 | 8.5 | 213 | 1 588 | 388.4 | 37.4 | 67 | 161 | 19.0 | 2.7 |
| Platte | 229.4 | 26 616 | 5 | 63 | 34.1 | 2.1 | 47 | 413 | 93.4 | 7.9 | 15 | 32 | 3.8 | 0.6 |
| Sheridan | 198.8 | 7 259 | 40 | D | D | D | 176 | 1 769 | 478.2 | 43.7 | 66 | 234 | 32.3 | 6.2 |
| Sublette | 170.6 | 24 633 | 7 | D | D | D | 43 | 364 | 82.8 | 8.9 | 32 | 143 | 23.0 | 3.5 |
| Sweetwater | 156.8 | 4 130 | 62 | 573 | 437.5 | 32.0 | 202 | 2 753 | 898.2 | 69.7 | 74 | 426 | 105.3 | 18.8 |
| Teton | 67.5 | 3 547 | 32 | D | D | D | 261 | 2 043 | 515.6 | 57.9 | 150 | 528 | 138.7 | 22.1 |
| Uinta | 114.1 | 5 724 | 28 | 225 | 159.4 | 12.3 | 101 | 1 262 | 414.0 | 25.7 | 33 | 138 | 14.2 | 3.1 |
| Washakie | 181.3 | 22 850 | 10 | 69 | 12.1 | 2.0 | 51 | 476 | 98.3 | 8.9 | 19 | 68 | 10.1 | 1.7 |
| Weston | 31.9 | 4 788 | 6 | 51 | 11.5 | 2.1 | 30 | 241 | 64.3 | 4.3 | 9 | 9 | 1.5 | 0.2 |

1. Merchant wholesalers, except manufacturers' sales branches and offices.    2. Employer establishments.

# Table B. States and Counties — Professional Services, Manufacturing, and Accommodation and Food Services

| STATE County | Professional, scientific, and technical services,[1] 2007 | | | | Manufacturing, 2007 | | | | Accommodation and food services, 2007 | | | |
|---|---|---|---|---|---|---|---|---|---|---|---|---|
| | Number of establish-ments | Number of employees | Receipts (mil dol) | Annual payroll (mil dol) | Number of establish-ments | Number of employees | Receipts (mil dol) | Annual payroll (mil dol) | Number of establish-ments | Number of employees | Sales (mil dol) | Annual payroll (mil dol) |
| | 147 | 148 | 149 | 150 | 151 | 152 | 153 | 154 | 155 | 156 | 157 | 158 |
| WYOMING—Cont'd | | | | | | | | | | | | |
| Crook | 12 | 22 | 3.2 | 0.8 | NA | NA | NA | NA | 31 | 147 | 6.1 | 1.5 |
| Fremont | 118 | 406 | 55.5 | 14.8 | NA | NA | NA | NA | 133 | 1 495 | 67.0 | 18.4 |
| Goshen | 20 | D | D | D | 19 | 500 | 147.9 | 14.2 | 31 | 362 | 11.8 | 2.7 |
| Hot Springs | 18 | 46 | 3.3 | 1.3 | NA | NA | NA | NA | 24 | 309 | 10.4 | 3.0 |
| Johnson | 45 | 147 | 15.2 | 5.3 | NA | NA | NA | NA | 43 | 400 | 20.7 | 5.8 |
| Laramie | 312 | 1 402 | 182.0 | 65.2 | 61 | 1 710 | 2 420.2 | 80.9 | 185 | 3 938 | 173.7 | 52.1 |
| Lincoln | 46 | 124 | 11.6 | 4.1 | 22 | 539 | D | 29.4 | 61 | 435 | 21.1 | 4.3 |
| Natrona | 271 | D | D | D | 94 | 2 525 | 1 230.6 | 114.9 | 185 | 3 853 | 168.0 | 50.0 |
| Niobrara | 4 | D | D | D | NA | NA | NA | NA | 13 | 69 | 3.1 | 0.7 |
| Park | 93 | 374 | 40.3 | 15.5 | 54 | 541 | 62.7 | 20.0 | 157 | 1 363 | 133.0 | 32.8 |
| Platte | 22 | 56 | 5.2 | 1.2 | NA | NA | NA | NA | 34 | 347 | 12.1 | 3.2 |
| Sheridan | 119 | D | D | D | NA | NA | NA | NA | 96 | 1 398 | 66.8 | 19.0 |
| Sublette | 54 | 125 | 14.3 | 4.6 | NA | NA | NA | NA | 46 | 225 | 19.7 | 3.9 |
| Sweetwater | 104 | 447 | 64.5 | 22.2 | 34 | 2 122 | D | 145.8 | 108 | 2 040 | 150.4 | 30.1 |
| Teton | 253 | D | D | D | NA | NA | NA | NA | 180 | 4 525 | 327.4 | 112.2 |
| Uinta | 51 | D | D | D | NA | NA | NA | NA | 51 | 773 | 35.5 | 8.1 |
| Washakie | 28 | 115 | 10.8 | 3.5 | NA | NA | NA | NA | 33 | 299 | 10.2 | 2.8 |
| Weston | 13 | D | D | D | NA | NA | NA | NA | 29 | 210 | 7.5 | 1.8 |

1. Establishment subject to federal tax.

Table B. States and Counties — **Health Care and Social Assistance, Other Services, and Federal Funds**

| STATE County | Health care and social assistance, 2007 | | | | Other services, 2007 | | | | Federal funds and grants, 2009–2010 | | | |
|---|---|---|---|---|---|---|---|---|---|---|---|---|
| | | | | | | | | | | Expenditures (mil dol) | | |
| | | | | | | | | | | | Direct payments for individuals[1] | |
| | Number of establishments | Number of employees | Receipts (mil dol) | Annual payroll (mil dol) | Number of establishments | Number of employees | Receipts (mil dol) | Annual payroll (mil dol) | Total | Social Security and government retirement | Medicare | Food Stamps and Supplemental Security Income |
| | 159 | 160 | 161 | 162 | 163 | 164 | 165 | 166 | 167 | 168 | 169 | 170 |
| WYOMING—Cont'd | | | | | | | | | | | | |
| Crook | 16 | D | D | D | 12 | D | D | D | 45.9 | 22.3 | 6.9 | 0.4 |
| Fremont | 129 | 1 842 | 148.8 | 58.2 | 85 | 340 | 32.4 | 8.8 | 331.3 | 122.4 | 54.8 | 12.6 |
| Goshen | 24 | 763 | 39.2 | 19.3 | 26 | 86 | 6.8 | 1.6 | 112.8 | 46.5 | 18.8 | 1.4 |
| Hot Springs | 16 | 358 | 26.5 | 10.9 | 16 | 63 | 4.0 | 1.0 | 46.0 | 22.2 | 10.4 | 0.9 |
| Johnson | 24 | 428 | 30.0 | 13.1 | 23 | 84 | 6.9 | 2.2 | 58.3 | 29.5 | 8.6 | 0.9 |
| Laramie | 281 | 6 040 | 563.1 | 232.9 | 180 | 947 | 83.0 | 25.0 | 1 699.6 | 348.0 | 94.1 | 16.7 |
| Lincoln | 52 | 635 | 44.9 | 18.2 | 37 | 94 | 11.4 | 2.0 | 100.8 | 48.0 | 14.2 | 1.7 |
| Natrona | 283 | 4 819 | 482.2 | 203.0 | 202 | 1 200 | 141.1 | 34.1 | 499.4 | 205.5 | 84.1 | 15.6 |
| Niobrara | 6 | D | D | D | 8 | D | D | D | 21.2 | 8.9 | 4.2 | 2.1 |
| Park | 108 | 1 569 | 144.9 | 58.6 | 81 | 296 | 23.6 | 5.3 | 264.6 | 105.4 | 33.0 | 4.4 |
| Platte | 23 | 403 | 25.7 | 10.9 | 19 | 58 | 5.0 | 0.8 | 115.1 | 36.8 | 14.6 | 1.7 |
| Sheridan | 106 | 2 320 | 219.6 | 100.3 | 72 | 346 | 39.4 | 7.4 | 288.9 | 113.1 | 33.2 | 4.1 |
| Sublette | 20 | 192 | 13.2 | 5.7 | 29 | 150 | 25.8 | 6.6 | 40.7 | 19.1 | 4.9 | 0.5 |
| Sweetwater | 98 | 1 091 | 115.3 | 36.8 | 94 | 448 | 54.2 | 14.5 | 191.1 | 93.0 | 35.2 | 3.3 |
| Teton | 114 | D | D | D | 94 | 461 | 67.4 | 14.5 | 132.2 | 37.6 | 10.8 | 0.5 |
| Uinta | 69 | 1 403 | 97.1 | 39.5 | 47 | 143 | 13.3 | 2.9 | 78.9 | 44.8 | 11.7 | 5.2 |
| Washakie | 25 | 675 | 47.6 | 19.9 | 30 | 112 | 6.9 | 1.9 | 81.9 | 29.0 | 15.6 | 1.1 |
| Weston | 17 | 382 | 20.2 | 8.4 | 12 | 41 | 3.7 | 0.8 | 74.1 | 23.7 | 10.2 | 0.9 |

1. State totals may include programs not allocated by county.

# Table B. States and Counties — Federal Funds, Residential Construction, and Local Government Finances

| STATE County | Federal funds and grants, 2009–2010 (cont.) | | | | | | | Value of residential construction authorized by building permits, 2011 | | Local government finances, 2007 | | | | |
|---|---|---|---|---|---|---|---|---|---|---|---|---|---|---|
| | Expenditures (mil dol) (cont.) | | | | | | | | | General revenue | | | | |
| | | Procurement contract awards | | Grants[1] | | | | | | | | Taxes | | |
| | | | | | | | | | | | | | Per capita[2] (dollars) | |
| | Salaries and wages | Defense | Other | Medicaid and other health-related | Nutrition and family welfare | Education | Other | New con-struction ($1,000) | Number of housing units | Total (mil dol) | Inter-govern-mental (mil dol) | Total (mil dol) | Total | Property |
| | 171 | 172 | 173 | 174 | 175 | 176 | 177 | 178 | 179 | 180 | 181 | 182 | 183 | 184 |
| WYOMING—Cont'd | | | | | | | | | | | | | | |
| Crook | 4.3 | 0.0 | 1.6 | 4.7 | 0.8 | 0.4 | 3.1 | 1 700 | 14 | 46.2 | 28.3 | 9.7 | 1 543 | 1 147 |
| Fremont | 29.8 | 0.7 | 10.6 | 40.3 | 9.6 | 22.7 | 11.6 | 3 030 | 21 | 235.5 | 150.8 | 58.9 | 1 572 | 1 458 |
| Goshen | 11.2 | 0.0 | 1.0 | 23.1 | 2.3 | 0.9 | 0.1 | 960 | 2 | 70.5 | 51.5 | 9.9 | 826 | 564 |
| Hot Springs | 1.0 | 0.0 | 0.2 | 8.1 | 0.7 | 0.3 | 1.8 | 125 | 1 | 45.5 | 18.4 | 11.5 | 2 519 | 2 140 |
| Johnson | 8.0 | 0.0 | 0.9 | 4.6 | 0.8 | 1.4 | 1.4 | 810 | 3 | 77.7 | 26.5 | 32.1 | 3 940 | 3 393 |
| Laramie | 342.8 | 87.9 | 58.5 | 123.4 | 32.6 | 51.0 | 504.2 | 50 748 | 279 | 582.4 | 242.9 | 90.9 | 1 052 | 576 |
| Lincoln | 8.9 | 0.0 | 3.4 | 5.8 | 2.0 | 0.7 | 13.9 | 8 270 | 40 | 132.3 | 54.4 | 46.1 | 2 848 | 2 451 |
| Natrona | 60.4 | 6.7 | 26.2 | 43.2 | 9.6 | 5.5 | 33.5 | 53 589 | 402 | 354.6 | 203.8 | 86.7 | 1 209 | 798 |
| Niobrara | 1.1 | 0.0 | 0.7 | 2.3 | 0.4 | 0.2 | 0.1 | 95 | 3 | 18.6 | 9.4 | 4.5 | 1 975 | 1 494 |
| Park | 39.0 | 0.0 | 47.6 | 19.7 | 3.2 | 1.6 | 1.7 | 21 078 | 113 | 203.2 | 87.4 | 42.3 | 1 562 | 1 381 |
| Platte | 15.4 | 10.5 | 18.0 | 8.1 | 5.7 | 0.6 | 0.4 | 1 813 | 10 | 49.0 | 31.2 | 10.2 | 1 215 | 959 |
| Sheridan | 50.5 | 3.7 | 27.3 | 31.3 | 4.2 | 1.1 | 6.9 | 24 249 | 158 | 198.3 | 80.8 | 45.2 | 1 615 | 1 076 |
| Sublette | 7.5 | 0.0 | 3.0 | 1.2 | 0.7 | 0.4 | 0.6 | 4 110 | 25 | 167.7 | 35.9 | 118.2 | 14 919 | 14 764 |
| Sweetwater | 19.7 | 0.7 | 4.3 | 16.4 | 5.7 | 1.6 | 5.9 | 18 501 | 122 | 358.3 | 89.5 | 164.7 | 4 192 | 2 944 |
| Teton | 19.1 | 1.6 | 49.8 | 3.7 | 2.2 | 0.9 | 3.5 | 97 487 | 118 | 212.3 | 35.0 | 70.4 | 3 520 | 2 230 |
| Uinta | 5.7 | 0.0 | 1.0 | 3.6 | 4.2 | 1.1 | 1.1 | 6 651 | 34 | 118.2 | 49.4 | 54.9 | 2 717 | 2 309 |
| Washakie | 14.9 | 0.1 | 5.2 | 9.6 | 3.9 | 0.6 | 0.6 | 1 857 | 14 | 49.8 | 34.1 | 10.1 | 1 286 | 990 |
| Weston | 2.9 | 26.7 | 0.5 | 5.8 | 0.9 | 0.4 | 0.5 | 496 | 4 | 42.6 | 23.7 | 8.8 | 1 287 | 1 029 |

1. State totals may include programs not allocated by county.    2. Based on the resident population estimated as of July 1 of the year shown.

# Table B. States and Counties — Local Government Finances, Government Employment, and Voting

| STATE County | Local government finances, 2007 (cont.) | | | | | | | | | Government employment, 2011 | | | Presidential election,[2] 2012 | | |
| | Direct general expenditure | | | | | | | Debt outstanding | | | | | Percent of vote cast: | | |
| | | | Percent of total for: | | | | | | | | | | | | |
| | Total (mil dol) | Per capita[1] (dollars) | Education | Health and hospitals | Police protection | Public welfare | Highways | Total (mil dol) | Per capita[1] (dollars) | Federal civilian | Federal military | State and local | Democratic | Republican | All other |
| | 185 | 186 | 187 | 188 | 189 | 190 | 191 | 192 | 193 | 194 | 195 | 196 | 197 | 198 | 199 |
| **WYOMING—Cont'd** | | | | | | | | | | | | | | | |
| Crook | 45.4 | 7 218 | 54.0 | 14.6 | 2.9 | 0.1 | 5.0 | 2.8 | 442 | 94 | 40 | 627 | 16.6 | 80.6 | 2.8 |
| Fremont | 209.7 | 5 594 | 68.5 | 1.3 | 4.0 | 0.3 | 2.2 | 31.1 | 831 | 479 | 231 | 5 369 | 34.2 | 63.0 | 2.8 |
| Goshen | 64.6 | 5 389 | 67.6 | 2.2 | 4.3 | 0.3 | 4.0 | 11.7 | 974 | 87 | 77 | 1 416 | 31.0 | 66.7 | 2.3 |
| Hot Springs | 47.0 | 10 315 | 42.9 | 31.7 | 2.5 | 0.3 | 2.7 | 17.5 | 3 852 | 13 | 27 | 576 | 24.3 | 72.0 | 3.7 |
| Johnson | 74.4 | 9 140 | 48.2 | 21.6 | 2.9 | 0.1 | 10.5 | 19.5 | 2 395 | 132 | 49 | 861 | 20.9 | 76.6 | 2.6 |
| Laramie | 565.4 | 6 548 | 41.9 | 29.9 | 2.9 | 0.3 | 4.0 | 169.5 | 1 963 | 2 664 | 3 610 | 11 261 | 38.6 | 59.0 | 2.4 |
| Lincoln | 126.1 | 7 797 | 50.0 | 21.1 | 3.3 | 0.1 | 4.0 | 57.6 | 3 564 | 122 | 103 | 1 653 | 21.3 | 75.7 | 3.0 |
| Natrona | 342.8 | 4 778 | 60.3 | 1.0 | 4.9 | 0.4 | 3.5 | 80.2 | 1 118 | 696 | 435 | 5 065 | 31.5 | 65.8 | 2.7 |
| Niobrara | 17.9 | 7 903 | 38.1 | 26.9 | 3.0 | 0.1 | 10.4 | 14.0 | 6 175 | 14 | 14 | 441 | 18.9 | 78.7 | 2.5 |
| Park | 199.8 | 7 379 | 50.8 | 22.8 | 2.6 | 0.0 | 4.0 | 45.4 | 1 675 | 807 | 163 | 2 731 | 25.1 | 72.3 | 2.6 |
| Platte | 51.9 | 6 182 | 46.2 | 2.7 | 2.7 | 0.1 | 3.2 | 60.8 | 7 239 | 128 | 50 | 831 | 30.9 | 65.8 | 3.3 |
| Sheridan | 188.7 | 6 739 | 47.2 | 27.4 | 3.0 | 0.1 | 3.6 | 37.3 | 1 334 | 750 | 166 | 2 631 | 29.8 | 67.9 | 2.3 |
| Sublette | 176.7 | 22 302 | 51.4 | 5.5 | 2.4 | 1.5 | 13.1 | 12.0 | 1 511 | 127 | 58 | 942 | 21.5 | 76.1 | 2.4 |
| Sweetwater | 334.9 | 8 521 | 41.6 | 21.8 | 4.4 | 0.4 | 6.4 | 239.5 | 6 094 | 242 | 251 | 4 383 | 34.5 | 62.0 | 3.5 |
| Teton | 179.5 | 8 976 | 23.0 | 32.2 | 4.6 | 0.7 | 4.5 | 45.3 | 2 267 | 421 | 122 | 1 849 | 60.7 | 37.1 | 2.3 |
| Uinta | 128.7 | 6 374 | 59.9 | 1.2 | 4.7 | 0.1 | 4.5 | 82.5 | 4 083 | 71 | 119 | 2 077 | 27.6 | 68.7 | 3.6 |
| Washakie | 38.7 | 4 951 | 59.3 | 1.6 | 4.7 | 1.8 | 3.1 | 10.3 | 1 322 | 131 | 48 | 760 | 25.5 | 72.3 | 2.2 |
| Weston | 41.0 | 5 979 | 40.8 | 28.1 | 3.6 | 0.5 | 8.3 | 4.7 | 685 | 52 | 40 | 756 | 19.4 | 77.2 | 3.4 |

1. Based on the resident population estimated as of July 1 of the year shown. 2. © 2013 Election Data Services, Inc. All rights reserved.

Items 185—199

# Metropolitan Areas

(For explanation of symbols, see page viii)

# Metropolitan Area Highlights and Rankings

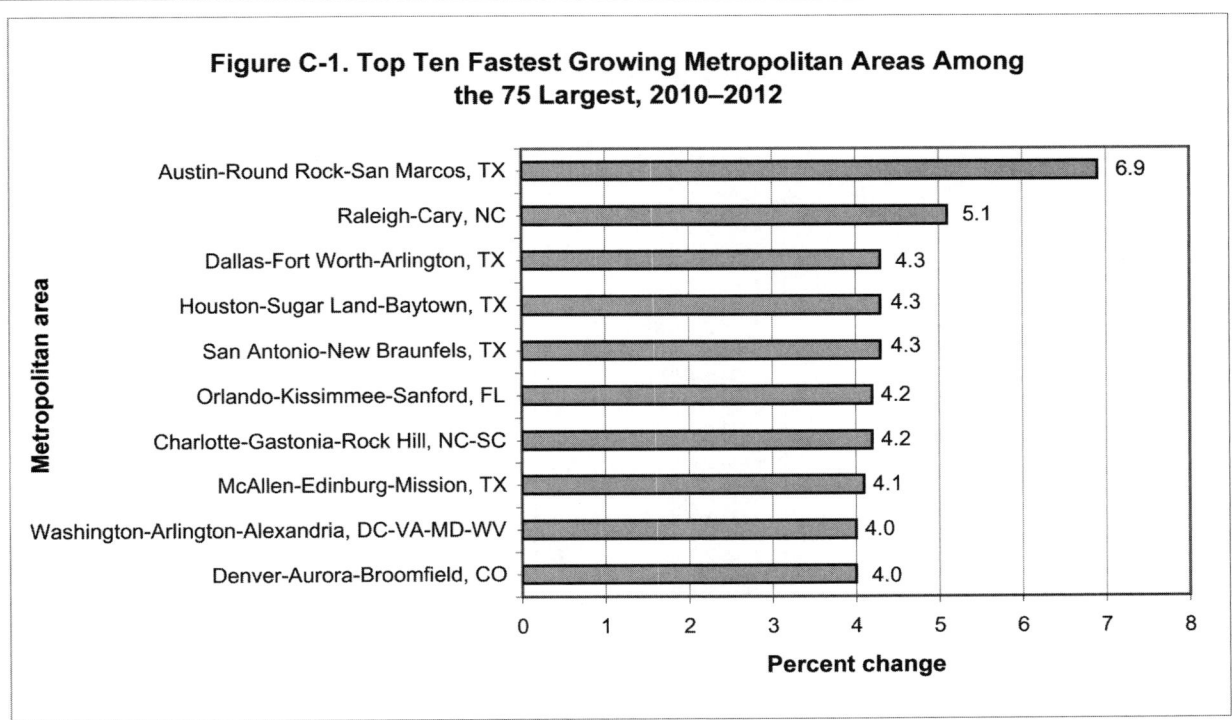

**Figure C-1. Top Ten Fastest Growing Metropolitan Areas Among the 75 Largest, 2010–2012**

In 2012, 83.9 percent of Americans lived in metropolitan areas, but these metropolitan areas made up a mere 26 percent of the nation's land area. In 2013, the Census Bureau released data for new metropolitan and micropolitan areas based on the 2010 census. These new delineations are listed in Appendix C, together with their 2010 census populations and 2012 estimated populations. However, Table C continues to use the 2009 delineations until more data are available for the new areas.

With nearly 19.2 million people, the New York metropolitan area was the largest, followed by Los Angeles with a population of almost 13.1 million. Chicago ranked third with 9.5 million people. Another 11 metropolitan areas had more than 4 million residents (Dallas, Houston, Philadelphia, Washington, Miami, Atlanta, Boston, San Francisco, Riverside, Phoenix, and Detroit), while 37 other metropolitan areas had between 1 million and 4 million people. Over 54 percent of the U.S. population lived in these 51 metropolitan areas with one million or more residents.

Ten metropolitan areas grew by 5 percent or more between 2010 and 2012. Midland, TX, had the highest growth rate, increasing by 7.0 percent to a 2012 population of 146,645 residents. Among the 75 largest metropolitan areas, Austin-Round Rock-San Marcos, TX had the largest increase at 6.9 percent followed by Raleigh-Cary, NC at 5.1 percent. Three of the most populous metropolitan areas lost population since 2010. All were areas located in the Great Lakes region (Detroit, MI; Buffalo, NY; and Cleveland, OH).

Among metropolitan areas, New York and Los Angeles shared the top spots for density as well as for total population.

With 1,106.3 persons per square kilometer, the New York metropolitan area is only slightly more densely populated than the Los Angeles metropolitan area, which had nearly 1,039.5 persons per square kilometer. At the other extreme, 4 of the largest metropolitan areas had fewer than 50 persons per square kilometer. All four of these had large land areas and were located in western states (Albuquerque, NM; Bakersfield, CA; Tucson, AZ; and Salt Lake City, UT).

In 2012, 52 metropolitan areas had an unemployment rate at 10 percent or higher. In contrast, 131 metropolitan areas had an unemployment rate at 10 percent or higher in 2010. Topping the list are El Centro, CA and Yuma, AZ, two metropolitan areas with large agricultural workforces and unemployment rates over 25 percent. Eight of the 10 metropolitan areas with the highest unemployment were in California. Ten of the 75 most populous metropolitan areas had unemployment rates higher than 10 percent and two had unemployment rates over 15 percent. Twenty-three metropolitan areas had unemployment rates below 5 percent in 2012. Many of them were relatively small areas. Bismark, ND had the lowest unemployment rate among all metropolitan areas at 3.0 percent, followed by Midland, TX at 3.5 percent.

# 75 Largest Metropolitan Areas by 2012 Population
## Selected Rankings

| | Population, 2012 | | | | Total land area, 2010 | |
|---|---|---|---|---|---|---|
| Population rank | Metropolitan area | Population [col 2] | Population rank | Land area rank | Metropolitan area | Land area (square kilometers) [col 1] |
| 1 | New York-Northern New Jersey-Long Island, NY-NJ-PA | 19 160 024 | 12 | 1 | Riverside-San Bernardino-Ontario, CA | 70 612 |
| 2 | Los Angeles-Long Beach-Santa Ana, CA | 13 052 921 | 13 | 2 | Phoenix-Mesa-Glendale, AZ | 37 725 |
| 3 | Chicago-Joliet-Naperville, IL-IN-WI | 9 522 434 | 48 | 3 | Salt Lake City, UT | 24 748 |
| 4 | Dallas-Fort Worth-Arlington, TX | 6 645 678 | 57 | 4 | Albuquerque, NM | 24 042 |
| 5 | Houston-Sugar Land-Baytown, TX | 6 204 161 | 52 | 5 | Tucson, AZ | 23 794 |
| 6 | Philadelphia-Camden-Wilmington, PA-NJ-DE-MD | 6 018 800 | 4 | 6 | Dallas-Fort Worth-Arlington, TX | 23 122 |
| 7 | Washington-Arlington-Alexandria, DC-VA-MD-WV | 5 804 975 | 5 | 7 | Houston-Sugar Land-Baytown, TX | 22 863 |
| 8 | Miami-Fort Lauderdale-Pompano Beach, FL | 5 762 717 | 19 | 8 | St. Louis, MO-IL | 22 334 |
| 9 | Atlanta-Sandy Springs-Marietta, GA | 5 439 950 | 21 | 9 | Denver-Aurora-Broomfield, CO | 21 616 |
| 10 | Boston-Cambridge-Quincy, MA-NH | 4 640 802 | 9 | 10 | Atlanta-Sandy Springs-Marietta, GA | 21 597 |
| 11 | San Francisco-Oakland-Fremont, CA | 4 455 560 | 61 | 11 | Bakersfield-Delano, CA | 21 062 |
| 12 | Riverside-San Bernardino-Ontario, CA | 4 350 096 | 30 | 12 | Las Vegas-Paradise, NV | 20 439 |
| 13 | Phoenix-Mesa-Glendale, AZ | 4 329 534 | 28 | 13 | Kansas City, MO-KS | 20 273 |
| 14 | Detroit-Warren-Livonia, MI | 4 292 060 | 24 | 14 | San Antonio-New Braunfels, TX | 18 940 |
| 15 | Seattle-Tacoma-Bellevue, WA | 3 552 157 | 3 | 15 | Chicago-Joliet-Naperville, IL-IN-WI | 18 640 |
| 16 | Minneapolis-St. Paul-Bloomington, MN | 3 353 724 | 1 | 16 | New York-Northern New Jersey-Long Island, NY-NJ-PA | 17 319 |
| 17 | San Diego-Carlsbad-San Marcos, CA | 3 177 063 | 23 | 17 | Portland-Vancouver-Hillsboro, OR-WA | 17 311 |
| 18 | Tampa-St. Petersburg-Clearwater, FL | 2 842 878 | 54 | 18 | Tulsa, OK | 16 237 |
| 19 | St. Louis, MO-IL | 2 820 889 | 16 | 19 | Minneapolis-St. Paul-Bloomington, MN | 15 610 |
| 20 | Baltimore-Towson, MD | 2 753 149 | 55 | 20 | Fresno, CA | 15 431 |
| 21 | Denver-Aurora-Broomfield, CO | 2 645 209 | 15 | 21 | Seattle-Tacoma-Bellevue, WA | 15 209 |
| 22 | Pittsburgh, PA | 2 360 733 | 37 | 22 | Nashville-Davidson—Murfreesboro—Franklin, TN | 14 734 |
| 23 | Portland-Vancouver-Hillsboro, OR-WA | 2 289 800 | 44 | 23 | Richmond, VA | 14 724 |
| 24 | San Antonio-New Braunfels, TX | 2 234 003 | 7 | 24 | Washington-Arlington-Alexandria, DC-VA-MD-WV | 14 500 |
| 25 | Orlando-Kissimmee-Sanford, FL | 2 223 674 | 43 | 25 | Oklahoma City, OK | 14 275 |
| 26 | Sacramento—Arden-Arcade—Roseville, CA | 2 196 482 | 22 | 26 | Pittsburgh, PA | 13 679 |
| 27 | Cincinnati-Middletown, OH-KY-IN | 2 144 210 | 49 | 27 | Birmingham-Hoover, AL | 13 674 |
| 28 | Kansas City, MO-KS | 2 064 630 | 26 | 28 | Sacramento—Arden-Arcade—Roseville, CA | 13 194 |
| 29 | Cleveland-Elyria-Mentor, OH | 2 063 535 | 8 | 29 | Miami-Fort Lauderdale-Pompano Beach, FL | 13 150 |
| 30 | Las Vegas-Paradise, NV | 2 000 759 | 2 | 30 | Los Angeles-Long Beach-Santa Ana, CA | 12 557 |
| 31 | San Jose-Sunnyvale-Santa Clara, CA | 1 894 388 | 6 | 31 | Philadelphia-Camden-Wilmington, PA-NJ-DE-MD | 11 919 |
| 32 | Columbus, OH | 1 878 714 | 41 | 32 | Memphis, TN-MS-AR | 11 857 |
| 33 | Austin-Round Rock-San Marcos, TX | 1 834 303 | 27 | 33 | Cincinnati-Middletown, OH-KY-IN | 11 375 |
| 34 | Charlotte-Gastonia-Rock Hill, NC-SC | 1 831 084 | 58 | 34 | Omaha-Council Bluffs, NE-IA | 11 266 |
| 35 | Indianapolis-Carmel, IN | 1 798 634 | 33 | 35 | Austin-Round Rock-San Marcos, TX | 10 929 |
| 36 | Virginia Beach-Norfolk-Newport News, VA-NC | 1 694 900 | 17 | 36 | San Diego-Carlsbad-San Marcos, CA | 10 895 |
| 37 | Nashville-Davidson—Murfreesboro—Franklin, TN | 1 644 703 | 42 | 37 | Louisville-Jefferson County, KY-IN | 10 647 |
| 38 | Providence-New Bedford-Fall River, RI-MA | 1 601 374 | 73 | 38 | Little Rock-North Little Rock-Conway, AR | 10 581 |
| 39 | Milwaukee-Waukesha-West Allis, WI | 1 566 981 | 66 | 39 | Baton Rouge, LA | 10 430 |
| 40 | Jacksonville, FL | 1 377 850 | 32 | 40 | Columbus, OH | 10 275 |
| 41 | Memphis, TN-MS-AR | 1 332 960 | 14 | 41 | Detroit-Warren-Livonia, MI | 10 071 |
| 42 | Louisville-Jefferson County, KY-IN | 1 301 116 | 35 | 42 | Indianapolis-Carmel, IN | 9 983 |
| 43 | Oklahoma City, OK | 1 296 565 | 70 | 43 | Columbia, SC | 9 590 |
| 44 | Richmond, VA | 1 282 305 | 10 | 44 | Boston-Cambridge-Quincy, MA-NH | 9 032 |
| 45 | Hartford-West Hartford-East Hartford, CT | 1 214 400 | 25 | 45 | Orlando-Kissimmee-Sanford, FL | 9 009 |
| 46 | New Orleans-Metairie-Kenner, LA | 1 205 374 | 40 | 46 | Jacksonville, FL | 8 291 |
| 47 | Raleigh-Cary, NC | 1 188 564 | 34 | 47 | Charlotte-Gastonia-Rock Hill, NC-SC | 7 991 |
| 48 | Salt Lake City, UT | 1 161 715 | 46 | 48 | New Orleans-Metairie-Kenner, LA | 7 667 |
| 49 | Birmingham-Hoover, AL | 1 136 650 | 51 | 49 | Rochester, NY | 7 584 |
| 50 | Buffalo-Niagara Falls, NY | 1 134 210 | 59 | 50 | Albany-Schenectady-Troy, NY | 7 282 |
| 51 | Rochester, NY | 1 056 940 | 69 | 51 | Grand Rapids-Wyoming, MI | 7 212 |
| 52 | Tucson, AZ | 992 394 | 31 | 52 | San Jose-Sunnyvale-Santa Clara, CA | 6 938 |
| 53 | Honolulu, HI | 976 372 | 36 | 53 | Virginia Beach-Norfolk-Newport News, VA-NC | 6 811 |
| 54 | Tulsa, OK | 951 880 | 20 | 54 | Baltimore-Towson, MD | 6 738 |
| 55 | Fresno, CA | 947 895 | 18 | 55 | Tampa-St. Petersburg-Clearwater, FL | 6 510 |
| 56 | Bridgeport-Stamford-Norwalk, CT | 933 835 | 11 | 56 | San Francisco-Oakland-Fremont, CA | 6 399 |
| 57 | Albuquerque, NM | 901 700 | 47 | 57 | Raleigh-Cary, NC | 5 486 |
| 58 | Omaha-Council Bluffs, NE-IA | 885 624 | 29 | 58 | Cleveland-Elyria-Mentor, OH | 5 173 |
| 59 | Albany-Schenectady-Troy, NY | 874 646 | 71 | 59 | Greensboro-High Point, NC | 5 164 |
| 60 | New Haven-Milford, CT | 862 813 | 74 | 60 | Knoxville, TN | 4 809 |
| 61 | Bakersfield-Delano, CA | 856 158 | 63 | 61 | Oxnard-Thousand Oaks-Ventura, CA | 4 774 |
| 62 | Dayton, OH | 842 858 | 62 | 62 | Dayton, OH | 4 418 |
| 63 | Oxnard-Thousand Oaks-Ventura, CA | 835 981 | 38 | 63 | Providence-New Bedford-Fall River, RI-MA | 4 110 |
| 64 | El Paso, TX | 827 398 | 67 | 64 | McAllen-Edinburg-Mission, TX | 4 069 |
| 65 | Allentown-Bethlehem-Easton, PA-NJ | 827 171 | 50 | 65 | Buffalo-Niagara Falls, NY | 4 053 |
| 66 | Baton Rouge, LA | 815 298 | 45 | 66 | Hartford-West Hartford-East Hartford, CT | 3 923 |
| 67 | McAllen-Edinburg-Mission, TX | 806 552 | 68 | 67 | Worcester, MA | 3 913 |
| 68 | Worcester, MA | 806 163 | 39 | 68 | Milwaukee-Waukesha-West Allis, WI | 3 768 |
| 69 | Grand Rapids-Wyoming, MI | 785 352 | 65 | 69 | Allentown-Bethlehem-Easton, PA-NJ | 3 764 |
| 70 | Columbia, SC | 784 745 | 75 | 70 | Stockton, CA | 3 604 |
| 71 | Greensboro-High Point, NC | 736 065 | 72 | 71 | North Port-Bradenton-Sarasota, FL | 3 364 |
| 72 | North Port-Bradenton-Sarasota, FL | 720 042 | 64 | 72 | El Paso, TX | 2 623 |
| 73 | Little Rock-North Little Rock-Conway, AR | 717 666 | 56 | 73 | Bridgeport-Stamford-Norwalk, CT | 1 618 |
| 74 | Knoxville, TN | 709 824 | 60 | 74 | New Haven-Milford, CT | 1 566 |
| 75 | Stockton, CA | 702 612 | 53 | 75 | Honolulu, HI | 1 556 |

# 75 Largest Metropolitan Areas by 2012 Population
## Selected Rankings

| Population density, 2012 | | | | Percent population change, 2010–2012 | | | |
| --- | --- | --- | --- | --- | --- | --- | --- |
| Population rank | Density rank | Metropolitan area | Density (per square kilometer) [col 4] | Population rank | Percent change rank | Metropolitan area | Percent change [col 23] |
| 1 | 1 | New York-Northern New Jersey-Long Island, NY-NJ-PA | 1 106 | 33 | 1 | Austin-Round Rock-San Marcos, TX | 6.9 |
| 2 | 2 | Los Angeles-Long Beach-Santa Ana, CA | 1 040 | 47 | 2 | Raleigh-Cary, NC | 5.1 |
| 11 | 3 | San Francisco-Oakland-Fremont, CA | 696 | 4 | 3 | Dallas-Fort Worth-Arlington, TX | 4.3 |
| 53 | 4 | Honolulu, HI | 628 | 5 | 3 | Houston-Sugar Land-Baytown, TX | 4.3 |
| 56 | 5 | Bridgeport-Stamford-Norwalk, CT | 577 | 24 | 3 | San Antonio-New Braunfels, TX | 4.3 |
| 60 | 6 | New Haven-Milford, CT | 551 | 25 | 6 | Orlando-Kissimmee-Sanford, FL | 4.2 |
| 10 | 7 | Boston-Cambridge-Quincy, MA-NH | 514 | 34 | 6 | Charlotte-Gastonia-Rock Hill, NC-SC | 4.2 |
| 3 | 8 | Chicago-Joliet-Naperville, IL-IN-WI | 511 | 67 | 8 | McAllen-Edinburg-Mission, TX | 4.1 |
| 6 | 9 | Philadelphia-Camden-Wilmington, PA-NJ-DE-MD | 505 | 7 | 9 | Washington-Arlington-Alexandria, DC-VA-MD-WV | 4.0 |
| 8 | 10 | Miami-Fort Lauderdale-Pompano Beach, FL | 438 | 21 | 9 | Denver-Aurora-Broomfield, CO | 4.0 |
| 18 | 11 | Tampa-St. Petersburg-Clearwater, FL | 437 | 8 | 11 | Miami-Fort Lauderdale-Pompano Beach, FL | 3.6 |
| 14 | 12 | Detroit-Warren-Livonia, MI | 426 | 43 | 12 | Oklahoma City, OK | 3.5 |
| 39 | 13 | Milwaukee-Waukesha-West Allis, WI | 416 | 37 | 13 | Nashville-Davidson—Murfreesboro—Franklin, TN | 3.4 |
| 20 | 14 | Baltimore-Towson, MD | 409 | 13 | 14 | Phoenix-Mesa-Glendale, AZ | 3.3 |
| 7 | 15 | Washington-Arlington-Alexandria, DC-VA-MD-WV | 400 | 15 | 14 | Seattle-Tacoma-Bellevue, WA | 3.3 |
| 29 | 16 | Cleveland-Elyria-Mentor, OH | 399 | 48 | 14 | Salt Lake City, UT | 3.3 |
| 38 | 17 | Providence-New Bedford-Fall River, RI-MA | 390 | 64 | 14 | El Paso, TX | 3.3 |
| 64 | 18 | El Paso, TX | 315 | 9 | 18 | Atlanta-Sandy Springs-Marietta, GA | 3.2 |
| 45 | 19 | Hartford-West Hartford-East Hartford, CT | 310 | 46 | 18 | New Orleans-Metairie-Kenner, LA | 3.2 |
| 17 | 20 | San Diego-Carlsbad-San Marcos, CA | 292 | 31 | 20 | San Jose-Sunnyvale-Santa Clara, CA | 3.1 |
| 4 | 21 | Dallas-Fort Worth-Arlington, TX | 287 | 12 | 21 | Riverside-San Bernardino-Ontario, CA | 3.0 |
| 50 | 22 | Buffalo-Niagara Falls, NY | 280 | 23 | 22 | Portland-Vancouver-Hillsboro, OR-WA | 2.9 |
| 31 | 23 | San Jose-Sunnyvale-Santa Clara, CA | 273 | 11 | 23 | San Francisco-Oakland-Fremont, CA | 2.8 |
| 5 | 24 | Houston-Sugar Land-Baytown, TX | 271 | 17 | 24 | San Diego-Carlsbad-San Marcos, CA | 2.6 |
| 9 | 25 | Atlanta-Sandy Springs-Marietta, GA | 252 | 73 | 24 | Little Rock-North Little Rock-Conway, AR | 2.6 |
| 36 | 26 | Virginia Beach-Norfolk-Newport News, VA-NC | 249 | 30 | 26 | Las Vegas-Paradise, NV | 2.5 |
| 25 | 27 | Orlando-Kissimmee-Sanford, FL | 247 | 72 | 26 | North Port-Bradenton-Sarasota, FL | 2.5 |
| 15 | 28 | Seattle-Tacoma-Bellevue, WA | 234 | 75 | 26 | Stockton, CA | 2.5 |
| 34 | 29 | Charlotte-Gastonia-Rock Hill, NC-SC | 229 | 35 | 29 | Indianapolis-Carmel, IN | 2.4 |
| 65 | 30 | Allentown-Bethlehem-Easton, PA-NJ | 220 | 40 | 29 | Jacksonville, FL | 2.4 |
| 47 | 31 | Raleigh-Cary, NC | 217 | 53 | 29 | Honolulu, HI | 2.4 |
| 16 | 32 | Minneapolis-St. Paul-Bloomington, MN | 215 | 16 | 32 | Minneapolis-St. Paul-Bloomington, MN | 2.3 |
| 72 | 33 | North Port-Bradenton-Sarasota, FL | 214 | 32 | 32 | Columbus, OH | 2.3 |
| 68 | 34 | Worcester, MA | 206 | 58 | 32 | Omaha-Council Bluffs, NE-IA | 2.3 |
| 67 | 35 | McAllen-Edinburg-Mission, TX | 198 | 26 | 35 | Sacramento—Arden-Arcade—Roseville, CA | 2.2 |
| 75 | 36 | Stockton, CA | 195 | 70 | 35 | Columbia, SC | 2.2 |
| 62 | 37 | Dayton, OH | 191 | 18 | 37 | Tampa-St. Petersburg-Clearwater, FL | 2.1 |
| 27 | 38 | Cincinnati-Middletown, OH-KY-IN | 189 | 61 | 38 | Bakersfield-Delano, CA | 2.0 |
| 32 | 39 | Columbus, OH | 183 | 10 | 39 | Boston-Cambridge-Quincy, MA-NH | 1.9 |
| 35 | 40 | Indianapolis-Carmel, IN | 180 | 44 | 39 | Richmond, VA | 1.9 |
| 63 | 41 | Oxnard-Thousand Oaks-Ventura, CA | 175 | 55 | 39 | Fresno, CA | 1.9 |
| 22 | 42 | Pittsburgh, PA | 173 | 56 | 39 | Bridgeport-Stamford-Norwalk, CT | 1.9 |
| 33 | 43 | Austin-Round Rock-San Marcos, TX | 168 | 2 | 43 | Los Angeles-Long Beach-Santa Ana, CA | 1.7 |
| 26 | 44 | Sacramento—Arden-Arcade—Roseville, CA | 167 | 71 | 43 | Greensboro-High Point, NC | 1.7 |
| 40 | 45 | Jacksonville, FL | 166 | 74 | 43 | Knoxville, TN | 1.7 |
| 46 | 46 | New Orleans-Metairie-Kenner, LA | 157 | 20 | 46 | Baltimore-Towson, MD | 1.6 |
| 74 | 47 | Knoxville, TN | 148 | 57 | 46 | Albuquerque, NM | 1.6 |
| 71 | 48 | Greensboro-High Point, NC | 143 | 66 | 46 | Baton Rouge, LA | 1.6 |
| 51 | 49 | Rochester, NY | 139 | 54 | 49 | Tulsa, OK | 1.5 |
| 23 | 50 | Portland-Vancouver-Hillsboro, OR-WA | 132 | 63 | 49 | Oxnard-Thousand Oaks-Ventura, CA | 1.5 |
| 19 | 51 | St. Louis, MO-IL | 126 | 1 | 51 | New York-Northern New Jersey-Long Island, NY-NJ-PA | 1.4 |
| 21 | 52 | Denver-Aurora-Broomfield, CO | 122 | 28 | 51 | Kansas City, MO-KS | 1.4 |
| 42 | 53 | Louisville-Jefferson County, KY-IN | 122 | 36 | 51 | Virginia Beach-Norfolk-Newport News, VA-NC | 1.4 |
| 59 | 54 | Albany-Schenectady-Troy, NY | 120 | 42 | 51 | Louisville-Jefferson County, KY-IN | 1.4 |
| 24 | 55 | San Antonio-New Braunfels, TX | 118 | 69 | 51 | Grand Rapids-Wyoming, MI | 1.4 |
| 13 | 56 | Phoenix-Mesa-Glendale, AZ | 115 | 41 | 56 | Memphis, TN-MS-AR | 1.3 |
| 41 | 57 | Memphis, TN-MS-AR | 112 | 52 | 57 | Tucson, AZ | 1.2 |
| 37 | 58 | Nashville-Davidson—Murfreesboro—Franklin, TN | 112 | 68 | 58 | Worcester, MA | 1.0 |
| 69 | 59 | Grand Rapids-Wyoming, MI | 109 | 6 | 59 | Philadelphia-Camden-Wilmington, PA-NJ-DE-MD | 0.9 |
| 28 | 60 | Kansas City, MO-KS | 102 | 49 | 60 | Birmingham-Hoover, AL | 0.8 |
| 30 | 61 | Las Vegas-Paradise, NV | 98 | 27 | 61 | Cincinnati-Middletown, OH-KY-IN | 0.7 |
| 43 | 62 | Oklahoma City, OK | 91 | 39 | 61 | Milwaukee-Waukesha-West Allis, WI | 0.7 |
| 44 | 63 | Richmond, VA | 87 | 65 | 61 | Allentown-Bethlehem-Easton, PA-NJ | 0.7 |
| 49 | 64 | Birmingham-Hoover, AL | 83 | 3 | 64 | Chicago-Joliet-Naperville, IL-IN-WI | 0.6 |
| 70 | 65 | Columbia, SC | 82 | 59 | 65 | Albany-Schenectady-Troy, NY | 0.5 |
| 58 | 66 | Omaha-Council Bluffs, NE-IA | 79 | 19 | 66 | St. Louis, MO-IL | 0.3 |
| 66 | 67 | Baton Rouge, LA | 78 | 22 | 67 | Pittsburgh, PA | 0.2 |
| 73 | 68 | Little Rock-North Little Rock-Conway, AR | 68 | 45 | 67 | Hartford-West Hartford-East Hartford, CT | 0.2 |
| 12 | 69 | Riverside-San Bernardino-Ontario, CA | 62 | 51 | 67 | Rochester, NY | 0.2 |
| 55 | 70 | Fresno, CA | 61 | 62 | 67 | Dayton, OH | 0.2 |
| 54 | 71 | Tulsa, OK | 59 | 38 | 71 | Providence-New Bedford-Fall River, RI-MA | 0.0 |
| 48 | 72 | Salt Lake City, UT | 47 | 60 | 71 | New Haven-Milford, CT | 0.0 |
| 52 | 73 | Tucson, AZ | 42 | 14 | 73 | Detroit-Warren-Livonia, MI | -0.1 |
| 61 | 74 | Bakersfield-Delano, CA | 41 | 50 | 73 | Buffalo-Niagara Falls, NY | -0.1 |
| 57 | 75 | Albuquerque, NM | 38 | 29 | 75 | Cleveland-Elyria-Mentor, OH | -0.7 |

# 75 Largest Metropolitan Areas by 2012 Population
## Selected Rankings

| Percent White, not Hispanic or Latino, alone or in combination, 2011 | | | | Percent Black, not Hispanic or Latino, alone or in combination, 2011 | | | |
|---|---|---|---|---|---|---|---|
| Population rank | White rank | Metropolitan area | Percent White [col 5] | Population rank | Black rank | Metropolitan area | Percent Black [col 6] |
| 22 | 1 | Pittsburgh, PA | 88.2 | 41 | 1 | Memphis, TN-MS-AR | 46.1 |
| 74 | 2 | Knoxville, TN | 88.0 | 66 | 2 | Baton Rouge, LA | 36.1 |
| 59 | 3 | Albany-Schenectady-Troy, NY | 84.3 | 46 | 3 | New Orleans-Metairie-Kenner, LA | 34.7 |
| 27 | 4 | Cincinnati-Middletown, OH-KY-IN | 83.0 | 70 | 4 | Columbia, SC | 33.9 |
| 68 | 5 | Worcester, MA | 82.2 | 9 | 5 | Atlanta-Sandy Springs-Marietta, GA | 33.0 |
| 38 | 6 | Providence-New Bedford-Fall River, RI-MA | 81.4 | 36 | 6 | Virginia Beach-Norfolk-Newport News, VA-NC | 32.0 |
| 69 | 7 | Grand Rapids-Wyoming, MI | 81.1 | 44 | 7 | Richmond, VA | 30.5 |
| 62 | 8 | Dayton, OH | 80.7 | 20 | 8 | Baltimore-Towson, MD | 29.7 |
| 50 | 9 | Buffalo-Niagara Falls, NY | 80.6 | 49 | 9 | Birmingham-Hoover, AL | 28.8 |
| 16 | 10 | Minneapolis-St. Paul-Bloomington, MN | 80.5 | 7 | 10 | Washington-Arlington-Alexandria, DC-VA-MD-WV | 26.5 |
| 42 | 11 | Louisville-Jefferson County, KY-IN | 80.3 | 71 | 10 | Greensboro-High Point, NC | 26.5 |
| 58 | 12 | Omaha-Council Bluffs, NE-IA | 80.2 | 34 | 12 | Charlotte-Gastonia-Rock Hill, NC-SC | 24.7 |
| 72 | 12 | North Port-Bradenton-Sarasota, FL | 80.2 | 14 | 13 | Detroit-Warren-Livonia, MI | 23.6 |
| 51 | 14 | Rochester, NY | 79.4 | 73 | 14 | Little Rock-North Little Rock-Conway, AR | 22.9 |
| 65 | 15 | Allentown-Bethlehem-Easton, PA-NJ | 79.2 | 40 | 15 | Jacksonville, FL | 22.3 |
| 23 | 16 | Portland-Vancouver-Hillsboro, OR-WA | 79.0 | 6 | 16 | Philadelphia-Camden-Wilmington, PA-NJ-DE-MD | 21.2 |
| 32 | 17 | Columbus, OH | 77.8 | 47 | 17 | Raleigh-Cary, NC | 20.9 |
| 19 | 18 | St. Louis, MO-IL | 76.6 | 29 | 18 | Cleveland-Elyria-Mentor, OH | 20.7 |
| 10 | 19 | Boston-Cambridge-Quincy, MA-NH | 76.5 | 8 | 19 | Miami-Fort Lauderdale-Pompano Beach, FL | 20.5 |
| 28 | 20 | Kansas City, MO-KS | 76.3 | 19 | 20 | St. Louis, MO-IL | 19.0 |
| 48 | 20 | Salt Lake City, UT | 76.3 | 3 | 21 | Chicago-Joliet-Naperville, IL-IN-WI | 17.6 |
| 35 | 22 | Indianapolis-Carmel, IN | 76.1 | 39 | 22 | Milwaukee-Waukesha-West Allis, WI | 17.4 |
| 37 | 23 | Nashville-Davidson—Murfreesboro—Franklin, TN | 75.3 | 5 | 23 | Houston-Sugar Land-Baytown, TX | 17.2 |
| 29 | 24 | Cleveland-Elyria-Mentor, OH | 73.1 | 1 | 24 | New York-Northern New Jersey-Long Island, NY-NJ-PA | 17.0 |
| 54 | 25 | Tulsa, OK | 72.8 | 25 | 25 | Orlando-Kissimmee-Sanford, FL | 16.2 |
| 45 | 26 | Hartford-West Hartford-East Hartford, CT | 72.5 | 32 | 25 | Columbus, OH | 16.2 |
| 15 | 27 | Seattle-Tacoma-Bellevue, WA | 71.5 | 62 | 25 | Dayton, OH | 16.2 |
| 43 | 28 | Oklahoma City, OK | 70.9 | 37 | 28 | Nashville-Davidson—Murfreesboro—Franklin, TN | 16.0 |
| 73 | 29 | Little Rock-North Little Rock-Conway, AR | 70.7 | 35 | 29 | Indianapolis-Carmel, IN | 15.9 |
| 39 | 30 | Milwaukee-Waukesha-West Allis, WI | 70.2 | 4 | 30 | Dallas-Fort Worth-Arlington, TX | 15.4 |
| 14 | 31 | Detroit-Warren-Livonia, MI | 69.4 | 42 | 31 | Louisville-Jefferson County, KY-IN | 14.7 |
| 60 | 32 | New Haven-Milford, CT | 68.6 | 28 | 32 | Kansas City, MO-KS | 13.4 |
| 18 | 33 | Tampa-St. Petersburg-Clearwater, FL | 68.3 | 27 | 33 | Cincinnati-Middletown, OH-KY-IN | 12.9 |
| 21 | 34 | Denver-Aurora-Broomfield, CO | 67.5 | 60 | 33 | New Haven-Milford, CT | 12.9 |
| 40 | 35 | Jacksonville, FL | 67.3 | 50 | 35 | Buffalo-Niagara Falls, NY | 12.8 |
| 56 | 36 | Bridgeport-Stamford-Norwalk, CT | 67.1 | 18 | 36 | Tampa-St. Petersburg-Clearwater, FL | 12.4 |
| 6 | 37 | Philadelphia-Camden-Wilmington, PA-NJ-DE-MD | 66.1 | 51 | 37 | Rochester, NY | 12.1 |
| 49 | 38 | Birmingham-Hoover, AL | 65.6 | 43 | 38 | Oklahoma City, OK | 11.7 |
| 47 | 39 | Raleigh-Cary, NC | 64.7 | 30 | 39 | Las Vegas-Paradise, NV | 11.2 |
| 71 | 40 | Greensboro-High Point, NC | 63.1 | 45 | 40 | Hartford-West Hartford-East Hartford, CT | 11.1 |
| 34 | 41 | Charlotte-Gastonia-Rock Hill, NC-SC | 62.3 | 56 | 41 | Bridgeport-Stamford-Norwalk, CT | 11.0 |
| 44 | 42 | Richmond, VA | 61.5 | 54 | 42 | Tulsa, OK | 9.6 |
| 20 | 43 | Baltimore-Towson, MD | 61.4 | 22 | 43 | Pittsburgh, PA | 9.3 |
| 13 | 44 | Phoenix-Mesa-Glendale, AZ | 59.9 | 69 | 44 | Grand Rapids-Wyoming, MI | 9.1 |
| 36 | 45 | Virginia Beach-Norfolk-Newport News, VA-NC | 59.5 | 11 | 45 | San Francisco-Oakland-Fremont, CA | 9.0 |
| 70 | 45 | Columbia, SC | 59.5 | 58 | 46 | Omaha-Council Bluffs, NE-IA | 8.8 |
| 66 | 47 | Baton Rouge, LA | 58.6 | 16 | 47 | Minneapolis-St. Paul-Bloomington, MN | 8.5 |
| 26 | 48 | Sacramento—Arden-Arcade—Roseville, CA | 58.5 | 59 | 47 | Albany-Schenectady-Troy, NY | 8.5 |
| 52 | 49 | Tucson, AZ | 56.4 | 26 | 49 | Sacramento—Arden-Arcade—Roseville, CA | 8.3 |
| 3 | 50 | Chicago-Joliet-Naperville, IL-IN-WI | 55.9 | 12 | 50 | Riverside-San Bernardino-Ontario, CA | 7.9 |
| 33 | 51 | Austin-Round Rock-San Marcos, TX | 55.8 | 75 | 50 | Stockton, CA | 7.9 |
| 46 | 52 | New Orleans-Metairie-Kenner, LA | 54.7 | 10 | 52 | Boston-Cambridge-Quincy, MA-NH | 7.8 |
| 25 | 53 | Orlando-Kissimmee-Sanford, FL | 54.2 | 33 | 52 | Austin-Round Rock-San Marcos, TX | 7.8 |
| 9 | 54 | Atlanta-Sandy Springs-Marietta, GA | 51.9 | 2 | 54 | Los Angeles-Long Beach-Santa Ana, CA | 7.3 |
| 4 | 55 | Dallas-Fort Worth-Arlington, TX | 51.1 | 74 | 54 | Knoxville, TN | 7.3 |
| 17 | 56 | San Diego-Carlsbad-San Marcos, CA | 50.6 | 72 | 56 | North Port-Bradenton-Sarasota, FL | 7.1 |
| 7 | 57 | Washington-Arlington-Alexandria, DC-VA-MD-WV | 50.5 | 15 | 57 | Seattle-Tacoma-Bellevue, WA | 6.9 |
| 63 | 58 | Oxnard-Thousand Oaks-Ventura, CA | 50.1 | 24 | 58 | San Antonio-New Braunfels, TX | 6.7 |
| 30 | 59 | Las Vegas-Paradise, NV | 50.0 | 21 | 59 | Denver-Aurora-Broomfield, CO | 6.1 |
| 1 | 60 | New York-Northern New Jersey-Long Island, NY-NJ-PA | 49.6 | 61 | 60 | Bakersfield-Delano, CA | 6.0 |
| 41 | 61 | Memphis, TN-MS-AR | 47.0 | 17 | 61 | San Diego-Carlsbad-San Marcos, CA | 5.7 |
| 11 | 62 | San Francisco-Oakland-Fremont, CA | 45.1 | 38 | 61 | Providence-New Bedford-Fall River, RI-MA | 5.7 |
| 57 | 63 | Albuquerque, NM | 43.3 | 13 | 63 | Phoenix-Mesa-Glendale, AZ | 5.5 |
| 5 | 64 | Houston-Sugar Land-Baytown, TX | 40.4 | 55 | 64 | Fresno, CA | 5.3 |
| 61 | 65 | Bakersfield-Delano, CA | 39.6 | 65 | 65 | Allentown-Bethlehem-Easton, PA-NJ | 5.2 |
| 75 | 66 | Stockton, CA | 38.0 | 68 | 66 | Worcester, MA | 4.5 |
| 12 | 67 | Riverside-San Bernardino-Ontario, CA | 37.8 | 52 | 67 | Tucson, AZ | 4.0 |
| 31 | 68 | San Jose-Sunnyvale-Santa Clara, CA | 37.4 | 23 | 68 | Portland-Vancouver-Hillsboro, OR-WA | 3.6 |
| 24 | 69 | San Antonio-New Braunfels, TX | 37.0 | 53 | 69 | Honolulu, HI | 3.5 |
| 8 | 70 | Miami-Fort Lauderdale-Pompano Beach, FL | 35.6 | 64 | 70 | El Paso, TX | 3.2 |
| 55 | 71 | Fresno, CA | 33.9 | 31 | 71 | San Jose-Sunnyvale-Santa Clara, CA | 3.0 |
| 2 | 72 | Los Angeles-Long Beach-Santa Ana, CA | 33.1 | 57 | 72 | Albuquerque, NM | 2.9 |
| 53 | 73 | Honolulu, HI | 32.6 | 63 | 73 | Oxnard-Thousand Oaks-Ventura, CA | 2.1 |
| 64 | 74 | El Paso, TX | 14.3 | 48 | 74 | Salt Lake City, UT | 1.9 |
| 67 | 75 | McAllen-Edinburg-Mission, TX | 7.9 | 67 | 75 | McAllen-Edinburg-Mission, TX | 0.5 |

# 75 Largest Metropolitan Areas by 2012 Population
## Selected Rankings

| Percent American Indian, Alaska Native, alone or in combination, 2011 | | | | Percent Asian and Pacific Islander, alone or in combination, 2011 | | | |
|---|---|---|---|---|---|---|---|
| Population rank | American Indian Alaska native rank | Metropolitan area | Percent American Indian, Alaska Native [col 7] | Population rank | Asian and Pacific Islander rank | Metropolitan area | Percent Asian and Pacific Islander [col 8] |
| 54 | 1 | Tulsa, OK | 12.5 | 53 | 1 | Honolulu, HI | 78.5 |
| 43 | 2 | Oklahoma City, OK | 6.8 | 31 | 2 | San Jose-Sunnyvale-Santa Clara, CA | 34.0 |
| 57 | 3 | Albuquerque, NM | 5.8 | 11 | 3 | San Francisco-Oakland-Fremont, CA | 26.8 |
| 52 | 4 | Tucson, AZ | 3.0 | 75 | 4 | Stockton, CA | 16.8 |
| 13 | 5 | Phoenix-Mesa-Glendale, AZ | 2.4 | 2 | 5 | Los Angeles-Long Beach-Santa Ana, CA | 16.3 |
| 15 | 6 | Seattle-Tacoma-Bellevue, WA | 2.1 | 26 | 6 | Sacramento—Arden-Arcade—Roseville, CA | 15.2 |
| 23 | 7 | Portland-Vancouver-Hillsboro, OR-WA | 1.7 | 15 | 7 | Seattle-Tacoma-Bellevue, WA | 15.0 |
| 26 | 8 | Sacramento—Arden-Arcade—Roseville, CA | 1.6 | 17 | 8 | San Diego-Carlsbad-San Marcos, CA | 13.4 |
| 53 | 8 | Honolulu, HI | 1.6 | 30 | 9 | Las Vegas-Paradise, NV | 11.5 |
| 61 | 10 | Bakersfield-Delano, CA | 1.4 | 1 | 10 | New York-Northern New Jersey-Long Island, NY-NJ-PA | 11.1 |
| 16 | 11 | Minneapolis-St. Paul-Bloomington, MN | 1.3 | 7 | 11 | Washington-Arlington-Alexandria, DC-VA-MD-WV | 10.8 |
| 28 | 12 | Kansas City, MO-KS | 1.2 | 55 | 12 | Fresno, CA | 10.6 |
| 55 | 12 | Fresno, CA | 1.2 | 63 | 13 | Oxnard-Thousand Oaks-Ventura, CA | 8.4 |
| 75 | 12 | Stockton, CA | 1.2 | 23 | 14 | Portland-Vancouver-Hillsboro, OR-WA | 8.0 |
| 21 | 15 | Denver-Aurora-Broomfield, CO | 1.1 | 12 | 15 | Riverside-San Bernardino-Ontario, CA | 7.6 |
| 48 | 15 | Salt Lake City, UT | 1.1 | 10 | 16 | Boston-Cambridge-Quincy, MA-NH | 7.5 |
| 50 | 15 | Buffalo-Niagara Falls, NY | 1.1 | 5 | 17 | Houston-Sugar Land-Baytown, TX | 7.3 |
| 73 | 15 | Little Rock-North Little Rock-Conway, AR | 1.1 | 16 | 18 | Minneapolis-St. Paul-Bloomington, MN | 6.7 |
| 12 | 19 | Riverside-San Bernardino-Ontario, CA | 1.0 | 3 | 19 | Chicago-Joliet-Naperville, IL-IN-WI | 6.4 |
| 17 | 19 | San Diego-Carlsbad-San Marcos, CA | 1.0 | 4 | 20 | Dallas-Fort Worth-Arlington, TX | 6.2 |
| 30 | 19 | Las Vegas-Paradise, NV | 1.0 | 6 | 21 | Philadelphia-Camden-Wilmington, PA-NJ-DE-MD | 5.7 |
| 36 | 19 | Virginia Beach-Norfolk-Newport News, VA-NC | 1.0 | 48 | 21 | Salt Lake City, UT | 5.7 |
| 58 | 19 | Omaha-Council Bluffs, NE-IA | 1.0 | 9 | 23 | Atlanta-Sandy Springs-Marietta, GA | 5.6 |
| 69 | 19 | Grand Rapids-Wyoming, MI | 1.0 | 20 | 23 | Baltimore-Towson, MD | 5.6 |
| 71 | 19 | Greensboro-High Point, NC | 1.0 | 33 | 23 | Austin-Round Rock-San Marcos, TX | 5.6 |
| 4 | 26 | Dallas-Fort Worth-Arlington, TX | 0.9 | 56 | 26 | Bridgeport-Stamford-Norwalk, CT | 5.5 |
| 11 | 26 | San Francisco-Oakland-Fremont, CA | 0.9 | 47 | 27 | Raleigh-Cary, NC | 5.2 |
| 14 | 26 | Detroit-Warren-Livonia, MI | 0.9 | 61 | 28 | Bakersfield-Delano, CA | 5.1 |
| 34 | 26 | Charlotte-Gastonia-Rock Hill, NC-SC | 0.9 | 25 | 29 | Orlando-Kissimmee-Sanford, FL | 4.9 |
| 38 | 26 | Providence-New Bedford-Fall River, RI-MA | 0.9 | 36 | 29 | Virginia Beach-Norfolk-Newport News, VA-NC | 4.9 |
| 39 | 26 | Milwaukee-Waukesha-West Allis, WI | 0.9 | 68 | 31 | Worcester, MA | 4.8 |
| 44 | 26 | Richmond, VA | 0.9 | 21 | 32 | Denver-Aurora-Broomfield, CO | 4.7 |
| 47 | 26 | Raleigh-Cary, NC | 0.9 | 45 | 33 | Hartford-West Hartford-East Hartford, CT | 4.6 |
| 7 | 34 | Washington-Arlington-Alexandria, DC-VA-MD-WV | 0.8 | 40 | 34 | Jacksonville, FL | 4.5 |
| 20 | 34 | Baltimore-Towson, MD | 0.8 | 13 | 35 | Phoenix-Mesa-Glendale, AZ | 4.4 |
| 32 | 34 | Columbus, OH | 0.8 | 14 | 36 | Detroit-Warren-Livonia, MI | 4.1 |
| 33 | 34 | Austin-Round Rock-San Marcos, TX | 0.8 | 59 | 36 | Albany-Schenectady-Troy, NY | 4.1 |
| 40 | 34 | Jacksonville, FL | 0.8 | 60 | 36 | New Haven-Milford, CT | 4.1 |
| 46 | 34 | New Orleans-Metairie-Kenner, LA | 0.8 | 32 | 39 | Columbus, OH | 3.9 |
| 62 | 34 | Dayton, OH | 0.8 | 44 | 39 | Richmond, VA | 3.9 |
| 63 | 34 | Oxnard-Thousand Oaks-Ventura, CA | 0.8 | 34 | 41 | Charlotte-Gastonia-Rock Hill, NC-SC | 3.8 |
| 70 | 34 | Columbia, SC | 0.8 | 18 | 42 | Tampa-St. Petersburg-Clearwater, FL | 3.7 |
| 74 | 34 | Knoxville, TN | 0.8 | 43 | 43 | Oklahoma City, OK | 3.6 |
| 9 | 44 | Atlanta-Sandy Springs-Marietta, GA | 0.7 | 39 | 44 | Milwaukee-Waukesha-West Allis, WI | 3.5 |
| 18 | 44 | Tampa-St. Petersburg-Clearwater, FL | 0.7 | 52 | 44 | Tucson, AZ | 3.5 |
| 19 | 44 | St. Louis, MO-IL | 0.7 | 71 | 44 | Greensboro-High Point, NC | 3.5 |
| 31 | 44 | San Jose-Sunnyvale-Santa Clara, CA | 0.7 | 38 | 47 | Providence-New Bedford-Fall River, RI-MA | 3.3 |
| 37 | 44 | Nashville-Davidson—Murfreesboro—Franklin, TN | 0.7 | 46 | 48 | New Orleans-Metairie-Kenner, LA | 3.2 |
| 42 | 44 | Louisville-Jefferson County, KY-IN | 0.7 | 51 | 48 | Rochester, NY | 3.2 |
| 49 | 44 | Birmingham-Hoover, AL | 0.7 | 28 | 50 | Kansas City, MO-KS | 3.1 |
| 51 | 44 | Rochester, NY | 0.7 | 65 | 51 | Allentown-Bethlehem-Easton, PA-NJ | 3.0 |
| 59 | 44 | Albany-Schenectady-Troy, NY | 0.7 | 8 | 52 | Miami-Fort Lauderdale-Pompano Beach, FL | 2.9 |
| 2 | 53 | Los Angeles-Long Beach-Santa Ana, CA | 0.6 | 35 | 52 | Indianapolis-Carmel, IN | 2.9 |
| 5 | 53 | Houston-Sugar Land-Baytown, TX | 0.6 | 37 | 52 | Nashville-Davidson—Murfreesboro—Franklin, TN | 2.9 |
| 6 | 53 | Philadelphia-Camden-Wilmington, PA-NJ-DE-MD | 0.6 | 24 | 55 | San Antonio-New Braunfels, TX | 2.8 |
| 24 | 53 | San Antonio-New Braunfels, TX | 0.6 | 50 | 55 | Buffalo-Niagara Falls, NY | 2.8 |
| 25 | 53 | Orlando-Kissimmee-Sanford, FL | 0.6 | 58 | 55 | Omaha-Council Bluffs, NE-IA | 2.8 |
| 27 | 53 | Cincinnati-Middletown, OH-KY-IN | 0.6 | 19 | 58 | St. Louis, MO-IL | 2.7 |
| 29 | 53 | Cleveland-Elyria-Mentor, OH | 0.6 | 57 | 58 | Albuquerque, NM | 2.7 |
| 35 | 53 | Indianapolis-Carmel, IN | 0.6 | 62 | 60 | Dayton, OH | 2.5 |
| 41 | 53 | Memphis, TN-MS-AR | 0.6 | 27 | 61 | Cincinnati-Middletown, OH-KY-IN | 2.4 |
| 60 | 53 | New Haven-Milford, CT | 0.6 | 29 | 61 | Cleveland-Elyria-Mentor, OH | 2.4 |
| 66 | 53 | Baton Rouge, LA | 0.6 | 54 | 61 | Tulsa, OK | 2.4 |
| 68 | 53 | Worcester, MA | 0.6 | 69 | 61 | Grand Rapids-Wyoming, MI | 2.4 |
| 1 | 65 | New York-Northern New Jersey-Long Island, NY-NJ-PA | 0.5 | 41 | 65 | Memphis, TN-MS-AR | 2.3 |
| 3 | 65 | Chicago-Joliet-Naperville, IL-IN-WI | 0.5 | 70 | 65 | Columbia, SC | 2.3 |
| 10 | 65 | Boston-Cambridge-Quincy, MA-NH | 0.5 | 22 | 67 | Pittsburgh, PA | 2.2 |
| 22 | 65 | Pittsburgh, PA | 0.5 | 66 | 67 | Baton Rouge, LA | 2.2 |
| 45 | 65 | Hartford-West Hartford-East Hartford, CT | 0.5 | 42 | 69 | Louisville-Jefferson County, KY-IN | 2.0 |
| 64 | 65 | El Paso, TX | 0.5 | 72 | 69 | North Port-Bradenton-Sarasota, FL | 2.0 |
| 72 | 65 | North Port-Bradenton-Sarasota, FL | 0.5 | 73 | 69 | Little Rock-North Little Rock-Conway, AR | 2.0 |
| 56 | 72 | Bridgeport-Stamford-Norwalk, CT | 0.4 | 74 | 72 | Knoxville, TN | 1.9 |
| 65 | 72 | Allentown-Bethlehem-Easton, PA-NJ | 0.4 | 49 | 73 | Birmingham-Hoover, AL | 1.6 |
| 8 | 74 | Miami-Fort Lauderdale-Pompano Beach, FL | 0.3 | 64 | 74 | El Paso, TX | 1.5 |
| 67 | 75 | McAllen-Edinburg-Mission, TX | 0.1 | 67 | 75 | McAllen-Edinburg-Mission, TX | 1.0 |

# 75 Largest Metropolitan Areas by 2012 Population
## Selected Rankings

| | | Percent Hispanic or Latino,[1] 2011 | | | | | Percent under 18 years old, 2011 | |
|---|---|---|---|---|---|---|---|---|
| Population rank | Hispanic or Latino rank | Metropolitan area | Percent Hispanic or Latino [col 9] | Population rank | Under 18 years old rank | Metropolitan area | Percent Under 18 years old [cols 10 and 11] |
| 67 | 1 | McAllen-Edinburg-Mission, TX | 90.7 | 67 | 1 | McAllen-Edinburg-Mission, TX | 34.4 |
| 64 | 2 | El Paso, TX | 81.4 | 61 | 2 | Bakersfield-Delano, CA | 29.9 |
| 24 | 3 | San Antonio-New Braunfels, TX | 54.2 | 64 | 3 | El Paso, TX | 29.7 |
| 55 | 4 | Fresno, CA | 50.9 | 55 | 4 | Fresno, CA | 29.6 |
| 61 | 5 | Bakersfield-Delano, CA | 50.0 | 48 | 5 | Salt Lake City, UT | 29.2 |
| 12 | 6 | Riverside-San Bernardino-Ontario, CA | 47.9 | 75 | 6 | Stockton, CA | 28.9 |
| 57 | 7 | Albuquerque, NM | 47.1 | 12 | 7 | Riverside-San Bernardino-Ontario, CA | 28.3 |
| 2 | 8 | Los Angeles-Long Beach-Santa Ana, CA | 44.8 | 5 | 8 | Houston-Sugar Land-Baytown, TX | 27.7 |
| 8 | 9 | Miami-Fort Lauderdale-Pompano Beach, FL | 41.8 | 4 | 8 | Dallas-Fort Worth-Arlington, TX | 27.7 |
| 63 | 10 | Oxnard-Thousand Oaks-Ventura, CA | 40.9 | 24 | 10 | San Antonio-New Braunfels, TX | 26.6 |
| 75 | 11 | Stockton, CA | 39.4 | 9 | 11 | Atlanta-Sandy Springs-Marietta, GA | 26.2 |
| 5 | 12 | Houston-Sugar Land-Baytown, TX | 35.9 | 41 | 11 | Memphis, TN-MS-AR | 26.2 |
| 52 | 13 | Tucson, AZ | 35.1 | 58 | 13 | Omaha-Council Bluffs, NE-IA | 26.1 |
| 17 | 14 | San Diego-Carlsbad-San Marcos, CA | 32.5 | 35 | 14 | Indianapolis-Carmel, IN | 26.0 |
| 33 | 15 | Austin-Round Rock-San Marcos, TX | 31.8 | 47 | 14 | Raleigh-Cary, NC | 26.0 |
| 13 | 16 | Phoenix-Mesa-Glendale, AZ | 29.9 | 13 | 16 | Phoenix-Mesa-Glendale, AZ | 25.9 |
| 30 | 17 | Las Vegas-Paradise, NV | 29.7 | 34 | 17 | Charlotte-Gastonia-Rock Hill, NC-SC | 25.7 |
| 4 | 18 | Dallas-Fort Worth-Arlington, TX | 28.1 | 69 | 18 | Grand Rapids-Wyoming, MI | 25.6 |
| 31 | 19 | San Jose-Sunnyvale-Santa Clara, CA | 28.0 | 28 | 19 | Kansas City, MO-KS | 25.4 |
| 25 | 20 | Orlando-Kissimmee-Sanford, FL | 25.9 | 54 | 20 | Tulsa, OK | 25.3 |
| 1 | 21 | New York-Northern New Jersey-Long Island, NY-NJ-PA | 23.3 | 63 | 20 | Oxnard-Thousand Oaks-Ventura, CA | 25.3 |
| 21 | 22 | Denver-Aurora-Broomfield, CO | 22.7 | 33 | 22 | Austin-Round Rock-San Marcos, TX | 25.1 |
| 11 | 23 | San Francisco-Oakland-Fremont, CA | 22.0 | 43 | 23 | Oklahoma City, OK | 24.9 |
| 3 | 24 | Chicago-Joliet-Naperville, IL-IN-WI | 21.1 | 30 | 24 | Las Vegas-Paradise, NV | 24.8 |
| 26 | 25 | Sacramento—Arden-Arcade—Roseville, CA | 20.5 | 3 | 24 | Chicago-Joliet-Naperville, IL-IN-WI | 24.8 |
| 56 | 26 | Bridgeport-Stamford-Norwalk, CT | 17.4 | 16 | 26 | Minneapolis-St. Paul-Bloomington, MN | 24.7 |
| 48 | 27 | Salt Lake City, UT | 17.0 | 21 | 26 | Denver-Aurora-Broomfield, CO | 24.7 |
| 18 | 28 | Tampa-St. Petersburg-Clearwater, FL | 16.6 | 27 | 26 | Cincinnati-Middletown, OH-KY-IN | 24.7 |
| 60 | 29 | New Haven-Milford, CT | 15.4 | 32 | 29 | Columbus, OH | 24.6 |
| 7 | 30 | Washington-Arlington-Alexandria, DC-VA-MD-WV | 14.1 | 26 | 30 | Sacramento—Arden-Arcade—Roseville, CA | 24.4 |
| 65 | 31 | Allentown-Bethlehem-Easton, PA-NJ | 13.5 | 56 | 31 | Bridgeport-Stamford-Norwalk, CT | 24.3 |
| 45 | 32 | Hartford-West Hartford-East Hartford, CT | 12.9 | 57 | 31 | Albuquerque, NM | 24.3 |
| 43 | 33 | Oklahoma City, OK | 11.7 | 66 | 31 | Baton Rouge, LA | 24.3 |
| 72 | 34 | North Port-Bradenton-Sarasota, FL | 11.4 | 73 | 31 | Little Rock-North Little Rock-Conway, AR | 24.3 |
| 23 | 35 | Portland-Vancouver-Hillsboro, OR-WA | 11.1 | 39 | 31 | Milwaukee-Waukesha-West Allis, WI | 24.3 |
| 9 | 36 | Atlanta-Sandy Springs-Marietta, GA | 10.6 | 37 | 36 | Nashville-Davidson—Murfreesboro—Franklin, TN | 24.2 |
| 38 | 36 | Providence-New Bedford-Fall River, RI-MA | 10.6 | 2 | 37 | Los Angeles-Long Beach-Santa Ana, CA | 24.1 |
| 47 | 38 | Raleigh-Cary, NC | 10.3 | 31 | 37 | San Jose-Sunnyvale-Santa Clara, CA | 24.1 |
| 34 | 39 | Charlotte-Gastonia-Rock Hill, NC-SC | 10.1 | 14 | 39 | Detroit-Warren-Livonia, MI | 23.8 |
| 39 | 40 | Milwaukee-Waukesha-West Allis, WI | 9.7 | 49 | 39 | Birmingham-Hoover, AL | 23.8 |
| 68 | 41 | Worcester, MA | 9.6 | 42 | 41 | Louisville-Jefferson County, KY-IN | 23.7 |
| 10 | 42 | Boston-Cambridge-Quincy, MA-NH | 9.3 | 7 | 42 | Washington-Arlington-Alexandria, DC-VA-MD-WV | 23.6 |
| 15 | 43 | Seattle-Tacoma-Bellevue, WA | 9.2 | 19 | 43 | St. Louis, MO-IL | 23.5 |
| 58 | 43 | Omaha-Council Bluffs, NE-IA | 9.2 | 40 | 43 | Jacksonville, FL | 23.5 |
| 54 | 45 | Tulsa, OK | 8.7 | 23 | 45 | Portland-Vancouver-Hillsboro, OR-WA | 23.3 |
| 69 | 46 | Grand Rapids-Wyoming, MI | 8.6 | 70 | 45 | Columbia, SC | 23.3 |
| 53 | 47 | Honolulu, HI | 8.5 | 17 | 47 | San Diego-Carlsbad-San Marcos, CA | 23.2 |
| 28 | 48 | Kansas City, MO-KS | 8.3 | 46 | 47 | New Orleans-Metairie-Kenner, LA | 23.2 |
| 6 | 49 | Philadelphia-Camden-Wilmington, PA-NJ-DE-MD | 8.1 | 71 | 47 | Greensboro-High Point, NC | 23.2 |
| 46 | 50 | New Orleans-Metairie-Kenner, LA | 8.0 | 36 | 47 | Virginia Beach-Norfolk-Newport News, VA-NC | 23.2 |
| 71 | 51 | Greensboro-High Point, NC | 7.8 | 25 | 51 | Orlando-Kissimmee-Sanford, FL | 23.1 |
| 40 | 52 | Jacksonville, FL | 7.2 | 6 | 52 | Philadelphia-Camden-Wilmington, PA-NJ-DE-MD | 23.0 |
| 37 | 53 | Nashville-Davidson—Murfreesboro—Franklin, TN | 6.8 | 44 | 52 | Richmond, VA | 23.0 |
| 35 | 54 | Indianapolis-Carmel, IN | 6.4 | 68 | 52 | Worcester, MA | 23.0 |
| 51 | 54 | Rochester, NY | 6.4 | 20 | 55 | Baltimore-Towson, MD | 22.7 |
| 36 | 56 | Virginia Beach-Norfolk-Newport News, VA-NC | 5.6 | 29 | 55 | Cleveland-Elyria-Mentor, OH | 22.7 |
| 16 | 57 | Minneapolis-St. Paul-Bloomington, MN | 5.5 | 52 | 55 | Tucson, AZ | 22.7 |
| 41 | 58 | Memphis, TN-MS-AR | 5.2 | 1 | 58 | New York-Northern New Jersey-Long Island, NY-NJ-PA | 22.6 |
| 44 | 58 | Richmond, VA | 5.2 | 15 | 59 | Seattle-Tacoma-Bellevue, WA | 22.5 |
| 70 | 58 | Columbia, SC | 5.2 | 62 | 59 | Dayton, OH | 22.5 |
| 73 | 61 | Little Rock-North Little Rock-Conway, AR | 5.0 | 65 | 61 | Allentown-Bethlehem-Easton, PA-NJ | 22.3 |
| 20 | 62 | Baltimore-Towson, MD | 4.8 | 51 | 62 | Rochester, NY | 22.1 |
| 29 | 62 | Cleveland-Elyria-Mentor, OH | 4.8 | 53 | 63 | Honolulu, HI | 22.0 |
| 49 | 64 | Birmingham-Hoover, AL | 4.4 | 45 | 64 | Hartford-West Hartford-East Hartford, CT | 21.9 |
| 59 | 64 | Albany-Schenectady-Troy, NY | 4.4 | 60 | 64 | New Haven-Milford, CT | 21.9 |
| 50 | 66 | Buffalo-Niagara Falls, NY | 4.3 | 74 | 66 | Knoxville, TN | 21.5 |
| 42 | 67 | Louisville-Jefferson County, KY-IN | 4.1 | 8 | 67 | Miami-Fort Lauderdale-Pompano Beach, FL | 21.3 |
| 14 | 68 | Detroit-Warren-Livonia, MI | 4.0 | 10 | 67 | Boston-Cambridge-Quincy, MA-NH | 21.3 |
| 32 | 69 | Columbus, OH | 3.7 | 38 | 69 | Providence-New Bedford-Fall River, RI-MA | 21.2 |
| 66 | 70 | Baton Rouge, LA | 3.6 | 50 | 69 | Buffalo-Niagara Falls, NY | 21.2 |
| 74 | 71 | Knoxville, TN | 3.5 | 11 | 71 | San Francisco-Oakland-Fremont, CA | 21.0 |
| 19 | 72 | St. Louis, MO-IL | 2.7 | 59 | 72 | Albany-Schenectady-Troy, NY | 20.9 |
| 27 | 72 | Cincinnati-Middletown, OH-KY-IN | 2.7 | 18 | 73 | Tampa-St. Petersburg-Clearwater, FL | 20.8 |
| 62 | 74 | Dayton, OH | 2.2 | 22 | 74 | Pittsburgh, PA | 19.9 |
| 22 | 75 | Pittsburgh, PA | 1.4 | 72 | 75 | North Port-Bradenton-Sarasota, FL | 17.7 |

1. May be of any race.

# 75 Largest Metropolitan Areas by 2012 Population
## Selected Rankings

| | Percent 65 years old and over, 2011 | | | | Percent female-headed family households, 2010 | | |
| --- | --- | --- | --- | --- | --- | --- | --- |
| Population rank | 65 years old and over rank | Metropolitan area | Percent 65 years old and over [cols 17 + 18] | Population rank | Female households rank | Metropolitan area | Percent female households [col 30] |
| 72 | 1 | North Port-Bradenton-Sarasota, FL | 28.0 | 41 | 1 | Memphis, TN-MS-AR | 20.3 |
| 18 | 2 | Tampa-St. Petersburg-Clearwater, FL | 17.4 | 64 | 1 | El Paso, TX | 20.3 |
| 22 | 3 | Pittsburgh, PA | 17.3 | 67 | 3 | McAllen-Edinburg-Mission, TX | 18.8 |
| 8 | 4 | Miami-Fort Lauderdale-Pompano Beach, FL | 16.0 | 46 | 4 | New Orleans-Metairie-Kenner, LA | 17.4 |
| 52 | 5 | Tucson, AZ | 15.9 | 66 | 5 | Baton Rouge, LA | 17.0 |
| 50 | 6 | Buffalo-Niagara Falls, NY | 15.8 | 55 | 6 | Fresno, CA | 16.9 |
| 65 | 7 | Allentown-Bethlehem-Easton, PA-NJ | 15.4 | 8 | 7 | Miami-Fort Lauderdale-Pompano Beach, FL | 15.8 |
| 29 | 7 | Cleveland-Elyria-Mentor, OH | 15.4 | 36 | 7 | Virginia Beach-Norfolk-Newport News, VA-NC | 15.8 |
| 62 | 7 | Dayton, OH | 15.4 | 70 | 7 | Columbia, SC | 15.8 |
| 74 | 10 | Knoxville, TN | 15.0 | 61 | 10 | Bakersfield-Delano, CA | 15.7 |
| 53 | 11 | Honolulu, HI | 14.8 | 24 | 11 | San Antonio-New Braunfels, TX | 15.5 |
| 38 | 12 | Providence-New Bedford-Fall River, RI-MA | 14.6 | 75 | 12 | Stockton, CA | 15.4 |
| 60 | 12 | New Haven-Milford, CT | 14.6 | 1 | 13 | New York-Northern New Jersey-Long Island, NY-NJ-PA | 15.3 |
| 45 | 14 | Hartford-West Hartford-East Hartford, CT | 14.5 | 9 | 13 | Atlanta-Sandy Springs-Marietta, GA | 15.3 |
| 51 | 15 | Rochester, NY | 14.4 | 14 | 13 | Detroit-Warren-Livonia, MI | 15.3 |
| 59 | 16 | Albany-Schenectady-Troy, NY | 14.3 | 49 | 13 | Birmingham-Hoover, AL | 15.3 |
| 56 | 17 | Bridgeport-Stamford-Norwalk, CT | 13.7 | 20 | 17 | Baltimore-Towson, MD | 15.2 |
| 19 | 18 | St. Louis, MO-IL | 13.5 | 6 | 18 | Philadelphia-Camden-Wilmington, PA-NJ-DE-MD | 14.8 |
| 6 | 19 | Philadelphia-Camden-Wilmington, PA-NJ-DE-MD | 13.4 | 40 | 18 | Jacksonville, FL | 14.8 |
| 71 | 19 | Greensboro-High Point, NC | 13.4 | 12 | 20 | Riverside-San Bernardino-Ontario, CA | 14.7 |
| 14 | 19 | Detroit-Warren-Livonia, MI | 13.4 | 29 | 20 | Cleveland-Elyria-Mentor, OH | 14.7 |
| 1 | 22 | New York-Northern New Jersey-Long Island, NY-NJ-PA | 13.3 | 44 | 20 | Richmond, VA | 14.7 |
| 10 | 22 | Boston-Cambridge-Quincy, MA-NH | 13.3 | 25 | 23 | Orlando-Kissimmee-Sanford, FL | 14.6 |
| 49 | 24 | Birmingham-Hoover, AL | 13.2 | 2 | 24 | Los Angeles-Long Beach-Santa Ana, CA | 14.5 |
| 54 | 25 | Tulsa, OK | 13.1 | 60 | 24 | New Haven-Milford, CT | 14.5 |
| 42 | 26 | Louisville-Jefferson County, KY-IN | 13.0 | 71 | 26 | Greensboro-High Point, NC | 14.4 |
| 11 | 27 | San Francisco-Oakland-Fremont, CA | 12.9 | 73 | 26 | Little Rock-North Little Rock-Conway, AR | 14.4 |
| 68 | 27 | Worcester, MA | 12.9 | 5 | 28 | Houston-Sugar Land-Baytown, TX | 14.3 |
| 20 | 29 | Baltimore-Towson, MD | 12.8 | 34 | 29 | Charlotte-Gastonia-Rock Hill, NC-SC | 14.1 |
| 39 | 30 | Milwaukee-Waukesha-West Allis, WI | 12.7 | 42 | 30 | Louisville-Jefferson County, KY-IN | 13.9 |
| 13 | 31 | Phoenix-Mesa-Glendale, AZ | 12.6 | 57 | 31 | Albuquerque, NM | 13.8 |
| 25 | 31 | Orlando-Kissimmee-Sanford, FL | 12.6 | 3 | 32 | Chicago-Joliet-Naperville, IL-IN-WI | 13.7 |
| 57 | 31 | Albuquerque, NM | 12.6 | 19 | 32 | St. Louis, MO-IL | 13.7 |
| 40 | 34 | Jacksonville, FL | 12.5 | 38 | 32 | Providence-New Bedford-Fall River, RI-MA | 13.7 |
| 44 | 34 | Richmond, VA | 12.5 | 62 | 35 | Dayton, OH | 13.6 |
| 26 | 36 | Sacramento—Arden-Arcade—Roseville, CA | 12.4 | 30 | 36 | Las Vegas-Paradise, NV | 13.5 |
| 27 | 36 | Cincinnati-Middletown, OH-KY-IN | 12.4 | 35 | 36 | Indianapolis-Carmel, IN | 13.5 |
| 46 | 36 | New Orleans-Metairie-Kenner, LA | 12.4 | 50 | 36 | Buffalo-Niagara Falls, NY | 13.5 |
| 73 | 39 | Little Rock-North Little Rock-Conway, AR | 12.3 | 4 | 39 | Dallas-Fort Worth-Arlington, TX | 13.4 |
| 28 | 40 | Kansas City, MO-KS | 12.2 | 39 | 39 | Milwaukee-Waukesha-West Allis, WI | 13.4 |
| 63 | 41 | Oxnard-Thousand Oaks-Ventura, CA | 12.1 | 51 | 41 | Rochester, NY | 13.2 |
| 43 | 42 | Oklahoma City, OK | 11.9 | 45 | 42 | Hartford-West Hartford-East Hartford, CT | 13.1 |
| 69 | 42 | Grand Rapids-Wyoming, MI | 11.9 | 26 | 43 | Sacramento—Arden-Arcade—Roseville, CA | 13.0 |
| 30 | 44 | Las Vegas-Paradise, NV | 11.8 | 27 | 43 | Cincinnati-Middletown, OH-KY-IN | 13.0 |
| 36 | 44 | Virginia Beach-Norfolk-Newport News, VA-NC | 11.8 | 18 | 45 | Tampa-St. Petersburg-Clearwater, FL | 12.9 |
| 23 | 46 | Portland-Vancouver-Hillsboro, OR-WA | 11.7 | 32 | 45 | Columbus, OH | 12.9 |
| 70 | 46 | Columbia, SC | 11.7 | 37 | 47 | Nashville-Davidson—Murfreesboro—Franklin, TN | 12.8 |
| 3 | 48 | Chicago-Joliet-Naperville, IL-IN-WI | 11.6 | 52 | 47 | Tucson, AZ | 12.8 |
| 17 | 49 | San Diego-Carlsbad-San Marcos, CA | 11.5 | 43 | 49 | Oklahoma City, OK | 12.7 |
| 2 | 50 | Los Angeles-Long Beach-Santa Ana, CA | 11.3 | 53 | 49 | Honolulu, HI | 12.7 |
| 31 | 50 | San Jose-Sunnyvale-Santa Clara, CA | 11.3 | 54 | 51 | Tulsa, OK | 12.6 |
| 15 | 52 | Seattle-Tacoma-Bellevue, WA | 11.2 | 7 | 52 | Washington-Arlington-Alexandria, DC-VA-MD-WV | 12.5 |
| 58 | 52 | Omaha-Council Bluffs, NE-IA | 11.2 | 13 | 53 | Phoenix-Mesa-Glendale, AZ | 12.4 |
| 24 | 54 | San Antonio-New Braunfels, TX | 11.1 | 28 | 53 | Kansas City, MO-KS | 12.4 |
| 35 | 55 | Indianapolis-Carmel, IN | 11.0 | 56 | 55 | Bridgeport-Stamford-Norwalk, CT | 12.3 |
| 66 | 55 | Baton Rouge, LA | 11.0 | 68 | 56 | Worcester, MA | 12.2 |
| 16 | 57 | Minneapolis-St. Paul-Bloomington, MN | 10.9 | 17 | 57 | San Diego-Carlsbad-San Marcos, CA | 12.1 |
| 37 | 57 | Nashville-Davidson—Murfreesboro—Franklin, TN | 10.9 | 69 | 58 | Grand Rapids-Wyoming, MI | 12.0 |
| 41 | 59 | Memphis, TN-MS-AR | 10.8 | 10 | 59 | Boston-Cambridge-Quincy, MA-NH | 11.9 |
| 32 | 60 | Columbus, OH | 10.7 | 63 | 60 | Oxnard-Thousand Oaks-Ventura, CA | 11.8 |
| 12 | 61 | Riverside-San Bernardino-Ontario, CA | 10.6 | 47 | 61 | Raleigh-Cary, NC | 11.7 |
| 75 | 61 | Stockton, CA | 10.6 | 58 | 61 | Omaha-Council Bluffs, NE-IA | 11.7 |
| 21 | 63 | Denver-Aurora-Broomfield, CO | 10.4 | 59 | 61 | Albany-Schenectady-Troy, NY | 11.7 |
| 34 | 63 | Charlotte-Gastonia-Rock Hill, NC-SC | 10.4 | 65 | 61 | Allentown-Bethlehem-Easton, PA-NJ | 11.7 |
| 55 | 65 | Fresno, CA | 10.3 | 22 | 65 | Pittsburgh, PA | 11.4 |
| 64 | 65 | El Paso, TX | 10.3 | 74 | 66 | Knoxville, TN | 11.3 |
| 7 | 67 | Washington-Arlington-Alexandria, DC-VA-MD-WV | 10.2 | 11 | 67 | San Francisco-Oakland-Fremont, CA | 11.2 |
| 67 | 68 | McAllen-Edinburg-Mission, TX | 9.5 | 33 | 68 | Austin-Round Rock-San Marcos, TX | 10.9 |
| 9 | 69 | Atlanta-Sandy Springs-Marietta, GA | 9.3 | 31 | 69 | San Jose-Sunnyvale-Santa Clara, CA | 10.8 |
| 47 | 69 | Raleigh-Cary, NC | 9.3 | 48 | 70 | Salt Lake City, UT | 10.7 |
| 61 | 71 | Bakersfield-Delano, CA | 9.1 | 21 | 71 | Denver-Aurora-Broomfield, CO | 10.6 |
| 4 | 72 | Dallas-Fort Worth-Arlington, TX | 9.0 | 23 | 72 | Portland-Vancouver-Hillsboro, OR-WA | 10.5 |
| 5 | 73 | Houston-Sugar Land-Baytown, TX | 8.9 | 15 | 73 | Seattle-Tacoma-Bellevue, WA | 10.2 |
| 48 | 74 | Salt Lake City, UT | 8.8 | 16 | 73 | Minneapolis-St. Paul-Bloomington, MN | 10.2 |
| 33 | 75 | Austin-Round Rock-San Marcos, TX | 8.3 | 72 | 75 | North Port-Bradenton-Sarasota, FL | 9.6 |

# 75 Largest Metropolitan Areas by 2012 Population
## Selected Rankings

| Birth rate, 2011 | | | | Percent under 65 who have no health insurance, 2010 | | | |
|---|---|---|---|---|---|---|---|
| Population rank | Birth rate rank | Metropolitan area | Births (per 1,000 population) [col 36] | Population rank | No health insurance rank | Metropolitan area | Percent with no health insurance [col 40] |
| 67 | 1 | McAllen-Edinburg-Mission, TX | 21.2 | 67 | 1 | McAllen-Edinburg-Mission, TX | 38.1 |
| 48 | 2 | Salt Lake City, UT | 17.1 | 64 | 2 | El Paso, TX | 32.8 |
| 55 | 3 | Fresno, CA | 16.9 | 8 | 3 | Miami-Fort Lauderdale-Pompano Beach, FL | 30.9 |
| 61 | 3 | Bakersfield-Delano, CA | 16.9 | 5 | 4 | Houston-Sugar Land-Baytown, TX | 27.3 |
| 64 | 3 | El Paso, TX | 16.9 | 30 | 5 | Las Vegas-Paradise, NV | 25.4 |
| 5 | 6 | Houston-Sugar Land-Baytown, TX | 16.1 | 4 | 6 | Dallas-Fort Worth-Arlington, TX | 24.9 |
| 4 | 7 | Dallas-Fort Worth-Arlington, TX | 15.3 | 2 | 7 | Los Angeles-Long Beach-Santa Ana, CA | 24.5 |
| 75 | 8 | Stockton, CA | 15.2 | 72 | 8 | North Port-Bradenton-Sarasota, FL | 24.4 |
| 58 | 9 | Omaha-Council Bluffs, NE-IA | 15.1 | 25 | 9 | Orlando-Kissimmee-Sanford, FL | 23.9 |
| 43 | 10 | Oklahoma City, OK | 14.7 | 61 | 10 | Bakersfield-Delano, CA | 23.4 |
| 33 | 11 | Austin-Round Rock-San Marcos, TX | 14.6 | 12 | 11 | Riverside-San Bernardino-Ontario, CA | 23.0 |
| 41 | 11 | Memphis, TN-MS-AR | 14.6 | 24 | 11 | San Antonio-New Braunfels, TX | 23.0 |
| 24 | 13 | San Antonio-New Braunfels, TX | 14.5 | 18 | 13 | Tampa-St. Petersburg-Clearwater, FL | 22.5 |
| 35 | 13 | Indianapolis-Carmel, IN | 14.5 | 9 | 14 | Atlanta-Sandy Springs-Marietta, GA | 22.0 |
| 12 | 15 | Riverside-San Bernardino-Ontario, CA | 14.4 | 55 | 15 | Fresno, CA | 21.9 |
| 54 | 16 | Tulsa, OK | 14.3 | 33 | 16 | Austin-Round Rock-San Marcos, TX | 21.7 |
| 13 | 17 | Phoenix-Mesa-Glendale, AZ | 14.0 | 46 | 17 | New Orleans-Metairie-Kenner, LA | 21.4 |
| 17 | 17 | San Diego-Carlsbad-San Marcos, CA | 14.0 | 54 | 18 | Tulsa, OK | 21.3 |
| 30 | 17 | Las Vegas-Paradise, NV | 14.0 | 43 | 19 | Oklahoma City, OK | 20.7 |
| 66 | 17 | Baton Rouge, LA | 14.0 | 57 | 20 | Albuquerque, NM | 20.1 |
| 32 | 21 | Columbus, OH | 13.9 | 71 | 21 | Greensboro-High Point, NC | 19.6 |
| 7 | 22 | Washington-Arlington-Alexandria, DC-VA-MD-WV | 13.8 | 75 | 22 | Stockton, CA | 19.4 |
| 9 | 22 | Atlanta-Sandy Springs-Marietta, GA | 13.8 | 13 | 23 | Phoenix-Mesa-Glendale, AZ | 19.2 |
| 28 | 22 | Kansas City, MO-KS | 13.8 | 17 | 24 | San Diego-Carlsbad-San Marcos, CA | 19.1 |
| 34 | 25 | Charlotte-Gastonia-Rock Hill, NC-SC | 13.7 | 40 | 25 | Jacksonville, FL | 18.6 |
| 53 | 25 | Honolulu, HI | 13.7 | 34 | 26 | Charlotte-Gastonia-Rock Hill, NC-SC | 18.5 |
| 69 | 27 | Grand Rapids-Wyoming, MI | 13.6 | 66 | 27 | Baton Rouge, LA | 18.3 |
| 3 | 28 | Chicago-Joliet-Naperville, IL-IN-WI | 13.5 | 52 | 28 | Tucson, AZ | 18.2 |
| 21 | 28 | Denver-Aurora-Broomfield, CO | 13.5 | 63 | 28 | Oxnard-Thousand Oaks-Ventura, CA | 18.2 |
| 36 | 28 | Virginia Beach-Norfolk-Newport News, VA-NC | 13.5 | 73 | 30 | Little Rock-North Little Rock-Conway, AR | 17.9 |
| 49 | 28 | Birmingham-Hoover, AL | 13.5 | 41 | 31 | Memphis, TN-MS-AR | 17.8 |
| 73 | 28 | Little Rock-North Little Rock-Conway, AR | 13.5 | 70 | 31 | Columbia, SC | 17.8 |
| 27 | 33 | Cincinnati-Middletown, OH-KY-IN | 13.4 | 23 | 33 | Portland-Vancouver-Hillsboro, OR-WA | 17.7 |
| 47 | 33 | Raleigh-Cary, NC | 13.4 | 48 | 34 | Salt Lake City, UT | 17.6 |
| 2 | 35 | Los Angeles-Long Beach-Santa Ana, CA | 13.3 | 21 | 35 | Denver-Aurora-Broomfield, CO | 17.4 |
| 31 | 35 | San Jose-Sunnyvale-Santa Clara, CA | 13.3 | 3 | 36 | Chicago-Joliet-Naperville, IL-IN-WI | 16.7 |
| 37 | 35 | Nashville-Davidson—Murfreesboro—Franklin, TN | 13.3 | 35 | 37 | Indianapolis-Carmel, IN | 16.4 |
| 39 | 35 | Milwaukee-Waukesha-West Allis, WI | 13.3 | 47 | 37 | Raleigh-Cary, NC | 16.4 |
| 63 | 35 | Oxnard-Thousand Oaks-Ventura, CA | 13.3 | 37 | 39 | Nashville-Davidson—Murfreesboro—Franklin, TN | 16.3 |
| 16 | 40 | Minneapolis-St. Paul-Bloomington, MN | 13.2 | 42 | 40 | Louisville-Jefferson County, KY-IN | 15.8 |
| 46 | 41 | New Orleans-Metairie-Kenner, LA | 13.1 | 49 | 40 | Birmingham-Hoover, AL | 15.8 |
| 57 | 42 | Albuquerque, NM | 13.0 | 1 | 42 | New York-Northern New Jersey-Long Island, NY-NJ-PA | 15.2 |
| 1 | 43 | New York-Northern New Jersey-Long Island, NY-NJ-PA | 12.9 | 26 | 42 | Sacramento—Arden-Arcade—Roseville, CA | 15.2 |
| 40 | 43 | Jacksonville, FL | 12.9 | 44 | 44 | Richmond, VA | 15.1 |
| 42 | 45 | Louisville-Jefferson County, KY-IN | 12.8 | 14 | 45 | Detroit-Warren-Livonia, MI | 14.8 |
| 15 | 46 | Seattle-Tacoma-Bellevue, WA | 12.7 | 74 | 45 | Knoxville, TN | 14.8 |
| 23 | 46 | Portland-Vancouver-Hillsboro, OR-WA | 12.7 | 15 | 47 | Seattle-Tacoma-Bellevue, WA | 14.7 |
| 26 | 46 | Sacramento—Arden-Arcade—Roseville, CA | 12.7 | 28 | 48 | Kansas City, MO-KS | 14.5 |
| 70 | 49 | Columbia, SC | 12.6 | 62 | 49 | Dayton, OH | 14.4 |
| 6 | 50 | Philadelphia-Camden-Wilmington, PA-NJ-DE-MD | 12.4 | 11 | 50 | San Francisco-Oakland-Fremont, CA | 14.3 |
| 19 | 50 | St. Louis, MO-IL | 12.4 | 36 | 51 | Virginia Beach-Norfolk-Newport News, VA-NC | 14.2 |
| 20 | 50 | Baltimore-Towson, MD | 12.4 | 29 | 52 | Cleveland-Elyria-Mentor, OH | 14.1 |
| 52 | 50 | Tucson, AZ | 12.4 | 31 | 53 | San Jose-Sunnyvale-Santa Clara, CA | 14.0 |
| 44 | 54 | Richmond, VA | 12.1 | 69 | 53 | Grand Rapids-Wyoming, MI | 14.0 |
| 62 | 54 | Dayton, OH | 12.1 | 32 | 55 | Columbus, OH | 13.9 |
| 25 | 56 | Orlando-Kissimmee-Sanford, FL | 12.0 | 27 | 56 | Cincinnati-Middletown, OH-KY-IN | 13.7 |
| 11 | 57 | San Francisco-Oakland-Fremont, CA | 11.8 | 7 | 57 | Washington-Arlington-Alexandria, DC-VA-MD-WV | 13.0 |
| 71 | 57 | Greensboro-High Point, NC | 11.8 | 19 | 58 | St. Louis, MO-IL | 12.7 |
| 14 | 59 | Detroit-Warren-Livonia, MI | 11.7 | 58 | 59 | Omaha-Council Bluffs, NE-IA | 12.3 |
| 8 | 60 | Miami-Fort Lauderdale-Pompano Beach, FL | 11.6 | 65 | 60 | Allentown-Bethlehem-Easton, PA-NJ | 12.2 |
| 74 | 61 | Knoxville, TN | 11.4 | 6 | 61 | Philadelphia-Camden-Wilmington, PA-NJ-DE-MD | 12.0 |
| 10 | 62 | Boston-Cambridge-Quincy, MA-NH | 11.3 | 56 | 61 | Bridgeport-Stamford-Norwalk, CT | 12.0 |
| 29 | 62 | Cleveland-Elyria-Mentor, OH | 11.3 | 20 | 63 | Baltimore-Towson, MD | 11.7 |
| 68 | 62 | Worcester, MA | 11.3 | 39 | 64 | Milwaukee-Waukesha-West Allis, WI | 11.4 |
| 56 | 65 | Bridgeport-Stamford-Norwalk, CT | 11.2 | 38 | 65 | Providence-New Bedford-Fall River, RI-MA | 10.9 |
| 18 | 66 | Tampa-St. Petersburg-Clearwater, FL | 10.9 | 22 | 66 | Pittsburgh, PA | 10.6 |
| 51 | 66 | Rochester, NY | 10.9 | 60 | 67 | New Haven-Milford, CT | 10.5 |
| 60 | 68 | New Haven-Milford, CT | 10.7 | 51 | 68 | Rochester, NY | 10.4 |
| 65 | 68 | Allentown-Bethlehem-Easton, PA-NJ | 10.7 | 59 | 68 | Albany-Schenectady-Troy, NY | 10.4 |
| 38 | 70 | Providence-New Bedford-Fall River, RI-MA | 10.6 | 50 | 70 | Buffalo-Niagara Falls, NY | 10.2 |
| 50 | 71 | Buffalo-Niagara Falls, NY | 10.5 | 16 | 71 | Minneapolis-St. Paul-Bloomington, MN | 9.9 |
| 59 | 72 | Albany-Schenectady-Troy, NY | 10.4 | 45 | 72 | Hartford-West Hartford-East Hartford, CT | 9.5 |
| 45 | 73 | Hartford-West Hartford-East Hartford, CT | 10.2 | 53 | 73 | Honolulu, HI | 7.9 |
| 22 | 74 | Pittsburgh, PA | 10.0 | 10 | 74 | Boston-Cambridge-Quincy, MA-NH | 5.7 |
| 72 | 75 | North Port-Bradenton-Sarasota, FL | 8.8 | 68 | 75 | Worcester, MA | 4.8 |

# 75 Largest Metropolitan Areas by 2012 Population
## Selected Rankings

### Percent college graduates (bachelor's degree or more), 2007–2011

| Population rank | Percent college graduates rank | Metropolitan area | Percent college graduates [col 51] |
|---|---|---|---|
| 7 | 1 | Washington-Arlington-Alexandria, DC-VA-MD-WV | 47.5 |
| 31 | 2 | San Jose-Sunnyvale-Santa Clara, CA | 44.8 |
| 56 | 3 | Bridgeport-Stamford-Norwalk, CT | 44.0 |
| 11 | 4 | San Francisco-Oakland-Fremont, CA | 43.7 |
| 10 | 5 | Boston-Cambridge-Quincy, MA-NH | 42.6 |
| 47 | 6 | Raleigh-Cary, NC | 41.9 |
| 33 | 7 | Austin-Round Rock-San Marcos, TX | 39.9 |
| 21 | 8 | Denver-Aurora-Broomfield, CO | 38.3 |
| 16 | 9 | Minneapolis-St. Paul-Bloomington, MN | 37.9 |
| 15 | 10 | Seattle-Tacoma-Bellevue, WA | 37.2 |
| 1 | 11 | New York-Northern New Jersey-Long Island, NY-NJ-PA | 35.9 |
| 20 | 12 | Baltimore-Towson, MD | 35.1 |
| 45 | 13 | Hartford-West Hartford-East Hartford, CT | 34.8 |
| 9 | 14 | Atlanta-Sandy Springs-Marietta, GA | 34.7 |
| 17 | 15 | San Diego-Carlsbad-San Marcos, CA | 34.2 |
| 23 | 16 | Portland-Vancouver-Hillsboro, OR-WA | 33.9 |
| 3 | 17 | Chicago-Joliet-Naperville, IL-IN-WI | 33.8 |
| 68 | 18 | Worcester, MA | 33.3 |
| 32 | 19 | Columbus, OH | 33.0 |
| 59 | 19 | Albany-Schenectady-Troy, NY | 33.0 |
| 34 | 21 | Charlotte-Gastonia-Rock Hill, NC-SC | 32.7 |
| 6 | 22 | Philadelphia-Camden-Wilmington, PA-NJ-DE-MD | 32.6 |
| 28 | 23 | Kansas City, MO-KS | 32.5 |
| 60 | 24 | New Haven-Milford, CT | 32.3 |
| 58 | 25 | Omaha-Council Bluffs, NE-IA | 32.2 |
| 51 | 26 | Rochester, NY | 31.9 |
| 4 | 27 | Dallas-Fort Worth-Arlington, TX | 31.2 |
| 39 | 27 | Milwaukee-Waukesha-West Allis, WI | 31.2 |
| 44 | 27 | Richmond, VA | 31.2 |
| 53 | 27 | Honolulu, HI | 31.2 |
| 63 | 31 | Oxnard-Thousand Oaks-Ventura, CA | 31.0 |
| 2 | 32 | Los Angeles-Long Beach-Santa Ana, CA | 30.9 |
| 35 | 33 | Indianapolis-Carmel, IN | 30.8 |
| 48 | 34 | Salt Lake City, UT | 30.4 |
| 37 | 35 | Nashville-Davidson—Murfreesboro—Franklin, TN | 30.1 |
| 26 | 36 | Sacramento—Arden-Arcade—Roseville, CA | 30.0 |
| 70 | 37 | Columbia, SC | 29.8 |
| 19 | 38 | St. Louis, MO-IL | 29.6 |
| 52 | 39 | Tucson, AZ | 29.5 |
| 57 | 40 | Albuquerque, NM | 29.4 |
| 27 | 41 | Cincinnati-Middletown, OH-KY-IN | 29.0 |
| 8 | 42 | Miami-Fort Lauderdale-Pompano Beach, FL | 28.8 |
| 5 | 43 | Houston-Sugar Land-Baytown, TX | 28.7 |
| 22 | 43 | Pittsburgh, PA | 28.7 |
| 38 | 43 | Providence-New Bedford-Fall River, RI-MA | 28.7 |
| 74 | 46 | Knoxville, TN | 28.6 |
| 13 | 47 | Phoenix-Mesa-Glendale, AZ | 28.1 |
| 36 | 47 | Virginia Beach-Norfolk-Newport News, VA-NC | 28.1 |
| 50 | 49 | Buffalo-Niagara Falls, NY | 28.0 |
| 72 | 50 | North Port-Bradenton-Sarasota, FL | 27.9 |
| 25 | 51 | Orlando-Kissimmee-Sanford, FL | 27.8 |
| 43 | 52 | Oklahoma City, OK | 27.6 |
| 29 | 53 | Cleveland-Elyria-Mentor, OH | 27.5 |
| 14 | 54 | Detroit-Warren-Livonia, MI | 27.3 |
| 73 | 55 | Little Rock-North Little Rock-Conway, AR | 27.1 |
| 49 | 56 | Birmingham-Hoover, AL | 26.7 |
| 69 | 56 | Grand Rapids-Wyoming, MI | 26.7 |
| 40 | 58 | Jacksonville, FL | 26.4 |
| 65 | 59 | Allentown-Bethlehem-Easton, PA-NJ | 26.3 |
| 71 | 59 | Greensboro-High Point, NC | 26.3 |
| 46 | 61 | New Orleans-Metairie-Kenner, LA | 26.2 |
| 66 | 62 | Baton Rouge, LA | 26.0 |
| 18 | 63 | Tampa-St. Petersburg-Clearwater, FL | 25.9 |
| 24 | 64 | San Antonio-New Braunfels, TX | 25.4 |
| 54 | 64 | Tulsa, OK | 25.4 |
| 41 | 66 | Memphis, TN-MS-AR | 25.0 |
| 42 | 66 | Louisville-Jefferson County, KY-IN | 25.0 |
| 62 | 66 | Dayton, OH | 25.0 |
| 30 | 69 | Las Vegas-Paradise, NV | 22.0 |
| 64 | 70 | El Paso, TX | 19.8 |
| 12 | 71 | Riverside-San Bernardino-Ontario, CA | 19.6 |
| 55 | 72 | Fresno, CA | 19.5 |
| 75 | 73 | Stockton, CA | 17.6 |
| 67 | 74 | McAllen-Edinburg-Mission, TX | 15.3 |
| 61 | 75 | Bakersfield-Delano, CA | 14.6 |

### Median household income, 2007–2011

| Population rank | Median income rank | Metropolitan area | Median income (dollars) [col 55] |
|---|---|---|---|
| 7 | 1 | Washington-Arlington-Alexandria, DC-VA-MD-WV | 88 486 |
| 31 | 2 | San Jose-Sunnyvale-Santa Clara, CA | 88 339 |
| 56 | 3 | Bridgeport-Stamford-Norwalk, CT | 82 558 |
| 11 | 4 | San Francisco-Oakland-Fremont, CA | 76 911 |
| 63 | 5 | Oxnard-Thousand Oaks-Ventura, CA | 76 728 |
| 10 | 6 | Boston-Cambridge-Quincy, MA-NH | 71 878 |
| 53 | 7 | Honolulu, HI | 71 263 |
| 20 | 8 | Baltimore-Towson, MD | 67 891 |
| 45 | 9 | Hartford-West Hartford-East Hartford, CT | 67 695 |
| 15 | 10 | Seattle-Tacoma-Bellevue, WA | 67 023 |
| 16 | 11 | Minneapolis-St. Paul-Bloomington, MN | 66 157 |
| 68 | 12 | Worcester, MA | 65 772 |
| 1 | 13 | New York-Northern New Jersey-Long Island, NY-NJ-PA | 65 288 |
| 17 | 14 | San Diego-Carlsbad-San Marcos, CA | 63 857 |
| 60 | 15 | New Haven-Milford, CT | 62 497 |
| 21 | 16 | Denver-Aurora-Broomfield, CO | 61 734 |
| 6 | 17 | Philadelphia-Camden-Wilmington, PA-NJ-DE-MD | 61 496 |
| 47 | 18 | Raleigh-Cary, NC | 61 407 |
| 3 | 19 | Chicago-Joliet-Naperville, IL-IN-WI | 61 257 |
| 2 | 20 | Los Angeles-Long Beach-Santa Ana, CA | 60 667 |
| 26 | 21 | Sacramento—Arden-Arcade—Roseville, CA | 60 479 |
| 48 | 22 | Salt Lake City, UT | 59 930 |
| 33 | 23 | Austin-Round Rock-San Marcos, TX | 59 476 |
| 59 | 24 | Albany-Schenectady-Troy, NY | 59 339 |
| 36 | 25 | Virginia Beach-Norfolk-Newport News, VA-NC | 59 211 |
| 44 | 26 | Richmond, VA | 58 889 |
| 65 | 27 | Allentown-Bethlehem-Easton, PA-NJ | 58 054 |
| 9 | 28 | Atlanta-Sandy Springs-Marietta, GA | 57 783 |
| 4 | 29 | Dallas-Fort Worth-Arlington, TX | 57 658 |
| 23 | 30 | Portland-Vancouver-Hillsboro, OR-WA | 57 307 |
| 12 | 31 | Riverside-San Bernardino-Ontario, CA | 57 096 |
| 5 | 32 | Houston-Sugar Land-Baytown, TX | 56 876 |
| 28 | 33 | Kansas City, MO-KS | 56 613 |
| 58 | 34 | Omaha-Council Bluffs, NE-IA | 56 346 |
| 30 | 35 | Las Vegas-Paradise, NV | 55 961 |
| 38 | 36 | Providence-New Bedford-Fall River, RI-MA | 55 924 |
| 13 | 37 | Phoenix-Mesa-Glendale, AZ | 54 732 |
| 27 | 38 | Cincinnati-Middletown, OH-KY-IN | 54 651 |
| 34 | 39 | Charlotte-Gastonia-Rock Hill, NC-SC | 54 229 |
| 19 | 40 | St. Louis, MO-IL | 54 149 |
| 32 | 41 | Columbus, OH | 54 112 |
| 75 | 42 | Stockton, CA | 53 764 |
| 39 | 43 | Milwaukee-Waukesha-West Allis, WI | 53 618 |
| 35 | 44 | Indianapolis-Carmel, IN | 53 531 |
| 40 | 45 | Jacksonville, FL | 53 363 |
| 51 | 46 | Rochester, NY | 52 777 |
| 37 | 47 | Nashville-Davidson—Murfreesboro—Franklin, TN | 52 347 |
| 14 | 48 | Detroit-Warren-Livonia, MI | 52 244 |
| 25 | 49 | Orlando-Kissimmee-Sanford, FL | 50 433 |
| 24 | 50 | San Antonio-New Braunfels, TX | 50 318 |
| 69 | 51 | Grand Rapids-Wyoming, MI | 50 187 |
| 66 | 52 | Baton Rouge, LA | 50 146 |
| 22 | 53 | Pittsburgh, PA | 49 246 |
| 29 | 54 | Cleveland-Elyria-Mentor, OH | 49 024 |
| 8 | 55 | Miami-Fort Lauderdale-Pompano Beach, FL | 49 018 |
| 42 | 56 | Louisville-Jefferson County, KY-IN | 48 820 |
| 70 | 57 | Columbia, SC | 48 766 |
| 72 | 58 | North Port-Bradenton-Sarasota, FL | 48 745 |
| 57 | 59 | Albuquerque, NM | 48 663 |
| 43 | 60 | Oklahoma City, OK | 48 498 |
| 49 | 61 | Birmingham-Hoover, AL | 48 411 |
| 50 | 62 | Buffalo-Niagara Falls, NY | 48 332 |
| 61 | 63 | Bakersfield-Delano, CA | 48 021 |
| 62 | 64 | Dayton, OH | 47 864 |
| 54 | 65 | Tulsa, OK | 47 760 |
| 73 | 66 | Little Rock-North Little Rock-Conway, AR | 47 731 |
| 46 | 67 | New Orleans-Metairie-Kenner, LA | 47 566 |
| 41 | 68 | Memphis, TN-MS-AR | 47 344 |
| 55 | 69 | Fresno, CA | 46 903 |
| 18 | 70 | Tampa-St. Petersburg-Clearwater, FL | 46 890 |
| 74 | 71 | Knoxville, TN | 46 666 |
| 52 | 72 | Tucson, AZ | 46 341 |
| 71 | 73 | Greensboro-High Point, NC | 43 915 |
| 64 | 74 | El Paso, TX | 38 259 |
| 67 | 75 | McAllen-Edinburg-Mission, TX | 32 479 |

# 75 Largest Metropolitan Areas by 2012 Population
## Selected Rankings

### Percent of population below the poverty level, 2007–2011

| Population rank | Poverty rate rank | Metropolitan area | Poverty rate [col 59] |
|---|---|---|---|
| 67 | 1 | McAllen-Edinburg-Mission, TX | 35.3 |
| 64 | 2 | El Paso, TX | 25.0 |
| 55 | 3 | Fresno, CA | 23.4 |
| 61 | 4 | Bakersfield-Delano, CA | 21.4 |
| 41 | 5 | Memphis, TN-MS-AR | 18.7 |
| 52 | 6 | Tucson, AZ | 17.4 |
| 46 | 7 | New Orleans-Metairie-Kenner, LA | 16.8 |
| 75 | 8 | Stockton, CA | 16.7 |
| 57 | 9 | Albuquerque, NM | 16.5 |
| 71 | 10 | Greensboro-High Point, NC | 16.4 |
| 66 | 11 | Baton Rouge, LA | 16.1 |
| 24 | 12 | San Antonio-New Braunfels, TX | 16.0 |
| 14 | 13 | Detroit-Warren-Livonia, MI | 15.5 |
| 5 | 14 | Houston-Sugar Land-Baytown, TX | 15.4 |
| 8 | 15 | Miami-Fort Lauderdale-Pompano Beach, FL | 15.2 |
| 12 | 16 | Riverside-San Bernardino-Ontario, CA | 15.1 |
| 2 | 17 | Los Angeles-Long Beach-Santa Ana, CA | 15.0 |
| 43 | 18 | Oklahoma City, OK | 14.9 |
| 13 | 19 | Phoenix-Mesa-Glendale, AZ | 14.8 |
| 73 | 19 | Little Rock-North Little Rock-Conway, AR | 14.8 |
| 69 | 21 | Grand Rapids-Wyoming, MI | 14.7 |
| 49 | 22 | Birmingham-Hoover, AL | 14.6 |
| 70 | 22 | Columbia, SC | 14.6 |
| 32 | 24 | Columbus, OH | 14.5 |
| 62 | 24 | Dayton, OH | 14.5 |
| 29 | 26 | Cleveland-Elyria-Mentor, OH | 14.4 |
| 54 | 26 | Tulsa, OK | 14.4 |
| 42 | 28 | Louisville-Jefferson County, KY-IN | 14.1 |
| 33 | 29 | Austin-Round Rock-San Marcos, TX | 14.0 |
| 74 | 29 | Knoxville, TN | 14.0 |
| 4 | 31 | Dallas-Fort Worth-Arlington, TX | 13.9 |
| 18 | 31 | Tampa-St. Petersburg-Clearwater, FL | 13.9 |
| 39 | 31 | Milwaukee-Waukesha-West Allis, WI | 13.9 |
| 50 | 31 | Buffalo-Niagara Falls, NY | 13.9 |
| 37 | 35 | Nashville-Davidson—Murfreesboro—Franklin, TN | 13.6 |
| 9 | 36 | Atlanta-Sandy Springs-Marietta, GA | 13.5 |
| 26 | 37 | Sacramento—Arden-Arcade—Roseville, CA | 13.4 |
| 51 | 37 | Rochester, NY | 13.4 |
| 25 | 39 | Orlando-Kissimmee-Sanford, FL | 13.3 |
| 34 | 39 | Charlotte-Gastonia-Rock Hill, NC-SC | 13.3 |
| 1 | 41 | New York-Northern New Jersey-Long Island, NY-NJ-PA | 13.1 |
| 40 | 41 | Jacksonville, FL | 13.1 |
| 17 | 43 | San Diego-Carlsbad-San Marcos, CA | 13.0 |
| 30 | 44 | Las Vegas-Paradise, NV | 12.9 |
| 35 | 45 | Indianapolis-Carmel, IN | 12.8 |
| 3 | 46 | Chicago-Joliet-Naperville, IL-IN-WI | 12.7 |
| 23 | 47 | Portland-Vancouver-Hillsboro, OR-WA | 12.6 |
| 27 | 47 | Cincinnati-Middletown, OH-KY-IN | 12.6 |
| 38 | 49 | Providence-New Bedford-Fall River, RI-MA | 12.3 |
| 6 | 50 | Philadelphia-Camden-Wilmington, PA-NJ-DE-MD | 12.2 |
| 19 | 50 | St. Louis, MO-IL | 12.2 |
| 72 | 50 | North Port-Bradenton-Sarasota, FL | 12.2 |
| 21 | 53 | Denver-Aurora-Broomfield, CO | 11.9 |
| 22 | 53 | Pittsburgh, PA | 11.9 |
| 28 | 55 | Kansas City, MO-KS | 11.5 |
| 44 | 56 | Richmond, VA | 11.4 |
| 60 | 56 | New Haven-Milford, CT | 11.4 |
| 47 | 58 | Raleigh-Cary, NC | 11.2 |
| 58 | 58 | Omaha-Council Bluffs, NE-IA | 11.2 |
| 59 | 60 | Albany-Schenectady-Troy, NY | 10.8 |
| 36 | 61 | Virginia Beach-Norfolk-Newport News, VA-NC | 10.7 |
| 48 | 61 | Salt Lake City, UT | 10.7 |
| 15 | 63 | Seattle-Tacoma-Bellevue, WA | 10.5 |
| 11 | 64 | San Francisco-Oakland-Fremont, CA | 10.4 |
| 65 | 64 | Allentown-Bethlehem-Easton, PA-NJ | 10.4 |
| 20 | 66 | Baltimore-Towson, MD | 10.1 |
| 16 | 67 | Minneapolis-St. Paul-Bloomington, MN | 9.9 |
| 63 | 67 | Oxnard-Thousand Oaks-Ventura, CA | 9.9 |
| 68 | 67 | Worcester, MA | 9.9 |
| 10 | 70 | Boston-Cambridge-Quincy, MA-NH | 9.8 |
| 45 | 70 | Hartford-West Hartford-East Hartford, CT | 9.8 |
| 31 | 72 | San Jose-Sunnyvale-Santa Clara, CA | 9.3 |
| 53 | 72 | Honolulu, HI | 9.3 |
| 56 | 74 | Bridgeport-Stamford-Norwalk, CT | 8.3 |
| 7 | 75 | Washington-Arlington-Alexandria, DC-VA-MD-WV | 7.5 |

### Percent of children under 18 years old below the poverty level, 2007–2011

| Population rank | Poverty rate rank | Metropolitan area | Poverty rate [col 60] |
|---|---|---|---|
| 67 | 1 | McAllen-Edinburg-Mission, TX | 46.7 |
| 64 | 2 | El Paso, TX | 34.6 |
| 55 | 3 | Fresno, CA | 33.0 |
| 61 | 4 | Bakersfield-Delano, CA | 29.5 |
| 41 | 5 | Memphis, TN-MS-AR | 28.0 |
| 46 | 6 | New Orleans-Metairie-Kenner, LA | 24.2 |
| 52 | 7 | Tucson, AZ | 23.9 |
| 57 | 8 | Albuquerque, NM | 23.3 |
| 71 | 8 | Greensboro-High Point, NC | 23.3 |
| 24 | 10 | San Antonio-New Braunfels, TX | 22.5 |
| 5 | 11 | Houston-Sugar Land-Baytown, TX | 22.2 |
| 14 | 11 | Detroit-Warren-Livonia, MI | 22.2 |
| 75 | 13 | Stockton, CA | 22.0 |
| 29 | 14 | Cleveland-Elyria-Mentor, OH | 21.5 |
| 66 | 14 | Baton Rouge, LA | 21.5 |
| 54 | 16 | Tulsa, OK | 21.1 |
| 2 | 17 | Los Angeles-Long Beach-Santa Ana, CA | 20.8 |
| 62 | 17 | Dayton, OH | 20.8 |
| 13 | 19 | Phoenix-Mesa-Glendale, AZ | 20.7 |
| 73 | 19 | Little Rock-North Little Rock-Conway, AR | 20.7 |
| 49 | 21 | Birmingham-Hoover, AL | 20.6 |
| 8 | 22 | Miami-Fort Lauderdale-Pompano Beach, FL | 20.4 |
| 12 | 22 | Riverside-San Bernardino-Ontario, CA | 20.4 |
| 39 | 24 | Milwaukee-Waukesha-West Allis, WI | 20.3 |
| 69 | 24 | Grand Rapids-Wyoming, MI | 20.3 |
| 42 | 26 | Louisville-Jefferson County, KY-IN | 20.2 |
| 43 | 26 | Oklahoma City, OK | 20.2 |
| 50 | 28 | Buffalo-Niagara Falls, NY | 20.0 |
| 72 | 29 | North Port-Bradenton-Sarasota, FL | 19.9 |
| 4 | 30 | Dallas-Fort Worth-Arlington, TX | 19.7 |
| 18 | 31 | Tampa-St. Petersburg-Clearwater, FL | 19.4 |
| 32 | 32 | Columbus, OH | 19.0 |
| 37 | 33 | Nashville-Davidson—Murfreesboro—Franklin, TN | 18.9 |
| 70 | 34 | Columbia, SC | 18.8 |
| 74 | 35 | Knoxville, TN | 18.5 |
| 9 | 36 | Atlanta-Sandy Springs-Marietta, GA | 18.4 |
| 51 | 36 | Rochester, NY | 18.4 |
| 40 | 38 | Jacksonville, FL | 18.2 |
| 30 | 39 | Las Vegas-Paradise, NV | 18.1 |
| 1 | 40 | New York-Northern New Jersey-Long Island, NY-NJ-PA | 17.9 |
| 34 | 40 | Charlotte-Gastonia-Rock Hill, NC-SC | 17.9 |
| 3 | 42 | Chicago-Joliet-Naperville, IL-IN-WI | 17.8 |
| 25 | 42 | Orlando-Kissimmee-Sanford, FL | 17.8 |
| 35 | 42 | Indianapolis-Carmel, IN | 17.8 |
| 26 | 45 | Sacramento—Arden-Arcade—Roseville, CA | 17.5 |
| 33 | 45 | Austin-Round Rock-San Marcos, TX | 17.5 |
| 19 | 47 | St. Louis, MO-IL | 17.3 |
| 27 | 48 | Cincinnati-Middletown, OH-KY-IN | 17.1 |
| 17 | 49 | San Diego-Carlsbad-San Marcos, CA | 16.7 |
| 38 | 49 | Providence-New Bedford-Fall River, RI-MA | 16.7 |
| 6 | 51 | Philadelphia-Camden-Wilmington, PA-NJ-DE-MD | 16.3 |
| 22 | 51 | Pittsburgh, PA | 16.3 |
| 21 | 53 | Denver-Aurora-Broomfield, CO | 16.2 |
| 23 | 53 | Portland-Vancouver-Hillsboro, OR-WA | 16.2 |
| 28 | 55 | Kansas City, MO-KS | 16.0 |
| 60 | 55 | New Haven-Milford, CT | 16.0 |
| 36 | 57 | Virginia Beach-Norfolk-Newport News, VA-NC | 15.9 |
| 65 | 58 | Allentown-Bethlehem-Easton, PA-NJ | 15.4 |
| 44 | 59 | Richmond, VA | 15.2 |
| 58 | 60 | Omaha-Council Bluffs, NE-IA | 15.0 |
| 47 | 61 | Raleigh-Cary, NC | 14.4 |
| 59 | 62 | Albany-Schenectady-Troy, NY | 14.3 |
| 48 | 63 | Salt Lake City, UT | 13.3 |
| 63 | 63 | Oxnard-Thousand Oaks-Ventura, CA | 13.3 |
| 45 | 65 | Hartford-West Hartford-East Hartford, CT | 13.1 |
| 15 | 66 | Seattle-Tacoma-Bellevue, WA | 12.9 |
| 20 | 66 | Baltimore-Towson, MD | 12.9 |
| 16 | 68 | Minneapolis-St. Paul-Bloomington, MN | 12.7 |
| 68 | 69 | Worcester, MA | 12.5 |
| 11 | 70 | San Francisco-Oakland-Fremont, CA | 12.3 |
| 53 | 71 | Honolulu, HI | 11.9 |
| 31 | 72 | San Jose-Sunnyvale-Santa Clara, CA | 11.3 |
| 10 | 73 | Boston-Cambridge-Quincy, MA-NH | 11.2 |
| 56 | 74 | Bridgeport-Stamford-Norwalk, CT | 9.7 |
| 7 | 75 | Washington-Arlington-Alexandria, DC-VA-MD-WV | 9.1 |

# 75 Largest Metropolitan Areas by 2012 Population
## Selected Rankings

### Median value of owner-occupied housing units, 2007–2011

| Population rank | Median value rank | Metropolitan area | Median value (dollars) [col 91] |
|---|---|---|---|
| 31 | 1 | San Jose-Sunnyvale-Santa Clara, CA | 674 800 |
| 11 | 2 | San Francisco-Oakland-Fremont, CA | 627 000 |
| 53 | 3 | Honolulu, HI | 560 300 |
| 63 | 4 | Oxnard-Thousand Oaks-Ventura, CA | 515 900 |
| 2 | 5 | Los Angeles-Long Beach-Santa Ana, CA | 501 900 |
| 56 | 6 | Bridgeport-Stamford-Norwalk, CT | 466 700 |
| 17 | 7 | San Diego-Carlsbad-San Marcos, CA | 455 000 |
| 1 | 8 | New York-Northern New Jersey-Long Island, NY-NJ-PA | 440 400 |
| 7 | 9 | Washington-Arlington-Alexandria, DC-VA-MD-WV | 399 400 |
| 10 | 10 | Boston-Cambridge-Quincy, MA-NH | 373 500 |
| 15 | 11 | Seattle-Tacoma-Bellevue, WA | 352 800 |
| 26 | 12 | Sacramento—Arden-Arcade—Roseville, CA | 324 300 |
| 79 | 13 | Poughkeepsie-Newburgh-Middletown, NY | 306 800 |
| 20 | 14 | Baltimore-Towson, MD | 297 200 |
| 23 | 15 | Portland-Vancouver-Hillsboro, OR-WA | 284 400 |
| 12 | 16 | Riverside-San Bernardino-Ontario, CA | 281 600 |
| 38 | 17 | Providence-New Bedford-Fall River, RI-MA | 280 300 |
| 68 | 18 | Worcester, MA | 274 900 |
| 60 | 19 | New Haven-Milford, CT | 270 900 |
| 75 | 20 | Stockton, CA | 264 600 |
| 45 | 21 | Hartford-West Hartford-East Hartford, CT | 258 200 |
| 36 | 22 | Virginia Beach-Norfolk-Newport News, VA-NC | 246 500 |
| 21 | 23 | Denver-Aurora-Broomfield, CO | 246 200 |
| 3 | 24 | Chicago-Joliet-Naperville, IL-IN-WI | 245 700 |
| 6 | 25 | Philadelphia-Camden-Wilmington, PA-NJ-DE-MD | 245 000 |
| 48 | 26 | Salt Lake City, UT | 241 000 |
| 8 | 27 | Miami-Fort Lauderdale-Pompano Beach, FL | 236 900 |
| 55 | 28 | Fresno, CA | 236 400 |
| 16 | 29 | Minneapolis-St. Paul-Bloomington, MN | 234 000 |
| 95 | 30 | Provo-Orem, UT | 233 300 |
| 44 | 31 | Richmond, VA | 227 600 |
| 30 | 32 | Las Vegas-Paradise, NV | 226 200 |
| 89 | 33 | Madison, WI | 223 500 |
| 78 | 34 | Springfield, MA | 219 700 |
| 80 | 35 | Colorado Springs, CO | 217 600 |
| 65 | 36 | Allentown-Bethlehem-Easton, PA-NJ | 216 800 |
| 13 | 37 | Phoenix-Mesa-Glendale, AZ | 212 100 |
| 92 | 38 | Ogden-Clearfield, UT | 205 900 |
| 72 | 39 | North Port-Bradenton-Sarasota, FL | 205 700 |
| 39 | 40 | Milwaukee-Waukesha-West Allis, WI | 205 100 |
| 47 | 41 | Raleigh-Cary, NC | 202 900 |
| 25 | 42 | Orlando-Kissimmee-Sanford, FL | 201 100 |
| 61 | 43 | Bakersfield-Delano, CA | 196 000 |
| 59 | 44 | Albany-Schenectady-Troy, NY | 194 900 |
| 77 | 45 | Charleston-North Charleston-Summerville, SC | 192 000 |
| 52 | 46 | Tucson, AZ | 190 500 |
| 33 | 47 | Austin-Round Rock-San Marcos, TX | 186 300 |
| 9 | 48 | Atlanta-Sandy Springs-Marietta, GA | 184 900 |
| 85 | 49 | Boise City-Nampa, ID | 184 300 |
| 57 | 50 | Albuquerque, NM | 183 800 |
| 40 | 51 | Jacksonville, FL | 183 300 |
| 84 | 52 | Cape Coral-Fort Myers, FL | 181 000 |
| 46 | 53 | New Orleans-Metairie-Kenner, LA | 179 500 |
| 37 | 54 | Nashville-Davidson—Murfreesboro—Franklin, TN | 172 700 |
| 34 | 55 | Charlotte-Gastonia-Rock Hill, NC-SC | 171 400 |
| 18 | 56 | Tampa-St. Petersburg-Clearwater, FL | 169 900 |
| 94 | 57 | Harrisburg-Carlisle, PA | 166 200 |
| 32 | 58 | Columbus, OH | 163 500 |
| 19 | 59 | St. Louis, MO-IL | 160 400 |
| 28 | 60 | Kansas City, MO-KS | 159 600 |
| 27 | 61 | Cincinnati-Middletown, OH-KY-IN | 156 400 |
| 66 | 62 | Baton Rouge, LA | 154 700 |
| 88 | 63 | Des Moines-West Des Moines, IA | 153 700 |
| 74 | 64 | Knoxville, TN | 151 800 |
| 4 | 65 | Dallas-Fort Worth-Arlington, TX | 148 700 |
| 14 | 66 | Detroit-Warren-Livonia, MI | 148 500 |
| 29 | 67 | Cleveland-Elyria-Mentor, OH | 148 100 |
| 42 | 68 | Louisville-Jefferson County, KY-IN | 145 900 |
| 58 | 69 | Omaha-Council Bluffs, NE-IA | 144 800 |
| 35 | 70 | Indianapolis-Carmel, IN | 144 500 |
| 76 | 70 | Akron, OH | 144 500 |
| 49 | 72 | Birmingham-Hoover, AL | 144 100 |
| 69 | 73 | Grand Rapids-Wyoming, MI | 141 100 |
| 71 | 74 | Greensboro-High Point, NC | 140 900 |
| 5 | 75 | Houston-Sugar Land-Baytown, TX | 140 000 |

### Median gross rent of renter-occupied housing units, 2007–2011

| Population rank | Median gross rent | Metropolitan area | Median rent (dollars) [col 94] |
|---|---|---|---|
| 31 | 1 | San Jose-Sunnyvale-Santa Clara, CA | 1 454 |
| 63 | 2 | Oxnard-Thousand Oaks-Ventura, CA | 1 428 |
| 53 | 3 | Honolulu, HI | 1 381 |
| 7 | 4 | Washington-Arlington-Alexandria, DC-VA-MD-WV | 1 353 |
| 11 | 5 | San Francisco-Oakland-Fremont, CA | 1 344 |
| 17 | 6 | San Diego-Carlsbad-San Marcos, CA | 1 261 |
| 56 | 7 | Bridgeport-Stamford-Norwalk, CT | 1 249 |
| 2 | 8 | Los Angeles-Long Beach-Santa Ana, CA | 1 218 |
| 10 | 9 | Boston-Cambridge-Quincy, MA-NH | 1 163 |
| 1 | 10 | New York-Northern New Jersey-Long Island, NY-NJ-PA | 1 157 |
| 12 | 11 | Riverside-San Bernardino-Ontario, CA | 1 115 |
| 8 | 12 | Miami-Fort Lauderdale-Pompano Beach, FL | 1 108 |
| 20 | 13 | Baltimore-Towson, MD | 1 067 |
| 30 | 14 | Las Vegas-Paradise, NV | 1 049 |
| 26 | 15 | Sacramento—Arden-Arcade—Roseville, CA | 1 040 |
| 15 | 16 | Seattle-Tacoma-Bellevue, WA | 1 033 |
| 60 | 17 | New Haven-Milford, CT | 1 030 |
| 36 | 18 | Virginia Beach-Norfolk-Newport News, VA-NC | 1 020 |
| 25 | 19 | Orlando-Kissimmee-Sanford, FL | 1 018 |
| 75 | 20 | Stockton, CA | 993 |
| 72 | 21 | North Port-Bradenton-Sarasota, FL | 974 |
| 45 | 22 | Hartford-West Hartford-East Hartford, CT | 954 |
| 6 | 23 | Philadelphia-Camden-Wilmington, PA-NJ-DE-MD | 952 |
| 9 | 24 | Atlanta-Sandy Springs-Marietta, GA | 937 |
| 33 | 25 | Austin-Round Rock-San Marcos, TX | 936 |
| 40 | 25 | Jacksonville, FL | 936 |
| 13 | 27 | Phoenix-Mesa-Glendale, AZ | 934 |
| 3 | 28 | Chicago-Joliet-Naperville, IL-IN-WI | 931 |
| 18 | 29 | Tampa-St. Petersburg-Clearwater, FL | 928 |
| 44 | 30 | Richmond, VA | 921 |
| 46 | 31 | New Orleans-Metairie-Kenner, LA | 913 |
| 21 | 32 | Denver-Aurora-Broomfield, CO | 902 |
| 23 | 33 | Portland-Vancouver-Hillsboro, OR-WA | 886 |
| 68 | 34 | Worcester, MA | 883 |
| 4 | 35 | Dallas-Fort Worth-Arlington, TX | 874 |
| 38 | 36 | Providence-New Bedford-Fall River, RI-MA | 865 |
| 16 | 37 | Minneapolis-St. Paul-Bloomington, MN | 864 |
| 65 | 38 | Allentown-Bethlehem-Easton, PA-NJ | 863 |
| 5 | 39 | Houston-Sugar Land-Baytown, TX | 860 |
| 59 | 40 | Albany-Schenectady-Troy, NY | 859 |
| 47 | 41 | Raleigh-Cary, NC | 855 |
| 48 | 42 | Salt Lake City, UT | 852 |
| 55 | 43 | Fresno, CA | 850 |
| 61 | 44 | Bakersfield-Delano, CA | 840 |
| 34 | 45 | Charlotte-Gastonia-Rock Hill, NC-SC | 818 |
| 14 | 46 | Detroit-Warren-Livonia, MI | 808 |
| 41 | 47 | Memphis, TN-MS-AR | 802 |
| 37 | 48 | Nashville-Davidson—Murfreesboro—Franklin, TN | 799 |
| 24 | 49 | San Antonio-New Braunfels, TX | 792 |
| 39 | 50 | Milwaukee-Waukesha-West Allis, WI | 788 |
| 28 | 51 | Kansas City, MO-KS | 786 |
| 70 | 52 | Columbia, SC | 782 |
| 32 | 53 | Columbus, OH | 777 |
| 52 | 54 | Tucson, AZ | 769 |
| 66 | 55 | Baton Rouge, LA | 768 |
| 35 | 56 | Indianapolis-Carmel, IN | 763 |
| 49 | 56 | Birmingham-Hoover, AL | 763 |
| 51 | 58 | Rochester, NY | 762 |
| 19 | 59 | St. Louis, MO-IL | 757 |
| 58 | 60 | Omaha-Council Bluffs, NE-IA | 752 |
| 57 | 61 | Albuquerque, NM | 748 |
| 73 | 62 | Little Rock-North Little Rock-Conway, AR | 734 |
| 29 | 63 | Cleveland-Elyria-Mentor, OH | 725 |
| 62 | 64 | Dayton, OH | 718 |
| 27 | 65 | Cincinnati-Middletown, OH-KY-IN | 713 |
| 69 | 66 | Grand Rapids-Wyoming, MI | 710 |
| 43 | 67 | Oklahoma City, OK | 709 |
| 74 | 68 | Knoxville, TN | 704 |
| 54 | 69 | Tulsa, OK | 699 |
| 71 | 70 | Greensboro-High Point, NC | 695 |
| 50 | 71 | Buffalo-Niagara Falls, NY | 691 |
| 42 | 72 | Louisville-Jefferson County, KY-IN | 689 |
| 22 | 73 | Pittsburgh, PA | 672 |
| 64 | 74 | El Paso, TX | 660 |
| 67 | 75 | McAllen-Edinburg-Mission, TX | 620 |

# 75 Largest Metropolitan Areas by 2012 Population
## Selected Rankings

| | Unemployment rate, 2012 | | | | Percent of Votes for Barack Obama, 2012 | | |
|---|---|---|---|---|---|---|---|
| Population rank | Unemployment rate rank | Metropolitan area | Unemployment rate [col 100] | Population Rank | Vote for Obama rank | Metropolitan area | Percent of votes for Obama [col 197] |
| 55 | 1 | Fresno, CA | 15.2 | 11 | 1 | San Francisco-Oakland-Fremont, CA | 75.4 |
| 75 | 1 | Stockton, CA | 15.2 | 67 | 2 | McAllen-Edinburg-Mission, TX | 70.4 |
| 61 | 3 | Bakersfield-Delano, CA | 13.3 | 31 | 3 | San Jose-Sunnyvale-Santa Clara, CA | 69.8 |
| 12 | 4 | Riverside-San Bernardino-Ontario, CA | 12.1 | 53 | 4 | Honolulu, HI | 68.9 |
| 30 | 5 | Las Vegas-Paradise, NV | 11.2 | 7 | 5 | Washington-Arlington-Alexandria, DC-VA-MD-WV | 67.5 |
| 67 | 6 | McAllen-Edinburg-Mission, TX | 11.0 | 64 | 6 | El Paso, TX | 65.5 |
| 14 | 7 | Detroit-Warren-Livonia, MI | 10.5 | 1 | 7 | New York-Northern New Jersey-Long Island, NY-NJ-PA | 65.3 |
| 26 | 8 | Sacramento—Arden-Arcade—Roseville, CA | 10.4 | 6 | 8 | Philadelphia-Camden-Wilmington, PA-NJ-DE-MD | 64.0 |
| 2 | 9 | Los Angeles-Long Beach-Santa Ana, CA | 10.1 | 3 | 9 | Chicago-Joliet-Naperville, IL-IN-WI | 63.8 |
| 38 | 10 | Providence-New Bedford-Fall River, RI-MA | 10.0 | 15 | 10 | Seattle-Tacoma-Bellevue, WA | 63.6 |
| 71 | 11 | Greensboro-High Point, NC | 9.9 | 2 | 11 | Los Angeles-Long Beach-Santa Ana, CA | 63.4 |
| 34 | 12 | Charlotte-Gastonia-Rock Hill, NC-SC | 9.5 | 8 | 12 | Miami-Fort Lauderdale-Pompano Beach, FL | 62.6 |
| 64 | 13 | El Paso, TX | 9.3 | 29 | 13 | Cleveland-Elyria-Mentor, OH | 61.5 |
| 60 | 14 | New Haven-Milford, CT | 9.2 | 38 | 13 | Providence-New Bedford-Fall River, RI-MA | 61.5 |
| 41 | 15 | Memphis, TN-MS-AR | 9.0 | 45 | 15 | Hartford-West Hartford-East Hartford, CT | 60.7 |
| 63 | 15 | Oxnard-Thousand Oaks-Ventura, CA | 9.0 | 60 | 15 | New Haven-Milford, CT | 60.7 |
| 3 | 17 | Chicago-Joliet-Naperville, IL-IN-WI | 8.9 | 10 | 17 | Boston-Cambridge-Quincy, MA-NH | 60.1 |
| 17 | 17 | San Diego-Carlsbad-San Marcos, CA | 8.9 | 23 | 18 | Portland-Vancouver-Hillsboro, OR-WA | 60.0 |
| 1 | 19 | New York-Northern New Jersey-Long Island, NY-NJ-PA | 8.8 | 14 | 19 | Detroit-Warren-Livonia, MI | 59.5 |
| 9 | 19 | Atlanta-Sandy Springs-Marietta, GA | 8.8 | 20 | 20 | Baltimore-Towson, MD | 57.8 |
| 18 | 19 | Tampa-St. Petersburg-Clearwater, FL | 8.8 | 59 | 21 | Albany-Schenectady-Troy, NY | 57.0 |
| 6 | 22 | Philadelphia-Camden-Wilmington, PA-NJ-DE-MD | 8.6 | 30 | 22 | Las Vegas-Paradise, NV | 56.4 |
| 31 | 22 | San Jose-Sunnyvale-Santa Clara, CA | 8.6 | 50 | 23 | Buffalo-Niagara Falls, NY | 55.9 |
| 72 | 22 | North Port-Bradenton-Sarasota, FL | 8.6 | 75 | 24 | Stockton, CA | 55.8 |
| 8 | 25 | Miami-Fort Lauderdale-Pompano Beach, FL | 8.5 | 41 | 25 | Memphis, TN-MS-AR | 55.7 |
| 50 | 25 | Buffalo-Niagara Falls, NY | 8.5 | 21 | 26 | Denver-Aurora-Broomfield, CO | 55.5 |
| 65 | 25 | Allentown-Bethlehem-Easton, PA-NJ | 8.5 | 16 | 27 | Minneapolis-St. Paul-Bloomington, MN | 54.9 |
| 25 | 28 | Orlando-Kissimmee-Sanford, FL | 8.4 | 36 | 27 | Virginia Beach-Norfolk-Newport News, VA-NC | 54.9 |
| 40 | 29 | Jacksonville, FL | 8.3 | 56 | 27 | Bridgeport-Stamford-Norwalk, CT | 54.9 |
| 42 | 29 | Louisville-Jefferson County, KY-IN | 8.3 | 51 | 30 | Rochester, NY | 54.5 |
| 45 | 29 | Hartford-West Hartford-East Hartford, CT | 8.3 | 57 | 31 | Albuquerque, NM | 54.0 |
| 23 | 32 | Portland-Vancouver-Hillsboro, OR-WA | 8.2 | 68 | 32 | Worcester, MA | 53.7 |
| 11 | 33 | San Francisco-Oakland-Fremont, CA | 8.1 | 25 | 33 | Orlando-Kissimmee-Sanford, FL | 53.4 |
| 51 | 33 | Rochester, NY | 8.1 | 26 | 34 | Sacramento—Arden-Arcade—Roseville, CA | 53.1 |
| 70 | 35 | Columbia, SC | 8.0 | 32 | 35 | Columbus, OH | 52.8 |
| 21 | 36 | Denver-Aurora-Broomfield, CO | 7.9 | 17 | 36 | San Diego-Carlsbad-San Marcos, CA | 52.6 |
| 35 | 37 | Indianapolis-Carmel, IN | 7.8 | 52 | 36 | Tucson, AZ | 52.6 |
| 47 | 38 | Raleigh-Cary, NC | 7.7 | 19 | 38 | St. Louis, MO-IL | 52.5 |
| 19 | 39 | St. Louis, MO-IL | 7.6 | 63 | 39 | Oxnard-Thousand Oaks-Ventura, CA | 52.3 |
| 56 | 39 | Bridgeport-Stamford-Norwalk, CT | 7.6 | 39 | 40 | Milwaukee-Waukesha-West Allis, WI | 52.1 |
| 62 | 39 | Dayton, OH | 7.6 | 47 | 40 | Raleigh-Cary, NC | 52.1 |
| 59 | 42 | Albany-Schenectady-Troy, NY | 7.5 | 33 | 42 | Austin-Round Rock-San Marcos, TX | 51.9 |
| 68 | 42 | Worcester, MA | 7.5 | 44 | 43 | Richmond, VA | 51.7 |
| 15 | 44 | Seattle-Tacoma-Bellevue, WA | 7.4 | 12 | 44 | Riverside-San Bernardino-Ontario, CA | 51.0 |
| 39 | 44 | Milwaukee-Waukesha-West Allis, WI | 7.4 | 18 | 44 | Tampa-St. Petersburg-Clearwater, FL | 51.0 |
| 13 | 46 | Phoenix-Mesa-Glendale, AZ | 7.3 | 65 | 46 | Allentown-Bethlehem-Easton, PA-NJ | 50.6 |
| 52 | 46 | Tucson, AZ | 7.3 | 34 | 47 | Charlotte-Gastonia-Rock Hill, NC-SC | 50.3 |
| 57 | 46 | Albuquerque, NM | 7.3 | 70 | 48 | Columbia, SC | 50.2 |
| 20 | 49 | Baltimore-Towson, MD | 7.2 | 55 | 49 | Fresno, CA | 49.9 |
| 22 | 49 | Pittsburgh, PA | 7.2 | 71 | 50 | Greensboro-High Point, NC | 49.8 |
| 27 | 51 | Cincinnati-Middletown, OH-KY-IN | 7.1 | 9 | 51 | Atlanta-Sandy Springs-Marietta, GA | 49.7 |
| 29 | 51 | Cleveland-Elyria-Mentor, OH | 7.1 | 46 | 52 | New Orleans-Metairie-Kenner, LA | 49.0 |
| 5 | 53 | Houston-Sugar Land-Baytown, TX | 6.8 | 22 | 53 | Pittsburgh, PA | 48.8 |
| 69 | 53 | Grand Rapids-Wyoming, MI | 6.8 | 28 | 54 | Kansas City, MO-KS | 47.7 |
| 4 | 55 | Dallas-Fort Worth-Arlington, TX | 6.7 | 42 | 54 | Louisville-Jefferson County, KY-IN | 47.7 |
| 28 | 56 | Kansas City, MO-KS | 6.6 | 62 | 56 | Dayton, OH | 45.5 |
| 36 | 56 | Virginia Beach-Norfolk-Newport News, VA-NC | 6.6 | 24 | 57 | San Antonio-New Braunfels, TX | 45.3 |
| 37 | 56 | Nashville-Davidson—Murfreesboro—Franklin, TN | 6.6 | 35 | 58 | Indianapolis-Carmel, IN | 45.1 |
| 74 | 56 | Knoxville, TN | 6.6 | 72 | 59 | North Port-Bradenton-Sarasota, FL | 44.8 |
| 24 | 60 | San Antonio-New Braunfels, TX | 6.5 | 69 | 60 | Grand Rapids-Wyoming, MI | 44.7 |
| 46 | 60 | New Orleans-Metairie-Kenner, LA | 6.5 | 58 | 61 | Omaha-Council Bluffs, NE-IA | 44.0 |
| 73 | 60 | Little Rock-North Little Rock-Conway, AR | 6.5 | 5 | 62 | Houston-Sugar Land-Baytown, TX | 43.5 |
| 44 | 63 | Richmond, VA | 6.4 | 13 | 62 | Phoenix-Mesa-Glendale, AZ | 43.5 |
| 49 | 63 | Birmingham-Hoover, AL | 6.4 | 73 | 64 | Little Rock-North Little Rock-Conway, AR | 43.2 |
| 66 | 63 | Baton Rouge, LA | 6.4 | 66 | 65 | Baton Rouge, LA | 43.0 |
| 10 | 66 | Boston-Cambridge-Quincy, MA-NH | 6.1 | 4 | 66 | Dallas-Fort Worth-Arlington, TX | 42.1 |
| 32 | 66 | Columbus, OH | 6.1 | 27 | 67 | Cincinnati-Middletown, OH-KY-IN | 41.3 |
| 33 | 68 | Austin-Round Rock-San Marcos, TX | 5.8 | 37 | 67 | Nashville-Davidson—Murfreesboro—Franklin, TN | 41.3 |
| 7 | 69 | Washington-Arlington-Alexandria, DC-VA-MD-WV | 5.6 | 61 | 69 | Bakersfield-Delano, CA | 40.4 |
| 54 | 69 | Tulsa, OK | 5.6 | 40 | 70 | Jacksonville, FL | 40.0 |
| 16 | 71 | Minneapolis-St. Paul-Bloomington, MN | 5.5 | 49 | 71 | Birmingham-Hoover, AL | 39.3 |
| 48 | 71 | Salt Lake City, UT | 5.5 | 48 | 72 | Salt Lake City, UT | 37.9 |
| 53 | 73 | Honolulu, HI | 5.2 | 43 | 73 | Oklahoma City, OK | 36.5 |
| 43 | 74 | Oklahoma City, OK | 4.8 | 54 | 74 | Tulsa, OK | 33.9 |
| 58 | 75 | Omaha-Council Bluffs, NE-IA | 4.4 | 74 | 75 | Knoxville, TN | 31.9 |

# 75 Largest Metropolitan Areas by 2012 Population
## Selected Rankings

| | | Employment in manufacturing as a percent of total nonfarm employment, 2011 | | | | Employment in professional, scientific, and technical services as a percent of total nonfarm employment, 2011 | |
|---|---|---|---|---|---|---|---|
| Population rank | Manufacturing rank | Metropolitan area | Percent employed in manufacturing [col 107/ col 105] | Population rank | Professional services rank | Metropolitan area | Percent employed in services [col 110/ col 105] |
| 71 | 1 | Greensboro-High Point, NC | 18.4 | 7 | 1 | Washington-Arlington-Alexandria, DC-VA-MD-WV | 20.0 |
| 69 | 2 | Grand Rapids-Wyoming, MI | 17.4 | 31 | 2 | San Jose-Sunnyvale-Santa Clara, CA | 13.5 |
| 39 | 3 | Milwaukee-Waukesha-West Allis, WI | 15.4 | 11 | 3 | San Francisco-Oakland-Fremont, CA | 12.0 |
| 29 | 4 | Cleveland-Elyria-Mentor, OH | 13.8 | 17 | 4 | San Diego-Carlsbad-San Marcos, CA | 10.6 |
| 51 | 4 | Rochester, NY | 13.8 | 14 | 5 | Detroit-Warren-Livonia, MI | 10.0 |
| 54 | 6 | Tulsa, OK | 13.7 | 10 | 6 | Boston-Cambridge-Quincy, MA-NH | 9.9 |
| 62 | 7 | Dayton, OH | 13.4 | 33 | 6 | Austin-Round Rock-San Marcos, TX | 9.9 |
| 75 | 8 | Stockton, CA | 12.3 | 20 | 8 | Baltimore-Towson, MD | 9.8 |
| 38 | 9 | Providence-New Bedford-Fall River, RI-MA | 12.2 | 56 | 9 | Bridgeport-Stamford-Norwalk, CT | 9.3 |
| 42 | 9 | Louisville-Jefferson County, KY-IN | 12.2 | 1 | 10 | New York-Northern New Jersey-Long Island, NY-NJ-PA | 9.2 |
| 68 | 11 | Worcester, MA | 12.1 | 2 | 10 | Los Angeles-Long Beach-Santa Ana, CA | 9.2 |
| 45 | 11 | Hartford-West Hartford-East Hartford, CT | 12.1 | 9 | 12 | Atlanta-Sandy Springs-Marietta, GA | 9.1 |
| 70 | 13 | Columbia, SC | 11.8 | 21 | 13 | Denver-Aurora-Broomfield, CO | 8.9 |
| 50 | 14 | Buffalo-Niagara Falls, NY | 11.6 | 47 | 13 | Raleigh-Cary, NC | 8.9 |
| 14 | 14 | Detroit-Warren-Livonia, MI | 11.6 | 59 | 15 | Albany-Schenectady-Troy, NY | 8.8 |
| 27 | 16 | Cincinnati-Middletown, OH-KY-IN | 11.5 | 58 | 16 | Omaha-Council Bluffs, NE-IA | 8.7 |
| 2 | 17 | Los Angeles-Long Beach-Santa Ana, CA | 11.4 | 63 | 17 | Oxnard-Thousand Oaks-Ventura, CA | 8.6 |
| 65 | 18 | Allentown-Bethlehem-Easton, PA-NJ | 11.3 | 36 | 17 | Virginia Beach-Norfolk-Newport News, VA-NC | 8.6 |
| 60 | 19 | New Haven-Milford, CT | 11.1 | 57 | 19 | Albuquerque, NM | 8.4 |
| 16 | 20 | Minneapolis-St. Paul-Bloomington, MN | 11.0 | 5 | 20 | Houston-Sugar Land-Baytown, TX | 8.3 |
| 23 | 21 | Portland-Vancouver-Hillsboro, OR-WA | 10.8 | 6 | 20 | Philadelphia-Camden-Wilmington, PA-NJ-DE-MD | 8.3 |
| 31 | 22 | San Jose-Sunnyvale-Santa Clara, CA | 10.6 | 3 | 22 | Chicago-Joliet-Naperville, IL-IN-WI | 8.0 |
| 55 | 23 | Fresno, CA | 10.4 | 18 | 22 | Tampa-St. Petersburg-Clearwater, FL | 8.0 |
| 3 | 23 | Chicago-Joliet-Naperville, IL-IN-WI | 10.4 | 28 | 24 | Kansas City, MO-KS | 7.9 |
| 74 | 25 | Knoxville, TN | 10.2 | 15 | 25 | Seattle-Tacoma-Bellevue, WA | 7.7 |
| 35 | 26 | Indianapolis-Carmel, IN | 10.1 | 74 | 26 | Knoxville, TN | 7.5 |
| 63 | 26 | Oxnard-Thousand Oaks-Ventura, CA | 10.1 | 8 | 27 | Miami-Fort Lauderdale-Pompano Beach, FL | 7.4 |
| 12 | 28 | Riverside-San Bernardino-Ontario, CA | 9.9 | 25 | 27 | Orlando-Kissimmee-Sanford, FL | 7.4 |
| 15 | 29 | Seattle-Tacoma-Bellevue, WA | 9.7 | 40 | 29 | Jacksonville, FL | 7.3 |
| 36 | 30 | Virginia Beach-Norfolk-Newport News, VA-NC | 9.6 | 4 | 30 | Dallas-Fort Worth-Arlington, TX | 7.2 |
| 5 | 31 | Houston-Sugar Land-Baytown, TX | 9.4 | 62 | 30 | Dayton, OH | 7.2 |
| 4 | 31 | Dallas-Fort Worth-Arlington, TX | 9.4 | 16 | 30 | Minneapolis-St. Paul-Bloomington, MN | 7.2 |
| 56 | 33 | Bridgeport-Stamford-Norwalk, CT | 9.3 | 22 | 33 | Pittsburgh, PA | 7.1 |
| 48 | 34 | Salt Lake City, UT | 9.2 | 26 | 34 | Sacramento—Arden-Arcade—Roseville, CA | 7.0 |
| 28 | 35 | Kansas City, MO-KS | 9.1 | 19 | 34 | St. Louis, MO-IL | 7.0 |
| 22 | 36 | Pittsburgh, PA | 9.0 | 23 | 36 | Portland-Vancouver-Hillsboro, OR-WA | 6.9 |
| 37 | 37 | Nashville-Davidson—Murfreesboro—Franklin, TN | 8.9 | 46 | 37 | New Orleans-Metairie-Kenner, LA | 6.8 |
| 19 | 38 | St. Louis, MO-IL | 8.8 | 48 | 38 | Salt Lake City, UT | 6.7 |
| 49 | 38 | Birmingham-Hoover, AL | 8.8 | 66 | 39 | Baton Rouge, LA | 6.6 |
| 52 | 40 | Tucson, AZ | 8.7 | 44 | 40 | Richmond, VA | 6.3 |
| 34 | 41 | Charlotte-Gastonia-Rock Hill, NC-SC | 8.6 | 61 | 40 | Bakersfield-Delano, CA | 6.3 |
| 17 | 42 | San Diego-Carlsbad-San Marcos, CA | 8.4 | 27 | 42 | Cincinnati-Middletown, OH-KY-IN | 6.2 |
| 73 | 43 | Little Rock-North Little Rock-Conway, AR | 8.3 | 43 | 42 | Oklahoma City, OK | 6.2 |
| 58 | 44 | Omaha-Council Bluffs, NE-IA | 8.2 | 35 | 44 | Indianapolis-Carmel, IN | 6.1 |
| 32 | 45 | Columbus, OH | 8.0 | 32 | 44 | Columbus, OH | 6.1 |
| 6 | 46 | Philadelphia-Camden-Wilmington, PA-NJ-DE-MD | 7.6 | 45 | 44 | Hartford-West Hartford-East Hartford, CT | 6.1 |
| 44 | 47 | Richmond, VA | 7.5 | 13 | 44 | Phoenix-Mesa-Glendale, AZ | 6.1 |
| 41 | 48 | Memphis, TN-MS-AR | 7.4 | 72 | 48 | North Port-Bradenton-Sarasota, FL | 5.9 |
| 66 | 49 | Baton Rouge, LA | 7.3 | 70 | 49 | Columbia, SC | 5.8 |
| 10 | 50 | Boston-Cambridge-Quincy, MA-NH | 7.1 | 34 | 50 | Charlotte-Gastonia-Rock Hill, NC-SC | 5.7 |
| 11 | 51 | San Francisco-Oakland-Fremont, CA | 7.0 | 50 | 50 | Buffalo-Niagara Falls, NY | 5.7 |
| 64 | 52 | El Paso, TX | 6.9 | 29 | 52 | Cleveland-Elyria-Mentor, OH | 5.6 |
| 13 | 53 | Phoenix-Mesa-Glendale, AZ | 6.8 | 51 | 52 | Rochester, NY | 5.6 |
| 46 | 54 | New Orleans-Metairie-Kenner, LA | 6.7 | 53 | 54 | Honolulu, HI | 5.5 |
| 61 | 54 | Bakersfield-Delano, CA | 6.7 | 49 | 54 | Birmingham-Hoover, AL | 5.5 |
| 43 | 56 | Oklahoma City, OK | 6.6 | 68 | 54 | Worcester, MA | 5.5 |
| 33 | 57 | Austin-Round Rock-San Marcos, TX | 6.5 | 39 | 57 | Milwaukee-Waukesha-West Allis, WI | 5.4 |
| 9 | 57 | Atlanta-Sandy Springs-Marietta, GA | 6.5 | 37 | 57 | Nashville-Davidson—Murfreesboro—Franklin, TN | 5.4 |
| 72 | 59 | North Port-Bradenton-Sarasota, FL | 6.4 | 24 | 57 | San Antonio-New Braunfels, TX | 5.4 |
| 57 | 60 | Albuquerque, NM | 6.1 | 54 | 57 | Tulsa, OK | 5.4 |
| 24 | 60 | San Antonio-New Braunfels, TX | 6.1 | 55 | 61 | Fresno, CA | 5.3 |
| 59 | 62 | Albany-Schenectady-Troy, NY | 5.8 | 42 | 62 | Louisville-Jefferson County, KY-IN | 5.2 |
| 20 | 63 | Baltimore-Towson, MD | 5.7 | 52 | 63 | Tucson, AZ | 5.1 |
| 47 | 63 | Raleigh-Cary, NC | 5.7 | 30 | 64 | Las Vegas-Paradise, NV | 5.0 |
| 26 | 63 | Sacramento—Arden-Arcade—Roseville, CA | 5.7 | 60 | 65 | New Haven-Milford, CT | 4.9 |
| 18 | 66 | Tampa-St. Petersburg-Clearwater, FL | 5.6 | 73 | 66 | Little Rock-North Little Rock-Conway, AR | 4.8 |
| 21 | 67 | Denver-Aurora-Broomfield, CO | 5.5 | 38 | 66 | Providence-New Bedford-Fall River, RI-MA | 4.8 |
| 40 | 68 | Jacksonville, FL | 5.0 | 64 | 68 | El Paso, TX | 4.7 |
| 1 | 69 | New York-Northern New Jersey-Long Island, NY-NJ-PA | 4.9 | 69 | 69 | Grand Rapids-Wyoming, MI | 4.5 |
| 25 | 70 | Orlando-Kissimmee-Sanford, FL | 4.3 | 65 | 70 | Allentown-Bethlehem-Easton, PA-NJ | 4.2 |
| 8 | 71 | Miami-Fort Lauderdale-Pompano Beach, FL | 3.7 | 71 | 71 | Greensboro-High Point, NC | 3.7 |
| 67 | 72 | McAllen-Edinburg-Mission, TX | 3.2 | 41 | 72 | Memphis, TN-MS-AR | 3.5 |
| 53 | 73 | Honolulu, HI | 3.0 | 12 | 73 | Riverside-San Bernardino-Ontario, CA | 3.4 |
| 30 | 74 | Las Vegas-Paradise, NV | 2.7 | 67 | 74 | McAllen-Edinburg-Mission, TX | 3.0 |
| 7 | 75 | Washington-Arlington-Alexandria, DC-VA-MD-WV | 2.3 | 75 | 75 | Stockton, CA | 2.6 |

# 75 Largest Metropolitan Areas by 2012 Population
## Selected Rankings

| Per capita local government taxes, 2007 | | | | Violent crime rate, 2011 (violent crimes known to police) | | | |
|---|---|---|---|---|---|---|---|
| Popu-lation rank | Local taxes rank | Metropolitan area | Local per capita taxes (dollars) [col 183] | Popu-lation rank | Crime rate rank | Metropolitan area | Crime rate (per 100,000 population) [col 46] |
| 1 | 1 | New York-Northern New Jersey-Long Island, NY-NJ-PA | 3 848 | 41 | 1 | Memphis, TN-MS-AR | 1 001 |
| 7 | 2 | Washington-Arlington-Alexandria, DC-VA-MD-WV | 3 239 | 75 | 2 | Stockton, CA | 821 |
| 56 | 3 | Bridgeport-Stamford-Norwalk, CT | 3 019 | 73 | 3 | Little Rock-North Little Rock-Conway, AR | 744 |
| 11 | 4 | San Francisco-Oakland-Fremont, CA | 2 530 | 70 | 4 | Columbia, SC | 678 |
| 31 | 5 | San Jose-Sunnyvale-Santa Clara, CA | 2 453 | 35 | 5 | Indianapolis-Carmel, IN | 654 |
| 59 | 6 | Albany-Schenectady-Troy, NY | 2 386 | 37 | 6 | Nashville-Davidson—Murfreesboro—Franklin, TN | 652 |
| 8 | 7 | Miami-Fort Lauderdale-Pompano Beach, FL | 2 343 | 57 | 7 | Albuquerque, NM | 649 |
| 29 | 8 | Cleveland-Elyria-Mentor, OH | 2 304 | 30 | 8 | Las Vegas-Paradise, NV | 624 |
| 3 | 9 | Chicago-Joliet-Naperville, IL-IN-WI | 2 250 | 25 | 9 | Orlando-Kissimmee-Sanford, FL | 596 |
| 45 | 10 | Hartford-West Hartford-East Hartford, CT | 2 216 | 8 | 10 | Miami-Fort Lauderdale-Pompano Beach, FL | 595 |
| 51 | 11 | Rochester, NY | 2 189 | 66 | 11 | Baton Rouge, LA | 587 |
| 33 | 12 | Austin-Round Rock-San Marcos, TX | 2 139 | 14 | 12 | Detroit-Warren-Livonia, MI | 572 |
| 32 | 13 | Columbus, OH | 2 128 | 54 | 13 | Tulsa, OK | 557 |
| 6 | 14 | Philadelphia-Camden-Wilmington, PA-NJ-DE-MD | 2 126 | 55 | 14 | Fresno, CA | 553 |
| 72 | 15 | North Port-Bradenton-Sarasota, FL | 2 125 | 5 | 15 | Houston-Sugar Land-Baytown, TX | 551 |
| 60 | 16 | New Haven-Milford, CT | 2 086 | 6 | 16 | Philadelphia-Camden-Wilmington, PA-NJ-DE-MD | 548 |
| 21 | 17 | Denver-Aurora-Broomfield, CO | 2 077 | 49 | 17 | Birmingham-Hoover, AL | 540 |
| 4 | 18 | Dallas-Fort Worth-Arlington, TX | 2 072 | 43 | 18 | Oklahoma City, OK | 530 |
| 46 | 19 | New Orleans-Metairie-Kenner, LA | 2 019 | 40 | 19 | Jacksonville, FL | 524 |
| 50 | 20 | Buffalo-Niagara Falls, NY | 1 983 | 61 | 20 | Bakersfield-Delano, CA | 523 |
| 5 | 21 | Houston-Sugar Land-Baytown, TX | 1 954 | 11 | 21 | San Francisco-Oakland-Fremont, CA | 508 |
| 10 | 22 | Boston-Cambridge-Quincy, MA-NH | 1 947 | 39 | 22 | Milwaukee-Waukesha-West Allis, WI | 501 |
| 20 | 23 | Baltimore-Towson, MD | 1 938 | 72 | 23 | North Port-Bradenton-Sarasota, FL | 494 |
| 28 | 24 | Kansas City, MO-KS | 1 918 | 46 | 24 | New Orleans-Metairie-Kenner, LA | 491 |
| 15 | 25 | Seattle-Tacoma-Bellevue, WA | 1 856 | 28 | 25 | Kansas City, MO-KS | 477 |
| 65 | 26 | Allentown-Bethlehem-Easton, PA-NJ | 1 844 | 20 | 26 | Baltimore-Towson, MD | 473 |
| 17 | 27 | San Diego-Carlsbad-San Marcos, CA | 1 831 | 74 | 27 | Knoxville, TN | 463 |
| 62 | 28 | Dayton, OH | 1 774 | 50 | 28 | Buffalo-Niagara Falls, NY | 439 |
| 9 | 29 | Atlanta-Sandy Springs-Marietta, GA | 1 757 | 68 | 28 | Worcester, MA | 439 |
| 2 | 30 | Los Angeles-Long Beach-Santa Ana, CA | 1 755 | 18 | 30 | Tampa-St. Petersburg-Clearwater, FL | 435 |
| 36 | 31 | Virginia Beach-Norfolk-Newport News, VA-NC | 1 751 | 34 | 31 | Charlotte-Gastonia-Rock Hill, NC-SC | 432 |
| 25 | 32 | Orlando-Kissimmee-Sanford, FL | 1 744 | 52 | 31 | Tucson, AZ | 432 |
| 39 | 33 | Milwaukee-Waukesha-West Allis, WI | 1 735 | 42 | 33 | Louisville-Jefferson County, KY-IN | 426 |
| 27 | 34 | Cincinnati-Middletown, OH-KY-IN | 1 722 | 3 | 34 | Chicago-Joliet-Naperville, IL-IN-WI | 420 |
| 30 | 35 | Las Vegas-Paradise, NV | 1 720 | 26 | 34 | Sacramento—Arden-Arcade—Roseville, CA | 420 |
| 26 | 36 | Sacramento—Arden-Arcade—Roseville, CA | 1 718 | 1 | 36 | New York-Northern New Jersey-Long Island, NY-NJ-PA | 406 |
| 58 | 37 | Omaha-Council Bluffs, NE-IA | 1 711 | 2 | 37 | Los Angeles-Long Beach-Santa Ana, CA | 405 |
| 38 | 38 | Providence-New Bedford-Fall River, RI-MA | 1 695 | 29 | 37 | Cleveland-Elyria-Mentor, OH | 405 |
| 18 | 39 | Tampa-St. Petersburg-Clearwater, FL | 1 686 | 9 | 39 | Atlanta-Sandy Springs-Marietta, GA | 404 |
| 22 | 40 | Pittsburgh, PA | 1 645 | 24 | 40 | San Antonio-New Braunfels, TX | 398 |
| 63 | 41 | Oxnard-Thousand Oaks-Ventura, CA | 1 642 | 64 | 41 | El Paso, TX | 396 |
| 41 | 42 | Memphis, TN-MS-AR | 1 567 | 58 | 42 | Omaha-Council Bluffs, NE-IA | 385 |
| 19 | 43 | St. Louis, MO-IL | 1 565 | 60 | 43 | New Haven-Milford, CT | 384 |
| 66 | 43 | Baton Rouge, LA | 1 565 | 10 | 44 | Boston-Cambridge-Quincy, MA-NH | 377 |
| 14 | 45 | Detroit-Warren-Livonia, MI | 1 533 | 13 | 45 | Phoenix-Mesa-Glendale, AZ | 373 |
| 23 | 46 | Portland-Vancouver-Hillsboro, OR-WA | 1 529 | 32 | 46 | Columbus, OH | 371 |
| 44 | 47 | Richmond, VA | 1 523 | 4 | 47 | Dallas-Fort Worth-Arlington, TX | 359 |
| 49 | 48 | Birmingham-Hoover, AL | 1 502 | 12 | 48 | Riverside-San Bernardino-Ontario, CA | 355 |
| 13 | 49 | Phoenix-Mesa-Glendale, AZ | 1 490 | 71 | 48 | Greensboro-High Point, NC | 355 |
| 12 | 50 | Riverside-San Bernardino-Ontario, CA | 1 486 | 21 | 50 | Denver-Aurora-Broomfield, CO | 354 |
| 75 | 51 | Stockton, CA | 1 470 | 38 | 50 | Providence-New Bedford-Fall River, RI-MA | 354 |
| 37 | 52 | Nashville-Davidson—Murfreesboro—Franklin, TN | 1 455 | 17 | 52 | San Diego-Carlsbad-San Marcos, CA | 352 |
| 24 | 53 | San Antonio-New Braunfels, TX | 1 447 | 69 | 53 | Grand Rapids-Wyoming, MI | 344 |
| 34 | 54 | Charlotte-Gastonia-Rock Hill, NC-SC | 1 426 | 7 | 54 | Washington-Arlington-Alexandria, DC-VA-MD-WV | 335 |
| 40 | 55 | Jacksonville, FL | 1 415 | 15 | 55 | Seattle-Tacoma-Bellevue, WA | 324 |
| 35 | 56 | Indianapolis-Carmel, IN | 1 380 | 19 | 56 | St. Louis, MO-IL | 323 |
| 68 | 57 | Worcester, MA | 1 374 | 36 | 56 | Virginia Beach-Norfolk-Newport News, VA-NC | 323 |
| 48 | 58 | Salt Lake City, UT | 1 345 | 48 | 58 | Salt Lake City, UT | 309 |
| 52 | 59 | Tucson, AZ | 1 333 | 22 | 59 | Pittsburgh, PA | 301 |
| 16 | 60 | Minneapolis-St. Paul-Bloomington, MN | 1 299 | 67 | 60 | McAllen-Edinburg-Mission, TX | 295 |
| 61 | 61 | Bakersfield-Delano, CA | 1 292 | 45 | 61 | Hartford-West Hartford-East Hartford, CT | 294 |
| 74 | 62 | Knoxville, TN | 1 266 | 56 | 61 | Bridgeport-Stamford-Norwalk, CT | 294 |
| 70 | 63 | Columbia, SC | 1 243 | 27 | 63 | Cincinnati-Middletown, OH-KY-IN | 293 |
| 64 | 64 | El Paso, TX | 1 219 | 62 | 63 | Dayton, OH | 293 |
| 54 | 65 | Tulsa, OK | 1 193 | 51 | 65 | Rochester, NY | 290 |
| 47 | 66 | Raleigh-Cary, NC | 1 191 | 33 | 66 | Austin-Round Rock-San Marcos, TX | 287 |
| 55 | 67 | Fresno, CA | 1 189 | 59 | 67 | Albany-Schenectady-Troy, NY | 284 |
| 69 | 68 | Grand Rapids-Wyoming, MI | 1 170 | 16 | 68 | Minneapolis-St. Paul-Bloomington, MN | 270 |
| 43 | 69 | Oklahoma City, OK | 1 158 | 23 | 69 | Portland-Vancouver-Hillsboro, OR-WA | 259 |
| 42 | 70 | Louisville-Jefferson County, KY-IN | 1 130 | 31 | 70 | San Jose-Sunnyvale-Santa Clara, CA | 256 |
| 71 | 71 | Greensboro-High Point, NC | 1 107 | 53 | 71 | Honolulu, HI | 246 |
| 57 | 72 | Albuquerque, NM | 1 072 | 47 | 72 | Raleigh-Cary, NC | 243 |
| 53 | 73 | Honolulu, HI | 1 000 | 44 | 73 | Richmond, VA | 232 |
| 67 | 74 | McAllen-Edinburg-Mission, TX | 968 | 65 | 74 | Allentown-Bethlehem-Easton, PA-NJ | 217 |
| 73 | 75 | Little Rock-North Little Rock-Conway, AR | 762 | 63 | 75 | Oxnard-Thousand Oaks-Ventura, CA | 205 |

# All Metropolitan Areas
## Selected Rankings

| | Defense contracts, 2009–2010 | | | | Non-defense contracts, 2009–2010 | | |
|---|---|---|---|---|---|---|---|
| Popu-lation rank | Defense contracts rank | Metropolitan area | Defense contracts (millions of dollars) [col 172] | Popu-lation rank | Non-defense contracts rank | Metropolitan area | Non-defense contracts (millions of dollars) [col 173] |
| 7 | 1 | Washington-Arlington-Alexandria, DC-VA-MD-WV | 37 778.4 | 7 | 1 | Washington-Arlington-Alexandria, DC-VA-MD-WV | 43 559 |
| 4 | 2 | Dallas-Fort Worth-Arlington, TX | 15 187.7 | 2 | 2 | Los Angeles-Long Beach-Santa Ana, CA | 6 236 |
| 2 | 3 | Los Angeles-Long Beach-Santa Ana, CA | 12 663.2 | 1 | 3 | New York-Northern New Jersey-Long Island, NY-NJ-PA | 5 054 |
| 17 | 4 | San Diego-Carlsbad-San Marcos, CA | 11 593.0 | 11 | 4 | San Francisco-Oakland-Fremont, CA | 4 836 |
| 10 | 5 | Boston-Cambridge-Quincy, MA-NH | 10 905.4 | 6 | 5 | Philadelphia-Camden-Wilmington, PA-NJ-DE-MD | 4 628 |
| 19 | 6 | St. Louis, MO-IL | 9 200.0 | 5 | 6 | Houston-Sugar Land-Baytown, TX | 4 615 |
| 36 | 7 | Virginia Beach-Norfolk-Newport News, VA-NC | 9 027.1 | 74 | 7 | Knoxville, TN | 4 044 |
| 1 | 8 | New York-Northern New Jersey-Long Island, NY-NJ-PA | 8 653.9 | 3 | 8 | Chicago-Joliet-Naperville, IL-IN-WI | 3 872 |
| 237 | 9 | Oshkosh-Neenah, WI | 7 100.1 | 21 | 9 | Denver-Aurora-Broomfield, CO | 3 474 |
| 6 | 10 | Philadelphia-Camden-Wilmington, PA-NJ-DE-MD | 6 849.6 | 174 | 10 | Kennewick-Pasco-Richland, WA | 3 140 |
| 20 | 11 | Baltimore-Towson, MD | 5 598.5 | 9 | 11 | Atlanta-Sandy Springs-Marietta, GA | 3 094 |
| 52 | 12 | Tucson, AZ | 5 268.8 | 57 | 12 | Albuquerque, NM | 2 912 |
| 119 | 13 | Huntsville, AL | 5 254.2 | 10 | 13 | Boston-Cambridge-Quincy, MA-NH | 2 896 |
| 3 | 14 | Chicago-Joliet-Naperville, IL-IN-WI | 5 106.0 | 20 | 14 | Baltimore-Towson, MD | 2 795 |
| 9 | 15 | Atlanta-Sandy Springs-Marietta, GA | 4 883.8 | 90 | 15 | Augusta-Richmond County, GA-SC | 2 426 |
| 31 | 16 | San Jose-Sunnyvale-Santa Clara, CA | 4 727.3 | 28 | 16 | Kansas City, MO-KS | 2 234 |
| 26 | 17 | Sacramento—Arden-Arcade—Roseville, CA | 4 694.0 | 4 | 17 | Dallas-Fort Worth-Arlington, TX | 1 986 |
| 46 | 18 | New Orleans-Metairie-Kenner, LA | 4 493.1 | 22 | 18 | Pittsburgh, PA | 1 589 |
| 13 | 19 | Phoenix-Mesa-Glendale, AZ | 4 444.2 | 14 | 19 | Detroit-Warren-Livonia, MI | 1 376 |
| 56 | 20 | Bridgeport-Stamford-Norwalk, CT | 4 045.9 | 295 | 20 | Idaho Falls, ID | 1 362 |
| 24 | 21 | San Antonio-New Braunfels, TX | 4 014.7 | 17 | 21 | San Diego-Carlsbad-San Marcos, CA | 1 289 |
| 5 | 22 | Houston-Sugar Land-Baytown, TX | 3 886.9 | 97 | 22 | Palm Bay-Melbourne-Titusville, FL | 1 237 |
| 15 | 23 | Seattle-Tacoma-Bellevue, WA | 3 712.7 | 37 | 23 | Nashville-Davidson—Murfreesboro—Franklin, TN | 1 165 |
| 171 | 24 | Norwich-New London, CT | 3 520.5 | 36 | 24 | Virginia Beach-Norfolk-Newport News, VA-NC | 1 161 |
| 25 | 25 | Orlando-Kissimmee-Sanford, FL | 3 485.6 | 119 | 25 | Huntsville, AL | 1 130 |
| 45 | 26 | Hartford-West Hartford-East Hartford, CT | 3 420.8 | 16 | 26 | Minneapolis-St. Paul-Bloomington, MN | 1 118 |
| 42 | 27 | Louisville-Jefferson County, KY-IN | 3 130.3 | 15 | 27 | Seattle-Tacoma-Bellevue, WA | 1 081 |
| 80 | 28 | Colorado Springs, CO | 2 889.0 | 31 | 28 | San Jose-Sunnyvale-Santa Clara, CA | 1 076 |
| 14 | 29 | Detroit-Warren-Livonia, MI | 2 718.6 | 8 | 29 | Miami-Fort Lauderdale-Pompano Beach, FL | 1 068 |
| 12 | 30 | Riverside-San Bernardino-Ontario, CA | 2 713.9 | 18 | 30 | Tampa-St. Petersburg-Clearwater, FL | 1 042 |
| 77 | 31 | Charleston-North Charleston-Summerville, SC | 2 492.1 | 19 | 31 | St. Louis, MO-IL | 1 004 |
| 183 | 32 | Amarillo, TX | 2 428.8 | 33 | 32 | Austin-Round Rock-San Marcos, TX | 997 |
| 21 | 33 | Denver-Aurora-Broomfield, CO | 2 410.9 | 13 | 33 | Phoenix-Mesa-Glendale, AZ | 934 |
| 38 | 34 | Providence-New Bedford-Fall River, RI-MA | 2 362.0 | 30 | 34 | Las Vegas-Paradise, NV | 893 |
| 53 | 35 | Honolulu, HI | 2 218.2 | 100 | 35 | Durham-Chapel Hill, NC | 891 |
| 27 | 36 | Cincinnati-Middletown, OH-KY-IN | 2 211.5 | 29 | 36 | Cleveland-Elyria-Mentor, OH | 851 |
| 18 | 37 | Tampa-St. Petersburg-Clearwater, FL | 2 146.8 | 46 | 37 | New Orleans-Metairie-Kenner, LA | 802 |
| 97 | 38 | Palm Bay-Melbourne-Titusville, FL | 2 092.1 | 77 | 38 | Charleston-North Charleston-Summerville, SC | 725 |
| 22 | 39 | Pittsburgh, PA | 2 023.4 | 23 | 39 | Portland-Vancouver-Hillsboro, OR-WA | 683 |
| 51 | 40 | Rochester, NY | 1 939.3 | 183 | 40 | Amarillo, TX | 639 |
| 41 | 41 | Memphis, TN-MS-AR | 1 645.7 | 25 | 41 | Orlando-Kissimmee-Sanford, FL | 631 |
| 11 | 42 | San Francisco-Oakland-Fremont, CA | 1 586.8 | 281 | 42 | Coeur d'Alene, ID | 618 |
| 62 | 43 | Dayton, OH | 1 546.3 | 41 | 43 | Memphis, TN-MS-AR | 610 |
| 222 | 44 | Crestview-Fort Walton Beach-Destin, FL | 1 397.5 | 24 | 44 | San Antonio-New Braunfels, TX | 609 |
| 28 | 45 | Kansas City, MO-KS | 1 385.0 | 35 | 45 | Indianapolis-Carmel, IN | 553 |
| 35 | 46 | Indianapolis-Carmel, IN | 1 374.2 | 98 | 46 | Chattanooga, TN-GA | 534 |
| 16 | 47 | Minneapolis-St. Paul-Bloomington, MN | 1 360.4 | 157 | 47 | Boulder, CO | 533 |
| 113 | 48 | York-Hanover, PA | 1 323.7 | 182 | 48 | Gulfport-Biloxi, MS | 527 |
| 123 | 49 | Killeen-Temple-Fort Hood, TX | 1 306.7 | 43 | 49 | Oklahoma City, OK | 495 |
| 32 | 50 | Columbus, OH | 1 251.1 | 26 | 50 | Sacramento—Arden-Arcade—Roseville, CA | 489 |
| 139 | 51 | Fayetteville, NC | 1 230.5 | 27 | 51 | Cincinnati-Middletown, OH-KY-IN | 486 |
| 81 | 52 | Syracuse, NY | 1 191.0 | 32 | 52 | Columbus, OH | 468 |
| 282 | 53 | Johnstown, PA | 1 180.9 | 12 | 53 | Riverside-San Bernardino-Ontario, CA | 449 |
| 179 | 54 | Cedar Rapids, IA | 1 128.7 | 39 | 54 | Milwaukee-Waukesha-West Allis, WI | 445 |
| 150 | 55 | South Bend-Mishawaka, IN-MI | 1 124.3 | 52 | 55 | Tucson, AZ | 389 |
| 44 | 56 | Richmond, VA | 1 096.7 | 38 | 56 | Providence-New Bedford-Fall River, RI-MA | 384 |
| 102 | 57 | Portland-South Portland-Biddeford, ME | 1 094.4 | 70 | 57 | Columbia, SC | 378 |
| 152 | 58 | Columbus, GA-AL | 1 079.5 | 40 | 58 | Jacksonville, FL | 376 |
| 86 | 59 | Wichita, KS | 1 077.6 | 34 | 59 | Charlotte-Gastonia-Rock Hill, NC-SC | 375 |
| 8 | 60 | Miami-Fort Lauderdale-Pompano Beach, FL | 1 045.7 | 49 | 60 | Birmingham-Hoover, AL | 373 |
| 94 | 61 | Harrisburg-Carlisle, PA | 993.0 | 205 | 61 | Houma-Bayou Cane-Thibodaux, LA | 369 |
| 43 | 62 | Oklahoma City, OK | 987.1 | 64 | 62 | El Paso, TX | 360 |
| 40 | 63 | Jacksonville, FL | 970.7 | 294 | 63 | Morgantown, WV | 352 |
| 132 | 64 | Anchorage, AK | 964.8 | 53 | 64 | Honolulu, HI | 350 |
| 64 | 65 | El Paso, TX | 958.0 | 56 | 65 | Bridgeport-Stamford-Norwalk, CT | 347 |
| 48 | 66 | Salt Lake City, UT | 944.9 | 62 | 66 | Dayton, OH | 329 |
| 33 | 67 | Austin-Round Rock-San Marcos, TX | 924.6 | 44 | 67 | Richmond, VA | 328 |
| 226 | 68 | Jacksonville, NC | 920.0 | 132 | 68 | Anchorage, AK | 318 |
| 92 | 69 | Ogden-Clearfield, UT | 916.1 | 184 | 69 | Lynchburg, VA | 314 |
| 121 | 70 | Fort Wayne, IN | 905.2 | 48 | 70 | Salt Lake City, UT | 308 |
| 186 | 71 | Binghamton, NY | 902.7 | 105 | 71 | Lexington-Fayette, KY | 303 |
| 57 | 72 | Albuquerque, NM | 770.5 | 172 | 72 | Hagerstown-Martinsburg, MD-WV | 295 |
| 58 | 73 | Omaha-Council Bluffs, NE-IA | 735.9 | 58 | 73 | Omaha-Council Bluffs, NE-IA | 279 |
| 142 | 73 | Savannah, GA | 735.9 | 42 | 74 | Louisville-Jefferson County, KY-IN | 262 |
| 118 | 75 | Santa Barbara-Santa Maria-Goleta, CA | 701.1 | 59 | 75 | Albany-Schenectady-Troy, NY | 258 |

# 75 Metropolitan Areas with Highest Agricultural Sales
## Selected Rankings

| Value of agricultural products sold, 2007 | | | Number of farms, 2007 | | | |
|---|---|---|---|---|---|---|
| Value of sales rank | Metropolitan area | Value of sales (millions of dollars) [col 125] | Value of sales rank | Number of farms rank | Metropolitan area | Number of farms [col 113] |
| 1 | Fresno, CA | 3 730.5 | 55 | 1 | Dallas-Fort Worth-Arlington, TX | 25 402 |
| 2 | Visalia-Porterville, CA | 3 335.0 | 28 | 2 | Kansas City, MO-KS | 15 529 |
| 3 | Bakersfield-Delano, CA | 3 204.1 | 20 | 3 | St. Louis, MO-IL | 12 686 |
| 4 | Merced, CA | 2 330.4 | 73 | 4 | Oklahoma City, OK | 10 772 |
| 5 | Salinas, CA | 2 178.5 | 8 | 5 | Chicago-Naperville-Joliet, IL-IN-WI | 7 714 |
| 6 | Modesto, CA | 1 820.6 | 18 | 6 | Fayetteville-Springdale-Rogers, AR-MO | 7 401 |
| 7 | Riverside-San Bernardino-Ontario, CA | 1 755.7 | 32 | 7 | Columbus, OH | 7 050 |
| 8 | Chicago-Joliet-Naperville, IL-IN-WI | 1 715.6 | 21 | 8 | Philadelphia-Camden-Wilmington, PA-NJ-DE-MD | 6 987 |
| 9 | Miami-Fort Lauderdale-Pompano Beach, FL | 1 643.1 | 30 | 9 | Madison, WI | 6 729 |
| 10 | Phoenix-Mesa-Glendale, AZ | 1 613.3 | 23 | 10 | San Diego-Carlsbad-San Marcos, CA | 6 687 |
| 11 | Stockton, CA | 1 564.4 | 58 | 11 | Fort Smith, AR-OK | 6 111 |
| 12 | Greeley, CO | 1 539.1 | 47 | 12 | New York-Northern New Jersey-Long Island, NY-NJ-PA | 6 110 |
| 13 | Hanford-Corcoran, CA | 1 358.4 | 1 | 13 | Fresno, CA | 6 081 |
| 14 | Oxnard-Thousand Oaks-Ventura, CA | 1 316.3 | 19 | 14 | Omaha-Council Bluffs, NE-IA | 5 783 |
| 15 | El Centro, CA | 1 290.3 | 34 | 15 | Indianapolis-Carmel, IN | 5 756 |
| 16 | Lexington-Fayette, KY | 1 248.5 | 22 | 16 | Lancaster, PA | 5 462 |
| 17 | Yakima, WA | 1 203.8 | 2 | 17 | Visalia-Porterville, CA | 5 240 |
| 18 | Fayetteville-Springdale-Rogers, AR-MO | 1 123.0 | 29 | 18 | Boise City-Nampa, ID | 5 238 |
| 19 | Omaha-Council Bluffs, NE-IA | 1 102.6 | 31 | 19 | Sacramento—Arden-Arcade—Roseville, CA | 5 132 |
| 20 | St. Louis, MO-IL | 1 084.7 | 16 | 20 | Lexington-Fayette, KY | 4 988 |
| 21 | Philadelphia-Camden-Wilmington, PA-NJ-DE-MD | 1 084.2 | 42 | 21 | Tampa-St. Petersburg-Clearwater, FL | 4 955 |
| 22 | Lancaster, PA | 1 072.2 | 7 | 22 | Riverside-San Bernardino-Ontario, CA | 4 868 |
| 23 | San Diego-Carlsbad-San Marcos, CA | 1 054.2 | 35 | 23 | Des Moines-West Des Moines, IA | 4 782 |
| 24 | Kennewick-Pasco-Richland, WA | 992.9 | 61 | 24 | Wichita, KS | 4 774 |
| 25 | Madera-Chowchilla, CA | 990.1 | 48 | 25 | Grand Rapids-Wyoming, MI | 4 491 |
| 26 | Yuma, AZ | 960.0 | 9 | 26 | Miami-Fort Lauderdale-Pompano Beach, FL | 4 308 |
| 27 | Santa Barbara-Santa Maria-Goleta, CA | 951.3 | 43 | 27 | St. Cloud, MN | 4 287 |
| 28 | Kansas City, MO-KS | 818.6 | 6 | 28 | Modesto, CA | 4 114 |
| 29 | Boise City-Nampa, ID | 814.8 | 67 | 29 | Jackson, MS | 3 969 |
| 30 | Madison, WI | 795.2 | 33 | 30 | Salem, OR | 3 922 |
| 30 | Sacramento—Arden-Arcade—Roseville, CA | 795.2 | 12 | 31 | Greeley, CO | 3 921 |
| 32 | Columbus, OH | 780.1 | 36 | 32 | Davenport-Moline-Rock Island, IA-IL | 3 819 |
| 33 | Salem, OR | 733.4 | 44 | 33 | Cedar Rapids, IA | 3 781 |
| 34 | Indianapolis-Carmel, IN | 697.1 | 40 | 34 | Rochester, NY | 3 728 |
| 35 | Des Moines-West Des Moines, IA | 690.8 | 37 | 35 | Peoria, IL | 3 679 |
| 36 | Davenport-Moline-Rock Island, IA-IL | 686.2 | 11 | 36 | Stockton, CA | 3 624 |
| 37 | Peoria, IL | 676.2 | 17 | 37 | Yakima, WA | 3 540 |
| 38 | Los Angeles-Long Beach-Santa Ana, CA | 662.3 | 41 | 38 | Santa Rosa-Petaluma, CA | 3 429 |
| 39 | Sioux Falls, SD | 651.0 | 51 | 39 | Orlando-Kissimmee, FL | 3 415 |
| 40 | Rochester, NY | 649.8 | 39 | 40 | Sioux Falls, SD | 3 316 |
| 41 | Santa Rosa-Petaluma, CA | 647.6 | 52 | 41 | Green Bay, WI | 3 190 |
| 42 | Tampa-St. Petersburg-Clearwater, FL | 637.6 | 62 | 42 | Rochester, MN | 3 083 |
| 43 | St. Cloud, MN | 633.3 | 59 | 43 | Columbia, SC | 2 945 |
| 44 | Cedar Rapids, IA | 628.8 | 69 | 44 | Evansville, IN-KY | 2 841 |
| 45 | Champaign-Urbana, IL | 603.9 | 54 | 45 | San Luis Obispo-Paso Robles, CA | 2 784 |
| 46 | Grand Forks, ND-MN | 597.0 | 50 | 46 | Waterloo-Cedar Falls, IA | 2 737 |
| 47 | New York-Northern New Jersey-Long Island, NY-NJ-PA | 594.2 | 4 | 47 | Merced, CA | 2 607 |
| 48 | Grand Rapids-Wyoming, MI | 591.5 | 46 | 48 | Grand Forks, ND-MN | 2 582 |
| 49 | Sioux City, IA-NE-SD | 579.5 | 10 | 49 | Phoenix-Mesa-Scottsdale, AZ | 2 578 |
| 50 | Waterloo-Cedar Falls, IA | 573.3 | 64 | 50 | Iowa City, IA | 2 550 |
| 51 | Orlando-Kissimmee-Sanford, FL | 570.1 | 24 | 51 | Kennewick-Pasco-Richland, WA | 2 521 |
| 52 | Green Bay, WI | 564.5 | 49 | 52 | Sioux City, IA-NE-SD | 2 516 |
| 53 | Mankato, North Mankato, MN | 564.3 | 14 | 53 | Oxnard-Thousand Oaks-Ventura, CA | 2 437 |
| 54 | San Luis Obispo-Paso Robles, CA | 560.6 | 45 | 54 | Champaign-Urbana, IL | 2 393 |
| 55 | Dallas-Fort Worth-Arlington, TX | 554.8 | 3 | 55 | Bakersfield, CA | 2 117 |
| 56 | Amarillo, TX | 554.4 | 74 | 56 | Appleton, WI | 2 094 |
| 57 | Harrisonburg, VA | 534.1 | 70 | 57 | Yuba City, CA | 2 091 |
| 58 | Fort Smith, AR-OK | 510.4 | 53 | 58 | Mankato, North Mankato, MN | 2 074 |
| 59 | Columbia, SC | 505.4 | 38 | 59 | Los Angeles-Long Beach-Santa Ana, CA | 2 059 |
| 60 | Goldsboro, NC | 501.2 | 57 | 60 | Harrisonburg, VA | 1 970 |
| 61 | Wichita, KS | 498.6 | 56 | 61 | Amarillo, TX | 1 879 |
| 62 | Rochester, MN | 472.1 | 63 | 62 | Fargo, ND-MN | 1 834 |
| 63 | Fargo, ND-MN | 469.7 | 71 | 63 | Athens-Clarke County, GA | 1 784 |
| 64 | Iowa City, IA | 458.8 | 72 | 64 | Idaho Falls, ID | 1 752 |
| 64 | San Jose-Sunnyvale-Santa Clara, CA | 458.8 | 75 | 65 | Lafayette, IN | 1 737 |
| 66 | Pine Bluff, AR | 455.3 | 25 | 66 | Madera-Chowchilla, CA | 1 708 |
| 67 | Jackson, MS | 450.1 | 65 | 67 | San Jose-Sunnyvale-Santa Clara, CA | 1 693 |
| 68 | Santa Cruz-Watsonville, CA | 447.4 | 27 | 68 | Santa Barbara-Santa Maria-Goleta, CA | 1 597 |
| 69 | Evansville, IN-KY | 437.2 | 5 | 69 | Salinas, CA | 1 199 |
| 70 | Yuba City, CA | 430.5 | 13 | 70 | Hanford-Corcoran, CA | 1 129 |
| 71 | Athens-Clarke County, GA | 426.9 | 66 | 71 | Pine Bluff, AR | 1 114 |
| 72 | Idaho Falls, ID | 422.4 | 60 | 72 | Goldsboro, NC | 723 |
| 73 | Oklahoma City, OK | 413.5 | 68 | 73 | Santa Cruz-Watsonville, CA | 682 |
| 74 | Appleton, WI | 403.7 | 15 | 74 | El Centro, CA | 452 |
| 75 | Lafayette, IN | 402.6 | 26 | 74 | Yuma, AZ | 452 |

# 75 Metropolitan Areas with Highest Agricultural Sales
## Selected Rankings

| | Land in farms, 2007 | | | | | Average value of agricultural land and buildings per acre, 2007 | |
|---|---|---|---|---|---|---|---|
| Value of sales rank | Land in farms rank | Metropolitan area | Land in farms (1,000 acres) [col 117] | Value of sales rank | Value per Acre rank | Metropolitan area | Value per acre (1,000 acres) [col 123] |
| 28 | 1 | Kansas City, MO-KS | 3 607 | 14 | 1 | Oxnard-Thousand Oaks-Ventura, CA | 22 782 |
| 55 | 2 | Dallas-Fort Worth-Arlington, TX | 3 522 | 68 | 2 | Santa Cruz-Watsonville, CA | 22 423 |
| 20 | 3 | St. Louis, MO-IL | 3 076 | 23 | 3 | San Diego-Carlsbad-San Marcos, CA | 19 247 |
| 73 | 4 | Oklahoma City, OK | 2 665 | 41 | 4 | Santa Rosa-Petaluma, CA | 15 887 |
| 3 | 5 | Bakersfield, CA | 2 362 | 38 | 5 | Los Angeles-Long Beach-Santa Ana, CA | 13 165 |
| 61 | 6 | Wichita, KS | 2 346 | 21 | 6 | Philadelphia-Camden-Wilmington, PA-NJ-DE-MD | 10 868 |
| 8 | 7 | Chicago-Naperville-Joliet, IL-IN-WI | 2 291 | 11 | 7 | Stockton, CA | 10 168 |
| 56 | 8 | Amarillo, TX | 2 202 | 6 | 8 | Modesto, CA | 9 476 |
| 19 | 9 | Omaha-Council Bluffs, NE-IA | 2 159 | 22 | 9 | Lancaster, PA | 9 324 |
| 12 | 10 | Greeley, CO | 2 089 | 42 | 10 | Tampa-St. Petersburg-Clearwater, FL | 9 310 |
| 46 | 11 | Grand Forks, ND-MN | 1 925 | 26 | 11 | Yuma, AZ | 8 361 |
| 63 | 12 | Fargo, ND-MN | 1 653 | 7 | 12 | Riverside-San Bernardino-Ontario, CA | 8 310 |
| 17 | 13 | Yakima, WA | 1 649 | 2 | 13 | Visalia-Porterville, CA | 8 266 |
| 1 | 14 | Fresno, CA | 1 636 | 1 | 14 | Fresno, CA | 7 927 |
| 10 | 15 | Phoenix-Mesa-Scottsdale, AZ | 1 533 | 4 | 15 | Merced, CA | 7 210 |
| 32 | 16 | Columbus, OH | 1 522 | 27 | 16 | Santa Barbara-Santa Maria-Goleta, CA | 7 081 |
| 39 | 17 | Sioux Falls, SD | 1 489 | 9 | 17 | Miami-Fort Lauderdale-Pompano Beach, FL | 7 064 |
| 35 | 18 | Des Moines-West Des Moines, IA | 1 426 | 31 | 18 | Sacramento—Arden-Arcade—Roseville, CA | 6 933 |
| 54 | 19 | San Luis Obispo-Paso Robles, CA | 1 370 | 25 | 19 | Madera-Chowchilla, CA | 6 783 |
| 34 | 20 | Indianapolis-Carmel, IN | 1 354 | 33 | 20 | Salem, OR | 6 404 |
| 5 | 21 | Salinas, CA | 1 328 | 70 | 21 | Yuba City, CA | 6 365 |
| 29 | 22 | Boise City-Nampa, ID | 1 255 | 57 | 22 | Harrisonburg, VA | 6 150 |
| 37 | 23 | Peoria, IL | 1 251 | 13 | 23 | Hanford-Corcoran, CA | 5 465 |
| 24 | 24 | Kennewick-Pasco-Richland, WA | 1 242 | 15 | 24 | El Centro, CA | 5 290 |
| 36 | 25 | Davenport-Moline-Rock Island, IA-IL | 1 223 | 10 | 25 | Phoenix-Mesa-Scottsdale, AZ | 5 177 |
| 30 | 26 | Madison, WI | 1 217 | 16 | 26 | Lexington-Fayette, KY | 4 958 |
| 2 | 27 | Visalia-Porterville, CA | 1 169 | 5 | 27 | Salinas, CA | 4 645 |
| 49 | 28 | Sioux City, IA-NE-SD | 1 140 | 3 | 28 | Bakersfield, CA | 4 626 |
| 45 | 29 | Champaign-Urbana, IL | 1 088 | 71 | 29 | Athens-Clarke County, GA | 4 591 |
| 58 | 30 | Fort Smith, AR-OK | 1 075 | 54 | 30 | San Luis Obispo-Paso Robles, CA | 4 546 |
| 44 | 31 | Cedar Rapids, IA | 1 060 | 8 | 31 | Chicago-Naperville-Joliet, IL-IN-WI | 4 455 |
| 31 | 32 | Sacramento—Arden-Arcade—Roseville, CA | 1 048 | 51 | 32 | Orlando-Kissimmee, FL | 4 397 |
| 18 | 33 | Fayetteville-Springdale-Rogers, AR-MO | 1 041 | 45 | 33 | Champaign-Urbana, IL | 4 262 |
| 4 | 33 | Merced, CA | 1 041 | 60 | 34 | Goldsboro, NC | 4 160 |
| 69 | 35 | Evansville, IN-KY | 968 | 37 | 35 | Peoria, IL | 4 064 |
| 51 | 36 | Orlando-Kissimmee, FL | 939 | 34 | 36 | Indianapolis-Carmel, IN | 4 048 |
| 43 | 37 | St. Cloud, MN | 894 | 36 | 37 | Davenport-Moline-Rock Island, IA-IL | 3 957 |
| 65 | 38 | San Jose-Sunnyvale-Santa Clara, CA | 880 | 50 | 38 | Waterloo-Cedar Falls, IA | 3 926 |
| 67 | 39 | Jackson, MS | 872 | 30 | 39 | Madison, WI | 3 867 |
| 7 | 40 | Riverside-San Bernardino-Ontario, CA | 869 | 32 | 40 | Columbus, OH | 3 824 |
| 40 | 41 | Rochester, NY | 863 | 65 | 41 | San Jose-Sunnyvale-Santa Clara, CA | 3 786 |
| 50 | 42 | Waterloo-Cedar Falls, IA | 841 | 48 | 42 | Grand Rapids-Wyoming, MI | 3 781 |
| 16 | 43 | Lexington-Fayette, KY | 808 | 75 | 43 | Lafayette, IN | 3 772 |
| 62 | 44 | Rochester, MN | 806 | 74 | 44 | Appleton, WI | 3 745 |
| 6 | 45 | Modesto, CA | 789 | 64 | 45 | Iowa City, IA | 3 719 |
| 72 | 46 | Idaho Falls, ID | 778 | 18 | 46 | Fayetteville-Springdale-Rogers, AR-MO | 3 695 |
| 11 | 47 | Stockton, CA | 738 | 44 | 47 | Cedar Rapids, IA | 3 623 |
| 27 | 48 | Santa Barbara-Santa Maria-Goleta, CA | 727 | 53 | 48 | Mankato, North Mankato, MN | 3 480 |
| 48 | 49 | Grand Rapids-Wyoming, MI | 710 | 20 | 49 | St. Louis, MO-IL | 3 477 |
| 53 | 50 | Mankato, North Mankato, MN | 689 | 52 | 50 | Green Bay, WI | 3 448 |
| 13 | 51 | Hanford-Corcoran, CA | 681 | 62 | 51 | Rochester, MN | 3 407 |
| 75 | 51 | Lafayette, IN | 681 | 35 | 52 | Des Moines-West Des Moines, IA | 3 231 |
| 25 | 53 | Madera-Chowchilla, CA | 680 | 19 | 53 | Omaha-Council Bluffs, NE-IA | 3 094 |
| 21 | 54 | Philadelphia-Camden-Wilmington, PA-NJ-DE-MD | 679 | 59 | 54 | Columbia, SC | 3 092 |
| 64 | 55 | Iowa City, IA | 647 | 55 | 55 | Dallas-Fort Worth-Arlington, TX | 3 058 |
| 9 | 56 | Miami-Fort Lauderdale-Pompano Beach, FL | 601 | 69 | 56 | Evansville, IN-KY | 2 933 |
| 52 | 57 | Green Bay, WI | 569 | 29 | 57 | Boise City-Nampa, ID | 2 925 |
| 41 | 58 | Santa Rosa-Petaluma, CA | 531 | 43 | 58 | St. Cloud, MN | 2 875 |
| 70 | 59 | Yuba City, CA | 521 | 39 | 59 | Sioux Falls, SD | 2 538 |
| 66 | 60 | Pine Bluff, AR | 520 | 49 | 60 | Sioux City, IA-NE-SD | 2 457 |
| 59 | 61 | Columbia, SC | 507 | 24 | 61 | Kennewick-Pasco-Richland, WA | 2 244 |
| 33 | 62 | Salem, OR | 474 | 28 | 62 | Kansas City, MO-KS | 2 227 |
| 15 | 63 | El Centro, CA | 427 | 66 | 63 | Pine Bluff, AR | 2 221 |
| 42 | 63 | Tampa-St. Petersburg-Clearwater, FL | 427 | 40 | 64 | Rochester, NY | 2 151 |
| 22 | 65 | Lancaster, PA | 425 | 58 | 65 | Fort Smith, AR-OK | 2 089 |
| 74 | 66 | Appleton, WI | 399 | 67 | 66 | Jackson, MS | 2 075 |
| 47 | 67 | New York-Northern New Jersey-Long Island, NY-NJ-PA | 369 | 72 | 67 | Idaho Falls, ID | 2 047 |
| 23 | 68 | San Diego-Carlsbad-San Marcos, CA | 304 | 63 | 68 | Fargo, ND-MN | 1 609 |
| 14 | 69 | Oxnard-Thousand Oaks-Ventura, CA | 259 | 73 | 69 | Oklahoma City, OK | 1 601 |
| 57 | 70 | Harrisonburg, VA | 233 | 12 | 70 | Greeley, CO | 1 550 |
| 71 | 71 | Athens-Clarke County, GA | 222 | 17 | 71 | Yakima, WA | 1 530 |
| 26 | 72 | Yuma, AZ | 210 | 46 | 72 | Grand Forks, ND-MN | 1 311 |
| 38 | 73 | Los Angeles-Long Beach-Santa Ana, CA | 196 | 61 | 73 | Wichita, KS | 1 161 |
| 60 | 74 | Goldsboro, NC | 175 | 56 | 74 | Amarillo, TX | 873 |
| 68 | 75 | Santa Cruz-Watsonville, CA | 47 | 47 | X | New York-Northern New Jersey-Long Island, NY-NJ-PA | D |

Table C. Metropolitan Areas — **Land Area and Population**

| | | Population 2012 | | | | Population characteristics, 2011 | | | | | | | | | |
|---|---|---|---|---|---|---|---|---|---|---|---|---|---|---|---|
| | | | | | | Race alone or in combination, not Hispanic or Latino (percent) | | | | | Age (percent) | | | | |
| CBSA/ DIV code[1] | Area name | Land area,[2] 2010 (sq km) | Total persons | Rank | Per square kilometer | White | Black | Amer- ican Indian, Alaska Native | Asian and Pacific Islander | Percent Hispanic or Latino[3] | Under 5 years | 5 to 17 years | 18 to 24 years | 25 to 34 years | 35 to 44 years | 45 to 54 years |
| | | 1 | 2 | 3 | 4 | 5 | 6 | 7 | 8 | 9 | 10 | 11 | 12 | 13 | 14 | 15 |

1. CBSA = Core Based Statistical Area. DIV = Metropolitan Division. See Appendix A for explanation. See Appendix B for list of metropolitan areas identified by type. 2. Dry land or land partially or temporarily covered by water. 3. May be of any race.

Table C. Metropolitan Areas — **Population and Households**

| | Population, 2011 (cont.) | | | Population change and components of change, 2000–2012 | | | | | | | Households, 2010 | | | | |
|---|---|---|---|---|---|---|---|---|---|---|---|---|---|---|---|
| | Age (percent) (cont.) | | | | Total persons | | Percent change | | Components of change, 2010–2012 | | | | | | Percent |
| Area name | 55 to 64 years | 65 to 74 years | 75 years and over | Percent female | 2000 | 2010 | 2000– 2010 | 2010– 2012 | Births | Deaths | Net migration | Number | Percent change, 2000– 2010 | Persons per house- hold | Female family house- holder[1] | One person |
| | 16 | 17 | 18 | 19 | 20 | 21 | 22 | 23 | 24 | 25 | 26 | 27 | 28 | 29 | 30 | 31 |

1. No spouse present.

Table C. Metropolitan Areas — **Population, Vital Statistics, Medicare, and Crime**

| | Daytime population, 2007–2011 | | | Births, 2011 | | Deaths, 2011 | | Persons under 65 with no health insurance 2010 | | Medicare, 2012 | | | Serious crimes known to police,[2] 2011 | |
|---|---|---|---|---|---|---|---|---|---|---|---|---|---|---|
| | | | | | | | | | | | | | Total | |
| Area name | Persons in group quarters, 2009 | Number | Employ- ment/ residence ratio | Total | Rate[1] | Number | Rate[1] | Number | Percent | Enrolled in original Medicare | Enrolled in Medicare Advantage | Enrolled in a Medicare prescription drug plan | Number | Rate[3] |
| | 32 | 33 | 34 | 35 | 36 | 37 | 38 | 39 | 40 | 41 | 42 | 43 | 44 | 45 |

1. Per 1,000 estimated resident population. 2. Data for serious crimes have not been adjusted for underreporting; this may affect comparability between geographic areas and over time. 3. Per 100,000 population estimated by the FBI.

Table C. Metropolitan Areas — **Crime, Education, Money Income, and Poverty**

| | Serious crimes known to police, 2011 (cont.)[1] | | Education | | | | | Income and Poverty, 2007–2011 | | | | | | | |
|---|---|---|---|---|---|---|---|---|---|---|---|---|---|---|---|
| | Rate[2] | | School enrollment and attainment, 2007–2011 | | | | Local government expenditures,[5] 2009–2010 | | | | | | | Percent below poverty level | |
| | | | Enrollment[3] | | Attainment[4] (percent) | | | | | | | | Percent of house- | | |
| Area name | Violent | Property | Total | Percent private | High school grad- uate or less | Bach- elor's degree or more | Total current expendi- tures (mil dol) | Current expendi- tures per student (dollars) | Per capita income[6] (dollars) | Median house- hold income (dollars) | Percent of households with income of less than $25,000 | Percent of house- holds with income of $100,000 or more | holds with in- come of $200,000 or more | All persons | Related Children under 18 years | Related Children under 5 |
| | 46 | 47 | 48 | 49 | 50 | 51 | 52 | 53 | 54 | 55 | 56 | 57 | 58 | 59 | 60 | 61 |

1. Data for serious crimes have not been adjusted for underreporting; this may affect comparability between geographic areas and over time. 2. Per 100,000 population estimated by the FBI. 3. All persons 3 years old and over enrolled in nursery school through college. 4. Persons 25 years old and over. 5. Elementary and secondary education expenditures. 6. Based on resident population estimated as of July 1, 2009.

## Table C. Metropolitan Areas — **Personal Income**

| Area name | Personal income, 2011 | | | | | | | | | | | | |
|---|---|---|---|---|---|---|---|---|---|---|---|---|---|
| | | | Per capita[1] | | | | | | | Transfer payments | | | | |
| | | | | | | | | | | | Government payments to individuals | | | |
| | Total (mil dol) | Percent change, 2010–2011 | Dollars | Rank | Wages and salaries[2] (mil dol) | Proprietors' income (mil dol) | Dividends, interest, and rent (mil dol) | Total (mil dol) | Total (mil dol) | Social Security (mil dol) | Medical payments (mil dol) | Income mainte-nance (mil dol) | Unemploy-ment insurance (mil dol) |
| | 62 | 63 | 64 | 65 | 66 | 67 | 68 | 69 | 70 | 71 | 72 | 73 | 74 |

1. Based on the resident population estimated as of July 1 of the year shown.    2. Includes other labor income.

## Table C. Metropolitan Areas — **Earnings, Social Security, and Housing**

| Area name | Earnings, 2011 | | | | | | | | | Social Security beneficiaries, December 2011 | | | Housing units, 2010 | |
|---|---|---|---|---|---|---|---|---|---|---|---|---|---|---|
| | | | | Percent by selected industries | | | | | | | | | | |
| | | | Goods-related[1] | | Service-related and health | | | | | | | | Supple-mental Security Income recipients, December 2011 | |
| | Total (mil dol) | Farm | Total | Manu-facturing | Infor-mation, profes-sional, and technical services | Retail trade | Finance, insur-ance, and real estate | Health care and social services | Govern-ment | Number | Rate[2] | | Total | Percent change, 2000–2010 |
| | 75 | 76 | 77 | 78 | 79 | 80 | 81 | 82 | 83 | 84 | 85 | 86 | 87 | 88 |

1. Includes mining, construction, and manufacturing.    2. Per 1,000 resident population estimated as of July 1, 2011.

## Table C. Metropolitan Areas — **Housing, Labor Force, and Employment**

| Area name | Housing units, 2007–2011 | | | | | | | | | Civilian labor force, 2012 | | | | Civilian employment,[5] 2007–2011 | | |
|---|---|---|---|---|---|---|---|---|---|---|---|---|---|---|---|---|
| | | Occupied units | | | | | | | | | | Unemployment | | | Percent | |
| | | | Owner-occupied | | | | Renter-occupied | | | | | | | | | |
| | | | | Median owner cost as a percent of income | | | | | | | | | | | | |
| | Total | Percent | Median value[1] | With a mort-gage | Without a mort-gage | Median rent[2] | Median rent as a percent of in-come | Sub-stand-ard units[3] (percent) | | Total | Percent change, 2011–2012 | Total | Rate[4] | Total | Management, professional, and related occupations | Construction, production, and related occupations |
| | 89 | 90 | 91 | 92 | 93 | 94 | 95 | 96 | | 97 | 98 | 99 | 100 | 101 | 102 | 103 |

1. Specified owner-occupied units.    2. Specified renter-occupied units.    3. Overcrowded or lacking complete plumbing facilities.    4. Percent of civilian labor force.    5. Persons 16 years old and over.

## Table C. Metropolitan Areas — **Nonfarm Employment and Agriculture**

| Area name | Private nonfarm establishments, employment and payroll, 2011 | | | | | | | | | Agriculture, 2007 | | | |
|---|---|---|---|---|---|---|---|---|---|---|---|---|---|
| | | Employment | | | | | | Annual payroll | | Farms | | | |
| | | | | | | | | | | | Percent with: | | |
| | Number of establish-ments | Total | Health care and social assistance | Manufac-turing | Retail trade | Finance and insurance | Professional, scientific, and technical services | Total (mil dol) | Average per employee (dollars) | Number | Fewer than 50 acres | 500 acres or more | Farm operators whose principal occu-pation is farming (percent) |
| | 104 | 105 | 106 | 107 | 108 | 109 | 110 | 111 | 112 | 113 | 114 | 115 | 116 |

## Table C. Metropolitan Areas — **Agriculture**

| Area name | Agriculture, 2007 (cont.) | | | | | | | | | | | | | | | |
|---|---|---|---|---|---|---|---|---|---|---|---|---|---|---|---|---|
| | Land in farms | | | | | Value of land and buildings (dollars) | | | Value of products sold | | | | | Percent of farms with sales of: | | Government payments | |
| | | | Acres | | | | | | | | Percent from: | | | | | | |
| | Acreage (1,000) | Percent change, 2002–2007 | Average size of farm | Total irrigated (1,000) | Total cropland (1,000) | Average per farm | Average per acre | Value of machinery and equipment, average per farm (dollars) | Total (mil dol) | Average per farm (dollars) | Crops | Livestock and poultry products | $10,000 or more | $100,000 or more | Total ($1,000) | Percent of farms |
| | 117 | 118 | 119 | 120 | 121 | 122 | 123 | 124 | 125 | 126 | 127 | 128 | 129 | 130 | 131 | 132 |

## Table C. Metropolitan Areas — **Water Use, Wholesale Trade, Retail Trade, and Real Estate**

| Area name | Water use, 2005 | | Wholesale trade,[1] 2007 | | | | Retail trade, 2007 | | | | Real estate and rental and leasing, 2007 | | | |
|---|---|---|---|---|---|---|---|---|---|---|---|---|---|---|
| | Total water withdrawn (mil gal/day) | Gallons withdrawn per person | Number of establishments | Number of employees | Sales (mil dol) | Annual payroll (mil dol) | Number of establishments | Number of employees | Sales (mil dol) | Annual payroll (mil dol) | Number of establishments | Number of employees | Receipts (mil dol) | Annual payroll (mil dol) |
| | 133 | 134 | 135 | 136 | 137 | 138 | 139 | 140 | 141 | 142 | 143 | 144 | 145 | 146 |

1. Merchant wholesalers, except manufacturers' sales branches and offices.

## Table C. Metropolitan Areas — **Professional Services, Manufacturing, and Accommodation and Food Services**

| Area name | Professional, scientific, and technical services,[1] 2007 | | | | Manufacturing, 2007 | | | | Accommodation and food services, 2007 | | | |
|---|---|---|---|---|---|---|---|---|---|---|---|---|
| | Number of establishments | Number of employees | Sales (mil dol) | Annual payroll (mil dol) | Number of establishments | Number of employees | Sales (mil dol) | Annual payroll (mil dol) | Number of establishments | Number of employees | Sales (mil dol) | Annual payroll (mil dol) |
| | 147 | 148 | 149 | 150 | 151 | 152 | 153 | 154 | 155 | 156 | 157 | 158 |

1. Establishments subject to federal tax.

## Table C. Metropolitan Areas — **Health Care and Social Assistance, Other Services, and Federal Funds**

| Area name | Health care and social assistance,[1] 2007 | | | | Other services,[1] 2007 | | | | Federal funds and grants, 2009–2010 | | | |
|---|---|---|---|---|---|---|---|---|---|---|---|---|
| | | | | | | | | | Expenditures (mil dol) | | | |
| | | | | | | | | | | Direct payments for individuals | | |
| | Number of establishments | Number of employees | Receipts (mil dol) | Annual payroll (mil dol) | Number of establishments | Number of employees | Receipts (mil dol) | Annual payroll (mil dol) | Total | Social Security and government retirement | Medicare | Food stamps and Supplemental Security Income |
| | 159 | 160 | 161 | 162 | 163 | 164 | 165 | 166 | 167 | 168 | 169 | 170 |

1. Establishments subject to federal tax.

Table C. Metropolitan Areas — **Federal Funds, Residential Construction and Local Government Finances**

| Area name | Federal funds and grants, 2009–2010 (cont.) | | | | | | | Value of residential construction authorized by building permits, 2011 | | Local government finances, 2007 | | | | |
|---|---|---|---|---|---|---|---|---|---|---|---|---|---|---|
| | Expenditures (mil dol) (cont.) | | | | | | | | | General revenue | | | | |
| | Procurement contract awards | | | Grants | | | | | | | | Taxes | | |
| | | | | | | | | | | | | | Per capita[1] (dollars) | |
| | Salaries and wages | Defense | Other | Medicaid and other health-related | Nutrition and family welfare | Education | Other | New con-struction ($1,000) | Number of housing units | Total (mil dol) | Inter-govern-mental (mil dol) | Total (mil dol) | Total | Property |
| | 171 | 172 | 173 | 174 | 175 | 176 | 177 | 178 | 179 | 180 | 181 | 182 | 183 | 184 |

1. Based on the resident population estimated as of July 1 of the year shown.

Table C. Metropolitan Areas — **Local Government Finances, Government Employment, and Voting**

| Area name | Local government finances, 2007 (cont.) | | | | | | | | | Government employment, 2011 | | | Presidential election,[2] 2012 | | |
|---|---|---|---|---|---|---|---|---|---|---|---|---|---|---|---|
| | Direct general expenditure | | | | | | | Debt outstanding | | | | | Percent of vote cast: | | |
| | | | Percent of total for: | | | | | | | | | | | | |
| | Total (mil dol) | Per capita[1] (dollars) | Educa-tion | Health and hospitals | Police protec-tion | Public welfare | High-ways | Total (mil dol) | Per capita[1] (dollars) | Federal civilian | Federal military | State and local | Demo-cratic | Republi-can | All other |
| | 185 | 186 | 187 | 188 | 189 | 190 | 191 | 192 | 193 | 194 | 195 | 196 | 197 | 198 | 199 |

1. Based on the resident population estimated as of July 1 of the year shown.   2. © 2013 Election Data Services, Inc. All rights reserved.

# Table C. Metropolitan Areas — **Land Area and Population**

| CBSA/ DIV code[1] | Area name | Land area[2] 2010 (sq km) | Total persons | Rank | Per square kilometer | White | Black | American Indian, Alaska Native | Asian and Pacific Islander | Percent Hispanic or Latino[3] | Under 5 years | 5 to 17 years | 18 to 24 years | 25 to 34 years | 35 to 44 years | 45 to 54 years |
|---|---|---|---|---|---|---|---|---|---|---|---|---|---|---|---|---|
| | | 1 | 2 | 3 | 4 | 5 | 6 | 7 | 8 | 9 | 10 | 11 | 12 | 13 | 14 | 15 |
| 10180 | Abilene, TX | 7 106 | 166 963 | 241 | 23.5 | 69.0 | 8.0 | 0.9 | 2.0 | 21.8 | 7.0 | 16.5 | 12.9 | 14.1 | 11.4 | 13.3 |
| 10420 | Akron, OH | 2 331 | 702 262 | 76 | 301.3 | 83.9 | 13.2 | 0.7 | 2.5 | 1.6 | 5.6 | 16.4 | 10.7 | 11.9 | 12.3 | 15.2 |
| 10500 | Albany, GA | 5 005 | 157 399 | 254 | 31.4 | 44.1 | 52.7 | 0.6 | 1.4 | 2.4 | 7.2 | 18.5 | 11.4 | 12.8 | 12.2 | 13.5 |
| 10580 | Albany-Schenectady-Troy, NY | 7 282 | 874 646 | 59 | 120.1 | 84.3 | 8.5 | 0.7 | 4.1 | 4.4 | 5.3 | 15.6 | 11.1 | 12.3 | 12.6 | 15.4 |
| 10740 | Albuquerque, NM | 24 042 | 901 700 | 57 | 37.5 | 43.3 | 2.9 | 5.8 | 2.7 | 47.1 | 6.7 | 17.6 | 9.8 | 13.9 | 12.6 | 14.1 |
| 10780 | Alexandria, LA | 5 079 | 154 441 | 257 | 30.4 | 65.3 | 30.4 | 1.4 | 1.4 | 2.9 | 7.0 | 18.3 | 8.9 | 13.6 | 12.3 | 14.2 |
| 10900 | Allentown-Bethlehem-Easton, PA-NJ | 3 764 | 827 171 | 65 | 219.8 | 79.2 | 5.2 | 0.4 | 3.0 | 13.5 | 5.6 | 16.7 | 9.1 | 11.4 | 13.0 | 15.7 |
| 11020 | Altoona, PA | 1 362 | 127 121 | 306 | 93.3 | 96.5 | 2.3 | 0.4 | 0.9 | 1.0 | 5.7 | 15.3 | 9.3 | 11.2 | 12.0 | 14.5 |
| 11100 | Amarillo, TX | 9 451 | 255 518 | 183 | 27.0 | 64.6 | 6.6 | 1.1 | 3.0 | 26.2 | 7.6 | 18.7 | 10.7 | 14.2 | 12.3 | 13.3 |
| 11180 | Ames, IA | 1 484 | 91 140 | 356 | 61.4 | 87.9 | 3.2 | 0.5 | 6.9 | 3.1 | 5.2 | 12.2 | 30.2 | 13.6 | 9.1 | 10.0 |
| 11260 | Anchorage, AK | 68 149 | 392 535 | 132 | 5.8 | 72.7 | 5.9 | 11.2 | 10.5 | 6.9 | 7.5 | 18.8 | 10.7 | 15.2 | 13.1 | 15.0 |
| 11300 | Anderson, IN | 1 170 | 130 348 | 298 | 111.4 | 87.6 | 9.2 | 0.7 | 0.7 | 3.4 | 6.1 | 16.7 | 9.0 | 12.5 | 12.9 | 14.2 |
| 11340 | Anderson, SC | 1 853 | 189 355 | 223 | 102.2 | 79.5 | 17.1 | 0.6 | 1.1 | 3.1 | 6.3 | 17.4 | 8.5 | 11.6 | 13.1 | 14.6 |
| 11460 | Ann Arbor, MI | 1 828 | 350 946 | 145 | 192.0 | 74.4 | 14.1 | 1.0 | 9.4 | 4.2 | 5.3 | 14.8 | 18.4 | 13.8 | 12.3 | 13.2 |
| 11500 | Anniston-Oxford, AL | 1 569 | 117 296 | 319 | 74.8 | 74.6 | 21.3 | 1.0 | 1.2 | 3.4 | 6.1 | 16.7 | 10.6 | 12.5 | 12.2 | 14.1 |
| 11540 | Appleton, WI | 2 475 | 228 450 | 194 | 92.3 | 91.1 | 1.4 | 1.7 | 3.2 | 3.7 | 6.5 | 18.6 | 8.3 | 13.3 | 13.6 | 16.0 |
| 11700 | Asheville, NC | 5 265 | 432 406 | 117 | 82.1 | 87.3 | 5.4 | 1.0 | 1.4 | 6.6 | 5.4 | 14.7 | 7.8 | 12.1 | 12.7 | 14.1 |
| 12020 | Athens-Clarke County, GA | 2 654 | 196 425 | 217 | 74.0 | 68.9 | 20.1 | 0.5 | 3.9 | 8.1 | 5.9 | 14.6 | 22.3 | 13.9 | 11.4 | 11.5 |
| 12060 | Atlanta-Sandy Springs-Marietta, GA | 21 597 | 5 439 950 | 9 | 251.9 | 51.9 | 33.0 | 0.7 | 5.6 | 10.6 | 7.1 | 19.1 | 9.3 | 14.4 | 15.4 | 14.6 |
| 12100 | Atlantic City-Hammonton, NJ | 1 439 | 275 422 | 169 | 191.4 | 59.6 | 15.9 | 0.7 | 8.4 | 17.3 | 6.0 | 17.0 | 9.3 | 11.5 | 12.7 | 16.0 |
| 12220 | Auburn-Opelika, AL | 1 574 | 147 257 | 269 | 93.6 | 70.8 | 23.3 | 0.7 | 3.1 | 3.4 | 5.9 | 15.9 | 21.8 | 13.6 | 11.9 | 11.9 |
| 12260 | Augusta-Richmond County, GA-SC | 8 470 | 568 161 | 90 | 67.1 | 57.8 | 36.0 | 0.8 | 2.6 | 4.7 | 6.6 | 17.8 | 10.1 | 13.4 | 12.3 | 14.4 |
| 12420 | Austin-Round Rock-San Marcos, TX | 10 929 | 1 834 303 | 33 | 167.8 | 55.8 | 7.8 | 0.8 | 5.6 | 31.8 | 7.3 | 17.8 | 11.3 | 17.0 | 15.1 | 13.1 |
| 12540 | Bakersfield-Delano, CA | 21 062 | 856 158 | 61 | 40.6 | 39.6 | 6.0 | 1.4 | 5.1 | 50.0 | 8.6 | 21.3 | 11.3 | 14.7 | 12.8 | 12.7 |
| 12580 | Baltimore-Towson, MD | 6 738 | 2 753 149 | 20 | 408.6 | 61.4 | 29.7 | 0.8 | 5.6 | 4.8 | 6.2 | 16.5 | 9.8 | 13.7 | 13.0 | 15.4 |
| 12620 | Bangor, ME | 8 799 | 153 746 | 260 | 17.5 | 96.0 | 1.3 | 1.8 | 1.3 | 1.1 | 5.1 | 14.4 | 13.0 | 11.6 | 11.9 | 15.5 |
| 12700 | Barnstable Town, MA | 1 020 | 215 423 | 199 | 211.2 | 93.7 | 2.8 | 1.1 | 1.7 | 2.3 | 4.1 | 12.8 | 6.8 | 8.5 | 10.0 | 15.5 |
| 12940 | Baton Rouge, LA | 10 430 | 815 298 | 66 | 78.2 | 58.6 | 36.1 | 0.6 | 2.2 | 3.6 | 6.8 | 17.5 | 12.1 | 14.6 | 12.5 | 13.7 |
| 12980 | Battle Creek, MI | 1 829 | 135 099 | 292 | 73.9 | 82.2 | 12.4 | 1.4 | 2.1 | 4.6 | 6.3 | 17.6 | 9.3 | 11.6 | 12.1 | 14.6 |
| 13020 | Bay City, MI | 1 146 | 106 935 | 335 | 93.3 | 92.6 | 2.4 | 1.1 | 0.8 | 4.7 | 5.6 | 16.1 | 8.5 | 11.6 | 11.8 | 15.3 |
| 13140 | Beaumont-Port Arthur, TX | 5 440 | 389 980 | 133 | 71.7 | 59.2 | 24.8 | 0.8 | 2.9 | 13.5 | 6.8 | 17.6 | 9.8 | 13.6 | 12.4 | 14.6 |
| 13380 | Bellingham, WA | 5 457 | 205 262 | 210 | 37.6 | 84.1 | 1.7 | 3.7 | 5.7 | 8.2 | 5.5 | 14.9 | 15.1 | 12.8 | 11.6 | 13.1 |
| 13460 | Bend, OR | 7 817 | 162 277 | 246 | 20.8 | 90.0 | 0.7 | 1.8 | 2.0 | 7.7 | 5.9 | 16.7 | 7.2 | 12.5 | 13.2 | 14.1 |
| 13740 | Billings, MT | 12 127 | 162 009 | 247 | 13.4 | 90.4 | 1.2 | 4.8 | 1.3 | 4.6 | 6.5 | 16.7 | 8.6 | 13.4 | 11.8 | 14.7 |
| 13780 | Binghamton, NY | 3 171 | 248 538 | 186 | 78.4 | 89.8 | 4.7 | 0.6 | 3.7 | 3.1 | 5.2 | 15.3 | 11.6 | 11.5 | 11.0 | 15.5 |
| 13820 | Birmingham-Hoover, AL | 13 674 | 1 136 650 | 49 | 83.1 | 65.6 | 28.8 | 0.7 | 1.6 | 4.4 | 6.6 | 17.2 | 8.9 | 13.8 | 13.2 | 14.3 |
| 13900 | Bismarck, ND | 9 218 | 113 875 | 325 | 12.4 | 93.5 | 1.0 | 4.6 | 0.8 | 1.4 | 6.6 | 16.1 | 9.5 | 14.4 | 12.0 | 14.5 |
| 13980 | Blacksburg-Christiansburg-Radford, VA | 2 778 | 163 543 | 243 | 58.9 | 89.2 | 5.3 | 0.6 | 4.5 | 2.3 | 4.5 | 11.9 | 26.3 | 11.5 | 10.9 | 11.2 |
| 14020 | Bloomington, IN | 3 425 | 195 339 | 218 | 57.0 | 90.6 | 3.2 | 0.7 | 4.8 | 2.5 | 4.9 | 13.2 | 23.4 | 13.1 | 10.6 | 11.9 |
| 14060 | Bloomington-Normal, IL | 3 065 | 172 281 | 234 | 56.2 | 83.3 | 8.5 | 0.5 | 5.0 | 4.6 | 6.2 | 16.1 | 18.1 | 13.4 | 12.1 | 13.1 |
| 14260 | Boise City-Nampa, ID | 30 473 | 637 896 | 85 | 20.9 | 83.6 | 1.3 | 1.4 | 3.0 | 12.8 | 7.4 | 20.1 | 9.0 | 14.1 | 13.5 | 13.3 |
| 14460 | Boston-Cambridge-Quincy, MA-NH | 9 032 | 4 640 802 | 10 | 513.8 | 76.5 | 7.8 | 0.5 | 7.5 | 9.3 | 5.6 | 15.7 | 10.3 | 13.9 | 13.4 | 15.4 |
| 14460 | Boston-Quincy, MA Div | 2 884 | 1 926 030 | X | 667.8 | 70.7 | 13.0 | 0.6 | 7.5 | 9.9 | 5.6 | 15.2 | 11.5 | 14.9 | 13.2 | 14.5 |
| 14460 | Cambridge-Newton-Framingham, MA Div | 2 118 | 1 537 215 | X | 725.8 | 78.6 | 5.3 | 0.4 | 10.7 | 6.8 | 5.7 | 15.4 | 9.5 | 14.8 | 13.8 | 15.4 |
| 14460 | Peabody, MA Div | 1 276 | 755 618 | X | 592.2 | 76.8 | 3.5 | 0.3 | 3.6 | 16.9 | 5.8 | 16.9 | 8.9 | 11.5 | 13.1 | 16.1 |
| 14460 | Rockingham County-Strafford County, NH Div | 2 755 | 421 939 | X | 153.2 | 94.8 | 1.2 | 0.6 | 2.6 | 2.1 | 5.0 | 16.5 | 9.9 | 10.7 | 13.5 | 17.7 |
| 14500 | Boulder, CO | 1 881 | 305 318 | 157 | 162.3 | 80.7 | 1.4 | 0.9 | 5.4 | 13.7 | 5.4 | 15.4 | 15.2 | 13.0 | 13.5 | 14.5 |
| 14540 | Bowling Green, KY | 2 187 | 129 181 | 300 | 59.1 | 84.4 | 9.2 | 0.6 | 3.1 | 4.3 | 6.2 | 16.3 | 15.8 | 13.5 | 12.2 | 13.1 |
| 14740 | Bremerton-Silverdale, WA | 1 023 | 254 991 | 185 | 249.3 | 83.0 | 4.0 | 2.9 | 8.8 | 6.6 | 5.8 | 16.0 | 10.6 | 13.0 | 11.7 | 14.8 |
| 14860 | Bridgeport-Stamford-Norwalk, CT | 1 618 | 933 835 | 56 | 577.2 | 67.1 | 11.0 | 0.4 | 5.5 | 17.4 | 6.0 | 18.3 | 8.0 | 11.7 | 13.9 | 16.2 |
| 15180 | Brownsville-Harlingen, TX | 2 307 | 415 557 | 125 | 180.1 | 10.8 | 0.4 | 0.2 | 0.7 | 88.1 | 8.8 | 23.8 | 10.2 | 12.6 | 12.8 | 11.2 |
| 15260 | Brunswick, GA | 3 332 | 113 448 | 326 | 34.0 | 69.7 | 24.4 | 0.7 | 1.5 | 5.2 | 6.5 | 17.3 | 8.5 | 11.7 | 12.3 | 14.6 |
| 15380 | Buffalo-Niagara Falls, NY | 4 053 | 1 134 210 | 50 | 279.8 | 80.6 | 12.8 | 1.1 | 2.8 | 4.3 | 5.3 | 15.9 | 10.3 | 12.0 | 11.9 | 15.4 |
| 15500 | Burlington, NC | 1 098 | 153 920 | 259 | 140.2 | 68.1 | 19.5 | 0.9 | 1.6 | 11.4 | 6.2 | 17.1 | 10.5 | 11.3 | 13.4 | 14.4 |
| 15540 | Burlington-South Burlington, VT | 3 243 | 213 701 | 202 | 65.9 | 93.8 | 2.2 | 1.3 | 2.9 | 1.7 | 5.1 | 15.4 | 13.7 | 12.8 | 12.7 | 15.6 |
| 15940 | Canton-Massillon, OH | 2 512 | 403 455 | 129 | 160.6 | 90.2 | 8.4 | 0.8 | 1.0 | 1.6 | 5.7 | 16.9 | 8.7 | 11.1 | 12.0 | 15.1 |
| 15980 | Cape Coral-Fort Myers, FL | 2 032 | 645 293 | 84 | 317.6 | 71.6 | 8.5 | 0.5 | 1.9 | 18.6 | 5.2 | 14.2 | 7.6 | 10.5 | 11.1 | 13.0 |
| 16020 | Cape Girardeau-Jackson, MO-IL | 3 709 | 97 080 | 349 | 26.2 | 88.0 | 9.4 | 0.8 | 1.4 | 1.9 | 6.1 | 15.9 | 13.1 | 12.3 | 11.4 | 13.7 |
| 16180 | Carson City, NV | 375 | 54 838 | 366 | 146.2 | 71.6 | 2.5 | 2.8 | 3.1 | 22.0 | 5.8 | 15.3 | 8.5 | 12.0 | 12.2 | 15.1 |
| 16220 | Casper, WY | 13 831 | 78 621 | 363 | 5.7 | 90.3 | 1.6 | 1.6 | 1.1 | 7.1 | 7.0 | 16.7 | 9.5 | 14.7 | 12.0 | 14.3 |
| 16300 | Cedar Rapids, IA | 5 203 | 261 761 | 179 | 50.3 | 92.0 | 4.6 | 0.6 | 2.2 | 2.5 | 6.5 | 17.8 | 9.2 | 13.4 | 12.7 | 14.6 |
| 16580 | Champaign-Urbana, IL | 4 976 | 233 788 | 192 | 47.0 | 75.7 | 11.8 | 0.6 | 9.2 | 5.0 | 5.6 | 14.0 | 22.6 | 14.0 | 10.6 | 11.7 |

1. CBSA = Core Based Statistical Area. DIV = Metropolitan Division. See Appendix A for explanation. See Appendix B for list of metropolitan areas identified by type.   2. Dry land or land partially or temporarily covered by water.   3. May be of any race.

# Table C. Metropolitan Areas — **Population and Households**

| Area name | Population, 2011 (cont.) Age (percent) (cont.) 55 to 64 years | 65 to 74 years | 75 years and over | Percent female | Population change and components of change, 2000–2012 Total persons 2000 | 2010 | Percent change 2000–2010 | 2010–2012 | Components of change, 2010–2012 Births | Deaths | Net migration | Households, 2010 Number | Percent change, 2000–2010 | Persons per house-hold | Percent Female family house-holder[1] | One person |
|---|---|---|---|---|---|---|---|---|---|---|---|---|---|---|---|---|
| | 16 | 17 | 18 | 19 | 20 | 21 | 22 | 23 | 24 | 25 | 26 | 27 | 28 | 29 | 30 | 31 |
| Abilene, TX .......................... | 11.2 | 7.1 | 6.5 | 49.8 | 160 245 | 165 252 | 3.1 | 1.0 | 5 198 | 3 726 | 191 | 62 206 | 6.4 | 2.49 | 12.4 | 26.9 |
| Akron, OH ........................... | 13.6 | 7.4 | 7.0 | 51.5 | 694 960 | 703 200 | 1.2 | -0.1 | 16 796 | 15 056 | -2 449 | 285 003 | 3.9 | 2.40 | 13.0 | 29.0 |
| Albany, GA.......................... | 12.3 | 6.9 | 5.3 | 52.2 | 157 833 | 157 308 | -0.3 | 0.1 | 5 123 | 2 942 | -2 196 | 59 319 | 3.3 | 2.56 | 22.2 | 26.8 |
| Albany-Schenectady-Troy, NY ..................................... | 13.5 | 7.4 | 6.9 | 51.2 | 825 875 | 870 716 | 5.4 | 0.5 | 20 351 | 16 877 | 579 | 355 301 | 7.6 | 2.36 | 11.7 | 30.3 |
| Albuquerque, NM ................. | 12.6 | 7.1 | 5.5 | 50.8 | 729 649 | 887 077 | 21.6 | 1.6 | 26 000 | 14 967 | 3 702 | 347 366 | 23.6 | 2.51 | 13.8 | 28.5 |
| Alexandria, LA .................... | 12.2 | 7.7 | 5.9 | 50.7 | 145 035 | 153 922 | 6.1 | 0.3 | 4 715 | 3 383 | -748 | 57 897 | 6.8 | 2.53 | 17.7 | 26.8 |
| Allentown-Bethlehem-Easton, PA-NJ .................... | 13.2 | 7.7 | 7.7 | 51.2 | 740 395 | 821 173 | 10.9 | 0.7 | 19 760 | 16 997 | 3 414 | 315 712 | 10.5 | 2.53 | 11.7 | 25.7 |
| Altoona, PA ......................... | 14.3 | 8.8 | 9.0 | 51.4 | 129 144 | 127 089 | -1.6 | 0.0 | 3 184 | 3 621 | 446 | 52 159 | 1.2 | 2.37 | 11.7 | 29.6 |
| Amarillo, TX ........................ | 11.4 | 6.4 | 5.5 | 50.1 | 226 522 | 249 881 | 10.3 | 2.3 | 8 427 | 4 839 | 2 019 | 94 111 | 10.4 | 2.56 | 12.9 | 26.7 |
| Ames, IA ............................. | 9.5 | 5.1 | 5.0 | 48.2 | 79 981 | 89 542 | 12.0 | 1.8 | 2 113 | 1 095 | 597 | 34 736 | 18.2 | 2.34 | 6.2 | 28.3 |
| Anchorage, AK..................... | 12.0 | 5.0 | 2.8 | 49.1 | 319 605 | 380 821 | 19.2 | 3.1 | 13 680 | 4 001 | 1 961 | 139 156 | 20.6 | 2.67 | 11.0 | 24.3 |
| Anderson, IN ....................... | 13.0 | 8.4 | 7.3 | 50.0 | 133 358 | 131 636 | -1.3 | -1.0 | 3 540 | 3 227 | -1 562 | 51 927 | -2.1 | 2.41 | 13.6 | 28.3 |
| Anderson, SC....................... | 13.2 | 8.8 | 6.6 | 51.7 | 165 740 | 187 126 | 12.9 | 1.2 | 4 987 | 4 383 | 1 633 | 73 829 | 12.5 | 2.50 | 14.5 | 25.4 |
| Ann Arbor, MI...................... | 11.6 | 5.9 | 4.6 | 50.7 | 322 895 | 344 791 | 6.8 | 1.8 | 8 347 | 4 522 | 2 389 | 137 193 | 9.5 | 2.38 | 9.8 | 30.6 |
| Anniston-Oxford, AL............. | 13.3 | 8.2 | 6.4 | 51.9 | 112 249 | 118 572 | 5.6 | -1.1 | 3 169 | 3 059 | -1 333 | 47 331 | 4.5 | 2.44 | 15.2 | 27.7 |
| Appleton, WI ........................ | 11.9 | 6.3 | 5.7 | 50.1 | 201 602 | 225 666 | 11.9 | 1.2 | 6 238 | 3 379 | -64 | 88 223 | 16.9 | 2.52 | 8.4 | 24.9 |
| Asheville, NC ....................... | 14.5 | 10.1 | 8.6 | 51.7 | 369 171 | 424 858 | 15.1 | 1.8 | 9 776 | 10 156 | 7 887 | 179 917 | 16.6 | 2.30 | 10.4 | 29.5 |
| Athens-Clarke County, GA ... | 10.0 | 6.1 | 4.4 | 51.5 | 166 079 | 192 541 | 15.9 | 2.0 | 5 018 | 2 716 | 1 520 | 73 191 | 15.4 | 2.50 | 12.5 | 26.5 |
| Atlanta-Sandy Springs-Marietta, GA............................... | 10.9 | 5.6 | 3.7 | 51.3 | 4 247 981 | 5 268 860 | 24.0 | 3.2 | 164 184 | 72 636 | 77 164 | 1 937 225 | 24.6 | 2.68 | 15.3 | 25.3 |
| Atlantic City-Hammonton, NJ | 13.0 | 7.9 | 6.5 | 51.4 | 252 552 | 274 549 | 8.7 | 0.3 | 7 658 | 5 675 | -1 038 | 102 847 | 8.2 | 2.61 | 15.5 | 26.9 |
| Auburn-Opelika, AL.............. | 9.8 | 5.5 | 3.7 | 50.6 | 115 092 | 140 247 | 21.9 | 5.0 | 3 324 | 1 928 | 5 512 | 55 682 | 21.8 | 2.44 | 13.0 | 27.9 |
| Augusta-Richmond County, GA-SC................................. | 12.7 | 7.4 | 5.4 | 51.3 | 499 684 | 556 877 | 11.4 | 2.0 | 15 807 | 10 879 | 6 259 | 212 245 | 14.9 | 2.54 | 17.7 | 26.1 |
| Austin-Round Rock-San Marcos, TX .............................. | 10.0 | 4.9 | 3.4 | 49.9 | 1 249 763 | 1 716 289 | 37.3 | 6.9 | 56 812 | 18 688 | 78 081 | 650 459 | 37.9 | 2.58 | 10.9 | 27.3 |
| Bakersfield-Delano, CA......... | 9.5 | 5.3 | 3.8 | 48.4 | 661 645 | 839 631 | 26.9 | 2.0 | 33 060 | 12 046 | -4 358 | 254 610 | 22.0 | 3.15 | 15.7 | 19.3 |
| Baltimore-Towson, MD ......... | 12.6 | 6.9 | 5.9 | 51.8 | 2 552 994 | 2 710 489 | 6.2 | 1.6 | 75 162 | 51 187 | 19 037 | 1 038 765 | 6.6 | 2.54 | 15.2 | 27.4 |
| Bangor, ME .......................... | 13.9 | 7.8 | 7.0 | 50.7 | 144 919 | 153 923 | 6.2 | -0.1 | 3 384 | 3 224 | -324 | 62 966 | 8.4 | 2.33 | 10.3 | 28.0 |
| Barnstable Town, MA ........... | 17.0 | 12.8 | 12.6 | 52.4 | 222 230 | 215 888 | -2.9 | -0.2 | 3 903 | 6 222 | 2 078 | 95 755 | 1.0 | 2.21 | 9.6 | 31.8 |
| Baton Rouge, LA ................. | 11.7 | 6.4 | 4.6 | 50.9 | 705 973 | 802 484 | 13.7 | 1.6 | 25 144 | 14 261 | 1 892 | 300 022 | 16.9 | 2.59 | 17.0 | 25.7 |
| Battle Creek, MI.................... | 13.5 | 7.7 | 7.2 | 51.1 | 137 985 | 136 146 | -1.3 | -0.8 | 3 681 | 3 109 | -1 600 | 54 016 | -0.2 | 2.44 | 14.6 | 28.8 |
| Bay City, MI ......................... | 14.5 | 8.7 | 7.8 | 51.0 | 110 157 | 107 771 | -2.2 | -0.8 | 2 558 | 2 508 | -883 | 44 603 | 1.5 | 2.38 | 11.8 | 29.3 |
| Beaumont-Port Arthur, TX .... | 12.1 | 6.9 | 6.2 | 49.4 | 385 090 | 388 745 | 0.9 | 0.3 | 11 533 | 8 583 | -1 635 | 144 934 | 1.8 | 2.56 | 15.4 | 26.4 |
| Bellingham, WA ................... | 13.2 | 7.7 | 6.1 | 50.4 | 166 814 | 201 140 | 20.6 | 2.0 | 5 058 | 3 122 | 2 257 | 80 370 | 24.7 | 2.43 | 8.8 | 27.8 |
| Bend, OR ............................. | 14.7 | 9.2 | 6.4 | 50.6 | 115 367 | 157 733 | 36.7 | 2.9 | 3 810 | 2 747 | 3 362 | 64 090 | 40.6 | 2.44 | 9.4 | 24.1 |
| Billings, MT .......................... | 13.5 | 7.7 | 6.9 | 51.0 | 138 904 | 158 050 | 13.8 | 2.5 | 4 534 | 3 173 | 2 576 | 65 243 | 16.2 | 2.37 | 10.2 | 29.8 |
| Binghamton, NY................... | 13.4 | 8.1 | 8.4 | 50.9 | 252 320 | 251 725 | -0.2 | -1.3 | 5 612 | 5 614 | -3 109 | 102 517 | 2.0 | 2.35 | 11.7 | 30.9 |
| Birmingham-Hoover, AL........ | 12.8 | 7.3 | 5.9 | 51.8 | 1 052 238 | 1 128 047 | 7.2 | 0.8 | 34 801 | 24 796 | -1 396 | 441 924 | 7.2 | 2.50 | 15.3 | 27.4 |
| Bismarck, ND ....................... | 13.0 | 7.0 | 7.0 | 50.6 | 94 719 | 108 779 | 14.8 | 4.7 | 3 312 | 1 922 | 3 637 | 45 265 | 20.5 | 2.33 | 8.8 | 29.8 |
| Blacksburg-Christiansburg-Radford, VA ........................ | 11.0 | 7.1 | 5.5 | 49.5 | 151 272 | 162 958 | 7.7 | 0.4 | 3 212 | 2 829 | 189 | 63 793 | 9.2 | 2.35 | 9.2 | 27.7 |
| Bloomington, IN ................... | 11.0 | 6.5 | 5.4 | 50.1 | 175 506 | 192 714 | 9.8 | 1.4 | 4 193 | 3 225 | 1 658 | 76 837 | 12.1 | 2.31 | 8.4 | 30.6 |
| Bloomington-Normal, IL ........ | 10.7 | 5.4 | 4.9 | 51.4 | 150 433 | 169 572 | 12.7 | 1.6 | 4 660 | 2 439 | 551 | 65 104 | 14.7 | 2.44 | 9.6 | 28.1 |
| Boise City-Nampa, ID........... | 11.3 | 6.4 | 4.9 | 50.1 | 464 840 | 616 561 | 32.6 | 3.5 | 19 058 | 8 974 | 10 915 | 225 594 | 32.5 | 2.67 | 10.6 | 23.6 |
| Boston-Cambridge-Quincy, MA-NH ............................... | 12.4 | 6.9 | 6.4 | 51.6 | 4 391 344 | 4 552 402 | 3.7 | 1.9 | 115 667 | 76 938 | 51 463 | 1 760 584 | 4.8 | 2.50 | 11.9 | 28.5 |
| Boston-Quincy, MA Div ..... | 11.9 | 6.8 | 6.2 | 51.8 | 1 812 937 | 1 887 792 | 4.1 | 2.0 | 48 519 | 31 977 | 22 299 | 731 807 | 5.2 | 2.47 | 13.2 | 30.1 |
| Cambridge-Newton-Framingham, MA Div ........ | 12.3 | 6.8 | 6.5 | 51.3 | 1 465 396 | 1 503 085 | 2.6 | 2.3 | 39 522 | 24 376 | 19 677 | 580 688 | 3.5 | 2.49 | 10.1 | 27.8 |
| Peabody, MA Div .............. | 13.3 | 7.3 | 7.1 | 51.9 | 723 419 | 743 159 | 2.7 | 1.7 | 19 117 | 13 876 | 7 538 | 285 956 | 3.8 | 2.54 | 13.5 | 28.1 |
| Rockingham County-Strafford County, NH Div..... | 13.8 | 7.3 | 5.7 | 50.8 | 389 592 | 418 366 | 7.4 | 0.9 | 8 509 | 6 709 | 1 949 | 162 133 | 10.2 | 2.51 | 9.3 | 24.3 |
| Boulder, CO ......................... | 12.5 | 6.0 | 4.5 | 49.8 | 291 288 | 294 567 | 1.1 | 3.6 | 6 708 | 3 502 | 7 430 | 119 300 | 4.0 | 2.39 | 7.7 | 29.0 |
| Bowling Green, KY ............... | 11.2 | 6.7 | 5.0 | 51.0 | 104 166 | 125 953 | 20.9 | 2.6 | 3 538 | 2 219 | 1 904 | 48 531 | 21.3 | 2.46 | 11.7 | 27.4 |
| Bremerton-Silverdale, WA .... | 14.3 | 8.0 | 5.7 | 49.1 | 231 969 | 251 133 | 8.3 | 1.5 | 6 559 | 4 387 | 1 699 | 97 220 | 12.5 | 2.49 | 10.2 | 25.2 |
| Bridgeport-Stamford-Norwalk, CT ........................... | 12.1 | 7.0 | 6.7 | 51.3 | 882 567 | 916 829 | 3.9 | 1.9 | 23 078 | 14 370 | 8 674 | 335 545 | 3.5 | 2.68 | 12.3 | 24.9 |
| Brownsville-Harlingen, TX..... | 9.4 | 6.2 | 5.1 | 51.8 | 335 227 | 406 220 | 21.2 | 2.3 | 17 135 | 5 393 | -2 283 | 119 631 | 23.0 | 3.36 | 20.0 | 16.4 |
| Brunswick, GA ..................... | 13.9 | 9.1 | 6.2 | 52.0 | 93 044 | 112 370 | 20.8 | 1.0 | 3 019 | 2 321 | 371 | 44 630 | 21.1 | 2.48 | 15.5 | 26.8 |
| Buffalo-Niagara Falls, NY ..... | 13.4 | 7.8 | 8.0 | 51.7 | 1 170 111 | 1 135 509 | -3.0 | -0.1 | 26 763 | 26 462 | -1 023 | 473 720 | 1.1 | 2.33 | 13.5 | 32.7 |
| Burlington, NC ..................... | 12.2 | 7.8 | 7.0 | 52.4 | 130 800 | 151 131 | 15.5 | 1.8 | 3 935 | 3 214 | 2 147 | 59 960 | 16.2 | 2.45 | 14.5 | 27.8 |
| Burlington-South Burlington, VT ...................................... | 12.8 | 6.6 | 5.4 | 51.0 | 198 889 | 211 261 | 6.2 | 1.2 | 4 674 | 3 104 | 894 | 83 242 | 9.6 | 2.41 | 9.5 | 26.4 |
| Canton-Massillon, OH.......... | 14.1 | 8.5 | 8.0 | 51.5 | 406 934 | 404 422 | -0.6 | -0.2 | 9 665 | 9 439 | -1 062 | 162 474 | 1.9 | 2.43 | 12.4 | 27.8 |
| Cape Coral-Fort Myers, FL.... | 14.3 | 13.4 | 10.7 | 50.9 | 440 888 | 618 754 | 40.3 | 4.3 | 14 027 | 13 633 | 25 704 | 259 818 | 37.8 | 2.35 | 10.3 | 26.7 |
| Cape Girardeau-Jackson, MO-IL ................................. | 12.7 | 7.8 | 7.2 | 51.3 | 90 312 | 96 275 | 6.6 | 0.8 | 2 583 | 2 081 | 263 | 38 024 | 7.5 | 2.41 | 11.4 | 27.6 |
| Carson City, NV ................... | 14.0 | 9.1 | 7.9 | 48.2 | 52 457 | 55 274 | 5.4 | -0.8 | 1 467 | 1 391 | -487 | 21 427 | 6.2 | 2.41 | 12.0 | 30.4 |
| Casper, WY .......................... | 13.3 | 6.5 | 6.0 | 49.6 | 66 533 | 75 450 | 13.4 | 4.2 | 2 272 | 1 470 | 2 325 | 30 616 | 14.2 | 2.41 | 10.9 | 28.5 |
| Cedar Rapids, IA .................. | 12.2 | 7.1 | 6.6 | 50.4 | 237 230 | 257 940 | 8.7 | 1.5 | 7 185 | 4 632 | 1 264 | 104 617 | 11.2 | 2.40 | 9.6 | 28.6 |
| Champaign-Urbana, IL.......... | 10.4 | 5.7 | 5.4 | 50.2 | 210 275 | 231 891 | 10.3 | 0.8 | 5 925 | 3 492 | -511 | 93 123 | 12.6 | 2.31 | 9.7 | 32.3 |

1. No spouse present.

# Table C. Metropolitan Areas — **Population, Vital Statistics, Medicare, and Crime**

| Area name | Persons in group quarters, 2009 | Daytime population, 2007–2011 | | Births, 2011 | | Deaths, 2011 | | Persons under 65 with no health insurance 2010 | | Medicare, 2012 | | | Serious crimes known to police,[2] 2011 Total | |
|---|---|---|---|---|---|---|---|---|---|---|---|---|---|---|
| | | Number | Employment/ residence ratio | Total | Rate[1] | Number | Rate[1] | Number | Percent | Enrolled in original Medicare | Enrolled in Medicare Advantage | Enrolled in a Medicare prescription drug plan | Number | Rate[3] |
| | 32 | 33 | 34 | 35 | 36 | 37 | 38 | 39 | 40 | 41 | 42 | 43 | 44 | 45 |
| Abilene, TX ...................... | 10 369 | 164 985 | 1.01 | 2 424 | 14.6 | 1 658 | 10.0 | 32 060 | 23.9 | 27 500 | 3 308 | 12 149 | 5 613 | 3 327 |
| Akron, OH ........................ | 17 881 | 700 471 | 0.99 | 7 686 | 11.0 | 6 658 | 9.5 | 82 219 | 14.0 | 122 490 | 53 443 | 44 383 | 23 663 | 3 668 |
| Albany, GA ...................... | 5 578 | 158 495 | 1.01 | 2 310 | 14.6 | 1 389 | 8.8 | 26 823 | 20.0 | 25 329 | 4 895 | 11 093 | 7 697 | 4 860 |
| Albany-Schenectady-Troy, NY .................................. | 32 571 | 880 726 | 1.03 | 9 044 | 10.4 | 7 503 | 8.6 | 74 978 | 10.4 | 152 942 | 56 218 | 38 109 | 24 302 | 2 779 |
| Albuquerque, NM ................. | 14 850 | 871 108 | 0.99 | 11 693 | 13.0 | 6 590 | 7.3 | 154 655 | 20.1 | 139 340 | 64 353 | 33 715 | 42 017 | 4 684 |
| Alexandria, LA.................. | 7 438 | 155 481 | 1.04 | 2 186 | 14.1 | 1 509 | 9.8 | 25 336 | 19.9 | 28 663 | 3 379 | 14 924 | 7 614 | 4 998 |
| Allentown-Bethlehem-Easton, PA-NJ ......................... | 22 280 | 774 843 | 0.89 | 8 796 | 10.7 | 7 429 | 9.0 | 82 532 | 12.2 | 154 166 | 37 320 | 71 575 | 20 610 | 2 502 |
| Altoona, PA ...................... | 3 672 | 132 223 | 1.09 | 1 410 | 11.1 | 1 613 | 12.7 | 12 470 | 12.2 | 28 355 | 13 872 | 8 074 | 2 858 | 2 242 |
| Amarillo, TX ..................... | 9 044 | 246 067 | 0.99 | 3 884 | 15.3 | 2 131 | 8.4 | 53 381 | 25.1 | 36 268 | 4 700 | 16 986 | 11 636 | 4 561 |
| Ames, IA ......................... | 8 174 | 89 815 | 1.03 | 948 | 10.6 | 466 | 5.2 | 7 602 | 10.4 | 10 790 | 1 117 | 6 534 | 2 609 | 2 899 |
| Anchorage, AK .................. | 9 820 | 371 705 | 0.99 | 5 875 | 15.2 | 1 752 | 4.5 | 66 370 | 19.1 | 39 235 | 196 | 15 085 | NA | NA |
| Anderson, IN .................... | 6 277 | 120 319 | 0.80 | 1 591 | 12.1 | 1 382 | 10.5 | 17 850 | 16.9 | 26 401 | 4 415 | 9 543 | NA | NA |
| Anderson, SC .................... | 2 764 | 173 283 | 0.84 | 2 246 | 11.9 | 1 885 | 10.0 | 29 910 | 19.1 | 38 657 | 9 564 | 15 217 | 10 805 | 5 708 |
| Ann Arbor, MI ................... | 17 812 | 380 623 | 1.22 | 3 696 | 10.6 | 1 973 | 5.7 | 32 780 | 11.3 | 46 492 | 10 340 | 18 458 | 8 931 | 2 592 |
| Anniston-Oxford, AL............. | 2 919 | 123 392 | 1.12 | 1 385 | 11.8 | 1 344 | 11.4 | 15 920 | 16.1 | 24 795 | 2 726 | 9 891 | 5 693 | 4 778 |
| Appleton, WI .................... | 3 237 | 218 973 | 0.96 | 2 750 | 12.1 | 1 464 | 6.4 | 18 402 | 9.4 | 33 172 | 18 293 | 7 589 | 4 221 | 1 862 |
| Asheville, NC .................... | 10 813 | 424 800 | 1.02 | 4 384 | 10.2 | 4 478 | 10.4 | 70 539 | 20.7 | 97 524 | 17 266 | 43 270 | 11 726 | 2 739 |
| Athens-Clarke County, GA ... | 9 681 | 196 454 | 1.07 | 2 328 | 12.0 | 1 224 | 6.3 | 35 776 | 21.9 | 26 206 | 5 511 | 9 846 | 7 955 | 4 102 |
| Atlanta-Sandy Springs-Marietta, GA ....................... | 84 370 | 5 231 606 | 1.01 | 74 174 | 13.8 | 31 266 | 5.8 | 1 038 658 | 22.0 | 631 895 | 172 479 | 233 074 | 211 926 | 3 978 |
| Atlantic City-Hammonton, NJ | 6 046 | 281 872 | 1.07 | 3 411 | 12.4 | 2 555 | 9.3 | 35 980 | 15.5 | 48 213 | 5 279 | 26 583 | 10 788 | 3 916 |
| Auburn-Opelika, AL............. | 4 410 | 129 116 | 0.86 | 1 536 | 10.7 | 840 | 5.9 | 19 495 | 15.8 | 18 103 | 1 888 | 7 157 | 4 883 | 3 465 |
| Augusta-Richmond County, GA-SC ............................ | 17 233 | 553 458 | 1.01 | 6 433 | 11.4 | 4 796 | 8.5 | 87 123 | 18.4 | 92 125 | 21 187 | 31 357 | 26 321 | 4 725 |
| Austin-Round Rock-San Marcos, TX ........................... | 40 873 | 1 690 017 | 1.01 | 25 973 | 14.6 | 7 888 | 4.4 | 337 083 | 21.7 | 186 549 | 35 405 | 67 472 | 65 476 | 3 736 |
| Bakersfield-Delano, CA........ | 36 757 | 830 119 | 1.00 | 14 378 | 16.9 | 5 318 | 6.2 | 171 643 | 23.4 | 98 895 | 33 370 | 38 502 | 34 518 | 4 063 |
| Baltimore-Towson, MD ........ | 68 923 | 2 663 072 | 0.97 | 33 729 | 12.4 | 22 788 | 8.3 | 270 372 | 11.7 | 419 310 | 39 685 | 177 705 | 256 774 | 3 235 |
| Bangor, ME ...................... | 7 318 | 156 075 | 1.04 | 1 506 | 9.8 | 1 407 | 9.1 | 15 317 | 12.2 | 31 649 | 5 241 | 16 324 | 4 439 | 2 884 |
| Barnstable Town, MA .......... | 3 961 | 211 285 | 0.95 | 1 750 | 8.1 | 2 743 | 12.7 | 9 583 | 6.0 | 65 255 | 5 661 | 29 289 | 7 039 | 3 241 |
| Baton Rouge, LA ............... | 25 547 | 796 745 | 1.00 | 11 349 | 14.0 | 6 240 | 7.7 | 126 914 | 18.3 | 114 665 | 44 105 | 37 266 | 37 183 | 4 653 |
| Battle Creek, MI ............... | 4 275 | 142 445 | 1.10 | 1 649 | 12.2 | 1 321 | 9.7 | 17 249 | 15.2 | 27 326 | 4 752 | 14 011 | 5 958 | 4 434 |
| Bay City, MI ..................... | 1 438 | 98 251 | 0.80 | 1 142 | 10.7 | 1 121 | 10.5 | 12 490 | 13.9 | 23 232 | 4 679 | 9 902 | 2 409 | 2 237 |
| Beaumont-Port Arthur, TX ... | 17 002 | 396 190 | 1.06 | 5 344 | 13.7 | 3 805 | 9.7 | 81 090 | 25.2 | 64 740 | 16 338 | 26 675 | 17 540 | 4 419 |
| Bellingham, WA ................. | 5 704 | 194 290 | 0.95 | 2 270 | 11.1 | 1 366 | 6.7 | 28 264 | 16.6 | 34 937 | 12 233 | 11 469 | 6 436 | 3 150 |
| Bend, OR ......................... | 1 244 | 158 319 | 1.02 | 1 773 | 11.1 | 1 154 | 7.2 | 26 582 | 19.9 | 31 185 | 8 672 | 12 368 | 5 453 | 3 421 |
| Billings, MT ...................... | 3 748 | 157 349 | 1.01 | 2 001 | 12.5 | 1 364 | 8.5 | 23 677 | 17.8 | 27 702 | 5 900 | 12 728 | 5 956 | 3 735 |
| Binghamton, NY ................. | 10 664 | 252 549 | 1.01 | 2 539 | 10.2 | 2 491 | 10.0 | 23 617 | 11.7 | 51 590 | 14 608 | 19 174 | 7 196 | 2 846 |
| Birmingham-Hoover, AL........ | 24 287 | 1 126 588 | 1.01 | 15 283 | 13.5 | 10 862 | 9.6 | 151 245 | 15.8 | 200 536 | 76 608 | 52 506 | 50 792 | 4 723 |
| Bismarck, ND .................... | 3 360 | 105 678 | 0.97 | 1 456 | 13.1 | 843 | 7.6 | 8 977 | 9.7 | 18 364 | 2 837 | 11 793 | 2 919 | 2 639 |
| Blacksburg-Christiansburg-Radford, VA ..................... | 12 985 | 165 112 | 1.05 | 1 449 | 8.9 | 1 216 | 7.5 | 22 214 | 17.0 | 26 424 | 3 901 | 14 143 | 4 335 | 2 629 |
| Bloomington, IN .................. | 15 454 | 190 029 | 0.99 | 1 887 | 9.7 | 1 417 | 7.3 | 26 243 | 16.8 | 28 433 | 3 879 | 13 913 | 5 335 | 3 142 |
| Bloomington-Normal, IL ........ | 10 676 | 174 894 | 1.08 | 2 097 | 12.3 | 1 058 | 6.2 | 15 110 | 10.6 | 21 558 | 3 018 | 9 137 | 4 044 | 2 486 |
| Boise City-Nampa, ID .......... | 13 394 | 608 225 | 0.99 | 8 500 | 13.5 | 3 852 | 6.1 | 101 716 | 18.9 | 90 263 | 39 206 | 22 498 | 14 147 | 2 271 |
| Boston-Cambridge-Quincy, MA-NH ........................... | 159 463 | 4 679 621 | 1.07 | 51 666 | 11.3 | 33 523 | 7.3 | 218 339 | 5.7 | 738 381 | 118 137 | 324 922 | 110 552 | 2 488 |
| Boston-Quincy, MA Div....... | 76 660 | 2 034 692 | 1.17 | 21 577 | 11.3 | 14 000 | 7.4 | 82 316 | 5.2 | 299 090 | 43 824 | 134 025 | 52 921 | 2 879 |
| Cambridge-Newton-Framingham, MA Div ........ | 55 412 | 1 563 942 | 1.09 | 17 581 | 11.6 | 10 644 | 7.0 | 57 135 | 4.5 | 235 049 | 49 458 | 95 124 | 29 725 | 2 046 |
| Peabody, MA Div ........... | 16 472 | 688 149 | 0.86 | 8 653 | 11.6 | 6 121 | 8.2 | 34 862 | 5.5 | 132 964 | 21 598 | 62 687 | 18 566 | 2 483 |
| Rockingham County-Strafford County, NH Div. | 10 919 | 392 838 | 0.89 | 3 855 | 9.2 | 2 758 | 6.6 | 44 026 | 12.4 | 71 278 | 3 257 | 33 086 | 9 340 | 2 307 |
| Boulder, CO ...................... | 8 949 | 320 108 | 1.18 | 3 066 | 10.2 | 1 510 | 5.0 | 37 869 | 14.7 | 37 898 | 13 066 | 11 007 | 6 584 | 2 197 |
| Bowling Green, KY ............. | 6 533 | 128 738 | 1.08 | 1 577 | 12.4 | 965 | 7.6 | 20 239 | 19.1 | 19 575 | 3 003 | 11 330 | 3 614 | 2 850 |
| Bremerton-Silverdale, WA .... | 8 722 | 239 902 | 0.92 | 2 886 | 11.3 | 1 952 | 7.7 | 29 481 | 13.9 | 42 588 | 8 011 | 12 406 | 8 132 | 3 188 |
| Bridgeport-Stamford-Norwalk, CT .......................... | 19 168 | 938 416 | 1.06 | 10 396 | 11.2 | 6 191 | 6.7 | 93 423 | 12.0 | 140 054 | 29 898 | 61 036 | 20 089 | 2 230 |
| Brownsville-Harlingen, TX..... | 3 730 | 397 909 | 0.98 | 7 924 | 19.1 | 2 296 | 5.5 | 134 358 | 37.6 | 51 310 | 13 223 | 24 101 | 18 272 | 4 405 |
| Brunswick, GA ................... | 1 590 | 112 379 | 1.03 | 1 405 | 12.4 | 1 029 | 9.1 | 21 925 | 23.1 | 20 491 | 3 621 | 9 287 | 5 757 | 5 147 |
| Buffalo-Niagara Falls, NY ..... | 32 706 | 1 141 608 | 1.01 | 11 868 | 10.5 | 11 692 | 10.3 | 95 207 | 10.2 | 224 738 | 118 894 | 37 028 | 38 537 | 3 379 |
| Burlington, NC ................... | 4 229 | 140 829 | 0.88 | 1 836 | 12.0 | 1 424 | 9.3 | 26 845 | 21.3 | 27 822 | 11 764 | 9 142 | 6 647 | 4 343 |
| Burlington-South Burlington, VT .................................. | 10 324 | 216 614 | 1.06 | 2 053 | 9.7 | 1 321 | 6.2 | 15 578 | 8.8 | 33 205 | 2 338 | 16 673 | 6 126 | 2 897 |
| Canton-Massillon, OH.......... | 9 669 | 393 839 | 0.94 | 4 476 | 11.1 | 4 093 | 10.1 | 48 633 | 14.7 | 80 400 | 38 589 | 28 244 | 13 682 | 3 417 |
| Cape Coral-Fort Myers, FL... | 8 488 | 604 861 | 0.95 | 6 308 | 10.0 | 5 852 | 9.3 | 127 288 | 27.2 | 144 273 | 39 238 | 54 897 | 19 711 | 3 143 |
| Cape Girardeau-Jackson, MO-IL ............................. | 4 529 | 98 896 | 1.07 | 1 160 | 12.0 | 896 | 9.2 | 11 977 | 15.3 | 17 869 | 1 277 | 10 030 | 4 011 | 4 151 |
| Carson City, NV ................. | 3 625 | 61 847 | 1.28 | 662 | 11.9 | 614 | 11.1 | 10 283 | 24.0 | 11 199 | 838 | 5 341 | 1 423 | 2 553 |
| Casper, WY ...................... | 1 645 | 74 993 | 1.01 | 1 033 | 13.5 | 667 | 8.7 | 10 302 | 15.9 | 11 731 | 545 | 6 591 | 2 626 | 3 453 |
| Cedar Rapids, IA ............... | 6 783 | 260 391 | 1.03 | 3 262 | 12.5 | 2 026 | 7.8 | 19 590 | 9.0 | 42 594 | 10 301 | 21 495 | 6 783 | 2 642 |
| Champaign-Urbana, IL.......... | 16 611 | 236 145 | 1.05 | 2 680 | 11.5 | 1 546 | 6.7 | 27 951 | 14.6 | 30 453 | 5 621 | 10 037 | 6 892 | 3 048 |

1. Per 1,000 estimated resident population.    2. Data for serious crimes have not been adjusted for underreporting; this may affect comparability between geographic areas and over time.    3. Per 100,000 population estimated by the FBI.

# Table C. Metropolitan Areas — Crime, Education, Money Income, and Poverty

| Area name | Serious crimes known to police, 2011 (cont.)[1] Rate[2] Violent | Property | Education — School enrollment and attainment, 2007–2011 Enrollment[3] Total | Percent private | Attainment[4] (percent) High school graduate or less | Bachelor's degree or more | Local government expenditures,[5] 2009–2010 Total current expenditures (mil dol) | Current expenditures per student (dollars) | Income and Poverty, 2007–2011 Per capita income[6] (dollars) | Median household income (dollars) | Percent of households with income of less than $25,000 | Percent of households with income of $100,000 or more | Percent of households with income of $200,000 or more | Percent below poverty level All persons | Related Children under 18 years | Related Children under 5 |
|---|---|---|---|---|---|---|---|---|---|---|---|---|---|---|---|---|
| | 46 | 47 | 48 | 49 | 50 | 51 | 52 | 53 | 54 | 55 | 56 | 57 | 58 | 59 | 60 | 61 |
| Abilene, TX | 298 | 3 029 | 43 871 | 24.0 | 47.2 | 21.2 | 256.0 | 9 175 | 21 619 | 42 644 | 27.4 | 13.4 | 1.9 | 15.8 | 19.8 | 27.6 |
| Akron, OH | 340 | 3 328 | 191 007 | 15.4 | 43.9 | 28.3 | 1 118.3 | 10 897 | 26 823 | 49 485 | 24.8 | 18.1 | 3.1 | 14.4 | 20.4 | 27.9 |
| Albany, GA | 522 | 4 338 | 47 434 | 9.6 | 53.5 | 16.4 | 252.5 | 9 052 | 19 800 | 36 613 | 35.0 | 11.3 | 2.0 | 24.9 | 35.2 | 42.9 |
| Albany-Schenectady-Troy, NY | 284 | 2 495 | 228 650 | 21.5 | 38.3 | 33.0 | 1 898.5 | 15 062 | 30 719 | 59 339 | 20.0 | 24.8 | 3.8 | 10.8 | 14.3 | 19.4 |
| Albuquerque, NM | 649 | 4 036 | 242 816 | 13.7 | 38.7 | 29.4 | 1 236.9 | 8 967 | 25 902 | 48 663 | 25.1 | 18.8 | 3.0 | 16.5 | 23.3 | 27.1 |
| Alexandria, LA | 676 | 4 321 | 38 157 | 12.8 | 54.9 | 17.3 | 243.1 | 8 933 | 21 454 | 40 402 | 31.9 | 13.2 | 1.5 | 18.5 | 27.1 | 32.4 |
| Allentown-Bethlehem-Easton, PA-NJ | 217 | 2 284 | 205 632 | 23.6 | 48.6 | 26.3 | 1 575.3 | 12 757 | 28 727 | 58 054 | 20.1 | 23.5 | 3.9 | 10.4 | 15.4 | 19.8 |
| Altoona, PA | 263 | 1 979 | 27 643 | 14.4 | 58.7 | 17.3 | 220.4 | 12 099 | 23 561 | 43 243 | 29.0 | 11.9 | 1.8 | 13.8 | 20.1 | 24.6 |
| Amarillo, TX | 517 | 4 043 | 69 118 | 8.1 | 41.9 | 22.9 | 395.9 | 8 578 | 24 272 | 47 234 | 26.0 | 16.3 | 2.8 | 15.8 | 21.6 | 26.1 |
| Ames, IA | 280 | 2 619 | 38 204 | 4.1 | 23.6 | 47.7 | 98.8 | 9 218 | 25 890 | 49 733 | 25.8 | 18.3 | 3.0 | 19.0 | 10.7 | 13.7 |
| Anchorage, AK | NA | NA | 104 443 | 13.7 | 32.9 | 29.7 | 893.6 | 13 401 | 34 121 | 74 271 | 12.5 | 33.4 | 6.2 | 8.3 | 10.9 | 13.8 |
| Anderson, IN | NA | NA | 29 967 | 16.8 | 54.9 | 16.8 | 184.1 | 9 514 | 22 150 | 44 035 | 26.0 | 11.7 | 1.3 | 16.1 | 24.6 | 33.8 |
| Anderson, SC | 585 | 5 123 | 45 563 | 13.8 | 52.2 | 18.1 | 258.4 | 8 319 | 22 494 | 42 854 | 29.8 | 13.6 | 1.6 | 15.8 | 22.8 | 32.0 |
| Ann Arbor, MI | 310 | 2 283 | 125 661 | 10.7 | 22.4 | 51.0 | 527.7 | 11 760 | 32 529 | 59 737 | 21.2 | 28.2 | 6.0 | 14.2 | 13.3 | 18.1 |
| Anniston-Oxford, AL | 509 | 4 269 | 29 245 | 11.3 | 55.8 | 15.8 | 159.2 | 8 574 | 20 903 | 39 467 | 33.7 | 11.3 | 1.6 | 20.4 | 28.4 | 32.9 |
| Appleton, WI | 143 | 1 720 | 58 574 | 15.7 | 43.7 | 25.9 | 383.5 | 10 241 | 27 704 | 58 389 | 17.2 | 20.3 | 2.5 | 7.8 | 9.7 | 10.9 |
| Asheville, NC | 218 | 2 522 | 91 056 | 16.9 | 40.1 | 28.8 | 468.4 | 8 614 | 25 990 | 44 512 | 26.5 | 14.1 | 2.4 | 14.8 | 21.3 | 26.3 |
| Athens-Clarke County, GA | 377 | 3 725 | 71 003 | 9.8 | 42.3 | 34.3 | 283.2 | 10 821 | 21 875 | 40 951 | 33.5 | 15.7 | 3.0 | 25.8 | 25.4 | 31.2 |
| Atlanta-Sandy Springs-Marietta, GA | 404 | 3 574 | 1 479 032 | 18.2 | 38.0 | 34.7 | 8 780.5 | 9 451 | 29 051 | 57 783 | 19.8 | 24.8 | 5.3 | 13.5 | 18.4 | 21.4 |
| Atlantic City-Hammonton, NJ | 507 | 3 410 | 70 008 | 15.5 | 50.3 | 23.2 | 792.1 | 16 955 | 27 613 | 55 222 | 21.4 | 22.1 | 3.7 | 12.5 | 17.7 | 23.0 |
| Auburn-Opelika, AL | 210 | 3 255 | 52 053 | 9.9 | 41.5 | 31.2 | 180.2 | 8 881 | 23 015 | 42 320 | 32.1 | 14.4 | 2.1 | 19.8 | 18.3 | 22.9 |
| Augusta-Richmond County, GA-SC | 361 | 4 364 | 147 271 | 13.6 | 47.5 | 23.3 | 814.5 | 8 724 | 23 463 | 45 162 | 28.4 | 16.3 | 2.6 | 18.4 | 26.5 | 32.1 |
| Austin-Round Rock-San Marcos, TX | 287 | 3 449 | 481 420 | 12.2 | 31.9 | 39.9 | 2 597.2 | 8 842 | 30 886 | 59 476 | 19.1 | 26.0 | 5.6 | 14.0 | 17.5 | 20.3 |
| Bakersfield-Delano, CA | 523 | 3 540 | 244 546 | 8.7 | 55.3 | 14.6 | 1 600.0 | 9 190 | 20 167 | 48 021 | 26.1 | 18.6 | 2.7 | 21.4 | 29.5 | 33.8 |
| Baltimore-Towson, MD | 473 | 2 762 | 727 722 | 22.4 | 38.8 | 35.1 | 5 203.4 | 13 483 | 34 425 | 67 891 | 17.2 | 32.0 | 7.2 | 10.1 | 12.9 | 15.4 |
| Bangor, ME | 80 | 2 804 | 41 302 | 15.5 | 45.9 | 23.4 | 259.8 | 11 527 | 23 366 | 43 601 | 28.9 | 13.1 | 1.7 | 16.3 | 18.5 | 25.0 |
| Barnstable Town, MA | 454 | 2 787 | 42 693 | 19.4 | 29.9 | 40.5 | 379.8 | 13 954 | 36 000 | 60 525 | 18.4 | 25.4 | 5.0 | 8.4 | 11.3 | 10.3 |
| Baton Rouge, LA | 587 | 4 066 | 226 648 | 19.3 | 47.1 | 26.0 | 1 275.7 | 10 764 | 25 554 | 50 146 | 26.0 | 20.6 | 3.3 | 16.1 | 21.5 | 25.0 |
| Battle Creek, MI | 629 | 3 805 | 35 987 | 12.0 | 47.5 | 18.7 | 249.2 | 11 332 | 22 430 | 42 287 | 28.8 | 12.8 | 1.7 | 17.0 | 24.4 | 33.6 |
| Bay City, MI | 276 | 1 961 | 26 516 | 13.4 | 46.9 | 18.3 | 160.9 | 10 445 | 23 642 | 45 962 | 25.0 | 13.5 | 1.4 | 12.7 | 18.1 | 24.7 |
| Beaumont-Port Arthur, TX | 546 | 3 873 | 97 920 | 9.2 | 52.4 | 16.2 | 653.0 | 9 572 | 23 159 | 45 622 | 27.9 | 16.7 | 2.3 | 16.6 | 23.4 | 28.3 |
| Bellingham, WA | 196 | 2 954 | 56 875 | 13.3 | 31.7 | 31.8 | 244.7 | 9 146 | 26 273 | 51 389 | 23.5 | 17.5 | 2.6 | 15.2 | 15.5 | 21.3 |
| Bend, OR | 331 | 3 089 | 35 174 | 15.2 | 31.1 | 29.8 | 219.4 | 9 055 | 27 965 | 52 962 | 20.4 | 18.7 | 3.1 | 11.4 | 15.6 | 15.1 |
| Billings, MT | 263 | 3 472 | 36 445 | 12.8 | 39.5 | 29.3 | 218.8 | 9 385 | 27 188 | 49 952 | 23.1 | 17.0 | 2.6 | 11.4 | 14.8 | 23.0 |
| Binghamton, NY | 217 | 2 629 | 67 002 | 8.7 | 45.2 | 25.0 | 589.7 | 16 033 | 24 960 | 47 398 | 26.6 | 16.1 | 2.3 | 14.8 | 19.9 | 25.1 |
| Birmingham-Hoover, AL | 540 | 4 184 | 281 252 | 17.0 | 43.9 | 26.7 | 1 637.0 | 9 236 | 26 841 | 48 411 | 25.9 | 19.3 | 3.6 | 14.6 | 20.6 | 23.3 |
| Bismarck, ND | 222 | 2 417 | 26 401 | 19.5 | 33.8 | 29.7 | 147.2 | 9 681 | 29 383 | 55 933 | 20.4 | 20.0 | 2.6 | 8.8 | 10.7 | 16.4 |
| Blacksburg-Christiansburg-Radford, VA | 146 | 2 483 | 61 750 | 6.3 | 42.4 | 30.0 | 180.5 | 9 709 | 21 870 | 42 468 | 31.9 | 14.1 | 2.2 | 21.5 | 16.3 | 21.5 |
| Bloomington, IN | 206 | 2 936 | 72 185 | 7.7 | 42.2 | 31.6 | 208.2 | 9 328 | 22 104 | 40 490 | 32.8 | 12.9 | 2.2 | 21.6 | 17.4 | 24.1 |
| Bloomington-Normal, IL | 323 | 2 162 | 57 352 | 15.1 | 32.9 | 41.1 | 251.5 | 9 851 | 29 425 | 59 410 | 20.6 | 25.2 | 3.7 | 13.4 | 11.5 | 12.0 |
| Boise City-Nampa, ID | 211 | 2 061 | 172 103 | 13.5 | 36.6 | 28.5 | 773.5 | 6 923 | 24 503 | 50 899 | 21.6 | 17.3 | 2.9 | 13.8 | 17.5 | 21.7 |
| Boston-Cambridge-Quincy, MA-NH | 377 | 2 111 | 1 225 286 | 30.9 | 34.5 | 42.6 | 8 758.1 | 13 327 | 37 846 | 71 878 | 18.3 | 34.7 | 8.8 | 9.8 | 11.2 | 12.8 |
| Boston-Quincy, MA Div | 530 | 2 350 | 519 368 | 35.1 | 36.2 | 40.8 | 3 574.1 | 13 526 | 36 773 | 67 701 | 20.5 | 32.9 | 8.4 | 11.9 | 13.7 | 15.1 |
| Cambridge-Newton-Framingham, MA Div | 250 | 1 797 | 401 854 | 32.6 | 30.5 | 49.8 | 2 940.9 | 13 782 | 41 453 | 79 691 | 15.6 | 39.2 | 10.6 | 7.7 | 7.8 | 9.2 |
| Peabody, MA Div | 372 | 2 111 | 194 394 | 23.3 | 38.2 | 36.4 | 1 460.6 | 12 870 | 34 858 | 65 785 | 20.2 | 31.4 | 7.5 | 10.6 | 14.2 | 15.5 |
| Rockingham County-Strafford County, NH Div | 151 | 2 156 | 109 670 | 18.3 | 35.4 | 34.9 | 782.5 | 11 848 | 35 066 | 71 982 | 14.5 | 33.1 | 6.1 | 6.6 | 7.0 | 10.0 |
| Boulder, CO | 201 | 1 996 | 91 246 | 12.7 | 19.3 | 57.7 | 497.6 | 8 929 | 37 720 | 66 479 | 18.8 | 32.4 | 8.4 | 13.1 | 12.4 | 16.3 |
| Bowling Green, KY | 165 | 2 685 | 37 733 | 7.5 | 47.8 | 25.8 | 160.5 | 8 186 | 23 239 | 42 162 | 30.4 | 13.6 | 2.2 | 18.6 | 23.9 | 27.9 |
| Bremerton-Silverdale, WA | 307 | 2 881 | 59 704 | 14.4 | 31.0 | 28.7 | 365.0 | 9 864 | 30 913 | 61 112 | 16.9 | 25.1 | 3.9 | 9.8 | 11.9 | 15.9 |
| Bridgeport-Stamford-Norwalk, CT | 294 | 1 935 | 246 238 | 24.8 | 34.9 | 44.0 | 2 291.2 | 15 732 | 48 922 | 82 558 | 15.1 | 42.0 | 16.7 | 8.3 | 9.7 | 10.9 |
| Brownsville-Harlingen, TX | 293 | 4 112 | 125 727 | 5.0 | 61.4 | 14.6 | 919.3 | 9 197 | 14 183 | 32 156 | 40.1 | 10.1 | 1.6 | 34.9 | 47.5 | 51.2 |
| Brunswick, GA | 509 | 4 638 | 26 602 | 9.2 | 50.5 | 21.2 | 177.5 | 9 754 | 25 324 | 46 199 | 27.1 | 16.9 | 2.9 | 16.7 | 25.1 | 31.2 |
| Buffalo-Niagara Falls, NY | 439 | 2 940 | 296 942 | 18.6 | 42.0 | 28.0 | 2 363.6 | 14 289 | 26 924 | 48 332 | 26.5 | 18.2 | 2.8 | 13.9 | 20.0 | 25.6 |
| Burlington, NC | 421 | 3 922 | 38 543 | 19.0 | 48.0 | 21.6 | 181.8 | 7 599 | 23 477 | 44 430 | 27.5 | 13.9 | 2.2 | 16.1 | 24.8 | 30.8 |
| Burlington-South Burlington, VT | 182 | 2 714 | 59 433 | 16.3 | 34.8 | 39.3 | 463.6 | 14 949 | 31 042 | 60 552 | 18.5 | 23.7 | 4.4 | 10.7 | 11.4 | 15.6 |
| Canton-Massillon, OH | 296 | 3 121 | 103 416 | 17.5 | 52.7 | 20.1 | 621.0 | 9 800 | 24 038 | 45 171 | 26.2 | 13.9 | 2.1 | 13.6 | 20.7 | 26.5 |
| Cape Coral-Fort Myers, FL | 353 | 2 790 | 126 928 | 13.7 | 46.0 | 24.6 | 707.5 | 8 790 | 28 946 | 49 444 | 22.2 | 18.4 | 4.1 | 13.5 | 21.3 | 26.6 |
| Cape Girardeau-Jackson, MO-IL | 464 | 3 688 | 26 133 | 14.0 | 51.5 | 22.7 | 111.6 | 8 684 | 22 064 | 43 122 | 27.7 | 12.3 | 1.9 | 16.0 | 23.8 | 34.1 |
| Carson City, NV | 266 | 2 287 | 12 802 | 9.7 | 45.1 | 21.0 | 109.0 | 8 486 | 27 704 | 54 235 | 22.5 | 19.0 | 2.8 | 14.4 | 22.3 | 30.3 |
| Casper, WY | 247 | 3 205 | 19 223 | 10.8 | 38.4 | 21.6 | 173.5 | 14 792 | 29 620 | 53 519 | 18.9 | 21.1 | 3.5 | 8.4 | 10.0 | 13.9 |
| Cedar Rapids, IA | 186 | 2 456 | 68 858 | 18.8 | 37.5 | 27.6 | 445.6 | 10 331 | 28 493 | 55 196 | 19.5 | 20.4 | 2.8 | 9.4 | 10.7 | 14.9 |
| Champaign-Urbana, IL | 565 | 2 483 | 88 226 | 6.9 | 33.1 | 38.5 | 321.7 | 10 638 | 25 392 | 46 152 | 28.8 | 17.9 | 3.1 | 19.8 | 19.1 | 23.1 |

1. Data for serious crimes have not been adjusted for underreporting; this may affect comparability between geographic areas and over time. 2. Per 100,000 population estimated by the FBI. 3. All persons 3 years old and over enrolled in nursery school through college. 4. Persons 25 years old and over. 5. Elementary and secondary education expenditures. 6. Based on resident population estimated as of July 1, 2009.

# Table C. Metropolitan Areas — **Personal Income**

| Area name | \multicolumn{9}{c}{Personal income, 2011} |
| | Total (mil dol) | Percent change, 2010–2011 | Per capita[1] Dollars | Per capita[1] Rank | Wages and salaries[2] (mil dol) | Proprietors' income (mil dol) | Dividends, interest, and rent (mil dol) | Transfer payments Total (mil dol) | Government payments to individuals Total (mil dol) | Social Security (mil dol) | Medical payments (mil dol) | Income maintenance (mil dol) | Unemployment insurance (mil dol) |
|---|---|---|---|---|---|---|---|---|---|---|---|---|---|
| | 62 | 63 | 64 | 65 | 66 | 67 | 68 | 69 | 70 | 71 | 72 | 73 | 74 |
| Abilene, TX .......................... | 5 920 | 5.2 | 35 571 | 202 | 3 359 | 582 | 999 | 1 297 | 1 261 | 369 | 614 | 143 | 31 |
| Akron, OH ........................... | 28 066 | 5.1 | 40 011 | 106 | 17 467 | 1 815 | 3 806 | 5 759 | 5 604 | 1 775 | 2 385 | 627 | 210 |
| Albany, GA .......................... | 5 018 | 4.2 | 31 821 | 305 | 3 063 | 344 | 738 | 1 332 | 1 297 | 347 | 487 | 282 | 43 |
| Albany-Schenectady-Troy, NY .................................. | 39 168 | 4.2 | 44 944 | 42 | 26 150 | 2 806 | 6 993 | 7 097 | 6 904 | 2 336 | 2 826 | 670 | 308 |
| Albuquerque, NM ................. | 31 459 | 3.8 | 35 007 | 226 | 20 825 | 1 808 | 4 686 | 6 447 | 6 249 | 1 918 | 2 578 | 814 | 287 |
| Alexandria, LA..................... | 5 679 | 3.6 | 36 758 | 182 | 3 152 | 582 | 816 | 1 456 | 1 421 | 348 | 764 | 185 | 22 |
| Allentown-Bethlehem-Easton, PA-NJ ..................... | 33 075 | 4.4 | 40 095 | 104 | 19 006 | 2 014 | 5 034 | 6 711 | 6 528 | 2 376 | 2 833 | 553 | 424 |
| Altoona, PA ......................... | 4 386 | 4.8 | 34 511 | 244 | 2 824 | 270 | 619 | 1 224 | 1 196 | 363 | 520 | 111 | 75 |
| Amarillo, TX ........................ | 9 383 | 5.2 | 36 968 | 176 | 5 710 | 1 301 | 1 359 | 1 627 | 1 570 | 503 | 668 | 204 | 42 |
| Ames, IA ............................. | 3 356 | 6.2 | 37 429 | 164 | 2 325 | 399 | 527 | 453 | 433 | 163 | 162 | 39 | 13 |
| Anchorage, AK .................... | 18 914 | 5.5 | 48 810 | 21 | 12 940 | 2 094 | 2 778 | 2 648 | 2 565 | 535 | 977 | 308 | 130 |
| Anderson, IN ....................... | 3 992 | 3.4 | 30 421 | 336 | 1 791 | 233 | 440 | 1 143 | 1 114 | 426 | 462 | 119 | 50 |
| Anderson, SC ...................... | 5 854 | 4.5 | 31 059 | 329 | 2 780 | 362 | 716 | 1 494 | 1 453 | 583 | 530 | 179 | 40 |
| Ann Arbor, MI...................... | 14 204 | 6.8 | 40 821 | 89 | 11 879 | 810 | 2 327 | 2 071 | 1 994 | 772 | 759 | 190 | 94 |
| Anniston-Oxford, AL............. | 3 741 | 2.6 | 31 758 | 308 | 2 447 | 194 | 564 | 1 000 | 974 | 335 | 387 | 135 | 23 |
| Appleton, WI ........................ | 8 983 | 6.0 | 39 504 | 121 | 6 048 | 639 | 1 242 | 1 235 | 1 184 | 519 | 419 | 92 | 81 |
| Asheville, NC ....................... | 14 639 | 4.5 | 34 122 | 256 | 8 019 | 924 | 3 076 | 3 646 | 3 551 | 1 392 | 1 454 | 342 | 152 |
| Athens-Clarke County, GA .. | 6 051 | 3.8 | 31 302 | 324 | 4 063 | 319 | 1 136 | 1 134 | 1 092 | 376 | 402 | 165 | 44 |
| Atlanta-Sandy Springs-Marietta, GA ............................. | 212 830 | 5.6 | 39 713 | 116 | 151 417 | 20 562 | 29 687 | 29 152 | 27 966 | 9 347 | 10 223 | 4 509 | 1 409 |
| Atlantic City-Hammonton, NJ | 11 046 | 3.5 | 40 262 | 99 | 7 389 | 1 096 | 1 648 | 2 519 | 2 459 | 727 | 1 053 | 274 | 259 |
| Auburn-Opelika, AL.............. | 4 190 | 5.6 | 29 208 | 351 | 2 280 | 287 | 684 | 781 | 749 | 274 | 245 | 122 | 24 |
| Augusta-Richmond County, GA-SC ............................... | 19 463 | 4.9 | 34 640 | 238 | 12 821 | 944 | 2 760 | 4 372 | 4 250 | 1 342 | 1 633 | 663 | 145 |
| Austin-Round Rock-San Marcos, TX ............................. | 72 152 | 7.2 | 40 455 | 96 | 50 870 | 7 611 | 11 634 | 8 108 | 7 713 | 2 667 | 2 928 | 995 | 358 |
| Bakersfield-Delano, CA........ | 26 744 | 6.6 | 31 400 | 317 | 16 546 | 3 699 | 3 259 | 5 437 | 5 249 | 1 301 | 2 042 | 1 039 | 379 |
| Baltimore-Towson, MD ........ | 139 528 | 5.5 | 51 126 | 15 | 92 406 | 8 892 | 21 092 | 20 713 | 20 113 | 6 061 | 9 511 | 2 405 | 847 |
| Bangor, ME .......................... | 5 220 | 4.1 | 33 940 | 258 | 3 380 | 385 | 632 | 1 375 | 1 341 | 408 | 613 | 156 | 44 |
| Barnstable Town, MA ........... | 11 968 | 4.9 | 55 465 | 9 | 4 761 | 851 | 3 418 | 2 306 | 2 259 | 932 | 946 | 149 | 144 |
| Baton Rouge, LA .................. | 31 510 | 4.7 | 38 985 | 132 | 21 280 | 2 259 | 4 597 | 5 569 | 5 386 | 1 582 | 2 474 | 847 | 120 |
| Battle Creek, MI .................. | 4 544 | 2.7 | 33 541 | 265 | 3 188 | 195 | 589 | 1 241 | 1 211 | 409 | 479 | 187 | 46 |
| Bay City, MI ......................... | 3 614 | 5.3 | 33 737 | 262 | 1 810 | 191 | 533 | 1 036 | 1 012 | 369 | 405 | 117 | 40 |
| Beaumont-Port Arthur, TX .... | 15 082 | 5.7 | 38 620 | 140 | 9 796 | 1 108 | 2 204 | 3 526 | 3 437 | 975 | 1 781 | 375 | 120 |
| Bellingham, WA ................... | 7 759 | 5.4 | 38 098 | 153 | 4 345 | 662 | 1 698 | 1 458 | 1 413 | 492 | 500 | 173 | 88 |
| Bend, OR ............................. | 5 946 | 4.9 | 37 084 | 172 | 2 923 | 751 | 1 383 | 1 291 | 1 256 | 469 | 444 | 122 | 120 |
| Billings, MT .......................... | 6 309 | 5.8 | 39 405 | 123 | 4 189 | 441 | 1 183 | 1 043 | 1 008 | 384 | 381 | 92 | 31 |
| Binghamton, NY................... | 9 000 | 3.6 | 35 990 | 196 | 5 359 | 533 | 1 573 | 2 202 | 2 147 | 767 | 911 | 260 | 97 |
| Birmingham-Hoover, AL........ | 46 215 | 4.7 | 40 816 | 90 | 28 515 | 4 957 | 7 558 | 8 800 | 8 545 | 3 074 | 3 438 | 1 124 | 208 |
| Bismarck, ND ...................... | 4 709 | 7.9 | 42 468 | 71 | 3 265 | 325 | 740 | 728 | 704 | 253 | 294 | 57 | 18 |
| Blacksburg-Christiansburg-Radford, VA ....................... | 4 831 | 5.4 | 29 733 | 346 | 3 269 | 177 | 829 | 1 066 | 1 030 | 387 | 407 | 111 | 26 |
| Bloomington, IN ................... | 6 004 | 4.5 | 30 915 | 332 | 3 696 | 282 | 942 | 1 162 | 1 119 | 420 | 443 | 108 | 52 |
| Bloomington-Normal, IL ........ | 7 132 | 4.9 | 41 816 | 78 | 5 630 | 564 | 1 037 | 837 | 799 | 322 | 245 | 97 | 56 |
| Boise City-Nampa, ID .......... | 21 512 | 4.6 | 34 274 | 250 | 13 465 | 2 713 | 3 303 | 3 728 | 3 589 | 1 284 | 1 345 | 432 | 188 |
| Boston-Cambridge-Quincy, MA-NH ............................. | 265 794 | 5.2 | 57 893 | 7 | 194 531 | 25 563 | 44 496 | 35 789 | 34 773 | 10 173 | 16 890 | 3 922 | 2 242 |
| Boston-Quincy, MA Div....... | 111 030 | 5.2 | 58 316 | X | 90 781 | 13 756 | 17 257 | 16 457 | 16 036 | 3 984 | 8 422 | 1 897 | 1 021 |
| Cambridge-Newton-Framingham, MA Div ............ | 94 619 | 5.3 | 62 324 | X | 73 045 | 7 247 | 17 759 | 10 329 | 9 993 | 3 311 | 4 525 | 1 000 | 717 |
| Peabody, MA Div .............. | 39 850 | 5.3 | 53 209 | X | 19 668 | 2 567 | 6 688 | 6 425 | 6 260 | 1 823 | 2 966 | 807 | 435 |
| Rockingham County-Strafford County, NH Div..... | 20 295 | 4.9 | 48 315 | X | 11 037 | 1 994 | 2 793 | 2 577 | 2 484 | 1 055 | 977 | 218 | 70 |
| Boulder, CO ......................... | 15 536 | 5.2 | 51 893 | 13 | 11 351 | 1 556 | 3 481 | 1 408 | 1 341 | 521 | 510 | 100 | 89 |
| Bowling Green, KY ............... | 4 010 | 5.2 | 31 422 | 315 | 2 752 | 243 | 557 | 921 | 893 | 277 | 370 | 110 | 38 |
| Bremerton-Silverdale, WA .... | 10 842 | 4.7 | 42 580 | 68 | 6 213 | 494 | 2 090 | 1 808 | 1 754 | 552 | 647 | 175 | 105 |
| Bridgeport-Stamford-Norwalk, CT ............................. | 72 687 | 4.3 | 78 504 | 1 | 42 770 | 9 641 | 16 294 | 6 961 | 6 756 | 2 193 | 3 283 | 590 | 447 |
| Brownsville-Harlingen, TX..... | 9 623 | 4.6 | 23 236 | 365 | 5 112 | 790 | 1 027 | 3 180 | 3 086 | 545 | 1 482 | 765 | 109 |
| Brunswick, GA ..................... | 3 693 | 4.0 | 32 708 | 290 | 1 972 | 174 | 780 | 873 | 848 | 298 | 343 | 112 | 30 |
| Buffalo-Niagara Falls, NY .... | 45 499 | 4.4 | 40 121 | 103 | 28 639 | 3 005 | 7 106 | 10 223 | 9 972 | 3 416 | 4 240 | 1 174 | 449 |
| Burlington, NC ..................... | 4 808 | 4.7 | 31 363 | 321 | 2 670 | 310 | 760 | 1 160 | 1 126 | 417 | 453 | 130 | 68 |
| Burlington-South Burlington, VT ................................... | 9 320 | 5.0 | 43 853 | 51 | 6 772 | 754 | 1 427 | 1 507 | 1 460 | 478 | 653 | 182 | 48 |
| Canton-Massillon, OH.......... | 14 030 | 5.8 | 34 739 | 233 | 7 831 | 1 052 | 1 894 | 3 440 | 3 351 | 1 168 | 1 383 | 377 | 123 |
| Cape Coral-Fort Myers, FL... | 27 161 | 5.4 | 43 022 | 64 | 10 447 | 1 580 | 10 783 | 5 282 | 5 129 | 2 158 | 2 048 | 472 | 139 |
| Cape Girardeau-Jackson, MO-IL ................................ | 3 290 | 3.8 | 33 907 | 259 | 2 081 | 302 | 531 | 745 | 723 | 248 | 299 | 89 | 24 |
| Carson City, NV .................. | 2 208 | 2.7 | 39 833 | 113 | 1 596 | 240 | 462 | 435 | 422 | 146 | 176 | 40 | 30 |
| Casper, WY ......................... | 4 132 | 7.7 | 54 108 | 11 | 2 410 | 574 | 963 | 501 | 485 | 173 | 190 | 46 | 22 |
| Cedar Rapids, IA ................. | 11 075 | 6.9 | 42 503 | 69 | 7 868 | 966 | 1 716 | 1 723 | 1 666 | 650 | 645 | 158 | 85 |
| Champaign-Urbana, IL.......... | 8 654 | 3.4 | 37 246 | 169 | 5 670 | 748 | 1 682 | 1 177 | 1 126 | 389 | 380 | 156 | 84 |

1. Based on the resident population estimated as of July 1 of the year shown.  2. Includes other labor income.

# Table C. Metropolitan Areas — Earnings, Social Security, and Housing

| Area name | Earnings, 2011 | | | | | | | | | Social Security beneficiaries, December 2011 | | | Housing units, 2010 | |
|---|---|---|---|---|---|---|---|---|---|---|---|---|---|---|
| | | | Percent by selected industries | | | | | | | | | Supplemental Security Income recipients, December 2011 | | |
| | | | Goods-related[1] | | Service-related and health | | | | | | | | | |
| | Total (mil dol) | Farm | Total | Manu-facturing | Infor-mation, profes-sional, and technical services | Retail trade | Finance, insur-ance, and real estate | Health care and social services | Govern-ment | Number | Rate[2] | | Total | Percent change, 2000–2010 |
| | 75 | 76 | 77 | 78 | 79 | 80 | 81 | 82 | 83 | 84 | 85 | 86 | 87 | 88 |
| Abilene, TX .................... | 3 941 | 0.3 | 15.6 | 3.5 | 5.3 | 7.2 | 6.5 | 13.8 | 28.8 | 29 895 | 180 | 4 458 | 69 721 | 6.9 |
| Akron, OH ...................... | 19 282 | 0.1 | 19.9 | 15.0 | 8.3 | 6.5 | 5.9 | 13.6 | 14.9 | 130 255 | 186 | 15 620 | 312 581 | 7.4 |
| Albany, GA ..................... | 3 407 | 4.7 | 4.3 | D | 6.5 | 6.9 | 3.5 | 14.3 | 27.2 | 28 775 | 182 | 7 055 | 66 060 | 3.6 |
| Albany-Schenectady-Troy, NY .............................. | 28 955 | 0.2 | 13.2 | 6.9 | 13.4 | 6.2 | 8.2 | 11.9 | 26.0 | 168 710 | 194 | 20 634 | 393 297 | 8.1 |
| Albuquerque, NM ............. | 22 632 | 0.2 | 12.8 | 6.3 | 14.9 | 6.8 | 5.4 | 11.8 | 26.6 | 150 685 | 168 | 21 953 | 374 404 | 22.4 |
| Alexandria, LA ................. | 3 734 | 0.9 | 18.7 | 10.0 | 5.9 | 7.5 | 3.8 | 18.0 | 24.9 | 31 015 | 201 | 7 895 | 64 570 | 6.6 |
| Allentown-Bethlehem-Eas-ton, PA-NJ ..................... | 21 020 | 0.2 | 18.6 | 13.3 | 8.0 | 6.5 | 5.2 | 16.6 | 12.2 | 170 270 | 206 | 18 444 | 342 200 | 11.4 |
| Altoona, PA ..................... | 3 094 | 1.1 | 18.1 | 13.2 | 6.3 | 9.1 | 4.0 | 19.5 | 16.0 | 29 105 | 229 | 4 913 | 56 276 | 2.2 |
| Amarillo, TX .................... | 7 012 | 1.8 | 8.0 | D | 8.0 | 7.4 | 6.9 | 13.5 | 16.1 | 38 590 | 152 | 4 564 | 102 546 | 12.0 |
| Ames, IA ........................ | 2 724 | 3.9 | 20.7 | 15.7 | 5.1 | 5.0 | 2.9 | 7.6 | 40.1 | 11 415 | 127 | 655 | 36 789 | 20.1 |
| Anchorage, AK ................ | 15 034 | 0.0 | 13.2 | 0.9 | 12.0 | 5.9 | 6.2 | 11.7 | 28.6 | 42 450 | 110 | 7 283 | 154 361 | 20.9 |
| Anderson, IN ................... | 2 024 | 2.7 | 19.7 | 15.5 | 3.9 | 6.8 | 4.3 | 16.3 | 16.7 | 30 720 | 234 | 3 159 | 59 068 | 3.7 |
| Anderson, SC ................. | 3 142 | 0.1 | 30.5 | 24.2 | 3.7 | 9.6 | 3.9 | 8.1 | 21.6 | 44 645 | 237 | 4 170 | 84 774 | 15.8 |
| Ann Arbor, MI .................. | 12 689 | 0.2 | 12.0 | 9.7 | 14.6 | 4.7 | 4.2 | 11.1 | 35.5 | 50 220 | 144 | 5 129 | 147 573 | 12.7 |
| Anniston-Oxford, AL .......... | 2 641 | 0.1 | 15.6 | 13.1 | 5.5 | 7.2 | 2.6 | 9.2 | 36.4 | 28 520 | 242 | 4 689 | 53 289 | 3.8 |
| Appleton, WI ................... | 6 687 | 1.9 | 30.9 | 21.9 | 6.9 | 6.7 | 8.1 | 10.2 | 11.2 | 37 810 | 166 | 2 523 | 92 844 | 18.5 |
| Asheville, NC .................. | 8 942 | 0.7 | 19.1 | 13.3 | 6.2 | 8.6 | 5.5 | 18.1 | 17.9 | 106 065 | 247 | 9 853 | 213 637 | 21.8 |
| Athens-Clarke County, GA ... | 4 382 | 1.0 | 15.4 | 12.0 | 4.3 | 6.5 | 5.7 | 15.4 | 33.5 | 29 240 | 151 | 4 637 | 81 719 | 21.0 |
| Atlanta-Sandy Springs-Mari-etta, GA........................ | 171 979 | 0.0 | 12.2 | 7.3 | 18.3 | 5.8 | 10.0 | 8.5 | 12.7 | 692 525 | 129 | 99 264 | 2 165 495 | 31.7 |
| Atlantic City-Hammonton, NJ | 8 485 | 0.8 | 9.2 | 1.9 | 6.0 | 6.9 | 3.8 | 14.1 | 21.7 | 52 965 | 193 | 6 512 | 126 647 | 11.0 |
| Auburn-Opelika, AL........... | 2 567 | 0.1 | 17.2 | 11.7 | 5.1 | 7.5 | 4.5 | 7.2 | 37.1 | 20 920 | 146 | 3 298 | 62 391 | 24.0 |
| Augusta-Richmond County, GA-SC........................... | 13 765 | 0.4 | 16.5 | 10.2 | 7.8 | 6.1 | 3.6 | 10.1 | 30.8 | 104 665 | 186 | 16 247 | 236 949 | 15.8 |
| Austin-Round Rock-San Mar-cos, TX........................ | 58 481 | 0.1 | 17.3 | 9.7 | 16.9 | 6.1 | 8.2 | 9.0 | 17.6 | 196 015 | 110 | 25 172 | 706 505 | 42.4 |
| Bakersfield-Delano, CA........ | 20 245 | 9.5 | 19.2 | 5.1 | 5.8 | 5.7 | 3.2 | 8.0 | 23.3 | 109 465 | 129 | 33 616 | 284 367 | 22.8 |
| Baltimore-Towson, MD ....... | 101 298 | 0.1 | 12.3 | 5.7 | 14.5 | 5.2 | 7.6 | 12.4 | 24.6 | 438 960 | 161 | 64 615 | 1 132 251 | 8.0 |
| Bangor, ME ..................... | 3 765 | 0.3 | 11.5 | 6.3 | 5.8 | 10.0 | 4.0 | 21.9 | 21.2 | 34 310 | 223 | 5 359 | 73 860 | 10.5 |
| Barnstable Town, MA .......... | 5 612 | 0.1 | 11.4 | 2.4 | 10.2 | 10.2 | 5.7 | 18.2 | 19.1 | 66 520 | 308 | 3 642 | 160 281 | 9.0 |
| Baton Rouge, LA ................ | 23 539 | 0.4 | 25.6 | 11.9 | 8.9 | 6.1 | 6.0 | 10.1 | 19.4 | 125 755 | 156 | 25 740 | 329 729 | 16.7 |
| Battle Creek, MI ................ | 3 383 | 1.3 | 26.7 | 23.0 | D | 5.5 | 2.1 | 12.9 | 21.9 | 30 980 | 229 | 4 863 | 61 042 | 4.0 |
| Bay City, MI .................... | 2 001 | 2.8 | 16.2 | 12.8 | 12.9 | 8.5 | 4.2 | 17.3 | 17.2 | 26 970 | 252 | 3 099 | 48 220 | 3.9 |
| Beaumont-Port Arthur, TX .... | 10 904 | 0.2 | 39.1 | 23.3 | 7.3 | 6.7 | 3.6 | 10.5 | 13.6 | 73 400 | 188 | 12 777 | 162 334 | 3.6 |
| Bellingham, WA ............... | 5 007 | 2.9 | 22.7 | 13.7 | 9.6 | 8.4 | 4.7 | 11.5 | 19.0 | 37 155 | 182 | 4 221 | 90 665 | 22.7 |
| Bend, OR ....................... | 3 674 | -0.3 | 14.7 | 6.2 | 11.7 | 9.3 | 8.7 | 18.8 | 14.2 | 34 545 | 215 | 2 010 | 80 139 | 46.8 |
| Billings, MT .................... | 4 630 | 0.2 | 16.7 | 6.5 | 8.8 | 8.3 | 6.3 | 17.2 | 14.1 | 29 715 | 186 | 2 562 | 70 384 | 17.2 |
| Binghamton, NY ............... | 5 893 | 0.4 | 24.8 | 18.8 | 6.3 | 7.0 | 4.6 | 15.1 | 22.7 | 58 070 | 232 | 8 152 | 112 766 | 2.3 |
| Birmingham-Hoover, AL....... | 33 472 | -0.1 | 16.0 | 7.3 | 10.9 | 6.2 | 10.3 | 12.7 | 15.5 | 230 620 | 204 | 37 181 | 500 025 | 10.1 |
| Bismarck, ND .................. | 3 591 | 2.5 | 10.9 | 3.4 | 8.0 | 7.5 | 6.4 | 16.6 | 21.1 | 19 670 | 177 | 1 225 | 47 833 | 20.8 |
| Blacksburg-Christiansburg-Radford, VA ................... | 3 446 | 0.1 | D | 21.3 | D | 6.4 | 2.8 | D | 32.8 | 29 575 | 182 | 3 004 | 70 550 | 12.5 |
| Bloomington, IN ............... | 3 978 | 1.0 | 19.2 | 14.3 | 6.3 | 5.9 | 3.4 | 12.9 | 32.0 | 31 550 | 162 | 2 849 | 84 409 | 11.4 |
| Bloomington-Normal, IL ....... | 6 195 | 3.5 | 7.7 | 4.3 | D | 4.8 | 22.1 | 10.0 | 14.2 | 23 450 | 137 | 1 729 | 69 656 | 16.1 |
| Boise City-Nampa, ID ......... | 16 178 | 2.3 | 18.4 | 11.7 | 10.1 | 7.5 | 7.6 | 12.9 | 15.7 | 98 970 | 158 | 10 923 | 246 052 | 35.8 |
| Boston-Cambridge-Quincy, MA-NH ......................... | 220 095 | 0.0 | 13.2 | 8.8 | 20.7 | 4.3 | 14.1 | 12.4 | 10.5 | 745 470 | 162 | 114 214 | 1 883 206 | 7.5 |
| Boston-Quincy, MA Div....... | 104 537 | 0.0 | 7.9 | 3.8 | 17.3 | 3.8 | 22.2 | 15.0 | 11.2 | 299 680 | 157 | 58 641 | 786 042 | 7.8 |
| Cambridge-Newton-Fra-mingham, MA Div ......... | 80 292 | 0.1 | 16.2 | 11.9 | 29.0 | 3.6 | 6.5 | 8.6 | 8.8 | 232 645 | 153 | 27 571 | 612 004 | 6.1 |
| Peabody, MA Div .............. | 22 235 | 0.0 | 25.2 | 20.0 | 12.1 | 6.5 | 6.3 | 15.5 | 12.4 | 135 885 | 181 | 23 712 | 306 754 | 6.8 |
| Rockingham County-Straf-ford County, NH Div..... | 13 030 | 0.0 | 17.9 | 11.2 | 11.5 | 9.5 | 9.9 | 10.6 | 12.5 | 77 260 | 184 | 4 290 | 178 406 | 12.5 |
| Boulder, CO .................... | 12 907 | 0.1 | 16.3 | 12.5 | 30.3 | 4.8 | 6.4 | 9.4 | 15.2 | 37 330 | 125 | 2 445 | 127 071 | 14.0 |
| Bowling Green, KY ............ | 2 996 | 0.8 | 24.1 | 16.9 | 4.8 | 7.2 | 5.3 | 13.5 | 18.6 | 22 085 | 173 | 3 976 | 53 690 | 20.8 |
| Bremerton-Silverdale, WA .... | 6 708 | 0.2 | 6.0 | 1.6 | 7.1 | 6.0 | 3.0 | 9.9 | 56.2 | 44 170 | 173 | 5 014 | 107 367 | 15.9 |
| Bridgeport-Stamford-Nor-walk, CT ....................... | 52 411 | 0.0 | D | 9.7 | 14.4 | 5.2 | 28.0 | 8.4 | 7.1 | 143 870 | 155 | 11 577 | 361 221 | 6.4 |
| Brownsville-Harlingen, TX..... | 5 902 | 1.0 | 8.9 | 5.2 | 4.2 | 8.8 | 4.4 | 20.7 | 29.6 | 56 485 | 136 | 22 317 | 141 924 | 18.6 |
| Brunswick, GA ................. | 2 146 | 0.1 | 14.9 | 8.3 | D | 7.8 | 4.5 | 8.6 | 33.8 | 22 940 | 203 | 2 864 | 58 022 | 29.3 |
| Buffalo-Niagara Falls, NY .... | 31 644 | 0.3 | 17.8 | 12.8 | 9.3 | 6.5 | 7.4 | 13.3 | 20.2 | 250 170 | 221 | 35 562 | 519 094 | 1.5 |
| Burlington, NC ................. | 2 980 | 0.3 | 22.2 | 16.6 | 4.8 | 7.9 | 5.4 | 16.4 | 11.7 | 31 320 | 204 | 3 031 | 66 576 | 20.0 |
| Burlington-South Burlington, VT ............................... | 7 527 | 1.0 | 20.4 | 14.4 | 11.9 | 7.7 | 6.2 | 14.4 | 19.0 | 35 945 | 169 | 4 320 | 92 358 | 11.7 |
| Canton-Massillon, OH.......... | 8 883 | 0.6 | 28.2 | 20.6 | 5.1 | 7.9 | 5.8 | 16.7 | 13.1 | 87 425 | 216 | 9 376 | 178 913 | 5.2 |
| Cape Coral-Fort Myers, FL... | 12 027 | 0.2 | 10.5 | 2.8 | 11.6 | 10.1 | 7.2 | 12.2 | 20.6 | 153 955 | 244 | 10 863 | 371 099 | 51.2 |
| Cape Girardeau-Jackson, MO-IL ........................... | 2 383 | 0.9 | 16.7 | 10.8 | 5.7 | 8.2 | 4.7 | 25.7 | 15.2 | 20 040 | 207 | 2 586 | 42 500 | 7.5 |
| Carson City, NV ............... | 1 837 | 0.0 | D | 9.3 | 6.1 | 6.6 | 7.6 | 15.3 | 36.0 | 11 605 | 209 | 820 | 23 534 | 10.6 |
| Casper, WY ..................... | 2 984 | 0.2 | 31.6 | 4.4 | 5.5 | 6.4 | 5.7 | 13.1 | 13.1 | 12 935 | 169 | 1 168 | 33 807 | 13.1 |
| Cedar Rapids, IA .............. | 8 834 | 3.0 | 28.0 | 22.0 | 9.0 | 7.5 | 9.5 | 9.7 | 11.0 | 46 910 | 180 | 3 679 | 112 257 | 13.3 |
| Champaign-Urbana, IL......... | 6 417 | 5.9 | 11.4 | 7.2 | 7.8 | 5.1 | 4.7 | 12.0 | 36.0 | 31 350 | 135 | 3 220 | 101 120 | 14.7 |

1. Includes mining, construction, and manufacturing.   2. Per 1,000 resident population estimated as of July 1, 2011.

# Table C. Metropolitan Areas — **Housing, Labor Force, and Employment**

| | Housing units, 2007–2011 | | | | | | | | Civilian labor force, 2012 | | Unemployment | | Civilian employment,[5] 2007–2011 | | |
| | Occupied units | | | | | | | | | | | | | Percent | |
| | | | Owner-occupied | | | Renter-occupied | | | | | | | | | |
| | | | | Median owner cost as a percent of income | | | Median rent as a percent of income | Sub-standard units[3] (percent) | | Percent change, 2011–2012 | | | | Management, professional, and related occupations | Construction, production, and related occupations |
| Area name | Total | Percent | Median value[1] | With a mort-gage | Without a mort-gage | Median rent[2] | | | Total | | Total | Rate[4] | Total | | |
| --- | ---: | ---: | ---: | ---: | ---: | ---: | ---: | ---: | ---: | ---: | ---: | ---: | ---: | ---: | ---: |
| | 89 | 90 | 91 | 92 | 93 | 94 | 95 | 96 | 97 | 98 | 99 | 100 | 101 | 102 | 103 |
| Abilene, TX | 60 482 | 65.6 | 84 800 | 21.3 | 12.4 | 719 | 29.8 | 3.2 | 84 226 | -0.4 | 4 514 | 5.4 | 70 799 | 31.1 | 22.2 |
| Akron, OH | 283 244 | 69.0 | 144 500 | 23.3 | 13.7 | 738 | 31.0 | 1.2 | 372 177 | -1.0 | 25 268 | 6.8 | 338 863 | 35.3 | 21.8 |
| Albany, GA | 58 263 | 57.6 | 104 800 | 23.1 | 12.8 | 651 | 32.0 | 2.8 | 74 907 | -0.1 | 7 187 | 9.6 | 62 609 | 29.7 | 26.4 |
| Albany-Schenectady-Troy, NY | 345 936 | 66.3 | 194 900 | 23.3 | 13.8 | 859 | 29.0 | 1.5 | 445 504 | 0.8 | 33 555 | 7.5 | 435 832 | 40.5 | 16.1 |
| Albuquerque, NM | 340 666 | 68.1 | 183 800 | 24.5 | 10.1 | 748 | 30.1 | 3.3 | 397 857 | -0.1 | 29 193 | 7.3 | 403 879 | 38.1 | 18.3 |
| Alexandria, LA | 54 649 | 68.7 | 108 800 | 21.3 | 10.5 | 687 | 32.4 | 3.3 | 67 368 | -1.3 | 4 327 | 6.4 | 62 244 | 31.1 | 24.4 |
| Allentown-Bethlehem-Easton, PA-NJ | 313 091 | 72.6 | 216 800 | 25.5 | 15.1 | 863 | 30.7 | 1.8 | 433 264 | 1.9 | 36 966 | 8.5 | 389 580 | 34.9 | 23.5 |
| Altoona, PA | 51 771 | 72.3 | 101 500 | 21.1 | 12.8 | 587 | 28.8 | 0.9 | 64 939 | 0.5 | 4 649 | 7.2 | 57 571 | 29.9 | 25.8 |
| Amarillo, TX | 91 526 | 65.4 | 111 700 | 21.2 | 10.9 | 691 | 30.3 | 3.8 | 134 099 | -0.9 | 6 467 | 4.8 | 120 213 | 31.1 | 24.4 |
| Ames, IA | 34 613 | 54.9 | 159 900 | 21.0 | 10.3 | 714 | 32.8 | 1.4 | 48 064 | -1.1 | 1 898 | 3.9 | 49 190 | 44.5 | 16.7 |
| Anchorage, AK | 135 732 | 65.3 | 256 800 | 24.1 | 11.4 | 1 046 | 28.3 | 5.9 | 200 765 | 0.2 | 12 060 | 6.0 | 182 695 | 37.2 | 20.5 |
| Anderson, IN | 51 028 | 72.6 | 95 900 | 21.6 | 12.1 | 663 | 30.5 | 1.6 | 60 424 | -0.5 | 5 871 | 9.7 | 55 956 | 28.5 | 26.8 |
| Anderson, SC | 72 519 | 73.5 | 120 500 | 21.6 | 10.2 | 643 | 31.1 | 2.7 | 85 046 | -0.8 | 7 296 | 8.6 | 80 174 | 28.9 | 29.6 |
| Ann Arbor, MI | 134 165 | 62.4 | 208 800 | 24.1 | 13.4 | 879 | 33.1 | 1.2 | 182 258 | 0.5 | 10 346 | 5.7 | 168 734 | 50.1 | 12.5 |
| Anniston-Oxford, AL | 45 923 | 70.1 | 99 600 | 21.7 | 11.8 | 593 | 30.5 | 1.6 | 52 372 | -2.6 | 3 966 | 7.6 | 47 597 | 26.8 | 31.9 |
| Appleton, WI | 87 318 | 74.7 | 156 800 | 23.0 | 12.9 | 681 | 24.9 | 1.7 | 123 338 | -0.4 | 7 745 | 6.3 | 118 922 | 31.7 | 28.8 |
| Asheville, NC | 180 830 | 70.6 | 184 400 | 23.8 | 11.0 | 736 | 29.9 | 2.1 | 217 450 | 1.4 | 16 731 | 7.7 | 193 511 | 35.0 | 22.5 |
| Athens-Clarke County, GA | 66 676 | 58.6 | 166 100 | 23.5 | 11.0 | 744 | 34.7 | 2.7 | 113 316 | 1.1 | 7 594 | 6.7 | 85 451 | 39.4 | 19.2 |
| Atlanta-Sandy Springs-Marietta, GA | 1 890 208 | 67.3 | 184 900 | 24.9 | 11.4 | 937 | 31.4 | 2.9 | 2 736 475 | 1.2 | 241 322 | 8.8 | 2 488 056 | 38.8 | 19.6 |
| Atlantic City-Hammonton, NJ | 101 418 | 70.7 | 256 600 | 31.3 | 19.2 | 995 | 33.8 | 3.0 | 136 125 | 0.7 | 18 377 | 13.5 | 129 740 | 28.4 | 16.5 |
| Auburn-Opelika, AL | 55 176 | 63.2 | 144 100 | 23.3 | 12.6 | 707 | 33.6 | 2.0 | 68 739 | 1.2 | 4 316 | 6.3 | 62 255 | 36.8 | 23.8 |
| Augusta-Richmond County, GA-SC | 204 886 | 68.6 | 123 200 | 22.7 | 11.2 | 706 | 29.9 | 2.2 | 263 970 | -0.5 | 23 270 | 8.8 | 230 484 | 33.3 | 24.3 |
| Austin-Round Rock-San Marcos, TX | 637 294 | 58.8 | 186 300 | 23.7 | 12.5 | 936 | 30.4 | 4.1 | 963 883 | 1.9 | 55 629 | 5.8 | 860 326 | 43.3 | 16.6 |
| Bakersfield-Delano, CA | 250 999 | 60.1 | 196 000 | 27.9 | 11.3 | 840 | 32.8 | 9.3 | 396 657 | 3.1 | 52 681 | 13.3 | 312 748 | 26.0 | 32.4 |
| Baltimore-Towson, MD | 1 020 744 | 67.7 | 297 200 | 24.8 | 12.8 | 1 067 | 31.2 | 1.9 | 1 473 692 | 1.5 | 106 178 | 7.2 | 1 342 381 | 43.5 | 15.9 |
| Bangor, ME | 62 570 | 69.7 | 137 900 | 23.1 | 13.2 | 695 | 31.9 | 2.3 | 79 103 | 0.5 | 6 139 | 7.8 | 74 769 | 32.9 | 21.5 |
| Barnstable Town, MA | 96 775 | 79.8 | 384 200 | 29.8 | 16.2 | 1 099 | 34.4 | 1.5 | 121 351 | 0.8 | 8 953 | 7.4 | 102 352 | 37.2 | 18.5 |
| Baton Rouge, LA | 291 547 | 69.5 | 154 700 | 20.9 | 10.0 | 768 | 32.4 | 3.4 | 383 238 | 1.4 | 24 438 | 6.4 | 374 727 | 33.7 | 23.1 |
| Battle Creek, MI | 53 481 | 71.1 | 107 000 | 23.8 | 13.8 | 647 | 32.1 | 1.2 | 63 634 | -1.5 | 4 711 | 7.4 | 57 372 | 28.1 | 28.5 |
| Bay City, MI | 44 005 | 79.5 | 104 600 | 22.8 | 13.4 | 579 | 30.2 | 0.8 | 51 768 | -0.6 | 4 405 | 8.5 | 47 956 | 30.1 | 23.9 |
| Beaumont-Port Arthur, TX | 142 797 | 69.2 | 91 400 | 20.2 | 11.9 | 717 | 28.3 | 3.5 | 190 039 | -1.0 | 19 150 | 10.1 | 160 355 | 29.1 | 29.4 |
| Bellingham, WA | 79 003 | 62.9 | 290 400 | 27.9 | 12.4 | 842 | 32.4 | 2.7 | 105 360 | 0.2 | 7 948 | 7.5 | 96 968 | 34.3 | 21.6 |
| Bend, OR | 63 935 | 66.9 | 290 400 | 29.3 | 12.2 | 901 | 30.8 | 3.1 | 78 294 | -1.5 | 8 822 | 11.3 | 71 762 | 35.1 | 21.3 |
| Billings, MT | 64 528 | 70.3 | 174 200 | 22.6 | 11.6 | 675 | 27.5 | 1.7 | 88 764 | 2.4 | 3 894 | 4.4 | 81 442 | 32.1 | 22.6 |
| Binghamton, NY | 100 715 | 69.2 | 103 600 | 20.9 | 13.5 | 638 | 29.9 | 1.8 | 117 147 | -1.1 | 10 258 | 8.8 | 116 442 | 35.7 | 21.1 |
| Birmingham-Hoover, AL | 432 911 | 71.4 | 144 100 | 22.9 | 11.9 | 763 | 30.7 | 1.8 | 530 609 | -0.4 | 33 969 | 6.4 | 505 647 | 35.1 | 22.0 |
| Bismarck, ND | 44 355 | 72.7 | 151 700 | 21.1 | 11.3 | 593 | 24.8 | 1.3 | 61 354 | -1.5 | 1 820 | 3.0 | 60 167 | 35.6 | 20.9 |
| Blacksburg-Christiansburg-Radford, VA | 62 173 | 61.2 | 155 700 | 21.8 | 10.0 | 701 | 35.4 | 1.1 | 81 949 | 1.8 | 5 277 | 6.4 | 74 495 | 38.9 | 20.8 |
| Bloomington, IN | 74 488 | 61.6 | 127 700 | 21.4 | 11.0 | 725 | 38.5 | 1.9 | 95 356 | -0.8 | 7 187 | 7.5 | 88 747 | 38.7 | 21.6 |
| Bloomington-Normal, IL | 63 431 | 67.8 | 154 600 | 21.2 | 12.3 | 711 | 28.3 | 1.6 | 90 653 | -0.7 | 6 280 | 6.9 | 87 317 | 40.7 | 15.0 |
| Boise City-Nampa, ID | 223 931 | 69.9 | 184 300 | 24.8 | 10.4 | 777 | 29.5 | 3.0 | 306 006 | 2.0 | 21 131 | 6.9 | 279 055 | 36.9 | 21.0 |
| Boston-Cambridge-Quincy, MA-NH | 1 745 155 | 62.7 | 373 500 | 26.7 | 15.8 | 1 163 | 30.0 | 2.1 | 2 471 285 | 0.5 | 149 733 | 6.1 | 2 339 798 | 45.8 | 14.5 |
| Boston-Quincy, MA Div | 721 377 | 58.5 | 375 900 | 27.1 | 15.9 | 1 200 | 30.9 | 2.3 | 1 000 731 | 0.4 | 63 209 | 6.3 | 956 083 | 44.2 | 13.9 |
| Cambridge-Newton-Framingham, MA Div | 577 349 | 63.4 | 410 100 | 25.8 | 15.2 | 1 243 | 28.5 | 1.9 | 839 137 | 0.5 | 44 620 | 5.3 | 791 260 | 51.8 | 12.6 |
| Peabody, MA Div | 284 940 | 64.9 | 362 300 | 27.3 | 16.0 | 1 001 | 31.6 | 2.1 | 384 950 | 0.4 | 27 467 | 7.1 | 365 415 | 41.1 | 17.0 |
| Rockingham County-Strafford County, NH Div | 161 489 | 75.4 | 276 600 | 27.0 | 16.7 | 996 | 29.7 | 1.5 | 246 467 | 1.2 | 14 437 | 5.9 | 227 040 | 39.7 | 19.0 |
| Boulder, CO | 118 545 | 64.2 | 353 000 | 24.0 | 10.0 | 1 026 | 35.2 | 2.8 | 179 816 | 1.8 | 10 899 | 6.1 | 155 375 | 51.7 | 12.0 |
| Bowling Green, KY | 47 680 | 62.5 | 132 600 | 22.1 | 10.1 | 630 | 31.3 | 2.0 | 65 672 | 1.2 | 4 654 | 7.1 | 58 630 | 32.8 | 25.4 |
| Bremerton-Silverdale, WA | 96 683 | 67.7 | 284 300 | 26.1 | 12.1 | 958 | 30.4 | 2.3 | 120 076 | -1.5 | 8 907 | 7.4 | 107 386 | 37.5 | 21.0 |
| Bridgeport-Stamford-Norwalk, CT | 332 139 | 70.4 | 466 700 | 28.2 | 18.1 | 1 249 | 32.3 | 3.0 | 476 031 | -0.9 | 36 266 | 7.6 | 442 427 | 43.4 | 15.5 |
| Brownsville-Harlingen, TX | 114 881 | 68.3 | 76 000 | 26.3 | 13.7 | 614 | 32.2 | 11.8 | 162 955 | -0.2 | 17 070 | 10.5 | 140 754 | 26.9 | 22.8 |
| Brunswick, GA | 43 298 | 68.9 | 147 700 | 23.4 | 11.4 | 747 | 28.5 | 3.6 | 51 079 | 0.8 | 5 114 | 10.0 | 49 224 | 30.0 | 23.9 |
| Buffalo-Niagara Falls, NY | 468 067 | 66.8 | 116 800 | 21.9 | 14.5 | 691 | 31.2 | 1.2 | 573 270 | 0.2 | 48 517 | 8.5 | 531 830 | 35.9 | 18.9 |
| Burlington, NC | 59 948 | 68.6 | 136 000 | 23.3 | 11.3 | 728 | 29.4 | 3.1 | 73 885 | 1.4 | 6 978 | 9.4 | 70 846 | 30.7 | 26.4 |
| Burlington-South Burlington, VT | 83 744 | 68.4 | 246 600 | 25.7 | 15.2 | 979 | 32.8 | 1.5 | 123 192 | -0.1 | 5 148 | 4.2 | 115 535 | 42.0 | 17.6 |
| Canton-Massillon, OH | 161 557 | 71.4 | 125 500 | 22.8 | 12.3 | 640 | 29.6 | 1.4 | 198 217 | -0.9 | 14 581 | 7.4 | 185 216 | 30.5 | 25.4 |
| Cape Coral-Fort Myers, FL | 243 017 | 73.8 | 181 000 | 30.5 | 14.1 | 957 | 33.7 | 3.0 | 286 397 | 1.3 | 25 493 | 8.9 | 251 857 | 29.0 | 20.6 |
| Cape Girardeau-Jackson, MO-IL | 37 408 | 68.9 | 122 200 | 21.2 | 10.5 | 604 | 27.7 | 2.1 | 46 778 | -0.6 | 2 978 | 6.4 | 45 229 | 29.2 | 26.5 |
| Carson City, NV | 21 289 | 61.0 | 244 600 | 25.8 | 11.8 | 926 | 30.6 | 2.9 | 27 968 | -3.0 | 3 114 | 11.1 | 23 911 | 30.9 | 21.1 |
| Casper, WY | 29 850 | 69.8 | 177 700 | 21.2 | 10.0 | 731 | 26.7 | 1.2 | 43 900 | 2.7 | 2 137 | 4.9 | 38 731 | 30.2 | 27.5 |
| Cedar Rapids, IA | 104 425 | 74.5 | 137 100 | 20.9 | 12.0 | 615 | 26.4 | 1.3 | 144 218 | -1.7 | 7 710 | 5.3 | 134 852 | 35.4 | 23.3 |
| Champaign-Urbana, IL | 91 116 | 58.1 | 141 000 | 21.5 | 11.5 | 756 | 35.4 | 1.4 | 114 382 | -1.6 | 9 200 | 8.0 | 114 362 | 42.2 | 17.0 |

1. Specified owner-occupied units.  2. Specified renter-occupied units.  3. Overcrowded or lacking complete plumbing facilities.  4. Percent of civilian labor force.  5. Persons 16 years old and over.

# Table C. Metropolitan Areas — Nonfarm Employment and Agriculture

| Area name | Private nonfarm establishments, employment and payroll, 2011 | | | | | | | | | Agriculture, 2007 | | | |
|---|---|---|---|---|---|---|---|---|---|---|---|---|---|
| | Number of establish-ments | Employment | | | | | | Annual payroll | | Farms | | | |
| | | Total | Health care and social assistance | Manufac-turing | Retail trade | Finance and insurance | Professional, scientific, and technical services | Total (mil dol) | Average per employee (dollars) | Number | Fewer than 50 acres | 500 acres or more | Farm operators whose principal occu-pation is farming (percent) |
| | | | | | | | | | | | Percent with: | | |
| | 104 | 105 | 106 | 107 | 108 | 109 | 110 | 111 | 112 | 113 | 114 | 115 | 116 |
| Abilene, TX .......................... | 3 844 | 55 193 | 12 137 | 2 295 | 8 535 | 2 962 | 1 815 | 1 728 | 31 315 | 3 403 | 28.0 | 20.2 | 35.7 |
| Akron, OH .......................... | 16 402 | 277 410 | 50 262 | 36 071 | 36 960 | 10 453 | 16 872 | 11 704 | 42 190 | 1 196 | 63.3 | 2.5 | 41.6 |
| Albany, GA.......................... | 3 242 | 44 963 | 9 466 | 3 876 | 7 825 | 1 514 | 2 603 | 1 473 | 32 752 | 1 253 | 29.8 | 25.7 | 48.6 |
| Albany-Schenectady-Troy, NY .......................... | 21 027 | 325 375 | 62 268 | 19 235 | 45 707 | 20 429 | 27 041 | 13 490 | 41 461 | 2 364 | 39.3 | 5.1 | 52.3 |
| Albuquerque, NM ................ | 18 466 | 276 731 | 48 591 | 16 645 | 41 475 | 11 827 | 23 750 | 10 365 | 37 453 | 2 749 | 65.7 | 13.7 | 43.0 |
| Alexandria, LA .................... | 3 398 | 48 383 | 13 875 | 3 963 | 8 158 | 1 711 | 1 820 | 1 624 | 33 571 | 1 227 | 53.2 | 7.7 | 43.0 |
| Allentown-Bethlehem-Eas-ton, PA-NJ ...................... | 18 174 | 288 983 | 56 382 | 31 412 | 41 544 | 12 258 | 11 767 | 12 648 | 43 769 | 2 142 | 62.1 | 4.9 | 46.9 |
| Altoona, PA .......................... | 3 200 | 50 360 | 10 875 | 6 777 | 8 759 | 1 498 | 1 917 | 1 681 | 33 372 | 523 | 33.8 | 5.9 | 58.1 |
| Amarillo, TX ........................ | 6 018 | 90 682 | 16 673 | 7 880 | 13 965 | 5 414 | 2 804 | 3 287 | 36 251 | 1 879 | 26.6 | 38.1 | 39.4 |
| Ames, IA .............................. | 2 015 | 28 288 | 4 845 | 4 315 | 4 798 | 822 | 1 210 | 956 | 33 784 | 1 077 | 36.1 | 20.1 | 50.7 |
| Anchorage, AK.................... | 10 366 | 159 707 | 25 571 | 2 967 | 17 882 | 5 309 | 13 508 | 8 988 | 56 280 | 278 | 50.4 | 6.1 | 52.5 |
| Anderson, IN ...................... | 2 295 | 33 864 | 6 684 | 2 972 | 4 911 | 1 132 | 879 | 1 049 | 30 965 | 870 | 55.3 | 14.3 | 49.8 |
| Anderson, SC ...................... | 3 622 | 51 091 | 7 930 | 10 566 | 8 256 | 1 085 | 1 723 | 1 682 | 32 917 | 1 650 | 48.1 | 3.2 | 32.9 |
| Ann Arbor, MI ...................... | 7 889 | 134 317 | D | 11 757 | 16 106 | 4 127 | 11 483 | 6 610 | 49 214 | 1 300 | 54.9 | 6.1 | 45.2 |
| Anniston-Oxford, AL............ | 2 333 | 36 093 | 6 095 | 5 900 | 6 207 | 915 | 1 557 | 1 166 | 32 318 | 735 | 51.6 | 2.0 | 40.7 |
| Appleton, WI ........................ | 5 838 | 104 778 | 12 599 | 20 522 | 14 265 | 6 318 | 4 057 | 4 128 | 39 401 | 2 094 | 37.1 | 8.9 | 53.1 |
| Asheville, NC ...................... | 11 362 | 144 047 | 31 485 | 17 920 | 23 113 | 3 726 | 5 547 | 4 876 | 33 848 | 3 142 | 61.7 | 1.6 | 40.0 |
| Athens-Clarke County, GA ... | 4 402 | 54 616 | 11 264 | 6 035 | 9 495 | 1 729 | 2 404 | 1 779 | 32 566 | 1 784 | 47.1 | 4.4 | 39.0 |
| Atlanta-Sandy Springs-Mari-etta, GA .......................... | 128 050 | 2 004 006 | 228 951 | 125 613 | 245 002 | 105 714 | 166 568 | 97 811 | 48 808 | 8 518 | 56.1 | 2.9 | 40.8 |
| Atlantic City-Hammonton, NJ | 6 408 | 111 036 | 17 538 | 1 664 | 15 941 | 3 211 | 4 453 | 4 040 | 36 386 | 499 | 75.2 | 1.6 | 45.3 |
| Auburn-Opelika, AL.............. | 2 343 | 35 565 | 5 462 | 5 402 | 6 352 | 854 | 1 149 | 1 014 | 28 498 | 356 | 40.4 | 7.3 | 46.3 |
| Augusta-Richmond County, GA-SC.......................... | 10 218 | 173 863 | 33 037 | 21 622 | 24 874 | 4 840 | 8 429 | 6 795 | 39 080 | 2 634 | 42.2 | 7.6 | 38.2 |
| Austin-Round Rock-San Mar-cos, TX...................... | 41 924 | 653 617 | 81 835 | 36 452 | 89 288 | 32 226 | 64 489 | 31 583 | 48 320 | 8 706 | 47.4 | 8.3 | 37.2 |
| Bakersfield-Delano, CA........ | 11 982 | 179 232 | 27 475 | 11 773 | 28 115 | 6 180 | 11 567 | 7 421 | 41 405 | 2 117 | 43.0 | 24.7 | 57.4 |
| Baltimore-Towson, MD ........ | 64 425 | 1 062 322 | 184 021 | 57 336 | 134 781 | 52 846 | 111 969 | 51 400 | 48 385 | 3 836 | 55.4 | 5.9 | 47.1 |
| Bangor, ME ........................ | 4 127 | 57 082 | 13 792 | 3 937 | 10 760 | 1 939 | 1 885 | 1 948 | 34 132 | 706 | 41.4 | 9.1 | 49.9 |
| Barnstable Town, MA .......... | 8 116 | 68 452 | 15 427 | 2 001 | 14 293 | 2 258 | 4 613 | 2 766 | 40 410 | 406 | 93.3 | 0.0 | 53.4 |
| Baton Rouge, LA ................ | 17 725 | 305 691 | 47 440 | 22 547 | 41 862 | 14 518 | 20 322 | 12 962 | 42 401 | 2 987 | 51.1 | 10.1 | 38.9 |
| Battle Creek, MI .................. | 2 670 | 47 544 | 9 501 | 10 705 | 5 928 | 968 | 1 193 | 2 015 | 42 379 | 1 178 | 37.6 | 9.3 | 45.3 |
| Bay City, MI ........................ | 2 254 | 30 165 | 6 553 | 3 008 | 5 490 | 1 111 | 1 205 | 1 113 | 36 901 | 851 | 40.2 | 12.1 | 48.3 |
| Beaumont-Port Arthur, TX .... | 7 845 | 127 633 | 20 133 | 18 527 | 19 006 | 3 464 | 6 590 | 5 552 | 43 503 | 2 167 | 64.8 | 8.0 | 38.4 |
| Bellingham, WA .................. | 6 117 | 66 595 | 10 024 | 8 400 | 10 506 | 2 127 | 3 123 | 2 489 | 37 373 | 1 483 | 71.2 | 2.2 | 45.2 |
| Bend, OR ............................ | 5 695 | 51 078 | 9 461 | 3 464 | 9 045 | 2 020 | 2 636 | 1 756 | 34 369 | 1 405 | 77.9 | 2.3 | 40.8 |
| Billings, MT ........................ | 5 779 | 68 100 | 12 899 | 3 322 | 10 529 | 3 812 | 3 330 | 2 540 | 37 299 | 2 122 | 36.4 | 25.5 | 41.1 |
| Binghamton, NY .................. | 5 113 | 82 861 | 16 743 | 9 738 | 12 608 | 2 746 | 7 459 | 3 081 | 37 188 | 1 145 | 27.5 | 5.5 | 43.5 |
| Birmingham-Hoover, AL........ | 25 246 | 432 202 | 66 104 | 35 846 | 56 922 | 33 198 | 21 679 | 18 683 | 43 227 | 4 464 | 47.0 | 3.8 | 41.7 |
| Bismarck, ND ...................... | 3 484 | 52 709 | 12 010 | 1 718 | 8 018 | 2 547 | 2 726 | 1 954 | 37 072 | 1 862 | 16.4 | 43.3 | 50.4 |
| Blacksburg-Christiansburg-Radford, VA .................. | 3 193 | 44 767 | 5 876 | 10 176 | 7 791 | 1 332 | 2 538 | 1 583 | 35 366 | 1 387 | 37.4 | 6.3 | 40.9 |
| Bloomington, IN .................. | 3 854 | 55 964 | 9 757 | 8 671 | 8 748 | 1 714 | 2 470 | 1 802 | 32 200 | 1 850 | 43.4 | 6.3 | 40.8 |
| Bloomington-Normal, IL ........ | 3 694 | 76 610 | 8 662 | 4 093 | 9 367 | 22 699 | 2 882 | 3 553 | 46 383 | 1 513 | 35.1 | 30.5 | 53.7 |
| Boise City-Nampa, ID .......... | 15 991 | 210 528 | 34 878 | 23 954 | 27 670 | 10 432 | 11 489 | 8 107 | 38 506 | 5 238 | 70.9 | 7.1 | 41.4 |
| Boston-Cambridge-Quincy, MA-NH .......................... | 121 796 | 2 241 063 | 408 605 | 150 141 | 252 411 | 167 074 | 220 434 | 135 915 | 60 647 | 3 281 | 72.3 | 1.2 | 48.8 |
| Boston-Quincy, MA Div....... | X | X | X | X | X | X | X | X | X | 1 153 | 75.9 | 1.5 | 51.6 |
| Cambridge-Newton-Fra-mingham, MA Div ....... | X | X | X | X | X | X | X | X | X | 700 | 75.0 | 0.6 | 48.7 |
| Peabody, MA Div ................ | X | X | X | X | X | X | X | X | X | 531 | 75.7 | 1.9 | 45.2 |
| Rockingham County-Straf-ford County, NH Div..... | X | X | X | X | X | X | X | X | X | 897 | 63.5 | 0.9 | 47.4 |
| Boulder, CO ........................ | 11 419 | 131 872 | 18 598 | 13 934 | 16 536 | 4 125 | 24 315 | 6 982 | 52 946 | 746 | 67.2 | 6.4 | 38.6 |
| Bowling Green, KY .............. | 2 889 | 47 133 | 7 584 | 7 416 | 7 219 | 1 530 | 2 064 | 1 688 | 35 811 | 2 536 | 42.7 | 4.5 | 35.3 |
| Bremerton-Silverdale, WA.... | 5 541 | 55 525 | 12 827 | 1 750 | 10 425 | 1 956 | 4 049 | 2 009 | 36 177 | 664 | 91.3 | 0.3 | 45.5 |
| Bridgeport-Stamford-Nor-walk, CT .......................... | 26 725 | 398 342 | 62 118 | 33 141 | 48 321 | 38 774 | 34 556 | 31 040 | 77 922 | 310 | 71.0 | 2.6 | 47.4 |
| Brownsville-Harlingen, TX.... | 6 285 | 99 119 | 30 705 | 5 569 | 17 069 | 3 353 | 2 346 | 2 477 | 24 990 | 1 241 | 63.1 | 13.7 | 43.3 |
| Brunswick, GA .................... | 2 764 | 31 588 | 5 028 | 2 416 | 5 469 | 874 | 948 | 986 | 31 213 | 333 | 52.9 | 3.9 | 40.8 |
| Buffalo-Niagara Falls, NY .... | 26 813 | 464 080 | 83 675 | 50 584 | 63 470 | 28 711 | 27 280 | 17 862 | 38 490 | 2 080 | 47.4 | 5.0 | 51.7 |
| Burlington, NC...................... | 3 153 | 50 394 | 7 730 | 9 626 | 8 545 | 1 490 | 1 285 | 1 541 | 30 583 | 753 | 42.6 | 3.9 | 43.0 |
| Burlington-South Burlington, VT .......................... | 6 595 | 97 224 | 17 371 | 13 044 | 14 783 | 3 644 | 9 738 | 4 255 | 43 765 | 1 445 | 34.5 | 9.1 | 49.8 |
| Canton-Massillon, OH.......... | 8 801 | 139 427 | 27 878 | 24 057 | 20 733 | 6 320 | 4 588 | 4 766 | 34 185 | 2 074 | 47.8 | 4.0 | 46.0 |
| Cape Coral-Fort Myers, FL... | 15 629 | 171 148 | 28 466 | 4 070 | 33 882 | 5 465 | 9 306 | 5 809 | 33 942 | 944 | 86.4 | 4.1 | 37.7 |
| Cape Girardeau-Jackson, MO-IL .......................... | 2 694 | 39 488 | 11 309 | 3 975 | 6 374 | 1 240 | 1 034 | 1 296 | 32 816 | 2 445 | 25.8 | 10.5 | 43.8 |
| Carson City, NV .................. | 2 067 | 21 836 | 3 645 | 3 386 | 3 412 | 948 | 1 531 | 849 | 38 869 | 21 | 66.7 | 9.5 | 42.9 |
| Casper, WY ........................ | 2 902 | 32 295 | 5 015 | 1 925 | 4 806 | 1 159 | 1 613 | 1 425 | 44 125 | 413 | 28.8 | 41.4 | 46.2 |
| Cedar Rapids, IA ................ | 6 402 | 122 402 | 16 334 | 18 651 | 15 423 | 9 047 | 5 258 | 5 221 | 42 652 | 3 781 | 30.9 | 17.8 | 50.5 |
| Champaign-Urbana, IL.......... | 4 825 | 73 646 | 14 092 | 7 497 | 11 602 | 2 708 | 3 330 | 2 573 | 34 933 | 2 393 | 30.8 | 30.1 | 55.9 |

# Table C. Metropolitan Areas — **Agriculture**

| Area name | Land in farms: Acreage (1,000) | Percent change, 2002–2007 | Acres: Average size of farm | Total irrigated (1,000) | Total cropland (1,000) | Value of land and buildings (dollars): Average per farm | Average per acre | Value of machinery and equipment, average per farm (dollars) | Value of products sold: Total (mil dol) | Average per farm (dollars) | Percent from: Crops | Live-stock and poultry products | Percent of farms with sales of: $10,000 or more | $100,000 or more | Government payments: Total ($1,000) | Percent of farms |
|---|---|---|---|---|---|---|---|---|---|---|---|---|---|---|---|---|
| | 117 | 118 | 119 | 120 | 121 | 122 | 123 | 124 | 125 | 126 | 127 | 128 | 129 | 130 | 131 | 132 |
| Abilene, TX ...................... | 1 685 | 7.5 | 495 | 9.6 | 643.4 | 594 486 | 1 200 | 57 564 | 135.2 | 39 750 | 44.7 | 55.3 | 25.9 | 6.7 | 15 880 | 41.6 |
| Akron, OH ........................ | 98 | -16.9 | 82 | 0.7 | 67.4 | 422 112 | 5 156 | 62 626 | 43.6 | 36 444 | 71.9 | 28.2 | 32.7 | 6.4 | 888 | 16.9 |
| Albany, GA .......................... | 678 | 0.7 | 541 | 112.3 | 326.1 | 1 333 707 | 2 464 | 154 585 | 208.2 | 166 136 | 77.1 | 22.9 | 39.7 | 23.7 | 22 792 | 60.5 |
| Albany-Schenectady-Troy, NY ................................ | 336 | -9.4 | 142 | 2.8 | 183.7 | 451 426 | 3 173 | 79 550 | 156.8 | 66 329 | 33.9 | 66.1 | 39.6 | 10.5 | D | 21.5 |
| Albuquerque, NM ................. | 3 131 | D | 1 139 | 67.6 | 151.9 | 528 636 | 464 | 45 368 | 103.7 | 37 722 | 33.5 | 66.5 | 19.6 | 4.2 | 980 | 4.8 |
| Alexandria, LA ..................... | 229 | -3.4 | 187 | 10.3 | 128.5 | 440 346 | 2 359 | 77 519 | 90.5 | 73 821 | 85.8 | 14.2 | 32.9 | 10.4 | 4 489 | 17.6 |
| Allentown-Bethlehem-Easton, PA-NJ ....................... | 248 | -6.8 | 116 | 4.0 | 195.8 | 909 370 | 7 857 | 82 210 | 188.3 | 87 881 | 67.1 | 32.9 | 38.0 | 12.8 | 3 021 | 22.6 |
| Altoona, PA ......................... | 87 | 1.2 | 167 | 0.2 | 61.9 | 690 402 | 4 130 | 99 314 | 85.2 | 162 904 | 11.9 | 88.1 | 51.6 | 25.0 | 1 092 | 36.3 |
| Amarillo, TX ........................ | 2 202 | 10.5 | 1 172 | 74.2 | 834.9 | 1 023 528 | 873 | 89 962 | 554.4 | 294 973 | 17.6 | 82.4 | 38.5 | 17.9 | 17 243 | 54.0 |
| Ames, IA ............................. | 352 | -2.2 | 327 | 0.3 | 328.1 | 1 163 987 | 3 559 | 162 630 | 200.6 | 186 271 | 80.6 | 19.4 | 64.2 | 34.2 | 7 792 | 73.9 |
| Anchorage, AK ..................... | 38 | NA | 138 | 1.7 | 17.0 | 488 278 | 3 536 | 72 515 | 31.8 | 114 216 | 49.6 | 50.4 | 41.0 | 14.4 | 110 | 6.1 |
| Anderson, IN ....................... | 217 | -11.1 | 250 | 1.5 | 204.1 | 933 308 | 3 736 | 115 455 | 115.5 | 132 730 | 87.5 | 12.5 | 50.9 | 21.6 | 4 441 | 61.0 |
| Anderson, SC ....................... | 173 | -2.3 | 105 | 0.7 | 63.8 | 413 318 | 3 939 | 48 678 | 50.2 | 30 443 | 11.0 | 89.0 | 19.2 | 2.2 | 941 | 18.6 |
| Ann Arbor, MI ...................... | 167 | -4.6 | 128 | 2.7 | 133.1 | 642 197 | 5 003 | 83 247 | 73.2 | 56 305 | 74.9 | 25.1 | 37.3 | 12.4 | 2 193 | 32.6 |
| Anniston-Oxford, AL ............. | 76 | 1.3 | 104 | 1.7 | 26.0 | 329 225 | 3 176 | 56 359 | 69.1 | 93 961 | 14.8 | 85.2 | 25.3 | 7.8 | 391 | 13.3 |
| Appleton, WI ...................... | 399 | -3.6 | 191 | 0.3 | 336.1 | 713 808 | 3 745 | 129 107 | 403.7 | 192 768 | 20.5 | 79.5 | 59.2 | 29.9 | 6 348 | 68.6 |
| Asheville, NC ....................... | 233 | -20.2 | 74 | 3.1 | 71.2 | 511 435 | 6 897 | 49 059 | 122.9 | 39 130 | 76.3 | 23.7 | 23.0 | 3.7 | 1 146 | 9.6 |
| Athens-Clarke County, GA ... | 222 | 10.4 | 125 | 2.1 | 65.6 | 572 301 | 4 591 | 63 550 | 426.9 | 239 316 | D | D | 32.7 | 15.8 | 1 164 | 18.6 |
| Atlanta-Sandy Springs-Marietta, GA ............................ | 871 | -15.2 | 102 | D | 256.4 | 512 802 | 5 013 | 51 117 | D | D | 11.3 | D | 23.4 | 7.5 | D | 11.1 |
| Atlantic City-Hammonton, NJ | 30 | 0.0 | 61 | 11.7 | 18.6 | 902 470 | 14 827 | 113 651 | 128.3 | 257 192 | 98.0 | 2.0 | 44.9 | 20.6 | 349 | 5.0 |
| Auburn-Opelika, AL .............. | 63 | -14.9 | 177 | 0.8 | 13.9 | 534 602 | 3 012 | 57 383 | D | D | D | D | 28.7 | 2.8 | 497 | 16.3 |
| Augusta-Richmond County, GA-SC ............................. | 495 | -4.8 | 188 | 26.5 | 219.6 | 569 763 | 3 031 | 62 451 | 228.1 | 86 595 | D | D | 25.8 | 6.5 | 6 623 | 23.6 |
| Austin-Round Rock-San Marcos, TX ........................... | 1 746 | -7.5 | 201 | 6.9 | 492.5 | 544 782 | 2 716 | 45 522 | 309.9 | 35 596 | 30.0 | 70.0 | 21.9 | 3.3 | 7 611 | 13.2 |
| Bakersfield-Delano, CA ........ | 2 362 | -13.5 | 1 116 | 786.3 | 942.8 | 5 160 784 | 4 626 | 253 255 | 3 204.1 | 1 513 532 | 79.6 | 20.4 | 59.6 | 40.3 | 27 346 | 17.1 |
| Baltimore-Towson, MD ........ | 501 | -5.1 | 131 | 15.8 | 358.7 | 1 093 432 | 8 373 | 94 420 | 353.8 | 92 231 | 59.8 | 40.2 | 38.1 | 13.1 | 8 525 | 29.7 |
| Bangor, ME ........................ | 115 | 7.5 | 162 | 1.8 | 47.1 | 370 924 | 2 285 | 67 340 | 42.5 | 60 231 | 30.2 | 69.8 | 32.7 | 9.1 | 889 | 11.5 |
| Barnstable Town, MA .......... | 5 | -16.7 | 13 | 1.3 | 2.0 | 457 980 | 35 532 | 44 526 | 17.7 | 43 475 | 57.5 | 42.5 | 46.6 | 10.3 | 282 | 9.6 |
| Baton Rouge, LA .................. | 697 | -1.1 | 233 | D | 359.8 | 645 966 | 2 769 | 79 310 | 217.0 | 72 646 | 69.8 | 30.2 | 30.0 | 7.6 | 5 342 | 15.9 |
| Battle Creek, MI .................. | 228 | -5.0 | 194 | 9.3 | 175.1 | 583 048 | 3 012 | 81 935 | 89.8 | 76 244 | 60.6 | 39.4 | 37.4 | 13.1 | 3 170 | 49.6 |
| Bay City, MI ........................ | 186 | 0.0 | 219 | 4.1 | 166.7 | 616 830 | 2 818 | 117 055 | 77.2 | 90 744 | 89.2 | 10.8 | 49.9 | 20.7 | 2 424 | 67.0 |
| Beaumont-Port Arthur, TX .... | 488 | -7.9 | 225 | 18.4 | 190.9 | 384 081 | 1 705 | 50 777 | D | D | D | 59.0 | 18.5 | 3.6 | 3 752 | 8.4 |
| Bellingham, WA ................... | 103 | -30.4 | 69 | 35.0 | 73.7 | 773 740 | 11 186 | 95 287 | 326.5 | 220 128 | 30.6 | 69.4 | 36.2 | 16.8 | 1 050 | 19.7 |
| Bend, OR ............................ | 129 | -6.5 | 92 | 37.8 | 39.9 | 633 973 | 6 885 | 45 880 | 19.8 | 14 063 | 45.8 | 54.2 | 20.4 | 2.4 | 135 | 1.4 |
| Billings, MT ......................... | 2 409 | 3.7 | 1 135 | 150.9 | 482.2 | 1 126 609 | 992 | 77 324 | 209.9 | 98 922 | 26.2 | 73.8 | 39.0 | 13.1 | 5 338 | 32.3 |
| Binghamton, NY ................... | 193 | -15.0 | 169 | 0.5 | 97.4 | 303 050 | 1 794 | 66 246 | 66.6 | 58 122 | 15.7 | 84.3 | 30.9 | 11.3 | 1 807 | 27.9 |
| Birmingham-Hoover, AL........ | 527 | -4.4 | 118 | 6.1 | 159.4 | 362 781 | 3 074 | 55 331 | D | D | D | D | 28.9 | 7.3 | 1 828 | 11.3 |
| Bismarck, ND ...................... | 2 045 | -4.5 | 1 098 | 12.3 | 1 025.5 | 741 062 | 675 | 108 183 | 199.5 | 107 136 | 55.9 | 44.1 | 51.8 | 23.1 | 11 418 | 67.0 |
| Blacksburg-Christiansburg-Radford, VA .................... | 230 | -7.6 | 166 | 0.7 | 67.3 | 612 259 | 3 686 | 58 927 | 37.3 | 26 927 | 17.8 | 82.2 | 33.7 | 4.2 | 590 | 12.5 |
| Bloomington, IN ................... | 311 | -5.8 | 168 | 1.4 | 199.7 | 524 496 | 3 119 | 66 246 | 109.0 | 58 895 | 58.1 | 41.9 | 34.5 | 7.9 | 3 825 | 40.6 |
| Bloomington-Normal, IL ........ | 676 | -1.7 | 447 | 2.9 | 647.4 | 1 868 207 | 4 181 | 175 125 | 366.5 | 242 265 | 89.5 | 10.5 | 65.1 | 44.7 | 12 275 | 77.9 |
| Boise City-Nampa, ID ........... | 1 255 | -6.2 | 240 | 406.6 | 433.5 | 701 088 | 2 925 | 78 774 | 814.8 | 155 557 | 35.1 | 64.9 | 33.9 | 11.9 | 4 227 | 19.4 |
| Boston-Cambridge-Quincy, MA-NH ............................ | 182 | D | 56 | 15.0 | 71.7 | 793 133 | 14 266 | 59 302 | 235.2 | 71 717 | D | D | 37.0 | 11.4 | D | 5.9 |
| Boston-Quincy, MA Div....... | 61 | D | 53 | 12.1 | 21.6 | 841 609 | 15 813 | 60 468 | 92.6 | 80 334 | D | D | 46.3 | 15.4 | D | 8.1 |
| Cambridge-Newton-Framingham, MA Div ........ | 34 | 3.0 | 48 | 1.5 | 15.4 | 907 619 | 18 745 | 56 824 | 81.7 | 116 726 | 84.2 | 15.8 | 34.3 | 11.7 | D | 2.0 |
| Peabody, MA Div .............. | 28 | 0.0 | 52 | 0.9 | 12.2 | 971 091 | 18 526 | 59 475 | 25.0 | 47 122 | 75.9 | 24.1 | 33.9 | 10.0 | 276 | 4.0 |
| Rockingham County-Strafford County, NH Div..... | 59 | -9.2 | 66 | 0.5 | 22.6 | 536 131 | 8 108 | 59 634 | 35.9 | 40 075 | 71.1 | 28.9 | 29.0 | 6.9 | 342 | 7.2 |
| Boulder, CO ........................ | 138 | 27.8 | 185 | 33.9 | 54.4 | 588 686 | 3 190 | 66 628 | 34.0 | 45 626 | 76.4 | 23.6 | 31.2 | 6.8 | 376 | 11.1 |
| Bowling Green, KY ............... | 362 | 3.7 | 143 | 0.4 | 193.0 | 410 520 | 2 878 | 56 921 | 92.2 | 36 342 | 27.0 | 73.0 | 32.1 | 5.2 | 2 896 | 33.4 |
| Bremerton-Silverdale, WA .... | 15 | -6.3 | 23 | 0.9 | 3.7 | 429 990 | 18 668 | 31 903 | 7.0 | 10 520 | 75.5 | 24.6 | 17.2 | 1.2 | 88 | 2.6 |
| Bridgeport-Stamford-Norwalk, CT ......................... | 40 | 207.7 | 128 | 0.2 | 6.6 | 1 850 189 | 14 505 | 64 999 | 37.3 | 120 274 | 77.7 | 22.3 | 39.4 | 11.3 | 19 | 2.6 |
| Brownsville-Harlingen, TX..... | 349 | -0.3 | 282 | 101.1 | 226.1 | 544 393 | 1 933 | 73 172 | 112.4 | 90 532 | 93.5 | 6.5 | 33.1 | 11.9 | 7 614 | 41.6 |
| Brunswick, GA ..................... | 40 | -21.6 | 121 | 0.5 | 13.8 | 331 124 | 2 737 | 59 737 | 9.2 | 27 658 | 35.8 | 64.2 | 19.5 | 3.3 | D | 16.2 |
| Buffalo-Niagara Falls, NY ..... | 292 | -5.8 | 140 | 5.5 | 212.2 | 359 197 | 2 559 | 98 364 | 220.6 | 106 094 | 46.4 | 53.6 | 38.7 | 14.4 | 2 935 | 24.6 |
| Burlington, NC...................... | 88 | -10.2 | 117 | 1.6 | 35.9 | 538 124 | 4 610 | 60 524 | 42.6 | 56 598 | 19.2 | 80.8 | 34.3 | 10.5 | 459 | 18.2 |
| Burlington-South Burlington, VT ................................... | 281 | -0.7 | 194 | 0.6 | 127.6 | 572 197 | 2 947 | 87 799 | 207.7 | 143 718 | 12.1 | 87.9 | 47.1 | 20.6 | 2 563 | 23.7 |
| Canton-Massillon, OH........... | 255 | -5.2 | 123 | 1.5 | 166.8 | 496 200 | 4 037 | 80 553 | 164.4 | 79 265 | 30.2 | 69.8 | 39.0 | 11.2 | 2 375 | 30.7 |
| Cape Coral-Fort Myers, FL... | 86 | -31.7 | 91 | 14.6 | 22.0 | 982 569 | 10 818 | 39 788 | 116.1 | 122 945 | 97.1 | 2.9 | 26.2 | 6.1 | 142 | 1.2 |
| Cape Girardeau-Jackson, MO-IL ............................. | 558 | -1.6 | 228 | D | 333.7 | 533 823 | 2 339 | 65 475 | 117.4 | 48 002 | 59.1 | 40.9 | 40.6 | 8.8 | 5 674 | 52.1 |
| Carson City, NV ................... | 3 | -25.0 | 131 | D | 1.2 | 408 435 | 3 112 | 67 740 | 1.1 | 54 143 | D | D | 23.8 | 14.3 | 0 | 0.0 |
| Casper, WY ......................... | 2 181 | -24.0 | 5 282 | 40.3 | 49.6 | 1 762 052 | 334 | 92 949 | 32.7 | 79 186 | 16.5 | 83.5 | 47.0 | 17.4 | 1 623 | 19.4 |
| Cedar Rapids, IA .................. | 1 060 | -0.1 | 280 | 1.2 | 922.6 | 1 015 910 | 3 623 | 129 041 | 628.8 | 166 313 | 60.0 | 40.0 | 63.0 | 33.2 | 25 307 | 80.1 |
| Champaign-Urbana, IL........... | 1 088 | -2.9 | 455 | 7.6 | 1 054.3 | 1 938 330 | 4 262 | 182 960 | 603.9 | 252 333 | 93.2 | 6.8 | 72.4 | 45.4 | 20 145 | 86.4 |

# Table C. Metropolitan Areas — Water Use, Wholesale Trade, Retail Trade, and Real Estate

| Area name | Water use, 2005 | | Wholesale trade,[1] 2007 | | | | Retail trade, 2007 | | | | Real estate and rental and leasing, 2007 | | | |
|---|---|---|---|---|---|---|---|---|---|---|---|---|---|---|
| | Total water withdrawn (mil gal/day) | Gallons withdrawn per person | Number of establishments | Number of employees | Sales (mil dol) | Annual payroll (mil dol) | Number of establishments | Number of employees | Sales (mil dol) | Annual payroll (mil dol) | Number of establishments | Number of employees | Receipts (mil dol) | Annual payroll (mil dol) |
| | 133 | 134 | 135 | 136 | 137 | 138 | 139 | 140 | 141 | 142 | 143 | 144 | 145 | 146 |
| Abilene, TX | 32.1 | 202 | 193 | 1 967 | 2 268.2 | 73.8 | 669 | 9 119 | 2 345.6 | 198.3 | 179 | 691 | 138.2 | 20.3 |
| Akron, OH | 86.2 | 123 | 1 219 | 20 568 | 16 631.7 | 1 019.7 | 2 352 | 37 531 | 9 041.6 | 837.9 | 631 | 3 366 | 550.4 | 99.0 |
| Albany, GA | 230.7 | 1 417 | 215 | 2 662 | 1 564.5 | 101.7 | 713 | 8 401 | 1 873.5 | 169.0 | 191 | 816 | 105.1 | 20.8 |
| Albany-Schenectady-Troy, NY | 378.8 | 446 | 982 | 13 583 | 11 573.9 | 698.0 | 3 171 | 49 200 | 13 228.5 | 1 093.6 | 837 | 5 299 | 996.5 | 172.8 |
| Albuquerque, NM | 433.6 | 543 | 1 076 | 14 486 | 9 054.4 | 627.5 | 2 639 | 43 054 | 11 242.4 | 1 044.5 | 1 142 | 5 807 | 964.0 | 165.4 |
| Alexandria, LA | 531.4 | 3 591 | 160 | 1 971 | 871.4 | 72.0 | 632 | 8 233 | 1 984.9 | 175.8 | 142 | 742 | 93.3 | 18.7 |
| Allentown-Bethlehem-Easton, PA-NJ | 515.2 | 652 | 964 | 20 599 | 25 205.8 | 1 139.1 | 2 820 | 42 384 | 10 520.7 | 957.2 | 609 | 3 073 | 646.9 | 95.0 |
| Altoona, PA | 18.4 | 145 | 143 | 2 326 | 1 655.2 | 94.4 | 619 | 9 366 | 2 038.7 | 179.6 | 82 | 393 | 66.7 | 10.3 |
| Amarillo, TX | 129.9 | 544 | 295 | 5 106 | 4 256.4 | 208.3 | 952 | 13 887 | 4 007.6 | 308.9 | 293 | 1 331 | 220.1 | 38.7 |
| Ames, IA | 11.9 | 149 | 93 | 1 178 | 752.6 | 61.9 | 320 | 4 611 | 968.3 | 91.7 | 96 | 371 | 38.1 | 10.1 |
| Anchorage, AK | 114.4 | 325 | 444 | 6 534 | 5 323.2 | 318.7 | 1 156 | 19 042 | 5 336.6 | 528.6 | 450 | 2 688 | 490.9 | 100.8 |
| Anderson, IN | 15.6 | 119 | 89 | 1 535 | 848.2 | 73.7 | 431 | 5 542 | 1 234.9 | 108.0 | 103 | 434 | 61.5 | 10.2 |
| Anderson, SC | 163.6 | 932 | 204 | 2 685 | 2 839.5 | 111.1 | 755 | 8 901 | 2 004.7 | 178.1 | 140 | 502 | 97.1 | 14.2 |
| Ann Arbor, MI | 37.9 | 111 | 346 | 4 097 | 4 021.3 | 224.6 | 1 148 | 16 403 | 3 681.1 | 355.3 | 368 | 2 595 | 712.4 | 98.3 |
| Anniston-Oxford, AL | 29.0 | 258 | 114 | 2 074 | 2 821.7 | 80.5 | 552 | 6 854 | 1 543.0 | 139.1 | 93 | 459 | 66.3 | 10.2 |
| Appleton, WI | 108.1 | 502 | 356 | 5 551 | 4 551.6 | 275.0 | 910 | 15 207 | 3 293.1 | 308.8 | 170 | 882 | 161.0 | 25.2 |
| Asheville, NC | 366.2 | 932 | 502 | 5 464 | 3 758.5 | 222.2 | 1 972 | 24 609 | 5 974.9 | 545.7 | 650 | 2 118 | 361.0 | 66.0 |
| Athens-Clarke County, GA | 15.1 | 86 | 188 | 2 661 | 2 082.7 | 109.0 | 750 | 10 066 | 2 184.3 | 208.0 | 299 | 975 | 144.9 | 28.2 |
| Atlanta-Sandy Springs-Marietta, GA | 1 137.4 | 231 | 9 593 | 158 372 | 208 828.5 | 9 408.4 | 17 974 | 270 206 | 68 832.2 | 6 431.2 | 8 188 | 47 362 | 11 310.7 | 2 418.0 |
| Atlantic City-Hammonton, NJ | 51.4 | 190 | 222 | 3 376 | 1 707.0 | 153.3 | 1 291 | 17 258 | 4 429.4 | 428.6 | 287 | 1 867 | 378.7 | 56.9 |
| Auburn-Opelika, AL | 21.5 | 175 | 74 | D | D | D | 472 | 6 391 | 1 451.6 | 125.3 | 122 | 636 | 79.4 | 15.0 |
| Augusta-Richmond County, GA-SC | 436.4 | 839 | 433 | 4 840 | 6 428.9 | 222.6 | 1 989 | 25 509 | 6 159.3 | 545.1 | 508 | 2 512 | 401.4 | 64.3 |
| Austin-Round Rock-San Marcos, TX | 902.6 | 621 | 1 902 | 49 950 | 67 697.7 | 3 260.9 | 5 347 | 85 862 | 26 735.1 | 2 106.9 | 2 431 | 15 328 | 2 945.6 | 588.7 |
| Bakersfield-Delano, CA | 2 663.6 | 3 519 | 654 | 9 008 | 6 890.3 | 442.1 | 1 993 | 30 123 | 7 876.0 | 725.6 | 627 | 3 414 | 565.5 | 112.8 |
| Baltimore-Towson, MD | 1 521.7 | 573 | 3 400 | 56 795 | 45 872.4 | 3 139.0 | 9 536 | 141 052 | 36 583.9 | 3 462.3 | 3 126 | 22 029 | 5 938.1 | 951.3 |
| Bangor, ME | 45.1 | 307 | 179 | 2 391 | 1 551.7 | 91.7 | 777 | 10 842 | 2 983.9 | 241.6 | 172 | 782 | 124.9 | 21.8 |
| Barnstable Town, MA | 529.6 | 2 338 | 220 | 1 393 | 951.9 | 64.9 | 1 628 | 16 213 | 3 973.2 | 427.7 | 385 | 1 632 | 270.6 | 50.3 |
| Baton Rouge, LA | 1 711.4 | 2 332 | 1 018 | D | D | D | 2 955 | 42 265 | 10 269.6 | 925.2 | 790 | 4 107 | 773.4 | 129.2 |
| Battle Creek, MI | 35.6 | 255 | 117 | 1 177 | 862.9 | 48.4 | 531 | 7 074 | 1 571.3 | 136.0 | 95 | 475 | 62.7 | 11.7 |
| Bay City, MI | 629.6 | 5 774 | 108 | 1 326 | 1 255.5 | 55.1 | 430 | 5 580 | 1 301.0 | 115.5 | 77 | 316 | 39.9 | 6.0 |
| Beaumont-Port Arthur, TX | 1 465.0 | 3 820 | 390 | 5 724 | 6 727.5 | 279.7 | 1 467 | 20 141 | 5 437.5 | 453.8 | 373 | 1 811 | 374.9 | 60.0 |
| Bellingham, WA | 81.3 | 443 | 343 | 3 433 | 1 563.8 | 151.4 | 851 | 11 100 | 2 556.0 | 263.5 | 352 | 1 254 | 240.2 | 33.3 |
| Bend, OR | 206.6 | 1 462 | 264 | 2 142 | 1 372.8 | 96.6 | 867 | 10 952 | 2 809.1 | 271.9 | 452 | 1 782 | 229.7 | 48.2 |
| Billings, MT | 765.3 | 5 221 | 377 | 5 080 | 2 901.4 | 228.5 | 816 | 10 481 | 2 901.4 | 255.0 | 283 | 938 | 147.3 | 27.2 |
| Binghamton, NY | 125.5 | 505 | 243 | 4 513 | 2 868.2 | 176.0 | 904 | 13 259 | 2 875.2 | 264.9 | 169 | 1 138 | 195.2 | 31.5 |
| Birmingham-Hoover, AL | 1 934.9 | 1 775 | 1 946 | 30 000 | 29 323.4 | 1 528.0 | 4 676 | 62 472 | 15 876.1 | 1 402.5 | 1 167 | 9 929 | 1 714.4 | 357.8 |
| Bismarck, ND | 78.7 | 792 | 202 | 2 233 | 1 477.7 | 91.5 | 479 | 7 818 | 1 743.1 | 162.0 | 143 | 440 | 67.3 | 9.8 |
| Blacksburg-Christiansburg-Radford, VA | 377.9 | 2 502 | 98 | 834 | 412.3 | 29.2 | 600 | 8 010 | 1 702.0 | 166.6 | 153 | 692 | 107.3 | 18.1 |
| Bloomington, IN | 24.2 | 136 | 124 | 2 308 | 1 891.9 | 106.7 | 670 | 8 993 | 1 863.2 | 174.4 | 212 | 1 206 | 149.0 | 30.2 |
| Bloomington-Normal, IL | 16.0 | 100 | 195 | 3 322 | 5 883.8 | 180.4 | 608 | 9 660 | 2 231.4 | 197.0 | 153 | 934 | 139.2 | 24.9 |
| Boise City-Nampa, ID | 3 330.0 | 6 119 | 921 | 12 110 | 11 570.5 | 632.6 | 2 086 | 31 707 | 8 214.7 | 755.8 | 1 166 | 4 330 | 626.0 | 134.3 |
| Boston-Cambridge-Quincy, MA-NH | 2 211.5 | 501 | 6 813 | 119 540 | 117 889.5 | 8 202.0 | 17 098 | 252 997 | 62 993.3 | 6 370.9 | 5 163 | 38 734 | 12 365.6 | 1 975.4 |
| Boston-Quincy, MA Div | 380.8 | 212 | 2 667 | 45 484 | 40 858.2 | 2 896.0 | 6 996 | 101 159 | 25 422.3 | 2 592.9 | 2 351 | 21 098 | 7 628.9 | 1 225.5 |
| Cambridge-Newton-Framingham, MA Div | 388.9 | 267 | 2 464 | 51 935 | 54 648.1 | 3 879.8 | 5 306 | 80 413 | 19 661.1 | 2 036.6 | 1 690 | 12 621 | 3 802.7 | 571.3 |
| Peabody, MA Div | 505.2 | 684 | 963 | 13 443 | 14 341.3 | 890.2 | 2 690 | 38 874 | 9 822.1 | 962.0 | 647 | 3 045 | 584.1 | 109.8 |
| Rockingham County-Strafford County, NH Div | 936.7 | 2 262 | 719 | 8 678 | 8 041.9 | 536.0 | 2 106 | 32 551 | 8 087.8 | 779.4 | 475 | 1 970 | 349.9 | 68.8 |
| Boulder, CO | 203.7 | 726 | 493 | 6 003 | 5 023.0 | 503.9 | 1 244 | 17 620 | 4 039.3 | 444.5 | 669 | 2 365 | 441.7 | 83.2 |
| Bowling Green, KY | 20.9 | 189 | 151 | 2 199 | 2 357.6 | 84.1 | 562 | 7 706 | 1 723.7 | 153.7 | 133 | 1 113 | 114.4 | 28.7 |
| Bremerton-Silverdale, WA | 28.0 | 116 | 184 | 1 178 | 765.1 | 49.0 | 840 | 11 918 | 2 936.2 | 301.3 | 392 | 1 332 | 224.2 | 37.3 |
| Bridgeport-Stamford-Norwalk, CT | 652.0 | 722 | 1 514 | 26 495 | 102 548.3 | 2 145.5 | 3 770 | 53 738 | 15 702.2 | 1 648.8 | 1 174 | 7 465 | 2 283.4 | 450.7 |
| Brownsville-Harlingen, TX | 210.1 | 555 | 369 | 3 911 | 1 687.8 | 103.8 | 1 230 | 17 667 | 3 911.7 | 340.0 | 341 | 1 593 | 169.4 | 30.0 |
| Brunswick, GA | 116.0 | 1 178 | 117 | 841 | 712.8 | 37.2 | 613 | 5 777 | 1 528.2 | 131.0 | 210 | 746 | 98.2 | 20.8 |
| Buffalo-Niagara Falls, NY | 1 093.4 | 953 | 1 537 | 27 236 | 28 529.7 | 1 362.0 | 4 106 | 63 093 | 13 292.3 | 1 288.6 | 962 | 6 639 | 1 001.2 | 187.0 |
| Burlington, NC | 24.3 | 173 | 170 | 1 941 | 729.4 | 79.1 | 631 | 8 251 | 1 968.8 | 168.1 | 135 | 523 | 83.0 | 14.7 |
| Burlington-South Burlington, VT | 32.2 | 157 | 352 | 5 012 | 3 160.1 | 252.4 | 1 161 | 14 844 | 3 325.7 | 338.6 | 280 | 1 674 | 268.5 | 48.9 |
| Canton-Massillon, OH | 53.4 | 130 | 462 | 6 462 | 6 803.2 | 283.7 | 1 463 | 22 719 | 5 127.3 | 489.7 | 336 | 1 611 | 212.8 | 37.3 |
| Cape Coral-Fort Myers, FL | 709.1 | 1 291 | 722 | 6 704 | 3 136.0 | 278.9 | 2 624 | 38 417 | 9 193.1 | 923.2 | 1 307 | 5 643 | 1 000.1 | 171.3 |
| Cape Girardeau-Jackson, MO-IL | 48.9 | 529 | 161 | 2 392 | 1 944.1 | 89.0 | 502 | 6 629 | 1 435.4 | 130.8 | 123 | 447 | 65.0 | 10.2 |
| Carson City, NV | 9.9 | 177 | 110 | 628 | 466.6 | 34.9 | 262 | 3 698 | 991.5 | 99.5 | 147 | 569 | 73.4 | 16.0 |
| Casper, WY | 119.5 | 1 712 | 195 | 2 240 | 3 159.9 | 117.2 | 406 | 5 138 | 1 377.0 | 130.4 | 164 | 1 076 | 263.3 | 45.7 |
| Cedar Rapids, IA | 276.8 | 1 123 | 434 | 5 479 | 3 412.3 | 249.5 | 971 | 16 000 | 4 026.9 | 346.6 | 264 | 1 765 | 363.2 | 93.1 |
| Champaign-Urbana, IL | 47.9 | 222 | 249 | 4 262 | 4 179.3 | 174.1 | 773 | 12 055 | 2 578.2 | 232.8 | 246 | 1 707 | 352.3 | 51.7 |

1. Merchant wholesalers, except manufacturers' sales branches and offices.

# Table C. Metropolitan Areas — Professional Services, Manufacturing, and Accommodation and Food Services

| Area name | Professional, scientific, and technical services,[1] 2007 | | | | Manufacturing, 2007 | | | | Accommodation and food services, 2007 | | | |
|---|---|---|---|---|---|---|---|---|---|---|---|---|
| | Number of establish-ments | Number of employees | Sales (mil dol) | Annual payroll (mil dol) | Number of establish-ments | Number of employees | Sales (mil dol) | Annual payroll (mil dol) | Number of establish-ments | Number of employees | Sales (mil dol) | Annual payroll (mil dol) |
| | 147 | 148 | 149 | 150 | 151 | 152 | 153 | 154 | 155 | 156 | 157 | 158 |
| Abilene, TX .......................... | 299 | D | D | D | 122 | 2 733 | 872.6 | 98.4 | 317 | 6 881 | 258.4 | 72.4 |
| Akron, OH ........................... | 1 871 | D | D | D | 1 188 | 43 853 | 12 245.1 | 1 954.4 | 1 528 | 27 058 | 1 072.7 | 304.9 |
| Albany, GA .......................... | 257 | 1 638 | 184.3 | 66.3 | 121 | 6 359 | 3 634.3 | 293.1 | 261 | 4 659 | 190.0 | 47.7 |
| Albany-Schenectady-Troy, NY ..................................... | 2 360 | D | D | D | 644 | 21 188 | 7 638.7 | 1 042.7 | 2 110 | 29 445 | 1 417.6 | 404.0 |
| Albuquerque, NM .................. | 2 517 | D | D | D | 772 | 23 520 | 8 364.1 | 1 084.6 | 1 584 | 35 110 | 1 617.4 | 473.8 |
| Alexandria, LA ..................... | 289 | 1 767 | 208.0 | 69.4 | 90 | 4 781 | 4 348.7 | 203.9 | 228 | 4 326 | 176.7 | 45.0 |
| Allentown-Bethlehem-Easton, PA-NJ ..................... | 1 687 | D | D | D | 951 | 38 581 | 13 681.2 | 1 779.0 | 1 763 | 24 480 | 1 153.7 | 305.4 |
| Altoona, PA .......................... | 228 | D | D | D | 139 | 7 282 | 1 931.2 | 285.6 | 274 | 4 841 | 178.9 | 52.0 |
| Amarillo, TX ......................... | 485 | D | D | D | 209 | 8 141 | 4 404.5 | 316.3 | 527 | 10 352 | 460.4 | 121.7 |
| Ames, IA .............................. | 193 | D | D | D | 75 | 4 668 | 1 970.8 | 213.4 | 224 | 4 388 | 151.0 | 43.4 |
| Anchorage, AK ..................... | 1 224 | 9 898 | 1 669.9 | 623.5 | 230 | 2 522 | 527.6 | 99.9 | 905 | 15 805 | 1 047.0 | 314.1 |
| Anderson, IN ........................ | 202 | D | D | D | 118 | 4 652 | 1 046.9 | 191.8 | 246 | 4 343 | 155.1 | 43.6 |
| Anderson, SC........................ | 288 | D | D | D | 222 | 12 655 | 4 886.3 | 495.2 | 350 | 6 420 | 235.8 | 64.5 |
| Ann Arbor, MI ....................... | 1 215 | 14 248 | 1 788.8 | 1 017.4 | 324 | 15 543 | 5 331.8 | 881.4 | 679 | 13 734 | 613.5 | 180.4 |
| Anniston-Oxford, AL.............. | 171 | D | D | D | 141 | 6 961 | 2 680.0 | 279.3 | 224 | 5 129 | 186.5 | 51.5 |
| Appleton, WI ........................ | 412 | 4 621 | 494.8 | 195.4 | 415 | 22 900 | 8 157.8 | 1 044.1 | 524 | 9 585 | 336.2 | 93.5 |
| Asheville, NC ....................... | 1 181 | 5 910 | 636.1 | 259.1 | 517 | 21 057 | 6 271.5 | 863.5 | 1 042 | 20 002 | 966.0 | 282.4 |
| Athens-Clarke County, GA ... | 476 | D | D | D | 165 | 7 971 | 2 219.7 | 300.5 | 421 | 8 235 | 341.3 | 92.1 |
| Atlanta-Sandy Springs-Marietta, GA ............................... | 20 442 | D | D | D | 4 312 | 161 018 | 58 521.5 | 6 922.0 | 10 511 | 207 366 | 10 689.7 | 2 961.9 |
| Atlantic City-Hammonton, NJ | 648 | D | D | D | 140 | 2 974 | D | 113.8 | 862 | 56 370 | 6 093.0 | 1 505.4 |
| Auburn-Opelika, AL............... | 189 | D | D | D | 123 | D | D | D | 271 | 5 515 | 201.2 | 55.8 |
| Augusta-Richmond County, GA-SC.................................. | 939 | 7 751 | 952.3 | 400.6 | 348 | 24 428 | 12 650.6 | 1 145.3 | 921 | 18 737 | 730.0 | 197.2 |
| Austin-Round Rock-San Marcos, TX ............................... | 6 052 | D | D | D | 1 254 | 47 630 | 31 352.5 | 2 345.7 | 3 350 | 73 490 | 3 796.0 | 1 061.5 |
| Bakersfield-Delano, CA........ | 1 123 | D | D | D | 390 | 12 789 | 9 456.2 | 583.7 | 1 203 | 19 344 | 940.3 | 252.2 |
| Baltimore-Towson, MD ......... | 9 266 | D | D | D | 1 923 | 70 099 | 24 306.5 | 3 738.1 | 5 326 | 97 405 | 5 371.3 | 1 450.1 |
| Bangor, ME .......................... | 333 | D | D | D | 155 | 4 795 | 1 088.5 | 171.9 | 320 | 5 179 | 224.2 | 68.1 |
| Barnstable Town, MA ........... | 753 | D | D | D | 210 | 2 461 | 533.3 | 110.3 | 1 100 | 12 721 | 891.0 | 261.6 |
| Baton Rouge, LA .................. | 2 098 | 21 316 | 3 219.4 | 1 140.7 | 593 | 24 773 | D | 1 555.1 | 1 330 | 29 936 | 1 290.3 | 354.2 |
| Battle Creek, MI ................... | 209 | D | D | D | 179 | 11 532 | 4 954.0 | 537.5 | 284 | 4 558 | 182.0 | 54.1 |
| Bay City, MI ......................... | 174 | D | D | D | 126 | 3 532 | 1 107.2 | 191.2 | 238 | 3 973 | 134.7 | 41.3 |
| Beaumont-Port Arthur, TX .... | 669 | D | D | D | 334 | 21 563 | 55 089.6 | 1 369.4 | 610 | 12 226 | 510.0 | 142.0 |
| Bellingham, WA .................... | 670 | 3 562 | 419.2 | 163.4 | 334 | 10 165 | 11 809.7 | 467.2 | 505 | 8 461 | 407.9 | 116.2 |
| Bend, OR ............................. | 650 | D | D | D | 299 | 5 359 | 897.4 | 201.7 | 504 | 8 078 | 416.4 | 121.1 |
| Billings, MT .......................... | 597 | 3 280 | 381.0 | 140.5 | 199 | 4 019 | 5 749.0 | 192.4 | 418 | 8 244 | 380.3 | 102.9 |
| Binghamton, NY ................... | 386 | D | D | D | 248 | 12 807 | 3 061.1 | 547.3 | 590 | 8 663 | 359.2 | 102.8 |
| Birmingham-Hoover, AL........ | 2 807 | D | D | D | 1 124 | 43 380 | 14 083.7 | 1 858.2 | 1 941 | 37 945 | 1 780.0 | 490.8 |
| Bismarck, ND ....................... | 312 | D | D | D | 112 | 3 008 | 2 444.2 | 128.7 | 223 | 5 122 | 196.2 | 57.5 |
| Blacksburg-Christiansburg-Radford, VA ....................... | 318 | D | D | D | 144 | 12 277 | 4 578.7 | 563.8 | 320 | 6 166 | 237.7 | 67.2 |
| Bloomington, IN ................... | 345 | 3 106 | 341.1 | 119.1 | 165 | 8 676 | 2 098.3 | 358.6 | 407 | 8 252 | 317.8 | 87.3 |
| Bloomington-Normal, IL ........ | 338 | D | D | D | 115 | 5 497 | 2 578.8 | 270.5 | 375 | 8 558 | 336.1 | 97.4 |
| Boise City-Nampa, ID ........... | 1 896 | D | D | D | 686 | 31 240 | 7 792.3 | 1 593.2 | 1 214 | 22 484 | 955.9 | 263.5 |
| Boston-Cambridge-Quincy, MA-NH .............................. | 17 498 | 217 147 | 44 853.7 | 19 181.6 | 5 111 | 195 861 | 61 691.3 | 11 207.1 | 10 883 | 185 188 | 11 243.7 | 3 263.0 |
| Boston-Quincy, MA Div......... | 7 059 | 87 301 | 19 961.7 | 7 896.4 | 1 634 | 52 290 | 16 621.4 | 2 675.9 | 4 715 | 90 155 | 5 884.4 | 1 711.7 |
| Cambridge-Newton-Framingham, MA Div ............ | 6 883 | 106 332 | 21 264.5 | 9 828.5 | 1 853 | 72 842 | 22 482.6 | 4 609.2 | 3 372 | 54 344 | 3 250.2 | 932.3 |
| Peabody, MA Div ............. | 2 221 | D | D | D | 997 | 47 909 | 17 488.7 | 2 877.4 | 1 708 | 23 927 | 1 301.5 | 377.7 |
| Rockingham County-Strafford County, NH Div..... | 1 335 | D | D | D | 627 | 22 820 | 5 098.6 | 1 044.6 | 1 088 | 16 762 | 807.6 | 241.3 |
| Boulder, CO .......................... | 2 447 | 23 459 | 5 054.5 | 1 781.8 | 534 | 16 791 | 3 855.9 | 896.9 | 815 | 14 563 | 668.9 | 208.4 |
| Bowling Green, KY .............. | 214 | D | D | D | 123 | 9 585 | 4 553.4 | 420.7 | 230 | 5 598 | 237.5 | 65.3 |
| Bremerton-Silverdale, WA .... | 716 | D | D | D | 163 | 2 154 | D | 78.3 | 505 | 7 483 | 392.8 | 117.4 |
| Bridgeport-Stamford-Norwalk, CT ............................ | 3 778 | 38 942 | 7 103.5 | 3 058.3 | 1 029 | 42 123 | 20 028.4 | 2 455.4 | 2 094 | 27 883 | 1 861.9 | 523.1 |
| Brownsville-Harlingen, TX..... | 474 | D | D | D | 221 | D | D | D | 643 | 12 287 | 503.1 | 131.4 |
| Brunswick, GA ...................... | 288 | D | D | D | 90 | 2 703 | 1 039.9 | 128.0 | 301 | 8 019 | 422.4 | 168.9 |
| Buffalo-Niagara Falls, NY ..... | 2 438 | D | D | D | 1 381 | 58 267 | 19 306.9 | 2 971.5 | 2 602 | 45 852 | 2 125.2 | 585.3 |
| Burlington, NC....................... | 233 | D | D | D | 236 | 11 733 | 3 163.1 | 445.0 | 281 | 5 080 | 219.4 | 62.8 |
| Burlington-South Burlington, VT ..................................... | 796 | 6 254 | 963.7 | 364.3 | 267 | 14 916 | 6 278.4 | 825.9 | 548 | 8 285 | 406.9 | 118.1 |
| Canton-Massillon, OH.......... | 766 | D | D | D | 591 | 28 877 | 10 732.0 | 1 239.0 | 827 | 14 271 | 536.8 | 159.5 |
| Cape Coral-Fort Myers, FL... | 1 848 | 10 115 | 1 305.2 | 511.3 | 403 | 5 988 | 1 181.8 | 222.6 | 1 095 | 23 070 | 1 192.0 | 344.2 |
| Cape Girardeau-Jackson, MO-IL ................................ | 173 | D | D | D | 117 | D | 3 422.7 | D | 210 | 4 272 | 153.9 | 44.6 |
| Carson City, NV ................... | 381 | D | D | D | 143 | 3 528 | 621.6 | 141.7 | 167 | 2 664 | 127.7 | 37.8 |
| Casper, WY .......................... | 271 | D | D | D | 94 | 2 525 | 1 230.6 | 114.9 | 185 | 3 853 | 168.0 | 50.0 |
| Cedar Rapids, IA .................. | 568 | 4 799 | 591.8 | 251.1 | 297 | 19 479 | 8 586.7 | 1 183.3 | 564 | 10 050 | 373.0 | 108.5 |
| Champaign-Urbana, IL.......... | 513 | 3 125 | 317.1 | 134.5 | 178 | 10 029 | 3 636.3 | 375.3 | 569 | 10 437 | 395.9 | 110.4 |

1. Establishments subject to federal tax.

# Table C. Metropolitan Areas — Health Care and Social Assistance, Other Services, and Federal Funds

| Area name | Health care and social assistance,¹ 2007 | | | | Other services,¹ 2007 | | | | Federal funds and grants, 2009–2010 Expenditures (mil dol) | | | |
|---|---|---|---|---|---|---|---|---|---|---|---|---|
| | | | | | | | | | Total | Direct payments for individuals | | |
| | Number of establishments | Number of employees | Receipts (mil dol) | Annual payroll (mil dol) | Number of establishments | Number of employees | Receipts (mil dol) | Annual payroll (mil dol) | Total | Social Security and government retirement | Medicare | Food stamps and Supplemental Security Income |
| | 159 | 160 | 161 | 162 | 163 | 164 | 165 | 166 | 167 | 168 | 169 | 170 |
| Abilene, TX | 414 | 12 311 | 867.5 | 349.6 | 282 | 1 664 | 155.5 | 33.1 | 1 522.1 | 517.9 | 259.3 | 62.4 |
| Akron, OH | 1 747 | 45 542 | 4 061.5 | 1 663.5 | 1 385 | 9 299 | 848.2 | 233.6 | 5 424.2 | 1 904.7 | 1 318.8 | 260.5 |
| Albany, GA | 381 | 9 322 | 901.4 | 336.0 | 261 | 1 363 | 108.3 | 31.5 | 1 593.7 | 466.2 | 223.1 | 137.2 |
| Albany-Schenectady-Troy, NY | 2 387 | 59 709 | 5 105.9 | 2 166.3 | 1 562 | 11 148 | 1 149.1 | 327.4 | 15 440.0 | 2 615.5 | 1 260.0 | 237.9 |
| Albuquerque, NM | 1 980 | 47 563 | 4 218.4 | 1 840.5 | 1 252 | 8 779 | 735.2 | 228.6 | 10 866.1 | 2 763.5 | 828.3 | 308.1 |
| Alexandria, LA | 504 | 13 319 | 1 227.1 | 490.7 | 234 | 1 217 | 103.1 | 28.2 | 1 612.5 | 501.6 | 309.4 | 85.6 |
| Allentown-Bethlehem-Easton, PA-NJ | 2 303 | 52 271 | 5 144.4 | 2 080.5 | 1 597 | 9 216 | 808.4 | 228.4 | 6 417.2 | 2 552.6 | 1 716.2 | 181.3 |
| Altoona, PA | 403 | 10 162 | 909.5 | 373.1 | 299 | 1 686 | 115.7 | 33.5 | 1 300.8 | 508.9 | 337.5 | 63.5 |
| Amarillo, TX | 696 | 14 808 | 1 630.0 | 558.6 | 430 | 2 890 | 296.8 | 63.7 | 4 532.8 | 641.5 | 305.5 | 74.3 |
| Ames, IA | 172 | 5 026 | 415.3 | 172.4 | 148 | 1 096 | 212.9 | 28.7 | 1 268.6 | 195.3 | 80.6 | 12.0 |
| Anchorage, AK | 1 265 | 23 414 | 2 932.2 | 1 066.8 | 693 | 4 558 | 498.1 | 139.1 | 5 174.2 | 871.7 | 168.0 | 93.3 |
| Anderson, IN | 266 | 6 713 | 556.4 | 223.6 | 201 | 1 239 | 83.4 | 24.0 | 1 214.0 | 561.7 | 257.3 | 55.3 |
| Anderson, SC | 362 | 8 112 | 786.0 | 301.2 | 244 | 1 871 | 154.5 | 55.0 | 1 233.9 | 629.3 | 227.6 | 51.1 |
| Ann Arbor, MI | 958 | 34 745 | 3 715.8 | 1 627.0 | 557 | 3 917 | 443.2 | 122.6 | 3 527.0 | 780.4 | 357.0 | 71.1 |
| Anniston-Oxford, AL | 283 | 6 307 | 545.7 | 206.7 | 186 | 944 | 81.3 | 22.1 | 1 726.3 | 565.6 | 229.3 | 61.1 |
| Appleton, WI | 533 | 12 694 | 1 231.7 | 517.6 | 428 | 2 780 | 233.4 | 63.7 | 1 113.3 | 556.9 | 180.9 | 24.8 |
| Asheville, NC | 1 187 | 30 282 | 2 822.7 | 1 140.5 | 736 | 4 230 | 346.8 | 97.5 | 3 486.0 | 1 639.3 | 616.9 | 147.1 |
| Athens-Clarke County, GA | 502 | 9 685 | 949.3 | 406.1 | 288 | 2 216 | 236.0 | 46.0 | 1 291.2 | 448.1 | 174.0 | 68.2 |
| Atlanta-Sandy Springs-Marietta, GA | 11 642 | 213 216 | 23 772.3 | 8 863.9 | 8 707 | 63 724 | 7 448.4 | 2 039.4 | 40 616.0 | 11 173.4 | 4 215.5 | 1 600.6 |
| Atlantic City-Hammonton, NJ | 821 | 16 172 | 1 780.0 | 702.6 | 547 | 3 496 | 270.1 | 81.7 | 2 365.5 | 831.2 | 563.0 | 79.3 |
| Auburn-Opelika, AL | 221 | 6 157 | 469.5 | 191.8 | 152 | 748 | 49.7 | 14.2 | 762.5 | 321.6 | 107.1 | 38.7 |
| Augusta-Richmond County, GA-SC | 1 202 | 30 349 | 3 176.8 | 1 186.0 | 715 | 4 312 | 403.1 | 97.3 | 8 423.1 | 1 929.1 | 643.9 | 292.8 |
| Austin-Round Rock-San Marcos, TX | 3 713 | 65 629 | 7 015.6 | 2 738.4 | 2 745 | 23 514 | 2 463.8 | 746.5 | 19 767.6 | 3 272.5 | 966.8 | 320.3 |
| Bakersfield-Delano, CA | 1 456 | 25 119 | 2 746.4 | 1 042.9 | 857 | 5 637 | 569.1 | 145.0 | 5 744.5 | 1 632.6 | 1 074.6 | 328.6 |
| Baltimore-Towson, MD | 7 208 | 173 557 | 19 053.3 | 7 171.0 | 4 997 | 36 876 | 4 149.0 | 1 100.5 | 42 393.2 | 8 445.7 | 8 890.6 | 968.5 |
| Bangor, ME | 563 | 14 538 | 1 318.9 | 561.5 | 276 | 1 350 | 139.8 | 33.6 | 1 644.1 | 537.9 | 207.0 | 75.8 |
| Barnstable Town, MA | 807 | 15 247 | 1 466.2 | 620.7 | 601 | 3 279 | 334.9 | 88.2 | 2 650.7 | 1 059.0 | 647.7 | 45.7 |
| Baton Rouge, LA | 1 846 | 44 467 | 3 987.1 | 1 469.8 | 1 286 | 8 991 | 1 020.9 | 274.9 | 11 347.0 | 1 776.3 | 1 142.6 | 316.9 |
| Battle Creek, MI | 341 | 8 967 | 898.1 | 372.5 | 225 | 1 249 | 503.8 | 42.5 | 1 481.8 | 503.1 | 252.8 | 76.8 |
| Bay City, MI | 315 | 5 902 | 513.3 | 209.5 | 196 | 1 068 | 75.9 | 21.8 | 897.4 | 401.0 | 203.4 | 50.5 |
| Beaumont-Port Arthur, TX | 1 067 | 20 932 | 1 827.1 | 667.3 | 546 | 4 058 | 408.7 | 101.5 | 3 258.9 | 1 150.7 | 904.1 | 195.8 |
| Bellingham, WA | 636 | 9 730 | 862.9 | 348.7 | 390 | 2 155 | 207.5 | 59.0 | 1 279.8 | 567.6 | 165.5 | 57.7 |
| Bend, OR | 543 | 8 144 | 974.3 | 351.5 | 322 | 1 761 | 169.5 | 46.5 | 950.9 | 535.6 | 125.8 | 37.1 |
| Billings, MT | 530 | 11 746 | 1 181.9 | 481.4 | 396 | 2 015 | 200.9 | 49.3 | 1 203.6 | 486.3 | 179.4 | 34.3 |
| Binghamton, NY | 509 | 14 884 | 1 302.9 | 525.8 | 393 | 2 253 | 180.7 | 49.2 | 2 815.9 | 834.7 | 420.9 | 100.2 |
| Birmingham-Hoover, AL | 2 532 | 67 157 | 7 562.2 | 2 841.0 | 1 808 | 12 646 | 1 451.4 | 387.1 | 10 252.3 | 3 661.4 | 2 153.4 | 475.9 |
| Bismarck, ND | 277 | 10 100 | 791.4 | 358.3 | 307 | 1 965 | 177.7 | 49.9 | 1 625.9 | 320.6 | 119.5 | 19.5 |
| Blacksburg-Christiansburg-Radford, VA | 352 | 6 425 | 602.1 | 236.0 | 261 | 1 258 | 286.9 | 29.4 | 1 292.2 | 453.5 | 197.6 | 40.7 |
| Bloomington, IN | 398 | 9 059 | 775.2 | 333.4 | 292 | 2 362 | 632.3 | 60.8 | 1 461.9 | 495.9 | 186.9 | 41.7 |
| Bloomington-Normal, IL | 333 | 8 693 | 875.8 | 354.5 | 260 | 2 362 | 187.8 | 59.7 | 758.0 | 353.8 | 140.8 | 25.7 |
| Boise City-Nampa, ID | 1 697 | 31 482 | 2 897.6 | 1 212.9 | 1 042 | 5 975 | 489.1 | 149.9 | 4 516.3 | 1 573.1 | 405.9 | 151.6 |
| Boston-Cambridge-Quincy, MA-NH | 12 525 | 363 736 | 38 593.4 | 16 468.8 | 9 748 | 68 801 | 7 926.9 | 2 151.1 | 57 692.9 | 11 465.4 | 9 038.9 | 1 325.8 |
| Boston-Quincy, MA Div | 4 996 | 196 332 | 22 166.2 | 9 425.4 | 4 172 | 31 341 | 3 772.0 | 965.8 | 25 223.8 | 4 550.7 | 4 100.1 | 703.5 |
| Cambridge-Newton-Framingham, MA Div | 4 386 | 99 055 | 10 192.8 | 4 326.2 | 3 202 | 23 744 | 2 577.2 | 790.2 | 20 144.1 | 3 615.4 | 3 012.9 | 287.1 |
| Peabody, MA Div | 2 030 | 47 584 | 4 272.0 | 1 909.5 | 1 470 | 8 644 | 1 096.7 | 254.2 | 9 423.9 | 2 019.7 | 1 518.0 | 274.1 |
| Rockingham County-Strafford County, NH Div | 1 113 | 20 765 | 1 962.4 | 807.6 | 904 | 5 072 | 481.0 | 140.9 | 2 901.1 | 1 279.6 | 407.9 | 61.2 |
| Boulder, CO | 1 158 | 17 109 | 1 712.5 | 716.4 | 711 | 4 509 | 794.5 | 161.0 | 3 118.2 | 722.8 | 256.8 | 37.7 |
| Bowling Green, KY | 330 | 7 655 | 723.8 | 248.3 | 170 | 1 195 | 85.2 | 25.0 | 960.1 | 327.7 | 250.2 | 47.8 |
| Bremerton-Silverdale, WA | 659 | 12 424 | 1 169.6 | 482.9 | 392 | 2 004 | 157.5 | 48.0 | 4 004.4 | 1 088.8 | 231.7 | 79.6 |
| Bridgeport-Stamford-Norwalk, CT | 2 739 | 60 497 | 6 923.5 | 2 604.2 | 2 056 | 13 357 | 1 722.7 | 431.1 | 13 539.9 | 2 248.1 | 4 982.5 | 184.7 |
| Brownsville-Harlingen, TX | 925 | 27 384 | 1 711.7 | 686.6 | 424 | 2 214 | 140.9 | 36.3 | 2 895.6 | 668.7 | 441.3 | 326.4 |
| Brunswick, GA | 288 | 4 943 | 911.7 | 189.7 | 180 | 984 | 79.4 | 22.4 | 1 113.1 | 380.2 | 183.4 | 51.5 |
| Buffalo-Niagara Falls, NY | 3 234 | 83 751 | 7 057.8 | 2 815.2 | 2 120 | 14 710 | 1 200.3 | 353.0 | 10 696.4 | 4 017.3 | 2 172.2 | 485.5 |
| Burlington, NC | 335 | 6 483 | 549.1 | 227.9 | 201 | 1 165 | 93.5 | 27.7 | 925.3 | 465.3 | 191.6 | 35.2 |
| Burlington-South Burlington, VT | 683 | 15 754 | 1 488.8 | 590.1 | 485 | 2 339 | 195.7 | 60.4 | 2 414.8 | 514.0 | 194.6 | 54.4 |
| Canton-Massillon, OH | 1 035 | 27 536 | 2 171.5 | 939.1 | 772 | 5 203 | 433.8 | 121.3 | 3 022.6 | 1 347.1 | 733.2 | 146.4 |
| Cape Coral-Fort Myers, FL | 1 389 | 25 867 | 3 068.2 | 1 115.8 | 1 206 | 6 552 | 589.9 | 162.5 | 4 275.2 | 2 289.1 | 1 205.1 | 133.0 |
| Cape Girardeau-Jackson, MO-IL | 307 | 10 119 | 997.5 | 366.8 | 184 | 820 | 69.0 | 17.4 | 771.9 | 289.0 | 131.1 | 37.9 |
| Carson City, NV | 220 | 3 407 | 453.3 | 164.1 | 149 | 948 | 83.3 | 25.4 | 1 497.0 | 208.9 | 85.3 | 13.9 |
| Casper, WY | 283 | 4 819 | 482.2 | 203.0 | 202 | 1 200 | 141.1 | 34.1 | 499.4 | 205.5 | 84.1 | 15.6 |
| Cedar Rapids, IA | 636 | 14 920 | 1 253.2 | 527.7 | 494 | 2 818 | 266.2 | 68.4 | 2 861.1 | 713.8 | 293.0 | 59.9 |
| Champaign-Urbana, IL | 425 | 12 236 | 1 340.7 | 527.4 | 334 | 2 303 | 437.5 | 58.5 | 1 707.6 | 478.9 | 205.3 | 48.8 |

1. Establishments subject to federal tax.

| | Federal funds and grants, 2009–2010 (cont.) | | | | | | | Value of residential construction authorized by building permits, 2011 | | Local government finances, 2007 | | | | |
|---|---|---|---|---|---|---|---|---|---|---|---|---|---|---|
| | Expenditures (mil dol) (cont.) | | | | | | | | | General revenue | | | | |
| | Procurement contract awards | | | Grants | | | | | | | | Taxes | | |
| | | | | | | | | | | | | | Per capita[1] (dollars) | |
| Area name | Salaries and wages | Defense | Other | Medicaid and other health-related | Nutrition and family welfare | Education | Other | New construction ($1,000) | Number of housing units | Total (mil dol) | Inter-governmental (mil dol) | Total (mil dol) | Total | Property |
| | 171 | 172 | 173 | 174 | 175 | 176 | 177 | 178 | 179 | 180 | 181 | 182 | 183 | 184 |
| Abilene, TX | 319.2 | 74.7 | 9.7 | 168.4 | 28.6 | 6.8 | 17.5 | 28 029 | 159 | 470.3 | 202.9 | 186.0 | 1 167 | 854 |
| Akron, OH | 239.3 | 443.7 | 64.0 | 623.8 | 129.8 | 54.4 | 188.1 | 143 067 | 1 122 | 3 024.0 | 1 110.1 | 1 248.6 | 1 785 | 1 223 |
| Albany, GA | 176.9 | 112.3 | 64.4 | 231.4 | 51.4 | 23.1 | 18.1 | 21 956 | 206 | 550.1 | 247.8 | 204.8 | 1 248 | 771 |
| Albany-Schenectady-Troy, NY | 728.8 | 383.8 | 258.0 | 1 647.8 | 1 313.6 | 2 357.6 | 4 085.2 | 304 007 | 1 764 | 4 338.0 | 1 520.4 | 2 036.1 | 2 386 | 1 696 |
| Albuquerque, NM | 1 275.3 | 770.5 | 2 911.8 | 1 248.6 | 152.1 | 93.8 | 273.1 | 269 592 | 1 634 | 2 999.5 | 1 585.5 | 895.0 | 1 072 | 551 |
| Alexandria, LA | 276.2 | 11.0 | 90.0 | 217.3 | 35.6 | 14.0 | 45.7 | 52 915 | 376 | 476.7 | 234.0 | 178.8 | 1 194 | 433 |
| Allentown-Bethlehem-Easton, PA-NJ | 290.1 | 129.3 | 87.0 | 475.1 | 109.6 | 23.7 | 755.1 | 179 659 | 1 133 | 3 470.1 | 1 251.1 | 1 482.4 | 1 844 | 1 536 |
| Altoona, PA | 83.3 | 1.9 | 63.2 | 170.2 | 31.2 | 4.1 | 23.9 | 13 020 | 75 | 389.5 | 217.2 | 109.2 | 870 | 625 |
| Amarillo, TX | 143.6 | 2 428.8 | 638.8 | 123.3 | 36.1 | 12.4 | 50.9 | 156 587 | 703 | 772.5 | 278.6 | 337.7 | 1 394 | 1 070 |
| Ames, IA | 85.6 | 15.0 | 63.0 | 61.0 | 8.3 | 2.6 | 699.8 | 44 503 | 457 | 394.2 | 77.8 | 112.0 | 1 321 | 1 045 |
| Anchorage, AK | 1 152.4 | 964.8 | 317.7 | 347.8 | 96.0 | 52.1 | 1 036.5 | 131 625 | 524 | 1 504.4 | 673.5 | 577.6 | 1 594 | 1 354 |
| Anderson, IN | 33.7 | 4.5 | 13.0 | 160.5 | 19.5 | 3.3 | 93.3 | 14 735 | 75 | 356.2 | 165.7 | 101.0 | 769 | 650 |
| Anderson, SC | 86.7 | 14.6 | 6.6 | 132.5 | 19.3 | 15.9 | 25.4 | 49 797 | 280 | 424.3 | 186.7 | 168.4 | 936 | 819 |
| Ann Arbor, MI | 231.6 | 107.4 | 209.4 | 1 191.4 | 49.9 | 31.5 | 388.9 | 65 511 | 477 | 1 351.8 | 485.7 | 589.1 | 1 683 | 1 660 |
| Anniston-Oxford, AL | 233.1 | 415.3 | 58.5 | 104.4 | 16.3 | 9.1 | 7.4 | 10 862 | 83 | 507.7 | 186.6 | 103.4 | 915 | 334 |
| Appleton, WI | 72.0 | 50.5 | 22.8 | 115.4 | 22.7 | 10.6 | 23.0 | 87 068 | 648 | 890.5 | 410.2 | 315.7 | 1 448 | 1 413 |
| Asheville, NC | 257.4 | 34.7 | 134.3 | 437.0 | 65.4 | 31.7 | 48.2 | 205 237 | 1 001 | 1 444.9 | 558.6 | 469.0 | 1 160 | 845 |
| Athens-Clarke County, GA | 130.5 | 5.7 | 34.6 | 209.7 | 37.7 | 19.7 | 109.9 | 51 732 | 327 | 947.2 | 205.0 | 237.4 | 1 267 | 877 |
| Atlanta-Sandy Springs-Marietta, GA | 5 338.8 | 4 883.8 | 3 094.4 | 3 008.9 | 1 054.1 | 1 467.7 | 3 707.8 | 1 400 186 | 8 634 | 19 722.7 | 5 897.8 | 9 275.4 | 1 757 | 1 171 |
| Atlantic City-Hammonton, NJ | 301.1 | 40.6 | 95.9 | 278.6 | 51.5 | 10.0 | 40.2 | 64 738 | 390 | 1 515.6 | 456.0 | 828.2 | 3 060 | 2 999 |
| Auburn-Opelika, AL | 70.4 | 22.7 | 10.2 | 66.3 | 18.2 | 7.9 | 59.1 | 191 657 | 957 | 728.3 | 134.9 | 132.6 | 1 016 | 470 |
| Augusta-Richmond County, GA-SC | 1 841.2 | 308.0 | 2 426.2 | 622.2 | 107.1 | 46.4 | 88.9 | 372 784 | 2 385 | 1 604.4 | 689.3 | 568.4 | 1 075 | 726 |
| Austin-Round Rock-San Marcos, TX | 1 062.5 | 924.6 | 996.8 | 1 500.5 | 1 129.7 | 1 338.0 | 7 867.2 | 1 367 696 | 10 239 | 5 871.3 | 1 096.4 | 3 419.2 | 2 139 | 1 751 |
| Bakersfield-Delano, CA | 772.0 | 484.6 | 233.1 | 712.0 | 203.4 | 69.5 | 80.2 | 150 696 | 969 | 5 502.3 | 2 722.3 | 1 021.3 | 1 292 | 1 083 |
| Baltimore-Towson, MD | 5 294.7 | 5 598.5 | 2 795.0 | 5 324.4 | 670.0 | 800.7 | 3 035.1 | 912 375 | 6 153 | 10 299.2 | 3 623.0 | 5 170.4 | 1 938 | 979 |
| Bangor, ME | 173.7 | 131.4 | 69.6 | 254.0 | 28.6 | 10.5 | 90.0 | 36 853 | 369 | 413.1 | 167.1 | 177.0 | 1 190 | 1 173 |
| Barnstable Town, MA | 250.1 | 84.7 | 75.5 | 189.4 | 35.0 | 11.3 | 233.0 | 140 861 | 404 | 915.3 | 212.8 | 541.7 | 2 438 | 2 298 |
| Baton Rouge, LA | 395.4 | 326.2 | -77.6 | 764.4 | 331.9 | 475.7 | 5 723.7 | 526 894 | 3 135 | 2 588.1 | 848.0 | 1 205.4 | 1 565 | 592 |
| Battle Creek, MI | 156.6 | 156.0 | 60.6 | 190.7 | 37.0 | 11.3 | 11.6 | 7 704 | 49 | 634.9 | 350.7 | 166.3 | 1 217 | 1 073 |
| Bay City, MI | 40.3 | 1.8 | 13.8 | 103.8 | 22.2 | 5.9 | 6.3 | 14 849 | 91 | 514.5 | 250.3 | 131.3 | 1 221 | 1 199 |
| Beaumont-Port Arthur, TX | 214.5 | 49.8 | 42.8 | 494.6 | 65.0 | 15.3 | 50.9 | 131 886 | 1 179 | 1 383.2 | 423.7 | 634.6 | 1 687 | 1 368 |
| Bellingham, WA | 120.9 | 22.1 | 48.4 | 128.8 | 33.0 | 12.1 | 69.1 | 108 013 | 605 | 612.9 | 225.3 | 248.7 | 1 288 | 756 |
| Bend, OR | 84.9 | 4.7 | 24.7 | 59.4 | 15.8 | 6.7 | 33.8 | 105 512 | 459 | 589.4 | 201.9 | 249.0 | 1 617 | 1 353 |
| Billings, MT | 162.4 | 3.5 | 112.1 | 134.9 | 33.5 | 10.7 | 13.7 | 48 225 | 272 | 487.6 | 170.6 | 139.3 | 931 | 856 |
| Binghamton, NY | 78.3 | 902.7 | 21.3 | 268.4 | 68.8 | 22.7 | 70.9 | 15 084 | 117 | 1 283.1 | 575.4 | 516.8 | 2 097 | 1 385 |
| Birmingham-Hoover, AL | 970.2 | 291.3 | 373.3 | 1 229.2 | 154.1 | 84.7 | 470.7 | 388 781 | 2 362 | 4 025.7 | 1 389.6 | 1 664.7 | 1 502 | 599 |
| Bismarck, ND | 185.3 | 6.7 | 41.7 | 85.0 | 53.8 | 85.2 | 642.9 | 128 184 | 844 | 314.1 | 111.3 | 123.7 | 1 198 | 1 018 |
| Blacksburg-Christiansburg-Radford, VA | 56.6 | 148.9 | 35.6 | 141.3 | 17.5 | 10.2 | 144.8 | 44 913 | 330 | 391.6 | 180.6 | 139.2 | 883 | 604 |
| Bloomington, IN | 94.9 | 9.1 | 16.4 | 443.8 | 22.0 | 13.7 | 88.9 | 33 049 | 236 | 428.6 | 173.5 | 142.3 | 774 | 676 |
| Bloomington-Normal, IL | 67.4 | 0.3 | 18.6 | 56.5 | 18.9 | 5.3 | 21.8 | 62 499 | 620 | 542.8 | 157.7 | 275.3 | 1 676 | 1 372 |
| Boise City-Nampa, ID | 524.3 | 45.0 | 165.4 | 502.1 | 111.2 | 134.3 | 785.3 | 390 712 | 1 840 | 1 650.3 | 728.4 | 519.6 | 884 | 806 |
| Boston-Cambridge-Quincy, MA-NH | 3 497.6 | 10 905.4 | 2 895.5 | 10 529.5 | 976.2 | 1 129.9 | 4 630.0 | 1 327 032 | 6 139 | 19 175.6 | 7 604.7 | 8 730.3 | 1 947 | 1 885 |
| Boston-Quincy, MA Div | 1 700.4 | 924.2 | 1 218.4 | 6 916.5 | 589.5 | 684.0 | 2 868.1 | 555 996 | 2 727 | 8 898.4 | 4 131.0 | 3 591.8 | 1 933 | 1 848 |
| Cambridge-Newton-Framingham, MA Div | 1 248.1 | 5 847.4 | 1 415.4 | 2 508.9 | 213.3 | 356.0 | 1 452.4 | 454 991 | 1 823 | 6 250.8 | 1 991.3 | 3 083.9 | 2 093 | 2 040 |
| Peabody, MA Div | 269.8 | 3 843.8 | 150.9 | 900.1 | 132.3 | 59.5 | 163.4 | 164 567 | 725 | 2 602.3 | 1 061.9 | 1 210.2 | 1 651 | 1 609 |
| Rockingham County-Strafford County, NH Div | 279.4 | 290.0 | 110.8 | 204.0 | 41.1 | 30.4 | 146.1 | 151 479 | 864 | 1 424.2 | 420.5 | 844.3 | 2 019 | 1 990 |
| Boulder, CO | 317.0 | 183.9 | 532.6 | 216.3 | 30.3 | 21.4 | 757.2 | 132 006 | 661 | 1 187.5 | 282.9 | 670.7 | 2 311 | 1 403 |
| Bowling Green, KY | 64.9 | 1.9 | 22.2 | 94.7 | 20.5 | 11.0 | 60.5 | 73 158 | 843 | 258.0 | 112.2 | 111.8 | 963 | 444 |
| Bremerton-Silverdale, WA | 969.1 | 598.8 | 59.3 | 132.3 | 45.2 | 26.1 | 709.1 | 105 792 | 540 | 945.8 | 310.5 | 312.3 | 1 312 | 828 |
| Bridgeport-Stamford-Norwalk, CT | 303.9 | 4 045.9 | 346.9 | 869.6 | 127.7 | 52.2 | 278.3 | 322 224 | 937 | 4 018.8 | 884.0 | 2 701.7 | 3 019 | 2 940 |
| Brownsville-Harlingen, TX | 234.8 | 17.6 | 103.1 | 761.1 | 155.1 | 35.2 | 63.4 | 109 449 | 1 136 | 1 402.5 | 780.0 | 367.1 | 948 | 734 |
| Brunswick, GA | 209.9 | 12.0 | 123.1 | 79.7 | 27.1 | 9.4 | 18.8 | 89 567 | 396 | 582.6 | 107.4 | 194.1 | 1 907 | 1 222 |
| Buffalo-Niagara Falls, NY | 753.4 | 285.9 | 226.9 | 1 795.3 | 331.4 | 103.0 | 275.7 | 226 967 | 1 315 | 5 642.4 | 2 660.4 | 2 237.6 | 1 983 | 1 360 |
| Burlington, NC | 28.0 | 5.2 | 9.0 | 128.2 | 19.4 | 10.3 | 9.6 | 76 728 | 556 | 402.1 | 208.0 | 128.4 | 883 | 667 |
| Burlington-South Burlington, VT | 419.8 | 503.0 | 115.9 | 371.0 | 38.0 | 15.6 | 120.6 | 101 471 | 681 | 699.0 | 467.0 | 118.5 | 572 | 486 |
| Canton-Massillon, OH | 168.2 | 9.2 | 24.1 | 351.7 | 74.1 | 33.0 | 61.7 | 45 763 | 256 | 1 359.3 | 639.7 | 489.8 | 1 203 | 913 |
| Cape Coral-Fort Myers, FL | 190.7 | 4.9 | 41.8 | 138.2 | 62.1 | 27.1 | 94.8 | 313 138 | 1 587 | 3 868.3 | 890.3 | 1 485.2 | 2 515 | 2 088 |
| Cape Girardeau-Jackson, MO-IL | 61.4 | 11.5 | 9.7 | 147.6 | 12.4 | 6.6 | 30.0 | 19 257 | 122 | 214.6 | 87.5 | 90.2 | 966 | 537 |
| Carson City, NV | 66.8 | 14.4 | 10.5 | 71.7 | 107.2 | 177.7 | 730.6 | 2 424 | 13 | 198.2 | 99.8 | 49.3 | 897 | 577 |
| Casper, WY | 60.4 | 6.7 | 26.2 | 43.2 | 9.6 | 5.5 | 33.5 | 53 589 | 402 | 354.6 | 203.8 | 86.7 | 1 209 | 798 |
| Cedar Rapids, IA | 107.1 | 1 128.7 | 254.2 | 153.2 | 35.3 | 6.4 | 37.3 | 77 633 | 731 | 942.6 | 364.3 | 357.6 | 1 415 | 1 268 |
| Champaign-Urbana, IL | 140.1 | 32.8 | 47.5 | 253.8 | 30.2 | 19.8 | 377.6 | 69 320 | 518 | 716.8 | 278.6 | 307.3 | 1 391 | 1 167 |

1. Based on the resident population estimated as of July 1 of the year shown.

# Table C. Metropolitan Areas — Local Government Finances, Government Employment, and Voting

| Area name | Local government finances, 2007 (cont.) — Direct general expenditure | | | | | | | Debt outstanding | | Government employment, 2011 | | | Presidential election,[2] 2012 — Percent of vote cast: | | |
| --- | --- | --- | --- | --- | --- | --- | --- | --- | --- | --- | --- | --- | --- | --- | --- |
| | Total (mil dol) | Per capita[1] (dollars) | Education | Health and hospitals | Police protection | Public welfare | Highways | Total (mil dol) | Per capita[1] (dollars) | Federal civilian | Federal military | State and local | Democratic | Republican | All other |
| | 185 | 186 | 187 | 188 | 189 | 190 | 191 | 192 | 193 | 194 | 195 | 196 | 197 | 198 | 199 |
| Abilene, TX | 483.1 | 3 032 | 57.7 | 5.6 | 6.2 | 0.4 | 2.7 | 325.2 | 2 041 | 1 337 | 5 056 | 11 773 | 21.7 | 76.9 | 1.4 |
| Akron, OH | 3 049.0 | 4 360 | 38.9 | 10.8 | 5.8 | 5.8 | 5.3 | 2 396.6 | 3 427 | 2 288 | 1 822 | 46 696 | 56.0 | 42.5 | 1.5 |
| Albany, GA | 533.4 | 3 251 | 54.1 | 5.5 | 5.8 | 0.1 | 3.8 | 484.6 | 2 954 | 3 400 | 889 | 10 381 | 53.6 | 45.9 | 0.6 |
| Albany-Schenectady-Troy, NY | 4 414.1 | 5 173 | 47.6 | 3.3 | 3.7 | 11.9 | 4.2 | 4 465.8 | 5 233 | 6 871 | 3 107 | 92 882 | 57.0 | 41.0 | 2.0 |
| Albuquerque, NM | 2 712.4 | 3 248 | 50.0 | 0.6 | 8.2 | 2.0 | 6.4 | 2 515.3 | 3 012 | 15 743 | 6 164 | 66 361 | 54.0 | 41.0 | 5.0 |
| Alexandria, LA | 453.6 | 3 028 | 50.6 | 0.2 | 9.0 | 0.0 | 5.2 | 371.5 | 2 480 | 2 970 | 741 | 11 407 | 32.2 | 66.4 | 1.4 |
| Allentown-Bethlehem-Easton, PA-NJ | 3 616.8 | 4 499 | 52.6 | 2.7 | 3.1 | 9.4 | 2.8 | 5 776.8 | 7 186 | 2 347 | 2 084 | 38 911 | 50.6 | 48.1 | 1.4 |
| Altoona, PA | 382.8 | 3 050 | 55.8 | 0.2 | 2.5 | 7.8 | 5.2 | 430.7 | 3 431 | 1 019 | 324 | 8 002 | 32.4 | 66.3 | 1.3 |
| Amarillo, TX | 790.4 | 3 263 | 55.9 | 5.2 | 5.2 | 0.0 | 3.2 | 717.0 | 2 960 | 2 164 | 632 | 17 811 | 18.9 | 79.7 | 1.4 |
| Ames, IA | 363.8 | 4 292 | 28.6 | 44.0 | 3.1 | 0.7 | 3.6 | 190.7 | 2 251 | 1 123 | 399 | 18 261 | 55.6 | 41.7 | 2.7 |
| Anchorage, AK | 1 455.5 | 4 017 | 53.2 | 2.3 | 6.4 | 0.0 | 8.0 | 2 093.7 | 5 778 | 9 760 | 14 774 | 24 751 | NA | NA | NA |
| Anderson, IN | 426.4 | 3 247 | 50.8 | 0.3 | 4.1 | 3.0 | 3.4 | 373.2 | 2 842 | 257 | 435 | 5 787 | 46.6 | 51.1 | 2.3 |
| Anderson, SC | 416.3 | 2 313 | 65.6 | 1.5 | 6.3 | 0.0 | 2.4 | 418.4 | 2 325 | 336 | 805 | 11 187 | 31.0 | 67.5 | 1.5 |
| Ann Arbor, MI | 1 453.7 | 4 153 | 53.1 | 3.4 | 5.9 | 0.9 | 5.5 | 1 701.4 | 4 861 | 3 691 | 708 | 70 580 | 67.3 | 31.4 | 1.3 |
| Anniston-Oxford, AL | 494.3 | 4 370 | 38.2 | 35.3 | 3.6 | 0.2 | 4.0 | 141.5 | 1 251 | 5 206 | 670 | 8 059 | 33.5 | 65.3 | 1.2 |
| Appleton, WI | 951.8 | 4 365 | 53.8 | 4.3 | 4.5 | 4.9 | 8.9 | 934.0 | 4 284 | 692 | 645 | 11 453 | 47.2 | 51.2 | 1.6 |
| Asheville, NC | 1 464.8 | 3 623 | 38.3 | 18.5 | 4.1 | 6.0 | 1.3 | 696.1 | 1 722 | 3 795 | 1 153 | 23 712 | 48.4 | 49.8 | 1.8 |
| Athens-Clarke County, GA | 938.0 | 5 005 | 30.7 | 42.5 | 3.1 | 0.2 | 2.3 | 476.4 | 2 542 | 1 462 | 688 | 26 014 | 45.5 | 52.6 | 2.0 |
| Atlanta-Sandy Springs-Marietta, GA | 19 476.8 | 3 690 | 49.4 | 5.6 | 5.8 | 0.7 | 4.1 | 30 295.4 | 5 739 | 46 907 | 18 024 | 272 044 | 49.7 | 49.1 | 1.2 |
| Atlantic City-Hammonton, NJ | 1 447.7 | 5 349 | 53.0 | 0.9 | 7.2 | 2.0 | 2.4 | 1 176.7 | 4 348 | 2 795 | 893 | 20 356 | 58.0 | 41.1 | 0.9 |
| Auburn-Opelika, AL | 542.0 | 4 153 | 36.5 | 35.4 | 3.4 | 0.1 | 4.0 | 632.6 | 4 847 | 306 | 746 | 15 572 | 39.2 | 59.1 | 1.7 |
| Augusta-Richmond County, GA-SC | 1 685.7 | 3 190 | 51.5 | 9.8 | 4.8 | 0.2 | 2.8 | 2 485.7 | 4 703 | 8 934 | 11 921 | 38 880 | 45.5 | 53.5 | 1.1 |
| Austin-Round Rock-San Marcos, TX | 5 862.5 | 3 668 | 51.5 | 4.8 | 5.7 | 0.4 | 3.8 | 16 736.5 | 10 472 | 11 804 | 4 248 | 155 657 | 51.9 | 44.8 | 3.3 |
| Bakersfield-Delano, CA | 5 086.6 | 6 433 | 43.2 | 8.2 | 3.5 | 7.3 | 1.6 | 2 907.0 | 3 676 | 10 739 | 3 999 | 46 849 | 40.4 | 57.2 | 2.4 |
| Baltimore-Towson, MD | 10 472.5 | 3 925 | 51.2 | 2.3 | 7.3 | 0.6 | 4.3 | 8 728.9 | 3 272 | 80 747 | 25 760 | 174 746 | 57.8 | 39.8 | 2.4 |
| Bangor, ME | 434.5 | 2 920 | 52.8 | 0.4 | 4.1 | 0.5 | 4.6 | 271.7 | 1 826 | 1 299 | 497 | 13 170 | 50.2 | 47.3 | 2.5 |
| Barnstable Town, MA | 979.9 | 4 411 | 46.8 | 1.1 | 6.2 | 0.3 | 3.2 | 860.0 | 3 871 | 1 708 | 1 228 | 12 384 | 53.2 | 45.4 | 1.4 |
| Baton Rouge, LA | 2 346.3 | 3 047 | 45.4 | 5.2 | 6.7 | 0.2 | 5.6 | 3 202.0 | 4 158 | 3 013 | 4 010 | 71 866 | 43.0 | 55.4 | 1.6 |
| Battle Creek, MI | 649.8 | 4 756 | 50.9 | 14.2 | 3.9 | 2.4 | 4.3 | 580.6 | 4 250 | 2 890 | 310 | 7 418 | 50.2 | 48.6 | 1.2 |
| Bay City, MI | 497.3 | 4 625 | 48.5 | 16.6 | 3.8 | 4.2 | 5.0 | 312.7 | 2 909 | 259 | 236 | 5 555 | 52.2 | 46.7 | 1.1 |
| Beaumont-Port Arthur, TX | 1 279.1 | 3 400 | 48.4 | 3.8 | 6.2 | 0.5 | 3.2 | 2 405.7 | 6 394 | 2 187 | 1 103 | 22 897 | 39.0 | 60.1 | 0.9 |
| Bellingham, WA | 575.8 | 2 984 | 41.1 | 3.0 | 5.3 | 0.0 | 6.1 | 473.4 | 2 453 | 1 404 | 667 | 14 010 | 55.4 | 41.4 | 3.1 |
| Bend, OR | 590.3 | 3 832 | 42.3 | 3.4 | 7.3 | 0.5 | 6.4 | 840.1 | 5 454 | 900 | 450 | 7 439 | 45.1 | 51.8 | 3.0 |
| Billings, MT | 478.1 | 3 195 | 47.5 | 5.7 | 5.8 | 0.2 | 6.5 | 239.3 | 1 599 | 1 895 | 826 | 7 598 | 38.2 | 59.0 | 2.8 |
| Binghamton, NY | 1 347.2 | 5 467 | 47.6 | 2.9 | 2.6 | 10.8 | 4.6 | 1 079.9 | 4 382 | 762 | 423 | 22 022 | 49.5 | 48.4 | 2.2 |
| Birmingham-Hoover, AL | 4 040.7 | 3 646 | 46.0 | 4.2 | 6.0 | 0.1 | 5.3 | 9 265.7 | 8 361 | 9 086 | 5 802 | 70 760 | 39.3 | 59.6 | 1.1 |
| Bismarck, ND | 313.0 | 3 032 | 44.5 | 1.9 | 5.1 | 1.8 | 10.7 | 207.9 | 2 014 | 1 232 | 821 | 11 389 | 32.6 | 64.3 | 3.1 |
| Blacksburg-Christiansburg-Radford, VA | 371.9 | 2 360 | 47.0 | 2.1 | 6.6 | 4.5 | 4.7 | 401.0 | 2 544 | 460 | 565 | 19 551 | 44.7 | 52.6 | 2.7 |
| Bloomington, IN | 437.4 | 2 381 | 49.8 | 5.5 | 3.2 | 3.8 | 4.6 | 408.9 | 2 226 | 448 | 690 | 24 479 | 51.8 | 45.9 | 2.3 |
| Bloomington-Normal, IL | 563.9 | 3 434 | 44.5 | 1.2 | 5.4 | 1.4 | 5.2 | 651.5 | 3 968 | 711 | 347 | 14 579 | 43.4 | 54.4 | 2.1 |
| Boise City-Nampa, ID | 1 550.9 | 2 639 | 46.4 | 2.0 | 7.3 | 0.5 | 6.7 | 1 297.5 | 2 208 | 5 917 | 2 446 | 36 494 | 38.6 | 58.3 | 3.1 |
| Boston-Cambridge-Quincy, MA-NH | 17 835.4 | 3 979 | 50.4 | 5.2 | 5.7 | 1.0 | 2.7 | 16 972.0 | 3 786 | 38 308 | 15 319 | 259 028 | 60.1 | 38.2 | 1.7 |
| Boston-Quincy, MA Div | 7 572.1 | 4 075 | 46.6 | 2.5 | 7.0 | 1.3 | 2.5 | 10 257.6 | 5 520 | 19 683 | 6 368 | 125 300 | 61.9 | 36.5 | 1.6 |
| Cambridge-Newton-Framingham, MA Div | 6 127.7 | 4 159 | 50.3 | 11.8 | 4.4 | 0.3 | 2.7 | 3 686.3 | 2 502 | 13 699 | 5 270 | 72 788 | 62.6 | 35.4 | 2.0 |
| Peabody, MA Div | 2 691.9 | 3 672 | 57.7 | 0.4 | 4.9 | 0.1 | 2.6 | 2 237.1 | 3 052 | 3 473 | 2 039 | 35 922 | 57.4 | 41.1 | 1.5 |
| Rockingham County-Strafford County, NH Div | 1 443.7 | 3 453 | 56.5 | 0.4 | 5.8 | 4.6 | 3.8 | 790.9 | 1 892 | 1 453 | 1 642 | 25 018 | 49.6 | 48.9 | 1.5 |
| Boulder, CO | 1 157.4 | 3 987 | 40.7 | 0.9 | 7.7 | 2.8 | 6.3 | 2 072.2 | 7 139 | 2 142 | 911 | 28 805 | 69.7 | 27.8 | 2.5 |
| Bowling Green, KY | 257.4 | 2 219 | 52.4 | 0.9 | 6.6 | 0.1 | 4.5 | 849.4 | 7 322 | 685 | 419 | 10 636 | 37.4 | 61.0 | 1.6 |
| Bremerton-Silverdale, WA | 934.1 | 3 946 | 41.1 | 3.4 | 4.0 | 0.0 | 4.0 | 820.7 | 3 467 | 16 373 | 10 904 | 13 072 | 54.5 | 42.8 | 2.6 |
| Bridgeport-Stamford-Norwalk, CT | 3 883.2 | 4 339 | 56.0 | 0.9 | 5.8 | 0.7 | 2.3 | 3 327.6 | 3 718 | 2 982 | 1 822 | 43 482 | 54.9 | 44.2 | 0.9 |
| Brownsville-Harlingen, TX | 1 380.8 | 3 566 | 64.6 | 1.2 | 4.1 | 0.4 | 2.2 | 2 023.2 | 5 225 | 3 032 | 1 028 | 27 579 | 65.0 | 33.9 | 1.1 |
| Brunswick, GA | 549.2 | 5 396 | 32.4 | 37.6 | 4.0 | 0.1 | 2.0 | 467.0 | 4 588 | 1 865 | 410 | 8 292 | 34.6 | 64.4 | 1.0 |
| Buffalo-Niagara Falls, NY | 5 723.0 | 5 073 | 48.5 | 3.1 | 4.0 | 11.0 | 3.3 | 5 124.0 | 4 542 | 9 977 | 2 148 | 78 930 | 55.9 | 42.3 | 1.7 |
| Burlington, NC | 417.6 | 2 873 | 49.4 | 8.4 | 5.8 | 6.2 | 2.8 | 191.4 | 1 317 | 231 | 397 | 6 801 | 42.3 | 56.7 | 1.1 |
| Burlington-South Burlington, VT | 785.4 | 3 787 | 66.0 | 0.3 | 4.0 | 0.0 | 5.0 | 499.8 | 2 410 | 3 449 | 1 494 | 16 719 | 67.5 | 30.1 | 2.4 |
| Canton-Massillon, OH | 1 373.3 | 3 373 | 52.6 | 7.2 | 5.0 | 6.0 | 5.1 | 753.4 | 1 850 | 1 134 | 1 034 | 19 336 | 48.8 | 49.2 | 2.0 |
| Cape Coral-Fort Myers, FL | 3 524.7 | 5 968 | 29.1 | 19.2 | 4.5 | 0.4 | 5.9 | 4 370.1 | 7 400 | 2 422 | 1 297 | 34 191 | 41.4 | 57.9 | 0.7 |
| Cape Girardeau-Jackson, MO-IL | 229.4 | 2 459 | 61.1 | 1.2 | 4.3 | 0.1 | 7.4 | 185.6 | 1 989 | 486 | 331 | 6 758 | 28.9 | 69.3 | 1.8 |
| Carson City, NV | 199.1 | 3 625 | 39.8 | 3.2 | 11.6 | 1.0 | 5.7 | 200.1 | 3 642 | 547 | 147 | 8 973 | 44.1 | 53.1 | 2.7 |
| Casper, WY | 342.8 | 4 778 | 60.3 | 1.0 | 4.9 | 0.4 | 3.5 | 80.2 | 1 118 | 696 | 435 | 5 065 | 27.7 | 68.4 | 4.0 |
| Cedar Rapids, IA | 928.6 | 3 673 | 57.3 | 3.8 | 4.5 | 1.3 | 6.2 | 956.0 | 3 782 | 1 186 | 1 085 | 15 796 | 56.7 | 41.5 | 1.9 |
| Champaign-Urbana, IL | 689.4 | 3 120 | 49.3 | 2.5 | 5.6 | 3.9 | 6.0 | 375.4 | 1 699 | 1 343 | 500 | 36 349 | 49.0 | 48.3 | 2.7 |

1. Based on the resident population estimated as of July 1 of the year shown. 2. © 2013 Election Data Services, Inc. All rights reserved.

# Table C. Metropolitan Areas — Land Area and Population

| CBSA/ DIV code[1] | Area name | Land area,[2] 2010 (sq km) | Population 2012 | | | | Population characteristics, 2011 | | | | | | | | | | | |
|---|---|---|---|---|---|---|---|---|---|---|---|---|---|---|---|---|---|---|
| | | | Total persons | Rank | Per square kilometer | | Race alone or in combination, not Hispanic or Latino (percent) | | | | Percent Hispanic or Latino[3] | Age (percent) | | | | | |
| | | | | | | | White | Black | American Indian, Alaska Native | Asian and Pacific Islander | | Under 5 years | 5 to 17 years | 18 to 24 years | 25 to 34 years | 35 to 44 years | 45 to 54 years |
| | | 1 | 2 | 3 | 4 | | 5 | 6 | 7 | 8 | 9 | 10 | 11 | 12 | 13 | 14 | 15 |
| 16620 | Charleston, WV................. | 6 547 | 304 016 | 158 | 46.4 | | 93.1 | 5.8 | 0.7 | 1.1 | 0.9 | 5.8 | 15.7 | 7.5 | 12.1 | 12.8 | 15.0 |
| 16700 | Charleston-North Charleston-Summerville, SC..... | 6 703 | 697 439 | 77 | 104.0 | | 64.9 | 28.3 | 0.9 | 2.4 | 5.4 | 6.9 | 16.2 | 10.8 | 15.4 | 12.9 | 14.0 |
| 16740 | Charlotte-Gastonia-Rock Hill, NC-SC ............... | 7 991 | 1 831 084 | 34 | 229.1 | | 62.3 | 24.7 | 0.9 | 3.8 | 10.1 | 7.1 | 18.6 | 8.9 | 14.4 | 15.4 | 14.3 |
| 16820 | Charlottesville, VA ............. | 4 258 | 205 772 | 209 | 48.3 | | 78.3 | 13.5 | 0.6 | 4.9 | 4.9 | 5.7 | 14.5 | 14.2 | 13.6 | 11.8 | 13.7 |
| 16860 | Chattanooga, TN-GA .......... | 5 410 | 537 889 | 98 | 99.4 | | 80.6 | 14.6 | 0.8 | 1.8 | 3.7 | 6.0 | 16.1 | 9.5 | 12.6 | 13.0 | 14.4 |
| 16940 | Cheyenne, WY ................... | 6 956 | 94 483 | 354 | 13.6 | | 82.3 | 3.1 | 1.4 | 2.0 | 13.3 | 7.1 | 16.9 | 9.6 | 13.7 | 12.2 | 14.4 |
| 16980 | Chicago-Joliet-Naperville, IL-IN-WI ...................... | 18 640 | 9 522 434 | 3 | 510.9 | | 55.9 | 17.6 | 0.5 | 6.4 | 21.1 | 6.6 | 18.2 | 9.4 | 14.5 | 13.7 | 14.4 |
| 16980 | Chicago-Joliet-Naperville, IL Div ............................ | 11 921 | 7 945 578 | X | 666.5 | | 53.6 | 18.6 | 0.4 | 6.8 | 22.0 | 6.6 | 17.9 | 9.4 | 15.0 | 13.9 | 14.2 |
| 16980 | Gary, IN Div ...................... | 4 865 | 706 800 | X | 145.3 | | 65.9 | 18.9 | 0.6 | 1.6 | 14.3 | 6.4 | 18.5 | 8.9 | 12.5 | 12.7 | 14.7 |
| 16980 | Lake County-Kenosha County, IL-WI Div ......... | 1 854 | 870 056 | X | 469.3 | | 68.7 | 7.5 | 0.5 | 6.2 | 18.7 | 6.5 | 20.0 | 9.4 | 11.7 | 13.7 | 16.0 |
| 17020 | Chico, CA ......................... | 4 238 | 221 539 | 196 | 52.3 | | 77.6 | 2.4 | 3.0 | 5.9 | 14.7 | 5.5 | 15.0 | 15.8 | 11.9 | 10.3 | 12.5 |
| 17140 | Cincinnati-Middletown, OH-KY-IN ............................ | 11 375 | 2 144 210 | 27 | 188.5 | | 83.0 | 12.9 | 0.6 | 2.4 | 2.7 | 6.7 | 18.0 | 9.4 | 13.0 | 13.0 | 15.0 |
| 17300 | Clarksville, TN-KY.............. | 5 588 | 287 639 | 163 | 51.5 | | 72.3 | 19.6 | 1.1 | 3.0 | 7.0 | 8.6 | 18.7 | 12.0 | 16.7 | 12.7 | 12.1 |
| 17420 | Cleveland, TN ................... | 1 977 | 117 820 | 317 | 59.6 | | 90.5 | 4.4 | 0.9 | 1.2 | 4.4 | 5.8 | 16.9 | 10.0 | 12.1 | 13.3 | 14.4 |
| 17460 | Cleveland-Elyria-Mentor, OH ................................ | 5 173 | 2 063 535 | 29 | 398.9 | | 73.1 | 20.7 | 0.6 | 2.4 | 4.8 | 5.7 | 17.0 | 8.5 | 11.8 | 12.5 | 15.5 |
| 17660 | Coeur d'Alene, ID .............. | 3 222 | 142 357 | 281 | 44.2 | | 93.6 | 0.7 | 2.2 | 1.6 | 4.0 | 6.4 | 18.0 | 8.6 | 12.3 | 12.2 | 14.1 |
| 17780 | College Station-Bryan, TX ... | 5 439 | 234 501 | 191 | 43.1 | | 60.4 | 11.9 | 0.7 | 5.1 | 23.2 | 6.4 | 14.3 | 28.4 | 14.0 | 9.9 | 9.9 |
| 17820 | Colorado Springs, CO ........ | 6 951 | 668 353 | 80 | 96.2 | | 75.3 | 7.2 | 1.5 | 4.6 | 15.0 | 7.0 | 18.5 | 10.9 | 14.3 | 12.8 | 14.6 |
| 17860 | Columbia, MO ................... | 2 977 | 178 704 | 228 | 60.0 | | 83.8 | 10.4 | 1.0 | 4.4 | 3.1 | 6.1 | 14.7 | 21.0 | 14.8 | 11.2 | 12.1 |
| 17900 | Columbia, SC .................... | 9 590 | 784 745 | 70 | 81.8 | | 59.5 | 33.9 | 0.8 | 2.3 | 5.2 | 6.4 | 16.9 | 11.7 | 13.9 | 12.9 | 14.1 |
| 17980 | Columbus, GA-AL............... | 5 015 | 310 531 | 152 | 61.9 | | 51.4 | 41.2 | 0.9 | 2.6 | 6.1 | 7.3 | 17.7 | 11.4 | 14.7 | 12.3 | 13.5 |
| 18020 | Columbus, IN .................... | 1 054 | 79 129 | 362 | 75.1 | | 87.7 | 2.7 | 0.5 | 4.0 | 6.3 | 6.6 | 18.2 | 8.0 | 13.1 | 13.4 | 14.1 |
| 18140 | Columbus, OH ................... | 10 275 | 1 878 714 | 32 | 182.8 | | 77.8 | 16.2 | 0.8 | 3.9 | 3.7 | 6.9 | 17.7 | 10.2 | 14.8 | 13.9 | 14.3 |
| 18580 | Corpus Christi, TX ............. | 4 621 | 437 109 | 114 | 94.6 | | 36.6 | 3.6 | 0.6 | 2.0 | 58.2 | 6.9 | 18.8 | 9.9 | 13.3 | 12.0 | 13.8 |
| 18700 | Corvallis, OR..................... | 1 751 | 86 430 | 358 | 49.4 | | 85.8 | 1.6 | 1.7 | 7.6 | 6.7 | 4.3 | 12.8 | 24.6 | 11.7 | 9.7 | 11.7 |
| 18880 | Crestview-Fort Walton Beach-Destin, FL.......... | 2 409 | 190 083 | 222 | 78.9 | | 79.5 | 10.7 | 1.2 | 4.9 | 7.2 | 6.5 | 15.6 | 10.2 | 14.3 | 11.6 | 15.4 |
| 19060 | Cumberland, MD-WV.......... | 1 948 | 101 968 | 341 | 52.3 | | 91.0 | 7.7 | 0.5 | 1.0 | 1.3 | 4.8 | 13.5 | 12.4 | 11.6 | 12.1 | 14.1 |
| 19100 | Dallas-Fort Worth-Arlington, TX ................................ | 23 122 | 6 645 678 | 4 | 287.4 | | 51.1 | 15.4 | 0.9 | 6.2 | 28.1 | 7.7 | 20.0 | 9.3 | 14.9 | 14.8 | 14.1 |
| 19100 | Dallas-Plano-Irving, TX Div ............................ | 14 326 | 4 431 940 | X | 309.4 | | 48.1 | 16.5 | 0.8 | 6.8 | 29.3 | 7.7 | 20.0 | 9.3 | 15.1 | 15.1 | 14.0 |
| 19100 | Fort Worth-Arlington, TX Div ............................ | 8 796 | 2 213 738 | X | 251.7 | | 56.9 | 13.4 | 0.9 | 4.8 | 25.6 | 7.6 | 19.9 | 9.3 | 14.3 | 14.2 | 14.3 |
| 19140 | Dalton, GA ........................ | 1 644 | 142 751 | 280 | 86.8 | | 68.4 | 3.7 | 0.5 | 1.3 | 27.1 | 7.6 | 20.2 | 9.5 | 13.0 | 14.0 | 13.6 |
| 19180 | Danville, IL........................ | 2 327 | 80 727 | 361 | 34.7 | | 81.6 | 14.1 | 0.6 | 1.1 | 4.4 | 6.7 | 17.6 | 8.2 | 11.9 | 11.6 | 14.2 |
| 19260 | Danville, VA....................... | 2 621 | 105 803 | 336 | 40.4 | | 63.9 | 33.3 | 0.5 | 0.9 | 2.6 | 5.6 | 15.5 | 8.2 | 10.4 | 11.6 | 15.4 |
| 19340 | Davenport-Moline-Rock Island, IA-IL.................. | 5 879 | 382 630 | 134 | 65.1 | | 83.5 | 7.8 | 0.7 | 2.1 | 7.8 | 6.4 | 17.0 | 8.7 | 12.7 | 12.1 | 14.5 |
| 19380 | Dayton, OH ....................... | 4 418 | 842 858 | 62 | 190.8 | | 80.7 | 16.2 | 0.8 | 2.5 | 2.2 | 6.0 | 16.5 | 10.2 | 12.3 | 11.8 | 14.4 |
| 19460 | Decatur, AL....................... | 3 289 | 154 233 | 258 | 46.9 | | 79.1 | 12.7 | 3.2 | 0.8 | 6.5 | 6.2 | 17.4 | 8.3 | 12.3 | 13.1 | 15.2 |
| 19500 | Decatur, IL........................ | 1 504 | 110 122 | 332 | 73.2 | | 80.3 | 17.9 | 0.5 | 1.5 | 2.0 | 6.3 | 16.4 | 9.4 | 11.7 | 11.4 | 14.2 |
| 19660 | Deltona-Daytona Beach-Ormond Beach, FL........ | 2 852 | 496 950 | 103 | 174.2 | | 76.3 | 10.9 | 0.8 | 2.1 | 11.5 | 4.9 | 13.7 | 9.0 | 10.4 | 11.1 | 14.7 |
| 19740 | Denver-Aurora-Broomfield, CO .............................. | 21 616 | 2 645 209 | 21 | 122.4 | | 67.5 | 6.1 | 1.1 | 4.7 | 22.7 | 7.0 | 17.7 | 8.5 | 15.5 | 14.7 | 14.4 |
| 19780 | Des Moines-West Des Moines, IA.................... | 7 469 | 588 999 | 88 | 78.9 | | 84.9 | 5.7 | 0.6 | 3.7 | 6.8 | 7.5 | 18.4 | 8.5 | 15.2 | 13.8 | 13.9 |
| 19820 | Detroit-Warren-Livonia, MI... | 10 071 | 4 292 060 | 14 | 426.2 | | 69.4 | 23.6 | 0.9 | 4.1 | 4.0 | 5.9 | 17.9 | 8.8 | 11.9 | 13.4 | 15.5 |
| 19820 | Detroit-Livonia-Dearborn, MI Div ............................ | 1 585 | 1 792 365 | X | 1 130.8 | | 51.4 | 41.1 | 1.0 | 3.3 | 5.4 | 6.5 | 18.4 | 9.9 | 12.1 | 13.1 | 14.6 |
| 19820 | Warren-Troy-Farmington Hills, MI Div.............. | 8 486 | 2 499 695 | X | 294.6 | | 82.5 | 10.8 | 0.9 | 4.7 | 3.0 | 5.6 | 17.5 | 7.9 | 11.7 | 13.6 | 16.2 |
| 20020 | Dothan, AL........................ | 4 444 | 147 620 | 268 | 33.2 | | 72.4 | 23.9 | 1.0 | 1.0 | 3.1 | 6.3 | 17.4 | 8.1 | 12.2 | 12.7 | 14.3 |
| 20100 | Dover, DE ......................... | 1 518 | 167 626 | 240 | 110.4 | | 67.2 | 25.4 | 1.3 | 3.1 | 6.0 | 6.7 | 17.8 | 11.0 | 12.5 | 12.3 | 14.2 |
| 20220 | Dubuque, IA ...................... | 1 576 | 95 097 | 353 | 60.3 | | 93.8 | 3.2 | 0.4 | 1.6 | 2.0 | 6.3 | 17.1 | 10.3 | 12.2 | 11.3 | 14.4 |
| 20260 | Duluth, MN-WI ................... | 21 789 | 279 452 | 168 | 12.8 | | 93.7 | 2.1 | 3.7 | 1.4 | 1.3 | 5.5 | 14.7 | 11.8 | 11.9 | 11.0 | 14.8 |
| 20500 | Durham-Chapel Hill, NC ...... | 4 554 | 522 826 | 100 | 114.8 | | 56.8 | 27.8 | 0.9 | 5.1 | 11.3 | 6.5 | 15.5 | 12.5 | 15.1 | 13.5 | 13.4 |
| 20740 | Eau Claire, WI ................... | 4 264 | 163 599 | 242 | 38.4 | | 93.9 | 1.7 | 0.9 | 3.1 | 1.7 | 6.0 | 15.6 | 13.8 | 13.2 | 11.5 | 13.9 |
| 20940 | El Centro, CA..................... | 10 817 | 176 948 | 231 | 16.4 | | 14.1 | 3.1 | 1.1 | 1.8 | 80.6 | 7.9 | 20.9 | 11.2 | 14.0 | 12.9 | 12.6 |
| 21060 | Elizabethtown, KY.............. | 2 292 | 121 176 | 314 | 52.9 | | 81.6 | 12.4 | 1.0 | 3.0 | 4.9 | 7.0 | 18.3 | 9.6 | 13.6 | 13.2 | 15.1 |
| 21140 | Elkhart-Goshen, IN ............ | 1 200 | 199 619 | 215 | 166.3 | | 78.5 | 6.8 | 0.6 | 1.4 | 14.5 | 8.0 | 20.3 | 8.9 | 12.8 | 12.9 | 13.3 |
| 21300 | Elmira, NY......................... | 1 055 | 88 911 | 357 | 84.3 | | 89.2 | 7.9 | 0.7 | 1.8 | 2.7 | 5.9 | 16.2 | 9.1 | 12.0 | 12.1 | 15.4 |
| 21340 | El Paso, TX........................ | 2 623 | 827 398 | 64 | 315.4 | | 14.3 | 3.2 | 0.5 | 1.5 | 81.4 | 8.1 | 21.6 | 11.5 | 13.7 | 12.9 | 12.4 |
| 21500 | Erie, PA............................ | 2 070 | 280 646 | 166 | 135.6 | | 88.1 | 8.1 | 0.5 | 1.5 | 3.5 | 5.9 | 16.5 | 11.7 | 11.9 | 11.7 | 14.4 |
| 21660 | Eugene-Springfield, OR....... | 11 793 | 354 542 | 144 | 30.1 | | 87.5 | 1.7 | 2.6 | 4.3 | 7.6 | 5.1 | 14.3 | 13.4 | 12.8 | 11.4 | 13.1 |
| 21780 | Evansville, IN-KY................ | 5 915 | 360 474 | 143 | 60.9 | | 90.4 | 7.3 | 0.6 | 1.4 | 2.1 | 6.4 | 16.7 | 9.6 | 12.5 | 12.1 | 14.9 |
| 21820 | Fairbanks, AK .................... | 19 006 | 100 272 | 343 | 5.3 | | 78.7 | 6.0 | 10.5 | 4.9 | 6.3 | 8.0 | 17.3 | 13.5 | 17.1 | 12.4 | 13.4 |
| 22020 | Fargo, ND-MN ................... | 7 279 | 216 312 | 198 | 29.7 | | 91.9 | 2.6 | 1.9 | 2.7 | 2.6 | 6.8 | 15.1 | 16.9 | 16.1 | 11.8 | 12.3 |
| 22140 | Farmington, NM ................. | 14 279 | 128 529 | 301 | 9.0 | | 43.6 | 1.2 | 36.7 | 0.9 | 19.6 | 8.2 | 20.4 | 9.8 | 13.9 | 11.4 | 13.5 |
| 22180 | Fayetteville, NC ................. | 2 702 | 374 585 | 139 | 138.6 | | 49.4 | 37.0 | 3.3 | 3.7 | 10.2 | 8.6 | 18.4 | 12.4 | 16.6 | 12.4 | 12.6 |
| 22220 | Fayetteville-Springdale-Rogers, AR-MO............. | 8 192 | 482 200 | 107 | 58.9 | | 77.7 | 2.8 | 2.5 | 4.0 | 15.2 | 7.5 | 18.9 | 10.9 | 15.1 | 13.3 | 12.7 |

1. CBSA = Core Based Statistical Area. DIV = Metropolitan Division. See Appendix A for explanation. See Appendix B for list of metropolitan areas identified by type.   2. Dry land or land partially or temporarily covered by water.   3. May be of any race.

Table C. Metropolitan Areas — **Population and Households**

| Area name | Population, 2011 (cont.) Age (percent) (cont.) 55 to 64 years | 65 to 74 years | 75 years and over | Percent female | Population change and components of change, 2000–2012 Total persons 2000 | 2010 | Percent change 2000–2010 | 2010–2012 | Components of change, 2010–2012 Births | Deaths | Net migration | Households, 2010 Number | Percent change, 2000–2010 | Persons per household | Percent Female family householder[1] | One person |
|---|---|---|---|---|---|---|---|---|---|---|---|---|---|---|---|---|
| | 16 | 17 | 18 | 19 | 20 | 21 | 22 | 23 | 24 | 25 | 26 | 27 | 28 | 29 | 30 | 31 |
| Charleston, WV | 15.1 | 8.8 | 7.3 | 51.4 | 309 635 | 304 284 | -1.7 | -0.1 | 7 797 | 8 291 | 212 | 128 621 | -0.5 | 2.34 | 12.1 | 29.6 |
| Charleston-North Charleston-Summerville, SC | 12.1 | 7.1 | 4.7 | 51.1 | 549 033 | 664 607 | 21.1 | 4.9 | 20 451 | 11 261 | 22 911 | 259 987 | 25.0 | 2.49 | 15.1 | 26.4 |
| Charlotte-Gastonia-Rock Hill, NC-SC | 10.9 | 6.0 | 4.4 | 51.5 | 1 330 448 | 1 758 038 | 32.1 | 4.2 | 54 476 | 26 863 | 44 914 | 671 229 | 31.5 | 2.58 | 14.1 | 25.9 |
| Charlottesville, VA | 12.6 | 7.6 | 6.3 | 52.1 | 174 021 | 201 559 | 15.8 | 2.1 | 5 008 | 3 341 | 2 320 | 78 560 | 16.3 | 2.43 | 10.3 | 27.7 |
| Chattanooga, TN-GA | 13.6 | 8.3 | 6.7 | 51.6 | 476 531 | 528 143 | 10.8 | 1.8 | 14 040 | 11 400 | 7 044 | 210 867 | 11.2 | 2.44 | 13.4 | 27.6 |
| Cheyenne, WY | 13.2 | 7.2 | 5.7 | 49.8 | 81 607 | 91 738 | 12.4 | 3.0 | 2 791 | 1 640 | 1 610 | 37 576 | 17.7 | 2.40 | 10.7 | 29.1 |
| Chicago-Joliet-Naperville, IL-IN-WI | 11.6 | 6.3 | 5.3 | 51.1 | 9 098 316 | 9 461 105 | 4.0 | 0.6 | 283 016 | 151 322 | -69 948 | 3 475 726 | 6.0 | 2.68 | 13.7 | 27.2 |
| Chicago-Joliet-Naperville, IL Div | 11.4 | 6.2 | 5.3 | 51.2 | 7 628 412 | 7 883 147 | 3.3 | 0.8 | 239 562 | 124 847 | -51 963 | 2 903 474 | 5.4 | 2.67 | 13.8 | 27.9 |
| Gary, IN Div | 13.0 | 7.2 | 6.2 | 51.4 | 675 971 | 708 070 | 4.7 | -0.2 | 19 651 | 14 433 | -6 379 | 267 890 | 6.2 | 2.60 | 15.3 | 26.1 |
| Lake County-Kenosha County, IL-WI Div | 11.8 | 6.0 | 4.9 | 50.1 | 793 933 | 869 888 | 9.6 | 0.0 | 23 803 | 12 042 | -11 606 | 304 362 | 11.8 | 2.77 | 10.9 | 22.4 |
| Chico, CA | 13.4 | 8.1 | 7.5 | 50.5 | 203 171 | 220 000 | 8.3 | 0.7 | 5 493 | 4 863 | 1 024 | 87 618 | 10.1 | 2.45 | 11.6 | 27.9 |
| Cincinnati-Middletown, OH-KY-IN | 12.4 | 6.7 | 5.7 | 51.1 | 2 009 632 | 2 130 151 | 6.0 | 0.7 | 62 072 | 40 877 | -6 898 | 830 608 | 6.6 | 2.51 | 13.0 | 27.7 |
| Clarksville, TN-KY | 9.5 | 5.6 | 4.1 | 50.4 | 232 000 | 273 949 | 18.1 | 5.0 | 10 931 | 4 532 | 7 148 | 101 086 | 21.3 | 2.62 | 14.8 | 23.6 |
| Cleveland, TN | 12.7 | 8.8 | 6.1 | 51.2 | 104 015 | 115 788 | 11.3 | 1.8 | 2 964 | 2 522 | 1 585 | 44 600 | 9.5 | 2.53 | 12.1 | 24.0 |
| Cleveland-Elyria-Mentor, OH | 13.7 | 7.8 | 7.6 | 51.9 | 2 148 143 | 2 077 240 | -3.3 | -0.7 | 51 522 | 45 708 | -19 385 | 854 893 | 0.2 | 2.38 | 14.7 | 31.0 |
| Coeur d'Alene, ID | 13.6 | 8.6 | 6.3 | 50.6 | 108 685 | 138 494 | 27.4 | 2.8 | 3 825 | 2 676 | 2 649 | 54 200 | 31.2 | 2.53 | 10.0 | 24.3 |
| College Station-Bryan, TX | 8.2 | 4.9 | 4.0 | 49.5 | 184 885 | 228 660 | 23.7 | 2.6 | 6 750 | 2 873 | 1 929 | 85 102 | 25.6 | 2.52 | 11.1 | 26.6 |
| Colorado Springs, CO | 11.6 | 6.0 | 4.3 | 50.0 | 537 484 | 645 613 | 20.1 | 3.5 | 20 678 | 8 601 | 10 623 | 245 764 | 22.6 | 2.55 | 11.1 | 25.9 |
| Columbia, MO | 10.4 | 5.2 | 4.5 | 51.5 | 145 666 | 172 786 | 18.6 | 3.4 | 4 908 | 2 317 | 3 334 | 68 058 | 19.5 | 2.40 | 10.6 | 28.7 |
| Columbia, SC | 12.2 | 6.8 | 4.9 | 51.3 | 647 158 | 767 598 | 18.6 | 2.2 | 21 343 | 13 770 | 9 546 | 294 881 | 20.2 | 2.48 | 15.8 | 27.5 |
| Columbus, GA-AL | 11.4 | 6.5 | 5.2 | 51.0 | 281 768 | 294 865 | 4.6 | 5.3 | 10 806 | 6 111 | 10 826 | 113 239 | 8.9 | 2.50 | 19.9 | 28.2 |
| Columbus, IN | 12.4 | 8.0 | 6.3 | 50.5 | 71 435 | 76 794 | 7.5 | 3.0 | 2 283 | 1 538 | 1 603 | 29 860 | 6.9 | 2.53 | 10.7 | 25.3 |
| Columbus, OH | 11.4 | 6.0 | 4.7 | 50.9 | 1 612 694 | 1 836 536 | 13.9 | 2.3 | 56 922 | 30 735 | 16 151 | 723 572 | 13.7 | 2.47 | 12.9 | 28.4 |
| Corpus Christi, TX | 12.3 | 7.2 | 5.9 | 50.8 | 403 280 | 428 185 | 6.2 | 2.1 | 13 053 | 7 924 | 3 736 | 157 019 | 10.9 | 2.68 | 15.9 | 24.7 |
| Corvallis, OR | 12.8 | 6.6 | 5.7 | 49.8 | 78 153 | 85 579 | 9.5 | 1.0 | 1 654 | 1 201 | 386 | 34 317 | 13.8 | 2.35 | 7.3 | 28.2 |
| Crestview-Fort Walton Beach-Destin, FL | 12.2 | 7.9 | 6.3 | 49.7 | 170 498 | 180 822 | 6.1 | 5.1 | 5 800 | 3 408 | 6 820 | 72 379 | 9.2 | 2.43 | 11.8 | 26.1 |
| Cumberland, MD-WV | 13.5 | 9.6 | 8.3 | 48.8 | 102 008 | 103 299 | 1.3 | -1.3 | 2 232 | 2 738 | -776 | 40 727 | 1.5 | 2.33 | 10.7 | 30.3 |
| Dallas-Fort Worth-Arlington, TX | 10.2 | 5.3 | 3.7 | 50.7 | 5 161 544 | 6 371 773 | 23.4 | 4.3 | 215 517 | 83 968 | 140 426 | 2 298 498 | 22.2 | 2.74 | 13.4 | 24.8 |
| Dallas-Plano-Irving, TX Div | 10.0 | 5.2 | 3.6 | 50.6 | 3 451 226 | 4 235 751 | 22.7 | 4.6 | 144 392 | 53 437 | 103 837 | 1 526 087 | 21.6 | 2.74 | 13.5 | 25.2 |
| Fort Worth-Arlington, TX Div | 10.6 | 5.6 | 4.0 | 50.8 | 1 710 318 | 2 136 022 | 24.9 | 3.6 | 71 125 | 30 531 | 36 589 | 772 411 | 23.4 | 2.73 | 13.3 | 24.0 |
| Dalton, GA | 10.7 | 6.9 | 4.6 | 50.1 | 120 031 | 142 227 | 18.5 | 0.4 | 4 469 | 2 387 | -1 544 | 49 260 | 15.4 | 2.86 | 13.3 | 21.0 |
| Danville, IL | 13.4 | 8.6 | 7.8 | 50.4 | 83 919 | 81 625 | -2.7 | -1.1 | 2 416 | 2 102 | -1 199 | 32 655 | -2.2 | 2.41 | 14.7 | 29.8 |
| Danville, VA | 15.0 | 9.9 | 8.4 | 52.3 | 110 156 | 106 561 | -3.3 | -0.7 | 2 405 | 3 013 | -254 | 45 014 | -0.6 | 2.32 | 16.7 | 30.7 |
| Davenport-Moline-Rock Island, IA-IL | 13.5 | 8.0 | 7.3 | 50.9 | 376 019 | 379 690 | 1.0 | 0.8 | 10 883 | 7 900 | 56 | 155 175 | 3.6 | 2.39 | 11.7 | 29.4 |
| Dayton, OH | 13.2 | 8.1 | 7.3 | 51.6 | 848 153 | 841 502 | -0.8 | 0.2 | 22 195 | 18 636 | -1 836 | 343 971 | 1.5 | 2.38 | 13.6 | 29.9 |
| Decatur, AL | 12.9 | 8.5 | 6.1 | 50.8 | 145 867 | 153 829 | 5.5 | 0.3 | 4 154 | 3 509 | -168 | 60 684 | 6.2 | 2.50 | 12.8 | 25.5 |
| Decatur, IL | 14.1 | 8.3 | 8.2 | 52.1 | 114 706 | 110 768 | -3.4 | -0.6 | 3 180 | 2 605 | -1 181 | 45 855 | -1.5 | 2.33 | 14.1 | 30.9 |
| Deltona-Daytona Beach-Ormond Beach, FL | 14.7 | 11.1 | 10.4 | 51.2 | 443 343 | 494 593 | 11.6 | 0.5 | 10 484 | 13 460 | 5 602 | 208 236 | 12.7 | 2.31 | 12.1 | 29.5 |
| Denver-Aurora-Broomfield, CO | 11.8 | 5.9 | 4.5 | 50.2 | 2 157 756 | 2 543 482 | 17.9 | 4.0 | 78 196 | 34 717 | 56 996 | 1 004 696 | 19.0 | 2.50 | 10.6 | 29.1 |
| Des Moines-West Des Moines, IA | 11.4 | 6.1 | 5.3 | 50.9 | 481 394 | 569 633 | 18.3 | 3.4 | 18 608 | 9 276 | 9 869 | 223 268 | 17.9 | 2.50 | 10.4 | 27.1 |
| Detroit-Warren-Livonia, MI | 13.1 | 7.1 | 6.3 | 51.5 | 4 452 557 | 4 296 250 | -3.5 | -0.1 | 111 515 | 87 350 | -28 758 | 1 682 111 | -0.9 | 2.53 | 15.3 | 28.8 |
| Detroit-Livonia-Dearborn, MI Div | 12.6 | 6.6 | 6.2 | 51.9 | 2 061 162 | 1 820 584 | -11.7 | -1.5 | 52 969 | 39 989 | -42 025 | 702 749 | -8.5 | 2.56 | 20.7 | 30.7 |
| Warren-Troy-Farmington Hills, MI Div | 13.5 | 7.5 | 6.4 | 51.2 | 2 391 395 | 2 475 666 | 3.5 | 1.0 | 58 546 | 47 361 | 13 267 | 979 362 | 5.5 | 2.50 | 11.4 | 27.4 |
| Dothan, AL | 13.3 | 8.9 | 6.9 | 52.0 | 130 861 | 145 639 | 11.3 | 1.4 | 4 143 | 3 495 | 1 329 | 58 883 | 11.4 | 2.44 | 15.4 | 26.9 |
| Dover, DE | 11.7 | 8.1 | 5.8 | 51.8 | 126 697 | 162 310 | 28.1 | 3.3 | 5 098 | 3 170 | 3 304 | 60 278 | 27.6 | 2.62 | 14.9 | 23.6 |
| Dubuque, IA | 12.9 | 7.6 | 7.7 | 50.6 | 89 143 | 93 653 | 5.1 | 1.5 | 2 616 | 1 949 | 810 | 36 815 | 9.3 | 2.43 | 9.2 | 28.4 |
| Duluth, MN-WI | 14.6 | 8.0 | 7.7 | 49.7 | 275 486 | 279 771 | 1.6 | -0.1 | 6 510 | 6 324 | -411 | 116 876 | 3.9 | 2.28 | 9.7 | 31.8 |
| Durham-Chapel Hill, NC | 12.0 | 6.5 | 5.1 | 52.2 | 426 493 | 504 357 | 18.3 | 3.7 | 14 589 | 7 845 | 11 013 | 202 476 | 20.0 | 2.39 | 12.9 | 29.8 |
| Eau Claire, WI | 12.5 | 7.0 | 6.5 | 49.9 | 148 337 | 161 151 | 8.6 | 1.5 | 4 257 | 2 794 | 1 030 | 63 903 | 11.8 | 2.41 | 8.9 | 27.4 |
| El Centro, CA | 9.9 | 5.6 | 4.9 | 48.5 | 142 361 | 174 528 | 22.6 | 1.4 | 6 990 | 2 029 | -2 539 | 49 126 | 24.7 | 3.34 | 15.9 | 17.0 |
| Elizabethtown, KY | 11.6 | 6.5 | 5.2 | 50.2 | 107 547 | 119 736 | 11.3 | 1.2 | 4 035 | 2 271 | -399 | 45 468 | 14.3 | 2.55 | 12.8 | 24.7 |
| Elkhart-Goshen, IN | 11.4 | 6.6 | 5.8 | 50.7 | 182 791 | 197 559 | 8.1 | 1.0 | 6 830 | 3 343 | -1 425 | 70 244 | 6.2 | 2.76 | 12.6 | 22.7 |
| Elmira, NY | 13.6 | 7.9 | 7.9 | 50.2 | 91 070 | 88 830 | -2.5 | 0.1 | 2 225 | 2 091 | -6 | 35 462 | 1.2 | 2.37 | 13.0 | 30.3 |
| El Paso, TX | 9.5 | 5.5 | 4.8 | 51.4 | 679 622 | 800 647 | 17.8 | 3.3 | 31 019 | 10 553 | 6 485 | 256 557 | 22.2 | 3.06 | 20.3 | 19.8 |
| Erie, PA | 13.2 | 7.4 | 7.3 | 50.8 | 280 843 | 280 566 | -0.1 | 0.0 | 7 199 | 6 059 | -930 | 110 413 | 3.7 | 2.42 | 13.2 | 29.3 |
| Eugene-Springfield, OR | 14.5 | 8.4 | 7.0 | 50.9 | 322 959 | 351 715 | 8.9 | 0.8 | 7 719 | 6 932 | 2 143 | 145 966 | 11.9 | 2.35 | 10.6 | 28.8 |
| Evansville, IN-KY | 13.3 | 7.6 | 6.8 | 51.3 | 342 815 | 358 676 | 4.6 | 0.5 | 9 962 | 8 186 | 153 | 144 362 | 5.6 | 2.41 | 11.8 | 28.5 |
| Fairbanks, AK | 11.5 | 4.5 | 2.3 | 47.3 | 82 840 | 97 581 | 17.8 | 2.8 | 3 716 | 857 | -215 | 36 441 | 22.4 | 2.56 | 8.8 | 26.7 |
| Fargo, ND-MN | 10.6 | 5.1 | 5.3 | 49.9 | 174 367 | 208 777 | 19.7 | 3.6 | 6 616 | 2 943 | 3 802 | 86 178 | 23.1 | 2.32 | 8.6 | 31.4 |
| Farmington, NM | 11.4 | 6.3 | 5.0 | 50.3 | 113 801 | 130 044 | 14.3 | -1.2 | 4 464 | 2 008 | -3 991 | 44 404 | 17.7 | 2.89 | 15.6 | 21.9 |
| Fayetteville, NC | 9.8 | 5.4 | 3.9 | 51.4 | 336 609 | 366 383 | 8.8 | 2.2 | 15 577 | 5 532 | -1 952 | 138 963 | 17.0 | 2.56 | 19.0 | 25.8 |
| Fayetteville-Springdale-Rogers, AR-MO | 10.2 | 6.4 | 5.0 | 50.3 | 347 045 | 463 204 | 33.5 | 4.1 | 15 576 | 7 085 | 10 287 | 173 054 | 31.2 | 2.62 | 10.2 | 24.8 |

1. No spouse present.

# Table C. Metropolitan Areas — Population, Vital Statistics, Medicare, and Crime

| Area name | Persons in group quarters, 2009 | Daytime population, 2007–2011 Number | Employ-ment/residence ratio | Births, 2011 Total | Rate[1] | Deaths, 2011 Number | Rate[1] | Persons under 65 with no health insurance 2010 Number | Percent | Medicare, 2012 Enrolled in original Medicare | Enrolled in Medicare Advantage | Enrolled in a Medicare prescription drug plan | Serious crimes known to police,[2] 2011 Total Number | Rate[3] |
|---|---|---|---|---|---|---|---|---|---|---|---|---|---|---|
| | 32 | 33 | 34 | 35 | 36 | 37 | 38 | 39 | 40 | 41 | 42 | 43 | 44 | 45 |
| Charleston, WV | 3 658 | 316 947 | 1.10 | 3 540 | 11.7 | 3 648 | 12.0 | 39 943 | 15.8 | 66 244 | 18 803 | 26 236 | 9 010 | 3 423 |
| Charleston-North Charles-ton-Summerville, SC | 16 088 | 660 037 | 1.01 | 9 320 | 13.7 | 4 798 | 7.0 | 112 983 | 19.7 | 103 382 | 15 061 | 33 423 | 26 215 | 3 920 |
| Charlotte-Gastonia-Rock Hill, NC-SC | 29 251 | 1 782 522 | 1.06 | 24 619 | 13.7 | 11 581 | 6.5 | 288 918 | 18.5 | 236 745 | 43 836 | 105 213 | 66 872 | 3 846 |
| Charlottesville, VA | 10 813 | 208 948 | 1.10 | 2 279 | 11.2 | 1 417 | 7.0 | 24 885 | 15.1 | 33 048 | 2 833 | 17 205 | 4 441 | 2 177 |
| Chattanooga, TN-GA | 12 993 | 530 542 | 1.03 | 6 264 | 11.7 | 5 078 | 9.5 | 77 722 | 17.6 | 99 536 | 25 627 | 45 394 | 22 305 | 4 181 |
| Cheyenne, WY | 1 644 | 92 493 | 1.05 | 1 264 | 13.6 | 720 | 7.8 | 13 281 | 16.8 | 15 100 | 1 134 | 6 764 | 2 785 | 3 012 |
| Chicago-Joliet-Naperville, IL-IN-WI | 162 698 | 9 468 333 | 1.01 | 128 052 | 13.5 | 66 569 | 7.0 | 1 377 958 | 16.7 | 1 313 460 | 120 705 | 664 838 | 301 702 | 3 224 |
| Chicago-Joliet-Naperville, IL Div | 126 538 | 7 942 049 | 1.02 | 108 307 | 13.7 | 54 921 | 6.9 | 1 184 858 | 17.2 | 1 082 427 | 105 435 | 547 452 | 256 453 | 3 283 |
| Gary, IN Div | 10 850 | 667 299 | 0.87 | 8 837 | 12.5 | 6 468 | 9.1 | 96 637 | 16.0 | 116 550 | 7 171 | 61 456 | 26 430 | 3 887 |
| Lake County-Kenosha County, IL-WI Div | 25 310 | 858 985 | 0.98 | 10 908 | 12.5 | 5 180 | 5.9 | 96 463 | 12.8 | 114 483 | 8 099 | 55 930 | 18 819 | 2 174 |
| Chico, CA | 4 942 | 218 043 | 0.99 | 2 403 | 10.9 | 2 182 | 9.9 | 34 814 | 19.0 | 44 093 | 766 | 24 965 | 5 951 | 2 674 |
| Cincinnati-Middletown, OH-KY-IN | 46 438 | 2 123 940 | 1.00 | 28 550 | 13.4 | 17 926 | 8.4 | 250 192 | 13.7 | 334 964 | 118 938 | 135 991 | 79 481 | 3 760 |
| Clarksville, TN-KY | 8 975 | 266 673 | 0.98 | 4 818 | 17.3 | 1 992 | 7.2 | 36 410 | 15.2 | 35 357 | 5 365 | 15 480 | 9 036 | 3 291 |
| Cleveland, TN | 2 988 | 110 286 | 0.90 | 1 329 | 11.4 | 1 089 | 9.3 | 16 309 | 17.0 | 23 499 | 6 712 | 9 807 | 4 243 | 3 632 |
| Cleveland-Elyria-Mentor, OH | 43 431 | 2 131 394 | 1.05 | 23 371 | 11.3 | 20 027 | 9.7 | 243 802 | 14.1 | 378 095 | 133 401 | 162 121 | 57 032 | 3 091 |
| Coeur d'Alene, ID | 1 488 | 131 718 | 0.91 | 1 715 | 12.2 | 1 148 | 8.1 | 23 704 | 20.1 | 27 313 | 8 153 | 9 612 | 4 354 | 3 109 |
| College Station-Bryan, TX | 13 868 | 224 461 | 1.01 | 3 078 | 13.3 | 1 227 | 5.3 | 44 671 | 22.9 | 24 722 | 2 982 | 9 102 | 8 300 | 3 555 |
| Colorado Springs, CO | 19 273 | 631 615 | 0.99 | 9 070 | 13.7 | 3 749 | 5.7 | 91 884 | 16.2 | 85 463 | 22 285 | 20 896 | 21 635 | 3 298 |
| Columbia, MO | 9 712 | 173 741 | 1.03 | 2 158 | 12.3 | 1 014 | 5.8 | 20 991 | 14.2 | 22 599 | 2 480 | 12 096 | 6 299 | 3 632 |
| Columbia, SC | 35 637 | 766 044 | 1.03 | 9 771 | 12.6 | 5 984 | 7.7 | 115 158 | 17.8 | 116 374 | 19 908 | 40 235 | 36 206 | 4 662 |
| Columbus, GA-AL | 11 379 | 305 181 | 1.10 | 4 285 | 14.2 | 2 698 | 9.0 | 47 008 | 18.8 | 46 732 | 10 589 | 16 326 | 16 683 | 5 751 |
| Columbus, IN | 1 147 | 84 026 | 1.21 | 1 010 | 13.0 | 647 | 8.3 | 10 396 | 16.0 | 13 589 | 2 011 | 6 091 | 3 322 | 4 325 |
| Columbus, OH | 46 903 | 1 861 735 | 1.05 | 25 789 | 13.9 | 13 399 | 7.2 | 221 592 | 13.9 | 253 844 | 104 091 | 113 907 | 82 352 | 4 607 |
| Corpus Christi, TX | 6 931 | 428 730 | 1.01 | 6 016 | 13.9 | 3 450 | 8.0 | 87 475 | 23.8 | 68 343 | 27 911 | 17 832 | 21 007 | 4 805 |
| Corvallis, OR | 5 043 | 86 218 | 1.03 | 753 | 8.8 | 537 | 6.2 | 12 386 | 17.6 | 12 598 | 5 502 | 4 209 | 2 355 | 2 723 |
| Crestview-Fort Walton Beach-Destin, FL | 4 883 | 189 352 | 1.08 | 2 521 | 13.7 | 1 529 | 8.3 | 29 019 | 19.3 | 32 094 | 3 005 | 9 282 | 6 033 | 3 292 |
| Cumberland, MD-WV | 8 570 | 103 303 | 1.01 | 1 038 | 10.1 | 1 217 | 11.8 | 10 787 | 13.9 | 22 299 | 1 312 | 11 525 | 3 299 | 3 219 |
| Dallas-Fort Worth-Arlington, TX | 77 578 | 6 313 087 | 1.01 | 99 733 | 15.3 | 36 229 | 5.6 | 1 434 006 | 24.9 | 729 831 | 176 302 | 272 099 | 251 040 | 3 860 |
| Dallas-Plano-Irving, TX Div | 50 199 | 4 276 980 | 1.05 | 66 862 | 15.4 | 23 046 | 5.3 | 980 024 | 25.5 | 469 987 | 95 447 | 193 343 | 161 385 | 3 733 |
| Fort Worth-Arlington, TX Div | 27 379 | 2 036 107 | 0.93 | 32 871 | 15.1 | 13 183 | 6.0 | 453 982 | 23.7 | 259 844 | 80 855 | 78 756 | 89 655 | 4 114 |
| Dalton, GA | 1 256 | 149 743 | 1.15 | 2 050 | 14.4 | 1 061 | 7.4 | 33 064 | 26.3 | 21 377 | 2 532 | 12 587 | 4 503 | 3 179 |
| Danville, IL | 2 903 | 80 601 | 0.96 | 1 075 | 13.2 | 929 | 11.4 | 8 967 | 13.6 | 16 772 | 4 154 | 6 345 | 3 759 | 4 591 |
| Danville, VA | 2 322 | 103 341 | 0.92 | 1 103 | 10.4 | 1 336 | 12.6 | 15 492 | 18.0 | 25 283 | 4 814 | 13 846 | 3 048 | 2 827 |
| Davenport-Moline-Rock Island, IA-IL | 8 556 | 381 709 | 1.02 | 4 807 | 12.6 | 3 433 | 9.0 | 37 972 | 12.0 | 69 528 | 11 672 | 28 044 | 12 628 | 3 361 |
| Dayton, OH | 24 358 | 855 739 | 1.03 | 10 254 | 12.1 | 8 039 | 9.5 | 100 457 | 14.4 | 153 124 | 63 966 | 55 822 | 31 338 | 3 763 |
| Decatur, AL | 2 362 | 145 646 | 0.89 | 1 831 | 11.9 | 1 512 | 9.8 | 24 648 | 19.0 | 29 892 | 2 343 | 14 265 | 4 280 | 2 769 |
| Decatur, IL | 4 059 | 116 562 | 1.12 | 1 425 | 12.9 | 1 135 | 10.3 | 10 986 | 12.2 | 22 375 | 1 719 | 12 813 | 3 932 | 3 539 |
| Deltona-Daytona Beach-Ormond Beach, FL | 12 809 | 471 830 | 0.88 | 4 785 | 9.7 | 5 885 | 11.9 | 94 014 | 24.7 | 118 912 | 47 535 | 33 270 | 20 728 | 4 150 |
| Denver-Aurora-Broomfield, CO | 33 586 | 2 503 306 | 1.00 | 35 028 | 13.5 | 15 031 | 5.8 | 394 481 | 17.4 | 324 736 | 150 681 | 73 433 | 79 437 | 3 097 |
| Des Moines-West Des Moines, IA | 11 976 | 578 855 | 1.06 | 8 304 | 14.3 | 4 025 | 6.9 | 48 818 | 9.8 | 81 284 | 13 660 | 40 819 | 19 435 | 3 394 |
| Detroit-Warren-Livonia, MI | 48 644 | 4 336 018 | 1.01 | 50 037 | 11.7 | 38 303 | 8.9 | 545 249 | 14.8 | 731 533 | 186 221 | 313 435 | 147 279 | 3 431 |
| Detroit-Livonia-Dearborn, MI Div | 23 849 | 1 894 635 | 1.07 | 23 853 | 13.2 | 17 647 | 9.8 | 275 614 | 17.5 | 302 061 | 76 890 | 126 749 | 93 363 | 5 132 |
| Warren-Troy-Farmington Hills, MI Div | 24 795 | 2 441 383 | 0.97 | 26 184 | 10.5 | 20 656 | 8.3 | 269 635 | 12.8 | 429 472 | 109 331 | 186 686 | 53 916 | 2 179 |
| Dothan, AL | 1 844 | 144 632 | 1.01 | 1 815 | 12.4 | 1 529 | 10.4 | 21 280 | 17.4 | 30 863 | 3 746 | 14 292 | 4 890 | 3 342 |
| Dover, DE | 4 322 | 152 575 | 0.90 | 2 214 | 13.4 | 1 406 | 8.5 | 14 714 | 10.7 | 28 676 | 1 398 | 12 052 | 7 038 | 4 292 |
| Dubuque, IA | 4 268 | 100 539 | 1.15 | 1 187 | 12.5 | 842 | 8.9 | 6 468 | 8.5 | 17 192 | 6 906 | 10 615 | 2 046 | 2 173 |
| Duluth, MN-WI | 12 789 | 280 920 | 1.02 | 2 918 | 10.4 | 2 805 | 10.0 | 24 731 | 10.9 | 55 803 | 21 525 | 24 747 | 9 785 | 3 473 |
| Durham-Chapel Hill, NC | 20 898 | 542 194 | 1.19 | 6 582 | 12.8 | 3 375 | 6.6 | 79 017 | 18.4 | 73 204 | 14 253 | 29 403 | 21 566 | 4 222 |
| Eau Claire, WI | 7 338 | 163 178 | 1.04 | 1 883 | 11.6 | 1 226 | 7.5 | 13 082 | 9.8 | 28 009 | 7 924 | 10 718 | 3 658 | 2 260 |
| El Centro, CA | 10 684 | 170 192 | 0.98 | 3 062 | 17.3 | 844 | 4.8 | 33 176 | 22.6 | 25 128 | 1 915 | 15 836 | 6 156 | 3 647 |
| Elizabethtown, KY | 3 569 | 121 968 | 1.10 | 1 805 | 14.8 | 993 | 8.2 | 16 710 | 16.2 | 18 801 | 1 684 | 8 744 | 2 005 | 1 663 |
| Elkhart-Goshen, IN | 3 804 | 216 349 | 1.21 | 3 061 | 15.4 | 1 462 | 7.3 | 39 869 | 23.3 | 29 650 | 6 994 | 13 474 | 3 132 | 1 577 |
| Elmira, NY | 4 916 | 89 685 | 1.03 | 974 | 11.0 | 942 | 10.6 | 7 539 | 10.7 | 18 422 | 4 828 | 6 253 | 2 278 | 2 553 |
| El Paso, TX | 15 792 | 786 162 | 1.00 | 13 862 | 16.9 | 4 572 | 5.6 | 230 924 | 32.8 | 105 997 | 40 752 | 32 888 | 22 653 | 2 771 |
| Erie, PA | 12 875 | 284 438 | 1.04 | 3 185 | 11.3 | 2 685 | 9.6 | 27 235 | 11.9 | 52 228 | 22 892 | 18 247 | 8 260 | 2 935 |
| Eugene-Springfield, OR | 8 530 | 351 128 | 1.01 | 3 481 | 9.8 | 3 060 | 8.7 | 62 772 | 21.4 | 67 786 | 31 357 | 19 943 | 13 640 | 3 837 |
| Evansville, IN-KY | 10 795 | 366 776 | 1.06 | 4 417 | 12.3 | 3 596 | 10.0 | 44 079 | 14.8 | 65 863 | 15 855 | 29 841 | 9 472 | 3 433 |
| Fairbanks, AK | 4 313 | 95 302 | 0.98 | 1 639 | 16.5 | 383 | 3.9 | 17 920 | 20.3 | 8 430 | 34 | 2 762 | NA | NA |
| Fargo, ND-MN | 8 753 | 208 130 | 1.02 | 2 942 | 13.9 | 1 291 | 6.1 | 18 159 | 10.1 | 27 325 | 6 237 | 14 815 | 4 923 | 2 325 |
| Farmington, NM | 1 754 | 128 123 | 1.00 | 2 098 | 16.4 | 898 | 7.0 | 33 447 | 28.9 | 16 905 | 466 | 9 144 | 3 580 | 2 722 |
| Fayetteville, NC | 10 827 | 375 690 | 1.08 | 6 815 | 18.2 | 2 389 | 6.4 | 57 527 | 17.8 | 47 645 | 7 266 | 15 960 | 22 043 | 5 941 |
| Fayetteville-Springdale-Rogers, AR-MO | 9 860 | 459 991 | 1.02 | 6 877 | 14.5 | 3 061 | 6.5 | 86 949 | 21.5 | 68 588 | 16 419 | 27 223 | 13 554 | 2 940 |

1. Per 1,000 estimated resident population.    2. Data for serious crimes have not been adjusted for underreporting; this may affect comparability between geographic areas and over time.    3. Per 100,000 population estimated by the FBI.

# Table C. Metropolitan Areas — Crime, Education, Money Income, and Poverty

| Area name | Serious crimes known to police, 2011 (cont.)[1] Rate[2] Violent | Property | School enrollment and attainment, 2007–2011 Enrollment[3] Total | Percent private | Attainment[4] (percent) High school graduate or less | Bachelor's degree or more | Local government expenditures,[5] 2009–2010 Total current expenditures (mil dol) | Current expenditures per student (dollars) | Per capita income[6] (dollars) | Median household income (dollars) | Percent of households with income of less than $25,000 | Percent of households with income of $100,000 or more | Percent of households with income of $200,000 or more | Percent below poverty level All persons | Related Children under 18 years | Related Children under 5 |
|---|---|---|---|---|---|---|---|---|---|---|---|---|---|---|---|---|
| | 46 | 47 | 48 | 49 | 50 | 51 | 52 | 53 | 54 | 55 | 56 | 57 | 58 | 59 | 60 | 61 |
| Charleston, WV | 436 | 2 986 | 64 664 | 12.1 | 54.6 | 21.1 | 554.0 | 11 304 | 25 404 | 44 140 | 28.3 | 14.6 | 2.8 | 15.1 | 21.5 | 29.0 |
| Charleston-North Charleston-Summerville, SC | 457 | 3 463 | 173 142 | 18.0 | 39.9 | 30.2 | 843.8 | 8 716 | 26 961 | 51 332 | 23.7 | 19.4 | 3.5 | 15.1 | 21.5 | 25.4 |
| Charlotte-Gastonia-Rock Hill, NC-SC | 432 | 3 415 | 470 225 | 17.2 | 37.7 | 32.7 | 2 389.6 | 8 135 | 29 303 | 54 229 | 21.2 | 22.5 | 4.9 | 13.3 | 17.9 | 21.1 |
| Charlottesville, VA | 166 | 2 012 | 59 900 | 15.8 | 36.0 | 42.6 | 300.9 | 11 736 | 31 845 | 58 026 | 20.4 | 25.4 | 5.7 | 12.3 | 9.9 | 11.6 |
| Chattanooga, TN-GA | 498 | 3 682 | 127 258 | 19.5 | 47.0 | 23.1 | 622.6 | 8 564 | 24 824 | 44 164 | 28.1 | 15.3 | 2.8 | 15.6 | 22.8 | 29.0 |
| Cheyenne, WY | 244 | 2 767 | 23 348 | 11.1 | 35.6 | 24.4 | 199.1 | 14 036 | 28 648 | 54 156 | 19.1 | 19.2 | 2.7 | 9.4 | 12.9 | 18.6 |
| Chicago-Joliet-Naperville, IL-IN-WI | 420 | 2 805 | 2 622 121 | 21.0 | 39.3 | 33.8 | 19 114.5 | 11 977 | 30 989 | 61 257 | 19.8 | 27.2 | 6.1 | 12.7 | 17.8 | 19.9 |
| Chicago-Joliet-Naperville, IL Div | 456 | 2 827 | 2 181 114 | 21.8 | 38.8 | 34.6 | 15 791.9 | 12 124 | 30 959 | 61 045 | 20.0 | 27.1 | 6.1 | 13.0 | 18.1 | 19.8 |
| Gary, IN Div | 324 | 3 563 | 190 822 | 16.6 | 49.3 | 20.4 | 1 174.1 | 9 550 | 24 805 | 52 227 | 23.6 | 18.6 | 2.2 | 14.5 | 21.9 | 26.7 |
| Lake County-Kenosha County, IL-WI Div | 170 | 2 004 | 250 185 | 17.4 | 35.1 | 38.1 | 2 148.5 | 12 605 | 36 300 | 73 587 | 14.8 | 35.1 | 9.7 | 8.8 | 12.2 | 15.1 |
| Chico, CA | 259 | 2 415 | 67 176 | 8.0 | 36.8 | 24.0 | 304.9 | 9 840 | 23 431 | 42 971 | 29.2 | 14.9 | 1.9 | 19.8 | 24.1 | 27.1 |
| Cincinnati-Middletown, OH-KY-IN | 293 | 3 467 | 579 921 | 19.8 | 43.8 | 29.0 | 3 369.1 | 10 406 | 28 153 | 54 651 | 22.3 | 22.1 | 3.9 | 12.6 | 17.1 | 22.2 |
| Clarksville, TN-KY | 436 | 2 854 | 74 245 | 11.8 | 46.4 | 19.4 | 336.3 | 7 851 | 21 514 | 45 305 | 26.1 | 12.7 | 1.3 | 16.6 | 23.1 | 29.7 |
| Cleveland, TN | 616 | 3 015 | 28 763 | 22.6 | 54.1 | 17.3 | 133.8 | 7 368 | 21 181 | 39 964 | 30.4 | 10.6 | 1.8 | 17.0 | 21.6 | 24.0 |
| Cleveland-Elyria-Mentor, OH | 405 | 2 686 | 540 598 | 23.2 | 43.2 | 27.5 | 3 626.4 | 11 902 | 27 487 | 49 024 | 25.6 | 18.8 | 3.3 | 14.4 | 21.5 | 26.1 |
| Coeur d'Alene, ID | 301 | 2 809 | 33 981 | 14.1 | 37.4 | 23.1 | 133.0 | 6 295 | 24 766 | 48 075 | 23.1 | 13.7 | 2.3 | 12.8 | 15.2 | 20.3 |
| College Station-Bryan, TX | 359 | 3 197 | 92 739 | 5.7 | 42.4 | 33.8 | 286.2 | 8 779 | 21 341 | 37 899 | 37.2 | 15.8 | 3.3 | 27.8 | 25.6 | 30.0 |
| Colorado Springs, CO | 373 | 2 925 | 181 468 | 13.9 | 29.8 | 34.9 | 951.0 | 8 450 | 28 622 | 57 111 | 19.2 | 23.4 | 3.8 | 11.5 | 15.5 | 20.3 |
| Columbia, MO | 421 | 3 211 | 61 155 | 13.6 | 31.6 | 44.4 | 214.7 | 8 490 | 25 822 | 47 118 | 26.9 | 16.7 | 2.8 | 18.9 | 17.3 | 20.4 |
| Columbia, SC | 678 | 3 984 | 211 797 | 15.3 | 39.7 | 29.8 | 1 262.4 | 9 886 | 25 589 | 48 766 | 24.8 | 18.0 | 2.8 | 14.6 | 18.8 | 25.4 |
| Columbus, GA-AL | 412 | 5 339 | 82 809 | 11.0 | 46.6 | 20.5 | 461.8 | 9 373 | 22 652 | 41 680 | 30.4 | 13.8 | 2.4 | 17.9 | 24.9 | 28.5 |
| Columbus, IN | 167 | 4 158 | 19 535 | 15.8 | 45.2 | 27.2 | 131.4 | 10 724 | 27 518 | 53 692 | 20.5 | 20.1 | 3.0 | 11.4 | 17.0 | 23.6 |
| Columbus, OH | 371 | 4 236 | 510 310 | 17.6 | 39.6 | 33.0 | 3 332.3 | 11 168 | 28 371 | 54 112 | 22.2 | 21.9 | 4.0 | 14.5 | 19.0 | 23.4 |
| Corpus Christi, TX | 540 | 4 265 | 114 493 | 8.2 | 48.5 | 15.9 | 698.4 | 8 853 | 23 363 | 45 199 | 27.6 | 17.1 | 2.6 | 18.5 | 28.2 | 34.8 |
| Corvallis, OR | 120 | 2 603 | 32 263 | 7.6 | 22.3 | 47.4 | 80.8 | 9 026 | 26 370 | 47 716 | 29.5 | 21.6 | 3.7 | 21.0 | 14.9 | 15.0 |
| Crestview-Fort Walton Beach-Destin, FL | 427 | 2 865 | 44 391 | 11.2 | 37.0 | 26.9 | 248.3 | 8 614 | 28 505 | 54 140 | 19.7 | 20.5 | 4.0 | 11.7 | 18.7 | 23.7 |
| Cumberland, MD-WV | 325 | 2 894 | 23 596 | 9.8 | 58.7 | 15.0 | 183.5 | 13 482 | 21 135 | 37 804 | 31.6 | 11.9 | 1.2 | 15.2 | 19.5 | 24.9 |
| Dallas-Fort Worth-Arlington, TX | 359 | 3 502 | 1 761 317 | 13.6 | 40.0 | 31.2 | 10 187.0 | 8 369 | 29 006 | 57 658 | 19.4 | 25.4 | 5.5 | 13.9 | 19.7 | 22.9 |
| Dallas-Plano-Irving, TX Div | 337 | 3 396 | 1 176 125 | 13.4 | 39.1 | 33.2 | 6 983.7 | 8 493 | 29 662 | 58 345 | 19.3 | 26.4 | 6.1 | 14.0 | 19.8 | 23.0 |
| Fort Worth-Arlington, TX Div | 402 | 3 712 | 585 192 | 14.1 | 41.6 | 27.3 | 3 203.4 | 8 111 | 27 703 | 56 536 | 19.6 | 23.6 | 4.5 | 13.7 | 19.6 | 22.9 |
| Dalton, GA | 222 | 2 957 | 37 562 | 6.5 | 64.5 | 12.6 | 245.9 | 8 801 | 19 182 | 40 677 | 30.3 | 12.5 | 1.9 | 19.3 | 25.8 | 31.5 |
| Danville, IL | 585 | 4 006 | 18 928 | 8.2 | 53.9 | 14.0 | 142.0 | 10 319 | 21 000 | 40 463 | 30.4 | 10.2 | 1.0 | 18.8 | 30.8 | 38.9 |
| Danville, VA | 208 | 2 619 | 25 146 | 16.4 | 55.7 | 14.4 | 150.6 | 9 543 | 20 240 | 36 102 | 35.2 | 9.4 | 1.0 | 18.9 | 28.5 | 37.2 |
| Davenport-Moline-Rock Island, IA-IL | 415 | 2 946 | 95 493 | 17.6 | 42.4 | 24.9 | 619.3 | 10 087 | 26 702 | 49 605 | 23.5 | 16.9 | 2.8 | 12.2 | 18.0 | 21.6 |
| Dayton, OH | 293 | 3 470 | 237 813 | 21.5 | 42.7 | 25.0 | 1 389.5 | 11 289 | 25 830 | 47 864 | 25.3 | 16.9 | 2.3 | 14.5 | 20.8 | 26.3 |
| Decatur, AL | 221 | 2 548 | 36 499 | 11.1 | 53.3 | 17.5 | 233.6 | 9 373 | 22 683 | 44 207 | 27.6 | 14.6 | 1.4 | 14.8 | 21.8 | 26.0 |
| Decatur, IL | 512 | 3 027 | 27 712 | 20.9 | 48.0 | 20.8 | 181.8 | 10 710 | 25 797 | 45 987 | 26.1 | 15.7 | 2.9 | 15.0 | 24.4 | 30.1 |
| Deltona-Daytona Beach-Ormond Beach, FL | 501 | 3 649 | 112 287 | 20.4 | 45.4 | 20.8 | 520.8 | 8 358 | 24 536 | 44 169 | 27.4 | 13.5 | 2.3 | 15.0 | 22.9 | 28.6 |
| Denver-Aurora-Broomfield, CO | 354 | 2 742 | 651 257 | 16.3 | 32.6 | 38.3 | 3 816.6 | 8 907 | 32 980 | 61 734 | 18.6 | 27.4 | 5.6 | 11.9 | 16.2 | 19.7 |
| Des Moines-West Des Moines, IA | 280 | 3 114 | 148 171 | 20.8 | 36.0 | 33.4 | 959.5 | 9 874 | 30 012 | 59 381 | 18.2 | 23.5 | 3.8 | 9.8 | 13.0 | 17.1 |
| Detroit-Warren-Livonia, MI | 572 | 2 858 | 1 190 548 | 14.0 | 41.1 | 27.3 | 7 909.8 | 10 766 | 27 571 | 52 244 | 24.0 | 21.7 | 3.8 | 15.5 | 22.2 | 25.3 |
| Detroit-Livonia-Dearborn, MI Div | 1 048 | 4 084 | 526 320 | 12.6 | 48.1 | 20.6 | 3 524.7 | 10 877 | 22 351 | 41 886 | 31.5 | 15.6 | 2.3 | 22.7 | 32.9 | 36.3 |
| Warren-Troy-Farmington Hills, MI Div | 223 | 1 957 | 664 228 | 15.1 | 36.2 | 32.0 | 4 385.1 | 10 679 | 31 458 | 60 567 | 18.7 | 25.9 | 4.9 | 10.1 | 13.5 | 16.0 |
| Dothan, AL | 397 | 2 945 | 33 089 | 15.1 | 54.5 | 16.7 | 188.1 | 8 387 | 22 225 | 40 071 | 31.8 | 12.8 | 1.8 | 17.3 | 26.5 | 31.0 |
| Dover, DE | 626 | 3 666 | 44 495 | 16.2 | 48.9 | 20.0 | 285.9 | 11 346 | 24 374 | 54 783 | 21.2 | 18.3 | 1.8 | 12.4 | 20.0 | 25.3 |
| Dubuque, IA | 155 | 2 018 | 24 873 | 34.3 | 47.0 | 25.5 | 132.9 | 9 219 | 25 525 | 49 663 | 20.9 | 14.9 | 2.2 | 9.3 | 11.2 | 15.2 |
| Duluth, MN-WI | 198 | 3 275 | 70 402 | 13.1 | 38.8 | 24.5 | 420.0 | 10 938 | 25 355 | 46 133 | 27.0 | 14.7 | 1.8 | 14.9 | 18.1 | 24.2 |
| Durham-Chapel Hill, NC | 440 | 3 783 | 148 017 | 19.9 | 33.4 | 43.3 | 669.3 | 9 669 | 29 516 | 51 632 | 24.1 | 22.5 | 5.1 | 16.4 | 20.7 | 24.5 |
| Eau Claire, WI | 151 | 2 109 | 44 554 | 11.3 | 42.6 | 25.6 | 244.9 | 10 766 | 25 000 | 48 255 | 25.4 | 15.2 | 2.0 | 13.4 | 15.0 | 20.7 |
| El Centro, CA | 268 | 3 379 | 53 712 | 4.9 | 58.6 | 12.8 | 355.7 | 9 788 | 16 593 | 39 402 | 34.1 | 15.0 | 1.9 | 23.3 | 30.1 | 33.3 |
| Elizabethtown, KY | 100 | 1 563 | 31 193 | 10.6 | 48.7 | 18.2 | 159.9 | 8 304 | 23 088 | 47 310 | 25.1 | 15.2 | 1.9 | 14.5 | 24.4 | 25.5 |
| Elkhart-Goshen, IN | 42 | 1 535 | 51 936 | 15.6 | 56.8 | 17.9 | 344.9 | 9 737 | 21 879 | 47 308 | 22.9 | 12.9 | 2.0 | 15.7 | 24.0 | 28.2 |
| Elmira, NY | 198 | 2 355 | 21 510 | 17.3 | 48.9 | 20.8 | 190.2 | 15 176 | 24 299 | 46 589 | 28.0 | 15.6 | 2.4 | 16.5 | 26.9 | 28.9 |
| El Paso, TX | 396 | 2 375 | 258 970 | 7.0 | 52.4 | 19.8 | 1 583.7 | 8 890 | 17 618 | 38 259 | 33.4 | 12.6 | 1.9 | 25.0 | 34.6 | 36.8 |
| Erie, PA | 242 | 2 693 | 74 353 | 25.9 | 52.4 | 23.6 | 487.6 | 11 996 | 23 321 | 44 503 | 27.7 | 14.5 | 2.1 | 15.8 | 23.1 | 29.3 |
| Eugene-Springfield, OR | 282 | 3 556 | 94 306 | 11.6 | 35.0 | 27.8 | 448.6 | 9 720 | 24 105 | 42 621 | 29.1 | 13.7 | 2.2 | 17.4 | 17.2 | 20.8 |
| Evansville, IN-KY | 298 | 3 135 | 87 846 | 15.9 | 49.0 | 20.4 | 476.7 | 9 222 | 25 170 | 47 294 | 25.0 | 15.5 | 2.2 | 13.4 | 18.4 | 23.9 |
| Fairbanks, AK | NA | NA | 27 292 | 11.7 | 33.3 | 27.7 | 238.8 | 14 887 | 31 532 | 68 922 | 14.5 | 28.9 | 3.6 | 7.8 | 9.4 | 11.2 |
| Fargo, ND-MN | 239 | 2 086 | 62 083 | 14.8 | 29.5 | 34.8 | 280.8 | 9 718 | 27 893 | 50 091 | 24.0 | 18.1 | 3.3 | 13.1 | 12.3 | 15.3 |
| Farmington, NM | 625 | 2 097 | 33 196 | 6.1 | 51.9 | 15.2 | 216.2 | 9 093 | 21 471 | 49 024 | 24.8 | 17.1 | 2.1 | 19.7 | 25.7 | 30.5 |
| Fayetteville, NC | 484 | 5 457 | 108 467 | 12.7 | 39.5 | 21.0 | 522.8 | 8 546 | 22 383 | 45 016 | 25.8 | 14.6 | 1.8 | 17.2 | 23.3 | 24.7 |
| Fayetteville-Springdale-Rogers, AR-MO | 336 | 2 604 | 125 186 | 10.8 | 47.3 | 26.1 | 675.7 | 8 507 | 24 016 | 46 131 | 25.2 | 17.1 | 3.0 | 15.5 | 20.6 | 24.7 |

1. Data for serious crimes have not been adjusted for underreporting; this may affect comparability between geographic areas and over time. 2. Per 100,000 population estimated by the FBI. 3. All persons 3 years old and over enrolled in nursery school through college. 4. Persons 25 years old and over. 5. Elementary and secondary education expenditures. 6. Based on resident population estimated as of July 1, 2009.

Table C. Metropolitan Areas — **Personal Income**

| Area name | Personal income, 2011 | | | | | | | | | | | | |
|---|---|---|---|---|---|---|---|---|---|---|---|---|---|
| | | | Per capita[1] | | | | | | Transfer payments | | | | |
| | | | | | | | | | | Government payments to individuals | | | |
| | Total (mil dol) | Percent change, 2010–2011 | Dollars | Rank | Wages and salaries[2] (mil dol) | Proprietors' income (mil dol) | Dividends, interest, and rent (mil dol) | Total (mil dol) | Total (mil dol) | Social Security (mil dol) | Medical payments (mil dol) | Income maintenance (mil dol) | Unemployment insurance (mil dol) |
| | 62 | 63 | 64 | 65 | 66 | 67 | 68 | 69 | 70 | 71 | 72 | 73 | 74 |
| Charleston, WV | 11 949 | 5.0 | 39 348 | 125 | 8 257 | 1 036 | 1 381 | 2 891 | 2 824 | 1 021 | 1 205 | 302 | 64 |
| Charleston-North Charleston-Summerville, SC | 25 706 | 6.5 | 37 685 | 159 | 17 172 | 2 252 | 3 701 | 4 556 | 4 408 | 1 450 | 1 738 | 538 | 169 |
| Charlotte-Gastonia-Rock Hill, NC-SC | 72 220 | 6.4 | 40 223 | 100 | 54 215 | 6 976 | 9 483 | 11 058 | 10 661 | 3 622 | 4 114 | 1 473 | 797 |
| Charlottesville, VA | 9 042 | 5.7 | 44 350 | 47 | 5 859 | 763 | 2 021 | 1 245 | 1 200 | 484 | 499 | 114 | 27 |
| Chattanooga, TN-GA | 19 236 | 4.8 | 36 066 | 195 | 12 114 | 1 876 | 2 467 | 4 323 | 4 205 | 1 470 | 1 809 | 511 | 120 |
| Cheyenne, WY | 4 345 | 6.5 | 46 882 | 29 | 2 801 | 319 | 933 | 660 | 640 | 201 | 247 | 55 | 23 |
| Chicago-Joliet-Naperville, IL-IN-WI | 436 998 | 4.0 | 45 977 | 33 | 302 799 | 37 691 | 68 571 | 62 906 | 60 806 | 19 311 | 25 438 | 8 229 | 4 025 |
| Chicago-Joliet-Naperville, IL Div | 365 651 | 4.0 | 46 153 | X | 257 845 | 33 556 | 56 435 | 52 808 | 51 055 | 15 615 | 21 655 | 7 106 | 3 454 |
| Gary, IN Div | 26 058 | 4.7 | 36 770 | X | 14 921 | 1 520 | 2 996 | 5 340 | 5 184 | 1 898 | 2 098 | 660 | 218 |
| Lake County-Kenosha County, IL-WI Div | 45 289 | 4.1 | 51 847 | X | 30 033 | 2 615 | 9 140 | 4 757 | 4 567 | 1 797 | 1 685 | 463 | 353 |
| Chico, CA | 7 347 | 4.3 | 33 356 | 274 | 3 429 | 760 | 1 427 | 1 974 | 1 926 | 593 | 784 | 250 | 100 |
| Cincinnati-Middletown, OH-KY-IN | 87 485 | 4.9 | 40 918 | 88 | 59 375 | 6 276 | 12 868 | 15 409 | 14 936 | 4 920 | 6 167 | 1 720 | 629 |
| Clarksville, TN-KY | 11 015 | 9.9 | 39 666 | 117 | 8 053 | 684 | 1 107 | 1 804 | 1 751 | 496 | 635 | 258 | 64 |
| Cleveland, TN | 3 630 | 5.3 | 31 073 | 328 | 1 913 | 418 | 403 | 983 | 958 | 341 | 410 | 115 | 25 |
| Cleveland-Elyria-Mentor, OH | 87 622 | 5.3 | 42 365 | 73 | 59 931 | 7 650 | 12 434 | 17 847 | 17 389 | 5 429 | 7 685 | 2 147 | 575 |
| Coeur d'Alene, ID | 4 647 | 5.3 | 32 923 | 283 | 2 351 | 354 | 844 | 1 014 | 983 | 396 | 352 | 96 | 49 |
| College Station-Bryan, TX | 6 932 | 4.6 | 29 928 | 343 | 4 429 | 507 | 1 288 | 1 134 | 1 083 | 338 | 423 | 165 | 43 |
| Colorado Springs, CO | 26 409 | 6.8 | 39 994 | 109 | 18 458 | 1 491 | 3 934 | 4 122 | 3 984 | 1 149 | 1 456 | 399 | 234 |
| Columbia, MO | 6 567 | 5.6 | 37 350 | 168 | 4 543 | 444 | 1 061 | 1 111 | 1 073 | 323 | 481 | 108 | 32 |
| Columbia, SC | 27 471 | 4.3 | 35 350 | 212 | 19 181 | 1 715 | 3 439 | 5 352 | 5 182 | 1 721 | 1 933 | 651 | 191 |
| Columbus, GA-AL | 11 651 | 7.6 | 38 653 | 138 | 8 411 | 478 | 1 785 | 2 318 | 2 254 | 646 | 785 | 442 | 71 |
| Columbus, IN | 3 087 | 8.4 | 39 645 | 118 | 2 701 | 202 | 429 | 536 | 518 | 219 | 209 | 45 | 21 |
| Columbus, OH | 74 688 | 5.9 | 40 188 | 101 | 54 824 | 6 205 | 8 710 | 12 630 | 12 219 | 3 488 | 5 154 | 1 717 | 473 |
| Corpus Christi, TX | 16 655 | 6.1 | 38 609 | 141 | 10 025 | 2 003 | 2 273 | 3 529 | 3 433 | 899 | 1 698 | 494 | 102 |
| Corvallis, OR | 3 323 | 4.5 | 38 677 | 136 | 2 136 | 205 | 795 | 469 | 450 | 186 | 124 | 41 | 23 |
| Crestview-Fort Walton Beach-Destin, FL | 7 914 | 6.5 | 43 132 | 60 | 5 861 | 354 | 1 643 | 1 410 | 1 336 | 436 | 548 | 124 | 30 |
| Cumberland, MD-WV | 3 349 | 4.1 | 32 547 | 294 | 1 875 | 154 | 488 | 1 063 | 1 040 | 305 | 500 | 97 | 31 |
| Dallas-Fort Worth-Arlington, TX | 285 260 | 6.2 | 43 708 | 52 | 195 727 | 41 399 | 37 820 | 34 098 | 32 653 | 10 569 | 13 635 | 4 696 | 1 455 |
| Dallas-Plano-Irving, TX Div | 197 316 | 6.3 | 45 404 | X | 143 515 | 31 093 | 26 543 | 22 211 | 21 248 | 6 810 | 8 899 | 3 129 | 964 |
| Fort Worth-Arlington, TX Div | 87 944 | 6.2 | 40 327 | X | 52 212 | 10 306 | 11 277 | 11 887 | 11 404 | 3 759 | 4 736 | 1 568 | 491 |
| Dalton, GA | 3 890 | 3.3 | 27 249 | 358 | 3 079 | 255 | 519 | 935 | 903 | 307 | 359 | 134 | 41 |
| Danville, IL | 2 659 | 4.5 | 32 619 | 292 | 1 512 | 239 | 402 | 687 | 669 | 236 | 238 | 108 | 35 |
| Danville, VA | 3 308 | 4.1 | 31 297 | 325 | 1 693 | 172 | 514 | 989 | 966 | 358 | 387 | 141 | 23 |
| Davenport-Moline-Rock Island, IA-IL | 16 070 | 5.7 | 42 141 | 75 | 10 480 | 1 344 | 2 504 | 3 118 | 3 034 | 1 016 | 980 | 321 | 121 |
| Dayton, OH | 31 626 | 5.1 | 37 410 | 166 | 21 444 | 1 959 | 4 672 | 6 927 | 6 741 | 2 158 | 2 777 | 787 | 247 |
| Decatur, AL | 4 941 | 2.8 | 32 071 | 300 | 2 758 | 288 | 705 | 1 163 | 1 129 | 456 | 441 | 140 | 32 |
| Decatur, IL | 4 495 | 4.3 | 40 591 | 94 | 3 088 | 383 | 756 | 905 | 880 | 326 | 325 | 115 | 49 |
| Deltona-Daytona Beach-Ormond Beach, FL | 16 544 | 3.4 | 33 436 | 269 | 7 050 | 525 | 4 513 | 4 561 | 4 451 | 1 729 | 1 804 | 428 | 127 |
| Denver-Aurora-Broomfield, CO | 127 324 | 6.1 | 48 980 | 19 | 86 215 | 16 897 | 19 293 | 14 297 | 13 722 | 4 512 | 5 514 | 1 409 | 948 |
| Des Moines-West Des Moines, IA | 26 092 | 6.7 | 44 966 | 41 | 19 066 | 3 040 | 3 438 | 3 568 | 3 440 | 1 239 | 1 385 | 372 | 183 |
| Detroit-Warren-Livonia, MI | 171 473 | 6.1 | 40 009 | 107 | 115 601 | 12 482 | 22 239 | 36 482 | 35 534 | 11 979 | 15 034 | 4 856 | 1 885 |
| Detroit-Livonia-Dearborn, MI Div | 61 293 | 3.5 | 34 012 | X | 47 120 | 3 684 | 6 760 | 18 312 | 17 913 | 4 799 | 8 067 | 3 344 | 859 |
| Warren-Troy-Farmington Hills, MI Div | 110 179 | 7.5 | 44 360 | X | 68 481 | 8 798 | 15 479 | 18 170 | 17 621 | 7 180 | 6 967 | 1 512 | 1 026 |
| Dothan, AL | 5 079 | 3.6 | 34 654 | 237 | 2 633 | 342 | 818 | 1 219 | 1 186 | 431 | 456 | 173 | 25 |
| Dover, DE | 5 489 | 5.1 | 33 302 | 276 | 3 407 | 546 | 689 | 1 295 | 1 260 | 417 | 536 | 145 | 46 |
| Dubuque, IA | 3 680 | 8.0 | 38 886 | 134 | 2 712 | 321 | 652 | 687 | 666 | 253 | 284 | 60 | 26 |
| Duluth, MN-WI | 10 141 | 4.9 | 36 242 | 190 | 6 367 | 558 | 1 582 | 2 544 | 2 482 | 784 | 1 087 | 260 | 105 |
| Durham-Chapel Hill, NC | 21 435 | 4.5 | 41 785 | 79 | 20 388 | 1 529 | 3 734 | 3 253 | 3 139 | 1 091 | 1 299 | 363 | 175 |
| Eau Claire, WI | 5 874 | 3.8 | 36 111 | 192 | 3 757 | 582 | 960 | 1 107 | 1 071 | 401 | 439 | 97 | 56 |
| El Centro, CA | 5 020 | 4.2 | 28 351 | 356 | 2 782 | 624 | 511 | 1 380 | 1 341 | 265 | 518 | 283 | 168 |
| Elizabethtown, KY | 4 700 | 9.3 | 38 597 | 142 | 3 885 | 316 | 533 | 899 | 874 | 251 | 360 | 94 | 36 |
| Elkhart-Goshen, IN | 6 392 | 5.0 | 32 131 | 297 | 5 362 | 550 | 905 | 1 230 | 1 186 | 462 | 437 | 148 | 71 |
| Elmira, NY | 3 155 | 3.8 | 35 517 | 205 | 2 044 | 155 | 471 | 811 | 792 | 271 | 347 | 95 | 31 |
| El Paso, TX | 24 696 | 7.2 | 30 088 | 339 | 15 584 | 2 931 | 2 650 | 5 695 | 5 519 | 1 130 | 2 392 | 1 164 | 210 |
| Erie, PA | 9 756 | 6.4 | 34 721 | 234 | 6 345 | 498 | 1 365 | 2 538 | 2 476 | 783 | 1 065 | 299 | 171 |
| Eugene-Springfield, OR | 12 214 | 4.6 | 34 561 | 242 | 6 912 | 795 | 2 468 | 2 888 | 2 810 | 968 | 1 049 | 319 | 180 |
| Evansville, IN-KY | 13 639 | 5.1 | 37 899 | 156 | 9 186 | 1 049 | 2 124 | 2 739 | 2 659 | 1 003 | 1 115 | 263 | 100 |
| Fairbanks, AK | 4 228 | 7.8 | 42 626 | 67 | 3 450 | 242 | 625 | 646 | 626 | 116 | 258 | 68 | 31 |
| Fargo, ND-MN | 9 068 | 7.7 | 42 740 | 66 | 6 304 | 1 073 | 1 477 | 1 171 | 1 124 | 379 | 437 | 120 | 39 |
| Farmington, NM | 4 022 | 5.7 | 31 373 | 320 | 2 811 | 251 | 488 | 863 | 835 | 234 | 359 | 117 | 40 |
| Fayetteville, NC | 16 184 | 7.6 | 43 254 | 57 | 13 518 | 513 | 1 675 | 2 796 | 2 724 | 657 | 995 | 433 | 160 |
| Fayetteville-Springdale-Rogers, AR-MO | 16 172 | 5.4 | 34 130 | 255 | 11 343 | 1 042 | 2 767 | 2 633 | 2 529 | 984 | 948 | 296 | 90 |

1. Based on the resident population estimated as of July 1 of the year shown.  2. Includes other labor income.

Table C. Metropolitan Areas — **Earnings, Social Security, and Housing**

| Area name | Earnings, 2011 | | | | | | | | Social Security beneficiaries, December 2011 | | | Housing units, 2010 | |
|---|---|---|---|---|---|---|---|---|---|---|---|---|---|
| | | | | Percent by selected industries | | | | | | | | | |
| | | | Goods-related[1] | | Service-related and health | | | | | | | Supple-mental Security Income recipients, December 2011 | | |
| | Total (mil dol) | Farm | Total | Manu-facturing | Infor-mation, profes-sional, and technical services | Retail trade | Finance, insur-ance, and real estate | Health care and social services | Govern-ment | Number | Rate[2] | | Total | Percent change, 2000–2010 |
| | 75 | 76 | 77 | 78 | 79 | 80 | 81 | 82 | 83 | 84 | 85 | 86 | 87 | 88 |
| Charleston, WV | 9 293 | 0.0 | 21.1 | 5.1 | 10.2 | 5.7 | 6.2 | 14.2 | 17.9 | 75 600 | 249 | 12 989 | 141 585 | -0.1 |
| Charleston-North Charleston-Summerville, SC | 19 424 | 0.1 | 15.7 | 10.0 | 11.7 | 6.9 | 7.4 | 9.5 | 26.5 | 113 465 | 166 | 13 145 | 298 542 | 28.2 |
| Charlotte-Gastonia-Rock Hill, NC-SC | 61 192 | 0.3 | 14.1 | 8.7 | 13.0 | 6.2 | 15.5 | 7.6 | 11.9 | 264 235 | 147 | 30 527 | 737 775 | 35.0 |
| Charlottesville, VA | 6 623 | 0.0 | 10.0 | 3.7 | 13.8 | 5.4 | 6.1 | 9.9 | 34.4 | 34 705 | 170 | 2 628 | 89 134 | 20.7 |
| Chattanooga, TN-GA | 13 990 | 0.0 | 19.9 | 14.0 | 7.2 | 7.8 | 10.8 | 11.6 | 17.4 | 111 095 | 208 | 13 614 | 234 440 | 14.2 |
| Cheyenne, WY | 3 120 | 2.0 | 11.1 | 4.4 | 6.5 | 6.8 | 5.6 | 8.3 | 41.2 | 15 655 | 169 | 1 411 | 40 462 | 18.3 |
| Chicago-Joliet-Naperville, IL-IN-WI | 340 490 | 0.2 | 15.7 | 10.9 | 15.1 | 5.0 | 11.9 | 9.7 | 12.9 | 1 376 265 | 145 | 207 923 | 3 797 247 | 9.7 |
| Chicago-Joliet-Naperville, IL Div | 291 401 | 0.1 | 13.8 | 9.3 | 16.3 | 4.7 | 12.9 | 9.7 | 12.6 | 1 121 490 | 142 | 181 860 | 3 173 522 | 9.2 |
| Gary, IN Div | 16 441 | 1.4 | 32.9 | 21.7 | 4.4 | 7.2 | 3.3 | 13.9 | 12.4 | 132 920 | 188 | 15 176 | 294 127 | 9.1 |
| Lake County-Kenosha County, IL-WI Div | 32 648 | 0.1 | 23.6 | 20.1 | 9.6 | 6.9 | 7.5 | 8.0 | 15.4 | 121 855 | 139 | 10 887 | 329 598 | 15.2 |
| Chico, CA | 4 189 | 6.3 | 10.6 | 4.9 | 6.9 | 9.1 | 4.8 | 19.2 | 21.3 | 47 585 | 216 | 11 581 | 95 835 | 12.1 |
| Cincinnati-Middletown, OH-KY-IN | 65 650 | 0.2 | 18.0 | 13.0 | 10.1 | 5.6 | 9.0 | 12.0 | 12.5 | 363 850 | 170 | 46 023 | 917 396 | 10.1 |
| Clarksville, TN-KY | 8 736 | 0.9 | 11.5 | 7.8 | 4.0 | 4.2 | 2.2 | 5.2 | 60.7 | 41 305 | 149 | 6 529 | 114 145 | 24.0 |
| Cleveland, TN | 2 331 | -0.1 | 28.8 | 23.2 | 3.6 | 7.5 | 4.7 | D | 12.8 | 27 075 | 232 | 3 268 | 49 386 | 11.8 |
| Cleveland-Elyria-Mentor, OH | 67 582 | 0.2 | 19.4 | 15.2 | 10.9 | 5.3 | 9.3 | 13.6 | 14.1 | 398 230 | 193 | 60 068 | 955 756 | 4.9 |
| Coeur d'Alene, ID | 2 704 | 0.3 | 16.9 | 8.5 | 8.5 | 10.6 | 6.7 | 12.1 | 20.9 | 30 420 | 216 | 2 410 | 63 177 | 35.6 |
| College Station-Bryan, TX | 4 937 | 0.6 | 17.2 | 5.9 | D | 7.7 | 4.4 | 10.4 | 35.7 | 26 260 | 113 | 4 375 | 95 016 | 26.5 |
| Colorado Springs, CO | 19 948 | 0.0 | 9.5 | 4.8 | 14.7 | 5.8 | 6.3 | 7.9 | 38.7 | 91 725 | 139 | 7 962 | 265 495 | 24.8 |
| Columbia, MO | 4 987 | 0.6 | 9.1 | 4.3 | 7.0 | 7.6 | 7.5 | 11.2 | 37.5 | 24 800 | 141 | 2 919 | 74 133 | 21.5 |
| Columbia, SC | 20 896 | 0.2 | 14.0 | 8.9 | 9.5 | 6.5 | 8.6 | 9.6 | 28.2 | 130 835 | 168 | 15 491 | 331 470 | 23.1 |
| Columbus, GA-AL | 8 889 | 0.1 | 10.7 | 7.1 | 6.0 | 4.8 | 10.1 | 9.2 | 43.9 | 53 170 | 176 | 9 901 | 128 214 | 10.8 |
| Columbus, IN | 2 903 | 0.6 | 47.8 | 44.3 | 4.6 | 4.7 | 4.8 | 7.0 | 11.3 | 15 560 | 200 | 1 212 | 33 098 | 10.9 |
| Columbus, OH | 61 030 | 0.7 | 13.0 | 8.5 | 13.4 | 6.3 | 10.5 | 10.6 | 17.5 | 267 330 | 144 | 39 786 | 792 340 | 16.4 |
| Corpus Christi, TX | 12 028 | 1.1 | 28.0 | 8.2 | 5.9 | 6.1 | 4.3 | 12.2 | 21.2 | 75 415 | 175 | 16 109 | 182 909 | 13.8 |
| Corvallis, OR | 2 341 | 1.0 | 17.2 | 14.1 | 10.5 | 4.8 | 3.0 | 15.1 | 30.2 | 13 430 | 156 | 964 | 36 245 | 13.3 |
| Crestview-Fort Walton Beach-Destin, FL | 6 216 | 0.1 | 7.9 | 4.0 | 10.7 | 6.0 | 5.0 | 6.8 | 47.3 | 34 875 | 190 | 2 812 | 92 407 | 17.6 |
| Cumberland, MD-WV | 2 029 | 0.1 | 20.0 | 14.4 | D | 7.3 | 3.3 | 17.0 | 25.3 | 23 685 | 230 | 2 976 | 46 350 | 2.8 |
| Dallas-Fort Worth-Arlington, TX | 237 126 | 0.1 | 19.5 | 10.1 | 14.6 | 5.7 | 11.6 | 9.7 | 10.9 | 774 120 | 119 | 118 488 | 2 502 075 | 25.2 |
| Dallas-Plano-Irving, TX Div | 174 608 | 0.0 | 17.8 | 9.2 | 16.6 | 5.4 | 12.9 | 9.6 | 10.1 | 496 885 | 114 | 80 310 | 1 660 144 | 24.6 |
| Fort Worth-Arlington, TX Div | 62 518 | 0.1 | 24.2 | 12.8 | 8.8 | 6.7 | 8.0 | 9.9 | 12.9 | 277 235 | 127 | 38 178 | 841 931 | 26.5 |
| Dalton, GA | 3 334 | -0.3 | 38.8 | 36.9 | 8.0 | 7.4 | 2.2 | D | 11.1 | 24 490 | 172 | 3 388 | 55 878 | 24.0 |
| Danville, IL | 1 751 | 8.2 | 23.3 | 20.9 | D | 5.8 | 4.1 | 9.2 | 22.1 | 18 620 | 228 | 2 793 | 36 318 | -0.1 |
| Danville, VA | 1 865 | 0.9 | 27.9 | 23.4 | 3.1 | 8.3 | 3.2 | 13.8 | 18.6 | 29 030 | 275 | 4 582 | 53 745 | 5.1 |
| Davenport-Moline-Rock Island, IA-IL | 11 824 | 2.2 | 20.3 | 15.1 | 7.4 | 6.6 | 5.1 | 10.6 | 17.4 | 75 475 | 198 | 7 352 | 167 110 | 5.4 |
| Dayton, OH | 23 404 | 0.9 | 15.9 | 12.1 | 11.5 | 5.5 | 5.4 | 14.4 | 24.6 | 162 950 | 193 | 19 632 | 385 160 | 5.7 |
| Decatur, AL | 3 045 | 0.9 | 40.1 | 32.5 | 3.7 | 7.1 | 3.6 | D | 15.7 | 34 710 | 225 | 4 742 | 66 422 | 6.4 |
| Decatur, IL | 3 470 | 2.9 | 35.6 | 28.7 | 5.4 | 5.3 | 3.6 | 12.8 | 10.5 | 24 055 | 217 | 3 206 | 50 475 | 0.5 |
| Deltona-Daytona Beach-Ormond Beach, FL | 7 575 | 0.6 | 11.7 | 6.7 | 7.0 | 10.3 | 5.9 | 19.5 | 17.3 | 131 685 | 266 | 10 623 | 254 226 | 20.0 |
| Denver-Aurora-Broomfield, CO | 103 112 | 0.1 | 13.8 | 5.4 | 20.8 | 5.0 | 12.0 | 8.1 | 13.2 | 333 080 | 128 | 34 581 | 1 078 837 | 21.1 |
| Des Moines-West Des Moines, IA | 22 105 | 1.5 | 13.0 | 5.8 | 8.8 | 5.5 | 24.6 | 10.0 | 13.1 | 88 545 | 153 | 8 308 | 240 203 | 20.5 |
| Detroit-Warren-Livonia, MI | 128 083 | 0.1 | 19.6 | 15.2 | 15.6 | 5.7 | 6.8 | 12.6 | 11.8 | 827 065 | 193 | 125 963 | 1 886 537 | 5.0 |
| Detroit-Livonia-Dearborn, MI Div | 50 804 | 0.0 | 18.0 | 14.2 | 13.5 | 4.7 | 4.8 | 13.6 | 14.9 | 349 745 | 194 | 81 910 | 821 693 | -0.5 |
| Warren-Troy-Farmington Hills, MI Div | 77 279 | 0.1 | 20.6 | 15.8 | 17.0 | 6.5 | 8.2 | 11.9 | 9.8 | 477 320 | 192 | 44 053 | 1 064 844 | 9.7 |
| Dothan, AL | 2 975 | 1.4 | 15.3 | 8.4 | 4.6 | 9.9 | 4.1 | 14.9 | 19.4 | 35 250 | 241 | 5 901 | 66 897 | 12.0 |
| Dover, DE | 3 954 | 1.4 | 4.5 | D | 4.0 | 7.8 | 7.7 | 11.3 | 39.6 | 31 990 | 194 | 3 686 | 65 338 | 29.4 |
| Dubuque, IA | 3 033 | 3.4 | 24.8 | 19.0 | 9.8 | 6.9 | 7.8 | 14.1 | 8.4 | 19 135 | 202 | 1 548 | 38 951 | 9.7 |
| Duluth, MN-WI | 6 925 | 0.1 | 19.1 | 7.6 | 4.9 | 6.8 | 5.8 | 20.2 | 21.0 | 60 735 | 217 | 7 119 | 141 539 | 9.0 |
| Durham-Chapel Hill, NC | 21 918 | 0.2 | 23.8 | 21.1 | 13.5 | 3.6 | 6.7 | 13.0 | 19.4 | 78 705 | 153 | 9 199 | 222 760 | 23.7 |
| Eau Claire, WI | 4 340 | 2.2 | 21.6 | 15.0 | 5.0 | 8.2 | 6.1 | 17.4 | 14.5 | 31 195 | 192 | 3 068 | 69 336 | 15.0 |
| El Centro, CA | 3 406 | 14.4 | 6.2 | 3.9 | 2.3 | 7.1 | 2.4 | 4.4 | 39.3 | 27 115 | 153 | 10 547 | 56 067 | 27.7 |
| Elizabethtown, KY | 4 201 | 0.5 | 11.9 | 9.2 | 6.0 | 4.8 | 2.7 | 5.1 | 58.9 | 21 300 | 175 | 3 426 | 49 433 | 13.6 |
| Elkhart-Goshen, IN | 5 911 | 1.0 | 49.4 | 45.3 | 3.2 | 5.0 | 2.9 | 9.1 | 8.0 | 33 115 | 166 | 3 089 | 77 767 | 11.4 |
| Elmira, NY | 2 199 | 0.2 | 26.9 | 18.5 | 4.1 | 7.4 | 3.8 | 16.0 | 20.9 | 20 950 | 236 | 3 549 | 38 369 | 1.7 |
| El Paso, TX | 18 515 | 0.2 | 13.3 | 6.5 | 4.8 | 6.9 | 6.0 | 9.6 | 38.7 | 112 490 | 137 | 29 302 | 270 307 | 20.4 |
| Erie, PA | 6 843 | 0.3 | 27.5 | 23.4 | 5.0 | 7.0 | 7.0 | 17.7 | 15.2 | 59 165 | 211 | 11 092 | 119 138 | 4.2 |
| Eugene-Springfield, OR | 7 707 | 0.4 | 15.5 | 9.9 | 8.9 | 8.9 | 5.4 | 16.8 | 20.8 | 73 565 | 208 | 8 092 | 156 112 | 12.3 |
| Evansville, IN-KY | 10 236 | 2.0 | 30.5 | 21.3 | 5.5 | 6.0 | 3.3 | 13.5 | 10.1 | 74 475 | 207 | 8 238 | 159 314 | 7.8 |
| Fairbanks, AK | 3 692 | 0.2 | 13.3 | 1.4 | 4.2 | 5.4 | 2.8 | 8.0 | 51.6 | 9 220 | 93 | 1 127 | 41 783 | 25.5 |
| Fargo, ND-MN | 7 377 | 4.7 | 14.9 | 7.9 | 10.1 | 7.0 | 9.4 | 13.3 | 14.8 | 29 035 | 137 | 2 645 | 91 897 | 25.0 |
| Farmington, NM | 3 061 | 0.2 | 32.1 | 2.6 | 2.7 | 7.2 | 3.4 | 11.5 | 21.0 | 19 345 | 151 | 4 067 | 49 341 | 14.2 |
| Fayetteville, NC | 14 031 | 0.2 | 7.1 | 4.3 | 3.7 | 3.8 | 1.9 | 4.4 | 67.8 | 55 335 | 148 | 10 873 | 153 735 | 17.4 |
| Fayetteville-Springdale-Rogers, AR-MO | 12 385 | 0.4 | 15.6 | 10.9 | 7.6 | 6.2 | 5.8 | 9.0 | 13.9 | 77 345 | 163 | 8 362 | 198 298 | 37.3 |

1. Includes mining, construction, and manufacturing.    2. Per 1,000 resident population estimated as of July 1, 2011.

Table C. Metropolitan Areas — **Housing, Labor Force, and Employment**

| Area name | Housing units, 2007–2011 | | | | | | | | Civilian labor force, 2012 | | | | Civilian employment,[5] 2007–2011 | | |
| | Occupied units | | | | | | | | | | Unemployment | | | Percent | |
| | Owner-occupied | | | | | Renter-occupied | | | | | | | | | |
| | | | | Median owner cost as a percent of income | | | | | | | | | | | |
| | Total | Percent | Median value[1] | With a mortgage | Without a mortgage | Median rent[2] | Median rent as a percent of income | Substandard units[3] (percent) | Total | Percent change, 2011–2012 | Total | Rate[4] | Total | Management, professional, and related occupations | Construction, production, and related occupations |
| | 89 | 90 | 91 | 92 | 93 | 94 | 95 | 96 | 97 | 98 | 99 | 100 | 101 | 102 | 103 |
| Charleston, WV | 125 314 | 75.0 | 100 900 | 18.8 | 10.0 | 610 | 26.0 | 1.3 | 137 511 | -0.2 | 9 488 | 6.9 | 132 011 | 35.0 | 21.1 |
| Charleston-North Charleston-Summerville, SC | 250 406 | 66.2 | 192 000 | 25.7 | 12.7 | 899 | 31.3 | 2.1 | 335 882 | 1.1 | 25 042 | 7.5 | 306 458 | 34.7 | 22.0 |
| Charlotte-Gastonia-Rock Hill, NC-SC | 660 504 | 67.3 | 171 400 | 23.2 | 11.5 | 818 | 29.5 | 2.6 | 918 571 | 2.2 | 87 677 | 9.5 | 839 919 | 38.0 | 20.7 |
| Charlottesville, VA | 77 441 | 65.0 | 283 000 | 23.7 | 10.7 | 1 009 | 31.1 | 1.6 | 108 921 | -0.2 | 5 511 | 5.1 | 96 977 | 46.8 | 14.6 |
| Chattanooga, TN-GA | 207 386 | 69.1 | 140 000 | 22.9 | 10.8 | 680 | 30.0 | 2.4 | 261 563 | -0.1 | 19 505 | 7.5 | 240 601 | 33.6 | 23.7 |
| Cheyenne, WY | 36 566 | 68.7 | 174 100 | 23.2 | 10.0 | 698 | 24.8 | 1.5 | 45 331 | 1.1 | 2 769 | 6.1 | 44 510 | 34.4 | 22.2 |
| Chicago-Joliet-Naperville, IL-IN-WI | 3 427 501 | 67.3 | 245 700 | 27.5 | 14.7 | 931 | 31.3 | 3.6 | 4 888 916 | 0.9 | 433 427 | 8.9 | 4 485 101 | 37.2 | 20.7 |
| Chicago-Joliet-Naperville, IL Div | 2 863 197 | 66.0 | 257 200 | 28.1 | 14.9 | 943 | 31.4 | 3.8 | 4 117 620 | 1.0 | 365 712 | 8.9 | 3 753 893 | 37.5 | 20.3 |
| Gary, IN Div | 262 142 | 72.7 | 144 700 | 22.8 | 12.8 | 773 | 30.8 | 2.3 | 325 028 | 0.0 | 29 273 | 9.0 | 315 583 | 30.0 | 28.2 |
| Lake County-Kenosha County, IL-WI Div | 302 162 | 75.7 | 251 900 | 26.9 | 15.2 | 939 | 30.4 | 2.7 | 446 268 | -0.2 | 38 442 | 8.6 | 415 625 | 39.7 | 19.5 |
| Chico, CA | 85 219 | 60.3 | 254 900 | 29.0 | 12.8 | 878 | 35.7 | 4.0 | 102 063 | 0.1 | 12 493 | 12.2 | 87 965 | 34.2 | 19.6 |
| Cincinnati-Middletown, OH-KY-IN | 814 307 | 68.9 | 156 400 | 22.9 | 12.9 | 713 | 29.8 | 1.7 | 1 089 269 | -1.1 | 77 688 | 7.1 | 1 020 553 | 36.3 | 20.7 |
| Clarksville, TN-KY | 99 383 | 63.8 | 124 200 | 22.3 | 10.4 | 738 | 28.7 | 2.5 | 117 050 | 1.0 | 9 974 | 8.5 | 101 868 | 29.6 | 27.6 |
| Cleveland, TN | 43 744 | 69.4 | 131 900 | 23.6 | 10.6 | 649 | 31.4 | 2.9 | 57 787 | 3.0 | 4 459 | 7.7 | 49 937 | 27.8 | 31.7 |
| Cleveland-Elyria-Mentor, OH | 846 344 | 67.4 | 148 100 | 24.3 | 14.4 | 725 | 30.9 | 1.6 | 1 054 725 | -0.3 | 74 867 | 7.1 | 972 254 | 36.0 | 20.6 |
| Coeur d'Alene, ID | 55 301 | 70.7 | 212 300 | 26.8 | 11.7 | 783 | 29.9 | 2.5 | 71 444 | -0.4 | 6 023 | 8.4 | 63 339 | 31.9 | 24.1 |
| College Station-Bryan, TX | 80 073 | 50.7 | 135 000 | 22.2 | 11.2 | 780 | 40.3 | 4.4 | 114 238 | -1.4 | 6 498 | 5.7 | 103 521 | 38.2 | 19.6 |
| Colorado Springs, CO | 239 671 | 66.3 | 217 600 | 24.6 | 10.0 | 855 | 29.6 | 2.4 | 313 188 | -0.1 | 28 942 | 9.2 | 286 962 | 40.2 | 17.3 |
| Columbia, MO | 67 584 | 58.8 | 153 500 | 21.2 | 10.0 | 755 | 31.9 | 1.9 | 97 469 | 1.6 | 4 574 | 4.7 | 89 762 | 42.9 | 15.3 |
| Columbia, SC | 291 897 | 68.3 | 138 300 | 22.2 | 10.9 | 782 | 30.1 | 1.7 | 373 092 | 0.0 | 29 902 | 8.0 | 352 662 | 36.6 | 20.7 |
| Columbus, GA-AL | 109 628 | 59.9 | 131 300 | 23.6 | 11.7 | 749 | 31.0 | 2.2 | 132 287 | 0.4 | 11 845 | 9.0 | 115 448 | 32.6 | 21.2 |
| Columbus, IN | 30 037 | 72.5 | 135 400 | 19.9 | 11.4 | 757 | 26.4 | 2.2 | 41 105 | 4.1 | 2 630 | 6.4 | 36 775 | 37.9 | 25.4 |
| Columbus, OH | 705 771 | 63.7 | 163 500 | 23.4 | 12.8 | 777 | 29.5 | 2.2 | 969 548 | 0.3 | 59 348 | 6.1 | 898 193 | 39.2 | 18.1 |
| Corpus Christi, TX | 154 556 | 62.4 | 106 200 | 23.6 | 13.5 | 811 | 31.9 | 5.6 | 217 176 | 1.5 | 13 883 | 6.4 | 187 639 | 30.7 | 24.8 |
| Corvallis, OR | 33 427 | 57.4 | 268 200 | 24.2 | 11.0 | 757 | 38.7 | 2.4 | 44 422 | -0.7 | 2 728 | 6.1 | 40 603 | 46.4 | 16.0 |
| Crestview-Fort Walton Beach-Destin, FL | 71 609 | 66.9 | 196 800 | 26.1 | 11.3 | 981 | 31.9 | 2.2 | 98 219 | 0.5 | 6 120 | 6.2 | 82 776 | 35.0 | 18.6 |
| Cumberland, MD-WV | 39 872 | 70.9 | 120 700 | 21.9 | 12.3 | 552 | 28.8 | 1.7 | 50 173 | 0.0 | 4 017 | 8.0 | 42 802 | 27.8 | 26.6 |
| Dallas-Fort Worth-Arlington, TX | 2 246 574 | 62.5 | 148 700 | 23.6 | 13.0 | 874 | 29.2 | 4.7 | 3 339 583 | 1.1 | 222 749 | 6.7 | 3 055 554 | 36.8 | 21.6 |
| Dallas-Plano-Irving, TX Div | 1 489 863 | 61.2 | 157 100 | 23.9 | 12.9 | 884 | 29.1 | 4.9 | 2 224 665 | 1.1 | 149 831 | 6.7 | 2 045 513 | 37.8 | 20.7 |
| Fort Worth-Arlington, TX Div | 756 711 | 65.2 | 134 900 | 23.1 | 13.0 | 854 | 29.4 | 4.2 | 1 114 918 | 1.2 | 72 918 | 6.5 | 1 010 041 | 34.7 | 23.6 |
| Dalton, GA | 48 814 | 68.4 | 119 700 | 23.5 | 10.8 | 651 | 28.9 | 6.7 | 59 990 | -3.3 | 6 923 | 11.5 | 59 957 | 22.0 | 42.1 |
| Danville, IL | 31 979 | 71.1 | 76 100 | 20.6 | 12.1 | 597 | 29.8 | 1.6 | 36 356 | -0.9 | 3 602 | 9.9 | 34 065 | 25.3 | 32.3 |
| Danville, VA | 45 263 | 69.3 | 98 000 | 23.9 | 12.7 | 587 | 31.5 | 2.4 | 51 065 | -1.2 | 4 354 | 8.5 | 44 808 | 25.8 | 32.0 |
| Davenport-Moline-Rock Island, IA-IL | 154 412 | 72.2 | 122 400 | 21.3 | 12.1 | 637 | 27.7 | 1.5 | 200 153 | -1.0 | 14 269 | 7.1 | 183 076 | 32.4 | 25.5 |
| Dayton, OH | 343 789 | 66.3 | 127 900 | 22.9 | 13.4 | 718 | 31.1 | 1.4 | 403 961 | -1.7 | 30 513 | 7.6 | 383 079 | 35.2 | 22.1 |
| Decatur, AL | 59 660 | 73.6 | 112 600 | 20.8 | 10.9 | 575 | 25.7 | 2.0 | 72 086 | -1.6 | 5 226 | 7.2 | 67 279 | 28.1 | 32.6 |
| Decatur, IL | 44 568 | 70.1 | 92 300 | 19.7 | 11.4 | 634 | 29.1 | 1.6 | 53 617 | -1.4 | 5 689 | 10.6 | 49 050 | 30.9 | 26.4 |
| Deltona-Daytona Beach-Ormond Beach, FL | 197 382 | 75.0 | 172 100 | 28.7 | 14.6 | 890 | 35.9 | 1.5 | 252 690 | 0.2 | 22 340 | 8.8 | 207 221 | 30.6 | 20.3 |
| Denver-Aurora-Broomfield, CO | 989 823 | 65.6 | 246 200 | 24.9 | 10.3 | 902 | 30.3 | 2.9 | 1 417 427 | 1.1 | 112 562 | 7.9 | 1 294 355 | 40.5 | 18.1 |
| Des Moines-West Des Moines, IA | 221 804 | 72.3 | 153 700 | 21.8 | 12.2 | 729 | 27.6 | 2.2 | 311 535 | -0.5 | 16 445 | 5.3 | 300 120 | 39.1 | 17.9 |
| Detroit-Warren-Livonia, MI | 1 657 772 | 72.4 | 148 500 | 25.1 | 14.8 | 808 | 32.7 | 2.2 | 2 006 920 | -0.2 | 211 348 | 10.5 | 1 859 679 | 36.4 | 20.2 |
| Detroit-Livonia-Dearborn, MI Div | 681 674 | 66.6 | 110 000 | 26.3 | 15.6 | 775 | 36.4 | 3.1 | 816 059 | -0.4 | 95 160 | 11.7 | 704 477 | 31.0 | 22.6 |
| Warren-Troy-Farmington Hills, MI Div | 976 098 | 76.5 | 168 200 | 24.6 | 14.4 | 839 | 30.1 | 1.5 | 1 190 861 | 0.0 | 116 188 | 9.8 | 1 155 202 | 39.7 | 18.8 |
| Dothan, AL | 56 175 | 69.3 | 107 400 | 20.6 | 10.3 | 607 | 28.3 | 1.9 | 63 194 | -2.0 | 4 440 | 7.0 | 62 165 | 28.2 | 28.1 |
| Dover, DE | 57 629 | 72.4 | 208 300 | 25.7 | 11.8 | 954 | 32.0 | 2.0 | 75 502 | 0.3 | 5 703 | 7.6 | 70 155 | 32.6 | 24.4 |
| Dubuque, IA | 36 984 | 74.4 | 140 200 | 21.2 | 12.5 | 612 | 26.9 | 1.2 | 53 439 | -0.5 | 2 546 | 4.8 | 49 610 | 32.9 | 23.8 |
| Duluth, MN-WI | 119 437 | 71.9 | 144 000 | 22.8 | 12.1 | 635 | 31.6 | 1.8 | 144 804 | -0.8 | 9 660 | 6.7 | 133 074 | 33.2 | 22.2 |
| Durham-Chapel Hill, NC | 198 761 | 61.1 | 190 000 | 22.9 | 11.5 | 812 | 30.7 | 2.8 | 275 146 | 2.5 | 20 252 | 7.4 | 243 560 | 47.4 | 16.5 |
| Eau Claire, WI | 63 511 | 67.7 | 148 300 | 23.4 | 13.2 | 674 | 29.4 | 1.8 | 91 293 | 0.6 | 5 574 | 6.1 | 83 593 | 31.0 | 25.9 |
| El Centro, CA | 48 117 | 55.7 | 169 600 | 29.1 | 12.4 | 699 | 32.8 | 10.6 | 78 282 | 0.2 | 22 132 | 28.3 | 58 017 | 24.4 | 27.2 |
| Elizabethtown, KY | 42 918 | 66.2 | 130 300 | 21.2 | 10.0 | 662 | 27.0 | 1.7 | 56 903 | -0.2 | 4 473 | 7.9 | 46 804 | 31.8 | 25.9 |
| Elkhart-Goshen, IN | 70 088 | 73.2 | 126 600 | 22.7 | 11.7 | 716 | 30.6 | 3.1 | 91 830 | 1.5 | 8 788 | 9.6 | 89 772 | 25.2 | 37.5 |
| Elmira, NY | 35 528 | 67.1 | 89 400 | 19.2 | 13.3 | 673 | 29.8 | 1.2 | 39 964 | -1.0 | 3 462 | 8.7 | 38 820 | 33.2 | 22.3 |
| El Paso, TX | 247 305 | 63.6 | 108 000 | 24.1 | 11.7 | 660 | 31.0 | 7.6 | 324 613 | -0.5 | 30 309 | 9.3 | 308 988 | 28.9 | 23.4 |
| Erie, PA | 108 303 | 68.7 | 113 300 | 22.5 | 12.8 | 634 | 30.0 | 1.5 | 141 404 | 0.8 | 10 969 | 7.8 | 127 332 | 32.3 | 24.3 |
| Eugene-Springfield, OR | 144 806 | 60.2 | 230 900 | 26.9 | 12.7 | 793 | 33.6 | 2.1 | 177 073 | -1.7 | 15 225 | 8.6 | 157 787 | 34.1 | 21.7 |
| Evansville, IN-KY | 142 905 | 71.0 | 114 100 | 20.6 | 10.9 | 655 | 30.4 | 2.2 | 181 509 | -1.0 | 13 459 | 7.4 | 170 908 | 29.3 | 28.2 |
| Fairbanks, AK | 35 583 | 59.2 | 212 800 | 25.1 | 10.2 | 1 105 | 29.1 | 9.4 | 46 697 | 0.1 | 2 915 | 6.2 | 45 413 | 33.0 | 26.0 |
| Fargo, ND-MN | 85 829 | 58.1 | 130 300 | 21.9 | 11.3 | 631 | 28.4 | 1.3 | 119 465 | -0.4 | 4 245 | 3.6 | 118 469 | 35.9 | 21.8 |
| Farmington, NM | 42 215 | 74.5 | 154 200 | 20.8 | 10.0 | 704 | 24.5 | 10.3 | 56 035 | 0.8 | 3 836 | 6.8 | 52 807 | 25.9 | 31.8 |
| Fayetteville, NC | 132 925 | 59.5 | 123 800 | 23.6 | 12.3 | 816 | 29.2 | 2.4 | 164 654 | 0.7 | 16 721 | 10.2 | 134 192 | 31.9 | 22.1 |
| Fayetteville-Springdale-Rogers, AR-MO | 171 108 | 63.8 | 150 800 | 21.9 | 10.5 | 692 | 28.0 | 4.3 | 234 791 | 2.1 | 13 061 | 5.6 | 214 202 | 33.3 | 25.9 |

1. Specified owner-occupied units.   2. Specified renter-occupied units.   3. Overcrowded or lacking complete plumbing facilities.   4. Percent of civilian labor force.   5. Persons 16 years old and over.

Table C. Metropolitan Areas — **Nonfarm Employment and Agriculture**

| Area name | Private nonfarm establishments, employment and payroll, 2011 | | | | | | | | | Agriculture, 2007 | | | |
|---|---|---|---|---|---|---|---|---|---|---|---|---|---|
| | | Employment | | | | | | Annual payroll | | Farms | | | |
| | | | | | | | | | | | Percent with: | | |
| | Number of establishments | Total | Health care and social assistance | Manufacturing | Retail trade | Finance and insurance | Professional, scientific, and technical services | Total (mil dol) | Average per employee (dollars) | Number | Fewer than 50 acres | 500 acres or more | Farm operators whose principal occupation is farming (percent) |
| | 104 | 105 | 106 | 107 | 108 | 109 | 110 | 111 | 112 | 113 | 114 | 115 | 116 |
| Charleston, WV | 7 086 | 113 663 | 22 055 | 5 570 | 14 963 | 5 611 | 7 291 | 4 648 | 40 893 | 1 263 | 33.2 | 1.3 | 38.7 |
| Charleston-North Charleston-Summerville, SC | 16 376 | 235 543 | 34 358 | 20 338 | 35 481 | 8 105 | 17 659 | 9 085 | 38 569 | 1 023 | 55.5 | 6.7 | 43.7 |
| Charlotte-Gastonia-Rock Hill, NC-SC | 43 955 | 736 199 | 95 548 | 59 658 | 88 827 | 69 520 | 45 514 | 34 953 | 47 478 | 3 995 | 50.8 | 4.2 | 40.5 |
| Charlottesville, VA | 5 537 | 74 700 | 16 211 | 3 445 | 10 799 | 4 050 | 5 790 | 3 110 | 41 634 | 1 906 | 36.7 | 6.3 | 39.6 |
| Chattanooga, TN-GA | 10 913 | 204 531 | 30 984 | 32 067 | 25 978 | 13 335 | 8 191 | 7 422 | 36 288 | 2 358 | 49.7 | 3.1 | 38.8 |
| Cheyenne, WY | 2 780 | 30 566 | 6 413 | 1 361 | 5 242 | 1 654 | 1 481 | 1 110 | 36 320 | 844 | 20.9 | 39.7 | 39.6 |
| Chicago-Joliet-Naperville, IL-IN-WI | 236 012 | 3 845 021 | 557 622 | 384 510 | 437 848 | 222 127 | 301 315 | 199 965 | 52 006 | 7 714 | 51.5 | 17.5 | 49.8 |
| Chicago-Joliet-Naperville, IL Div | X | X | X | X | X | X | X | X | X | 4 732 | 52.5 | 17.5 | 51.8 |
| Gary, IN Div | X | X | X | X | X | X | X | X | X | 2 126 | 44.5 | 22.2 | 46.3 |
| Lake County-Kenosha County, IL-WI Div | X | X | X | X | X | X | X | X | X | 856 | 63.8 | 6.0 | 47.2 |
| Chico, CA | 4 606 | 53 193 | 12 880 | 3 836 | 9 326 | 2 307 | 2 527 | 1 776 | 33 380 | 2 048 | 64.5 | 7.9 | 51.6 |
| Cincinnati-Middletown, OH-KY-IN | 45 607 | 875 217 | 136 509 | 99 735 | 115 360 | 53 574 | 56 609 | 38 903 | 44 450 | 10 376 | 43.9 | 4.3 | 39.7 |
| Clarksville, TN-KY | 4 259 | 67 651 | 11 279 | 10 534 | 11 547 | 2 088 | 3 248 | 2 142 | 31 667 | 2 997 | 31.5 | 9.1 | 43.9 |
| Cleveland, TN | 2 065 | 37 156 | 5 234 | 7 443 | 4 979 | 1 646 | 818 | 1 262 | 33 976 | 1 264 | 54.0 | 2.9 | 43.4 |
| Cleveland-Elyria-Mentor, OH | 51 600 | 889 949 | 173 734 | 117 379 | 98 325 | 52 689 | 52 199 | 39 890 | 44 822 | 3 098 | 63.1 | 3.6 | 45.0 |
| Coeur d'Alene, ID | 4 293 | 42 855 | 8 376 | 3 819 | 7 670 | 1 985 | 2 635 | 1 426 | 33 277 | 826 | 57.9 | 8.0 | 40.0 |
| College Station-Bryan, TX | 4 316 | 59 124 | 8 796 | 5 036 | 10 958 | 1 576 | 3 149 | 1 851 | 31 311 | 4 494 | 34.9 | 10.3 | 40.0 |
| Colorado Springs, CO | 16 427 | 217 358 | 31 359 | 11 110 | 29 317 | 9 345 | 17 972 | 8 748 | 40 249 | 1 655 | 46.8 | 17.6 | 34.3 |
| Columbia, MO | 4 568 | 68 678 | 16 274 | 4 138 | 11 773 | 6 186 | 3 478 | 2 337 | 34 022 | 2 189 | 30.4 | 11.4 | 32.9 |
| Columbia, SC | 16 681 | 267 226 | 43 104 | 26 285 | 36 831 | 20 665 | 14 565 | 9 840 | 36 824 | 2 945 | 43.6 | 6.6 | 41.6 |
| Columbus, GA-AL | 5 666 | 93 386 | 14 908 | 10 866 | 13 890 | 11 271 | 4 771 | 3 297 | 35 306 | 924 | 39.7 | 10.6 | 37.4 |
| Columbus, IN | 1 845 | 40 314 | 4 901 | 9 783 | 4 778 | 974 | 3 152 | 1 677 | 41 597 | 668 | 46.0 | 13.6 | 39.7 |
| Columbus, OH | 38 781 | 757 339 | 119 580 | 57 032 | 94 137 | 70 528 | 50 517 | 33 608 | 44 376 | 7 050 | 49.0 | 11.0 | 41.0 |
| Corpus Christi, TX | 9 257 | 143 987 | 28 959 | 8 682 | 20 089 | 4 170 | 5 838 | 5 392 | 37 451 | 1 458 | 45.3 | 22.2 | 41.9 |
| Corvallis, OR | 2 003 | 25 118 | 5 027 | 3 141 | 3 540 | 605 | 2 202 | 1 012 | 40 283 | 906 | 73.3 | 4.5 | 41.1 |
| Crestview-Fort Walton Beach-Destin, FL | 4 961 | 58 506 | 8 381 | 2 552 | 11 500 | 2 540 | 5 634 | 2 027 | 34 642 | 567 | 47.6 | 3.5 | 36.3 |
| Cumberland, MD-WV | 2 099 | 30 930 | 7 287 | 4 734 | 4 897 | 1 165 | 795 | 950 | 30 731 | 795 | 32.1 | 3.5 | 38.6 |
| Dallas-Fort Worth-Arlington, TX | 141 069 | 2 566 469 | 311 599 | 222 308 | 301 383 | 183 904 | 190 758 | 127 846 | 49 814 | 25 402 | 61.3 | 4.8 | 34.9 |
| Dallas-Plano-Irving, TX Div | X | X | X | X | X | X | X | X | X | 14 567 | 59.4 | 5.1 | 35.3 |
| Fort Worth-Arlington, TX Div | X | X | X | X | X | X | X | X | X | 10 835 | 63.8 | 4.4 | 34.3 |
| Dalton, GA | 2 651 | 54 824 | 4 724 | 20 994 | 5 709 | 931 | 1 206 | 1 852 | 33 778 | 788 | 48.1 | 1.5 | 34.6 |
| Danville, IL | 1 492 | 23 300 | 4 723 | 4 798 | 3 483 | 1 137 | 420 | 835 | 35 835 | 1 014 | 38.7 | 27.3 | 52.4 |
| Danville, VA | 2 181 | 31 365 | 5 953 | 6 525 | 5 219 | 1 034 | 557 | 945 | 30 117 | 1 356 | 22.4 | 8.8 | 44.8 |
| Davenport-Moline-Rock Island, IA-IL | 9 091 | 156 875 | 23 500 | 23 315 | 21 701 | 6 450 | 6 360 | 6 394 | 40 757 | 3 819 | 36.6 | 20.5 | 51.8 |
| Dayton, OH | 17 241 | 311 621 | 62 584 | 42 163 | 40 783 | 10 166 | 22 675 | 12 576 | 40 356 | 3 809 | 54.7 | 10.8 | 43.4 |
| Decatur, AL | 3 061 | 47 380 | 6 605 | 12 472 | 6 647 | 1 534 | 2 143 | 1 787 | 37 710 | 3 058 | 46.9 | 3.9 | 38.9 |
| Decatur, IL | 2 478 | 45 784 | 7 430 | 7 510 | 5 529 | 1 366 | 1 221 | 1 835 | 40 078 | 708 | 44.1 | 27.0 | 54.5 |
| Deltona-Daytona Beach-Ormond Beach, FL | 11 693 | 126 547 | 26 001 | 7 432 | 23 274 | 4 413 | 6 279 | 3 993 | 31 553 | 1 243 | 84.5 | 2.4 | 46.7 |
| Denver-Aurora-Broomfield, CO | 73 419 | 1 049 564 | 129 487 | 55 589 | 120 052 | 60 120 | 98 276 | 53 880 | 51 335 | 4 928 | 50.0 | 16.0 | 33.1 |
| Des Moines-West Des Moines, IA | 14 709 | 274 567 | 36 910 | 17 480 | 35 548 | 48 000 | 15 836 | 12 138 | 44 206 | 4 782 | 37.0 | 16.3 | 42.1 |
| Detroit-Warren-Livonia, MI | 96 919 | 1 554 363 | 248 220 | 185 056 | 192 590 | 75 161 | 157 680 | 75 575 | 48 621 | 4 560 | 59.4 | 5.2 | 46.8 |
| Detroit-Livonia-Dearborn, MI Div | X | X | X | X | X | X | X | X | X | 313 | 78.0 | 1.9 | 46.6 |
| Warren-Troy-Farmington Hills, MI Div | X | X | X | X | X | X | X | X | X | 4 247 | 58.0 | 5.4 | 46.8 |
| Dothan, AL | 3 463 | 50 080 | 10 103 | 5 036 | 9 094 | 1 407 | 1 347 | 1 684 | 33 621 | 2 427 | 30.5 | 10.6 | 41.3 |
| Dover, DE | 3 177 | 48 100 | 9 061 | 5 000 | 8 831 | 1 139 | 2 026 | 1 667 | 34 648 | 825 | 57.0 | 9.3 | 58.4 |
| Dubuque, IA | 2 708 | 51 097 | 7 555 | 8 194 | 6 988 | 2 936 | 2 691 | 1 843 | 36 067 | 1 483 | 26.0 | 11.1 | 53.1 |
| Duluth, MN-WI | 7 113 | 103 674 | 27 393 | 7 009 | 15 850 | 4 237 | 3 561 | 3 725 | 35 928 | 1 579 | 21.8 | 8.2 | 43.8 |
| Durham-Chapel Hill, NC | 11 593 | 219 298 | 40 746 | 15 998 | 23 066 | 8 214 | 33 196 | 11 981 | 54 632 | 2 338 | 48.4 | 4.1 | 44.4 |
| Eau Claire, WI | 4 200 | 68 904 | 13 543 | 10 389 | 10 502 | 3 592 | 2 380 | 2 329 | 33 805 | 2 798 | 23.7 | 6.8 | 48.2 |
| El Centro, CA | 2 350 | 29 516 | 4 502 | 3 276 | 7 269 | D | 822 | 904 | 30 618 | 452 | 28.1 | 39.4 | 71.0 |
| Elizabethtown, KY | 2 510 | 35 969 | 6 382 | 5 414 | 6 143 | 1 570 | 1 954 | 1 082 | 30 072 | 2 399 | 40.7 | 5.3 | 40.3 |
| Elkhart-Goshen, IN | 4 830 | 102 109 | 9 733 | 49 226 | 8 774 | 1 837 | 1 925 | 3 669 | 35 932 | 1 617 | 64.1 | 4.5 | 37.3 |
| Elmira, NY | 1 834 | 33 442 | 6 814 | 5 893 | 5 289 | 1 163 | 779 | 1 185 | 35 423 | 373 | 22.3 | 7.8 | 49.1 |
| El Paso, TX | 13 494 | 210 200 | 36 929 | 14 083 | 35 069 | 6 567 | 9 644 | 6 254 | 29 755 | 590 | 78.3 | 7.5 | 47.6 |
| Erie, PA | 6 246 | 114 273 | 24 086 | 22 960 | 15 339 | D | 3 196 | 3 994 | 34 947 | 1 609 | 44.0 | 2.9 | 39.7 |
| Eugene-Springfield, OR | 9 437 | 112 024 | 21 525 | 11 911 | 18 322 | 4 550 | 5 625 | 3 898 | 34 793 | 3 335 | 75.5 | 2.8 | 37.5 |
| Evansville, IN-KY | 8 497 | 162 744 | 26 799 | 27 263 | 19 495 | 6 465 | 5 571 | 6 158 | 37 838 | 2 841 | 40.3 | 17.3 | 44.2 |
| Fairbanks, AK | 2 455 | 26 951 | 5 443 | 553 | 4 746 | 730 | 1 812 | 1 241 | 46 062 | 212 | 34.0 | 22.2 | 56.1 |
| Fargo, ND-MN | 6 266 | 108 022 | 18 886 | 9 519 | 15 127 | 7 441 | 4 818 | 4 151 | 38 431 | 1 834 | 17.7 | 41.8 | 59.5 |
| Farmington, NM | 2 833 | 37 637 | 6 556 | 1 341 | 6 406 | 1 027 | 1 315 | 1 598 | 42 463 | 1 897 | 85.7 | 2.2 | 55.4 |
| Fayetteville, NC | 6 018 | 99 571 | 19 707 | 8 145 | 16 851 | 2 641 | 7 522 | 3 188 | 32 021 | 749 | 44.1 | 10.5 | 48.3 |
| Fayetteville-Springdale-Rogers, AR-MO | 10 552 | 185 606 | 21 071 | 25 420 | 22 301 | 5 126 | 8 670 | 8 050 | 43 371 | 7 401 | 43.3 | 5.3 | 42.2 |

# Table C. Metropolitan Areas — **Agriculture**

| Area name | Land in farms Acreage (1,000) [117] | Percent change, 2002–2007 [118] | Average size of farm [119] | Total irrigated (1,000) [120] | Total cropland (1,000) [121] | Value of land and buildings — Average per farm [122] | Average per acre [123] | Value of machinery and equipment, average per farm (dollars) [124] | Value of products sold — Total (mil dol) [125] | Average per farm (dollars) [126] | Percent from: Crops [127] | Livestock and poultry products [128] | Percent of farms with sales of: $10,000 or more [129] | $100,000 or more [130] | Government payments Total ($1,000) [131] | Percent of farms [132] |
|---|---|---|---|---|---|---|---|---|---|---|---|---|---|---|---|---|
| Charleston, WV | 145 | 9.0 | 115 | 0.2 | 30.0 | 243 749 | 2 126 | 30 733 | 9.8 | 7 717 | 64.0 | 36.0 | 8.5 | 0.3 | 54 | 7.0 |
| Charleston-North Charleston-Summerville, SC | 159 | -1.9 | 156 | 3.8 | 60.0 | 671 668 | 4 310 | 68 000 | D | D | D | D | 22.2 | 6.8 | 1 754 | 19.5 |
| Charlotte-Gastonia-Rock Hill, NC-SC | 517 | -6.2 | 129 | 2.6 | 245.7 | 657 897 | 5 088 | 67 692 | D | D | D | D | 28.9 | 12.8 | 4 250 | 20.9 |
| Charlottesville, VA | 311 | -12.4 | 163 | 2.2 | 99.8 | 897 521 | 5 494 | 58 776 | 49.9 | 26 186 | 45.5 | 54.5 | 30.6 | 3.4 | 441 | 11.2 |
| Chattanooga, TN-GA | 261 | -6.5 | 111 | 0.5 | 98.3 | 471 016 | 4 258 | 57 563 | 168.7 | 71 593 | D | D | 22.2 | 6.0 | 529 | 9.5 |
| Cheyenne, WY | 1 692 | -3.6 | 2 004 | 53.0 | 345.6 | 971 638 | 485 | 88 824 | 124.1 | 147 031 | 17.5 | 82.5 | 37.3 | 14.5 | 4 352 | 38.7 |
| Chicago-Joliet-Naperville, IL-IN-WI | 2 291 | -1.8 | 297 | D | 2 144.9 | 1 323 210 | 4 455 | 144 387 | 1 715.6 | 222 402 | 72.1 | 27.9 | 53.0 | 30.5 | 44 684 | 53.1 |
| Chicago-Joliet-Naperville, IL Div | 1 398 | -4.9 | 295 | D | 1 325.3 | 1 425 731 | 4 826 | 151 220 | 1 022.5 | 216 069 | 81.9 | 18.1 | 54.2 | 31.9 | 29 017 | 50.9 |
| Gary, IN Div | 774 | 5.3 | 364 | 46.9 | 719.4 | 1 323 186 | 3 633 | 151 441 | 602.6 | 283 454 | 55.2 | 44.8 | 55.8 | 32.5 | 13 978 | 67.5 |
| Lake County-Kenosha County, IL-WI Div | 119 | -7.0 | 139 | 0.8 | 100.2 | 756 535 | 5 448 | 89 089 | 90.5 | 105 783 | 73.2 | 26.8 | 39.1 | 17.3 | 1 689 | 30.1 |
| Chico, CA | 374 | -2.1 | 183 | 202.2 | 222.7 | 1 371 244 | 7 513 | 108 816 | 342.8 | 167 366 | 96.5 | 3.5 | 53.6 | 25.5 | 14 780 | 14.3 |
| Cincinnati-Middletown, OH-KY-IN | 1 342 | -5.6 | 129 | 3.9 | 804.8 | 468 425 | 3 622 | 62 166 | 300.6 | 28 977 | 71.6 | 28.4 | 28.5 | 6.0 | 11 530 | 30.5 |
| Clarksville, TN-KY | 689 | 0.3 | 230 | 4.6 | 420.6 | 628 879 | 2 736 | 78 467 | 163.8 | 54 658 | D | D | 37.2 | 11.3 | 8 210 | 40.4 |
| Cleveland, TN | 128 | 1.6 | 101 | 0.3 | 58.3 | 482 893 | 4 769 | 57 935 | 123.6 | 97 734 | 4.8 | 95.2 | 28.1 | 11.7 | 288 | 9.7 |
| Cleveland-Elyria-Mentor, OH | 295 | -21.3 | 95 | 4.2 | 218.6 | 520 944 | 5 468 | 69 058 | 310.2 | 100 128 | 83.8 | 16.2 | 37.3 | 9.7 | D | 20.8 |
| Coeur d'Alene, ID | 131 | -14.9 | 158 | 11.0 | 71.2 | 642 680 | 4 057 | 52 170 | 16.4 | 19 834 | 75.1 | 24.9 | 18.8 | 3.6 | 869 | 17.4 |
| College Station-Bryan, TX | 1 092 | -10.0 | 243 | 45.0 | 272.5 | 554 744 | 2 283 | 61 563 | 226.9 | 50 502 | 22.1 | 77.9 | 33.2 | 5.0 | 5 052 | 7.3 |
| Colorado Springs, CO | 690 | -22.1 | 417 | 17.3 | 97.5 | 554 050 | 1 329 | 53 758 | 40.5 | 24 466 | 49.3 | 50.7 | 20.7 | 3.1 | D | 8.2 |
| Columbia, MO | 535 | -0.9 | 245 | 15.6 | 324.8 | 598 049 | 2 445 | 61 636 | 90.6 | 41 381 | 70.2 | 29.8 | 37.8 | 9.0 | 5 523 | 43.8 |
| Columbia, SC | 507 | 2.6 | 172 | 28.4 | 199.2 | 532 092 | 3 092 | 69 506 | 505.4 | 171 597 | 19.3 | 80.7 | 26.4 | 10.4 | 6 331 | 21.6 |
| Columbus, GA-AL | 214 | -12.3 | 231 | D | 54.2 | 607 141 | 2 627 | 54 032 | D | D | 27.4 | D | 21.0 | 4.7 | D | 18.3 |
| Columbus, IN | 166 | 3.1 | 249 | 10.2 | 148.3 | 945 855 | 3 798 | 108 015 | 69.5 | 104 009 | 87.5 | 12.5 | 48.4 | 19.3 | 3 817 | 64.7 |
| Columbus, OH | 1 522 | -6.9 | 216 | 3.7 | 1 298.1 | 825 409 | 3 824 | 102 450 | 780.1 | 110 652 | 70.8 | 29.2 | 42.4 | 17.6 | 30 532 | 51.4 |
| Corpus Christi, TX | 930 | 1.2 | 638 | 18.6 | D | 812 956 | 1 275 | 116 742 | 221.8 | 152 109 | 89.2 | 10.8 | 33.7 | 18.4 | D | 34.3 |
| Corvallis, OR | 115 | -11.5 | 126 | 23.3 | 79.2 | 675 605 | 5 343 | 81 023 | 74.6 | 82 301 | 84.4 | 15.6 | 23.3 | 7.8 | 342 | 7.7 |
| Crestview-Fort Walton Beach-Destin, FL | 66 | 20.0 | 116 | 0.4 | 24.3 | 628 564 | 5 410 | 38 958 | D | D | D | D | 13.1 | 3.4 | 1 641 | 36.2 |
| Cumberland, MD-WV | 115 | -4.2 | 144 | 0.5 | 32.1 | 474 725 | 3 293 | 37 716 | 18.7 | 23 433 | 16.7 | 83.3 | 22.0 | 3.3 | 254 | 17.4 |
| Dallas-Fort Worth-Arlington, TX | 3 522 | -5.7 | 139 | D | 1 348.2 | 424 036 | 3 058 | 46 883 | 554.8 | 21 835 | 47.0 | 53.0 | 19.1 | 2.5 | 10 149 | 8.3 |
| Dallas-Plano-Irving, TX Div | 2 152 | -3.1 | 148 | D | 947.7 | 417 101 | 2 823 | 48 138 | 330.3 | 22 668 | 50.1 | 49.9 | 18.7 | 2.7 | 8 451 | 10.7 |
| Fort Worth-Arlington, TX Div | 1 370 | -9.6 | 126 | 7.3 | 400.5 | 433 360 | 3 427 | 45 196 | 224.5 | 20 714 | 42.4 | 57.6 | 19.5 | 2.2 | 1 698 | 5.0 |
| Dalton, GA | 83 | -2.4 | 105 | 0.5 | 29.1 | 457 636 | 4 362 | 55 960 | 159.9 | 202 869 | 1.5 | 98.5 | 32.2 | 13.1 | 207 | 7.7 |
| Danville, IL | 457 | 1.6 | 451 | 0.7 | 428.1 | 1 781 695 | 3 950 | 178 307 | 224.0 | 220 876 | 95.5 | 4.5 | 61.3 | 37.7 | 8 500 | 78.9 |
| Danville, VA | 274 | NA | 202 | 4.2 | 103.6 | 638 676 | 3 157 | 73 087 | 62.6 | 46 198 | 37.4 | 62.6 | 32.1 | 7.9 | 1 494 | 34.1 |
| Davenport-Moline-Rock Island, IA-IL | 1 223 | 4.4 | 320 | 21.6 | 1 090.8 | 1 267 848 | 3 957 | 130 651 | 686.2 | 179 693 | 75.3 | 24.7 | 59.2 | 34.4 | 27 720 | 75.7 |
| Dayton, OH | 701 | 7.4 | 184 | 4.1 | 622.8 | 718 881 | 3 906 | 91 594 | 324.9 | 85 309 | 78.5 | 21.5 | 45.5 | 17.4 | 12 745 | 55.7 |
| Decatur, AL | 384 | 0.3 | 126 | 4.4 | 188.9 | 340 474 | 2 712 | 57 567 | 241.9 | 79 098 | 9.8 | 90.2 | 28.6 | 8.2 | 7 743 | 31.8 |
| Decatur, IL | 291 | -9.3 | 410 | 0.0 | 280.7 | 1 831 072 | 4 461 | 177 853 | 156.8 | 221 463 | 96.8 | 3.2 | 58.9 | 37.3 | 5 131 | 74.2 |
| Deltona-Daytona Beach-Ormond Beach, FL | 83 | -11.7 | 67 | 9.1 | 18.3 | 662 001 | 9 881 | 38 989 | 125.5 | 101 002 | 94.9 | 5.1 | 36.7 | 10.2 | 47 | 1.3 |
| Denver-Aurora-Broomfield, CO | 2 726 | D | 553 | D | 1 035.4 | 735 672 | 1 330 | 64 519 | 257.2 | 52 208 | D | D | 22.1 | 6.1 | D | 17.5 |
| Des Moines-West Des Moines, IA | 1 426 | -2.6 | 298 | 5.5 | 1 124.0 | 963 853 | 3 231 | 117 099 | 690.8 | 144 456 | 62.0 | 38.0 | 47.9 | 21.3 | 29 631 | 71.1 |
| Detroit-Warren-Livonia, MI | 545 | -8.9 | 120 | 9.6 | 427.9 | 560 530 | 4 688 | 81 252 | 261.8 | 57 401 | 78.2 | 21.8 | 31.8 | 10.9 | 4 843 | 21.5 |
| Detroit-Livonia-Dearborn, MI Div | 17 | -19.0 | 56 | 0.8 | 13.1 | 431 377 | 7 741 | 73 184 | 28.8 | 91 875 | 97.1 | 2.9 | 35.8 | 11.2 | 93 | 10.9 |
| Warren-Troy-Farmington Hills, MI Div | 528 | -8.5 | 124 | 8.7 | 414.8 | 570 048 | 4 587 | 81 846 | 233.0 | 54 860 | 75.9 | 24.1 | 31.5 | 10.9 | 4 750 | 22.3 |
| Dothan, AL | 591 | 4.2 | 244 | 21.3 | 284.6 | 490 989 | 2 016 | 67 033 | 225.9 | 93 065 | 27.9 | 72.1 | 34.0 | 11.3 | 19 609 | 59.8 |
| Dover, DE | 174 | -5.9 | 211 | 29.1 | 146.5 | 2 091 272 | 9 926 | 122 692 | 188.4 | 228 352 | D | D | 46.7 | 26.1 | 3 285 | 37.3 |
| Dubuque, IA | 311 | -1.6 | 210 | D | 237.4 | 711 542 | 3 395 | 119 819 | 271.1 | 182 789 | 23.6 | 76.4 | 65.3 | 37.2 | 7 841 | 81.2 |
| Duluth, MN-WI | 319 | -14.7 | 202 | 2.4 | 144.4 | 408 519 | 2 020 | 48 794 | 27.7 | 17 541 | 37.4 | 62.6 | 26.2 | 4.5 | 286 | 8.7 |
| Durham-Chapel Hill, NC | 289 | -7.1 | 124 | 3.7 | 119.3 | 594 313 | 4 809 | 57 227 | D | D | 18.3 | D | 32.7 | 11.8 | 1 898 | 18.6 |
| Eau Claire, WI | 559 | -3.3 | 200 | 6.6 | 357.9 | 519 857 | 2 603 | 86 606 | 249.6 | 89 197 | 21.6 | 78.4 | 46.6 | 21.9 | 7 217 | 65.8 |
| El Centro, CA | 427 | -16.9 | 945 | 376.5 | 396.7 | 5 001 024 | 5 290 | 413 760 | 1 290.3 | 2 854 542 | 54.5 | 45.5 | 83.2 | 61.9 | 4 885 | 29.2 |
| Elizabethtown, KY | 348 | -7.0 | 145 | 0.8 | 193.8 | 409 608 | 2 826 | 57 110 | 73.5 | 30 632 | 55.2 | 44.8 | 33.8 | 6.0 | 2 528 | 34.8 |
| Elkhart-Goshen, IN | 163 | -18.9 | 101 | 22.0 | 141.6 | 560 281 | 5 548 | 72 668 | 205.8 | 127 245 | 26.1 | 73.9 | 49.7 | 26.2 | 1 909 | 26.3 |
| Elmira, NY | 65 | -5.8 | 175 | 0.2 | 32.9 | 319 539 | 1 830 | 69 729 | 16.6 | 44 525 | 18.9 | 81.1 | 29.2 | 9.4 | 394 | 27.9 |
| El Paso, TX | 169 | 48.2 | 286 | 37.8 | 54.1 | 418 167 | 1 464 | 78 916 | 47.5 | 80 447 | 86.2 | 13.8 | 26.1 | 11.4 | 894 | 10.3 |
| Erie, PA | 173 | 4.2 | 108 | 1.4 | 101.7 | 430 926 | 4 005 | 62 976 | 71.3 | 44 303 | 69.0 | 31.0 | 31.7 | 11.4 | 1 348 | 16.7 |
| Eugene-Springfield, OR | 246 | 4.7 | 74 | 22.4 | 116.4 | 547 167 | 7 432 | 49 129 | 131.1 | 39 307 | 70.5 | 29.5 | 17.5 | 4.4 | 759 | 4.3 |
| Evansville, IN-KY | 968 | 4.0 | 341 | D | 826.2 | 998 966 | 2 933 | 130 927 | 437.2 | 153 889 | 76.0 | 24.0 | 47.4 | 23.7 | 15 625 | 68.4 |
| Fairbanks, AK | 111 | NA | 523 | 2.0 | 63.6 | 406 163 | 777 | 74 337 | 7.1 | 33 373 | 83.2 | 16.8 | 42.5 | 7.5 | 1 356 | 23.6 |
| Fargo, ND-MN | 1 653 | -4.3 | 901 | 17.6 | 1 535.9 | 1 449 652 | 1 609 | 228 729 | 469.7 | 256 095 | 89.9 | 10.1 | 57.9 | 41.1 | 24 398 | 81.0 |
| Farmington, NM | 1 631 | D | 860 | 78.4 | 107.4 | 268 195 | 312 | 37 574 | 57.2 | 30 152 | 82.6 | 17.4 | 8.9 | 1.3 | 900 | 4.6 |
| Fayetteville, NC | 149 | -3.2 | 198 | 3.9 | 80.0 | 627 065 | 3 161 | 79 354 | 157.9 | 210 816 | 16.7 | 83.3 | 35.9 | 18.6 | 2 654 | 38.6 |
| Fayetteville-Springdale-Rogers, AR-MO | 1 041 | -12.6 | 141 | 2.1 | 341.1 | 519 753 | 3 695 | 59 940 | 1 123.0 | 151 730 | 1.8 | 98.2 | 38.8 | 13.2 | 1 278 | 6.3 |

# Table C. Metropolitan Areas — Water Use, Wholesale Trade, Retail Trade, and Real Estate

| Area name | Water use, 2005 | | Wholesale trade,[1] 2007 | | | | Retail trade, 2007 | | | | Real estate and rental and leasing, 2007 | | | |
|---|---|---|---|---|---|---|---|---|---|---|---|---|---|---|
| | Total water withdrawn (mil gal/day) | Gallons withdrawn per person | Number of establishments | Number of employees | Sales (mil dol) | Annual payroll (mil dol) | Number of establishments | Number of employees | Sales (mil dol) | Annual payroll (mil dol) | Number of establishments | Number of employees | Receipts (mil dol) | Annual payroll (mil dol) |
| | 133 | 134 | 135 | 136 | 137 | 138 | 139 | 140 | 141 | 142 | 143 | 144 | 145 | 146 |
| Charleston, WV | 567.6 | 1 852 | 432 | 6 150 | 4 160.1 | 294.4 | 1 190 | 17 349 | 3 842.5 | 327.3 | 341 | 2 055 | 412.3 | 61.9 |
| Charleston-North Charleston-Summerville, SC | 713.8 | 1 200 | 760 | 11 530 | 8 645.0 | 556.3 | 2 799 | 37 845 | 8 752.8 | 841.3 | 1 044 | 5 212 | 936.0 | 169.8 |
| Charlotte-Gastonia-Rock Hill, NC-SC | 4 008.8 | 2 635 | 3 489 | 55 343 | 52 134.4 | 3 081.9 | 6 225 | 91 990 | 23 219.9 | 2 112.7 | 2 596 | 15 084 | 3 396.6 | 642.2 |
| Charlottesville, VA | 244.6 | 1 298 | 180 | 2 108 | 925.7 | 102.3 | 859 | 11 418 | 2 639.8 | 269.2 | 311 | 1 700 | 239.0 | 52.8 |
| Chattanooga, TN-GA | 1 674.6 | 3 403 | 708 | 8 176 | 4 895.3 | 357.8 | 2 094 | 27 398 | 6 586.1 | 607.2 | 501 | 2 682 | 410.3 | 107.2 |
| Cheyenne, WY | 272.5 | 3 200 | 116 | 1 017 | 828.8 | 46.2 | 360 | 5 603 | 1 720.5 | 133.4 | 134 | 519 | 94.2 | 14.3 |
| Chicago-Joliet-Naperville, IL-IN-WI | 9 495.4 | 1 006 | 16 000 | 265 925 | 346 250.0 | 16 552.3 | 30 234 | 475 144 | 129 111.8 | 11 514.3 | 11 251 | 75 220 | 19 819.5 | 3 666.0 |
| Chicago-Joliet-Naperville, IL Div | 6 106.4 | 775 | 13 725 | 219 797 | 282 205.5 | 13 219.7 | 24 781 | 387 591 | 97 414.1 | 9 183.2 | 9 612 | 67 343 | 18 193.2 | 3 353.8 |
| Gary, IN Div | 2 502.8 | 3 589 | 697 | 8 772 | 8 406.2 | 431.8 | 2 397 | 35 715 | 9 560.9 | 758.3 | 645 | 3 292 | 456.8 | 86.2 |
| Lake County-Kenosha County, IL-WI Div | 886.2 | 1 027 | 1 578 | 37 356 | 55 638.4 | 2 900.7 | 3 056 | 51 838 | 22 136.9 | 1 572.8 | 994 | 4 585 | 1 169.4 | 226.0 |
| Chico, CA | 789.9 | 3 688 | 182 | 1 934 | 868.1 | 76.0 | 798 | 11 316 | 2 400.7 | 256.8 | 264 | 1 462 | 158.8 | 32.6 |
| Cincinnati-Middletown, OH-KY-IN | 2 131.1 | 1 029 | 3 110 | 57 817 | 90 116.2 | 3 373.3 | 6 977 | 110 110 | 25 842.3 | 2 395.2 | 2 142 | 13 389 | 2 615.8 | 470.2 |
| Clarksville, TN-KY | 2 127.7 | 8 732 | 159 | 1 861 | 1 433.9 | 73.1 | 866 | 11 876 | 2 948.3 | 262.5 | 230 | 949 | 147.3 | 22.4 |
| Cleveland, TN | 24.1 | 223 | 79 | D | D | D | 444 | 4 970 | 1 232.3 | 113.5 | 90 | 478 | 89.7 | 12.8 |
| Cleveland-Elyria-Mentor, OH | 2 097.9 | 987 | 3 869 | 55 061 | 48 609.8 | 2 933.9 | 7 396 | 106 023 | 24 195.3 | 2 304.4 | 2 258 | 18 202 | 6 344.0 | 782.1 |
| Coeur d'Alene, ID | 73.2 | 573 | 163 | 1 625 | 915.7 | 67.8 | 609 | 7 398 | 2 175.2 | 187.5 | 249 | 876 | 155.3 | 27.4 |
| College Station-Bryan, TX | 103.9 | 548 | 155 | 1 882 | 1 013.5 | 70.2 | 748 | 10 070 | 2 418.2 | 209.7 | 241 | 1 240 | 208.1 | 34.5 |
| Colorado Springs, CO | 163.5 | 278 | 559 | 9 150 | 6 385.6 | 592.9 | 2 158 | 31 970 | 8 119.2 | 787.7 | 1 183 | 4 028 | 603.3 | 117.2 |
| Columbia, MO | 23.8 | 155 | 153 | 1 878 | 960.2 | 75.4 | 689 | 11 629 | 3 100.3 | 245.4 | 245 | 1 045 | 149.9 | 25.5 |
| Columbia, SC | 2 394.6 | 3 471 | 885 | 15 623 | 10 539.6 | 760.4 | 2 790 | 39 139 | 8 967.8 | 819.2 | 786 | 5 179 | 1 090.3 | 172.1 |
| Columbus, GA-AL | 94.5 | 333 | 235 | 3 163 | 1 999.3 | 132.6 | 1 097 | 15 393 | 3 468.3 | 313.1 | 321 | 1 822 | 321.8 | 60.6 |
| Columbus, IN | 21.2 | 289 | 95 | 1 166 | 891.8 | 61.2 | 375 | 5 133 | 1 075.2 | 106.7 | 74 | 319 | 50.1 | 8.9 |
| Columbus, OH | 331.6 | 194 | 2 220 | 45 650 | 57 654.2 | 2 373.1 | 5 712 | 101 313 | 26 892.3 | 2 381.3 | 2 091 | 12 876 | 2 513.7 | 468.5 |
| Corpus Christi, TX | 388.7 | 940 | 509 | 5 792 | 4 541.3 | 276.3 | 1 449 | 20 267 | 5 177.6 | 440.5 | 541 | 3 012 | 461.3 | 86.7 |
| Corvallis, OR | 45.1 | 573 | 57 | 585 | 430.5 | 24.0 | 275 | 3 559 | 685.2 | 73.0 | 119 | 543 | 58.1 | 11.3 |
| Crestview-Fort Walton Beach-Destin, FL | 26.4 | 140 | 130 | 710 | 702.4 | 34.8 | 903 | 12 427 | 3 031.0 | 272.4 | 398 | 1 772 | 260.5 | 57.0 |
| Cumberland, MD-WV | 48.8 | 484 | 64 | D | D | D | 391 | 5 051 | 1 088.8 | 91.1 | 70 | 266 | 38.1 | 6.3 |
| Dallas-Fort Worth-Arlington, TX | 2 382.2 | 409 | 9 458 | 167 324 | 206 962.4 | 9 823.0 | 19 069 | 301 443 | 85 651.3 | 7 513.7 | 7 342 | 57 889 | 13 368.4 | 2 812.1 |
| Dallas-Plano-Irving, TX Div | 1 817.6 | 467 | 6 819 | 120 653 | 161 092.6 | 7 061.1 | 12 704 | 200 693 | 57 367.2 | 5 049.6 | 5 272 | 45 640 | 10 407.7 | 2 341.2 |
| Fort Worth-Arlington, TX Div | 564.7 | 293 | 2 639 | 46 671 | 45 869.8 | 2 761.9 | 6 365 | 100 750 | 28 284.1 | 2 464.1 | 2 070 | 12 249 | 2 960.7 | 470.8 |
| Dalton, GA | 43.2 | 328 | 297 | 5 190 | 4 943.3 | 208.6 | 605 | 6 525 | 1 659.1 | 146.9 | 100 | 412 | 61.5 | 12.0 |
| Danville, IL | 17.1 | 208 | 81 | D | D | D | 281 | 3 443 | 757.9 | 68.5 | 59 | 254 | 34.3 | 6.6 |
| Danville, VA | 63.8 | 591 | 101 | 1 463 | 614.1 | 48.0 | 487 | 5 478 | 1 161.5 | 101.3 | 86 | 416 | 47.1 | 10.1 |
| Davenport-Moline-Rock Island, IA-IL | 1 214.1 | 3 226 | 597 | 8 829 | 9 543.2 | 377.1 | 1 492 | 22 567 | 5 127.2 | 480.3 | 357 | 2 521 | 378.9 | 62.4 |
| Dayton, OH | 304.9 | 361 | 947 | 14 608 | 12 999.4 | 702.0 | 2 781 | 43 291 | 10 397.4 | 916.9 | 830 | 4 827 | 711.2 | 152.0 |
| Decatur, AL | 192.2 | 1 296 | 194 | 2 297 | 1 356.1 | 94.0 | 631 | 6 676 | 1 804.6 | 144.0 | 109 | 448 | 63.1 | 11.4 |
| Decatur, IL | 40.4 | 366 | 123 | 1 251 | 738.5 | 57.2 | 432 | 6 231 | 1 450.6 | 132.5 | 91 | 454 | 64.6 | 12.6 |
| Deltona-Daytona Beach-Ormond Beach, FL | 171.2 | 346 | 516 | 5 110 | 2 897.3 | 188.5 | 1 970 | 26 205 | 6 099.9 | 575.9 | 842 | 3 978 | 531.8 | 101.5 |
| Denver-Aurora-Broomfield, CO | 703.0 | 298 | 4 366 | 69 932 | 75 213.8 | 4 051.4 | 8 476 | 129 655 | 34 016.1 | 3 309.8 | 4 608 | 25 955 | 5 102.5 | 1 132.5 |
| Des Moines-West Des Moines, IA | 69.6 | 133 | 1 007 | 15 770 | 12 947.7 | 773.9 | 2 118 | 35 904 | 8 120.5 | 790.2 | 655 | 3 810 | 754.6 | 137.3 |
| Detroit-Warren-Livonia, MI | 3 636.2 | 810 | 6 291 | 90 203 | 152 004.0 | 5 301.9 | 15 985 | 204 938 | 49 928.3 | 4 590.6 | 4 085 | 29 503 | 9 253.9 | 1 012.8 |
| Detroit-Livonia-Dearborn, MI Div | 1 858.7 | 930 | 1 974 | 34 186 | 64 988.9 | 1 867.3 | 6 361 | 68 272 | 17 275.8 | 1 451.0 | 1 276 | 7 929 | 5 528.0 | 241.0 |
| Warren-Troy-Farmington Hills, MI Div | 1 777.4 | 714 | 4 317 | 56 017 | 87 015.1 | 3 434.6 | 9 624 | 136 666 | 32 652.6 | 3 139.6 | 2 809 | 21 574 | 3 725.9 | 771.8 |
| Dothan, AL | 145.2 | 1 063 | 221 | 3 607 | 9 466.8 | 151.1 | 780 | 9 231 | 2 172.2 | 202.2 | 143 | 601 | 85.1 | 17.9 |
| Dover, DE | 37.6 | 261 | 113 | D | D | D | 632 | 9 614 | 2 589.2 | 224.6 | 127 | 604 | 91.0 | 22.0 |
| Dubuque, IA | 86.8 | 947 | 170 | 2 664 | 2 452.9 | 100.5 | 467 | 7 056 | 1 433.5 | 135.0 | 103 | 446 | 73.6 | 16.6 |
| Duluth, MN-WI | 306.6 | 1 113 | 296 | 4 396 | 3 324.6 | 176.0 | 1 313 | 16 792 | 3 622.4 | 344.6 | 266 | 1 146 | 180.9 | 25.6 |
| Durham-Chapel Hill, NC | 1 271.6 | 2 788 | 451 | 12 129 | 11 159.7 | 1 102.3 | 1 658 | 24 387 | 5 274.3 | 536.1 | 536 | 2 686 | 514.3 | 98.2 |
| Eau Claire, WI | 34.8 | 226 | 171 | 2 760 | 1 505.0 | 107.5 | 688 | 11 320 | 2 572.1 | 227.9 | 137 | 790 | 90.7 | 17.3 |
| El Centro, CA | 2 144.9 | 13 765 | 236 | 2 040 | 1 364.8 | 71.7 | 534 | 8 052 | 1 727.3 | 170.2 | 134 | 555 | 73.4 | 12.5 |
| Elizabethtown, KY | 15.2 | 137 | 72 | 661 | 375.2 | 20.3 | 464 | 6 229 | 1 498.7 | 136.1 | 106 | 459 | 57.1 | 9.3 |
| Elkhart-Goshen, IN | 36.5 | 187 | 418 | 6 711 | 4 123.4 | 293.6 | 727 | 9 710 | 2 416.9 | 219.0 | 180 | 813 | 109.4 | 20.4 |
| Elmira, NY | 15.7 | 175 | 95 | 1 221 | 425.6 | 48.6 | 388 | 5 580 | 1 207.2 | 111.0 | 79 | 410 | 65.6 | 10.7 |
| El Paso, TX | 267.3 | 370 | 1 012 | 9 918 | 7 291.8 | 362.0 | 2 334 | 33 948 | 8 460.9 | 683.1 | 672 | 3 599 | 629.2 | 106.8 |
| Erie, PA | 55.7 | 199 | 308 | 3 575 | 1 371.9 | 141.6 | 1 051 | 15 831 | 3 428.4 | 314.5 | 187 | 1 115 | 135.3 | 25.9 |
| Eugene-Springfield, OR | 213.9 | 638 | 515 | 6 214 | 3 806.1 | 269.5 | 1 403 | 20 408 | 4 452.2 | 456.9 | 569 | 2 554 | 380.1 | 59.6 |
| Evansville, IN-KY | 981.6 | 2 808 | 463 | 8 450 | 5 344.0 | 400.5 | 1 421 | 20 550 | 4 797.5 | 435.3 | 326 | 1 923 | 282.5 | 49.6 |
| Fairbanks, AK | 38.3 | 437 | 81 | 924 | 839.9 | 43.3 | 339 | 5 236 | 1 574.3 | 146.7 | 136 | 745 | 152.5 | 29.9 |
| Fargo, ND-MN | 25.4 | 137 | 480 | 7 639 | 5 309.3 | 354.9 | 843 | 14 809 | 3 515.8 | 311.1 | 308 | 1 809 | 243.8 | 49.0 |
| Farmington, NM | 332.7 | 2 636 | 167 | 1 684 | 1 253.7 | 84.8 | 482 | 6 671 | 1 742.0 | 155.5 | 120 | 879 | 211.5 | 45.2 |
| Fayetteville, NC | 46.2 | 134 | 187 | 2 362 | 1 180.6 | 96.3 | 1 140 | 16 425 | 4 019.1 | 351.4 | 350 | 1 723 | 256.5 | 49.4 |
| Fayetteville-Springdale-Rogers, AR-MO | 454.1 | 1 121 | 618 | 9 579 | 25 120.0 | 449.5 | 1 658 | 22 909 | 5 451.8 | 497.6 | 609 | 3 481 | 362.7 | 93.6 |

1. Merchant wholesalers, except manufacturers' sales branches and offices.

| Area name | Professional, scientific, and technical services,[1] 2007 | | | | Manufacturing, 2007 | | | | Accommodation and food services, 2007 | | | |
|---|---|---|---|---|---|---|---|---|---|---|---|---|
| | Number of establishments | Number of employees | Sales (mil dol) | Annual payroll (mil dol) | Number of establishments | Number of employees | Sales (mil dol) | Annual payroll (mil dol) | Number of establishments | Number of employees | Sales (mil dol) | Annual payroll (mil dol) |
| | 147 | 148 | 149 | 150 | 151 | 152 | 153 | 154 | 155 | 156 | 157 | 158 |
| Charleston, WV | 717 | 6 459 | 781.4 | 312.8 | 184 | 5 767 | 4 491.5 | 318.7 | 611 | 10 971 | 493.9 | 135.0 |
| Charleston-North Charleston-Summerville, SC | 1 821 | D | D | D | 493 | 22 043 | 13 226.8 | 1 041.9 | 1 406 | 31 250 | 1 647.9 | 448.6 |
| Charlotte-Gastonia-Rock Hill, NC-SC | 5 109 | D | D | D | 1 926 | 75 520 | 37 009.7 | 3 256.2 | 3 511 | 70 733 | 3 599.1 | 983.2 |
| Charlottesville, VA | 682 | D | D | D | 167 | 3 650 | 1 087.3 | D | 464 | 8 781 | 451.9 | 130.3 |
| Chattanooga, TN-GA | 947 | D | D | D | 653 | 37 654 | 11 406.2 | 1 484.4 | 1 014 | 19 768 | 823.0 | 238.8 |
| Cheyenne, WY | 312 | 1 402 | 182.0 | 65.2 | 61 | 1 710 | 2 420.2 | 80.9 | 185 | 3 938 | 173.7 | 52.1 |
| Chicago-Joliet-Naperville, IL-IN-WI | 32 985 | D | D | D | 12 022 | 482 380 | 177 305.4 | 24 319.0 | 19 142 | 351 200 | 20 892.1 | 5 611.5 |
| Chicago-Joliet-Naperville, IL Div | 28 421 | D | D | D | 10 275 | 386 223 | 127 798.4 | 18 049.7 | 15 897 | 294 630 | 18 056.4 | 4 851.0 |
| Gary, IN Div | 1 335 | D | D | D | 628 | 39 027 | 30 031.8 | 2 198.6 | 1 391 | 26 183 | 1 322.4 | 335.4 |
| Lake County-Kenosha County, IL-WI Div | 3 229 | D | D | D | 1 119 | 57 130 | 19 475.2 | 4 070.7 | 1 854 | 30 387 | 1 513.3 | 425.1 |
| Chico, CA | 426 | D | D | D | 224 | 4 404 | 987.4 | 150.6 | 429 | 7 708 | 355.8 | 96.7 |
| Cincinnati-Middletown, OH-KY-IN | 4 956 | D | D | D | 2 531 | 125 573 | 50 675.7 | 6 169.7 | 4 240 | 92 094 | 4 413.7 | 1 211.4 |
| Clarksville, TN-KY | 267 | D | D | D | 169 | 12 535 | 4 357.3 | 496.6 | 453 | 8 714 | 342.7 | 91.6 |
| Cleveland, TN | 162 | D | D | D | 144 | 9 807 | 4 730.9 | 340.2 | 187 | 3 386 | 139.2 | 38.1 |
| Cleveland-Elyria-Mentor, OH | 6 163 | 51 027 | 7 535.8 | 2 959.6 | 3 774 | 141 166 | 42 181.1 | 6 876.6 | 4 714 | 79 741 | 3 496.7 | 963.9 |
| Coeur d'Alene, ID | 438 | D | D | D | 246 | 4 401 | 992.2 | 163.3 | 363 | 6 773 | 303.7 | 96.0 |
| College Station-Bryan, TX | 418 | D | D | D | 134 | 5 316 | 1 059.6 | 181.9 | 427 | 9 138 | 368.3 | 98.0 |
| Colorado Springs, CO | 2 423 | D | D | D | 516 | 14 448 | 5 075.3 | 693.2 | 1 316 | 25 914 | 1 281.8 | 388.6 |
| Columbia, MO | 394 | D | D | D | 107 | 4 831 | 1 605.9 | 192.9 | 437 | 8 615 | 318.6 | 94.0 |
| Columbia, SC | 1 897 | 19 364 | 1 922.4 | 763.5 | 574 | 29 335 | 11 562.5 | 1 282.5 | 1 411 | 29 213 | 1 237.5 | 352.0 |
| Columbus, GA-AL | 453 | D | D | D | 201 | 10 451 | 3 354.4 | 404.7 | 551 | 12 099 | 529.9 | 150.0 |
| Columbus, IN | 157 | D | D | D | 143 | 11 711 | 4 843.9 | 502.9 | 160 | 3 416 | 139.7 | 39.9 |
| Columbus, OH | 4 707 | D | D | D | 1 523 | 69 841 | 34 330.4 | 3 346.4 | 3 790 | 78 561 | 3 448.1 | 993.4 |
| Corpus Christi, TX | 907 | D | D | D | 255 | 9 899 | D | D | 1 030 | 18 298 | 788.4 | 218.7 |
| Corvallis, OR | 282 | D | D | D | 92 | 4 322 | 590.5 | 209.8 | 206 | 3 197 | 134.0 | 37.2 |
| Crestview-Fort Walton Beach-Destin, FL | 637 | D | D | D | 98 | 3 858 | 656.7 | 166.4 | 431 | 10 619 | 491.9 | 148.9 |
| Cumberland, MD-WV | 140 | D | D | D | 74 | 4 299 | 1 123.9 | 195.6 | 227 | 3 386 | 146.1 | 39.7 |
| Dallas-Fort Worth-Arlington, TX | 17 686 | 176 361 | 32 628.1 | 12 124.7 | 6 102 | 304 809 | 104 883.8 | 15 172.3 | 11 100 | 237 408 | 12 349.0 | 3 442.0 |
| Dallas-Plano-Irving, TX Div | 13 181 | 142 565 | 27 891.2 | 10 170.3 | 3 929 | 193 957 | 59 178.0 | 9 573.4 | 7 521 | 157 394 | 8 289.5 | 2 327.1 |
| Fort Worth-Arlington, TX Div | 4 505 | 33 796 | 4 736.9 | 1 954.3 | 2 173 | 110 852 | 45 705.8 | 5 598.8 | 3 579 | 80 014 | 4 059.5 | 1 114.9 |
| Dalton, GA | 187 | D | D | D | 399 | 27 729 | 9 130.6 | 863.7 | 232 | 4 001 | 169.4 | 45.4 |
| Danville, IL | 93 | 396 | 44.7 | 12.9 | 100 | 5 458 | 2 576.4 | 239.7 | 156 | 2 370 | 85.0 | 24.6 |
| Danville, VA | 125 | D | D | D | 96 | 6 926 | 2 028.1 | 294.0 | 183 | 3 190 | 125.5 | 34.3 |
| Davenport-Moline-Rock Island, IA-IL | 766 | 5 999 | 759.2 | 267.7 | 423 | 25 175 | 11 531.2 | 1 137.5 | 902 | 16 365 | 695.8 | 189.7 |
| Dayton, OH | 1 848 | D | D | D | 1 214 | 52 046 | 18 851.0 | 2 360.1 | 1 677 | 33 676 | 1 325.8 | 392.4 |
| Decatur, AL | 262 | 1 563 | 124.4 | 50.4 | 223 | 13 563 | 9 505.9 | 668.3 | 249 | 4 299 | 177.4 | 47.5 |
| Decatur, IL | 181 | 1 185 | 125.8 | 51.1 | 112 | 8 762 | 9 590.8 | 409.4 | 219 | 4 733 | 170.9 | 52.0 |
| Deltona-Daytona Beach-Ormond Beach, FL | 1 353 | D | D | D | 369 | 9 491 | 1 948.6 | 366.2 | 1 006 | 19 359 | 899.2 | 245.8 |
| Denver-Aurora-Broomfield, CO | 12 019 | 91 413 | 17 642.7 | 6 530.9 | 2 443 | 67 646 | 24 222.8 | 3 445.5 | 5 380 | 108 481 | 5 759.1 | 1 667.2 |
| Des Moines-West Des Moines, IA | 1 616 | 13 296 | 1 965.3 | 705.0 | 471 | 21 153 | 8 439.5 | 919.1 | 1 307 | 23 794 | 976.7 | 285.2 |
| Detroit-Warren-Livonia, MI | 11 820 | 164 820 | 20 494.6 | 11 254.7 | 5 987 | 234 520 | 112 084.5 | 13 174.3 | 8 135 | 146 138 | 6 949.9 | 1 976.0 |
| Detroit-Livonia-Dearborn, MI Div | 2 880 | D | D | D | 1 729 | 87 991 | 55 896.9 | 5 545.3 | 3 215 | 57 836 | 3 112.4 | 857.5 |
| Warren-Troy-Farmington Hills, MI Div | 8 940 | D | D | D | 4 258 | 146 529 | 56 187.5 | 7 629.0 | 4 920 | 88 302 | 3 837.5 | 1 118.5 |
| Dothan, AL | 292 | D | D | D | 170 | 7 348 | 1 889.8 | 253.6 | 282 | 5 007 | 195.0 | 53.1 |
| Dover, DE | 248 | D | D | D | 87 | 5 253 | 2 361.8 | 213.8 | 236 | 5 352 | 447.9 | 76.2 |
| Dubuque, IA | 168 | D | D | D | 150 | 9 378 | 4 711.2 | 380.3 | 253 | 4 502 | 145.7 | 42.5 |
| Duluth, MN-WI | 529 | D | D | D | 310 | 8 551 | 3 487.9 | 370.8 | 812 | 12 944 | 607.7 | 148.9 |
| Durham-Chapel Hill, NC | 1 655 | 34 201 | 4 881.9 | 2 788.6 | 373 | 21 560 | 11 749.3 | 1 044.7 | 1 045 | 20 891 | 1 081.9 | 304.6 |
| Eau Claire, WI | 265 | 1 760 | 195.3 | 85.3 | 228 | 10 762 | 3 109.0 | 424.2 | 418 | 6 405 | 226.5 | 63.2 |
| El Centro, CA | 153 | D | D | D | 58 | 2 846 | 1 207.9 | 96.9 | 261 | 3 719 | 167.8 | 46.2 |
| Elizabethtown, KY | 156 | D | D | D | 99 | 6 206 | 1 882.3 | 245.1 | 194 | 4 712 | 174.5 | 54.5 |
| Elkhart-Goshen, IN | 338 | D | D | D | 852 | 64 309 | 15 779.8 | 2 508.4 | 385 | 7 395 | 272.4 | 76.0 |
| Elmira, NY | 115 | D | D | D | 93 | 6 348 | 1 280.8 | 285.8 | 198 | 3 151 | 123.1 | 35.2 |
| El Paso, TX | 1 151 | D | D | D | 588 | 16 091 | 14 423.5 | 617.6 | 1 269 | 24 563 | 1 031.3 | 268.5 |
| Erie, PA | 416 | D | D | D | 505 | 24 441 | 6 890.8 | 1 190.2 | 646 | 10 728 | 428.1 | 114.6 |
| Eugene-Springfield, OR | 988 | 5 097 | 554.6 | 217.5 | 606 | 20 273 | 6 219.9 | 853.6 | 920 | 13 385 | 607.7 | 171.5 |
| Evansville, IN-KY | 731 | D | D | D | 478 | 33 017 | 21 220.2 | 1 619.5 | 746 | 15 457 | 668.7 | 190.4 |
| Fairbanks, AK | 228 | 1 329 | 174.9 | 64.7 | 78 | 745 | D | 37.3 | 220 | 3 430 | 221.6 | 60.9 |
| Fargo, ND-MN | 483 | D | D | D | 249 | 9 191 | 2 797.2 | 346.6 | 452 | 10 382 | 399.7 | 117.5 |
| Farmington, NM | 239 | D | D | D | 91 | 1 649 | 668.7 | 64.3 | 192 | 4 108 | 173.2 | 45.8 |
| Fayetteville, NC | 528 | D | D | D | 126 | 10 561 | 3 758.8 | 450.1 | 609 | 13 292 | 526.3 | 144.2 |
| Fayetteville-Springdale-Rogers, AR-MO | 1 134 | D | D | D | 457 | 30 601 | 7 300.6 | 1 007.3 | 858 | 17 438 | 664.7 | 191.7 |

1. Establishments subject to federal tax.

| Area name | Health care and social assistance,[1] 2007 | | | | Other services,[1] 2007 | | | | Federal funds and grants, 2009–2010 Expenditures (mil dol) | | | |
|---|---|---|---|---|---|---|---|---|---|---|---|---|
| | | | | | | | | | | Direct payments for individuals | | |
| | Number of establishments | Number of employees | Receipts (mil dol) | Annual payroll (mil dol) | Number of establishments | Number of employees | Receipts (mil dol) | Annual payroll (mil dol) | Total | Social Security and government retirement | Medicare | Food stamps and Supplemental Security Income |
| | 159 | 160 | 161 | 162 | 163 | 164 | 165 | 166 | 167 | 168 | 169 | 170 |
| Charleston, WV | 951 | 19 734 | 1 929.5 | 704.0 | 524 | 3 801 | 356.9 | 95.5 | 4 374.4 | 1 171.2 | 581.5 | 163.9 |
| Charleston-North Charleston-Summerville, SC | 1 558 | 31 530 | 3 817.1 | 1 308.4 | 1 159 | 7 555 | 652.9 | 196.0 | 8 341.7 | 2 204.2 | 660.7 | 256.3 |
| Charlotte-Gastonia-Rock Hill, NC-SC | 3 703 | 89 158 | 8 873.9 | 3 640.6 | 2 734 | 18 931 | 2 657.5 | 525.1 | 9 160.6 | 4 103.5 | 1 442.0 | 472.4 |
| Charlottesville, VA | 502 | 14 902 | 1 872.9 | 662.2 | 384 | 3 223 | 623.6 | 112.0 | 1 876.0 | 608.5 | 230.4 | 39.3 |
| Chattanooga, TN-GA | 1 272 | 29 256 | 3 004.0 | 1 159.3 | 789 | 5 942 | 552.4 | 150.0 | 4 819.9 | 1 809.8 | 1 114.5 | 245.4 |
| Cheyenne, WY | 281 | 6 040 | 563.1 | 232.9 | 180 | 947 | 83.0 | 25.0 | 1 699.6 | 348.0 | 94.1 | 16.7 |
| Chicago-Joliet-Naperville, IL-IN-WI | 23 636 | 518 516 | 54 052.7 | 21 616.2 | 17 377 | 133 283 | 17 239.0 | 4 354.1 | 70 771.9 | 21 338.2 | 14 345.8 | 3 584.0 |
| Chicago-Joliet-Naperville, IL Div | 19 763 | 438 790 | 46 146.8 | 18 456.8 | 14 619 | 114 385 | 15 632.8 | 3 889.5 | 60 361.8 | 17 168.7 | 12 306.7 | 3 123.2 |
| Gary, IN Div | 1 654 | 40 530 | 3 833.0 | 1 495.6 | 1 260 | 8 871 | 726.0 | 216.3 | 5 168.5 | 2 173.9 | 1 213.4 | 322.5 |
| Lake County-Kenosha County, IL-WI Div | 2 219 | 39 196 | 4 072.9 | 1 663.8 | 1 498 | 10 027 | 880.2 | 248.3 | 5 241.6 | 1 995.6 | 825.7 | 138.3 |
| Chico, CA | 737 | 12 120 | 1 179.3 | 427.5 | 321 | 2 168 | 173.6 | 49.9 | 1 788.2 | 699.6 | 453.6 | 104.9 |
| Cincinnati-Middletown, OH-KY-IN | 4 833 | 129 504 | 12 087.4 | 5 143.1 | 3 426 | 24 021 | 2 390.8 | 645.9 | 17 400.1 | 5 605.3 | 3 371.5 | 700.1 |
| Clarksville, TN-KY | 481 | 10 538 | 859.8 | 317.0 | 316 | 1 915 | 135.1 | 39.2 | 7 603.2 | 881.1 | 381.0 | 95.5 |
| Cleveland, TN | 249 | 4 750 | 393.6 | 151.3 | 121 | 1 045 | 92.3 | 21.0 | 850.6 | 384.7 | 228.2 | 44.5 |
| Cleveland-Elyria-Mentor, OH | 5 520 | 159 804 | 14 974.6 | 6 459.7 | 4 195 | 28 804 | 2 837.6 | 766.6 | 19 049.7 | 6 140.7 | 4 697.2 | 1 029.6 |
| Coeur d'Alene, ID | 458 | 7 004 | 573.4 | 238.0 | 240 | 1 242 | 82.8 | 24.6 | 1 486.4 | 487.5 | 118.9 | 38.9 |
| College Station-Bryan, TX | 430 | 7 750 | 909.3 | 303.0 | 311 | 2 033 | 374.0 | 45.6 | 1 505.2 | 420.9 | 167.7 | 61.1 |
| Colorado Springs, CO | 1 796 | 27 724 | 2 934.4 | 1 110.6 | 1 127 | 8 222 | 1 328.2 | 259.3 | 11 194.6 | 2 150.8 | 478.3 | 140.3 |
| Columbia, MO | 593 | 16 310 | 1 710.0 | 622.4 | 334 | 2 107 | 185.0 | 52.6 | 1 272.5 | 389.5 | 184.1 | 47.2 |
| Columbia, SC | 1 596 | 39 169 | 4 070.4 | 1 614.8 | 1 327 | 8 711 | 803.3 | 233.4 | 8 993.9 | 2 317.7 | 696.9 | 258.1 |
| Columbus, GA-AL | 665 | 15 093 | 1 456.2 | 569.0 | 452 | 2 820 | 212.2 | 65.9 | 6 317.7 | 1 088.8 | 378.8 | 191.2 |
| Columbus, IN | 228 | 5 095 | 439.1 | 178.5 | 120 | 857 | 82.8 | 19.5 | 709.5 | 247.2 | 97.4 | 15.8 |
| Columbus, OH | 4 167 | 107 649 | 10 205.8 | 4 268.1 | 3 052 | 24 610 | 2 994.8 | 771.0 | 18 219.0 | 4 015.7 | 2 079.5 | 586.7 |
| Corpus Christi, TX | 1 152 | 26 350 | 2 241.9 | 859.7 | 698 | 4 703 | 492.1 | 130.7 | 3 990.3 | 1 248.9 | 670.1 | 246.1 |
| Corvallis, OR | 229 | 4 356 | 504.0 | 201.1 | 128 | 855 | 158.3 | 22.7 | 706.7 | 202.6 | 67.9 | 18.4 |
| Crestview-Fort Walton Beach-Destin, FL | 499 | 8 357 | 845.8 | 312.4 | 393 | 2 053 | 166.4 | 46.1 | 3 812.1 | 1 006.3 | 281.1 | 43.9 |
| Cumberland, MD-WV | 318 | 6 931 | 612.8 | 232.2 | 201 | 1 079 | 76.8 | 20.6 | 1 263.2 | 393.7 | 439.5 | 41.4 |
| Dallas-Fort Worth-Arlington, TX | 14 512 | 265 112 | 30 774.9 | 11 459.6 | 8 428 | 68 607 | 7 289.1 | 1 956.1 | 46 644.0 | 12 484.9 | 5 525.1 | 1 540.0 |
| Dallas-Plano-Irving, TX Div | 10 048 | 181 424 | 21 417.7 | 8 168.7 | 5 640 | 46 432 | 5 338.5 | 1 397.7 | 26 771.0 | 7 870.1 | 3 627.4 | 1 062.4 |
| Fort Worth-Arlington, TX Div | 4 464 | 83 688 | 9 357.2 | 3 290.9 | 2 788 | 22 175 | 1 950.6 | 558.4 | 19 873.0 | 4 614.8 | 1 897.8 | 477.6 |
| Dalton, GA | 228 | 4 281 | 480.5 | 183.3 | 166 | 839 | 77.6 | 24.0 | 696.4 | 326.3 | 145.8 | 40.2 |
| Danville, IL | 149 | 4 729 | 437.7 | 203.4 | 138 | 780 | 54.8 | 14.5 | 774.1 | 302.8 | 150.8 | 44.4 |
| Danville, VA | 265 | 5 275 | 437.9 | 175.7 | 193 | 920 | 72.0 | 18.3 | 899.5 | 396.9 | 180.1 | 49.1 |
| Davenport-Moline-Rock Island, IA-IL | 967 | 21 784 | 1 824.2 | 791.5 | 724 | 4 533 | 376.3 | 104.8 | 3 590.3 | 1 291.2 | 555.9 | 142.1 |
| Dayton, OH | 2 072 | 58 768 | 5 776.5 | 2 310.8 | 1 410 | 9 417 | 927.3 | 256.7 | 9 572.2 | 2 928.6 | 1 441.0 | 279.2 |
| Decatur, AL | 384 | 6 863 | 547.9 | 220.1 | 212 | 1 159 | 99.7 | 28.5 | 1 109.8 | 555.6 | 231.0 | 48.7 |
| Decatur, IL | 282 | 7 449 | 750.1 | 281.3 | 197 | 1 526 | 222.4 | 33.5 | 1 043.4 | 382.0 | 189.1 | 51.9 |
| Deltona-Daytona Beach-Ormond Beach, FL | 1 246 | 24 171 | 2 513.9 | 949.0 | 1 028 | 5 409 | 499.6 | 119.4 | 4 310.1 | 2 079.7 | 1 282.7 | 171.3 |
| Denver-Aurora-Broomfield, CO | 6 481 | 122 406 | 13 292.8 | 5 288.1 | 5 126 | 33 777 | 4 179.6 | 1 015.3 | 22 522.1 | 5 519.4 | 2 340.6 | 530.5 |
| Des Moines-West Des Moines, IA | 1 302 | 36 966 | 3 416.4 | 1 483.0 | 1 157 | 8 289 | 893.7 | 260.2 | 5 273.3 | 1 398.0 | 641.2 | 141.9 |
| Detroit-Warren-Livonia, MI | 12 227 | 241 649 | 24 485.3 | 10 037.1 | 7 434 | 46 504 | 5 094.0 | 1 259.1 | 38 663.6 | 13 116.2 | 8 958.2 | 2 311.2 |
| Detroit-Livonia-Dearborn, MI Div | 4 200 | 99 597 | 10 640.0 | 4 241.8 | 2 859 | 18 419 | 2 068.3 | 511.0 | 19 605.8 | 5 484.5 | 4 914.9 | 1 781.8 |
| Warren-Troy-Farmington Hills, MI Div | 8 027 | 142 052 | 13 845.3 | 5 795.3 | 4 575 | 28 085 | 3 025.7 | 748.1 | 19 057.8 | 7 631.7 | 4 043.3 | 529.4 |
| Dothan, AL | 390 | 10 440 | 987.5 | 395.0 | 238 | 1 230 | 115.9 | 27.3 | 1 173.3 | 554.3 | 232.7 | 67.0 |
| Dover, DE | 354 | 7 773 | 672.8 | 269.3 | 249 | 1 460 | 100.8 | 32.3 | 2 016.4 | 584.1 | 142.1 | 46.2 |
| Dubuque, IA | 242 | 7 056 | 592.0 | 264.0 | 208 | 1 505 | 102.2 | 27.4 | 640.7 | 284.2 | 148.6 | 20.4 |
| Duluth, MN-WI | 887 | 26 320 | 2 359.8 | 1 087.0 | 574 | 3 348 | 266.5 | 68.8 | 2 734.6 | 1 024.5 | 584.2 | 93.6 |
| Durham-Chapel Hill, NC | 1 263 | 39 491 | 4 277.7 | 1 577.9 | 769 | 5 961 | 1 025.2 | 213.4 | 6 636.7 | 1 195.1 | 501.1 | 143.4 |
| Eau Claire, WI | 441 | 13 010 | 1 218.0 | 539.6 | 313 | 1 747 | 150.7 | 42.7 | 1 101.3 | 461.9 | 202.0 | 42.7 |
| El Centro, CA | 265 | 4 257 | 394.1 | 142.6 | 163 | 1 046 | 83.2 | 25.1 | 1 240.1 | 314.4 | 226.8 | 84.2 |
| Elizabethtown, KY | 323 | 6 123 | 600.9 | 217.9 | 169 | 1 136 | 82.5 | 25.7 | 2 914.9 | 521.5 | 203.1 | 43.6 |
| Elkhart-Goshen, IN | 347 | 9 746 | 1 024.6 | 358.1 | 374 | 2 298 | 195.7 | 60.1 | 913.7 | 486.1 | 182.1 | 45.9 |
| Elmira, NY | 221 | 6 722 | 587.1 | 247.0 | 129 | 786 | 59.9 | 15.7 | 754.7 | 306.1 | 159.0 | 39.0 |
| El Paso, TX | 1 345 | 34 489 | 3 057.1 | 1 096.2 | 916 | 6 163 | 402.6 | 125.2 | 9 449.6 | 1 712.4 | 810.7 | 497.2 |
| Erie, PA | 893 | 21 880 | 1 847.7 | 783.0 | 563 | 3 529 | 242.4 | 70.2 | 2 238.2 | 876.3 | 576.3 | 134.9 |
| Eugene-Springfield, OR | 993 | 18 660 | 1 947.8 | 735.6 | 684 | 3 684 | 516.8 | 95.3 | 2 802.5 | 1 158.9 | 439.6 | 180.6 |
| Evansville, IN-KY | 971 | 24 277 | 2 270.7 | 859.5 | 646 | 4 383 | 377.5 | 110.8 | 2 764.7 | 1 122.3 | 636.0 | 128.2 |
| Fairbanks, AK | 267 | 4 867 | 570.5 | 223.9 | 195 | 1 081 | 106.8 | 31.3 | 1 546.6 | 196.7 | 45.0 | 19.0 |
| Fargo, ND-MN | 575 | 16 573 | 1 464.0 | 604.3 | 481 | 3 152 | 263.7 | 75.3 | 1 566.4 | 481.3 | 176.6 | 38.3 |
| Farmington, NM | 265 | 6 274 | 534.2 | 226.2 | 192 | 1 363 | 170.4 | 37.1 | 995.9 | 299.9 | 102.4 | 51.5 |
| Fayetteville, NC | 813 | 20 659 | 1 652.0 | 682.6 | 434 | 2 787 | 182.7 | 57.2 | 13 186.5 | 1 363.0 | 265.3 | 189.4 |
| Fayetteville-Springdale-Rogers, AR-MO | 945 | 18 182 | 1 764.3 | 701.8 | 617 | 4 171 | 425.2 | 104.0 | 2 474.5 | 1 130.6 | 367.0 | 85.8 |

1. Establishments subject to federal tax.

# Table C. Metropolitan Areas — Federal Funds, Residential Construction and Local Government Finances

| Area name | Federal funds and grants, 2009–2010 (cont.) | | | | | | | Value of residential construction authorized by building permits, 2011 | | Local government finances, 2007 | | | | |
|---|---|---|---|---|---|---|---|---|---|---|---|---|---|---|
| | Expenditures (mil dol) (cont.) | | | | | | | | | General revenue | | | | |
| | Procurement contract awards | | | Grants | | | | | | | | Taxes | | |
| | | | | | | | | | | | | | Per capita[1] (dollars) | |
| | Salaries and wages | Defense | Other | Medicaid and other health-related | Nutrition and family welfare | Education | Other | New construction ($1,000) | Number of housing units | Total (mil dol) | Inter-govern-mental (mil dol) | Total (mil dol) | Total | Property |
| | 171 | 172 | 173 | 174 | 175 | 176 | 177 | 178 | 179 | 180 | 181 | 182 | 183 | 184 |
| Charleston, WV | 298.8 | 24.7 | 59.9 | 398.7 | 158.0 | 180.3 | 1 240.5 | 47 195 | 295 | 823.4 | 358.3 | 307.6 | 1 012 | 762 |
| Charleston-North Charleston-Summerville, SC | 920.9 | 2 492.1 | 724.9 | 707.3 | 81.9 | 45.4 | 122.5 | 663 856 | 3 822 | 2 007.4 | 624.9 | 894.4 | 1 419 | 1 101 |
| Charlotte-Gastonia-Rock Hill, NC-SC | 766.7 | 113.0 | 374.8 | 869.0 | 195.7 | 101.8 | 477.8 | 1 086 065 | 6 446 | 7 982.4 | 2 334.7 | 2 355.2 | 1 426 | 1 095 |
| Charlottesville, VA | 178.2 | 199.2 | 56.3 | 395.8 | 14.7 | 22.8 | 103.0 | 163 749 | 1 008 | 643.4 | 258.7 | 308.2 | 1 599 | 1 115 |
| Chattanooga, TN-GA | 210.2 | 42.3 | 533.9 | 480.1 | 77.4 | 43.2 | 168.8 | 171 667 | 1 331 | 1 988.8 | 507.3 | 576.5 | 1 120 | 723 |
| Cheyenne, WY | 342.8 | 87.9 | 58.5 | 123.4 | 32.6 | 51.0 | 504.2 | 50 748 | 279 | 582.4 | 242.9 | 90.9 | 1 052 | 576 |
| Chicago-Joliet-Naperville, IL-IN-WI | 5 222.5 | 5 106.0 | 3 872.4 | 9 562.0 | 1 752.2 | 483.3 | 3 369.3 | 1 514 929 | 7 593 | 44 952.9 | 14 135.7 | 21 434.7 | 2 250 | 1 816 |
| Chicago-Joliet-Naperville, IL Div | 4 436.8 | 4 317.4 | 3 499.0 | 8 481.7 | 1 535.2 | 425.6 | 3 166.5 | 1 150 479 | 5 799 | 37 931.2 | 11 869.0 | 18 150.9 | 2 282 | 1 788 |
| Gary, IN Div | 210.2 | 36.9 | 42.1 | 787.3 | 123.7 | 21.8 | 125.2 | 185 057 | 939 | 2 974.2 | 1 124.2 | 1 038.6 | 1 486 | 1 411 |
| Lake County-Kenosha County, IL-WI Div | 575.4 | 751.7 | 331.3 | 293.1 | 93.3 | 36.0 | 77.6 | 179 393 | 855 | 4 047.5 | 1 142.5 | 2 245.2 | 2 571 | 2 400 |
| Chico, CA | 47.0 | 0.5 | 36.4 | 263.4 | 44.7 | 22.7 | 34.9 | 42 692 | 240 | 1 116.2 | 653.8 | 247.0 | 1 129 | 888 |
| Cincinnati-Middletown, OH-KY-IN | 1 308.5 | 2 211.5 | 486.1 | 2 376.1 | 347.8 | 131.5 | 381.8 | 583 161 | 3 369 | 8 511.5 | 3 081.7 | 3 674.7 | 1 722 | 1 165 |
| Clarksville, TN-KY | 5 297.1 | 557.0 | 38.9 | 177.9 | 39.1 | 21.3 | 15.7 | 207 284 | 2 001 | 565.5 | 255.1 | 201.0 | 768 | 474 |
| Cleveland, TN | 21.2 | 0.1 | 9.7 | 97.5 | 25.1 | 11.5 | 2.4 | 49 503 | 376 | 236.3 | 102.6 | 80.0 | 720 | 458 |
| Cleveland-Elyria-Mentor, OH | 1 434.0 | 251.6 | 851.4 | 2 898.7 | 430.4 | 172.6 | 690.8 | 360 472 | 1 767 | 11 419.1 | 4 261.7 | 4 831.1 | 2 304 | 1 502 |
| Coeur d'Alene, ID | 61.7 | 13.4 | 618.3 | 103.5 | 13.6 | 2.4 | 5.8 | 102 611 | 623 | 567.8 | 168.3 | 115.8 | 862 | 708 |
| College Station-Bryan, TX | 130.1 | 58.8 | 32.3 | 295.4 | 27.3 | 11.7 | 231.2 | 149 807 | 1 444 | 574.2 | 144.4 | 316.8 | 1 558 | 1 259 |
| Colorado Springs, CO | 4 748.0 | 2 889.0 | 109.3 | 235.8 | 70.4 | 62.1 | 68.2 | 615 427 | 2 275 | 2 475.6 | 754.9 | 790.1 | 1 297 | 720 |
| Columbia, MO | 113.9 | 8.9 | 49.9 | 202.3 | 20.2 | 29.0 | 144.1 | 131 201 | 1 052 | 467.8 | 146.6 | 209.0 | 1 288 | 755 |
| Columbia, SC | 2 012.5 | 557.6 | 378.4 | 725.7 | 234.5 | 301.2 | 1 226.8 | 416 357 | 2 897 | 2 478.4 | 790.7 | 890.3 | 1 243 | 1 088 |
| Columbus, GA-AL | 3 054.4 | 1 079.5 | 24.5 | 294.9 | 70.8 | 28.8 | 38.8 | 168 352 | 1 060 | 953.6 | 446.5 | 327.8 | 1 159 | 786 |
| Columbus, IN | 185.4 | 19.5 | 4.0 | 68.4 | 12.8 | 1.3 | 49.9 | 36 630 | 178 | 398.0 | 87.4 | 73.8 | 988 | 791 |
| Columbus, OH | 1 350.1 | 1 251.1 | 468.0 | 2 103.5 | 904.0 | 1 406.1 | 3 417.6 | 668 058 | 4 730 | 8 296.9 | 2 940.2 | 3 733.2 | 2 128 | 1 364 |
| Corpus Christi, TX | 348.3 | 487.8 | 78.3 | 618.6 | 102.9 | 19.9 | 52.3 | 159 546 | 1 142 | 1 488.4 | 505.3 | 671.1 | 1 619 | 1 285 |
| Corvallis, OR | 57.7 | 49.4 | 45.2 | 85.6 | 10.1 | 5.6 | 129.2 | 48 529 | 364 | 246.0 | 103.0 | 88.2 | 1 083 | 962 |
| Crestview-Fort Walton Beach-Destin, FL | 868.9 | 1 397.5 | 25.3 | 84.9 | 28.9 | 14.3 | 25.7 | 194 035 | 749 | 652.5 | 245.8 | 266.4 | 1 468 | 1 264 |
| Cumberland, MD-WV | 58.3 | 67.2 | 36.1 | 149.3 | 23.8 | 7.2 | 22.4 | 20 269 | 118 | 350.9 | 187.1 | 87.3 | 879 | 556 |
| Dallas-Fort Worth-Arlington, TX | 4 049.8 | 15 187.7 | 1 986.3 | 3 263.5 | 638.0 | 204.5 | 967.4 | 4 348 698 | 24 827 | 24 273.0 | 5 277.3 | 12 732.6 | 2 072 | 1 668 |
| Dallas-Plano-Irving, TX Div | 2 726.7 | 5 814.2 | 1 425.9 | 2 327.4 | 440.0 | 135.9 | 756.0 | 3 364 276 | 18 686 | 16 950.2 | 3 478.9 | 8 875.6 | 2 159 | 1 732 |
| Fort Worth-Arlington, TX Div | 1 323.1 | 9 373.6 | 560.4 | 936.1 | 198.0 | 68.6 | 211.4 | 984 422 | 6 141 | 7 322.8 | 1 798.4 | 3 857.0 | 1 897 | 1 538 |
| Dalton, GA | 31.9 | 13.1 | 10.1 | 75.1 | 22.7 | 11.8 | 0.9 | 6 865 | 63 | 458.4 | 197.7 | 150.6 | 1 124 | 582 |
| Danville, IL | 56.9 | 14.7 | 69.5 | 79.2 | 19.3 | 3.6 | 9.5 | 2 036 | 12 | 277.9 | 144.2 | 79.7 | 981 | 836 |
| Danville, VA | 23.4 | 0.9 | 8.6 | 171.4 | 18.4 | 8.8 | 11.8 | 13 786 | 142 | 306.8 | 176.9 | 92.7 | 877 | 606 |
| Davenport-Moline-Rock Island, IA-IL | 452.5 | 363.7 | 29.9 | 235.2 | 63.4 | 12.3 | 68.4 | 101 651 | 635 | 1 382.8 | 549.3 | 536.5 | 1 426 | 1 210 |
| Dayton, OH | 1 488.9 | 1 546.3 | 328.5 | 871.8 | 166.5 | 71.2 | 195.1 | 175 168 | 752 | 3 659.6 | 1 386.3 | 1 482.4 | 1 774 | 1 172 |
| Decatur, AL | 50.4 | 16.5 | 7.6 | 127.8 | 28.8 | 10.5 | 9.4 | 16 734 | 103 | 509.0 | 191.9 | 104.5 | 700 | 339 |
| Decatur, IL | 63.7 | 2.0 | 18.1 | 111.7 | 20.3 | 4.3 | 179.3 | 11 931 | 84 | 391.1 | 180.1 | 140.6 | 1 293 | 1 103 |
| Deltona-Daytona Beach-Ormond Beach, FL | 119.4 | 115.2 | 49.7 | 230.3 | 58.2 | 31.4 | 57.5 | 186 655 | 1 024 | 2 373.1 | 574.3 | 864.5 | 1 728 | 1 379 |
| Denver-Aurora-Broomfield, CO | 2 642.9 | 2 410.9 | 3 473.8 | 1 946.2 | 565.6 | 555.2 | 1 928.3 | 1 194 839 | 6 673 | 11 468.2 | 2 949.0 | 5 120.6 | 2 077 | 1 204 |
| Des Moines-West Des Moines, IA | 643.9 | 83.3 | 183.2 | 454.1 | 195.5 | 241.3 | 1 133.5 | 506 823 | 2 640 | 2 213.9 | 729.9 | 959.8 | 1 756 | 1 480 |
| Detroit-Warren-Livonia, MI | 2 388.3 | 2 718.6 | 1 375.8 | 4 764.8 | 915.4 | 348.0 | 1 126.4 | 708 015 | 3 366 | 20 217.9 | 8 914.1 | 6 850.1 | 1 533 | 1 368 |
| Detroit-Livonia-Dearborn, MI Div | 1 265.6 | 104.6 | 779.9 | 3 645.7 | 580.9 | 207.1 | 501.2 | 120 042 | 705 | 10 286.1 | 4 751.5 | 3 099.1 | 1 561 | 1 241 |
| Warren-Troy-Farmington Hills, MI Div | 1 122.7 | 2 614.0 | 595.9 | 1 119.0 | 334.5 | 140.9 | 625.3 | 587 973 | 2 661 | 9 931.8 | 4 162.6 | 3 751.0 | 1 511 | 1 469 |
| Dothan, AL | 45.3 | 12.9 | 10.0 | 151.4 | 26.7 | 12.7 | 12.5 | 54 515 | 288 | 601.3 | 168.0 | 106.8 | 766 | 243 |
| Dover, DE | 309.0 | 144.0 | 10.1 | 177.8 | 24.9 | 223.7 | 297.7 | 85 575 | 680 | 410.9 | 241.0 | 85.8 | 564 | 439 |
| Dubuque, IA | 35.9 | 3.8 | 5.3 | 77.2 | 14.0 | 3.3 | 28.3 | 62 319 | 410 | 300.1 | 111.3 | 128.9 | 1 395 | 1 009 |
| Duluth, MN-WI | 188.0 | 28.5 | 47.9 | 495.7 | 72.5 | 28.2 | 101.7 | 70 241 | 444 | 1 330.0 | 643.6 | 306.1 | 1 116 | 1 007 |
| Durham-Chapel Hill, NC | 417.5 | 142.6 | 891.2 | 2 120.9 | 73.3 | 67.3 | 977.5 | 322 589 | 1 924 | 1 863.9 | 910.1 | 672.6 | 1 402 | 1 125 |
| Eau Claire, WI | 85.0 | 21.9 | 11.4 | 182.0 | 25.8 | 10.8 | 15.4 | 49 196 | 364 | 595.2 | 283.0 | 211.9 | 1 343 | 1 232 |
| El Centro, CA | 178.5 | 47.7 | 59.2 | 199.4 | 50.0 | 23.2 | 20.8 | 37 648 | 257 | 1 139.1 | 670.3 | 166.9 | 1 031 | 684 |
| Elizabethtown, KY | 1 614.7 | 316.7 | 93.7 | 72.9 | 17.9 | 6.7 | 2.1 | 64 062 | 714 | 434.7 | 129.0 | 72.4 | 649 | 371 |
| Elkhart-Goshen, IN | 27.9 | 21.1 | -6.4 | 103.4 | 21.7 | 5.2 | 14.1 | 26 429 | 146 | 585.9 | 266.7 | 200.5 | 1 013 | 835 |
| Elmira, NY | 36.0 | 2.0 | 7.9 | 143.0 | 26.0 | 6.1 | 19.8 | 12 355 | 138 | 422.5 | 199.0 | 150.5 | 1 710 | 1 109 |
| El Paso, TX | 3 576.5 | 958.0 | 360.1 | 892.5 | 190.6 | 57.3 | 171.8 | 576 503 | 4 153 | 2 916.2 | 1 424.5 | 895.6 | 1 219 | 955 |
| Erie, PA | 120.8 | 41.5 | 43.0 | 264.1 | 59.0 | 12.5 | 38.0 | 38 019 | 311 | 1 069.7 | 529.9 | 326.3 | 1 169 | 941 |
| Eugene-Springfield, OR | 163.3 | 29.0 | 45.5 | 481.3 | 53.8 | 48.9 | 125.5 | 98 962 | 670 | 1 336.0 | 563.3 | 401.7 | 1 169 | 991 |
| Evansville, IN-KY | 147.1 | 145.7 | 26.9 | 358.1 | 57.3 | 14.2 | 47.5 | 90 235 | 559 | 1 027.7 | 399.3 | 357.8 | 1 023 | 867 |
| Fairbanks, AK | 343.6 | 493.1 | 116.7 | 114.0 | 33.8 | 18.3 | 135.5 | 7 484 | 39 | 327.0 | 164.7 | 114.5 | 1 174 | 1 041 |
| Fargo, ND-MN | 211.1 | 72.0 | 194.5 | 134.8 | 31.2 | 8.1 | 103.0 | 175 499 | 1 536 | 687.5 | 252.6 | 234.1 | 1 217 | 1 010 |
| Farmington, NM | 106.8 | 1.2 | 79.4 | 196.6 | 23.1 | 38.8 | 10.4 | 35 045 | 213 | 501.8 | 314.6 | 117.3 | 958 | 569 |
| Fayetteville, NC | 9 438.9 | 1 230.5 | 77.3 | 339.3 | 73.0 | 44.0 | 41.5 | 344 884 | 2 807 | 1 031.7 | 550.7 | 305.2 | 875 | 656 |
| Fayetteville-Springdale-Rogers, AR-MO | 208.5 | 159.6 | 125.3 | 185.1 | 42.9 | 26.3 | 83.7 | 256 362 | 1 206 | 1 154.1 | 594.6 | 330.8 | 759 | 275 |

1. Based on the resident population estimated as of July 1 of the year shown.

# Table C. Metropolitan Areas — Local Government Finances, Government Employment, and Voting

| Area name | Local government finances, 2007 (cont.) | | | | | | | Debt outstanding | | Government employment, 2011 | | | Presidential election,[2] 2012 | | |
|---|---|---|---|---|---|---|---|---|---|---|---|---|---|---|---|
| | Direct general expenditure | | | | | | | | | | | | Percent of vote cast: | | |
| | | | Percent of total for: | | | | | | | | | | | | |
| | Total (mil dol) | Per capita[1] (dollars) | Educa-tion | Health and hospitals | Police protec-tion | Public welfare | High-ways | Total (mil dol) | Per capita[1] (dollars) | Federal civilian | Federal military | State and local | Demo-cratic | Republi-can | All other |
| | 185 | 186 | 187 | 188 | 189 | 190 | 191 | 192 | 193 | 194 | 195 | 196 | 197 | 198 | 199 |
| Charleston, WV | 847.2 | 2 787 | 55.8 | 5.0 | 4.8 | 0.0 | 2.3 | 541.3 | 1 781 | 2 326 | 1 560 | 25 334 | 39.0 | 59.1 | 1.9 |
| Charleston-North Charles-ton-Summerville, SC | 2 017.4 | 3 202 | 48.2 | 0.9 | 6.7 | 0.3 | 3.0 | 4 766.3 | 7 564 | 9 940 | 13 233 | 49 306 | 46.5 | 51.8 | 1.6 |
| Charlotte-Gastonia-Rock Hill, NC-SC | 7 764.6 | 4 701 | 33.6 | 27.9 | 4.2 | 2.8 | 2.0 | 10 865.6 | 6 579 | 6 923 | 5 158 | 110 654 | 50.3 | 48.5 | 1.2 |
| Charlottesville, VA | 625.9 | 3 247 | 52.0 | 3.2 | 5.2 | 6.6 | 1.1 | 476.2 | 2 470 | 1 369 | 1 014 | 31 037 | 56.4 | 41.9 | 1.7 |
| Chattanooga, TN-GA | 1 815.0 | 3 527 | 35.2 | 26.7 | 5.4 | 1.3 | 2.8 | 1 825.0 | 3 547 | 6 296 | 1 778 | 30 530 | 36.6 | 61.6 | 1.7 |
| Cheyenne, WY | 565.4 | 6 548 | 41.9 | 29.9 | 2.9 | 0.3 | 4.0 | 169.5 | 1 963 | 2 664 | 3 610 | 11 261 | 36.2 | 60.5 | 3.3 |
| Chicago-Joliet-Naperville, IL-IN-WI | 44 542.0 | 4 676 | 42.7 | 3.8 | 7.0 | 1.4 | 4.2 | 64 743.2 | 6 797 | 56 758 | 33 722 | 507 190 | 63.8 | 34.8 | 1.5 |
| Chicago-Joliet-Naperville, IL Div | 37 373.2 | 4 700 | 41.3 | 3.6 | 7.3 | 1.1 | 4.3 | 58 210.7 | 7 320 | 48 754 | 16 253 | 426 473 | 65.3 | 33.2 | 1.5 |
| Gary, IN Div | 3 159.2 | 4 520 | 43.8 | 7.6 | 5.2 | 4.4 | 2.3 | 2 856.6 | 4 087 | 2 017 | 2 347 | 35 300 | 59.7 | 38.9 | 1.4 |
| Lake County-Kenosha County, IL-WI Div | 4 009.6 | 4 592 | 54.7 | 2.4 | 5.8 | 1.9 | 4.3 | 3 675.9 | 4 210 | 5 987 | 15 122 | 45 417 | 53.9 | 44.7 | 1.4 |
| Chico, CA | 1 112.9 | 5 087 | 41.0 | 5.4 | 4.3 | 12.0 | 2.7 | 441.7 | 2 019 | 577 | 352 | 14 393 | 47.0 | 49.0 | 4.0 |
| Cincinnati-Middletown, OH-KY-IN | 8 496.8 | 3 982 | 42.4 | 4.2 | 5.8 | 7.3 | 3.9 | 12 281.8 | 5 756 | 16 880 | 5 941 | 113 851 | 41.3 | 57.2 | 1.6 |
| Clarksville, TN-KY | 565.4 | 2 159 | 52.4 | 1.6 | 6.2 | 0.1 | 4.4 | 8 398.1 | 32 076 | 6 799 | 34 803 | 13 681 | 41.3 | 57.3 | 1.4 |
| Cleveland, TN | 256.2 | 2 306 | 49.8 | 11.4 | 7.6 | 0.2 | 5.5 | 250.4 | 2 253 | 292 | 391 | 5 461 | 23.5 | 75.0 | 1.4 |
| Cleveland-Elyria-Mentor, OH | 10 918.1 | 5 208 | 38.9 | 11.4 | 5.4 | 4.6 | 3.5 | 12 728.5 | 6 071 | 18 916 | 5 764 | 116 659 | 61.5 | 37.2 | 1.2 |
| Coeur d'Alene, ID | 541.9 | 4 031 | 32.3 | 34.0 | 3.6 | 0.5 | 4.0 | 219.9 | 1 636 | 575 | 534 | 9 378 | 31.5 | 65.8 | 2.7 |
| College Station-Bryan, TX | 611.2 | 3 005 | 53.8 | 1.9 | 5.3 | 0.4 | 4.6 | 872.2 | 4 289 | 910 | 601 | 32 893 | 31.5 | 66.4 | 2.0 |
| Colorado Springs, CO | 2 508.2 | 4 118 | 43.3 | 16.5 | 5.4 | 1.8 | 4.4 | 3 894.9 | 6 395 | 13 426 | 41 086 | 36 320 | 38.3 | 59.2 | 2.6 |
| Columbia, MO | 495.0 | 3 050 | 48.1 | 2.2 | 4.3 | 1.5 | 7.1 | 543.3 | 3 347 | 2 242 | 637 | 29 035 | 49.3 | 48.0 | 2.7 |
| Columbia, SC | 2 597.8 | 3 628 | 53.2 | 19.9 | 4.2 | 0.1 | 1.0 | 2 873.8 | 4 014 | 10 448 | 12 560 | 67 483 | 50.2 | 48.5 | 1.4 |
| Columbus, GA-AL | 928.5 | 3 284 | 52.8 | 6.0 | 5.2 | 1.7 | 3.7 | 879.4 | 3 110 | 6 805 | 23 095 | 17 675 | 54.1 | 45.1 | 0.7 |
| Columbus, IN | 413.6 | 5 533 | 28.0 | 41.7 | 2.3 | 1.9 | 2.1 | 184.1 | 2 463 | 185 | 259 | 6 148 | 36.2 | 61.7 | 2.1 |
| Columbus, OH | 8 067.9 | 4 599 | 41.3 | 7.3 | 6.2 | 4.8 | 3.9 | 9 305.9 | 5 305 | 14 778 | 5 245 | 150 424 | 52.8 | 45.6 | 1.6 |
| Corpus Christi, TX | 1 531.8 | 3 697 | 52.3 | 5.3 | 5.7 | 0.2 | 4.0 | 1 743.5 | 4 208 | 6 785 | 4 547 | 27 037 | 44.8 | 53.9 | 1.3 |
| Corvallis, OR | 227.5 | 2 794 | 43.3 | 9.9 | 8.6 | 0.0 | 4.9 | 279.5 | 3 432 | 596 | 294 | 13 863 | 62.0 | 33.5 | 4.5 |
| Crestview-Fort Walton Beach-Destin, FL | 652.0 | 3 592 | 50.0 | 1.8 | 7.1 | 0.3 | 4.7 | 355.6 | 1 959 | 8 138 | 15 242 | 7 959 | 24.7 | 74.0 | 1.3 |
| Cumberland, MD-WV | 356.2 | 3 586 | 58.7 | 1.8 | 2.8 | 6.1 | 3.4 | 185.0 | 1 863 | 613 | 377 | 7 746 | 31.0 | 66.3 | 2.6 |
| Dallas-Fort Worth-Arlington, TX | 23 865.9 | 3 884 | 46.3 | 8.9 | 5.5 | 0.2 | 4.7 | 52 759.4 | 8 586 | 46 136 | 16 611 | 341 396 | 42.1 | 56.5 | 1.4 |
| Dallas-Plano-Irving, TX Div | 16 867.6 | 4 103 | 45.6 | 8.5 | 5.3 | 0.2 | 4.8 | 36 914.4 | 8 978 | 30 832 | 10 711 | 234 399 | 44.4 | 54.2 | 1.4 |
| Fort Worth-Arlington, TX Div | 6 998.3 | 3 441 | 47.8 | 10.0 | 6.2 | 0.1 | 4.3 | 15 845.1 | 7 792 | 15 304 | 5 900 | 106 997 | 37.7 | 60.8 | 1.4 |
| Dalton, GA | 471.5 | 3 518 | 53.5 | 9.6 | 3.7 | 0.2 | 4.6 | 316.0 | 2 358 | 259 | 430 | 6 609 | 25.6 | 72.9 | 1.5 |
| Danville, IL | 256.8 | 3 163 | 54.1 | 1.5 | 6.1 | 3.3 | 6.8 | 94.9 | 1 168 | 1 481 | 164 | 4 519 | 42.5 | 55.7 | 1.8 |
| Danville, VA | 293.0 | 2 770 | 51.7 | 0.5 | 5.4 | 8.9 | 3.1 | 259.0 | 2 448 | 223 | 331 | 6 622 | 45.3 | 53.1 | 1.5 |
| Davenport-Moline-Rock Island, IA-IL | 1 368.0 | 3 637 | 49.8 | 4.7 | 6.2 | 1.4 | 5.2 | 928.7 | 2 469 | 7 215 | 1 511 | 20 332 | 56.7 | 41.8 | 1.5 |
| Dayton, OH | 3 498.8 | 4 187 | 47.0 | 3.9 | 7.0 | 6.0 | 4.5 | 3 117.3 | 3 731 | 19 117 | 7 552 | 46 686 | 45.5 | 52.8 | 1.7 |
| Decatur, AL | 533.1 | 3 571 | 43.9 | 19.2 | 5.2 | 0.4 | 3.2 | 637.0 | 4 267 | 401 | 748 | 8 157 | 29.1 | 69.6 | 1.3 |
| Decatur, IL | 379.7 | 3 492 | 50.8 | 2.2 | 6.6 | 0.3 | 7.8 | 200.6 | 1 845 | 344 | 229 | 5 619 | 46.6 | 51.8 | 1.7 |
| Deltona-Daytona Beach-Ormond Beach, FL | 2 294.2 | 4 585 | 36.0 | 21.7 | 6.6 | 0.5 | 3.7 | 3 233.2 | 6 461 | 1 282 | 1 065 | 19 931 | 48.9 | 50.1 | 1.0 |
| Denver-Aurora-Broomfield, CO | 11 502.8 | 4 667 | 33.5 | 6.9 | 5.7 | 3.1 | 4.5 | 24 034.4 | 9 751 | 28 509 | 9 733 | 156 973 | 55.5 | 42.2 | 2.2 |
| Des Moines-West Des Moines, IA | 2 310.0 | 4 226 | 49.8 | 7.5 | 4.4 | 1.1 | 5.6 | 2 610.0 | 4 775 | 6 202 | 2 555 | 36 475 | 53.3 | 44.9 | 1.8 |
| Detroit-Warren-Livonia, MI | 20 226.1 | 4 527 | 46.8 | 4.7 | 6.1 | 2.9 | 4.5 | 28 206.6 | 6 314 | 28 682 | 8 983 | 173 960 | 59.5 | 39.5 | 0.9 |
| Detroit-Livonia-Dearborn, MI Div | 10 151.2 | 5 114 | 39.6 | 3.2 | 6.4 | 4.6 | 3.5 | 17 567.5 | 8 850 | 14 759 | 3 834 | 84 981 | 73.0 | 26.2 | 0.8 |
| Warren-Troy-Farmington Hills, MI Div | 10 074.8 | 4 058 | 54.1 | 6.2 | 5.8 | 1.1 | 5.4 | 10 639.1 | 4 286 | 13 923 | 5 149 | 88 979 | 50.9 | 48.1 | 1.0 |
| Dothan, AL | 602.5 | 4 319 | 31.7 | 40.5 | 4.4 | 1.6 | 4.3 | 441.8 | 3 167 | 435 | 721 | 10 109 | 28.2 | 71.0 | 0.8 |
| Dover, DE | 421.6 | 2 769 | 68.9 | 0.9 | 5.1 | 0.0 | 1.8 | 243.8 | 1 601 | 1 994 | 4 429 | 17 154 | 51.7 | 46.8 | 1.5 |
| Dubuque, IA | 294.8 | 3 192 | 47.5 | 4.1 | 5.2 | 2.1 | 9.1 | 144.0 | 1 559 | 253 | 410 | 4 296 | 56.5 | 41.8 | 1.7 |
| Duluth, MN-WI | 1 357.6 | 4 949 | 34.9 | 9.3 | 5.2 | 8.0 | 9.0 | 1 399.6 | 5 102 | 1 701 | 1 140 | 23 353 | 63.5 | 34.0 | 2.5 |
| Durham-Chapel Hill, NC | 1 883.6 | 3 927 | 36.3 | 5.0 | 5.3 | 19.6 | 1.9 | 1 603.3 | 3 343 | 5 858 | 1 528 | 55 517 | 69.0 | 29.7 | 1.3 |
| Eau Claire, WI | 603.2 | 3 822 | 51.8 | 5.0 | 4.8 | 5.9 | 10.3 | 893.1 | 5 659 | 572 | 456 | 11 102 | 53.5 | 45.0 | 1.5 |
| El Centro, CA | 1 068.8 | 6 603 | 47.6 | 16.7 | 3.8 | 7.4 | 2.8 | 843.5 | 5 211 | 2 527 | 539 | 15 219 | 60.6 | 37.7 | 1.7 |
| Elizabethtown, KY | 419.1 | 3 755 | 34.9 | 45.8 | 2.1 | 0.1 | 2.1 | 357.2 | 3 200 | 6 948 | 11 858 | 7 347 | 36.0 | 62.5 | 1.6 |
| Elkhart-Goshen, IN | 815.9 | 4 122 | 53.1 | 1.4 | 3.8 | 2.4 | 2.6 | 702.5 | 3 549 | 255 | 659 | 8 153 | 36.0 | 62.5 | 1.6 |
| Elmira, NY | 429.2 | 4 877 | 43.9 | 2.8 | 3.2 | 18.3 | 6.8 | 316.2 | 3 593 | 239 | 146 | 6 617 | 48.1 | 50.4 | 1.5 |
| El Paso, TX | 2 885.0 | 3 927 | 57.2 | 12.5 | 4.4 | 0.3 | 2.0 | 3 658.4 | 4 980 | 12 869 | 27 488 | 54 284 | 65.5 | 33.1 | 1.3 |
| Erie, PA | 1 050.1 | 3 763 | 47.5 | 8.1 | 2.5 | 8.8 | 2.8 | 1 590.5 | 5 699 | 1 570 | 761 | 16 123 | 57.4 | 41.3 | 1.3 |
| Eugene-Springfield, OR | 1 242.2 | 3 615 | 45.9 | 4.6 | 6.9 | 2.5 | 5.0 | 1 385.2 | 4 031 | 1 702 | 1 078 | 27 814 | 59.7 | 36.4 | 3.9 |
| Evansville, IN-KY | 1 134.3 | 3 243 | 43.5 | 1.4 | 4.9 | 2.1 | 3.7 | 1 566.4 | 4 479 | 1 328 | 1 196 | 17 442 | 40.4 | 57.8 | 1.8 |
| Fairbanks, AK | 291.2 | 2 987 | 60.0 | 1.2 | 2.8 | 0.0 | 3.6 | 185.0 | 1 898 | 3 444 | 9 784 | 8 050 | NA | NA | NA |
| Fargo, ND-MN | 707.0 | 3 674 | 41.0 | 1.8 | 4.4 | 4.0 | 11.2 | 1 269.6 | 6 598 | 2 378 | 1 368 | 15 420 | 48.6 | 48.4 | 3.0 |
| Farmington, NM | 519.0 | 4 239 | 59.6 | 0.9 | 5.4 | 1.2 | 4.5 | 941.0 | 7 686 | 1 602 | 356 | 9 228 | 34.3 | 62.4 | 3.3 |
| Fayetteville, NC | 1 031.1 | 2 955 | 52.4 | 4.3 | 6.8 | 8.7 | 1.5 | 565.1 | 1 620 | 14 563 | 53 610 | 25 269 | 59.3 | 39.7 | 1.0 |
| Fayetteville-Springdale-Rog-ers, AR-MO | 1 243.2 | 2 853 | 57.0 | 1.9 | 4.8 | 0.0 | 7.2 | 1 666.4 | 3 824 | 2 390 | 2 036 | 25 625 | 33.4 | 63.6 | 3.0 |

1. Based on the resident population estimated as of July 1 of the year shown.  2. © 2013 Election Data Services, Inc. All rights reserved.

# Table C. Metropolitan Areas — Land Area and Population

| CBSA/ DIV code[1] | Area name | Land area,[2] 2010 (sq km) | Population 2012 | | | Race alone or in combination, not Hispanic or Latino (percent) | | | | Percent Hispanic or Latino[3] | Age (percent) | | | | | |
|---|---|---|---|---|---|---|---|---|---|---|---|---|---|---|---|---|
| | | | Total persons | Rank | Per square kilometer | White | Black | American Indian, Alaska Native | Asian and Pacific Islander | | Under 5 years | 5 to 17 years | 18 to 24 years | 25 to 34 years | 35 to 44 years | 45 to 54 years |
| | | 1 | 2 | 3 | 4 | 5 | 6 | 7 | 8 | 9 | 10 | 11 | 12 | 13 | 14 | 15 |
| 22380 | Flagstaff, AZ | 48 223 | 136 011 | 288 | 2.8 | 57.0 | 2.0 | 27.1 | 2.5 | 13.9 | 6.6 | 16.5 | 18.8 | 13.2 | 11.1 | 12.7 |
| 22420 | Flint, MI | 1 650 | 418 408 | 124 | 253.6 | 74.6 | 21.9 | 1.4 | 1.4 | 3.1 | 6.3 | 18.2 | 9.0 | 11.7 | 12.7 | 15.0 |
| 22500 | Florence, SC | 3 525 | 206 087 | 208 | 58.5 | 55.2 | 41.8 | 0.7 | 1.2 | 2.2 | 6.6 | 17.7 | 9.5 | 11.9 | 12.7 | 14.1 |
| 22520 | Florence-Muscle Shoals, AL | 3 264 | 146 988 | 270 | 45.0 | 84.1 | 13.0 | 1.0 | 0.9 | 2.3 | 5.6 | 15.9 | 9.9 | 11.3 | 12.1 | 14.3 |
| 22540 | Fond du Lac, WI | 1 864 | 101 843 | 342 | 54.6 | 92.6 | 1.7 | 0.8 | 1.4 | 4.5 | 5.9 | 16.6 | 8.9 | 12.3 | 12.3 | 15.5 |
| 22660 | Fort Collins-Loveland, CO | 6 724 | 310 487 | 153 | 46.2 | 85.8 | 1.4 | 1.1 | 2.9 | 10.8 | 5.6 | 15.2 | 14.7 | 13.9 | 12.0 | 13.5 |
| 22900 | Fort Smith, AR-OK | 10 350 | 298 566 | 159 | 28.8 | 79.3 | 4.5 | 9.0 | 2.7 | 8.5 | 6.8 | 18.4 | 8.9 | 12.3 | 12.5 | 14.2 |
| 23060 | Fort Wayne, IN | 3 525 | 421 406 | 121 | 119.5 | 81.2 | 11.4 | 0.7 | 2.9 | 6.0 | 7.2 | 19.2 | 9.2 | 13.0 | 12.7 | 14.1 |
| 23420 | Fresno, CA | 15 431 | 947 895 | 55 | 61.4 | 33.9 | 5.3 | 1.2 | 10.6 | 50.9 | 8.5 | 21.1 | 11.6 | 14.4 | 12.2 | 12.2 |
| 23460 | Gadsden, AL | 1 386 | 104 392 | 338 | 75.3 | 80.0 | 15.9 | 0.9 | 0.9 | 3.5 | 6.0 | 16.9 | 8.6 | 11.6 | 13.1 | 14.1 |
| 23540 | Gainesville, FL | 3 172 | 268 232 | 175 | 84.6 | 66.8 | 19.9 | 0.8 | 6.1 | 8.6 | 5.3 | 12.4 | 24.2 | 13.9 | 10.1 | 11.5 |
| 23580 | Gainesville, GA | 1 017 | 185 416 | 225 | 182.3 | 63.6 | 8.0 | 0.6 | 2.2 | 26.8 | 7.7 | 20.0 | 9.4 | 13.4 | 14.0 | 13.3 |
| 24020 | Glens Falls, NY | 4 398 | 128 472 | 302 | 29.2 | 95.0 | 2.4 | 0.7 | 1.0 | 2.2 | 5.0 | 15.4 | 8.2 | 11.2 | 12.7 | 16.2 |
| 24140 | Goldsboro, NC | 1 432 | 124 246 | 309 | 86.8 | 56.8 | 32.3 | 0.9 | 1.8 | 10.1 | 6.9 | 17.7 | 10.0 | 13.4 | 12.3 | 14.1 |
| 24220 | Grand Forks, ND-MN | 8 825 | 98 888 | 344 | 11.2 | 90.6 | 2.2 | 3.1 | 2.2 | 3.9 | 6.3 | 14.5 | 18.4 | 13.6 | 10.2 | 12.9 |
| 24300 | Grand Junction, CO | 8 622 | 147 848 | 267 | 17.1 | 84.1 | 1.0 | 1.4 | 1.5 | 13.6 | 6.8 | 16.6 | 9.8 | 13.3 | 13.2 | 13.7 |
| 24340 | Grand Rapids-Wyoming, MI | 7 212 | 785 352 | 69 | 108.9 | 81.1 | 9.1 | 1.0 | 2.4 | 8.6 | 7.0 | 18.6 | 9.9 | 13.7 | 12.6 | 14.3 |
| 24500 | Great Falls, MT | 6 988 | 81 723 | 359 | 11.7 | 90.0 | 2.0 | 5.9 | 1.7 | 3.6 | 6.8 | 15.9 | 10.3 | 13.1 | 10.9 | 14.3 |
| 24540 | Greeley, CO | 10 327 | 263 691 | 177 | 25.5 | 68.5 | 1.3 | 1.1 | 1.9 | 28.5 | 7.7 | 19.8 | 10.9 | 13.8 | 13.7 | 13.3 |
| 24580 | Green Bay, WI | 4 844 | 311 098 | 151 | 64.2 | 87.1 | 2.6 | 2.7 | 2.8 | 6.4 | 6.6 | 17.6 | 9.3 | 13.2 | 12.8 | 15.4 |
| 24660 | Greensboro-High Point, NC | 5 164 | 736 065 | 71 | 142.5 | 63.1 | 26.5 | 1.0 | 3.5 | 7.8 | 6.1 | 17.1 | 10.4 | 12.5 | 13.6 | 14.5 |
| 24780 | Greenville, NC | 2 377 | 193 983 | 220 | 81.6 | 57.2 | 35.1 | 0.7 | 2.1 | 6.6 | 6.6 | 15.7 | 17.8 | 14.1 | 12.2 | 12.4 |
| 24860 | Greenville-Mauldin-Easley, SC | 5 168 | 653 498 | 82 | 126.5 | 74.1 | 17.5 | 0.6 | 2.2 | 7.0 | 6.7 | 16.6 | 11.2 | 12.7 | 13.1 | 14.1 |
| 25060 | Gulfport-Biloxi, MS | 3 867 | 257 312 | 182 | 66.5 | 72.2 | 20.9 | 1.1 | 3.1 | 4.8 | 7.1 | 17.2 | 10.3 | 13.7 | 12.4 | 14.5 |
| 25180 | Hagerstown-Martinsburg, MD-WV | 2 611 | 273 749 | 172 | 104.8 | 86.8 | 9.5 | 0.7 | 1.7 | 3.5 | 6.2 | 17.1 | 8.1 | 12.8 | 13.9 | 15.4 |
| 25260 | Hanford-Corcoran, CA | 3 599 | 151 364 | 263 | 42.1 | 36.8 | 7.5 | 1.3 | 5.2 | 51.4 | 8.4 | 19.2 | 11.6 | 16.8 | 14.2 | 13.2 |
| 25420 | Harrisburg-Carlisle, PA | 4 201 | 553 980 | 94 | 131.9 | 82.0 | 11.0 | 0.5 | 3.5 | 4.9 | 5.8 | 16.0 | 9.4 | 12.6 | 12.6 | 15.1 |
| 25500 | Harrisonburg, VA | 2 244 | 128 372 | 303 | 57.2 | 84.4 | 4.3 | 0.4 | 2.6 | 9.7 | 5.5 | 14.5 | 21.8 | 11.6 | 10.8 | 12.2 |
| 25540 | Hartford-West Hartford-East Hartford, CT | 3 923 | 1 214 400 | 45 | 309.6 | 72.5 | 11.1 | 0.5 | 4.6 | 12.9 | 5.3 | 16.6 | 9.8 | 12.0 | 12.8 | 15.9 |
| 25620 | Hattiesburg, MS | 4 171 | 146 766 | 271 | 35.2 | 67.3 | 29.1 | 0.6 | 1.3 | 2.9 | 7.3 | 17.3 | 14.2 | 14.5 | 12.1 | 12.5 |
| 25860 | Hickory-Lenoir-Morganton, NC | 4 241 | 363 627 | 141 | 85.7 | 83.5 | 7.8 | 0.7 | 3.0 | 6.5 | 5.7 | 17.0 | 8.2 | 11.1 | 13.8 | 15.2 |
| 25980 | Hinesville-Fort Stewart, GA | 2 305 | 81 519 | 360 | 35.4 | 49.1 | 39.2 | 1.1 | 3.4 | 10.7 | 10.4 | 19.8 | 13.8 | 17.3 | 12.0 | 11.8 |
| 26100 | Holland-Grand Haven, MI | 1 459 | 269 099 | 173 | 184.8 | 86.7 | 2.1 | 0.7 | 3.1 | 8.8 | 6.6 | 19.0 | 12.7 | 11.9 | 12.3 | 14.0 |
| 26180 | Honolulu, HI | 1 556 | 976 372 | 53 | 627.5 | 32.6 | 3.5 | 1.6 | 78.5 | 8.5 | 6.5 | 15.5 | 10.3 | 14.6 | 12.8 | 13.4 |
| 26300 | Hot Springs, AR | 1 755 | 96 903 | 350 | 55.2 | 85.4 | 9.0 | 1.5 | 1.1 | 5.0 | 5.6 | 15.3 | 7.8 | 10.9 | 11.2 | 13.7 |
| 26380 | Houma-Bayou Cane-Thibodaux, LA | 5 957 | 208 922 | 205 | 35.1 | 74.3 | 17.2 | 4.9 | 1.3 | 4.1 | 7.2 | 17.9 | 10.1 | 13.9 | 12.4 | 14.9 |
| 26420 | Houston-Sugar Land-Baytown, TX | 22 863 | 6 204 161 | 5 | 271.4 | 40.4 | 17.2 | 0.6 | 7.3 | 35.9 | 7.9 | 19.8 | 9.5 | 15.1 | 14.3 | 13.8 |
| 26580 | Huntington-Ashland, WV-KY-OH | 4 519 | 286 603 | 164 | 63.4 | 95.3 | 3.5 | 0.7 | 0.9 | 1.0 | 5.8 | 15.6 | 9.5 | 12.2 | 12.7 | 14.1 |
| 26620 | Huntsville, AL | 3 526 | 430 734 | 119 | 122.2 | 70.2 | 22.7 | 1.5 | 2.8 | 4.9 | 6.2 | 17.2 | 9.7 | 13.4 | 13.1 | 16.0 |
| 26820 | Idaho Falls, ID | 7 665 | 133 368 | 295 | 17.4 | 86.5 | 0.8 | 1.0 | 1.4 | 11.5 | 9.6 | 22.4 | 8.3 | 14.5 | 11.5 | 12.3 |
| 26900 | Indianapolis-Carmel, IN | 9 983 | 1 798 634 | 35 | 180.2 | 76.1 | 15.9 | 0.6 | 2.9 | 6.4 | 7.2 | 18.8 | 8.8 | 14.3 | 13.8 | 14.6 |
| 26980 | Iowa City, IA | 3 064 | 158 231 | 252 | 51.6 | 85.9 | 5.1 | 0.6 | 5.4 | 4.9 | 6.1 | 14.1 | 20.4 | 15.9 | 11.3 | 11.7 |
| 27060 | Ithaca, NY | 1 229 | 102 554 | 339 | 83.4 | 81.3 | 4.8 | 0.9 | 11.2 | 4.6 | 4.1 | 11.4 | 28.8 | 12.8 | 9.6 | 11.2 |
| 27100 | Jackson, MI | 1 817 | 160 309 | 251 | 88.2 | 87.7 | 9.3 | 1.0 | 1.1 | 3.1 | 5.7 | 17.0 | 9.3 | 11.7 | 12.9 | 15.4 |
| 27140 | Jackson, MS | 9 651 | 548 605 | 96 | 56.8 | 48.7 | 48.2 | 0.4 | 1.3 | 2.2 | 7.1 | 18.6 | 10.1 | 14.2 | 12.8 | 13.9 |
| 27180 | Jackson, TN | 2 183 | 115 827 | 322 | 53.1 | 63.3 | 32.9 | 0.6 | 1.3 | 3.3 | 6.6 | 16.9 | 11.9 | 12.3 | 12.0 | 14.0 |
| 27260 | Jacksonville, FL | 8 291 | 1 377 850 | 40 | 166.2 | 67.3 | 22.3 | 0.8 | 4.5 | 7.2 | 6.4 | 17.1 | 9.5 | 13.6 | 13.3 | 15.0 |
| 27340 | Jacksonville, NC | 1 975 | 183 263 | 226 | 92.8 | 71.2 | 17.0 | 1.4 | 3.4 | 10.5 | 9.7 | 15.4 | 22.6 | 17.1 | 10.1 | 9.8 |
| 27500 | Janesville, WI | 1 860 | 160 418 | 250 | 86.2 | 86.0 | 5.9 | 0.7 | 1.5 | 7.8 | 6.4 | 18.2 | 8.6 | 12.7 | 13.0 | 14.9 |
| 27620 | Jefferson City, MO | 5 822 | 150 151 | 266 | 25.8 | 88.8 | 8.2 | 0.9 | 1.4 | 2.3 | 6.3 | 16.9 | 9.7 | 13.3 | 13.0 | 15.0 |
| 27740 | Johnson City, TN | 2 211 | 200 684 | 213 | 90.8 | 93.1 | 3.6 | 0.7 | 1.1 | 2.7 | 5.3 | 14.7 | 10.3 | 12.1 | 12.9 | 14.4 |
| 27780 | Johnstown, PA | 1 783 | 141 584 | 282 | 79.4 | 94.0 | 4.5 | 0.3 | 0.8 | 1.5 | 4.9 | 14.4 | 9.8 | 10.6 | 11.8 | 14.8 |
| 27860 | Jonesboro, AR | 3 796 | 124 042 | 310 | 32.7 | 82.3 | 12.8 | 0.9 | 1.3 | 4.2 | 7.1 | 17.7 | 11.8 | 14.0 | 12.4 | 12.8 |
| 27900 | Joplin, MO | 3 272 | 174 327 | 232 | 53.3 | 88.9 | 2.5 | 3.1 | 2.0 | 6.2 | 7.2 | 18.3 | 9.7 | 13.0 | 12.2 | 13.6 |
| 28020 | Kalamazoo-Portage, MI | 3 028 | 330 034 | 149 | 109.0 | 82.6 | 10.8 | 1.3 | 2.5 | 5.6 | 6.1 | 16.7 | 14.3 | 12.5 | 11.7 | 13.5 |
| 28100 | Kankakee-Bradley, IL | 1 752 | 113 040 | 327 | 64.5 | 74.4 | 16.0 | 0.6 | 1.4 | 9.2 | 6.6 | 18.4 | 10.2 | 12.5 | 12.4 | 14.0 |
| 28140 | Kansas City, MO-KS | 20 273 | 2 064 630 | 28 | 101.8 | 76.3 | 13.4 | 1.2 | 3.1 | 8.3 | 7.0 | 18.4 | 8.2 | 14.2 | 13.3 | 14.7 |
| 28420 | Kennewick-Pasco-Richland, WA | 7 621 | 268 243 | 174 | 35.2 | 66.3 | 2.0 | 1.4 | 3.4 | 28.8 | 8.4 | 20.6 | 9.4 | 14.4 | 12.5 | 12.9 |
| 28660 | Killeen-Temple-Fort Hood, TX | 7 293 | 420 375 | 123 | 57.6 | 56.1 | 20.4 | 1.1 | 4.7 | 21.0 | 8.7 | 19.2 | 11.9 | 17.2 | 12.8 | 12.1 |
| 28700 | Kingsport-Bristol-Bristol, TN-VA | 5 206 | 309 006 | 156 | 59.4 | 95.6 | 2.6 | 0.7 | 0.8 | 1.4 | 5.1 | 15.2 | 7.7 | 10.6 | 13.1 | 15.0 |
| 28740 | Kingston, NY | 2 912 | 181 791 | 227 | 62.4 | 83.1 | 6.7 | 0.9 | 2.4 | 9.0 | 4.8 | 14.8 | 10.1 | 11.1 | 12.8 | 16.6 |
| 28940 | Knoxville, TN | 4 809 | 709 824 | 74 | 147.6 | 88.0 | 7.3 | 0.8 | 1.9 | 3.5 | 5.7 | 15.8 | 10.5 | 12.5 | 12.9 | 14.4 |

1. CBSA = Core Based Statistical Area. DIV = Metropolitan Division. See Appendix A for explanation. See Appendix B for list of metropolitan areas identified by type. 2. Dry land or land partially or temporarily covered by water. 3. May be of any race.

# Table C. Metropolitan Areas — **Population and Households**

| | Population, 2011 (cont.) | | | | Population change and components of change, 2000–2012 | | | | | | | Households, 2010 | | | | |
|---|---|---|---|---|---|---|---|---|---|---|---|---|---|---|---|---|
| | Age (percent) (cont.) | | | | Total persons | | Percent change | | Components of change, 2010–2012 | | | | | | Percent | |
| Area name | 55 to 64 years | 65 to 74 years | 75 years and over | Percent female | 2000 | 2010 | 2000–2010 | 2010–2012 | Births | Deaths | Net migration | Number | Percent change, 2000–2010 | Persons per house-hold | Female family house-holder[1] | One person |
| | 16 | 17 | 18 | 19 | 20 | 21 | 22 | 23 | 24 | 25 | 26 | 27 | 28 | 29 | 30 | 31 |
| Flagstaff, AZ......................... | 11.6 | 5.9 | 3.4 | 50.6 | 116 320 | 134 421 | 15.6 | 1.2 | 3 998 | 1 606 | -831 | 46 711 | 15.5 | 2.69 | 12.7 | 24.5 |
| Flint, MI.............................. | 13.0 | 7.5 | 6.6 | 51.8 | 436 141 | 425 790 | -2.4 | -1.7 | 11 503 | 9 257 | -9 625 | 169 202 | -0.4 | 2.48 | 17.2 | 28.4 |
| Florence, SC......................... | 13.5 | 8.3 | 5.7 | 52.9 | 193 155 | 205 566 | 6.4 | 0.3 | 5 789 | 4 987 | -184 | 79 184 | 8.6 | 2.54 | 19.9 | 26.2 |
| Florence-Muscle Shoals, AL. | 13.7 | 9.4 | 7.8 | 52.1 | 142 950 | 147 137 | 2.9 | -0.1 | 3 541 | 3 913 | 292 | 61 453 | 5.0 | 2.36 | 12.7 | 28.9 |
| Fond du Lac, WI.................. | 13.3 | 7.7 | 7.7 | 50.8 | 97 296 | 101 633 | 4.5 | 0.2 | 2 504 | 2 008 | -210 | 40 697 | 10.2 | 2.41 | 8.5 | 27.6 |
| Fort Collins-Loveland, CO .... | 12.8 | 6.9 | 5.4 | 50.4 | 251 494 | 299 630 | 19.1 | 3.6 | 7 555 | 4 130 | 7 247 | 120 295 | 23.8 | 2.42 | 8.2 | 25.9 |
| Fort Smith, AR-OK.............. | 12.5 | 8.2 | 6.1 | 50.6 | 273 170 | 298 592 | 9.3 | 0.0 | 7 918 | 6 665 | -1 181 | 115 169 | 10.2 | 2.55 | 12.5 | 25.9 |
| Fort Wayne, IN..................... | 12.2 | 6.6 | 5.9 | 51.1 | 390 156 | 416 257 | 6.7 | 1.2 | 13 649 | 7 588 | -776 | 161 632 | 7.1 | 2.53 | 12.5 | 27.5 |
| Fresno, CA.......................... | 9.8 | 5.5 | 4.8 | 50.0 | 799 407 | 930 450 | 16.4 | 1.9 | 36 236 | 13 970 | -4 730 | 289 391 | 14.4 | 3.15 | 16.9 | 19.8 |
| Gadsden, AL........................ | 14.0 | 8.8 | 7.1 | 51.6 | 103 459 | 104 430 | 0.9 | 0.0 | 2 810 | 3 229 | 447 | 42 036 | 1.0 | 2.43 | 14.3 | 28.1 |
| Gainesville, FL..................... | 11.1 | 6.4 | 5.2 | 51.4 | 232 392 | 264 275 | 13.7 | 1.5 | 6 793 | 4 201 | 1 456 | 106 637 | 15.2 | 2.34 | 12.7 | 29.8 |
| Gainesville, GA.................... | 10.7 | 6.7 | 4.8 | 49.9 | 139 277 | 179 684 | 29.0 | 3.2 | 5 900 | 2 809 | 2 388 | 60 691 | 28.1 | 2.91 | 12.4 | 20.3 |
| Glens Falls, NY.................... | 14.7 | 9.0 | 7.7 | 49.7 | 124 345 | 128 923 | 3.7 | -0.3 | 2 804 | 2 830 | -363 | 52 132 | 8.2 | 2.40 | 10.9 | 27.4 |
| Goldsboro, NC...................... | 12.2 | 7.6 | 5.8 | 51.1 | 113 329 | 122 623 | 8.2 | 1.3 | 3 696 | 2 656 | 636 | 47 831 | 12.2 | 2.50 | 16.7 | 27.4 |
| Grand Forks, ND-MN............ | 11.6 | 6.2 | 6.2 | 49.0 | 97 478 | 98 461 | 1.0 | 0.4 | 2 901 | 1 812 | -655 | 40 121 | 7.0 | 2.32 | 9.1 | 31.5 |
| Grand Junction, CO............ | 13.4 | 8.1 | 7.2 | 50.3 | 116 255 | 146 723 | 26.2 | 0.8 | 4 277 | 2 889 | -218 | 58 095 | 26.8 | 2.46 | 10.0 | 26.5 |
| Grand Rapids-Wyoming, MI.................................. | 11.8 | 6.3 | 5.6 | 50.4 | 740 482 | 774 160 | 4.5 | 1.4 | 23 761 | 12 805 | 352 | 290 340 | 6.7 | 2.60 | 12.0 | 25.3 |
| Great Falls, MT.................... | 13.0 | 8.3 | 7.4 | 50.1 | 80 357 | 81 327 | 1.2 | 0.5 | 2 658 | 1 646 | -601 | 33 809 | 3.9 | 2.33 | 10.2 | 30.5 |
| Greeley, CO......................... | 11.0 | 5.8 | 4.1 | 49.8 | 180 936 | 252 825 | 39.7 | 4.3 | 8 437 | 3 165 | 5 448 | 89 349 | 41.3 | 2.76 | 9.9 | 21.5 |
| Green Bay, WI..................... | 12.4 | 6.8 | 5.9 | 50.2 | 282 599 | 306 241 | 8.4 | 1.6 | 8 948 | 4 846 | 877 | 122 037 | 12.1 | 2.45 | 9.5 | 27.2 |
| Greensboro-High Point, NC.. | 12.4 | 7.4 | 6.0 | 52.0 | 643 430 | 723 801 | 12.5 | 1.7 | 19 081 | 14 146 | 7 523 | 290 694 | 13.4 | 2.43 | 14.4 | 28.6 |
| Greenville, NC..................... | 10.8 | 5.8 | 4.5 | 52.1 | 152 772 | 189 510 | 24.0 | 2.4 | 5 386 | 3 062 | 2 128 | 74 890 | 26.4 | 2.41 | 15.8 | 29.6 |
| Greenville-Mauldin-Easley, SC................................... | 12.2 | 7.7 | 5.7 | 51.2 | 559 940 | 636 986 | 13.8 | 2.6 | 18 974 | 12 391 | 9 976 | 247 284 | 13.9 | 2.49 | 13.4 | 26.6 |
| Gulfport-Biloxi, MS.............. | 12.3 | 7.3 | 5.3 | 50.2 | 246 190 | 248 820 | 1.1 | 3.4 | 7 753 | 4 867 | 5 457 | 95 021 | 2.0 | 2.54 | 16.3 | 26.1 |
| Hagerstown-Martinsburg, MD-WV............................. | 12.9 | 7.6 | 6.0 | 49.7 | 222 771 | 269 140 | 20.8 | 1.7 | 7 064 | 5 412 | 2 979 | 102 845 | 20.4 | 2.52 | 11.8 | 25.3 |
| Hanford-Corcoran, CA......... | 8.7 | 4.6 | 3.5 | 43.6 | 129 461 | 152 982 | 18.2 | -1.1 | 5 792 | 1 758 | -5 743 | 41 233 | 19.8 | 3.19 | 15.9 | 17.5 |
| Harrisburg-Carlisle, PA......... | 13.7 | 7.7 | 7.1 | 51.2 | 509 074 | 549 475 | 7.9 | 0.8 | 14 185 | 10 936 | 1 471 | 222 281 | 9.8 | 2.38 | 11.3 | 29.3 |
| Harrisonburg, VA................. | 10.6 | 6.6 | 6.3 | 51.8 | 108 193 | 125 228 | 15.7 | 2.5 | 3 098 | 2 032 | 1 852 | 45 165 | 17.3 | 2.57 | 9.5 | 24.4 |
| Hartford-West Hartford-East Hartford, CT................. | 13.1 | 7.4 | 7.1 | 51.3 | 1 148 618 | 1 212 381 | 5.6 | 0.2 | 27 456 | 22 698 | -2 483 | 472 533 | 6.0 | 2.46 | 13.1 | 28.1 |
| Hattiesburg, MS.................. | 10.4 | 6.6 | 5.0 | 52.0 | 123 812 | 142 842 | 15.4 | 2.7 | 4 580 | 2 700 | 1 911 | 54 962 | 19.5 | 2.53 | 16.3 | 26.9 |
| Hickory-Lenoir-Morganton, NC.................................. | 13.6 | 8.9 | 6.5 | 50.5 | 341 851 | 365 497 | 6.9 | -0.5 | 8 492 | 8 261 | -2 069 | 144 504 | 7.9 | 2.47 | 12.2 | 26.1 |
| Hinesville-Fort Stewart, GA .. | 8.5 | 4.2 | 2.3 | 50.5 | 71 914 | 77 917 | 8.3 | 4.6 | 3 665 | 808 | 592 | 27 178 | 18.4 | 2.76 | 20.9 | 21.0 |
| Holland-Grand Haven, MI ..... | 11.4 | 6.5 | 5.6 | 51.0 | 238 314 | 263 801 | 10.7 | 2.0 | 7 282 | 3 730 | 1 870 | 93 775 | 14.8 | 2.73 | 8.4 | 20.9 |
| Honolulu, HI........................ | 12.1 | 7.4 | 7.4 | 49.8 | 876 156 | 953 207 | 8.8 | 2.4 | 29 935 | 15 810 | 9 490 | 311 047 | 8.6 | 2.95 | 12.7 | 22.8 |
| Hot Springs, AR.................. | 14.6 | 11.4 | 9.7 | 51.5 | 88 068 | 96 024 | 9.0 | 0.9 | 2 451 | 2 850 | 1 192 | 40 994 | 8.4 | 2.29 | 11.9 | 29.6 |
| Houma-Bayou Cane-Thibo-daux, LA...................... | 11.5 | 6.9 | 5.1 | 50.7 | 194 477 | 208 178 | 7.0 | 0.4 | 6 600 | 3 954 | -1 850 | 75 577 | 11.1 | 2.71 | 14.8 | 22.0 |
| Houston-Sugar Land-Bay-town, TX....................... | 10.7 | 5.3 | 3.6 | 50.2 | 4 715 407 | 5 946 800 | 26.1 | 4.3 | 208 359 | 77 011 | 125 726 | 2 072 625 | 25.1 | 2.83 | 14.3 | 23.5 |
| Huntington-Ashland, WV-KY-OH............................ | 13.7 | 9.0 | 7.4 | 51.1 | 288 649 | 287 702 | -0.3 | -0.4 | 7 188 | 7 495 | -702 | 118 002 | 0.3 | 2.37 | 12.3 | 28.9 |
| Huntsville, AL...................... | 11.9 | 7.1 | 5.3 | 50.7 | 342 376 | 417 593 | 22.0 | 3.1 | 11 843 | 7 468 | 8 684 | 166 146 | 23.4 | 2.45 | 12.5 | 27.8 |
| Idaho Falls, ID..................... | 10.6 | 6.1 | 4.8 | 50.0 | 101 677 | 130 374 | 28.2 | 2.3 | 5 362 | 1 980 | -441 | 44 775 | 29.2 | 2.88 | 9.6 | 21.1 |
| Indianapolis-Carmel, IN ........ | 11.4 | 6.1 | 4.9 | 51.2 | 1 525 104 | 1 756 241 | 15.2 | 2.4 | 57 395 | 30 037 | 14 779 | 680 257 | 14.4 | 2.53 | 13.5 | 27.0 |
| Iowa City, IA....................... | 10.7 | 5.3 | 4.7 | 50.1 | 131 676 | 152 586 | 15.9 | 3.7 | 4 427 | 1 930 | 3 114 | 61 456 | 17.9 | 2.35 | 7.6 | 30.0 |
| Ithaca, NY.......................... | 11.1 | 5.9 | 5.2 | 50.7 | 96 501 | 101 564 | 5.2 | 1.0 | 1 953 | 1 399 | 425 | 38 967 | 7.0 | 2.27 | 8.7 | 33.3 |
| Jackson, MI......................... | 13.4 | 7.6 | 6.0 | 49.0 | 158 422 | 160 248 | 1.2 | 0.0 | 4 084 | 3 365 | -598 | 60 771 | 4.5 | 2.48 | 13.3 | 27.1 |
| Jackson, MS........................ | 11.8 | 6.4 | 5.0 | 52.3 | 497 197 | 539 057 | 8.4 | 1.8 | 16 819 | 10 521 | 3 072 | 201 054 | 11.4 | 2.60 | 19.8 | 26.4 |
| Jackson, TN........................ | 12.5 | 7.5 | 6.2 | 52.4 | 107 377 | 115 425 | 7.5 | 0.3 | 3 315 | 2 388 | -503 | 44 281 | 7.4 | 2.48 | 17.2 | 27.1 |
| Jacksonville, FL................... | 12.6 | 7.1 | 5.4 | 51.3 | 1 122 750 | 1 345 596 | 19.8 | 2.4 | 39 092 | 24 809 | 17 998 | 524 146 | 21.2 | 2.52 | 14.8 | 26.0 |
| Jacksonville, NC.................. | 7.6 | 4.5 | 3.2 | 46.2 | 150 355 | 177 772 | 18.2 | 3.1 | 9 499 | 1 931 | -2 172 | 60 092 | 24.9 | 2.66 | 13.1 | 20.3 |
| Janesville, WI...................... | 12.5 | 7.3 | 6.5 | 50.9 | 152 307 | 160 331 | 5.3 | 0.1 | 4 347 | 3 023 | -1 236 | 62 905 | 7.3 | 2.50 | 12.3 | 26.3 |
| Jefferson City, MO.............. | 12.8 | 7.0 | 5.9 | 48.9 | 140 052 | 149 807 | 7.0 | 0.2 | 3 893 | 2 821 | -689 | 56 915 | 10.2 | 2.45 | 10.5 | 27.7 |
| Johnson City, TN................ | 13.7 | 9.4 | 7.1 | 51.1 | 181 607 | 198 716 | 9.4 | 1.0 | 4 615 | 4 828 | 2 215 | 83 245 | 10.7 | 2.31 | 11.1 | 29.4 |
| Johnstown, PA..................... | 14.9 | 8.9 | 9.8 | 51.2 | 152 598 | 143 679 | -5.8 | -1.5 | 3 036 | 4 080 | -978 | 58 950 | -2.6 | 2.30 | 10.9 | 31.2 |
| Jonesboro, AR..................... | 11.2 | 7.3 | 5.7 | 51.2 | 107 762 | 121 026 | 12.3 | 2.5 | 3 773 | 2 655 | 1 867 | 47 045 | 11.1 | 2.49 | 14.2 | 26.5 |
| Joplin, MO.......................... | 11.9 | 7.7 | 6.4 | 50.9 | 157 322 | 175 518 | 11.6 | -0.7 | 5 486 | 3 659 | -3 252 | 67 660 | 9.9 | 2.54 | 11.7 | 26.0 |
| Kalamazoo-Portage, MI ........ | 12.3 | 6.8 | 6.0 | 50.9 | 314 866 | 326 589 | 3.7 | 1.1 | 9 022 | 6 147 | 652 | 129 538 | 6.6 | 2.45 | 11.9 | 28.3 |
| Kankakee-Bradley, IL............ | 12.2 | 7.2 | 6.5 | 50.9 | 103 833 | 113 449 | 9.3 | -0.4 | 3 263 | 2 399 | -1 255 | 41 511 | 8.7 | 2.61 | 14.7 | 25.5 |
| Kansas City, MO-KS............ | 12.1 | 6.6 | 5.6 | 51.0 | 1 836 038 | 2 035 334 | 10.9 | 1.4 | 63 000 | 35 761 | 2 167 | 799 637 | 11.4 | 2.51 | 12.4 | 27.8 |
| Kennewick-Pasco-Richland, WA.................................. | 11.3 | 6.0 | 4.5 | 49.2 | 191 822 | 253 340 | 32.1 | 5.9 | 9 594 | 3 615 | 8 757 | 88 549 | 30.8 | 2.82 | 11.7 | 22.2 |
| Killeen-Temple-Fort Hood, TX................................. | 9.0 | 5.1 | 3.9 | 50.6 | 330 714 | 405 300 | 22.6 | 3.7 | 16 662 | 5 517 | 3 861 | 144 119 | 28.7 | 2.68 | 14.4 | 23.4 |
| Kingsport-Bristol-Bristol, TN-VA................................. | 14.6 | 10.5 | 8.1 | 51.3 | 298 484 | 309 544 | 3.7 | -0.2 | 6 739 | 8 142 | 937 | 130 138 | 4.9 | 2.33 | 11.1 | 28.4 |
| Kingston, NY....................... | 14.5 | 8.3 | 7.1 | 50.3 | 177 749 | 182 493 | 2.7 | -0.4 | 3 682 | 3 502 | -905 | 71 049 | 5.3 | 2.40 | 11.4 | 29.0 |
| Knoxville, TN....................... | 13.2 | 8.4 | 6.6 | 51.4 | 616 079 | 698 030 | 13.3 | 1.7 | 17 836 | 15 105 | 9 206 | 284 984 | 12.6 | 2.39 | 11.3 | 28.1 |

1. No spouse present.

| Area name | Persons in group quarters, 2009 | Daytime population, 2007–2011 Number | Employ- ment/ residence ratio | Births, 2011 Total | Rate[1] | Deaths, 2011 Number | Rate[1] | Persons under 65 with no health insurance 2010 Number | Percent | Medicare, 2012 Enrolled in original Medicare | Enrolled in Medicare Advantage | Enrolled in a Medicare prescription drug plan | Serious crimes known to police,[2] 2011 Total Number | Rate[3] |
|---|---|---|---|---|---|---|---|---|---|---|---|---|---|---|
| | 32 | 33 | 34 | 35 | 36 | 37 | 38 | 39 | 40 | 41 | 42 | 43 | 44 | 45 |
| Flagstaff, AZ | 8 834 | 133 248 | 1.00 | 1 802 | 13.4 | 703 | 5.2 | 24 623 | 21.4 | 15 235 | 1 810 | 7 223 | 5 150 | 3 778 |
| Flint, MI | 5 973 | 414 570 | 0.91 | 5 222 | 12.4 | 4 102 | 9.7 | 44 805 | 12.3 | 79 974 | 22 869 | 28 955 | 19 615 | 4 620 |
| Florence, SC | 4 573 | 209 354 | 1.06 | 2 637 | 12.8 | 2 131 | 10.3 | 33 150 | 19.0 | 38 438 | 2 944 | 20 667 | 11 648 | 5 601 |
| Florence-Muscle Shoals, AL. | 2 365 | 142 930 | 0.94 | 1 548 | 10.5 | 1 705 | 11.6 | 18 034 | 15.0 | 32 480 | 2 798 | 15 550 | 3 991 | 2 699 |
| Fond du Lac, WI | 3 589 | 96 618 | 0.91 | 1 154 | 11.3 | 860 | 8.4 | 8 507 | 10.2 | 18 345 | 7 638 | 5 918 | 1 808 | 1 771 |
| Fort Collins-Loveland, CO .... | 8 530 | 288 186 | 0.95 | 3 380 | 11.1 | 1 739 | 5.7 | 40 267 | 15.6 | 45 017 | 10 985 | 16 058 | 8 273 | 2 714 |
| Fort Smith, AR-OK | 5 254 | 297 366 | 1.01 | 3 932 | 13.1 | 2 918 | 9.7 | 60 237 | 23.8 | 57 454 | 13 678 | 25 077 | 9 697 | 3 228 |
| Fort Wayne, IN | 7 015 | 424 576 | 1.05 | 6 075 | 14.5 | 3 299 | 7.9 | 60 416 | 16.8 | 66 165 | 27 235 | 25 973 | 12 193 | 3 083 |
| Fresno, CA | 17 523 | 924 213 | 1.01 | 15 958 | 16.9 | 6 161 | 6.5 | 181 235 | 21.9 | 116 513 | 29 070 | 56 155 | 45 521 | 4 912 |
| Gadsden, AL | 2 085 | 98 896 | 0.87 | 1 232 | 11.8 | 1 443 | 13.8 | 15 817 | 18.3 | 23 394 | 3 938 | 8 759 | 5 111 | 4 871 |
| Gainesville, FL | 15 048 | 276 354 | 1.11 | 3 013 | 11.3 | 1 864 | 7.0 | 45 362 | 20.5 | 37 637 | 4 622 | 15 384 | 10 807 | 4 034 |
| Gainesville, GA | 3 141 | 177 119 | 0.99 | 2 672 | 14.6 | 1 238 | 6.8 | 40 656 | 25.8 | 27 125 | 6 504 | 11 250 | 4 789 | 2 631 |
| Glens Falls, NY | 3 902 | 125 170 | 0.94 | 1 252 | 9.7 | 1 236 | 9.6 | 13 299 | 12.7 | 26 968 | 9 229 | 7 479 | 2 336 | 1 804 |
| Goldsboro, NC | 3 219 | 118 492 | 0.95 | 1 615 | 13.1 | 1 192 | 9.6 | 21 224 | 20.4 | 21 170 | 1 402 | 10 320 | 5 612 | 4 624 |
| Grand Forks, ND-MN | 5 546 | 100 106 | 1.04 | 1 270 | 13.0 | 807 | 8.2 | 8 657 | 10.6 | 14 626 | 3 455 | 8 176 | 2 472 | 2 521 |
| Grand Junction, CO | 3 631 | 142 401 | 0.97 | 1 943 | 13.2 | 1 280 | 8.7 | 24 352 | 20.0 | 26 618 | 9 850 | 8 269 | 4 482 | 3 017 |
| Grand Rapids-Wyoming, MI | 18 037 | 799 575 | 1.07 | 10 571 | 13.6 | 5 599 | 7.2 | 93 320 | 14.0 | 120 421 | 49 883 | 41 529 | 20 237 | 2 632 |
| Great Falls, MT | 2 562 | 81 221 | 1.01 | 1 154 | 14.1 | 716 | 8.7 | 12 461 | 18.6 | 15 626 | 3 586 | 6 262 | 3 153 | 3 843 |
| Greeley, CO | 5 895 | 224 405 | 0.79 | 3 788 | 14.6 | 1 326 | 5.1 | 42 498 | 19.0 | 31 698 | 8 121 | 12 095 | 6 018 | 2 384 |
| Green Bay, WI | 7 088 | 313 258 | 1.05 | 3 996 | 12.9 | 2 114 | 6.8 | 28 050 | 10.7 | 49 041 | 21 063 | 14 060 | 5 895 | 1 917 |
| Greensboro-High Point, NC.. | 17 845 | 748 208 | 1.03 | 8 593 | 11.8 | 6 267 | 8.6 | 120 395 | 19.6 | 124 972 | 49 518 | 40 546 | 30 677 | 4 187 |
| Greenville, NC | 8 846 | 184 488 | 0.98 | 2 445 | 12.7 | 1 357 | 7.0 | 29 925 | 18.4 | 26 483 | 1 144 | 14 593 | NA | NA |
| Greenville-Mauldin-Easley, SC | 21 309 | 644 260 | 1.05 | 9 631 | 14.9 | 5 385 | 8.3 | 109 365 | 20.5 | 114 315 | 30 274 | 43 126 | 27 110 | 4 207 |
| Gulfport-Biloxi, MS | 7 287 | 261 544 | 1.14 | 3 419 | 13.5 | 2 079 | 8.2 | 48 855 | 23.1 | 41 845 | 5 141 | 17 679 | 9 482 | 4 282 |
| Hagerstown-Martinsburg, MD-WV | 9 458 | 246 392 | 0.83 | 3 171 | 11.7 | 2 393 | 8.8 | 32 546 | 14.4 | 47 163 | 5 742 | 20 299 | 6 669 | 2 474 |
| Hanford-Corcoran, CA | 21 580 | 151 680 | 0.99 | 2 528 | 16.4 | 770 | 5.0 | 23 607 | 19.6 | 14 582 | 1 635 | 7 702 | 3 978 | 2 570 |
| Harrisburg-Carlisle, PA | 20 267 | 593 943 | 1.18 | 6 298 | 11.4 | 4 750 | 8.6 | 50 515 | 11.1 | 99 010 | 40 479 | 27 929 | 13 709 | 2 504 |
| Harrisonburg, VA | 9 054 | 129 667 | 1.10 | 1 373 | 10.8 | 881 | 7.0 | 20 316 | 20.1 | 19 213 | 2 858 | 10 597 | 1 814 | 1 431 |
| Hartford-West Hartford-East Hartford, CT | 49 429 | 1 241 240 | 1.06 | 12 329 | 10.2 | 9 836 | 8.1 | 95 126 | 9.5 | 208 089 | 49 479 | 90 078 | 28 128 | 2 752 |
| Hattiesburg, MS | 4 041 | 144 362 | 1.05 | 2 060 | 14.2 | 1 139 | 7.8 | 24 863 | 20.2 | 22 153 | 3 221 | 11 528 | 3 008 | 2 295 |
| Hickory-Lenoir-Morganton, NC | 7 889 | 361 908 | 0.99 | 3 889 | 10.7 | 3 560 | 9.8 | 61 155 | 20.0 | 72 765 | 14 315 | 35 877 | 13 682 | 3 770 |
| Hinesville-Fort Stewart, GA .. | 2 907 | 76 901 | 0.97 | 1 619 | 20.1 | 378 | 4.7 | 13 264 | 19.2 | 6 305 | 1 098 | 2 078 | 2 401 | 3 637 |
| Holland-Grand Haven, MI ..... | 8 261 | 250 834 | 0.90 | 3 154 | 11.8 | 1 595 | 6.0 | 26 637 | 11.9 | 40 141 | 20 938 | 11 336 | 5 225 | 1 982 |
| Honolulu, HI | 35 300 | 944 728 | 1.00 | 13 246 | 13.7 | 6 870 | 7.1 | 63 196 | 7.9 | 156 177 | 71 793 | 37 658 | 32 982 | 3 423 |
| Hot Springs, AR | 2 166 | 96 154 | 1.01 | 1 100 | 11.3 | 1 241 | 12.8 | 17 327 | 23.2 | 25 698 | 4 274 | 11 396 | 5 477 | 5 661 |
| Houma-Bayou Cane-Thibo- daux, LA | 3 104 | 209 228 | 1.02 | 2 997 | 14.4 | 1 740 | 8.3 | 39 720 | 22.0 | 33 514 | 5 319 | 17 842 | 7 616 | 3 625 |
| Houston-Sugar Land-Bay- town, TX | 77 956 | 5 848 993 | 1.00 | 97 795 | 16.1 | 33 432 | 5.5 | 1 471 666 | 27.3 | 652 800 | 186 110 | 222 786 | 251 645 | 4 145 |
| Huntington-Ashland, WV- KY-OH | 7 643 | 289 606 | 1.02 | 3 287 | 11.4 | 3 275 | 11.4 | 39 344 | 16.8 | 64 003 | 14 544 | 30 384 | 7 855 | 2 762 |
| Huntsville, AL | 10 949 | 434 239 | 1.13 | 5 152 | 12.1 | 3 201 | 7.5 | 52 101 | 14.6 | 66 900 | 8 259 | 22 338 | 15 270 | 3 639 |
| Idaho Falls, ID | 1 283 | 128 990 | 1.02 | 2 428 | 18.4 | 854 | 6.5 | 21 127 | 18.2 | 17 750 | 3 616 | 7 880 | 2 975 | 2 256 |
| Indianapolis-Carmel, IN | 32 080 | 1 769 076 | 1.04 | 25 734 | 14.5 | 12 907 | 7.3 | 251 494 | 16.4 | 248 645 | 54 110 | 103 218 | 71 251 | 4 678 |
| Iowa City, IA | 8 167 | 158 452 | 1.09 | 1 975 | 12.8 | 851 | 5.5 | 13 124 | 10.0 | 19 030 | 2 327 | 9 489 | 3 219 | 2 099 |
| Ithaca, NY | 13 232 | 111 396 | 1.21 | 910 | 8.9 | 587 | 5.8 | 9 233 | 11.9 | 13 637 | 2 267 | 4 107 | NA | NA |
| Jackson, MI | 9 672 | 155 570 | 0.92 | 1 815 | 11.4 | 1 496 | 9.4 | 17 963 | 14.0 | 30 074 | 6 482 | 13 727 | 4 111 | 2 602 |
| Jackson, MS | 16 906 | 545 867 | 1.04 | 7 534 | 13.8 | 4 551 | 8.3 | 86 517 | 18.7 | 83 946 | 15 535 | 40 313 | 20 153 | 4 091 |
| Jackson, TN | 5 680 | 126 194 | 1.24 | 1 522 | 13.2 | 1 017 | 8.8 | 15 132 | 15.9 | 20 552 | 2 290 | 11 654 | 5 597 | 4 806 |
| Jacksonville, FL | 26 921 | 1 340 435 | 1.01 | 17 601 | 12.9 | 10 910 | 8.0 | 215 663 | 18.6 | 215 423 | 45 782 | 80 551 | 57 374 | 4 207 |
| Jacksonville, NC | 17 805 | 173 961 | 1.01 | 4 202 | 23.4 | 848 | 4.7 | 23 749 | 16.0 | 18 319 | 1 017 | 7 182 | 5 846 | 3 247 |
| Janesville, WI | 2 934 | 149 230 | 0.85 | 1 937 | 12.1 | 1 308 | 8.2 | 16 472 | 12.1 | 28 071 | 6 525 | 12 558 | 5 270 | 3 273 |
| Jefferson City, MO | 10 596 | 152 492 | 1.05 | 1 750 | 11.6 | 1 243 | 8.3 | 16 258 | 13.4 | 24 759 | 1 944 | 12 026 | 4 192 | 2 788 |
| Johnson City, TN | 6 545 | 195 471 | 0.98 | 2 056 | 10.3 | 2 109 | 10.6 | 25 759 | 16.0 | 43 200 | 16 087 | 14 478 | 6 748 | 3 365 |
| Johnstown, PA | 8 092 | 141 871 | 0.96 | 1 325 | 9.2 | 1 803 | 12.5 | 13 128 | 12.0 | 33 452 | 19 994 | 7 757 | 3 249 | 2 333 |
| Jonesboro, AR | 3 920 | 122 243 | 1.05 | 1 690 | 13.8 | 1 156 | 9.4 | 21 072 | 20.6 | 21 757 | 2 676 | 12 591 | 5 135 | 4 333 |
| Joplin, MO | 3 358 | 179 240 | 1.06 | 2 482 | 14.0 | 1 635 | 9.2 | 29 693 | 20.0 | 31 441 | 5 398 | 15 611 | 7 042 | 3 998 |
| Kalamazoo-Portage, MI | 9 332 | 325 282 | 1.00 | 4 010 | 12.2 | 2 708 | 8.3 | 39 304 | 14.1 | 55 054 | 14 888 | 23 590 | 10 323 | 3 163 |
| Kankakee-Bradley, IL | 5 107 | 108 996 | 0.92 | 1 493 | 13.1 | 1 088 | 9.6 | 13 722 | 14.5 | 19 597 | 541 | 11 050 | 3 460 | 3 354 |
| Kansas City, MO-KS | 32 031 | 2 037 265 | 1.02 | 28 301 | 13.8 | 15 596 | 7.6 | 256 301 | 14.5 | 309 525 | 80 806 | 114 399 | 79 327 | 3 882 |
| Kennewick-Pasco-Richland, WA | 3 272 | 245 849 | 0.99 | 4 194 | 15.9 | 1 582 | 6.0 | 39 868 | 17.7 | 34 419 | 4 681 | 16 257 | 7 479 | 2 907 |
| Killeen-Temple-Fort Hood, TX | 19 745 | 396 266 | 0.99 | 7 250 | 17.6 | 2 375 | 5.8 | 74 504 | 21.1 | 48 185 | 11 456 | 11 704 | 12 996 | 3 158 |
| Kingsport-Bristol-Bristol, TN- VA | 5 797 | 308 830 | 1.00 | 3 046 | 9.8 | 3 529 | 11.4 | 38 997 | 15.7 | 76 586 | 35 628 | 23 123 | 11 345 | 3 629 |
| Kingston, NY | 11 773 | 165 550 | 0.80 | 1 631 | 8.9 | 1 523 | 8.3 | 19 515 | 13.1 | 34 889 | 6 879 | 12 468 | 3 770 | 2 057 |
| Knoxville, TN | 16 190 | 722 591 | 1.09 | 8 009 | 11.4 | 6 517 | 9.3 | 86 170 | 14.8 | 133 029 | 48 523 | 41 668 | 30 259 | 4 296 |

1. Per 1,000 estimated resident population.   2. Data for serious crimes have not been adjusted for underreporting; this may affect comparability between geographic areas and over time.   3. Per 100,000 population estimated by the FBI.

# Table C. Metropolitan Areas — Crime, Education, Money Income, and Poverty

| Area name | Rate[2] Violent | Rate[2] Property | Enrollment[3] Total | Enrollment Percent private | Attainment[4] (percent) High school graduate or less | Attainment Bachelor's degree or more | Local government expenditures,[5] 2009–2010 Total current expenditures (mil dol) | Current expenditures per student (dollars) | Per capita income[6] (dollars) | Median household income (dollars) | Percent of households with income of less than $25,000 | Percent of households with income of $100,000 or more | Percent of households with income of $200,000 or more | Percent below poverty level All persons | Related Children under 18 years | Related Children under 5 |
|---|---|---|---|---|---|---|---|---|---|---|---|---|---|---|---|---|
| | 46 | 47 | 48 | 49 | 50 | 51 | 52 | 53 | 54 | 55 | 56 | 57 | 58 | 59 | 60 | 61 |
| Flagstaff, AZ | 414 | 3 363 | 44 837 | 4.6 | 35.6 | 31.5 | 178.0 | 8 848 | 22 607 | 49 615 | 25.2 | 18.6 | 2.5 | 19.8 | 22.6 | 24.6 |
| Flint, MI | 834 | 3 786 | 119 919 | 10.8 | 45.5 | 18.9 | 796.8 | 10 462 | 22 577 | 43 418 | 28.4 | 14.3 | 1.5 | 18.8 | 27.7 | 33.9 |
| Florence, SC | 656 | 4 945 | 52 199 | 14.1 | 54.8 | 18.9 | 309.4 | 9 074 | 21 710 | 40 565 | 30.7 | 13.0 | 1.9 | 19.7 | 29.3 | 36.5 |
| Florence-Muscle Shoals, AL. | 228 | 2 472 | 34 943 | 10.7 | 52.1 | 20.0 | 198.7 | 9 203 | 22 321 | 39 927 | 32.9 | 12.2 | 1.9 | 17.0 | 24.1 | 32.0 |
| Fond du Lac, WI | 180 | 1 591 | 25 298 | 20.3 | 50.8 | 18.7 | 144.4 | 10 750 | 25 934 | 52 717 | 21.6 | 15.2 | 2.1 | 9.5 | 11.8 | 16.6 |
| Fort Collins-Loveland, CO .... | 198 | 2 516 | 90 582 | 9.9 | 25.6 | 43.1 | 363.7 | 8 467 | 30 276 | 57 215 | 21.0 | 23.6 | 3.9 | 13.4 | 12.4 | 16.6 |
| Fort Smith, AR-OK | 419 | 2 809 | 73 337 | 7.7 | 54.4 | 15.2 | 449.8 | 8 496 | 20 503 | 39 344 | 31.8 | 11.2 | 1.7 | 19.3 | 28.8 | 34.4 |
| Fort Wayne, IN | 231 | 2 853 | 115 584 | 20.5 | 43.7 | 24.5 | 621.5 | 9 398 | 24 816 | 49 808 | 21.9 | 15.5 | 2.3 | 12.6 | 17.5 | 19.5 |
| Fresno, CA | 553 | 4 359 | 286 887 | 7.5 | 50.4 | 19.5 | 1 808.3 | 9 436 | 20 638 | 46 903 | 27.4 | 18.6 | 3.0 | 23.4 | 33.0 | 37.4 |
| Gadsden, AL | 488 | 4 383 | 23 450 | 11.5 | 50.5 | 15.3 | 133.7 | 8 137 | 20 818 | 37 772 | 33.2 | 12.1 | 1.3 | 18.0 | 26.2 | 36.7 |
| Gainesville, FL | 598 | 3 436 | 97 110 | 8.8 | 32.8 | 39.0 | 266.1 | 8 404 | 24 769 | 41 198 | 32.7 | 16.9 | 3.7 | 23.2 | 20.2 | 24.6 |
| Gainesville, GA | 156 | 2 475 | 45 355 | 12.3 | 52.8 | 22.1 | 276.1 | 8 555 | 24 572 | 52 050 | 20.5 | 19.5 | 3.7 | 15.1 | 21.7 | 24.3 |
| Glens Falls, NY | 155 | 1 649 | 28 925 | 14.7 | 48.8 | 22.5 | 313.9 | 16 133 | 26 153 | 51 894 | 22.0 | 16.5 | 2.3 | 11.3 | 15.6 | 21.5 |
| Goldsboro, NC | 447 | 4 176 | 31 958 | 12.8 | 49.4 | 16.0 | 153.7 | 7 839 | 21 135 | 41 751 | 29.6 | 11.7 | 1.4 | 20.2 | 29.4 | 32.8 |
| Grand Forks, ND-MN | 205 | 2 316 | 31 137 | 7.9 | 35.4 | 29.1 | 137.2 | 10 076 | 25 317 | 46 951 | 27.4 | 15.5 | 2.4 | 15.2 | 14.3 | 21.7 |
| Grand Junction, CO | 304 | 2 713 | 36 430 | 12.0 | 40.6 | 26.1 | 186.3 | 8 206 | 27 680 | 52 986 | 22.0 | 19.2 | 3.1 | 12.7 | 15.5 | 20.2 |
| Grand Rapids-Wyoming, MI | 344 | 2 288 | 216 878 | 19.2 | 41.7 | 26.7 | 1 405.6 | 10 352 | 24 657 | 50 187 | 23.4 | 17.0 | 2.8 | 14.7 | 20.3 | 24.6 |
| Great Falls, MT | 250 | 3 593 | 19 192 | 15.8 | 40.4 | 22.8 | 111.9 | 9 557 | 23 554 | 44 074 | 26.7 | 12.2 | 1.6 | 13.8 | 20.4 | 26.0 |
| Greeley, CO | 293 | 2 091 | 73 290 | 9.0 | 41.6 | 25.6 | 301.1 | 8 184 | 25 233 | 55 825 | 20.9 | 22.0 | 3.0 | 13.8 | 17.3 | 21.5 |
| Green Bay, WI | 165 | 1 752 | 80 035 | 15.6 | 46.0 | 23.3 | 540.6 | 10 664 | 26 997 | 52 944 | 21.3 | 17.3 | 2.6 | 10.7 | 14.3 | 19.7 |
| Greensboro-High Point, NC.. | 355 | 3 832 | 189 449 | 12.6 | 45.7 | 26.3 | 974.2 | 8 654 | 24 858 | 43 915 | 27.1 | 15.6 | 2.8 | 16.4 | 23.3 | 28.1 |
| Greenville, NC | NA | NA | 64 433 | 8.7 | 43.2 | 25.8 | 226.6 | 8 465 | 22 079 | 39 937 | 33.7 | 13.9 | 2.5 | 23.4 | 27.9 | 36.8 |
| Greenville-Mauldin-Easley, SC | 540 | 3 667 | 168 072 | 19.8 | 45.1 | 27.4 | 754.8 | 7 801 | 24 651 | 45 888 | 27.3 | 16.7 | 2.8 | 15.8 | 22.3 | 29.0 |
| Gulfport-Biloxi, MS | 232 | 4 050 | 61 219 | 14.3 | 45.0 | 20.5 | 331.4 | 8 879 | 23 027 | 44 170 | 28.0 | 14.9 | 2.1 | 17.2 | 25.4 | 32.6 |
| Hagerstown-Martinsburg, MD-WV | 265 | 2 210 | 64 217 | 13.2 | 54.2 | 18.9 | 495.5 | 11 796 | 26 011 | 51 729 | 22.6 | 19.0 | 2.1 | 11.5 | 15.6 | 20.4 |
| Hanford-Corcoran, CA | 350 | 2 220 | 42 092 | 10.8 | 55.4 | 12.5 | 253.4 | 8 847 | 18 296 | 48 838 | 23.5 | 18.9 | 1.8 | 19.3 | 28.7 | 34.0 |
| Harrisburg-Carlisle, PA | 307 | 2 197 | 133 553 | 19.5 | 47.7 | 28.3 | 885.4 | 12 246 | 29 310 | 56 821 | 18.5 | 21.2 | 3.3 | 9.9 | 14.4 | 18.4 |
| Harrisonburg, VA | 118 | 1 314 | 41 259 | 12.4 | 53.7 | 26.2 | 164.6 | 9 950 | 22 630 | 47 222 | 24.6 | 15.1 | 2.4 | 17.6 | 15.0 | 19.7 |
| Hartford-West Hartford-East Hartford, CT | 294 | 2 457 | 327 599 | 18.0 | 39.4 | 34.8 | 2 747.4 | 13 910 | 34 716 | 67 695 | 18.0 | 31.2 | 6.6 | 9.8 | 13.1 | 17.7 |
| Hattiesburg, MS | 103 | 2 192 | 42 032 | 14.6 | 42.1 | 27.1 | 194.1 | 8 511 | 22 782 | 40 427 | 33.8 | 14.1 | 2.5 | 22.2 | 27.1 | 29.5 |
| Hickory-Lenoir-Morganton, NC | 222 | 3 494 | 88 110 | 10.8 | 53.9 | 16.4 | 451.5 | 7 837 | 21 414 | 40 519 | 30.2 | 11.0 | 1.8 | 15.8 | 21.5 | 24.7 |
| Hinesville-Fort Stewart, GA .. | 354 | 3 283 | 23 944 | 10.1 | 47.5 | 15.7 | 116.3 | 8 931 | 19 264 | 43 443 | 27.2 | 9.7 | 1.1 | 17.9 | 25.2 | 29.4 |
| Holland-Grand Haven, MI ..... | 148 | 1 834 | 81 270 | 18.7 | 40.3 | 29.4 | 432.7 | 9 918 | 25 197 | 55 661 | 18.9 | 19.4 | 2.7 | 10.1 | 10.7 | 11.6 |
| Honolulu, HI | 246 | 3 177 | 239 307 | 26.0 | 37.4 | 31.2 | 2 118.0 | 11 754 | 30 016 | 71 263 | 14.9 | 32.6 | 6.1 | 9.3 | 11.9 | 13.1 |
| Hot Springs, AR | 492 | 5 169 | 20 676 | 10.0 | 47.3 | 20.6 | 128.7 | 9 000 | 22 955 | 38 210 | 33.0 | 11.6 | 2.4 | 18.5 | 27.6 | 30.4 |
| Houma-Bayou Cane-Thibodaux, LA | 313 | 3 312 | 52 263 | 17.7 | 66.2 | 14.0 | 319.0 | 9 434 | 23 910 | 48 740 | 27.1 | 18.5 | 2.6 | 16.4 | 24.0 | 28.8 |
| Houston-Sugar Land-Baytown, TX | 551 | 3 594 | 1 640 798 | 11.4 | 43.7 | 28.7 | 9 937.7 | 8 485 | 28 483 | 56 876 | 21.0 | 25.8 | 6.2 | 15.4 | 22.2 | 25.3 |
| Huntington-Ashland, WV-KY-OH | 188 | 2 574 | 68 526 | 8.9 | 55.0 | 17.3 | 466.4 | 10 525 | 21 201 | 37 537 | 34.2 | 11.1 | 1.5 | 19.2 | 25.4 | 32.5 |
| Huntsville, AL | 455 | 3 184 | 111 060 | 16.0 | 37.2 | 34.1 | 581.6 | 9 097 | 29 415 | 54 733 | 22.6 | 24.7 | 4.3 | 12.7 | 17.7 | 22.6 |
| Idaho Falls, ID | 194 | 2 062 | 36 276 | 13.4 | 37.1 | 25.4 | 164.5 | 6 075 | 22 754 | 51 729 | 20.3 | 17.5 | 2.5 | 10.6 | 12.8 | 16.6 |
| Indianapolis-Carmel, IN | 654 | 4 024 | 466 465 | 18.9 | 41.7 | 30.8 | 2 857.2 | 9 576 | 28 168 | 53 531 | 21.3 | 21.3 | 4.0 | 12.8 | 17.8 | 21.4 |
| Iowa City, IA | 241 | 1 857 | 54 412 | 8.6 | 26.9 | 45.4 | 173.4 | 9 125 | 28 151 | 53 322 | 24.8 | 19.8 | 3.5 | 16.7 | 13.2 | 13.1 |
| Ithaca, NY | NA | NA | 42 374 | 56.1 | 28.2 | 49.8 | 201.8 | 17 039 | 26 199 | 49 789 | 26.4 | 21.2 | 3.7 | 20.4 | 15.5 | 16.4 |
| Jackson, MI | 391 | 2 211 | 41 367 | 15.4 | 45.8 | 17.9 | 271.5 | 10 758 | 22 227 | 47 169 | 25.9 | 14.5 | 1.6 | 15.1 | 22.2 | 30.0 |
| Jackson, MS | 412 | 3 679 | 155 624 | 18.6 | 40.1 | 29.3 | 686.4 | 7 769 | 24 208 | 46 182 | 27.3 | 17.6 | 3.4 | 17.9 | 25.3 | 28.2 |
| Jackson, TN | 738 | 4 067 | 31 790 | 27.6 | 50.5 | 22.5 | 130.1 | 8 101 | 22 535 | 40 573 | 30.7 | 12.7 | 2.7 | 19.0 | 28.2 | 32.4 |
| Jacksonville, FL | 524 | 3 683 | 352 676 | 19.3 | 41.1 | 26.4 | 1 750.6 | 8 519 | 27 899 | 53 363 | 21.3 | 20.3 | 3.7 | 13.1 | 18.2 | 21.3 |
| Jacksonville, NC | 237 | 3 011 | 42 507 | 13.4 | 41.3 | 18.0 | 184.0 | 7 642 | 21 391 | 45 457 | 23.9 | 12.2 | 1.5 | 13.8 | 18.7 | 19.4 |
| Janesville, WI | 244 | 3 029 | 41 547 | 13.4 | 49.9 | 19.5 | 309.3 | 10 993 | 24 119 | 50 532 | 22.2 | 15.2 | 1.5 | 13.3 | 18.5 | 23.4 |
| Jefferson City, MO | 314 | 2 474 | 38 128 | 24.2 | 47.7 | 25.3 | 169.3 | 7 670 | 24 540 | 52 659 | 21.9 | 15.7 | 1.6 | 11.0 | 14.0 | 20.2 |
| Johnson City, TN | 327 | 3 038 | 48 401 | 10.7 | 50.7 | 22.9 | 211.2 | 7 753 | 22 484 | 38 002 | 33.3 | 12.1 | 2.3 | 19.0 | 24.8 | 29.8 |
| Johnstown, PA | 264 | 2 070 | 32 539 | 20.3 | 59.7 | 17.4 | 206.3 | 10 841 | 21 925 | 41 202 | 30.2 | 10.2 | 1.3 | 14.2 | 22.6 | 28.3 |
| Jonesboro, AR | 382 | 3 951 | 31 982 | 7.2 | 54.4 | 20.6 | 179.0 | 8 471 | 21 375 | 38 063 | 34.4 | 12.4 | 2.3 | 21.5 | 31.0 | 34.3 |
| Joplin, MO | 311 | 3 687 | 44 356 | 12.6 | 49.9 | 19.0 | 224.6 | 7 554 | 21 173 | 40 260 | 30.2 | 10.6 | 1.6 | 17.6 | 25.3 | 32.5 |
| Kalamazoo-Portage, MI | 362 | 2 802 | 100 846 | 10.8 | 37.5 | 29.6 | 539.1 | 10 254 | 24 746 | 45 679 | 27.4 | 16.5 | 2.7 | 18.7 | 22.1 | 29.1 |
| Kankakee-Bradley, IL | 392 | 2 963 | 30 792 | 19.0 | 49.6 | 17.3 | 199.3 | 10 178 | 23 190 | 49 266 | 24.2 | 16.7 | 1.7 | 15.0 | 21.3 | 23.9 |
| Kansas City, MO-KS | 477 | 3 405 | 532 853 | 18.0 | 37.3 | 32.5 | 3 313.8 | 9 787 | 29 321 | 56 613 | 20.0 | 23.0 | 3.9 | 11.5 | 16.0 | 20.2 |
| Kennewick-Pasco-Richland, WA | 256 | 2 651 | 67 256 | 10.0 | 42.2 | 24.2 | 439.5 | 8 957 | 24 993 | 56 407 | 20.3 | 22.6 | 3.2 | 14.8 | 21.6 | 25.1 |
| Killeen-Temple-Fort Hood, TX | 335 | 2 823 | 112 107 | 10.2 | 42.0 | 19.7 | 654.8 | 8 376 | 22 306 | 49 300 | 21.8 | 15.3 | 2.0 | 14.7 | 22.0 | 25.3 |
| Kingsport-Bristol-Bristol, TN-VA | 347 | 3 282 | 66 543 | 14.1 | 54.1 | 18.4 | 382.5 | 8 602 | 22 735 | 38 931 | 32.4 | 11.0 | 1.8 | 16.5 | 22.2 | 26.0 |
| Kingston, NY | 183 | 1 874 | 44 559 | 15.1 | 41.5 | 29.3 | 497.9 | 19 283 | 29 692 | 58 808 | 19.9 | 24.4 | 4.3 | 12.1 | 14.8 | 17.3 |
| Knoxville, TN | 463 | 3 833 | 168 998 | 15.6 | 43.4 | 28.6 | 795.6 | 8 114 | 26 667 | 46 666 | 26.1 | 16.7 | 3.2 | 14.0 | 18.5 | 23.8 |

1. Data for serious crimes have not been adjusted for underreporting; this may affect comparability between geographic areas and over time. 2. Per 100,000 population estimated by the FBI. 3. All persons 3 years old and over enrolled in nursery school through college. 4. Persons 25 years old and over. 5. Elementary and secondary education expenditures. 6. Based on resident population estimated as of July 1, 2009.

# Table C. Metropolitan Areas — **Personal Income**

| | | Personal income, 2011 | | | | | | | | | | | |
|---|---|---|---|---|---|---|---|---|---|---|---|---|---|
| | | Per capita[1] | | | | | Transfer payments | | | | | | |
| | | | | | | | | Government payments to individuals | | | | | |
| Area name | Total (mil dol) | Percent change, 2010–2011 | Dollars | Rank | Wages and salaries[2] (mil dol) | Proprietors' income (mil dol) | Dividends, interest, and rent (mil dol) | Total (mil dol) | Total (mil dol) | Social Security (mil dol) | Medical payments (mil dol) | Income mainte- nance (mil dol) | Unemploy- ment insurance (mil dol) |
| | 62 | 63 | 64 | 65 | 66 | 67 | 68 | 69 | 70 | 71 | 72 | 73 | 74 |
| Flagstaff, AZ.......................... | 4 621 | 3.9 | 34 353 | 247 | 2 901 | 352 | 750 | 947 | 917 | 207 | 434 | 125 | 32 |
| Flint, MI............................... | 13 108 | 4.6 | 31 057 | 330 | 6 908 | 698 | 1 573 | 4 291 | 4 198 | 1 340 | 1 673 | 679 | 169 |
| Florence, SC......................... | 6 754 | 3.0 | 32 762 | 287 | 4 271 | 367 | 834 | 1 903 | 1 857 | 542 | 786 | 306 | 61 |
| Florence-Muscle Shoals, AL. | 4 719 | 3.1 | 32 038 | 301 | 2 458 | 340 | 758 | 1 240 | 1 207 | 490 | 450 | 136 | 32 |
| Fond du Lac, WI................... | 3 766 | 4.5 | 36 897 | 178 | 2 255 | 288 | 571 | 717 | 695 | 272 | 293 | 47 | 35 |
| Fort Collins-Loveland, CO .... | 12 150 | 6.1 | 39 767 | 115 | 7 329 | 898 | 2 320 | 1 684 | 1 617 | 610 | 623 | 126 | 97 |
| Fort Smith, AR-OK................ | 9 537 | 3.7 | 31 782 | 306 | 5 408 | 782 | 1 529 | 2 488 | 2 421 | 807 | 1 037 | 297 | 71 |
| Fort Wayne, IN..................... | 14 698 | 5.5 | 35 042 | 223 | 10 496 | 1 044 | 2 162 | 2 824 | 2 731 | 1 045 | 1 057 | 312 | 132 |
| Fresno, CA........................... | 29 741 | 4.2 | 31 542 | 313 | 17 073 | 3 419 | 4 265 | 7 111 | 6 902 | 1 446 | 2 939 | 1 390 | 518 |
| Gadsden, AL......................... | 3 321 | 2.8 | 31 844 | 304 | 1 555 | 220 | 462 | 967 | 944 | 347 | 386 | 116 | 20 |
| Gainesville, FL..................... | 9 455 | 3.6 | 35 497 | 206 | 6 708 | 385 | 1 830 | 1 768 | 1 709 | 537 | 711 | 213 | 37 |
| Gainesville, GA..................... | 5 858 | 6.6 | 32 001 | 303 | 3 833 | 402 | 1 010 | 1 108 | 1 067 | 410 | 402 | 135 | 40 |
| Glens Falls, NY.................... | 4 801 | 4.7 | 37 216 | 170 | 2 655 | 252 | 910 | 1 102 | 1 073 | 403 | 454 | 102 | 52 |
| Goldsboro, NC...................... | 3 865 | 5.8 | 31 245 | 327 | 2 421 | 149 | 498 | 992 | 965 | 287 | 413 | 138 | 38 |
| Grand Forks, ND-MN.......... | 3 862 | 5.9 | 39 382 | 124 | 2 563 | 419 | 601 | 657 | 635 | 199 | 274 | 68 | 20 |
| Grand Junction, CO............. | 5 173 | 5.1 | 35 169 | 219 | 3 056 | 372 | 970 | 1 026 | 993 | 349 | 382 | 96 | 61 |
| Grand Rapids-Wyoming, MI.................................... | 27 305 | 6.6 | 35 024 | 225 | 19 569 | 2 677 | 3 649 | 5 190 | 5 017 | 1 863 | 1 829 | 734 | 248 |
| Great Falls, MT.................... | 3 228 | 4.0 | 39 448 | 122 | 1 965 | 299 | 604 | 630 | 612 | 211 | 240 | 56 | 18 |
| Greeley, CO.......................... | 7 756 | 7.2 | 29 986 | 340 | 4 513 | 786 | 1 119 | 1 349 | 1 292 | 425 | 526 | 141 | 92 |
| Green Bay, WI...................... | 12 084 | 4.3 | 39 046 | 129 | 9 043 | 958 | 1 946 | 1 871 | 1 803 | 735 | 651 | 173 | 115 |
| Greensboro-High Point, NC.. | 25 880 | 4.6 | 35 405 | 210 | 18 115 | 1 754 | 4 084 | 5 474 | 5 312 | 1 872 | 2 081 | 667 | 340 |
| Greenville, NC...................... | 6 188 | 5.1 | 32 111 | 299 | 3 833 | 328 | 826 | 1 378 | 1 336 | 371 | 562 | 206 | 71 |
| Greenville-Mauldin-Easley, SC.................................... | 22 684 | 5.4 | 35 038 | 224 | 15 966 | 1 382 | 3 099 | 4 700 | 4 557 | 1 725 | 1 778 | 505 | 153 |
| Gulfport-Biloxi, MS.............. | 8 853 | 1.8 | 34 922 | 228 | 6 246 | 604 | 1 308 | 2 004 | 1 920 | 578 | 909 | 232 | 40 |
| Hagerstown-Martinsburg, MD-WV.............................. | 9 395 | 5.0 | 34 604 | 239 | 5 116 | 455 | 1 236 | 1 926 | 1 866 | 683 | 729 | 213 | 79 |
| Hanford-Corcoran, CA......... | 4 522 | 9.7 | 29 407 | 349 | 2 678 | 702 | 544 | 887 | 854 | 182 | 362 | 155 | 64 |
| Harrisburg-Carlisle, PA........ | 22 751 | 4.8 | 41 148 | 86 | 18 682 | 1 483 | 3 378 | 4 164 | 4 042 | 1 458 | 1 687 | 322 | 232 |
| Harrisonburg, VA.................. | 3 964 | 4.9 | 31 324 | 323 | 2 890 | 293 | 720 | 690 | 662 | 273 | 245 | 78 | 19 |
| Hartford-West Hartford-East Hartford, CT....................... | 64 401 | 5.1 | 53 081 | 12 | 45 420 | 6 156 | 11 209 | 9 871 | 9 603 | 3 144 | 4 471 | 881 | 664 |
| Hattiesburg, MS................... | 4 544 | 4.3 | 31 248 | 326 | 2 743 | 418 | 645 | 1 078 | 1 045 | 323 | 468 | 141 | 23 |
| Hickory-Lenoir-Morganton, NC.................................... | 11 249 | 4.5 | 30 857 | 334 | 6 592 | 788 | 1 632 | 2 997 | 2 916 | 1 078 | 1 171 | 333 | 182 |
| Hinesville-Fort Stewart, GA .. | 2 154 | 7.1 | 26 726 | 361 | 3 181 | 46 | 269 | 432 | 418 | 85 | 148 | 90 | 21 |
| Holland-Grand Haven, MI ..... | 8 995 | 5.7 | 33 777 | 261 | 5 482 | 436 | 1 463 | 1 481 | 1 422 | 638 | 477 | 119 | 84 |
| Honolulu, HI......................... | 44 927 | 6.0 | 46 624 | 31 | 31 532 | 2 664 | 7 782 | 6 328 | 6 125 | 2 101 | 2 401 | 859 | 297 |
| Hot Springs, AR.................. | 3 434 | 4.8 | 35 355 | 211 | 1 531 | 213 | 874 | 1 007 | 985 | 375 | 429 | 88 | 22 |
| Houma-Bayou Cane-Thibo- daux, LA........................... | 8 843 | 4.1 | 42 393 | 72 | 5 603 | 1 085 | 1 146 | 1 497 | 1 436 | 482 | 666 | 194 | 23 |
| Houston-Sugar Land-Bay- town, TX........................... | 289 790 | 7.9 | 47 612 | 27 | 192 865 | 47 331 | 38 272 | 33 311 | 31 944 | 9 372 | 14 349 | 4 802 | 1 365 |
| Huntington-Ashland, WV- KY-OH.............................. | 9 437 | 3.9 | 32 811 | 284 | 5 799 | 423 | 1 060 | 2 784 | 2 720 | 876 | 1 110 | 344 | 73 |
| Huntsville, AL....................... | 17 073 | 4.9 | 40 126 | 102 | 14 274 | 942 | 2 712 | 2 588 | 2 493 | 944 | 900 | 296 | 78 |
| Idaho Falls, ID..................... | 4 427 | 5.1 | 33 520 | 266 | 2 143 | 625 | 640 | 773 | 744 | 259 | 307 | 98 | 30 |
| Indianapolis-Carmel, IN ........ | 72 161 | 5.5 | 40 572 | 95 | 52 591 | 6 321 | 9 132 | 11 549 | 11 155 | 3 922 | 4 132 | 1 307 | 538 |
| Iowa City, IA........................ | 6 393 | 7.5 | 41 277 | 84 | 4 763 | 569 | 1 024 | 767 | 732 | 285 | 275 | 82 | 29 |
| Ithaca, NY............................ | 3 689 | 4.2 | 36 263 | 189 | 2 870 | 213 | 750 | 602 | 579 | 205 | 220 | 63 | 31 |
| Jackson, MI.......................... | 5 015 | 5.4 | 31 396 | 318 | 2 922 | 256 | 677 | 1 313 | 1 278 | 476 | 497 | 161 | 56 |
| Jackson, MS......................... | 20 476 | 4.7 | 37 544 | 161 | 13 289 | 2 230 | 2 674 | 4 102 | 3 977 | 1 231 | 1 726 | 649 | 81 |
| Jackson, TN.......................... | 3 951 | 4.7 | 34 237 | 251 | 2 792 | 396 | 488 | 964 | 939 | 295 | 387 | 140 | 31 |
| Jacksonville, FL.................... | 55 375 | 4.6 | 40 709 | 92 | 35 754 | 3 274 | 10 491 | 9 740 | 9 440 | 3 075 | 3 829 | 1 204 | 335 |
| Jacksonville, NC .................. | 8 296 | 5.1 | 46 163 | 32 | 7 095 | 186 | 761 | 1 007 | 978 | 243 | 362 | 134 | 46 |
| Janesville, WI....................... | 5 332 | 4.3 | 33 305 | 275 | 3 090 | 260 | 841 | 1 180 | 1 145 | 440 | 436 | 129 | 86 |
| Jefferson City, MO............... | 5 335 | 3.5 | 35 453 | 208 | 3 759 | 444 | 775 | 1 020 | 987 | 363 | 427 | 96 | 30 |
| Johnson City, TN ................. | 6 543 | 5.3 | 32 745 | 288 | 3 652 | 412 | 844 | 1 748 | 1 704 | 599 | 722 | 184 | 42 |
| Johnstown, PA...................... | 4 716 | 4.1 | 32 810 | 285 | 2 658 | 272 | 644 | 1 508 | 1 476 | 471 | 691 | 117 | 95 |
| Jonesboro, AR...................... | 3 948 | 5.5 | 32 141 | 296 | 2 296 | 450 | 507 | 995 | 968 | 304 | 427 | 126 | 29 |
| Joplin, MO............................ | 5 555 | 4.5 | 31 408 | 316 | 3 644 | 378 | 813 | 1 362 | 1 323 | 435 | 599 | 157 | 38 |
| Kalamazoo-Portage, MI ........ | 11 419 | 4.7 | 34 792 | 229 | 7 257 | 582 | 1 864 | 2 474 | 2 401 | 865 | 930 | 335 | 112 |
| Kankakee-Bradley, IL............ | 3 771 | 3.2 | 33 171 | 278 | 2 057 | 198 | 524 | 888 | 863 | 285 | 356 | 112 | 58 |
| Kansas City, MO-KS............. | 88 392 | 4.6 | 43 062 | 62 | 60 275 | 9 046 | 12 939 | 13 748 | 13 294 | 4 670 | 5 784 | 1 346 | 582 |
| Kennewick-Pasco-Richland, WA.................................... | 9 652 | 6.0 | 36 544 | 184 | 6 698 | 792 | 1 323 | 1 715 | 1 657 | 508 | 631 | 243 | 94 |
| Killeen-Temple-Fort Hood, TX.................................... | 16 476 | 7.3 | 40 029 | 105 | 12 206 | 822 | 1 810 | 2 630 | 2 550 | 631 | 904 | 343 | 112 |
| Kingsport-Bristol-Bristol, TN- VA.................................... | 10 234 | 5.2 | 33 035 | 282 | 6 253 | 542 | 1 468 | 2 886 | 2 818 | 1 110 | 1 148 | 308 | 61 |
| Kingston, NY........................ | 7 223 | 3.7 | 39 589 | 120 | 3 004 | 378 | 1 400 | 1 548 | 1 508 | 531 | 682 | 150 | 69 |
| Knoxville, TN........................ | 26 037 | 5.0 | 36 958 | 177 | 17 668 | 2 694 | 3 567 | 5 279 | 5 123 | 1 961 | 2 071 | 591 | 154 |

1. Based on the resident population estimated as of July 1 of the year shown.    2. Includes other labor income.

# Table C. Metropolitan Areas — **Earnings, Social Security, and Housing**

| | Earnings, 2011 | | | | | | | | | Social Security beneficiaries, December 2011 | | | | Housing units, 2010 | |
| | | Percent by selected industries | | | | | | | | | | | | | |
| | | | Goods-related[1] | | Service-related and health | | | | | | | | | | |
| Area name | Total (mil dol) | Farm | Total | Manu-facturing | Infor-mation, profes-sional, and technical services | Retail trade | Finance, insur-ance, and real estate | Health care and social services | Govern-ment | Number | Rate[2] | Supple-mental Security Income recipients, December 2011 | Total | Percent change, 2000–2010 |
| | 75 | 76 | 77 | 78 | 79 | 80 | 81 | 82 | 83 | 84 | 85 | 86 | 87 | 88 |
| Flagstaff, AZ | 3 253 | 0.3 | 14.6 | 10.2 | 3.6 | 7.2 | 4.6 | 16.2 | 32.3 | 16 695 | 124 | 2 832 | 63 321 | 18.5 |
| Flint, MI | 7 606 | 0.2 | 16.2 | 12.3 | 8.6 | 8.4 | 6.1 | 18.6 | 18.6 | 94 095 | 223 | 16 331 | 192 180 | 4.7 |
| Florence, SC | 4 638 | 0.3 | 20.6 | 17.1 | 6.2 | 7.8 | 11.5 | 12.5 | 19.2 | 43 900 | 213 | 8 590 | 88 963 | 10.1 |
| Florence-Muscle Shoals, AL. | 2 798 | 2.4 | 23.3 | 15.4 | 3.7 | 10.0 | 4.0 | 12.7 | 23.1 | 37 495 | 255 | 5 060 | 69 549 | 6.3 |
| Fond du Lac, WI | 2 542 | 3.8 | 33.3 | 25.0 | 4.2 | 6.7 | 4.6 | 13.2 | 12.8 | 20 080 | 197 | 1 366 | 43 910 | 11.8 |
| Fort Collins-Loveland, CO .... | 8 227 | 0.4 | 21.6 | 13.6 | 13.5 | 6.8 | 5.7 | 13.0 | 20.0 | 46 310 | 152 | 2 536 | 132 722 | 25.9 |
| Fort Smith, AR-OK | 6 190 | 0.6 | 27.3 | 17.9 | D | 7.1 | 4.2 | D | 17.6 | 67 290 | 224 | 10 862 | 128 891 | 11.7 |
| Fort Wayne, IN | 11 539 | 0.6 | 26.2 | 20.4 | 7.1 | 6.0 | 7.1 | 15.6 | 11.0 | 74 850 | 178 | 7 854 | 178 124 | 9.7 |
| Fresno, CA | 20 492 | 7.9 | 12.0 | 7.1 | 6.3 | 6.8 | 5.5 | 12.8 | 21.9 | 121 670 | 129 | 42 186 | 315 531 | 16.6 |
| Gadsden, AL | 1 776 | -0.7 | 21.5 | 16.4 | 4.1 | 8.4 | 4.8 | D | 16.8 | 27 415 | 263 | 4 729 | 47 454 | 3.3 |
| Gainesville, FL | 7 093 | 0.5 | 7.5 | 4.3 | 7.6 | 6.2 | 5.5 | 17.2 | 39.5 | 41 185 | 155 | 5 858 | 120 073 | 18.9 |
| Gainesville, GA | 4 234 | 0.1 | 24.6 | 19.3 | 4.1 | 6.9 | 8.0 | 15.1 | 12.9 | 30 295 | 165 | 2 812 | 68 825 | 34.8 |
| Glens Falls, NY | 2 908 | 0.9 | 22.1 | 15.5 | D | 8.3 | 4.4 | 14.1 | 21.1 | 30 575 | 237 | 3 343 | 67 570 | 9.6 |
| Goldsboro, NC | 2 570 | 2.2 | 16.9 | 10.8 | 3.1 | 6.4 | 3.5 | 11.5 | 37.4 | 24 185 | 196 | 4 673 | 52 949 | 11.9 |
| Grand Forks, ND-MN | 2 983 | 8.0 | 12.4 | 6.2 | 4.6 | 8.0 | 4.0 | 15.6 | 28.1 | 15 730 | 160 | 1 317 | 43 954 | 6.2 |
| Grand Junction, CO | 3 428 | 0.2 | 21.0 | 4.1 | 6.8 | 8.0 | 6.7 | 15.1 | 17.4 | 28 070 | 191 | 2 288 | 62 644 | 28.6 |
| Grand Rapids-Wyoming, MI | 22 247 | 1.2 | 24.4 | 19.7 | 8.2 | 6.7 | 8.6 | 13.8 | 10.0 | 136 205 | 175 | 18 232 | 323 764 | 10.5 |
| Great Falls, MT | 2 264 | 0.6 | 9.8 | 2.8 | 6.4 | 7.8 | 7.4 | 16.3 | 30.2 | 17 085 | 209 | 1 859 | 37 276 | 5.8 |
| Greeley, CO | 5 299 | 4.0 | 30.1 | 11.7 | 4.4 | 6.0 | 6.0 | 8.6 | 14.5 | 33 650 | 130 | 3 292 | 96 281 | 45.5 |
| Green Bay, WI | 10 000 | 1.9 | 23.1 | 18.0 | D | 5.5 | 8.2 | 12.5 | 11.8 | 55 135 | 178 | 5 264 | 137 212 | 16.0 |
| Greensboro-High Point, NC.. | 19 869 | 0.2 | 22.3 | 17.2 | 8.2 | 6.6 | 8.9 | 11.7 | 12.9 | 139 535 | 191 | 16 319 | 322 754 | 17.4 |
| Greenville, NC | 4 161 | 1.3 | 15.2 | 10.9 | 4.3 | 7.1 | 4.5 | 12.4 | 37.3 | 30 125 | 156 | 6 432 | 83 203 | 26.6 |
| Greenville-Mauldin-Easley, SC | 17 348 | -0.1 | 20.6 | 15.5 | 10.7 | 7.0 | 6.3 | 9.1 | 14.8 | 128 565 | 199 | 13 172 | 277 415 | 16.1 |
| Gulfport-Biloxi, MS | 6 850 | 0.0 | D | 6.2 | 6.3 | 6.5 | 3.5 | 6.5 | 38.3 | 47 185 | 186 | 7 372 | 114 182 | 7.7 |
| Hagerstown-Martinsburg, MD-WV | 5 571 | 0.7 | 16.3 | 10.8 | 7.2 | 8.9 | 8.5 | 14.0 | 24.0 | 51 850 | 191 | 5 534 | 115 329 | 22.7 |
| Hanford-Corcoran, CA | 3 380 | 18.1 | 10.7 | 8.3 | 2.0 | 4.4 | 1.8 | 8.2 | 42.3 | 16 130 | 105 | 4 711 | 43 867 | 20.0 |
| Harrisburg-Carlisle, PA | 20 165 | 0.5 | 12.2 | 7.6 | 9.4 | 5.2 | 9.1 | 14.0 | 21.6 | 107 055 | 194 | 10 243 | 240 818 | 11.0 |
| Harrisonburg, VA | 3 183 | 2.5 | 26.4 | 19.7 | 7.7 | 7.9 | 3.8 | 11.8 | 17.5 | 21 030 | 166 | 1 651 | 51 104 | 24.6 |
| Hartford-West Hartford-East Hartford, CT | 51 575 | 0.1 | 17.2 | 12.6 | 10.6 | 5.0 | 19.9 | 12.0 | 15.2 | 219 435 | 181 | 22 372 | 507 049 | 7.5 |
| Hattiesburg, MS | 3 161 | 0.5 | 12.9 | 6.7 | D | 9.4 | 4.7 | 18.0 | 27.2 | 25 920 | 178 | 4 681 | 61 878 | 22.6 |
| Hickory-Lenoir-Morganton, NC | 7 380 | 0.7 | 29.8 | 26.0 | D | 7.3 | 3.6 | 12.2 | 16.4 | 82 880 | 227 | 7 308 | 162 613 | 12.2 |
| Hinesville-Fort Stewart, GA .. | 3 227 | 0.1 | 5.1 | 3.8 | 1.3 | 1.9 | 1.1 | 1.2 | 83.0 | 7 460 | 93 | 1 380 | 32 770 | 25.0 |
| Holland-Grand Haven, MI ..... | 5 918 | 2.4 | 39.5 | 34.8 | 5.1 | 5.1 | 3.8 | 6.9 | 15.3 | 44 880 | 169 | 2 650 | 102 495 | 18.0 |
| Honolulu, HI | 34 196 | 0.2 | 8.5 | 1.9 | 7.9 | 5.2 | 5.6 | 9.5 | 39.2 | 159 550 | 166 | 17 144 | 336 899 | 6.6 |
| Hot Springs, AR | 1 744 | 0.3 | 13.5 | 6.3 | 5.9 | 11.7 | 6.2 | 22.7 | 16.9 | 28 795 | 296 | 3 636 | 50 548 | 12.4 |
| Houma-Bayou Cane-Thibo-daux, LA | 6 687 | 0.5 | 27.1 | 12.1 | 4.1 | 5.7 | 5.7 | 7.8 | 11.6 | 38 305 | 184 | 8 117 | 82 469 | 10.0 |
| Houston-Sugar Land-Bay-town, TX | 240 196 | 0.1 | 29.5 | 10.7 | 12.8 | 4.7 | 7.3 | 7.2 | 10.0 | 693 750 | 114 | 132 214 | 2 308 205 | 28.3 |
| Huntington-Ashland, WV-KY-OH | 6 222 | -0.1 | 18.2 | 11.8 | 5.3 | 7.5 | 3.3 | 21.4 | 19.3 | 68 625 | 239 | 14 754 | 131 132 | 1.0 |
| Huntsville, AL | 15 217 | 0.6 | 14.8 | 11.3 | 23.7 | 5.3 | 2.8 | 6.3 | 32.4 | 71 970 | 169 | 8 715 | 181 424 | 23.2 |
| Idaho Falls, ID | 2 768 | 5.6 | 13.2 | 5.8 | 10.3 | 9.4 | 4.8 | 15.0 | 13.7 | 20 110 | 152 | 2 176 | 48 453 | 31.8 |
| Indianapolis-Carmel, IN | 58 912 | 0.4 | 20.4 | 14.2 | 10.7 | 5.8 | 8.6 | 12.6 | 13.7 | 279 495 | 157 | 31 048 | 757 441 | 17.5 |
| Iowa City, IA | 5 332 | 3.5 | 12.2 | 7.4 | 6.2 | 5.5 | 4.0 | 7.4 | 41.8 | 20 210 | 130 | 1 826 | 65 483 | 20.4 |
| Ithaca, NY | 3 083 | 0.8 | 11.2 | 8.0 | 7.5 | 5.2 | 3.4 | D | 13.3 | 14 545 | 143 | 1 747 | 41 674 | 7.9 |
| Jackson, MI | 3 177 | 1.0 | 21.8 | 18.2 | 4.4 | 6.9 | 3.2 | 14.7 | 17.8 | 34 465 | 216 | 4 288 | 69 458 | 10.4 |
| Jackson, MS | 15 519 | 0.4 | 14.7 | 6.6 | 8.9 | 6.8 | 8.6 | 12.6 | 23.1 | 95 320 | 175 | 18 722 | 222 584 | 13.2 |
| Jackson, TN | 3 189 | 1.1 | 24.2 | 16.5 | D | 7.8 | 3.8 | 12.7 | 22.0 | 23 340 | 202 | 3 617 | 48 857 | 10.1 |
| Jacksonville, FL | 39 028 | 0.1 | 9.9 | 5.4 | 10.8 | 6.9 | 13.3 | 12.4 | 18.5 | 235 230 | 173 | 29 020 | 598 490 | 26.0 |
| Jacksonville, NC | 7 280 | 0.3 | 3.0 | 0.6 | 1.9 | 3.2 | 1.3 | 2.3 | 81.1 | 20 805 | 116 | 2 650 | 68 226 | 22.4 |
| Janesville, WI | 3 350 | 2.4 | 23.2 | 17.5 | 4.3 | 9.2 | 3.4 | 16.5 | 15.5 | 32 180 | 201 | 3 582 | 68 422 | 10.0 |
| Jefferson City, MO | 4 203 | 2.2 | 14.3 | 7.4 | 7.7 | 6.2 | 4.6 | D | 33.2 | 28 730 | 191 | 2 737 | 63 555 | 12.0 |
| Johnson City, TN | 4 063 | -0.1 | 17.1 | 12.0 | 6.0 | 8.0 | 5.1 | D | 22.7 | 48 550 | 243 | 5 987 | 93 830 | 14.5 |
| Johnstown, PA | 2 930 | 0.3 | 13.9 | 8.4 | 8.3 | 7.9 | 5.5 | 21.6 | 18.6 | 37 310 | 260 | 5 123 | 65 650 | -0.2 |
| Jonesboro, AR | 2 746 | 4.9 | 18.6 | 13.6 | 3.8 | 7.7 | 5.7 | 19.4 | 17.6 | 25 345 | 206 | 5 504 | 51 438 | 11.4 |
| Joplin, MO | 4 023 | 1.2 | 22.2 | 17.8 | 3.7 | 8.6 | 3.8 | 15.3 | 12.5 | 35 915 | 203 | 4 446 | 74 981 | 11.1 |
| Kalamazoo-Portage, MI | 7 840 | 2.0 | 25.2 | 20.6 | 6.2 | 6.0 | 6.8 | 15.0 | 15.7 | 62 600 | 191 | 8 180 | 146 792 | 10.2 |
| Kankakee-Bradley, IL | 2 256 | 4.4 | 20.2 | 16.2 | D | 7.6 | 4.7 | 18.1 | 17.5 | 21 340 | 188 | 2 731 | 45 246 | 11.4 |
| Kansas City, MO-KS | 69 320 | 0.4 | 14.6 | 9.0 | 17.1 | 5.8 | 9.8 | 10.3 | 15.8 | 336 385 | 164 | 32 497 | 883 099 | 15.0 |
| Kennewick-Pasco-Richland, WA | 7 490 | 6.2 | 12.6 | 5.6 | 17.8 | 5.8 | 2.9 | 8.3 | 17.0 | 36 875 | 140 | 4 985 | 93 041 | 29.1 |
| Killeen-Temple-Fort Hood, TX | 13 028 | 0.1 | 7.2 | 2.9 | 4.6 | 4.3 | 2.3 | 8.4 | 61.2 | 54 210 | 132 | 8 408 | 159 366 | 30.5 |
| Kingsport-Bristol-Bristol, TN-VA | 6 795 | -0.2 | D | 26.3 | 4.5 | 7.5 | 3.5 | D | 12.5 | 87 355 | 282 | 10 761 | 146 978 | 7.9 |
| Kingston, NY | 3 382 | 0.7 | 11.9 | 6.9 | 6.0 | 10.0 | 4.3 | 13.4 | 30.8 | 38 440 | 211 | 4 554 | 83 638 | 7.8 |
| Knoxville, TN | 20 362 | 0.0 | 18.3 | 11.0 | 12.5 | 7.6 | 6.1 | 13.7 | 15.0 | 146 470 | 208 | 16 627 | 315 615 | 14.3 |

1. Includes mining, construction, and manufacturing.   2. Per 1,000 resident population estimated as of July 1, 2011.

# Table C. Metropolitan Areas — Housing, Labor Force, and Employment

| Area name | Housing units, 2007–2011 | | | | | | | | Civilian labor force, 2012 | | | | Civilian employment,[5] 2007–2011 | | |
|---|---|---|---|---|---|---|---|---|---|---|---|---|---|---|---|
| | Occupied units | | | | | | | | | | Unemployment | | | Percent | |
| | | | Owner-occupied | | | Renter-occupied | | | | | | | | | |
| | | | | Median owner cost as a percent of income | | | | | | | | | | | |
| | Total | Percent | Median value[1] | With a mortgage | Without a mortgage | Median rent[2] | Median rent as a percent of income | Substandard units[3] (percent) | Total | Percent change, 2011–2012 | Total | Rate[4] | Total | Management, professional, and related occupations | Construction, production, and related occupations |
| | 89 | 90 | 91 | 92 | 93 | 94 | 95 | 96 | 97 | 98 | 99 | 100 | 101 | 102 | 103 |
| Flagstaff, AZ | 45 266 | 61.3 | 246 600 | 25.6 | 10.0 | 927 | 32.2 | 9.4 | 72 988 | -1.0 | 5 936 | 8.1 | 65 122 | 32.2 | 20.3 |
| Flint, MI | 166 479 | 71.0 | 109 000 | 24.8 | 14.1 | 685 | 34.6 | 1.9 | 184 149 | -1.1 | 17 414 | 9.5 | 164 803 | 30.2 | 24.0 |
| Florence, SC | 77 787 | 68.3 | 99 900 | 21.3 | 10.3 | 617 | 29.8 | 2.6 | 93 278 | -0.3 | 9 370 | 10.0 | 86 599 | 30.7 | 25.6 |
| Florence-Muscle Shoals, AL. | 60 637 | 71.8 | 104 200 | 21.5 | 11.3 | 579 | 30.6 | 1.4 | 69 322 | -1.2 | 4 851 | 7.0 | 61 620 | 27.8 | 29.1 |
| Fond du Lac, WI | 40 832 | 71.7 | 145 200 | 23.6 | 13.5 | 650 | 27.6 | 1.8 | 54 769 | -0.5 | 3 596 | 6.6 | 52 953 | 26.7 | 33.4 |
| Fort Collins-Loveland, CO | 118 791 | 67.0 | 244 600 | 25.1 | 10.0 | 887 | 33.8 | 1.6 | 180 713 | 1.2 | 11 637 | 6.4 | 154 002 | 42.9 | 17.2 |
| Fort Smith, AR-OK | 112 570 | 68.6 | 95 600 | 20.3 | 10.9 | 573 | 28.1 | 3.3 | 133 028 | -0.2 | 10 238 | 7.7 | 124 318 | 27.2 | 32.2 |
| Fort Wayne, IN | 160 073 | 72.2 | 113 700 | 20.5 | 10.0 | 640 | 26.7 | 1.7 | 204 886 | -1.1 | 16 856 | 8.2 | 194 158 | 32.8 | 25.9 |
| Fresno, CA | 285 338 | 55.0 | 236 400 | 27.9 | 10.9 | 850 | 33.7 | 10.7 | 442 453 | -0.3 | 67 426 | 15.2 | 367 858 | 28.5 | 28.5 |
| Gadsden, AL | 41 160 | 73.3 | 102 000 | 22.3 | 13.1 | 600 | 28.5 | 2.2 | 45 402 | -0.9 | 3 275 | 7.2 | 40 621 | 29.5 | 31.0 |
| Gainesville, FL | 103 551 | 56.0 | 179 100 | 24.8 | 11.5 | 876 | 38.0 | 2.4 | 141 552 | 1.2 | 9 496 | 6.7 | 122 405 | 44.2 | 12.5 |
| Gainesville, GA | 60 939 | 69.6 | 174 400 | 25.0 | 11.1 | 838 | 30.5 | 5.3 | 90 910 | 1.7 | 6 814 | 7.5 | 80 531 | 28.9 | 34.2 |
| Glens Falls, NY | 53 074 | 71.6 | 164 800 | 24.3 | 14.2 | 785 | 30.7 | 1.7 | 67 507 | -0.1 | 5 572 | 8.3 | 61 050 | 31.1 | 26.3 |
| Goldsboro, NC | 47 027 | 63.0 | 107 200 | 22.9 | 12.0 | 646 | 28.8 | 2.7 | 55 038 | 1.3 | 4 925 | 8.9 | 50 590 | 29.3 | 30.2 |
| Grand Forks, ND-MN | 39 202 | 60.6 | 136 000 | 21.1 | 12.1 | 639 | 30.4 | 1.1 | 54 282 | -1.3 | 2 286 | 4.2 | 52 422 | 33.7 | 22.3 |
| Grand Junction, CO | 58 288 | 71.9 | 222 800 | 24.4 | 10.0 | 837 | 29.9 | 3.2 | 78 619 | -0.1 | 7 235 | 9.2 | 69 053 | 33.0 | 25.4 |
| Grand Rapids-Wyoming, MI | 291 565 | 73.5 | 141 100 | 23.8 | 13.1 | 710 | 31.1 | 2.2 | 390 584 | 1.3 | 26 423 | 6.8 | 360 534 | 32.8 | 25.7 |
| Great Falls, MT | 33 134 | 67.0 | 151 200 | 23.2 | 11.8 | 564 | 24.8 | 2.6 | 40 281 | 0.2 | 2 165 | 5.4 | 36 731 | 31.2 | 22.6 |
| Greeley, CO | 88 242 | 71.1 | 193 300 | 25.4 | 11.2 | 801 | 31.9 | 4.4 | 124 972 | 1.2 | 10 915 | 8.7 | 119 511 | 32.8 | 26.4 |
| Green Bay, WI | 122 010 | 69.9 | 157 700 | 23.7 | 13.3 | 658 | 27.4 | 2.2 | 172 743 | -0.1 | 11 197 | 6.5 | 156 310 | 31.1 | 27.5 |
| Greensboro-High Point, NC. | 284 797 | 66.2 | 140 900 | 23.5 | 11.3 | 695 | 30.0 | 2.6 | 374 408 | 0.7 | 37 102 | 9.9 | 335 532 | 32.4 | 25.6 |
| Greenville, NC | 71 576 | 57.0 | 124 100 | 23.2 | 14.2 | 689 | 33.9 | 2.6 | 99 070 | 2.7 | 9 239 | 9.3 | 86 012 | 36.3 | 21.8 |
| Greenville-Mauldin-Easley, SC | 242 048 | 68.7 | 139 500 | 21.8 | 10.2 | 693 | 29.8 | 1.8 | 315 921 | -0.3 | 23 725 | 7.5 | 285 928 | 34.2 | 24.5 |
| Gulfport-Biloxi, MS | 92 633 | 67.9 | 144 500 | 24.5 | 11.9 | 841 | 32.6 | 3.4 | 116 170 | -0.8 | 10 047 | 8.6 | 106 865 | 29.4 | 24.3 |
| Hagerstown-Martinsburg, MD-WV | 101 959 | 70.2 | 206 000 | 24.6 | 11.6 | 769 | 29.9 | 1.8 | 125 495 | 1.4 | 9 849 | 7.8 | 126 038 | 30.4 | 25.8 |
| Hanford-Corcoran, CA | 40 716 | 54.6 | 208 100 | 27.1 | 10.2 | 864 | 29.7 | 8.9 | 60 886 | -0.1 | 9 321 | 15.3 | 52 895 | 24.2 | 35.0 |
| Harrisburg-Carlisle, PA | 220 557 | 69.4 | 166 200 | 22.8 | 12.4 | 794 | 26.9 | 1.4 | 288 316 | 1.2 | 20 784 | 7.2 | 274 218 | 36.7 | 20.9 |
| Harrisonburg, VA | 44 890 | 63.2 | 203 000 | 23.9 | 10.0 | 789 | 29.4 | 3.6 | 67 014 | -0.4 | 3 943 | 5.9 | 57 919 | 30.7 | 29.6 |
| Hartford-West Hartford-East Hartford, CT | 469 622 | 68.8 | 258 200 | 25.1 | 15.8 | 954 | 30.5 | 2.0 | 639 837 | -1.3 | 53 046 | 8.3 | 604 839 | 41.4 | 17.2 |
| Hattiesburg, MS | 53 978 | 65.2 | 126 300 | 22.4 | 11.6 | 696 | 33.3 | 2.8 | 68 724 | 0.0 | 5 513 | 8.0 | 62 788 | 34.3 | 23.7 |
| Hickory-Lenoir-Morganton, NC | 138 715 | 73.7 | 118 700 | 22.2 | 11.1 | 614 | 29.0 | 2.6 | 169 360 | -0.2 | 18 550 | 11.0 | 160 507 | 27.4 | 33.6 |
| Hinesville-Fort Stewart, GA | 27 655 | 53.0 | 119 100 | 23.5 | 10.5 | 811 | 28.4 | 2.8 | 33 435 | -0.9 | 3 045 | 9.1 | 27 875 | 26.9 | 27.9 |
| Holland-Grand Haven, MI | 93 777 | 79.1 | 158 900 | 23.5 | 12.5 | 747 | 30.6 | 2.3 | 129 921 | 0.8 | 8 851 | 6.8 | 127 025 | 33.1 | 27.7 |
| Honolulu, HI | 307 248 | 56.9 | 560 300 | 28.9 | 10.0 | 1 381 | 33.5 | 9.1 | 457 990 | -0.4 | 23 651 | 5.2 | 441 581 | 35.3 | 17.8 |
| Hot Springs, AR | 40 002 | 70.1 | 128 400 | 23.9 | 10.8 | 693 | 30.5 | 2.6 | 42 431 | 0.6 | 3 183 | 7.5 | 39 255 | 30.3 | 23.5 |
| Houma-Bayou Cane-Thibodaux, LA | 73 514 | 75.8 | 122 400 | 19.8 | 10.0 | 697 | 28.5 | 5.0 | 103 869 | 2.1 | 4 670 | 4.5 | 91 682 | 26.8 | 34.1 |
| Houston-Sugar Land-Baytown, TX | 2 005 544 | 63.1 | 140 000 | 23.3 | 12.2 | 860 | 29.5 | 6.0 | 3 038 369 | 1.8 | 205 638 | 6.8 | 2 764 951 | 35.6 | 24.0 |
| Huntington-Ashland, WV-KY-OH | 115 539 | 70.0 | 93 600 | 20.2 | 10.6 | 586 | 30.8 | 1.6 | 127 300 | -1.2 | 9 408 | 7.4 | 114 034 | 31.7 | 23.1 |
| Huntsville, AL | 159 690 | 71.5 | 154 500 | 19.7 | 10.0 | 682 | 27.9 | 2.0 | 211 801 | -1.0 | 13 195 | 6.2 | 191 874 | 41.4 | 20.4 |
| Idaho Falls, ID | 44 004 | 75.1 | 157 600 | 22.9 | 10.0 | 694 | 29.4 | 2.7 | 63 654 | 1.1 | 3 832 | 6.0 | 58 011 | 34.8 | 23.8 |
| Indianapolis-Carmel, IN | 667 753 | 67.8 | 144 500 | 21.9 | 11.3 | 763 | 29.8 | 1.7 | 905 398 | 0.8 | 70 517 | 7.8 | 841 339 | 37.1 | 20.7 |
| Iowa City, IA | 60 715 | 62.6 | 168 900 | 22.0 | 11.1 | 756 | 33.9 | 2.0 | 91 508 | -1.0 | 3 544 | 3.9 | 85 114 | 42.5 | 16.9 |
| Ithaca, NY | 38 531 | 55.3 | 165 900 | 22.5 | 13.2 | 888 | 34.1 | 1.9 | 57 036 | 0.5 | 3 416 | 6.0 | 50 316 | 50.0 | 14.4 |
| Jackson, MI | 60 257 | 75.0 | 123 200 | 23.9 | 13.3 | 708 | 31.6 | 2.0 | 70 432 | -1.4 | 6 012 | 8.5 | 67 007 | 29.0 | 26.7 |
| Jackson, MS | 196 364 | 68.1 | 129 000 | 22.1 | 10.4 | 784 | 32.4 | 3.4 | 272 087 | 0.1 | 19 992 | 7.3 | 241 795 | 36.1 | 20.8 |
| Jackson, TN | 42 150 | 67.8 | 112 000 | 23.4 | 11.6 | 706 | 35.7 | 2.2 | 58 106 | -0.2 | 4 788 | 8.2 | 49 626 | 31.5 | 25.7 |
| Jacksonville, FL | 506 217 | 68.2 | 183 300 | 26.2 | 11.8 | 936 | 31.5 | 2.1 | 696 351 | 0.7 | 57 551 | 8.3 | 621 442 | 34.2 | 19.3 |
| Jacksonville, NC | 57 571 | 57.2 | 144 300 | 24.9 | 11.8 | 858 | 29.4 | 2.6 | 68 568 | 1.8 | 5 979 | 8.7 | 57 441 | 29.7 | 23.2 |
| Janesville, WI | 62 745 | 72.8 | 139 000 | 24.1 | 13.9 | 727 | 31.3 | 1.4 | 78 820 | 0.1 | 6 644 | 8.4 | 76 424 | 28.6 | 30.8 |
| Jefferson City, MO | 57 093 | 71.9 | 131 600 | 19.9 | 10.0 | 581 | 23.8 | 1.6 | 76 180 | -1.5 | 4 294 | 5.6 | 72 536 | 35.9 | 22.3 |
| Johnson City, TN | 82 150 | 68.9 | 123 700 | 23.0 | 10.7 | 592 | 29.1 | 1.3 | 100 299 | -1.5 | 7 330 | 7.3 | 86 989 | 32.9 | 23.1 |
| Johnstown, PA | 58 428 | 73.7 | 87 600 | 20.4 | 13.5 | 525 | 27.1 | 0.9 | 68 583 | 0.4 | 6 011 | 8.8 | 61 595 | 29.5 | 25.6 |
| Jonesboro, AR | 46 242 | 61.4 | 97 100 | 19.6 | 11.0 | 599 | 30.5 | 2.6 | 59 782 | 0.9 | 4 124 | 6.9 | 52 833 | 32.1 | 26.9 |
| Joplin, MO | 66 393 | 68.5 | 99 500 | 21.7 | 11.4 | 623 | 29.3 | 3.3 | 86 279 | -0.5 | 5 205 | 6.0 | 79 297 | 28.1 | 28.5 |
| Kalamazoo-Portage, MI | 128 449 | 68.4 | 139 300 | 23.4 | 13.3 | 687 | 34.7 | 1.4 | 160 635 | -1.4 | 12 147 | 7.6 | 150 510 | 34.7 | 22.8 |
| Kankakee-Bradley, IL | 41 086 | 69.9 | 147 700 | 24.8 | 14.0 | 755 | 32.2 | 2.2 | 55 825 | -0.4 | 6 176 | 11.1 | 50 002 | 28.9 | 28.0 |
| Kansas City, MO-KS | 792 861 | 68.2 | 159 600 | 22.6 | 12.5 | 786 | 28.5 | 1.9 | 1 043 558 | -0.3 | 69 394 | 6.6 | 1 003 959 | 38.1 | 19.9 |
| Kennewick-Pasco-Richland, WA | 85 244 | 68.9 | 167 500 | 21.3 | 10.0 | 743 | 28.8 | 4.2 | 132 482 | -1.1 | 11 753 | 8.9 | 110 265 | 33.5 | 27.9 |
| Killeen-Temple-Fort Hood, TX | 129 748 | 58.8 | 114 500 | 22.6 | 11.5 | 839 | 28.3 | 3.1 | 170 188 | -0.2 | 12 748 | 7.5 | 149 925 | 31.3 | 22.5 |
| Kingsport-Bristol-Bristol, TN-VA | 130 899 | 74.6 | 113 500 | 22.1 | 10.4 | 562 | 27.8 | 1.7 | 146 988 | -1.3 | 10 739 | 7.3 | 131 512 | 30.2 | 27.9 |
| Kingston, NY | 70 034 | 69.3 | 242 500 | 27.3 | 17.8 | 984 | 32.8 | 2.1 | 87 050 | -0.4 | 7 681 | 8.8 | 88 944 | 37.5 | 19.5 |
| Knoxville, TN | 286 362 | 69.6 | 151 800 | 22.6 | 10.3 | 704 | 29.3 | 1.8 | 366 378 | -1.2 | 24 170 | 6.6 | 326 638 | 36.3 | 20.3 |

1. Specified owner-occupied units.   2. Specified renter-occupied units.   3. Overcrowded or lacking complete plumbing facilities.   4. Percent of civilian labor force.   5. Persons 16 years old and over.

# Table C. Metropolitan Areas — Nonfarm Employment and Agriculture

| | Private nonfarm establishments, employment and payroll, 2011 | | | | | | | | | Agriculture, 2007 | | | |
| | | Employment | | | | | | Annual payroll | | Farms | | | |
| | | | | | | | | | | | Percent with: | | |
| Area name | Number of establishments | Total | Health care and social assistance | Manufacturing | Retail trade | Finance and insurance | Professional, scientific, and technical services | Total (mil dol) | Average per employee (dollars) | Number | Fewer than 50 acres | 500 acres or more | Farm operators whose principal occupation is farming (percent) |
| | 104 | 105 | 106 | 107 | 108 | 109 | 110 | 111 | 112 | 113 | 114 | 115 | 116 |
| Flagstaff, AZ.................... | 3 529 | 44 547 | 7 756 | D | 7 698 | 916 | 1 576 | 1 494 | 33 527 | 1 597 | 94.3 | 2.8 | 67.3 |
| Flint, MI........................ | 7 810 | 111 270 | 25 591 | 9 658 | 19 288 | 5 219 | 3 383 | 4 137 | 37 179 | 988 | 61.3 | 5.3 | 47.5 |
| Florence, SC.................. | 4 228 | 71 925 | 16 250 | 8 661 | 10 927 | 4 811 | 2 612 | 2 511 | 34 905 | 1 044 | 37.3 | 15.2 | 41.7 |
| Florence-Muscle Shoals, AL. | 3 225 | 43 459 | 7 076 | 7 346 | 8 171 | 1 534 | 1 804 | 1 332 | 30 645 | 2 433 | 47.1 | 5.3 | 33.9 |
| Fond du Lac, WI............. | 2 393 | 38 783 | 5 881 | 7 846 | 5 297 | 1 752 | 1 089 | 1 356 | 34 965 | 1 643 | 30.3 | 8.9 | 51.6 |
| Fort Collins-Loveland, CO .... | 9 356 | 104 622 | 17 593 | 10 073 | 16 860 | 3 356 | 9 334 | 4 110 | 39 289 | 1 757 | 60.8 | 9.2 | 34.1 |
| Fort Smith, AR-OK............... | 6 228 | 100 616 | 17 692 | 20 343 | 13 338 | 3 275 | 2 390 | 3 310 | 32 892 | 6 111 | 38.8 | 7.0 | 41.6 |
| Fort Wayne, IN.................... | 10 252 | 179 021 | 33 093 | 31 354 | 21 870 | 9 168 | 7 476 | 6 890 | 38 486 | 3 159 | 54.8 | 9.5 | 36.9 |
| Fresno, CA........................ | 15 700 | 227 628 | 40 047 | 23 958 | 32 546 | 9 704 | 11 174 | 8 465 | 37 190 | 6 081 | 61.3 | 10.8 | 57.1 |
| Gadsden, AL...................... | 1 979 | 28 470 | 7 041 | 4 709 | 4 410 | 1 004 | 630 | 892 | 31 344 | 1 004 | 52.7 | 2.1 | 33.5 |
| Gainesville, FL.................. | 5 929 | 82 177 | 21 226 | 3 259 | 13 392 | 4 134 | 4 933 | 2 862 | 34 822 | 2 101 | 69.9 | 5.1 | 40.9 |
| Gainesville, GA.................. | 3 860 | 59 760 | 11 062 | 15 344 | 7 860 | 1 761 | 1 691 | 2 292 | 38 359 | 799 | 60.6 | 1.6 | 40.3 |
| Glens Falls, NY.................. | 3 398 | 40 930 | 8 367 | 7 156 | 7 683 | 1 483 | 1 101 | 1 464 | 35 779 | 929 | 32.6 | 12.4 | 48.5 |
| Goldsboro, NC.................. | 2 169 | 34 069 | 7 727 | 5 151 | 5 546 | 1 130 | 755 | 1 033 | 30 330 | 723 | 42.9 | 13.4 | 58.1 |
| Grand Forks, ND-MN.......... | 2 624 | 40 519 | 9 070 | 3 720 | 6 860 | 1 200 | 1 467 | 1 345 | 33 197 | 2 582 | 12.9 | 35.4 | 49.3 |
| Grand Junction, CO............ | 4 529 | 49 509 | 9 330 | 2 305 | 8 363 | 1 843 | 2 842 | 1 840 | 37 159 | 1 767 | 71.0 | 6.6 | 36.6 |
| Grand Rapids-Wyoming, MI... | 17 952 | 331 099 | 50 828 | 58 477 | 36 836 | 14 032 | 13 812 | 13 282 | 40 116 | 4 491 | 45.4 | 6.9 | 42.6 |
| Great Falls, MT.................. | 2 429 | 29 151 | 6 485 | 1 059 | 5 029 | 1 960 | 1 292 | 943 | 32 347 | 1 112 | 30.5 | 33.3 | 44.6 |
| Greeley, CO...................... | 5 125 | 66 594 | 8 121 | 11 464 | 8 040 | 3 597 | 2 184 | 2 883 | 43 293 | 3 921 | 34.4 | 18.1 | 40.9 |
| Green Bay, WI.................. | 7 523 | 145 623 | 20 556 | 28 015 | 15 970 | D | 5 509 | 6 029 | 41 404 | 3 190 | 37.1 | 6.7 | 49.7 |
| Greensboro-High Point, NC.. | 17 328 | 303 511 | 41 520 | 52 091 | 35 262 | 14 812 | 11 000 | 11 553 | 38 065 | 3 327 | 49.3 | 3.4 | 43.9 |
| Greenville, NC.................. | 3 751 | 57 706 | 15 904 | 4 968 | 9 352 | 1 857 | 1 822 | 1 914 | 33 173 | 727 | 37.0 | 19.5 | 59.3 |
| Greenville-Mauldin-Easley, SC | 14 950 | 249 787 | 31 565 | 37 150 | 30 341 | 8 753 | 17 958 | 9 318 | 37 302 | 2 759 | 57.3 | 2.6 | 32.1 |
| Gulfport-Biloxi, MS............. | 5 137 | 83 497 | 14 484 | 4 147 | 13 141 | 3 303 | 4 419 | 2 986 | 35 756 | 976 | 54.6 | 3.2 | 37.3 |
| Hagerstown-Martinsburg, MD-WV | 5 229 | 78 623 | 15 537 | 8 189 | 13 589 | 5 782 | 3 006 | 2 750 | 34 975 | 1 889 | 51.0 | 3.4 | 44.4 |
| Hanford-Corcoran, CA......... | 1 599 | 22 896 | 4 757 | 3 771 | 4 049 | 543 | 451 | 783 | 34 201 | 1 129 | 53.3 | 17.7 | 57.8 |
| Harrisburg-Carlisle, PA........ | 13 352 | 262 415 | 48 918 | 16 058 | 32 019 | 19 445 | 15 089 | 10 664 | 40 637 | 3 388 | 46.9 | 3.7 | 43.2 |
| Harrisonburg, VA............... | 2 958 | 48 399 | 6 921 | 8 889 | 7 594 | 1 298 | 1 253 | 1 628 | 33 628 | 1 970 | 43.3 | 3.3 | 51.3 |
| Hartford-West Hartford-East Hartford, CT................... | 29 007 | 519 722 | 98 219 | 59 870 | 63 229 | 57 531 | 33 707 | 27 008 | 51 967 | 1 667 | 68.0 | 1.6 | 45.7 |
| Hattiesburg, MS................ | 3 305 | 49 462 | 11 688 | 4 410 | 9 261 | 1 776 | 1 729 | 1 572 | 31 779 | 1 238 | 42.6 | 3.1 | 37.8 |
| Hickory-Lenoir-Morganton, NC | 7 476 | 123 517 | 18 886 | 38 236 | 15 683 | 2 391 | 2 525 | 4 175 | 33 799 | 2 304 | 57.8 | 2.1 | 39.5 |
| Hinesville-Fort Stewart, GA .. | 882 | 12 262 | 1 867 | 1 449 | 2 100 | 297 | 949 | 404 | 32 918 | 135 | 45.9 | 10.4 | 40.7 |
| Holland-Grand Haven, MI ..... | 5 633 | 90 369 | 10 887 | 27 181 | 9 535 | 2 226 | 3 210 | 3 383 | 37 433 | 1 451 | 59.4 | 4.9 | 43.2 |
| Honolulu, HI..................... | 21 139 | 337 092 | 48 373 | 9 595 | 44 633 | 16 351 | 20 755 | 13 376 | 39 681 | 967 | 90.6 | 1.6 | 71.5 |
| Hot Springs, AR................ | 2 663 | 31 328 | 7 135 | 2 319 | 5 748 | 930 | 1 528 | 891 | 28 452 | 439 | 56.9 | 2.1 | 38.3 |
| Houma-Bayou Cane-Thibodaux, LA................... | 4 780 | 76 257 | 10 806 | 7 504 | 11 355 | 2 315 | 2 832 | 3 356 | 44 006 | 609 | 46.6 | 12.0 | 44.7 |
| Houston-Sugar Land-Baytown, TX................... | 123 784 | 2 218 263 | 282 618 | 197 530 | 259 582 | 91 327 | 179 775 | 124 898 | 56 304 | 15 451 | 58.5 | 6.8 | 35.5 |
| Huntington-Ashland, WV-KY-OH....................... | 5 730 | 92 081 | 25 396 | 9 659 | 14 780 | 2 550 | 3 409 | 3 376 | 36 664 | 2 330 | 32.1 | 2.5 | 37.2 |
| Huntsville, AL................... | 9 225 | 163 109 | 22 355 | 19 017 | 21 471 | D | 35 119 | 7 361 | 45 129 | 2 539 | 50.1 | 6.5 | 39.2 |
| Idaho Falls, ID.................. | 3 613 | 46 049 | 7 282 | 3 034 | 7 338 | 1 290 | 0 | 1 760 | 38 231 | 1 752 | 53.6 | 17.4 | 40.9 |
| Indianapolis-Carmel, IN ....... | 42 086 | 752 263 | 117 741 | 67 835 | 88 241 | 42 945 | 46 536 | 33 687 | 44 780 | 5 756 | 58.1 | 12.0 | 42.9 |
| Iowa City, IA..................... | 3 716 | 65 159 | 17 698 | 5 855 | 9 439 | 2 392 | 1 822 | 2 217 | 34 022 | 2 550 | 28.5 | 15.8 | 52.8 |
| Ithaca, NY........................ | 2 326 | 45 545 | 5 223 | 2 736 | 5 058 | 1 071 | 2 562 | 1 657 | 36 375 | 588 | 40.5 | 9.0 | 45.9 |
| Jackson, MI...................... | 2 995 | 46 046 | 9 210 | 7 864 | 7 023 | 1 354 | 2 271 | 1 856 | 40 318 | 1 184 | 50.3 | 6.1 | 40.2 |
| Jackson, MS..................... | 12 524 | 199 082 | 40 950 | 15 919 | 27 992 | 11 370 | 9 884 | 7 419 | 37 266 | 3 969 | 33.1 | 8.0 | 37.1 |
| Jackson, TN..................... | 2 795 | 52 750 | 11 911 | 8 222 | 7 308 | 1 306 | 1 185 | 1 792 | 33 963 | 1 190 | 33.2 | 8.5 | 37.0 |
| Jacksonville, FL................ | 33 538 | 483 329 | 76 140 | 24 681 | 67 009 | 47 173 | 27 953 | 20 133 | 41 654 | 1 732 | 76.0 | 3.3 | 43.0 |
| Jacksonville, NC................ | 2 710 | 32 898 | 5 703 | 820 | 7 600 | 1 059 | 1 661 | 852 | 25 884 | 401 | 51.1 | 5.5 | 59.1 |
| Janesville, WI................... | 3 236 | 49 944 | 8 625 | 7 886 | 8 638 | 1 675 | 1 095 | 1 847 | 36 989 | 1 556 | 45.5 | 9.6 | 47.6 |
| Jefferson City, MO............. | 3 548 | 49 670 | 8 995 | 5 493 | 7 545 | 2 473 | 2 133 | 1 810 | 36 435 | 4 925 | 23.3 | 8.7 | 39.6 |
| Johnson City, TN............... | 3 772 | 61 796 | 15 139 | 7 205 | 10 468 | 3 094 | 2 421 | 1 987 | 32 147 | 2 252 | 59.8 | 1.8 | 39.1 |
| Johnstown, PA.................. | 3 381 | 50 282 | 12 250 | 5 544 | 6 977 | 2 168 | 3 161 | 1 609 | 31 992 | 656 | 37.0 | 5.6 | 38.6 |
| Jonesboro, AR.................. | 2 760 | 39 987 | 8 805 | 6 211 | 7 228 | 1 323 | 981 | 1 315 | 32 883 | 1 154 | 34.9 | 34.3 | 55.4 |
| Joplin, MO....................... | 4 196 | 70 174 | 15 496 | 11 784 | 9 724 | 1 754 | 1 518 | 2 357 | 33 590 | 2 959 | 35.6 | 6.5 | 42.5 |
| Kalamazoo-Portage, MI ....... | 6 867 | 119 365 | 20 952 | 17 204 | 15 274 | 6 205 | 7 731 | 4 978 | 41 700 | 2 086 | 51.6 | 5.5 | 46.7 |
| Kankakee-Bradley, IL.......... | 2 361 | 35 778 | 7 376 | 4 890 | 5 557 | 1 372 | 744 | 1 213 | 33 905 | 835 | 34.9 | 26.6 | 51.0 |
| Kansas City, MO-KS............ | 49 878 | 859 449 | 127 435 | 74 255 | 105 494 | 57 903 | 66 735 | 38 378 | 44 654 | 15 529 | 37.0 | 10.1 | 38.7 |
| Kennewick-Pasco-Richland, WA | 5 277 | 76 768 | 11 626 | 5 768 | 12 063 | 2 026 | 10 484 | 3 542 | 46 137 | 2 521 | 60.2 | 15.9 | 47.8 |
| Killeen-Temple-Fort Hood, TX | 5 907 | 96 133 | 22 809 | 6 317 | 15 697 | 3 164 | 4 572 | 3 281 | 34 135 | 4 689 | 41.4 | 13.9 | 37.5 |
| Kingsport-Bristol-Bristol, TN-VA | 6 031 | 105 053 | 17 489 | 25 014 | 15 066 | 3 025 | 3 000 | 4 221 | 40 178 | 6 150 | 49.8 | 2.3 | 38.6 |
| Kingston, NY.................... | 4 663 | 44 056 | 8 949 | 3 590 | 8 872 | 2 419 | 1 496 | 1 432 | 32 508 | 501 | 42.1 | 5.0 | 57.1 |
| Knoxville, TN.................... | 15 843 | 294 413 | 45 650 | 29 967 | 41 303 | 13 592 | 22 503 | 11 849 | 40 246 | 4 178 | 55.7 | 1.8 | 39.7 |

# Table C. Metropolitan Areas — **Agriculture**

| | Agriculture, 2007 (cont.) | | | | | | | | | | | | | | |
| Area name | Land in farms | | | | | Value of land and buildings (dollars) | | Value of machinery and equipment, average per farm (dollars) | Value of products sold | | | | Percent of farms with sales of: | | Government payments | |
| | Acreage (1,000) | Percent change, 2002–2007 | Average size of farm | Total irrigated (1,000) | Total cropland (1,000) | Average per farm | Average per acre | | Total (mil dol) | Average per farm (dollars) | Percent from: | | $10,000 or more | $100,000 or more | Total ($1,000) | Percent of farms |
| | | | | | | | | | | | Crops | Live-stock and poultry products | | | | |
| | 117 | 118 | 119 | 120 | 121 | 122 | 123 | 124 | 125 | 126 | 127 | 128 | 129 | 130 | 131 | 132 |
|---|---|---|---|---|---|---|---|---|---|---|---|---|---|---|---|---|
| Flagstaff, AZ | 6 102 | D | 3 821 | 2.2 | 20.5 | 752 116 | 197 | 22 738 | D | D | D | D | 7.4 | 1.9 | 372 | 3.0 |
| Flint, MI | 129 | -9.8 | 131 | 1.1 | 106.6 | 488 344 | 3 733 | 82 249 | 58.8 | 59 489 | 81.3 | 18.7 | 31.4 | 9.2 | 1 569 | 31.6 |
| Florence, SC | 331 | -0.6 | 317 | 6.6 | 227.0 | 683 855 | 2 155 | 105 826 | 108.9 | 104 282 | 56.6 | 43.4 | 35.1 | 12.8 | 7 670 | 54.5 |
| Florence-Muscle Shoals, AL | 357 | 5.0 | 147 | 3.5 | 168.3 | 332 283 | 2 267 | 52 669 | 87.4 | 35 921 | 29.0 | 71.0 | 26.6 | 5.1 | 7 242 | 34.6 |
| Fond du Lac, WI | 336 | -2.3 | 204 | 0.9 | 279.9 | 721 664 | 3 532 | 127 243 | 290.4 | 176 760 | 24.0 | 76.0 | 56.1 | 30.6 | 5 413 | 77.6 |
| Fort Collins-Loveland, CO | 490 | -6.1 | 279 | 63.4 | 120.0 | 695 145 | 2 494 | 63 923 | 128.1 | 72 921 | 38.9 | 61.1 | 26.0 | 6.8 | 803 | 9.0 |
| Fort Smith, AR-OK | 1 075 | -0.6 | 176 | 14.6 | 369.7 | 367 435 | 2 089 | 58 848 | 510.4 | 83 515 | 7.7 | 92.3 | 34.4 | 9.2 | 3 595 | 8.6 |
| Fort Wayne, IN | 586 | -14.2 | 185 | 1.8 | 532.9 | 702 875 | 3 790 | 87 713 | 314.6 | 99 583 | 68.4 | 31.6 | 45.2 | 18.7 | 11 658 | 65.5 |
| Fresno, CA | 1 636 | -15.2 | 269 | 984.5 | 1 102.2 | 2 132 914 | 7 927 | 147 707 | 3 730.5 | 613 476 | 67.0 | 33.0 | 71.6 | 33.6 | 24 737 | 9.2 |
| Gadsden, AL | 94 | 4.4 | 94 | 0.6 | 29.6 | 282 306 | 3 009 | 44 457 | 66.2 | 65 893 | 5.3 | 94.7 | 23.2 | 7.0 | 518 | 11.2 |
| Gainesville, FL | 244 | -19.7 | 116 | 21.2 | 98.5 | 825 789 | 7 113 | 49 698 | 168.8 | 80 317 | 48.1 | 51.9 | 27.3 | 5.4 | 1 777 | 8.2 |
| Gainesville, GA | 57 | -8.1 | 72 | 0.2 | 15.4 | 532 486 | 7 426 | 53 349 | 181.5 | 227 193 | 0.6 | 99.4 | 31.0 | 19.3 | 213 | 11.3 |
| Glens Falls, NY | 211 | -0.9 | 228 | 0.5 | 113.3 | 497 142 | 2 184 | 99 374 | D | D | D | D | 47.4 | 19.6 | 2 189 | 25.0 |
| Goldsboro, NC | 175 | 2.3 | 242 | 6.7 | 131.7 | 1 008 378 | 4 160 | 163 067 | 501.2 | 693 189 | 15.0 | 85.0 | 59.2 | 38.0 | 3 902 | 50.5 |
| Grand Forks, ND-MN | 1 925 | 3.1 | 746 | 27.5 | 1 730.3 | 977 778 | 1 311 | 202 134 | 597.0 | 231 221 | 92.3 | 7.7 | 45.9 | 30.7 | 31 811 | 85.2 |
| Grand Junction, CO | 373 | -3.1 | 211 | 64.3 | 131.2 | 703 108 | 3 335 | 57 102 | 61.2 | 34 652 | 49.4 | 50.6 | 28.1 | 5.7 | 476 | 7.9 |
| Grand Rapids-Wyoming, MI | 710 | -1.5 | 158 | 27.7 | 534.3 | 597 908 | 3 781 | 85 735 | 591.5 | 131 710 | 42.1 | 57.9 | 36.0 | 13.4 | 7 836 | 38.5 |
| Great Falls, MT | 1 380 | -0.6 | 1 241 | 35.6 | 506.6 | 1 130 619 | 911 | 85 783 | 83.6 | 75 148 | 49.0 | 51.0 | 37.5 | 15.3 | 5 971 | 52.2 |
| Greeley, CO | 2 089 | 15.3 | 533 | 327.8 | 987.9 | 825 561 | 1 550 | 123 541 | 1 539.1 | 392 520 | 17.7 | 82.3 | 39.8 | 16.4 | 15 403 | 39.4 |
| Green Bay, WI | 569 | -3.6 | 178 | 1.9 | 449.5 | 614 546 | 3 448 | 113 064 | 564.5 | 176 960 | 16.0 | 84.0 | 47.8 | 25.7 | 7 816 | 60.5 |
| Greensboro-High Point, NC | 361 | -10.6 | 108 | 7.7 | 153.4 | 503 144 | 4 638 | 59 080 | 286.2 | 86 024 | 21.3 | 78.7 | 29.9 | 11.8 | 1 349 | 15.6 |
| Greenville, NC | 264 | -7.0 | 363 | 8.5 | 198.8 | 1 235 199 | 3 405 | 146 616 | 368.7 | 507 165 | 31.8 | 68.2 | 59.7 | 37.1 | 8 024 | 55.6 |
| Greenville-Mauldin-Easley, SC | 254 | -8.0 | 92 | 3.0 | 83.3 | 401 523 | 4 362 | 43 659 | 65.6 | 23 776 | D | D | 15.6 | 2.1 | 1 088 | 8.9 |
| Gulfport-Biloxi, MS | 116 | -3.3 | 118 | 0.6 | 26.7 | 380 352 | 3 212 | 49 307 | 14.0 | 14 340 | D | D | 19.3 | 1.9 | 969 | 13.2 |
| Hagerstown-Martinsburg, MD-WV | 212 | -5.8 | 112 | 1.1 | 127.8 | 775 919 | 6 927 | 64 246 | 107.3 | 56 780 | 33.1 | 66.9 | 31.8 | 12.4 | 1 194 | 21.3 |
| Hanford-Corcoran, CA | 681 | 5.4 | 603 | 421.6 | 512.9 | 3 295 061 | 5 465 | 245 730 | 1 358.4 | 1 203 198 | 48.0 | 52.0 | 63.7 | 41.9 | 23 258 | 35.5 |
| Harrisburg-Carlisle, PA | 391 | 6.5 | 115 | 1.7 | 281.6 | 644 383 | 5 579 | 73 842 | 320.8 | 94 670 | 17.6 | 82.4 | 38.9 | 17.4 | 5 105 | 34.4 |
| Harrisonburg, VA | 233 | NA | 118 | 4.8 | 114.5 | 727 644 | 6 150 | 84 927 | 534.1 | 271 138 | 3.8 | 96.2 | 54.7 | 31.6 | 1 356 | 16.1 |
| Hartford-West Hartford-East Hartford, CT | 109 | 3.8 | 66 | 7.0 | 53.8 | 926 360 | 14 108 | 73 912 | 227.0 | 136 118 | 88.4 | 11.6 | 35.6 | 11.1 | 836 | 4.7 |
| Hattiesburg, MS | 160 | 3.2 | 129 | 1.8 | 42.3 | 352 911 | 2 736 | 55 212 | 61.8 | 49 899 | 18.6 | 81.4 | 26.6 | 5.7 | 2 742 | 24.7 |
| Hickory-Lenoir-Morganton, NC | 189 | -7.4 | 82 | 5.3 | 83.9 | 441 797 | 5 399 | 55 330 | 198.9 | 86 295 | 24.3 | 75.7 | 28.9 | 12.2 | 835 | 10.2 |
| Hinesville-Fort Stewart, GA | 23 | -42.5 | 167 | 0.5 | 6.1 | 355 065 | 2 129 | 71 386 | 5.5 | 40 978 | 15.4 | 84.6 | 18.5 | 3.7 | 154 | 15.6 |
| Holland-Grand Haven, MI | 171 | 3.6 | 118 | 15.2 | 130.0 | 683 668 | 5 817 | 97 890 | 391.1 | 269 533 | 59.3 | 40.7 | 51.8 | 24.7 | 1 463 | 24.9 |
| Honolulu, HI | 60 | -15.5 | 62 | 8.4 | 18.9 | 1 106 333 | 17 710 | 61 269 | 126.6 | 130 897 | 84.4 | 15.6 | 48.2 | 15.1 | 294 | 1.8 |
| Hot Springs, AR | 39 | -15.2 | 90 | 0.1 | 11.4 | 329 321 | 3 662 | 37 905 | 12.2 | 27 886 | 19.4 | 80.6 | 19.1 | 3.4 | 41 | 3.2 |
| Houma-Bayou Cane-Thibodaux, LA | 285 | 39.7 | 467 | 3.6 | 85.2 | 772 453 | 1 653 | 105 878 | 69.9 | 114 755 | 44.9 | 55.1 | 39.6 | 10.0 | 192 | 5.4 |
| Houston-Sugar Land-Baytown, TX | 2 710 | -9.0 | 175 | 59.5 | 949.7 | 458 301 | 2 613 | 52 832 | 398.6 | 25 802 | 62.1 | 37.9 | 21.1 | 3.3 | 14 455 | 7.1 |
| Huntington-Ashland, WV-KY-OH | 274 | -2.1 | 118 | 0.1 | 71.2 | 264 161 | 2 248 | 40 040 | 13.8 | 5 878 | 35.4 | 64.6 | 11.7 | 0.5 | 392 | 14.1 |
| Huntsville, AL | 436 | 2.8 | 172 | 13.9 | 272.8 | 458 553 | 2 667 | 64 462 | 108.3 | 42 646 | 56.1 | 43.9 | 28.4 | 6.6 | 13 226 | 34.3 |
| Idaho Falls, ID | 778 | -0.6 | 444 | 366.3 | 523.7 | 909 499 | 2 047 | 125 875 | 422.4 | 241 055 | 55.7 | 44.3 | 43.1 | 18.4 | 8 152 | 43.4 |
| Indianapolis-Carmel, IN | 1 354 | -2.0 | 235 | D | 1 210.5 | 952 245 | 4 048 | 100 975 | 697.1 | 121 101 | D | D | 40.9 | 17.8 | 22 173 | 48.8 |
| Iowa City, IA | 647 | 1.9 | 254 | 3.2 | 550.8 | 943 716 | 3 719 | 118 547 | 458.8 | 179 906 | 43.8 | 56.2 | 60.2 | 33.9 | 18 196 | 77.6 |
| Ithaca, NY | 109 | 7.9 | 185 | 0.3 | 67.3 | 418 353 | 2 262 | 94 081 | 60.2 | 102 355 | 25.4 | 74.6 | 39.6 | 17.0 | 955 | 30.4 |
| Jackson, MI | 182 | -5.7 | 154 | 3.8 | 135.1 | 534 327 | 3 490 | 73 640 | 56.9 | 48 039 | 55.8 | 44.2 | 31.0 | 8.6 | 2 030 | 32.3 |
| Jackson, MS | 872 | 1.0 | 220 | 4.4 | 257.1 | 455 853 | 2 075 | 59 209 | 450.1 | 113 423 | 9.4 | 90.6 | 25.8 | 8.2 | 11 269 | 30.2 |
| Jackson, TN | 249 | 3.3 | 209 | 1.6 | 170.8 | 563 817 | 2 697 | 68 294 | 33.2 | 27 837 | 77.8 | 22.2 | 20.4 | 5.7 | 6 382 | 62.7 |
| Jacksonville, FL | 160 | D | 92 | 18.3 | 39.9 | 647 007 | 7 010 | 41 530 | 61.8 | 35 693 | D | D | 17.6 | 4.5 | 108 | 2.7 |
| Jacksonville, NC | 55 | -14.1 | 138 | 5.2 | 38.1 | 628 054 | 4 562 | 84 654 | 159.1 | 396 646 | 11.8 | 88.2 | 46.4 | 32.4 | 1 271 | 34.7 |
| Janesville, WI | 344 | 0.0 | 221 | 15.6 | 298.2 | 891 333 | 4 028 | 113 908 | 195.6 | 125 720 | 62.2 | 37.8 | 46.9 | 21.7 | 7 095 | 71.7 |
| Jefferson City, MO | 1 044 | -6.5 | 212 | 5.3 | 468.7 | 489 787 | 2 310 | 59 835 | 293.2 | 59 531 | 21.4 | 78.6 | 45.7 | 8.2 | 5 979 | 35.3 |
| Johnson City, TN | 163 | -9.4 | 72 | 1.0 | 82.7 | 376 273 | 5 208 | 53 999 | 46.2 | 20 533 | 24.2 | 75.8 | 22.1 | 3.0 | D | 13.4 |
| Johnstown, PA | 88 | 0.0 | 134 | 0.0 | 54.6 | 466 056 | 3 477 | 62 980 | 23.2 | 35 317 | 47.2 | 52.8 | 26.1 | 6.9 | 756 | 32.0 |
| Jonesboro, AR | 678 | -7.4 | 587 | 506.5 | 624.7 | 1 375 169 | 2 342 | 221 904 | 313.1 | 271 313 | 98.0 | 2.0 | 53.6 | 37.1 | 30 648 | 59.9 |
| Joplin, MO | 505 | -9.3 | 171 | 6.3 | 243.7 | 411 304 | 2 411 | 59 052 | 328.3 | 110 931 | 14.8 | 85.2 | 39.8 | 8.7 | 3 847 | 23.5 |
| Kalamazoo-Portage, MI | 330 | 1.9 | 158 | 61.8 | 251.0 | 670 849 | 4 238 | 105 030 | 352.8 | 169 093 | 77.0 | 23.0 | 41.0 | 17.0 | 3 410 | 25.3 |
| Kankakee-Bradley, IL | 386 | 11.2 | 462 | 16.0 | 376.2 | 2 000 617 | 4 330 | 187 468 | 244.1 | 292 277 | 88.8 | 11.2 | 70.2 | 41.8 | 5 988 | 75.0 |
| Kansas City, MO-KS | 3 607 | -2.0 | 232 | D | 2 182.2 | 517 348 | 2 227 | 63 988 | 818.6 | 52 715 | D | D | 36.2 | 8.7 | 35 030 | 43.3 |
| Kennewick-Pasco-Richland, WA | 1 242 | -2.4 | 493 | 398.8 | 944.4 | 1 105 169 | 2 244 | 139 043 | 992.9 | 393 864 | 85.9 | 14.1 | 43.4 | 26.1 | 13 302 | 18.0 |
| Killeen-Temple-Fort Hood, TX | 1 336 | -1.5 | 285 | 4.0 | 375.4 | 590 850 | 2 073 | 54 366 | 115.8 | 24 711 | 35.2 | 64.8 | 26.0 | 3.7 | 3 143 | 16.0 |
| Kingsport-Bristol-Bristol, TN-VA | 586 | -6.1 | 95 | 0.9 | 199.3 | 373 200 | 3 918 | 47 743 | 92.9 | 15 106 | 18.1 | 81.9 | 22.0 | 2.2 | 1 444 | 16.4 |
| Kingston, NY | 75 | -9.6 | 150 | 4.7 | 31.7 | 598 130 | 3 985 | 92 909 | 65.6 | 130 928 | 89.7 | 10.3 | 42.9 | 15.8 | 284 | 11.0 |
| Knoxville, TN | 344 | -8.8 | 82 | 1.4 | 162.8 | 442 163 | 5 363 | 57 759 | 105.5 | 25 252 | D | D | 17.7 | 1.7 | 394 | 8.1 |

## Table C. Metropolitan Areas — Water Use, Wholesale Trade, Retail Trade, and Real Estate

| Area name | Water use, 2005 | | Wholesale trade,[1] 2007 | | | | Retail trade, 2007 | | | | Real estate and rental and leasing, 2007 | | | |
|---|---|---|---|---|---|---|---|---|---|---|---|---|---|---|
| | Total water withdrawn (mil gal/day) | Gallons withdrawn per person | Number of establishments | Number of employees | Sales (mil dol) | Annual payroll (mil dol) | Number of establishments | Number of employees | Sales (mil dol) | Annual payroll (mil dol) | Number of establishments | Number of employees | Receipts (mil dol) | Annual payroll (mil dol) |
| | 133 | 134 | 135 | 136 | 137 | 138 | 139 | 140 | 141 | 142 | 143 | 144 | 145 | 146 |
| Flagstaff, AZ | 48.0 | 387 | 110 | 1 422 | 604.8 | 49.4 | 674 | 7 861 | 1 691.7 | 169.3 | 237 | 754 | 187.5 | 24.2 |
| Flint, MI | 20.4 | 46 | 351 | 7 069 | 4 820.8 | 427.9 | 1 614 | 21 531 | 4 836.7 | 440.5 | 339 | 1 813 | 270.2 | 47.7 |
| Florence, SC | 835.7 | 4 211 | 248 | 3 648 | 2 359.2 | 136.4 | 1 027 | 11 963 | 2 765.4 | 233.1 | 170 | 815 | 182.6 | 21.2 |
| Florence-Muscle Shoals, AL. | 1 380.3 | 9 697 | 178 | 2 425 | 1 138.6 | 77.1 | 683 | 8 102 | 1 952.9 | 167.1 | 124 | 556 | 68.1 | 12.5 |
| Fond du Lac, WI | 13.5 | 136 | 115 | 1 827 | 1 577.9 | 88.3 | 407 | 5 999 | 1 277.7 | 118.3 | 77 | 305 | 34.3 | 5.3 |
| Fort Collins-Loveland, CO | 504.4 | 1 855 | 359 | 5 978 | 4 107.4 | 407.8 | 1 306 | 17 510 | 3 922.9 | 402.7 | 562 | 2 181 | 327.1 | 63.6 |
| Fort Smith, AR-OK | 85.2 | 299 | 333 | 4 053 | 2 385.7 | 146.1 | 1 072 | 13 267 | 3 157.1 | 268.5 | 268 | 1 326 | 212.0 | 40.6 |
| Fort Wayne, IN | 63.8 | 158 | 719 | 11 763 | 14 384.5 | 465.5 | 1 569 | 24 077 | 5 339.0 | 493.8 | 466 | 2 102 | 343.2 | 58.9 |
| Fresno, CA | 3 260.2 | 3 715 | 941 | 14 594 | 9 307.3 | 671.5 | 2 579 | 38 046 | 9 808.3 | 905.0 | 755 | 4 478 | 695.2 | 132.1 |
| Gadsden, AL | 173.9 | 1 685 | 102 | 1 288 | 588.0 | 43.9 | 453 | 4 786 | 1 114.8 | 92.7 | 79 | 428 | 68.7 | 12.1 |
| Gainesville, FL | 74.8 | 291 | 217 | 2 742 | 1 510.4 | 110.2 | 1 010 | 14 849 | 3 204.7 | 304.8 | 405 | 2 086 | 316.2 | 60.0 |
| Gainesville, GA | 108.6 | 655 | 317 | 4 112 | 5 520.4 | 189.9 | 630 | 8 134 | 2 220.7 | 206.5 | 229 | 558 | 125.5 | 18.4 |
| Glens Falls, NY | 22.2 | 173 | 114 | 1 081 | 686.6 | 43.9 | 658 | 7 833 | 1 867.8 | 182.4 | 106 | 435 | 72.7 | 11.5 |
| Goldsboro, NC | 45.1 | 394 | 117 | 2 092 | 1 268.6 | 81.9 | 501 | 5 759 | 1 388.0 | 113.7 | 70 | 288 | 35.3 | 6.6 |
| Grand Forks, ND-MN | 36.3 | 374 | 154 | 1 840 | 1 302.3 | 71.5 | 458 | 7 262 | 1 536.0 | 141.6 | 75 | 511 | 62.7 | 10.7 |
| Grand Junction, CO | 926.3 | 7 132 | 254 | 2 766 | 1 385.8 | 117.9 | 693 | 8 856 | 2 389.5 | 223.8 | 323 | 1 101 | 246.9 | 40.1 |
| Grand Rapids-Wyoming, MI | 118.9 | 154 | 1 267 | 26 437 | 19 901.8 | 1 391.8 | 2 698 | 38 265 | 9 136.1 | 811.4 | 729 | D | D | D |
| Great Falls, MT | 189.2 | 2 378 | 132 | 1 225 | 758.4 | 47.8 | 388 | 5 507 | 1 302.3 | 121.0 | 137 | 378 | 56.3 | 8.3 |
| Greeley, CO | 773.0 | 3 377 | 275 | 3 811 | 3 471.5 | 167.5 | 650 | 8 735 | 2 246.1 | 212.9 | 227 | 838 | 115.6 | 23.7 |
| Green Bay, WI | 1 356.8 | 4 561 | 459 | 6 744 | 4 622.3 | 312.9 | 1 187 | 17 523 | 3 948.8 | 358.1 | 273 | 1 697 | 238.1 | 47.1 |
| Greensboro-High Point, NC.. | 362.1 | 537 | 1 555 | 23 166 | 20 428.2 | 1 158.6 | 2 782 | 38 394 | 9 248.9 | 890.9 | 824 | 5 046 | 1 517.8 | 158.0 |
| Greenville, NC | 34.8 | 214 | 165 | 1 845 | 1 003.8 | 76.7 | 713 | 9 221 | 2 273.8 | 195.3 | 205 | 860 | 129.8 | 27.2 |
| Greenville-Mauldin-Easley, SC | 106.2 | 180 | 986 | 13 096 | 14 081.9 | 664.8 | 2 386 | 31 461 | 7 560.2 | 690.4 | 735 | 3 680 | 822.0 | 132.3 |
| Gulfport-Biloxi, MS | 209.3 | 820 | 213 | 2 013 | 1 042.5 | 86.9 | 1 002 | 13 198 | 3 477.1 | 302.9 | 295 | 1 075 | 191.1 | 31.4 |
| Hagerstown-Martinsburg, MD-WV | 95.4 | 380 | 208 | 3 151 | 1 990.0 | 135.4 | 999 | 14 220 | 3 444.5 | 302.5 | 239 | 1 016 | 180.2 | 25.4 |
| Hanford-Corcoran, CA | 1 380.4 | 9 625 | 67 | D | D | D | 326 | 4 267 | 1 035.9 | 93.9 | 95 | 343 | 55.4 | 7.2 |
| Harrisburg-Carlisle, PA | 219.4 | 420 | 627 | 15 518 | 14 070.1 | 784.1 | 2 125 | 33 703 | 7 947.8 | 725.1 | 462 | 3 430 | 807.8 | 123.9 |
| Harrisonburg, VA | 44.3 | 397 | 129 | 2 364 | 1 562.3 | 92.4 | 601 | 8 250 | 1 920.8 | 200.1 | 127 | 1 285 | 172.7 | 37.5 |
| Hartford-West Hartford-East Hartford, CT | 387.4 | 326 | 1 515 | 27 480 | 25 182.0 | 1 561.2 | 4 578 | 66 748 | 17 156.2 | 1 646.9 | 1 188 | 7 661 | 1 500.4 | 298.6 |
| Hattiesburg, MS | 75.2 | 570 | 131 | 1 692 | 1 410.5 | 54.7 | 739 | 9 647 | 3 173.8 | 199.3 | 166 | 609 | 82.4 | 16.4 |
| Hickory-Lenoir-Morganton, NC | 1 217.8 | 3 424 | 471 | 9 323 | 6 434.0 | 395.2 | 1 441 | 16 856 | 4 209.6 | 366.9 | 320 | 1 098 | 190.5 | 29.5 |
| Hinesville-Fort Stewart, GA .. | 17.0 | 247 | 13 | D | D | D | 204 | 2 004 | 556.7 | 42.0 | 55 | 238 | 29.4 | 5.9 |
| Holland-Grand Haven, MI ..... | 854.5 | 3 346 | 372 | 3 682 | 2 973.4 | 164.1 | 830 | 10 670 | 2 367.8 | 220.4 | 186 | 891 | 107.9 | 23.9 |
| Honolulu, HI | 1 593.3 | 1 760 | 1 419 | 16 288 | 10 152.0 | 679.6 | 3 058 | 46 613 | 11 518.3 | 1 144.1 | 1 294 | 9 867 | 2 660.2 | 399.9 |
| Hot Springs, AR | 19.9 | 212 | 107 | 1 402 | 1 176.0 | 55.9 | 523 | 5 898 | 1 443.4 | 126.9 | 158 | 614 | 88.0 | 14.6 |
| Houma-Bayou Cane-Thibodaux, LA | 67.9 | 340 | 298 | 4 019 | 2 119.2 | 180.6 | 796 | 11 724 | 2 832.9 | 259.9 | 256 | 2 290 | 487.9 | 103.0 |
| Houston-Sugar Land-Baytown, TX | 4 287.5 | 812 | 8 790 | 138 496 | 283 564.2 | 8 341.6 | 16 938 | 251 088 | 69 984.2 | 6 074.4 | 6 455 | 47 101 | 11 098.2 | 2 018.8 |
| Huntington-Ashland, WV-KY-OH | 150.1 | 525 | 257 | 3 409 | 3 931.5 | 136.9 | 1 179 | 16 402 | 3 527.9 | 306.9 | 233 | 888 | 132.8 | 20.9 |
| Huntsville, AL | 2 084.4 | 5 654 | 496 | 6 679 | 4 298.8 | 350.3 | 1 594 | 21 451 | 5 161.9 | 479.9 | 487 | 2 247 | 369.3 | 69.3 |
| Idaho Falls, ID | 2 990.0 | 26 358 | 196 | 3 945 | 2 780.6 | 145.9 | 568 | 7 849 | 1 963.8 | 167.4 | 155 | 548 | 91.8 | 12.2 |
| Indianapolis-Carmel, IN | 666.8 | 406 | 2 817 | 44 273 | 39 808.4 | 2 236.5 | 5 955 | 94 406 | 22 908.2 | 2 182.8 | 2 163 | 14 833 | 2 732.4 | 557.0 |
| Iowa City, IA | 49.5 | 357 | 151 | 1 665 | 1 156.8 | 66.9 | 639 | 9 417 | 1 848.1 | 185.7 | 157 | 720 | 143.4 | 21.7 |
| Ithaca, NY | 254.2 | 2 541 | 60 | 498 | 256.7 | 19.8 | 372 | 5 068 | 1 018.3 | 106.1 | 95 | 748 | 116.2 | 19.8 |
| Jackson, MI | 22.6 | 138 | 168 | 2 011 | 2 085.7 | 90.1 | 582 | 7 462 | 1 690.9 | 153.6 | 118 | 608 | 64.9 | 12.5 |
| Jackson, MS | 92.9 | 178 | 805 | 13 008 | 10 469.1 | 588.3 | 2 125 | 28 700 | 6 842.9 | 630.8 | 594 | 3 156 | 700.8 | 106.6 |
| Jackson, TN | 22.0 | 199 | 186 | 2 313 | 1 440.9 | 96.3 | 564 | 7 507 | 1 814.1 | 162.9 | 115 | 787 | 102.8 | 19.6 |
| Jacksonville, FL | 891.1 | 697 | 1 813 | 28 131 | 29 028.3 | 1 440.2 | 5 190 | 74 132 | 18 173.6 | 1 692.3 | 2 141 | 10 977 | 2 447.5 | 444.5 |
| Jacksonville, NC | 18.6 | 122 | 47 | 281 | 113.6 | 11.5 | 550 | 7 276 | 1 913.9 | 154.2 | 185 | 757 | 108.4 | 17.2 |
| Janesville, WI | 96.0 | 609 | 150 | 3 305 | 2 902.1 | 161.6 | 579 | 9 269 | 2 439.8 | 216.8 | 126 | 432 | 92.6 | 10.3 |
| Jefferson City, MO | 110.5 | 768 | 133 | 3 192 | 1 023.1 | 97.7 | 606 | 7 808 | 1 827.3 | 158.6 | 116 | 360 | 53.0 | 8.1 |
| Johnson City, TN | 50.4 | 267 | 170 | 2 294 | 1 353.5 | 82.3 | 749 | 10 577 | 2 449.9 | 216.8 | 162 | 1 079 | 128.8 | 20.4 |
| Johnstown, PA | 18.6 | 125 | 139 | 1 641 | 656.9 | 53.3 | 588 | 7 207 | 1 626.5 | 137.9 | 99 | 584 | 65.8 | 16.7 |
| Jonesboro, AR | 1 182.3 | 10 548 | 163 | 1 921 | 1 206.1 | 77.8 | 587 | 7 419 | 1 634.1 | 139.8 | 115 | 545 | 79.7 | 13.2 |
| Joplin, MO | 39.5 | 238 | 207 | 3 128 | 1 709.4 | 106.4 | 799 | 10 096 | 2 573.1 | 208.2 | 182 | 835 | 95.0 | 19.2 |
| Kalamazoo-Portage, MI | 226.9 | 710 | 358 | 5 456 | 3 870.0 | 340.7 | 1 180 | 16 579 | 3 365.5 | 327.5 | 271 | 2 701 | 239.3 | 72.0 |
| Kankakee-Bradley, IL | 35.3 | 327 | 129 | 2 274 | 1 410.4 | 94.0 | 389 | 5 737 | 1 258.5 | 118.1 | 105 | 342 | 63.5 | 9.5 |
| Kansas City, MO-KS | 1 615.9 | 830 | 3 403 | 64 263 | 66 226.3 | 2 953.3 | 6 840 | 110 941 | 27 215.8 | 2 521.7 | 2 726 | 15 815 | 3 167.4 | 531.1 |
| Kennewick-Pasco-Richland, WA | 1 394.5 | 6 311 | 231 | 2 843 | 2 702.3 | 127.9 | 762 | 11 477 | 2 910.5 | 280.3 | 270 | 1 276 | 244.8 | 37.2 |
| Killeen-Temple-Fort Hood, TX | 115.7 | 329 | 168 | 3 345 | 4 520.1 | 143.8 | 1 125 | 14 902 | 3 999.7 | 334.1 | 377 | 1 704 | 232.0 | 44.9 |
| Kingsport-Bristol-Bristol, TN-VA | 1 320.1 | 4 382 | 329 | 5 782 | 5 204.9 | 272.3 | 1 238 | 15 165 | 3 555.5 | 316.0 | 242 | 997 | 198.3 | 26.6 |
| Kingston, NY | 472.5 | 2 586 | 160 | D | D | D | 794 | 9 242 | 2 241.1 | 216.3 | 209 | 676 | 125.2 | 18.4 |
| Knoxville, TN | 672.4 | 1 026 | 1 042 | 15 943 | 17 370.7 | 853.9 | 2 757 | 45 019 | 11 164.5 | 1 065.4 | 744 | 4 016 | 756.1 | 124.0 |

1. Merchant wholesalers, except manufacturers' sales branches and offices.

| Area name | Professional, scientific, and technical services,[1] 2007 | | | | Manufacturing, 2007 | | | | Accommodation and food services, 2007 | | | |
|---|---|---|---|---|---|---|---|---|---|---|---|---|
| | Number of establish-ments | Number of employees | Sales (mil dol) | Annual payroll (mil dol) | Number of establish-ments | Number of employees | Sales (mil dol) | Annual payroll (mil dol) | Number of establish-ments | Number of employees | Sales (mil dol) | Annual payroll (mil dol) |
| | 147 | 148 | 149 | 150 | 151 | 152 | 153 | 154 | 155 | 156 | 157 | 158 |
| Flagstaff, AZ | 322 | D | D | D | 109 | 4 219 | 1 526.8 | 240.5 | 531 | 11 181 | 717.7 | 181.9 |
| Flint, MI | 694 | D | D | D | 309 | 14 878 | 12 579.5 | 1 099.6 | 762 | 13 583 | 528.7 | 151.9 |
| Florence, SC | 287 | D | D | D | 182 | 11 892 | 5 318.7 | 546.2 | 374 | 7 173 | 303.9 | 81.7 |
| Florence-Muscle Shoals, AL. | 270 | D | D | D | 203 | 7 312 | 3 166.8 | 301.3 | 249 | 5 128 | 198.5 | 56.3 |
| Fond du Lac, WI | 157 | 1 320 | 101.9 | 65.4 | 151 | 9 745 | 2 903.2 | 392.3 | 242 | 4 001 | 131.5 | 37.5 |
| Fort Collins-Loveland, CO .... | 1 327 | 7 876 | 867.5 | 387.3 | 420 | 11 764 | 3 226.8 | 664.5 | 807 | 14 244 | 604.4 | 181.9 |
| Fort Smith, AR-OK | 498 | D | D | D | 337 | 25 540 | 7 272.0 | 816.0 | 477 | 8 222 | 332.1 | 90.5 |
| Fort Wayne, IN | 978 | 7 253 | 753.3 | 346.6 | 694 | 38 250 | 22 548.5 | 1 837.4 | 803 | 16 997 | 598.0 | 182.2 |
| Fresno, CA | 1 564 | D | D | D | 646 | 26 898 | 7 827.3 | 1 018.0 | 1 460 | 25 553 | 1 147.2 | 320.9 |
| Gadsden, AL | 156 | 876 | 76.6 | 26.8 | 118 | 5 430 | 1 253.0 | 203.7 | 177 | 3 381 | 138.0 | 38.1 |
| Gainesville, FL | 810 | 5 326 | 629.8 | 265.2 | 154 | 4 028 | 1 068.9 | 178.6 | 543 | 11 333 | 502.1 | 135.7 |
| Gainesville, GA | 419 | D | D | D | 265 | 17 296 | 6 069.0 | 602.5 | 272 | 4 930 | 224.1 | 62.5 |
| Glens Falls, NY | 250 | 1 196 | 113.7 | 43.9 | 176 | 7 263 | 1 962.7 | 302.9 | 529 | 5 579 | 325.0 | 97.8 |
| Goldsboro, NC | 143 | 825 | 65.7 | 22.8 | 84 | 6 147 | 1 474.8 | 221.7 | 197 | 3 485 | 132.1 | 36.2 |
| Grand Forks, ND-MN | 157 | D | D | D | 94 | 4 495 | 1 519.4 | 152.9 | 247 | 5 190 | 177.8 | 51.3 |
| Grand Junction, CO | 547 | D | D | D | 177 | 2 691 | 539.6 | 104.9 | 301 | 6 307 | 268.8 | 77.6 |
| Grand Rapids-Wyoming, MI | 1 821 | D | D | D | 1 344 | 69 520 | 18 393.9 | 3 337.5 | 1 382 | 27 437 | 1 027.0 | 312.3 |
| Great Falls, MT | 199 | D | D | D | 81 | 1 094 | 670.9 | 44.8 | 247 | 3 997 | 174.3 | 48.6 |
| Greeley, CO | 462 | D | D | D | 284 | 10 186 | 4 193.7 | 451.8 | 379 | 6 099 | 217.2 | 63.8 |
| Green Bay, WI | 588 | D | D | D | 552 | 29 482 | 10 130.5 | 1 245.0 | 769 | 14 107 | 507.2 | 146.5 |
| Greensboro-High Point, NC.. | 1 814 | D | D | D | 1 194 | 63 505 | 31 456.5 | 2 461.3 | 1 432 | 27 982 | 1 260.5 | 353.3 |
| Greenville, NC | 318 | 1 778 | 200.8 | 77.8 | 107 | 7 017 | 2 053.5 | 268.5 | 315 | 7 345 | 299.9 | 81.0 |
| Greenville-Mauldin-Easley, SC | 1 611 | 14 533 | 2 147.8 | 825.9 | 825 | 41 280 | 13 843.6 | 1 672.0 | 1 304 | 24 444 | 1 014.4 | 282.4 |
| Gulfport-Biloxi, MS | 504 | D | D | D | 165 | 4 713 | D | 219.0 | 458 | 20 051 | 1 771.6 | 473.7 |
| Hagerstown-Martinsburg, MD-WV | 382 | D | D | D | 201 | 10 289 | 3 522.3 | 464.8 | 494 | 8 122 | 397.6 | 105.1 |
| Hanford-Corcoran, CA | 101 | 535 | 52.9 | 16.9 | 73 | 4 291 | 2 107.7 | 148.7 | 171 | 4 209 | 360.1 | 77.5 |
| Harrisburg-Carlisle, PA | 1 390 | 14 474 | 2 081.9 | 808.0 | 450 | 20 726 | 7 695.4 | 876.1 | 1 264 | 22 498 | 1 101.3 | 315.8 |
| Harrisonburg, VA | 233 | D | D | D | 134 | 10 112 | 6 183.8 | 399.8 | 257 | 6 326 | 230.7 | 73.8 |
| Hartford-West Hartford-East Hartford, CT | 2 900 | D | D | D | 1 813 | 77 946 | 19 374.0 | 4 299.5 | 2 577 | 41 547 | 2 104.5 | 622.3 |
| Hattiesburg, MS | 292 | D | D | D | 110 | 5 737 | 1 282.6 | 198.1 | 281 | 6 813 | 263.6 | 73.3 |
| Hickory-Lenoir-Morganton, NC | 584 | D | D | D | 845 | 50 686 | 10 725.5 | 1 618.2 | 645 | 11 611 | 466.1 | 127.1 |
| Hinesville-Fort Stewart, GA .. | 57 | D | D | D | 19 | 1 183 | 704.0 | 58.3 | 101 | 1 767 | 64.7 | 16.5 |
| Holland-Grand Haven, MI ..... | 515 | D | D | D | 584 | 31 912 | 9 210.9 | 1 395.5 | 381 | 7 551 | 277.2 | 83.8 |
| Honolulu, HI | 2 433 | 18 508 | 2 686.9 | 1 056.8 | 684 | 10 996 | 8 201.9 | 398.9 | 2 347 | 57 064 | 4 123.8 | 1 126.5 |
| Hot Springs, AR | 218 | D | D | D | 119 | 2 786 | 661.7 | 99.9 | 265 | 5 080 | 203.3 | 62.2 |
| Houma-Bayou Cane-Thibo-daux, LA | 441 | D | D | D | 185 | 8 372 | 1 729.9 | 360.7 | 397 | 7 226 | 339.8 | 95.2 |
| Houston-Sugar Land-Bay-town, TX | 15 662 | 181 596 | 34 284.2 | 13 772.5 | 5 484 | 222 142 | 238 606.5 | 12 175.3 | 9 616 | 197 339 | 10 225.1 | 2 740.7 |
| Huntington-Ashland, WV-KY-OH | 400 | D | D | D | 213 | 10 799 | 15 159.1 | 562.3 | 537 | 10 187 | 386.3 | 107.4 |
| Huntsville, AL | 1 374 | 32 363 | 5 761.6 | 2 244.1 | 391 | 27 771 | 9 598.0 | 1 303.6 | 739 | 15 537 | 664.5 | 184.8 |
| Idaho Falls, ID | 426 | D | D | D | 177 | 3 649 | 796.3 | 119.1 | 224 | 4 062 | 160.9 | 43.1 |
| Indianapolis-Carmel, IN | 4 907 | 43 194 | 6 898.8 | 2 701.5 | 1 803 | 88 795 | 35 647.6 | 4 407.4 | 3 598 | 75 084 | 3 413.5 | 1 004.1 |
| Iowa City, IA | 293 | D | D | D | 122 | 6 712 | 8 945.4 | 263.8 | 370 | 8 130 | 373.5 | 97.1 |
| Ithaca, NY | 273 | D | D | D | 92 | 3 152 | 742.8 | 137.3 | 308 | 3 742 | 177.7 | 51.9 |
| Jackson, MI | 235 | D | D | D | 284 | 9 250 | 2 783.0 | 403.6 | 300 | 4 999 | 185.4 | 53.5 |
| Jackson, MS | 1 398 | 10 281 | 1 536.4 | 535.8 | 403 | 19 953 | 10 509.1 | 813.4 | 990 | 19 771 | 818.4 | 218.5 |
| Jackson, TN | 206 | D | D | D | 137 | 10 111 | 4 567.9 | 452.1 | 235 | 5 780 | 216.4 | 58.5 |
| Jacksonville, FL | 4 453 | 33 141 | 4 168.3 | 1 671.0 | 869 | 31 029 | 13 029.4 | 1 460.0 | 2 713 | 53 981 | 2 747.5 | 786.4 |
| Jacksonville, NC | 210 | D | D | D | 43 | 1 016 | 253.0 | 31.8 | 310 | 6 265 | 287.9 | 71.5 |
| Janesville, WI | 199 | D | D | D | 236 | 13 527 | 12 381.6 | 720.3 | 383 | 5 673 | 211.7 | 58.6 |
| Jefferson City, MO | 303 | 1 653 | 192.6 | 69.2 | 160 | 5 992 | 2 357.6 | 239.2 | 267 | 4 426 | 173.1 | 50.2 |
| Johnson City, TN | 285 | D | D | D | 212 | 10 146 | 2 222.9 | 367.4 | 348 | 7 873 | 302.0 | 90.3 |
| Johnstown, PA | 221 | D | D | D | 146 | 5 409 | 1 439.8 | 199.6 | 307 | 4 135 | 156.0 | 40.9 |
| Jonesboro, AR | 194 | D | D | D | 139 | 7 289 | 2 002.3 | 259.0 | 215 | 4 324 | 158.3 | 44.2 |
| Joplin, MO | 269 | D | D | D | 269 | 13 785 | 3 983.2 | 490.7 | 352 | 6 754 | 251.9 | 73.1 |
| Kalamazoo-Portage, MI | 647 | D | D | D | 434 | 21 099 | 8 458.8 | 1 065.0 | 675 | 13 767 | 495.2 | 153.7 |
| Kankakee-Bradley, IL | 169 | D | D | D | 115 | 5 633 | 3 418.9 | 280.8 | 229 | D | D | D |
| Kansas City, MO-KS | 6 155 | D | D | D | 2 033 | 82 421 | 38 876.0 | 4 091.7 | 3 882 | 84 322 | 4 368.5 | 1 184.5 |
| Kennewick-Pasco-Richland, WA | 470 | D | D | D | 190 | 5 975 | 2 049.7 | 241.7 | 447 | 6 634 | 305.7 | 89.1 |
| Killeen-Temple-Fort Hood, TX | 427 | D | D | D | 179 | 7 848 | 2 146.6 | 278.0 | 610 | 10 940 | 462.9 | 120.2 |
| Kingsport-Bristol-Bristol, TN-VA | 463 | 2 941 | 300.8 | 109.1 | 320 | 27 089 | 9 083.1 | 1 150.5 | 568 | 11 315 | 434.2 | 122.1 |
| Kingston, NY | 455 | D | D | D | 202 | D | D | 165.3 | 533 | 6 542 | 321.4 | 103.9 |
| Knoxville, TN | 1 736 | D | D | D | 771 | 35 786 | 13 322.3 | 1 686.2 | 1 308 | 30 600 | 1 310.9 | 390.5 |

1. Establishments subject to federal tax.

# Table C. Metropolitan Areas — Health Care and Social Assistance, Other Services, and Federal Funds

| Area name | Health care and social assistance,[1] 2007 | | | | Other services,[1] 2007 | | | | Federal funds and grants, 2009–2010 Expenditures (mil dol) | | | |
|---|---|---|---|---|---|---|---|---|---|---|---|---|
| | | | | | | | | | | Direct payments for individuals | | |
| | Number of establishments | Number of employees | Receipts (mil dol) | Annual payroll (mil dol) | Number of establishments | Number of employees | Receipts (mil dol) | Annual payroll (mil dol) | Total | Social Security and government retirement | Medicare | Food stamps and Supplemental Security Income |
| | 159 | 160 | 161 | 162 | 163 | 164 | 165 | 166 | 167 | 168 | 169 | 170 |
| Flagstaff, AZ | 389 | 6 628 | 878.6 | 305.9 | 247 | 1 493 | 100.8 | 32.2 | 1 357.4 | 341.8 | 109.5 | 63.7 |
| Flint, MI | 1 261 | 25 790 | 2 505.1 | 1 005.4 | 648 | 3 695 | 418.1 | 103.4 | 3 751.3 | 1 495.5 | 857.8 | 303.7 |
| Florence, SC | 437 | 14 058 | 1 532.9 | 574.6 | 291 | 1 792 | 155.3 | 40.5 | 1 741.4 | 661.7 | 299.5 | 137.8 |
| Florence-Muscle Shoals, AL. | 405 | 7 284 | 660.9 | 251.0 | 219 | 1 393 | 120.9 | 31.9 | 1 276.6 | 647.5 | 269.2 | 53.4 |
| Fond du Lac, WI | 266 | 6 180 | 607.2 | 223.9 | 193 | 1 206 | 88.4 | 24.4 | 626.2 | 314.9 | 134.3 | 14.8 |
| Fort Collins-Loveland, CO .... | 908 | 15 177 | 1 400.5 | 610.6 | 612 | 3 123 | 286.8 | 77.2 | 1 879.7 | 719.3 | 236.7 | 38.7 |
| Fort Smith, AR-OK | 683 | 17 336 | 1 343.8 | 568.0 | 363 | 1 756 | 145.1 | 39.7 | 2 326.1 | 997.8 | 443.1 | 128.6 |
| Fort Wayne, IN | 1 114 | 31 151 | 2 944.2 | 1 142.1 | 825 | 5 686 | 457.1 | 140.9 | 3 457.0 | 1 110.1 | 468.8 | 125.3 |
| Fresno, CA | 2 099 | 36 707 | 4 150.8 | 1 713.0 | 1 069 | 7 309 | 704.7 | 191.7 | 5 953.8 | 1 736.7 | 991.7 | 468.5 |
| Gadsden, AL | 302 | 6 515 | 626.7 | 229.8 | 121 | 691 | 54.0 | 15.8 | 966.6 | 420.9 | 248.2 | 51.1 |
| Gainesville, FL | 729 | 20 958 | 2 363.5 | 926.2 | 390 | 2 806 | 658.1 | 88.3 | 2 490.7 | 709.9 | 467.3 | 111.2 |
| Gainesville, GA | 398 | 8 599 | 1 046.7 | 384.6 | 272 | 1 384 | 136.1 | 36.5 | 1 157.9 | 440.8 | 154.3 | 39.2 |
| Glens Falls, NY | 365 | 7 916 | 610.9 | 283.2 | 220 | 1 029 | 97.8 | 27.8 | 927.4 | 452.4 | 183.3 | 33.8 |
| Goldsboro, NC | 294 | 7 587 | 573.0 | 248.6 | 159 | 949 | 70.0 | 20.5 | 1 332.9 | 419.7 | 161.2 | 59.5 |
| Grand Forks, ND-MN | 244 | 8 510 | 646.2 | 281.6 | 215 | 1 471 | 98.5 | 28.9 | 1 009.3 | 247.1 | 135.8 | 22.5 |
| Grand Junction, CO | 425 | 8 480 | 847.4 | 336.2 | 317 | 1 599 | 160.1 | 42.3 | 1 064.5 | 462.6 | 163.9 | 33.6 |
| Grand Rapids-Wyoming, MI | 1 755 | 44 696 | 4 274.2 | 1 694.3 | 1 354 | 8 877 | 832.6 | 219.4 | 4 504.9 | 1 946.7 | 827.8 | 239.2 |
| Great Falls, MT | 269 | 6 050 | 517.8 | 206.6 | 166 | 845 | 65.4 | 18.8 | 1 022.7 | 329.7 | 119.7 | 23.9 |
| Greeley, CO | 429 | 8 538 | 763.1 | 292.3 | 340 | 1 513 | 161.2 | 40.0 | 1 076.8 | 454.9 | 177.6 | 43.9 |
| Green Bay, WI | 695 | 21 052 | 2 104.4 | 821.4 | 554 | 3 268 | 251.0 | 70.0 | 1 805.7 | 812.2 | 296.5 | 64.4 |
| Greensboro-High Point, NC.. | 1 655 | 38 752 | 3 478.4 | 1 436.9 | 1 186 | 6 684 | 843.5 | 177.2 | 5 119.3 | 2 098.7 | 829.8 | 223.7 |
| Greenville, NC | 482 | 15 787 | 1 448.3 | 594.0 | 198 | 1 108 | 110.0 | 22.0 | 1 235.2 | 448.0 | 183.4 | 90.7 |
| Greenville-Mauldin-Easley, SC | 1 298 | 28 740 | 2 888.9 | 1 162.6 | 952 | 6 658 | 603.3 | 176.5 | 4 289.6 | 1 916.9 | 675.7 | 188.5 |
| Gulfport-Biloxi, MS | 515 | 14 123 | 1 610.8 | 615.9 | 349 | 1 983 | 201.4 | 52.9 | 3 461.0 | 905.3 | 418.3 | 107.2 |
| Hagerstown-Martinsburg, MD-WV | 617 | 14 608 | 1 323.3 | 582.3 | 431 | 2 659 | 229.8 | 65.5 | 2 296.6 | 887.3 | 459.1 | 62.0 |
| Hanford-Corcoran, CA | 204 | 4 106 | 433.8 | 153.1 | 105 | 582 | 47.0 | 13.4 | 994.5 | 260.9 | 141.1 | 49.3 |
| Harrisburg-Carlisle, PA | 1 485 | 43 317 | 3 960.3 | 1 674.8 | 1 290 | 9 051 | 1 003.3 | 273.6 | 12 034.5 | 1 934.0 | 923.3 | 116.9 |
| Harrisonburg, VA | 245 | 6 349 | 549.2 | 229.3 | 237 | 1 233 | 118.5 | 30.4 | 576.5 | 273.7 | 111.4 | 17.8 |
| Hartford-West Hartford-East Hartford, CT | 3 459 | 91 507 | 8 632.4 | 3 847.9 | 2 515 | 18 825 | 1 935.7 | 541.0 | 19 348.8 | 3 326.8 | 7 193.4 | 350.2 |
| Hattiesburg, MS | 329 | 10 401 | 1 074.6 | 453.7 | 167 | 1 033 | 73.2 | 20.9 | 1 387.3 | 420.5 | 184.6 | 64.4 |
| Hickory-Lenoir-Morganton, NC | 761 | 17 609 | 1 598.0 | 630.1 | 483 | 2 583 | 257.5 | 67.2 | 2 224.3 | 1 148.6 | 427.1 | 100.2 |
| Hinesville-Fort Stewart, GA .. | 70 | D | D | D | 72 | 438 | 31.4 | 9.2 | 526.0 | 203.4 | 38.6 | 32.6 |
| Holland-Grand Haven, MI ..... | 500 | 9 536 | 761.6 | 294.0 | 425 | 2 575 | 240.5 | 67.4 | 1 266.2 | 660.2 | 197.4 | 28.4 |
| Honolulu, HI | 2 473 | 47 727 | 5 055.4 | 2 047.9 | 2 083 | 15 228 | 1 462.7 | 388.7 | 17 392.9 | 3 117.6 | 1 100.2 | 333.7 |
| Hot Springs, AR | 276 | 6 590 | 613.4 | 244.4 | 179 | 1 309 | 80.6 | 26.6 | 1 017.6 | 513.5 | 231.6 | 44.9 |
| Houma-Bayou Cane-Thibodaux, LA | 440 | 9 563 | 954.4 | 373.8 | 288 | 2 161 | 280.2 | 78.5 | 1 780.1 | 533.5 | 330.2 | 99.6 |
| Houston-Sugar Land-Baytown, TX | 12 477 | 255 500 | 27 871.1 | 10 593.2 | 7 954 | 67 524 | 7 692.8 | 2 123.5 | 36 145.6 | 10 541.6 | 5 383.2 | 1 984.7 |
| Huntington-Ashland, WV-KY-OH | 868 | 23 995 | 2 299.4 | 929.8 | 447 | 2 666 | 274.7 | 69.0 | 3 042.9 | 1 164.2 | 666.4 | 191.4 |
| Huntsville, AL | 1 001 | 20 402 | 2 020.2 | 828.1 | 569 | 4 019 | 619.4 | 103.1 | 10 321.0 | 1 562.5 | 387.8 | 120.4 |
| Idaho Falls, ID | 497 | 7 331 | 626.0 | 235.0 | 183 | 978 | 87.0 | 23.0 | 2 103.3 | 312.1 | 100.4 | 38.8 |
| Indianapolis-Carmel, IN | 4 211 | 106 787 | 11 177.8 | 4 309.3 | 3 135 | 24 557 | 3 592.7 | 713.3 | 16 770.2 | 4 427.5 | 2 079.9 | 519.9 |
| Iowa City, IA | 423 | 16 714 | 1 562.4 | 607.3 | 263 | 1 529 | 193.2 | 38.7 | 1 203.5 | 313.8 | 114.4 | 20.8 |
| Ithaca, NY | 250 | 4 919 | 388.7 | 152.9 | 149 | 945 | 129.2 | 21.6 | 939.3 | 220.0 | 84.8 | 21.6 |
| Jackson, MI | 379 | 8 717 | 810.5 | 346.6 | 241 | 1 528 | 147.0 | 41.2 | 1 149.7 | 513.5 | 248.9 | 66.6 |
| Jackson, MS | 1 282 | 38 253 | 3 760.2 | 1 403.3 | 875 | 5 548 | 542.3 | 151.7 | 6 208.0 | 1 464.1 | 675.3 | 265.8 |
| Jackson, TN | 328 | 11 033 | 1 055.1 | 448.2 | 160 | 993 | 75.7 | 26.9 | 1 011.8 | 335.9 | 268.4 | 54.4 |
| Jacksonville, FL | 3 270 | 69 014 | 7 365.5 | 2 800.4 | 2 485 | 15 941 | 2 498.5 | 501.2 | 12 558.3 | 4 491.2 | 2 326.4 | 464.7 |
| Jacksonville, NC | 246 | 5 465 | 433.8 | 163.4 | 213 | 1 136 | 68.0 | 21.4 | 2 938.6 | 575.1 | 92.7 | 52.6 |
| Janesville, WI | 330 | 9 276 | 878.5 | 337.0 | 285 | 1 578 | 108.7 | 30.6 | 1 258.0 | 478.3 | 210.7 | 48.9 |
| Jefferson City, MO | 374 | 9 056 | 781.7 | 308.8 | 341 | 1 987 | 199.9 | 56.9 | 3 845.0 | 431.2 | 215.2 | 32.7 |
| Johnson City, TN | 429 | 13 218 | 1 334.8 | 525.0 | 267 | 1 476 | 101.5 | 31.8 | 1 862.8 | 764.6 | 427.8 | 92.1 |
| Johnstown, PA | 545 | 11 825 | 872.0 | 383.6 | 320 | 1 590 | 114.3 | 28.9 | 2 819.4 | 606.4 | 492.3 | 63.8 |
| Jonesboro, AR | 346 | 8 212 | 792.6 | 294.5 | 161 | 887 | 71.6 | 18.0 | 953.8 | 358.2 | 156.0 | 58.1 |
| Joplin, MO | 507 | 12 259 | 1 089.4 | 435.8 | 344 | 1 675 | 117.3 | 34.6 | 1 283.1 | 512.7 | 258.5 | 60.8 |
| Kalamazoo-Portage, MI | 754 | 20 517 | 1 978.8 | 776.7 | 523 | 3 982 | 511.7 | 103.0 | 2 745.9 | 926.9 | 419.8 | 125.9 |
| Kankakee-Bradley, IL | 290 | 6 260 | 618.8 | 228.6 | 193 | 1 080 | 105.7 | 26.6 | 794.0 | 326.4 | 202.6 | 42.4 |
| Kansas City, MO-KS | 4 880 | 116 844 | 11 601.6 | 4 734.2 | 3 655 | 24 541 | 3 112.4 | 683.1 | 18 387.4 | 5 715.0 | 2 909.5 | 538.7 |
| Kennewick-Pasco-Richland, WA | 613 | 9 790 | 952.5 | 374.4 | 325 | 1 808 | 151.3 | 44.5 | 4 614.1 | 660.7 | 186.0 | 95.1 |
| Killeen-Temple-Fort Hood, TX | 558 | 19 898 | 2 047.3 | 834.3 | 504 | 3 083 | 239.7 | 66.9 | 12 413.6 | 1 384.1 | 303.9 | 108.9 |
| Kingsport-Bristol-Bristol, TN-VA | 726 | 17 368 | 1 714.0 | 650.5 | 433 | 2 909 | 354.4 | 66.8 | 3 110.1 | 1 292.0 | 664.2 | 145.3 |
| Kingston, NY | 520 | D | D | D | 316 | 1 559 | 117.0 | 30.2 | 1 284.7 | 551.4 | 269.0 | 46.9 |
| Knoxville, TN | 1 705 | 42 022 | 4 132.4 | 1 651.0 | 1 143 | 7 707 | 793.7 | 215.5 | 9 945.5 | 2 450.3 | 1 340.5 | 276.8 |

1. Establishments subject to federal tax.

Table C. Metropolitan Areas

# Table C. Metropolitan Areas — Federal Funds, Residential Construction and Local Government Finances

| Area name | Federal funds and grants, 2009–2010 (cont.) | | | | | | | Value of residential construction authorized by building permits, 2011 | | Local government finances, 2007 | | | | |
| | Expenditures (mil dol) (cont.) | | | | | | | | | General revenue | | | | |
| | Procurement contract awards | | | Grants | | | | | | | | | Taxes | |
| | | | | | | | | | | | | | Per capita[1] (dollars) | |
| | Salaries and wages | Defense | Other | Medicaid and other health-related | Nutrition and family welfare | Education | Other | New construction ($1,000) | Number of housing units | Total (mil dol) | Inter-govern-mental (mil dol) | Total (mil dol) | Total | Property |
| | 171 | 172 | 173 | 174 | 175 | 176 | 177 | 178 | 179 | 180 | 181 | 182 | 183 | 184 |
| Flagstaff, AZ | 171.0 | 6.3 | 128.3 | 330.2 | 40.9 | 50.2 | 48.2 | 18 820 | 100 | 557.6 | 231.7 | 219.0 | 1 718 | 965 |
| Flint, MI | 129.6 | 8.1 | 36.2 | 510.6 | 112.4 | 40.8 | 46.5 | 12 723 | 66 | 2 037.0 | 976.1 | 403.5 | 928 | 864 |
| Florence, SC | 91.3 | 5.2 | 16.8 | 368.5 | 43.4 | 21.2 | 28.1 | 47 921 | 389 | 542.7 | 250.7 | 185.6 | 934 | 735 |
| Florence-Muscle Shoals, AL | 49.8 | 8.0 | 30.9 | 125.0 | 18.9 | 12.5 | 19.4 | 20 721 | 240 | 814.4 | 194.3 | 115.9 | 810 | 344 |
| Fond du Lac, WI | 23.2 | 7.1 | 5.1 | 78.8 | 14.5 | 6.4 | 4.9 | 29 161 | 237 | 412.3 | 176.1 | 143.4 | 1 447 | 1 409 |
| Fort Collins-Loveland, CO | 212.8 | 26.2 | 223.3 | 157.5 | 30.1 | 13.6 | 166.3 | 211 693 | 1 192 | 1 133.2 | 287.5 | 531.6 | 1 848 | 1 167 |
| Fort Smith, AR-OK | 189.4 | 42.1 | 36.0 | 332.0 | 48.7 | 29.4 | 26.3 | 77 386 | 590 | 781.9 | 449.3 | 193.3 | 667 | 243 |
| Fort Wayne, IN | 220.6 | 905.2 | 172.3 | 268.8 | 58.0 | 12.6 | 46.7 | 133 116 | 743 | 1 213.8 | 451.0 | 429.4 | 1 047 | 853 |
| Fresno, CA | 601.7 | 72.9 | 167.6 | 992.0 | 274.8 | 96.6 | 252.1 | 278 260 | 1 622 | 4 901.8 | 2 877.0 | 1 069.3 | 1 189 | 832 |
| Gadsden, AL | 42.2 | 4.3 | 15.2 | 119.3 | 15.8 | 11.8 | 10.7 | 11 975 | 99 | 268.4 | 133.0 | 101.5 | 983 | 266 |
| Gainesville, FL | 225.4 | 16.6 | 159.3 | 454.4 | 42.2 | 25.1 | 173.7 | 64 155 | 464 | 922.3 | 333.5 | 315.3 | 1 226 | 950 |
| Gainesville, GA | 62.2 | 264.1 | 41.1 | 74.7 | 41.3 | 9.3 | 3.2 | 36 666 | 228 | 1 091.0 | 200.0 | 285.5 | 1 585 | 843 |
| Glens Falls, NY | 34.9 | 1.6 | 8.3 | 144.7 | 36.5 | 8.9 | 8.6 | 45 235 | 242 | 680.5 | 266.1 | 307.3 | 2 384 | 1 757 |
| Goldsboro, NC | 302.7 | 74.2 | 4.5 | 202.6 | 29.5 | 13.7 | 13.4 | 27 492 | 205 | 330.8 | 188.2 | 88.4 | 779 | 555 |
| Grand Forks, ND-MN | 172.8 | 69.5 | 29.0 | 118.7 | 29.0 | 12.2 | 86.1 | 51 914 | 391 | 381.6 | 163.9 | 114.7 | 1 174 | 940 |
| Grand Junction, CO | 89.3 | 38.4 | 99.1 | 98.5 | 13.1 | 8.5 | 20.1 | 67 323 | 359 | 480.7 | 186.9 | 192.8 | 1 387 | 752 |
| Grand Rapids-Wyoming, MI | 327.2 | 89.0 | 103.8 | 550.7 | 124.2 | 47.0 | 108.0 | 161 633 | 900 | 2 911.5 | 1 413.0 | 909.1 | 1 170 | 1 052 |
| Great Falls, MT | 238.8 | 90.2 | 17.2 | 136.8 | 15.5 | 7.4 | 11.5 | 25 926 | 144 | 227.1 | 110.8 | 63.8 | 781 | 755 |
| Greeley, CO | 57.0 | 27.5 | 23.5 | 135.0 | 20.5 | 17.0 | 66.4 | 179 964 | 889 | 851.6 | 256.5 | 359.0 | 1 473 | 1 074 |
| Green Bay, WI | 122.1 | 51.1 | 61.2 | 228.2 | 46.9 | 19.8 | 39.2 | 110 487 | 880 | 1 263.2 | 571.8 | 458.2 | 1 522 | 1 402 |
| Greensboro-High Point, NC | 447.9 | 216.2 | 195.0 | 550.3 | 103.2 | 83.3 | 122.8 | 227 679 | 2 047 | 2 202.4 | 1 008.7 | 773.2 | 1 107 | 868 |
| Greenville, NC | 55.1 | 13.8 | 9.4 | 263.5 | 29.6 | 18.4 | 28.3 | 48 869 | 345 | 516.9 | 268.3 | 144.5 | 838 | 612 |
| Greenville-Mauldin-Easley, SC | 270.1 | 338.4 | 36.7 | 397.4 | 73.3 | 41.9 | 178.6 | 431 941 | 1 749 | 2 461.3 | 561.9 | 569.1 | 927 | 788 |
| Gulfport-Biloxi, MS | 787.5 | 344.6 | 527.2 | 159.7 | 47.4 | 10.5 | 100.6 | 199 586 | 1 669 | 1 611.7 | 774.5 | 264.0 | 1 140 | 955 |
| Hagerstown-Martinsburg, MD-WV | 278.7 | 36.5 | 294.8 | 168.0 | 37.3 | 11.6 | 23.9 | 96 486 | 529 | 759.6 | 303.4 | 298.4 | 1 143 | 755 |
| Hanford-Corcoran, CA | 195.1 | 28.9 | 66.6 | 129.2 | 37.8 | 20.1 | 11.0 | 28 528 | 222 | 632.3 | 386.7 | 115.8 | 778 | 616 |
| Harrisburg-Carlisle, PA | 713.5 | 993.0 | 196.5 | 674.2 | 660.6 | 2 787.2 | 2 720.3 | 201 273 | 1 113 | 2 312.2 | 863.1 | 901.8 | 1 705 | 1 200 |
| Harrisonburg, VA | 35.3 | 23.2 | 14.6 | 48.7 | 8.2 | 6.0 | 15.8 | 40 316 | 248 | 322.0 | 145.0 | 126.0 | 1 072 | 672 |
| Hartford-West Hartford-East Hartford, CT | 703.2 | 3 420.8 | 245.8 | 1 592.4 | 345.7 | 315.6 | 1 586.1 | 176 557 | 1 123 | 4 648.4 | 1 604.0 | 2 635.0 | 2 216 | 2 179 |
| Hattiesburg, MS | 317.7 | 88.2 | 14.3 | 128.8 | 26.3 | 9.8 | 74.5 | 7 629 | 64 | 710.9 | 196.5 | 120.0 | 869 | 796 |
| Hickory-Lenoir-Morganton, NC | 104.1 | 8.7 | 25.1 | 255.0 | 52.7 | 34.5 | 19.3 | 79 387 | 380 | 1 152.9 | 543.0 | 273.7 | 759 | 554 |
| Hinesville-Fort Stewart, GA | 121.4 | 34.9 | 2.0 | 34.1 | 16.8 | 15.0 | 11.1 | 41 449 | 201 | 230.2 | 110.9 | 70.7 | 984 | 534 |
| Holland-Grand Haven, MI | 41.7 | 105.5 | 62.4 | 68.2 | 32.7 | 11.3 | 12.0 | 96 405 | 611 | 809.0 | 388.8 | 287.7 | 1 110 | 1 090 |
| Honolulu, HI | 7 676.7 | 2 218.2 | 350.0 | 983.8 | 208.1 | 288.2 | 929.3 | 369 974 | 1 724 | 1 503.1 | 212.0 | 905.8 | 1 000 | 754 |
| Hot Springs, AR | 42.3 | 22.1 | 39.0 | 77.7 | 12.8 | 8.8 | 7.4 | 7 174 | 37 | 219.2 | 115.5 | 56.9 | 591 | 174 |
| Houma-Bayou Cane-Thibo-daux, LA | 50.7 | 123.7 | 369.0 | 161.3 | 38.4 | 18.9 | 31.2 | 93 952 | 390 | 953.3 | 312.6 | 273.7 | 1 361 | 458 |
| Houston-Sugar Land-Bay-town, TX | 2 793.3 | 3 886.9 | 4 615.0 | 4 191.9 | 649.4 | 245.9 | 1 067.8 | 4 831 151 | 31 271 | 21 578.3 | 5 384.7 | 10 996.2 | 1 954 | 1 628 |
| Huntington-Ashland, WV-KY-OH | 231.9 | 16.5 | 95.0 | 464.8 | 62.1 | 26.7 | 69.0 | 27 848 | 269 | 755.9 | 408.5 | 217.7 | 766 | 552 |
| Huntsville, AL | 1 360.8 | 5 254.2 | 1 129.8 | 207.8 | 35.0 | 35.6 | 106.2 | 281 084 | 2 019 | 1 841.8 | 755.2 | 363.9 | 941 | 411 |
| Idaho Falls, ID | 69.2 | 66.5 | 1 362.0 | 97.5 | 19.8 | 1.9 | 5.4 | 38 624 | 272 | 312.2 | 168.7 | 78.2 | 655 | 628 |
| Indianapolis-Carmel, IN | 1 921.8 | 1 374.2 | 552.5 | 1 448.4 | 507.1 | 513.8 | 2 464.1 | 804 377 | 5 259 | 6 662.6 | 2 171.5 | 2 338.9 | 1 380 | 1 160 |
| Iowa City, IA | 133.2 | 11.9 | 66.3 | 427.3 | 14.5 | 13.0 | 42.8 | 124 921 | 762 | 436.9 | 136.4 | 202.0 | 1 373 | 1 223 |
| Ithaca, NY | 39.8 | 18.9 | 15.5 | 210.4 | 23.7 | 11.1 | 260.2 | 23 137 | 153 | 478.3 | 175.8 | 213.9 | 2 117 | 1 557 |
| Jackson, MI | 65.1 | 17.2 | 7.3 | 140.0 | 36.5 | 10.9 | 9.0 | 8 432 | 57 | 577.7 | 311.0 | 149.1 | 915 | 851 |
| Jackson, MS | 552.5 | 355.4 | 182.9 | 696.7 | 255.0 | 328.5 | 1 232.7 | 253 299 | 1 360 | 1 530.0 | 760.6 | 488.4 | 914 | 859 |
| Jackson, TN | 85.2 | 0.1 | 8.9 | 161.1 | 20.2 | 12.0 | 13.5 | 31 904 | 174 | 870.2 | 118.1 | 143.4 | 1 273 | 643 |
| Jacksonville, FL | 1 747.8 | 970.7 | 376.4 | 912.4 | 195.3 | 112.9 | 276.8 | 758 705 | 3 911 | 5 029.7 | 1 751.1 | 1 840.9 | 1 415 | 1 070 |
| Jacksonville, NC | 1 099.6 | 920.0 | 8.7 | 89.1 | 25.9 | 15.1 | 19.2 | 226 082 | 2 031 | 491.5 | 204.5 | 109.0 | 670 | 440 |
| Janesville, WI | 40.5 | 204.4 | 16.2 | 176.1 | 29.3 | 13.4 | 15.9 | 18 301 | 99 | 656.4 | 360.8 | 202.7 | 1 270 | 1 232 |
| Jefferson City, MO | 214.4 | 10.2 | 19.7 | 248.6 | 250.4 | 407.1 | 1 971.0 | 35 176 | 211 | 297.6 | 99.9 | 142.1 | 976 | 633 |
| Johnson City, TN | 138.1 | 11.9 | 95.6 | 225.1 | 25.4 | 18.6 | 18.4 | 58 799 | 399 | 451.5 | 167.7 | 171.7 | 887 | 450 |
| Johnstown, PA | 158.9 | 1 180.9 | 28.1 | 180.3 | 33.8 | 6.0 | 41.5 | 12 027 | 62 | 524.9 | 265.3 | 128.6 | 887 | 691 |
| Jonesboro, AR | 64.8 | 11.5 | 11.4 | 152.9 | 16.6 | 10.6 | 17.4 | 62 728 | 765 | 298.5 | 174.8 | 73.3 | 630 | 299 |
| Joplin, MO | 87.9 | 37.8 | 31.3 | 189.0 | 27.0 | 16.7 | 24.8 | 29 399 | 310 | 411.9 | 157.3 | 155.2 | 906 | 487 |
| Kalamazoo-Portage, MI | 163.3 | 39.0 | 32.9 | 344.9 | 70.7 | 24.7 | 504.2 | 71 368 | 351 | 1 302.3 | 629.0 | 384.4 | 1 189 | 1 162 |
| Kankakee-Bradley, IL | 53.7 | 0.2 | 4.7 | 96.5 | 20.0 | 5.2 | 18.9 | 11 642 | 62 | 374.3 | 178.8 | 129.3 | 1 168 | 1 106 |
| Kansas City, MO-KS | 2 972.4 | 1 385.0 | 2 234.4 | 1 524.5 | 244.3 | 112.0 | 358.3 | 634 706 | 3 287 | 8 632.1 | 2 284.3 | 3 808.5 | 1 918 | 1 190 |
| Kennewick-Pasco-Richland, WA | 122.9 | 36.1 | 3 139.6 | 130.5 | 42.7 | 13.4 | 122.8 | 366 432 | 1 697 | 1 005.6 | 476.4 | 253.7 | 1 108 | 632 |
| Killeen-Temple-Fort Hood, TX | 8 731.2 | 1 306.7 | 94.3 | 202.2 | 43.8 | 83.8 | 36.5 | 302 664 | 2 208 | 1 235.5 | 571.8 | 365.0 | 986 | 763 |
| Kingsport-Bristol-Bristol, TN-VA | 108.5 | 205.9 | 33.2 | 422.3 | 54.2 | 24.5 | 108.2 | 56 224 | 385 | 838.2 | 378.5 | 297.7 | 980 | 632 |
| Kingston, NY | 54.7 | 6.1 | 10.4 | 260.8 | 43.2 | 12.7 | 10.8 | 46 577 | 230 | 984.4 | 317.9 | 535.2 | 2 943 | 2 321 |
| Knoxville, TN | 421.6 | 195.2 | 4 044.3 | 678.1 | 87.9 | 53.8 | 190.8 | 225 976 | 1 180 | 2 114.5 | 588.5 | 862.9 | 1 266 | 739 |

1. Based on the resident population estimated as of July 1 of the year shown.

# Table C. Metropolitan Areas — Local Government Finances, Government Employment, and Voting

| | Local government finances, 2007 (cont.) | | | | | | | | | Government employment, 2011 | | | Presidential election,[2] 2012 | | |
| | Direct general expenditure | | | | | | | Debt outstanding | | | | | Percent of vote cast: | | |
| | | | | Percent of total for: | | | | | | | | | | | |
| Area name | Total (mil dol) | Per capita[1] (dollars) | Educa-tion | Health and hospitals | Police protec-tion | Public welfare | High-ways | Total (mil dol) | Per capita[1] (dollars) | Federal civilian | Federal military | State and local | Demo-cratic | Republi-can | All other |
| | 185 | 186 | 187 | 188 | 189 | 190 | 191 | 192 | 193 | 194 | 195 | 196 | 197 | 198 | 199 |
| Flagstaff, AZ | 485.8 | 3 812 | 39.5 | 2.6 | 9.4 | 1.2 | 10.3 | 462.9 | 3 632 | 3 014 | 304 | 13 358 | 56.6 | 41.0 | 2.4 |
| Flint, MI | 2 071.2 | 4 764 | 47.7 | 24.0 | 4.0 | 0.9 | 3.3 | 1 026.1 | 2 360 | 1 282 | 780 | 21 383 | 63.6 | 35.4 | 1.1 |
| Florence, SC | 520.5 | 2 619 | 61.4 | 7.0 | 5.8 | 0.2 | 2.2 | 381.2 | 1 918 | 808 | 885 | 15 215 | 49.9 | 49.2 | 0.9 |
| Florence-Muscle Shoals, AL. | 550.8 | 3 847 | 42.0 | 30.7 | 3.5 | 0.1 | 4.3 | 459.8 | 3 212 | 1 370 | 717 | 8 956 | 35.8 | 62.6 | 1.6 |
| Fond du Lac, WI | 425.1 | 4 289 | 50.7 | 12.4 | 4.9 | 4.6 | 6.8 | 370.8 | 3 740 | 213 | 285 | 5 527 | 41.9 | 56.8 | 1.3 |
| Fort Collins-Loveland, CO .... | 1 068.3 | 3 715 | 36.2 | 4.8 | 7.0 | 2.5 | 11.5 | 1 529.2 | 5 317 | 2 594 | 848 | 25 232 | 51.5 | 45.7 | 2.8 |
| Fort Smith, AR-OK | 750.1 | 2 589 | 62.5 | 0.7 | 4.3 | 0.1 | 7.1 | 771.8 | 2 664 | 1 637 | 1 303 | 17 935 | 28.5 | 69.6 | 1.8 |
| Fort Wayne, IN | 1 349.4 | 3 291 | 50.4 | 0.8 | 4.4 | 2.7 | 3.2 | 996.9 | 2 431 | 1 986 | 1 432 | 19 944 | 38.8 | 59.5 | 1.6 |
| Fresno, CA | 4 984.7 | 5 543 | 47.6 | 6.2 | 5.4 | 9.9 | 3.3 | 3 891.0 | 4 326 | 10 253 | 1 633 | 54 961 | 49.9 | 48.1 | 2.0 |
| Gadsden, AL | 274.7 | 2 661 | 50.8 | 1.8 | 7.6 | 0.2 | 3.9 | 247.2 | 2 395 | 343 | 506 | 5 120 | 30.0 | 68.3 | 1.6 |
| Gainesville, FL | 906.1 | 3 524 | 42.3 | 2.6 | 8.4 | 0.7 | 3.4 | 1 732.8 | 6 740 | 4 455 | 611 | 38 461 | 55.8 | 42.6 | 1.6 |
| Gainesville, GA | 1 105.6 | 6 136 | 27.0 | 44.1 | 2.1 | 0.6 | 1.6 | 1 620.4 | 8 994 | 487 | 552 | 9 706 | 21.2 | 77.4 | 1.4 |
| Glens Falls, NY | 688.4 | 5 341 | 50.1 | 3.7 | 2.1 | 10.4 | 7.1 | 503.6 | 3 907 | 317 | 213 | 9 768 | 50.1 | 47.9 | 1.9 |
| Goldsboro, NC | 315.2 | 2 775 | 55.2 | 3.9 | 4.3 | 8.1 | 1.0 | 122.6 | 1 080 | 1 235 | 5 025 | 8 369 | 45.4 | 53.8 | 0.8 |
| Grand Forks, ND-MN | 380.7 | 3 897 | 37.4 | 0.8 | 4.1 | 5.7 | 9.4 | 558.3 | 5 715 | 1 302 | 1 929 | 11 596 | 46.5 | 50.7 | 2.8 |
| Grand Junction, CO | 515.5 | 3 707 | 37.5 | 1.5 | 9.2 | 4.5 | 14.9 | 409.8 | 2 946 | 1 510 | 401 | 8 049 | 32.7 | 65.1 | 2.2 |
| Grand Rapids-Wyoming, MI | 3 051.8 | 3 929 | 55.2 | 5.6 | 3.9 | 2.1 | 5.1 | 4 164.6 | 5 362 | 3 270 | 1 507 | 29 874 | 44.7 | 54.1 | 1.3 |
| Great Falls, MT | 225.3 | 2 755 | 48.3 | 2.4 | 8.2 | 0.6 | 3.2 | 95.4 | 1 166 | 1 787 | 3 522 | 4 147 | 44.1 | 53.1 | 2.9 |
| Greeley, CO | 813.1 | 3 336 | 41.4 | 2.0 | 5.9 | 2.3 | 7.6 | 908.7 | 3 728 | 587 | 702 | 14 811 | 42.3 | 55.0 | 2.6 |
| Green Bay, WI | 1 301.3 | 4 321 | 48.7 | 4.5 | 5.2 | 6.0 | 9.3 | 1 740.6 | 5 780 | 1 206 | 905 | 19 834 | 47.9 | 50.9 | 1.2 |
| Greensboro-High Point, NC.. | 2 356.0 | 3 373 | 47.2 | 4.7 | 6.1 | 5.8 | 2.5 | 2 002.0 | 2 866 | 4 246 | 1 957 | 40 384 | 49.8 | 49.1 | 1.1 |
| Greenville, NC | 523.4 | 3 035 | 48.5 | 4.9 | 6.2 | 7.8 | 1.4 | 396.8 | 2 300 | 486 | 520 | 25 209 | 52.4 | 46.6 | 1.0 |
| Greenville-Mauldin-Easley, SC | 2 605.7 | 4 245 | 36.3 | 34.3 | 3.4 | 0.1 | 2.4 | 4 795.1 | 7 812 | 2 125 | 2 854 | 39 247 | 33.9 | 64.3 | 1.8 |
| Gulfport-Biloxi, MS | 1 506.0 | 6 505 | 32.5 | 19.8 | 4.3 | 0.1 | 3.5 | 1 124.6 | 4 857 | 8 121 | 11 098 | 15 639 | 33.0 | 65.7 | 1.3 |
| Hagerstown-Martinsburg, MD-WV | 730.9 | 2 798 | 59.4 | 2.1 | 4.1 | 0.5 | 3.5 | 630.4 | 2 413 | 4 601 | 1 155 | 14 216 | 39.0 | 58.7 | 2.4 |
| Hanford-Corcoran, CA | 609.8 | 4 096 | 45.4 | 5.7 | 5.8 | 8.7 | 3.3 | 264.9 | 1 780 | 1 218 | 5 679 | 11 546 | 41.3 | 56.2 | 2.4 |
| Harrisburg-Carlisle, PA | 2 390.2 | 4 519 | 51.8 | 5.0 | 3.2 | 7.9 | 2.4 | 4 104.3 | 7 760 | 7 761 | 2 185 | 55 515 | 45.3 | 53.3 | 1.4 |
| Harrisonburg, VA | 374.7 | 3 188 | 54.9 | 2.5 | 4.7 | 6.2 | 4.0 | 555.6 | 4 726 | 356 | 399 | 9 986 | 37.1 | 60.9 | 2.0 |
| Hartford-West Hartford-East Hartford, CT | 4 694.5 | 3 948 | 58.9 | 0.7 | 5.0 | 0.8 | 3.5 | 2 515.2 | 2 115 | 6 224 | 2 419 | 92 037 | 60.7 | 38.1 | 1.2 |
| Hattiesburg, MS | 704.5 | 5 100 | 31.2 | 47.6 | 2.9 | 0.1 | 4.2 | 523.9 | 3 792 | 831 | 1 240 | 13 987 | 33.4 | 65.4 | 1.2 |
| Hickory-Lenoir-Morganton, NC | 1 148.6 | 3 186 | 46.7 | 19.9 | 4.0 | 7.8 | 1.3 | 490.0 | 1 359 | 818 | 945 | 23 149 | 33.7 | 64.7 | 1.6 |
| Hinesville-Fort Stewart, GA .. | 234.3 | 3 264 | 54.1 | 14.0 | 4.6 | 0.3 | 3.7 | 46.3 | 645 | 4 426 | 19 268 | 3 696 | 59.6 | 39.4 | 1.0 |
| Holland-Grand Haven, MI | 823.2 | 3 176 | 56.8 | 5.0 | 3.3 | 1.0 | 7.2 | 1 132.8 | 4 370 | 418 | 558 | 14 475 | 32.3 | 66.6 | 1.1 |
| Honolulu, HI | 1 403.3 | 1 550 | 0.0 | 2.0 | 13.7 | 0.0 | 9.7 | 4 105.7 | 4 534 | 32 059 | 54 454 | 66 778 | 68.9 | 29.8 | 1.3 |
| Hot Springs, AR | 214.2 | 2 223 | 58.7 | 0.3 | 6.5 | 0.0 | 3.5 | 179.2 | 1 860 | 534 | 418 | 4 400 | 33.9 | 63.9 | 2.2 |
| Houma-Bayou Cane-Thibo-daux, LA | 891.5 | 4 432 | 34.7 | 33.0 | 3.9 | 0.3 | 2.6 | 379.5 | 1 887 | 427 | 1 042 | 13 044 | 26.6 | 71.4 | 2.0 |
| Houston-Sugar Land-Bay-town, TX | 21 951.1 | 3 900 | 47.7 | 8.1 | 5.7 | 0.3 | 3.5 | 55 754.3 | 9 906 | 27 919 | 14 990 | 335 052 | 43.5 | 55.3 | 1.3 |
| Huntington-Ashland, WV-KY-OH | 728.0 | 2 563 | 59.0 | 2.5 | 4.1 | 2.4 | 2.7 | 582.5 | 2 051 | 3 087 | 1 237 | 17 100 | 40.6 | 57.5 | 1.9 |
| Huntsville, AL | 1 656.3 | 4 284 | 33.6 | 38.0 | 4.1 | 0.1 | 3.1 | 2 142.7 | 5 542 | 20 863 | 3 394 | 29 086 | 37.6 | 60.8 | 1.5 |
| Idaho Falls, ID | 298.3 | 2 498 | 55.1 | 1.3 | 5.0 | 0.4 | 6.2 | 186.7 | 1 564 | 816 | 500 | 6 223 | 20.5 | 77.2 | 2.2 |
| Indianapolis-Carmel, IN | 7 797.8 | 4 600 | 41.1 | 15.5 | 3.5 | 1.8 | 2.2 | 11 019.6 | 6 501 | 16 382 | 6 302 | 106 945 | 45.1 | 53.1 | 1.9 |
| Iowa City, IA | 508.5 | 3 458 | 33.2 | 7.3 | 3.9 | 0.5 | 5.1 | 753.4 | 5 124 | 1 810 | 703 | 33 128 | 64.1 | 33.6 | 2.2 |
| Ithaca, NY | 492.8 | 4 876 | 48.5 | 4.3 | 2.7 | 7.5 | 7.6 | 461.8 | 4 570 | 300 | 186 | 6 295 | 68.7 | 28.0 | 3.2 |
| Jackson, MI | 646.7 | 3 968 | 55.8 | 6.7 | 2.6 | 3.5 | 7.1 | 487.5 | 2 991 | 344 | 295 | 8 596 | 46.5 | 52.3 | 1.2 |
| Jackson, MS | 1 529.8 | 2 865 | 54.4 | 1.5 | 6.3 | 0.4 | 6.5 | 1 746.0 | 3 269 | 5 930 | 3 380 | 52 991 | 50.4 | 48.8 | 0.8 |
| Jackson, TN | 970.9 | 8 618 | 14.1 | 68.8 | 2.2 | 0.0 | 1.0 | 1 414.9 | 12 559 | 498 | 388 | 12 404 | 42.4 | 56.6 | 0.9 |
| Jacksonville, FL | 4 872.0 | 3 745 | 44.3 | 1.1 | 5.8 | 2.0 | 3.6 | 15 196.7 | 11 682 | 17 435 | 18 273 | 59 150 | 40.0 | 59.1 | 0.9 |
| Jacksonville, NC | 512.9 | 3 152 | 44.1 | 27.9 | 3.7 | 5.4 | 0.7 | 286.7 | 1 762 | 6 891 | 51 050 | 7 953 | 35.9 | 62.7 | 1.4 |
| Janesville, WI | 655.8 | 4 109 | 49.7 | 6.8 | 6.1 | 7.0 | 6.4 | 520.8 | 3 262 | 292 | 448 | 8 539 | 61.0 | 37.8 | 1.2 |
| Jefferson City, MO | 308.9 | 2 120 | 56.3 | 2.6 | 6.0 | 0.0 | 6.9 | 301.3 | 2 068 | 839 | 543 | 25 621 | 30.8 | 67.4 | 1.8 |
| Johnson City, TN | 407.4 | 2 105 | 50.3 | 7.6 | 5.6 | 0.5 | 5.5 | 998.4 | 5 158 | 2 654 | 712 | 15 011 | 27.8 | 70.4 | 1.8 |
| Johnstown, PA | 556.4 | 3 838 | 53.9 | 5.1 | 3.3 | 8.7 | 4.5 | 684.2 | 4 719 | 1 235 | 422 | 8 646 | 32.9 | 64.5 | 2.6 |
| Jonesboro, AR | 298.1 | 2 561 | 59.8 | 0.6 | 5.3 | 0.0 | 6.2 | 479.6 | 4 120 | 434 | 534 | 9 389 | 27.4 | 70.5 | 2.2 |
| Joplin, MO | 432.5 | 2 525 | 58.0 | 6.7 | 5.8 | 0.1 | 7.2 | 359.1 | 2 096 | 474 | 619 | 9 389 | 27.4 | 70.5 | 2.2 |
| Kalamazoo-Portage, MI | 1 304.4 | 4 035 | 49.8 | 17.1 | 5.7 | 0.9 | 5.4 | 1 509.8 | 4 670 | 996 | 611 | 18 534 | 54.7 | 44.1 | 1.2 |
| Kankakee-Bradley, IL | 395.4 | 3 571 | 54.9 | 1.0 | 6.0 | 0.1 | 5.7 | 256.7 | 2 319 | 251 | 228 | 6 161 | 47.5 | 50.8 | 1.7 |
| Kansas City, MO-KS | 8 688.9 | 4 376 | 42.2 | 8.6 | 6.7 | 0.4 | 4.5 | 15 122.7 | 7 617 | 28 616 | 11 609 | 126 753 | 47.7 | 50.4 | 1.9 |
| Kennewick-Pasco-Richland, WA | 926.6 | 4 046 | 46.7 | 18.5 | 3.7 | 0.0 | 5.2 | 7 695.8 | 33 607 | 1 311 | 791 | 16 948 | 35.8 | 61.8 | 2.4 |
| Killeen-Temple-Fort Hood, TX | 1 194.4 | 3 228 | 60.7 | 3.6 | 4.1 | 0.4 | 2.6 | 1 820.3 | 4 920 | 11 780 | 48 888 | 26 443 | 38.3 | 60.4 | 1.3 |
| Kingsport-Bristol-Bristol, TN-VA | 771.3 | 2 540 | 49.3 | 2.9 | 6.1 | 2.4 | 4.0 | 654.6 | 2 155 | 1 073 | 1 043 | 15 238 | 26.4 | 72.0 | 1.6 |
| Kingston, NY | 971.0 | 5 340 | 51.6 | 2.6 | 3.4 | 12.6 | 4.9 | 738.4 | 4 060 | 420 | 318 | 13 491 | 60.3 | 37.4 | 2.3 |
| Knoxville, TN | 2 067.5 | 3 034 | 37.6 | 9.4 | 5.7 | 0.3 | 2.4 | 5 792.1 | 8 499 | 5 158 | 2 467 | 46 747 | 31.9 | 66.3 | 1.9 |

1. Based on the resident population estimated as of July 1 of the year shown.    2. © 2013 Election Data Services, Inc. All rights reserved.

Table C. Metropolitan Areas — **Land Area and Population**

| CBSA/ DIV code[1] | Area name | Land area,[2] 2010 (sq km) | Total persons | Rank | Per square kilometer | White | Black | American Indian, Alaska Native | Asian and Pacific Islander | Percent Hispanic or Latino[3] | Under 5 years | 5 to 17 years | 18 to 24 years | 25 to 34 years | 35 to 44 years | 45 to 54 years |
|---|---|---|---|---|---|---|---|---|---|---|---|---|---|---|---|---|
| | | 1 | 2 | 3 | 4 | 5 | 6 | 7 | 8 | 9 | 10 | 11 | 12 | 13 | 14 | 15 |
| 29020 | Kokomo, IN | 1 434 | 98 544 | 345 | 68.7 | 90.2 | 7.0 | 0.7 | 1.3 | 2.6 | 5.9 | 17.2 | 7.8 | 11.3 | 12.2 | 14.9 |
| 29100 | La Crosse, WI-MN | 2 600 | 135 298 | 290 | 52.0 | 93.0 | 2.0 | 0.7 | 4.2 | 1.5 | 5.8 | 15.3 | 14.7 | 12.5 | 11.1 | 13.8 |
| 29140 | Lafayette, IN | 3 311 | 206 412 | 207 | 62.3 | 83.3 | 4.4 | 0.6 | 6.2 | 7.2 | 6.3 | 14.7 | 22.9 | 13.5 | 10.8 | 11.3 |
| 29180 | Lafayette, LA | 2 606 | 279 781 | 167 | 107.4 | 67.7 | 27.4 | 0.7 | 1.7 | 3.7 | 7.1 | 17.6 | 11.4 | 15.1 | 12.5 | 14.1 |
| 29340 | Lake Charles, LA | 6 083 | 201 195 | 212 | 33.1 | 71.3 | 25.1 | 1.0 | 1.4 | 2.7 | 7.1 | 18.0 | 10.0 | 13.6 | 11.9 | 14.3 |
| 29420 | Lake Havasu City-Kingman, AZ | 34 476 | 203 334 | 211 | 5.9 | 80.5 | 1.4 | 2.8 | 1.9 | 15.2 | 5.3 | 14.9 | 6.9 | 9.3 | 9.7 | 13.8 |
| 29460 | Lakeland-Winter Haven, FL. | 4 656 | 616 158 | 87 | 132.3 | 65.3 | 15.1 | 0.7 | 2.2 | 18.1 | 6.3 | 16.9 | 8.9 | 11.9 | 12.0 | 13.1 |
| 29540 | Lancaster, PA | 2 444 | 526 823 | 99 | 215.6 | 85.7 | 4.0 | 0.4 | 2.3 | 8.9 | 6.8 | 17.8 | 9.6 | 11.9 | 11.9 | 14.3 |
| 29620 | Lansing-East Lansing, MI | 4 397 | 465 732 | 109 | 105.9 | 80.5 | 10.3 | 1.2 | 4.5 | 6.2 | 5.6 | 15.9 | 16.4 | 12.7 | 11.4 | 13.6 |
| 29700 | Laredo, TX | 8 706 | 259 172 | 180 | 29.8 | 3.7 | 0.3 | 0.1 | 0.6 | 95.4 | 9.8 | 25.0 | 11.0 | 13.8 | 13.7 | 10.9 |
| 29740 | Las Cruces, NM | 9 861 | 214 445 | 201 | 21.7 | 30.7 | 1.7 | 1.2 | 1.5 | 65.9 | 7.5 | 19.0 | 12.9 | 13.5 | 11.1 | 12.4 |
| 29820 | Las Vegas-Paradise, NV | 20 439 | 2 000 759 | 30 | 97.9 | 50.0 | 11.2 | 1.0 | 11.5 | 29.7 | 7.0 | 17.8 | 9.2 | 15.0 | 14.5 | 13.5 |
| 29940 | Lawrence, KS | 1 181 | 112 864 | 329 | 95.6 | 83.9 | 5.4 | 3.4 | 5.2 | 5.5 | 5.4 | 13.1 | 26.0 | 15.4 | 10.7 | 10.7 |
| 30020 | Lawton, OK | 2 769 | 126 390 | 308 | 45.6 | 63.1 | 19.2 | 7.4 | 4.4 | 11.5 | 7.7 | 17.4 | 13.5 | 16.7 | 12.0 | 12.7 |
| 30140 | Lebanon, PA | 937 | 135 251 | 291 | 144.3 | 87.2 | 2.2 | 0.4 | 1.5 | 9.7 | 6.2 | 16.5 | 8.4 | 11.3 | 12.3 | 14.6 |
| 30300 | Lewiston, ID-WA | 3 844 | 61 419 | 365 | 16.0 | 91.7 | 0.8 | 5.1 | 1.5 | 3.1 | 5.7 | 15.9 | 9.1 | 11.9 | 11.0 | 14.0 |
| 30340 | Lewiston-Auburn, ME | 1 212 | 107 609 | 334 | 88.8 | 93.6 | 4.4 | 1.2 | 1.2 | 1.6 | 6.3 | 16.0 | 9.2 | 12.2 | 12.9 | 15.7 |
| 30460 | Lexington-Fayette, KY | 3 803 | 485 023 | 105 | 127.5 | 80.6 | 11.8 | 0.6 | 2.9 | 5.9 | 6.5 | 16.0 | 12.4 | 14.9 | 13.5 | 13.8 |
| 30620 | Lima, OH | 1 042 | 105 141 | 337 | 100.9 | 84.6 | 13.6 | 0.6 | 1.1 | 2.5 | 6.3 | 17.4 | 10.7 | 11.7 | 11.5 | 14.2 |
| 30700 | Lincoln, NE | 3 649 | 310 342 | 154 | 85.0 | 86.8 | 4.5 | 1.1 | 4.1 | 5.8 | 6.9 | 16.0 | 15.1 | 14.8 | 11.9 | 12.6 |
| 30780 | Little Rock-North Little Rock-Conway, AR | 10 581 | 717 666 | 73 | 67.8 | 70.7 | 22.9 | 1.1 | 2.0 | 5.0 | 6.8 | 17.5 | 9.9 | 14.6 | 13.1 | 13.8 |
| 30860 | Logan, UT-ID | 4 736 | 128 306 | 304 | 27.1 | 86.9 | 0.9 | 0.9 | 3.0 | 9.7 | 9.7 | 21.6 | 17.9 | 15.2 | 10.3 | 9.2 |
| 30980 | Longview, TX | 4 611 | 216 679 | 197 | 47.0 | 66.6 | 17.9 | 1.0 | 1.2 | 14.9 | 7.1 | 17.7 | 9.6 | 13.2 | 12.1 | 13.3 |
| 31020 | Longview, WA | 2 953 | 101 996 | 340 | 34.5 | 88.0 | 1.2 | 3.1 | 2.6 | 8.1 | 6.2 | 17.7 | 8.2 | 11.3 | 12.0 | 14.4 |
| 31100 | Los Angeles-Long Beach-Santa Ana, CA | 12 557 | 13 052 921 | 2 | 1 039.5 | 33.1 | 7.3 | 0.6 | 16.3 | 44.8 | 6.5 | 17.6 | 10.6 | 14.8 | 14.4 | 14.1 |
| 31100 | Los Angeles-Long Beach-Glendale, CA Div | 10 510 | 9 962 789 | X | 947.9 | 29.2 | 8.9 | 0.6 | 15.2 | 48.1 | 6.6 | 17.5 | 10.8 | 15.1 | 14.4 | 13.9 |
| 31100 | Santa Ana-Anaheim-Irvine, CA Div | 2 048 | 3 090 132 | X | 1 508.9 | 45.6 | 2.0 | 0.6 | 20.1 | 34.1 | 6.3 | 17.8 | 10.1 | 13.8 | 14.3 | 14.7 |
| 31140 | Louisville-Jefferson County, KY-IN | 10 647 | 1 301 116 | 42 | 122.2 | 80.3 | 14.7 | 0.7 | 2.0 | 4.1 | 6.4 | 17.3 | 8.6 | 13.5 | 13.2 | 15.1 |
| 31180 | Lubbock, TX | 4 651 | 291 886 | 161 | 62.8 | 57.3 | 7.6 | 0.7 | 2.5 | 33.0 | 7.3 | 17.0 | 17.4 | 14.3 | 10.8 | 12.0 |
| 31340 | Lynchburg, VA | 5 492 | 255 342 | 184 | 46.5 | 78.4 | 18.4 | 0.8 | 1.8 | 2.2 | 5.4 | 15.4 | 12.6 | 11.0 | 11.7 | 14.5 |
| 31420 | Macon, GA | 4 462 | 232 723 | 193 | 52.2 | 52.1 | 44.2 | 0.6 | 1.7 | 2.7 | 6.8 | 18.0 | 9.9 | 12.5 | 12.2 | 14.4 |
| 31460 | Madera-Chowchilla, CA | 5 535 | 152 218 | 261 | 27.5 | 38.8 | 3.9 | 1.9 | 2.5 | 54.5 | 7.8 | 20.4 | 10.5 | 13.8 | 12.5 | 12.6 |
| 31540 | Madison, WI | 7 059 | 583 869 | 89 | 82.7 | 85.1 | 5.6 | 0.8 | 5.0 | 5.6 | 6.0 | 15.6 | 12.7 | 15.4 | 13.0 | 14.1 |
| 31700 | Manchester-Nashua, NH | 2 269 | 402 922 | 130 | 177.6 | 89.0 | 2.5 | 0.6 | 4.0 | 5.5 | 5.8 | 17.2 | 8.6 | 12.4 | 13.9 | 17.0 |
| 31740 | Manhattan, KS | 4 754 | 135 823 | 289 | 28.6 | 78.9 | 9.9 | 1.5 | 5.0 | 8.3 | 8.2 | 15.2 | 24.3 | 17.4 | 9.6 | 9.2 |
| 31860 | Mankato, North Mankato, MN | 3 098 | 98 020 | 347 | 31.6 | 92.1 | 3.1 | 0.7 | 2.5 | 3.0 | 6.0 | 14.2 | 20.6 | 13.7 | 10.3 | 12.0 |
| 31900 | Mansfield, OH | 1 283 | 122 673 | 311 | 95.6 | 88.3 | 10.4 | 0.7 | 1.0 | 1.5 | 5.9 | 16.3 | 8.5 | 11.9 | 12.3 | 14.7 |
| 32580 | McAllen-Edinburg-Mission, TX | 4 069 | 806 552 | 67 | 198.2 | 7.9 | 0.5 | 0.1 | 1.0 | 90.7 | 9.7 | 24.7 | 10.8 | 13.8 | 13.2 | 10.4 |
| 32780 | Medford, OR | 7 209 | 206 412 | 206 | 28.6 | 85.6 | 1.1 | 2.3 | 2.5 | 11.2 | 5.8 | 15.7 | 8.6 | 11.6 | 11.2 | 13.7 |
| 32820 | Memphis, TN-MS-AR | 11 857 | 1 332 960 | 41 | 112.4 | 47.0 | 46.1 | 0.6 | 2.3 | 5.2 | 7.1 | 19.1 | 9.9 | 13.7 | 13.3 | 14.2 |
| 32900 | Merced, CA | 5 012 | 262 305 | 178 | 52.3 | 32.8 | 3.9 | 0.9 | 8.6 | 55.7 | 8.5 | 22.6 | 11.9 | 13.8 | 12.3 | 12.1 |
| 33100 | Miami-Fort Lauderdale-Pompano Beach, FL | 13 150 | 5 762 717 | 8 | 438.2 | 35.6 | 20.5 | 0.3 | 2.9 | 41.8 | 5.8 | 15.5 | 9.1 | 12.9 | 13.9 | 15.0 |
| 33100 | Fort Lauderdale-Pompano Beach-Deerfield Beach, FL Div | 3 133 | 1 815 137 | X | 579.4 | 44.2 | 26.9 | 0.5 | 4.2 | 25.8 | 5.9 | 16.1 | 8.6 | 13.1 | 14.0 | 15.8 |
| 33100 | Miami-Miami Beach-Kendall, FL Div | 4 915 | 2 591 035 | X | 527.2 | 16.5 | 17.5 | 0.2 | 1.9 | 64.5 | 5.9 | 15.5 | 10.0 | 13.7 | 14.7 | 14.9 |
| 33100 | West Palm Beach-Boca Raton-Boynton Beach, FL Div | 5 102 | 1 356 545 | X | 265.9 | 60.5 | 17.7 | 0.4 | 3.1 | 19.6 | 5.3 | 14.9 | 8.0 | 11.2 | 12.2 | 14.1 |
| 33140 | Michigan City-La Porte, IN .. | 1 550 | 111 246 | 330 | 71.8 | 82.9 | 11.8 | 0.7 | 0.8 | 5.6 | 6.0 | 16.5 | 8.5 | 13.0 | 12.8 | 15.0 |
| 33260 | Midland, TX | 2 332 | 146 645 | 272 | 62.9 | 53.1 | 6.8 | 0.8 | 1.6 | 38.8 | 8.2 | 19.2 | 9.9 | 15.0 | 11.7 | 13.8 |
| 33340 | Milwaukee-Waukesha-West Allis, WI | 3 768 | 1 566 981 | 39 | 415.9 | 70.2 | 17.4 | 0.9 | 3.5 | 9.7 | 6.6 | 17.7 | 9.5 | 13.7 | 12.6 | 14.8 |
| 33460 | Minneapolis-St. Paul-Bloomington, MN | 15 610 | 3 353 724 | 16 | 214.8 | 80.5 | 8.5 | 1.3 | 6.7 | 5.5 | 6.8 | 17.9 | 8.9 | 14.8 | 13.6 | 15.3 |
| 33540 | Missoula, MT | 6 717 | 110 977 | 331 | 16.5 | 92.9 | 0.9 | 4.0 | 2.0 | 2.8 | 5.6 | 13.9 | 15.6 | 15.8 | 11.5 | 12.9 |
| 33660 | Mobile, AL | 3 184 | 413 936 | 126 | 130.0 | 59.9 | 35.3 | 1.4 | 2.3 | 2.5 | 6.8 | 18.0 | 10.0 | 13.0 | 12.2 | 14.2 |
| 33700 | Modesto, CA | 3 872 | 521 726 | 101 | 134.7 | 48.3 | 3.2 | 1.4 | 7.3 | 42.6 | 7.7 | 20.6 | 10.5 | 13.7 | 12.8 | 13.3 |
| 33740 | Monroe, LA | 3 852 | 177 782 | 230 | 46.2 | 61.2 | 35.9 | 0.6 | 1.2 | 2.2 | 7.2 | 18.5 | 10.8 | 13.4 | 12.0 | 13.2 |
| 33780 | Monroe, MI | 1 423 | 151 048 | 264 | 106.1 | 93.8 | 2.9 | 0.8 | 0.9 | 3.1 | 5.7 | 18.0 | 8.4 | 10.9 | 12.8 | 16.3 |
| 33860 | Montgomery, AL | 7 027 | 377 149 | 136 | 53.7 | 52.1 | 43.3 | 0.7 | 2.0 | 3.2 | 6.6 | 18.0 | 10.9 | 13.6 | 13.1 | 13.9 |
| 34060 | Morgantown, WV | 2 613 | 134 164 | 294 | 51.3 | 92.7 | 3.8 | 0.6 | 2.8 | 1.7 | 4.8 | 11.9 | 21.8 | 14.9 | 11.3 | 12.1 |
| 34100 | Morristown, TN | 1 854 | 137 643 | 285 | 74.2 | 89.6 | 3.5 | 0.7 | 0.8 | 6.7 | 6.0 | 16.7 | 8.6 | 11.2 | 13.2 | 14.5 |
| 34580 | Mount Vernon-Anacortes, WA | 4 484 | 118 222 | 316 | 26.4 | 78.2 | 1.1 | 2.7 | 2.9 | 17.3 | 6.4 | 17.0 | 8.4 | 12.1 | 11.7 | 13.6 |
| 34620 | Muncie, IN | 1 016 | 117 364 | 318 | 115.5 | 89.7 | 8.0 | 0.7 | 1.7 | 1.9 | 5.4 | 14.3 | 20.1 | 10.7 | 10.6 | 12.4 |
| 34740 | Muskegon-Norton Shores, MI | 1 293 | 170 182 | 236 | 131.6 | 79.3 | 15.6 | 1.6 | 1.0 | 4.9 | 6.5 | 17.9 | 9.1 | 12.4 | 12.2 | 14.9 |
| 34820 | Myrtle Beach-North Myrtle Beach-Conway, SC | 2 937 | 282 285 | 165 | 96.1 | 78.5 | 14.3 | 0.9 | 1.6 | 6.3 | 5.6 | 14.4 | 9.5 | 12.4 | 12.1 | 13.5 |
| 34900 | Napa, CA | 1 938 | 139 045 | 284 | 71.7 | 57.5 | 2.3 | 1.1 | 8.4 | 32.9 | 5.9 | 17.0 | 8.9 | 12.4 | 12.8 | 14.4 |

1. CBSA = Core Based Statistical Area. DIV = Metropolitan Division. See Appendix A for explanation. See Appendix B for list of metropolitan areas identified by type.   2. Dry land or land partially or temporarily covered by water.   3. May be of any race.

# Table C. Metropolitan Areas — **Population and Households**

| Area name | 55 to 64 years | 65 to 74 years | 75 years and over | Percent female | 2000 | 2010 | 2000–2010 | 2010–2012 | Births | Deaths | Net migration | Number | Percent change, 2000–2010 | Persons per house-hold | Female family house-holder[1] | One person |
|---|---|---|---|---|---|---|---|---|---|---|---|---|---|---|---|---|
| | 16 | 17 | 18 | 19 | 20 | 21 | 22 | 23 | 24 | 25 | 26 | 27 | 28 | 29 | 30 | 31 |
| Kokomo, IN ...................... | 13.8 | 9.3 | 7.6 | 51.6 | 101 541 | 98 688 | -2.8 | -0.1 | 2 450 | 2 378 | -240 | 40 677 | -1.4 | 2.39 | 12.6 | 28.8 |
| La Crosse, WI-MN ............... | 12.5 | 7.0 | 7.1 | 51.0 | 126 838 | 133 665 | 5.4 | 1.2 | 3 418 | 2 541 | 761 | 53 986 | 9.7 | 2.37 | 8.6 | 29.2 |
| Lafayette, IN..................... | 10.0 | 5.6 | 4.9 | 49.1 | 178 541 | 201 789 | 13.0 | 2.3 | 5 553 | 3 010 | 2 109 | 76 911 | 15.7 | 2.43 | 9.5 | 28.6 |
| Lafayette, LA..................... | 11.4 | 6.0 | 4.7 | 51.2 | 239 086 | 273 738 | 14.5 | 2.2 | 8 967 | 4 710 | 1 863 | 106 243 | 18.7 | 2.52 | 15.4 | 26.9 |
| Lake Charles, LA ............... | 12.3 | 7.2 | 5.6 | 51.2 | 193 568 | 199 607 | 3.1 | 0.8 | 6 324 | 4 338 | -320 | 76 571 | 6.0 | 2.56 | 15.7 | 25.9 |
| Lake Havasu City-Kingman, AZ .............................. | 16.1 | 14.4 | 9.6 | 49.9 | 155 032 | 200 186 | 29.1 | 1.6 | 4 681 | 5 863 | 4 268 | 82 539 | 31.4 | 2.39 | 10.4 | 26.7 |
| Lakeland-Winter Haven, FL ... | 12.5 | 10.2 | 8.1 | 51.0 | 483 924 | 602 095 | 24.4 | 2.3 | 16 386 | 13 083 | 11 078 | 227 485 | 21.5 | 2.59 | 13.7 | 23.8 |
| Lancaster, PA ..................... | 12.4 | 7.6 | 7.7 | 51.1 | 470 658 | 519 445 | 10.4 | 1.4 | 15 896 | 10 240 | 1 815 | 193 602 | 12.2 | 2.62 | 9.6 | 24.2 |
| Lansing-East Lansing, MI ..... | 12.4 | 6.6 | 5.5 | 51.3 | 447 728 | 464 036 | 3.6 | 0.4 | 11 433 | 7 600 | -2 253 | 183 422 | 6.4 | 2.42 | 11.7 | 28.9 |
| Laredo, TX ........................ | 7.7 | 4.5 | 3.5 | 51.4 | 193 117 | 250 304 | 29.6 | 3.5 | 12 204 | 2 676 | -582 | 67 106 | 32.3 | 3.68 | 20.9 | 13.4 |
| Las Cruces, NM ................. | 11.0 | 7.1 | 5.6 | 50.9 | 174 682 | 209 233 | 19.8 | 2.5 | 7 408 | 3 234 | 1 084 | 75 532 | 26.8 | 2.71 | 16.0 | 24.2 |
| Las Vegas-Paradise, NV ...... | 11.3 | 7.2 | 4.6 | 49.7 | 1 375 765 | 1 951 269 | 41.8 | 2.5 | 60 960 | 29 877 | 18 588 | 715 365 | 39.7 | 2.70 | 13.5 | 25.3 |
| Lawrence, KS ..................... | 9.8 | 4.8 | 4.3 | 49.8 | 99 962 | 110 826 | 10.9 | 1.8 | 2 754 | 1 335 | 616 | 43 576 | 13.2 | 2.34 | 8.6 | 29.8 |
| Lawton, OK ........................ | 9.7 | 5.7 | 4.6 | 48.4 | 114 996 | 124 098 | 7.9 | 1.8 | 4 546 | 2 124 | -178 | 44 982 | 13.0 | 2.53 | 14.5 | 27.1 |
| Lebanon, PA ...................... | 13.5 | 8.6 | 8.5 | 51.2 | 120 327 | 133 568 | 11.0 | 1.3 | 3 639 | 3 127 | 1 212 | 52 258 | 12.3 | 2.49 | 10.1 | 25.9 |
| Lewiston, ID-WA ................ | 13.8 | 9.6 | 8.9 | 51.0 | 57 961 | 60 888 | 5.0 | 0.9 | 1 522 | 1 571 | 601 | 25 477 | 7.7 | 2.35 | 10.9 | 28.9 |
| Lewiston-Auburn, ME............ | 13.3 | 7.5 | 6.8 | 51.0 | 103 793 | 107 702 | 3.8 | -0.1 | 2 972 | 2 229 | -808 | 44 315 | 5.4 | 2.37 | 12.0 | 28.3 |
| Lexington-Fayette, KY ......... | 11.7 | 6.3 | 5.0 | 50.9 | 408 326 | 472 099 | 15.6 | 2.7 | 13 949 | 7 876 | 6 871 | 190 142 | 16.0 | 2.39 | 12.4 | 29.3 |
| Lima, OH........................... | 13.2 | 7.6 | 7.4 | 49.6 | 108 473 | 106 331 | -2.0 | -1.1 | 2 873 | 2 428 | -1 639 | 40 619 | -0.1 | 2.47 | 13.8 | 28.7 |
| Lincoln, NE........................ | 11.4 | 5.9 | 5.4 | 49.9 | 266 787 | 302 157 | 13.3 | 2.7 | 9 700 | 4 502 | 3 014 | 119 639 | 13.7 | 2.40 | 9.5 | 29.8 |
| Little Rock-North Little Rock-Conway, AR .................. | 12.1 | 7.0 | 5.3 | 51.4 | 610 518 | 699 757 | 14.6 | 2.6 | 21 743 | 13 299 | 9 350 | 279 225 | 15.8 | 2.45 | 14.4 | 27.7 |
| Logan, UT-ID ..................... | 7.6 | 4.5 | 3.9 | 50.3 | 102 720 | 125 442 | 22.1 | 2.3 | 5 868 | 1 298 | -1 738 | 38 801 | 25.1 | 3.14 | 7.6 | 16.5 |
| Longview, TX ...................... | 12.2 | 7.6 | 6.6 | 50.0 | 194 042 | 214 369 | 10.5 | 1.1 | 6 859 | 5 047 | 528 | 79 199 | 8.0 | 2.58 | 13.7 | 25.8 |
| Longview, WA..................... | 14.2 | 9.0 | 7.0 | 50.5 | 92 948 | 102 410 | 10.2 | -0.4 | 2 772 | 2 189 | -998 | 40 244 | 12.3 | 2.51 | 11.8 | 25.8 |
| Los Angeles-Long Beach-Santa Ana, CA.............. | 10.8 | 6.1 | 5.2 | 50.6 | 12 365 627 | 12 828 837 | 3.7 | 1.7 | 390 725 | 173 334 | 10 008 | 4 233 985 | 4.1 | 2.98 | 14.5 | 23.4 |
| Los Angeles-Long Beach-Glendale, CA Div............ | 10.7 | 6.0 | 5.2 | 50.7 | 9 519 338 | 9 818 605 | 3.1 | 1.5 | 302 441 | 133 505 | -22 066 | 3 241 204 | 3.4 | 2.98 | 15.3 | 24.2 |
| Santa Ana-Anaheim-Irvine, CA Div..................... | 11.1 | 6.4 | 5.5 | 50.5 | 2 846 289 | 3 010 232 | 5.8 | 2.7 | 88 284 | 39 829 | 32 074 | 992 781 | 6.1 | 2.99 | 11.6 | 20.9 |
| Louisville-Jefferson County, KY-IN .......................... | 12.9 | 7.1 | 5.9 | 51.2 | 1 161 975 | 1 283 566 | 10.5 | 1.4 | 36 995 | 25 799 | 6 645 | 514 214 | 11.2 | 2.45 | 13.9 | 28.3 |
| Lubbock, TX ...................... | 10.1 | 6.0 | 5.2 | 50.6 | 249 700 | 284 890 | 14.1 | 2.5 | 9 254 | 5 318 | 3 015 | 108 018 | 13.7 | 2.53 | 13.5 | 27.4 |
| Lynchburg, VA .................... | 13.4 | 8.8 | 7.2 | 51.8 | 228 616 | 252 634 | 10.5 | 1.1 | 6 095 | 5 477 | 1 931 | 99 602 | 11.0 | 2.41 | 12.6 | 27.0 |
| Macon, GA ........................ | 12.8 | 7.4 | 5.8 | 52.0 | 222 368 | 232 293 | 4.5 | 0.2 | 7 034 | 5 410 | -1 331 | 88 999 | 5.5 | 2.52 | 19.4 | 27.8 |
| Madera-Chowchilla, CA ....... | 10.8 | 6.7 | 4.9 | 51.8 | 123 109 | 150 865 | 22.5 | 0.9 | 5 411 | 2 102 | -1 931 | 43 317 | 19.8 | 3.28 | 13.3 | 16.7 |
| Madison, WI ...................... | 12.1 | 6.0 | 5.2 | 50.3 | 501 774 | 568 593 | 13.3 | 2.7 | 15 656 | 7 935 | 7 381 | 236 032 | 16.5 | 2.35 | 8.5 | 29.9 |
| Manchester-Nashua, NH ...... | 12.9 | 6.7 | 5.6 | 50.5 | 380 841 | 400 721 | 5.2 | 0.5 | 9 948 | 6 430 | -1 175 | 155 466 | 7.6 | 2.53 | 10.5 | 25.3 |
| Manhattan, KS ................... | 7.9 | 4.2 | 4.0 | 48.7 | 108 899 | 127 081 | 16.6 | 6.9 | 5 556 | 1 580 | 4 672 | 46 364 | 17.8 | 2.52 | 10.9 | 25.8 |
| Mankato, North Mankato, MN ................................ | 11.1 | 6.0 | 6.1 | 49.9 | 85 712 | 96 740 | 12.9 | 1.3 | 2 544 | 1 542 | 290 | 36 646 | 15.6 | 2.44 | 8.5 | 27.1 |
| Mansfield, OH .................... | 13.8 | 8.7 | 7.9 | 49.3 | 128 852 | 124 475 | -3.4 | -1.4 | 3 098 | 2 914 | -1 980 | 48 921 | -1.2 | 2.40 | 12.5 | 28.8 |
| McAllen-Edinburg-Mission, TX ................................. | 7.9 | 5.2 | 4.3 | 51.2 | 569 463 | 774 769 | 36.1 | 4.1 | 36 410 | 8 534 | 3 827 | 216 471 | 38.0 | 3.55 | 18.8 | 14.0 |
| Medford, OR ...................... | 15.2 | 9.7 | 8.4 | 51.3 | 181 269 | 203 206 | 12.1 | 1.6 | 5 160 | 4 712 | 2 774 | 83 076 | 16.1 | 2.40 | 11.0 | 27.7 |
| Memphis, TN-MS-AR........... | 11.9 | 6.1 | 4.7 | 52.0 | 1 205 204 | 1 316 100 | 9.2 | 1.3 | 43 110 | 24 845 | -1 336 | 491 198 | 9.5 | 2.63 | 20.3 | 26.4 |
| Merced, CA ........................ | 9.1 | 5.3 | 4.3 | 49.6 | 210 554 | 255 793 | 21.5 | 2.5 | 9 841 | 3 454 | 127 | 75 642 | 18.5 | 3.32 | 15.8 | 17.4 |
| Miami-Fort Lauderdale-Pompano Beach, FL............. | 11.8 | 8.0 | 8.0 | 51.5 | 5 007 564 | 5 564 635 | 11.1 | 3.6 | 147 680 | 104 274 | 155 462 | 2 097 626 | 10.1 | 2.62 | 15.8 | 27.0 |
| Fort Lauderdale-Pompano Beach-Deerfield Beach, FL Div.............. | 12.2 | 7.3 | 7.0 | 51.5 | 1 623 018 | 1 748 066 | 7.7 | 3.8 | 46 965 | 32 473 | 53 032 | 686 047 | 4.8 | 2.52 | 15.3 | 28.8 |
| Miami-Miami Beach-Kendall, FL Div................. | 11.2 | 7.5 | 6.7 | 51.4 | 2 253 362 | 2 496 435 | 10.8 | 3.8 | 70 089 | 41 938 | 66 334 | 867 352 | 11.7 | 2.83 | 18.8 | 23.5 |
| West Palm Beach-Boca Raton-Boynton Beach, FL Div ....................... | 12.4 | 10.0 | 11.8 | 51.6 | 1 131 184 | 1 320 134 | 16.7 | 2.8 | 30 626 | 29 863 | 36 096 | 544 227 | 14.8 | 2.39 | 11.7 | 30.1 |
| Michigan City-La Porte, IN.... | 13.8 | 8.0 | 6.5 | 48.3 | 110 106 | 111 467 | 1.2 | -0.2 | 2 988 | 2 509 | -681 | 42 331 | 3.1 | 2.48 | 12.8 | 27.3 |
| Midland, TX........................ | 11.3 | 5.5 | 5.4 | 50.7 | 116 009 | 136 872 | 18.0 | 7.1 | 5 112 | 2 260 | 6 735 | 50 845 | 18.9 | 2.66 | 12.8 | 24.8 |
| Milwaukee-Waukesha-West Allis, WI ........................ | 12.3 | 6.4 | 6.3 | 51.3 | 1 500 741 | 1 555 908 | 3.7 | 0.7 | 46 088 | 28 748 | -5 958 | 622 087 | 5.9 | 2.45 | 13.4 | 29.9 |
| Minneapolis-St. Paul-Bloomington, MN ........... | 11.8 | 5.9 | 5.0 | 50.6 | 2 968 806 | 3 279 833 | 10.5 | 2.3 | 97 842 | 45 451 | 21 897 | 1 272 677 | 12.0 | 2.53 | 10.2 | 27.5 |
| Missoula, MT...................... | 13.0 | 6.7 | 5.1 | 49.6 | 95 802 | 109 299 | 14.1 | 1.5 | 2 657 | 1 696 | 752 | 45 926 | 19.5 | 2.30 | 9.2 | 30.3 |
| Mobile, AL......................... | 12.5 | 7.5 | 5.7 | 52.0 | 399 843 | 412 992 | 3.3 | 0.2 | 12 955 | 9 222 | -2 660 | 158 435 | 5.5 | 2.56 | 18.8 | 26.5 |
| Modesto, CA ...................... | 10.5 | 5.9 | 5.0 | 50.5 | 446 997 | 514 453 | 15.1 | 1.4 | 17 531 | 7 997 | -2 174 | 165 180 | 13.8 | 3.08 | 14.6 | 19.3 |
| Monroe, LA ........................ | 11.8 | 7.1 | 6.0 | 52.0 | 170 053 | 176 441 | 3.8 | 0.8 | 5 789 | 3 942 | -432 | 67 835 | 5.9 | 2.51 | 19.4 | 27.8 |
| Monroe, MI ........................ | 14.1 | 7.6 | 6.2 | 50.7 | 145 945 | 152 021 | 4.2 | -0.6 | 3 641 | 2 856 | -1 772 | 58 230 | 8.3 | 2.59 | 11.1 | 23.5 |
| Montgomery, AL................... | 11.7 | 6.9 | 5.3 | 52.0 | 346 528 | 374 536 | 8.1 | 0.7 | 11 664 | 7 459 | -1 618 | 142 855 | 10.1 | 2.52 | 18.5 | 27.4 |
| Morgantown, WV ................ | 11.6 | 6.5 | 5.2 | 48.5 | 111 200 | 129 709 | 16.6 | 3.4 | 2 926 | 2 187 | 3 683 | 52 672 | 17.1 | 2.28 | 8.4 | 30.0 |
| Morristown, TN................... | 13.4 | 9.9 | 6.5 | 50.9 | 123 081 | 136 608 | 11.0 | 0.8 | 3 469 | 3 366 | 925 | 53 453 | 9.9 | 2.51 | 11.0 | 24.3 |
| Mount Vernon-Anacortes, WA ............................. | 14.2 | 9.2 | 7.4 | 50.4 | 102 979 | 116 901 | 13.5 | 1.1 | 3 282 | 2 458 | 487 | 45 557 | 17.3 | 2.53 | 10.1 | 25.6 |
| Muncie, IN......................... | 11.5 | 8.0 | 7.0 | 52.0 | 118 769 | 117 671 | -0.9 | -0.3 | 2 822 | 2 607 | -453 | 46 516 | -1.3 | 2.34 | 12.2 | 29.6 |
| Muskegon-Norton Shores, MI .............................. | 13.2 | 7.4 | 6.5 | 50.3 | 170 200 | 172 188 | 1.2 | -1.2 | 4 856 | 3 651 | -3 186 | 65 616 | 3.6 | 2.53 | 15.4 | 26.4 |
| Myrtle Beach-North Myrtle Beach-Conway, SC ....... | 14.7 | 11.0 | 6.8 | 51.1 | 196 629 | 269 291 | 37.0 | 4.8 | 6 877 | 5 978 | 11 922 | 112 225 | 37.2 | 2.37 | 12.5 | 26.8 |
| Napa, CA........................... | 13.3 | 8.0 | 7.3 | 50.1 | 124 279 | 136 484 | 9.8 | 1.9 | 3 636 | 2 683 | 1 621 | 48 876 | 7.7 | 2.69 | 10.3 | 25.3 |

1. No spouse present.

| Area name | Daytime population, 2007–2011 | | | Births, 2011 | | Deaths, 2011 | | Persons under 65 with no health insurance 2010 | | Medicare, 2012 | | | Serious crimes known to police,[2] 2011 Total | |
|---|---|---|---|---|---|---|---|---|---|---|---|---|---|---|
| | Persons in group quarters, 2009 | Number | Employ-ment/residence ratio | Total | Rate[1] | Number | Rate[1] | Number | Percent | Enrolled in original Medicare | Enrolled in Medicare Advantage | Enrolled in a Medicare prescription drug plan | Number | Rate[3] |
| | 32 | 33 | 34 | 35 | 36 | 37 | 38 | 39 | 40 | 41 | 42 | 43 | 44 | 45 |
| Kokomo, IN | 1 487 | 101 392 | 1.06 | 1 082 | 11.0 | 1 029 | 10.4 | 12 526 | 15.4 | 20 895 | 2 142 | 8 767 | 3 661 | 3 691 |
| La Crosse, WI-MN | 5 452 | 137 438 | 1.06 | 1 529 | 11.4 | 1 106 | 8.2 | 10 711 | 9.7 | 22 865 | 9 614 | 8 183 | 3 340 | 2 512 |
| Lafayette, IN | 14 661 | 205 570 | 1.06 | 2 503 | 12.3 | 1 295 | 6.4 | 30 753 | 18.4 | 26 081 | 4 054 | 12 873 | 5 735 | 2 922 |
| Lafayette, LA | 5 851 | 286 782 | 1.12 | 4 076 | 14.7 | 2 032 | 7.3 | 48 675 | 20.3 | 38 385 | 3 287 | 20 681 | 11 586 | 4 322 |
| Lake Charles, LA | 3 796 | 205 368 | 1.09 | 2 863 | 14.3 | 1 873 | 9.3 | 31 415 | 18.3 | 33 423 | 4 204 | 15 648 | 8 559 | 4 422 |
| Lake Havasu City-Kingman, AZ | 2 629 | 187 900 | 0.82 | 2 099 | 10.4 | 2 485 | 12.3 | 30 734 | 20.4 | 52 571 | 11 869 | 19 362 | 6 872 | 3 385 |
| Lakeland-Winter Haven, FL | 12 261 | 572 976 | 0.89 | 7 412 | 12.2 | 5 683 | 9.3 | 117 796 | 24.4 | 123 620 | 48 914 | 35 375 | 22 649 | 3 711 |
| Lancaster, PA | 12 638 | 504 605 | 0.95 | 7 141 | 13.6 | 4 511 | 8.6 | 62 229 | 14.4 | 93 711 | 30 137 | 38 606 | 11 495 | 2 206 |
| Lansing-East Lansing, MI | 20 717 | 475 780 | 1.05 | 5 097 | 11.0 | 3 327 | 7.2 | 47 164 | 12.1 | 71 411 | 16 759 | 27 450 | 12 384 | 2 718 |
| Laredo, TX | 3 479 | 246 569 | 1.01 | 5 698 | 22.2 | 1 112 | 4.3 | 83 761 | 36.8 | 26 319 | 2 066 | 14 962 | 12 078 | 4 726 |
| Las Cruces, NM | 4 581 | 202 060 | 0.96 | 3 281 | 15.4 | 1 387 | 6.5 | 46 450 | 25.9 | 31 650 | 8 023 | 12 972 | 7 564 | 3 575 |
| Las Vegas-Paradise, NV | 21 992 | 1 941 134 | 1.01 | 27 563 | 14.0 | 13 168 | 6.7 | 435 139 | 25.4 | 262 493 | 95 037 | 69 557 | 63 044 | 3 204 |
| Lawrence, KS | 8 792 | 104 277 | 0.90 | 1 227 | 10.9 | 567 | 5.1 | 16 404 | 17.7 | 13 176 | 1 319 | 6 969 | 4 946 | 4 435 |
| Lawton, OK | 10 343 | 125 766 | 1.07 | 2 068 | 16.4 | 930 | 7.4 | 19 859 | 19.3 | 16 061 | 540 | 6 241 | 6 768 | 5 396 |
| Lebanon, PA | 3 657 | 120 612 | 0.81 | 1 621 | 12.1 | 1 385 | 10.3 | 13 095 | 12.1 | 27 145 | 9 312 | 9 394 | 2 498 | 1 923 |
| Lewiston, ID-WA | 1 140 | 60 899 | 1.01 | 681 | 11.1 | 683 | 11.1 | 7 817 | 15.9 | 14 062 | 2 658 | 6 238 | 2 247 | 3 644 |
| Lewiston-Auburn, ME | 2 760 | 105 431 | 0.95 | 1 331 | 12.4 | 986 | 9.2 | 10 386 | 11.6 | 21 818 | 4 007 | 11 640 | 3 351 | 3 112 |
| Lexington-Fayette, KY | 16 922 | 492 960 | 1.12 | 6 288 | 13.1 | 3 373 | 7.0 | 72 396 | 17.9 | 69 529 | 14 901 | 33 419 | 21 012 | 4 435 |
| Lima, OH | 5 934 | 113 689 | 1.16 | 1 334 | 12.6 | 1 063 | 10.0 | 12 063 | 14.1 | 19 752 | 4 766 | 10 261 | 4 393 | 4 128 |
| Lincoln, NE | 15 112 | 304 718 | 1.03 | 4 277 | 14.0 | 1 941 | 6.3 | 29 837 | 11.7 | 41 841 | 3 193 | 23 214 | 11 823 | 3 980 |
| Little Rock-North Little Rock-Conway, AR | 14 285 | 705 272 | 1.04 | 9 610 | 13.5 | 5 719 | 8.1 | 108 343 | 17.9 | 118 757 | 15 838 | 53 062 | 41 866 | 5 962 |
| Logan, UT-ID | 3 696 | 119 585 | 0.95 | 2 645 | 20.7 | 555 | 4.4 | 18 547 | 16.6 | 12 514 | 4 690 | 4 043 | 1 457 | 1 140 |
| Longview, TX | 10 140 | 218 638 | 1.07 | 3 136 | 14.5 | 2 143 | 9.9 | 45 030 | 25.6 | 37 332 | 5 772 | 17 078 | 8 187 | 3 760 |
| Longview, WA | 1 207 | 98 937 | 0.93 | 1 234 | 12.0 | 971 | 9.5 | 13 984 | 16.3 | 21 545 | 9 208 | 6 564 | 3 773 | 3 627 |
| Los Angeles-Long Beach-Santa Ana, CA | 210 917 | 13 005 564 | 1.04 | 171 737 | 13.3 | 75 587 | 5.8 | 2 775 414 | 24.5 | 1 664 072 | 691 474 | 580 895 | 342 419 | 2 638 |
| Los Angeles-Long Beach-Glendale, CA Div | 171 681 | 9 934 403 | 1.03 | 133 239 | 13.5 | 58 426 | 5.9 | 2 248 384 | 25.9 | 1 254 353 | 508 040 | 457 962 | 274 252 | 2 761 |
| Santa Ana-Anaheim-Irvine, CA Div | 39 236 | 3 071 161 | 1.06 | 38 498 | 12.6 | 17 161 | 5.6 | 527 030 | 19.9 | 409 719 | 183 434 | 122 933 | 68 167 | 2 238 |
| Louisville-Jefferson County, KY-IN | 25 265 | 1 275 902 | 1.00 | 16 542 | 12.8 | 11 142 | 8.6 | 173 616 | 15.8 | 221 197 | 43 181 | 114 664 | 53 372 | 4 248 |
| Lubbock, TX | 11 099 | 283 028 | 1.02 | 4 342 | 15.0 | 2 335 | 8.1 | 55 431 | 22.7 | 39 723 | 8 056 | 17 208 | 15 619 | 5 369 |
| Lynchburg, VA | 12 915 | 245 282 | 0.95 | 2 679 | 10.5 | 2 343 | 9.2 | 33 448 | 16.5 | 51 897 | 8 420 | 27 609 | 104 635 | 3 814 |
| Macon, GA | 7 802 | 237 268 | 1.06 | 3 192 | 13.7 | 2 377 | 10.2 | 37 794 | 19.3 | 41 424 | 10 890 | 16 511 | 13 848 | 5 916 |
| Madera-Chowchilla, CA | 8 624 | 147 407 | 0.95 | 2 376 | 15.5 | 880 | 5.8 | 28 784 | 22.8 | 20 908 | 6 371 | 8 419 | 4 604 | 3 016 |
| Madison, WI | 14 515 | 591 937 | 1.09 | 6 974 | 12.1 | 3 411 | 5.9 | 44 186 | 8.9 | 80 030 | 16 471 | 42 607 | 15 970 | 2 803 |
| Manchester-Nashua, NH | 7 759 | 383 112 | 0.92 | 4 448 | 11.1 | 2 731 | 6.8 | 41 402 | 11.9 | 64 086 | 2 433 | 31 753 | 10 242 | 2 709 |
| Manhattan, KS | 10 273 | 127 940 | 1.07 | 2 448 | 18.8 | 701 | 5.4 | 14 744 | 13.6 | 12 865 | 887 | 6 139 | 2 869 | 2 255 |
| Mankato, North Mankato, MN | 7 249 | 97 533 | 1.03 | 1 122 | 11.5 | 671 | 6.9 | 8 029 | 10.1 | 14 188 | 6 198 | 7 743 | 2 965 | 3 042 |
| Mansfield, OH | 7 263 | 125 908 | 1.01 | 1 484 | 12.0 | 1 273 | 10.3 | 14 686 | 15.0 | 25 283 | 5 805 | 13 398 | 5 666 | 4 618 |
| McAllen-Edinburg-Mission, TX | 6 982 | 746 649 | 0.96 | 16 884 | 21.2 | 3 641 | 4.6 | 265 156 | 38.1 | 83 728 | 16 274 | 47 002 | 33 632 | 4 251 |
| Medford, OR | 3 492 | 202 368 | 1.00 | 2 293 | 11.2 | 2 012 | 9.8 | 36 877 | 22.3 | 44 994 | 13 742 | 15 851 | 7 638 | 3 719 |
| Memphis, TN-MS-AR | 24 145 | 1 327 095 | 1.03 | 19 393 | 14.6 | 10 778 | 8.1 | 205 378 | 17.8 | 186 706 | 33 694 | 87 881 | 71 972 | 5 586 |
| Merced, CA | 4 896 | 241 565 | 0.87 | 4 260 | 16.4 | 1 510 | 5.8 | 49 697 | 21.7 | 30 697 | 2 251 | 17 116 | 10 541 | 4 073 |
| Miami-Fort Lauderdale-Pompano Beach, FL | 76 921 | 5 542 086 | 1.01 | 65 977 | 11.6 | 45 537 | 8.0 | 1 428 998 | 30.9 | 931 659 | 443 877 | 290 569 | 269 152 | 4 772 |
| Fort Lauderdale-Pompano Beach-Deerfield Beach, FL Div | 16 892 | 1 677 174 | 0.92 | 20 927 | 11.8 | 14 331 | 8.1 | 401 954 | 27.1 | 265 352 | 132 273 | 69 763 | 78 781 | 4 446 |
| Miami-Miami Beach-Kendall, FL Div | 40 057 | 2 539 249 | 1.06 | 31 317 | 12.3 | 18 117 | 7.1 | 758 908 | 35.8 | 394 991 | 220 104 | 121 905 | 138 000 | 5 454 |
| West Palm Beach-Boca Raton-Boynton Beach, FL Div | 19 972 | 1 325 663 | 1.03 | 13 733 | 10.3 | 13 089 | 9.8 | 268 136 | 26.3 | 271 316 | 91 500 | 98 901 | 52 371 | 3 914 |
| Michigan City-La Porte, IN | 6 623 | 107 014 | 0.91 | 1 330 | 11.9 | 1 140 | 10.2 | 13 878 | 15.6 | 19 969 | 1 511 | 10 952 | 4 098 | 3 776 |
| Midland, TX | 1 678 | 139 452 | 1.07 | 2 216 | 15.8 | 990 | 7.1 | 29 402 | 24.4 | 17 266 | 1 894 | 8 463 | 4 215 | 3 016 |
| Milwaukee-Waukesha-West Allis, WI | 33 087 | 1 591 680 | 1.06 | 20 839 | 13.3 | 12 455 | 8.0 | 151 655 | 11.4 | 245 420 | 76 067 | 86 822 | 58 422 | 3 841 |
| Minneapolis-St. Paul-Bloomington, MN | 64 055 | 3 291 394 | 1.02 | 43 858 | 13.2 | 19 562 | 5.9 | 286 918 | 9.9 | 446 033 | 226 606 | 147 583 | 102 832 | 3 114 |
| Missoula, MT | 3 634 | 113 055 | 1.08 | 1 177 | 10.7 | 744 | 6.8 | 19 173 | 20.5 | 16 967 | 1 798 | 8 226 | 3 501 | 3 175 |
| Mobile, AL | 6 808 | 419 942 | 1.06 | 5 734 | 13.9 | 4 069 | 9.9 | 66 095 | 18.6 | 72 730 | 28 422 | 19 094 | 22 472 | 5 415 |
| Modesto, CA | 6 305 | 494 508 | 0.91 | 7 713 | 14.9 | 3 467 | 6.7 | 89 607 | 19.6 | 72 342 | 27 902 | 27 190 | 21 671 | 4 163 |
| Monroe, LA | 5 949 | 178 578 | 1.04 | 2 620 | 14.7 | 1 709 | 9.6 | 34 048 | 22.9 | 29 373 | 4 472 | 15 204 | 8 396 | 4 808 |
| Monroe, MI | 1 462 | 131 438 | 0.68 | 1 658 | 10.9 | 1 246 | 8.2 | 14 322 | 11.0 | 26 714 | 6 701 | 10 736 | 3 972 | 2 769 |
| Montgomery, AL | 15 116 | 382 132 | 1.06 | 4 982 | 13.2 | 3 276 | 8.7 | 47 910 | 15.2 | 62 957 | 16 726 | 16 198 | 16 416 | 4 362 |
| Morgantown, WV | 9 640 | 134 674 | 1.12 | 1 260 | 9.5 | 932 | 7.0 | 18 426 | 17.4 | 18 540 | 3 984 | 8 255 | 2 651 | 2 162 |
| Morristown, TN | 2 663 | 129 652 | 0.89 | 1 568 | 11.4 | 1 462 | 10.6 | 20 953 | 18.6 | 30 195 | 11 197 | 10 863 | 5 324 | 3 862 |
| Mount Vernon-Anacortes, WA | 1 624 | 116 436 | 1.00 | 1 479 | 12.5 | 1 085 | 9.2 | 17 920 | 18.4 | 23 701 | 7 741 | 7 673 | 5 302 | 4 465 |
| Muncie, IN | 8 830 | 118 733 | 1.03 | 1 277 | 10.9 | 1 126 | 9.6 | 15 957 | 17.2 | 22 066 | 2 776 | 10 231 | 3 954 | 3 343 |
| Muskegon-Norton Shores, MI | 6 345 | 166 624 | 0.91 | 2 209 | 12.9 | 1 622 | 9.5 | 21 459 | 14.9 | 33 780 | 11 553 | 14 204 | 7 574 | 4 402 |
| Myrtle Beach-North Myrtle Beach-Conway, SC | 2 952 | 268 281 | 1.03 | 3 103 | 11.2 | 2 523 | 9.1 | 57 872 | 26.2 | 62 135 | 6 862 | 26 409 | 17 088 | 6 273 |
| Napa, CA | 4 918 | 141 419 | 1.10 | 1 565 | 11.3 | 1 209 | 8.8 | 21 105 | 18.7 | 25 080 | 9 183 | 7 274 | 3 251 | 2 354 |

1. Per 1,000 estimated resident population.   2. Data for serious crimes have not been adjusted for underreporting; this may affect comparability between geographic areas and over time.   3. Per 100,000 population estimated by the FBI.

# Table C. Metropolitan Areas — Crime, Education, Money Income, and Poverty

| Area name | Serious crimes known to police, 2011 (cont.)[1] Rate[2] Violent | Property | School enrollment and attainment, 2007–2011 Enrollment[3] Total | Percent private | Attainment[4] (percent) High school graduate or less | Bach-elor's degree or more | Local government expenditures,[5] 2009–2010 Total current expenditures (mil dol) | Current expenditures per student (dollars) | Per capita income[6] (dollars) | Median house-hold income (dollars) | Percent of households with income of less than $25,000 | Percent of house-holds with income of $100,000 or more | Percent of house-holds with in-come of $200,000 or more | Percent below poverty level All persons | Related Children under 18 years | Related Children under 5 |
|---|---|---|---|---|---|---|---|---|---|---|---|---|---|---|---|---|
| | 46 | 47 | 48 | 49 | 50 | 51 | 52 | 53 | 54 | 55 | 56 | 57 | 58 | 59 | 60 | 61 |
| Kokomo, IN | 264 | 3 427 | 24 381 | 9.2 | 51.2 | 19.0 | 157.7 | 9 685 | 23 847 | 46 295 | 25.0 | 13.7 | 1.5 | 14.0 | 21.1 | 29.3 |
| La Crosse, WI-MN | 165 | 2 347 | 38 527 | 15.1 | 38.2 | 27.9 | 230.2 | 11 319 | 25 696 | 50 836 | 24.1 | 16.2 | 2.2 | 13.2 | 13.1 | 13.3 |
| Lafayette, IN | 277 | 2 645 | 75 335 | 8.8 | 41.6 | 32.1 | 243.8 | 9 399 | 22 985 | 44 422 | 29.2 | 15.0 | 2.3 | 19.3 | 17.6 | 22.1 |
| Lafayette, LA | 556 | 3 766 | 75 870 | 20.8 | 49.9 | 24.3 | 380.7 | 9 938 | 26 520 | 47 309 | 28.1 | 19.5 | 4.2 | 16.5 | 20.5 | 21.9 |
| Lake Charles, LA | 497 | 3 925 | 51 609 | 13.2 | 53.7 | 18.9 | 343.6 | 10 040 | 24 036 | 44 232 | 28.4 | 16.7 | 2.6 | 16.8 | 23.2 | 27.7 |
| Lake Havasu City-Kingman, AZ | 201 | 3 183 | 41 353 | 10.6 | 50.0 | 12.2 | 176.9 | 6 735 | 21 457 | 40 573 | 28.7 | 9.7 | 1.5 | 16.8 | 25.9 | 29.6 |
| Lakeland-Winter Haven, FL | 417 | 3 294 | 140 435 | 15.8 | 54.6 | 18.0 | 819.6 | 8 670 | 21 952 | 44 398 | 26.5 | 12.6 | 1.9 | 16.4 | 25.9 | 31.4 |
| Lancaster, PA | 180 | 2 026 | 126 925 | 26.4 | 56.0 | 23.2 | 879.7 | 12 872 | 26 141 | 55 816 | 19.1 | 19.2 | 2.9 | 9.9 | 14.0 | 16.4 |
| Lansing-East Lansing, MI | 370 | 2 349 | 153 405 | 10.2 | 34.4 | 31.5 | 761.3 | 10 612 | 25 329 | 50 168 | 24.7 | 18.1 | 2.6 | 16.1 | 17.3 | 23.0 |
| Laredo, TX | 480 | 4 245 | 86 000 | 4.8 | 57.7 | 17.1 | 592.3 | 8 834 | 14 465 | 37 868 | 33.6 | 12.3 | 1.5 | 30.6 | 41.5 | 46.7 |
| Las Cruces, NM | 367 | 3 208 | 66 132 | 4.7 | 45.5 | 25.5 | 359.0 | 8 852 | 19 077 | 37 223 | 35.5 | 12.8 | 1.9 | 25.6 | 35.9 | 41.8 |
| Las Vegas-Paradise, NV | 624 | 2 580 | 470 628 | 11.0 | 46.0 | 22.0 | 2 536.8 | 8 262 | 27 330 | 55 961 | 19.0 | 21.5 | 3.7 | 12.9 | 18.1 | 20.3 |
| Lawrence, KS | 360 | 4 075 | 45 225 | 11.1 | 25.3 | 48.8 | 128.2 | 9 252 | 25 654 | 47 063 | 27.6 | 18.2 | 3.0 | 19.0 | 11.9 | 19.1 |
| Lawton, OK | 698 | 4 698 | 33 151 | 6.3 | 45.7 | 20.4 | 175.7 | 7 809 | 21 746 | 45 947 | 26.4 | 12.9 | 1.9 | 16.9 | 23.8 | 30.7 |
| Lebanon, PA | 172 | 1 750 | 30 301 | 22.7 | 60.4 | 18.7 | 192.8 | 10 262 | 26 238 | 53 474 | 20.6 | 17.5 | 2.3 | 9.6 | 14.4 | 18.2 |
| Lewiston, ID-WA | 146 | 3 498 | 13 879 | 9.6 | 46.2 | 18.3 | 83.6 | 9 337 | 24 329 | 43 520 | 26.6 | 11.9 | 1.7 | 12.5 | 18.6 | 26.5 |
| Lewiston-Auburn, ME | 156 | 2 956 | 26 169 | 18.2 | 52.3 | 18.6 | 180.5 | 11 411 | 23 663 | 45 699 | 26.5 | 13.6 | 1.4 | 14.2 | 19.4 | 28.8 |
| Lexington-Fayette, KY | 381 | 4 054 | 131 109 | 17.1 | 38.5 | 33.6 | 597.1 | 8 970 | 27 825 | 49 226 | 26.0 | 19.2 | 3.5 | 16.9 | 22.0 | 27.1 |
| Lima, OH | 469 | 3 659 | 28 494 | 18.3 | 54.4 | 15.7 | 161.0 | 10 479 | 21 878 | 43 323 | 29.1 | 12.6 | 1.5 | 18.0 | 28.2 | 33.2 |
| Lincoln, NE | 331 | 3 648 | 92 718 | 18.8 | 30.4 | 35.4 | 429.7 | 10 116 | 26 615 | 51 419 | 22.7 | 18.3 | 2.8 | 13.9 | 16.4 | 21.7 |
| Little Rock-North Little Rock-Conway, AR | 744 | 5 219 | 185 480 | 16.4 | 42.8 | 27.1 | 1 012.9 | 9 236 | 25 907 | 47 731 | 25.4 | 17.1 | 2.8 | 14.8 | 20.7 | 23.8 |
| Logan, UT-ID | 48 | 1 093 | 46 517 | 7.2 | 32.3 | 33.5 | 157.1 | 6 044 | 20 004 | 48 002 | 21.7 | 14.0 | 2.0 | 15.2 | 15.3 | 19.4 |
| Longview, TX | 380 | 3 380 | 52 606 | 12.1 | 49.5 | 17.7 | 358.8 | 9 335 | 23 118 | 45 436 | 26.6 | 15.0 | 2.8 | 15.2 | 22.2 | 29.5 |
| Longview, WA | 309 | 3 319 | 24 438 | 12.0 | 43.7 | 15.0 | 152.1 | 8 753 | 23 575 | 46 461 | 25.8 | 15.6 | 1.7 | 17.5 | 25.1 | 34.6 |
| Los Angeles-Long Beach-Santa Ana, CA | 405 | 2 233 | 3 666 965 | 15.3 | 42.4 | 30.9 | 20 251.1 | 9 681 | 29 466 | 60 667 | 20.4 | 28.4 | 7.2 | 15.0 | 20.8 | 22.6 |
| Los Angeles-Long Beach-Glendale, CA Div | 464 | 2 297 | 2 807 907 | 15.4 | 44.8 | 29.2 | 15 936.9 | 10 026 | 27 954 | 56 266 | 22.3 | 25.8 | 6.3 | 16.3 | 22.8 | 24.6 |
| Santa Ana-Anaheim-Irvine, CA Div | 214 | 2 024 | 859 058 | 14.9 | 34.9 | 36.2 | 4 314.2 | 8 589 | 34 416 | 75 762 | 14.3 | 37.0 | 9.9 | 10.9 | 14.2 | 15.9 |
| Louisville-Jefferson County, KY-IN | 426 | 3 821 | 322 500 | 20.3 | 45.6 | 25.0 | 1 788.4 | 9 372 | 26 338 | 48 820 | 24.6 | 17.8 | 3.1 | 14.1 | 20.2 | 24.6 |
| Lubbock, TX | 676 | 4 694 | 93 429 | 9.7 | 43.0 | 27.0 | 420.2 | 8 863 | 23 213 | 43 784 | 29.6 | 15.1 | 3.0 | 19.3 | 22.9 | 29.0 |
| Lynchburg, VA | 359 | 3 454 | 68 439 | 34.5 | 49.3 | 22.3 | 323.7 | 9 238 | 23 797 | 45 512 | 26.7 | 14.6 | 2.1 | 15.0 | 19.9 | 26.6 |
| Macon, GA | 388 | 5 528 | 62 910 | 19.2 | 53.3 | 20.2 | 342.3 | 9 108 | 21 836 | 39 888 | 33.1 | 14.7 | 2.6 | 21.0 | 29.2 | 34.5 |
| Madera-Chowchilla, CA | 523 | 2 493 | 41 313 | 6.6 | 55.8 | 14.0 | 264.2 | 8 913 | 18 817 | 47 724 | 23.8 | 17.9 | 2.6 | 19.8 | 28.9 | 32.7 |
| Madison, WI | 219 | 2 584 | 163 689 | 12.6 | 29.5 | 41.7 | 935.2 | 11 507 | 32 324 | 61 163 | 18.1 | 24.3 | 4.1 | 11.5 | 11.6 | 14.4 |
| Manchester-Nashua, NH | 265 | 2 443 | 102 227 | 24.6 | 37.1 | 34.6 | 681.9 | 11 390 | 33 653 | 70 591 | 15.5 | 31.7 | 5.7 | 7.5 | 9.8 | 13.0 |
| Manhattan, KS | 294 | 1 961 | 44 599 | 7.4 | 30.2 | 35.2 | 175.4 | 9 239 | 21 959 | 45 122 | 27.1 | 13.9 | 2.1 | 17.4 | 13.7 | 18.7 |
| Mankato, North Mankato, MN | 144 | 2 898 | 31 187 | 17.3 | 34.7 | 30.9 | 136.2 | 11 120 | 24 711 | 51 895 | 22.0 | 16.3 | 1.9 | 16.4 | 13.1 | 18.5 |
| Mansfield, OH | 183 | 4 435 | 29 992 | 19.0 | 56.7 | 15.1 | 201.4 | 12 112 | 21 966 | 43 098 | 26.0 | 12.4 | 1.2 | 13.4 | 19.5 | 27.4 |
| McAllen-Edinburg-Mission, TX | 295 | 3 956 | 249 749 | 4.3 | 63.9 | 15.3 | 1 906.6 | 9 180 | 13 821 | 32 479 | 40.1 | 10.4 | 1.6 | 35.3 | 46.7 | 48.3 |
| Medford, OR | 295 | 3 425 | 45 575 | 10.6 | 39.7 | 23.7 | 262.8 | 9 334 | 24 263 | 43 386 | 27.7 | 13.1 | 2.0 | 15.8 | 20.5 | 26.8 |
| Memphis, TN-MS-AR | 1 001 | 4 585 | 368 535 | 18.1 | 44.8 | 25.0 | 1 924.5 | 8 451 | 24 675 | 47 344 | 26.8 | 18.1 | 3.5 | 18.7 | 28.0 | 33.4 |
| Merced, CA | 544 | 3 529 | 81 303 | 6.0 | 58.5 | 12.3 | 522.4 | 9 286 | 18 304 | 43 945 | 28.3 | 15.5 | 2.7 | 23.0 | 31.0 | 37.0 |
| Miami-Fort Lauderdale-Pompano Beach, FL | 595 | 4 176 | 1 380 482 | 21.2 | 44.6 | 28.8 | 7 092.7 | 9 129 | 27 556 | 49 018 | 25.5 | 20.6 | 4.8 | 15.2 | 20.4 | 22.4 |
| Fort Lauderdale-Pompano Beach-Deerfield Beach, FL Div | 490 | 3 956 | 451 218 | 22.2 | 41.0 | 29.9 | 2 379.6 | 9 290 | 28 720 | 51 782 | 23.2 | 21.8 | 4.5 | 13.0 | 16.8 | 18.8 |
| Miami-Miami Beach-Kendall, FL Div | 724 | 4 730 | 634 419 | 21.1 | 50.1 | 26.2 | 3 118.1 | 9 017 | 23 348 | 43 957 | 29.4 | 17.7 | 4.1 | 17.9 | 23.2 | 24.3 |
| West Palm Beach-Boca Raton-Boynton Beach, FL Div | 492 | 3 422 | 294 845 | 20.2 | 39.5 | 32.2 | 1 595.0 | 9 113 | 33 960 | 52 951 | 22.3 | 23.5 | 6.3 | 13.3 | 20.0 | 23.5 |
| Michigan City-La Porte, IN | 165 | 3 611 | 27 440 | 13.0 | 53.0 | 17.0 | 180.3 | 9 868 | 22 968 | 46 934 | 25.7 | 14.3 | 1.8 | 15.2 | 23.8 | 30.4 |
| Midland, TX | 286 | 2 731 | 36 604 | 14.3 | 43.5 | 23.7 | 198.7 | 8 436 | 31 986 | 57 807 | 19.4 | 24.7 | 7.3 | 11.5 | 15.6 | 18.1 |
| Milwaukee-Waukesha-West Allis, WI | 501 | 3 340 | 424 882 | 24.4 | 39.6 | 31.2 | 2 777.8 | 11 715 | 28 969 | 53 618 | 22.8 | 21.8 | 3.8 | 13.9 | 20.3 | 23.7 |
| Minneapolis-St. Paul-Bloomington, MN | 270 | 2 843 | 895 334 | 19.0 | 31.0 | 37.9 | 5 706.7 | 10 713 | 33 577 | 66 157 | 16.4 | 28.8 | 5.7 | 9.9 | 12.7 | 14.9 |
| Missoula, MT | 264 | 2 911 | 31 424 | 10.4 | 31.8 | 38.1 | 130.7 | 9 912 | 25 418 | 43 895 | 29.5 | 15.9 | 2.6 | 17.6 | 15.1 | 18.6 |
| Mobile, AL | 608 | 4 807 | 110 308 | 20.5 | 50.7 | 20.1 | 562.1 | 8 712 | 22 306 | 42 187 | 30.6 | 13.7 | 2.3 | 19.2 | 28.2 | 35.6 |
| Modesto, CA | 477 | 3 686 | 150 625 | 9.2 | 52.2 | 16.4 | 992.0 | 9 450 | 21 820 | 50 671 | 24.2 | 19.1 | 2.7 | 18.0 | 24.6 | 28.4 |
| Monroe, LA | 602 | 4 205 | 47 406 | 9.7 | 51.6 | 21.7 | 315.1 | 10 113 | 22 186 | 39 490 | 32.5 | 15.2 | 2.4 | 22.0 | 34.8 | 43.6 |
| Monroe, MI | 245 | 2 524 | 39 518 | 13.6 | 49.6 | 17.1 | 261.4 | 9 891 | 25 774 | 55 826 | 20.0 | 20.1 | 1.9 | 10.4 | 15.0 | 22.1 |
| Montgomery, AL | 297 | 4 065 | 101 706 | 21.2 | 45.1 | 27.1 | 484.2 | 8 539 | 24 526 | 47 146 | 26.5 | 17.7 | 2.8 | 17.1 | 25.0 | 32.8 |
| Morgantown, WV | 310 | 1 852 | 41 600 | 6.1 | 49.9 | 29.2 | 169.4 | 11 226 | 22 784 | 42 100 | 33.7 | 14.7 | 2.6 | 19.5 | 14.4 | 15.7 |
| Morristown, TN | 348 | 3 515 | 30 643 | 13.3 | 61.2 | 13.5 | 151.4 | 7 137 | 20 115 | 37 380 | 33.5 | 9.7 | 1.5 | 18.5 | 26.0 | 38.8 |
| Mount Vernon-Anacortes, WA | 201 | 4 264 | 26 396 | 10.8 | 37.1 | 23.7 | 192.3 | 10 128 | 27 447 | 55 555 | 19.7 | 19.1 | 2.5 | 12.0 | 17.1 | 17.9 |
| Muncie, IN | 509 | 2 834 | 38 767 | 5.0 | 51.1 | 22.2 | 151.1 | 9 196 | 21 132 | 38 730 | 32.3 | 10.9 | 1.7 | 20.6 | 22.1 | 30.3 |
| Muskegon-Norton Shores, MI | 426 | 3 976 | 44 454 | 10.2 | 48.3 | 16.8 | 321.3 | 10 444 | 20 222 | 40 298 | 30.7 | 11.0 | 1.2 | 18.5 | 25.1 | 36.0 |
| Myrtle Beach-North Myrtle Beach-Conway, SC | 670 | 5 603 | 55 419 | 8.5 | 47.1 | 21.9 | 375.2 | 9 929 | 24 531 | 42 877 | 27.2 | 12.6 | 2.2 | 16.7 | 26.2 | 30.8 |
| Napa, CA | 327 | 2 027 | 33 403 | 16.6 | 37.7 | 30.7 | 214.7 | 10 564 | 35 309 | 68 641 | 15.5 | 33.3 | 8.8 | 9.8 | 12.7 | 12.8 |

1. Data for serious crimes have not been adjusted for underreporting; this may affect comparability between geographic areas and over time.   2. Per 100,000 population estimated by the FBI.   3. All persons 3 years old and over enrolled in nursery school through college.   4. Persons 25 years old and over.   5. Elementary and secondary education expenditures.   6. Based on resident population estimated as of July 1, 2009.

# Table C. Metropolitan Areas — **Personal Income**

| Area name | Total (mil dol) | Percent change, 2010–2011 | Per capita[1] Dollars | Rank | Wages and salaries[2] (mil dol) | Proprietors' income (mil dol) | Dividends, interest, and rent (mil dol) | Transfer payments Total (mil dol) | Govt payments to individuals Total (mil dol) | Social Security (mil dol) | Medical payments (mil dol) | Income mainte-nance (mil dol) | Unemploy-ment insurance (mil dol) |
|---|---|---|---|---|---|---|---|---|---|---|---|---|---|
| | 62 | 63 | 64 | 65 | 66 | 67 | 68 | 69 | 70 | 71 | 72 | 73 | 74 |
| Kokomo, IN | 3 266 | 6.5 | 33 126 | 281 | 2 297 | 185 | 435 | 875 | 853 | 348 | 343 | 85 | 35 |
| La Crosse, WI-MN | 5 135 | 3.9 | 38 184 | 151 | 3 589 | 330 | 863 | 917 | 887 | 324 | 370 | 71 | 37 |
| Lafayette, IN | 6 464 | 7.3 | 31 747 | 310 | 4 705 | 576 | 961 | 1 049 | 1 004 | 407 | 339 | 111 | 53 |
| Lafayette, LA | 12 253 | 6.0 | 44 184 | 48 | 8 587 | 1 729 | 2 014 | 1 754 | 1 686 | 523 | 732 | 251 | 34 |
| Lake Charles, LA | 7 295 | 5.5 | 36 324 | 188 | 4 922 | 505 | 1 135 | 1 496 | 1 450 | 486 | 654 | 190 | 28 |
| Lake Havasu City-Kingman, AZ | 5 291 | 4.3 | 26 145 | 362 | 2 013 | 342 | 831 | 1 782 | 1 737 | 766 | 619 | 181 | 44 |
| Lakeland-Winter Haven, FL | 20 385 | 4.4 | 33 447 | 267 | 9 663 | 1 136 | 4 412 | 4 799 | 4 660 | 1 763 | 1 802 | 655 | 137 |
| Lancaster, PA | 19 653 | 4.1 | 37 535 | 162 | 11 350 | 1 934 | 3 390 | 3 681 | 3 566 | 1 428 | 1 467 | 298 | 202 |
| Lansing-East Lansing, MI | 16 049 | 3.3 | 34 505 | 245 | 11 604 | 951 | 2 031 | 3 249 | 3 146 | 1 157 | 1 191 | 404 | 153 |
| Laredo, TX | 6 409 | 7.5 | 24 985 | 364 | 3 864 | 792 | 584 | 1 665 | 1 608 | 266 | 712 | 470 | 46 |
| Las Cruces, NM | 6 400 | 3.3 | 29 963 | 341 | 3 443 | 532 | 833 | 1 631 | 1 584 | 389 | 681 | 290 | 66 |
| Las Vegas-Paradise, NV | 70 289 | 3.8 | 35 680 | 200 | 46 205 | 5 616 | 12 488 | 11 561 | 11 127 | 3 753 | 4 063 | 1 421 | 1 083 |
| Lawrence, KS | 3 746 | 4.4 | 33 379 | 271 | 2 182 | 169 | 631 | 568 | 544 | 198 | 192 | 66 | 29 |
| Lawton, OK | 4 653 | 4.6 | 36 985 | 175 | 3 596 | 165 | 501 | 850 | 825 | 219 | 281 | 114 | 19 |
| Lebanon, PA | 5 169 | 5.1 | 38 489 | 146 | 2 422 | 321 | 735 | 1 049 | 1 019 | 400 | 417 | 84 | 59 |
| Lewiston, ID-WA | 2 201 | 3.8 | 35 796 | 199 | 1 220 | 205 | 389 | 558 | 544 | 202 | 222 | 62 | 10 |
| Lewiston-Auburn, ME | 3 887 | 3.9 | 36 192 | 191 | 2 328 | 259 | 417 | 1 031 | 1 007 | 285 | 491 | 137 | 31 |
| Lexington-Fayette, KY | 18 098 | 5.7 | 37 763 | 158 | 13 349 | 1 552 | 2 787 | 3 091 | 2 985 | 1 011 | 1 021 | 333 | 131 |
| Lima, OH | 3 369 | 5.2 | 31 750 | 309 | 2 580 | 340 | 452 | 869 | 845 | 283 | 333 | 106 | 32 |
| Lincoln, NE | 11 959 | 6.0 | 39 018 | 131 | 8 523 | 900 | 2 053 | 1 751 | 1 683 | 603 | 658 | 172 | 48 |
| Little Rock-North Little Rock-Conway, AR | 28 324 | 5.2 | 39 899 | 112 | 19 037 | 2 055 | 4 736 | 5 398 | 5 242 | 1 728 | 2 196 | 603 | 158 |
| Logan, UT-ID | 3 520 | 4.1 | 27 594 | 357 | 2 249 | 252 | 578 | 561 | 532 | 177 | 185 | 79 | 18 |
| Longview, TX | 8 397 | 7.3 | 38 756 | 135 | 5 318 | 1 146 | 1 177 | 1 753 | 1 705 | 533 | 837 | 190 | 45 |
| Longview, WA | 3 341 | 3.1 | 32 607 | 293 | 1 913 | 223 | 540 | 969 | 947 | 333 | 351 | 138 | 45 |
| Los Angeles-Long Beach-Santa Ana, CA | 575 045 | 4.5 | 44 423 | 46 | 380 978 | 63 507 | 101 202 | 92 812 | 89 948 | 20 455 | 43 644 | 13 352 | 5 567 |
| Los Angeles-Long Beach-Glendale, CA Div | 420 913 | 4.4 | 42 564 | X | 281 652 | 47 450 | 72 720 | 74 863 | 72 675 | 14 962 | 36 600 | 11 530 | 4 275 |
| Santa Ana-Anaheim-Irvine, CA Div | 154 132 | 4.8 | 50 440 | X | 99 325 | 16 057 | 28 482 | 17 949 | 17 273 | 5 493 | 7 044 | 1 822 | 1 291 |
| Louisville-Jefferson County, KY-IN | 50 546 | 5.1 | 39 037 | 130 | 32 821 | 4 151 | 7 452 | 9 623 | 9 336 | 3 272 | 3 807 | 1 059 | 437 |
| Lubbock, TX | 10 026 | 3.3 | 34 573 | 241 | 5 886 | 1 048 | 1 647 | 2 113 | 2 049 | 547 | 1 052 | 262 | 52 |
| Lynchburg, VA | 8 556 | 4.2 | 33 664 | 263 | 4 985 | 394 | 1 415 | 2 091 | 2 035 | 751 | 821 | 214 | 41 |
| Macon, GA | 8 281 | 4.2 | 35 554 | 203 | 4 741 | 503 | 1 263 | 2 007 | 1 955 | 568 | 789 | 351 | 63 |
| Madera-Chowchilla, CA | 4 378 | 7.6 | 28 631 | 354 | 2 137 | 767 | 627 | 1 014 | 980 | 283 | 391 | 165 | 70 |
| Madison, WI | 26 497 | 5.9 | 45 964 | 34 | 20 000 | 1 916 | 4 531 | 3 224 | 3 096 | 1 232 | 1 180 | 297 | 159 |
| Manchester-Nashua, NH | 19 274 | 4.6 | 47 981 | 25 | 13 051 | 1 599 | 2 391 | 2 528 | 2 439 | 965 | 957 | 281 | 71 |
| Manhattan, KS | 5 678 | 7.8 | 43 593 | 55 | 4 774 | 207 | 732 | 593 | 568 | 181 | 193 | 81 | 25 |
| Mankato, North Mankato, MN | 3 638 | 7.2 | 37 424 | 165 | 2 369 | 441 | 600 | 621 | 599 | 199 | 236 | 60 | 29 |
| Mansfield, OH | 3 794 | 4.2 | 30 714 | 335 | 2 352 | 176 | 524 | 1 062 | 1 034 | 363 | 426 | 121 | 41 |
| McAllen-Edinburg-Mission, TX | 17 248 | 4.5 | 21 620 | 366 | 9 093 | 2 119 | 1 588 | 5 478 | 5 302 | 830 | 2 383 | 1 523 | 216 |
| Medford, OR | 7 087 | 4.0 | 34 602 | 240 | 3 606 | 685 | 1 512 | 1 771 | 1 725 | 634 | 637 | 196 | 117 |
| Memphis, TN-MS-AR | 51 198 | 4.2 | 38 622 | 139 | 35 288 | 5 676 | 5 499 | 9 517 | 9 224 | 2 698 | 3 671 | 1 877 | 337 |
| Merced, CA | 7 406 | 6.5 | 28 497 | 355 | 3 250 | 1 204 | 929 | 1 936 | 1 878 | 385 | 848 | 346 | 141 |
| Miami-Fort Lauderdale-Pompano Beach, FL | 244 224 | 4.6 | 43 072 | 61 | 135 605 | 19 026 | 60 111 | 44 952 | 43 693 | 12 129 | 21 461 | 6 070 | 1 470 |
| Fort Lauderdale-Pompano Beach-Deerfield Beach, FL Div | 76 134 | 4.7 | 42 768 | X | 41 961 | 5 063 | 16 493 | 12 604 | 12 208 | 3 730 | 5 547 | 1 527 | 466 |
| Miami-Miami Beach-Kendall, FL Div | 96 658 | 4.8 | 37 834 | X | 62 315 | 9 284 | 15 697 | 21 415 | 20 847 | 4 224 | 11 247 | 3 605 | 700 |
| West Palm Beach-Boca Raton-Boynton Beach, FL Div | 71 432 | 4.4 | 53 500 | X | 31 330 | 4 679 | 27 921 | 10 933 | 10 637 | 4 174 | 4 668 | 939 | 304 |
| Michigan City-La Porte, IN | 3 525 | 5.4 | 31 650 | 312 | 2 053 | 205 | 465 | 845 | 821 | 319 | 322 | 95 | 37 |
| Midland, TX | 9 144 | 14.6 | 65 173 | 2 | 5 160 | 2 393 | 1 302 | 827 | 796 | 250 | 350 | 132 | 21 |
| Milwaukee-Waukesha-West Allis, WI | 69 691 | 4.1 | 44 610 | 43 | 49 448 | 5 249 | 10 729 | 11 900 | 11 555 | 3 802 | 4 876 | 1 722 | 618 |
| Minneapolis-St. Paul-Bloomington, MN | 161 468 | 5.7 | 48 657 | 24 | 117 454 | 11 574 | 25 709 | 21 886 | 21 151 | 6 714 | 9 509 | 2 203 | 1 098 |
| Missoula, MT | 3 876 | 4.1 | 35 190 | 218 | 2 598 | 351 | 750 | 686 | 662 | 233 | 237 | 69 | 28 |
| Mobile, AL | 13 524 | 3.9 | 32 779 | 286 | 9 608 | 961 | 1 896 | 3 467 | 3 347 | 1 075 | 1 334 | 582 | 91 |
| Modesto, CA | 16 652 | 4.2 | 32 115 | 298 | 8 661 | 1 689 | 2 344 | 3 845 | 3 731 | 964 | 1 572 | 577 | 312 |
| Monroe, LA | 6 013 | 3.8 | 33 846 | 260 | 3 491 | 610 | 885 | 1 449 | 1 409 | 396 | 631 | 248 | 28 |
| Monroe, MI | 5 403 | 6.3 | 35 647 | 201 | 2 119 | 252 | 658 | 1 127 | 1 093 | 441 | 426 | 110 | 54 |
| Montgomery, AL | 13 800 | 3.8 | 36 450 | 185 | 9 223 | 1 119 | 1 977 | 2 900 | 2 816 | 898 | 1 034 | 526 | 72 |
| Morgantown, WV | 4 659 | 5.1 | 35 226 | 217 | 3 500 | 378 | 545 | 903 | 873 | 275 | 391 | 77 | 23 |
| Morristown, TN | 4 029 | 3.9 | 29 306 | 350 | 2 055 | 290 | 474 | 1 233 | 1 202 | 429 | 501 | 146 | 43 |
| Mount Vernon-Anacortes, WA | 4 552 | 4.4 | 38 543 | 144 | 2 396 | 294 | 985 | 1 017 | 991 | 347 | 379 | 111 | 64 |
| Muncie, IN | 3 549 | 4.1 | 30 164 | 338 | 2 092 | 252 | 492 | 955 | 929 | 343 | 372 | 106 | 40 |
| Muskegon-Norton Shores, MI | 5 099 | 4.8 | 29 766 | 345 | 2 911 | 243 | 621 | 1 530 | 1 492 | 519 | 582 | 253 | 66 |
| Myrtle Beach-North Myrtle Beach-Conway, SC | 8 055 | 4.3 | 29 148 | 352 | 4 553 | 510 | 1 413 | 2 301 | 2 240 | 927 | 781 | 235 | 108 |
| Napa, CA | 7 077 | 6.1 | 51 253 | 14 | 4 098 | 583 | 1 533 | 985 | 955 | 333 | 416 | 62 | 62 |

1. Based on the resident population estimated as of July 1 of the year shown. 2. Includes other labor income.

Table C. Metropolitan Areas — **Earnings, Social Security, and Housing**

| Area name | Earnings, 2011 | | | | | | | | | Social Security beneficiaries, December 2011 | | Supplemental Security Income recipients, December 2011 | Housing units, 2010 | |
|---|---|---|---|---|---|---|---|---|---|---|---|---|---|---|
| | | | Percent by selected industries | | | | | | | | | | | |
| | | | Goods-related[1] | | Service-related and health | | | | | | | | | |
| | Total (mil dol) | Farm | Total | Manu-facturing | Infor-mation, profes-sional, and technical services | Retail trade | Finance, insur-ance, and real estate | Health care and social services | Govern-ment | Number | Rate[2] | | Total | Percent change, 2000–2010 |
| | 75 | 76 | 77 | 78 | 79 | 80 | 81 | 82 | 83 | 84 | 85 | 86 | 87 | 88 |
| Kokomo, IN | 2 482 | 2.7 | 44.4 | 41.6 | 3.4 | 6.3 | 3.2 | D | 15.8 | 24 240 | 246 | 2 368 | 45 677 | 2.8 |
| La Crosse, WI-MN | 3 919 | 1.4 | D | 13.6 | 5.2 | 6.5 | 6.5 | 21.7 | 14.8 | 24 845 | 185 | 2 397 | 57 003 | 10.4 |
| Lafayette, IN | 5 282 | 3.5 | 25.8 | 22.3 | 4.9 | 5.5 | 4.6 | 12.8 | 26.9 | 29 460 | 145 | 2 297 | 84 505 | 19.3 |
| Lafayette, LA | 10 316 | 0.2 | 31.1 | 7.4 | 9.3 | 6.3 | 7.3 | 13.4 | 10.1 | 42 285 | 152 | 7 823 | 115 597 | 17.6 |
| Lake Charles, LA | 5 427 | 0.1 | 32.7 | 19.8 | 7.1 | 6.0 | 3.6 | 12.0 | 15.7 | 37 430 | 186 | 6 157 | 85 651 | 5.3 |
| Lake Havasu City-Kingman, AZ | 2 355 | 0.8 | 12.8 | 6.3 | 4.1 | 13.1 | 5.4 | 21.9 | 19.6 | 58 670 | 290 | 4 208 | 110 911 | 38.5 |
| Lakeland-Winter Haven, FL.. | 10 799 | 1.0 | 14.7 | 9.0 | 5.9 | 8.6 | 8.1 | 14.4 | 15.0 | 137 250 | 225 | 18 193 | 281 214 | 24.2 |
| Lancaster, PA | 13 284 | 2.9 | 27.6 | 17.5 | 7.2 | 7.4 | 5.3 | 14.0 | 9.6 | 101 500 | 194 | 9 551 | 202 952 | 12.8 |
| Lansing-East Lansing, MI | 12 555 | 1.4 | 15.3 | 11.3 | D | 5.4 | 8.3 | 12.3 | 30.4 | 80 910 | 174 | 9 506 | 199 026 | 9.4 |
| Laredo, TX | 4 656 | 0.6 | 9.9 | 0.7 | 4.0 | 8.7 | 4.5 | 10.7 | 29.2 | 28 850 | 112 | 12 046 | 73 496 | 33.1 |
| Las Cruces, NM | 3 974 | 4.9 | 9.9 | 4.5 | 8.2 | 5.9 | 3.4 | 13.7 | 34.6 | 34 360 | 161 | 7 422 | 81 492 | 25.0 |
| Las Vegas-Paradise, NV | 51 822 | 0.0 | 9.4 | 2.7 | 8.8 | 7.4 | 7.0 | 8.7 | 16.2 | 283 050 | 144 | 33 124 | 840 343 | 50.1 |
| Lawrence, KS | 2 351 | 0.2 | 14.8 | 8.8 | 9.6 | 7.0 | 4.8 | 7.4 | 34.8 | 14 085 | 126 | 1 242 | 46 731 | 16.1 |
| Lawton, OK | 3 761 | 0.0 | 11.0 | 7.8 | 2.8 | 4.6 | 3.0 | 4.4 | 62.4 | 18 415 | 146 | 3 077 | 50 739 | 11.7 |
| Lebanon, PA | 2 744 | 2.8 | 23.3 | 18.5 | 5.3 | 7.7 | 2.7 | 13.7 | 20.1 | 29 640 | 221 | 2 330 | 55 592 | 12.7 |
| Lewiston, ID-WA | 1 426 | 2.6 | 19.4 | 13.8 | 4.8 | 8.8 | 7.1 | 16.8 | 19.0 | 15 670 | 255 | 1 750 | 27 310 | 7.9 |
| Lewiston-Auburn, ME | 2 587 | 0.4 | 19.3 | 12.0 | 7.2 | 8.3 | 7.2 | 21.2 | 11.4 | 24 015 | 224 | 3 810 | 49 090 | 6.8 |
| Lexington-Fayette, KY | 14 901 | 1.1 | 20.6 | 15.1 | 10.1 | 6.8 | 5.0 | 9.6 | 20.9 | 75 740 | 158 | 11 596 | 209 138 | 19.3 |
| Lima, OH | 2 921 | 2.2 | 28.9 | 24.8 | 3.7 | 7.1 | 3.0 | 19.8 | 13.3 | 21 615 | 204 | 2 961 | 44 999 | 1.7 |
| Lincoln, NE | 9 423 | 1.6 | 14.1 | 9.0 | 9.0 | 6.1 | 9.2 | 13.3 | 22.5 | 43 825 | 143 | 4 529 | 127 750 | 15.5 |
| Little Rock-North Little Rock-Conway, AR | 21 092 | 0.4 | 12.8 | 6.0 | 10.9 | 7.0 | 7.6 | 11.9 | 25.2 | 133 455 | 188 | 23 677 | 306 882 | 17.2 |
| Logan, UT-ID | 2 501 | 2.5 | 28.7 | 23.2 | 7.1 | 7.1 | 3.6 | 8.9 | 23.6 | 13 705 | 107 | 940 | 41 552 | 26.3 |
| Longview, TX | 6 465 | 0.2 | 36.3 | 12.8 | 6.8 | 7.7 | 4.3 | 11.1 | 9.2 | 41 440 | 191 | 6 525 | 87 318 | 7.6 |
| Longview, WA | 2 136 | 0.1 | 34.4 | 21.4 | 3.7 | 7.2 | 3.0 | 13.7 | 15.4 | 24 305 | 237 | 3 433 | 43 450 | 12.5 |
| Los Angeles-Long Beach-Santa Ana, CA | 444 484 | 0.0 | 14.3 | 9.9 | 19.6 | 5.9 | 9.6 | 9.5 | 13.0 | 1 572 525 | 121 | 491 097 | 4 493 983 | 6.0 |
| Los Angeles-Long Beach-Glendale, CA Div | 329 102 | 0.0 | 12.9 | 9.1 | 21.3 | 5.7 | 8.5 | 9.8 | 14.1 | 1 181 910 | 120 | 418 384 | 3 445 076 | 5.3 |
| Santa Ana-Anaheim-Irvine, CA Div | 115 382 | 0.0 | 18.5 | 12.0 | 14.8 | 6.3 | 12.8 | 8.9 | 10.0 | 390 615 | 128 | 72 713 | 1 048 907 | 8.2 |
| Louisville-Jefferson County, KY-IN | 36 972 | 0.2 | 18.4 | 13.2 | 8.7 | 5.7 | 10.1 | 13.7 | 13.9 | 245 375 | 190 | 36 082 | 559 837 | 13.7 |
| Lubbock, TX | 6 934 | 0.0 | 11.0 | 3.7 | 7.6 | 9.0 | 8.0 | 16.6 | 23.4 | 42 940 | 148 | 6 655 | 117 966 | 13.7 |
| Lynchburg, VA | 5 379 | -0.2 | D | 19.6 | 10.4 | 7.0 | 6.0 | 12.4 | 13.8 | 57 675 | 227 | 6 383 | 112 515 | 14.7 |
| Macon, GA | 5 244 | 0.3 | 11.8 | 7.3 | 6.8 | 7.9 | 11.0 | 19.5 | 15.6 | 46 235 | 199 | 9 280 | 101 587 | 8.0 |
| Madera-Chowchilla, CA | 2 904 | 21.7 | 10.5 | 7.1 | 3.5 | 5.7 | 1.7 | 14.5 | 22.4 | 22 985 | 150 | 4 751 | 49 140 | 21.7 |
| Madison, WI | 21 915 | 1.3 | 14.8 | 9.8 | 13.4 | 6.2 | 10.3 | 9.4 | 23.8 | 87 210 | 151 | 8 059 | 252 878 | 18.9 |
| Manchester-Nashua, NH | 14 650 | 0.0 | 22.1 | 16.7 | 14.7 | 8.2 | 10.7 | 11.7 | 10.8 | 70 455 | 175 | 6 474 | 166 053 | 10.7 |
| Manhattan, KS | 4 981 | 0.6 | 7.6 | 3.6 | D | 4.0 | 2.7 | D | 66.6 | 14 515 | 111 | 1 308 | 51 355 | 20.4 |
| Mankato, North Mankato, MN | 2 810 | 8.7 | 20.0 | 15.3 | D | 6.9 | 4.3 | 13.8 | 17.6 | 15 365 | 158 | 1 320 | 39 075 | 17.7 |
| Mansfield, OH | 2 528 | 1.2 | 26.6 | 21.5 | 5.1 | 8.9 | 3.6 | 15.1 | 18.9 | 27 500 | 223 | 3 156 | 54 599 | 2.9 |
| McAllen-Edinburg-Mission, TX | 11 212 | 0.4 | 9.1 | 2.4 | 4.3 | 10.3 | 4.4 | 20.6 | 26.4 | 93 105 | 117 | 41 579 | 248 287 | 28.9 |
| Medford, OR | 4 291 | 0.3 | 16.3 | 8.2 | 7.1 | 10.9 | 5.4 | 18.4 | 16.1 | 48 955 | 239 | 4 158 | 90 937 | 20.1 |
| Memphis, TN-MS-AR | 40 964 | 0.5 | 14.8 | 9.8 | 5.5 | 6.6 | 7.6 | 11.0 | 15.3 | 210 525 | 159 | 45 340 | 550 896 | 14.6 |
| Merced, CA | 4 453 | 20.1 | 12.9 | 9.1 | 3.5 | 6.6 | 2.4 | 9.5 | 23.7 | 33 570 | 129 | 11 172 | 83 698 | 22.1 |
| Miami-Fort Lauderdale-Pompano Beach, FL | 154 631 | 0.3 | 8.1 | 3.5 | 13.5 | 7.9 | 11.0 | 11.7 | 15.0 | 953 030 | 168 | 205 725 | 2 464 417 | 14.6 |
| Fort Lauderdale-Pompano Beach-Deerfield Beach, FL Div | 47 024 | 0.0 | 9.0 | 3.9 | 14.1 | 8.8 | 10.4 | 10.3 | 15.5 | 284 245 | 160 | 39 670 | 810 388 | 9.4 |
| Miami-Miami Beach-Kendall, FL Div | 71 598 | 0.3 | 7.4 | 3.2 | 13.2 | 7.3 | 10.6 | 11.7 | 15.8 | 381 305 | 149 | 145 629 | 989 435 | 16.1 |
| West Palm Beach-Boca Raton-Boynton Beach, FL Div | 36 009 | 0.7 | 8.3 | 3.5 | 13.4 | 7.7 | 12.8 | 13.7 | 12.5 | 287 480 | 215 | 20 426 | 664 594 | 19.4 |
| Michigan City-La Porte, IN.... | 2 258 | 2.8 | 29.0 | 22.3 | 3.2 | 6.9 | 3.2 | 14.0 | 16.8 | 22 925 | 206 | 2 164 | 48 448 | 6.2 |
| Midland, TX | 7 553 | 0.0 | 52.8 | 3.6 | 6.2 | 4.3 | 4.5 | 4.8 | 6.8 | 18 855 | 134 | 2 335 | 54 351 | 13.1 |
| Milwaukee-Waukesha-West Allis, WI | 54 697 | 0.1 | 21.9 | 17.7 | 10.3 | 5.1 | 10.1 | 13.0 | 11.1 | 271 275 | 174 | 44 220 | 669 879 | 8.4 |
| Minneapolis-St. Paul-Bloomington, MN | 129 028 | 0.3 | 16.6 | 12.2 | 13.2 | 4.9 | 12.3 | 10.3 | 12.4 | 471 950 | 142 | 55 077 | 1 354 973 | 15.8 |
| Missoula, MT | 2 949 | 0.0 | 9.7 | 3.2 | 9.0 | 9.0 | 6.4 | 17.9 | 20.7 | 18 020 | 164 | 2 039 | 50 106 | 21.3 |
| Mobile, AL | 10 569 | 0.2 | 20.2 | 12.3 | 8.3 | 6.6 | 9.0 | 11.2 | 17.3 | 84 270 | 204 | 14 844 | 178 196 | 7.9 |
| Modesto, CA | 10 350 | 8.5 | 18.9 | 14.2 | 4.2 | 7.7 | 4.1 | 16.5 | 16.8 | 77 895 | 150 | 21 600 | 179 503 | 19.0 |
| Monroe, LA | 4 101 | 0.7 | 4.7 | D | 10.1 | 8.4 | 7.7 | 15.6 | 18.5 | 31 930 | 180 | 7 407 | 75 827 | 6.8 |
| Monroe, MI | 2 371 | 2.0 | 23.9 | 17.2 | D | 6.6 | 2.9 | 10.1 | 13.8 | 30 795 | 203 | 2 577 | 62 971 | 11.5 |
| Montgomery, AL | 10 342 | 0.6 | 17.3 | 11.1 | 8.4 | 6.2 | 6.4 | 9.7 | 30.8 | 71 555 | 189 | 14 742 | 161 573 | 11.7 |
| Morgantown, WV | 3 878 | -0.1 | 18.6 | 9.0 | 7.8 | 5.4 | 4.7 | 17.3 | 30.1 | 20 530 | 155 | 3 028 | 58 335 | 16.3 |
| Morristown, TN | 2 344 | 0.2 | D | 26.9 | 2.7 | 8.5 | 3.2 | D | 14.7 | 34 690 | 252 | 4 388 | 61 356 | 14.2 |
| Mount Vernon-Anacortes, WA | 2 690 | 2.7 | 24.9 | 16.3 | 4.8 | 10.1 | 5.3 | 8.5 | 24.2 | 25 415 | 215 | 2 308 | 51 473 | 20.6 |
| Muncie, IN | 2 344 | 1.5 | 13.7 | 9.6 | 7.0 | 8.0 | 5.6 | 20.5 | 23.7 | 25 105 | 213 | 2 858 | 52 357 | 2.6 |
| Muskegon-Norton Shores, MI | 3 154 | 1.1 | 29.9 | 25.4 | 4.1 | 10.5 | 3.5 | 17.5 | 16.1 | 39 145 | 229 | 6 221 | 73 561 | 7.3 |
| Myrtle Beach-North Myrtle Beach-Conway, SC | 5 062 | -0.2 | 10.9 | 3.5 | 6.4 | 12.0 | 11.2 | 11.1 | 18.0 | 69 015 | 250 | 5 422 | 185 992 | 52.3 |
| Napa, CA | 4 681 | 2.4 | 25.2 | 19.5 | 6.9 | 5.6 | 5.3 | 11.6 | 15.9 | 25 100 | 182 | 2 654 | 54 759 | 12.8 |

1. Includes mining, construction, and manufacturing.   2. Per 1,000 resident population estimated as of July 1, 2011.

# Table C. Metropolitan Areas — Housing, Labor Force, and Employment

| Area name | Housing units, 2007–2011 Occupied units Owner-occupied Total | Percent | Median value[1] | Median owner cost as a percent of income With a mortgage | Without a mortgage | Renter-occupied Median rent[2] | Median rent as a percent of income | Sub-standard units[3] (percent) | Civilian labor force, 2012 Total | Percent change, 2011–2012 | Unemployment Total | Rate[4] | Civilian employment,[5] 2007–2011 Total | Percent Management, professional, and related occupations | Construction, production, and related occupations |
|---|---|---|---|---|---|---|---|---|---|---|---|---|---|---|---|
| | 89 | 90 | 91 | 92 | 93 | 94 | 95 | 96 | 97 | 98 | 99 | 100 | 101 | 102 | 103 |
| Kokomo, IN | 40 852 | 72.0 | 105 700 | 20.2 | 10.5 | 640 | 29.8 | 1.5 | 42 483 | 0.3 | 3 921 | 9.2 | 41 864 | 28.6 | 29.8 |
| La Crosse, WI-MN | 53 514 | 67.6 | 151 700 | 22.8 | 13.5 | 681 | 29.2 | 1.6 | 76 854 | 0.4 | 4 195 | 5.5 | 71 354 | 33.6 | 24.1 |
| Lafayette, IN | 76 815 | 58.2 | 123 700 | 21.2 | 10.0 | 743 | 34.3 | 2.0 | 97 971 | 1.1 | 7 272 | 7.4 | 96 188 | 37.7 | 23.1 |
| Lafayette, LA | 103 419 | 67.6 | 145 500 | 19.8 | 10.0 | 714 | 28.2 | 2.7 | 140 927 | 2.7 | 6 649 | 4.7 | 132 396 | 31.9 | 23.0 |
| Lake Charles, LA | 74 522 | 71.7 | 116 600 | 19.6 | 10.0 | 711 | 29.1 | 2.5 | 95 154 | 1.7 | 5 618 | 5.9 | 88 197 | 28.5 | 27.2 |
| Lake Havasu City-Kingman, AZ | 80 389 | 71.2 | 158 200 | 27.9 | 11.5 | 831 | 31.4 | 3.8 | 85 127 | -2.4 | 8 394 | 9.9 | 73 759 | 24.7 | 23.1 |
| Lakeland-Winter Haven, FL | 221 975 | 71.7 | 133 200 | 26.7 | 13.0 | 858 | 33.1 | 3.7 | 271 538 | 0.4 | 26 542 | 9.8 | 244 360 | 29.0 | 25.2 |
| Lancaster, PA | 192 681 | 70.1 | 187 300 | 24.2 | 12.8 | 828 | 29.2 | 2.2 | 268 804 | 0.7 | 17 824 | 6.6 | 252 430 | 31.1 | 29.2 |
| Lansing-East Lansing, MI | 180 136 | 67.2 | 143 600 | 23.8 | 12.7 | 737 | 33.1 | 1.4 | 232 959 | -1.4 | 16 726 | 7.2 | 220 424 | 37.7 | 18.7 |
| Laredo, TX | 65 796 | 63.9 | 106 500 | 28.3 | 15.0 | 722 | 33.9 | 17.7 | 100 354 | 0.7 | 7 086 | 7.1 | 97 544 | 25.3 | 22.6 |
| Las Cruces, NM | 72 748 | 66.1 | 141 900 | 23.8 | 11.3 | 657 | 33.7 | 4.4 | 93 195 | 0.9 | 6 653 | 7.1 | 85 170 | 32.2 | 22.0 |
| Las Vegas-Paradise, NV | 701 836 | 57.0 | 226 200 | 29.4 | 11.6 | 1 049 | 31.0 | 5.0 | 992 403 | -0.7 | 111 425 | 11.2 | 904 125 | 26.5 | 18.6 |
| Lawrence, KS | 43 238 | 51.9 | 179 900 | 23.3 | 12.3 | 811 | 34.5 | 2.0 | 61 614 | -0.4 | 3 251 | 5.3 | 60 345 | 43.2 | 15.3 |
| Lawton, OK | 44 179 | 57.6 | 106 300 | 20.8 | 10.1 | 706 | 27.5 | 3.2 | 47 772 | -1.0 | 3 151 | 6.6 | 47 646 | 31.1 | 24.7 |
| Lebanon, PA | 51 899 | 73.6 | 160 800 | 22.9 | 12.7 | 672 | 28.5 | 2.4 | 74 910 | 1.7 | 4 813 | 6.4 | 63 590 | 29.3 | 27.7 |
| Lewiston, ID-WA | 25 046 | 68.7 | 165 900 | 23.3 | 10.9 | 629 | 28.0 | 1.6 | 28 894 | -0.8 | 2 006 | 6.9 | 27 877 | 29.3 | 26.1 |
| Lewiston-Auburn, ME | 43 968 | 67.2 | 157 100 | 24.5 | 16.4 | 682 | 29.3 | 1.8 | 58 224 | 0.6 | 4 298 | 7.4 | 52 591 | 31.2 | 24.1 |
| Lexington-Fayette, KY | 189 717 | 60.7 | 158 600 | 21.5 | 10.0 | 708 | 29.1 | 2.1 | 242 819 | 0.8 | 16 028 | 6.6 | 234 308 | 38.8 | 19.8 |
| Lima, OH | 40 703 | 70.0 | 105 400 | 21.6 | 12.3 | 626 | 31.6 | 1.7 | 48 784 | -2.0 | 3 793 | 7.8 | 47 059 | 26.2 | 27.7 |
| Lincoln, NE | 119 268 | 62.3 | 145 800 | 22.4 | 11.3 | 686 | 28.5 | 1.9 | 175 527 | 2.1 | 6 219 | 3.5 | 162 864 | 38.4 | 19.6 |
| Little Rock-North Little Rock-Conway, AR | 271 327 | 65.9 | 132 200 | 20.7 | 10.5 | 734 | 29.9 | 2.4 | 345 930 | 0.7 | 22 446 | 6.5 | 327 491 | 36.1 | 21.2 |
| Logan, UT-ID | 38 728 | 65.5 | 183 000 | 24.3 | 10.0 | 656 | 28.1 | 4.1 | 66 724 | -0.6 | 2 954 | 4.4 | 57 829 | 34.2 | 25.3 |
| Longview, TX | 78 077 | 69.5 | 102 900 | 20.4 | 10.8 | 694 | 26.3 | 4.5 | 116 140 | 1.2 | 6 759 | 5.8 | 93 888 | 27.4 | 30.6 |
| Longview, WA | 39 793 | 67.3 | 193 800 | 25.5 | 11.8 | 705 | 34.2 | 3.1 | 43 067 | 0.0 | 4 687 | 10.9 | 41 229 | 28.2 | 31.1 |
| Los Angeles-Long Beach-Santa Ana, CA | 4 205 682 | 50.8 | 501 900 | 32.0 | 10.8 | 1 218 | 33.9 | 11.8 | 6 498 351 | -0.4 | 656 667 | 10.1 | 5 942 695 | 36.1 | 20.3 |
| Los Angeles-Long Beach-Glendale, CA Div | 3 218 518 | 47.8 | 478 300 | 32.6 | 11.0 | 1 161 | 34.2 | 12.5 | 4 879 674 | -1.0 | 533 951 | 10.9 | 4 501 382 | 35.0 | 21.2 |
| Santa Ana-Anaheim-Irvine, CA Div | 987 164 | 60.3 | 575 100 | 30.5 | 10.1 | 1 463 | 32.9 | 9.6 | 1 618 677 | 1.2 | 122 716 | 7.6 | 1 441 313 | 39.6 | 17.3 |
| Louisville-Jefferson County, KY-IN | 502 720 | 69.3 | 145 900 | 22.3 | 11.0 | 689 | 28.7 | 1.9 | 632 665 | 0.2 | 52 258 | 8.3 | 601 740 | 33.4 | 24.7 |
| Lubbock, TX | 105 025 | 59.7 | 104 100 | 21.7 | 11.6 | 746 | 32.6 | 4.3 | 146 472 | -0.4 | 8 070 | 5.5 | 136 255 | 32.2 | 20.1 |
| Lynchburg, VA | 98 428 | 71.7 | 157 300 | 22.8 | 10.0 | 667 | 30.1 | 1.5 | 120 835 | -0.7 | 8 052 | 6.7 | 116 096 | 32.3 | 25.4 |
| Macon, GA | 84 807 | 64.9 | 120 000 | 23.7 | 12.3 | 712 | 35.1 | 2.3 | 114 444 | 1.0 | 10 888 | 9.5 | 94 134 | 32.4 | 23.1 |
| Madera-Chowchilla, CA | 42 032 | 62.2 | 245 500 | 31.5 | 11.7 | 861 | 31.5 | 11.1 | 68 167 | 0.7 | 9 295 | 13.6 | 52 804 | 23.3 | 35.6 |
| Madison, WI | 232 350 | 63.3 | 223 500 | 25.0 | 12.7 | 853 | 29.5 | 1.9 | 345 720 | -0.2 | 17 225 | 5.0 | 315 868 | 44.8 | 16.4 |
| Manchester-Nashua, NH | 153 471 | 68.3 | 265 100 | 26.6 | 16.5 | 1 019 | 29.5 | 2.0 | 229 472 | 0.7 | 13 040 | 5.7 | 213 830 | 40.5 | 19.6 |
| Manhattan, KS | 45 121 | 51.4 | 150 900 | 21.5 | 11.2 | 798 | 30.1 | 5.4 | 62 444 | 0.5 | 3 176 | 5.1 | 54 671 | 37.7 | 20.0 |
| Mankato, North Mankato, MN | 36 292 | 69.2 | 165 000 | 23.3 | 11.7 | 691 | 31.2 | 1.2 | 57 948 | -0.6 | 2 790 | 4.8 | 54 608 | 31.9 | 23.5 |
| Mansfield, OH | 48 593 | 70.2 | 110 900 | 22.6 | 12.1 | 609 | 27.5 | 1.6 | 57 622 | -3.3 | 4 803 | 8.3 | 54 088 | 27.1 | 31.0 |
| McAllen-Edinburg-Mission, TX | 209 796 | 70.1 | 75 500 | 25.6 | 13.7 | 620 | 34.3 | 14.8 | 316 032 | -0.3 | 34 702 | 11.0 | 275 737 | 25.4 | 24.0 |
| Medford, OR | 83 897 | 61.8 | 262 500 | 29.2 | 14.1 | 844 | 34.8 | 2.8 | 100 207 | -0.8 | 10 871 | 10.8 | 87 663 | 30.9 | 21.7 |
| Memphis, TN-MS-AR | 477 904 | 64.4 | 136 700 | 24.2 | 12.5 | 802 | 33.2 | 3.2 | 615 739 | -0.5 | 55 236 | 9.0 | 590 112 | 32.8 | 23.2 |
| Merced, CA | 74 079 | 55.2 | 197 700 | 29.7 | 10.7 | 806 | 34.1 | 9.6 | 111 322 | 0.8 | 18 935 | 17.0 | 94 066 | 22.5 | 35.9 |
| Miami-Fort Lauderdale-Pompano Beach, FL | 2 013 933 | 65.0 | 236 900 | 33.4 | 17.4 | 1 108 | 37.5 | 4.3 | 2 949 802 | 1.6 | 251 752 | 8.5 | 2 556 466 | 32.9 | 18.4 |
| Fort Lauderdale-Pompano Beach-Deerfield Beach, FL Div | 665 037 | 68.2 | 225 300 | 32.7 | 18.6 | 1 162 | 36.5 | 3.5 | 1 015 805 | 1.7 | 75 388 | 7.4 | 845 492 | 35.2 | 16.4 |
| Miami-Miami Beach-Kendall, FL Div | 825 337 | 57.6 | 246 800 | 35.2 | 17.0 | 1 053 | 38.7 | 5.7 | 1 299 265 | 1.5 | 120 533 | 9.3 | 1 131 458 | 30.3 | 20.6 |
| West Palm Beach-Boca Raton-Boynton Beach, FL Div | 523 559 | 72.6 | 236 600 | 32.0 | 16.7 | 1 148 | 36.3 | 2.9 | 634 732 | 1.6 | 55 831 | 8.8 | 579 516 | 34.7 | 16.7 |
| Michigan City-La Porte, IN | 42 255 | 75.0 | 120 500 | 22.1 | 11.4 | 686 | 30.5 | 2.2 | 49 828 | -0.9 | 4 986 | 10.0 | 48 341 | 26.6 | 30.8 |
| Midland, TX | 49 534 | 70.2 | 133 100 | 20.0 | 11.1 | 855 | 28.0 | 3.9 | 90 130 | 7.2 | 3 125 | 3.5 | 67 256 | 31.0 | 26.1 |
| Milwaukee-Waukesha-West Allis, WI | 616 639 | 62.3 | 205 100 | 24.8 | 14.7 | 788 | 30.4 | 2.2 | 795 351 | -0.3 | 59 066 | 7.4 | 762 414 | 37.0 | 21.1 |
| Minneapolis-St. Paul-Bloomington, MN | 1 271 957 | 72.0 | 234 000 | 24.6 | 12.0 | 864 | 29.9 | 2.4 | 1 857 426 | 0.5 | 102 153 | 5.5 | 1 723 465 | 41.7 | 17.9 |
| Missoula, MT | 44 946 | 60.5 | 239 000 | 25.7 | 11.3 | 718 | 33.7 | 2.5 | 58 869 | 1.0 | 3 465 | 5.9 | 56 776 | 35.7 | 17.5 |
| Mobile, AL | 155 638 | 67.9 | 124 100 | 23.2 | 12.5 | 723 | 34.0 | 2.8 | 186 408 | -2.6 | 15 617 | 8.4 | 173 345 | 29.8 | 25.7 |
| Modesto, CA | 164 933 | 60.8 | 232 000 | 30.7 | 12.3 | 962 | 34.6 | 7.2 | 239 461 | 0.3 | 36 324 | 15.2 | 205 958 | 26.6 | 30.9 |
| Monroe, LA | 64 734 | 63.9 | 109 500 | 20.0 | 10.0 | 639 | 31.4 | 3.1 | 81 364 | 1.0 | 5 684 | 7.0 | 76 164 | 31.1 | 22.8 |
| Monroe, MI | 58 200 | 80.4 | 156 600 | 24.1 | 13.2 | 755 | 29.9 | 1.7 | 69 315 | -0.4 | 5 543 | 8.0 | 68 242 | 27.2 | 31.1 |
| Montgomery, AL | 140 389 | 68.3 | 128 700 | 22.4 | 11.0 | 773 | 31.9 | 2.8 | 168 320 | -1.0 | 12 626 | 7.5 | 162 860 | 34.2 | 22.0 |
| Morgantown, WV | 48 174 | 64.0 | 132 200 | 19.1 | 10.0 | 656 | 33.3 | 1.5 | 67 046 | 1.7 | 3 528 | 5.3 | 59 076 | 37.0 | 22.0 |
| Morristown, TN | 52 923 | 74.3 | 115 000 | 23.0 | 11.4 | 614 | 29.1 | 1.8 | 62 927 | -1.5 | 6 051 | 9.6 | 57 606 | 24.0 | 35.3 |
| Mount Vernon-Anacortes, WA | 45 475 | 68.9 | 280 800 | 28.8 | 12.8 | 911 | 30.5 | 3.9 | 56 435 | -0.5 | 5 214 | 9.2 | 51 185 | 30.9 | 27.6 |
| Muncie, IN | 46 162 | 65.9 | 92 200 | 21.2 | 12.3 | 650 | 34.9 | 1.3 | 54 245 | 1.1 | 5 161 | 9.5 | 50 644 | 30.7 | 21.3 |
| Muskegon-Norton Shores, MI | 65 272 | 74.8 | 108 700 | 24.3 | 13.5 | 642 | 34.5 | 1.8 | 83 069 | 0.4 | 7 293 | 8.8 | 68 790 | 26.8 | 30.0 |
| Myrtle Beach-North Myrtle Beach-Conway, SC | 112 358 | 70.9 | 170 600 | 26.5 | 12.1 | 808 | 33.0 | 5.1 | 129 445 | 0.0 | 13 243 | 10.2 | 121 926 | 26.9 | 19.8 |
| Napa, CA | 49 640 | 63.3 | 521 700 | 30.0 | 11.7 | 1 279 | 32.4 | 6.6 | 77 843 | 1.9 | 6 080 | 7.8 | 64 899 | 35.6 | 23.4 |

1. Specified owner-occupied units.  2. Specified renter-occupied units.  3. Overcrowded or lacking complete plumbing facilities.  4. Percent of civilian labor force.  5. Persons 16 years old and over.

Table C. Metropolitan Areas — **Nonfarm Employment and Agriculture**

| | Private nonfarm establishments, employment and payroll, 2011 | | | | | | | | | Agriculture, 2007 | | | |
|---|---|---|---|---|---|---|---|---|---|---|---|---|---|
| | | Employment | | | | | | Annual payroll | | Farms | | | |
| | | | | | | | | | | | | Percent with: | |
| Area name | Number of establishments | Total | Health care and social assistance | Manufacturing | Retail trade | Finance and insurance | Professional, scientific, and technical services | Total (mil dol) | Average per employee (dollars) | Number | Fewer than 50 acres | 500 acres or more | Farm operators whose principal occupation is farming (percent) |
| | 104 | 105 | 106 | 107 | 108 | 109 | 110 | 111 | 112 | 113 | 114 | 115 | 116 |
| Kokomo, IN .................... | 2 089 | 31 770 | 6 161 | 8 148 | 5 270 | 732 | 821 | 1 301 | 40 937 | 1 059 | 46.6 | 18.5 | 51.5 |
| La Crosse, WI-MN ............... | 3 396 | 61 775 | 11 805 | 7 205 | 8 784 | 3 027 | 1 764 | 2 129 | 34 459 | 1 886 | 20.3 | 9.1 | 46.8 |
| Lafayette, IN.................... | 3 893 | 65 748 | 9 767 | 14 914 | 9 558 | 2 917 | 2 398 | 2 469 | 37 551 | 1 737 | 43.0 | 21.1 | 46.7 |
| Lafayette, LA................... | 8 892 | 133 949 | 23 024 | 9 148 | 17 279 | 3 891 | 8 653 | 5 654 | 42 212 | 1 068 | 72.3 | 6.3 | 38.6 |
| Lake Charles, LA................ | 4 369 | 69 486 | 12 315 | 8 166 | 10 671 | 1 890 | 3 455 | 2 673 | 38 466 | 1 310 | 48.7 | 12.5 | 38.0 |
| Lake Havasu City-Kingman, AZ .............................. | 3 600 | 39 743 | 8 726 | 2 552 | 9 782 | 1 039 | 1 081 | 1 202 | 30 233 | 334 | 57.8 | 21.6 | 48.8 |
| Lakeland-Winter Haven, FL .. | 10 718 | 161 846 | 26 544 | 13 582 | 23 278 | 11 011 | 8 813 | 5 855 | 36 176 | 2 768 | 66.2 | 6.4 | 42.5 |
| Lancaster, PA ................... | 12 041 | 210 772 | 34 089 | 33 619 | 30 183 | 6 710 | 10 343 | 7 903 | 37 494 | 5 462 | 46.6 | 1.7 | 64.1 |
| Lansing-East Lansing, MI ..... | 9 466 | 153 970 | 27 919 | 19 192 | 21 809 | 11 777 | 7 411 | 6 016 | 39 071 | 3 409 | 47.6 | 9.0 | 43.8 |
| Laredo, TX....................... | 4 779 | 66 417 | 13 988 | 700 | 12 550 | 2 432 | 1 619 | 1 772 | 26 682 | 663 | 15.7 | 41.3 | 34.1 |
| Las Cruces, NM.................. | 3 630 | 49 011 | 12 400 | 2 329 | 7 981 | 1 705 | 3 924 | 1 410 | 28 765 | 1 762 | 80.5 | 5.6 | 41.4 |
| Las Vegas-Paradise, NV ...... | 39 343 | 730 747 | 68 513 | 18 806 | 94 270 | 24 510 | 39 059 | 27 824 | 38 076 | 193 | 74.6 | 5.2 | 40.4 |
| Lawrence, KS.................... | 2 601 | 37 058 | 5 960 | 3 281 | 6 111 | 979 | 1 899 | 1 031 | 27 816 | 1 040 | 38.8 | 9.2 | 35.4 |
| Lawton, OK...................... | 2 194 | 32 151 | 6 357 | 3 459 | 5 396 | 1 851 | 1 293 | 1 008 | 31 355 | 1 126 | 24.5 | 21.0 | 42.6 |
| Lebanon, PA ..................... | 2 610 | 43 384 | 7 539 | 8 889 | 6 425 | 869 | 1 067 | 1 472 | 33 920 | 1 193 | 52.9 | 1.4 | 54.8 |
| Lewiston, ID-WA ................ | 1 551 | 20 493 | 4 162 | 3 001 | 3 469 | 1 360 | 668 | 679 | 33 116 | 665 | 36.8 | 31.7 | 51.6 |
| Lewiston-Auburn, ME........... | 2 749 | 43 155 | 9 557 | 5 317 | 6 188 | 3 108 | 1 879 | 1 545 | 35 801 | 378 | 47.9 | 5.3 | 52.4 |
| Lexington-Fayette, KY ......... | 11 644 | 196 010 | 32 456 | 24 308 | 26 949 | 6 277 | 11 542 | 7 803 | 39 810 | 4 988 | 43.2 | 7.4 | 45.8 |
| Lima, OH......................... | 2 516 | 46 301 | 11 626 | 7 595 | 6 055 | 1 195 | 938 | 1 612 | 34 810 | 946 | 40.7 | 13.1 | 37.8 |
| Lincoln, NE...................... | 8 208 | 130 701 | 22 978 | 12 694 | 17 268 | 10 251 | 9 182 | 4 778 | 36 556 | 2 591 | 39.9 | 17.8 | 43.9 |
| Little Rock-North Little Rock-Conway, AR ..... | 17 486 | 277 352 | 60 008 | 20 809 | 37 200 | 14 810 | 12 700 | 10 740 | 38 722 | 3 763 | 44.2 | 9.0 | 40.1 |
| Logan, UT-ID .................... | 3 321 | 38 370 | 5 425 | 10 785 | 5 920 | 1 055 | 2 428 | 1 156 | 30 125 | 1 934 | 45.6 | 11.9 | 38.3 |
| Longview, TX .................... | 5 337 | 79 914 | 13 384 | 9 630 | 11 462 | 2 708 | 3 173 | 3 073 | 38 456 | 3 514 | 43.7 | 6.0 | 36.1 |
| Longview, WA.................... | 2 149 | 30 312 | 5 634 | 5 974 | 4 678 | 877 | 838 | 1 272 | 41 954 | 481 | 67.8 | 1.9 | 44.3 |
| Los Angeles-Long Beach-Santa Ana, CA ..... | 331 734 | 4 949 519 | 630 391 | 505 918 | 518 153 | 236 709 | 542 189 | 247 676 | 50 040 | 2 059 | 86.2 | 2.8 | 36.6 |
| Los Angeles-Long Beach-Glendale, CA Div ........ | X | X | X | X | X | X | X | X | X | 1 734 | 86.9 | 2.8 | 35.8 |
| Santa Ana-Anaheim-Irvine, CA Div ....... | X | X | X | X | X | X | X | X | X | 325 | 82.8 | 2.8 | 40.9 |
| Louisville-Jefferson County, KY-IN ................ | 29 228 | 517 444 | 82 035 | 60 891 | 62 204 | 32 106 | 25 538 | 20 628 | 39 865 | 10 328 | 44.8 | 4.8 | 40.8 |
| Lubbock, TX ..................... | 6 943 | 105 974 | 23 197 | 5 342 | 16 806 | 4 914 | 3 972 | 3 341 | 31 530 | 1 576 | 31.8 | 29.4 | 43.8 |
| Lynchburg, VA ................... | 5 829 | 94 216 | 13 765 | 16 538 | 13 515 | 4 030 | 5 433 | 3 501 | 37 162 | 2 897 | 30.5 | 6.9 | 39.1 |
| Macon, GA....................... | 5 172 | 80 941 | 16 389 | 5 504 | 12 033 | 8 702 | 2 723 | 2 840 | 35 089 | 842 | 37.2 | 7.8 | 47.5 |
| Madera-Chowchilla, CA ....... | 1 882 | 25 329 | 5 759 | 3 171 | 3 344 | 462 | 489 | 885 | 34 932 | 1 708 | 46.4 | 13.1 | 54.4 |
| Madison, WI...................... | 15 105 | 277 027 | 45 961 | 28 085 | 36 557 | 22 741 | 19 760 | 11 999 | 43 315 | 6 729 | 38.2 | 8.0 | 44.6 |
| Manchester-Nashua, NH ...... | 10 635 | 176 356 | 27 983 | 25 924 | 26 664 | 6 348 | 10 541 | 8 716 | 49 422 | 615 | 57.9 | 1.8 | 48.1 |
| Manhattan, KS................... | 2 697 | 35 947 | 6 168 | 2 347 | 7 640 | 1 345 | 1 382 | 1 036 | 28 831 | 1 604 | 21.0 | 26.5 | 46.4 |
| Mankato, North Mankato, MN ............................. | 2 564 | 45 646 | 11 199 | 6 999 | 6 802 | 1 228 | 1 192 | 1 564 | 34 269 | 2 074 | 27.1 | 20.9 | 55.5 |
| Mansfield, OH.................... | 2 673 | 42 132 | 7 460 | 7 881 | 6 516 | 1 057 | 1 017 | 1 298 | 30 805 | 1 009 | 43.0 | 4.5 | 41.8 |
| McAllen-Edinburg-Mission, TX ............................. | 11 206 | 169 833 | 54 623 | 5 039 | 34 056 | 6 345 | 6 273 | 4 425 | 26 053 | 2 151 | 61.6 | 14.9 | 44.1 |
| Medford, OR ..................... | 5 704 | 63 060 | 11 480 | 5 288 | 11 071 | 2 489 | 2 292 | 2 120 | 33 623 | 1 976 | 69.5 | 3.5 | 45.5 |
| Memphis, TN-MS-AR........... | 25 131 | 509 410 | 76 411 | 35 185 | 60 403 | 20 705 | 17 331 | 21 487 | 42 179 | 4 220 | 37.7 | 13.9 | 40.9 |
| Merced, CA ...................... | 2 830 | 39 914 | 6 604 | 8 468 | 7 652 | 1 049 | 828 | 1 356 | 33 969 | 2 607 | 55.7 | 12.6 | 59.5 |
| Miami-Fort Lauderdale-Pompano Beach, FL ........... | 172 255 | 1 856 135 | 289 320 | 63 694 | 282 518 | 97 332 | 142 310 | 79 353 | 42 752 | 4 308 | 91.5 | 2.1 | 51.6 |
| Fort Lauderdale-Pompano Beach-Deerfield Beach, FL Div .............. | X | X | X | X | X | X | X | X | X | 547 | 92.3 | 0.5 | 50.3 |
| Miami-Miami Beach-Kendall, FL Div................ | X | X | X | X | X | X | X | X | X | 2 498 | 93.2 | 0.9 | 50.4 |
| West Palm Beach-Boca Raton-Boynton Beach, FL Div .............. | X | X | X | X | X | X | X | X | X | 1 263 | 87.8 | 5.3 | 54.4 |
| Michigan City-La Porte, IN.... | 2 387 | 33 833 | 5 079 | 7 267 | 5 678 | 802 | 963 | 1 104 | 32 623 | 869 | 51.6 | 18.1 | 44.3 |
| Midland, TX...................... | 4 655 | 65 689 | 7 619 | 2 382 | 8 054 | 1 888 | 3 672 | 3 588 | 54 621 | 601 | 51.1 | 16.5 | 28.6 |
| Milwaukee-Waukesha-West Allis, WI ...................... | 37 705 | 745 662 | 123 169 | 112 411 | 78 747 | 55 975 | 45 840 | 34 707 | 46 546 | 2 115 | 50.4 | 6.0 | 49.8 |
| Minneapolis-St. Paul-Bloomington, MN ........... | 89 280 | 1 596 823 | 257 543 | 169 490 | 173 517 | 117 804 | 113 212 | 82 743 | 51 817 | 11 672 | 43.8 | 6.9 | 42.4 |
| Missoula, MT..................... | 4 081 | 46 175 | 10 255 | 1 366 | 7 908 | 1 924 | 2 971 | 1 427 | 30 896 | 699 | 59.2 | 8.0 | 30.3 |
| Mobile, AL........................ | 8 659 | 149 033 | 22 199 | 16 198 | 20 241 | 5 537 | 9 726 | 5 845 | 39 218 | 876 | 60.8 | 4.8 | 39.7 |
| Modesto, CA..................... | 8 289 | 122 473 | 22 718 | 18 407 | 21 417 | 3 639 | 4 803 | 4 806 | 39 237 | 4 114 | 69.4 | 6.1 | 54.1 |
| Monroe, LA....................... | 4 479 | 66 473 | 13 798 | 6 391 | 9 833 | 5 322 | 3 961 | 2 055 | 30 913 | 928 | 43.1 | 6.1 | 42.9 |
| Monroe, MI....................... | 2 333 | 34 779 | 5 347 | 6 243 | 5 038 | 867 | 1 822 | 1 360 | 39 104 | 1 119 | 52.4 | 10.0 | 44.2 |
| Montgomery, AL.................. | 7 586 | 125 522 | 19 329 | 17 345 | 18 647 | 5 108 | 6 805 | 4 636 | 36 935 | 2 066 | 34.9 | 15.8 | 40.9 |
| Morgantown, WV ................ | 2 743 | 45 865 | 13 416 | 4 018 | 6 880 | 897 | 2 675 | 1 721 | 37 514 | 1 505 | 27.8 | 3.8 | 42.9 |
| Morristown, TN................... | 2 173 | 38 131 | 5 495 | 11 232 | 6 212 | 860 | 519 | 1 230 | 32 245 | 2 934 | 49.6 | 1.5 | 40.8 |
| Mount Vernon-Anacortes, WA ............................. | 3 358 | 36 338 | 7 060 | 5 036 | 6 882 | 1 523 | 1 315 | 1 365 | 37 575 | 1 215 | 74.7 | 4.4 | 39.4 |
| Muncie, IN........................ | 2 396 | 36 601 | 9 247 | 3 622 | 6 198 | 2 088 | 1 425 | 1 156 | 31 582 | 659 | 58.0 | 11.1 | 48.1 |
| Muskegon-Norton Shores, MI ............................. | 3 268 | 49 204 | 9 330 | 11 499 | 7 964 | 1 084 | 1 492 | 1 766 | 35 898 | 525 | 52.2 | 5.7 | 45.3 |
| Myrtle Beach-North Myrtle Beach-Conway, SC ....... | 8 048 | 93 009 | 10 255 | 2 868 | 20 232 | 3 516 | 2 910 | 2 511 | 26 999 | 914 | 37.1 | 7.5 | 46.2 |
| Napa, CA......................... | 3 880 | 56 022 | 10 768 | 10 262 | 6 593 | 1 281 | 1 603 | 2 563 | 45 741 | 1 638 | 73.0 | 5.3 | 41.4 |

# Table C. Metropolitan Areas — **Agriculture**

| Area name | Agriculture, 2007 (cont.) | | | | | | | | | | | | | | | |
|---|---|---|---|---|---|---|---|---|---|---|---|---|---|---|---|---|
| | Land in farms | | | | | Value of land and buildings (dollars) | | | Value of products sold | | | | Percent of farms with sales of: | | Government payments | |
| | | | Acres | | | | | Value of machinery and equipment, average per farm (dollars) | | | Percent from: | | | | | |
| | Acreage (1,000) | Percent change, 2002–2007 | Average size of farm | Total irrigated (1,000) | Total cropland (1,000) | Average per farm | Average per acre | | Total (mil dol) | Average per farm (dollars) | Crops | Live-stock and poultry products | $10,000 or more | $100,000 or more | Total ($1,000) | Percent of farms |
| | 117 | 118 | 119 | 120 | 121 | 122 | 123 | 124 | 125 | 126 | 127 | 128 | 129 | 130 | 131 | 132 |
| Kokomo, IN | 328 | 6.5 | 310 | 0.1 | 311.0 | 1 280 954 | 4 134 | 137 159 | 192.9 | 182 117 | 74.7 | 25.3 | 61.0 | 29.5 | 6 409 | 74.7 |
| La Crosse, WI-MN | 410 | -4.2 | 217 | 1.0 | 215.2 | 601 091 | 2 767 | 91 513 | 151.8 | 80 485 | 30.1 | 69.9 | 45.7 | 18.9 | 5 821 | 73.2 |
| Lafayette, IN | 681 | 1.6 | 392 | 9.9 | 640.5 | 1 479 765 | 3 772 | 156 954 | 402.6 | 231 741 | 77.5 | 22.5 | 58.7 | 32.9 | 13 820 | 67.5 |
| Lafayette, LA | 146 | -6.4 | 137 | 11.5 | 108.2 | 393 405 | 2 872 | 71 694 | 61.4 | 57 501 | 89.8 | 10.2 | 23.1 | 6.3 | 1 731 | 15.2 |
| Lake Charles, LA | 584 | 5.8 | 446 | 24.0 | 180.5 | 794 338 | 1 782 | 59 362 | 27.9 | 21 276 | 44.4 | 55.6 | 27.3 | 4.5 | 4 251 | 29.3 |
| Lake Havasu City-Kingman, AZ | 858 | 8.2 | 2 570 | 17.1 | 31.2 | 1 450 681 | 564 | 57 373 | 18.6 | 55 784 | 65.2 | 34.8 | 28.1 | 5.1 | 761 | 4.5 |
| Lakeland-Winter Haven, FL | 549 | -12.4 | 198 | 98.4 | 136.3 | 1 417 168 | 7 144 | 57 381 | 399.0 | 144 132 | 91.1 | 8.9 | 62.7 | 22.8 | 211 | 1.7 |
| Lancaster, PA | 425 | 3.2 | 78 | 5.4 | 326.6 | 726 059 | 9 324 | 83 136 | 1 072.2 | 196 293 | 13.9 | 86.1 | 69.5 | 44.3 | 4 547 | 23.0 |
| Lansing-East Lansing, MI | 680 | 0.1 | 199 | 8.1 | 565.9 | 695 306 | 3 486 | 97 308 | 320.7 | 94 101 | 54.4 | 45.6 | 40.1 | 14.7 | 8 980 | 47.3 |
| Laredo, TX | 1 856 | -9.2 | 2 799 | 5.1 | 58.8 | 2 090 515 | 747 | 57 689 | 24.7 | 37 297 | 1.2 | 98.8 | 26.4 | 5.4 | 298 | 5.0 |
| Las Cruces, NM | 589 | 1.4 | 334 | 79.0 | 95.8 | 636 656 | 1 903 | 77 539 | 388.8 | 220 651 | 43.2 | 56.8 | 36.8 | 9.9 | 2 338 | 13.1 |
| Las Vegas-Paradise, NV | 88 | 27.5 | 458 | 6.5 | 6.2 | 1 391 798 | 3 039 | 64 840 | 10.2 | 53 062 | 46.1 | 53.9 | 21.2 | 7.3 | 91 | 6.7 |
| Lawrence, KS | 221 | 10.0 | 212 | 1.8 | 134.7 | 408 136 | 1 924 | 66 492 | 41.3 | 39 675 | 67.8 | 32.2 | 34.3 | 7.9 | 1 994 | 44.2 |
| Lawton, OK | 498 | 17.2 | 442 | 1.4 | 160.7 | 506 837 | 1 147 | 52 948 | 38.8 | 34 484 | 22.7 | 77.3 | 36.7 | 6.0 | 3 169 | 40.0 |
| Lebanon, PA | 113 | -9.6 | 95 | 1.3 | 89.6 | 791 376 | 8 319 | 100 682 | 257.1 | 215 505 | 8.6 | 91.4 | 51.6 | 33.4 | 1 495 | 29.2 |
| Lewiston, ID-WA | 627 | 0.5 | 943 | 0.9 | 284.0 | 1 121 528 | 1 189 | 112 883 | 72.1 | 108 374 | D | D | 37.1 | 19.8 | 7 352 | 50.7 |
| Lewiston-Auburn, ME | 51 | -8.9 | 135 | 0.5 | 23.1 | 402 339 | 2 991 | 112 469 | 68.4 | 181 071 | 11.2 | 88.8 | 36.2 | 16.4 | 487 | 15.1 |
| Lexington-Fayette, KY | 808 | 2.3 | 162 | 2.6 | 368.2 | 802 819 | 4 958 | 67 341 | 1 248.5 | 250 275 | 5.7 | 94.3 | 42.0 | 14.1 | 2 541 | 18.4 |
| Lima, OH | 187 | -0.5 | 198 | 0.4 | 170.4 | 708 676 | 3 581 | 86 747 | 87.6 | 92 629 | 73.7 | 26.3 | 54.1 | 20.6 | 3 921 | 79.7 |
| Lincoln, NE | 754 | -7.3 | 291 | 143.0 | 596.0 | 737 329 | 2 534 | 103 101 | 347.8 | 134 255 | 62.4 | 37.6 | 46.4 | 22.4 | 13 648 | 70.7 |
| Little Rock-North Little Rock-Conway, AR | 808 | -6.6 | 215 | 248.7 | 487.0 | 539 290 | 2 510 | 76 088 | 257.4 | 68 389 | 59.6 | 40.4 | 30.9 | 8.5 | 14 229 | 18.7 |
| Logan, UT-ID | 476 | -2.9 | 246 | 129.7 | 275.5 | 649 863 | 2 638 | 94 283 | 214.9 | 111 077 | 18.7 | 81.3 | 44.1 | 14.8 | 4 993 | 41.1 |
| Longview, TX | 544 | 5.4 | 155 | 2.6 | 139.1 | 365 068 | 2 357 | 49 264 | 108.8 | 30 969 | 22.0 | 78.0 | 22.4 | 3.1 | 293 | 2.0 |
| Longview, WA | 31 | -22.5 | 64 | 3.0 | 10.9 | 485 875 | 7 612 | 51 689 | 26.5 | 55 006 | 40.2 | 59.8 | 18.3 | 5.6 | 29 | 1.9 |
| Los Angeles-Long Beach-Santa Ana, CA | 196 | 9.5 | 95 | 38.7 | 63.8 | 1 252 511 | 13 165 | 82 634 | 662.3 | 321 646 | 96.0 | 4.0 | 31.2 | 13.6 | 176 | 1.9 |
| Los Angeles-Long Beach-Glendale, CA Div | 108 | -2.7 | 63 | 29.7 | 49.2 | 877 388 | 14 027 | 67 008 | 325.9 | 187 935 | 92.7 | 7.3 | 27.8 | 11.2 | 138 | 1.6 |
| Santa Ana-Anaheim-Irvine, CA Div | 87 | 27.9 | 269 | 9.0 | 14.6 | 3 253 936 | 12 095 | 166 005 | 336.4 | 1 035 046 | 99.2 | 0.8 | 49.5 | 26.8 | 38 | 3.4 |
| Louisville-Jefferson County, KY-IN | 1 417 | -1.6 | 137 | 6.0 | 809.9 | 491 673 | 3 584 | 60 403 | 392.9 | 38 040 | D | D | 33.3 | 6.8 | 12 481 | 32.2 |
| Lubbock, TX | 1 068 | 2.0 | 678 | 269.4 | 704.8 | 634 326 | 936 | 143 751 | 301.7 | 191 466 | D | D | 40.0 | 26.0 | 29 437 | 64.3 |
| Lynchburg, VA | 517 | NA | 178 | 1.5 | 166.8 | 675 462 | 3 785 | 61 428 | 64.0 | 22 126 | 15.2 | 84.8 | 30.4 | 3.4 | 1 391 | 19.3 |
| Macon, GA | 169 | -17.6 | 200 | 7.2 | 51.4 | 621 040 | 3 100 | 65 938 | 86.0 | 102 137 | 22.1 | 77.9 | 28.3 | 8.3 | 1 119 | 14.4 |
| Madera-Chowchilla, CA | 680 | -0.3 | 398 | 281.7 | 290.7 | 2 699 315 | 6 783 | 139 667 | 990.1 | 579 696 | 63.2 | 36.8 | 64.8 | 38.8 | 4 608 | 11.3 |
| Madison, WI | 1 217 | -1.1 | 181 | 14.1 | 861.0 | 699 298 | 3 867 | 100 029 | 795.2 | 118 177 | 31.5 | 68.5 | 43.3 | 19.6 | 22 912 | 65.3 |
| Manchester-Nashua, NH | 50 | 25.0 | 82 | 0.8 | 13.1 | 560 697 | 6 864 | 55 096 | 17.1 | 27 800 | 67.6 | 32.4 | 24.6 | 5.4 | 60 | 4.6 |
| Manhattan, KS | 809 | -6.7 | 504 | 28.3 | 328.5 | 614 890 | 1 219 | 86 189 | 157.4 | 98 155 | 41.4 | 58.6 | 51.5 | 17.3 | 5 323 | 65.3 |
| Mankato, North Mankato, MN | 689 | 3.9 | 332 | D | 625.7 | 1 156 641 | 3 480 | 167 231 | 564.3 | 272 058 | 44.5 | 55.5 | 65.1 | 43.1 | 14 000 | 80.3 |
| Mansfield, OH | 147 | -7.5 | 145 | 0.1 | 110.2 | 525 268 | 3 616 | 77 684 | 72.8 | 72 127 | 52.6 | 47.4 | 41.8 | 18.3 | 1 934 | 41.3 |
| McAllen-Edinburg-Mission, TX | 723 | 21.9 | 336 | 169.3 | 404.3 | 732 730 | 2 181 | 88 682 | 314.3 | 146 098 | 91.8 | 8.2 | 35.1 | 11.0 | 10 723 | 19.6 |
| Medford, OR | 244 | -3.2 | 124 | 56.4 | 56.5 | 721 613 | 5 843 | 44 133 | 79.1 | 40 042 | 64.8 | 35.2 | 21.3 | 3.0 | 458 | 2.6 |
| Memphis, TN-MS-AR | 1 496 | -3.9 | 355 | 243.3 | 1 069.9 | 853 535 | 2 407 | 99 029 | 350.2 | 82 999 | D | D | 28.0 | 10.9 | 37 241 | 43.3 |
| Merced, CA | 1 041 | 3.5 | 399 | 514.2 | 537.7 | 2 879 524 | 7 210 | 198 153 | 2 330.4 | 893 904 | 37.7 | 62.3 | 72.7 | 39.6 | 11 968 | 19.8 |
| Miami-Fort Lauderdale-Pompano Beach, FL | 601 | -7.5 | 140 | 428.4 | 509.3 | 986 213 | 7 064 | 67 777 | 1 643.1 | 381 412 | D | D | 45.8 | 17.4 | 8 585 | 7.6 |
| Fort Lauderdale-Pompano Beach-Deerfield Beach, FL Div | 9 | -62.5 | 16 | 1.7 | 4.9 | 424 408 | 26 571 | 32 949 | 50.3 | 91 945 | 97.0 | 3.0 | 29.4 | 10.2 | 680 | 5.5 |
| Miami-Miami Beach-Kendall, FL Div | 67 | -25.6 | 27 | 39.0 | 53.8 | 742 119 | 27 648 | 45 341 | 661.1 | 264 652 | D | D | 51.5 | 18.3 | 5 450 | 8.9 |
| West Palm Beach-Boca Raton-Boynton Beach, FL Div | 526 | -1.9 | 416 | 387.8 | 450.7 | 1 712 306 | 4 114 | 127 234 | 931.7 | 737 713 | 99.1 | 0.9 | 41.7 | 18.8 | 2 455 | 6.1 |
| Michigan City-La Porte, IN | 256 | 5.3 | 295 | 47.8 | 231.9 | 1 077 366 | 3 655 | 131 009 | 152.3 | 175 237 | 67.4 | 32.6 | 49.0 | 26.6 | 5 128 | 59.7 |
| Midland, TX | 457 | 26.2 | 760 | 8.3 | 90.0 | 660 020 | 869 | 59 919 | 15.4 | 25 621 | 77.7 | 22.3 | 18.5 | 5.5 | 2 750 | 29.8 |
| Milwaukee-Waukesha-West Allis, WI | 293 | -5.2 | 138 | 2.4 | 236.0 | 715 564 | 5 173 | 96 063 | 222.0 | 104 961 | 45.5 | 54.5 | 44.9 | 19.6 | 4 444 | 48.3 |
| Minneapolis-St. Paul-Bloomington, MN | 1 920 | D | 165 | 105.9 | 1 445.8 | 674 933 | 4 103 | 93 603 | D | D | D | D | 39.7 | 14.9 | D | 52.0 |
| Missoula, MT | 282 | 9.3 | 403 | 16.6 | 27.9 | 895 806 | 2 221 | 39 176 | 7.6 | 10 840 | 35.8 | 64.2 | 16.9 | 2.9 | 102 | 6.4 |
| Mobile, AL | 114 | 12.9 | 130 | 3.5 | 44.2 | 414 764 | 3 197 | 69 495 | 83.2 | 94 946 | 90.1 | 9.9 | 29.3 | 10.0 | 2 538 | 12.9 |
| Modesto, CA | 789 | -0.1 | 192 | 375.0 | 351.2 | 1 817 304 | 9 476 | 119 526 | 1 820.6 | 442 529 | 40.4 | 59.6 | 61.4 | 28.7 | 4 379 | 10.0 |
| Monroe, LA | 153 | -8.4 | 165 | 7.4 | 69.1 | 419 611 | 2 550 | 67 543 | 167.4 | 180 404 | 8.4 | 91.6 | 33.1 | 14.7 | 2 197 | 15.5 |
| Monroe, MI | 208 | -4.1 | 186 | 6.5 | 189.5 | 710 533 | 3 826 | 102 813 | 130.1 | 116 237 | 93.8 | 6.2 | 51.4 | 18.8 | 3 127 | 48.9 |
| Montgomery, AL | 623 | -1.4 | 302 | 6.9 | 187.7 | 591 570 | 1 961 | 66 400 | 131.3 | 63 485 | D | D | 32.2 | 7.6 | 5 709 | 25.4 |
| Morgantown, WV | 212 | 4.4 | 141 | 0.1 | 63.0 | 350 475 | 2 494 | 43 631 | 16.7 | 11 111 | 19.0 | 81.0 | 23.7 | 1.1 | 92 | 6.2 |
| Morristown, TN | 263 | -2.2 | 90 | D | 127.9 | 370 697 | 4 138 | 48 951 | 76.0 | 25 928 | D | D | 22.5 | 2.6 | 248 | 8.0 |
| Mount Vernon-Anacortes, WA | 109 | -4.4 | 89 | 16.3 | 69.8 | 602 607 | 6 746 | 80 332 | 256.2 | 210 904 | 68.0 | 32.0 | 26.5 | 10.8 | 630 | 8.9 |
| Muncie, IN | 154 | -18.9 | 234 | 0.5 | 143.4 | 824 551 | 3 518 | 95 643 | 68.6 | 104 109 | 88.2 | 11.8 | 44.6 | 18.7 | 2 670 | 58.4 |
| Muskegon-Norton Shores, MI | 80 | 8.1 | 152 | 9.8 | 58.1 | 601 241 | 3 962 | 100 785 | 91.2 | 173 669 | 44.2 | 55.8 | 34.1 | 14.5 | 790 | 23.0 |
| Myrtle Beach-North Myrtle Beach-Conway, SC | 164 | -12.8 | 179 | 1.3 | 97.3 | 619 386 | 3 460 | 77 868 | 65.9 | 72 046 | 65.9 | 34.1 | 29.3 | 10.7 | 2 240 | 47.4 |
| Napa, CA | 223 | -6.3 | 136 | 51.6 | 66.2 | 3 696 510 | 27 122 | 76 502 | 376.9 | 230 078 | 98.7 | 1.3 | 72.6 | 31.2 | 233 | 1.6 |

# Table C. Metropolitan Areas — Water Use, Wholesale Trade, Retail Trade, and Real Estate

| Area name | Water use, 2005 | | Wholesale trade,[1] 2007 | | | | Retail trade, 2007 | | | | Real estate and rental and leasing, 2007 | | | |
|---|---|---|---|---|---|---|---|---|---|---|---|---|---|---|
| | Total water withdrawn (mil gal/day) | Gallons withdrawn per person | Number of establishments | Number of employees | Sales (mil dol) | Annual payroll (mil dol) | Number of establishments | Number of employees | Sales (mil dol) | Annual payroll (mil dol) | Number of establishments | Number of employees | Receipts (mil dol) | Annual payroll (mil dol) |
| | 133 | 134 | 135 | 136 | 137 | 138 | 139 | 140 | 141 | 142 | 143 | 144 | 145 | 146 |
| Kokomo, IN | 23.1 | 228 | 92 | 767 | 604.1 | 35.3 | 426 | 5 665 | 1 330.7 | 117.4 | 98 | 355 | 49.7 | 8.0 |
| La Crosse, WI-MN | 72.8 | 565 | 167 | 2 890 | 3 248.0 | 110.6 | 526 | 9 273 | 1 952.1 | 178.1 | 131 | 614 | 84.0 | 15.2 |
| Lafayette, IN | 42.7 | 233 | 153 | 1 613 | 1 510.1 | 68.4 | 668 | 10 651 | 2 232.6 | 205.4 | 213 | 1 099 | 190.2 | 35.7 |
| Lafayette, LA | 104.8 | 423 | 555 | 8 890 | 4 254.2 | 439.7 | 1 178 | 17 005 | 4 221.9 | 374.8 | 480 | 4 046 | 1 092.4 | 214.4 |
| Lake Charles, LA | 341.6 | 1 752 | 227 | 2 617 | 2 260.2 | 109.9 | 853 | 11 942 | 2 812.8 | 249.6 | 215 | 1 053 | 231.5 | 35.6 |
| Lake Havasu City-Kingman, AZ | 138.6 | 741 | 129 | 1 060 | 458.3 | 36.1 | 730 | 10 672 | 2 837.7 | 248.0 | 280 | 876 | 133.3 | 22.7 |
| Lakeland-Winter Haven, FL | 219.3 | 405 | 696 | 9 822 | 16 436.7 | 407.0 | 1 876 | 25 321 | 6 420.1 | 586.4 | 741 | 3 423 | 517.8 | 95.9 |
| Lancaster, PA | 102.6 | 209 | 690 | 13 363 | 12 187.5 | 500.4 | 2 000 | 30 083 | 6 542.3 | 644.4 | 348 | 2 223 | 420.1 | 74.3 |
| Lansing-East Lansing, MI | 259.7 | 570 | 424 | 6 358 | 7 545.2 | 290.1 | 1 590 | 23 293 | 5 115.0 | 468.3 | 456 | 3 348 | 399.8 | 88.9 |
| Laredo, TX | 88.8 | 395 | 374 | 2 742 | 1 593.4 | 86.1 | 819 | 12 864 | 2 913.5 | 235.4 | 205 | 724 | 119.6 | 18.9 |
| Las Cruces, NM | 465.2 | 2 456 | 127 | 1 136 | 507.3 | 36.0 | 536 | 7 881 | 1 925.6 | 159.5 | 229 | 1 009 | 143.2 | 22.2 |
| Las Vegas-Paradise, NV | 607.7 | 355 | 2 002 | 27 453 | 16 605.7 | 1 380.0 | 5 744 | 99 817 | 26 676.6 | 2 656.9 | 3 356 | 25 654 | 5 235.4 | 925.5 |
| Lawrence, KS | 22.0 | 213 | 95 | 842 | 455.7 | 32.8 | 407 | 6 121 | 1 202.2 | 110.5 | 170 | 711 | 93.4 | 17.5 |
| Lawton, OK | 22.6 | 204 | 63 | 550 | 213.4 | 15.5 | 435 | 5 540 | 1 206.8 | 108.0 | 135 | 484 | 66.7 | 10.9 |
| Lebanon, PA | 124.5 | 992 | 117 | 3 287 | 2 859.9 | 124.1 | 451 | 6 611 | 1 488.6 | 144.1 | 68 | 271 | 43.5 | 7.3 |
| Lewiston, ID-WA | 34.1 | 576 | 62 | 701 | 716.5 | 27.2 | 273 | 3 586 | 911.8 | 90.5 | 64 | 241 | 29.6 | 5.9 |
| Lewiston-Auburn, ME | 15.8 | 146 | 114 | 1 321 | 471.9 | 53.1 | 489 | 6 386 | 1 704.3 | 145.2 | 119 | 509 | 82.0 | 13.4 |
| Lexington-Fayette, KY | 304.9 | 709 | 595 | 13 415 | 12 467.8 | 813.9 | 1 831 | 29 937 | 6 901.1 | 679.3 | 647 | 2 907 | 484.7 | 85.2 |
| Lima, OH | 27.5 | 259 | 151 | 3 397 | 2 326.7 | 119.2 | 464 | 6 950 | 1 577.5 | 133.6 | 105 | 481 | 67.1 | 12.2 |
| Lincoln, NE | 159.7 | 567 | 339 | 4 425 | 3 189.9 | 190.8 | 1 108 | 17 746 | 3 772.5 | 356.2 | 376 | 1 575 | 252.8 | 43.4 |
| Little Rock-North Little Rock-Conway, AR | 662.0 | 1 029 | 1 092 | 18 488 | 22 361.1 | 842.0 | 2 709 | 37 562 | 9 186.1 | 813.6 | 904 | 4 417 | 768.4 | 131.5 |
| Logan, UT-ID | 484.3 | 4 177 | 147 | 1 033 | 462.1 | 36.1 | 440 | 5 855 | 1 208.6 | 106.1 | 202 | 590 | 65.5 | 13.5 |
| Longview, TX | 2 527.0 | 12 541 | 329 | 4 261 | 2 354.8 | 175.2 | 942 | 11 426 | 2 976.2 | 264.8 | 217 | 1 437 | 302.8 | 58.5 |
| Longview, WA | 147.8 | 1 518 | 94 | 1 379 | 1 538.5 | 66.8 | 360 | 5 018 | 1 219.7 | 117.1 | 117 | 442 | 54.3 | 9.7 |
| Los Angeles-Long Beach-Santa Ana, CA | 4 528.7 | 350 | 31 642 | 415 986 | 465 512.5 | 22 339.7 | 40 170 | 577 963 | 164 134.4 | 15 153.5 | 19 651 | 134 213 | 37 478.6 | 6 290.8 |
| Los Angeles-Long Beach-Glendale, CA Div | 3 811.1 | 384 | 23 856 | 294 204 | 313 461.3 | 14 526.0 | 30 179 | 418 153 | 119 111.8 | 10 849.2 | 14 085 | 90 847 | 26 790.4 | 4 129.2 |
| Santa Ana-Anaheim-Irvine, CA Div | 717.6 | 240 | 7 786 | 121 782 | 152 051.1 | 7 813.7 | 9 991 | 159 810 | 45 022.5 | 4 304.3 | 5 566 | 43 366 | 10 688.2 | 2 161.6 |
| Louisville-Jefferson County, KY-IN | 1 138.4 | 942 | 1 750 | 25 858 | 26 461.4 | 1 224.5 | 4 423 | 64 772 | 15 331.4 | 1 422.8 | 1 404 | 8 538 | 2 222.0 | 300.4 |
| Lubbock, TX | 330.1 | 1 275 | 455 | 5 970 | 4 832.8 | 257.8 | 1 064 | 16 919 | 3 948.7 | 348.5 | 383 | 2 264 | 239.8 | 51.4 |
| Lynchburg, VA | 50.7 | 214 | 223 | 2 763 | 1 577.0 | 104.5 | 1 039 | 13 775 | 3 187.2 | 286.2 | 288 | 908 | 128.4 | 25.9 |
| Macon, GA | 138.2 | 604 | 282 | 3 641 | 2 805.9 | 160.5 | 1 011 | 12 921 | 2 769.7 | 271.2 | 259 | 1 310 | 235.5 | 36.9 |
| Madera-Chowchilla, CA | 834.8 | 5 846 | 89 | 745 | 397.6 | 30.6 | 368 | 3 883 | 1 010.2 | 89.3 | 100 | 409 | 36.7 | 9.4 |
| Madison, WI | 336.8 | 627 | 779 | 13 290 | 8 758.7 | 632.4 | 2 113 | 39 786 | 9 471.6 | 934.2 | 744 | 5 106 | 684.1 | 156.7 |
| Manchester-Nashua, NH | 58.6 | 146 | 649 | 8 676 | 6 030.9 | 601.8 | 1 657 | 27 793 | 7 647.3 | 678.7 | 443 | 2 664 | 554.7 | 96.4 |
| Manhattan, KS | 58.7 | 551 | 71 | 1 128 | 456.5 | 33.9 | 464 | 6 783 | 1 307.7 | 122.8 | 160 | 678 | 75.7 | 14.1 |
| Mankato, North Mankato, MN | 38.7 | 436 | 131 | 1 827 | 1 568.3 | 79.4 | 441 | 7 099 | 1 376.3 | 126.3 | 105 | 766 | 85.0 | 16.1 |
| Mansfield, OH | 16.3 | 128 | 149 | 2 499 | 1 190.3 | 90.3 | 497 | 7 387 | 1 489.5 | 145.8 | 108 | 571 | 59.2 | 12.3 |
| McAllen-Edinburg-Mission, TX | 394.4 | 581 | 744 | 8 485 | 5 117.1 | 286.5 | 2 132 | 32 803 | 7 898.8 | 635.3 | 491 | 2 289 | 366.9 | 53.2 |
| Medford, OR | 352.8 | 1 806 | 249 | 2 459 | 1 176.6 | 97.8 | 991 | 12 243 | 3 422.4 | 290.1 | 360 | 1 563 | 205.4 | 36.5 |
| Memphis, TN-MS-AR | 965.3 | 766 | 1 841 | 38 271 | 49 114.8 | 2 074.1 | 4 479 | 64 473 | 15 818.3 | 1 491.0 | 1 285 | 9 229 | 1 675.3 | 351.1 |
| Merced, CA | 1 624.9 | 6 723 | 113 | 1 674 | 1 673.3 | 65.9 | 578 | 8 005 | 2 001.3 | 179.9 | 153 | 641 | 85.6 | 15.1 |
| Miami-Fort Lauderdale-Pompano Beach, FL | 3 972.7 | 732 | 15 850 | 137 754 | 139 829.9 | 6 580.6 | 23 239 | 304 024 | 84 738.4 | 7 682.8 | 11 250 | 55 949 | 11 006.6 | 2 137.1 |
| Fort Lauderdale-Pompano Beach-Deerfield Beach, FL Div | 1 837.9 | 1 056 | 4 706 | 43 584 | 49 935.2 | 2 118.6 | 7 382 | 104 336 | 30 886.3 | 2 710.6 | 3 624 | 18 044 | 3 555.6 | 648.1 |
| Miami-Miami Beach-Kendall, FL Div | 602.3 | 249 | 8 654 | 72 193 | 72 464.3 | 3 269.7 | 10 293 | 123 559 | 34 530.5 | 3 055.6 | 4 935 | 25 546 | 5 367.9 | 985.2 |
| West Palm Beach-Boca Raton-Boynton Beach, FL Div | 1 532.5 | 1 211 | 2 490 | 21 977 | 17 430.4 | 1 192.3 | 5 564 | 76 129 | 19 321.7 | 1 916.5 | 2 691 | 12 359 | 2 083.2 | 503.8 |
| Michigan City-La Porte, IN | 37.3 | 338 | 142 | 1 718 | 1 002.8 | 69.2 | 495 | 6 054 | 1 363.6 | 114.9 | 102 | 438 | 60.4 | 11.1 |
| Midland, TX | 31.1 | 256 | 286 | 3 717 | 2 745.6 | 184.8 | 551 | 7 744 | 2 276.7 | 183.9 | 227 | 1 418 | 270.7 | 56.8 |
| Milwaukee-Waukesha-West Allis, WI | 1 576.1 | 1 042 | 2 654 | 46 102 | 40 493.1 | 2 541.1 | 5 012 | 86 028 | 18 898.8 | 1 853.3 | 1 474 | 9 657 | 1 673.8 | 337.7 |
| Minneapolis-St. Paul-Bloomington, MN | 1 868.9 | 595 | 6 087 | 104 304 | 117 099.0 | 7 100.9 | 10 933 | 188 242 | 46 284.7 | 4 394.6 | 5 034 | 31 686 | 8 295.0 | 1 148.4 |
| Missoula, MT | 112.7 | 1 126 | 195 | 2 019 | 1 073.9 | 76.4 | 587 | 8 668 | 2 179.4 | 194.6 | 227 | 952 | 126.3 | 21.6 |
| Mobile, AL | 1 130.9 | 2 817 | 619 | 7 671 | 4 340.3 | 336.5 | 1 644 | 22 271 | 5 225.5 | 483.4 | 448 | 2 460 | 417.2 | 77.8 |
| Modesto, CA | 1 457.9 | 2 884 | 451 | 6 078 | 4 402.7 | 277.0 | 1 500 | 23 394 | 5 661.9 | 561.1 | 500 | 2 988 | 472.6 | 90.3 |
| Monroe, LA | 83.0 | 485 | 217 | 3 179 | 2 033.7 | 111.2 | 809 | 10 259 | 2 369.7 | 208.0 | 198 | 874 | 151.1 | 27.7 |
| Monroe, MI | 1 846.7 | 11 997 | 107 | 1 716 | 1 841.4 | 77.2 | 427 | 5 637 | 1 465.3 | 120.3 | 95 | 373 | 48.8 | 7.5 |
| Montgomery, AL | 134.2 | 376 | 413 | 6 975 | 5 264.2 | 293.8 | 1 448 | 19 572 | 4 558.3 | 428.6 | 389 | 2 617 | 329.4 | 79.0 |
| Morgantown, WV | 279.9 | 2 445 | 73 | 573 | 511.5 | 22.0 | 487 | 7 365 | 1 510.8 | 127.9 | 151 | 625 | 82.7 | 15.5 |
| Morristown, TN | 21.3 | 163 | 93 | 1 692 | 751.0 | 67.8 | 505 | 6 220 | 1 688.8 | 133.3 | 97 | 387 | 54.0 | 8.1 |
| Mount Vernon-Anacortes, WA | 44.2 | 390 | 140 | 1 641 | 926.6 | 66.9 | 616 | 7 788 | 2 134.8 | 200.4 | 181 | 653 | 105.5 | 18.3 |
| Muncie, IN | 17.7 | 152 | 111 | 1 231 | 1 215.5 | 47.5 | 484 | 6 563 | 1 516.8 | 130.8 | 113 | 575 | 89.0 | 17.2 |
| Muskegon-Norton Shores, MI | 323.1 | 1 840 | 133 | 1 816 | 2 250.8 | 91.1 | 608 | 7 878 | 1 656.7 | 154.5 | 112 | 484 | 67.0 | 12.0 |
| Myrtle Beach-North Myrtle Beach-Conway, SC | 171.2 | 754 | 277 | 2 299 | 952.4 | 84.4 | 1 810 | 21 072 | 4 967.2 | 459.4 | 708 | 5 839 | 829.9 | 187.4 |
| Napa, CA | 51.8 | 390 | 172 | 2 036 | 2 858.5 | 134.0 | 537 | 6 463 | 1 665.0 | 180.7 | 206 | 893 | 153.0 | 31.1 |

1. Merchant wholesalers, except manufacturers' sales branches and offices.

## Table C. Metropolitan Areas — **Professional Services, Manufacturing, and Accommodation and Food Services**

| Area name | Professional, scientific, and technical services,[1] 2007 | | | | Manufacturing, 2007 | | | | Accommodation and food services, 2007 | | | |
|---|---|---|---|---|---|---|---|---|---|---|---|---|
| | Number of establishments | Number of employees | Sales (mil dol) | Annual payroll (mil dol) | Number of establishments | Number of employees | Sales (mil dol) | Annual payroll (mil dol) | Number of establishments | Number of employees | Sales (mil dol) | Annual payroll (mil dol) |
| | 147 | 148 | 149 | 150 | 151 | 152 | 153 | 154 | 155 | 156 | 157 | 158 |
| Kokomo, IN | 154 | D | D | D | 100 | 13 074 | 3 285.3 | 914.9 | 213 | 4 220 | 160.3 | 47.2 |
| La Crosse, WI-MN | 253 | D | D | D | 189 | 7 756 | 1 930.6 | 274.0 | 355 | 6 275 | 222.5 | 64.8 |
| Lafayette, IN | 334 | D | D | D | 172 | 16 830 | 13 018.7 | 780.3 | 432 | 8 989 | 337.0 | 98.2 |
| Lafayette, LA | 1 213 | D | D | D | 344 | 10 151 | 2 361.6 | 403.1 | 590 | 13 477 | 629.8 | 167.0 |
| Lake Charles, LA | 455 | D | D | D | 134 | 8 358 | 31 622.3 | 592.2 | 332 | 10 366 | 879.9 | 181.9 |
| Lake Havasu City-Kingman, AZ | 251 | D | D | D | 164 | 3 814 | 1 350.0 | 139.6 | 381 | 6 380 | 274.3 | 77.3 |
| Lakeland-Winter Haven, FL | 1 093 | 6 654 | 781.8 | 310.5 | 438 | 16 160 | 7 178.0 | 697.4 | 765 | 16 084 | 699.6 | 199.4 |
| Lancaster, PA | 939 | D | D | D | 920 | 40 077 | 13 269.9 | 1 735.9 | 935 | 17 060 | 763.9 | 221.2 |
| Lansing-East Lansing, MI | 1 087 | 7 810 | 928.7 | 375.1 | 385 | 20 365 | 14 472.8 | 1 187.2 | 901 | 17 436 | 652.2 | 194.7 |
| Laredo, TX | 309 | D | D | D | 89 | 914 | 242.4 | 30.7 | 360 | 7 489 | 317.3 | 86.5 |
| Las Cruces, NM | 315 | D | D | D | 141 | 2 349 | 931.9 | 84.2 | 298 | 5 955 | 238.7 | 64.9 |
| Las Vegas-Paradise, NV | 5 282 | 43 063 | 6 982.5 | 2 498.8 | 1 096 | 26 478 | 7 180.7 | 1 086.3 | 3 797 | 266 845 | 24 857.8 | 7 431.8 |
| Lawrence, KS | 285 | D | D | D | 88 | 3 848 | 976.5 | 143.0 | 299 | 5 937 | 213.7 | 60.1 |
| Lawton, OK | 175 | D | D | D | 48 | 3 549 | 1 232.4 | 171.0 | 204 | 4 330 | 154.5 | 46.4 |
| Lebanon, PA | 193 | D | D | D | 213 | 9 655 | 2 393.6 | 363.3 | 241 | 3 075 | 125.3 | 35.3 |
| Lewiston, ID-WA | 109 | D | D | D | 62 | 3 312 | 964.6 | 166.3 | 134 | 2 278 | 87.5 | 27.6 |
| Lewiston-Auburn, ME | 182 | D | D | D | 158 | 6 945 | 2 186.2 | 300.2 | 226 | 3 422 | 149.7 | 44.0 |
| Lexington-Fayette, KY | 1 347 | D | D | D | 459 | 30 392 | 17 925.5 | 1 502.4 | 960 | 22 013 | 985.7 | 286.2 |
| Lima, OH | 170 | D | D | D | 136 | 8 661 | 10 009.0 | 475.9 | 219 | 4 469 | 173.2 | 47.4 |
| Lincoln, NE | 804 | 8 361 | 1 112.3 | 386.2 | 272 | 14 390 | 4 541.2 | 577.4 | 685 | 12 466 | 486.1 | 136.3 |
| Little Rock-North Little Rock-Conway, AR | 2 013 | D | D | D | 615 | 24 783 | 8 828.2 | 1 033.8 | 1 238 | 25 036 | 1 087.4 | 307.0 |
| Logan, UT-ID | 363 | D | D | D | 234 | 10 810 | 3 685.3 | 420.5 | 155 | 2 921 | 101.0 | 31.2 |
| Longview, TX | 436 | D | D | D | 250 | 12 506 | 4 642.8 | 522.3 | 380 | 7 316 | 296.7 | 86.3 |
| Longview, WA | 150 | D | D | D | 128 | 7 001 | 2 914.7 | 356.7 | 215 | 2 782 | 124.0 | 36.2 |
| Los Angeles-Long Beach-Santa Ana, CA | 44 767 | 571 476 | 79 845.9 | 31 400.9 | 20 509 | 628 771 | 202 475.6 | 29 161.5 | 26 330 | 481 517 | 28 486.0 | 7 936.8 |
| Los Angeles-Long Beach-Glendale, CA Div | 30 754 | D | D | D | 15 158 | 451 656 | 153 343.7 | 20 520.1 | 19 476 | 339 815 | 20 238.1 | 5 570.1 |
| Santa Ana-Anaheim-Irvine, CA Div | 14 013 | D | D | D | 5 351 | 177 115 | 49 131.9 | 8 641.4 | 6 854 | 141 702 | 8 247.8 | 2 366.7 |
| Louisville-Jefferson County, KY-IN | 3 134 | D | D | D | 1 400 | 75 811 | 34 623.8 | 3 457.3 | 2 284 | 52 254 | 2 548.0 | 717.8 |
| Lubbock, TX | 585 | 3 410 | 374.5 | 128.7 | 258 | D | D | 204.5 | 587 | 13 168 | 541.3 | 142.7 |
| Lynchburg, VA | 518 | D | D | D | 302 | 18 731 | 5 973.9 | 898.0 | 431 | 7 932 | 297.0 | 89.0 |
| Macon, GA | 486 | D | D | D | 187 | 6 403 | 1 838.2 | 266.2 | 470 | 8 618 | 346.1 | 92.6 |
| Madera-Chowchilla, CA | 124 | D | D | D | 116 | 4 143 | 1 452.9 | 170.3 | 192 | 2 265 | 125.1 | 33.1 |
| Madison, WI | 1 715 | D | D | D | 727 | 33 367 | 9 107.7 | 1 525.6 | 1 459 | 28 022 | 1 106.8 | 321.9 |
| Manchester-Nashua, NH | 1 347 | D | D | D | 633 | 31 243 | 7 707.6 | 1 944.4 | 875 | 15 987 | 732.3 | 224.9 |
| Manhattan, KS | 235 | D | D | D | 68 | 3 040 | 685.6 | 109.7 | 263 | 5 139 | 189.2 | 52.9 |
| Mankato, North Mankato, MN | 169 | D | D | D | 140 | 8 903 | 3 601.1 | 309.0 | 214 | 4 840 | 164.5 | 48.6 |
| Mansfield, OH | 194 | 1 044 | 110.4 | 41.0 | 192 | 11 080 | 3 563.7 | 555.3 | 277 | 4 802 | 178.9 | 52.5 |
| McAllen-Edinburg-Mission, TX | 793 | D | D | D | 276 | 6 007 | 1 503.2 | 183.5 | 896 | 17 219 | 758.0 | 186.5 |
| Medford, OR | 491 | D | D | D | 324 | 6 115 | 2 037.5 | 228.8 | 590 | 7 946 | 372.9 | 108.9 |
| Memphis, TN-MS-AR | 2 273 | 18 556 | 2 378.9 | 973.1 | 1 017 | 43 692 | 22 469.6 | 1 988.6 | 2 257 | 62 998 | 3 489.6 | 954.9 |
| Merced, CA | 170 | D | D | D | 122 | 9 208 | 3 954.2 | 348.6 | 302 | 5 130 | 219.4 | 55.2 |
| Miami-Fort Lauderdale-Pompano Beach, FL | 27 747 | 141 555 | 22 331.1 | 8 589.8 | 5 041 | 83 698 | 20 748.5 | 3 370.1 | 10 669 | 218 145 | 13 303.6 | 3 719.0 |
| Fort Lauderdale-Pompano Beach-Deerfield Beach, FL Div | 9 509 | 46 243 | 6 635.1 | 2 550.4 | 1 734 | 29 333 | 7 160.8 | 1 185.5 | 3 693 | 70 373 | 4 209.1 | 1 140.1 |
| Miami-Miami Beach-Kendall, FL Div | 11 294 | 60 310 | 9 603.2 | 3 755.1 | 2 312 | 40 446 | 9 347.1 | 1 556.0 | 4 358 | 91 230 | 6 005.9 | 1 659.8 |
| West Palm Beach-Boca Raton-Boynton Beach, FL Div | 6 944 | 35 002 | 6 092.8 | 2 284.2 | 995 | 13 919 | 4 240.7 | 628.6 | 2 618 | 56 542 | 3 088.6 | 919.0 |
| Michigan City-La Porte, IN | 169 | D | D | D | 184 | 8 808 | 2 364.0 | 363.9 | 259 | 5 254 | 389.7 | 80.1 |
| Midland, TX | 436 | D | D | D | 140 | 2 366 | 533.8 | 95.2 | 254 | 5 324 | 259.2 | 69.3 |
| Milwaukee-Waukesha-West Allis, WI | 3 967 | 40 641 | 5 592.7 | 2 312.5 | 2 740 | 130 675 | 41 284.2 | 6 590.5 | 3 194 | 59 644 | 2 465.0 | 701.4 |
| Minneapolis-St. Paul-Bloomington, MN | 13 279 | 119 276 | 18 443.4 | 7 620.1 | 4 997 | 200 650 | 63 158.2 | 10 420.0 | 6 326 | 138 810 | 6 590.5 | 1 980.6 |
| Missoula, MT | 458 | D | D | D | 112 | 2 159 | 674.9 | 93.8 | 332 | 6 209 | 269.1 | 70.0 |
| Mobile, AL | 901 | D | D | D | 385 | 16 776 | 12 407.2 | 840.9 | 652 | 13 252 | 562.4 | 155.0 |
| Modesto, CA | 701 | D | D | D | 443 | 24 127 | 9 476.0 | 1 032.9 | 842 | 13 881 | 615.1 | 171.7 |
| Monroe, LA | 462 | D | D | D | 146 | 6 927 | D | D | 302 | 6 798 | 260.5 | 70.4 |
| Monroe, MI | 147 | 944 | 84.3 | 39.6 | 143 | 8 555 | 3 503.0 | 440.6 | 274 | 4 682 | 171.5 | 47.8 |
| Montgomery, AL | 817 | 7 278 | 1 020.9 | 377.5 | 318 | 18 749 | D | D | 653 | 13 159 | 539.5 | 150.2 |
| Morgantown, WV | 231 | D | D | D | 98 | 3 918 | 1 480.9 | 173.7 | 266 | 5 401 | 205.1 | 56.4 |
| Morristown, TN | 130 | D | D | D | 194 | 16 517 | 4 248.2 | 566.4 | 192 | 3 821 | 145.6 | 41.0 |
| Mount Vernon-Anacortes, WA | 305 | D | D | D | 205 | 6 387 | 8 918.2 | 294.5 | 347 | 4 734 | 251.0 | 74.1 |
| Muncie, IN | 169 | D | D | D | 150 | 5 268 | 1 280.6 | 232.7 | 216 | 4 981 | 160.8 | 48.3 |
| Muskegon-Norton Shores, MI | 239 | D | D | D | 290 | 13 271 | 3 675.8 | 609.1 | 344 | 5 763 | 221.0 | 64.6 |
| Myrtle Beach-North Myrtle Beach-Conway, SC | 660 | D | D | D | 168 | 4 103 | 894.8 | 166.8 | 1 178 | 25 931 | 1 483.8 | 396.2 |
| Napa, CA | 419 | D | D | D | 436 | 13 165 | 4 529.3 | 632.4 | 363 | 8 904 | 620.4 | 195.4 |

1. Establishments subject to federal tax.

# Table C. Metropolitan Areas — Health Care and Social Assistance, Other Services, and Federal Funds

| Area name | Health care and social assistance,[1] 2007 | | | | Other services,[1] 2007 | | | | Federal funds and grants, 2009–2010 Expenditures (mil dol) | | | |
|---|---|---|---|---|---|---|---|---|---|---|---|---|
| | | | | | | | | | | Direct payments for individuals | | |
| | Number of establishments | Number of employees | Receipts (mil dol) | Annual payroll (mil dol) | Number of establishments | Number of employees | Receipts (mil dol) | Annual payroll (mil dol) | Total | Social Security and government retirement | Medicare | Food stamps and Supplemental Security Income |
| | 159 | 160 | 161 | 162 | 163 | 164 | 165 | 166 | 167 | 168 | 169 | 170 |
| Kokomo, IN | 253 | 6 193 | 571.4 | 216.9 | 160 | 838 | 66.4 | 17.2 | 797.8 | 408.1 | 173.6 | 36.4 |
| La Crosse, WI-MN | 315 | 11 491 | 1 137.5 | 453.6 | 275 | 2 041 | 137.7 | 43.2 | 912.4 | 382.2 | 154.9 | 33.9 |
| Lafayette, IN | 364 | 9 594 | 935.2 | 353.2 | 299 | 1 980 | 249.4 | 49.5 | 1 245.0 | 438.5 | 172.5 | 35.2 |
| Lafayette, LA | 1 020 | 20 357 | 1 929.3 | 708.9 | 494 | 3 590 | 324.0 | 89.9 | 1 650.0 | 597.0 | 321.3 | 87.5 |
| Lake Charles, LA | 520 | 11 058 | 1 037.5 | 352.5 | 284 | 1 733 | 176.7 | 47.0 | 1 486.8 | 554.2 | 344.6 | 73.7 |
| Lake Havasu City-Kingman, AZ | 456 | 7 612 | 911.1 | 284.4 | 315 | 1 895 | 129.4 | 38.0 | 1 474.8 | 868.4 | 294.3 | 80.2 |
| Lakeland-Winter Haven, FL | 971 | 24 347 | 2 613.7 | 926.8 | 727 | 3 850 | 323.5 | 94.6 | 4 156.6 | 1 954.4 | 1 105.1 | 266.6 |
| Lancaster, PA | 1 062 | 32 573 | 2 878.0 | 1 163.1 | 1 042 | 6 812 | 587.2 | 157.1 | 2 993.7 | 1 497.6 | 683.1 | 94.5 |
| Lansing-East Lansing, MI | 1 182 | 24 945 | 2 329.6 | 970.0 | 864 | 6 760 | 748.4 | 209.1 | 7 633.8 | 1 242.4 | 575.8 | 160.3 |
| Laredo, TX | 441 | 12 142 | 723.4 | 284.3 | 257 | 1 465 | 124.3 | 28.6 | 1 613.9 | 325.1 | 210.5 | 164.0 |
| Las Cruces, NM | 474 | 10 748 | 798.2 | 323.2 | 230 | 1 237 | 94.1 | 27.7 | 2 062.5 | 567.9 | 160.8 | 130.9 |
| Las Vegas-Paradise, NV | 3 978 | 67 163 | 8 517.4 | 3 017.6 | 2 313 | 18 791 | 1 602.5 | 473.7 | 11 254.2 | 4 651.5 | 1 579.7 | 494.2 |
| Lawrence, KS | 283 | 5 331 | 375.5 | 163.3 | 190 | 1 429 | 277.4 | 33.7 | 689.9 | 246.9 | 76.3 | 18.1 |
| Lawton, OK | 274 | 6 219 | 580.1 | 223.7 | 170 | 879 | 63.3 | 15.2 | 3 180.5 | 477.1 | 114.1 | 56.3 |
| Lebanon, PA | 266 | 7 662 | 626.6 | 286.9 | 233 | 1 059 | 93.0 | 25.2 | 1 398.6 | 491.7 | 205.8 | 22.5 |
| Lewiston, ID-WA | 190 | 3 784 | 356.0 | 121.9 | 119 | 607 | 39.9 | 11.6 | 601.9 | 253.9 | 98.8 | 29.9 |
| Lewiston-Auburn, ME | 421 | 9 495 | 872.4 | 355.7 | 203 | 945 | 69.8 | 21.2 | 874.9 | 352.8 | 171.4 | 57.0 |
| Lexington-Fayette, KY | 1 323 | 31 132 | 3 415.2 | 1 316.8 | 844 | 6 104 | 586.4 | 171.1 | 4 087.5 | 1 191.4 | 707.8 | 141.8 |
| Lima, OH | 330 | 11 408 | 999.0 | 417.5 | 213 | 1 448 | 93.3 | 27.9 | 1 079.7 | 526.6 | 182.7 | 48.5 |
| Lincoln, NE | 874 | 22 175 | 1 978.1 | 811.0 | 700 | 4 372 | 561.1 | 121.1 | 2 912.4 | 761.2 | 239.2 | 56.6 |
| Little Rock-North Little Rock-Conway, AR | 2 041 | 48 896 | 5 101.1 | 1 964.0 | 1 188 | 7 197 | 810.6 | 191.3 | 8 126.7 | 2 228.2 | 843.6 | 257.0 |
| Logan, UT-ID | 326 | 4 717 | 376.9 | 135.6 | 181 | 847 | 65.3 | 15.8 | 747.8 | 208.0 | 109.7 | 17.0 |
| Longview, TX | 534 | 11 452 | 1 080.6 | 387.2 | 338 | 2 189 | 221.1 | 60.5 | 1 537.7 | 651.5 | 375.8 | 82.0 |
| Longview, WA | 249 | 5 122 | 487.3 | 198.6 | 146 | 894 | 75.9 | 22.8 | 779.0 | 356.7 | 134.8 | 53.8 |
| Los Angeles-Long Beach-Santa Ana, CA | 37 695 | 577 980 | 69 501.3 | 25 483.8 | 21 200 | 152 375 | 18 866.4 | 4 337.0 | 100 586.1 | 22 206.6 | 21 974.1 | 4 892.8 |
| Los Angeles-Long Beach-Glendale, CA Div | 27 728 | 444 806 | 53 200.9 | 19 568.8 | 16 089 | 117 748 | 15 230.4 | 3 369.6 | 82 544.3 | 16 317.2 | 17 792.2 | 4 259.6 |
| Santa Ana-Anaheim-Irvine, CA Div | 9 967 | 133 174 | 16 300.4 | 5 915.0 | 5 111 | 34 627 | 3 636.0 | 967.4 | 18 041.8 | 5 889.5 | 4 181.8 | 633.2 |
| Louisville-Jefferson County, KY-IN | 3 257 | 77 550 | 7 682.4 | 2 918.7 | 2 130 | 17 244 | 1 652.4 | 425.7 | 12 859.1 | 3 768.3 | 2 625.1 | 312.8 |
| Lubbock, TX | 824 | D | D | D | 481 | 3 383 | 298.8 | 78.1 | 1 967.8 | 661.0 | 480.5 | 109.8 |
| Lynchburg, VA | 532 | 12 079 | 1 026.4 | 439.4 | 458 | 2 354 | 175.5 | 53.0 | 2 163.5 | 932.7 | 289.5 | 77.0 |
| Macon, GA | 637 | 16 562 | 1 755.5 | 639.9 | 371 | 2 066 | 213.6 | 57.3 | 2 105.7 | 762.1 | 419.8 | 165.4 |
| Madera-Chowchilla, CA | 221 | 5 836 | 554.7 | 255.8 | 119 | 609 | 48.9 | 12.9 | 847.3 | 327.4 | 188.3 | 45.6 |
| Madison, WI | 1 357 | 42 786 | 4 355.3 | 1 777.5 | 1 189 | 8 991 | 1 398.4 | 275.2 | 6 991.6 | 1 352.1 | 517.4 | 92.8 |
| Manchester-Nashua, NH | 1 020 | 26 771 | 2 503.8 | 1 065.3 | 828 | 5 317 | 501.5 | 155.6 | 3 353.3 | 1 143.0 | 408.1 | 88.2 |
| Manhattan, KS | 269 | 6 429 | 444.4 | 185.2 | 232 | 1 950 | 303.8 | 56.0 | 3 855.4 | 306.1 | 88.7 | 23.0 |
| Mankato, North Mankato, MN | 270 | 9 523 | 694.8 | 321.8 | 220 | 1 326 | 205.1 | 28.4 | 594.8 | 231.8 | 106.4 | 14.4 |
| Mansfield, OH | 354 | 7 670 | 663.5 | 263.1 | 238 | 1 533 | 109.3 | 29.3 | 950.7 | 414.3 | 216.4 | 47.1 |
| McAllen-Edinburg-Mission, TX | 1 655 | 44 931 | 2 877.2 | 1 137.1 | 573 | 3 257 | 238.5 | 61.9 | 4 297.2 | 973.0 | 654.8 | 575.5 |
| Medford, OR | 627 | 11 160 | 1 173.9 | 434.7 | 357 | 2 107 | 182.0 | 56.9 | 1 624.4 | 769.7 | 250.3 | 87.8 |
| Memphis, TN-MS-AR | 2 702 | 71 899 | 7 409.8 | 2 946.3 | 1 730 | 14 358 | 1 988.2 | 402.3 | 12 902.4 | 3 385.4 | 2 450.0 | 852.8 |
| Merced, CA | 443 | 6 048 | 592.2 | 235.3 | 209 | 899 | 73.9 | 19.3 | 1 519.8 | 461.0 | 273.2 | 126.0 |
| Miami-Fort Lauderdale-Pompano Beach, FL | 18 858 | 276 188 | 34 308.5 | 11 820.3 | 12 419 | 68 297 | 7 169.9 | 1 706.1 | 50 255.7 | 13 113.2 | 18 594.2 | 2 809.5 |
| Fort Lauderdale-Pompano Beach-Deerfield Beach, FL Div | 5 732 | 88 155 | 10 883.5 | 3 647.7 | 4 174 | 22 705 | 2 171.8 | 586.7 | 12 480.1 | 4 158.7 | 4 960.3 | 545.3 |
| Miami-Miami Beach-Kendall, FL Div | 8 311 | 120 152 | 15 042.3 | 5 194.3 | 5 065 | 27 878 | 3 185.8 | 659.3 | 27 110.5 | 4 568.7 | 9 894.6 | 1 956.9 |
| West Palm Beach-Boca Raton-Boynton Beach, FL Div | 4 815 | 67 881 | 8 382.6 | 2 978.3 | 3 180 | 17 714 | 1 812.2 | 460.1 | 10 665.1 | 4 385.8 | 3 739.3 | 307.3 |
| Michigan City-La Porte, IN | 236 | 4 900 | 521.2 | 188.2 | 207 | 1 172 | 74.6 | 22.2 | 756.1 | 357.8 | 183.6 | 38.0 |
| Midland, TX | 359 | 5 999 | 697.2 | 241.4 | 255 | 2 469 | 287.0 | 65.5 | 638.5 | 281.9 | 156.8 | 40.0 |
| Milwaukee-Waukesha-West Allis, WI | 4 879 | 118 780 | 11 226.9 | 4 710.5 | 2 926 | 21 389 | 2 254.9 | 615.4 | 12 331.2 | 4 184.9 | 2 473.3 | 805.6 |
| Minneapolis-St. Paul-Bloomington, MN | 8 405 | 227 776 | 22 299.0 | 9 658.7 | 6 589 | 49 916 | 5 202.8 | 1 332.5 | 24 336.5 | 7 306.3 | 3 955.4 | 737.5 |
| Missoula, MT | 451 | 8 022 | 754.8 | 278.6 | 288 | 1 618 | 150.7 | 37.8 | 818.8 | 299.5 | 93.6 | 28.0 |
| Mobile, AL | 741 | 23 845 | 2 160.0 | 894.7 | 666 | 4 681 | 412.6 | 116.5 | 3 934.1 | 1 327.4 | 768.5 | 269.2 |
| Modesto, CA | 1 108 | 21 628 | 2 662.6 | 967.7 | 650 | 4 205 | 380.9 | 119.5 | 3 048.2 | 1 091.0 | 705.9 | 198.7 |
| Monroe, LA | 616 | 13 311 | 1 181.0 | 416.2 | 245 | 1 573 | 138.5 | 38.1 | 1 379.0 | 464.3 | 339.1 | 93.8 |
| Monroe, MI | 284 | 4 733 | 381.3 | 158.7 | 195 | 1 172 | 93.7 | 30.3 | 885.2 | 468.7 | 218.6 | 37.2 |
| Montgomery, AL | 917 | 19 608 | 1 977.5 | 741.6 | 654 | 4 413 | 398.6 | 115.6 | 5 924.7 | 1 336.2 | 530.9 | 201.9 |
| Morgantown, WV | 272 | 11 546 | 1 169.3 | 421.2 | 186 | 1 190 | 177.2 | 27.3 | 1 418.0 | 328.1 | 153.2 | 40.1 |
| Morristown, TN | 245 | 5 377 | 439.6 | 165.3 | 148 | 651 | 47.5 | 13.2 | 1 201.5 | 523.4 | 304.0 | 66.0 |
| Mount Vernon-Anacortes, WA | 342 | 6 346 | 614.5 | 241.6 | 237 | 1 158 | 94.1 | 27.6 | 846.6 | 417.2 | 158.3 | 40.4 |
| Muncie, IN | 316 | 10 078 | 836.1 | 335.6 | 203 | 1 206 | 119.8 | 26.7 | 932.8 | 377.0 | 182.0 | 52.1 |
| Muskegon-Norton Shores, MI | 398 | 9 463 | 864.8 | 374.1 | 283 | 1 440 | 116.0 | 27.8 | 1 299.3 | 564.9 | 261.1 | 96.9 |
| Myrtle Beach-North Myrtle Beach-Conway, SC | 611 | 9 079 | 976.0 | 358.7 | 512 | 3 110 | 265.6 | 65.3 | 1 722.0 | 1 023.9 | 245.0 | 78.9 |
| Napa, CA | 425 | 10 004 | 1 150.0 | 502.2 | 219 | 1 172 | 142.5 | 38.4 | 1 011.6 | 412.9 | 312.3 | 21.3 |

1. Establishments subject to federal tax.

Table C. Metropolitan Areas —

# Federal Funds, Residential Construction and Local Government Finances

| Area name | Federal funds and grants, 2009–2010 (cont.) Expenditures (mil dol) (cont.) Procurement contract awards Salaries and wages | Defense | Other | Grants Medicaid and other health-related | Nutrition and family welfare | Education | Other | Value of residential construction authorized by building permits, 2011 New construction ($1,000) | Number of housing units | Local government finances, 2007 General revenue Total (mil dol) | Inter-govern-mental (mil dol) | Taxes Total (mil dol) | Per capita¹ (dollars) Total | Property |
|---|---|---|---|---|---|---|---|---|---|---|---|---|---|---|
| | 171 | 172 | 173 | 174 | 175 | 176 | 177 | 178 | 179 | 180 | 181 | 182 | 183 | 184 |
| Kokomo, IN | 36.6 | 0.5 | 6.2 | 91.5 | 15.9 | 1.9 | 10.3 | 5 623 | 39 | 491.0 | 132.6 | 135.5 | 1 357 | 1 261 |
| La Crosse, WI-MN | 57.8 | 39.6 | 32.3 | 132.2 | 23.0 | 8.4 | 13.6 | 41 764 | 300 | 583.4 | 280.8 | 190.1 | 1 452 | 1 339 |
| Lafayette, IN | 72.0 | 17.6 | 20.1 | 161.1 | 19.6 | 10.3 | 237.1 | 175 918 | 1 244 | 487.5 | 185.1 | 198.8 | 1 035 | 907 |
| Lafayette, LA | 152.3 | 32.3 | 33.5 | 235.6 | 44.1 | 29.8 | 45.2 | 122 017 | 859 | 756.1 | 266.3 | 352.8 | 1 375 | 463 |
| Lake Charles, LA | 101.2 | 45.8 | 72.8 | 152.0 | 34.0 | 17.1 | 53.6 | 149 147 | 1 195 | 909.3 | 276.6 | 410.3 | 2 138 | 820 |
| Lake Havasu City-Kingman, AZ | 36.4 | 6.0 | 15.3 | 84.6 | 25.0 | 12.8 | 29.3 | 39 177 | 196 | 613.2 | 254.1 | 253.3 | 1 299 | 749 |
| Lakeland-Winter Haven, FL | 153.2 | 49.3 | 24.1 | 306.9 | 97.8 | 47.9 | 49.1 | 211 033 | 1 156 | 2 004.3 | 841.8 | 655.6 | 1 141 | 856 |
| Lancaster, PA | 177.0 | 44.0 | 95.9 | 238.2 | 63.5 | 13.4 | 51.1 | 159 827 | 1 204 | 1 635.2 | 540.9 | 714.1 | 1 433 | 1 148 |
| Lansing-East Lansing, MI | 337.4 | 520.7 | 133.6 | 654.4 | 529.6 | 843.4 | 2 401.7 | 77 154 | 416 | 1 965.3 | 944.4 | 592.5 | 1 298 | 1 211 |
| Laredo, TX | 205.4 | 2.8 | 40.7 | 421.4 | 132.8 | 21.3 | 39.6 | 115 842 | 956 | 1 057.5 | 514.3 | 342.7 | 1 470 | 1 182 |
| Las Cruces, NM | 218.7 | 309.3 | 203.7 | 273.0 | 47.7 | 15.0 | 64.9 | 126 380 | 644 | 633.2 | 389.2 | 159.6 | 803 | 331 |
| Las Vegas-Paradise, NV | 1 452.3 | 443.1 | 893.0 | 790.9 | 162.4 | 87.6 | 466.0 | 582 848 | 5 147 | 9 530.4 | 3 523.8 | 3 157.6 | 1 720 | 1 078 |
| Lawrence, KS | 52.4 | 12.5 | 18.6 | 110.8 | 13.8 | 27.9 | 77.8 | 60 365 | 490 | 429.5 | 85.5 | 157.0 | 1 384 | 1 048 |
| Lawton, OK | 1 851.8 | 466.2 | 26.4 | 87.4 | 25.3 | 20.5 | 22.5 | 44 884 | 280 | 403.3 | 143.2 | 85.4 | 751 | 385 |
| Lebanon, PA | 423.9 | 36.7 | 83.5 | 61.2 | 14.6 | 2.2 | 45.5 | 28 862 | 175 | 428.2 | 136.1 | 157.2 | 1 229 | 937 |
| Lewiston, ID-WA | 23.1 | 2.1 | 17.7 | 97.9 | 15.0 | 10.1 | 14.8 | 11 786 | 65 | 183.8 | 92.4 | 50.3 | 837 | 752 |
| Lewiston-Auburn, ME | 46.5 | 1.1 | 5.4 | 178.8 | 17.7 | 6.3 | 18.2 | 16 550 | 148 | 330.4 | 146.7 | 142.8 | 1 337 | 1 325 |
| Lexington-Fayette, KY | 282.5 | 463.2 | 303.2 | 452.3 | 62.5 | 38.5 | 144.5 | 181 383 | 1 501 | 1 117.4 | 312.8 | 612.1 | 1 369 | 563 |
| Lima, OH | 41.1 | 87.4 | 6.3 | 108.5 | 24.3 | 8.3 | 9.2 | 7 851 | 51 | 397.7 | 197.7 | 129.4 | 1 230 | 858 |
| Lincoln, NE | 331.7 | 19.0 | 91.4 | 284.1 | 116.2 | 160.7 | 773.3 | 139 807 | 1 059 | 991.2 | 253.8 | 510.4 | 1 747 | 1 314 |
| Little Rock-North Little Rock-Conway, AR | 1 183.4 | 450.3 | 248.2 | 659.1 | 232.4 | 306.1 | 1 519.3 | 355 528 | 3 230 | 1 928.9 | 964.9 | 507.6 | 762 | 335 |
| Logan, UT-ID | 42.2 | 52.6 | 24.8 | 55.4 | 20.6 | 24.0 | 150.7 | 67 780 | 542 | 305.4 | 137.4 | 89.2 | 737 | 448 |
| Longview, TX | 53.5 | 1.4 | 12.0 | 278.3 | 36.1 | 6.3 | 13.1 | 52 621 | 477 | 684.5 | 247.3 | 323.1 | 1 587 | 1 246 |
| Longview, WA | 46.3 | 17.2 | 6.0 | 92.5 | 19.4 | 18.2 | 16.7 | 22 148 | 113 | 372.1 | 160.5 | 105.3 | 1 048 | 664 |
| Los Angeles-Long Beach-Santa Ana, CA | 5 900.3 | 12 663.2 | 6 235.7 | 15 628.9 | 3 451.2 | 1 018.7 | 4 302.2 | 2 997 275 | 14 247 | 76 654.5 | 35 407.6 | 22 598.3 | 1 755 | 1 172 |
| Los Angeles-Long Beach-Glendale, CA Div | 4 489.4 | 10 637.0 | 5 805.2 | 13 950.6 | 2 840.6 | 852.6 | 3 697.1 | 2 177 034 | 9 895 | 61 779.9 | 29 562.5 | 17 192.0 | 1 740 | 1 120 |
| Santa Ana-Anaheim-Irvine, CA Div | 1 410.9 | 2 026.2 | 430.5 | 1 678.3 | 610.6 | 166.1 | 605.1 | 820 241 | 4 352 | 14 874.7 | 5 845.1 | 5 406.3 | 1 804 | 1 344 |
| Louisville-Jefferson County, KY-IN | 879.2 | 3 130.3 | 262.0 | 1 080.2 | 187.5 | 115.7 | 203.5 | 356 862 | 2 397 | 3 732.4 | 1 234.0 | 1 393.9 | 1 130 | 680 |
| Lubbock, TX | 156.8 | 13.8 | 17.6 | 258.3 | 44.1 | 10.3 | 111.7 | 176 126 | 1 507 | 1 022.6 | 296.9 | 348.0 | 1 302 | 987 |
| Lynchburg, VA | 93.9 | 115.4 | 313.5 | 178.1 | 26.4 | 16.5 | 19.3 | 88 861 | 529 | 694.5 | 336.2 | 252.0 | 1 034 | 693 |
| Macon, GA | 193.1 | 12.5 | 48.2 | 292.4 | 51.5 | 28.6 | 39.4 | 36 321 | 396 | 763.2 | 282.5 | 328.4 | 1 429 | 839 |
| Madera-Chowchilla, CA | 44.6 | 0.9 | 7.9 | 144.3 | 33.6 | 9.9 | 14.9 | 31 281 | 291 | 598.1 | 351.0 | 131.1 | 895 | 715 |
| Madison, WI | 475.5 | 166.8 | 239.4 | 1 033.9 | 300.7 | 454.4 | 2 195.6 | 252 247 | 1 443 | 2 389.4 | 852.4 | 1 084.8 | 1 952 | 1 800 |
| Manchester-Nashua, NH | 369.5 | 700.2 | 111.2 | 271.3 | 39.2 | 22.6 | 101.1 | 102 043 | 702 | 1 330.6 | 420.3 | 697.9 | 1 735 | 1 686 |
| Manhattan, KS | 2 861.5 | 324.0 | 20.9 | 68.4 | 20.4 | 21.0 | 79.4 | 104 444 | 767 | 384.0 | 148.0 | 142.3 | 1 252 | 898 |
| Mankato, North Mankato, MN | 62.3 | 6.1 | 6.6 | 78.1 | 15.4 | 5.5 | 15.5 | 42 403 | 281 | 351.9 | 167.7 | 79.0 | 864 | 782 |
| Mansfield, OH | 57.7 | 7.8 | 8.2 | 119.8 | 24.8 | 10.7 | 23.4 | 7 097 | 42 | 490.3 | 239.1 | 173.6 | 1 381 | 907 |
| McAllen-Edinburg-Mission, TX | 296.2 | -35.5 | 207.6 | 1 025.4 | 205.3 | 97.6 | 84.4 | 408 214 | 3 105 | 2 583.5 | 1 512.6 | 687.4 | 968 | 774 |
| Medford, OR | 132.1 | 13.7 | 104.2 | 176.9 | 31.5 | 14.5 | 25.0 | 62 135 | 362 | 629.4 | 302.0 | 211.7 | 1 062 | 872 |
| Memphis, TN-MS-AR | 1 028.2 | 1 645.7 | 609.7 | 1 896.3 | 321.0 | 102.5 | 281.0 | 353 120 | 2 210 | 4 881.4 | 1 759.5 | 2 007.0 | 1 567 | 1 117 |
| Merced, CA | 54.0 | 54.7 | 64.5 | 260.0 | 73.7 | 26.1 | 48.7 | 29 805 | 157 | 1 419.6 | 825.1 | 251.4 | 1 024 | 823 |
| Miami-Fort Lauderdale-Pompano Beach, FL | 2 948.1 | 1 045.7 | 1 068.1 | 6 789.3 | 807.8 | 329.4 | 1 575.7 | 1 307 935 | 7 532 | 31 511.9 | 8 246.7 | 12 682.0 | 2 343 | 1 884 |
| Fort Lauderdale-Pompano Beach-Deerfield Beach, FL Div | 672.6 | 202.1 | 285.6 | 601.0 | 203.9 | 104.8 | 326.9 | 279 497 | 2 444 | 10 074.0 | 2 472.5 | 3 722.3 | 2 115 | 1 746 |
| Miami-Miami Beach-Kendall, FL Div | 1 812.5 | 396.7 | 472.7 | 5 786.5 | 443.0 | 166.9 | 1 018.8 | 311 632 | 2 618 | 14 420.4 | 4 219.0 | 5 277.1 | 2 211 | 1 651 |
| West Palm Beach-Boca Raton-Boynton Beach, FL Div | 463.0 | 446.9 | 309.7 | 401.8 | 160.8 | 57.8 | 230.1 | 716 805 | 2 470 | 7 017.5 | 1 555.2 | 3 682.6 | 2 908 | 2 513 |
| Michigan City-La Porte, IN | 37.9 | 4.2 | 5.8 | 86.8 | 17.7 | 2.6 | 5.0 | 23 132 | 143 | 386.6 | 163.7 | 106.7 | 972 | 806 |
| Midland, TX | 57.0 | 0.2 | 10.5 | 53.0 | 9.0 | 4.2 | 10.7 | 96 880 | 539 | 587.8 | 144.8 | 231.6 | 1 832 | 1 400 |
| Milwaukee-Waukesha-West Allis, WI | 782.7 | 292.8 | 444.9 | 2 037.7 | 337.5 | 127.8 | 604.5 | 314 325 | 1 593 | 6 708.0 | 2 770.3 | 2 679.2 | 1 735 | 1 624 |
| Minneapolis-St. Paul-Bloomington, MN | 2 228.8 | 1 360.4 | 1 118.0 | 3 320.3 | 616.7 | 540.8 | 2 098.8 | 1 165 292 | 5 148 | 14 119.4 | 6 409.0 | 4 167.3 | 1 299 | 1 192 |
| Missoula, MT | 103.8 | 5.5 | 52.8 | 117.3 | 17.7 | 8.6 | 58.9 | 40 339 | 563 | 266.9 | 105.7 | 114.6 | 1 085 | 1 048 |
| Mobile, AL | 317.4 | 507.9 | 65.7 | 333.9 | 74.8 | 37.7 | 104.8 | 143 429 | 1 541 | 1 348.0 | 605.0 | 535.3 | 1 324 | 417 |
| Modesto, CA | 93.7 | 18.4 | 33.7 | 535.9 | 145.3 | 36.1 | 78.6 | 28 290 | 164 | 2 994.5 | 1 529.2 | 678.5 | 1 327 | 984 |
| Monroe, LA | 77.4 | 10.1 | 13.3 | 228.6 | 29.8 | 18.7 | 42.2 | 64 385 | 405 | 575.8 | 259.6 | 242.1 | 1 405 | 443 |
| Monroe, MI | 23.8 | 1.1 | 5.6 | 72.5 | 25.0 | 10.1 | 4.8 | 19 319 | 110 | 529.2 | 247.3 | 182.9 | 1 191 | 1 160 |
| Montgomery, AL | 832.7 | 422.8 | 97.4 | 439.2 | 213.3 | 392.7 | 1 334.0 | 139 557 | 972 | 918.9 | 453.6 | 331.1 | 905 | 254 |
| Morgantown, WV | 205.4 | 23.4 | 352.2 | 162.4 | 16.4 | 10.1 | 82.0 | 31 172 | 399 | 254.5 | 106.6 | 83.9 | 712 | 544 |
| Morristown, TN | 33.1 | 25.4 | 10.4 | 164.9 | 24.8 | 11.4 | 6.7 | 23 405 | 134 | 256.2 | 115.8 | 95.5 | 710 | 357 |
| Mount Vernon-Anacortes, WA | 29.4 | 19.2 | 34.2 | 69.5 | 23.5 | 15.8 | 19.7 | 35 595 | 179 | 655.4 | 196.6 | 178.4 | 1 533 | 973 |
| Muncie, IN | 56.0 | 0.4 | 20.6 | 156.3 | 21.6 | 4.4 | 25.1 | 10 358 | 82 | 304.8 | 150.1 | 87.5 | 758 | 697 |
| Muskegon-Norton Shores, MI | 41.1 | 37.2 | 6.6 | 195.6 | 44.5 | 17.7 | 13.4 | 16 817 | 95 | 697.5 | 353.7 | 177.1 | 1 016 | 945 |
| Myrtle Beach-North Myrtle Beach-Conway, SC | 64.1 | 6.7 | 8.1 | 151.2 | 30.3 | 14.0 | 29.6 | 265 401 | 1 776 | 984.4 | 221.7 | 404.4 | 1 618 | 1 288 |
| Napa, CA | 22.6 | 24.8 | 9.1 | 102.5 | 32.0 | 10.9 | 35.0 | 55 850 | 154 | 773.9 | 256.2 | 327.3 | 2 469 | 1 962 |

1. Based on the resident population estimated as of July 1 of the year shown.

# Table C. Metropolitan Areas — Local Government Finances, Government Employment, and Voting

| Area name | Local government finances, 2007 (cont.) | | | | | | | | | Government employment, 2011 | | | Presidential election,[2] 2012 | | |
|---|---|---|---|---|---|---|---|---|---|---|---|---|---|---|---|
| | Direct general expenditure | | | | | | | Debt outstanding | | | | | Percent of vote cast: | | |
| | | | Percent of total for: | | | | | | | | | | | | |
| | Total (mil dol) | Per capita[1] (dollars) | Education | Health and hospitals | Police protection | Public welfare | Highways | Total (mil dol) | Per capita[1] (dollars) | Federal civilian | Federal military | State and local | Democratic | Republican | All other |
| | 185 | 186 | 187 | 188 | 189 | 190 | 191 | 192 | 193 | 194 | 195 | 196 | 197 | 198 | 199 |
| Kokomo, IN | 508.6 | 5 094 | 33.5 | 32.9 | 4.0 | 1.8 | 2.7 | 278.2 | 2 786 | 288 | 327 | 7 072 | 40.2 | 57.5 | 2.3 |
| La Crosse, WI-MN | 590.4 | 4 509 | 48.2 | 2.7 | 4.5 | 14.4 | 6.4 | 455.7 | 3 480 | 546 | 399 | 10 414 | 56.8 | 41.5 | 1.7 |
| Lafayette, IN | 532.0 | 2 768 | 49.1 | 1.0 | 3.0 | 3.5 | 6.9 | 493.7 | 2 569 | 638 | 725 | 24 255 | 44.6 | 52.8 | 2.5 |
| Lafayette, LA | 703.2 | 2 742 | 45.6 | 1.6 | 7.5 | 0.0 | 5.8 | 1 097.8 | 4 280 | 1 085 | 1 343 | 15 782 | 33.2 | 65.0 | 1.8 |
| Lake Charles, LA | 827.7 | 4 313 | 38.3 | 6.9 | 6.2 | 0.2 | 6.3 | 1 011.3 | 5 269 | 584 | 1 053 | 14 806 | 33.7 | 64.5 | 1.9 |
| Lake Havasu City-Kingman, AZ | 607.7 | 3 117 | 33.3 | 2.7 | 8.5 | 0.8 | 7.5 | 509.9 | 2 616 | 510 | 437 | 7 505 | 27.9 | 70.2 | 1.9 |
| Lakeland-Winter Haven, FL | 1 985.5 | 3 455 | 50.8 | 2.7 | 6.7 | 0.9 | 6.0 | 2 648.1 | 4 607 | 1 184 | 1 223 | 27 652 | 46.1 | 52.9 | 1.0 |
| Lancaster, PA | 1 704.0 | 3 419 | 57.0 | 3.5 | 4.3 | 3.6 | 3.2 | 3 018.1 | 6 055 | 1 307 | 1 331 | 19 732 | 39.8 | 58.7 | 1.5 |
| Lansing-East Lansing, MI | 2 008.5 | 4 400 | 51.0 | 8.1 | 4.5 | 2.1 | 4.5 | 2 287.2 | 5 011 | 2 154 | 1 099 | 54 201 | 57.2 | 41.5 | 1.3 |
| Laredo, TX | 1 026.5 | 4 402 | 63.3 | 1.1 | 5.2 | 0.5 | 0.9 | 1 283.2 | 5 504 | 3 347 | 569 | 18 226 | 76.6 | 22.6 | 0.9 |
| Las Cruces, NM | 605.1 | 3 044 | 58.2 | 3.1 | 4.2 | 0.8 | 2.8 | 401.1 | 2 018 | 4 062 | 600 | 17 062 | 55.9 | 41.1 | 3.0 |
| Las Vegas-Paradise, NV | 8 762.7 | 4 772 | 34.3 | 7.6 | 8.9 | 2.7 | 10.3 | 18 303.4 | 10 011 | 11 751 | 15 034 | 81 839 | 56.4 | 41.8 | 1.8 |
| Lawrence, KS | 378.9 | 3 339 | 32.9 | 31.9 | 6.2 | 0.1 | 3.9 | 522.0 | 4 600 | 473 | 527 | 14 179 | 61.0 | 36.3 | 2.8 |
| Lawton, OK | 395.6 | 3 476 | 46.6 | 31.8 | 4.1 | 0.0 | 1.7 | 141.9 | 1 247 | 4 546 | 13 312 | 9 678 | 41.5 | 58.5 | 0.0 |
| Lebanon, PA | 452.1 | 3 535 | 52.0 | 5.2 | 2.3 | 12.1 | 2.9 | 710.8 | 5 558 | 2 583 | 343 | 5 453 | 35.2 | 63.4 | 1.4 |
| Lewiston, ID-WA | 181.9 | 3 029 | 45.9 | 4.8 | 6.0 | 0.4 | 7.7 | 50.5 | 841 | 256 | 216 | 4 964 | 39.1 | 58.4 | 2.5 |
| Lewiston-Auburn, ME | 325.1 | 3 043 | 50.6 | 0.2 | 3.6 | 0.2 | 4.5 | 321.5 | 3 010 | 291 | 339 | 5 111 | 54.8 | 42.1 | 3.1 |
| Lexington-Fayette, KY | 1 059.4 | 2 369 | 46.4 | 2.8 | 6.9 | 1.8 | 1.8 | 2 323.0 | 5 195 | 4 580 | 1 616 | 46 099 | 43.8 | 54.0 | 2.2 |
| Lima, OH | 390.5 | 3 711 | 48.9 | 3.1 | 5.8 | 6.2 | 4.3 | 181.4 | 1 724 | 330 | 272 | 6 172 | 37.1 | 61.2 | 1.7 |
| Lincoln, NE | 1 056.5 | 3 616 | 48.1 | 3.2 | 4.2 | 2.1 | 7.6 | 1 828.3 | 6 257 | 2 931 | 1 284 | 30 891 | 47.7 | 50.0 | 2.3 |
| Little Rock-North Little Rock-Conway, AR | 1 994.7 | 2 993 | 50.9 | 3.1 | 6.1 | 0.0 | 4.5 | 2 059.1 | 3 090 | 9 561 | 8 356 | 62 369 | 43.2 | 54.5 | 2.3 |
| Logan, UT-ID | 286.8 | 2 369 | 50.8 | 6.8 | 5.0 | 0.3 | 5.1 | 227.7 | 1 880 | 390 | 574 | 11 175 | 13.7 | 84.0 | 2.3 |
| Longview, TX | 618.6 | 3 038 | 64.0 | 3.9 | 4.8 | 0.1 | 3.1 | 611.7 | 3 004 | 461 | 481 | 11 280 | 26.4 | 72.7 | 0.9 |
| Longview, WA | 352.0 | 3 503 | 42.9 | 4.2 | 5.1 | 0.0 | 6.6 | 638.1 | 6 351 | 233 | 303 | 5 466 | 50.9 | 46.5 | 2.6 |
| Los Angeles-Long Beach-Santa Ana, CA | 71 175.2 | 5 528 | 39.2 | 8.4 | 7.3 | 7.5 | 3.1 | 95 156.9 | 7 390 | 60 960 | 23 419 | 653 504 | 63.4 | 34.1 | 2.5 |
| Los Angeles-Long Beach-Glendale, CA Div | 56 883.7 | 5 758 | 38.2 | 9.7 | 7.3 | 8.0 | 2.9 | 73 718.0 | 7 462 | 49 343 | 18 152 | 518 252 | 69.7 | 27.8 | 2.5 |
| Santa Ana-Anaheim-Irvine, CA Div | 14 291.5 | 4 769 | 43.2 | 3.0 | 7.4 | 5.6 | 4.0 | 21 438.8 | 7 153 | 11 617 | 5 267 | 135 252 | 45.6 | 51.9 | 2.5 |
| Louisville-Jefferson County, KY-IN | 3 603.5 | 2 921 | 45.4 | 11.4 | 4.3 | 0.9 | 3.1 | 6 352.1 | 5 149 | 9 718 | 4 473 | 69 987 | 47.7 | 50.7 | 1.6 |
| Lubbock, TX | 1 062.0 | 3 975 | 40.1 | 29.8 | 4.8 | 0.1 | 3.0 | 1 365.7 | 5 111 | 1 347 | 705 | 25 646 | 28.9 | 69.5 | 1.6 |
| Lynchburg, VA | 693.9 | 2 849 | 52.4 | 2.8 | 5.7 | 6.0 | 2.4 | 382.9 | 1 572 | 730 | 813 | 13 665 | 34.6 | 63.8 | 1.6 |
| Macon, GA | 761.9 | 3 315 | 48.5 | 5.7 | 7.3 | 0.4 | 3.7 | 742.6 | 3 231 | 1 184 | 799 | 13 875 | 51.4 | 47.8 | 0.8 |
| Madera-Chowchilla, CA | 691.1 | 4 717 | 49.3 | 3.3 | 3.4 | 8.0 | 4.8 | 386.0 | 2 635 | 315 | 242 | 10 184 | 40.2 | 57.3 | 2.5 |
| Madison, WI | 2 415.8 | 4 348 | 45.6 | 2.0 | 5.6 | 8.8 | 6.6 | 2 676.5 | 4 817 | 5 366 | 1 706 | 81 186 | 69.5 | 29.1 | 1.4 |
| Manchester-Nashua, NH | 1 345.6 | 3 345 | 51.1 | 0.7 | 5.8 | 3.9 | 4.3 | 1 045.4 | 2 599 | 3 886 | 1 358 | 18 230 | 49.7 | 48.6 | 1.6 |
| Manhattan, KS | 365.2 | 3 214 | 48.0 | 14.2 | 5.5 | 0.0 | 5.4 | 366.4 | 3 224 | 4 227 | 19 589 | 14 758 | 38.2 | 59.1 | 2.7 |
| Mankato, North Mankato, MN | 363.6 | 3 975 | 38.7 | 4.0 | 4.4 | 5.1 | 15.1 | 359.8 | 3 933 | 362 | 407 | 7 953 | 52.9 | 43.9 | 3.2 |
| Mansfield, OH | 479.8 | 3 818 | 47.7 | 7.1 | 5.3 | 5.5 | 6.8 | 143.1 | 1 139 | 630 | 314 | 7 476 | 39.3 | 58.7 | 2.0 |
| McAllen-Edinburg-Mission, TX | 2 724.7 | 3 835 | 70.2 | 1.7 | 3.5 | 0.8 | 2.3 | 2 783.8 | 3 918 | 3 478 | 1 814 | 49 745 | 70.4 | 28.6 | 1.0 |
| Medford, OR | 598.7 | 3 004 | 44.0 | 6.5 | 7.5 | 0.0 | 7.3 | 575.5 | 2 887 | 1 697 | 576 | 9 471 | 45.8 | 50.5 | 3.7 |
| Memphis, TN-MS-AR | 5 015.8 | 3 917 | 49.4 | 8.0 | 7.8 | 0.8 | 3.2 | 7 650.1 | 5 974 | 14 753 | 6 269 | 75 723 | 55.7 | 43.4 | 0.9 |
| Merced, CA | 1 437.0 | 5 853 | 49.3 | 3.6 | 3.8 | 9.6 | 3.0 | 688.0 | 2 802 | 762 | 413 | 16 040 | 53.2 | 44.4 | 2.4 |
| Miami-Fort Lauderdale-Pompano Beach, FL | 31 624.3 | 5 842 | 32.5 | 12.1 | 7.3 | 2.4 | 2.0 | 36 405.7 | 6 725 | 34 316 | 13 988 | 271 279 | 62.6 | 36.9 | 0.5 |
| Fort Lauderdale-Pompano Beach-Deerfield Beach, FL Div | 10 081.9 | 5 730 | 30.6 | 21.2 | 8.5 | 1.5 | 1.6 | 9 068.5 | 5 154 | 8 017 | 3 888 | 90 936 | 67.2 | 32.3 | 0.5 |
| Miami-Miami Beach-Kendall, FL Div | 14 688.6 | 6 153 | 33.7 | 10.0 | 6.5 | 3.0 | 2.0 | 20 249.0 | 8 482 | 19 938 | 7 405 | 124 157 | 61.6 | 37.9 | 0.4 |
| West Palm Beach-Boca Raton-Boynton Beach, FL Div | 6 853.8 | 5 412 | 32.9 | 3.3 | 7.3 | 2.4 | 2.4 | 7 088.2 | 5 597 | 6 361 | 2 695 | 56 186 | 58.2 | 41.2 | 0.6 |
| Michigan City-La Porte, IN | 352.4 | 3 210 | 57.1 | 1.3 | 2.1 | 2.0 | 7.3 | 269.9 | 2 459 | 176 | 388 | 7 038 | 55.2 | 42.6 | 2.2 |
| Midland, TX | 564.0 | 4 462 | 39.4 | 32.9 | 4.4 | 0.0 | 1.9 | 394.8 | 3 123 | 565 | 312 | 8 058 | 18.6 | 80.0 | 1.4 |
| Milwaukee-Waukesha-West Allis, WI | 6 855.1 | 4 439 | 44.2 | 7.1 | 7.3 | 4.7 | 5.5 | 7 487.8 | 4 848 | 10 613 | 4 730 | 78 739 | 52.1 | 46.9 | 1.0 |
| Minneapolis-St. Paul-Bloomington, MN | 14 634.1 | 4 561 | 42.4 | 6.5 | 5.4 | 6.7 | 6.7 | 21 879.2 | 6 820 | 20 991 | 12 872 | 211 636 | 54.9 | 42.8 | 2.3 |
| Missoula, MT | 281.7 | 2 666 | 46.3 | 3.9 | 5.5 | 0.7 | 4.4 | 200.7 | 1 900 | 1 393 | 560 | 9 205 | 57.4 | 39.6 | 3.0 |
| Mobile, AL | 1 241.0 | 3 069 | 48.4 | 3.3 | 6.9 | 0.5 | 4.8 | 1 144.8 | 2 831 | 2 693 | 2 988 | 24 641 | 45.0 | 54.2 | 0.8 |
| Modesto, CA | 2 929.4 | 5 730 | 52.0 | 7.3 | 4.7 | 8.4 | 2.9 | 3 299.0 | 6 453 | 876 | 825 | 25 147 | 50.0 | 47.3 | 2.7 |
| Monroe, LA | 543.3 | 3 154 | 49.5 | 2.9 | 5.6 | 0.1 | 4.8 | 396.9 | 2 304 | 576 | 842 | 12 775 | 37.5 | 61.2 | 1.3 |
| Monroe, MI | 519.5 | 3 382 | 55.8 | 6.3 | 3.9 | 0.7 | 7.7 | 565.9 | 3 684 | 239 | 280 | 5 231 | 49.8 | 48.9 | 1.3 |
| Montgomery, AL | 1 000.6 | 2 734 | 48.9 | 1.2 | 6.9 | 0.3 | 5.9 | 696.7 | 1 904 | 7 001 | 4 670 | 33 625 | 49.8 | 49.5 | 0.7 |
| Morgantown, WV | 261.5 | 2 220 | 59.2 | 2.9 | 4.9 | 0.3 | 1.6 | 262.4 | 2 228 | 1 867 | 663 | 17 058 | 39.3 | 58.0 | 2.7 |
| Morristown, TN | 258.8 | 1 923 | 61.3 | 2.7 | 5.2 | 0.1 | 3.6 | 199.2 | 1 480 | 342 | 460 | 6 953 | 24.8 | 73.7 | 1.5 |
| Mount Vernon-Anacortes, WA | 668.9 | 5 747 | 25.6 | 41.8 | 3.1 | 0.0 | 3.7 | 488.5 | 4 197 | 408 | 348 | 10 563 | 51.9 | 45.4 | 2.7 |
| Muncie, IN | 373.1 | 3 232 | 51.4 | 1.3 | 3.9 | 4.7 | 2.7 | 233.5 | 2 023 | 335 | 394 | 10 472 | 50.4 | 47.3 | 2.4 |
| Muskegon-Norton Shores, MI | 748.6 | 4 293 | 53.1 | 10.7 | 3.7 | 2.9 | 4.2 | 815.1 | 4 674 | 338 | 340 | 7 823 | 58.3 | 40.5 | 1.1 |
| Myrtle Beach-North Myrtle Beach-Conway, SC | 982.5 | 3 931 | 45.9 | 11.4 | 5.3 | 0.3 | 2.6 | 1 240.3 | 4 963 | 605 | 1 180 | 14 513 | 34.6 | 64.2 | 1.2 |
| Napa, CA | 789.2 | 5 954 | 41.2 | 5.1 | 6.7 | 3.7 | 4.4 | 766.1 | 5 779 | 358 | 219 | 9 515 | 63.0 | 34.3 | 2.8 |

1. Based on the resident population estimated as of July 1 of the year shown.   2. © 2013 Election Data Services, Inc. All rights reserved.

Table C. Metropolitan Areas — **Land Area and Population**

| CBSA/ DIV code[1] | Area name | Land area,[2] 2010 (sq km) | Population 2012 Total persons | Rank | Per square kilometer | Race alone or in combination, not Hispanic or Latino (percent) White | Black | American Indian, Alaska Native | Asian and Pacific Islander | Percent Hispanic or Latino[3] | Age (percent) Under 5 years | 5 to 17 years | 18 to 24 years | 25 to 34 years | 35 to 44 years | 45 to 54 years |
|---|---|---|---|---|---|---|---|---|---|---|---|---|---|---|---|---|
| | | 1 | 2 | 3 | 4 | 5 | 6 | 7 | 8 | 9 | 10 | 11 | 12 | 13 | 14 | 15 |
| 34940 | Naples-Marco Island, FL | 5 176 | 332 427 | 148 | 64.2 | 65.9 | 6.7 | 0.4 | 1.5 | 26.3 | 5.2 | 14.0 | 6.9 | 10.1 | 10.7 | 12.5 |
| 34980 | Nashville-Davidson—Murfreesboro—Franklin, TN | 14 734 | 1 644 703 | 37 | 111.6 | 75.3 | 16.0 | 0.7 | 2.9 | 6.8 | 6.8 | 17.4 | 9.7 | 14.9 | 14.1 | 14.6 |
| 35300 | New Haven-Milford, CT | 1 566 | 862 813 | 60 | 551.0 | 68.6 | 12.9 | 0.6 | 4.1 | 15.4 | 5.5 | 16.4 | 9.9 | 12.7 | 12.8 | 15.3 |
| 35380 | New Orleans-Metairie-Kenner, LA | 7 667 | 1 205 374 | 46 | 157.2 | 54.7 | 34.7 | 0.8 | 3.2 | 8.0 | 6.6 | 16.6 | 9.6 | 14.6 | 12.5 | 14.7 |
| 35620 | New York-Northern New Jersey-Long Island, NY-NJ-PA | 17 319 | 19 160 024 | 1 | 1 106.3 | 49.6 | 17.0 | 0.5 | 11.1 | 23.3 | 6.2 | 16.4 | 9.4 | 14.4 | 13.8 | 14.7 |
| 35620 | Edison-New Brunswick, NJ Div | 4 424 | 2 360 602 | X | 533.6 | 68.0 | 7.5 | 0.4 | 12.2 | 13.2 | 6.0 | 17.3 | 8.5 | 11.8 | 13.3 | 15.7 |
| 35620 | Nassau-Suffolk, NY Div | 3 100 | 2 848 506 | X | 918.9 | 69.0 | 9.4 | 0.5 | 6.3 | 16.1 | 5.6 | 17.6 | 8.8 | 11.0 | 13.3 | 16.3 |
| 35620 | Newark-Union, NJ-PA Div | 5 649 | 2 161 110 | X | 382.6 | 55.1 | 21.3 | 0.5 | 6.1 | 18.4 | 6.1 | 17.8 | 8.5 | 12.1 | 14.2 | 16.1 |
| 35620 | New York-White Plains-Wayne, NY-NJ Div | 4 146 | 11 789 806 | X | 2 843.7 | 40.1 | 20.0 | 0.5 | 12.9 | 28.0 | 6.4 | 15.6 | 9.8 | 16.2 | 13.9 | 13.9 |
| 35660 | Niles-Benton Harbor, MI | 1 470 | 156 067 | 255 | 106.2 | 77.8 | 16.4 | 1.1 | 2.1 | 4.7 | 6.1 | 17.0 | 8.5 | 11.1 | 11.9 | 14.9 |
| 35840 | North Port-Bradenton-Sarasota, FL | 3 364 | 720 042 | 72 | 214.0 | 80.2 | 7.1 | 0.5 | 2.0 | 11.4 | 4.6 | 13.1 | 6.4 | 9.1 | 10.3 | 13.4 |
| 35980 | Norwich-New London, CT | 1 722 | 274 170 | 171 | 159.2 | 80.4 | 6.8 | 1.7 | 5.2 | 8.8 | 5.3 | 16.0 | 9.9 | 12.1 | 12.6 | 16.2 |
| 36100 | Ocala, FL | 4 104 | 335 125 | 147 | 81.7 | 74.7 | 12.8 | 0.8 | 1.8 | 11.2 | 5.1 | 14.0 | 7.2 | 9.8 | 10.5 | 13.1 |
| 36140 | Ocean City, NJ | 651 | 96 304 | 351 | 147.9 | 87.9 | 5.2 | 0.5 | 1.4 | 6.4 | 4.8 | 13.7 | 8.0 | 9.7 | 10.1 | 15.3 |
| 36220 | Odessa, TX | 2 325 | 144 325 | 278 | 62.1 | 40.6 | 4.5 | 0.8 | 1.1 | 53.9 | 9.0 | 20.0 | 11.2 | 14.8 | 11.9 | 12.8 |
| 36260 | Ogden-Clearfield, UT | 3 844 | 562 270 | 92 | 146.3 | 84.2 | 1.7 | 0.9 | 3.2 | 12.1 | 9.4 | 22.9 | 9.7 | 15.5 | 12.4 | 11.6 |
| 36420 | Oklahoma City, OK | 14 275 | 1 296 565 | 43 | 90.8 | 70.9 | 11.7 | 6.8 | 3.6 | 11.7 | 7.3 | 17.6 | 10.8 | 14.9 | 12.5 | 13.5 |
| 36500 | Olympia, WA | 1 870 | 258 332 | 181 | 138.1 | 82.3 | 4.0 | 2.6 | 8.4 | 7.4 | 6.1 | 16.5 | 9.3 | 13.8 | 12.8 | 14.2 |
| 36540 | Omaha-Council Bluffs, NE-IA | 11 266 | 885 624 | 58 | 78.6 | 80.2 | 8.8 | 1.0 | 2.8 | 9.2 | 7.5 | 18.6 | 9.2 | 14.9 | 12.9 | 14.0 |
| 36740 | Orlando-Kissimmee-Sanford, FL | 9 009 | 2 223 674 | 25 | 246.8 | 54.2 | 16.2 | 0.6 | 4.9 | 25.9 | 6.1 | 17.0 | 10.9 | 14.1 | 13.7 | 14.3 |
| 36780 | Oshkosh-Neenah, WI | 1 125 | 168 794 | 237 | 150.0 | 91.6 | 2.3 | 1.0 | 2.8 | 3.6 | 5.9 | 15.5 | 11.5 | 13.5 | 12.5 | 15.2 |
| 36980 | Owensboro, KY | 2 327 | 116 030 | 321 | 49.9 | 92.4 | 5.3 | 0.4 | 0.9 | 2.4 | 6.7 | 17.6 | 8.5 | 12.2 | 12.4 | 14.7 |
| 37100 | Oxnard-Thousand Oaks-Ventura, CA | 4 774 | 835 981 | 63 | 175.1 | 50.1 | 2.1 | 0.8 | 8.4 | 40.9 | 6.6 | 18.7 | 10.0 | 12.9 | 13.2 | 14.8 |
| 37340 | Palm Bay-Melbourne-Titusville, FL | 2 631 | 547 307 | 97 | 208.0 | 79.1 | 10.8 | 0.8 | 3.1 | 8.4 | 4.8 | 14.6 | 7.9 | 10.2 | 10.9 | 16.4 |
| 37380 | Palm Coast, FL | 1 257 | 98 359 | 346 | 78.2 | 77.2 | 11.8 | 0.7 | 2.9 | 9.0 | 4.8 | 14.6 | 6.3 | 9.2 | 11.0 | 13.1 |
| 37460 | Panama City-Lynn Haven-Panama City Beach, FL | 1 964 | 171 903 | 235 | 87.5 | 81.1 | 12.0 | 1.4 | 3.2 | 5.1 | 6.2 | 15.5 | 9.4 | 13.3 | 12.4 | 15.4 |
| 37620 | Parkersburg-Marietta-Vienna, WV-OH | 3 525 | 161 618 | 248 | 45.8 | 97.2 | 1.8 | 0.7 | 0.8 | 0.8 | 5.4 | 15.8 | 8.1 | 11.1 | 12.4 | 15.3 |
| 37700 | Pascagoula, MS | 3 112 | 163 228 | 244 | 52.5 | 73.2 | 20.6 | 0.8 | 2.3 | 4.5 | 6.8 | 18.6 | 8.8 | 12.9 | 13.2 | 14.8 |
| 37860 | Pensacola-Ferry Pass-Brent, FL | 4 320 | 461 227 | 110 | 106.8 | 74.6 | 17.9 | 1.7 | 3.8 | 4.8 | 6.2 | 15.9 | 11.4 | 12.9 | 11.9 | 14.9 |
| 37900 | Peoria, IL | 6 399 | 380 447 | 135 | 59.5 | 85.5 | 10.3 | 0.6 | 2.4 | 3.0 | 6.5 | 17.3 | 8.8 | 12.9 | 12.4 | 14.0 |
| 37980 | Philadelphia-Camden-Wilmington, PA-NJ-DE-MD | 11 919 | 6 018 800 | 6 | 505.0 | 66.1 | 21.2 | 0.6 | 5.7 | 8.1 | 6.1 | 16.9 | 10.0 | 13.2 | 12.9 | 15.1 |
| 37980 | Camden, NJ Div | 3 475 | 1 254 461 | X | 361.0 | 69.9 | 16.7 | 0.6 | 5.2 | 9.6 | 6.0 | 17.5 | 8.9 | 12.3 | 13.4 | 15.9 |
| 37980 | Philadelphia, PA Div | 5 583 | 4 050 793 | X | 725.6 | 64.6 | 22.7 | 0.6 | 6.2 | 7.6 | 6.2 | 16.6 | 10.2 | 13.5 | 12.6 | 14.8 |
| 37980 | Wilmington, DE-MD-NJ Div | 2 861 | 713 546 | X | 249.4 | 67.9 | 21.1 | 0.7 | 4.2 | 8.0 | 6.1 | 17.0 | 10.4 | 12.9 | 13.2 | 15.3 |
| 38060 | Phoenix-Mesa-Glendale, AZ | 37 725 | 4 329 534 | 13 | 114.8 | 59.9 | 5.5 | 2.4 | 4.4 | 29.9 | 7.2 | 18.7 | 9.7 | 14.2 | 13.5 | 13.0 |
| 38220 | Pine Bluff, AR | 5 258 | 97 451 | 348 | 18.5 | 49.6 | 47.9 | 0.7 | 1.0 | 2.0 | 6.1 | 16.9 | 10.7 | 12.9 | 12.2 | 14.5 |
| 38300 | Pittsburgh, PA | 13 679 | 2 360 733 | 22 | 172.6 | 88.2 | 9.3 | 0.5 | 2.2 | 1.4 | 5.1 | 14.8 | 9.1 | 12.0 | 12.0 | 15.4 |
| 38340 | Pittsfield, MA | 2 400 | 130 016 | 299 | 54.2 | 92.2 | 3.6 | 0.6 | 1.9 | 3.5 | 4.5 | 14.6 | 9.6 | 10.0 | 11.2 | 15.8 |
| 38540 | Pocatello, ID | 6 517 | 91 578 | 355 | 14.1 | 86.0 | 1.1 | 3.4 | 2.4 | 9.0 | 8.1 | 19.2 | 12.6 | 14.6 | 11.0 | 11.6 |
| 38860 | Portland-South Portland-Biddeford, ME | 5 386 | 518 117 | 102 | 96.2 | 94.8 | 2.0 | 0.9 | 2.1 | 1.6 | 5.1 | 15.5 | 8.4 | 11.6 | 13.1 | 16.5 |
| 38900 | Portland-Vancouver-Hillsboro, OR-WA | 17 311 | 2 289 800 | 23 | 132.3 | 79.0 | 3.6 | 1.7 | 8.0 | 11.1 | 6.4 | 16.9 | 8.6 | 15.1 | 14.5 | 14.1 |
| 38940 | Port St. Lucie, FL | 2 889 | 432 683 | 116 | 149.8 | 68.7 | 14.7 | 0.6 | 2.0 | 15.3 | 5.2 | 15.2 | 7.3 | 10.1 | 11.4 | 14.3 |
| 39100 | Poughkeepsie-Newburgh-Middletown, NY | 4 163 | 671 834 | 79 | 161.4 | 72.1 | 10.4 | 0.7 | 3.7 | 15.1 | 6.1 | 18.4 | 10.5 | 11.0 | 13.2 | 16.1 |
| 39140 | Prescott, AZ | 21 040 | 212 637 | 203 | 10.1 | 83.0 | 1.0 | 2.2 | 1.6 | 13.9 | 4.7 | 13.8 | 7.0 | 8.8 | 9.4 | 13.6 |
| 39300 | Providence-New Bedford-Fall River, RI-MA | 4 110 | 1 601 374 | 38 | 389.6 | 81.4 | 5.7 | 0.9 | 3.3 | 10.6 | 5.4 | 15.8 | 10.9 | 12.1 | 12.9 | 15.4 |
| 39340 | Provo-Orem, UT | 13 975 | 550 845 | 95 | 39.4 | 85.7 | 0.9 | 0.9 | 3.7 | 10.9 | 10.9 | 23.9 | 16.6 | 16.1 | 11.3 | 8.3 |
| 39380 | Pueblo, CO | 6 180 | 160 852 | 249 | 26.0 | 55.1 | 2.2 | 1.3 | 1.2 | 41.6 | 6.5 | 17.7 | 9.5 | 12.1 | 11.7 | 13.6 |
| 39460 | Punta Gorda, FL | 1 762 | 162 449 | 245 | 92.2 | 86.9 | 6.1 | 0.6 | 1.8 | 5.9 | 3.3 | 10.5 | 5.5 | 7.0 | 8.4 | 12.9 |
| 39540 | Racine, WI | 861 | 194 797 | 219 | 226.2 | 75.9 | 11.9 | 0.8 | 1.5 | 11.7 | 6.5 | 18.1 | 8.1 | 12.2 | 12.8 | 16.0 |
| 39580 | Raleigh-Cary, NC | 5 486 | 1 188 564 | 47 | 216.7 | 64.7 | 20.9 | 0.9 | 5.2 | 10.3 | 7.1 | 18.9 | 9.2 | 14.5 | 15.9 | 14.6 |
| 39660 | Rapid City, SD | 16 181 | 130 399 | 297 | 8.1 | 85.9 | 2.1 | 9.7 | 1.7 | 3.9 | 7.3 | 17.1 | 9.7 | 13.9 | 11.4 | 14.1 |
| 39740 | Reading, PA | 2 218 | 413 491 | 127 | 186.4 | 77.4 | 4.9 | 0.4 | 1.7 | 16.8 | 6.0 | 17.4 | 10.2 | 11.3 | 12.7 | 15.1 |
| 39820 | Redding, CA | 9 778 | 178 586 | 229 | 18.3 | 85.2 | 1.6 | 4.2 | 3.9 | 8.8 | 5.7 | 16.3 | 9.0 | 11.5 | 10.8 | 14.5 |
| 39900 | Reno-Sparks, NV | 17 004 | 433 843 | 115 | 25.5 | 67.9 | 2.9 | 2.0 | 7.2 | 22.6 | 6.5 | 16.7 | 10.4 | 13.5 | 12.4 | 14.3 |
| 40060 | Richmond, VA | 14 724 | 1 282 305 | 44 | 87.1 | 61.5 | 30.5 | 0.9 | 3.9 | 5.2 | 6.1 | 16.9 | 9.7 | 13.4 | 13.4 | 15.2 |
| 40140 | Riverside-San Bernardino-Ontario, CA | 70 612 | 4 350 096 | 12 | 61.6 | 37.8 | 7.9 | 1.0 | 7.6 | 47.9 | 7.5 | 20.8 | 10.9 | 13.5 | 13.2 | 13.4 |
| 40220 | Roanoke, VA | 4 840 | 310 118 | 155 | 64.1 | 81.8 | 13.8 | 0.6 | 2.1 | 3.3 | 5.7 | 15.5 | 8.5 | 11.3 | 12.6 | 15.2 |
| 40340 | Rochester, MN | 4 184 | 188 773 | 224 | 45.1 | 87.1 | 4.5 | 0.6 | 5.2 | 4.2 | 7.1 | 18.0 | 7.5 | 14.4 | 12.4 | 15.2 |
| 40380 | Rochester, NY | 7 584 | 1 056 940 | 51 | 139.4 | 79.4 | 12.1 | 0.7 | 3.2 | 6.4 | 5.6 | 16.5 | 10.9 | 12.0 | 12.1 | 15.3 |
| 40420 | Rockford, IL | 2 057 | 346 009 | 146 | 168.2 | 74.4 | 11.6 | 0.6 | 2.7 | 12.7 | 6.6 | 18.6 | 8.4 | 12.2 | 13.1 | 14.7 |
| 40580 | Rocky Mount, NC | 2 708 | 151 662 | 262 | 56.0 | 48.5 | 45.3 | 0.9 | 1.0 | 5.5 | 6.2 | 17.5 | 8.8 | 11.4 | 12.4 | 15.0 |
| 40660 | Rome, GA | 1 321 | 96 177 | 352 | 72.8 | 74.2 | 15.2 | 0.6 | 1.7 | 9.7 | 6.6 | 17.3 | 10.5 | 12.2 | 12.8 | 13.9 |

1.  CBSA = Core Based Statistical Area. DIV = Metropolitan Division. See Appendix A for explanation. See Appendix B for list of metropolitan areas identified by type.    2.  Dry land or land partially or temporarily covered by water.    3.  May be of any race.

# Table C. Metropolitan Areas — Population and Households

| Area name | 55 to 64 years | 65 to 74 years | 75 years and over | Percent female | Total persons 2000 | Total persons 2010 | Percent change 2000–2010 | Percent change 2010–2012 | Births | Deaths | Net migration | Number | Percent change, 2000–2010 | Persons per household | Female family householder[1] | One person |
|---|---|---|---|---|---|---|---|---|---|---|---|---|---|---|---|---|
| | 16 | 17 | 18 | 19 | 20 | 21 | 22 | 23 | 24 | 25 | 26 | 27 | 28 | 29 | 30 | 31 |
| Naples-Marco Island, FL....... | 13.3 | 14.6 | 12.6 | 50.6 | 251 377 | 321 520 | 27.9 | 3.4 | 7 357 | 6 565 | 9 897 | 133 179 | 29.3 | 2.38 | 8.6 | 26.7 |
| Nashville-Davidson—Murfreesboro—Franklin, TN ........ | 11.7 | 6.3 | 4.6 | 51.1 | 1 311 789 | 1 589 934 | 21.2 | 3.4 | 48 303 | 27 065 | 33 036 | 615 374 | 20.6 | 2.52 | 12.8 | 26.8 |
| New Haven-Milford, CT ........ | 12.7 | 7.3 | 7.3 | 51.8 | 824 008 | 862 477 | 4.7 | 0.0 | 20 519 | 16 825 | -3 171 | 334 502 | 4.8 | 2.49 | 14.5 | 28.9 |
| New Orleans-Metairie-Kenner, LA .......... | 12.9 | 6.9 | 5.5 | 51.4 | 1 316 510 | 1 167 764 | -11.3 | 3.2 | 34 939 | 22 829 | 24 818 | 455 146 | -8.7 | 2.52 | 17.4 | 28.4 |
| New York-Northern New Jersey-Long Island, NY-NJ-PA........ | 11.9 | 7.0 | 6.3 | 51.8 | 18 323 002 | 18 897 109 | 3.1 | 1.4 | 545 525 | 301 487 | 20 688 | 6 918 950 | 3.6 | 2.67 | 15.3 | 27.6 |
| Edison-New Brunswick, NJ Div.................. | 12.5 | 7.7 | 7.4 | 51.3 | 2 173 869 | 2 340 249 | 7.7 | 0.9 | 60 606 | 44 773 | 5 262 | 854 039 | 6.8 | 2.69 | 10.6 | 24.7 |
| Nassau-Suffolk, NY Div ..... | 12.8 | 7.5 | 7.1 | 51.2 | 2 753 913 | 2 832 882 | 2.9 | 0.6 | 69 367 | 49 899 | -2 914 | 948 450 | 3.5 | 2.93 | 11.7 | 20.4 |
| Newark-Union, NJ-PA Div... | 12.3 | 6.8 | 6.0 | 51.3 | 2 098 843 | 2 147 727 | 2.3 | 0.6 | 54 751 | 35 000 | -6 660 | 776 210 | 3.3 | 2.71 | 14.6 | 24.8 |
| New York-White Plains-Wayne, NY-NJ Div....... | 11.4 | 6.7 | 5.9 | 52.1 | 11 296 377 | 11 576 251 | 2.5 | 1.8 | 360 801 | 171 815 | 25 000 | 4 340 251 | 3.1 | 2.61 | 17.2 | 30.2 |
| Niles-Benton Harbor, MI ....... | 13.9 | 8.8 | 7.9 | 51.3 | 162 453 | 156 813 | -3.5 | -0.5 | 4 274 | 3 669 | -1 451 | 63 054 | -0.8 | 2.43 | 13.6 | 28.7 |
| North Port-Bradenton-Sarasota, FL ........ | 15.0 | 14.1 | 13.9 | 52.0 | 589 959 | 702 281 | 19.0 | 2.5 | 13 950 | 18 866 | 22 697 | 311 475 | 18.7 | 2.22 | 9.6 | 30.5 |
| Norwich-New London, CT..... | 13.3 | 7.7 | 6.8 | 50.1 | 259 088 | 274 055 | 5.8 | 0.0 | 6 180 | 5 172 | -800 | 107 057 | 7.2 | 2.44 | 11.8 | 27.6 |
| Ocala, FL ........ | 14.1 | 14.4 | 11.8 | 52.1 | 258 916 | 331 298 | 28.0 | 1.2 | 7 551 | 9 483 | 5 875 | 137 726 | 29.0 | 2.35 | 12.0 | 26.7 |
| Ocean City, NJ ........ | 16.3 | 11.7 | 10.3 | 51.4 | 102 326 | 97 265 | -4.9 | -1.0 | 2 069 | 2 822 | -138 | 40 812 | -3.2 | 2.32 | 11.0 | 31.2 |
| Odessa, TX ........ | 10.2 | 5.5 | 4.5 | 50.4 | 121 123 | 137 130 | 13.2 | 5.2 | 5 597 | 2 588 | 4 100 | 48 688 | 11.0 | 2.77 | 15.4 | 24.5 |
| Ogden-Clearfield, UT ........... | 9.3 | 5.0 | 4.2 | 49.8 | 442 656 | 547 184 | 23.6 | 2.8 | 22 227 | 6 575 | -543 | 175 113 | 26.0 | 3.09 | 10.4 | 18.0 |
| Oklahoma City, OK .............. | 11.6 | 6.6 | 5.3 | 50.7 | 1 095 421 | 1 252 987 | 14.4 | 3.5 | 41 124 | 23 323 | 25 052 | 489 654 | 13.9 | 2.49 | 12.7 | 27.8 |
| Olympia, WA ........ | 13.9 | 7.6 | 5.8 | 51.1 | 207 355 | 252 264 | 21.7 | 2.4 | 6 897 | 4 052 | 3 266 | 100 650 | 23.3 | 2.46 | 11.4 | 25.9 |
| Omaha-Council Bluffs, NE-IA........ | 11.6 | 6.0 | 5.2 | 50.6 | 767 041 | 865 350 | 12.8 | 2.3 | 30 091 | 13 954 | 4 370 | 334 379 | 13.5 | 2.54 | 11.7 | 27.5 |
| Orlando-Kissimmee-Sanford, FL ........ | 11.3 | 7.0 | 5.6 | 51.0 | 1 644 561 | 2 134 411 | 29.8 | 4.2 | 58 751 | 33 385 | 63 564 | 798 445 | 27.7 | 2.62 | 14.6 | 24.1 |
| Oshkosh-Neenah, WI........... | 12.4 | 6.8 | 6.8 | 49.7 | 156 763 | 166 994 | 6.5 | 1.1 | 4 273 | 3 130 | 673 | 67 875 | 11.0 | 2.34 | 9.1 | 29.9 |
| Owensboro, KY........ | 13.0 | 8.0 | 6.9 | 51.3 | 109 875 | 114 752 | 4.4 | 1.1 | 3 484 | 2 624 | 434 | 45 737 | 5.8 | 2.45 | 12.4 | 27.6 |
| Oxnard-Thousand Oaks-Ventura, CA........ | 11.8 | 6.5 | 5.6 | 50.3 | 753 197 | 823 318 | 9.3 | 1.5 | 25 125 | 11 582 | -733 | 266 920 | 9.7 | 3.04 | 11.8 | 19.9 |
| Palm Bay-Melbourne-Titusville, FL ........ | 14.4 | 10.8 | 10.0 | 51.1 | 476 230 | 543 376 | 14.1 | 0.7 | 11 209 | 13 404 | 6 286 | 229 692 | 15.9 | 2.33 | 11.8 | 28.4 |
| Palm Coast, FL........ | 15.7 | 14.6 | 10.7 | 51.9 | 49 832 | 95 696 | 92.0 | 2.8 | 1 823 | 2 256 | 3 082 | 39 186 | 84.0 | 2.42 | 11.0 | 23.1 |
| Panama City-Lynn Haven-Panama City Beach, FL | 12.9 | 8.2 | 6.6 | 50.5 | 148 217 | 168 852 | 13.9 | 1.8 | 4 881 | 3 652 | 1 824 | 68 438 | 14.8 | 2.41 | 13.0 | 27.5 |
| Parkersburg-Marietta-Vienna, WV-OH ........... | 14.6 | 9.7 | 7.6 | 51.2 | 164 624 | 162 056 | -1.6 | -0.3 | 3 781 | 4 193 | 33 | 67 410 | 1.2 | 2.35 | 10.8 | 28.0 |
| Pascagoula, MS........ | 12.2 | 7.7 | 5.0 | 50.5 | 150 564 | 162 246 | 7.8 | 0.6 | 4 567 | 3 304 | -254 | 60 187 | 10.6 | 2.66 | 15.7 | 22.9 |
| Pensacola-Ferry Pass-Brent, FL........ | 12.8 | 8.0 | 6.1 | 50.2 | 412 153 | 448 991 | 8.9 | 2.7 | 12 736 | 9 441 | 8 976 | 173 148 | 11.8 | 2.46 | 14.7 | 26.4 |
| Peoria, IL........ | 13.2 | 7.7 | 7.3 | 51.1 | 366 899 | 379 186 | 3.3 | 0.3 | 10 873 | 8 317 | -1 181 | 151 801 | 5.7 | 2.44 | 11.8 | 28.2 |
| Philadelphia-Camden-Wilmington, PA-NJ-DE-MD. | 12.4 | 6.9 | 6.5 | 51.7 | 5 687 147 | 5 965 343 | 4.9 | 0.9 | 165 969 | 117 080 | 5 750 | 2 260 312 | 5.9 | 2.56 | 14.8 | 27.4 |
| Camden, NJ Div.............. | 12.6 | 7.0 | 6.3 | 51.4 | 1 186 999 | 1 250 679 | 5.4 | 0.3 | 32 276 | 23 440 | -4 807 | 461 569 | 7.1 | 2.66 | 13.9 | 24.6 |
| Philadelphia, PA Div........ | 12.3 | 6.9 | 6.7 | 51.9 | 3 849 647 | 4 008 994 | 4.1 | 1.0 | 114 129 | 80 698 | 8 996 | 1 533 935 | 5.1 | 2.53 | 15.2 | 28.6 |
| Wilmington, DE-MD-NJ Div. | 12.4 | 6.9 | 5.8 | 51.3 | 650 501 | 705 670 | 8.5 | 1.1 | 19 564 | 12 942 | 1 561 | 264 808 | 8.3 | 2.59 | 14.4 | 25.5 |
| Phoenix-Mesa-Glendale, AZ. | 10.9 | 7.1 | 5.5 | 50.2 | 3 251 876 | 4 192 887 | 28.9 | 3.3 | 131 706 | 62 501 | 66 343 | 1 537 173 | 28.7 | 2.68 | 12.4 | 25.4 |
| Pine Bluff, AR ........ | 13.0 | 7.6 | 6.1 | 49.2 | 107 341 | 100 258 | -6.6 | -2.8 | 2 621 | 2 388 | -3 076 | 36 496 | -4.2 | 2.50 | 19.9 | 27.6 |
| Pittsburgh, PA ........ | 14.4 | 8.4 | 8.9 | 51.6 | 2 431 087 | 2 356 285 | -3.1 | 0.2 | 53 243 | 60 455 | 12 953 | 1 001 627 | 0.6 | 2.29 | 11.4 | 31.9 |
| Pittsfield, MA ........ | 15.4 | 9.4 | 9.6 | 51.8 | 134 953 | 131 219 | -2.8 | -0.9 | 2 496 | 3 088 | -514 | 56 090 | 0.2 | 2.23 | 11.5 | 33.0 |
| Pocatello, ID........ | 11.4 | 6.3 | 5.2 | 50.1 | 83 103 | 90 656 | 9.1 | 1.0 | 3 387 | 1 552 | -898 | 33 323 | 12.0 | 2.67 | 10.7 | 24.5 |
| Portland-South Portland-Biddeford, ME ........ | 14.6 | 8.1 | 7.1 | 51.4 | 487 568 | 514 098 | 5.4 | 0.8 | 11 200 | 10 104 | 3 033 | 213 436 | 8.5 | 2.35 | 9.7 | 28.3 |
| Portland-Vancouver-Hillsboro, OR-WA ........ | 12.7 | 6.5 | 5.2 | 50.6 | 1 927 881 | 2 226 009 | 15.5 | 2.9 | 62 399 | 34 744 | 35 797 | 867 794 | 16.4 | 2.52 | 10.5 | 27.0 |
| Port St. Lucie, FL........ | 13.6 | 11.7 | 11.2 | 51.0 | 319 426 | 424 107 | 32.8 | 2.0 | 9 389 | 10 187 | 9 166 | 172 422 | 30.4 | 2.42 | 11.3 | 26.7 |
| Poughkeepsie-Newburgh-Middletown, NY.............. | 12.3 | 6.8 | 5.7 | 50.1 | 621 517 | 670 301 | 7.8 | 0.2 | 17 693 | 10 814 | -5 146 | 233 890 | 9.1 | 2.73 | 11.7 | 23.9 |
| Prescott, AZ........ | 17.6 | 14.4 | 10.8 | 51.0 | 167 517 | 211 033 | 26.0 | 0.8 | 4 120 | 5 439 | 2 896 | 90 903 | 29.5 | 2.28 | 9.0 | 29.1 |
| Providence-New Bedford-Fall River, RI-MA ........ | 12.8 | 7.3 | 7.3 | 51.6 | 1 582 997 | 1 600 852 | 1.1 | 0.0 | 37 714 | 32 009 | -4 897 | 626 610 | 2.1 | 2.46 | 13.7 | 28.9 |
| Provo-Orem, UT........ | 6.4 | 3.7 | 3.0 | 49.8 | 376 774 | 526 810 | 39.8 | 4.6 | 26 964 | 4 614 | 1 686 | 143 695 | 40.3 | 3.57 | 8.1 | 11.7 |
| Pueblo, CO........ | 13.3 | 8.1 | 7.4 | 50.8 | 141 472 | 159 063 | 12.4 | 1.1 | 4 282 | 3 567 | 1 146 | 62 972 | 15.4 | 2.46 | 14.1 | 28.9 |
| Punta Gorda, FL........ | 17.3 | 18.5 | 16.6 | 51.4 | 141 627 | 159 978 | 13.0 | 1.5 | 2 167 | 5 096 | 5 571 | 73 370 | 14.9 | 2.14 | 8.5 | 28.5 |
| Racine, WI........ | 12.9 | 7.1 | 6.3 | 50.4 | 188 831 | 195 408 | 3.5 | -0.3 | 5 589 | 3 557 | -2 608 | 75 651 | 6.8 | 2.52 | 13.0 | 26.4 |
| Raleigh-Cary, NC........ | 10.6 | 5.5 | 3.8 | 51.2 | 797 071 | 1 130 490 | 41.8 | 5.1 | 34 612 | 13 824 | 36 730 | 430 577 | 40.5 | 2.57 | 11.7 | 25.6 |
| Rapid City, SD........ | 13.0 | 7.2 | 6.4 | 49.7 | 112 818 | 126 382 | 12.0 | 3.2 | 4 088 | 2 050 | 2 007 | 51 154 | 17.7 | 2.40 | 11.2 | 28.0 |
| Reading, PA........ | 12.6 | 7.4 | 7.3 | 50.9 | 373 638 | 411 442 | 10.1 | 0.5 | 11 060 | 8 098 | -710 | 154 356 | 9.0 | 2.59 | 12.0 | 24.5 |
| Redding, CA........ | 14.9 | 9.7 | 7.6 | 50.9 | 163 256 | 177 223 | 8.6 | 0.8 | 4 659 | 4 356 | 993 | 70 346 | 10.9 | 2.48 | 12.2 | 25.9 |
| Reno-Sparks, NV........ | 13.1 | 7.6 | 5.0 | 49.6 | 342 885 | 425 417 | 24.1 | 2.0 | 12 358 | 7 173 | 3 238 | 165 187 | 23.7 | 2.54 | 11.2 | 27.2 |
| Richmond, VA........ | 12.9 | 7.0 | 5.5 | 51.6 | 1 096 957 | 1 258 251 | 14.7 | 1.9 | 34 149 | 22 475 | 12 263 | 488 330 | 14.9 | 2.50 | 14.7 | 26.6 |
| Riverside-San Bernardino-Ontario, CA........ | 10.1 | 5.9 | 4.7 | 50.2 | 3 254 821 | 4 224 851 | 29.8 | 3.0 | 143 043 | 60 027 | 41 819 | 1 297 878 | 25.4 | 3.20 | 14.7 | 18.5 |
| Roanoke, VA........ | 14.6 | 8.9 | 7.7 | 51.7 | 288 309 | 308 707 | 7.1 | 0.5 | 7 501 | 7 368 | 1 147 | 128 454 | 7.6 | 2.34 | 12.5 | 29.6 |
| Rochester, MN........ | 11.8 | 7.1 | 6.4 | 50.9 | 163 618 | 186 011 | 13.7 | 1.5 | 6 020 | 2 812 | -514 | 73 362 | 17.4 | 2.49 | 8.5 | 26.5 |
| Rochester, NY........ | 13.2 | 7.5 | 6.9 | 51.4 | 1 037 831 | 1 054 323 | 1.6 | -0.0 | 25 911 | 20 266 | -2 790 | 420 554 | 5.9 | 2.41 | 13.2 | 29.2 |
| Rockford, IL........ | 12.5 | 7.5 | 6.4 | 51.0 | 320 204 | 349 431 | 9.1 | -1.0 | 9 831 | 6 678 | -6 531 | 134 006 | 9.3 | 2.57 | 13.5 | 26.4 |
| Rocky Mount, NC........ | 14.1 | 8.3 | 6.4 | 52.4 | 143 026 | 152 392 | 6.5 | -0.5 | 4 067 | 3 453 | -1 347 | 59 462 | 10.0 | 2.50 | 18.9 | 27.3 |
| Rome, GA........ | 12.3 | 7.8 | 6.6 | 51.5 | 90 565 | 96 317 | 6.4 | -0.1 | 2 772 | 2 259 | -604 | 35 930 | 5.6 | 2.58 | 14.8 | 26.0 |

1. No spouse present.

# Table C. Metropolitan Areas — Population, Vital Statistics, Medicare, and Crime

| Area name | Persons in group quarters, 2009 | Daytime population, 2007–2011 Number | Daytime population, 2007–2011 Employment/residence ratio | Births, 2011 Total | Births, 2011 Rate[1] | Deaths, 2011 Number | Deaths, 2011 Rate[1] | Persons under 65 with no health insurance 2010 Number | Persons under 65 with no health insurance 2010 Percent | Medicare, 2012 Enrolled in original Medicare | Medicare, 2012 Enrolled in Medicare Advantage | Medicare, 2012 Enrolled in a Medicare prescription drug plan | Serious crimes known to police,[2] 2011 Total Number | Serious crimes known to police,[2] 2011 Total Rate[3] |
|---|---|---|---|---|---|---|---|---|---|---|---|---|---|---|
| | 32 | 33 | 34 | 35 | 36 | 37 | 38 | 39 | 40 | 41 | 42 | 43 | 44 | 45 |
| Naples-Marco Island, FL...... | 4 546 | 327 765 | 1.06 | 3 371 | 10.3 | 2 742 | 8.4 | 68 849 | 29.5 | 75 607 | 11 864 | 35 265 | 7 105 | 2 180 |
| Nashville-Davidson—Murfreesboro—Franklin, TN | 38 454 | 1 595 941 | 1.04 | 21 555 | 13.3 | 11 688 | 7.2 | 226 446 | 16.3 | 226 629 | 78 790 | 73 408 | 63 804 | 3 977 |
| New Haven-Milford, CT ....... | 29 198 | 826 521 | 0.92 | 9 190 | 10.7 | 7 322 | 8.5 | 75 254 | 10.5 | 147 093 | 37 341 | 59 155 | 27 127 | 3 347 |
| New Orleans-Metairie-Kenner, LA | 19 379 | 1 174 767 | 1.07 | 15 558 | 13.1 | 9 928 | 8.3 | 216 372 | 21.4 | 187 025 | 88 958 | 51 808 | 45 764 | 3 883 |
| New York-Northern New Jersey-Long Island, NY-NJ-PA.......................... | 394 769 | 18 986 849 | 1.02 | 245 327 | 12.9 | 132 991 | 7.0 | 2 459 195 | 15.2 | 2 880 771 | 722 369 | 1 208 384 | 408 239 | 2 152 |
| Edison-New Brunswick, NJ Div............................ | 42 638 | 2 212 128 | 0.89 | 27 422 | 11.7 | 19 802 | 8.4 | 254 283 | 12.9 | 406 763 | 57 411 | 205 814 | 48 779 | 2 077 |
| Nassau-Suffolk, NY Div ...... | 51 072 | 2 653 906 | 0.88 | 31 266 | 11.0 | 21 773 | 7.7 | 280 004 | 11.7 | 488 780 | 100 084 | 167 614 | 50 192 | 1 765 |
| Newark-Union, NJ-PA Div...... | 46 231 | 2 141 059 | 1.00 | 25 038 | 11.6 | 15 353 | 7.1 | 284 546 | 15.4 | 319 017 | 48 940 | 157 600 | 53 006 | 2 460 |
| New York-White Plains-Wayne, NY-NJ Div...... | 254 828 | 11 979 756 | 1.09 | 161 601 | 13.8 | 76 063 | 6.5 | 1 640 362 | 16.4 | 1 666 211 | 515 934 | 677 356 | 256 262 | 2 205 |
| Niles-Benton Harbor, MI ....... | 3 527 | 156 218 | 0.99 | 1 901 | 12.1 | 1 588 | 10.1 | 20 054 | 15.5 | 32 144 | 6 467 | 16 769 | 3 673 | 2 380 |
| North Port-Bradenton-Sarasota, FL | 10 439 | 695 236 | 0.98 | 6 244 | 8.8 | 8 204 | 11.6 | 122 666 | 24.4 | 189 486 | 44 225 | 74 896 | 29 515 | 4 146 |
| Norwich-New London, CT..... | 12 782 | 276 925 | 1.03 | 2 735 | 10.0 | 2 286 | 8.4 | 21 416 | 9.6 | 47 859 | 7 226 | 21 829 | NA | NA |
| Ocala, FL........................ | 8 239 | 322 875 | 0.94 | 3 402 | 10.2 | 4 144 | 12.5 | 59 070 | 24.7 | 95 234 | 31 651 | 29 994 | 10 049 | 2 992 |
| Ocean City, NJ................ | 2 628 | 95 455 | 0.96 | 941 | 9.7 | 1 260 | 13.0 | 10 988 | 14.7 | 24 569 | 2 664 | 14 010 | 4 853 | 4 973 |
| Odessa, TX.................... | 2 175 | 133 797 | 0.97 | 2 677 | 19.1 | 1 154 | 8.2 | 35 639 | 29.5 | 17 409 | 2 240 | 8 799 | 5 189 | 3 706 |
| Ogden-Clearfield, UT........... | 5 802 | 496 855 | 0.83 | 10 055 | 18.1 | 2 867 | 5.2 | 69 961 | 14.1 | 62 500 | 21 053 | 13 638 | 15 250 | 2 734 |
| Oklahoma City, OK ........... | 31 897 | 1 242 497 | 1.01 | 18 778 | 14.7 | 9 874 | 7.7 | 224 347 | 20.7 | 188 334 | 36 252 | 77 201 | 61 078 | 4 823 |
| Olympia, WA .................. | 4 222 | 234 842 | 0.88 | 3 015 | 11.8 | 1 815 | 7.1 | 30 150 | 13.9 | 43 614 | 13 840 | 11 137 | 7 694 | 3 003 |
| Omaha-Council Bluffs, NE-IA.................................. | 17 599 | 860 082 | 1.01 | 13 219 | 15.1 | 6 036 | 6.9 | 93 010 | 12.3 | 122 903 | 24 695 | 56 277 | 32 672 | 3 748 |
| Orlando-Kissimmee-Sanford, FL.................... | 44 468 | 2 172 256 | 1.06 | 26 060 | 12.0 | 14 503 | 6.7 | 439 851 | 23.9 | 324 793 | 110 396 | 99 525 | 92 130 | 4 258 |
| Oshkosh-Neenah, WI............ | 8 239 | 175 043 | 1.11 | 1 911 | 11.4 | 1 364 | 8.1 | 13 679 | 10.0 | 27 364 | 13 406 | 7 547 | 3 516 | 2 096 |
| Owensboro, KY................ | 2 753 | 114 902 | 1.01 | 1 554 | 13.5 | 1 140 | 9.9 | 14 621 | 15.3 | 23 345 | 3 226 | 13 636 | 3 231 | 2 796 |
| Oxnard-Thousand Oaks-Ventura, CA............................ | 10 600 | 773 434 | 0.89 | 11 060 | 13.3 | 5 083 | 6.1 | 130 774 | 18.2 | 119 422 | 32 899 | 44 034 | 15 874 | 1 906 |
| Palm Bay-Melbourne-Titusville, FL........................... | 7 735 | 534 591 | 0.97 | 4 943 | 9.1 | 5 854 | 10.8 | 87 870 | 20.7 | 126 864 | 40 824 | 33 306 | 21 417 | 3 888 |
| Palm Coast, FL.................. | 684 | 84 343 | 0.71 | 854 | 8.8 | 953 | 9.8 | 16 774 | 23.3 | 27 612 | 9 159 | 8 073 | 2 375 | 2 448 |
| Panama City-Lynn Haven-Panama City Beach, FL | 3 817 | 170 160 | 1.03 | 2 209 | 13.0 | 1 610 | 9.5 | 31 413 | 22.2 | 31 841 | 3 674 | 12 870 | 8 339 | 4 872 |
| Parkersburg-Marietta-Vienna, WV-OH ............. | 3 450 | 163 616 | 1.02 | 1 712 | 10.6 | 1 823 | 11.2 | 20 640 | 15.7 | 36 435 | 6 084 | 20 118 | 3 091 | 1 934 |
| Pascagoula, MS................ | 1 854 | 153 136 | 0.89 | 2 081 | 12.8 | 1 456 | 8.9 | 29 025 | 20.7 | 27 632 | 4 642 | 12 163 | 5 623 | 3 453 |
| Pensacola-Ferry Pass-Brent, FL.................................. | 22 203 | 434 820 | 0.93 | 5 700 | 12.6 | 4 198 | 9.3 | 73 534 | 20.1 | 84 398 | 18 087 | 26 538 | 18 717 | 4 113 |
| Peoria, IL.......................... | 9 190 | 383 414 | 1.03 | 4 940 | 13.0 | 3 670 | 9.7 | 35 603 | 11.3 | 67 548 | 12 012 | 27 660 | 11 218 | 3 152 |
| Philadelphia-Camden-Wilmington, PA-NJ-DE-MD. | 167 826 | 5 909 237 | 0.99 | 74 382 | 12.4 | 51 613 | 8.6 | 602 828 | 12.0 | 978 093 | 257 101 | 409 446 | 197 515 | 3 302 |
| Camden, NJ Div............. | 24 851 | 1 158 918 | 0.85 | 14 477 | 11.6 | 10 278 | 8.2 | 131 633 | 12.3 | 205 916 | 36 991 | 102 602 | 37 901 | 3 020 |
| Philadelphia, PA Div........ | 123 013 | 4 050 824 | 1.03 | 51 261 | 12.7 | 35 646 | 8.8 | 405 492 | 12.0 | 660 274 | 213 099 | 250 295 | 132 866 | 3 310 |
| Wilmington, DE-MD-NJ Div. | 19 962 | 699 495 | 0.99 | 8 644 | 12.2 | 5 689 | 8.0 | 65 703 | 10.9 | 111 903 | 7 011 | 56 549 | 26 748 | 3 755 |
| Phoenix-Mesa-Glendale, AZ. | 79 422 | 4 141 336 | 1.00 | 59 738 | 14.0 | 26 891 | 6.3 | 693 519 | 19.2 | 591 457 | 246 060 | 156 738 | 170 047 | 4 002 |
| Pine Bluff, AR.................. | 9 027 | 100 424 | 1.00 | 1 213 | 12.3 | 1 071 | 10.8 | 14 195 | 18.2 | 18 418 | 3 189 | 9 191 | 5 763 | 5 810 |
| Pittsburgh, PA ................. | 62 679 | 2 373 185 | 1.01 | 23 690 | 10.0 | 26 950 | 11.4 | 200 675 | 10.6 | 489 049 | 300 879 | 84 246 | 52 145 | 2 218 |
| Pittsfield, MA .................. | 6 159 | 133 770 | 1.04 | 1 110 | 8.5 | 1 365 | 10.5 | 5 247 | 5.1 | 30 253 | 868 | 17 708 | 3 587 | 2 834 |
| Pocatello, ID................... | 1 839 | 88 544 | 0.98 | 1 550 | 16.9 | 667 | 7.3 | 14 811 | 18.8 | 13 352 | 4 057 | 5 807 | 2 825 | 3 082 |
| Portland-South Portland-Biddeford, ME........................ | 12 560 | 514 104 | 1.00 | 4 954 | 9.6 | 4 443 | 8.6 | 47 023 | 11.0 | 100 974 | 17 773 | 45 370 | 13 950 | 2 714 |
| Portland-Vancouver-Hillsboro, OR-WA.................. | 38 319 | 2 206 674 | 1.00 | 28 672 | 12.7 | 15 161 | 6.7 | 344 892 | 17.7 | 325 583 | 172 797 | 74 229 | 76 099 | 3 387 |
| Port St. Lucie, FL................. | 6 986 | 397 478 | 0.86 | 4 225 | 9.9 | 4 438 | 10.4 | 82 599 | 25.5 | 99 186 | 25 698 | 36 602 | 13 544 | 3 151 |
| Poughkeepsie-Newburgh-Middletown, NY.............. | 32 195 | 621 526 | 0.85 | 7 976 | 11.9 | 4 788 | 7.1 | 64 620 | 11.5 | 104 110 | 15 163 | 37 989 | 14 470 | 2 183 |
| Prescott, AZ................... | 3 525 | 207 260 | 0.96 | 1 885 | 8.9 | 2 309 | 10.9 | 31 553 | 20.0 | 61 531 | 14 132 | 22 010 | 5 283 | 2 468 |
| Providence-New Bedford-Fall River, RI-MA ......... | 58 531 | 1 534 605 | 0.91 | 17 019 | 10.6 | 14 079 | 8.8 | 145 207 | 10.9 | 296 890 | 81 457 | 121 707 | 47 111 | 2 939 |
| Provo-Orem, UT................ | 14 034 | 492 168 | 0.91 | 12 100 | 22.4 | 1 963 | 3.6 | 73 124 | 15.1 | 43 474 | 17 517 | 13 271 | 12 316 | 2 294 |
| Pueblo, CO ................... | 4 321 | 156 303 | 0.97 | 1 961 | 12.2 | 1 561 | 9.7 | 22 972 | 17.4 | 31 674 | 9 408 | 11 331 | 8 014 | 4 952 |
| Punta Gorda, FL ................. | 3 012 | 155 871 | 0.92 | 974 | 6.1 | 2 208 | 13.8 | 23 632 | 22.9 | 52 998 | 13 670 | 19 170 | 4 433 | 2 734 |
| Racine, WI .................... | 4 995 | 182 113 | 0.86 | 2 535 | 13.0 | 1 537 | 7.9 | 16 950 | 10.3 | 33 781 | 10 056 | 11 415 | 6 095 | 3 106 |
| Raleigh-Cary, NC................ | 24 394 | 1 087 486 | 0.97 | 15 559 | 13.4 | 5 951 | 5.1 | 165 539 | 16.4 | 138 849 | 24 064 | 54 793 | 32 304 | 2 828 |
| Rapid City, SD ................ | 3 372 | 124 899 | 1.00 | 1 852 | 14.4 | 860 | 6.7 | 15 590 | 14.5 | 23 441 | 3 714 | 10 107 | 4 260 | 3 330 |
| Reading, PA ................... | 12 023 | 388 020 | 0.89 | 4 987 | 12.1 | 3 538 | 8.6 | 42 425 | 12.4 | 73 643 | 24 976 | 29 274 | 10 176 | 2 465 |
| Redding, CA................... | 2 654 | 178 424 | 1.02 | 2 052 | 11.5 | 1 884 | 10.6 | 25 788 | 17.7 | 42 098 | 2 415 | 22 619 | 6 256 | 3 489 |
| Reno-Sparks, NV.............. | 5 277 | 422 349 | 1.00 | 5 473 | 12.7 | 3 122 | 7.3 | 91 271 | 24.6 | 67 780 | 19 184 | 20 434 | 11 927 | 2 780 |
| Richmond, VA .................. | 36 912 | 1 245 559 | 1.00 | 15 340 | 12.1 | 9 821 | 7.7 | 162 329 | 15.1 | 198 172 | 36 498 | 84 375 | 33 987 | 2 669 |
| Riverside-San Bernardino-Ontario, CA........................ | 75 883 | 3 951 038 | 0.86 | 61 923 | 14.4 | 26 097 | 6.1 | 860 020 | 23.0 | 531 029 | 267 802 | 135 026 | 135 648 | 3 173 |
| Roanoke, VA.................. | 7 928 | 318 878 | 1.08 | 3 370 | 10.9 | 3 201 | 10.4 | 39 342 | 15.5 | 65 599 | 12 263 | 31 169 | 8 770 | 2 807 |
| Rochester, MN................ | 3 165 | 192 352 | 1.08 | 2 625 | 14.0 | 1 191 | 6.3 | 13 893 | 8.7 | 29 294 | 9 387 | 10 371 | 3 583 | 1 946 |
| Rochester, NY................ | 39 346 | 1 063 947 | 1.02 | 11 493 | 10.9 | 8 843 | 8.4 | 90 761 | 10.4 | 194 401 | 115 871 | 37 660 | 30 474 | 2 877 |
| Rockford, IL................... | 4 995 | 345 329 | 0.98 | 4 441 | 12.7 | 2 894 | 8.3 | 45 345 | 15.2 | 60 568 | 11 611 | 26 980 | 13 608 | 4 050 |
| Rocky Mount, NC............. | 3 640 | 149 531 | 0.97 | 1 903 | 12.5 | 1 501 | 9.9 | 23 363 | 18.3 | 28 988 | 2 221 | 17 131 | 6 727 | 4 401 |
| Rome, GA .................... | 3 733 | 100 097 | 1.10 | 1 280 | 13.3 | 1 008 | 10.5 | 17 347 | 21.9 | 18 019 | 3 176 | 9 277 | 4 210 | 4 314 |

1. Per 1,000 estimated resident population.   2. Data for serious crimes have not been adjusted for underreporting; this may affect comparability between geographic areas and over time.   3. Per 100,000 population estimated by the FBI.

# Table C. Metropolitan Areas — Crime, Education, Money Income, and Poverty

| Area name | Serious crimes known to police, 2011 (cont.)[1] Rate[2] Violent | Property | School enrollment and attainment, 2007–2011 Enrollment[3] Total | Percent private | Attainment[4] (percent) High school graduate or less | Bachelor's degree or more | Local government expenditures,[5] 2009–2010 Total current expenditures (mil dol) | Current expenditures per student (dollars) | Per capita income[6] (dollars) | Median household income (dollars) | Percent of households with income of less than $25,000 | Percent of households with income of $100,000 or more | Percent of households with income of $200,000 or more | Percent below poverty level All persons | Related Children under 18 years | Related Children under 5 |
|---|---|---|---|---|---|---|---|---|---|---|---|---|---|---|---|---|
| | 46 | 47 | 48 | 49 | 50 | 51 | 52 | 53 | 54 | 55 | 56 | 57 | 58 | 59 | 60 | 61 |
| Naples-Marco Island, FL....... | 315 | 1 865 | 62 128 | 15.1 | 42.3 | 31.6 | 431.1 | 10 092 | 37 335 | 56 876 | 18.2 | 25.6 | 8.2 | 13.5 | 22.0 | 27.0 |
| Nashville-Davidson—Mur-freesboro—Franklin, TN | 652 | 3 325 | 410 535 | 22.3 | 42.7 | 30.1 | 1 979.4 | 8 201 | 28 182 | 52 347 | 21.6 | 20.1 | 4.2 | 13.6 | 18.9 | 23.9 |
| New Haven-Milford, CT ....... | 384 | 2 964 | 229 599 | 24.5 | 42.7 | 32.3 | 1 926.2 | 15 047 | 32 509 | 62 497 | 20.4 | 28.7 | 5.9 | 11.4 | 16.0 | 18.6 |
| New Orleans-Metairie-Kenner, LA ......................... | 491 | 3 393 | 293 954 | 29.9 | 46.0 | 26.2 | 1 767.2 | 12 196 | 26 587 | 47 566 | 26.9 | 19.3 | 3.9 | 16.8 | 24.2 | 28.4 |
| New York-Northern New Jersey-Long Island, NY-NJ-PA................................. | 406 | 1 746 | 4 884 378 | 24.9 | 42.2 | 35.9 | 50 759.9 | 18 609 | 35 450 | 65 288 | 20.5 | 32.3 | 9.1 | 13.1 | 17.9 | 19.6 |
| Edison-New Brunswick, NJ Div.................................. | 151 | 1 926 | 604 102 | 22.2 | 39.3 | 37.1 | 5 651.3 | 15 706 | 37 301 | 77 143 | 14.6 | 37.6 | 9.4 | 7.2 | 9.7 | 12.5 |
| Nassau-Suffolk, NY Div ..... | 154 | 1 610 | 754 895 | 21.0 | 38.1 | 36.6 | 9 617.6 | 20 774 | 39 291 | 91 139 | 11.2 | 45.3 | 12.2 | 5.5 | 6.4 | 7.6 |
| Newark-Union, NJ-PA Div... | 388 | 2 072 | 573 019 | 19.8 | 41.0 | 36.5 | 6 248.5 | 17 639 | 37 743 | 72 850 | 16.9 | 36.2 | 10.9 | 9.6 | 13.0 | 15.5 |
| New York-White Plains-Wayne, NY-NJ Div...... | 523 | 1 682 | 2 952 362 | 27.4 | 44.0 | 35.5 | 29 242.5 | 18 857 | 33 707 | 56 570 | 24.4 | 27.7 | 8.1 | 16.7 | 23.7 | 24.5 |
| Niles-Benton Harbor, MI ....... | 369 | 2 010 | 40 082 | 20.0 | 44.5 | 23.7 | 278.2 | 10 457 | 24 490 | 42 488 | 29.6 | 14.6 | 2.5 | 16.7 | 25.5 | 31.6 |
| North Port-Bradenton-Sarasota, FL................... | 494 | 3 652 | 132 605 | 16.1 | 42.0 | 27.9 | 817.0 | 9 701 | 30 718 | 48 745 | 23.1 | 18.5 | 4.0 | 12.2 | 19.9 | 25.0 |
| Norwich-New London, CT..... | NA | NA | 67 666 | 17.5 | 41.2 | 30.9 | 580.4 | 14 411 | 33 478 | 67 010 | 15.4 | 29.4 | 5.2 | 7.7 | 10.2 | 13.1 |
| Ocala, FL.............................. | 497 | 2 496 | 64 937 | 16.8 | 52.6 | 16.8 | 362.4 | 8 627 | 22 328 | 40 103 | 28.4 | 10.3 | 1.9 | 16.5 | 26.6 | 34.9 |
| Ocean City, NJ...................... | 317 | 4 656 | 19 181 | 16.8 | 47.3 | 27.1 | 252.7 | 18 802 | 33 796 | 55 315 | 19.4 | 23.8 | 4.0 | 9.6 | 13.2 | 16.6 |
| Odessa, TX........................... | 679 | 3 027 | 37 244 | 8.0 | 56.7 | 13.3 | 217.0 | 7 773 | 24 010 | 50 056 | 25.6 | 17.2 | 3.2 | 16.2 | 21.9 | 24.1 |
| Ogden-Clearfield, UT ........... | 150 | 2 584 | 169 838 | 9.1 | 33.3 | 28.8 | 719.1 | 5 987 | 24 807 | 62 340 | 14.7 | 23.1 | 3.2 | 9.1 | 10.9 | 12.1 |
| Oklahoma City, OK .............. | 530 | 4 293 | 340 030 | 12.3 | 40.5 | 27.6 | 1 542.6 | 7 515 | 26 056 | 48 498 | 24.6 | 18.0 | 3.2 | 14.9 | 20.2 | 24.2 |
| Olympia, WA......................... | 229 | 2 774 | 62 524 | 12.2 | 30.7 | 32.5 | 375.5 | 9 274 | 30 331 | 63 129 | 17.2 | 24.4 | 3.0 | 10.5 | 12.6 | 19.1 |
| Omaha-Council Bluffs, NE-IA............................................ | 385 | 3 363 | 242 451 | 20.4 | 35.4 | 32.2 | 1 456.4 | 10 121 | 28 458 | 56 346 | 20.0 | 21.8 | 3.6 | 11.2 | 15.0 | 18.3 |
| Orlando-Kissimmee-Sanford, FL....................... | 596 | 3 663 | 577 747 | 18.3 | 41.4 | 27.8 | 2 682.6 | 8 107 | 25 725 | 50 433 | 21.8 | 18.6 | 3.5 | 13.3 | 17.8 | 20.6 |
| Oshkosh-Neenah, WI........... | 191 | 1 905 | 44 595 | 12.0 | 45.3 | 24.3 | 242.3 | 10 477 | 26 880 | 51 596 | 21.7 | 16.6 | 2.6 | 11.1 | 13.1 | 18.6 |
| Owensboro, KY..................... | 145 | 2 652 | 28 799 | 15.9 | 54.0 | 17.3 | 173.6 | 9 079 | 22 319 | 44 518 | 28.0 | 12.3 | 1.5 | 14.4 | 21.3 | 23.5 |
| Oxnard-Thousand Oaks-Ventura, CA........................ | 205 | 1 701 | 231 620 | 15.1 | 36.9 | 31.0 | 1 205.4 | 8 523 | 32 740 | 76 728 | 14.2 | 37.2 | 8.8 | 9.9 | 13.3 | 15.4 |
| Palm Bay-Melbourne-Titusville, FL | 592 | 3 296 | 124 912 | 19.6 | 39.5 | 26.4 | 578.8 | 7 993 | 27 927 | 50 068 | 22.5 | 18.6 | 3.2 | 11.2 | 15.9 | 20.0 |
| Palm Coast, FL..................... | 321 | 2 128 | 19 259 | 15.8 | 43.8 | 22.0 | 103.1 | 7 846 | 24 455 | 48 708 | 22.8 | 13.9 | 2.3 | 13.3 | 21.2 | 30.6 |
| Panama City-Lynn Haven-Panama City Beach, FL | 535 | 4 338 | 38 882 | 11.4 | 44.7 | 21.0 | 208.8 | 8 062 | 25 370 | 48 225 | 22.6 | 15.5 | 2.0 | 12.4 | 17.3 | 17.5 |
| Parkersburg-Marietta-Vienna, WV-OH ............. | 262 | 1 673 | 37 863 | 14.1 | 52.0 | 16.6 | 263.2 | 10 768 | 23 037 | 42 395 | 29.7 | 12.8 | 1.8 | 16.0 | 22.8 | 30.8 |
| Pascagoula, MS.................... | 298 | 3 154 | 41 397 | 10.3 | 49.4 | 17.5 | 249.1 | 8 662 | 23 128 | 48 968 | 24.8 | 15.7 | 2.2 | 14.9 | 20.7 | 25.4 |
| Pensacola-Ferry Pass-Brent, FL.............................. | 527 | 3 586 | 114 856 | 19.1 | 41.5 | 24.1 | 539.0 | 8 143 | 24 689 | 48 075 | 24.1 | 16.3 | 2.7 | 14.8 | 22.2 | 27.5 |
| Peoria, IL.............................. | 399 | 2 753 | 97 985 | 19.9 | 41.7 | 25.5 | 603.6 | 10 295 | 28 213 | 53 219 | 21.5 | 19.7 | 3.3 | 11.8 | 17.0 | 21.3 |
| Philadelphia-Camden-Wilmington, PA-NJ-DE-MD. | 548 | 2 754 | 1 610 503 | 28.0 | 43.2 | 32.6 | 12 550.0 | 14 580 | 32 046 | 61 496 | 20.6 | 28.4 | 6.2 | 12.2 | 16.3 | 18.5 |
| Camden, NJ Div................. | 351 | 2 669 | 335 705 | 18.4 | 43.4 | 30.1 | 3 386.2 | 16 282 | 32 720 | 70 221 | 15.8 | 32.1 | 5.9 | 8.5 | 11.7 | 14.3 |
| Philadelphia, PA Div .......... | 609 | 2 701 | 1 082 464 | 32.0 | 43.1 | 33.9 | 7 857.0 | 14 259 | 31 985 | 58 308 | 22.5 | 27.2 | 6.5 | 13.7 | 18.2 | 20.0 |
| Wilmington, DE-MD-NJ Div. | 551 | 3 204 | 192 334 | 22.5 | 43.1 | 29.6 | 1 306.7 | 12 840 | 31 192 | 64 003 | 17.6 | 28.7 | 5.0 | 10.5 | 14.0 | 17.5 |
| Phoenix-Mesa-Glendale, AZ. | 373 | 3 629 | 1 117 619 | 11.5 | 38.3 | 28.1 | 5 718.5 | 7 770 | 27 097 | 54 732 | 20.4 | 22.0 | 4.2 | 14.8 | 20.7 | 23.9 |
| Pine Bluff, AR ...................... | 774 | 5 036 | 27 055 | 6.5 | 58.1 | 15.5 | 151.9 | 9 399 | 18 548 | 37 158 | 35.2 | 10.8 | 1.0 | 22.5 | 33.4 | 40.1 |
| Pittsburgh, PA ..................... | 301 | 1 917 | 557 599 | 21.5 | 45.8 | 28.7 | 4 067.3 | 12 715 | 28 345 | 49 246 | 25.5 | 18.5 | 3.4 | 11.9 | 16.3 | 20.7 |
| Pittsfield, MA....................... | 415 | 2 419 | 30 545 | 20.3 | 42.6 | 30.2 | 255.6 | 14 267 | 29 387 | 48 705 | 26.0 | 17.8 | 3.3 | 11.8 | 15.6 | 26.4 |
| Pocatello, ID........................ | 211 | 2 872 | 27 000 | 8.2 | 37.0 | 26.1 | 107.7 | 6 877 | 21 185 | 45 080 | 26.1 | 12.5 | 1.3 | 14.5 | 18.3 | 24.1 |
| Portland-South Portland-Biddeford, ME ................... | 131 | 2 583 | 122 352 | 19.4 | 36.7 | 34.7 | 901.0 | 12 369 | 30 487 | 56 961 | 20.2 | 21.6 | 3.6 | 9.9 | 12.5 | 15.3 |
| Portland-Vancouver-Hillsboro, OR-WA.................. | 259 | 3 128 | 563 761 | 17.5 | 32.4 | 33.9 | 3 168.6 | 9 404 | 29 736 | 57 307 | 19.8 | 23.1 | 4.2 | 12.6 | 16.2 | 18.3 |
| Port St. Lucie, FL................. | 345 | 2 806 | 92 667 | 14.6 | 47.0 | 22.3 | 490.4 | 8 600 | 27 552 | 47 306 | 23.5 | 17.8 | 3.7 | 13.7 | 21.6 | 24.4 |
| Poughkeepsie-Newburgh-Middletown, NY.............. | 241 | 1 942 | 193 864 | 24.8 | 41.4 | 30.2 | 1 907.5 | 17 351 | 30 978 | 70 694 | 16.2 | 32.8 | 5.7 | 10.5 | 15.0 | 20.9 |
| Prescott, AZ......................... | 349 | 2 119 | 42 907 | 13.5 | 36.8 | 24.2 | 187.3 | 7 306 | 26 028 | 44 084 | 26.2 | 13.8 | 2.3 | 14.9 | 21.7 | 28.4 |
| Providence-New Bedford-Fall River, RI-MA............. | 354 | 2 585 | 420 804 | 23.8 | 45.5 | 28.7 | 2 998.9 | 13 312 | 29 342 | 55 924 | 23.5 | 24.2 | 4.1 | 12.3 | 16.7 | 20.3 |
| Provo-Orem, UT ................... | 75 | 2 218 | 202 903 | 26.8 | 24.8 | 35.4 | 676.9 | 5 670 | 20 746 | 59 104 | 17.0 | 21.6 | 3.3 | 12.9 | 10.5 | 12.1 |
| Pueblo, CO .......................... | 517 | 4 435 | 41 911 | 10.5 | 43.2 | 21.5 | 225.7 | 8 281 | 22 056 | 41 273 | 30.9 | 12.1 | 1.8 | 17.8 | 25.1 | 32.8 |
| Punta Gorda, FL .................. | 244 | 2 490 | 25 935 | 16.0 | 47.0 | 20.9 | 152.4 | 8 995 | 26 902 | 45 112 | 24.6 | 12.4 | 1.9 | 11.4 | 19.1 | 24.1 |
| Racine, WI............................ | 231 | 2 874 | 50 372 | 18.2 | 46.7 | 22.5 | 347.1 | 11 155 | 26 953 | 54 356 | 21.0 | 19.9 | 3.0 | 11.7 | 17.5 | 19.3 |
| Raleigh-Cary, NC................. | 243 | 2 585 | 317 502 | 17.5 | 30.4 | 41.9 | 1 455.5 | 7 754 | 30 983 | 61 407 | 17.7 | 27.3 | 5.3 | 11.2 | 14.4 | 17.3 |
| Rapid City, SD ..................... | 410 | 2 921 | 32 107 | 12.4 | 37.5 | 26.5 | 161.5 | 8 291 | 25 982 | 48 155 | 21.8 | 14.8 | 2.9 | 12.9 | 17.9 | 26.6 |
| Reading, PA ......................... | 306 | 2 160 | 106 675 | 16.4 | 55.0 | 22.1 | 873.9 | 12 450 | 26 332 | 54 823 | 20.7 | 20.1 | 2.8 | 13.1 | 19.4 | 24.0 |
| Redding, CA......................... | 726 | 2 763 | 44 667 | 16.0 | 38.8 | 19.7 | 274.2 | 9 882 | 23 691 | 44 058 | 28.2 | 14.8 | 2.7 | 17.2 | 22.4 | 28.5 |
| Reno-Sparks, NV.................. | 377 | 2 403 | 110 447 | 9.9 | 38.5 | 26.9 | 562.4 | 8 615 | 30 021 | 55 860 | 20.1 | 22.8 | 4.1 | 12.9 | 17.2 | 21.8 |
| Richmond, VA....................... | 232 | 2 437 | 323 506 | 15.6 | 41.7 | 31.2 | 1 954.9 | 9 676 | 30 321 | 58 889 | 18.6 | 24.4 | 4.7 | 11.4 | 15.2 | 18.3 |
| Riverside-San Bernardino-Ontario, CA......................... | 355 | 2 818 | 1 264 539 | 11.4 | 47.5 | 19.6 | 7 022.7 | 8 349 | 23 264 | 57 096 | 20.3 | 23.8 | 3.8 | 15.1 | 20.4 | 23.5 |
| Roanoke, VA......................... | 272 | 2 536 | 71 758 | 17.6 | 45.1 | 25.2 | 439.9 | 9 766 | 27 048 | 49 540 | 23.1 | 16.6 | 2.7 | 12.2 | 17.7 | 22.1 |
| Rochester, MN...................... | 158 | 1 789 | 47 150 | 16.0 | 32.3 | 35.9 | 275.1 | 8 901 | 32 428 | 64 453 | 16.1 | 27.0 | 4.8 | 7.9 | 9.1 | 9.8 |
| Rochester, NY....................... | 290 | 2 588 | 286 372 | 22.8 | 39.1 | 31.9 | 2 585.2 | 15 891 | 27 096 | 52 777 | 22.9 | 19.7 | 2.9 | 13.4 | 18.4 | 21.6 |
| Rockford, IL.......................... | 741 | 3 309 | 90 955 | 19.6 | 49.5 | 21.0 | 644.3 | 10 970 | 24 819 | 49 724 | 25.0 | 16.9 | 3.0 | 15.8 | 24.0 | 31.6 |
| Rocky Mount, NC.................. | 501 | 3 900 | 39 274 | 11.0 | 54.9 | 15.9 | 219.9 | 8 354 | 21 450 | 40 667 | 32.2 | 12.4 | 1.7 | 18.4 | 27.7 | 37.4 |
| Rome, GA............................. | 498 | 3 816 | 25 556 | 22.1 | 54.9 | 18.1 | 169.5 | 10 511 | 21 213 | 43 129 | 30.8 | 13.4 | 2.4 | 18.9 | 25.6 | 29.0 |

1. Data for serious crimes have not been adjusted for underreporting; this may affect comparability between geographic areas and over time.  2. Per 100,000 population estimated by the FBI.  3. All persons 3 years old and over enrolled in nursery school through college.  4. Persons 25 years old and over.  5. Elementary and secondary education expenditures.  6. Based on resident population estimated as of July 1, 2009.

# Table C. Metropolitan Areas — **Personal Income**

| Area name | Personal income, 2011 | | | | | | | | | | | | |
|---|---|---|---|---|---|---|---|---|---|---|---|---|---|
| | | Per capita[1] | | | | | | Transfer payments | | | | | |
| | | | | | | | | | | Government payments to individuals | | | |
| | Total (mil dol) | Percent change, 2010–2011 | Dollars | Rank | Wages and salaries[2] (mil dol) | Proprietors' income (mil dol) | Dividends, interest, and rent (mil dol) | Total (mil dol) | Total (mil dol) | Social Security (mil dol) | Medical payments (mil dol) | Income mainte-nance (mil dol) | Unemploy-ment insurance (mil dol) |
| | 62 | 63 | 64 | 65 | 66 | 67 | 68 | 69 | 70 | 71 | 72 | 73 | 74 |
| Naples-Marco Island, FL | 19 447 | 5.1 | 59 264 | 6 | 6 457 | 1 182 | 10 308 | 2 550 | 2 464 | 1 153 | 925 | 203 | 60 |
| Nashville-Davidson—Murfreesboro—Franklin, TN | 68 129 | 5.3 | 42 129 | 76 | 44 245 | 11 678 | 8 210 | 10 416 | 10 058 | 3 430 | 4 223 | 1 307 | 392 |
| New Haven-Milford, CT | 42 606 | 4.8 | 49 478 | 18 | 23 506 | 3 469 | 7 064 | 7 650 | 7 459 | 2 204 | 3 628 | 743 | 522 |
| New Orleans-Metairie-Kenner, LA | 51 935 | 4.0 | 43 603 | 54 | 32 915 | 5 672 | 8 734 | 8 836 | 8 491 | 2 599 | 3 903 | 1 258 | 170 |
| New York-Northern New Jersey-Long Island, NY-NJ-PA | 1 079 532 | 4.5 | 56 770 | 8 | 706 377 | 121 200 | 173 428 | 173 563 | 169 356 | 41 988 | 89 329 | 20 246 | 9 370 |
| Edison-New Brunswick, NJ Div | 124 200 | 4.0 | 52 862 | X | 69 658 | 9 747 | 19 918 | 18 003 | 17 483 | 6 513 | 7 217 | 1 098 | 1 555 |
| Nassau-Suffolk, NY Div | 169 583 | 3.5 | 59 644 | X | 83 628 | 14 309 | 32 593 | 23 102 | 22 473 | 8 031 | 10 517 | 1 596 | 1 003 |
| Newark-Union, NJ-PA Div | 123 143 | 4.1 | 57 196 | X | 75 078 | 12 313 | 19 521 | 16 748 | 16 272 | 4 966 | 7 132 | 1 751 | 1 478 |
| New York-White Plains-Wayne, NY-NJ Div | 662 607 | 5.0 | 56 778 | X | 478 014 | 84 832 | 101 396 | 115 710 | 113 128 | 22 478 | 64 463 | 15 801 | 5 334 |
| Niles-Benton Harbor, MI | 5 623 | 3.3 | 35 830 | 198 | 3 239 | 372 | 856 | 1 435 | 1 400 | 495 | 590 | 190 | 58 |
| North Port-Bradenton-Sarasota, FL | 33 859 | 4.4 | 47 732 | 26 | 12 437 | 2 139 | 12 751 | 6 554 | 6 387 | 2 819 | 2 618 | 464 | 133 |
| Norwich-New London, CT | 12 978 | 3.6 | 47 452 | 28 | 8 816 | 782 | 2 588 | 2 150 | 2 091 | 713 | 935 | 169 | 155 |
| Ocala, FL | 10 877 | 4.3 | 32 709 | 289 | 4 185 | 395 | 2 602 | 3 300 | 3 226 | 1 370 | 1 230 | 331 | 71 |
| Ocean City, NJ | 4 704 | 2.9 | 48 694 | 23 | 1 893 | 371 | 1 073 | 1 128 | 1 107 | 385 | 491 | 74 | 107 |
| Odessa, TX | 5 378 | 14.8 | 38 385 | 149 | 4 014 | 439 | 547 | 922 | 891 | 244 | 433 | 139 | 26 |
| Ogden-Clearfield, UT | 18 976 | 5.8 | 34 134 | 254 | 10 707 | 1 197 | 2 652 | 2 553 | 2 431 | 800 | 856 | 323 | 111 |
| Oklahoma City, OK | 51 124 | 7.6 | 40 002 | 108 | 33 535 | 6 282 | 7 502 | 8 293 | 8 012 | 2 692 | 3 220 | 1 019 | 189 |
| Olympia, WA | 10 585 | 4.8 | 41 251 | 85 | 5 554 | 598 | 1 643 | 1 940 | 1 884 | 649 | 631 | 193 | 120 |
| Omaha-Council Bluffs, NE-IA | 39 005 | 5.5 | 44 470 | 45 | 26 106 | 4 124 | 6 470 | 5 622 | 5 429 | 1 776 | 2 325 | 589 | 154 |
| Orlando-Kissimmee-Sanford, FL | 77 159 | 4.8 | 35 535 | 204 | 53 447 | 5 166 | 12 365 | 14 921 | 14 440 | 4 592 | 5 988 | 2 035 | 547 |
| Oshkosh-Neenah, WI | 6 447 | 4.0 | 38 444 | 147 | 5 296 | 352 | 1 058 | 1 047 | 1 010 | 422 | 394 | 78 | 55 |
| Owensboro, KY | 3 999 | 6.0 | 34 677 | 235 | 2 398 | 324 | 587 | 984 | 959 | 341 | 390 | 105 | 34 |
| Oxnard-Thousand Oaks-Ventura, CA | 38 141 | 4.5 | 45 855 | 35 | 20 450 | 2 641 | 6 824 | 5 055 | 4 872 | 1 639 | 1 910 | 486 | 386 |
| Palm Bay-Melbourne-Titusville, FL | 20 671 | 3.6 | 38 028 | 155 | 11 580 | 944 | 4 287 | 4 801 | 4 681 | 1 866 | 1 889 | 382 | 147 |
| Palm Coast, FL | 3 230 | 6.5 | 33 170 | 279 | 802 | 22 | 935 | 871 | 849 | 419 | 288 | 69 | 21 |
| Panama City-Lynn Haven-Panama City Beach, FL | 6 296 | 3.2 | 37 068 | 173 | 3 887 | 299 | 1 202 | 1 441 | 1 371 | 436 | 579 | 160 | 43 |
| Parkersburg-Marietta-Vienna, WV-OH | 5 304 | 4.8 | 32 694 | 291 | 3 317 | 295 | 702 | 1 518 | 1 482 | 532 | 628 | 159 | 42 |
| Pascagoula, MS | 5 584 | 2.3 | 34 304 | 249 | 3 429 | 237 | 785 | 1 237 | 1 192 | 422 | 532 | 138 | 29 |
| Pensacola-Ferry Pass-Brent, FL | 16 352 | 5.3 | 36 079 | 194 | 9 393 | 572 | 2 741 | 3 664 | 3 531 | 1 159 | 1 446 | 419 | 82 |
| Peoria, IL | 16 580 | 8.6 | 43 684 | 53 | 11 554 | 997 | 2 894 | 2 654 | 2 570 | 1 029 | 943 | 299 | 152 |
| Philadelphia-Camden-Wilmington, PA-NJ-DE-MD | 291 970 | 4.4 | 48 723 | 22 | 186 923 | 26 146 | 43 324 | 51 408 | 50 083 | 14 856 | 23 669 | 5 428 | 3 403 |
| Camden, NJ Div | 56 051 | 3.5 | 44 772 | X | 31 040 | 3 650 | 7 332 | 10 288 | 10 012 | 3 216 | 4 224 | 933 | 978 |
| Philadelphia, PA Div | 204 090 | 4.3 | 50 631 | X | 132 808 | 20 220 | 31 412 | 35 699 | 34 807 | 9 888 | 17 009 | 3 995 | 2 175 |
| Wilmington, DE-MD-NJ Div | 31 829 | 6.4 | 44 857 | X | 23 075 | 2 275 | 4 580 | 5 421 | 5 264 | 1 752 | 2 437 | 500 | 250 |
| Phoenix-Mesa-Glendale, AZ | 157 026 | 5.3 | 36 833 | 180 | 102 929 | 13 742 | 23 476 | 28 496 | 27 554 | 8 895 | 11 221 | 2 903 | 806 |
| Pine Bluff, AR | 3 053 | 2.3 | 30 866 | 333 | 1 887 | 159 | 373 | 869 | 847 | 244 | 324 | 139 | 29 |
| Pittsburgh, PA | 106 146 | 5.6 | 44 982 | 40 | 67 975 | 9 468 | 15 100 | 22 220 | 21 697 | 7 377 | 10 134 | 1 744 | 1 163 |
| Pittsfield, MA | 5 803 | 4.4 | 44 483 | 44 | 3 142 | 372 | 1 227 | 1 407 | 1 378 | 425 | 681 | 149 | 77 |
| Pocatello, ID | 2 652 | 4.4 | 28 998 | 353 | 1 641 | 179 | 363 | 633 | 612 | 181 | 218 | 83 | 24 |
| Portland-South Portland-Biddeford, ME | 22 675 | 5.1 | 43 960 | 50 | 14 675 | 1 722 | 3 591 | 4 000 | 3 886 | 1 373 | 1 769 | 362 | 125 |
| Portland-Vancouver-Hillsboro, OR-WA | 93 449 | 6.3 | 41 302 | 82 | 63 844 | 6 744 | 15 868 | 14 946 | 14 445 | 4 788 | 5 303 | 1 744 | 1 097 |
| Port St. Lucie, FL | 16 414 | 4.7 | 38 362 | 150 | 6 158 | 708 | 5 872 | 3 778 | 3 684 | 1 483 | 1 543 | 337 | 106 |
| Poughkeepsie-Newburgh-Middletown, NY | 28 585 | 4.3 | 42 482 | 70 | 14 711 | 1 425 | 4 355 | 5 012 | 4 864 | 1 658 | 2 185 | 471 | 237 |
| Prescott, AZ | 6 248 | 3.9 | 29 490 | 348 | 2 438 | 316 | 1 684 | 1 832 | 1 785 | 890 | 586 | 129 | 42 |
| Providence-New Bedford-Fall River, RI-MA | 69 116 | 4.4 | 43 192 | 58 | 39 659 | 4 304 | 10 194 | 14 758 | 14 404 | 4 114 | 6 706 | 1 705 | 1 034 |
| Provo-Orem, UT | 13 975 | 6.6 | 25 841 | 363 | 8 882 | 1 482 | 1 807 | 2 166 | 2 046 | 639 | 753 | 305 | 83 |
| Pueblo, CO | 5 099 | 5.5 | 31 760 | 307 | 2 872 | 305 | 753 | 1 414 | 1 378 | 376 | 597 | 182 | 64 |
| Punta Gorda, FL | 5 644 | 4.7 | 35 161 | 220 | 1 866 | 250 | 1 851 | 1 725 | 1 687 | 785 | 683 | 97 | 30 |
| Racine, WI | 7 508 | 3.7 | 38 425 | 148 | 4 247 | 319 | 1 222 | 1 399 | 1 356 | 535 | 533 | 152 | 84 |
| Raleigh-Cary, NC | 47 275 | 6.1 | 40 631 | 93 | 31 081 | 3 206 | 6 549 | 6 207 | 5 950 | 2 073 | 2 346 | 682 | 452 |
| Rapid City, SD | 5 299 | 7.2 | 41 286 | 83 | 3 115 | 438 | 1 252 | 901 | 874 | 322 | 325 | 94 | 10 |
| Reading, PA | 15 552 | 4.5 | 37 675 | 160 | 9 259 | 990 | 2 310 | 3 244 | 3 152 | 1 123 | 1 321 | 328 | 205 |
| Redding, CA | 6 305 | 3.3 | 35 466 | 207 | 3 042 | 532 | 1 169 | 1 890 | 1 851 | 572 | 808 | 206 | 107 |
| Reno-Sparks, NV | 17 922 | 4.4 | 41 718 | 80 | 10 549 | 1 372 | 4 562 | 2 674 | 2 579 | 954 | 933 | 260 | 232 |
| Richmond, VA | 54 641 | 5.8 | 43 046 | 63 | 38 274 | 3 575 | 8 718 | 8 449 | 8 169 | 2 991 | 3 340 | 1 004 | 216 |
| Riverside-San Bernardino-Ontario, CA | 128 982 | 4.4 | 29 961 | 342 | 65 492 | 8 632 | 18 189 | 27 395 | 26 447 | 7 199 | 10 402 | 4 272 | 2 088 |
| Roanoke, VA | 12 081 | 4.9 | 39 115 | 128 | 8 120 | 692 | 2 201 | 2 492 | 2 424 | 911 | 924 | 248 | 50 |
| Rochester, MN | 8 288 | 1.0 | 44 174 | 49 | 6 304 | 540 | 1 305 | 1 238 | 1 196 | 424 | 542 | 103 | 54 |
| Rochester, NY | 43 987 | 4.3 | 41 683 | 81 | 27 669 | 3 537 | 7 325 | 9 258 | 9 024 | 3 018 | 4 024 | 1 097 | 389 |
| Rockford, IL | 11 914 | 3.6 | 34 201 | 252 | 7 817 | 646 | 1 912 | 2 434 | 2 357 | 931 | 800 | 334 | 183 |
| Rocky Mount, NC | 4 775 | 3.2 | 31 380 | 319 | 2 821 | 292 | 662 | 1 378 | 1 345 | 400 | 558 | 214 | 80 |
| Rome, GA | 3 183 | 3.6 | 33 159 | 280 | 1 897 | 201 | 497 | 806 | 785 | 266 | 303 | 109 | 28 |

1. Based on the resident population estimated as of July 1 of the year shown.   2. Includes other labor income.

## Table C. Metropolitan Areas — Earnings, Social Security, and Housing

| Area name | Earnings, 2011 | | | | | | | | | Social Security beneficiaries, December 2011 | | Housing units, 2010 | | |
| | | | Percent by selected industries | | | | | | | | | | | |
| | | | Goods-related[1] | | Service-related and health | | | | | | | | | |
| | Total (mil dol) | Farm | Total | Manu-facturing | Infor-mation, profes-sional, and technical services | Retail trade | Finance, insur-ance, and real estate | Health care and social services | Govern-ment | Number | Rate[2] | Supple-mental Security Income recipients, December 2011 | Total | Percent change, 2000–2010 |
| | 75 | 76 | 77 | 78 | 79 | 80 | 81 | 82 | 83 | 84 | 85 | 86 | 87 | 88 |
| Naples-Marco Island, FL...... | 7 639 | 1.9 | 11.3 | 2.5 | 8.2 | 9.3 | 11.5 | 15.3 | 11.6 | 77 900 | 237 | 3 314 | 197 298 | 36.5 |
| Nashville-Davidson—Mur-freesboro—Franklin, TN | 55 923 | 0.0 | 13.6 | 7.9 | 11.5 | 6.8 | 8.6 | 19.9 | 11.1 | 251 455 | 155 | 29 129 | 667 655 | 22.9 |
| New Haven-Milford, CT ........ | 26 975 | 0.1 | 16.4 | 11.0 | 10.6 | 6.1 | 7.5 | 16.2 | 14.8 | 155 530 | 181 | 18 536 | 362 004 | 6.2 |
| New Orleans-Metairie-Ken-ner, LA .......... | 38 587 | 0.1 | 19.3 | 8.2 | 11.1 | 5.8 | 6.2 | 9.4 | 16.6 | 202 790 | 170 | 42 805 | 538 239 | -1.9 |
| New York-Northern New Jer-sey-Long Island, NY-NJ-PA... | 827 577 | 0.0 | 8.4 | 4.3 | 18.3 | 5.0 | 21.0 | 10.4 | 12.7 | 2 952 500 | 155 | 611 681 | 7 527 752 | 6.2 |
| Edison-New Brunswick, NJ Div.................. | 79 404 | 0.1 | 13.8 | 8.4 | 18.3 | 6.9 | 8.6 | 10.8 | 13.7 | 433 065 | 184 | 29 471 | 954 389 | 9.0 |
| Nassau-Suffolk, NY Div ...... | 97 936 | 0.1 | 12.1 | 6.0 | 13.6 | 7.2 | 10.6 | 15.2 | 18.0 | 522 740 | 184 | 40 952 | 1 038 331 | 5.9 |
| Newark-Union, NJ-PA Div... | 87 390 | 0.0 | 14.8 | 10.2 | 16.5 | 5.7 | 10.8 | 10.1 | 15.2 | 336 040 | 156 | 45 449 | 852 179 | 5.9 |
| New York-White Plains-Wayne, NY-NJ Div....... | 562 846 | 0.0 | 6.0 | 2.6 | 19.4 | 4.2 | 26.2 | 9.5 | 11.2 | 1 660 655 | 142 | 495 809 | 4 682 853 | 5.7 |
| Niles-Benton Harbor, MI ...... | 3 611 | 1.9 | 33.0 | 29.1 | 4.4 | 5.9 | 4.2 | 11.9 | 13.8 | 36 210 | 231 | 4 993 | 76 922 | 4.7 |
| North Port-Bradenton-Sara-sota, FL................ | 14 575 | 1.3 | 12.9 | 6.1 | 11.3 | 9.3 | 9.3 | 16.7 | 12.1 | 200 355 | 282 | 9 447 | 401 103 | 25.1 |
| Norwich-New London, CT..... | 9 597 | 0.4 | 21.6 | 17.0 | 8.9 | 5.5 | 3.2 | 11.0 | 31.1 | 50 970 | 186 | 3 686 | 120 994 | 9.3 |
| Ocala, FL ...................... | 4 580 | -0.2 | 14.8 | 8.6 | 6.5 | 10.8 | 5.8 | 15.9 | 22.3 | 104 990 | 316 | 8 314 | 164 050 | 33.7 |
| Ocean City, NJ.................. | 2 264 | 0.2 | 10.2 | 1.4 | 5.2 | 11.1 | 6.2 | 12.1 | 28.5 | 27 115 | 281 | 1 831 | 98 309 | 8.0 |
| Odessa, TX ...................... | 4 452 | 0.0 | 38.7 | 8.2 | 4.9 | 6.1 | 4.6 | 6.6 | 11.8 | 19 435 | 139 | 3 809 | 53 027 | 7.1 |
| Ogden-Clearfield, UT .......... | 11 904 | 0.1 | 20.2 | 12.7 | 7.9 | 7.1 | 5.0 | 9.4 | 30.8 | 64 535 | 116 | 5 665 | 186 763 | 27.3 |
| Oklahoma City, OK.............. | 39 817 | 0.2 | 21.7 | 6.5 | 8.6 | 6.4 | 6.5 | 11.0 | 22.6 | 206 460 | 162 | 26 981 | 539 077 | 14.2 |
| Olympia, WA ...................... | 6 152 | 0.4 | 8.0 | 3.2 | 6.1 | 7.2 | 4.5 | 13.2 | 40.0 | 47 985 | 187 | 4 924 | 108 182 | 24.8 |
| Omaha-Council Bluffs, NE-IA.................. | 30 230 | 1.6 | 13.6 | 6.4 | 11.7 | 5.6 | 10.5 | 10.8 | 16.0 | 131 085 | 149 | 13 645 | 362 327 | 16.3 |
| Orlando-Kissimmee-Sanford, FL............. | 58 613 | 0.2 | 9.8 | 4.9 | 13.3 | 7.4 | 9.8 | 11.4 | 12.4 | 358 420 | 165 | 51 688 | 942 312 | 37.9 |
| Oshkosh-Neenah, WI........... | 5 648 | 0.6 | 39.3 | 34.6 | 6.0 | 4.4 | 4.5 | 10.7 | 11.8 | 30 920 | 184 | 2 313 | 73 329 | 13.3 |
| Owensboro, KY................... | 2 721 | 3.8 | D | 20.8 | 3.5 | 7.2 | 5.9 | 8.8 | 20.4 | 26 695 | 231 | 4 242 | 49 450 | 6.5 |
| Oxnard-Thousand Oaks-Ven-tura, CA.......... | 23 091 | 3.3 | 21.6 | 15.7 | 9.9 | 6.7 | 9.7 | 8.9 | 17.3 | 120 935 | 145 | 16 571 | 281 695 | 11.9 |
| Palm Bay-Melbourne-Titus-ville, FL ............ | 12 524 | 0.1 | 19.3 | 15.3 | 11.1 | 6.7 | 4.5 | 13.4 | 18.4 | 138 755 | 255 | 10 439 | 269 864 | 21.5 |
| Palm Coast, FL .................. | 824 | 1.0 | 8.1 | 4.5 | 10.2 | 11.2 | 4.0 | 15.7 | 25.5 | 30 310 | 311 | 1 567 | 48 595 | 98.7 |
| Panama City-Lynn Haven-Panama City Beach, FL | 4 186 | 0.0 | 11.0 | 4.7 | 9.6 | 8.1 | 5.2 | 11.0 | 31.6 | 35 190 | 207 | 4 463 | 99 650 | 27.0 |
| Parkersburg-Marietta-Vienna, WV-OH............ | 3 612 | 0.0 | 22.3 | 15.3 | 4.6 | 8.5 | 5.1 | 16.3 | 18.7 | 40 915 | 252 | 6 298 | 75 203 | 1.6 |
| Pascagoula, MS................... | 3 666 | 0.0 | 45.4 | 35.7 | 5.4 | 5.2 | 2.6 | 6.2 | 21.3 | 32 285 | 198 | 3 925 | 69 397 | 17.2 |
| Pensacola-Ferry Pass-Brent, FL............................ | 9 966 | 0.4 | 9.6 | 4.1 | 8.6 | 7.0 | 5.6 | 15.1 | 33.2 | 93 540 | 206 | 11 981 | 201 463 | 15.9 |
| Peoria, IL............................ | 12 551 | 2.6 | 31.6 | 26.4 | 10.6 | 4.8 | 4.4 | 13.7 | 10.3 | 74 180 | 195 | 7 018 | 164 283 | 7.2 |
| Philadelphia-Camden-Wil-mington, PA-NJ-DE-MD. | 213 069 | 0.1 | 12.9 | 7.5 | 16.8 | 5.4 | 11.2 | 13.7 | 12.5 | 1 043 910 | 174 | 176 916 | 2 433 611 | 6.7 |
| Camden, NJ Div................. | 34 691 | 0.3 | 15.4 | 9.5 | 10.7 | 8.0 | 8.0 | 13.8 | 18.9 | 225 625 | 180 | 25 315 | 490 354 | 7.5 |
| Philadelphia, PA Div .......... | 153 029 | 0.1 | 13.2 | 7.8 | 18.5 | 4.8 | 11.1 | 14.0 | 11.0 | 695 485 | 173 | 138 787 | 1 657 226 | 5.8 |
| Wilmington, DE-MD-NJ Div. | 25 350 | 0.3 | 5.1 | D | 14.8 | 4.9 | 16.4 | 12.0 | 13.3 | 122 800 | 173 | 12 814 | 286 031 | 10.0 |
| Phoenix-Mesa-Glendale, AZ. | 116 671 | 0.5 | 15.0 | 8.6 | 10.7 | 8.1 | 11.0 | 12.0 | 13.5 | 647 090 | 152 | 62 384 | 1 798 501 | 35.1 |
| Pine Bluff, AR .................... | 2 046 | 3.2 | 21.4 | 16.0 | D | 6.0 | 3.6 | 11.6 | 31.7 | 20 600 | 208 | 5 282 | 41 930 | -2.8 |
| Pittsburgh, PA .................... | 77 443 | 0.0 | 17.4 | 9.4 | 12.7 | 6.0 | 8.3 | 14.0 | 10.9 | 537 735 | 228 | 69 684 | 1 102 048 | 2.2 |
| Pittsfield, MA...................... | 3 514 | 0.0 | 18.3 | 11.4 | 9.2 | 8.2 | 6.6 | 19.6 | 13.6 | 32 465 | 249 | 4 231 | 68 508 | 3.3 |
| Pocatello, ID....................... | 1 819 | 2.2 | 18.4 | 11.9 | D | 7.0 | 5.3 | 14.2 | 24.3 | 14 215 | 155 | 1 868 | 36 135 | 13.1 |
| Portland-South Portland-Bid-deford, ME ............ | 16 398 | 0.2 | 5.7 | D | 10.1 | 7.2 | 10.4 | 14.8 | 17.2 | 106 125 | 206 | 9 537 | 262 718 | 12.6 |
| Portland-Vancouver-Hills-boro, OR-WA ................ | 70 589 | 0.5 | 20.2 | 14.4 | 12.2 | 5.8 | 7.2 | 11.4 | 14.1 | 347 575 | 154 | 40 869 | 925 076 | 17.0 |
| Port St. Lucie, FL............... | 6 866 | 0.9 | 9.9 | 4.4 | 8.7 | 10.1 | 6.4 | 16.8 | 17.4 | 107 550 | 251 | 7 530 | 215 160 | 37.3 |
| Poughkeepsie-Newburgh-Middletown, NY.............. | 16 136 | 0.2 | 16.3 | 11.3 | 7.6 | 8.2 | 4.3 | 14.7 | 27.3 | 115 825 | 172 | 12 700 | 255 663 | 11.7 |
| Prescott, AZ........................ | 2 754 | 0.3 | 14.9 | 5.4 | 5.0 | 10.6 | 5.9 | 15.7 | 23.1 | 66 330 | 313 | 3 456 | 110 432 | 35.1 |
| Providence-New Bedford-Fall River, RI-MA ........ | 43 964 | 0.1 | 16.5 | 11.2 | 9.6 | 6.6 | 8.1 | 15.3 | 17.3 | 318 840 | 199 | 52 566 | 693 923 | 5.7 |
| Provo-Orem, UT ................. | 10 363 | 0.5 | 17.7 | 10.5 | 18.2 | 8.0 | 5.4 | 9.9 | 13.7 | 48 965 | 91 | 4 375 | 151 852 | 41.8 |
| Pueblo, CO........................ | 3 178 | 0.3 | 19.1 | 10.8 | 4.2 | 7.9 | 3.7 | 19.2 | 22.8 | 32 820 | 204 | 6 001 | 69 526 | 18.0 |
| Punta Gorda, FL................. | 2 116 | 1.0 | 7.2 | 1.3 | 6.5 | 13.0 | 6.0 | 24.8 | 17.9 | 57 175 | 356 | 2 399 | 100 632 | 26.2 |
| Racine, WI.......................... | 4 566 | 0.6 | 39.5 | 34.9 | 5.4 | 5.6 | 4.3 | 12.5 | 13.2 | 38 435 | 197 | 4 860 | 82 164 | 10.0 |
| Raleigh-Cary, NC................ | 34 287 | 0.2 | 13.8 | 7.4 | 18.5 | 6.2 | 8.7 | 9.4 | 16.6 | 150 820 | 130 | 16 908 | 466 095 | 41.5 |
| Rapid City, SD.................... | 3 552 | 2.5 | 11.1 | 3.7 | 6.1 | 8.0 | 5.8 | 16.8 | 27.8 | 25 405 | 198 | 2 235 | 55 949 | 18.0 |
| Reading, PA........................ | 10 250 | 0.9 | 26.1 | 19.9 | 7.4 | 7.5 | 5.1 | 13.7 | 13.7 | 80 995 | 196 | 9 957 | 164 827 | 9.7 |
| Redding, CA........................ | 3 574 | 0.6 | 10.7 | 3.9 | 6.4 | 10.2 | 4.6 | 19.3 | 22.6 | 45 995 | 259 | 9 959 | 77 313 | 12.4 |
| Reno-Sparks, NV ............... | 11 921 | 0.1 | 13.7 | 6.8 | 9.4 | 6.8 | 8.8 | 11.4 | 17.0 | 71 810 | 167 | 6 227 | 186 831 | 28.4 |
| Richmond, VA..................... | 41 849 | 0.2 | 11.9 | 6.6 | D | 5.3 | D | 9.9 | 20.4 | 217 430 | 171 | 26 743 | 531 648 | 17.4 |
| Riverside-San Bernardino-Ontario, CA.................. | 74 124 | 0.7 | 15.0 | 7.8 | 6.1 | 9.1 | 4.4 | 11.4 | 24.9 | 568 170 | 132 | 129 015 | 1 500 344 | 26.5 |
| Roanoke, VA....................... | 8 812 | 0.1 | D | 13.8 | 7.3 | 6.4 | 6.6 | D | 15.1 | 69 430 | 225 | 7 491 | 144 987 | 11.9 |
| Rochester, MN.................... | 6 844 | 2.6 | 17.0 | 12.9 | 3.5 | 4.8 | 3.1 | 47.0 | 9.5 | 31 345 | 167 | 2 482 | 78 439 | 20.4 |
| Rochester, NY..................... | 31 205 | 0.8 | 20.9 | 15.3 | 10.8 | 6.1 | 5.8 | 12.5 | 16.2 | 215 975 | 205 | 31 987 | 455 397 | 6.6 |
| Rockford, IL........................ | 8 463 | 0.6 | 30.4 | 25.4 | 4.8 | 6.6 | 5.7 | 16.0 | 12.6 | 67 105 | 193 | 7 487 | 145 935 | 12.4 |
| Rocky Mount, NC................ | 3 113 | 2.3 | 26.3 | 21.2 | D | 7.6 | 4.4 | D | 18.4 | 32 845 | 216 | 6 250 | 67 124 | 9.9 |
| Rome, GA........................... | 2 098 | 0.1 | 19.3 | 16.8 | 6.1 | 5.8 | 4.2 | 25.9 | 16.0 | 20 530 | 214 | 3 078 | 40 551 | 10.7 |

1. Includes mining, construction, and manufacturing.    2. Per 1,000 resident population estimated as of July 1, 2011.

Table C. Metropolitan Areas — **Housing, Labor Force, and Employment**

| Area name | Housing units, 2007–2011 | | | | | | | | Civilian labor force, 2012 | | Unemployment | | Civilian employment,[5] 2007–2011 | | |
|---|---|---|---|---|---|---|---|---|---|---|---|---|---|---|---|
| | Occupied units | | | | | | | | | | | | | Percent | |
| | | | Owner-occupied | | | Renter-occupied | | | | | | | | | |
| | | | | Median owner cost as a percent of income | | | | | | | | | | | |
| | Total | Percent | Median value[1] | With a mortgage | Without a mortgage | Median rent[2] | Median rent as a percent of income | Substandard units[3] (percent) | Total | Percent change, 2011–2012 | Total | Rate[4] | Total | Management, professional, and related occupations | Construction, production, and related occupations |
| | 89 | 90 | 91 | 92 | 93 | 94 | 95 | 96 | 97 | 98 | 99 | 100 | 101 | 102 | 103 |
| Naples-Marco Island, FL...... | 119 554 | 76.1 | 317 200 | 32.5 | 14.4 | 1 045 | 34.3 | 3.5 | 150 903 | 2.0 | 12 824 | 8.5 | 130 779 | 29.1 | 20.7 |
| Nashville-Davidson—Murfreesboro—Franklin, TN | 604 098 | 67.7 | 172 700 | 23.8 | 10.4 | 799 | 29.8 | 2.3 | 850 823 | 1.4 | 56 129 | 6.6 | 767 694 | 36.8 | 20.9 |
| New Haven-Milford, CT ....... | 330 396 | 64.8 | 270 900 | 27.2 | 18.5 | 1 030 | 33.2 | 2.4 | 448 745 | -0.9 | 41 181 | 9.2 | 424 782 | 39.0 | 19.0 |
| New Orleans-Metairie-Kenner, LA ...................... | 440 908 | 63.8 | 179 500 | 24.4 | 11.6 | 913 | 34.4 | 3.2 | 544 740 | 0.8 | 35 589 | 6.5 | 530 075 | 34.4 | 22.2 |
| New York-Northern New Jersey-Long Island, NY-NJ-PA................... | 6 818 735 | 52.6 | 440 400 | 29.6 | 17.8 | 1 157 | 31.4 | 6.4 | 9 555 948 | 1.1 | 839 668 | 8.8 | 8 923 656 | 39.7 | 16.5 |
| Edison-New Brunswick, NJ Div. | 848 844 | 74.8 | 355 600 | 28.6 | 18.9 | 1 230 | 31.5 | 2.7 | 1 234 123 | 1.7 | 109 189 | 8.8 | 1 109 506 | 42.1 | 17.2 |
| Nassau-Suffolk, NY Div ...... | 939 992 | 81.3 | 446 400 | 30.5 | 19.4 | 1 455 | 33.9 | 2.6 | 1 480 344 | 0.9 | 109 104 | 7.4 | 1 378 820 | 40.3 | 16.6 |
| Newark-Union, NJ-PA Div... | 765 822 | 63.4 | 394 400 | 29.0 | 18.5 | 1 098 | 31.4 | 5.2 | 1 107 933 | 0.9 | 102 599 | 9.3 | 1 032 809 | 40.3 | 18.2 |
| New York-White Plains-Wayne, NY-NJ Div....... | 4 264 077 | 39.9 | 486 100 | 29.9 | 16.3 | 1 141 | 31.2 | 8.2 | 5 733 548 | 1.1 | 518 776 | 9.0 | 5 402 521 | 38.9 | 15.9 |
| Niles-Benton Harbor, MI ...... | 61 678 | 73.3 | 135 400 | 23.0 | 12.8 | 619 | 32.9 | 2.0 | 72 468 | -1.4 | 6 528 | 9.0 | 69 139 | 31.7 | 24.2 |
| North Port-Bradenton-Sarasota, FL | 300 574 | 74.8 | 205 700 | 30.2 | 14.3 | 974 | 34.0 | 2.0 | 305 212 | 1.3 | 26 327 | 8.6 | 284 663 | 32.7 | 18.9 |
| Norwich-New London, CT..... | 107 115 | 69.4 | 265 700 | 25.8 | 15.0 | 987 | 28.8 | 1.7 | 147 124 | -2.3 | 12 468 | 8.5 | 133 983 | 37.5 | 18.2 |
| Ocala, FL | 133 977 | 78.4 | 142 000 | 28.3 | 12.9 | 839 | 35.6 | 2.1 | 133 573 | -0.2 | 13 296 | 10.0 | 119 756 | 27.6 | 22.6 |
| Ocean City, NJ | 44 788 | 74.3 | 332 400 | 29.7 | 17.8 | 1 001 | 33.1 | 1.7 | 58 190 | 1.7 | 7 793 | 13.4 | 43 734 | 33.6 | 19.5 |
| Odessa, TX | 48 318 | 66.9 | 83 100 | 19.0 | 10.7 | 686 | 25.0 | 6.3 | 83 462 | 6.2 | 3 515 | 4.2 | 62 748 | 22.4 | 33.8 |
| Ogden-Clearfield, UT .......... | 174 223 | 75.7 | 205 900 | 23.7 | 10.0 | 787 | 27.0 | 2.5 | 260 794 | -0.2 | 15 297 | 5.9 | 244 272 | 36.1 | 22.4 |
| Oklahoma City, OK ............. | 476 275 | 66.1 | 125 900 | 21.7 | 10.9 | 709 | 29.4 | 2.8 | 594 801 | 1.7 | 28 775 | 4.8 | 594 362 | 35.1 | 21.5 |
| Olympia, WA .................... | 100 147 | 67.4 | 259 500 | 26.1 | 11.7 | 974 | 29.0 | 2.8 | 126 669 | -0.8 | 9 871 | 7.8 | 115 691 | 41.0 | 17.3 |
| Omaha-Council Bluffs, NE-IA | 330 614 | 68.1 | 144 800 | 22.3 | 12.8 | 752 | 28.4 | 2.0 | 462 718 | 1.0 | 20 520 | 4.4 | 443 739 | 37.1 | 19.8 |
| Orlando-Kissimmee-Sanford, FL | 770 401 | 65.3 | 201 100 | 29.2 | 13.2 | 1 018 | 35.0 | 2.5 | 1 147 605 | 1.6 | 96 654 | 8.4 | 1 012 288 | 34.1 | 17.5 |
| Oshkosh-Neenah, WI........... | 66 861 | 68.2 | 140 800 | 22.8 | 13.7 | 635 | 26.4 | 1.1 | 94 345 | -0.5 | 6 002 | 6.4 | 84 627 | 30.0 | 26.5 |
| Owensboro, KY | 44 353 | 72.0 | 102 200 | 19.7 | 10.0 | 581 | 26.7 | 1.6 | 59 322 | 1.5 | 4 058 | 6.8 | 50 461 | 28.6 | 31.6 |
| Oxnard-Thousand Oaks-Ventura, CA | 264 982 | 65.8 | 515 900 | 30.3 | 11.1 | 1 428 | 33.1 | 6.7 | 440 649 | 1.0 | 39 865 | 9.0 | 384 192 | 37.3 | 20.8 |
| Palm Bay-Melbourne-Titusville, FL ...................... | 219 669 | 75.3 | 171 200 | 27.4 | 12.8 | 909 | 32.7 | 1.7 | 268 281 | -0.3 | 24 746 | 9.2 | 233 820 | 36.5 | 19.4 |
| Palm Coast, FL ................... | 36 232 | 81.2 | 201 300 | 31.5 | 13.6 | 1 068 | 34.6 | 1.4 | 35 348 | 0.8 | 4 096 | 11.6 | 35 423 | 34.6 | 18.4 |
| Panama City-Lynn Haven-Panama City Beach, FL | 68 819 | 65.7 | 168 400 | 25.9 | 12.0 | 924 | 29.9 | 2.3 | 90 582 | -0.3 | 7 484 | 8.3 | 76 890 | 31.4 | 21.6 |
| Parkersburg-Marietta-Vienna, WV-OH ......... | 66 129 | 75.3 | 104 300 | 20.2 | 10.0 | 570 | 29.8 | 1.7 | 75 411 | -1.4 | 5 516 | 7.3 | 68 857 | 30.1 | 26.3 |
| Pascagoula, MS | 58 254 | 73.5 | 124 700 | 22.8 | 10.9 | 833 | 31.4 | 2.8 | 71 351 | -1.2 | 7 069 | 9.9 | 68 547 | 29.6 | 28.8 |
| Pensacola-Ferry Pass-Brent, FL | 167 884 | 70.3 | 155 100 | 25.9 | 11.9 | 866 | 32.9 | 2.3 | 215 127 | 0.1 | 17 521 | 8.1 | 189 622 | 32.1 | 20.0 |
| Peoria, IL | 151 075 | 73.5 | 125 900 | 20.8 | 12.0 | 672 | 27.9 | 1.6 | 202 019 | 0.2 | 15 960 | 7.9 | 177 598 | 35.6 | 22.7 |
| Philadelphia-Camden-Wilmington, PA-NJ-DE-MD. | 2 225 487 | 69.3 | 245 000 | 25.5 | 15.1 | 952 | 31.9 | 1.9 | 3 019 454 | 1.3 | 259 084 | 8.6 | 2 823 907 | 40.6 | 17.4 |
| Camden, NJ Div................. | 459 612 | 74.9 | 240 700 | 27.0 | 18.1 | 1 001 | 32.7 | 1.8 | 668 942 | 0.6 | 66 425 | 9.9 | 606 842 | 39.1 | 18.0 |
| Philadelphia, PA Div ........... | 1 505 061 | 67.2 | 245 900 | 25.1 | 14.9 | 935 | 31.8 | 1.9 | 1 992 185 | 1.6 | 165 565 | 8.3 | 1 873 968 | 41.3 | 16.7 |
| Wilmington, DE-MD-NJ Div. | 260 869 | 71.3 | 249 800 | 24.4 | 12.0 | 980 | 31.4 | 2.1 | 358 327 | 0.7 | 27 094 | 7.6 | 343 097 | 39.2 | 19.6 |
| Phoenix-Mesa-Glendale, AZ. | 1 515 297 | 66.1 | 212 100 | 26.4 | 11.2 | 934 | 30.9 | 4.4 | 2 037 028 | -0.4 | 147 826 | 7.3 | 1 864 273 | 35.7 | 19.2 |
| Pine Bluff, AR .................... | 35 427 | 66.2 | 76 400 | 19.9 | 11.9 | 617 | 32.1 | 2.8 | 43 057 | -1.8 | 3 946 | 9.2 | 38 047 | 27.7 | 28.4 |
| Pittsburgh, PA ................... | 985 980 | 70.9 | 121 100 | 21.7 | 13.3 | 672 | 28.6 | 1.0 | 1 255 395 | 1.9 | 90 027 | 7.2 | 1 123 383 | 37.0 | 20.0 |
| Pittsfield, MA | 55 793 | 69.0 | 208 100 | 25.4 | 14.8 | 750 | 30.0 | 1.2 | 71 631 | -1.2 | 4 817 | 6.7 | 62 741 | 35.9 | 18.9 |
| Pocatello, ID | 32 642 | 71.1 | 139 800 | 23.3 | 10.3 | 589 | 28.8 | 2.6 | 43 697 | -0.3 | 3 096 | 7.1 | 41 333 | 32.5 | 24.8 |
| Portland-South Portland-Biddeford, ME | 212 310 | 71.0 | 237 600 | 25.6 | 14.8 | 873 | 30.5 | 1.7 | 292 327 | 0.8 | 17 957 | 6.1 | 268 599 | 39.2 | 19.5 |
| Portland-Vancouver-Hillsboro, OR-WA | 859 996 | 62.7 | 284 400 | 26.9 | 13.0 | 886 | 30.4 | 3.2 | 1 186 739 | -0.1 | 96 800 | 8.2 | 1 072 516 | 39.0 | 19.9 |
| Port St. Lucie, FL................ | 163 216 | 76.5 | 175 100 | 32.0 | 14.4 | 1 023 | 34.6 | 2.1 | 190 380 | 0.6 | 19 608 | 10.3 | 170 281 | 30.2 | 21.0 |
| Poughkeepsie-Newburgh-Middletown, NY............. | 232 090 | 70.4 | 306 800 | 28.3 | 17.3 | 1 079 | 32.8 | 3.3 | 319 155 | -0.1 | 25 946 | 8.1 | 313 848 | 37.5 | 19.5 |
| Prescott, AZ ...................... | 90 309 | 71.8 | 216 900 | 28.7 | 12.0 | 831 | 31.6 | 3.4 | 92 545 | -0.7 | 7 951 | 8.6 | 86 200 | 30.4 | 20.6 |
| Providence-New Bedford-Fall River, RI-MA | 621 011 | 62.7 | 280 300 | 27.3 | 16.0 | 865 | 30.2 | 2.0 | 850 871 | -0.4 | 85 407 | 10.0 | 781 982 | 35.6 | 20.2 |
| Provo-Orem, UT ................. | 141 896 | 69.4 | 233 300 | 25.4 | 10.0 | 807 | 29.6 | 4.7 | 229 813 | 2.2 | 12 734 | 5.5 | 223 297 | 38.6 | 18.8 |
| Pueblo, CO ....................... | 61 858 | 68.5 | 140 700 | 25.4 | 12.0 | 679 | 34.3 | 2.0 | 75 795 | -0.7 | 8 089 | 10.7 | 65 675 | 30.5 | 21.3 |
| Punta Gorda, FL................. | 71 059 | 80.3 | 166 700 | 31.1 | 14.2 | 928 | 32.4 | 1.1 | 70 478 | 0.4 | 6 199 | 8.8 | 56 092 | 30.5 | 19.9 |
| Racine, WI ........................ | 75 599 | 69.8 | 177 300 | 25.0 | 14.3 | 731 | 30.0 | 1.8 | 97 131 | -0.2 | 8 279 | 8.5 | 92 504 | 31.3 | 28.1 |
| Raleigh-Cary, NC ............... | 417 485 | 68.2 | 202 900 | 22.5 | 10.5 | 855 | 28.9 | 2.6 | 601 392 | 2.8 | 46 521 | 7.7 | 554 964 | 45.8 | 16.2 |
| Rapid City, SD ................... | 50 239 | 67.2 | 153 600 | 24.4 | 12.2 | 698 | 28.1 | 1.9 | 67 213 | -0.4 | 3 033 | 4.5 | 61 941 | 33.7 | 21.6 |
| Reading, PA ...................... | 153 780 | 72.9 | 174 000 | 24.3 | 14.6 | 782 | 30.3 | 2.1 | 206 060 | 1.0 | 16 556 | 8.0 | 195 640 | 31.2 | 27.4 |
| Redding, CA ...................... | 69 147 | 65.3 | 246 800 | 30.2 | 13.0 | 882 | 35.8 | 3.5 | 81 245 | -1.5 | 10 896 | 13.4 | 69 420 | 33.3 | 20.0 |
| Reno-Sparks, NV ............... | 162 644 | 60.0 | 256 700 | 28.5 | 12.5 | 922 | 31.0 | 4.3 | 224 433 | -1.3 | 24 454 | 10.9 | 207 081 | 32.6 | 19.8 |
| Richmond, VA .................... | 476 146 | 68.9 | 227 600 | 24.3 | 11.1 | 921 | 30.4 | 1.8 | 665 401 | 0.9 | 42 431 | 6.4 | 606 603 | 38.6 | 19.2 |
| Riverside-San Bernardino-Ontario, CA.................... | 1 271 718 | 66.8 | 281 600 | 31.7 | 12.8 | 1 115 | 35.0 | 8.3 | 1 805 353 | 0.6 | 218 592 | 12.1 | 1 684 000 | 28.8 | 25.6 |
| Roanoke, VA ..................... | 129 157 | 71.2 | 168 600 | 23.5 | 10.6 | 705 | 27.7 | 1.7 | 158 172 | 0.3 | 9 612 | 6.1 | 148 585 | 34.6 | 22.9 |
| Rochester, MN ................... | 72 699 | 78.0 | 170 500 | 22.5 | 11.0 | 750 | 28.3 | 1.6 | 105 204 | 1.1 | 4 899 | 4.7 | 99 636 | 44.5 | 18.3 |
| Rochester, NY ................... | 413 238 | 69.0 | 126 600 | 22.8 | 14.2 | 762 | 32.7 | 1.7 | 523 789 | 0.1 | 42 294 | 8.1 | 498 677 | 39.1 | 19.5 |
| Rockford, IL ...................... | 130 975 | 71.0 | 134 900 | 24.1 | 13.9 | 707 | 31.9 | 2.2 | 165 984 | -0.7 | 18 979 | 11.4 | 156 993 | 29.6 | 28.0 |
| Rocky Mount, NC ............... | 59 487 | 63.4 | 101 800 | 23.6 | 14.2 | 691 | 30.0 | 2.4 | 70 928 | -0.8 | 9 199 | 13.0 | 64 982 | 27.4 | 30.4 |
| Rome, GA ......................... | 34 823 | 66.8 | 120 000 | 23.4 | 12.1 | 687 | 32.1 | 3.4 | 48 706 | 0.8 | 4 857 | 10.0 | 40 675 | 30.6 | 27.6 |

1. Specified owner-occupied units.  2. Specified renter-occupied units.  3. Overcrowded or lacking complete plumbing facilities.  4. Percent of civilian labor force.  5. Persons 16 years old and over.

# Table C. Metropolitan Areas — Nonfarm Employment and Agriculture

| Area name | Private nonfarm establishments, employment and payroll, 2011 | | | | | | | | | Agriculture, 2007 | | | |
|---|---|---|---|---|---|---|---|---|---|---|---|---|---|
| | Number of establish-ments | Employment | | | | | | Annual payroll | | Farms | | | |
| | | Total | Health care and social assistance | Manufac-turing | Retail trade | Finance and insurance | Professional, scientific, and technical services | Total (mil dol) | Average per employee (dollars) | Number | Percent with: | | Farm operators whose principal occu-pation is farming (percent) |
| | | | | | | | | | | | Fewer than 50 acres | 500 acres or more | |
| | 104 | 105 | 106 | 107 | 108 | 109 | 110 | 111 | 112 | 113 | 114 | 115 | 116 |
| Naples-Marco Island, FL....... | 9 888 | 101 687 | 16 716 | 2 287 | 18 565 | 3 601 | 4 494 | 3 869 | 38 044 | 322 | 70.5 | 9.9 | 53.1 |
| Nashville-Davidson—Murfreesboro—Franklin, TN | 37 102 | 665 865 | 109 314 | 55 456 | 81 383 | 38 039 | 35 272 | 30 000 | 45 054 | 14 063 | 45.7 | 3.6 | 37.0 |
| New Haven-Milford, CT ....... | 19 261 | 325 467 | 71 493 | 32 012 | 41 737 | 11 717 | 16 868 | 15 243 | 46 834 | 573 | 70.5 | 1.4 | 50.6 |
| New Orleans-Metairie-Kenner, LA .......................... | 28 991 | 453 437 | 70 145 | 28 386 | 59 386 | 18 959 | 31 278 | 20 171 | 44 486 | 986 | 64.7 | 9.8 | 47.0 |
| New York-Northern New Jersey-Long Island, NY-NJ-PA............................. | 534 157 | 7 353 468 | 1 346 083 | 339 377 | 835 239 | 554 334 | 673 082 | 477 984 | 65 001 | 6 110 | 78.5 | 2.0 | 43.9 |
| Edison-New Brunswick, NJ Div......................... | X | X | X | X | X | X | X | X | X | 1 868 | 83.1 | 2.5 | 44.5 |
| Nassau-Suffolk, NY Div ...... | X | X | X | X | X | X | X | X | X | 644 | 75.5 | 1.1 | 62.3 |
| Newark-Union, NJ-PA Div... | X | X | X | X | X | X | X | X | X | 3 187 | 75.6 | 2.0 | 39.6 |
| New York-White Plains-Wayne, NY-NJ Div...... | X | X | X | X | X | X | X | X | X | 411 | 84.9 | 1.2 | 46.2 |
| Niles-Benton Harbor, MI ...... | 3 623 | 51 085 | 8 849 | 7 659 | 6 838 | 1 273 | 2 186 | 1 881 | 36 820 | 1 300 | 57.8 | 5.5 | 49.1 |
| North Port-Bradenton-Sarasota, FL.......................... | 19 980 | 204 743 | 38 627 | 12 384 | 36 089 | 8 277 | 12 453 | 7 045 | 34 408 | 1 099 | 67.8 | 8.2 | 43.7 |
| Norwich-New London, CT..... | 5 675 | 105 276 | 16 975 | D | 13 882 | 2 104 | 9 185 | 4 777 | 45 377 | 793 | 58.9 | 1.5 | 44.6 |
| Ocala, FL .......................... | 6 638 | 72 006 | 14 822 | 5 087 | 14 947 | 2 400 | 3 764 | 2 267 | 31 489 | 3 496 | 81.9 | 1.9 | 50.6 |
| Ocean City, NJ .................. | 3 801 | 24 667 | 4 666 | 415 | 5 904 | 1 138 | 997 | 907 | 36 769 | 201 | 80.6 | 1.0 | 50.7 |
| Odessa, TX ....................... | 3 313 | 53 018 | 7 851 | 3 803 | 7 340 | 1 283 | 2 008 | 2 448 | 46 172 | 301 | 74.4 | 13.0 | 29.2 |
| Ogden-Clearfield, UT ........... | 11 273 | 140 221 | 19 370 | 20 074 | 23 512 | 6 082 | 11 084 | 4 807 | 34 283 | 1 813 | 75.3 | 4.3 | 34.5 |
| Oklahoma City, OK .............. | 33 111 | 462 555 | 75 499 | 29 751 | 60 147 | 24 142 | 27 508 | 18 555 | 40 114 | 10 772 | 35.8 | 11.7 | 39.6 |
| Olympia, WA ..................... | 5 733 | 63 511 | 11 842 | 2 520 | 11 917 | 2 444 | 5 930 | 2 300 | 36 222 | 1 288 | 76.9 | 2.0 | 40.5 |
| Omaha-Council Bluffs, NE-IA.................................... | 22 087 | 391 405 | 57 687 | 30 220 | 51 861 | 37 521 | 23 361 | 16 119 | 41 184 | 5 783 | 33.6 | 24.5 | 54.7 |
| Orlando-Kissimmee-Sanford, FL..................... | 54 922 | 881 329 | 103 919 | 37 472 | 122 460 | 36 901 | 55 636 | 33 343 | 37 833 | 3 415 | 80.0 | 4.1 | 43.0 |
| Oshkosh-Neenah, WI........... | 3 525 | 85 684 | 14 136 | 24 047 | 7 633 | 3 137 | 2 756 | 3 717 | 43 378 | 1 001 | 39.6 | 8.1 | 44.5 |
| Owensboro, KY.................. | 2 553 | 45 060 | 8 156 | 8 000 | 6 182 | 2 537 | 1 432 | 1 564 | 34 701 | 1 810 | 37.2 | 11.6 | 45.1 |
| Oxnard-Thousand Oaks-Ventura, CA........................ | 19 576 | 238 849 | 31 190 | 22 133 | 37 550 | 15 911 | 21 092 | 11 285 | 47 246 | 2 437 | 77.8 | 4.1 | 47.7 |
| Palm Bay-Melbourne-Titusville, FL........................... | 12 746 | 166 490 | 28 831 | 19 054 | 24 999 | 5 932 | 17 352 | 6 814 | 40 930 | 531 | 79.8 | 4.9 | 46.7 |
| Palm Coast, FL.................. | 1 733 | 15 813 | 2 511 | 715 | 3 079 | 507 | 428 | 434 | 27 460 | 82 | 47.6 | 24.4 | 53.7 |
| Panama City-Lynn Haven-Panama City Beach, FL | 4 374 | 55 989 | 9 357 | 3 468 | 10 235 | 2 053 | 3 362 | 1 821 | 32 517 | 133 | 69.2 | 2.3 | 38.3 |
| Parkersburg-Marietta-Vienna, WV-OH .............. | 3 715 | 58 632 | 12 850 | 7 245 | 9 353 | 1 824 | 1 786 | 1 988 | 33 907 | 2 242 | 28.4 | 2.4 | 39.2 |
| Pascagoula, MS ................. | 2 542 | 49 793 | 6 100 | D | 6 149 | 1 081 | 1 704 | 2 195 | 44 074 | 1 058 | 58.1 | 2.6 | 38.8 |
| Pensacola-Ferry Pass-Brent, FL................................ | 8 961 | 117 584 | 21 595 | 4 093 | 20 000 | 5 775 | 6 652 | 4 085 | 34 737 | 1 319 | 58.3 | 4.7 | 36.0 |
| Peoria, IL.......................... | 8 549 | 163 926 | 27 680 | 19 836 | 19 186 | 6 394 | 6 266 | 8 094 | 49 375 | 3 679 | 33.9 | 21.6 | 52.4 |
| Philadelphia-Camden-Wilmington, PA-NJ-DE-MD. | 143 604 | 2 449 574 | 458 552 | 172 072 | 295 786 | 161 337 | 190 461 | 124 663 | 50 892 | 6 987 | 66.2 | 4.1 | 48.9 |
| Camden, NJ Div................. | X | X | X | X | X | X | X | X | X | 1 816 | 76.8 | 3.4 | 46.3 |
| Philadelphia, PA Div .......... | X | X | X | X | X | X | X | X | X | 3 482 | 64.2 | 2.9 | 49.2 |
| Wilmington, DE-MD-NJ Div. | X | X | X | X | X | X | X | X | X | 1 689 | 58.8 | 7.5 | 51.2 |
| Phoenix-Mesa-Glendale, AZ. | 86 667 | 1 493 276 | 206 154 | 96 754 | 206 918 | 109 039 | 94 817 | 64 767 | 43 373 | 2 578 | 71.2 | 12.5 | 51.2 |
| Pine Bluff, AR .................... | 1 642 | 25 139 | 5 149 | 5 344 | 3 714 | 904 | 1 215 | 845 | 33 600 | 1 114 | 35.6 | 19.7 | 53.9 |
| Pittsburgh, PA ................... | 59 052 | 1 058 939 | 190 274 | 90 841 | 128 256 | 56 211 | 78 069 | 46 649 | 44 053 | 7 926 | 39.8 | 2.8 | 39.7 |
| Pittsfield, MA .................... | 3 985 | 53 110 | 11 512 | 5 138 | 8 611 | 2 200 | 0 | 2 085 | 39 265 | 522 | 49.8 | 4.8 | 48.7 |
| Pocatello, ID ..................... | 2 102 | 25 707 | 4 888 | 2 870 | 4 685 | 1 307 | 1 404 | 800 | 31 128 | 1 273 | 43.4 | 24.7 | 39.6 |
| Portland-South Portland-Biddeford, ME ..................... | 17 062 | 217 441 | 42 645 | 21 791 | 32 633 | 15 332 | 12 553 | 8 771 | 40 338 | 1 521 | 55.1 | 2.1 | 43.9 |
| Portland-Vancouver-Hillsboro, OR-WA ................ | 62 085 | 863 546 | 121 870 | 92 273 | 102 720 | 40 829 | 61 530 | 41 024 | 47 506 | 11 457 | 78.7 | 2.0 | 41.0 |
| Port St. Lucie, FL............... | 9 748 | 102 950 | 19 251 | 4 404 | 23 136 | 3 064 | 4 635 | 3 434 | 33 359 | 857 | 67.4 | 11.2 | 44.3 |
| Poughkeepsie-Newburgh-Middletown, NY.............. | 16 526 | 198 898 | 38 470 | 18 488 | 36 355 | 6 881 | 9 769 | 7 869 | 39 563 | 1 298 | 46.3 | 5.2 | 58.3 |
| Prescott, AZ ...................... | 5 495 | 50 662 | 10 876 | 2 621 | 10 369 | 1 308 | 1 521 | 1 546 | 30 518 | 756 | 63.0 | 13.8 | 46.2 |
| Providence-New Bedford-Fall River, RI-MA ........... | 40 607 | 596 268 | 123 707 | 67 174 | 82 584 | 29 601 | 28 709 | 24 847 | 41 671 | 1 996 | 69.7 | 0.7 | 49.5 |
| Provo-Orem, UT.................. | 10 907 | 159 245 | 19 992 | 15 433 | 22 533 | 4 303 | 12 694 | 5 695 | 35 763 | 2 510 | 69.4 | 8.2 | 33.5 |
| Pueblo, CO ....................... | 3 093 | 45 865 | 12 205 | 4 201 | 7 887 | 1 190 | 1 595 | 1 493 | 32 552 | 881 | 41.2 | 23.7 | 38.7 |
| Punta Gorda, FL ................ | 3 542 | 32 974 | 8 492 | 308 | 7 993 | 1 183 | 1 268 | 970 | 29 415 | 242 | 57.9 | 13.6 | 49.2 |
| Racine, WI ........................ | 4 037 | 66 884 | 10 739 | 14 394 | 8 481 | 1 852 | 2 333 | 2 776 | 41 506 | 652 | 53.7 | 7.5 | 44.6 |
| Raleigh-Cary, NC ............... | 28 873 | 418 514 | 56 220 | 22 736 | 59 006 | 21 552 | 37 060 | 18 669 | 44 608 | 2 665 | 49.9 | 6.6 | 46.6 |
| Rapid City, SD ................... | 4 251 | 48 367 | 9 736 | 2 436 | 8 570 | 2 835 | 2 064 | 1 669 | 34 506 | 1 534 | 18.8 | 49.1 | 55.6 |
| Reading, PA ...................... | 8 177 | 144 686 | 24 270 | 28 859 | 20 528 | 6 038 | 6 163 | 5 930 | 40 988 | 1 980 | 48.5 | 4.0 | 54.5 |
| Redding, CA....................... | 4 205 | 46 057 | 10 416 | 1 934 | 8 859 | 1 856 | 2 035 | 1 593 | 34 584 | 1 473 | 69.5 | 8.5 | 46.8 |
| Reno-Sparks, NV................ | 11 629 | 163 921 | 22 337 | 12 676 | 21 783 | 6 249 | 9 207 | 6 608 | 40 311 | 398 | 67.6 | 6.0 | 37.7 |
| Richmond, VA .................... | 30 539 | 479 531 | 68 016 | 31 715 | 65 058 | 42 741 | 35 188 | 21 970 | 45 815 | 4 330 | 41.6 | 8.7 | 41.3 |
| Riverside-San Bernardino-Ontario, CA .................... | 64 625 | 980 475 | 144 542 | 91 041 | 159 955 | 26 754 | 33 409 | 34 870 | 35 564 | 4 868 | 85.8 | 2.8 | 48.1 |
| Roanoke, VA ..................... | 8 062 | 131 880 | 23 717 | 15 028 | 18 000 | 9 108 | 6 170 | 5 094 | 38 626 | 2 219 | 37.4 | 6.1 | 42.5 |
| Rochester, MN ................... | 4 376 | 86 211 | D | 10 394 | 11 550 | 2 074 | 2 638 | 3 619 | 41 978 | 3 083 | 33.1 | 13.2 | 49.5 |
| Rochester, NY.................... | 23 577 | 421 950 | 75 270 | 54 762 | 57 115 | 14 712 | 23 103 | 16 989 | 40 264 | 3 728 | 40.1 | 10.2 | 54.8 |
| Rockford, IL....................... | 7 388 | 129 111 | 21 170 | 28 994 | 15 978 | 4 332 | 4 724 | 5 093 | 39 450 | 1 400 | 56.1 | 13.4 | 48.9 |
| Rocky Mount, NC................ | 2 921 | 49 335 | 8 086 | D | 7 006 | 1 992 | 1 126 | 1 730 | 35 062 | 787 | 39.3 | 17.5 | 53.0 |
| Rome, GA .......................... | 1 927 | 32 780 | 7 971 | 6 095 | 4 129 | D | 746 | 1 127 | 34 393 | 553 | 42.0 | 6.5 | 40.0 |

# Table C. Metropolitan Areas — **Agriculture**

| Area name | Agriculture, 2007 (cont.) | | | | | | | | | | | | | | | |
|---|---|---|---|---|---|---|---|---|---|---|---|---|---|---|---|---|
| | Land in farms | | | | | Value of land and buildings (dollars) | | Value of machinery and equipment, average per farm (dollars) | Value of products sold | | | | Percent of farms with sales of: | | Government payments | |
| | | | Acres | | | | | | | | Percent from: | | | | | |
| | Acreage (1,000) | Percent change, 2002– 2007 | Average size of farm | Total irrigated (1,000) | Total cropland (1,000) | Average per farm | Average per acre | | Total (mil dol) | Average per farm (dollars) | Crops | Live-stock and poultry products | $10,000 or more | $100,000 or more | Total ($1,000) | Percent of farms |
| | 117 | 118 | 119 | 120 | 121 | 122 | 123 | 124 | 125 | 126 | 127 | 128 | 129 | 130 | 131 | 132 |
| Naples-Marco Island, FL....... | 110 | -39.2 | 341 | 31.4 | 69.9 | 2 039 523 | 5 974 | 87 700 | 278.8 | 865 907 | 98.5 | 1.5 | 40.7 | 20.5 | 132 | 4.3 |
| Nashville-Davidson—Murfreesboro—Franklin, TN | 1 701 | -12.3 | 121 | 6.4 | 786.1 | 473 528 | 3 914 | 53 869 | 285.1 | 20 270 | 47.4 | 52.6 | 24.0 | 3.2 | 4 289 | 14.6 |
| New Haven-Milford, CT ....... | 46 | 76.9 | 80 | 1.5 | 13.8 | 1 061 198 | 13 310 | 64 600 | 90.2 | 157 370 | 90.3 | 9.7 | 36.8 | 12.7 | 344 | 6.1 |
| New Orleans-Metairie-Kenner, LA ......................... | 228 | D | 231 | D | D | D | D | D | D | D | D | 57.3 | 31.2 | 7.8 | 1 041 | 9.5 |
| New York-Northern New Jersey-Long Island, NY-NJ-PA.......................... | 369 | D | 60 | D | D | D | D | D | 594.2 | 97 267 | 84.8 | 15.0 | 32.4 | 11.1 | D | 5.7 |
| Edison-New Brunswick, NJ Div .............................. | 105 | -10.3 | 56 | 10.1 | 65.3 | 1 217 607 | 21 579 | 64 385 | 177.7 | 95 125 | 78.5 | 21.5 | 33.5 | 10.3 | 708 | 4.6 |
| Nassau-Suffolk, NY Div ...... | 36 | 2.9 | 55 | 13.8 | 26.6 | 1 165 722 | 21 034 | 174 458 | 258.7 | 401 758 | 91.5 | 8.5 | 69.9 | 37.0 | 253 | 8.5 |
| Newark-Union, NJ-PA Div... | 210 | D | 66 | 2.9 | 111.8 | 1 068 544 | 16 203 | 48 059 | 123.9 | 38 913 | 81.5 | 18.5 | 23.5 | 5.6 | D | 6.3 |
| New York-White Plains-Wayne, NY-NJ Div....... | 17 | D | 42 | D | D | D | D | D | 33.9 | 82 387 | 78.1 | 17.9 | 38.4 | 17.0 | D | 1.7 |
| Niles-Benton Harbor, MI ....... | 169 | -2.9 | 130 | 18.4 | 138.6 | 600 093 | 4 616 | 102 068 | 136.3 | 104 815 | 90.5 | 9.5 | 47.3 | 17.0 | 2 241 | 27.4 |
| North Port-Bradenton-Sarasota, FL ......................... | 286 | -32.4 | 260 | 53.1 | 86.0 | 1 695 414 | 6 512 | 71 523 | 342.8 | 311 954 | D | D | 36.8 | 14.3 | 90 | 0.8 |
| Norwich-New London, CT..... | 63 | 6.8 | 80 | 0.6 | 25.1 | 953 549 | 11 931 | 52 855 | 110.1 | 138 799 | 46.5 | 53.5 | 29.8 | 8.1 | 479 | 9.6 |
| Ocala, FL .......................... | 267 | -1.5 | 76 | 9.7 | 59.9 | 725 733 | 9 518 | 46 830 | 173.7 | 49 697 | 15.7 | 84.3 | 22.6 | 5.9 | 476 | 1.3 |
| Ocean City, NJ ................... | 8 | -20.0 | 40 | 2.3 | 4.3 | 637 097 | 16 055 | 59 369 | 14.6 | 72 567 | 96.2 | 3.8 | 35.8 | 8.0 | 20 | 4.0 |
| Odessa, TX ......................... | 424 | -15.9 | 1 408 | 1.1 | 7.0 | 560 521 | 398 | 43 889 | 3.6 | 11 824 | 27.5 | 72.5 | 15.3 | 3.3 | 109 | 4.3 |
| Ogden-Clearfield, UT .......... | 457 | D | 252 | 55.7 | 67.0 | 663 693 | 2 635 | 60 361 | 81.8 | 45 119 | 54.5 | 45.5 | 25.0 | 6.3 | 781 | 8.7 |
| Oklahoma City, OK ............. | 2 665 | 3.1 | 247 | 22.0 | 1 001.8 | 396 265 | 1 601 | 56 498 | 413.5 | 38 386 | 21.5 | 78.5 | 31.1 | 5.4 | 11 165 | 23.2 |
| Olympia, WA ...................... | 81 | 9.5 | 63 | 6.9 | 26.3 | 535 414 | 8 554 | 56 688 | 117.9 | 91 526 | 36.5 | 63.5 | 18.9 | 4.7 | 297 | 2.8 |
| Omaha-Council Bluffs, NE-IA ...................................... | 2 159 | -11.4 | 373 | D | 1 877.8 | 1 154 999 | 3 094 | 138 136 | 1 102.6 | 190 674 | 67.9 | 32.1 | 58.8 | 33.9 | 36 293 | 71.9 |
| Orlando-Kissimmee-Sanford, FL ....................... | 939 | -6.8 | 275 | 60.1 | 104.3 | 1 209 527 | 4 397 | 50 079 | 570.1 | 166 958 | D | D | 42.1 | 13.6 | D | 0.8 |
| Oshkosh-Neenah, WI........... | 164 | -3.5 | 164 | 0.3 | 133.3 | 563 264 | 3 438 | 93 394 | 107.8 | 107 654 | 28.6 | 71.4 | 45.2 | 19.2 | 2 690 | 69.9 |
| Owensboro, KY ................... | 464 | 2.7 | 256 | D | 357.1 | 744 187 | 2 902 | 97 802 | 289.3 | 159 815 | 47.8 | 52.2 | 43.0 | 17.6 | 5 154 | 55.5 |
| Oxnard-Thousand Oaks-Ventura, CA .......................... | 259 | -22.0 | 106 | 91.3 | 113.9 | 2 421 700 | 22 782 | 95 150 | 1 316.3 | 540 137 | 99.0 | 1.0 | 62.2 | 25.2 | 554 | 1.9 |
| Palm Bay-Melbourne-Titusville, FL .......................... | 167 | -11.2 | 315 | 20.5 | 22.1 | 1 238 223 | 3 936 | 56 362 | 46.7 | 87 913 | 85.2 | 14.8 | 50.1 | 9.0 | 21 | 1.5 |
| Palm Coast, FL ................... | 58 | -14.7 | 712 | 6.8 | 8.7 | 2 833 332 | 3 979 | 88 146 | 35.1 | 428 537 | 97.6 | 2.4 | 43.9 | 20.7 | 27 | 4.9 |
| Panama City-Lynn Haven-Panama City Beach, FL | 12 | 9.1 | 94 | D | 2.7 | 718 873 | 7 667 | 33 325 | 5.0 | 37 812 | 92.3 | 7.7 | 19.5 | 2.3 | 5 | 4.5 |
| Parkersburg-Marietta-Vienna, WV-OH .............. | 280 | -0.7 | 125 | D | 95.2 | 286 437 | 2 293 | 42 158 | D | D | 38.2 | D | 17.8 | 2.5 | D | 10.6 |
| Pascagoula, MS .................. | 110 | 3.8 | 104 | 0.9 | 41.8 | 330 052 | 3 186 | 57 467 | 25.4 | 24 009 | 64.8 | 35.2 | 24.2 | 4.2 | 2 012 | 15.0 |
| Pensacola-Ferry Pass-Brent, FL ...................................... | 152 | 2.7 | 115 | 5.1 | 85.6 | 602 464 | 5 223 | 52 955 | 52.7 | 39 967 | 84.5 | 15.5 | 24.6 | 6.7 | 6 999 | 40.0 |
| Peoria, IL............................ | 1 251 | -1.4 | 340 | 37.4 | 1 137.3 | 1 382 199 | 4 064 | 133 647 | 676.2 | 183 812 | 86.8 | 13.2 | 61.9 | 35.8 | 23 316 | 75.7 |
| Philadelphia-Camden-Wilmington, PA-NJ-DE-MD. | 679 | D | 97 | D | 489.0 | 1 056 233 | 10 868 | 89 344 | 1 084.2 | 155 149 | D | D | 39.9 | 16.4 | D | 16.7 |
| Camden, NJ Div ............. | 141 | -18.0 | 78 | 28.2 | 93.4 | 1 037 852 | 13 347 | 70 900 | 198.8 | 109 438 | 94.1 | 5.9 | 36.9 | 13.1 | 1 473 | 8.1 |
| Philadelphia, PA Div ...... | 289 | D | 83 | D | 205.5 | 871 207 | 10 486 | 92 411 | 663.9 | 190 647 | D | D | 41.1 | 18.4 | D | 16.0 |
| Wilmington, DE-MD-NJ Div. | 249 | 1.6 | 147 | 21.8 | 190.1 | 1 457 443 | 9 904 | 102 852 | 221.5 | 131 115 | D | D | 40.6 | 15.7 | 4 005 | 27.4 |
| Phoenix-Mesa-Glendale, AZ. | 1 533 | -14.3 | 594 | 414.5 | 523.3 | 3 078 081 | 5 177 | 154 163 | 1 613.3 | 625 796 | 39.1 | 60.9 | 36.4 | 19.1 | 34 774 | 16.6 |
| Pine Bluff, AR .................... | 520 | 1.8 | 467 | D | 400.2 | 1 036 953 | 2 221 | 161 530 | 455.3 | 408 683 | 38.4 | 61.6 | 47.5 | 30.0 | 15 857 | 44.2 |
| Pittsburgh, PA ................... | 876 | -3.5 | 111 | 2.4 | 484.0 | 469 623 | 4 247 | 62 321 | 228.4 | 28 817 | 50.5 | 49.5 | 26.0 | 5.6 | 4 518 | 18.1 |
| Pittsfield, MA ..................... | 66 | -4.3 | 127 | 0.2 | 22.6 | 1 113 751 | 8 762 | 54 632 | 20.6 | 39 466 | 37.5 | 62.5 | 28.4 | 8.2 | 205 | 6.1 |
| Pocatello, ID....................... | 773 | -1.2 | 607 | 153.3 | 536.0 | 749 754 | 1 235 | 102 779 | 198.4 | 155 841 | 77.3 | 22.7 | 28.6 | 12.1 | 11 923 | 42.2 |
| Portland-South Portland-Biddeford, ME ..................... | 130 | -1.5 | 85 | 1.7 | 46.9 | 398 209 | 4 671 | 56 909 | 43.3 | 28 439 | D | D | 27.5 | 7.3 | 641 | 7.6 |
| Portland-Vancouver-Hillsboro, OR-WA ................. | 662 | -7.4 | 58 | 95.1 | 389.4 | 631 364 | 10 932 | 59 345 | D | D | D | D | 26.3 | 8.3 | 3 387 | 6.6 |
| Port St. Lucie, FL ............... | 283 | -33.9 | 330 | 117.8 | 114.6 | 2 016 864 | 6 111 | 74 821 | 302.8 | 353 315 | 88.7 | 11.3 | 43.8 | 18.9 | 473 | 4.7 |
| Poughkeepsie-Newburgh-Middletown, NY............. | 183 | -16.8 | 141 | 5.9 | 93.2 | 762 975 | 5 402 | 95 761 | 118.6 | 91 382 | 62.9 | 37.1 | 49.0 | 18.3 | 1 161 | 18.6 |
| Prescott, AZ ...................... | 639 | -11.3 | 845 | 7.9 | 25.3 | 1 503 944 | 1 779 | 52 064 | D | D | D | D | 26.2 | 5.0 | 282 | 3.6 |
| Providence-New Bedford-Fall River, RI-MA .......... | 107 | 10.3 | 54 | 6.2 | 39.7 | 885 545 | 16 508 | 61 580 | 110.1 | 55 186 | 83.7 | 16.3 | 36.5 | 9.8 | 1 298 | 8.2 |
| Provo-Orem, UT.................. | 606 | -1.1 | 241 | 104.6 | 183.5 | 710 678 | 2 943 | 66 251 | 201.5 | 80 297 | 38.3 | 61.7 | 28.8 | 6.3 | 2 550 | 14.5 |
| Pueblo, CO ......................... | 911 | 17.7 | 1 034 | 24.6 | 73.5 | 692 240 | 670 | 68 533 | 49.3 | 55 904 | 32.2 | 67.8 | 29.3 | 8.3 | 1 667 | 18.8 |
| Punta Gorda, FL ................. | 166 | -13.5 | 686 | 20.0 | 28.7 | 2 224 000 | 3 241 | 61 849 | 65.6 | 270 921 | 89.5 | 10.5 | 39.7 | 16.5 | 306 | 2.5 |
| Racine, WI ......................... | 120 | -3.2 | 185 | 3.5 | 105.0 | 883 553 | 4 782 | 131 796 | 101.9 | 156 324 | 61.3 | 38.7 | 45.1 | 18.3 | 2 081 | 52.8 |
| Raleigh-Cary, NC ............... | 392 | -5.5 | 147 | 14.9 | 223.3 | 725 673 | 4 934 | 74 020 | 293.4 | 110 049 | 51.6 | 48.4 | 32.7 | 12.0 | 7 406 | 34.3 |
| Rapid City, SD ................... | 3 394 | -1.3 | 2 212 | 14.5 | 800.7 | 1 254 455 | 567 | 104 686 | 134.4 | 87 644 | 28.9 | 71.1 | 52.7 | 22.6 | 9 241 | 43.8 |
| Reading, PA ....................... | 222 | 2.8 | 112 | 1.3 | 170.8 | 772 086 | 6 882 | 101 016 | 367.8 | 185 778 | 45.0 | 55.0 | 52.5 | 24.8 | 3 280 | 33.0 |
| Redding, CA........................ | 391 | 17.1 | 265 | 48.7 | 40.2 | 837 861 | 3 158 | 43 514 | 44.7 | 30 329 | D | D | 22.6 | 4.1 | 252 | 3.8 |
| Reno-Sparks, NV ................ | 486 | D | 1 221 | D | 19.0 | 971 262 | 793 | 66 029 | D | D | D | 44.7 | 21.6 | 4.5 | 284 | 2.0 |
| Richmond, VA .................... | 850 | NA | 196 | 13.8 | 412.4 | 849 890 | 4 331 | 78 561 | 288.8 | 66 707 | D | D | 28.8 | 8.1 | 8 946 | 25.0 |
| Riverside-San Bernardino-Ontario, CA .................... | 869 | -20.0 | 179 | 197.0 | 255.8 | 1 483 376 | 8 310 | 72 148 | 1 755.7 | 360 662 | 49.6 | 50.4 | 46.0 | 15.3 | 6 980 | 2.9 |
| Roanoke, VA ...................... | 325 | NA | 147 | 1.0 | 114.3 | 614 239 | 4 189 | 67 391 | 77.9 | 35 114 | 17.2 | 82.8 | 30.1 | 5.5 | 1 019 | 15.6 |
| Rochester, MN ................... | 806 | -0.9 | 262 | D | 635.3 | 891 032 | 3 407 | 130 622 | 472.1 | 153 129 | 48.1 | 51.9 | 54.5 | 28.3 | 14 620 | 72.6 |
| Rochester, NY .................... | 863 | 6.7 | 231 | 8.8 | 650.6 | 497 601 | 2 151 | 124 029 | 649.8 | 174 326 | 57.8 | 42.2 | 47.8 | 22.1 | 10 289 | 37.2 |
| Rockford, IL........................ | 321 | -5.0 | 229 | 2.2 | 291.4 | 1 062 738 | 4 638 | 98 406 | 171.3 | 122 371 | 83.9 | 16.1 | 43.6 | 23.6 | 7 779 | 55.8 |
| Rocky Mount, NC ............... | 293 | -9.6 | 373 | 13.2 | 198.2 | 1 105 896 | 2 967 | 131 295 | 290.8 | 369 551 | 48.3 | 51.7 | 45.5 | 29.6 | 8 386 | 50.6 |
| Rome, GA ........................... | 85 | -6.6 | 153 | 1.1 | 28.0 | 565 269 | 3 695 | 63 954 | 49.4 | 89 351 | 5.9 | 94.1 | 26.6 | 8.0 | 769 | 16.8 |

| Area name | Water use, 2005 | | Wholesale trade,[1] 2007 | | | | Retail trade, 2007 | | | | Real estate and rental and leasing, 2007 | | | |
|---|---|---|---|---|---|---|---|---|---|---|---|---|---|---|
| | Total water withdrawn (mil gal/day) | Gallons withdrawn per person | Number of establishments | Number of employees | Sales (mil dol) | Annual payroll (mil dol) | Number of establishments | Number of employees | Sales (mil dol) | Annual payroll (mil dol) | Number of establishments | Number of employees | Receipts (mil dol) | Annual payroll (mil dol) |
| | 133 | 134 | 135 | 136 | 137 | 138 | 139 | 140 | 141 | 142 | 143 | 144 | 145 | 146 |
| Naples-Marco Island, FL | 193.2 | 608 | 385 | 2 933 | 1 838.1 | 145.5 | 1 500 | 20 122 | 5 186.5 | 535.5 | 958 | 2 874 | 552.3 | 118.0 |
| Nashville-Davidson—Murfreesboro—Franklin, TN | 1 212.4 | 852 | 2 155 | 39 397 | 37 880.7 | 1 939.0 | 5 869 | 84 667 | 21 088.0 | 1 997.6 | 1 846 | 12 182 | 2 703.5 | 420.2 |
| New Haven-Milford, CT | 342.7 | 405 | 1 130 | 16 584 | 12 043.2 | 939.9 | 3 172 | 46 058 | 11 785.3 | 1 112.5 | 780 | 5 470 | 1 611.1 | 192.9 |
| New Orleans-Metairie-Kenner, LA | 5 738.2 | 4 349 | 1 773 | 22 985 | 23 831.4 | 1 136.4 | 4 311 | 61 162 | 15 554.7 | 1 496.4 | 1 268 | 9 069 | 1 700.0 | 318.0 |
| New York-Northern New Jersey-Long Island, NY-NJ-PA | 11 840.4 | 632 | 40 354 | 526 717 | 643 078.2 | 33 175.4 | 75 619 | 856 298 | 237 554.8 | 23 310.4 | 33 481 | 186 514 | 57 284.2 | 9 294.6 |
| Edison-New Brunswick, NJ Div | 2 341.1 | 1 016 | 4 153 | 75 469 | 98 802.1 | 5 226.4 | 8 886 | 129 943 | 35 419.5 | 3 348.5 | 2 375 | 14 060 | 3 870.6 | 603.2 |
| Nassau-Suffolk, NY Div | 2 059.5 | 733 | 7 000 | 85 309 | 78 816.5 | 4 752.1 | 13 106 | 168 238 | 47 632.6 | 4 491.6 | 4 314 | 18 290 | 4 787.8 | 825.4 |
| Newark-Union, NJ-PA Div | 196.8 | 91 | 3 902 | 69 907 | 78 972.4 | 5 003.3 | 8 275 | 101 421 | 28 129.1 | 2 673.6 | 2 477 | 18 407 | 4 667.5 | 938.9 |
| New York-White Plains-Wayne, NY-NJ Div | 7 243.0 | 631 | 25 299 | 296 032 | 386 487.3 | 18 193.6 | 45 352 | 456 696 | 126 373.6 | 12 796.7 | 24 315 | 135 757 | 43 958.3 | 6 927.1 |
| Niles-Benton Harbor, MI | 2 327.2 | 14 311 | 171 | 2 063 | 1 789.3 | 77.3 | 609 | 7 360 | 1 622.8 | 153.9 | 189 | 796 | 105.6 | 19.3 |
| North Port-Bradenton-Sarasota, FL | 182.4 | 271 | 955 | 7 671 | 4 500.5 | 333.2 | 2 927 | 39 824 | 9 474.3 | 943.1 | 1 479 | 5 402 | 929.9 | 169.3 |
| Norwich-New London, CT | 2 259.1 | 8 473 | 174 | 2 286 | 1 698.6 | 120.1 | 1 123 | 15 660 | 3 883.0 | 390.4 | 232 | D | D | D |
| Ocala, FL | 54.4 | 179 | 370 | 4 691 | 2 421.0 | 182.3 | 1 208 | 16 639 | 4 218.8 | 379.2 | 466 | 1 598 | 217.9 | 39.9 |
| Ocean City, NJ | 217.6 | 2 191 | 71 | D | D | D | 746 | 6 103 | 1 584.9 | 164.8 | 258 | 836 | 177.1 | 27.0 |
| Odessa, TX | 64.0 | 511 | 319 | 4 654 | 2 324.3 | 247.5 | 476 | 6 660 | 2 090.6 | 167.6 | 157 | 1 383 | 338.4 | 74.3 |
| Ogden-Clearfield, UT | 437.4 | 874 | 502 | 6 539 | 4 660.3 | 261.8 | 1 517 | 24 999 | 6 070.9 | 537.6 | 752 | 2 215 | 322.2 | 50.7 |
| Oklahoma City, OK | 204.6 | 177 | 1 770 | 25 698 | 36 154.4 | 1 182.1 | 4 391 | 61 143 | 15 683.4 | 1 371.5 | 1 650 | 10 607 | 1 631.5 | 370.3 |
| Olympia, WA | 46.2 | 202 | 203 | 2 083 | 1 227.6 | 100.1 | 822 | 12 136 | 3 103.0 | 313.2 | 323 | 1 234 | 238.8 | 31.6 |
| Omaha-Council Bluffs, NE-IA | 2 087.6 | 2 567 | 1 376 | 20 154 | 20 914.4 | 1 059.6 | 2 857 | 51 994 | 13 053.0 | 1 153.4 | 1 018 | 6 713 | 1 146.9 | 215.1 |
| Orlando-Kissimmee-Sanford, FL | 559.3 | 286 | 3 281 | 42 454 | 48 564.7 | 2 007.3 | 8 295 | 126 325 | 32 378.4 | 2 870.5 | 4 241 | 36 652 | 7 857.9 | 1 398.3 |
| Oshkosh-Neenah, WI | 76.6 | 480 | 184 | 3 375 | 1 487.3 | 137.1 | 540 | 8 027 | 1 796.5 | 162.1 | 125 | 756 | 97.5 | 19.6 |
| Owensboro, KY | 491.6 | 4 405 | 117 | 1 452 | 933.7 | 52.5 | 488 | 6 298 | 1 359.0 | 129.7 | 85 | 537 | 51.3 | 11.2 |
| Oxnard-Thousand Oaks-Ventura, CA | 1 198.6 | 1 506 | 1 170 | 17 854 | 34 976.8 | 1 218.5 | 2 766 | 40 773 | 11 083.6 | 1 074.8 | 1 051 | 5 064 | 1 006.1 | 196.0 |
| Palm Bay-Melbourne-Titusville, FL | 957.3 | 1 799 | 606 | 4 267 | 2 639.7 | 179.3 | 2 073 | 28 911 | 6 594.0 | 630.4 | 777 | 2 795 | 401.1 | 74.8 |
| Palm Coast, FL | 19.3 | 245 | 59 | 298 | 92.9 | 10.9 | 208 | 2 899 | 684.1 | 66.3 | 195 | 508 | 66.9 | 13.8 |
| Panama City-Lynn Haven-Panama City Beach, FL | 291.9 | 1 805 | 193 | 1 736 | 868.3 | 72.1 | 816 | 10 186 | 2 472.0 | 227.1 | 314 | 1 172 | 167.7 | 33.6 |
| Parkersburg-Marietta-Vienna, WV-OH | 1 113.5 | 6 851 | 181 | 1 709 | 1 045.4 | 54.8 | 711 | 9 986 | 2 425.5 | 194.1 | 135 | 667 | 117.0 | 18.1 |
| Pascagoula, MS | 57.7 | 367 | 71 | 626 | 318.8 | 19.5 | 534 | 6 244 | 1 536.6 | 132.4 | 114 | 388 | 50.5 | 9.6 |
| Pensacola-Ferry Pass-Brent, FL | 358.0 | 813 | 415 | 4 592 | 2 718.6 | 182.1 | 1 596 | 21 249 | 5 163.6 | 471.0 | 591 | 2 008 | 333.3 | 55.7 |
| Peoria, IL | 676.4 | 1 832 | 490 | 8 246 | 16 183.5 | 445.1 | 1 404 | 20 008 | 4 598.1 | 430.9 | 352 | 1 589 | 259.4 | 42.4 |
| Philadelphia-Camden-Wilmington, PA-NJ-DE-MD | 5 258.7 | 903 | 8 743 | 144 877 | 160 429.2 | 9 316.9 | 20 970 | 316 013 | 84 725.2 | 7 790.6 | 5 693 | 43 149 | 19 440.1 | 1 911.9 |
| Camden, NJ Div | 235.2 | 189 | 1 802 | D | D | D | 4 494 | 69 542 | 17 217.0 | 1 694.6 | 1 046 | D | D | D |
| Philadelphia, PA Div | 1 814.1 | 466 | 6 137 | 91 849 | 87 723.7 | 6 056.8 | 13 900 | 207 225 | 57 105.7 | 5 162.6 | 3 686 | D | D | D |
| Wilmington, DE-MD-NJ Div | 3 209.4 | 4 671 | 804 | D | D | D | 2 576 | 39 246 | 10 402.5 | 933.5 | 961 | 4 251 | 10 805.6 | 167.8 |
| Phoenix-Mesa-Glendale, AZ | 3 256.2 | 842 | 5 216 | 83 170 | 75 372.4 | 4 476.5 | 11 992 | 226 298 | 60 721.4 | 5 507.8 | 6 325 | 38 676 | 7 904.0 | 1 582.1 |
| Pine Bluff, AR | 556.6 | 5 308 | 79 | D | D | D | 363 | 4 353 | 937.2 | 84.6 | 83 | 259 | 47.9 | 6.8 |
| Pittsburgh, PA | 2 311.9 | 969 | 3 251 | 46 323 | 51 610.7 | 2 308.7 | 8 858 | 132 058 | 32 663.5 | 2 755.0 | 2 016 | 13 928 | 2 677.3 | 508.2 |
| Pittsfield, MA | 35.6 | 270 | 124 | 1 334 | 529.3 | 58.1 | 766 | 8 942 | 1 901.8 | 208.8 | 128 | 770 | 123.3 | 22.9 |
| Pocatello, ID | 747.1 | 8 697 | 95 | 864 | 557.6 | 32.0 | 373 | 5 185 | 1 149.7 | 101.6 | 103 | 350 | 54.0 | 7.1 |
| Portland-South Portland-Biddeford, ME | 253.2 | 492 | 775 | 9 597 | 6 901.6 | 435.9 | 2 637 | 34 309 | 7 984.1 | 803.3 | 900 | 3 763 | 622.5 | 126.8 |
| Portland-Vancouver-Hillsboro, OR-WA | 787.1 | 376 | 4 056 | 57 847 | 62 236.2 | 3 234.9 | 7 404 | 113 736 | 29 223.1 | 2 847.1 | 3 702 | 20 226 | 3 772.1 | 729.1 |
| Port St. Lucie, FL | 1 491.0 | 3 912 | 524 | 3 753 | 2 145.5 | 159.2 | 1 514 | 24 047 | 6 168.1 | 578.3 | 653 | 2 609 | 377.2 | 72.5 |
| Poughkeepsie-Newburgh-Middletown, NY | 893.8 | 1 338 | 771 | 11 008 | 9 421.6 | 523.3 | 2 681 | 36 977 | 9 328.4 | 873.6 | 811 | 3 435 | 667.5 | 108.3 |
| Prescott, AZ | 91.5 | 460 | 201 | 1 728 | 886.6 | 63.9 | 920 | 11 795 | 2 695.4 | 266.6 | 469 | 1 776 | 293.9 | 55.4 |
| Providence-New Bedford-Fall River, RI-MA | 1 462.2 | 901 | 2 123 | 34 240 | 24 749.2 | 1 829.5 | 6 499 | 87 944 | 20 934.2 | 2 061.9 | 1 705 | 8 944 | 1 844.9 | 297.8 |
| Provo-Orem, UT | 476.2 | 1 024 | 476 | 6 412 | 3 188.4 | 292.2 | 1 391 | 24 306 | 5 884.3 | 523.1 | 755 | 2 462 | 334.4 | 60.1 |
| Pueblo, CO | 301.3 | 1 991 | 96 | 959 | 472.8 | 41.6 | 548 | 8 064 | 1 864.6 | 192.4 | 165 | 667 | 94.9 | 18.3 |
| Punta Gorda, FL | 40.1 | 260 | 114 | 658 | 279.3 | 25.1 | 582 | 8 761 | 1 898.1 | 187.9 | 289 | 877 | 120.7 | 22.1 |
| Racine, WI | 42.3 | 216 | 213 | 3 442 | 4 657.4 | 166.2 | 654 | 10 082 | 2 230.0 | 198.7 | 140 | 596 | 64.5 | 13.4 |
| Raleigh-Cary, NC | 164.0 | 173 | 1 546 | 22 231 | 20 942.0 | 1 361.4 | 3 899 | 58 236 | 14 941.7 | 1 340.3 | 1 502 | 7 839 | 1 990.0 | 337.6 |
| Rapid City, SD | 44.7 | 378 | 208 | 2 259 | 1 289.7 | 90.5 | 686 | 8 604 | 2 162.1 | 194.1 | 187 | 771 | 128.2 | 18.1 |
| Reading, PA | 61.0 | 154 | 448 | 7 216 | 7 091.9 | 358.9 | 1 327 | 20 433 | 4 953.2 | 466.8 | 273 | 1 384 | 210.2 | 39.4 |
| Redding, CA | 236.2 | 1 313 | 196 | 1 936 | 1 166.0 | 77.5 | 722 | 10 287 | 2 526.4 | 260.1 | 225 | 1 201 | 128.2 | 26.1 |
| Reno-Sparks, NV | 120.6 | 306 | 688 | 11 434 | 8 716.2 | 521.2 | 1 577 | 25 079 | 6 674.2 | 672.1 | 765 | 4 008 | 705.9 | 129.4 |
| Richmond, VA | 4 085.9 | 3 475 | 1 756 | 29 714 | 27 573.3 | 1 520.7 | 4 622 | 69 570 | 17 888.3 | 1 591.0 | 1 470 | 9 303 | 1 929.3 | 370.1 |
| Riverside-San Bernardino-Ontario, CA | 1 843.5 | 471 | 4 401 | 63 310 | 59 701.7 | 2 764.3 | 10 338 | 173 855 | 45 863.8 | 4 276.1 | 3 960 | 21 722 | 4 366.9 | 731.4 |
| Roanoke, VA | 54.3 | 185 | 527 | 7 785 | 5 305.7 | 343.0 | 1 338 | 18 897 | 4 121.3 | 413.8 | 411 | 2 288 | 328.2 | 61.1 |
| Rochester, MN | 55.8 | 315 | 176 | 2 638 | 1 541.0 | 140.9 | 774 | 11 860 | 2 484.6 | 254.6 | 179 | 859 | 120.6 | 22.2 |
| Rochester, NY | 714.5 | 688 | 1 305 | 19 642 | 11 387.3 | 1 047.8 | 3 547 | 56 071 | 12 056.1 | 1 185.1 | 1 029 | 7 181 | 1 158.2 | 213.5 |
| Rockford, IL | 52.0 | 153 | 469 | 5 939 | 4 056.5 | 256.1 | 1 154 | 17 650 | 4 306.9 | 383.0 | 270 | 1 653 | 219.2 | 47.5 |
| Rocky Mount, NC | 37.5 | 258 | 148 | 4 535 | 3 152.0 | 137.1 | 636 | 7 312 | 1 595.9 | 144.6 | 123 | 533 | 96.0 | 13.9 |
| Rome, GA | 588.9 | 6 252 | 101 | 1 410 | 692.1 | 52.5 | 431 | 4 718 | 1 039.8 | 94.0 | 82 | 353 | 58.0 | 10.1 |

1. Merchant wholesalers, except manufacturers' sales branches and offices.

# Table C. Metropolitan Areas — **Professional Services, Manufacturing, and Accommodation and Food Services**

| Area name | Professional, scientific, and technical services,[1] 2007 | | | | Manufacturing, 2007 | | | | Accommodation and food services, 2007 | | | |
|---|---|---|---|---|---|---|---|---|---|---|---|---|
| | Number of establishments | Number of employees | Sales (mil dol) | Annual payroll (mil dol) | Number of establishments | Number of employees | Sales (mil dol) | Annual payroll (mil dol) | Number of establishments | Number of employees | Sales (mil dol) | Annual payroll (mil dol) |
| | 147 | 148 | 149 | 150 | 151 | 152 | 153 | 154 | 155 | 156 | 157 | 158 |
| Naples-Marco Island, FL | 1 271 | D | D | D | 228 | 3 035 | 606.7 | 109.5 | 704 | 17 421 | 1 037.2 | 308.3 |
| Nashville-Davidson—Murfreesboro—Franklin, TN | 3 653 | D | D | D | 1 583 | 74 547 | D | 3 135.7 | 3 096 | 69 674 | 3 463.8 | 987.1 |
| New Haven-Milford, CT | 2 015 | D | D | D | 1 289 | 40 188 | 10 493.0 | 1 976.9 | 1 920 | 24 768 | 1 345.9 | 371.7 |
| New Orleans-Metairie-Kenner, LA | 3 710 | 28 673 | 4 672.5 | 1 655.4 | 764 | 35 267 | D | 1 939.1 | 2 830 | 60 410 | 3 677.0 | 1 043.7 |
| New York-Northern New Jersey-Long Island, NY-NJ-PA | 67 946 | 672 812 | 135 779.9 | 54 004.4 | 18 482 | 449 307 | 144 942.5 | 21 711.5 | 41 108 | 538 990 | 39 932.8 | 10 809.3 |
| Edison-New Brunswick, NJ Div | 9 804 | D | D | D | 2 010 | D | D | 3 789.0 | 5 055 | 66 830 | 3 787.7 | 1 016.2 |
| Nassau-Suffolk, NY Div | 12 596 | D | D | D | 3 577 | D | D | 4 056.0 | 6 466 | 79 474 | 4 815.7 | 1 331.5 |
| Newark-Union, NJ-PA Div | 7 888 | 102 853 | 16 262.9 | 7 903.4 | 2 552 | 87 290 | 38 292.3 | 5 050.9 | 4 595 | 58 397 | 3 637.6 | 982.3 |
| New York-White Plains-Wayne, NY-NJ Div | 37 658 | D | D | D | 10 343 | 202 733 | 58 514.0 | 8 815.6 | 24 992 | 334 289 | 27 691.8 | 7 479.3 |
| Niles-Benton Harbor, MI | 287 | D | D | D | 332 | 10 831 | 2 298.3 | 474.7 | 413 | 5 519 | 219.5 | 64.1 |
| North Port-Bradenton-Sarasota, FL | 2 687 | D | D | D | 630 | 17 798 | 4 351.7 | 763.1 | 1 335 | 26 200 | 1 288.2 | 381.4 |
| Norwich-New London, CT | 555 | D | D | D | 201 | D | D | 848.8 | 690 | 30 404 | 3 444.7 | 856.8 |
| Ocala, FL | 698 | 3 459 | 361.6 | 132.0 | 221 | 8 904 | 1 841.5 | 320.9 | 443 | 7 784 | 353.1 | 100.0 |
| Ocean City, NJ | 250 | D | D | D | 81 | 662 | D | 18.9 | 832 | 5 615 | 517.0 | 144.9 |
| Odessa, TX | 224 | D | D | D | 240 | 4 814 | 2 049.7 | 222.0 | 245 | 5 213 | 228.6 | 59.4 |
| Ogden-Clearfield, UT | 1 278 | D | D | D | 529 | 22 140 | 9 104.3 | 909.8 | 737 | 14 674 | 541.1 | 149.1 |
| Oklahoma City, OK | 3 836 | D | D | D | 1 138 | 32 649 | 10 181.0 | 1 278.9 | 2 428 | 52 115 | 2 111.7 | 588.3 |
| Olympia, WA | 598 | D | D | D | 189 | 3 118 | 870.1 | 120.7 | 497 | 7 612 | 346.7 | 102.7 |
| Omaha-Council Bluffs, NE-IA | 2 196 | D | D | D | 748 | 33 757 | 14 272.2 | 1 377.6 | 1 826 | 37 671 | 1 782.4 | 479.4 |
| Orlando-Kissimmee-Sanford, FL | 7 667 | D | D | D | 1 473 | 43 017 | 14 027.0 | 2 060.2 | 4 190 | 126 780 | 8 735.7 | 2 143.5 |
| Oshkosh-Neenah, WI | 250 | D | D | D | 319 | 23 777 | 9 198.9 | 1 149.8 | 377 | 6 071 | 212.1 | 58.4 |
| Owensboro, KY | 182 | D | D | D | 135 | 9 342 | 4 765.0 | 424.3 | 196 | 4 171 | 152.7 | 45.9 |
| Oxnard-Thousand Oaks-Ventura, CA | 2 597 | 16 457 | 6 370.8 | 1 032.7 | 954 | 33 602 | 8 769.0 | 1 643.4 | 1 602 | 29 832 | 1 478.2 | 422.9 |
| Palm Bay-Melbourne-Titusville, FL | 1 683 | 19 711 | 3 364.7 | 1 589.6 | 473 | 22 772 | 6 767.6 | 1 172.5 | 1 019 | 19 057 | 855.5 | 240.1 |
| Palm Coast, FL | 197 | 674 | 105.6 | 46.6 | 52 | 1 031 | 235.7 | 29.9 | 131 | 2 401 | 114.8 | 31.6 |
| Panama City-Lynn Haven-Panama City Beach, FL | 406 | D | D | D | 116 | 3 702 | 1 254.3 | 153.4 | 442 | 9 154 | 480.4 | 135.8 |
| Parkersburg-Marietta-Vienna, WV-OH | 249 | 1 975 | 180.3 | 69.4 | 178 | 9 219 | 5 203.7 | 474.0 | 364 | 6 463 | 249.0 | 72.6 |
| Pascagoula, MS | 221 | D | D | D | 96 | 14 386 | D | 672.2 | 254 | 4 509 | 191.5 | 50.2 |
| Pensacola-Ferry Pass-Brent, FL | 1 042 | 8 005 | 936.0 | 379.3 | 246 | 5 710 | 2 191.9 | 271.1 | 718 | 14 399 | 629.0 | 173.6 |
| Peoria, IL | 679 | D | D | D | 362 | D | D | D | 920 | 15 634 | 733.7 | 193.3 |
| Philadelphia-Camden-Wilmington, PA-NJ-DE-MD | 18 282 | 190 964 | 32 765.7 | 13 547.2 | 5 881 | 224 483 | 122 509.8 | 12 018.5 | 12 138 | 185 109 | 9 991.3 | 2 727.1 |
| Camden, NJ Div | 3 525 | D | D | D | 1 180 | 48 041 | 25 901.8 | 2 543.0 | 2 398 | 35 317 | 1 715.2 | 470.0 |
| Philadelphia, PA Div | 12 688 | D | D | D | 4 182 | 150 767 | 73 597.8 | 7 873.8 | 8 407 | 126 476 | 7 062.3 | 1 932.9 |
| Wilmington, DE-MD-NJ Div | 2 069 | D | D | D | 519 | 25 675 | 23 010.2 | 1 601.7 | 1 333 | 23 316 | 1 213.8 | 324.2 |
| Phoenix-Mesa-Glendale, AZ | 11 954 | 100 017 | 14 346.2 | 5 938.7 | 3 520 | 124 958 | 42 332.0 | 6 195.2 | 7 078 | 162 741 | 8 750.9 | 2 534.5 |
| Pine Bluff, AR | 99 | D | D | D | 69 | 5 260 | 1 477.9 | 173.9 | 156 | 2 324 | 91.7 | 23.9 |
| Pittsburgh, PA | 5 990 | D | D | D | 2 755 | 101 747 | 38 078.2 | 4 809.8 | 5 348 | 93 669 | 3 940.7 | 1 134.7 |
| Pittsfield, MA | 366 | D | D | D | 173 | 6 204 | 1 425.5 | 317.1 | 516 | 7 600 | 401.9 | 125.6 |
| Pocatello, ID | 170 | D | D | D | 66 | 3 320 | 1 206.5 | 130.5 | 197 | 3 126 | 120.4 | 32.5 |
| Portland-South Portland-Biddeford, ME | 1 868 | D | D | D | 715 | 26 666 | 6 744.0 | 1 187.9 | 1 733 | 23 504 | 1 285.5 | 383.2 |
| Portland-Vancouver-Hillsboro, OR-WA | 7 698 | D | D | D | 3 281 | 110 749 | 47 590.7 | 5 358.2 | 5 340 | 83 103 | 4 170.4 | 1 226.8 |
| Port St. Lucie, FL | 1 178 | D | D | D | 295 | 6 106 | 1 772.6 | 231.8 | 665 | 13 151 | 547.4 | 161.6 |
| Poughkeepsie-Newburgh-Middletown, NY | 1 679 | D | D | D | 554 | 23 458 | 6 176.5 | 1 584.1 | 1 493 | 16 927 | 879.4 | 240.4 |
| Prescott, AZ | 584 | D | D | D | 233 | 3 618 | 764.0 | 143.6 | 578 | 8 737 | 456.5 | 126.2 |
| Providence-New Bedford-Fall River, RI-MA | 4 206 | D | D | D | 2 628 | 88 819 | 20 939.6 | 4 034.3 | 4 132 | 65 292 | 3 033.9 | 883.7 |
| Provo-Orem, UT | 1 442 | 16 746 | 1 354.1 | 509.0 | 530 | 18 472 | 4 867.1 | 815.1 | 564 | 11 935 | 458.8 | 130.2 |
| Pueblo, CO | 251 | D | D | D | 106 | 3 838 | 1 705.8 | 180.3 | 344 | 5 602 | 220.9 | 61.8 |
| Punta Gorda, FL | 366 | D | D | D | 64 | 430 | 103.7 | 14.6 | 240 | 4 322 | 178.0 | 53.2 |
| Racine, WI | 346 | D | D | D | 345 | 17 183 | 7 863.3 | 890.8 | 388 | 6 239 | 242.7 | 66.1 |
| Raleigh-Cary, NC | 4 380 | 36 371 | 5 527.1 | 2 270.9 | 810 | 27 491 | 17 544.0 | 1 263.7 | 2 087 | 41 492 | 1 945.2 | 537.0 |
| Rapid City, SD | 326 | D | D | D | 163 | 3 201 | 713.8 | 112.3 | 412 | 6 538 | 320.0 | 88.8 |
| Reading, PA | 735 | 6 289 | 1 449.0 | 389.4 | 550 | 32 597 | 8 461.8 | 1 487.9 | 715 | 11 030 | 446.0 | 124.4 |
| Redding, CA | 400 | D | D | D | 167 | 2 794 | 662.9 | 117.1 | 403 | 5 862 | 281.0 | 74.9 |
| Reno-Sparks, NV | 1 696 | 10 101 | 1 444.2 | 549.1 | 507 | 15 502 | 5 884.3 | 765.8 | 1 003 | 35 540 | 2 404.2 | 730.6 |
| Richmond, VA | 3 401 | 30 395 | 4 176.1 | 1 861.6 | 1 035 | 42 516 | 22 849.0 | 2 196.1 | 2 319 | 45 274 | 2 090.9 | 583.5 |
| Riverside-San Bernardino-Ontario, CA | 5 662 | 35 199 | 4 326.5 | 1 583.0 | 3 668 | 122 090 | 32 530.9 | 4 855.0 | 6 404 | 128 663 | 7 590.0 | 2 021.0 |
| Roanoke, VA | 744 | 5 864 | 808.4 | 288.7 | 346 | 17 968 | 4 915.0 | 733.0 | 628 | 12 451 | 520.1 | 156.6 |
| Rochester, MN | 334 | D | D | D | 160 | 12 447 | 4 212.7 | 711.4 | 395 | 8 214 | 355.7 | 101.7 |
| Rochester, NY | 2 433 | D | D | D | 1 333 | 66 957 | 21 530.8 | 3 036.9 | 2 170 | 33 119 | 1 412.2 | 409.7 |
| Rockford, IL | 727 | 4 914 | 534.9 | 217.9 | 756 | 33 901 | 13 467.0 | 1 742.1 | 662 | 11 409 | 492.4 | 135.5 |
| Rocky Mount, NC | 222 | 1 232 | 133.0 | 48.1 | 145 | 12 735 | 4 183.1 | 500.7 | 266 | 5 058 | 200.2 | 55.2 |
| Rome, GA | 174 | 703 | 80.1 | 24.8 | 109 | 7 726 | 3 346.1 | 312.7 | 198 | 3 423 | 144.3 | 38.1 |

1. Establishments subject to federal tax.

# Table C. Metropolitan Areas — Health Care and Social Assistance, Other Services, and Federal Funds

| Area name | Health care and social assistance,[1] 2007 | | | | Other services,[1] 2007 | | | | Federal funds and grants, 2009–2010 Expenditures (mil dol) | | | |
|---|---|---|---|---|---|---|---|---|---|---|---|---|
| | | | | | | | | | | Direct payments for individuals | | |
| | Number of establishments | Number of employees | Receipts (mil dol) | Annual payroll (mil dol) | Number of establishments | Number of employees | Receipts (mil dol) | Annual payroll (mil dol) | Total | Social Security and government retirement | Medicare | Food stamps and Supplemental Security Income |
| | 159 | 160 | 161 | 162 | 163 | 164 | 165 | 166 | 167 | 168 | 169 | 170 |
| Naples-Marco Island, FL...... | 914 | 14 861 | 1 796.1 | 703.8 | 828 | 4 364 | 393.3 | 113.0 | 2 069.4 | 1 202.8 | 492.5 | 54.2 |
| Nashville-Davidson—Murfreesboro—Franklin, TN | 3 820 | 89 796 | 10 518.5 | 3 917.0 | 2 529 | 20 895 | 1 944.3 | 614.7 | 15 209.1 | 3 935.9 | 2 386.8 | 513.4 |
| New Haven-Milford, CT ........ | 2 371 | 68 663 | 6 467.8 | 2 792.6 | 1 772 | 10 629 | 948.2 | 288.9 | 11 538.3 | 2 403.0 | 5 657.1 | 291.9 |
| New Orleans-Metairie-Kenner, LA ......................... | 3 027 | 61 663 | 6 835.2 | 2 484.5 | 1 935 | 12 290 | 1 654.5 | 360.5 | 15 844.0 | 3 119.2 | 2 819.8 | 697.8 |
| New York-Northern New Jersey-Long Island, NY-NJ-PA.................... | 55 243 | 1 255 893 | 130 730.9 | 54 812.1 | 44 877 | 256 021 | 41 257.8 | 8 606.9 | 169 410.6 | 44 503.5 | 38 973.7 | 8 037.3 |
| Edison-New Brunswick, NJ Div.................................. | 6 848 | 125 226 | 13 035.7 | 5 180.4 | 4 877 | 27 864 | 3 369.7 | 824.0 | 19 043.9 | 7 014.8 | 4 236.9 | 289.6 |
| Nassau-Suffolk, NY Div ...... | 10 014 | 179 244 | 19 852.0 | 8 240.8 | 7 604 | 37 690 | 3 737.3 | 1 042.6 | 23 918.0 | 8 659.2 | 5 576.1 | 398.7 |
| Newark-Union, NJ-PA Div... | 6 504 | 131 899 | 13 247.6 | 5 867.9 | 4 926 | 28 360 | 3 128.5 | 837.8 | 17 359.5 | 5 300.6 | 4 068.9 | 627.9 |
| New York-White Plains-Wayne, NY-NJ Div...... | 31 877 | 819 524 | 84 595.6 | 35 523.0 | 27 470 | 162 107 | 31 022.2 | 5 902.6 | 109 089.3 | 23 528.9 | 25 091.9 | 6 721.1 |
| Niles-Benton Harbor, MI ....... | 394 | 8 821 | 701.7 | 282.8 | 281 | 1 468 | 112.2 | 35.1 | 1 365.2 | 568.7 | 292.2 | 90.6 |
| North Port-Bradenton-Sarasota, FL............................. | 2 244 | 35 836 | 3 772.8 | 1 384.5 | 1 431 | 7 361 | 577.6 | 160.1 | 6 387.1 | 3 283.7 | 1 962.4 | 154.7 |
| Norwich-New London, CT..... | 703 | 16 048 | 1 467.8 | 617.5 | 479 | 2 549 | 234.3 | 59.3 | 6 569.1 | 887.6 | 1 336.7 | 55.3 |
| Ocala, FL............................. | 817 | 14 493 | 1 590.4 | 566.1 | 467 | 2 408 | 201.6 | 51.4 | 2 844.7 | 1 621.9 | 717.0 | 121.2 |
| Ocean City, NJ..................... | 268 | D | D | D | 288 | 1 124 | 91.2 | 29.5 | 961.9 | 429.9 | 310.1 | 20.2 |
| Odessa, TX........................... | 300 | 6 988 | 644.3 | 248.5 | 246 | 2 115 | 283.6 | 64.3 | 749.5 | 287.9 | 194.9 | 70.3 |
| Ogden-Clearfield, UT .......... | 1 154 | 18 393 | 1 597.3 | 620.7 | 715 | 4 457 | 326.2 | 97.2 | 5 112.2 | 1 524.7 | 679.8 | 110.4 |
| Oklahoma City, OK.............. | 3 832 | 73 078 | 8 033.8 | 2 723.7 | 2 034 | 12 913 | 1 348.9 | 318.7 | 12 811.2 | 3 852.5 | 1 467.4 | 439.1 |
| Olympia, WA........................ | 710 | 11 596 | 1 238.4 | 447.6 | 464 | 2 812 | 273.7 | 88.2 | 4 306.4 | 924.1 | 232.8 | 71.1 |
| Omaha-Council Bluffs, NE-IA........................................ | 2 141 | 53 429 | 5 209.5 | 2 133.1 | 1 591 | 10 887 | 1 256.8 | 284.8 | 7 087.1 | 2 428.1 | 957.7 | 217.3 |
| Orlando-Kissimmee-Sanford, FL...................... | 4 863 | 92 989 | 9 853.3 | 3 908.8 | 3 611 | 24 032 | 2 345.8 | 664.8 | 16 831.3 | 6 109.2 | 3 077.5 | 687.8 |
| Oshkosh-Neenah, WI........... | 430 | 12 589 | 1 344.9 | 476.6 | 290 | 2 355 | 199.8 | 61.9 | 8 060.3 | 447.7 | 214.4 | 25.8 |
| Owensboro, KY.................... | 324 | 8 026 | 662.0 | 252.7 | 178 | 1 207 | 78.7 | 25.0 | 952.5 | 379.4 | 268.7 | 53.5 |
| Oxnard-Thousand Oaks-Ventura, CA........................... | 2 317 | 29 522 | 3 140.0 | 1 200.9 | 1 196 | 7 303 | 839.6 | 195.9 | 5 559.1 | 1 945.1 | 1 102.6 | 147.1 |
| Palm Bay-Melbourne-Titusville, FL .......................... | 1 417 | 26 415 | 2 796.8 | 1 085.6 | 1 039 | 4 868 | 395.3 | 121.0 | 8 154.8 | 2 539.4 | 1 110.3 | 165.0 |
| Palm Coast, FL.................... | 149 | 1 807 | 175.1 | 70.7 | 126 | 484 | 35.2 | 9.4 | 631.4 | 469.7 | 101.0 | 17.6 |
| Panama City-Lynn Haven-Panama City Beach, FL | 493 | 9 501 | 985.3 | 354.0 | 315 | 1 767 | 122.2 | 38.1 | 2 261.4 | 730.5 | 337.2 | 74.5 |
| Parkersburg-Marietta-Vienna, WV-OH ............. | 460 | 11 253 | 924.5 | 346.7 | 307 | 1 568 | 127.0 | 28.9 | 1 521.5 | 632.8 | 305.8 | 79.7 |
| Pascagoula, MS.................... | 318 | 5 980 | 622.4 | 243.8 | 175 | 849 | 71.7 | 19.9 | 1 226.4 | 531.3 | 216.1 | 54.2 |
| Pensacola-Ferry Pass-Brent, FL............................ | 983 | 23 199 | 2 412.9 | 894.2 | 649 | 3 468 | 283.2 | 86.2 | 4 928.0 | 2 006.9 | 877.4 | 198.1 |
| Peoria, IL............................. | 845 | 27 673 | 2 527.2 | 1 059.6 | 669 | 5 352 | 467.9 | 180.5 | 2 779.0 | 1 119.8 | 587.3 | 116.8 |
| Philadelphia-Camden-Wilmington, PA-NJ-DE-MD. | 16 323 | 415 348 | 42 566.2 | 17 480.6 | 11 395 | 74 963 | 9 790.7 | 2 169.8 | 62 636.7 | 17 098.9 | 14 133.7 | 2 440.0 |
| Camden, NJ Div.................. | 3 328 | 68 999 | 7 081.3 | 2 808.5 | 2 319 | 14 328 | 1 135.9 | 363.6 | 11 837.1 | 3 792.6 | 2 214.6 | 306.7 |
| Philadelphia, PA Div | 11 159 | 300 011 | 30 720.5 | 12 542.3 | 7 826 | 52 579 | 7 889.0 | 1 584.7 | 45 563.0 | 11 294.6 | 10 871.2 | 1 925.8 |
| Wilmington, DE-MD-NJ Div. | 1 836 | 46 338 | 4 764.4 | 2 129.9 | 1 250 | 8 056 | 765.9 | 221.5 | 5 236.6 | 2 011.7 | 1 047.8 | 207.4 |
| Phoenix-Mesa-Glendale, AZ. | 10 008 | 180 870 | 20 217.1 | 7 822.2 | 5 750 | 47 116 | 4 481.5 | 1 223.9 | 33 532.2 | 10 122.3 | 4 348.1 | 1 242.3 |
| Pine Bluff, AR...................... | 289 | 4 791 | 411.5 | 150.4 | 116 | 763 | 57.6 | 22.0 | 1 329.6 | 350.7 | 171.3 | 83.9 |
| Pittsburgh, PA...................... | 7 734 | 184 576 | 17 470.8 | 6 919.7 | 5 279 | 31 880 | 3 755.4 | 782.5 | 28 473.6 | 8 645.4 | 7 805.0 | 938.1 |
| Pittsfield, MA........................ | 450 | 10 869 | 981.1 | 429.8 | 309 | 1 742 | 142.3 | 38.5 | 1 352.8 | 459.3 | 357.1 | 48.0 |
| Pocatello, ID........................ | 303 | 4 956 | 404.5 | 152.6 | 145 | 712 | 63.4 | 15.2 | 652.9 | 258.0 | 77.9 | 40.3 |
| Portland-South Portland-Biddeford, ME........................ | 2 031 | 40 747 | 3 487.0 | 1 505.2 | 1 188 | 6 117 | 543.7 | 147.9 | 5 091.1 | 1 706.7 | 636.1 | 159.0 |
| Portland-Vancouver-Hillsboro, OR-WA................. | 6 374 | 114 594 | 12 607.5 | 5 005.4 | 4 041 | 24 286 | 2 985.0 | 726.9 | 15 688.0 | 5 585.8 | 2 331.1 | 707.8 |
| Port St. Lucie, FL................. | 1 087 | 17 254 | 1 857.4 | 671.3 | 734 | 3 709 | 288.0 | 85.8 | 3 198.9 | 1 722.0 | 978.4 | 116.3 |
| Poughkeepsie-Newburgh-Middletown, NY.............. | 1 901 | 37 055 | 3 337.4 | 1 453.5 | 1 354 | 6 464 | 697.6 | 167.1 | 5 175.0 | 1 860.0 | 890.1 | 146.7 |
| Prescott, AZ ........................ | 737 | 10 268 | 930.0 | 370.7 | 386 | 1 822 | 141.9 | 41.0 | 1 624.2 | 996.3 | 244.7 | 51.4 |
| Providence-New Bedford-Fall River, RI-MA .......... | 4 642 | 118 319 | 10 073.1 | 4 455.6 | 3 434 | 20 277 | 1 914.7 | 504.6 | 17 257.8 | 4 687.4 | 3 140.9 | 646.5 |
| Provo-Orem, UT................... | 1 035 | 19 210 | 1 648.7 | 644.1 | 547 | 3 039 | 245.4 | 64.4 | 2 575.7 | 749.3 | 496.5 | 67.6 |
| Pueblo, CO........................... | 410 | 11 085 | 872.7 | 388.5 | 237 | 1 160 | 92.3 | 25.4 | 1 440.6 | 554.1 | 256.1 | 92.2 |
| Punta Gorda, FL .................. | 474 | 7 731 | 897.1 | 308.2 | 275 | 1 186 | 90.0 | 24.7 | 1 438.9 | 829.2 | 490.9 | 31.4 |
| Racine, WI............................ | 417 | 11 897 | 946.4 | 478.0 | 343 | 2 167 | 162.7 | 49.1 | 1 319.4 | 599.0 | 262.3 | 65.9 |
| Raleigh-Cary, NC................. | 2 601 | 52 345 | 4 949.4 | 2 062.5 | 1 869 | 13 363 | 1 516.1 | 408.2 | 9 618.5 | 2 418.0 | 752.5 | 224.0 |
| Rapid City, SD..................... | 365 | 9 404 | 977.3 | 381.2 | 304 | 1 674 | 145.6 | 37.7 | 1 394.5 | 472.0 | 115.4 | 40.5 |
| Reading, PA.......................... | 799 | 21 887 | 2 014.4 | 848.1 | 781 | 4 670 | 398.8 | 108.0 | 2 648.7 | 1 186.8 | 686.4 | 108.4 |
| Redding, CA.......................... | 661 | 10 015 | 1 124.5 | 420.3 | 320 | 1 697 | 168.2 | 43.3 | 1 678.2 | 724.9 | 355.0 | 93.5 |
| Reno-Sparks, NV.................. | 1 113 | 19 938 | 2 642.3 | 1 000.5 | 765 | 5 594 | 703.9 | 148.9 | 3 495.6 | 1 167.4 | 382.4 | 99.1 |
| Richmond, VA....................... | 2 937 | 70 736 | 7 079.7 | 2 874.6 | 2 496 | 16 629 | 2 014.7 | 481.3 | 13 630.3 | 3 963.6 | 1 482.6 | 386.0 |
| Riverside-San Bernardino-Ontario, CA.................... | 7 225 | 129 700 | 14 971.5 | 5 514.6 | 4 810 | 32 342 | 2 927.7 | 850.7 | 24 553.0 | 8 445.0 | 5 113.2 | 1 239.8 |
| Roanoke, VA......................... | 763 | 22 840 | 2 378.1 | 928.0 | 685 | 3 976 | 299.1 | 92.3 | 2 553.1 | 1 133.3 | 428.3 | 83.7 |
| Rochester, MN...................... | 421 | 19 262 | 2 036.4 | 829.5 | 345 | D | D | D | 1 037.0 | 445.4 | 213.1 | 30.7 |
| Rochester, NY....................... | 2 454 | 69 515 | 5 675.0 | 2 437.8 | 1 693 | 9 937 | 967.1 | 253.1 | 10 403.0 | 3 204.2 | 1 672.7 | 380.0 |
| Rockford, IL........................... | 734 | 20 112 | 1 949.3 | 814.3 | 617 | 4 043 | 332.5 | 97.7 | 2 108.5 | 967.7 | 385.0 | 105.5 |
| Rocky Mount, NC.................. | 343 | 9 283 | 711.5 | 306.7 | 213 | 1 198 | 197.6 | 29.8 | 1 296.2 | 490.9 | 220.3 | 98.5 |
| Rome, GA............................. | 259 | 7 910 | 785.1 | 310.9 | 108 | D | D | D | 705.5 | 304.8 | 152.1 | 42.4 |

1. Establishments subject to federal tax.

Table C. Metropolitan Areas —

# Federal Funds, Residential Construction and Local Government Finances

| Area name | Salaries and wages | Defense | Other | Medicaid and other health-related | Nutrition and family welfare | Education | Other | New construction ($1,000) | Number of housing units | Total (mil dol) | Inter-govern-mental (mil dol) | Total (mil dol) | Total | Property |
|---|---|---|---|---|---|---|---|---|---|---|---|---|---|---|
| | 171 | 172 | 173 | 174 | 175 | 176 | 177 | 178 | 179 | 180 | 181 | 182 | 183 | 184 |
| Naples-Marco Island, FL........ | 53.2 | 61.7 | 19.9 | 63.1 | 62.5 | 11.5 | 14.8 | 425 480 | 1 320 | 1 632.7 | 314.3 | 935.7 | 2 963 | 2 487 |
| Nashville-Davidson—Murfreesboro—Franklin, TN.. | 1 180.6 | 181.3 | 1 164.5 | 1 846.6 | 433.2 | 1 019.0 | 2 008.7 | 1 011 473 | 5 394 | 4 745.9 | 1 342.2 | 2 214.3 | 1 455 | 860 |
| New Haven-Milford, CT........ | 480.1 | 79.2 | 179.4 | 1 810.1 | 129.2 | 70.3 | 256.3 | 85 098 | 689 | 3 404.4 | 1 294.9 | 1 764.1 | 2 086 | 2 046 |
| New Orleans-Metairie-Kenner, LA........ | 1 168.6 | 4 493.1 | 801.8 | 1 624.5 | 252.9 | 163.4 | 479.0 | 382 874 | 2 328 | 5 638.9 | 1 775.8 | 2 079.9 | 2 019 | 830 |
| New York-Northern New Jersey-Long Island, NY-NJ-PA | 10 184.2 | 8 653.9 | 5 053.8 | 35 663.7 | 4 029.2 | 1 370.2 | 8 116.6 | 3 252 738 | 21 539 | 137 447.6 | 42 994.4 | 72 397.9 | 3 848 | 2 306 |
| Edison-New Brunswick, NJ Div | 1 218.1 | 3 237.4 | 533.7 | 1 434.3 | 280.3 | 55.6 | 382.2 | 587 017 | 3 602 | 10 162.1 | 2 541.4 | 6 010.9 | 2 591 | 2 541 |
| Nassau-Suffolk, NY Div........ | 1 557.6 | 2 458.4 | 1 208.9 | 2 726.0 | 529.3 | 152.2 | 305.0 | 528 052 | 1 709 | 18 984.9 | 4 839.8 | 11 977.9 | 4 340 | 3 390 |
| Newark-Union, NJ-PA Div.... | 1 319.5 | 1 240.5 | 596.6 | 2 285.1 | 371.6 | 88.1 | 1 091.1 | 390 985 | 2 255 | 10 053.9 | 3 015.0 | 5 675.5 | 2 666 | 2 593 |
| New York-White Plains-Wayne, NY-NJ Div........ | 6 089.0 | 1 717.5 | 2 714.5 | 29 218.3 | 2 848.1 | 1 074.3 | 6 338.3 | 1 746 684 | 13 973 | 98 246.7 | 32 598.2 | 48 733.6 | 4 198 | 1 948 |
| Niles-Benton Harbor, MI ...... | 31.8 | 2.9 | 16.0 | 249.9 | 36.3 | 15.7 | 32.6 | 30 856 | 136 | 590.1 | 307.2 | 173.2 | 1 085 | 1 060 |
| North Port-Bradenton-Sarasota, FL | 228.4 | 224.2 | 38.9 | 186.0 | 76.7 | 35.0 | 126.0 | 475 878 | 2 385 | 3 477.2 | 617.2 | 1 460.5 | 2 125 | 1 736 |
| Norwich-New London, CT...... | 342.9 | 3 520.5 | 55.9 | 234.1 | 35.3 | 19.9 | 33.0 | 41 551 | 209 | 1 033.0 | 375.8 | 540.4 | 2 021 | 1 959 |
| Ocala, FL........ | 57.6 | 15.9 | 17.1 | 163.8 | 42.2 | 18.5 | 24.2 | 74 066 | 361 | 968.0 | 357.1 | 320.2 | 986 | 783 |
| Ocean City, NJ........ | 75.3 | 7.4 | 17.1 | 61.7 | 15.9 | 4.0 | 5.8 | 120 273 | 452 | 633.6 | 155.7 | 372.3 | 3 861 | 3 709 |
| Odessa, TX ........ | 28.1 | 0.0 | 3.8 | 92.7 | 28.4 | 8.5 | 16.4 | 90 369 | 740 | 609.9 | 162.7 | 189.3 | 1 461 | 1 149 |
| Ogden-Clearfield, UT ............ | 1 158.6 | 916.1 | 181.2 | 333.0 | 71.7 | 13.4 | 35.9 | 331 187 | 1 849 | 1 432.6 | 590.7 | 482.8 | 931 | 616 |
| Oklahoma City, OK ................ | 2 251.8 | 987.1 | 495.3 | 930.8 | 376.1 | 352.9 | 1 416.5 | 578 376 | 3 261 | 3 651.6 | 1 168.8 | 1 381.7 | 1 158 | 587 |
| Olympia, WA ........ | 122.2 | 119.1 | 24.2 | 287.1 | 340.4 | 673.5 | 1 437.6 | 215 611 | 1 028 | 882.4 | 347.7 | 334.2 | 1 401 | 841 |
| Omaha-Council Bluffs, NE-IA | 1 043.8 | 735.9 | 278.9 | 844.4 | 134.8 | 66.5 | 165.9 | 434 195 | 3 133 | 3 077.0 | 980.9 | 1 419.8 | 1 711 | 1 290 |
| Orlando-Kissimmee-Sanford, FL........ | 1 044.0 | 3 485.6 | 630.6 | 708.6 | 240.5 | 135.8 | 287.2 | 1 340 405 | 6 505 | 9 424.9 | 2 900.8 | 3 544.8 | 1 744 | 1 210 |
| Oshkosh-Neenah, WI............ | 82.1 | 7 100.1 | 11.7 | 112.5 | 23.6 | 7.7 | 10.5 | 49 954 | 385 | 566.0 | 263.6 | 202.6 | 1 249 | 1 209 |
| Owensboro, KY........ | 39.5 | 2.2 | 7.7 | 85.2 | 28.5 | 7.1 | 29.5 | 21 456 | 278 | 351.9 | 133.1 | 96.1 | 857 | 499 |
| Oxnard-Thousand Oaks-Ventura, CA........ | 602.1 | 681.1 | 175.4 | 445.3 | 153.9 | 52.6 | 159.5 | 116 433 | 568 | 4 288.6 | 1 876.2 | 1 310.9 | 1 642 | 1 348 |
| Palm Bay-Melbourne-Titusville, FL........ | 617.8 | 2 092.1 | 1 237.4 | 154.1 | 63.8 | 28.4 | 65.6 | 235 830 | 882 | 1 940.6 | 575.9 | 770.6 | 1 437 | 1 095 |
| Palm Coast, FL........ | 13.8 | 0.4 | 3.2 | 7.1 | 6.8 | 2.9 | 4.1 | 47 584 | 152 | 366.4 | 107.4 | 156.2 | 1 767 | 1 578 |
| Panama City-Lynn Haven-Panama City Beach, FL.. | 420.0 | 425.6 | 56.4 | 109.4 | 33.1 | 14.2 | 12.5 | 41 970 | 343 | 877.5 | 228.1 | 282.9 | 1 725 | 1 267 |
| Parkersburg-Marietta-Vienna, WV-OH........ | 180.8 | 16.5 | 40.7 | 170.0 | 27.4 | 15.0 | 19.8 | 14 654 | 102 | 450.9 | 202.8 | 152.6 | 950 | 716 |
| Pascagoula, MS........ | 113.9 | 118.1 | 48.0 | 59.2 | 26.4 | 8.7 | 37.9 | 47 162 | 303 | 849.6 | 289.0 | 161.9 | 1 065 | 997 |
| Pensacola-Ferry Pass-Brent, FL........ | 514.0 | 532.2 | 163.6 | 369.4 | 82.4 | 36.1 | 55.4 | 173 572 | 1 205 | 1 509.6 | 673.1 | 457.5 | 1 009 | 739 |
| Peoria, IL........ | 231.5 | 253.7 | 53.1 | 204.5 | 57.5 | 11.0 | 57.1 | 109 334 | 470 | 1 316.6 | 517.7 | 512.6 | 1 381 | 1 173 |
| Philadelphia-Camden-Wilmington, PA-NJ-DE-MD........ | 4 899.5 | 6 849.6 | 4 627.6 | 8 409.3 | 994.8 | 282.1 | 1 866.0 | 966 393 | 6 979 | 28 819.0 | 11 352.5 | 12 391.9 | 2 126 | 1 483 |
| Camden, NJ Div ........ | 1 268.2 | 2 149.8 | 645.7 | 885.0 | 186.8 | 50.0 | 130.6 | 215 351 | 1 859 | 5 997.4 | 2 118.1 | 2 704.2 | 2 170 | 2 136 |
| Philadelphia, PA Div ........... | 3 218.2 | 4 616.2 | 3 811.0 | 6 800.0 | 678.8 | 195.1 | 1 463.3 | 631 637 | 4 039 | 20 605.5 | 8 216.6 | 8 909.8 | 2 292 | 1 384 |
| Wilmington, DE-MD-NJ Div.. | 413.1 | 83.5 | 170.8 | 724.4 | 129.2 | 37.0 | 272.1 | 119 405 | 1 081 | 2 216.2 | 1 017.9 | 777.8 | 1 121 | 869 |
| Phoenix-Mesa-Glendale, AZ.. | 1 920.1 | 4 444.2 | 933.6 | 4 349.4 | 869.5 | 777.1 | 2 408.9 | 1 820 813 | 9 081 | 16 700.4 | 6 455.8 | 6 225.7 | 1 490 | 852 |
| Pine Bluff, AR........ | 97.1 | 256.5 | 43.4 | 217.3 | 24.2 | 16.3 | 19.7 | 6 766 | 69 | 252.5 | 164.5 | 54.5 | 537 | 233 |
| Pittsburgh, PA........ | 1 614.9 | 2 023.4 | 1 588.6 | 3 906.8 | 463.7 | 114.7 | 752.5 | 628 557 | 2 914 | 10 276.0 | 4 522.4 | 3 874.9 | 1 645 | 1 213 |
| Pittsfield, MA........ | 54.6 | 111.3 | 29.3 | 202.4 | 27.1 | 12.7 | 31.0 | 26 265 | 122 | 442.7 | 189.6 | 203.0 | 1 564 | 1 520 |
| Pocatello, ID........ | 60.4 | 0.4 | 12.2 | 107.3 | 15.0 | 3.2 | 19.5 | 10 669 | 83 | 365.2 | 117.2 | 69.3 | 791 | 749 |
| Portland-South Portland-Biddeford, ME ........ | 543.2 | 1 094.4 | 91.1 | 511.4 | 73.5 | 18.6 | 157.1 | 211 717 | 1 112 | 1 706.5 | 484.1 | 939.3 | 1 831 | 1 800 |
| Portland-Vancouver-Hillsboro, OR-WA........ | 1 546.5 | 563.3 | 683.2 | 2 366.8 | 330.4 | 152.2 | 1 053.1 | 1 016 236 | 5 213 | 8 948.6 | 3 360.4 | 3 325.9 | 1 529 | 1 096 |
| Port St. Lucie, FL........ | 83.6 | 5.7 | 21.7 | 118.8 | 48.1 | 20.8 | 32.8 | 161 173 | 539 | 1 906.0 | 533.3 | 861.7 | 2 154 | 1 803 |
| Poughkeepsie-Newburgh-Middletown, NY........ | 954.9 | 199.0 | 95.0 | 702.7 | 140.0 | 41.9 | 69.4 | 204 659 | 1 190 | 3 554.2 | 1 219.8 | 1 833.3 | 2 737 | 2 083 |
| Prescott, AZ........ | 70.5 | 1.1 | 46.3 | 147.1 | 24.0 | 12.9 | 5.6 | 67 532 | 302 | 692.9 | 249.7 | 293.3 | 1 380 | 903 |
| Providence-New Bedford-Fall River, RI-MA........ | 1 149.9 | 2 362.0 | 383.6 | 2 795.2 | 379.8 | 314.4 | 942.4 | 215 060 | 1 178 | 5 688.9 | 2 261.4 | 2 713.2 | 1 695 | 1 641 |
| Provo-Orem, UT........ | 166.8 | 497.2 | 27.7 | 244.7 | 56.4 | 13.7 | 131.0 | 383 332 | 1 932 | 1 329.0 | 554.5 | 433.7 | 879 | 577 |
| Pueblo, CO........ | 85.8 | 42.0 | 20.4 | 258.3 | 33.6 | 16.6 | 39.7 | 20 893 | 118 | 490.8 | 226.0 | 183.4 | 1 187 | 747 |
| Punta Gorda, FL ........ | 26.1 | 0.8 | 5.5 | 16.6 | 19.3 | 4.9 | 5.5 | 52 752 | 312 | 668.6 | 125.2 | 347.4 | 2 273 | 1 705 |
| Racine, WI........ | 53.3 | 54.5 | 10.7 | 196.2 | 34.6 | 13.0 | 18.6 | 28 343 | 107 | 724.8 | 359.2 | 255.6 | 1 310 | 1 266 |
| Raleigh-Cary, NC ........ | 704.4 | 186.1 | 205.3 | 889.8 | 554.7 | 1 091.9 | 2 278.7 | 1 036 867 | 6 366 | 3 468.0 | 1 311.5 | 1 247.8 | 1 191 | 886 |
| Rapid City, SD ........ | 350.4 | 134.8 | 40.6 | 81.2 | 21.6 | 16.4 | 64.0 | 59 802 | 412 | 380.7 | 116.8 | 185.8 | 1 545 | 1 097 |
| Reading, PA........ | 146.1 | 65.2 | 29.9 | 225.9 | 52.4 | 11.3 | 78.4 | 44 516 | 306 | 1 848.0 | 724.3 | 738.8 | 1 838 | 1 472 |
| Redding, CA........ | 96.8 | 3.9 | 75.2 | 199.0 | 50.8 | 18.4 | 30.1 | 23 168 | 138 | 953.9 | 513.4 | 222.1 | 1 238 | 962 |
| Reno-Sparks, NV ........ | 274.7 | 674.8 | 135.5 | 292.4 | 58.6 | 35.3 | 315.8 | 136 153 | 556 | 1 810.5 | 781.1 | 633.6 | 1 544 | 1 089 |
| Richmond, VA ........ | 2 084.2 | 1 096.7 | 328.0 | 1 076.9 | 347.9 | 606.5 | 2 004.6 | 457 865 | 2 709 | 4 384.5 | 1 802.0 | 1 847.3 | 1 523 | 1 110 |
| Riverside-San Bernardino-Ontario, CA........ | 2 362.5 | 2 713.9 | 448.8 | 2 202.6 | 737.4 | 265.9 | 551.6 | 914 752 | 4 736 | 23 957.5 | 11 947.5 | 6 066.6 | 1 486 | 1 093 |
| Roanoke, VA........ | 228.5 | 129.4 | 143.0 | 224.4 | 37.9 | 20.0 | 34.9 | 93 007 | 510 | 1 019.9 | 454.7 | 446.5 | 1 506 | 975 |
| Rochester, MN........ | 107.6 | 3.4 | 40.9 | 103.4 | 24.0 | 10.3 | 20.9 | 74 187 | 332 | 732.5 | 332.8 | 194.1 | 1 072 | 950 |
| Rochester, NY........ | 460.4 | 1 939.3 | 253.2 | 1 509.4 | 264.4 | 160.4 | 296.8 | 254 464 | 1 523 | 5 326.6 | 2 262.9 | 2 255.8 | 2 189 | 1 636 |
| Rockford, IL........ | 124.3 | 153.5 | 25.4 | 185.1 | 38.1 | 11.8 | 38.9 | 23 902 | 168 | 1 207.5 | 495.5 | 500.1 | 1 419 | 1 257 |
| Rocky Mount, NC........ | 61.0 | 16.0 | 10.3 | 271.1 | 38.7 | 12.9 | 17.2 | 26 959 | 192 | 469.2 | 269.9 | 120.1 | 825 | 623 |
| Rome, GA........ | 35.5 | 0.0 | 8.9 | 86.1 | 19.0 | 7.5 | 5.0 | 9 546 | 109 | 530.9 | 181.6 | 115.9 | 1 212 | 720 |

1. Based on the resident population estimated as of July 1 of the year shown.

# Table C. Metropolitan Areas — Local Government Finances, Government Employment, and Voting

| Area name | Local government finances, 2007 (cont.) | | | | | | | | | Government employment, 2011 | | | Presidential election,[2] 2012 | | |
| | Direct general expenditure | | | | | | | Debt outstanding | | | | | Percent of vote cast: | | |
| | | | Percent of total for: | | | | | | | | | | | | |
| | Total (mil dol) | Per capita[1] (dollars) | Educa-tion | Health and hospitals | Police protec-tion | Public welfare | High-ways | Total (mil dol) | Per capita[1] (dollars) | Federal civilian | Federal military | State and local | Demo-cratic | Republi-can | All other |
|---|---|---|---|---|---|---|---|---|---|---|---|---|---|---|---|
| | 185 | 186 | 187 | 188 | 189 | 190 | 191 | 192 | 193 | 194 | 195 | 196 | 197 | 198 | 199 |
| Naples-Marco Island, FL | 1 757.0 | 5 563 | 38.1 | 2.3 | 8.8 | 0.2 | 8.2 | 3 007.6 | 9 523 | 663 | 641 | 12 121 | 34.7 | 64.7 | 0.6 |
| Nashville-Davidson—Mur-freesboro—Franklin, TN | 4 675.5 | 3 073 | 40.6 | 7.5 | 7.2 | 0.9 | 3.9 | 7 627.7 | 5 013 | 12 771 | 5 930 | 87 986 | 41.3 | 57.2 | 1.5 |
| New Haven-Milford, CT | 3 336.5 | 3 946 | 57.5 | 0.9 | 4.8 | 0.5 | 3.5 | 2 951.8 | 3 491 | 5 572 | 1 890 | 44 780 | 60.7 | 38.3 | 1.0 |
| New Orleans-Metairie-Ken-ner, LA | 4 944.9 | 4 799 | 29.5 | 19.0 | 6.8 | 0.3 | 3.3 | 6 274.4 | 6 089 | 12 411 | 8 879 | 74 839 | 49.0 | 49.0 | 2.0 |
| New York-Northern New Jer-sey-Long Island, NY-NJ-PA | 129 641.2 | 6 890 | 37.4 | 7.4 | 5.9 | 10.1 | 2.4 | 165 011.4 | 8 770 | 112 972 | 36 761 | 1 124 031 | 65.3 | 33.7 | 1.0 |
| Edison-New Brunswick, NJ Div | 10 703.2 | 4 614 | 55.7 | 0.9 | 5.7 | 2.5 | 3.1 | 9 930.7 | 4 281 | 11 725 | 5 737 | 127 485 | 51.1 | 47.8 | 1.1 |
| Nassau-Suffolk, NY Div | 19 216.3 | 6 963 | 50.0 | 5.5 | 7.0 | 5.4 | 3.3 | 14 662.0 | 5 313 | 17 417 | 5 285 | 170 695 | 52.2 | 46.7 | 1.1 |
| Newark-Union, NJ-PA Div | 10 538.2 | 4 951 | 51.3 | 1.7 | 6.7 | 2.4 | 2.3 | 8 940.1 | 4 200 | 17 417 | 4 602 | 142 530 | 60.0 | 39.1 | 0.9 |
| New York-White Plains-Wayne, NY-NJ Div | 89 183.5 | 7 683 | 30.9 | 9.3 | 5.6 | 12.9 | 2.2 | 131 478.5 | 11 327 | 66 413 | 21 137 | 683 321 | 74.2 | 24.8 | 0.9 |
| Niles-Benton Harbor, MI | 592.1 | 3 710 | 53.6 | 7.8 | 5.6 | 1.1 | 4.9 | 334.7 | 2 098 | 332 | 312 | 8 674 | 46.2 | 52.7 | 1.1 |
| North Port-Bradenton-Sara-sota, FL | 3 398.0 | 4 945 | 35.1 | 15.0 | 5.8 | 0.8 | 5.3 | 3 541.2 | 5 153 | 1 821 | 1 430 | 24 259 | 44.8 | 54.3 | 0.9 |
| Norwich-New London, CT | 1 092.9 | 4 087 | 63.7 | 0.4 | 4.8 | 0.6 | 5.1 | 682.5 | 2 553 | 2 570 | 7 841 | 33 032 | 58.3 | 40.1 | 1.6 |
| Ocala, FL | 959.0 | 2 952 | 50.3 | 1.7 | 10.2 | 0.7 | 8.4 | 760.8 | 2 342 | 719 | 652 | 16 595 | 41.4 | 57.7 | 0.9 |
| Ocean City, NJ | 730.0 | 7 570 | 37.5 | 1.2 | 5.3 | 3.6 | 5.2 | 626.5 | 6 497 | 442 | 1 189 | 8 544 | 45.2 | 53.8 | 1.0 |
| Odessa, TX | 554.0 | 4 275 | 41.9 | 34.4 | 3.8 | 0.0 | 2.2 | 306.9 | 2 369 | 165 | 311 | 9 386 | 25.0 | 73.8 | 1.2 |
| Ogden-Clearfield, UT | 1 470.7 | 2 837 | 50.9 | 2.6 | 5.9 | 2.0 | 3.8 | 1 208.1 | 2 331 | 19 591 | 6 305 | 28 114 | 20.9 | 77.0 | 2.1 |
| Oklahoma City, OK | 3 744.3 | 3 139 | 43.8 | 8.9 | 6.6 | 0.2 | 5.7 | 3 308.0 | 2 773 | 28 426 | 12 416 | 93 122 | 36.5 | 63.5 | 0.0 |
| Olympia, WA | 845.2 | 3 543 | 48.3 | 5.0 | 3.8 | 0.0 | 5.0 | 708.9 | 2 972 | 904 | 826 | 34 763 | 58.3 | 38.8 | 2.9 |
| Omaha-Council Bluffs, NE-IA | 2 988.8 | 3 601 | 50.4 | 3.2 | 5.4 | 0.6 | 5.1 | 5 775.9 | 6 960 | 9 450 | 9 431 | 53 718 | 44.0 | 54.0 | 2.0 |
| Orlando-Kissimmee-Sanford, FL | 9 060.4 | 4 458 | 41.7 | 3.3 | 6.3 | 0.8 | 5.7 | 14 883.2 | 7 323 | 12 015 | 4 568 | 101 302 | 53.4 | 45.7 | 0.9 |
| Oshkosh-Neenah, WI | 592.7 | 3 655 | 40.8 | 2.6 | 5.6 | 11.6 | 8.2 | 694.9 | 4 285 | 467 | 478 | 11 758 | 51.0 | 47.2 | 1.8 |
| Owensboro, KY | 348.4 | 3 108 | 42.4 | 1.7 | 3.8 | 0.1 | 3.3 | 1 772.3 | 15 809 | 318 | 393 | 9 803 | 38.6 | 59.5 | 1.9 |
| Oxnard-Thousand Oaks-Ven-tura, CA | 4 176.2 | 5 231 | 39.4 | 8.7 | 7.5 | 4.3 | 4.1 | 2 696.6 | 3 378 | 7 412 | 5 963 | 35 211 | 52.3 | 45.3 | 2.5 |
| Palm Bay-Melbourne-Titus-ville, FL | 1 977.4 | 3 688 | 44.4 | 8.3 | 6.0 | 0.3 | 4.8 | 2 145.2 | 4 001 | 6 420 | 2 903 | 22 499 | 43.1 | 55.8 | 1.1 |
| Palm Coast, FL | 414.3 | 4 686 | 35.3 | 1.3 | 4.2 | 0.2 | 7.2 | 447.0 | 5 057 | 144 | 190 | 3 535 | 45.9 | 53.3 | 0.8 |
| Panama City-Lynn Haven-Panama City Beach, FL | 846.1 | 5 159 | 36.6 | 29.6 | 5.2 | 0.0 | 3.0 | 797.3 | 4 862 | 3 862 | 3 698 | 10 763 | 27.6 | 71.2 | 1.2 |
| Parkersburg-Marietta-Vienna, WV-OH | 457.5 | 2 848 | 58.1 | 4.3 | 5.2 | 2.8 | 5.2 | 493.0 | 3 069 | 2 440 | 654 | 8 294 | 35.8 | 62.3 | 1.8 |
| Pascagoula, MS | 775.8 | 5 103 | 33.0 | 35.3 | 2.9 | 0.1 | 4.1 | 501.4 | 3 298 | 961 | 1 318 | 10 784 | 29.4 | 69.5 | 1.1 |
| Pensacola-Ferry Pass-Brent, FL | 1 540.3 | 3 397 | 46.8 | 3.8 | 6.2 | 0.3 | 4.3 | 1 882.3 | 4 151 | 6 913 | 13 854 | 21 090 | 33.7 | 65.2 | 1.1 |
| Peoria, IL | 1 281.4 | 3 452 | 47.8 | 1.5 | 5.7 | 1.3 | 6.8 | 770.8 | 2 077 | 2 304 | 808 | 18 861 | 44.2 | 53.9 | 1.9 |
| Philadelphia-Camden-Wil-mington, PA-NJ-DE-MD | 28 218.2 | 4 842 | 48.3 | 6.5 | 5.1 | 4.8 | 2.0 | 42 828.0 | 7 349 | 54 730 | 22 768 | 288 792 | 64.0 | 34.9 | 1.1 |
| Camden, NJ Div | 6 100.4 | 4 895 | 57.2 | 1.9 | 4.8 | 2.6 | 2.1 | 6 980.2 | 5 601 | 8 803 | 7 665 | 71 929 | 61.4 | 37.5 | 1.1 |
| Philadelphia, PA Div | 19 685.3 | 5 063 | 44.3 | 8.6 | 5.0 | 6.1 | 1.9 | 33 740.4 | 8 679 | 41 033 | 11 465 | 175 043 | 65.2 | 33.8 | 1.0 |
| Wilmington, DE-MD-NJ Div | 2 432.4 | 3 505 | 59.0 | 1.0 | 7.5 | 0.7 | 2.0 | 2 107.4 | 3 037 | 4 894 | 3 638 | 41 820 | 61.2 | 37.2 | 1.6 |
| Phoenix-Mesa-Glendale, AZ | 16 103.8 | 3 853 | 40.8 | 4.4 | 7.5 | 1.9 | 5.6 | 27 140.8 | 6 494 | 22 214 | 13 652 | 210 945 | 43.5 | 54.7 | 1.8 |
| Pine Bluff, AR | 272.4 | 2 684 | 65.1 | 0.2 | 5.8 | 0.0 | 3.9 | 149.3 | 1 471 | 1 925 | 457 | 8 974 | 57.4 | 40.8 | 1.8 |
| Pittsburgh, PA | 9 931.6 | 4 216 | 47.2 | 6.4 | 3.4 | 7.5 | 3.5 | 17 650.1 | 7 492 | 18 398 | 6 508 | 106 628 | 48.8 | 50.0 | 1.2 |
| Pittsfield, MA | 500.5 | 3 856 | 60.3 | 0.5 | 3.4 | 0.1 | 5.3 | 347.1 | 2 674 | 389 | 344 | 8 146 | 75.7 | 22.1 | 2.2 |
| Pocatello, ID | 381.5 | 4 355 | 26.9 | 40.5 | 4.4 | 0.4 | 6.1 | 157.0 | 1 793 | 592 | 347 | 8 145 | 37.2 | 60.0 | 2.8 |
| Portland-South Portland-Bid-deford, ME | 1 662.1 | 3 239 | 50.0 | 0.8 | 5.0 | 1.7 | 5.9 | 1 279.4 | 2 493 | 8 074 | 4 513 | 28 666 | 59.9 | 37.6 | 2.4 |
| Portland-Vancouver-Hills-boro, OR-WA | 8 842.2 | 4 065 | 39.3 | 4.1 | 5.2 | 2.4 | 6.2 | 14 538.1 | 6 684 | 18 118 | 6 943 | 122 296 | 60.0 | 36.6 | 3.3 |
| Port St. Lucie, FL | 1 904.6 | 4 760 | 41.5 | 2.2 | 6.8 | 1.0 | 8.7 | 2 616.8 | 6 540 | 1 023 | 915 | 17 800 | 47.5 | 51.7 | 0.7 |
| Poughkeepsie-Newburgh-Middletown, NY | 3 631.4 | 5 421 | 54.2 | 3.6 | 3.5 | 9.0 | 3.7 | 2 540.4 | 3 792 | 6 519 | 7 208 | 42 466 | 52.5 | 46.0 | 1.5 |
| Prescott, AZ | 676.3 | 3 181 | 35.2 | 1.6 | 7.3 | 4.9 | 10.7 | 475.8 | 2 237 | 1 447 | 467 | 9 170 | 33.8 | 64.3 | 1.9 |
| Providence-New Bedford-Fall River, RI-MA | 5 733.3 | 3 581 | 56.9 | 0.4 | 6.5 | 0.4 | 2.6 | 3 764.5 | 2 352 | 11 436 | 8 820 | 80 174 | 61.5 | 36.5 | 2.0 |
| Provo-Orem, UT | 1 237.3 | 2 508 | 51.4 | 3.5 | 5.9 | 0.3 | 4.4 | 2 038.0 | 4 131 | 1 000 | 2 469 | 27 432 | 9.8 | 88.3 | 2.0 |
| Pueblo, CO | 498.3 | 3 224 | 43.3 | 0.9 | 6.1 | 4.6 | 4.6 | 446.2 | 2 887 | 1 008 | 450 | 11 850 | 55.8 | 41.9 | 2.3 |
| Punta Gorda, FL | 645.6 | 4 225 | 30.2 | 3.1 | 8.6 | 1.3 | 9.5 | 627.2 | 4 104 | 326 | 315 | 5 679 | 42.4 | 56.7 | 0.9 |
| Racine, WI | 733.5 | 3 760 | 46.9 | 4.9 | 8.3 | 6.0 | 7.2 | 719.6 | 3 688 | 366 | 546 | 8 789 | 51.3 | 47.7 | 1.0 |
| Raleigh-Cary, NC | 3 752.7 | 3 582 | 43.6 | 7.3 | 4.5 | 4.6 | 2.5 | 13 091.7 | 12 496 | 5 535 | 3 618 | 86 421 | 52.1 | 46.4 | 1.5 |
| Rapid City, SD | 368.4 | 3 063 | 46.2 | 2.2 | 6.3 | 0.3 | 7.4 | 239.5 | 1 991 | 2 963 | 4 309 | 7 596 | 32.7 | 64.8 | 2.6 |
| Reading, PA | 1 817.4 | 4 521 | 55.4 | 4.1 | 3.6 | 7.3 | 2.6 | 3 268.4 | 8 131 | 1 098 | 1 063 | 22 637 | 48.7 | 49.7 | 1.5 |
| Redding, CA | 983.2 | 5 480 | 41.0 | 6.6 | 5.0 | 9.3 | 2.5 | 684.3 | 3 814 | 1 396 | 295 | 11 443 | 33.8 | 63.0 | 3.2 |
| Reno-Sparks, NV | 1 655.6 | 4 035 | 33.3 | 1.4 | 7.4 | 3.7 | 6.5 | 3 087.6 | 7 526 | 3 505 | 1 175 | 24 003 | 50.7 | 47.2 | 2.1 |
| Richmond, VA | 4 321.0 | 3 562 | 48.2 | 3.3 | 7.3 | 4.4 | 3.1 | 4 536.1 | 3 740 | 16 506 | 12 548 | 98 903 | 51.7 | 46.9 | 1.4 |
| Riverside-San Bernardino-Ontario, CA | 23 139.3 | 5 669 | 41.5 | 9.1 | 5.7 | 6.7 | 4.1 | 23 606.5 | 5 784 | 21 393 | 25 281 | 211 242 | 51.0 | 46.7 | 2.3 |
| Roanoke, VA | 1 031.0 | 3 477 | 47.6 | 0.5 | 6.0 | 6.5 | 2.6 | 1 016.8 | 3 429 | 3 875 | 988 | 17 393 | 41.6 | 56.1 | 2.3 |
| Rochester, MN | 773.7 | 4 273 | 37.9 | 1.6 | 4.5 | 9.3 | 6.5 | 1 736.2 | 9 588 | 1 014 | 707 | 9 154 | 49.0 | 48.2 | 2.8 |
| Rochester, NY | 5 606.0 | 5 440 | 49.1 | 3.8 | 3.5 | 11.4 | 3.6 | 3 829.8 | 3 716 | 4 501 | 1 829 | 70 419 | 54.5 | 43.6 | 1.9 |
| Rockford, IL | 1 254.9 | 3 562 | 47.7 | 1.3 | 5.6 | 2.7 | 5.4 | 954.7 | 2 710 | 1 074 | 706 | 15 598 | 51.0 | 47.2 | 1.8 |
| Rocky Mount, NC | 475.2 | 3 264 | 52.2 | 5.7 | 5.3 | 8.1 | 1.4 | 88.0 | 604 | 418 | 395 | 10 830 | 56.5 | 42.9 | 0.6 |
| Rome, GA | 541.5 | 5 663 | 32.4 | 42.5 | 2.6 | 0.1 | 2.8 | 233.9 | 2 446 | 230 | 292 | 6 257 | 29.4 | 69.2 | 1.4 |

1. Based on the resident population estimated as of July 1 of the year shown.  2. © 2013 Election Data Services, Inc. All rights reserved.

Table C. Metropolitan Areas — **Land Area and Population**

| CBSA/ DIV code[1] | Area name | Land area,[2] 2010 (sq km) | Total persons | Rank | Per square kilometer | White | Black | American Indian, Alaska Native | Asian and Pacific Islander | Percent Hispanic or Latino[3] | Under 5 years | 5 to 17 years | 18 to 24 years | 25 to 34 years | 35 to 44 years | 45 to 54 years |
|---|---|---|---|---|---|---|---|---|---|---|---|---|---|---|---|---|
| | | | **Population 2012** | | | **Population characteristics, 2011** | | | | | | | | | | |
| | | | | | | Race alone or in combination, not Hispanic or Latino (percent) | | | | | Age (percent) | | | | | |
| | | 1 | 2 | 3 | 4 | 5 | 6 | 7 | 8 | 9 | 10 | 11 | 12 | 13 | 14 | 15 |
| 40900 | Sacramento—Arden-Arcade—Roseville, CA. | 13 194 | 2 196 482 | 26 | 166.5 | 58.5 | 8.3 | 1.6 | 15.2 | 20.5 | 6.5 | 17.9 | 10.5 | 13.6 | 12.9 | 14.2 |
| 40980 | Saginaw-Saginaw Township North, MI | 2 072 | 198 353 | 216 | 95.7 | 72.0 | 19.6 | 0.8 | 1.5 | 7.8 | 5.9 | 17.2 | 10.6 | 11.1 | 11.7 | 14.4 |
| 41060 | St. Cloud, MN | 4 536 | 190 471 | 221 | 42.0 | 92.1 | 3.6 | 0.7 | 2.4 | 2.7 | 6.5 | 16.6 | 15.0 | 13.6 | 11.4 | 13.7 |
| 41100 | St. George, UT | 6 284 | 144 809 | 276 | 23.0 | 86.8 | 0.9 | 1.7 | 2.4 | 10.0 | 8.7 | 21.4 | 9.2 | 13.1 | 10.1 | 9.5 |
| 41140 | St. Joseph, MO-KS | 4 288 | 127 927 | 305 | 29.8 | 89.0 | 6.2 | 1.0 | 1.2 | 4.4 | 6.4 | 16.3 | 10.3 | 13.3 | 12.3 | 14.7 |
| 41180 | St. Louis, MO-IL | 22 334 | 2 820 889 | 19 | 126.3 | 76.6 | 19.0 | 0.7 | 2.7 | 2.7 | 6.2 | 17.3 | 9.1 | 13.4 | 12.5 | 15.3 |
| 41420 | Salem, OR | 4 981 | 396 338 | 131 | 79.6 | 72.9 | 1.4 | 2.3 | 3.6 | 22.4 | 7.2 | 18.7 | 10.3 | 13.2 | 12.2 | 12.7 |
| 41500 | Salinas, CA | 8 497 | 426 762 | 120 | 50.2 | 34.2 | 3.4 | 0.8 | 8.0 | 56.1 | 8.0 | 18.8 | 11.0 | 15.1 | 13.0 | 12.6 |
| 41540 | Salisbury, MD | 1 798 | 126 900 | 307 | 70.6 | 64.8 | 29.2 | 0.7 | 2.9 | 4.4 | 6.0 | 15.1 | 15.3 | 12.4 | 11.4 | 14.0 |
| 41620 | Salt Lake City, UT | 24 748 | 1 161 715 | 48 | 46.9 | 76.3 | 1.9 | 1.1 | 5.7 | 17.0 | 8.6 | 20.6 | 10.0 | 16.9 | 13.4 | 11.9 |
| 41660 | San Angelo, TX | 6 665 | 114 854 | 324 | 17.2 | 58.3 | 4.5 | 0.8 | 1.6 | 36.1 | 7.0 | 16.5 | 13.4 | 13.9 | 10.8 | 12.8 |
| 41700 | San Antonio-New Braunfels, TX | 18 940 | 2 234 003 | 24 | 118.0 | 37.0 | 6.7 | 0.6 | 2.8 | 54.2 | 7.3 | 19.3 | 10.4 | 14.1 | 13.2 | 13.5 |
| 41740 | San Diego-Carlsbad-San Marcos, CA. | 10 895 | 3 177 063 | 17 | 291.6 | 50.6 | 5.7 | 1.0 | 13.4 | 32.5 | 6.6 | 16.6 | 11.7 | 15.4 | 13.4 | 13.7 |
| 41780 | Sandusky, OH | 652 | 76 398 | 364 | 117.2 | 87.1 | 10.1 | 0.7 | 0.9 | 3.5 | 5.3 | 16.5 | 7.5 | 10.6 | 11.7 | 15.5 |
| 41860 | San Francisco-Oakland-Fremont, CA. | 6 399 | 4 455 560 | 11 | 696.3 | 45.1 | 9.0 | 0.9 | 26.8 | 22.0 | 5.9 | 15.1 | 8.7 | 15.1 | 14.9 | 14.8 |
| 41860 | Oakland-Fremont-Hayward, CA Div. | 3 768 | 2 634 317 | X | 699.1 | 42.6 | 11.9 | 1.0 | 25.0 | 23.6 | 6.3 | 16.8 | 9.2 | 14.0 | 14.5 | 14.9 |
| 41860 | San Francisco-San Mateo-Redwood City, CA Div | 2 630 | 1 821 243 | X | 692.5 | 48.9 | 4.8 | 0.7 | 29.3 | 19.6 | 5.4 | 12.6 | 7.9 | 16.7 | 15.4 | 14.7 |
| 41940 | San Jose-Sunnyvale-Santa Clara, CA | 6 938 | 1 894 388 | 31 | 273.0 | 37.4 | 3.0 | 0.7 | 34.0 | 28.0 | 6.9 | 17.2 | 8.8 | 15.0 | 15.4 | 14.7 |
| 42020 | San Luis Obispo-Paso Robles, CA | 8 543 | 274 804 | 170 | 32.2 | 72.4 | 2.6 | 1.3 | 4.9 | 21.3 | 4.9 | 13.5 | 15.9 | 11.5 | 10.7 | 13.7 |
| 42060 | Santa Barbara-Santa Maria-Goleta, CA | 7 084 | 431 249 | 118 | 60.9 | 49.1 | 2.3 | 1.0 | 6.4 | 43.4 | 6.4 | 16.2 | 16.2 | 13.2 | 11.6 | 12.6 |
| 42100 | Santa Cruz-Watsonville, CA | 1 153 | 266 776 | 176 | 231.4 | 61.5 | 1.6 | 1.2 | 6.1 | 32.7 | 5.7 | 15.0 | 14.8 | 12.4 | 12.3 | 14.2 |
| 42140 | Santa Fe, NM | 4 945 | 146 375 | 274 | 29.6 | 44.8 | 1.0 | 3.0 | 1.6 | 50.9 | 5.5 | 15.2 | 7.5 | 11.5 | 12.3 | 15.0 |
| 42220 | Santa Rosa-Petaluma, CA .. | 4 081 | 491 829 | 104 | 120.5 | 68.2 | 2.1 | 1.6 | 5.6 | 25.4 | 5.8 | 16.0 | 9.4 | 12.8 | 12.3 | 14.8 |
| 42340 | Savannah, GA | 3 471 | 361 941 | 142 | 104.3 | 58.4 | 34.5 | 0.7 | 2.8 | 5.3 | 7.0 | 16.9 | 11.8 | 15.4 | 12.5 | 13.3 |
| 42540 | Scranton--Wilkes-Barre, PA. | 4 524 | 563 629 | 91 | 124.6 | 89.6 | 3.3 | 0.4 | 1.6 | 6.2 | 5.2 | 15.0 | 9.6 | 11.3 | 12.3 | 14.9 |
| 42660 | Seattle-Tacoma-Bellevue, WA | 15 209 | 3 552 157 | 15 | 233.6 | 71.5 | 6.9 | 2.1 | 15.0 | 9.2 | 6.5 | 16.0 | 9.3 | 15.5 | 14.6 | 14.9 |
| 42660 | Seattle-Bellevue-Everett, WA Div | 10 885 | 2 740 476 | X | 251.8 | 70.5 | 6.4 | 1.9 | 16.4 | 9.2 | 6.3 | 15.6 | 9.0 | 15.8 | 15.0 | 15.0 |
| 42660 | Tacoma, WA Div | 4 324 | 811 681 | X | 187.7 | 75.0 | 8.8 | 2.6 | 10.4 | 9.4 | 6.9 | 17.4 | 10.4 | 14.5 | 13.2 | 14.4 |
| 42680 | Sebastian-Vero Beach, FL .. | 1 302 | 140 567 | 283 | 108.0 | 77.8 | 9.4 | 0.5 | 1.7 | 11.6 | 4.6 | 14.0 | 6.7 | 9.0 | 9.9 | 13.4 |
| 43100 | Sheboygan, WI | 1 324 | 115 009 | 323 | 86.9 | 87.8 | 1.9 | 0.8 | 5.1 | 5.6 | 6.1 | 17.5 | 7.7 | 12.0 | 12.6 | 16.0 |
| 43300 | Sherman-Denison, TX | 2 416 | 121 935 | 313 | 50.5 | 79.9 | 6.7 | 2.3 | 1.4 | 11.8 | 6.4 | 17.4 | 9.3 | 11.4 | 11.8 | 14.7 |
| 43340 | Shreveport-Bossier City, LA | 6 719 | 406 253 | 128 | 60.5 | 55.7 | 39.4 | 1.0 | 1.7 | 3.6 | 7.2 | 17.7 | 9.7 | 14.3 | 12.0 | 13.6 |
| 43580 | Sioux City, IA-NE-SD | 5 371 | 144 014 | 279 | 26.8 | 77.9 | 3.2 | 2.1 | 2.8 | 15.9 | 7.7 | 19.2 | 9.6 | 12.7 | 12.0 | 13.5 |
| 43620 | Sioux Falls, SD | 6 671 | 237 251 | 189 | 35.6 | 90.1 | 3.7 | 2.7 | 1.8 | 3.6 | 7.9 | 17.9 | 9.0 | 15.8 | 12.9 | 14.0 |
| 43780 | South Bend-Mishawaka, IN-MI | 2 455 | 318 586 | 150 | 129.8 | 79.5 | 12.8 | 1.0 | 2.3 | 6.8 | 6.4 | 17.8 | 10.7 | 12.3 | 12.1 | 13.9 |
| 43900 | Spartanburg, SC | 2 093 | 288 745 | 162 | 138.0 | 70.9 | 21.4 | 0.6 | 2.4 | 6.1 | 6.7 | 17.5 | 10.0 | 11.9 | 13.2 | 14.2 |
| 44060 | Spokane, WA | 4 568 | 475 735 | 108 | 104.1 | 89.5 | 2.8 | 2.6 | 4.0 | 4.7 | 6.3 | 16.6 | 11.2 | 13.5 | 12.0 | 14.1 |
| 44100 | Springfield, IL | 3 063 | 211 993 | 204 | 69.2 | 85.0 | 12.4 | 0.6 | 2.1 | 1.9 | 6.2 | 17.2 | 8.3 | 12.9 | 12.4 | 15.1 |
| 44140 | Springfield, MA | 4 775 | 697 258 | 78 | 146.0 | 75.4 | 6.7 | 0.6 | 3.2 | 15.8 | 5.3 | 16.0 | 13.1 | 11.4 | 11.8 | 14.8 |
| 44180 | Springfield, MO | 7 788 | 444 617 | 112 | 57.1 | 93.0 | 3.0 | 1.5 | 1.8 | 2.8 | 6.4 | 16.5 | 12.0 | 13.4 | 12.1 | 13.5 |
| 44220 | Springfield, OH | 1 029 | 137 206 | 286 | 133.3 | 87.4 | 10.2 | 0.9 | 1.1 | 2.8 | 6.2 | 17.2 | 9.1 | 11.1 | 11.8 | 14.3 |
| 44300 | State College, PA | 2 875 | 155 171 | 256 | 54.0 | 88.6 | 3.6 | 0.4 | 6.2 | 2.7 | 4.2 | 11.2 | 30.5 | 11.6 | 10.0 | 11.2 |
| 44600 | Steubenville-Weirton, WV-OH | 1 503 | 122 547 | 312 | 81.5 | 94.4 | 4.8 | 0.6 | 0.7 | 1.1 | 4.8 | 14.9 | 8.8 | 10.0 | 11.8 | 15.2 |
| 44700 | Stockton, CA | 3 604 | 702 612 | 75 | 195.0 | 38.0 | 7.9 | 1.2 | 16.8 | 39.4 | 7.8 | 21.1 | 10.4 | 13.3 | 13.1 | 13.3 |
| 44940 | Sumter, SC | 1 723 | 108 052 | 333 | 62.7 | 48.2 | 47.4 | 0.8 | 1.8 | 3.5 | 7.3 | 17.9 | 11.0 | 13.2 | 11.7 | 13.8 |
| 45060 | Syracuse, NY | 6 177 | 660 934 | 81 | 107.0 | 85.3 | 8.9 | 1.2 | 3.0 | 3.6 | 5.7 | 16.7 | 11.7 | 11.8 | 11.9 | 15.4 |
| 45220 | Tallahassee, FL | 6 184 | 375 371 | 138 | 60.7 | 58.7 | 33.1 | 0.8 | 3.0 | 6.2 | 5.5 | 14.2 | 20.3 | 13.6 | 11.3 | 12.6 |
| 45300 | Tampa-St. Petersburg-Clearwater, FL | 6 510 | 2 842 878 | 18 | 436.7 | 68.3 | 12.4 | 0.7 | 3.7 | 16.6 | 5.6 | 15.2 | 8.6 | 12.3 | 12.8 | 14.9 |
| 45460 | Terre Haute, IN | 3 794 | 172 493 | 233 | 45.5 | 91.4 | 6.0 | 0.8 | 1.6 | 2.0 | 5.6 | 15.9 | 12.4 | 12.6 | 12.4 | 13.9 |
| 45500 | Texarkana, TX-Texarkana, AR | 3 912 | 136 782 | 287 | 35.0 | 68.7 | 24.7 | 1.4 | 1.1 | 5.8 | 6.6 | 17.5 | 8.9 | 13.5 | 12.8 | 14.0 |
| 45780 | Toledo, OH | 4 192 | 650 050 | 83 | 155.1 | 79.1 | 14.5 | 0.7 | 1.8 | 5.9 | 6.3 | 16.9 | 11.5 | 12.2 | 12.0 | 14.4 |
| 45820 | Topeka, KS | 8 372 | 234 566 | 190 | 28.0 | 82.0 | 8.0 | 2.5 | 1.5 | 9.0 | 6.7 | 18.0 | 8.1 | 12.5 | 11.5 | 14.6 |
| 45940 | Trenton-Ewing, NJ | 582 | 368 303 | 140 | 632.8 | 55.3 | 20.2 | 0.5 | 10.0 | 15.5 | 5.9 | 16.5 | 11.0 | 12.7 | 13.8 | 15.1 |
| 46060 | Tucson, AZ | 23 794 | 992 394 | 52 | 41.7 | 56.4 | 4.0 | 3.0 | 3.5 | 35.1 | 6.3 | 16.4 | 11.0 | 13.0 | 11.6 | 13.1 |
| 46140 | Tulsa, OK | 16 237 | 951 880 | 54 | 58.6 | 72.8 | 9.6 | 12.5 | 2.4 | 8.7 | 7.0 | 18.3 | 9.1 | 13.5 | 12.7 | 14.0 |
| 46220 | Tuscaloosa, AL | 6 767 | 222 860 | 195 | 32.9 | 61.8 | 34.2 | 0.6 | 1.5 | 2.9 | 6.0 | 15.5 | 19.0 | 13.0 | 11.3 | 12.2 |
| 46340 | Tyler, TX | 2 387 | 214 821 | 200 | 90.0 | 62.7 | 18.3 | 0.8 | 1.6 | 17.9 | 7.1 | 18.4 | 10.6 | 13.0 | 12.0 | 12.8 |
| 46540 | Utica-Rome, NY | 6 796 | 298 064 | 160 | 43.9 | 88.2 | 5.6 | 0.6 | 2.9 | 4.1 | 5.6 | 16.0 | 9.8 | 11.4 | 11.9 | 15.2 |
| 46660 | Valdosta, GA | 4 116 | 144 343 | 277 | 35.1 | 58.1 | 34.9 | 0.8 | 2.0 | 5.9 | 7.6 | 16.9 | 16.5 | 14.3 | 11.7 | 12.3 |
| 46700 | Vallejo-Fairfield, CA | 2 128 | 420 757 | 122 | 197.7 | 44.6 | 16.0 | 1.4 | 18.9 | 24.6 | 6.4 | 17.6 | 9.9 | 13.5 | 12.8 | 15.1 |
| 47020 | Victoria, TX | 5 804 | 118 229 | 315 | 20.4 | 48.3 | 5.7 | 0.5 | 1.8 | 44.4 | 7.2 | 18.9 | 8.9 | 12.6 | 11.5 | 14.0 |
| 47220 | Vineland-Millville-Bridgeton, NJ | 1 253 | 157 785 | 253 | 125.9 | 51.3 | 19.9 | 1.4 | 1.8 | 27.6 | 6.9 | 17.0 | 9.5 | 14.4 | 13.8 | 14.1 |

1. CBSA = Core Based Statistical Area. DIV = Metropolitan Division. See Appendix A for explanation. See Appendix B for list of metropolitan areas identified by type.   2. Dry land or land partially or temporarily covered by water.   3. May be of any race.

Table C. Metropolitan Areas — **Population and Households**

| Area name | Population, 2011 (cont.) | | | | Population change and components of change, 2000–2012 | | | | | | | Households, 2010 | | | | |
|---|---|---|---|---|---|---|---|---|---|---|---|---|---|---|---|---|
| | Age (percent) (cont.) | | | | Total persons | | Percent change | | Components of change, 2010–2012 | | | | | | Percent | |
| | 55 to 64 years | 65 to 74 years | 75 years and over | Percent female | 2000 | 2010 | 2000–2010 | 2010–2012 | Births | Deaths | Net migration | Number | Percent change, 2000–2010 | Persons per household | Female family householder[1] | One person |
| | 16 | 17 | 18 | 19 | 20 | 21 | 22 | 23 | 24 | 25 | 26 | 27 | 28 | 29 | 30 | 31 |
| Sacramento—Arden-Arcade—Roseville, CA .. | 11.9 | 6.7 | 5.7 | 51.0 | 1 796 857 | 2 149 127 | 19.6 | 2.2 | 62 968 | 34 455 | 18 708 | 787 667 | 18.4 | 2.68 | 13.0 | 24.8 |
| Saginaw-Saginaw Township North, MI | 13.6 | 8.2 | 7.4 | 51.6 | 210 039 | 200 169 | -4.7 | -0.9 | 5 204 | 4 476 | -2 473 | 79 011 | -1.8 | 2.44 | 16.0 | 28.2 |
| St. Cloud, MN | 10.9 | 6.2 | 6.1 | 49.6 | 167 392 | 189 093 | 13.0 | 0.7 | 5 520 | 2 655 | -1 510 | 71 311 | 17.5 | 2.52 | 8.5 | 25.4 |
| St. George, UT | 10.4 | 9.4 | 8.2 | 50.5 | 90 354 | 138 115 | 52.9 | 4.8 | 5 236 | 2 359 | 3 649 | 46 334 | 54.8 | 2.94 | 8.4 | 18.8 |
| St. Joseph, MO-KS | 12.3 | 7.4 | 6.9 | 48.8 | 122 336 | 127 329 | 4.1 | 0.5 | 3 622 | 2 770 | -344 | 48 184 | 3.6 | 2.46 | 12.0 | 28.1 |
| St. Louis, MO-IL | 12.7 | 7.1 | 6.4 | 51.6 | 2 698 687 | 2 812 896 | 4.2 | 0.3 | 77 806 | 55 897 | -13 501 | 1 119 020 | 6.7 | 2.46 | 13.7 | 28.5 |
| Salem, OR | 12.2 | 7.2 | 6.3 | 50.3 | 347 214 | 390 738 | 12.5 | 1.4 | 11 954 | 7 146 | 844 | 141 245 | 13.3 | 2.68 | 12.0 | 24.6 |
| Salinas, CA | 10.6 | 5.7 | 5.2 | 48.6 | 401 762 | 415 057 | 3.3 | 2.8 | 15 665 | 5 200 | 1 500 | 125 946 | 3.9 | 3.15 | 12.7 | 21.7 |
| Salisbury, MD | 12.3 | 7.4 | 6.1 | 51.0 | 109 391 | 125 203 | 14.5 | 1.4 | 3 395 | 2 649 | 964 | 46 008 | 13.4 | 2.50 | 15.2 | 26.5 |
| Salt Lake City, UT | 9.7 | 5.0 | 3.8 | 49.7 | 968 858 | 1 124 197 | 16.0 | 3.3 | 43 701 | 13 815 | 7 904 | 373 583 | 17.4 | 2.97 | 10.7 | 21.6 |
| San Angelo, TX | 11.7 | 7.2 | 6.7 | 50.9 | 105 781 | 111 823 | 5.7 | 2.7 | 3 465 | 2 230 | 1 808 | 42 984 | 6.9 | 2.48 | 13.3 | 28.1 |
| San Antonio-New Braunfels, TX | 11.0 | 6.2 | 4.9 | 50.9 | 1 711 703 | 2 142 508 | 25.2 | 4.3 | 69 681 | 33 067 | 54 182 | 763 022 | 26.9 | 2.74 | 15.5 | 24.3 |
| San Diego-Carlsbad-San Marcos, CA | 11.0 | 6.0 | 5.5 | 49.8 | 2 813 833 | 3 095 313 | 10.0 | 2.6 | 100 498 | 44 443 | 26 655 | 1 086 865 | 9.3 | 2.75 | 12.1 | 24.0 |
| Sandusky, OH | 15.2 | 9.4 | 8.3 | 51.1 | 79 551 | 77 079 | -3.1 | -0.9 | 1 719 | 1 962 | -406 | 31 860 | 0.4 | 2.37 | 12.9 | 28.6 |
| San Francisco-Oakland-Fremont, CA | 12.5 | 6.9 | 6.0 | 50.6 | 4 123 740 | 4 335 391 | 5.1 | 2.8 | 117 478 | 63 943 | 67 916 | 1 627 360 | 4.9 | 2.61 | 11.2 | 28.0 |
| Oakland-Fremont-Hayward, CA Div | 12.2 | 6.6 | 5.4 | 51.0 | 2 392 557 | 2 559 296 | 7.0 | 2.9 | 72 223 | 36 803 | 40 354 | 920 502 | 6.1 | 2.73 | 12.7 | 24.7 |
| San Francisco-San Mateo-Redwood City, CA Div. | 13.0 | 7.4 | 6.8 | 50.1 | 1 731 183 | 1 776 095 | 2.6 | 2.5 | 45 255 | 27 140 | 27 562 | 706 858 | 3.3 | 2.45 | 9.3 | 32.3 |
| San Jose-Sunnyvale-Santa Clara, CA | 10.8 | 6.1 | 5.2 | 49.8 | 1 735 819 | 1 836 911 | 5.8 | 3.1 | 56 170 | 21 621 | 23 866 | 621 009 | 6.7 | 2.91 | 10.8 | 21.6 |
| San Luis Obispo-Paso Robles, CA | 14.1 | 8.2 | 7.4 | 48.8 | 246 681 | 269 637 | 9.3 | 1.9 | 5 889 | 4 832 | 4 171 | 102 016 | 10.0 | 2.48 | 9.3 | 26.2 |
| Santa Barbara-Santa Maria-Goleta, CA | 10.8 | 6.5 | 6.6 | 49.8 | 399 347 | 423 895 | 6.1 | 1.7 | 13 255 | 6 452 | 725 | 142 104 | 4.0 | 2.86 | 10.9 | 24.8 |
| Santa Cruz-Watsonville, CA | 14.0 | 6.4 | 5.2 | 50.2 | 255 602 | 262 382 | 2.7 | 1.7 | 7 241 | 3 803 | 1 030 | 94 355 | 3.5 | 2.66 | 10.5 | 26.4 |
| Santa Fe, NM | 17.0 | 9.9 | 6.1 | 51.2 | 129 292 | 144 170 | 11.5 | 1.5 | 3 226 | 2 193 | 1 249 | 61 963 | 18.1 | 2.28 | 11.0 | 33.7 |
| Santa Rosa-Petaluma, CA | 14.6 | 7.8 | 6.6 | 50.8 | 458 614 | 483 878 | 5.5 | 1.6 | 12 465 | 8 672 | 4 199 | 185 825 | 7.8 | 2.55 | 10.6 | 27.3 |
| Savannah, GA | 11.4 | 6.7 | 5.1 | 51.3 | 293 000 | 347 611 | 18.6 | 4.1 | 11 431 | 6 290 | 9 179 | 131 868 | 18.7 | 2.53 | 16.5 | 26.2 |
| Scranton--Wilkes-Barre, PA.. | 13.9 | 8.7 | 9.1 | 51.3 | 560 625 | 563 631 | 0.5 | 0.0 | 12 669 | 15 433 | 2 975 | 230 395 | 1.2 | 2.36 | 12.5 | 31.2 |
| Seattle-Tacoma-Bellevue, WA | 12.1 | 6.2 | 5.0 | 50.1 | 3 043 878 | 3 439 809 | 13.0 | 3.3 | 99 729 | 50 203 | 63 037 | 1 357 475 | 13.4 | 2.49 | 10.2 | 28.4 |
| Seattle-Bellevue-Everett, WA Div | 12.2 | 6.1 | 5.0 | 50.1 | 2 343 058 | 2 644 584 | 12.9 | 3.6 | 74 818 | 37 083 | 58 278 | 1 057 557 | 13.0 | 2.46 | 9.4 | 29.3 |
| Tacoma, WA Div | 11.9 | 6.3 | 4.9 | 50.3 | 700 820 | 795 225 | 13.5 | 2.1 | 24 911 | 13 120 | 4 759 | 299 918 | 15.0 | 2.59 | 13.0 | 25.1 |
| Sebastian-Vero Beach, FL.... | 14.7 | 13.4 | 14.2 | 51.7 | 112 947 | 138 028 | 22.2 | 1.8 | 2 830 | 3 932 | 3 578 | 60 176 | 22.5 | 2.26 | 9.8 | 29.8 |
| Sheboygan, WI | 13.4 | 7.4 | 7.3 | 49.7 | 112 646 | 115 507 | 2.5 | -0.4 | 2 883 | 2 286 | -1 118 | 46 390 | 6.5 | 2.42 | 8.6 | 27.9 |
| Sherman-Denison, TX | 13.2 | 8.8 | 7.1 | 51.3 | 110 595 | 120 877 | 9.3 | 0.9 | 3 352 | 2 848 | 625 | 46 905 | 9.5 | 2.53 | 12.2 | 25.5 |
| Shreveport-Bossier City, LA . | 12.3 | 7.2 | 6.1 | 52.0 | 375 965 | 398 604 | 6.0 | 1.9 | 13 151 | 8 716 | 3 254 | 157 916 | 9.4 | 2.47 | 18.8 | 28.9 |
| Sioux City, IA-NE-SD | 12.2 | 6.8 | 6.3 | 50.4 | 143 053 | 143 577 | 0.4 | 0.3 | 4 874 | 2 767 | -1 657 | 54 396 | 1.5 | 2.58 | 11.9 | 27.0 |
| Sioux Falls, SD | 11.3 | 5.8 | 5.6 | 50.1 | 187 093 | 228 261 | 22.0 | 3.9 | 8 221 | 3 712 | 4 447 | 89 297 | 23.2 | 2.48 | 9.6 | 27.4 |
| South Bend-Mishawaka, IN-MI | 13.0 | 7.0 | 6.8 | 51.2 | 316 663 | 319 224 | 0.8 | -0.2 | 8 973 | 6 490 | -3 141 | 123 673 | 2.7 | 2.49 | 13.1 | 28.3 |
| Spartanburg, SC | 12.7 | 8.0 | 5.8 | 51.5 | 253 791 | 284 307 | 12.0 | 1.6 | 8 154 | 6 155 | 2 520 | 109 246 | 11.8 | 2.53 | 15.1 | 26.2 |
| Spokane, WA | 13.0 | 7.1 | 6.2 | 50.5 | 417 939 | 471 221 | 12.7 | 1.0 | 13 068 | 8 907 | 457 | 187 167 | 14.4 | 2.44 | 11.2 | 28.6 |
| Springfield, IL | 13.8 | 7.5 | 6.6 | 52.0 | 201 437 | 210 170 | 4.3 | 0.9 | 5 697 | 4 620 | 786 | 88 126 | 5.4 | 2.34 | 13.0 | 31.4 |
| Springfield, MA | 13.4 | 7.2 | 7.0 | 52.1 | 680 014 | 692 942 | 1.9 | 0.6 | 16 229 | 13 464 | 1 770 | 269 091 | 3.2 | 2.44 | 15.2 | 29.5 |
| Springfield, MO | 11.9 | 7.6 | 6.6 | 51.1 | 368 374 | 436 712 | 18.6 | 1.8 | 12 550 | 8 741 | 4 059 | 174 584 | 20.2 | 2.42 | 10.4 | 27.4 |
| Springfield, OH | 14.0 | 8.8 | 7.6 | 51.5 | 144 742 | 138 333 | -4.4 | -0.8 | 3 627 | 3 625 | -1 111 | 55 244 | -2.5 | 2.45 | 14.1 | 27.7 |
| State College, PA | 9.9 | 6.0 | 5.4 | 48.1 | 135 758 | 153 990 | 13.4 | 0.8 | 2 803 | 2 118 | 562 | 57 573 | 16.7 | 2.38 | 6.4 | 28.7 |
| Steubenville-Weirton, WV-OH | 15.9 | 9.5 | 9.1 | 51.8 | 132 008 | 124 454 | -5.7 | -1.5 | 2 450 | 3 812 | -518 | 52 426 | -3.8 | 2.31 | 12.0 | 30.0 |
| Stockton, CA | 10.4 | 5.8 | 4.8 | 50.1 | 563 598 | 685 306 | 21.6 | 2.5 | 24 244 | 10 484 | 3 590 | 215 007 | 18.4 | 3.12 | 15.4 | 19.7 |
| Sumter, SC | 11.8 | 7.5 | 5.8 | 51.8 | 104 646 | 107 456 | 2.7 | 0.6 | 3 392 | 2 231 | -547 | 40 398 | 7.1 | 2.59 | 20.2 | 25.8 |
| Syracuse, NY | 12.9 | 7.1 | 6.8 | 51.4 | 650 154 | 662 577 | 1.9 | -0.2 | 16 502 | 12 581 | -5 302 | 261 840 | 3.9 | 2.43 | 13.0 | 29.2 |
| Tallahassee, FL | 11.7 | 6.2 | 4.6 | 51.5 | 320 304 | 367 413 | 14.7 | 2.2 | 9 124 | 5 503 | 2 931 | 144 033 | 14.7 | 2.40 | 15.0 | 28.9 |
| Tampa-St. Petersburg-Clearwater, FL | 13.2 | 9.0 | 8.4 | 51.5 | 2 395 997 | 2 783 243 | 16.2 | 2.1 | 69 160 | 64 784 | 55 937 | 1 151 263 | 14.1 | 2.37 | 12.9 | 29.9 |
| Terre Haute, IN | 12.7 | 7.6 | 6.7 | 49.2 | 170 943 | 172 425 | 0.9 | 0.0 | 4 387 | 4 099 | -159 | 66 250 | 0.7 | 2.42 | 12.3 | 28.8 |
| Texarkana, TX-Texarkana, AR | 12.4 | 7.9 | 6.3 | 49.9 | 129 749 | 136 027 | 4.8 | 0.6 | 4 013 | 3 127 | -69 | 51 888 | 6.6 | 2.47 | 16.8 | 27.6 |
| Toledo, OH | 13.1 | 7.1 | 6.5 | 51.4 | 659 188 | 651 429 | -1.2 | -0.2 | 17 350 | 13 687 | -5 220 | 263 001 | 1.2 | 2.41 | 14.1 | 29.9 |
| Topeka, KS | 13.6 | 7.9 | 7.1 | 51.1 | 224 551 | 233 870 | 4.2 | 0.3 | 6 836 | 5 005 | -1 071 | 94 483 | 5.4 | 2.42 | 11.5 | 29.2 |
| Trenton-Ewing, NJ | 12.1 | 6.7 | 6.3 | 51.1 | 350 761 | 366 513 | 4.5 | 0.5 | 9 548 | 6 295 | -1 516 | 133 155 | 5.8 | 2.61 | 14.2 | 29.2 |
| Tucson, AZ | 12.8 | 8.6 | 7.3 | 50.8 | 843 746 | 980 263 | 16.2 | 1.2 | 26 942 | 18 947 | 4 363 | 388 660 | 16.9 | 2.46 | 12.8 | 29.2 |
| Tulsa, OK | 12.2 | 7.3 | 5.8 | 50.9 | 859 532 | 937 478 | 9.1 | 1.5 | 29 222 | 18 985 | 4 096 | 367 091 | 8.9 | 2.51 | 12.6 | 27.3 |
| Tuscaloosa, AL | 11.5 | 6.2 | 5.3 | 51.7 | 192 034 | 219 461 | 14.3 | 1.5 | 6 231 | 4 378 | 1 603 | 86 178 | 15.1 | 2.42 | 15.8 | 29.4 |
| Tyler, TX | 11.6 | 7.7 | 6.7 | 51.6 | 174 706 | 209 714 | 20.0 | 2.4 | 6 711 | 4 215 | 2 637 | 79 055 | 20.3 | 2.60 | 13.3 | 25.3 |
| Utica-Rome, NY | 13.5 | 8.2 | 8.4 | 50.4 | 299 896 | 299 397 | -0.2 | -0.4 | 7 260 | 6 990 | -1 537 | 119 352 | 2.7 | 2.38 | 12.7 | 30.7 |
| Valdosta, GA | 10.2 | 6.1 | 4.5 | 50.9 | 119 560 | 139 588 | 16.8 | 3.4 | 4 879 | 2 542 | 2 365 | 51 141 | 19.9 | 2.60 | 16.7 | 24.6 |
| Vallejo-Fairfield, CA | 12.9 | 6.6 | 5.1 | 50.0 | 394 542 | 413 344 | 4.8 | 1.8 | 11 802 | 6 487 | 2 142 | 141 758 | 8.7 | 2.83 | 14.7 | 21.9 |
| Victoria, TX | 12.6 | 7.8 | 6.5 | 50.7 | 111 663 | 115 384 | 3.3 | 2.5 | 3 641 | 2 270 | 1 499 | 42 821 | 6.6 | 2.65 | 13.7 | 24.3 |
| Vineland-Millville-Bridgeton, NJ | 11.4 | 6.9 | 5.9 | 48.6 | 146 438 | 156 898 | 7.1 | 0.6 | 4 982 | 3 114 | -922 | 51 931 | 5.7 | 2.79 | 18.6 | 24.0 |

1. No spouse present.

| Area name | Persons in group quarters, 2009 | Daytime population, 2007–2011 Number | Employment/residence ratio | Births, 2011 Total | Rate[1] | Deaths, 2011 Number | Rate[1] | Persons under 65 with no health insurance 2010 Number | Percent | Medicare, 2012 Enrolled in original Medicare | Enrolled in Medicare Advantage | Enrolled in a Medicare prescription drug plan | Serious crimes known to police,[2] 2011 Total Number | Rate[3] |
|---|---|---|---|---|---|---|---|---|---|---|---|---|---|---|
| | 32 | 33 | 34 | 35 | 36 | 37 | 38 | 39 | 40 | 41 | 42 | 43 | 44 | 45 |
| Sacramento—Arden-Arcade—Roseville, CA .. | 35 946 | 2 129 231 | 1.00 | 27 593 | 12.7 | 14 934 | 6.9 | 285 013 | 15.2 | 331 533 | 137 496 | 93 034 | 70 568 | 3 245 |
| Saginaw-Saginaw Township North, MI | 7 116 | 211 417 | 1.13 | 2 362 | 11.9 | 1 980 | 9.9 | 23 415 | 14.3 | 40 535 | 9 390 | 16 059 | 6 452 | 3 226 |
| St. Cloud, MN | 9 261 | 192 028 | 1.04 | 2 485 | 13.1 | 1 152 | 6.1 | 16 400 | 10.3 | 28 088 | 13 475 | 12 339 | 4 776 | 2 596 |
| St. George, UT | 1 853 | 137 118 | 1.00 | 2 408 | 17.0 | 980 | 6.9 | 23 224 | 20.7 | 26 296 | 8 105 | 8 425 | 2 422 | 1 720 |
| St. Joseph, MO-KS | 8 674 | 127 196 | 1.01 | 1 655 | 13.0 | 1 208 | 9.5 | 14 577 | 14.4 | 22 143 | 1 391 | 12 204 | 5 179 | 4 052 |
| St. Louis, MO-IL | 56 232 | 2 810 361 | 1.01 | 34 833 | 12.4 | 24 577 | 8.7 | 304 126 | 12.7 | 471 631 | 127 547 | 186 202 | 69 214 | 2 799 |
| Salem, OR | 12 314 | 383 600 | 0.97 | 5 470 | 13.9 | 3 183 | 8.1 | 68 987 | 20.9 | 65 187 | 36 458 | 15 920 | 11 960 | 3 029 |
| Salinas, CA | 18 702 | 410 839 | 1.00 | 6 808 | 16.1 | 2 259 | 5.4 | 86 376 | 24.3 | 53 521 | 510 | 28 688 | 11 844 | 2 820 |
| Salisbury, MD | 10 054 | 123 686 | 0.99 | 1 509 | 12.0 | 1 187 | 9.5 | 15 092 | 15.0 | 20 614 | 569 | 10 215 | 4 631 | 3 664 |
| Salt Lake City, UT | 14 477 | 1 175 855 | 1.12 | 19 631 | 17.1 | 5 957 | 5.2 | 178 944 | 17.6 | 122 676 | 48 030 | 35 850 | 51 031 | 4 455 |
| San Angelo, TX | 5 165 | 110 612 | 1.00 | 1 573 | 13.9 | 952 | 8.4 | 22 446 | 24.4 | 19 418 | 2 168 | 8 069 | 4 297 | 3 763 |
| San Antonio-New Braunfels, TX | 49 032 | 2 094 371 | 0.99 | 31 812 | 14.5 | 14 326 | 6.5 | 431 384 | 23.0 | 310 024 | 102 070 | 76 044 | 110 774 | 5 066 |
| San Diego-Carlsbad-San Marcos, CA | 101 966 | 3 086 589 | 1.02 | 44 076 | 14.0 | 19 373 | 6.2 | 511 168 | 19.1 | 426 740 | 175 340 | 118 221 | 76 111 | 2 430 |
| Sandusky, OH | 1 677 | 78 540 | 1.04 | 769 | 10.0 | 864 | 11.3 | 8 691 | 13.8 | 16 421 | 3 412 | 7 924 | 2 164 | 2 817 |
| San Francisco-Oakland-Fremont, CA | 89 917 | 4 364 588 | 1.03 | 51 720 | 11.8 | 27 781 | 6.3 | 535 814 | 14.3 | 652 142 | 267 601 | 208 205 | 157 316 | 3 586 |
| Oakland-Fremont-Hayward, CA Div. | 47 756 | 2 434 114 | 0.92 | 31 661 | 12.2 | 15 989 | 6.2 | 329 301 | 14.7 | 363 258 | 155 609 | 110 252 | 97 345 | 3 759 |
| San Francisco-San Mateo-Redwood City, CA Div. | 42 161 | 1 930 474 | 1.19 | 20 059 | 11.2 | 11 792 | 6.6 | 206 513 | 13.7 | 288 884 | 111 992 | 97 953 | 59 971 | 3 337 |
| San Jose-Sunnyvale-Santa Clara, CA | 30 639 | 1 912 398 | 1.11 | 24 727 | 13.3 | 9 351 | 5.0 | 226 244 | 14.0 | 236 568 | 82 316 | 89 162 | 44 644 | 2 402 |
| San Luis Obispo-Paso Robles, CA | 17 006 | 265 139 | 0.98 | 2 632 | 9.7 | 2 078 | 7.6 | 38 754 | 18.2 | 49 939 | 4 578 | 23 671 | 6 876 | 2 520 |
| Santa Barbara-Santa Maria-Goleta, CA | 17 782 | 432 395 | 1.07 | 5 842 | 13.7 | 2 845 | 6.7 | 75 530 | 21.3 | 65 093 | 8 905 | 32 993 | 10 740 | 2 504 |
| Santa Cruz-Watsonville, CA . | 10 969 | 247 440 | 0.90 | 3 191 | 12.1 | 1 693 | 6.4 | 41 184 | 18.3 | 37 946 | 2 657 | 20 889 | 9 913 | 3 734 |
| Santa Fe, NM | 2 613 | 147 181 | 1.06 | 1 411 | 9.7 | 924 | 6.3 | 27 496 | 22.8 | 27 576 | 7 076 | 10 665 | 5 783 | 3 967 |
| Santa Rosa-Petaluma, CA.... | 10 043 | 459 121 | 0.91 | 5 444 | 11.2 | 3 769 | 7.7 | 72 057 | 17.5 | 84 235 | 31 997 | 26 994 | 10 009 | 2 044 |
| Savannah, GA | 13 596 | 351 519 | 1.06 | 5 044 | 14.2 | 2 715 | 7.6 | 60 078 | 20.3 | 50 970 | 13 353 | 18 360 | 13 940 | 3 958 |
| Scranton--Wilkes-Barre, PA.. | 20 456 | 563 033 | 1.00 | 5 632 | 10.0 | 6 880 | 12.2 | 56 963 | 12.7 | 123 096 | 29 102 | 58 131 | 14 031 | 2 501 |
| Seattle-Tacoma-Bellevue, WA | 65 473 | 3 450 936 | 1.03 | 44 416 | 12.7 | 22 136 | 6.3 | 446 419 | 14.7 | 475 840 | 153 241 | 154 882 | 140 077 | 4 009 |
| Seattle-Bellevue-Everett, WA Div. | 47 528 | 2 704 764 | 1.07 | 33 459 | 12.4 | 16 300 | 6.1 | 340 166 | 14.5 | 357 892 | 121 716 | 118 417 | 105 179 | 3 916 |
| Tacoma, WA Div | 17 945 | 746 172 | 0.88 | 10 957 | 13.6 | 5 836 | 7.2 | 106 253 | 15.3 | 117 948 | 31 525 | 36 465 | 34 898 | 4 321 |
| Sebastian-Vero Beach, FL... | 1 794 | 138 314 | 1.02 | 1 266 | 9.1 | 1 730 | 12.5 | 25 651 | 25.9 | 39 180 | 6 824 | 16 140 | 4 409 | 3 151 |
| Sheboygan, WI | 3 023 | 115 371 | 1.00 | 1 316 | 11.4 | 1 014 | 8.8 | 9 552 | 9.9 | 20 523 | 7 332 | 6 158 | 2 551 | 2 199 |
| Sherman-Denison, TX | 2 214 | 115 432 | 0.91 | 1 542 | 12.7 | 1 224 | 10.1 | 27 565 | 27.4 | 23 719 | 2 559 | 10 189 | 4 244 | 3 439 |
| Shreveport-Bossier City, LA . | 8 423 | 405 352 | 1.05 | 5 822 | 14.4 | 3 778 | 9.4 | 69 768 | 20.5 | 66 391 | 9 623 | 27 618 | 16 394 | 4 169 |
| Sioux City, IA-NE-SD | 3 055 | 144 737 | 1.03 | 2 188 | 15.2 | 1 201 | 8.3 | 18 224 | 14.9 | 23 066 | 4 964 | 12 021 | 4 775 | 3 427 |
| Sioux Falls, SD | 7 040 | 229 325 | 1.03 | 3 693 | 15.9 | 1 567 | 6.7 | 23 016 | 11.5 | 34 786 | 5 277 | 19 383 | 6 046 | 2 621 |
| South Bend-Mishawaka, IN-MI | 11 746 | 316 400 | 0.98 | 4 037 | 12.7 | 2 853 | 9.0 | 44 969 | 17.0 | 53 950 | 13 724 | 22 150 | 12 603 | 4 013 |
| Spartanburg, SC | 7 986 | 288 786 | 1.06 | 3 845 | 13.4 | 2 660 | 9.3 | 53 232 | 22.2 | 54 324 | 17 325 | 19 615 | 11 802 | 4 103 |
| Spokane, WA | 14 692 | 475 343 | 1.04 | 5 873 | 12.4 | 3 964 | 8.4 | 64 130 | 16.1 | 81 479 | 26 081 | 26 857 | 26 235 | 5 481 |
| Springfield, IL | 4 120 | 220 273 | 1.11 | 2 520 | 11.9 | 2 067 | 9.8 | 19 983 | 11.2 | 37 149 | 2 316 | 14 825 | 11 252 | 5 673 |
| Springfield, MA | 37 104 | 673 857 | 0.94 | 7 283 | 10.5 | 5 914 | 8.5 | 32 881 | 5.8 | 130 204 | 26 200 | 55 070 | 23 112 | 3 400 |
| Springfield, MO | 14 413 | 436 037 | 1.02 | 5 603 | 12.7 | 3 833 | 8.7 | 62 447 | 17.2 | 80 419 | 31 750 | 26 592 | 21 973 | 5 013 |
| Springfield, OH | 2 798 | 129 245 | 0.84 | 1 674 | 12.2 | 1 599 | 11.6 | 17 234 | 15.1 | 27 540 | 12 559 | 13 286 | 6 020 | 4 358 |
| State College, PA | 16 989 | 159 852 | 1.10 | 1 256 | 8.1 | 907 | 5.9 | 15 163 | 12.6 | 20 403 | 8 939 | 6 785 | 2 640 | 1 709 |
| Steubenville-Weirton, WV-OH | 3 310 | 118 635 | 0.89 | 1 153 | 9.4 | 1 714 | 13.9 | 14 949 | 15.2 | 28 232 | 8 927 | 13 757 | 2 029 | 1 727 |
| Stockton, CA | 14 354 | 652 426 | 0.89 | 10 557 | 15.2 | 4 525 | 6.5 | 117 928 | 19.4 | 91 198 | 27 878 | 38 034 | 34 836 | 5 024 |
| Sumter, SC | 2 774 | 106 588 | 0.99 | 1 571 | 14.6 | 966 | 9.0 | 17 636 | 19.4 | 18 568 | 2 328 | 7 434 | 4 886 | 4 495 |
| Syracuse, NY | 27 156 | 669 588 | 1.03 | 7 446 | 11.2 | 5 460 | 8.2 | 64 164 | 11.7 | 117 908 | 32 142 | 35 919 | 17 297 | 2 608 |
| Tallahassee, FL | 21 922 | 369 972 | 1.03 | 4 159 | 11.2 | 2 371 | 6.4 | 56 577 | 18.3 | 49 326 | 19 249 | 12 561 | 16 173 | 4 350 |
| Tampa-St. Petersburg-Clearwater, FL | 49 245 | 2 765 289 | 1.00 | 30 923 | 10.9 | 28 605 | 10.1 | 509 932 | 22.5 | 547 313 | 236 937 | 143 230 | 99 775 | 3 537 |
| Terre Haute, IN | 12 393 | 174 528 | 1.03 | 1 906 | 11.0 | 1 791 | 10.4 | 23 453 | 17.1 | 31 604 | 2 923 | 17 097 | 6 552 | 4 369 |
| Texarkana, TX-Texarkana, AR | 7 686 | 137 899 | 1.05 | 1 785 | 13.1 | 1 370 | 10.0 | 23 437 | 21.3 | 24 915 | 3 407 | 10 921 | 7 341 | 5 308 |
| Toledo, OH | 17 825 | 666 311 | 1.05 | 8 101 | 12.5 | 6 047 | 9.3 | 79 694 | 14.5 | 111 676 | 38 872 | 54 032 | 21 037 | 3 553 |
| Topeka, KS | 5 049 | 230 173 | 0.98 | 3 048 | 13.0 | 2 203 | 9.4 | 29 646 | 15.1 | 44 483 | 2 759 | 23 132 | 10 667 | 4 603 |
| Trenton-Ewing, NJ | 18 805 | 416 053 | 1.30 | 4 378 | 11.9 | 2 746 | 7.5 | 41 627 | 13.7 | 59 625 | 8 274 | 34 467 | 9 614 | 2 614 |
| Tucson, AZ | 24 139 | 973 775 | 1.00 | 12 223 | 12.4 | 8 255 | 8.3 | 147 455 | 18.2 | 173 473 | 77 507 | 40 065 | 28 227 | 2 839 |
| Tulsa, OK | 15 486 | 934 855 | 1.02 | 13 581 | 14.3 | 8 231 | 8.7 | 172 467 | 21.3 | 154 100 | 43 142 | 60 383 | 38 501 | 4 063 |
| Tuscaloosa, AL | 10 802 | 219 504 | 1.03 | 2 744 | 12.4 | 1 894 | 8.5 | 32 242 | 17.5 | 36 645 | 3 031 | 15 556 | 8 469 | 4 067 |
| Tyler, TX | 4 127 | 215 600 | 1.10 | 3 086 | 14.5 | 1 824 | 8.5 | 48 073 | 27.2 | 37 397 | 5 395 | 16 742 | 7 765 | 3 626 |
| Utica-Rome, NY | 14 831 | 297 522 | 0.99 | 3 215 | 10.8 | 3 080 | 10.3 | 26 048 | 10.9 | 62 137 | 17 602 | 21 466 | 7 274 | 2 456 |
| Valdosta, GA | 6 670 | 139 754 | 1.04 | 2 160 | 15.2 | 1 132 | 8.0 | 27 789 | 23.4 | 19 564 | 3 295 | 9 114 | 4 843 | 3 457 |
| Vallejo-Fairfield, CA | 12 452 | 369 815 | 0.77 | 5 121 | 12.3 | 2 852 | 6.8 | 51 013 | 14.3 | 60 671 | 26 820 | 11 498 | 13 889 | 3 321 |
| Victoria, TX | 1 850 | 117 306 | 1.05 | 1 706 | 14.7 | 996 | 8.6 | 23 895 | 24.4 | 20 143 | 2 101 | 9 667 | 5 084 | 4 367 |
| Vineland-Millville-Bridgeton, NJ | 12 111 | 155 401 | 0.99 | 2 297 | 14.6 | 1 360 | 8.7 | 24 925 | 19.6 | 25 707 | 3 591 | 15 969 | 5 995 | 3 808 |

1. Per 1,000 estimated resident population.     2. Data for serious crimes have not been adjusted for underreporting; this may affect comparability between geographic areas and over time.     3. Per 100,000 population estimated by the FBI.

# Table C. Metropolitan Areas — Crime, Education, Money Income, and Poverty

| Area name | Serious crimes known to police, 2011 (cont.)[1] Rate[2] Violent | Property | Education — School enrollment and attainment, 2007–2011 Enrollment[3] Total | Percent private | Attainment[4] (percent) High school graduate or less | Bachelor's degree or more | Local government expenditures,[5] 2009–2010 Total current expenditures (mil dol) | Current expenditures per student (dollars) | Income and Poverty, 2007–2011 Per capita income[6] (dollars) | Median household income (dollars) | Percent of households with income of less than $25,000 | Percent of households with income of $100,000 or more | Percent of households with income of $200,000 or more | Percent below poverty level All persons | Related Children under 18 years | Related Children under 5 |
|---|---|---|---|---|---|---|---|---|---|---|---|---|---|---|---|---|
| | 46 | 47 | 48 | 49 | 50 | 51 | 52 | 53 | 54 | 55 | 56 | 57 | 58 | 59 | 60 | 61 |
| Sacramento—Arden-Arcade—Roseville, CA | 420 | 2 825 | 623 119 | 12.6 | 34.3 | 30.0 | 3 121.5 | 8 707 | 29 279 | 60 479 | 19.0 | 26.5 | 4.8 | 13.4 | 17.5 | 20.1 |
| Saginaw-Saginaw Township North, MI | 780 | 2 446 | 55 007 | 12.1 | 48.8 | 18.6 | 333.4 | 10 365 | 22 257 | 43 258 | 29.0 | 13.6 | 1.9 | 18.6 | 27.6 | 34.4 |
| St. Cloud, MN | 184 | 2 412 | 56 729 | 18.4 | 41.9 | 22.8 | 284.8 | 9 993 | 25 042 | 52 625 | 22.0 | 16.5 | 2.2 | 12.9 | 13.1 | 16.2 |
| St. George, UT | 146 | 1 574 | 39 884 | 11.2 | 36.1 | 24.9 | 169.8 | 6 262 | 21 447 | 50 307 | 19.8 | 13.9 | 2.2 | 11.9 | 15.7 | 14.7 |
| St. Joseph, MO-KS | 275 | 3 777 | 31 396 | 13.1 | 53.5 | 18.5 | 160.5 | 8 749 | 22 277 | 45 051 | 26.1 | 12.9 | 1.4 | 13.8 | 18.6 | 25.3 |
| St. Louis, MO-IL | 323 | 2 476 | 755 131 | 24.3 | 39.3 | 29.6 | 4 583.3 | 10 835 | 28 955 | 54 149 | 22.2 | 21.6 | 3.9 | 12.2 | 17.3 | 20.5 |
| Salem, OR | 226 | 2 803 | 101 520 | 14.6 | 42.8 | 22.1 | 667.9 | 9 883 | 22 694 | 47 574 | 24.3 | 15.2 | 2.0 | 16.4 | 23.9 | 28.2 |
| Salinas, CA | 465 | 2 356 | 116 010 | 10.2 | 50.0 | 23.2 | 692.4 | 9 755 | 25 508 | 59 737 | 18.2 | 25.9 | 5.4 | 15.1 | 21.5 | 22.9 |
| Salisbury, MD | 526 | 3 138 | 37 566 | 10.5 | 51.2 | 23.1 | 232.3 | 13 263 | 24 157 | 49 668 | 24.3 | 16.5 | 2.7 | 15.9 | 18.6 | 24.0 |
| Salt Lake City, UT | 309 | 4 116 | 333 521 | 13.2 | 35.2 | 30.4 | 1 336.6 | 6 180 | 25 922 | 59 930 | 17.1 | 23.3 | 4.0 | 10.7 | 13.3 | 15.1 |
| San Angelo, TX | 252 | 3 511 | 28 663 | 8.8 | 48.4 | 22.1 | 169.2 | 9 082 | 22 977 | 43 498 | 28.0 | 14.2 | 2.2 | 15.7 | 22.9 | 24.9 |
| San Antonio-New Braunfels, TX | 398 | 4 668 | 605 437 | 13.6 | 43.5 | 25.4 | 3 511.9 | 8 626 | 24 545 | 50 318 | 24.2 | 19.3 | 3.5 | 16.0 | 22.5 | 25.5 |
| San Diego-Carlsbad-San Marcos, CA | 352 | 2 079 | 861 453 | 14.2 | 34.1 | 34.2 | 4 543.7 | 9 134 | 30 955 | 63 857 | 18.2 | 29.3 | 6.5 | 13.0 | 16.7 | 17.4 |
| Sandusky, OH | 245 | 2 572 | 17 846 | 14.0 | 51.7 | 20.0 | 166.5 | 13 402 | 25 704 | 47 466 | 24.9 | 16.6 | 2.5 | 12.6 | 17.5 | 23.8 |
| San Francisco-Oakland-Fremont, CA | 508 | 3 078 | 1 101 162 | 19.7 | 30.6 | 43.7 | 5 325.6 | 9 549 | 40 786 | 76 911 | 16.4 | 38.8 | 11.8 | 10.4 | 12.3 | 12.7 |
| Oakland-Fremont-Hayward, CA Div. | 568 | 3 191 | 693 271 | 15.9 | 32.8 | 39.8 | 3 369.9 | 8 842 | 36 250 | 74 055 | 16.7 | 36.9 | 10.0 | 11.0 | 13.7 | 14.3 |
| San Francisco-San Mateo-Redwood City, CA Div. | 422 | 2 916 | 407 891 | 26.3 | 27.8 | 48.9 | 1 955.7 | 11 077 | 47 313 | 81 066 | 16.1 | 41.3 | 14.2 | 9.4 | 9.6 | 9.8 |
| San Jose-Sunnyvale-Santa Clara, CA | 256 | 2 146 | 504 793 | 19.9 | 30.3 | 44.8 | 2 641.9 | 9 558 | 40 264 | 88 339 | 13.3 | 44.6 | 14.4 | 9.3 | 11.3 | 11.7 |
| San Luis Obispo-Paso Robles, CA | 249 | 2 271 | 75 632 | 9.9 | 33.0 | 30.8 | 314.7 | 9 089 | 30 204 | 58 630 | 20.7 | 25.7 | 4.9 | 13.2 | 12.2 | 10.6 |
| Santa Barbara-Santa Maria-Goleta, CA | 386 | 2 118 | 130 843 | 10.8 | 37.6 | 31.3 | 604.3 | 9 161 | 30 330 | 61 896 | 18.6 | 28.8 | 6.7 | 14.2 | 16.9 | 18.3 |
| Santa Cruz-Watsonville, CA | 440 | 3 294 | 77 725 | 11.3 | 31.9 | 31.6 | 369.1 | 9 485 | 32 975 | 66 030 | 18.8 | 31.3 | 8.0 | 13.7 | 15.0 | 16.9 |
| Santa Fe, NM | 370 | 3 597 | 33 388 | 22.1 | 33.7 | 39.6 | 145.6 | 8 944 | 32 680 | 53 698 | 24.1 | 22.8 | 5.3 | 15.6 | 23.2 | 25.6 |
| Santa Rosa-Petaluma, CA | 348 | 1 697 | 122 769 | 12.5 | 34.3 | 31.8 | 667.0 | 9 393 | 33 119 | 64 343 | 17.7 | 28.8 | 6.2 | 10.7 | 13.0 | 17.4 |
| Savannah, GA | 340 | 3 618 | 96 251 | 21.3 | 42.9 | 27.5 | 480.0 | 8 985 | 25 512 | 49 033 | 24.9 | 18.1 | 3.0 | 16.3 | 22.8 | 26.7 |
| Scranton--Wilkes-Barre, PA | 270 | 2 231 | 131 254 | 27.3 | 52.6 | 21.7 | 879.3 | 11 411 | 24 357 | 44 319 | 28.0 | 14.5 | 2.2 | 13.7 | 21.1 | 27.1 |
| Seattle-Tacoma-Bellevue, WA | 324 | 3 685 | 844 653 | 17.7 | 30.3 | 37.2 | 4 669.7 | 9 417 | 35 061 | 67 023 | 16.2 | 30.3 | 6.3 | 10.5 | 12.9 | 15.4 |
| Seattle-Bellevue-Everett, WA Div. | 296 | 3 620 | 641 840 | 18.2 | 27.8 | 41.2 | 3 455.8 | 9 436 | 37 146 | 69 822 | 15.7 | 32.4 | 7.2 | 10.2 | 12.1 | 14.8 |
| Tacoma, WA Div. | 420 | 3 901 | 202 813 | 15.9 | 39.2 | 23.6 | 1 213.9 | 9 362 | 28 179 | 58 824 | 18.0 | 22.9 | 3.1 | 11.6 | 15.0 | 17.6 |
| Sebastian-Vero Beach, FL | 322 | 2 830 | 26 630 | 15.1 | 42.0 | 26.4 | 148.7 | 8 378 | 31 732 | 46 363 | 25.4 | 18.7 | 5.5 | 13.4 | 21.9 | 25.0 |
| Sheboygan, WI | 136 | 2 063 | 29 252 | 17.3 | 47.9 | 21.6 | 212.1 | 10 824 | 25 830 | 52 993 | 20.0 | 16.3 | 1.8 | 8.2 | 11.3 | 16.3 |
| Sherman-Denison, TX | 272 | 3 166 | 29 281 | 13.2 | 47.7 | 19.8 | 188.2 | 8 947 | 23 818 | 46 993 | 25.1 | 15.4 | 2.5 | 14.4 | 19.7 | 25.3 |
| Shreveport-Bossier City, LA | 614 | 3 555 | 103 013 | 11.7 | 49.5 | 21.6 | 742.3 | 10 957 | 24 298 | 42 398 | 30.5 | 15.3 | 2.9 | 18.3 | 28.2 | 32.7 |
| Sioux City, IA-NE-SD | 299 | 3 128 | 38 012 | 17.3 | 50.0 | 19.8 | 273.2 | 10 378 | 23 367 | 47 348 | 24.9 | 14.5 | 1.9 | 13.8 | 20.3 | 31.9 |
| Sioux Falls, SD | 217 | 2 404 | 57 656 | 17.9 | 37.7 | 30.0 | 291.0 | 8 149 | 28 003 | 55 754 | 19.0 | 18.0 | 3.1 | 9.1 | 10.9 | 15.3 |
| South Bend-Mishawaka, IN-MI | 346 | 3 667 | 92 150 | 29.0 | 46.5 | 24.6 | 488.8 | 10 216 | 23 358 | 45 226 | 26.0 | 15.2 | 2.4 | 15.5 | 22.6 | 27.2 |
| Spartanburg, SC | 500 | 3 604 | 71 887 | 15.6 | 50.6 | 20.4 | 436.9 | 9 305 | 22 275 | 43 563 | 29.1 | 13.9 | 1.9 | 16.2 | 22.2 | 26.8 |
| Spokane, WA | 343 | 5 138 | 124 927 | 17.9 | 32.8 | 28.6 | 709.4 | 9 525 | 25 752 | 49 257 | 24.6 | 16.4 | 2.9 | 14.4 | 16.5 | 19.1 |
| Springfield, IL | 873 | 4 800 | 54 004 | 17.8 | 38.1 | 30.6 | 346.9 | 10 471 | 28 993 | 53 682 | 22.1 | 20.8 | 2.8 | 13.0 | 19.0 | 24.4 |
| Springfield, MA | 501 | 2 898 | 198 559 | 19.0 | 44.2 | 28.7 | 1 368.4 | 13 063 | 26 522 | 51 751 | 25.8 | 20.4 | 3.0 | 15.1 | 21.6 | 27.1 |
| Springfield, MO | 426 | 4 587 | 114 093 | 17.6 | 43.5 | 25.0 | 514.3 | 7 812 | 22 999 | 43 042 | 28.0 | 12.3 | 2.0 | 15.9 | 21.5 | 27.2 |
| Springfield, OH | 294 | 4 064 | 35 562 | 19.4 | 52.5 | 16.6 | 210.6 | 9 731 | 22 434 | 44 037 | 27.6 | 13.2 | 1.4 | 16.9 | 25.3 | 34.2 |
| State College, PA | 111 | 1 598 | 61 436 | 8.0 | 40.3 | 39.8 | 174.5 | 12 831 | 24 514 | 48 262 | 26.4 | 18.3 | 3.4 | 18.9 | 11.7 | 13.9 |
| Steubenville-Weirton, WV-OH | 129 | 1 598 | 27 760 | 17.5 | 56.7 | 14.8 | 191.2 | 11 086 | 22 263 | 39 581 | 30.9 | 10.9 | 1.2 | 15.8 | 25.5 | 33.9 |
| Stockton, CA | 821 | 4 203 | 204 621 | 12.3 | 50.0 | 17.6 | 1 160.3 | 8 545 | 22 857 | 53 764 | 21.5 | 22.5 | 3.5 | 16.7 | 22.0 | 24.8 |
| Sumter, SC | 1 135 | 3 359 | 28 078 | 15.1 | 50.4 | 17.8 | 147.2 | 8 478 | 19 686 | 40 542 | 29.7 | 10.5 | 1.2 | 18.3 | 27.0 | 33.1 |
| Syracuse, NY | 284 | 2 324 | 186 187 | 22.1 | 42.3 | 28.6 | 1 679.8 | 15 653 | 26 567 | 51 606 | 23.6 | 19.9 | 2.9 | 13.8 | 19.1 | 24.4 |
| Tallahassee, FL | 661 | 3 688 | 127 454 | 12.5 | 37.3 | 35.0 | 381.8 | 7 888 | 24 619 | 45 011 | 29.4 | 17.4 | 2.7 | 22.2 | 24.0 | 28.3 |
| Tampa-St. Petersburg-Clearwater, FL | 435 | 3 101 | 652 994 | 16.7 | 43.7 | 25.9 | 3 314.6 | 8 531 | 27 105 | 46 890 | 25.2 | 17.0 | 3.2 | 13.9 | 19.4 | 23.4 |
| Terre Haute, IN | 191 | 4 178 | 46 334 | 12.4 | 52.4 | 18.3 | 250.0 | 9 357 | 21 122 | 42 170 | 29.0 | 12.4 | 1.6 | 16.4 | 22.9 | 29.9 |
| Texarkana, TX-Texarkana, AR | 659 | 4 648 | 33 387 | 7.4 | 51.3 | 16.7 | 225.1 | 9 162 | 21 852 | 42 229 | 31.7 | 13.1 | 2.0 | 19.0 | 28.8 | 32.1 |
| Toledo, OH | 538 | 3 014 | 187 535 | 15.6 | 45.1 | 23.5 | 1 214.9 | 11 641 | 24 684 | 45 495 | 28.0 | 15.9 | 2.5 | 17.1 | 23.2 | 28.7 |
| Topeka, KS | 379 | 4 223 | 60 361 | 14.7 | 43.2 | 26.8 | 370.9 | 9 680 | 25 949 | 49 634 | 22.7 | 16.5 | 2.3 | 13.2 | 18.7 | 25.7 |
| Trenton-Ewing, NJ | 436 | 2 178 | 104 725 | 24.6 | 39.0 | 38.0 | 1 016.6 | 16 192 | 36 721 | 73 883 | 17.0 | 36.5 | 10.7 | 10.7 | 15.0 | 17.7 |
| Tucson, AZ | 432 | 2 407 | 264 429 | 11.5 | 36.4 | 29.5 | 1 170.4 | 7 953 | 25 477 | 46 341 | 26.4 | 17.2 | 3.0 | 17.4 | 23.9 | 27.9 |
| Tulsa, OK | 557 | 3 506 | 242 721 | 16.0 | 42.3 | 25.4 | 1 248.1 | 7 682 | 26 029 | 47 760 | 24.8 | 17.3 | 3.1 | 14.4 | 21.1 | 25.6 |
| Tuscaloosa, AL | 456 | 3 611 | 67 888 | 9.3 | 48.5 | 24.0 | 278.6 | 8 631 | 21 703 | 41 368 | 32.0 | 14.1 | 2.1 | 20.9 | 27.0 | 29.7 |
| Tyler, TX | 365 | 3 261 | 56 751 | 12.1 | 42.1 | 24.5 | 287.4 | 8 653 | 25 787 | 46 615 | 25.7 | 18.0 | 3.9 | 15.5 | 21.1 | 26.2 |
| Utica-Rome, NY | 232 | 2 224 | 74 238 | 14.2 | 47.6 | 21.1 | 680.4 | 14 964 | 24 010 | 47 060 | 26.4 | 15.4 | 1.9 | 15.0 | 24.0 | 30.8 |
| Valdosta, GA | 343 | 3 114 | 40 606 | 7.5 | 51.2 | 20.2 | 210.5 | 9 325 | 20 014 | 38 678 | 32.3 | 11.4 | 1.7 | 22.6 | 29.5 | 32.5 |
| Vallejo-Fairfield, CA | 431 | 2 890 | 113 107 | 12.7 | 37.8 | 24.2 | 566.6 | 8 397 | 29 367 | 69 914 | 15.4 | 31.0 | 5.3 | 10.8 | 14.4 | 18.8 |
| Victoria, TX | 494 | 3 873 | 28 687 | 12.0 | 50.5 | 16.2 | 187.8 | 9 142 | 24 221 | 48 531 | 25.2 | 17.6 | 2.7 | 16.8 | 25.5 | 34.9 |
| Vineland-Millville-Bridgeton, NJ | 494 | 3 314 | 38 055 | 10.5 | 62.8 | 14.0 | 460.8 | 16 950 | 22 636 | 52 004 | 24.4 | 19.5 | 2.5 | 15.7 | 23.9 | 26.1 |

1. Data for serious crimes have not been adjusted for underreporting; this may affect comparability between geographic areas and over time.   2. Per 100,000 population estimated by the FBI.   3. All persons 3 years old and over enrolled in nursery school through college.   4. Persons 25 years old and over.   5. Elementary and secondary education expenditures.   6. Based on resident population estimated as of July 1, 2009.

# Table C. Metropolitan Areas — **Personal Income**

| | Personal income, 2011 | | | | | | | Transfer payments | | | | | |
| | | | Per capita[1] | | | | | | Government payments to individuals | | | | |
| Area name | Total (mil dol) | Percent change, 2010–2011 | Dollars | Rank | Wages and salaries[2] (mil dol) | Proprietors' income (mil dol) | Dividends, interest, and rent (mil dol) | Total (mil dol) | Total (mil dol) | Social Security (mil dol) | Medical payments (mil dol) | Income mainte-nance (mil dol) | Unemploy-ment insurance (mil dol) |
|---|---|---|---|---|---|---|---|---|---|---|---|---|---|
| | 62 | 63 | 64 | 65 | 66 | 67 | 68 | 69 | 70 | 71 | 72 | 73 | 74 |
| Sacramento—Arden-Arcade—Roseville, CA .. | 88 670 | 4.2 | 40 745 | 91 | 57 736 | 6 748 | 14 299 | 16 321 | 15 840 | 4 403 | 6 792 | 1 963 | 1 119 |
| Saginaw-Saginaw Township North, MI | 6 372 | 5.0 | 32 007 | 302 | 4 270 | 374 | 827 | 1 888 | 1 844 | 650 | 744 | 304 | 72 |
| St. Cloud, MN | 6 699 | 5.3 | 35 253 | 216 | 4 741 | 596 | 1 084 | 1 269 | 1 227 | 377 | 492 | 118 | 67 |
| St. George, UT | 3 848 | 4.9 | 27 159 | 359 | 1 955 | 298 | 916 | 911 | 880 | 379 | 305 | 97 | 28 |
| St. Joseph, MO-KS | 4 362 | 5.0 | 34 189 | 253 | 2 709 | 389 | 570 | 966 | 937 | 312 | 428 | 100 | 30 |
| St. Louis, MO-IL | 120 763 | 4.7 | 42 864 | 65 | 80 028 | 8 426 | 20 846 | 20 735 | 20 112 | 7 126 | 8 576 | 2 212 | 837 |
| Salem, OR | 13 180 | 4.1 | 33 378 | 272 | 7 363 | 1 120 | 2 108 | 3 175 | 3 087 | 941 | 1 276 | 422 | 197 |
| Salinas, CA | 17 356 | 4.1 | 41 138 | 87 | 9 941 | 1 963 | 3 688 | 2 601 | 2 509 | 696 | 1 011 | 316 | 215 |
| Salisbury, MD | 4 218 | 3.4 | 33 601 | 264 | 2 616 | 250 | 668 | 1 028 | 1 000 | 300 | 454 | 128 | 46 |
| Salt Lake City, UT | 45 373 | 5.8 | 39 595 | 119 | 36 510 | 4 277 | 7 480 | 5 519 | 5 266 | 1 789 | 1 980 | 727 | 221 |
| San Angelo, TX | 4 258 | 6.6 | 37 532 | 163 | 2 408 | 354 | 855 | 857 | 833 | 260 | 389 | 94 | 20 |
| San Antonio-New Braunfels, TX | 80 732 | 6.5 | 36 781 | 181 | 50 420 | 8 471 | 11 523 | 15 065 | 14 586 | 3 976 | 6 353 | 2 076 | 441 |
| San Diego-Carlsbad-San Marcos, CA | 146 956 | 5.3 | 46 800 | 30 | 98 688 | 11 353 | 26 732 | 20 650 | 19 978 | 5 529 | 8 394 | 2 198 | 1 481 |
| Sandusky, OH | 2 929 | 5.1 | 38 161 | 152 | 1 717 | 243 | 441 | 686 | 669 | 241 | 280 | 64 | 24 |
| San Francisco-Oakland-Fremont, CA | 269 588 | 6.0 | 61 395 | 3 | 177 202 | 24 998 | 51 510 | 29 743 | 28 772 | 8 612 | 12 748 | 2 910 | 2 045 |
| Oakland-Fremont-Hayward, CA Div. | 136 687 | 5.4 | 52 653 | X | 78 499 | 9 504 | 23 191 | 17 847 | 17 273 | 4 884 | 7 802 | 1 846 | 1 294 |
| San Francisco-San Mateo-Redwood City, CA Div. | 132 901 | 6.6 | 74 037 | X | 98 703 | 15 495 | 28 319 | 11 897 | 11 500 | 3 728 | 4 946 | 1 065 | 751 |
| San Jose-Sunnyvale-Santa Clara, CA | 113 844 | 9.0 | 61 028 | 4 | 104 826 | 6 863 | 19 444 | 10 859 | 10 446 | 3 108 | 4 454 | 1 042 | 861 |
| San Luis Obispo-Paso Robles, CA | 10 966 | 5.1 | 40 322 | 97 | 5 544 | 1 067 | 2 866 | 1 759 | 1 699 | 690 | 604 | 142 | 100 |
| Santa Barbara-Santa Maria-Goleta, CA | 19 303 | 5.4 | 45 219 | 38 | 11 211 | 1 854 | 5 384 | 2 574 | 2 480 | 882 | 925 | 259 | 144 |
| Santa Cruz-Watsonville, CA | 12 920 | 5.5 | 48 883 | 20 | 5 289 | 1 207 | 2 696 | 1 686 | 1 627 | 511 | 642 | 160 | 142 |
| Santa Fe, NM | 6 310 | 4.2 | 43 325 | 56 | 3 373 | 514 | 1 594 | 1 023 | 991 | 388 | 390 | 98 | 41 |
| Santa Rosa-Petaluma, CA | 22 127 | 5.5 | 45 331 | 37 | 10 879 | 1 961 | 5 067 | 3 330 | 3 222 | 1 181 | 1 299 | 244 | 232 |
| Savannah, GA | 14 337 | 6.4 | 40 321 | 98 | 8 702 | 725 | 2 327 | 2 529 | 2 451 | 751 | 880 | 332 | 88 |
| Scranton--Wilkes-Barre, PA | 20 777 | 3.9 | 36 889 | 179 | 12 043 | 1 270 | 3 079 | 5 429 | 5 305 | 1 746 | 2 311 | 466 | 380 |
| Seattle-Tacoma-Bellevue, WA | 178 307 | 6.2 | 50 944 | 17 | 130 462 | 15 455 | 28 549 | 22 772 | 22 006 | 6 899 | 7 734 | 2 512 | 1 852 |
| Seattle-Bellevue-Everett, WA Div. | 145 189 | 6.6 | 53 931 | X | 111 118 | 13 366 | 24 059 | 16 806 | 16 212 | 5 198 | 5 686 | 1 770 | 1 383 |
| Tacoma, WA Div. | 33 118 | 4.7 | 40 992 | X | 19 344 | 2 089 | 4 490 | 5 966 | 5 794 | 1 701 | 2 048 | 743 | 469 |
| Sebastian-Vero Beach, FL | 7 080 | 5.1 | 50 977 | 16 | 2 247 | 299 | 3 434 | 1 358 | 1 327 | 589 | 545 | 98 | 34 |
| Sheboygan, WI | 4 596 | 3.3 | 39 910 | 111 | 3 036 | 452 | 751 | 750 | 724 | 320 | 266 | 59 | 50 |
| Sherman-Denison, TX | 4 056 | 5.3 | 33 404 | 270 | 2 112 | 251 | 641 | 1 028 | 1 001 | 337 | 458 | 95 | 28 |
| Shreveport-Bossier City, LA . | 15 700 | 5.6 | 38 899 | 133 | 9 906 | 1 578 | 2 625 | 3 057 | 2 969 | 891 | 1 285 | 482 | 54 |
| Sioux City, IA-NE-SD | 5 334 | 5.0 | 37 025 | 174 | 3 388 | 690 | 809 | 992 | 960 | 328 | 407 | 119 | 39 |
| Sioux Falls, SD | 10 480 | 7.9 | 45 087 | 39 | 6 846 | 1 389 | 2 010 | 1 271 | 1 220 | 498 | 494 | 123 | 16 |
| South Bend-Mishawaka, IN-MI | 11 499 | 4.8 | 36 083 | 193 | 6 643 | 1 318 | 1 698 | 2 321 | 2 251 | 841 | 871 | 281 | 109 |
| Spartanburg, SC | 9 085 | 4.2 | 31 670 | 311 | 6 418 | 664 | 1 268 | 2 183 | 2 119 | 813 | 803 | 241 | 74 |
| Spokane, WA | 17 027 | 4.3 | 35 940 | 197 | 11 127 | 1 001 | 3 033 | 3 880 | 3 776 | 1 133 | 1 456 | 514 | 206 |
| Springfield, IL | 9 130 | 4.2 | 43 158 | 59 | 6 522 | 758 | 1 530 | 1 472 | 1 425 | 541 | 526 | 185 | 77 |
| Springfield, MA | 27 711 | 3.8 | 39 975 | 110 | 15 391 | 1 425 | 3 937 | 7 203 | 7 050 | 1 691 | 3 594 | 1 030 | 417 |
| Springfield, MO | 14 658 | 4.7 | 33 302 | 276 | 8 725 | 1 604 | 2 415 | 3 231 | 3 134 | 1 106 | 1 306 | 329 | 97 |
| Springfield, OH | 4 788 | 4.7 | 34 777 | 230 | 2 282 | 253 | 580 | 1 287 | 1 256 | 385 | 564 | 157 | 41 |
| State College, PA | 5 469 | 5.3 | 35 347 | 213 | 4 138 | 398 | 888 | 868 | 834 | 307 | 291 | 47 | 49 |
| Steubenville-Weirton, WV-OH | 3 862 | 4.0 | 31 339 | 322 | 1 995 | 197 | 470 | 1 247 | 1 219 | 435 | 535 | 125 | 43 |
| Stockton, CA | 21 592 | 3.8 | 31 013 | 331 | 11 201 | 1 905 | 3 091 | 5 398 | 5 244 | 1 201 | 2 431 | 786 | 432 |
| Sumter, SC | 3 215 | 3.6 | 29 915 | 344 | 2 196 | 135 | 401 | 900 | 878 | 253 | 318 | 158 | 32 |
| Syracuse, NY | 25 619 | 3.6 | 38 668 | 137 | 16 767 | 1 737 | 3 905 | 5 442 | 5 295 | 1 812 | 2 252 | 650 | 256 |
| Tallahassee, FL | 12 845 | 3.0 | 34 740 | 232 | 8 572 | 713 | 2 419 | 2 229 | 2 145 | 705 | 754 | 340 | 61 |
| Tampa-St. Petersburg-Clearwater, FL | 110 901 | 4.5 | 39 261 | 126 | 65 592 | 6 664 | 24 887 | 23 302 | 22 632 | 7 870 | 9 687 | 2 505 | 658 |
| Terre Haute, IN | 5 428 | 3.6 | 31 439 | 314 | 3 298 | 428 | 747 | 1 395 | 1 357 | 469 | 584 | 151 | 58 |
| Texarkana, TX-Texarkana, AR | 4 749 | 4.4 | 34 776 | 231 | 2 800 | 405 | 722 | 1 158 | 1 127 | 323 | 531 | 154 | 32 |
| Toledo, OH | 23 629 | 5.0 | 36 338 | 187 | 16 045 | 2 044 | 2 975 | 5 638 | 5 495 | 1 591 | 2 430 | 714 | 199 |
| Topeka, KS | 8 861 | 5.4 | 37 765 | 157 | 5 848 | 487 | 1 331 | 1 846 | 1 794 | 626 | 692 | 204 | 82 |
| Trenton-Ewing, NJ | 19 985 | 4.6 | 54 445 | 10 | 17 518 | 1 965 | 3 178 | 3 086 | 3 005 | 926 | 1 362 | 317 | 239 |
| Tucson, AZ | 34 596 | 4.0 | 34 961 | 227 | 19 827 | 1 948 | 6 608 | 8 192 | 7 974 | 2 491 | 3 761 | 838 | 183 |
| Tulsa, OK | 39 996 | 7.6 | 42 236 | 74 | 23 785 | 6 158 | 6 405 | 6 708 | 6 499 | 2 343 | 2 656 | 744 | 171 |
| Tuscaloosa, AL | 7 600 | 4.3 | 34 305 | 248 | 4 945 | 564 | 1 170 | 1 647 | 1 597 | 537 | 639 | 241 | 41 |
| Tyler, TX | 8 218 | 5.2 | 38 515 | 145 | 4 829 | 1 118 | 1 536 | 1 628 | 1 578 | 536 | 703 | 173 | 46 |
| Utica-Rome, NY | 10 567 | 3.3 | 35 406 | 209 | 6 148 | 673 | 1 651 | 2 766 | 2 700 | 874 | 1 217 | 330 | 111 |
| Valdosta, GA | 4 323 | 4.6 | 30 377 | 337 | 2 711 | 288 | 670 | 1 002 | 972 | 262 | 392 | 168 | 33 |
| Vallejo-Fairfield, CA | 15 859 | 3.7 | 38 078 | 154 | 8 538 | 688 | 2 279 | 2 808 | 2 717 | 810 | 1 021 | 316 | 239 |
| Victoria, TX | 4 627 | 7.7 | 39 808 | 114 | 2 739 | 647 | 680 | 942 | 916 | 285 | 441 | 114 | 24 |
| Vineland-Millville-Bridgeton, NJ | 5 541 | 4.1 | 35 272 | 215 | 3 298 | 406 | 671 | 1 499 | 1 464 | 389 | 662 | 201 | 141 |

1. Based on the resident population estimated as of July 1 of the year shown.   2. Includes other labor income.

# Table C. Metropolitan Areas — Earnings, Social Security, and Housing

| Area name | Earnings, 2011 | | | | | | | | | Social Security beneficiaries, December 2011 | | Supplemental Security Income recipients, December 2011 | Housing units, 2010 | |
|---|---|---|---|---|---|---|---|---|---|---|---|---|---|---|
| | Total (mil dol) | Percent by selected industries | | | | | | | | Number | Rate[2] | | Total | Percent change, 2000–2010 |
| | | Farm | Goods-related[1] | | Service-related and health | | | | Govern-ment | | | | | |
| | | | Total | Manu-facturing | Infor-mation, profes-sional, and technical services | Retail trade | Finance, insur-ance, and real estate | Health care and social services | | | | | | |
| | 75 | 76 | 77 | 78 | 79 | 80 | 81 | 82 | 83 | 84 | 85 | 86 | 87 | 88 |
| Sacramento—Arden-Arcade—Roseville, CA.. | 64 484 | 0.6 | 10.6 | 4.8 | 12.1 | 6.4 | 7.4 | 11.5 | 31.8 | 336 980 | 155 | 78 677 | 871 793 | 21.9 |
| Saginaw-Saginaw Township North, MI | 4 644 | 1.7 | 24.1 | 19.9 | 6.5 | 7.5 | 5.5 | 17.4 | 15.6 | 46 925 | 236 | 8 388 | 86 844 | 1.6 |
| St. Cloud, MN | 5 337 | 4.5 | 23.2 | 15.7 | D | 7.2 | 5.3 | 15.9 | 16.1 | 30 570 | 161 | 2 611 | 78 114 | 22.5 |
| St. George, UT | 2 253 | -0.2 | 14.4 | 4.9 | 6.3 | 10.6 | 6.4 | 18.1 | 16.8 | 28 455 | 201 | 1 193 | 57 734 | 58.3 |
| St. Joseph, MO-KS | 3 098 | 2.9 | 28.4 | 22.6 | 4.8 | 7.3 | 5.3 | 13.2 | 16.0 | 24 445 | 192 | 2 831 | 53 638 | 6.1 |
| St. Louis, MO-IL | 88 453 | 0.5 | 16.5 | 10.7 | D | 5.7 | 7.9 | 12.2 | 13.8 | 517 905 | 184 | 59 662 | 1 236 222 | 9.1 |
| Salem, OR | 8 483 | 3.1 | 12.4 | 6.5 | 4.9 | 6.7 | 5.7 | 16.7 | 29.6 | 72 350 | 183 | 8 606 | 151 250 | 14.0 |
| Salinas, CA | 11 904 | 8.6 | 7.0 | 3.4 | 6.3 | 6.0 | 3.6 | 7.7 | 27.4 | 55 480 | 132 | 9 314 | 139 048 | 5.6 |
| Salisbury, MD | 2 866 | 1.1 | 14.1 | 8.0 | 6.4 | 8.1 | 4.1 | 19.0 | 22.1 | 23 205 | 185 | 3 050 | 52 322 | 17.6 |
| Salt Lake City, UT | 40 788 | 0.0 | 17.2 | 9.7 | 11.8 | 7.3 | 11.1 | 8.0 | 16.4 | 132 090 | 115 | 13 352 | 410 031 | 19.8 |
| San Angelo, TX | 2 762 | 0.6 | 19.6 | 9.4 | D | 6.9 | 5.2 | 14.7 | 28.6 | 21 070 | 186 | 2 921 | 47 427 | 5.8 |
| San Antonio-New Braunfels, TX | 58 891 | 0.1 | 13.4 | 5.1 | 9.7 | 6.9 | 10.6 | 10.6 | 24.6 | 337 690 | 154 | 62 425 | 837 999 | 29.2 |
| San Diego-Carlsbad-San Marcos, CA | 110 042 | 0.4 | 13.5 | 8.5 | 17.2 | 5.4 | 6.9 | 8.4 | 26.4 | 427 485 | 136 | 83 160 | 1 164 786 | 12.0 |
| Sandusky, OH | 1 961 | 0.8 | 27.0 | 22.5 | 3.3 | 7.1 | 3.4 | 14.5 | 16.5 | 17 550 | 229 | 1 508 | 37 845 | 5.4 |
| San Francisco-Oakland-Fre-mont, CA | 202 200 | 0.1 | 12.4 | 7.4 | 23.6 | 5.1 | 11.9 | 9.1 | 13.3 | 618 015 | 141 | 141 614 | 1 741 999 | 8.4 |
| Oakland-Fremont-Hayward, CA Div | 88 002 | 0.1 | 18.0 | 11.4 | 17.0 | 5.8 | 6.4 | 12.4 | 14.7 | 351 750 | 135 | 79 463 | 982 812 | 9.8 |
| San Francisco-San Mateo-Redwood City, CA Div. | 114 198 | 0.1 | 8.1 | 4.4 | 28.6 | 4.7 | 16.1 | 6.6 | 12.3 | 266 265 | 148 | 62 151 | 759 187 | 6.6 |
| San Jose-Sunnyvale-Santa Clara, CA | 111 688 | 0.1 | 29.5 | 26.5 | 29.9 | 4.3 | 4.3 | 6.8 | 7.1 | 218 640 | 117 | 49 304 | 649 790 | 9.1 |
| San Luis Obispo-Paso Robles, CA | 6 611 | 1.9 | 14.9 | 6.3 | 8.9 | 8.7 | 5.0 | 11.7 | 21.5 | 51 645 | 190 | 5 230 | 117 315 | 14.7 |
| Santa Barbara-Santa Maria-Goleta, CA | 13 065 | 3.5 | 15.0 | 8.4 | 13.9 | 6.4 | 5.4 | 10.7 | 21.2 | 66 610 | 156 | 9 642 | 152 834 | 6.9 |
| Santa Cruz-Watsonville, CA . | 6 496 | 5.0 | 15.1 | 7.2 | 9.2 | 7.5 | 4.4 | 13.8 | 18.8 | 38 925 | 147 | 5 854 | 104 476 | 5.7 |
| Santa Fe, NM | 3 887 | 0.0 | 7.5 | 1.4 | 10.2 | 9.2 | 8.2 | 13.9 | 29.5 | 29 065 | 200 | 2 759 | 71 267 | 23.5 |
| Santa Rosa-Petaluma, CA.... | 12 840 | 1.2 | 22.1 | 14.3 | 11.7 | 7.6 | 6.0 | 13.8 | 14.5 | 85 465 | 175 | 9 784 | 204 572 | 11.7 |
| Savannah, GA | 9 426 | 0.1 | 19.3 | 15.1 | 5.2 | 6.6 | 4.1 | 12.3 | 23.5 | 56 430 | 159 | 7 781 | 151 049 | 23.2 |
| Scranton--Wilkes-Barre, PA.. | 13 314 | 0.0 | 17.7 | 12.2 | 7.6 | 8.0 | 6.3 | 16.3 | 14.6 | 136 755 | 243 | 17 188 | 258 834 | 2.4 |
| Seattle-Tacoma-Bellevue, WA | 145 917 | 0.1 | 17.7 | 12.3 | 20.8 | 6.0 | 6.8 | 9.2 | 16.7 | 488 490 | 140 | 66 629 | 1 463 295 | 16.5 |
| Seattle-Bellevue-Everett, WA Div | 124 484 | 0.1 | 18.6 | 13.3 | 23.5 | 6.0 | 7.2 | 8.4 | 12.9 | 361 235 | 134 | 48 166 | 1 137 920 | 16.3 |
| Tacoma, WA Div | 21 434 | 0.1 | 12.5 | 6.1 | 5.0 | 5.9 | 4.2 | 13.7 | 39.1 | 127 255 | 158 | 18 463 | 325 375 | 17.4 |
| Sebastian-Vero Beach, FL.... | 2 547 | 1.6 | 10.1 | 4.3 | 9.4 | 10.9 | 7.4 | 18.6 | 13.6 | 41 905 | 302 | 2 032 | 76 346 | 31.9 |
| Sheboygan, WI | 3 488 | 1.5 | 44.6 | 39.9 | 3.0 | 5.6 | 5.8 | 12.4 | 9.7 | 23 110 | 201 | 1 659 | 50 766 | 10.5 |
| Sherman-Denison, TX | 2 363 | 0.7 | 27.9 | 19.8 | 4.2 | 8.7 | 6.7 | 17.8 | 14.2 | 25 705 | 212 | 2 910 | 53 727 | 11.2 |
| Shreveport-Bossier City, LA . | 11 484 | 0.1 | 20.9 | 6.8 | 5.6 | 7.3 | 4.6 | 13.4 | 25.1 | 72 120 | 179 | 17 288 | 173 669 | 8.7 |
| Sioux City, IA-NE-SD | 4 078 | 7.9 | 20.2 | 14.6 | 4.4 | 6.8 | 5.4 | 13.0 | 13.5 | 25 520 | 177 | 2 379 | 58 083 | 2.0 |
| Sioux Falls, SD | 8 235 | 5.9 | 14.0 | 8.2 | 7.3 | 7.3 | 13.4 | 18.3 | 10.0 | 37 465 | 161 | 2 879 | 95 862 | 26.8 |
| South Bend-Mishawaka, IN-MI | 7 960 | 1.5 | 23.3 | 19.0 | 8.3 | 5.9 | 5.8 | 14.0 | 11.6 | 60 895 | 191 | 6 551 | 140 736 | 7.5 |
| Spartanburg, SC | 7 082 | 0.2 | 30.2 | 25.5 | 5.3 | 6.2 | 5.9 | 8.8 | 17.2 | 62 070 | 216 | 7 049 | 122 628 | 14.6 |
| Spokane, WA | 12 128 | 0.2 | 14.2 | 8.0 | 7.8 | 8.0 | 7.9 | 17.4 | 20.6 | 86 990 | 184 | 13 051 | 201 434 | 15.1 |
| Springfield, IL | 7 281 | 3.4 | 7.1 | 2.8 | 7.3 | 5.5 | 7.3 | 19.0 | 33.1 | 41 545 | 196 | 5 108 | 95 555 | 5.3 |
| Springfield, MA | 16 817 | 0.1 | 16.1 | 10.8 | 6.4 | 6.9 | 7.8 | 17.2 | 20.9 | 137 750 | 199 | 36 103 | 288 536 | 4.4 |
| Springfield, MO | 10 329 | 0.2 | 14.6 | 9.5 | 8.0 | 8.4 | 6.7 | 17.0 | 14.7 | 88 645 | 201 | 9 553 | 192 346 | 22.9 |
| Springfield, OH | 2 535 | 2.1 | 20.5 | 16.8 | 3.7 | 7.0 | 6.5 | 15.7 | 15.8 | 29 770 | 216 | 3 777 | 61 419 | 0.6 |
| State College, PA | 4 536 | 0.2 | 12.5 | 5.7 | 9.5 | 5.9 | 3.6 | 9.6 | 45.9 | 21 940 | 142 | 1 574 | 63 297 | 19.1 |
| Steubenville-Weirton, WV-OH | 2 192 | 0.1 | D | 21.2 | 4.2 | 6.8 | 3.1 | D | 14.1 | 32 060 | 260 | 4 049 | 58 334 | -1.4 |
| Stockton, CA | 13 106 | 5.3 | 14.6 | 9.0 | 4.3 | 7.6 | 4.7 | 13.1 | 20.0 | 96 410 | 138 | 29 095 | 233 755 | 23.6 |
| Sumter, SC | 2 330 | 0.1 | 19.9 | 13.8 | 4.1 | 5.6 | 2.7 | 10.7 | 39.6 | 21 455 | 200 | 4 144 | 46 011 | 10.2 |
| Syracuse, NY | 18 504 | 0.6 | 16.6 | 11.4 | 9.6 | 6.5 | 7.4 | 12.9 | 19.4 | 132 735 | 200 | 19 449 | 287 712 | 3.5 |
| Tallahassee, FL | 9 284 | 0.4 | 6.4 | 2.4 | 13.2 | 6.1 | 6.4 | 11.9 | 38.7 | 53 805 | 146 | 9 208 | 163 078 | 19.3 |
| Tampa-St. Petersburg-Clear-water, FL | 72 256 | 0.3 | 10.6 | 5.9 | 14.0 | 7.8 | 11.4 | 14.3 | 15.0 | 601 695 | 213 | 69 496 | 1 353 158 | 18.3 |
| Terre Haute, IN | 3 726 | 2.7 | 26.3 | 20.4 | 3.4 | 6.7 | 3.7 | 14.4 | 18.7 | 36 035 | 209 | 4 453 | 74 136 | 2.2 |
| Texarkana, TX-Texarkana, AR | 3 205 | 0.9 | 13.5 | 8.4 | D | 8.0 | 6.4 | 15.3 | 29.2 | 27 475 | 201 | 6 027 | 57 774 | 6.6 |
| Toledo, OH | 18 089 | 1.0 | 24.2 | 18.1 | 6.7 | 6.9 | 5.1 | 14.5 | 16.0 | 119 725 | 184 | 19 312 | 301 322 | 5.5 |
| Topeka, KS | 6 335 | 0.9 | 12.9 | 7.4 | D | 5.3 | 9.0 | 14.0 | 26.0 | 47 535 | 203 | 5 536 | 103 809 | 7.7 |
| Trenton-Ewing, NJ | 19 483 | 0.0 | 8.0 | 5.1 | 19.8 | 3.9 | 12.8 | 9.5 | 22.4 | 63 800 | 174 | 8 983 | 143 169 | 7.4 |
| Tucson, AZ | 21 775 | 0.1 | 16.0 | 10.5 | 9.7 | 6.6 | 6.4 | 15.1 | 25.7 | 187 530 | 190 | 19 295 | 440 909 | 20.2 |
| Tulsa, OK | 29 943 | 0.1 | 27.6 | 12.5 | 8.2 | 6.2 | 6.7 | 10.6 | 10.4 | 172 070 | 182 | 20 945 | 409 820 | 11.9 |
| Tuscaloosa, AL | 5 509 | 1.0 | 28.7 | 18.0 | 5.8 | 6.3 | 3.7 | 8.8 | 27.9 | 42 775 | 193 | 8 987 | 97 534 | 15.7 |
| Tyler, TX | 5 947 | 0.3 | 21.5 | 7.5 | 8.7 | 8.6 | 5.8 | 22.7 | 12.2 | 40 205 | 188 | 5 222 | 87 309 | 21.8 |
| Utica-Rome, NY | 6 821 | 0.9 | 14.0 | 9.9 | 6.4 | 8.4 | 7.1 | 15.7 | 29.9 | 69 345 | 232 | 10 524 | 137 561 | 2.0 |
| Valdosta, GA | 2 999 | 2.2 | 5.1 | 0.6 | 4.5 | 7.9 | D | 11.2 | 37.3 | 22 535 | 158 | 4 541 | 57 434 | 19.2 |
| Vallejo-Fairfield, CA | 9 226 | 1.0 | 20.1 | 11.0 | 4.2 | 7.2 | 4.7 | 15.7 | 27.8 | 63 110 | 152 | 12 361 | 152 698 | 13.5 |
| Victoria, TX | 3 386 | 0.9 | 36.5 | 17.5 | D | 10.0 | 4.5 | 11.6 | 12.8 | 22 445 | 193 | 3 410 | 50 537 | 8.4 |
| Vineland-Millville-Bridgeton, NJ | 3 704 | 2.0 | 21.9 | 15.3 | 3.4 | 7.3 | 2.8 | 13.5 | 28.0 | 29 120 | 185 | 5 362 | 55 834 | 5.6 |

1. Includes mining, construction, and manufacturing.   2. Per 1,000 resident population estimated as of July 1, 2011.

# Table C. Metropolitan Areas — Housing, Labor Force, and Employment

| Area name | Housing units, 2007–2011 Occupied units — Owner-occupied Total | Percent | Median value[1] | Median owner cost as a percent of income With a mortgage | Without a mortgage | Renter-occupied Median rent[2] | Median rent as a percent of income | Sub-stand-ard units[3] (percent) | Civilian labor force, 2012 Total | Percent change, 2011–2012 | Unemployment Total | Rate[4] | Civilian employment,[5] 2007–2011 Total | Percent Management, professional, and related occupations | Construction, production, and related occupations |
|---|---|---|---|---|---|---|---|---|---|---|---|---|---|---|---|
| | 89 | 90 | 91 | 92 | 93 | 94 | 95 | 96 | 97 | 98 | 99 | 100 | 101 | 102 | 103 |
| Sacramento—Arden-Arcade—Roseville, CA .. | 780 384 | 62.0 | 324 300 | 29.5 | 11.3 | 1 040 | 33.1 | 4.4 | 1 048 167 | 0.4 | 109 305 | 10.4 | 954 292 | 38.7 | 16.7 |
| Saginaw-Saginaw Township North, MI ...................... | 76 828 | 73.6 | 106 400 | 23.7 | 13.5 | 697 | 34.6 | 1.5 | 90 451 | -1.1 | 7 761 | 8.6 | 80 749 | 29.6 | 22.2 |
| St. Cloud, MN ..................... | 71 608 | 72.4 | 171 100 | 24.1 | 12.1 | 687 | 30.4 | 1.8 | 108 094 | 0.2 | 6 107 | 5.6 | 100 003 | 30.2 | 26.9 |
| St. George, UT..................... | 46 088 | 70.1 | 235 300 | 29.0 | 10.0 | 918 | 30.3 | 4.3 | 57 958 | 1.1 | 4 071 | 7.0 | 54 003 | 30.7 | 22.7 |
| St. Joseph, MO-KS................. | 47 351 | 68.9 | 108 900 | 20.3 | 11.4 | 628 | 27.7 | 1.5 | 72 438 | 1.1 | 4 070 | 5.6 | 59 223 | 29.0 | 28.3 |
| St. Louis, MO-IL................... | 1 109 777 | 71.5 | 160 400 | 22.7 | 12.3 | 757 | 29.9 | 1.6 | 1 418 358 | -1.5 | 107 603 | 7.6 | 1 351 427 | 36.6 | 19.9 |
| Salem, OR ......................... | 140 952 | 62.2 | 212 000 | 27.1 | 12.8 | 760 | 31.1 | 4.6 | 193 341 | -1.3 | 18 037 | 9.3 | 166 008 | 31.7 | 26.2 |
| Salinas, CA ........................ | 125 217 | 51.4 | 497 400 | 32.8 | 10.6 | 1 160 | 31.6 | 12.0 | 226 510 | 2.1 | 25 743 | 11.4 | 175 425 | 27.6 | 30.3 |
| Salisbury, MD...................... | 44 979 | 65.1 | 190 200 | 25.5 | 14.2 | 928 | 33.3 | 2.9 | 64 049 | -0.1 | 5 697 | 8.9 | 56 242 | 32.4 | 23.3 |
| Salt Lake City, UT................. | 370 396 | 68.4 | 241 000 | 24.8 | 10.0 | 852 | 29.3 | 3.9 | 602 375 | 0.7 | 33 168 | 5.5 | 546 437 | 35.3 | 21.7 |
| San Angelo, TX.................... | 42 075 | 67.3 | 90 700 | 21.2 | 12.0 | 687 | 29.6 | 3.3 | 56 087 | 0.6 | 2 963 | 5.3 | 50 130 | 29.4 | 22.3 |
| San Antonio-New Braunfels, TX .............................. | 741 249 | 64.8 | 127 200 | 22.7 | 11.6 | 792 | 29.6 | 4.7 | 1 026 243 | 0.6 | 66 367 | 6.5 | 942 292 | 34.4 | 20.6 |
| San Diego-Carlsbad-San Marcos, CA .................... | 1 064 048 | 55.2 | 455 000 | 31.2 | 10.7 | 1 261 | 33.6 | 6.1 | 1 599 133 | 1.1 | 142 810 | 8.9 | 1 382 856 | 39.8 | 16.5 |
| Sandusky, OH...................... | 31 642 | 71.4 | 138 000 | 23.5 | 13.4 | 689 | 28.7 | 1.4 | 40 622 | -3.3 | 2 962 | 7.3 | 35 328 | 30.5 | 25.7 |
| San Francisco-Oakland-Fremont, CA .......................... | 1 604 706 | 55.5 | 627 000 | 30.4 | 10.5 | 1 344 | 30.0 | 6.0 | 2 323 878 | 1.9 | 188 375 | 8.1 | 2 136 586 | 45.4 | 14.5 |
| Oakland-Fremont-Hayward, CA Div. ........................ | 907 085 | 60.1 | 531 300 | 30.5 | 10.7 | 1 251 | 31.5 | 5.3 | 1 311 637 | 1.3 | 118 130 | 9.0 | 1 201 619 | 43.5 | 16.4 |
| San Francisco-San Mateo-Redwood City, CA Div. ... | 697 621 | 49.4 | 779 400 | 30.2 | 10.3 | 1 452 | 28.7 | 6.9 | 1 012 241 | 2.7 | 70 245 | 6.9 | 934 967 | 47.9 | 12.0 |
| San Jose-Sunnyvale-Santa Clara, CA ...................... | 616 437 | 58.8 | 674 800 | 29.8 | 10.0 | 1 454 | 28.4 | 7.5 | 937 594 | 1.9 | 80 328 | 8.6 | 875 469 | 48.8 | 15.6 |
| San Luis Obispo-Paso Robles, CA ...................... | 101 993 | 60.4 | 480 200 | 31.1 | 11.5 | 1 165 | 36.4 | 3.2 | 143 069 | 2.6 | 11 531 | 8.1 | 121 788 | 36.0 | 17.6 |
| Santa Barbara-Santa Maria-Goleta, CA ..................... | 141 635 | 53.6 | 523 800 | 30.7 | 10.7 | 1 303 | 34.4 | 8.7 | 229 464 | 1.6 | 18 289 | 8.0 | 195 736 | 35.5 | 21.9 |
| Santa Cruz-Watsonville, CA . | 93 834 | 59.4 | 613 500 | 32.8 | 11.9 | 1 325 | 33.8 | 7.3 | 151 139 | 1.0 | 16 848 | 11.1 | 127 947 | 40.7 | 19.9 |
| Santa Fe, NM...................... | 60 594 | 70.6 | 293 900 | 26.9 | 10.1 | 892 | 31.8 | 3.9 | 75 698 | 0.7 | 4 158 | 5.5 | 71 194 | 42.1 | 15.5 |
| Santa Rosa-Petaluma, CA.... | 184 170 | 61.5 | 477 300 | 31.6 | 12.5 | 1 223 | 33.0 | 5.2 | 256 878 | 0.2 | 22 005 | 8.6 | 232 866 | 35.2 | 20.3 |
| Savannah, GA...................... | 129 219 | 62.2 | 172 400 | 24.7 | 11.9 | 903 | 31.8 | 2.0 | 182 096 | 1.9 | 15 191 | 8.3 | 153 316 | 33.2 | 23.0 |
| Scranton--Wilkes-Barre, PA.. | 228 556 | 68.5 | 126 600 | 23.1 | 14.9 | 639 | 28.0 | 1.3 | 284 864 | 1.1 | 26 864 | 9.4 | 260 731 | 30.6 | 25.1 |
| Seattle-Tacoma-Bellevue, WA ............................... | 1 354 240 | 62.0 | 352 800 | 27.4 | 13.2 | 1 033 | 29.5 | 2.9 | 1 890 684 | 0.2 | 140 774 | 7.4 | 1 716 431 | 42.2 | 18.3 |
| Seattle-Bellevue-Everett, WA Div. ........................ | 1 056 401 | 61.6 | 379 300 | 27.3 | 13.2 | 1 058 | 29.2 | 2.9 | 1 505 221 | 0.3 | 106 429 | 7.1 | 1 363 711 | 44.8 | 16.8 |
| Tacoma, WA Div................. | 297 839 | 63.1 | 265 200 | 27.9 | 13.3 | 948 | 30.9 | 2.8 | 385 463 | -0.3 | 34 345 | 8.9 | 352 720 | 32.4 | 23.7 |
| Sebastian-Vero Beach, FL.... | 57 467 | 76.3 | 179 300 | 28.5 | 14.2 | 889 | 36.4 | 2.1 | 63 435 | 0.3 | 6 747 | 10.6 | 54 526 | 30.6 | 22.1 |
| Sheboygan, WI .................... | 46 318 | 72.4 | 154 300 | 23.0 | 14.0 | 647 | 26.6 | 1.8 | 61 249 | -1.3 | 4 038 | 6.6 | 58 977 | 28.1 | 32.5 |
| Sherman-Denison, TX ........... | 45 878 | 69.0 | 102 300 | 23.3 | 13.2 | 736 | 27.9 | 3.4 | 57 766 | -0.9 | 4 147 | 7.2 | 53 936 | 30.7 | 26.2 |
| Shreveport-Bossier City, LA . | 152 558 | 65.3 | 121 300 | 21.5 | 10.0 | 706 | 31.2 | 2.9 | 184 004 | -0.5 | 11 786 | 6.4 | 174 442 | 30.3 | 23.8 |
| Sioux City, IA-NE-SD.......... | 54 228 | 68.5 | 97 800 | 20.3 | 12.1 | 622 | 28.5 | 2.9 | 76 441 | -0.6 | 4 061 | 5.3 | 72 136 | 27.5 | 30.1 |
| Sioux Falls, SD ................... | 88 307 | 68.4 | 150 300 | 22.0 | 10.0 | 679 | 26.7 | 1.6 | 131 705 | 1.3 | 5 381 | 4.1 | 125 719 | 34.1 | 22.5 |
| South Bend-Mishawaka, IN-MI............................... | 120 984 | 72.8 | 119 000 | 22.1 | 11.8 | 694 | 29.9 | 1.7 | 150 010 | -1.6 | 14 005 | 9.3 | 144 838 | 33.1 | 24.7 |
| Spartanburg, SC .................. | 106 055 | 70.6 | 118 800 | 22.2 | 10.0 | 650 | 29.9 | 2.2 | 136 513 | 1.9 | 12 279 | 9.0 | 122 472 | 30.3 | 28.7 |
| Spokane, WA ...................... | 185 983 | 64.7 | 192 800 | 24.7 | 11.1 | 733 | 31.2 | 1.9 | 229 965 | -0.3 | 19 882 | 8.6 | 212 594 | 35.2 | 18.7 |
| Springfield, IL..................... | 87 381 | 71.5 | 120 600 | 20.9 | 11.4 | 700 | 29.6 | 1.7 | 114 980 | -1.3 | 8 671 | 7.5 | 104 843 | 39.4 | 14.9 |
| Springfield, MA.................... | 267 237 | 64.7 | 219 700 | 25.0 | 15.4 | 793 | 32.1 | 2.4 | 345 068 | -0.5 | 26 014 | 7.5 | 324 443 | 36.5 | 20.3 |
| Springfield, MO.................... | 173 882 | 65.7 | 129 300 | 22.0 | 10.7 | 654 | 29.4 | 2.2 | 221 091 | 0.0 | 13 528 | 6.1 | 204 025 | 32.2 | 22.6 |
| Springfield, OH.................... | 54 771 | 69.8 | 110 400 | 22.3 | 13.0 | 642 | 30.8 | 1.7 | 67 726 | -1.9 | 4 934 | 7.3 | 59 996 | 28.4 | 27.7 |
| State College, PA ................ | 56 134 | 59.4 | 181 400 | 22.6 | 12.0 | 817 | 35.5 | 2.8 | 75 989 | 0.1 | 4 454 | 5.9 | 72 984 | 42.3 | 18.3 |
| Steubenville-Weirton, WV-OH................................ | 51 646 | 75.2 | 86 100 | 20.2 | 11.2 | 546 | 28.8 | 1.0 | 54 980 | -1.2 | 5 468 | 9.9 | 52 484 | 26.9 | 28.1 |
| Stockton, CA ...................... | 212 902 | 60.7 | 264 600 | 31.4 | 11.3 | 993 | 34.5 | 8.2 | 298 468 | -0.5 | 45 264 | 15.2 | 269 072 | 28.2 | 29.0 |
| Sumter, SC ........................ | 39 273 | 66.5 | 100 900 | 21.9 | 11.9 | 671 | 27.2 | 2.4 | 44 701 | -0.9 | 4 608 | 10.3 | 40 200 | 27.5 | 29.9 |
| Syracuse, NY ..................... | 255 911 | 68.2 | 119 300 | 22.0 | 14.0 | 725 | 30.1 | 1.6 | 320 040 | -0.5 | 27 553 | 8.6 | 308 777 | 37.2 | 19.7 |
| Tallahassee, FL ................... | 141 848 | 59.6 | 173 400 | 24.5 | 11.6 | 891 | 38.5 | 3.7 | 188 041 | -1.2 | 13 976 | 7.4 | 172 163 | 42.2 | 14.3 |
| Tampa-St. Petersburg-Clearwater, FL ....................... | 1 120 102 | 68.8 | 169 900 | 28.3 | 14.3 | 928 | 33.3 | 2.2 | 1 325 428 | 1.3 | 116 864 | 8.8 | 1 240 882 | 35.6 | 17.8 |
| Terre Haute, IN................... | 64 232 | 70.4 | 86 300 | 19.8 | 11.6 | 620 | 29.1 | 2.1 | 78 651 | -0.6 | 8 092 | 10.3 | 74 807 | 29.5 | 26.8 |
| Texarkana, TX-Texarkana, AR .............................. | 49 876 | 66.8 | 90 800 | 20.2 | 10.6 | 659 | 29.5 | 2.5 | 65 126 | -1.5 | 4 394 | 6.7 | 56 845 | 28.3 | 28.1 |
| Toledo, OH......................... | 261 798 | 67.3 | 128 100 | 23.4 | 13.6 | 658 | 31.2 | 1.1 | 317 396 | -0.9 | 25 018 | 7.9 | 299 080 | 32.2 | 24.8 |
| Topeka, KS ........................ | 95 380 | 69.6 | 117 200 | 21.7 | 11.9 | 673 | 28.2 | 2.4 | 120 837 | -1.1 | 7 588 | 6.3 | 113 932 | 34.7 | 21.8 |
| Trenton-Ewing, NJ ............... | 129 933 | 67.5 | 302 100 | 25.9 | 16.9 | 1 083 | 30.7 | 2.9 | 210 019 | 1.5 | 16 472 | 7.8 | 175 761 | 42.9 | 15.3 |
| Tucson, AZ ........................ | 382 366 | 64.0 | 190 500 | 25.5 | 11.7 | 769 | 31.8 | 4.1 | 462 748 | -1.2 | 33 581 | 7.3 | 420 203 | 36.3 | 17.6 |
| Tulsa, OK .......................... | 364 262 | 67.4 | 125 000 | 21.6 | 11.3 | 699 | 28.8 | 3.0 | 445 190 | 0.9 | 25 026 | 5.6 | 440 602 | 33.5 | 24.0 |
| Tuscaloosa, AL ................... | 77 926 | 65.0 | 141 200 | 22.6 | 11.3 | 735 | 34.8 | 2.1 | 101 487 | -0.2 | 7 047 | 6.9 | 94 386 | 31.4 | 27.8 |
| Tyler, TX ........................... | 77 934 | 68.9 | 119 800 | 22.2 | 12.5 | 783 | 31.9 | 4.6 | 102 902 | -0.8 | 7 189 | 7.0 | 93 762 | 31.9 | 23.5 |
| Utica-Rome, NY .................. | 118 038 | 68.9 | 101 300 | 21.1 | 13.9 | 647 | 29.5 | 1.6 | 136 273 | -1.0 | 11 859 | 8.7 | 133 891 | 34.4 | 21.1 |
| Valdosta, GA ...................... | 49 577 | 60.6 | 126 500 | 24.2 | 10.7 | 723 | 32.3 | 3.0 | 67 965 | 1.7 | 5 832 | 8.6 | 57 601 | 27.8 | 25.2 |
| Vallejo-Fairfield, CA ............. | 139 312 | 64.9 | 340 100 | 30.0 | 10.1 | 1 222 | 32.8 | 4.4 | 217 024 | 0.8 | 21 995 | 10.1 | 181 725 | 33.6 | 21.4 |
| Victoria, TX ....................... | 42 882 | 69.2 | 101 200 | 21.2 | 11.8 | 693 | 28.7 | 4.7 | 61 182 | 0.5 | 3 460 | 5.7 | 51 824 | 29.0 | 28.6 |
| Vineland-Millville-Bridgeton, NJ..................................... | 50 868 | 68.4 | 177 800 | 27.2 | 17.1 | 914 | 35.2 | 3.9 | 69 538 | -0.7 | 9 824 | 14.1 | 64 661 | 26.2 | 28.1 |

1. Specified owner-occupied units.    2. Specified renter-occupied units.    3. Overcrowded or lacking complete plumbing facilities.    4. Percent of civilian labor force.    5. Persons 16 years old and over.

# Table C. Metropolitan Areas — Nonfarm Employment and Agriculture

| Area name | Private nonfarm establishments, employment and payroll, 2011 | | | | | | | | | Agriculture, 2007 | | | |
| | Number of establishments | Employment | | | | | | Annual payroll | | Farms | | | Farm operators whose principal occupation is farming (percent) |
| | | Total | Health care and social assistance | Manufacturing | Retail trade | Finance and insurance | Professional, scientific, and technical services | Total (mil dol) | Average per employee (dollars) | Number | Percent with: Fewer than 50 acres | 500 acres or more | |
| | 104 | 105 | 106 | 107 | 108 | 109 | 110 | 111 | 112 | 113 | 114 | 115 | 116 |
|---|---|---|---|---|---|---|---|---|---|---|---|---|---|
| Sacramento—Arden-Arcade—Roseville, CA.. | 44 300 | 625 535 | 102 112 | 31 614 | 89 330 | 37 303 | 47 676 | 27 278 | 43 607 | 5 132 | 71.4 | 7.0 | 47.0 |
| Saginaw-Saginaw Township North, MI | 4 375 | 75 555 | 16 457 | 10 186 | 12 677 | 2 764 | 2 303 | 2 745 | 36 337 | 1 533 | 43.4 | 10.0 | 48.3 |
| St. Cloud, MN | 5 164 | 89 930 | 17 322 | 14 472 | 12 635 | 3 832 | 3 810 | 3 261 | 36 267 | 4 287 | 25.7 | 8.2 | 53.9 |
| St. George, UT | 3 844 | 36 114 | 6 809 | 1 896 | 7 194 | 1 194 | 1 619 | 1 052 | 29 117 | 593 | 60.4 | 13.2 | 31.0 |
| St. Joseph, MO-KS | 3 049 | 48 762 | 8 397 | 11 559 | 6 804 | 2 144 | 1 148 | 1 700 | 34 861 | 3 420 | 27.0 | 14.2 | 41.2 |
| St. Louis, MO-IL | 69 374 | 1 174 986 | 180 359 | 98 811 | 143 984 | 62 029 | 85 520 | 52 322 | 44 530 | 12 686 | 38.6 | 13.5 | 42.6 |
| Salem, OR | 8 813 | 103 917 | 21 071 | 9 811 | 17 026 | 3 785 | 4 224 | 3 419 | 32 901 | 3 922 | 68.1 | 5.4 | 45.5 |
| Salinas, CA | 8 216 | 96 528 | 14 125 | 5 653 | 16 108 | 3 152 | 7 822 | 3 907 | 40 473 | 1 199 | 45.0 | 24.9 | 64.1 |
| Salisbury, MD | 2 858 | 40 447 | 9 606 | 3 264 | 7 050 | 1 215 | 1 521 | 1 435 | 35 486 | 837 | 46.2 | 9.3 | 50.9 |
| Salt Lake City, UT | 31 390 | 530 264 | 59 896 | 47 768 | 62 859 | 35 499 | 36 652 | 22 526 | 42 481 | 1 595 | 66.1 | 10.6 | 32.0 |
| San Angelo, TX | 2 636 | 36 567 | 7 247 | 3 137 | 6 191 | 1 314 | 1 298 | 1 185 | 32 403 | 1 336 | 43.3 | 27.5 | 38.1 |
| San Antonio-New Braunfels, TX | 40 516 | 731 665 | 119 277 | 41 940 | 98 206 | 59 478 | 41 347 | 28 808 | 39 373 | 14 552 | 44.0 | 10.1 | 39.6 |
| San Diego-Carlsbad-San Marcos, CA | 75 837 | 1 128 909 | 145 431 | 94 413 | 138 742 | 51 882 | 121 359 | 55 585 | 49 237 | 6 687 | 91.1 | 1.3 | 37.8 |
| Sandusky, OH | 1 879 | 28 036 | 5 163 | 5 603 | 4 461 | 633 | 654 | 1 013 | 36 130 | 403 | 47.9 | 11.7 | 42.7 |
| San Francisco-Oakland-Fremont, CA | 117 920 | 1 758 043 | 237 581 | 109 481 | 189 949 | 107 537 | 208 112 | 118 655 | 67 493 | 1 749 | 63.7 | 12.9 | 44.3 |
| Oakland-Fremont-Hayward, CA Div | X | X | X | X | X | X | X | X | X | 1 159 | 67.7 | 10.4 | 39.9 |
| San Francisco-San Mateo-Redwood City, CA Div. | X | X | X | X | X | X | X | X | X | 590 | 55.8 | 18.0 | 53.1 |
| San Jose-Sunnyvale-Santa Clara, CA | 45 462 | 874 495 | 92 962 | 91 571 | 79 941 | 25 213 | 122 166 | 78 579 | 89 857 | 1 693 | 68.5 | 11.7 | 50.1 |
| San Luis Obispo-Paso Robles, CA | 7 720 | 81 045 | 14 881 | 5 318 | 13 530 | 2 572 | 4 645 | 2 954 | 36 443 | 2 784 | 56.7 | 12.5 | 49.6 |
| Santa Barbara-Santa Maria-Goleta, CA | 11 064 | 133 803 | 19 329 | 12 222 | 18 824 | 4 332 | 12 312 | 6 178 | 46 175 | 1 597 | 64.9 | 11.1 | 50.9 |
| Santa Cruz-Watsonville, CA . | 6 673 | 68 341 | 11 831 | 4 509 | 11 100 | 2 021 | 4 546 | 2 863 | 41 899 | 682 | 77.7 | 2.2 | 61.9 |
| Santa Fe, NM | 4 714 | 45 353 | 8 956 | 679 | 9 100 | 1 953 | 2 463 | 1 741 | 38 382 | 489 | 66.9 | 13.5 | 42.7 |
| Santa Rosa-Petaluma, CA.... | 13 080 | 144 934 | 22 539 | 17 447 | 22 520 | 7 322 | 8 273 | 6 500 | 44 845 | 3 429 | 72.4 | 5.3 | 47.3 |
| Savannah, GA | 8 321 | 130 217 | 20 575 | 14 190 | 18 160 | 3 545 | 5 811 | 4 789 | 36 779 | 313 | 46.6 | 9.3 | 38.3 |
| Scranton--Wilkes-Barre, PA.. | 13 150 | 226 988 | 46 353 | 27 942 | 32 943 | 10 706 | 8 223 | 7 716 | 33 994 | 1 676 | 37.6 | 2.3 | 34.1 |
| Seattle-Tacoma-Bellevue, WA | 95 613 | 1 467 406 | 203 659 | 138 987 | 163 435 | 59 193 | 112 845 | 84 722 | 57 736 | 4 908 | 85.5 | 0.9 | 41.1 |
| Seattle-Bellevue-Everett, WA Div | X | X | X | X | X | X | X | X | X | 3 460 | 85.8 | 1.0 | 40.8 |
| Tacoma, WA Div | X | X | X | X | X | X | X | X | X | 1 448 | 84.6 | 0.4 | 41.9 |
| Sebastian-Vero Beach, FL.... | 3 840 | 37 876 | 7 588 | 1 806 | 7 851 | 1 222 | 1 554 | 1 282 | 33 846 | 415 | 68.7 | 9.6 | 50.1 |
| Sheboygan, WI | 2 674 | 49 695 | 6 975 | 15 547 | 6 082 | 1 948 | 1 270 | 1 889 | 38 021 | 1 059 | 42.0 | 9.4 | 53.7 |
| Sherman-Denison, TX | 2 464 | 38 460 | 8 781 | 6 571 | 6 097 | 2 206 | 816 | 1 239 | 32 217 | 2 723 | 55.3 | 4.9 | 35.1 |
| Shreveport-Bossier City, LA . | 9 128 | 150 661 | 32 463 | 9 458 | 21 986 | 4 808 | 5 222 | 5 460 | 36 239 | 1 737 | 49.6 | 10.5 | 43.9 |
| Sioux City, IA-NE-SD | 3 748 | 65 462 | 9 858 | 12 480 | 8 659 | 2 922 | 1 319 | 2 242 | 34 252 | 2 516 | 23.8 | 27.0 | 52.7 |
| Sioux Falls, SD | 6 921 | 122 295 | 25 429 | 13 045 | 16 609 | 13 495 | 4 217 | 4 649 | 38 019 | 3 316 | 28.1 | 29.0 | 56.3 |
| South Bend-Mishawaka, IN-MI | 6 656 | 119 238 | 19 316 | 16 329 | 15 828 | 4 254 | 4 223 | 4 285 | 35 941 | 1 523 | 49.2 | 10.8 | 42.7 |
| Spartanburg, SC | 6 142 | 110 969 | 14 011 | 22 512 | 13 535 | 2 224 | 3 731 | 4 183 | 37 697 | 1 242 | 53.8 | 2.4 | 39.7 |
| Spokane, WA | 12 151 | 169 532 | 34 231 | 13 925 | 24 570 | 10 416 | 8 312 | 6 569 | 38 750 | 2 502 | 54.8 | 10.6 | 36.3 |
| Springfield, IL | 5 312 | 82 922 | 20 978 | 2 916 | 12 368 | 5 308 | 4 146 | 3 178 | 38 321 | 1 564 | 45.3 | 22.8 | 47.7 |
| Springfield, MA | 14 682 | 238 868 | 58 848 | 27 574 | 32 868 | 11 630 | 9 300 | 8 983 | 37 608 | 1 960 | 55.7 | 2.1 | 47.7 |
| Springfield, MO | 10 981 | 165 634 | 32 180 | 14 256 | 23 947 | 8 722 | 6 732 | 5 461 | 32 973 | 8 122 | 38.0 | 6.2 | 39.6 |
| Springfield, OH | 2 388 | 39 851 | 8 187 | 5 431 | 5 699 | 2 420 | 1 215 | 1 266 | 31 773 | 744 | 53.5 | 14.1 | 42.9 |
| State College, PA | 3 169 | 43 808 | 7 532 | 4 100 | 7 963 | 1 402 | 3 380 | 1 481 | 33 808 | 1 146 | 40.2 | 4.3 | 44.2 |
| Steubenville-Weirton, WV-OH | 2 303 | 35 755 | 7 467 | 6 093 | 5 237 | 990 | 833 | 1 181 | 33 027 | 688 | 28.8 | 4.5 | 49.0 |
| Stockton, CA | 10 697 | 159 882 | 26 540 | 18 011 | 23 929 | 5 301 | 4 347 | 6 016 | 37 627 | 3 624 | 64.1 | 8.6 | 55.9 |
| Sumter, SC | 1 784 | 28 937 | 5 321 | 5 671 | 4 458 | 851 | 743 | 845 | 29 197 | 554 | 43.0 | 12.8 | 49.6 |
| Syracuse, NY | 15 264 | 249 854 | 43 574 | 24 511 | 35 324 | 13 818 | 14 107 | 9 700 | 38 822 | 2 075 | 31.4 | 10.4 | 54.7 |
| Tallahassee, FL | 8 540 | 103 140 | 20 298 | 3 334 | 17 857 | 4 880 | 9 788 | 3 632 | 35 214 | 1 498 | 56.7 | 6.9 | 37.3 |
| Tampa-St. Petersburg-Clearwater, FL | 69 369 | 947 930 | 160 560 | 49 117 | 136 646 | 70 660 | 78 196 | 38 925 | 41 063 | 4 955 | 82.2 | 2.7 | 44.5 |
| Terre Haute, IN | 3 673 | 58 503 | 11 060 | 11 872 | 8 709 | 1 559 | 1 476 | 2 035 | 34 791 | 1 924 | 48.0 | 16.2 | 46.9 |
| Texarkana, TX-Texarkana, AR | 2 859 | 42 260 | 7 749 | 4 297 | 7 921 | 1 422 | 1 440 | 1 338 | 31 665 | 2 211 | 46.9 | 8.7 | 38.1 |
| Toledo, OH | 14 469 | 265 476 | 51 923 | 36 685 | 32 270 | 7 696 | 11 844 | 10 112 | 38 089 | 2 893 | 45.8 | 12.9 | 42.6 |
| Topeka, KS | 5 314 | 83 710 | 20 299 | 6 456 | 11 133 | 5 494 | 4 043 | 3 146 | 37 578 | 4 901 | 26.6 | 15.6 | 38.7 |
| Trenton-Ewing, NJ | 9 615 | 177 336 | 29 150 | 6 704 | 19 037 | 14 006 | 20 014 | 10 705 | 60 363 | 311 | 70.7 | 2.3 | 40.8 |
| Tucson, AZ | 20 059 | 300 956 | 57 630 | 25 633 | 46 397 | 11 901 | 16 042 | 11 231 | 37 317 | 622 | 74.0 | 12.1 | 41.2 |
| Tulsa, OK | 23 852 | 373 676 | 59 555 | 47 195 | 45 353 | 17 200 | 19 751 | 16 113 | 43 120 | 9 916 | 39.6 | 10.8 | 38.1 |
| Tuscaloosa, AL | 4 254 | 73 352 | 12 177 | 12 737 | 10 397 | 1 777 | 2 290 | 2 824 | 38 506 | 1 408 | 30.5 | 14.9 | 44.5 |
| Tyler, TX | 5 504 | 86 101 | 21 611 | 7 513 | 11 864 | 3 114 | 3 916 | 3 315 | 38 504 | 2 514 | 53.1 | 4.5 | 35.0 |
| Utica-Rome, NY | 6 033 | 98 365 | 22 789 | 12 875 | 13 756 | 7 220 | 3 481 | 3 348 | 34 031 | 1 685 | 24.6 | 8.7 | 58.1 |
| Valdosta, GA | 3 051 | 40 127 | 7 533 | 3 268 | 6 890 | 1 161 | 1 268 | 1 129 | 28 138 | 1 093 | 39.2 | 13.4 | 37.3 |
| Vallejo-Fairfield, CA | 6 629 | 97 762 | 19 352 | 8 897 | 17 381 | 3 490 | 3 697 | 4 149 | 42 438 | 890 | 62.0 | 12.1 | 52.8 |
| Victoria, TX | 2 819 | 39 621 | 7 297 | 5 000 | 6 588 | 1 265 | 1 215 | 1 669 | 42 127 | 2 725 | 33.5 | 17.9 | 40.3 |
| Vineland-Millville-Bridgeton, NJ | 2 923 | 44 881 | 8 717 | 7 588 | 7 230 | 1 320 | 1 068 | 1 678 | 37 378 | 615 | 62.0 | 5.7 | 52.7 |

# Table C. Metropolitan Areas — **Agriculture**

| | Agriculture, 2007 (cont.) | | | | | | | | | | | | | | |
|---|---|---|---|---|---|---|---|---|---|---|---|---|---|---|---|
| | Land in farms | | | | Value of land and buildings (dollars) | | | Value of products sold | | | | Percent of farms with sales of: | | Government payments | |
| | | | Acres | | | | | | | Percent from: | | | | | |
| Area name | Acreage (1,000) | Percent change, 2002–2007 | Average size of farm | Total irrigated (1,000) | Total cropland (1,000) | Average per farm | Average per acre | Value of machinery and equipment, average per farm (dollars) | Total (mil dol) | Average per farm (dollars) | Crops | Live-stock and poultry products | $10,000 or more | $100,000 or more | Total ($1,000) | Percent of farms |
| | 117 | 118 | 119 | 120 | 121 | 122 | 123 | 124 | 125 | 126 | 127 | 128 | 129 | 130 | 131 | 132 |
| Sacramento—Arden-Arcade—Roseville, CA | 1 048 | -5.8 | 204 | 399.9 | 510.5 | 1 415 346 | 6 933 | 79 048 | 795.2 | 154 964 | 76.9 | 23.1 | 34.9 | 12.3 | 14 924 | 10.3 |
| Saginaw-Saginaw Township North, MI | 324 | -0.3 | 212 | 1.8 | 287.2 | 599 832 | 2 835 | 100 851 | 142.5 | 92 959 | 88.8 | 11.2 | 49.5 | 17.6 | 5 355 | 70.8 |
| St. Cloud, MN | 894 | 1.9 | 209 | 56.1 | 664.5 | 599 831 | 2 875 | 126 760 | 633.3 | 147 727 | 15.1 | 84.9 | 55.7 | 29.3 | 15 029 | 69.0 |
| St. George, UT | 174 | -19.8 | 294 | 13.8 | 42.8 | 915 375 | 3 116 | 56 838 | 9.8 | 16 587 | 39.0 | 61.0 | 26.1 | 3.4 | 268 | 10.3 |
| St. Joseph, MO-KS | 944 | 10.5 | 276 | D | 655.8 | 598 249 | 2 166 | 71 963 | 239.0 | 69 838 | 74.4 | 25.6 | 45.6 | 14.8 | 13 979 | 68.8 |
| St. Louis, MO-IL | 3 076 | 0.7 | 242 | 12 | 2 338.3 | 842 983 | 3 477 | 97 692 | 1 084.7 | 85 517 | 73.1 | 26.9 | 41.7 | 16.7 | 40 472 | 54.5 |
| Salem, OR | 474 | -7.1 | 121 | 113.0 | 345.2 | 774 463 | 6 404 | 100 949 | 733.4 | 186 999 | 81.5 | 18.5 | 34.6 | 16.5 | 2 483 | 11.8 |
| Salinas, CA | 1 328 | 5.3 | 1 108 | 233.0 | 311.1 | 5 144 255 | 4 645 | 305 191 | 2 178.5 | 1 816 906 | 98.2 | 1.8 | 59.8 | 37.9 | 1 316 | 7.8 |
| Salisbury, MD | 153 | 5.5 | 183 | 7.3 | 87.1 | 1 099 106 | 6 009 | 99 176 | 390.4 | 466 417 | 14.2 | 85.8 | 55.1 | 38.6 | 3 031 | 56.6 |
| Salt Lake City, UT | 775 | -11.2 | 486 | 58.4 | 83.2 | 852 923 | 1 755 | 55 518 | 79.5 | 49 814 | 34.0 | 66.0 | 25.7 | 6.5 | 394 | 4.8 |
| San Angelo, TX | 1 548 | 12.1 | 1 159 | 35.0 | 235.5 | 1 036 726 | 895 | 76 156 | 139.1 | 104 093 | 36.5 | 63.6 | 28.7 | 12.2 | 6 309 | 25.4 |
| San Antonio-New Braunfels, TX | 3 534 | -3.0 | 243 | 94.3 | 810.4 | 554 483 | 2 283 | 44 811 | 330.7 | 22 717 | 49.5 | 50.5 | 19.4 | 2.4 | 8 675 | 11.3 |
| San Diego-Carlsbad-San Marcos, CA | 304 | -25.5 | 45 | 62.2 | 102.5 | 874 683 | 19 247 | 40 032 | 1 054.2 | 157 646 | 91.2 | 8.8 | 42.0 | 10.8 | 342 | 0.5 |
| Sandusky, OH | 84 | -11.6 | 209 | 0.2 | 75.3 | 833 263 | 3 994 | 133 276 | 40.4 | 100 166 | 87.1 | 12.9 | 55.8 | 21.1 | 1 615 | 55.3 |
| San Francisco-Oakland-Fremont, CA | 542 | D | 310 | 42.3 | 88.8 | 1 700 623 | 5 488 | 70 494 | 315.3 | 180 236 | 73.9 | 26.1 | 41.1 | 14.7 | 1 185 | 5.3 |
| Oakland-Fremont-Hayward, CA Div | 352 | 2.3 | 303 | 37.1 | 66.4 | 1 522 267 | 5 018 | 63 521 | 121.2 | 104 545 | 77.4 | 22.6 | 36.7 | 11.2 | 557 | 4.2 |
| San Francisco-San Mateo-Redwood City, CA Div | 190 | D | 323 | 5.2 | 22.4 | 2 050 985 | 6 357 | 84 191 | 194.1 | 328 924 | 71.6 | 28.4 | 49.7 | 21.5 | 628 | 7.3 |
| San Jose-Sunnyvale-Santa Clara, CA | 880 | -2.1 | 520 | 52.6 | 88.5 | 1 967 370 | 3 786 | 88 895 | 458.8 | 270 991 | 89.1 | 10.9 | 41.2 | 13.8 | 528 | 4.5 |
| San Luis Obispo-Paso Robles, CA | 1 370 | 3.9 | 492 | 98.9 | 299.6 | 2 236 326 | 4 546 | 69 792 | 560.6 | 201 367 | 93.2 | 6.8 | 46.3 | 15.9 | 4 492 | 8.2 |
| Santa Barbara-Santa Maria-Goleta, CA | 727 | -4.0 | 455 | 95.1 | 125.0 | 3 223 533 | 7 081 | 104 111 | 951.3 | 595 696 | 96.0 | 4.0 | 57.2 | 25.9 | 132 | 1.0 |
| Santa Cruz-Watsonville, CA | 47 | -29.9 | 70 | 19.6 | 23.6 | 1 561 362 | 22 423 | 101 383 | 447.4 | 656 037 | 96.9 | 3.1 | 59.4 | 30.4 | 40 | 0.7 |
| Santa Fe, NM | 569 | -16.8 | 1 164 | 50.0 | 21.5 | 778 559 | 669 | 42 309 | 12.6 | 25 796 | 68.1 | 31.9 | 20.2 | 3.5 | 49 | 4.5 |
| Santa Rosa-Petaluma, CA | 531 | -15.3 | 155 | 78.3 | 134.4 | 2 459 725 | 15 887 | 68 139 | 647.6 | 188 854 | 65.2 | 34.8 | 56.9 | 20.6 | 711 | 2.6 |
| Savannah, GA | 65 | -17.7 | 208 | D | 22.4 | 599 680 | 2 887 | 69 752 | 12.8 | 40 965 | 86.4 | 13.6 | 24.6 | 6.1 | D | 23.3 |
| Scranton--Wilkes-Barre, PA | 184 | 9.5 | 110 | 0.8 | 101.4 | 466 597 | 4 243 | 56 554 | 47.9 | 28 558 | 60.5 | 39.5 | 23.2 | 7.0 | 1 714 | 26.9 |
| Seattle-Tacoma-Bellevue, WA | 174 | 3.6 | 35 | 13.3 | 72.3 | 491 170 | 13 870 | 43 251 | 336.3 | 68 519 | 40.7 | 59.3 | 21.6 | 5.6 | 1 014 | 2.8 |
| Seattle-Bellevue-Everett, WA Div | 126 | 14.5 | 36 | 8.8 | 55.0 | 493 504 | 13 539 | 43 681 | 252.9 | 73 089 | 41.4 | 58.6 | 23.9 | 6.0 | 946 | 3.4 |
| Tacoma, WA Div | 48 | -15.8 | 33 | 4.5 | 17.3 | 485 594 | 14 748 | 42 222 | 83.4 | 57 598 | 38.8 | 61.2 | 16.1 | 4.5 | 68 | 1.2 |
| Sebastian-Vero Beach, FL | 157 | -17.8 | 379 | 66.9 | 81.3 | 1 986 694 | 5 245 | 104 511 | 136.1 | 327 911 | D | D | 61.0 | 24.1 | 68 | 3.6 |
| Sheboygan, WI | 192 | -1.5 | 181 | 0.1 | 157.6 | 700 484 | 3 869 | 124 039 | 166.9 | 157 569 | 20.3 | 79.7 | 54.3 | 26.3 | 2 134 | 59.2 |
| Sherman-Denison, TX | 400 | -9.3 | 147 | 3.1 | 166.5 | 446 159 | 3 034 | 48 025 | 52.8 | 19 405 | 56.5 | 43.5 | 21.0 | 3.0 | 1 251 | 11.1 |
| Shreveport-Bossier City, LA | 422 | 1.7 | 243 | 10.4 | 151.3 | 544 328 | 2 240 | 67 978 | 68.2 | 39 278 | 50.7 | 49.3 | 27.6 | 6.2 | 5 373 | 13.1 |
| Sioux City, IA-NE-SD | 1 140 | -0.6 | 453 | 92.4 | 973.2 | 1 112 904 | 2 457 | 142 988 | 579.5 | 230 334 | 57.2 | 42.8 | 59.9 | 34.3 | 21 110 | 79.3 |
| Sioux Falls, SD | 1 489 | 4.6 | 449 | 30.4 | 1 227.3 | 1 139 529 | 2 538 | 141 650 | 651.0 | 196 351 | 58.4 | 41.6 | 66.2 | 37.8 | 19 796 | 73.7 |
| South Bend-Mishawaka, IN-MI | 369 | 4.2 | 242 | 64.0 | 315.4 | 866 012 | 3 575 | 109 273 | 191.4 | 125 673 | 68.3 | 31.7 | 43.7 | 19.0 | 5 913 | 57.1 |
| Spartanburg, SC | 110 | -12.7 | 89 | 2.1 | 41.5 | 432 985 | 4 892 | 41 123 | 26.3 | 21 171 | 57.4 | 42.6 | 18.0 | 2.7 | 499 | 10.6 |
| Spokane, WA | 626 | -2.6 | 250 | 13.5 | 394.9 | 588 545 | 2 351 | 65 660 | 117.1 | 46 789 | 84.2 | 15.8 | 23.6 | 8.3 | 5 929 | 24.5 |
| Springfield, IL | 687 | 10.3 | 439 | 3.6 | 636.1 | 1 702 347 | 3 877 | 167 151 | 374.7 | 239 628 | 94.1 | 5.9 | 49.8 | 33.0 | 12 252 | 69.8 |
| Springfield, MA | 169 | 3.7 | 86 | 3.9 | 61.2 | 755 959 | 8 764 | 60 526 | 121.1 | 61 835 | 71.1 | 28.9 | 35.1 | 10.9 | 1 447 | 10.9 |
| Springfield, MO | 1 266 | -10.3 | 156 | 2.0 | 509.0 | 400 097 | 2 568 | 44 928 | 267.6 | 32 953 | 8.6 | 91.4 | 37.3 | 6.3 | 2 242 | 10.7 |
| Springfield, OH | 177 | 7.3 | 238 | 1.5 | 153.5 | 911 967 | 3 826 | 112 592 | 137.0 | 184 200 | 67.1 | 32.9 | 44.9 | 21.5 | 3 093 | 53.4 |
| State College, PA | 148 | -10.3 | 130 | 0.6 | 86.1 | 660 008 | 5 095 | 60 906 | 69.7 | 60 786 | 25.1 | 74.9 | 39.4 | 17.2 | 1 266 | 26.8 |
| Steubenville-Weirton, WV-OH | 95 | 8.0 | 137 | D | 39.9 | 312 292 | 2 273 | 51 411 | 10.7 | 15 494 | 36.9 | 63.1 | 25.4 | 3.6 | 376 | 20.6 |
| Stockton, CA | 738 | -9.2 | 204 | 454.0 | 492.0 | 2 069 142 | 10 168 | 127 313 | 1 564.4 | 431 665 | 63.4 | 36.6 | 65.5 | 33.9 | 4 444 | 8.5 |
| Sumter, SC | 153 | 12.5 | 277 | 9.5 | 88.8 | 552 862 | 1 996 | 91 687 | 88.8 | 160 338 | 37.3 | 62.7 | 25.6 | 11.0 | 4 016 | 54.0 |
| Syracuse, NY | 439 | 2.6 | 212 | 3.2 | 271.2 | 417 445 | 1 973 | 107 941 | 263.0 | 126 769 | 29.9 | 70.1 | 47.4 | 20.7 | 4 215 | 29.5 |
| Tallahassee, FL | 314 | 9.8 | 209 | 6.1 | 64.1 | 908 795 | 4 341 | 45 544 | 124.1 | 82 911 | 89.1 | 10.9 | 24.5 | 3.1 | 1 682 | 20.7 |
| Tampa-St. Petersburg-Clearwater, FL | 427 | -18.0 | 86 | 42.2 | D | 803 173 | 9 310 | 46 114 | 637.6 | 128 671 | 79.1 | 20.9 | 30.5 | 9.2 | D | 1.2 |
| Terre Haute, IN | 589 | 4.6 | 306 | D | 507.9 | 947 330 | 3 096 | 118 263 | 250.0 | 129 906 | 90.2 | 9.8 | 46.3 | 23.0 | 9 485 | 69.2 |
| Texarkana, TX-Texarkana, AR | 467 | 0.2 | 211 | 5.0 | 197.4 | 392 245 | 1 859 | 55 289 | 97.1 | 43 934 | 30.7 | 69.3 | 28.3 | 5.7 | 2 579 | 11.0 |
| Toledo, OH | 638 | -8.2 | 220 | 2.3 | 597.8 | 757 544 | 3 438 | 109 471 | 353.5 | 122 226 | 78.3 | 21.7 | 57.2 | 23.1 | 12 203 | 73.6 |
| Topeka, KS | 1 682 | 1.0 | 343 | D | 759.0 | 429 700 | 1 252 | 66 304 | 263.4 | 53 761 | 50.3 | 49.7 | 41.6 | 10.9 | 11 453 | 51.8 |
| Trenton-Ewing, NJ | 22 | -12.0 | 70 | 1.0 | 15.4 | 1 314 520 | 18 813 | 64 690 | 18.6 | 59 955 | 80.5 | 19.5 | 41.2 | 11.9 | 286 | 13.2 |
| Tucson, AZ | D | D | D | 35.7 | 49.6 | 1 951 879 | D | 80 179 | 67.5 | 108 521 | 73.2 | 26.8 | 27.2 | 9.8 | 3 771 | 6.6 |
| Tulsa, OK | 3 025 | 6.4 | 305 | 11.6 | 693.3 | 437 580 | 1 434 | 47 276 | 288.6 | 29 106 | 18.3 | 81.7 | 27.6 | 3.6 | 3 734 | 13.4 |
| Tuscaloosa, AL | 416 | 6.1 | 295 | 1.6 | 110.1 | 562 865 | 1 907 | 72 824 | 106.2 | 75 450 | D | D | 28.0 | 9.0 | 3 429 | 29.8 |
| Tyler, TX | 302 | 5.2 | 120 | 2.7 | 91.8 | 377 217 | 3 136 | 53 392 | 68.0 | 27 049 | 62.5 | 37.5 | 23.3 | 2.8 | 68 | 1.7 |
| Utica-Rome, NY | 332 | -12.6 | 197 | 0.5 | 186.9 | 365 662 | 1 854 | 91 371 | 152.2 | 90 358 | 21.3 | 78.7 | 48.8 | 21.4 | 3 069 | 34.4 |
| Valdosta, GA | 324 | -9.5 | 297 | 35.6 | 148.1 | 883 515 | 2 977 | 90 995 | 138.7 | 126 913 | 82.4 | 17.6 | 34.9 | 14.5 | 8 745 | 42.0 |
| Vallejo-Fairfield, CA | 358 | 2.0 | 403 | 146.0 | 154.9 | 1 985 813 | 4 934 | 99 718 | 244.3 | 274 489 | 83.1 | 16.9 | 41.0 | 19.3 | 2 289 | 17.4 |
| Victoria, TX | 1 194 | -5.8 | 438 | 7.3 | 281.9 | 696 286 | 1 589 | 65 633 | 92.4 | 33 907 | 52.2 | 47.8 | 31.8 | 6.2 | 5 771 | 15.6 |
| Vineland-Millville-Bridgeton, NJ | 69 | -2.8 | 113 | 18.4 | 52.3 | 1 056 005 | 9 346 | 118 184 | 156.9 | 255 185 | 97.4 | 2.6 | 48.0 | 22.9 | 413 | 9.3 |

| Area name | Total water withdrawn (mil gal/day) | Gallons withdrawn per person | Number of establishments | Number of employees | Sales (mil dol) | Annual payroll (mil dol) | Number of establishments | Number of employees | Sales (mil dol) | Annual payroll (mil dol) | Number of establishments | Number of employees | Receipts (mil dol) | Annual payroll (mil dol) |
|---|---|---|---|---|---|---|---|---|---|---|---|---|---|---|
| | Water use, 2005 | | Wholesale trade,[1] 2007 | | | | Retail trade, 2007 | | | | Real estate and rental and leasing, 2007 | | | |
| | 133 | 134 | 135 | 136 | 137 | 138 | 139 | 140 | 141 | 142 | 143 | 144 | 145 | 146 |
| Sacramento—Arden-Arcade—Roseville, CA .. | 1 768.3 | 866 | 2 204 | 35 604 | 34 925.8 | 1 714.1 | 6 166 | 99 917 | 25 165.5 | 2 583.3 | 2 808 | 17 197 | 2 790.3 | 601.2 |
| Saginaw-Saginaw Township North, MI | 20.2 | 97 | 204 | 2 542 | 1 254.6 | 101.7 | 973 | 12 584 | 2 534.3 | 243.3 | 149 | 751 | 101.8 | 17.4 |
| St. Cloud, MN | 73.6 | 406 | 240 | 5 488 | 2 437.8 | 233.9 | 842 | 13 555 | 2 918.8 | 265.7 | 206 | 1 126 | 121.3 | 27.4 |
| St. George, UT | 98.9 | 778 | 157 | 1 320 | 590.8 | 50.8 | 593 | 8 035 | 2 087.8 | 185.9 | 367 | 856 | 122.0 | 20.0 |
| St. Joseph, MO-KS | 106.1 | 870 | 143 | 1 858 | 1 467.5 | 73.4 | 486 | 7 006 | 1 671.9 | 147.9 | 144 | 526 | 63.5 | 10.9 |
| St. Louis, MO-IL | 3 968.1 | 1 428 | 4 337 | 60 274 | 70 978.7 | 3 325.4 | 9 989 | 148 889 | 35 738.2 | 3 661.6 | 3 266 | 20 731 | 3 990.4 | 720.7 |
| Salem, OR | 327.4 | 872 | 392 | 4 456 | 3 860.8 | 188.0 | 1 259 | 18 547 | 4 391.6 | 438.1 | 556 | 2 924 | 359.1 | 69.7 |
| Salinas, CA | 1 129.2 | 2 740 | 453 | 6 994 | 6 581.3 | 375.2 | 1 497 | 18 392 | 4 541.1 | 487.8 | 487 | 2 423 | 500.6 | 86.6 |
| Salisbury, MD | 24.4 | 210 | 148 | 2 475 | 1 536.2 | 119.1 | 506 | 7 890 | 1 886.0 | 175.6 | 173 | 745 | 112.5 | 23.4 |
| Salt Lake City, UT | 651.7 | 611 | 2 115 | 35 199 | 28 056.2 | 1 760.8 | 3 818 | 65 130 | 17 922.2 | 1 612.3 | 2 390 | 12 775 | 2 257.2 | 427.5 |
| San Angelo, TX | 44.9 | 426 | 134 | 1 215 | 597.9 | 43.8 | 452 | 6 052 | 1 558.2 | 132.7 | 135 | 631 | 76.0 | 15.8 |
| San Antonio-New Braunfels, TX | 969.3 | 513 | 2 007 | 31 051 | 22 838.4 | 1 418.0 | 5 913 | 95 964 | 27 169.2 | 2 233.7 | 2 164 | 13 556 | 2 433.7 | 464.0 |
| San Diego-Carlsbad-San Marcos, CA | 4 085.1 | 1 393 | 4 569 | 64 810 | 49 017.1 | 4 804.4 | 9 948 | 151 425 | 38 710.6 | 3 889.2 | 5 810 | 33 067 | 7 190.2 | 1 345.2 |
| Sandusky, OH | 35.2 | 448 | 72 | 1 038 | 599.0 | 38.9 | 351 | 5 086 | 1 034.9 | 101.8 | 79 | 360 | 40.9 | 8.8 |
| San Francisco-Oakland-Fremont, CA | 3 707.1 | 893 | 7 079 | 100 925 | 111 769.0 | 6 831.0 | 14 412 | 210 050 | 56 860.9 | 6 077.9 | 7 206 | 45 485 | 12 223.8 | 2 307.7 |
| Oakland-Fremont-Hayward, CA Div | 1 850.9 | 750 | 3 979 | 63 505 | 69 710.8 | 4 032.4 | 7 325 | 113 400 | 29 672.8 | 3 125.0 | 3 484 | 19 990 | 4 688.8 | 820.5 |
| San Francisco-San Mateo-Redwood City, CA Div | 1 856.2 | 1 101 | 3 100 | 37 420 | 42 058.2 | 2 798.7 | 7 087 | 96 650 | 27 188.1 | 2 952.9 | 3 722 | 25 495 | 7 535.0 | 1 487.2 |
| San Jose-Sunnyvale-Santa Clara, CA | 365.5 | 208 | 2 973 | 87 492 | 89 981.1 | 8 953.8 | 5 421 | 87 932 | 26 844.4 | 2 947.0 | 2 664 | 14 946 | 5 189.2 | 752.0 |
| San Luis Obispo-Paso Robles, CA | 2 774.1 | 10 858 | 319 | 2 511 | 1 213.5 | 110.5 | 1 262 | 14 652 | 3 548.4 | 353.6 | 475 | 2 050 | 293.4 | 56.7 |
| Santa Barbara-Santa Maria-Goleta, CA | 239.6 | 598 | 491 | 6 446 | 5 371.5 | 391.5 | 1 605 | 20 281 | 4 983.4 | 524.4 | 681 | 3 452 | 620.7 | 119.5 |
| Santa Cruz-Watsonville, CA | 73.7 | 295 | 315 | 7 288 | 6 357.7 | 497.9 | 981 | 12 454 | 3 725.4 | 316.0 | 380 | 1 793 | 311.1 | 58.6 |
| Santa Fe, NM | 47.4 | 336 | 158 | 1 377 | 1 155.0 | 64.9 | 887 | 9 949 | 2 426.3 | 261.6 | 311 | 1 092 | 206.0 | 40.8 |
| Santa Rosa-Petaluma, CA | 114.3 | 245 | 676 | 9 568 | 6 887.4 | 606.1 | 1 925 | 26 177 | 6 427.2 | 718.5 | 718 | 3 237 | 604.1 | 114.2 |
| Savannah, GA | 395.2 | 1 259 | 410 | 5 287 | 4 771.8 | 262.0 | 1 491 | 18 989 | 4 551.8 | 422.8 | 487 | 2 223 | 387.6 | 68.7 |
| Scranton--Wilkes-Barre, PA.. | 156.7 | 285 | 650 | 10 799 | 6 226.5 | 431.6 | 2 383 | 34 129 | 8 691.1 | 694.7 | 393 | 2 628 | 385.5 | 72.1 |
| Seattle-Tacoma-Bellevue, WA | 554.0 | 173 | 6 002 | 87 932 | 85 085.5 | 5 055.2 | 11 549 | 176 728 | 55 952.6 | 4 867.7 | 6 187 | 33 954 | 7 698.4 | 1 345.0 |
| Seattle-Bellevue-Everett, WA Div | 355.5 | 145 | 5 191 | 75 356 | 76 985.3 | 4 534.1 | 9 243 | 140 913 | 46 211.0 | 3 915.4 | 5 093 | 28 259 | 6 727.9 | 1 183.7 |
| Tacoma, WA Div | 198.5 | 263 | 811 | 12 576 | 8 100.2 | 521.0 | 2 306 | 35 815 | 9 741.6 | 952.3 | 1 094 | 5 695 | 970.6 | 161.2 |
| Sebastian-Vero Beach, FL... | 285.7 | 2 197 | 158 | D | D | D | 699 | 9 096 | 1 851.7 | 203.3 | 260 | 945 | 146.5 | 24.1 |
| Sheboygan, WI | 402.3 | 3 510 | 105 | 1 605 | 1 160.4 | 79.3 | 427 | 6 386 | 1 398.7 | 131.5 | 80 | 372 | 73.8 | 12.1 |
| Sherman-Denison, TX | 23.6 | 202 | 120 | 1 170 | 779.0 | 39.7 | 497 | 6 333 | 1 594.7 | 140.4 | 114 | 456 | 69.9 | 11.1 |
| Shreveport-Bossier City, LA . | 904.0 | 2 359 | 477 | 7 147 | 7 498.1 | 319.2 | 1 557 | 21 638 | 5 633.3 | 483.8 | 422 | 2 432 | 362.4 | 65.1 |
| Sioux City, IA-NE-SD | 1 031.4 | 7 234 | 233 | 3 172 | 2 454.4 | 134.4 | 608 | 9 140 | 2 023.5 | 174.2 | 132 | 680 | 106.0 | 18.0 |
| Sioux Falls, SD | 58.7 | 282 | 467 | 6 144 | 4 507.6 | 282.7 | 1 035 | 16 679 | 4 364.2 | 370.8 | 245 | 1 577 | 238.5 | 46.2 |
| South Bend-Mishawaka, IN-MI | 78.0 | 245 | 457 | 7 008 | 4 395.1 | 310.9 | 1 072 | 17 506 | 3 866.8 | 367.4 | 267 | 1 498 | 225.2 | 44.4 |
| Spartanburg, SC | 100.7 | 377 | 488 | 7 196 | 6 641.4 | 322.7 | 1 089 | 13 937 | 3 638.4 | 309.0 | 279 | 1 279 | 220.8 | 45.1 |
| Spokane, WA | 191.7 | 435 | 757 | 10 996 | 8 498.9 | 459.0 | 1 712 | 26 853 | 6 741.2 | 697.7 | 662 | 3 426 | 630.3 | 105.1 |
| Springfield, IL | 415.3 | 2 021 | 238 | 3 191 | 2 215.7 | 132.0 | 842 | 12 798 | 2 931.6 | 255.8 | 235 | 1 069 | 163.0 | 25.2 |
| Springfield, MA | 238.8 | 347 | 654 | 10 229 | 9 587.3 | 476.6 | 2 560 | 34 910 | 7 905.8 | 789.4 | 587 | 2 817 | 463.1 | 86.4 |
| Springfield, MO | 242.3 | 609 | 651 | 10 134 | 7 331.5 | 409.9 | 1 781 | 25 165 | 6 142.0 | 548.1 | 589 | 3 103 | 379.1 | 73.9 |
| Springfield, OH | 27.9 | 196 | 103 | 1 977 | 1 944.3 | 76.1 | 460 | 6 625 | 1 398.7 | 131.7 | 101 | 485 | 64.0 | 10.9 |
| State College, PA | 101.6 | 723 | 98 | D | D | D | 548 | 8 014 | 1 604.3 | 151.0 | 129 | 922 | 184.7 | 26.2 |
| Steubenville-Weirton, WV-OH | 2 413.4 | 19 084 | 85 | 979 | 929.8 | 35.8 | 443 | 5 421 | 1 118.1 | 105.3 | 82 | 351 | 42.2 | 7.4 |
| Stockton, CA | 1 483.5 | 2 234 | 630 | 11 301 | 12 465.7 | 516.6 | 1 756 | 27 329 | 7 109.7 | 653.0 | 634 | 3 363 | 577.5 | 104.4 |
| Sumter, SC | 24.9 | 236 | 83 | 943 | 403.4 | 31.3 | 417 | 4 919 | 1 021.5 | 91.8 | 87 | 308 | 36.7 | 6.8 |
| Syracuse, NY | 1 409.6 | 2 163 | 944 | 15 728 | 22 145.7 | 723.5 | 2 368 | 35 712 | 8 023.1 | 762.2 | 763 | 3 899 | 714.7 | 134.0 |
| Tallahassee, FL | 84.1 | 234 | 321 | 3 407 | 1 440.2 | 137.2 | 1 298 | 19 641 | 4 230.5 | 396.2 | 505 | 2 565 | 381.4 | 71.7 |
| Tampa-St. Petersburg-Clearwater, FL | 4 714.6 | 1 788 | 4 201 | 52 123 | 50 581.7 | 2 349.9 | 10 024 | 148 740 | 40 337.4 | 3 561.3 | 4 391 | 22 538 | 3 987.4 | 813.4 |
| Terre Haute, IN | 1 678.6 | 9 988 | 163 | 1 732 | 1 101.7 | 61.0 | 705 | 10 036 | 2 312.1 | 199.5 | 129 | 720 | 88.0 | 19.5 |
| Texarkana, TX-Texarkana, AR | 247.3 | 1 848 | 163 | 2 018 | 2 198.6 | 78.0 | 629 | 7 921 | 1 943.1 | 172.0 | 123 | 549 | 77.8 | 13.0 |
| Toledo, OH | 944.2 | 1 438 | 892 | 12 516 | 9 268.5 | 548.4 | 2 419 | 35 261 | 8 219.6 | 751.0 | 652 | 3 780 | 1 120.0 | 131.0 |
| Topeka, KS | 49.5 | 216 | 232 | 2 556 | 1 239.4 | 100.8 | 926 | 11 716 | 2 569.8 | 237.7 | 269 | 1 133 | 167.2 | 31.8 |
| Trenton-Ewing, NJ | 691.6 | 1 888 | 414 | 10 266 | 9 049.0 | 851.9 | 1 412 | 20 683 | 5 089.1 | 505.0 | 357 | D | D | D |
| Tucson, AZ | 306.8 | 332 | 855 | 9 543 | 4 838.2 | 398.8 | 2 982 | 51 830 | 11 928.5 | 1 208.9 | 1 449 | 8 133 | 1 211.7 | 251.8 |
| Tulsa, OK | 190.0 | 214 | 1 475 | 21 606 | 20 496.6 | 1 139.0 | 3 152 | 45 953 | 11 623.2 | 996.3 | 1 169 | 8 958 | 1 468.7 | 289.3 |
| Tuscaloosa, AL | 463.0 | 2 352 | 171 | 1 916 | 885.9 | 82.3 | 858 | 11 097 | 2 566.2 | 233.5 | 204 | 1 182 | 175.5 | 32.2 |
| Tyler, TX | 45.5 | 239 | 291 | 3 019 | 1 516.0 | 135.4 | 855 | 12 347 | 3 110.1 | 287.8 | 229 | 1 447 | 204.5 | 41.3 |
| Utica-Rome, NY | 57.7 | 194 | 246 | 2 877 | 1 356.0 | 109.0 | 1 091 | 14 414 | 3 254.1 | 309.9 | 250 | 1 014 | 172.0 | 22.4 |
| Valdosta, GA | 43.3 | 346 | 169 | 1 987 | 992.0 | 67.3 | 632 | 7 478 | 1 938.4 | 152.4 | 144 | 803 | 84.6 | 19.3 |
| Vallejo-Fairfield, CA | 467.9 | 1 137 | 293 | 5 152 | 3 639.4 | 246.4 | 1 167 | 19 117 | 4 828.0 | 482.7 | 404 | 1 913 | 347.9 | 58.5 |
| Victoria, TX | 77.3 | 682 | 139 | 1 759 | 948.2 | 78.5 | 496 | 7 072 | 1 793.8 | 157.5 | 142 | 944 | 175.3 | 37.9 |
| Vineland-Millville-Bridgeton, NJ | 58.1 | 379 | 173 | 2 807 | 1 753.1 | 103.9 | 564 | 7 602 | 1 952.7 | 185.4 | 125 | 540 | 88.3 | 16.2 |

1. Merchant wholesalers, except manufacturers' sales branches and offices.

Table C. Metropolitan Areas —

# Professional Services, Manufacturing, and Accommodation and Food Services

| Area name | Professional, scientific, and technical services,[1] 2007 | | | | Manufacturing, 2007 | | | | Accommodation and food services, 2007 | | | |
|---|---|---|---|---|---|---|---|---|---|---|---|---|
| | Number of establish-ments | Number of employees | Sales (mil dol) | Annual payroll (mil dol) | Number of establish-ments | Number of employees | Sales (mil dol) | Annual payroll (mil dol) | Number of establish-ments | Number of employees | Sales (mil dol) | Annual payroll (mil dol) |
| | 147 | 148 | 149 | 150 | 151 | 152 | 153 | 154 | 155 | 156 | 157 | 158 |
| Sacramento—Arden-Arcade—Roseville, CA .. | 5 856 | 50 677 | 7 296.2 | 3 360.2 | 1 598 | 44 504 | 12 821.8 | 1 859.3 | 4 304 | 77 056 | 4 168.6 | 1 100.2 |
| Saginaw-Saginaw Township North, MI ..................... | 355 | 3 009 | 429.9 | 121.3 | 219 | 11 437 | 4 604.8 | 659.0 | 383 | 8 620 | 337.3 | 102.2 |
| St. Cloud, MN ...................... | 351 | D | D | D | 330 | 17 503 | 4 584.6 | 694.0 | 452 | 8 241 | 293.3 | 83.6 |
| St. George, UT .................... | 432 | D | D | D | 154 | 3 225 | 609.6 | 117.4 | 279 | 5 631 | 254.5 | 74.5 |
| St. Joseph, MO-KS .............. | 209 | D | D | D | 126 | 9 871 | 4 934.8 | 413.4 | 232 | 4 492 | 165.7 | 48.5 |
| St. Louis, MO-IL ................. | 7 330 | D | D | D | 2 976 | 132 161 | 67 121.1 | 6 916.2 | 5 835 | 121 229 | 5 558.7 | 1 586.9 |
| Salem, OR ......................... | 826 | 4 270 | 445.6 | 172.5 | 448 | 12 783 | 3 262.0 | 438.1 | 773 | 13 231 | 768.8 | 195.6 |
| Salinas, CA ....................... | 818 | D | D | D | 301 | 7 333 | 2 227.6 | 268.4 | 983 | 18 026 | 1 197.1 | 345.4 |
| Salisbury, MD..................... | 251 | D | D | D | 100 | D | 1 124.3 | D | 225 | 4 300 | 194.7 | 53.2 |
| Salt Lake City, UT.............. | 4 111 | 34 053 | 4 964.4 | 1 944.3 | 1 560 | 53 639 | 19 597.6 | 2 442.0 | 2 048 | 46 050 | 2 138.6 | 635.8 |
| San Angelo, TX................... | 188 | D | D | D | 121 | 2 932 | 877.8 | 114.0 | 210 | 4 301 | 180.1 | 50.1 |
| San Antonio-New Braunfels, TX ................................. | 4 284 | 35 667 | 5 087.5 | 1 997.8 | 1 332 | 48 294 | 15 945.7 | 1 869.9 | 3 944 | 86 014 | 4 291.7 | 1 200.1 |
| San Diego-Carlsbad-San Marcos, CA..................... | 11 972 | 117 497 | 18 834.7 | 7 694.0 | 3 182 | 102 168 | 27 541.1 | 5 244.6 | 6 599 | 144 287 | 9 551.5 | 2 567.2 |
| Sandusky, OH..................... | 132 | D | D | D | 110 | 7 149 | 2 329.9 | 344.9 | 279 | 5 661 | 254.7 | 69.0 |
| San Francisco-Oakland-Fremont, CA........................ | 18 729 | 225 698 | 44 312.5 | 17 801.0 | 4 462 | 143 318 | 77 651.2 | 8 277.1 | 11 166 | 184 046 | 12 142.9 | 3 499.3 |
| Oakland-Fremont-Hayward, CA Div. | 8 416 | D | D | D | 2 703 | 99 553 | 57 258.3 | 5 791.5 | 5 162 | 75 932 | 4 370.0 | 1 203.1 |
| San Francisco-San Mateo-Redwood City, CA Div. | 10 313 | D | D | D | 1 759 | 43 765 | 20 392.9 | 2 485.6 | 6 004 | 108 114 | 7 772.9 | 2 296.2 |
| San Jose-Sunnyvale-Santa Clara, CA.......................... | 7 885 | 123 833 | 21 593.3 | 13 561.5 | 2 683 | 145 580 | 45 719.1 | 10 397.9 | 4 190 | 69 623 | 4 197.8 | 1 173.9 |
| San Luis Obispo-Paso Robles, CA...................... | 930 | 5 709 | 593.8 | 222.6 | 377 | 6 517 | 2 548.2 | 260.4 | 850 | 14 903 | 767.9 | 219.7 |
| Santa Barbara-Santa Maria-Goleta, CA........................ | 1 359 | D | D | D | 505 | 13 149 | 3 174.1 | 676.8 | 1 029 | 21 380 | 1 361.5 | 360.1 |
| Santa Cruz-Watsonville, CA . | 914 | D | D | D | 329 | 6 689 | 1 502.4 | 301.6 | 657 | 9 774 | 513.8 | 148.8 |
| Santa Fe, NM..................... | 693 | D | D | D | 153 | 980 | D | 34.5 | 398 | 9 203 | 540.4 | 166.3 |
| Santa Rosa-Petaluma, CA.... | 1 538 | D | D | D | 885 | 24 077 | 5 841.9 | 1 201.2 | 1 173 | 17 739 | 1 005.4 | 283.8 |
| Savannah, GA..................... | 816 | D | D | D | 226 | 15 650 | 8 463.5 | 899.2 | 921 | 18 424 | 933.8 | 252.9 |
| Scranton--Wilkes-Barre, PA.. | 1 107 | 9 715 | 844.2 | 340.5 | 649 | 32 526 | 11 135.4 | 1 238.4 | 1 369 | 19 758 | 825.7 | 225.5 |
| Seattle-Tacoma-Bellevue, WA ................................. | 11 939 | D | D | D | 4 024 | 165 676 | 64 901.7 | 8 809.4 | 8 615 | 134 167 | 7 701.2 | 2 239.4 |
| Seattle-Bellevue-Everett, WA Div. | 10 553 | D | D | D | 3 356 | 145 350 | 59 943.1 | 7 915.2 | 7 037 | 110 091 | 6 528.7 | 1 906.7 |
| Tacoma, WA Div................. | 1 386 | D | D | D | 668 | 20 326 | 4 958.6 | 894.2 | 1 578 | 24 076 | 1 172.5 | 332.7 |
| Sebastian-Vero Beach, FL.... | 473 | 2 076 | 235.3 | 97.2 | 99 | 2 179 | 413.0 | 87.7 | 232 | 4 557 | 190.5 | 56.2 |
| Sheboygan, WI .................... | 176 | 1 743 | 209.1 | 70.5 | 246 | 18 774 | 6 126.1 | 816.0 | 271 | 4 869 | 193.0 | 54.8 |
| Sherman-Denison, TX .......... | 220 | 1 086 | 92.5 | 34.5 | 132 | 6 148 | 2 542.8 | 293.7 | 226 | 4 001 | 167.7 | 48.6 |
| Shreveport-Bossier City, LA . | 788 | 5 212 | 593.9 | 206.3 | 303 | 12 519 | 8 801.5 | 615.0 | 692 | 22 372 | 1 397.5 | 352.7 |
| Sioux City, IA-NE-SD........... | 245 | D | D | D | 166 | D | D | 408.9 | 351 | 5 692 | 199.2 | 57.4 |
| Sioux Falls, SD .................. | 556 | D | D | D | 264 | 13 300 | 4 044.2 | 541.4 | 510 | 10 672 | 423.2 | 127.4 |
| South Bend-Mishawaka, IN-MI..................................... | 616 | D | D | D | 512 | 20 781 | 8 722.3 | 975.8 | 618 | 11 918 | 466.8 | 134.1 |
| Spartanburg, SC ................. | 467 | D | D | D | 462 | 26 108 | 11 731.8 | 1 204.9 | 528 | 10 002 | 411.5 | 113.6 |
| Spokane, WA...................... | 1 231 | 8 631 | 1 157.2 | 432.4 | 589 | 17 412 | 3 895.4 | 730.7 | 993 | 17 046 | 780.2 | 232.2 |
| Springfield, IL .................... | 594 | 4 726 | 567.6 | 230.3 | 123 | 3 172 | 683.4 | 137.1 | 543 | 9 450 | 373.8 | 112.2 |
| Springfield, MA................... | 1 366 | D | D | D | 941 | 32 853 | 8 264.3 | 1 501.5 | 1 502 | 22 047 | 967.5 | 283.7 |
| Springfield, MO .................. | 1 033 | D | D | D | 538 | 18 405 | 4 428.8 | 664.6 | 881 | 18 123 | 691.8 | 202.4 |
| Springfield, OH................... | 163 | D | D | D | 182 | 7 164 | 2 494.3 | 299.2 | 241 | 4 574 | 173.1 | 49.6 |
| State College, PA ............... | 376 | D | D | D | 150 | 4 341 | 1 216.5 | 181.0 | 301 | 5 961 | 240.1 | 68.8 |
| Steubenville-Weirton, WV-OH..................................... | 161 | D | D | D | 83 | 8 433 | 5 467.0 | 428.3 | 308 | 3 446 | 131.6 | 34.2 |
| Stockton, CA...................... | 801 | D | D | D | 585 | 23 442 | 8 272.5 | 938.6 | 1 079 | 15 195 | 745.8 | 199.3 |
| Sumter, SC ........................ | 139 | D | D | D | 82 | 7 707 | 1 922.0 | 253.3 | 149 | 3 173 | 109.4 | 29.8 |
| Syracuse, NY ..................... | 1 462 | 15 052 | 2 395.7 | 845.1 | 633 | 29 539 | 10 634.2 | 1 467.2 | 1 527 | 22 740 | 989.9 | 286.6 |
| Tallahassee, FL .................. | 1 488 | 10 506 | 1 982.0 | 684.9 | 152 | 4 293 | 1 027.4 | 177.7 | 684 | 14 779 | 597.7 | 161.9 |
| Tampa-St. Petersburg-Clearwater, FL .......................... | 10 175 | 74 476 | 10 297.6 | 4 104.9 | 2 323 | 65 945 | 18 564.6 | 2 763.0 | 4 995 | 99 165 | 5 143.5 | 1 423.0 |
| Terre Haute, IN .................. | 279 | D | D | D | 190 | 11 628 | 4 552.6 | 519.3 | 372 | 6 181 | 244.5 | 67.0 |
| Texarkana, TX-Texarkana, AR .................................. | 208 | D | D | D | 94 | 4 825 | 2 442.1 | 233.0 | 232 | 4 856 | 210.2 | 62.1 |
| Toledo, OH ......................... | 1 251 | D | D | D | 927 | 49 565 | 28 585.1 | 2 557.9 | 1 567 | 28 162 | 1 055.8 | 305.4 |
| Topeka, KS ........................ | 534 | D | D | D | 156 | 6 810 | 2 418.2 | 300.1 | 442 | 8 874 | 456.5 | 110.9 |
| Trenton-Ewing, NJ .............. | 1 646 | 30 900 | 5 790.4 | 2 345.3 | 293 | 9 352 | D | 420.1 | 834 | 12 103 | 695.8 | 197.7 |
| Tucson, AZ ......................... | 2 692 | 16 250 | 1 886.4 | 777.8 | 760 | 30 567 | 10 365.2 | 1 877.0 | 1 758 | 42 002 | 2 135.2 | 601.8 |
| Tulsa, OK ........................... | 2 815 | 18 151 | 2 527.6 | 937.0 | 1 448 | 55 034 | 21 574.6 | 2 496.5 | 1 809 | 34 896 | 1 421.1 | 399.5 |
| Tuscaloosa, AL ................... | 370 | 2 599 | 225.7 | 84.7 | 171 | 14 378 | 11 142.2 | 755.9 | 395 | 8 389 | 331.8 | 88.6 |
| Tyler, TX ............................ | 548 | D | D | D | 224 | 10 737 | 5 423.5 | 474.5 | 339 | 7 563 | 337.3 | 93.6 |
| Utica-Rome, NY .................. | 462 | D | D | D | 329 | 13 713 | 3 798.2 | 547.0 | 662 | 7 136 | 314.7 | 89.3 |
| Valdosta, GA ...................... | 230 | D | D | D | 128 | 4 881 | 2 326.4 | 180.1 | 272 | 5 615 | 212.7 | 56.2 |
| Vallejo-Fairfield, CA ............ | 598 | D | D | D | 296 | 10 357 | 8 377.3 | 578.9 | 731 | 12 523 | 573.3 | 153.4 |
| Victoria, TX ........................ | 198 | D | D | D | 99 | 5 007 | 11 902.9 | 346.6 | 242 | 3 777 | 155.8 | 41.7 |
| Vineland-Millville-Bridgeton, NJ..................................... | 231 | D | D | D | 175 | 9 037 | 2 591.4 | 341.6 | 262 | 3 263 | 155.1 | 40.0 |

1. Establishments subject to federal tax.

| Area name | Health care and social assistance,[1] 2007 | | | | Other services,[1] 2007 | | | | Federal funds and grants, 2009–2010 Expenditures (mil dol) | | | |
|---|---|---|---|---|---|---|---|---|---|---|---|---|
| | | | | | | | | | | Direct payments for individuals | | |
| | Number of establishments | Number of employees | Receipts (mil dol) | Annual payroll (mil dol) | Number of establishments | Number of employees | Receipts (mil dol) | Annual payroll (mil dol) | Total | Social Security and government retirement | Medicare | Food stamps and Supplemental Security Income |
| | 159 | 160 | 161 | 162 | 163 | 164 | 165 | 166 | 167 | 168 | 169 | 170 |
| Sacramento—Arden-Arcade—Roseville, CA .. | 5 027 | 96 068 | 12 292.4 | 4 739.2 | 3 314 | 28 694 | 4 276.2 | 1 121.0 | 32 388.0 | 5 596.7 | 2 668.6 | 786.4 |
| Saginaw-Saginaw Township North, MI | 584 | 16 811 | 1 512.5 | 605.3 | 369 | 2 191 | 178.2 | 46.5 | 1 822.0 | 749.9 | 366.7 | 145.4 |
| St. Cloud, MN | 487 | 15 066 | 1 357.3 | 637.4 | 450 | 2 917 | 216.5 | 62.0 | 1 217.3 | 513.9 | 200.2 | 30.0 |
| St. George, UT | 393 | 6 648 | 628.5 | 250.2 | 198 | 1 116 | 95.0 | 27.4 | 1 063.0 | 435.9 | 120.4 | 18.5 |
| St. Joseph, MO-KS | 352 | 8 067 | 744.7 | 298.8 | 235 | 1 391 | 120.4 | 40.7 | 959.9 | 374.6 | 220.9 | 48.9 |
| St. Louis, MO-IL | 7 544 | 170 320 | 15 882.5 | 6 161.2 | 5 193 | 35 614 | 3 393.0 | 1 003.8 | 34 277.1 | 8 588.8 | 4 849.7 | 1 079.3 |
| Salem, OR | 1 047 | 17 339 | 1 580.1 | 655.6 | 596 | 2 876 | 235.9 | 70.3 | 4 403.2 | 1 106.7 | 448.1 | 159.9 |
| Salinas, CA | 970 | 13 789 | 1 876.6 | 723.7 | 556 | 3 651 | 425.9 | 104.6 | 3 298.5 | 932.2 | 553.5 | 91.2 |
| Salisbury, MD | 386 | 8 982 | 823.2 | 368.0 | 207 | 1 303 | 112.1 | 32.0 | 1 054.9 | 352.7 | 339.7 | 38.8 |
| Salt Lake City, UT | 2 844 | 55 193 | 5 899.6 | 2 256.9 | 2 059 | 14 359 | 1 381.6 | 383.3 | 9 696.7 | 2 187.2 | 1 579.4 | 230.4 |
| San Angelo, TX | 260 | 6 778 | 590.2 | 245.3 | 214 | 1 170 | 107.2 | 26.8 | 1 016.3 | 355.2 | 152.9 | 39.9 |
| San Antonio-New Braunfels, TX | 4 849 | 109 941 | 10 646.6 | 3 893.2 | 3 063 | 21 362 | 1 732.3 | 509.8 | 23 110.7 | 6 821.9 | 2 454.8 | 850.4 |
| San Diego-Carlsbad-San Marcos, CA | 7 924 | 133 893 | 15 954.7 | 5 872.9 | 5 176 | 37 084 | 3 732.5 | 1 015.3 | 37 302.9 | 7 771.6 | 4 652.8 | 790.1 |
| Sandusky, OH | 195 | 4 986 | 434.3 | 162.8 | 155 | 815 | 49.6 | 14.5 | 666.7 | 297.9 | 153.9 | 23.6 |
| San Francisco-Oakland-Fremont, CA | 13 103 | 221 320 | 28 727.4 | 11 570.0 | 8 537 | 59 689 | 12 556.2 | 2 072.7 | 40 303.3 | 9 748.0 | 7 459.6 | 1 259.6 |
| Oakland-Fremont-Hayward, CA Div. | 6 975 | 118 515 | 15 333.8 | 6 289.8 | 4 270 | 28 823 | 3 413.6 | 946.9 | 21 436.0 | 5 551.9 | 4 046.2 | 768.4 |
| San Francisco-San Mateo-Redwood City, CA Div. | 6 128 | 102 805 | 13 393.6 | 5 280.3 | 4 267 | 30 866 | 9 142.6 | 1 125.8 | 18 867.3 | 4 196.0 | 3 413.4 | 491.3 |
| San Jose-Sunnyvale-Santa Clara, CA | 5 161 | 88 995 | 12 403.9 | 4 736.6 | 2 970 | 19 637 | 2 838.4 | 664.1 | 16 250.0 | 3 352.8 | 2 115.6 | 474.5 |
| San Luis Obispo-Paso Robles, CA | 864 | 14 341 | 1 341.2 | 546.4 | 464 | 2 808 | 222.0 | 60.3 | 1 783.4 | 769.8 | 416.5 | 44.5 |
| Santa Barbara-Santa Maria-Goleta, CA | 1 322 | 19 124 | 2 076.4 | 784.0 | 767 | 5 005 | 816.9 | 141.4 | 3 677.4 | 1 037.4 | 621.1 | 91.6 |
| Santa Cruz-Watsonville, CA . | 863 | 11 416 | 1 441.4 | 505.0 | 452 | 2 702 | 258.2 | 72.1 | 1 598.2 | 550.8 | 387.8 | 56.7 |
| Santa Fe, NM | 518 | 8 465 | 809.4 | 318.0 | 341 | 1 849 | 231.0 | 54.1 | 2 153.9 | 470.9 | 117.4 | 28.7 |
| Santa Rosa-Petaluma, CA.... | 1 516 | 23 219 | 2 623.9 | 1 065.9 | 873 | 4 877 | 508.1 | 138.8 | 3 142.9 | 1 300.7 | 800.3 | 86.8 |
| Savannah, GA | 767 | 20 019 | 2 012.8 | 825.9 | 538 | 3 467 | 306.5 | 91.1 | 7 185.6 | 1 002.3 | 481.0 | 172.6 |
| Scranton--Wilkes-Barre, PA.. | 1 761 | 43 009 | 3 621.4 | 1 482.7 | 1 034 | 5 467 | 429.8 | 114.6 | 5 883.8 | 2 071.6 | 1 750.2 | 187.4 |
| Seattle-Tacoma-Bellevue, WA | 10 071 | 189 085 | 21 143.3 | 8 376.0 | 6 953 | 43 575 | 6 464.1 | 1 357.4 | 33 849.9 | 8 520.3 | 3 411.8 | 1 062.3 |
| Seattle-Bellevue-Everett, WA Div. | 8 191 | 147 038 | 16 748.1 | 6 594.7 | 5 652 | 35 082 | 5 661.0 | 1 106.2 | 21 905.7 | 6 023.9 | 2 674.5 | 748.0 |
| Tacoma, WA Div | 1 880 | 42 047 | 4 395.2 | 1 781.3 | 1 301 | 8 493 | 803.1 | 251.2 | 11 944.2 | 2 496.4 | 737.4 | 314.3 |
| Sebastian-Vero Beach, FL.... | 446 | 7 230 | 836.4 | 300.9 | 264 | 1 169 | 97.0 | 26.7 | 1 224.1 | 654.7 | 422.4 | 26.9 |
| Sheboygan, WI | 292 | 6 709 | 501.4 | 242.7 | 217 | 1 093 | 76.8 | 20.2 | 765.1 | 334.6 | 141.0 | 18.9 |
| Sherman-Denison, TX | 382 | 8 254 | 706.2 | 279.6 | 165 | 820 | 59.1 | 16.6 | 868.6 | 401.2 | 214.3 | 37.4 |
| Shreveport-Bossier City, LA . | 1 033 | 28 793 | 2 713.9 | 1 122.7 | 606 | 4 172 | 316.2 | 89.5 | 3 640.2 | 1 181.0 | 667.8 | 210.2 |
| Sioux City, IA-NE-SD | 424 | 9 421 | 834.8 | 325.4 | 270 | 1 736 | 142.1 | 42.6 | 1 304.1 | 388.9 | 224.3 | 38.0 |
| Sioux Falls, SD | 599 | 22 420 | 2 079.8 | 952.0 | 456 | 2 690 | 227.0 | 62.2 | 1 894.1 | 607.9 | 190.6 | 38.4 |
| South Bend-Mishawaka, IN-MI | 728 | 18 605 | 1 990.8 | 718.8 | 581 | 4 088 | 431.2 | 102.9 | 3 311.7 | 885.6 | 469.8 | 117.5 |
| Spartanburg, SC | 510 | 13 349 | 1 287.4 | 520.8 | 433 | 2 920 | 283.9 | 69.8 | 1 826.7 | 951.9 | 320.5 | 93.8 |
| Spokane, WA | 1 424 | 33 424 | 3 273.7 | 1 325.9 | 863 | 5 436 | 479.1 | 132.2 | 4 074.6 | 1 547.5 | 616.2 | 199.1 |
| Springfield, IL | 477 | D | D | D | 501 | 3 555 | 387.4 | 109.6 | 5 593.0 | 614.6 | 333.0 | 70.0 |
| Springfield, MA | 1 778 | 49 008 | 4 274.5 | 1 849.1 | 1 268 | 7 575 | 627.2 | 185.4 | 5 994.5 | 1 959.1 | 1 294.3 | 411.1 |
| Springfield, MO | 981 | 30 796 | 2 692.2 | 1 152.4 | 851 | 5 346 | 465.0 | 133.8 | 2 936.9 | 1 339.5 | 510.3 | 127.7 |
| Springfield, OH | 319 | 8 186 | 619.8 | 258.2 | 237 | 1 402 | 188.1 | 38.4 | 1 247.9 | 511.9 | 288.8 | 64.5 |
| State College, PA | 332 | 6 543 | 549.7 | 238.6 | 228 | 1 270 | 100.7 | 27.6 | 1 405.5 | 336.6 | 165.5 | 19.1 |
| Steubenville-Weirton, WV-OH | 306 | 7 421 | 547.3 | 226.1 | 207 | 1 016 | 61.2 | 16.7 | 1 287.0 | 589.5 | 370.1 | 65.6 |
| Stockton, CA | 1 351 | 26 658 | 3 045.8 | 1 141.3 | 879 | 5 576 | 462.8 | 144.6 | 4 164.3 | 1 413.7 | 851.2 | 287.4 |
| Sumter, SC | 180 | 4 812 | 469.3 | 172.7 | 152 | 1 141 | 69.7 | 21.7 | 1 422.2 | 401.7 | 121.4 | 78.0 |
| Syracuse, NY | 1 658 | 42 157 | 4 003.5 | 1 689.2 | 1 158 | 7 158 | 629.1 | 177.8 | 6 233.8 | 2 021.2 | 948.9 | 239.4 |
| Tallahassee, FL | 783 | 19 119 | 1 879.5 | 713.5 | 721 | 4 825 | 727.3 | 168.1 | 9 141.2 | 900.3 | 548.5 | 153.8 |
| Tampa-St. Petersburg-Clearwater, FL | 7 869 | 147 093 | 16 779.4 | 6 161.0 | 5 037 | 31 222 | 2 816.9 | 781.2 | 26 756.0 | 9 642.6 | 7 343.4 | 1 026.2 |
| Terre Haute, IN | 477 | 10 700 | 1 051.3 | 353.2 | 284 | 1 811 | 133.1 | 36.3 | 1 548.2 | 563.4 | 340.2 | 63.4 |
| Texarkana, TX-Texarkana, AR | 373 | 8 177 | 736.6 | 290.9 | 193 | 1 214 | 93.7 | 26.5 | 1 482.9 | 504.7 | 273.1 | 77.5 |
| Toledo, OH | 1 698 | 48 747 | 4 266.3 | 1 830.8 | 1 176 | 7 730 | 687.5 | 181.6 | 5 031.9 | 1 769.6 | 1 309.4 | 317.7 |
| Topeka, KS | 593 | 18 560 | 1 465.1 | 651.6 | 489 | 3 159 | 303.2 | 85.6 | 3 278.0 | 883.0 | 318.8 | 69.5 |
| Trenton-Ewing, NJ | 1 147 | 26 724 | 2 609.3 | 1 180.7 | 860 | 6 084 | 828.6 | 214.7 | 6 657.9 | 1 020.4 | 810.3 | 91.2 |
| Tucson, AZ | 2 672 | 51 151 | 5 459.8 | 2 073.5 | 1 494 | 12 045 | 1 020.6 | 289.4 | 14 248.6 | 3 301.3 | 1 318.0 | 381.9 |
| Tulsa, OK | 2 622 | 53 658 | 5 098.5 | 2 001.8 | 1 502 | 8 672 | 926.6 | 228.3 | 6 426.0 | 2 693.1 | 1 268.7 | 327.7 |
| Tuscaloosa, AL | 422 | 12 490 | 1 066.5 | 494.1 | 257 | 1 789 | 137.5 | 39.0 | 1 920.5 | 638.8 | 332.0 | 112.0 |
| Tyler, TX | 636 | 19 044 | 2 002.7 | 784.8 | 334 | 2 556 | 192.7 | 71.9 | 1 498.6 | 640.5 | 307.9 | 66.0 |
| Utica-Rome, NY | 727 | 22 040 | 1 606.9 | 754.0 | 513 | 3 534 | 223.8 | 66.2 | 2 843.0 | 1 047.0 | 559.4 | 124.5 |
| Valdosta, GA | 359 | 7 813 | 638.7 | 260.9 | 190 | 867 | 69.4 | 22.6 | 1 241.8 | 363.7 | 165.4 | 77.9 |
| Vallejo-Fairfield, CA | 861 | 18 135 | 2 136.5 | 895.9 | 541 | 3 240 | 324.0 | 92.5 | 3 454.6 | 1 261.9 | 407.1 | 118.6 |
| Victoria, TX | 364 | 7 029 | 635.6 | 252.9 | 212 | 1 417 | 134.2 | 38.7 | 846.5 | 340.3 | 178.3 | 49.1 |
| Vineland-Millville-Bridgeton, NJ | 399 | 8 351 | 820.8 | 333.3 | 273 | 1 439 | 103.0 | 31.1 | 1 295.5 | 434.9 | 354.9 | 63.3 |

1. Establishments subject to federal tax.

## Table C. Metropolitan Areas — Federal Funds, Residential Construction and Local Government Finances

| Area name | Federal funds and grants, 2009–2010 (cont.) | | | | | | | Value of residential construction authorized by building permits, 2011 | | Local government finances, 2007 | | | | |
| | Expenditures (mil dol) (cont.) | | | | | | | | | General revenue | | | | |
| | Procurement contract awards | | | Grants | | | | | | | | Taxes | | |
| | | | | | | | | | | | | | Per capita[1] (dollars) | |
| | Salaries and wages | Defense | Other | Medicaid and other health-related | Nutrition and family welfare | Education | Other | New construction ($1,000) | Number of housing units | Total (mil dol) | Inter-governmental (mil dol) | Total (mil dol) | Total | Property |
| | 171 | 172 | 173 | 174 | 175 | 176 | 177 | 178 | 179 | 180 | 181 | 182 | 183 | 184 |
| Sacramento—Arden-Arcade—Roseville, CA ... | 1 258.0 | 4 694.0 | 488.7 | 2 822.1 | 2 812.7 | 3 074.1 | 7 628.0 | 599 810 | 2 491 | 12 365.1 | 5 339.3 | 3 593.5 | 1 718 | 1 250 |
| Saginaw-Saginaw Township North, MI | 102.1 | 16.2 | 31.3 | 262.1 | 58.9 | 19.0 | 55.0 | 22 763 | 177 | 749.6 | 432.9 | 168.2 | 831 | 732 |
| St. Cloud, MN | 128.5 | 1.0 | 56.7 | 145.4 | 29.5 | 9.5 | 15.5 | 57 644 | 368 | 700.6 | 350.7 | 171.0 | 921 | 821 |
| St. George, UT | 377.3 | 0.4 | 27.3 | 27.9 | 11.5 | 4.2 | 17.9 | 166 770 | 893 | 442.8 | 162.8 | 155.0 | 1 158 | 767 |
| St. Joseph, MO-KS | 55.1 | 15.2 | 11.3 | 141.7 | 13.9 | 7.8 | 27.9 | 19 135 | 118 | 356.0 | 132.5 | 136.5 | 1 107 | 738 |
| St. Louis, MO-IL | 3 503.0 | 9 200.0 | 1 003.6 | 3 653.4 | 402.0 | 188.9 | 1 190.5 | 827 350 | 4 407 | 9 708.2 | 3 240.8 | 4 387.9 | 1 565 | 1 087 |
| Salem, OR | 264.8 | 29.4 | 39.4 | 500.6 | 268.0 | 300.5 | 1 189.4 | 82 731 | 431 | 1 336.4 | 696.3 | 376.1 | 973 | 839 |
| Salinas, CA | 588.4 | 385.9 | 170.6 | 285.9 | 114.4 | 35.1 | 93.0 | 38 140 | 156 | 2 775.3 | 1 150.3 | 709.4 | 1 740 | 1 280 |
| Salisbury, MD | 45.6 | 14.1 | 12.5 | 144.6 | 27.2 | 11.5 | 26.7 | 26 032 | 169 | 466.8 | 215.7 | 157.0 | 1 313 | 764 |
| Salt Lake City, UT | 1 280.0 | 944.9 | 308.1 | 1 146.3 | 236.3 | 230.7 | 1 350.0 | 577 123 | 3 457 | 3 574.8 | 1 081.5 | 1 479.5 | 1 345 | 918 |
| San Angelo, TX | 205.4 | 64.0 | 5.5 | 112.7 | 22.8 | 3.8 | 16.9 | 24 414 | 145 | 298.8 | 127.6 | 122.6 | 1 135 | 849 |
| San Antonio-New Braunfels, TX | 4 647.3 | 4 014.7 | 609.1 | 2 319.4 | 360.0 | 130.9 | 353.0 | 1 005 586 | 7 127 | 7 279.7 | 2 504.1 | 2 880.3 | 1 447 | 1 208 |
| San Diego-Carlsbad-San Marcos, CA | 4 765.8 | 11 593.0 | 1 288.7 | 3 866.8 | 677.8 | 239.4 | 990.5 | 1 089 286 | 5 370 | 16 065.9 | 6 632.0 | 5 448.0 | 1 831 | 1 394 |
| Sandusky, OH | 33.6 | 25.3 | 35.8 | 47.4 | 16.2 | 5.5 | 21.0 | 8 940 | 48 | 382.6 | 124.9 | 143.7 | 1 859 | 1 381 |
| San Francisco-Oakland-Fremont, CA | 3 330.8 | 1 586.8 | 4 836.0 | 7 369.9 | 858.4 | 412.3 | 2 633.7 | 1 534 982 | 5 783 | 29 510.4 | 10 613.2 | 10 634.5 | 2 530 | 1 716 |
| Oakland-Fremont-Hayward, CA Div | 1 581.8 | 604.4 | 3 307.2 | 3 306.1 | 508.0 | 216.3 | 1 140.6 | 707 513 | 3 033 | 17 127.4 | 6 717.7 | 5 452.8 | 2 195 | 1 558 |
| San Francisco-San Mateo-Redwood City, CA Div.. | 1 749.0 | 982.4 | 1 528.9 | 4 063.7 | 350.4 | 196.0 | 1 493.1 | 827 468 | 2 750 | 12 383.1 | 3 895.5 | 5 181.6 | 3 012 | 1 945 |
| San Jose-Sunnyvale-Santa Clara, CA | 965.3 | 4 727.3 | 1 076.4 | 2 027.3 | 346.7 | 119.6 | 793.4 | 709 971 | 3 097 | 11 689.2 | 3 794.5 | 4 423.8 | 2 453 | 1 836 |
| San Luis Obispo-Paso Robles, CA | 126.0 | 56.0 | 25.0 | 176.0 | 70.7 | 13.3 | 44.4 | 92 274 | 306 | 1 183.8 | 434.3 | 521.1 | 1 986 | 1 598 |
| Santa Barbara-Santa Maria-Goleta, CA | 416.1 | 701.1 | 65.0 | 332.1 | 93.3 | 38.4 | 201.3 | 80 063 | 231 | 2 499.6 | 956.2 | 791.8 | 1 959 | 1 459 |
| Santa Cruz-Watsonville, CA .. | 53.2 | 9.7 | 19.4 | 275.4 | 54.0 | 21.4 | 116.7 | 35 096 | 208 | 1 409.1 | 614.7 | 454.6 | 1 806 | 1 403 |
| Santa Fe, NM | 136.2 | 45.2 | 43.5 | 254.6 | 123.5 | 151.5 | 743.4 | 12 536 | 94 | 511.3 | 237.0 | 184.0 | 1 287 | 676 |
| Santa Rosa-Petaluma, CA..... | 203.3 | 47.1 | 78.1 | 359.9 | 84.6 | 26.4 | 103.0 | 131 369 | 632 | 2 520.7 | 903.4 | 933.6 | 2 010 | 1 589 |
| Savannah, GA | 4 120.0 | 735.9 | 33.3 | 290.7 | 75.2 | 32.7 | 48.3 | 193 019 | 1 625 | 1 837.4 | 356.0 | 665.4 | 2 020 | 1 229 |
| Scranton--Wilkes-Barre, PA ... | 378.7 | 374.1 | 138.6 | 617.0 | 104.1 | 16.3 | 79.6 | 81 763 | 439 | 1 760.0 | 694.0 | 737.4 | 1 342 | 984 |
| Seattle-Tacoma-Bellevue, WA | 8 503.9 | 3 712.7 | 1 080.6 | 4 499.1 | 522.2 | 184.9 | 1 830.8 | 2 214 497 | 11 230 | 15 920.4 | 5 052.5 | 6 142.1 | 1 856 | 1 024 |
| Seattle-Bellevue-Everett, WA Div | 2 219.0 | 3 067.7 | 936.9 | 3 774.8 | 388.0 | 128.0 | 1 553.8 | 1 733 744 | 8 664 | 12 963.1 | 3 851.1 | 5 048.3 | 1 990 | 1 063 |
| Tacoma, WA Div | 6 284.9 | 644.9 | 143.8 | 724.3 | 134.3 | 56.9 | 277.0 | 480 753 | 2 566 | 2 957.3 | 1 201.4 | 1 093.9 | 1 415 | 896 |
| Sebastian-Vero Beach, FL... | 33.2 | 0.1 | 10.4 | 38.1 | 17.6 | 6.6 | 5.8 | 126 231 | 372 | 581.3 | 109.6 | 324.0 | 2 458 | 1 835 |
| Sheboygan, WI | 28.1 | 38.1 | 90.0 | 78.4 | 16.4 | 5.6 | 4.7 | 15 459 | 73 | 493.2 | 225.5 | 180.9 | 1 580 | 1 523 |
| Sherman-Denison, TX | 25.3 | 6.5 | 10.0 | 123.9 | 16.0 | 2.7 | 7.8 | 10 054 | 76 | 363.4 | 126.4 | 155.6 | 1 311 | 1 087 |
| Shreveport-Bossier City, LA... | 623.1 | 159.8 | 51.1 | 471.2 | 81.4 | 41.1 | 60.2 | 231 436 | 1 401 | 1 399.9 | 501.5 | 690.8 | 1 782 | 773 |
| Sioux City, IA-NE-SD | 97.2 | 282.0 | 20.2 | 138.8 | 26.6 | 8.4 | 21.4 | 40 308 | 176 | 563.8 | 234.6 | 225.0 | 1 576 | 1 152 |
| Sioux Falls, SD | 219.2 | 43.2 | 105.8 | 136.4 | 21.0 | 4.3 | 133.5 | 148 187 | 1 129 | 621.7 | 172.8 | 333.9 | 1 470 | 979 |
| South Bend-Mishawaka, IN-MI | 153.0 | 1 124.3 | 30.7 | 305.7 | 42.5 | 12.3 | 88.7 | 68 581 | 467 | 1 024.5 | 447.0 | 349.8 | 1 105 | 1 047 |
| Spartanburg, SC | 85.6 | 4.8 | 10.7 | 239.6 | 37.1 | 19.4 | 22.2 | 61 288 | 532 | 1 277.3 | 308.7 | 290.4 | 1 054 | 930 |
| Spokane, WA | 486.6 | 237.7 | 134.2 | 482.5 | 91.6 | 32.6 | 129.8 | 257 698 | 1 785 | 1 575.8 | 697.5 | 548.2 | 1 202 | 709 |
| Springfield, IL | 273.0 | 25.2 | 32.9 | 282.4 | 396.1 | 940.2 | 2 563.2 | 71 720 | 391 | 703.6 | 275.4 | 294.0 | 1 423 | 1 249 |
| Springfield, MA | 504.7 | 106.5 | 148.1 | 987.3 | 147.3 | 65.5 | 212.3 | 108 339 | 512 | 2 455.1 | 1 318.8 | 895.3 | 1 312 | 1 282 |
| Springfield, MO | 266.1 | 8.9 | 49.1 | 380.3 | 52.2 | 26.8 | 70.6 | 148 290 | 1 304 | 1 129.9 | 390.1 | 448.9 | 1 069 | 592 |
| Springfield, OH | 72.3 | 22.3 | 5.4 | 188.8 | 27.6 | 11.8 | 28.5 | 14 749 | 142 | 580.8 | 303.3 | 164.6 | 1 172 | 789 |
| State College, PA | 72.0 | 236.8 | 68.0 | 179.8 | 22.9 | 11.9 | 192.3 | 46 699 | 259 | 400.8 | 139.2 | 181.2 | 1 253 | 907 |
| Steubenville-Weirton, WV-OH | 31.6 | 5.3 | 7.4 | 148.6 | 24.2 | 9.6 | 16.9 | 2 529 | 19 | 431.3 | 217.5 | 120.0 | 979 | 725 |
| Stockton, CA | 285.9 | 93.9 | 65.0 | 739.1 | 153.5 | 47.5 | 89.5 | 182 054 | 933 | 3 836.6 | 1 957.0 | 986.4 | 1 470 | 1 065 |
| Sumter, SC | 294.5 | 176.0 | 76.3 | 180.0 | 28.4 | 13.9 | 15.1 | 36 527 | 345 | 256.0 | 124.9 | 98.3 | 946 | 684 |
| Syracuse, NY | 396.9 | 1 191.0 | 214.4 | 750.9 | 169.9 | 60.5 | 143.1 | 150 812 | 1 220 | 3 396.8 | 1 536.9 | 1 316.2 | 2 040 | 1 452 |
| Tallahassee, FL | 208.5 | 42.3 | 40.9 | 840.5 | 644.2 | 2 166.6 | 3 343.5 | 127 660 | 1 039 | 1 355.6 | 555.3 | 430.0 | 1 220 | 891 |
| Tampa-St. Petersburg-Clearwater, FL | 2 400.1 | 2 146.8 | 1 042.0 | 1 538.0 | 387.1 | 194.4 | 429.2 | 1 424 723 | 6 342 | 11 250.7 | 3 906.6 | 4 592.7 | 1 686 | 1 317 |
| Terre Haute, IN | 146.0 | 25.6 | 58.2 | 241.3 | 31.6 | 6.1 | 22.0 | 32 589 | 423 | 500.3 | 219.1 | 135.5 | 800 | 695 |
| Texarkana, TX-Texarkana, AR | 172.1 | 133.4 | 12.9 | 216.0 | 26.5 | 7.0 | 21.0 | 26 956 | 361 | 391.7 | 196.8 | 122.5 | 912 | 648 |
| Toledo, OH | 291.9 | 38.5 | 53.0 | 734.3 | 126.6 | 59.5 | 126.1 | 105 458 | 603 | 2 991.3 | 1 130.6 | 1 237.8 | 1 901 | 1 213 |
| Topeka, KS | 316.1 | 24.9 | 58.2 | 270.5 | 146.0 | 227.5 | 898.3 | 45 370 | 264 | 852.0 | 320.2 | 344.7 | 1 507 | 1 173 |
| Trenton-Ewing, NJ | 320.8 | 177.4 | 175.7 | 690.6 | 349.7 | 578.2 | 2 175.8 | 62 982 | 400 | 1 979.0 | 683.1 | 990.7 | 2 711 | 2 675 |
| Tucson, AZ | 1 074.4 | 5 268.8 | 388.9 | 1 668.4 | 174.1 | 107.4 | 341.9 | 458 236 | 2 242 | 3 481.7 | 1 650.1 | 1 289.2 | 1 333 | 911 |
| Tulsa, OK | 462.0 | 251.7 | 209.3 | 628.1 | 170.8 | 74.5 | 181.9 | 473 139 | 3 565 | 2 611.2 | 945.7 | 1 080.9 | 1 193 | 646 |
| Tuscaloosa, AL | 113.4 | 122.9 | 152.0 | 228.7 | 36.6 | 21.5 | 82.9 | 99 338 | 743 | 940.5 | 286.9 | 173.6 | 846 | 330 |
| Tyler, TX | 80.8 | 56.3 | 30.8 | 223.4 | 25.1 | 8.5 | 17.5 | 33 578 | 262 | 557.5 | 164.4 | 281.6 | 1 417 | 1 075 |
| Utica-Rome, NY | 236.6 | 162.1 | 24.0 | 490.4 | 81.2 | 27.4 | 40.5 | 43 011 | 254 | 1 456.9 | 721.1 | 524.4 | 1 778 | 1 162 |
| Valdosta, GA | 286.4 | 89.1 | 5.1 | 135.3 | 34.1 | 12.8 | 12.6 | 51 963 | 660 | 401.3 | 173.1 | 166.7 | 1 281 | 653 |
| Vallejo-Fairfield, CA | 689.1 | 363.8 | 49.4 | 264.2 | 71.7 | 24.2 | 163.2 | 81 456 | 387 | 2 176.4 | 1 047.1 | 670.5 | 1 641 | 1 187 |
| Victoria, TX | 41.5 | 16.9 | 6.0 | 138.5 | 22.7 | 4.7 | 6.3 | 23 921 | 148 | 552.0 | 112.4 | 208.7 | 1 834 | 1 545 |
| Vineland-Millville-Bridgeton, NJ | 61.2 | 42.0 | 14.4 | 232.9 | 41.0 | 11.5 | 17.7 | 19 117 | 182 | 758.8 | 469.5 | 192.0 | 1 234 | 1 205 |

1. Based on the resident population estimated as of July 1 of the year shown.

# Table C. Metropolitan Areas — Local Government Finances, Government Employment, and Voting

| Area name | Local government finances, 2007 (cont.) | | | | | | | | | Government employment, 2011 | | | Presidential election,[2] 2012 | | |
| | Direct general expenditure | | | | | | | Debt outstanding | | | | | Percent of vote cast: | | |
| | | | Percent of total for: | | | | | | | | | | | | |
| | Total (mil dol) | Per capita[1] (dollars) | Education | Health and hospitals | Police protection | Public welfare | Highways | Total (mil dol) | Per capita[1] (dollars) | Federal civilian | Federal military | State and local | Democratic | Republican | All other |
|---|---|---|---|---|---|---|---|---|---|---|---|---|---|---|---|
| | 185 | 186 | 187 | 188 | 189 | 190 | 191 | 192 | 193 | 194 | 195 | 196 | 197 | 198 | 199 |
| Sacramento—Arden-Arcade—Roseville, CA.. | 12 885.3 | 6 162 | 34.6 | 5.1 | 5.0 | 7.6 | 6.8 | 20 284.8 | 9 700 | 14 089 | 4 180 | 230 920 | 53.1 | 44.2 | 2.7 |
| Saginaw-Saginaw Township North, MI | 770.9 | 3 811 | 48.9 | 13.1 | 4.2 | 0.7 | 5.5 | 503.7 | 2 490 | 1 513 | 388 | 9 919 | 55.5 | 43.6 | 1.0 |
| St. Cloud, MN | 688.3 | 3 709 | 42.4 | 7.1 | 4.7 | 4.5 | 12.6 | 1 258.3 | 6 781 | 2 140 | 720 | 11 716 | 42.5 | 54.9 | 2.6 |
| St. George, UT | 406.0 | 3 035 | 48.1 | 2.7 | 6.5 | 0.0 | 5.3 | 645.9 | 4 828 | 553 | 643 | 6 660 | 15.4 | 82.8 | 1.8 |
| St. Joseph, MO-KS | 355.6 | 2 883 | 51.1 | 1.7 | 4.1 | 0.1 | 6.0 | 518.3 | 4 202 | 620 | 466 | 9 269 | 39.8 | 57.8 | 2.4 |
| St. Louis, MO-IL | 9 511.1 | 3 392 | 50.8 | 2.5 | 6.7 | 0.5 | 5.3 | 11 371.8 | 4 056 | 30 046 | 14 146 | 142 922 | 52.5 | 45.8 | 1.7 |
| Salem, OR | 1 367.8 | 3 537 | 53.1 | 6.6 | 5.3 | 0.3 | 4.7 | 1 736.6 | 4 491 | 1 490 | 1 114 | 38 145 | 46.7 | 50.1 | 3.2 |
| Salinas, CA | 2 680.5 | 6 576 | 35.2 | 21.3 | 4.5 | 4.9 | 4.8 | 1 456.7 | 3 574 | 5 938 | 6 491 | 25 118 | 67.1 | 30.3 | 2.6 |
| Salisbury, MD | 455.6 | 3 809 | 57.5 | 0.9 | 4.8 | 3.9 | 4.3 | 271.1 | 2 267 | 365 | 431 | 10 318 | 47.2 | 50.9 | 1.9 |
| Salt Lake City, UT | 3 281.7 | 2 983 | 40.0 | 1.5 | 6.6 | 1.6 | 4.7 | 6 352.8 | 5 775 | 12 560 | 5 558 | 87 780 | 37.9 | 59.0 | 3.1 |
| San Angelo, TX | 287.2 | 2 657 | 53.7 | 3.9 | 6.3 | 0.3 | 3.0 | 218.1 | 2 017 | 1 440 | 3 699 | 7 612 | 25.1 | 73.4 | 1.5 |
| San Antonio-New Braunfels, TX | 7 423.0 | 3 729 | 52.6 | 11.1 | 5.0 | 1.0 | 2.7 | 16 637.3 | 8 358 | 35 526 | 35 945 | 125 041 | 45.3 | 53.3 | 1.4 |
| San Diego-Carlsbad-San Marcos, CA | 16 037.1 | 5 391 | 40.2 | 9.0 | 6.0 | 6.5 | 2.9 | 17 352.6 | 5 833 | 47 046 | 107 893 | 178 469 | 52.6 | 45.0 | 2.4 |
| Sandusky, OH | 363.6 | 4 702 | 49.0 | 2.2 | 5.8 | 6.0 | 4.2 | 235.3 | 3 043 | 306 | 195 | 5 209 | 55.3 | 43.0 | 1.7 |
| San Francisco-Oakland-Fremont, CA | 29 792.9 | 7 087 | 26.1 | 13.6 | 5.6 | 6.0 | 3.5 | 45 709.5 | 10 873 | 33 913 | 9 210 | 265 055 | 75.4 | 21.8 | 2.8 |
| Oakland-Fremont-Hayward, CA Div | 17 899.6 | 7 206 | 28.1 | 11.5 | 5.3 | 5.4 | 3.7 | 27 119.1 | 10 918 | 14 721 | 5 591 | 136 289 | 73.6 | 23.7 | 2.8 |
| San Francisco-San Mateo-Redwood City, CA Div | 11 893.4 | 6 915 | 23.1 | 16.8 | 6.0 | 7.0 | 3.3 | 18 590.5 | 10 808 | 19 192 | 3 619 | 128 766 | 77.7 | 19.3 | 3.0 |
| San Jose-Sunnyvale-Santa Clara, CA | 11 417.7 | 6 330 | 33.0 | 16.3 | 5.0 | 5.5 | 3.1 | 15 026.0 | 8 331 | 10 195 | 3 300 | 78 604 | 69.8 | 27.5 | 2.7 |
| San Luis Obispo-Paso Robles, CA | 1 122.2 | 4 276 | 38.3 | 5.7 | 6.4 | 8.8 | 5.0 | 704.1 | 2 683 | 612 | 490 | 19 818 | 48.8 | 47.7 | 3.5 |
| Santa Barbara-Santa Maria-Goleta, CA | 2 477.1 | 6 129 | 37.4 | 14.0 | 5.5 | 5.4 | 4.7 | 1 475.7 | 3 651 | 3 997 | 3 410 | 30 458 | 57.6 | 39.6 | 2.8 |
| Santa Cruz-Watsonville, CA | 1 495.0 | 5 939 | 37.8 | 6.0 | 4.3 | 8.0 | 3.1 | 1 194.1 | 4 743 | 514 | 421 | 17 440 | 75.6 | 20.0 | 4.4 |
| Santa Fe, NM | 462.7 | 3 237 | 43.5 | 3.0 | 6.5 | 3.1 | 5.8 | 626.5 | 4 382 | 1 030 | 404 | 16 666 | 73.5 | 22.4 | 4.1 |
| Santa Rosa-Petaluma, CA.... | 2 662.5 | 5 733 | 35.4 | 8.3 | 6.4 | 4.9 | 4.3 | 2 522.0 | 5 430 | 1 568 | 1 411 | 24 775 | 71.1 | 25.3 | 3.6 |
| Savannah, GA | 1 841.7 | 5 592 | 26.0 | 31.0 | 5.7 | 0.2 | 4.1 | 1 351.0 | 4 102 | 3 206 | 7 423 | 19 908 | 48.3 | 50.7 | 1.1 |
| Scranton--Wilkes-Barre, PA.. | 1 850.3 | 3 368 | 50.1 | 0.3 | 3.2 | 3.8 | 4.3 | 2 109.4 | 3 839 | 4 355 | 1 465 | 26 786 | 56.0 | 42.7 | 1.3 |
| Seattle-Tacoma-Bellevue, WA | 15 163.6 | 4 582 | 34.2 | 9.4 | 4.9 | 0.7 | 4.7 | 26 380.5 | 7 972 | 36 730 | 51 474 | 227 454 | 63.6 | 34.0 | 2.4 |
| Seattle-Bellevue-Everett, WA Div | 12 137.2 | 4 786 | 31.4 | 10.8 | 4.9 | 0.7 | 4.5 | 22 184.6 | 8 747 | 23 502 | 13 909 | 182 184 | 66.0 | 31.5 | 2.4 |
| Tacoma, WA Div | 3 026.4 | 3 914 | 45.2 | 3.8 | 5.1 | 0.4 | 5.5 | 4 196.0 | 5 427 | 13 228 | 37 565 | 45 270 | 54.4 | 43.3 | 2.3 |
| Sebastian-Vero Beach, FL.... | 528.1 | 4 006 | 35.5 | 3.8 | 7.4 | 0.6 | 7.4 | 540.1 | 4 097 | 383 | 271 | 5 030 | 38.5 | 60.8 | 0.7 |
| Sheboygan, WI | 509.8 | 4 452 | 52.0 | 6.2 | 5.0 | 8.7 | 7.4 | 481.1 | 4 202 | 207 | 338 | 5 552 | 44.6 | 54.4 | 1.1 |
| Sherman-Denison, TX | 365.4 | 3 079 | 62.8 | 2.5 | 4.5 | 0.1 | 3.3 | 392.7 | 3 309 | 335 | 270 | 6 122 | 25.2 | 73.2 | 1.6 |
| Shreveport-Bossier City, LA | 1 329.4 | 3 430 | 49.7 | 1.4 | 7.7 | 0.0 | 3.7 | 1 303.1 | 3 362 | 4 816 | 7 583 | 29 509 | 44.2 | 54.7 | 1.2 |
| Sioux City, IA-NE-SD | 550.9 | 3 858 | 55.5 | 2.1 | 5.4 | 0.9 | 8.0 | 440.9 | 3 088 | 899 | 628 | 8 629 | 47.0 | 51.1 | 1.9 |
| Sioux Falls, SD | 633.3 | 2 788 | 47.1 | 1.8 | 5.3 | 0.6 | 7.1 | 677.5 | 2 982 | 2 562 | 1 545 | 10 039 | 42.7 | 55.4 | 2.0 |
| South Bend-Mishawaka, IN-MI | 1 086.4 | 3 431 | 52.1 | 1.6 | 4.5 | 4.0 | 2.8 | 1 075.8 | 3 397 | 1 091 | 1 054 | 15 899 | 49.6 | 49.0 | 1.4 |
| Spartanburg, SC | 1 311.4 | 4 760 | 35.2 | 42.2 | 3.2 | 0.4 | 1.5 | 2 196.7 | 7 973 | 466 | 1 227 | 18 854 | 37.7 | 60.9 | 1.3 |
| Spokane, WA | 1 516.3 | 3 324 | 49.0 | 4.6 | 5.4 | 0.1 | 5.0 | 957.6 | 2 099 | 4 603 | 4 272 | 30 670 | 45.7 | 51.5 | 2.8 |
| Springfield, IL | 678.9 | 3 286 | 54.4 | 1.2 | 8.2 | 1.8 | 6.0 | 1 083.5 | 5 245 | 1 960 | 484 | 26 413 | 44.0 | 53.9 | 2.1 |
| Springfield, MA | 2 453.2 | 3 594 | 60.9 | 0.6 | 4.6 | 0.5 | 3.4 | 2 059.7 | 3 017 | 5 567 | 2 007 | 50 020 | 65.1 | 32.6 | 2.4 |
| Springfield, MO | 1 107.5 | 2 637 | 50.6 | 7.4 | 8.0 | 0.8 | 9.7 | 1 408.4 | 3 353 | 2 528 | 1 541 | 25 127 | 33.1 | 64.8 | 2.1 |
| Springfield, OH | 533.2 | 3 795 | 49.5 | 6.3 | 6.0 | 8.4 | 3.9 | 240.3 | 1 711 | 577 | 351 | 6 543 | 48.8 | 49.6 | 1.6 |
| State College, PA | 425.6 | 2 942 | 51.8 | 4.4 | 3.0 | 7.7 | 5.2 | 425.5 | 2 942 | 443 | 486 | 45 055 | 49.1 | 48.8 | 2.1 |
| Steubenville-Weirton, WV-OH | 401.6 | 3 276 | 45.8 | 8.5 | 4.4 | 7.7 | 4.8 | 150.3 | 1 226 | 289 | 444 | 5 729 | 44.1 | 53.8 | 2.1 |
| Stockton, CA | 3 766.6 | 5 613 | 43.4 | 8.4 | 5.5 | 8.1 | 2.8 | 3 448.9 | 5 140 | 4 042 | 1 182 | 31 404 | 55.8 | 42.0 | 2.2 |
| Sumter, SC | 251.4 | 2 418 | 60.8 | 1.6 | 6.9 | 0.0 | 2.4 | 433.8 | 4 174 | 1 311 | 5 341 | 5 832 | 58.3 | 40.7 | 0.9 |
| Syracuse, NY | 3 517.6 | 5 451 | 48.9 | 3.6 | 3.3 | 10.4 | 4.8 | 3 224.4 | 4 997 | 4 732 | 1 263 | 49 126 | 57.6 | 40.6 | 1.8 |
| Tallahassee, FL | 1 366.3 | 3 878 | 44.0 | 1.1 | 6.7 | 0.1 | 9.9 | 3 225.4 | 9 155 | 1 937 | 825 | 59 458 | 59.9 | 39.1 | 1.0 |
| Tampa-St. Petersburg-Clearwater, FL | 10 560.7 | 3 877 | 40.6 | 2.3 | 7.3 | 2.3 | 3.6 | 12 459.9 | 4 574 | 22 572 | 12 680 | 124 522 | 51.0 | 47.9 | 1.1 |
| Terre Haute, IN | 546.5 | 3 227 | 50.2 | 4.6 | 2.9 | 2.0 | 3.9 | 387.4 | 2 287 | 1 346 | 595 | 11 344 | 44.8 | 53.1 | 2.1 |
| Texarkana, TX-Texarkana, AR | 375.5 | 2 798 | 65.5 | 0.5 | 5.8 | 0.2 | 3.7 | 440.7 | 3 284 | 4 928 | 408 | 8 701 | 29.0 | 70.0 | 1.0 |
| Toledo, OH | 3 079.3 | 4 730 | 42.4 | 6.6 | 5.6 | 5.8 | 4.8 | 2 810.0 | 4 317 | 2 500 | 1 809 | 46 063 | 59.8 | 38.4 | 1.9 |
| Topeka, KS | 836.3 | 3 657 | 54.8 | 1.8 | 5.7 | 0.3 | 4.2 | 1 208.8 | 5 286 | 3 746 | 1 243 | 24 648 | 44.9 | 52.7 | 2.4 |
| Trenton-Ewing, NJ | 2 085.4 | 5 706 | 53.1 | 1.0 | 5.4 | 4.4 | 1.3 | 1 899.1 | 5 197 | 2 407 | 794 | 45 697 | 68.0 | 30.8 | 1.2 |
| Tucson, AZ | 3 541.9 | 3 662 | 35.0 | 8.9 | 8.4 | 2.7 | 6.5 | 4 775.0 | 4 937 | 12 629 | 8 681 | 61 835 | 52.6 | 45.7 | 1.6 |
| Tulsa, OK | 2 623.3 | 2 896 | 51.8 | 2.9 | 5.4 | 1.0 | 3.7 | 4 063.4 | 4 486 | 4 710 | 3 960 | 48 793 | 33.9 | 66.1 | 0.0 |
| Tuscaloosa, AL | 979.3 | 4 772 | 32.5 | 41.0 | 4.0 | 0.0 | 5.1 | 616.7 | 3 005 | 1 731 | 1 086 | 23 555 | 45.3 | 53.6 | 1.1 |
| Tyler, TX | 599.0 | 3 015 | 63.3 | 5.0 | 4.6 | 0.4 | 3.7 | 786.9 | 3 960 | 861 | 484 | 12 094 | 27.0 | 72.0 | 1.0 |
| Utica-Rome, NY | 1 465.7 | 4 971 | 51.2 | 2.6 | 2.9 | 11.1 | 7.1 | 1 424.5 | 4 831 | 2 644 | 555 | 29 299 | 46.4 | 51.8 | 1.8 |
| Valdosta, GA | 427.8 | 3 287 | 53.0 | 8.2 | 6.0 | 0.5 | 8.9 | 68.6 | 527 | 1 195 | 4 931 | 11 769 | 43.8 | 55.3 | 0.8 |
| Vallejo-Fairfield, CA | 2 178.6 | 5 332 | 37.7 | 4.8 | 8.0 | 6.8 | 5.1 | 2 079.0 | 5 088 | 4 068 | 7 280 | 20 059 | 63.5 | 34.2 | 2.3 |
| Victoria, TX | 516.2 | 4 536 | 44.7 | 26.2 | 4.7 | 0.4 | 3.0 | 576.5 | 5 066 | 276 | 319 | 8 170 | 31.7 | 67.1 | 1.3 |
| Vineland-Millville-Bridgeton, NJ | 747.9 | 4 808 | 62.4 | 2.2 | 3.5 | 3.7 | 1.8 | 357.1 | 2 296 | 632 | 326 | 13 662 | 61.6 | 37.4 | 1.0 |

1. Based on the resident population estimated as of July 1 of the year shown.  2. © 2013 Election Data Services, Inc. All rights reserved.

## Table C. Metropolitan Areas — **Land Area and Population**

| CBSA/ DIV code[1] | Area name | Land area,[2] 2010 (sq km) | Total persons | Rank | Per square kilometer | White | Black | American Indian, Alaska Native | Asian and Pacific Islander | Percent Hispanic or Latino[3] | Under 5 years | 5 to 17 years | 18 to 24 years | 25 to 34 years | 35 to 44 years | 45 to 54 years |
|---|---|---|---|---|---|---|---|---|---|---|---|---|---|---|---|---|
| | | | Population 2012 | | | Race alone or in combination, not Hispanic or Latino (percent) | | | | | Age (percent) | | | | | |
| | | | | | | | | | | Population characteristics, 2011 | | | | | | |
| | | 1 | 2 | 3 | 4 | 5 | 6 | 7 | 8 | 9 | 10 | 11 | 12 | 13 | 14 | 15 |
| 47260 | Virginia Beach-Norfolk-Newport News, VA-NC ........ | 6 811 | 1 694 900 | 36 | 248.8 | 59.5 | 32.0 | 1.0 | 4.9 | 5.6 | 6.5 | 16.7 | 11.9 | 14.5 | 12.4 | 14.7 |
| 47300 | Visalia-Porterville, CA .......... | 12 495 | 451 977 | 111 | 36.2 | 33.2 | 1.6 | 1.3 | 4.1 | 61.3 | 9.2 | 23.1 | 10.8 | 14.0 | 12.3 | 11.7 |
| 47380 | Waco, TX ............................ | 2 686 | 238 707 | 188 | 88.9 | 59.4 | 15.1 | 0.7 | 2.0 | 24.2 | 7.0 | 18.1 | 15.0 | 12.8 | 11.2 | 12.5 |
| 47580 | Warner Robins, GA ............. | 973 | 146 136 | 275 | 150.2 | 61.9 | 29.8 | 0.8 | 3.7 | 6.2 | 7.1 | 19.2 | 9.6 | 14.6 | 13.2 | 15.0 |
| 47900 | Washington-Arlington-Alexandria, DC-VA-MD-WV. | 14 500 | 5 804 975 | 7 | 400.3 | 50.5 | 26.5 | 0.8 | 10.8 | 14.1 | 6.7 | 16.9 | 9.1 | 15.6 | 14.8 | 15.1 |
| 47900 | Bethesda-Rockvilee-Frederick, MD Div .............. | 2 982 | 1 244 291 | X | 417.3 | 56.3 | 16.6 | 0.6 | 13.5 | 15.6 | 6.5 | 17.5 | 7.8 | 13.4 | 14.3 | 15.7 |
| 47900 | Washington-Arlington-Alexandria, DC-VA-MD-WV Div ..................... | 11 517 | 4 560 684 | X | 396.0 | 48.9 | 29.3 | 0.8 | 10.1 | 13.7 | 6.8 | 16.8 | 9.5 | 16.1 | 14.9 | 14.9 |
| 47940 | Waterloo-Cedar Falls, IA ..... | 3 893 | 168 747 | 238 | 43.3 | 88.2 | 7.9 | 0.5 | 1.8 | 3.3 | 6.2 | 15.4 | 15.1 | 12.6 | 10.7 | 12.6 |
| 48140 | Wausau, WI ........................ | 4 001 | 134 735 | 293 | 33.7 | 91.0 | 1.1 | 0.8 | 5.9 | 2.3 | 6.4 | 17.7 | 7.8 | 12.4 | 12.7 | 15.5 |
| 48300 | Wenatchee-East Wenatchee, WA ..................... | 12 276 | 113 037 | 328 | 9.2 | 70.5 | 0.6 | 1.6 | 1.6 | 27.4 | 7.1 | 18.5 | 8.6 | 12.0 | 11.5 | 13.8 |
| 48540 | Wheeling, WV-OH .............. | 2 443 | 146 420 | 273 | 59.9 | 95.3 | 4.0 | 0.5 | 0.8 | 0.8 | 5.1 | 14.5 | 8.9 | 11.2 | 11.8 | 15.0 |
| 48620 | Wichita, KS ........................ | 10 746 | 628 242 | 86 | 58.5 | 76.1 | 8.8 | 2.0 | 4.1 | 11.8 | 7.6 | 19.2 | 9.3 | 13.7 | 12.1 | 14.0 |
| 48660 | Wichita Falls, TX ................ | 6 785 | 150 829 | 265 | 22.2 | 72.4 | 9.7 | 1.4 | 2.5 | 15.8 | 6.6 | 16.4 | 12.9 | 13.6 | 11.3 | 13.8 |
| 48700 | Williamsport, PA ................. | 3 182 | 117 168 | 320 | 36.8 | 93.2 | 5.5 | 0.5 | 0.9 | 1.5 | 5.5 | 15.1 | 10.8 | 11.5 | 11.7 | 15.0 |
| 48900 | Wilmington, NC .................. | 4 942 | 375 686 | 137 | 76.0 | 78.8 | 14.9 | 1.1 | 1.4 | 5.5 | 5.5 | 14.2 | 10.1 | 12.7 | 12.5 | 13.4 |
| 49020 | Winchester, VA-WV ............ | 2 753 | 130 907 | 296 | 47.6 | 85.7 | 5.9 | 0.7 | 1.7 | 7.6 | 6.2 | 17.6 | 8.7 | 12.3 | 13.2 | 15.4 |
| 49180 | Winston-Salem, NC ............. | 3 771 | 484 437 | 106 | 128.5 | 67.4 | 20.9 | 0.7 | 1.9 | 10.6 | 6.4 | 17.3 | 9.3 | 12.1 | 13.3 | 14.7 |
| 49340 | Worcester, MA ................... | 3 913 | 806 163 | 68 | 206.0 | 82.2 | 4.5 | 0.6 | 4.8 | 9.6 | 5.8 | 17.2 | 9.7 | 11.8 | 13.7 | 16.3 |
| 49420 | Yakima, WA ........................ | 11 125 | 246 977 | 187 | 22.2 | 48.6 | 1.2 | 4.6 | 1.8 | 45.8 | 8.9 | 21.5 | 10.1 | 11.8 | 11.9 | 12.1 |
| 49620 | York-Hanover, PA................ | 2 342 | 437 846 | 113 | 187.0 | 87.3 | 6.3 | 0.5 | 1.7 | 5.8 | 6.0 | 17.1 | 8.4 | 11.7 | 13.5 | 15.7 |
| 49660 | Youngstown-Warren-Boardman, OH-PA ..................... | 4 409 | 558 206 | 93 | 126.6 | 85.6 | 11.7 | 0.6 | 1.0 | 2.8 | 5.3 | 16.2 | 8.6 | 10.6 | 11.8 | 15.0 |
| 49700 | Yuba City, CA ..................... | 3 197 | 167 948 | 239 | 52.5 | 56.4 | 3.3 | 2.8 | 13.5 | 27.9 | 7.8 | 20.0 | 10.0 | 14.0 | 12.2 | 13.2 |
| 49740 | Yuma, AZ ............................ | 14 281 | 200 022 | 214 | 14.0 | 35.6 | 2.3 | 1.5 | 1.7 | 60.1 | 7.6 | 20.0 | 11.4 | 12.7 | 11.4 | 11.4 |

1. CBSA = Core Based Statistical Area. DIV = Metropolitan Division. See Appendix A for explanation. See Appendix B for list of metropolitan areas identified by type.   2. Dry land or land partially or temporarily covered by water.   3. May be of any race.

Table C. Metropolitan Areas — **Population and Households**

| Area name | Population, 2011 (cont.) | | | | Population change and components of change, 2000–2012 | | | | | | | Households, 2010 | | | | |
|---|---|---|---|---|---|---|---|---|---|---|---|---|---|---|---|---|
| | Age (percent) (cont.) | | | | Total persons | | Percent change | | Components of change, 2010–2012 | | | | | | Percent | |
| | 55 to 64 years | 65 to 74 years | 75 years and over | Percent female | 2000 | 2010 | 2000–2010 | 2010–2012 | Births | Deaths | Net migration | Number | Percent change, 2000–2010 | Persons per house-hold | Female family house-holder[1] | One person |
| | 16 | 17 | 18 | 19 | 20 | 21 | 22 | 23 | 24 | 25 | 26 | 27 | 28 | 29 | 30 | 31 |
| Virginia Beach-Norfolk-Newport News, VA-NC ........ | 11.5 | 6.6 | 5.2 | 51.0 | 1 576 370 | 1 671 683 | 6.0 | 1.4 | 50 800 | 28 639 | 1 105 | 628 572 | 8.3 | 2.55 | 15.8 | 25.0 |
| Visalia-Porterville, CA .......... | 9.3 | 5.3 | 4.3 | 49.8 | 368 021 | 442 179 | 20.2 | 2.2 | 18 591 | 6 062 | -2 643 | 130 352 | 18.1 | 3.36 | 16.1 | 16.6 |
| Waco, TX ........................... | 10.9 | 6.5 | 6.0 | 51.3 | 213 517 | 234 906 | 10.0 | 1.6 | 7 606 | 4 448 | 701 | 86 892 | 10.2 | 2.60 | 14.7 | 26.2 |
| Warner Robins, GA............... | 10.8 | 6.0 | 4.4 | 51.3 | 110 765 | 139 900 | 26.3 | 4.5 | 4 584 | 2 357 | 3 878 | 53 051 | 29.7 | 2.61 | 16.2 | 24.0 |
| Washington-Arlington-Alexandria, DC-VA-MD-WV .. | 11.5 | 5.9 | 4.3 | 51.3 | 4 796 183 | 5 582 170 | 16.4 | 4.0 | 177 072 | 69 316 | 114 172 | 2 074 730 | 15.2 | 2.64 | 12.5 | 27.0 |
| Bethesda-Rockvilee-Frederick, MD Div ............... | 12.5 | 6.6 | 5.8 | 51.7 | 1 068 618 | 1 205 162 | 12.8 | 3.2 | 35 663 | 15 362 | 18 972 | 441 886 | 12.0 | 2.70 | 11.1 | 24.4 |
| Washington-Arlington-Alexandria, DC-VA-MD-WV Div..................... | 11.3 | 5.7 | 3.9 | 51.1 | 3 727 565 | 4 377 008 | 17.4 | 4.2 | 141 409 | 53 954 | 95 200 | 1 632 844 | 16.2 | 2.63 | 12.9 | 27.7 |
| Waterloo-Cedar Falls, IA ...... | 12.6 | 7.4 | 7.3 | 51.2 | 163 706 | 167 819 | 2.5 | 0.6 | 4 570 | 3 399 | -155 | 66 986 | 5.4 | 2.39 | 10.4 | 28.2 |
| Wausau, WI ......................... | 13.1 | 7.4 | 7.0 | 49.8 | 125 834 | 134 063 | 6.5 | 0.5 | 3 644 | 2 407 | -605 | 53 176 | 11.5 | 2.49 | 8.5 | 25.8 |
| Wenatchee-East Wenatchee, WA ..................... | 13.3 | 8.2 | 7.1 | 50.0 | 99 219 | 110 884 | 11.8 | 1.9 | 3 389 | 2 070 | 827 | 41 721 | 13.5 | 2.63 | 10.0 | 24.4 |
| Wheeling, WV-OH................. | 15.7 | 8.9 | 8.9 | 50.7 | 153 172 | 147 950 | -3.4 | -1.0 | 3 306 | 4 203 | -556 | 61 462 | -1.3 | 2.29 | 11.5 | 31.1 |
| Wichita, KS ......................... | 11.9 | 6.3 | 6.0 | 50.5 | 571 166 | 623 061 | 9.1 | 0.8 | 21 463 | 11 648 | -4 578 | 240 359 | 9.0 | 2.55 | 11.8 | 27.9 |
| Wichita Falls, TX ................. | 11.6 | 7.2 | 6.6 | 48.9 | 151 524 | 151 306 | -0.1 | -0.3 | 4 333 | 3 314 | -1 507 | 56 873 | 1.4 | 2.45 | 12.8 | 28.5 |
| Williamsport, PA.................. | 13.8 | 8.2 | 8.3 | 51.0 | 120 044 | 116 111 | -3.3 | 0.9 | 2 737 | 2 883 | 1 261 | 46 700 | -0.6 | 2.37 | 10.8 | 28.2 |
| Wilmington, NC .................... | 14.6 | 10.3 | 6.6 | 51.3 | 274 532 | 362 315 | 32.0 | 3.7 | 8 687 | 7 251 | 11 721 | 152 676 | 33.1 | 2.32 | 11.6 | 28.0 |
| Winchester, VA-WV .............. | 12.7 | 8.0 | 6.0 | 50.2 | 102 997 | 128 472 | 24.7 | 1.9 | 3 423 | 2 394 | 1 432 | 49 066 | 22.5 | 2.57 | 10.5 | 24.5 |
| Winston-Salem, NC .............. | 12.8 | 7.7 | 6.4 | 52.2 | 421 961 | 477 717 | 13.2 | 1.4 | 12 976 | 9 270 | 3 162 | 192 310 | 13.3 | 2.43 | 13.8 | 28.8 |
| Worcester, MA ..................... | 12.6 | 6.6 | 6.3 | 50.7 | 750 963 | 798 552 | 6.3 | 1.0 | 19 999 | 14 691 | 2 576 | 303 080 | 6.7 | 2.55 | 12.2 | 26.2 |
| Yakima, WA ......................... | 10.6 | 6.4 | 5.3 | 49.9 | 222 581 | 243 231 | 9.3 | 1.5 | 9 711 | 4 129 | -1 789 | 80 592 | 8.9 | 2.97 | 14.7 | 21.6 |
| York-Hanover, PA ................ | 13.3 | 7.7 | 6.6 | 50.6 | 381 751 | 434 972 | 13.9 | 0.7 | 11 254 | 8 190 | -80 | 168 372 | 13.6 | 2.53 | 10.6 | 23.7 |
| Youngstown-Warren-Boardman, OH-PA ..................... | 14.7 | 8.8 | 9.1 | 51.4 | 602 964 | 565 773 | -6.2 | -1.3 | 12 353 | 15 234 | -4 419 | 231 165 | -3.0 | 2.37 | 13.9 | 30.3 |
| Yuba City, CA ...................... | 11.0 | 6.5 | 5.3 | 50.0 | 139 149 | 166 892 | 19.9 | 0.6 | 5 830 | 2 668 | -2 100 | 55 744 | 17.2 | 2.95 | 13.4 | 21.1 |
| Yuma, AZ............................. | 9.6 | 8.8 | 7.0 | 49.4 | 160 026 | 195 751 | 22.3 | 2.2 | 7 132 | 3 079 | 200 | 64 767 | 20.3 | 2.93 | 13.8 | 19.6 |

1. No spouse present.

# Table C. Metropolitan Areas — Population, Vital Statistics, Medicare, and Crime

| Area name | Persons in group quarters, 2009 | Daytime population, 2007–2011 | | Births, 2011 | | Deaths, 2011 | | Persons under 65 with no health insurance 2010 | | Medicare, 2012 | | | Serious crimes known to police,[2] 2011 Total | |
|---|---|---|---|---|---|---|---|---|---|---|---|---|---|---|
| | | Number | Employ-ment/ residence ratio | Total | Rate[1] | Number | Rate[1] | Number | Percent | Enrolled in original Medicare | Enrolled in Medicare Advantage | Enrolled in a Medicare prescription drug plan | Number | Rate[3] |
| | 32 | 33 | 34 | 35 | 36 | 37 | 38 | 39 | 40 | 41 | 42 | 43 | 44 | 45 |
| Virginia Beach-Norfolk-Newport News, VA-NC ........ | 69 128 | 1 674 241 | 1.01 | 22 692 | 13.5 | 12 648 | 7.5 | 201 509 | 14.2 | 244 431 | 35 845 | 81 837 | 60 889 | 3 599 |
| Visalia-Porterville, CA .......... | 4 772 | 428 077 | 0.95 | 8 115 | 18.1 | 2 640 | 5.9 | 92 846 | 23.3 | 53 227 | 5 706 | 30 514 | 17 153 | 3 834 |
| Waco, TX ............................. | 9 085 | 238 229 | 1.06 | 3 362 | 14.1 | 1 930 | 8.1 | 47 444 | 23.9 | 36 846 | 7 576 | 15 078 | 10 675 | 4 451 |
| Warner Robins, GA............... | 1 599 | 140 118 | 1.04 | 1 992 | 13.8 | 1 012 | 7.0 | 22 375 | 18.0 | 19 719 | 2 431 | 5 573 | 6 417 | 4 527 |
| Washington-Arlington-Alexandria, DC-VA-MD-WV .. | 102 275 | 5 680 991 | 1.06 | 78 603 | 13.8 | 30 368 | 5.3 | 641 718 | 13.0 | 663 335 | 66 403 | 213 916 | 153 710 | 2 720 |
| Bethesda-Rockvilee-Frederick, MD Div .............. | 13 082 | 1 142 415 | 0.92 | 15 983 | 13.0 | 6 692 | 5.5 | 131 022 | 12.5 | 163 440 | 13 282 | 56 176 | 24 789 | 2 038 |
| Washington-Arlington-Alexandria, DC-VA-MD-WV Div | 89 193 | 4 538 576 | 1.10 | 62 620 | 14.0 | 23 676 | 5.3 | 510 696 | 13.1 | 499 895 | 53 121 | 157 740 | 128 921 | 2 907 |
| Waterloo-Cedar Falls, IA ...... | 7 839 | 173 563 | 1.08 | 2 061 | 12.2 | 1 525 | 9.1 | 14 047 | 10.3 | 29 863 | 3 879 | 14 701 | 4 021 | 2 384 |
| Wausau, WI ......................... | 1 655 | 135 968 | 1.04 | 1 618 | 12.0 | 1 032 | 7.7 | 11 640 | 10.2 | 22 880 | 9 317 | 6 342 | 2 615 | 1 942 |
| Wenatchee-East Wenatchee, WA ...................... | 1 118 | 108 560 | 0.98 | 1 546 | 13.7 | 918 | 8.2 | 19 755 | 21.1 | 20 477 | 3 487 | 8 970 | 3 111 | 2 762 |
| Wheeling, WV-OH................ | 6 899 | 149 602 | 1.03 | 1 517 | 10.3 | 1 855 | 12.6 | 17 288 | 15.0 | 31 870 | 13 124 | 12 095 | 2 836 | 1 990 |
| Wichita, KS ......................... | 11 281 | 620 234 | 1.02 | 9 526 | 15.2 | 5 105 | 8.2 | 89 254 | 16.6 | 94 666 | 14 187 | 50 302 | 28 235 | 4 515 |
| Wichita Falls, TX................. | 12 143 | 151 055 | 1.01 | 2 013 | 13.4 | 1 444 | 9.6 | 28 757 | 24.1 | 25 477 | 1 854 | 11 605 | 6 232 | 4 034 |
| Williamsport, PA.................. | 5 437 | 117 808 | 1.03 | 1 208 | 10.3 | 1 283 | 11.0 | 11 636 | 12.6 | 23 740 | 6 728 | 11 574 | 2 809 | 2 412 |
| Wilmington, NC .................... | 8 631 | 356 655 | 1.00 | 3 888 | 10.5 | 3 175 | 8.6 | 57 653 | 19.4 | 75 980 | 7 053 | 36 391 | 14 433 | 3 989 |
| Winchester, VA-WV ............. | 2 451 | 126 170 | 0.98 | 1 533 | 11.8 | 998 | 7.7 | 19 240 | 17.7 | 22 122 | 2 406 | 10 176 | 3 235 | 2 493 |
| Winston-Salem, NC .............. | 10 976 | 476 249 | 1.01 | 5 920 | 12.3 | 4 003 | 8.3 | 74 636 | 18.6 | 84 543 | 40 387 | 23 184 | 23 513 | 4 889 |
| Worcester, MA .................... | 27 045 | 743 234 | 0.87 | 9 069 | 11.3 | 6 500 | 8.1 | 32 633 | 4.8 | 131 791 | 44 547 | 46 423 | 20 832 | 2 617 |
| Yakima, WA ........................ | 3 485 | 239 966 | 1.00 | 4 427 | 17.9 | 1 848 | 7.5 | 57 694 | 27.0 | 36 363 | 7 514 | 16 457 | 11 237 | 4 549 |
| York-Hanover, PA ................ | 8 430 | 397 480 | 0.84 | 5 039 | 11.5 | 3 559 | 8.1 | 40 797 | 11.1 | 77 853 | 24 728 | 27 150 | 10 046 | 2 302 |
| Youngstown-Warren-Boardman, OH-PA .................. | 18 460 | 560 404 | 0.97 | 5 730 | 10.2 | 6 733 | 12.0 | 63 621 | 14.1 | 123 111 | 54 330 | 46 599 | 19 496 | 3 485 |
| Yuba City, CA ...................... | 2 231 | 153 680 | 0.80 | 2 566 | 15.3 | 1 149 | 6.9 | 29 769 | 20.3 | 25 301 | 886 | 14 142 | 5 400 | 3 198 |
| Yuma, AZ............................ | 5 921 | 192 794 | 0.98 | 3 179 | 15.8 | 1 317 | 6.6 | 38 228 | 23.9 | 28 024 | 5 931 | 10 204 | 4 437 | 2 570 |

1. Per 1,000 estimated resident population.   2. Data for serious crimes have not been adjusted for underreporting; this may affect comparability between geographic areas and over time.   3. Per 100,000 population estimated by the FBI.

## Table C. Metropolitan Areas — Crime, Education, Money Income, and Poverty

| Area name | Serious crimes known to police, 2011 (cont.)[1] Rate[2] Violent | Property | Education — School enrollment and attainment, 2007–2011 Enrollment[3] Total | Percent private | Attainment[4] (percent) High school graduate or less | Bachelor's degree or more | Local government expenditures,[5] 2009–2010 Total current expenditures (mil dol) | Current expenditures per student (dollars) | Income and Poverty, 2007–2011 Per capita income[6] (dollars) | Median household income (dollars) | Percent of households with income of less than $25,000 | Percent of households with income of $100,000 or more | Percent of households with income of $200,000 or more | Percent below poverty level All persons | Related Children under 18 years | Related Children under 5 |
|---|---|---|---|---|---|---|---|---|---|---|---|---|---|---|---|---|
| | 46 | 47 | 48 | 49 | 50 | 51 | 52 | 53 | 54 | 55 | 56 | 57 | 58 | 59 | 60 | 61 |
| Virginia Beach-Norfolk-Newport News, VA-NC | 323 | 3 276 | 462 281 | 16.0 | 37.8 | 28.1 | 2 755.9 | 10 170 | 28 718 | 59 211 | 18.0 | 23.4 | 3.5 | 10.7 | 15.9 | 19.9 |
| Visalia-Porterville, CA | 426 | 3 408 | 135 054 | 6.7 | 56.4 | 12.9 | 908.6 | 9 372 | 17 986 | 43 550 | 27.5 | 15.6 | 2.3 | 23.8 | 32.6 | 35.8 |
| Waco, TX | 469 | 3 981 | 71 628 | 24.8 | 47.2 | 21.6 | 385.4 | 9 010 | 21 630 | 41 656 | 30.9 | 14.9 | 2.4 | 21.7 | 28.5 | 36.1 |
| Warner Robins, GA | 332 | 4 196 | 41 780 | 9.7 | 41.4 | 24.5 | 237.7 | 8 874 | 25 329 | 55 738 | 19.4 | 19.3 | 2.3 | 12.7 | 18.6 | 23.3 |
| Washington-Arlington-Alexandria, DC-VA-MD-WV | 335 | 2 385 | 1 516 970 | 22.9 | 29.7 | 47.5 | 11 436.3 | 13 358 | 43 018 | 88 486 | 11.1 | 44.1 | 12.7 | 7.5 | 9.1 | 10.1 |
| Bethesda-Rockvilee-Frederick, MD Div | 188 | 1 850 | 325 286 | 23.9 | 25.5 | 53.0 | 2 697.7 | 14 832 | 46 021 | 92 796 | 10.0 | 46.5 | 14.6 | 6.1 | 7.4 | 8.5 |
| Washington-Arlington-Alexandria, DC-VA-MD-WV Div | 375 | 2 532 | 1 191 684 | 22.6 | 30.8 | 45.9 | 8 738.7 | 12 961 | 42 189 | 87 395 | 11.5 | 43.4 | 12.2 | 7.9 | 9.6 | 10.5 |
| Waterloo-Cedar Falls, IA | 333 | 2 050 | 49 152 | 13.5 | 43.6 | 25.2 | 269.9 | 10 580 | 24 684 | 47 138 | 25.0 | 15.2 | 2.1 | 15.0 | 19.0 | 23.4 |
| Wausau, WI | 149 | 1 794 | 33 548 | 12.9 | 49.4 | 21.2 | 221.7 | 11 175 | 26 763 | 54 316 | 19.4 | 17.4 | 2.4 | 9.4 | 12.9 | 17.5 |
| Wenatchee-East Wenatchee, WA | 158 | 2 604 | 26 702 | 8.8 | 46.3 | 21.1 | 187.8 | 9 512 | 24 187 | 49 573 | 21.2 | 16.2 | 2.7 | 14.0 | 20.0 | 24.1 |
| Wheeling, WV-OH | 258 | 1 733 | 33 603 | 16.8 | 54.8 | 17.3 | 216.6 | 11 495 | 22 580 | 39 516 | 30.9 | 11.0 | 1.3 | 15.2 | 22.0 | 25.8 |
| Wichita, KS | 575 | 3 940 | 172 498 | 16.4 | 40.0 | 27.2 | 996.2 | 9 484 | 25 679 | 50 122 | 23.1 | 17.8 | 2.6 | 13.1 | 18.1 | 24.0 |
| Wichita Falls, TX | 357 | 3 677 | 37 753 | 8.0 | 50.1 | 19.7 | 226.8 | 8 997 | 23 588 | 45 882 | 24.8 | 14.0 | 2.5 | 13.6 | 18.1 | 22.4 |
| Williamsport, PA | 179 | 2 233 | 27 977 | 15.4 | 55.3 | 18.8 | 204.5 | 12 444 | 22 301 | 43 788 | 27.5 | 11.6 | 1.5 | 14.2 | 21.6 | 30.2 |
| Wilmington, NC | 336 | 3 653 | 85 260 | 12.4 | 38.7 | 29.7 | 408.2 | 8 810 | 27 947 | 46 868 | 26.0 | 17.4 | 3.3 | 15.6 | 21.7 | 25.2 |
| Winchester, VA-WV | 196 | 2 297 | 31 210 | 15.7 | 53.8 | 22.2 | 213.0 | 10 258 | 26 534 | 52 164 | 23.1 | 21.2 | 3.1 | 12.0 | 15.1 | 18.5 |
| Winston-Salem, NC | 478 | 4 411 | 119 558 | 17.9 | 45.1 | 26.9 | 653.9 | 8 758 | 25 488 | 45 847 | 25.9 | 16.6 | 3.1 | 15.8 | 23.7 | 28.4 |
| Worcester, MA | 439 | 2 177 | 215 834 | 22.7 | 40.1 | 33.3 | 1 593.9 | 12 050 | 31 470 | 65 772 | 19.3 | 29.6 | 5.4 | 9.9 | 12.5 | 16.1 |
| Yakima, WA | 327 | 4 222 | 65 411 | 8.6 | 55.7 | 16.0 | 486.6 | 9 591 | 19 730 | 44 419 | 27.1 | 13.8 | 1.8 | 21.4 | 30.4 | 34.3 |
| York-Hanover, PA | 304 | 1 998 | 103 352 | 19.3 | 54.4 | 21.6 | 769.2 | 11 468 | 28 042 | 58 586 | 17.9 | 21.8 | 2.8 | 9.4 | 12.8 | 17.4 |
| Youngstown-Warren-Boardman, OH-PA | 264 | 3 220 | 134 593 | 15.4 | 55.6 | 19.0 | 940.2 | 11 220 | 22 642 | 41 931 | 29.5 | 11.8 | 1.4 | 15.9 | 25.6 | 32.2 |
| Yuba City, CA | 405 | 2 793 | 46 963 | 8.8 | 46.9 | 16.3 | 294.2 | 8 529 | 21 418 | 48 857 | 23.6 | 17.1 | 2.2 | 17.4 | 24.5 | 29.2 |
| Yuma, AZ | 329 | 2 241 | 52 208 | 6.7 | 54.1 | 13.9 | 243.1 | 6 437 | 18 778 | 41 441 | 28.0 | 11.2 | 1.4 | 20.8 | 29.3 | 28.6 |

1. Data for serious crimes have not been adjusted for underreporting; this may affect comparability between geographic areas and over time.   2. Per 100,000 population estimated by the FBI.   3. All persons 3 years old and over enrolled in nursery school through college.   4. Persons 25 years old and over.   5. Elementary and secondary education expenditures.   6. Based on resident population estimated as of July 1, 2009.

## Table C. Metropolitan Areas — **Personal Income**

| | Personal income, 2011 | | | | | | | | | | | | |
|---|---|---|---|---|---|---|---|---|---|---|---|---|---|
| | | | Per capita[1] | | | | | | Transfer payments | | | | |
| | | | | | | | | | | Government payments to individuals | | | |
| Area name | Total (mil dol) | Percent change, 2010–2011 | Dollars | Rank | Wages and salaries[2] (mil dol) | Proprietors' income (mil dol) | Dividends, interest, and rent (mil dol) | Total (mil dol) | Total (mil dol) | Social Security (mil dol) | Medical payments (mil dol) | Income mainte-nance (mil dol) | Unemploy-ment insurance (mil dol) |
| | 62 | 63 | 64 | 65 | 66 | 67 | 68 | 69 | 70 | 71 | 72 | 73 | 74 |
| Virginia Beach-Norfolk-Newport News, VA-NC .......... | 70 516 | 5.0 | 41 976 | 77 | 50 603 | 3 477 | 10 470 | 11 218 | 10 866 | 3 399 | 4 224 | 1 411 | 288 |
| Visalia-Porterville, CA .......... | 13 316 | 7.3 | 29 640 | 347 | 6 564 | 2 160 | 1 764 | 3 322 | 3 222 | 660 | 1 389 | 672 | 230 |
| Waco, TX ........................... | 8 098 | 3.8 | 33 943 | 257 | 5 153 | 732 | 1 171 | 1 691 | 1 638 | 501 | 640 | 231 | 50 |
| Warner Robins, GA.............. | 4 990 | 5.3 | 34 674 | 236 | 4 075 | 218 | 674 | 895 | 864 | 243 | 344 | 133 | 31 |
| Washington-Arlington-Alex-andria, DC-VA-MD-WV .. | 338 498 | 5.3 | 59 345 | 5 | 272 419 | 26 768 | 49 644 | 29 408 | 28 156 | 8 529 | 12 417 | 3 156 | 1 242 |
| Bethesda-Rockvilee-Fred-erick, MD Div .............. | 80 085 | 4.8 | 65 293 | X | 47 419 | 7 550 | 14 556 | 6 307 | 6 037 | 2 173 | 2 616 | 517 | 273 |
| Washington-Arlington-Alex-andria, DC-VA-MD-WV Div ................................. | 258 413 | 5.4 | 57 715 | X | 225 001 | 19 218 | 35 088 | 23 101 | 22 119 | 6 355 | 9 802 | 2 639 | 969 |
| Waterloo-Cedar Falls, IA ...... | 6 596 | 8.3 | 39 195 | 127 | 4 496 | 659 | 1 006 | 1 236 | 1 198 | 447 | 491 | 126 | 46 |
| Wausau, WI ........................ | 5 002 | 3.2 | 37 214 | 171 | 3 361 | 420 | 752 | 858 | 828 | 337 | 313 | 76 | 56 |
| Wenatchee-East Wenat-chee, WA ......................... | 3 953 | 5.0 | 35 152 | 221 | 2 184 | 313 | 800 | 885 | 860 | 292 | 341 | 104 | 46 |
| Wheeling, WV-OH................ | 5 064 | 5.6 | 34 406 | 246 | 3 000 | 391 | 776 | 1 379 | 1 346 | 467 | 596 | 135 | 38 |
| Wichita, KS ........................ | 24 125 | 4.7 | 38 568 | 143 | 16 030 | 2 742 | 3 219 | 4 288 | 4 150 | 1 449 | 1 654 | 557 | 236 |
| Wichita Falls, TX................. | 5 510 | 4.1 | 36 671 | 183 | 3 077 | 757 | 888 | 1 135 | 1 103 | 349 | 502 | 120 | 30 |
| Williamsport, PA................. | 4 119 | 8.0 | 35 283 | 214 | 2 689 | 224 | 637 | 970 | 944 | 344 | 386 | 91 | 61 |
| Wilmington, NC................... | 12 770 | 5.6 | 34 543 | 243 | 6 974 | 1 041 | 2 430 | 3 036 | 2 955 | 1 147 | 1 175 | 276 | 161 |
| Winchester, VA-WV ............ | 4 559 | 5.6 | 35 048 | 222 | 2 926 | 253 | 739 | 798 | 769 | 315 | 285 | 89 | 22 |
| Winston-Salem, NC ............. | 17 554 | 5.3 | 36 416 | 186 | 11 423 | 1 332 | 3 046 | 3 583 | 3 476 | 1 284 | 1 412 | 378 | 207 |
| Worcester, MA .................... | 36 494 | 5.0 | 45 548 | 36 | 19 659 | 2 344 | 4 560 | 6 390 | 6 213 | 1 832 | 2 884 | 740 | 478 |
| Yakima, WA ........................ | 8 247 | 5.3 | 33 371 | 273 | 4 366 | 1 029 | 1 287 | 2 107 | 2 053 | 489 | 896 | 406 | 106 |
| York-Hanover, PA................ | 16 326 | 4.9 | 37 380 | 167 | 9 565 | 816 | 2 422 | 3 069 | 2 972 | 1 193 | 1 151 | 258 | 202 |
| Youngstown-Warren-Board-man, OH-PA ................. | 18 818 | 4.9 | 33 440 | 268 | 10 553 | 1 178 | 2 721 | 5 518 | 5 393 | 1 817 | 2 394 | 603 | 201 |
| Yuba City, CA ..................... | 5 428 | 4.4 | 32 404 | 295 | 2 577 | 731 | 776 | 1 399 | 1 363 | 320 | 615 | 197 | 101 |
| Yuma, AZ............................ | 5 442 | 4.9 | 27 091 | 360 | 3 236 | 547 | 616 | 1 405 | 1 362 | 353 | 533 | 242 | 112 |

1. Based on the resident population estimated as of July 1 of the year shown.   2. Includes other labor income.

Table C. Metropolitan Areas — **Earnings, Social Security, and Housing**

| Area name | Earnings, 2011 | | | | | | | | | Social Security beneficiaries, December 2011 | | | Housing units, 2010 | |
|---|---|---|---|---|---|---|---|---|---|---|---|---|---|---|
| | | Percent by selected industries | | | | | | | | | | | | |
| | | | Goods-related[1] | | Service-related and health | | | | | | | Supplemental Security Income recipients, December 2011 | | Percent change, 2000–2010 |
| | Total (mil dol) | Farm | Total | Manufacturing | Information, professional, and technical services | Retail trade | Finance, insurance, and real estate | Health care and social services | Government | Number | Rate[2] | | Total | |
| | 75 | 76 | 77 | 78 | 79 | 80 | 81 | 82 | 83 | 84 | 85 | 86 | 87 | 88 |
| Virginia Beach-Norfolk-Newport News, VA-NC ........ | 54 080 | 0.1 | 11.3 | 6.5 | D | 5.0 | D | 8.3 | 40.1 | 263 990 | 157 | 32 483 | 686 297 | 10.2 |
| Visalia-Porterville, CA .......... | 8 724 | 17.3 | 11.5 | 7.6 | 3.6 | 7.1 | 3.0 | 7.0 | 22.2 | 58 550 | 130 | 18 887 | 141 696 | 18.4 |
| Waco, TX ........................... | 5 886 | 0.2 | 25.0 | 17.9 | 5.4 | 6.0 | 10.8 | 11.1 | 17.0 | 40 475 | 170 | 7 048 | 95 124 | 12.2 |
| Warner Robins, GA.............. | 4 293 | 0.1 | 8.7 | 6.5 | 7.3 | 5.0 | 2.1 | 5.1 | 61.0 | 21 090 | 147 | 3 172 | 58 325 | 31.0 |
| Washington-Arlington-Alexandria, DC-VA-MD-WV .. | 299 187 | 0.0 | 5.8 | 1.6 | 27.1 | 3.3 | 5.9 | 6.2 | 29.7 | 551 715 | 97 | 56 082 | 2 213 752 | 17.1 |
| Bethesda-Rockvilee-Frederick, MD Div .............. | 54 969 | 0.1 | 10.1 | 3.5 | 25.1 | 4.5 | 9.3 | 8.9 | 23.4 | 151 460 | 123 | 15 355 | 466 041 | 14.3 |
| Washington-Arlington-Alexandria, DC-VA-MD-WV Div.................................. | 244 219 | 0.0 | D | 1.2 | 27.5 | D | 5.2 | 5.6 | 31.1 | 400 255 | 89 | 40 727 | 1 747 711 | 17.9 |
| Waterloo-Cedar Falls, IA ...... | 5 155 | 5.7 | 29.6 | 24.8 | 4.1 | 6.0 | 6.3 | D | 15.4 | 32 820 | 195 | 3 357 | 71 332 | 7.4 |
| Wausau, WI ........................ | 3 781 | 2.2 | 28.1 | 23.1 | 6.1 | 7.1 | 10.2 | 13.4 | 11.4 | 25 455 | 189 | 2 081 | 57 734 | 14.6 |
| Wenatchee-East Wenatchee, WA ......................... | 2 496 | 9.0 | 11.8 | 5.8 | 5.1 | 8.3 | 3.8 | 15.8 | 22.4 | 22 170 | 197 | 2 029 | 51 469 | 18.7 |
| Wheeling, WV-OH................ | 3 391 | 0.0 | 25.7 | 10.7 | D | 8.3 | 5.0 | D | 15.7 | 35 440 | 241 | 4 670 | 69 542 | 0.5 |
| Wichita, KS ........................ | 18 772 | 1.1 | 30.6 | 25.3 | 5.9 | 6.2 | 4.0 | D | 14.3 | 104 825 | 168 | 12 101 | 263 043 | 10.3 |
| Wichita Falls, TX................. | 3 834 | 0.7 | 23.6 | 9.4 | D | 6.8 | 4.8 | 12.3 | 28.3 | 28 090 | 187 | 4 177 | 64 823 | 4.3 |
| Williamsport, PA.................. | 2 913 | 0.5 | 31.1 | 20.0 | 5.2 | 6.8 | 3.9 | 14.3 | 17.8 | 26 575 | 228 | 3 401 | 52 500 | 0.1 |
| Wilmington, NC ................... | 8 015 | 0.6 | 18.3 | 8.7 | 10.9 | 8.5 | 6.9 | 11.1 | 19.3 | 83 300 | 225 | 7 448 | 205 642 | 35.4 |
| Winchester, VA-WV ............. | 3 179 | -0.1 | D | 14.8 | D | 9.1 | 4.4 | 17.6 | 19.7 | 24 090 | 185 | 2 281 | 56 906 | 26.2 |
| Winston-Salem, NC ............. | 12 754 | 0.4 | 18.3 | 14.1 | 8.2 | 7.4 | 9.3 | 15.9 | 10.8 | 94 165 | 195 | 9 439 | 214 375 | 17.1 |
| Worcester, MA .................... | 22 003 | 0.0 | 18.8 | 13.5 | 9.8 | 6.0 | 8.5 | 15.7 | 15.4 | 139 380 | 174 | 22 887 | 326 788 | 9.6 |
| Yakima, WA ........................ | 5 395 | 16.1 | 11.9 | 7.7 | 3.5 | 7.0 | 3.3 | 14.2 | 19.1 | 39 930 | 162 | 7 311 | 85 474 | 8.0 |
| York-Hanover, PA................ | 10 382 | 0.6 | 29.2 | 21.0 | 7.3 | 6.5 | 3.8 | 13.5 | 14.4 | 85 795 | 196 | 8 197 | 178 671 | 14.0 |
| Youngstown-Warren-Boardman, OH-PA .................. | 11 730 | 0.4 | 25.7 | 19.9 | 4.7 | 8.5 | 4.7 | 16.5 | 15.3 | 136 560 | 243 | 18 575 | 259 729 | 1.2 |
| Yuba City, CA ..................... | 3 308 | 11.6 | 9.3 | 4.1 | 3.8 | 7.0 | 2.8 | 11.6 | 33.7 | 27 450 | 164 | 8 027 | 61 493 | 20.7 |
| Yuma, AZ............................ | 3 783 | 9.0 | 6.6 | 2.7 | 5.8 | 6.6 | 3.3 | 10.5 | 36.0 | 31 300 | 156 | 4 102 | 87 850 | 18.5 |

1. Includes mining, construction, and manufacturing.     2. Per 1,000 resident population estimated as of July 1, 2011.

# Table C. Metropolitan Areas — Housing, Labor Force, and Employment

| Area name | Housing units, 2007–2011 | | | | | | | | Civilian labor force, 2012 | | | | Civilian employment,[5] 2007–2011 | | |
|---|---|---|---|---|---|---|---|---|---|---|---|---|---|---|---|
| | Occupied units | | | | | | | | | | Unemployment | | | Percent | |
| | | Owner-occupied | | | | Renter-occupied | | | | | | | | | |
| | | | | Median owner cost as a percent of income | | | Median rent as a percent of income | Sub-stand-ard units[3] (percent) | | Percent change, 2011–2012 | | | | Management, professional, and related occupations | Construction, production, and related occupations |
| | Total | Percent | Median value[1] | With a mort-gage | Without a mort-gage | Median rent[2] | | | Total | | Total | Rate[4] | Total | | |
| | 89 | 90 | 91 | 92 | 93 | 94 | 95 | 96 | 97 | 98 | 99 | 100 | 101 | 102 | 103 |
| Virginia Beach-Norfolk-Newport News, VA-NC | 620 286 | 64.4 | 246 500 | 26.5 | 12.6 | 1 020 | 31.3 | 2.3 | 826 075 | -0.1 | 54 143 | 6.6 | 766 189 | 36.4 | 20.6 |
| Visalia-Porterville, CA | 128 324 | 58.9 | 191 500 | 28.5 | 11.5 | 781 | 31.7 | 11.8 | 207 634 | -0.5 | 32 860 | 15.8 | 167 498 | 23.7 | 36.6 |
| Waco, TX | 83 851 | 60.0 | 104 800 | 22.4 | 12.7 | 757 | 33.5 | 3.8 | 116 314 | -0.4 | 7 593 | 6.5 | 104 761 | 31.8 | 24.3 |
| Warner Robins, GA | 50 871 | 68.1 | 134 200 | 20.9 | 10.0 | 783 | 27.8 | 2.5 | 71 633 | 0.3 | 5 450 | 7.6 | 61 407 | 38.3 | 22.2 |
| Washington-Arlington-Alexandria, DC-VA-MD-WV | 2 035 320 | 65.6 | 399 400 | 25.2 | 10.8 | 1 353 | 29.2 | 2.8 | 3 182 006 | 1.1 | 176 941 | 5.6 | 2 925 934 | 50.8 | 12.9 |
| Bethesda-Rockvilee-Frederick, MD Div | 440 482 | 70.2 | 435 100 | 24.8 | 11.2 | 1 436 | 30.3 | 2.5 | 663 230 | 0.7 | 34 985 | 5.3 | 639 324 | 53.8 | 11.1 |
| Washington-Arlington-Alexandria, DC-VA-MD-WV Div | 1 594 838 | 64.3 | 391 000 | 25.3 | 10.7 | 1 330 | 29.0 | 2.9 | 2 518 776 | 1.2 | 141 956 | 5.6 | 2 286 610 | 49.9 | 13.3 |
| Waterloo-Cedar Falls, IA | 66 506 | 71.5 | 123 300 | 20.5 | 11.3 | 632 | 30.6 | 1.7 | 94 782 | -0.3 | 4 848 | 5.1 | 83 749 | 31.5 | 25.6 |
| Wausau, WI | 52 865 | 74.5 | 141 700 | 22.4 | 12.5 | 663 | 25.8 | 2.5 | 71 412 | -1.7 | 5 136 | 7.2 | 69 504 | 31.3 | 30.7 |
| Wenatchee-East Wenatchee, WA | 40 799 | 68.3 | 240 700 | 25.0 | 10.8 | 718 | 26.9 | 4.4 | 62 630 | 1.8 | 4 796 | 7.7 | 49 618 | 28.2 | 30.9 |
| Wheeling, WV-OH | 61 286 | 74.6 | 87 100 | 19.5 | 11.0 | 506 | 27.7 | 0.9 | 67 536 | -1.2 | 5 030 | 7.4 | 64 048 | 28.4 | 25.3 |
| Wichita, KS | 238 268 | 68.5 | 118 000 | 21.1 | 11.4 | 660 | 28.5 | 2.3 | 302 447 | -1.1 | 20 512 | 6.8 | 295 456 | 33.7 | 25.5 |
| Wichita Falls, TX | 55 607 | 67.8 | 88 400 | 21.6 | 12.5 | 698 | 28.1 | 2.7 | 72 384 | -1.3 | 4 434 | 6.1 | 65 096 | 29.5 | 25.8 |
| Williamsport, PA | 46 604 | 69.5 | 125 400 | 23.2 | 14.3 | 629 | 29.8 | 1.3 | 64 026 | 3.1 | 4 988 | 7.8 | 54 441 | 28.4 | 29.4 |
| Wilmington, NC | 151 686 | 67.9 | 205 600 | 25.6 | 12.6 | 840 | 32.7 | 2.6 | 183 639 | 1.6 | 17 934 | 9.8 | 164 562 | 33.9 | 21.4 |
| Winchester, VA-WV | 49 133 | 68.9 | 226 600 | 24.8 | 11.9 | 886 | 29.5 | 2.2 | 67 398 | 0.6 | 4 003 | 5.9 | 61 213 | 33.1 | 27.6 |
| Winston-Salem, NC | 187 608 | 69.8 | 145 300 | 22.6 | 10.7 | 675 | 30.1 | 2.9 | 244 516 | 1.6 | 21 881 | 8.9 | 215 509 | 35.6 | 23.6 |
| Worcester, MA | 299 089 | 67.2 | 274 900 | 25.0 | 14.8 | 883 | 29.3 | 1.8 | 402 240 | -0.5 | 30 197 | 7.5 | 395 271 | 40.3 | 19.2 |
| Yakima, WA | 79 565 | 63.5 | 154 800 | 24.4 | 11.3 | 693 | 30.3 | 7.2 | 125 257 | 1.9 | 12 243 | 9.8 | 97 922 | 26.3 | 33.9 |
| York-Hanover, PA | 167 568 | 76.2 | 178 400 | 24.5 | 14.1 | 782 | 28.4 | 1.3 | 228 725 | 1.5 | 17 698 | 7.7 | 216 693 | 31.5 | 28.3 |
| Youngstown-Warren-Boardman, OH-PA | 231 913 | 73.1 | 99 400 | 22.8 | 13.4 | 600 | 30.8 | 1.4 | 265 560 | -1.1 | 21 389 | 8.1 | 242 243 | 28.7 | 26.6 |
| Yuba City, CA | 55 553 | 60.2 | 216 400 | 28.9 | 11.5 | 850 | 31.6 | 7.6 | 70 582 | -0.2 | 12 245 | 17.3 | 63 412 | 28.0 | 28.8 |
| Yuma, AZ | 69 993 | 70.4 | 138 600 | 27.1 | 10.5 | 775 | 31.2 | 8.3 | 92 015 | 2.0 | 25 277 | 27.5 | 68 215 | 25.5 | 28.0 |

1. Specified owner-occupied units.   2. Specified renter-occupied units.   3. Overcrowded or lacking complete plumbing facilities.   4. Percent of civilian labor force.   5. Persons 16 years old and over.

# Table C. Metropolitan Areas — Nonfarm Employment and Agriculture

| Area name | Private nonfarm establishments, employment and payroll, 2011 | | | | | | | | | Agriculture, 2007 | | | |
|---|---|---|---|---|---|---|---|---|---|---|---|---|---|
| | | Employment | | | | | | Annual payroll | | Farms | | | |
| | | | | | | | | | | | | Percent with: | |
| | Number of establish-ments | Total | Health care and social assistance | Manufac-turing | Retail trade | Finance and insurance | Professional, scientific, and technical services | Total (mil dol) | Average per employee (dollars) | Number | Fewer than 50 acres | 500 acres or more | Farm operators whose principal occupation is farming (percent) |
| | 104 | 105 | 106 | 107 | 108 | 109 | 110 | 111 | 112 | 113 | 114 | 115 | 116 |
| Virginia Beach-Norfolk-Newport News, VA-NC ........ | 36 830 | 583 529 | 83 911 | 53 984 | 86 540 | 25 429 | 48 785 | 21 935 | 37 591 | 1 500 | 60.3 | 11.5 | 51.5 |
| Visalia-Porterville, CA .......... | 6 109 | 83 911 | 14 497 | 12 035 | 14 400 | 3 037 | 2 498 | 2 916 | 34 746 | 5 240 | 64.3 | 8.0 | 53.2 |
| Waco, TX .............................. | 4 938 | 95 918 | 17 706 | 13 785 | 11 675 | 4 692 | 2 478 | 3 099 | 32 314 | 2 798 | 52.9 | 7.0 | 34.8 |
| Warner Robins, GA............... | 2 280 | 34 278 | 6 020 | 3 840 | 6 495 | 1 087 | 3 749 | 1 032 | 30 093 | 298 | 54.0 | 5.7 | 51.0 |
| Washington-Arlington-Alexandria, DC-VA-MD-WV .. | 140 830 | 2 431 159 | 283 572 | 50 079 | 258 557 | 99 618 | 504 923 | 144 870 | 59 589 | 8 257 | 54.6 | 5.0 | 45.3 |
| Bethesda-Rockvilee-Frederick, MD Div .............. | X | X | X | X | X | X | X | X | X | 2 003 | 51.5 | 5.6 | 48.0 |
| Washington-Arlington-Alexandria, DC-VA-MD-WV Div.................................. | X | X | X | X | X | X | X | X | X | 6 254 | 55.6 | 4.8 | 44.4 |
| Waterloo-Cedar Falls, IA ...... | 4 113 | 75 898 | 15 002 | 15 449 | 10 641 | 3 752 | 3 117 | 2 763 | 36 407 | 2 737 | 32.9 | 18.9 | 52.8 |
| Wausau, WI ........................ | 3 371 | 59 017 | 9 463 | 15 384 | 7 872 | 4 737 | 2 035 | 2 210 | 37 454 | 2 545 | 25.3 | 6.4 | 53.8 |
| Wenatchee-East Wenatchee, WA .................... | 3 044 | 31 815 | 6 103 | 2 049 | 5 574 | 1 056 | 1 418 | 1 112 | 34 967 | 1 934 | 58.3 | 14.4 | 55.6 |
| Wheeling, WV-OH................ | 3 432 | 55 380 | 13 019 | 2 999 | 8 496 | 2 180 | 2 264 | 1 774 | 32 027 | 1 674 | 25.8 | 3.5 | 38.3 |
| Wichita, KS ........................ | 14 404 | 242 354 | 40 529 | 47 333 | 30 472 | 9 853 | 10 487 | 9 878 | 40 760 | 4 774 | 23.1 | 44.6 | |
| Wichita Falls, TX................. | 3 469 | 48 365 | 11 110 | 4 851 | 7 983 | 1 807 | 1 342 | 1 520 | 31 430 | 2 102 | 25.6 | 26.4 | 42.7 |
| Williamsport, PA.................. | 2 867 | 46 228 | 8 119 | 8 348 | 7 377 | 1 395 | 1 748 | 1 578 | 34 134 | 1 211 | 32.6 | 3.1 | 41.4 |
| Wilmington, NC .................. | 9 762 | 113 948 | 20 402 | 8 708 | 19 081 | 3 756 | 5 806 | 4 019 | 35 271 | 694 | 56.9 | 7.5 | 48.7 |
| Winchester, VA-WV ............. | 3 026 | 45 668 | 8 570 | 6 658 | 7 596 | 1 625 | 1 949 | 1 724 | 37 746 | 1 353 | 41.1 | 7.3 | 39.0 |
| Winston-Salem, NC ............. | 10 158 | 181 219 | 35 833 | 18 735 | 22 907 | 11 090 | 7 617 | 7 494 | 41 355 | 3 260 | 52.3 | 2.4 | 44.5 |
| Worcester, MA .................... | 17 421 | 270 224 | 58 058 | 31 454 | 37 697 | 15 657 | 15 263 | 12 170 | 45 036 | 1 547 | 59.4 | 0.8 | 44.6 |
| Yakima, WA ........................ | 4 583 | 61 150 | 12 954 | 7 576 | 9 876 | 1 558 | 1 815 | 2 086 | 34 108 | 3 540 | 69.8 | 6.0 | 51.6 |
| York-Hanover, PA................ | 8 519 | 155 366 | 22 789 | 32 027 | 21 341 | 3 824 | 5 770 | 6 062 | 39 018 | 2 370 | 58.9 | 5.2 | 45.2 |
| Youngstown-Warren-Boardman, OH-PA................ | 12 650 | 200 256 | 41 673 | 30 348 | 29 451 | 6 296 | 5 920 | 6 826 | 34 084 | 2 758 | 38.8 | 4.1 | 46.8 |
| Yuba City, CA .................... | 2 475 | 27 681 | 5 409 | 1 941 | 5 467 | 953 | 1 042 | 992 | 35 839 | 2 091 | 55.7 | 11.5 | 55.7 |
| Yuma, AZ............................ | 2 897 | 39 826 | 6 409 | 2 629 | 7 786 | 1 160 | 1 207 | 1 169 | 29 364 | 452 | 60.6 | 19.5 | 57.5 |

# Table C. Metropolitan Areas — **Agriculture**

| | Agriculture, 2007 (cont.) | | | | | | | | | | | | | | |
| Area name | Land in farms | | | | Value of land and buildings (dollars) | | Value of machinery and equipment, average per farm (dollars) | Value of products sold | | | | Percent of farms with sales of: | | Government payments | |
| | | | Acres | | | | | | | Percent from: | | | | | |
| | Acreage (1,000) | Percent change, 2002–2007 | Average size of farm | Total irrigated (1,000) | Total cropland (1,000) | Average per farm | Average per acre | | Total (mil dol) | Average per farm (dollars) | Crops | Livestock and poultry products | $10,000 or more | $100,000 or more | Total ($1,000) | Percent of farms |
| | 117 | 118 | 119 | 120 | 121 | 122 | 123 | 124 | 125 | 126 | 127 | 128 | 129 | 130 | 131 | 132 |
| Virginia Beach-Norfolk-Newport News, VA-NC | 326 | D | 217 | 3.4 | 246.5 | 968 267 | 4 457 | 103 337 | 167.5 | 111 603 | 66.5 | 18.2 | 37.8 | 16.7 | 9 008 | 33.7 |
| Visalia-Porterville, CA | 1 169 | -16.1 | 223 | 550.3 | 638.8 | 1 843 502 | 8 266 | 125 007 | 3 335.0 | 636 453 | 36.2 | 63.8 | 69.9 | 32.8 | 20 335 | 11.3 |
| Waco, TX | 530 | -1.5 | 189 | 2.9 | 241.6 | 390 384 | 2 062 | 49 514 | 104.7 | 37 431 | 39.8 | 60.2 | 21.9 | 3.7 | 2 612 | 16.0 |
| Warner Robins, GA | 47 | -37.3 | 157 | 4.5 | 20.3 | 577 908 | 3 692 | 64 949 | 15.6 | 52 339 | 44.8 | 55.2 | 28.9 | 6.4 | 1 095 | 24.2 |
| Washington-Arlington-Alexandria, DC-VA-MD-WV | 1 050 | D | 127 | 10.1 | 556.5 | 924 408 | 7 271 | 70 848 | 343.0 | 41 536 | D | D | 28.6 | 6.6 | 7 164 | 17.0 |
| Bethesda-Rockvilee-Frederick, MD Div | 270 | -0.4 | 135 | 2.3 | 192.2 | 1 165 883 | 8 659 | 95 938 | 160.2 | 79 994 | 38.2 | 61.8 | 37.5 | 13.1 | 3 899 | 30.6 |
| Washington-Arlington-Alexandria, DC-VA-MD-WV Div | 780 | D | 125 | 7.8 | 364.3 | 847 070 | 6 791 | 62 812 | 182.8 | 29 219 | D | D | 25.7 | 4.5 | 3 265 | 12.6 |
| Waterloo-Cedar Falls, IA | 841 | -1.5 | 307 | 0.5 | 787.0 | 1 206 628 | 3 926 | 155 560 | 573.3 | 209 491 | 66.4 | 33.6 | 67.1 | 38.9 | 21 637 | 80.3 |
| Wausau, WI | 491 | -7.5 | 193 | 7.1 | 323.6 | 526 977 | 2 734 | 100 135 | 307.4 | 120 800 | 14.8 | 85.2 | 54.9 | 29.0 | 4 727 | 50.3 |
| Wenatchee-East Wenatchee, WA | 977 | -1.4 | 505 | 47.6 | 583.0 | 857 223 | 1 697 | 81 409 | 402.2 | 207 946 | 97.5 | 2.5 | 61.4 | 31.2 | 11 939 | 21.3 |
| Wheeling, WV-OH | 256 | 0.4 | 153 | 0.1 | 83.6 | 308 242 | 2 018 | 42 010 | 20.1 | 11 972 | 23.5 | 76.5 | 17.9 | 2.2 | 211 | 9.4 |
| Wichita, KS | 2 346 | 1.2 | 491 | 94.5 | 1 564.7 | 570 428 | 1 161 | 98 717 | 498.6 | 104 442 | 39.7 | 60.3 | 42.9 | 15.4 | 21 492 | 58.7 |
| Wichita Falls, TX | 1 500 | 0.5 | 714 | 8.7 | 356.9 | 803 795 | 1 126 | 71 421 | 145.1 | 69 035 | 18.2 | 81.8 | 42.4 | 12.5 | 4 070 | 31.7 |
| Williamsport, PA | 160 | -9.6 | 132 | 1.7 | 88.0 | 458 300 | 3 459 | 61 706 | 53.4 | 44 080 | 38.7 | 61.3 | 33.8 | 11.5 | 1 832 | 39.9 |
| Wilmington, NC | 110 | D | 159 | 8.0 | 66.0 | 680 116 | 4 288 | 85 287 | 215.9 | 311 147 | 34.1 | 65.9 | 36.9 | 17.1 | 926 | 23.8 |
| Winchester, VA-WV | 227 | NA | 168 | 0.3 | 71.4 | 880 815 | 5 239 | 60 379 | 60.5 | 44 720 | 38.5 | 61.5 | 28.2 | 6.1 | 593 | 14.0 |
| Winston-Salem, NC | 310 | -11.9 | 95 | 2.0 | 150.4 | 488 299 | 5 141 | 52 156 | 154.7 | 47 453 | 32.0 | 68.0 | 26.5 | 7.2 | 1 124 | 12.7 |
| Worcester, MA | 106 | 1.9 | 69 | 0.9 | 35.6 | 810 727 | 11 792 | 50 355 | 80.6 | 52 069 | 55.5 | 44.5 | 29.2 | 6.9 | 1 034 | 7.6 |
| Yakima, WA | 1 649 | -1.8 | 466 | 267.6 | 344.5 | 712 970 | 1 530 | 97 908 | 1 203.8 | 340 058 | 65.4 | 34.6 | 52.6 | 21.8 | 4 705 | 9.2 |
| York-Hanover, PA | 293 | 2.8 | 123 | 1.0 | 225.4 | 701 059 | 5 680 | 81 789 | 212.6 | 89 719 | 47.1 | 52.9 | 38.4 | 13.9 | 2 722 | 22.7 |
| Youngstown-Warren-Boardman, OH-PA | 361 | -1.6 | 131 | 0.9 | 245.3 | 443 488 | 3 387 | 73 223 | 147.4 | 53 427 | 44.1 | 55.9 | 41.7 | 11.6 | 3 529 | 36.9 |
| Yuba City, CA | 521 | -14.0 | 249 | 302.7 | 345.4 | 1 585 064 | 6 365 | 123 374 | 430.5 | 205 890 | 94.4 | 5.6 | 57.5 | 27.5 | 21 983 | 22.9 |
| Yuma, AZ | 210 | -9.1 | 466 | 174.2 | 193.1 | 3 893 483 | 8 361 | 373 336 | 960.0 | 2 123 823 | D | D | 60.0 | 37.4 | 4 395 | 20.8 |

| Area name | Water use, 2005 | | Wholesale trade,[1] 2007 | | | | Retail trade, 2007 | | | | Real estate and rental and leasing, 2007 | | | |
|---|---|---|---|---|---|---|---|---|---|---|---|---|---|---|
| | Total water withdrawn (mil gal/day) | Gallons withdrawn per person | Number of establish-ments | Number of employees | Sales (mil dol) | Annual payroll (mil dol) | Number of establish-ments | Number of employees | Sales (mil dol) | Annual payroll (mil dol) | Number of establish-ments | Number of employees | Receipts (mil dol) | Annual payroll (mil dol) |
| | 133 | 134 | 135 | 136 | 137 | 138 | 139 | 140 | 141 | 142 | 143 | 144 | 145 | 146 |
| Virginia Beach-Norfolk-New-port News, VA-NC ......... | 3 909.7 | 2 373 | 1 552 | 26 377 | 15 913.8 | 1 074.5 | 6 285 | 94 923 | 20 958.7 | 2 050.9 | 2 237 | 16 873 | 2 359.8 | 532.6 |
| Visalia-Porterville, CA ......... | 2 275.0 | 5 537 | 393 | 4 748 | 3 850.6 | 190.4 | 1 140 | 16 005 | 3 900.9 | 367.4 | 294 | 1 260 | 189.1 | 32.3 |
| Waco, TX ...................... | 198.4 | 883 | 275 | 3 629 | 5 947.1 | 137.7 | 872 | 11 703 | 2 942.6 | 248.7 | 211 | 1 408 | 281.7 | 54.3 |
| Warner Robins, GA.............. | 29.4 | 233 | 54 | 408 | 168.7 | 13.8 | 452 | 6 600 | 1 524.3 | 143.9 | 133 | 510 | 72.6 | 12.5 |
| Washington-Arlington-Alex-andria, DC-VA-MD-WV .. | 6 669.1 | 1 271 | 4 397 | 71 935 | 67 941.6 | 4 616.7 | 16 959 | 271 527 | 69 885.5 | 7 074.5 | 7 153 | 57 318 | 15 438.3 | 3 048.1 |
| Bethesda-Rockvilee-Fred-erick, MD Div .............. | 692.6 | 603 | 1 111 | 17 102 | 12 148.6 | 1 204.2 | 3 742 | 60 739 | 16 322.1 | 1 654.7 | 1 732 | 16 740 | 4 566.7 | 922.2 |
| Washington-Arlington-Alex-andria, DC-VA-MD-WV Div..................... | 5 976.5 | 1 458 | 3 286 | 54 833 | 55 793.0 | 3 412.5 | 13 217 | 210 788 | 53 563.4 | 5 419.9 | 5 421 | 40 578 | 10 871.6 | 2 125.9 |
| Waterloo-Cedar Falls, IA ...... | 43.1 | 266 | 204 | 3 004 | 1 836.9 | 117.2 | 683 | 10 226 | 2 307.2 | 208.9 | 177 | 809 | 135.5 | 24.1 |
| Wausau, WI ...................... | 232.9 | 1 806 | 207 | 3 190 | 1 295.2 | 131.0 | 505 | 10 000 | 2 139.1 | 196.5 | 99 | 473 | 75.4 | 11.9 |
| Wenatchee-East Wenat-chee, WA ..................... | 130.1 | 1 242 | 155 | 2 596 | 1 104.7 | 90.0 | 505 | 5 984 | 1 435.6 | 145.4 | 146 | 628 | 86.4 | 15.6 |
| Wheeling, WV-OH.............. | 1 004.1 | 6 754 | 137 | 2 276 | 3 518.2 | 80.9 | 640 | 8 930 | 1 811.2 | 171.2 | 126 | 681 | 70.0 | 14.6 |
| Wichita, KS ...................... | 161.0 | 274 | 834 | 10 875 | 19 098.8 | 548.8 | 2 159 | 30 972 | 7 547.8 | 670.3 | 712 | 3 670 | 533.8 | 98.5 |
| Wichita Falls, TX.................. | 115.7 | 791 | 196 | 2 078 | 1 324.4 | 86.6 | 589 | 7 894 | 1 832.9 | 164.9 | 189 | 856 | 102.9 | 19.6 |
| Williamsport, PA.................. | 14.5 | 123 | 128 | 2 740 | 961.1 | 85.9 | 519 | 6 968 | 1 458.4 | 130.8 | 94 | 444 | 80.7 | 11.4 |
| Wilmington, NC .................. | 1 617.4 | 5 132 | 475 | 5 031 | 2 958.2 | 217.1 | 1 657 | 20 685 | 5 161.5 | 471.5 | 703 | 2 829 | 460.8 | 92.0 |
| Winchester, VA-WV ............. | 11.0 | 95 | 142 | 2 623 | 1 507.8 | 117.7 | 557 | 8 428 | 2 231.6 | 192.4 | 143 | 569 | 108.2 | 20.4 |
| Winston-Salem, NC .............. | 1 310.4 | 2 921 | 592 | 8 954 | 6 313.2 | 381.7 | 1 810 | 24 580 | 6 075.9 | 548.7 | 497 | 2 240 | 786.5 | 67.4 |
| Worcester, MA ..................... | 446.5 | 570 | 998 | 15 838 | 12 545.8 | 991.7 | 2 738 | 40 506 | 10 057.2 | 971.0 | 673 | 3 794 | 692.2 | 138.6 |
| Yakima, WA ...................... | 658.3 | 2 843 | 282 | 5 725 | 3 343.5 | 221.6 | 780 | 9 900 | 2 425.6 | 239.5 | 255 | 977 | 151.6 | 23.7 |
| York-Hanover, PA.................. | 2 596.5 | 6 352 | 429 | 7 690 | 5 321.6 | 341.6 | 1 344 | 21 762 | 4 942.7 | 455.6 | 285 | 2 158 | 294.5 | 75.5 |
| Youngstown-Warren-Board-man, OH-PA .................. | 245.0 | 413 | 634 | 9 060 | 6 195.8 | 355.6 | 2 352 | 31 815 | 6 785.7 | 625.9 | 447 | 2 936 | 398.2 | 78.5 |
| Yuba City, CA ..................... | 1 185.4 | 7 598 | 109 | D | D | D | 430 | 6 136 | 1 489.0 | 147.0 | 136 | 723 | 80.9 | 15.5 |
| Yuma, AZ ...................... | 1 166.1 | 6 433 | 139 | 1 984 | 1 209.3 | 77.5 | 540 | 8 905 | 2 004.6 | 180.2 | 190 | 734 | 119.2 | 17.5 |

1. Merchant wholesalers, except manufacturers' sales branches and offices.

| Area name | Professional, scientific, and technical services,[1] 2007 | | | | Manufacturing, 2007 | | | | Accommodation and food services, 2007 | | | |
|---|---|---|---|---|---|---|---|---|---|---|---|---|
| | Number of establishments | Number of employees | Sales (mil dol) | Annual payroll (mil dol) | Number of establishments | Number of employees | Sales (mil dol) | Annual payroll (mil dol) | Number of establishments | Number of employees | Sales (mil dol) | Annual payroll (mil dol) |
| | 147 | 148 | 149 | 150 | 151 | 152 | 153 | 154 | 155 | 156 | 157 | 158 |
| Virginia Beach-Norfolk-Newport News, VA-NC | 3 957 | 50 947 | 6 937.7 | 2 714.0 | 1 000 | 57 622 | 16 143.4 | 2 588.4 | 3 631 | 74 162 | 3 403.5 | 953.9 |
| Visalia-Porterville, CA | 446 | D | D | D | 278 | 12 443 | 5 016.0 | 458.3 | 558 | 8 282 | 379.4 | 102.8 |
| Waco, TX | 352 | D | D | D | 255 | 13 971 | 5 888.9 | 550.4 | 468 | 9 123 | 375.3 | 100.9 |
| Warner Robins, GA | 281 | D | D | D | 64 | 2 511 | 1 422.9 | 97.2 | 248 | 5 246 | 206.1 | 54.8 |
| Washington-Arlington-Alexandria, DC-VA-MD-WV | 27 953 | 447 594 | 94 021.2 | 36 863.4 | 2 453 | 63 946 | 17 576.7 | 3 312.5 | 11 141 | 219 832 | 14 530.1 | 4 019.5 |
| Bethesda-Rockvilee-Frederick, MD Div | 6 399 | 78 940 | 14 969.5 | 5 972.7 | 640 | 17 874 | 6 267.8 | 982.7 | 2 145 | 37 600 | 2 229.3 | 614.1 |
| Washington-Arlington-Alexandria, DC-VA-MD-WV Div | 21 554 | 368 654 | 79 051.7 | 30 890.8 | 1 813 | 46 072 | 11 308.9 | 2 329.7 | 8 996 | 182 232 | 12 300.9 | 3 405.3 |
| Waterloo-Cedar Falls, IA | 295 | D | D | D | 215 | 15 137 | 6 723.9 | 652.4 | 355 | 6 885 | 215.6 | 65.2 |
| Wausau, WI | 235 | D | D | D | 250 | 18 678 | D | 765.6 | 321 | 4 813 | 173.7 | 48.8 |
| Wenatchee-East Wenatchee, WA | 226 | D | D | D | 121 | 2 168 | 700.7 | 88.3 | 327 | 4 080 | 201.6 | 60.4 |
| Wheeling, WV-OH | 271 | 1 967 | 250.1 | 77.0 | 129 | 3 032 | 994.2 | 122.1 | 316 | 5 713 | 215.8 | 61.3 |
| Wichita, KS | 1 288 | D | D | D | 724 | 60 130 | 25 390.9 | 3 212.5 | 1 266 | 24 281 | 950.5 | 275.0 |
| Wichita Falls, TX | 252 | D | D | D | 155 | 6 336 | 1 548.8 | 271.7 | 306 | 6 775 | 258.8 | 81.0 |
| Williamsport, PA | 183 | 1 367 | 102.9 | 39.6 | 183 | 10 240 | 3 358.2 | 408.7 | 277 | 3 721 | 147.9 | 40.0 |
| Wilmington, NC | 1 118 | D | D | D | 312 | 9 167 | 4 808.7 | 441.9 | 923 | 16 719 | 711.6 | 204.1 |
| Winchester, VA-WV | 274 | D | D | D | 128 | 8 970 | 3 459.9 | D | 267 | 4 790 | 208.6 | 59.1 |
| Winston-Salem, NC | 1 123 | D | D | D | 480 | 24 818 | 18 942.7 | 1 095.6 | 890 | 16 714 | 738.1 | 204.7 |
| Worcester, MA | 1 888 | 14 149 | 2 693.0 | 917.8 | 1 099 | 39 334 | 10 706.1 | 1 953.9 | 1 691 | 24 156 | 1 150.7 | 330.8 |
| Yakima, WA | 320 | D | D | D | 255 | 8 696 | 2 686.1 | 304.4 | 427 | 5 287 | 245.6 | 70.8 |
| York-Hanover, PA | 726 | 5 437 | 620.4 | 240.9 | 600 | 38 016 | 11 957.4 | 1 669.8 | 736 | 13 112 | 527.9 | 146.4 |
| Youngstown-Warren-Boardman, OH-PA | 937 | D | D | D | 840 | 37 611 | 14 779.7 | 1 879.9 | 1 249 | 20 511 | 752.6 | 213.9 |
| Yuba City, CA | 199 | D | D | D | 116 | 2 470 | 664.9 | 94.6 | 238 | 3 553 | 153.1 | 42.1 |
| Yuma, AZ | 208 | D | D | D | 82 | 2 856 | 891.6 | 88.0 | 316 | 5 942 | 271.9 | 69.6 |

1. Establishments subject to federal tax.

| Area name | Health care and social assistance,[1] 2007 | | | | Other services,[1] 2007 | | | | Federal funds and grants, 2009–2010 | | | |
|---|---|---|---|---|---|---|---|---|---|---|---|---|
| | | | | | | | | | | Expenditures (mil dol) | | |
| | | | | | | | | | | | Direct payments for individuals | |
| | Number of establish-ments | Number of employees | Receipts (mil dol) | Annual payroll (mil dol) | Number of establish-ments | Number of employees | Receipts (mil dol) | Annual payroll (mil dol) | Total | Social Security and government retirement | Medicare | Food stamps and Supplemental Security Income |
| | 159 | 160 | 161 | 162 | 163 | 164 | 165 | 166 | 167 | 168 | 169 | 170 |
| Virginia Beach-Norfolk-Newport News, VA-NC ......... | 3 385 | 79 324 | 7 792.4 | 3 220.5 | 2 998 | 20 356 | 2 143.1 | 526.1 | 27 891.6 | 6 512.0 | 1 823.6 | 595.0 |
| Visalia-Porterville, CA .......... | 806 | 13 734 | 1 295.3 | 493.8 | 384 | 2 298 | 208.1 | 62.9 | 2 559.9 | 749.5 | 525.0 | 196.5 |
| Waco, TX ...................... | 525 | 15 510 | 1 219.3 | 504.2 | 394 | 2 615 | 244.7 | 64.2 | 2 019.0 | 701.0 | 261.8 | 104.5 |
| Warner Robins, GA.............. | 256 | 4 784 | 461.8 | 176.5 | 166 | 932 | 67.1 | 17.0 | 2 499.9 | 601.1 | 113.9 | 48.8 |
| Washington-Arlington-Alexandria, DC-VA-MD-WV.. | 14 178 | 259 815 | 29 523.9 | 11 613.2 | 12 486 | 132 740 | 30 096.7 | 6 657.7 | 169 492.6 | 18 118.3 | 6 322.7 | 1 058.9 |
| Bethesda-Rockvilee-Frederick, MD Div ............... | 3 907 | 64 067 | 7 490.2 | 2 943.8 | 2 339 | 19 995 | 3 645.3 | 832.2 | 23 309.8 | 3 499.7 | 1 752.6 | 152.4 |
| Washington-Arlington-Alexandria, DC-VA-MD-WV Div.................... | 10 271 | 195 748 | 22 033.7 | 8 669.4 | 10 147 | 112 745 | 26 451.4 | 5 825.5 | 146 182.8 | 14 618.6 | 4 570.1 | 906.5 |
| Waterloo-Cedar Falls, IA ...... | 423 | 12 317 | 963.0 | 414.7 | 294 | 1 978 | 150.9 | 42.3 | 1 272.3 | 498.1 | 278.7 | 58.3 |
| Wausau, WI ...................... | 345 | 9 438 | 926.4 | 379.0 | 253 | 1 591 | 139.1 | 36.2 | 828.7 | 350.2 | 152.5 | 30.7 |
| Wenatchee-East Wenatchee, WA .................... | 261 | 5 526 | 547.9 | 248.4 | 204 | 806 | 69.8 | 16.6 | 800.5 | 341.5 | 128.7 | 34.5 |
| Wheeling, WV-OH.................. | 485 | 11 961 | 937.5 | 371.9 | 310 | 1 787 | 124.8 | 34.2 | 1 326.9 | 532.8 | 347.6 | 70.6 |
| Wichita, KS ...................... | 1 608 | 39 696 | 3 939.7 | 1 452.5 | 1 046 | 6 775 | 604.3 | 180.6 | 5 408.5 | 1 715.4 | 819.7 | 181.4 |
| Wichita Falls, TX ................ | 399 | 10 734 | 840.2 | 336.2 | 284 | 1 544 | 144.7 | 35.7 | 1 642.4 | 545.0 | 239.6 | 56.9 |
| Williamsport, PA.................. | 285 | 8 065 | 675.8 | 272.5 | 244 | 1 521 | 150.1 | 33.0 | 969.5 | 391.6 | 250.7 | 45.6 |
| Wilmington, NC .................. | 950 | 22 009 | 2 105.9 | 882.9 | 626 | 3 672 | 293.5 | 81.2 | 2 725.5 | 1 375.4 | 381.9 | 128.4 |
| Winchester, VA-WV ............ | 352 | 7 680 | 775.7 | 341.1 | 202 | 1 181 | 104.3 | 31.5 | 805.7 | 406.7 | 115.3 | 25.3 |
| Winston-Salem, NC ............. | 971 | 32 257 | 3 051.8 | 1 188.7 | 749 | 4 549 | 435.8 | 106.7 | 3 416.7 | 1 475.9 | 563.7 | 150.9 |
| Worcester, MA .................. | 1 945 | 55 586 | 5 551.2 | 2 200.6 | 1 346 | 7 695 | 772.5 | 224.3 | 6 321.4 | 2 028.3 | 1 564.3 | 283.5 |
| Yakima, WA ...................... | 537 | 11 636 | 1 119.8 | 441.2 | 297 | 1 767 | 132.9 | 33.9 | 1 822.9 | 574.3 | 269.3 | 140.3 |
| York-Hanover, PA................ | 925 | 20 265 | 1 931.3 | 790.7 | 746 | 5 098 | 582.7 | 115.6 | 3 882.1 | 1 330.7 | 554.7 | 77.2 |
| Youngstown-Warren-Boardman, OH-PA .................. | 1 768 | 38 812 | 3 155.1 | 1 254.2 | 1 030 | 6 263 | 474.1 | 130.4 | 5 279.6 | 2 133.5 | 1 498.1 | 305.0 |
| Yuba City, CA .................... | 347 | 5 793 | 722.4 | 228.5 | 186 | 991 | 95.8 | 26.5 | 1 364.9 | 439.3 | 245.3 | 74.0 |
| Yuma, AZ............................ | 329 | 6 463 | 654.6 | 235.7 | 208 | 1 217 | 85.2 | 26.0 | 1 761.7 | 495.9 | 212.6 | 96.0 |

1. Establishments subject to federal tax.

| Area name | Federal funds and grants, 2009–2010 (cont.) | | | | | | | Value of residential construction authorized by building permits, 2011 | | Local government finances, 2007 | | | | |
|---|---|---|---|---|---|---|---|---|---|---|---|---|---|---|
| | Expenditures (mil dol) (cont.) | | | | | | | | | General revenue | | | | |
| | Procurement contract awards | | | Grants | | | | | | | | Taxes | | |
| | | | | | | | | | | | | | Per capita[1] (dollars) | |
| | Salaries and wages | Defense | Other | Medicaid and other health-related | Nutrition and family welfare | Education | Other | New construction ($1,000) | Number of housing units | Total (mil dol) | Inter-govern-mental (mil dol) | Total (mil dol) | Total | Property |
| | 171 | 172 | 173 | 174 | 175 | 176 | 177 | 178 | 179 | 180 | 181 | 182 | 183 | 184 |
| Virginia Beach-Norfolk-Newport News, VA-NC | 6 402.6 | 9 027.1 | 1 160.6 | 956.1 | 193.2 | 158.4 | 377.7 | 719 348 | 5 559 | 7 247.2 | 2 801.2 | 2 903.9 | 1 751 | 1 205 |
| Visalia-Porterville, CA | 77.9 | 12.8 | 73.0 | 569.1 | 116.0 | 40.5 | 68.2 | 135 666 | 922 | 2 844.1 | 1 469.6 | 387.4 | 919 | 613 |
| Waco, TX | 190.6 | 256.7 | 34.8 | 300.0 | 33.5 | 11.5 | 35.7 | 99 673 | 523 | 1 359.6 | 479.5 | 300.6 | 1 318 | 1 012 |
| Warner Robins, GA | 982.5 | 572.7 | 67.4 | 55.7 | 25.1 | 7.4 | 2.1 | 107 962 | 653 | 597.5 | 168.8 | 172.5 | 1 316 | 721 |
| Washington-Arlington-Alexandria, DC-VA-MD-WV | 42 792.8 | 37 778.4 | 43 558.9 | 4 596.1 | 818.6 | 1 006.4 | 9 991.6 | 2 937 160 | 19 657 | 30 893.9 | 8 530.0 | 17 190.3 | 3 239 | 1 718 |
| Bethesda-Rockvilee-Frederick, MD Div | 5 396.8 | 3 125.5 | 7 314.8 | 959.1 | 122.4 | 34.3 | 758.4 | 563 051 | 3 156 | 5 574.5 | 1 195.3 | 3 543.9 | 3 067 | 1 344 |
| Washington-Arlington-Alexandria, DC-VA-MD-WV Div | 37 396.1 | 34 652.9 | 36 244.1 | 3 637.0 | 696.3 | 972.1 | 9 233.2 | 2 374 110 | 16 501 | 25 319.4 | 7 334.7 | 13 646.4 | 3 287 | 1 822 |
| Waterloo-Cedar Falls, IA | 89.6 | 15.3 | 33.8 | 155.2 | 28.1 | 8.8 | 45.7 | 67 540 | 410 | 647.1 | 248.3 | 232.8 | 1 426 | 1 116 |
| Wausau, WI | 72.1 | 2.2 | 42.5 | 122.5 | 19.4 | 6.0 | 6.0 | 46 349 | 276 | 538.7 | 241.1 | 193.6 | 1 489 | 1 374 |
| Wenatchee-East Wenatchee, WA | 53.0 | 15.3 | 14.1 | 85.1 | 22.8 | 5.7 | 45.4 | 46 183 | 246 | 453.8 | 196.7 | 129.3 | 1 207 | 764 |
| Wheeling, WV-OH | 77.3 | 9.4 | 18.9 | 157.8 | 30.9 | 11.4 | 35.2 | 4 086 | 27 | 506.2 | 234.9 | 152.9 | 1 051 | 670 |
| Wichita, KS | 704.2 | 1 077.6 | 157.4 | 412.3 | 97.8 | 29.0 | 92.2 | 163 647 | 1 062 | 2 115.8 | 918.4 | 811.5 | 1 361 | 965 |
| Wichita Falls, TX | 380.1 | 181.1 | 9.6 | 145.0 | 28.1 | 6.0 | 16.8 | 31 765 | 170 | 421.3 | 140.7 | 189.1 | 1 277 | 979 |
| Williamsport, PA | 64.5 | 20.3 | 16.9 | 107.0 | 24.2 | 4.8 | 20.0 | 17 260 | 156 | 397.9 | 173.9 | 143.6 | 1 229 | 892 |
| Wilmington, NC | 138.8 | 124.3 | 45.3 | 309.2 | 45.6 | 20.2 | 91.2 | 350 169 | 1 831 | 1 715.5 | 427.5 | 465.3 | 1 370 | 996 |
| Winchester, VA-WV | 128.5 | 9.2 | 19.0 | 66.2 | 9.3 | 7.3 | 4.6 | 106 882 | 452 | 384.4 | 149.2 | 180.8 | 1 492 | 986 |
| Winston-Salem, NC | 153.7 | 53.4 | 79.2 | 642.9 | 61.2 | 44.4 | 83.4 | 153 284 | 1 412 | 1 392.4 | 652.4 | 490.6 | 1 059 | 816 |
| Worcester, MA | 313.7 | 165.3 | 113.1 | 1 290.4 | 135.6 | 62.6 | 243.3 | 151 118 | 791 | 2 659.9 | 1 294.8 | 1 073.9 | 1 374 | 1 341 |
| Yakima, WA | 134.0 | 62.6 | 30.9 | 333.3 | 103.9 | 48.1 | 58.2 | 76 321 | 438 | 808.0 | 483.0 | 196.6 | 844 | 524 |
| York-Hanover, PA | 216.5 | 1 323.7 | 41.4 | 211.8 | 48.0 | 7.3 | 31.6 | 103 376 | 638 | 1 629.2 | 579.2 | 662.4 | 1 573 | 1 241 |
| Youngstown-Warren-Boardman, OH-PA | 231.8 | 53.1 | 43.2 | 681.6 | 131.5 | 47.8 | 68.1 | 54 754 | 256 | 2 072.6 | 1 071.0 | 708.0 | 1 241 | 892 |
| Yuba City, CA | 244.2 | 12.9 | 19.5 | 201.4 | 42.0 | 19.3 | 13.9 | 21 870 | 146 | 886.8 | 481.6 | 202.7 | 1 235 | 967 |
| Yuma, AZ | 235.1 | 324.8 | 45.2 | 209.7 | 51.8 | 19.1 | 30.8 | 49 179 | 360 | 669.9 | 368.7 | 193.9 | 1 017 | 548 |

1. Based on the resident population estimated as of July 1 of the year shown.

| Area name | Total (mil dol) | Per capita[1] (dollars) | Educa- tion | Health and hospitals | Police protec- tion | Public welfare | High- ways | Total (mil dol) | Per capita[1] (dollars) | Federal civilian | Federal military | State and local | Demo- cratic | Republi- can | All other |
|---|---|---|---|---|---|---|---|---|---|---|---|---|---|---|---|
| | | | | | | | | | | | | | | | |
| | 185 | 186 | 187 | 188 | 189 | 190 | 191 | 192 | 193 | 194 | 195 | 196 | 197 | 198 | 199 |
| Virginia Beach-Norfolk-Newport News, VA-NC ........ | 6 951.5 | 4 191 | 45.4 | 6.5 | 4.9 | 4.1 | 3.1 | 7 717.4 | 4 653 | 51 340 | 92 962 | 108 957 | 54.9 | 43.7 | 1.4 |
| Visalia-Porterville, CA .......... | 2 828.2 | 6 709 | 40.6 | 21.2 | 3.1 | 8.7 | 2.8 | 1 178.2 | 2 795 | 1 250 | 713 | 30 018 | 41.3 | 56.3 | 2.4 |
| Waco, TX ............................. | 1 351.0 | 5 922 | 29.1 | 1.9 | 3.4 | 0.3 | 1.4 | 15 878.1 | 69 603 | 3 068 | 603 | 14 314 | 34.5 | 64.3 | 1.3 |
| Warner Robins, GA.............. | 604.1 | 4 611 | 46.0 | 28.7 | 3.8 | 0.2 | 4.5 | 126.5 | 966 | 16 881 | 4 236 | 9 261 | 39.1 | 59.8 | 1.1 |
| Washington-Arlington-Alex- andria, DC-VA-MD-WV .. | 29 967.0 | 5 647 | 40.6 | 3.8 | 5.4 | 9.5 | 2.2 | 35 715.8 | 6 730 | 400 781 | 69 123 | 308 418 | 67.5 | 30.9 | 1.6 |
| Bethesda-Rockvilee-Fred- erick, MD Div .............. | 5 432.0 | 4 701 | 50.8 | 2.6 | 4.7 | 3.1 | 3.9 | 4 556.8 | 3 943 | 52 945 | 8 917 | 51 669 | 66.1 | 31.8 | 2.2 |
| Washington-Arlington-Alex- andria, DC-VA-MD-WV Div................................ | 24 534.9 | 5 911 | 38.4 | 4.0 | 5.6 | 10.9 | 1.8 | 31 159.1 | 7 506 | 347 836 | 60 206 | 256 749 | 67.9 | 30.6 | 1.5 |
| Waterloo-Cedar Falls, IA ...... | 689.5 | 4 222 | 51.3 | 10.0 | 4.0 | 0.8 | 7.3 | 451.5 | 2 765 | 628 | 712 | 14 423 | 56.3 | 42.1 | 1.6 |
| Wausau, WI ......................... | 586.2 | 4 511 | 46.6 | 14.1 | 4.0 | 3.7 | 9.8 | 477.0 | 3 670 | 499 | 377 | 7 104 | 46.3 | 52.4 | 1.3 |
| Wenatchee-East Wenat- chee, WA ....................... | 384.6 | 3 588 | 47.9 | 11.0 | 4.4 | 0.0 | 7.6 | 1 742.9 | 16 263 | 897 | 332 | 7 838 | 38.7 | 59.0 | 2.3 |
| Wheeling, WV-OH................ | 494.1 | 3 397 | 45.1 | 1.5 | 5.0 | 5.1 | 6.3 | 442.1 | 3 040 | 661 | 559 | 9 556 | 40.8 | 57.2 | 2.1 |
| Wichita, KS .......................... | 1 966.0 | 3 296 | 52.1 | 4.0 | 6.4 | 0.5 | 4.8 | 3 636.4 | 6 097 | 5 943 | 5 515 | 35 365 | 37.6 | 60.0 | 2.4 |
| Wichita Falls, TX.................. | 393.0 | 2 653 | 54.0 | 5.2 | 6.5 | 0.6 | 4.6 | 702.9 | 4 745 | 2 220 | 5 640 | 10 488 | 23.5 | 75.0 | 1.5 |
| Williamsport, PA.................. | 377.8 | 3 234 | 55.4 | 0.0 | 2.6 | 4.4 | 4.6 | 503.7 | 4 312 | 435 | 296 | 9 455 | 32.7 | 65.9 | 1.4 |
| Wilmington, NC.................... | 1 772.3 | 5 220 | 26.1 | 35.9 | 4.3 | 4.0 | 1.1 | 1 606.9 | 4 733 | 1 424 | 1 294 | 24 920 | 43.3 | 55.4 | 1.3 |
| Winchester, VA-WV ............. | 391.4 | 3 230 | 62.3 | 1.1 | 4.3 | 3.2 | 1.4 | 407.6 | 3 364 | 1 716 | 462 | 7 220 | 36.7 | 61.0 | 2.3 |
| Winston-Salem, NC ............. | 1 412.8 | 3 050 | 48.0 | 5.7 | 5.7 | 5.7 | 2.1 | 1 361.0 | 2 939 | 1 788 | 1 290 | 23 574 | 46.3 | 52.4 | 1.2 |
| Worcester, MA ..................... | 2 872.2 | 3 676 | 59.7 | 0.6 | 4.3 | 0.1 | 3.5 | 2 447.7 | 3 133 | 2 599 | 2 109 | 48 411 | 53.7 | 44.3 | 2.0 |
| Yakima, WA ......................... | 822.6 | 3 529 | 56.3 | 1.4 | 4.6 | 1.2 | 5.4 | 518.4 | 2 224 | 1 315 | 837 | 15 922 | 43.2 | 54.9 | 2.0 |
| York-Hanover, PA ................ | 1 595.0 | 3 788 | 45.1 | 4.3 | 2.9 | 10.1 | 2.6 | 2 349.1 | 5 579 | 4 584 | 1 407 | 16 679 | 38.7 | 59.9 | 1.4 |
| Youngstown-Warren-Board- man, OH-PA ..................... | 2 082.9 | 3 650 | 54.9 | 5.2 | 5.3 | 5.1 | 3.9 | 1 393.7 | 2 442 | 2 086 | 1 463 | 28 689 | 59.5 | 39.0 | 1.5 |
| Yuba City, CA ...................... | 897.1 | 5 466 | 51.6 | 4.8 | 4.7 | 8.4 | 2.7 | 443.3 | 2 701 | 1 568 | 3 998 | 9 725 | 39.2 | 58.0 | 2.8 |
| Yuma, AZ............................. | 749.5 | 3 933 | 47.7 | 1.1 | 6.0 | 0.3 | 6.6 | 534.1 | 2 803 | 3 797 | 4 321 | 10 979 | 43.0 | 55.7 | 1.3 |

1. Based on the resident population estimated as of July 1 of the year shown.    2. © 2013 Election Data Services, Inc. All rights reserved.

PART D.

# Cities of 25,000 or More

(For explanation of symbols, see page viii)

Page

# City Highlights and Rankings

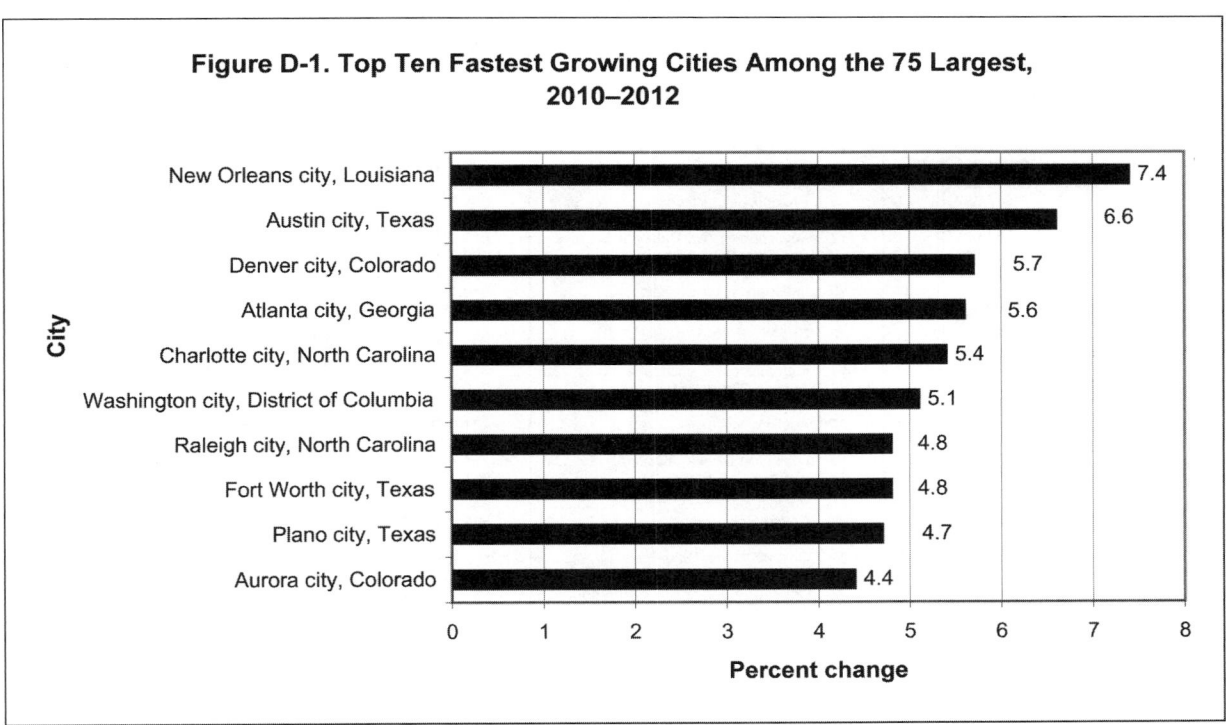

**Figure D-1. Top Ten Fastest Growing Cities Among the 75 Largest, 2010–2012**

| City | Percent change |
|------|----------------|
| New Orleans city, Louisiana | 7.4 |
| Austin city, Texas | 6.6 |
| Denver city, Colorado | 5.7 |
| Atlanta city, Georgia | 5.6 |
| Charlotte city, North Carolina | 5.4 |
| Washington city, District of Columbia | 5.1 |
| Raleigh city, North Carolina | 4.8 |
| Fort Worth city, Texas | 4.8 |
| Plano city, Texas | 4.7 |
| Aurora city, Colorado | 4.4 |

In 2012, 9 cities had more than 1 million residents, led by New York City with over 8.3 million people, Los Angeles with 3.8 million people, and Chicago with 2.7 million people. California had 13 cities among the nation's 75 most populous, as well as 4 among the top 15 (Los Angeles, San Diego, San Jose, and San Francisco). Texas had 9 cities in the top 75, and also had 4 among the top 15 (Houston, San Antonio, Dallas, and Austin).

Among the largest cities, six had growth rates exceeding 5 percent from 2010 to 2012. Many of these cities were in the south. However, Denver, CO ranked third with a growth rate of 5.7 percent. New Orleans had the highest growth rate at 7.4 percent. Texas had three cities in the top ten (Austin, Fort Worth, Plano) while North Carolina (Charlotte, Raleigh) and Colorado (Denver, Aurora) each had two.

Among the 75 largest cities, six lost population between 2010 and 2012. Detroit, Cleveland, and Toledo each lost more than 1 percent of their populations. Though New Orleans lost 29.1 percent of its population between 2000 and 2010, it actually grew by nearly two-thirds between 2006 and 2010, after losing more than half of its population after Hurricane Katrina in 2005. It was the fastest growing city from 2010 to 2012, but its 2012 population is still 85,000 short of its pre-Katrina total.

Among all cities of 25,000 or more, 262 cities had unemployment rates of 10 percent or more, significantly lower than two years earlier when 555 cities had an unemployment rate of 10 percent or more. Twenty of the twenty-five cities with the highest unemployment rates were located in California.

Among the largest cities, Detroit, MI had the highest unemployment rate at 18.6 percent followed by Stockton, CA at 18.3 percent while Lincoln and Omaha, NE had the lowest unemployment rates at 3.4 percent and 4.6 percent respectively. Thirty-one cities had unemployment rates of 4 percent or lower. Five of the ten cities with the lowest unemployment rates were in North Dakota.

While the 2010 census provides updated counts of the population and basic demographic characteristics, updated information on social and economic characteristics is now obtained through the ongoing American Community Survey (ACS). Between the 2000 census and the late-decade information from the ACS, housing values increased dramatically in many cities, while the median household income increased less markedly. Among the largest cities, the same five cities topped the rankings for median household income in 2000 and 2007–2011: Plano, San Jose, Henderson, Anchorage, and San Francisco. San Francisco retains its spot at the top with an estimated median housing value of $767,300 up from $396,400 in 2000.

In the 2007–2011 time period in 17 of the largest cities, more than 10 percent of the residents had moved there during the previous year. Some cities have large shifts because of student or military population groups: Pittsburgh, PA lost 8.6 percent of its population from 2000 to 2010 but 11.1 percent of its population were new residents in the 2007–2011 time period, reflecting the 18.9 percent of residents who were between the ages of 18 and 24, well above the 10.0 percent national average.

# 75 Largest Cities by 2012 Population
## Selected Rankings

| Population, 2012 | | | Land area, 2010 | | | | Population density, 2012 | | | |
|---|---|---|---|---|---|---|---|---|---|---|
| Population rank | City | Population [col 2] | Population rank | Land area rank | City | Land area (square kilometers) [col 1] | Population rank | Density rank | City | Density (per square kilometer) [col 4] |
| 1 | New York city, New York | 8 336 697 | 63 | 1 | Anchorage municipality, Alaska | 4 415.1 | 1 | 1 | New York city, New York | 10 636 |
| 2 | Los Angeles city, California | 3 857 799 | 12 | 2 | Jacksonville city, Florida | 1 934.7 | 14 | 2 | San Francisco city, California | 6 803 |
| 3 | Chicago city, Illinois | 2 714 856 | 29 | 3 | Oklahoma City city, Oklahoma | 1 570.6 | 75 | 3 | Jersey City city, New Jersey | 6 643 |
| 4 | Houston city, Texas | 2 160 821 | 4 | 4 | Houston city, Texas | 1 552.9 | 21 | 4 | Boston city, Massachusetts | 5 092 |
| 5 | Philadelphia city, Pennsylvania | 1 547 607 | 6 | 5 | Phoenix city, Arizona | 1 338.3 | 57 | 5 | Santa Ana city, California | 4 687 |
| 6 | Phoenix city, Arizona | 1 488 750 | 25 | 6 | Nashville-Davidson, Tennessee | 1 305.4 | 3 | 6 | Chicago city, Illinois | 4 605 |
| 7 | San Antonio city, Texas | 1 382 951 | 2 | 7 | Los Angeles city, California | 1 213.9 | 5 | 7 | Philadelphia city, Pennsylvania | 4 456 |
| 8 | San Diego city, California | 1 338 348 | 7 | 8 | San Antonio city, Texas | 1 193.8 | 44 | 8 | Miami city, Florida | 4 455 |
| 9 | Dallas city, Texas | 1 241 162 | 27 | 9 | Louisville/Jefferson, Kentucky | 985.3 | 68 | 9 | Newark city, New Jersey | 4 437 |
| 10 | San Jose city, California | 982 765 | 13 | 10 | Indianapolis city, Indiana | 949.1 | 24 | 10 | Washington city, District of Columbia | 4 000 |
| 11 | Austin city, Texas | 842 592 | 9 | 11 | Dallas city, Texas | 881.9 | 36 | 11 | Long Beach city, California | 3 591 |
| 12 | Jacksonville city, Florida | 836 507 | 16 | 12 | Fort Worth city, Texas | 880.1 | 2 | 12 | Los Angeles city, California | 3 178 |
| 13 | Indianapolis city, Indiana | 834 852 | 8 | 13 | San Diego city, California | 842.2 | 26 | 13 | Baltimore city, Maryland | 2 964 |
| 14 | San Francisco city, California | 825 863 | 20 | 14 | Memphis city, Tennessee | 816.0 | 22 | 14 | Seattle city, Washington | 2 919 |
| 15 | Columbus city, Ohio | 809 798 | 37 | 15 | Kansas City city, Missouri | 815.7 | 47 | 15 | Minneapolis city, Minnesota | 2 810 |
| 16 | Fort Worth city, Texas | 777 992 | 1 | 16 | New York city, New York | 783.8 | 45 | 16 | Oakland city, California | 2 773 |
| 17 | Charlotte city, North Carolina | 775 202 | 11 | 17 | Austin city, Texas | 771.6 | 55 | 17 | Anaheim city, California | 2 659 |
| 18 | Detroit city, Michigan | 701 475 | 17 | 18 | Charlotte city, North Carolina | 771.0 | 73 | 18 | Buffalo city, New York | 2 480 |
| 19 | El Paso city, Texas | 672 538 | 62 | 19 | Lexington-Fayette, Kentucky | 734.7 | 30 | 19 | Milwaukee city, Wisconsin | 2 405 |
| 20 | Memphis city, Tennessee | 655 155 | 19 | 20 | El Paso city, Texas | 661.1 | 54 | 20 | Urban Honolulu CDP, Hawaii | 2 204 |
| 21 | Boston city, Massachusetts | 636 479 | 39 | 21 | Virginia Beach city, Virginia | 645.0 | 66 | 21 | St. Paul city, Minnesota | 2 160 |
| 22 | Seattle city, Washington | 634 535 | 3 | 22 | Chicago city, Illinois | 589.6 | 10 | 22 | San Jose city, California | 2 150 |
| 23 | Denver city, Colorado | 634 265 | 33 | 23 | Tucson city, Arizona | 587.2 | 61 | 23 | Pittsburgh city, Pennsylvania | 2 135 |
| 24 | Washington, District of Columbia | 632 323 | 15 | 24 | Columbus city, Ohio | 562.5 | 58 | 24 | St. Louis city, Missouri | 1 985 |
| 25 | Nashville-Davidson, Tennessee | 624 496 | 46 | 25 | Tulsa city, Oklahoma | 509.6 | 18 | 25 | Detroit city, Michigan | 1 952 |
| 26 | Baltimore city, Maryland | 621 342 | 41 | 26 | Colorado Springs city, Colorado | 503.9 | 48 | 26 | Cleveland city, Ohio | 1 943 |
| 27 | Louisville/Jefferson, Kentucky | 605 110 | 32 | 27 | Albuquerque city, New Mexico | 486.2 | 35 | 27 | Sacramento city, California | 1 875 |
| 28 | Portland city, Oregon | 603 106 | 10 | 28 | San Jose city, California | 457.2 | 64 | 28 | Stockton city, California | 1 866 |
| 29 | Oklahoma City city, Oklahoma | 599 199 | 51 | 29 | New Orleans city, Louisiana | 438.8 | 28 | 29 | Portland city, Oregon | 1 745 |
| 30 | Milwaukee city, Wisconsin | 598 916 | 60 | 30 | Corpus Christi city, Texas | 416.0 | 34 | 30 | Fresno city, California | 1 744 |
| 31 | Las Vegas city, Nevada | 596 424 | 49 | 31 | Wichita city, Kansas | 412.6 | 31 | 31 | Las Vegas city, Nevada | 1 695 |
| 32 | Albuquerque city, New Mexico | 555 417 | 56 | 32 | Aurora city, Colorado | 400.8 | 23 | 32 | Denver city, Colorado | 1 601 |
| 33 | Tucson city, Arizona | 524 295 | 23 | 33 | Denver city, Colorado | 396.3 | 8 | 33 | San Diego city, California | 1 589 |
| 34 | Fresno city, California | 505 882 | 42 | 34 | Raleigh city, North Carolina | 370.1 | 50 | 34 | Arlington city, Texas | 1 513 |
| 35 | Sacramento city, California | 475 516 | 52 | 35 | Bakersfield city, California | 368.2 | 59 | 35 | Riverside city, California | 1 492 |
| 36 | Long Beach city, California | 467 892 | 18 | 36 | Detroit city, Michigan | 359.4 | 65 | 36 | Cincinnati city, Ohio | 1 469 |
| 37 | Kansas City city, Missouri | 464 310 | 38 | 37 | Mesa city, Arizona | 353.4 | 70 | 37 | Plano city, Texas | 1 468 |
| 38 | Mesa city, Arizona | 452 084 | 31 | 38 | Las Vegas city, Nevada | 351.8 | 15 | 38 | Columbus city, Ohio | 1 440 |
| 39 | Virginia Beach city, Virginia | 447 021 | 5 | 39 | Philadelphia city, Pennsylvania | 347.3 | 9 | 39 | Dallas city, Texas | 1 407 |
| 40 | Atlanta city, Georgia | 443 775 | 28 | 40 | Portland city, Oregon | 345.6 | 4 | 40 | Houston city, Texas | 1 392 |
| 41 | Colorado Springs city, Colorado | 431 834 | 40 | 41 | Atlanta city, Georgia | 344.9 | 67 | 41 | Toledo city, Ohio | 1 359 |
| 42 | Raleigh city, North Carolina | 423 179 | 43 | 42 | Omaha city, Nebraska | 329.2 | 40 | 42 | Atlanta city, Georgia | 1 287 |
| 43 | Omaha city, Nebraska | 421 570 | 69 | 43 | Greensboro city, North Carolina | 327.7 | 43 | 43 | Omaha city, Nebraska | 1 281 |
| 44 | Miami city, Florida | 413 892 | 53 | 44 | Tampa city, Florida | 293.7 | 38 | 44 | Mesa city, Arizona | 1 279 |
| 45 | Oakland city, California | 400 740 | 34 | 45 | Fresno city, California | 290.0 | 53 | 45 | Tampa city, Florida | 1 184 |
| 46 | Tulsa city, Oklahoma | 393 987 | 74 | 46 | Fort Wayne city, Indiana | 286.5 | 7 | 46 | San Antonio city, Texas | 1 158 |
| 47 | Minneapolis city, Minnesota | 392 880 | 71 | 47 | Henderson city, Nevada | 279.0 | 72 | 47 | Lincoln city, Nebraska | 1 150 |
| 48 | Cleveland city, Ohio | 390 928 | 35 | 48 | Sacramento city, California | 253.6 | 42 | 48 | Raleigh city, North Carolina | 1 143 |
| 49 | Wichita city, Kansas | 385 577 | 30 | 49 | Milwaukee city, Wisconsin | 249.0 | 32 | 49 | Albuquerque city, New Mexico | 1 142 |
| 50 | Arlington city, Texas | 375 600 | 50 | 50 | Arlington city, Texas | 248.3 | 6 | 50 | Phoenix city, Arizona | 1 112 |
| 51 | New Orleans city, Louisiana | 369 250 | 72 | 51 | Lincoln city, Nebraska | 230.8 | 11 | 51 | Austin city, Texas | 1 092 |
| 52 | Bakersfield city, California | 358 597 | 22 | 52 | Seattle city, Washington | 217.4 | 19 | 52 | El Paso city, Texas | 1 017 |
| 53 | Tampa city, Florida | 347 645 | 59 | 53 | Riverside city, California | 210.2 | 17 | 53 | Charlotte city, North Carolina | 1 006 |
| 54 | Urban Honolulu CDP, Hawaii | 345 610 | 26 | 54 | Baltimore city, Maryland | 209.6 | 52 | 54 | Bakersfield city, California | 974 |
| 55 | Anaheim city, California | 343 248 | 67 | 55 | Toledo city, Ohio | 209.0 | 71 | 55 | Henderson city, Nevada | 952 |
| 56 | Aurora city, Colorado | 339 030 | 65 | 56 | Cincinnati city, Ohio | 201.9 | 49 | 56 | Wichita city, Kansas | 935 |
| 57 | Santa Ana city, California | 330 920 | 48 | 57 | Cleveland city, Ohio | 201.2 | 33 | 57 | Tucson city, Arizona | 893 |
| 58 | St. Louis city, Missouri | 318 172 | 70 | 58 | Plano city, Texas | 185.4 | 13 | 58 | Indianapolis city, Indiana | 892 |
| 59 | Riverside city, California | 313 673 | 58 | 59 | St. Louis city, Missouri | 160.3 | 74 | 59 | Fort Wayne city, Indiana | 889 |
| 60 | Corpus Christi city, Texas | 312 195 | 64 | 60 | Stockton city, California | 159.7 | 16 | 60 | Fort Worth city, Texas | 884 |
| 61 | Pittsburgh city, Pennsylvania | 306 211 | 24 | 61 | Washington city, District of Columbia | 158.1 | 41 | 61 | Colorado Springs city, Colorado | 857 |
| 62 | Lexington-Fayette, Kentucky | 305 489 | 54 | 62 | Urban Honolulu CDP, Hawaii | 156.8 | 56 | 62 | Aurora city, Colorado | 846 |
| 63 | Anchorage municipality, Alaska | 298 610 | 45 | 63 | Oakland city, California | 144.5 | 69 | 63 | Greensboro city, North Carolina | 846 |
| 64 | Stockton city, California | 297 984 | 61 | 64 | Pittsburgh city, Pennsylvania | 143.4 | 51 | 64 | New Orleans city, Louisiana | 842 |
| 65 | Cincinnati city, Ohio | 296 550 | 47 | 65 | Minneapolis city, Minnesota | 139.8 | 20 | 65 | Memphis city, Tennessee | 803 |
| 66 | St. Paul city, Minnesota | 290 770 | 66 | 66 | St. Paul city, Minnesota | 134.6 | 46 | 66 | Tulsa city, Oklahoma | 773 |
| 67 | Toledo city, Ohio | 284 012 | 36 | 67 | Long Beach city, California | 130.3 | 60 | 67 | Corpus Christi city, Texas | 751 |
| 68 | Newark city, New Jersey | 277 727 | 55 | 68 | Anaheim city, California | 129.1 | 27 | 68 | Louisville/Jefferson, Kentucky | 718 |
| 69 | Greensboro city, North Carolina | 277 080 | 21 | 69 | Boston city, Massachusetts | 125.0 | 39 | 69 | Virginia Beach city, Virginia | 693 |
| 70 | Plano city, Texas | 272 068 | 14 | 70 | San Francisco city, California | 121.4 | 37 | 70 | Kansas City city, Missouri | 569 |
| 71 | Henderson city, Nevada | 265 679 | 73 | 71 | Buffalo city, New York | 104.6 | 25 | 71 | Nashville-Davidson, Tennessee | 508 |
| 72 | Lincoln city, Nebraska | 265 404 | 44 | 72 | Miami city, Florida | 92.9 | 12 | 72 | Jacksonville city, Florida | 432 |
| 73 | Buffalo city, New York | 259 384 | 57 | 73 | Santa Ana city, California | 70.6 | 62 | 73 | Lexington-Fayette, Kentucky | 416 |
| 74 | Fort Wayne city, Indiana | 254 555 | 68 | 74 | Newark city, New Jersey | 62.6 | 29 | 74 | Oklahoma City city, Oklahoma | 382 |
| 75 | Jersey City city, New Jersey | 254 441 | 75 | 75 | Jersey City city, New Jersey | 38.3 | 63 | 75 | Anchorage municipality, Alaska | 68 |

# 75 Largest Cities by 2012 Population
## Selected Rankings

| Percent population change, 2010–2012 | | | | Percent White, alone or in combination, 2010 | | | | Percent Black, alone or in combination, 2010 | | | |
|---|---|---|---|---|---|---|---|---|---|---|---|
| Popu-lation rank | Percent change rank | City | Percent change [col 26] | Popu-lation rank | White rank | City | Percent White [col 5] | Popu-lation rank | Black rank | City | Percent Black [col 6] |
| 51 | 1 | New Orleans city, Louisiana | 7.4 | 72 | 1 | Lincoln city, Nebraska | 85.3 | 18 | 1 | Detroit city, Michigan | 83.6 |
| 11 | 2 | Austin city, Texas | 6.6 | 28 | 2 | Portland city, Oregon | 75.5 | 26 | 2 | Baltimore city, Maryland | 64.4 |
| 23 | 3 | Denver city, Colorado | 5.7 | 62 | 3 | Lexington-Fayette, Kentucky | 74.9 | 20 | 3 | Memphis city, Tennessee | 63.8 |
| 40 | 4 | Atlanta city, Georgia | 5.6 | 41 | 4 | Colorado Springs city, Colorado | 73.7 | 51 | 4 | New Orleans city, Louisiana | 60.4 |
| 17 | 5 | Charlotte city, North Carolina | 5.4 | 74 | 5 | Fort Wayne city, Indiana | 72.8 | 40 | 5 | Atlanta city, Georgia | 54.4 |
| 24 | 6 | Washington city, District of Columbia | 5.1 | 27 | 6 | Louisville/Jefferson, Kentucky | 72.2 | 48 | 6 | Cleveland city, Ohio | 53.9 |
| 16 | 7 | Fort Worth city, Texas | 4.8 | 71 | 7 | Henderson city, Nevada | 71.6 | 24 | 7 | Washington city, District of Columbia | 51.3 |
| 42 | 7 | Raleigh city, North Carolina | 4.8 | 22 | 8 | Seattle city, Washington | 70.1 | 68 | 8 | Newark city, New Jersey | 50.6 |
| 70 | 9 | Plano city, Texas | 4.7 | 43 | 9 | Omaha city, Nebraska | 69.8 | 58 | 9 | St. Louis city, Missouri | 50.3 |
| 56 | 10 | Aurora city, Colorado | 4.4 | 63 | 10 | Anchorage municipality, Alaska | 68.5 | 65 | 10 | Cincinnati city, Ohio | 46.2 |
| 22 | 11 | Seattle city, Washington | 4.3 | 49 | 11 | Wichita city, Kansas | 67.3 | 5 | 11 | Philadelphia city, Pennsylvania | 43.4 |
| 7 | 12 | San Antonio city, Texas | 4.2 | 39 | 12 | Virginia Beach city, Virginia | 67.2 | 69 | 12 | Greensboro city, North Carolina | 41.6 |
| 41 | 13 | Colorado Springs city, Colorado | 3.7 | 61 | 13 | Pittsburgh city, Pennsylvania | 66.7 | 30 | 13 | Milwaukee city, Wisconsin | 40.9 |
| 9 | 14 | Dallas city, Texas | 3.6 | 38 | 14 | Mesa city, Arizona | 66.0 | 73 | 14 | Buffalo city, New York | 39.0 |
| 19 | 14 | El Paso city, Texas | 3.6 | 67 | 15 | Toledo city, Ohio | 64.0 | 17 | 15 | Charlotte city, North Carolina | 35.6 |
| 44 | 14 | Miami city, Florida | 3.6 | 47 | 16 | Minneapolis city, Minnesota | 63.1 | 3 | 16 | Chicago city, Illinois | 33.0 |
| 53 | 14 | Tampa city, Florida | 3.6 | 46 | 17 | Tulsa city, Oklahoma | 62.0 | 12 | 17 | Jacksonville city, Florida | 31.2 |
| 25 | 18 | Nashville-Davidson, Tennessee | 3.5 | 15 | 18 | Columbus city, Ohio | 61.7 | 37 | 18 | Kansas City city, Missouri | 31.0 |
| 28 | 19 | Portland city, Oregon | 3.3 | 13 | 19 | Indianapolis city, Indiana | 60.7 | 42 | 19 | Raleigh city, North Carolina | 29.8 |
| 29 | 19 | Oklahoma City city, Oklahoma | 3.3 | 70 | 20 | Plano city, Texas | 60.2 | 15 | 20 | Columbus city, Ohio | 29.6 |
| 62 | 19 | Lexington-Fayette, Kentucky | 3.3 | 29 | 21 | Oklahoma City city, Oklahoma | 60.0 | 45 | 21 | Oakland city, California | 29.2 |
| 10 | 22 | San Jose city, California | 3.2 | 25 | 22 | Nashville-Davidson, Tennessee | 59.0 | 67 | 22 | Toledo city, Ohio | 28.9 |
| 52 | 22 | Bakersfield city, California | 3.2 | 66 | 23 | St. Paul city, Minnesota | 58.6 | 13 | 23 | Indianapolis city, Indiana | 28.6 |
| 59 | 22 | Riverside city, California | 3.2 | 12 | 24 | Jacksonville city, Florida | 56.9 | 25 | 24 | Nashville-Davidson, Tennessee | 28.5 |
| 21 | 25 | Boston city, Massachusetts | 3.1 | 37 | 25 | Kansas City city, Missouri | 56.8 | 61 | 25 | Pittsburgh city, Pennsylvania | 27.3 |
| 71 | 25 | Henderson city, Nevada | 3.1 | 42 | 26 | Raleigh city, North Carolina | 54.8 | 53 | 26 | Tampa city, Florida | 25.8 |
| 4 | 27 | Houston city, Texas | 3.0 | 23 | 27 | Denver city, Colorado | 53.9 | 9 | 27 | Dallas city, Texas | 25.1 |
| 43 | 28 | Omaha city, Nebraska | 2.9 | 11 | 28 | Austin city, Texas | 50.3 | 75 | 28 | Jersey City city, New Jersey | 24.9 |
| 6 | 29 | Phoenix city, Arizona | 2.8 | 31 | 29 | Las Vegas city, Nevada | 50.2 | 21 | 29 | Boston city, Massachusetts | 23.8 |
| 8 | 29 | San Diego city, California | 2.8 | 65 | 30 | Cincinnati city, Ohio | 50.0 | 1 | 30 | New York city, New York | 23.6 |
| 38 | 29 | Mesa city, Arizona | 2.8 | 56 | 31 | Aurora city, Colorado | 49.9 | 4 | 30 | Houston city, Texas | 23.6 |
| 50 | 29 | Arlington city, Texas | 2.8 | 33 | 32 | Tucson city, Arizona | 48.9 | 27 | 32 | Louisville/Jefferson, Kentucky | 21.8 |
| 75 | 29 | Jersey City city, New Jersey | 2.8 | 21 | 33 | Boston city, Massachusetts | 48.5 | 39 | 33 | Virginia Beach city, Virginia | 20.6 |
| 15 | 34 | Columbus city, Ohio | 2.7 | 6 | 34 | Phoenix city, Arizona | 48.0 | 47 | 34 | Minneapolis city, Minnesota | 20.4 |
| 47 | 34 | Minneapolis city, Minnesota | 2.7 | 53 | 35 | Tampa city, Florida | 47.9 | 50 | 35 | Arlington city, Texas | 19.3 |
| 69 | 34 | Greensboro city, North Carolina | 2.7 | 8 | 36 | San Diego city, California | 47.8 | 16 | 36 | Fort Worth city, Texas | 19.2 |
| 72 | 34 | Lincoln city, Nebraska | 2.7 | 73 | 37 | Buffalo city, New York | 47.7 | 46 | 37 | Tulsa city, Oklahoma | 17.4 |
| 14 | 38 | San Francisco city, California | 2.6 | 69 | 38 | Greensboro city, North Carolina | 47.1 | 66 | 38 | St. Paul city, Minnesota | 17.3 |
| 45 | 38 | Oakland city, California | 2.6 | 50 | 39 | Arlington city, Texas | 46.5 | 74 | 39 | Fort Wayne city, Indiana | 17.1 |
| 54 | 40 | Urban Honolulu CDP, Hawaii | 2.5 | 17 | 40 | Charlotte city, North Carolina | 46.4 | 56 | 40 | Aurora city, Colorado | 17.0 |
| 60 | 41 | Corpus Christi city, Texas | 2.3 | 14 | 41 | San Francisco city, California | 44.6 | 44 | 41 | Miami city, Florida | 16.7 |
| 63 | 41 | Anchorage municipality, Alaska | 2.3 | 58 | 42 | St. Louis city, Missouri | 43.8 | 29 | 42 | Oklahoma City city, Oklahoma | 16.4 |
| 31 | 43 | Las Vegas city, Nevada | 2.2 | 32 | 43 | Albuquerque city, New Mexico | 43.7 | 35 | 43 | Sacramento city, California | 15.9 |
| 39 | 44 | Virginia Beach city, Virginia | 2.1 | 16 | 44 | Fort Worth city, Texas | 43.0 | 62 | 44 | Lexington-Fayette, Kentucky | 15.6 |
| 55 | 44 | Anaheim city, California | 2.1 | 52 | 45 | Bakersfield city, California | 39.6 | 43 | 45 | Omaha city, Nebraska | 14.9 |
| 64 | 44 | Stockton city, California | 2.1 | 30 | 46 | Milwaukee city, Wisconsin | 38.8 | 36 | 46 | Long Beach city, California | 14.1 |
| 1 | 47 | New York city, New York | 2.0 | 5 | 47 | Philadelphia city, Pennsylvania | 38.1 | 49 | 47 | Wichita city, Kansas | 12.8 |
| 34 | 47 | Fresno city, California | 2.0 | 35 | 48 | Sacramento city, California | 37.7 | 64 | 47 | Stockton city, California | 12.8 |
| 57 | 47 | Santa Ana city, California | 2.0 | 40 | 49 | Atlanta city, Georgia | 37.4 | 31 | 49 | Las Vegas city, Nevada | 11.8 |
| 66 | 47 | St. Paul city, Minnesota | 2.0 | 24 | 50 | Washington city, District of Columbia | 36.3 | 23 | 50 | Denver city, Colorado | 10.8 |
| 35 | 51 | Sacramento city, California | 1.9 | 59 | 51 | Riverside city, California | 35.9 | 2 | 51 | Los Angeles city, California | 9.8 |
| 12 | 52 | Jacksonville city, Florida | 1.8 | 48 | 52 | Cleveland city, Ohio | 34.9 | 22 | 52 | Seattle city, Washington | 9.1 |
| 13 | 52 | Indianapolis city, Indiana | 1.8 | 1 | 53 | New York city, New York | 34.3 | 52 | 53 | Bakersfield city, California | 8.5 |
| 2 | 54 | Los Angeles city, California | 1.7 | 60 | 54 | Corpus Christi city, Texas | 34.1 | 34 | 54 | Fresno city, California | 8.4 |
| 32 | 55 | Albuquerque city, New Mexico | 1.6 | 3 | 55 | Chicago city, Illinois | 32.7 | 11 | 55 | Austin city, Texas | 8.3 |
| 5 | 56 | Philadelphia city, Pennsylvania | 1.4 | 34 | 56 | Fresno city, California | 31.6 | 70 | 56 | Plano city, Texas | 8.0 |
| 20 | 57 | Memphis city, Tennessee | 1.3 | 36 | 57 | Long Beach city, California | 31.4 | 28 | 57 | Portland city, Oregon | 7.4 |
| 27 | 57 | Louisville/Jefferson, Kentucky | 1.3 | 51 | 57 | New Orleans city, Louisiana | 31.4 | 59 | 57 | Riverside city, California | 7.4 |
| 36 | 59 | Long Beach city, California | 1.2 | 10 | 59 | San Jose city, California | 30.9 | 8 | 59 | San Diego city, California | 7.3 |
| 37 | 60 | Kansas City city, Missouri | 1.0 | 2 | 60 | Los Angeles city, California | 30.3 | 41 | 59 | Colorado Springs city, Colorado | 7.3 |
| 33 | 61 | Tucson city, Arizona | 0.8 | 9 | 61 | Dallas city, Texas | 29.6 | 63 | 61 | Anchorage municipality, Alaska | 7.1 |
| 49 | 61 | Wichita city, Kansas | 0.8 | 26 | 62 | Baltimore city, Maryland | 29.2 | 6 | 62 | Phoenix city, Arizona | 6.8 |
| 3 | 63 | Chicago city, Illinois | 0.7 | 55 | 63 | Anaheim city, California | 29.0 | 7 | 62 | San Antonio city, Texas | 6.8 |
| 30 | 63 | Milwaukee city, Wisconsin | 0.7 | 45 | 64 | Oakland city, California | 28.6 | 14 | 64 | San Francisco city, California | 6.7 |
| 46 | 65 | Tulsa city, Oklahoma | 0.5 | 20 | 65 | Memphis city, Tennessee | 28.3 | 71 | 65 | Henderson city, Nevada | 5.9 |
| 74 | 66 | Fort Wayne city, Indiana | 0.3 | 7 | 66 | San Antonio city, Texas | 27.6 | 33 | 66 | Tucson city, Arizona | 5.3 |
| 61 | 67 | Pittsburgh city, Pennsylvania | 0.2 | 54 | 67 | Urban Honolulu CDP, Hawaii | 26.5 | 72 | 67 | Lincoln city, Nebraska | 5.0 |
| 68 | 67 | Newark city, New Jersey | 0.2 | 4 | 68 | Houston city, Texas | 26.4 | 60 | 68 | Corpus Christi city, Texas | 4.2 |
| 26 | 69 | Baltimore city, Maryland | 0.1 | 64 | 69 | Stockton city, California | 25.3 | 38 | 69 | Mesa city, Arizona | 4.0 |
| 65 | 70 | Cincinnati city, Ohio | -0.1 | 75 | 70 | Jersey City city, New Jersey | 22.7 | 10 | 70 | San Jose city, California | 3.4 |
| 58 | 71 | St. Louis city, Missouri | -0.4 | 19 | 71 | El Paso city, Texas | 14.9 | 32 | 71 | Albuquerque city, New Mexico | 3.3 |
| 73 | 72 | Buffalo city, New York | -0.7 | 68 | 72 | Newark city, New Jersey | 12.5 | 19 | 72 | El Paso city, Texas | 3.1 |
| 67 | 73 | Toledo city, Ohio | -1.1 | 44 | 73 | Miami city, Florida | 12.3 | 55 | 73 | Anaheim city, California | 2.8 |
| 48 | 74 | Cleveland city, Ohio | -1.5 | 57 | 74 | Santa Ana city, California | 9.8 | 54 | 74 | Urban Honolulu CDP, Hawaii | 2.3 |
| 18 | 75 | Detroit city, Michigan | -1.7 | 18 | 75 | Detroit city, Michigan | 8.9 | 57 | 75 | Santa Ana city, California | 1.1 |

# 75 Largest Cities by 2012 Population
## Selected Rankings

| Percent American Indian, Alaska Native, 2010 | | | | Percent Asian and Pacific Islander, 2010 | | | | Percent Hispanic or Latino,[1] 2010 | | | |
|---|---|---|---|---|---|---|---|---|---|---|---|
| Population rank | American Indian, Alaska Native rank | City | Percent American Indian, Alaska Native [col 7] | Population rank | Asian and Pacific Islander rank | City | Percent Asian and Pacific Islander [col 8] | Population rank | Hispanic or Latino rank | City | Percent Hispanic or Latino [col 10] |
| 63 | 1 | Anchorage municipality, Alaska | 11.5 | 54 | 1 | Urban Honolulu CDP, Hawaii | 65.9 | 19 | 1 | El Paso city, Texas | 80.7 |
| 46 | 2 | Tulsa city, Oklahoma | 8.5 | 14 | 2 | San Francisco city, California | 35.2 | 57 | 2 | Santa Ana city, California | 78.2 |
| 29 | 3 | Oklahoma City city, Oklahoma | 5.6 | 10 | 3 | San Jose city, California | 33.7 | 44 | 3 | Miami city, Florida | 70.0 |
| 32 | 4 | Albuquerque city, New Mexico | 4.5 | 75 | 4 | Jersey City city, New Jersey | 24.8 | 7 | 4 | San Antonio city, Texas | 63.2 |
| 47 | 5 | Minneapolis city, Minnesota | 2.8 | 64 | 5 | Stockton city, California | 22.6 | 60 | 5 | Corpus Christi city, Texas | 59.7 |
| 38 | 6 | Mesa city, Arizona | 2.5 | 35 | 6 | Sacramento city, California | 20.2 | 55 | 6 | Anaheim city, California | 52.8 |
| 33 | 7 | Tucson city, Arizona | 2.3 | 45 | 7 | Oakland city, California | 18.4 | 59 | 7 | Riverside city, California | 49.0 |
| 6 | 8 | Phoenix city, Arizona | 2.1 | 70 | 8 | Plano city, Texas | 18.1 | 2 | 8 | Los Angeles city, California | 48.5 |
| 49 | 8 | Wichita city, Kansas | 2.1 | 8 | 9 | San Diego city, California | 17.7 | 34 | 9 | Fresno city, California | 46.9 |
| 28 | 10 | Portland city, Oregon | 1.9 | 22 | 10 | Seattle city, Washington | 16.3 | 32 | 10 | Albuquerque city, New Mexico | 46.7 |
| 66 | 10 | St. Paul city, Minnesota | 1.9 | 55 | 11 | Anaheim city, California | 15.8 | 52 | 11 | Bakersfield city, California | 45.5 |
| 22 | 12 | Seattle city, Washington | 1.7 | 66 | 11 | St. Paul city, Minnesota | 15.8 | 4 | 12 | Houston city, Texas | 43.8 |
| 35 | 12 | Sacramento city, California | 1.7 | 36 | 13 | Long Beach city, California | 14.0 | 9 | 13 | Dallas city, Texas | 42.4 |
| 41 | 14 | Colorado Springs city, Colorado | 1.5 | 1 | 14 | New York city, New York | 13.6 | 33 | 14 | Tucson city, Arizona | 41.6 |
| 52 | 15 | Bakersfield city, California | 1.4 | 34 | 15 | Fresno city, California | 13.3 | 6 | 15 | Phoenix city, Arizona | 40.8 |
| 34 | 16 | Fresno city, California | 1.3 | 2 | 16 | Los Angeles city, California | 12.3 | 36 | 15 | Long Beach city, California | 40.8 |
| 56 | 16 | Aurora city, Colorado | 1.3 | 57 | 17 | Santa Ana city, California | 10.8 | 64 | 17 | Stockton city, California | 40.3 |
| 64 | 16 | Stockton city, California | 1.3 | 63 | 18 | Anchorage municipality, Alaska | 9.9 | 11 | 18 | Austin city, Texas | 35.1 |
| 23 | 19 | Denver city, Colorado | 1.2 | 21 | 19 | Boston city, Massachusetts | 9.7 | 16 | 19 | Fort Worth city, Texas | 34.1 |
| 30 | 19 | Milwaukee city, Wisconsin | 1.2 | 71 | 20 | Henderson city, Nevada | 8.9 | 68 | 20 | Newark city, New Jersey | 33.8 |
| 37 | 19 | Kansas City city, Missouri | 1.2 | 28 | 21 | Portland city, Oregon | 8.7 | 10 | 21 | San Jose city, California | 33.2 |
| 43 | 19 | Omaha city, Nebraska | 1.2 | 59 | 22 | Riverside city, California | 8.2 | 23 | 22 | Denver city, Colorado | 31.8 |
| 45 | 19 | Oakland city, California | 1.2 | 39 | 23 | Virginia Beach city, Virginia | 7.5 | 31 | 23 | Las Vegas city, Nevada | 31.5 |
| 54 | 19 | Urban Honolulu CDP, Hawaii | 1.2 | 50 | 24 | Arlington city, Texas | 7.4 | 3 | 24 | Chicago city, Illinois | 28.9 |
| 72 | 19 | Lincoln city, Nebraska | 1.2 | 31 | 25 | Las Vegas city, Nevada | 7.3 | 8 | 25 | San Diego city, California | 28.8 |
| 73 | 19 | Buffalo city, New York | 1.2 | 11 | 26 | Austin city, Texas | 7.1 | 56 | 26 | Aurora city, Colorado | 28.7 |
| 69 | 27 | Greensboro city, North Carolina | 1.1 | 5 | 27 | Philadelphia city, Pennsylvania | 6.9 | 1 | 27 | New York city, New York | 28.6 |
| 71 | 27 | Henderson city, Nevada | 1.1 | 52 | 28 | Bakersfield city, California | 6.7 | 75 | 28 | Jersey City city, New Jersey | 27.6 |
| 18 | 29 | Detroit city, Michigan | 1.0 | 4 | 29 | Houston city, Texas | 6.5 | 50 | 29 | Arlington city, Texas | 27.4 |
| 31 | 29 | Las Vegas city, Nevada | 1.0 | 47 | 29 | Minneapolis city, Minnesota | 6.5 | 35 | 30 | Sacramento city, California | 26.9 |
| 39 | 29 | Virginia Beach city, Virginia | 1.0 | 3 | 31 | Chicago city, Illinois | 6.0 | 38 | 31 | Mesa city, Arizona | 26.4 |
| 12 | 32 | Jacksonville city, Florida | 0.9 | 56 | 32 | Aurora city, Colorado | 5.9 | 45 | 32 | Oakland city, California | 25.4 |
| 15 | 32 | Columbus city, Ohio | 0.9 | 17 | 33 | Charlotte city, North Carolina | 5.5 | 53 | 33 | Tampa city, Florida | 23.1 |
| 26 | 32 | Baltimore city, Maryland | 0.9 | 49 | 33 | Wichita city, Kansas | 5.5 | 21 | 34 | Boston city, Massachusetts | 17.5 |
| 36 | 32 | Long Beach city, California | 0.9 | 12 | 35 | Jacksonville city, Florida | 5.1 | 30 | 35 | Milwaukee city, Wisconsin | 17.3 |
| 50 | 32 | Arlington city, Texas | 0.9 | 42 | 36 | Raleigh city, North Carolina | 5.0 | 29 | 36 | Oklahoma City city, Oklahoma | 17.2 |
| 58 | 32 | St. Louis city, Missouri | 0.9 | 61 | 36 | Pittsburgh city, Pennsylvania | 5.0 | 41 | 37 | Colorado Springs city, Colorado | 16.1 |
| 59 | 32 | Riverside city, California | 0.9 | 15 | 38 | Columbus city, Ohio | 4.7 | 49 | 38 | Wichita city, Kansas | 15.3 |
| 67 | 32 | Toledo city, Ohio | 0.9 | 29 | 39 | Oklahoma City city, Oklahoma | 4.6 | 14 | 39 | San Francisco city, California | 15.1 |
| 74 | 32 | Fort Wayne city, Indiana | 0.9 | 69 | 40 | Greensboro city, North Carolina | 4.5 | 71 | 40 | Henderson city, Nevada | 14.9 |
| 8 | 41 | San Diego city, California | 0.8 | 72 | 41 | Lincoln city, Nebraska | 4.4 | 70 | 41 | Plano city, Texas | 14.7 |
| 14 | 41 | San Francisco city, California | 0.8 | 24 | 42 | Washington city, District of Columbia | 4.3 | 46 | 42 | Tulsa city, Oklahoma | 14.1 |
| 16 | 41 | Fort Worth city, Texas | 0.8 | 41 | 42 | Colorado Springs city, Colorado | 4.3 | 17 | 43 | Charlotte city, North Carolina | 13.1 |
| 17 | 41 | Charlotte city, North Carolina | 0.8 | 16 | 44 | Fort Worth city, Texas | 4.2 | 43 | 43 | Omaha city, Nebraska | 13.1 |
| 24 | 41 | Washington city, District of Columbia | 0.8 | 23 | 45 | Denver city, Colorado | 4.1 | 5 | 45 | Philadelphia city, Pennsylvania | 12.3 |
| 48 | 41 | Cleveland city, Ohio | 0.8 | 53 | 45 | Tampa city, Florida | 4.1 | 42 | 46 | Raleigh city, North Carolina | 11.4 |
| 65 | 41 | Cincinnati city, Ohio | 0.8 | 30 | 47 | Milwaukee city, Wisconsin | 3.9 | 47 | 47 | Minneapolis city, Minnesota | 10.5 |
| 70 | 41 | Plano city, Texas | 0.8 | 62 | 48 | Lexington-Fayette, Kentucky | 3.8 | 73 | 47 | Buffalo city, New York | 10.5 |
| 5 | 49 | Philadelphia city, Pennsylvania | 0.7 | 74 | 48 | Fort Wayne city, Indiana | 3.8 | 37 | 49 | Kansas City city, Missouri | 10.0 |
| 10 | 49 | San Jose city, California | 0.7 | 6 | 50 | Phoenix city, Arizona | 3.7 | 48 | 49 | Cleveland city, Ohio | 10.0 |
| 11 | 49 | Austin city, Texas | 0.7 | 40 | 50 | Atlanta city, Georgia | 3.7 | 25 | 51 | Nashville-Davidson, Tennessee | 9.8 |
| 13 | 49 | Indianapolis city, Indiana | 0.7 | 25 | 52 | Nashville-Davidson, Tennessee | 3.6 | 66 | 52 | St. Paul city, Minnesota | 9.6 |
| 21 | 49 | Boston city, Massachusetts | 0.7 | 73 | 52 | Buffalo city, New York | 3.6 | 13 | 53 | Indianapolis city, Indiana | 9.4 |
| 25 | 49 | Nashville-Davidson, Tennessee | 0.7 | 33 | 54 | Tucson city, Arizona | 3.5 | 28 | 53 | Portland city, Oregon | 9.4 |
| 27 | 49 | Louisville/Jefferson, Kentucky | 0.7 | 58 | 55 | St. Louis city, Missouri | 3.4 | 24 | 55 | Washington city, District of Columbia | 9.1 |
| 40 | 49 | Atlanta city, Georgia | 0.7 | 9 | 56 | Dallas city, Texas | 3.2 | 74 | 56 | Fort Wayne city, Indiana | 8.0 |
| 42 | 49 | Raleigh city, North Carolina | 0.7 | 32 | 56 | Albuquerque city, New Mexico | 3.2 | 12 | 57 | Jacksonville city, Florida | 7.7 |
| 61 | 49 | Pittsburgh city, Pennsylvania | 0.7 | 51 | 56 | New Orleans city, Louisiana | 3.2 | 63 | 58 | Anchorage municipality, Alaska | 7.6 |
| 75 | 49 | Jersey City city, New Jersey | 0.7 | 37 | 59 | Kansas City city, Missouri | 3.0 | 69 | 59 | Greensboro city, North Carolina | 7.5 |
| 9 | 60 | Dallas city, Texas | 0.6 | 43 | 60 | Omaha city, Nebraska | 2.9 | 67 | 60 | Toledo city, Ohio | 7.4 |
| 51 | 60 | New Orleans city, Louisiana | 0.6 | 7 | 61 | San Antonio city, Texas | 2.8 | 62 | 61 | Lexington-Fayette, Kentucky | 6.9 |
| 53 | 60 | Tampa city, Florida | 0.6 | 26 | 61 | Baltimore city, Maryland | 2.8 | 18 | 62 | Detroit city, Michigan | 6.8 |
| 62 | 60 | Lexington-Fayette, Kentucky | 0.6 | 46 | 61 | Tulsa city, Oklahoma | 2.8 | 22 | 63 | Seattle city, Washington | 6.6 |
| 68 | 60 | Newark city, New Jersey | 0.6 | 27 | 64 | Louisville/Jefferson, Kentucky | 2.6 | 39 | 63 | Virginia Beach city, Virginia | 6.6 |
| 1 | 65 | New York city, New York | 0.5 | 13 | 65 | Indianapolis city, Indiana | 2.5 | 20 | 65 | Memphis city, Tennessee | 6.5 |
| 2 | 65 | Los Angeles city, California | 0.5 | 38 | 65 | Mesa city, Arizona | 2.5 | 72 | 66 | Lincoln city, Nebraska | 6.3 |
| 3 | 65 | Chicago city, Illinois | 0.5 | 65 | 67 | Cincinnati city, Ohio | 2.3 | 15 | 67 | Columbus city, Ohio | 5.6 |
| 7 | 65 | San Antonio city, Texas | 0.5 | 48 | 68 | Cleveland city, Ohio | 2.1 | 54 | 68 | Urban Honolulu CDP, Hawaii | 5.4 |
| 20 | 65 | Memphis city, Tennessee | 0.5 | 60 | 68 | Corpus Christi city, Texas | 2.1 | 40 | 69 | Atlanta city, Georgia | 5.2 |
| 55 | 65 | Anaheim city, California | 0.5 | 20 | 70 | Memphis city, Tennessee | 1.8 | 51 | 69 | New Orleans city, Louisiana | 5.2 |
| 60 | 65 | Corpus Christi city, Texas | 0.5 | 68 | 70 | Newark city, New Jersey | 1.8 | 27 | 71 | Louisville/Jefferson, Kentucky | 4.4 |
| 4 | 72 | Houston city, Texas | 0.4 | 67 | 72 | Toledo city, Ohio | 1.5 | 26 | 72 | Baltimore city, Maryland | 4.2 |
| 19 | 72 | El Paso city, Texas | 0.4 | 19 | 73 | El Paso city, Texas | 1.4 | 58 | 73 | St. Louis city, Missouri | 3.5 |
| 57 | 74 | Santa Ana city, California | 0.3 | 18 | 74 | Detroit city, Michigan | 1.3 | 65 | 74 | Cincinnati city, Ohio | 2.8 |
| 44 | 75 | Miami city, Florida | 0.2 | 44 | 75 | Miami city, Florida | 1.2 | 61 | 75 | Pittsburgh city, Pennsylvania | 2.3 |

# 75 Largest Cities by 2012 Population
## Selected Rankings

| Percent under 18 years old, 2010 | | | | Percent 65 years old and over, 2010 | | | | Percent high school graduate or less, 2007–2011 | | | |
|---|---|---|---|---|---|---|---|---|---|---|---|
| Population rank | Under 18 years old rank | City | Percent under 18 years old [col 12 and 13] | Population rank | 65 years old and over rank | City | Percent 65 years old and over [col 19 and 20] | Population rank | Percent high school graduate or less rank | City | Percent high school graduate or less [col 40] |
| 52 | 1 | Bakersfield city, California | 31.5 | 54 | 1 | Urban Honolulu CDP, Hawaii | 17.9 | 57 | 1 | Santa Ana city, California | 69.1 |
| 57 | 2 | Santa Ana city, California | 30.7 | 44 | 2 | Miami city, Florida | 16.0 | 68 | 2 | Newark city, New Jersey | 65.8 |
| 34 | 3 | Fresno city, California | 30.1 | 71 | 3 | Henderson city, Nevada | 14.2 | 44 | 3 | Miami city, Florida | 59.9 |
| 64 | 4 | Stockton city, California | 29.9 | 38 | 4 | Mesa city, Arizona | 14.1 | 48 | 4 | Cleveland city, Ohio | 57.9 |
| 16 | 5 | Fort Worth city, Texas | 29.3 | 61 | 5 | Pittsburgh city, Pennsylvania | 13.7 | 18 | 5 | Detroit city, Michigan | 56.3 |
| 19 | 6 | El Paso city, Texas | 29.2 | 14 | 6 | San Francisco city, California | 13.6 | 5 | 6 | Philadelphia city, Pennsylvania | 55.2 |
| 6 | 7 | Phoenix city, Arizona | 28.3 | 27 | 7 | Louisville/Jefferson, Kentucky | 13.4 | 64 | 7 | Stockton city, California | 51.1 |
| 50 | 8 | Arlington city, Texas | 27.9 | 46 | 8 | Tulsa city, Oklahoma | 12.4 | 26 | 8 | Baltimore city, Maryland | 51.0 |
| 55 | 9 | Anaheim city, California | 27.4 | 5 | 9 | Philadelphia city, Pennsylvania | 12.1 | 30 | 8 | Milwaukee city, Wisconsin | 51.0 |
| 56 | 9 | Aurora city, Colorado | 27.4 | 32 | 9 | Albuquerque city, New Mexico | 12.1 | 55 | 10 | Anaheim city, California | 50.7 |
| 30 | 11 | Milwaukee city, Wisconsin | 27.1 | 1 | 11 | New York city, New York | 12.1 | 67 | 11 | Toledo city, Ohio | 50.5 |
| 59 | 12 | Riverside city, California | 26.8 | 67 | 11 | Toledo city, Ohio | 12.1 | 19 | 12 | El Paso city, Texas | 49.3 |
| 7 | 12 | San Antonio city, Texas | 26.8 | 31 | 13 | Las Vegas city, Nevada | 12.0 | 34 | 13 | Fresno city, California | 49.0 |
| 18 | 14 | Detroit city, Michigan | 26.6 | 48 | 13 | Cleveland city, Ohio | 12.0 | 9 | 14 | Dallas city, Texas | 48.6 |
| 9 | 15 | Dallas city, Texas | 26.5 | 74 | 13 | Fort Wayne city, Indiana | 12.0 | 4 | 15 | Houston city, Texas | 48.5 |
| 49 | 15 | Wichita city, Kansas | 26.5 | 33 | 16 | Tucson city, Arizona | 11.9 | 20 | 16 | Memphis city, Tennessee | 48.1 |
| 74 | 17 | Fort Wayne city, Indiana | 26.4 | 60 | 16 | Corpus Christi city, Texas | 11.9 | 73 | 16 | Buffalo city, New York | 48.1 |
| 38 | 18 | Mesa city, Arizona | 26.3 | 26 | 18 | Baltimore city, Maryland | 11.7 | 52 | 18 | Bakersfield city, California | 47.4 |
| 70 | 19 | Plano city, Texas | 25.9 | 18 | 19 | Detroit city, Michigan | 11.5 | 31 | 19 | Las Vegas city, Nevada | 47.3 |
| 20 | 19 | Memphis city, Tennessee | 25.9 | 49 | 19 | Wichita city, Kansas | 11.5 | 59 | 20 | Riverside city, California | 46.7 |
| 63 | 19 | Anchorage municipality, Alaska | 25.9 | 69 | 19 | Greensboro city, North Carolina | 11.5 | 60 | 21 | Corpus Christi city, Texas | 46.3 |
| 4 | 22 | Houston city, Texas | 25.8 | 73 | 22 | Buffalo city, New York | 11.4 | 1 | 22 | New York city, New York | 45.9 |
| 60 | 22 | Corpus Christi city, Texas | 25.8 | 24 | 23 | Washington city, District of Columbia | 11.4 | 7 | 22 | San Antonio city, Texas | 45.9 |
| 31 | 24 | Las Vegas city, Nevada | 25.6 | 43 | 23 | Omaha city, Nebraska | 11.4 | 2 | 24 | Los Angeles city, California | 45.7 |
| 68 | 25 | Newark city, New Jersey | 25.5 | 29 | 25 | Oklahoma City city, Oklahoma | 11.3 | 16 | 24 | Fort Worth city, Texas | 45.7 |
| 29 | 26 | Oklahoma City city, Oklahoma | 25.4 | 19 | 26 | El Paso city, Texas | 11.2 | 13 | 26 | Indianapolis city, Indiana | 45.6 |
| 17 | 27 | Charlotte city, North Carolina | 25.3 | 45 | 27 | Oakland city, California | 11.1 | 6 | 27 | Phoenix city, Arizona | 44.5 |
| 43 | 28 | Omaha city, Nebraska | 25.1 | 12 | 28 | Jacksonville city, Florida | 11.0 | 58 | 27 | St. Louis city, Missouri | 44.5 |
| 66 | 28 | St. Paul city, Minnesota | 25.1 | 37 | 28 | Kansas City city, Missouri | 11.0 | 3 | 29 | Chicago city, Illinois | 43.6 |
| 13 | 30 | Indianapolis city, Indiana | 25.0 | 51 | 28 | New Orleans city, Louisiana | 11.0 | 12 | 30 | Jacksonville city, Florida | 43.0 |
| 41 | 30 | Colorado Springs city, Colorado | 25.0 | 58 | 28 | St. Louis city, Missouri | 11.0 | 65 | 30 | Cincinnati city, Ohio | 43.0 |
| 10 | 32 | San Jose city, California | 24.9 | 41 | 32 | Colorado Springs city, Colorado | 10.9 | 74 | 32 | Fort Wayne city, Indiana | 42.4 |
| 35 | 32 | Sacramento city, California | 24.9 | 53 | 33 | Tampa city, Florida | 10.9 | 53 | 33 | Tampa city, Florida | 42.2 |
| 36 | 32 | Long Beach city, California | 24.9 | 65 | 34 | Cincinnati city, Ohio | 10.8 | 51 | 34 | New Orleans city, Louisiana | 41.9 |
| 48 | 35 | Cleveland city, Ohio | 24.6 | 8 | 35 | San Diego city, California | 10.7 | 61 | 35 | Pittsburgh city, Pennsylvania | 41.8 |
| 46 | 36 | Tulsa city, Oklahoma | 24.5 | 22 | 35 | Seattle city, Washington | 10.7 | 27 | 36 | Louisville/Jefferson, Kentucky | 41.5 |
| 37 | 37 | Kansas City city, Missouri | 24.1 | 72 | 35 | Lincoln city, Nebraska | 10.7 | 56 | 37 | Aurora city, Colorado | 41.3 |
| 67 | 37 | Toledo city, Ohio | 24.1 | 39 | 38 | Virginia Beach city, Virginia | 10.6 | 29 | 38 | Oklahoma City city, Oklahoma | 41.1 |
| 39 | 37 | Virginia Beach city, Virginia | 24.1 | 13 | 39 | Indianapolis city, Indiana | 10.6 | 33 | 39 | Tucson city, Arizona | 41.0 |
| 32 | 40 | Albuquerque city, New Mexico | 24.0 | 35 | 39 | Sacramento city, California | 10.6 | 49 | 40 | Wichita city, Kansas | 40.7 |
| 12 | 41 | Jacksonville city, Florida | 23.9 | 25 | 41 | Nashville-Davidson, Tennessee | 10.5 | 38 | 41 | Mesa city, Arizona | 40.6 |
| 73 | 42 | Buffalo city, New York | 23.6 | 62 | 41 | Lexington-Fayette, Kentucky | 10.5 | 36 | 42 | Long Beach city, California | 40.2 |
| 33 | 43 | Tucson city, Arizona | 23.4 | 2 | 43 | Los Angeles city, California | 10.4 | 75 | 42 | Jersey City city, New Jersey | 40.2 |
| 27 | 44 | Louisville/Jefferson, Kentucky | 23.2 | 20 | 43 | Memphis city, Tennessee | 10.4 | 46 | 44 | Tulsa city, Oklahoma | 40.1 |
| 15 | 44 | Columbus city, Ohio | 23.2 | 23 | 43 | Denver city, Colorado | 10.4 | 37 | 45 | Kansas City city, Missouri | 39.8 |
| 3 | 46 | Chicago city, Illinois | 23.1 | 28 | 43 | Portland city, Oregon | 10.4 | 25 | 46 | Nashville-Davidson, Tennessee | 39.6 |
| 42 | 46 | Raleigh city, North Carolina | 23.1 | 7 | 47 | San Antonio city, Texas | 10.4 | 50 | 47 | Arlington city, Texas | 39.4 |
| 2 | 48 | Los Angeles city, California | 23.0 | 3 | 48 | Chicago city, Illinois | 10.3 | 15 | 48 | Columbus city, Ohio | 39.2 |
| 71 | 49 | Henderson city, Nevada | 22.7 | 10 | 49 | San Jose city, California | 10.0 | 35 | 49 | Sacramento city, California | 39.1 |
| 69 | 49 | Greensboro city, North Carolina | 22.7 | 21 | 49 | Boston city, Massachusetts | 10.0 | 21 | 50 | Boston city, Massachusetts | 38.7 |
| 72 | 49 | Lincoln city, Nebraska | 22.7 | 64 | 49 | Stockton city, California | 10.0 | 45 | 51 | Oakland city, California | 38.6 |
| 53 | 52 | Tampa city, Florida | 22.6 | 40 | 52 | Atlanta city, Georgia | 9.9 | 54 | 51 | Urban Honolulu CDP, Hawaii | 38.6 |
| 5 | 53 | Philadelphia city, Pennsylvania | 22.5 | 34 | 53 | Fresno city, California | 9.4 | 66 | 53 | St. Paul city, Minnesota | 37.2 |
| 65 | 54 | Cincinnati city, Ohio | 22.2 | 55 | 54 | Anaheim city, California | 9.3 | 69 | 54 | Greensboro city, North Carolina | 37.0 |
| 11 | 54 | Austin city, Texas | 22.2 | 36 | 55 | Long Beach city, California | 9.2 | 43 | 55 | Omaha city, Nebraska | 36.9 |
| 25 | 56 | Nashville-Davidson, Tennessee | 21.7 | 4 | 56 | Houston city, Texas | 9.1 | 10 | 56 | San Jose city, California | 36.7 |
| 1 | 57 | New York city, New York | 21.6 | 66 | 57 | St. Paul city, Minnesota | 9.0 | 32 | 57 | Albuquerque city, New Mexico | 36.0 |
| 23 | 58 | Denver city, Colorado | 21.5 | 75 | 57 | Jersey City city, New Jersey | 9.0 | 23 | 58 | Denver city, Colorado | 35.1 |
| 26 | 58 | Baltimore city, Maryland | 21.5 | 30 | 59 | Milwaukee city, Wisconsin | 8.9 | 71 | 59 | Henderson city, Nevada | 34.4 |
| 8 | 60 | San Diego city, California | 21.4 | 9 | 60 | Dallas city, Texas | 8.9 | 40 | 60 | Atlanta city, Georgia | 34.0 |
| 45 | 61 | Oakland city, California | 21.3 | 56 | 60 | Aurora city, Colorado | 8.9 | 62 | 61 | Lexington-Fayette, Kentucky | 32.7 |
| 51 | 61 | New Orleans city, Louisiana | 21.3 | 70 | 62 | Plano city, Texas | 8.8 | 24 | 62 | Washington city, District of Columbia | 32.4 |
| 62 | 63 | Lexington-Fayette, Kentucky | 21.2 | 15 | 63 | Columbus city, Ohio | 8.6 | 17 | 63 | Charlotte city, North Carolina | 32.3 |
| 75 | 63 | Jersey City city, New Jersey | 21.2 | 59 | 63 | Riverside city, California | 8.6 | 63 | 64 | Anchorage municipality, Alaska | 31.1 |
| 58 | 65 | St. Louis city, Missouri | 21.1 | 68 | 63 | Newark city, New Jersey | 8.6 | 39 | 65 | Virginia Beach city, Virginia | 31.0 |
| 47 | 66 | Minneapolis city, Minnesota | 20.2 | 6 | 66 | Phoenix city, Arizona | 8.5 | 11 | 66 | Austin city, Texas | 30.8 |
| 40 | 67 | Atlanta city, Georgia | 19.4 | 17 | 66 | Charlotte city, North Carolina | 8.5 | 47 | 67 | Minneapolis city, Minnesota | 30.4 |
| 28 | 68 | Portland city, Oregon | 19.1 | 52 | 68 | Bakersfield city, California | 8.4 | 72 | 68 | Lincoln city, Nebraska | 30.2 |
| 44 | 69 | Miami city, Florida | 18.4 | 16 | 69 | Fort Worth city, Texas | 8.2 | 8 | 69 | San Diego city, California | 30.1 |
| 54 | 70 | Urban Honolulu CDP, Hawaii | 17.4 | 42 | 69 | Raleigh city, North Carolina | 8.2 | 41 | 70 | Colorado Springs city, Colorado | 29.5 |
| 24 | 71 | Washington city, District of Columbia | 16.7 | 50 | 69 | Arlington city, Texas | 8.2 | 28 | 71 | Portland city, Oregon | 29.0 |
| 21 | 71 | Boston city, Massachusetts | 16.7 | 47 | 72 | Minneapolis city, Minnesota | 8.0 | 14 | 72 | San Francisco city, California | 28.7 |
| 61 | 73 | Pittsburgh city, Pennsylvania | 16.2 | 63 | 73 | Anchorage municipality, Alaska | 7.3 | 42 | 73 | Raleigh city, North Carolina | 26.1 |
| 22 | 74 | Seattle city, Washington | 15.4 | 11 | 74 | Austin city, Texas | 7.0 | 70 | 74 | Plano city, Texas | 20.7 |
| 14 | 75 | San Francisco city, California | 13.4 | 57 | 75 | Santa Ana city, California | 6.8 | 22 | 75 | Seattle city, Washington | 19.7 |

# 75 Largest Cities by 2012 Population
## Selected Rankings

| Percent college graduates (bachelor's degree or more), 2007–2011 | | | | Percent female-headed family households, 2010 | | | | Percent of households composed of one person, 2010 | | | |
|---|---|---|---|---|---|---|---|---|---|---|---|
| Population rank | Percent college graduate rank | City | Percent college graduates [col 41] | Population rank | Female households rank | City | Percent female households [col 29] | Population rank | One-person household rank | City | Percent one-person households [col 30] |
| 22 | 1 | Seattle city, Washington | 55.8 | 18 | 1 | Detroit city, Michigan | 31.4 | 24 | 1 | Washington city, District of Columbia | 44.0 |
| 70 | 2 | Plano city, Texas | 54.0 | 68 | 2 | Newark city, New Jersey | 28.9 | 40 | 1 | Atlanta city, Georgia | 44.0 |
| 14 | 3 | San Francisco city, California | 51.4 | 20 | 3 | Memphis city, Tennessee | 25.3 | 65 | 3 | Cincinnati city, Ohio | 43.4 |
| 24 | 4 | Washington city, District of Columbia | 50.5 | 48 | 3 | Cleveland city, Ohio | 25.3 | 58 | 4 | St. Louis city, Missouri | 42.6 |
| 42 | 5 | Raleigh city, North Carolina | 47.3 | 26 | 5 | Baltimore city, Maryland | 23.8 | 61 | 5 | Pittsburgh city, Pennsylvania | 41.7 |
| 40 | 6 | Atlanta city, Georgia | 46.1 | 30 | 6 | Milwaukee city, Wisconsin | 22.6 | 22 | 6 | Seattle city, Washington | 41.3 |
| 47 | 7 | Minneapolis city, Minnesota | 44.7 | 5 | 7 | Philadelphia city, Pennsylvania | 22.5 | 23 | 7 | Denver city, Colorado | 40.6 |
| 11 | 8 | Austin city, Texas | 44.5 | 73 | 8 | Buffalo city, New York | 22.0 | 47 | 8 | Minneapolis city, Minnesota | 40.3 |
| 21 | 9 | Boston city, Massachusetts | 42.8 | 51 | 9 | New Orleans city, Louisiana | 20.9 | 73 | 9 | Buffalo city, New York | 39.7 |
| 28 | 10 | Portland city, Oregon | 42.0 | 19 | 10 | El Paso city, Texas | 20.7 | 48 | 10 | Cleveland city, Ohio | 39.5 |
| 23 | 11 | Denver city, Colorado | 41.3 | 67 | 11 | Toledo city, Ohio | 19.9 | 14 | 11 | San Francisco city, California | 38.6 |
| 8 | 12 | San Diego city, California | 41.0 | 58 | 12 | St. Louis city, Missouri | 19.4 | 21 | 12 | Boston city, Massachusetts | 37.1 |
| 75 | 13 | Jersey City city, New Jersey | 40.6 | 34 | 13 | Fresno city, California | 19.3 | 26 | 13 | Baltimore city, Maryland | 36.1 |
| 17 | 14 | Charlotte city, North Carolina | 39.6 | 65 | 14 | Cincinnati city, Ohio | 19.1 | 51 | 14 | New Orleans city, Louisiana | 35.9 |
| 62 | 15 | Lexington-Fayette, Kentucky | 39.3 | 64 | 15 | Stockton city, California | 18.9 | 66 | 15 | St. Paul city, Minnesota | 35.8 |
| 45 | 16 | Oakland city, California | 37.2 | 1 | 16 | New York city, New York | 18.7 | 15 | 16 | Columbus city, Ohio | 35.1 |
| 66 | 16 | St. Paul city, Minnesota | 37.2 | 75 | 17 | Jersey City city, New Jersey | 18.2 | 3 | 17 | Chicago city, Illinois | 35.0 |
| 10 | 18 | San Jose city, California | 36.6 | 44 | 18 | Miami city, Florida | 18.1 | 67 | 18 | Toledo city, Ohio | 34.8 |
| 41 | 19 | Colorado Springs city, Colorado | 36.1 | 3 | 19 | Chicago city, Illinois | 17.7 | 37 | 19 | Kansas City city, Missouri | 34.7 |
| 72 | 20 | Lincoln city, Nebraska | 36.0 | 7 | 20 | San Antonio city, Texas | 17.6 | 25 | 20 | Nashville-Davidson, Tennessee | 34.5 |
| 69 | 21 | Greensboro city, North Carolina | 35.0 | 13 | 21 | Indianapolis city, Indiana | 17.2 | 28 | 20 | Portland city, Oregon | 34.5 |
| 25 | 22 | Nashville-Davidson, Tennessee | 34.4 | 12 | 22 | Jacksonville city, Florida | 17.1 | 46 | 20 | Tulsa city, Oklahoma | 34.5 |
| 61 | 22 | Pittsburgh city, Pennsylvania | 34.4 | 53 | 23 | Tampa city, Florida | 16.8 | 5 | 23 | Philadelphia city, Pennsylvania | 34.1 |
| 1 | 24 | New York city, New York | 33.7 | 60 | 24 | Corpus Christi city, Texas | 16.6 | 11 | 24 | Austin city, Texas | 34.0 |
| 54 | 25 | Urban Honolulu CDP, Hawaii | 33.6 | 40 | 25 | Atlanta city, Georgia | 16.5 | 18 | 24 | Detroit city, Michigan | 34.0 |
| 3 | 26 | Chicago city, Illinois | 32.9 | 69 | 25 | Greensboro city, North Carolina | 16.5 | 9 | 26 | Dallas city, Texas | 33.9 |
| 15 | 27 | Columbus city, Ohio | 32.3 | 24 | 27 | Washington city, District of Columbia | 16.4 | 45 | 26 | Oakland city, California | 33.9 |
| 39 | 27 | Virginia Beach city, Virginia | 32.3 | 36 | 27 | Long Beach city, California | 16.4 | 69 | 28 | Greensboro city, North Carolina | 33.8 |
| 51 | 27 | New Orleans city, Louisiana | 32.3 | 21 | 29 | Boston city, Massachusetts | 16.3 | 30 | 29 | Milwaukee city, Wisconsin | 33.6 |
| 63 | 27 | Anchorage municipality, Alaska | 32.3 | 4 | 30 | Houston city, Texas | 16.2 | 53 | 29 | Tampa city, Florida | 33.6 |
| 32 | 31 | Albuquerque city, New Mexico | 32.2 | 52 | 30 | Bakersfield city, California | 16.2 | 44 | 31 | Miami city, Florida | 33.3 |
| 53 | 31 | Tampa city, Florida | 32.2 | 37 | 32 | Kansas City city, Missouri | 16.1 | 33 | 32 | Tucson city, Arizona | 33.1 |
| 43 | 33 | Omaha city, Nebraska | 32.1 | 57 | 32 | Santa Ana city, California | 16.1 | 54 | 33 | Urban Honolulu CDP, Hawaii | 32.9 |
| 65 | 34 | Cincinnati city, Ohio | 31.0 | 9 | 34 | Dallas city, Texas | 16.0 | 42 | 34 | Raleigh city, North Carolina | 32.8 |
| 2 | 35 | Los Angeles city, California | 30.5 | 15 | 35 | Columbus city, Ohio | 15.9 | 62 | 35 | Lexington-Fayette, Kentucky | 32.7 |
| 71 | 36 | Henderson city, Nevada | 30.4 | 35 | 36 | Sacramento city, California | 15.8 | 43 | 36 | Omaha city, Nebraska | 32.3 |
| 37 | 37 | Kansas City city, Missouri | 30.1 | 45 | 37 | Oakland city, California | 15.7 | 20 | 37 | Memphis city, Tennessee | 32.2 |
| 46 | 38 | Tulsa city, Oklahoma | 29.5 | 17 | 38 | Charlotte city, North Carolina | 15.6 | 13 | 38 | Indianapolis city, Indiana | 32.1 |
| 27 | 39 | Louisville/Jefferson, Kentucky | 29.2 | 27 | 39 | Louisville/Jefferson, Kentucky | 15.4 | 1 | 39 | New York city, New York | 32.0 |
| 35 | 39 | Sacramento city, California | 29.2 | 33 | 39 | Tucson city, Arizona | 15.4 | 27 | 39 | Louisville/Jefferson, Kentucky | 32.0 |
| 50 | 41 | Arlington city, Texas | 28.9 | 16 | 41 | Fort Worth city, Texas | 15.3 | 32 | 41 | Albuquerque city, New Mexico | 31.9 |
| 9 | 42 | Dallas city, Texas | 28.8 | 59 | 42 | Riverside city, California | 15.1 | 72 | 42 | Lincoln city, Nebraska | 31.3 |
| 36 | 43 | Long Beach city, California | 28.7 | 50 | 43 | Arlington city, Texas | 15.0 | 74 | 43 | Fort Wayne city, Indiana | 31.2 |
| 4 | 44 | Houston city, Texas | 28.4 | 2 | 44 | Los Angeles city, California | 14.9 | 49 | 44 | Wichita city, Kansas | 31.1 |
| 29 | 45 | Oklahoma City city, Oklahoma | 27.9 | 6 | 44 | Phoenix city, Arizona | 14.9 | 4 | 45 | Houston city, Texas | 31.0 |
| 49 | 45 | Wichita city, Kansas | 27.9 | 61 | 44 | Pittsburgh city, Pennsylvania | 14.9 | 29 | 46 | Oklahoma City city, Oklahoma | 30.5 |
| 58 | 47 | St. Louis city, Missouri | 27.7 | 55 | 47 | Anaheim city, California | 14.8 | 35 | 46 | Sacramento city, California | 30.5 |
| 13 | 48 | Indianapolis city, Indiana | 27.2 | 66 | 47 | St. Paul city, Minnesota | 14.8 | 17 | 48 | Charlotte city, North Carolina | 30.3 |
| 56 | 49 | Aurora city, Colorado | 26.1 | 74 | 47 | Fort Wayne city, Indiana | 14.8 | 75 | 49 | Jersey City city, New Jersey | 30.2 |
| 16 | 50 | Fort Worth city, Texas | 25.9 | 25 | 50 | Nashville-Davidson, Tennessee | 14.7 | 41 | 50 | Colorado Springs city, Colorado | 29.6 |
| 26 | 51 | Baltimore city, Maryland | 25.8 | 46 | 51 | Tulsa city, Oklahoma | 14.6 | 36 | 51 | Long Beach city, California | 28.5 |
| 74 | 52 | Fort Wayne city, Indiana | 25.5 | 32 | 52 | Albuquerque city, New Mexico | 14.3 | 2 | 52 | Los Angeles city, California | 28.3 |
| 6 | 53 | Phoenix city, Arizona | 25.4 | 56 | 53 | Aurora city, Colorado | 14.2 | 12 | 53 | Jacksonville city, Florida | 28.2 |
| 33 | 54 | Tucson city, Arizona | 24.5 | 31 | 54 | Las Vegas city, Nevada | 14.1 | 8 | 54 | San Diego city, California | 28.0 |
| 12 | 55 | Jacksonville city, Florida | 24.2 | 29 | 55 | Oklahoma City city, Oklahoma | 13.9 | 68 | 55 | Newark city, New Jersey | 27.9 |
| 7 | 56 | San Antonio city, Texas | 23.9 | 39 | 55 | Virginia Beach city, Virginia | 13.9 | 56 | 56 | Aurora city, Colorado | 27.7 |
| 38 | 57 | Mesa city, Arizona | 23.5 | 43 | 57 | Omaha city, Nebraska | 13.7 | 6 | 57 | Phoenix city, Arizona | 27.1 |
| 55 | 58 | Anaheim city, California | 23.4 | 42 | 58 | Raleigh city, North Carolina | 13.5 | 7 | 58 | San Antonio city, Texas | 26.9 |
| 20 | 59 | Memphis city, Tennessee | 23.1 | 49 | 59 | Wichita city, Kansas | 13.1 | 38 | 59 | Mesa city, Arizona | 26.6 |
| 5 | 60 | Philadelphia city, Pennsylvania | 22.6 | 10 | 60 | San Jose city, California | 12.6 | 16 | 60 | Fort Worth city, Texas | 26.5 |
| 73 | 61 | Buffalo city, New York | 22.5 | 38 | 60 | Mesa city, Arizona | 12.6 | 31 | 61 | Las Vegas city, Nevada | 26.0 |
| 44 | 62 | Miami city, Florida | 22.4 | 62 | 62 | Lexington-Fayette, Kentucky | 12.3 | 60 | 62 | Corpus Christi city, Texas | 25.6 |
| 19 | 63 | El Paso city, Texas | 21.9 | 54 | 63 | Urban Honolulu CDP, Hawaii | 12.1 | 50 | 63 | Arlington city, Texas | 24.9 |
| 59 | 63 | Riverside city, California | 21.9 | 47 | 64 | Minneapolis city, Minnesota | 11.7 | 63 | 63 | Anchorage municipality, Alaska | 24.9 |
| 31 | 65 | Las Vegas city, Nevada | 21.5 | 63 | 64 | Anchorage municipality, Alaska | 11.7 | 70 | 65 | Plano city, Texas | 24.4 |
| 30 | 66 | Milwaukee city, Wisconsin | 21.3 | 41 | 66 | Colorado Springs city, Colorado | 11.6 | 71 | 66 | Henderson city, Nevada | 24.2 |
| 60 | 67 | Corpus Christi city, Texas | 21.2 | 8 | 67 | San Diego city, California | 11.4 | 39 | 67 | Virginia Beach city, Virginia | 23.3 |
| 34 | 68 | Fresno city, California | 20.1 | 11 | 68 | Austin city, Texas | 11.0 | 34 | 68 | Fresno city, California | 22.1 |
| 52 | 69 | Bakersfield city, California | 19.8 | 71 | 68 | Henderson city, Nevada | 11.0 | 19 | 69 | El Paso city, Texas | 21.5 |
| 67 | 70 | Toledo city, Ohio | 17.3 | 23 | 70 | Denver city, Colorado | 10.6 | 64 | 69 | Stockton city, California | 21.5 |
| 64 | 71 | Stockton city, California | 17.1 | 72 | 71 | Lincoln city, Nebraska | 10.2 | 59 | 71 | Riverside city, California | 19.9 |
| 48 | 72 | Cleveland city, Ohio | 13.8 | 28 | 72 | Portland city, Oregon | 10.1 | 10 | 72 | San Jose city, California | 19.7 |
| 68 | 73 | Newark city, New Jersey | 12.5 | 70 | 73 | Plano city, Texas | 9.7 | 52 | 73 | Bakersfield city, California | 19.6 |
| 18 | 74 | Detroit city, Michigan | 12.2 | 14 | 74 | San Francisco city, California | 8.3 | 55 | 74 | Anaheim city, California | 17.8 |
| 57 | 75 | Santa Ana city, California | 11.7 | 22 | 75 | Seattle city, Washington | 7.3 | 57 | 75 | Santa Ana city, California | 12.6 |

# 75 Largest Cities by 2012 Population
## Selected Rankings

### Median household income, 2007–2011

| Population rank | Median income rank | City | Median income (dollars) [col 43] |
|---|---|---|---|
| 70 | 1 | Plano city, Texas | 82 901 |
| 10 | 2 | San Jose city, California | 80 764 |
| 63 | 3 | Anchorage municipality, Alaska | 75 485 |
| 14 | 4 | San Francisco city, California | 72 947 |
| 71 | 5 | Henderson city, Nevada | 67 934 |
| 39 | 6 | Virginia Beach city, Virginia | 65 910 |
| 8 | 7 | San Diego city, California | 63 739 |
| 22 | 8 | Seattle city, Washington | 61 856 |
| 24 | 9 | Washington, District of Columbia | 61 835 |
| 55 | 10 | Anaheim city, California | 59 330 |
| 59 | 11 | Riverside city, California | 57 555 |
| 75 | 12 | Jersey City city, New Jersey | 57 520 |
| 54 | 13 | Urban Honolulu CDP, Hawaii | 56 939 |
| 52 | 14 | Bakersfield city, California | 54 656 |
| 57 | 15 | Santa Ana city, California | 54 399 |
| 31 | 16 | Las Vegas city, Nevada | 54 174 |
| 41 | 17 | Colorado Springs city, Colorado | 53 747 |
| 17 | 18 | Charlotte city, North Carolina | 53 146 |
| 36 | 19 | Long Beach city, California | 52 945 |
| 42 | 20 | Raleigh city, North Carolina | 52 819 |
| 50 | 21 | Arlington city, Texas | 52 699 |
| 21 | 22 | Boston city, Massachusetts | 51 739 |
| 11 | 23 | Austin city, Texas | 51 596 |
| 1 | 24 | New York city, New York | 51 270 |
| 45 | 25 | Oakland city, California | 51 144 |
| 35 | 26 | Sacramento city, California | 50 781 |
| 56 | 27 | Aurora city, Colorado | 50 468 |
| 16 | 28 | Fort Worth city, Texas | 50 456 |
| 28 | 29 | Portland city, Oregon | 50 177 |
| 2 | 30 | Los Angeles city, California | 50 028 |
| 38 | 31 | Mesa city, Arizona | 49 872 |
| 12 | 32 | Jacksonville city, Florida | 49 192 |
| 72 | 33 | Lincoln city, Nebraska | 49 114 |
| 6 | 34 | Phoenix city, Arizona | 48 596 |
| 62 | 35 | Lexington-Fayette, Kentucky | 48 306 |
| 23 | 36 | Denver city, Colorado | 47 499 |
| 47 | 37 | Minneapolis city, Minnesota | 47 478 |
| 3 | 38 | Chicago city, Illinois | 47 371 |
| 64 | 39 | Stockton city, California | 47 365 |
| 32 | 40 | Albuquerque city, New Mexico | 47 333 |
| 43 | 41 | Omaha city, Nebraska | 46 978 |
| 25 | 42 | Nashville-Davidson, Tennessee | 46 737 |
| 27 | 43 | Louisville/Jefferson, Kentucky | 46 298 |
| 40 | 44 | Atlanta city, Georgia | 45 946 |
| 66 | 45 | St. Paul city, Minnesota | 45 939 |
| 49 | 46 | Wichita city, Kansas | 45 625 |
| 60 | 47 | Corpus Christi city, Texas | 45 267 |
| 37 | 48 | Kansas City city, Missouri | 45 246 |
| 29 | 49 | Oklahoma City city, Oklahoma | 44 973 |
| 74 | 50 | Fort Wayne city, Indiana | 44 597 |
| 4 | 51 | Houston city, Texas | 44 124 |
| 7 | 52 | San Antonio city, Texas | 43 961 |
| 53 | 53 | Tampa city, Florida | 43 957 |
| 34 | 54 | Fresno city, California | 43 440 |
| 15 | 55 | Columbus city, Ohio | 43 348 |
| 13 | 56 | Indianapolis city, Indiana | 42 772 |
| 9 | 57 | Dallas city, Texas | 42 259 |
| 69 | 58 | Greensboro city, North Carolina | 41 973 |
| 46 | 59 | Tulsa city, Oklahoma | 40 268 |
| 26 | 60 | Baltimore city, Maryland | 40 100 |
| 19 | 61 | El Paso city, Texas | 39 442 |
| 33 | 62 | Tucson city, Arizona | 37 448 |
| 51 | 63 | New Orleans city, Louisiana | 37 325 |
| 61 | 64 | Pittsburgh city, Pennsylvania | 37 161 |
| 20 | 65 | Memphis city, Tennessee | 37 072 |
| 5 | 66 | Philadelphia city, Pennsylvania | 36 957 |
| 30 | 67 | Milwaukee city, Wisconsin | 35 851 |
| 68 | 68 | Newark city, New Jersey | 35 696 |
| 58 | 69 | St. Louis city, Missouri | 34 402 |
| 67 | 70 | Toledo city, Ohio | 34 170 |
| 65 | 71 | Cincinnati city, Ohio | 34 104 |
| 44 | 72 | Miami city, Florida | 30 270 |
| 73 | 73 | Buffalo city, New York | 30 230 |
| 18 | 74 | Detroit city, Michigan | 27 862 |
| 48 | 75 | Cleveland city, Ohio | 27 470 |

### Median value of owner-occupied housing units, 2007–2011

| Population rank | Median value rank | City | Median value (dollars) [col 52] |
|---|---|---|---|
| 14 | 1 | San Francisco city, California | 767 300 |
| 10 | 2 | San Jose city, California | 605 400 |
| 54 | 3 | Urban Honolulu CDP, Hawaii | 545 700 |
| 1 | 4 | New York city, New York | 514 900 |
| 2 | 5 | Los Angeles city, California | 513 600 |
| 45 | 6 | Oakland city, California | 492 200 |
| 36 | 7 | Long Beach city, California | 478 400 |
| 8 | 8 | San Diego city, California | 477 100 |
| 55 | 9 | Anaheim city, California | 457 800 |
| 22 | 10 | Seattle city, Washington | 453 000 |
| 24 | 11 | Washington, District of Columbia | 442 600 |
| 21 | 12 | Boston city, Massachusetts | 381 900 |
| 57 | 13 | Santa Ana city, California | 371 700 |
| 75 | 14 | Jersey City city, New Jersey | 353 000 |
| 59 | 15 | Riverside city, California | 299 600 |
| 28 | 16 | Portland city, Oregon | 292 800 |
| 68 | 17 | Newark city, New Jersey | 282 400 |
| 39 | 18 | Virginia Beach city, Virginia | 276 500 |
| 63 | 19 | Anchorage municipality, Alaska | 276 200 |
| 35 | 20 | Sacramento city, California | 275 800 |
| 71 | 20 | Henderson city, Nevada | 275 800 |
| 22 | 22 | Chicago city, Illinois | 260 800 |
| 44 | 23 | Miami city, Florida | 257 500 |
| 23 | 24 | Denver city, Colorado | 243 400 |
| 40 | 25 | Atlanta city, Georgia | 228 000 |
| 34 | 26 | Fresno city, California | 223 900 |
| 47 | 27 | Minneapolis city, Minnesota | 223 400 |
| 64 | 28 | Stockton city, California | 222 200 |
| 31 | 29 | Las Vegas city, Nevada | 222 000 |
| 52 | 30 | Bakersfield city, California | 218 200 |
| 70 | 31 | Plano city, Texas | 214 700 |
| 41 | 32 | Colorado Springs city, Colorado | 212 700 |
| 11 | 33 | Austin city, Texas | 209 900 |
| 42 | 34 | Raleigh city, North Carolina | 205 200 |
| 6 | 35 | Phoenix city, Arizona | 201 000 |
| 66 | 36 | St. Paul city, Minnesota | 198 100 |
| 32 | 37 | Albuquerque city, New Mexico | 191 300 |
| 53 | 38 | Tampa city, Florida | 189 400 |
| 51 | 39 | New Orleans city, Louisiana | 183 500 |
| 56 | 40 | Aurora city, Colorado | 182 800 |
| 38 | 41 | Mesa city, Arizona | 178 900 |
| 17 | 42 | Charlotte city, North Carolina | 174 100 |
| 12 | 43 | Jacksonville city, Florida | 166 400 |
| 25 | 44 | Nashville-Davidson, Tennessee | 166 300 |
| 33 | 45 | Tucson city, Arizona | 163 900 |
| 26 | 46 | Baltimore city, Maryland | 163 700 |
| 62 | 47 | Lexington-Fayette, Kentucky | 161 100 |
| 27 | 48 | Louisville/Jefferson, Kentucky | 147 900 |
| 69 | 49 | Greensboro city, North Carolina | 147 800 |
| 72 | 50 | Lincoln city, Nebraska | 141 200 |
| 5 | 51 | Philadelphia city, Pennsylvania | 140 700 |
| 30 | 52 | Milwaukee city, Wisconsin | 139 000 |
| 15 | 53 | Columbus city, Ohio | 137 400 |
| 37 | 54 | Kansas City city, Missouri | 136 900 |
| 43 | 55 | Omaha city, Nebraska | 132 700 |
| 50 | 56 | Arlington city, Texas | 131 800 |
| 9 | 57 | Dallas city, Texas | 129 600 |
| 29 | 58 | Oklahoma City city, Oklahoma | 129 300 |
| 65 | 59 | Cincinnati city, Ohio | 129 100 |
| 4 | 60 | Houston city, Texas | 124 400 |
| 58 | 61 | St. Louis city, Missouri | 123 300 |
| 16 | 62 | Fort Worth city, Texas | 121 900 |
| 13 | 63 | Indianapolis city, Indiana | 120 900 |
| 46 | 64 | Tulsa city, Oklahoma | 118 700 |
| 49 | 65 | Wichita city, Kansas | 114 800 |
| 19 | 66 | El Paso city, Texas | 114 200 |
| 7 | 67 | San Antonio city, Texas | 111 900 |
| 60 | 68 | Corpus Christi city, Texas | 111 300 |
| 74 | 69 | Fort Wayne city, Indiana | 100 500 |
| 20 | 70 | Memphis city, Tennessee | 99 000 |
| 67 | 71 | Toledo city, Ohio | 93 300 |
| 61 | 72 | Pittsburgh city, Pennsylvania | 87 800 |
| 48 | 73 | Cleveland city, Ohio | 84 300 |
| 18 | 74 | Detroit city, Michigan | 71 100 |
| 73 | 75 | Buffalo city, New York | 66 200 |

### Median gross rent of renter-occupied housing units, 2007–2011

| Population rank | Median rent rank | City | Median rent (dollars) [col 56] |
|---|---|---|---|
| 10 | 1 | San Jose city, California | 1 390 |
| 14 | 2 | San Francisco city, California | 1 388 |
| 55 | 3 | Anaheim city, California | 1 314 |
| 8 | 4 | San Diego city, California | 1 294 |
| 57 | 5 | Santa Ana city, California | 1 269 |
| 21 | 6 | Boston city, Massachusetts | 1 238 |
| 71 | 7 | Henderson city, Nevada | 1 193 |
| 39 | 8 | Virginia Beach city, Virginia | 1 191 |
| 54 | 9 | Urban Honolulu CDP, Hawaii | 1 185 |
| 24 | 10 | Washington city, District of Columbia | 1 135 |
| 2 | 11 | Los Angeles city, California | 1 127 |
| 75 | 11 | Jersey City city, New Jersey | 1 127 |
| 1 | 13 | New York city, New York | 1 125 |
| 59 | 14 | Riverside city, California | 1 115 |
| 36 | 15 | Long Beach city, California | 1 075 |
| 63 | 16 | Anchorage municipality, Alaska | 1 058 |
| 45 | 17 | Oakland city, California | 1 042 |
| 31 | 18 | Las Vegas city, Nevada | 1 016 |
| 70 | 19 | Plano city, Texas | 1 012 |
| 22 | 20 | Seattle city, Washington | 1 003 |
| 35 | 21 | Sacramento city, California | 978 |
| 68 | 22 | Newark city, New Jersey | 941 |
| 52 | 23 | Bakersfield city, California | 937 |
| 64 | 24 | Stockton city, California | 936 |
| 51 | 25 | New Orleans city, Louisiana | 924 |
| 53 | 26 | Tampa city, Florida | 923 |
| 11 | 27 | Austin city, Texas | 920 |
| 3 | 28 | Chicago city, Illinois | 916 |
| 12 | 29 | Jacksonville city, Florida | 910 |
| 40 | 29 | Atlanta city, Georgia | 910 |
| 44 | 29 | Miami city, Florida | 910 |
| 26 | 32 | Baltimore city, Maryland | 889 |
| 56 | 33 | Aurora city, Colorado | 888 |
| 38 | 34 | Mesa city, Arizona | 876 |
| 34 | 35 | Fresno city, California | 862 |
| 6 | 36 | Phoenix city, Arizona | 860 |
| 28 | 37 | Portland city, Oregon | 855 |
| 42 | 37 | Raleigh city, North Carolina | 855 |
| 5 | 39 | Philadelphia city, Pennsylvania | 850 |
| 17 | 39 | Charlotte city, North Carolina | 850 |
| 23 | 41 | Denver city, Colorado | 832 |
| 16 | 42 | Fort Worth city, Texas | 827 |
| 50 | 43 | Arlington city, Texas | 823 |
| 60 | 43 | Corpus Christi city, Texas | 823 |
| 4 | 45 | Houston city, Texas | 820 |
| 41 | 46 | Colorado Springs city, Colorado | 812 |
| 9 | 47 | Dallas city, Texas | 811 |
| 25 | 48 | Nashville-Davidson, Tennessee | 798 |
| 47 | 49 | Minneapolis city, Minnesota | 793 |
| 20 | 50 | Memphis city, Tennessee | 786 |
| 66 | 51 | St. Paul city, Minnesota | 778 |
| 15 | 52 | Columbus city, Ohio | 776 |
| 7 | 53 | San Antonio city, Texas | 775 |
| 18 | 54 | Detroit city, Michigan | 761 |
| 30 | 55 | Milwaukee city, Wisconsin | 754 |
| 37 | 56 | Kansas City city, Missouri | 752 |
| 32 | 57 | Albuquerque city, New Mexico | 738 |
| 13 | 58 | Indianapolis city, Indiana | 737 |
| 43 | 59 | Omaha city, Nebraska | 735 |
| 61 | 60 | Pittsburgh city, Pennsylvania | 724 |
| 62 | 61 | Lexington-Fayette, Kentucky | 722 |
| 69 | 61 | Greensboro city, North Carolina | 722 |
| 33 | 63 | Tucson city, Arizona | 714 |
| 29 | 64 | Oklahoma City city, Oklahoma | 699 |
| 46 | 65 | Tulsa city, Oklahoma | 697 |
| 58 | 66 | St. Louis city, Missouri | 690 |
| 27 | 67 | Louisville/Jefferson, Kentucky | 689 |
| 72 | 67 | Lincoln city, Nebraska | 689 |
| 73 | 69 | Buffalo city, New York | 666 |
| 19 | 70 | El Paso city, Texas | 661 |
| 49 | 71 | Wichita city, Kansas | 650 |
| 48 | 72 | Cleveland city, Ohio | 646 |
| 74 | 73 | Fort Wayne city, Indiana | 638 |
| 67 | 74 | Toledo city, Ohio | 629 |
| 65 | 75 | Cincinnati city, Ohio | 617 |

# 75 Largest Cities by 2012 Population
## Selected Rankings

| Percent of population below the poverty level, 2007–2011 | | | | Unemployment rate, 2012 | | | | Percent change in civilian labor force, 2011–2012 | | | |
|---|---|---|---|---|---|---|---|---|---|---|---|
| Popu-lation rank | Poverty rate rank | City | Poverty rate [col 46] | Popu-lation rank | Unem-ployment rate rank | City | Unem-ployment rate [col 64] | Popu-lation rank | Percent change rank | City | Percent change [col 62] |
| 18 | 1 | Detroit city, Michigan | 31.1 | 18 | 1 | Detroit city, Michigan | 18.6 | 52 | 5.9 | Bakersfield city, California | 5.9 |
| 48 | 2 | Cleveland city, Ohio | 27.9 | 64 | 2 | Stockton city, California | 18.3 | 17 | 5.0 | Charlotte city, North Carolina | 5.0 |
| 73 | 3 | Buffalo city, New York | 26.1 | 68 | 3 | Newark city, New Jersey | 15.0 | 42 | 4.5 | Raleigh city, North Carolina | 4.5 |
| 68 | 4 | Newark city, New Jersey | 23.5 | 34 | 4 | Fresno city, California | 14.3 | 72 | 4.2 | Lincoln city, Nebraska | 4.2 |
| 44 | 5 | Miami city, Florida | 22.8 | 45 | 5 | Oakland city, California | 13.7 | 24 | 4.1 | Washington city, District of Columbia | 4.1 |
| 30 | 6 | Milwaukee city, Wisconsin | 22.6 | 35 | 6 | Sacramento city, California | 12.4 | 11 | 3.7 | Austin city, Texas | 3.7 |
| 65 | 7 | Cincinnati city, Ohio | 21.8 | 59 | 7 | Riverside city, California | 12.3 | 14 | 3.7 | San Francisco city, California | 3.7 |
| 20 | 8 | Memphis city, Tennessee | 21.3 | 2 | 8 | Los Angeles city, California | 12.1 | 29 | 3.7 | Oklahoma City city, Oklahoma | 3.7 |
| 58 | 9 | St. Louis city, Missouri | 21.0 | 36 | 9 | Long Beach city, California | 12.0 | 60 | 3.4 | Corpus Christi city, Texas | 3.4 |
| 34 | 10 | Fresno city, California | 20.7 | 57 | 9 | Santa Ana city, California | 12.0 | 61 | 3.4 | Pittsburgh city, Pennsylvania | 3.4 |
| 67 | 10 | Toledo city, Ohio | 20.7 | 31 | 11 | Las Vegas city, Nevada | 11.6 | 13 | 3.2 | Indianapolis city, Indiana | 3.2 |
| 5 | 12 | Philadelphia city, Pennsylvania | 20.5 | 40 | 12 | Atlanta city, Georgia | 11.2 | 4 | 3.1 | Houston city, Texas | 3.1 |
| 51 | 12 | New Orleans city, Louisiana | 20.5 | 73 | 13 | Buffalo city, New York | 10.9 | 25 | 3.1 | Nashville-Davidson, Tennessee | 3.1 |
| 19 | 14 | El Paso city, Texas | 20.1 | 75 | 13 | Jersey City city, New Jersey | 10.9 | 53 | 3.0 | Tampa city, Florida | 3.0 |
| 9 | 15 | Dallas city, Texas | 19.6 | 5 | 15 | Philadelphia city, Pennsylvania | 10.8 | 16 | 2.8 | Fort Worth city, Texas | 2.8 |
| 40 | 16 | Atlanta city, Georgia | 19.5 | 71 | 16 | Henderson city, Nevada | 10.5 | 10 | 2.7 | San Jose city, California | 2.7 |
| 4 | 17 | Houston city, Texas | 18.2 | 44 | 17 | Miami city, Florida | 10.3 | 50 | 2.7 | Arlington city, Texas | 2.7 |
| 64 | 18 | Stockton city, California | 18.0 | 20 | 18 | Memphis city, Tennessee | 10.2 | 43 | 2.6 | Omaha city, Nebraska | 2.6 |
| 26 | 19 | Baltimore city, Maryland | 17.7 | 26 | 18 | Baltimore city, Maryland | 10.2 | 3 | 2.5 | Chicago city, Illinois | 2.5 |
| 3 | 20 | Chicago city, Illinois | 17.6 | 3 | 20 | Chicago city, Illinois | 10.1 | 44 | 2.5 | Miami city, Florida | 2.5 |
| 66 | 21 | St. Paul city, Minnesota | 17.0 | 30 | 20 | Milwaukee city, Wisconsin | 10.1 | 12 | 2.4 | Jacksonville city, Florida | 2.4 |
| 15 | 22 | Columbus city, Ohio | 16.6 | 55 | 22 | Anaheim city, California | 9.7 | 15 | 2.4 | Columbus city, Ohio | 2.4 |
| 57 | 22 | Santa Ana city, California | 16.6 | 48 | 23 | Cleveland city, Ohio | 9.5 | 47 | 2.4 | Minneapolis city, Minnesota | 2.4 |
| 2 | 24 | Los Angeles city, California | 16.5 | 10 | 24 | San Jose city, California | 9.4 | 62 | 2.3 | Lexington-Fayette, Kentucky | 2.3 |
| 33 | 24 | Tucson city, Arizona | 16.5 | 52 | 25 | Bakersfield city, California | 9.3 | 70 | 2.3 | Plano city, Texas | 2.3 |
| 1 | 26 | New York city, New York | 16.4 | 58 | 25 | St. Louis city, Missouri | 9.3 | 7 | 2.2 | San Antonio city, Texas | 2.2 |
| 21 | 27 | Boston city, Massachusetts | 16.0 | 1 | 27 | New York city, New York | 9.2 | 66 | 2.2 | St. Paul city, Minnesota | 2.2 |
| 45 | 27 | Oakland city, California | 16.0 | 41 | 27 | Colorado Springs city, Colorado | 9.2 | 75 | 2.2 | Jersey City city, New Jersey | 2.2 |
| 6 | 29 | Phoenix city, Arizona | 15.9 | 53 | 27 | Tampa city, Florida | 9.2 | 26 | 2.1 | Baltimore city, Maryland | 2.1 |
| 47 | 30 | Minneapolis city, Minnesota | 15.8 | 69 | 30 | Greensboro city, North Carolina | 9.1 | 5 | 2.0 | Philadelphia city, Pennsylvania | 2.0 |
| 36 | 31 | Long Beach city, California | 15.5 | 8 | 31 | San Diego city, California | 8.9 | 39 | 1.9 | Virginia Beach city, Virginia | 1.9 |
| 53 | 32 | Tampa city, Florida | 15.4 | 24 | 31 | Washington city, District of Columbia | 8.9 | 40 | 1.9 | Atlanta city, Georgia | 1.9 |
| 61 | 32 | Pittsburgh city, Pennsylvania | 15.4 | 13 | 33 | Indianapolis city, Indiana | 8.8 | 9 | 1.8 | Dallas city, Texas | 1.8 |
| 7 | 34 | San Antonio city, Texas | 15.1 | 74 | 33 | Fort Wayne city, Indiana | 8.8 | 56 | 1.8 | Aurora city, Colorado | 1.8 |
| 46 | 34 | Tulsa city, Oklahoma | 15.1 | 12 | 35 | Jacksonville city, Florida | 8.6 | 69 | 1.8 | Greensboro city, North Carolina | 1.8 |
| 13 | 36 | Indianapolis city, Indiana | 14.7 | 19 | 35 | El Paso city, Texas | 8.6 | 1 | 1.7 | New York city, New York | 1.7 |
| 52 | 36 | Bakersfield city, California | 14.7 | 27 | 35 | Louisville/Jefferson, Kentucky | 8.6 | 27 | 1.7 | Louisville/Jefferson, Kentucky | 1.7 |
| 16 | 38 | Fort Worth city, Texas | 14.5 | 67 | 35 | Toledo, Ohio | 8.6 | 8 | 1.6 | San Diego city, California | 1.6 |
| 60 | 38 | Corpus Christi city, Texas | 14.5 | 23 | 39 | Denver city, Colorado | 8.5 | 46 | 1.6 | Tulsa city, Oklahoma | 1.6 |
| 23 | 40 | Denver city, Colorado | 14.2 | 56 | 39 | Aurora city, Colorado | 8.5 | 23 | 1.5 | Denver city, Colorado | 1.5 |
| 35 | 41 | Sacramento city, California | 14.1 | 17 | 41 | Charlotte city, North Carolina | 8.2 | 51 | 1.5 | New Orleans city, Louisiana | 1.5 |
| 24 | 42 | Washington city, District of Columbia | 13.9 | 33 | 42 | Tucson city, Arizona | 8.0 | 21 | 1.3 | Boston city, Massachusetts | 1.3 |
| 75 | 42 | Jersey City city, New Jersey | 13.9 | 51 | 43 | New Orleans city, Louisiana | 7.8 | 22 | 1.3 | Seattle city, Washington | 1.3 |
| 37 | 44 | Kansas City city, Missouri | 13.8 | 65 | 44 | Cincinnati city, Ohio | 7.7 | 45 | 1.1 | Oakland city, California | 1.1 |
| 25 | 45 | Nashville-Davidson, Tennessee | 13.5 | 6 | 45 | Phoenix city, Arizona | 7.6 | 55 | 1.1 | Anaheim city, California | 1.1 |
| 29 | 46 | Oklahoma City city, Oklahoma | 13.3 | 28 | 45 | Portland city, Oregon | 7.6 | 48 | 0.8 | Cleveland city, Ohio | 0.8 |
| 56 | 47 | Aurora city, Colorado | 13.1 | 61 | 45 | Pittsburgh city, Pennsylvania | 7.6 | 28 | 0.7 | Portland city, Oregon | 0.7 |
| 11 | 48 | Austin city, Texas | 13.0 | 49 | 48 | Wichita city, Kansas | 7.5 | 37 | 0.6 | Kansas City city, Missouri | 0.6 |
| 69 | 49 | Greensboro city, North Carolina | 12.8 | 37 | 49 | Kansas City city, Missouri | 7.4 | 73 | 0.6 | Buffalo city, New York | 0.6 |
| 32 | 50 | Albuquerque city, New Mexico | 12.5 | 9 | 50 | Dallas city, Texas | 7.3 | 32 | 0.5 | Albuquerque city, New Mexico | 0.5 |
| 74 | 51 | Fort Wayne city, Indiana | 12.3 | 14 | 50 | San Francisco city, California | 7.3 | 57 | 0.5 | Santa Ana city, California | 0.5 |
| 49 | 52 | Wichita city, Kansas | 12.1 | 38 | 52 | Mesa city, Arizona | 7.0 | 59 | 0.5 | Riverside city, California | 0.5 |
| 50 | 52 | Arlington city, Texas | 12.1 | 4 | 53 | Houston city, Texas | 6.9 | 68 | 0.5 | Newark city, New Jersey | 0.5 |
| 27 | 54 | Louisville/Jefferson, Kentucky | 12.0 | 42 | 53 | Raleigh city, North Carolina | 6.9 | 30 | 0.4 | Milwaukee city, Wisconsin | 0.4 |
| 62 | 55 | Lexington-Fayette, Kentucky | 11.8 | 32 | 55 | Albuquerque city, New Mexico | 6.8 | 34 | 0.3 | Fresno city, California | 0.3 |
| 28 | 56 | Portland city, Oregon | 11.7 | 16 | 56 | Fort Worth city, Texas | 6.7 | 41 | 0.3 | Colorado Springs city, Colorado | 0.3 |
| 43 | 57 | Omaha city, Nebraska | 11.4 | 25 | 57 | Nashville-Davidson, Tennessee | 6.6 | 65 | 0.3 | Cincinnati city, Ohio | 0.3 |
| 55 | 57 | Anaheim city, California | 11.4 | 7 | 58 | San Antonio city, Texas | 6.5 | 67 | 0.3 | Toledo city, Ohio | 0.3 |
| 12 | 59 | Jacksonville city, Florida | 11.3 | 21 | 59 | Boston city, Massachusetts | 6.4 | 35 | 0.0 | Sacramento city, California | 0.0 |
| 17 | 59 | Charlotte city, North Carolina | 11.3 | 22 | 59 | Seattle city, Washington | 6.4 | 54 | 0.0 | Urban Honolulu CDP, Hawaii | 0.0 |
| 31 | 61 | Las Vegas city, Nevada | 11.0 | 50 | 59 | Arlington city, Texas | 6.4 | 63 | 0.0 | Anchorage municipality, Alaska | 0.0 |
| 59 | 62 | Riverside city, California | 10.9 | 62 | 62 | Lexington-Fayette, Kentucky | 6.3 | 71 | 0.0 | Henderson city, Nevada | 0.0 |
| 42 | 63 | Raleigh city, North Carolina | 10.7 | 15 | 63 | Columbus city, Ohio | 6.2 | 31 | -0.3 | Las Vegas city, Nevada | -0.3 |
| 8 | 64 | San Diego city, California | 9.9 | 66 | 63 | St. Paul city, Minnesota | 6.2 | 19 | -0.5 | El Paso city, Texas | -0.5 |
| 38 | 65 | Mesa city, Arizona | 9.8 | 60 | 65 | Corpus Christi city, Texas | 6.0 | 20 | -0.5 | Memphis city, Tennessee | -0.5 |
| 41 | 66 | Colorado Springs city, Colorado | 9.3 | 70 | 65 | Plano city, Texas | 6.0 | 74 | -0.6 | Fort Wayne city, Indiana | -0.6 |
| 72 | 67 | Lincoln city, Nebraska | 9.1 | 39 | 67 | Virginia Beach city, Virginia | 5.6 | 64 | -0.7 | Stockton city, California | -0.7 |
| 10 | 68 | San Jose city, California | 7.9 | 47 | 68 | Minneapolis city, Minnesota | 5.5 | 6 | -1.0 | Phoenix city, Arizona | -1.0 |
| 14 | 69 | San Francisco city, California | 7.6 | 11 | 69 | Austin city, Texas | 5.4 | 18 | -1.1 | Detroit city, Michigan | -1.1 |
| 54 | 70 | Urban Honolulu CDP, Hawaii | 7.5 | 63 | 69 | Anchorage municipality, Alaska | 5.4 | 36 | -1.2 | Long Beach city, California | -1.2 |
| 22 | 71 | Seattle city, Washington | 6.8 | 46 | 71 | Tulsa city, Oklahoma | 5.3 | 38 | -1.2 | Mesa city, Arizona | -1.2 |
| 71 | 72 | Henderson city, Nevada | 5.5 | 29 | 72 | Oklahoma City city, Oklahoma | 4.8 | 2 | -1.3 | Los Angeles city, California | -1.3 |
| 63 | 73 | Anchorage municipality, Alaska | 5.4 | 43 | 73 | Omaha city, Nebraska | 4.6 | 58 | -1.5 | St. Louis city, Missouri | -1.5 |
| 39 | 74 | Virginia Beach city, Virginia | 5.2 | 72 | 74 | Lincoln city, Nebraska | 3.4 | 33 | -2.1 | Tucson city, Arizona | -2.1 |
| 70 | 75 | Plano city, Texas | 5.1 | 54 | 75 | Urban Honolulu CDP, Hawaii | NA | 49 | -2.5 | Wichita city, Kansas | -2.5 |

# 75 Largest Cities by 2012 Population
## Selected Rankings

| Per capita local government taxes, 2007 | | | | Per capita city government debt outstanding, 2007 | | | | Violent crime rate, 2011 (violent crimes known to police) | | | |
|---|---|---|---|---|---|---|---|---|---|---|---|
| Popu-lation rank | Local taxes rank | City | Local per capita taxes (dollars) [col 121] | Popu-lation rank | Debt rank | City | Debt per capita (dollars) [col 138] | Popu-lation rank | Violent crime rate rank | City | Violent crimes (per 100 000 population) [col 37] |
| 1 | 24 | Washington city, District of Columbia | 8 826 | 24 | 1 | Washington city, District of Columbia | 14 497 | 18 | 1 | Detroit city, Michigan | 2 139 |
| 2 | 1 | New York city, New York | 4 611 | 40 | 2 | Atlanta city, Georgia | 13 604 | 58 | 2 | St. Louis city, Missouri | 1 857 |
| 3 | 14 | San Francisco city, California | 3 154 | 12 | 3 | Jacksonville city, Florida | 13 560 | 45 | 3 | Oakland city, California | 1 683 |
| 4 | 21 | Boston city, Massachusetts | 2 168 | 14 | 4 | San Francisco city, California | 11 380 | 20 | 4 | Memphis city, Tennessee | 1 584 |
| 5 | 5 | Philadelphia city, Pennsylvania | 1 971 | 1 | 5 | New York city, New York | 10 961 | 40 | 5 | Atlanta city, Georgia | 1 433 |
| 6 | 25 | Nashville-Davidson, Tennessee | 1 966 | 23 | 6 | Denver city, Colorado | 8 576 | 26 | 6 | Baltimore city, Maryland | 1 418 |
| 7 | 39 | Virginia Beach city, Virginia | 1 941 | 18 | 7 | Detroit city, Michigan | 8 410 | 64 | 7 | Stockton city, California | 1 408 |
| 8 | 26 | Baltimore city, Maryland | 1 680 | 51 | 8 | New Orleans city, Louisiana | 8 088 | 48 | 8 | Cleveland city, Ohio | 1 368 |
| 9 | 63 | Anchorage municipality, Alaska | 1 677 | 47 | 9 | Minneapolis city, Minnesota | 7 883 | 73 | 9 | Buffalo city, New York | 1 238 |
| 10 | 51 | New Orleans city, Louisiana | 1 636 | 9 | 10 | Dallas city, Texas | 7 136 | 37 | 10 | Kansas City city, Missouri | 1 204 |
| 11 | 37 | Kansas City city, Missouri | 1 493 | 45 | 11 | Oakland city, California | 7 000 | 44 | 11 | Miami city, Florida | 1 198 |
| 12 | 45 | Oakland city, California | 1 466 | 25 | 12 | Nashville-Davidson, Tennessee | 6 531 | 5 | 12 | Philadelphia city, Pennsylvania | 1 193 |
| 13 | 23 | Denver city, Colorado | 1 454 | 11 | 13 | Austin city, Texas | 6 251 | 25 | 13 | Nashville-Davidson, Tennessee | 1 184 |
| 14 | 22 | Seattle city, Washington | 1 287 | 48 | 14 | Cleveland city, Ohio | 5 976 | 68 | 14 | Newark city, New Jersey | 1 166 |
| 14 | 58 | St. Louis city, Missouri | 1 287 | 63 | 15 | Anchorage municipality, Alaska | 5 936 | 24 | 15 | Washington city, District of Columbia | 1 130 |
| 16 | 65 | Cincinnati city, Ohio | 1 275 | 22 | 16 | Seattle city, Washington | 5 869 | 30 | 16 | Milwaukee city, Wisconsin | 1 111 |
| 17 | 13 | Indianapolis city, Indiana | 1 170 | 3 | 17 | Chicago city, Illinois | 5 693 | 13 | 17 | Indianapolis city, Indiana | 1 101 |
| 18 | 61 | Pittsburgh city, Pennsylvania | 1 064 | 13 | 18 | Indianapolis city, Indiana | 5 681 | 65 | 18 | Cincinnati city, Ohio | 1 035 |
| 19 | 47 | Minneapolis city, Minnesota | 1 009 | 4 | 19 | Houston city, Texas | 5 510 | 46 | 19 | Tulsa city, Oklahoma | 1 000 |
| 20 | 2 | Los Angeles city, California | 1 008 | 37 | 20 | Kansas City city, Missouri | 5 478 | 67 | 20 | Toledo city, Ohio | 998 |
| 21 | 8 | San Diego city, California | 981 | 41 | 21 | Colorado Springs city, Colorado | 5 325 | 3 | 21 | Chicago city, Illinois | 992 |
| 22 | 48 | Cleveland city, Ohio | 968 | 50 | 22 | Arlington city, Texas | 5 239 | 4 | 22 | Houston city, Texas | 975 |
| 23 | 18 | Detroit city, Michigan | 948 | 55 | 23 | Anaheim city, California | 5 128 | 47 | 23 | Minneapolis city, Minnesota | 965 |
| 24 | 20 | Memphis city, Tennessee | 930 | 17 | 24 | Charlotte city, North Carolina | 5 110 | 29 | 24 | Oklahoma City city, Oklahoma | 871 |
| 25 | 12 | Jacksonville city, Florida | 925 | 7 | 25 | San Antonio city, Texas | 4 825 | 21 | 25 | Boston city, Massachusetts | 845 |
| 26 | 62 | Lexington-Fayette, Kentucky | 911 | 10 | 26 | San Jose city, California | 4 747 | 63 | 26 | Anchorage municipality, Alaska | 804 |
| 27 | 35 | Sacramento city, California | 887 | 58 | 27 | St. Louis city, Missouri | 4 715 | 61 | 27 | Pittsburgh city, Pennsylvania | 802 |
| 28 | 29 | Oklahoma City city, Oklahoma | 876 | 5 | 28 | Philadelphia city, Pennsylvania | 4 683 | 51 | 28 | New Orleans city, Louisiana | 792 |
| 29 | 68 | Newark city, New Jersey | 866 | 28 | 29 | Portland city, Oregon | 4 674 | 49 | 29 | Wichita city, Kansas | 770 |
| 30 | 10 | San Jose city, California | 856 | 6 | 30 | Phoenix city, Arizona | 4 563 | 75 | 30 | Jersey City city, New Jersey | 767 |
| 31 | 53 | Tampa city, Florida | 851 | 53 | 31 | Tampa city, Florida | 4 553 | 32 | 31 | Albuquerque city, New Mexico | 763 |
| 32 | 44 | Miami city, Florida | 844 | 36 | 32 | Long Beach city, California | 4 494 | 31 | 32 | Las Vegas city, Nevada | 741 |
| 33 | 55 | Anaheim city, California | 828 | 20 | 33 | Memphis city, Tennessee | 4 380 | 35 | 33 | Sacramento city, California | 711 |
| 34 | 28 | Portland city, Oregon | 820 | 59 | 34 | Riverside city, California | 4 368 | 9 | 34 | Dallas city, Texas | 681 |
| 35 | 40 | Atlanta city, Georgia | 796 | 2 | 35 | Los Angeles city, California | 4 317 | 15 | 35 | Columbus city, Ohio | 664 |
| 36 | 15 | Columbus city, Ohio | 790 | 26 | 36 | Baltimore city, Maryland | 3 839 | 14 | 36 | San Francisco city, California | 660 |
| 37 | 70 | Plano city, Texas | 781 | 35 | 37 | Sacramento city, California | 3 747 | 53 | 37 | Tampa city, Florida | 655 |
| 38 | 59 | Riverside city, California | 769 | 46 | 38 | Tulsa city, Oklahoma | 3 678 | 66 | 37 | St. Paul city, Minnesota | 655 |
| 39 | 9 | Dallas city, Texas | 757 | 72 | 39 | Lincoln city, Nebraska | 3 649 | 33 | 39 | Tucson city, Arizona | 652 |
| 40 | 4 | Houston city, Texas | 728 | 61 | 40 | Pittsburgh city, Pennsylvania | 3 263 | 60 | 40 | Corpus Christi city, Texas | 638 |
| 41 | 36 | Long Beach city, California | 720 | 66 | 41 | St. Paul city, Minnesota | 3 154 | 1 | 41 | New York city, New York | 624 |
| 42 | 3 | Chicago city, Illinois | 719 | 39 | 42 | Virginia Beach city, Virginia | 3 128 | 12 | 42 | Jacksonville city, Florida | 621 |
| 42 | 16 | Fort Worth city, Texas | 719 | 60 | 43 | Corpus Christi city, Texas | 3 047 | 27 | 43 | Louisville/Jefferson, Kentucky | 614 |
| 44 | 56 | Aurora city, Colorado | 703 | 75 | 44 | Jersey City city, New Jersey | 2 955 | 36 | 44 | Long Beach city, California | 611 |
| 45 | 67 | Toledo city, Ohio | 698 | 56 | 45 | Aurora city, Colorado | 2 852 | 23 | 45 | Denver city, Colorado | 609 |
| 46 | 64 | Stockton city, California | 691 | 62 | 46 | Lexington-Fayette, Kentucky | 2 739 | 17 | 46 | Charlotte city, North Carolina | 606 |
| 47 | 6 | Phoenix city, Arizona | 687 | 42 | 47 | Raleigh city, North Carolina | 2 596 | 16 | 47 | Fort Worth city, Texas | 605 |
| 48 | 75 | Jersey City city, New Jersey | 684 | 38 | 48 | Mesa city, Arizona | 2 522 | 22 | 48 | Seattle city, Washington | 593 |
| 49 | 46 | Tulsa city, Oklahoma | 681 | 8 | 49 | San Diego city, California | 2 450 | 34 | 49 | Fresno city, California | 582 |
| 50 | 32 | Albuquerque city, New Mexico | 680 | 15 | 50 | Columbus city, Ohio | 2 445 | 43 | 50 | Omaha city, Nebraska | 560 |
| 51 | 43 | Omaha city, Nebraska | 660 | 73 | 51 | Buffalo city, New York | 2 443 | 6 | 51 | Phoenix city, Arizona | 552 |
| 52 | 11 | Austin city, Texas | 634 | 64 | 52 | Stockton city, California | 2 424 | 52 | 52 | Bakersfield city, California | 531 |
| 53 | 57 | Santa Ana city, California | 624 | 21 | 53 | Boston city, Massachusetts | 2 404 | 69 | 53 | Greensboro city, North Carolina | 523 |
| 54 | 17 | Charlotte city, North Carolina | 614 | 49 | 54 | Wichita city, Kansas | 2 268 | 2 | 54 | Los Angeles city, California | 522 |
| 55 | 50 | Arlington city, Texas | 604 | 65 | 55 | Cincinnati city, Ohio | 2 181 | 7 | 55 | San Antonio city, Texas | 519 |
| 56 | 69 | Greensboro city, North Carolina | 601 | 33 | 56 | Tucson city, Arizona | 2 162 | 28 | 56 | Portland city, Oregon | 515 |
| 57 | 73 | Buffalo city, New York | 600 | 30 | 57 | Milwaukee city, Wisconsin | 2 101 | 50 | 57 | Arlington city, Texas | 502 |
| 58 | 71 | Henderson city, Nevada | 593 | 34 | 58 | Fresno city, California | 2 000 | 62 | 58 | Lexington-Fayette, Kentucky | 457 |
| 59 | 60 | Corpus Christi city, Texas | 569 | 29 | 59 | Oklahoma City city, Oklahoma | 1 980 | 56 | 59 | Aurora city, Colorado | 441 |
| 60 | 72 | Lincoln city, Nebraska | 566 | 43 | 60 | Omaha city, Nebraska | 1 941 | 41 | 60 | Colorado Springs city, Colorado | 440 |
| 61 | 41 | Colorado Springs city, Colorado | 558 | 32 | 61 | Albuquerque city, New Mexico | 1 837 | 19 | 61 | El Paso city, Texas | 431 |
| 62 | 34 | Fresno city, California | 553 | 19 | 62 | El Paso city, Texas | 1 812 | 11 | 62 | Austin city, Texas | 430 |
| 63 | 52 | Bakersfield city, California | 522 | 69 | 63 | Greensboro city, North Carolina | 1 804 | 59 | 63 | Riverside city, California | 426 |
| 64 | 33 | Tucson city, Arizona | 514 | 16 | 64 | Fort Worth city, Texas | 1 735 | 42 | 64 | Raleigh city, North Carolina | 422 |
| 65 | 19 | El Paso city, Texas | 490 | 68 | 65 | Newark city, New Jersey | 1 677 | 38 | 65 | Mesa city, Arizona | 413 |
| 65 | 74 | Fort Wayne city, Indiana | 490 | 71 | 66 | Henderson city, Nevada | 1 622 | 57 | 66 | Santa Ana city, California | 400 |
| 67 | 42 | Raleigh city, North Carolina | 473 | 44 | 67 | Miami city, Florida | 1 328 | 8 | 67 | San Diego city, California | 388 |
| 68 | 7 | San Antonio city, Texas | 461 | 57 | 68 | Santa Ana city, California | 1 243 | 55 | 68 | Anaheim city, California | 377 |
| 69 | 66 | St. Paul city, Minnesota | 457 | 70 | 69 | Plano city, Texas | 1 221 | 72 | 69 | Lincoln city, Nebraska | 371 |
| 70 | 49 | Wichita city, Kansas | 451 | 67 | 70 | Toledo city, Ohio | 1 219 | 10 | 70 | San Jose city, California | 335 |
| 71 | 31 | Las Vegas city, Nevada | 450 | 74 | 71 | Fort Wayne city, Indiana | 1 189 | 74 | 71 | Fort Wayne city, Indiana | 308 |
| 72 | 30 | Milwaukee city, Wisconsin | 410 | 31 | 72 | Las Vegas city, Nevada | 631 | 71 | 72 | Henderson city, Nevada | 220 |
| 73 | 38 | Mesa city, Arizona | 391 | 52 | 73 | Bakersfield city, California | 382 | 39 | 73 | Virginia Beach city, Virginia | 177 |
| NA | 27 | Louisville/Jefferson, Kentucky | NA | 27 | 74 | Louisville/Jefferson, Kentucky | NA | 70 | 74 | Plano city, Texas | 164 |
| NA | 54 | Urban Honolulu CDP, Hawaii | NA | 54 | 74 | Urban Honolulu CDP, Hawaii | NA | 54 | NA | Urban Honolulu CDP, Hawaii | NA |

# All Cities
## Selected Rankings

| Defense procurement contracts for all cities, 2009–2010 | | | | Non-defense procurement contracts for all cities, 2009–2010 | | | | Federal grants, 2009–2010 | | | |
|---|---|---|---|---|---|---|---|---|---|---|---|
| Popu-lation rank | Defense contract rank | City | Defense contracts (millions of dollars) [col 108] | Popu-lation rank | Non-defense contract rank | City | Non-defense contracts (millions of dollars) [col 109] | Popu-lation rank | Grants rank | City | Grants (millions of dollars) [col 110] |
| 16 | 1 | Fort Worth city, Texas | 7 742.9 | 24 | 1 | Washington city, District of Columbia | 16 598.9 | 1 | 1 | New York city, New York | 34 534.2 |
| 504 | 2 | Oshkosh city, Wisconsin | 7 026.8 | 4 | 2 | Houston city, Texas | 4 174.0 | 24 | 2 | Washington city, District of Columbia | 10 872.0 |
| 33 | 3 | Tucson city, Arizona | 5 200.9 | 1 241 | 3 | Oak Ridge city, Tennessee | 3 380.3 | 35 | 3 | Sacramento city, California | 9 252.3 |
| 8 | 4 | San Diego city, California | 4 772.4 | 704 | 4 | Richland city, Washington | 3 100.3 | 11 | 4 | Austin city, Texas | 7 296.9 |
| 125 | 5 | Huntsville city, Alabama | 4 741.0 | 32 | 5 | Albuquerque city, New Mexico | 2 752.9 | 21 | 5 | Boston city, Massachusetts | 6 428.2 |
| 24 | 6 | Washington city, District of Columbia | 4 651.0 | 1 217 | 6 | Aiken city, South Carolina | 2 319.8 | 744 | 6 | Harrisburg city, Pennsylvania | 4 756.8 |
| 169 | 7 | Sunnyvale city, California | 3 983.8 | 1 | 7 | New York city, New York | 2 225.2 | 124 | 7 | Tallahassee city, Florida | 4 447.5 |
| 36 | 8 | Long Beach city, California | 3 814.0 | 543 | 8 | Rockville city, Maryland | 2 072.2 | 296 | 8 | Albany city, New York | 4 416.7 |
| 605 | 9 | Marietta city, Georgia | 3 485.4 | 40 | 9 | Atlanta city, Georgia | 1 859.6 | 3 | 9 | Chicago city, Illinois | 4 225.5 |
| 77 | 10 | Orlando city, Florida | 3 058.4 | 373 | 10 | Livermore city, California | 1 571.9 | 40 | 10 | Atlanta city, Georgia | 4 102.9 |
| 58 | 11 | St. Louis city, Missouri | 3 022.3 | 326 | 11 | Santa Monica city, California | 1 456.1 | 26 | 11 | Baltimore city, Maryland | 4 036.3 |
| 129 | 12 | Newport News city, Virginia | 3 012.1 | 611 | 12 | Idaho Falls city, Idaho | 1 344.4 | 15 | 12 | Columbus city, Ohio | 3 619.3 |
| 500 | 13 | Rancho Cordova city, California | 2 999.6 | 37 | 13 | Kansas City city, Missouri | 1 268.1 | 2 | 13 | Los Angeles city, California | 3 310.9 |
| 7 | 14 | San Antonio city, Texas | 2 791.9 | 8 | 14 | San Diego city, California | 897.1 | 22 | 14 | Seattle city, Washington | 3 027.0 |
| 118 | 15 | Amarillo city, Texas | 2 394.6 | 5 | 15 | Philadelphia city, Pennsylvania | 882.3 | 5 | 15 | Philadelphia city, Pennsylvania | 2 976.3 |
| 51 | 16 | New Orleans city, Louisiana | 2 386.5 | 231 | 16 | Berkeley city, California | 795.6 | 42 | 16 | Raleigh city, North Carolina | 2 880.8 |
| 128 | 17 | Grand Prairie city, Texas | 2 252.0 | 3 | 17 | Chicago city, Illinois | 726.4 | 234 | 17 | Lansing city, Michigan | 2 770.2 |
| 191 | 18 | Sterling Heights city, Michigan | 2 108.9 | 168 | 18 | Alexandria city, Virginia | 721.1 | 82 | 18 | Madison city, Wisconsin | 2 762.3 |
| 79 | 19 | Norfolk city, Virginia | 2 099.7 | 14 | 19 | San Francisco city, California | 706.1 | 14 | 19 | San Francisco city, California | 2 739.5 |
| 39 | 20 | Virginia Beach city, Virginia | 1 962.6 | 31 | 20 | Las Vegas city, Nevada | 696.6 | 8 | 20 | San Diego city, California | 2 736.8 |
| 41 | 21 | Colorado Springs city, Colorado | 1 892.4 | 26 | 21 | Baltimore city, Maryland | 688.6 | 90 | 21 | Baton Rouge city, Louisiana | 2 574.9 |
| 6 | 22 | Phoenix city, Arizona | 1 873.8 | 21 | 22 | Boston city, Massachusetts | 614.8 | 25 | 22 | Nashville-Davidson, Tennessee | 2 476.4 |
| 65 | 23 | Cincinnati city, Ohio | 1 784.8 | 806 | 23 | Coeur d'Alene city, Idaho | 602.7 | 13 | 23 | Indianapolis city, Indiana | 2 170.3 |
| 101 | 24 | Rochester city, New York | 1 754.9 | 23 | 24 | Denver city, Colorado | 566.3 | 4 | 24 | Houston city, Texas | 2 135.2 |
| 798 | 25 | Leesburg town, Virginia | 1 640.9 | 546 | 25 | Gaithersburg city, Maryland | 548.3 | 226 | 25 | Springfield city, Illinois | 2 100.1 |
| 4 | 26 | Houston city, Texas | 1 530.1 | 118 | 26 | Amarillo city, Texas | 537.6 | 6 | 26 | Phoenix city, Arizona | 2 074.8 |
| 20 | 27 | Memphis city, Tennessee | 1 513.6 | 204 | 27 | Charleston city, South Carolina | 505.0 | 102 | 27 | Richmond city, Virginia | 2 033.0 |
| 212 | 28 | Kent city, Washington | 1 475.2 | 20 | 28 | Memphis city, Tennessee | 495.9 | 367 | 28 | Trenton city, New Jersey | 1 913.7 |
| 640 | 29 | Taunton city, Massachusetts | 1 386.7 | 1 019 | 29 | Leavenworth city, Kansas | 487.8 | 23 | 29 | Denver city, Colorado | 1 880.5 |
| 328 | 30 | Lynn city, Massachusetts | 1 384.5 | 137 | 30 | Chattanooga city, Tennessee | 483.1 | 58 | 30 | St. Louis city, Missouri | 1 828.5 |
| 1 391 | 31 | Greenville city, Texas | 1 345.3 | 22 | 31 | Seattle city, Washington | 482.7 | 773 | 31 | Olympia city, Washington | 1 715.6 |
| 13 | 32 | Indianapolis city, Indiana | 1 289.4 | 51 | 32 | New Orleans city, Louisiana | 481.2 | 61 | 32 | Pittsburgh city, Pennsylvania | 1 697.2 |
| 749 | 33 | Poway city, California | 1 275.1 | 77 | 33 | Orlando city, Florida | 472.0 | 123 | 33 | Salt Lake City city, Utah | 1 688.1 |
| 837 | 34 | York city, Pennsylvania | 1 207.2 | 1 374 | 34 | Batavia city, Illinois | 440.2 | 28 | 34 | Portland city, Oregon | 1 443.6 |
| 38 | 35 | Mesa city, Arizona | 1 145.0 | 25 | 35 | Nashville-Davidson, Tennessee | 438.7 | 262 | 35 | Cambridge city, Massachusetts | 1 398.8 |
| 831 | 36 | Littleton city, Colorado | 1 138.3 | 279 | 36 | Boulder city, Colorado | 436.4 | 227 | 36 | Ann Arbor city, Michigan | 1 384.4 |
| 737 | 37 | West Sacramento city, California | 1 131.2 | 262 | 37 | Cambridge city, Massachusetts | 435.6 | 83 | 37 | Durham city, North Carolina | 1 372.5 |
| 196 | 38 | Cedar Rapids city, Iowa | 1 097.7 | 233 | 38 | Murfreesboro city, Tennessee | 429.3 | 841 | 38 | Jefferson City city, Missouri | 1 371.9 |
| 22 | 39 | Seattle city, Washington | 1 044.2 | 18 | 39 | Detroit city, Michigan | 428.2 | 29 | 39 | Oklahoma City city, Oklahoma | 1 360.0 |
| 425 | 40 | Melbourne city, Florida | 1 040.8 | 9 | 40 | Dallas city, Texas | 425.0 | 117 | 40 | Little Rock city, Arkansas | 1 319.0 |
| 53 | 41 | Tampa city, Florida | 998.2 | 11 | 41 | Austin city, Texas | 418.7 | 104 | 41 | Des Moines city, Iowa | 1 314.5 |
| 49 | 42 | Wichita city, Kansas | 988.4 | 28 | 42 | Portland city, Oregon | 408.9 | 66 | 42 | St. Paul city, Minnesota | 1 309.5 |
| 957 | 43 | Hurst city, Texas | 976.0 | 1 104 | 43 | Menlo Park city, California | 390.8 | 154 | 43 | Salem city, Oregon | 1 226.4 |
| 63 | 44 | Anchorage municipality, Alaska | 963.9 | 125 | 44 | Huntsville city, Alabama | 384.8 | 134 | 44 | Jackson city, Mississippi | 1 183.5 |
| 1 101 | 45 | Deer Park city, Texas | 952.9 | 6 | 45 | Phoenix city, Arizona | 378.1 | 47 | 45 | Minneapolis city, Minnesota | 1 161.7 |
| 29 | 46 | Oklahoma City city, Oklahoma | 921.8 | 127 | 46 | Knoxville city, Tennessee | 372.9 | 48 | 46 | Cleveland city, Ohio | 1 129.0 |
| 286 | 47 | South Bend city, Indiana | 876.9 | 7 | 47 | San Antonio city, Texas | 366.0 | 189 | 47 | Columbia city, South Carolina | 1 115.1 |
| 12 | 48 | Jacksonville city, Florida | 845.0 | 13 | 48 | Indianapolis city, Indiana | 356.9 | 713 | 48 | Charleston city, West Virginia | 1 101.6 |
| 168 | 49 | Alexandria city, Virginia | 834.3 | 48 | 49 | Cleveland city, Ohio | 355.4 | 105 | 49 | Montgomery city, Alabama | 1 069.9 |
| 74 | 50 | Fort Wayne city, Indiana | 822.0 | 2 | 50 | Los Angeles city, California | 343.7 | 1 313 | 50 | Frankfort city, Kentucky | 1 068.1 |
| 176 | 51 | McKinney city, Texas | 815.7 | 53 | 51 | Tampa city, Florida | 342.0 | 68 | 51 | Newark city, New Jersey | 1 054.9 |
| 495 | 52 | Redondo Beach city, California | 815.6 | 1 172 | 52 | Morgantown city, West Virginia | 321.4 | 44 | 52 | Miami city, Florida | 1 039.2 |
| 155 | 53 | Palmdale city, California | 804.4 | 65 | 53 | Cincinnati city, Ohio | 302.2 | 9 | 53 | Dallas city, Texas | 991.8 |
| 225 | 54 | Independence city, Missouri | 793.9 | 507 | 54 | Palo Alto city, California | 300.6 | 190 | 54 | New Haven city, Connecticut | 971.6 |
| 890 | 55 | Manassas city, Virginia | 746.3 | 47 | 55 | Minneapolis city, Minnesota | 296.3 | 208 | 55 | Hartford city, Connecticut | 932.8 |
| 40 | 56 | Atlanta city, Georgia | 702.4 | 83 | 56 | Durham city, North Carolina | 279.9 | 602 | 56 | Chapel Hill town, North Carolina | 914.9 |
| 2 | 57 | Los Angeles city, California | 675.7 | 63 | 57 | Anchorage municipality, Alaska | 278.6 | 133 | 57 | Providence city, Rhode Island | 881.9 |
| 262 | 58 | Cambridge city, Massachusetts | 660.7 | 506 | 58 | Frederick city, Maryland | 275.4 | 100 | 58 | Birmingham city, Alabama | 842.1 |
| 945 | 59 | Annapolis city, Maryland | 658.8 | 17 | 59 | Charlotte city, North Carolina | 270.5 | 30 | 59 | Milwaukee city, Wisconsin | 819.7 |
| 938 | 60 | Woburn city, Massachusetts | 654.8 | 261 | 60 | Richmond city, California | 265.9 | 101 | 60 | Rochester city, New York | 797.7 |
| 323 | 61 | Sparks city, Nevada | 633.3 | 15 | 61 | Columbus city, Ohio | 262.5 | 51 | 61 | New Orleans city, Louisiana | 772.0 |
| 1 | 62 | New York city, New York | 611.4 | 29 | 62 | Oklahoma City city, Oklahoma | 257.6 | 7 | 62 | San Antonio city, Texas | 738.5 |
| 352 | 63 | Nashua city, New Hampshire | 583.6 | 184 | 63 | Hampton city, Virginia | 252.2 | 279 | 63 | Boulder city, Colorado | 717.6 |
| 94 | 64 | Scottsdale city, Arizona | 568.2 | 100 | 64 | Birmingham city, Alabama | 236.4 | 65 | 64 | Cincinnati city, Ohio | 699.6 |
| 3 | 65 | Chicago city, Illinois | 543.6 | 196 | 65 | Cedar Rapids city, Iowa | 233.2 | 72 | 65 | Lincoln city, Nebraska | 697.7 |
| 848 | 66 | Dublin city, Ohio | 538.7 | 425 | 66 | Melbourne city, Florida | 231.8 | 45 | 66 | Oakland city, California | 695.2 |
| 15 | 67 | Columbus city, Ohio | 535.1 | 62 | 67 | Lexington-Fayette, Kentucky | 230.9 | 197 | 67 | Topeka city, Kansas | 673.4 |
| 123 | 68 | Salt Lake City city, Utah | 529.1 | 61 | 68 | Pittsburgh city, Pennsylvania | 225.0 | 18 | 68 | Detroit city, Michigan | 653.1 |
| 1 277 | 69 | Monroeville municipality, Pennsylvan | 523.5 | 16 | 69 | Fort Worth city, Texas | 221.8 | 231 | 69 | Berkeley city, California | 638.0 |
| 744 | 70 | Harrisburg city, Pennsylvania | 522.5 | 43 | 70 | Omaha city, Nebraska | 217.4 | 945 | 70 | Annapolis city, Maryland | 608.0 |
| 47 | 71 | Minneapolis city, Minnesota | 516.9 | 44 | 71 | Miami city, Florida | 216.9 | 481 | 71 | Santa Fe city, New Mexico | 598.5 |
| 14 | 72 | San Francisco city, California | 508.7 | 260 | 72 | Round Rock city, Texas | 213.9 | 20 | 72 | Memphis city, Tennessee | 587.3 |
| 234 | 73 | Lansing city, Michigan | 508.2 | 12 | 73 | Jacksonville city, Florida | 213.6 | 99 | 73 | Boise City city, Idaho | 583.7 |
| 1 199 | 74 | Clearfield city, Utah | 493.4 | 19 | 74 | El Paso city, Texas | 206.7 | 33 | 74 | Tucson city, Arizona | 579.6 |
| 184 | 75 | Hampton city, Virginia | 482.7 | 963 | 75 | Lancaster city, Texas | 206.2 | 63 | 75 | Anchorage municipality, Alaska | 576.9 |

## Table D. Cities — **Land Area and Population**

| STATE Place code | City | Population, 2012 | | | | Race alone or in combination, not of Hispanic origin (percent), 2010 | | | | | | | |
|---|---|---|---|---|---|---|---|---|---|---|---|---|---|
| | | | | | | | Race alone or in combination | | | | | | |
| | | Land area,[1] 2010 (sq km) | Total persons | Rank | Per square kilometer | White | Black | American Indian, Alaska Native | Asian | Hawaiian Pacific Islander | Percent Hispanic or Latino[2], 2010 | Percent Foreign born 2007–2011 | |
| | | 1 | 2 | 3 | 4 | 5 | 6 | 7 | 8 | 9 | 10 | 11 | |

1. Dry land or land partially or temporarily covered by water.　2. May be of any race.

## Table D. Cities — **Population**

| City | Age of population (percent), 2010 | | | | | | | | | | | Population | | | |
|---|---|---|---|---|---|---|---|---|---|---|---|---|---|---|---|
| | | | | | | | | | | | | Census counts | | Percent change | |
| | Under 5 years | 5 to 17 years | 18 to 24 years | 25 to 34 years | 35 to 44 years | 45 to 54 years | 55 to 64 years | 65 to 74 years | 75 years and over | Median age | Percent female | 2000 | 2010 | 2000–2010 | 2010–2012 |
| | 12 | 13 | 14 | 15 | 16 | 17 | 18 | 19 | 20 | 21 | 22 | 23 | 24 | 25 | 26 |

## Table D. Cities — **Households, Group Quarters, Crime, and Education**

| City | Households, 2010 | | | | Persons in group quarters, 2010 | | | | Serious crimes known to police,[2] 2011 | | | | Educational attainment, 2007–2011 | | |
|---|---|---|---|---|---|---|---|---|---|---|---|---|---|---|---|
| | | Percent | | | | Institutional | | | Total | | Rate[3] | | | Attainment[4] (percent) | |
| | Number | Persons per house-hold | Female family house-holder[1] | One-person | Total | Total | Persons in nursing facilities | Non-institu-tional | Number | Rate[3] | Violent | Property | Population age 25 and older | High school graduate or less | Bachelor's degree or more |
| | 27 | 28 | 29 | 30 | 31 | 32 | 33 | 34 | 35 | 36 | 37 | 38 | 39 | 40 | 41 |

1. No spouse present.　2. Data for serious crimes have not been adjusted for underreporting. This may affect comparability between geographic areas and over time.　3. Per 100,000 population estimated by the FBI.　4. Persons 25 years old and over.

## Table D. Cities — **Income, Poverty, and Housing**

| City | Money income, 2007–2011 | | | | | Housing units, 2010 | | | Occupied Housing units 2007–2011 | | | | |
|---|---|---|---|---|---|---|---|---|---|---|---|---|---|
| | | Households | | | | | | | | Owner-occupied | | Median owner costs as a percent of income | |
| | Per capita income[1] (dollars) | Median income | Percent with income of $200,000 or more | Percent with income of less than $25,000 | Families with income below poverty (percent) | Total | Percent change, 2000–2010 | Vacant units for sale or rent[2] | Total | Percent | Median value[3] (dollars) | With a mortgage[4] | Without a mortgage[5] |
| | 42 | 43 | 44 | 45 | 46 | 47 | 48 | 49 | 50 | 51 | 52 | 53 | 54 |

1. Based on population estimated by the American Community Survey.　2. Includes units rented or sold but not occupied.　3. Specified owner-occupied units; $1,000,000 represents $1,000,000 or more　4. 50.0 represents 50 percent or more.　5. 10.0 represents 10 percent or less.

## Table D. Cities — **Housing, Labor Force, and Employment**

| City | Occupied housing units, 2007–2011 (cont.) | | | | | Migration, 2007–2011 | | Civilian labor force, 2012 | | | | Civilian employment[4], 2007–2011 | | | |
|---|---|---|---|---|---|---|---|---|---|---|---|---|---|---|---|
| | | | | | | | | | | Unemployment | | | Percent | | |
| | Percent renter occupied | Median gross rent[1] | Median rent as a percent of income[2] | Percent with no vehicle available | Percent who lived in the same house one year ago | Percent who lived outside this city one year ago | Total | Total | Percent change, 2011–2012 | Total | Rate[3] | Population age 16 and older | In labor force | Full-year full-time worker | Households with no workers (percent) |
| | 55 | 56 | 57 | 58 | 59 | 60 | 61 | 62 | 63 | 64 | | 65 | 66 | 67 | 68 |

1. $2,000 represents $2,000 or more.  2. 50.0 represents 50 percent or more.  3. Percent of civilian labor force.  4. Persons 16 years old and over.

## Table D. Cities — **Construction, Wholesale Trade, and Retail Trade**

| City | Value of residential construction authorized by building permits, 2011 | | | Wholesale trade,[1] 2007 | | | | Retail trade,[2] 2007 | | | |
|---|---|---|---|---|---|---|---|---|---|---|---|
| | New construction ($1,000) | Number of housing units | Percent single family | Number of establish-ments | Number of employees | Sales (mil dol) | Annual payroll (mil dol) | Number of establish-ments | Number of employees | Sales (mil dol) | Annual payroll (mil dol) |
| | 69 | 70 | 71 | 72 | 73 | 74 | 75 | 76 | 77 | 78 | 79 |

1. Merchant wholesalers except manufacturers' sales branches and offices.  2. Establishments with payroll.

## Table D. Cities — **Real Estate, Professional Services, and Manufacturing**

| City | Real estate and rental and leasing, 2007 | | | | Professional, scientific, and technical services,[1] 2007 | | | | Manufacturing, 2007 | | | |
|---|---|---|---|---|---|---|---|---|---|---|---|---|
| | Number of establish-ments | Number of employees | Receipts (mil dol) | Annual payroll (mil dol) | Number of establish-ments | Number of employees | Receipts (mil dol) | Annual payroll (mil dol) | Number of establish-ments | Number of employees | Receipts (mil dol) | Annual payroll (mil dol) |
| | 80 | 81 | 82 | 83 | 84 | 85 | 86 | 87 | 88 | 89 | 90 | 91 |

1. Establishments subject to federal tax.

## Table D. Cities — **Accommodation and Food Services, Arts, Entertainment, and Recreation, and Health Care and Social Assistance**

| City | Accommodation and food services, 2007 | | | | Arts, entertainment, and recreation,[1] 2007 | | | | Health care and social assistance,[1] 2007 | | | |
|---|---|---|---|---|---|---|---|---|---|---|---|---|
| | Number of establish-ments | Number of employees | Sales (mil dol) | Annual payroll (mil dol) | Number of establish-ments | Number of employees | Receipts (mil dol) | Annual payroll (mil dol) | Number of establish-ments | Number of employees | Receipts (mil dol) | Annual payroll (mil dol) |
| | 92 | 93 | 94 | 95 | 96 | 97 | 98 | 99 | 100 | 101 | 102 | 103 |

1. Establishments subject to federal tax.

## Table D. Cities — **Other Services and Federal Funds**

| City | Other services[1], 2007 | | | | Selected federal funds, 2009–2010 (mil dol) | | | | | | | | | |
|---|---|---|---|---|---|---|---|---|---|---|---|---|---|---|
| | | | | | Procurement contracts | | Grants | | | | | | | |
| | Number of establish-ments | Number of employees | Receipts (mil dol) | Annual payroll (mil dol) | Defense | Other | Total[2] | Medicaid and other health related | Nutrition and family welfare | Energy and envi-ronment | Disasters and emergency prepared-ness | Housing and community develop-ment | Employment and training |
| | 104 | 105 | 106 | 107 | 108 | 109 | 110 | 111 | 112 | 113 | 114 | 115 | 116 |

1. Establishments subject to federal tax.    2. Includes program categories not shown separately. State totals include additional categories not allocated by city.

## Table D. Cities — **City Government Finances**

| City | City government finances, 2007 | | | | | | | | | |
|---|---|---|---|---|---|---|---|---|---|---|
| | General revenue | | | | | | | General expenditure | | |
| | Intergovernmental | | | Taxes | | | | | Per capita[1] (dollars) | |
| | | | | | Per capita[1] (dollars) | | | | | |
| | Total (mil dol) | Total (mil dol) | Percent from state government | Total (mil dol) | Total | Property | Sales and gross receipts | Total (mil dol) | Total | Capital outlays |
| | 117 | 118 | 119 | 120 | 121 | 122 | 123 | 124 | 125 | 126 |

1. Based on population estimated as of July 1 of the year shown.

## Table D. Cities — **City Government Finances**

| City | City government finances, 2007 (cont.) | | | | | | | | | |
|---|---|---|---|---|---|---|---|---|---|---|
| | General expenditure (cont.) | | | | | | | | | |
| | Percent of total for: | | | | | | | | | |
| | Public welfare | Highways | Parking facilities | Education | Health and hospitals | Police protection | Sewerage and sanitation | Parks and recreation | Housing and community development | Interest on debt |
| | 127 | 128 | 129 | 130 | 131 | 132 | 133 | 134 | 135 | 136 |

## Table D. Cities — **City Government Finances, City Government Employment, and Climate**

| City | City government finances, 2007 (cont.) | | | | Climate[2] | | | | | | | |
|---|---|---|---|---|---|---|---|---|---|---|---|---|
| | Debt outstanding | | | | Average daily temperature (degrees Fahrenheit) | | | | | | | |
| | | | | | Mean | | Limits | | | | | |
| | Total (mil dol) | Per capita[1] (dollars) | Debt issued during year | City government employment, 2011 | January | July | January[3] | July[4] | Annual precipitation (inches) | Heating degree days | Cooling degree days |
| | 137 | 138 | 139 | 140 | 141 | 142 | 143 | 144 | 145 | 146 | 147 |

1. Based on the population estimated as of July 1 of the year shown.    2. Represents normal values based on the 30-year period, 1971–2000.    3. Average daily minimum.    4. Average daily maximum.

# Table D. Cities — **Land Area and Population**

| STATE Place code | City | Land area,[1] 2010 (sq km) | Population, 2012 Total persons | Rank | Per square kilometer | White | Black | American Indian, Alaska Native | Asian | Hawaiian Pacific Islander | Percent Hispanic or Latino[2], 2010 | Percent Foreign born 2007–2011 |
|---|---|---|---|---|---|---|---|---|---|---|---|---|
| | | 1 | 2 | 3 | 4 | 5 | 6 | 7 | 8 | 9 | 10 | 11 |
| 00 00000 | United States............. | 9 147 592.7 | 313 914 040 | X | 34.3 | 65.4 | 13.0 | 1.3 | 5.4 | 0.3 | 16.3 | 12.8 |
| 01 00000 | ALABAMA ................ | 131 170.8 | 4 822 023 | X | 36.8 | 68.2 | 26.6 | 1.1 | 1.4 | 0.1 | 3.9 | 3.4 |
| 01 00820 | Alabaster ...................... | 64.9 | 30 991 | 1 175 | 477.5 | 76.1 | 14.0 | 0.7 | 1.2 | 0.1 | 9.0 | 6.6 |
| 01 03076 | Auburn ........................... | 150.4 | 56 908 | 628 | 378.4 | 74.7 | 16.9 | 0.7 | 5.9 | 0.1 | 2.9 | 7.9 |
| 01 05980 | Bessemer ...................... | 103.2 | 27 289 | 1 334 | 264.4 | 24.2 | 71.6 | 0.6 | 0.3 | 0.0 | 4.1 | 1.8 |
| 01 07000 | Birmingham ................... | 378.3 | 212 038 | 100 | 560.5 | 21.7 | 73.7 | 0.5 | 1.2 | 0.1 | 3.6 | 3.4 |
| 01 20104 | Decatur ......................... | 139.0 | 55 996 | 642 | 402.8 | 64.4 | 22.5 | 1.1 | 1.1 | 0.1 | 12.4 | 8.4 |
| 01 21184 | Dothan........................... | 231.5 | 67 382 | 499 | 291.1 | 62.9 | 33.2 | 0.8 | 1.4 | 0.1 | 2.9 | 2.7 |
| 01 24184 | Enterprise ..................... | 80.9 | 27 789 | 1 300 | 343.5 | 67.9 | 21.4 | 1.2 | 2.8 | 0.3 | 8.8 | 6.5 |
| 01 26896 | Florence........................ | 67.3 | 39 447 | 922 | 586.1 | 75.2 | 20.2 | 0.9 | 1.6 | 0.1 | 3.6 | 2.7 |
| 01 28696 | Gadsden........................ | 96.3 | 36 674 | 997 | 380.8 | 57.4 | 37.2 | 0.7 | 0.7 | 0.1 | 5.4 | 3.4 |
| 01 35800 | Homewood .................... | 21.7 | 25 262 | 1 429 | 1 164.1 | 72.9 | 17.5 | 0.4 | 2.7 | 0.1 | 7.3 | 10.5 |
| 01 35896 | Hoover ........................... | 122.2 | 83 412 | 375 | 682.6 | 73.6 | 15.2 | 0.5 | 5.7 | 0.1 | 6.0 | 10.8 |
| 01 37000 | Huntsville...................... | 541.5 | 183 739 | 126 | 339.3 | 59.8 | 31.9 | 1.3 | 3.0 | 0.2 | 5.8 | 6.5 |
| 01 45784 | Madison ........................ | 76.7 | 44 972 | 815 | 586.3 | 73.3 | 15.2 | 1.1 | 8.0 | 0.2 | 4.3 | 7.9 |
| 01 50000 | Mobile ........................... | 360.3 | 194 822 | 120 | 540.7 | 44.8 | 51.1 | 0.7 | 2.1 | 0.1 | 2.4 | 3.8 |
| 01 51000 | Montgomery ................. | 413.3 | 205 293 | 105 | 496.7 | 36.9 | 57.1 | 0.5 | 2.6 | 0.1 | 3.9 | 4.3 |
| 01 57048 | Opelika.......................... | 154.3 | 27 825 | 1 298 | 180.3 | 50.0 | 44.0 | 0.5 | 1.9 | 0.1 | 4.4 | 5.5 |
| 01 59472 | Phenix City ................... | 71.9 | 36 185 | 1 009 | 503.3 | 48.4 | 47.2 | 0.8 | 1.1 | 0.3 | 4.0 | 1.8 |
| 01 62328 | Prattville....................... | 85.1 | 34 873 | 1 048 | 409.8 | 78.3 | 17.2 | 0.9 | 2.0 | 0.1 | 3.1 | 2.8 |
| 01 77256 | Tuscaloosa.................... | 156.0 | 93 357 | 318 | 598.4 | 53.3 | 41.9 | 0.5 | 2.1 | 0.1 | 3.0 | 5.0 |
| 01 78552 | Vestavia Hills............... | 50.3 | 34 090 | 1 071 | 677.7 | 89.6 | 4.0 | 0.4 | 4.2 | 0.0 | 2.5 | 5.6 |
| 02 00000 | ALASKA ................ | 1 477 953.2 | 731 449 | X | 0.5 | 69.8 | 4.3 | 18.8 | 6.8 | 1.5 | 5.5 | 6.9 |
| 02 03000 | Anchorage..................... | 4 415.1 | 298 610 | 63 | 67.6 | 68.5 | 7.1 | 11.5 | 9.9 | 2.6 | 7.6 | 9.1 |
| 02 24230 | Fairbanks...................... | 82.1 | 32 312 | 1 128 | 393.6 | 67.7 | 10.6 | 13.4 | 5.0 | 1.2 | 9.0 | 6.8 |
| 02 36400 | Juneau........................... | 6 998.0 | 32 556 | 1 118 | 4.7 | 74.7 | 1.7 | 18.1 | 8.8 | 1.3 | 5.1 | 6.0 |
| 04 00000 | ARIZONA ................ | 294 207.3 | 6 553 255 | X | 22.3 | 59.4 | 4.4 | 4.6 | 3.3 | 0.3 | 29.6 | 13.9 |
| 04 02830 | Apache Junction............ | 90.6 | 36 613 | 999 | 404.1 | 82.6 | 1.6 | 1.5 | 1.1 | 0.2 | 14.4 | 7.7 |
| 04 04720 | Avondale....................... | 118.1 | 78 256 | 411 | 662.6 | 35.8 | 9.8 | 1.4 | 4.1 | 0.6 | 50.3 | 15.6 |
| 04 07940 | Buckeye......................... | 971.9 | 54 542 | 663 | 56.1 | 51.6 | 7.5 | 1.7 | 2.3 | 0.3 | 38.3 | 10.8 |
| 04 08220 | Bullhead City ................ | 153.8 | 39 571 | 918 | 257.3 | 72.6 | 1.6 | 1.4 | 1.8 | 0.3 | 23.7 | 9.9 |
| 04 10530 | Casa Grande................. | 284.0 | 49 974 | 728 | 176.0 | 51.2 | 4.9 | 4.1 | 2.1 | 0.3 | 39.0 | 11.7 |
| 04 12000 | Chandler........................ | 166.8 | 245 628 | 80 | 1 472.6 | 63.7 | 5.4 | 1.6 | 9.2 | 0.4 | 21.9 | 13.4 |
| 04 22220 | El Mirage ...................... | 26.0 | 32 574 | 1 116 | 1 252.8 | 43.3 | 7.2 | 1.6 | 2.2 | 0.4 | 47.6 | 19.9 |
| 04 23620 | Flagstaff........................ | 165.4 | 67 468 | 498 | 407.9 | 66.5 | 2.3 | 12.0 | 2.7 | 0.4 | 18.4 | 8.4 |
| 04 23760 | Florence ........................ | 135.9 | 26 754 | 1 360 | 196.9 | 47.3 | 6.7 | 14.6 | 1.1 | 0.1 | 31.2 | 25.2 |
| 04 27400 | Gilbert........................... | 176.0 | 221 140 | 97 | 1 256.5 | 75.0 | 4.0 | 1.1 | 6.9 | 0.4 | 14.9 | 9.3 |
| 04 27820 | Glendale........................ | 155.3 | 232 143 | 87 | 1 494.8 | 53.3 | 6.6 | 1.7 | 4.5 | 0.3 | 35.5 | 16.1 |
| 04 28380 | Goodyear....................... | 495.9 | 69 648 | 480 | 140.4 | 60.2 | 7.3 | 1.4 | 5.1 | 0.3 | 27.8 | 11.5 |
| 04 37620 | Kingman........................ | 90.2 | 28 336 | 1 280 | 314.1 | 83.1 | 1.5 | 2.3 | 2.1 | 0.5 | 12.5 | 5.3 |
| 04 39370 | Lake Havasu City........... | 115.1 | 52 819 | 681 | 458.9 | 85.3 | 0.9 | 1.4 | 1.4 | 0.2 | 12.1 | 5.1 |
| 04 44270 | Marana .......................... | 314.6 | 36 756 | 995 | 116.8 | 70.6 | 2.9 | 1.4 | 4.5 | 0.3 | 22.1 | 9.0 |
| 04 44410 | Maricopa....................... | 123.0 | 44 803 | 817 | 364.3 | 60.2 | 10.6 | 2.1 | 5.0 | 0.5 | 24.4 | 11.8 |
| 04 46000 | Mesa.............................. | 353.4 | 452 084 | 38 | 1 279.2 | 66.0 | 4.0 | 2.5 | 2.5 | 0.5 | 26.4 | 13.4 |
| 04 51600 | Oro Valley ..................... | 92.0 | 41 388 | 879 | 449.9 | 83.4 | 1.8 | 0.7 | 3.9 | 0.3 | 11.5 | 8.3 |
| 04 54050 | Peoria............................ | 451.7 | 159 789 | 150 | 353.8 | 73.9 | 3.9 | 1.2 | 3.9 | 0.3 | 18.6 | 8.7 |
| 04 55000 | Phoenix.......................... | 1 338.3 | 1 488 750 | 6 | 1 112.4 | 48.0 | 6.8 | 2.1 | 3.7 | 0.3 | 40.8 | 21.5 |
| 04 57380 | Prescott......................... | 107.1 | 40 308 | 901 | 376.4 | 88.3 | 0.9 | 1.5 | 1.7 | 0.2 | 8.6 | 7.0 |
| 04 57450 | Prescott Valley .............. | 100.1 | 39 114 | 934 | 390.7 | 80.3 | 1.2 | 1.6 | 1.5 | 0.3 | 16.7 | 8.8 |
| 04 58150 | Queen Creek ................. | 72.6 | 27 963 | 1 290 | 385.2 | 75.9 | 4.1 | 0.9 | 3.6 | 0.3 | 17.3 | 5.1 |
| 04 62140 | Sahuarita...................... | 80.4 | 26 289 | 1 381 | 327.0 | 62.4 | 3.4 | 1.2 | 2.8 | 0.4 | 32.0 | 8.4 |
| 04 63470 | San Luis ....................... | 83.0 | 26 418 | 1 376 | 318.3 | 1.0 | 0.1 | 0.1 | 0.2 | 0.0 | 98.7 | 43.5 |
| 04 65000 | Scottsdale..................... | 476.4 | 223 514 | 94 | 469.2 | 85.2 | 2.1 | 1.0 | 4.2 | 0.2 | 8.8 | 10.7 |
| 04 66820 | Sierra Vista................... | 394.4 | 46 351 | 797 | 117.5 | 66.3 | 9.9 | 1.6 | 5.9 | 1.0 | 19.4 | 10.0 |
| 04 71510 | Surprise ........................ | 273.9 | 121 287 | 215 | 442.8 | 73.2 | 5.8 | 1.0 | 3.4 | 0.4 | 18.5 | 8.7 |
| 04 73000 | Tempe........................... | 103.4 | 166 842 | 144 | 1 613.6 | 64.4 | 6.6 | 3.0 | 6.6 | 0.6 | 21.1 | 14.9 |
| 04 77000 | Tucson .......................... | 587.2 | 524 295 | 33 | 892.9 | 48.9 | 5.3 | 2.3 | 3.5 | 0.3 | 41.6 | 15.8 |
| 04 85540 | Yuma............................. | 311.5 | 95 429 | 309 | 306.4 | 39.2 | 3.2 | 1.5 | 2.3 | 0.3 | 54.8 | 19.6 |
| 05 00000 | ARKANSAS............... | 134 771.3 | 2 949 131 | X | 21.9 | 76.0 | 15.9 | 1.5 | 1.5 | 0.2 | 6.4 | 4.4 |
| 05 04840 | Bella Vista .................... | 114.6 | 27 347 | 1 331 | 238.6 | 95.1 | 0.8 | 1.7 | 0.7 | 0.1 | 2.6 | 2.1 |
| 05 05290 | Benton........................... | 57.6 | 32 117 | 1 132 | 557.6 | 88.0 | 6.6 | 1.0 | 1.1 | 0.1 | 4.5 | 2.7 |
| 05 05320 | Bentonville.................... | 81.0 | 38 284 | 957 | 472.6 | 78.9 | 2.8 | 2.1 | 9.0 | 0.3 | 8.7 | 10.4 |
| 05 15190 | Conway ......................... | 117.4 | 62 939 | 546 | 536.1 | 76.6 | 16.4 | 1.0 | 2.4 | 0.3 | 5.1 | 5.3 |
| 05 23290 | Fayetteville................... | 139.5 | 76 899 | 427 | 551.2 | 83.2 | 6.8 | 2.1 | 3.7 | 0.3 | 6.4 | 5.9 |
| 05 24550 | Fort Smith..................... | 160.5 | 87 443 | 349 | 544.8 | 67.4 | 10.1 | 3.2 | 5.8 | 0.1 | 16.5 | 12.5 |
| 05 33400 | Hot Springs ................... | 90.7 | 35 478 | 1 032 | 391.2 | 74.1 | 18.1 | 1.4 | 1.2 | 0.1 | 7.5 | 6.6 |

1. Dry land or land partially or temporarily covered by water.    2. May be of any race.

# Table D. Cities — **Population**

| City | Age of population (percent), 2010 | | | | | | | | | | | Population | | | |
|---|---|---|---|---|---|---|---|---|---|---|---|---|---|---|---|
| | | | | | | | | | | | | Census counts | | Percent change | |
| | Under 5 years | 5 to 17 years | 18 to 24 years | 25 to 34 years | 35 to 44 years | 45 to 54 years | 55 to 64 years | 65 to 74 years | 75 years and over | Median age | Percent female | 2000 | 2010 | 2000–2010 | 2010–2012 |
| | 12 | 13 | 14 | 15 | 16 | 17 | 18 | 19 | 20 | 21 | 22 | 23 | 24 | 25 | 26 |
| United States............ | 6.5 | 17.5 | 9.9 | 13.3 | 13.3 | 14.6 | 11.8 | 7.0 | 6.0 | 37.2 | 50.8 | 281 421 906 | 308 745 538 | 9.7 | 1.7 |
| ALABAMA ............... | 6.4 | 17.3 | 10.0 | 12.7 | 13.0 | 14.5 | 12.3 | 7.8 | 6.0 | 37.9 | 51.5 | 4 447 100 | 4 779 745 | 7.5 | 0.9 |
| Alabaster.................. | 7.5 | 20.7 | 7.1 | 13.7 | 16.9 | 14.7 | 10.2 | 5.3 | 3.8 | 35.6 | 50.7 | 22 619 | 30 359 | 34.2 | 2.1 |
| Auburn..................... | 4.9 | 12.5 | 38.0 | 13.4 | 9.7 | 8.2 | 6.3 | 3.6 | 3.2 | 23.3 | 49.9 | 42 987 | 53 496 | 24.2 | 6.4 |
| Bessemer.................. | 7.1 | 17.6 | 9.2 | 12.8 | 11.2 | 14.0 | 13.0 | 7.0 | 8.0 | 38.0 | 53.3 | 29 672 | 27 463 | -7.5 | -0.6 |
| Birmingham .............. | 6.9 | 14.7 | 12.4 | 15.6 | 11.5 | 14.3 | 12.3 | 6.2 | 6.2 | 35.4 | 53.2 | 242 820 | 212 288 | -12.6 | -0.1 |
| Decatur.................... | 6.7 | 17.4 | 9.0 | 13.4 | 12.7 | 14.2 | 12.1 | 8.0 | 6.5 | 37.9 | 51.9 | 53 929 | 55 677 | 3.3 | 0.6 |
| Dothan...................... | 6.9 | 17.6 | 8.5 | 13.3 | 12.8 | 14.0 | 12.3 | 7.8 | 6.9 | 38.0 | 52.7 | 57 737 | 65 926 | 13.4 | 2.2 |
| Enterprise................. | 7.5 | 17.9 | 9.3 | 16.1 | 13.0 | 12.4 | 10.9 | 6.8 | 6.1 | 34.4 | 51.0 | 21 178 | 26 615 | 25.4 | 4.4 |
| Florence................... | 5.9 | 14.2 | 15.4 | 12.3 | 10.4 | 12.7 | 11.8 | 8.5 | 8.8 | 37.1 | 53.8 | 36 264 | 39 339 | 8.4 | 0.3 |
| Gadsden................... | 6.4 | 16.0 | 9.7 | 12.6 | 12.5 | 13.4 | 12.6 | 8.2 | 8.6 | 39.3 | 52.5 | 38 978 | 36 878 | -5.4 | -0.6 |
| Homewood ................ | 7.3 | 15.4 | 17.4 | 18.2 | 12.6 | 11.3 | 8.6 | 3.9 | 5.2 | 29.8 | 53.1 | 25 043 | 25 167 | 0.5 | 0.4 |
| Hoover...................... | 6.8 | 18.2 | 7.8 | 14.6 | 14.1 | 14.7 | 11.9 | 6.3 | 5.6 | 37.0 | 51.9 | 62 742 | 81 113 | 30.1 | 2.8 |
| Huntsville.................. | 6.2 | 15.3 | 12.5 | 14.3 | 11.9 | 14.5 | 11.2 | 7.6 | 6.6 | 36.5 | 51.4 | 158 216 | 180 176 | 13.8 | 2.0 |
| Madison.................... | 6.2 | 22.2 | 7.5 | 11.5 | 14.9 | 18.9 | 10.5 | 5.0 | 3.2 | 37.0 | 50.7 | 29 329 | 42 938 | 46.4 | 4.7 |
| Mobile...................... | 6.7 | 17.4 | 11.2 | 13.8 | 11.5 | 13.9 | 11.7 | 7.0 | 6.7 | 35.7 | 53.0 | 198 915 | 195 092 | -1.9 | -0.1 |
| Montgomery .............. | 7.2 | 17.7 | 11.7 | 14.6 | 12.7 | 13.4 | 10.8 | 6.2 | 5.6 | 34.0 | 53.0 | 201 568 | 205 600 | 2.1 | -0.1 |
| Opelika.................... | 7.7 | 17.7 | 8.9 | 15.0 | 13.0 | 13.7 | 11.7 | 6.9 | 5.3 | 35.5 | 52.5 | 23 498 | 26 401 | 12.7 | 5.4 |
| Phenix City............... | 8.3 | 18.6 | 10.4 | 15.3 | 12.6 | 12.7 | 10.2 | 6.3 | 5.5 | 33.1 | 53.3 | 28 265 | 32 869 | 16.1 | 10.1 |
| Prattville.................. | 6.5 | 20.6 | 8.5 | 12.4 | 15.4 | 14.5 | 10.1 | 7.0 | 4.9 | 36.3 | 52.3 | 24 303 | 33 983 | 39.7 | 2.6 |
| Tuscaloosa............... | 5.0 | 12.4 | 31.9 | 12.9 | 9.1 | 9.8 | 9.1 | 4.9 | 4.9 | 25.4 | 51.9 | 77 906 | 90 898 | 16.1 | 2.7 |
| Vestavia Hills............ | 6.4 | 18.9 | 6.0 | 12.2 | 13.8 | 14.7 | 12.7 | 7.0 | 8.3 | 39.7 | 52.4 | 24 476 | 34 059 | 39.0 | 0.1 |
| ALASKA .................. | 7.6 | 18.8 | 10.5 | 14.5 | 13.1 | 15.6 | 12.1 | 5.0 | 2.8 | 33.8 | 48.0 | 626 932 | 710 231 | 13.3 | 3.0 |
| Anchorage................. | 7.5 | 18.4 | 11.2 | 15.6 | 13.4 | 15.3 | 11.3 | 4.6 | 2.7 | 32.9 | 49.2 | 260 283 | 291 826 | 12.1 | 2.3 |
| Fairbanks.................. | 9.6 | 16.3 | 16.7 | 19.1 | 11.2 | 10.9 | 8.9 | 4.1 | 3.2 | 27.9 | 46.8 | 30 224 | 31 535 | 4.3 | 2.5 |
| Juneau...................... | 6.3 | 17.1 | 8.9 | 13.8 | 13.8 | 17.4 | 14.2 | 5.5 | 2.9 | 38.1 | 49.0 | 30 711 | 31 275 | 1.8 | 4.1 |
| ARIZONA ................ | 7.1 | 18.4 | 9.9 | 13.4 | 12.9 | 13.2 | 11.4 | 7.8 | 6.0 | 35.9 | 50.3 | 5 130 632 | 6 392 015 | 24.6 | 2.5 |
| Apache Junction........... | 5.4 | 14.4 | 6.6 | 9.7 | 10.7 | 12.9 | 14.2 | 14.7 | 11.4 | 47.5 | 51.4 | 31 814 | 35 838 | 12.7 | 2.2 |
| Avondale .................. | 9.3 | 23.3 | 11.7 | 15.9 | 15.0 | 11.7 | 7.7 | 3.6 | 1.9 | 28.6 | 50.4 | 35 883 | 76 227 | 112.5 | 2.7 |
| Buckeye.................... | 9.1 | 21.5 | 8.7 | 18.8 | 15.7 | 10.7 | 8.9 | 5.0 | 1.7 | 30.7 | 45.4 | 6 537 | 50 903 | 678.3 | 7.1 |
| Bullhead City.............. | 5.4 | 14.2 | 7.4 | 8.9 | 9.8 | 14.3 | 16.1 | 14.7 | 9.3 | 48.2 | 50.6 | 33 769 | 39 540 | 17.1 | 0.1 |
| Casa Grande.............. | 7.9 | 20.0 | 8.5 | 12.3 | 11.7 | 11.5 | 12.2 | 9.6 | 6.2 | 36.0 | 51.5 | 25 224 | 48 583 | 92.6 | 2.9 |
| Chandler................... | 7.6 | 20.0 | 8.8 | 15.0 | 16.6 | 14.7 | 9.6 | 4.7 | 3.1 | 34.1 | 50.9 | 176 581 | 236 127 | 33.7 | 4.0 |
| El Mirage.................. | 10.5 | 25.0 | 9.7 | 17.7 | 14.2 | 9.9 | 6.7 | 4.2 | 2.2 | 28.1 | 50.4 | 7 609 | 31 797 | 317.9 | 2.4 |
| Flagstaff................... | 6.1 | 14.5 | 26.2 | 15.6 | 11.1 | 11.2 | 9.0 | 3.9 | 2.5 | 26.6 | 50.6 | 52 894 | 65 870 | 24.5 | 2.4 |
| Florence................... | 1.8 | 5.1 | 13.8 | 26.3 | 21.2 | 14.4 | 8.2 | 5.7 | 3.4 | 36.2 | 17.9 | 17 054 | 25 526 | 49.7 | 4.8 |
| Gilbert..................... | 8.5 | 23.6 | 8.0 | 14.8 | 17.1 | 13.6 | 8.4 | 4.1 | 2.0 | 31.9 | 50.8 | 109 697 | 208 340 | 90.0 | 6.1 |
| Glendale................... | 7.6 | 20.4 | 11.4 | 13.7 | 13.2 | 14.1 | 10.4 | 5.3 | 3.9 | 32.5 | 50.9 | 218 812 | 226 480 | 3.6 | 2.5 |
| Goodyear................... | 7.3 | 19.7 | 9.1 | 14.0 | 15.6 | 12.7 | 10.8 | 7.5 | 3.4 | 34.9 | 53.1 | 18 911 | 65 241 | 245.2 | 6.8 |
| Kingman.................... | 6.4 | 16.9 | 8.3 | 10.9 | 11.3 | 13.8 | 13.4 | 10.7 | 8.4 | 41.7 | 51.1 | 20 069 | 28 068 | 39.9 | 1.0 |
| Lake Havasu City......... | 4.5 | 13.4 | 6.1 | 8.9 | 10.0 | 14.2 | 16.1 | 15.5 | 11.4 | 50.3 | 50.6 | 41 938 | 52 532 | 25.2 | 0.5 |
| Marana..................... | 7.8 | 17.8 | 6.2 | 14.0 | 14.4 | 12.4 | 12.6 | 10.2 | 4.7 | 37.7 | 50.1 | 13 556 | 34 578 | 157.9 | 6.3 |
| Maricopa................... | 10.7 | 21.9 | 6.3 | 19.0 | 16.0 | 10.8 | 9.1 | 4.7 | 1.6 | 31.2 | 50.4 | 1 040 | 43 482 | 4 081.0 | 3.0 |
| Mesa........................ | 7.7 | 18.6 | 10.0 | 14.2 | 12.6 | 12.6 | 10.3 | 7.3 | 6.8 | 34.6 | 50.8 | 396 375 | 439 627 | 10.8 | 2.8 |
| Oro Valley................. | 3.9 | 15.3 | 6.1 | 7.0 | 10.7 | 15.3 | 15.7 | 13.6 | 12.5 | 49.8 | 52.4 | 29 700 | 41 011 | 38.1 | 0.9 |
| Peoria...................... | 6.4 | 19.6 | 8.4 | 11.6 | 14.1 | 14.5 | 11.1 | 7.4 | 6.9 | 38.1 | 52.0 | 108 364 | 154 098 | 42.2 | 3.7 |
| Phoenix .................... | 8.3 | 20.0 | 10.4 | 15.5 | 14.3 | 13.5 | 9.6 | 4.9 | 3.6 | 32.2 | 49.8 | 1 321 045 | 1 447 552 | 9.4 | 2.8 |
| Prescott.................... | 3.1 | 10.4 | 9.8 | 7.4 | 7.9 | 12.6 | 17.9 | 15.9 | 14.9 | 54.1 | 50.8 | 33 938 | 39 828 | 17.4 | 1.2 |
| Prescott Valley ........... | 6.9 | 17.2 | 8.3 | 11.6 | 11.0 | 12.9 | 13.0 | 10.7 | 8.4 | 40.6 | 51.5 | 23 535 | 38 822 | 65.0 | 0.8 |
| Queen Creek.............. | 10.4 | 27.0 | 6.7 | 15.0 | 17.2 | 11.1 | 7.4 | 3.8 | 1.4 | 29.8 | 49.9 | 4 316 | 26 361 | 510.8 | 6.1 |
| Sahuarita .................. | 9.5 | 20.3 | 5.4 | 16.0 | 14.1 | 9.0 | 11.0 | 10.0 | 4.7 | 34.4 | 51.2 | 3 242 | 25 259 | 679.1 | 4.1 |
| San Luis ................... | 9.2 | 27.7 | 12.4 | 12.5 | 13.8 | 12.2 | 6.4 | 3.6 | 2.3 | 25.5 | 50.5 | 15 322 | 25 505 | 66.5 | 3.6 |
| Scottsdale................. | 4.2 | 13.6 | 6.8 | 12.2 | 12.8 | 15.5 | 15.0 | 10.8 | 9.2 | 45.4 | 51.7 | 202 705 | 217 383 | 7.2 | 2.8 |
| Sierra Vista............... | 7.5 | 15.5 | 12.5 | 16.9 | 12.0 | 11.2 | 9.7 | 8.0 | 6.6 | 33.1 | 49.1 | 37 775 | 45 129 | 16.2 | 2.7 |
| Surprise.................... | 7.9 | 19.5 | 6.1 | 13.7 | 13.8 | 9.4 | 10.7 | 11.9 | 7.1 | 36.8 | 51.7 | 30 848 | 117 519 | 281.0 | 3.2 |
| Tempe...................... | 5.0 | 11.8 | 25.8 | 18.1 | 10.6 | 11.1 | 9.1 | 4.7 | 3.7 | 28.1 | 47.9 | 158 625 | 161 746 | 2.0 | 3.2 |
| Tucson...................... | 6.9 | 16.5 | 14.3 | 15.0 | 12.2 | 12.8 | 10.6 | 6.1 | 5.8 | 33.0 | 50.5 | 486 699 | 520 116 | 6.9 | 0.8 |
| Yuma....................... | 7.9 | 20.3 | 12.7 | 13.8 | 12.2 | 11.6 | 8.9 | 6.8 | 5.8 | 31.3 | 49.2 | 77 515 | 93 106 | 20.1 | 2.5 |
| ARKANSAS............... | 6.8 | 17.6 | 9.7 | 12.9 | 12.6 | 14.0 | 12.0 | 8.0 | 6.4 | 37.4 | 50.9 | 2 673 400 | 2 915 919 | 9.1 | 1.1 |
| Bella Vista................. | 5.5 | 12.4 | 3.7 | 10.8 | 11.1 | 11.4 | 13.7 | 16.6 | 15.0 | 50.8 | 52.0 | 16 582 | 26 461 | 59.6 | 3.3 |
| Benton ..................... | 7.6 | 19.2 | 7.9 | 15.3 | 14.1 | 12.8 | 10.4 | 6.7 | 6.0 | 35.0 | 51.6 | 21 906 | 30 683 | 40.1 | 4.7 |
| Bentonville................. | 9.2 | 21.9 | 8.1 | 18.8 | 16.0 | 11.9 | 6.9 | 3.7 | 3.4 | 30.6 | 51.0 | 19 730 | 35 301 | 78.9 | 8.5 |
| Conway .................... | 7.0 | 15.6 | 22.8 | 15.6 | 11.6 | 10.6 | 7.9 | 4.5 | 4.3 | 27.3 | 51.7 | 43 167 | 58 905 | 36.5 | 6.8 |
| Fayetteville ............... | 6.0 | 12.5 | 26.2 | 18.6 | 11.1 | 9.8 | 8.0 | 3.9 | 3.9 | 27.2 | 49.7 | 58 047 | 73 580 | 26.8 | 4.5 |
| Fort Smith................. | 7.6 | 17.8 | 10.7 | 13.7 | 12.4 | 13.9 | 11.1 | 6.6 | 6.1 | 35.1 | 51.3 | 80 268 | 86 217 | 7.4 | 1.4 |
| Hot Springs ............... | 6.0 | 14.5 | 8.5 | 11.9 | 10.7 | 13.6 | 13.4 | 9.6 | 11.7 | 43.5 | 52.7 | 35 750 | 35 193 | -1.6 | 0.8 |

# Table D. Cities — Households, Group Quarters, Crime, and Education

| City | Households, 2010 | | | | Persons in group quarters, 2010 | | | | Serious crimes known to police,[2] 2011 | | | | Educational attainment, 2007–2011 | | |
|---|---|---|---|---|---|---|---|---|---|---|---|---|---|---|---|
| | | | Percent | | | Institutional | | | Total | | Rate[3] | | | Attainment[4] (percent) | |
| | Number | Persons per household | Female family householder[1] | One-person | Total | Total | Persons in nursing facilities | Non-institu- tional | Number | Rate[3] | Violent | Property | Population age 25 and older | High school graduate or less | Bachelor's degree or more |
| | 27 | 28 | 29 | 30 | 31 | 32 | 33 | 34 | 35 | 36 | 37 | 38 | 39 | 40 | 41 |
| United States | 116 716 292 | 2.58 | 13.1 | 26.7 | 7 987 323 | 3 993 659 | 1 502 264 | 3 993 664 | 10 266 737 | 3 295 | 386 | 2 909 | 202 048 123 | 43.2 | 28.2 |
| ALABAMA | 1 883 791 | 2.48 | 15.3 | 27.4 | 115 816 | 67 004 | 22 995 | 48 812 | 193 364 | 4 026 | 420 | 3 606 | 3 138 078 | 49.5 | 22.0 |
| Alabaster | 10 628 | 2.83 | 10.1 | 18.7 | 300 | 297 | 293 | 3 | 715 | 2 344 | 193 | 2 151 | 19 650 | 32.4 | 33.1 |
| Auburn | 22 111 | 2.24 | 8.8 | 33.8 | 3 827 | 130 | 130 | 3 697 | 2 295 | 4 279 | 283 | 3 995 | 22 556 | 20.9 | 60.0 |
| Bessemer | 10 711 | 2.48 | 29.7 | 30.9 | 871 | 519 | 472 | 352 | 3 738 | 13 549 | 1 682 | 11 867 | 18 747 | 56.2 | 12.4 |
| Birmingham | 89 382 | 2.27 | 25.0 | 37.7 | 9 035 | 3 300 | 1 559 | 5 735 | 21 004 | 9 849 | 1 483 | 8 366 | 142 471 | 46.7 | 21.3 |
| Decatur | 22 576 | 2.42 | 15.6 | 29.9 | 966 | 767 | 246 | 199 | 2 306 | 4 121 | 352 | 3 769 | 37 575 | 48.4 | 21.5 |
| Dothan | 26 845 | 2.39 | 17.7 | 28.8 | 1 369 | 1 171 | 484 | 198 | 3 080 | 4 680 | 521 | 4 159 | 43 104 | 45.8 | 23.0 |
| Enterprise | 10 513 | 2.50 | 13.9 | 25.6 | 279 | 245 | 245 | 34 | 1 203 | 4 507 | 457 | 4 050 | 16 810 | 39.0 | 27.2 |
| Florence | 17 267 | 2.18 | 15.0 | 35.5 | 1 701 | 524 | 370 | 1 177 | 1 680 | 4 252 | 223 | 4 030 | 25 471 | 45.1 | 25.7 |
| Gadsden | 15 171 | 2.31 | 19.5 | 34.9 | 1 752 | 1 189 | 380 | 563 | 3 272 | 8 835 | 807 | 8 028 | 25 101 | 53.3 | 15.5 |
| Homewood | 10 092 | 2.31 | 12.2 | 34.4 | 1 864 | 18 | 0 | 1 846 | 1 046 | 4 136 | 225 | 3 911 | 14 487 | 21.3 | 59.3 |
| Hoover | 32 478 | 2.50 | 10.0 | 25.8 | 408 | 393 | 361 | 15 | 2 254 | 2 748 | 72 | 2 676 | 54 066 | 19.5 | 55.3 |
| Huntsville | 77 033 | 2.25 | 14.5 | 34.7 | 6 786 | 1 924 | 874 | 4 862 | 11 267 | 6 226 | 839 | 5 387 | 118 126 | 33.1 | 37.9 |
| Madison | 16 111 | 2.65 | 9.9 | 23.4 | 270 | 270 | 225 | 0 | 1 005 | 2 329 | 239 | 2 091 | 26 263 | 18.0 | 56.7 |
| Mobile | 78 959 | 2.40 | 21.6 | 32.2 | 5 598 | 2 632 | 1 196 | 2 966 | 15 269 | 6 062 | 643 | 5 419 | 125 299 | 43.9 | 25.9 |
| Montgomery | 81 486 | 2.44 | 21.8 | 31.1 | 6 879 | 2 967 | 1 005 | 3 912 | 11 451 | 5 538 | 342 | 5 197 | 129 379 | 41.7 | 31.3 |
| Opelika | 10 523 | 2.46 | 20.1 | 28.2 | 572 | 481 | 141 | 91 | 2 151 | 8 085 | 432 | 7 653 | 17 325 | 49.2 | 24.5 |
| Phenix City | 13 243 | 2.44 | 23.9 | 30.1 | 557 | 494 | 203 | 63 | 2 399 | 7 274 | 649 | 6 625 | 20 178 | 49.7 | 16.2 |
| Prattville | 12 711 | 2.64 | 14.0 | 22.9 | 398 | 362 | 181 | 36 | 1 349 | 3 953 | 176 | 3 778 | 20 527 | 40.2 | 28.0 |
| Tuscaloosa | 36 185 | 2.23 | 16.2 | 35.4 | 9 659 | 942 | 144 | 8 717 | 4 834 | 5 318 | 475 | 4 843 | 47 078 | 41.1 | 32.7 |
| Vestavia Hills | 13 987 | 2.42 | 7.7 | 29.3 | 141 | 138 | 138 | 3 | 549 | 1 605 | 73 | 1 532 | 23 237 | 13.2 | 67.3 |
| ALASKA | 258 058 | 2.65 | 10.7 | 25.6 | 26 352 | 6 458 | 1 626 | 19 894 | 23 411 | 3 239 | 606 | 2 633 | 438 805 | 35.9 | 27.2 |
| Anchorage | 107 332 | 2.64 | 11.7 | 24.9 | 8 450 | 2 828 | 1 137 | 5 622 | 11 843 | 3 988 | 804 | 3 184 | 180 063 | 31.1 | 32.3 |
| Fairbanks | 11 534 | 2.52 | 12.2 | 29.9 | 2 518 | 427 | 81 | 2 091 | 1 409 | 4 391 | 552 | 3 839 | 18 052 | 38.9 | 20.4 |
| Juneau | 12 187 | 2.49 | 10.4 | 26.9 | 887 | 408 | 57 | 479 | 1 384 | 4 349 | 500 | 3 849 | 20 975 | 27.0 | 36.4 |
| ARIZONA | 2 380 990 | 2.63 | 12.4 | 26.1 | 139 384 | 84 788 | 13 819 | 54 596 | 256 733 | 3 960 | 406 | 3 555 | 4 087 214 | 39.5 | 26.4 |
| Apache Junction | 15 574 | 2.28 | 10.7 | 31.4 | 283 | 120 | 120 | 163 | 1 340 | 3 687 | 237 | 3 450 | 25 691 | 51.0 | 11.8 |
| Avondale | 23 386 | 3.25 | 17.0 | 15.5 | 160 | 146 | 132 | 14 | 4 165 | 5 387 | 318 | 5 069 | 40 703 | 49.2 | 20.1 |
| Buckeye | 14 424 | 3.17 | 11.7 | 15.2 | 5 094 | 5 084 | 0 | 10 | 1 384 | 2 682 | 83 | 2 599 | 27 659 | 45.9 | 18.6 |
| Bullhead City | 16 761 | 2.35 | 12.2 | 27.8 | 166 | 96 | 93 | 70 | 1 548 | 3 860 | 142 | 3 718 | 29 103 | 51.8 | 13.6 |
| Casa Grande | 17 651 | 2.74 | 14.0 | 22.3 | 282 | 47 | 3 | 235 | 2 896 | 5 879 | 471 | 5 408 | 27 908 | 45.1 | 18.9 |
| Chandler | 86 924 | 2.71 | 11.8 | 22.7 | 546 | 136 | 94 | 410 | 8 097 | 3 381 | 284 | 3 097 | 146 989 | 26.0 | 39.6 |
| El Mirage | 9 416 | 3.38 | 17.9 | 14.8 | 13 | 0 | 0 | 13 | 1 136 | 3 523 | 295 | 3 228 | 16 009 | 54.8 | 12.0 |
| Flagstaff | 22 836 | 2.53 | 11.8 | 25.6 | 8 076 | 668 | 114 | 7 408 | 3 271 | 4 897 | 394 | 4 503 | 34 166 | 26.8 | 42.0 |
| Florence | 3 330 | 2.35 | 10.1 | 26.2 | 17 700 | 17 700 | 0 | 0 | 225 | 869 | 131 | 738 | 19 813 | 59.5 | 5.8 |
| Gilbert | 69 372 | 3.00 | 10.6 | 16.1 | 304 | 4 | 0 | 300 | 4 065 | 1 923 | 86 | 1 837 | 120 723 | 22.1 | 38.0 |
| Glendale | 79 114 | 2.82 | 16.0 | 24.0 | 3 257 | 1 000 | 836 | 2 257 | 15 852 | 6 894 | 484 | 6 410 | 138 698 | 43.3 | 21.4 |
| Goodyear | 21 491 | 2.86 | 9.9 | 16.0 | 3 828 | 3 670 | 164 | 158 | 1 968 | 2 973 | 163 | 2 810 | 39 699 | 32.5 | 27.9 |
| Kingman | 11 217 | 2.44 | 11.7 | 27.9 | 699 | 541 | 132 | 158 | 1 621 | 5 695 | 355 | 5 340 | 19 574 | 46.0 | 15.2 |
| Lake Havasu City | 23 168 | 2.26 | 8.8 | 26.6 | 201 | 151 | 142 | 50 | 1 366 | 2 564 | 184 | 2 380 | 38 551 | 43.7 | 14.8 |
| Marana | 13 073 | 2.63 | 8.5 | 18.7 | 520 | 499 | 0 | 21 | 1 421 | 4 008 | 135 | 3 872 | 22 727 | 25.8 | 38.0 |
| Maricopa | 14 359 | 3.03 | 10.9 | 15.6 | 0 | 0 | 0 | 0 | 1 039 | 2 356 | 136 | 2 220 | 24 523 | 30.7 | 27.8 |
| Mesa | 165 374 | 2.63 | 12.6 | 26.6 | 3 538 | 1 344 | 928 | 2 194 | 16 954 | 3 808 | 413 | 3 395 | 284 236 | 40.6 | 23.5 |
| Oro Valley | 17 804 | 2.30 | 6.9 | 25.1 | 68 | 63 | 42 | 5 | 768 | 1 847 | 58 | 1 789 | 30 276 | 19.6 | 48.0 |
| Peoria | 57 457 | 2.66 | 11.6 | 23.5 | 1 227 | 868 | 826 | 359 | 5 075 | 3 248 | 193 | 3 055 | 100 271 | 34.7 | 26.6 |
| Phoenix | 514 806 | 2.77 | 14.9 | 27.1 | 21 738 | 13 589 | 2 696 | 8 149 | 72 568 | 4 950 | 552 | 4 398 | 890 425 | 44.5 | 25.4 |
| Prescott | 18 611 | 2.03 | 7.5 | 35.1 | 2 008 | 675 | 474 | 1 333 | 1 429 | 3 537 | 423 | 3 113 | 31 146 | 29.5 | 35.4 |
| Prescott Valley | 15 364 | 2.51 | 11.4 | 23.9 | 209 | 158 | 118 | 51 | 893 | 2 268 | 287 | 1 981 | 25 510 | 39.4 | 17.0 |
| Queen Creek | 7 720 | 3.41 | 8.4 | 10.4 | 16 | 0 | 0 | 16 | NA | NA | NA | NA | 13 493 | 25.1 | 32.6 |
| Sahuarita | 9 020 | 2.79 | 8.5 | 16.3 | 63 | 44 | 44 | 19 | 463 | 1 807 | 55 | 1 753 | 15 131 | 26.0 | 34.8 |
| San Luis | 5 953 | 4.20 | 19.8 | 5.7 | 524 | 502 | 0 | 22 | NA | NA | NA | NA | 13 410 | 70.8 | 7.8 |
| Scottsdale | 101 273 | 2.14 | 7.6 | 34.4 | 1 159 | 686 | 622 | 473 | 7 124 | 3 231 | 181 | 3 050 | 164 650 | 19.2 | 52.2 |
| Sierra Vista | 17 059 | 2.39 | 10.7 | 28.9 | 3 037 | 233 | 217 | 2 804 | 1 471 | 3 305 | 326 | 2 979 | 28 165 | 29.4 | 29.2 |
| Surprise | 43 272 | 2.71 | 9.8 | 19.0 | 274 | 89 | 80 | 185 | 2 727 | 2 288 | 110 | 2 178 | 71 438 | 32.7 | 27.5 |
| Tempe | 66 000 | 2.30 | 10.7 | 32.3 | 10 188 | 298 | 280 | 9 890 | 9 720 | 5 927 | 480 | 5 447 | 94 081 | 25.3 | 41.3 |
| Tucson | 205 390 | 2.43 | 15.4 | 33.1 | 20 706 | 9 920 | 1 798 | 10 786 | 11 165 | 2 117 | 652 | 1 465 | 326 587 | 41.0 | 24.5 |
| Yuma | 30 714 | 2.86 | 15.5 | 21.8 | 5 128 | 3 291 | 308 | 1 837 | 4 230 | 2 725 | 358 | 2 367 | 53 856 | 47.0 | 16.5 |
| ARKANSAS | 1 147 084 | 2.47 | 13.4 | 27.1 | 78 931 | 47 287 | 18 532 | 31 644 | 124 424 | 4 235 | 481 | 3 754 | 1 904 692 | 52.5 | 19.6 |
| Bella Vista | 11 729 | 2.24 | 4.8 | 23.4 | 133 | 133 | 133 | 0 | 204 | 765 | 83 | 683 | 19 913 | 29.7 | 35.3 |
| Benton | 11 834 | 2.55 | 13.5 | 24.3 | 493 | 462 | 289 | 31 | 1 591 | 5 147 | 395 | 4 752 | 19 711 | 43.2 | 25.8 |
| Bentonville | 13 253 | 2.64 | 11.6 | 25.1 | 258 | 179 | 160 | 79 | 855 | 2 404 | 239 | 2 165 | 21 291 | 35.2 | 36.3 |
| Conway | 22 399 | 2.45 | 12.8 | 27.0 | 4 038 | 1 118 | 372 | 2 920 | 2 975 | 5 012 | 416 | 4 596 | 30 907 | 35.0 | 35.0 |
| Fayetteville | 30 726 | 2.17 | 9.6 | 36.5 | 6 818 | 1 124 | 405 | 5 694 | 3 367 | 4 542 | 403 | 4 138 | 40 737 | 28.5 | 43.8 |
| Fort Smith | 34 352 | 2.45 | 14.3 | 31.2 | 1 930 | 1 083 | 592 | 847 | 5 320 | 6 125 | 693 | 5 432 | 55 614 | 50.1 | 20.7 |
| Hot Springs | 15 575 | 2.15 | 14.5 | 38.5 | 1 692 | 1 127 | 578 | 565 | 3 179 | 8 965 | 919 | 8 046 | 25 381 | 50.0 | 19.5 |

1. No spouse present.  2. Data for serious crimes have not been adjusted for underreporting. This may affect comparability between geographic areas and over time.  3. Per 100,000 population estimated by the FBI.  4. Persons 25 years old and over.

## Table D. Cities — Income, Poverty, and Housing

| City | Money income, 2007–2011 | | | | | Housing units, 2010 | | | Occupied Housing units 2007–2011 | | | | |
|---|---|---|---|---|---|---|---|---|---|---|---|---|---|
| | | Households | | | Families with income below poverty (percent) | | | | Owner-occupied | | | Median owner costs as a percent of income | |
| | Per capita income[1] (dollars) | Median income | Percent with income of $200,000 or more | Percent with income of less than $25,000 | | Total | Percent change, 2000–2010 | Vacant units for sale or rent[2] | Total | Percent | Median value[3] (dollars) | With a mortgage[4] | Without a mortgage[5] |
| | 42 | 43 | 44 | 45 | 46 | 47 | 48 | 49 | 50 | 51 | 52 | 53 | 54 |
| United States............. | 27 915 | 52 762 | 4.5 | 23.2 | 10.5 | 131 704 730 | 13.6 | 14 988 438 | 114 761 359 | 66.1 | 186 200 | 25.0 | 12.6 |
| ALABAMA ................. | 23 483 | 42 934 | 2.5 | 30.1 | 13.4 | 2 171 853 | 10.6 | 288 062 | 1 831 269 | 70.7 | 120 800 | 22.2 | 11.7 |
| Alabaster................... | 28 510 | 72 902 | 2.5 | 11.5 | 4.8 | 11 295 | 28.3 | 667 | 10 567 | 85.2 | 167 600 | 22.5 | 10.4 |
| Auburn...................... | 23 840 | 37 460 | 2.9 | 37.8 | 8.7 | 24 646 | 22.7 | 2 535 | 21 466 | 45.2 | 214 800 | 23.4 | 12.6 |
| Bessemer.................. | 17 085 | 29 600 | 0.5 | 45.4 | 20.3 | 12 369 | -3.2 | 1 658 | 11 195 | 59.8 | 86 800 | 27.5 | 15.6 |
| Birmingham.............. | 19 962 | 31 898 | 1.6 | 40.6 | 22.5 | 108 981 | -2.9 | 19 599 | 89 822 | 51.2 | 87 100 | 26.7 | 14.9 |
| Decatur.................... | 23 871 | 43 049 | 1.9 | 30.0 | 14.2 | 24 538 | 2.2 | 1 962 | 22 364 | 61.3 | 125 500 | 19.8 | 10.0 |
| Dothan..................... | 24 906 | 42 836 | 3.1 | 29.7 | 13.5 | 29 274 | 12.6 | 2 429 | 25 228 | 61.6 | 138 000 | 20.3 | 10.0 |
| Enterprise................. | 25 097 | 48 103 | 2.0 | 26.8 | 14.0 | 11 616 | 20.2 | 1 103 | 9 721 | 66.4 | 151 300 | 21.2 | 10.0 |
| Florence................... | 21 942 | 32 122 | 1.8 | 40.9 | 18.1 | 19 299 | 9.1 | 2 032 | 17 409 | 58.7 | 108 500 | 22.3 | 11.0 |
| Gadsden................... | 18 843 | 28 419 | 1.7 | 44.6 | 23.8 | 17 672 | -5.9 | 2 501 | 15 494 | 60.7 | 73 100 | 23.5 | 14.8 |
| Homewood................ | 30 114 | 61 436 | 4.5 | 19.4 | 4.9 | 11 385 | 0.5 | 1 293 | 9 317 | 57.3 | 293 200 | 24.9 | 11.0 |
| Hoover..................... | 39 183 | 75 831 | 8.6 | 12.2 | 4.1 | 35 474 | 31.2 | 2 996 | 30 808 | 69.2 | 266 200 | 22.4 | 10.0 |
| Huntsville................. | 29 635 | 48 043 | 4.1 | 27.1 | 12.2 | 84 949 | 15.4 | 7 916 | 74 073 | 60.4 | 151 200 | 20.0 | 10.0 |
| Madison................... | 40 054 | 89 770 | 9.9 | 10.2 | 4.2 | 17 203 | 43.1 | 1 092 | 15 289 | 74.1 | 231 100 | 18.1 | 10.0 |
| Mobile..................... | 23 362 | 38 240 | 3.3 | 33.5 | 18.1 | 89 127 | 3.5 | 10 168 | 77 019 | 58.8 | 124 900 | 23.9 | 13.0 |
| Montgomery ............. | 24 588 | 43 674 | 3.0 | 29.5 | 17.0 | 92 115 | 6.1 | 10 629 | 79 473 | 60.8 | 120 300 | 22.8 | 10.6 |
| Opelika.................... | 23 004 | 39 048 | 1.8 | 35.0 | 16.7 | 11 751 | 14.4 | 1 228 | 10 912 | 66.0 | 132 600 | 22.6 | 13.8 |
| Phenix City............... | 19 960 | 34 700 | 0.8 | 37.3 | 20.7 | 15 198 | 15.0 | 1 955 | 12 711 | 55.0 | 112 400 | 25.1 | 12.0 |
| Prattville.................. | 26 644 | 60 617 | 2.3 | 16.8 | 6.6 | 13 541 | 40.7 | 830 | 11 857 | 71.4 | 147 500 | 20.8 | 10.0 |
| Tuscaloosa............... | 20 800 | 34 359 | 2.9 | 39.2 | 18.4 | 40 842 | 16.8 | 4 657 | 31 984 | 47.6 | 158 400 | 24.6 | 10.3 |
| Vestavia Hills.............. | 52 790 | 86 509 | 14.9 | 11.8 | 2.6 | 14 952 | 40.8 | 965 | 13 655 | 73.0 | 330 600 | 20.7 | 10.0 |
| ALASKA .................. | 31 944 | 69 014 | 4.9 | 14.7 | 6.5 | 306 967 | 17.6 | 48 909 | 252 920 | 64.3 | 235 100 | 23.8 | 11.1 |
| Anchorage................ | 35 580 | 75 485 | 6.8 | 11.7 | 5.4 | 113 032 | 12.6 | 5 700 | 105 123 | 61.4 | 276 200 | 24.0 | 11.4 |
| Fairbanks................. | 27 522 | 55 409 | 2.3 | 19.0 | 7.3 | 13 056 | 5.2 | 1 522 | 12 215 | 37.5 | 197 900 | 27.3 | 11.3 |
| Juneau..................... | 37 294 | 77 465 | 4.9 | 10.3 | 4.4 | 13 055 | 6.3 | 868 | 12 379 | 64.5 | 299 100 | 25.0 | 12.1 |
| ARIZONA ................. | 25 784 | 50 752 | 3.5 | 23.0 | 11.7 | 2 844 526 | 29.9 | 463 536 | 2 344 215 | 66.6 | 197 400 | 26.2 | 11.1 |
| Apache Junction........... | 21 665 | 40 010 | 0.7 | 30.6 | 11.2 | 22 564 | -1.0 | 6 990 | 15 099 | 79.7 | 102 200 | 26.7 | 12.6 |
| Avondale.................. | 20 843 | 59 953 | 1.4 | 16.1 | 13.0 | 27 001 | 136.6 | 3 615 | 22 019 | 63.8 | 164 900 | 26.7 | 12.7 |
| Buckeye................... | 21 542 | 63 935 | 2.4 | 15.2 | 12.3 | 18 207 | NA | 3 783 | 13 576 | 71.7 | 168 000 | 27.0 | 10.0 |
| Bullhead City............. | 20 952 | 38 930 | 1.4 | 30.5 | 13.9 | 23 464 | 27.5 | 6 703 | 16 822 | 63.9 | 123 800 | 30.0 | 12.8 |
| Casa Grande............. | 21 110 | 44 467 | 1.3 | 23.7 | 14.5 | 22 400 | 104.8 | 4 749 | 16 864 | 66.9 | 135 000 | 27.6 | 13.8 |
| Chandler................... | 32 942 | 71 343 | 5.3 | 11.8 | 5.8 | 94 404 | 41.7 | 7 480 | 86 139 | 66.2 | 255 100 | 23.8 | 10.0 |
| El Mirage.................. | 16 238 | 48 084 | 0.3 | 20.8 | 19.2 | 11 326 | NA | 1 910 | 8 518 | 68.6 | 126 100 | 29.9 | 13.3 |
| Flagstaff................... | 23 232 | 48 758 | 2.2 | 25.8 | 10.7 | 26 254 | 22.5 | 3 418 | 22 360 | 47.7 | 294 400 | 25.2 | 10.0 |
| Florence................... | 10 391 | 42 561 | 1.3 | 22.6 | 6.5 | 5 224 | 60.5 | 1 894 | 3 056 | 71.8 | 116 700 | 26.8 | 10.0 |
| Gilbert..................... | 31 376 | 80 090 | 5.4 | 9.1 | 4.8 | 74 907 | 102.2 | 5 535 | 66 420 | 74.2 | 266 100 | 24.8 | 10.0 |
| Glendale.................. | 23 181 | 51 570 | 2.6 | 22.6 | 13.5 | 90 505 | 13.6 | 11 391 | 79 710 | 61.1 | 183 300 | 25.2 | 12.1 |
| Goodyear.................. | 28 111 | 72 500 | 3.7 | 10.9 | 6.0 | 25 027 | 275.6 | 3 536 | 19 896 | 73.5 | 242 500 | 25.3 | 10.0 |
| Kingman................... | 22 638 | 47 045 | 1.4 | 25.1 | 10.2 | 12 724 | 48.6 | 1 507 | 10 702 | 66.2 | 146 400 | 24.3 | 10.0 |
| Lake Havasu City......... | 25 099 | 44 069 | 2.3 | 23.6 | 8.7 | 32 327 | 40.6 | 9 159 | 22 526 | 71.6 | 223 100 | 30.2 | 11.7 |
| Marana.................... | 31 085 | 70 705 | 3.8 | 9.9 | 3.4 | 14 726 | 160.3 | 1 653 | 12 079 | 76.9 | 242 100 | 26.4 | 10.0 |
| Maricopa.................. | 25 091 | 65 556 | 1.3 | 11.5 | 2.3 | 17 240 | NA | 2 881 | 13 530 | 80.3 | 154 900 | 28.1 | 13.5 |
| Mesa....................... | 24 872 | 49 872 | 2.4 | 21.2 | 9.8 | 201 173 | 14.5 | 35 799 | 166 526 | 64.0 | 178 900 | 25.6 | 11.0 |
| Oro Valley................ | 39 303 | 71 561 | 6.7 | 12.7 | 4.2 | 20 340 | 45.2 | 2 536 | 17 006 | 77.4 | 308 600 | 24.8 | 10.2 |
| Peoria...................... | 29 352 | 64 270 | 3.8 | 15.1 | 6.1 | 64 818 | 51.9 | 7 361 | 55 585 | 75.6 | 216 800 | 26.4 | 11.2 |
| Phoenix.................... | 24 365 | 48 596 | 3.7 | 24.8 | 15.9 | 590 149 | 19.0 | 75 343 | 516 084 | 58.5 | 201 000 | 27.2 | 12.2 |
| Prescott.................... | 29 581 | 43 867 | 2.9 | 27.3 | 7.4 | 22 159 | 27.1 | 3 548 | 18 911 | 66.0 | 291 000 | 27.5 | 11.9 |
| Prescott Valley............ | 21 269 | 44 086 | 1.3 | 24.1 | 10.7 | 17 494 | 84.5 | 2 130 | 14 512 | 65.6 | 189 200 | 26.6 | 11.5 |
| Queen Creek............. | 28 663 | 83 601 | 7.0 | 6.9 | 5.0 | 8 557 | NA | 837 | 6 981 | 83.8 | 264 500 | 28.8 | 10.0 |
| Sahuarita.................. | 28 391 | 72 781 | 1.2 | 9.8 | 3.7 | 10 615 | NA | 1 595 | 8 196 | 82.4 | 224 300 | 24.2 | 10.7 |
| San Luis................... | 8 450 | 28 548 | 0.0 | 43.0 | 32.9 | 6 525 | 95.8 | 572 | 6 422 | 76.1 | 123 300 | 32.7 | 14.2 |
| Scottsdale................. | 51 276 | 71 816 | 12.8 | 15.8 | 4.6 | 124 001 | 18.2 | 22 728 | 100 912 | 70.6 | 430 500 | 26.5 | 11.6 |
| Sierra Vista................ | 27 383 | 56 671 | 2.3 | 17.4 | 5.9 | 18 742 | 20.0 | 1 683 | 17 033 | 57.1 | 200 300 | 21.0 | 10.0 |
| Surprise................... | 25 192 | 60 687 | 1.5 | 13.4 | 6.4 | 52 586 | 222.5 | 9 314 | 39 719 | 77.8 | 219 800 | 27.6 | 10.7 |
| Tempe..................... | 26 561 | 48 618 | 3.3 | 25.7 | 12.6 | 73 462 | 9.6 | 7 462 | 64 074 | 46.0 | 233 400 | 24.0 | 10.0 |
| Tucson..................... | 20 460 | 37 448 | 1.1 | 33.2 | 16.5 | 229 762 | 9.5 | 24 372 | 204 990 | 52.3 | 163 900 | 25.8 | 12.7 |
| Yuma....................... | 20 786 | 44 113 | 1.7 | 26.1 | 15.5 | 38 626 | 10.2 | 7 912 | 33 968 | 60.7 | 155 700 | 24.9 | 11.4 |
| ARKANSAS............... | 21 833 | 40 149 | 2.0 | 31.4 | 13.8 | 1 316 299 | 12.2 | 169 215 | 1 121 386 | 67.5 | 105 100 | 21.0 | 11.0 |
| Bella Vista................ | 32 703 | 61 266 | 3.6 | 12.2 | 3.9 | 13 241 | 49.2 | 1 512 | 10 917 | 88.7 | 158 700 | 19.5 | 10.0 |
| Benton..................... | 24 939 | 49 858 | 2.3 | 26.0 | 9.4 | 12 902 | 38.9 | 1 068 | 11 389 | 68.9 | 131 500 | 21.0 | 13.0 |
| Bentonville............... | 30 017 | 54 194 | 5.6 | 19.2 | 7.8 | 14 693 | 84.9 | 1 440 | 13 014 | 58.6 | 168 200 | 20.6 | 10.0 |
| Conway.................... | 23 616 | 44 745 | 3.0 | 30.6 | 10.8 | 24 402 | 41.2 | 2 003 | 21 330 | 52.0 | 147 400 | 19.6 | 10.0 |
| Fayetteville............... | 25 341 | 35 970 | 2.9 | 35.0 | 13.3 | 36 188 | 42.9 | 5 462 | 31 009 | 41.1 | 177 900 | 21.9 | 10.0 |
| Fort Smith................. | 22 824 | 37 340 | 3.1 | 34.0 | 17.1 | 37 899 | 7.2 | 3 547 | 34 008 | 56.1 | 113 700 | 20.4 | 11.1 |
| Hot Springs ............... | 20 828 | 31 643 | 1.5 | 40.3 | 17.0 | 18 947 | 1.2 | 3 372 | 15 427 | 56.1 | 112 000 | 24.9 | 12.8 |

1. Based on population estimated by the American Community Survey.　2. Includes units rented or sold but not occupied.　3. Specified owner-occupied units; $1,000,000 represents $1,000,000 or more　4. 50.0 represents 50 percent or more.　5. 10.0 represents 10 percent or less.

# Table D. Cities — Housing, Labor Force, and Employment

| City | Occupied housing units, 2007–2011 (cont.) | | | | Migration, 2007–2011 | | Civilian labor force, 2012 | | | | Civilian employment[4], 2007–2011 | | | |
|---|---|---|---|---|---|---|---|---|---|---|---|---|---|---|
| | | | | | | | | | Unemployment | | | Percent | | |
| | Percent renter occupied | Median gross rent[1] | Median rent as a percent of income[2] | Percent with no vehicle available | Percent who lived in the same house one year ago | Percent who lived outside this city one year ago | Total | Percent change, 2011–2012 | Total | Rate[3] | Population age 16 and older | In labor force | Full-year full-time worker | Households with no workers (percent) |
| | 55 | 56 | 57 | 58 | 59 | 60 | 61 | 62 | 63 | 64 | 65 | 66 | 67 | 68 |
| United States | 33.9 | 871 | 30.9 | 8.9 | 84.6 | 10.3 | 155 049 194 | 0.3 | 12 512 946 | 8.1 | 241 302 749 | 64.8 | 40.0 | 26.3 |
| ALABAMA | 29.3 | 674 | 30.7 | 6.4 | 84.5 | 10.8 | 2 156 301 | -1.3 | 157 119 | 7.3 | 3 748 844 | 60.3 | 38.0 | 31.1 |
| Alabaster | 14.8 | 1 031 | 24.1 | 1.9 | 86.3 | 9.8 | 16 742 | 0.3 | 741 | 4.4 | 22 540 | 73.3 | 50.8 | 16.3 |
| Auburn | 54.8 | 735 | 37.1 | 3.8 | 63.0 | 20.7 | 25 189 | 2.2 | 1 665 | 6.6 | 44 486 | 57.7 | 27.9 | 28.6 |
| Bessemer | 40.2 | 650 | 38.4 | 16.3 | 86.3 | 7.1 | 9 938 | -2.2 | 939 | 9.4 | 22 171 | 53.7 | 34.5 | 40.6 |
| Birmingham | 48.8 | 706 | 34.8 | 14.4 | 77.2 | 9.3 | 90 207 | -1.1 | 7 626 | 8.5 | 172 551 | 60.8 | 35.4 | 33.1 |
| Decatur | 38.7 | 573 | 26.8 | 6.8 | 84.8 | 7.8 | 26 258 | -1.1 | 1 882 | 7.2 | 43 801 | 64.5 | 41.2 | 30.4 |
| Dothan | 38.4 | 631 | 28.2 | 7.3 | 83.2 | 8.2 | 28 577 | -2.8 | 1 998 | 7.0 | 50 681 | 61.1 | 40.0 | 29.5 |
| Enterprise | 33.6 | 667 | 28.0 | 7.8 | 80.5 | 13.1 | 10 880 | -3.0 | 628 | 5.8 | 20 047 | 60.6 | 37.1 | 28.1 |
| Florence | 41.3 | 551 | 32.5 | 8.2 | 79.2 | 11.6 | 17 928 | 0.3 | 1 262 | 7.0 | 32 241 | 57.5 | 32.9 | 36.9 |
| Gadsden | 39.3 | 572 | 30.1 | 9.6 | 81.2 | 8.9 | 14 130 | -0.5 | 1 290 | 9.1 | 29 447 | 50.7 | 30.0 | 43.8 |
| Homewood | 42.7 | 874 | 29.8 | 3.5 | 73.7 | 21.5 | 13 948 | 0.5 | 613 | 4.4 | 20 203 | 69.3 | 41.2 | 19.0 |
| Hoover | 30.8 | 948 | 28.6 | 2.3 | 81.6 | 13.0 | 43 966 | 0.9 | 1 867 | 4.2 | 61 944 | 70.0 | 47.1 | 19.3 |
| Huntsville | 39.6 | 686 | 29.2 | 6.8 | 79.8 | 9.3 | 90 741 | -1.4 | 5 747 | 6.3 | 144 249 | 65.8 | 40.5 | 27.0 |
| Madison | 25.9 | 823 | 23.6 | 2.0 | 84.2 | 12.5 | 24 180 | -0.5 | 1 147 | 4.7 | 31 204 | 72.2 | 49.3 | 11.7 |
| Mobile | 41.2 | 733 | 34.4 | 9.0 | 84.3 | 6.0 | 87 025 | -2.7 | 7 549 | 8.7 | 153 910 | 60.7 | 37.5 | 31.3 |
| Montgomery | 39.2 | 783 | 33.2 | 8.4 | 78.6 | 7.3 | 93 235 | -1.3 | 7 106 | 7.6 | 159 390 | 63.7 | 39.9 | 27.4 |
| Opelika | 34.0 | 620 | 32.6 | 10.0 | 82.6 | 8.8 | 12 456 | 1.9 | 917 | 7.4 | 20 757 | 64.4 | 40.7 | 27.9 |
| Phenix City | 45.0 | 685 | 31.2 | 8.9 | 74.4 | 13.9 | 14 519 | 1.5 | 1 051 | 7.2 | 24 418 | 63.2 | 37.1 | 29.5 |
| Prattville | 28.6 | 864 | 28.0 | 4.6 | 82.4 | 12.0 | 16 117 | -0.7 | 923 | 5.7 | 24 625 | 66.6 | 43.3 | 22.7 |
| Tuscaloosa | 52.4 | 736 | 39.2 | 9.4 | 73.0 | 14.1 | 42 237 | -0.1 | 3 013 | 7.1 | 74 075 | 54.5 | 30.3 | 32.6 |
| Vestavia Hills | 27.0 | 1 016 | 28.2 | 5.5 | 85.2 | 13.4 | 15 822 | 0.8 | 669 | 4.2 | 26 491 | 65.7 | 45.4 | 24.4 |
| ALASKA | 35.7 | 1 017 | 27.5 | 9.6 | 79.3 | 11.9 | 366 297 | 1.6 | 25 586 | 7.0 | 536 544 | 71.7 | 38.2 | 20.1 |
| Anchorage | 38.6 | 1 058 | 28.1 | 6.1 | 77.9 | 8.5 | 157 001 | 0.0 | 8 551 | 5.4 | 221 420 | 74.4 | 43.0 | 16.4 |
| Fairbanks | 62.5 | 1 120 | 29.7 | 9.8 | 66.7 | 23.1 | 13 140 | 2.1 | 936 | 7.1 | 24 172 | 71.7 | 35.8 | 23.0 |
| Juneau | 35.5 | 1 135 | 26.1 | 8.8 | 79.9 | 8.9 | 18 427 | 0.0 | 895 | 4.9 | 24 892 | 74.7 | 45.6 | 16.3 |
| ARIZONA | 33.4 | 881 | 30.9 | 6.7 | 80.1 | 11.9 | 3 030 238 | -1.1 | 251 659 | 8.3 | 4 895 581 | 61.8 | 38.3 | 28.4 |
| Apache Junction | 20.3 | 723 | 32.5 | 9.7 | 87.2 | 8.3 | 15 407 | -1.9 | 1 688 | 11.0 | 28 724 | 48.9 | 28.6 | 49.1 |
| Avondale | 36.2 | 1 115 | 27.7 | 3.5 | 77.2 | 15.4 | 36 590 | -1.2 | 3 093 | 8.5 | 51 152 | 71.4 | 49.6 | 14.1 |
| Buckeye | 28.3 | 1 096 | 29.7 | 2.9 | 74.3 | 18.1 | 21 344 | -1.1 | 2 002 | 9.4 | 33 219 | 59.8 | 42.8 | 18.9 |
| Bullhead City | 36.1 | 826 | 31.3 | 6.7 | 75.1 | 12.5 | 18 110 | -2.3 | 1 650 | 9.1 | 32 975 | 52.4 | 30.2 | 44.4 |
| Casa Grande | 33.1 | 822 | 31.1 | 7.6 | 75.1 | 12.2 | 21 056 | -0.9 | 2 104 | 10.0 | 34 228 | 61.1 | 35.8 | 31.6 |
| Chandler | 33.8 | 1 064 | 27.5 | 3.5 | 78.1 | 14.3 | 132 522 | -0.6 | 7 869 | 5.9 | 175 319 | 75.3 | 50.6 | 15.5 |
| El Mirage | 31.4 | 1 125 | 34.0 | 2.6 | 82.5 | 14.3 | 14 328 | -0.8 | 1 239 | 8.6 | 19 832 | 68.0 | 40.9 | 13.8 |
| Flagstaff | 52.3 | 981 | 36.3 | 5.3 | 71.3 | 15.4 | 39 936 | 1.5 | 2 281 | 5.7 | 53 192 | 72.5 | 35.1 | 16.8 |
| Florence | 28.2 | 764 | 24.7 | 4.5 | 55.4 | 41.4 | 3 333 | -6.6 | 616 | 18.5 | 23 008 | 9.4 | 6.2 | 55.2 |
| Gilbert | 25.8 | 1 277 | 27.9 | 1.7 | 77.9 | 15.5 | 114 341 | -0.4 | 6 110 | 5.3 | 142 913 | 76.0 | 49.8 | 12.5 |
| Glendale | 38.9 | 860 | 32.3 | 8.3 | 79.9 | 14.2 | 116 644 | -1.2 | 8 793 | 7.5 | 172 506 | 68.0 | 41.6 | 22.1 |
| Goodyear | 26.5 | 1 164 | 28.8 | 2.5 | 78.9 | 17.5 | 28 901 | -1.0 | 2 355 | 8.1 | 45 888 | 64.0 | 43.1 | 20.3 |
| Kingman | 33.8 | 855 | 29.5 | 6.5 | 73.1 | 13.2 | 12 673 | -3.5 | 1 378 | 10.9 | 22 827 | 56.7 | 32.5 | 35.8 |
| Lake Havasu City | 28.4 | 859 | 31.9 | 3.8 | 83.3 | 7.2 | 22 741 | -4.8 | 2 407 | 10.6 | 43 431 | 52.3 | 30.3 | 42.1 |
| Marana | 23.1 | 1 167 | 26.2 | 2.8 | 78.7 | 15.8 | 16 492 | -2.0 | 1 008 | 6.1 | 25 358 | 62.7 | 41.5 | 25.8 |
| Maricopa | 19.7 | 1 204 | 32.1 | 2.9 | 77.6 | 17.1 | 19 991 | -1.3 | 1 790 | 9.0 | 27 039 | 71.1 | 52.2 | 13.4 |
| Mesa | 36.0 | 876 | 31.1 | 6.8 | 80.7 | 10.8 | 222 505 | -1.2 | 15 493 | 7.0 | 342 034 | 63.9 | 39.8 | 28.9 |
| Oro Valley | 22.6 | 1 070 | 26.0 | 1.6 | 83.2 | 13.3 | 18 257 | -1.7 | 1 090 | 6.0 | 33 739 | 52.3 | 31.9 | 41.5 |
| Peoria | 24.4 | 1 128 | 32.8 | 5.0 | 84.9 | 10.5 | 76 347 | -1.3 | 5 129 | 6.7 | 116 995 | 66.3 | 44.3 | 25.0 |
| Phoenix | 41.5 | 860 | 31.5 | 9.0 | 78.2 | 8.5 | 727 540 | -1.0 | 54 993 | 7.6 | 1 085 662 | 67.4 | 44.5 | 20.7 |
| Prescott | 34.0 | 788 | 34.2 | 6.9 | 78.8 | 13.0 | 17 073 | -0.3 | 1 540 | 9.0 | 34 987 | 49.3 | 25.7 | 45.9 |
| Prescott Valley | 34.4 | 865 | 31.4 | 4.5 | 79.1 | 15.7 | 17 204 | -0.1 | 1 618 | 9.4 | 29 551 | 61.3 | 33.4 | 32.7 |
| Queen Creek | 16.2 | 1 470 | 27.2 | 0.7 | 76.3 | 15.1 | NA | NA | NA | NA | 16 236 | 72.2 | 48.1 | 13.3 |
| Sahuarita | 17.6 | 1 197 | 27.3 | 1.1 | 82.9 | 13.6 | 11 913 | -1.4 | 758 | 6.4 | 16 808 | 63.8 | 43.0 | 27.1 |
| San Luis | 23.9 | 492 | 27.5 | 12.1 | 89.8 | 8.5 | 16 851 | 50.5 | 10 760 | 63.9 | 17 456 | 46.3 | 21.8 | 35.8 |
| Scottsdale | 29.4 | 1 122 | 28.7 | 4.6 | 83.3 | 10.9 | 119 458 | -0.7 | 6 779 | 5.7 | 185 267 | 63.7 | 41.3 | 28.7 |
| Sierra Vista | 42.9 | 912 | 26.6 | 6.6 | 72.2 | 20.0 | 20 360 | -4.6 | 1 567 | 7.7 | 34 399 | 63.4 | 33.7 | 29.4 |
| Surprise | 22.2 | 1 212 | 31.4 | 2.3 | 80.1 | 14.3 | 43 751 | -1.5 | 3 724 | 8.5 | 80 292 | 58.0 | 36.2 | 32.9 |
| Tempe | 54.0 | 912 | 31.8 | 8.5 | 69.3 | 20.8 | 99 227 | -0.7 | 6 191 | 6.2 | 137 413 | 70.4 | 38.8 | 21.7 |
| Tucson | 47.7 | 714 | 33.3 | 11.6 | 75.0 | 9.2 | 250 410 | -2.1 | 20 048 | 8.0 | 414 895 | 62.4 | 34.7 | 28.1 |
| Yuma | 39.3 | 831 | 31.4 | 6.3 | 75.5 | 12.1 | 45 381 | -1.3 | 7 935 | 17.5 | 68 989 | 62.7 | 36.0 | 28.6 |
| ARKANSAS | 32.5 | 637 | 29.6 | 6.5 | 82.4 | 11.5 | 1 355 851 | 1.5 | 98 834 | 7.3 | 2 267 563 | 60.6 | 38.3 | 30.8 |
| Bella Vista | 11.3 | 1 068 | 33.2 | 0.8 | 86.7 | 10.2 | 9 753 | 4.7 | 700 | 7.2 | 21 347 | 51.1 | 35.6 | 41.5 |
| Benton | 31.1 | 719 | 30.9 | 7.3 | 79.5 | 15.2 | 15 392 | 2.3 | 925 | 6.0 | 23 203 | 65.9 | 43.7 | 26.2 |
| Bentonville | 41.4 | 704 | 24.6 | 5.5 | 73.4 | 19.8 | 18 829 | 5.6 | 985 | 5.2 | 25 242 | 68.8 | 50.8 | 15.8 |
| Conway | 48.0 | 695 | 31.4 | 5.0 | 70.0 | 15.5 | 30 822 | 3.4 | 1 977 | 6.4 | 45 652 | 67.6 | 39.5 | 21.3 |
| Fayetteville | 58.9 | 663 | 31.5 | 7.0 | 65.2 | 19.3 | 39 426 | 5.3 | 2 213 | 5.6 | 60 612 | 68.1 | 37.4 | 23.6 |
| Fort Smith | 43.9 | 578 | 28.9 | 7.0 | 81.6 | 8.1 | 40 813 | 0.0 | 2 991 | 7.3 | 66 529 | 61.1 | 40.4 | 28.4 |
| Hot Springs | 43.9 | 661 | 32.8 | 13.6 | 79.0 | 11.3 | 15 303 | 2.6 | 1 316 | 8.6 | 29 385 | 54.5 | 30.0 | 40.2 |

1. $2,000 represents $2,000 or more.  2. 50.0 represents 50 percent or more.  3. Percent of civilian labor force.  4. Persons 16 years old and over.

| City | Value of residential construction authorized by building permits, 2011 | | | Wholesale trade,[1] 2007 | | | | Retail trade,[2] 2007 | | | |
|---|---|---|---|---|---|---|---|---|---|---|---|
| | New construction ($1,000) | Number of housing units | Percent single family | Number of establish-ments | Number of employees | Sales (mil dol) | Annual payroll (mil dol) | Number of establish-ments | Number of employees | Sales (mil dol) | Annual payroll (mil dol) |
| | 69 | 70 | 71 | 72 | 73 | 74 | 75 | 76 | 77 | 78 | 79 |
| United States............. | 105 268 541 | 624 061 | 67.1 | 369 387 | 5 098 545 | 4 174 286.5 | 260 532.1 | 1 128 112 | 15 515 396 | 3 917 663.5 | 362 818.7 |
| ALABAMA ................. | 1 704 064 | 11 667 | 75.9 | 4 824 | 70 469 | 52 252.8 | 3 032.2 | 19 722 | 238 922 | 57 344.9 | 5 112.0 |
| Alabaster...................... | 5 106 | 30 | 100.0 | 38 | 330 | 306.5 | 14.6 | 98 | 1 700 | 388.7 | 42.6 |
| Auburn......................... | 146 277 | 711 | 69.6 | 22 | 200 | 88.3 | 6.8 | 207 | 3 148 | 672.4 | 62.5 |
| Bessemer..................... | 459 | 3 | 100.0 | 70 | 1 208 | 769.1 | 60.9 | 211 | 2 550 | 633.2 | 60.2 |
| Birmingham.................. | 28 859 | 226 | 53.5 | 537 | 11 374 | 6 667.8 | 523.1 | 1 137 | 15 093 | 4 690.4 | 358.1 |
| Decatur........................ | 9 115 | 47 | 100.0 | 82 | 1 163 | 793.0 | 51.6 | 355 | 4 319 | 1 159.6 | 97.5 |
| Dothan......................... | 42 965 | 206 | 100.0 | 140 | D | D | D | 551 | 7 329 | 1 790.2 | 167.1 |
| Enterprise.................... | 22 085 | 210 | 42.9 | 10 | 58 | 15.3 | 1.7 | 177 | 2 196 | 570.2 | 49.3 |
| Florence ...................... | 9 388 | 111 | 49.5 | 50 | 443 | 143.3 | 13.0 | 307 | 4 425 | 951.7 | 87.0 |
| Gadsden....................... | 651 | 9 | 100.0 | 38 | 331 | 168.7 | 11.6 | 276 | 3 364 | 722.6 | 63.6 |
| Homewood.................... | 18 741 | 130 | 6.2 | 78 | 864 | 670.5 | 43.7 | 257 | 3 891 | 662.8 | 82.8 |
| Hoover......................... | 103 888 | 637 | 60.4 | 81 | 1 092 | 1 045.4 | 90.8 | 418 | 8 411 | 2 117.6 | 197.0 |
| Huntsville..................... | 53 307 | 1 022 | 99.6 | 238 | 3 505 | 2 425.2 | 166.1 | 1 016 | 15 593 | 3 675.8 | 351.6 |
| Madison....................... | 124 427 | 374 | 100.0 | 48 | 634 | 382.7 | 33.7 | 133 | 2 066 | 530.8 | 48.2 |
| Mobile......................... | 57 320 | 681 | 17.6 | 350 | 4 591 | 2 311.0 | 208.0 | 1 004 | 15 513 | 3 557.8 | 341.6 |
| Montgomery ................ | 36 893 | 288 | 60.4 | 263 | 4 995 | 3 039.3 | 211.3 | 952 | 13 945 | 3 132.0 | 304.9 |
| Opelika ....................... | 18 956 | 91 | 100.0 | 30 | 671 | 659.2 | 26.9 | 207 | 2 792 | 675.1 | 54.1 |
| Phenix City.................. | 60 559 | 317 | 99.4 | 13 | 205 | 74.1 | 8.9 | 114 | 1 077 | 233.2 | 21.2 |
| Prattville...................... | 24 365 | 106 | 100.0 | 21 | 123 | 39.5 | 4.2 | 169 | 2 312 | 598.2 | 58.4 |
| Tuscaloosa................... | 70 786 | 574 | 37.1 | 85 | 1 051 | 473.6 | 45.0 | 504 | 7 545 | 1 693.2 | 159.4 |
| Vestavia Hills.............. | 21 682 | 64 | 100.0 | 37 | 686 | 443.4 | 46.9 | 146 | 1 689 | 388.4 | 38.3 |
| ALASKA ..................... | 203 975 | 877 | 81.3 | 658 | 8 262 | 4 563.6 | 391.6 | 2 641 | 34 977 | 9 303.4 | 936.8 |
| Anchorage.................... | 117 246 | 447 | 77.0 | 339 | 5 498 | 2 914.0 | 261.0 | 923 | 15 842 | 4 482.7 | 441.8 |
| Fairbanks..................... | 0 | 0 | 0.0 | 51 | 714 | 355.1 | 33.4 | 244 | 4 031 | 1 185.6 | 113.4 |
| Juneau......................... | NA | NA | NA | 33 | D | D | D | 172 | 1 933 | 465.3 | 52.0 |
| ARIZONA ................... | 2 580 351 | 13 007 | 79.2 | 5 874 | 84 029 | 57 573.5 | 4 116.4 | 19 384 | 337 529 | 86 758.8 | 8 010.8 |
| Apache Junction............ | 6 740 | 57 | 100.0 | 17 | 66 | 24.7 | 1.8 | 96 | 2 181 | 447.5 | 45.4 |
| Avondale...................... | 7 614 | 32 | 100.0 | 14 | 181 | 73.4 | 11.3 | 126 | 4 287 | 1 601.3 | 126.1 |
| Buckeye....................... | 104 401 | 507 | 100.0 | 9 | D | D | D | 48 | 449 | 215.2 | 14.2 |
| Bullhead City................ | 5 153 | 20 | 100.0 | 9 | 70 | 26.1 | 2.5 | 146 | 2 668 | 570.7 | 58.1 |
| Casa Grande................ | 6 927 | 70 | 94.3 | 23 | 374 | 139.4 | 12.8 | 195 | 2 981 | 676.7 | 64.4 |
| Chandler...................... | 270 239 | 1 062 | 62.6 | 220 | 4 198 | 4 585.9 | 291.8 | 694 | 15 714 | 3 608.3 | 353.3 |
| El Mirage ..................... | 0 | 0 | 0.0 | 5 | 43 | 17.9 | 1.7 | 25 | 487 | 89.1 | 10.0 |
| Flagstaff...................... | 8 463 | 47 | 95.7 | 66 | 856 | 405.9 | 29.8 | 362 | 5 566 | 1 174.4 | 119.0 |
| Florence ...................... | 12 239 | 112 | 100.0 | NA | NA | NA | NA | 17 | 104 | 30.0 | 2.8 |
| Gilbert......................... | 249 014 | 1 541 | 100.0 | 147 | 1 450 | 649.3 | 59.7 | 441 | 8 466 | 2 079.1 | 207.2 |
| Glendale...................... | 34 580 | 141 | 100.0 | 135 | 2 079 | 1 013.5 | 70.0 | 714 | 15 566 | 3 627.8 | 332.3 |
| Goodyear..................... | 174 696 | 592 | 100.0 | 17 | D | D | D | 109 | 2 955 | 631.7 | 61.4 |
| Kingman....................... | 6 264 | 36 | 100.0 | 19 | 240 | 136.9 | 9.5 | 154 | 3 085 | 993.6 | 72.5 |
| Lake Havasu City......... | 16 937 | 90 | 100.0 | 58 | 361 | 97.5 | 10.8 | 272 | 3 279 | 862.8 | 82.4 |
| Marana........................ | 93 460 | 337 | 100.0 | 21 | 255 | 98.8 | 12.1 | 98 | 3 098 | 748.7 | 72.1 |
| Maricopa...................... | 21 327 | 120 | 100.0 | 7 | D | D | D | 30 | 524 | 149.6 | 11.2 |
| Mesa........................... | 149 233 | 503 | 100.0 | 301 | 3 372 | 2 037.3 | 174.1 | 1 507 | 28 855 | 6 294.5 | 653.9 |
| Oro Valley ................... | 25 807 | 59 | 100.0 | 11 | 38 | 11.8 | 1.3 | 79 | 1 999 | 395.9 | 37.0 |
| Peoria......................... | 56 710 | 430 | 100.0 | 56 | 368 | 251.2 | 14.8 | 353 | 8 143 | 2 340.4 | 216.9 |
| Phoenix....................... | 284 342 | 1 628 | 58.5 | 1 946 | 34 585 | 23 670.5 | 1 650.7 | 4 266 | 77 534 | 21 859.5 | 1 913.7 |
| Prescott....................... | 23 010 | 87 | 100.0 | 64 | 509 | 276.5 | 22.0 | 318 | 5 205 | 1 227.5 | 121.5 |
| Prescott Valley............. | 7 955 | 41 | 100.0 | 29 | 611 | 393.1 | 22.4 | 109 | 1 274 | 281.2 | 28.8 |
| Queen Creek................ | 38 868 | 116 | 100.0 | 15 | 94 | 42.8 | 2.6 | 36 | 1 033 | 241.1 | 21.9 |
| Sahuarita..................... | 52 497 | 187 | 100.0 | 3 | 22 | 3.5 | 1.0 | 19 | 766 | 168.0 | 19.1 |
| San Luis...................... | 10 416 | 67 | 100.0 | 5 | 25 | 7.0 | 0.8 | 34 | 383 | 77.2 | 6.3 |
| Scottsdale.................... | 118 115 | 405 | 36.5 | 538 | 5 811 | 3 445.5 | 314.3 | 1 378 | 22 923 | 6 645.4 | 664.9 |
| Sierra Vista.................. | 43 972 | 186 | 100.0 | 13 | 120 | 28.4 | 3.5 | 163 | 3 284 | 726.4 | 73.8 |
| Surprise....................... | 54 860 | 219 | 100.0 | 23 | 97 | 20.4 | 3.5 | 147 | 4 064 | 888.2 | 85.7 |
| Tempe ......................... | 20 062 | 467 | 4.1 | 511 | 11 117 | 7 286.1 | 722.2 | 847 | 16 389 | 6 172.5 | 447.5 |
| Tucson......................... | 123 288 | 874 | 34.6 | 473 | 5 730 | 2 124.6 | 224.0 | 2 080 | 37 716 | 8 647.0 | 887.8 |
| Yuma........................... | 23 913 | 123 | 100.0 | 79 | 1 318 | 817.9 | 51.8 | 391 | 7 294 | 1 683.6 | 153.0 |
| ARKANSAS............... | 861 479 | 6 800 | 60.9 | 2 977 | 38 988 | 29 659.8 | 1 536.3 | 11 906 | 140 018 | 32 974.3 | 2 889.2 |
| Bella Vista ................... | 3 135 | 17 | 100.0 | 6 | 18 | 2.9 | 0.4 | 30 | 415 | 66.9 | 8.6 |
| Benton......................... | 24 715 | 148 | 100.0 | 17 | 106 | 75.4 | 3.6 | 146 | 1 839 | 488.4 | 38.7 |
| Bentonville................... | 85 702 | 371 | 93.0 | 63 | 1 624 | 447.3 | 52.9 | 134 | 2 038 | 703.3 | 55.6 |
| Conway........................ | 31 096 | 166 | 91.6 | 47 | 438 | 229.7 | 17.6 | 301 | 4 595 | 1 077.3 | 91.8 |
| Fayetteville.................. | 58 327 | 273 | 99.3 | 60 | 798 | 440.2 | 30.6 | 430 | 7 281 | 1 646.9 | 147.5 |
| Fort Smith.................... | 44 807 | 288 | 68.1 | 172 | 2 275 | 1 216.1 | 90.0 | 545 | 7 273 | 1 667.4 | 152.7 |
| Hot Springs ................. | 7 024 | 35 | 100.0 | 48 | 325 | 120.6 | 10.3 | 386 | 4 741 | 1 184.0 | 104.4 |

1. Merchant wholesalers except manufacturers' sales branches and offices.     2. Establishments with payroll.

| City | Real estate and rental and leasing, 2007 | | | | Professional, scientific, and technical services,[1] 2007 | | | | Manufacturing, 2007 | | | |
|---|---|---|---|---|---|---|---|---|---|---|---|---|
| | Number of establishments | Number of employees | Receipts (mil dol) | Annual payroll (mil dol) | Number of establishments | Number of employees | Receipts (mil dol) | Annual payroll (mil dol) | Number of establishments | Number of employees | Receipts (mil dol) | Annual payroll (mil dol) |
| | 80 | 81 | 82 | 83 | 84 | 85 | 86 | 87 | 88 | 89 | 90 | 91 |
| United States.............. | 384 297 | 2 188 479 | 485 058.6 | 84 764.9 | 842 607 | 7 678 304 | 1 220 434.1 | 489 965.4 | 332 536 | 13 395 670 | 5 319 456.3 | 613 768.6 |
| ALABAMA ................. | 4 554 | 27 100 | 4 073.2 | 823.4 | 9 437 | 92 759 | 13 623.2 | 4 996.4 | 4 928 | 271 986 | 112 858.8 | 11 351.6 |
| Alabaster ..................... | 11 | 53 | 8.5 | 1.4 | 60 | 600 | 268.2 | 31.4 | 25 | 1 094 | 287.6 | 45.8 |
| Auburn ........................ | 62 | 357 | 44.4 | 8.8 | 105 | D | D | D | 55 | 3 672 | 869.0 | 135.3 |
| Bessemer .................... | 35 | 131 | 17.5 | 4.1 | 75 | D | D | D | 51 | 1 780 | 373.1 | 70.3 |
| Birmingham ................. | 339 | 3 706 | 526.1 | 145.8 | 901 | D | D | D | 305 | 15 835 | 4 724.8 | 749.4 |
| Decatur........................ | 74 | 290 | 39.9 | 6.7 | 159 | 970 | 80.9 | 31.8 | 90 | 4 463 | 2 650.1 | 204.3 |
| Dothan ........................ | 115 | D | D | D | 222 | D | D | D | 102 | 5 180 | 1 153.6 | 183.0 |
| Enterprise ................... | 49 | 223 | 24.7 | 5.6 | 57 | 346 | 41.8 | 10.4 | 18 | 856 | 318.4 | 24.8 |
| Florence ..................... | 62 | 255 | 40.5 | 7.2 | 154 | D | D | D | 64 | 2 700 | 987.2 | 100.3 |
| Gadsden...................... | 46 | 226 | 41.0 | 5.6 | 118 | 626 | 51.3 | 19.9 | 58 | 4 239 | 977.8 | 167.6 |
| Homewood .................. | 65 | 438 | 76.0 | 16.7 | 183 | 1 545 | 241.3 | 79.7 | 27 | 1 297 | 594.3 | 57.6 |
| Hoover........................ | 97 | 720 | 247.7 | 25.5 | 280 | 2 269 | 460.3 | 136.1 | NA | NA | NA | NA |
| Huntsville.................... | 330 | 1 720 | 277.8 | 54.7 | 997 | 28 335 | 5 091.5 | 1 988.4 | 195 | 21 059 | 8 209.6 | 1 028.7 |
| Madison ...................... | 59 | 253 | 48.2 | 7.9 | 130 | D | D | D | 33 | 1 205 | D | 50.1 |
| Mobile ........................ | 324 | 1 729 | 282.3 | 51.3 | 739 | D | D | D | 156 | 7 341 | 2 338.8 | 362.5 |
| Montgomery ................ | 292 | 2 333 | 288.1 | 71.5 | 633 | 6 216 | 876.2 | 335.8 | 176 | 11 155 | 6 943.7 | 499.7 |
| Opelika ....................... | 38 | 175 | 21.3 | 3.6 | 69 | D | D | D | 47 | 2 801 | D | 112.5 |
| Phenix City ................. | 38 | 136 | 18.5 | 2.7 | 42 | 205 | 13.8 | 4.6 | 29 | 1 659 | D | 93.5 |
| Prattville..................... | 32 | 124 | 19.3 | 3.4 | 57 | D | D | D | 21 | 1 335 | D | D |
| Tuscaloosa.................. | 142 | 925 | 142.0 | 26.0 | 262 | 1 978 | 180.0 | 66.7 | 64 | 5 390 | 2 115.6 | 216.1 |
| Vestavia Hills............... | 67 | D | D | D | 147 | D | D | D | NA | NA | NA | NA |
| ALASKA ................... | 852 | 4 370 | 840.6 | 160.2 | 1 799 | 12 509 | 2 006.8 | 745.4 | 544 | 13 298 | 8 204.0 | 489.5 |
| Anchorage................... | 378 | 2 416 | 453.5 | 94.0 | 1 092 | D | D | D | 194 | 2 305 | D | D |
| Fairbanks..................... | 91 | 518 | 116.9 | 22.9 | 140 | D | D | D | NA | NA | NA | NA |
| Juneau........................ | 58 | 241 | 41.1 | 5.9 | 95 | D | D | D | NA | NA | NA | NA |
| ARIZONA ................. | 9 441 | 52 627 | 10 077.6 | 1 994.3 | 16 563 | 128 188 | 17 617.1 | 7 239.5 | 5 074 | 172 438 | 57 977.8 | 8 774.3 |
| Apache Junction........... | 42 | 123 | 23.5 | 3.8 | 30 | 122 | 9.7 | 2.7 | NA | NA | NA | NA |
| Avondale ..................... | 54 | 228 | 32.6 | 8.6 | 44 | 200 | 20.6 | 6.2 | NA | NA | NA | NA |
| Buckeye....................... | 15 | 58 | 46.9 | 2.3 | 22 | 149 | 22.1 | 7.1 | NA | NA | NA | NA |
| Bullhead City ............... | 65 | 231 | 33.9 | 6.0 | 51 | D | D | D | NA | NA | NA | NA |
| Casa Grande................ | 61 | 244 | 40.4 | 7.3 | 49 | D | D | D | 28 | 1 624 | 1 040.0 | 73.6 |
| Chandler...................... | 301 | 1 171 | 228.0 | 37.7 | 610 | 7 138 | 373.9 | 490.9 | 162 | 8 577 | 3 956.0 | 502.4 |
| El Mirage .................... | 7 | 15 | 3.2 | 0.4 | 6 | D | D | D | NA | NA | NA | NA |
| Flagstaff...................... | 156 | 533 | 105.5 | 17.1 | 255 | D | D | D | 72 | 3 429 | 1 314.2 | 213.1 |
| Florence ..................... | 4 | 11 | 0.7 | 0.2 | 7 | D | D | D | NA | NA | NA | NA |
| Gilbert......................... | 307 | 1 003 | 185.2 | 34.7 | 462 | D | D | D | 115 | 2 941 | 415.9 | 94.5 |
| Glendale...................... | 250 | 1 208 | 202.9 | 30.9 | 302 | D | D | D | 159 | 3 904 | 913.0 | 193.7 |
| Goodyear..................... | 61 | 166 | 33.7 | 5.6 | 67 | 355 | 36.6 | 15.1 | 20 | 760 | 185.5 | 30.2 |
| Kingman ...................... | 53 | 181 | 26.5 | 5.7 | 65 | D | D | D | NA | NA | NA | NA |
| Lake Havasu City......... | 108 | 307 | 55.8 | 8.0 | 100 | 350 | 45.3 | 14.5 | 78 | 1 399 | 238.6 | 49.8 |
| Marana ........................ | 40 | 107 | 14.6 | 3.2 | 53 | 205 | 20.4 | 7.0 | 28 | 783 | 243.7 | 39.1 |
| Maricopa...................... | 14 | 33 | 3.2 | 0.6 | 29 | 83 | 5.5 | 3.7 | NA | NA | NA | NA |
| Mesa........................... | 594 | 2 834 | 524.9 | 80.1 | 1 081 | 7 105 | 708.1 | 301.8 | 257 | 8 764 | 3 072.5 | 585.6 |
| Oro Valley ................... | 72 | D | D | D | 125 | 481 | 49.4 | 24.4 | 13 | D | D | D |
| Peoria......................... | 152 | 710 | 114.5 | 25.1 | 218 | D | D | D | 54 | 1 341 | 267.8 | 45.3 |
| Phoenix ....................... | 2 227 | 17 353 | 3 261.0 | 746.4 | 5 038 | 46 488 | 7 094.6 | 2 922.4 | 1 626 | 57 398 | 16 926.9 | 2 733.3 |
| Prescott ...................... | 188 | 444 | 81.9 | 11.5 | 237 | D | D | D | 71 | 1 536 | 267.6 | 61.2 |
| Prescott Valley ............ | 54 | 187 | 39.0 | 6.2 | 50 | 200 | 12.2 | 4.4 | 42 | 856 | 214.5 | 31.9 |
| Queen Creek............... | 31 | 46 | 4.2 | 0.8 | 50 | 117 | 11.2 | 3.2 | NA | NA | NA | NA |
| Sahuarita .................... | 5 | 17 | 1.4 | 0.3 | 11 | 27 | 2.3 | 0.8 | NA | NA | NA | NA |
| San Luis ..................... | 10 | 22 | 3.4 | 0.4 | 5 | D | D | D | NA | NA | NA | NA |
| Scottsdale.................... | 1 102 | 5 637 | 1 992.0 | 335.8 | 1 970 | D | D | D | 252 | 8 620 | 4 806.6 | 611.1 |
| Sierra Vista.................. | 62 | 337 | 44.3 | 9.1 | 102 | D | D | D | NA | NA | NA | NA |
| Surprise ...................... | 55 | 445 | 48.1 | 6.8 | 83 | 437 | 27.5 | 11.1 | NA | NA | NA | NA |
| Tempe ......................... | 451 | 3 423 | 768.9 | 138.5 | 1 005 | 10 930 | 1 321.4 | 606.0 | 453 | 17 621 | 5 877.6 | 835.4 |
| Tucson......................... | 865 | 5 832 | 834.2 | 176.8 | 1 759 | 12 057 | 1 416.0 | 567.6 | 459 | 10 964 | 3 446.1 | 489.9 |
| Yuma........................... | 143 | 572 | 90.3 | 13.2 | 169 | D | D | D | 53 | 2 662 | 830.4 | 82.6 |
| ARKANSAS.............. | 3 162 | 14 115 | 1 968.1 | 374.9 | 5 588 | D | D | D | 3 088 | 184 568 | 60 735.6 | 6 518.4 |
| Bella Vista ................... | 36 | 73 | 7.9 | 1.7 | 35 | 69 | 6.5 | 2.0 | NA | NA | NA | NA |
| Benton......................... | 33 | 106 | 14.5 | 2.0 | 62 | 210 | 15.8 | 5.7 | 29 | 571 | 124.3 | D |
| Bentonville................... | 66 | 223 | 32.1 | 5.2 | 186 | 2 300 | 191.4 | 135.6 | 25 | 1 074 | 293.8 | 57.6 |
| Conway ....................... | 98 | 336 | 48.7 | 8.8 | 159 | 614 | 62.3 | 19.0 | 56 | 5 036 | 1 540.8 | 207.2 |
| Fayetteville .................. | 160 | 1 797 | 126.9 | 48.4 | 354 | D | D | D | 59 | 5 223 | 1 309.7 | 178.0 |
| Fort Smith.................... | 150 | 675 | 128.8 | 20.2 | 265 | D | D | D | 160 | 18 247 | 5 080.4 | 589.3 |
| Hot Springs ................. | 97 | 491 | 68.5 | 11.7 | 150 | D | D | D | 47 | D | D | D |

1. Establishments subject to federal tax.

**Accommodation and Food Services, Arts, Entertainment, and Recreation, and Health Care and Social Assistance**

| City | Accommodation and food services, 2007 | | | | Arts, entertainment, and recreation,[1] 2007 | | | | Health care and social assistance,[1] 2007 | | | |
|---|---|---|---|---|---|---|---|---|---|---|---|---|
| | Number of establish-ments | Number of employees | Sales (mil dol) | Annual payroll (mil dol) | Number of establish-ments | Number of employees | Receipts (mil dol) | Annual payroll (mil dol) | Number of establish-ments | Number of employees | Receipts (mil dol) | Annual payroll (mil dol) |
| | 92 | 93 | 94 | 95 | 96 | 97 | 98 | 99 | 100 | 101 | 102 | 103 |
| United States............. | 634 361 | 11 600 751 | 613 795.7 | 170 826.8 | 100 656 | 1 496 869 | 151 958.0 | 45 916.0 | 647 120 | 8 322 326 | 818 394.6 | 330 887.7 |
| ALABAMA ................ | 8 093 | 150 791 | 6 426.3 | 1 751.4 | 843 | 11 475 | 950.1 | 188.1 | 8 502 | 134 925 | 12 637.2 | 5 167.2 |
| Alabaster ..................... | 44 | 737 | 38.4 | 10.0 | 5 | D | D | D | 83 | D | D | D |
| Auburn.......................... | 168 | 3 419 | 123.1 | 32.7 | 14 | D | D | D | 79 | D | D | D |
| Bessemer...................... | 75 | 1 427 | 62.3 | 16.5 | 11 | 128 | 12.8 | 3.2 | 87 | D | D | D |
| Birmingham.................. | 549 | 11 539 | 587.7 | 165.0 | 45 | 749 | 61.4 | 13.4 | 738 | 13 898 | 1 705.5 | 701.3 |
| Decatur......................... | 144 | 3 009 | 122.4 | 33.1 | 10 | D | D | D | 219 | 2 770 | 259.0 | 97.8 |
| Dothan.......................... | 208 | 4 333 | 174.0 | 47.8 | 17 | D | D | D | 255 | D | D | D |
| Enterprise .................... | 74 | 1 401 | 47.5 | 12.4 | 8 | D | D | D | 73 | D | D | D |
| Florence ...................... | 113 | 3 145 | 118.7 | 36.0 | 14 | D | D | D | 190 | D | D | D |
| Gadsden....................... | 105 | 2 299 | 94.6 | 27.3 | 7 | D | D | D | 185 | 4 572 | 514.5 | 182.6 |
| Homewood .................. | 121 | 2 962 | 142.5 | 38.8 | 5 | D | D | D | 177 | D | D | D |
| Hoover.......................... | 176 | 4 257 | 224.0 | 64.5 | 20 | 292 | 18.5 | 4.3 | 196 | D | D | D |
| Huntsville..................... | 480 | 10 921 | 471.9 | 133.4 | 48 | D | D | D | 593 | D | D | D |
| Madison........................ | 89 | 1 580 | 72.7 | 19.3 | 9 | 102 | 3.1 | 1.0 | 85 | 1 270 | 93.5 | 36.5 |
| Mobile.......................... | 461 | 10 113 | 427.5 | 122.1 | 42 | 485 | 23.4 | 6.5 | 470 | 10 484 | 983.1 | 458.6 |
| Montgomery ................ | 456 | 9 565 | 395.9 | 110.4 | 31 | D | D | D | 572 | 8 657 | 931.2 | 356.1 |
| Opelika ........................ | 75 | 1 893 | 71.4 | 21.3 | 3 | D | D | D | 83 | D | D | D |
| Phenix City.................. | 65 | 1 156 | 45.9 | 11.8 | 5 | D | D | D | 49 | D | D | D |
| Prattville...................... | 87 | 2 054 | 83.3 | 23.7 | 6 | D | D | D | 61 | D | D | D |
| Tuscaloosa................... | 276 | 6 318 | 260.7 | 68.7 | 17 | 266 | 11.8 | 4.4 | 219 | 2 808 | 282.4 | 122.7 |
| Vestavia Hills............... | 66 | 1 218 | 50.4 | 13.5 | 14 | 257 | 14.0 | 5.6 | 88 | D | D | D |
| ALASKA .................. | 1 996 | 25 638 | 1 851.3 | 529.8 | 392 | 3 738 | 291.8 | 55.1 | 1 603 | 15 416 | 1 820.6 | 714.2 |
| Anchorage.................... | 720 | 14 031 | 933.3 | 283.9 | 109 | D | D | D | 851 | 9 685 | 1 181.7 | 451.7 |
| Fairbanks..................... | 139 | 2 569 | 155.7 | 43.1 | 26 | 765 | 25.6 | 5.0 | 131 | D | D | D |
| Juneau.......................... | 97 | 1 228 | 86.9 | 21.6 | 24 | D | D | D | 87 | 648 | 65.7 | 25.4 |
| ARIZONA ................ | 11 610 | 250 716 | 13 268.5 | 3 766.3 | 1 510 | 39 112 | 3 816.4 | 1 171.2 | 13 643 | 154 061 | 16 655.7 | 6 572.3 |
| Apache Junction............ | 58 | 915 | 36.3 | 8.5 | 8 | 161 | 6.2 | 1.5 | 39 | D | D | D |
| Avondale ..................... | 97 | 2 113 | 94.6 | 26.1 | 11 | D | D | D | 85 | D | D | D |
| Buckeye........................ | 25 | 271 | 17.2 | 4.1 | 5 | D | D | D | 9 | D | D | D |
| Bullhead City............... | 80 | 1 240 | 54.6 | 15.3 | 7 | 231 | 5.9 | 3.3 | 106 | D | D | D |
| Casa Grande................ | 80 | 1 758 | 75.2 | 20.4 | 7 | 94 | 4.9 | 1.5 | 107 | 1 424 | 127.8 | 52.1 |
| Chandler....................... | 456 | 10 153 | 500.9 | 153.6 | 48 | 2 316 | 314.3 | 66.6 | 557 | 5 196 | 540.8 | 186.1 |
| El Mirage ..................... | 7 | 47 | 2.4 | 0.7 | 1 | D | D | D | 4 | D | D | D |
| Flagstaff....................... | 269 | 5 546 | 294.5 | 77.3 | 30 | 630 | 23.8 | 9.3 | 292 | 2 407 | 259.8 | 107.0 |
| Florence ...................... | 18 | 379 | 28.7 | 5.5 | 4 | D | D | D | 11 | D | D | D |
| Gilbert.......................... | 248 | 4 450 | 191.2 | 54.5 | 35 | D | D | D | 421 | D | D | D |
| Glendale....................... | 394 | 7 516 | 340.7 | 97.5 | 37 | 1 444 | 97.7 | 69.9 | 514 | 6 077 | 747.4 | 291.7 |
| Goodyear...................... | 76 | 2 167 | 105.1 | 32.5 | 10 | D | D | D | 101 | D | D | D |
| Kingman........................ | 93 | 1 716 | 75.6 | 21.0 | 9 | D | D | D | 104 | D | D | D |
| Lake Havasu City......... | 136 | 2 574 | 104.7 | 30.3 | 14 | 255 | 12.2 | 3.0 | 161 | D | D | D |
| Marana.......................... | 88 | 1 903 | 76.6 | 20.9 | 12 | D | D | D | 38 | D | D | D |
| Maricopa....................... | 30 | 457 | 18.3 | 5.0 | 2 | D | D | D | 22 | D | D | D |
| Mesa............................. | 788 | 16 920 | 753.2 | 210.0 | 79 | 1 677 | 80.5 | 22.6 | 1 096 | 12 584 | 1 403.7 | 543.9 |
| Oro Valley ................... | 52 | 1 630 | 81.8 | 23.1 | 9 | 221 | 6.7 | 3.7 | 93 | 1 323 | 142.7 | 53.6 |
| Peoria........................... | 217 | 6 006 | 258.5 | 78.5 | 30 | 623 | 30.9 | 11.3 | 293 | 3 900 | 350.9 | 152.0 |
| Phoenix ........................ | 2 600 | 61 385 | 3 644.4 | 1 027.3 | 333 | 7 211 | 729.6 | 285.8 | 3 232 | 39 166 | 4 469.4 | 1 897.0 |
| Prescott........................ | 164 | 2 528 | 111.2 | 32.8 | 14 | 109 | 3.9 | 1.3 | 294 | 2 682 | 241.5 | 92.7 |
| Prescott Valley............. | 72 | 993 | 40.6 | 12.0 | 8 | 258 | 10.8 | 3.0 | 90 | 783 | 53.9 | 19.6 |
| Queen Creek................ | 34 | 527 | 25.6 | 6.8 | 7 | D | D | D | 55 | 508 | 31.7 | 15.5 |
| Sahuarita ..................... | 14 | 217 | 7.8 | 2.0 | 3 | D | D | D | 10 | D | D | D |
| San Luis ...................... | 14 | 234 | 11.0 | 2.4 | 1 | D | D | D | 7 | D | D | D |
| Scottsdale..................... | 705 | 22 206 | 1 314.3 | 403.3 | 160 | 4 435 | 306.6 | 102.6 | 1 272 | 10 821 | 1 295.3 | 516.9 |
| Sierra Vista.................. | 99 | 1 854 | 86.8 | 24.2 | 5 | D | D | D | 124 | 1 347 | 122.3 | 52.1 |
| Surprise ....................... | 112 | 2 720 | 115.1 | 34.8 | 11 | D | D | D | 111 | D | D | D |
| Tempe........................... | 566 | 11 197 | 606.8 | 163.2 | 61 | 1 420 | 292.7 | 159.2 | 495 | 7 572 | 960.3 | 306.7 |
| Tucson.......................... | 1 210 | 27 059 | 1 214.9 | 347.5 | 137 | 1 582 | 74.6 | 22.6 | 1 476 | 18 451 | 1 869.0 | 784.8 |
| Yuma............................ | 232 | 5 084 | 230.0 | 60.3 | 13 | D | D | D | 259 | 3 240 | 305.6 | 116.7 |
| ARKANSAS............... | 5 112 | 89 933 | 3 559.8 | 994.1 | 607 | 6 136 | 346.2 | 92.6 | 5 718 | 77 215 | 7 150.8 | 2 895.5 |
| Bella Vista ................... | 19 | 178 | 8.6 | 2.3 | 2 | D | D | D | 22 | 298 | 18.7 | 8.7 |
| Benton.......................... | 55 | 856 | 33.3 | 9.5 | 9 | 55 | 2.8 | 0.8 | 79 | D | D | D |
| Bentonville................... | 123 | 2 275 | 88.5 | 26.5 | 11 | 182 | 7.6 | 2.5 | 97 | 1 531 | 173.6 | 63.5 |
| Conway......................... | 135 | 3 325 | 122.3 | 33.0 | 15 | D | D | D | 194 | 2 488 | 202.1 | 81.4 |
| Fayetteville................... | 281 | 5 943 | 231.9 | 66.1 | 23 | 284 | 11.2 | 4.5 | 245 | 3 139 | 355.4 | 136.7 |
| Fort Smith.................... | 233 | 4 785 | 197.0 | 54.0 | 16 | D | D | D | 294 | 5 620 | 516.1 | 248.4 |
| Hot Springs ................. | 188 | 4 262 | 168.9 | 52.6 | 34 | D | D | D | 186 | 3 079 | 342.2 | 140.0 |

1. Establishments subject to federal tax.

# Table D. Cities — **Other Services and Federal Funds**

| City | Other services[1], 2007 | | | | Selected federal funds, 2009–2010 (mil dol) | | | | | | | | |
| | | | | | Procurement contracts | | Grants | | | | | | |
| | Number of establishments | Number of employees | Receipts (mil dol) | Annual payroll (mil dol) | Defense | Other | Total[2] | Medicaid and other health related | Nutrition and family welfare | Energy and environment | Disasters and emergency preparedness | Housing and community development | Employment and training |
| | 104 | 105 | 106 | 107 | 108 | 109 | 110 | 111 | 112 | 113 | 114 | 115 | 116 |
| United States.............. | 432 302 | 2 598 622 | 219 837.5 | 66 828.9 | 329 872.9 | 184 951.4 | 675 282.4 | 357 482.0 | 74 796.2 | 26 084.7 | 6 668.4 | 35 873.9 | 9 977.6 |
| ALABAMA ................ | 5 606 | 33 791 | 3 102.5 | 851.5 | 8 140.1 | 2 341.6 | 9 273.4 | 4 946.9 | 949.1 | 370.3 | 46.6 | 382.0 | 137.5 |
| Alabaster ...................... | 37 | D | D | D | 185.2 | 0.0 | 0.0 | 0.0 | 0.0 | 0.0 | 0.0 | 0.0 | 0.0 |
| Auburn.......................... | 62 | 367 | 20.2 | 6.6 | 21.3 | 2.9 | 68.0 | 6.3 | 5.9 | 4.8 | 0.0 | 2.9 | 0.0 |
| Bessemer...................... | 54 | 492 | 62.3 | 15.5 | 4.8 | 0.1 | 66.8 | 0.0 | 0.0 | 0.0 | 0.0 | 7.2 | 0.0 |
| Birmingham .................. | 409 | 3 825 | 367.7 | 123.2 | 42.8 | 236.4 | 842.1 | 481.8 | 17.6 | 167.6 | 2.2 | 87.1 | 1.2 |
| Decatur......................... | 96 | D | D | D | 7.9 | 0.3 | 20.0 | 0.2 | 12.1 | 0.0 | 0.0 | 7.3 | 0.0 |
| Dothan.......................... | 153 | D | D | D | 3.9 | 0.8 | 17.9 | 0.5 | 7.0 | 0.0 | 0.0 | 5.1 | 3.0 |
| Enterprise..................... | 48 | D | D | D | 41.2 | 7.9 | 3.1 | 0.0 | 0.0 | 0.0 | 0.0 | 0.8 | 0.0 |
| Florence ...................... | 87 | D | D | D | 0.9 | 1.1 | 8.2 | 0.8 | 1.2 | 0.0 | 0.0 | 5.4 | 0.0 |
| Gadsden........................ | 56 | D | D | D | 0.1 | 8.6 | 21.8 | 7.1 | 2.0 | 0.1 | 0.0 | 3.4 | 0.0 |
| Homewood .................. | 65 | 440 | 38.9 | 12.7 | 5.8 | 14.3 | 0.0 | 0.0 | 0.0 | 0.0 | 0.0 | 0.0 | 0.0 |
| Hoover.......................... | 91 | 570 | 54.3 | 17.8 | 0.2 | 0.4 | 0.4 | 0.0 | 0.0 | 0.0 | 0.0 | 0.0 | 0.0 |
| Huntsville..................... | 289 | 2 629 | 502.4 | 71.1 | 4 741.0 | 384.8 | 108.8 | 15.4 | 3.4 | 13.8 | 0.0 | 14.6 | 0.0 |
| Madison........................ | 38 | 206 | 12.6 | 3.9 | 187.0 | 12.2 | 0.2 | 0.0 | 0.0 | 0.0 | 0.0 | 0.0 | 0.0 |
| Mobile.......................... | 345 | 2 892 | 177.2 | 65.0 | 466.9 | 42.9 | 109.9 | 39.3 | 0.4 | 3.9 | 2.0 | 38.3 | 0.0 |
| Montgomery .................. | 311 | D | D | D | 406.5 | 68.6 | 1 069.9 | 127.5 | 156.2 | 85.9 | -3.5 | 71.2 | 127.3 |
| Opelika ........................ | 43 | 175 | 14.6 | 3.9 | 1.4 | 1.1 | 5.1 | 0.0 | 0.0 | 0.0 | 0.0 | 5.0 | 0.0 |
| Phenix City .................. | 50 | D | D | D | 0.6 | 0.3 | 8.1 | 0.0 | 1.9 | 0.2 | 0.0 | 5.2 | 0.0 |
| Prattville...................... | 43 | D | D | D | 0.0 | 0.0 | 1.9 | 0.0 | 0.0 | 0.6 | 0.0 | 0.4 | 0.0 |
| Tuscaloosa.................. | 118 | 1 122 | 76.9 | 25.5 | 120.1 | 142.6 | 115.1 | 24.6 | 6.7 | 15.0 | 0.0 | 9.4 | 0.5 |
| Vestavia Hills................ | 60 | 422 | 25.1 | 9.8 | 0.0 | 0.0 | 0.0 | 0.0 | 0.0 | 0.0 | 0.0 | 0.0 | 0.0 |
| ALASKA ................ | 871 | 4 874 | 477.0 | 145.2 | 1 776.3 | 687.9 | 3 465.2 | 1 065.9 | 283.0 | 260.3 | 15.8 | 174.4 | 56.0 |
| Anchorage.................... | 394 | 2 642 | 241.2 | 78.2 | 963.9 | 278.6 | 576.9 | 39.1 | 18.2 | 26.9 | 3.3 | 73.1 | 9.0 |
| Fairbanks...................... | 88 | 648 | 60.5 | 19.8 | 77.8 | 66.1 | 114.2 | 25.3 | 7.0 | 22.5 | 0.0 | 10.8 | 0.0 |
| Juneau.......................... | 47 | 228 | 18.1 | 5.1 | 2.0 | 41.2 | 466.9 | 34.6 | 45.0 | 114.2 | 0.2 | 19.5 | 43.7 |
| ARIZONA ................ | 7 444 | 52 045 | 3 940.2 | 1 230.9 | 10 831.4 | 1 981.7 | 14 361.0 | 8 500.6 | 1 460.7 | 449.2 | 12.7 | 710.9 | 146.4 |
| Apache Junction............ | 43 | 143 | 10.2 | 3.0 | 0.0 | 0.0 | 0.0 | 0.0 | 0.0 | 0.0 | 0.0 | 0.0 | 0.0 |
| Avondale ..................... | 43 | 322 | 19.7 | 6.8 | 0.0 | 0.0 | 0.5 | 0.0 | 0.0 | 0.0 | -0.9 | 0.5 | 0.0 |
| Buckeye........................ | 7 | D | D | D | 0.0 | 0.1 | 4.6 | 0.0 | 0.0 | 0.0 | 4.2 | 0.0 | 0.0 |
| Bullhead City ................ | 40 | 223 | 16.9 | 4.8 | 0.0 | 1.5 | 0.3 | 0.0 | 0.0 | 0.3 | 0.0 | 3.7 | 0.0 |
| Casa Grande................ | 58 | 426 | 23.6 | 7.5 | 0.0 | 0.0 | 9.8 | 1.9 | 0.0 | 2.1 | 0.0 | 3.7 | 0.0 |
| Chandler....................... | 237 | 2 032 | 136.7 | 53.4 | 189.0 | 9.0 | 10.1 | 0.1 | 0.0 | 2.3 | 0.0 | 6.8 | 0.0 |
| El Mirage ..................... | 18 | 79 | 5.8 | 1.7 | 0.0 | 0.0 | 2.2 | 0.0 | 0.0 | 0.0 | 0.7 | 0.0 | 0.0 |
| Flagstaff....................... | 132 | 890 | 58.7 | 18.8 | 3.8 | 14.4 | 80.1 | 11.3 | 14.7 | 11.3 | 0.8 | 4.1 | 0.2 |
| Florence ...................... | 4 | D | D | D | 0.0 | 37.0 | 5.9 | 0.0 | 0.0 | 0.0 | 0.0 | 0.8 | 0.0 |
| Gilbert.......................... | 198 | 1 083 | 68.4 | 19.9 | 48.0 | 23.4 | 5.8 | 0.0 | 0.0 | 1.8 | 3.0 | 0.8 | 0.0 |
| Glendale....................... | 297 | 1 597 | 127.0 | 40.4 | 29.7 | 2.3 | 17.2 | 0.0 | 0.0 | 2.4 | 0.0 | 13.0 | 0.0 |
| Goodyear...................... | 35 | 181 | 9.2 | 3.3 | 61.9 | 0.2 | 0.6 | 0.0 | 0.0 | 0.5 | 0.0 | 0.0 | 0.0 |
| Kingman........................ | 51 | 438 | 32.0 | 10.0 | 5.3 | 2.5 | 2.3 | 0.0 | 0.0 | 0.0 | 0.0 | 1.6 | 0.0 |
| Lake Havasu City......... | 122 | 689 | 47.7 | 14.3 | 0.6 | 4.2 | 0.4 | 0.0 | 0.0 | 0.0 | 0.0 | 0.0 | 0.0 |
| Marana ........................ | 57 | D | D | D | 1.7 | 0.5 | 5.2 | 2.4 | 0.0 | 0.0 | 0.0 | 0.0 | 0.0 |
| Maricopa...................... | 12 | D | D | D | 0.0 | 0.0 | 2.0 | 0.2 | 0.0 | 0.4 | 0.0 | 0.7 | 0.0 |
| Mesa............................ | 596 | 5 247 | 320.5 | 103.4 | 1 145.0 | 66.1 | 41.5 | 0.7 | 0.3 | 0.6 | 4.0 | 17.6 | 0.0 |
| Oro Valley .................... | 47 | D | D | D | 1.1 | 0.7 | 0.0 | 0.0 | 0.0 | 0.0 | 0.0 | 0.0 | 0.0 |
| Peoria.......................... | 185 | 1 009 | 80.0 | 22.2 | 1.3 | 5.3 | 4.7 | 0.0 | 0.0 | 3.1 | 0.0 | 1.5 | 0.0 |
| Phoenix ....................... | 1 829 | 15 911 | 1 318.6 | 380.6 | 1 873.8 | 378.1 | 2 074.8 | 173.1 | 364.3 | 121.2 | -0.1 | 374.0 | 123.1 |
| Prescott........................ | 115 | 552 | 41.8 | 12.6 | 0.3 | 8.4 | 4.4 | 0.9 | 0.0 | 0.5 | 0.0 | 0.3 | 0.0 |
| Prescott Valley ............. | 54 | 207 | 15.9 | 5.2 | 0.0 | 0.1 | 0.6 | 0.0 | 0.0 | 0.0 | 0.0 | 0.0 | 0.0 |
| Queen Creek................ | 26 | 114 | 9.2 | 3.0 | 0.0 | 0.0 | 0.4 | 0.0 | 0.0 | 0.0 | 0.0 | 0.0 | 0.0 |
| Sahuarita...................... | 6 | D | D | D | 0.1 | 0.0 | 0.0 | 0.0 | 0.0 | 0.0 | 0.0 | 0.0 | 0.0 |
| San Luis ...................... | 4 | D | D | D | 47.0 | 1.6 | 1.7 | 0.0 | 0.0 | 0.0 | 0.0 | 0.0 | 0.0 |
| Scottsdale.................... | 531 | 3 388 | 257.0 | 85.0 | 568.2 | 133.2 | 90.6 | 21.2 | 2.7 | 4.4 | 0.0 | 10.2 | 0.1 |
| Sierra Vista.................. | 41 | 252 | 14.5 | 4.7 | 192.8 | 8.4 | 2.1 | 0.0 | 0.0 | 0.2 | 0.0 | 0.0 | 0.0 |
| Surprise ....................... | 76 | 425 | 48.0 | 17.1 | 0.1 | 0.1 | 6.5 | 4.3 | 0.0 | 1.1 | 0.0 | 0.8 | 0.0 |
| Tempe.......................... | 286 | 2 437 | 202.4 | 69.8 | 362.3 | 34.6 | 251.2 | 36.1 | 0.0 | 80.0 | 0.6 | 12.0 | 0.0 |
| Tucson......................... | 810 | 5 535 | 417.7 | 133.5 | 5 200.9 | 160.7 | 579.6 | 208.8 | 28.7 | 54.1 | 0.1 | 99.6 | 3.9 |
| Yuma............................ | 125 | 728 | 52.3 | 16.8 | 19.4 | 20.7 | 31.9 | 0.6 | 8.5 | 3.1 | 0.0 | 9.6 | 0.1 |
| ARKANSAS................ | 3 325 | 18 421 | 1 407.7 | 426.5 | 1 137.5 | 613.5 | 6 843.0 | 3 731.0 | 680.6 | 109.3 | 76.9 | 265.1 | 100.8 |
| Bella Vista ................... | 7 | D | D | D | NA | NA | NA | NA | NA | NA | NA | NA | NA |
| Benton.......................... | 50 | 237 | 20.4 | 5.9 | -0.1 | 0.0 | 6.6 | 0.0 | 3.2 | 0.0 | 0.0 | 3.4 | 0.0 |
| Bentonville................... | 54 | 638 | 28.3 | 20.8 | 0.0 | 0.2 | 4.2 | 0.8 | 0.0 | 1.1 | 0.0 | 0.2 | 0.0 |
| Conway......................... | 79 | D | D | D | 0.3 | 0.7 | 38.0 | 0.1 | 6.4 | 0.0 | 24.1 | 2.1 | 0.0 |
| Fayetteville .................. | 118 | 765 | 43.4 | 14.6 | 7.9 | 55.8 | 87.3 | 9.4 | 4.5 | 9.6 | 0.6 | 3.9 | 0.0 |
| Fort Smith.................... | 140 | D | D | D | 5.6 | 12.8 | 17.4 | 1.6 | 0.5 | 0.9 | 0.0 | 8.7 | 0.0 |
| Hot Springs .................. | 84 | 411 | 25.3 | 8.5 | 2.3 | 1.5 | 4.9 | 0.0 | 0.0 | 0.0 | 0.0 | 4.0 | 0.0 |

1. Establishments subject to federal tax.   2. Includes program categories not shown separately. State totals include additional categories not allocated by city.

# Table D. Cities — **City Government Finances**

| City | City government finances, 2007 | | | | | | | | | |
|---|---|---|---|---|---|---|---|---|---|---|
| | General revenue | | | | | | | General expenditure | | |
| | | Intergovernmental | | Taxes | | | | | Per capita[1] (dollars) | |
| | | | | | Per capita[1] (dollars) | | | | | |
| | Total (mil dol) | Total (mil dol) | Percent from state government | Total (mil dol) | Total | Property | Sales and gross receipts | Total (mil dol) | Total | Capital outlays |
| | 117 | 118 | 119 | 120 | 121 | 122 | 123 | 124 | 125 | 126 |
| United States............. | X | X | X | X | X | X | X | X | X | X |
| ALABAMA ................ | X | X | X | X | X | X | X | X | X | X |
| Alabaster ...................... | 41.1 | 2.6 | 100.0 | 17.4 | 606 | 85 | 451 | 36.0 | 1 254 | 331 |
| Auburn ......................... | 73.2 | 2.4 | 60.3 | 52.3 | 963 | 241 | 578 | 51.2 | 943 | 212 |
| Bessemer ..................... | 50.1 | 6.1 | 58.8 | 35.8 | 1 248 | 222 | 863 | 49.7 | 1 736 | 270 |
| Birmingham .................. | 490.6 | 42.5 | 38.5 | 380.5 | 1 656 | 239 | 1 059 | 398.2 | 1 733 | 130 |
| Decatur ........................ | 87.2 | 10.5 | 100.0 | 41.3 | 741 | 44 | 697 | 94.8 | 1 702 | 214 |
| Dothan ......................... | 63.6 | 3.2 | 16.0 | 49.0 | 748 | 42 | 706 | 74.5 | 1 138 | 66 |
| Enterprise .................... | 25.0 | 2.4 | 96.3 | 17.7 | 726 | 113 | 614 | 25.9 | 1 059 | 203 |
| Florence ...................... | 62.4 | 12.3 | 94.6 | 40.0 | 1 069 | 262 | 807 | 51.6 | 1 377 | 100 |
| Gadsden ...................... | 63.0 | 3.0 | 26.1 | 48.4 | 1 311 | 108 | 849 | 64.6 | 1 749 | 54 |
| Homewood ................... | 53.7 | 0.4 | 100.0 | 45.3 | 1 893 | 612 | 1 281 | 27.2 | 1 137 | 65 |
| Hoover ......................... | 104.5 | 5.2 | 57.0 | 82.9 | 1 186 | 126 | 1 034 | 94.3 | 1 349 | 162 |
| Huntsville..................... | 305.0 | 23.1 | 69.7 | 200.8 | 1 172 | 235 | 937 | 212.8 | 1 242 | 104 |
| Madison ....................... | 32.9 | 1.9 | 84.2 | 22.8 | 597 | 138 | 459 | 40.8 | 1 066 | 313 |
| Mobile ......................... | 357.5 | 25.8 | 27.4 | 247.1 | 1 291 | 68 | 1 051 | 266.4 | 1 392 | 178 |
| Montgomery ................ | 240.4 | 32.7 | 45.4 | 175.6 | 860 | 131 | 729 | 212.7 | 1 042 | 97 |
| Opelika ........................ | 50.8 | 4.7 | 12.7 | 35.6 | 1 377 | 260 | 812 | 42.4 | 1 640 | 293 |
| Phenix City .................. | 32.7 | 2.0 | 71.6 | 20.8 | 679 | 130 | 548 | 33.6 | 1 097 | 287 |
| Prattville ...................... | 28.8 | 0.4 | 0.0 | 20.5 | 639 | 56 | 583 | 25.1 | 784 | 0 |
| Tuscaloosa ................... | 120.8 | 29.2 | 43.6 | 65.0 | 732 | 115 | 608 | 108.9 | 1 227 | 213 |
| Vestavia Hills................ | 33.3 | 2.5 | 53.3 | 25.6 | 825 | 374 | 451 | 30.2 | 973 | 81 |
| ALASKA ...................... | X | X | X | X | X | X | X | X | X | X |
| Anchorage .................... | 1 143.1 | 467.0 | 93.0 | 469.1 | 1 677 | 1 461 | 217 | 1 089.1 | 3 894 | 733 |
| Fairbanks..................... | 43.2 | 8.5 | 84.9 | 17.3 | 500 | 337 | 163 | 35.3 | 1 023 | 192 |
| Juneau ......................... | 246.3 | 57.4 | 90.9 | 80.7 | 2 631 | 1 223 | 1 407 | 235.9 | 7 686 | 1 599 |
| ARIZONA ................. | X | X | X | X | X | X | X | X | X | X |
| Apache Junction........... | 38.5 | 17.6 | 100.0 | 17.0 | 533 | 0 | 533 | 32.6 | 1 021 | 0 |
| Avondale...................... | 110.0 | 25.2 | 94.0 | 61.4 | 770 | 55 | 715 | 101.8 | 1 276 | 380 |
| Buckeye....................... | 45.8 | 5.2 | 95.9 | 33.7 | 1 125 | 195 | 925 | 30.6 | 1 020 | 9 |
| Bullhead City ............... | 58.8 | 22.2 | 100.0 | 19.2 | 468 | 4 | 464 | 49.0 | 1 195 | 12 |
| Casa Grande................ | 76.6 | 14.7 | 82.9 | 37.4 | 982 | 65 | 917 | 58.2 | 1 525 | 269 |
| Chandler....................... | 313.2 | 88.1 | 92.8 | 143.4 | 582 | 109 | 473 | 381.3 | 1 548 | 543 |
| El Mirage ..................... | 31.2 | 12.3 | 100.0 | 9.1 | 343 | 83 | 260 | 22.7 | 860 | 0 |
| Flagstaff....................... | 149.2 | 39.5 | 78.1 | 66.6 | 1 114 | 291 | 823 | 117.9 | 1 973 | 271 |
| Florence ...................... | 20.4 | 8.5 | 95.5 | 5.6 | 314 | 17 | 297 | 15.8 | 887 | 134 |
| Gilbert.......................... | 287.2 | 73.0 | 78.8 | 153.1 | 738 | 89 | 649 | 260.9 | 1 257 | 603 |
| Glendale....................... | 367.8 | 126.9 | 82.9 | 138.6 | 547 | 52 | 496 | 301.9 | 1 192 | 32 |
| Goodyear...................... | 206.2 | 103.1 | 100.0 | 68.3 | 1 293 | 234 | 1 059 | 152.2 | 2 880 | 1 545 |
| Kingman ....................... | 43.1 | 16.3 | 100.0 | 15.3 | 552 | 16 | 537 | 40.1 | 1 447 | 245 |
| Lake Havasu City.......... | 88.2 | 27.4 | 82.8 | 33.4 | 590 | 116 | 475 | 146.4 | 2 586 | 1 399 |
| Marana ........................ | 67.7 | 16.6 | 63.8 | 42.7 | 1 340 | 0 | 1 340 | 104.6 | 3 283 | 1 674 |
| Maricopa...................... | 54.9 | 8.3 | 100.0 | 29.5 | 778 | 58 | 720 | 17.4 | 459 | 181 |
| Mesa............................ | 538.7 | 190.6 | 82.6 | 177.0 | 391 | 0 | 378 | 618.8 | 1 366 | 224 |
| Oro Valley .................... | 58.4 | 31.8 | 95.2 | 16.1 | 400 | 41 | 294 | 58.8 | 1 463 | 766 |
| Peoria .......................... | 260.1 | 64.5 | 73.9 | 101.0 | 688 | 122 | 566 | 290.9 | 1 983 | 824 |
| Phoenix ........................ | 3 081.9 | 1 018.4 | 63.4 | 1 066.6 | 687 | 137 | 549 | 2 912.4 | 1 876 | 764 |
| Prescott ....................... | 107.7 | 17.9 | 94.2 | 37.2 | 880 | 67 | 813 | 85.1 | 2 014 | 752 |
| Prescott Valley ............. | 46.0 | 13.3 | 100.0 | 16.4 | 435 | 0 | 435 | 50.1 | 1 327 | 449 |
| Queen Creek................ | 42.4 | 4.2 | 99.3 | 24.3 | 1 030 | 0 | 1 030 | 89.9 | 3 806 | 2 191 |
| Sahuarita ..................... | 39.3 | 9.6 | 93.8 | 23.3 | 1 444 | 0 | 1 444 | 76.8 | 4 755 | 1 789 |
| San Luis ...................... | 18.6 | 8.9 | 96.3 | 4.8 | 203 | 0 | 203 | 63.6 | 2 671 | 1 837 |
| Scottsdale..................... | 575.0 | 92.5 | 92.4 | 268.2 | 1 138 | 215 | 923 | 402.9 | 1 710 | 317 |
| Sierra Vista.................. | 57.4 | 19.2 | 91.6 | 23.9 | 554 | 115 | 439 | 51.5 | 1 195 | 77 |
| Surprise ....................... | 215.8 | 57.2 | 98.5 | 72.5 | 799 | 59 | 741 | 221.6 | 2 442 | 1 493 |
| Tempe .......................... | 385.3 | 136.0 | 40.9 | 167.8 | 964 | 159 | 805 | 312.3 | 1 794 | 400 |
| Tucson.......................... | 749.7 | 284.2 | 71.1 | 270.4 | 514 | 72 | 443 | 643.4 | 1 224 | 177 |
| Yuma............................ | 125.9 | 38.6 | 91.0 | 53.6 | 604 | 83 | 521 | 148.8 | 1 677 | 593 |
| ARKANSAS................ | X | X | X | X | X | X | X | X | X | X |
| Bella Vista ................... | NA | NA | NA | NA | NA | NA | NA | NA | NA | NA |
| Benton ......................... | 18.2 | 2.7 | 60.0 | 11.0 | 388 | 51 | 337 | 21.8 | 769 | 183 |
| Bentonville.................... | 47.1 | 7.2 | 39.6 | 20.8 | 615 | 116 | 499 | 46.2 | 1 369 | 557 |
| Conway ........................ | 69.6 | 4.1 | 66.1 | 29.1 | 511 | 37 | 474 | 55.1 | 966 | 136 |
| Fayetteville................... | 104.0 | 22.1 | 40.3 | 43.7 | 605 | 43 | 562 | 131.8 | 1 825 | 869 |
| Fort Smith.................... | 125.0 | 28.4 | 40.6 | 58.7 | 696 | 119 | 577 | 106.0 | 1 257 | 426 |
| Hot Springs ................. | 65.0 | 8.6 | 89.3 | 30.6 | 782 | 1 | 781 | 54.3 | 1 389 | 273 |

1. Based on population estimated as of July 1 of the year shown.

## Table D. Cities — City Government Finances

| City | City government finances, 2006 (cont.) | | | | | | | | | |
| | General expenditure (cont.) | | | | | | | | | |
| | Percent of total for: | | | | | | | | | |
| | Public welfare | Highways | Parking facilities | Education | Health and hospitals | Police protection | Sewerage and sanitation | Parks and recreation | Housing and community development | Interest on debt |
| | 127 | 128 | 129 | 130 | 131 | 132 | 133 | 134 | 135 | 136 |
| United States | X | X | X | X | X | X | X | X | X | X |
| ALABAMA | X | X | X | X | X | X | X | X | X | X |
| Alabaster | 0.0 | 9.2 | 0.0 | 0.0 | 0.0 | 13.6 | 15.9 | 7.6 | 0.0 | 9.0 |
| Auburn | 0.1 | 7.2 | 0.0 | 0.0 | 0.4 | 14.3 | 15.8 | 18.7 | 0.0 | 7.3 |
| Bessemer | 2.5 | 4.3 | 0.0 | 2.1 | 0.0 | 18.9 | 7.9 | 2.2 | 4.6 | 1.7 |
| Birmingham | 0.0 | 18.6 | 2.4 | 0.3 | 0.4 | 16.7 | 5.4 | 6.4 | 0.2 | 6.0 |
| Decatur | 0.1 | 2.8 | 0.0 | 0.0 | 0.7 | 11.7 | 15.3 | 6.7 | 2.9 | 13.9 |
| Dothan | 0.1 | 6.6 | 0.0 | 4.0 | 1.0 | 19.0 | 18.4 | 12.8 | 0.0 | 0.0 |
| Enterprise | 0.5 | 10.7 | 0.0 | 17.9 | 2.2 | 15.2 | 17.6 | 9.0 | 0.0 | 3.5 |
| Florence | 0.0 | 9.5 | 0.1 | 14.8 | 0.7 | 15.0 | 6.5 | 8.8 | 0.9 | 9.5 |
| Gadsden | 0.0 | 1.2 | 0.0 | 0.9 | 0.0 | 13.0 | 11.1 | 8.9 | 2.2 | 5.3 |
| Homewood | 0.0 | 0.0 | 0.0 | 0.0 | 0.2 | 27.9 | 7.5 | 11.1 | 0.0 | 9.0 |
| Hoover | 0.0 | 6.3 | 0.0 | 7.5 | 0.3 | 19.3 | 6.8 | 12.1 | 0.3 | 5.5 |
| Huntsville | 0.0 | 4.1 | 0.9 | 0.0 | 0.6 | 15.8 | 10.0 | 8.5 | 5.1 | 11.9 |
| Madison | 0.0 | 38.1 | 0.0 | 0.0 | 0.0 | 11.5 | 0.0 | 4.8 | 0.0 | 12.5 |
| Mobile | 0.0 | 5.6 | 4.2 | 0.0 | 0.2 | 20.4 | 11.4 | 10.9 | 0.0 | 6.4 |
| Montgomery | 0.0 | 13.1 | 0.1 | 1.1 | 0.1 | 18.6 | 0.9 | 14.1 | 2.3 | 4.0 |
| Opelika | 0.0 | 14.1 | 0.0 | 10.4 | 0.2 | 14.9 | 12.6 | 6.4 | 0.4 | 7.5 |
| Phenix City | 0.1 | 9.5 | 0.0 | 0.0 | 0.2 | 14.1 | 14.6 | 16.9 | 0.0 | 6.4 |
| Prattville | 0.0 | 3.6 | 0.0 | 0.0 | 0.0 | 21.9 | 17.9 | 7.2 | 0.0 | 4.7 |
| Tuscaloosa | 0.0 | 10.5 | 0.0 | 0.0 | 0.2 | 20.6 | 18.9 | 4.0 | 3.1 | 2.5 |
| Vestavia Hills | 0.0 | 3.7 | 0.0 | 2.5 | 0.6 | 15.1 | 8.1 | 9.2 | 0.1 | 4.8 |
| ALASKA | X | X | X | X | X | X | X | X | X | X |
| Anchorage | 0.0 | 8.8 | 0.6 | 52.0 | 2.2 | 7.8 | 5.8 | 6.1 | 0.0 | 2.9 |
| Fairbanks | 0.0 | 23.5 | 0.6 | 0.0 | 0.0 | 19.9 | 1.0 | 0.0 | 0.0 | 1.8 |
| Juneau | 0.0 | 3.9 | 0.1 | 34.6 | 27.8 | 5.6 | 4.2 | 3.7 | 1.1 | 2.4 |
| ARIZONA | X | X | X | X | X | X | X | X | X | X |
| Apache Junction | 0.0 | 25.6 | 0.0 | 0.0 | 0.0 | 24.8 | 0.0 | 12.3 | 5.3 | 0.9 |
| Avondale | 0.5 | 12.1 | 0.0 | 0.0 | 1.2 | 15.9 | 21.0 | 8.8 | 4.3 | 3.7 |
| Buckeye | 0.0 | 6.2 | 0.0 | 0.0 | 0.0 | 25.2 | 20.5 | 2.3 | 0.0 | 1.2 |
| Bullhead City | 0.0 | 19.9 | 0.0 | 0.0 | 0.0 | 27.2 | 7.1 | 4.4 | 0.5 | 3.1 |
| Casa Grande | 0.0 | 8.6 | 0.0 | 0.0 | 0.0 | 17.8 | 16.1 | 6.5 | 4.3 | 2.2 |
| Chandler | 0.0 | 22.9 | 0.0 | 0.0 | 0.0 | 17.2 | 6.2 | 0.1 | 4.8 | 4.2 |
| El Mirage | 0.0 | 6.5 | 0.0 | 0.0 | 0.0 | 32.4 | 17.4 | 3.7 | 5.5 | 1.9 |
| Flagstaff | 0.0 | 23.6 | 0.0 | 0.0 | 0.0 | 12.3 | 15.3 | 0.0 | 10.8 | 2.5 |
| Florence | 0.0 | 10.7 | 0.0 | 0.0 | 0.0 | 12.1 | 23.5 | 7.0 | 1.3 | 1.1 |
| Gilbert | 0.0 | 14.1 | 0.0 | 0.0 | 0.0 | 11.9 | 16.5 | 21.1 | 0.5 | 3.7 |
| Glendale | 0.2 | 8.6 | 0.0 | 0.0 | 0.0 | 18.7 | 13.0 | 6.0 | 2.5 | 7.8 |
| Goodyear | 0.0 | 7.8 | 0.0 | 0.0 | 0.0 | 7.5 | 12.7 | 2.3 | 4.0 | 3.5 |
| Kingman | 0.0 | 22.9 | 0.0 | 0.0 | 0.0 | 21.3 | 9.8 | 9.9 | 0.0 | 2.1 |
| Lake Havasu City | 0.0 | 5.4 | 0.0 | 0.0 | 0.0 | 8.3 | 55.5 | 6.5 | 0.3 | 3.8 |
| Marana | 0.0 | 47.7 | 0.0 | 0.0 | 0.0 | 9.7 | 0.0 | 5.7 | 0.2 | 2.2 |
| Maricopa | 0.0 | 11.9 | 0.0 | 0.0 | 0.0 | 14.0 | 0.0 | 7.4 | 2.6 | 0.0 |
| Mesa | 0.6 | 9.9 | 0.0 | 0.0 | 0.0 | 24.4 | 16.1 | 8.4 | 3.1 | 7.0 |
| Oro Valley | 0.0 | 58.0 | 0.0 | 0.0 | 0.0 | 19.5 | 0.0 | 3.8 | 0.0 | 2.1 |
| Peoria | 0.0 | 8.3 | 0.0 | 0.2 | 0.0 | 9.2 | 27.4 | 12.0 | 0.7 | 2.8 |
| Phoenix | 0.4 | 8.1 | 0.2 | 0.7 | 0.0 | 15.4 | 17.6 | 13.3 | 4.4 | 6.7 |
| Prescott | 0.0 | 25.1 | 0.1 | 0.0 | 0.0 | 14.2 | 19.2 | 6.3 | 3.9 | 1.9 |
| Prescott Valley | 0.0 | 23.4 | 0.0 | 0.0 | 0.0 | 14.1 | 12.6 | 5.0 | 0.5 | 8.8 |
| Queen Creek | 0.0 | 24.3 | 0.0 | 0.0 | 0.0 | 3.0 | 16.8 | 4.8 | 0.0 | 1.4 |
| Sahuarita | 0.0 | 37.5 | 0.0 | 0.0 | 0.0 | 4.6 | 9.8 | 11.2 | 0.3 | 1.9 |
| San Luis | 0.0 | 4.4 | 0.0 | 0.0 | 0.0 | 5.3 | 17.0 | 3.8 | 0.8 | 4.7 |
| Scottsdale | 0.0 | 14.6 | 0.0 | 0.0 | 0.0 | 19.4 | 15.3 | 10.4 | 1.8 | 9.5 |
| Sierra Vista | 0.0 | 23.1 | 0.0 | 0.0 | 0.0 | 21.9 | 14.2 | 11.4 | 3.1 | 2.3 |
| Surprise | 0.0 | 9.7 | 0.0 | 0.0 | 0.0 | 22.2 | 31.7 | 7.2 | 0.3 | 1.1 |
| Tempe | 0.0 | 6.2 | 0.0 | 0.0 | 0.3 | 21.5 | 16.0 | 15.1 | 8.5 | 5.1 |
| Tucson | 0.0 | 8.5 | 0.0 | 0.0 | 0.0 | 19.3 | 6.3 | 7.5 | 16.3 | 3.8 |
| Yuma | 0.0 | 19.6 | 0.0 | 0.0 | 0.0 | 18.3 | 17.3 | 11.2 | 1.3 | 4.0 |
| ARKANSAS | X | X | X | X | X | X | X | X | X | X |
| Bella Vista | NA | NA | NA | NA | NA | NA | NA | NA | NA | NA |
| Benton | 0.0 | 14.8 | 0.0 | 0.0 | 1.7 | 18.0 | 16.1 | 6.4 | 2.1 | 1.4 |
| Bentonville | 0.0 | 34.8 | 0.0 | 0.0 | 0.0 | 9.0 | 12.5 | 3.3 | 0.0 | 1.2 |
| Conway | 0.0 | 2.9 | 0.0 | 0.0 | 0.0 | 17.7 | 23.9 | 2.6 | 1.1 | 12.8 |
| Fayetteville | 0.0 | 8.7 | 0.5 | 0.0 | 0.7 | 9.5 | 51.0 | 2.9 | 0.8 | 5.1 |
| Fort Smith | 0.0 | 23.7 | 0.3 | 0.0 | 0.1 | 12.0 | 25.3 | 3.0 | 1.8 | 1.6 |
| Hot Springs | 0.0 | 7.7 | 0.2 | 0.0 | 1.0 | 18.4 | 31.4 | 3.7 | 1.2 | 2.5 |

# Table D. Cities — City Government Finances, City Government Employment, and Climate

| | City government finances, 2007 (cont.) | | | | Climate[2] | | | | | | |
| | Debt outstanding | | | | Average daily temperature (degrees Fahrenheit) | | | | | | |
| | | | | | Mean | | Limits | | | | |
| City | Total (mil dol) | Per capita[1] (dollars) | Debt issued during year | City government employment, 2011 | January | July | January[3] | July[4] | Annual precipitation (inches) | Heating degree days | Cooling degree days |
| | 137 | 138 | 139 | 140 | 141 | 142 | 143 | 144 | 145 | 146 | 147 |
|---|---|---|---|---|---|---|---|---|---|---|---|
| United States............. | X | X | X | X | X | X | X | X | X | X | X |
| ALABAMA ............... | X | X | X | X | X | X | X | X | X | X | X |
| Alabaster ...................... | 72.3 | 2 520 | 15.2 | 232 | NA | NA | NA | NA | NA | NA | NA |
| Auburn ......................... | 216.2 | 3 978 | 15.6 | 536 | 44.7 | 79.9 | 34.2 | 89.7 | 52.63 | 2 507 | 1 932 |
| Bessemer ..................... | 43.0 | 1 501 | 1.5 | 533 | 42.9 | 81.0 | 30.8 | 93.6 | 59.38 | 2 766 | 1 943 |
| Birmingham .................. | 930.7 | 4 050 | 329.2 | 4 749 | 42.6 | 80.2 | 32.3 | 90.6 | 53.99 | 2 823 | 1 881 |
| Decatur........................ | 226.6 | 4 066 | 5.3 | 706 | 38.9 | 79.2 | 29.1 | 90.3 | 55.31 | 3 469 | 1 609 |
| Dothan......................... | 56.6 | 865 | 0.0 | 977 | 47.7 | 81.3 | 36.2 | 93.3 | 56.61 | 2 058 | 2 264 |
| Enterprise .................... | 20.8 | 854 | 1.3 | 559 | NA | NA | NA | NA | NA | NA | NA |
| Florence ...................... | 125.0 | 3 337 | 1.9 | 811 | 39.9 | 80.2 | 30.7 | 90.6 | 55.80 | 3 236 | 1 789 |
| Gadsden....................... | 86.2 | 2 335 | 0.0 | 710 | 40.3 | 79.8 | 29.9 | 90.5 | 56.10 | 3 220 | 1 716 |
| Homewood .................. | 50.1 | 2 095 | 0.0 | 353 | 42.6 | 80.2 | 32.3 | 90.6 | 53.99 | 2 823 | 1 881 |
| Hoover......................... | 118.3 | 1 693 | 0.0 | 669 | 42.9 | 81.0 | 30.8 | 93.6 | 59.38 | 2 766 | 1 943 |
| Huntsville ..................... | 684.0 | 3 992 | 68.1 | 2 631 | 39.8 | 79.5 | 30.7 | 89.4 | 57.51 | 3 262 | 1 671 |
| Madison ....................... | 103.9 | 2 714 | 0.8 | 421 | 46.6 | 81.8 | 35.5 | 92.7 | 54.77 | 2 194 | 2 252 |
| Mobile......................... | 536.0 | 2 800 | 66.0 | 2 964 | 50.1 | 81.5 | 39.5 | 91.2 | 66.29 | 1 681 | 2 539 |
| Montgomery ................. | 201.1 | 985 | 37.1 | 2 885 | 46.6 | 81.8 | 35.5 | 92.7 | 54.77 | 2 194 | 2 252 |
| Opelika ........................ | 93.8 | 3 631 | 1.9 | 362 | NA | NA | NA | NA | NA | NA | NA |
| Phenix City................... | 123.2 | 4 017 | 50.8 | 372 | 46.8 | 82.0 | 36.6 | 91.7 | 48.57 | 2 154 | 2 296 |
| Prattville...................... | 60.6 | 1 891 | 33.0 | 345 | NA | NA | NA | NA | NA | NA | NA |
| Tuscaloosa ................... | 193.3 | 2 179 | 41.5 | 1 279 | 42.9 | 80.4 | 32.5 | 90.8 | 54.99 | 2 787 | 1 893 |
| Vestavia Hills................ | 32.2 | 1 037 | 0.0 | 251 | NA | NA | NA | NA | NA | NA | NA |
| ALASKA .................... | X | X | X | X | X | X | X | X | X | X | X |
| Anchorage.................... | 1 660.0 | 5 936 | 127.7 | 9 848 | 15.8 | 58.4 | 9.3 | 65.3 | 16.08 | 10 470 | 3 |
| Fairbanks...................... | 11.4 | 331 | 0.0 | 193 | -9.7 | 62.4 | -19.0 | 73.0 | 10.34 | 13 980 | 74 |
| Juneau......................... | 182.5 | 5 946 | 50.1 | 1 924 | 25.7 | 56.8 | 20.7 | 64.3 | 58.33 | 8 574 | 0 |
| ARIZONA ................... | X | X | X | X | X | X | X | X | X | X | X |
| Apache Junction............ | 16.7 | 524 | 6.1 | NA | 52.7 | 89.5 | 40.0 | 104.3 | 12.29 | 1 542 | 3 443 |
| Avondale ..................... | 87.2 | 1 093 | 21.0 | 512 | 54.7 | 93.5 | 41.3 | 107.6 | 9.03 | 1 173 | 4 166 |
| Buckeye....................... | 29.9 | 998 | 15.0 | NA | NA | NA | NA | NA | NA | NA | NA |
| Bullhead City................ | 56.4 | 1 377 | 0.0 | NA | 54.4 | 95.6 | 43.3 | 111.7 | 5.84 | 1 164 | 4 508 |
| Casa Grande................. | 25.0 | 656 | 0.5 | NA | 52.4 | 90.4 | 37.3 | 105.1 | 9.22 | 1 572 | 3 554 |
| Chandler...................... | 446.1 | 1 810 | 134.9 | 1 628 | 54.3 | 91.3 | 41.5 | 105.7 | 9.23 | 1 271 | 3 798 |
| El Mirage ..................... | 20.4 | 771 | 12.5 | 163 | NA | NA | NA | NA | NA | NA | NA |
| Flagstaff....................... | 147.8 | 2 474 | 50.1 | 777 | 29.7 | 66.1 | 16.5 | 82.2 | 22.91 | 6 999 | 126 |
| Florence ...................... | 14.4 | 807 | 0.4 | NA | NA | NA | NA | NA | NA | NA | NA |
| Gilbert......................... | 450.4 | 2 170 | 146.2 | 1 112 | 54.3 | 91.3 | 41.5 | 105.7 | 9.23 | 1 271 | 3 798 |
| Glendale...................... | 864.6 | 3 415 | 177.8 | 1 846 | 52.5 | 90.6 | 39.2 | 104.2 | 7.78 | 1 535 | 3 488 |
| Goodyear..................... | 189.5 | 3 585 | 42.9 | 524 | NA | NA | NA | NA | NA | NA | NA |
| Kingman ...................... | 21.8 | 786 | 3.7 | NA | NA | NA | NA | NA | NA | NA | NA |
| Lake Havasu City......... | 197.8 | 3 494 | 37.0 | NA | 53.9 | 95.2 | 42.9 | 107.5 | 6.25 | 1 230 | 4 523 |
| Marana........................ | 64.5 | 2 025 | 29.0 | NA | NA | NA | NA | NA | NA | NA | NA |
| Maricopa...................... | 0.0 | 0 | 0.0 | NA | NA | NA | NA | NA | NA | NA | NA |
| Mesa........................... | 1 142.4 | 2 522 | 230.4 | 3 657 | 54.3 | 91.3 | 41.5 | 105.7 | 9.23 | 1 271 | 3 798 |
| Oro Valley .................... | 72.1 | 1 794 | 9.6 | NA | 50.6 | 86.3 | 34.6 | 100.7 | 12.40 | 1 831 | 2 810 |
| Peoria ......................... | 403.4 | 2 749 | 214.4 | 1 177 | 54.7 | 93.5 | 41.3 | 107.6 | 9.03 | 1 173 | 4 166 |
| Phoenix ....................... | 7 082.8 | 4 563 | 958.8 | 13 924 | 54.2 | 92.8 | 43.4 | 104.2 | 8.29 | 1 125 | 4 189 |
| Prescott ....................... | 54.6 | 1 292 | 8.9 | 533 | 37.1 | 73.4 | 23.3 | 88.3 | 19.19 | 4 849 | 742 |
| Prescott Valley ............. | 69.4 | 1 836 | 0.0 | 182 | NA | NA | NA | NA | NA | NA | NA |
| Queen Creek ................ | 81.2 | 3 440 | 81.2 | NA | NA | NA | NA | NA | NA | NA | NA |
| Sahuarita ..................... | 28.3 | 1 750 | 0.0 | NA | NA | NA | NA | NA | NA | NA | NA |
| San Luis ...................... | 73.3 | 3 079 | 5.5 | 191 | NA | NA | NA | NA | NA | NA | NA |
| Scottsdale.................... | 968.8 | 4 111 | 221.5 | 2 476 | 54.2 | 92.8 | 43.4 | 104.2 | 8.29 | 1 125 | 4 189 |
| Sierra Vista.................. | 25.5 | 593 | 1.6 | 392 | 47.7 | 79.1 | 33.7 | 92.6 | 14.02 | 2 369 | 1 739 |
| Surprise ...................... | 103.0 | 1 135 | 52.0 | 743 | 54.7 | 93.5 | 41.3 | 107.6 | 9.03 | 1 173 | 4 166 |
| Tempe ......................... | 604.1 | 3 470 | 168.5 | 1 766 | 54.1 | 89.9 | 40.1 | 103.6 | 9.36 | 1 390 | 3 655 |
| Tucson......................... | 1 136.0 | 2 162 | 303.3 | 4 941 | 54.0 | 88.5 | 41.9 | 100.5 | 12.00 | 1 333 | 3 501 |
| Yuma.......................... | 157.2 | 1 773 | 0.0 | 956 | 58.1 | 94.1 | 46.2 | 107.3 | 3.01 | 782 | 4 540 |
| ARKANSAS............... | X | X | X | X | X | X | X | X | X | X | X |
| Bella Vista ................... | NA | NA | NA | NA | NA | NA | NA | NA | NA | NA | NA |
| Benton......................... | 51.0 | 1 800 | 26.5 | 261 | NA | NA | NA | NA | NA | NA | NA |
| Bentonville................... | 34.8 | 1 030 | 5.0 | 426 | NA | NA | NA | NA | NA | NA | NA |
| Conway........................ | 179.3 | 3 145 | 33.1 | 472 | 38.3 | 82.1 | 28.1 | 92.4 | 48.67 | 3 320 | 1 961 |
| Fayetteville................... | 172.8 | 2 393 | 61.0 | 701 | 34.3 | 78.9 | 24.2 | 89.1 | 46.02 | 4 166 | 1 439 |
| Fort Smith.................... | 239.4 | 2 837 | 87.2 | 867 | 38.0 | 82.2 | 27.8 | 92.9 | 43.87 | 3 437 | 1 929 |
| Hot Springs ................. | 42.3 | 1 083 | 4.8 | 599 | 40.2 | 82.2 | 29.6 | 94.3 | 57.69 | 3 133 | 1 993 |

1. Based on the population estimated as of July 1 of the year shown.   2. Represents normal values based on the 30-year period, 1971–2000.   3. Average daily minimum.   4. Average daily maximum.

# Table D. Cities — **Land Area and Population**

| STATE Place code | City | Land area,[1] 2010 (sq km) | Population, 2012 | | | | Race alone or in combination, not of Hispanic origin (percent), 2010 | | | | | | Percent Hispanic or Latino[2], 2010 | Percent Foreign born 2007–2011 |
| | | | | | | | Race alone or in combination | | | | | | | |
| | | | Total persons | Rank | Per square kilometer | White | Black | American Indian, Alaska Native | Asian | Hawaiian Pacific Islander | | | | |
| | | 1 | 2 | 3 | 4 | 5 | 6 | 7 | 8 | 9 | | | 10 | 11 |
| | **ARKANSAS—Cont'd** | | | | | | | | | | | | | |
| 05 34750 | Jacksonville ................... | 72.8 | 28 657 | 1 267 | 393.6 | 57.7 | 34.4 | 1.4 | 2.9 | 0.2 | | | 6.7 | 3.9 |
| 05 35710 | Jonesboro..................... | 206.9 | 70 187 | 472 | 339.2 | 74.4 | 19.3 | 0.8 | 1.8 | 0.1 | | | 5.2 | 4.3 |
| 05 41000 | Little Rock ................... | 308.7 | 196 537 | 118 | 636.7 | 47.7 | 42.9 | 0.7 | 3.0 | 0.1 | | | 6.8 | 7.5 |
| 05 50450 | North Little Rock .......... | 133.4 | 64 633 | 529 | 484.5 | 53.0 | 40.6 | 1.0 | 1.3 | 0.1 | | | 5.7 | 4.2 |
| 05 53390 | Paragould .................... | 80.8 | 27 016 | 1 343 | 334.4 | 95.5 | 1.2 | 1.0 | 0.5 | 0.1 | | | 2.8 | 1.4 |
| 05 55310 | Pine Bluff.................... | 115.5 | 47 035 | 789 | 407.2 | 22.1 | 76.1 | 0.5 | 0.7 | 0.0 | | | 1.5 | 1.4 |
| 05 60410 | Rogers........................ | 98.3 | 58 895 | 596 | 599.1 | 63.4 | 1.7 | 1.5 | 2.9 | 0.4 | | | 31.5 | 19.3 |
| 05 61670 | Russellville ................. | 73.2 | 28 616 | 1 272 | 390.9 | 80.7 | 6.1 | 1.2 | 1.9 | 0.1 | | | 11.7 | 6.2 |
| 05 63800 | Sherwood .................... | 53.4 | 29 824 | 1 220 | 558.5 | 75.2 | 19.4 | 1.0 | 2.1 | 0.1 | | | 4.0 | 4.7 |
| 05 66080 | Springdale .................. | 108.3 | 73 123 | 452 | 675.2 | 54.2 | 2.1 | 1.6 | 2.3 | 5.9 | | | 35.4 | 24.6 |
| 05 68810 | Texarkana .................... | 107.9 | 30 049 | 1 211 | 278.5 | 62.8 | 33.9 | 1.1 | 0.8 | 0.1 | | | 2.8 | 1.7 |
| 05 74540 | West Memphis .............. | 73.7 | 25 686 | 1 406 | 348.5 | 34.3 | 63.9 | 0.4 | 0.5 | 0.0 | | | 1.6 | 0.5 |
| 06 00000 | **CALIFORNIA............** | 403 466.3 | 38 041 430 | X | 94.3 | 42.3 | 6.5 | 1.0 | 14.3 | 0.6 | | | 37.6 | 27.2 |
| 06 00296 | Adelanto ..................... | 145.1 | 31 239 | 1 163 | 215.3 | 18.8 | 21.1 | 1.0 | 2.2 | 0.8 | | | 58.3 | 20.7 |
| 06 00562 | Alameda ...................... | 27.5 | 75 641 | 435 | 2 750.6 | 50.0 | 7.6 | 1.2 | 34.6 | 1.0 | | | 11.0 | 28.1 |
| 06 00884 | Alhambra ..................... | 19.8 | 84 322 | 369 | 4 258.7 | 11.1 | 1.6 | 0.4 | 53.7 | 0.3 | | | 34.4 | 53.0 |
| 06 00947 | Aliso Viejo .................. | 19.4 | 49 493 | 740 | 2 551.2 | 65.6 | 2.5 | 0.6 | 17.7 | 0.6 | | | 17.1 | 23.6 |
| 06 02000 | Anaheim ...................... | 129.1 | 343 248 | 55 | 2 658.8 | 29.0 | 2.8 | 0.5 | 15.8 | 0.7 | | | 52.8 | 38.4 |
| 06 02252 | Antioch ....................... | 73.4 | 105 508 | 266 | 1 437.4 | 39.2 | 18.6 | 1.5 | 12.3 | 1.2 | | | 31.7 | 21.6 |
| 06 02364 | Apple Valley ................ | 189.6 | 70 700 | 469 | 372.9 | 58.0 | 9.8 | 1.5 | 3.6 | 0.6 | | | 29.2 | 8.1 |
| 06 02462 | Arcadia ....................... | 28.3 | 57 497 | 617 | 2 031.7 | 27.1 | 1.4 | 0.4 | 60.5 | 0.3 | | | 12.1 | 49.0 |
| 06 03064 | Atascadero .................. | 66.4 | 28 814 | 1 263 | 433.9 | 79.1 | 2.5 | 1.7 | 3.2 | 0.3 | | | 15.6 | 5.3 |
| 06 03162 | Atwater ...................... | 15.8 | 28 742 | 1 264 | 1 819.1 | 37.6 | 4.6 | 1.1 | 5.7 | 0.5 | | | 52.6 | 22.3 |
| 06 03386 | Azusa......................... | 25.0 | 47 407 | 779 | 1 896.3 | 20.5 | 3.2 | 0.5 | 9.3 | 0.3 | | | 67.6 | 31.2 |
| 06 03526 | Bakersfield................... | 368.2 | 358 597 | 52 | 973.9 | 39.6 | 8.5 | 1.4 | 6.7 | 0.2 | | | 45.5 | 18.8 |
| 06 03666 | Baldwin Park ............... | 17.2 | 76 419 | 431 | 4 443.0 | 4.6 | 1.0 | 0.2 | 14.2 | 0.2 | | | 80.1 | 46.7 |
| 06 03820 | Banning ...................... | 59.8 | 30 310 | 1 205 | 506.9 | 45.1 | 7.7 | 2.0 | 5.7 | 0.2 | | | 41.1 | 20.0 |
| 06 04758 | Beaumont .................... | 80.1 | 39 455 | 921 | 492.6 | 44.9 | 6.6 | 1.4 | 8.6 | 0.4 | | | 40.3 | 19.2 |
| 06 04870 | Bell .......................... | 6.5 | 35 820 | 1 020 | 5 510.8 | 5.2 | 0.7 | 0.3 | 0.9 | 0.0 | | | 93.1 | 46.1 |
| 06 04982 | Bellflower.................... | 15.8 | 77 356 | 420 | 4 895.9 | 21.0 | 14.4 | 0.7 | 12.3 | 1.1 | | | 52.3 | 29.3 |
| 06 04996 | Bell Gardens ............... | 6.4 | 42 757 | 853 | 6 680.8 | 2.8 | 0.5 | 0.3 | 0.6 | 0.1 | | | 95.7 | 45.0 |
| 06 05108 | Belmont ...................... | 12.0 | 26 491 | 1 373 | 2 207.6 | 65.5 | 2.2 | 0.7 | 23.1 | 1.4 | | | 11.5 | 26.5 |
| 06 05290 | Benicia....................... | 33.5 | 27 426 | 1 324 | 818.7 | 70.4 | 6.7 | 1.5 | 13.6 | 1.0 | | | 12.0 | 11.3 |
| 06 06000 | Berkeley...................... | 27.1 | 115 403 | 232 | 4 258.4 | 58.9 | 11.1 | 1.0 | 22.3 | 0.4 | | | 10.8 | 21.9 |
| 06 06308 | Beverly Hills ............... | 14.8 | 34 622 | 1 059 | 2 339.3 | 82.8 | 2.6 | 0.4 | 12.3 | 0.3 | | | 5.7 | 37.7 |
| 06 08100 | Brea.......................... | 31.3 | 40 330 | 900 | 1 288.5 | 54.8 | 1.7 | 0.7 | 19.7 | 0.5 | | | 25.0 | 21.9 |
| 06 08142 | Brentwood ................... | 38.3 | 53 673 | 673 | 1 401.4 | 57.9 | 7.4 | 1.2 | 10.0 | 0.9 | | | 26.8 | 14.6 |
| 06 08786 | Buena Park .................. | 27.3 | 82 155 | 384 | 3 009.3 | 29.5 | 4.0 | 0.6 | 27.8 | 0.8 | | | 39.3 | 36.6 |
| 06 08954 | Burbank ...................... | 44.9 | 104 391 | 271 | 2 325.0 | 61.0 | 3.0 | 0.6 | 13.4 | 0.3 | | | 24.5 | 33.3 |
| 06 09066 | Burlingame .................. | 11.4 | 29 660 | 1 228 | 2 601.8 | 63.6 | 1.6 | 0.4 | 22.8 | 0.7 | | | 13.8 | 27.4 |
| 06 09710 | Calexico...................... | 21.7 | 39 310 | 927 | 1 811.5 | 1.7 | 0.1 | 0.1 | 1.1 | 0.0 | | | 96.8 | 45.7 |
| 06 10046 | Camarillo .................... | 50.6 | 65 968 | 514 | 1 303.7 | 64.5 | 2.3 | 0.8 | 11.9 | 0.5 | | | 22.9 | 16.0 |
| 06 10345 | Campbell ..................... | 15.0 | 40 272 | 903 | 2 684.8 | 61.8 | 3.6 | 0.9 | 18.6 | 0.7 | | | 18.4 | 22.2 |
| 06 11194 | Carlsbad ..................... | 97.7 | 109 318 | 247 | 1 118.9 | 77.7 | 1.7 | 0.6 | 9.1 | 0.5 | | | 13.3 | 13.9 |
| 06 11530 | Carson........................ | 48.5 | 93 002 | 321 | 1 917.6 | 9.0 | 24.3 | 0.6 | 26.6 | 3.0 | | | 38.6 | 34.8 |
| 06 12048 | Cathedral City .............. | 55.7 | 52 655 | 684 | 945.3 | 33.5 | 2.6 | 0.8 | 5.3 | 0.2 | | | 58.8 | 34.1 |
| 06 12524 | Ceres......................... | 20.8 | 45 719 | 805 | 2 198.0 | 33.3 | 2.7 | 1.5 | 7.6 | 1.0 | | | 56.0 | 25.9 |
| 06 12552 | Cerritos ...................... | 22.6 | 49 629 | 736 | 2 196.0 | 18.4 | 7.2 | 0.4 | 63.7 | 0.7 | | | 12.0 | 46.7 |
| 06 13014 | Chico......................... | 85.3 | 87 714 | 348 | 1 028.3 | 76.9 | 2.9 | 2.2 | 5.5 | 0.5 | | | 15.4 | 8.4 |
| 06 13210 | Chino......................... | 76.8 | 80 164 | 401 | 1 043.8 | 29.1 | 6.3 | 0.7 | 11.1 | 0.3 | | | 53.8 | 23.9 |
| 06 13214 | Chino Hills................... | 115.7 | 76 457 | 430 | 660.8 | 35.6 | 4.9 | 0.5 | 31.8 | 0.4 | | | 29.1 | 27.7 |
| 06 13392 | Chula Vista................... | 128.5 | 252 422 | 76 | 1 964.4 | 22.5 | 4.9 | 0.6 | 15.6 | 0.8 | | | 58.2 | 31.4 |
| 06 13588 | Citrus Heights............... | 36.9 | 84 870 | 365 | 2 300.0 | 75.9 | 4.1 | 1.9 | 4.6 | 0.7 | | | 16.5 | 13.0 |
| 06 13756 | Claremont.................... | 34.6 | 35 457 | 1 033 | 1 024.8 | 62.0 | 5.3 | 0.8 | 15.1 | 0.4 | | | 19.8 | 17.5 |
| 06 14218 | Clovis......................... | 60.3 | 98 632 | 295 | 1 635.7 | 59.9 | 3.1 | 1.7 | 11.8 | 0.4 | | | 25.6 | 11.4 |
| 06 14260 | Coachella .................... | 75.0 | 42 734 | 854 | 569.8 | 2.5 | 0.4 | 0.2 | 0.5 | 0.0 | | | 96.4 | 41.6 |
| 06 14890 | Colton ........................ | 39.7 | 53 123 | 678 | 1 338.1 | 14.2 | 9.7 | 0.6 | 5.3 | 0.4 | | | 71.0 | 25.5 |
| 06 15044 | Compton...................... | 25.9 | 97 559 | 299 | 3 766.8 | 1.2 | 32.9 | 0.5 | 0.4 | 0.8 | | | 65.0 | 30.6 |
| 06 16000 | Concord ...................... | 79.1 | 124 711 | 210 | 1 576.6 | 53.7 | 4.1 | 1.1 | 13.2 | 1.0 | | | 30.6 | 26.5 |
| 06 16350 | Corona........................ | 100.6 | 158 391 | 153 | 1 574.5 | 40.1 | 6.2 | 0.7 | 11.1 | 0.6 | | | 43.6 | 24.9 |
| 06 16532 | Costa Mesa .................. | 40.5 | 111 918 | 238 | 2 763.4 | 54.1 | 1.7 | 0.7 | 9.2 | 0.8 | | | 35.8 | 26.4 |
| 06 16742 | Covina ........................ | 18.2 | 48 346 | 766 | 2 656.4 | 31.5 | 4.3 | 0.7 | 12.6 | 0.4 | | | 52.4 | 20.6 |
| 06 17568 | Culver City................... | 13.2 | 39 313 | 926 | 2 978.3 | 51.4 | 10.7 | 0.8 | 17.0 | 0.5 | | | 23.2 | 25.7 |
| 06 17610 | Cupertino .................... | 29.2 | 60 009 | 584 | 2 055.1 | 31.7 | 0.8 | 0.4 | 65.8 | 0.3 | | | 3.6 | 49.8 |
| 06 17750 | Cypress ...................... | 17.0 | 48 779 | 758 | 2 869.4 | 46.3 | 3.6 | 0.8 | 33.2 | 0.8 | | | 18.4 | 28.1 |
| 06 17918 | Daly City..................... | 19.9 | 103 690 | 274 | 5 210.6 | 15.8 | 4.0 | 0.4 | 57.2 | 1.2 | | | 23.7 | 52.2 |
| 06 17946 | Dana Point ................... | 16.8 | 34 048 | 1 073 | 2 026.7 | 78.4 | 1.1 | 1.0 | 4.2 | 0.3 | | | 17.0 | 13.1 |
| 06 17988 | Danville...................... | 46.7 | 43 088 | 846 | 922.7 | 81.2 | 1.2 | 0.5 | 12.9 | 0.4 | | | 6.8 | 12.2 |
| 06 18100 | Davis .......................... | 25.6 | 65 993 | 512 | 2 577.9 | 62.7 | 2.8 | 0.9 | 24.6 | 0.4 | | | 12.5 | 19.1 |

1. Dry land or land partially or temporarily covered by water.     2. May be of any race.

| City | Age of population (percent), 2010 | | | | | | | | | | | Population | | | |
|---|---|---|---|---|---|---|---|---|---|---|---|---|---|---|---|
| | | | | | | | | | | | | Census counts | | Percent change | |
| | Under 5 years | 5 to 17 years | 18 to 24 years | 25 to 34 years | 35 to 44 years | 45 to 54 years | 55 to 64 years | 65 to 74 years | 75 years and over | Median age | Percent female | 2000 | 2010 | 2000–2010 | 2010–2012 |
| | 12 | 13 | 14 | 15 | 16 | 17 | 18 | 19 | 20 | 21 | 22 | 23 | 24 | 25 | 26 |
| **ARKANSAS—Cont'd** | | | | | | | | | | | | | | | |
| Jacksonville | 8.9 | 18.0 | 13.1 | 15.5 | 11.9 | 12.3 | 9.9 | 5.9 | 4.4 | 30.8 | 50.7 | 29 916 | 28 364 | -5.2 | 1.0 |
| Jonesboro | 7.6 | 17.2 | 15.0 | 15.3 | 11.6 | 11.7 | 9.8 | 6.2 | 5.7 | 31.3 | 51.7 | 55 515 | 67 261 | 21.2 | 4.4 |
| Little Rock | 7.0 | 17.2 | 9.5 | 16.3 | 13.2 | 13.8 | 11.8 | 5.8 | 5.5 | 35.1 | 52.3 | 183 133 | 193 524 | 5.7 | 1.6 |
| North Little Rock | 7.4 | 16.8 | 9.5 | 15.2 | 12.5 | 13.8 | 11.8 | 6.4 | 6.6 | 35.9 | 52.7 | 60 433 | 62 304 | 3.1 | 3.7 |
| Paragould | 7.4 | 18.3 | 9.4 | 13.6 | 12.9 | 12.9 | 11.0 | 7.6 | 7.0 | 36.0 | 52.0 | 22 017 | 26 113 | 18.6 | 3.5 |
| Pine Bluff | 7.3 | 18.2 | 13.4 | 13.0 | 11.4 | 13.4 | 11.0 | 6.2 | 6.2 | 33.4 | 52.5 | 55 085 | 49 083 | -10.9 | -4.2 |
| Rogers | 9.1 | 21.5 | 9.1 | 15.3 | 14.7 | 12.6 | 8.4 | 4.7 | 4.6 | 31.7 | 51.0 | 38 829 | 55 966 | 44.1 | 5.2 |
| Russellville | 7.2 | 14.5 | 22.4 | 13.2 | 10.6 | 10.8 | 9.1 | 6.2 | 6.2 | 29.1 | 51.1 | 23 682 | 27 917 | 17.9 | 2.5 |
| Sherwood | 7.0 | 17.1 | 8.0 | 15.1 | 13.8 | 13.9 | 12.5 | 7.4 | 5.2 | 37.0 | 52.6 | 21 511 | 29 523 | 37.2 | 1.0 |
| Springdale | 10.3 | 22.3 | 9.8 | 16.5 | 13.5 | 11.1 | 7.6 | 4.7 | 4.1 | 29.6 | 50.3 | 45 798 | 70 382 | 52.4 | 3.9 |
| Texarkana | 7.5 | 16.3 | 9.8 | 14.6 | 12.5 | 13.3 | 12.2 | 7.3 | 6.3 | 36.2 | 51.2 | 26 448 | 29 911 | 13.1 | 0.5 |
| West Memphis | 8.7 | 21.1 | 9.8 | 12.9 | 11.8 | 13.5 | 10.8 | 6.4 | 5.0 | 32.9 | 53.8 | 27 666 | 26 245 | -5.1 | -2.1 |
| **CALIFORNIA** | 6.8 | 18.2 | 10.5 | 14.3 | 13.9 | 14.1 | 10.8 | 6.1 | 5.3 | 35.2 | 50.3 | 33 871 648 | 37 253 956 | 10.0 | 2.1 |
| Adelanto | 10.3 | 26.8 | 12.3 | 15.7 | 13.5 | 10.7 | 6.2 | 2.8 | 1.6 | 25.3 | 48.6 | 18 130 | 31 765 | 75.2 | -1.7 |
| Alameda | 5.7 | 15.1 | 7.4 | 12.9 | 15.6 | 16.1 | 13.8 | 6.9 | 6.6 | 40.7 | 52.2 | 72 259 | 73 812 | 2.1 | 2.5 |
| Alhambra | 5.2 | 13.7 | 9.5 | 15.1 | 14.9 | 15.1 | 12.2 | 6.9 | 7.4 | 39.3 | 52.7 | 85 804 | 83 089 | -3.2 | 1.5 |
| Aliso Viejo | 7.7 | 18.2 | 7.8 | 16.0 | 19.8 | 16.8 | 8.3 | 3.3 | 2.1 | 35.1 | 51.9 | 40 166 | 47 823 | 19.1 | 3.5 |
| Anaheim | 7.7 | 19.7 | 10.9 | 15.5 | 14.6 | 13.3 | 9.2 | 5.1 | 4.2 | 32.4 | 50.3 | 328 014 | 336 265 | 2.5 | 2.1 |
| Antioch | 7.1 | 21.0 | 10.3 | 13.0 | 13.8 | 15.3 | 10.6 | 5.1 | 3.7 | 33.8 | 51.3 | 90 532 | 102 365 | 13.1 | 3.1 |
| Apple Valley | 6.9 | 21.0 | 9.4 | 10.7 | 11.1 | 13.7 | 11.7 | 8.5 | 6.9 | 37.0 | 51.0 | 54 239 | 69 139 | 27.5 | 2.3 |
| Arcadia | 4.3 | 17.5 | 7.3 | 9.9 | 13.9 | 17.5 | 13.3 | 8.2 | 8.2 | 43.1 | 52.3 | 53 054 | 56 364 | 6.2 | 2.0 |
| Atascadero | 5.9 | 15.5 | 8.1 | 13.4 | 12.1 | 16.5 | 15.4 | 7.1 | 5.9 | 41.0 | 49.2 | 26 411 | 28 310 | 7.2 | 1.8 |
| Atwater | 8.9 | 23.1 | 10.5 | 14.2 | 12.4 | 11.8 | 8.7 | 5.9 | 4.5 | 30.0 | 51.1 | 23 113 | 28 168 | 21.9 | 2.0 |
| Azusa | 7.5 | 19.2 | 16.7 | 14.5 | 13.9 | 11.9 | 8.5 | 4.4 | 3.3 | 29.3 | 51.0 | 44 712 | 46 361 | 3.7 | 2.3 |
| Bakersfield | 9.0 | 22.5 | 10.8 | 14.7 | 13.2 | 12.4 | 8.9 | 4.7 | 3.7 | 30.0 | 51.0 | 247 057 | 347 574 | 40.6 | 3.2 |
| Baldwin Park | 7.8 | 22.1 | 11.7 | 14.6 | 14.1 | 12.5 | 9.2 | 4.6 | 3.4 | 30.5 | 50.4 | 75 837 | 75 390 | -0.6 | 1.4 |
| Banning | 6.2 | 16.7 | 9.2 | 11.1 | 9.3 | 10.9 | 10.7 | 11.6 | 14.3 | 42.3 | 51.7 | 23 562 | 29 603 | 25.6 | 2.4 |
| Beaumont | 9.1 | 21.0 | 7.9 | 16.1 | 13.9 | 11.1 | 10.4 | 6.8 | 3.8 | 32.5 | 51.2 | 11 384 | 36 877 | 223.9 | 7.0 |
| Bell | 8.8 | 23.2 | 11.6 | 15.9 | 14.5 | 11.5 | 7.7 | 3.9 | 2.9 | 28.9 | 49.6 | 36 664 | 35 477 | -3.2 | 1.0 |
| Bellflower | 7.6 | 20.8 | 11.1 | 14.9 | 14.3 | 13.2 | 9.5 | 4.9 | 3.7 | 31.9 | 51.4 | 72 878 | 76 616 | 5.1 | 1.0 |
| Bell Gardens | 9.3 | 24.7 | 12.4 | 15.9 | 14.3 | 11.2 | 6.9 | 3.2 | 2.0 | 27.3 | 50.1 | 44 054 | 42 072 | -4.5 | 1.6 |
| Belmont | 6.6 | 14.3 | 6.5 | 13.0 | 16.5 | 15.9 | 12.3 | 7.4 | 7.5 | 40.9 | 51.2 | 25 123 | 25 844 | 2.8 | 2.5 |
| Benicia | 4.8 | 18.6 | 7.1 | 9.7 | 12.9 | 18.1 | 16.4 | 7.4 | 5.0 | 42.9 | 51.9 | 26 865 | 26 997 | 0.5 | 1.6 |
| Berkeley | 3.7 | 8.6 | 26.9 | 15.7 | 11.1 | 10.9 | 11.3 | 6.6 | 5.1 | 31.0 | 51.1 | 102 743 | 112 583 | 9.6 | 2.5 |
| Beverly Hills | 3.8 | 15.7 | 7.4 | 12.3 | 12.7 | 15.6 | 13.4 | 9.0 | 10.1 | 43.6 | 54.3 | 33 784 | 34 109 | 1.0 | 1.5 |
| Brea | 5.5 | 17.6 | 9.3 | 12.5 | 14.7 | 16.0 | 11.9 | 6.8 | 5.8 | 38.7 | 51.2 | 35 410 | 39 282 | 10.9 | 2.7 |
| Brentwood | 7.0 | 24.2 | 7.5 | 10.5 | 16.7 | 14.4 | 8.4 | 6.5 | 4.9 | 35.6 | 51.5 | 23 302 | 51 624 | 120.9 | 4.0 |
| Buena Park | 6.5 | 18.8 | 10.7 | 14.0 | 14.2 | 15.0 | 10.3 | 5.6 | 5.0 | 35.1 | 50.7 | 78 282 | 80 529 | 2.9 | 2.0 |
| Burbank | 5.0 | 14.9 | 8.7 | 15.5 | 16.0 | 15.7 | 11.0 | 6.8 | 6.6 | 38.9 | 51.6 | 100 316 | 103 340 | 3.0 | 1.0 |
| Burlingame | 6.5 | 15.2 | 5.2 | 13.7 | 17.1 | 16.3 | 12.0 | 6.7 | 7.3 | 40.5 | 52.5 | 28 158 | 28 806 | 2.3 | 3.0 |
| Calexico | 7.7 | 23.4 | 11.0 | 11.4 | 12.8 | 12.6 | 9.5 | 6.0 | 5.5 | 31.8 | 52.7 | 27 109 | 38 572 | 42.3 | 1.9 |
| Camarillo | 5.7 | 17.5 | 7.9 | 11.6 | 12.8 | 15.1 | 12.3 | 8.0 | 9.2 | 40.8 | 51.6 | 57 077 | 65 221 | 14.2 | 1.1 |
| Campbell | 6.6 | 14.5 | 7.6 | 16.2 | 16.4 | 16.5 | 11.1 | 5.7 | 5.5 | 38.3 | 51.0 | 38 138 | 39 349 | 3.2 | 2.3 |
| Carlsbad | 6.0 | 18.1 | 6.4 | 11.6 | 15.0 | 16.3 | 12.5 | 6.8 | 7.3 | 40.4 | 51.1 | 78 247 | 105 459 | 34.6 | 3.7 |
| Carson | 5.7 | 18.2 | 10.9 | 12.0 | 13.2 | 14.3 | 11.9 | 8.1 | 5.6 | 37.6 | 52.1 | 89 730 | 91 714 | 2.2 | 1.4 |
| Cathedral City | 6.9 | 20.1 | 9.6 | 12.1 | 13.2 | 13.6 | 10.1 | 7.7 | 6.6 | 36.0 | 48.6 | 42 647 | 51 200 | 20.1 | 2.8 |
| Ceres | 8.7 | 23.5 | 11.2 | 14.2 | 13.4 | 12.8 | 8.5 | 4.5 | 3.3 | 29.4 | 50.5 | 34 609 | 45 190 | 31.2 | 1.2 |
| Cerritos | 3.9 | 16.5 | 8.3 | 10.0 | 12.7 | 15.3 | 15.6 | 11.3 | 6.4 | 44.0 | 51.9 | 51 488 | 49 041 | -4.8 | 1.2 |
| Chico | 5.7 | 13.8 | 23.9 | 15.2 | 10.7 | 10.5 | 9.5 | 4.9 | 5.7 | 28.6 | 50.4 | 59 954 | 86 186 | 43.8 | 1.8 |
| Chino | 6.7 | 18.6 | 10.9 | 16.6 | 15.6 | 14.5 | 9.8 | 4.4 | 2.9 | 33.2 | 48.6 | 67 168 | 77 983 | 16.1 | 2.8 |
| Chino Hills | 5.8 | 21.3 | 9.6 | 11.1 | 15.9 | 18.0 | 11.2 | 4.4 | 2.7 | 36.6 | 50.6 | 66 787 | 74 799 | 12.0 | 2.2 |
| Chula Vista | 7.2 | 20.8 | 10.1 | 13.7 | 15.2 | 13.8 | 9.2 | 5.3 | 4.7 | 33.7 | 51.6 | 173 556 | 243 916 | 40.5 | 3.5 |
| Citrus Heights | 6.7 | 16.4 | 10.2 | 15.1 | 12.5 | 14.2 | 11.6 | 6.8 | 6.5 | 36.2 | 51.5 | 85 071 | 83 301 | -2.1 | 1.9 |
| Claremont | 3.7 | 14.8 | 19.4 | 8.8 | 11.1 | 13.4 | 12.3 | 7.7 | 8.8 | 38.6 | 53.1 | 33 998 | 34 926 | 2.7 | 1.5 |
| Clovis | 7.2 | 20.9 | 10.0 | 13.1 | 13.6 | 14.0 | 10.7 | 5.6 | 5.0 | 34.1 | 51.8 | 68 468 | 95 631 | 39.7 | 3.1 |
| Coachella | 11.0 | 27.8 | 12.0 | 16.4 | 12.8 | 10.1 | 5.4 | 2.8 | 1.7 | 24.5 | 50.2 | 22 724 | 40 704 | 79.1 | 5.0 |
| Colton | 9.4 | 22.6 | 12.2 | 15.8 | 12.9 | 11.9 | 8.2 | 3.9 | 3.1 | 28.4 | 51.0 | 47 662 | 52 155 | 9.4 | 1.9 |
| Compton | 9.2 | 23.9 | 12.3 | 14.4 | 13.1 | 12.0 | 7.5 | 4.2 | 3.3 | 28.0 | 51.3 | 93 493 | 96 455 | 3.2 | 1.1 |
| Concord | 6.8 | 16.1 | 9.0 | 15.3 | 14.0 | 15.2 | 11.7 | 6.3 | 5.5 | 37.0 | 50.3 | 121 780 | 122 110 | 0.2 | 2.1 |
| Corona | 7.4 | 22.5 | 10.2 | 13.2 | 15.9 | 14.8 | 8.7 | 4.3 | 3.0 | 32.5 | 50.8 | 124 966 | 152 374 | 21.9 | 3.9 |
| Costa Mesa | 6.5 | 15.0 | 11.7 | 19.2 | 15.6 | 13.6 | 9.2 | 4.8 | 4.4 | 33.6 | 49.1 | 108 724 | 109 960 | 1.1 | 1.8 |
| Covina | 6.3 | 18.6 | 10.6 | 13.5 | 14.0 | 14.9 | 10.6 | 5.9 | 5.7 | 35.7 | 51.7 | 46 837 | 47 796 | 2.0 | 1.2 |
| Culver City | 5.3 | 13.5 | 7.0 | 15.2 | 16.0 | 15.5 | 12.6 | 7.3 | 7.7 | 40.5 | 52.9 | 38 816 | 38 883 | 0.2 | 1.1 |
| Cupertino | 5.4 | 22.1 | 5.6 | 8.6 | 18.2 | 17.3 | 10.2 | 6.2 | 6.3 | 39.9 | 50.7 | 50 546 | 58 565 | 15.3 | 2.5 |
| Cypress | 5.0 | 18.8 | 9.8 | 10.3 | 14.2 | 17.5 | 11.6 | 7.3 | 5.6 | 39.9 | 51.5 | 46 229 | 47 802 | 3.4 | 2.0 |
| Daly City | 5.4 | 13.9 | 10.4 | 15.7 | 13.6 | 14.6 | 12.9 | 7.2 | 6.3 | 38.3 | 50.6 | 103 621 | 101 047 | -2.4 | 2.6 |
| Dana Point | 4.7 | 13.2 | 7.6 | 12.1 | 12.7 | 16.9 | 15.9 | 9.0 | 8.0 | 44.8 | 50.5 | 35 110 | 33 343 | -5.0 | 2.1 |
| Danville | 4.9 | 21.8 | 5.0 | 5.7 | 13.4 | 19.8 | 15.0 | 8.1 | 6.3 | 44.5 | 51.7 | 41 715 | 41 988 | 0.8 | 2.6 |
| Davis | 3.7 | 12.7 | 33.2 | 13.0 | 9.6 | 10.4 | 9.0 | 4.5 | 4.0 | 25.2 | 52.5 | 60 308 | 65 622 | 8.8 | 0.6 |

| City | Households, 2010 | | | | Persons in group quarters, 2010 | | | | Serious crimes known to police,[2] 2011 | | | | Educational attainment, 2007–2011 | | |
|---|---|---|---|---|---|---|---|---|---|---|---|---|---|---|---|
| | | | Percent | | | Institutional | | | Total | | Rate[3] | | | Attainment[4] (percent) | |
| | Number | Persons per household | Female family householder[1] | One-person | Total | Total | Persons in nursing facilities | Non-institutional | Number | Rate[3] | Violent | Property | Population age 25 and older | High school graduate or less | Bachelor's degree or more |
| | 27 | 28 | 29 | 30 | 31 | 32 | 33 | 34 | 35 | 36 | 37 | 38 | 39 | 40 | 41 |
| ARKANSAS—Cont'd | | | | | | | | | | | | | | | |
| Jacksonville | 10 936 | 2.52 | 18.5 | 27.1 | 847 | 100 | 98 | 747 | 1 826 | 6 389 | 822 | 5 567 | 17 300 | 49.8 | 17.0 |
| Jonesboro | 26 111 | 2.45 | 15.3 | 28.3 | 3 412 | 1 238 | 800 | 2 174 | 3 707 | 5 470 | 496 | 4 974 | 39 575 | 43.8 | 28.8 |
| Little Rock | 82 018 | 2.30 | 17.5 | 34.8 | 4 543 | 2 781 | 1 074 | 1 762 | 18 458 | 9 466 | 1 495 | 7 971 | 126 103 | 33.0 | 38.2 |
| North Little Rock | 26 530 | 2.32 | 19.4 | 34.2 | 870 | 638 | 583 | 232 | 6 144 | 9 787 | 975 | 8 812 | 41 115 | 43.8 | 25.3 |
| Paragould | 10 288 | 2.48 | 14.6 | 26.3 | 550 | 391 | 226 | 159 | 1 962 | 7 457 | 456 | 7 001 | 16 562 | 60.5 | 12.5 |
| Pine Bluff | 18 071 | 2.49 | 27.7 | 31.3 | 3 999 | 2 512 | 429 | 1 487 | 4 689 | 9 482 | 1 381 | 8 100 | 30 132 | 52.9 | 18.6 |
| Rogers | 19 675 | 2.82 | 11.8 | 23.8 | 450 | 312 | 312 | 138 | 2 517 | 4 464 | 385 | 4 079 | 32 179 | 48.8 | 27.1 |
| Russellville | 10 318 | 2.39 | 14.4 | 30.1 | 3 251 | 448 | 277 | 2 803 | 1 204 | 4 280 | 359 | 3 921 | 16 025 | 48.2 | 23.9 |
| Sherwood | 12 207 | 2.41 | 13.9 | 27.0 | 85 | 85 | 85 | 0 | 1 131 | 3 802 | 501 | 3 301 | 19 841 | 38.9 | 28.5 |
| Springdale | 22 805 | 3.02 | 13.3 | 21.5 | 830 | 678 | 577 | 152 | 3 035 | 4 316 | 454 | 3 862 | 39 180 | 60.2 | 17.3 |
| Texarkana | 12 032 | 2.36 | 19.9 | 29.8 | 1 468 | 1 251 | 300 | 217 | 2 518 | 8 353 | 813 | 7 540 | 19 677 | 52.9 | 15.0 |
| West Memphis | 9 835 | 2.61 | 29.2 | 28.1 | 608 | 505 | 206 | 103 | 3 255 | 12 309 | 2 329 | 9 980 | 15 702 | 62.4 | 9.6 |
| CALIFORNIA | 12 577 498 | 2.90 | 13.3 | 23.3 | 819 816 | 397 142 | 111 884 | 422 674 | 1 128 845 | 2 995 | 411 | 2 584 | 23 797 844 | 40.3 | 30.2 |
| Adelanto | 7 809 | 3.84 | 23.8 | 11.7 | 1 753 | 1 723 | 0 | 30 | 1 049 | 3 264 | 510 | 2 754 | 14 990 | 62.3 | 6.9 |
| Alameda | 30 123 | 2.40 | 12.0 | 31.0 | 1 496 | 639 | 639 | 857 | 2 105 | 2 819 | 277 | 2 542 | 52 329 | 25.3 | 46.6 |
| Alhambra | 29 217 | 2.82 | 16.5 | 22.2 | 614 | 482 | 455 | 132 | 2 043 | 2 430 | 181 | 2 249 | 60 581 | 42.5 | 30.7 |
| Aliso Viejo | 18 204 | 2.60 | 10.8 | 24.3 | 469 | 19 | 19 | 450 | 467 | 965 | 62 | 903 | 31 401 | 17.4 | 53.9 |
| Anaheim | 98 294 | 3.38 | 14.8 | 17.8 | 3 557 | 1 537 | 1 376 | 2 020 | 9 774 | 2 873 | 377 | 2 496 | 206 814 | 50.7 | 23.4 |
| Antioch | 32 252 | 3.15 | 17.7 | 16.4 | 664 | 260 | 229 | 404 | 4 691 | 4 529 | 790 | 3 739 | 60 276 | 42.7 | 19.5 |
| Apple Valley | 23 598 | 2.91 | 15.0 | 20.1 | 461 | 300 | 104 | 161 | 2 109 | 3 015 | 224 | 2 791 | 42 436 | 44.5 | 16.6 |
| Arcadia | 19 592 | 2.83 | 12.4 | 19.7 | 862 | 223 | 220 | 639 | 1 767 | 3 099 | 119 | 2 979 | 39 497 | 23.0 | 53.3 |
| Atascadero | 10 737 | 2.51 | 11.0 | 23.3 | 1 324 | 1 100 | 91 | 224 | 769 | 2 685 | 234 | 2 451 | 19 533 | 29.4 | 30.0 |
| Atwater | 8 838 | 3.18 | 17.6 | 18.3 | 102 | 71 | 63 | 31 | 1 359 | 4 769 | 453 | 4 316 | 16 133 | 52.7 | 12.7 |
| Azusa | 12 716 | 3.43 | 17.9 | 17.6 | 2 802 | 111 | 97 | 2 691 | 1 287 | 2 744 | 510 | 2 234 | 25 158 | 51.8 | 20.2 |
| Bakersfield | 111 132 | 3.10 | 16.2 | 19.6 | 3 395 | 1 301 | 749 | 2 094 | 16 706 | 4 752 | 531 | 4 221 | 195 975 | 47.4 | 19.8 |
| Baldwin Park | 17 189 | 4.36 | 19.5 | 8.6 | 406 | 318 | 276 | 88 | 1 843 | 2 416 | 317 | 2 099 | 43 939 | 68.9 | 12.2 |
| Banning | 10 838 | 2.61 | 13.7 | 28.5 | 1 365 | 1 111 | 177 | 254 | 869 | 2 901 | 531 | 2 371 | 21 464 | 56.2 | 17.1 |
| Beaumont | 11 801 | 3.08 | 12.3 | 16.2 | 474 | 211 | 137 | 263 | 1 069 | 2 865 | 239 | 2 627 | 22 135 | 40.3 | 26.2 |
| Bell | 8 870 | 3.93 | 21.2 | 10.9 | 579 | 89 | 89 | 490 | 1 092 | 3 042 | 811 | 2 232 | 19 809 | 79.9 | 5.4 |
| Bellflower | 23 651 | 3.21 | 20.3 | 19.5 | 739 | 340 | 329 | 399 | 2 118 | 2 732 | 369 | 2 363 | 45 674 | 52.1 | 17.4 |
| Bell Gardens | 9 655 | 4.31 | 22.2 | 7.8 | 424 | 299 | 299 | 125 | 964 | 2 265 | 399 | 1 865 | 22 538 | 80.9 | 4.9 |
| Belmont | 10 575 | 2.39 | 7.8 | 27.5 | 514 | 120 | 120 | 394 | 470 | 1 798 | 61 | 1 737 | 18 336 | 16.6 | 56.1 |
| Benicia | 10 686 | 2.52 | 11.9 | 24.6 | 26 | 0 | 0 | 26 | 449 | 1 644 | 146 | 1 497 | 18 845 | 21.1 | 40.1 |
| Berkeley | 46 029 | 2.17 | 8.4 | 36.7 | 12 849 | 419 | 237 | 12 430 | 5 546 | 4 869 | 423 | 4 446 | 69 074 | 13.5 | 69.0 |
| Beverly Hills | 14 869 | 2.29 | 9.1 | 36.3 | 121 | 0 | 0 | 121 | 1 032 | 2 990 | 168 | 2 822 | 24 350 | 19.8 | 58.5 |
| Brea | 14 266 | 2.75 | 11.3 | 21.5 | 69 | 0 | 0 | 69 | 1 477 | 3 716 | 146 | 3 570 | 26 555 | 26.3 | 41.9 |
| Brentwood | 16 494 | 3.11 | 11.1 | 15.9 | 146 | 5 | 5 | 141 | 1 198 | 2 300 | 227 | 2 073 | 29 469 | 31.8 | 28.0 |
| Buena Park | 23 686 | 3.37 | 16.0 | 14.3 | 814 | 261 | 242 | 553 | 2 109 | 2 588 | 282 | 2 306 | 50 313 | 42.5 | 27.1 |
| Burbank | 41 940 | 2.45 | 11.9 | 30.6 | 573 | 282 | 268 | 291 | 2 746 | 2 626 | 183 | 2 444 | 74 078 | 31.1 | 36.2 |
| Burlingame | 12 361 | 2.29 | 8.4 | 34.6 | 449 | 294 | 294 | 155 | 690 | 2 367 | 175 | 2 192 | 20 797 | 19.1 | 54.1 |
| Calexico | 10 116 | 3.80 | 22.9 | 11.9 | 100 | 0 | 0 | 100 | 1 506 | 3 859 | 287 | 3 572 | 21 155 | 61.5 | 13.5 |
| Camarillo | 24 504 | 2.64 | 9.7 | 24.4 | 496 | 341 | 227 | 155 | 961 | 1 457 | 120 | 1 337 | 43 996 | 25.7 | 37.8 |
| Campbell | 16 163 | 2.42 | 10.8 | 29.7 | 201 | 122 | 114 | 79 | 1 474 | 3 702 | 241 | 3 461 | 27 598 | 23.3 | 45.9 |
| Carlsbad | 41 345 | 2.53 | 9.2 | 23.9 | 915 | 456 | 451 | 459 | 2 180 | 2 046 | 197 | 1 849 | 71 034 | 17.7 | 51.3 |
| Carson | 25 432 | 3.56 | 18.8 | 14.8 | 1 303 | 133 | 49 | 1 170 | 2 936 | 3 164 | 478 | 2 686 | 59 887 | 42.7 | 25.4 |
| Cathedral City | 17 047 | 2.99 | 13.4 | 25.2 | 295 | 32 | 32 | 263 | 2 009 | 3 878 | 436 | 3 442 | 32 481 | 55.2 | 15.6 |
| Ceres | 12 692 | 3.55 | 17.4 | 12.5 | 353 | 60 | 38 | 293 | 1 856 | 4 039 | 357 | 3 682 | 26 119 | 62.2 | 9.2 |
| Cerritos | 15 526 | 3.15 | 12.1 | 11.6 | 104 | 18 | 18 | 86 | 1 845 | 3 718 | 169 | 3 549 | 34 203 | 24.9 | 48.2 |
| Chico | 34 805 | 2.38 | 11.4 | 29.9 | 3 178 | 587 | 577 | 2 591 | 2 360 | 2 706 | 281 | 2 425 | 47 901 | 26.0 | 34.4 |
| Chino | 20 772 | 3.41 | 14.6 | 13.7 | 7 064 | 6 900 | 3 | 164 | 2 319 | 2 939 | 313 | 2 626 | 49 528 | 50.4 | 19.0 |
| Chino Hills | 22 941 | 3.25 | 10.4 | 11.8 | 155 | 147 | 0 | 8 | 1 046 | 1 382 | 90 | 1 292 | 46 646 | 25.6 | 42.9 |
| Chula Vista | 75 515 | 3.21 | 16.6 | 16.7 | 1 736 | 1 080 | 538 | 656 | 5 677 | 2 300 | 271 | 2 029 | 145 740 | 38.8 | 26.7 |
| Citrus Heights | 32 686 | 2.53 | 14.3 | 27.1 | 486 | 182 | 131 | 304 | 3 667 | 4 351 | 396 | 3 955 | 56 377 | 38.2 | 18.5 |
| Claremont | 11 608 | 2.57 | 10.5 | 25.5 | 5 124 | 198 | 192 | 4 926 | 882 | 2 496 | 91 | 2 405 | 21 498 | 18.9 | 56.0 |
| Clovis | 33 419 | 2.85 | 13.6 | 21.0 | 388 | 258 | 221 | 130 | 4 144 | 4 283 | 218 | 4 065 | 57 882 | 32.4 | 30.0 |
| Coachella | 8 998 | 4.52 | 21.4 | 5.2 | 58 | 0 | 0 | 58 | 1 973 | 4 791 | 670 | 4 121 | 18 992 | 79.3 | 4.8 |
| Colton | 14 971 | 3.46 | 21.6 | 16.4 | 330 | 245 | 243 | 85 | 1 747 | 3 311 | 358 | 2 953 | 28 918 | 57.0 | 13.2 |
| Compton | 23 062 | 4.15 | 27.6 | 12.9 | 755 | 112 | 84 | 643 | 3 932 | 4 029 | 1 093 | 2 936 | 51 218 | 68.3 | 7.0 |
| Concord | 44 278 | 2.73 | 12.7 | 23.5 | 1 047 | 535 | 469 | 512 | 4 233 | 3 427 | 348 | 3 079 | 82 797 | 36.8 | 31.0 |
| Corona | 44 950 | 3.38 | 13.3 | 14.4 | 511 | 282 | 268 | 229 | 3 554 | 2 305 | 130 | 2 176 | 90 558 | 40.6 | 24.7 |
| Costa Mesa | 39 946 | 2.68 | 10.9 | 27.4 | 2 970 | 738 | 581 | 2 232 | 3 765 | 3 384 | 208 | 3 177 | 74 122 | 32.3 | 34.3 |
| Covina | 15 855 | 2.99 | 17.8 | 19.9 | 435 | 367 | 341 | 68 | 1 861 | 3 848 | 294 | 3 555 | 30 294 | 40.0 | 23.1 |
| Culver City | 16 779 | 2.30 | 11.2 | 33.7 | 311 | 227 | 227 | 84 | 1 815 | 4 614 | 371 | 4 243 | 28 866 | 20.9 | 50.3 |
| Cupertino | 20 181 | 2.87 | 6.9 | 17.6 | 337 | 276 | 258 | 61 | 757 | 1 283 | 78 | 1 205 | 39 061 | 10.0 | 75.5 |
| Cypress | 15 654 | 3.02 | 14.1 | 15.3 | 502 | 0 | 0 | 502 | 917 | 1 896 | 124 | 1 772 | 31 500 | 27.6 | 37.4 |
| Daly City | 31 090 | 3.23 | 15.0 | 18.8 | 681 | 408 | 397 | 273 | 2 064 | 2 017 | 180 | 1 838 | 70 647 | 35.9 | 33.6 |
| Dana Point | 14 182 | 2.33 | 8.7 | 28.3 | 241 | 81 | 77 | 160 | 680 | 2 015 | 157 | 1 858 | 24 678 | 21.9 | 46.3 |
| Danville | 15 420 | 2.71 | 7.4 | 18.2 | 243 | 187 | 183 | 56 | 519 | 1 220 | 61 | 1 159 | 28 140 | 11.0 | 62.8 |
| Davis | 24 873 | 2.55 | 7.6 | 23.9 | 2 100 | 277 | 203 | 1 823 | 1 603 | 2 414 | 172 | 2 243 | 32 486 | 11.7 | 69.3 |

1. No spouse present.   2. Data for serious crimes have not been adjusted for underreporting. This may affect comparability between geographic areas and over time.   3. Per 100,000 population estimated by the FBI.   4. Persons 25 years old and over.

## Table D. Cities — Income, Poverty, and Housing

| City | Money income, 2007–2011 | | | | | Housing units, 2010 | | | Occupied Housing units 2007–2011 | | | | |
|---|---|---|---|---|---|---|---|---|---|---|---|---|---|
| | Households | | | | Families with income below poverty (percent) | | | | Owner-occupied | | | Median owner costs as a percent of income | |
| | Per capita income[1] (dollars) | Median income | Percent with income of $200,000 or more | Percent with income of less than $25,000 | | Total | Percent change, 2000–2010 | Vacant units for sale or rent[2] | Total | Percent | Median value[3] (dollars) | With a mortgage[4] | Without a mortgage[5] |
| | 42 | 43 | 44 | 45 | 46 | 47 | 48 | 49 | 50 | 51 | 52 | 53 | 54 |
| **ARKANSAS—Cont'd** | | | | | | | | | | | | | |
| Jacksonville | 21 157 | 41 190 | 1.1 | 27.4 | 15.5 | 12 412 | 4.8 | 1 476 | 10 975 | 52.0 | 111 100 | 22.4 | 10.8 |
| Jonesboro | 23 442 | 38 415 | 3.3 | 34.8 | 19.0 | 28 321 | 16.5 | 2 210 | 25 457 | 54.6 | 130 900 | 19.5 | 10.0 |
| Little Rock | 29 575 | 44 392 | 4.8 | 28.3 | 13.5 | 91 288 | 7.5 | 9 270 | 79 284 | 57.2 | 149 300 | 22.1 | 11.8 |
| North Little Rock | 24 171 | 39 228 | 2.3 | 34.1 | 16.9 | 29 437 | 6.8 | 2 907 | 25 804 | 52.7 | 118 100 | 19.9 | 11.7 |
| Paragould | 18 744 | 37 717 | 0.5 | 36.2 | 13.5 | 11 070 | 12.9 | 782 | 10 150 | 57.2 | 95 400 | 20.5 | 10.6 |
| Pine Bluff | 16 656 | 31 600 | 1.0 | 41.3 | 23.2 | 20 923 | -6.2 | 2 852 | 17 587 | 55.5 | 68 600 | 21.3 | 13.5 |
| Rogers | 24 832 | 50 205 | 4.2 | 22.1 | 10.7 | 22 022 | 47.9 | 2 347 | 19 382 | 60.1 | 157 800 | 22.7 | 10.9 |
| Russellville | 19 916 | 37 107 | 1.8 | 35.0 | 18.9 | 11 124 | 8.9 | 806 | 10 151 | 53.3 | 112 600 | 20.3 | 10.0 |
| Sherwood | 27 739 | 55 859 | 2.0 | 19.8 | 8.3 | 12 924 | 40.5 | 717 | 11 847 | 68.6 | 142 000 | 21.5 | 10.0 |
| Springdale | 18 645 | 41 753 | 1.9 | 26.7 | 17.4 | 25 614 | 50.4 | 2 809 | 22 678 | 54.9 | 143 500 | 22.3 | 10.9 |
| Texarkana | 21 396 | 40 351 | 1.3 | 34.9 | 16.4 | 13 375 | 13.5 | 1 343 | 11 596 | 59.3 | 96 600 | 20.5 | 11.0 |
| West Memphis | 16 748 | 29 167 | 0.9 | 43.1 | 32.0 | 10 966 | -0.5 | 1 131 | 10 162 | 49.8 | 89 500 | 24.3 | 13.9 |
| **CALIFORNIA** | 29 634 | 61 632 | 6.9 | 19.8 | 10.8 | 13 680 081 | 12.0 | 1 102 583 | 12 433 172 | 56.7 | 421 600 | 30.9 | 11.3 |
| Adelanto | 11 771 | 42 208 | 0.4 | 31.7 | 25.6 | 9 086 | 62.6 | 1 277 | 7 060 | 62.4 | 118 500 | 34.6 | 12.7 |
| Alameda | 39 160 | 75 832 | 9.1 | 15.5 | 7.6 | 32 351 | 2.2 | 2 228 | 29 087 | 49.2 | 642 200 | 30.0 | 10.3 |
| Alhambra | 24 849 | 52 717 | 3.3 | 21.5 | 11.1 | 30 915 | 2.8 | 1 698 | 28 824 | 41.5 | 505 600 | 32.3 | 10.9 |
| Aliso Viejo | 44 646 | 99 095 | 11.1 | 5.8 | 2.2 | 18 867 | 13.6 | 663 | 18 077 | 63.5 | 512 300 | 29.9 | 10.0 |
| Anaheim | 23 109 | 59 330 | 4.1 | 17.6 | 11.4 | 104 237 | 4.7 | 5 943 | 98 952 | 49.1 | 457 800 | 31.6 | 10.2 |
| Antioch | 25 264 | 66 479 | 5.0 | 16.2 | 10.3 | 34 849 | 15.5 | 2 597 | 30 968 | 65.5 | 302 700 | 32.4 | 10.3 |
| Apple Valley | 23 229 | 50 664 | 2.7 | 25.6 | 14.2 | 26 117 | 29.5 | 2 519 | 22 851 | 71.4 | 230 300 | 29.4 | 13.7 |
| Arcadia | 38 518 | 77 221 | 12.2 | 16.0 | 8.3 | 20 686 | 3.5 | 1 094 | 19 378 | 61.6 | 793 100 | 31.3 | 10.9 |
| Atascadero | 32 153 | 68 502 | 3.3 | 15.0 | 6.5 | 11 505 | 16.8 | 768 | 11 134 | 66.6 | 427 900 | 30.6 | 10.0 |
| Atwater | 18 562 | 40 752 | 2.9 | 26.2 | 21.9 | 9 771 | 20.8 | 933 | 8 431 | 51.5 | 162 800 | 29.4 | 11.1 |
| Azusa | 19 119 | 53 826 | 2.3 | 22.2 | 14.0 | 13 386 | 3.6 | 670 | 12 539 | 52.4 | 359 300 | 33.2 | 12.6 |
| Bakersfield | 23 141 | 54 656 | 3.5 | 22.2 | 14.7 | 120 725 | 36.9 | 9 593 | 107 096 | 59.0 | 218 200 | 28.6 | 11.5 |
| Baldwin Park | 15 534 | 52 094 | 1.9 | 20.1 | 14.3 | 17 736 | 1.8 | 547 | 17 374 | 62.5 | 322 500 | 35.8 | 10.0 |
| Banning | 21 150 | 37 373 | 1.4 | 29.8 | 14.0 | 12 144 | 24.7 | 1 306 | 12 319 | 70.3 | 197 200 | 32.7 | 14.1 |
| Beaumont | 26 458 | 66 132 | 3.4 | 16.8 | 7.5 | 12 908 | 203.1 | 1 107 | 12 039 | 76.7 | 251 500 | 33.2 | 12.3 |
| Bell | 12 436 | 37 121 | 0.1 | 30.4 | 22.7 | 9 217 | 0.0 | 347 | 8 891 | 27.3 | 314 500 | 35.4 | 10.3 |
| Bellflower | 20 591 | 50 244 | 1.5 | 22.8 | 10.7 | 24 897 | 2.9 | 1 246 | 24 132 | 38.7 | 386 200 | 32.5 | 11.1 |
| Bell Gardens | 12 026 | 38 971 | 0.4 | 29.3 | 23.6 | 9 986 | 2.0 | 331 | 9 940 | 25.9 | 331 000 | 36.2 | 12.6 |
| Belmont | 51 115 | 100 417 | 18.7 | 8.0 | 2.3 | 11 028 | 3.8 | 453 | 10 291 | 58.1 | 896 300 | 30.0 | 10.0 |
| Benicia | 41 854 | 90 338 | 10.2 | 10.6 | 3.9 | 11 306 | 7.1 | 620 | 10 599 | 70.8 | 466 000 | 28.1 | 10.0 |
| Berkeley | 38 896 | 60 908 | 10.7 | 24.8 | 7.2 | 49 454 | 5.5 | 3 425 | 44 904 | 43.5 | 720 100 | 28.0 | 10.5 |
| Beverly Hills | 75 234 | 85 560 | 21.0 | 15.4 | 5.2 | 16 394 | 3.4 | 1 525 | 14 334 | 41.3 | 1 000 000 | 39.7 | 13.4 |
| Brea | 36 195 | 81 278 | 7.8 | 13.0 | 3.6 | 14 785 | 11.4 | 519 | 14 277 | 64.8 | 567 200 | 27.8 | 10.0 |
| Brentwood | 32 030 | 87 642 | 7.7 | 10.6 | 5.3 | 17 523 | 125.6 | 1 029 | 15 493 | 77.3 | 412 100 | 33.1 | 13.3 |
| Buena Park | 23 470 | 64 809 | 4.0 | 14.9 | 7.5 | 24 623 | 3.1 | 937 | 22 627 | 58.7 | 444 300 | 31.0 | 10.4 |
| Burbank | 33 651 | 66 024 | 5.5 | 18.1 | 6.0 | 44 309 | 3.4 | 2 369 | 41 056 | 43.9 | 596 500 | 32.5 | 10.0 |
| Burlingame | 52 634 | 79 760 | 15.8 | 12.8 | 5.6 | 13 027 | 1.3 | 666 | 12 098 | 48.7 | 1 000 000 | 33.0 | 11.1 |
| Calexico | 14 317 | 35 988 | 2.5 | 34.2 | 24.0 | 10 651 | 52.5 | 535 | 9 598 | 55.3 | 173 700 | 32.1 | 13.6 |
| Camarillo | 37 840 | 84 168 | 9.5 | 11.7 | 4.0 | 25 702 | 17.2 | 1 198 | 23 455 | 71.7 | 510 700 | 28.8 | 11.0 |
| Campbell | 44 354 | 82 687 | 11.7 | 13.0 | 4.0 | 16 950 | 3.7 | 787 | 16 205 | 52.8 | 680 400 | 29.6 | 10.6 |
| Carlsbad | 42 712 | 85 743 | 11.9 | 13.3 | 6.8 | 44 673 | 32.5 | 3 328 | 39 964 | 66.4 | 633 200 | 30.4 | 11.0 |
| Carson | 24 026 | 70 416 | 4.1 | 13.5 | 5.4 | 26 226 | 3.6 | 794 | 24 919 | 75.7 | 384 300 | 31.2 | 10.0 |
| Cathedral City | 21 734 | 45 088 | 3.2 | 25.6 | 15.2 | 20 995 | 17.9 | 3 948 | 17 419 | 64.6 | 232 300 | 35.6 | 17.0 |
| Ceres | 17 688 | 48 550 | 1.0 | 25.2 | 15.9 | 13 673 | 26.6 | 981 | 13 238 | 64.3 | 205 300 | 33.9 | 13.6 |
| Cerritos | 32 610 | 87 853 | 9.2 | 10.2 | 4.9 | 15 859 | 1.6 | 333 | 14 993 | 81.0 | 620 000 | 29.2 | 10.0 |
| Chico | 23 611 | 41 632 | 1.7 | 30.4 | 12.6 | 37 050 | 52.1 | 2 245 | 33 891 | 44.9 | 295 700 | 28.2 | 12.5 |
| Chino | 22 918 | 73 400 | 3.9 | 14.4 | 5.3 | 21 797 | 21.0 | 1 025 | 20 240 | 72.1 | 378 900 | 33.0 | 10.9 |
| Chino Hills | 35 157 | 101 905 | 10.8 | 6.6 | 3.6 | 23 617 | 15.8 | 676 | 22 280 | 81.6 | 536 500 | 29.3 | 10.0 |
| Chula Vista | 25 419 | 65 526 | 3.7 | 16.9 | 8.0 | 79 416 | 33.4 | 3 901 | 73 633 | 59.5 | 401 000 | 34.4 | 10.0 |
| Citrus Heights | 25 778 | 54 575 | 1.1 | 18.2 | 9.5 | 35 075 | 0.4 | 2 389 | 32 615 | 58.0 | 236 600 | 29.9 | 12.9 |
| Claremont | 37 539 | 81 715 | 12.2 | 13.9 | 3.9 | 12 156 | 5.0 | 548 | 11 547 | 65.7 | 578 600 | 28.5 | 10.0 |
| Clovis | 27 749 | 65 300 | 3.6 | 17.6 | 7.6 | 35 306 | 40.4 | 1 887 | 32 540 | 63.5 | 284 500 | 27.7 | 11.4 |
| Coachella | 12 219 | 43 357 | 1.0 | 27.7 | 23.4 | 9 903 | 98.8 | 905 | 8 790 | 66.9 | 171 300 | 33.5 | 13.9 |
| Colton | 16 385 | 41 788 | 1.3 | 26.8 | 18.7 | 16 350 | 3.6 | 1 379 | 15 076 | 55.1 | 206 600 | 31.1 | 12.6 |
| Compton | 13 595 | 43 311 | 0.3 | 27.4 | 21.3 | 24 523 | 3.1 | 1 461 | 23 353 | 54.6 | 288 000 | 37.1 | 13.4 |
| Concord | 31 338 | 65 769 | 5.0 | 16.2 | 7.8 | 47 125 | 4.8 | 2 847 | 45 069 | 63.2 | 418 500 | 31.8 | 12.0 |
| Corona | 27 825 | 79 877 | 5.9 | 11.7 | 7.2 | 47 174 | 20.2 | 2 224 | 43 509 | 69.7 | 381 400 | 30.8 | 10.3 |
| Costa Mesa | 33 800 | 65 471 | 6.2 | 16.0 | 9.5 | 42 120 | 4.3 | 2 174 | 40 720 | 41.6 | 617 000 | 31.0 | 10.0 |
| Covina | 26 055 | 67 638 | 2.7 | 15.5 | 8.5 | 16 576 | 0.9 | 721 | 15 132 | 59.8 | 411 000 | 29.9 | 10.4 |
| Culver City | 42 832 | 75 596 | 9.4 | 15.7 | 4.6 | 17 491 | 2.1 | 712 | 16 744 | 57.1 | 623 100 | 31.5 | 11.9 |
| Cupertino | 51 965 | 124 825 | 25.7 | 9.1 | 2.6 | 21 027 | 12.4 | 846 | 20 176 | 64.2 | 1 000 000 | 29.2 | 10.0 |
| Cypress | 32 815 | 82 954 | 7.9 | 10.3 | 4.7 | 16 068 | 0.3 | 414 | 15 456 | 71.0 | 558 800 | 28.1 | 10.3 |
| Daly City | 28 649 | 75 399 | 5.9 | 12.2 | 4.8 | 32 588 | 4.3 | 1 498 | 31 115 | 57.2 | 585 600 | 32.1 | 10.0 |
| Dana Point | 51 431 | 83 306 | 15.4 | 11.9 | 5.1 | 15 938 | 1.8 | 1 756 | 14 170 | 59.7 | 785 500 | 31.2 | 10.8 |
| Danville | 61 002 | 133 360 | 27.6 | 5.8 | 2.9 | 15 934 | 3.9 | 514 | 15 175 | 84.5 | 877 000 | 30.4 | 10.8 |
| Davis | 33 256 | 61 182 | 8.7 | 26.1 | 8.8 | 25 869 | 9.6 | 996 | 23 899 | 44.6 | 560 500 | 23.7 | 10.0 |

1. Based on population estimated by the American Community Survey.   2. Includes units rented or sold but not occupied.   3. Specified owner-occupied units; $1,000,000 represents $1,000,000 or more   4. 50.0 represents 50 percent or more.   5. 10.0 represents 10 percent or less.

# Table D. Cities — Housing, Labor Force, and Employment

| City | Occupied housing units, 2007–2011 (cont.) | | | | Migration, 2007–2011 | | Civilian labor force, 2012 | | Unemployment | | Civilian employment[4], 2007–2011 | Percent | | |
|---|---|---|---|---|---|---|---|---|---|---|---|---|---|---|
| | Percent renter occupied | Median gross rent[1] | Median rent as a percent of income[2] | Percent with no vehicle available | Percent who lived in the same house one year ago | Percent who lived outside this city one year ago | Total | Percent change, 2011–2012 | Total | Rate[3] | Population age 16 and older | In labor force | Full-year full-time worker | Households with no workers (percent) |
| | 55 | 56 | 57 | 58 | 59 | 60 | 61 | 62 | 63 | 64 | 65 | 66 | 67 | 68 |
| **ARKANSAS—Cont'd** | | | | | | | | | | | | | | |
| Jacksonville | 48.0 | 671 | 27.4 | 10.4 | 75.1 | 16.9 | 11 810 | 1.2 | 959 | 8.1 | 21 635 | 65.9 | 38.8 | 25.5 |
| Jonesboro | 45.4 | 622 | 31.4 | 9.7 | 72.6 | 10.6 | 34 929 | 3.9 | 2 340 | 6.7 | 51 065 | 64.9 | 38.0 | 29.9 |
| Little Rock | 42.8 | 761 | 31.3 | 7.8 | 80.0 | 7.5 | 96 244 | 3.1 | 6 497 | 6.8 | 150 001 | 68.8 | 44.3 | 24.8 |
| North Little Rock | 47.3 | 760 | 34.2 | 11.3 | 77.7 | 13.3 | 30 070 | 2.9 | 2 039 | 6.8 | 48 116 | 63.7 | 41.6 | 30.4 |
| Paragould | 42.8 | 606 | 28.3 | 8.0 | 78.8 | 8.9 | 11 994 | 2.0 | 1 064 | 8.9 | 20 044 | 60.2 | 39.7 | 33.8 |
| Pine Bluff | 44.5 | 630 | 35.4 | 12.2 | 78.8 | 9.4 | 20 182 | -0.7 | 2 181 | 10.8 | 38 157 | 57.9 | 31.1 | 35.0 |
| Rogers | 39.9 | 777 | 27.7 | 5.8 | 81.0 | 11.3 | 28 261 | 5.4 | 1 637 | 5.8 | 39 814 | 68.8 | 46.1 | 19.3 |
| Russellville | 46.7 | 630 | 31.8 | 7.9 | 75.2 | 15.5 | 13 667 | 1.2 | 962 | 7.0 | 22 092 | 64.3 | 34.0 | 26.2 |
| Sherwood | 31.4 | 756 | 26.7 | 4.2 | 83.3 | 13.9 | 15 771 | 3.5 | 786 | 5.0 | 22 963 | 68.2 | 46.5 | 21.1 |
| Springdale | 45.1 | 674 | 29.4 | 6.2 | 76.0 | 11.2 | 34 841 | 5.2 | 1 786 | 5.1 | 47 304 | 70.1 | 46.7 | 20.2 |
| Texarkana | 40.7 | 670 | 29.7 | 9.0 | 76.5 | 12.2 | 14 298 | 1.4 | 1 018 | 7.1 | 23 073 | 60.7 | 39.3 | 32.9 |
| West Memphis | 50.2 | 642 | 36.4 | 14.1 | 73.1 | 10.8 | 10 439 | 1.4 | 1 316 | 12.6 | 19 344 | 62.4 | 37.1 | 32.0 |
| **CALIFORNIA** | 43.3 | 1 185 | 33.0 | 7.7 | 84.2 | 9.7 | 18 494 881 | 1.0 | 1 934 533 | 10.5 | 28 796 402 | 64.7 | 38.0 | 24.1 |
| Adelanto | 37.6 | 1 034 | 44.0 | 7.7 | 70.9 | 22.5 | 6 864 | -1.1 | 1 261 | 18.4 | 19 761 | 51.3 | 29.3 | 28.5 |
| Alameda | 50.8 | 1 291 | 27.8 | 8.4 | 82.9 | 11.0 | 40 708 | 3.0 | 2 514 | 6.2 | 60 041 | 68.7 | 41.7 | 22.4 |
| Alhambra | 58.5 | 1 165 | 33.0 | 8.4 | 88.9 | 8.4 | 45 288 | -0.7 | 4 274 | 9.4 | 69 607 | 64.1 | 41.7 | 19.0 |
| Aliso Viejo | 36.5 | 1 842 | 29.8 | 1.7 | 81.4 | 14.7 | 28 062 | 2.4 | 1 121 | 4.0 | 36 197 | 80.0 | 56.6 | 10.1 |
| Anaheim | 50.9 | 1 314 | 35.8 | 6.9 | 83.2 | 9.6 | 177 182 | 1.1 | 17 256 | 9.7 | 252 387 | 68.7 | 42.6 | 18.8 |
| Antioch | 34.5 | 1 279 | 34.8 | 5.6 | 81.3 | 8.8 | 50 175 | 1.7 | 5 108 | 10.2 | 75 988 | 65.7 | 37.4 | 21.4 |
| Apple Valley | 28.6 | 986 | 42.0 | 5.1 | 83.0 | 10.5 | 26 144 | 0.0 | 3 422 | 13.1 | 51 339 | 56.6 | 30.5 | 35.2 |
| Arcadia | 38.4 | 1 390 | 31.1 | 5.1 | 88.9 | 9.0 | 27 627 | -0.1 | 1 726 | 6.2 | 45 388 | 61.7 | 41.0 | 22.4 |
| Atascadero | 33.4 | 1 084 | 34.1 | 3.6 | 83.1 | 11.7 | 15 943 | 4.6 | 1 052 | 6.6 | 23 033 | 63.8 | 37.8 | 23.7 |
| Atwater | 48.5 | 896 | 31.2 | 8.7 | 80.5 | 8.6 | 13 070 | 1.6 | 2 265 | 17.3 | 20 118 | 59.6 | 32.6 | 30.8 |
| Azusa | 47.6 | 1 191 | 34.9 | 6.6 | 84.4 | 10.9 | 21 319 | -1.2 | 2 532 | 11.9 | 35 351 | 68.5 | 39.4 | 16.4 |
| Bakersfield | 41.0 | 937 | 32.6 | 7.2 | 79.1 | 8.1 | 166 292 | 5.9 | 15 437 | 9.3 | 245 826 | 65.2 | 38.6 | 22.5 |
| Baldwin Park | 37.5 | 1 182 | 34.9 | 5.0 | 89.6 | 7.8 | 33 463 | -1.5 | 4 564 | 13.6 | 56 079 | 63.8 | 36.9 | 15.1 |
| Banning | 29.7 | 898 | 39.1 | 8.2 | 86.3 | 9.5 | 12 025 | 0.2 | 1 684 | 14.0 | 24 324 | 43.5 | 25.9 | 50.7 |
| Beaumont | 23.3 | 948 | 36.8 | 3.4 | 84.9 | 10.2 | 7 027 | 0.2 | 980 | 13.9 | 25 475 | 62.4 | 41.0 | 24.3 |
| Bell | 72.7 | 979 | 33.9 | 11.3 | 91.6 | 7.2 | 15 938 | -1.7 | 2 307 | 14.5 | 25 114 | 59.9 | 38.3 | 18.1 |
| Bellflower | 61.3 | 1 141 | 32.8 | 7.4 | 86.9 | 10.0 | 36 477 | -1.1 | 4 048 | 11.1 | 56 711 | 65.1 | 43.7 | 22.1 |
| Bell Gardens | 74.1 | 1 052 | 34.1 | 10.8 | 91.5 | 5.8 | 17 471 | -2.2 | 3 032 | 17.4 | 28 932 | 63.0 | 40.4 | 15.9 |
| Belmont | 41.9 | 1 453 | 24.3 | 3.3 | 86.3 | 11.8 | 15 200 | 4.7 | 875 | 5.8 | 20 742 | 70.3 | 45.1 | 20.5 |
| Benicia | 29.2 | 1 314 | 29.0 | 2.4 | 87.9 | 7.9 | 17 101 | 2.3 | 1 081 | 6.3 | 21 736 | 68.3 | 42.3 | 21.9 |
| Berkeley | 56.5 | 1 214 | 35.9 | 20.1 | 73.0 | 16.9 | 59 965 | 2.4 | 5 140 | 8.6 | 97 979 | 58.5 | 29.5 | 29.0 |
| Beverly Hills | 58.7 | 1 841 | 31.4 | 7.5 | 88.0 | 8.9 | 19 055 | -0.4 | 1 452 | 7.6 | 28 068 | 62.2 | 38.1 | 25.2 |
| Brea | 35.2 | 1 395 | 28.6 | 4.8 | 86.7 | 10.3 | 21 577 | 2.1 | 1 121 | 5.2 | 31 178 | 67.5 | 41.6 | 19.8 |
| Brentwood | 22.7 | 1 637 | 34.8 | 1.1 | 86.1 | 10.6 | 11 126 | 2.4 | 886 | 8.0 | 35 125 | 65.1 | 39.3 | 21.8 |
| Buena Park | 41.3 | 1 357 | 35.4 | 4.4 | 85.3 | 11.7 | 42 739 | 1.1 | 4 053 | 9.5 | 61 809 | 64.3 | 39.5 | 18.1 |
| Burbank | 56.1 | 1 330 | 30.4 | 7.9 | 85.5 | 9.7 | 59 923 | -0.6 | 5 322 | 8.9 | 84 546 | 68.4 | 43.8 | 22.1 |
| Burlingame | 51.3 | 1 424 | 28.6 | 6.6 | 87.8 | 9.7 | 16 486 | 5.0 | 804 | 4.9 | 23 013 | 68.3 | 43.4 | 20.0 |
| Calexico | 44.7 | 716 | 36.0 | 11.9 | 90.2 | 2.3 | 15 730 | 1.5 | 4 926 | 31.3 | 27 374 | 58.5 | 26.7 | 27.7 |
| Camarillo | 28.3 | 1 580 | 32.6 | 3.6 | 85.0 | 8.7 | 32 522 | 2.7 | 2 099 | 6.5 | 50 828 | 65.0 | 39.2 | 26.8 |
| Campbell | 47.2 | 1 403 | 28.0 | 5.6 | 85.1 | 12.3 | 23 359 | 3.2 | 1 688 | 7.2 | 31 674 | 72.8 | 47.1 | 18.5 |
| Carlsbad | 33.6 | 1 568 | 33.2 | 3.0 | 84.2 | 12.0 | 48 642 | 2.2 | 2 878 | 5.9 | 80 792 | 65.2 | 39.7 | 24.4 |
| Carson | 24.3 | 1 275 | 29.5 | 4.2 | 89.4 | 8.0 | 45 902 | -1.0 | 5 064 | 11.0 | 72 589 | 65.8 | 40.5 | 19.6 |
| Cathedral City | 35.4 | 1 084 | 35.5 | 5.8 | 82.4 | 8.0 | 27 073 | 0.5 | 3 242 | 12.0 | 38 890 | 63.7 | 36.1 | 27.8 |
| Ceres | 35.7 | 908 | 36.8 | 6.0 | 81.5 | 12.9 | 18 850 | -0.1 | 3 547 | 18.8 | 32 637 | 67.0 | 35.6 | 25.3 |
| Cerritos | 19.0 | 1 856 | 35.8 | 2.6 | 90.5 | 7.3 | 28 662 | -0.1 | 1 710 | 6.0 | 40 534 | 60.1 | 39.5 | 22.9 |
| Chico | 55.1 | 922 | 36.7 | 8.0 | 67.1 | 13.4 | 33 315 | 0.6 | 3 796 | 11.4 | 71 556 | 63.8 | 28.7 | 29.5 |
| Chino | 27.9 | 1 261 | 34.2 | 3.8 | 79.5 | 16.6 | 34 705 | 0.5 | 3 710 | 10.7 | 61 562 | 60.6 | 36.7 | 16.9 |
| Chino Hills | 18.4 | 1 771 | 33.4 | 1.8 | 89.8 | 7.0 | 39 568 | 1.5 | 2 395 | 6.1 | 56 674 | 72.1 | 44.7 | 11.6 |
| Chula Vista | 40.5 | 1 242 | 36.6 | 5.6 | 87.3 | 7.8 | 93 908 | 1.3 | 9 790 | 10.4 | 178 489 | 66.6 | 40.2 | 20.3 |
| Citrus Heights | 42.0 | 1 026 | 29.8 | 6.0 | 79.4 | 14.9 | 50 495 | 1.2 | 3 738 | 7.4 | 67 384 | 67.1 | 39.2 | 26.2 |
| Claremont | 34.3 | 1 191 | 32.1 | 7.0 | 83.2 | 14.1 | 16 314 | 0.0 | 935 | 5.7 | 29 017 | 59.4 | 30.0 | 27.6 |
| Clovis | 36.5 | 975 | 31.5 | 5.7 | 86.0 | 9.8 | 42 988 | 1.8 | 3 538 | 8.2 | 71 025 | 66.0 | 39.3 | 22.8 |
| Coachella | 33.1 | 856 | 38.9 | 4.5 | 85.2 | 8.2 | 12 655 | -0.8 | 2 438 | 19.3 | 25 066 | 70.1 | 36.6 | 15.7 |
| Colton | 44.9 | 990 | 38.4 | 6.8 | 86.5 | 9.7 | 24 945 | 0.0 | 3 223 | 12.9 | 37 037 | 65.7 | 36.5 | 21.5 |
| Compton | 45.4 | 980 | 38.5 | 8.5 | 88.0 | 7.5 | 36 739 | -2.5 | 6 822 | 18.6 | 67 069 | 61.9 | 36.1 | 23.2 |
| Concord | 36.8 | 1 208 | 34.7 | 6.6 | 86.1 | 8.1 | 71 490 | 1.9 | 6 951 | 9.7 | 96 720 | 70.0 | 40.0 | 21.4 |
| Corona | 30.3 | 1 284 | 34.4 | 3.5 | 84.9 | 9.9 | 86 915 | 1.1 | 7 842 | 9.0 | 112 026 | 70.7 | 42.9 | 13.4 |
| Costa Mesa | 58.4 | 1 479 | 31.2 | 4.9 | 83.0 | 10.6 | 67 161 | 1.8 | 4 557 | 6.8 | 88 789 | 73.6 | 45.0 | 17.7 |
| Covina | 40.2 | 1 202 | 31.9 | 4.7 | 86.8 | 11.1 | 25 683 | -0.4 | 1 984 | 7.7 | 36 753 | 68.8 | 39.9 | 19.0 |
| Culver City | 42.9 | 1 478 | 29.3 | 6.3 | 85.3 | 12.2 | 24 260 | -0.4 | 1 822 | 7.5 | 31 966 | 69.6 | 45.2 | 24.6 |
| Cupertino | 35.8 | 2 000 | 23.4 | 3.8 | 86.1 | 10.2 | 25 223 | 3.8 | 1 370 | 5.4 | 44 052 | 61.5 | 42.2 | 20.5 |
| Cypress | 29.0 | 1 474 | 31.3 | 4.0 | 89.2 | 8.7 | 27 504 | 1.5 | 2 204 | 8.0 | 38 147 | 65.3 | 40.7 | 17.8 |
| Daly City | 42.8 | 1 455 | 32.5 | 8.2 | 86.3 | 10.0 | 56 578 | 4.1 | 4 728 | 8.4 | 83 664 | 68.8 | 43.1 | 18.5 |
| Dana Point | 40.3 | 1 781 | 34.9 | 2.1 | 85.0 | 11.2 | 22 464 | 2.1 | 1 233 | 5.5 | 27 952 | 67.3 | 42.3 | 24.6 |
| Danville | 15.5 | 2 000 | 30.7 | 2.8 | 90.7 | 7.5 | 23 724 | 3.3 | 1 120 | 4.7 | 31 688 | 64.0 | 41.3 | 21.6 |
| Davis | 55.4 | 1 248 | 43.4 | 7.3 | 68.4 | 15.9 | 38 534 | 0.2 | 2 837 | 7.4 | 55 359 | 63.0 | 28.3 | 23.4 |

1. $2,000 represents $2,000 or more.  2. 50.0 represents 50 percent or more.  3. Percent of civilian labor force.  4. Persons 16 years old and over.

| City | New construction ($1,000) | Number of housing units | Percent single family | Number of establishments | Number of employees | Sales (mil dol) | Annual payroll (mil dol) | Number of establishments | Number of employees | Sales (mil dol) | Annual payroll (mil dol) |
|---|---|---|---|---|---|---|---|---|---|---|---|
| | Value of residential construction authorized by building permits, 2011 | | | Wholesale trade,[1] 2007 | | | | Retail trade,[2] 2007 | | | |
| | 69 | 70 | 71 | 72 | 73 | 74 | 75 | 76 | 77 | 78 | 79 |
| **ARKANSAS—Cont'd** | | | | | | | | | | | |
| Jacksonville | 3 416 | 31 | 100.0 | 15 | 163 | 49.7 | 6.1 | 101 | 1 594 | 347.2 | 37.9 |
| Jonesboro | 57 039 | 676 | 45.0 | 104 | 1 204 | 495.5 | 50.2 | 440 | 6 193 | 1 335.6 | 119.1 |
| Little Rock | 131 397 | 1 329 | 24.5 | 387 | 7 632 | 3 999.3 | 339.0 | 1 008 | 14 560 | 3 359.2 | 330.4 |
| North Little Rock | 59 043 | 809 | 19.3 | 192 | 3 792 | 7 809.5 | 175.7 | 422 | 6 705 | 1 509.5 | 132.7 |
| Paragould | 12 172 | 135 | 60.7 | 31 | 269 | 82.1 | 7.8 | 161 | 1 554 | 336.8 | 31.3 |
| Pine Bluff | 1 655 | 12 | 83.3 | 52 | 394 | 211.9 | 13.7 | 280 | 3 646 | 798.7 | 74.2 |
| Rogers | 33 991 | 187 | 94.7 | 55 | 1 124 | 314.2 | 42.1 | 308 | 4 921 | 995.1 | 104.2 |
| Russellville | 5 234 | 68 | 75.0 | 50 | 331 | 204.6 | 13.3 | 251 | 3 290 | 852.8 | 68.1 |
| Sherwood | 13 719 | 82 | 100.0 | 30 | 173 | 78.8 | 7.4 | 92 | 1 480 | 579.7 | 39.2 |
| Springdale | 29 738 | 128 | 95.3 | 148 | 1 706 | 865.2 | 73.6 | 259 | 3 536 | 875.2 | 87.6 |
| Texarkana | 8 099 | 45 | 77.8 | 41 | D | D | D | 133 | 1 438 | 397.2 | 30.2 |
| West Memphis | 573 | 4 | 100.0 | 32 | 383 | 668.7 | 17.8 | 122 | 1 805 | 586.5 | 36.5 |
| CALIFORNIA | 9 638 517 | 45 471 | 47.7 | 53 963 | 745 785 | 598 456.5 | 42 334.5 | 114 438 | 1 683 023 | 455 032.3 | 44 328.9 |
| Adelanto | 8 375 | 24 | 100.0 | 5 | 48 | 25.2 | 2.3 | 13 | 205 | 52.2 | 5.0 |
| Alameda | 8 201 | 24 | 100.0 | 62 | 1 405 | 2 014.7 | 146.9 | 180 | 2 258 | 517.3 | 58.6 |
| Alhambra | 23 977 | 100 | 12.0 | 261 | 1 088 | 561.3 | 36.6 | 249 | 4 014 | 1 491.5 | 113.4 |
| Aliso Viejo | 28 052 | 126 | 83.3 | 65 | 1 903 | 1 273.0 | 136.9 | 69 | 1 078 | 662.8 | 28.8 |
| Anaheim | 21 914 | 147 | 27.9 | 797 | 12 461 | 7 962.1 | 580.1 | 866 | 14 042 | 3 679.3 | 367.0 |
| Antioch | 39 686 | 149 | 100.0 | 27 | 261 | 162.8 | 17.6 | 253 | 4 315 | 957.1 | 104.2 |
| Apple Valley | 3 429 | 22 | 100.0 | 15 | 32 | 12.6 | 1.6 | 106 | 2 213 | 493.0 | 49.0 |
| Arcadia | 15 987 | 110 | 26.4 | 293 | 1 233 | 619.7 | 45.8 | 330 | 4 965 | 900.1 | 98.0 |
| Atascadero | 4 315 | 27 | 88.9 | 24 | 121 | 32.3 | 4.8 | 126 | 1 556 | 356.3 | 36.8 |
| Atwater | 404 | 3 | 100.0 | 2 | D | D | D | 54 | 632 | 151.9 | 15.1 |
| Azusa | 58 426 | 153 | 100.0 | 73 | 890 | 404.0 | 41.7 | 96 | 1 162 | 427.0 | 31.2 |
| Bakersfield | 92 313 | 422 | 100.0 | 274 | 4 127 | 3 299.9 | 193.0 | 1 062 | 19 677 | 5 104.1 | 487.2 |
| Baldwin Park | 8 649 | 47 | 100.0 | 145 | 1 044 | 546.8 | 41.1 | 134 | 2 451 | 643.9 | 59.8 |
| Banning | 0 | 0 | 0.0 | 13 | 452 | 95.9 | 13.1 | 63 | 771 | 233.2 | 20.8 |
| Beaumont | 25 704 | 169 | 100.0 | 4 | 6 | 1.2 | 0.2 | 53 | 1 109 | 298.1 | 27.8 |
| Bell | 0 | 0 | 0.0 | 51 | 747 | 639.5 | 40.5 | 62 | 664 | 212.4 | 21.0 |
| Bellflower | 478 | 3 | 100.0 | 39 | 244 | 76.3 | 8.7 | 189 | 1 676 | 438.2 | 45.2 |
| Bell Gardens | 5 193 | 68 | 4.4 | 37 | 534 | 155.8 | 18.7 | 72 | 854 | 186.6 | 21.5 |
| Belmont | 1 755 | 3 | 100.0 | 19 | D | D | D | 56 | 916 | 363.8 | 36.2 |
| Benicia | 28 | 1 | 100.0 | 79 | 1 468 | 859.1 | 78.5 | 74 | 868 | 175.5 | 29.9 |
| Berkeley | 1 600 | 42 | 9.5 | 118 | 1 394 | 620.3 | 66.8 | 506 | 5 975 | 1 274.6 | 168.3 |
| Beverly Hills | 48 833 | 58 | 34.5 | 137 | 741 | 725.7 | 63.6 | 443 | 6 018 | 2 512.0 | 269.8 |
| Brea | 6 601 | 36 | 25.0 | 262 | 5 315 | 4 709.8 | 258.2 | 329 | 6 144 | 1 079.6 | 123.2 |
| Brentwood | 21 618 | 104 | 100.0 | 18 | 63 | 24.4 | 3.5 | 128 | 1 969 | 463.2 | 48.6 |
| Buena Park | 5 113 | 22 | 100.0 | 175 | 2 543 | 1 770.0 | 120.4 | 230 | 4 538 | 1 649.8 | 136.1 |
| Burbank | 5 231 | 21 | 28.6 | 213 | 3 581 | 6 364.4 | 219.5 | 426 | 8 247 | 2 276.9 | 195.5 |
| Burlingame | 11 859 | 19 | 100.0 | 153 | 1 040 | 935.4 | 61.1 | 201 | 2 425 | 819.4 | 94.5 |
| Calexico | 8 500 | 52 | 0.0 | 73 | 414 | 346.7 | 9.8 | 195 | 2 591 | 545.2 | 50.6 |
| Camarillo | 431 | 1 | 100.0 | 132 | 1 651 | 647.2 | 87.2 | 299 | 4 855 | 1 276.2 | 134.9 |
| Campbell | 10 135 | 48 | 50.0 | 82 | 906 | 470.0 | 57.2 | 174 | 3 008 | 691.4 | 79.6 |
| Carlsbad | 86 733 | 317 | 84.2 | 247 | 3 622 | 2 305.2 | 225.1 | 513 | 8 049 | 2 270.1 | 236.3 |
| Carson | NA | NA | NA | 369 | 6 927 | 4 918.7 | 335.5 | 237 | 4 830 | 1 703.9 | 180.3 |
| Cathedral City | 466 | 2 | 100.0 | 22 | 108 | 44.2 | 5.0 | 160 | 2 478 | 962.7 | 83.7 |
| Ceres | 94 | 1 | 100.0 | 19 | 289 | 205.6 | 11.0 | 88 | 1 633 | 402.9 | 38.0 |
| Cerritos | 0 | 0 | 0.0 | 257 | 4 835 | 5 247.7 | 288.1 | 266 | 8 177 | 2 681.5 | 232.4 |
| Chico | 20 548 | 126 | 69.8 | 86 | 983 | 434.1 | 38.3 | 464 | 8 018 | 1 642.3 | 174.1 |
| Chino | 46 922 | 185 | 80.0 | 390 | 4 599 | 2 468.8 | 197.2 | 236 | 4 455 | 952.0 | 95.7 |
| Chino Hills | 5 370 | 24 | 100.0 | 72 | 159 | 79.2 | 5.6 | 124 | 2 311 | 597.7 | 53.7 |
| Chula Vista | 137 298 | 723 | 59.2 | 297 | 2 045 | 1 156.6 | 83.7 | 651 | 11 801 | 2 754.1 | 271.1 |
| Citrus Heights | 4 237 | 18 | 88.9 | 21 | 31 | 12.0 | 1.5 | 309 | 5 362 | 1 151.8 | 113.7 |
| Claremont | 673 | 3 | 100.0 | 35 | 116 | 84.1 | 6.1 | 89 | 1 021 | 442.8 | 37.0 |
| Clovis | 70 391 | 320 | 100.0 | 41 | 175 | 87.6 | 7.3 | 286 | 5 804 | 1 569.5 | 137.9 |
| Coachella | 9 053 | 87 | 100.0 | 18 | 352 | 178.2 | 19.4 | 57 | 695 | 197.7 | 15.2 |
| Colton | 91 | 1 | 100.0 | 42 | 647 | 420.2 | 29.7 | 111 | 2 120 | 645.5 | 66.5 |
| Compton | 2 679 | 25 | 100.0 | 122 | 3 251 | 2 195.2 | 176.3 | 158 | 1 124 | 267.9 | 30.0 |
| Concord | 1 086 | 2 | 100.0 | 135 | 1 302 | 553.7 | 69.4 | 505 | 8 856 | 2 578.5 | 256.5 |
| Corona | 66 773 | 463 | 11.9 | 299 | 5 283 | 6 720.2 | 280.7 | 485 | 8 950 | 2 418.9 | 229.8 |
| Costa Mesa | 6 802 | 31 | 67.7 | 336 | 4 639 | 4 176.2 | 303.2 | 740 | 14 696 | 3 875.8 | 401.4 |
| Covina | 3 030 | 32 | 0.0 | 82 | 524 | 250.8 | 20.3 | 193 | 3 013 | 765.3 | 81.6 |
| Culver City | 7 000 | 28 | 0.0 | 150 | 3 233 | 1 965.9 | 206.2 | 334 | 5 847 | 1 605.6 | 163.6 |
| Cupertino | 18 504 | 51 | 100.0 | 66 | 1 194 | 1 139.3 | 96.5 | 157 | 3 266 | 3 703.0 | 77.2 |
| Cypress | 1 887 | 10 | 100.0 | 110 | 3 530 | 7 669.6 | 262.6 | 104 | 2 011 | 597.4 | 51.5 |
| Daly City | 10 644 | 48 | 16.7 | 25 | D | D | D | 217 | 4 005 | 943.2 | 90.9 |
| Dana Point | 12 484 | 14 | 100.0 | 44 | 150 | 188.7 | 10.1 | 123 | 1 115 | 351.7 | 32.0 |
| Danville | 9 742 | 17 | 76.5 | 42 | 156 | 105.6 | 7.8 | 131 | 1 324 | 316.8 | 35.1 |
| Davis | 26 126 | 123 | 43.9 | 15 | 170 | 171.6 | 10.3 | 146 | 2 061 | 480.5 | 50.8 |

1. Merchant wholesalers except manufacturers' sales branches and offices.   2. Establishments with payroll.

# Table D. Cities — **Real Estate, Professional Services, and Manufacturing**

| City | Real estate and rental and leasing, 2007 | | | | Professional, scientific, and technical services,[1] 2007 | | | | Manufacturing, 2007 | | | |
|---|---|---|---|---|---|---|---|---|---|---|---|---|
| | Number of establish-ments | Number of employees | Receipts (mil dol) | Annual payroll (mil dol) | Number of establish-ments | Number of employees | Receipts (mil dol) | Annual payroll (mil dol) | Number of establish-ments | Number of employees | Receipts (mil dol) | Annual payroll (mil dol) |
| | 80 | 81 | 82 | 83 | 84 | 85 | 86 | 87 | 88 | 89 | 90 | 91 |
| ARKANSAS—Cont'd | | | | | | | | | | | | |
| Jacksonville | 43 | 157 | 15.5 | 3.1 | 33 | D | D | D | 30 | 1 192 | 378.6 | 48.5 |
| Jonesboro | 99 | 468 | 73.2 | 11.7 | 157 | D | D | D | 101 | 6 186 | 1 703.7 | 221.2 |
| Little Rock | 414 | 2 643 | 455.0 | 87.8 | 1 173 | D | D | D | 188 | 8 669 | 3 918.1 | 402.2 |
| North Little Rock | 89 | 434 | 142.9 | 11.6 | 193 | 1 544 | 122.6 | 47.6 | 80 | 2 500 | 767.0 | 106.4 |
| Paragould | 27 | D | D | D | 51 | 355 | 19.7 | 7.9 | 36 | 3 648 | D | D |
| Pine Bluff | 60 | 182 | 35.5 | 5.1 | 73 | D | D | D | 44 | D | 1 151.5 | 119.0 |
| Rogers | 98 | 529 | 69.3 | 17.7 | 179 | 1 816 | 220.4 | 82.8 | 68 | 5 922 | 1 607.5 | 207.5 |
| Russellville | 66 | 213 | 42.0 | 5.4 | 100 | D | D | D | 52 | 4 024 | 1 318.0 | D |
| Sherwood | 29 | 105 | 17.7 | 3.1 | 55 | 431 | 45.9 | 16.5 | NA | NA | NA | NA |
| Springdale | 94 | 397 | 56.6 | 9.9 | 150 | 947 | 89.5 | 39.7 | 107 | 9 022 | 2 131.7 | 289.8 |
| Texarkana | 21 | 66 | 10.5 | 1.5 | 37 | D | D | D | 26 | D | D | D |
| West Memphis | 27 | 136 | 17.8 | 4.4 | 41 | D | D | D | 31 | D | D | 38.1 |
| CALIFORNIA | 51 597 | 312 488 | 76 805.0 | 13 446.7 | 111 954 | 1 231 372 | 194 406.3 | 80 738.1 | 44 296 | 1 448 485 | 491 372.1 | 71 247.3 |
| Adelanto | 10 | 21 | 2.0 | 0.3 | 5 | 46 | 4.7 | 1.6 | 43 | 1 829 | 385.8 | 71.9 |
| Alameda | 113 | D | D | D | 247 | 2 254 | 642.6 | 202.3 | 59 | 2 567 | 1 219.3 | 186.1 |
| Alhambra | 116 | 597 | 66.1 | 17.8 | 245 | D | D | D | 98 | 1 944 | 393.7 | 69.4 |
| Aliso Viejo | 69 | 1 013 | 135.4 | 58.0 | 234 | D | D | D | 35 | 1 437 | 558.2 | 78.1 |
| Anaheim | 377 | 3 858 | 677.4 | 168.9 | 717 | D | D | D | 818 | 30 787 | 7 648.1 | 1 479.1 |
| Antioch | 64 | 311 | 46.4 | 9.3 | 106 | 777 | 65.6 | 27.0 | NA | NA | NA | NA |
| Apple Valley | 55 | 268 | 41.7 | 7.1 | 63 | 267 | 25.3 | 9.3 | NA | NA | NA | NA |
| Arcadia | 150 | 540 | 135.8 | 17.3 | 282 | 1 726 | 388.6 | 92.9 | 67 | 1 044 | 192.5 | 43.4 |
| Atascadero | 37 | 123 | 21.4 | 2.8 | 84 | D | D | D | NA | NA | NA | NA |
| Atwater | 16 | 66 | 7.6 | 1.2 | 12 | D | D | D | 11 | 519 | 158.6 | 17.5 |
| Azusa | 36 | 189 | 30.9 | 6.9 | 22 | 127 | 7.0 | 2.9 | 123 | 4 986 | 1 444.6 | 247.7 |
| Bakersfield | 358 | 1 956 | 309.4 | 63.4 | 752 | D | D | D | 152 | 2 514 | 820.8 | 102.6 |
| Baldwin Park | 29 | 124 | 20.9 | 3.5 | 28 | 129 | 9.1 | 2.8 | 119 | 2 207 | 383.0 | 79.0 |
| Banning | 30 | 202 | 18.6 | 5.0 | 12 | 61 | 4.4 | 1.8 | 22 | 890 | 176.6 | 21.9 |
| Beaumont | 19 | 67 | 11.8 | 1.8 | 21 | 53 | 5.6 | 2.1 | 18 | 543 | 131.7 | 18.7 |
| Bell | 19 | D | D | D | 9 | D | D | D | 23 | 1 004 | 396.6 | 43.9 |
| Bellflower | 82 | 367 | 37.4 | 10.9 | 74 | 420 | 28.1 | 12.2 | NA | NA | NA | NA |
| Bell Gardens | 9 | 54 | 3.8 | 0.9 | 9 | 53 | 4.7 | 1.4 | 57 | 1 020 | 237.6 | 38.8 |
| Belmont | 52 | 482 | 49.1 | 18.4 | 95 | 309 | 60.9 | 22.4 | NA | NA | NA | NA |
| Benicia | 51 | 273 | 58.6 | 10.9 | 103 | 640 | 93.4 | 35.6 | 84 | 2 520 | D | 193.3 |
| Berkeley | 181 | 766 | 185.4 | 25.5 | 589 | 3 864 | 750.5 | 256.3 | 155 | 4 733 | D | 262.9 |
| Beverly Hills | 498 | 2 568 | 851.9 | 146.9 | 1 017 | D | D | D | NA | NA | NA | NA |
| Brea | 107 | 520 | 134.1 | 30.3 | 257 | 2 326 | 360.5 | 131.6 | 172 | 6 822 | 1 690.6 | 299.4 |
| Brentwood | 54 | 223 | 36.9 | 6.4 | 74 | 356 | 33.1 | 14.9 | NA | NA | NA | NA |
| Buena Park | 65 | 239 | 52.0 | 7.3 | 129 | 1 124 | 161.8 | 51.2 | 106 | 4 906 | 1 671.4 | 226.0 |
| Burbank | 239 | 2 543 | 810.8 | 127.0 | 527 | 144 144 | 6 976.0 | 3 869.3 | 220 | 5 429 | 1 028.5 | 249.5 |
| Burlingame | 149 | 1 025 | 219.0 | 34.9 | 264 | D | D | D | 60 | 1 678 | 364.3 | 83.6 |
| Calexico | 26 | 137 | 11.4 | 2.7 | 32 | 119 | 8.9 | 3.3 | NA | NA | NA | NA |
| Camarillo | 103 | 714 | 125.9 | 28.1 | 268 | D | D | D | 145 | 6 110 | 1 530.4 | 316.3 |
| Campbell | 108 | 592 | 121.2 | 23.5 | 296 | D | D | D | 111 | 1 977 | 371.5 | 109.9 |
| Carlsbad | 342 | 1 883 | 328.5 | 71.5 | 760 | D | D | D | 178 | 11 834 | 3 775.2 | 733.4 |
| Carson | 68 | 4 455 | 1 141.3 | 210.4 | 117 | 1 859 | 356.6 | 121.8 | 263 | 12 324 | 12 083.3 | 621.0 |
| Cathedral City | 54 | 308 | 53.0 | 7.8 | 45 | 142 | 13.0 | 4.6 | NA | NA | NA | NA |
| Ceres | 38 | 144 | 20.9 | 3.3 | 20 | 171 | 12.4 | 4.8 | 30 | 613 | 122.0 | 21.2 |
| Cerritos | 97 | 411 | 115.7 | 12.7 | 178 | 3 990 | 304.0 | 113.1 | 155 | 3 548 | 852.2 | 145.3 |
| Chico | 147 | 947 | 107.5 | 20.9 | 297 | D | D | D | 84 | 2 009 | 504.6 | 70.8 |
| Chino | 76 | 381 | 71.6 | 13.0 | 128 | 912 | 103.2 | 34.0 | 244 | 9 023 | 1 902.9 | 332.3 |
| Chino Hills | 52 | 125 | 33.0 | 3.6 | 144 | 371 | 39.3 | 13.7 | NA | NA | NA | NA |
| Chula Vista | 307 | 1 156 | 215.9 | 31.9 | 331 | D | D | D | 160 | 4 237 | 1 233.2 | 274.0 |
| Citrus Heights | 88 | 441 | 64.2 | 10.6 | 135 | 1 196 | 102.9 | 40.1 | NA | NA | NA | NA |
| Claremont | 60 | D | D | D | 147 | D | D | D | 27 | 803 | 118.3 | 26.8 |
| Clovis | 81 | 292 | 59.4 | 7.2 | 168 | 1 084 | 117.6 | 41.7 | 51 | 3 547 | 719.2 | 151.1 |
| Coachella | 13 | 56 | 6.5 | 0.9 | 5 | D | D | D | 15 | 551 | 108.3 | 25.4 |
| Colton | 29 | 187 | 29.2 | 5.3 | 50 | 505 | 57.4 | 21.6 | 57 | 4 043 | 1 157.0 | 128.9 |
| Compton | 19 | 180 | 98.4 | 3.4 | 21 | D | D | D | 133 | 4 940 | 1 083.7 | 176.9 |
| Concord | 166 | 1 014 | 242.2 | 42.4 | 323 | D | D | D | 120 | 2 705 | 528.6 | 122.9 |
| Corona | 200 | 909 | 184.9 | 38.2 | 315 | 2 105 | 211.0 | 115.0 | 372 | 16 971 | 4 279.7 | 708.0 |
| Costa Mesa | 294 | 2 676 | 686.1 | 128.6 | 764 | D | D | D | 258 | 7 604 | 1 962.7 | 386.2 |
| Covina | 102 | 542 | 75.7 | 20.5 | 159 | 682 | 79.5 | 27.8 | 103 | 1 833 | 393.7 | 72.8 |
| Culver City | 129 | 1 305 | 161.9 | 53.7 | 384 | D | D | D | 82 | 2 384 | 566.7 | 118.5 |
| Cupertino | 91 | D | D | D | 394 | 2 692 | 609.6 | 283.6 | 46 | 1 786 | 669.8 | 148.0 |
| Cypress | 68 | 255 | 40.7 | 8.3 | 131 | 1 949 | 649.1 | 150.4 | 44 | 1 683 | 431.2 | 97.9 |
| Daly City | 63 | 290 | 96.3 | 10.2 | 81 | 262 | 25.0 | 8.3 | NA | NA | NA | NA |
| Dana Point | 79 | 233 | 70.0 | 10.0 | 185 | 699 | 108.8 | 43.7 | NA | NA | NA | NA |
| Danville | 108 | 399 | 110.9 | 20.8 | 201 | 854 | 159.2 | 59.5 | NA | NA | NA | NA |
| Davis | 112 | 640 | 69.0 | 18.2 | 197 | D | D | D | NA | NA | NA | NA |

1. Establishments subject to federal tax.

# Table D. Cities — Accommodation and Food Services, Arts, Entertainment, and Recreation, and Health Care and Social Assistance

| City | Accommodation and food services, 2007 | | | | Arts, entertainment, and recreation,[1] 2007 | | | | Health care and social assistance,[1] 2007 | | | |
|---|---|---|---|---|---|---|---|---|---|---|---|---|
| | Number of establish-ments | Number of employees | Sales (mil dol) | Annual payroll (mil dol) | Number of establish-ments | Number of employees | Receipts (mil dol) | Annual payroll (mil dol) | Number of establish-ments | Number of employees | Receipts (mil dol) | Annual payroll (mil dol) |
| | 92 | 93 | 94 | 95 | 96 | 97 | 98 | 99 | 100 | 101 | 102 | 103 |
| ARKANSAS—Cont'd | | | | | | | | | | | | |
| Jacksonville | 49 | 1 016 | 39.8 | 11.0 | 6 | D | D | D | 55 | D | D | D |
| Jonesboro | 171 | 3 866 | 144.0 | 40.7 | 12 | D | D | D | 246 | D | D | D |
| Little Rock | 522 | 11 312 | 532.7 | 154.3 | 60 | 872 | 55.2 | 15.2 | 846 | 10 964 | 1 447.6 | 595.8 |
| North Little Rock | 201 | 4 206 | 184.5 | 51.3 | 24 | D | D | D | 222 | D | D | D |
| Paragould | 57 | 967 | 37.5 | 10.4 | 3 | D | D | D | 66 | D | D | D |
| Pine Bluff | 115 | 1 912 | 77.6 | 20.3 | 5 | D | D | D | 191 | D | D | D |
| Rogers | 120 | 3 283 | 142.1 | 42.5 | 13 | D | D | D | 126 | D | D | D |
| Russellville | 98 | 2 144 | 74.6 | 19.9 | 7 | D | D | D | 110 | D | D | D |
| Sherwood | 32 | 477 | 19.8 | 5.4 | 2 | D | D | D | 56 | D | D | D |
| Springdale | 130 | 2 893 | 105.9 | 30.8 | 15 | 123 | 4.2 | 1.6 | 135 | D | D | D |
| Texarkana | 58 | 1 113 | 42.1 | 12.2 | 4 | D | D | D | 52 | D | D | D |
| West Memphis | 64 | 1 304 | 51.9 | 14.6 | 8 | D | D | D | 68 | 790 | 64.5 | 25.8 |
| CALIFORNIA | 75 989 | 1 366 926 | 80 852.8 | 22 374.8 | 18 025 | 243 993 | 31 778.7 | 10 364.4 | 84 335 | 883 552 | 102 703.1 | 38 944.0 |
| Adelanto | 16 | 143 | 8.9 | 2.2 | 4 | D | D | D | 3 | D | D | D |
| Alameda | 191 | 1 983 | 107.6 | 30.4 | 30 | D | D | D | 176 | 1 562 | 178.8 | 68.7 |
| Alhambra | 204 | 3 116 | 143.1 | 41.0 | 11 | D | D | D | 255 | 2 512 | 270.4 | 84.3 |
| Aliso Viejo | 63 | 964 | 53.5 | 15.7 | 12 | D | D | D | 105 | D | D | D |
| Anaheim | 686 | 22 020 | 1 405.3 | 438.7 | 74 | D | D | D | 781 | 9 799 | 1 159.6 | 435.0 |
| Antioch | 152 | 2 528 | 121.3 | 33.8 | 15 | D | D | D | 200 | 2 204 | 343.5 | 102.3 |
| Apple Valley | 67 | 1 035 | 49.5 | 13.4 | 6 | D | D | D | 172 | D | D | D |
| Arcadia | 189 | 3 531 | 180.3 | 48.8 | 72 | 1 913 | 208.8 | 54.4 | 371 | D | D | D |
| Atascadero | 60 | 850 | 36.6 | 10.6 | 7 | D | D | D | 78 | D | D | D |
| Atwater | 38 | 583 | 27.9 | 6.7 | 4 | D | D | D | 24 | D | D | D |
| Azusa | 84 | 936 | 44.6 | 11.6 | 4 | D | D | D | 43 | D | D | D |
| Bakersfield | 631 | 12 254 | 593.1 | 163.4 | 61 | 1 638 | 57.0 | 19.3 | 871 | 10 618 | 1 240.1 | 440.9 |
| Baldwin Park | 81 | 1 198 | 66.5 | 15.9 | 2 | D | D | D | 67 | D | D | D |
| Banning | 50 | 821 | 39.2 | 10.8 | 2 | D | D | D | 49 | 738 | 76.2 | 21.9 |
| Beaumont | 36 | 448 | 25.0 | 7.8 | 4 | 162 | 6.6 | 3.0 | 32 | D | D | D |
| Bell | 52 | 794 | 41.8 | 10.7 | 1 | D | D | D | 23 | D | D | D |
| Bellflower | 109 | 1 262 | 61.8 | 16.9 | 11 | 108 | 5.8 | 1.8 | 144 | D | D | D |
| Bell Gardens | 61 | 774 | 48.5 | 10.6 | 2 | D | D | D | 27 | 489 | 35.6 | 15.2 |
| Belmont | 53 | 722 | 45.8 | 12.4 | 8 | D | D | D | 49 | 407 | 33.4 | 12.8 |
| Benicia | 61 | 908 | 35.4 | 9.7 | 11 | 142 | 3.7 | 1.0 | 56 | 305 | 41.4 | 10.5 |
| Berkeley | 424 | 5 666 | 323.8 | 96.2 | 63 | 970 | 131.3 | 28.9 | 401 | 2 931 | 392.5 | 160.7 |
| Beverly Hills | 214 | 7 899 | 648.9 | 196.1 | 846 | 5 001 | 2 182.7 | 890.5 | 980 | 5 865 | 1 104.5 | 350.9 |
| Brea | 155 | 4 055 | 211.1 | 61.8 | 14 | D | D | D | 135 | D | D | D |
| Brentwood | 86 | 1 194 | 58.6 | 15.4 | 9 | 308 | 12.3 | 4.6 | 70 | 443 | 37.9 | 15.1 |
| Buena Park | 189 | 3 086 | 173.2 | 45.5 | 15 | D | D | D | 142 | 1 327 | 162.9 | 42.7 |
| Burbank | 289 | 6 989 | 427.3 | 113.2 | 276 | D | D | D | 411 | D | D | D |
| Burlingame | 144 | 3 984 | 286.5 | 85.2 | 20 | 246 | 21.1 | 4.1 | 149 | D | D | D |
| Calexico | 65 | 955 | 44.8 | 11.8 | 4 | D | D | D | 26 | 106 | 8.6 | 3.2 |
| Camarillo | 165 | 3 002 | 146.2 | 39.4 | 26 | D | D | D | 207 | 1 806 | 158.3 | 59.9 |
| Campbell | 126 | 2 267 | 130.9 | 36.7 | 13 | D | D | D | 134 | D | D | D |
| Carlsbad | 220 | 6 891 | 551.8 | 148.8 | 56 | 1 133 | 88.2 | 30.8 | 214 | 2 106 | 244.2 | 81.3 |
| Carson | 145 | 2 422 | 124.0 | 32.9 | 21 | D | D | D | 131 | 977 | 78.4 | 27.3 |
| Cathedral City | 90 | 1 441 | 69.5 | 21.2 | 12 | 336 | 19.1 | 5.5 | 58 | 583 | 38.4 | 18.2 |
| Ceres | 67 | 1 061 | 50.0 | 13.5 | 2 | D | D | D | 44 | D | D | D |
| Cerritos | 148 | 2 850 | 145.8 | 42.8 | 10 | 158 | 11.3 | 2.3 | 162 | 1 948 | 196.8 | 76.6 |
| Chico | 268 | 5 112 | 207.8 | 57.9 | 24 | 780 | 21.7 | 7.1 | 371 | 3 703 | 333.5 | 116.6 |
| Chino | 131 | 2 579 | 115.8 | 32.4 | 18 | D | D | D | 145 | 1 724 | 208.7 | 65.6 |
| Chino Hills | 110 | 1 681 | 81.2 | 20.9 | 16 | D | D | D | 104 | D | D | D |
| Chula Vista | 383 | 6 389 | 333.5 | 93.3 | 34 | 799 | 65.8 | 13.5 | 464 | 3 697 | 383.6 | 139.9 |
| Citrus Heights | 129 | 2 660 | 120.5 | 33.5 | 11 | D | D | D | 154 | 1 834 | 144.0 | 58.7 |
| Claremont | 79 | 1 238 | 64.4 | 18.6 | 13 | D | D | D | 120 | 1 035 | 80.3 | 32.7 |
| Clovis | 182 | 3 223 | 132.4 | 36.9 | 15 | 141 | 8.4 | 1.9 | 166 | D | D | D |
| Coachella | 42 | 538 | 27.8 | 6.8 | 2 | D | D | D | 10 | 55 | 2.9 | 1.3 |
| Colton | 94 | 1 311 | 60.3 | 16.9 | 5 | D | D | D | 82 | D | D | D |
| Compton | 77 | 1 270 | 86.5 | 21.5 | 4 | 6 | 0.4 | 0.1 | 61 | 451 | 35.6 | 13.7 |
| Concord | 272 | 4 480 | 241.0 | 66.2 | 26 | 716 | 41.5 | 11.7 | 345 | 3 376 | 349.0 | 144.8 |
| Corona | 300 | 5 785 | 247.7 | 69.3 | 38 | D | D | D | 293 | 2 858 | 287.7 | 98.5 |
| Costa Mesa | 402 | 8 460 | 512.1 | 142.0 | 46 | 544 | 47.8 | 11.6 | 310 | 3 058 | 274.3 | 103.9 |
| Covina | 117 | 1 886 | 91.8 | 23.3 | 10 | D | D | D | 185 | 2 824 | 236.0 | 104.6 |
| Culver City | 173 | 2 837 | 189.5 | 51.2 | 139 | 897 | 185.1 | 89.6 | 164 | 3 302 | 257.0 | 105.5 |
| Cupertino | 141 | 2 774 | 163.1 | 47.9 | 14 | 238 | 13.5 | 5.3 | 170 | 1 499 | 145.4 | 54.4 |
| Cypress | 109 | 2 044 | 105.4 | 27.9 | 22 | D | D | D | 105 | D | D | D |
| Daly City | 137 | 2 424 | 142.2 | 39.1 | 9 | D | D | D | 225 | D | D | D |
| Dana Point | 107 | 3 837 | 290.5 | 84.6 | 27 | D | D | D | 73 | D | D | D |
| Danville | 88 | 1 370 | 69.8 | 20.9 | 16 | 445 | 36.2 | 11.5 | 116 | 880 | 96.5 | 35.9 |
| Davis | 164 | D | D | D | 17 | D | D | D | 119 | 1 072 | 165.6 | 42.3 |

1. Establishments subject to federal tax.

| City | Other services[1], 2007 | | | | Selected federal funds, 2009–2010 (mil dol) | | | | | | | | |
|---|---|---|---|---|---|---|---|---|---|---|---|---|---|
| | | | | | Procurement contracts | | Grants | | | | | | |
| | Number of establishments | Number of employees | Receipts (mil dol) | Annual payroll (mil dol) | Defense | Other | Total[2] | Medicaid and other health related | Nutrition and family welfare | Energy and environment | Disasters and emergency preparedness | Housing and community development | Employment and training |
| | 104 | 105 | 106 | 107 | 108 | 109 | 110 | 111 | 112 | 113 | 114 | 115 | 116 |
| ARKANSAS—Cont'd | | | | | | | | | | | | | |
| Jacksonville | 33 | D | D | D | 32.8 | 0.0 | 6.4 | 0.0 | 0.0 | 0.0 | 0.0 | 4.1 | 0.0 |
| Jonesboro | 100 | D | D | D | 5.6 | 5.3 | 15.3 | 0.4 | 0.1 | 0.8 | 0.0 | 8.7 | 0.0 |
| Little Rock | 322 | 2 405 | 179.6 | 53.0 | 49.0 | 77.6 | 1 319.0 | 200.9 | 139.7 | 56.3 | 0.3 | 137.9 | 89.5 |
| North Little Rock | 133 | 762 | 57.5 | 17.0 | 1.7 | 113.9 | 42.2 | 0.6 | 0.3 | 11.8 | 2.4 | 16.2 | 0.0 |
| Paragould | 40 | D | D | D | 0.9 | 0.1 | 2.7 | 0.1 | 0.0 | 0.0 | 0.0 | 2.2 | 0.0 |
| Pine Bluff | 67 | D | D | D | 19.0 | 2.7 | 32.2 | 4.9 | 2.6 | 0.8 | 0.0 | 5.6 | 0.0 |
| Rogers | 84 | 518 | 26.4 | 9.0 | 4.9 | 6.6 | 4.3 | 0.1 | 3.0 | 0.6 | 0.0 | 0.5 | 0.0 |
| Russellville | 68 | 344 | 22.9 | 7.6 | 0.0 | 1.5 | 17.1 | 0.0 | 7.9 | 0.1 | 0.0 | 3.6 | 0.0 |
| Sherwood | 43 | 193 | 16.7 | 4.8 | 0.1 | 0.1 | 0.5 | 0.0 | 0.0 | 0.0 | 0.0 | 0.0 | 0.0 |
| Springdale | 102 | 824 | 54.2 | 21.6 | 141.5 | 5.9 | 7.3 | 3.2 | 0.0 | 0.0 | 0.0 | 1.5 | 0.0 |
| Texarkana | 27 | D | D | D | 1.9 | 2.8 | 4.9 | 0.3 | 0.1 | 0.0 | 0.0 | 2.2 | 0.0 |
| West Memphis | 46 | D | D | D | 1.4 | 0.1 | 10.6 | 1.5 | 0.0 | 0.0 | 0.0 | 3.8 | 3.4 |
| CALIFORNIA | 47 780 | 308 788 | 30 937.3 | 8 721.2 | 41 323.3 | 16 213.6 | 78 868.9 | 41 931.1 | 11 743.7 | 2 723.1 | 148.7 | 4 890.8 | 1 299.6 |
| Adelanto | 6 | D | D | D | 2.6 | 0.1 | 0.6 | 0.0 | 0.0 | 0.1 | 0.0 | 0.0 | 0.1 |
| Alameda | 98 | 386 | 33.9 | 11.1 | 56.9 | 93.2 | 50.0 | 1.8 | 2.2 | 19.0 | 0.0 | 26.3 | 0.0 |
| Alhambra | 105 | 453 | 45.7 | 10.9 | 0.1 | 0.6 | 5.9 | 0.0 | 0.0 | 0.0 | 0.0 | 2.4 | 0.0 |
| Aliso Viejo | 43 | D | D | D | 4.3 | -1.9 | 1.4 | 1.4 | 0.0 | 0.0 | 0.0 | 0.0 | 0.0 |
| Anaheim | 376 | 2 850 | 270.6 | 85.3 | 204.9 | 9.5 | 102.7 | 0.8 | 0.1 | 18.7 | 0.0 | 79.8 | 0.0 |
| Antioch | 98 | 716 | 62.0 | 18.9 | 0.8 | 1.4 | 7.4 | 0.0 | 0.0 | 3.8 | 0.0 | 1.5 | 0.0 |
| Apple Valley | 32 | 174 | 10.5 | 4.5 | 0.7 | 3.8 | 19.9 | 0.0 | 0.0 | 18.0 | 0.0 | 1.4 | 0.0 |
| Arcadia | 99 | 432 | 36.6 | 9.9 | 3.9 | 32.2 | 99.1 | 86.1 | 0.0 | 10.1 | 0.0 | 0.0 | 0.0 |
| Atascadero | 37 | 165 | 13.9 | 4.2 | 1.2 | 0.5 | 0.0 | 0.0 | 0.0 | 0.0 | 0.0 | 0.0 | 0.0 |
| Atwater | 20 | D | D | D | 28.3 | 30.9 | 0.2 | 0.0 | 0.0 | 0.0 | 0.0 | 0.0 | 0.0 |
| Azusa | 70 | 292 | 27.0 | 7.9 | 29.8 | 5.2 | 0.9 | 0.8 | 0.0 | 0.1 | 0.0 | 0.0 | 0.0 |
| Bakersfield | 351 | 2 690 | 231.1 | 65.2 | 13.5 | 44.4 | 99.8 | 0.4 | 22.9 | 1.7 | 0.0 | 38.3 | 5.0 |
| Baldwin Park | 48 | D | D | D | 2.2 | 1.5 | 10.2 | 0.9 | 0.0 | 0.6 | 0.0 | 7.3 | 0.0 |
| Banning | 30 | 148 | 9.6 | 3.3 | 0.1 | 0.0 | 4.6 | 1.9 | 0.2 | 0.6 | 0.0 | 0.0 | 0.0 |
| Beaumont | 31 | D | D | D | 0.0 | 0.0 | 0.0 | 0.0 | 0.0 | 0.0 | 0.0 | 0.0 | 0.0 |
| Bell | 27 | D | D | D | 0.0 | 0.0 | 0.8 | 0.0 | 0.0 | 0.1 | 0.0 | 0.0 | 0.0 |
| Bellflower | 135 | 606 | 61.7 | 18.6 | 2.2 | -0.1 | 2.9 | 0.0 | 0.0 | 0.0 | 0.0 | 2.5 | 0.0 |
| Bell Gardens | 35 | 177 | 18.1 | 4.5 | 0.6 | 0.1 | 0.0 | 0.0 | 0.0 | 0.0 | 0.0 | 0.0 | 0.0 |
| Belmont | 48 | 261 | 23.7 | 7.1 | 0.3 | 0.2 | 72.7 | -0.2 | 0.0 | 0.0 | 0.0 | 70.1 | 2.6 |
| Benicia | 50 | 558 | 86.6 | 23.1 | 99.4 | 5.2 | 4.4 | 0.0 | 0.0 | 0.0 | 0.0 | 4.4 | 0.0 |
| Berkeley | 194 | 1 512 | 103.3 | 57.1 | 1.4 | 795.6 | 638.0 | 323.8 | 6.3 | 33.6 | 0.5 | 31.9 | 0.2 |
| Beverly Hills | 266 | 1 963 | 218.2 | 56.2 | 0.3 | 1.8 | 1.3 | 1.2 | 0.0 | 0.0 | 0.0 | 0.1 | 0.0 |
| Brea | 109 | 1 028 | 93.4 | 31.6 | 24.0 | 5.7 | 0.1 | 0.0 | 0.0 | 0.1 | 0.0 | 0.0 | 0.0 |
| Brentwood | 58 | 373 | 35.3 | 10.4 | 0.0 | 0.0 | 0.0 | 0.0 | 0.0 | 0.0 | 0.0 | 0.0 | 0.0 |
| Buena Park | 76 | D | D | D | 3.4 | 0.2 | 1.8 | 0.0 | 0.0 | 0.7 | 0.0 | 1.1 | 0.0 |
| Burbank | 250 | 2 210 | 195.8 | 78.5 | 12.2 | 3.6 | 33.1 | 0.0 | 0.0 | 20.0 | 0.0 | 11.0 | 0.0 |
| Burlingame | 114 | 671 | 54.9 | 17.9 | 107.8 | 0.4 | 16.2 | 14.8 | 0.0 | 0.0 | 0.0 | 1.1 | 0.0 |
| Calexico | 20 | D | D | D | 0.0 | 1.2 | 3.1 | 0.0 | 0.0 | 0.0 | 0.0 | 2.2 | 0.0 |
| Camarillo | 104 | 832 | 88.8 | 26.1 | 55.1 | 5.2 | 9.3 | 0.3 | 0.4 | 0.3 | 0.0 | 0.5 | 0.0 |
| Campbell | 171 | 999 | 91.2 | 29.2 | 2.9 | 9.3 | 15.4 | 0.0 | 0.3 | 15.0 | 0.0 | 0.1 | 0.0 |
| Carlsbad | 133 | 1 245 | 109.3 | 30.4 | 159.1 | 11.3 | 11.3 | 2.7 | 0.0 | 0.0 | 0.0 | 7.3 | 0.0 |
| Carson | 110 | 1 136 | 138.1 | 34.1 | 425.5 | 1.7 | 11.1 | 1.0 | 0.6 | 0.1 | 0.0 | 1.2 | 0.0 |
| Cathedral City | 89 | 612 | 49.5 | 15.2 | 0.0 | 0.0 | 0.6 | 0.0 | 0.0 | 0.0 | 0.0 | 0.0 | 0.0 |
| Ceres | 50 | D | D | D | 1.0 | 0.3 | 0.1 | 0.0 | 0.0 | 0.0 | 0.0 | 0.0 | 0.0 |
| Cerritos | 63 | 630 | 69.5 | 18.5 | 2.8 | 5.5 | 0.2 | 0.0 | 0.0 | 0.0 | 0.0 | 0.1 | 0.0 |
| Chico | 155 | 779 | 68.6 | 19.2 | 0.4 | 27.3 | 39.1 | 1.7 | 0.2 | 1.7 | 0.0 | 14.8 | 4.3 |
| Chino | 118 | 1 486 | 114.1 | 49.7 | 1.8 | 61.8 | 22.7 | 0.0 | 0.0 | 21.8 | 0.0 | 0.8 | 0.0 |
| Chino Hills | 62 | 334 | 15.5 | 5.1 | 0.1 | 0.5 | 1.3 | 0.0 | 0.0 | 0.6 | 0.0 | 0.5 | 0.0 |
| Chula Vista | 216 | 1 585 | 135.5 | 38.4 | 24.5 | 13.6 | 17.6 | 0.0 | 0.2 | 1.9 | 0.0 | 3.6 | 0.4 |
| Citrus Heights | 83 | 673 | 80.3 | 17.9 | 0.0 | 3.7 | 1.5 | 0.0 | 0.0 | 0.4 | 0.0 | 1.1 | 0.0 |
| Claremont | 31 | 139 | 9.2 | 3.2 | 1.6 | 0.1 | 21.3 | 12.4 | 0.5 | 0.2 | 0.0 | 0.0 | 0.0 |
| Clovis | 120 | 657 | 52.3 | 15.5 | 0.0 | 11.6 | 1.5 | 0.4 | 0.0 | 0.1 | 0.0 | 0.7 | 0.0 |
| Coachella | 11 | D | D | D | 94.9 | 2.4 | 1.1 | 0.0 | 0.3 | 0.4 | 0.0 | 0.0 | 0.0 |
| Colton | 52 | 671 | 55.9 | 15.1 | 0.1 | 0.4 | 0.7 | 0.0 | 0.0 | 0.5 | 0.0 | 0.0 | 0.0 |
| Compton | 62 | 392 | 23.2 | 7.7 | 5.3 | 0.7 | 12.6 | -0.2 | 0.0 | 0.9 | 0.0 | 11.2 | 0.0 |
| Concord | 221 | 1 246 | 141.4 | 42.7 | 24.8 | 5.7 | 10.7 | 0.0 | 0.0 | 3.6 | 0.0 | 1.9 | 0.0 |
| Corona | 221 | 1 312 | 129.4 | 36.3 | 60.1 | 3.1 | 4.5 | 0.3 | 0.0 | 0.0 | 0.0 | 3.5 | 0.0 |
| Costa Mesa | 332 | 2 166 | 222.6 | 67.8 | 52.1 | 19.4 | 10.8 | 0.3 | 0.0 | 1.1 | 0.1 | 3.3 | 0.0 |
| Covina | 117 | 711 | 71.0 | 20.0 | 1.9 | 0.0 | 3.0 | 0.0 | 0.0 | 2.1 | 0.0 | 0.0 | 0.0 |
| Culver City | 136 | 2 856 | 115.9 | 49.9 | 1.8 | 7.6 | 18.4 | 0.2 | 0.0 | 0.5 | 0.0 | 1.8 | 0.0 |
| Cupertino | 58 | 398 | 23.9 | 8.8 | 5.1 | 2.8 | 2.8 | 2.3 | 0.0 | 0.0 | 0.0 | 0.5 | 0.0 |
| Cypress | 77 | 472 | 58.4 | 14.7 | 3.9 | 0.1 | 0.0 | 0.0 | 0.0 | 0.0 | 0.0 | 0.0 | 0.0 |
| Daly City | 84 | 505 | 40.1 | 12.4 | 0.0 | -0.7 | 2.0 | 0.1 | 0.0 | 0.0 | 0.0 | 1.9 | 0.0 |
| Dana Point | 50 | 347 | 53.3 | 8.7 | 0.4 | 0.1 | 0.1 | 0.0 | 0.0 | 0.0 | 0.0 | 0.0 | 0.0 |
| Danville | 63 | 297 | 22.9 | 6.6 | 0.3 | 2.0 | 0.2 | 0.0 | 0.0 | 0.0 | 0.0 | 0.0 | 0.0 |
| Davis | 51 | 248 | 22.8 | 7.3 | 3.6 | 6.0 | 475.8 | 368.0 | 0.4 | 28.4 | 0.0 | 1.6 | 0.0 |

1. Establishments subject to federal tax.    2. Includes program categories not shown separately. State totals include additional categories not allocated by city.

# Table D. Cities — City Government Finances

| City | General revenue Total (mil dol) | Intergovernmental Total (mil dol) | Intergovernmental Percent from state government | Taxes Total (mil dol) | Taxes Per capita¹ (dollars) Total | Taxes Per capita¹ Property | Taxes Per capita¹ Sales and gross receipts | General expenditure Total (mil dol) | General expenditure Per capita¹ (dollars) Total | General expenditure Per capita¹ Capital outlays |
|---|---|---|---|---|---|---|---|---|---|---|
| | 117 | 118 | 119 | 120 | 121 | 122 | 123 | 124 | 125 | 126 |
| **ARKANSAS—Cont'd** | | | | | | | | | | |
| Jacksonville .................. | 78.4 | 9.6 | 37.7 | 9.3 | 299 | 30 | 269 | 70.2 | 2 251 | 89 |
| Jonesboro .................. | 62.7 | 16.0 | 28.2 | 20.5 | 324 | 51 | 273 | 58.6 | 928 | 97 |
| Little Rock .................. | 304.1 | 66.2 | 10.1 | 103.6 | 553 | 189 | 364 | 350.4 | 1 869 | 482 |
| North Little Rock .......... | 91.9 | 19.1 | 21.9 | 50.9 | 856 | 131 | 726 | 112.7 | 1 894 | 705 |
| Paragould .................. | 25.9 | 5.3 | 39.8 | 6.4 | 260 | 29 | 230 | 20.6 | 841 | 46 |
| Pine Bluff .................. | 41.3 | 12.5 | 38.3 | 15.7 | 309 | 66 | 243 | 43.1 | 850 | 59 |
| Rogers .................. | 68.1 | 17.5 | 33.6 | 27.9 | 507 | 67 | 440 | 53.3 | 971 | 339 |
| Russellville .................. | 23.9 | 5.0 | 35.0 | 13.3 | 499 | 15 | 484 | 17.5 | 656 | 109 |
| Sherwood .................. | 23.4 | 5.5 | 30.6 | 10.4 | 429 | 16 | 413 | 20.4 | 846 | 98 |
| Springdale .................. | 70.3 | 15.9 | 29.3 | 34.1 | 510 | 74 | 436 | 72.0 | 1 076 | 483 |
| Texarkana .................. | 25.3 | 5.5 | 40.0 | 11.3 | 382 | 110 | 272 | 22.0 | 744 | 17 |
| West Memphis .............. | 25.4 | 5.3 | 59.2 | 11.5 | 419 | 21 | 399 | 26.9 | 979 | 37 |
| **CALIFORNIA** ............ | X | X | X | X | X | X | X | X | X | X |
| Adelanto .................. | 27.8 | 2.9 | 100.0 | 9.0 | 325 | 181 | 138 | 28.7 | 1 035 | 37 |
| Alameda .................. | 138.7 | 16.3 | 80.0 | 72.9 | 1 037 | 578 | 398 | 170.8 | 2 430 | 649 |
| Alhambra .................. | 95.6 | 13.2 | 51.9 | 49.8 | 577 | 311 | 261 | 100.8 | 1 168 | 309 |
| Aliso Viejo .................. | 19.4 | 3.2 | 100.0 | 13.7 | 332 | 162 | 137 | 20.3 | 489 | 179 |
| Anaheim .................. | 578.9 | 100.5 | 26.9 | 275.9 | 828 | 348 | 474 | 663.2 | 1 990 | 514 |
| Antioch .................. | 77.4 | 8.2 | 86.0 | 44.4 | 446 | 285 | 155 | 80.5 | 808 | 217 |
| Apple Valley ................ | 55.6 | 3.8 | 94.0 | 30.7 | 436 | 221 | 144 | 55.1 | 784 | 273 |
| Arcadia .................. | 61.6 | 4.0 | 65.4 | 40.9 | 728 | 357 | 363 | 63.6 | 1 132 | 171 |
| Atascadero .................. | 37.4 | 5.7 | 92.4 | 22.6 | 805 | 428 | 222 | 33.9 | 1 211 | 532 |
| Atwater .................. | 23.7 | 4.0 | 45.7 | 10.1 | 373 | 242 | 93 | 27.5 | 1 020 | 292 |
| Azusa .................. | 60.1 | 3.5 | 71.9 | 34.4 | 739 | 339 | 373 | 78.8 | 1 690 | 332 |
| Bakersfield .................. | 387.1 | 37.4 | 37.1 | 164.8 | 522 | 279 | 237 | 303.3 | 960 | 192 |
| Baldwin Park .............. | 42.5 | 7.7 | 58.7 | 25.9 | 333 | 202 | 128 | 41.9 | 538 | 47 |
| Banning .................. | 34.3 | 6.7 | 85.9 | 12.8 | 440 | 258 | 179 | 38.7 | 1 331 | 356 |
| Beaumont .................. | 38.0 | 1.9 | 100.0 | 7.0 | 230 | 60 | 147 | 30.3 | 1 004 | 430 |
| Bell .................. | 27.3 | 2.4 | 68.7 | 18.2 | 493 | 307 | 184 | 61.5 | 1 668 | 878 |
| Bellflower .................. | 36.2 | 4.8 | 73.6 | 25.5 | 348 | 161 | 184 | 35.5 | 483 | 114 |
| Bell Gardens ............... | 36.8 | 3.1 | 81.7 | 25.5 | 568 | 179 | 388 | 31.7 | 706 | 59 |
| Belmont .................. | 39.0 | 2.3 | 92.5 | 25.3 | 1 026 | 741 | 267 | 39.7 | 1 610 | 114 |
| Benicia .................. | 51.1 | 3.4 | 95.8 | 30.8 | 1 171 | 572 | 560 | 43.7 | 1 659 | 314 |
| Berkeley .................. | 295.4 | 25.5 | 84.7 | 133.1 | 1 313 | 641 | 485 | 290.6 | 2 867 | 113 |
| Beverly Hills ................ | 210.8 | 5.5 | 73.5 | 134.6 | 3 892 | 1 119 | 2 739 | 163.3 | 4 720 | 376 |
| Brea .................. | 93.9 | 6.1 | 77.4 | 57.4 | 1 495 | 1 000 | 488 | 86.6 | 2 257 | 497 |
| Brentwood .................. | 95.7 | 2.9 | 100.0 | 37.3 | 770 | 463 | 145 | 110.6 | 2 282 | 750 |
| Buena Park .................. | 100.0 | 14.1 | 34.3 | 70.0 | 883 | 514 | 364 | 70.2 | 886 | 119 |
| Burbank .................. | 299.5 | 31.2 | 33.7 | 145.0 | 1 404 | 774 | 621 | 301.8 | 2 922 | 778 |
| Burlingame .................. | 57.4 | 2.1 | 100.0 | 34.4 | 1 247 | 408 | 820 | 58.8 | 2 133 | 582 |
| Calexico .................. | 37.3 | 6.2 | 39.7 | 16.6 | 442 | 143 | 268 | 38.1 | 1 013 | 53 |
| Camarillo .................. | 73.9 | 9.7 | 56.9 | 37.8 | 599 | 315 | 274 | 69.9 | 1 108 | 312 |
| Campbell .................. | 43.1 | 2.0 | 91.6 | 28.7 | 760 | 435 | 308 | 43.3 | 1 149 | 167 |
| Carlsbad .................. | 212.4 | 21.0 | 43.0 | 113.3 | 1 187 | 559 | 614 | 183.9 | 1 926 | 613 |
| Carson .................. | 115.0 | 10.1 | 74.2 | 78.2 | 843 | 477 | 359 | 100.4 | 1 082 | 190 |
| Cathedral City .............. | 72.8 | 8.8 | 88.4 | 46.3 | 885 | 645 | 228 | 68.6 | 1 311 | 239 |
| Ceres .................. | 39.9 | 2.9 | 91.4 | 23.4 | 547 | 241 | 242 | 38.5 | 902 | 269 |
| Cerritos .................. | 116.3 | 2.7 | 100.0 | 69.9 | 1 354 | 831 | 516 | 117.7 | 2 279 | 185 |
| Chico .................. | 112.5 | 9.2 | 51.3 | 73.7 | 887 | 487 | 394 | 117.9 | 1 418 | 597 |
| Chino .................. | 127.7 | 7.6 | 88.7 | 54.3 | 655 | 426 | 222 | 132.1 | 1 595 | 219 |
| Chino Hills .................. | 88.0 | 5.8 | 92.6 | 22.4 | 301 | 137 | 156 | 86.5 | 1 163 | 499 |
| Chula Vista .................. | 238.6 | 18.9 | 77.4 | 130.6 | 601 | 286 | 308 | 277.7 | 1 277 | 212 |
| Citrus Heights.............. | 59.8 | 16.6 | 82.0 | 36.1 | 428 | 203 | 222 | 44.5 | 527 | 96 |
| Claremont.................. | 40.9 | 2.7 | 94.5 | 23.2 | 664 | 296 | 356 | 38.6 | 1 104 | 152 |
| Clovis .................. | 108.6 | 7.5 | 69.5 | 49.2 | 542 | 268 | 268 | 108.9 | 1 199 | 323 |
| Coachella .................. | 40.1 | 8.7 | 78.7 | 16.9 | 435 | 248 | 141 | 47.9 | 1 236 | 334 |
| Colton .................. | 61.0 | 4.4 | 71.1 | 35.0 | 689 | 399 | 279 | 58.9 | 1 159 | 218 |
| Compton.................. | 86.0 | 15.9 | 29.5 | 44.7 | 474 | 186 | 282 | 91.4 | 968 | 33 |
| Concord .................. | 141.0 | 9.5 | 86.2 | 81.7 | 676 | 366 | 305 | 123.4 | 1 021 | 205 |
| Corona.................. | 234.4 | 14.5 | 65.5 | 128.6 | 855 | 490 | 327 | 254.2 | 1 691 | 263 |
| Costa Mesa.................. | 126.6 | 9.1 | 69.5 | 93.4 | 857 | 383 | 468 | 106.6 | 978 | 85 |
| Covina .................. | 50.4 | 4.3 | 89.1 | 33.6 | 712 | 362 | 342 | 47.5 | 1 005 | 173 |
| Culver City.................. | 163.8 | 17.2 | 60.7 | 100.2 | 2 578 | 1 002 | 1 479 | 129.8 | 3 341 | 463 |
| Cupertino.................. | 53.7 | 2.5 | 66.7 | 34.7 | 651 | 268 | 353 | 54.8 | 1 028 | 149 |
| Cypress .................. | 51.7 | 4.1 | 79.4 | 36.2 | 768 | 422 | 339 | 46.7 | 990 | 276 |
| Daly City.................. | 104.8 | 13.8 | 40.4 | 53.4 | 529 | 301 | 218 | 102.1 | 1 012 | 105 |
| Dana Point .................. | 34.1 | 2.7 | 100.0 | 26.6 | 746 | 257 | 472 | 37.3 | 1 046 | 352 |
| Danville.................. | 37.4 | 2.8 | 100.0 | 23.7 | 578 | 323 | 194 | 32.1 | 783 | 187 |
| Davis .................. | 102.2 | 17.7 | 93.2 | 49.1 | 783 | 384 | 307 | 99.6 | 1 587 | 261 |

1. Based on population estimated as of July 1 of the year shown.

# Table D. Cities — **City Government Finances**

| City | City government finances, 2006 (cont.) | | | | | | | | | |
|---|---|---|---|---|---|---|---|---|---|---|
| | General expenditure (cont.) | | | | | | | | | |
| | Percent of total for: | | | | | | | | | |
| | Public welfare | Highways | Parking facilities | Education | Health and hospitals | Police protection | Sewerage and sanitation | Parks and recreation | Housing and community development | Interest on debt |
| | 127 | 128 | 129 | 130 | 131 | 132 | 133 | 134 | 135 | 136 |
| ARKANSAS—Cont'd | | | | | | | | | | |
| Jacksonville | 0.0 | 3.1 | 0.0 | 0.0 | 63.8 | 7.2 | 10.1 | 3.2 | 0.5 | 0.9 |
| Jonesboro | 0.0 | 16.8 | 0.0 | 0.0 | 0.6 | 15.8 | 14.6 | 3.8 | 0.1 | 18.5 |
| Little Rock | 0.0 | 9.4 | 0.2 | 0.0 | 4.4 | 14.7 | 18.5 | 10.2 | 1.0 | 4.3 |
| North Little Rock | 0.0 | 5.6 | 0.0 | 0.0 | 0.4 | 14.3 | 12.4 | 34.7 | 1.0 | 1.7 |
| Paragould | 0.3 | 7.9 | 0.0 | 0.0 | 0.7 | 12.2 | 17.9 | 6.0 | 0.0 | 5.3 |
| Pine Bluff | 0.0 | 8.2 | 0.0 | 0.0 | 0.8 | 24.1 | 19.2 | 8.9 | 3.8 | 1.8 |
| Rogers | 0.0 | 4.8 | 0.0 | 0.0 | 0.0 | 12.4 | 25.7 | 5.5 | 0.0 | 4.4 |
| Russellville | 0.3 | 22.6 | 0.0 | 0.0 | 0.0 | 22.2 | 14.5 | 3.8 | 0.0 | 1.9 |
| Sherwood | 0.0 | 12.3 | 0.0 | 0.0 | 1.6 | 21.2 | 21.1 | 9.0 | 0.0 | 1.2 |
| Springdale | 0.0 | 36.7 | 0.0 | 0.0 | 0.4 | 13.2 | 8.8 | 11.0 | 0.9 | 2.6 |
| Texarkana | 0.0 | 8.5 | 0.0 | 0.0 | 0.4 | 29.1 | 21.8 | 0.9 | 3.0 | 1.9 |
| West Memphis | 0.0 | 9.6 | 0.0 | 0.0 | 0.7 | 21.8 | 11.9 | 4.5 | 1.3 | 3.6 |
| CALIFORNIA | X | X | X | X | X | X | X | X | X | X |
| Adelanto | 0.0 | 3.7 | 0.0 | 0.0 | 0.6 | 16.5 | 8.4 | 1.9 | 5.5 | 9.5 |
| Alameda | 0.0 | 4.6 | 0.0 | 0.0 | 9.5 | 14.9 | 3.0 | 6.1 | 16.7 | 2.8 |
| Alhambra | 0.0 | 7.0 | 1.6 | 0.0 | 2.6 | 20.9 | 9.4 | 7.4 | 20.0 | 5.2 |
| Aliso Viejo | 0.0 | 8.3 | 0.0 | 0.0 | 0.4 | 26.2 | 0.0 | 0.3 | 0.5 | 0.0 |
| Anaheim | 0.0 | 6.9 | 0.0 | 0.0 | 0.1 | 15.8 | 7.1 | 14.1 | 18.5 | 10.5 |
| Antioch | 0.0 | 21.3 | 0.0 | 0.0 | 1.0 | 32.0 | 5.0 | 9.6 | 10.6 | 4.9 |
| Apple Valley | 0.0 | 21.0 | 0.0 | 0.0 | 1.8 | 15.6 | 13.5 | 8.4 | 18.2 | 1.3 |
| Arcadia | 0.0 | 7.7 | 0.0 | 0.0 | 3.6 | 22.2 | 1.5 | 3.9 | 3.4 | 2.3 |
| Atascadero | 0.0 | 14.5 | 0.0 | 0.0 | 0.0 | 15.3 | 9.5 | 19.1 | 12.2 | 2.3 |
| Atwater | 0.0 | 6.4 | 0.0 | 0.0 | 0.0 | 16.0 | 25.1 | 3.7 | 5.5 | 1.5 |
| Azusa | 0.0 | 4.8 | 0.0 | 0.0 | 0.5 | 17.8 | 5.4 | 4.6 | 20.5 | 5.1 |
| Bakersfield | 0.0 | 6.2 | 0.0 | 0.0 | 0.0 | 21.4 | 15.2 | 9.8 | 1.3 | 2.1 |
| Baldwin Park | 0.0 | 10.6 | 0.0 | 0.0 | 0.0 | 36.2 | 0.8 | 5.4 | 17.4 | 4.9 |
| Banning | 0.0 | 2.8 | 0.0 | 0.0 | 0.4 | 24.3 | 17.0 | 13.4 | 17.5 | 3.1 |
| Beaumont | 0.0 | 2.5 | 0.0 | 0.0 | 0.4 | 15.4 | 10.1 | 3.5 | 4.1 | 16.4 |
| Bell | 0.0 | 2.8 | 0.0 | 0.0 | 0.0 | 14.4 | 3.2 | 4.1 | 12.1 | 5.5 |
| Bellflower | 0.0 | 17.7 | 0.0 | 0.0 | 0.0 | 28.6 | 0.0 | 12.3 | 17.6 | 6.2 |
| Bell Gardens | 0.0 | 10.0 | 0.0 | 0.0 | 0.0 | 38.0 | 4.3 | 20.1 | 3.6 | 6.6 |
| Belmont | 0.0 | 5.3 | 0.0 | 0.0 | 0.0 | 20.5 | 16.1 | 8.2 | 12.5 | 4.8 |
| Benicia | 0.0 | 17.7 | 0.0 | 0.0 | 0.0 | 20.4 | 13.0 | 13.0 | 0.1 | 4.3 |
| Berkeley | 0.0 | 5.6 | 2.3 | 0.0 | 10.3 | 15.9 | 13.0 | 6.1 | 11.9 | 2.1 |
| Beverly Hills | 0.0 | 6.7 | 5.1 | 0.0 | 3.4 | 21.0 | 15.5 | 9.9 | 0.1 | 5.1 |
| Brea | 0.0 | 13.0 | 0.0 | 0.0 | 3.4 | 26.8 | 3.5 | 9.9 | 13.7 | 11.5 |
| Brentwood | 0.0 | 26.9 | 0.0 | 0.0 | 0.0 | 11.4 | 14.1 | 9.4 | 9.3 | 11.3 |
| Buena Park | 0.0 | 15.2 | 0.0 | 0.0 | 0.3 | 30.7 | 4.4 | 6.8 | 14.5 | 2.3 |
| Burbank | 0.0 | 7.2 | 0.3 | 0.0 | 4.0 | 12.8 | 7.9 | 4.8 | 24.7 | 4.5 |
| Burlingame | 0.0 | 22.7 | 1.9 | 0.0 | 0.0 | 14.1 | 14.0 | 9.9 | 0.0 | 2.5 |
| Calexico | 0.0 | 7.6 | 0.0 | 0.0 | 0.4 | 17.7 | 14.5 | 3.3 | 7.7 | 0.5 |
| Camarillo | 0.0 | 27.5 | 0.0 | 0.0 | 0.2 | 18.0 | 15.7 | 0.4 | 10.0 | 3.8 |
| Campbell | 0.0 | 11.4 | 0.0 | 0.0 | 0.0 | 26.3 | 0.0 | 14.1 | 13.9 | 3.0 |
| Carlsbad | 0.0 | 12.9 | 0.0 | 0.0 | 0.1 | 13.6 | 9.7 | 23.5 | 3.8 | 2.9 |
| Carson | 0.0 | 12.4 | 0.0 | 0.0 | 0.4 | 19.5 | 0.1 | 17.6 | 18.0 | 5.4 |
| Cathedral City | 0.0 | 6.9 | 0.0 | 0.0 | 3.0 | 17.8 | 0.7 | 0.0 | 24.8 | 11.8 |
| Ceres | 0.0 | 12.2 | 0.0 | 0.0 | 0.0 | 22.8 | 12.3 | 9.3 | 10.6 | 7.7 |
| Cerritos | 0.0 | 8.8 | 0.0 | 0.0 | 0.1 | 10.4 | 4.2 | 14.7 | 9.2 | 14.5 |
| Chico | 0.0 | 4.9 | 0.9 | 0.0 | 0.8 | 17.9 | 6.6 | 5.5 | 31.4 | 5.9 |
| Chino | 0.0 | 8.3 | 0.0 | 0.0 | 4.4 | 19.7 | 13.7 | 10.8 | 15.3 | 6.8 |
| Chino Hills | 0.0 | 28.7 | 0.0 | 0.0 | 0.3 | 11.7 | 8.9 | 21.8 | 0.0 | 5.2 |
| Chula Vista | 0.0 | 8.7 | 0.1 | 0.0 | 1.4 | 18.8 | 8.1 | 8.8 | 4.1 | 8.9 |
| Citrus Heights | 0.0 | 26.9 | 0.0 | 0.0 | 1.2 | 36.6 | 1.0 | 0.0 | 2.5 | 5.0 |
| Claremont | 0.0 | 9.3 | 0.0 | 0.0 | 1.4 | 24.5 | 13.1 | 9.3 | 11.6 | 3.7 |
| Clovis | 0.0 | 8.7 | 0.0 | 0.0 | 1.4 | 21.4 | 28.2 | 5.5 | 4.1 | 4.1 |
| Coachella | 0.0 | 30.2 | 0.0 | 0.0 | 0.3 | 12.4 | 7.0 | 0.9 | 9.6 | 7.1 |
| Colton | 0.0 | 15.7 | 0.0 | 0.0 | 0.0 | 24.5 | 7.7 | 7.4 | 6.5 | 8.4 |
| Compton | 0.0 | 10.2 | 0.0 | 0.0 | 1.0 | 16.3 | 9.4 | 2.3 | 10.6 | 2.7 |
| Concord | 0.0 | 16.2 | 0.0 | 0.0 | 0.0 | 31.2 | 13.9 | 13.4 | 7.6 | 3.1 |
| Corona | 0.0 | 8.5 | 0.1 | 0.0 | 0.9 | 14.9 | 10.2 | 4.8 | 18.1 | 9.8 |
| Costa Mesa | 0.0 | 6.5 | 0.0 | 0.0 | 0.8 | 37.1 | 0.1 | 4.0 | 3.9 | 1.1 |
| Covina | 0.0 | 7.1 | 0.2 | 0.0 | 0.4 | 26.1 | 11.8 | 4.9 | 12.6 | 5.0 |
| Culver City | 0.0 | 5.0 | 0.1 | 0.0 | 2.7 | 22.5 | 10.8 | 5.0 | 15.6 | 8.7 |
| Cupertino | 0.0 | 23.9 | 0.0 | 0.0 | 0.4 | 12.7 | 3.9 | 16.4 | 0.9 | 4.1 |
| Cypress | 0.0 | 14.3 | 0.0 | 0.0 | 0.2 | 27.6 | 1.8 | 24.2 | 14.1 | 3.3 |
| Daly City | 0.0 | 6.0 | 0.0 | 0.0 | 0.0 | 21.9 | 12.2 | 16.1 | 3.1 | 1.5 |
| Dana Point | 0.0 | 26.0 | 0.0 | 0.0 | 0.6 | 20.9 | 0.0 | 20.5 | 1.1 | 0.0 |
| Danville | 0.0 | 17.5 | 0.0 | 0.0 | 0.5 | 19.1 | 0.0 | 9.3 | 2.8 | 2.6 |
| Davis | 0.0 | 11.9 | 0.0 | 0.0 | 0.0 | 13.8 | 16.1 | 28.4 | 8.6 | 2.0 |

— **City Government Finances, City Government Employment, and Climate**

| City | City government finances, 2007 (cont.) | | | | Climate[2] | | | | | | |
|---|---|---|---|---|---|---|---|---|---|---|---|
| | Debt outstanding | | | | Average daily temperature (degrees Fahrenheit) | | | | | | |
| | | | | | Mean | | Limits | | | | |
| | Total (mil dol) | Per capita[1] (dollars) | Debt issued during year | City government employment, 2011 | January | July | January[3] | July[4] | Annual precipitation (inches) | Heating degree days | Cooling degree days |
| | 137 | 138 | 139 | 140 | 141 | 142 | 143 | 144 | 145 | 146 | 147 |
| **ARKANSAS—Cont'd** | | | | | | | | | | | |
| Jacksonville | 17.4 | 558 | 4.5 | 352 | 38.2 | 79.9 | 27.4 | 91.1 | 50.56 | 3 470 | 1 699 |
| Jonesboro | 313.8 | 4 966 | 5.9 | 676 | 35.6 | 81.6 | 25.8 | 92.3 | 46.18 | 3 737 | 1 858 |
| Little Rock | 380.2 | 2 028 | 23.1 | 2 854 | 40.1 | 82.4 | 30.8 | 92.8 | 50.93 | 3 084 | 2 086 |
| North Little Rock | 141.8 | 2 384 | 12.0 | 951 | 40.1 | 82.4 | 30.8 | 92.8 | 50.93 | 3 084 | 2 086 |
| Paragould | 46.8 | 1 910 | 0.0 | 289 | NA | NA | NA | NA | NA | NA | NA |
| Pine Bluff | 21.0 | 415 | 0.0 | 424 | 40.8 | 82.4 | 31.5 | 92.4 | 52.48 | 2 935 | 2 099 |
| Rogers | 104.7 | 1 905 | 15.4 | 469 | 32.9 | 77.5 | 22.0 | 88.8 | 46.92 | 4 483 | 1 269 |
| Russellville | 7.3 | 275 | 0.0 | 242 | NA | NA | NA | NA | NA | NA | NA |
| Sherwood | 6.2 | 255 | 0.0 | 257 | NA | NA | NA | NA | NA | NA | NA |
| Springdale | 136.4 | 2 039 | 127.6 | 568 | 34.3 | 78.9 | 24.2 | 89.1 | 46.02 | 4 166 | 1 439 |
| Texarkana | 54.5 | 1 839 | 0.7 | 234 | 44.3 | 82.7 | 35.6 | 92.7 | 47.38 | 2 421 | 2 280 |
| West Memphis | 30.3 | 1 104 | 0.0 | 379 | 37.5 | 81.5 | 28.5 | 90.9 | 52.80 | 3 417 | 1 903 |
| **CALIFORNIA** | X | X | X | X | X | X | X | X | X | X | X |
| Adelanto | 63.7 | 2 301 | 8.0 | NA | NA | NA | NA | NA | NA | NA | NA |
| Alameda | 137.2 | 1 953 | 4.0 | NA | 50.9 | 64.9 | 44.7 | 72.7 | 22.94 | 2 400 | 377 |
| Alhambra | 109.4 | 1 267 | 0.0 | 437 | 56.3 | 75.6 | 42.6 | 89.0 | 18.56 | 1 295 | 1 575 |
| Aliso Viejo | 0.0 | 0 | 0.0 | NA | 56.7 | 72.4 | 47.2 | 82.3 | 14.03 | 1 465 | 1 183 |
| Anaheim | 1 708.8 | 5 128 | 537.1 | 2 507 | 56.9 | 73.2 | 45.2 | 84.0 | 11.23 | 1 286 | 1 294 |
| Antioch | 73.0 | 733 | 0.0 | 326 | 45.7 | 74.4 | 37.8 | 90.7 | 13.33 | 2 714 | 1 179 |
| Apple Valley | 21.6 | 307 | 9.0 | NA | 45.5 | 80.0 | 31.4 | 99.1 | 6.20 | 2 929 | 1 735 |
| Arcadia | 33.9 | 603 | 0.0 | NA | 56.3 | 75.6 | 42.6 | 89.0 | 18.56 | 1 295 | 1 575 |
| Atascadero | 15.1 | 537 | 1.0 | NA | 47.3 | 71.6 | 33.1 | 91.3 | 14.71 | 2 932 | 785 |
| Atwater | 13.3 | 492 | 10.8 | NA | NA | NA | NA | NA | NA | NA | NA |
| Azusa | 208.2 | 4 467 | 126.7 | NA | 54.6 | 73.8 | 41.5 | 88.7 | 16.96 | 1 727 | 1 191 |
| Bakersfield | 120.5 | 382 | 1.3 | 1 410 | 47.8 | 83.1 | 39.3 | 96.9 | 6.49 | 2 120 | 2 286 |
| Baldwin Park | 89.4 | 1 149 | 12.8 | 239 | 56.3 | 75.6 | 42.6 | 89.0 | 18.56 | 1 295 | 1 575 |
| Banning | 55.5 | 1 911 | 30.0 | NA | NA | NA | NA | NA | NA | NA | NA |
| Beaumont | 146.6 | 4 852 | 31.1 | NA | NA | NA | NA | NA | NA | NA | NA |
| Bell | 83.3 | 2 260 | 0.0 | NA | 58.8 | 76.6 | 47.9 | 88.9 | 14.44 | 949 | 1 837 |
| Bellflower | 37.5 | 511 | 2.6 | NA | 57.0 | 73.8 | 46.0 | 82.9 | 12.94 | 1 211 | 1 186 |
| Bell Gardens | 72.0 | 1 606 | 0.4 | NA | 58.8 | 76.6 | 47.9 | 88.9 | 14.44 | 949 | 1 837 |
| Belmont | 45.3 | 1 837 | 0.0 | NA | 48.1 | 69.7 | 36.4 | 88.2 | 28.71 | 2 769 | 569 |
| Benicia | 79.2 | 3 007 | 0.0 | NA | 46.3 | 71.2 | 38.8 | 87.4 | 19.58 | 2 757 | 786 |
| Berkeley | 192.0 | 1 894 | 0.0 | 1 773 | 50.0 | 62.8 | 43.6 | 70.4 | 25.40 | 2 857 | 142 |
| Beverly Hills | 273.6 | 7 908 | 117.1 | 606 | 57.9 | 69.5 | 49.4 | 76.9 | 18.68 | 1 379 | 893 |
| Brea | 232.9 | 6 067 | 0.0 | NA | 56.9 | 73.2 | 45.2 | 84.0 | 11.23 | 1 286 | 1 294 |
| Brentwood | 216.8 | 4 475 | 0.0 | NA | NA | NA | NA | NA | NA | NA | NA |
| Buena Park | 51.8 | 653 | 0.0 | 326 | 57.0 | 73.8 | 46.0 | 82.9 | 12.94 | 1 211 | 1 186 |
| Burbank | 423.1 | 4 096 | 52.9 | 1 349 | 54.8 | 75.5 | 42.0 | 88.9 | 17.49 | 1 575 | 1 455 |
| Burlingame | 36.3 | 1 317 | 33.0 | NA | 50.0 | 62.7 | 42.9 | 70.5 | 23.35 | 2 720 | 184 |
| Calexico | 5.9 | 158 | 0.0 | NA | 55.8 | 91.4 | 41.3 | 107.0 | 2.96 | 1 080 | 3 952 |
| Camarillo | 108.7 | 1 723 | 27.6 | NA | 55.7 | 66.0 | 45.3 | 74.0 | 13.61 | 1 961 | 389 |
| Campbell | 33.6 | 891 | 0.0 | NA | 48.7 | 70.3 | 38.8 | 85.4 | 22.64 | 2 641 | 613 |
| Carlsbad | 108.5 | 1 137 | 0.0 | 793 | 54.7 | 67.6 | 45.4 | 72.1 | 11.13 | 2 009 | 505 |
| Carson | 165.3 | 1 781 | 61.0 | 516 | 56.3 | 69.4 | 46.2 | 77.6 | 14.79 | 1 526 | 742 |
| Cathedral City | 250.3 | 4 787 | 115.8 | NA | 57.3 | 92.1 | 44.2 | 108.2 | 5.23 | 951 | 4 224 |
| Ceres | 55.1 | 1 290 | 38.1 | NA | 47.2 | 77.7 | 40.1 | 93.6 | 13.12 | 2 358 | 1 570 |
| Cerritos | 267.4 | 5 177 | 1.0 | NA | 57.0 | 73.8 | 46.0 | 82.9 | 12.94 | 1 211 | 1 186 |
| Chico | 150.4 | 1 810 | 0.0 | NA | 44.5 | 76.9 | 35.2 | 93.0 | 26.23 | 2 945 | 1 334 |
| Chino | 247.0 | 2 982 | 89.5 | 442 | 54.6 | 73.8 | 41.5 | 88.7 | 16.96 | 1 727 | 1 191 |
| Chino Hills | 185.4 | 2 493 | 49.7 | 175 | 56.9 | 73.2 | 45.2 | 84.0 | 11.23 | 1 286 | 1 294 |
| Chula Vista | 850.8 | 3 912 | 26.8 | 1 112 | 57.3 | 70.1 | 46.1 | 76.1 | 9.95 | 1 321 | 862 |
| Citrus Heights | 50.2 | 595 | 0.0 | 208 | 46.9 | 77.7 | 39.2 | 94.8 | 24.61 | 2 532 | 1 528 |
| Claremont | 29.3 | 837 | 0.0 | NA | 54.6 | 73.8 | 41.5 | 88.7 | 16.96 | 1 727 | 1 191 |
| Clovis | 281.4 | 3 098 | 68.5 | 511 | 46.0 | 81.4 | 38.4 | 96.6 | 11.23 | 2 447 | 1 963 |
| Coachella | 102.3 | 2 641 | 10.1 | NA | NA | NA | NA | NA | NA | NA | NA |
| Colton | 90.2 | 1 776 | 0.4 | NA | 54.4 | 79.6 | 41.8 | 96.0 | 16.43 | 1 599 | 1 937 |
| Compton | 97.7 | 1 034 | 53.1 | 409 | 57.0 | 73.8 | 46.0 | 82.9 | 12.94 | 1 211 | 1 186 |
| Concord | 117.8 | 975 | 0.6 | 455 | 46.3 | 71.2 | 38.8 | 87.4 | 19.58 | 2 757 | 786 |
| Corona | 621.6 | 4 135 | 61.4 | 752 | 54.7 | 75.9 | 41.5 | 92.0 | 12.00 | 1 599 | 1 534 |
| Costa Mesa | 57.0 | 523 | 30.0 | 515 | 55.9 | 67.3 | 48.2 | 71.4 | 11.65 | 1 719 | 543 |
| Covina | 59.5 | 1 260 | 0.3 | NA | 54.6 | 73.8 | 41.5 | 88.7 | 16.96 | 1 727 | 1 191 |
| Culver City | 199.1 | 5 125 | 1.6 | NA | 56.7 | 70.8 | 46.1 | 80.0 | 13.32 | 1 344 | 959 |
| Cupertino | 50.1 | 940 | 0.0 | NA | 48.7 | 70.3 | 38.8 | 85.4 | 22.64 | 2 641 | 613 |
| Cypress | 51.1 | 1 084 | 29.9 | NA | 57.0 | 73.8 | 46.0 | 82.9 | 12.94 | 1 211 | 1 186 |
| Daly City | 56.1 | 556 | 0.0 | 585 | 50.6 | 57.3 | 44.6 | 61.1 | 19.77 | 3 665 | 17 |
| Dana Point | 0.0 | 0 | 0.0 | NA | 55.4 | 68.7 | 43.9 | 77.3 | 13.56 | 1 756 | 666 |
| Danville | 14.8 | 360 | 0.0 | NA | 47.5 | 72.4 | 39.3 | 85.2 | 23.96 | 3 267 | 983 |
| Davis | 49.0 | 782 | 21.1 | NA | 45.2 | 74.3 | 37.1 | 92.7 | 19.05 | 2 853 | 1 127 |

1. Based on the population estimated as of July 1 of the year shown.  2. Represents normal values based on the 30-year period, 1971–2000.  3. Average daily minimum.  4. Average daily maximum.

| STATE Place code | City | Land area,[1] 2010 (sq km) | Population, 2012 Total persons | Rank | Per square kilometer | Race alone or in combination, not of Hispanic origin (percent), 2010 — White | Black | American Indian, Alaska Native | Asian | Hawaiian Pacific Islander | Percent Hispanic or Latino[2], 2010 | Percent Foreign born 2007–2011 |
|---|---|---|---|---|---|---|---|---|---|---|---|---|
| | | 1 | 2 | 3 | 4 | 5 | 6 | 7 | 8 | 9 | 10 | 11 |
| | CALIFORNIA—Cont'd | | | | | | | | | | | |
| 06 18394 | Delano | 37.0 | 52 426 | 688 | 1 416.9 | 8.0 | 7.7 | 0.4 | 12.8 | 0.2 | 71.5 | 37.6 |
| 06 18996 | Desert Hot Springs | 61.2 | 27 745 | 1 303 | 453.3 | 36.2 | 8.6 | 1.2 | 3.0 | 0.5 | 52.6 | 25.3 |
| 06 19192 | Diamond Bar | 38.5 | 56 363 | 635 | 1 464.0 | 22.9 | 4.4 | 0.4 | 53.8 | 0.5 | 20.1 | 42.7 |
| 06 19766 | Downey | 32.1 | 112 873 | 237 | 3 516.3 | 18.5 | 3.7 | 0.4 | 7.2 | 0.3 | 70.7 | 35.2 |
| 06 20018 | Dublin | 38.6 | 48 775 | 759 | 1 263.6 | 48.0 | 10.0 | 0.9 | 29.7 | 1.1 | 14.5 | 23.4 |
| 06 20956 | East Palo Alto | 6.5 | 28 867 | 1 262 | 4 441.1 | 7.4 | 16.8 | 0.7 | 4.6 | 8.2 | 64.5 | 41.4 |
| 06 21712 | El Cajon | 37.4 | 101 435 | 283 | 2 712.2 | 60.8 | 7.3 | 1.2 | 5.9 | 1.0 | 28.2 | 27.6 |
| 06 21782 | El Centro | 28.7 | 43 107 | 845 | 1 502.0 | 14.0 | 2.3 | 0.4 | 2.1 | 0.1 | 81.6 | 30.5 |
| 06 22020 | Elk Grove | 109.3 | 159 038 | 152 | 1 455.1 | 42.2 | 12.7 | 1.3 | 29.3 | 2.0 | 18.0 | 22.5 |
| 06 22230 | El Monte | 24.8 | 115 111 | 233 | 4 641.6 | 5.2 | 0.5 | 0.2 | 25.2 | 0.1 | 69.0 | 52.9 |
| 06 22300 | El Paso de Robles (Paso Robles) | 49.5 | 30 556 | 1 193 | 617.3 | 60.9 | 2.4 | 1.2 | 2.5 | 0.3 | 34.5 | 14.7 |
| 06 22678 | Encinitas | 48.7 | 60 994 | 568 | 1 252.4 | 81.1 | 0.9 | 0.7 | 5.5 | 0.4 | 13.7 | 13.2 |
| 06 22804 | Escondido | 95.3 | 147 575 | 165 | 1 548.5 | 42.1 | 2.7 | 0.9 | 6.9 | 0.4 | 48.9 | 28.3 |
| 06 23042 | Eureka | 24.3 | 26 961 | 1 345 | 1 109.5 | 78.0 | 2.7 | 6.2 | 5.1 | 1.0 | 11.6 | 6.9 |
| 06 23182 | Fairfield | 96.8 | 107 684 | 256 | 1 112.4 | 40.0 | 17.7 | 1.6 | 17.9 | 2.0 | 27.3 | 21.6 |
| 06 24638 | Folsom | 56.8 | 73 384 | 447 | 1 292.0 | 69.3 | 6.1 | 1.0 | 14.4 | 0.5 | 11.2 | 14.8 |
| 06 24680 | Fontana | 109.9 | 201 812 | 110 | 1 836.3 | 16.6 | 9.9 | 0.6 | 7.1 | 0.4 | 66.8 | 30.9 |
| 06 25338 | Foster City | 9.7 | 32 129 | 1 131 | 3 312.3 | 45.3 | 2.2 | 0.4 | 48.1 | 1.0 | 6.5 | 40.6 |
| 06 25380 | Fountain Valley | 23.4 | 56 464 | 634 | 2 413.0 | 51.9 | 1.2 | 0.7 | 35.2 | 0.7 | 13.1 | 29.1 |
| 06 26000 | Fremont | 200.6 | 221 986 | 96 | 1 106.6 | 29.9 | 3.8 | 0.7 | 53.8 | 1.0 | 14.8 | 43.1 |
| 06 27000 | Fresno | 290.0 | 505 882 | 34 | 1 744.4 | 31.6 | 8.4 | 1.3 | 13.3 | 0.3 | 46.9 | 21.3 |
| 06 28000 | Fullerton | 57.9 | 138 574 | 183 | 2 393.3 | 40.1 | 2.5 | 0.6 | 24.0 | 0.5 | 34.4 | 31.1 |
| 06 28168 | Gardena | 15.1 | 59 490 | 588 | 3 939.7 | 10.8 | 24.8 | 0.6 | 27.2 | 1.1 | 37.7 | 33.8 |
| 06 29000 | Garden Grove | 46.5 | 174 389 | 136 | 3 750.3 | 23.9 | 1.3 | 0.4 | 38.1 | 0.9 | 36.9 | 44.6 |
| 06 29504 | Gilroy | 41.8 | 50 660 | 721 | 1 212.0 | 33.2 | 1.9 | 0.8 | 7.9 | 0.4 | 57.8 | 24.5 |
| 06 30000 | Glendale | 78.9 | 194 478 | 122 | 2 464.9 | 64.6 | 1.5 | 0.3 | 18.8 | 0.4 | 17.4 | 54.8 |
| 06 30014 | Glendora | 50.2 | 50 719 | 718 | 1 010.3 | 59.2 | 2.1 | 0.6 | 9.3 | 0.4 | 30.7 | 15.5 |
| 06 30378 | Goleta | 20.5 | 30 289 | 1 206 | 1 477.5 | 55.9 | 1.9 | 0.9 | 10.5 | 0.2 | 32.9 | 24.6 |
| 06 31960 | Hanford | 43.0 | 54 324 | 667 | 1 263.3 | 43.2 | 5.3 | 1.1 | 5.1 | 0.3 | 47.1 | 16.4 |
| 06 32548 | Hawthorne | 15.8 | 85 681 | 361 | 5 422.8 | 11.4 | 27.7 | 0.5 | 7.4 | 1.4 | 52.9 | 34.5 |
| 06 33000 | Hayward | 117.4 | 149 392 | 162 | 1 272.5 | 21.3 | 12.4 | 1.0 | 24.2 | 4.2 | 40.7 | 37.6 |
| 06 33182 | Hemet | 72.1 | 81 046 | 392 | 1 124.1 | 54.0 | 7.0 | 1.5 | 3.7 | 0.6 | 35.8 | 13.9 |
| 06 33434 | Hesperia | 189.3 | 92 062 | 325 | 486.3 | 42.7 | 6.1 | 1.0 | 2.6 | 0.4 | 48.9 | 14.5 |
| 06 33588 | Highland | 48.6 | 54 154 | 668 | 1 114.3 | 32.7 | 11.7 | 1.0 | 8.3 | 0.5 | 48.1 | 21.4 |
| 06 34120 | Hollister | 18.9 | 36 096 | 1 013 | 1 909.8 | 30.4 | 1.0 | 0.9 | 3.2 | 0.2 | 65.7 | 24.3 |
| 06 36000 | Huntington Beach | 69.3 | 194 708 | 121 | 2 809.6 | 70.1 | 1.3 | 0.9 | 13.0 | 0.7 | 17.1 | 16.3 |
| 06 36056 | Huntington Park | 7.8 | 58 673 | 601 | 7 522.2 | 1.7 | 0.4 | 0.1 | 0.6 | 0.0 | 97.1 | 51.6 |
| 06 36294 | Imperial Beach | 10.8 | 26 845 | 1 356 | 2 485.6 | 38.9 | 5.1 | 1.2 | 8.3 | 1.1 | 49.0 | 19.8 |
| 06 36448 | Indio | 75.6 | 79 302 | 403 | 1 049.0 | 27.7 | 2.3 | 0.5 | 2.3 | 0.1 | 67.8 | 26.9 |
| 06 36546 | Inglewood | 23.5 | 111 182 | 239 | 4 731.1 | 3.7 | 44.2 | 0.8 | 1.7 | 0.5 | 50.6 | 28.1 |
| 06 36770 | Irvine | 171.2 | 229 985 | 91 | 1 343.4 | 49.2 | 2.2 | 0.4 | 42.7 | 0.4 | 9.2 | 34.8 |
| 06 39220 | Laguna Hills | 17.3 | 30 951 | 1 177 | 1 789.1 | 64.9 | 1.7 | 0.6 | 15.1 | 0.4 | 20.6 | 23.7 |
| 06 39248 | Laguna Niguel | 38.4 | 64 452 | 532 | 1 678.4 | 75.7 | 1.5 | 0.6 | 11.1 | 0.4 | 13.9 | 21.2 |
| 06 39290 | La Habra | 19.1 | 61 392 | 565 | 3 214.2 | 31.6 | 1.7 | 0.6 | 10.0 | 0.3 | 57.2 | 26.7 |
| 06 39486 | Lake Elsinore | 93.8 | 55 288 | 650 | 589.4 | 40.1 | 5.8 | 1.0 | 6.6 | 0.6 | 48.4 | 20.5 |
| 06 39496 | Lake Forest | 46.1 | 78 853 | 407 | 1 710.5 | 60.0 | 2.0 | 0.7 | 15.1 | 0.6 | 24.6 | 23.9 |
| 06 39892 | Lakewood | 24.4 | 80 833 | 394 | 3 312.8 | 43.6 | 9.3 | 0.9 | 17.9 | 1.4 | 30.1 | 20.5 |
| 06 40004 | La Mesa | 23.5 | 58 160 | 608 | 2 474.9 | 65.1 | 8.6 | 1.2 | 7.3 | 0.9 | 20.5 | 13.0 |
| 06 40032 | La Mirada | 20.3 | 49 001 | 754 | 2 413.8 | 39.6 | 2.4 | 0.6 | 18.8 | 0.6 | 39.7 | 24.5 |
| 06 40130 | Lancaster | 244.2 | 159 055 | 151 | 651.3 | 36.5 | 21.4 | 1.2 | 5.1 | 0.4 | 38.0 | 13.2 |
| 06 40340 | La Puente | 9.0 | 40 272 | 903 | 4 474.7 | 4.9 | 1.3 | 0.3 | 8.5 | 0.2 | 85.1 | 41.8 |
| 06 40354 | La Quinta | 91.0 | 38 783 | 944 | 426.2 | 64.6 | 2.0 | 0.6 | 3.7 | 0.2 | 30.3 | 14.2 |
| 06 40830 | La Verne | 21.8 | 31 348 | 1 156 | 1 438.0 | 57.4 | 3.7 | 0.9 | 8.7 | 0.4 | 31.0 | 13.4 |
| 06 40886 | Lawndale | 5.1 | 33 122 | 1 102 | 6 494.5 | 17.8 | 10.1 | 0.6 | 10.7 | 1.3 | 61.0 | 39.0 |
| 06 41124 | Lemon Grove | 10.1 | 25 961 | 1 392 | 2 570.4 | 37.4 | 14.6 | 1.1 | 7.7 | 1.5 | 41.2 | 16.7 |
| 06 41474 | Lincoln | 52.1 | 44 390 | 822 | 852.0 | 73.6 | 1.9 | 1.3 | 7.6 | 0.6 | 17.7 | 11.8 |
| 06 41992 | Livermore | 65.2 | 83 547 | 374 | 1 281.4 | 67.8 | 2.5 | 1.0 | 10.4 | 0.6 | 20.9 | 17.2 |
| 06 42202 | Lodi | 35.3 | 63 301 | 543 | 1 793.2 | 55.3 | 0.9 | 1.2 | 7.8 | 0.4 | 36.4 | 19.0 |
| 06 42524 | Lompoc | 30.0 | 43 260 | 841 | 1 442.0 | 38.7 | 6.4 | 1.6 | 4.7 | 0.6 | 50.8 | 24.7 |
| 06 43000 | Long Beach | 130.3 | 467 892 | 36 | 3 590.9 | 31.4 | 14.1 | 0.9 | 14.0 | 1.4 | 40.8 | 26.8 |
| 06 43280 | Los Altos | 16.8 | 29 929 | 1 217 | 1 781.5 | 71.5 | 0.7 | 0.3 | 26.9 | 0.3 | 3.9 | 23.0 |
| 06 44000 | Los Angeles | 1 213.9 | 3 857 799 | 2 | 3 178.0 | 30.3 | 9.8 | 0.5 | 12.3 | 0.3 | 48.5 | 39.4 |
| 06 44028 | Los Banos | 25.9 | 36 747 | 996 | 1 418.8 | 27.9 | 3.7 | 0.9 | 3.5 | 0.6 | 64.9 | 25.2 |
| 06 44112 | Los Gatos | 28.7 | 30 141 | 1 210 | 1 050.2 | 80.4 | 1.2 | 0.7 | 13.5 | 0.4 | 7.2 | 16.5 |
| 06 44574 | Lynwood | 12.5 | 70 709 | 468 | 5 656.7 | 2.4 | 9.9 | 0.2 | 0.6 | 0.3 | 86.6 | 41.0 |
| 06 45022 | Madera | 40.9 | 62 624 | 548 | 1 531.1 | 17.8 | 3.0 | 0.9 | 2.4 | 0.1 | 76.7 | 30.6 |
| 06 45400 | Manhattan Beach | 10.2 | 35 738 | 1 025 | 3 503.7 | 83.1 | 1.3 | 0.5 | 11.6 | 0.4 | 6.9 | 9.4 |
| 06 45484 | Manteca | 45.9 | 71 067 | 465 | 1 548.3 | 49.8 | 4.8 | 1.4 | 8.6 | 0.9 | 37.7 | 16.3 |
| 06 46114 | Martinez | 31.4 | 36 673 | 998 | 1 167.9 | 72.6 | 4.5 | 1.7 | 10.3 | 0.8 | 14.7 | 12.4 |
| 06 46492 | Maywood | 3.1 | 27 659 | 1 311 | 8 922.3 | 1.9 | 0.2 | 0.1 | 0.3 | 0.1 | 97.4 | 48.6 |
| 06 46842 | Menifee | 120.4 | 81 474 | 390 | 676.7 | 56.4 | 5.5 | 1.1 | 5.9 | 0.7 | 33.0 | 15.0 |

1. Dry land or land partially or temporarily covered by water.  2. May be of any race.

| City | Age of population (percent), 2010 | | | | | | | | | Median age | Percent female | Population — Census counts | | Percent change | |
|---|---|---|---|---|---|---|---|---|---|---|---|---|---|---|---|
| | Under 5 years | 5 to 17 years | 18 to 24 years | 25 to 34 years | 35 to 44 years | 45 to 54 years | 55 to 64 years | 65 to 74 years | 75 years and over | | | 2000 | 2010 | 2000–2010 | 2010–2012 |
| | 12 | 13 | 14 | 15 | 16 | 17 | 18 | 19 | 20 | 21 | 22 | 23 | 24 | 25 | 26 |
| CALIFORNIA—Cont'd | | | | | | | | | | | | | | | |
| Delano | 8.0 | 20.5 | 14.7 | 18.0 | 14.6 | 11.5 | 6.7 | 3.4 | 2.7 | 28.5 | 40.1 | 38 824 | 53 041 | 36.6 | -1.2 |
| Desert Hot Springs | 9.0 | 22.1 | 10.5 | 13.7 | 12.9 | 13.4 | 8.9 | 5.6 | 4.0 | 31.0 | 49.9 | 16 582 | 27 049 | 56.4 | 2.6 |
| Diamond Bar | 4.3 | 17.1 | 10.1 | 11.0 | 13.5 | 17.8 | 14.6 | 7.2 | 4.4 | 41.0 | 51.2 | 56 287 | 55 544 | -1.3 | 1.5 |
| Downey | 7.0 | 19.8 | 10.8 | 14.7 | 14.8 | 12.9 | 9.5 | 5.2 | 5.2 | 33.3 | 51.5 | 107 323 | 111 772 | 4.1 | 1.0 |
| Dublin | 7.4 | 15.0 | 8.0 | 18.9 | 19.3 | 14.8 | 9.3 | 4.7 | 2.6 | 35.3 | 47.9 | 29 973 | 46 036 | 53.6 | 5.9 |
| East Palo Alto | 9.3 | 22.6 | 12.4 | 17.5 | 14.1 | 11.1 | 7.1 | 3.4 | 2.5 | 28.1 | 49.3 | 29 506 | 28 155 | -4.6 | 2.5 |
| El Cajon | 7.6 | 18.1 | 11.3 | 14.7 | 12.9 | 14.3 | 10.1 | 5.6 | 5.4 | 33.7 | 51.1 | 94 869 | 99 476 | 4.9 | 2.0 |
| El Centro | 7.9 | 21.9 | 11.3 | 12.7 | 12.3 | 13.2 | 10.1 | 5.7 | 5.0 | 31.8 | 51.4 | 37 835 | 42 598 | 12.6 | 1.2 |
| Elk Grove | 7.2 | 22.9 | 8.6 | 12.2 | 15.7 | 15.2 | 9.8 | 4.8 | 3.5 | 34.3 | 51.6 | 59 984 | 153 015 | 155.1 | 3.9 |
| El Monte | 7.9 | 20.5 | 11.3 | 15.2 | 14.2 | 12.4 | 9.2 | 5.1 | 4.3 | 31.6 | 49.8 | 115 965 | 113 475 | -2.1 | 1.4 |
| El Paso de Robles (Paso Robles) | 7.8 | 18.5 | 9.5 | 13.8 | 12.6 | 13.5 | 10.9 | 6.6 | 6.8 | 35.3 | 51.3 | 24 297 | 29 793 | 22.6 | 2.6 |
| Encinitas | 5.4 | 15.3 | 6.3 | 13.4 | 14.5 | 16.9 | 15.4 | 6.6 | 6.3 | 41.5 | 50.5 | 58 014 | 59 518 | 2.6 | 2.5 |
| Escondido | 8.1 | 19.6 | 10.7 | 15.0 | 13.5 | 13.1 | 9.6 | 5.1 | 5.3 | 32.5 | 50.5 | 133 559 | 143 913 | 7.8 | 2.5 |
| Eureka | 6.1 | 13.9 | 11.4 | 16.9 | 12.6 | 14.0 | 13.3 | 6.3 | 5.5 | 36.2 | 48.6 | 26 128 | 27 191 | 4.1 | -0.8 |
| Fairfield | 7.4 | 19.7 | 10.7 | 13.9 | 13.5 | 14.4 | 10.1 | 5.4 | 4.8 | 33.7 | 50.8 | 96 178 | 105 323 | 9.5 | 2.2 |
| Folsom | 6.1 | 18.2 | 7.4 | 14.1 | 17.8 | 16.6 | 10.2 | 5.1 | 4.5 | 37.6 | 46.7 | 51 884 | 72 203 | 39.2 | 1.6 |
| Fontana | 8.6 | 24.3 | 11.7 | 14.5 | 14.9 | 12.7 | 7.6 | 3.4 | 2.2 | 28.7 | 50.3 | 128 929 | 196 069 | 52.1 | 2.9 |
| Foster City | 6.8 | 15.8 | 5.0 | 14.6 | 17.5 | 14.6 | 12.3 | 8.1 | 5.3 | 39.3 | 51.7 | 28 803 | 30 567 | 6.1 | 5.1 |
| Fountain Valley | 4.6 | 16.4 | 8.4 | 10.5 | 13.5 | 15.7 | 13.2 | 10.4 | 7.2 | 42.6 | 51.3 | 54 978 | 55 313 | 0.6 | 2.1 |
| Fremont | 7.1 | 17.7 | 7.3 | 14.7 | 16.5 | 15.8 | 10.6 | 5.6 | 4.5 | 36.8 | 50.3 | 203 413 | 214 089 | 5.2 | 3.7 |
| Fresno | 8.9 | 21.2 | 12.7 | 15.3 | 12.1 | 11.6 | 9.0 | 4.9 | 4.5 | 29.3 | 50.9 | 427 652 | 496 009 | 15.7 | 2.0 |
| Fullerton | 5.9 | 17.4 | 13.0 | 14.0 | 14.0 | 14.3 | 9.7 | 5.8 | 5.9 | 34.8 | 50.9 | 126 003 | 135 126 | 7.3 | 2.6 |
| Gardena | 6.3 | 16.5 | 9.1 | 13.9 | 14.4 | 14.2 | 11.5 | 7.2 | 6.9 | 37.9 | 51.9 | 57 746 | 58 829 | 1.9 | 1.1 |
| Garden Grove | 6.7 | 18.9 | 10.2 | 13.2 | 15.5 | 14.6 | 10.1 | 5.9 | 4.9 | 35.6 | 50.1 | 165 196 | 170 883 | 3.4 | 2.1 |
| Gilroy | 8.5 | 22.2 | 9.2 | 13.8 | 15.1 | 13.5 | 9.2 | 4.8 | 3.6 | 32.4 | 50.4 | 41 464 | 48 821 | 17.7 | 3.8 |
| Glendale | 4.8 | 13.9 | 8.7 | 14.2 | 14.2 | 16.0 | 12.7 | 8.0 | 7.6 | 41.0 | 52.3 | 194 973 | 191 719 | -1.7 | 1.4 |
| Glendora | 5.0 | 18.5 | 9.8 | 10.5 | 13.1 | 16.5 | 12.4 | 7.4 | 6.8 | 40.2 | 51.6 | 49 415 | 50 073 | 1.3 | 1.3 |
| Goleta | 5.5 | 15.6 | 12.7 | 14.3 | 12.3 | 14.8 | 11.2 | 6.3 | 7.3 | 36.5 | 49.7 | 55 204 | 29 888 | -45.9 | 1.3 |
| Hanford | 9.1 | 21.9 | 10.2 | 14.6 | 12.7 | 12.3 | 9.3 | 5.2 | 4.7 | 30.9 | 51.0 | 41 686 | 53 967 | 29.5 | 0.7 |
| Hawthorne | 8.0 | 19.4 | 11.3 | 17.1 | 15.0 | 13.1 | 8.7 | 4.3 | 3.1 | 31.5 | 51.7 | 84 112 | 84 293 | 0.2 | 1.6 |
| Hayward | 7.5 | 17.1 | 11.1 | 16.5 | 14.0 | 13.4 | 10.3 | 5.3 | 4.8 | 33.5 | 50.7 | 140 030 | 144 342 | 3.0 | 3.5 |
| Hemet | 7.2 | 18.6 | 8.7 | 11.3 | 10.7 | 10.8 | 10.5 | 9.8 | 12.4 | 39.0 | 52.9 | 58 812 | 78 658 | 33.7 | 3.0 |
| Hesperia | 8.4 | 23.9 | 10.5 | 13.1 | 12.7 | 13.0 | 9.3 | 5.2 | 3.9 | 30.5 | 50.4 | 62 582 | 90 173 | 44.1 | 2.1 |
| Highland | 8.4 | 23.5 | 11.1 | 12.4 | 13.6 | 13.9 | 9.4 | 4.8 | 3.0 | 30.6 | 51.3 | 44 605 | 53 104 | 19.1 | 2.0 |
| Hollister | 8.5 | 23.2 | 10.1 | 14.0 | 14.4 | 13.9 | 8.4 | 3.8 | 3.6 | 30.8 | 50.3 | 34 413 | 34 928 | 1.5 | 3.3 |
| Huntington Beach | 5.1 | 15.5 | 8.4 | 13.8 | 14.7 | 15.9 | 12.6 | 8.1 | 6.1 | 40.2 | 50.4 | 189 594 | 190 986 | 0.7 | 1.9 |
| Huntington Park | 8.8 | 23.0 | 12.0 | 15.8 | 15.0 | 11.2 | 7.6 | 4.0 | 2.7 | 28.9 | 50.1 | 61 348 | 58 114 | -5.3 | 1.0 |
| Imperial Beach | 7.5 | 17.9 | 13.8 | 16.1 | 12.8 | 13.4 | 9.4 | 4.8 | 4.2 | 31.0 | 49.7 | 26 992 | 26 324 | -2.5 | 2.0 |
| Indio | 8.5 | 21.6 | 9.5 | 14.2 | 13.0 | 11.2 | 9.6 | 7.6 | 4.8 | 32.2 | 50.7 | 49 116 | 76 038 | 54.8 | 4.3 |
| Inglewood | 7.3 | 19.4 | 10.8 | 14.7 | 14.1 | 14.1 | 10.2 | 5.6 | 3.7 | 33.4 | 52.5 | 112 580 | 109 673 | -2.6 | 1.4 |
| Irvine | 5.7 | 15.9 | 14.3 | 15.8 | 15.6 | 14.0 | 10.1 | 5.1 | 3.6 | 33.9 | 51.3 | 143 072 | 211 906 | 48.4 | 8.5 |
| Laguna Hills | 5.2 | 17.1 | 8.6 | 11.4 | 13.7 | 17.0 | 14.1 | 6.9 | 5.9 | 40.8 | 51.2 | 31 178 | 30 347 | -2.7 | 2.0 |
| Laguna Niguel | 5.1 | 17.4 | 7.5 | 9.8 | 13.5 | 19.0 | 14.7 | 7.5 | 5.5 | 42.8 | 51.5 | 61 891 | 62 964 | 1.8 | 2.4 |
| La Habra | 7.2 | 19.4 | 10.5 | 14.7 | 14.1 | 13.6 | 9.5 | 5.4 | 5.5 | 33.6 | 50.8 | 58 974 | 60 245 | 2.1 | 1.9 |
| Lake Elsinore | 9.2 | 23.6 | 10.2 | 15.0 | 15.4 | 13.0 | 7.9 | 3.6 | 2.2 | 29.8 | 49.9 | 28 928 | 52 214 | 79.1 | 5.9 |
| Lake Forest | 6.3 | 18.5 | 8.8 | 13.4 | 15.2 | 17.1 | 11.6 | 5.4 | 3.8 | 37.2 | 50.3 | 58 707 | 77 266 | 31.6 | 2.1 |
| Lakewood | 6.1 | 18.3 | 9.5 | 12.6 | 15.0 | 15.7 | 11.5 | 5.9 | 5.5 | 37.5 | 51.5 | 79 345 | 80 048 | 0.9 | 1.0 |
| La Mesa | 6.3 | 13.2 | 11.2 | 16.3 | 13.1 | 14.5 | 11.2 | 6.0 | 8.2 | 37.1 | 52.4 | 54 749 | 57 065 | 4.2 | 1.9 |
| La Mirada | 5.1 | 16.0 | 14.6 | 11.0 | 13.0 | 14.3 | 10.9 | 7.3 | 7.9 | 37.9 | 52.0 | 46 783 | 48 527 | 3.7 | 1.0 |
| Lancaster | 8.0 | 22.1 | 11.9 | 14.1 | 13.1 | 14.0 | 8.7 | 4.5 | 3.6 | 30.4 | 49.9 | 118 718 | 156 633 | 31.9 | 1.5 |
| La Puente | 7.5 | 21.2 | 11.7 | 14.5 | 14.3 | 13.1 | 8.6 | 5.1 | 4.1 | 31.5 | 50.1 | 41 063 | 39 816 | -3.0 | 1.1 |
| La Quinta | 4.8 | 17.1 | 6.7 | 8.6 | 11.9 | 14.5 | 15.5 | 13.3 | 7.5 | 45.6 | 51.7 | 23 694 | 37 467 | 58.1 | 3.5 |
| La Verne | 4.4 | 16.9 | 10.0 | 10.1 | 11.4 | 16.4 | 13.9 | 8.7 | 8.2 | 42.9 | 52.7 | 31 638 | 31 063 | -1.8 | 0.9 |
| Lawndale | 7.5 | 19.7 | 11.4 | 16.3 | 15.9 | 13.5 | 8.7 | 4.1 | 2.8 | 31.9 | 49.7 | 31 711 | 32 769 | 3.3 | 1.1 |
| Lemon Grove | 7.0 | 18.5 | 10.2 | 14.3 | 13.0 | 14.8 | 11.1 | 5.4 | 5.7 | 35.0 | 51.2 | 24 918 | 25 320 | 1.6 | 2.5 |
| Lincoln | 7.8 | 16.5 | 5.5 | 12.7 | 12.6 | 9.5 | 11.9 | 14.2 | 9.3 | 40.5 | 51.9 | 11 205 | 42 889 | 282.1 | 3.5 |
| Livermore | 6.6 | 18.9 | 7.6 | 12.3 | 15.5 | 17.7 | 11.0 | 5.8 | 4.5 | 38.3 | 50.4 | 73 345 | 80 968 | 10.4 | 3.2 |
| Lodi | 7.9 | 19.9 | 9.4 | 13.7 | 11.9 | 13.2 | 10.4 | 6.3 | 7.2 | 34.3 | 51.2 | 56 999 | 62 134 | 9.0 | 1.9 |
| Lompoc | 7.6 | 18.8 | 10.5 | 14.5 | 14.3 | 14.7 | 9.6 | 5.3 | 4.6 | 33.9 | 46.5 | 41 103 | 42 438 | 3.2 | 1.9 |
| Long Beach | 7.0 | 17.9 | 11.7 | 15.9 | 14.6 | 13.6 | 10.0 | 5.0 | 4.2 | 33.2 | 51.0 | 461 522 | 462 257 | 0.2 | 1.2 |
| Los Altos | 5.4 | 20.7 | 3.5 | 4.7 | 13.5 | 18.6 | 13.7 | 9.5 | 10.5 | 46.2 | 51.8 | 27 693 | 28 970 | 4.6 | 3.3 |
| Los Angeles | 6.6 | 16.4 | 11.5 | 16.8 | 15.0 | 13.3 | 9.9 | 5.5 | 4.9 | 34.1 | 50.2 | 3 694 820 | 3 792 627 | 2.6 | 1.7 |
| Los Banos | 9.0 | 24.6 | 10.3 | 13.0 | 13.7 | 12.6 | 8.2 | 4.7 | 3.8 | 29.8 | 50.2 | 25 869 | 35 972 | 39.1 | 2.2 |
| Los Gatos | 4.7 | 17.6 | 4.9 | 8.5 | 14.4 | 18.7 | 13.3 | 9.1 | 8.8 | 45.0 | 52.1 | 28 592 | 29 437 | 2.9 | 2.4 |
| Lynwood | 9.1 | 23.9 | 12.5 | 15.7 | 14.7 | 11.4 | 7.3 | 3.4 | 2.0 | 27.8 | 51.4 | 69 845 | 69 772 | -0.1 | 1.3 |
| Madera | 10.7 | 24.0 | 12.6 | 15.7 | 12.5 | 9.9 | 7.0 | 4.0 | 3.5 | 26.6 | 49.0 | 43 207 | 61 416 | 42.1 | 2.0 |
| Manhattan Beach | 5.8 | 19.1 | 5.0 | 11.5 | 15.7 | 17.5 | 12.9 | 7.2 | 5.5 | 40.9 | 49.9 | 33 852 | 35 135 | 3.8 | 1.7 |
| Manteca | 7.7 | 21.2 | 9.8 | 13.1 | 13.8 | 14.6 | 9.8 | 5.6 | 4.3 | 33.6 | 50.8 | 49 258 | 67 193 | 36.2 | 5.8 |
| Martinez | 5.0 | 15.5 | 7.9 | 12.1 | 13.6 | 18.4 | 15.4 | 7.3 | 4.8 | 42.2 | 50.8 | 35 866 | 35 823 | -0.1 | 2.4 |
| Maywood | 9.4 | 23.1 | 12.4 | 16.5 | 15.0 | 10.5 | 7.0 | 3.6 | 2.4 | 27.9 | 48.9 | 28 083 | 27 395 | -2.4 | 1.0 |
| Menifee | 6.9 | 19.0 | 8.3 | 12.0 | 12.2 | 12.3 | 10.4 | 9.3 | 9.6 | 38.1 | 51.9 | NA | 77 519 | NA | 5.1 |

# Table D. Cities — Households, Group Quarters, Crime, and Education

| City | Households, 2010 Number | Persons per house-hold | Percent Female family householder[1] | One-person | Persons in group quarters, 2010 Total | Institutional Total | Persons in nursing facilities | Non-institu-tional | Serious crimes known to police,[2] 2011 Total Number | Rate[3] | Rate[3] Violent | Property | Educational attainment, 2007–2011 Population age 25 and older | High school graduate or less | Bachelor's degree or more |
|---|---|---|---|---|---|---|---|---|---|---|---|---|---|---|---|
| | 27 | 28 | 29 | 30 | 31 | 32 | 33 | 34 | 35 | 36 | 37 | 38 | 39 | 40 | 41 |
| **CALIFORNIA—Cont'd** | | | | | | | | | | | | | | | |
| Delano | 10 260 | 4.11 | 20.4 | 9.6 | 10 897 | 10 719 | 189 | 178 | 1 864 | 3 473 | 410 | 3 063 | 29 844 | 74.7 | 7.1 |
| Desert Hot Springs | 8 650 | 2.98 | 18.5 | 23.9 | 118 | 0 | 0 | 118 | 1 797 | 6 848 | 1 273 | 5 575 | 14 475 | 58.3 | 11.8 |
| Diamond Bar | 17 880 | 3.10 | 12.1 | 12.9 | 129 | 27 | 22 | 102 | 836 | 1 488 | 103 | 1 384 | 38 646 | 23.6 | 48.8 |
| Downey | 33 936 | 3.27 | 18.5 | 16.9 | 683 | 561 | 534 | 122 | 4 266 | 3 772 | 345 | 3 427 | 69 933 | 53.1 | 18.8 |
| Dublin | 14 913 | 2.70 | 9.3 | 21.5 | 5 774 | 5 682 | 0 | 92 | 721 | 1 548 | 170 | 1 378 | 30 238 | 25.3 | 45.1 |
| East Palo Alto | 6 940 | 4.03 | 21.8 | 17.2 | 154 | 4 | 0 | 150 | 1 087 | 3 816 | 923 | 2 893 | 15 797 | 62.3 | 15.8 |
| El Cajon | 34 134 | 2.84 | 16.6 | 23.1 | 2 482 | 1 350 | 1 339 | 1 132 | 2 997 | 2 978 | 526 | 2 452 | 60 998 | 49.6 | 17.1 |
| El Centro | 13 108 | 3.19 | 21.7 | 18.8 | 816 | 520 | 98 | 296 | 2 449 | 5 682 | 383 | 5 299 | 24 345 | 52.4 | 15.8 |
| Elk Grove | 47 927 | 3.18 | 13.7 | 15.1 | 669 | 209 | 133 | 460 | 3 793 | 2 450 | 338 | 2 112 | 88 483 | 28.6 | 32.9 |
| El Monte | 27 814 | 4.04 | 19.0 | 11.3 | 1 080 | 763 | 618 | 317 | 2 707 | 2 358 | 367 | 1 991 | 69 879 | 72.0 | 11.1 |
| El Paso de Robles (Paso Robles) | 10 833 | 2.73 | 12.4 | 22.9 | 169 | 5 | 0 | 164 | 927 | 3 075 | 315 | 2 760 | 18 432 | 40.1 | 22.2 |
| Encinitas | 24 082 | 2.45 | 8.1 | 26.2 | 528 | 405 | 405 | 123 | 1 177 | 1 955 | 232 | 1 722 | 42 735 | 18.9 | 54.5 |
| Escondido | 45 484 | 3.12 | 13.4 | 20.9 | 2 119 | 786 | 657 | 1 333 | 3 705 | 2 545 | 340 | 2 205 | 87 624 | 48.0 | 22.2 |
| Eureka | 11 150 | 2.27 | 13.0 | 35.6 | 1 883 | 449 | 8 | 1 434 | 1 766 | 6 419 | 443 | 5 976 | 18 568 | 39.7 | 21.7 |
| Fairfield | 34 484 | 2.98 | 15.1 | 19.7 | 2 489 | 1 268 | 332 | 1 221 | 3 399 | 3 190 | 399 | 2 791 | 62 394 | 39.1 | 22.3 |
| Folsom | 24 951 | 2.61 | 8.8 | 23.2 | 6 960 | 6 772 | 96 | 188 | 1 594 | 2 182 | 115 | 2 067 | 48 647 | 27.0 | 42.0 |
| Fontana | 49 116 | 3.98 | 16.4 | 9.8 | 444 | 228 | 194 | 216 | 4 955 | 2 498 | 363 | 2 135 | 107 457 | 54.0 | 15.0 |
| Foster City | 12 016 | 2.53 | 8.0 | 23.4 | 109 | 57 | 57 | 52 | 421 | 1 361 | 84 | 1 277 | 21 626 | 14.0 | 63.0 |
| Fountain Valley | 18 648 | 2.94 | 11.3 | 18.5 | 437 | 180 | 160 | 257 | 1 358 | 2 427 | 141 | 2 285 | 39 626 | 28.6 | 36.8 |
| Fremont | 71 004 | 2.99 | 10.0 | 16.3 | 1 651 | 682 | 662 | 969 | 4 336 | 2 002 | 177 | 1 825 | 144 757 | 29.3 | 49.9 |
| Fresno | 158 349 | 3.07 | 19.3 | 22.1 | 8 867 | 4 552 | 1 825 | 4 315 | 28 336 | 5 662 | 582 | 5 079 | 280 985 | 49.0 | 20.1 |
| Fullerton | 45 391 | 2.91 | 12.1 | 21.5 | 3 077 | 759 | 629 | 2 318 | 3 856 | 2 820 | 224 | 2 596 | 85 692 | 31.7 | 37.9 |
| Gardena | 20 558 | 2.82 | 19.1 | 25.0 | 794 | 672 | 631 | 122 | 1 734 | 2 913 | 472 | 2 441 | 40 095 | 44.7 | 22.8 |
| Garden Grove | 46 037 | 3.67 | 14.9 | 14.1 | 1 941 | 707 | 624 | 1 234 | 3 836 | 2 219 | 260 | 1 959 | 108 621 | 52.3 | 19.3 |
| Gilroy | 14 175 | 3.39 | 15.6 | 15.1 | 806 | 164 | 128 | 642 | 1 586 | 3 211 | 413 | 2 798 | 28 696 | 45.6 | 23.8 |
| Glendale | 72 269 | 2.63 | 12.3 | 24.9 | 1 429 | 1 206 | 1 181 | 223 | 3 710 | 1 913 | 133 | 1 780 | 138 618 | 34.7 | 39.0 |
| Glendora | 17 141 | 2.88 | 13.3 | 19.0 | 765 | 573 | 519 | 192 | 1 374 | 2 712 | 128 | 2 584 | 32 578 | 32.9 | 29.4 |
| Goleta | 10 903 | 2.72 | 9.8 | 25.1 | 201 | 178 | 170 | 23 | 423 | 1 399 | 132 | 1 267 | 19 583 | 27.7 | 43.6 |
| Hanford | 17 492 | 3.03 | 16.2 | 19.9 | 899 | 616 | 296 | 283 | 1 621 | 2 969 | 319 | 2 650 | 32 112 | 45.7 | 17.9 |
| Hawthorne | 28 486 | 2.94 | 22.4 | 25.0 | 539 | 331 | 311 | 208 | 2 747 | 3 221 | 731 | 2 491 | 51 096 | 52.1 | 16.2 |
| Hayward | 45 365 | 3.12 | 16.5 | 20.6 | 2 724 | 770 | 723 | 1 954 | 4 361 | 2 989 | 397 | 2 593 | 92 322 | 49.2 | 23.6 |
| Hemet | 30 092 | 2.59 | 14.5 | 30.3 | 614 | 459 | 421 | 155 | 3 833 | 4 816 | 454 | 4 363 | 51 404 | 51.5 | 14.0 |
| Hesperia | 26 431 | 3.41 | 16.0 | 15.3 | 28 | 6 | 6 | 22 | 2 562 | 2 808 | 343 | 2 465 | 49 696 | 56.6 | 9.6 |
| Highland | 15 471 | 3.42 | 18.6 | 14.6 | 172 | 96 | 96 | 76 | 1 693 | 3 151 | 439 | 2 712 | 29 710 | 50.2 | 19.7 |
| Hollister | 9 860 | 3.53 | 15.3 | 13.4 | 115 | 106 | 102 | 9 | 779 | 2 204 | 447 | 1 757 | 20 677 | 54.7 | 15.0 |
| Huntington Beach | 74 285 | 2.55 | 10.3 | 24.9 | 890 | 403 | 391 | 487 | 4 995 | 2 599 | 211 | 2 387 | 134 909 | 24.1 | 40.4 |
| Huntington Park | 14 597 | 3.96 | 22.0 | 11.3 | 255 | 7 | 0 | 248 | 2 587 | 4 400 | 828 | 3 572 | 32 423 | 78.6 | 6.1 |
| Imperial Beach | 9 112 | 2.82 | 18.7 | 22.5 | 619 | 0 | 0 | 619 | 576 | 2 163 | 537 | 1 626 | 15 622 | 48.2 | 16.1 |
| Indio | 23 378 | 3.21 | 15.3 | 16.5 | 949 | 584 | 135 | 365 | 3 040 | 3 952 | 559 | 3 393 | 43 820 | 52.5 | 17.7 |
| Inglewood | 36 389 | 2.97 | 24.7 | 25.7 | 1 502 | 515 | 405 | 987 | 3 390 | 3 055 | 728 | 2 327 | 68 010 | 49.8 | 17.5 |
| Irvine | 78 978 | 2.61 | 9.6 | 23.4 | 6 556 | 588 | 55 | 5 968 | 3 400 | 1 582 | 56 | 1 526 | 130 067 | 13.2 | 65.0 |
| Laguna Hills | 10 469 | 2.86 | 9.4 | 19.5 | 369 | 136 | 136 | 233 | 642 | 2 091 | 147 | 1 945 | 20 888 | 27.0 | 44.5 |
| Laguna Niguel | 24 232 | 2.59 | 9.4 | 22.2 | 248 | 0 | 0 | 248 | 709 | 1 113 | 67 | 1 045 | 44 362 | 16.0 | 53.3 |
| La Habra | 18 977 | 3.16 | 15.3 | 19.2 | 340 | 171 | 167 | 169 | 1 571 | 2 578 | 330 | 2 248 | 37 521 | 47.1 | 21.2 |
| Lake Elsinore | 14 788 | 3.48 | 14.0 | 13.2 | 432 | 208 | 0 | 224 | 1 733 | 3 305 | 233 | 3 073 | 27 662 | 49.1 | 17.3 |
| Lake Forest | 26 224 | 2.93 | 10.3 | 18.6 | 515 | 216 | 216 | 299 | 1 036 | 1 325 | 114 | 1 211 | 51 847 | 24.6 | 42.2 |
| Lakewood | 26 543 | 3.01 | 15.0 | 17.8 | 109 | 0 | 0 | 109 | 2 113 | 2 609 | 264 | 2 345 | 52 348 | 35.9 | 27.3 |
| La Mesa | 24 512 | 2.30 | 12.7 | 32.7 | 657 | 533 | 512 | 124 | 1 760 | 3 048 | 393 | 2 655 | 38 735 | 27.6 | 34.4 |
| La Mirada | 14 681 | 3.11 | 11.8 | 17.3 | 2 857 | 271 | 271 | 2 586 | 888 | 1 809 | 165 | 1 644 | 30 378 | 38.9 | 27.8 |
| Lancaster | 46 992 | 3.16 | 20.2 | 19.7 | 8 259 | 6 775 | 486 | 1 484 | 4 067 | 2 566 | 537 | 2 029 | 90 437 | 48.9 | 16.5 |
| La Puente | 9 451 | 4.21 | 19.3 | 10.5 | 43 | 0 | 0 | 43 | 751 | 1 864 | 390 | 1 475 | 23 515 | 68.2 | 10.2 |
| La Quinta | 14 820 | 2.52 | 9.7 | 21.3 | 57 | 7 | 7 | 50 | 1 616 | 4 263 | 496 | 3 767 | 25 896 | 30.1 | 34.4 |
| La Verne | 11 261 | 2.70 | 12.8 | 22.4 | 676 | 175 | 104 | 501 | 710 | 2 259 | 200 | 2 059 | 21 171 | 29.9 | 31.7 |
| Lawndale | 9 681 | 3.37 | 18.7 | 18.2 | 175 | 17 | 0 | 158 | 622 | 1 876 | 528 | 1 348 | 19 417 | 56.3 | 16.1 |
| Lemon Grove | 8 434 | 2.96 | 16.8 | 22.9 | 346 | 146 | 129 | 200 | 553 | 2 159 | 535 | 1 624 | 15 966 | 48.5 | 15.1 |
| Lincoln | 16 479 | 2.59 | 7.3 | 21.3 | 115 | 85 | 85 | 30 | 516 | 1 191 | 67 | 1 124 | 28 470 | 26.8 | 30.6 |
| Livermore | 29 134 | 2.76 | 9.7 | 20.6 | 510 | 121 | 121 | 389 | 2 043 | 2 494 | 326 | 2 168 | 53 264 | 27.6 | 36.8 |
| Lodi | 22 097 | 2.78 | 13.2 | 25.1 | 677 | 490 | 470 | 187 | 2 675 | 4 255 | 375 | 3 880 | 38 943 | 48.5 | 19.2 |
| Lompoc | 13 355 | 2.90 | 15.4 | 24.7 | 3 656 | 3 557 | 163 | 99 | 1 246 | 2 902 | 641 | 2 262 | 25 355 | 53.3 | 13.9 |
| Long Beach | 163 531 | 2.78 | 16.4 | 28.5 | 8 277 | 2 956 | 2 370 | 5 321 | 15 673 | 3 351 | 611 | 2 740 | 289 444 | 40.2 | 28.7 |
| Los Altos | 10 745 | 2.68 | 5.6 | 19.4 | 227 | 193 | 193 | 34 | 275 | 938 | 20 | 918 | 20 295 | 7.4 | 76.7 |
| Los Angeles | 1 318 168 | 2.81 | 14.9 | 28.3 | 84 601 | 26 415 | 13 845 | 58 186 | 106 375 | 2 772 | 522 | 2 250 | 2 472 041 | 45.7 | 30.5 |
| Los Banos | 10 259 | 3.49 | 14.4 | 15.1 | 181 | 78 | 78 | 103 | 1 345 | 3 696 | 462 | 3 234 | 19 009 | 62.5 | 10.1 |
| Los Gatos | 12 355 | 2.35 | 7.7 | 29.9 | 350 | 258 | 238 | 92 | 669 | 2 248 | 141 | 2 107 | 20 956 | 11.5 | 66.2 |
| Lynwood | 14 680 | 4.57 | 22.2 | 7.2 | 2 652 | 2 203 | 370 | 449 | 2 002 | 2 836 | 863 | 1 973 | 38 003 | 77.6 | 4.6 |
| Madera | 15 938 | 3.82 | 18.3 | 14.9 | 591 | 173 | 173 | 418 | 1 848 | 2 974 | 653 | 2 321 | 31 943 | 65.5 | 10.1 |
| Manhattan Beach | 14 038 | 2.50 | 6.4 | 25.8 | 28 | 0 | 0 | 28 | 935 | 2 630 | 124 | 2 506 | 24 253 | 8.3 | 73.0 |
| Manteca | 21 618 | 3.08 | 13.9 | 18.0 | 495 | 345 | 341 | 150 | 2 573 | 3 790 | 303 | 3 487 | 40 079 | 48.9 | 14.8 |
| Martinez | 14 287 | 2.42 | 12.3 | 27.4 | 1 296 | 1 061 | 268 | 235 | 906 | 2 500 | 188 | 2 312 | 25 476 | 27.4 | 34.5 |
| Maywood | 6 559 | 4.16 | 19.1 | 9.1 | 119 | 119 | 119 | 0 | 513 | 1 851 | 559 | 1 292 | 14 667 | 81.6 | 3.4 |
| Menifee | 27 461 | 2.82 | 10.0 | 24.0 | 188 | 107 | 106 | 81 | 1 664 | 2 122 | 68 | 2 054 | 49 853 | 45.3 | 17.4 |

1. No spouse present.   2. Data for serious crimes have not been adjusted for underreporting. This may affect comparability between geographic areas and over time.   3. Per 100,000 population estimated by the FBI.   4. Persons 25 years old and over.

# Table D. Cities — Income, Poverty, and Housing

| City | Money income, 2007–2011 | | | | | Housing units, 2010 | | | Occupied Housing units 2007–2011 | | | | |
|---|---|---|---|---|---|---|---|---|---|---|---|---|---|
| | | Households | | | Families with income below poverty (percent) | | | | Owner-occupied | | | Median owner costs as a percent of income | |
| | Per capita income[1] (dollars) | Median income | Percent with income of $200,000 or more | Percent with income of less than $25,000 | | Total | Percent change, 2000–2010 | Vacant units for sale or rent[2] | Total | Percent | Median value[3] (dollars) | With a mortgage[4] | Without a mortgage[5] |
| | 42 | 43 | 44 | 45 | 46 | 47 | 48 | 49 | 50 | 51 | 52 | 53 | 54 |
| CALIFORNIA—Cont'd | | | | | | | | | | | | | |
| Delano | 10 957 | 37 810 | 1.4 | 30.7 | 25.4 | 10 713 | 21.0 | 453 | 10 249 | 55.4 | 162 300 | 30.9 | 11.1 |
| Desert Hot Springs | 15 671 | 34 606 | 0.6 | 32.2 | 20.8 | 10 902 | 55.2 | 2 252 | 8 522 | 51.4 | 163 500 | 33.5 | 15.3 |
| Diamond Bar | 35 771 | 90 153 | 9.6 | 8.6 | 3.7 | 18 455 | 2.8 | 575 | 17 627 | 82.7 | 548 200 | 29.8 | 10.0 |
| Downey | 23 241 | 59 773 | 3.2 | 17.6 | 9.1 | 35 601 | 2.4 | 1 665 | 33 374 | 51.8 | 470 700 | 32.7 | 10.2 |
| Dublin | 41 197 | 111 481 | 15.0 | 6.5 | 2.1 | 15 782 | 59.6 | 869 | 14 131 | 63.9 | 624 000 | 29.0 | 11.8 |
| East Palo Alto | 18 014 | 50 137 | 4.1 | 19.8 | 15.1 | 7 819 | 10.8 | 879 | 7 079 | 43.5 | 447 600 | 38.9 | 12.9 |
| El Cajon | 21 132 | 47 303 | 2.6 | 27.2 | 18.0 | 35 850 | 1.9 | 1 716 | 32 378 | 42.4 | 363 200 | 31.5 | 10.5 |
| El Centro | 18 273 | 38 297 | 2.0 | 37.1 | 23.4 | 14 476 | 17.8 | 1 368 | 13 092 | 49.6 | 181 500 | 26.8 | 12.1 |
| Elk Grove | 29 188 | 78 564 | 6.3 | 9.9 | 6.9 | 50 634 | 167.9 | 2 707 | 45 317 | 75.1 | 312 300 | 29.8 | 10.7 |
| El Monte | 14 464 | 41 820 | 1.1 | 27.9 | 19.7 | 29 069 | 4.8 | 1 255 | 28 022 | 41.2 | 371 600 | 35.6 | 10.8 |
| El Paso de Robles (Paso Robles) | 26 547 | 57 927 | 3.6 | 17.2 | 8.0 | 11 426 | 30.1 | 593 | 10 670 | 59.7 | 390 100 | 32.1 | 12.2 |
| Encinitas | 47 346 | 88 458 | 14.6 | 13.5 | 6.5 | 25 740 | 7.8 | 1 658 | 23 047 | 65.2 | 710 200 | 30.2 | 10.0 |
| Escondido | 23 194 | 50 597 | 4.1 | 21.3 | 12.2 | 48 044 | 6.8 | 2 560 | 44 918 | 53.3 | 367 300 | 32.8 | 12.7 |
| Eureka | 22 972 | 36 081 | 1.3 | 35.9 | 12.3 | 11 891 | 2.6 | 741 | 11 127 | 48.3 | 278 300 | 28.2 | 10.0 |
| Fairfield | 26 785 | 68 037 | 4.5 | 15.1 | 8.6 | 37 184 | 16.7 | 2 700 | 32 359 | 62.0 | 341 600 | 31.6 | 10.0 |
| Folsom | 37 187 | 95 143 | 9.1 | 9.1 | 2.4 | 26 109 | 45.5 | 1 158 | 23 657 | 71.9 | 431 900 | 26.8 | 14.0 |
| Fontana | 19 297 | 64 058 | 2.5 | 15.2 | 11.6 | 51 857 | 44.5 | 2 741 | 47 253 | 69.5 | 294 800 | 33.9 | 10.5 |
| Foster City | 53 384 | 115 053 | 20.0 | 7.2 | 2.8 | 12 458 | 3.7 | 442 | 11 505 | 59.4 | 867 200 | 26.6 | 10.0 |
| Fountain Valley | 35 487 | 81 661 | 8.1 | 12.2 | 4.6 | 19 164 | 3.7 | 516 | 18 795 | 71.9 | 626 900 | 29.2 | 10.0 |
| Fremont | 38 752 | 98 513 | 12.7 | 9.9 | 3.4 | 73 989 | 6.5 | 2 985 | 69 589 | 64.3 | 624 500 | 28.3 | 10.0 |
| Fresno | 19 978 | 43 440 | 2.6 | 30.4 | 20.7 | 171 288 | 15.0 | 12 939 | 156 724 | 49.3 | 223 900 | 28.5 | 11.4 |
| Fullerton | 30 967 | 69 432 | 7.5 | 16.7 | 9.0 | 47 869 | 7.0 | 2 478 | 44 781 | 54.0 | 540 900 | 30.3 | 10.0 |
| Gardena | 22 969 | 46 961 | 2.1 | 27.1 | 12.8 | 21 472 | 2.1 | 914 | 21 242 | 47.6 | 385 500 | 32.9 | 11.0 |
| Garden Grove | 21 066 | 60 036 | 3.2 | 18.7 | 11.8 | 47 755 | 2.0 | 1 718 | 45 597 | 57.7 | 439 000 | 31.7 | 10.0 |
| Gilroy | 28 719 | 75 483 | 7.9 | 16.8 | 7.8 | 14 854 | 22.1 | 679 | 14 403 | 62.1 | 527 700 | 33.7 | 12.4 |
| Glendale | 30 107 | 54 087 | 6.7 | 25.0 | 11.2 | 76 269 | 3.5 | 4 000 | 71 189 | 39.4 | 624 100 | 32.6 | 12.3 |
| Glendora | 32 851 | 75 939 | 6.8 | 11.7 | 3.8 | 17 778 | 3.5 | 637 | 16 568 | 70.0 | 489 800 | 30.5 | 11.0 |
| Goleta | 34 263 | 72 870 | 6.7 | 12.7 | 3.7 | 11 473 | -43.6 | 570 | 11 068 | 53.7 | 707 500 | 29.0 | 10.0 |
| Hanford | 22 383 | 54 421 | 1.9 | 19.4 | 11.5 | 18 493 | 25.4 | 1 001 | 16 816 | 59.5 | 215 100 | 25.4 | 11.1 |
| Hawthorne | 19 862 | 45 622 | 1.6 | 26.1 | 16.0 | 29 869 | 1.0 | 1 383 | 28 379 | 26.2 | 461 800 | 35.8 | 10.0 |
| Hayward | 24 987 | 62 115 | 3.9 | 17.6 | 8.7 | 48 296 | 5.1 | 2 931 | 44 507 | 54.8 | 381 100 | 33.2 | 10.3 |
| Hemet | 19 236 | 34 273 | 1.4 | 37.0 | 16.4 | 35 305 | 19.8 | 5 213 | 30 440 | 62.3 | 139 100 | 32.1 | 15.5 |
| Hesperia | 17 589 | 48 624 | 1.3 | 23.3 | 15.8 | 29 004 | 36.2 | 2 573 | 25 088 | 68.7 | 193 700 | 33.1 | 11.9 |
| Highland | 22 494 | 59 419 | 5.2 | 19.2 | 14.7 | 16 578 | 10.9 | 1 107 | 14 757 | 66.2 | 303 300 | 28.3 | 11.1 |
| Hollister | 22 433 | 62 570 | 3.1 | 19.9 | 11.5 | 10 401 | 4.5 | 541 | 10 307 | 59.2 | 344 600 | 34.2 | 13.5 |
| Huntington Beach | 42 127 | 80 901 | 10.4 | 12.3 | 4.7 | 78 003 | 2.9 | 3 718 | 75 183 | 61.2 | 663 900 | 29.8 | 10.6 |
| Huntington Park | 12 461 | 36 788 | 1.3 | 32.4 | 24.4 | 15 151 | -1.2 | 554 | 14 454 | 28.4 | 351 900 | 38.5 | 10.0 |
| Imperial Beach | 20 175 | 45 480 | 1.6 | 28.0 | 14.7 | 9 882 | 1.5 | 770 | 9 064 | 31.0 | 389 400 | 30.3 | 10.0 |
| Indio | 21 293 | 52 199 | 3.2 | 25.0 | 16.1 | 28 971 | 71.4 | 5 593 | 22 851 | 64.4 | 248 500 | 32.5 | 13.1 |
| Inglewood | 20 187 | 44 021 | 1.7 | 27.3 | 18.2 | 38 429 | -0.5 | 2 040 | 36 774 | 36.6 | 372 300 | 36.2 | 11.6 |
| Irvine | 43 102 | 92 599 | 13.9 | 13.9 | 5.1 | 83 899 | 56.2 | 4 921 | 74 711 | 52.7 | 661 700 | 28.9 | 10.0 |
| Laguna Hills | 44 751 | 85 971 | 15.3 | 11.5 | 4.8 | 11 046 | -2.5 | 577 | 10 651 | 75.9 | 591 500 | 30.7 | 10.0 |
| Laguna Niguel | 51 491 | 100 480 | 19.4 | 9.4 | 3.5 | 25 312 | 5.9 | 1 080 | 23 927 | 75.6 | 714 200 | 30.3 | 10.6 |
| La Habra | 24 589 | 63 356 | 4.9 | 17.0 | 10.1 | 19 924 | 2.0 | 947 | 18 468 | 56.4 | 422 800 | 30.6 | 11.0 |
| Lake Elsinore | 21 642 | 63 771 | 2.9 | 16.5 | 9.8 | 16 253 | 70.6 | 1 465 | 14 199 | 68.7 | 247 800 | 34.9 | 17.0 |
| Lake Forest | 39 844 | 94 632 | 11.4 | 8.6 | 3.7 | 27 088 | 31.6 | 864 | 26 888 | 71.1 | 543 600 | 27.8 | 11.8 |
| Lakewood | 29 838 | 78 360 | 3.7 | 10.4 | 4.2 | 27 470 | 0.7 | 927 | 26 030 | 72.0 | 460 000 | 29.4 | 10.0 |
| La Mesa | 29 958 | 54 519 | 2.4 | 21.3 | 8.7 | 26 167 | 5.1 | 1 655 | 23 720 | 47.3 | 396 400 | 30.5 | 10.8 |
| La Mirada | 28 468 | 81 913 | 5.2 | 13.5 | 3.1 | 15 092 | 1.9 | 411 | 14 361 | 78.9 | 466 700 | 28.7 | 10.0 |
| Lancaster | 20 739 | 52 290 | 2.7 | 26.1 | 17.3 | 51 835 | 24.4 | 4 843 | 46 255 | 62.2 | 214 800 | 31.0 | 13.3 |
| La Puente | 15 762 | 52 042 | 1.1 | 17.6 | 10.1 | 9 761 | 1.0 | 310 | 9 579 | 59.1 | 328 300 | 34.1 | 10.0 |
| La Quinta | 45 172 | 77 790 | 13.3 | 13.5 | 4.2 | 23 489 | 99.7 | 8 669 | 14 105 | 75.1 | 396 600 | 31.1 | 12.8 |
| La Verne | 32 335 | 77 088 | 6.8 | 17.2 | 6.3 | 11 686 | 3.5 | 425 | 10 849 | 77.8 | 483 300 | 29.4 | 13.8 |
| Lawndale | 18 895 | 48 813 | 1.6 | 24.6 | 12.3 | 10 151 | 2.8 | 470 | 9 955 | 31.4 | 400 500 | 34.3 | 10.8 |
| Lemon Grove | 22 061 | 50 353 | 1.7 | 26.6 | 13.8 | 8 868 | 1.2 | 434 | 8 462 | 56.6 | 336 800 | 33.2 | 10.9 |
| Lincoln | 33 260 | 75 071 | 3.5 | 13.7 | 4.5 | 17 457 | 322.6 | 978 | 15 678 | 80.3 | 371 200 | 35.1 | 12.6 |
| Livermore | 41 741 | 96 322 | 12.0 | 11.1 | 4.3 | 30 342 | 14.3 | 1 208 | 28 552 | 71.8 | 544 300 | 29.3 | 10.0 |
| Lodi | 25 011 | 49 318 | 3.9 | 23.8 | 12.6 | 23 792 | 11.2 | 1 695 | 22 033 | 55.7 | 286 000 | 27.8 | 13.6 |
| Lompoc | 19 851 | 47 592 | 1.6 | 24.1 | 15.4 | 14 416 | 5.8 | 1 061 | 13 028 | 48.1 | 286 000 | 30.0 | 10.2 |
| Long Beach | 26 986 | 52 945 | 4.7 | 23.6 | 15.5 | 176 032 | 2.5 | 12 501 | 161 932 | 41.4 | 478 400 | 31.4 | 10.0 |
| Los Altos | 77 267 | 151 856 | 37.1 | 6.1 | 1.3 | 11 204 | 4.4 | 459 | 10 710 | 84.5 | 1 000 000 | 28.8 | 10.5 |
| Los Angeles | 28 222 | 50 028 | 6.3 | 26.4 | 16.5 | 1 413 995 | 5.7 | 95 827 | 1 312 983 | 38.4 | 513 600 | 34.9 | 12.5 |
| Los Banos | 18 092 | 51 478 | 3.2 | 24.4 | 19.2 | 11 375 | 40.9 | 1 116 | 9 798 | 61.5 | 185 500 | 32.7 | 11.4 |
| Los Gatos | 69 134 | 122 875 | 27.2 | 8.6 | 2.7 | 13 050 | 5.2 | 695 | 11 933 | 64.2 | 1 000 000 | 28.0 | 10.0 |
| Lynwood | 12 443 | 43 782 | 0.3 | 27.1 | 19.6 | 15 277 | 1.8 | 597 | 15 270 | 48.1 | 350 100 | 37.6 | 11.5 |
| Madera | 14 685 | 41 991 | 1.2 | 29.6 | 21.6 | 17 049 | 34.7 | 1 111 | 15 848 | 50.9 | 188 700 | 32.2 | 11.2 |
| Manhattan Beach | 81 472 | 132 752 | 32.6 | 6.9 | 2.5 | 14 929 | -1.1 | 891 | 13 827 | 68.3 | 1 000 000 | 26.2 | 10.0 |
| Manteca | 23 823 | 60 963 | 1.8 | 15.3 | 6.7 | 23 132 | 36.9 | 1 514 | 21 618 | 64.3 | 260 000 | 32.3 | 12.2 |
| Martinez | 38 311 | 79 705 | 7.6 | 13.8 | 5.3 | 14 976 | 2.3 | 689 | 14 461 | 67.1 | 464 500 | 29.9 | 10.0 |
| Maywood | 12 210 | 38 155 | 0.2 | 31.5 | 24.6 | 6 766 | 1.0 | 207 | 6 430 | 26.5 | 320 600 | 34.1 | 10.0 |
| Menifee | 24 159 | 54 068 | 2.0 | 20.2 | 6.4 | 30 269 | NA | 2 808 | 26 097 | 80.3 | 228 100 | 34.4 | 13.7 |

1. Based on population estimated by the American Community Survey.   2. Includes units rented or sold but not occupied.   3. Specified owner-occupied units; $1,000,000 represents $1,000,000 or more   4. 50.0 represents 50 percent or more.   5. 10.0 represents 10 percent or less.

# Table D. Cities — Housing, Labor Force, and Employment

| City | Occupied housing units, 2007–2011 (cont.) | | | | Migration, 2007–2011 | | Civilian labor force, 2012 | | | | Civilian employment[4], 2007–2011 | | | |
|---|---|---|---|---|---|---|---|---|---|---|---|---|---|---|
| | | | | | | | | | Unemployment | | | Percent | | |
| | Percent renter occupied | Median gross rent[1] | Median rent as a percent of income[2] | Percent with no vehicle available | Percent who lived in the same house one year ago | Percent who lived outside this city one year ago | Total | Percent change, 2011–2012 | Total | Rate[3] | Population age 16 and older | In labor force | Full-year full-time worker | Households with no workers (percent) |
| | 55 | 56 | 57 | 58 | 59 | 60 | 61 | 62 | 63 | 64 | 65 | 66 | 67 | 68 |
| CALIFORNIA—Cont'd | | | | | | | | | | | | | | |
| Delano | 44.6 | 729 | 33.6 | 8.5 | 76.0 | 15.8 | 20 612 | -1.2 | 6 795 | 33.0 | 38 264 | 47.1 | 23.1 | 22.9 |
| Desert Hot Springs | 48.6 | 871 | 35.0 | 9.6 | 76.5 | 13.2 | 9 775 | -0.4 | 1 684 | 17.2 | 18 044 | 60.9 | 34.1 | 32.1 |
| Diamond Bar | 17.3 | 1 737 | 36.2 | 1.8 | 89.9 | 7.7 | 32 146 | -0.4 | 2 516 | 7.8 | 45 676 | 64.9 | 44.0 | 15.0 |
| Downey | 48.2 | 1 182 | 32.6 | 4.4 | 86.8 | 8.7 | 53 492 | -0.6 | 4 710 | 8.8 | 85 182 | 65.9 | 41.3 | 19.2 |
| Dublin | 36.1 | 1 749 | 25.8 | 2.7 | 77.2 | 18.0 | 15 704 | 3.2 | 857 | 5.5 | 35 587 | 65.2 | 44.4 | 11.2 |
| East Palo Alto | 56.5 | 1 186 | 37.3 | 9.3 | 84.1 | 12.0 | 13 778 | 2.2 | 2 198 | 16.0 | 20 803 | 68.9 | 38.2 | 15.5 |
| El Cajon | 57.6 | 1 051 | 35.6 | 9.1 | 79.5 | 12.5 | 54 170 | 1.0 | 6 587 | 12.2 | 75 653 | 63.3 | 34.0 | 26.4 |
| El Centro | 50.4 | 723 | 36.6 | 13.0 | 83.1 | 7.8 | 22 682 | 1.5 | 6 087 | 26.8 | 30 317 | 60.1 | 32.1 | 30.4 |
| Elk Grove | 24.9 | 1 446 | 33.9 | 2.5 | 84.9 | 8.5 | 35 267 | 0.9 | 3 018 | 8.6 | 106 216 | 70.8 | 43.9 | 16.4 |
| El Monte | 58.8 | 1 061 | 37.9 | 9.9 | 89.0 | 6.6 | 51 854 | -1.5 | 7 000 | 13.5 | 86 805 | 61.6 | 37.0 | 18.0 |
| El Paso de Robles (Paso Robles) | 40.3 | 1 072 | 32.8 | 6.1 | 79.3 | 11.1 | 13 542 | 3.7 | 1 299 | 9.6 | 22 197 | 63.6 | 35.5 | 27.0 |
| Encinitas | 34.8 | 1 667 | 31.2 | 3.2 | 85.4 | 11.1 | 39 615 | 2.1 | 2 513 | 6.3 | 48 255 | 68.5 | 39.8 | 20.5 |
| Escondido | 46.7 | 1 139 | 37.0 | 7.4 | 86.4 | 6.6 | 74 579 | 1.5 | 6 932 | 9.3 | 108 004 | 65.1 | 37.7 | 22.3 |
| Eureka | 51.7 | 770 | 33.6 | 10.6 | 79.2 | 12.1 | 11 716 | -0.6 | 1 305 | 11.1 | 22 501 | 58.8 | 31.3 | 33.4 |
| Fairfield | 38.0 | 1 196 | 32.9 | 4.6 | 78.8 | 12.0 | 49 973 | 1.1 | 5 544 | 11.1 | 79 435 | 69.1 | 37.3 | 20.2 |
| Folsom | 28.1 | 1 282 | 27.6 | 3.4 | 82.5 | 12.8 | 27 176 | 1.8 | 1 299 | 4.8 | 56 179 | 61.1 | 38.9 | 18.2 |
| Fontana | 30.5 | 1 106 | 36.1 | 3.9 | 83.9 | 10.3 | 62 330 | 0.1 | 7 762 | 12.5 | 137 000 | 68.6 | 39.7 | 14.4 |
| Foster City | 40.6 | 1 971 | 24.5 | 2.7 | 83.5 | 13.2 | 17 226 | 4.9 | 851 | 4.9 | 23 816 | 67.8 | 45.6 | 18.3 |
| Fountain Valley | 28.1 | 1 492 | 32.0 | 4.9 | 89.8 | 7.9 | 33 124 | 1.9 | 2 092 | 6.3 | 45 754 | 63.5 | 39.4 | 23.2 |
| Fremont | 35.7 | 1 494 | 26.3 | 4.6 | 86.2 | 8.3 | 111 868 | 3.0 | 7 263 | 6.5 | 165 260 | 67.1 | 44.7 | 20.0 |
| Fresno | 50.7 | 862 | 35.2 | 11.3 | 80.9 | 6.0 | 232 258 | 0.3 | 33 244 | 14.3 | 359 155 | 63.3 | 33.8 | 28.7 |
| Fullerton | 46.0 | 1 336 | 33.4 | 4.6 | 81.7 | 12.8 | 71 943 | 1.4 | 6 125 | 8.5 | 105 360 | 66.8 | 39.6 | 20.9 |
| Gardena | 52.4 | 1 031 | 33.7 | 9.3 | 89.9 | 8.4 | 29 415 | -0.9 | 3 016 | 10.3 | 46 537 | 63.2 | 39.6 | 26.1 |
| Garden Grove | 42.3 | 1 326 | 36.1 | 5.3 | 87.9 | 8.0 | 85 886 | 1.1 | 8 143 | 9.5 | 131 866 | 64.4 | 38.3 | 19.6 |
| Gilroy | 37.9 | 1 222 | 33.2 | 6.4 | 85.5 | 6.7 | 21 854 | 1.8 | 2 764 | 12.6 | 34 321 | 71.6 | 40.8 | 19.5 |
| Glendale | 60.6 | 1 244 | 38.6 | 11.2 | 88.1 | 7.2 | 103 941 | -0.8 | 9 919 | 9.5 | 160 511 | 62.2 | 36.9 | 24.8 |
| Glendora | 30.0 | 1 355 | 29.9 | 4.7 | 89.7 | 7.8 | 27 747 | 0.0 | 1 581 | 5.7 | 39 862 | 63.1 | 37.9 | 21.5 |
| Goleta | 46.3 | 1 582 | 31.7 | 4.8 | 84.6 | 12.6 | 18 020 | 5.8 | 709 | 3.9 | 24 041 | 71.3 | 42.2 | 22.0 |
| Hanford | 40.5 | 895 | 29.0 | 8.1 | 83.5 | 7.7 | 23 983 | 1.8 | 3 216 | 13.4 | 39 393 | 65.5 | 39.1 | 22.3 |
| Hawthorne | 73.8 | 996 | 31.2 | 10.1 | 87.1 | 9.7 | 42 306 | -1.7 | 6 016 | 14.2 | 62 215 | 67.2 | 43.9 | 18.4 |
| Hayward | 45.2 | 1 246 | 33.0 | 7.5 | 82.4 | 10.4 | 71 701 | 2.0 | 7 207 | 10.1 | 111 895 | 69.2 | 40.4 | 22.1 |
| Hemet | 37.7 | 948 | 43.6 | 11.1 | 74.3 | 14.3 | 27 582 | -0.1 | 4 248 | 15.4 | 59 560 | 48.3 | 25.0 | 49.7 |
| Hesperia | 31.3 | 1 067 | 37.5 | 3.9 | 83.6 | 10.5 | 30 598 | -0.5 | 4 700 | 15.4 | 62 745 | 59.4 | 33.4 | 28.0 |
| Highland | 33.8 | 963 | 35.0 | 6.0 | 84.2 | 10.3 | 23 058 | -0.4 | 3 476 | 15.1 | 37 309 | 64.7 | 38.1 | 20.1 |
| Hollister | 40.8 | 1 177 | 33.5 | 5.2 | 83.3 | 8.5 | 17 447 | -3.4 | 2 709 | 15.5 | 25 215 | 69.0 | 38.8 | 19.7 |
| Huntington Beach | 38.8 | 1 506 | 30.0 | 3.5 | 87.0 | 8.1 | 123 195 | 1.9 | 7 620 | 6.2 | 156 297 | 68.6 | 42.0 | 22.6 |
| Huntington Park | 71.6 | 890 | 36.2 | 16.9 | 90.1 | 6.3 | 26 831 | -2.0 | 4 371 | 16.3 | 41 654 | 66.5 | 40.7 | 13.9 |
| Imperial Beach | 69.0 | 1 111 | 34.9 | 12.3 | 77.9 | 15.1 | 14 312 | 0.6 | 2 047 | 14.3 | 20 053 | 64.4 | 33.1 | 24.5 |
| Indio | 35.6 | 957 | 35.6 | 5.8 | 78.0 | 11.5 | 28 252 | 0.3 | 3 745 | 13.3 | 53 742 | 64.6 | 36.4 | 28.0 |
| Inglewood | 63.4 | 1 033 | 35.9 | 10.3 | 88.5 | 8.0 | 54 127 | -1.6 | 7 403 | 13.7 | 82 846 | 65.0 | 40.0 | 25.0 |
| Irvine | 47.3 | 1 813 | 29.4 | 3.7 | 78.5 | 14.4 | 84 319 | 2.0 | 4 800 | 5.7 | 166 893 | 65.5 | 42.4 | 17.7 |
| Laguna Hills | 24.1 | 1 766 | 41.0 | 4.8 | 86.2 | 12.4 | 18 040 | 1.9 | 1 158 | 6.4 | 25 020 | 66.7 | 39.7 | 19.3 |
| Laguna Niguel | 24.4 | 1 765 | 33.1 | 2.5 | 88.2 | 9.5 | 37 915 | 2.0 | 2 241 | 5.9 | 50 600 | 67.6 | 43.4 | 19.3 |
| La Habra | 43.6 | 1 256 | 33.7 | 5.5 | 85.2 | 9.2 | 32 013 | 1.3 | 2 745 | 8.6 | 45 421 | 68.5 | 43.4 | 19.7 |
| Lake Elsinore | 31.3 | 1 223 | 34.5 | 4.5 | 77.8 | 13.8 | 17 782 | 0.6 | 2 111 | 11.9 | 35 228 | 68.3 | 40.1 | 17.2 |
| Lake Forest | 28.9 | 1 678 | 30.0 | 2.7 | 87.7 | 9.3 | 37 043 | 2.1 | 1 942 | 5.2 | 60 158 | 73.9 | 50.1 | 14.1 |
| Lakewood | 28.0 | 1 445 | 29.8 | 3.4 | 89.1 | 9.4 | 44 425 | -0.3 | 3 145 | 7.1 | 62 247 | 69.6 | 46.1 | 18.3 |
| La Mesa | 52.7 | 1 172 | 33.6 | 7.8 | 76.7 | 18.9 | 34 745 | 1.9 | 2 594 | 7.5 | 46 463 | 67.5 | 38.8 | 27.3 |
| La Mirada | 21.1 | 1 336 | 39.1 | 3.8 | 88.6 | 9.5 | 24 195 | -0.2 | 1 613 | 6.7 | 38 803 | 62.3 | 37.8 | 23.9 |
| Lancaster | 37.8 | 1 113 | 39.1 | 6.9 | 85.4 | 8.2 | 56 160 | -1.9 | 8 629 | 15.4 | 111 720 | 56.8 | 37.7 | 27.2 |
| La Puente | 40.9 | 1 144 | 35.8 | 7.7 | 91.1 | 5.2 | 19 081 | -1.4 | 2 452 | 12.9 | 29 706 | 63.2 | 40.9 | 16.9 |
| La Quinta | 24.9 | 1 480 | 32.8 | 3.5 | 86.5 | 9.4 | 15 257 | 1.6 | 980 | 6.4 | 29 209 | 59.6 | 33.4 | 32.3 |
| La Verne | 22.2 | 1 194 | 31.0 | 5.7 | 89.1 | 8.9 | 18 172 | -0.1 | 1 145 | 6.3 | 25 457 | 62.3 | 35.1 | 27.5 |
| Lawndale | 68.6 | 1 308 | 37.4 | 7.7 | 87.7 | 9.9 | 16 345 | -1.0 | 1 774 | 10.9 | 24 388 | 68.2 | 39.5 | 19.9 |
| Lemon Grove | 43.4 | 1 052 | 37.3 | 6.8 | 91.0 | 7.8 | 14 153 | 1.2 | 1 581 | 11.2 | 19 560 | 62.0 | 37.2 | 27.8 |
| Lincoln | 19.7 | 1 514 | 34.1 | 2.7 | 85.4 | 11.2 | 7 885 | -1.2 | 1 330 | 16.9 | 31 476 | 54.1 | 33.2 | 40.2 |
| Livermore | 28.2 | 1 367 | 29.0 | 3.9 | 87.4 | 7.9 | 41 954 | 3.1 | 2 458 | 5.9 | 61 939 | 70.8 | 45.3 | 19.6 |
| Lodi | 44.3 | 990 | 36.4 | 7.6 | 83.9 | 5.9 | 31 757 | 1.2 | 3 661 | 11.5 | 46 955 | 61.0 | 35.2 | 30.3 |
| Lompoc | 51.9 | 948 | 34.2 | 9.2 | 81.1 | 9.8 | 21 128 | 2.6 | 2 967 | 14.0 | 31 923 | 58.9 | 34.3 | 26.1 |
| Long Beach | 58.6 | 1 075 | 33.0 | 10.9 | 80.6 | 9.6 | 236 642 | -1.2 | 28 483 | 12.0 | 357 639 | 67.5 | 38.9 | 22.6 |
| Los Altos | 15.5 | 2 000 | 25.6 | 3.2 | 91.2 | 8.3 | 13 207 | 4.1 | 563 | 4.3 | 21 935 | 58.9 | 37.4 | 27.5 |
| Los Angeles | 61.6 | 1 127 | 35.1 | 13.0 | 85.6 | 5.3 | 1 910 998 | -1.3 | 230 864 | 12.1 | 3 002 210 | 66.5 | 39.4 | 23.1 |
| Los Banos | 38.5 | 1 029 | 37.9 | 6.3 | 79.5 | 8.8 | 13 937 | 1.5 | 2 490 | 17.9 | 24 532 | 65.5 | 32.7 | 24.6 |
| Los Gatos | 35.8 | 1 738 | 27.2 | 3.4 | 84.3 | 11.2 | 15 956 | 3.7 | 881 | 5.5 | 22 951 | 61.9 | 41.0 | 27.5 |
| Lynwood | 51.9 | 989 | 40.2 | 7.2 | 89.4 | 8.5 | 27 969 | -2.2 | 4 823 | 17.2 | 50 190 | 58.8 | 36.7 | 15.0 |
| Madera | 49.1 | 838 | 33.1 | 9.2 | 84.0 | 6.1 | 24 453 | -2.7 | 4 684 | 19.2 | 41 393 | 59.4 | 31.4 | 37.2 |
| Manhattan Beach | 31.7 | 2 000 | 24.8 | 2.5 | 87.9 | 8.9 | 22 131 | 0.3 | 855 | 3.9 | 27 070 | 68.1 | 46.0 | 19.5 |
| Manteca | 35.7 | 1 117 | 31.5 | 4.0 | 81.3 | 11.5 | 27 518 | 0.7 | 3 640 | 13.2 | 48 298 | 69.6 | 38.7 | 23.1 |
| Martinez | 32.9 | 1 290 | 31.8 | 4.5 | 87.3 | 9.7 | 22 372 | 2.6 | 1 610 | 7.2 | 29 753 | 67.9 | 41.9 | 21.3 |
| Maywood | 73.5 | 962 | 34.4 | 15.1 | 91.1 | 6.0 | 12 286 | -2.0 | 1 952 | 15.9 | 19 246 | 65.1 | 39.2 | 16.2 |
| Menifee | 19.7 | 1 231 | 43.0 | 3.6 | 80.2 | 14.8 | 23 828 | 0.3 | 3 117 | 13.1 | 57 877 | 58.6 | 33.4 | 36.8 |

1. $2,000 represents $2,000 or more.  2. 50.0 represents 50 percent or more.  3. Percent of civilian labor force.  4. Persons 16 years old and over.

| City | Value of residential construction authorized by building permits, 2011 | | | Wholesale trade,[1] 2007 | | | | Retail trade,[2] 2007 | | | |
|---|---|---|---|---|---|---|---|---|---|---|---|
| | New construction ($1,000) | Number of housing units | Percent single family | Number of establishments | Number of employees | Sales (mil dol) | Annual payroll (mil dol) | Number of establishments | Number of employees | Sales (mil dol) | Annual payroll (mil dol) |
| | 69 | 70 | 71 | 72 | 73 | 74 | 75 | 76 | 77 | 78 | 79 |
| CALIFORNIA—Cont'd | | | | | | | | | | | |
| Delano | 2 799 | 30 | 100.0 | 16 | 247 | 208.8 | 11.4 | 81 | 1 072 | 258.9 | 23.8 |
| Desert Hot Springs | 0 | 0 | 0.0 | NA | NA | NA | NA | 38 | 639 | 120.9 | 13.9 |
| Diamond Bar | 4 841 | 20 | 100.0 | 203 | 698 | 463.5 | 31.6 | 125 | 1 576 | 391.9 | 34.2 |
| Downey | 0 | 0 | 0.0 | 96 | 947 | 376.1 | 37.7 | 320 | 5 367 | 1 216.2 | 132.1 |
| Dublin | 269 890 | 819 | 33.7 | 57 | 503 | 251.8 | 25.5 | 185 | 3 939 | 1 249.9 | 114.8 |
| East Palo Alto | 220 | 2 | 100.0 | 5 | D | D | D | 22 | 819 | 220.2 | 19.4 |
| El Cajon | 2 232 | 11 | 100.0 | 129 | 1 243 | 459.1 | 47.3 | 508 | 7 503 | 1 968.4 | 193.6 |
| El Centro | 693 | 2 | 100.0 | 48 | 363 | 202.2 | 13.6 | 213 | 3 848 | 756.0 | 81.7 |
| Elk Grove | 81 792 | 525 | 48.0 | 54 | D | D | D | 274 | 6 684 | 1 950.0 | 177.9 |
| El Monte | 9 510 | 100 | 32.0 | 339 | 1 976 | 858.9 | 66.1 | 300 | 4 461 | 2 140.4 | 153.6 |
| El Paso de Robles (Paso Robles) | 11 561 | 42 | 100.0 | 38 | 317 | 166.6 | 16.0 | 172 | 2 401 | 634.7 | 59.1 |
| Encinitas | 24 445 | 89 | 100.0 | 91 | 423 | 155.1 | 18.1 | 302 | 4 309 | 1 082.8 | 105.9 |
| Escondido | 21 771 | 144 | 22.2 | 160 | 1 328 | 642.0 | 64.8 | 593 | 10 151 | 2 698.3 | 267.6 |
| Eureka | 0 | 0 | 0.0 | 48 | 469 | 159.3 | 18.5 | 274 | 3 689 | 968.6 | 87.4 |
| Fairfield | 29 802 | 181 | 100.0 | 62 | 1 616 | 681.9 | 68.9 | 344 | 5 687 | 1 346.3 | 135.0 |
| Folsom | 23 141 | 99 | 59.6 | 33 | 405 | 824.8 | 31.4 | 288 | 6 074 | 1 766.7 | 157.2 |
| Fontana | 26 672 | 136 | 100.0 | 138 | 3 302 | 2 405.0 | 148.0 | 336 | 6 599 | 1 852.5 | 167.8 |
| Foster City | 52 385 | 300 | 0.0 | 42 | D | D | D | 37 | 885 | 279.6 | 25.2 |
| Fountain Valley | 6 208 | 26 | 100.0 | 124 | 1 925 | 6 251.7 | 138.8 | 250 | 3 805 | 1 283.1 | 99.9 |
| Fremont | 81 859 | 506 | 25.1 | 500 | 10 709 | 11 312.2 | 801.9 | 456 | 8 160 | 2 721.8 | 254.5 |
| Fresno | 158 223 | 891 | 79.2 | 533 | 8 235 | 4 831.4 | 362.0 | 1 658 | 25 728 | 6 358.8 | 611.1 |
| Fullerton | 2 244 | 13 | 53.8 | 235 | 3 219 | 2 275.7 | 143.4 | 401 | 6 034 | 1 608.6 | 152.9 |
| Gardena | 4 216 | 23 | 82.6 | 185 | 1 875 | 1 049.5 | 84.3 | 182 | 2 702 | 757.4 | 78.7 |
| Garden Grove | 11 775 | 70 | 44.3 | 246 | 2 541 | 1 379.0 | 113.2 | 418 | 4 760 | 1 410.7 | 119.5 |
| Gilroy | 59 432 | 169 | 100.0 | 53 | 649 | 274.0 | 31.3 | 330 | 4 907 | 1 141.0 | 112.9 |
| Glendale | 35 140 | 239 | 4.6 | 244 | 2 112 | 894.2 | 97.0 | 734 | 11 451 | 3 224.0 | 298.7 |
| Glendora | 1 562 | 3 | 100.0 | 43 | 471 | 145.0 | 25.6 | 141 | 2 500 | 727.6 | 66.6 |
| Goleta | 291 | 2 | 100.0 | 63 | 1 662 | 1 166.2 | 124.9 | 125 | 2 346 | 668.3 | 62.1 |
| Hanford | 6 871 | 49 | 100.0 | 27 | 376 | 164.6 | 16.4 | 201 | 3 186 | 733.0 | 68.4 |
| Hawthorne | 10 842 | 59 | 1.7 | 75 | 1 423 | 549.2 | 57.6 | 176 | 3 460 | 1 039.2 | 88.4 |
| Hayward | 48 993 | 223 | 100.0 | 493 | 7 787 | 4 967.5 | 403.8 | 443 | 6 868 | 1 785.7 | 188.8 |
| Hemet | 15 970 | 62 | 100.0 | 28 | 149 | 30.6 | 4.5 | 243 | 4 614 | 876.4 | 115.1 |
| Hesperia | 0 | 0 | 0.0 | 43 | 324 | 274.5 | 12.1 | 186 | 1 977 | 508.7 | 48.0 |
| Highland | 3 651 | 16 | 100.0 | 12 | 186 | 38.3 | 4.7 | 60 | 677 | 160.5 | 15.6 |
| Hollister | 7 088 | 27 | 100.0 | 22 | 547 | 128.8 | 25.4 | 102 | 1 393 | 315.0 | 37.3 |
| Huntington Beach | 20 353 | 69 | 34.8 | 457 | 6 703 | 4 698.0 | 426.4 | 596 | 9 070 | 2 364.8 | 230.3 |
| Huntington Park | 0 | 0 | 0.0 | 60 | 1 113 | 463.0 | 44.3 | 219 | 2 514 | 652.2 | 63.7 |
| Imperial Beach | 757 | 6 | 33.3 | 4 | 13 | 2.6 | 0.3 | 39 | 271 | 68.1 | 6.0 |
| Indio | 47 378 | 214 | 100.0 | 45 | 567 | 237.5 | 26.6 | 171 | 2 797 | 789.3 | 80.3 |
| Inglewood | 455 | 4 | 100.0 | 91 | 1 825 | 958.0 | 69.2 | 263 | 3 849 | 1 099.6 | 88.5 |
| Irvine | 388 293 | 2 633 | 32.5 | 902 | 18 358 | 33 740.7 | 1 324.0 | 636 | 13 736 | 4 566.8 | 438.6 |
| Laguna Hills | 0 | 0 | 0.0 | 85 | 548 | 252.3 | 30.3 | 226 | 3 124 | 571.1 | 62.9 |
| Laguna Niguel | 4 330 | 11 | 100.0 | 94 | 374 | 161.5 | 19.2 | 174 | 3 853 | 1 304.3 | 117.1 |
| La Habra | 2 485 | 8 | 100.0 | 69 | 560 | 235.4 | 24.7 | 183 | 3 446 | 971.7 | 85.4 |
| Lake Elsinore | 20 396 | 180 | 37.2 | 42 | 290 | 69.0 | 9.7 | 171 | 2 938 | 773.2 | 71.4 |
| Lake Forest | 880 | 3 | 100.0 | 218 | 3 761 | 2 875.0 | 244.4 | 241 | 3 826 | 1 225.8 | 103.0 |
| Lakewood | 0 | 0 | 0.0 | 36 | 174 | 46.5 | 4.6 | 241 | 5 437 | 1 056.0 | 109.0 |
| La Mesa | 4 762 | 22 | 100.0 | 25 | 124 | 37.6 | 4.6 | 264 | 4 631 | 1 236.3 | 117.5 |
| La Mirada | 0 | 0 | 0.0 | 123 | 3 364 | 5 047.9 | 187.2 | 104 | 1 554 | 424.5 | 42.6 |
| Lancaster | 42 076 | 175 | 100.0 | 65 | 905 | 928.6 | 40.1 | 343 | 6 023 | 1 754.4 | 156.5 |
| La Puente | 297 | 2 | 100.0 | 33 | 230 | 97.5 | 6.4 | 113 | 1 205 | 227.3 | 27.3 |
| La Quinta | 15 481 | 41 | 100.0 | 21 | 57 | 20.1 | 2.1 | 108 | 3 127 | 784.7 | 72.6 |
| La Verne | 494 | 2 | 100.0 | 92 | 1 036 | 472.0 | 48.2 | 94 | 1 380 | 288.3 | 31.0 |
| Lawndale | 605 | 3 | 100.0 | 17 | 150 | 43.2 | 5.1 | 93 | 871 | 253.5 | 22.5 |
| Lemon Grove | 4 697 | 59 | 5.1 | 15 | 123 | 31.9 | 4.3 | 76 | 1 266 | 402.1 | 36.0 |
| Lincoln | 19 449 | 92 | 100.0 | 17 | 244 | 115.7 | 11.0 | 52 | 848 | 193.5 | 20.5 |
| Livermore | 22 418 | 98 | 61.2 | 159 | 3 337 | 2 130.0 | 206.4 | 240 | 4 278 | 1 315.2 | 138.0 |
| Lodi | 738 | 5 | 100.0 | 49 | 331 | 436.0 | 13.8 | 236 | 3 617 | 853.9 | 91.7 |
| Lompoc | 0 | 0 | 0.0 | 7 | 47 | 8.3 | 1.6 | 128 | 1 725 | 385.3 | 39.2 |
| Long Beach | 41 093 | 298 | 22.1 | 331 | 4 884 | 7 337.1 | 286.7 | 1 012 | 13 851 | 4 320.9 | 323.2 |
| Los Altos | 39 850 | 67 | 65.7 | 24 | 50 | 36.8 | 2.3 | 113 | 1 163 | 265.0 | 35.1 |
| Los Angeles | 1 105 322 | 5 947 | 8.8 | 8 693 | 84 842 | 49 819.9 | 3 788.8 | 11 880 | 140 076 | 36 672.8 | 3 602.7 |
| Los Banos | 0 | 0 | 0.0 | 9 | 81 | 62.2 | 3.2 | 94 | 1 487 | 350.9 | 33.3 |
| Los Gatos | 15 213 | 19 | 100.0 | 44 | 540 | 321.5 | 42.8 | 187 | 2 387 | 721.0 | 68.4 |
| Lynwood | 11 500 | 99 | 0.0 | 41 | 709 | 334.4 | 32.8 | 132 | 1 345 | 274.1 | 27.1 |
| Madera | 10 971 | 121 | 41.3 | 28 | 271 | 169.0 | 11.8 | 175 | 2 363 | 518.9 | 52.2 |
| Manhattan Beach | 36 161 | 54 | 96.3 | 38 | D | D | D | 182 | 3 187 | 721.9 | 71.8 |
| Manteca | 64 337 | 464 | 67.2 | 27 | 285 | 163.7 | 13.0 | 174 | 2 826 | 679.6 | 72.1 |
| Martinez | 860 | 3 | 100.0 | 23 | 143 | 38.1 | 5.1 | 72 | 1 256 | 312.0 | 35.6 |
| Maywood | 0 | 0 | 0.0 | 23 | 409 | 171.1 | 15.3 | 50 | 563 | 104.2 | 13.0 |
| Menifee | 68 949 | 283 | 100.0 | NA | NA | NA | NA | NA | NA | NA | NA |

1. Merchant wholesalers except manufacturers' sales branches and offices.  2. Establishments with payroll.

# Table D. Cities — **Real Estate, Professional Services, and Manufacturing**

| City | Real estate and rental and leasing, 2007 | | | | Professional, scientific, and technical services,[1] 2007 | | | | Manufacturing, 2007 | | | |
|---|---|---|---|---|---|---|---|---|---|---|---|---|
| | Number of establishments | Number of employees | Receipts (mil dol) | Annual payroll (mil dol) | Number of establishments | Number of employees | Receipts (mil dol) | Annual payroll (mil dol) | Number of establishments | Number of employees | Receipts (mil dol) | Annual payroll (mil dol) |
| | 80 | 81 | 82 | 83 | 84 | 85 | 86 | 87 | 88 | 89 | 90 | 91 |
| CALIFORNIA—Cont'd | | | | | | | | | | | | |
| Delano | 21 | 58 | 9.0 | 1.2 | 20 | D | D | D | NA | NA | NA | NA |
| Desert Hot Springs | 14 | 155 | 14.7 | 4.7 | 11 | 292 | 5.9 | 3.6 | NA | NA | NA | NA |
| Diamond Bar | 100 | 322 | 53.7 | 9.1 | 245 | 1 342 | 198.1 | 64.2 | 24 | 968 | 319.5 | 43.8 |
| Downey | 197 | 1 217 | 154.0 | 31.0 | 142 | D | D | D | 95 | 2 738 | 1 141.7 | 109.9 |
| Dublin | 52 | 319 | 75.6 | 13.5 | 150 | 1 184 | 190.8 | 81.2 | 23 | 1 430 | D | 92.8 |
| East Palo Alto | 15 | 44 | 24.3 | 1.7 | 16 | D | D | D | NA | NA | NA | NA |
| El Cajon | 175 | 843 | 150.8 | 24.0 | 208 | 1 303 | 125.5 | 47.8 | 183 | 5 660 | 999.1 | 233.7 |
| El Centro | 58 | 221 | 31.6 | 4.9 | 84 | D | D | D | NA | NA | NA | NA |
| Elk Grove | 103 | 368 | 67.1 | 10.6 | 177 | 835 | 88.8 | 35.9 | 39 | 1 155 | 281.5 | 48.0 |
| El Monte | 73 | 499 | 46.6 | 13.8 | 122 | D | D | D | 182 | 4 537 | 806.7 | 180.9 |
| El Paso de Robles (Paso Robles) | 55 | 164 | 30.4 | 5.0 | 95 | 392 | 59.7 | 16.9 | 85 | 2 418 | 489.5 | 98.4 |
| Encinitas | 217 | 473 | 114.6 | 18.8 | 474 | D | D | D | NA | NA | NA | NA |
| Escondido | 197 | 948 | 482.9 | 42.2 | 386 | D | D | D | 197 | 3 321 | 572.2 | 126.4 |
| Eureka | 68 | 297 | 53.6 | 9.3 | 111 | D | D | D | 34 | 557 | 117.4 | 19.6 |
| Fairfield | 97 | 401 | 85.5 | 12.9 | 162 | 1 148 | 111.2 | 50.0 | 62 | 2 642 | 1 358.5 | 139.8 |
| Folsom | 120 | 494 | 100.5 | 17.6 | 276 | D | D | D | 33 | 502 | 110.7 | 24.9 |
| Fontana | 88 | 598 | 115.6 | 21.7 | 78 | D | D | D | 127 | 6 095 | 1 839.3 | 231.3 |
| Foster City | 48 | 609 | 161.2 | 47.4 | 182 | D | D | D | 20 | D | D | D |
| Fountain Valley | 102 | 412 | 77.4 | 15.6 | 289 | 2 186 | 455.1 | 136.3 | 99 | 2 926 | 3 201.1 | 154.1 |
| Fremont | 281 | 1 441 | 407.7 | 56.8 | 948 | D | D | D | 343 | 22 496 | 8 724.6 | 1 577.6 |
| Fresno | 487 | 3 393 | 507.9 | 104.2 | 1 154 | D | D | D | 366 | 13 192 | 3 965.6 | 495.9 |
| Fullerton | 183 | 1 097 | 221.8 | 37.8 | 394 | D | D | D | 226 | 6 982 | 2 128.2 | 287.8 |
| Gardena | 50 | 392 | 35.0 | 8.4 | 68 | 375 | 43.2 | 13.2 | 276 | 5 692 | 1 426.1 | 220.4 |
| Garden Grove | 133 | 743 | 109.4 | 24.5 | 277 | D | D | D | 333 | 8 131 | 1 705.1 | 324.1 |
| Gilroy | 52 | D | D | D | 75 | D | D | D | 59 | 1 846 | 566.1 | 81.6 |
| Glendale | 309 | 2 441 | 1 049.5 | 150.9 | 806 | 7 801 | 1 854.0 | 543.7 | 240 | 5 156 | 606.6 | 206.8 |
| Glendora | 80 | 252 | 49.2 | 7.9 | 130 | 1 107 | 89.7 | 39.6 | 35 | 965 | 388.8 | 36.1 |
| Goleta | 56 | 348 | 44.6 | 10.3 | 155 | D | D | D | 123 | 5 686 | 1 658.8 | 376.2 |
| Hanford | 49 | 215 | 30.6 | 4.7 | 58 | 337 | 31.3 | 10.4 | 28 | 962 | 343.5 | 38.9 |
| Hawthorne | 69 | 340 | 42.3 | 8.5 | 69 | 869 | 149.5 | 44.9 | 81 | 2 976 | 516.3 | 116.4 |
| Hayward | 167 | 1 207 | 241.9 | 46.1 | 256 | D | D | D | 340 | 12 570 | 3 295.8 | 580.8 |
| Hemet | 74 | 399 | 55.8 | 9.0 | 93 | 525 | 49.8 | 16.9 | 28 | 970 | 185.3 | 33.5 |
| Hesperia | 51 | 220 | 39.4 | 6.6 | 67 | 543 | 34.6 | 11.5 | 73 | 718 | 112.3 | 28.1 |
| Highland | 22 | 75 | 12.4 | 1.5 | 29 | 93 | 9.9 | 3.3 | NA | NA | NA | NA |
| Hollister | 39 | 91 | 11.5 | 2.5 | 41 | 151 | 17.4 | 4.9 | 38 | 1 639 | 355.5 | 53.6 |
| Huntington Beach | 341 | 1 692 | 337.7 | 57.9 | 797 | D | D | D | 380 | 13 155 | 4 423.5 | 849.2 |
| Huntington Park | 24 | 123 | 17.4 | 2.8 | 35 | 244 | 21.4 | 5.6 | 127 | 3 412 | 561.9 | 106.0 |
| Imperial Beach | 26 | 96 | 13.7 | 2.4 | 16 | 73 | 4.8 | 1.7 | NA | NA | NA | NA |
| Indio | 56 | 365 | 57.0 | 9.7 | 67 | D | D | D | 41 | 774 | 124.5 | 29.3 |
| Inglewood | 77 | 650 | 108.3 | 19.0 | 58 | D | D | D | 69 | 2 184 | 438.0 | 102.0 |
| Irvine | 622 | 8 462 | 1 739.3 | 462.0 | 2 428 | D | D | D | 433 | 29 937 | 8 761.5 | 1 704.0 |
| Laguna Hills | 92 | 843 | 127.8 | 37.4 | 364 | 1 726 | 250.2 | 94.4 | 72 | 583 | D | 26.7 |
| Laguna Niguel | 150 | 571 | 115.5 | 20.0 | 315 | 1 410 | 292.8 | 79.1 | NA | NA | NA | NA |
| La Habra | 57 | 262 | 44.4 | 6.8 | 84 | 468 | 39.8 | 17.3 | 70 | 1 250 | 215.0 | 46.7 |
| Lake Elsinore | 44 | 162 | 60.6 | 4.9 | 49 | 307 | 29.0 | 9.1 | 62 | 892 | 121.0 | 31.7 |
| Lake Forest | 124 | 1 203 | 200.1 | 52.9 | 399 | 3 383 | 452.7 | 208.1 | 111 | 4 953 | 1 238.8 | 238.2 |
| Lakewood | 52 | 296 | 73.2 | 7.8 | 64 | 236 | 20.3 | 8.3 | NA | NA | NA | NA |
| La Mesa | 161 | 985 | 117.1 | 29.4 | 256 | 1 343 | 140.5 | 55.2 | NA | NA | NA | NA |
| La Mirada | 40 | 341 | 83.0 | 16.8 | 62 | 646 | 75.8 | 33.0 | 58 | 2 726 | 859.9 | 118.6 |
| Lancaster | 116 | 654 | 114.8 | 17.8 | 144 | D | D | D | 56 | 1 192 | 258.6 | 50.2 |
| La Puente | 21 | 72 | 11.6 | 1.9 | 17 | D | D | D | NA | NA | NA | NA |
| La Quinta | 81 | 204 | 42.5 | 7.5 | 92 | 419 | 60.2 | 20.6 | NA | NA | NA | NA |
| La Verne | 30 | 145 | 20.8 | 4.0 | 68 | 281 | 30.9 | 10.0 | 54 | 1 398 | 294.6 | 54.6 |
| Lawndale | 24 | 324 | 62.5 | 9.6 | 35 | D | D | D | NA | NA | NA | NA |
| Lemon Grove | 22 | 99 | 19.5 | 1.8 | 25 | 118 | 8.1 | 3.2 | NA | NA | NA | NA |
| Lincoln | 27 | 82 | 15.9 | 2.0 | 46 | D | D | D | 24 | 868 | 214.2 | 40.7 |
| Livermore | 109 | 593 | 179.4 | 27.5 | 192 | D | D | D | 150 | 5 221 | 1 803.8 | 299.9 |
| Lodi | 91 | 928 | 67.0 | 22.0 | 114 | 670 | 63.6 | 24.5 | 92 | 3 433 | 687.1 | 114.1 |
| Lompoc | 35 | 151 | 22.3 | 4.7 | 37 | D | D | D | NA | NA | NA | NA |
| Long Beach | 504 | 3 206 | 1 099.2 | 134.4 | 1 005 | D | D | D | 273 | 12 425 | 6 198.3 | 856.7 |
| Los Altos | 88 | 371 | 127.7 | 19.8 | 270 | D | D | D | NA | NA | NA | NA |
| Los Angeles | 5 912 | 38 870 | 13 742.3 | 1 904.9 | 14 157 | 178 164 | 27 271.5 | 10 738.3 | 6 118 | 129 537 | 41 805.6 | 5 391.5 |
| Los Banos | 23 | 57 | 10.4 | 1.1 | 23 | 130 | 12.7 | 4.9 | 11 | 604 | 412.9 | 25.9 |
| Los Gatos | 106 | 726 | 822.5 | 80.5 | 288 | 1 360 | 251.1 | 102.4 | 31 | 620 | 112.6 | 32.6 |
| Lynwood | 15 | 63 | 10.0 | 2.9 | 16 | D | D | D | 57 | 1 630 | 374.1 | 58.6 |
| Madera | 37 | 120 | 16.0 | 3.5 | 33 | D | D | D | 41 | D | 394.6 | 58.2 |
| Manhattan Beach | 134 | 556 | 81.0 | 23.8 | 281 | 1 119 | 194.8 | 92.1 | NA | NA | NA | NA |
| Manteca | 65 | 236 | 37.9 | 6.2 | 49 | 239 | 19.4 | 6.6 | 32 | 941 | 293.7 | 41.3 |
| Martinez | 48 | 176 | 29.1 | 6.0 | 92 | D | D | D | 26 | 949 | D | D |
| Maywood | 3 | D | D | D | 5 | D | D | D | NA | NA | NA | NA |
| Menifee | NA | NA | NA | NA | NA | NA | NA | NA | NA | NA | NA | NA |

1. Establishments subject to federal tax.

**Accommodation and Food Services, Arts, Entertainment, and Recreation, and Health Care and Social Assistance**

| City | Accommodation and food services, 2007 | | | | Arts, entertainment, and recreation,[1] 2007 | | | | Health care and social assistance,[1] 2007 | | | |
|---|---|---|---|---|---|---|---|---|---|---|---|---|
| | Number of establish-ments | Number of employees | Sales (mil dol) | Annual payroll (mil dol) | Number of establish-ments | Number of employees | Receipts (mil dol) | Annual payroll (mil dol) | Number of establish-ments | Number of employees | Receipts (mil dol) | Annual payroll (mil dol) |
| | 92 | 93 | 94 | 95 | 96 | 97 | 98 | 99 | 100 | 101 | 102 | 103 |
| **CALIFORNIA—Cont'd** | | | | | | | | | | | | |
| Delano | 43 | 495 | 25.9 | 5.8 | 2 | D | D | D | 69 | 807 | 64.8 | 25.3 |
| Desert Hot Springs | 33 | 353 | 18.2 | 4.4 | 1 | D | D | D | 13 | D | D | D |
| Diamond Bar | 116 | 1 377 | 64.7 | 17.4 | 10 | D | D | D | 161 | 1 223 | 108.4 | 36.2 |
| Downey | 202 | 3 424 | 181.5 | 50.4 | 13 | 197 | 14.7 | 3.6 | 293 | 4 008 | 455.3 | 174.0 |
| Dublin | 123 | 2 287 | 135.8 | 36.5 | 12 | D | D | D | 79 | 653 | 59.1 | 23.4 |
| East Palo Alto | 13 | 668 | 41.9 | 17.8 | 2 | D | D | D | 14 | 133 | 21.1 | 11.3 |
| El Cajon | 244 | 3 526 | 171.3 | 45.9 | 17 | D | D | D | 232 | 3 318 | 265.9 | 109.4 |
| El Centro | 107 | 1 857 | 81.9 | 23.3 | 3 | D | D | D | 119 | 741 | 81.9 | 32.4 |
| Elk Grove | 208 | 4 110 | 169.6 | 47.7 | 18 | D | D | D | 225 | 2 184 | 294.2 | 72.5 |
| El Monte | 161 | 1 526 | 84.0 | 19.9 | 5 | D | D | D | 146 | 1 865 | 146.7 | 55.5 |
| El Paso de Robles (Paso Robles) | 113 | 2 193 | 98.0 | 29.4 | 14 | D | D | D | 62 | 521 | 32.8 | 11.7 |
| Encinitas | 193 | 3 638 | 180.1 | 50.6 | 44 | D | D | D | 318 | 2 422 | 296.9 | 101.7 |
| Escondido | 276 | 4 149 | 211.6 | 57.8 | 30 | 564 | 28.3 | 8.1 | 305 | 3 511 | 332.5 | 140.6 |
| Eureka | 133 | 1 928 | 91.8 | 25.5 | 11 | D | D | D | 109 | 1 086 | 91.9 | 34.4 |
| Fairfield | 193 | 3 467 | 162.3 | 42.3 | 18 | D | D | D | 218 | 2 200 | 295.1 | 93.8 |
| Folsom | 200 | 3 442 | 159.1 | 48.0 | 23 | 505 | 24.1 | 6.1 | 197 | D | D | D |
| Fontana | 202 | 3 325 | 158.0 | 42.1 | 13 | 245 | 15.2 | 4.0 | 132 | D | D | D |
| Foster City | 60 | 1 236 | 78.6 | 22.8 | 10 | D | D | D | 63 | 537 | 66.6 | 25.2 |
| Fountain Valley | 146 | 2 093 | 115.3 | 30.1 | 18 | D | D | D | 357 | D | D | D |
| Fremont | 384 | 5 456 | 296.6 | 80.7 | 37 | 719 | 41.9 | 12.6 | 552 | 6 413 | 787.1 | 303.6 |
| Fresno | 944 | 17 909 | 813.6 | 229.4 | 92 | 2 061 | 116.1 | 32.3 | 1 326 | 15 864 | 1 749.4 | 729.6 |
| Fullerton | 293 | 5 125 | 253.5 | 69.2 | 22 | 384 | 33.1 | 7.4 | 339 | D | D | D |
| Gardena | 180 | 1 842 | 102.2 | 24.9 | 10 | D | D | D | 153 | 1 940 | 225.3 | 74.4 |
| Garden Grove | 359 | 5 564 | 344.2 | 89.8 | 20 | D | D | D | 447 | 4 441 | 450.7 | 157.0 |
| Gilroy | 120 | 2 070 | 103.3 | 28.0 | 11 | D | D | D | 124 | 1 231 | 151.3 | 45.8 |
| Glendale | 376 | 5 760 | 324.0 | 86.6 | 131 | 658 | 94.5 | 30.5 | 842 | 6 977 | 780.0 | 281.9 |
| Glendora | 94 | 1 298 | 68.3 | 18.9 | 21 | D | D | D | 189 | D | D | D |
| Goleta | 91 | 1 862 | 93.0 | 24.4 | 9 | 140 | 9.4 | 2.9 | 109 | 812 | 85.8 | 35.4 |
| Hanford | 97 | D | D | D | 8 | D | D | D | 120 | 1 197 | 106.9 | 44.7 |
| Hawthorne | 129 | 1 840 | 103.2 | 24.1 | 11 | D | D | D | 114 | 1 812 | 165.8 | 62.3 |
| Hayward | 306 | 3 593 | 210.5 | 51.6 | 17 | D | D | D | 234 | 4 312 | 575.6 | 254.5 |
| Hemet | 139 | 2 340 | 113.2 | 32.3 | 14 | D | D | D | 208 | D | D | D |
| Hesperia | 107 | 1 653 | 86.2 | 21.9 | 8 | D | D | D | 68 | 470 | 39.0 | 13.9 |
| Highland | 35 | 490 | 24.3 | 6.0 | 3 | D | D | D | 46 | D | D | D |
| Hollister | 63 | 783 | 36.4 | 10.3 | 11 | D | D | D | 68 | D | D | D |
| Huntington Beach | 416 | 7 878 | 445.0 | 125.1 | 51 | 645 | 43.6 | 9.2 | 567 | 4 484 | 495.4 | 191.9 |
| Huntington Park | 100 | 1 634 | 86.2 | 21.3 | 3 | D | D | D | 113 | D | D | D |
| Imperial Beach | 39 | 380 | 20.1 | 4.7 | 3 | D | D | D | 19 | 149 | 12.1 | 3.7 |
| Indio | 104 | D | D | D | 12 | D | D | D | 105 | 1 484 | 182.1 | 70.4 |
| Inglewood | 159 | 2 285 | 129.6 | 33.2 | 39 | D | D | D | 276 | 2 691 | 358.4 | 113.6 |
| Irvine | 534 | 12 383 | 755.8 | 204.4 | 68 | 2 360 | 160.2 | 39.2 | 752 | 7 108 | 1 063.8 | 393.9 |
| Laguna Hills | 110 | 2 363 | 115.5 | 36.1 | 7 | D | D | D | 298 | D | D | D |
| Laguna Niguel | 119 | 1 814 | 98.1 | 27.1 | 21 | D | D | D | 202 | 1 077 | 117.8 | 39.4 |
| La Habra | 131 | 2 001 | 99.6 | 27.2 | 6 | D | D | D | 99 | D | D | D |
| Lake Elsinore | 104 | 1 622 | 73.1 | 21.0 | 11 | 234 | 12.1 | 4.7 | 47 | D | D | D |
| Lake Forest | 186 | 3 615 | 172.7 | 49.2 | 25 | D | D | D | 158 | D | D | D |
| Lakewood | 156 | 3 150 | 155.5 | 41.3 | 10 | 263 | 14.8 | 3.5 | 139 | 1 708 | 223.7 | 80.5 |
| La Mesa | 146 | 3 359 | 155.6 | 51.9 | 13 | D | D | D | 293 | D | D | D |
| La Mirada | 92 | 1 443 | 77.7 | 19.3 | 10 | D | D | D | 111 | 1 301 | 123.1 | 45.4 |
| Lancaster | 222 | 3 733 | 178.1 | 45.9 | 19 | D | D | D | 367 | 5 511 | 701.4 | 213.3 |
| La Puente | 81 | 685 | 36.6 | 9.2 | 2 | D | D | D | 52 | D | D | D |
| La Quinta | 74 | 3 505 | 219.2 | 70.3 | 21 | D | D | D | 58 | 269 | 30.7 | 10.3 |
| La Verne | 78 | 1 239 | 58.1 | 17.0 | 8 | 169 | 10.4 | 2.6 | 45 | 321 | 32.1 | 11.3 |
| Lawndale | 47 | 599 | 34.4 | 8.8 | 5 | 13 | 2.7 | 0.7 | 55 | 236 | 22.0 | 6.1 |
| Lemon Grove | 51 | D | D | D | 4 | 45 | 1.3 | 0.4 | 38 | 592 | 35.2 | 15.8 |
| Lincoln | 55 | 637 | 28.7 | 8.3 | 8 | D | D | D | 52 | 487 | 93.1 | 25.7 |
| Livermore | 159 | 2 296 | 132.0 | 36.2 | 16 | D | D | D | 141 | 1 241 | 151.1 | 50.6 |
| Lodi | 148 | 2 020 | 90.6 | 24.3 | 10 | D | D | D | 180 | D | D | D |
| Lompoc | 85 | 1 275 | 59.1 | 14.9 | 5 | 23 | 0.8 | 0.2 | 64 | D | D | D |
| Long Beach | 852 | 17 187 | 924.8 | 266.0 | 77 | 1 597 | 106.8 | 25.8 | 1 007 | 12 146 | 1 257.0 | 485.9 |
| Los Altos | 56 | 959 | 67.1 | 17.2 | 14 | 120 | 6.9 | 4.4 | 137 | 1 012 | 114.6 | 46.7 |
| Los Angeles | 7 609 | 130 390 | 8 271.8 | 2 279.2 | 6 627 | 31 958 | 8 263.6 | 3 056.4 | 9 129 | 98 549 | 11 732.8 | 4 226.3 |
| Los Banos | 53 | 957 | 42.7 | 10.8 | 7 | D | D | D | 39 | 245 | 23.3 | 9.4 |
| Los Gatos | 121 | 2 281 | 125.9 | 41.6 | 17 | D | D | D | 289 | D | D | D |
| Lynwood | 72 | 1 036 | 59.4 | 13.4 | 1 | D | D | D | 105 | D | D | D |
| Madera | 74 | 890 | 46.9 | 11.2 | 8 | D | D | D | 110 | D | D | D |
| Manhattan Beach | 141 | 3 357 | 206.9 | 57.6 | 57 | 322 | 50.5 | 19.2 | 158 | D | D | D |
| Manteca | 116 | 1 654 | 86.5 | 22.9 | 11 | 316 | 12.0 | 3.6 | 100 | 2 172 | 333.3 | 123.2 |
| Martinez | 73 | 777 | 43.2 | 10.5 | 6 | 51 | 5.9 | 0.9 | 37 | D | D | D |
| Maywood | 34 | 393 | 21.1 | 5.2 | 1 | D | D | D | 30 | D | D | D |
| Menifee | NA | NA | NA | NA | NA | NA | NA | NA | NA | NA | NA | NA |

1. Establishments subject to federal tax.

# Table D. Cities — Other Services and Federal Funds

| City | Other services[1], 2007 | | | | Selected federal funds, 2009–2010 (mil dol) | | | | | | | | |
| | Number of establish-ments | Number of employees | Receipts (mil dol) | Annual payroll (mil dol) | Procurement contracts | | Grants | | | | | | |
| | | | | | Defense | Other | Total[2] | Medicaid and other health related | Nutrition and family welfare | Energy and environment | Disasters and emergency prepared-ness | Housing and community develop-ment | Employment and training |
| | 104 | 105 | 106 | 107 | 108 | 109 | 110 | 111 | 112 | 113 | 114 | 115 | 116 |
| **CALIFORNIA—Cont'd** | | | | | | | | | | | | | |
| Delano | 18 | 103 | 10.3 | 4.7 | 0.0 | 1.0 | 2.0 | 0.0 | 0.0 | 1.1 | 0.0 | 0.9 | 0.0 |
| Desert Hot Springs | 15 | 28 | 6.2 | 0.6 | 0.1 | 0.0 | 0.2 | 0.0 | 0.0 | 0.0 | 0.0 | 0.0 | 0.0 |
| Diamond Bar | 75 | 247 | 17.4 | 5.0 | 22.9 | 5.5 | 74.1 | 0.0 | 0.0 | 74.1 | 0.0 | 0.0 | 0.0 |
| Downey | 140 | 818 | 73.1 | 18.9 | 0.6 | 1.3 | 215.7 | 1.8 | 210.1 | 0.0 | 0.0 | 3.1 | 0.0 |
| Dublin | 80 | 511 | 52.9 | 16.6 | 29.0 | 2.9 | 1.3 | 0.0 | 0.0 | 0.0 | 0.0 | 0.3 | 0.0 |
| East Palo Alto | 8 | D | D | D | 0.0 | 0.0 | 0.2 | 0.0 | 0.0 | 0.0 | 0.0 | 0.0 | 0.0 |
| El Cajon | 162 | 974 | 90.4 | 23.7 | 13.8 | 2.5 | 8.8 | 0.2 | 0.2 | 0.9 | 0.0 | 1.9 | 0.0 |
| El Centro | 59 | D | D | D | 0.5 | 39.7 | 3.9 | 0.7 | 0.0 | 0.2 | 0.0 | 0.2 | 0.0 |
| Elk Grove | 112 | 610 | 52.1 | 15.4 | 0.1 | 6.1 | 4.8 | 0.0 | 0.0 | 2.7 | 0.0 | 0.0 | 0.0 |
| El Monte | 134 | 704 | 58.4 | 16.1 | 8.5 | 0.3 | 8.1 | 0.0 | 0.0 | 6.6 | 0.0 | -0.3 | 0.5 |
| El Paso de Robles (Paso Robles) | 43 | 249 | 23.4 | 6.7 | 0.3 | 0.0 | 0.2 | 0.0 | 0.0 | 0.0 | 0.0 | 0.2 | 0.0 |
| Encinitas | 127 | 785 | 64.2 | 20.8 | 7.5 | 1.6 | 6.8 | 4.2 | 0.0 | 0.5 | 0.0 | 1.7 | 0.0 |
| Escondido | 240 | 1 349 | 137.9 | 39.1 | 4.7 | 1.8 | 10.7 | 2.3 | 0.0 | 0.1 | 0.0 | 5.4 | 0.3 |
| Eureka | 85 | 497 | 41.9 | 12.5 | 1.4 | 3.7 | 15.4 | 1.2 | 0.5 | 1.8 | 0.0 | 6.4 | 0.6 |
| Fairfield | 123 | 699 | 60.2 | 18.2 | 103.4 | 5.9 | 24.3 | 1.1 | 0.2 | 1.2 | 0.0 | 11.9 | 0.0 |
| Folsom | 77 | 505 | 41.5 | 12.8 | 98.6 | 116.2 | 5.1 | 0.7 | 0.0 | 2.9 | 0.0 | 0.1 | 0.0 |
| Fontana | 165 | 1 149 | 92.5 | 29.4 | 0.6 | 0.4 | 6.7 | 0.0 | 0.0 | 1.7 | 0.0 | 3.1 | 0.0 |
| Foster City | 21 | 123 | 7.9 | 2.7 | 7.4 | 16.3 | 0.0 | 0.0 | 0.0 | 0.0 | 0.0 | 0.0 | 0.0 |
| Fountain Valley | 102 | 610 | 61.1 | 18.0 | 7.8 | 3.0 | 2.7 | 0.0 | 0.0 | 0.5 | 0.0 | 0.5 | 1.6 |
| Fremont | 265 | 2 159 | 168.7 | 61.8 | 24.0 | 31.7 | 27.9 | 9.2 | 10.6 | 2.3 | 0.0 | 4.0 | 0.0 |
| Fresno | 578 | 4 197 | 371.4 | 107.5 | 23.3 | 98.8 | 274.9 | 4.4 | 31.9 | 18.0 | 0.0 | 129.9 | 3.9 |
| Fullerton | 183 | 732 | 73.0 | 19.1 | 245.8 | 1.3 | 32.7 | 4.8 | 7.4 | 1.8 | 0.0 | 2.6 | 0.0 |
| Gardena | 124 | 778 | 65.2 | 21.1 | 7.2 | 0.2 | 1.4 | 0.0 | 0.0 | 0.0 | 0.0 | 1.0 | 0.0 |
| Garden Grove | 243 | 1 117 | 89.5 | 24.3 | 6.2 | 0.4 | 33.0 | 0.7 | 0.0 | 0.5 | 0.0 | 30.7 | 0.0 |
| Gilroy | 68 | 431 | 41.1 | 12.9 | 0.5 | 0.3 | 2.7 | 0.0 | 0.0 | 0.0 | 0.0 | 1.8 | 0.0 |
| Glendale | 308 | 2 041 | 156.6 | 58.0 | 129.7 | 9.8 | 51.0 | 0.7 | 0.0 | 22.6 | 0.0 | 21.0 | 0.0 |
| Glendora | 97 | D | D | D | 0.4 | 0.6 | 8.6 | 0.0 | 0.0 | 0.7 | 0.0 | 0.4 | 0.0 |
| Goleta | 62 | D | D | D | 311.5 | 21.9 | 23.7 | 0.8 | 10.4 | 3.0 | 0.0 | 0.6 | 0.0 |
| Hanford | 48 | D | D | D | 0.0 | 0.0 | 16.9 | 0.0 | 6.5 | 0.0 | 0.0 | 6.4 | 0.0 |
| Hawthorne | 103 | 405 | 39.8 | 9.7 | 8.4 | 22.3 | 6.6 | 0.0 | 0.0 | 0.0 | 0.0 | 6.2 | 0.1 |
| Hayward | 209 | 1 653 | 158.1 | 44.1 | 25.8 | 7.0 | 115.3 | 7.1 | 0.0 | 7.0 | 0.0 | 85.3 | 0.0 |
| Hemet | 89 | 446 | 29.7 | 7.8 | 0.7 | 0.3 | 1.9 | 0.0 | 0.0 | 0.9 | 0.0 | 0.8 | 0.0 |
| Hesperia | 85 | 449 | 41.3 | 11.6 | 0.6 | 0.1 | 8.2 | 0.0 | 0.0 | 0.0 | 0.0 | 0.8 | 0.0 |
| Highland | 33 | 191 | 11.4 | 3.8 | 1.4 | 0.3 | 0.7 | 0.0 | 0.0 | 0.2 | 0.0 | 0.0 | 0.0 |
| Hollister | 48 | D | D | D | 1.4 | 1.5 | 1.4 | 0.7 | 0.0 | 0.0 | 0.0 | 0.0 | 0.0 |
| Huntington Beach | 342 | 1 994 | 153.9 | 46.6 | 476.1 | 55.3 | 12.4 | 0.0 | 0.0 | 8.1 | 0.0 | 2.5 | 0.0 |
| Huntington Park | 47 | D | D | D | 0.0 | 0.0 | 4.4 | 0.0 | 0.0 | 0.0 | 0.0 | 4.3 | 0.0 |
| Imperial Beach | 18 | 75 | 4.7 | 1.4 | 5.6 | 22.0 | 1.1 | 0.7 | 0.0 | 0.1 | 0.0 | 0.0 | 0.0 |
| Indio | 61 | 366 | 37.7 | 9.9 | 0.1 | 0.3 | 11.2 | 0.0 | 0.0 | 1.0 | 0.0 | 9.3 | 0.0 |
| Inglewood | 143 | 993 | 78.1 | 22.3 | 61.8 | 22.9 | 25.9 | 0.3 | 0.0 | 1.0 | 0.0 | 13.0 | 0.0 |
| Irvine | 278 | 2 176 | 188.5 | 62.3 | 305.8 | 62.9 | 367.0 | 279.2 | 0.0 | 19.7 | 0.0 | 4.6 | 0.0 |
| Laguna Hills | 71 | 470 | 34.4 | 10.7 | 7.7 | 0.3 | 0.0 | 0.0 | 0.0 | 0.0 | 0.0 | 0.0 | 0.0 |
| Laguna Niguel | 86 | 538 | 45.0 | 14.6 | 1.9 | 14.3 | 0.7 | 0.1 | 0.0 | 0.0 | 0.0 | 0.7 | 0.0 |
| La Habra | 123 | 653 | 61.8 | 16.5 | 0.0 | 0.0 | 2.1 | 0.1 | 0.0 | 0.0 | 0.0 | 1.7 | 0.0 |
| Lake Elsinore | 51 | 341 | 21.9 | 6.9 | 18.0 | 0.3 | 2.9 | 0.0 | 0.0 | 1.9 | 0.0 | 0.0 | 0.0 |
| Lake Forest | 112 | 768 | 84.2 | 22.2 | 20.9 | 3.9 | 14.1 | 0.0 | 0.0 | 0.7 | 12.2 | 0.9 | 0.0 |
| Lakewood | 70 | D | D | D | 0.4 | 0.5 | 3.1 | 0.0 | 0.0 | 0.4 | 0.0 | 2.3 | 0.0 |
| La Mesa | 118 | 697 | 44.3 | 13.7 | 0.0 | 0.5 | 2.1 | 0.0 | 0.0 | 0.9 | 0.0 | 1.1 | 0.0 |
| La Mirada | 33 | 309 | 14.2 | 6.4 | 26.7 | 1.4 | 0.1 | 0.0 | 0.0 | 0.0 | 0.0 | 0.0 | 0.0 |
| Lancaster | 150 | 917 | 74.2 | 21.2 | 9.7 | 0.8 | 19.1 | 1.2 | 0.0 | 0.0 | 0.0 | 2.0 | 0.0 |
| La Puente | 41 | 147 | 8.8 | 2.4 | 3.8 | 0.7 | 0.0 | 0.0 | 0.0 | 0.0 | 0.0 | 0.0 | 0.0 |
| La Quinta | 29 | 217 | 9.3 | 3.6 | 0.2 | 0.0 | 1.7 | 0.0 | 0.0 | 0.0 | 0.0 | 0.0 | 0.0 |
| La Verne | 42 | D | D | D | 88.9 | 1.8 | 1.0 | 0.0 | 0.0 | 0.0 | 0.0 | 0.0 | 0.0 |
| Lawndale | 64 | D | D | D | 0.1 | 0.2 | 0.5 | 0.0 | 0.0 | 0.0 | 0.0 | 0.0 | 0.0 |
| Lemon Grove | 52 | 223 | 21.5 | 5.6 | 0.4 | 0.0 | 0.6 | 0.0 | 0.0 | 0.0 | 0.0 | 0.1 | 0.0 |
| Lincoln | 29 | D | D | D | 2.6 | 0.2 | 0.0 | 0.0 | 0.0 | 0.0 | 0.0 | 0.0 | 0.0 |
| Livermore | 117 | 630 | 63.7 | 22.8 | 16.0 | 1 571.9 | 23.1 | 4.7 | 0.0 | 1.8 | 0.0 | 9.0 | 0.0 |
| Lodi | 112 | 637 | 54.5 | 17.5 | 0.7 | 17.9 | 3.3 | 0.0 | 0.0 | 0.0 | 0.0 | 1.6 | 0.0 |
| Lompoc | 44 | 223 | 20.9 | 5.5 | 11.9 | 11.5 | 41.0 | 0.0 | 0.0 | 0.0 | 0.0 | 36.7 | 0.0 |
| Long Beach | 538 | 4 265 | 470.4 | 114.9 | 3 814.0 | 38.3 | 569.9 | 11.7 | 18.4 | 368.0 | 0.0 | 117.2 | 1.2 |
| Los Altos | 44 | 189 | 13.2 | 4.8 | 0.6 | 0.2 | 8.9 | 6.7 | 0.0 | 0.3 | 0.0 | 0.0 | 0.0 |
| Los Angeles | 5 424 | 36 122 | 3 211.8 | 885.5 | 675.7 | 343.7 | 3 310.9 | 1 453.2 | 28.8 | 157.1 | 0.3 | 901.5 | 15.4 |
| Los Banos | 22 | D | D | D | 0.0 | 8.7 | 1.9 | 0.0 | 0.0 | 1.9 | 0.0 | 0.0 | 0.0 |
| Los Gatos | 97 | 515 | 40.0 | 11.5 | 0.3 | 0.8 | 24.0 | 1.2 | 0.0 | 21.3 | 0.0 | 0.0 | 0.0 |
| Lynwood | 46 | 190 | 20.6 | 4.4 | 1.3 | 0.3 | 3.6 | 0.1 | 0.0 | 0.6 | 0.0 | 2.4 | 0.0 |
| Madera | 51 | 278 | 25.0 | 6.2 | 0.0 | 0.1 | 14.8 | 2.3 | 3.3 | 0.1 | 0.0 | 7.2 | 0.0 |
| Manhattan Beach | 76 | 474 | 31.4 | 9.1 | 0.1 | 7.4 | 0.5 | 0.4 | 0.0 | 0.0 | 0.0 | 0.1 | 0.0 |
| Manteca | 80 | 333 | 25.5 | 7.4 | 0.7 | 0.7 | 1.5 | 0.0 | 0.0 | 0.5 | 0.0 | 0.0 | 0.0 |
| Martinez | 47 | 232 | 23.6 | 7.7 | 4.4 | 42.1 | 127.6 | 2.2 | 20.8 | 3.6 | 0.0 | 98.8 | 0.0 |
| Maywood | 22 | D | D | D | 0.0 | 0.0 | 0.0 | 0.0 | 0.0 | 0.0 | 0.0 | 0.0 | 0.0 |
| Menifee | NA | NA | NA | NA | NA | NA | NA | NA | NA | NA | NA | NA | NA |

1. Establishments subject to federal tax.　2. Includes program categories not shown separately. State totals include additional categories not allocated by city.

| City | General revenue | | | | | | | General expenditure | | |
|---|---|---|---|---|---|---|---|---|---|---|
| | | Intergovernmental | | Taxes | | | | | Per capita[1] (dollars) | |
| | | | | | Per capita[1] (dollars) | | | | | |
| | Total (mil dol) | Total (mil dol) | Percent from state government | Total (mil dol) | Total | Property | Sales and gross receipts | Total (mil dol) | Total | Capital outlays |
| | 117 | 118 | 119 | 120 | 121 | 122 | 123 | 124 | 125 | 126 |
| CALIFORNIA—Cont'd | | | | | | | | | | |
| Delano | 34.3 | 11.2 | 86.3 | 15.0 | 286 | 176 | 90 | 31.0 | 592 | 53 |
| Desert Hot Springs | 23.5 | 2.4 | 90.3 | 16.6 | 682 | 260 | 231 | 30.1 | 1 238 | 441 |
| Diamond Bar | 29.4 | 8.4 | 96.2 | 14.0 | 245 | 89 | 130 | 25.1 | 437 | 106 |
| Downey | 95.8 | 11.6 | 67.7 | 56.6 | 524 | 253 | 267 | 89.7 | 829 | 38 |
| Dublin | 69.8 | 2.7 | 86.5 | 49.2 | 1 120 | 538 | 377 | 64.8 | 1 473 | 364 |
| East Palo Alto | 32.2 | 2.2 | 68.5 | 22.3 | 675 | 492 | 173 | 24.9 | 753 | 79 |
| El Cajon | 101.7 | 11.2 | 87.6 | 59.9 | 648 | 358 | 285 | 101.8 | 1 100 | 155 |
| El Centro | 137.1 | 9.6 | 52.3 | 30.3 | 764 | 374 | 352 | 124.8 | 3 147 | 389 |
| Elk Grove | 139.6 | 9.1 | 66.9 | 95.0 | 724 | 287 | 431 | 186.5 | 1 422 | 413 |
| El Monte | 90.0 | 13.8 | 65.4 | 67.2 | 550 | 274 | 267 | 93.3 | 763 | 103 |
| El Paso de Robles (Paso Robles) | 50.0 | 3.7 | 81.5 | 34.3 | 1 198 | 579 | 611 | 38.3 | 1 338 | 271 |
| Encinitas | 78.2 | 5.2 | 97.0 | 46.8 | 780 | 552 | 219 | 83.2 | 1 388 | 422 |
| Escondido | 192.4 | 17.0 | 56.2 | 91.6 | 672 | 422 | 244 | 165.4 | 1 214 | 245 |
| Eureka | 35.2 | 4.1 | 75.6 | 22.0 | 867 | 376 | 488 | 41.3 | 1 625 | 206 |
| Fairfield | 166.4 | 23.9 | 41.8 | 103.9 | 999 | 568 | 425 | 140.4 | 1 350 | 342 |
| Folsom | 132.2 | 6.7 | 89.5 | 82.8 | 1 229 | 448 | 687 | 138.9 | 2 060 | 730 |
| Fontana | 268.3 | 26.7 | 77.8 | 166.9 | 909 | 634 | 269 | 324.3 | 1 768 | 789 |
| Foster City | 60.1 | 1.2 | 100.0 | 38.7 | 1 339 | 1 079 | 251 | 65.8 | 2 275 | 343 |
| Fountain Valley | 57.9 | 4.4 | 84.6 | 37.7 | 679 | 409 | 266 | 47.1 | 849 | 99 |
| Fremont | 237.2 | 28.4 | 74.3 | 161.7 | 803 | 485 | 254 | 231.2 | 1 148 | 348 |
| Fresno | 574.0 | 102.4 | 51.1 | 260.3 | 553 | 297 | 252 | 568.8 | 1 209 | 295 |
| Fullerton | 145.8 | 11.7 | 64.3 | 77.5 | 587 | 379 | 200 | 127.7 | 967 | 174 |
| Gardena | 69.7 | 9.4 | 66.8 | 51.9 | 883 | 202 | 507 | 69.1 | 1 177 | 115 |
| Garden Grove | 166.3 | 44.0 | 24.4 | 90.7 | 548 | 332 | 212 | 155.5 | 939 | 117 |
| Gilroy | 75.8 | 6.0 | 45.2 | 37.5 | 764 | 265 | 372 | 86.3 | 1 758 | 754 |
| Glendale | 328.1 | 59.2 | 23.4 | 146.9 | 746 | 383 | 357 | 366.2 | 1 859 | 648 |
| Glendora | 46.3 | 5.6 | 91.8 | 29.7 | 597 | 389 | 202 | 51.6 | 1 038 | 350 |
| Goleta | 25.9 | 5.1 | 91.5 | 17.5 | 592 | 272 | 245 | 24.2 | 821 | 102 |
| Hanford | 52.9 | 8.9 | 85.4 | 21.8 | 439 | 257 | 140 | 48.0 | 968 | 323 |
| Hawthorne | 118.7 | 48.5 | 24.9 | 50.9 | 603 | 263 | 335 | 144.4 | 1 710 | 504 |
| Hayward | 172.5 | 17.7 | 88.7 | 98.9 | 702 | 398 | 251 | 204.5 | 1 451 | 567 |
| Hemet | 85.1 | 14.4 | 78.5 | 38.3 | 545 | 336 | 202 | 84.2 | 1 197 | 183 |
| Hesperia | 62.7 | 12.2 | 93.0 | 38.9 | 455 | 190 | 186 | 68.1 | 796 | 187 |
| Highland | 34.2 | 7.5 | 81.5 | 17.2 | 336 | 220 | 61 | 36.4 | 709 | 340 |
| Hollister | 39.1 | 1.5 | 72.8 | 21.6 | 619 | 497 | 113 | 50.1 | 1 434 | 616 |
| Huntington Beach | 236.2 | 25.7 | 89.1 | 131.0 | 679 | 335 | 338 | 217.2 | 1 126 | 162 |
| Huntington Park | 60.9 | 7.9 | 60.7 | 34.6 | 564 | 339 | 223 | 67.6 | 1 103 | 333 |
| Imperial Beach | 28.2 | 1.3 | 95.1 | 14.4 | 545 | 432 | 108 | 34.7 | 1 313 | 151 |
| Indio | 127.9 | 4.5 | 68.5 | 55.0 | 655 | 320 | 327 | 110.8 | 1 320 | 328 |
| Inglewood | 147.0 | 8.8 | 73.3 | 84.9 | 749 | 319 | 375 | 141.6 | 1 249 | 59 |
| Irvine | 318.3 | 23.5 | 65.3 | 152.7 | 759 | 326 | 433 | 281.2 | 1 398 | 259 |
| Laguna Hills | 27.2 | 4.4 | 28.3 | 17.9 | 561 | 304 | 248 | 28.5 | 893 | 347 |
| Laguna Niguel | 43.4 | 3.9 | 91.2 | 32.8 | 509 | 297 | 205 | 38.7 | 601 | 213 |
| La Habra | 57.3 | 9.6 | 80.8 | 33.8 | 571 | 287 | 276 | 51.4 | 868 | 105 |
| Lake Elsinore | 91.6 | 1.9 | 99.6 | 29.1 | 596 | 217 | 248 | 93.1 | 1 906 | 518 |
| Lake Forest | 48.5 | 3.8 | 79.8 | 38.1 | 503 | 259 | 238 | 37.3 | 492 | 79 |
| Lakewood | 60.0 | 5.9 | 54.1 | 38.6 | 488 | 273 | 212 | 60.8 | 770 | 125 |
| La Mesa | 53.3 | 4.9 | 86.3 | 30.9 | 573 | 305 | 257 | 54.1 | 1 002 | 175 |
| La Mirada | 53.7 | 3.7 | 52.7 | 38.1 | 765 | 488 | 272 | 68.5 | 1 376 | 692 |
| Lancaster | 189.6 | 15.7 | 69.5 | 134.8 | 939 | 629 | 303 | 185.6 | 1 292 | 309 |
| La Puente | 16.8 | 2.8 | 69.2 | 10.1 | 246 | 132 | 100 | 14.1 | 345 | 24 |
| La Quinta | 141.9 | 5.2 | 99.4 | 110.1 | 2 553 | 2 076 | 376 | 136.6 | 3 165 | 828 |
| La Verne | 44.6 | 5.9 | 98.9 | 25.8 | 778 | 478 | 288 | 40.5 | 1 224 | 208 |
| Lawndale | 22.2 | 3.1 | 61.8 | 15.9 | 505 | 262 | 239 | 18.1 | 573 | 107 |
| Lemon Grove | 22.2 | 1.6 | 77.7 | 13.8 | 573 | 333 | 236 | 22.6 | 938 | 69 |
| Lincoln | 72.8 | 8.9 | 94.5 | 28.9 | 686 | 231 | 416 | 129.0 | 3 063 | 1 929 |
| Livermore | 142.8 | 7.4 | 73.1 | 66.0 | 830 | 476 | 342 | 151.5 | 1 905 | 389 |
| Lodi | 68.4 | 7.9 | 77.4 | 41.2 | 668 | 277 | 351 | 55.5 | 900 | 127 |
| Lompoc | 52.0 | 6.0 | 69.9 | 22.9 | 565 | 257 | 271 | 58.8 | 1 454 | 285 |
| Long Beach | 1 535.0 | 175.9 | 38.1 | 335.7 | 720 | 403 | 312 | 1 327.1 | 2 845 | 352 |
| Los Altos | 34.4 | 2.0 | 92.9 | 20.6 | 735 | 410 | 300 | 42.4 | 1 513 | 136 |
| Los Angeles | 8 472.8 | 682.8 | 50.7 | 3 866.6 | 1 008 | 443 | 494 | 7 602.3 | 1 983 | 365 |
| Los Banos | 39.3 | 3.7 | 70.4 | 20.2 | 580 | 328 | 162 | 45.8 | 1 314 | 576 |
| Los Gatos | 43.8 | 2.4 | 97.2 | 30.5 | 1 046 | 614 | 406 | 38.5 | 1 318 | 181 |
| Lynwood | 51.6 | 7.6 | 82.1 | 31.1 | 442 | 264 | 172 | 63.1 | 897 | 122 |
| Madera | 54.9 | 4.8 | 54.8 | 26.9 | 482 | 268 | 150 | 73.9 | 1 322 | 672 |
| Manhattan Beach | 65.6 | 2.3 | 100.0 | 39.5 | 1 082 | 597 | 462 | 81.2 | 2 222 | 291 |
| Manteca | 124.1 | 12.1 | 95.7 | 41.1 | 641 | 481 | 160 | 111.0 | 1 733 | 680 |
| Martinez | 25.5 | 2.9 | 97.4 | 17.0 | 485 | 295 | 185 | 23.7 | 674 | 44 |
| Maywood | 18.5 | 4.7 | 54.2 | 9.5 | 336 | 237 | 92 | 23.7 | 834 | 234 |
| Menifee | NA | NA | NA | NA | NA | NA | NA | NA | NA | NA |

1. Based on population estimated as of July 1 of the year shown.

| City | Public welfare | Highways | Parking facilities | Education | Health and hospitals | Police protection | Sewerage and sanitation | Parks and recreation | Housing and community development | Interest on debt |
|---|---|---|---|---|---|---|---|---|---|---|
| | 127 | 128 | 129 | 130 | 131 | 132 | 133 | 134 | 135 | 136 |
| CALIFORNIA—Cont'd | | | | | | | | | | |
| Delano | 0.0 | 4.5 | 0.0 | 0.0 | 1.0 | 40.8 | 10.5 | 6.4 | 5.9 | 4.5 |
| Desert Hot Springs | 0.0 | 19.5 | 0.0 | 0.0 | 1.0 | 19.0 | 0.0 | 11.8 | 16.6 | 3.6 |
| Diamond Bar | 0.0 | 23.6 | 0.0 | 0.0 | 0.4 | 0.0 | 1.5 | 22.1 | 2.4 | 2.0 |
| Downey | 0.0 | 7.4 | 0.0 | 0.0 | 3.0 | 29.5 | 2.0 | 11.5 | 4.1 | 3.7 |
| Dublin | 0.0 | 13.0 | 0.0 | 0.0 | 0.7 | 18.3 | 2.5 | 26.0 | 0.9 | 0.5 |
| East Palo Alto | 0.0 | 6.0 | 0.0 | 0.0 | 0.0 | 39.8 | 7.1 | 2.4 | 9.8 | 11.5 |
| El Cajon | 0.0 | 9.7 | 0.0 | 0.0 | 5.9 | 34.1 | 11.1 | 5.0 | 9.7 | 3.1 |
| El Centro | 0.0 | 7.8 | 0.0 | 0.0 | 57.3 | 6.4 | 8.7 | 2.0 | 4.4 | 2.0 |
| Elk Grove | 0.0 | 53.2 | 0.0 | 0.0 | 0.3 | 16.4 | 4.7 | 0.8 | 0.3 | 2.9 |
| El Monte | 0.0 | 9.1 | 0.1 | 0.0 | 0.1 | 31.4 | 0.0 | 6.1 | 12.0 | 6.0 |
| El Paso de Robles (Paso Robles) | 0.0 | 18.6 | 0.0 | 0.0 | 0.0 | 23.0 | 7.5 | 14.5 | 3.3 | 5.4 |
| Encinitas | 0.0 | 9.9 | 0.0 | 0.0 | 1.2 | 12.6 | 4.6 | 22.2 | 1.3 | 0.5 |
| Escondido | 0.0 | 11.2 | 0.0 | 0.0 | 0.4 | 27.3 | 16.8 | 6.8 | 3.9 | 4.0 |
| Eureka | 0.0 | 9.4 | 0.0 | 0.0 | 0.0 | 19.8 | 8.9 | 7.3 | 15.5 | 5.2 |
| Fairfield | 0.0 | 27.3 | 0.0 | 0.0 | 0.5 | 20.1 | 0.0 | 8.8 | 12.7 | 6.0 |
| Folsom | 0.0 | 25.5 | 0.0 | 0.0 | 0.5 | 14.4 | 8.1 | 12.0 | 6.8 | 3.7 |
| Fontana | 0.0 | 20.8 | 0.0 | 0.0 | 0.7 | 11.8 | 3.6 | 1.5 | 33.4 | 9.8 |
| Foster City | 0.0 | 2.6 | 0.0 | 0.0 | 0.0 | 12.9 | 5.6 | 8.3 | 12.0 | 3.6 |
| Fountain Valley | 0.0 | 14.6 | 0.0 | 0.0 | 4.8 | 28.8 | 7.0 | 6.6 | 6.3 | 4.4 |
| Fremont | 0.0 | 13.7 | 0.0 | 0.0 | 4.1 | 23.4 | 2.3 | 8.0 | 8.8 | 6.0 |
| Fresno | 0.0 | 9.9 | 1.0 | 0.0 | 1.7 | 23.6 | 18.5 | 8.5 | 3.9 | 7.7 |
| Fullerton | 0.0 | 6.5 | 0.0 | 0.0 | 4.9 | 28.0 | 8.0 | 6.0 | 10.1 | 8.3 |
| Gardena | 0.0 | 5.0 | 0.0 | 0.0 | 3.6 | 54.3 | 0.5 | 4.4 | 1.3 | 2.3 |
| Garden Grove | 0.0 | 9.4 | 0.0 | 0.0 | 3.9 | 25.8 | 5.9 | 4.0 | 25.0 | 5.7 |
| Gilroy | 0.0 | 3.5 | 0.0 | 0.0 | 0.4 | 20.5 | 3.5 | 1.2 | 44.5 | 1.8 |
| Glendale | 0.0 | 8.0 | 1.5 | 0.0 | 0.3 | 14.3 | 12.0 | 5.1 | 25.8 | 1.3 |
| Glendora | 0.0 | 9.7 | 0.0 | 0.0 | 0.3 | 23.7 | 0.2 | 9.0 | 32.9 | 5.3 |
| Goleta | 0.0 | 15.2 | 0.0 | 0.0 | 1.6 | 24.1 | 0.0 | 2.8 | 12.2 | 0.6 |
| Hanford | 0.0 | 15.0 | 0.0 | 0.0 | 0.3 | 15.4 | 18.9 | 22.5 | 3.4 | 4.4 |
| Hawthorne | 0.0 | 13.3 | 0.0 | 0.0 | 0.0 | 22.6 | 0.7 | 2.4 | 31.6 | 4.6 |
| Hayward | 0.0 | 8.8 | 0.0 | 0.0 | 0.8 | 22.6 | 23.5 | 0.9 | 11.0 | 2.0 |
| Hemet | 0.0 | 20.5 | 0.0 | 0.0 | 0.2 | 24.4 | 17.4 | 1.2 | 10.6 | 1.1 |
| Hesperia | 0.0 | 12.9 | 0.0 | 0.0 | 2.4 | 15.1 | 0.0 | 0.9 | 19.3 | 4.8 |
| Highland | 0.0 | 11.0 | 0.0 | 0.0 | 3.2 | 16.3 | 0.0 | 4.9 | 7.2 | 5.8 |
| Hollister | 0.0 | 36.4 | 0.0 | 0.0 | 0.8 | 10.7 | 25.1 | 2.6 | 2.0 | 4.9 |
| Huntington Beach | 0.0 | 14.0 | 0.9 | 0.0 | 2.8 | 26.3 | 9.0 | 9.8 | 1.9 | 3.9 |
| Huntington Park | 0.0 | 21.7 | 0.8 | 0.0 | 0.3 | 21.6 | 2.8 | 3.6 | 11.9 | 7.2 |
| Imperial Beach | 0.0 | 10.7 | 0.0 | 0.0 | 0.7 | 32.0 | 18.5 | 4.7 | 16.1 | 4.6 |
| Indio | 0.0 | 52.9 | 0.0 | 0.0 | 3.7 | 15.1 | 0.0 | 2.3 | 4.3 | 1.6 |
| Inglewood | 0.0 | 6.3 | 0.3 | 0.0 | 1.8 | 25.3 | 8.7 | 5.5 | 17.1 | 4.3 |
| Irvine | 0.0 | 25.6 | 0.0 | 0.0 | 0.8 | 18.3 | 0.0 | 13.3 | 4.2 | 15.4 |
| Laguna Hills | 0.0 | 27.0 | 0.0 | 0.0 | 0.1 | 20.7 | 0.0 | 26.7 | 0.0 | 2.9 |
| Laguna Niguel | 0.0 | 31.8 | 0.0 | 0.0 | 0.7 | 20.0 | 0.0 | 20.5 | 0.2 | 0.0 |
| La Habra | 0.0 | 14.7 | 0.0 | 0.0 | 3.2 | 26.5 | 6.5 | 15.3 | 5.0 | 2.9 |
| Lake Elsinore | 0.0 | 8.1 | 0.0 | 0.0 | 0.2 | 8.6 | 0.0 | 8.3 | 10.6 | 23.8 |
| Lake Forest | 0.0 | 25.2 | 0.0 | 0.0 | 0.7 | 26.7 | 0.0 | 10.9 | 9.2 | 1.1 |
| Lakewood | 0.0 | 16.4 | 0.0 | 0.0 | 0.3 | 18.5 | 7.6 | 19.4 | 12.8 | 4.6 |
| La Mesa | 0.0 | 10.3 | 0.2 | 0.0 | 0.2 | 23.9 | 19.9 | 8.5 | 0.9 | 5.6 |
| La Mirada | 0.0 | 13.2 | 0.0 | 0.0 | 0.1 | 11.4 | 0.0 | 45.8 | 14.0 | 7.7 |
| Lancaster | 0.0 | 18.0 | 0.0 | 0.0 | 0.2 | 10.3 | 0.0 | 7.3 | 40.7 | 9.0 |
| La Puente | 0.0 | 2.7 | 0.0 | 0.0 | 1.2 | 31.0 | 1.5 | 11.0 | 9.2 | 2.9 |
| La Quinta | 0.0 | 8.7 | 0.0 | 0.0 | 0.3 | 6.3 | 0.0 | 5.7 | 47.4 | 14.2 |
| La Verne | 0.0 | 11.6 | 0.0 | 0.0 | 4.6 | 27.4 | 1.7 | 7.2 | 14.9 | 5.3 |
| Lawndale | 0.0 | 15.2 | 0.0 | 0.0 | 0.9 | 22.9 | 0.2 | 15.3 | 11.2 | 3.5 |
| Lemon Grove | 0.0 | 9.2 | 0.0 | 0.0 | 0.7 | 20.0 | 14.2 | 7.1 | 12.4 | 4.4 |
| Lincoln | 0.0 | 4.3 | 0.0 | 0.0 | 0.0 | 4.9 | 11.2 | 2.2 | 1.3 | 7.2 |
| Livermore | 0.0 | 14.8 | 0.0 | 0.0 | 0.5 | 15.7 | 13.3 | 2.8 | 4.9 | 4.6 |
| Lodi | 0.0 | 6.0 | 0.0 | 0.0 | 0.5 | 24.9 | 15.2 | 9.2 | 1.2 | 0.1 |
| Lompoc | 0.0 | 9.4 | 0.0 | 0.0 | 0.6 | 28.0 | 29.2 | 6.8 | 3.5 | 1.6 |
| Long Beach | 0.0 | 5.1 | 0.0 | 0.0 | 4.3 | 17.3 | 5.5 | 8.1 | 7.5 | 7.5 |
| Los Altos | 0.0 | 6.7 | 0.0 | 0.0 | 6.1 | 37.4 | 12.2 | 7.5 | 2.2 | 0.1 |
| Los Angeles | 0.0 | 7.7 | 0.3 | 0.0 | 2.6 | 17.3 | 9.0 | 5.1 | 4.8 | 5.7 |
| Los Banos | 0.0 | 18.2 | 0.0 | 0.0 | 0.5 | 16.1 | 22.1 | 18.5 | 5.5 | 2.8 |
| Los Gatos | 0.0 | 8.2 | 0.0 | 0.0 | 0.4 | 31.3 | 0.6 | 7.2 | 15.4 | 4.2 |
| Lynwood | 0.0 | 14.4 | 0.0 | 0.0 | 0.8 | 19.9 | 0.0 | 16.7 | 6.4 | 3.8 |
| Madera | 0.0 | 12.8 | 0.0 | 0.0 | 1.4 | 12.0 | 37.7 | 5.0 | 9.4 | 3.6 |
| Manhattan Beach | 0.0 | 24.1 | 2.9 | 0.0 | 4.5 | 29.3 | 6.3 | 9.9 | 0.0 | 0.6 |
| Manteca | 0.0 | 19.6 | 0.0 | 0.0 | 0.2 | 11.6 | 24.9 | 5.2 | 18.2 | 6.3 |
| Martinez | 0.0 | 14.2 | 1.3 | 0.0 | 0.0 | 38.3 | 0.0 | 14.7 | 0.1 | 0.5 |
| Maywood | 0.0 | 4.1 | 0.0 | 0.0 | 0.2 | 42.4 | 0.0 | 3.7 | 35.3 | 1.7 |
| Menifee | NA | NA | NA | NA | NA | NA | NA | NA | NA | NA |

| City | City government finances, 2007 (cont.) | | | City government employment, 2011 | Climate[2] | | | | | | |
|---|---|---|---|---|---|---|---|---|---|---|---|
| | Debt outstanding | | | | Average daily temperature (degrees Fahrenheit) | | | | | | |
| | | | | | Mean | | Limits | | | | |
| | Total (mil dol) | Per capita[1] (dollars) | Debt issued during year | | January | July | January[3] | July[4] | Annual precipitation (inches) | Heating degree days | Cooling degree days |
| | 137 | 138 | 139 | 140 | 141 | 142 | 143 | 144 | 145 | 146 | 147 |
| CALIFORNIA—Cont'd | | | | | | | | | | | |
| Delano | 22.0 | 420 | 0.0 | NA | 46.6 | 81.1 | 36.5 | 99.0 | 7.34 | 2 434 | 1 990 |
| Desert Hot Springs | 21.6 | 889 | 7.0 | NA | NA | NA | NA | NA | NA | NA | NA |
| Diamond Bar | 13.3 | 231 | 0.0 | NA | 54.6 | 73.8 | 41.5 | 88.7 | 16.96 | 1 727 | 1 191 |
| Downey | 41.1 | 380 | 0.0 | 537 | 57.0 | 73.8 | 46.0 | 82.9 | 12.94 | 1 211 | 1 186 |
| Dublin | 8.1 | 183 | 0.0 | NA | 47.2 | 72.0 | 37.4 | 89.1 | 14.82 | 2 755 | 858 |
| East Palo Alto | 68.7 | 2 077 | 1.4 | NA | 49.0 | 68.0 | 40.4 | 78.8 | 15.71 | 2 584 | 452 |
| El Cajon | 80.5 | 870 | 15.8 | 458 | 54.9 | 74.7 | 41.6 | 87.0 | 11.96 | 1 560 | 1 371 |
| El Centro | 70.1 | 1 767 | 32.1 | 972 | 55.8 | 91.4 | 41.3 | 107.0 | 2.96 | 1 080 | 3 852 |
| Elk Grove | 105.2 | 802 | 0.2 | 279 | 46.3 | 75.4 | 38.8 | 92.4 | 17.93 | 2 666 | 1 248 |
| El Monte | 125.1 | 1 023 | 4.2 | 296 | 56.3 | 75.6 | 42.6 | 89.0 | 18.56 | 1 295 | 1 575 |
| El Paso de Robles (Paso Robles) | 52.8 | 1 842 | 1.2 | NA | NA | NA | NA | NA | NA | NA | NA |
| Encinitas | 50.6 | 844 | 0.0 | NA | 55.5 | 75.1 | 42.5 | 88.6 | 15.10 | 1 464 | 1 436 |
| Escondido | 280.1 | 2 056 | 159.0 | 936 | 55.5 | 75.1 | 42.5 | 88.6 | 15.10 | 1 464 | 1 436 |
| Eureka | 35.1 | 1 381 | 0.0 | 283 | 47.9 | 58.1 | 40.8 | 63.3 | 38.10 | 4 430 | 7 |
| Fairfield | 202.4 | 1 946 | 0.0 | 547 | 46.1 | 72.6 | 37.5 | 88.8 | 23.46 | 2 649 | 975 |
| Folsom | 174.2 | 2 584 | 16.9 | 526 | 46.9 | 77.7 | 39.2 | 94.8 | 24.61 | 2 532 | 1 528 |
| Fontana | 636.4 | 3 468 | 41.0 | 797 | 56.6 | 78.3 | 45.3 | 95.0 | 14.77 | 1 364 | 1 901 |
| Foster City | 29.0 | 1 004 | 0.0 | NA | 48.4 | 68.0 | 39.1 | 80.8 | 20.16 | 2 764 | 422 |
| Fountain Valley | 33.6 | 605 | 0.0 | NA | 58.0 | 72.9 | 46.6 | 87.7 | 13.84 | 1 153 | 1 299 |
| Fremont | 421.0 | 2 091 | 0.0 | 887 | 49.8 | 68.0 | 42.0 | 78.3 | 14.85 | 2 367 | 530 |
| Fresno | 940.9 | 2 000 | 22.5 | 3 666 | 46.0 | 81.4 | 38.4 | 96.6 | 11.23 | 2 447 | 1 963 |
| Fullerton | 199.6 | 1 512 | 74.6 | 731 | 56.9 | 73.2 | 45.2 | 84.0 | 11.23 | 1 286 | 1 294 |
| Gardena | 35.7 | 607 | 0.0 | NA | 56.3 | 69.4 | 46.2 | 77.6 | 14.79 | 1 526 | 742 |
| Garden Grove | 161.9 | 978 | 3.9 | 750 | 58.0 | 72.9 | 46.6 | 87.7 | 13.84 | 1 153 | 1 299 |
| Gilroy | 31.8 | 647 | 0.0 | NA | 49.7 | 72.0 | 39.4 | 88.3 | 20.60 | 2 278 | 913 |
| Glendale | 240.2 | 1 219 | 0.0 | 1 853 | 54.8 | 75.5 | 42.0 | 88.9 | 17.49 | 1 575 | 1 455 |
| Glendora | 55.0 | 1 106 | 0.0 | NA | 54.6 | 73.8 | 41.5 | 88.7 | 16.96 | 1 727 | 1 191 |
| Goleta | 1.9 | 64 | 0.0 | NA | 53.1 | 67.0 | 40.8 | 76.7 | 16.93 | 2 121 | 482 |
| Hanford | 48.7 | 983 | 0.5 | 262 | 44.7 | 79.6 | 35.7 | 95.9 | 8.58 | 2 749 | 1 724 |
| Hawthorne | 182.0 | 2 156 | 31.2 | 286 | 57.1 | 69.3 | 48.6 | 75.3 | 13.15 | 1 274 | 679 |
| Hayward | 215.2 | 1 527 | 54.6 | 813 | 49.7 | 64.6 | 41.7 | 75.2 | 26.30 | 2 810 | 261 |
| Hemet | 21.7 | 308 | 3.9 | NA | 52.4 | 79.9 | 38.4 | 97.8 | 12.55 | 1 914 | 1 903 |
| Hesperia | 94.4 | 1 103 | 0.0 | 191 | 45.5 | 80.0 | 31.4 | 99.1 | 6.20 | 2 929 | 1 735 |
| Highland | 87.8 | 1 711 | 43.0 | NA | 54.4 | 79.6 | 41.8 | 96.0 | 16.43 | 1 599 | 1 937 |
| Hollister | 43.8 | 1 255 | 0.0 | NA | 49.5 | 66.6 | 37.8 | 80.9 | 13.61 | 2 724 | 405 |
| Huntington Beach | 315.7 | 1 637 | 15.0 | 1 165 | 55.9 | 67.3 | 48.2 | 71.4 | 11.65 | 1 719 | 543 |
| Huntington Park | 278.0 | 4 533 | 27.9 | NA | 58.3 | 74.2 | 48.5 | 83.8 | 15.14 | 928 | 1 506 |
| Imperial Beach | 24.9 | 941 | 0.0 | NA | 57.3 | 70.1 | 46.1 | 76.1 | 9.95 | 1 321 | 862 |
| Indio | 157.6 | 1 878 | 101.1 | 253 | 56.8 | 92.8 | 42.0 | 107.1 | 3.15 | 903 | 4 388 |
| Inglewood | 195.5 | 1 724 | 6.1 | 714 | 57.1 | 69.3 | 48.6 | 75.3 | 13.15 | 1 274 | 679 |
| Irvine | 1 155.2 | 5 743 | 187.3 | 909 | 54.5 | 72.1 | 41.4 | 83.8 | 13.87 | 1 794 | 1 102 |
| Laguna Hills | 20.5 | 641 | 0.0 | NA | 56.7 | 72.4 | 47.2 | 82.3 | 14.03 | 1 465 | 1 183 |
| Laguna Niguel | 0.0 | 0 | 0.0 | NA | 55.4 | 68.7 | 43.9 | 77.3 | 13.56 | 1 756 | 666 |
| La Habra | 32.9 | 555 | 0.0 | NA | 56.9 | 73.2 | 45.2 | 84.0 | 11.23 | 1 286 | 1 294 |
| Lake Elsinore | 415.9 | 8 512 | 58.7 | NA | 52.2 | 79.6 | 38.3 | 98.1 | 12.09 | 1 924 | 1 874 |
| Lake Forest | 10.1 | 134 | 0.0 | 80 | 56.7 | 72.4 | 47.2 | 82.3 | 14.03 | 1 465 | 1 183 |
| Lakewood | 45.8 | 581 | 3.1 | 256 | 57.0 | 73.8 | 46.0 | 82.9 | 12.94 | 1 211 | 1 186 |
| La Mesa | 74.4 | 1 378 | 0.2 | 263 | 57.1 | 73.0 | 45.7 | 83.6 | 13.75 | 1 313 | 1 261 |
| La Mirada | 117.5 | 2 360 | 0.0 | NA | 58.8 | 76.6 | 47.9 | 88.9 | 14.44 | 949 | 1 837 |
| Lancaster | 435.9 | 3 035 | 40.0 | 382 | 43.9 | 80.8 | 31.0 | 95.5 | 7.40 | 3 241 | 1 733 |
| La Puente | 13.4 | 327 | 4.8 | NA | 58.8 | 76.6 | 47.9 | 88.9 | 14.44 | 949 | 1 837 |
| La Quinta | 357.4 | 8 285 | 0.1 | NA | NA | NA | NA | NA | NA | NA | NA |
| La Verne | 41.6 | 1 255 | 0.4 | 190 | 54.6 | 73.8 | 41.5 | 88.7 | 16.96 | 1 727 | 1 191 |
| Lawndale | 13.2 | 419 | 0.0 | NA | 57.1 | 69.3 | 48.6 | 75.3 | 13.15 | 1 274 | 679 |
| Lemon Grove | 32.4 | 1 348 | 14.1 | NA | NA | NA | NA | NA | NA | NA | NA |
| Lincoln | 193.6 | 4 596 | 118.8 | NA | NA | NA | NA | NA | NA | NA | NA |
| Livermore | 177.5 | 2 232 | 10.4 | 420 | 47.2 | 72.0 | 37.4 | 89.1 | 14.82 | 2 755 | 858 |
| Lodi | 1.9 | 31 | 0.0 | 483 | 46.1 | 73.8 | 37.5 | 91.1 | 18.22 | 2 710 | 1 057 |
| Lompoc | 62.3 | 1 540 | 24.5 | NA | 53.7 | 64.5 | 41.4 | 75.4 | 15.85 | 2 250 | 322 |
| Long Beach | 2 096.3 | 4 494 | 110.5 | 5 983 | 57.0 | 73.8 | 46.0 | 82.9 | 12.94 | 1 211 | 1 186 |
| Los Altos | 0.4 | 14 | 0.0 | NA | 49.0 | 68.0 | 40.4 | 78.8 | 15.71 | 2 584 | 452 |
| Los Angeles | 16 553.5 | 4 317 | 2 050.5 | 51 270 | 58.3 | 74.2 | 48.5 | 83.8 | 15.14 | 928 | 1 506 |
| Los Banos | 30.7 | 881 | 17.5 | NA | 45.9 | 78.1 | 36.8 | 94.6 | 9.95 | 2 570 | 1 547 |
| Los Gatos | 12.4 | 426 | 0.0 | NA | 48.7 | 70.3 | 38.8 | 85.4 | 22.64 | 2 641 | 613 |
| Lynwood | 46.5 | 661 | 0.0 | NA | 58.3 | 74.2 | 48.5 | 83.8 | 15.14 | 928 | 1 506 |
| Madera | 79.2 | 1 417 | 2.9 | NA | 45.7 | 79.6 | 37.2 | 96.5 | 11.94 | 2 670 | 1 706 |
| Manhattan Beach | 46.3 | 1 268 | 6.8 | NA | 57.1 | 69.3 | 48.6 | 75.3 | 13.15 | 1 274 | 679 |
| Manteca | 218.4 | 3 411 | 22.7 | NA | 46.0 | 77.3 | 38.1 | 93.8 | 13.84 | 2 563 | 1 456 |
| Martinez | 11.3 | 323 | 0.0 | NA | 46.3 | 71.2 | 38.8 | 87.4 | 19.58 | 2 757 | 786 |
| Maywood | 29.2 | 1 027 | 21.7 | NA | 58.3 | 74.2 | 48.5 | 83.8 | 15.14 | 928 | 1 506 |
| Menifee | NA | NA | NA | NA | NA | NA | NA | NA | NA | NA | NA |

1. Based on the population estimated as of July 1 of the year shown.  2. Represents normal values based on the 30-year period, 1971–2000.  3. Average daily minimum.  4. Average daily maximum.

| STATE Place code | City | Land area,[1] 2010 (sq km) | Total persons | Rank | Per square kilometer | White | Black | American Indian, Alaska Native | Asian | Hawaiian Pacific Islander | Percent Hispanic or Latino[2], 2010 | Percent Foreign born 2007–2011 |
|---|---|---|---|---|---|---|---|---|---|---|---|---|
| | | 1 | 2 | 3 | 4 | 5 | 6 | 7 | 8 | 9 | 10 | 11 |
| | **CALIFORNIA—Cont'd** | | | | | | | | | | | |
| 06 46870 | Menlo Park | 25.4 | 32 881 | 1 106 | 1 294.5 | 65.0 | 5.3 | 0.6 | 12.4 | 1.7 | 18.4 | 23.4 |
| 06 46898 | Merced | 60.4 | 80 793 | 395 | 1 337.6 | 31.9 | 6.6 | 1.2 | 12.6 | 0.3 | 49.6 | 21.3 |
| 06 47766 | Milpitas | 35.2 | 68 800 | 487 | 1 954.5 | 16.8 | 3.4 | 0.6 | 64.3 | 0.9 | 16.8 | 48.3 |
| 06 48256 | Mission Viejo | 45.9 | 95 290 | 313 | 2 076.0 | 72.0 | 1.8 | 0.6 | 11.4 | 0.4 | 17.0 | 19.0 |
| 06 48354 | Modesto | 95.5 | 203 547 | 106 | 2 131.4 | 52.0 | 4.7 | 1.5 | 7.9 | 1.5 | 35.5 | 16.6 |
| 06 48648 | Monrovia | 35.2 | 36 955 | 985 | 1 049.9 | 43.2 | 7.2 | 0.9 | 12.2 | 0.4 | 38.4 | 25.6 |
| 06 48788 | Montclair | 14.3 | 37 528 | 969 | 2 624.3 | 15.3 | 5.1 | 0.5 | 9.5 | 0.3 | 70.2 | 37.1 |
| 06 48816 | Montebello | 21.6 | 63 305 | 542 | 2 930.8 | 9.0 | 0.7 | 0.3 | 11.0 | 0.2 | 79.3 | 38.2 |
| 06 48872 | Monterey | 21.9 | 29 003 | 1 257 | 1 324.3 | 74.6 | 3.5 | 1.2 | 10.2 | 0.8 | 13.7 | 20.8 |
| 06 48914 | Monterey Park | 19.9 | 60 937 | 569 | 3 062.2 | 5.8 | 0.5 | 0.3 | 67.5 | 0.2 | 26.9 | 54.0 |
| 06 49138 | Moorpark | 32.6 | 35 088 | 1 041 | 1 076.3 | 59.7 | 1.9 | 0.7 | 8.6 | 0.3 | 31.4 | 18.3 |
| 06 49270 | Moreno Valley | 132.8 | 199 552 | 113 | 1 502.7 | 20.9 | 18.7 | 0.9 | 7.0 | 0.7 | 54.4 | 25.0 |
| 06 49278 | Morgan Hill | 33.4 | 39 420 | 924 | 1 180.2 | 53.3 | 2.4 | 0.9 | 11.9 | 0.7 | 34.0 | 19.4 |
| 06 49670 | Mountain View | 31.1 | 76 621 | 428 | 2 463.7 | 49.1 | 2.6 | 0.5 | 28.5 | 0.8 | 21.7 | 38.4 |
| 06 50076 | Murrieta | 87.0 | 106 810 | 259 | 1 227.7 | 58.8 | 6.1 | 1.0 | 11.1 | 0.7 | 25.9 | 14.0 |
| 06 50258 | Napa | 46.2 | 78 340 | 409 | 1 695.7 | 58.9 | 0.8 | 1.1 | 3.0 | 0.3 | 37.6 | 23.1 |
| 06 50398 | National City | 18.9 | 59 387 | 590 | 3 142.2 | 13.0 | 5.2 | 0.6 | 19.0 | 1.0 | 63.0 | 43.0 |
| 06 50916 | Newark | 35.9 | 43 621 | 838 | 1 215.1 | 30.6 | 5.1 | 0.7 | 29.9 | 2.4 | 35.2 | 36.8 |
| 06 51182 | Newport Beach | 61.7 | 87 068 | 352 | 1 411.2 | 84.5 | 0.9 | 0.5 | 8.7 | 0.3 | 7.2 | 13.4 |
| 06 51560 | Norco | 36.2 | 27 393 | 1 327 | 756.7 | 58.0 | 7.2 | 1.2 | 3.8 | 0.3 | 31.1 | 12.8 |
| 06 52526 | Norwalk | 25.1 | 106 278 | 264 | 4 234.2 | 13.1 | 4.2 | 0.5 | 12.3 | 0.5 | 70.1 | 36.9 |
| 06 52582 | Novato | 71.1 | 53 301 | 676 | 749.7 | 68.7 | 3.4 | 0.8 | 8.3 | 0.4 | 21.3 | 19.2 |
| 06 53000 | Oakland | 144.5 | 400 740 | 45 | 2 773.3 | 28.6 | 29.2 | 1.2 | 18.4 | 0.8 | 25.4 | 27.5 |
| 06 53070 | Oakley | 41.1 | 37 278 | 974 | 907.0 | 50.7 | 8.0 | 1.4 | 7.9 | 0.7 | 34.9 | 16.6 |
| 06 53322 | Oceanside | 106.8 | 171 293 | 137 | 1 603.9 | 51.2 | 5.3 | 0.9 | 8.3 | 1.8 | 35.9 | 21.7 |
| 06 53896 | Ontario | 129.4 | 167 211 | 143 | 1 292.2 | 19.2 | 6.4 | 0.5 | 5.5 | 0.4 | 69.0 | 29.2 |
| 06 53980 | Orange | 64.2 | 139 419 | 182 | 2 171.6 | 48.5 | 1.8 | 0.6 | 12.3 | 0.4 | 38.1 | 26.7 |
| 06 54652 | Oxnard | 69.7 | 201 555 | 111 | 2 891.8 | 16.1 | 2.8 | 0.5 | 8.0 | 0.4 | 73.5 | 37.5 |
| 06 54806 | Pacifica | 32.8 | 38 189 | 960 | 1 164.3 | 59.8 | 3.3 | 1.0 | 22.3 | 1.4 | 16.8 | 21.2 |
| 06 55156 | Palmdale | 274.4 | 155 650 | 156 | 567.2 | 26.2 | 15.3 | 0.9 | 4.9 | 0.3 | 54.4 | 25.0 |
| 06 55184 | Palm Desert | 69.4 | 50 013 | 724 | 720.6 | 71.6 | 2.0 | 0.6 | 4.0 | 0.2 | 22.8 | 17.9 |
| 06 55254 | Palm Springs | 243.8 | 45 907 | 801 | 188.3 | 65.0 | 4.7 | 1.2 | 5.0 | 0.3 | 25.3 | 20.8 |
| 06 55282 | Palo Alto | 61.9 | 66 363 | 508 | 1 072.1 | 64.0 | 2.2 | 0.4 | 30.0 | 0.4 | 6.2 | 32.2 |
| 06 55520 | Paradise | 47.4 | 26 216 | 1 386 | 553.1 | 90.3 | 0.7 | 2.5 | 1.8 | 0.3 | 7.0 | 4.6 |
| 06 55618 | Paramount | 12.3 | 54 680 | 660 | 4 445.5 | 6.1 | 11.5 | 0.4 | 3.2 | 0.9 | 78.6 | 38.5 |
| 06 56000 | Pasadena | 59.5 | 138 547 | 184 | 2 328.5 | 41.1 | 11.1 | 0.6 | 15.8 | 0.3 | 33.7 | 31.3 |
| 06 56700 | Perris | 81.3 | 71 326 | 462 | 877.3 | 12.3 | 12.4 | 0.6 | 4.0 | 0.6 | 71.8 | 28.2 |
| 06 56784 | Petaluma | 37.3 | 58 921 | 595 | 1 579.7 | 72.0 | 1.8 | 1.0 | 5.8 | 0.5 | 21.5 | 17.0 |
| 06 56924 | Pico Rivera | 21.5 | 63 522 | 540 | 2 954.5 | 5.5 | 0.7 | 0.3 | 2.5 | 0.1 | 91.2 | 33.0 |
| 06 57456 | Pittsburg | 44.6 | 65 664 | 518 | 1 472.3 | 22.6 | 18.7 | 1.0 | 17.3 | 1.5 | 42.4 | 32.1 |
| 06 57526 | Placentia | 17.0 | 51 673 | 701 | 3 039.6 | 46.4 | 2.0 | 0.6 | 16.1 | 0.3 | 36.4 | 26.7 |
| 06 57764 | Pleasant Hill | 18.3 | 33 831 | 1 078 | 1 848.7 | 71.7 | 2.7 | 0.9 | 16.2 | 0.5 | 12.1 | 19.9 |
| 06 57792 | Pleasanton | 62.5 | 72 338 | 458 | 1 157.4 | 64.0 | 2.1 | 0.7 | 25.8 | 0.5 | 10.3 | 22.9 |
| 06 58072 | Pomona | 59.4 | 150 812 | 161 | 2 538.9 | 13.5 | 7.3 | 0.5 | 9.0 | 0.3 | 70.5 | 34.3 |
| 06 58240 | Porterville | 45.6 | 55 023 | 653 | 1 206.6 | 31.7 | 1.1 | 1.5 | 5.0 | 0.2 | 61.9 | 20.5 |
| 06 58520 | Poway | 101.2 | 49 071 | 751 | 484.9 | 71.9 | 2.0 | 0.9 | 12.0 | 0.5 | 15.7 | 15.8 |
| 06 59444 | Rancho Cordova | 86.8 | 66 997 | 501 | 771.9 | 56.2 | 11.9 | 1.7 | 14.1 | 1.4 | 19.7 | 24.4 |
| 06 59451 | Rancho Cucamonga | 103.2 | 170 746 | 140 | 1 654.5 | 45.0 | 9.8 | 0.7 | 11.6 | 0.6 | 34.9 | 18.0 |
| 06 59514 | Rancho Palos Verdes | 34.9 | 42 323 | 862 | 1 212.7 | 59.5 | 2.9 | 0.4 | 31.8 | 0.4 | 8.5 | 28.6 |
| 06 59587 | Rancho Santa Margarita | 33.6 | 48 879 | 756 | 1 454.7 | 70.0 | 2.4 | 0.6 | 11.2 | 0.5 | 18.6 | 16.0 |
| 06 59920 | Redding | 154.5 | 90 755 | 332 | 587.4 | 84.6 | 2.0 | 3.8 | 4.2 | 0.4 | 8.7 | 5.6 |
| 06 59962 | Redlands | 93.6 | 69 916 | 477 | 747.0 | 56.3 | 5.7 | 0.9 | 8.8 | 0.6 | 30.3 | 15.1 |
| 06 60018 | Redondo Beach | 16.1 | 67 693 | 496 | 4 204.5 | 69.0 | 3.5 | 0.7 | 14.8 | 0.7 | 15.2 | 18.4 |
| 06 60102 | Redwood City | 50.3 | 79 009 | 406 | 1 570.8 | 46.5 | 2.8 | 0.6 | 12.5 | 1.4 | 38.8 | 31.2 |
| 06 60466 | Rialto | 57.9 | 101 740 | 281 | 1 757.2 | 13.6 | 16.5 | 0.6 | 2.5 | 0.5 | 67.6 | 27.0 |
| 06 60620 | Richmond | 77.9 | 106 516 | 262 | 1 367.3 | 19.1 | 27.5 | 0.9 | 14.7 | 0.7 | 39.5 | 32.4 |
| 06 60704 | Ridgecrest | 53.8 | 28 325 | 1 281 | 526.5 | 72.1 | 4.9 | 2.0 | 5.8 | 0.9 | 17.9 | 8.0 |
| 06 62000 | Riverside | 210.2 | 313 673 | 59 | 1 492.3 | 35.9 | 7.4 | 0.9 | 8.2 | 0.6 | 49.0 | 24.0 |
| 06 62364 | Rocklin | 50.6 | 59 030 | 594 | 1 166.6 | 78.9 | 2.0 | 1.3 | 9.4 | 0.6 | 11.5 | 10.4 |
| 06 62546 | Rohnert Park | 18.1 | 41 232 | 881 | 2 278.0 | 69.7 | 2.7 | 1.6 | 6.8 | 0.9 | 22.1 | 15.8 |
| 06 62896 | Rosemead | 13.4 | 54 393 | 665 | 4 059.2 | 5.2 | 0.4 | 0.2 | 60.9 | 0.1 | 33.8 | 57.3 |
| 06 62938 | Roseville | 93.8 | 124 519 | 211 | 1 327.5 | 74.1 | 2.6 | 1.3 | 10.2 | 0.5 | 14.6 | 12.1 |
| 06 64000 | Sacramento | 253.6 | 475 516 | 35 | 1 875.1 | 37.7 | 15.9 | 1.7 | 20.2 | 2.1 | 26.9 | 22.3 |
| 06 64224 | Salinas | 60.0 | 154 484 | 157 | 2 574.7 | 16.7 | 2.0 | 0.6 | 6.7 | 0.5 | 75.0 | 37.4 |
| 06 65000 | San Bernardino | 153.3 | 213 295 | 98 | 1 391.4 | 20.5 | 15.4 | 0.9 | 4.5 | 0.5 | 60.0 | 23.8 |
| 06 65028 | San Bruno | 14.2 | 42 165 | 866 | 2 969.4 | 38.6 | 2.6 | 0.7 | 27.6 | 4.4 | 29.2 | 37.1 |
| 06 65042 | San Buenaventura (Ventura) | 56.1 | 107 734 | 255 | 1 920.4 | 62.4 | 2.0 | 1.4 | 4.5 | 0.4 | 31.8 | 14.9 |
| 06 65070 | San Carlos | 14.3 | 29 092 | 1 255 | 2 034.4 | 76.8 | 1.2 | 0.6 | 14.4 | 0.5 | 10.1 | 18.3 |
| 06 65084 | San Clemente | 48.5 | 64 882 | 525 | 1 337.8 | 78.3 | 0.9 | 0.9 | 5.1 | 0.3 | 16.8 | 11.9 |
| 06 66000 | San Diego | 842.2 | 1 338 348 | 8 | 1 589.1 | 47.8 | 7.3 | 0.8 | 17.7 | 0.8 | 28.8 | 25.8 |
| 06 66070 | San Dimas | 39.0 | 33 737 | 1 082 | 865.1 | 54.6 | 3.6 | 0.8 | 11.6 | 0.3 | 31.4 | 21.9 |

1. Dry land or land partially or temporarily covered by water.  2. May be of any race.

# Table D. Cities — **Population**

| City | Under 5 years | 5 to 17 years | 18 to 24 years | 25 to 34 years | 35 to 44 years | 45 to 54 years | 55 to 64 years | 65 to 74 years | 75 years and over | Median age | Percent female | Census counts 2000 | Census counts 2010 | Percent change 2000–2010 | Percent change 2010–2012 |
|---|---|---|---|---|---|---|---|---|---|---|---|---|---|---|---|
| | 12 | 13 | 14 | 15 | 16 | 17 | 18 | 19 | 20 | 21 | 22 | 23 | 24 | 25 | 26 |
| CALIFORNIA—Cont'd | | | | | | | | | | | | | | | |
| Menlo Park | 7.7 | 16.7 | 5.7 | 14.1 | 15.8 | 14.7 | 11.1 | 6.7 | 7.6 | 38.7 | 51.6 | 30 785 | 32 026 | 4.0 | 2.7 |
| Merced | 9.4 | 22.4 | 13.3 | 14.7 | 11.8 | 11.1 | 8.6 | 4.6 | 4.2 | 28.1 | 50.9 | 63 893 | 78 958 | 23.6 | 2.3 |
| Milpitas | 6.9 | 16.0 | 8.8 | 16.3 | 16.3 | 15.2 | 10.9 | 5.7 | 3.8 | 36.1 | 48.9 | 62 698 | 66 790 | 6.5 | 3.0 |
| Mission Viejo | 4.9 | 17.9 | 8.4 | 9.7 | 13.5 | 17.8 | 13.2 | 7.7 | 6.8 | 42.2 | 51.2 | 93 102 | 93 310 | 0.2 | 2.1 |
| Modesto | 7.4 | 19.5 | 10.4 | 13.7 | 12.7 | 13.7 | 11.0 | 6.1 | 5.6 | 34.2 | 51.3 | 188 856 | 201 188 | 6.5 | 1.2 |
| Monrovia | 6.5 | 16.8 | 8.4 | 14.1 | 15.2 | 15.3 | 12.1 | 6.2 | 5.4 | 37.9 | 52.2 | 36 929 | 36 590 | -0.9 | 1.0 |
| Montclair | 8.1 | 21.3 | 11.7 | 15.1 | 14.0 | 12.5 | 8.9 | 4.9 | 3.6 | 30.7 | 50.2 | 33 049 | 36 664 | 10.9 | 2.4 |
| Montebello | 6.9 | 18.9 | 10.3 | 14.3 | 13.8 | 12.3 | 9.8 | 6.6 | 7.0 | 34.7 | 51.7 | 62 150 | 62 500 | 0.6 | 1.3 |
| Monterey | 5.1 | 10.2 | 13.8 | 18.1 | 12.4 | 12.4 | 12.5 | 7.2 | 8.3 | 36.9 | 49.7 | 29 674 | 27 810 | -6.3 | 4.3 |
| Monterey Park | 4.5 | 13.6 | 8.6 | 12.1 | 13.8 | 15.4 | 12.7 | 8.5 | 10.8 | 43.1 | 52.0 | 60 051 | 60 269 | 0.4 | 1.1 |
| Moorpark | 6.6 | 20.9 | 10.5 | 12.3 | 13.3 | 17.7 | 11.5 | 4.2 | 2.9 | 34.7 | 50.4 | 31 415 | 34 421 | 9.6 | 1.9 |
| Moreno Valley | 8.4 | 24.0 | 12.2 | 14.5 | 13.3 | 13.0 | 8.5 | 3.9 | 2.4 | 28.6 | 51.2 | 142 381 | 193 365 | 35.8 | 3.2 |
| Morgan Hill | 7.4 | 21.2 | 7.7 | 11.4 | 15.0 | 16.5 | 11.3 | 5.7 | 3.8 | 36.8 | 50.5 | 33 556 | 37 882 | 12.9 | 4.1 |
| Mountain View | 7.1 | 12.6 | 7.3 | 21.1 | 17.5 | 13.9 | 9.9 | 5.6 | 5.0 | 35.9 | 49.1 | 70 708 | 74 066 | 4.7 | 3.4 |
| Murrieta | 7.0 | 23.4 | 9.6 | 11.9 | 15.3 | 14.7 | 8.1 | 5.2 | 4.9 | 33.4 | 51.2 | 44 282 | 103 422 | 133.7 | 3.3 |
| Napa | 6.6 | 17.9 | 8.7 | 13.6 | 13.6 | 14.1 | 11.8 | 6.8 | 6.9 | 37.4 | 50.7 | 72 585 | 76 948 | 6.0 | 1.8 |
| National City | 6.9 | 18.6 | 16.2 | 14.7 | 12.4 | 12.0 | 8.6 | 5.0 | 5.6 | 30.2 | 48.7 | 54 260 | 58 578 | 8.0 | 1.4 |
| Newark | 7.4 | 18.0 | 9.0 | 15.0 | 14.8 | 14.7 | 10.5 | 6.3 | 4.3 | 35.4 | 50.2 | 42 471 | 42 573 | 0.2 | 2.5 |
| Newport Beach | 3.8 | 13.5 | 7.8 | 13.7 | 12.5 | 15.8 | 13.9 | 9.8 | 9.1 | 44.0 | 50.7 | 70 032 | 85 186 | 21.6 | 2.2 |
| Norco | 4.5 | 15.7 | 10.3 | 13.2 | 15.9 | 19.0 | 11.7 | 6.4 | 3.2 | 39.5 | 42.2 | 24 157 | 27 063 | 12.0 | 1.2 |
| Norwalk | 7.0 | 20.6 | 11.4 | 14.4 | 14.1 | 13.1 | 9.5 | 5.4 | 4.5 | 32.5 | 50.4 | 103 298 | 105 549 | 2.2 | 0.7 |
| Novato | 5.9 | 16.7 | 6.5 | 10.6 | 13.9 | 15.9 | 14.8 | 8.7 | 7.0 | 42.6 | 51.7 | 47 630 | 51 904 | 9.0 | 2.7 |
| Oakland | 6.7 | 14.6 | 9.3 | 17.4 | 15.6 | 13.6 | 11.7 | 5.9 | 5.2 | 36.2 | 51.5 | 399 484 | 390 719 | -2.2 | 2.6 |
| Oakley | 7.5 | 23.0 | 10.0 | 13.6 | 15.1 | 15.1 | 9.1 | 4.1 | 2.7 | 32.0 | 50.3 | 25 619 | 35 432 | 38.3 | 5.2 |
| Oceanside | 7.0 | 16.9 | 11.4 | 14.5 | 12.9 | 14.0 | 10.5 | 6.1 | 6.8 | 35.2 | 50.7 | 161 029 | 167 086 | 3.8 | 2.5 |
| Ontario | 8.4 | 21.8 | 11.8 | 15.9 | 14.3 | 12.7 | 8.4 | 4.0 | 2.8 | 29.9 | 50.2 | 158 007 | 163 924 | 3.7 | 2.0 |
| Orange | 6.4 | 17.2 | 12.0 | 14.7 | 14.3 | 14.4 | 10.3 | 5.7 | 5.0 | 34.8 | 49.6 | 128 821 | 136 416 | 5.9 | 2.2 |
| Oxnard | 8.9 | 20.9 | 12.1 | 15.8 | 13.5 | 12.0 | 8.5 | 4.6 | 3.7 | 29.9 | 49.3 | 170 358 | 197 899 | 16.2 | 1.8 |
| Pacifica | 5.4 | 15.3 | 7.6 | 12.2 | 14.7 | 17.4 | 15.2 | 7.0 | 5.2 | 41.5 | 51.1 | 38 390 | 37 231 | -3.0 | 2.6 |
| Palmdale | 8.3 | 24.8 | 11.2 | 12.2 | 14.0 | 14.3 | 8.6 | 3.9 | 2.7 | 29.7 | 51.2 | 116 670 | 152 750 | 30.9 | 1.9 |
| Palm Desert | 4.2 | 11.4 | 6.9 | 9.0 | 9.1 | 12.1 | 14.6 | 15.8 | 17.1 | 53.0 | 53.0 | 41 155 | 48 445 | 17.7 | 3.2 |
| Palm Springs | 3.9 | 9.9 | 5.8 | 8.9 | 10.5 | 17.2 | 17.5 | 14.0 | 12.6 | 51.6 | 43.6 | 42 807 | 44 552 | 4.1 | 3.0 |
| Palo Alto | 5.4 | 18.0 | 4.9 | 11.9 | 14.8 | 16.1 | 11.8 | 7.9 | 9.2 | 41.9 | 51.1 | 58 598 | 64 408 | 9.9 | 3.0 |
| Paradise | 4.4 | 12.8 | 7.1 | 8.8 | 9.6 | 15.2 | 17.1 | 11.1 | 13.9 | 50.2 | 52.5 | 26 408 | 26 217 | -0.7 | 0.0 |
| Paramount | 8.7 | 23.9 | 11.8 | 15.5 | 14.6 | 11.7 | 7.6 | 3.9 | 2.4 | 28.6 | 51.4 | 55 266 | 54 098 | -2.1 | 1.1 |
| Pasadena | 6.0 | 13.3 | 9.2 | 18.1 | 15.0 | 13.7 | 11.1 | 6.9 | 6.7 | 37.2 | 51.2 | 133 936 | 137 122 | 2.4 | 1.0 |
| Perris | 10.0 | 27.0 | 11.6 | 14.9 | 14.5 | 11.1 | 6.1 | 3.0 | 1.9 | 25.9 | 50.4 | 36 189 | 68 386 | 89.0 | 4.3 |
| Petaluma | 6.0 | 17.2 | 7.9 | 11.9 | 14.1 | 16.5 | 13.3 | 6.9 | 6.2 | 40.3 | 50.9 | 54 548 | 57 941 | 6.2 | 1.7 |
| Pico Rivera | 6.8 | 19.9 | 11.1 | 13.6 | 13.7 | 13.1 | 9.7 | 6.1 | 6.1 | 34.0 | 51.2 | 63 428 | 62 942 | -0.8 | 0.9 |
| Pittsburg | 7.9 | 19.6 | 10.8 | 15.3 | 13.7 | 13.7 | 10.5 | 5.0 | 3.6 | 32.5 | 51.3 | 56 769 | 63 260 | 11.4 | 3.8 |
| Placentia | 6.6 | 18.0 | 10.3 | 13.6 | 14.0 | 13.9 | 11.1 | 6.9 | 5.6 | 36.0 | 50.8 | 46 488 | 50 590 | 8.7 | 2.1 |
| Pleasant Hill | 5.5 | 14.3 | 9.6 | 12.9 | 13.9 | 15.9 | 14.0 | 6.7 | 7.2 | 40.7 | 51.5 | 32 837 | 33 110 | 1.0 | 2.2 |
| Pleasanton | 5.6 | 21.5 | 6.2 | 9.0 | 15.5 | 19.3 | 11.9 | 6.3 | 4.6 | 40.5 | 51.0 | 63 654 | 70 317 | 10.4 | 2.9 |
| Pomona | 8.1 | 21.4 | 13.5 | 14.8 | 13.6 | 12.5 | 8.6 | 4.2 | 3.4 | 29.5 | 50.0 | 149 473 | 149 058 | -0.3 | 1.2 |
| Porterville | 9.9 | 23.7 | 10.9 | 14.2 | 12.1 | 11.3 | 8.6 | 5.0 | 4.4 | 28.8 | 50.5 | 39 615 | 54 165 | 36.7 | 1.6 |
| Poway | 5.1 | 19.9 | 8.2 | 9.7 | 12.2 | 18.6 | 13.9 | 6.7 | 5.7 | 41.3 | 50.7 | 48 044 | 47 811 | -0.5 | 2.6 |
| Rancho Cordova | 8.3 | 18.0 | 9.9 | 16.8 | 13.4 | 13.5 | 9.9 | 5.7 | 4.6 | 33.1 | 51.1 | 55 060 | 64 805 | 17.6 | 3.4 |
| Rancho Cucamonga | 6.2 | 19.6 | 10.5 | 14.4 | 15.0 | 15.7 | 10.8 | 4.7 | 3.2 | 34.5 | 50.6 | 127 743 | 165 350 | 29.4 | 3.3 |
| Rancho Palos Verdes | 3.7 | 18.5 | 5.6 | 5.2 | 11.7 | 18.3 | 13.7 | 11.6 | 11.6 | 47.8 | 51.5 | 41 145 | 41 643 | 1.2 | 1.6 |
| Rancho Santa Margarita | 6.3 | 22.7 | 7.9 | 11.8 | 16.9 | 19.5 | 9.3 | 3.2 | 2.5 | 36.0 | 51.1 | 47 214 | 47 853 | 1.4 | 2.1 |
| Redding | 6.3 | 16.6 | 10.5 | 13.1 | 11.1 | 13.6 | 12.5 | 8.1 | 8.3 | 38.5 | 51.6 | 80 865 | 89 861 | 11.1 | 1.0 |
| Redlands | 6.0 | 17.6 | 11.9 | 13.0 | 12.3 | 14.0 | 12.1 | 6.5 | 6.5 | 36.2 | 52.4 | 63 591 | 68 667 | 8.1 | 1.8 |
| Redondo Beach | 6.3 | 13.0 | 6.3 | 16.4 | 18.3 | 17.0 | 12.3 | 6.0 | 4.5 | 39.3 | 50.2 | 63 261 | 66 748 | 5.5 | 1.4 |
| Redwood City | 7.5 | 16.2 | 7.8 | 15.7 | 16.6 | 14.9 | 10.8 | 5.6 | 5.0 | 36.7 | 50.2 | 75 402 | 76 802 | 1.9 | 2.9 |
| Rialto | 8.7 | 24.2 | 12.3 | 13.7 | 13.3 | 12.4 | 8.4 | 4.1 | 2.8 | 28.3 | 51.4 | 91 873 | 99 170 | 7.9 | 2.6 |
| Richmond | 7.4 | 17.5 | 10.0 | 15.4 | 14.3 | 13.8 | 11.4 | 5.9 | 4.3 | 34.8 | 51.3 | 99 216 | 103 670 | 4.5 | 2.7 |
| Ridgecrest | 8.2 | 19.1 | 9.6 | 14.6 | 11.4 | 13.9 | 10.9 | 6.8 | 5.6 | 33.8 | 49.9 | 24 927 | 27 616 | 10.8 | 2.6 |
| Riverside | 7.2 | 19.6 | 15.5 | 14.3 | 12.8 | 12.9 | 9.0 | 4.6 | 4.0 | 30.0 | 50.6 | 255 166 | 303 871 | 19.1 | 3.2 |
| Rocklin | 6.3 | 21.1 | 9.3 | 11.2 | 15.4 | 15.8 | 10.0 | 5.8 | 5.2 | 36.7 | 51.6 | 36 330 | 56 904 | 56.8 | 3.7 |
| Rohnert Park | 5.6 | 15.3 | 16.7 | 14.6 | 12.3 | 14.8 | 11.3 | 4.9 | 4.4 | 33.0 | 51.2 | 42 236 | 40 992 | -3.0 | 0.6 |
| Rosemead | 5.4 | 17.3 | 9.7 | 13.2 | 14.6 | 15.0 | 11.8 | 6.7 | 6.2 | 38.1 | 50.7 | 53 505 | 53 764 | 0.5 | 1.2 |
| Roseville | 6.8 | 19.5 | 7.9 | 13.3 | 14.8 | 14.3 | 10.1 | 6.4 | 7.0 | 36.8 | 52.1 | 79 921 | 118 790 | 48.6 | 4.8 |
| Sacramento | 7.5 | 17.4 | 11.2 | 16.6 | 13.2 | 12.8 | 10.7 | 5.5 | 5.1 | 33.0 | 51.3 | 407 018 | 466 488 | 14.6 | 1.9 |
| Salinas | 9.5 | 21.8 | 12.0 | 16.5 | 13.4 | 11.5 | 7.8 | 3.8 | 3.7 | 28.8 | 49.5 | 151 060 | 150 498 | -0.4 | 2.6 |
| San Bernardino | 9.3 | 22.7 | 12.7 | 14.1 | 12.7 | 12.4 | 8.2 | 4.3 | 3.6 | 28.5 | 50.7 | 185 401 | 209 952 | 13.2 | 1.6 |
| San Bruno | 6.0 | 15.0 | 8.7 | 15.0 | 14.3 | 15.7 | 12.7 | 6.8 | 5.9 | 38.8 | 50.7 | 40 165 | 41 117 | 2.4 | 2.5 |
| San Buenaventura (Ventura) | 5.8 | 16.7 | 9.0 | 13.4 | 13.7 | 15.8 | 12.4 | 6.5 | 6.8 | 39.0 | 50.6 | 100 916 | 106 421 | 5.5 | 1.2 |
| San Carlos | 6.6 | 17.0 | 4.1 | 9.7 | 17.3 | 17.6 | 13.5 | 7.4 | 6.9 | 42.6 | 51.7 | 27 718 | 28 406 | 2.5 | 2.4 |
| San Clemente | 6.5 | 18.0 | 7.9 | 11.3 | 14.7 | 16.1 | 12.5 | 7.0 | 6.2 | 39.7 | 49.8 | 49 936 | 63 515 | 27.2 | 2.2 |
| San Diego | 6.2 | 15.2 | 13.1 | 17.6 | 14.1 | 13.2 | 10.1 | 5.5 | 5.2 | 33.6 | 49.5 | 1 223 400 | 1 301 621 | 6.9 | 2.8 |
| San Dimas | 4.4 | 16.6 | 9.8 | 10.6 | 12.0 | 16.4 | 14.7 | 8.7 | 6.8 | 42.6 | 52.5 | 34 980 | 33 371 | -4.6 | 1.1 |

# Table D. Cities — Households, Group Quarters, Crime, and Education

| City | Households, 2010 | | | | Persons in group quarters, 2010 | | | | Serious crimes known to police,[2] 2011 | | | | Educational attainment, 2007–2011 | | |
| | | | Percent | | | Institutional | | | Total | | Rate[3] | | | Attainment[4] (percent) | |
| | Number | Persons per house-hold | Female family house-holder[1] | One-person | Total | Total | Persons in nursing facilities | Non-institutional | Number | Rate[3] | Violent | Property | Population age 25 and older | High school graduate or less | Bachelor's degree or more |
| | 27 | 28 | 29 | 30 | 31 | 32 | 33 | 34 | 35 | 36 | 37 | 38 | 39 | 40 | 41 |
| CALIFORNIA—Cont'd | | | | | | | | | | | | | | | |
| Menlo Park | 12 347 | 2.53 | 8.4 | 29.7 | 845 | 246 | 236 | 599 | 666 | 2 055 | 151 | 1 904 | 22 674 | 16.2 | 68.8 |
| Merced | 24 899 | 3.13 | 19.8 | 21.5 | 1 080 | 588 | 343 | 492 | 3 662 | 4 584 | 630 | 3 954 | 42 759 | 51.0 | 15.5 |
| Milpitas | 19 184 | 3.34 | 11.9 | 12.9 | 2 698 | 2 594 | 34 | 104 | 1 926 | 2 850 | 151 | 2 699 | 45 212 | 33.8 | 39.3 |
| Mission Viejo | 33 208 | 2.78 | 8.9 | 19.0 | 942 | 83 | 66 | 859 | 1 295 | 1 372 | 84 | 1 288 | 64 479 | 21.6 | 44.0 |
| Modesto | 69 107 | 2.87 | 15.6 | 23.0 | 2 955 | 1 766 | 1 169 | 1 189 | 10 307 | 5 064 | 694 | 4 370 | 124 691 | 47.8 | 18.7 |
| Monrovia | 13 762 | 2.65 | 15.1 | 26.5 | 156 | 95 | 76 | 61 | 979 | 2 645 | 203 | 2 442 | 24 988 | 33.8 | 33.5 |
| Montclair | 9 523 | 3.81 | 18.7 | 13.0 | 396 | 181 | 181 | 215 | 1 885 | 5 082 | 515 | 4 567 | 22 087 | 59.4 | 13.1 |
| Montebello | 19 012 | 3.27 | 21.2 | 17.6 | 400 | 361 | 350 | 39 | 2 011 | 3 180 | 275 | 2 905 | 40 936 | 57.4 | 16.7 |
| Monterey | 12 184 | 2.08 | 7.4 | 39.2 | 2 503 | 293 | 293 | 2 210 | 1 378 | 4 897 | 668 | 4 229 | 19 691 | 20.4 | 49.8 |
| Monterey Park | 19 963 | 3.01 | 16.2 | 18.2 | 230 | 189 | 186 | 41 | 1 141 | 1 871 | 167 | 1 704 | 43 228 | 46.9 | 27.9 |
| Moorpark | 10 484 | 3.28 | 10.6 | 12.8 | 0 | 0 | 0 | 0 | 392 | 1 126 | 78 | 1 048 | 21 444 | 30.2 | 37.6 |
| Moreno Valley | 51 592 | 3.74 | 19.4 | 11.8 | 554 | 83 | 27 | 471 | 6 494 | 3 319 | 374 | 2 945 | 104 092 | 52.4 | 14.7 |
| Morgan Hill | 12 326 | 3.04 | 11.9 | 16.2 | 386 | 222 | 144 | 164 | 732 | 1 910 | 110 | 1 800 | 23 274 | 29.7 | 38.8 |
| Mountain View | 31 957 | 2.31 | 7.7 | 34.3 | 265 | 120 | 107 | 145 | 1 506 | 2 010 | 204 | 1 806 | 53 673 | 21.2 | 59.4 |
| Murrieta | 32 749 | 3.15 | 11.6 | 15.9 | 429 | 138 | 56 | 291 | 1 600 | 1 528 | 100 | 1 428 | 58 417 | 32.3 | 29.2 |
| Napa | 28 166 | 2.69 | 11.4 | 26.5 | 1 237 | 669 | 343 | 568 | 1 839 | 2 363 | 288 | 2 075 | 51 595 | 43.3 | 26.2 |
| National City | 15 502 | 3.41 | 22.2 | 17.4 | 5 752 | 411 | 411 | 5 341 | 2 186 | 3 688 | 628 | 3 061 | 35 367 | 59.8 | 13.1 |
| Newark | 12 972 | 3.27 | 13.2 | 15.0 | 145 | 0 | 0 | 145 | 1 556 | 3 612 | 395 | 3 218 | 28 629 | 45.5 | 26.9 |
| Newport Beach | 38 751 | 2.19 | 6.7 | 33.1 | 402 | 251 | 221 | 151 | 2 339 | 2 714 | 135 | 2 579 | 62 414 | 12.1 | 63.4 |
| Norco | 7 023 | 3.23 | 11.1 | 14.7 | 4 397 | 4 322 | 0 | 75 | 683 | 2 494 | 124 | 2 370 | 18 345 | 47.5 | 17.7 |
| Norwalk | 27 110 | 3.83 | 18.6 | 12.6 | 1 615 | 1 300 | 474 | 315 | 2 645 | 2 477 | 347 | 2 129 | 64 907 | 54.7 | 15.1 |
| Novato | 20 279 | 2.53 | 11.0 | 26.4 | 626 | 177 | 175 | 449 | 1 100 | 2 095 | 206 | 1 889 | 36 949 | 26.1 | 42.5 |
| Oakland | 153 791 | 2.49 | 15.7 | 33.9 | 8 138 | 2 463 | 1 349 | 5 675 | 27 556 | 6 971 | 1 683 | 5 288 | 268 205 | 38.6 | 37.2 |
| Oakley | 10 727 | 3.29 | 13.2 | 14.2 | 103 | 28 | 6 | 75 | 605 | 1 688 | 220 | 1 467 | 20 588 | 48.2 | 13.5 |
| Oceanside | 59 238 | 2.80 | 11.7 | 23.8 | 936 | 134 | 91 | 802 | 4 469 | 2 644 | 367 | 2 277 | 107 428 | 39.0 | 24.5 |
| Ontario | 44 931 | 3.63 | 17.6 | 15.0 | 758 | 347 | 347 | 411 | 5 351 | 3 226 | 297 | 2 929 | 96 193 | 57.1 | 14.0 |
| Orange | 43 367 | 3.00 | 12.1 | 19.6 | 6 253 | 3 666 | 299 | 2 587 | 2 809 | 2 035 | 114 | 1 921 | 88 129 | 36.2 | 33.1 |
| Oxnard | 49 797 | 3.95 | 15.3 | 14.2 | 1 434 | 502 | 465 | 932 | 4 118 | 2 057 | 309 | 1 748 | 114 422 | 57.7 | 15.2 |
| Pacifica | 13 967 | 2.65 | 11.4 | 22.4 | 182 | 118 | 115 | 64 | 528 | 1 402 | 117 | 1 285 | 27 001 | 25.3 | 38.5 |
| Palmdale | 42 952 | 3.55 | 18.2 | 13.6 | 199 | 41 | 0 | 158 | 4 058 | 2 626 | 508 | 2 118 | 81 513 | 51.9 | 15.4 |
| Palm Desert | 23 117 | 2.08 | 9.4 | 34.4 | 308 | 210 | 210 | 98 | 2 223 | 4 535 | 155 | 4 380 | 38 470 | 29.1 | 32.8 |
| Palm Springs | 22 746 | 1.93 | 8.7 | 44.0 | 539 | 196 | 190 | 343 | 2 560 | 5 679 | 568 | 5 111 | 36 475 | 34.0 | 32.5 |
| Palo Alto | 26 493 | 2.41 | 7.0 | 30.1 | 583 | 378 | 323 | 205 | 1 312 | 2 014 | 98 | 1 915 | 45 045 | 7.6 | 79.4 |
| Paradise | 11 893 | 2.17 | 11.0 | 34.0 | 408 | 269 | 246 | 139 | 540 | 2 036 | 294 | 1 742 | 20 112 | 33.9 | 20.7 |
| Paramount | 13 881 | 3.87 | 22.4 | 13.7 | 310 | 283 | 283 | 27 | 1 876 | 3 427 | 466 | 2 962 | 30 026 | 72.3 | 8.2 |
| Pasadena | 55 270 | 2.42 | 11.1 | 34.1 | 3 493 | 1 021 | 890 | 2 472 | 4 107 | 2 960 | 314 | 2 647 | 98 084 | 30.9 | 46.5 |
| Perris | 16 365 | 4.16 | 19.1 | 8.8 | 240 | 100 | 71 | 140 | 2 291 | 3 311 | 241 | 3 070 | 33 735 | 64.4 | 9.0 |
| Petaluma | 21 737 | 2.63 | 10.4 | 24.7 | 724 | 363 | 363 | 361 | 1 024 | 1 747 | 239 | 1 508 | 39 242 | 31.8 | 35.4 |
| Pico Rivera | 16 566 | 3.77 | 20.1 | 13.7 | 454 | 415 | 415 | 39 | 1 811 | 2 844 | 382 | 2 462 | 39 524 | 65.5 | 10.4 |
| Pittsburg | 19 527 | 3.22 | 18.3 | 17.6 | 291 | 138 | 123 | 153 | 2 050 | 3 203 | 227 | 2 976 | 38 375 | 50.0 | 16.3 |
| Placentia | 16 365 | 3.07 | 12.6 | 17.6 | 337 | 84 | 73 | 253 | 973 | 1 903 | 160 | 1 743 | 31 794 | 33.5 | 34.9 |
| Pleasant Hill | 13 708 | 2.38 | 9.9 | 28.7 | 463 | 312 | 291 | 151 | 1 521 | 4 535 | 215 | 4 320 | 23 970 | 20.8 | 47.0 |
| Pleasanton | 25 245 | 2.77 | 8.0 | 19.3 | 456 | 136 | 129 | 320 | 1 274 | 1 792 | 83 | 1 709 | 45 752 | 18.4 | 55.5 |
| Pomona | 38 477 | 3.77 | 18.1 | 15.1 | 4 138 | 1 356 | 1 166 | 2 782 | 5 371 | 3 561 | 615 | 2 947 | 83 477 | 60.2 | 15.3 |
| Porterville | 15 644 | 3.39 | 18.9 | 17.1 | 1 147 | 940 | 931 | 207 | 2 163 | 3 947 | 412 | 3 535 | 30 022 | 54.6 | 11.9 |
| Poway | 16 128 | 2.93 | 10.4 | 15.3 | 550 | 266 | 260 | 284 | 709 | 1 466 | 194 | 1 271 | 32 054 | 23.8 | 45.0 |
| Rancho Cordova | 23 448 | 2.75 | 16.3 | 24.8 | 325 | 155 | 143 | 170 | 2 228 | 3 400 | 494 | 2 905 | 40 832 | 38.6 | 24.3 |
| Rancho Cucamonga | 54 383 | 2.98 | 13.8 | 18.3 | 3 124 | 2 988 | 73 | 136 | 4 208 | 2 517 | 175 | 2 341 | 103 493 | 31.3 | 29.7 |
| Rancho Palos Verdes | 15 561 | 2.65 | 7.8 | 18.9 | 340 | 27 | 27 | 313 | 586 | 1 391 | 85 | 1 305 | 29 704 | 12.6 | 65.5 |
| Rancho Santa Margarita | 16 665 | 2.87 | 10.2 | 19.2 | 2 | 0 | 0 | 2 | 400 | 826 | 66 | 760 | 29 497 | 17.0 | 48.1 |
| Redding | 36 130 | 2.43 | 13.3 | 28.6 | 2 020 | 882 | 543 | 1 138 | 4 097 | 4 506 | 771 | 3 735 | 58 918 | 35.3 | 23.4 |
| Redlands | 24 764 | 2.68 | 13.7 | 24.6 | 2 368 | 512 | 485 | 1 856 | 2 818 | 4 051 | 283 | 3 768 | 43 231 | 29.9 | 37.2 |
| Redondo Beach | 29 011 | 2.29 | 8.7 | 31.9 | 431 | 64 | 64 | 367 | 1 769 | 2 619 | 249 | 2 371 | 48 955 | 16.7 | 57.5 |
| Redwood City | 27 957 | 2.69 | 11.2 | 26.5 | 1 547 | 1 139 | 53 | 408 | 1 664 | 2 141 | 228 | 1 913 | 51 579 | 34.2 | 40.1 |
| Rialto | 25 202 | 3.92 | 20.5 | 12.5 | 447 | 193 | 153 | 254 | 3 458 | 3 446 | 478 | 2 968 | 54 351 | 64.8 | 8.4 |
| Richmond | 36 093 | 2.83 | 19.2 | 26.4 | 1 583 | 913 | 172 | 670 | 5 581 | 5 319 | 986 | 4 333 | 66 962 | 44.9 | 26.2 |
| Ridgecrest | 10 781 | 2.54 | 12.5 | 27.6 | 196 | 87 | 87 | 109 | 637 | 2 280 | 415 | 1 865 | 17 591 | 31.8 | 25.7 |
| Riverside | 91 932 | 3.18 | 15.1 | 19.9 | 11 549 | 2 624 | 1 153 | 8 925 | 10 941 | 3 559 | 426 | 3 133 | 175 632 | 46.7 | 21.9 |
| Rocklin | 20 800 | 2.71 | 10.5 | 21.2 | 637 | 181 | 176 | 456 | 1 154 | 2 002 | 108 | 1 894 | 35 395 | 20.9 | 41.7 |
| Rohnert Park | 15 808 | 2.57 | 11.9 | 26.4 | 397 | 6 | 6 | 391 | 994 | 2 398 | 466 | 1 932 | 25 530 | 35.8 | 24.3 |
| Rosemead | 14 247 | 3.74 | 17.6 | 12.2 | 413 | 278 | 208 | 135 | 1 310 | 2 408 | 313 | 2 096 | 37 047 | 62.2 | 14.8 |
| Roseville | 45 059 | 2.62 | 10.9 | 24.5 | 847 | 369 | 361 | 478 | 3 789 | 3 153 | 206 | 2 946 | 76 317 | 26.2 | 34.9 |
| Sacramento | 174 624 | 2.62 | 15.8 | 30.5 | 8 314 | 4 046 | 1 367 | 4 268 | 21 917 | 4 644 | 711 | 3 933 | 297 212 | 39.1 | 29.2 |
| Salinas | 40 387 | 3.66 | 16.9 | 17.1 | 2 465 | 1 807 | 531 | 658 | 5 607 | 3 684 | 733 | 2 951 | 84 078 | 63.1 | 13.0 |
| San Bernardino | 59 283 | 3.42 | 22.8 | 18.9 | 7 325 | 4 247 | 878 | 3 078 | 10 322 | 4 860 | 876 | 3 984 | 116 461 | 60.0 | 12.7 |
| San Bruno | 14 701 | 2.77 | 12.4 | 24.9 | 398 | 82 | 72 | 316 | 1 004 | 2 414 | 209 | 2 204 | 28 528 | 32.7 | 34.6 |
| San Buenaventura (Ventura) | 40 438 | 2.57 | 12.2 | 27.1 | 2 493 | 1 738 | 293 | 755 | 3 646 | 3 386 | 303 | 3 083 | 71 889 | 32.2 | 31.6 |
| San Carlos | 11 524 | 2.46 | 7.2 | 25.8 | 91 | 12 | 12 | 79 | NA | NA | NA | NA | 20 427 | 15.5 | 58.8 |
| San Clemente | 23 906 | 2.65 | 7.9 | 21.7 | 273 | 28 | 0 | 245 | 934 | 1 453 | 86 | 1 368 | 41 778 | 18.5 | 46.7 |
| San Diego | 483 092 | 2.60 | 11.4 | 28.0 | 51 956 | 7 050 | 2 902 | 44 906 | 34 813 | 2 644 | 388 | 2 256 | 847 910 | 30.1 | 41.0 |
| San Dimas | 12 030 | 2.73 | 12.2 | 22.2 | 540 | 220 | 128 | 320 | 640 | 1 896 | 231 | 1 665 | 23 258 | 29.5 | 31.9 |

1. No spouse present.   2. Data for serious crimes have not been adjusted for underreporting. This may affect comparability between geographic areas and over time.   3. Per 100,000 population estimated by the FBI.   4. Persons 25 years old and over.

# Table D. Cities — Income, Poverty, and Housing

| City | Money income, 2007–2011 | | | | | Housing units, 2010 | | | Occupied Housing units 2007–2011 | | | | |
|---|---|---|---|---|---|---|---|---|---|---|---|---|---|
| | | Households | | | | | | | | Owner-occupied | | Median owner costs as a percent of income | |
| | Per capita income[1] (dollars) | Median income | Percent with income of $200,000 or more | Percent with income of less than $25,000 | Families with income below poverty (percent) | Total | Percent change, 2000–2010 | Vacant units for sale or rent[2] | Total | Percent | Median value[3] (dollars) | With a mortgage[4] | Without a mortgage[5] |
| | 42 | 43 | 44 | 45 | 46 | 47 | 48 | 49 | 50 | 51 | 52 | 53 | 54 |
| CALIFORNIA—Cont'd | | | | | | | | | | | | | |
| Menlo Park | 68 967 | 111 244 | 26.8 | 9.5 | 2.8 | 13 085 | 2.7 | 738 | 12 726 | 56.1 | 1 000 000 | 28.5 | 10.0 |
| Merced | 17 120 | 37 025 | 1.8 | 33.6 | 23.1 | 27 446 | 27.4 | 2 547 | 24 016 | 42.9 | 172 100 | 27.3 | 11.3 |
| Milpitas | 32 465 | 94 589 | 10.9 | 10.8 | 4.8 | 19 806 | 14.0 | 622 | 18 673 | 66.6 | 578 100 | 28.9 | 10.0 |
| Mission Viejo | 41 436 | 96 420 | 12.1 | 9.0 | 2.5 | 34 228 | 4.0 | 1 020 | 32 968 | 79.1 | 592 000 | 28.6 | 10.0 |
| Modesto | 22 886 | 49 852 | 2.9 | 25.0 | 14.9 | 75 044 | 11.5 | 5 937 | 67 979 | 57.4 | 230 300 | 30.5 | 11.4 |
| Monrovia | 32 084 | 68 071 | 5.9 | 18.4 | 7.3 | 14 473 | 3.9 | 711 | 13 497 | 49.4 | 540 200 | 31.8 | 10.0 |
| Montclair | 17 173 | 50 959 | 2.1 | 20.3 | 15.3 | 9 911 | 8.0 | 388 | 9 322 | 60.1 | 283 000 | 33.6 | 10.0 |
| Montebello | 21 253 | 52 496 | 2.6 | 23.2 | 13.1 | 19 768 | 1.8 | 756 | 18 967 | 48.6 | 437 600 | 32.4 | 11.9 |
| Monterey | 36 148 | 62 720 | 5.7 | 19.4 | 4.9 | 13 584 | 1.2 | 1 400 | 12 356 | 34.1 | 715 400 | 29.0 | 10.7 |
| Monterey Park | 23 639 | 51 736 | 3.2 | 24.6 | 10.5 | 20 850 | 3.3 | 887 | 19 254 | 54.3 | 486 000 | 29.8 | 10.0 |
| Moorpark | 36 375 | 103 009 | 12.6 | 6.9 | 3.0 | 10 738 | 18.1 | 254 | 10 378 | 80.2 | 572 500 | 30.7 | 10.4 |
| Moreno Valley | 18 246 | 56 768 | 2.0 | 19.3 | 15.8 | 55 559 | 34.0 | 3 967 | 49 731 | 65.7 | 235 300 | 33.6 | 11.7 |
| Morgan Hill | 39 433 | 94 301 | 17.5 | 12.0 | 7.4 | 12 859 | 15.7 | 533 | 12 066 | 74.3 | 631 900 | 31.0 | 10.6 |
| Mountain View | 51 635 | 91 446 | 15.8 | 14.1 | 4.7 | 33 881 | 4.5 | 1 924 | 31 469 | 42.2 | 786 000 | 25.7 | 11.2 |
| Murrieta | 29 198 | 80 792 | 5.8 | 10.4 | 4.7 | 35 294 | 136.5 | 2 545 | 30 162 | 72.8 | 320 600 | 30.9 | 13.7 |
| Napa | 30 783 | 62 642 | 6.0 | 17.8 | 8.3 | 30 149 | 8.6 | 1 983 | 28 779 | 58.8 | 475 200 | 30.0 | 11.4 |
| National City | 16 611 | 36 907 | 1.2 | 32.9 | 18.4 | 16 762 | 8.0 | 1 260 | 16 060 | 34.8 | 307 900 | 34.7 | 11.3 |
| Newark | 29 375 | 81 777 | 5.8 | 11.3 | 5.0 | 13 414 | 2.0 | 442 | 13 007 | 72.2 | 491 400 | 32.5 | 10.4 |
| Newport Beach | 80 872 | 108 946 | 25.4 | 11.9 | 4.4 | 44 193 | 18.4 | 5 442 | 38 048 | 55.1 | 1 000 000 | 31.8 | 10.0 |
| Norco | 27 361 | 84 812 | 8.3 | 11.9 | 6.0 | 7 322 | 17.7 | 299 | 7 105 | 82.5 | 460 800 | 30.8 | 10.6 |
| Norwalk | 19 379 | 60 090 | 1.7 | 17.5 | 9.4 | 28 083 | 1.9 | 953 | 27 443 | 66.0 | 359 900 | 32.5 | 10.0 |
| Novato | 41 575 | 78 628 | 10.1 | 14.7 | 3.8 | 21 158 | 11.5 | 879 | 20 396 | 67.8 | 633 200 | 32.4 | 11.2 |
| Oakland | 31 675 | 51 144 | 6.9 | 27.4 | 16.0 | 169 710 | 7.7 | 15 919 | 154 537 | 41.9 | 492 200 | 32.9 | 12.5 |
| Oakley | 27 742 | 78 102 | 4.4 | 15.9 | 6.1 | 11 484 | 44.0 | 757 | 10 548 | 78.4 | 276 700 | 30.9 | 14.1 |
| Oceanside | 27 674 | 63 394 | 3.7 | 16.1 | 8.0 | 64 435 | 8.3 | 5 197 | 57 825 | 58.9 | 390 500 | 32.4 | 11.3 |
| Ontario | 19 123 | 55 902 | 1.6 | 16.3 | 12.5 | 47 449 | 5.2 | 2 518 | 45 283 | 57.8 | 294 300 | 32.0 | 11.0 |
| Orange | 32 797 | 78 654 | 9.2 | 13.0 | 6.7 | 45 111 | 8.0 | 1 744 | 42 752 | 62.4 | 567 100 | 31.1 | 10.0 |
| Oxnard | 20 612 | 60 191 | 3.2 | 18.1 | 12.4 | 52 772 | 16.8 | 2 975 | 51 362 | 55.3 | 387 500 | 32.8 | 11.0 |
| Pacifica | 42 933 | 93 436 | 10.4 | 8.4 | 2.4 | 14 523 | 1.9 | 556 | 14 153 | 69.2 | 635 800 | 30.3 | 10.0 |
| Palmdale | 19 193 | 55 213 | 2.9 | 19.9 | 15.4 | 46 544 | 25.3 | 3 592 | 40 465 | 67.8 | 227 300 | 32.2 | 12.9 |
| Palm Desert | 42 179 | 53 940 | 7.4 | 20.0 | 5.7 | 37 073 | 32.1 | 13 956 | 23 792 | 69.5 | 352 100 | 33.4 | 16.2 |
| Palm Springs | 38 054 | 45 989 | 5.6 | 26.3 | 8.9 | 34 794 | 12.3 | 12 048 | 23 088 | 57.5 | 319 500 | 33.1 | 17.0 |
| Palo Alto | 72 199 | 122 532 | 29.6 | 10.7 | 2.9 | 28 216 | 7.9 | 1 723 | 25 797 | 57.4 | 1 000 000 | 24.8 | 10.0 |
| Paradise | 25 132 | 42 363 | 1.1 | 30.8 | 10.0 | 12 981 | 5.4 | 1 088 | 11 519 | 72.3 | 237 100 | 28.9 | 14.0 |
| Paramount | 14 293 | 42 831 | 0.5 | 26.6 | 19.5 | 14 571 | -0.4 | 690 | 14 240 | 45.2 | 301 600 | 35.8 | 10.5 |
| Pasadena | 39 825 | 67 920 | 9.6 | 19.0 | 8.3 | 59 551 | 10.0 | 4 281 | 54 492 | 45.4 | 638 400 | 29.9 | 11.9 |
| Perris | 14 333 | 49 812 | 0.7 | 23.4 | 22.1 | 17 906 | 70.5 | 1 541 | 16 100 | 67.6 | 189 400 | 37.0 | 13.2 |
| Petaluma | 35 111 | 76 185 | 7.3 | 14.2 | 5.7 | 22 736 | 11.8 | 999 | 21 454 | 68.4 | 493 800 | 30.5 | 10.9 |
| Pico Rivera | 18 428 | 55 632 | 1.5 | 19.3 | 10.5 | 17 109 | 1.8 | 543 | 16 596 | 68.7 | 375 600 | 30.6 | 10.0 |
| Pittsburg | 23 344 | 57 965 | 3.2 | 18.6 | 11.6 | 21 126 | 14.9 | 1 599 | 18 900 | 61.1 | 292 500 | 32.4 | 13.5 |
| Placentia | 30 451 | 78 364 | 7.1 | 14.0 | 7.9 | 16 872 | 9.4 | 507 | 15 740 | 66.5 | 549 900 | 29.5 | 10.0 |
| Pleasant Hill | 42 497 | 78 765 | 11.6 | 13.5 | 4.2 | 14 321 | 2.0 | 613 | 13 657 | 60.7 | 577 400 | 28.0 | 11.3 |
| Pleasanton | 50 745 | 118 713 | 21.0 | 7.8 | 2.9 | 26 053 | 8.6 | 808 | 24 222 | 69.3 | 747 400 | 27.7 | 10.0 |
| Pomona | 17 113 | 50 893 | 1.8 | 22.8 | 15.5 | 40 685 | 2.7 | 2 208 | 38 491 | 54.5 | 311 300 | 34.2 | 11.9 |
| Porterville | 16 705 | 39 933 | 1.2 | 33.6 | 21.6 | 16 734 | 31.4 | 1 090 | 16 068 | 58.6 | 166 100 | 27.3 | 12.5 |
| Poway | 41 445 | 94 872 | 12.3 | 9.2 | 2.9 | 16 715 | 5.6 | 587 | 15 931 | 76.3 | 556 800 | 27.0 | 10.0 |
| Rancho Cordova | 24 967 | 53 878 | 2.2 | 19.0 | 12.5 | 25 479 | 18.5 | 2 031 | 23 084 | 55.7 | 233 400 | 29.8 | 10.9 |
| Rancho Cucamonga | 32 738 | 78 782 | 6.5 | 10.7 | 4.0 | 56 618 | 34.1 | 2 235 | 54 194 | 66.5 | 407 600 | 30.1 | 12.0 |
| Rancho Palos Verdes | 58 045 | 116 643 | 24.2 | 9.3 | 3.5 | 16 179 | 3.3 | 618 | 15 083 | 80.7 | 997 300 | 28.6 | 10.0 |
| Rancho Santa Margarita | 41 787 | 104 167 | 12.9 | 6.9 | 2.8 | 17 260 | 3.7 | 595 | 16 286 | 72.4 | 571 500 | 29.5 | 12.9 |
| Redding | 23 548 | 43 157 | 2.6 | 28.7 | 14.4 | 38 679 | 14.5 | 2 549 | 35 398 | 55.6 | 255 400 | 29.0 | 13.3 |
| Redlands | 32 586 | 68 015 | 7.2 | 17.5 | 8.1 | 26 634 | 7.1 | 1 870 | 24 257 | 61.3 | 340 600 | 26.7 | 10.0 |
| Redondo Beach | 51 703 | 94 982 | 15.1 | 12.5 | 3.3 | 30 609 | 3.6 | 1 598 | 28 456 | 52.1 | 745 000 | 27.7 | 10.0 |
| Redwood City | 39 927 | 77 111 | 13.7 | 13.9 | 6.3 | 29 167 | 0.8 | 1 210 | 27 934 | 53.6 | 798 100 | 30.4 | 11.0 |
| Rialto | 15 967 | 50 452 | 1.3 | 20.7 | 14.4 | 27 203 | 5.4 | 2 001 | 24 214 | 64.4 | 231 000 | 33.1 | 10.7 |
| Richmond | 25 358 | 54 554 | 3.8 | 22.6 | 15.0 | 39 328 | 8.8 | 3 235 | 35 884 | 53.0 | 352 600 | 33.6 | 10.6 |
| Ridgecrest | 28 181 | 59 830 | 2.7 | 20.0 | 9.6 | 11 915 | 4.8 | 1 134 | 10 722 | 62.0 | 191 100 | 20.3 | 11.4 |
| Riverside | 22 806 | 57 555 | 3.8 | 19.8 | 10.9 | 98 444 | 14.4 | 6 512 | 90 246 | 58.9 | 299 600 | 30.8 | 10.0 |
| Rocklin | 34 658 | 79 675 | 6.1 | 13.4 | 3.5 | 22 010 | 52.4 | 1 210 | 20 857 | 68.8 | 369 700 | 29.1 | 12.5 |
| Rohnert Park | 28 203 | 56 950 | 3.0 | 20.1 | 5.8 | 16 551 | 4.6 | 743 | 15 976 | 54.1 | 348 300 | 33.1 | 13.8 |
| Rosemead | 17 869 | 47 964 | 1.6 | 22.6 | 12.9 | 14 805 | 3.4 | 558 | 14 413 | 49.4 | 460 900 | 37.1 | 10.0 |
| Roseville | 34 047 | 75 245 | 6.0 | 13.8 | 5.0 | 47 757 | 49.3 | 2 698 | 44 217 | 66.4 | 356 500 | 28.5 | 12.4 |
| Sacramento | 25 744 | 50 781 | 3.2 | 24.5 | 14.1 | 190 911 | 16.5 | 16 287 | 175 288 | 50.0 | 275 800 | 30.0 | 10.6 |
| Salinas | 18 060 | 50 568 | 1.7 | 22.6 | 17.3 | 42 651 | 7.7 | 2 264 | 40 685 | 45.4 | 340 600 | 35.6 | 10.0 |
| San Bernardino | 15 762 | 40 161 | 1.5 | 31.3 | 23.4 | 65 401 | 3.1 | 6 118 | 60 614 | 51.7 | 202 400 | 32.2 | 11.4 |
| San Bruno | 34 102 | 77 468 | 6.7 | 11.6 | 5.5 | 15 356 | 2.7 | 655 | 14 796 | 58.2 | 624 500 | 31.8 | 10.1 |
| San Buenaventura (Ventura) | 31 775 | 66 226 | 4.7 | 18.2 | 7.4 | 42 827 | 7.5 | 2 389 | 40 238 | 55.5 | 483 500 | 29.0 | 10.0 |
| San Carlos | 60 313 | 118 865 | 24.7 | 7.6 | 2.2 | 12 018 | 3.6 | 494 | 11 279 | 72.6 | 940 900 | 27.4 | 11.2 |
| San Clemente | 47 894 | 89 289 | 15.3 | 11.1 | 5.3 | 25 966 | 25.7 | 2 060 | 23 601 | 66.7 | 802 500 | 32.8 | 10.4 |
| San Diego | 33 135 | 63 739 | 7.1 | 19.3 | 9.9 | 516 033 | 9.9 | 32 941 | 474 217 | 49.2 | 477 100 | 29.9 | 10.0 |
| San Dimas | 33 731 | 74 610 | 8.5 | 14.8 | 4.2 | 12 506 | -0.6 | 476 | 11 789 | 72.7 | 456 600 | 27.8 | 11.4 |

1. Based on population estimated by the American Community Survey.    2. Includes units rented or sold but not occupied.    3. Specified owner-occupied units; $1,000,000 represents $1,000,000 or more    4. 50.0 represents 50 percent or more.    5. 10.0 represents 10 percent or less.

# Table D. Cities — Housing, Labor Force, and Employment

| City | Occupied housing units, 2007–2011 (cont.) | | | | Migration, 2007–2011 | | Civilian labor force, 2012 | | | | Civilian employment[4], 2007–2011 | | | |
|---|---|---|---|---|---|---|---|---|---|---|---|---|---|---|
| | | | | | | | | | Unemployment | | | Percent | | |
| | Percent renter occupied | Median gross rent[1] | Median rent as a percent of income[2] | Percent with no vehicle available | Percent who lived in the same house one year ago | Percent who lived outside this city one year ago | Total | Percent change, 2011–2012 | Total | Rate[3] | Population age 16 and older | In labor force | Full-year full-time worker | Households with no workers (percent) |
| | 55 | 56 | 57 | 58 | 59 | 60 | 61 | 62 | 63 | 64 | 65 | 66 | 67 | 68 |
| CALIFORNIA—Cont'd | | | | | | | | | | | | | | |
| Menlo Park | 43.9 | 1 758 | 25.4 | 5.1 | 84.5 | 12.3 | 16 600 | 4.8 | 898 | 5.4 | 24 952 | 67.3 | 42.2 | 23.3 |
| Merced | 57.1 | 774 | 34.5 | 11.5 | 77.7 | 7.9 | 32 946 | 1.8 | 5 551 | 16.8 | 55 784 | 59.6 | 31.1 | 31.6 |
| Milpitas | 33.4 | 1 634 | 29.9 | 3.5 | 83.9 | 12.1 | 32 982 | 2.8 | 2 862 | 8.7 | 52 465 | 63.9 | 42.3 | 16.8 |
| Mission Viejo | 20.9 | 1 759 | 34.2 | 3.0 | 89.8 | 7.7 | 55 476 | 2.1 | 3 044 | 5.5 | 74 605 | 66.8 | 43.1 | 20.5 |
| Modesto | 42.6 | 981 | 34.8 | 8.3 | 80.0 | 8.2 | 102 880 | 1.3 | 13 490 | 13.1 | 151 547 | 61.7 | 34.6 | 28.8 |
| Monrovia | 50.6 | 1 287 | 29.1 | 6.1 | 85.7 | 10.7 | 20 583 | -0.8 | 1 984 | 9.6 | 29 126 | 69.3 | 44.5 | 18.8 |
| Montclair | 39.9 | 1 082 | 32.4 | 7.5 | 84.9 | 11.8 | 16 179 | 0.3 | 1 855 | 11.5 | 27 495 | 64.2 | 36.7 | 18.4 |
| Montebello | 51.4 | 1 100 | 32.6 | 10.5 | 89.7 | 8.0 | 28 797 | -1.3 | 3 516 | 12.2 | 48 089 | 61.4 | 39.9 | 24.5 |
| Monterey | 65.9 | 1 302 | 29.5 | 8.4 | 72.3 | 23.5 | 18 257 | 12.8 | 935 | 5.1 | 24 142 | 67.6 | 30.0 | 28.4 |
| Monterey Park | 45.7 | 1 170 | 35.9 | 11.0 | 90.3 | 6.9 | 29 238 | -0.5 | 2 419 | 8.3 | 50 323 | 57.0 | 36.7 | 26.9 |
| Moorpark | 19.8 | 1 762 | 35.3 | 2.0 | 90.4 | 6.9 | 19 079 | 2.2 | 1 610 | 8.4 | 25 871 | 72.9 | 48.4 | 11.8 |
| Moreno Valley | 34.3 | 1 291 | 39.2 | 4.5 | 83.9 | 8.0 | 90 632 | 0.1 | 12 843 | 14.2 | 134 668 | 64.7 | 36.5 | 17.7 |
| Morgan Hill | 25.7 | 1 485 | 33.5 | 1.8 | 87.5 | 7.7 | 18 212 | 2.2 | 1 981 | 10.9 | 27 642 | 70.3 | 41.6 | 17.9 |
| Mountain View | 57.8 | 1 477 | 24.7 | 7.1 | 78.2 | 16.6 | 43 636 | 3.5 | 2 715 | 6.2 | 60 198 | 73.4 | 47.5 | 19.3 |
| Murrieta | 27.2 | 1 475 | 32.5 | 2.2 | 79.9 | 14.8 | 28 299 | 1.3 | 2 287 | 8.1 | 72 306 | 67.3 | 39.0 | 20.1 |
| Napa | 41.2 | 1 226 | 33.3 | 6.5 | 85.1 | 6.1 | 46 458 | 5.4 | 3 791 | 8.2 | 60 457 | 67.0 | 38.8 | 24.4 |
| National City | 65.2 | 906 | 35.2 | 15.9 | 85.2 | 9.5 | 25 058 | 0.0 | 4 297 | 17.1 | 44 447 | 61.7 | 32.7 | 26.1 |
| Newark | 27.8 | 1 468 | 29.0 | 3.6 | 91.6 | 5.5 | 22 876 | 2.5 | 1 918 | 8.4 | 33 370 | 68.8 | 45.3 | 22.1 |
| Newport Beach | 44.9 | 1 876 | 27.8 | 3.1 | 81.5 | 12.5 | 44 963 | 2.3 | 2 129 | 4.7 | 71 199 | 65.5 | 41.1 | 24.3 |
| Norco | 17.5 | 1 765 | 33.9 | 3.7 | 85.5 | 12.3 | 14 109 | 0.9 | 1 407 | 10.0 | 22 027 | 55.7 | 32.8 | 20.8 |
| Norwalk | 34.0 | 1 215 | 34.0 | 6.7 | 90.4 | 6.1 | 48 999 | -1.1 | 5 661 | 11.6 | 80 493 | 64.3 | 40.5 | 19.1 |
| Novato | 32.2 | 1 484 | 33.7 | 4.8 | 86.9 | 8.1 | 27 609 | 3.8 | 2 071 | 7.5 | 41 210 | 67.0 | 37.9 | 25.3 |
| Oakland | 58.1 | 1 042 | 32.7 | 17.8 | 83.4 | 8.1 | 206 009 | 1.1 | 28 175 | 13.7 | 313 483 | 65.4 | 37.1 | 27.7 |
| Oakley | 21.6 | 1 445 | 39.8 | 4.3 | 88.0 | 9.9 | 14 043 | 2.8 | 910 | 6.5 | 25 361 | 66.5 | 38.1 | 19.9 |
| Oceanside | 41.1 | 1 341 | 33.8 | 5.6 | 81.1 | 10.9 | 87 702 | 1.7 | 7 459 | 8.5 | 131 409 | 66.4 | 38.1 | 24.8 |
| Ontario | 42.2 | 1 215 | 33.9 | 5.3 | 84.5 | 9.4 | 82 034 | 0.1 | 10 427 | 12.7 | 122 388 | 69.4 | 38.4 | 16.7 |
| Orange | 37.6 | 1 436 | 31.7 | 4.9 | 83.5 | 10.9 | 73 738 | 1.7 | 5 155 | 7.0 | 106 980 | 68.3 | 42.2 | 18.3 |
| Oxnard | 44.7 | 1 238 | 35.2 | 6.1 | 86.3 | 4.8 | 92 281 | 1.2 | 11 337 | 12.3 | 144 638 | 67.0 | 38.6 | 19.5 |
| Pacifica | 30.8 | 1 639 | 28.6 | 3.5 | 87.6 | 9.1 | 23 552 | 4.2 | 1 820 | 7.7 | 30 333 | 71.2 | 47.3 | 18.4 |
| Palmdale | 32.2 | 1 130 | 41.1 | 4.9 | 84.7 | 8.7 | 55 632 | -1.5 | 7 548 | 13.6 | 104 803 | 62.7 | 36.5 | 20.5 |
| Palm Desert | 30.5 | 1 157 | 33.1 | 7.2 | 83.5 | 12.8 | 25 881 | 1.4 | 1 885 | 7.3 | 42 479 | 51.7 | 27.3 | 45.5 |
| Palm Springs | 42.5 | 949 | 31.2 | 7.3 | 80.5 | 11.9 | 27 179 | 1.0 | 2 589 | 9.5 | 39 848 | 55.5 | 30.9 | 40.8 |
| Palo Alto | 42.6 | 1 795 | 25.0 | 6.0 | 82.5 | 12.7 | 32 694 | 4.0 | 1 468 | 4.5 | 50 367 | 64.3 | 42.2 | 24.8 |
| Paradise | 27.7 | 791 | 39.0 | 7.3 | 86.4 | 7.0 | 11 793 | 1.1 | 1 121 | 9.5 | 22 655 | 48.5 | 26.3 | 45.2 |
| Paramount | 54.8 | 1 136 | 38.7 | 5.9 | 89.0 | 7.7 | 24 797 | -2.0 | 3 952 | 15.9 | 38 419 | 63.0 | 39.6 | 17.7 |
| Pasadena | 54.6 | 1 324 | 30.7 | 10.2 | 81.8 | 12.7 | 75 705 | -0.5 | 6 322 | 8.4 | 114 153 | 67.0 | 41.8 | 24.5 |
| Perris | 32.4 | 1 191 | 39.5 | 4.9 | 81.5 | 12.1 | 20 318 | -0.7 | 3 846 | 18.9 | 43 737 | 65.4 | 32.7 | 20.2 |
| Petaluma | 31.6 | 1 397 | 34.0 | 5.4 | 87.1 | 7.4 | 31 485 | 1.8 | 2 458 | 7.8 | 45 231 | 70.2 | 41.4 | 20.8 |
| Pico Rivera | 31.3 | 1 170 | 36.4 | 6.6 | 91.2 | 6.5 | 28 930 | -0.9 | 2 951 | 10.2 | 48 765 | 60.8 | 40.0 | 21.8 |
| Pittsburg | 38.9 | 1 262 | 36.4 | 5.9 | 82.4 | 9.7 | 31 099 | 0.6 | 4 432 | 14.3 | 47 467 | 65.7 | 36.5 | 21.5 |
| Placentia | 33.5 | 1 436 | 34.7 | 3.5 | 85.6 | 11.3 | 28 262 | 1.8 | 1 905 | 6.7 | 38 769 | 67.7 | 40.4 | 19.1 |
| Pleasant Hill | 39.3 | 1 420 | 30.7 | 5.9 | 82.8 | 14.1 | 20 771 | 2.6 | 1 516 | 7.3 | 27 539 | 66.5 | 38.1 | 24.9 |
| Pleasanton | 30.7 | 1 625 | 25.5 | 2.8 | 86.7 | 9.5 | 36 090 | 3.5 | 1 639 | 4.5 | 52 847 | 68.9 | 44.8 | 19.9 |
| Pomona | 45.5 | 1 087 | 36.5 | 6.9 | 84.3 | 9.9 | 66 444 | -1.3 | 8 081 | 12.2 | 108 849 | 63.8 | 37.2 | 19.6 |
| Porterville | 41.4 | 709 | 33.3 | 7.7 | 84.5 | 6.3 | 21 474 | -0.2 | 3 122 | 14.5 | 37 142 | 63.2 | 34.9 | 27.9 |
| Poway | 23.7 | 1 388 | 31.3 | 4.9 | 87.0 | 8.6 | 28 685 | 2.3 | 1 520 | 5.3 | 37 857 | 67.6 | 43.1 | 20.0 |
| Rancho Cordova | 44.3 | 973 | 33.0 | 7.4 | 75.8 | 14.4 | 30 889 | 0.0 | 3 738 | 12.1 | 49 132 | 68.3 | 40.0 | 23.4 |
| Rancho Cucamonga | 33.5 | 1 422 | 32.5 | 3.1 | 82.2 | 12.0 | 76 967 | 1.1 | 6 015 | 7.8 | 126 922 | 71.0 | 43.0 | 16.2 |
| Rancho Palos Verdes | 19.3 | 2 000 | 32.7 | 2.8 | 89.6 | 9.2 | 21 126 | 0.4 | 790 | 3.7 | 33 264 | 55.8 | 34.6 | 29.7 |
| Rancho Santa Margarita | 27.6 | 1 667 | 32.0 | 3.7 | 87.9 | 8.3 | 29 304 | 2.2 | 1 419 | 4.8 | 35 302 | 74.7 | 49.6 | 10.8 |
| Redding | 44.4 | 894 | 36.5 | 8.7 | 79.2 | 9.5 | 40 683 | -2.1 | 4 766 | 11.7 | 71 105 | 59.3 | 30.2 | 35.4 |
| Redlands | 38.7 | 1 078 | 29.0 | 6.0 | 84.2 | 9.9 | 36 829 | 0.9 | 3 223 | 8.8 | 53 882 | 64.1 | 38.1 | 24.6 |
| Redondo Beach | 47.9 | 1 636 | 28.3 | 3.6 | 85.2 | 10.4 | 44 718 | 0.0 | 2 597 | 5.8 | 54 295 | 73.8 | 48.2 | 18.1 |
| Redwood City | 46.4 | 1 404 | 32.0 | 4.8 | 85.4 | 9.7 | 43 702 | 4.5 | 2 932 | 6.7 | 58 409 | 70.4 | 44.6 | 19.3 |
| Rialto | 35.6 | 1 097 | 38.7 | 5.4 | 81.9 | 12.0 | 43 936 | -0.5 | 6 717 | 15.3 | 70 156 | 64.8 | 35.5 | 19.0 |
| Richmond | 47.0 | 1 160 | 33.2 | 9.6 | 80.4 | 12.3 | 54 153 | 0.5 | 7 884 | 14.6 | 79 491 | 66.3 | 38.5 | 27.2 |
| Ridgecrest | 38.0 | 777 | 26.3 | 6.5 | 79.3 | 9.8 | 16 958 | 6.4 | 1 288 | 7.6 | 20 905 | 63.8 | 39.2 | 27.8 |
| Riverside | 41.1 | 1 115 | 34.9 | 5.5 | 81.0 | 9.0 | 166 104 | 0.5 | 20 509 | 12.3 | 230 980 | 63.5 | 36.0 | 22.1 |
| Rocklin | 31.2 | 1 289 | 32.8 | 3.8 | 83.2 | 11.2 | 27 135 | 1.3 | 1 833 | 6.8 | 42 142 | 70.8 | 42.8 | 22.3 |
| Rohnert Park | 45.9 | 1 223 | 35.1 | 5.0 | 80.3 | 12.3 | 25 029 | 1.6 | 2 100 | 8.4 | 33 257 | 69.9 | 37.3 | 24.0 |
| Rosemead | 50.6 | 1 153 | 38.4 | 7.4 | 93.1 | 4.1 | 24 781 | -0.8 | 2 387 | 9.6 | 43 597 | 59.7 | 37.5 | 18.1 |
| Roseville | 33.6 | 1 204 | 31.0 | 4.2 | 81.1 | 11.4 | 56 239 | 0.6 | 5 320 | 9.5 | 89 485 | 67.0 | 41.9 | 25.8 |
| Sacramento | 50.0 | 978 | 32.7 | 10.1 | 77.0 | 10.5 | 215 755 | 0.0 | 26 703 | 12.4 | 360 929 | 65.0 | 36.7 | 28.4 |
| Salinas | 54.6 | 1 060 | 33.4 | 7.6 | 83.7 | 4.9 | 78 826 | 5.7 | 12 569 | 15.9 | 105 899 | 67.3 | 35.6 | 20.1 |
| San Bernardino | 48.3 | 924 | 38.6 | 10.8 | 78.4 | 11.5 | 84 726 | -0.6 | 13 578 | 16.0 | 150 565 | 58.4 | 33.4 | 27.9 |
| San Bruno | 41.8 | 1 564 | 28.1 | 4.7 | 86.7 | 11.1 | 23 130 | 4.7 | 1 347 | 5.8 | 33 025 | 72.1 | 45.8 | 20.8 |
| San Buenaventura (Ventura) | 44.5 | 1 354 | 32.2 | 5.1 | 84.1 | 8.7 | 62 541 | 2.2 | 5 109 | 8.2 | 84 167 | 66.7 | 39.2 | 25.7 |
| San Carlos | 27.4 | 1 546 | 26.5 | 3.9 | 89.0 | 8.1 | 16 139 | 5.0 | 733 | 4.5 | 22 360 | 68.5 | 43.4 | 21.4 |
| San Clemente | 33.3 | 1 658 | 31.7 | 2.8 | 85.9 | 9.2 | 29 517 | 1.9 | 1 812 | 6.1 | 48 048 | 67.0 | 40.8 | 22.2 |
| San Diego | 50.8 | 1 294 | 32.5 | 7.2 | 80.8 | 8.9 | 713 852 | 1.6 | 63 723 | 8.9 | 1 050 528 | 67.1 | 39.3 | 22.6 |
| San Dimas | 27.3 | 1 480 | 34.2 | 5.3 | 86.9 | 11.3 | 19 895 | -0.2 | 1 274 | 6.4 | 27 396 | 63.9 | 42.0 | 24.3 |

1. $2,000 represents $2,000 or more.   2. 50.0 represents 50 percent or more.   3. Percent of civilian labor force.   4. Persons 16 years old and over.

# Table D. Cities — Construction, Wholesale Trade, and Retail Trade

| City | Value of residential construction authorized by building permits, 2011 | | | Wholesale trade,[1] 2007 | | | | Retail trade,[2] 2007 | | | |
|---|---|---|---|---|---|---|---|---|---|---|---|
| | New construction ($1,000) | Number of housing units | Percent single family | Number of establishments | Number of employees | Sales (mil dol) | Annual payroll (mil dol) | Number of establishments | Number of employees | Sales (mil dol) | Annual payroll (mil dol) |
| | 69 | 70 | 71 | 72 | 73 | 74 | 75 | 76 | 77 | 78 | 79 |
| **CALIFORNIA—Cont'd** | | | | | | | | | | | |
| Menlo Park | 7 199 | 10 | 100.0 | 45 | 640 | 411.0 | 50.2 | 115 | 1 483 | 354.3 | 48.2 |
| Merced | 6 415 | 70 | 0.0 | 32 | 818 | 1 204.2 | 35.7 | 270 | 4 509 | 1 057.5 | 103.5 |
| Milpitas | 42 543 | 373 | 1.9 | 146 | 5 498 | 4 231.2 | 512.4 | 312 | 5 088 | 993.9 | 103.3 |
| Mission Viejo | 5 747 | 42 | 100.0 | 117 | 1 385 | 598.4 | 89.7 | 372 | 7 291 | 1 727.6 | 181.8 |
| Modesto | 3 123 | 13 | 100.0 | 108 | 1 147 | 1 311.9 | 52.7 | 737 | 12 116 | 2 599.3 | 268.2 |
| Monrovia | 0 | 0 | 0.0 | 82 | 931 | 475.8 | 43.6 | 135 | 2 753 | 907.2 | 81.3 |
| Montclair | 0 | 0 | 0.0 | 77 | 699 | 257.8 | 24.1 | 260 | 5 046 | 1 136.0 | 123.1 |
| Montebello | 655 | 4 | 0.0 | 106 | 1 635 | 759.0 | 64.7 | 212 | 3 782 | 820.0 | 80.0 |
| Monterey | 6 332 | 12 | 58.3 | 45 | 1 701 | 2 172.2 | 94.1 | 227 | 2 684 | 512.9 | 70.4 |
| Monterey Park | 2 432 | 7 | 100.0 | 228 | 1 354 | 653.7 | 47.5 | 222 | 1 937 | 477.2 | 41.1 |
| Moorpark | 7 026 | 14 | 100.0 | 54 | 731 | 401.8 | 34.6 | 60 | 1 013 | 192.8 | 20.3 |
| Moreno Valley | 6 606 | 23 | 100.0 | 30 | 147 | 62.1 | 5.5 | 310 | 5 564 | 1 853.2 | 129.5 |
| Morgan Hill | 28 540 | 97 | 100.0 | 63 | 2 221 | 1 332.4 | 144.7 | 112 | 1 584 | 418.3 | 40.2 |
| Mountain View | 70 440 | 323 | 19.5 | 125 | 3 295 | 2 750.6 | 373.0 | 262 | 4 609 | 1 290.1 | 131.9 |
| Murrieta | 21 307 | 107 | 62.6 | 79 | 409 | 238.2 | 19.1 | 229 | 4 293 | 1 073.7 | 98.0 |
| Napa | 16 294 | 84 | 69.0 | 67 | 557 | 302.7 | 28.3 | 324 | 4 411 | 1 129.0 | 116.3 |
| National City | 1 516 | 8 | 100.0 | 96 | 940 | 946.4 | 43.8 | 322 | 5 688 | 1 483.3 | 150.3 |
| Newark | 0 | 0 | 0.0 | 57 | 1 734 | 755.4 | 79.0 | 195 | 3 705 | 781.8 | 76.5 |
| Newport Beach | 55 002 | 78 | 82.1 | 224 | 2 091 | 2 564.4 | 174.1 | 467 | 7 369 | 2 614.3 | 250.3 |
| Norco | 0 | 0 | 0.0 | 28 | 244 | 123.5 | 8.6 | 98 | 1 659 | 521.0 | 51.1 |
| Norwalk | 497 | 3 | 100.0 | 85 | 769 | 385.1 | 31.9 | 163 | 3 410 | 1 160.4 | 98.5 |
| Novato | 24 164 | 135 | 38.5 | 87 | 1 259 | 596.3 | 90.1 | 188 | 2 919 | 969.4 | 90.4 |
| Oakland | 45 058 | 290 | 14.1 | 424 | 5 473 | 3 541.5 | 277.3 | 1 099 | 11 176 | 2 987.1 | 314.0 |
| Oakley | 20 640 | 77 | 100.0 | 8 | D | D | D | 49 | 499 | 141.3 | 12.0 |
| Oceanside | 38 506 | 134 | 79.1 | 144 | 1 516 | 502.5 | 54.4 | 400 | 6 645 | 1 688.3 | 159.2 |
| Ontario | 6 443 | 52 | 69.2 | 596 | 12 375 | 13 263.9 | 539.7 | 583 | 10 441 | 3 160.6 | 268.2 |
| Orange | 23 053 | 68 | 7.4 | 349 | 4 806 | 6 253.9 | 253.2 | 608 | 7 997 | 2 101.9 | 211.0 |
| Oxnard | 31 486 | 214 | 26.2 | 193 | 4 187 | 2 837.6 | 207.0 | 458 | 7 877 | 2 348.6 | 212.2 |
| Pacifica | 1 688 | 4 | 50.0 | 8 | D | D | D | 65 | 663 | 177.5 | 15.9 |
| Palmdale | 22 057 | 107 | 100.0 | 34 | 259 | 51.3 | 8.1 | 314 | 7 319 | 1 670.4 | 163.2 |
| Palm Desert | 44 403 | 108 | 79.6 | 76 | 559 | 195.2 | 23.0 | 472 | 6 874 | 1 538.1 | 163.9 |
| Palm Springs | 29 579 | 111 | 94.6 | 50 | 249 | 106.3 | 10.8 | 222 | 2 753 | 643.7 | 71.4 |
| Palo Alto | 64 523 | 136 | 60.3 | 70 | 941 | 1 584.9 | 64.0 | 340 | 5 719 | 1 535.7 | 182.6 |
| Paradise | 7 183 | 44 | 100.0 | 6 | 17 | 6.1 | 0.6 | 83 | 878 | 168.5 | 19.7 |
| Paramount | 3 133 | 19 | 100.0 | 239 | 1 965 | 1 163.4 | 79.6 | 120 | 1 710 | 423.9 | 42.3 |
| Pasadena | 6 990 | 25 | 84.0 | 150 | D | D | D | 652 | 10 857 | 2 707.8 | 280.7 |
| Perris | 7 485 | 63 | 100.0 | 15 | 234 | 78.2 | 9.6 | 79 | 2 638 | 537.3 | 61.0 |
| Petaluma | 26 409 | 155 | 56.1 | 100 | 1 460 | 795.8 | 110.7 | 289 | 3 803 | 947.3 | 104.1 |
| Pico Rivera | 338 | 1 | 100.0 | 108 | 2 268 | 1 218.7 | 90.6 | 116 | 2 611 | 927.7 | 55.6 |
| Pittsburg | 22 137 | 130 | 100.0 | 33 | 398 | 217.9 | 21.3 | 123 | 2 535 | 650.0 | 69.6 |
| Placentia | 3 624 | 20 | 55.0 | 128 | 1 105 | 480.1 | 55.3 | 104 | 1 354 | 384.5 | 38.6 |
| Pleasant Hill | 1 869 | 6 | 100.0 | 26 | 146 | 113.8 | 9.1 | 140 | 2 472 | 510.8 | 54.8 |
| Pleasanton | 14 535 | 41 | 100.0 | 138 | 2 228 | 3 957.5 | 172.4 | 355 | 6 810 | 1 605.1 | 179.6 |
| Pomona | 461 | 4 | 100.0 | 302 | 3 199 | 1 629.7 | 139.6 | 291 | 4 139 | 1 102.6 | 100.4 |
| Porterville | 9 865 | 50 | 100.0 | 23 | 140 | 44.6 | 5.5 | 158 | 2 448 | 540.1 | 56.2 |
| Poway | 4 844 | 10 | 100.0 | 106 | 2 104 | 1 444.6 | 146.8 | 147 | 3 097 | 1 002.8 | 90.6 |
| Rancho Cordova | 40 044 | 148 | 100.0 | 102 | 1 053 | 453.8 | 56.8 | 191 | 2 828 | 543.9 | 68.7 |
| Rancho Cucamonga | 64 130 | 376 | 48.9 | 292 | 3 728 | 3 078.3 | 170.4 | 444 | 8 301 | 1 803.6 | 175.4 |
| Rancho Palos Verdes | 3 149 | 15 | 100.0 | 33 | 119 | 123.8 | 6.1 | 56 | 481 | 112.6 | 11.0 |
| Rancho Santa Margarita | 0 | 0 | 0.0 | 68 | 622 | 345.4 | 32.1 | 86 | 2 005 | 608.4 | 54.1 |
| Redding | 10 708 | 72 | 43.1 | 129 | 1 429 | 724.2 | 58.5 | 500 | 7 820 | 1 953.9 | 199.2 |
| Redlands | 5 027 | 34 | 100.0 | 49 | 650 | 174.7 | 25.1 | 253 | 5 303 | 1 581.1 | 133.4 |
| Redondo Beach | 16 943 | 58 | 100.0 | 63 | 295 | 102.2 | 12.6 | 303 | 4 570 | 815.7 | 101.6 |
| Redwood City | 22 920 | 116 | 70.7 | 73 | 1 243 | 1 189.7 | 114.5 | 245 | 4 925 | 1 613.7 | 175.2 |
| Rialto | 6 763 | 82 | 8.5 | 47 | 698 | 766.6 | 38.3 | 130 | 2 420 | 524.4 | 52.7 |
| Richmond | 12 239 | 98 | 27.6 | 94 | 1 871 | 1 127.9 | 94.9 | 261 | 4 139 | 1 024.6 | 103.5 |
| Ridgecrest | 6 814 | 51 | 100.0 | 6 | 33 | 12.0 | 1.6 | 96 | 1 442 | 298.2 | 32.1 |
| Riverside | 35 075 | 279 | 15.4 | 312 | 5 066 | 2 854.9 | 229.3 | 922 | 16 855 | 4 757.5 | 439.1 |
| Rocklin | 30 171 | 82 | 100.0 | 71 | 1 433 | 855.4 | 88.0 | 142 | 1 927 | 545.9 | 60.0 |
| Rohnert Park | 0 | 0 | 0.0 | 31 | 475 | 225.3 | 24.9 | 114 | 2 220 | 610.8 | 57.4 |
| Rosemead | 2 446 | 12 | 100.0 | 113 | 447 | 220.5 | 11.1 | 172 | 2 201 | 453.9 | 42.0 |
| Roseville | 91 310 | 411 | 100.0 | 107 | 2 175 | 2 233.8 | 109.0 | 549 | 13 868 | 3 923.2 | 372.1 |
| Sacramento | 39 251 | 295 | 20.7 | 488 | 9 008 | 8 940.1 | 402.1 | 1 282 | 20 067 | 4 307.5 | 486.9 |
| Salinas | 3 166 | 25 | 28.0 | 159 | 2 031 | 1 588.9 | 111.7 | 507 | 7 654 | 1 933.2 | 194.9 |
| San Bernardino | 6 688 | 24 | 100.0 | 142 | 2 655 | 2 265.4 | 96.8 | 592 | 10 661 | 2 845.1 | 268.5 |
| San Bruno | 7 948 | 15 | 100.0 | 23 | 224 | 340.5 | 9.9 | 133 | 2 403 | 512.7 | 53.7 |
| San Buenaventura (Ventura) | 22 999 | 199 | 60.8 | 179 | 1 885 | 747.8 | 91.9 | 568 | 7 907 | 1 980.7 | 201.9 |
| San Carlos | 2 426 | 2 | 100.0 | 101 | 933 | 455.6 | 55.6 | 148 | 1 669 | 494.5 | 51.8 |
| San Clemente | 8 005 | 13 | 100.0 | 162 | 2 010 | 914.9 | 107.7 | 197 | 2 185 | 580.7 | 56.7 |
| San Diego | 438 493 | 2 692 | 16.8 | 1 902 | 33 209 | 21 927.7 | 3 017.4 | 4 368 | 65 695 | 16 525.8 | 1 687.8 |
| San Dimas | 2 152 | 6 | 100.0 | 81 | 570 | 371.3 | 25.4 | 116 | 2 583 | 542.0 | 53.3 |

1. Merchant wholesalers except manufacturers' sales branches and offices.  2. Establishments with payroll.

| City | Real estate and rental and leasing, 2007 | | | | Professional, scientific, and technical services,[1] 2007 | | | | Manufacturing, 2007 | | | |
|---|---|---|---|---|---|---|---|---|---|---|---|---|
| | Number of establish-ments | Number of employees | Receipts (mil dol) | Annual payroll (mil dol) | Number of establish-ments | Number of employees | Receipts (mil dol) | Annual payroll (mil dol) | Number of establish-ments | Number of employees | Receipts (mil dol) | Annual payroll (mil dol) |
| | 80 | 81 | 82 | 83 | 84 | 85 | 86 | 87 | 88 | 89 | 90 | 91 |
| CALIFORNIA—Cont'd | | | | | | | | | | | | |
| Menlo Park | 95 | 454 | 126.4 | 21.7 | 307 | D | D | D | 60 | 3 102 | 1 095.0 | 191.9 |
| Merced | 69 | 374 | 50.3 | 9.8 | 103 | D | D | D | 35 | 1 979 | 605.7 | 81.5 |
| Milpitas | 88 | 520 | 167.2 | 13.8 | 220 | D | D | D | 179 | 16 051 | 4 831.9 | 1 432.6 |
| Mission Viejo | 186 | 884 | 233.6 | 43.4 | 408 | 1 545 | 232.4 | 84.2 | 61 | 1 038 | 548.0 | 66.0 |
| Modesto | 235 | 1 251 | 245.9 | 39.0 | 445 | D | D | D | 97 | 6 161 | 2 924.1 | 326.1 |
| Monrovia | 51 | 522 | 106.1 | 36.3 | 142 | 1 940 | 373.2 | 132.3 | 112 | 2 832 | 501.9 | 119.4 |
| Montclair | 41 | 191 | 38.1 | 6.3 | 34 | 214 | 17.8 | 6.7 | 83 | 999 | 177.7 | 36.4 |
| Montebello | 74 | 524 | 133.6 | 20.7 | 70 | 983 | 75.6 | 18.0 | 102 | 6 193 | 955.2 | 244.4 |
| Monterey | 98 | 592 | 79.0 | 17.6 | 260 | D | D | D | 49 | 836 | 152.3 | 38.4 |
| Monterey Park | 82 | 747 | 59.0 | 16.7 | 174 | D | D | D | 47 | 895 | 165.8 | 35.9 |
| Moorpark | 23 | 102 | 22.5 | 4.4 | 94 | 318 | 59.1 | 17.1 | 58 | 3 026 | 661.5 | 128.9 |
| Moreno Valley | 80 | 334 | 73.9 | 9.5 | 79 | 590 | 37.4 | 15.2 | 21 | 1 255 | 248.5 | 45.0 |
| Morgan Hill | 82 | 215 | 59.0 | 9.7 | 145 | 3 503 | 132.1 | 56.7 | 93 | 3 607 | 922.0 | 216.8 |
| Mountain View | 137 | 738 | 159.6 | 27.2 | 541 | 15 440 | 3 164.0 | 1 548.6 | 148 | 6 514 | 1 751.4 | 430.6 |
| Murrieta | 128 | 373 | 72.4 | 13.9 | 185 | 700 | 92.0 | 34.9 | 69 | 914 | 124.9 | 32.5 |
| Napa | 99 | 419 | 69.7 | 13.8 | 247 | D | D | D | 112 | 3 299 | D | 177.9 |
| National City | 59 | 339 | 76.2 | 11.0 | 62 | 546 | 42.4 | 16.1 | 93 | 2 215 | 332.1 | 78.7 |
| Newark | 42 | D | D | D | 111 | 1 979 | 496.8 | 184.0 | 78 | 3 754 | 954.3 | 196.3 |
| Newport Beach | 702 | 6 702 | 3 369.6 | 519.1 | 1 294 | D | D | D | 92 | 3 369 | 495.2 | 167.2 |
| Norco | 34 | 154 | 25.2 | 5.3 | 59 | 1 004 | 97.8 | 35.7 | 34 | 630 | 81.0 | 28.8 |
| Norwalk | 62 | 364 | 58.3 | 10.6 | 68 | D | D | D | 60 | 990 | 188.2 | 33.9 |
| Novato | 113 | 721 | 95.0 | 23.1 | 266 | D | D | D | 57 | 515 | 99.6 | 24.4 |
| Oakland | 475 | 2 942 | 763.2 | 112.0 | 1 442 | 14 607 | 2 039.2 | 1 104.7 | 407 | 8 970 | 1 797.7 | 387.0 |
| Oakley | 20 | 62 | 14.0 | 2.8 | 24 | 110 | 10.7 | 3.3 | NA | NA | NA | NA |
| Oceanside | 163 | 823 | 142.3 | 21.8 | 297 | 1 217 | 134.4 | 44.5 | 171 | 3 973 | 698.2 | 138.2 |
| Ontario | 194 | 1 535 | 680.8 | 72.8 | 246 | D | D | D | 443 | 17 492 | 4 945.1 | 655.4 |
| Orange | 299 | 2 198 | 485.8 | 100.3 | 741 | D | D | D | 294 | 8 054 | 1 721.4 | 334.9 |
| Oxnard | 148 | 672 | 128.8 | 24.9 | 224 | D | D | D | 185 | 11 928 | 3 490.0 | 567.8 |
| Pacifica | 31 | 80 | 14.0 | 2.1 | 64 | 218 | 30.7 | 10.3 | NA | NA | NA | NA |
| Palmdale | 119 | 591 | 66.0 | 10.5 | 109 | 1 048 | 171.5 | 53.7 | 44 | 5 026 | 1 277.9 | 342.5 |
| Palm Desert | 180 | 780 | 159.4 | 33.1 | 312 | D | D | D | NA | NA | NA | NA |
| Palm Springs | 151 | 850 | 167.7 | 22.9 | 186 | 767 | 125.7 | 38.9 | 32 | 737 | D | D |
| Palo Alto | 193 | 1 215 | 917.6 | 104.4 | 775 | 12 475 | 3 061.8 | 1 523.5 | 72 | 6 530 | 2 767.7 | 496.3 |
| Paradise | 35 | 224 | 16.6 | 4.5 | 34 | 118 | 10.0 | 2.7 | NA | NA | NA | NA |
| Paramount | 31 | 231 | 28.4 | 6.2 | 37 | 251 | 23.7 | 8.6 | 228 | 4 847 | 1 554.7 | 226.4 |
| Pasadena | 322 | 1 812 | 421.8 | 93.7 | 1 182 | D | D | D | 104 | 1 467 | 327.1 | 71.2 |
| Perris | 30 | 189 | 34.3 | 5.7 | 24 | 97 | 14.9 | 4.4 | 40 | 2 894 | 462.4 | 104.2 |
| Petaluma | 93 | 463 | 83.4 | 17.5 | 214 | D | D | D | 115 | 4 248 | 1 213.7 | 206.5 |
| Pico Rivera | 45 | 244 | 40.6 | 7.3 | 34 | 219 | 23.7 | 6.4 | 77 | 1 631 | 434.7 | 62.4 |
| Pittsburg | 39 | 308 | 43.7 | 11.9 | 46 | 297 | 29.6 | 10.7 | 45 | 2 112 | 1 526.5 | 138.0 |
| Placentia | 59 | 285 | 58.0 | 9.7 | 115 | 534 | 63.6 | 23.0 | 134 | 2 644 | 478.8 | 103.9 |
| Pleasant Hill | 63 | 265 | 78.6 | 14.8 | 149 | 723 | 109.2 | 41.5 | NA | NA | NA | NA |
| Pleasanton | 189 | 1 017 | 360.2 | 45.0 | 528 | 5 335 | 958.7 | 409.3 | 89 | 2 608 | 590.2 | 159.2 |
| Pomona | 87 | 640 | 125.3 | 21.7 | 125 | D | D | D | 244 | 7 424 | 1 829.3 | 264.4 |
| Porterville | 37 | 124 | 22.6 | 3.0 | 50 | 229 | 18.5 | 5.2 | 24 | 1 117 | 243.3 | 34.7 |
| Poway | 93 | 490 | 69.6 | 19.0 | 253 | 1 756 | 253.1 | 106.7 | 103 | 5 111 | 1 317.6 | 256.8 |
| Rancho Cordova | 86 | 470 | 71.5 | 16.5 | 207 | D | D | D | 93 | 5 233 | 1 016.2 | 296.5 |
| Rancho Cucamonga | 235 | 1 170 | 244.9 | 43.5 | 371 | D | D | D | 266 | 9 878 | 3 182.4 | 409.2 |
| Rancho Palos Verdes | 66 | D | D | D | 140 | 1 012 | 98.3 | 47.0 | NA | NA | NA | NA |
| Rancho Santa Marga-rita | 72 | 368 | 52.3 | 15.4 | 197 | D | D | D | 48 | 1 846 | 544.8 | 100.0 |
| Redding | 155 | 795 | 90.3 | 18.3 | 310 | D | D | D | 84 | 929 | 172.1 | 34.4 |
| Redlands | 99 | 460 | 87.2 | 14.0 | 214 | D | D | D | 53 | 1 234 | 194.3 | 42.5 |
| Redondo Beach | 117 | 340 | 66.6 | 12.0 | 298 | D | D | D | 37 | D | D | D |
| Redwood City | 121 | 915 | 184.8 | 37.6 | 412 | D | D | D | 79 | 3 813 | 985.3 | 214.3 |
| Rialto | 47 | 190 | 33.9 | 5.1 | 36 | 225 | 16.4 | 7.0 | 75 | 2 720 | 596.0 | 98.3 |
| Richmond | 84 | 431 | 85.6 | 13.3 | 122 | D | D | D | 121 | 4 313 | D | 250.1 |
| Ridgecrest | 22 | 118 | 14.9 | 2.9 | 56 | 826 | 96.7 | 40.9 | NA | NA | NA | NA |
| Riverside | 334 | 1 953 | 402.7 | 66.4 | 636 | D | D | D | 303 | 9 480 | 2 569.9 | 380.9 |
| Rocklin | 77 | D | D | D | 156 | 1 485 | 242.8 | 86.0 | 38 | 710 | 143.4 | 27.8 |
| Rohnert Park | 52 | 320 | 52.9 | 14.3 | 66 | 403 | 40.0 | 18.5 | 44 | 968 | 194.9 | 45.1 |
| Rosemead | 32 | 99 | 13.5 | 2.5 | 68 | 278 | 26.2 | 7.7 | 59 | 1 038 | 191.4 | 30.1 |
| Roseville | 235 | 2 824 | 473.3 | 103.0 | 467 | 4 209 | 671.5 | 243.5 | 69 | 4 969 | 2 114.7 | 176.5 |
| Sacramento | 591 | 4 017 | 687.3 | 181.3 | 1 766 | D | D | D | 388 | 11 961 | 3 985.5 | 442.8 |
| Salinas | 132 | 613 | 152.1 | 18.8 | 221 | D | D | D | 102 | 3 523 | 1 232.1 | 124.9 |
| San Bernardino | 143 | 704 | 112.9 | 20.1 | 264 | D | D | D | 131 | 3 008 | 837.0 | 115.1 |
| San Bruno | 33 | 284 | 35.7 | 8.3 | 69 | 509 | 93.1 | 46.5 | NA | NA | NA | NA |
| San Buenaventura (Ven-tura) | 196 | 1 134 | 168.1 | 32.7 | 493 | D | D | D | 162 | 2 579 | 457.1 | 108.9 |
| San Carlos | 74 | 271 | 74.3 | 14.4 | 216 | D | D | D | 121 | 2 443 | 846.7 | 134.7 |
| San Clemente | 122 | 486 | 449.9 | 34.6 | 372 | 1 843 | 270.9 | 112.3 | 97 | 1 844 | 431.5 | 86.3 |
| San Diego | 2 902 | 20 071 | 4 600.7 | 905.2 | 7 038 | 90 341 | 15 331.3 | 6 345.2 | 1 213 | 45 502 | 12 989.0 | 2 520.1 |
| San Dimas | 67 | 560 | 70.5 | 14.1 | 144 | 1 959 | 343.6 | 94.5 | 85 | 1 805 | 1 850.9 | 74.6 |

1. Establishments subject to federal tax.

| City | Accommodation and food services, 2007 | | | | Arts, entertainment, and recreation,[1] 2007 | | | | Health care and social assistance,[1] 2007 | | | |
|---|---|---|---|---|---|---|---|---|---|---|---|---|
| | Number of establishments | Number of employees | Sales (mil dol) | Annual payroll (mil dol) | Number of establishments | Number of employees | Receipts (mil dol) | Annual payroll (mil dol) | Number of establishments | Number of employees | Receipts (mil dol) | Annual payroll (mil dol) |
| | 92 | 93 | 94 | 95 | 96 | 97 | 98 | 99 | 100 | 101 | 102 | 103 |
| **CALIFORNIA—Cont'd** | | | | | | | | | | | | |
| Menlo Park | 96 | 1 375 | 92.0 | 28.9 | 21 | 112 | 10.0 | 3.4 | 111 | 910 | 94.0 | 43.0 |
| Merced | 139 | 2 582 | 104.9 | 26.4 | 9 | D | D | D | 241 | 2 195 | 218.1 | 80.2 |
| Milpitas | 259 | 4 520 | 278.8 | 76.6 | 23 | D | D | D | 173 | 1 390 | 227.8 | 62.0 |
| Mission Viejo | 187 | 2 980 | 148.4 | 42.3 | 25 | D | D | D | 397 | D | D | D |
| Modesto | 416 | 7 813 | 338.5 | 95.4 | 30 | 585 | 27.3 | 7.9 | 616 | 10 051 | 1 245.5 | 477.3 |
| Monrovia | 92 | 1 770 | 91.1 | 25.6 | 19 | D | D | D | 75 | 1 045 | 155.8 | 77.7 |
| Montclair | 89 | 1 881 | 84.3 | 23.9 | 5 | D | D | D | 81 | 1 379 | 131.1 | 52.6 |
| Montebello | 124 | 1 796 | 97.0 | 25.0 | 7 | D | D | D | 172 | D | D | D |
| Monterey | 216 | 5 359 | 374.3 | 113.1 | 23 | D | D | D | 277 | D | D | D |
| Monterey Park | 162 | 2 162 | 109.3 | 30.2 | 6 | D | D | D | 250 | 3 310 | 428.0 | 144.2 |
| Moorpark | 51 | 951 | 47.0 | 13.8 | 11 | 154 | 8.9 | 3.4 | 25 | D | D | D |
| Moreno Valley | 200 | 3 684 | 176.0 | 48.0 | 9 | D | D | D | 203 | 1 559 | 154.2 | 54.7 |
| Morgan Hill | 103 | 1 292 | 70.2 | 20.0 | 11 | D | D | D | 78 | D | D | D |
| Mountain View | 278 | 3 796 | 275.1 | 71.6 | 25 | 278 | 30.8 | 6.1 | 290 | D | D | D |
| Murrieta | 142 | 2 097 | 96.1 | 27.1 | 28 | D | D | D | 189 | D | D | D |
| Napa | 176 | 3 429 | 213.4 | 63.2 | 19 | 265 | 12.2 | 3.6 | 241 | 2 343 | 295.7 | 117.4 |
| National City | 175 | 2 429 | 132.9 | 32.8 | 6 | 96 | 8.7 | 1.9 | 136 | 1 301 | 117.5 | 38.0 |
| Newark | 139 | 1 956 | 113.3 | 30.4 | 4 | D | D | D | 65 | 351 | 40.5 | 13.4 |
| Newport Beach | 354 | 10 889 | 695.8 | 219.1 | 99 | 1 175 | 123.8 | 38.7 | 777 | D | D | D |
| Norco | 75 | 1 125 | 57.5 | 14.8 | 6 | D | D | D | 32 | 272 | 26.0 | 9.8 |
| Norwalk | 137 | 1 805 | 89.4 | 22.3 | 7 | 327 | 11.0 | 3.8 | 125 | D | D | D |
| Novato | 115 | 1 834 | 93.0 | 26.6 | 21 | D | D | D | 146 | 1 267 | 174.3 | 65.0 |
| Oakland | 826 | 11 240 | 749.5 | 200.1 | 77 | 1 953 | 350.4 | 203.5 | 892 | 11 401 | 1 454.0 | 755.9 |
| Oakley | 24 | 295 | 15.4 | 3.5 | 6 | D | D | D | 18 | D | D | D |
| Oceanside | 294 | 4 866 | 243.4 | 66.3 | 36 | 862 | 57.4 | 16.3 | 249 | 2 099 | 232.3 | 78.5 |
| Ontario | 309 | 7 496 | 417.5 | 112.7 | 29 | 547 | 45.5 | 11.0 | 181 | 2 562 | 232.1 | 86.0 |
| Orange | 364 | 7 252 | 390.7 | 102.7 | 47 | D | D | D | 603 | 7 938 | 945.9 | 402.6 |
| Oxnard | 266 | 4 962 | 225.8 | 58.4 | 28 | 542 | 38.4 | 11.1 | 391 | 3 732 | 404.5 | 151.1 |
| Pacifica | 70 | 667 | 37.1 | 9.5 | 11 | 121 | 4.6 | 1.4 | 40 | D | D | D |
| Palmdale | 177 | 3 649 | 181.9 | 50.5 | 14 | D | D | D | 158 | 1 293 | 128.1 | 45.3 |
| Palm Desert | 196 | 5 865 | 321.5 | 98.0 | 34 | 1 171 | 88.1 | 27.9 | 193 | 1 730 | 186.4 | 66.9 |
| Palm Springs | 252 | 4 927 | 298.3 | 88.8 | 31 | 1 398 | 221.0 | 36.7 | 244 | 4 290 | 633.4 | 200.8 |
| Palo Alto | 271 | 5 585 | 348.6 | 107.0 | 24 | 458 | 18.4 | 6.6 | 333 | D | D | D |
| Paradise | 44 | 546 | 21.4 | 6.7 | 7 | D | D | D | 99 | D | D | D |
| Paramount | 80 | 706 | 41.8 | 9.6 | 3 | 29 | 2.1 | 0.5 | 83 | D | D | D |
| Pasadena | 449 | 10 635 | 623.8 | 182.1 | 137 | 1 009 | 107.9 | 40.3 | 720 | 9 243 | 1 140.8 | 431.9 |
| Perris | 62 | 906 | 52.7 | 11.4 | 5 | D | D | D | 40 | 256 | 35.6 | 14.1 |
| Petaluma | 169 | 2 351 | 132.5 | 36.0 | 31 | D | D | D | 174 | 1 602 | 195.5 | 63.8 |
| Pico Rivera | 105 | 1 467 | 81.5 | 20.7 | 3 | D | D | D | 73 | 867 | 68.2 | 25.9 |
| Pittsburg | 82 | 1 331 | 69.9 | 18.6 | 3 | D | D | D | 65 | 576 | 48.0 | 22.1 |
| Placentia | 106 | 1 359 | 74.3 | 18.0 | 9 | D | D | D | 99 | 1 365 | 130.9 | 51.6 |
| Pleasant Hill | 80 | 1 507 | 89.3 | 23.0 | 15 | 184 | 11.5 | 4.3 | 109 | 1 173 | 88.0 | 34.7 |
| Pleasanton | 230 | 4 001 | 242.3 | 67.8 | 35 | 827 | 59.3 | 22.5 | 257 | 2 449 | 436.5 | 135.5 |
| Pomona | 202 | 3 080 | 165.7 | 43.7 | 15 | D | D | D | 261 | 3 419 | 318.8 | 119.2 |
| Porterville | 77 | 1 176 | 48.8 | 13.6 | 6 | D | D | D | 132 | 1 451 | 113.3 | 41.5 |
| Poway | 109 | 1 692 | 81.7 | 21.8 | 30 | D | D | D | 139 | D | D | D |
| Rancho Cordova | 136 | 1 756 | 95.5 | 23.6 | 11 | 164 | 9.2 | 2.1 | 84 | D | D | D |
| Rancho Cucamonga | 315 | 6 865 | 341.0 | 94.7 | 32 | D | D | D | 285 | 3 533 | 296.7 | 109.6 |
| Rancho Palos Verdes | 53 | D | D | D | 12 | D | D | D | 99 | D | D | D |
| Rancho Santa Margarita | 90 | 1 795 | 86.1 | 25.3 | 23 | D | D | D | 94 | D | D | D |
| Redding | 256 | 4 780 | 220.6 | 59.6 | 24 | D | D | D | 467 | 4 993 | 487.2 | 188.5 |
| Redlands | 173 | 3 330 | 160.5 | 45.8 | 22 | D | D | D | 242 | 2 509 | 353.7 | 106.8 |
| Redondo Beach | 188 | 3 470 | 196.2 | 57.0 | 39 | D | D | D | 184 | 1 080 | 187.4 | 53.8 |
| Redwood City | 226 | 3 120 | 214.5 | 58.0 | 24 | 550 | 33.7 | 10.5 | 249 | 2 861 | 454.6 | 206.5 |
| Rialto | 96 | 1 424 | 68.7 | 18.1 | 6 | D | D | D | 100 | 967 | 65.3 | 24.6 |
| Richmond | 128 | 1 199 | 64.5 | 16.6 | 24 | D | D | D | 137 | 2 358 | 292.7 | 133.4 |
| Ridgecrest | 55 | 897 | 45.5 | 12.1 | 4 | D | D | D | 51 | D | D | D |
| Riverside | 531 | 9 412 | 456.5 | 129.8 | 51 | 830 | 46.3 | 12.1 | 693 | 11 292 | 1 314.8 | 526.5 |
| Rocklin | 104 | 1 631 | 71.4 | 21.0 | 15 | D | D | D | 119 | D | D | D |
| Rohnert Park | 97 | 1 862 | 94.9 | 26.5 | 13 | D | D | D | 77 | 708 | 81.4 | 23.3 |
| Rosemead | 130 | 1 733 | 87.6 | 24.2 | 5 | 130 | 17.5 | 2.8 | 109 | D | D | D |
| Roseville | 333 | 7 021 | 344.2 | 97.8 | 31 | 839 | 38.5 | 11.7 | 377 | 5 257 | 807.8 | 302.2 |
| Sacramento | 1 055 | 19 705 | 1 021.4 | 294.9 | 90 | 2 939 | 327.9 | 106.1 | 1 025 | 13 515 | 1 875.7 | 756.7 |
| Salinas | 268 | 3 602 | 190.0 | 49.7 | 12 | 160 | 16.9 | 3.2 | 289 | 2 817 | 332.7 | 125.4 |
| San Bernardino | 343 | 6 514 | 330.5 | 87.1 | 27 | D | D | D | 356 | 4 923 | 421.0 | 165.9 |
| San Bruno | 104 | 1 427 | 83.3 | 23.0 | 7 | D | D | D | 66 | 648 | 112.5 | 26.5 |
| San Buenaventura (Ventura) | 333 | 5 799 | 309.8 | 87.1 | 50 | 764 | 41.5 | 11.6 | 442 | 3 917 | 406.7 | 162.4 |
| San Carlos | 87 | 919 | 57.2 | 16.5 | 8 | 10 | 1.6 | 0.4 | 90 | 523 | 46.9 | 17.7 |
| San Clemente | 158 | 2 374 | 122.4 | 31.1 | 28 | D | D | D | 185 | 981 | 111.1 | 37.6 |
| San Diego | 3 345 | 77 459 | 5 154.5 | 1 402.6 | 422 | 9 206 | 988.9 | 403.7 | 3 258 | 34 412 | 4 510.9 | 1 730.2 |
| San Dimas | 69 | 1 208 | 64.7 | 15.1 | 12 | 261 | 31.8 | 6.6 | 100 | D | D | D |

1. Establishments subject to federal tax.

## Table D. Cities — Other Services and Federal Funds

| City | Other services[1], 2007 | | | | Selected federal funds, 2009–2010 (mil dol) | | | | | | | | |
| | | | | | Procurement contracts | | Grants | | | | | | |
| | Number of establish-ments | Number of employees | Receipts (mil dol) | Annual payroll (mil dol) | Defense | Other | Total[2] | Medicaid and other health related | Nutrition and family welfare | Energy and envi-ronment | Disasters and emergency prepared-ness | Housing and community develop-ment | Employment and training |
| | 104 | 105 | 106 | 107 | 108 | 109 | 110 | 111 | 112 | 113 | 114 | 115 | 116 |
| CALIFORNIA—Cont'd | | | | | | | | | | | | | |
| Menlo Park | 60 | D | D | D | 115.3 | 390.8 | 90.9 | 31.9 | 0.0 | 30.5 | 0.0 | 0.0 | 0.0 |
| Merced | 67 | 343 | 28.9 | 8.7 | 0.0 | 2.4 | 66.1 | 12.0 | 8.7 | 1.6 | 0.0 | 22.0 | 0.0 |
| Milpitas | 99 | 1 017 | 172.5 | 35.0 | 8.7 | 31.6 | 4.8 | 0.0 | 0.0 | 4.0 | 0.0 | 0.7 | 0.0 |
| Mission Viejo | 156 | 972 | 89.8 | 24.5 | 1.7 | 2.9 | 4.0 | 0.0 | 0.2 | 0.9 | 0.0 | 0.5 | 0.0 |
| Modesto | 258 | 1 621 | 130.7 | 38.0 | 7.8 | 3.1 | 117.6 | 0.0 | 43.0 | 3.8 | 1.8 | 61.3 | 0.0 |
| Monrovia | 70 | 465 | 71.3 | 11.1 | 191.1 | 3.3 | 4.4 | 0.2 | 0.0 | 0.0 | 0.0 | 0.0 | 0.0 |
| Montclair | 76 | D | D | D | 1.6 | 1.4 | 0.1 | 0.0 | 0.0 | 0.0 | 0.0 | 0.1 | 0.0 |
| Montebello | 90 | 694 | 48.6 | 16.3 | 0.6 | 13.8 | 7.1 | 0.0 | 0.0 | 0.6 | 0.0 | 0.3 | 0.0 |
| Monterey | 60 | 484 | 31.3 | 11.5 | 253.3 | 55.1 | 15.9 | 0.0 | 0.3 | 1.2 | 0.0 | 0.8 | 0.0 |
| Monterey Park | 72 | D | D | D | 5.2 | 9.3 | 496.2 | 1.1 | 0.0 | 0.0 | 0.0 | 320.2 | 0.2 |
| Moorpark | 16 | 110 | 8.9 | 2.8 | 25.9 | 0.1 | 2.9 | 0.0 | 0.0 | 0.0 | 0.0 | 0.0 | 0.0 |
| Moreno Valley | 120 | 619 | 43.7 | 12.6 | 0.2 | 1.1 | 9.3 | 0.5 | 0.0 | 1.7 | 0.0 | 4.4 | 0.0 |
| Morgan Hill | 66 | 341 | 35.2 | 10.8 | 5.0 | 0.0 | 0.0 | 0.0 | 0.0 | 0.0 | 0.0 | 0.0 | 0.0 |
| Mountain View | 154 | 944 | 113.8 | 32.0 | 49.8 | 89.6 | 26.5 | 10.3 | 0.0 | 2.8 | 0.0 | 1.2 | 0.0 |
| Murrieta | 143 | 862 | 78.0 | 21.9 | 3.6 | 0.2 | 1.3 | 0.0 | 0.0 | 0.9 | 0.0 | 0.0 | 0.0 |
| Napa | 127 | 681 | 64.3 | 22.7 | 24.4 | 3.9 | 31.9 | 0.9 | 9.1 | 0.5 | 0.0 | 12.2 | 0.0 |
| National City | 119 | 698 | 60.9 | 20.3 | 8.8 | 0.9 | 25.3 | 0.0 | 13.9 | 0.0 | 0.0 | 11.1 | 0.0 |
| Newark | 61 | D | D | D | 0.3 | 73.4 | 1.2 | 0.2 | 0.0 | 0.0 | 0.0 | 0.0 | 0.0 |
| Newport Beach | 197 | 1 320 | 115.4 | 33.3 | 10.2 | 6.1 | 1.2 | 0.0 | 0.0 | 0.0 | 0.0 | 0.9 | 0.0 |
| Norco | 54 | 309 | 38.1 | 8.2 | 67.4 | 0.7 | 8.1 | 0.0 | 0.0 | 0.8 | 0.0 | 0.0 | 0.0 |
| Norwalk | 67 | 338 | 30.9 | 7.9 | 5.7 | 2.1 | 16.8 | 0.0 | 0.0 | 0.0 | 0.0 | 11.6 | 0.0 |
| Novato | 91 | 671 | 86.1 | 28.5 | 14.3 | 8.3 | 29.1 | 27.5 | 0.0 | 0.4 | 0.0 | 0.7 | 0.0 |
| Oakland | 600 | 3 665 | 318.9 | 93.0 | 156.1 | 110.4 | 695.2 | 171.2 | 16.7 | 10.3 | -0.2 | 236.4 | 7.8 |
| Oakley | 22 | D | D | D | 0.0 | 12.7 | 0.1 | 0.0 | 0.0 | 0.0 | 0.0 | 0.1 | 0.0 |
| Oceanside | 184 | 1 195 | 100.1 | 30.5 | 11.3 | 2.0 | 55.4 | 0.0 | 0.0 | 0.0 | 0.0 | 17.7 | 0.0 |
| Ontario | 212 | 2 110 | 192.3 | 62.0 | 14.3 | 4.7 | 9.0 | 0.3 | 0.0 | 1.5 | 1.4 | 4.4 | 0.0 |
| Orange | 289 | 1 813 | 158.1 | 43.5 | 35.0 | 4.6 | 54.7 | 2.5 | 0.0 | 4.6 | 0.0 | 2.4 | 0.0 |
| Oxnard | 179 | 947 | 91.2 | 24.9 | 24.0 | 40.6 | 66.6 | 0.0 | 11.1 | 22.5 | 0.0 | 25.1 | 0.0 |
| Pacifica | 36 | 127 | 10.8 | 3.2 | 1.1 | 0.1 | 4.4 | 0.0 | 0.0 | 4.4 | 0.0 | 0.0 | 0.0 |
| Palmdale | 109 | 615 | 48.4 | 12.0 | 804.4 | 5.9 | 9.3 | 0.0 | 0.0 | 1.2 | 0.0 | 3.9 | 0.2 |
| Palm Desert | 118 | 796 | 54.3 | 17.7 | 0.3 | 0.4 | 3.5 | 0.0 | 0.0 | 0.2 | 0.0 | 0.9 | 0.0 |
| Palm Springs | 76 | 372 | 29.7 | 9.6 | 5.8 | 4.0 | 2.8 | 0.1 | 0.1 | 0.5 | 0.0 | 0.5 | 0.0 |
| Palo Alto | 102 | 974 | 86.7 | 30.2 | 115.2 | 300.6 | 153.1 | 29.2 | 0.0 | 16.6 | 0.0 | 1.1 | 0.0 |
| Paradise | 37 | 121 | 13.5 | 3.0 | 0.0 | 0.0 | 1.9 | 0.0 | 0.0 | 0.0 | 0.0 | 0.2 | 0.0 |
| Paramount | 65 | 684 | 80.6 | 26.6 | 1.2 | 0.3 | 4.0 | 0.0 | 0.0 | 0.3 | 0.0 | 3.7 | 0.0 |
| Pasadena | 305 | 2 180 | 374.8 | 77.3 | 71.5 | 25.2 | 357.5 | 123.7 | 11.5 | 39.8 | 0.0 | 20.1 | 10.0 |
| Perris | 29 | D | D | D | 0.4 | 2.7 | 11.7 | 0.0 | 0.0 | 11.6 | 0.0 | 0.0 | 0.0 |
| Petaluma | 104 | 543 | 48.1 | 15.2 | 8.8 | 16.5 | 11.5 | 1.3 | 0.0 | 3.6 | 0.0 | 0.6 | 0.0 |
| Pico Rivera | 69 | 685 | 56.6 | 17.2 | 1.1 | 0.0 | 9.1 | 0.0 | 0.0 | 0.0 | 0.0 | 6.6 | 0.0 |
| Pittsburg | 61 | 347 | 31.0 | 9.1 | -0.6 | 0.2 | 17.9 | 0.6 | 0.0 | 0.0 | 0.0 | 16.7 | 0.0 |
| Placentia | 69 | 419 | 32.3 | 9.7 | 6.0 | 4.5 | 58.8 | 0.0 | 0.0 | 0.2 | 0.0 | 0.0 | 0.0 |
| Pleasant Hill | 43 | 281 | 20.5 | 5.9 | 0.0 | 0.2 | 0.6 | 0.0 | 0.0 | 0.0 | 0.0 | 0.2 | 0.0 |
| Pleasanton | 133 | 834 | 91.4 | 29.9 | 6.0 | 7.7 | 6.3 | 1.4 | 0.0 | 3.6 | 0.0 | 0.4 | 0.0 |
| Pomona | 148 | 923 | 85.0 | 25.4 | 11.8 | 9.8 | 28.9 | 5.2 | 0.0 | 1.5 | 0.0 | 16.3 | 0.0 |
| Porterville | 38 | 230 | 17.0 | 10.4 | 3.0 | 8.3 | 16.4 | 6.3 | 0.0 | 0.7 | 0.0 | 5.0 | 0.1 |
| Poway | 91 | 562 | 43.2 | 13.0 | 1 275.1 | 29.7 | 0.2 | 0.1 | 0.0 | 0.0 | 0.0 | 0.0 | 0.0 |
| Rancho Cordova | 79 | 394 | 34.9 | 11.2 | 2 999.6 | 15.8 | 82.7 | 0.5 | 9.6 | 42.5 | 0.0 | 0.9 | 0.0 |
| Rancho Cucamonga | 209 | 1 245 | 150.7 | 37.9 | 83.6 | 3.1 | 6.3 | 0.5 | 0.0 | 1.6 | 0.0 | 2.1 | 0.0 |
| Rancho Palos Verdes | 31 | 221 | 31.6 | 9.1 | 1.1 | 0.0 | 0.4 | 0.0 | 0.0 | 0.4 | 0.0 | 0.0 | 0.0 |
| Rancho Santa Marga-rita | 47 | 408 | 27.7 | 8.1 | 4.0 | 0.6 | 0.3 | 0.0 | 0.0 | 0.0 | 0.0 | 0.3 | 0.0 |
| Redding | 195 | 1 095 | 90.5 | 27.9 | 3.7 | 18.2 | 48.4 | 5.1 | 11.7 | 1.7 | 0.0 | 15.3 | 0.0 |
| Redlands | 102 | 606 | 42.2 | 12.8 | 28.0 | 12.0 | 4.4 | 0.5 | 0.1 | 1.3 | 0.0 | 1.3 | 0.0 |
| Redondo Beach | 124 | 846 | 145.3 | 28.7 | 815.6 | 9.2 | 7.9 | 0.0 | 0.0 | 0.0 | 0.0 | 6.6 | 0.0 |
| Redwood City | 123 | 1 049 | 247.6 | 43.6 | 20.1 | 22.4 | 23.7 | -0.9 | 0.1 | 10.6 | 0.0 | 4.7 | 0.0 |
| Rialto | 73 | 331 | 41.5 | 9.9 | 0.3 | 0.1 | 3.2 | 0.0 | 0.0 | 1.5 | 0.0 | 1.4 | 0.0 |
| Richmond | 86 | 406 | 45.6 | 13.2 | 10.3 | 265.9 | 26.3 | -0.1 | 0.0 | 1.2 | 0.0 | 23.5 | 0.5 |
| Ridgecrest | 30 | 150 | 11.8 | 3.3 | 26.4 | 1.4 | 1.7 | 0.0 | 0.0 | 0.2 | 0.0 | 0.0 | 0.0 |
| Riverside | 396 | 2 521 | 214.2 | 67.0 | 4.7 | 29.7 | 264.7 | 34.3 | 37.8 | 18.0 | 0.7 | 103.8 | 0.0 |
| Rocklin | 72 | D | D | D | 6.6 | 1.6 | 0.8 | 0.0 | 0.0 | 0.0 | 0.0 | 0.4 | 0.0 |
| Rohnert Park | 50 | 299 | 26.6 | 7.9 | 0.4 | 4.9 | 5.4 | 0.0 | -0.1 | 1.4 | 0.0 | 1.2 | 0.0 |
| Rosemead | 92 | 374 | 30.7 | 6.8 | 15.5 | 4.7 | 66.4 | 0.0 | 0.0 | 65.1 | 0.0 | 1.2 | 0.0 |
| Roseville | 172 | D | D | D | 3.2 | 3.8 | 7.3 | 0.0 | 0.0 | 0.0 | 0.0 | 5.2 | 0.0 |
| Sacramento | 627 | 4 186 | 392.7 | 116.6 | 68.3 | 89.3 | 9 252.3 | 776.5 | 2 433.3 | 603.2 | 19.9 | 274.6 | 1 167.3 |
| Salinas | 157 | 1 027 | 103.9 | 28.1 | 41.4 | 4.0 | 78.4 | 3.9 | 12.6 | 3.7 | 0.0 | 44.8 | 0.0 |
| San Bernardino | 209 | 1 287 | 113.9 | 31.6 | 61.8 | 18.4 | 222.1 | 15.2 | 35.4 | 14.9 | 0.0 | 96.1 | 4.4 |
| San Bruno | 56 | 259 | 31.4 | 9.4 | 38.6 | 10.4 | 1.2 | 0.0 | 0.0 | 0.2 | 0.0 | 0.0 | 0.0 |
| San Buenaventura (Ven-tura) | 194 | 1 086 | 104.6 | 29.4 | 36.2 | 28.0 | 22.3 | 0.0 | 0.0 | 1.4 | 0.0 | 18.6 | 0.0 |
| San Carlos | 95 | 778 | 71.7 | 26.6 | 14.8 | 66.7 | 45.2 | 0.2 | 0.3 | 0.0 | 0.0 | 0.0 | 0.0 |
| San Clemente | 86 | 454 | 34.0 | 9.5 | 9.8 | 3.9 | 2.4 | 0.1 | 0.0 | 0.3 | 0.0 | 1.7 | 0.0 |
| San Diego | 1 982 | 13 678 | 1 183.4 | 360.3 | 4 772.4 | 897.1 | 2 736.8 | 1 750.2 | 83.0 | 234.4 | 0.3 | 321.2 | 8.8 |
| San Dimas | 55 | D | D | D | 2.3 | 6.6 | 0.0 | 0.0 | 0.0 | 0.0 | 0.0 | 0.0 | 0.0 |

1. Establishments subject to federal tax.    2. Includes program categories not shown separately. State totals include additional categories not allocated by city.

## Table D. Cities — City Government Finances

| City | General revenue Total (mil dol) | Intergovernmental Total (mil dol) | Intergovernmental Percent from state government | Taxes Total (mil dol) | Taxes Per capita[1] (dollars) Total | Taxes Per capita[1] (dollars) Property | Taxes Per capita[1] (dollars) Sales and gross receipts | General expenditure Total (mil dol) | General expenditure Per capita[1] (dollars) Total | General expenditure Per capita[1] (dollars) Capital outlays |
|---|---|---|---|---|---|---|---|---|---|---|
| | 117 | 118 | 119 | 120 | 121 | 122 | 123 | 124 | 125 | 126 |
| **CALIFORNIA—Cont'd** | | | | | | | | | | |
| Menlo Park | 62.6 | 3.5 | 90.6 | 36.1 | 1 206 | 775 | 412 | 47.1 | 1 571 | 217 |
| Merced | 108.6 | 10.3 | 68.7 | 42.9 | 558 | 308 | 238 | 115.0 | 1 495 | 409 |
| Milpitas | 143.3 | 5.0 | 55.3 | 78.4 | 1 174 | 744 | 424 | 156.7 | 2 347 | 667 |
| Mission Viejo | 76.4 | 8.9 | 57.3 | 58.0 | 613 | 378 | 230 | 82.3 | 870 | 184 |
| Modesto | 234.2 | 22.6 | 50.1 | 128.3 | 629 | 211 | 414 | 231.2 | 1 134 | 232 |
| Monrovia | 50.8 | 7.3 | 94.2 | 32.8 | 872 | 552 | 311 | 54.4 | 1 447 | 277 |
| Montclair | 52.4 | 5.7 | 82.3 | 36.5 | 1 004 | 538 | 462 | 62.8 | 1 728 | 719 |
| Montebello | 99.7 | 18.4 | 78.0 | 59.7 | 959 | 482 | 460 | 71.4 | 1 146 | 260 |
| Monterey | 88.5 | 4.3 | 88.5 | 43.4 | 1 525 | 513 | 1 004 | 89.2 | 3 131 | 447 |
| Monterey Park | 64.6 | 9.0 | 56.3 | 38.3 | 622 | 386 | 230 | 61.9 | 1 007 | 142 |
| Moorpark | 39.5 | 2.0 | 79.2 | 22.9 | 633 | 351 | 143 | 33.0 | 913 | 253 |
| Moreno Valley | 162.5 | 16.2 | 80.0 | 83.0 | 440 | 207 | 225 | 141.5 | 749 | 94 |
| Morgan Hill | 81.5 | 5.1 | 43.2 | 49.5 | 1 317 | 940 | 219 | 85.1 | 2 263 | 1 247 |
| Mountain View | 165.0 | 5.4 | 80.7 | 91.7 | 1 302 | 765 | 408 | 167.2 | 2 374 | 524 |
| Murrieta | 85.7 | 8.6 | 99.9 | 49.9 | 551 | 299 | 244 | 140.2 | 1 548 | 983 |
| Napa | 110.9 | 18.5 | 35.5 | 57.8 | 779 | 385 | 388 | 101.0 | 1 360 | 239 |
| National City | 80.9 | 18.9 | 31.7 | 46.8 | 796 | 443 | 347 | 77.1 | 1 312 | 355 |
| Newark | 41.0 | 2.6 | 89.1 | 30.6 | 733 | 346 | 374 | 43.8 | 1 050 | 60 |
| Newport Beach | 173.5 | 10.9 | 85.9 | 119.9 | 1 507 | 931 | 576 | 179.5 | 2 257 | 532 |
| Norco | 48.6 | 2.9 | 99.0 | 27.9 | 1 036 | 756 | 231 | 57.3 | 2 128 | 766 |
| Norwalk | 84.6 | 23.1 | 40.0 | 51.2 | 493 | 238 | 253 | 78.8 | 760 | 93 |
| Novato | 52.1 | 3.5 | 76.9 | 34.4 | 660 | 444 | 194 | 53.7 | 1 030 | 268 |
| Oakland | 1 265.9 | 166.6 | 49.0 | 588.4 | 1 466 | 796 | 439 | 1 509.3 | 3 759 | 1 206 |
| Oakley | 36.9 | 2.3 | 70.0 | 21.2 | 696 | 300 | 146 | 44.7 | 1 469 | 786 |
| Oceanside | 237.2 | 38.5 | 100.0 | 102.1 | 605 | 386 | 214 | 231.7 | 1 374 | 188 |
| Ontario | 369.2 | 21.7 | 80.2 | 188.9 | 1 105 | 553 | 547 | 301.1 | 1 761 | 313 |
| Orange | 157.1 | 16.7 | 89.8 | 104.8 | 781 | 430 | 342 | 148.7 | 1 107 | 283 |
| Oxnard | 289.6 | 27.5 | 89.2 | 113.3 | 613 | 401 | 207 | 350.5 | 1 897 | 646 |
| Pacifica | 39.2 | 3.2 | 97.9 | 19.6 | 526 | 347 | 170 | 42.2 | 1 131 | 23 |
| Palmdale | 174.9 | 18.7 | 88.7 | 125.5 | 891 | 473 | 241 | 158.1 | 1 122 | 131 |
| Palm Desert | 210.6 | 3.5 | 73.8 | 133.0 | 2 621 | 1 894 | 713 | 242.2 | 4 774 | 1 985 |
| Palm Springs | 157.2 | 27.1 | 17.6 | 80.3 | 1 677 | 825 | 772 | 153.1 | 3 195 | 746 |
| Palo Alto | 199.2 | 6.5 | 49.6 | 70.3 | 1 206 | 463 | 642 | 205.0 | 3 519 | 469 |
| Paradise | 14.6 | 3.5 | 96.6 | 9.2 | 348 | 259 | 77 | 17.5 | 660 | 172 |
| Paramount | 43.9 | 6.6 | 77.8 | 31.3 | 563 | 324 | 236 | 38.0 | 683 | 112 |
| Pasadena | 367.4 | 41.2 | 70.0 | 175.7 | 1 225 | 558 | 659 | 372.0 | 2 594 | 619 |
| Perris | 79.4 | 2.4 | 92.9 | 48.2 | 899 | 395 | 494 | 63.2 | 1 179 | 350 |
| Petaluma | 107.2 | 9.6 | 75.3 | 49.5 | 909 | 530 | 356 | 154.9 | 2 842 | 1 593 |
| Pico Rivera | 52.2 | 12.2 | 54.3 | 31.0 | 489 | 259 | 228 | 52.8 | 832 | 48 |
| Pittsburg | 129.9 | 15.0 | 89.4 | 67.8 | 1 085 | 916 | 164 | 170.6 | 2 729 | 864 |
| Placentia | 36.0 | 3.6 | 95.8 | 24.7 | 497 | 291 | 200 | 41.8 | 842 | 61 |
| Pleasant Hill | 30.7 | 2.2 | 79.7 | 24.3 | 744 | 372 | 347 | 28.0 | 857 | 133 |
| Pleasanton | 146.5 | 5.6 | 81.9 | 79.8 | 1 199 | 771 | 415 | 140.9 | 2 117 | 362 |
| Pomona | 176.5 | 28.6 | 37.3 | 107.9 | 707 | 377 | 316 | 185.7 | 1 217 | 217 |
| Porterville | 52.0 | 7.9 | 77.1 | 24.0 | 466 | 149 | 233 | 46.9 | 910 | 206 |
| Poway | 106.9 | 2.7 | 90.8 | 67.2 | 1 379 | 1 045 | 298 | 104.2 | 2 140 | 439 |
| Rancho Cordova | 76.9 | 3.5 | 97.7 | 62.6 | 1 027 | 262 | 758 | 59.5 | 976 | 300 |
| Rancho Cucamonga | 243.3 | 9.9 | 82.8 | 180.5 | 1 060 | 797 | 255 | 190.1 | 1 117 | 196 |
| Rancho Palos Verdes | 26.8 | 2.4 | 89.8 | 18.6 | 449 | 249 | 192 | 24.5 | 591 | 92 |
| Rancho Santa Marga-rita | 19.7 | 2.8 | 85.7 | 15.0 | 302 | 149 | 146 | 17.5 | 352 | 91 |
| Redding | 184.9 | 35.8 | 37.7 | 71.7 | 799 | 400 | 330 | 189.2 | 2 108 | 861 |
| Redlands | 108.3 | 15.7 | 70.3 | 55.0 | 787 | 406 | 374 | 96.9 | 1 386 | 288 |
| Redondo Beach | 101.1 | 6.9 | 83.1 | 58.8 | 878 | 424 | 408 | 99.3 | 1 482 | 83 |
| Redwood City | 134.3 | 11.5 | 89.3 | 78.5 | 1 066 | 608 | 448 | 156.8 | 2 130 | 603 |
| Rialto | 112.6 | 7.7 | 73.1 | 66.6 | 675 | 356 | 315 | 119.8 | 1 213 | 406 |
| Richmond | 224.2 | 39.6 | 32.3 | 135.1 | 1 331 | 744 | 516 | 227.8 | 2 245 | 363 |
| Ridgecrest | 24.6 | 1.6 | 96.5 | 15.0 | 590 | 363 | 222 | 17.6 | 691 | 159 |
| Riverside | 412.5 | 39.4 | 67.5 | 226.5 | 769 | 421 | 335 | 544.4 | 1 849 | 677 |
| Rocklin | 73.4 | 8.9 | 71.5 | 38.9 | 754 | 351 | 241 | 79.6 | 1 542 | 310 |
| Rohnert Park | 63.6 | 2.1 | 100.0 | 31.5 | 777 | 527 | 246 | 85.2 | 2 102 | 457 |
| Rosemead | 30.6 | 3.1 | 69.2 | 17.4 | 318 | 156 | 127 | 25.2 | 461 | 79 |
| Roseville | 423.8 | 25.2 | 79.0 | 104.8 | 964 | 461 | 494 | 382.7 | 3 519 | 1 569 |
| Sacramento | 901.1 | 92.5 | 90.2 | 408.3 | 887 | 416 | 444 | 1 046.7 | 2 274 | 763 |
| Salinas | 131.3 | 19.9 | 57.6 | 91.1 | 635 | 260 | 372 | 125.5 | 875 | 185 |
| San Bernardino | 266.7 | 30.8 | 58.0 | 146.4 | 734 | 339 | 386 | 247.6 | 1 242 | 125 |
| San Bruno | 49.3 | 2.6 | 100.0 | 23.6 | 591 | 276 | 299 | 56.1 | 1 402 | 77 |
| San Buenaventura (Ventura) | 131.0 | 11.2 | 80.7 | 74.4 | 721 | 305 | 411 | 129.0 | 1 250 | 213 |
| San Carlos | 41.3 | 3.4 | 100.0 | 23.5 | 871 | 543 | 316 | 37.8 | 1 401 | 187 |
| San Clemente | 84.9 | 8.7 | 63.3 | 41.3 | 675 | 427 | 236 | 79.3 | 1 295 | 454 |
| San Diego | 2 537.8 | 375.5 | 42.5 | 1 242.6 | 981 | 532 | 399 | 2 069.4 | 1 634 | 236 |
| San Dimas | 33.6 | 2.7 | 64.2 | 24.0 | 681 | 371 | 305 | 39.7 | 1 125 | 225 |

1. Based on population estimated as of July 1 of the year shown.

| City | Public welfare | Highways | Parking facilities | Education | Health and hospitals | Police protection | Sewerage and sanitation | Parks and recreation | Housing and community development | Interest on debt |
|---|---|---|---|---|---|---|---|---|---|---|
| | 127 | 128 | 129 | 130 | 131 | 132 | 133 | 134 | 135 | 136 |
| **CALIFORNIA—Cont'd** | | | | | | | | | | |
| Menlo Park | 0.0 | 10.2 | 1.1 | 0.0 | 0.0 | 23.7 | 4.1 | 18.1 | 11.7 | 8.0 |
| Merced | 0.0 | 11.1 | 0.0 | 0.0 | 0.3 | 18.1 | 12.2 | 17.1 | 12.3 | 2.2 |
| Milpitas | 0.0 | 5.8 | 0.0 | 0.0 | 7.6 | 12.8 | 5.4 | 4.5 | 35.7 | 6.0 |
| Mission Viejo | 0.0 | 23.1 | 0.0 | 0.0 | 1.4 | 15.5 | 0.0 | 24.7 | 5.7 | 3.1 |
| Modesto | 0.0 | 11.7 | 0.5 | 0.0 | 0.5 | 23.6 | 11.7 | 12.3 | 10.7 | 1.9 |
| Monrovia | 0.0 | 6.8 | 0.0 | 0.0 | 2.6 | 21.7 | 2.5 | 19.8 | 9.3 | 6.4 |
| Montclair | 0.0 | 7.4 | 0.0 | 0.0 | 1.0 | 32.2 | 5.8 | 2.3 | 20.7 | 4.3 |
| Montebello | 0.0 | 6.3 | 0.0 | 0.0 | 0.0 | 25.7 | 4.3 | 17.2 | 8.5 | 6.3 |
| Monterey | 0.0 | 19.0 | 5.5 | 0.0 | 0.0 | 12.4 | 2.4 | 17.0 | 2.7 | 3.5 |
| Monterey Park | 0.0 | 5.8 | 0.0 | 0.0 | 0.9 | 21.6 | 9.6 | 6.0 | 11.4 | 5.2 |
| Moorpark | 0.0 | 19.7 | 0.0 | 0.0 | 0.9 | 16.2 | 0.4 | 8.3 | 18.4 | 4.2 |
| Moreno Valley | 0.0 | 18.7 | 0.0 | 0.0 | 3.0 | 24.5 | 0.0 | 9.2 | 9.6 | 2.8 |
| Morgan Hill | 0.0 | 9.5 | 0.0 | 0.0 | 0.1 | 11.2 | 10.4 | 8.5 | 39.1 | 1.4 |
| Mountain View | 0.0 | 5.5 | 5.6 | 0.0 | 0.0 | 11.6 | 15.2 | 18.4 | 0.8 | 1.9 |
| Murrieta | 0.0 | 21.3 | 0.0 | 0.0 | 0.0 | 12.8 | 0.0 | 9.5 | 6.5 | 2.7 |
| Napa | 0.0 | 14.7 | 0.7 | 0.0 | 2.5 | 17.5 | 16.0 | 8.9 | 16.7 | 2.6 |
| National City | 0.0 | 3.3 | 0.0 | 0.0 | 0.8 | 24.3 | 8.0 | 3.9 | 24.0 | 3.8 |
| Newark | 0.0 | 12.4 | 0.0 | 0.0 | 10.0 | 31.6 | 0.5 | 16.9 | 0.5 | 1.5 |
| Newport Beach | 0.0 | 7.9 | 0.0 | 0.0 | 3.0 | 24.5 | 2.2 | 22.4 | 3.2 | 6.4 |
| Norco | 0.0 | 5.9 | 0.0 | 0.0 | 4.1 | 20.3 | 19.4 | 11.7 | 16.9 | 8.0 |
| Norwalk | 0.0 | 19.5 | 0.5 | 0.0 | 6.2 | 16.1 | 0.0 | 10.2 | 17.2 | 9.0 |
| Novato | 0.0 | 25.3 | 0.0 | 0.0 | 0.9 | 22.0 | 0.0 | 13.1 | 5.6 | 12.4 |
| Oakland | 0.0 | 4.0 | 0.7 | 0.0 | 3.7 | 12.4 | 2.3 | 2.9 | 7.9 | 8.4 |
| Oakley | 0.0 | 31.5 | 0.0 | 0.0 | 0.2 | 12.8 | 0.0 | 10.0 | 18.4 | 1.9 |
| Oceanside | 0.0 | 7.3 | 0.4 | 0.0 | 0.1 | 19.5 | 19.4 | 6.3 | 13.6 | 4.8 |
| Ontario | 0.0 | 6.6 | 0.0 | 0.0 | 0.2 | 18.7 | 11.9 | 10.9 | 9.7 | 4.1 |
| Orange | 0.0 | 13.9 | 0.0 | 0.0 | 3.9 | 23.3 | 6.6 | 6.1 | 12.1 | 2.3 |
| Oxnard | 0.0 | 10.3 | 0.2 | 0.0 | 0.0 | 18.8 | 30.1 | 13.8 | 4.5 | 5.9 |
| Pacifica | 0.0 | 11.4 | 0.0 | 0.0 | 1.1 | 22.6 | 18.9 | 9.0 | 0.5 | 2.8 |
| Palmdale | 0.0 | 14.3 | 0.0 | 0.0 | 0.4 | 11.1 | 0.0 | 9.3 | 33.8 | 9.4 |
| Palm Desert | 0.0 | 12.5 | 0.0 | 0.0 | 0.5 | 5.0 | 0.0 | 8.2 | 50.9 | 9.1 |
| Palm Springs | 0.0 | 4.5 | 0.2 | 0.0 | 0.9 | 14.5 | 3.3 | 16.2 | 4.9 | 6.3 |
| Palo Alto | 0.0 | 7.6 | 0.1 | 0.0 | 0.2 | 10.9 | 28.5 | 10.8 | 0.1 | 1.3 |
| Paradise | 0.0 | 31.8 | 0.0 | 0.0 | 0.0 | 24.6 | 2.1 | 0.0 | 2.5 | 2.0 |
| Paramount | 0.0 | 18.4 | 0.0 | 0.0 | 0.0 | 26.2 | 0.0 | 12.1 | 15.9 | 7.2 |
| Pasadena | 0.0 | 8.4 | 2.5 | 0.0 | 4.6 | 14.3 | 3.5 | 7.3 | 5.9 | 11.1 |
| Perris | 0.0 | 18.0 | 0.0 | 0.0 | 0.7 | 8.4 | 2.5 | 7.6 | 10.8 | 15.0 |
| Petaluma | 0.0 | 17.2 | 0.0 | 0.0 | 1.9 | 10.2 | 40.3 | 4.3 | 12.3 | 3.1 |
| Pico Rivera | 0.0 | 19.4 | 0.0 | 0.0 | 0.0 | 17.2 | 0.0 | 12.1 | 24.4 | 7.1 |
| Pittsburg | 0.0 | 12.9 | 0.0 | 0.0 | 0.5 | 8.3 | 2.7 | 2.2 | 52.8 | 11.7 |
| Placentia | 0.0 | 11.7 | 0.0 | 0.0 | 0.0 | 30.0 | 7.2 | 8.5 | 6.5 | 8.0 |
| Pleasant Hill | 0.0 | 24.8 | 0.0 | 0.0 | 0.4 | 37.1 | 0.3 | 0.0 | 12.3 | 3.1 |
| Pleasanton | 0.0 | 9.6 | 0.0 | 0.0 | 1.2 | 18.3 | 8.0 | 17.4 | 0.8 | 3.7 |
| Pomona | 0.0 | 10.8 | 0.0 | 0.0 | 0.2 | 30.3 | 6.9 | 3.6 | 23.0 | 6.3 |
| Porterville | 0.0 | 7.5 | 0.1 | 0.0 | 0.3 | 15.7 | 27.8 | 9.5 | 4.6 | 5.7 |
| Poway | 0.0 | 10.5 | 0.0 | 0.0 | 0.2 | 8.8 | 7.1 | 6.1 | 18.7 | 18.1 |
| Rancho Cordova | 0.0 | 2.6 | 0.0 | 0.0 | 0.7 | 23.4 | 0.0 | 0.0 | 5.2 | 1.9 |
| Rancho Cucamonga | 0.0 | 19.7 | 0.0 | 0.0 | 1.4 | 12.5 | 0.5 | 4.0 | 17.0 | 13.1 |
| Rancho Palos Verdes | 0.0 | 12.0 | 0.0 | 0.0 | 1.3 | 12.8 | 1.5 | 10.3 | 1.4 | 5.7 |
| Rancho Santa Margarita | 0.0 | 35.2 | 0.0 | 0.0 | 0.2 | 33.5 | 0.0 | 10.0 | 0.0 | 0.0 |
| Redding | 0.0 | 1.3 | 0.0 | 0.0 | 0.3 | 12.5 | 18.8 | 10.1 | 10.5 | 3.2 |
| Redlands | 0.0 | 10.2 | 0.0 | 0.0 | 3.6 | 25.2 | 18.3 | 7.7 | 4.9 | 2.0 |
| Redondo Beach | 0.0 | 7.6 | 0.0 | 0.0 | 4.0 | 25.8 | 5.7 | 5.3 | 7.6 | 2.5 |
| Redwood City | 0.0 | 12.6 | 1.3 | 0.0 | 0.5 | 17.4 | 10.6 | 6.1 | 6.7 | 4.5 |
| Rialto | 0.0 | 7.6 | 0.0 | 0.0 | 3.2 | 19.0 | 11.2 | 7.7 | 26.9 | 5.1 |
| Richmond | 0.0 | 16.7 | 0.0 | 0.0 | 0.5 | 19.4 | 4.8 | 6.9 | 21.7 | 7.8 |
| Ridgecrest | 0.0 | 27.3 | 0.0 | 0.0 | 0.0 | 34.0 | 5.4 | 12.4 | 7.3 | 2.5 |
| Riverside | 0.0 | 12.1 | 0.6 | 0.0 | 0.0 | 15.4 | 6.9 | 6.7 | 9.5 | 4.2 |
| Rocklin | 0.0 | 8.3 | 0.0 | 0.0 | 0.0 | 16.1 | 0.0 | 19.3 | 8.8 | 6.4 |
| Rohnert Park | 0.0 | 4.8 | 0.0 | 0.0 | 1.2 | 29.1 | 15.6 | 7.0 | 15.0 | 0.9 |
| Rosemead | 0.0 | 15.3 | 0.0 | 0.0 | 0.1 | 19.7 | 0.0 | 0.3 | 23.5 | 6.0 |
| Roseville | 0.0 | 29.4 | 0.0 | 0.0 | 0.0 | 7.7 | 17.9 | 7.0 | 5.8 | 7.3 |
| Sacramento | 0.0 | 11.8 | 1.4 | 0.0 | 1.5 | 12.6 | 8.3 | 9.0 | 5.5 | 10.7 |
| Salinas | 0.0 | 16.5 | 1.0 | 0.0 | 2.9 | 30.7 | 3.4 | 8.0 | 3.3 | 2.5 |
| San Bernardino | 0.0 | 9.0 | 0.0 | 0.0 | 1.2 | 23.4 | 17.2 | 3.4 | 6.9 | 6.5 |
| San Bruno | 0.0 | 7.3 | 0.0 | 0.0 | 0.0 | 18.0 | 16.2 | 7.4 | 1.3 | 0.8 |
| San Buenaventura (Ventura) | 0.0 | 13.5 | 0.0 | 0.0 | 0.9 | 24.3 | 9.9 | 11.0 | 2.3 | 2.7 |
| San Carlos | 0.0 | 6.0 | 0.0 | 0.0 | 0.0 | 20.3 | 13.0 | 13.4 | 7.7 | 2.9 |
| San Clemente | 0.0 | 18.3 | 0.0 | 0.0 | 2.4 | 12.7 | 18.8 | 19.8 | 1.2 | 2.3 |
| San Diego | 0.0 | 6.7 | 0.1 | 0.0 | 2.4 | 18.1 | 15.1 | 8.9 | 16.4 | 6.8 |
| San Dimas | 0.0 | 13.5 | 0.1 | 0.0 | 0.3 | 25.4 | 0.1 | 8.5 | 16.9 | 3.2 |

| City | City government finances, 2007 (cont.) | | | | Climate[2] | | | | | | |
| | Debt outstanding | | | | Average daily temperature (degrees Fahrenheit) | | | | | | |
| | | | | | Mean | | Limits | | | | |
| | Total (mil dol) | Per capita[1] (dollars) | Debt issued during year | City government employment, 2011 | January | July | January[3] | July[4] | Annual precipitation (inches) | Heating degree days | Cooling degree days |
| | 137 | 138 | 139 | 140 | 141 | 142 | 143 | 144 | 145 | 146 | 147 |
| CALIFORNIA—Cont'd | | | | | | | | | | | |
| Menlo Park | 93.0 | 3 103 | 0.0 | NA | 49.0 | 68.0 | 40.4 | 78.8 | 15.71 | 2 584 | 452 |
| Merced | 69.2 | 901 | 0.0 | 485 | 46.3 | 78.6 | 37.5 | 96.5 | 12.50 | 2 602 | 1 578 |
| Milpitas | 309.2 | 4 631 | 26.2 | 422 | 50.5 | 70.9 | 41.7 | 84.3 | 15.08 | 2 171 | 811 |
| Mission Viejo | 58.9 | 623 | 0.2 | 186 | 56.7 | 72.4 | 47.2 | 82.3 | 14.03 | 1 465 | 1 183 |
| Modesto | 247.7 | 1 214 | 37.3 | 1 206 | 47.2 | 77.7 | 40.1 | 93.6 | 13.12 | 2 358 | 1 570 |
| Monrovia | 82.9 | 2 206 | 19.5 | NA | 56.1 | 75.3 | 44.3 | 89.4 | 21.09 | 1 398 | 1 558 |
| Montclair | 51.2 | 1 408 | 13.4 | NA | 54.6 | 73.8 | 41.5 | 88.7 | 16.96 | 1 727 | 1 191 |
| Montebello | 83.7 | 1 344 | 8.9 | NA | 58.8 | 76.6 | 47.9 | 88.9 | 14.44 | 949 | 1 837 |
| Monterey | 71.7 | 2 519 | 0.0 | NA | 51.6 | 60.2 | 43.4 | 68.1 | 20.35 | 3 092 | 74 |
| Monterey Park | 75.3 | 1 224 | 2.6 | NA | 56.3 | 75.6 | 42.6 | 89.0 | 18.56 | 1 295 | 1 575 |
| Moorpark | 30.1 | 832 | 11.7 | NA | 54.7 | 68.3 | 41.2 | 80.7 | 18.41 | 1 911 | 602 |
| Moreno Valley | 67.4 | 357 | 0.5 | 691 | 54.2 | 77.4 | 42.0 | 93.5 | 10.67 | 1 674 | 1 697 |
| Morgan Hill | 39.7 | 1 056 | 1.8 | NA | 43.5 | 70.7 | 37.5 | 78.2 | 23.73 | 4 566 | 747 |
| Mountain View | 78.4 | 1 112 | 0.0 | NA | 49.0 | 68.0 | 40.4 | 78.8 | 15.71 | 2 584 | 452 |
| Murrieta | 74.0 | 817 | 0.0 | 340 | 52.2 | 79.6 | 38.3 | 98.1 | 12.09 | 1 924 | 1 874 |
| Napa | 85.8 | 1 156 | 47.4 | NA | 47.9 | 68.6 | 39.2 | 82.6 | 26.46 | 2 689 | 529 |
| National City | 62.0 | 1 054 | 0.0 | NA | 57.3 | 70.1 | 46.1 | 76.1 | 9.95 | 1 321 | 862 |
| Newark | 14.5 | 347 | 0.0 | NA | 49.8 | 68.0 | 42.0 | 78.3 | 14.85 | 2 367 | 530 |
| Newport Beach | 301.2 | 3 786 | 0.0 | 837 | 55.9 | 67.3 | 48.2 | 71.4 | 11.65 | 1 719 | 543 |
| Norco | 147.5 | 5 480 | 0.0 | NA | NA | NA | NA | NA | NA | NA | NA |
| Norwalk | 158.1 | 1 524 | 2.5 | 338 | 57.0 | 73.8 | 46.0 | 82.9 | 12.94 | 1 211 | 1 186 |
| Novato | 216.7 | 4 160 | 5.4 | 191 | 48.8 | 67.7 | 41.3 | 80.9 | 34.29 | 2 621 | 451 |
| Oakland | 2 810.4 | 7 000 | 230.1 | 4 228 | 50.9 | 64.9 | 44.7 | 72.7 | 22.94 | 2 400 | 377 |
| Oakley | 16.5 | 543 | 8.5 | NA | 45.7 | 74.4 | 37.8 | 90.7 | 13.33 | 2 714 | 1 179 |
| Oceanside | 313.7 | 1 861 | 0.7 | 982 | 54.7 | 67.6 | 45.4 | 72.1 | 11.13 | 2 009 | 505 |
| Ontario | 292.8 | 1 713 | 0.0 | 1 074 | 54.6 | 73.8 | 41.5 | 88.7 | 16.96 | 1 727 | 1 191 |
| Orange | 122.2 | 910 | 0.0 | 697 | 58.0 | 72.9 | 46.6 | 82.7 | 13.84 | 1 153 | 1 299 |
| Oxnard | 454.3 | 2 459 | 44.7 | 1 284 | 55.6 | 65.9 | 45.5 | 72.7 | 15.62 | 1 936 | 403 |
| Pacifica | 47.4 | 1 271 | 0.0 | NA | 49.4 | 62.8 | 42.9 | 71.1 | 20.11 | 2 862 | 142 |
| Palmdale | 252.0 | 1 789 | 38.0 | 290 | 46.6 | 81.7 | 34.3 | 97.5 | 7.36 | 2 704 | 1 998 |
| Palm Desert | 598.6 | 11 799 | 334.9 | NA | 56.8 | 92.8 | 42.0 | 107.1 | 3.15 | 903 | 4 388 |
| Palm Springs | 181.4 | 3 787 | 2.0 | NA | 57.3 | 92.1 | 44.2 | 108.2 | 5.23 | 951 | 4 224 |
| Palo Alto | 51.5 | 884 | 0.0 | 924 | 49.0 | 68.0 | 40.4 | 78.8 | 15.71 | 2 584 | 452 |
| Paradise | 6.3 | 240 | 1.5 | NA | 45.7 | 77.8 | 37.7 | 91.7 | 56.20 | 3 145 | 1 464 |
| Paramount | 61.7 | 1 109 | 0.0 | NA | 57.0 | 73.8 | 46.0 | 82.9 | 12.94 | 1 211 | 1 186 |
| Pasadena | 679.0 | 4 735 | 21.6 | 1 518 | 56.1 | 75.3 | 44.3 | 89.4 | 21.09 | 1 398 | 1 558 |
| Perris | 299.6 | 5 591 | 68.3 | NA | 51.2 | 78.3 | 36.1 | 97.8 | 11.40 | 2 123 | 1 710 |
| Petaluma | 183.7 | 3 371 | 108.8 | NA | 48.4 | 67.3 | 38.9 | 82.7 | 25.85 | 2 741 | 385 |
| Pico Rivera | 154.3 | 2 433 | 1.2 | NA | 58.3 | 74.2 | 48.5 | 83.8 | 15.14 | 928 | 1 506 |
| Pittsburg | 598.2 | 9 570 | 208.7 | NA | 45.7 | 74.4 | 37.8 | 90.7 | 13.33 | 2 714 | 1 179 |
| Placentia | 54.6 | 1 099 | 0.0 | NA | 58.0 | 72.9 | 46.6 | 82.7 | 13.84 | 1 153 | 1 299 |
| Pleasant Hill | 32.0 | 979 | 0.0 | NA | 46.3 | 71.2 | 38.8 | 87.4 | 19.58 | 2 757 | 786 |
| Pleasanton | 139.6 | 2 097 | 3.1 | NA | 47.2 | 72.0 | 37.4 | 89.1 | 14.82 | 2 755 | 858 |
| Pomona | 290.7 | 1 905 | 60.9 | 644 | 54.6 | 73.8 | 41.5 | 88.7 | 16.96 | 1 727 | 1 191 |
| Porterville | 62.3 | 1 208 | 0.0 | NA | 48.7 | 82.8 | 39.4 | 98.1 | 11.40 | 2 053 | 2 246 |
| Poway | 317.8 | 6 524 | 25.1 | NA | 55.3 | 70.9 | 43.5 | 80.8 | 11.97 | 1 808 | 979 |
| Rancho Cordova | 27.7 | 455 | 0.3 | NA | 48.2 | 77.4 | 41.3 | 93.8 | 19.87 | 2 226 | 1 597 |
| Rancho Cucamonga | 521.2 | 3 061 | 58.3 | 566 | 56.6 | 78.3 | 45.3 | 95.0 | 14.77 | 1 364 | 1 901 |
| Rancho Palos Verdes | 22.4 | 540 | 1.2 | NA | 56.3 | 69.4 | 46.2 | 77.6 | 14.79 | 1 526 | 742 |
| Rancho Santa Margarita | 0.0 | 0 | 0.0 | NA | 56.7 | 72.4 | 47.2 | 82.3 | 14.03 | 1 465 | 1 183 |
| Redding | 286.3 | 3 189 | 39.7 | 749 | 45.5 | 81.3 | 35.5 | 98.5 | 33.52 | 2 961 | 1 741 |
| Redlands | 74.5 | 1 065 | 0.0 | NA | 52.9 | 78.0 | 40.4 | 94.4 | 13.62 | 1 904 | 1 714 |
| Redondo Beach | 69.8 | 1 041 | 0.0 | 519 | 57.1 | 69.3 | 48.6 | 75.3 | 13.15 | 1 274 | 679 |
| Redwood City | 212.4 | 2 886 | 15.2 | NA | 48.4 | 68.0 | 39.1 | 80.8 | 20.16 | 2 764 | 422 |
| Rialto | 179.2 | 1 816 | 25.0 | 385 | 54.4 | 79.6 | 41.8 | 96.0 | 16.43 | 1 599 | 1 937 |
| Richmond | 485.0 | 4 781 | 0.0 | 861 | 50.0 | 62.7 | 42.9 | 70.5 | 23.35 | 2 720 | 184 |
| Ridgecrest | 18.6 | 730 | 0.0 | NA | NA | NA | NA | NA | NA | NA | NA |
| Riverside | 1 286.2 | 4 368 | 301.0 | 2 217 | 55.3 | 78.7 | 42.7 | 94.1 | 10.22 | 1 475 | 1 863 |
| Rocklin | 102.2 | 1 980 | 15.9 | NA | 46.9 | 77.7 | 39.2 | 94.8 | 24.61 | 2 532 | 1 528 |
| Rohnert Park | 95.2 | 2 349 | 63.1 | NA | 48.7 | 67.6 | 39.5 | 82.2 | 31.01 | 2 694 | 526 |
| Rosemead | 37.5 | 687 | 24.2 | NA | 56.3 | 75.6 | 42.6 | 89.0 | 18.56 | 1 295 | 1 575 |
| Roseville | 972.8 | 8 945 | 208.9 | 1 119 | 46.9 | 77.7 | 39.2 | 94.8 | 24.61 | 2 532 | 1 528 |
| Sacramento | 1 724.6 | 3 747 | 278.3 | 4 210 | 46.3 | 75.4 | 38.8 | 92.4 | 17.93 | 2 666 | 1 248 |
| Salinas | 53.1 | 370 | 0.0 | 557 | 51.2 | 63.2 | 41.3 | 71.3 | 12.91 | 2 770 | 210 |
| San Bernardino | 395.7 | 1 985 | 8.1 | 1 514 | 54.4 | 79.6 | 41.8 | 96.0 | 16.43 | 1 599 | 1 937 |
| San Bruno | 8.7 | 218 | 0.0 | 250 | 49.4 | 62.8 | 42.9 | 71.1 | 20.11 | 2 862 | 142 |
| San Buenaventura (Ventura) | 98.8 | 957 | 0.4 | 676 | 55.6 | 65.9 | 45.5 | 72.7 | 15.62 | 1 936 | 403 |
| San Carlos | 29.6 | 1 097 | 0.0 | NA | 48.4 | 68.0 | 39.1 | 80.8 | 20.16 | 2 764 | 422 |
| San Clemente | 29.7 | 485 | 0.0 | NA | 55.4 | 68.7 | 43.9 | 77.3 | 13.56 | 1 756 | 666 |
| San Diego | 3 103.5 | 2 450 | 501.5 | 9 501 | 57.8 | 70.9 | 49.7 | 75.8 | 10.77 | 1 063 | 866 |
| San Dimas | 41.5 | 1 177 | 0.0 | NA | 54.6 | 73.8 | 41.5 | 88.7 | 16.96 | 1 727 | 1 191 |

1. Based on the population estimated as of July 1 of the year shown.   2. Represents normal values based on the 30-year period, 1971–2000.   3. Average daily minimum.   4. Average daily maximum.

# Table D. Cities — **Land Area and Population**

| STATE Place code | City | Land area,[1] 2010 (sq km) | Population, 2012 | | | Race alone or in combination, not of Hispanic origin (percent), 2010 | | | | | Percent Hispanic or Latino[2] 2010 | Percent Foreign born 2007–2011 |
| | | | | | | Race alone or in combination | | | | | | |
| | | | Total persons | Rank | Per square kilometer | White | Black | American Indian, Alaska Native | Asian | Hawaiian Pacific Islander | | |
| | | 1 | 2 | 3 | 4 | 5 | 6 | 7 | 8 | 9 | 10 | 11 |
| | **CALIFORNIA—Cont'd** | | | | | | | | | | | |
| 06 67000 | San Francisco | 121.4 | 825 863 | 14 | 6 802.8 | 44.6 | 6.7 | 0.8 | 35.2 | 0.7 | 15.1 | 35.6 |
| 06 67042 | San Gabriel | 10.7 | 40 150 | 908 | 3 752.3 | 12.4 | 1.0 | 0.3 | 61.5 | 0.2 | 25.7 | 54.4 |
| 06 67112 | San Jacinto | 66.6 | 45 384 | 811 | 681.4 | 37.1 | 7.2 | 1.7 | 3.7 | 0.4 | 52.3 | 22.4 |
| 06 68000 | San Jose | 457.2 | 982 765 | 10 | 2 149.5 | 30.9 | 3.4 | 0.7 | 33.7 | 0.7 | 33.2 | 38.6 |
| 06 68028 | San Juan Capistrano | 36.6 | 35 360 | 1 035 | 966.1 | 57.3 | 0.6 | 0.8 | 3.7 | 0.3 | 38.7 | 25.1 |
| 06 68084 | San Leandro | 34.6 | 86 890 | 354 | 2 511.3 | 29.5 | 13.0 | 0.9 | 31.2 | 1.2 | 27.4 | 34.0 |
| 06 68154 | San Luis Obispo | 33.1 | 45 878 | 802 | 1 386.0 | 78.4 | 1.5 | 1.0 | 6.8 | 0.4 | 14.7 | 10.3 |
| 06 68196 | San Marcos | 63.1 | 86 752 | 355 | 1 374.8 | 51.3 | 2.8 | 0.7 | 10.8 | 0.7 | 36.6 | 24.1 |
| 06 68252 | San Mateo | 31.4 | 99 670 | 291 | 3 174.2 | 49.5 | 2.7 | 0.5 | 21.2 | 2.7 | 26.6 | 33.5 |
| 06 68294 | San Pablo | 6.8 | 29 720 | 1 225 | 4 370.6 | 11.4 | 16.4 | 0.8 | 15.9 | 0.9 | 56.5 | 43.2 |
| 06 68364 | San Rafael | 42.7 | 58 502 | 602 | 1 370.1 | 61.3 | 2.4 | 0.7 | 7.5 | 0.4 | 30.0 | 27.9 |
| 06 68378 | San Ramon | 46.8 | 73 927 | 444 | 1 579.6 | 52.1 | 3.4 | 0.6 | 38.7 | 0.6 | 8.7 | 28.9 |
| 06 69000 | Santa Ana | 70.6 | 330 920 | 57 | 4 687.3 | 9.8 | 1.1 | 0.3 | 10.8 | 0.3 | 78.2 | 49.2 |
| 06 69070 | Santa Barbara | 50.4 | 89 639 | 337 | 1 778.6 | 56.5 | 1.7 | 0.9 | 4.4 | 0.2 | 38.0 | 25.0 |
| 06 69084 | Santa Clara | 47.7 | 119 311 | 220 | 2 501.3 | 38.9 | 3.2 | 0.6 | 40.1 | 0.9 | 19.4 | 39.7 |
| 06 69088 | Santa Clarita | 136.5 | 179 013 | 132 | 1 311.5 | 58.4 | 3.6 | 0.7 | 9.9 | 0.4 | 29.5 | 21.0 |
| 06 69112 | Santa Cruz | 33.0 | 62 041 | 556 | 1 880.0 | 70.3 | 2.5 | 1.4 | 9.7 | 0.5 | 19.4 | 12.3 |
| 06 69196 | Santa Maria | 58.9 | 101 459 | 282 | 1 722.6 | 22.8 | 1.5 | 0.7 | 5.4 | 0.3 | 70.4 | 34.4 |
| 06 70000 | Santa Monica | 21.8 | 91 812 | 327 | 4 211.6 | 73.3 | 4.6 | 0.7 | 11.2 | 0.3 | 13.1 | 22.8 |
| 06 70042 | Santa Paula | 11.9 | 29 963 | 1 215 | 2 517.9 | 19.1 | 0.4 | 0.7 | 0.8 | 0.1 | 79.5 | 29.6 |
| 06 70098 | Santa Rosa | 107.0 | 170 685 | 141 | 1 595.2 | 62.3 | 3.1 | 1.9 | 6.3 | 0.7 | 28.6 | 19.5 |
| 06 70224 | Santee | 42.1 | 55 343 | 649 | 1 314.6 | 76.8 | 2.7 | 1.3 | 5.5 | 1.0 | 16.3 | 8.7 |
| 06 70280 | Saratoga | 32.1 | 30 677 | 1 184 | 955.7 | 54.3 | 0.6 | 0.3 | 43.9 | 0.3 | 3.5 | 36.7 |
| 06 70742 | Seaside | 23.9 | 33 878 | 1 077 | 1 417.5 | 36.0 | 9.8 | 1.2 | 12.2 | 2.3 | 43.4 | 31.0 |
| 06 72016 | Simi Valley | 107.4 | 125 793 | 204 | 1 171.3 | 65.4 | 1.8 | 1.0 | 10.9 | 0.4 | 23.3 | 19.7 |
| 06 72520 | Soledad | 11.4 | 26 478 | 1 374 | 2 322.6 | 13.8 | 11.2 | 0.7 | 3.0 | 0.4 | 71.1 | 32.3 |
| 06 73080 | South Gate | 18.7 | 95 304 | 312 | 5 096.5 | 3.6 | 0.7 | 0.2 | 0.7 | 0.1 | 94.8 | 45.1 |
| 06 73220 | South Pasadena | 8.8 | 25 860 | 1 396 | 2 938.6 | 46.9 | 3.6 | 0.4 | 33.6 | 0.2 | 18.6 | 28.7 |
| 06 73262 | South San Francisco | 23.7 | 65 547 | 519 | 2 765.7 | 24.2 | 2.9 | 0.6 | 38.5 | 2.5 | 34.0 | 42.9 |
| 06 73962 | Stanton | 8.2 | 38 915 | 942 | 4 745.7 | 23.1 | 2.2 | 0.6 | 23.9 | 0.8 | 50.8 | 42.2 |
| 06 75000 | Stockton | 159.7 | 297 984 | 64 | 1 865.9 | 25.3 | 12.8 | 1.3 | 22.6 | 1.0 | 40.3 | 26.5 |
| 06 75630 | Suisun City | 10.6 | 28 644 | 1 270 | 2 702.3 | 34.3 | 22.5 | 1.6 | 22.4 | 2.5 | 24.0 | 23.0 |
| 06 77000 | Sunnyvale | 57.0 | 146 197 | 170 | 2 564.9 | 37.1 | 2.3 | 0.6 | 43.1 | 0.7 | 18.9 | 44.1 |
| 06 78120 | Temecula | 78.1 | 105 208 | 267 | 1 347.1 | 60.4 | 4.8 | 1.2 | 11.8 | 0.7 | 24.7 | 15.7 |
| 06 78148 | Temple City | 10.4 | 36 099 | 1 012 | 3 471.1 | 24.0 | 0.9 | 0.3 | 56.7 | 0.3 | 19.3 | 45.4 |
| 06 78252 | Thousand Oaks | 142.5 | 128 412 | 195 | 901.1 | 72.6 | 1.6 | 0.6 | 10.4 | 0.3 | 16.8 | 18.1 |
| 06 80000 | Torrance | 53.0 | 147 027 | 167 | 2 774.1 | 45.7 | 3.2 | 0.6 | 37.2 | 0.8 | 16.1 | 30.3 |
| 06 80238 | Tracy | 57.0 | 84 669 | 367 | 1 485.4 | 39.8 | 8.0 | 1.1 | 17.1 | 1.4 | 36.9 | 25.9 |
| 06 80644 | Tulare | 54.2 | 60 933 | 570 | 1 124.2 | 36.4 | 3.9 | 1.2 | 2.5 | 0.3 | 57.5 | 20.7 |
| 06 80812 | Turlock | 43.8 | 69 733 | 479 | 1 592.1 | 55.3 | 2.0 | 1.1 | 7.0 | 0.8 | 36.4 | 25.3 |
| 06 80854 | Tustin | 28.7 | 78 049 | 413 | 2 719.5 | 37.0 | 2.5 | 0.5 | 21.9 | 0.6 | 39.7 | 34.4 |
| 06 80994 | Twentynine Palms | 153.2 | 25 713 | 1 404 | 167.8 | 64.6 | 9.6 | 2.1 | 5.7 | 2.0 | 20.8 | 6.6 |
| 06 81204 | Union City | 50.4 | 71 763 | 461 | 1 423.9 | 17.7 | 6.9 | 0.6 | 54.3 | 2.0 | 22.9 | 46.2 |
| 06 81344 | Upland | 40.5 | 75 209 | 439 | 1 857.0 | 45.9 | 7.5 | 0.7 | 9.4 | 0.4 | 38.0 | 19.0 |
| 06 81554 | Vacaville | 73.5 | 93 899 | 316 | 1 277.5 | 58.9 | 11.5 | 1.6 | 8.3 | 1.1 | 22.9 | 12.1 |
| 06 81666 | Vallejo | 79.4 | 117 796 | 225 | 1 483.6 | 28.3 | 23.7 | 1.5 | 27.1 | 1.8 | 22.6 | 27.5 |
| 06 82590 | Victorville | 189.5 | 120 336 | 217 | 635.0 | 30.6 | 17.7 | 1.5 | 4.8 | 0.6 | 47.8 | 16.9 |
| 06 82954 | Visalia | 93.9 | 127 081 | 199 | 1 353.4 | 45.9 | 2.2 | 1.4 | 5.9 | 0.2 | 46.0 | 14.2 |
| 06 82984 | Vista | 48.4 | 96 047 | 304 | 1 984.4 | 43.0 | 3.8 | 0.9 | 5.5 | 1.1 | 48.4 | 26.2 |
| 06 83332 | Walnut | 23.3 | 30 011 | 1 212 | 1 288.0 | 13.9 | 3.0 | 0.3 | 65.0 | 0.5 | 19.1 | 48.6 |
| 06 83364 | Walnut Creek | 51.2 | 65 695 | 516 | 1 283.1 | 76.6 | 2.1 | 0.6 | 14.8 | 0.4 | 8.6 | 22.1 |
| 06 83542 | Wasco | 24.4 | 25 495 | 1 418 | 1 044.9 | 14.8 | 7.2 | 0.6 | 0.8 | 0.0 | 76.7 | 26.7 |
| 06 83668 | Watsonville | 17.3 | 51 881 | 698 | 2 998.9 | 14.6 | 0.6 | 0.6 | 3.5 | 0.1 | 81.4 | 41.9 |
| 06 84200 | West Covina | 41.6 | 107 440 | 257 | 2 582.7 | 16.5 | 4.5 | 0.5 | 26.4 | 0.3 | 53.2 | 34.9 |
| 06 84410 | West Hollywood | 4.9 | 34 781 | 1 052 | 7 098.2 | 80.4 | 3.9 | 0.7 | 6.8 | 0.3 | 10.5 | 30.2 |
| 06 84550 | Westminster | 26.0 | 91 377 | 328 | 3 514.5 | 27.4 | 1.1 | 0.6 | 48.7 | 0.7 | 23.6 | 45.8 |
| 06 84816 | West Sacramento | 55.5 | 49 523 | 739 | 892.3 | 51.1 | 5.5 | 1.8 | 12.6 | 1.9 | 31.4 | 22.7 |
| 06 85292 | Whittier | 37.9 | 86 177 | 358 | 2 273.8 | 29.2 | 1.1 | 0.5 | 4.1 | 0.2 | 65.7 | 20.0 |
| 06 85446 | Wildomar | 61.4 | 33 192 | 1 100 | 540.6 | 56.1 | 3.7 | 1.4 | 5.7 | 0.5 | 35.3 | 18.0 |
| 06 85922 | Windsor | 18.8 | 27 144 | 1 340 | 1 443.8 | 63.0 | 1.2 | 1.8 | 4.2 | 0.5 | 31.8 | 14.5 |
| 06 86328 | Woodland | 39.6 | 56 271 | 636 | 1 421.0 | 43.9 | 1.7 | 1.4 | 7.1 | 0.5 | 47.4 | 21.3 |
| 06 86832 | Yorba Linda | 50.5 | 66 735 | 504 | 1 321.5 | 68.1 | 1.6 | 0.6 | 17.5 | 0.3 | 14.4 | 17.1 |
| 06 86972 | Yuba City | 37.8 | 65 105 | 523 | 1 722.4 | 50.2 | 3.0 | 2.1 | 18.9 | 0.6 | 28.4 | 25.4 |
| 06 87042 | Yucaipa | 72.2 | 52 265 | 692 | 723.9 | 67.8 | 2.0 | 1.3 | 3.5 | 0.3 | 27.1 | 10.6 |
| 08 00000 | **COLORADO** | 268 431.3 | 5 187 582 | X | 19.3 | 71.8 | 4.5 | 1.3 | 3.5 | 0.2 | 20.7 | 9.7 |
| 08 03455 | Arvada | 91.0 | 109 745 | 246 | 1 206.0 | 82.8 | 1.2 | 0.9 | 2.7 | 0.1 | 13.7 | 4.5 |
| 08 04000 | Aurora | 400.8 | 339 030 | 56 | 845.9 | 49.9 | 17.0 | 1.3 | 5.9 | 0.5 | 28.7 | 20.4 |
| 08 07850 | Boulder | 63.9 | 101 808 | 280 | 1 593.2 | 85.0 | 1.3 | 0.8 | 6.0 | 0.2 | 8.7 | 10.9 |
| 08 08675 | Brighton | 51.8 | 34 636 | 1 058 | 668.6 | 56.3 | 1.5 | 1.1 | 1.7 | 0.1 | 40.5 | 11.5 |
| 08 09280 | Broomfield | 85.6 | 58 298 | 607 | 681.1 | 81.1 | 1.3 | 0.9 | 7.1 | 0.2 | 11.1 | 8.3 |

1. Dry land or land partially or temporarily covered by water.    2. May be of any race.

# Table D. Cities — **Population**

| City | Age of population (percent), 2010 | | | | | | | | | | | Population | | | |
|---|---|---|---|---|---|---|---|---|---|---|---|---|---|---|---|
| | | | | | | | | | | | | Census counts | | Percent change | |
| | Under 5 years | 5 to 17 years | 18 to 24 years | 25 to 34 years | 35 to 44 years | 45 to 54 years | 55 to 64 years | 65 to 74 years | 75 years and over | Median age | Percent female | 2000 | 2010 | 2000–2010 | 2010–2012 |
| | 12 | 13 | 14 | 15 | 16 | 17 | 18 | 19 | 20 | 21 | 22 | 23 | 24 | 25 | 26 |
| CALIFORNIA—Cont'd | | | | | | | | | | | | | | | |
| San Francisco | 4.4 | 9.0 | 9.6 | 20.9 | 16.6 | 13.9 | 12.0 | 6.7 | 6.9 | 38.5 | 49.3 | 776 733 | 805 235 | 3.7 | 2.6 |
| San Gabriel | 5.2 | 14.6 | 9.0 | 13.2 | 15.4 | 16.5 | 12.2 | 6.7 | 7.3 | 40.3 | 51.8 | 39 804 | 39 718 | -0.2 | 1.1 |
| San Jacinto | 8.8 | 23.9 | 10.0 | 13.9 | 13.0 | 11.6 | 8.2 | 5.6 | 5.0 | 30.3 | 51.1 | 23 779 | 44 199 | 85.9 | 2.7 |
| San Jose | 7.3 | 17.6 | 9.5 | 15.4 | 15.8 | 14.4 | 10.1 | 5.6 | 4.4 | 35.2 | 49.7 | 894 943 | 952 562 | 5.7 | 3.2 |
| San Juan Capistrano | 6.2 | 18.4 | 8.9 | 10.6 | 12.0 | 14.9 | 13.4 | 8.1 | 7.5 | 40.2 | 50.4 | 33 826 | 34 623 | 2.3 | 2.1 |
| San Leandro | 6.2 | 16.1 | 8.3 | 13.4 | 14.2 | 15.6 | 12.4 | 6.5 | 7.2 | 39.3 | 52.0 | 79 452 | 84 950 | 6.9 | 2.3 |
| San Luis Obispo | 3.3 | 8.9 | 34.7 | 13.2 | 8.1 | 10.1 | 9.6 | 5.3 | 6.8 | 26.5 | 47.8 | 44 174 | 45 170 | 2.1 | 1.6 |
| San Marcos | 8.4 | 19.4 | 11.0 | 14.4 | 15.8 | 12.2 | 8.7 | 5.1 | 5.0 | 32.9 | 51.1 | 54 977 | 83 650 | 52.4 | 3.7 |
| San Mateo | 6.8 | 14.1 | 7.1 | 15.5 | 16.1 | 14.7 | 11.4 | 6.7 | 7.7 | 38.9 | 51.2 | 92 482 | 97 207 | 5.1 | 2.5 |
| San Pablo | 8.3 | 20.0 | 11.1 | 15.8 | 14.1 | 12.9 | 9.0 | 4.5 | 4.3 | 31.6 | 50.3 | 30 215 | 29 134 | -3.6 | 2.0 |
| San Rafael | 6.2 | 13.1 | 8.6 | 14.6 | 14.7 | 14.0 | 13.0 | 7.5 | 8.3 | 40.2 | 50.1 | 56 063 | 57 717 | 2.9 | 1.4 |
| San Ramon | 7.9 | 21.7 | 4.9 | 11.7 | 19.9 | 16.1 | 10.0 | 5.1 | 2.7 | 37.1 | 50.9 | 44 722 | 72 211 | 61.3 | 2.4 |
| Santa Ana | 8.9 | 21.8 | 12.1 | 16.6 | 14.9 | 11.6 | 7.3 | 3.9 | 2.9 | 29.1 | 48.9 | 337 977 | 324 528 | -4.0 | 2.0 |
| Santa Barbara | 5.5 | 13.2 | 12.2 | 16.6 | 13.1 | 13.0 | 12.2 | 6.6 | 7.6 | 36.8 | 50.4 | 92 325 | 88 409 | -4.2 | 1.4 |
| Santa Clara | 7.8 | 13.5 | 10.7 | 19.8 | 16.2 | 12.9 | 9.1 | 5.1 | 4.9 | 34.1 | 49.5 | 102 361 | 116 493 | 13.8 | 2.4 |
| Santa Clarita | 6.3 | 19.9 | 10.0 | 12.3 | 14.9 | 16.4 | 10.8 | 5.4 | 4.1 | 36.2 | 50.7 | 151 088 | 176 320 | 16.7 | 1.5 |
| Santa Cruz | 3.9 | 9.7 | 29.1 | 13.6 | 11.5 | 12.0 | 11.3 | 4.8 | 4.1 | 29.9 | 49.4 | 54 593 | 59 948 | 9.8 | 3.5 |
| Santa Maria | 9.9 | 21.5 | 12.2 | 16.3 | 12.3 | 10.8 | 7.5 | 4.5 | 4.9 | 28.6 | 49.5 | 77 423 | 99 553 | 28.6 | 1.9 |
| Santa Monica | 4.1 | 9.9 | 7.2 | 19.4 | 16.9 | 15.0 | 12.6 | 7.4 | 7.6 | 40.4 | 51.8 | 84 084 | 89 736 | 6.7 | 2.3 |
| Santa Paula | 8.7 | 21.1 | 11.2 | 14.3 | 13.1 | 11.8 | 9.3 | 5.5 | 5.0 | 31.1 | 49.5 | 28 598 | 29 321 | 2.5 | 2.2 |
| Santa Rosa | 6.8 | 16.6 | 9.5 | 15.0 | 12.8 | 13.8 | 12.0 | 6.4 | 7.1 | 36.7 | 51.2 | 147 595 | 167 834 | 13.7 | 1.7 |
| Santee | 6.6 | 17.2 | 9.5 | 13.7 | 14.0 | 16.3 | 12.0 | 6.0 | 4.8 | 37.2 | 51.7 | 52 975 | 53 415 | 0.8 | 3.6 |
| Saratoga | 3.3 | 20.7 | 4.6 | 4.2 | 11.4 | 21.0 | 14.4 | 10.2 | 10.1 | 47.8 | 51.1 | 29 843 | 29 935 | 0.3 | 2.5 |
| Seaside | 8.9 | 18.1 | 13.4 | 16.7 | 14.1 | 11.7 | 8.5 | 4.3 | 4.3 | 30.6 | 49.9 | 31 696 | 33 025 | 4.2 | 2.6 |
| Simi Valley | 6.1 | 18.9 | 8.9 | 12.4 | 14.9 | 16.5 | 11.7 | 6.1 | 4.5 | 37.8 | 50.9 | 111 351 | 124 239 | 11.6 | 1.3 |
| Soledad | 6.1 | 15.9 | 9.5 | 18.6 | 20.8 | 16.3 | 8.1 | 2.7 | 1.9 | 34.9 | 29.8 | 11 263 | 25 740 | 128.5 | 2.9 |
| South Gate | 8.4 | 22.7 | 12.0 | 15.4 | 14.3 | 11.9 | 8.3 | 4.2 | 2.8 | 29.4 | 50.9 | 96 375 | 94 396 | -2.1 | 1.0 |
| South Pasadena | 5.2 | 18.2 | 6.2 | 12.7 | 16.3 | 17.1 | 12.2 | 6.6 | 5.5 | 40.1 | 52.5 | 24 292 | 25 619 | 5.5 | 0.9 |
| South San Francisco | 6.2 | 15.5 | 8.9 | 15.0 | 14.3 | 15.1 | 12.0 | 6.7 | 6.4 | 38.1 | 50.6 | 60 552 | 63 664 | 5.1 | 3.0 |
| Stanton | 7.9 | 19.7 | 10.6 | 14.6 | 15.0 | 13.1 | 9.0 | 5.2 | 4.8 | 33.0 | 50.5 | 37 403 | 38 192 | 2.1 | 1.9 |
| Stockton | 8.4 | 21.5 | 11.7 | 13.8 | 12.5 | 12.1 | 9.9 | 5.4 | 4.6 | 30.8 | 51.0 | 243 771 | 291 729 | 19.7 | 2.1 |
| Suisun City | 7.5 | 20.0 | 10.5 | 14.9 | 13.0 | 15.0 | 11.3 | 4.7 | 3.0 | 33.0 | 50.8 | 26 118 | 28 111 | 7.6 | 1.9 |
| Sunnyvale | 8.0 | 14.4 | 6.7 | 19.6 | 16.7 | 13.8 | 9.6 | 5.8 | 5.4 | 35.6 | 49.6 | 131 760 | 140 060 | 6.3 | 4.4 |
| Temecula | 7.0 | 23.6 | 9.3 | 12.0 | 15.9 | 15.7 | 8.7 | 4.5 | 3.3 | 33.4 | 51.0 | 57 716 | 100 146 | 73.4 | 5.1 |
| Temple City | 4.5 | 16.7 | 8.1 | 10.9 | 14.4 | 16.7 | 13.7 | 7.9 | 7.2 | 42.0 | 52.5 | 33 377 | 35 558 | 6.5 | 1.5 |
| Thousand Oaks | 5.2 | 18.5 | 8.1 | 9.8 | 13.7 | 17.0 | 13.0 | 7.9 | 6.8 | 41.5 | 51.1 | 117 005 | 126 683 | 8.3 | 1.4 |
| Torrance | 5.2 | 16.7 | 7.5 | 11.5 | 14.8 | 17.4 | 12.0 | 7.3 | 7.7 | 41.3 | 51.4 | 137 946 | 145 438 | 5.4 | 1.1 |
| Tracy | 8.0 | 24.2 | 9.0 | 12.5 | 16.2 | 14.9 | 8.3 | 4.0 | 2.9 | 32.3 | 50.4 | 56 929 | 82 922 | 45.7 | 2.1 |
| Tulare | 9.4 | 23.9 | 10.5 | 14.5 | 12.9 | 11.5 | 8.2 | 4.9 | 4.2 | 29.1 | 50.9 | 43 994 | 59 312 | 34.7 | 2.7 |
| Turlock | 7.5 | 19.9 | 11.8 | 14.1 | 12.6 | 12.8 | 9.6 | 5.8 | 5.8 | 32.5 | 51.3 | 55 810 | 68 549 | 22.8 | 1.7 |
| Tustin | 7.6 | 19.2 | 9.1 | 16.8 | 16.4 | 13.6 | 8.9 | 4.8 | 3.7 | 33.4 | 51.4 | 67 504 | 75 540 | 11.9 | 3.3 |
| Twentynine Palms | 11.1 | 14.5 | 30.0 | 17.4 | 8.1 | 7.3 | 5.8 | 3.3 | 2.5 | 23.5 | 43.7 | 14 764 | 25 048 | 69.7 | 2.7 |
| Union City | 6.8 | 17.4 | 9.3 | 14.6 | 14.7 | 14.2 | 11.9 | 6.3 | 4.8 | 36.2 | 50.6 | 66 869 | 69 524 | 4.0 | 3.2 |
| Upland | 6.2 | 18.3 | 10.2 | 13.8 | 13.2 | 14.5 | 11.7 | 6.5 | 5.5 | 36.1 | 51.8 | 68 393 | 73 732 | 7.8 | 2.0 |
| Vacaville | 6.0 | 17.3 | 9.7 | 14.2 | 14.3 | 16.7 | 11.5 | 5.5 | 4.9 | 37.2 | 47.1 | 88 625 | 92 422 | 4.3 | 1.6 |
| Vallejo | 6.5 | 16.7 | 10.1 | 13.4 | 12.5 | 15.1 | 13.6 | 6.6 | 5.4 | 37.9 | 51.5 | 116 760 | 115 940 | -0.7 | 1.6 |
| Victorville | 8.9 | 23.9 | 10.5 | 15.0 | 13.9 | 12.0 | 7.7 | 4.5 | 3.6 | 29.5 | 49.9 | 64 029 | 115 921 | 81.0 | 3.8 |
| Visalia | 8.6 | 21.4 | 10.0 | 14.6 | 12.6 | 12.5 | 9.8 | 5.5 | 4.8 | 31.6 | 51.2 | 91 565 | 124 462 | 35.9 | 2.1 |
| Vista | 8.0 | 18.8 | 12.5 | 16.2 | 13.2 | 13.3 | 8.7 | 4.3 | 4.9 | 31.1 | 49.8 | 89 857 | 93 854 | 4.4 | 2.3 |
| Walnut | 3.5 | 17.4 | 10.6 | 9.5 | 11.4 | 18.7 | 16.7 | 7.7 | 4.5 | 43.1 | 51.0 | 30 004 | 29 172 | -2.8 | 2.9 |
| Walnut Creek | 4.1 | 12.6 | 5.6 | 11.8 | 11.8 | 14.1 | 13.4 | 10.5 | 16.1 | 47.9 | 53.7 | 64 296 | 64 174 | -0.2 | 2.4 |
| Wasco | 8.6 | 20.1 | 14.4 | 19.0 | 14.7 | 11.4 | 6.6 | 3.0 | 2.1 | 28.3 | 38.4 | 21 263 | 25 552 | 20.1 | -0.2 |
| Watsonville | 9.5 | 22.0 | 11.7 | 15.7 | 13.3 | 11.4 | 8.2 | 4.1 | 4.2 | 29.2 | 50.2 | 44 265 | 51 199 | 15.7 | 1.3 |
| West Covina | 6.0 | 18.6 | 10.7 | 13.4 | 13.8 | 14.2 | 11.2 | 6.4 | 5.7 | 36.0 | 51.8 | 105 080 | 106 098 | 1.0 | 1.3 |
| West Hollywood | 1.9 | 2.7 | 7.0 | 26.8 | 20.4 | 15.5 | 10.8 | 6.7 | 8.2 | 40.4 | 43.8 | 35 716 | 34 399 | -3.7 | 1.1 |
| Westminster | 5.9 | 17.4 | 9.6 | 11.8 | 15.0 | 14.6 | 11.4 | 7.8 | 6.4 | 38.7 | 50.6 | 88 207 | 89 694 | 1.7 | 1.9 |
| West Sacramento | 8.4 | 18.3 | 9.1 | 16.5 | 14.5 | 13.1 | 10.2 | 5.3 | 4.5 | 33.6 | 50.6 | 31 615 | 48 744 | 54.2 | 1.6 |
| Whittier | 6.7 | 18.7 | 10.8 | 13.3 | 13.4 | 14.0 | 10.4 | 5.6 | 6.1 | 35.4 | 51.5 | 83 680 | 85 331 | 2.0 | 1.0 |
| Wildomar | 7.1 | 20.8 | 10.1 | 12.5 | 13.4 | 15.4 | 10.0 | 5.6 | 5.0 | 34.6 | 50.6 | 14 064 | 32 220 | 128.8 | 3.0 |
| Windsor | 6.8 | 21.2 | 8.3 | 11.2 | 14.3 | 16.2 | 11.1 | 5.5 | 5.5 | 37.0 | 50.9 | 22 744 | 26 801 | 17.8 | 1.3 |
| Woodland | 7.9 | 19.6 | 10.0 | 14.3 | 13.2 | 13.6 | 10.5 | 5.6 | 5.3 | 33.7 | 50.8 | 49 151 | 55 468 | 12.9 | 1.4 |
| Yorba Linda | 4.8 | 19.8 | 8.7 | 8.8 | 12.7 | 18.5 | 14.8 | 7.0 | 4.8 | 41.7 | 51.3 | 58 918 | 64 234 | 9.0 | 3.9 |
| Yuba City | 8.1 | 20.1 | 10.2 | 14.2 | 12.8 | 12.8 | 10.0 | 6.3 | 5.4 | 33.0 | 50.5 | 36 758 | 64 925 | 76.6 | 0.3 |
| Yucaipa | 6.6 | 19.6 | 8.7 | 11.6 | 12.8 | 15.5 | 11.9 | 6.9 | 6.4 | 37.8 | 50.8 | 41 207 | 51 371 | 24.7 | 1.7 |
| COLORADO | 6.8 | 17.5 | 9.7 | 14.4 | 13.9 | 14.8 | 11.9 | 6.2 | 4.8 | 36.1 | 49.9 | 4 301 261 | 5 029 196 | 16.9 | 3.1 |
| Arvada | 5.9 | 17.5 | 7.8 | 11.8 | 13.4 | 16.4 | 13.4 | 7.6 | 6.3 | 40.5 | 51.2 | 102 153 | 106 468 | 4.2 | 3.1 |
| Aurora | 8.4 | 19.0 | 9.3 | 16.2 | 14.5 | 13.4 | 10.4 | 5.1 | 3.8 | 33.2 | 50.8 | 276 393 | 324 598 | 17.6 | 4.4 |
| Boulder | 4.1 | 9.8 | 29.1 | 16.0 | 11.7 | 10.8 | 9.6 | 4.6 | 4.3 | 28.7 | 48.7 | 94 673 | 97 468 | 2.9 | 4.5 |
| Brighton | 8.6 | 21.3 | 8.9 | 15.7 | 15.1 | 12.6 | 8.9 | 4.9 | 3.9 | 32.2 | 49.4 | 20 905 | 33 366 | 59.5 | 3.8 |
| Broomfield | 7.1 | 19.2 | 7.7 | 13.9 | 16.0 | 15.5 | 10.8 | 5.6 | 4.3 | 36.4 | 50.4 | 38 272 | 55 870 | 46.0 | 4.3 |

# Table D. Cities — Households, Group Quarters, Crime, and Education

| City | Households, 2010 Number | Persons per household | Percent — Female family householder[1] | Percent — One-person | Persons in group quarters, 2010 Total | Institutional Total | Persons in nursing facilities | Non-institutional | Serious crimes known to police[2] 2011 — Total Number | Rate[3] | Violent | Property | Population age 25 and older | High school graduate or less | Bachelor's degree or more |
|---|---|---|---|---|---|---|---|---|---|---|---|---|---|---|---|
| | 27 | 28 | 29 | 30 | 31 | 32 | 33 | 34 | 35 | 36 | 37 | 38 | 39 | 40 | 41 |
| **CALIFORNIA—Cont'd** | | | | | | | | | | | | | | | |
| San Francisco | 345 811 | 2.26 | 8.3 | 38.6 | 24 264 | 5 362 | 2 942 | 18 902 | 38 260 | 4 696 | 660 | 4 037 | 616 042 | 28.7 | 51.4 |
| San Gabriel | 12 542 | 3.13 | 15.6 | 16.9 | 452 | 418 | 395 | 34 | 660 | 1 642 | 266 | 1 376 | 28 637 | 46.9 | 29.0 |
| San Jacinto | 13 152 | 3.34 | 16.1 | 18.7 | 228 | 59 | 43 | 169 | 1 580 | 3 533 | 264 | 3 269 | 24 645 | 54.3 | 10.7 |
| San Jose | 301 366 | 3.09 | 12.6 | 19.7 | 13 322 | 3 780 | 2 190 | 9 542 | 25 178 | 2 631 | 335 | 2 296 | 616 157 | 36.7 | 36.6 |
| San Juan Capistrano | 11 394 | 3.03 | 9.6 | 20.9 | 87 | 0 | 0 | 87 | 506 | 1 446 | 160 | 1 286 | 22 555 | 35.6 | 33.4 |
| San Leandro | 30 717 | 2.74 | 14.7 | 26.8 | 650 | 368 | 364 | 282 | 3 572 | 4 156 | 427 | 3 729 | 57 557 | 44.3 | 26.2 |
| San Luis Obispo | 19 193 | 2.29 | 7.0 | 32.4 | 1 182 | 215 | 206 | 967 | 1 916 | 4 197 | 294 | 3 904 | 21 970 | 23.9 | 45.2 |
| San Marcos | 27 202 | 3.05 | 11.2 | 19.0 | 844 | 108 | 108 | 736 | 1 657 | 1 955 | 275 | 1 680 | 49 901 | 38.1 | 29.3 |
| San Mateo | 38 233 | 2.51 | 10.0 | 30.7 | 1 316 | 341 | 306 | 975 | 1 978 | 2 011 | 250 | 1 761 | 69 328 | 28.8 | 43.1 |
| San Pablo | 8 761 | 3.28 | 19.6 | 21.2 | 441 | 373 | 373 | 68 | 1 598 | 5 420 | 868 | 4 552 | 17 449 | 63.5 | 11.7 |
| San Rafael | 22 764 | 2.44 | 8.8 | 32.7 | 2 119 | 805 | 497 | 1 314 | 1 673 | 2 865 | 343 | 2 523 | 41 487 | 30.0 | 45.3 |
| San Ramon | 25 284 | 2.85 | 7.9 | 18.5 | 75 | 23 | 0 | 52 | 896 | 1 227 | 37 | 1 190 | 45 521 | 13.2 | 60.8 |
| Santa Ana | 73 174 | 4.37 | 16.1 | 12.6 | 4 658 | 3 243 | 895 | 1 415 | 7 888 | 2 402 | 400 | 2 002 | 185 418 | 69.1 | 11.7 |
| Santa Barbara | 35 449 | 2.45 | 9.7 | 33.7 | 1 627 | 455 | 375 | 1 172 | 3 075 | 3 438 | 357 | 3 081 | 60 598 | 29.4 | 42.1 |
| Santa Clara | 43 021 | 2.63 | 9.5 | 25.4 | 3 196 | 336 | 318 | 2 860 | 3 110 | 2 639 | 150 | 2 489 | 77 637 | 24.8 | 49.2 |
| Santa Clarita | 59 507 | 2.94 | 11.6 | 19.6 | 1 410 | 129 | 111 | 1 281 | 2 830 | 1 586 | 147 | 1 440 | 111 139 | 32.9 | 31.7 |
| Santa Cruz | 21 657 | 2.39 | 8.5 | 31.3 | 8 289 | 379 | 2 | 7 910 | 3 836 | 6 325 | 791 | 5 533 | 33 803 | 21.6 | 52.2 |
| Santa Maria | 26 908 | 3.66 | 14.7 | 18.9 | 1 007 | 419 | 263 | 588 | 3 145 | 3 122 | 711 | 2 412 | 54 096 | 57.6 | 13.7 |
| Santa Monica | 46 917 | 1.87 | 7.5 | 48.4 | 2 126 | 827 | 783 | 1 299 | 3 340 | 3 679 | 406 | 3 272 | 70 368 | 15.2 | 64.0 |
| Santa Paula | 8 347 | 3.50 | 15.2 | 15.9 | 133 | 89 | 89 | 44 | 605 | 2 039 | 438 | 1 601 | 17 270 | 59.7 | 11.8 |
| Santa Rosa | 63 590 | 2.59 | 12.1 | 28.3 | 3 410 | 1 713 | 830 | 1 697 | 4 388 | 2 584 | 402 | 2 183 | 109 528 | 36.5 | 29.4 |
| Santee | 19 306 | 2.72 | 13.5 | 20.6 | 966 | 889 | 274 | 77 | 1 109 | 2 052 | 244 | 1 808 | 34 851 | 36.6 | 20.0 |
| Saratoga | 10 734 | 2.77 | 5.7 | 16.2 | 199 | 165 | 161 | 34 | 230 | 760 | 53 | 707 | 21 470 | 7.4 | 75.9 |
| Seaside | 10 093 | 3.16 | 14.2 | 19.1 | 1 127 | 0 | 0 | 1 127 | 745 | 2 230 | 335 | 1 894 | 19 649 | 46.2 | 19.8 |
| Simi Valley | 41 237 | 3.00 | 11.3 | 17.2 | 660 | 178 | 123 | 482 | 1 813 | 1 442 | 92 | 1 350 | 81 168 | 32.9 | 31.3 |
| Soledad | 3 664 | 4.27 | 16.0 | 8.2 | 10 103 | 10 103 | 55 | 0 | 325 | 1 248 | 284 | 964 | 17 855 | 72.8 | 4.3 |
| South Gate | 23 278 | 4.05 | 20.2 | 9.8 | 88 | 72 | 72 | 16 | 3 473 | 3 636 | 607 | 3 029 | 53 813 | 74.8 | 6.6 |
| South Pasadena | 10 467 | 2.43 | 12.1 | 29.4 | 163 | 155 | 151 | 8 | 513 | 1 979 | 127 | 1 852 | 17 791 | 11.6 | 64.0 |
| South San Francisco | 20 938 | 3.01 | 13.8 | 20.5 | 579 | 51 | 18 | 528 | 1 465 | 2 276 | 214 | 2 061 | 43 503 | 38.5 | 31.0 |
| Stanton | 10 825 | 3.50 | 16.6 | 18.1 | 350 | 258 | 240 | 92 | 770 | 1 993 | 365 | 1 628 | 23 595 | 58.9 | 16.7 |
| Stockton | 90 605 | 3.16 | 18.9 | 21.5 | 5 734 | 1 838 | 1 558 | 3 896 | 19 618 | 6 647 | 1 408 | 5 239 | 168 544 | 51.1 | 17.1 |
| Suisun City | 8 918 | 3.15 | 16.6 | 16.2 | 44 | 17 | 5 | 27 | 741 | 2 605 | 176 | 2 430 | 17 594 | 39.2 | 21.3 |
| Sunnyvale | 53 384 | 2.61 | 8.7 | 25.2 | 849 | 469 | 457 | 380 | 2 120 | 1 496 | 106 | 1 390 | 97 984 | 21.7 | 56.9 |
| Temecula | 31 781 | 3.15 | 11.8 | 13.8 | 129 | 8 | 0 | 121 | 2 501 | 2 470 | 94 | 2 376 | 58 441 | 30.7 | 29.7 |
| Temple City | 11 606 | 3.03 | 14.8 | 17.0 | 422 | 393 | 388 | 29 | 394 | 1 095 | 139 | 956 | 24 833 | 36.1 | 35.9 |
| Thousand Oaks | 45 836 | 2.73 | 9.3 | 21.2 | 1 742 | 352 | 348 | 1 390 | 1 925 | 1 502 | 107 | 1 395 | 83 937 | 21.6 | 48.8 |
| Torrance | 56 001 | 2.58 | 11.0 | 25.8 | 1 146 | 640 | 578 | 506 | 2 952 | 2 006 | 126 | 1 880 | 102 732 | 26.0 | 43.7 |
| Tracy | 24 331 | 3.40 | 13.1 | 13.7 | 316 | 247 | 245 | 69 | 2 316 | 2 761 | 164 | 2 596 | 47 246 | 44.2 | 21.7 |
| Tulare | 17 720 | 3.33 | 18.0 | 16.2 | 278 | 216 | 216 | 62 | 2 553 | 4 257 | 572 | 3 685 | 33 046 | 57.8 | 11.1 |
| Turlock | 22 772 | 2.96 | 13.9 | 20.9 | 1 207 | 520 | 445 | 687 | 2 959 | 4 266 | 531 | 3 736 | 41 433 | 47.9 | 22.9 |
| Tustin | 25 203 | 2.98 | 13.9 | 20.5 | 520 | 180 | 150 | 340 | 1 610 | 2 107 | 127 | 1 980 | 47 522 | 33.1 | 38.6 |
| Twentynine Palms | 8 095 | 2.68 | 12.9 | 21.1 | 3 347 | 0 | 0 | 3 347 | 602 | 2 376 | 312 | 2 064 | 11 319 | 42.5 | 16.8 |
| Union City | 20 433 | 3.38 | 13.5 | 13.4 | 518 | 96 | 75 | 422 | 2 098 | 2 983 | 442 | 2 541 | 45 541 | 38.3 | 37.4 |
| Upland | 25 823 | 2.83 | 15.6 | 20.0 | 682 | 377 | 359 | 305 | 2 397 | 3 213 | 245 | 2 968 | 48 039 | 33.7 | 29.8 |
| Vacaville | 31 092 | 2.71 | 13.1 | 22.7 | 8 022 | 7 989 | 171 | 33 | 1 872 | 2 002 | 209 | 1 793 | 61 994 | 38.5 | 21.4 |
| Vallejo | 40 559 | 2.82 | 17.8 | 24.3 | 1 663 | 533 | 483 | 1 130 | 6 147 | 5 240 | 770 | 4 470 | 77 459 | 38.6 | 24.5 |
| Victorville | 32 558 | 3.40 | 19.9 | 15.6 | 5 103 | 4 762 | 294 | 341 | 4 617 | 3 937 | 585 | 3 352 | 61 832 | 52.0 | 11.2 |
| Visalia | 41 349 | 2.98 | 15.7 | 20.3 | 1 326 | 720 | 408 | 606 | 5 607 | 4 453 | 386 | 4 067 | 73 467 | 42.9 | 20.1 |
| Vista | 29 317 | 3.13 | 13.7 | 19.7 | 2 045 | 1 384 | 588 | 661 | 2 412 | 2 541 | 408 | 2 133 | 57 017 | 47.6 | 19.7 |
| Walnut | 8 533 | 3.41 | 11.5 | 7.3 | 34 | 12 | 10 | 22 | 394 | 1 335 | 136 | 1 199 | 19 710 | 22.5 | 49.5 |
| Walnut Creek | 30 443 | 2.08 | 6.8 | 39.0 | 1 002 | 826 | 826 | 176 | 2 093 | 3 224 | 106 | 3 117 | 49 554 | 14.9 | 60.3 |
| Wasco | 5 131 | 3.86 | 19.3 | 11.2 | 5 720 | 5 710 | 0 | 10 | NA | NA | NA | NA | 14 820 | 77.3 | 4.4 |
| Watsonville | 13 528 | 3.75 | 17.6 | 18.2 | 528 | 206 | 201 | 322 | 1 886 | 3 641 | 542 | 3 098 | 28 559 | 69.2 | 10.1 |
| West Covina | 31 596 | 3.34 | 17.1 | 15.2 | 674 | 323 | 299 | 351 | 3 529 | 3 288 | 261 | 3 027 | 67 714 | 41.2 | 26.8 |
| West Hollywood | 22 511 | 1.52 | 3.8 | 59.7 | 109 | 0 | 0 | 109 | 1 774 | 5 097 | 968 | 4 129 | 30 564 | 18.4 | 55.4 |
| Westminster | 26 164 | 3.40 | 14.1 | 16.2 | 670 | 289 | 197 | 381 | 2 752 | 3 032 | 273 | 2 759 | 60 341 | 50.5 | 20.0 |
| West Sacramento | 17 421 | 2.78 | 14.8 | 24.5 | 338 | 92 | 82 | 246 | 1 548 | 3 139 | 349 | 2 790 | 29 737 | 41.9 | 24.9 |
| Whittier | 28 273 | 2.96 | 16.1 | 21.6 | 1 635 | 552 | 434 | 1 083 | 2 802 | 3 246 | 387 | 2 859 | 53 861 | 41.6 | 23.3 |
| Wildomar | 9 992 | 3.22 | 11.8 | 16.0 | 42 | 4 | 4 | 38 | 765 | 2 350 | 141 | 2 209 | 18 846 | 44.0 | 16.8 |
| Windsor | 8 970 | 2.98 | 10.1 | 19.4 | 51 | 0 | 0 | 51 | 398 | 1 468 | 240 | 1 228 | 16 714 | 37.8 | 26.3 |
| Woodland | 18 721 | 2.91 | 14.1 | 21.9 | 985 | 829 | 323 | 156 | 1 366 | 2 434 | 317 | 2 117 | 34 667 | 45.1 | 24.1 |
| Yorba Linda | 21 576 | 2.97 | 8.5 | 14.5 | 190 | 93 | 93 | 97 | 868 | 1 336 | 75 | 1 260 | 42 266 | 18.2 | 46.9 |
| Yuba City | 21 550 | 2.99 | 13.8 | 22.1 | 580 | 455 | 247 | 125 | 2 005 | 3 052 | 320 | 2 733 | 39 859 | 46.0 | 19.2 |
| Yucaipa | 18 231 | 2.79 | 12.2 | 23.0 | 554 | 327 | 242 | 227 | 1 018 | 1 959 | 227 | 1 732 | 32 857 | 38.0 | 21.8 |
| **COLORADO** | 1 972 868 | 2.49 | 10.1 | 27.9 | 115 878 | 61 591 | 18 079 | 54 287 | 149 744 | 2 927 | 320 | 2 606 | 3 265 425 | 33.3 | 36.3 |
| Arvada | 42 701 | 2.48 | 10.7 | 26.3 | 506 | 343 | 314 | 163 | 2 709 | 2 502 | 151 | 2 351 | 72 260 | 32.9 | 33.6 |
| Aurora | 121 901 | 2.65 | 14.2 | 27.7 | 2 556 | 1 850 | 1 145 | 706 | 11 359 | 3 434 | 441 | 2 993 | 202 570 | 41.3 | 26.1 |
| Boulder | 41 302 | 2.16 | 5.5 | 35.8 | 8 105 | 1 080 | 531 | 7 025 | 2 737 | 2 762 | 248 | 2 514 | 55 548 | 11.8 | 70.3 |
| Brighton | 10 788 | 2.95 | 12.5 | 20.9 | 1 546 | 1 518 | 197 | 28 | 1 188 | 3 501 | 265 | 3 236 | 20 023 | 50.3 | 17.8 |
| Broomfield | 21 414 | 2.60 | 8.0 | 23.9 | 282 | 279 | 207 | 3 | 1 136 | 1 998 | 58 | 1 940 | 35 739 | 22.7 | 45.6 |

1. No spouse present.   2. Data for serious crimes have not been adjusted for underreporting. This may affect comparability between geographic areas and over time.   3. Per 100,000 population estimated by the FBI.   4. Persons 25 years old and over.

## Table D. Cities — Income, Poverty, and Housing

| City | Money income, 2007–2011 | | | | | Housing units, 2010 | | | Occupied Housing units 2007–2011 | | | | |
|---|---|---|---|---|---|---|---|---|---|---|---|---|---|
| | Per capita income[1] (dollars) | Households | | | Families with income below poverty (percent) | | | | | Owner-occupied | | Median owner costs as a percent of income | |
| | | Median income | Percent with income of $200,000 or more | Percent with income of less than $25,000 | | Total | Percent change, 2000–2010 | Vacant units for sale or rent[2] | Total | Percent | Median value[3] (dollars) | With a mortgage[4] | Without a mortgage[5] |
| | 42 | 43 | 44 | 45 | 46 | 47 | 48 | 49 | 50 | 51 | 52 | 53 | 54 |
| **CALIFORNIA—Cont'd** | | | | | | | | | | | | | |
| San Francisco | 46 777 | 72 947 | 12.6 | 20.7 | 7.6 | 376 942 | 8.8 | 31 131 | 338 366 | 37.1 | 767 300 | 30.2 | 10.0 |
| San Gabriel | 25 432 | 57 666 | 5.4 | 22.2 | 11.0 | 13 237 | 3.0 | 695 | 12 140 | 51.2 | 563 400 | 29.4 | 10.3 |
| San Jacinto | 17 692 | 47 645 | 1.4 | 27.4 | 15.1 | 14 977 | 58.7 | 1 825 | 12 828 | 67.6 | 162 200 | 34.0 | 12.8 |
| San Jose | 33 770 | 80 764 | 11.0 | 14.6 | 7.9 | 314 038 | 11.5 | 12 672 | 301 001 | 59.5 | 605 400 | 30.5 | 10.0 |
| San Juan Capistrano | 39 097 | 73 806 | 13.9 | 15.3 | 8.7 | 11 940 | 5.3 | 546 | 11 481 | 76.3 | 598 900 | 35.5 | 13.7 |
| San Leandro | 27 878 | 61 857 | 3.4 | 18.3 | 8.1 | 32 419 | 3.6 | 1 702 | 29 550 | 57.0 | 437 200 | 32.3 | 10.9 |
| San Luis Obispo | 25 775 | 42 528 | 3.6 | 34.1 | 6.8 | 20 553 | 6.3 | 1 360 | 18 485 | 38.2 | 561 700 | 28.9 | 10.0 |
| San Marcos | 25 282 | 55 815 | 4.9 | 18.1 | 8.7 | 28 641 | 51.5 | 1 439 | 26 165 | 61.4 | 409 200 | 33.3 | 14.2 |
| San Mateo | 45 248 | 86 772 | 12.7 | 11.3 | 3.6 | 40 014 | 4.7 | 1 781 | 37 439 | 53.6 | 740 600 | 29.6 | 10.8 |
| San Pablo | 17 044 | 45 305 | 0.1 | 27.8 | 17.3 | 9 571 | 2.5 | 810 | 8 688 | 47.0 | 245 700 | 36.2 | 12.5 |
| San Rafael | 42 499 | 71 343 | 11.7 | 16.0 | 6.7 | 24 011 | 4.6 | 1 247 | 23 660 | 52.1 | 768 400 | 29.9 | 10.5 |
| San Ramon | 50 962 | 124 014 | 21.5 | 5.6 | 2.8 | 26 222 | 50.5 | 938 | 24 360 | 71.6 | 731 300 | 29.8 | 10.0 |
| Santa Ana | 16 564 | 54 399 | 2.3 | 18.3 | 16.6 | 76 896 | 3.3 | 3 722 | 73 662 | 48.8 | 371 700 | 33.8 | 10.0 |
| Santa Barbara | 37 087 | 63 401 | 8.4 | 19.2 | 9.0 | 37 820 | 1.7 | 2 371 | 35 103 | 41.8 | 926 100 | 32.8 | 10.9 |
| Santa Clara | 39 523 | 89 004 | 10.9 | 13.9 | 5.9 | 45 147 | 14.0 | 2 126 | 42 316 | 45.8 | 629 800 | 28.2 | 10.0 |
| Santa Clarita | 33 322 | 83 579 | 7.4 | 12.1 | 4.8 | 62 055 | 18.3 | 2 548 | 58 102 | 71.6 | 424 400 | 30.3 | 12.5 |
| Santa Cruz | 31 898 | 63 110 | 8.4 | 23.6 | 6.2 | 23 316 | 8.6 | 1 659 | 21 626 | 45.4 | 695 400 | 30.0 | 10.0 |
| Santa Maria | 18 915 | 51 664 | 2.3 | 21.2 | 14.0 | 28 294 | 24.0 | 1 386 | 26 750 | 51.1 | 297 400 | 31.8 | 11.5 |
| Santa Monica | 58 933 | 71 400 | 12.7 | 20.0 | 6.4 | 50 912 | 6.4 | 3 995 | 46 937 | 27.9 | 987 300 | 28.7 | 11.2 |
| Santa Paula | 19 713 | 53 359 | 3.0 | 23.5 | 13.2 | 8 749 | 4.5 | 402 | 8 361 | 56.5 | 355 700 | 31.7 | 11.3 |
| Santa Rosa | 30 085 | 60 850 | 5.0 | 19.4 | 8.7 | 67 396 | 17.2 | 3 806 | 62 090 | 54.8 | 419 100 | 30.3 | 12.5 |
| Santee | 28 242 | 69 828 | 2.6 | 14.3 | 5.9 | 20 048 | 6.6 | 742 | 18 407 | 70.5 | 350 400 | 30.6 | 13.6 |
| Saratoga | 71 223 | 155 182 | 39.4 | 7.4 | 2.1 | 11 123 | 4.3 | 389 | 10 712 | 85.2 | 1 000 000 | 29.7 | 10.0 |
| Seaside | 22 262 | 58 403 | 1.8 | 15.8 | 9.8 | 10 872 | -1.2 | 779 | 10 206 | 43.7 | 509 800 | 34.2 | 10.2 |
| Simi Valley | 35 467 | 89 452 | 8.9 | 10.0 | 4.6 | 42 506 | 13.9 | 1 269 | 40 550 | 74.1 | 493 000 | 30.3 | 10.8 |
| Soledad | 9 971 | 53 140 | 1.6 | 19.7 | 15.7 | 3 876 | 52.4 | 212 | 3 602 | 58.2 | 264 700 | 34.2 | 11.0 |
| South Gate | 14 039 | 41 990 | 0.8 | 25.7 | 19.2 | 24 160 | -0.5 | 882 | 23 718 | 44.3 | 339 900 | 37.0 | 10.0 |
| South Pasadena | 50 185 | 84 914 | 14.6 | 12.0 | 4.4 | 11 118 | 2.5 | 651 | 10 318 | 48.0 | 834 400 | 28.0 | 10.0 |
| South San Francisco | 31 563 | 75 543 | 6.8 | 13.4 | 3.4 | 21 814 | 8.2 | 876 | 21 084 | 59.9 | 626 200 | 32.4 | 10.0 |
| Stanton | 20 558 | 51 933 | 2.2 | 18.9 | 12.8 | 11 283 | 3.1 | 458 | 11 455 | 50.4 | 312 000 | 31.9 | 12.7 |
| Stockton | 20 082 | 47 365 | 2.5 | 25.7 | 18.0 | 99 637 | 21.3 | 9 032 | 89 816 | 53.3 | 222 200 | 31.7 | 10.8 |
| Suisun City | 26 148 | 71 411 | 3.2 | 12.1 | 6.6 | 9 454 | 16.0 | 536 | 8 939 | 71.2 | 283 400 | 31.1 | 10.5 |
| Sunnyvale | 44 617 | 93 292 | 13.5 | 11.2 | 4.0 | 55 791 | 3.8 | 2 407 | 53 155 | 48.3 | 710 600 | 27.3 | 10.0 |
| Temecula | 28 274 | 76 276 | 5.1 | 13.1 | 7.4 | 34 004 | 78.8 | 2 223 | 30 761 | 69.4 | 342 000 | 32.5 | 12.7 |
| Temple City | 26 779 | 65 445 | 5.8 | 15.5 | 7.1 | 12 117 | 3.5 | 511 | 11 207 | 62.5 | 585 200 | 31.0 | 10.0 |
| Thousand Oaks | 46 093 | 100 373 | 16.0 | 10.9 | 4.6 | 47 497 | 10.6 | 1 661 | 44 979 | 74.0 | 644 000 | 28.8 | 12.4 |
| Torrance | 36 370 | 75 885 | 7.3 | 15.4 | 5.0 | 58 377 | 4.3 | 2 376 | 55 433 | 57.0 | 641 400 | 30.4 | 10.0 |
| Tracy | 26 846 | 76 739 | 5.0 | 13.0 | 6.7 | 25 963 | 43.9 | 1 632 | 23 613 | 67.4 | 314 900 | 32.2 | 12.5 |
| Tulare | 17 922 | 46 274 | 1.8 | 24.1 | 15.1 | 18 863 | 32.6 | 1 143 | 17 351 | 58.5 | 183 900 | 27.6 | 12.8 |
| Turlock | 22 289 | 50 862 | 2.1 | 25.2 | 10.9 | 24 627 | 29.3 | 1 855 | 22 780 | 55.7 | 242 600 | 28.1 | 13.2 |
| Tustin | 32 854 | 73 231 | 9.8 | 14.0 | 7.5 | 26 476 | 3.9 | 1 273 | 24 945 | 52.6 | 540 500 | 30.7 | 11.5 |
| Twentynine Palms | 21 546 | 43 412 | 0.7 | 24.1 | 10.2 | 9 431 | 38.9 | 1 336 | 7 612 | 35.5 | 166 300 | 24.1 | 10.0 |
| Union City | 29 612 | 82 634 | 7.9 | 12.4 | 5.9 | 21 258 | 12.7 | 825 | 20 161 | 69.4 | 536 200 | 30.3 | 10.0 |
| Upland | 29 614 | 67 449 | 5.9 | 15.7 | 7.3 | 27 355 | 7.4 | 1 532 | 25 347 | 59.3 | 450 800 | 28.3 | 10.0 |
| Vacaville | 29 687 | 73 302 | 6.0 | 12.4 | 6.6 | 32 814 | 14.4 | 1 722 | 30 435 | 65.6 | 335 400 | 28.2 | 11.1 |
| Vallejo | 27 375 | 62 325 | 4.3 | 20.9 | 11.8 | 44 433 | 7.9 | 3 874 | 40 458 | 60.9 | 299 900 | 31.3 | 10.0 |
| Victorville | 17 249 | 52 357 | 1.5 | 24.0 | 18.2 | 36 655 | 61.8 | 4 097 | 30 806 | 63.6 | 172 500 | 30.8 | 14.0 |
| Visalia | 23 571 | 54 019 | 3.0 | 21.6 | 12.4 | 44 205 | 34.8 | 2 856 | 39 986 | 62.2 | 212 500 | 27.7 | 11.9 |
| Vista | 21 478 | 50 777 | 1.9 | 17.5 | 11.2 | 30 986 | 3.5 | 1 669 | 29 073 | 51.3 | 380 800 | 33.8 | 12.0 |
| Walnut | 34 045 | 101 358 | 12.3 | 8.1 | 4.1 | 8 753 | 4.3 | 220 | 8 259 | 90.0 | 634 100 | 29.0 | 10.0 |
| Walnut Creek | 52 727 | 84 722 | 13.2 | 12.7 | 2.0 | 32 681 | 3.8 | 2 238 | 30 018 | 67.5 | 614 000 | 26.5 | 14.8 |
| Wasco | 11 498 | 40 295 | 1.2 | 31.3 | 24.2 | 5 477 | 28.2 | 346 | 5 122 | 56.3 | 157 200 | 27.5 | 10.0 |
| Watsonville | 16 407 | 46 073 | 0.9 | 26.4 | 18.6 | 14 089 | 19.7 | 561 | 13 800 | 47.0 | 389 800 | 38.6 | 12.4 |
| West Covina | 26 006 | 68 308 | 4.1 | 14.5 | 6.4 | 32 705 | 2.2 | 1 109 | 31 372 | 65.8 | 426 100 | 30.7 | 10.0 |
| West Hollywood | 53 227 | 52 303 | 6.1 | 27.4 | 8.2 | 24 588 | 2.0 | 2 077 | 22 706 | 22.9 | 637 900 | 31.9 | 24.6 |
| Westminster | 23 201 | 56 867 | 4.1 | 21.6 | 11.7 | 27 650 | 2.7 | 1 486 | 27 092 | 55.8 | 491 500 | 31.6 | 10.0 |
| West Sacramento | 24 621 | 54 040 | 1.9 | 24.6 | 14.4 | 18 681 | 54.1 | 1 260 | 17 079 | 59.2 | 275 500 | 30.7 | 10.9 |
| Whittier | 28 031 | 68 055 | 5.0 | 16.5 | 7.8 | 29 591 | 1.9 | 1 318 | 27 337 | 57.2 | 473 400 | 31.0 | 10.0 |
| Wildomar | 24 255 | 63 519 | 4.1 | 16.4 | 8.6 | 10 806 | 128.0 | 814 | 9 545 | 75.0 | 267 000 | 35.2 | 11.8 |
| Windsor | 31 009 | 77 157 | 6.5 | 10.7 | 2.3 | 9 549 | 23.4 | 579 | 8 985 | 75.7 | 424 200 | 29.9 | 17.0 |
| Woodland | 26 416 | 56 859 | 3.2 | 20.3 | 8.0 | 19 806 | 15.8 | 1 085 | 19 363 | 58.0 | 319 500 | 28.4 | 10.0 |
| Yorba Linda | 49 485 | 115 291 | 19.8 | 7.7 | 1.8 | 22 305 | 14.2 | 729 | 21 360 | 84.5 | 724 600 | 29.6 | 10.0 |
| Yuba City | 21 566 | 48 830 | 2.0 | 24.0 | 12.2 | 23 174 | 66.6 | 1 624 | 21 711 | 57.7 | 227 400 | 28.3 | 12.6 |
| Yucaipa | 26 985 | 59 596 | 4.2 | 18.8 | 8.0 | 19 642 | 21.9 | 1 411 | 17 227 | 76.2 | 272 500 | 28.3 | 14.0 |
| **COLORADO** | 30 816 | 57 685 | 4.8 | 20.2 | 8.7 | 2 212 898 | 22.4 | 240 030 | 1 941 193 | 66.8 | 236 700 | 25.0 | 10.2 |
| Arvada | 31 808 | 67 302 | 3.7 | 15.3 | 5.6 | 44 427 | 12.1 | 1 726 | 42 214 | 74.3 | 239 700 | 24.7 | 10.7 |
| Aurora | 24 257 | 50 468 | 2.0 | 22.9 | 13.1 | 131 040 | 20.1 | 9 139 | 121 198 | 61.0 | 182 800 | 26.4 | 10.7 |
| Boulder | 37 349 | 54 051 | 8.7 | 26.6 | 7.1 | 43 479 | 6.6 | 2 177 | 40 985 | 49.5 | 484 800 | 23.7 | 10.0 |
| Brighton | 24 423 | 64 585 | 2.2 | 14.1 | 6.7 | 11 387 | 63.0 | 599 | 10 402 | 72.8 | 195 100 | 26.8 | 12.0 |
| Broomfield | 36 783 | 76 531 | 6.9 | 12.3 | 4.2 | 22 646 | 57.8 | 1 232 | 20 841 | 72.1 | 270 500 | 23.2 | 12.0 |

1. Based on population estimated by the American Community Survey.   2. Includes units rented or sold but not occupied.   3. Specified owner-occupied units; $1,000,000 represents $1,000,000 or more   4. 50.0 represents 50 percent or more.   5. 10.0 represents 10 percent or less.

# Table D. Cities — Housing, Labor Force, and Employment

| City | Occupied housing units, 2007–2011 (cont.) | | | | Migration, 2007–2011 | | Civilian labor force, 2012 | | Unemployment | | Civilian employment[4], 2007–2011 | | | |
|---|---|---|---|---|---|---|---|---|---|---|---|---|---|---|
| | | | | | | | | | | | | Percent | | |
| | Percent renter occupied | Median gross rent[1] | Median rent as a percent of income[2] | Percent with no vehicle available | Percent who lived in the same house one year ago | Percent who lived outside this city one year ago | Total | Percent change, 2011–2012 | Total | Rate[3] | Population age 16 and older | In labor force | Full-year full-time worker | Households with no workers (percent) |
| | 55 | 56 | 57 | 58 | 59 | 60 | 61 | 62 | 63 | 64 | 65 | 66 | 67 | 68 |
| CALIFORNIA—Cont'd | | | | | | | | | | | | | | |
| San Francisco | 62.9 | 1 388 | 27.9 | 30.1 | 84.0 | 7.5 | 477 632 | 3.7 | 34 859 | 7.3 | 702 526 | 68.9 | 43.7 | 25.0 |
| San Gabriel | 48.8 | 1 227 | 34.8 | 7.0 | 87.7 | 9.9 | 20 471 | -0.7 | 1 839 | 9.0 | 33 101 | 61.6 | 39.8 | 19.7 |
| San Jacinto | 32.4 | 1 051 | 36.8 | 6.4 | 79.3 | 13.6 | 12 843 | -0.6 | 2 363 | 18.4 | 30 165 | 58.6 | 30.3 | 32.2 |
| San Jose | 40.5 | 1 390 | 30.7 | 5.4 | 85.9 | 6.0 | 477 829 | 2.7 | 44 762 | 9.4 | 730 135 | 68.1 | 41.9 | 18.6 |
| San Juan Capistrano | 23.7 | 1 773 | 42.8 | 5.1 | 88.0 | 7.5 | 17 841 | 1.8 | 1 195 | 6.7 | 26 674 | 63.3 | 38.7 | 27.3 |
| San Leandro | 43.0 | 1 182 | 30.3 | 6.8 | 86.5 | 9.2 | 42 486 | 2.3 | 3 780 | 8.9 | 66 727 | 67.0 | 41.8 | 23.2 |
| San Luis Obispo | 61.8 | 1 195 | 49.9 | 7.9 | 63.1 | 16.7 | 28 841 | 3.9 | 2 558 | 8.9 | 40 428 | 60.9 | 26.5 | 28.1 |
| San Marcos | 38.6 | 1 259 | 36.9 | 4.1 | 85.1 | 10.6 | 31 775 | 1.6 | 2 837 | 8.9 | 60 309 | 62.2 | 37.3 | 24.3 |
| San Mateo | 46.4 | 1 538 | 27.6 | 7.3 | 86.4 | 9.4 | 51 882 | 4.8 | 2 766 | 5.3 | 78 190 | 70.6 | 45.8 | 22.5 |
| San Pablo | 53.0 | 1 066 | 40.0 | 15.6 | 80.3 | 12.2 | 14 280 | -0.4 | 2 566 | 18.0 | 21 703 | 66.5 | 33.5 | 25.8 |
| San Rafael | 47.9 | 1 415 | 33.4 | 6.8 | 83.0 | 12.0 | 32 001 | 3.8 | 2 408 | 7.5 | 47 356 | 66.9 | 38.4 | 24.6 |
| San Ramon | 28.4 | 1 632 | 24.9 | 2.7 | 84.5 | 11.7 | 28 975 | 3.6 | 1 073 | 3.7 | 50 795 | 74.3 | 50.2 | 12.2 |
| Santa Ana | 51.2 | 1 269 | 34.1 | 6.7 | 82.2 | 7.5 | 162 407 | 0.5 | 19 553 | 12.0 | 237 040 | 68.4 | 40.6 | 13.4 |
| Santa Barbara | 58.2 | 1 424 | 35.0 | 10.0 | 79.1 | 11.0 | 57 771 | 5.3 | 3 240 | 5.6 | 73 937 | 68.3 | 39.8 | 26.4 |
| Santa Clara | 54.2 | 1 487 | 25.6 | 5.2 | 79.3 | 15.9 | 58 717 | 3.1 | 4 525 | 7.7 | 91 709 | 68.1 | 43.0 | 20.5 |
| Santa Clarita | 28.4 | 1 494 | 32.6 | 4.6 | 85.2 | 9.8 | 88 794 | -0.2 | 5 968 | 6.7 | 134 186 | 70.8 | 42.5 | 19.1 |
| Santa Cruz | 54.6 | 1 369 | 39.1 | 8.9 | 69.9 | 17.0 | 32 834 | 3.1 | 3 051 | 9.3 | 51 555 | 63.6 | 28.3 | 26.9 |
| Santa Maria | 48.9 | 1 100 | 33.4 | 7.5 | 80.9 | 6.3 | 41 590 | 3.1 | 5 173 | 12.4 | 69 488 | 64.8 | 36.2 | 24.1 |
| Santa Monica | 72.1 | 1 447 | 28.7 | 9.9 | 82.2 | 13.3 | 56 991 | -0.7 | 5 145 | 9.0 | 78 351 | 69.9 | 41.3 | 26.2 |
| Santa Paula | 43.5 | 1 094 | 34.9 | 8.1 | 87.4 | 6.0 | 15 183 | 0.6 | 2 263 | 14.9 | 21 826 | 64.2 | 34.7 | 28.1 |
| Santa Rosa | 45.2 | 1 193 | 32.5 | 6.5 | 81.3 | 8.3 | 81 585 | 1.6 | 6 969 | 8.5 | 130 413 | 66.5 | 36.4 | 26.8 |
| Santee | 29.5 | 1 242 | 30.4 | 4.4 | 87.5 | 10.1 | 33 577 | 1.9 | 2 513 | 7.5 | 42 178 | 67.0 | 40.7 | 23.0 |
| Saratoga | 14.8 | 1 698 | 26.8 | 4.4 | 92.7 | 5.8 | 13 879 | 4.1 | 587 | 4.2 | 23 996 | 56.0 | 38.0 | 30.7 |
| Seaside | 56.3 | 1 465 | 33.4 | 6.8 | 75.1 | 18.4 | 17 118 | 11.7 | 1 143 | 6.7 | 24 968 | 72.5 | 34.2 | 16.5 |
| Simi Valley | 25.9 | 1 679 | 30.1 | 3.6 | 88.3 | 6.0 | 71 097 | 2.4 | 5 295 | 7.4 | 96 251 | 71.0 | 45.7 | 17.3 |
| Soledad | 41.8 | 1 030 | 33.3 | 8.4 | 78.7 | 16.4 | 6 104 | 6.6 | 881 | 14.4 | 21 109 | 34.4 | 18.2 | 18.2 |
| South Gate | 55.7 | 987 | 36.3 | 8.7 | 90.8 | 6.4 | 41 400 | -1.6 | 5 774 | 13.9 | 69 280 | 63.4 | 39.6 | 17.1 |
| South Pasadena | 52.0 | 1 399 | 25.6 | 2.6 | 86.1 | 11.5 | 15 151 | 0.0 | 823 | 5.4 | 20 214 | 71.4 | 46.4 | 19.4 |
| South San Francisco | 40.1 | 1 462 | 30.7 | 7.8 | 88.5 | 7.2 | 33 105 | 4.1 | 2 742 | 8.3 | 50 468 | 67.8 | 45.0 | 22.3 |
| Stanton | 49.6 | 1 262 | 35.6 | 7.4 | 87.7 | 9.9 | 18 763 | 0.5 | 2 297 | 12.2 | 28 992 | 67.7 | 40.4 | 19.7 |
| Stockton | 46.7 | 936 | 36.4 | 9.1 | 78.8 | 6.9 | 125 917 | -0.7 | 23 002 | 18.3 | 212 365 | 61.5 | 32.9 | 28.0 |
| Suisun City | 28.8 | 1 411 | 36.9 | 3.6 | 80.5 | 16.1 | 15 128 | 1.3 | 1 581 | 10.5 | 21 218 | 70.1 | 40.5 | 16.7 |
| Sunnyvale | 51.7 | 1 483 | 22.4 | 4.4 | 83.0 | 12.2 | 78 041 | 3.3 | 5 626 | 7.2 | 110 523 | 70.7 | 46.5 | 17.4 |
| Temecula | 30.6 | 1 431 | 34.0 | 2.7 | 82.1 | 12.1 | 37 933 | 1.2 | 3 167 | 8.3 | 71 722 | 68.8 | 39.3 | 17.2 |
| Temple City | 37.5 | 1 333 | 33.5 | 3.5 | 89.1 | 8.3 | 17 981 | -0.3 | 1 274 | 7.1 | 28 776 | 62.2 | 40.4 | 19.3 |
| Thousand Oaks | 26.0 | 1 766 | 31.3 | 3.7 | 87.1 | 8.4 | 72 623 | 2.5 | 5 085 | 7.0 | 98 920 | 67.0 | 40.2 | 22.2 |
| Torrance | 43.0 | 1 394 | 29.9 | 5.4 | 88.0 | 7.2 | 79 011 | 0.0 | 4 306 | 5.4 | 117 667 | 66.1 | 42.0 | 23.2 |
| Tracy | 32.6 | 1 353 | 31.9 | 4.2 | 80.6 | 10.3 | 32 730 | 1.7 | 3 111 | 9.5 | 57 675 | 71.3 | 41.0 | 15.3 |
| Tulare | 41.5 | 903 | 32.4 | 6.0 | 86.6 | 4.0 | 23 962 | 0.0 | 3 244 | 13.5 | 40 978 | 61.3 | 39.3 | 24.0 |
| Turlock | 44.3 | 942 | 34.5 | 7.2 | 79.8 | 9.7 | 29 095 | 1.7 | 3 360 | 11.5 | 52 304 | 64.7 | 34.9 | 26.9 |
| Tustin | 47.4 | 1 445 | 33.0 | 3.9 | 81.3 | 13.3 | 42 269 | 1.6 | 3 156 | 7.5 | 57 378 | 72.8 | 45.4 | 16.6 |
| Twentynine Palms | 64.5 | 927 | 31.0 | 6.1 | 57.8 | 29.5 | 6 140 | -0.3 | 882 | 14.4 | 20 118 | 73.1 | 19.7 | 21.9 |
| Union City | 30.6 | 1 359 | 32.0 | 5.4 | 89.8 | 7.6 | 35 023 | 2.5 | 2 961 | 8.5 | 53 744 | 66.5 | 42.4 | 22.2 |
| Upland | 40.7 | 1 165 | 32.2 | 4.2 | 85.2 | 11.2 | 40 101 | 1.0 | 3 296 | 8.2 | 57 670 | 66.4 | 39.9 | 20.5 |
| Vacaville | 34.4 | 1 313 | 31.9 | 4.5 | 82.7 | 9.8 | 46 142 | 2.0 | 3 483 | 7.5 | 72 922 | 61.3 | 36.2 | 21.9 |
| Vallejo | 39.1 | 1 168 | 34.6 | 8.1 | 82.5 | 7.6 | 66 298 | 0.8 | 8 266 | 12.5 | 91 696 | 64.4 | 37.1 | 26.5 |
| Victorville | 36.4 | 1 091 | 38.3 | 5.8 | 79.1 | 13.3 | 30 013 | -0.3 | 4 322 | 14.4 | 77 388 | 56.0 | 31.7 | 26.5 |
| Visalia | 37.8 | 928 | 32.7 | 7.8 | 83.3 | 6.2 | 55 543 | 0.7 | 5 494 | 9.9 | 88 847 | 63.7 | 40.4 | 24.8 |
| Vista | 48.7 | 1 234 | 35.1 | 3.9 | 84.0 | 11.7 | 49 973 | 1.4 | 4 966 | 9.9 | 71 635 | 64.1 | 37.7 | 21.8 |
| Walnut | 10.0 | 1 900 | 37.9 | 1.7 | 92.3 | 5.5 | 16 372 | 0.1 | 871 | 5.3 | 24 279 | 61.4 | 41.4 | 15.5 |
| Walnut Creek | 32.5 | 1 388 | 27.6 | 8.6 | 83.8 | 12.5 | 35 021 | 2.9 | 2 123 | 6.1 | 54 663 | 60.6 | 37.9 | 34.6 |
| Wasco | 43.7 | 595 | 30.1 | 7.7 | 71.9 | 19.1 | 9 128 | 1.3 | 2 220 | 24.3 | 19 327 | 42.5 | 24.3 | 25.4 |
| Watsonville | 53.0 | 1 054 | 34.9 | 7.7 | 85.3 | 5.6 | 23 691 | -2.3 | 5 500 | 23.2 | 36 597 | 66.3 | 32.1 | 23.2 |
| West Covina | 34.2 | 1 341 | 33.6 | 5.3 | 87.0 | 9.3 | 55 006 | -0.8 | 5 306 | 9.6 | 82 795 | 65.4 | 39.5 | 20.2 |
| West Hollywood | 77.1 | 1 260 | 31.3 | 15.9 | 80.4 | 16.9 | 26 847 | -0.7 | 2 484 | 9.3 | 33 262 | 74.3 | 44.5 | 27.8 |
| Westminster | 44.2 | 1 300 | 39.0 | 6.2 | 86.6 | 9.9 | 46 640 | 1.4 | 3 941 | 8.4 | 71 026 | 62.2 | 37.2 | 22.6 |
| West Sacramento | 40.8 | 890 | 32.2 | 7.7 | 78.7 | 11.4 | 16 687 | -3.4 | 2 931 | 17.6 | 36 086 | 67.2 | 38.5 | 26.7 |
| Whittier | 42.8 | 1 147 | 31.5 | 6.3 | 87.4 | 8.5 | 43 306 | -0.4 | 3 387 | 7.8 | 65 885 | 65.5 | 41.2 | 22.0 |
| Wildomar | 25.0 | 1 369 | 34.8 | 3.3 | 82.7 | 12.0 | NA | NA | NA | NA | 23 008 | 66.4 | 37.3 | 21.4 |
| Windsor | 24.3 | 1 585 | 32.7 | 4.6 | 89.9 | 5.4 | 12 549 | 1.9 | 955 | 7.6 | 19 833 | 70.9 | 42.7 | 22.8 |
| Woodland | 42.0 | 955 | 31.8 | 8.1 | 80.7 | 8.6 | 28 957 | -2.0 | 3 901 | 13.5 | 42 711 | 65.9 | 39.1 | 25.3 |
| Yorba Linda | 15.5 | 1 799 | 34.7 | 3.3 | 89.0 | 7.4 | 35 658 | 2.2 | 1 793 | 5.0 | 50 106 | 67.8 | 43.6 | 18.4 |
| Yuba City | 42.3 | 863 | 32.0 | 7.3 | 80.6 | 8.2 | 20 063 | 0.5 | 3 921 | 19.5 | 48 537 | 63.8 | 32.6 | 30.0 |
| Yucaipa | 23.8 | 987 | 33.4 | 4.2 | 86.3 | 7.8 | 21 930 | 0.7 | 2 107 | 9.6 | 39 028 | 63.0 | 37.1 | 27.2 |
| COLORADO | 33.2 | 883 | 30.7 | 5.7 | 80.8 | 12.7 | 2 743 264 | 1.6 | 219 729 | 8.0 | 3 888 310 | 69.7 | 42.6 | 21.9 |
| Arvada | 25.7 | 916 | 29.3 | 4.8 | 84.5 | 11.1 | 59 054 | 1.7 | 4 698 | 8.0 | 83 897 | 70.8 | 45.2 | 22.7 |
| Aurora | 39.0 | 888 | 33.6 | 6.6 | 78.7 | 11.2 | 179 797 | 1.8 | 15 281 | 8.5 | 241 425 | 72.0 | 45.6 | 19.9 |
| Boulder | 50.5 | 1 067 | 41.6 | 7.8 | 63.2 | 20.9 | 61 423 | 3.2 | 3 461 | 5.6 | 85 592 | 66.3 | 31.3 | 22.6 |
| Brighton | 27.2 | 923 | 27.4 | 4.0 | 82.1 | 12.8 | 16 395 | 1.4 | 1 629 | 9.9 | 24 111 | 67.5 | 43.8 | 16.9 |
| Broomfield | 27.9 | 1 037 | 28.2 | 3.3 | 82.2 | 13.2 | 31 506 | 2.6 | 2 249 | 7.1 | 41 746 | 74.0 | 49.0 | 16.9 |

1. $2,000 represents $2,000 or more.    2. 50.0 represents 50 percent or more.    3. Percent of civilian labor force.    4. Persons 16 years old and over.

| City | Value of residential construction authorized by building permits, 2011 | | | Wholesale trade,[1] 2007 | | | | Retail trade,[2] 2007 | | | |
|---|---|---|---|---|---|---|---|---|---|---|---|
| | New construction ($1,000) | Number of housing units | Percent single family | Number of establish-ments | Number of employees | Sales (mil dol) | Annual payroll (mil dol) | Number of establish-ments | Number of employees | Sales (mil dol) | Annual payroll (mil dol) |
| | 69 | 70 | 71 | 72 | 73 | 74 | 75 | 76 | 77 | 78 | 79 |
| CALIFORNIA—Cont'd | | | | | | | | | | | |
| San Francisco | 481 144 | 1 818 | 1.7 | 1 195 | 11 786 | 10 562.2 | 668.1 | 3 710 | 45 079 | 12 400.0 | 1 395.9 |
| San Gabriel | 2 996 | 9 | 100.0 | 146 | 726 | 220.1 | 21.5 | 221 | 1 651 | 440.4 | 35.5 |
| San Jacinto | 1 811 | 13 | 100.0 | 13 | 167 | 60.0 | 5.9 | 54 | 744 | 195.6 | 19.5 |
| San Jose | 172 285 | 1 045 | 7.9 | 1 098 | 21 549 | 30 166.7 | 1 922.0 | 2 397 | 41 343 | 11 482.4 | 1 666.4 |
| San Juan Capistrano .... | 5 055 | 14 | 100.0 | 62 | 414 | 318.7 | 21.9 | 150 | 1 883 | 535.9 | 53.9 |
| San Leandro | 2 482 | 8 | 100.0 | 263 | 5 151 | 2 428.6 | 271.5 | 320 | 5 597 | 1 557.9 | 151.9 |
| San Luis Obispo | 4 109 | 26 | 30.8 | 74 | 855 | 312.9 | 38.2 | 382 | 5 357 | 1 283.3 | 125.4 |
| San Marcos | 79 033 | 407 | 40.0 | 155 | 1 757 | 800.0 | 72.7 | 263 | 4 611 | 1 224.6 | 129.9 |
| San Mateo | 4 858 | 26 | 19.2 | 101 | 887 | 438.3 | 69.3 | 408 | 7 320 | 1 652.2 | 203.4 |
| San Pablo | 101 | 1 | 100.0 | 8 | D | D | D | 82 | 956 | 222.8 | 23.1 |
| San Rafael | 0 | 0 | 0.0 | 138 | 1 523 | 1 049.6 | 82.9 | 373 | 5 583 | 1 657.5 | 178.3 |
| San Ramon | 0 | 0 | 0.0 | 90 | 956 | 2 534.8 | 75.7 | 136 | 2 546 | 679.1 | 70.4 |
| Santa Ana | 24 783 | 167 | 25.1 | 560 | 7 262 | 2 881.5 | 372.9 | 920 | 13 893 | 3 346.1 | 372.8 |
| Santa Barbara | 11 354 | 45 | 33.3 | 111 | 1 330 | 558.9 | 51.8 | 617 | 7 579 | 1 729.6 | 205.3 |
| Santa Clara | 26 514 | 161 | 21.1 | 399 | 12 368 | 7 464.8 | 1 298.6 | 403 | 5 602 | 1 806.7 | 192.1 |
| Santa Clarita | 33 591 | 80 | 100.0 | 194 | 3 053 | 6 452.9 | 169.3 | 531 | 10 207 | 2 903.2 | 251.6 |
| Santa Cruz | 5 470 | 19 | 100.0 | 48 | 927 | 622.4 | 62.2 | 287 | 3 601 | 830.5 | 95.0 |
| Santa Maria | 6 722 | 42 | 52.4 | 108 | 1 218 | 673.7 | 52.3 | 349 | 5 531 | 1 448.8 | 139.3 |
| Santa Monica | 123 546 | 395 | 6.8 | 171 | 3 840 | 3 259.4 | 191.9 | 750 | 10 025 | 4 944.7 | 340.1 |
| Santa Paula | 3 057 | 21 | 4.8 | 14 | D | D | D | 64 | 724 | 168.6 | 17.7 |
| Santa Rosa | 48 764 | 255 | 72.5 | 157 | 2 514 | 1 522.5 | 155.8 | 729 | 11 971 | 2 977.2 | 334.8 |
| Santee | 30 770 | 160 | 50.0 | 51 | 447 | 152.8 | 15.8 | 131 | 2 835 | 672.9 | 64.2 |
| Saratoga | 25 991 | 33 | 100.0 | 24 | 145 | 75.9 | 7.5 | 51 | 542 | 108.8 | 13.1 |
| Seaside | 0 | 0 | 0.0 | 13 | 62 | 33.6 | 2.0 | 96 | 1 871 | 563.3 | 53.1 |
| Simi Valley | 1 987 | 6 | 100.0 | 140 | 2 137 | 852.5 | 100.5 | 468 | 6 857 | 1 689.6 | 159.3 |
| Soledad | 4 232 | 16 | 100.0 | 5 | D | D | D | 31 | 290 | 72.7 | 6.3 |
| South Gate | 912 | 7 | 100.0 | 64 | 915 | 717.4 | 41.2 | 185 | 2 518 | 787.0 | 61.8 |
| South Pasadena | 1 943 | 7 | 100.0 | 27 | 122 | 163.5 | 8.6 | 66 | 837 | 192.3 | 21.8 |
| South San Francisco | 23 953 | 109 | 0.0 | 332 | 5 350 | 3 150.1 | 339.0 | 193 | 2 676 | 791.9 | 83.3 |
| Stanton | 0 | 0 | 0.0 | 34 | 331 | 100.0 | 13.4 | 117 | 1 293 | 347.5 | 34.1 |
| Stockton | 26 058 | 127 | 100.0 | 248 | 4 783 | 3 701.8 | 199.4 | 759 | 13 076 | 3 340.1 | 301.2 |
| Suisun City | 0 | 0 | 0.0 | 4 | D | D | D | 33 | 520 | 172.5 | 13.9 |
| Sunnyvale | 83 445 | 490 | 43.1 | 228 | 12 043 | 10 557.8 | 1 587.1 | 316 | 5 524 | 1 863.1 | 159.2 |
| Temecula | 55 632 | 288 | 100.0 | 166 | 2 804 | 2 112.1 | 104.6 | 480 | 8 447 | 2 371.3 | 206.5 |
| Temple City | 12 632 | 32 | 100.0 | 80 | 327 | 112.2 | 7.6 | 110 | 964 | 180.6 | 18.5 |
| Thousand Oaks | 16 949 | 39 | 46.2 | 184 | 2 385 | 1 462.0 | 170.5 | 594 | 9 292 | 2 853.8 | 273.1 |
| Torrance | 3 390 | 13 | 61.5 | 586 | 6 226 | 13 175.4 | 321.5 | 762 | 14 145 | 4 877.8 | 371.1 |
| Tracy | 2 952 | 11 | 100.0 | 59 | 981 | 1 101.0 | 57.9 | 269 | 4 306 | 1 106.0 | 101.3 |
| Tulare | 28 161 | 267 | 58.1 | 41 | 541 | 182.3 | 21.7 | 185 | 2 838 | 662.4 | 65.4 |
| Turlock | 4 014 | 28 | 100.0 | 53 | 667 | 265.9 | 27.9 | 238 | 4 092 | 987.2 | 96.9 |
| Tustin | 46 766 | 334 | 29.0 | 195 | 2 709 | 1 343.4 | 160.8 | 286 | 4 961 | 1 849.9 | 147.2 |
| Twentynine Palms | 3 516 | 34 | 94.1 | 4 | 15 | 4.1 | 0.4 | 31 | 326 | 93.8 | 7.4 |
| Union City | 7 494 | 59 | 3.4 | 140 | 3 814 | 2 905.4 | 235.0 | 120 | 2 716 | 665.3 | 84.4 |
| Upland | 11 797 | 54 | 90.7 | 103 | 665 | 188.4 | 25.7 | 280 | 4 124 | 918.8 | 94.8 |
| Vacaville | 33 768 | 140 | 100.0 | 35 | D | D | D | 348 | 6 010 | 1 430.5 | 135.5 |
| Vallejo | 5 577 | 25 | 100.0 | 29 | 599 | 398.7 | 30.0 | 269 | 4 432 | 1 192.8 | 123.9 |
| Victorville | 25 484 | 152 | 73.7 | 39 | 217 | 169.9 | 11.0 | 372 | 7 457 | 1 939.5 | 173.1 |
| Visalia | 58 722 | 279 | 97.1 | 134 | 1 334 | 1 566.1 | 60.2 | 468 | 7 658 | 1 943.0 | 177.9 |
| Vista | 18 624 | 71 | 83.1 | 196 | 3 485 | 1 694.8 | 169.6 | 294 | 4 914 | 1 246.6 | 135.0 |
| Walnut | 42 943 | 85 | 100.0 | 265 | 988 | 611.5 | 36.0 | 106 | 1 082 | 209.7 | 21.2 |
| Walnut Creek | 14 139 | 61 | 13.1 | 74 | 484 | 583.0 | 31.0 | 356 | 7 089 | 1 918.4 | 231.7 |
| Wasco | 7 607 | 94 | 24.5 | 3 | 28 | 12.7 | 1.0 | 39 | 432 | 82.4 | 8.3 |
| Watsonville | 3 682 | 40 | 52.5 | 71 | 1 494 | 1 081.9 | 78.0 | 166 | 2 627 | 1 540.4 | 69.6 |
| West Covina | 1 676 | 4 | 100.0 | 72 | 182 | 100.2 | 5.0 | 284 | 6 118 | 1 563.9 | 144.7 |
| West Hollywood | 3 868 | 19 | 21.1 | 121 | 771 | 369.9 | 44.2 | 348 | 4 397 | 1 285.7 | 130.6 |
| Westminster | 2 511 | 9 | 100.0 | 103 | 487 | 229.8 | 16.1 | 442 | 6 101 | 1 625.6 | 147.8 |
| West Sacramento | 13 097 | 59 | 100.0 | 143 | 4 622 | 5 685.7 | 203.3 | 127 | 2 296 | 523.6 | 57.7 |
| Whittier | 2 637 | 24 | 45.8 | 74 | 414 | 157.1 | 15.2 | 228 | 3 661 | 815.0 | 80.5 |
| Wildomar | 2 176 | 17 | 100.0 | 5 | D | D | D | 31 | 367 | 126.7 | 10.3 |
| Windsor | 3 578 | 22 | 100.0 | 23 | 322 | 80.1 | 17.0 | 52 | 1 120 | 278.9 | 29.6 |
| Woodland | 15 159 | 66 | 100.0 | 74 | 1 020 | 528.8 | 43.6 | 178 | 2 748 | 586.0 | 60.6 |
| Yorba Linda | 32 131 | 118 | 100.0 | 112 | 1 614 | 1 021.1 | 120.1 | 119 | 1 878 | 578.0 | 49.5 |
| Yuba City | 3 090 | 14 | 100.0 | 45 | 527 | 199.3 | 21.4 | 262 | 4 323 | 983.7 | 100.0 |
| Yucaipa | 4 671 | 35 | 100.0 | 19 | 96 | 33.7 | 3.4 | 86 | 973 | 229.5 | 23.4 |
| COLORADO | 2 859 669 | 13 502 | 64.6 | 5 850 | 81 144 | 53 599.0 | 4 191.0 | 19 428 | 261 962 | 65 896.8 | 6 537.5 |
| Arvada | 74 806 | 549 | 31.1 | 83 | 661 | 532.6 | 33.6 | 279 | 4 037 | 958.8 | 97.7 |
| Aurora | 150 621 | 694 | 72.3 | 237 | 6 062 | 5 839.6 | 295.2 | 909 | 16 098 | 3 664.5 | 366.7 |
| Boulder | 25 438 | 115 | 51.3 | 194 | 2 414 | 1 131.8 | 212.2 | 614 | 8 421 | 1 919.5 | 224.0 |
| Brighton | 8 814 | 45 | 100.0 | 28 | 465 | 378.0 | 19.6 | 87 | 1 757 | 476.5 | 45.7 |
| Broomfield | 65 583 | 229 | 100.0 | 68 | D | D | D | 279 | 5 355 | 1 139.8 | 111.3 |

1. Merchant wholesalers except manufacturers' sales branches and offices.  2. Establishments with payroll.

# Table D. Cities — Real Estate, Professional Services, and Manufacturing

| City | Real estate and rental and leasing, 2007 | | | | Professional, scientific, and technical services,[1] 2007 | | | | Manufacturing, 2007 | | | |
|---|---|---|---|---|---|---|---|---|---|---|---|---|
| | Number of establishments | Number of employees | Receipts (mil dol) | Annual payroll (mil dol) | Number of establishments | Number of employees | Receipts (mil dol) | Annual payroll (mil dol) | Number of establishments | Number of employees | Receipts (mil dol) | Annual payroll (mil dol) |
| | 80 | 81 | 82 | 83 | 84 | 85 | 86 | 87 | 88 | 89 | 90 | 91 |
| CALIFORNIA—Cont'd | | | | | | | | | | | | |
| San Francisco | 1 843 | 14 332 | 4 309.7 | 984.3 | 5 600 | D | D | D | 788 | 11 339 | 2 077.5 | 422.5 |
| San Gabriel | 92 | 510 | 75.2 | 10.6 | 119 | 349 | 40.1 | 12.1 | NA | NA | NA | NA |
| San Jacinto | 23 | 104 | 15.6 | 2.5 | 23 | 180 | 16.0 | 6.1 | 34 | 640 | 83.7 | 20.0 |
| San Jose | 1 124 | 6 677 | 1 637.4 | 278.1 | 2 771 | 44 768 | 5 497.4 | 5 265.1 | 960 | 43 662 | 17 377.9 | 2 967.7 |
| San Juan Capistrano | 88 | 399 | 78.5 | 21.9 | 211 | 897 | 145.9 | 46.3 | 30 | 1 086 | 229.5 | 49.9 |
| San Leandro | 130 | 2 372 | 426.1 | 89.7 | 127 | 1 010 | 141.5 | 58.7 | 211 | 6 620 | 2 061.6 | 285.8 |
| San Luis Obispo | 137 | 802 | 106.9 | 23.6 | 330 | D | D | D | 64 | 979 | 166.6 | 39.3 |
| San Marcos | 106 | 500 | 100.0 | 19.2 | 221 | D | D | D | 188 | 4 916 | 1 141.6 | 220.2 |
| San Mateo | 205 | 1 065 | 462.8 | 76.1 | 526 | D | D | D | 57 | 579 | D | 27.1 |
| San Pablo | 25 | 78 | 16.0 | 2.2 | 11 | D | D | D | NA | NA | NA | NA |
| San Rafael | 167 | 1 019 | 535.4 | 46.9 | 518 | D | D | D | 88 | 832 | 154.4 | 32.8 |
| San Ramon | 125 | 897 | 192.4 | 41.4 | 439 | 5 264 | 996.0 | 429.9 | NA | NA | NA | NA |
| Santa Ana | 347 | 2 868 | 443.7 | 125.3 | 1 012 | 10 987 | 1 650.8 | 664.6 | 875 | 23 728 | 5 339.9 | 954.4 |
| Santa Barbara | 269 | 1 408 | 293.0 | 53.3 | 684 | 4 647 | 897.8 | 307.6 | 117 | 1 326 | 233.3 | 58.4 |
| Santa Clara | 193 | 1 411 | 364.6 | 77.7 | 850 | D | D | D | 542 | 18 177 | 5 296.3 | 1 306.0 |
| Santa Clarita | 225 | 1 012 | 186.3 | 31.6 | 501 | D | D | D | 246 | 9 292 | 1 860.4 | 463.1 |
| Santa Cruz | 89 | 415 | 87.5 | 11.7 | 306 | D | D | D | 100 | 1 600 | 310.9 | 69.0 |
| Santa Maria | 93 | 523 | 84.5 | 17.7 | 159 | 1 195 | 133.3 | 59.3 | 100 | 3 020 | 666.8 | 110.3 |
| Santa Monica | 438 | 3 095 | 1 205.9 | 194.7 | 1 192 | D | D | D | 100 | 1 201 | 256.0 | 46.2 |
| Santa Paula | 26 | 138 | 26.8 | 5.2 | 25 | 146 | 17.2 | 6.4 | 23 | 563 | 123.8 | 23.4 |
| Santa Rosa | 274 | 1 267 | 267.8 | 44.1 | 606 | D | D | D | 182 | 7 583 | 1 124.2 | 481.8 |
| Santee | 73 | 252 | 41.4 | 7.7 | 88 | D | D | D | 88 | 1 401 | 232.1 | 54.0 |
| Saratoga | 82 | 226 | 90.5 | 10.9 | 159 | 504 | 77.1 | 29.6 | NA | NA | NA | NA |
| Seaside | 15 | 97 | 12.4 | 2.7 | 18 | D | D | D | NA | NA | NA | NA |
| Simi Valley | 127 | 501 | 75.8 | 14.1 | 360 | 2 001 | 422.4 | 124.7 | 158 | 4 012 | 831.6 | 181.1 |
| Soledad | 7 | 25 | 2.5 | 0.4 | 4 | 28 | 1.5 | 0.6 | NA | NA | NA | NA |
| South Gate | 52 | 251 | 172.4 | 8.3 | 36 | 310 | 34.2 | 12.1 | 146 | 6 065 | 2 260.3 | 245.7 |
| South Pasadena | 46 | 163 | 26.9 | 5.3 | 158 | D | D | D | NA | NA | NA | NA |
| South San Francisco | 94 | 979 | 164.4 | 36.3 | 178 | D | D | D | 130 | 13 709 | D | 975.8 |
| Stanton | 27 | 157 | 27.3 | 3.2 | 30 | 176 | 12.9 | 5.0 | 76 | 978 | 131.3 | 37.8 |
| Stockton | 280 | 1 569 | 250.5 | 54.3 | 403 | D | D | D | 204 | 7 622 | 2 506.6 | 303.1 |
| Suisun City | 15 | 50 | 8.8 | 1.1 | 20 | 168 | 46.6 | 8.6 | NA | NA | NA | NA |
| Sunnyvale | 147 | 1 184 | 298.2 | 56.2 | 741 | 17 893 | 3 543.1 | 1 623.4 | 276 | 40 837 | 10 241.2 | 3 029.2 |
| Temecula | 196 | 747 | 132.9 | 32.2 | 377 | D | D | D | 129 | 7 716 | 1 929.2 | 377.3 |
| Temple City | 52 | 170 | 24.6 | 5.3 | 69 | 232 | 20.2 | 6.6 | NA | NA | NA | NA |
| Thousand Oaks | 290 | 1 294 | 359.1 | 67.4 | 787 | 5 177 | 4 358.1 | 359.6 | 132 | 3 373 | 1 113.9 | 234.1 |
| Torrance | 352 | 2 184 | 420.2 | 72.2 | 897 | D | D | D | 280 | 14 673 | 5 621.3 | 816.0 |
| Tracy | 77 | 235 | 139.0 | 7.7 | 112 | 514 | 45.8 | 16.2 | 53 | 2 512 | 1 063.0 | 111.1 |
| Tulare | 45 | 166 | 37.8 | 4.5 | 48 | 258 | 38.9 | 16.0 | 32 | 1 786 | 1 165.2 | 76.4 |
| Turlock | 62 | 334 | 37.0 | 8.1 | 71 | 515 | 46.9 | 16.5 | 77 | 3 762 | 1 605.0 | 137.5 |
| Tustin | 206 | 1 196 | 179.1 | 42.3 | 560 | D | D | D | 131 | 4 401 | 1 654.1 | 215.4 |
| Twentynine Palms | 16 | 113 | 9.5 | 1.5 | 11 | 92 | 11.3 | 2.5 | NA | NA | NA | NA |
| Union City | 48 | 395 | 116.3 | 19.7 | 106 | 433 | 70.0 | 23.9 | 90 | 4 149 | 1 088.0 | 218.8 |
| Upland | 106 | 965 | 366.5 | 57.1 | 220 | 1 498 | 182.5 | 73.1 | 116 | 1 078 | 210.7 | 44.4 |
| Vacaville | 90 | 565 | 95.9 | 17.0 | 121 | 639 | 77.3 | 25.9 | 54 | 3 414 | 1 054.7 | 172.3 |
| Vallejo | 92 | 413 | 59.8 | 10.2 | 123 | D | D | D | NA | NA | NA | NA |
| Victorville | 93 | 711 | 92.8 | 19.9 | 104 | D | D | D | 31 | 1 272 | 501.8 | 60.3 |
| Visalia | 131 | 695 | 104.6 | 20.8 | 259 | D | D | D | 81 | 2 657 | 617.4 | 99.6 |
| Vista | 142 | 599 | 105.7 | 20.1 | 252 | D | D | D | 197 | 8 746 | 2 730.7 | 347.4 |
| Walnut | 41 | 118 | 30.7 | 6.3 | 108 | 337 | 47.9 | 12.8 | NA | NA | NA | NA |
| Walnut Creek | 243 | 1 439 | 313.9 | 73.7 | 747 | 6 760 | 1 399.6 | 566.2 | 39 | 1 144 | 531.9 | 57.3 |
| Wasco | 10 | 41 | 4.8 | 0.9 | 5 | 22 | 2.1 | 0.4 | NA | NA | NA | NA |
| Watsonville | 59 | 253 | 46.3 | 9.1 | 79 | D | D | D | 74 | 1 982 | 459.4 | 80.2 |
| West Covina | 84 | 703 | 78.6 | 16.4 | 149 | 1 355 | 101.9 | 42.6 | NA | NA | NA | NA |
| West Hollywood | 137 | 982 | 434.5 | 42.1 | 372 | D | D | D | 105 | 1 104 | 195.3 | 34.8 |
| Westminster | 91 | 425 | 83.1 | 12.3 | 161 | 667 | 111.9 | 21.7 | | | | |
| West Sacramento | 69 | 565 | 120.6 | 24.9 | 88 | D | D | D | 59 | 1 962 | 588.0 | 84.2 |
| Whittier | 101 | 372 | 49.3 | 10.1 | 178 | 1 074 | 102.4 | 41.9 | 61 | 1 287 | 214.3 | 48.3 |
| Wildomar | 12 | 112 | 7.9 | 2.6 | 23 | 68 | 4.4 | 1.6 | NA | NA | NA | NA |
| Windsor | 27 | 214 | 42.1 | 7.3 | 54 | 290 | 36.4 | 8.2 | 26 | 814 | 136.5 | 33.2 |
| Woodland | 60 | 273 | 47.9 | 8.3 | 77 | D | D | D | 68 | 2 896 | 841.2 | 108.0 |
| Yorba Linda | 130 | 449 | 119.5 | 18.0 | 219 | 1 135 | 143.0 | 46.8 | 64 | 1 638 | 713.1 | 113.6 |
| Yuba City | 89 | 589 | 58.4 | 12.7 | 112 | D | D | D | 55 | 1 245 | 421.8 | D |
| Yucaipa | 47 | 196 | 27.9 | 5.4 | 66 | 270 | 35.6 | 8.9 | NA | NA | NA | NA |
| COLORADO | 10 011 | 47 568 | 8 460.9 | 1 793.0 | 22 522 | 156 859 | 28 932.6 | 10 515.7 | 5 288 | 137 880 | 46 332.0 | 6 789.7 |
| Arvada | 131 | 415 | 47.3 | 10.8 | 371 | 1 675 | 191.6 | 79.8 | 105 | 2 239 | 508.7 | 106.5 |
| Aurora | 335 | 1 555 | 325.3 | 58.5 | 620 | D | D | D | 132 | 3 144 | 767.2 | 137.4 |
| Boulder | 321 | 1 336 | 270.6 | 50.7 | 1 196 | D | D | D | 216 | 7 933 | 2 193.3 | 442.8 |
| Brighton | 34 | 127 | 14.7 | 3.2 | 52 | D | D | D | NA | NA | NA | NA |
| Broomfield | 91 | 525 | 105.3 | 15.3 | 271 | D | D | D | 85 | 3 939 | 2 255.5 | 192.9 |

1. Establishments subject to federal tax.

— **Accommodation and Food Services, Arts, Entertainment, and Recreation, and Health Care and Social Assistance**

| City | Accommodation and food services, 2007 | | | | Arts, entertainment, and recreation,[1] 2007 | | | | Health care and social assistance,[1] 2007 | | | |
|---|---|---|---|---|---|---|---|---|---|---|---|---|
| | Number of establishments | Number of employees | Sales (mil dol) | Annual payroll (mil dol) | Number of establishments | Number of employees | Receipts (mil dol) | Annual payroll (mil dol) | Number of establishments | Number of employees | Receipts (mil dol) | Annual payroll (mil dol) |
| | 92 | 93 | 94 | 95 | 96 | 97 | 98 | 99 | 100 | 101 | 102 | 103 |
| **CALIFORNIA—Cont'd** | | | | | | | | | | | | |
| San Francisco | 3 525 | 66 365 | 5 039.2 | 1 496.8 | 325 | 6 697 | 871.5 | 300.1 | 2 252 | 15 376 | 2 123.6 | 823.6 |
| San Gabriel | 167 | 1 318 | 71.6 | 18.5 | 5 | D | D | D | 178 | D | D | D |
| San Jacinto | 34 | 396 | 21.0 | 5.5 | 1 | D | D | D | 18 | 147 | 11.1 | 3.5 |
| San Jose | 1 793 | 30 188 | 1 714.6 | 474.1 | 134 | 4 474 | 403.1 | 160.8 | 2 010 | 22 791 | 2 620.3 | 1 078.0 |
| San Juan Capistrano | 71 | 1 287 | 68.5 | 20.5 | 18 | D | D | D | 117 | 2 632 | 275.7 | 125.0 |
| San Leandro | 173 | 2 162 | 118.5 | 32.1 | 15 | D | D | D | 225 | 2 637 | 291.7 | 110.7 |
| San Luis Obispo | 196 | 4 507 | 223.9 | 63.6 | 18 | 182 | 7.8 | 2.6 | 276 | 3 411 | 416.4 | 160.2 |
| San Marcos | 158 | 2 632 | 122.5 | 36.1 | 15 | D | D | D | 113 | 1 113 | 109.6 | 43.8 |
| San Mateo | 277 | 4 506 | 306.4 | 87.0 | 37 | 726 | 85.5 | 18.6 | 382 | 2 552 | 303.3 | 110.0 |
| San Pablo | 53 | 516 | 29.8 | 7.4 | 3 | D | D | D | 31 | 752 | 61.7 | 29.4 |
| San Rafael | 197 | 2 335 | 136.4 | 38.8 | 62 | 466 | 66.6 | 14.5 | 220 | 2 573 | 303.2 | 162.2 |
| San Ramon | 127 | 2 434 | 161.8 | 44.6 | 15 | 405 | 30.1 | 7.8 | 248 | 2 948 | 377.5 | 136.7 |
| Santa Ana | 518 | 7 690 | 447.4 | 119.2 | 29 | 333 | 28.7 | 6.2 | 745 | 8 689 | 960.6 | 384.0 |
| Santa Barbara | 400 | 7 984 | 447.1 | 124.4 | 59 | 843 | 43.6 | 17.8 | 457 | 3 945 | 519.1 | 194.7 |
| Santa Clara | 369 | 6 250 | 455.3 | 121.2 | 33 | 1 811 | 296.7 | 168.3 | 200 | D | D | D |
| Santa Clarita | 328 | 6 417 | 301.5 | 84.6 | 108 | 893 | 67.2 | 21.2 | 391 | 3 664 | 445.3 | 132.8 |
| Santa Cruz | 230 | 3 745 | 193.0 | 55.4 | 23 | 962 | 55.8 | 19.7 | 166 | 1 544 | 191.5 | 72.0 |
| Santa Maria | 168 | 2 993 | 150.5 | 41.7 | 14 | 249 | 9.0 | 2.7 | 262 | 2 144 | 212.7 | 78.0 |
| Santa Monica | 401 | 10 715 | 791.3 | 221.9 | 719 | 2 419 | 684.4 | 272.9 | 821 | 6 413 | 941.3 | 308.2 |
| Santa Paula | 45 | 522 | 22.0 | 5.6 | 3 | D | D | D | 39 | 298 | 29.4 | 10.3 |
| Santa Rosa | 394 | 5 911 | 300.2 | 84.4 | 50 | 756 | 35.2 | 12.0 | 609 | 7 234 | 941.9 | 398.9 |
| Santee | 89 | 1 522 | 68.4 | 20.6 | 10 | 186 | 9.7 | 3.1 | 57 | 486 | 38.7 | 14.8 |
| Saratoga | 51 | 561 | 38.5 | 11.4 | 6 | 84 | 5.4 | 2.4 | 86 | 561 | 50.2 | 19.5 |
| Seaside | 62 | 950 | 56.6 | 16.4 | 4 | D | D | D | 15 | 110 | 7.8 | 2.6 |
| Simi Valley | 252 | 4 191 | 204.9 | 59.3 | 53 | D | D | D | 270 | 2 059 | 216.9 | 79.9 |
| Soledad | 21 | 222 | 12.8 | 2.8 | 1 | D | D | D | 7 | D | D | D |
| South Gate | 113 | 1 137 | 62.2 | 15.0 | 5 | D | D | D | 74 | 744 | 74.1 | 24.9 |
| South Pasadena | 48 | 787 | 39.7 | 11.5 | 30 | D | D | D | 90 | D | D | D |
| South San Francisco | 203 | 3 466 | 289.6 | 73.7 | 16 | 131 | 11.4 | 2.9 | 160 | 2 413 | 272.2 | 141.7 |
| Stanton | 85 | 918 | 51.9 | 12.5 | 7 | D | D | D | 27 | D | D | D |
| Stockton | 471 | 6 765 | 343.5 | 89.5 | 37 | 687 | 40.0 | 14.5 | 602 | 8 582 | 972.7 | 367.3 |
| Suisun City | 29 | 411 | 17.5 | 4.5 | 4 | D | D | D | 26 | 85 | 6.1 | 2.2 |
| Sunnyvale | 327 | 4 318 | 276.7 | 75.2 | 25 | D | D | D | 302 | 3 741 | 375.3 | 188.1 |
| Temecula | 287 | 6 255 | 304.0 | 87.2 | 30 | D | D | D | 270 | 1 763 | 187.3 | 62.1 |
| Temple City | 65 | 845 | 40.0 | 11.2 | 11 | 20 | 1.0 | 0.3 | 93 | 968 | 69.1 | 23.5 |
| Thousand Oaks | 308 | 6 796 | 347.9 | 102.6 | 99 | 832 | 57.7 | 18.8 | 549 | 5 540 | 680.5 | 250.1 |
| Torrance | 432 | 8 920 | 503.2 | 140.5 | 59 | D | D | D | 936 | 8 131 | 1 136.1 | 353.8 |
| Tracy | 152 | 2 127 | 101.5 | 28.6 | 17 | D | D | D | 144 | D | D | D |
| Tulare | 95 | 1 184 | 59.7 | 16.0 | 8 | D | D | D | 88 | D | D | D |
| Turlock | 141 | 2 382 | 105.5 | 28.9 | 11 | D | D | D | 155 | D | D | D |
| Tustin | 201 | 3 407 | 176.4 | 55.2 | 20 | D | D | D | 343 | 2 771 | 292.5 | 109.9 |
| Twentynine Palms | 33 | 402 | 23.8 | 5.5 | 5 | D | D | D | 7 | D | D | D |
| Union City | 115 | 1 770 | 90.6 | 25.6 | 6 | D | D | D | 115 | 936 | 72.0 | 32.8 |
| Upland | 158 | 2 259 | 107.2 | 30.3 | 26 | D | D | D | 315 | D | D | D |
| Vacaville | 160 | 3 544 | 154.3 | 42.4 | 15 | D | D | D | 149 | 1 864 | 237.0 | 80.2 |
| Vallejo | 201 | 2 874 | 145.6 | 38.1 | 22 | D | D | D | 231 | 4 519 | 435.2 | 283.4 |
| Victorville | 199 | 3 777 | 182.0 | 49.9 | 13 | D | D | D | 171 | 3 260 | 325.6 | 113.8 |
| Visalia | 221 | 4 420 | 187.1 | 53.2 | 15 | D | D | D | 322 | 3 294 | 336.7 | 132.3 |
| Vista | 182 | 2 368 | 103.0 | 28.2 | 20 | D | D | D | 215 | 2 532 | 241.3 | 97.0 |
| Walnut | 67 | 641 | 32.8 | 8.2 | 4 | D | D | D | 70 | 722 | 43.8 | 19.6 |
| Walnut Creek | 202 | 4 666 | 258.8 | 76.6 | 35 | 524 | 30.4 | 9.6 | 412 | D | D | D |
| Wasco | 21 | D | D | D | 1 | D | D | D | 12 | D | D | D |
| Watsonville | 99 | 1 238 | 69.4 | 18.1 | 6 | D | D | D | 119 | 1 349 | 180.9 | 74.5 |
| West Covina | 200 | 3 635 | 177.5 | 49.0 | 15 | D | D | D | 281 | D | D | D |
| West Hollywood | 205 | 6 211 | 423.7 | 124.8 | 473 | D | D | D | 214 | 1 009 | 128.8 | 44.6 |
| Westminster | 232 | 2 780 | 139.3 | 39.2 | 17 | D | D | D | 275 | 2 164 | 229.7 | 75.3 |
| West Sacramento | 91 | D | D | D | 9 | D | D | D | 47 | D | D | D |
| Whittier | 168 | 2 970 | 144.0 | 41.9 | 11 | D | D | D | 309 | D | D | D |
| Wildomar | 20 | 245 | 13.0 | 3.3 | 8 | 155 | 4.9 | 1.3 | 45 | D | D | D |
| Windsor | 46 | 632 | 32.4 | 9.2 | 4 | 90 | 4.9 | 1.7 | 40 | 213 | 18.4 | 6.5 |
| Woodland | 109 | D | D | D | 10 | D | D | D | 90 | 1 126 | 108.6 | 54.9 |
| Yorba Linda | 87 | 1 706 | 78.6 | 24.6 | 22 | D | D | D | 153 | 1 228 | 139.0 | 44.4 |
| Yuba City | 126 | 2 274 | 90.7 | 25.6 | 13 | D | D | D | 202 | D | D | D |
| Yucaipa | 57 | 820 | 35.0 | 9.6 | 10 | D | D | D | 82 | 1 165 | 77.1 | 31.2 |
| **COLORADO** | 12 075 | 231 721 | 11 440.4 | 3 408.2 | 1 957 | 41 153 | 3 253.2 | 1 051.0 | 11 557 | 127 029 | 12 599.1 | 5 234.2 |
| Arvada | 169 | 2 963 | 128.1 | 35.4 | 19 | D | D | D | 187 | 1 382 | 121.1 | 46.1 |
| Aurora | 529 | 9 480 | 444.8 | 128.3 | 40 | 568 | 31.4 | 9.1 | 545 | 8 884 | 875.7 | 339.9 |
| Boulder | 402 | 8 121 | 390.5 | 120.6 | 90 | 944 | 59.9 | 15.1 | 510 | 3 719 | 352.1 | 158.3 |
| Brighton | 69 | 1 279 | 52.9 | 15.5 | 7 | D | D | D | 53 | D | D | D |
| Broomfield | 137 | 3 370 | 163.4 | 53.3 | 25 | D | D | D | 101 | 866 | 71.7 | 30.1 |

1. Establishments subject to federal tax.

| City | Other services[1], 2007 | | | | Selected federal funds, 2009–2010 (mil dol) | | | | | | | | |
|---|---|---|---|---|---|---|---|---|---|---|---|---|---|
| | | | | | Procurement contracts | | Grants | | | | | | |
| | Number of establishments | Number of employees | Receipts (mil dol) | Annual payroll (mil dol) | Defense | Other | Total[2] | Medicaid and other health related | Nutrition and family welfare | Energy and environment | Disasters and emergency preparedness | Housing and community development | Employment and training |
| | 104 | 105 | 106 | 107 | 108 | 109 | 110 | 111 | 112 | 113 | 114 | 115 | 116 |
| CALIFORNIA—Cont'd | | | | | | | | | | | | | |
| San Francisco | 1 489 | 9 487 | 843.1 | 247.3 | 508.7 | 706.1 | 2 739.5 | 1 362.4 | 24.6 | 66.6 | 0.7 | 216.3 | 16.2 |
| San Gabriel | 79 | 448 | 40.7 | 13.3 | 2.9 | 0.1 | 0.0 | 0.0 | 0.0 | 0.0 | 0.0 | 0.0 | 0.0 |
| San Jacinto | 27 | 80 | 7.9 | 1.9 | 0.2 | 0.0 | 1.9 | 0.0 | 0.2 | 0.4 | 0.0 | 0.0 | 0.0 |
| San Jose | 1 100 | 7 036 | 896.0 | 232.2 | 170.9 | 80.3 | 541.1 | 19.9 | 22.7 | 47.6 | 1.2 | 311.8 | 19.2 |
| San Juan Capistrano | 46 | 295 | 21.0 | 6.7 | 2.6 | 0.9 | 0.0 | 0.0 | 0.0 | 0.0 | 0.0 | 0.0 | 0.0 |
| San Leandro | 158 | 1 201 | 182.8 | 46.2 | 12.3 | 8.3 | 20.6 | 13.5 | 0.5 | 1.9 | 0.0 | 0.8 | 0.4 |
| San Luis Obispo | 112 | 648 | 55.4 | 14.9 | 20.1 | 1.3 | 70.7 | 1.4 | 27.7 | 2.7 | 0.0 | 21.1 | 0.1 |
| San Marcos | 132 | 776 | 72.6 | 22.9 | 8.7 | 0.5 | 18.7 | 9.8 | 0.0 | 0.7 | 0.0 | 0.8 | 0.0 |
| San Mateo | 213 | 1 052 | 104.9 | 30.2 | 23.9 | 2.0 | 14.2 | 8.2 | 0.0 | 0.4 | 0.0 | 1.6 | 0.0 |
| San Pablo | 35 | D | D | D | 0.0 | 0.0 | 3.1 | 1.1 | 0.0 | 0.0 | 0.0 | 0.0 | 0.0 |
| San Rafael | 192 | 1 222 | 154.4 | 52.2 | 1.5 | 3.2 | 55.1 | 3.7 | 4.1 | 4.5 | 0.0 | 36.3 | 0.0 |
| San Ramon | 107 | 706 | 67.5 | 22.2 | 25.0 | 1.7 | 1.5 | 0.0 | 0.0 | 0.0 | 0.0 | 0.0 | 0.0 |
| Santa Ana | 415 | 2 658 | 254.6 | 69.5 | 60.7 | 18.0 | 259.8 | 8.2 | 34.3 | 4.5 | 0.0 | 196.4 | 0.7 |
| Santa Barbara | 201 | 1 315 | 101.0 | 29.0 | 20.0 | 5.6 | 182.2 | 38.7 | 0.2 | 18.0 | 0.0 | 35.8 | 0.2 |
| Santa Clara | 227 | 1 477 | 162.3 | 48.2 | 290.7 | 4.9 | 34.6 | 3.2 | 0.9 | 21.9 | 0.0 | 2.9 | 0.0 |
| Santa Clarita | 244 | 1 784 | 171.0 | 45.8 | 61.2 | 6.9 | 21.2 | 1.0 | 0.0 | 2.1 | 0.0 | 2.7 | 0.0 |
| Santa Cruz | 103 | 618 | 56.7 | 17.0 | 1.1 | 6.1 | 168.3 | 52.7 | 4.9 | 8.3 | 0.0 | 51.4 | 0.0 |
| Santa Maria | 122 | 776 | 76.5 | 20.6 | 96.6 | 3.5 | 9.9 | 0.9 | 0.0 | 0.0 | 4.4 | 0.1 | 0.0 |
| Santa Monica | 328 | 2 365 | 196.0 | 53.0 | 7.5 | 1 456.1 | 184.0 | 70.6 | 0.0 | 3.6 | 0.0 | 21.8 | 5.0 |
| Santa Paula | 26 | D | D | D | 0.1 | 0.1 | 6.2 | 0.0 | 0.0 | 0.1 | 0.0 | 5.6 | 0.0 |
| Santa Rosa | 264 | 1 588 | 154.1 | 47.2 | 6.5 | 2.2 | 91.5 | 5.1 | 5.8 | 13.8 | 0.0 | 48.0 | 4.2 |
| Santee | 91 | 562 | 68.3 | 18.5 | 2.6 | 0.7 | 2.2 | 0.0 | 0.0 | 1.2 | 0.0 | 0.5 | 0.0 |
| Saratoga | 32 | D | D | D | 4.0 | 0.0 | 4.9 | 0.0 | 0.0 | 3.8 | 0.0 | 0.0 | 0.0 |
| Seaside | 49 | 202 | 23.9 | 6.4 | 31.3 | 93.5 | 9.2 | 0.0 | 0.0 | 0.1 | 0.0 | 0.4 | 0.0 |
| Simi Valley | 179 | D | D | D | 34.6 | 42.0 | 3.9 | 0.0 | 0.0 | 0.0 | 0.0 | 0.8 | 0.0 |
| Soledad | 4 | D | D | D | 0.0 | 0.0 | 1.2 | 0.0 | 0.0 | 0.0 | 0.0 | 0.0 | 0.0 |
| South Gate | 74 | 316 | 28.4 | 8.4 | 3.0 | 0.0 | 8.5 | 0.0 | 0.0 | 0.0 | 0.0 | 8.4 | 0.0 |
| South Pasadena | 32 | D | D | D | 0.1 | 1.0 | 1.4 | 1.1 | 0.0 | 0.0 | 0.0 | 0.0 | 0.0 |
| South San Francisco | 117 | 1 419 | 136.2 | 46.5 | 92.1 | 45.5 | 12.3 | 4.3 | 6.7 | 0.0 | 0.2 | 0.8 | 0.0 |
| Stanton | 58 | 266 | 27.1 | 7.1 | 1.4 | 0.0 | 0.0 | 0.0 | 0.0 | 0.0 | 0.0 | 0.0 | 0.0 |
| Stockton | 322 | 2 500 | 194.9 | 65.0 | 35.8 | 8.2 | 108.9 | 1.1 | 24.8 | 7.3 | 0.0 | 51.0 | 0.5 |
| Suisun City | 20 | D | D | D | 0.3 | 0.0 | 3.1 | 0.0 | 0.2 | 0.0 | 0.0 | 2.9 | 0.0 |
| Sunnyvale | 154 | 874 | 120.6 | 33.0 | 3 983.8 | 31.8 | 29.9 | 6.9 | 0.0 | 17.0 | 0.0 | 2.1 | 0.3 |
| Temecula | 185 | 997 | 80.7 | 22.7 | 5.2 | 18.4 | 9.7 | 0.2 | 0.3 | 7.6 | 0.0 | 0.0 | 0.0 |
| Temple City | 53 | 239 | 15.7 | 3.5 | 0.0 | 0.0 | 0.0 | 0.0 | 0.0 | 0.0 | 0.0 | 0.0 | 0.0 |
| Thousand Oaks | 217 | 1 172 | 105.8 | 29.1 | 97.1 | 18.1 | 50.1 | 0.1 | 0.0 | 15.0 | 0.0 | 31.5 | 0.0 |
| Torrance | 257 | 1 669 | 166.5 | 55.5 | 132.8 | 34.4 | 73.2 | 37.7 | 0.3 | 10.8 | 0.0 | 6.8 | 0.0 |
| Tracy | 96 | 434 | 37.9 | 10.0 | 24.7 | 3.5 | 1.9 | 0.0 | 0.0 | 0.6 | 0.0 | 0.0 | 0.0 |
| Tulare | 58 | 338 | 35.7 | 9.3 | 0.0 | 0.4 | 4.9 | 1.9 | 0.0 | 1.2 | 0.0 | 1.0 | 0.0 |
| Turlock | 84 | 716 | 50.8 | 16.7 | 3.2 | 8.2 | 8.3 | 0.0 | 0.0 | 0.6 | 0.0 | 2.5 | 0.0 |
| Tustin | 113 | 893 | 95.6 | 28.2 | 40.3 | 12.9 | 3.0 | 0.7 | 0.0 | 0.6 | 0.0 | 0.9 | 0.0 |
| Twentynine Palms | 13 | D | D | D | 400.8 | 0.1 | 1.4 | 0.0 | 0.0 | 0.1 | 0.0 | 0.0 | 0.0 |
| Union City | 61 | 542 | 88.2 | 19.1 | 7.7 | 1.0 | 5.6 | 2.5 | 0.0 | 0.0 | 0.0 | 0.7 | 0.0 |
| Upland | 152 | 769 | 63.9 | 18.5 | 0.4 | 2.1 | 8.3 | 1.5 | 0.0 | 0.0 | 0.0 | 6.6 | 0.0 |
| Vacaville | 94 | 515 | 41.7 | 11.8 | 3.5 | 1.3 | 16.0 | 0.0 | 0.0 | 0.1 | 0.0 | 10.7 | 0.0 |
| Vallejo | 119 | 615 | 50.8 | 15.9 | 19.9 | 22.6 | 121.9 | 3.8 | 0.2 | 1.0 | 0.0 | 27.1 | 0.0 |
| Victorville | 108 | 753 | 95.8 | 19.1 | 19.0 | 10.3 | 11.6 | 0.2 | 0.0 | 1.0 | 0.0 | 1.3 | 0.0 |
| Visalia | 159 | 1 096 | 94.8 | 26.2 | 0.1 | 1.8 | 64.4 | 0.1 | 18.0 | 1.4 | 0.0 | 25.3 | 9.3 |
| Vista | 127 | 759 | 75.1 | 22.4 | 34.3 | 2.6 | 8.0 | 3.0 | 0.0 | 0.8 | 0.0 | 0.0 | 0.0 |
| Walnut | 69 | D | D | D | 3.8 | 0.2 | 5.0 | 0.0 | 0.0 | 0.0 | 0.0 | 0.0 | 2.2 |
| Walnut Creek | 161 | 1 121 | 101.5 | 31.4 | 4.3 | 5.7 | 3.2 | 0.8 | 0.0 | 1.8 | 0.0 | 0.4 | 0.0 |
| Wasco | 11 | 33 | 3.5 | 0.7 | 0.0 | 0.0 | 3.6 | 0.0 | 0.0 | 3.6 | 0.0 | 0.0 | 0.0 |
| Watsonville | 68 | 234 | 23.8 | 6.0 | 0.0 | 3.4 | 4.2 | 1.5 | 0.0 | 0.0 | 0.0 | 1.8 | 0.0 |
| West Covina | 98 | 518 | 35.9 | 9.7 | 5.2 | 2.7 | 28.7 | 3.0 | 7.1 | 2.4 | 0.0 | 1.3 | 0.0 |
| West Hollywood | 165 | 1 107 | 82.2 | 21.3 | 0.0 | 0.1 | 1.2 | 0.3 | 0.0 | 0.0 | 0.0 | 0.0 | 0.0 |
| Westminster | 139 | 614 | 61.5 | 15.8 | 0.5 | 0.5 | 1.3 | 0.0 | 0.0 | 0.8 | 0.0 | 0.0 | 0.0 |
| West Sacramento | 78 | 576 | 68.6 | 20.1 | 1 131.2 | 5.6 | 4.0 | 0.0 | 0.0 | 0.0 | 0.0 | 3.0 | 0.1 |
| Whittier | 125 | D | D | D | 3.9 | 1.2 | 8.5 | 0.0 | 0.0 | 0.9 | 0.0 | 1.5 | 0.0 |
| Wildomar | 13 | D | D | D | NA | NA | NA | NA | NA | NA | NA | NA | NA |
| Windsor | 29 | 142 | 12.8 | 4.1 | 0.1 | 0.8 | 0.2 | 0.0 | 0.0 | 0.0 | 0.0 | 0.0 | 0.0 |
| Woodland | 86 | 535 | 41.5 | 11.9 | 4.3 | 0.3 | 23.7 | 0.0 | 3.9 | 0.9 | 0.0 | 12.5 | 0.0 |
| Yorba Linda | 83 | 484 | 48.7 | 13.4 | 7.3 | 8.7 | 2.4 | 0.0 | 0.0 | 1.7 | 0.0 | 0.0 | 0.0 |
| Yuba City | 94 | D | D | D | 0.2 | 7.7 | 11.4 | 3.7 | 0.0 | 0.0 | 0.0 | 5.6 | 0.0 |
| Yucaipa | 43 | 192 | 15.0 | 3.7 | 12.2 | 0.3 | 4.9 | 0.0 | 0.0 | 4.7 | 0.0 | 0.0 | 0.0 |
| COLORADO | 7 904 | 45 358 | 3 811.5 | 1 178.5 | 5 631.6 | 4 735.5 | 8 792.9 | 3 665.3 | 967.6 | 568.8 | 7.7 | 399.6 | 130.0 |
| Arvada | 167 | 856 | 56.6 | 17.6 | 10.3 | 51.8 | 4.9 | 0.0 | 0.0 | 0.5 | 0.0 | 4.3 | 0.0 |
| Aurora | 379 | 2 366 | 197.5 | 58.5 | 33.2 | 66.2 | 393.2 | 357.7 | 1.2 | 3.1 | 0.0 | 19.1 | 0.0 |
| Boulder | 220 | 1 480 | 127.3 | 44.8 | 161.0 | 436.4 | 717.6 | 104.6 | 1.2 | 151.8 | 0.0 | 17.1 | 0.0 |
| Brighton | 56 | 292 | 28.0 | 8.3 | 0.1 | 0.0 | 6.3 | 0.0 | 3.1 | 1.4 | 0.0 | 1.6 | 0.0 |
| Broomfield | 76 | 577 | 92.6 | 37.8 | 24.7 | 7.1 | 15.3 | 0.3 | 0.0 | 0.0 | 0.0 | 0.2 | 0.0 |

1. Establishments subject to federal tax.   2. Includes program categories not shown separately. State totals include additional categories not allocated by city.

# Table D. Cities — City Government Finances

| | City government finances, 2007 | | | | | | | | | |
|---|---|---|---|---|---|---|---|---|---|---|
| | General revenue | | | | | | | General expenditure | | |
| | | Intergovernmental | | Taxes | | | | | Per capita[1] (dollars) | |
| | | | | | Per capita[1] (dollars) | | | | | |
| City | Total (mil dol) | Total (mil dol) | Percent from state government | Total (mil dol) | Total | Property | Sales and gross receipts | Total (mil dol) | Total | Capital outlays |
| | 117 | 118 | 119 | 120 | 121 | 122 | 123 | 124 | 125 | 126 |
| CALIFORNIA—Cont'd | | | | | | | | | | |
| San Francisco | 5 978.3 | 2 003.3 | 73.3 | 2 412.5 | 3 154 | 1 542 | 905 | 5 225.2 | 6 831 | 577 |
| San Gabriel | 31.6 | 2.4 | 86.6 | 22.9 | 564 | 313 | 232 | 29.2 | 719 | 44 |
| San Jacinto | 38.4 | 2.3 | 89.6 | 22.1 | 593 | 300 | 134 | 30.4 | 816 | 83 |
| San Jose | 1 620.0 | 150.8 | 48.7 | 804.1 | 856 | 450 | 334 | 1 727.5 | 1 838 | 476 |
| San Juan Capistrano | 46.3 | 3.6 | 77.3 | 28.0 | 809 | 507 | 282 | 37.9 | 1 094 | 155 |
| San Leandro | 127.6 | 10.4 | 87.4 | 83.9 | 1 079 | 506 | 514 | 118.5 | 1 525 | 181 |
| San Luis Obispo | 76.6 | 7.1 | 77.8 | 43.3 | 994 | 344 | 619 | 62.8 | 1 444 | 230 |
| San Marcos | 165.0 | 5.2 | 88.7 | 102.4 | 1 307 | 980 | 252 | 168.8 | 2 156 | 765 |
| San Mateo | 141.3 | 10.9 | 66.2 | 86.5 | 943 | 522 | 290 | 165.7 | 1 805 | 586 |
| San Pablo | 46.3 | 2.6 | 65.6 | 34.9 | 1 136 | 590 | 543 | 41.4 | 1 348 | 570 |
| San Rafael | 84.8 | 6.2 | 69.8 | 54.2 | 974 | 494 | 454 | 85.0 | 1 528 | 139 |
| San Ramon | 68.4 | 4.6 | 84.4 | 39.1 | 798 | 498 | 283 | 88.9 | 1 817 | 738 |
| Santa Ana | 382.2 | 79.8 | 42.1 | 211.9 | 624 | 337 | 283 | 414.2 | 1 220 | 259 |
| Santa Barbara | 234.8 | 33.5 | 34.9 | 95.6 | 1 109 | 497 | 605 | 209.5 | 2 430 | 473 |
| Santa Clara | 259.0 | 24.7 | 93.1 | 110.9 | 1 010 | 554 | 444 | 231.4 | 2 109 | 463 |
| Santa Clarita | 165.5 | 13.6 | 64.3 | 113.0 | 665 | 203 | 456 | 105.6 | 621 | 186 |
| Santa Cruz | 123.4 | 11.2 | 72.7 | 55.7 | 1 007 | 479 | 508 | 122.7 | 2 218 | 403 |
| Santa Maria | 122.6 | 14.5 | 62.8 | 61.8 | 722 | 233 | 375 | 127.3 | 1 486 | 437 |
| Santa Monica | 531.7 | 51.2 | 58.0 | 276.6 | 3 172 | 1 126 | 1 972 | 387.2 | 4 439 | 830 |
| Santa Paula | 26.5 | 3.6 | 84.0 | 12.4 | 432 | 299 | 99 | 29.6 | 1 033 | 208 |
| Santa Rosa | 262.3 | 16.8 | 62.0 | 119.7 | 776 | 311 | 441 | 250.5 | 1 624 | 303 |
| Santee | 65.6 | 9.7 | 35.2 | 37.3 | 702 | 423 | 180 | 65.9 | 1 240 | 542 |
| Saratoga | 18.5 | 1.3 | 78.3 | 12.7 | 419 | 273 | 126 | 21.3 | 704 | 88 |
| Seaside | 35.6 | 2.8 | 56.9 | 27.1 | 808 | 477 | 329 | 39.0 | 1 161 | 391 |
| Simi Valley | 120.6 | 15.4 | 33.4 | 76.0 | 631 | 386 | 238 | 116.6 | 968 | 254 |
| Soledad | 19.3 | 1.2 | 71.3 | 6.4 | 228 | 169 | 57 | 13.4 | 478 | 62 |
| South Gate | 82.0 | 16.8 | 29.1 | 35.6 | 367 | 213 | 152 | 82.5 | 850 | 210 |
| South Pasadena | 27.2 | 6.0 | 40.1 | 15.2 | 388 | 203 | 203 | 24.2 | 986 | 189 |
| South San Francisco | 137.8 | 5.3 | 86.5 | 72.9 | 1 179 | 784 | 367 | 110.7 | 1 789 | 310 |
| Stanton | 35.7 | 2.6 | 70.9 | 24.3 | 646 | 450 | 178 | 39.6 | 1 053 | 444 |
| Stockton | 397.4 | 57.6 | 63.5 | 198.6 | 691 | 326 | 361 | 346.6 | 1 207 | 155 |
| Suisun City | 42.2 | 5.0 | 34.2 | 24.6 | 911 | 741 | 163 | 39.1 | 1 446 | 504 |
| Sunnyvale | 229.7 | 19.6 | 39.6 | 100.1 | 763 | 371 | 369 | 226.7 | 1 729 | 100 |
| Temecula | 131.9 | 20.5 | 65.8 | 78.1 | 824 | 381 | 374 | 117.7 | 1 242 | 398 |
| Temple City | 17.4 | 2.1 | 79.0 | 11.1 | 293 | 151 | 131 | 13.0 | 341 | 6 |
| Thousand Oaks | 154.5 | 9.1 | 74.8 | 91.9 | 745 | 381 | 356 | 158.6 | 1 286 | 170 |
| Torrance | 248.9 | 24.5 | 64.3 | 161.4 | 1 141 | 376 | 759 | 221.8 | 1 568 | 210 |
| Tracy | 136.1 | 8.6 | 72.4 | 63.0 | 791 | 421 | 363 | 148.2 | 1 860 | 758 |
| Tulare | 83.4 | 4.1 | 78.2 | 44.0 | 796 | 257 | 343 | 68.4 | 1 236 | 137 |
| Turlock | 87.2 | 10.7 | 69.8 | 43.9 | 645 | 319 | 213 | 85.8 | 1 259 | 538 |
| Tustin | 89.4 | 6.8 | 46.7 | 63.1 | 891 | 473 | 407 | 101.5 | 1 432 | 488 |
| Twentynine Palms | 11.8 | 1.2 | 86.6 | 9.5 | 305 | 176 | 115 | 9.8 | 315 | 72 |
| Union City | 83.9 | 5.7 | 74.9 | 58.2 | 830 | 518 | 254 | 94.9 | 1 354 | 390 |
| Upland | 93.0 | 5.9 | 87.8 | 39.4 | 543 | 373 | 158 | 91.3 | 1 260 | 180 |
| Vacaville | 177.5 | 34.2 | 33.1 | 89.5 | 971 | 615 | 352 | 170.3 | 1 850 | 670 |
| Vallejo | 223.0 | 48.6 | 28.5 | 85.4 | 739 | 320 | 386 | 243.5 | 2 107 | 255 |
| Victorville | 172.4 | 27.2 | 21.9 | 81.1 | 756 | 297 | 317 | 198.2 | 1 849 | 347 |
| Visalia | 156.9 | 24.5 | 34.7 | 77.6 | 654 | 253 | 395 | 152.4 | 1 285 | 472 |
| Vista | 112.8 | 10.6 | 81.9 | 57.2 | 629 | 393 | 230 | 103.1 | 1 135 | 233 |
| Walnut | 38.2 | 2.2 | 87.3 | 29.8 | 963 | 865 | 94 | 36.5 | 1 180 | 34 |
| Walnut Creek | 80.2 | 3.2 | 78.2 | 49.9 | 789 | 377 | 382 | 78.1 | 1 235 | 160 |
| Wasco | 31.8 | 3.8 | 36.0 | 6.1 | 252 | 156 | 95 | 15.4 | 635 | 88 |
| Watsonville | 81.7 | 15.2 | 75.1 | 37.4 | 752 | 458 | 270 | 102.9 | 2 067 | 679 |
| West Covina | 102.2 | 8.0 | 84.9 | 63.6 | 598 | 367 | 227 | 117.5 | 1 105 | 396 |
| West Hollywood | 94.5 | 2.7 | 96.4 | 50.0 | 1 386 | 562 | 811 | 69.1 | 1 915 | 216 |
| Westminster | 95.8 | 9.0 | 59.1 | 71.0 | 801 | 532 | 266 | 85.2 | 961 | 166 |
| West Sacramento | 139.8 | 4.8 | 56.7 | 78.4 | 1 687 | 948 | 731 | 143.7 | 3 091 | 1 428 |
| Whittier | 82.1 | 6.5 | 78.8 | 44.3 | 535 | 254 | 274 | 79.6 | 961 | 54 |
| Wildomar | NA | NA | NA | NA | NA | NA | NA | NA | NA | NA |
| Windsor | 29.8 | 2.0 | 100.0 | 17.8 | 703 | 404 | 240 | 24.4 | 965 | 241 |
| Woodland | 80.7 | 4.5 | 82.5 | 55.1 | 1 027 | 320 | 696 | 101.0 | 1 881 | 864 |
| Yorba Linda | 77.8 | 3.0 | 74.3 | 50.2 | 767 | 572 | 185 | 78.3 | 1 197 | 225 |
| Yuba City | 62.3 | 3.9 | 80.5 | 38.0 | 622 | 293 | 210 | 76.7 | 1 253 | 351 |
| Yucaipa | 36.5 | 2.0 | 83.8 | 23.7 | 474 | 222 | 100 | 31.8 | 636 | 167 |
| COLORADO | X | X | X | X | X | X | X | X | X | X |
| Arvada | 133.9 | 15.0 | 27.4 | 65.8 | 619 | 98 | 521 | 119.4 | 1 123 | 279 |
| Aurora | 361.9 | 35.8 | 46.6 | 219.3 | 703 | 104 | 599 | 379.3 | 1 216 | 138 |
| Boulder | 194.7 | 19.2 | 100.0 | 125.9 | 1 346 | 227 | 1 119 | 194.8 | 2 083 | 303 |
| Brighton | 43.4 | 3.3 | 43.6 | 20.2 | 658 | 76 | 577 | 36.1 | 1 176 | 435 |
| Broomfield | 155.8 | 10.6 | 38.8 | 90.4 | 1 684 | 559 | 1 125 | 101.8 | 1 897 | 105 |

1. Based on population estimated as of July 1 of the year shown.

| City | Public welfare | Highways | Parking facilities | Education | Health and hospitals | Police protection | Sewerage and sanitation | Parks and recreation | Housing and community development | Interest on debt |
|---|---|---|---|---|---|---|---|---|---|---|
| | | | | | City government finances, 2006 (cont.) | | | | | |
| | | | | | General expenditure (cont.) | | | | | |
| | | | | | Percent of total for: | | | | | |
| | 127 | 128 | 129 | 130 | 131 | 132 | 133 | 134 | 135 | 136 |
| CALIFORNIA—Cont'd | | | | | | | | | | |
| San Francisco .............. | 11.3 | 3.8 | 1.9 | 2.1 | 26.8 | 6.6 | 3.3 | 4.2 | 3.2 | 7.2 |
| San Gabriel ................. | 0.0 | 7.5 | 0.0 | 0.0 | 0.0 | 33.1 | 0.2 | 9.9 | 0.4 | 0.7 |
| San Jacinto .................. | 0.0 | 9.5 | 0.0 | 0.0 | 0.0 | 23.2 | 8.1 | 5.6 | 15.0 | 7.0 |
| San Jose ..................... | 0.0 | 6.6 | 0.6 | 0.0 | 0.6 | 13.8 | 13.1 | 8.9 | 7.0 | 11.9 |
| San Juan Capistrano .... | 0.0 | 14.1 | 0.0 | 0.0 | 0.0 | 14.2 | 8.4 | 16.9 | 11.8 | 5.5 |
| San Leandro................. | 0.0 | 8.8 | 0.3 | 0.0 | 1.2 | 22.2 | 6.9 | 7.8 | 9.6 | 2.0 |
| San Luis Obispo............ | 0.0 | 7.5 | 5.5 | 0.0 | 0.0 | 19.3 | 12.9 | 11.7 | 2.0 | 3.5 |
| San Marcos ................. | 0.0 | 16.8 | 0.0 | 0.0 | 1.8 | 12.2 | 0.0 | 8.5 | 27.2 | 14.1 |
| San Mateo................... | 0.0 | 7.0 | 0.9 | 0.0 | 0.3 | 17.4 | 16.6 | 7.8 | 12.9 | 5.6 |
| San Pablo.................... | 0.0 | 22.9 | 0.0 | 0.0 | 0.0 | 26.2 | 0.0 | 5.4 | 20.9 | 10.7 |
| San Rafael .................. | 0.0 | 10.5 | 2.9 | 0.0 | 5.2 | 22.3 | 0.0 | 11.1 | 2.8 | 2.1 |
| San Ramon .................. | 0.0 | 8.9 | 0.0 | 0.0 | 0.0 | 13.9 | 0.1 | 15.1 | 16.9 | 3.8 |
| Santa Ana ................... | 0.0 | 14.3 | 1.0 | 0.0 | 0.9 | 24.8 | 4.1 | 5.7 | 14.1 | 7.4 |
| Santa Barbara.............. | 0.0 | 15.3 | 2.7 | 0.0 | 7.8 | 15.0 | 1.5 | 9.8 | 8.0 | 2.1 |
| Santa Clara ................. | 0.0 | 8.5 | 0.6 | 0.0 | 1.4 | 16.7 | 12.0 | 7.9 | 13.6 | 4.6 |
| Santa Clarita ............... | 0.0 | 38.1 | 0.0 | 0.0 | 0.0 | 13.5 | 1.0 | 9.4 | 3.4 | 1.2 |
| Santa Cruz .................. | 0.0 | 9.8 | 1.5 | 0.0 | 1.7 | 14.8 | 19.7 | 14.7 | 8.6 | 2.9 |
| Santa Maria ................. | 0.0 | 32.2 | 0.0 | 0.0 | 0.0 | 15.3 | 19.7 | 7.1 | 1.4 | 1.7 |
| Santa Monica .............. | 0.0 | 8.6 | 0.1 | 0.0 | 6.3 | 17.1 | 8.7 | 10.7 | 13.4 | 2.5 |
| Santa Paula ................. | 0.0 | 11.4 | 0.0 | 0.0 | 0.5 | 17.8 | 19.0 | 6.8 | 16.0 | 0.8 |
| Santa Rosa .................. | 0.0 | 10.5 | 1.8 | 0.0 | 0.8 | 17.5 | 17.1 | 11.2 | 4.7 | 7.8 |
| Santee ........................ | 0.0 | 32.2 | 0.0 | 0.0 | 3.3 | 16.5 | 0.0 | 2.6 | 14.8 | 1.7 |
| Saratoga ..................... | 0.0 | 22.7 | 0.0 | 0.0 | 2.7 | 15.9 | 0.0 | 12.6 | 0.3 | 3.5 |
| Seaside ....................... | 0.0 | 10.8 | 0.0 | 0.0 | 0.3 | 23.1 | 0.0 | 4.0 | 13.3 | 5.1 |
| Simi Valley .................. | 0.0 | 14.5 | 0.0 | 0.0 | 0.9 | 24.4 | 12.7 | 0.5 | 15.6 | 5.3 |
| Soledad ...................... | 0.0 | 17.3 | 0.0 | 0.0 | 2.0 | 18.5 | 19.8 | 2.7 | 4.4 | 3.0 |
| South Gate .................. | 1.0 | 19.4 | 0.0 | 0.0 | 0.5 | 25.6 | 4.6 | 5.4 | 6.1 | 11.4 |
| South Pasadena............ | 0.0 | 21.6 | 0.0 | 0.0 | 2.3 | 26.0 | 3.0 | 5.0 | 2.9 | 0.5 |
| South San Francisco..... | 0.0 | 15.8 | 0.4 | 0.0 | 5.8 | 16.3 | 12.6 | 7.1 | 9.9 | 6.7 |
| Stanton ....................... | 0.0 | 10.3 | 0.0 | 0.0 | 0.2 | 18.9 | 1.7 | 3.8 | 45.7 | 5.1 |
| Stockton ...................... | 0.0 | 5.2 | 1.1 | 0.0 | 1.1 | 28.3 | 12.8 | 7.2 | 8.7 | 3.5 |
| Suisun City .................. | 0.0 | 9.9 | 0.0 | 0.0 | 0.0 | 11.3 | 0.0 | 6.3 | 54.3 | 8.2 |
| Sunnyvale.................... | 0.0 | 6.7 | 0.7 | 0.0 | 0.2 | 12.6 | 27.5 | 8.2 | 2.6 | 1.8 |
| Temecula..................... | 0.0 | 30.8 | 0.0 | 0.0 | 0.1 | 14.1 | 0.0 | 16.8 | 12.4 | 2.2 |
| Temple City ................. | 0.0 | 13.8 | 0.9 | 0.0 | 1.7 | 26.3 | 0.1 | 14.4 | 5.8 | 3.9 |
| Thousand Oaks............. | 0.0 | 14.6 | 0.0 | 0.0 | 0.5 | 14.4 | 10.5 | 5.6 | 16.5 | 4.1 |
| Torrance ...................... | 0.0 | 8.3 | 0.0 | 0.0 | 3.8 | 25.2 | 5.8 | 8.3 | 3.4 | 2.7 |
| Tracy .......................... | 0.0 | 8.2 | 0.0 | 0.0 | 3.7 | 12.0 | 26.8 | 8.1 | 8.2 | 7.3 |
| Tulare ......................... | 0.0 | 12.6 | 0.0 | 0.0 | 1.4 | 14.3 | 22.3 | 6.1 | 18.1 | 4.9 |
| Turlock ........................ | 0.0 | 15.8 | 0.0 | 0.0 | 0.4 | 15.5 | 21.7 | 4.4 | 14.2 | 2.7 |
| Tustin.......................... | 0.0 | 27.2 | 0.0 | 0.0 | 0.1 | 21.0 | 0.0 | 6.0 | 20.9 | 5.8 |
| Twentynine Palms........ | 0.0 | 29.9 | 0.0 | 0.0 | 3.3 | 25.1 | 0.0 | 15.7 | 5.0 | 0.8 |
| Union City ................... | 0.0 | 6.2 | 0.0 | 0.0 | 0.4 | 19.4 | 1.7 | 15.5 | 19.3 | 7.7 |
| Upland ........................ | 0.0 | 15.7 | 0.0 | 0.0 | 1.5 | 17.3 | 14.0 | 2.4 | 19.1 | 3.5 |
| Vacaville ..................... | 0.0 | 13.0 | 0.0 | 0.0 | 4.4 | 15.4 | 9.1 | 5.6 | 29.2 | 6.6 |
| Vallejo......................... | 0.0 | 8.3 | 0.0 | 0.0 | 0.1 | 16.5 | 7.2 | 23.4 | 10.6 | 2.9 |
| Victorville .................... | 0.0 | 10.8 | 0.0 | 0.0 | 0.4 | 8.3 | 10.6 | 6.1 | 4.8 | 8.4 |
| Visalia ........................ | 0.0 | 21.3 | 0.0 | 0.0 | 0.0 | 15.7 | 12.1 | 5.3 | 3.3 | 1.7 |
| Vista .......................... | 0.0 | 8.3 | 0.0 | 0.0 | 3.9 | 15.0 | 21.6 | 10.0 | 8.0 | 3.0 |
| Walnut ........................ | 0.0 | 10.2 | 0.0 | 0.0 | 0.7 | 8.3 | 0.0 | 9.4 | 51.6 | 10.2 |
| Walnut Creek ............... | 0.0 | 11.3 | 2.5 | 0.0 | 0.0 | 24.6 | 0.0 | 25.9 | 3.1 | 0.6 |
| Wasco......................... | 0.0 | 18.0 | 0.0 | 0.0 | 1.5 | 17.8 | 23.9 | 0.2 | 5.6 | 2.2 |
| Watsonville.................. | 0.0 | 15.0 | 0.0 | 0.0 | 0.5 | 14.0 | 16.4 | 5.1 | 15.8 | 1.8 |
| West Covina ................ | 0.0 | 10.4 | 0.4 | 0.0 | 3.3 | 22.9 | 0.0 | 25.9 | 10.0 | 4.1 |
| West Hollywood ........... | 0.0 | 13.2 | 9.2 | 0.0 | 8.6 | 14.7 | 2.3 | 5.2 | 13.0 | 1.4 |
| Westminster ................ | 0.0 | 11.7 | 0.0 | 0.0 | 1.0 | 29.6 | 0.0 | 4.9 | 19.6 | 2.2 |
| West Sacramento......... | 0.0 | 16.0 | 0.0 | 0.0 | 0.3 | 10.4 | 12.2 | 8.2 | 12.0 | 10.1 |
| Whittier ...................... | 0.0 | 9.8 | 0.0 | 0.0 | 0.0 | 35.7 | 12.0 | 15.2 | 4.9 | 3.3 |
| Wildomar ..................... | NA | NA | NA | NA | NA | NA | NA | NA | NA | NA |
| Windsor ...................... | 0.0 | 25.4 | 0.0 | 0.0 | 0.8 | 19.6 | 0.0 | 3.7 | 6.5 | 3.9 |
| Woodland ..................... | 0.0 | 25.0 | 0.0 | 0.0 | 0.0 | 14.3 | 9.8 | 17.7 | 1.6 | 3.7 |
| Yorba Linda.................. | 0.0 | 28.5 | 0.0 | 0.0 | 0.4 | 12.3 | 5.3 | 15.5 | 14.6 | 6.1 |
| Yuba City..................... | 0.0 | 4.5 | 0.0 | 0.0 | 0.4 | 25.2 | 8.9 | 5.1 | 7.7 | 2.8 |
| Yucaipa ...................... | 0.0 | 39.5 | 0.0 | 0.0 | 2.6 | 16.3 | 0.0 | 9.2 | 1.2 | 5.7 |
| COLORADO.............. | X | X | X | X | X | X | X | X | X | X |
| Arvada......................... | 0.0 | 10.8 | 0.0 | 0.0 | 0.0 | 18.0 | 9.8 | 22.8 | 3.8 | 2.5 |
| Aurora.......................... | 0.0 | 13.4 | 0.0 | 0.0 | 0.0 | 18.7 | 9.3 | 9.5 | 2.7 | 2.4 |
| Boulder........................ | 0.0 | 13.2 | 1.3 | 0.0 | 0.0 | 12.5 | 14.8 | 12.4 | 8.8 | 4.4 |
| Brighton ...................... | 0.0 | 25.0 | 0.0 | 0.0 | 0.4 | 14.1 | 12.0 | 15.7 | 1.3 | 2.8 |
| Broomfield ................... | 9.2 | 10.0 | 0.0 | 0.0 | 1.7 | 12.1 | 4.8 | 11.2 | 0.1 | 18.1 |

| City | City government finances, 2007 (cont.) Debt outstanding Total (mil dol) | Per capita[1] (dollars) | Debt issued during year | City government employment, 2011 | Climate[2] Average daily temperature (degrees Fahrenheit) Mean January | July | Limits January[3] | July[4] | Annual precipitation (inches) | Heating degree days | Cooling degree days |
|---|---|---|---|---|---|---|---|---|---|---|---|
| | 137 | 138 | 139 | 140 | 141 | 142 | 143 | 144 | 145 | 146 | 147 |
| CALIFORNIA—Cont'd | | | | | | | | | | | |
| San Francisco | 8 705.7 | 11 380 | 960.8 | 28 660 | 52.3 | 61.3 | 46.4 | 68.2 | 22.28 | 2 597 | 163 |
| San Gabriel | 2.3 | 56 | 0.3 | NA | 56.3 | 75.6 | 42.6 | 89.0 | 18.56 | 1 295 | 1 575 |
| San Jacinto | 41.3 | 1 109 | 0.0 | NA | NA | NA | NA | NA | NA | NA | NA |
| San Jose | 4 461.3 | 4 747 | 909.0 | 5 929 | 50.5 | 70.9 | 41.7 | 84.3 | 15.08 | 2 171 | 811 |
| San Juan Capistrano | 40.1 | 1 159 | 0.0 | NA | 55.4 | 68.7 | 43.9 | 77.3 | 13.56 | 1 756 | 666 |
| San Leandro | 68.4 | 880 | 23.4 | 377 | 50.0 | 62.8 | 43.6 | 70.4 | 25.40 | 2 857 | 142 |
| San Luis Obispo | 85.9 | 1 975 | 16.9 | NA | 53.3 | 66.5 | 41.9 | 80.3 | 24.36 | 2 138 | 476 |
| San Marcos | 517.2 | 6 607 | 14.1 | 276 | 56.4 | 71.6 | 45.1 | 82.2 | 13.69 | 1 514 | 1 047 |
| San Mateo | 190.7 | 2 078 | 46.1 | 615 | 48.4 | 68.0 | 39.1 | 80.8 | 20.16 | 2 764 | 422 |
| San Pablo | 91.9 | 2 995 | 36.2 | NA | 48.8 | 67.7 | 41.3 | 80.9 | 34.29 | 2 621 | 451 |
| San Rafael | 55.6 | 999 | 6.2 | NA | 48.8 | 67.7 | 41.3 | 80.9 | 34.29 | 2 621 | 451 |
| San Ramon | 105.3 | 2 152 | 55.2 | NA | 47.2 | 72.0 | 37.4 | 89.1 | 14.82 | 2 755 | 858 |
| Santa Ana | 422.2 | 1 243 | 0.0 | 1 578 | 58.0 | 72.9 | 46.6 | 87.7 | 13.84 | 1 153 | 1 299 |
| Santa Barbara | 138.7 | 1 609 | 0.0 | 1 132 | 53.1 | 67.0 | 40.8 | 76.7 | 16.93 | 2 121 | 482 |
| Santa Clara | 470.3 | 4 285 | 0.0 | 981 | 50.5 | 70.9 | 41.7 | 84.3 | 15.08 | 2 171 | 811 |
| Santa Clarita | 52.7 | 310 | 13.8 | 448 | 50.3 | 74.1 | 36.1 | 94.2 | 13.96 | 2 502 | 1 139 |
| Santa Cruz | 154.6 | 2 794 | 4.1 | 731 | 50.6 | 63.7 | 40.2 | 74.8 | 30.67 | 2 836 | 162 |
| Santa Maria | 94.6 | 1 104 | 0.0 | 513 | 51.6 | 63.5 | 39.3 | 73.5 | 14.01 | 2 783 | 121 |
| Santa Monica | 236.6 | 2 713 | 1.1 | 2 147 | 57.0 | 65.5 | 50.2 | 68.8 | 13.27 | 1 810 | 429 |
| Santa Paula | 35.4 | 1 235 | 0.0 | NA | 54.7 | 68.3 | 41.2 | 80.7 | 18.41 | 1 911 | 602 |
| Santa Rosa | 509.5 | 3 303 | 68.3 | 1 165 | 48.7 | 67.6 | 39.5 | 82.2 | 31.01 | 2 694 | 526 |
| Santee | 25.1 | 472 | 0.0 | NA | 57.1 | 73.0 | 45.7 | 83.6 | 13.75 | 1 313 | 1 261 |
| Saratoga | 13.9 | 458 | 0.0 | NA | 50.5 | 70.9 | 41.7 | 84.3 | 15.08 | 2 171 | 811 |
| Seaside | 45.5 | 1 355 | 7.2 | NA | 51.6 | 60.2 | 43.4 | 68.1 | 20.35 | 3 092 | 74 |
| Simi Valley | 240.4 | 1 995 | 0.0 | 606 | 53.7 | 76.0 | 39.5 | 95.0 | 17.79 | 1 822 | 1 485 |
| Soledad | 10.1 | 359 | 0.0 | NA | NA | NA | NA | NA | NA | NA | NA |
| South Gate | 212.3 | 2 186 | 0.0 | 338 | 58.3 | 74.2 | 48.5 | 83.8 | 15.14 | 928 | 1 506 |
| South Pasadena | 10.6 | 432 | 0.1 | NA | NA | NA | NA | NA | NA | NA | NA |
| South San Francisco | 160.4 | 2 593 | 0.0 | NA | 49.4 | 62.8 | 42.9 | 71.1 | 20.11 | 2 862 | 142 |
| Stanton | 46.3 | 1 233 | 0.0 | NA | 58.0 | 72.9 | 46.6 | 87.7 | 13.84 | 1 153 | 1 299 |
| Stockton | 696.3 | 2 424 | 191.5 | 1 579 | 46.0 | 77.3 | 38.1 | 93.8 | 13.84 | 2 563 | 1 456 |
| Suisun City | 87.4 | 3 239 | 0.0 | NA | 46.1 | 72.6 | 37.5 | 88.8 | 23.46 | 2 649 | 975 |
| Sunnyvale | 98.7 | 752 | 2.2 | 978 | 50.5 | 70.9 | 41.7 | 84.3 | 15.08 | 2 171 | 811 |
| Temecula | 76.5 | 808 | 21.1 | 190 | 51.2 | 78.3 | 36.1 | 97.8 | 11.40 | 2 123 | 1 710 |
| Temple City | 12.2 | 320 | 0.0 | NA | 56.3 | 75.6 | 42.6 | 89.0 | 18.56 | 1 295 | 1 575 |
| Thousand Oaks | 173.8 | 1 409 | 0.0 | 454 | 53.7 | 76.0 | 39.5 | 95.0 | 17.79 | 1 822 | 1 485 |
| Torrance | 120.3 | 851 | 0.0 | 1 406 | 56.3 | 69.4 | 46.2 | 77.6 | 14.79 | 1 526 | 742 |
| Tracy | 285.3 | 3 579 | 0.0 | 420 | 47.1 | 76.4 | 38.5 | 92.5 | 12.51 | 2 421 | 1 470 |
| Tulare | 128.5 | 2 323 | 6.3 | NA | 45.8 | 79.3 | 37.4 | 93.8 | 11.03 | 2 588 | 1 685 |
| Turlock | 68.4 | 1 004 | 0.0 | NA | 46.4 | 77.6 | 39.0 | 93.3 | 12.43 | 2 519 | 1 506 |
| Tustin | 122.9 | 1 734 | 25.0 | 340 | 54.5 | 72.1 | 41.4 | 83.8 | 13.87 | 1 794 | 1 102 |
| Twentynine Palms | 1.2 | 38 | 0.4 | NA | 50.0 | 88.4 | 36.1 | 105.8 | 4.57 | 1 910 | 3 064 |
| Union City | 138.8 | 1 981 | 0.0 | NA | 49.8 | 68.0 | 42.0 | 78.3 | 14.85 | 2 367 | 530 |
| Upland | 61.0 | 842 | 15.0 | NA | 54.6 | 73.8 | 41.5 | 88.7 | 16.96 | 1 727 | 1 191 |
| Vacaville | 188.4 | 2 046 | 19.3 | 608 | 47.2 | 77.3 | 38.8 | 95.8 | 24.55 | 2 410 | 1 498 |
| Vallejo | 353.6 | 3 060 | 46.5 | 583 | 46.3 | 71.2 | 38.8 | 87.4 | 19.58 | 2 757 | 786 |
| Victorville | 411.0 | 3 833 | 244.1 | 385 | 45.5 | 80.0 | 31.4 | 99.1 | 6.20 | 2 929 | 1 735 |
| Visalia | 55.3 | 467 | 6.2 | 608 | 45.8 | 79.3 | 37.4 | 93.8 | 11.03 | 2 588 | 1 685 |
| Vista | 103.1 | 1 135 | 0.0 | 304 | 56.4 | 71.6 | 45.1 | 82.2 | 13.69 | 1 514 | 1 047 |
| Walnut | 78.3 | 2 533 | 0.0 | NA | 54.6 | 73.8 | 41.5 | 88.7 | 16.96 | 1 727 | 1 191 |
| Walnut Creek | 10.7 | 169 | 0.0 | NA | 47.5 | 72.4 | 39.3 | 85.2 | 23.96 | 3 267 | 983 |
| Wasco | 7.4 | 306 | 0.3 | NA | NA | NA | NA | NA | NA | NA | NA |
| Watsonville | 44.9 | 902 | 0.0 | NA | 49.7 | 62.4 | 38.7 | 72.0 | 23.25 | 3 080 | 123 |
| West Covina | 132.0 | 1 240 | 23.9 | 453 | 56.3 | 75.6 | 42.6 | 89.0 | 18.56 | 1 295 | 1 575 |
| West Hollywood | 32.8 | 908 | 0.0 | NA | 58.3 | 74.2 | 48.5 | 83.8 | 15.14 | 928 | 1 506 |
| Westminster | 37.4 | 422 | 0.1 | 291 | 58.0 | 72.9 | 46.6 | 82.7 | 13.84 | 1 153 | 1 299 |
| West Sacramento | 400.4 | 8 612 | 8.6 | NA | 46.3 | 75.4 | 38.8 | 92.4 | 17.93 | 2 666 | 1 248 |
| Whittier | 102.2 | 1 233 | 37.3 | 430 | 56.3 | 75.6 | 42.6 | 89.0 | 18.56 | 1 295 | 1 575 |
| Wildomar | NA | NA | NA | NA | NA | NA | NA | NA | NA | NA | NA |
| Windsor | 39.1 | 1 543 | 0.0 | NA | NA | NA | NA | NA | NA | NA | NA |
| Woodland | 116.9 | 2 178 | 6.9 | NA | 45.7 | 76.4 | 37.6 | 94.0 | 20.78 | 2 683 | 1 417 |
| Yorba Linda | 104.2 | 1 592 | 1.8 | NA | 56.9 | 73.2 | 45.2 | 84.0 | 11.23 | 1 286 | 1 294 |
| Yuba City | 68.1 | 1 113 | 25.2 | NA | 46.3 | 78.9 | 37.8 | 96.3 | 22.07 | 2 488 | 1 687 |
| Yucaipa | 45.3 | 906 | 0.4 | NA | 52.9 | 78.0 | 40.4 | 94.4 | 13.62 | 1 904 | 1 714 |
| COLORADO | X | X | X | X | X | X | X | X | X | X | X |
| Arvada | 70.4 | 662 | 0.0 | 650 | 31.2 | 71.5 | 15.6 | 88.3 | 18.17 | 5 988 | 496 |
| Aurora | 889.2 | 2 852 | 189.0 | 2 595 | 29.2 | 73.4 | 15.2 | 88.0 | 15.81 | 6 128 | 696 |
| Boulder | 224.2 | 2 396 | 20.5 | 1 196 | 32.5 | 71.6 | 19.2 | 87.2 | 19.93 | 5 687 | 552 |
| Brighton | 28.1 | 914 | 0.0 | 261 | NA | NA | NA | NA | NA | NA | NA |
| Broomfield | 352.8 | 6 571 | 0.0 | 706 | 32.5 | 71.6 | 19.2 | 87.2 | 19.93 | 5 687 | 552 |

1. Based on the population estimated as of July 1 of the year shown.   2. Represents normal values based on the 30-year period, 1971–2000.   3. Average daily minimum.   4. Average daily maximum.

# Table D. Cities — **Land Area and Population**

| STATE Place code | City | Land area,[1] 2010 (sq km) | Total persons | Rank | Per square kilometer | White | Black | American Indian, Alaska Native | Asian | Hawaiian Pacific Islander | Percent Hispanic or Latino[2], 2010 | Percent Foreign born 2007–2011 |
|---|---|---|---|---|---|---|---|---|---|---|---|---|
| | | | Population, 2012 | | | Race alone or in combination, not of Hispanic origin (percent), 2010 | | | | | | |
| | | 1 | 2 | 3 | 4 | 5 | 6 | 7 | 8 | 9 | 10 | 11 |
| | **COLORADO—Cont'd** | | | | | | | | | | | |
| 08 12415 | Castle Rock | 87.5 | 51 348 | 708 | 586.8 | 86.6 | 1.6 | 0.9 | 2.6 | 0.2 | 10.0 | 5.8 |
| 08 12815 | Centennial | 74.4 | 103 743 | 273 | 1 394.4 | 84.4 | 4.0 | 0.8 | 5.3 | 0.3 | 7.4 | 7.6 |
| 08 16000 | Colorado Springs | 503.9 | 431 834 | 41 | 857.0 | 73.7 | 7.3 | 1.5 | 4.3 | 0.5 | 16.1 | 7.9 |
| 08 16495 | Commerce City | 88.8 | 48 421 | 764 | 545.3 | 47.4 | 3.4 | 1.1 | 2.8 | 0.2 | 46.8 | 17.7 |
| 08 20000 | Denver | 396.3 | 634 265 | 23 | 1 600.5 | 53.9 | 10.8 | 1.2 | 4.1 | 0.2 | 31.8 | 16.4 |
| 08 24785 | Englewood | 17.0 | 31 177 | 1 167 | 1 833.9 | 77.0 | 2.7 | 1.6 | 2.5 | 0.3 | 18.1 | 9.9 |
| 08 27425 | Fort Collins | 140.6 | 148 612 | 163 | 1 057.0 | 85.1 | 1.6 | 1.1 | 3.9 | 0.2 | 10.1 | 6.0 |
| 08 27865 | Fountain | 62.1 | 26 891 | 1 351 | 433.0 | 66.4 | 12.1 | 2.0 | 3.9 | 1.1 | 19.4 | 6.2 |
| 08 31660 | Grand Junction | 99.0 | 59 899 | 585 | 605.0 | 83.5 | 1.1 | 1.2 | 1.6 | 0.2 | 13.9 | 4.0 |
| 08 32155 | Greeley | 120.6 | 95 357 | 310 | 790.7 | 60.6 | 1.7 | 0.9 | 1.7 | 0.2 | 36.0 | 11.5 |
| 08 43000 | Lakewood | 111.1 | 145 516 | 172 | 1 309.8 | 72.5 | 1.8 | 1.3 | 3.7 | 0.2 | 22.0 | 8.9 |
| 08 45255 | Littleton | 33.6 | 43 775 | 833 | 1 302.8 | 83.4 | 1.8 | 1.1 | 2.8 | 0.1 | 12.4 | 8.7 |
| 08 45970 | Longmont | 67.8 | 88 669 | 343 | 1 307.8 | 70.8 | 1.2 | 1.0 | 3.9 | 0.1 | 24.6 | 14.4 |
| 08 46465 | Loveland | 87.0 | 70 223 | 470 | 807.2 | 86.2 | 0.9 | 1.0 | 1.4 | 0.1 | 11.7 | 4.5 |
| 08 54330 | Northglenn | 19.2 | 36 891 | 989 | 1 921.4 | 62.7 | 2.6 | 1.3 | 4.2 | 0.2 | 30.6 | 10.5 |
| 08 57630 | Parker | 53.0 | 47 169 | 783 | 890.0 | 86.5 | 2.0 | 0.8 | 4.3 | 0.2 | 8.2 | 4.4 |
| 08 62000 | Pueblo | 138.9 | 107 772 | 254 | 775.9 | 46.3 | 2.5 | 1.2 | 1.0 | 0.1 | 49.8 | 4.3 |
| 08 77290 | Thornton | 90.2 | 124 140 | 212 | 1 376.3 | 61.6 | 2.2 | 1.0 | 5.1 | 0.2 | 31.7 | 10.5 |
| 08 83835 | Westminster | 81.7 | 109 169 | 248 | 1 336.2 | 71.9 | 1.8 | 1.0 | 6.1 | 0.2 | 20.7 | 10.5 |
| 08 84440 | Wheat Ridge | 24.1 | 30 717 | 1 183 | 1 274.6 | 75.6 | 1.4 | 1.4 | 2.0 | 0.2 | 20.9 | 6.9 |
| 09 00000 | **CONNECTICUT** | 12 541.6 | 3 590 347 | X | 286.3 | 72.6 | 10.2 | 0.6 | 4.3 | 0.1 | 13.4 | 13.3 |
| 09 08000 | Bridgeport | 41.4 | 146 425 | 168 | 3 536.8 | 23.9 | 33.5 | 0.6 | 3.7 | 0.2 | 38.2 | 26.3 |
| 09 08420 | Bristol | 68.4 | 60 603 | 577 | 886.0 | 84.7 | 4.5 | 0.6 | 2.3 | 0.1 | 9.6 | 9.7 |
| 09 18430 | Danbury | 108.5 | 82 807 | 377 | 763.2 | 59.3 | 7.2 | 0.5 | 7.2 | 0.1 | 25.0 | 30.7 |
| 09 37000 | Hartford | 45.0 | 124 893 | 209 | 2 775.4 | 16.8 | 36.6 | 0.7 | 3.1 | 0.2 | 43.4 | 22.1 |
| 09 46450 | Meriden | 61.6 | 60 638 | 575 | 984.4 | 60.3 | 9.4 | 0.7 | 2.4 | 0.1 | 28.9 | 10.4 |
| 09 47290 | Middletown | 106.2 | 47 325 | 780 | 445.6 | 74.0 | 13.9 | 0.8 | 5.6 | 0.1 | 8.3 | 10.5 |
| 09 47500 | Milford | 57.4 | 51 488 | 704 | 908.1 | 86.6 | 2.8 | 0.4 | 5.9 | 0.1 | 5.2 | 10.5 |
| 09 49880 | Naugatuck | 42.2 | 31 774 | 1 143 | 752.9 | 82.3 | 5.4 | 0.5 | 3.3 | 0.1 | 9.2 | 12.2 |
| 09 50370 | New Britain | 34.7 | 73 153 | 450 | 2 108.2 | 49.4 | 12.1 | 0.5 | 2.8 | 0.1 | 36.8 | 20.1 |
| 09 52000 | New Haven | 48.4 | 130 741 | 191 | 2 701.3 | 33.4 | 34.9 | 0.9 | 5.2 | 0.1 | 27.4 | 16.7 |
| 09 52280 | New London | 14.5 | 27 707 | 1 307 | 1 910.8 | 51.9 | 18.0 | 1.9 | 3.4 | 0.4 | 28.3 | 16.6 |
| 09 55990 | Norwalk | 59.2 | 87 190 | 351 | 1 472.8 | 56.9 | 14.2 | 0.4 | 5.2 | 0.1 | 24.3 | 22.0 |
| 09 56200 | Norwich | 72.7 | 40 502 | 893 | 557.1 | 67.5 | 12.1 | 2.3 | 8.3 | 0.3 | 12.6 | 14.3 |
| 09 68100 | Shelton | 79.3 | 40 261 | 905 | 507.7 | 87.6 | 2.6 | 0.4 | 4.1 | 0.0 | 5.9 | 11.9 |
| 09 73000 | Stamford | 97.5 | 125 109 | 208 | 1 283.2 | 54.4 | 13.8 | 0.3 | 8.5 | 0.1 | 23.8 | 37.5 |
| 09 76500 | Torrington | 103.0 | 35 808 | 1 022 | 347.7 | 86.5 | 3.2 | 0.7 | 2.4 | 0.1 | 8.8 | 7.0 |
| 09 80000 | Waterbury | 73.9 | 109 915 | 244 | 1 487.3 | 47.2 | 19.6 | 0.8 | 2.1 | 0.2 | 31.2 | 14.4 |
| 09 82800 | West Haven | 27.8 | 55 404 | 648 | 1 992.9 | 58.7 | 19.8 | 0.6 | 4.3 | 0.2 | 18.3 | 13.7 |
| 10 00000 | **DELAWARE** | 5 046.7 | 917 092 | X | 181.7 | 67.0 | 22.1 | 0.9 | 3.7 | 0.1 | 8.2 | 8.3 |
| 10 21200 | Dover | 60.0 | 37 089 | 978 | 618.2 | 48.1 | 43.6 | 1.4 | 3.5 | 0.2 | 6.6 | 6.4 |
| 10 50670 | Newark | 23.8 | 32 367 | 1 125 | 1 360.0 | 81.1 | 7.3 | 0.5 | 8.1 | 0.1 | 4.8 | 11.6 |
| 10 77580 | Wilmington | 28.2 | 71 292 | 463 | 2 528.1 | 29.0 | 58.1 | 0.8 | 1.2 | 0.1 | 12.4 | 6.6 |
| 11 00000 | **DISTRICT OF COLUMBIA** | 158.1 | 632 323 | X | 3 999.5 | 36.3 | 51.3 | 0.8 | 4.3 | 0.1 | 9.1 | 13.3 |
| 11 50000 | Washington | 158.1 | 632 323 | 24 | 3 999.5 | 36.3 | 51.3 | 0.8 | 4.3 | 0.1 | 9.1 | 13.3 |
| 12 00000 | **FLORIDA** | 138 887.5 | 19 317 568 | X | 139.1 | 59.1 | 15.9 | 0.6 | 2.9 | 0.2 | 22.5 | 19.2 |
| 12 00950 | Altamonte Springs | 23.3 | 41 920 | 871 | 1 799.1 | 58.8 | 13.9 | 0.7 | 3.9 | 0.2 | 24.3 | 14.8 |
| 12 01700 | Apopka | 80.9 | 44 474 | 821 | 549.7 | 50.9 | 20.6 | 0.5 | 3.8 | 0.2 | 25.4 | 17.7 |
| 12 02681 | Aventura | 6.9 | 36 981 | 984 | 5 359.6 | 58.6 | 3.7 | 0.1 | 2.1 | 0.1 | 35.8 | 44.9 |
| 12 07300 | Boca Raton | 76.0 | 87 836 | 347 | 1 155.7 | 80.1 | 5.4 | 0.3 | 2.9 | 0.1 | 11.9 | 18.2 |
| 12 07525 | Bonita Springs | 100.0 | 46 340 | 798 | 463.4 | 75.6 | 0.8 | 0.3 | 1.2 | 0.1 | 22.5 | 21.3 |
| 12 07875 | Boynton Beach | 41.9 | 70 101 | 475 | 1 673.1 | 54.6 | 30.6 | 0.4 | 2.6 | 0.2 | 12.8 | 24.9 |
| 12 07950 | Bradenton | 36.7 | 50 672 | 720 | 1 380.7 | 65.8 | 16.5 | 0.6 | 1.3 | 0.1 | 17.0 | 12.7 |
| 12 10275 | Cape Coral | 273.7 | 161 248 | 147 | 589.1 | 74.8 | 4.4 | 0.5 | 1.9 | 0.1 | 19.5 | 14.7 |
| 12 11050 | Casselberry | 18.1 | 26 449 | 1 375 | 1 461.3 | 66.5 | 8.0 | 0.8 | 3.6 | 0.2 | 22.6 | 10.1 |
| 12 12875 | Clearwater | 66.2 | 108 732 | 251 | 1 642.5 | 72.5 | 11.4 | 0.6 | 2.6 | 0.2 | 14.2 | 15.9 |
| 12 12925 | Clermont | 35.3 | 29 421 | 1 239 | 833.5 | 62.0 | 14.5 | 0.8 | 5.4 | 0.3 | 17.8 | 14.4 |
| 12 13275 | Coconut Creek | 30.7 | 55 001 | 654 | 1 791.6 | 61.1 | 14.0 | 0.3 | 4.5 | 0.2 | 20.4 | 27.3 |
| 12 14125 | Cooper City | 20.8 | 32 345 | 1 127 | 1 555.0 | 66.2 | 5.2 | 0.4 | 6.4 | 0.1 | 22.8 | 22.3 |
| 12 14250 | Coral Gables | 33.5 | 49 411 | 741 | 1 475.0 | 40.9 | 2.8 | 0.1 | 3.2 | 0.0 | 53.6 | 36.3 |
| 12 14400 | Coral Springs | 61.6 | 125 287 | 207 | 2 033.9 | 53.0 | 18.3 | 0.4 | 5.9 | 0.2 | 23.5 | 26.1 |
| 12 15968 | Cutler Bay | 25.5 | 42 221 | 864 | 1 655.7 | 29.5 | 13.8 | 0.3 | 3.0 | 0.2 | 54.5 | 33.9 |
| 12 16335 | Dania Beach | 21.0 | 30 574 | 1 190 | 1 455.9 | 53.7 | 21.8 | 0.5 | 2.5 | 0.1 | 22.4 | 28.5 |
| 12 16475 | Davie | 90.4 | 95 489 | 307 | 1 056.3 | 58.0 | 8.1 | 0.5 | 5.3 | 0.2 | 29.1 | 25.1 |
| 12 16525 | Daytona Beach | 151.3 | 62 035 | 557 | 410.0 | 55.9 | 36.0 | 0.8 | 2.6 | 0.1 | 6.2 | 9.9 |

1. Dry land or land partially or temporarily covered by water.    2. May be of any race.

## Table D. Cities — **Population**

| City | Age of population (percent), 2010 | | | | | | | | | | | Population | | | |
|------|------|------|------|------|------|------|------|------|------|------|------|------|------|------|------|
| | | | | | | | | | | | | Census counts | | Percent change | |
| | Under 5 years | 5 to 17 years | 18 to 24 years | 25 to 34 years | 35 to 44 years | 45 to 54 years | 55 to 64 years | 65 to 74 years | 75 years and over | Median age | Percent female | 2000 | 2010 | 2000– 2010 | 2010– 2012 |
| | 12 | 13 | 14 | 15 | 16 | 17 | 18 | 19 | 20 | 21 | 22 | 23 | 24 | 25 | 26 |
| COLORADO—Cont'd | | | | | | | | | | | | | | | |
| Castle Rock | 9.2 | 23.2 | 5.7 | 14.0 | 19.0 | 14.1 | 8.6 | 4.0 | 2.2 | 33.8 | 50.4 | 20 224 | 48 254 | 138.5 | 6.4 |
| Centennial | 5.3 | 19.8 | 6.7 | 10.2 | 13.6 | 17.8 | 14.7 | 6.8 | 5.0 | 41.1 | 50.8 | NA | 100 340 | NA | 3.4 |
| Colorado Springs | 7.1 | 17.9 | 10.5 | 14.6 | 13.0 | 14.9 | 11.1 | 5.9 | 5.0 | 34.9 | 51.0 | 360 890 | 416 433 | 15.4 | 3.7 |
| Commerce City | 10.9 | 22.2 | 7.7 | 18.7 | 15.6 | 11.1 | 8.1 | 3.5 | 2.3 | 30.4 | 49.6 | 20 991 | 45 919 | 118.7 | 5.4 |
| Denver | 7.3 | 14.2 | 10.4 | 20.5 | 15.0 | 12.1 | 10.3 | 5.4 | 5.0 | 33.7 | 50.0 | 554 636 | 600 024 | 8.2 | 5.7 |
| Englewood | 6.4 | 11.9 | 9.7 | 18.8 | 13.8 | 15.6 | 11.3 | 5.5 | 6.9 | 37.1 | 50.0 | 31 727 | 30 255 | -4.6 | 3.0 |
| Fort Collins | 5.7 | 14.2 | 21.4 | 16.9 | 12.1 | 11.7 | 9.3 | 4.5 | 4.3 | 29.6 | 50.1 | 118 652 | 144 000 | 21.4 | 3.2 |
| Fountain | 10.2 | 23.5 | 9.5 | 17.8 | 15.5 | 11.8 | 6.5 | 3.5 | 1.8 | 28.7 | 50.8 | 15 197 | 25 885 | 70.1 | 3.9 |
| Grand Junction | 6.5 | 14.7 | 12.5 | 14.3 | 11.2 | 13.1 | 12.1 | 7.3 | 8.3 | 36.7 | 50.6 | 41 986 | 59 095 | 39.5 | 1.4 |
| Greeley | 7.8 | 18.0 | 16.9 | 13.9 | 11.5 | 11.3 | 9.8 | 5.4 | 5.3 | 29.8 | 50.9 | 76 930 | 92 865 | 20.7 | 2.7 |
| Lakewood | 6.0 | 14.8 | 9.7 | 14.3 | 12.8 | 15.3 | 12.6 | 7.6 | 6.9 | 39.2 | 51.1 | 144 126 | 142 980 | -0.8 | 1.8 |
| Littleton | 5.7 | 15.9 | 7.8 | 12.7 | 12.9 | 16.2 | 13.0 | 7.5 | 8.2 | 41.3 | 51.7 | 40 340 | 41 737 | 3.5 | 4.9 |
| Longmont | 7.2 | 19.0 | 7.9 | 13.5 | 14.7 | 15.3 | 11.2 | 6.0 | 5.2 | 36.6 | 50.7 | 71 093 | 86 281 | 21.3 | 2.8 |
| Loveland | 6.8 | 17.2 | 7.9 | 13.4 | 12.9 | 14.6 | 12.4 | 7.8 | 7.1 | 38.7 | 51.7 | 50 608 | 66 853 | 32.1 | 5.0 |
| Northglenn | 7.5 | 18.0 | 10.7 | 16.6 | 13.2 | 13.4 | 9.2 | 6.2 | 5.1 | 33.1 | 50.2 | 31 575 | 35 761 | 13.3 | 3.2 |
| Parker | 8.7 | 24.2 | 5.7 | 13.7 | 20.3 | 14.5 | 8.0 | 3.3 | 1.5 | 33.6 | 50.6 | 23 558 | 45 297 | 92.3 | 4.1 |
| Pueblo | 6.9 | 17.1 | 10.5 | 12.7 | 11.5 | 13.3 | 12.2 | 7.3 | 8.4 | 37.5 | 51.2 | 102 121 | 106 543 | 4.4 | 1.2 |
| Thornton | 8.6 | 20.9 | 9.0 | 16.6 | 16.1 | 13.1 | 9.2 | 4.0 | 2.5 | 32.0 | 50.5 | 82 384 | 118 796 | 44.2 | 4.5 |
| Westminster | 7.0 | 17.0 | 9.5 | 16.2 | 14.2 | 15.3 | 11.5 | 5.2 | 3.9 | 35.1 | 50.4 | 100 940 | 106 129 | 5.1 | 2.9 |
| Wheat Ridge | 5.4 | 13.3 | 7.1 | 13.6 | 12.2 | 16.1 | 13.6 | 8.1 | 10.5 | 43.7 | 51.4 | 32 913 | 30 190 | -8.3 | 1.7 |
| CONNECTICUT | 5.7 | 17.2 | 9.1 | 11.8 | 13.6 | 16.1 | 12.4 | 7.1 | 7.0 | 40.0 | 51.3 | 3 405 565 | 3 574 097 | 4.9 | 0.5 |
| Bridgeport | 7.4 | 17.6 | 12.4 | 16.1 | 13.8 | 13.3 | 9.3 | 5.3 | 4.8 | 32.6 | 51.5 | 139 529 | 144 236 | 3.4 | 1.5 |
| Bristol | 5.6 | 15.8 | 7.9 | 13.5 | 13.9 | 16.0 | 12.2 | 7.1 | 7.8 | 40.3 | 51.8 | 60 062 | 60 477 | 0.7 | 0.2 |
| Danbury | 6.7 | 14.4 | 10.6 | 16.4 | 15.4 | 14.6 | 10.8 | 5.7 | 5.4 | 36.2 | 50.9 | 74 848 | 80 898 | 8.1 | 2.4 |
| Hartford | 7.6 | 18.2 | 15.4 | 15.5 | 12.6 | 12.6 | 9.2 | 5.0 | 3.8 | 30.2 | 51.7 | 121 578 | 124 775 | 2.6 | 0.1 |
| Meriden | 6.7 | 17.2 | 8.5 | 14.1 | 13.6 | 15.1 | 11.9 | 6.3 | 6.6 | 37.7 | 51.6 | 58 244 | 60 868 | 4.5 | -0.4 |
| Middletown | 5.4 | 13.7 | 13.1 | 15.3 | 13.4 | 14.6 | 11.3 | 6.5 | 6.7 | 37.0 | 51.4 | 43 167 | 47 648 | 10.4 | -0.7 |
| Milford | 4.7 | 15.3 | 6.7 | 11.5 | 14.3 | 17.2 | 14.1 | 8.3 | 8.0 | 43.5 | 51.8 | 52 305 | 51 271 | 0.9 | 0.4 |
| Naugatuck | 5.9 | 17.2 | 8.6 | 14.1 | 14.3 | 16.3 | 11.6 | 6.3 | 5.7 | 38.2 | 51.0 | 30 989 | 31 862 | 2.8 | -0.3 |
| New Britain | 6.9 | 16.4 | 14.3 | 15.6 | 11.9 | 12.7 | 10.2 | 5.2 | 6.7 | 32.6 | 51.5 | 71 538 | 73 206 | 2.3 | -0.1 |
| New Haven | 7.1 | 15.7 | 16.8 | 19.0 | 12.6 | 11.2 | 8.4 | 5.0 | 4.3 | 29.9 | 51.8 | 123 626 | 129 773 | 5.0 | 0.7 |
| New London | 6.0 | 14.4 | 21.3 | 14.5 | 11.6 | 12.3 | 10.0 | 5.0 | 5.0 | 30.3 | 50.6 | 25 671 | 27 620 | 7.6 | 0.3 |
| Norwalk | 6.9 | 15.2 | 7.3 | 15.7 | 15.5 | 15.2 | 11.4 | 6.7 | 6.1 | 38.2 | 51.0 | 82 951 | 85 621 | 3.2 | 1.8 |
| Norwich | 6.3 | 16.1 | 9.3 | 14.4 | 13.3 | 15.2 | 12.2 | 6.4 | 6.7 | 38.0 | 51.6 | 36 117 | 40 493 | 12.1 | 0.0 |
| Shelton | 4.7 | 16.4 | 6.7 | 9.7 | 13.6 | 17.6 | 13.9 | 8.8 | 8.6 | 44.4 | 51.5 | 38 101 | 39 559 | 3.8 | 1.8 |
| Stamford | 6.8 | 14.8 | 7.8 | 17.4 | 15.1 | 14.2 | 10.8 | 6.4 | 6.8 | 37.1 | 50.7 | 117 083 | 122 643 | 4.7 | 2.0 |
| Torrington | 5.7 | 15.3 | 7.7 | 11.9 | 13.4 | 16.9 | 12.9 | 7.2 | 8.9 | 42.4 | 51.0 | 35 202 | 36 383 | 3.4 | -1.6 |
| Waterbury | 7.2 | 18.4 | 10.1 | 14.1 | 13.3 | 13.9 | 10.4 | 6.1 | 6.5 | 35.2 | 52.4 | 107 271 | 110 366 | 2.9 | -0.4 |
| West Haven | 5.9 | 14.9 | 13.1 | 14.1 | 13.1 | 14.7 | 11.7 | 6.2 | 6.3 | 36.6 | 51.6 | 52 360 | 55 564 | 6.1 | -0.3 |
| DELAWARE | 6.2 | 16.7 | 10.1 | 12.4 | 12.9 | 14.9 | 12.4 | 8.1 | 6.3 | 38.8 | 51.6 | 783 600 | 897 934 | 14.6 | 2.1 |
| Dover | 6.6 | 15.0 | 18.8 | 13.7 | 10.3 | 11.6 | 9.5 | 6.9 | 7.5 | 31.3 | 53.6 | 32 135 | 36 041 | 12.2 | 2.9 |
| Newark | 2.8 | 7.9 | 48.0 | 9.4 | 6.9 | 8.0 | 7.6 | 4.8 | 4.6 | 22.2 | 53.3 | 28 547 | 31 454 | 10.2 | 2.9 |
| Wilmington | 7.3 | 17.0 | 10.0 | 16.6 | 13.3 | 13.9 | 10.3 | 6.0 | 5.6 | 34.3 | 52.5 | 72 664 | 70 852 | -2.5 | 0.6 |
| DISTRICT OF COLUMBIA | 5.4 | 11.3 | 14.5 | 20.7 | 13.4 | 12.6 | 10.6 | 6.1 | 5.3 | 33.8 | 52.8 | 572 059 | 601 723 | 5.2 | 5.1 |
| Washington | 5.4 | 11.3 | 14.5 | 20.7 | 13.4 | 12.6 | 10.6 | 6.1 | 5.3 | 33.8 | 52.8 | 572 059 | 601 723 | 5.2 | 5.1 |
| FLORIDA | 5.7 | 15.6 | 9.3 | 12.2 | 12.9 | 14.6 | 12.4 | 9.2 | 8.1 | 40.7 | 51.1 | 15 982 378 | 18 802 690 | 17.6 | 2.7 |
| Altamonte Springs | 5.9 | 14.0 | 10.3 | 19.1 | 14.1 | 13.3 | 10.7 | 6.5 | 6.0 | 35.5 | 53.0 | 41 200 | 41 544 | 0.7 | 0.9 |
| Apopka | 8.1 | 19.3 | 7.9 | 14.1 | 16.0 | 14.1 | 10.5 | 5.8 | 4.2 | 35.4 | 51.5 | 26 642 | 41 604 | 55.9 | 6.9 |
| Aventura | 5.4 | 10.1 | 5.5 | 13.5 | 14.3 | 11.8 | 13.0 | 11.7 | 14.9 | 46.1 | 54.2 | 25 267 | 35 762 | 41.5 | 3.4 |
| Boca Raton | 3.9 | 13.3 | 11.2 | 9.5 | 11.5 | 15.7 | 14.0 | 10.2 | 10.8 | 45.4 | 51.1 | 74 764 | 84 392 | 12.9 | 4.1 |
| Bonita Springs | 4.4 | 9.4 | 5.6 | 10.2 | 9.0 | 11.2 | 16.5 | 20.1 | 13.7 | 55.2 | 49.6 | 32 797 | 43 914 | 33.9 | 5.5 |
| Boynton Beach | 5.8 | 13.5 | 8.0 | 13.6 | 13.2 | 13.5 | 11.0 | 9.2 | 12.2 | 41.9 | 52.8 | 60 389 | 68 217 | 13.0 | 2.8 |
| Bradenton | 6.5 | 15.0 | 8.4 | 11.7 | 10.9 | 12.5 | 12.0 | 9.1 | 14.0 | 42.8 | 53.4 | 49 504 | 49 560 | 0.1 | 2.2 |
| Cape Coral | 5.4 | 17.1 | 7.1 | 10.7 | 13.4 | 15.4 | 14.0 | 10.0 | 7.0 | 42.4 | 51.2 | 102 286 | 154 305 | 50.9 | 4.5 |
| Casselberry | 5.4 | 14.2 | 11.6 | 15.5 | 13.2 | 14.0 | 12.0 | 7.6 | 6.5 | 37.5 | 51.6 | 22 629 | 26 241 | 16.0 | 0.8 |
| Clearwater | 5.3 | 13.4 | 8.3 | 12.4 | 12.2 | 14.9 | 13.7 | 9.5 | 10.3 | 43.8 | 51.7 | 108 787 | 108 258 | -1.0 | 0.4 |
| Clermont | 5.7 | 17.8 | 7.6 | 10.8 | 13.8 | 12.4 | 11.9 | 11.7 | 8.4 | 40.9 | 52.7 | 9 333 | 28 748 | 208.0 | 2.3 |
| Coconut Creek | 5.7 | 15.8 | 7.3 | 13.5 | 14.8 | 14.2 | 10.2 | 6.9 | 11.6 | 40.3 | 53.4 | 43 566 | 52 936 | 21.4 | 3.9 |
| Cooper City | 4.7 | 21.1 | 8.7 | 8.4 | 13.5 | 20.6 | 14.2 | 5.2 | 3.6 | 41.0 | 51.6 | 27 939 | 28 548 | 2.2 | 13.3 |
| Coral Gables | 4.7 | 13.2 | 16.6 | 10.6 | 13.2 | 14.0 | 12.0 | 8.1 | 7.5 | 38.8 | 52.7 | 42 249 | 46 776 | 10.7 | 5.6 |
| Coral Springs | 5.8 | 20.8 | 9.4 | 12.0 | 14.8 | 17.3 | 12.0 | 4.6 | 3.3 | 36.5 | 51.9 | 117 549 | 121 098 | 3.0 | 3.5 |
| Cutler Bay | 6.8 | 18.9 | 9.0 | 13.3 | 16.2 | 15.4 | 9.8 | 5.9 | 4.7 | 36.3 | 51.7 | NA | 40 286 | NA | 4.8 |
| Dania Beach | 5.9 | 12.8 | 8.2 | 14.4 | 13.8 | 16.3 | 13.7 | 8.3 | 6.5 | 41.0 | 50.7 | 20 061 | 29 639 | 47.7 | 3.2 |
| Davie | 5.7 | 17.7 | 10.4 | 13.2 | 13.9 | 17.0 | 11.5 | 5.9 | 4.7 | 37.5 | 51.6 | 75 720 | 91 992 | 21.5 | 3.8 |
| Daytona Beach | 5.2 | 10.5 | 17.9 | 11.8 | 9.8 | 13.5 | 12.7 | 9.0 | 9.6 | 39.8 | 50.0 | 64 112 | 61 005 | -4.8 | 1.7 |

# Table D. Cities — Households, Group Quarters, Crime, and Education

| City | Households, 2010 Number | Persons per household | Percent Female family householder[1] | Percent One-person | Persons in group quarters, 2010 Total | Institutional Total | Persons in nursing facilities | Non-institutional | Serious crimes known to police[2] 2011 Total Number | Rate[3] | Rate[3] Violent | Property | Educational attainment, 2007–2011 Population age 25 and older | Attainment[4] (percent) High school graduate or less | Bachelor's degree or more |
|---|---|---|---|---|---|---|---|---|---|---|---|---|---|---|---|
| | 27 | 28 | 29 | 30 | 31 | 32 | 33 | 34 | 35 | 36 | 37 | 38 | 39 | 40 | 41 |
| COLORADO—Cont'd | | | | | | | | | | | | | | | |
| Castle Rock | 16 688 | 2.86 | 8.5 | 17.7 | 460 | 390 | 108 | 70 | 511 | 1 041 | 61 | 980 | 29 080 | 21.4 | 45.1 |
| Centennial | 37 449 | 2.63 | 9.0 | 20.5 | 1 701 | 1 559 | 307 | 142 | 1 515 | 1 483 | 159 | 1 325 | 68 456 | 18.1 | 53.3 |
| Colorado Springs | 167 788 | 2.44 | 11.6 | 29.6 | 7 629 | 3 467 | 1 657 | 4 162 | 17 738 | 4 187 | 440 | 3 746 | 265 705 | 29.5 | 36.1 |
| Commerce City | 14 479 | 3.15 | 13.1 | 17.4 | 351 | 191 | 191 | 160 | 1 397 | 2 991 | 362 | 2 629 | 25 763 | 51.1 | 19.8 |
| Denver | 263 107 | 2.22 | 10.6 | 40.6 | 15 981 | 6 518 | 2 333 | 9 463 | 26 211 | 4 293 | 609 | 3 684 | 402 665 | 35.1 | 41.3 |
| Englewood | 14 375 | 2.08 | 11.1 | 40.1 | 291 | 238 | 238 | 53 | 1 778 | 5 776 | 221 | 5 555 | 21 707 | 41.4 | 30.1 |
| Fort Collins | 57 829 | 2.37 | 8.1 | 28.4 | 7 085 | 1 437 | 514 | 5 648 | 4 659 | 3 180 | 263 | 2 917 | 82 187 | 19.1 | 51.5 |
| Fountain | 8 724 | 2.96 | 15.6 | 16.8 | 0 | 0 | 0 | 0 | 567 | 2 156 | 106 | 2 050 | 14 028 | 36.0 | 21.5 |
| Grand Junction | 24 311 | 2.29 | 9.7 | 32.6 | 2 884 | 1 077 | 395 | 1 807 | 2 849 | 4 781 | 433 | 4 348 | 38 261 | 36.1 | 30.6 |
| Greeley | 33 427 | 2.63 | 11.9 | 26.9 | 4 853 | 1 627 | 627 | 3 226 | 3 562 | 3 769 | 458 | 3 311 | 53 379 | 42.6 | 26.4 |
| Lakewood | 61 986 | 2.27 | 11.9 | 33.5 | 2 171 | 1 552 | 1 064 | 619 | 6 809 | 4 681 | 423 | 4 258 | 100 229 | 33.8 | 35.8 |
| Littleton | 18 312 | 2.25 | 9.5 | 34.7 | 491 | 448 | 313 | 43 | 1 176 | 2 769 | 127 | 2 642 | 29 107 | 24.5 | 42.9 |
| Longmont | 33 252 | 2.58 | 10.7 | 26.8 | 639 | 498 | 482 | 141 | 2 185 | 2 489 | 256 | 2 233 | 54 677 | 33.0 | 37.8 |
| Loveland | 27 153 | 2.44 | 10.6 | 26.7 | 510 | 416 | 414 | 94 | 1 832 | 2 693 | 157 | 2 536 | 44 073 | 32.5 | 33.1 |
| Northglenn | 13 492 | 2.64 | 14.6 | 26.2 | 129 | 129 | 129 | 0 | 1 107 | 3 040 | 250 | 2 790 | 22 721 | 51.7 | 17.1 |
| Parker | 15 917 | 2.84 | 8.8 | 18.9 | 28 | 0 | 0 | 28 | 586 | 1 272 | 93 | 1 178 | 26 615 | 16.5 | 48.0 |
| Pueblo | 43 290 | 2.37 | 16.4 | 33.1 | 4 045 | 3 050 | 1 444 | 995 | 6 342 | 5 848 | 744 | 5 104 | 70 355 | 46.4 | 19.0 |
| Thornton | 41 359 | 2.86 | 12.2 | 20.1 | 462 | 430 | 430 | 32 | 4 133 | 3 420 | 575 | 2 845 | 71 464 | 40.5 | 26.4 |
| Westminster | 42 041 | 2.51 | 10.9 | 26.4 | 467 | 448 | 348 | 19 | 3 058 | 2 832 | 227 | 2 606 | 68 691 | 33.8 | 33.2 |
| Wheat Ridge | 13 976 | 2.12 | 11.6 | 38.4 | 554 | 434 | 381 | 120 | 1 409 | 4 591 | 411 | 4 180 | 22 050 | 39.7 | 28.4 |
| CONNECTICUT | 1 371 087 | 2.52 | 12.9 | 27.3 | 118 152 | 49 370 | 26 371 | 68 782 | 87 376 | 2 440 | 273 | 2 167 | 2 413 922 | 39.6 | 35.7 |
| Bridgeport | 51 255 | 2.72 | 24.2 | 29.0 | 4 838 | 1 960 | 759 | 2 878 | 7 054 | 4 882 | 1 001 | 3 880 | 88 795 | 60.7 | 15.2 |
| Bristol | 25 320 | 2.35 | 12.8 | 30.4 | 849 | 637 | 611 | 212 | 1 622 | 2 677 | 198 | 2 479 | 42 935 | 50.3 | 21.7 |
| Danbury | 28 907 | 2.66 | 11.8 | 26.4 | 3 953 | 1 904 | 538 | 2 049 | 1 752 | 2 162 | 202 | 1 959 | 55 055 | 48.0 | 30.0 |
| Hartford | 45 124 | 2.57 | 30.0 | 33.1 | 8 951 | 2 194 | 777 | 6 757 | 7 141 | 5 713 | 1 311 | 4 401 | 72 918 | 62.8 | 14.3 |
| Meriden | 23 977 | 2.50 | 17.0 | 29.4 | 955 | 688 | 660 | 267 | 1 865 | 3 058 | 236 | 2 822 | 40 801 | 52.2 | 19.9 |
| Middletown | 19 863 | 2.21 | 13.0 | 35.7 | 3 731 | 998 | 552 | 2 733 | 1 100 | 2 304 | 161 | 2 143 | 32 115 | 41.2 | 33.4 |
| Milford | 21 708 | 2.41 | 9.9 | 29.3 | 472 | 355 | 344 | 117 | 1 788 | 3 383 | 66 | 3 316 | 37 782 | 35.3 | 38.6 |
| Naugatuck | 12 339 | 2.56 | 13.5 | 25.4 | 267 | 236 | 236 | 31 | 642 | 2 011 | 100 | 1 911 | 22 038 | 47.0 | 23.2 |
| New Britain | 28 158 | 2.49 | 20.7 | 31.0 | 3 194 | 790 | 557 | 2 404 | 3 295 | 4 493 | 447 | 4 045 | 46 367 | 58.6 | 17.5 |
| New Haven | 48 877 | 2.43 | 22.4 | 35.4 | 11 220 | 1 774 | 768 | 9 446 | 8 261 | 6 354 | 1 350 | 5 004 | 78 081 | 47.8 | 32.1 |
| New London | 10 373 | 2.30 | 18.4 | 38.0 | 3 713 | 225 | 225 | 3 488 | 1 138 | 4 113 | 1 164 | 2 949 | 16 479 | 51.5 | 22.2 |
| Norwalk | 33 217 | 2.55 | 13.0 | 28.6 | 797 | 461 | 405 | 336 | 2 243 | 2 615 | 382 | 2 233 | 63 166 | 37.1 | 40.2 |
| Norwich | 16 599 | 2.41 | 17.2 | 31.3 | 514 | 219 | 205 | 295 | 989 | 2 438 | 328 | 2 110 | 27 307 | 49.9 | 20.6 |
| Shelton | 15 325 | 2.55 | 9.0 | 24.2 | 502 | 446 | 442 | 56 | 552 | 1 393 | 68 | 1 325 | 28 481 | 39.3 | 34.4 |
| Stamford | 47 357 | 2.56 | 12.2 | 28.9 | 1 280 | 662 | 653 | 618 | 2 392 | 1 947 | 316 | 1 631 | 85 306 | 36.7 | 43.9 |
| Torrington | 15 243 | 2.33 | 12.1 | 31.9 | 838 | 611 | 559 | 227 | 826 | 2 266 | 170 | 2 096 | 26 123 | 51.6 | 19.7 |
| Waterbury | 42 761 | 2.54 | 22.3 | 30.7 | 1 938 | 1 149 | 886 | 789 | 4 930 | 4 459 | 325 | 4 134 | 70 641 | 57.1 | 17.2 |
| West Haven | 21 112 | 2.50 | 16.7 | 29.9 | 2 857 | 458 | 362 | 2 399 | 1 510 | 2 713 | 440 | 2 272 | 37 483 | 50.4 | 23.0 |
| DELAWARE | 342 297 | 2.55 | 14.2 | 25.6 | 24 413 | 11 673 | 4 591 | 12 740 | 36 014 | 3 970 | 559 | 3 411 | 595 938 | 44.3 | 28.0 |
| Dover | 13 771 | 2.35 | 19.0 | 33.6 | 3 745 | 569 | 340 | 3 176 | 2 562 | 7 035 | 862 | 6 173 | 20 675 | 41.3 | 26.5 |
| Newark | 9 834 | 2.47 | 6.5 | 26.8 | 7 128 | 0 | 0 | 7 128 | 1 097 | 3 452 | 428 | 3 024 | 14 202 | 23.4 | 51.9 |
| Wilmington | 28 615 | 2.36 | 24.8 | 38.1 | 3 226 | 2 324 | 531 | 902 | 4 937 | 6 897 | 1 587 | 5 310 | 47 703 | 49.8 | 25.3 |
| DISTRICT OF COLUMBIA | 266 707 | 2.11 | 16.4 | 44.0 | 40 021 | 7 339 | 3 064 | 32 682 | 37 065 | 5 998 | 1 202 | 4 796 | 407 576 | 32.4 | 50.5 |
| Washington | 266 707 | 2.11 | 16.4 | 44.0 | 40 021 | 7 339 | 3 064 | 32 682 | 35 297 | 5 712 | 1 130 | 4 581 | 407 576 | 32.4 | 50.5 |
| FLORIDA | 7 420 802 | 2.48 | 13.5 | 27.2 | 421 709 | 254 506 | 73 372 | 167 203 | 769 399 | 4 037 | 515 | 3 522 | 12 949 216 | 44.6 | 26.0 |
| Altamonte Springs | 19 126 | 2.15 | 15.3 | 37.6 | 448 | 444 | 444 | 4 | 1 468 | 3 490 | 411 | 3 079 | 29 697 | 32.3 | 32.6 |
| Apopka | 14 360 | 2.88 | 13.9 | 17.9 | 178 | 118 | 118 | 60 | 1 701 | 4 040 | 492 | 3 548 | 26 899 | 35.2 | 28.6 |
| Aventura | 17 892 | 1.99 | 9.0 | 39.3 | 96 | 96 | 96 | 0 | 2 178 | 6 008 | 188 | 5 821 | 27 235 | 28.4 | 48.5 |
| Boca Raton | 36 778 | 2.20 | 8.3 | 32.2 | 3 444 | 430 | 415 | 3 014 | 2 854 | 3 336 | 208 | 3 128 | 60 946 | 23.6 | 50.7 |
| Bonita Springs | 20 017 | 2.19 | 5.3 | 27.0 | 157 | 12 | 0 | 145 | NA | NA | NA | NA | 35 296 | 43.1 | 28.5 |
| Boynton Beach | 29 104 | 2.31 | 13.1 | 34.3 | 1 000 | 649 | 630 | 351 | 3 732 | 5 397 | 563 | 4 835 | 49 967 | 43.0 | 25.6 |
| Bradenton | 21 405 | 2.23 | 14.6 | 36.5 | 1 757 | 1 074 | 966 | 683 | 2 527 | 5 032 | 721 | 4 311 | 35 189 | 49.9 | 21.3 |
| Cape Coral | 60 767 | 2.53 | 12.0 | 21.4 | 445 | 350 | 307 | 95 | 4 225 | 2 701 | 150 | 2 551 | 106 060 | 46.9 | 20.6 |
| Casselberry | 11 430 | 2.29 | 14.8 | 32.5 | 51 | 12 | 5 | 39 | 1 221 | 4 590 | 617 | 3 974 | 18 308 | 44.0 | 22.6 |
| Clearwater | 47 638 | 2.19 | 12.5 | 36.5 | 3 584 | 1 011 | 1 000 | 2 573 | 4 930 | 4 517 | 734 | 3 783 | 78 395 | 42.7 | 26.9 |
| Clermont | 11 216 | 2.54 | 11.6 | 23.5 | 199 | 177 | 177 | 22 | 989 | 3 395 | 213 | 3 182 | 19 395 | 35.7 | 28.4 |
| Coconut Creek | 22 754 | 2.32 | 12.3 | 32.8 | 146 | 138 | 65 | 8 | 1 597 | 2 978 | 209 | 2 769 | 37 484 | 38.2 | 31.6 |
| Cooper City | 9 628 | 2.96 | 13.5 | 12.2 | 40 | 0 | 0 | 40 | 691 | 2 388 | 142 | 2 246 | 18 123 | 26.9 | 40.4 |
| Coral Gables | 17 946 | 2.35 | 9.8 | 29.2 | 4 540 | 1 | 0 | 4 539 | 2 389 | 5 038 | 194 | 4 844 | 29 305 | 16.4 | 64.4 |
| Coral Springs | 41 814 | 2.89 | 16.7 | 17.3 | 359 | 227 | 222 | 132 | 3 271 | 2 665 | 192 | 2 473 | 77 603 | 32.4 | 35.3 |
| Cutler Bay | 13 338 | 3.00 | 16.3 | 17.7 | 338 | 245 | 199 | 93 | 2 114 | 5 177 | 473 | 4 704 | 24 471 | 37.4 | 30.5 |
| Dania Beach | 12 877 | 2.28 | 15.3 | 33.0 | 329 | 294 | 87 | 35 | 2 014 | 6 704 | 589 | 6 115 | 21 061 | 45.8 | 23.2 |
| Davie | 34 315 | 2.64 | 14.6 | 23.0 | 1 355 | 86 | 50 | 1 269 | 3 984 | 4 273 | 383 | 3 890 | 59 423 | 36.3 | 30.8 |
| Daytona Beach | 27 314 | 2.05 | 15.1 | 41.1 | 5 048 | 1 094 | 1 059 | 3 954 | 5 103 | 8 252 | 1 350 | 6 902 | 41 020 | 46.9 | 21.1 |

1. No spouse present.   2. Data for serious crimes have not been adjusted for underreporting. This may affect comparability between geographic areas and over time.   3. Per 100,000 population estimated by the FBI.   4. Persons 25 years old and over.

## Table D. Cities — Income, Poverty, and Housing

| City | Money income, 2007–2011 | | | | | Housing units, 2010 | | | Occupied Housing units 2007–2011 | | | | |
|---|---|---|---|---|---|---|---|---|---|---|---|---|---|
| | Per capita income[1] (dollars) | Median income | Percent with income of $200,000 or more | Percent with income of less than $25,000 | Families with income below poverty (percent) | Total | Percent change, 2000–2010 | Vacant units for sale or rent[2] | Total | Percent | Median value[3] (dollars) | With a mortgage[4] | Without a mortgage[5] |
| | 42 | 43 | 44 | 45 | 46 | 47 | 48 | 49 | 50 | 51 | 52 | 53 | 54 |
| COLORADO—Cont'd | | | | | | | | | | | | | |
| Castle Rock................. | 35 267 | 85 009 | 7.7 | 9.8 | 4.3 | 17 626 | 135.5 | 938 | 16 455 | 76.2 | 278 000 | 24.8 | 11.3 |
| Centennial................... | 40 654 | 88 474 | 10.3 | 8.1 | 3.3 | 38 779 | NA | 1 330 | 37 299 | 84.4 | 289 300 | 23.0 | 10.0 |
| Colorado Springs ......... | 28 952 | 53 747 | 3.6 | 21.2 | 9.3 | 179 607 | 20.7 | 11 819 | 164 100 | 61.1 | 212 700 | 24.1 | 10.0 |
| Commerce City ............ | 22 107 | 60 045 | 1.4 | 18.2 | 12.9 | 15 452 | 123.7 | 973 | 13 647 | 72.9 | 195 200 | 28.1 | 13.2 |
| Denver........................ | 32 051 | 47 499 | 5.1 | 26.7 | 14.2 | 285 797 | 13.7 | 22 690 | 258 132 | 51.7 | 243 400 | 25.2 | 10.6 |
| Englewood................... | 26 882 | 43 962 | 2.0 | 26.7 | 10.8 | 15 478 | 4.0 | 1 103 | 14 405 | 48.7 | 214 700 | 26.1 | 13.4 |
| Fort Collins................. | 28 081 | 51 446 | 3.8 | 25.1 | 7.0 | 60 503 | 26.7 | 2 674 | 56 429 | 56.5 | 242 300 | 24.0 | 10.0 |
| Fountain...................... | 21 771 | 56 643 | 0.0 | 17.2 | 8.7 | 9 371 | 80.1 | 647 | 8 409 | 70.6 | 180 700 | 26.0 | 10.0 |
| Grand Junction............. | 27 654 | 48 257 | 2.5 | 25.4 | 9.6 | 26 170 | 38.7 | 1 859 | 24 502 | 63.0 | 231 200 | 24.4 | 10.0 |
| Greeley....................... | 21 574 | 43 466 | 2.2 | 30.4 | 15.2 | 36 323 | 25.9 | 2 896 | 33 265 | 58.7 | 168 700 | 25.4 | 11.5 |
| Lakewood.................... | 31 327 | 54 918 | 3.4 | 20.0 | 8.8 | 65 758 | 5.3 | 3 772 | 62 122 | 59.3 | 236 900 | 24.9 | 10.0 |
| Littleton...................... | 34 815 | 57 329 | 6.3 | 21.6 | 7.1 | 19 434 | 7.1 | 1 122 | 18 064 | 63.1 | 266 200 | 24.1 | 10.0 |
| Longmont .................... | 28 680 | 56 278 | 4.1 | 19.6 | 10.0 | 35 008 | 27.6 | 1 756 | 32 655 | 63.4 | 234 700 | 25.1 | 10.0 |
| Loveland..................... | 28 258 | 54 763 | 2.3 | 20.1 | 7.1 | 28 557 | 40.5 | 1 404 | 27 085 | 67.4 | 212 200 | 25.0 | 10.0 |
| Northglenn................... | 23 445 | 52 188 | 1.7 | 21.1 | 12.2 | 14 274 | 17.5 | 782 | 12 971 | 56.5 | 191 200 | 26.4 | 12.7 |
| Parker........................ | 35 270 | 92 917 | 6.1 | 7.8 | 2.6 | 16 533 | 97.8 | 616 | 15 729 | 75.8 | 288 800 | 25.2 | 10.0 |
| Pueblo ....................... | 20 284 | 34 750 | 1.4 | 36.5 | 17.4 | 47 593 | 10.4 | 4 303 | 43 076 | 61.6 | 118 400 | 25.6 | 12.1 |
| Thornton..................... | 26 746 | 66 827 | 1.9 | 13.3 | 7.4 | 43 230 | 46.6 | 1 871 | 39 582 | 72.4 | 212 100 | 25.2 | 11.3 |
| Westminster ................ | 30 532 | 64 076 | 3.5 | 15.9 | 8.0 | 43 968 | 11.4 | 1 927 | 40 859 | 65.5 | 224 900 | 24.6 | 10.0 |
| Wheat Ridge ............... | 29 093 | 48 777 | 1.8 | 24.4 | 9.1 | 14 868 | -0.7 | 892 | 13 847 | 56.8 | 235 700 | 25.0 | 11.1 |
| CONNECTICUT ........ | 37 627 | 69 243 | 8.7 | 17.6 | 6.7 | 1 487 891 | 7.4 | 116 804 | 1 360 115 | 68.9 | 293 100 | 26.5 | 17.0 |
| Bridgeport.................... | 19 979 | 40 947 | 1.5 | 32.9 | 18.0 | 57 012 | 4.9 | 5 757 | 51 014 | 44.6 | 228 300 | 35.5 | 22.8 |
| Bristol......................... | 30 197 | 60 032 | 2.7 | 17.7 | 6.4 | 27 011 | 3.4 | 1 691 | 25 127 | 66.7 | 217 100 | 25.5 | 17.7 |
| Danbury...................... | 30 838 | 65 656 | 5.4 | 16.9 | 6.6 | 31 154 | 9.2 | 2 247 | 29 465 | 62.5 | 330 100 | 29.4 | 15.4 |
| Hartford ...................... | 16 959 | 29 107 | 1.4 | 44.1 | 29.9 | 51 822 | 2.3 | 6 698 | 46 048 | 25.0 | 186 000 | 33.0 | 18.9 |
| Meriden ...................... | 27 647 | 53 722 | 2.4 | 22.2 | 12.1 | 25 892 | 5.1 | 1 915 | 23 783 | 62.9 | 205 400 | 28.9 | 17.1 |
| Middletown .................. | 31 850 | 59 966 | 3.8 | 21.2 | 7.5 | 21 223 | 7.7 | 1 360 | 19 875 | 56.2 | 239 000 | 25.9 | 16.0 |
| Milford ........................ | 39 736 | 79 828 | 8.7 | 12.9 | 2.7 | 23 074 | 5.1 | 1 366 | 20 818 | 77.5 | 335 900 | 27.3 | 20.9 |
| Naugatuck ................... | 28 801 | 63 414 | 1.9 | 18.6 | 7.7 | 13 061 | 5.8 | 722 | 12 386 | 69.2 | 221 400 | 26.9 | 18.7 |
| New Britain.................. | 20 768 | 39 838 | 0.6 | 32.2 | 16.9 | 31 226 | 0.2 | 3 068 | 28 659 | 43.3 | 174 000 | 30.6 | 19.9 |
| New Haven.................. | 22 814 | 39 094 | 2.8 | 35.4 | 20.8 | 54 967 | 3.8 | 6 090 | 49 247 | 31.1 | 228 600 | 29.4 | 19.9 |
| New London ................ | 22 386 | 45 509 | 1.7 | 25.1 | 14.1 | 11 840 | 2.4 | 1 467 | 10 517 | 37.9 | 204 400 | 28.8 | 16.5 |
| Norwalk ...................... | 45 122 | 76 384 | 10.7 | 14.6 | 5.5 | 35 415 | 4.9 | 2 198 | 36 463 | 65.1 | 460 200 | 31.7 | 19.7 |
| Norwich ...................... | 26 563 | 51 225 | 2.2 | 23.2 | 10.2 | 18 659 | 12.4 | 2 060 | 16 308 | 57.3 | 205 300 | 27.5 | 18.0 |
| Shelton ....................... | 40 441 | 83 128 | 10.0 | 11.7 | 2.5 | 16 146 | 9.8 | 821 | 14 912 | 82.5 | 375 900 | 27.2 | 17.2 |
| Stamford...................... | 44 595 | 78 201 | 14.5 | 15.8 | 7.5 | 50 573 | 6.9 | 3 216 | 45 478 | 56.4 | 571 400 | 28.4 | 18.4 |
| Torrington .................... | 27 449 | 48 742 | 2.1 | 25.6 | 8.8 | 16 761 | 3.8 | 1 518 | 15 560 | 66.4 | 187 500 | 27.6 | 18.5 |
| Waterbury ................... | 22 004 | 41 499 | 1.3 | 31.7 | 17.1 | 47 991 | 2.5 | 5 230 | 42 599 | 49.6 | 164 000 | 28.8 | 22.5 |
| West Haven................. | 26 601 | 53 057 | 2.5 | 20.6 | 8.7 | 22 446 | 0.5 | 1 334 | 21 535 | 57.7 | 229 600 | 31.2 | 20.1 |
| DELAWARE ............. | 29 659 | 59 317 | 4.4 | 18.7 | 7.6 | 405 885 | 18.3 | 63 588 | 332 837 | 73.0 | 244 100 | 24.7 | 11.3 |
| Dover.......................... | 22 508 | 47 754 | 1.9 | 25.3 | 14.0 | 15 024 | 12.5 | 1 253 | 12 603 | 55.7 | 193 900 | 26.5 | 11.2 |
| Newark ....................... | 24 580 | 50 309 | 4.6 | 31.3 | 3.6 | 10 475 | 12.5 | 641 | 10 058 | 54.9 | 285 900 | 20.5 | 10.0 |
| Wilmington .................. | 25 590 | 39 019 | 3.7 | 33.7 | 20.2 | 32 820 | 2.1 | 4 205 | 29 293 | 47.6 | 183 400 | 24.6 | 14.5 |
| DISTRICT OF COLUMBIA ................. | 43 993 | 61 835 | 10.5 | 23.0 | 13.9 | 296 719 | 8.0 | 30 012 | 260 136 | 42.8 | 442 600 | 24.7 | 10.7 |
| Washington ................. | 43 993 | 61 835 | 10.5 | 23.0 | 13.9 | 296 719 | 8.0 | 30 012 | 260 136 | 42.8 | 442 600 | 24.7 | 10.7 |
| FLORIDA................... | 26 733 | 47 827 | 3.7 | 24.8 | 10.6 | 8 989 580 | 23.1 | 1 568 778 | 7 140 096 | 69.0 | 188 600 | 29.4 | 14.1 |
| Altamonte Springs........ | 26 626 | 47 942 | 1.6 | 19.8 | 8.1 | 22 088 | 9.5 | 2 962 | 17 396 | 50.4 | 182 700 | 29.0 | 14.2 |
| Apopka....................... | 27 176 | 58 996 | 3.7 | 16.6 | 8.8 | 15 707 | 55.9 | 1 347 | 14 675 | 81.4 | 207 700 | 29.7 | 12.6 |
| Aventura..................... | 49 755 | 62 579 | 10.1 | 22.9 | 7.1 | 26 120 | 30.5 | 8 228 | 16 719 | 70.5 | 325 000 | 33.4 | 25.2 |
| Boca Raton ................. | 49 491 | 71 414 | 13.4 | 16.0 | 5.6 | 44 539 | 18.3 | 7 761 | 35 615 | 72.3 | 395 800 | 31.3 | 15.5 |
| Bonita Springs............. | 39 964 | 53 274 | 8.0 | 18.5 | 8.9 | 31 716 | 35.2 | 11 699 | 18 708 | 79.4 | 269 300 | 31.7 | 13.3 |
| Boynton Beach............. | 26 887 | 45 156 | 1.8 | 25.9 | 10.8 | 36 289 | 18.6 | 7 185 | 28 799 | 67.2 | 172 700 | 32.9 | 17.5 |
| Bradenton.................... | 23 120 | 41 877 | 1.2 | 27.6 | 11.8 | 26 767 | 7.3 | 5 362 | 21 145 | 56.7 | 161 800 | 29.1 | 14.5 |
| Cape Coral .................. | 24 489 | 51 407 | 1.8 | 20.2 | 9.3 | 78 948 | 72.7 | 18 181 | 56 002 | 74.9 | 181 900 | 31.6 | 16.1 |
| Casselberry ................. | 23 758 | 43 864 | 0.8 | 26.8 | 12.1 | 12 708 | 22.5 | 1 278 | 10 411 | 66.4 | 162 600 | 31.4 | 14.1 |
| Clearwater................... | 27 409 | 41 986 | 3.0 | 29.6 | 11.2 | 59 156 | 4.3 | 11 518 | 46 781 | 62.9 | 179 900 | 30.1 | 17.7 |
| Clermont ..................... | 27 412 | 56 291 | 2.5 | 17.9 | 5.4 | 12 730 | NA | 1 514 | 10 728 | 74.5 | 213 000 | 28.9 | 13.2 |
| Coconut Creek ............ | 28 445 | 50 990 | 2.0 | 21.0 | 5.8 | 25 926 | 17.1 | 3 172 | 22 193 | 70.9 | 182 700 | 31.3 | 26.3 |
| Cooper City ................. | 35 171 | 91 650 | 8.4 | 7.2 | 2.9 | 9 912 | 7.4 | 284 | 9 361 | 88.7 | 340 300 | 28.9 | 13.0 |
| Coral Gables ............... | 51 934 | 88 167 | 21.6 | 17.0 | 4.4 | 20 266 | 13.9 | 2 320 | 16 349 | 68.6 | 650 200 | 30.5 | 15.5 |
| Coral Springs .............. | 31 201 | 70 610 | 7.0 | 14.2 | 6.3 | 45 433 | 10.0 | 3 619 | 40 799 | 67.6 | 311 600 | 30.2 | 14.4 |
| Cutler Bay ................... | 25 960 | 65 188 | 4.4 | 16.6 | 8.4 | 14 620 | NA | 1 282 | 12 236 | 75.4 | 246 000 | 30.5 | 12.4 |
| Dania Beach................ | 24 065 | 44 608 | 1.3 | 28.5 | 13.0 | 15 671 | 44.1 | 2 794 | 12 291 | 56.3 | 186 300 | 29.5 | 20.4 |
| Davie.......................... | 30 874 | 58 313 | 6.4 | 20.1 | 7.9 | 37 306 | 19.6 | 2 991 | 32 973 | 74.6 | 245 000 | 29.7 | 16.9 |
| Daytona Beach............. | 19 108 | 29 533 | 1.4 | 43.4 | 21.1 | 33 920 | 1.6 | 6 606 | 25 923 | 49.8 | 150 200 | 31.8 | 14.8 |

1. Based on population estimated by the American Community Survey.    2. Includes units rented or sold but not occupied.    3. Specified owner-occupied units; $1,000,000 represents $1,000,000 or more    4. 50.0 represents 50 percent or more.    5. 10.0 represents 10 percent or less.

# Table D. Cities — Housing, Labor Force, and Employment

| City | Occupied housing units, 2007–2011 (cont.) | | | | Migration, 2007–2011 | | Civilian labor force, 2012 | | Unemployment | | Civilian employment[4], 2007–2011 | Percent | | |
|---|---|---|---|---|---|---|---|---|---|---|---|---|---|---|
| | Percent renter occupied | Median gross rent[1] | Median rent as a percent of income[2] | Percent with no vehicle available | Percent who lived in the same house one year ago | Percent who lived outside this city one year ago | Total | Percent change, 2011–2012 | Total | Rate[3] | Population age 16 and older | In labor force | Full-year full-time worker | Households with no workers (percent) |
| | 55 | 56 | 57 | 58 | 59 | 60 | 61 | 62 | 63 | 64 | 65 | 66 | 67 | 68 |
| COLORADO—Cont'd | | | | | | | | | | | | | | |
| Castle Rock | 23.8 | 1 069 | 30.0 | 2.6 | 80.7 | 11.2 | 27 807 | 2.3 | 1 861 | 6.7 | 33 042 | 78.2 | 52.2 | 11.9 |
| Centennial | 15.6 | 1 228 | 28.4 | 2.2 | 87.5 | 11.3 | 56 839 | 2.2 | 4 411 | 7.8 | 78 967 | 72.5 | 46.6 | 16.1 |
| Colorado Springs | 38.9 | 812 | 29.3 | 6.4 | 76.0 | 11.4 | 208 443 | 0.3 | 19 197 | 9.2 | 317 599 | 69.5 | 40.7 | 22.7 |
| Commerce City | 27.1 | 906 | 31.8 | 5.2 | 81.9 | 13.3 | 20 303 | 0.1 | 2 222 | 10.9 | 30 196 | 73.0 | 46.9 | 16.9 |
| Denver | 48.3 | 832 | 30.2 | 12.4 | 77.2 | 11.4 | 328 933 | 1.5 | 27 880 | 8.5 | 475 050 | 71.1 | 43.6 | 23.9 |
| Englewood | 51.3 | 772 | 30.8 | 10.4 | 77.2 | 18.4 | 17 598 | 1.4 | 1 561 | 8.9 | 24 914 | 74.0 | 44.4 | 24.0 |
| Fort Collins | 43.5 | 890 | 36.0 | 5.1 | 71.0 | 15.4 | 88 253 | 3.5 | 5 579 | 6.3 | 116 720 | 71.5 | 37.6 | 20.2 |
| Fountain | 29.4 | 1 048 | 33.3 | 3.2 | 78.0 | 18.6 | 11 699 | 0.4 | 1 263 | 10.8 | 17 452 | 70.7 | 42.4 | 17.1 |
| Grand Junction | 37.0 | 814 | 31.7 | 7.7 | 75.1 | 14.3 | 31 893 | 0.6 | 3 386 | 10.6 | 46 718 | 63.7 | 38.8 | 30.0 |
| Greeley | 41.3 | 710 | 33.1 | 7.7 | 75.3 | 13.1 | 44 753 | 3.8 | 3 999 | 8.9 | 71 301 | 64.9 | 38.4 | 26.3 |
| Lakewood | 40.7 | 894 | 29.9 | 6.6 | 78.5 | 14.4 | 81 391 | 1.5 | 6 542 | 8.0 | 117 555 | 68.3 | 42.4 | 24.4 |
| Littleton | 36.9 | 866 | 30.1 | 6.8 | 81.2 | 14.2 | 24 039 | 1.9 | 1 703 | 7.1 | 33 716 | 66.7 | 41.2 | 26.9 |
| Longmont | 36.6 | 924 | 31.6 | 5.2 | 80.5 | 10.2 | 50 273 | 2.4 | 3 686 | 7.3 | 64 681 | 70.2 | 40.9 | 21.1 |
| Loveland | 32.6 | 882 | 30.7 | 4.9 | 82.9 | 10.0 | 38 767 | 2.2 | 2 879 | 7.4 | 51 670 | 67.7 | 41.3 | 25.2 |
| Northglenn | 43.5 | 920 | 29.2 | 5.0 | 81.9 | 14.8 | 20 154 | 1.6 | 1 870 | 9.3 | 27 673 | 71.4 | 45.4 | 20.9 |
| Parker | 24.2 | 1 113 | 27.3 | 2.3 | 82.3 | 11.5 | 26 282 | 2.4 | 1 784 | 6.8 | 30 609 | 80.9 | 55.7 | 10.5 |
| Pueblo | 38.4 | 648 | 35.2 | 10.4 | 80.5 | 7.5 | 48 622 | 0.8 | 5 662 | 11.6 | 83 706 | 58.0 | 33.0 | 36.4 |
| Thornton | 27.6 | 991 | 31.1 | 3.5 | 84.2 | 12.3 | 67 643 | 1.8 | 5 672 | 8.4 | 84 624 | 76.2 | 50.9 | 13.0 |
| Westminster | 34.5 | 973 | 28.9 | 4.3 | 81.9 | 14.7 | 63 475 | 1.7 | 5 021 | 7.9 | 81 898 | 75.2 | 48.4 | 17.6 |
| Wheat Ridge | 43.2 | 796 | 31.3 | 7.7 | 78.5 | 18.4 | 16 011 | 1.8 | 1 563 | 9.8 | 25 432 | 64.3 | 40.0 | 29.6 |
| CONNECTICUT | 31.1 | 1 020 | 31.4 | 8.8 | 88.0 | 8.5 | 1 879 452 | -1.0 | 157 058 | 8.4 | 2 839 677 | 68.2 | 41.4 | 24.3 |
| Bridgeport | 55.4 | 1 032 | 36.4 | 21.3 | 84.5 | 6.1 | 66 715 | -1.6 | 8 337 | 12.5 | 109 755 | 66.9 | 37.6 | 28.3 |
| Bristol | 33.3 | 896 | 28.7 | 6.7 | 87.8 | 6.6 | 33 679 | -2.6 | 2 913 | 8.6 | 48 821 | 70.2 | 44.1 | 26.6 |
| Danbury | 37.5 | 1 210 | 31.9 | 9.1 | 87.0 | 8.2 | 45 898 | 0.2 | 3 153 | 6.9 | 64 828 | 72.3 | 43.5 | 20.0 |
| Hartford | 75.0 | 837 | 36.3 | 35.2 | 77.1 | 10.2 | 50 414 | -2.7 | 7 826 | 15.5 | 95 933 | 62.0 | 31.0 | 35.2 |
| Meriden | 37.1 | 916 | 33.3 | 10.9 | 86.1 | 6.4 | 32 491 | -1.3 | 3 254 | 10.0 | 48 005 | 68.7 | 42.3 | 26.1 |
| Middletown | 43.8 | 944 | 28.1 | 9.3 | 82.0 | 11.2 | 26 514 | -2.0 | 2 110 | 8.0 | 39 217 | 67.5 | 41.6 | 24.4 |
| Milford | 22.5 | 1 377 | 28.6 | 4.4 | 89.2 | 6.2 | 30 108 | -0.3 | 2 242 | 7.4 | 42 529 | 71.8 | 46.3 | 21.4 |
| Naugatuck | 30.8 | 966 | 29.3 | 5.5 | 91.1 | 6.0 | 16 792 | -1.7 | 1 688 | 10.1 | 25 215 | 72.7 | 43.9 | 24.5 |
| New Britain | 56.7 | 869 | 32.6 | 15.9 | 83.5 | 7.8 | 35 970 | -2.7 | 4 173 | 11.6 | 57 953 | 66.7 | 36.9 | 28.5 |
| New Haven | 68.9 | 1 055 | 34.6 | 28.1 | 77.3 | 11.1 | 58 705 | -1.5 | 7 118 | 12.1 | 103 744 | 65.4 | 33.7 | 30.6 |
| New London | 62.1 | 903 | 28.3 | 18.7 | 72.3 | 16.5 | 14 211 | -1.1 | 1 626 | 11.4 | 22 693 | 67.4 | 35.4 | 27.5 |
| Norwalk | 34.9 | 1 274 | 31.7 | 8.1 | 89.4 | 5.9 | 49 273 | -0.8 | 3 458 | 7.0 | 69 748 | 72.4 | 47.7 | 20.9 |
| Norwich | 42.7 | 930 | 30.4 | 11.4 | 82.6 | 7.9 | 22 177 | -2.1 | 2 085 | 9.4 | 31 761 | 69.7 | 40.7 | 25.2 |
| Shelton | 17.5 | 1 101 | 27.4 | 4.9 | 92.1 | 5.6 | 22 679 | -0.4 | 1 686 | 7.4 | 32 049 | 67.2 | 43.2 | 22.8 |
| Stamford | 43.6 | 1 503 | 32.0 | 11.6 | 86.4 | 6.7 | 68 126 | 0.2 | 4 764 | 7.0 | 97 816 | 73.2 | 43.4 | 19.0 |
| Torrington | 33.6 | 811 | 32.1 | 10.3 | 88.3 | 5.1 | 19 662 | -2.7 | 1 817 | 9.2 | 29 664 | 66.6 | 39.5 | 30.4 |
| Waterbury | 50.4 | 881 | 35.7 | 17.5 | 86.6 | 4.7 | 50 743 | -1.3 | 6 649 | 13.1 | 84 738 | 63.7 | 37.1 | 31.9 |
| West Haven | 42.3 | 1 025 | 34.0 | 11.2 | 86.4 | 9.3 | 31 252 | -1.1 | 3 018 | 9.7 | 44 675 | 70.3 | 41.2 | 23.5 |
| DELAWARE | 27.0 | 975 | 31.5 | 6.6 | 85.8 | 12.0 | 444 042 | 1.5 | 31 598 | 7.1 | 709 757 | 64.7 | 41.2 | 26.1 |
| Dover | 44.3 | 926 | 31.5 | 10.3 | 76.4 | 14.3 | 16 342 | -0.7 | 1 421 | 8.7 | 28 492 | 61.9 | 34.1 | 27.6 |
| Newark | 45.1 | 977 | 47.9 | 11.5 | 62.0 | 24.7 | 16 019 | 1.6 | 956 | 6.0 | 28 203 | 52.4 | 24.5 | 28.7 |
| Wilmington | 52.4 | 872 | 33.0 | 24.3 | 77.4 | 11.8 | 31 437 | 0.8 | 3 178 | 10.1 | 56 147 | 63.7 | 38.9 | 30.6 |
| DISTRICT OF COLUMBIA | 57.2 | 1 135 | 29.7 | 36.1 | 80.4 | 9.5 | 361 610 | 4.1 | 32 340 | 8.9 | 502 503 | 67.2 | 44.5 | 25.4 |
| Washington | 57.2 | 1 135 | 29.7 | 36.1 | 80.4 | 9.5 | 361 610 | 4.1 | 32 340 | 8.9 | 502 503 | 67.2 | 44.5 | 25.4 |
| FLORIDA | 31.0 | 981 | 34.8 | 6.6 | 83.5 | 12.4 | 9 368 500 | 2.2 | 806 808 | 8.6 | 15 169 949 | 61.1 | 37.6 | 31.2 |
| Altamonte Springs | 49.6 | 974 | 29.5 | 5.9 | 78.8 | 15.2 | 26 672 | 3.4 | 1 988 | 7.5 | 34 528 | 72.6 | 47.3 | 19.3 |
| Apopka | 18.6 | 971 | 36.3 | 4.6 | 87.8 | 9.1 | 22 696 | 3.9 | 1 730 | 7.6 | 31 494 | 70.8 | 49.0 | 17.9 |
| Aventura | 29.5 | 1 667 | 35.5 | 8.0 | 80.4 | 16.3 | 18 181 | 3.1 | 1 202 | 6.6 | 29 840 | 55.1 | 35.5 | 38.1 |
| Boca Raton | 27.7 | 1 393 | 36.8 | 4.3 | 83.9 | 10.6 | 43 326 | 3.1 | 3 024 | 7.0 | 71 954 | 62.4 | 38.2 | 29.0 |
| Bonita Springs | 20.6 | 1 003 | 33.5 | 3.0 | 86.5 | 8.4 | 19 485 | 2.7 | 1 441 | 7.4 | 38 364 | 47.3 | 28.3 | 48.2 |
| Boynton Beach | 32.8 | 1 209 | 34.8 | 6.6 | 83.0 | 12.7 | 33 539 | 2.7 | 2 862 | 8.5 | 56 885 | 63.7 | 38.0 | 35.5 |
| Bradenton | 43.3 | 913 | 36.5 | 8.5 | 79.4 | 11.7 | 21 836 | 2.4 | 1 938 | 8.9 | 41 169 | 59.8 | 36.0 | 37.3 |
| Cape Coral | 25.1 | 1 055 | 35.3 | 2.7 | 81.4 | 10.2 | 78 477 | 1.3 | 6 960 | 8.9 | 121 645 | 63.2 | 37.7 | 30.0 |
| Casselberry | 33.6 | 985 | 34.0 | 4.6 | 85.8 | 11.2 | 15 292 | 4.0 | 1 205 | 7.9 | 21 774 | 67.7 | 41.7 | 23.7 |
| Clearwater | 37.1 | 936 | 35.5 | 9.3 | 84.9 | 9.6 | 52 988 | 2.5 | 4 164 | 7.9 | 89 967 | 59.9 | 38.8 | 35.3 |
| Clermont | 25.5 | 1 028 | 35.2 | 3.1 | 80.8 | 12.5 | 13 957 | 3.7 | 1 006 | 7.2 | 21 921 | 61.3 | 36.3 | 33.7 |
| Coconut Creek | 29.1 | 1 336 | 33.0 | 5.6 | 82.3 | 12.9 | 30 367 | 3.2 | 2 035 | 6.7 | 42 543 | 64.5 | 43.0 | 29.7 |
| Cooper City | 11.3 | 1 774 | 35.5 | 1.1 | 91.6 | 7.2 | 18 168 | 3.2 | 1 092 | 6.0 | 22 401 | 71.9 | 44.8 | 13.8 |
| Coral Gables | 31.4 | 1 251 | 31.0 | 4.9 | 79.8 | 16.0 | 28 059 | 4.0 | 1 648 | 5.9 | 39 271 | 56.8 | 36.6 | 22.9 |
| Coral Springs | 32.4 | 1 305 | 34.3 | 4.3 | 85.1 | 9.5 | 75 463 | 3.2 | 5 076 | 6.7 | 93 567 | 73.7 | 46.0 | 14.2 |
| Cutler Bay | 24.6 | 1 353 | 34.1 | 7.6 | 88.3 | 10.5 | 23 705 | 3.1 | 1 900 | 8.0 | 29 809 | 66.4 | 46.4 | 19.7 |
| Dania Beach | 43.7 | 1 112 | 34.8 | 7.3 | 79.1 | 18.8 | 18 022 | 3.9 | 1 139 | 6.3 | 24 121 | 68.2 | 42.0 | 26.9 |
| Davie | 25.4 | 1 172 | 34.3 | 5.0 | 84.7 | 11.4 | 57 060 | 3.9 | 3 493 | 6.1 | 72 155 | 70.1 | 44.9 | 20.3 |
| Daytona Beach | 50.2 | 782 | 38.3 | 14.4 | 78.1 | 16.3 | 31 529 | 1.6 | 2 961 | 9.4 | 53 514 | 51.9 | 26.7 | 42.1 |

1. $2,000 represents $2,000 or more.   2. 50.0 represents 50 percent or more.   3. Percent of civilian labor force.   4. Persons 16 years old and over.

| City | Value of residential construction authorized by building permits, 2011 | | | Wholesale trade,[1] 2007 | | | | Retail trade,[2] 2007 | | | |
|---|---|---|---|---|---|---|---|---|---|---|---|
| | New construction ($1,000) | Number of housing units | Percent single family | Number of establish-ments | Number of employees | Sales (mil dol) | Annual payroll (mil dol) | Number of establish-ments | Number of employees | Sales (mil dol) | Annual payroll (mil dol) |
| | 69 | 70 | 71 | 72 | 73 | 74 | 75 | 76 | 77 | 78 | 79 |
| COLORADO—Cont'd | | | | | | | | | | | |
| Castle Rock | 70 841 | 321 | 87.2 | 26 | 163 | 48.3 | 7.6 | 210 | 2 869 | 636.9 | 69.8 |
| Centennial | 3 432 | 14 | 100.0 | 190 | 2 740 | 1 970.0 | 181.8 | 264 | 3 983 | 1 942.9 | 128.6 |
| Colorado Springs | NA | NA | NA | 358 | 4 471 | 2 482.4 | 225.2 | 1 741 | 27 411 | 7 027.3 | 678.4 |
| Commerce City | 17 005 | 116 | 96.6 | 129 | 2 820 | 2 015.9 | 154.2 | 101 | 1 496 | 458.6 | 40.5 |
| Denver | 316 561 | 2 685 | 26.2 | 1 174 | 21 245 | 14 920.9 | 1 064.5 | 2 271 | 27 979 | 6 835.4 | 752.6 |
| Englewood | 1 200 | 7 | 100.0 | 106 | 1 845 | 667.0 | 97.4 | 226 | 2 968 | 1 598.1 | 80.7 |
| Fort Collins | 86 750 | 714 | 36.1 | 101 | 933 | 371.7 | 50.1 | 595 | 9 642 | 2 152.3 | 222.3 |
| Fountain | NA | NA | NA | 3 | D | D | D | 42 | 1 070 | 242.8 | 24.6 |
| Grand Junction | NA | NA | NA | 160 | 1 856 | 921.5 | 79.3 | 535 | 7 495 | 2 002.3 | 191.5 |
| Greeley | 6 121 | 42 | 95.2 | 92 | 1 115 | 606.1 | 53.0 | 341 | 5 563 | 1 222.6 | 122.4 |
| Lakewood | 33 812 | 116 | 100.0 | 129 | 877 | 475.8 | 46.9 | 695 | 10 817 | 2 671.8 | 271.3 |
| Littleton | 2 029 | 3 | 100.0 | 67 | 961 | 288.2 | 43.2 | 255 | 4 575 | 1 688.6 | 150.0 |
| Longmont | 19 091 | 114 | 49.1 | 66 | 736 | 669.5 | 57.5 | 309 | 4 761 | 1 054.5 | 106.4 |
| Loveland | 38 635 | 193 | 83.4 | 62 | 900 | 387.1 | 39.3 | 350 | 5 218 | 1 211.7 | 117.8 |
| Northglenn | 0 | 0 | 0.0 | 17 | 280 | 65.2 | 8.9 | 91 | 1 559 | 366.2 | 41.0 |
| Parker | 56 649 | 192 | 96.4 | 33 | 396 | 127.9 | 9.8 | 135 | 2 460 | 629.4 | 57.2 |
| Pueblo | NA | NA | NA | 57 | 525 | 244.0 | 23.3 | 441 | 6 907 | 1 563.9 | 163.8 |
| Thornton | 56 515 | 260 | 94.2 | 28 | 207 | 118.2 | 16.7 | 194 | 5 057 | 1 267.0 | 131.7 |
| Westminster | 32 262 | 96 | 100.0 | 64 | 1 011 | 452.4 | 71.0 | 358 | 6 595 | 1 421.5 | 140.0 |
| Wheat Ridge | 8 200 | 88 | 0.0 | 61 | 570 | 178.5 | 29.3 | 186 | 2 402 | 637.7 | 69.8 |
| CONNECTICUT | 679 237 | 3 173 | 68.1 | 3 848 | 58 291 | 107 917.0 | 3 587.9 | 13 807 | 196 133 | 52 165.5 | 5 160.4 |
| Bridgeport | 5 680 | 126 | 15.1 | 125 | 1 732 | 794.3 | 94.8 | 313 | 3 555 | 1 122.2 | 112.3 |
| Bristol | 3 052 | 21 | 90.5 | 37 | 600 | 253.4 | 27.9 | 178 | 3 046 | 803.3 | 74.9 |
| Danbury | 22 278 | 103 | 100.0 | 99 | 1 041 | 1 037.3 | 65.0 | 473 | 8 219 | 2 176.7 | 217.6 |
| Hartford | 3 785 | 29 | 93.1 | 130 | 2 759 | 1 413.4 | 128.1 | 381 | 3 620 | 1 299.1 | 110.2 |
| Meriden | 1 022 | 12 | 100.0 | 36 | 451 | 169.2 | 22.6 | 257 | 3 907 | 828.6 | 78.9 |
| Middletown | 2 304 | 15 | 100.0 | 40 | 761 | 262.0 | 34.4 | 139 | 1 868 | 526.7 | 52.8 |
| Milford | 7 558 | 96 | 16.7 | 113 | 1 763 | 840.5 | 94.4 | 332 | 5 958 | 1 546.1 | 138.4 |
| Naugatuck | 1 270 | 10 | 100.0 | 27 | 429 | 240.6 | 25.8 | 71 | 1 066 | 275.4 | 24.0 |
| New Britain | 331 | 3 | 100.0 | 43 | 613 | 407.4 | 26.7 | 164 | 2 079 | 589.8 | 55.9 |
| New Haven | 13 834 | 229 | 47.2 | 78 | 1 042 | 1 077.9 | 51.7 | 345 | 3 366 | 907.2 | 88.0 |
| New London | 4 624 | 28 | 100.0 | 13 | 254 | 266.3 | 12.4 | 124 | 1 542 | 505.4 | 50.1 |
| Norwalk | 12 208 | 67 | 26.9 | 139 | 2 437 | 2 929.7 | 143.4 | 389 | 6 949 | 2 164.2 | 230.5 |
| Norwich | 1 353 | 9 | 55.6 | 18 | 450 | 248.3 | 27.0 | 151 | 2 134 | 517.6 | 51.4 |
| Shelton | 5 440 | 35 | 100.0 | 57 | 1 235 | 977.3 | 91.3 | 109 | 1 984 | 648.5 | 64.0 |
| Stamford | 35 016 | 207 | 14.5 | 222 | 4 587 | 64 886.5 | 568.9 | 492 | 6 157 | 1 596.1 | 186.7 |
| Torrington | 821 | 3 | 100.0 | 37 | 294 | 197.4 | 15.2 | 175 | 2 621 | 725.5 | 65.8 |
| Waterbury | 2 013 | 28 | 100.0 | 95 | 1 000 | 622.9 | 52.7 | 442 | 6 706 | 1 526.4 | 152.7 |
| West Haven | 341 | 3 | 100.0 | 62 | 1 148 | 486.8 | 58.0 | 129 | 1 487 | 443.1 | 40.9 |
| DELAWARE | 370 169 | 2 954 | 82.6 | 819 | 9 065 | 5 727.4 | 416.9 | 3 907 | 55 432 | 14 202.1 | 1 322.8 |
| Dover | 16 630 | 119 | 39.5 | 38 | 730 | 216.4 | 27.0 | 300 | 4 944 | 1 291.4 | 103.9 |
| Newark | 3 923 | 45 | 82.2 | 37 | 355 | 349.5 | 22.5 | 161 | 2 956 | 894.9 | 79.9 |
| Wilmington | 1 899 | 71 | 25.4 | 100 | 1 016 | 700.0 | 46.7 | 331 | 4 128 | 1 105.7 | 109.5 |
| DISTRICT OF COLUMBIA | 609 369 | 4 612 | 4.9 | 316 | 3 680 | 2 118.0 | 216.4 | 1 827 | 19 117 | 3 843.7 | 485.9 |
| Washington | 609 368 | 4 612 | 4.9 | 316 | 3 680 | 2 118.0 | 216.4 | 1 827 | 19 117 | 3 843.7 | 485.9 |
| FLORIDA | 8 814 610 | 42 360 | 75.2 | 27 442 | 279 300 | 221 641.5 | 12 566.1 | 73 794 | 1 016 290 | 262 341.1 | 24 049.7 |
| Altamonte Springs | 1 927 | 20 | 0.0 | 83 | 1 081 | 328.1 | 37.1 | 372 | 6 966 | 1 503.8 | 152.0 |
| Apopka | 58 639 | 189 | 100.0 | 55 | 464 | 128.6 | 14.4 | 144 | 2 082 | 567.7 | 48.8 |
| Aventura | 0 | 0 | 0.0 | 106 | 429 | 929.8 | 22.1 | 327 | 6 995 | 1 390.1 | 145.2 |
| Boca Raton | 72 144 | 218 | 100.0 | 421 | 4 906 | 5 249.8 | 314.8 | 746 | 10 183 | 2 348.5 | 272.7 |
| Bonita Springs | 80 525 | 379 | 62.0 | 38 | 410 | 188.3 | 15.0 | 228 | 2 762 | 663.1 | 73.7 |
| Boynton Beach | 20 360 | 234 | 91.5 | 119 | 963 | 457.4 | 42.8 | 356 | 6 019 | 1 191.8 | 118.8 |
| Bradenton | 10 049 | 67 | 34.3 | 42 | 574 | 322.4 | 27.0 | 216 | 2 930 | 718.4 | 71.5 |
| Cape Coral | 33 718 | 277 | 97.1 | 98 | 422 | 115.5 | 13.4 | 391 | 5 407 | 1 228.0 | 122.7 |
| Casselberry | 1 705 | 10 | 100.0 | 35 | 118 | 36.1 | 4.1 | 153 | 2 618 | 578.9 | 56.6 |
| Clearwater | 6 727 | 20 | 100.0 | 184 | 1 773 | 902.4 | 90.8 | 675 | 11 269 | 2 938.8 | 260.9 |
| Clermont | NA | NA | NA | 18 | 120 | 34.7 | 4.4 | 131 | 2 935 | 703.2 | 63.6 |
| Coconut Creek | 13 028 | 64 | 100.0 | 80 | 394 | 327.5 | 20.1 | 131 | 3 121 | 1 437.4 | 110.3 |
| Cooper City | 48 318 | 657 | 54.3 | 50 | 169 | 81.3 | 7.2 | 86 | 1 556 | 278.8 | 29.7 |
| Coral Gables | 52 300 | 509 | 3.1 | 169 | 1 124 | 7 011.7 | 93.3 | 316 | 4 545 | 1 436.4 | 151.2 |
| Coral Springs | 1 364 | 4 | 100.0 | 208 | 2 019 | 1 009.5 | 63.4 | 508 | 8 734 | 1 900.2 | 184.9 |
| Cutler Bay | 5 252 | 81 | 87.7 | NA | NA | NA | NA | NA | NA | NA | NA |
| Dania Beach | 2 911 | 29 | 100.0 | 134 | 1 054 | 581.3 | 52.2 | 193 | 2 053 | 564.1 | 55.5 |
| Davie | 9 666 | 80 | 81.3 | 253 | 1 589 | 633.3 | 76.0 | 412 | 6 288 | 2 010.5 | 170.0 |
| Daytona Beach | 73 127 | 545 | 24.0 | 96 | 1 054 | 447.8 | 40.5 | 500 | 7 644 | 1 810.6 | 168.7 |

1. Merchant wholesalers except manufacturers' sales branches and offices.  2. Establishments with payroll.

# Table D. Cities — Real Estate, Professional Services, and Manufacturing

| City | Real estate and rental and leasing, 2007 | | | | Professional, scientific, and technical services,[1] 2007 | | | | Manufacturing, 2007 | | | |
|---|---|---|---|---|---|---|---|---|---|---|---|---|
| | Number of establish-ments | Number of employees | Receipts (mil dol) | Annual payroll (mil dol) | Number of establish-ments | Number of employees | Receipts (mil dol) | Annual payroll (mil dol) | Number of establish-ments | Number of employees | Receipts (mil dol) | Annual payroll (mil dol) |
| | 80 | 81 | 82 | 83 | 84 | 85 | 86 | 87 | 88 | 89 | 90 | 91 |
| COLORADO—Cont'd | | | | | | | | | | | | |
| Castle Rock | 93 | 237 | 36.3 | 6.4 | 158 | 422 | 54.4 | 19.6 | NA | NA | NA | NA |
| Centennial | 246 | 1 688 | 336.3 | 67.2 | 719 | 4 300 | 772.7 | 283.7 | 76 | 1 451 | 436.5 | 75.6 |
| Colorado Springs | 942 | 3 364 | 521.5 | 99.7 | 1 871 | D | D | D | 379 | 11 518 | 3 819.9 | 577.9 |
| Commerce City | 48 | 380 | 111.1 | 18.6 | 35 | 189 | 20.8 | 7.2 | 78 | 2 424 | 4 019.7 | 125.9 |
| Denver | 1 451 | 11 600 | 2 536.4 | 623.7 | 3 856 | D | D | D | 840 | 19 480 | 5 189.9 | 826.0 |
| Englewood | 79 | 414 | 57.5 | 15.6 | 172 | D | D | D | 147 | 4 032 | 988.4 | 183.5 |
| Fort Collins | 289 | 1 274 | 185.2 | 34.0 | 768 | D | D | D | 126 | 5 852 | 2 179.3 | 367.0 |
| Fountain | 15 | 61 | 6.4 | 1.0 | 18 | 62 | 4.5 | 1.0 | 11 | 563 | 296.2 | 16.6 |
| Grand Junction | 232 | 830 | 203.1 | 32.2 | 373 | D | D | D | 106 | 2 082 | D | 83.0 |
| Greeley | 133 | 586 | 80.7 | 17.2 | 198 | D | D | D | 69 | 3 814 | 1 821.0 | 135.7 |
| Lakewood | 264 | 1 089 | 177.1 | 36.2 | 816 | D | D | D | 111 | 2 598 | 744.5 | 118.9 |
| Littleton | 113 | 466 | 58.7 | 12.6 | 351 | D | D | D | 34 | D | D | D |
| Longmont | 137 | 479 | 84.2 | 13.6 | 350 | 2 353 | 410.7 | 168.9 | 119 | 3 102 | 587.8 | 125.0 |
| Loveland | 112 | 462 | 60.1 | 13.4 | 210 | 1 108 | 125.1 | 41.4 | 92 | 2 885 | 563.6 | 181.6 |
| Northglenn | 44 | 257 | 19.8 | 5.4 | 51 | 179 | 14.9 | 6.0 | 36 | 804 | 128.4 | 29.5 |
| Parker | 66 | 176 | 26.2 | 4.1 | 186 | 580 | 80.1 | 28.7 | NA | NA | NA | NA |
| Pueblo | 121 | 581 | 85.1 | 16.5 | 202 | D | D | D | 59 | 2 046 | D | 104.6 |
| Thornton | 77 | 276 | 49.7 | 7.0 | 160 | 983 | 152.9 | 53.3 | NA | NA | NA | NA |
| Westminster | 158 | 584 | 87.6 | 17.1 | 335 | D | D | D | 52 | 813 | 271.7 | 41.2 |
| Wheat Ridge | 52 | 175 | 24.0 | 4.0 | 180 | 913 | 127.0 | 56.4 | 49 | 1 101 | 248.3 | 56.1 |
| CONNECTICUT | 3 609 | 22 455 | 5 686.6 | 994.0 | 9 828 | 101 384 | 15 771.7 | 7 988.8 | 4 924 | 190 790 | 58 404.9 | 10 345.1 |
| Bridgeport | 96 | 507 | 156.6 | 17.3 | 200 | D | D | D | 199 | 4 736 | 946.8 | 211.8 |
| Bristol | 40 | 138 | 30.1 | 4.1 | 74 | 416 | 38.5 | 17.2 | 148 | 3 675 | 719.2 | 160.1 |
| Danbury | 84 | 1 956 | 287.6 | 107.9 | 238 | 3 976 | 398.7 | 219.9 | 100 | 5 096 | 1 736.9 | 311.6 |
| Hartford | 174 | 1 562 | 257.6 | 77.4 | 404 | 7 844 | 1 666.5 | 639.6 | 80 | 1 314 | 242.9 | 51.5 |
| Meriden | 49 | 404 | 63.4 | 10.7 | 78 | 781 | 82.0 | 37.4 | 73 | 2 974 | 652.6 | 160.9 |
| Middletown | 49 | 404 | 140.7 | 21.6 | 113 | D | D | D | 64 | 3 390 | 1 668.0 | 199.8 |
| Milford | 60 | 910 | 863.6 | 43.0 | 187 | 2 126 | 224.6 | 95.9 | 167 | 3 477 | 1 102.4 | 190.5 |
| Naugatuck | 15 | 48 | 9.2 | 1.1 | 39 | 151 | 15.3 | 6.4 | 52 | 1 488 | 355.7 | 72.1 |
| New Britain | 45 | 153 | 30.0 | 4.7 | 94 | D | D | D | 103 | 3 382 | 713.2 | 157.6 |
| New Haven | 137 | 956 | 159.9 | 34.4 | 390 | D | D | D | 79 | 2 999 | 584.0 | 125.1 |
| New London | 27 | 166 | 21.2 | 6.3 | 106 | D | D | D | NA | NA | NA | NA |
| Norwalk | 100 | 386 | 92.2 | 18.1 | 374 | D | D | D | 131 | 3 220 | 991.2 | 207.6 |
| Norwich | 41 | 159 | 22.0 | 3.9 | 64 | 453 | 40.9 | 16.6 | 34 | 981 | 176.7 | 46.1 |
| Shelton | 44 | 263 | 93.5 | 19.3 | 152 | D | D | D | 74 | 4 316 | 1 195.7 | 301.0 |
| Stamford | 232 | 1 856 | 569.9 | 126.1 | 701 | D | D | D | 125 | 4 371 | 2 200.5 | 224.2 |
| Torrington | 28 | 123 | 15.9 | 4.1 | 65 | 254 | 30.4 | 8.9 | 63 | 1 998 | 415.4 | 90.4 |
| Waterbury | 89 | 352 | 87.1 | 12.0 | 159 | D | D | D | 177 | 4 187 | 1 009.4 | 186.5 |
| West Haven | 44 | 179 | 36.3 | 5.5 | 64 | D | D | D | 50 | 1 549 | 377.9 | 72.7 |
| DELAWARE | 1 248 | 5 807 | 11 057.2 | 222.4 | 2 383 | D | D | D | 673 | 34 866 | 25 679.9 | 1 759.7 |
| Dover | 60 | 388 | 60.5 | 15.5 | 143 | D | D | D | 26 | D | 1 413.5 | D |
| Newark | 66 | D | D | D | 117 | D | D | D | 36 | 4 372 | 3 070.0 | 311.7 |
| Wilmington | 244 | 861 | 2 285.7 | 39.0 | 567 | D | D | D | 77 | 1 578 | 397.2 | 76.2 |
| DISTRICT OF COLUMBIA | 1 140 | 9 663 | 2 747.8 | 624.8 | 4 373 | 82 107 | 24 177.7 | 8 660.6 | 137 | 2 015 | 332.8 | 80.8 |
| Washington | 1 140 | 9 663 | 2 747.8 | 624.8 | 4 373 | 82 107 | 24 177.7 | 8 660.6 | 137 | 2 015 | 332.8 | 80.8 |
| FLORIDA | 33 653 | 170 859 | 32 235.4 | 6 094.2 | 69 083 | 427 536 | 61 599.8 | 24 264.5 | 14 324 | 355 386 | 104 832.9 | 15 227.2 |
| Altamonte Springs | 142 | 783 | 137.5 | 28.1 | 332 | 2 172 | 264.2 | 98.0 | NA | NA | NA | NA |
| Apopka | 44 | 162 | 23.2 | 3.9 | 103 | 360 | 36.8 | 12.0 | 35 | 878 | 173.2 | 38.2 |
| Aventura | 174 | 828 | 217.1 | 32.1 | 261 | 864 | 145.1 | 55.0 | NA | NA | NA | NA |
| Boca Raton | 516 | 3 740 | 555.0 | 179.9 | 1 544 | D | D | D | 150 | 1 997 | 385.2 | 95.3 |
| Bonita Springs | 124 | 475 | 112.6 | 22.1 | 199 | 976 | 168.4 | 52.0 | NA | NA | NA | NA |
| Boynton Beach | 115 | 462 | 96.6 | 13.6 | 271 | 906 | 101.8 | 35.7 | 73 | 777 | 108.1 | 27.8 |
| Bradenton | 97 | 355 | 55.7 | 10.4 | 248 | D | D | D | 26 | 618 | 100.0 | 19.1 |
| Cape Coral | 295 | 637 | 82.1 | 15.5 | 347 | 1 318 | 136.9 | 48.8 | 85 | 745 | 101.2 | 27.9 |
| Casselberry | 59 | 295 | 49.1 | 9.0 | 108 | 411 | 50.5 | 15.3 | NA | NA | NA | NA |
| Clearwater | 286 | 1 151 | 198.5 | 39.5 | 772 | D | D | D | 112 | 1 301 | 219.6 | 49.6 |
| Clermont | 80 | 235 | 33.8 | 5.9 | 103 | 408 | 37.0 | 14.6 | NA | NA | NA | NA |
| Coconut Creek | 42 | D | D | D | 145 | 368 | 38.8 | 12.7 | NA | NA | NA | NA |
| Cooper City | 44 | 99 | 23.2 | 3.0 | 136 | 376 | 43.9 | 13.3 | NA | NA | NA | NA |
| Coral Gables | 385 | 2 418 | 403.9 | 89.7 | 1 424 | D | D | D | 45 | 512 | D | 27.7 |
| Coral Springs | 241 | 905 | 209.2 | 38.2 | 801 | 2 940 | 341.6 | 111.9 | 84 | 903 | 166.0 | 36.4 |
| Cutler Bay | NA | NA | NA | NA | NA | NA | NA | NA | NA | NA | NA | NA |
| Dania Beach | 69 | 204 | 52.4 | 7.2 | 154 | 638 | 85.1 | 29.9 | 59 | 792 | 131.8 | 29.5 |
| Davie | 219 | 875 | 213.1 | 35.0 | 503 | D | D | D | 99 | 2 449 | 331.4 | 113.3 |
| Daytona Beach | 158 | 1 515 | 209.2 | 41.9 | 333 | D | D | D | 62 | 1 382 | 316.3 | 58.7 |

1. Establishments subject to federal tax.

# Accommodation and Food Services, Arts, Entertainment, and Recreation, and Health Care and Social Assistance

| City | Accommodation and food services, 2007 | | | | Arts, entertainment, and recreation,[1] 2007 | | | | Health care and social assistance,[1] 2007 | | | |
|---|---|---|---|---|---|---|---|---|---|---|---|---|
| | Number of establishments | Number of employees | Sales (mil dol) | Annual payroll (mil dol) | Number of establishments | Number of employees | Receipts (mil dol) | Annual payroll (mil dol) | Number of establishments | Number of employees | Receipts (mil dol) | Annual payroll (mil dol) |
| | 92 | 93 | 94 | 95 | 96 | 97 | 98 | 99 | 100 | 101 | 102 | 103 |
| COLORADO—Cont'd | | | | | | | | | | | | |
| Castle Rock | 93 | 1 680 | 67.3 | 21.3 | 14 | D | D | D | 92 | 818 | 55.7 | 25.0 |
| Centennial | 168 | 2 680 | 125.4 | 36.1 | 33 | D | D | D | 305 | 2 419 | 230.1 | 98.7 |
| Colorado Springs | 1 008 | 20 874 | 1 011.9 | 309.4 | 146 | 1 492 | 81.9 | 22.5 | 1 354 | 14 224 | 1 406.1 | 583.1 |
| Commerce City | 52 | 814 | 37.1 | 11.3 | 4 | D | D | D | 14 | 262 | 17.1 | 7.7 |
| Denver | 1 778 | 38 701 | 2 279.0 | 656.3 | 204 | 4 981 | 626.2 | 320.9 | 1 595 | 22 442 | 2 562.4 | 1 047.8 |
| Englewood | 104 | 1 469 | 65.7 | 19.6 | 13 | D | D | D | 218 | 4 579 | 651.1 | 259.0 |
| Fort Collins | 392 | 8 324 | 328.0 | 99.9 | 52 | 813 | 35.1 | 9.8 | 486 | 5 257 | 531.3 | 223.6 |
| Fountain | 37 | 528 | 25.4 | 6.7 | 3 | 53 | 2.1 | 0.8 | 11 | 121 | 12.0 | 4.3 |
| Grand Junction | 210 | 4 746 | 211.3 | 61.0 | 34 | 733 | 18.4 | 6.8 | 313 | D | D | D |
| Greeley | 187 | 3 828 | 134.5 | 40.7 | 20 | 197 | 7.0 | 1.8 | 228 | 3 326 | 273.9 | 116.4 |
| Lakewood | 350 | 7 742 | 347.4 | 108.1 | 44 | 727 | 30.9 | 10.1 | 440 | 5 841 | 504.5 | 226.8 |
| Littleton | 127 | 2 229 | 94.6 | 29.3 | 19 | 160 | 7.5 | 2.6 | 203 | 2 238 | 244.2 | 114.8 |
| Longmont | 183 | 3 285 | 144.5 | 45.6 | 27 | 226 | 6.4 | 1.9 | 226 | 2 350 | 201.4 | 91.1 |
| Loveland | 181 | 3 274 | 128.6 | 37.4 | 26 | D | D | D | 180 | 1 842 | 177.5 | 68.7 |
| Northglenn | 56 | 1 516 | 69.3 | 20.6 | 8 | D | D | D | 42 | 495 | 38.7 | 16.4 |
| Parker | 98 | 2 117 | 87.9 | 26.0 | 12 | D | D | D | 107 | D | D | D |
| Pueblo | 282 | 4 840 | 194.1 | 55.0 | 24 | D | D | D | 318 | D | D | D |
| Thornton | 143 | 3 048 | 135.5 | 38.8 | 17 | D | D | D | 162 | 2 845 | 316.5 | 120.2 |
| Westminster | 234 | 5 207 | 259.6 | 82.5 | 26 | D | D | D | 206 | 2 579 | 232.4 | 108.6 |
| Wheat Ridge | 99 | 1 553 | 67.1 | 18.8 | 16 | 100 | 5.0 | 1.3 | 167 | 1 666 | 189.4 | 91.7 |
| CONNECTICUT | 7 941 | 132 001 | 9 138.4 | 2 483.1 | 1 206 | 14 325 | 1 834.8 | 457.0 | 7 687 | 122 425 | 11 534.8 | 5 062.3 |
| Bridgeport | 193 | D | D | D | 17 | 315 | 30.7 | 6.9 | 214 | 3 925 | 364.7 | 161.7 |
| Bristol | 101 | 1 251 | 62.1 | 16.9 | 12 | 169 | 30.8 | 7.7 | 108 | D | D | D |
| Danbury | 208 | 3 248 | 200.3 | 54.3 | 16 | D | D | D | 195 | D | D | D |
| Hartford | 350 | 5 163 | 294.9 | 84.8 | 15 | 746 | 123.7 | 57.6 | 248 | 4 850 | 714.9 | 346.3 |
| Meriden | 120 | 1 402 | 72.5 | 19.9 | 3 | D | D | D | 95 | 1 616 | 145.8 | 62.3 |
| Middletown | 117 | 1 238 | 83.4 | 21.3 | 8 | 84 | 3.8 | 0.8 | 118 | 2 491 | 245.4 | 114.5 |
| Milford | 184 | 2 470 | 129.0 | 35.9 | 20 | 229 | 19.1 | 6.2 | 134 | 2 416 | 231.6 | 101.7 |
| Naugatuck | 51 | 398 | 20.1 | 5.1 | 4 | D | D | D | 39 | 1 081 | 50.8 | 23.7 |
| New Britain | 81 | 1 091 | 49.1 | 14.8 | 8 | D | D | D | 104 | 1 366 | 193.4 | 84.7 |
| New Haven | 331 | 3 739 | 266.0 | 66.2 | 17 | 340 | 80.9 | 7.8 | 277 | 4 295 | 431.1 | 209.7 |
| New London | 94 | D | D | D | 13 | 113 | 11.6 | 4.8 | 85 | D | D | D |
| Norwalk | 238 | 2 777 | 207.0 | 54.0 | 53 | 720 | 101.8 | 30.9 | 196 | 2 901 | 283.3 | 124.4 |
| Norwich | 89 | D | D | D | 9 | D | D | D | 120 | 1 890 | 195.3 | 74.7 |
| Shelton | 95 | 1 683 | 99.2 | 30.4 | 10 | D | D | D | 92 | 1 923 | 223.7 | 72.7 |
| Stamford | 349 | 4 437 | 353.1 | 106.8 | 57 | D | D | D | 340 | 3 368 | 424.1 | 169.5 |
| Torrington | 90 | 1 114 | 56.6 | 15.6 | 7 | D | D | D | 102 | 1 834 | 170.1 | 70.4 |
| Waterbury | 215 | 2 848 | 138.7 | 40.8 | 16 | 161 | 8.6 | 2.1 | 242 | 6 276 | 552.2 | 252.4 |
| West Haven | 118 | 1 358 | 74.5 | 20.9 | 6 | D | D | D | 61 | D | D | D |
| DELAWARE | 1 850 | 32 194 | 1 910.8 | 468.8 | 291 | 3 722 | 349.3 | 82.6 | 1 877 | 25 319 | 2 620.7 | 1 155.8 |
| Dover | 123 | 3 732 | 378.6 | 57.0 | 16 | D | D | D | 165 | 2 272 | 205.7 | 90.6 |
| Newark | 124 | 2 513 | 138.6 | 32.2 | 12 | 135 | 7.1 | 2.4 | 161 | 2 563 | 334.4 | 151.5 |
| Wilmington | 212 | 3 315 | 198.1 | 56.4 | 27 | 380 | 31.7 | 10.0 | 253 | 3 791 | 521.9 | 218.2 |
| DISTRICT OF COLUMBIA | 2 148 | 52 998 | 4 278.2 | 1 238.4 | 198 | 4 721 | 612.3 | 240.4 | 1 419 | 19 710 | 2 098.8 | 944.4 |
| Washington | 2 148 | 52 998 | 4 278.2 | 1 238.4 | 198 | 4 721 | 612.3 | 240.4 | 1 419 | 19 710 | 2 098.8 | 944.4 |
| FLORIDA | 35 012 | 746 214 | 41 922.1 | 11 470.0 | 6 629 | 133 359 | 13 402.7 | 3 497.8 | 46 687 | 538 050 | 61 636.7 | 22 586.4 |
| Altamonte Springs | 161 | 4 366 | 219.1 | 65.5 | 19 | D | D | D | 220 | D | D | D |
| Apopka | 67 | 1 112 | 51.9 | 14.0 | 11 | D | D | D | 71 | 537 | 59.9 | 29.4 |
| Aventura | 86 | 3 455 | 237.0 | 69.0 | 24 | 120 | 12.7 | 2.7 | 219 | 2 603 | 439.8 | 131.2 |
| Boca Raton | 398 | 10 638 | 682.8 | 202.2 | 92 | 661 | 78.8 | 14.1 | 700 | 7 297 | 935.2 | 341.9 |
| Bonita Springs | 107 | 1 978 | 104.5 | 29.3 | 36 | 1 146 | 72.5 | 27.6 | 112 | 813 | 114.8 | 32.5 |
| Boynton Beach | 150 | 3 081 | 138.0 | 43.5 | 24 | D | D | D | 283 | D | D | D |
| Bradenton | 123 | 2 196 | 103.9 | 27.6 | 24 | 220 | 10.9 | 4.0 | 262 | 5 984 | 765.1 | 241.2 |
| Cape Coral | 178 | 2 822 | 125.9 | 36.0 | 40 | 246 | 18.9 | 3.9 | 232 | 2 145 | 263.6 | 85.2 |
| Casselberry | 76 | 1 251 | 49.8 | 14.8 | 13 | 225 | 10.4 | 2.5 | 56 | 612 | 45.1 | 20.2 |
| Clearwater | 358 | 6 966 | 361.3 | 102.3 | 57 | 771 | 43.8 | 12.5 | 474 | 5 699 | 634.8 | 264.1 |
| Clermont | 85 | 1 862 | 80.7 | 23.8 | 15 | D | D | D | 101 | D | D | D |
| Coconut Creek | 51 | 537 | 27.9 | 7.8 | 20 | D | D | D | 82 | D | D | D |
| Cooper City | 49 | 875 | 33.0 | 10.0 | 32 | 174 | 15.5 | 5.6 | 97 | D | D | D |
| Coral Gables | 210 | 4 645 | 292.2 | 93.0 | 42 | 237 | 25.3 | 10.0 | 454 | D | D | D |
| Coral Springs | 275 | 4 595 | 246.9 | 64.7 | 67 | 623 | 35.6 | 10.3 | 497 | D | D | D |
| Cutler Bay | NA | NA | NA | NA | NA | NA | NA | NA | NA | NA | NA | NA |
| Dania Beach | 80 | 1 646 | 106.4 | 26.9 | 25 | D | D | D | 37 | D | D | D |
| Davie | 217 | 3 335 | 175.4 | 46.0 | 62 | D | D | D | 190 | 1 187 | 140.7 | 36.3 |
| Daytona Beach | 267 | 6 442 | 337.1 | 85.5 | 34 | D | D | D | 229 | 3 544 | 356.4 | 160.1 |

1. Establishments subject to federal tax.

## Table D. Cities — **Other Services and Federal Funds**

| City | Other services[1], 2007 | | | | Selected federal funds, 2009–2010 (mil dol) | | | | | | | | |
|---|---|---|---|---|---|---|---|---|---|---|---|---|---|
| | | | | | Procurement contracts | | Grants | | | | | | |
| | Number of establishments | Number of employees | Receipts (mil dol) | Annual payroll (mil dol) | Defense | Other | Total[2] | Medicaid and other health related | Nutrition and family welfare | Energy and environment | Disasters and emergency preparedness | Housing and community development | Employment and training |
| | 104 | 105 | 106 | 107 | 108 | 109 | 110 | 111 | 112 | 113 | 114 | 115 | 116 |
| COLORADO—Cont'd | | | | | | | | | | | | | |
| Castle Rock | 79 | 405 | 29.4 | 9.8 | 0.1 | 4.2 | 4.3 | 0.0 | 0.0 | 3.0 | 0.0 | 0.9 | 0.0 |
| Centennial | 167 | 872 | 94.6 | 27.4 | 127.9 | 54.3 | 0.8 | 0.0 | 0.0 | 0.0 | 0.1 | 0.0 | 0.0 |
| Colorado Springs | 690 | 4 198 | 324.7 | 101.7 | 1 892.4 | 69.8 | 97.7 | 8.0 | 9.4 | 2.6 | 0.1 | 25.3 | 0.1 |
| Commerce City | 81 | 684 | 79.1 | 20.8 | 0.1 | 0.5 | 28.5 | 0.0 | 0.0 | 0.0 | 0.0 | 14.7 | 0.0 |
| Denver | 1 131 | 8 938 | 732.5 | 229.9 | 166.6 | 566.3 | 1 880.5 | 293.6 | 329.1 | 135.1 | 3.5 | 206.0 | 109.6 |
| Englewood | 142 | 874 | 89.8 | 29.5 | 185.1 | 92.0 | 54.6 | 6.4 | 4.9 | -0.2 | 0.0 | 3.9 | 0.0 |
| Fort Collins | 221 | 1 252 | 84.2 | 28.3 | 8.5 | 129.5 | 235.6 | 70.8 | 3.2 | 42.3 | 0.6 | 10.0 | 0.4 |
| Fountain | 13 | D | D | D | 4.1 | 0.0 | 14.5 | 0.0 | 0.0 | 0.0 | 0.0 | 1.8 | 0.0 |
| Grand Junction | 198 | 1 227 | 116.9 | 31.8 | 35.0 | 90.9 | 17.2 | 0.4 | 0.0 | 5.7 | 0.0 | 6.3 | 0.0 |
| Greeley | 123 | 633 | 48.7 | 14.5 | 0.4 | 7.4 | 18.6 | 1.6 | 0.0 | 0.2 | 0.0 | 7.0 | 0.0 |
| Lakewood | 271 | 1 301 | 99.1 | 33.3 | 5.7 | 150.2 | 61.8 | 0.4 | 1.0 | 39.3 | 0.0 | 12.2 | 3.6 |
| Littleton | 101 | 497 | 42.2 | 12.9 | 1 138.3 | 2.3 | 31.8 | 1.7 | 0.0 | 25.3 | 0.0 | 4.4 | 0.0 |
| Longmont | 149 | 794 | 53.8 | 17.9 | 0.2 | 5.0 | 113.9 | 1.9 | 1.4 | 0.9 | 0.0 | 4.6 | 0.0 |
| Loveland | 127 | 733 | 53.6 | 18.1 | 8.9 | 21.1 | 9.2 | 0.0 | 0.9 | 0.8 | 0.0 | 4.6 | 0.0 |
| Northglenn | 54 | D | D | D | 0.0 | 0.1 | 0.7 | 0.0 | 0.0 | 0.0 | 0.0 | 0.0 | 0.0 |
| Parker | 100 | 489 | 35.6 | 11.4 | 3.8 | 0.6 | 0.0 | 0.0 | 0.0 | 0.0 | 0.0 | 0.0 | 0.0 |
| Pueblo | 141 | 724 | 56.4 | 15.6 | 31.4 | 15.0 | 51.8 | 6.5 | 0.0 | 8.0 | 2.7 | 17.3 | 0.0 |
| Thornton | 83 | 699 | 48.3 | 19.7 | 0.8 | 1.3 | 1.0 | 0.0 | 0.0 | 0.0 | 0.0 | 0.6 | 0.0 |
| Westminster | 123 | 783 | 46.8 | 15.8 | 4.9 | 0.4 | 2.0 | 0.4 | 0.0 | 0.0 | 0.0 | 0.7 | 0.0 |
| Wheat Ridge | 108 | 512 | 48.1 | 14.7 | 6.9 | 9.5 | 23.0 | 2.7 | 0.2 | 7.2 | 0.0 | 11.8 | 0.0 |
| CONNECTICUT | 5 911 | 36 724 | 3 068.8 | 980.2 | 11 113.6 | 843.0 | 8 298.9 | 4 768.8 | 847.6 | 189.2 | 20.4 | 522.2 | 140.6 |
| Bridgeport | 159 | 760 | 72.3 | 19.3 | 107.8 | 2.9 | 79.4 | 7.4 | 8.9 | 2.7 | 0.0 | 41.9 | 8.1 |
| Bristol | 97 | 427 | 33.7 | 9.7 | 0.4 | 0.3 | 7.8 | 0.0 | 0.0 | 0.0 | 0.0 | 7.7 | 0.0 |
| Danbury | 160 | 1 023 | 90.8 | 28.0 | 85.0 | 14.6 | 23.2 | 0.2 | 1.8 | 11.0 | 0.0 | 9.2 | 0.0 |
| Hartford | 208 | 2 359 | 139.9 | 47.3 | 27.7 | 25.5 | 932.8 | 134.3 | 178.1 | 40.2 | 8.6 | 195.4 | 2.1 |
| Meriden | 78 | 385 | 28.6 | 10.0 | 11.4 | 1.2 | 10.8 | 0.2 | 0.1 | 0.0 | 0.0 | 9.3 | 0.0 |
| Middletown | 77 | 380 | 51.2 | 11.6 | 60.8 | 1.0 | 29.0 | 9.7 | 0.0 | 0.2 | 0.0 | 9.4 | 0.0 |
| Milford | 133 | 782 | 61.5 | 19.8 | 0.0 | 0.0 | 5.7 | 0.6 | 0.0 | 2.1 | 0.0 | 3.0 | 0.0 |
| Naugatuck | 38 | 192 | 14.1 | 4.4 | 3.4 | 0.2 | 2.7 | 0.0 | 0.0 | 0.0 | 0.0 | 2.4 | 0.0 |
| New Britain | 81 | 335 | 29.7 | 9.5 | 1.5 | 3.2 | 26.4 | 1.0 | 3.0 | 1.5 | 0.0 | 11.6 | 0.1 |
| New Haven | 174 | 967 | 76.8 | 24.4 | 7.1 | 38.5 | 971.6 | 803.8 | 6.8 | 16.1 | 0.0 | 68.5 | 0.0 |
| New London | 48 | 314 | 23.1 | 7.7 | 4.7 | 38.1 | 5.9 | 0.0 | 0.0 | 0.0 | 0.0 | 4.2 | 0.0 |
| Norwalk | 186 | 1 017 | 99.2 | 29.4 | 170.1 | 3.6 | 28.6 | 0.0 | 1.7 | 2.3 | 0.0 | 16.9 | 0.0 |
| Norwich | 72 | 515 | 32.3 | 10.9 | 0.4 | 1.1 | 18.4 | 0.4 | 0.1 | 10.6 | 0.0 | 6.5 | 0.0 |
| Shelton | 59 | 351 | 22.4 | 7.3 | 2.3 | 2.8 | 0.7 | 0.0 | 0.0 | 0.2 | 0.0 | 0.4 | 0.0 |
| Stamford | 221 | 1 431 | 125.4 | 39.5 | 38.4 | 19.8 | 40.5 | 0.2 | 2.7 | 5.5 | 0.0 | 28.1 | 0.0 |
| Torrington | 73 | 542 | 30.5 | 21.9 | 2.4 | 0.0 | 3.5 | 0.2 | 0.0 | 0.3 | 0.0 | 2.0 | 0.0 |
| Waterbury | 152 | 1 092 | 72.9 | 25.4 | 4.3 | 0.7 | 39.2 | 1.8 | 4.1 | 6.5 | 0.0 | 24.1 | 0.0 |
| West Haven | 81 | 368 | 37.3 | 11.0 | 7.9 | 58.9 | 15.2 | 0.0 | 1.3 | 0.5 | 0.0 | 12.0 | 0.0 |
| DELAWARE | 1 256 | 7 893 | 569.1 | 195.3 | 218.1 | 144.5 | 2 055.2 | 983.3 | 207.3 | 105.0 | 8.3 | 78.2 | 27.7 |
| Dover | 65 | 626 | 34.4 | 12.0 | 120.2 | 2.2 | 332.0 | 4.2 | 0.8 | 30.1 | 2.4 | 27.1 | 0.0 |
| Newark | 64 | 430 | 20.4 | 7.9 | 20.6 | 7.1 | 157.8 | 51.6 | 6.6 | 16.4 | 0.0 | 1.0 | 0.0 |
| Wilmington | 148 | 1 043 | 76.4 | 27.8 | 21.9 | 74.2 | 183.3 | 28.1 | 12.4 | 45.7 | 0.0 | 49.8 | 25.1 |
| DISTRICT OF COLUMBIA | 969 | 7 011 | 566.2 | 170.4 | 4 651.0 | 16 598.9 | 10 872.0 | 2 282.6 | 377.8 | 865.6 | 16.8 | 342.6 | 226.0 |
| Washington | 969 | 7 011 | 566.2 | 170.4 | 4 651.0 | 16 598.9 | 10 872.0 | 2 282.6 | 377.8 | 865.6 | 16.8 | 342.6 | 226.0 |
| FLORIDA | 28 522 | 149 369 | 11 718.0 | 3 529.5 | 12 814.2 | 5 166.5 | 28 066.3 | 14 386.2 | 3 377.4 | 807.6 | 110.2 | 1 635.9 | 393.6 |
| Altamonte Springs | 109 | 640 | 41.0 | 13.5 | 0.3 | 0.5 | 0.4 | 0.0 | 0.0 | 0.1 | 0.0 | 0.0 | 0.0 |
| Apopka | 59 | 293 | 20.8 | 6.2 | 170.0 | 1.5 | 0.0 | 0.0 | 0.0 | 0.0 | 0.0 | 0.0 | 0.0 |
| Aventura | 65 | 411 | 23.1 | 7.5 | 0.0 | 0.0 | 0.0 | 0.0 | 0.0 | 0.0 | 0.0 | 0.0 | 0.0 |
| Boca Raton | 347 | 1 954 | 142.7 | 47.5 | 75.3 | 12.6 | 29.9 | 7.7 | 0.0 | 4.0 | 0.0 | 6.4 | 0.0 |
| Bonita Springs | 68 | 318 | 18.8 | 6.6 | 0.7 | 0.1 | 49.6 | 0.0 | 0.0 | 24.3 | 0.0 | 0.0 | 0.0 |
| Boynton Beach | 133 | 772 | 52.7 | 15.5 | 0.9 | 4.6 | 1.6 | 0.1 | 0.0 | 0.0 | 0.0 | 1.3 | 0.0 |
| Bradenton | 95 | 393 | 28.6 | 8.9 | 11.3 | 1.2 | 34.0 | 0.4 | 5.3 | 2.5 | 0.0 | 14.3 | 0.0 |
| Cape Coral | 203 | 831 | 65.3 | 18.4 | 0.9 | 1.0 | 2.1 | 0.0 | 0.0 | 1.4 | 0.0 | 0.7 | 0.0 |
| Casselberry | 63 | 299 | 22.9 | 6.8 | 0.2 | 0.0 | 0.9 | 0.4 | 0.0 | 0.4 | 0.0 | 0.0 | 0.0 |
| Clearwater | 240 | 1 253 | 100.1 | 30.8 | 357.4 | 11.5 | 31.9 | 2.8 | -0.1 | 5.0 | 0.0 | 19.5 | 0.5 |
| Clermont | 45 | 211 | 13.6 | 4.1 | 3.0 | 5.8 | 0.0 | 0.0 | 0.0 | 0.0 | 0.0 | 0.0 | 0.0 |
| Coconut Creek | 65 | 276 | 37.0 | 8.5 | 0.0 | 0.0 | 0.4 | 0.0 | 0.0 | 0.0 | 0.0 | 0.3 | 0.0 |
| Cooper City | 43 | D | D | D | 0.0 | 0.0 | 0.0 | 0.0 | 0.0 | 0.0 | 0.0 | 0.0 | 0.0 |
| Coral Gables | 132 | 653 | 48.9 | 15.4 | 0.4 | 0.7 | 285.1 | 244.8 | 0.7 | 0.1 | 0.0 | 0.1 | 0.0 |
| Coral Springs | 242 | 1 001 | 76.5 | 20.8 | 8.2 | 21.1 | 0.9 | 0.0 | 0.0 | 0.0 | 0.0 | 0.9 | 0.0 |
| Cutler Bay | NA | NA | NA | NA | NA | NA | NA | NA | NA | NA | NA | NA | NA |
| Dania Beach | 102 | 583 | 57.8 | 16.3 | 10.5 | 4.3 | 0.0 | 0.0 | 0.0 | 0.0 | 0.0 | 0.0 | 0.0 |
| Davie | 216 | 1 096 | 105.3 | 29.2 | 4.1 | 1.4 | 4.5 | 0.0 | 0.0 | 1.3 | 0.0 | 0.7 | 0.0 |
| Daytona Beach | 132 | 853 | 51.7 | 15.1 | 71.3 | 27.3 | 38.4 | 1.2 | 0.1 | 1.3 | 0.0 | 11.4 | 0.0 |

1. Establishments subject to federal tax.  2. Includes program categories not shown separately. State totals include additional categories not allocated by city.

| City | City government finances, 2007 | | | | | | | | | |
|---|---|---|---|---|---|---|---|---|---|---|
| | General revenue | | | | | | | General expenditure | | |
| | | Intergovernmental | | Taxes | | | | | Per capita[1] (dollars) | |
| | | | | | Per capita[1] (dollars) | | | | | |
| | Total (mil dol) | Total (mil dol) | Percent from state government | Total (mil dol) | Total | Property | Sales and gross receipts | Total (mil dol) | Total | Capital outlays |
| | 117 | 118 | 119 | 120 | 121 | 122 | 123 | 124 | 125 | 126 |
| COLORADO—Cont'd | | | | | | | | | | |
| Castle Rock | 89.5 | 3.3 | 100.0 | 63.0 | 1 484 | 84 | 1 400 | 66.1 | 1 557 | 405 |
| Centennial | 44.8 | 8.1 | 59.9 | 30.4 | 306 | 81 | 225 | 44.8 | 452 | 39 |
| Colorado Springs | 936.7 | 58.8 | 43.7 | 209.9 | 558 | 57 | 501 | 881.4 | 2 341 | 517 |
| Commerce City | 54.6 | 4.0 | 28.2 | 44.5 | 1 087 | 102 | 985 | 34.5 | 843 | 0 |
| Denver | 1 963.0 | 226.0 | 17.5 | 855.5 | 1 454 | 369 | 974 | 2 147.9 | 3 651 | 545 |
| Englewood | 53.2 | 3.0 | 47.6 | 29.9 | 920 | 119 | 801 | 68.7 | 2 111 | 566 |
| Fort Collins | 250.4 | 39.9 | 8.3 | 108.0 | 806 | 119 | 688 | 243.1 | 1 815 | 545 |
| Fountain | 22.8 | 1.0 | 90.1 | 8.6 | 438 | 131 | 307 | 11.2 | 575 | 16 |
| Grand Junction | 109.5 | 15.2 | 47.6 | 53.8 | 1 112 | 146 | 966 | 135.5 | 2 799 | 1 084 |
| Greeley | 107.2 | 13.4 | 10.6 | 53.5 | 593 | 92 | 501 | 116.1 | 1 285 | 391 |
| Lakewood | 137.4 | 16.8 | 49.3 | 84.0 | 598 | 61 | 485 | 118.6 | 845 | 107 |
| Littleton | 64.5 | 15.4 | 15.6 | 30.5 | 751 | 88 | 663 | 67.5 | 1 661 | 103 |
| Longmont | 105.8 | 7.7 | 68.4 | 61.5 | 723 | 164 | 559 | 114.7 | 1 349 | 347 |
| Loveland | 103.0 | 7.2 | 95.8 | 63.6 | 988 | 115 | 872 | 77.6 | 1 205 | 303 |
| Northglenn | 34.7 | 3.6 | 28.9 | 19.7 | 588 | 148 | 441 | 31.3 | 933 | 253 |
| Parker | 50.4 | 5.9 | 26.1 | 31.3 | 732 | 30 | 700 | 52.3 | 1 223 | 584 |
| Pueblo | 116.6 | 15.3 | 37.4 | 59.9 | 577 | 89 | 489 | 113.3 | 1 092 | 299 |
| Thornton | 157.0 | 13.1 | 56.1 | 86.6 | 781 | 157 | 624 | 110.2 | 994 | 196 |
| Westminster | 161.3 | 14.1 | 33.5 | 83.7 | 788 | 54 | 734 | 238.3 | 2 244 | 806 |
| Wheat Ridge | 27.9 | 3.6 | 100.0 | 18.2 | 591 | 127 | 455 | 33.4 | 1 082 | 119 |
| CONNECTICUT | X | X | X | X | X | X | X | X | X | X |
| Bridgeport | 650.6 | 357.6 | 94.1 | 238.7 | 1 747 | 1 714 | 25 | 568.2 | 4 157 | 382 |
| Bristol | 200.0 | 69.9 | 98.1 | 107.0 | 1 756 | 1 704 | 28 | 228.4 | 3 750 | 553 |
| Danbury | 224.3 | 60.4 | 98.7 | 138.9 | 1 753 | 1 691 | 62 | 211.8 | 2 674 | 521 |
| Hartford | 748.2 | 489.7 | 98.2 | 238.2 | 1 912 | 1 851 | 40 | 731.7 | 5 874 | 704 |
| Meriden | 207.5 | 84.0 | 98.7 | 104.4 | 1 763 | 1 752 | 12 | 204.1 | 3 446 | 209 |
| Middletown | 172.8 | 75.1 | 99.7 | 84.4 | 1 766 | 1 750 | 9 | 189.2 | 3 959 | 1 373 |
| Milford | 176.4 | 24.4 | 98.2 | 132.2 | 2 462 | 2 395 | 33 | 176.4 | 3 286 | 215 |
| Naugatuck | 99.8 | 34.7 | 98.2 | 57.1 | 1 789 | 1 755 | 34 | 103.7 | 3 249 | 4 |
| New Britain | 265.1 | 137.8 | 97.2 | 100.3 | 1 420 | 1 369 | 51 | 231.3 | 3 273 | 452 |
| New Haven | 712.4 | 444.0 | 97.5 | 186.1 | 1 502 | 1 458 | 19 | 641.2 | 5 174 | 736 |
| New London | 109.1 | 57.0 | 96.8 | 38.0 | 1 467 | 1 418 | 25 | 135.7 | 5 236 | 1 427 |
| Norwalk | 308.6 | 44.9 | 97.4 | 225.6 | 2 704 | 2 584 | 119 | 266.1 | 3 189 | 127 |
| Norwich | 123.8 | 52.9 | 99.8 | 53.3 | 1 462 | 1 436 | 0 | 129.5 | 3 555 | 195 |
| Shelton | 111.3 | 16.7 | 98.5 | 85.6 | 2 140 | 2 068 | 72 | 130.4 | 3 259 | 829 |
| Stamford | 479.5 | 79.4 | 93.8 | 348.9 | 2 945 | 2 811 | 89 | 516.6 | 4 360 | 796 |
| Torrington | 114.0 | 36.1 | 99.9 | 64.7 | 1 826 | 1 826 | 0 | 110.1 | 3 107 | 162 |
| Waterbury | 415.7 | 183.4 | 96.5 | 200.6 | 1 872 | 1 816 | 25 | 449.0 | 4 190 | 162 |
| West Haven | 159.9 | 64.8 | 100.0 | 86.3 | 1 639 | 1 628 | 11 | 154.2 | 2 928 | 41 |
| DELAWARE | X | X | X | X | X | X | X | X | X | X |
| Dover | 38.4 | 5.2 | 69.8 | 16.4 | 458 | 362 | 75 | 46.7 | 1 304 | 172 |
| Newark | 19.5 | 2.5 | 74.2 | 7.4 | 246 | 127 | 58 | 26.1 | 870 | 57 |
| Wilmington | 169.4 | 47.0 | 11.1 | 86.8 | 1 191 | 415 | 91 | 197.9 | 2 716 | 361 |
| DISTRICT OF COLUMBIA | X | X | X | X | X | X | X | X | X | X |
| Washington | 9 507.7 | 2 775.7 | 0.0 | 5 192.2 | 8 826 | 2 577 | 2 464 | 8 740.9 | 14 858 | 2 403 |
| FLORIDA | X | X | X | X | X | X | X | X | X | X |
| Altamonte Springs | 53.5 | 5.2 | 97.1 | 26.9 | 668 | 233 | 435 | 49.9 | 1 238 | 462 |
| Apopka | 49.7 | 17.1 | 49.4 | 20.5 | 548 | 182 | 366 | 46.3 | 1 238 | 444 |
| Aventura | 42.8 | 10.7 | 69.7 | 26.9 | 912 | 478 | 434 | 36.5 | 1 239 | 347 |
| Boca Raton | 221.0 | 52.2 | 22.5 | 121.0 | 1 416 | 768 | 648 | 205.9 | 2 410 | 353 |
| Bonita Springs | 35.1 | 7.2 | 100.0 | 13.3 | 314 | 170 | 144 | 40.4 | 955 | 654 |
| Boynton Beach | 133.5 | 23.1 | 46.6 | 56.2 | 827 | 491 | 336 | 122.5 | 1 804 | 371 |
| Bradenton | 65.5 | 15.7 | 42.9 | 21.9 | 410 | 236 | 171 | 63.4 | 1 186 | 182 |
| Cape Coral | 270.8 | 35.9 | 68.3 | 103.1 | 657 | 485 | 172 | 230.4 | 1 468 | 524 |
| Casselberry | 30.5 | 5.1 | 68.4 | 13.0 | 523 | 251 | 272 | 29.3 | 1 181 | 70 |
| Clearwater | 213.4 | 49.2 | 75.8 | 75.6 | 709 | 451 | 258 | 200.8 | 1 883 | 336 |
| Clermont | 34.5 | 3.1 | 88.9 | 11.8 | 911 | 437 | 474 | 31.7 | 2 446 | 865 |
| Coconut Creek | 56.1 | 14.6 | 38.4 | 26.2 | 521 | 289 | 232 | 41.7 | 829 | 81 |
| Cooper City | 37.9 | 10.2 | 28.9 | 18.5 | 633 | 355 | 277 | 38.0 | 1 295 | 73 |
| Coral Gables | 135.3 | 8.0 | 74.7 | 91.4 | 2 171 | 1 469 | 702 | 130.4 | 3 097 | 212 |
| Coral Springs | 129.1 | 34.6 | 43.7 | 58.7 | 462 | 256 | 198 | 145.3 | 1 145 | 109 |
| Cutler Bay | 10.1 | 2.4 | 100.0 | 7.6 | 260 | 123 | 137 | 8.2 | 281 | 5 |
| Dania Beach | 39.2 | 3.2 | 99.1 | 23.8 | 840 | 556 | 205 | 42.5 | 1 503 | 146 |
| Davie | 95.6 | 26.0 | 99.0 | 50.9 | 563 | 275 | 289 | 105.5 | 1 168 | 132 |
| Daytona Beach | 125.0 | 24.5 | 55.9 | 51.1 | 794 | 456 | 338 | 103.7 | 1 611 | 169 |

1. Based on population estimated as of July 1 of the year shown.

# Table D. Cities — **City Government Finances**

| City | Public welfare | Highways | Parking facilities | Education | Health and hospitals | Police protection | Sewerage and sanitation | Parks and recreation | Housing and community development | Interest on debt |
|---|---|---|---|---|---|---|---|---|---|---|
| | 127 | 128 | 129 | 130 | 131 | 132 | 133 | 134 | 135 | 136 |
| **COLORADO—Cont'd** | | | | | | | | | | |
| Castle Rock | 0.0 | 22.0 | 0.0 | 0.0 | 0.0 | 8.9 | 17.5 | 20.2 | 0.0 | 1.9 |
| Centennial | 0.0 | 20.8 | 0.0 | 0.0 | 0.0 | 37.4 | 0.0 | 0.0 | 0.0 | 0.1 |
| Colorado Springs | 0.0 | 8.5 | 0.3 | 0.0 | 45.9 | 9.1 | 9.4 | 2.7 | 0.8 | 2.5 |
| Commerce City | 0.0 | 14.0 | 0.0 | 0.0 | 0.0 | 30.5 | 0.0 | 13.9 | 6.4 | 0.0 |
| Denver | 5.2 | 2.8 | 0.0 | 0.0 | 6.6 | 7.6 | 6.2 | 5.7 | 3.0 | 2.5 |
| Englewood | 0.0 | 5.1 | 0.0 | 0.0 | 0.0 | 12.9 | 39.4 | 10.7 | 2.0 | 4.9 |
| Fort Collins | 0.0 | 29.8 | 0.0 | 0.0 | 0.0 | 16.0 | 5.8 | 16.1 | 0.2 | 2.7 |
| Fountain | 0.0 | 12.7 | 0.0 | 0.0 | 7.0 | 36.0 | 0.0 | 7.5 | 0.1 | 0.0 |
| Grand Junction | 0.0 | 40.7 | 1.6 | 0.0 | 0.0 | 13.3 | 8.8 | 10.4 | 1.7 | 2.2 |
| Greeley | 0.0 | 11.7 | 0.7 | 0.0 | 0.4 | 17.2 | 5.4 | 21.4 | 0.8 | 3.2 |
| Lakewood | 0.0 | 14.3 | 0.0 | 0.0 | 0.4 | 27.7 | 3.4 | 14.7 | 0.5 | 2.3 |
| Littleton | 0.5 | 8.3 | 0.3 | 0.0 | 0.4 | 14.2 | 10.3 | 3.7 | 0.1 | 3.5 |
| Longmont | 0.0 | 18.1 | 0.0 | 0.0 | 0.0 | 15.4 | 14.1 | 15.9 | 2.3 | 1.6 |
| Loveland | 0.0 | 9.7 | 0.0 | 0.0 | 0.0 | 16.1 | 20.5 | 13.1 | 0.4 | 1.1 |
| Northglenn | 0.0 | 19.6 | 0.0 | 0.0 | 0.0 | 23.4 | 18.2 | 7.7 | 4.0 | 0.3 |
| Parker | 0.0 | 29.1 | 0.0 | 0.0 | 0.0 | 14.6 | 1.7 | 27.9 | 0.0 | 1.5 |
| Pueblo | 0.0 | 8.8 | 0.2 | 0.0 | 0.0 | 20.3 | 8.0 | 5.1 | 3.5 | 2.1 |
| Thornton | 0.0 | 9.9 | 0.0 | 0.0 | 1.9 | 17.2 | 11.8 | 13.4 | 0.0 | 4.8 |
| Westminster | 0.0 | 3.2 | 0.0 | 0.0 | 0.0 | 8.0 | 12.5 | 8.0 | 19.2 | 4.0 |
| Wheat Ridge | 0.0 | 19.9 | 0.0 | 0.0 | 0.0 | 24.3 | 0.0 | 19.0 | 3.9 | 0.8 |
| **CONNECTICUT** | X | X | X | X | X | X | X | X | X | X |
| Bridgeport | 0.3 | 2.0 | 0.3 | 53.7 | 1.7 | 7.4 | 4.5 | 1.1 | 2.4 | 7.4 |
| Bristol | 0.0 | 4.4 | 0.0 | 56.1 | 3.7 | 5.3 | 4.7 | 1.9 | 0.0 | 0.8 |
| Danbury | 0.0 | 2.8 | 0.8 | 59.0 | 1.7 | 9.9 | 2.6 | 0.6 | 0.3 | 2.2 |
| Hartford | 1.8 | 1.9 | 0.5 | 61.4 | 1.1 | 4.7 | 2.1 | 0.1 | 5.5 | 1.2 |
| Meriden | 2.1 | 1.6 | 0.0 | 56.7 | 1.5 | 5.0 | 3.5 | 1.4 | 0.5 | 2.1 |
| Middletown | 0.0 | 8.5 | 0.1 | 54.1 | 1.0 | 5.0 | 10.3 | 1.2 | 0.2 | 1.1 |
| Milford | 0.5 | 2.1 | 0.0 | 55.8 | 1.4 | 5.4 | 6.6 | 0.6 | 0.6 | 1.4 |
| Naugatuck | 0.0 | 1.5 | 0.0 | 56.9 | 6.8 | 4.7 | 1.3 | 1.5 | 0.1 | 3.6 |
| New Britain | 0.5 | 2.0 | 0.0 | 60.5 | 0.6 | 5.8 | 4.2 | 3.9 | 1.4 | 0.0 |
| New Haven | 0.6 | 1.6 | 0.3 | 62.8 | 0.6 | 5.4 | 1.0 | 0.0 | 3.2 | 2.9 |
| New London | 0.0 | 1.0 | 0.3 | 60.6 | 0.1 | 6.9 | 7.1 | 1.3 | 2.1 | 0.9 |
| Norwalk | 0.1 | 0.1 | 1.1 | 62.0 | 0.2 | 7.1 | 2.3 | 5.3 | 0.4 | 3.4 |
| Norwich | 1.4 | 11.3 | 0.0 | 54.7 | 0.0 | 8.4 | 6.1 | 1.9 | 1.7 | 1.1 |
| Shelton | 0.0 | 2.0 | 0.0 | 50.8 | 0.3 | 4.5 | 4.1 | 1.1 | 0.0 | 1.2 |
| Stamford | 0.0 | 1.0 | 1.1 | 59.0 | 1.0 | 8.8 | 6.6 | 1.4 | 0.0 | 3.4 |
| Torrington | 0.3 | 4.0 | 0.0 | 58.2 | 3.0 | 6.3 | 3.6 | 1.3 | 0.4 | 1.5 |
| Waterbury | 0.0 | 6.1 | 0.0 | 51.8 | 0.7 | 5.5 | 4.7 | 0.8 | 1.0 | 1.6 |
| West Haven | 0.1 | 6.5 | 0.0 | 55.2 | 0.6 | 8.0 | 5.0 | 0.5 | 0.8 | 3.9 |
| **DELAWARE** | X | X | X | X | X | X | X | X | X | X |
| Dover | 0.0 | 6.7 | 0.2 | 0.0 | 0.4 | 26.0 | 14.2 | 3.1 | 1.0 | 0.2 |
| Newark | 0.0 | 9.3 | 1.8 | 0.0 | 0.0 | 28.9 | 22.7 | 8.2 | 2.5 | 0.5 |
| Wilmington | 0.0 | 3.9 | 2.3 | 0.0 | 0.0 | 24.1 | 7.4 | 5.3 | 3.9 | 2.9 |
| **DISTRICT OF COLUMBIA** | X | X | X | X | X | X | X | X | X | X |
| Washington | 24.7 | 1.2 | 0.0 | 17.7 | 6.1 | 5.7 | 6.0 | 4.2 | 5.1 | 4.3 |
| **FLORIDA** | X | X | X | X | X | X | X | X | X | X |
| Altamonte Springs | 0.0 | 34.4 | 0.0 | 0.0 | 0.0 | 18.0 | 4.5 | 11.0 | 0.0 | 0.9 |
| Apopka | 0.0 | 9.9 | 0.0 | 0.0 | 0.0 | 13.6 | 17.2 | 3.7 | 0.0 | 0.4 |
| Aventura | 0.0 | 15.7 | 0.0 | 13.3 | 0.0 | 31.3 | 1.4 | 6.0 | 0.0 | 4.8 |
| Boca Raton | 0.0 | 7.6 | 0.0 | 0.0 | 0.0 | 16.9 | 9.3 | 16.9 | 1.1 | 2.5 |
| Bonita Springs | 0.0 | 54.2 | 0.0 | 0.0 | 0.9 | 2.1 | 0.0 | 20.7 | 7.0 | 4.1 |
| Boynton Beach | 0.0 | 1.2 | 0.0 | 0.0 | 0.0 | 17.1 | 22.4 | 9.1 | 1.4 | 0.6 |
| Bradenton | 4.4 | 3.7 | 11.5 | 0.0 | 0.0 | 16.5 | 16.6 | 3.8 | 13.9 | 0.1 |
| Cape Coral | 0.0 | 16.0 | 0.0 | 1.7 | 0.0 | 14.2 | 7.6 | 23.7 | 0.5 | 1.7 |
| Casselberry | 0.0 | 7.7 | 0.0 | 0.0 | 0.3 | 17.9 | 26.4 | 6.6 | 0.0 | 1.5 |
| Clearwater | 0.2 | 5.2 | 1.8 | 0.0 | 0.0 | 17.0 | 20.6 | 15.0 | 0.9 | 2.6 |
| Clermont | 0.0 | 2.6 | 0.0 | 0.0 | 0.2 | 12.9 | 19.0 | 32.0 | 0.5 | 4.2 |
| Coconut Creek | 0.0 | 4.4 | 0.0 | 0.0 | 0.0 | 29.1 | 2.4 | 14.2 | 0.1 | 3.3 |
| Cooper City | 0.0 | 3.6 | 0.1 | 0.0 | 0.0 | 19.8 | 12.4 | 33.7 | 0.0 | 0.7 |
| Coral Gables | 0.0 | 2.5 | 2.6 | 0.0 | 0.0 | 27.7 | 15.8 | 5.4 | 0.5 | 1.8 |
| Coral Springs | 0.0 | 4.3 | 0.0 | 0.0 | 5.5 | 24.5 | 6.1 | 11.2 | 0.0 | 1.8 |
| Cutler Bay | 0.0 | 0.0 | 0.0 | 0.0 | 0.0 | 65.2 | 0.0 | 7.9 | 0.0 | 0.0 |
| Dania Beach | 0.0 | 4.7 | 0.0 | 0.0 | 0.0 | 18.8 | 18.7 | 10.3 | 0.0 | 1.5 |
| Davie | 0.0 | 21.0 | 0.0 | 0.0 | 0.0 | 26.8 | 0.0 | 4.8 | 4.7 | 2.0 |
| Daytona Beach | 0.0 | 11.8 | 0.3 | 0.0 | 0.2 | 27.1 | 18.5 | 8.9 | 2.4 | 3.8 |

# Table D. Cities — City Government Finances, City Government Employment, and Climate

| | City government finances, 2007 (cont.) | | | | Climate[2] | | | | | | |
| | Debt outstanding | | | | Average daily temperature (degrees Fahrenheit) | | | | | | |
| | | | | | Mean | | Limits | | | | |
| City | Total (mil dol) | Per capita[1] (dollars) | Debt issued during year | City government employment, 2011 | January | July | January[3] | July[4] | Annual precipitation (inches) | Heating degree days | Cooling degree days |
| | 137 | 138 | 139 | 140 | 141 | 142 | 143 | 144 | 145 | 146 | 147 |
| COLORADO—Cont'd | | | | | | | | | | | |
| Castle Rock | 48.6 | 1 145 | 9.7 | NA | NA | NA | NA | NA | NA | NA | NA |
| Centennial | 3.1 | 31 | 0.0 | 53 | NA | NA | NA | NA | NA | NA | NA |
| Colorado Springs | 2 004.3 | 5 325 | 144.5 | 6 852 | 28.1 | 69.6 | 14.5 | 84.4 | 17.40 | 6 480 | 404 |
| Commerce City | 154.5 | 3 774 | 122.8 | NA | NA | NA | NA | NA | NA | NA | NA |
| Denver | 5 045.8 | 8 576 | 931.0 | 12 233 | 31.2 | 71.5 | 15.6 | 88.3 | 18.17 | 5 988 | 496 |
| Englewood | 94.0 | 2 889 | 0.1 | 493 | 28.2 | 70.2 | 12.7 | 85.8 | 17.06 | 6 773 | 435 |
| Fort Collins | 240.9 | 1 799 | 1.7 | 1 410 | 28.2 | 71.5 | 14.5 | 86.2 | 13.98 | 6 256 | 524 |
| Fountain | 11.8 | 605 | 0.0 | 215 | NA | NA | NA | NA | NA | NA | NA |
| Grand Junction | 77.9 | 1 609 | 15.3 | 689 | 27.4 | 77.5 | 16.8 | 91.9 | 9.06 | 5 489 | 1 098 |
| Greeley | 166.2 | 1 840 | 25.0 | 977 | 27.8 | 74.0 | 15.6 | 88.7 | 14.22 | 5 980 | 759 |
| Lakewood | 96.2 | 685 | 52.1 | 1 037 | 28.2 | 70.2 | 12.7 | 85.8 | 17.06 | 6 773 | 435 |
| Littleton | 70.9 | 1 745 | 0.0 | NA | 28.2 | 70.2 | 12.7 | 85.8 | 17.06 | 6 773 | 435 |
| Longmont | 72.0 | 847 | 21.0 | 871 | 27.1 | 72.2 | 12.0 | 88.9 | 14.15 | 6 415 | 587 |
| Loveland | 22.3 | 347 | 0.0 | 677 | 28.2 | 71.5 | 14.5 | 86.2 | 13.98 | 6 256 | 524 |
| Northglenn | 22.3 | 666 | 0.0 | NA | 30.0 | 72.0 | 16.2 | 87.9 | 13.25 | 6 074 | 590 |
| Parker | 20.4 | 476 | 17.0 | 274 | NA | NA | NA | NA | NA | NA | NA |
| Pueblo | 112.1 | 1 080 | 19.2 | 862 | 30.8 | 77.0 | 14.7 | 93.8 | 12.60 | 5 346 | 997 |
| Thornton | 211.8 | 1 910 | 0.0 | 842 | 30.0 | 72.0 | 16.2 | 87.9 | 13.25 | 6 074 | 590 |
| Westminster | 275.2 | 2 591 | 52.0 | 976 | 29.2 | 73.4 | 15.2 | 88.0 | 15.81 | 6 128 | 696 |
| Wheat Ridge | 12.5 | 404 | 0.1 | 285 | 31.2 | 71.5 | 15.6 | 88.3 | 18.17 | 5 988 | 496 |
| CONNECTICUT | X | X | X | X | X | X | X | X | X | X | X |
| Bridgeport | 696.7 | 5 097 | 0.0 | 4 234 | 29.9 | 74.0 | 22.9 | 81.9 | 44.15 | 5 466 | 789 |
| Bristol | 59.8 | 981 | 21.6 | 1 688 | 23.4 | 70.5 | 12.6 | 83.3 | 51.03 | 6 825 | 395 |
| Danbury | 124.0 | 1 565 | 31.6 | 1 784 | 26.5 | 72.5 | 17.6 | 83.9 | 51.77 | 6 159 | 597 |
| Hartford | 235.5 | 1 890 | 0.0 | 5 259 | 25.9 | 73.6 | 16.3 | 83.8 | 44.29 | 6 121 | 654 |
| Meriden | 110.9 | 1 872 | 20.2 | 1 674 | 28.3 | 73.4 | 20.3 | 84.2 | 52.35 | 5 791 | 669 |
| Middletown | 41.4 | 866 | 7.9 | 1 602 | 29.9 | 74.0 | 22.9 | 81.9 | 44.15 | 5 466 | 789 |
| Milford | 59.2 | 1 103 | 0.0 | 1 998 | 29.9 | 74.0 | 22.9 | 81.9 | 44.15 | 5 466 | 789 |
| Naugatuck | 90.7 | 2 840 | 0.0 | 888 | 29.9 | 74.0 | 22.9 | 81.9 | 44.15 | 5 466 | 789 |
| New Britain | 244.4 | 3 459 | 13.6 | 2 126 | 28.3 | 73.4 | 20.3 | 84.2 | 52.35 | 5 791 | 669 |
| New Haven | 584.4 | 4 716 | 109.1 | 5 020 | 25.9 | 72.5 | 16.9 | 82.8 | 52.73 | 6 271 | 558 |
| New London | 41.8 | 1 611 | 12.2 | 762 | 28.9 | 71.8 | 20.0 | 80.7 | 48.72 | 5 799 | 511 |
| Norwalk | 236.7 | 2 837 | 25.0 | 2 749 | 27.8 | 73.4 | 18.8 | 84.2 | 48.38 | 5 854 | 652 |
| Norwich | 36.3 | 996 | 0.0 | 988 | 27.6 | 73.2 | 17.3 | 83.8 | 52.78 | 5 916 | 627 |
| Shelton | 60.8 | 1 518 | 27.4 | 931 | 29.9 | 74.0 | 22.9 | 81.9 | 44.15 | 5 466 | 789 |
| Stamford | 493.1 | 4 162 | 0.0 | 3 817 | 28.7 | 73.5 | 19.2 | 85.4 | 52.79 | 5 582 | 692 |
| Torrington | 44.9 | 1 266 | 26.3 | 907 | 23.6 | 69.5 | 13.9 | 80.7 | 54.59 | 6 839 | 323 |
| Waterbury | 177.0 | 1 651 | 27.8 | 4 021 | 25.9 | 72.5 | 16.9 | 82.8 | 52.73 | 6 271 | 558 |
| West Haven | 142.9 | 2 713 | 0.0 | 1 423 | 25.9 | 72.5 | 16.9 | 82.8 | 52.73 | 6 271 | 558 |
| DELAWARE | X | X | X | X | X | X | X | X | X | X | X |
| Dover | 27.4 | 765 | 0.0 | 371 | 35.3 | 77.8 | 26.9 | 87.4 | 46.28 | 4 212 | 1 262 |
| Newark | 19.2 | 639 | 0.0 | 257 | 32.5 | 76.4 | 23.5 | 87.6 | 45.35 | 4 746 | 1 047 |
| Wilmington | 147.8 | 2 028 | 0.0 | 1 263 | 31.5 | 76.6 | 23.7 | 86.0 | 42.81 | 4 888 | 1 125 |
| DISTRICT OF COLUMBIA | X | X | X | X | X | X | X | X | X | X | X |
| Washington | 8 528.4 | 14 497 | 1 853.9 | 32 391 | 34.9 | 79.2 | 27.3 | 88.3 | 39.35 | 4 055 | 1 531 |
| FLORIDA | X | X | X | X | X | X | X | X | X | X | X |
| Altamonte Springs | 6.6 | 163 | 0.0 | NA | 58.7 | 81.5 | 47.0 | 91.9 | 51.31 | 799 | 3 017 |
| Apopka | 29.0 | 775 | 1.5 | NA | 58.7 | 81.5 | 47.0 | 91.9 | 51.31 | 799 | 3 017 |
| Aventura | 35.3 | 1 196 | 0.0 | NA | 67.9 | 82.7 | 62.6 | 87.0 | 46.60 | 141 | 4 090 |
| Boca Raton | 169.8 | 1 989 | 0.0 | 1 388 | 67.2 | 83.3 | 57.8 | 91.8 | 57.27 | 219 | 4 241 |
| Bonita Springs | 32.2 | 762 | 0.0 | NA | 64.3 | 82.0 | 53.4 | 91.2 | 51.90 | 316 | 3 646 |
| Boynton Beach | 99.6 | 1 466 | 11.3 | 813 | 66.2 | 82.5 | 57.3 | 90.1 | 61.39 | 246 | 3 999 |
| Bradenton | 34.4 | 643 | 3.6 | 478 | 61.6 | 81.9 | 50.9 | 91.3 | 54.12 | 538 | 3 327 |
| Cape Coral | 366.9 | 2 337 | 60.4 | 1 434 | 62.7 | 81.3 | 50.3 | 91.3 | 50.07 | 427 | 3 287 |
| Casselberry | 27.7 | 1 118 | 0.0 | NA | NA | NA | NA | NA | NA | NA | NA |
| Clearwater | 258.6 | 2 425 | 28.8 | 1 664 | 61.3 | 82.5 | 52.4 | 89.7 | 44.77 | 591 | 3 482 |
| Clermont | 28.9 | 2 224 | 5.3 | 264 | NA | NA | NA | NA | NA | NA | NA |
| Coconut Creek | 37.5 | 746 | 0.0 | 334 | 67.2 | 83.3 | 57.8 | 91.8 | 57.27 | 219 | 4 241 |
| Cooper City | 20.7 | 705 | 1.3 | NA | 67.5 | 82.6 | 59.2 | 89.8 | 64.19 | 167 | 4 120 |
| Coral Gables | 60.6 | 1 438 | 6.0 | 748 | 67.9 | 82.7 | 62.6 | 87.0 | 46.60 | 141 | 4 090 |
| Coral Springs | 110.4 | 871 | 0.0 | 835 | 67.2 | 83.3 | 57.8 | 91.8 | 57.27 | 219 | 4 241 |
| Cutler Bay | 2.7 | 92 | 0.0 | NA | NA | NA | NA | NA | NA | NA | NA |
| Dania Beach | 14.5 | 512 | 1.5 | 113 | NA | NA | NA | NA | NA | NA | NA |
| Davie | 110.3 | 1 221 | 41.5 | 621 | 66.2 | 82.5 | 57.3 | 90.1 | 61.39 | 246 | 3 999 |
| Daytona Beach | 181.6 | 2 822 | 0.0 | 911 | 57.1 | 81.2 | 44.5 | 91.2 | 57.03 | 954 | 2 819 |

1. Based on the population estimated as of July 1 of the year shown.   2. Represents normal values based on the 30-year period, 1971–2000.   3. Average daily minimum.   4. Average daily maximum.

# Table D. Cities — **Land Area and Population**

| STATE Place code | City | Land area,[1] 2010 (sq km) | Population, 2012 | | | Race alone or in combination, not of Hispanic origin (percent), 2010 | | | | | Percent Hispanic or Latino[2], 2010 | Percent Foreign born 2007–2011 |
| | | | Total persons | Rank | Per square kilometer | White | Black | American Indian, Alaska Native | Asian | Hawaiian Pacific Islander | | |
| | | 1 | 2 | 3 | 4 | 5 | 6 | 7 | 8 | 9 | 10 | 11 |
| | **FLORIDA—Cont'd** | | | | | | | | | | | |
| 12 16725 | Deerfield Beach | 39.1 | 77 439 | 417 | 1 980.5 | 57.4 | 25.8 | 0.4 | 1.9 | 0.2 | 14.2 | 31.8 |
| 12 16875 | DeLand | 45.6 | 27 447 | 1 321 | 601.9 | 68.4 | 17.5 | 0.8 | 2.1 | 0.1 | 12.7 | 7.6 |
| 12 17100 | Delray Beach | 40.9 | 62 357 | 551 | 1 524.6 | 60.0 | 28.4 | 0.4 | 2.2 | 0.3 | 9.5 | 20.2 |
| 12 17200 | Deltona | 97.2 | 85 442 | 362 | 879.0 | 58.4 | 10.4 | 0.8 | 1.6 | 0.1 | 30.2 | 9.1 |
| 12 17935 | Doral | 35.9 | 48 134 | 770 | 1 340.8 | 15.0 | 1.8 | 0.1 | 3.7 | 0.0 | 79.5 | 60.8 |
| 12 18575 | Dunedin | 26.8 | 35 444 | 1 034 | 1 322.5 | 88.6 | 3.7 | 0.6 | 2.0 | 0.2 | 5.9 | 9.6 |
| 12 24000 | Fort Lauderdale | 90.0 | 170 747 | 139 | 1 897.2 | 53.4 | 31.2 | 0.5 | 1.9 | 0.2 | 13.7 | 21.7 |
| 12 24125 | Fort Myers | 103.5 | 65 725 | 515 | 635.0 | 45.8 | 32.3 | 0.5 | 1.9 | 0.2 | 20.0 | 17.1 |
| 12 24300 | Fort Pierce | 53.3 | 42 645 | 856 | 800.1 | 36.2 | 41.4 | 0.7 | 1.1 | 0.2 | 21.6 | 19.7 |
| 12 25175 | Gainesville | 158.8 | 126 047 | 203 | 793.7 | 59.8 | 23.6 | 0.7 | 7.8 | 0.2 | 10.0 | 12.3 |
| 12 27322 | Greenacres | 15.0 | 38 467 | 950 | 2 564.5 | 41.8 | 16.9 | 0.3 | 3.4 | 0.2 | 38.3 | 34.0 |
| 12 28452 | Hallandale Beach | 10.9 | 38 327 | 956 | 3 516.2 | 48.4 | 18.2 | 0.3 | 1.8 | 0.1 | 31.8 | 44.3 |
| 12 30000 | Hialeah | 55.6 | 231 941 | 88 | 4 171.6 | 4.3 | 0.6 | 0.1 | 0.4 | 0.0 | 94.7 | 73.4 |
| 12 32000 | Hollywood | 70.9 | 145 236 | 173 | 2 048.5 | 48.5 | 16.2 | 0.4 | 2.9 | 0.2 | 32.6 | 32.2 |
| 12 32275 | Homestead | 39.2 | 63 190 | 545 | 1 612.0 | 16.7 | 19.1 | 0.3 | 1.5 | 0.3 | 62.9 | 36.5 |
| 12 35000 | Jacksonville | 1 934.7 | 836 507 | 12 | 432.4 | 56.9 | 31.2 | 0.9 | 5.1 | 0.2 | 7.7 | 9.3 |
| 12 35875 | Jupiter | 55.6 | 57 221 | 621 | 1 029.2 | 83.6 | 1.7 | 0.4 | 2.5 | 0.1 | 12.7 | 13.6 |
| 12 36950 | Kissimmee | 54.9 | 63 369 | 541 | 1 154.3 | 27.2 | 10.3 | 0.4 | 3.7 | 0.2 | 58.9 | 25.1 |
| 12 38250 | Lakeland | 169.1 | 99 999 | 290 | 591.4 | 64.5 | 21.4 | 0.7 | 2.1 | 0.2 | 12.6 | 9.9 |
| 12 39075 | Lake Worth | 15.2 | 35 986 | 1 024 | 2 354.3 | 39.0 | 19.8 | 1.2 | 1.2 | 0.2 | 39.6 | 41.7 |
| 12 39425 | Largo | 45.6 | 77 878 | 414 | 1 707.9 | 82.3 | 6.1 | 0.7 | 3.1 | 0.3 | 9.0 | 12.0 |
| 12 39525 | Lauderdale Lakes | 9.5 | 33 772 | 1 081 | 3 554.9 | 12.0 | 81.3 | 0.5 | 1.7 | 0.6 | 5.4 | 48.1 |
| 12 39550 | Lauderhill | 22.1 | 69 100 | 485 | 3 126.7 | 14.5 | 76.4 | 0.4 | 2.2 | 0.4 | 7.4 | 35.7 |
| 12 43125 | Margate | 22.9 | 55 026 | 652 | 2 402.9 | 47.2 | 26.1 | 0.4 | 4.7 | 0.3 | 22.2 | 30.5 |
| 12 43975 | Melbourne | 87.7 | 77 048 | 426 | 878.5 | 77.3 | 11.0 | 0.9 | 4.0 | 0.2 | 8.9 | 9.5 |
| 12 45000 | Miami | 92.9 | 413 892 | 44 | 4 455.2 | 12.3 | 16.7 | 0.2 | 1.2 | 0.1 | 70.0 | 58.4 |
| 12 45025 | Miami Beach | 19.8 | 90 588 | 335 | 4 575.2 | 41.4 | 3.5 | 0.3 | 2.2 | 0.1 | 53.0 | 51.1 |
| 12 45060 | Miami Gardens | 47.2 | 110 754 | 240 | 2 346.5 | 3.0 | 74.4 | 0.3 | 0.8 | 0.3 | 22.0 | 29.0 |
| 12 45100 | Miami Lakes | 14.6 | 30 396 | 1 199 | 2 081.9 | 14.8 | 2.6 | 0.1 | 1.6 | 0.0 | 81.1 | 49.8 |
| 12 45975 | Miramar | 76.5 | 128 729 | 194 | 1 682.7 | 12.6 | 45.0 | 0.3 | 6.0 | 0.3 | 36.9 | 42.5 |
| 12 49425 | North Lauderdale | 11.9 | 42 413 | 860 | 3 564.1 | 17.2 | 53.8 | 0.4 | 3.7 | 0.4 | 25.8 | 42.4 |
| 12 49450 | North Miami | 21.8 | 60 565 | 579 | 2 778.2 | 12.9 | 58.0 | 0.5 | 2.1 | 0.5 | 27.1 | 50.5 |
| 12 49475 | North Miami Beach | 12.5 | 42 971 | 849 | 3 437.7 | 19.1 | 40.6 | 0.4 | 3.9 | 0.6 | 36.6 | 51.7 |
| 12 49675 | North Port | 257.9 | 58 378 | 605 | 226.4 | 82.9 | 7.6 | 0.6 | 1.4 | 0.1 | 8.7 | 11.2 |
| 12 50575 | Oakland Park | 19.3 | 42 832 | 852 | 2 219.3 | 46.3 | 26.1 | 0.5 | 2.5 | 0.3 | 25.6 | 29.9 |
| 12 50750 | Ocala | 116.1 | 56 945 | 626 | 490.5 | 64.6 | 21.3 | 0.7 | 3.0 | 0.1 | 11.7 | 8.0 |
| 12 51075 | Ocoee | 38.1 | 38 354 | 954 | 1 006.7 | 54.9 | 17.8 | 0.6 | 6.5 | 0.3 | 20.8 | 17.8 |
| 12 53000 | Orlando | 265.2 | 249 562 | 77 | 941.0 | 42.8 | 27.8 | 0.6 | 4.4 | 0.2 | 25.4 | 18.8 |
| 12 53150 | Ormond Beach | 82.7 | 38 376 | 951 | 464.0 | 90.0 | 3.6 | 0.6 | 2.7 | 0.1 | 4.1 | 7.8 |
| 12 53575 | Oviedo | 39.4 | 35 291 | 1 036 | 895.7 | 71.1 | 8.7 | 0.5 | 4.7 | 0.1 | 16.3 | 9.1 |
| 12 54000 | Palm Bay | 170.2 | 104 124 | 272 | 611.8 | 66.0 | 18.5 | 0.8 | 2.5 | 0.2 | 14.1 | 14.5 |
| 12 54075 | Palm Beach Gardens | 142.7 | 49 889 | 730 | 349.6 | 83.2 | 4.8 | 0.3 | 3.6 | 0.1 | 8.9 | 15.9 |
| 12 54200 | Palm Coast | 232.8 | 77 374 | 419 | 332.4 | 74.3 | 13.2 | 0.6 | 3.0 | 0.2 | 10.0 | 15.3 |
| 12 54700 | Panama City | 75.8 | 36 167 | 1 010 | 477.1 | 70.6 | 22.9 | 1.2 | 2.3 | 0.2 | 5.1 | 6.0 |
| 12 55775 | Pembroke Pines | 85.8 | 160 306 | 148 | 1 868.4 | 34.0 | 19.5 | 0.3 | 5.7 | 0.2 | 41.4 | 36.4 |
| 12 55925 | Pensacola | 58.4 | 52 340 | 689 | 896.2 | 65.9 | 28.6 | 1.2 | 2.6 | 0.2 | 3.3 | 5.4 |
| 12 56975 | Pinellas Park | 40.2 | 49 686 | 735 | 1 236.0 | 76.9 | 5.1 | 0.8 | 7.9 | 0.2 | 10.7 | 14.8 |
| 12 57425 | Plantation | 56.3 | 88 016 | 346 | 1 563.3 | 55.0 | 20.6 | 0.4 | 4.8 | 0.2 | 20.4 | 26.5 |
| 12 57550 | Plant City | 70.4 | 35 903 | 1 018 | 510.0 | 54.6 | 15.2 | 0.7 | 1.8 | 0.1 | 28.8 | 16.6 |
| 12 58050 | Pompano Beach | 62.2 | 102 984 | 276 | 1 655.7 | 51.7 | 29.0 | 0.4 | 1.6 | 0.2 | 17.5 | 25.2 |
| 12 58575 | Port Orange | 69.1 | 56 766 | 632 | 821.5 | 89.5 | 3.7 | 0.7 | 2.8 | 0.1 | 4.5 | 7.2 |
| 12 58716 | Port St. Lucie | 295.1 | 168 716 | 142 | 571.7 | 63.0 | 16.7 | 0.6 | 2.5 | 0.2 | 18.4 | 17.6 |
| 12 60975 | Riviera Beach | 22.1 | 33 129 | 1 101 | 1 499.0 | 23.8 | 66.3 | 0.6 | 2.7 | 0.3 | 7.4 | 15.4 |
| 12 62100 | Royal Palm Beach | 29.0 | 35 162 | 1 040 | 1 212.5 | 52.5 | 22.9 | 0.4 | 5.0 | 0.2 | 20.4 | 20.7 |
| 12 62625 | St. Cloud | 46.0 | 39 171 | 931 | 851.5 | 63.5 | 5.4 | 0.6 | 2.3 | 0.2 | 29.2 | 10.4 |
| 12 63000 | St. Petersburg | 159.9 | 246 541 | 78 | 1 541.8 | 65.9 | 24.5 | 0.7 | 3.8 | 0.1 | 6.6 | 10.2 |
| 12 63650 | Sanford | 59.5 | 54 651 | 661 | 918.5 | 46.5 | 30.5 | 0.9 | 3.3 | 0.2 | 20.2 | 11.3 |
| 12 64175 | Sarasota | 38.0 | 52 811 | 682 | 1 389.8 | 66.9 | 15.4 | 0.6 | 1.7 | 0.1 | 16.6 | 17.1 |
| 12 69700 | Sunrise | 46.9 | 88 843 | 342 | 1 894.3 | 37.9 | 32.1 | 0.4 | 4.8 | 0.3 | 25.6 | 37.5 |
| 12 70600 | Tallahassee | 259.6 | 186 971 | 125 | 720.2 | 54.9 | 35.5 | 0.7 | 4.2 | 0.1 | 6.3 | 8.0 |
| 12 70675 | Tamarac | 30.1 | 62 557 | 549 | 2 078.3 | 49.9 | 23.2 | 0.3 | 3.1 | 0.2 | 24.3 | 29.6 |
| 12 71000 | Tampa | 293.7 | 347 645 | 53 | 1 183.7 | 47.9 | 25.8 | 0.6 | 4.1 | 0.2 | 23.1 | 14.9 |
| 12 71900 | Titusville | 76.1 | 43 940 | 827 | 577.4 | 78.2 | 14.1 | 1.1 | 1.8 | 0.2 | 6.5 | 6.0 |
| 12 75812 | Wellington | 116.3 | 58 679 | 600 | 504.5 | 66.1 | 10.8 | 0.3 | 4.6 | 0.2 | 19.4 | 18.7 |
| 12 76582 | Weston | 65.2 | 67 641 | 497 | 1 037.4 | 45.9 | 4.5 | 0.3 | 5.2 | 0.1 | 44.9 | 40.2 |
| 12 76600 | West Palm Beach | 143.2 | 101 903 | 279 | 711.6 | 42.6 | 32.5 | 0.5 | 2.7 | 0.3 | 22.6 | 27.3 |
| 12 78250 | Winter Garden | 39.9 | 37 063 | 981 | 928.9 | 55.6 | 16.4 | 0.5 | 6.1 | 0.3 | 22.0 | 16.2 |
| 12 78275 | Winter Haven | 81.1 | 34 975 | 1 044 | 431.3 | 59.2 | 27.9 | 0.5 | 2.3 | 0.2 | 11.0 | 10.6 |
| 12 78300 | Winter Park | 22.5 | 28 924 | 1 260 | 1 285.5 | 83.0 | 7.9 | 0.5 | 2.9 | 0.1 | 7.0 | 7.6 |
| 12 78325 | Winter Springs | 38.0 | 33 540 | 1 087 | 882.6 | 76.9 | 5.8 | 0.6 | 3.0 | 0.1 | 15.0 | 10.7 |

1. Dry land or land partially or temporarily covered by water.    2. May be of any race.

| City | Age of population (percent), 2010 | | | | | | | | | | | Population | | | |
|---|---|---|---|---|---|---|---|---|---|---|---|---|---|---|---|
| | | | | | | | | | | | | Census counts | | Percent change | |
| | Under 5 years | 5 to 17 years | 18 to 24 years | 25 to 34 years | 35 to 44 years | 45 to 54 years | 55 to 64 years | 65 to 74 years | 75 years and over | Median age | Percent female | 2000 | 2010 | 2000–2010 | 2010–2012 |
| | 12 | 13 | 14 | 15 | 16 | 17 | 18 | 19 | 20 | 21 | 22 | 23 | 24 | 25 | 26 |
| FLORIDA—Cont'd | | | | | | | | | | | | | | | |
| Deerfield Beach............. | 5.6 | 12.4 | 7.6 | 13.8 | 12.9 | 14.2 | 12.1 | 9.9 | 11.6 | 43.3 | 51.7 | 64 583 | 75 018 | 16.2 | 3.2 |
| DeLand........................ | 6.2 | 14.8 | 13.5 | 10.7 | 11.3 | 12.0 | 11.1 | 8.7 | 11.7 | 39.1 | 54.6 | 20 904 | 27 029 | 29.3 | 1.5 |
| Delray Beach................ | 4.7 | 11.4 | 8.0 | 12.4 | 12.1 | 14.4 | 13.3 | 10.2 | 13.5 | 46.0 | 51.9 | 60 020 | 60 580 | 0.8 | 2.9 |
| Deltona....................... | 6.2 | 19.0 | 8.6 | 12.4 | 13.9 | 15.3 | 11.5 | 7.1 | 5.9 | 37.8 | 51.3 | 69 543 | 85 182 | 22.5 | 0.3 |
| Doral.......................... | 7.7 | 20.6 | 8.4 | 15.4 | 20.6 | 14.1 | 7.3 | 4.0 | 2.1 | 34.0 | 51.9 | 20 438 | 45 709 | 123.6 | 5.3 |
| Dunedin....................... | 3.7 | 11.1 | 5.7 | 9.0 | 10.8 | 15.6 | 16.1 | 12.9 | 15.0 | 51.3 | 53.6 | 35 691 | 35 321 | -1.0 | 0.3 |
| Fort Lauderdale............ | 5.2 | 12.4 | 8.1 | 14.4 | 14.0 | 16.6 | 14.0 | 8.4 | 6.9 | 42.2 | 47.2 | 152 397 | 165 504 | 8.6 | 3.2 |
| Fort Myers.................... | 7.3 | 15.4 | 10.8 | 15.4 | 12.9 | 12.6 | 11.2 | 7.8 | 6.6 | 35.8 | 49.9 | 48 208 | 62 292 | 29.2 | 5.5 |
| Fort Pierce................... | 8.2 | 17.7 | 10.5 | 12.8 | 11.5 | 13.2 | 10.9 | 7.8 | 7.5 | 35.7 | 50.7 | 37 516 | 41 852 | 10.9 | 1.9 |
| Gainesville................... | 4.4 | 8.9 | 36.8 | 16.9 | 8.1 | 8.5 | 8.0 | 4.1 | 4.2 | 24.9 | 51.6 | 95 447 | 124 364 | 30.3 | 1.4 |
| Greenacres................... | 7.3 | 17.5 | 8.8 | 14.5 | 14.3 | 11.9 | 9.3 | 7.6 | 8.9 | 36.3 | 52.5 | 27 569 | 37 578 | 36.3 | 2.4 |
| Hallandale Beach......... | 5.2 | 10.2 | 6.5 | 12.7 | 13.2 | 13.5 | 13.7 | 12.0 | 13.1 | 46.7 | 52.5 | 34 282 | 37 113 | 8.3 | 3.3 |
| Hialeah....................... | 5.0 | 14.2 | 9.1 | 11.2 | 15.1 | 15.0 | 11.2 | 9.9 | 9.2 | 42.2 | 51.7 | 226 419 | 224 667 | -0.8 | 3.2 |
| Hollywood.................... | 5.9 | 14.4 | 7.9 | 13.1 | 14.7 | 16.3 | 12.7 | 7.7 | 7.4 | 41.1 | 51.0 | 139 357 | 140 769 | 1.0 | 3.2 |
| Homestead................... | 10.5 | 20.7 | 10.8 | 19.0 | 15.1 | 10.6 | 6.8 | 3.7 | 2.8 | 29.1 | 49.6 | 31 909 | 60 509 | 89.6 | 4.4 |
| Jacksonville................. | 7.0 | 16.9 | 10.5 | 14.9 | 13.6 | 14.8 | 11.4 | 6.1 | 4.9 | 35.5 | 51.5 | 735 617 | 821 784 | 11.7 | 1.8 |
| Jupiter........................ | 4.5 | 14.9 | 6.6 | 11.2 | 13.2 | 16.1 | 13.6 | 10.4 | 9.6 | 44.7 | 50.3 | 39 328 | 55 276 | 40.2 | 3.5 |
| Kissimmee.................... | 7.4 | 18.3 | 11.2 | 15.2 | 14.6 | 14.0 | 9.8 | 5.8 | 3.6 | 33.5 | 51.4 | 47 814 | 59 649 | 24.8 | 6.2 |
| Lakeland...................... | 6.2 | 14.8 | 11.4 | 12.3 | 10.9 | 12.0 | 11.7 | 9.8 | 10.9 | 39.8 | 53.1 | 78 452 | 97 430 | 24.2 | 2.6 |
| Lake Worth.................. | 7.4 | 14.8 | 11.0 | 16.8 | 14.3 | 14.3 | 10.2 | 5.9 | 5.4 | 35.0 | 46.0 | 35 133 | 34 910 | -0.6 | 2.5 |
| Largo.......................... | 4.5 | 11.1 | 7.1 | 11.4 | 11.2 | 14.5 | 14.1 | 12.3 | 13.7 | 48.2 | 52.8 | 69 371 | 77 849 | 11.9 | 0.0 |
| Lauderdale Lakes.......... | 7.0 | 17.7 | 9.9 | 12.4 | 11.8 | 13.4 | 12.1 | 8.6 | 7.0 | 37.6 | 54.1 | 31 705 | 32 653 | 2.8 | 3.4 |
| Lauderhill.................... | 7.7 | 17.9 | 10.0 | 13.8 | 13.2 | 13.8 | 10.7 | 6.5 | 6.4 | 35.5 | 54.2 | 57 585 | 66 887 | 16.2 | 3.3 |
| Margate...................... | 5.7 | 14.7 | 7.9 | 12.2 | 13.2 | 14.4 | 12.8 | 9.6 | 9.5 | 42.3 | 53.2 | 53 909 | 53 284 | -1.2 | 3.3 |
| Melbourne ................... | 5.1 | 13.1 | 10.3 | 12.3 | 11.1 | 15.5 | 12.5 | 9.4 | 10.5 | 43.3 | 51.5 | 71 382 | 76 201 | 6.6 | 1.1 |
| Miami......................... | 6.0 | 12.4 | 9.4 | 16.5 | 14.9 | 14.0 | 10.8 | 8.0 | 8.0 | 38.8 | 50.2 | 362 470 | 399 508 | 10.2 | 3.6 |
| Miami Beach................ | 4.2 | 8.5 | 7.4 | 19.8 | 18.1 | 14.7 | 11.0 | 7.8 | 8.4 | 40.3 | 47.6 | 87 933 | 87 784 | -0.2 | 3.2 |
| Miami Gardens............. | 6.9 | 20.0 | 11.9 | 13.0 | 12.9 | 13.2 | 10.9 | 6.9 | 4.3 | 33.5 | 53.2 | NA | 107 163 | NA | 3.4 |
| Miami Lakes................ | 5.1 | 18.0 | 9.1 | 11.8 | 16.1 | 16.6 | 10.3 | 7.3 | 5.9 | 38.9 | 52.8 | 22 676 | 29 364 | 29.5 | 3.5 |
| Miramar...................... | 7.4 | 21.6 | 9.5 | 13.6 | 17.1 | 15.1 | 8.7 | 4.3 | 2.6 | 33.6 | 52.8 | 72 739 | 122 041 | 67.8 | 5.5 |
| North Lauderdale ......... | 8.2 | 20.7 | 10.9 | 17.0 | 14.7 | 13.5 | 8.5 | 4.0 | 2.5 | 30.9 | 52.2 | 32 264 | 41 055 | 27.1 | 3.3 |
| North Miami................. | 6.9 | 16.9 | 12.8 | 14.3 | 13.6 | 14.4 | 11.2 | 5.8 | 4.3 | 34.4 | 51.9 | 59 880 | 58 763 | -1.8 | 3.1 |
| North Miami Beach ....... | 6.4 | 17.1 | 10.6 | 14.2 | 13.4 | 15.5 | 11.6 | 6.2 | 5.0 | 36.4 | 52.1 | 40 786 | 41 523 | 1.8 | 3.5 |
| North Port.................... | 6.2 | 18.0 | 6.6 | 11.2 | 13.5 | 13.7 | 13.0 | 10.7 | 7.1 | 40.9 | 51.2 | 22 797 | 57 337 | 151.6 | 1.8 |
| Oakland Park ............... | 6.3 | 13.9 | 8.4 | 15.4 | 16.2 | 18.2 | 11.9 | 5.7 | 4.0 | 38.8 | 46.5 | 30 966 | 41 389 | 33.6 | 3.5 |
| Ocala.......................... | 7.0 | 15.4 | 10.5 | 13.3 | 12.3 | 13.5 | 10.7 | 7.8 | 9.4 | 38.2 | 52.4 | 45 943 | 56 324 | 22.6 | 1.1 |
| Ocoee......................... | 7.1 | 20.6 | 8.5 | 13.1 | 16.4 | 15.6 | 10.0 | 4.9 | 3.7 | 35.4 | 51.2 | 24 391 | 35 731 | 45.9 | 7.3 |
| Orlando....................... | 7.1 | 14.9 | 11.2 | 20.6 | 15.1 | 12.8 | 9.0 | 4.9 | 4.5 | 32.8 | 51.4 | 185 951 | 238 304 | 28.2 | 4.7 |
| Ormond Beach.............. | 3.7 | 13.5 | 6.0 | 7.4 | 10.7 | 15.6 | 15.8 | 12.9 | 14.3 | 50.7 | 52.8 | 36 301 | 38 164 | 5.1 | 0.6 |
| Oviedo........................ | 5.6 | 22.6 | 10.8 | 10.6 | 15.9 | 17.6 | 9.5 | 4.3 | 3.1 | 35.3 | 50.8 | 26 316 | 33 468 | 26.7 | 5.4 |
| Palm Bay..................... | 6.2 | 17.7 | 8.6 | 11.8 | 12.3 | 15.8 | 12.2 | 8.4 | 6.9 | 39.8 | 51.7 | 79 413 | 103 190 | 29.9 | 0.9 |
| Palm Beach Gardens.... | 4.4 | 12.0 | 5.4 | 11.6 | 12.1 | 14.1 | 15.2 | 13.3 | 12.0 | 48.3 | 53.1 | 35 058 | 48 454 | 38.2 | 3.0 |
| Palm Coast.................. | 5.4 | 16.1 | 6.4 | 10.1 | 11.9 | 12.8 | 14.4 | 13.3 | 9.7 | 45.1 | 52.2 | 32 732 | 75 197 | 129.7 | 2.9 |
| Panama City................ | 6.2 | 14.5 | 10.2 | 13.7 | 12.2 | 14.8 | 12.1 | 7.5 | 8.8 | 39.7 | 50.9 | 36 417 | 35 505 | 0.2 | 1.9 |
| Pembroke Pines............ | 5.7 | 18.1 | 8.4 | 11.7 | 14.7 | 15.9 | 10.7 | 6.8 | 8.0 | 39.5 | 53.8 | 137 427 | 154 750 | 12.6 | 3.6 |
| Pensacola.................... | 5.5 | 14.1 | 9.3 | 12.7 | 11.2 | 15.3 | 14.3 | 8.6 | 9.1 | 42.6 | 52.6 | 56 255 | 51 923 | -7.7 | 0.8 |
| Pinellas Park................ | 5.3 | 14.2 | 7.6 | 12.7 | 13.2 | 15.4 | 13.0 | 9.8 | 8.8 | 42.7 | 51.4 | 45 658 | 49 120 | 7.5 | 1.2 |
| Plantation.................... | 5.8 | 15.6 | 7.9 | 14.0 | 14.4 | 15.7 | 13.0 | 7.2 | 6.2 | 39.7 | 52.6 | 82 934 | 84 877 | 2.4 | 3.7 |
| Plant City.................... | 8.1 | 20.2 | 9.7 | 14.1 | 13.2 | 13.0 | 10.3 | 6.4 | 5.0 | 33.3 | 51.6 | 29 915 | 34 682 | 16.1 | 3.5 |
| Pompano Beach............ | 5.7 | 12.6 | 8.4 | 13.3 | 13.3 | 15.5 | 12.3 | 8.6 | 10.3 | 42.7 | 49.0 | 78 191 | 99 844 | 27.7 | 3.1 |
| Port Orange................. | 4.2 | 13.9 | 8.1 | 10.1 | 11.2 | 14.8 | 15.2 | 11.8 | 10.7 | 46.9 | 51.8 | 45 823 | 56 505 | 22.3 | 0.5 |
| Port St. Lucie .............. | 6.2 | 18.3 | 7.5 | 11.4 | 14.1 | 14.8 | 11.9 | 8.8 | 7.0 | 39.8 | 51.4 | 88 769 | 164 640 | 85.4 | 2.5 |
| Riviera Beach............... | 7.2 | 17.8 | 9.9 | 12.1 | 12.8 | 14.0 | 11.4 | 8.3 | 6.6 | 37.5 | 52.2 | 29 884 | 32 488 | 8.7 | 2.0 |
| Royal Palm Beach ........ | 6.4 | 20.7 | 8.6 | 10.8 | 15.2 | 16.7 | 10.8 | 5.6 | 5.2 | 37.7 | 52.2 | 21 523 | 34 140 | 58.6 | 3.0 |
| St. Cloud..................... | 6.8 | 19.4 | 8.6 | 12.9 | 14.4 | 14.3 | 10.3 | 7.1 | 6.2 | 36.8 | 52.1 | 20 074 | 36 035 | 75.3 | 8.7 |
| St. Petersburg ............. | 5.4 | 14.1 | 8.7 | 12.9 | 13.5 | 16.3 | 13.4 | 7.9 | 7.8 | 41.6 | 51.9 | 248 232 | 244 769 | -1.4 | 0.7 |
| Sanford....................... | 8.0 | 18.1 | 11.2 | 16.9 | 13.7 | 13.3 | 9.6 | 5.0 | 4.3 | 32.4 | 52.0 | 38 291 | 53 653 | 39.9 | 1.9 |
| Sarasota...................... | 5.2 | 11.7 | 10.7 | 11.7 | 11.3 | 13.7 | 13.3 | 10.4 | 12.1 | 44.5 | 51.4 | 52 715 | 52 006 | -1.5 | 1.5 |
| Sunrise........................ | 6.0 | 16.4 | 8.6 | 13.3 | 14.4 | 14.9 | 11.3 | 6.9 | 8.2 | 39.1 | 53.5 | 85 779 | 84 439 | -1.6 | 5.2 |
| Tallahassee.................. | 5.5 | 11.7 | 30.0 | 16.3 | 10.0 | 9.7 | 8.6 | 4.3 | 3.8 | 26.1 | 52.9 | 150 624 | 181 382 | 20.4 | 3.1 |
| Tamarac...................... | 5.0 | 11.6 | 6.0 | 12.2 | 12.3 | 12.5 | 12.9 | 10.9 | 16.5 | 47.1 | 55.4 | 55 588 | 60 506 | 8.7 | 3.4 |
| Tampa......................... | 6.4 | 16.2 | 12.5 | 15.4 | 14.0 | 14.2 | 10.4 | 5.8 | 5.1 | 34.6 | 51.1 | 303 447 | 335 709 | 10.6 | 3.6 |
| Titusville...................... | 5.7 | 14.9 | 8.0 | 11.1 | 11.2 | 15.6 | 12.9 | 10.3 | 10.2 | 44.3 | 51.9 | 40 670 | 43 761 | 7.6 | 0.4 |
| Wellington.................... | 5.1 | 21.9 | 7.8 | 8.8 | 15.1 | 18.1 | 12.6 | 6.3 | 4.2 | 39.9 | 51.8 | 38 216 | 56 712 | 47.9 | 3.5 |
| Weston ....................... | 5.4 | 25.3 | 7.6 | 7.8 | 18.0 | 18.7 | 9.2 | 4.6 | 3.4 | 37.9 | 51.5 | 49 286 | 65 333 | 32.6 | 3.5 |
| West Palm Beach ......... | 6.4 | 13.5 | 10.2 | 15.9 | 13.0 | 13.3 | 11.8 | 8.4 | 7.6 | 38.1 | 51.3 | 82 103 | 99 923 | 21.7 | 2.0 |
| Winter Garden.............. | 7.8 | 20.3 | 7.9 | 14.4 | 16.9 | 13.9 | 9.2 | 5.1 | 4.5 | 34.7 | 51.6 | 14 351 | 34 684 | 140.9 | 6.9 |
| Winter Haven ............... | 6.5 | 15.8 | 7.9 | 11.8 | 10.9 | 12.2 | 12.6 | 10.8 | 11.5 | 42.3 | 53.7 | 26 487 | 33 874 | 27.9 | 3.3 |
| Winter Park.................. | 4.3 | 14.0 | 11.3 | 9.8 | 11.4 | 15.4 | 13.8 | 8.7 | 11.2 | 44.3 | 53.2 | 24 090 | 27 852 | 15.6 | 3.8 |
| Winter Springs............. | 4.4 | 18.1 | 8.3 | 10.7 | 13.2 | 17.7 | 14.2 | 7.5 | 5.9 | 41.8 | 52.1 | 31 666 | 33 282 | 5.1 | 0.8 |

# Table D. Cities — Households, Group Quarters, Crime, and Education

| City | Households, 2010 Number | Persons per house-hold | Percent Female family house-holder[1] | Percent One-person | Persons in group quarters, 2010 Total | Institutional Total | Persons in nursing facilities | Non-institutional | Serious crimes known to police,[2] 2011 Total Number | Rate[3] | Rate[3] Violent | Property | Population age 25 and older | Attainment[4] (percent) High school graduate or less | Bachelor's degree or more |
|---|---|---|---|---|---|---|---|---|---|---|---|---|---|---|---|
| | 27 | 28 | 29 | 30 | 31 | 32 | 33 | 34 | 35 | 36 | 37 | 38 | 39 | 40 | 41 |
| **FLORIDA—Cont'd** | | | | | | | | | | | | | | | |
| Deerfield Beach | 33 370 | 2.22 | 12.7 | 37.0 | 1 046 | 863 | 229 | 183 | 2 781 | 3 657 | 481 | 3 176 | 55 926 | 52.5 | 21.6 |
| DeLand | 10 746 | 2.29 | 14.9 | 35.1 | 2 377 | 595 | 587 | 1 782 | 1 575 | 5 748 | 507 | 5 241 | 17 284 | 43.8 | 25.6 |
| Delray Beach | 27 193 | 2.18 | 10.6 | 38.3 | 1 114 | 584 | 539 | 530 | 3 787 | 6 173 | 919 | 5 254 | 45 877 | 36.4 | 34.8 |
| Deltona | 30 223 | 2.81 | 15.3 | 18.1 | 166 | 127 | 127 | 39 | NA | NA | NA | NA | 56 492 | 50.5 | 13.8 |
| Doral | 15 244 | 3.00 | 15.5 | 14.9 | 6 | 0 | 0 | 6 | 2 402 | 5 185 | 168 | 5 017 | 26 903 | 21.0 | 55.8 |
| Dunedin | 17 618 | 1.98 | 9.5 | 39.9 | 385 | 344 | 338 | 41 | 1 029 | 2 874 | 316 | 2 559 | 27 840 | 39.4 | 26.6 |
| Fort Lauderdale | 74 786 | 2.17 | 12.3 | 39.4 | 3 418 | 1 861 | 324 | 1 557 | 11 757 | 7 008 | 933 | 6 075 | 122 812 | 40.4 | 32.7 |
| Fort Myers | 24 968 | 2.37 | 17.9 | 33.1 | 3 236 | 2 520 | 598 | 716 | 3 788 | 5 999 | 1 219 | 4 779 | 41 607 | 51.9 | 21.3 |
| Fort Pierce | 15 850 | 2.59 | 20.6 | 30.6 | 577 | 455 | 314 | 122 | 3 071 | 7 285 | 1 143 | 6 141 | 26 922 | 63.9 | 12.8 |
| Gainesville | 51 029 | 2.19 | 12.4 | 34.5 | 12 493 | 1 796 | 748 | 10 697 | 6 268 | 4 973 | 724 | 4 249 | 59 653 | 29.8 | 43.4 |
| Greenacres | 14 384 | 2.61 | 16.5 | 27.9 | 51 | 5 | 5 | 46 | 1 386 | 3 639 | 570 | 3 069 | 25 788 | 49.9 | 20.6 |
| Hallandale Beach | 18 301 | 2.02 | 12.4 | 40.9 | 101 | 0 | 0 | 101 | 2 242 | 5 960 | 845 | 5 114 | 28 317 | 47.2 | 25.0 |
| Hialeah | 71 205 | 3.13 | 20.1 | 16.4 | 1 493 | 727 | 700 | 766 | 8 353 | 3 668 | 378 | 3 290 | 163 231 | 66.3 | 13.4 |
| Hollywood | 58 438 | 2.39 | 14.3 | 32.3 | 1 203 | 608 | 476 | 595 | 8 449 | 5 921 | 463 | 5 459 | 99 688 | 43.7 | 28.3 |
| Homestead | 18 996 | 3.16 | 22.6 | 18.1 | 450 | 227 | 223 | 223 | 4 281 | 6 979 | 1 577 | 5 403 | 32 679 | 56.1 | 18.4 |
| Jacksonville | 323 106 | 2.48 | 17.1 | 28.2 | 19 747 | 8 158 | 3 155 | 11 589 | 41 295 | 4 949 | 621 | 4 328 | 533 912 | 43.0 | 24.2 |
| Jupiter | 23 920 | 2.29 | 9.4 | 29.6 | 393 | 131 | 131 | 262 | 1 259 | 2 252 | 261 | 1 991 | 39 763 | 31.0 | 41.9 |
| Kissimmee | 20 726 | 2.85 | 21.1 | 20.0 | 595 | 317 | 54 | 278 | 3 957 | 6 541 | 980 | 5 561 | 37 351 | 54.3 | 14.4 |
| Lakeland | 40 758 | 2.29 | 15.2 | 32.8 | 4 126 | 1 140 | 1 094 | 2 986 | 5 695 | 5 767 | 555 | 5 212 | 66 690 | 48.3 | 23.5 |
| Lake Worth | 12 958 | 2.65 | 13.1 | 33.1 | 618 | 518 | 409 | 100 | 2 250 | 6 358 | 1 125 | 5 234 | 23 757 | 59.8 | 19.4 |
| Largo | 38 022 | 2.02 | 11.2 | 39.6 | 1 026 | 941 | 836 | 85 | 3 421 | 4 347 | 474 | 3 873 | 60 079 | 50.0 | 19.2 |
| Lauderdale Lakes | 11 891 | 2.71 | 26.1 | 27.5 | 392 | 387 | 363 | 5 | 2 085 | 6 311 | 1 035 | 5 276 | 21 970 | 57.5 | 16.2 |
| Lauderhill | 24 826 | 2.67 | 25.9 | 28.2 | 592 | 225 | 225 | 367 | 3 712 | 5 475 | 944 | 4 531 | 43 074 | 50.0 | 19.5 |
| Margate | 21 483 | 2.47 | 14.2 | 30.8 | 169 | 6 | 6 | 163 | 1 419 | 2 627 | 265 | 2 363 | 38 522 | 50.9 | 22.0 |
| Melbourne | 34 040 | 2.17 | 13.4 | 35.7 | 2 125 | 746 | 713 | 1 379 | 4 760 | 6 173 | 973 | 5 201 | 55 335 | 39.9 | 26.3 |
| Miami | 158 317 | 2.47 | 18.1 | 33.3 | 8 161 | 5 133 | 1 526 | 3 028 | 27 770 | 6 858 | 1 198 | 5 661 | 283 881 | 59.9 | 22.4 |
| Miami Beach | 47 168 | 1.84 | 8.4 | 49.0 | 1 026 | 534 | 473 | 492 | 10 472 | 11 770 | 997 | 10 773 | 68 424 | 34.0 | 42.9 |
| Miami Gardens | 32 219 | 3.28 | 32.3 | 17.6 | 1 367 | 64 | 11 | 1 303 | 6 396 | 5 888 | 920 | 4 968 | 65 695 | 58.6 | 15.1 |
| Miami Lakes | 10 253 | 2.86 | 14.6 | 19.3 | 28 | 0 | 0 | 28 | 706 | 2 372 | 235 | 2 137 | 19 276 | 32.2 | 34.1 |
| Miramar | 37 420 | 3.26 | 22.2 | 13.5 | 87 | 24 | 11 | 63 | 3 722 | 3 009 | 416 | 2 593 | 71 926 | 35.5 | 32.8 |
| North Lauderdale | 12 977 | 3.16 | 25.0 | 18.8 | 31 | 0 | 0 | 31 | 1 454 | 3 497 | 560 | 2 936 | 24 767 | 57.8 | 14.0 |
| North Miami | 19 275 | 2.96 | 21.8 | 25.2 | 1 640 | 539 | 539 | 1 101 | 3 665 | 6 151 | 1 015 | 5 135 | 36 545 | 56.6 | 17.9 |
| North Miami Beach | 14 412 | 2.86 | 21.0 | 25.1 | 236 | 151 | 148 | 85 | 2 311 | 5 491 | 753 | 4 738 | 27 671 | 51.0 | 22.8 |
| North Port | 22 431 | 2.55 | 11.2 | 21.6 | 119 | 100 | 100 | 19 | 1 533 | 2 637 | 275 | 2 362 | 37 449 | 46.5 | 16.7 |
| Oakland Park | 17 499 | 2.35 | 15.0 | 34.0 | 205 | 19 | 0 | 186 | 2 510 | 5 987 | 775 | 5 211 | 30 430 | 45.6 | 23.3 |
| Ocala | 23 103 | 2.30 | 17.0 | 34.2 | 3 281 | 2 856 | 922 | 425 | 3 512 | 6 153 | 627 | 5 525 | 37 039 | 47.3 | 21.9 |
| Ocoee | 11 792 | 2.99 | 14.6 | 16.3 | 287 | 225 | 225 | 62 | 1 676 | 4 647 | 441 | 4 206 | 22 590 | 41.1 | 27.7 |
| Orlando | 102 521 | 2.29 | 16.9 | 34.6 | 3 294 | 1 227 | 1 009 | 2 067 | 19 736 | 8 171 | 1 073 | 7 098 | 155 968 | 39.5 | 31.9 |
| Ormond Beach | 17 062 | 2.21 | 9.8 | 30.3 | 458 | 434 | 434 | 24 | 1 664 | 4 305 | 691 | 3 614 | 29 261 | 32.5 | 31.1 |
| Oviedo | 11 125 | 2.99 | 12.1 | 12.7 | 103 | 94 | 94 | 9 | 588 | 1 740 | 240 | 1 500 | 19 914 | 26.1 | 39.7 |
| Palm Bay | 39 482 | 2.60 | 15.3 | 23.0 | 430 | 331 | 320 | 99 | 3 340 | 3 193 | 575 | 2 619 | 68 666 | 48.6 | 17.1 |
| Palm Beach Gardens | 22 804 | 2.11 | 8.8 | 31.4 | 235 | 205 | 154 | 30 | 1 760 | 3 584 | 206 | 3 378 | 36 857 | 25.7 | 47.0 |
| Palm Coast | 29 805 | 2.51 | 11.7 | 21.3 | 319 | 282 | 144 | 37 | NA | NA | NA | NA | 52 862 | 43.8 | 21.2 |
| Panama City | 14 792 | 2.28 | 16.8 | 34.1 | 2 782 | 2 453 | 553 | 329 | 2 597 | 7 023 | 854 | 6 168 | 24 432 | 46.0 | 19.8 |
| Pembroke Pines | 56 873 | 2.70 | 15.0 | 24.0 | 1 397 | 1 187 | 125 | 210 | 5 254 | 3 350 | 198 | 3 152 | 106 290 | 36.4 | 31.4 |
| Pensacola | 23 592 | 2.17 | 15.7 | 36.3 | 727 | 284 | 224 | 443 | 3 357 | 6 378 | 728 | 5 651 | 38 069 | 35.6 | 33.9 |
| Pinellas Park | 20 623 | 2.32 | 13.3 | 31.1 | 1 165 | 510 | 337 | 655 | 3 129 | 6 290 | 629 | 5 661 | 36 023 | 50.4 | 18.5 |
| Plantation | 34 190 | 2.47 | 13.6 | 26.3 | 363 | 307 | 304 | 56 | 4 205 | 4 883 | 339 | 4 544 | 59 927 | 28.0 | 42.5 |
| Plant City | 12 239 | 2.82 | 17.5 | 22.2 | 185 | 118 | 118 | 67 | 1 553 | 4 413 | 517 | 3 896 | 21 278 | 56.1 | 17.1 |
| Pompano Beach | 42 182 | 2.27 | 13.3 | 36.7 | 4 267 | 3 680 | 415 | 587 | 6 441 | 6 364 | 906 | 5 458 | 74 212 | 51.9 | 23.4 |
| Port Orange | 24 841 | 2.25 | 10.8 | 29.2 | 167 | 118 | 102 | 49 | 1 523 | 2 681 | 151 | 2 529 | 41 694 | 45.3 | 23.0 |
| Port St. Lucie | 60 902 | 2.69 | 12.9 | 19.5 | 711 | 330 | 322 | 381 | 4 232 | 2 536 | 222 | 2 314 | 107 940 | 50.4 | 18.0 |
| Riviera Beach | 12 380 | 2.60 | 24.3 | 28.2 | 323 | 134 | 134 | 189 | 2 448 | 7 434 | 1 585 | 5 849 | 20 797 | 51.3 | 21.1 |
| Royal Palm Beach | 11 556 | 2.93 | 15.8 | 16.9 | 236 | 229 | 119 | 7 | 1 093 | 3 159 | 272 | 2 887 | 20 844 | 36.4 | 27.7 |
| St. Cloud | 12 565 | 2.76 | 15.6 | 20.9 | 448 | 375 | 349 | 73 | 1 058 | 2 967 | 376 | 2 591 | 22 553 | 47.4 | 19.0 |
| St. Petersburg | 108 815 | 2.19 | 15.1 | 36.2 | 6 607 | 2 719 | 2 364 | 3 888 | 15 335 | 6 181 | 1 021 | 5 160 | 175 039 | 41.7 | 27.8 |
| Sanford | 20 118 | 2.59 | 21.1 | 27.5 | 1 531 | 996 | 180 | 535 | 3 563 | 6 562 | 606 | 5 956 | 33 475 | 45.9 | 21.2 |
| Sarasota | 23 142 | 2.09 | 12.6 | 40.2 | 3 582 | 1 632 | 738 | 1 950 | 3 739 | 7 105 | 975 | 6 130 | 38 438 | 45.5 | 27.2 |
| Sunrise | 32 493 | 2.58 | 17.0 | 27.3 | 578 | 506 | 496 | 72 | 3 859 | 4 509 | 314 | 4 194 | 58 241 | 43.6 | 24.6 |
| Tallahassee | 74 815 | 2.23 | 14.4 | 34.1 | 14 623 | 3 231 | 718 | 11 392 | 11 024 | 5 996 | 903 | 5 093 | 93 334 | 26.4 | 46.5 |
| Tamarac | 28 415 | 2.12 | 14.1 | 37.3 | 261 | 234 | 234 | 27 | 1 671 | 2 728 | 260 | 2 469 | 47 003 | 45.6 | 23.8 |
| Tampa | 135 955 | 2.38 | 16.8 | 33.6 | 12 282 | 2 138 | 876 | 10 144 | 12 621 | 3 709 | 655 | 3 054 | 218 275 | 42.2 | 32.2 |
| Titusville | 19 017 | 2.28 | 14.5 | 31.7 | 473 | 344 | 344 | 129 | 1 904 | 4 292 | 609 | 3 684 | 31 189 | 44.2 | 19.2 |
| Wellington | 19 659 | 2.87 | 12.2 | 15.9 | 2 | 0 | 0 | 2 | 1 532 | 2 675 | 250 | 2 425 | 34 697 | 28.7 | 40.2 |
| Weston | 21 220 | 3.08 | 12.1 | 13.0 | 0 | 0 | 0 | 0 | 816 | 1 232 | 112 | 1 120 | 39 236 | 17.8 | 58.1 |
| West Palm Beach | 42 912 | 2.26 | 14.8 | 36.5 | 2 943 | 1 196 | 1 093 | 1 747 | 6 152 | 6 074 | 759 | 5 315 | 69 752 | 41.6 | 29.9 |
| Winter Garden | 11 875 | 2.87 | 14.7 | 19.0 | 497 | 483 | 483 | 14 | 1 365 | 3 896 | 508 | 3 388 | 20 361 | 36.9 | 32.7 |
| Winter Haven | 14 323 | 2.32 | 15.8 | 32.5 | 598 | 491 | 490 | 107 | 2 159 | 6 288 | 880 | 5 408 | 23 005 | 54.0 | 17.1 |
| Winter Park | 12 228 | 2.15 | 9.0 | 36.5 | 1 609 | 338 | 338 | 1 271 | 947 | 3 354 | 273 | 3 082 | 19 461 | 22.0 | 52.1 |
| Winter Springs | 13 101 | 2.54 | 12.5 | 22.1 | 31 | 31 | 0 | 0 | 476 | 1 411 | 205 | 1 206 | 22 354 | 29.6 | 38.7 |

1. No spouse present.   2. Data for serious crimes have not been adjusted for underreporting. This may affect comparability between geographic areas and over time.   3. Per 100,000 population estimated by the FBI.   4. Persons 25 years old and over.

# Table D. Cities — Income, Poverty, and Housing

| City | Money income, 2007–2011 | | | | | Housing units, 2010 | | | Occupied Housing units 2007–2011 | | | | |
|---|---|---|---|---|---|---|---|---|---|---|---|---|---|
| | Households | | | | Families with income below poverty (percent) | | | | Owner-occupied | | | Median owner costs as a percent of income | |
| | Per capita income[1] (dollars) | Median income | Percent with income of $200,000 or more | Percent with income of less than $25,000 | | Total | Percent change, 2000–2010 | Vacant units for sale or rent[2] | Total | Percent | Median value[3] (dollars) | With a mortgage[4] | Without a mortgage[5] |
| | 42 | 43 | 44 | 45 | 46 | 47 | 48 | 49 | 50 | 51 | 52 | 53 | 54 |
| FLORIDA—Cont'd | | | | | | | | | | | | | |
| Deerfield Beach | 24 019 | 38 822 | 1.5 | 32.5 | 13.9 | 42 671 | 14.3 | 9 301 | 32 255 | 67.8 | 149 200 | 34.2 | 20.4 |
| DeLand | 21 048 | 36 527 | 1.5 | 36.8 | 15.4 | 12 610 | 35.6 | 1 864 | 9 947 | 60.6 | 167 900 | 29.1 | 17.2 |
| Delray Beach | 37 964 | 49 823 | 6.6 | 23.7 | 9.8 | 34 156 | 7.9 | 6 963 | 27 075 | 66.1 | 234 700 | 32.8 | 18.2 |
| Deltona | 20 864 | 50 420 | 1.2 | 20.6 | 9.4 | 34 089 | 28.4 | 3 866 | 28 862 | 84.8 | 166 000 | 29.3 | 13.2 |
| Doral | 29 321 | 71 656 | 7.5 | 11.6 | 6.6 | 17 785 | 89.4 | 2 541 | 13 641 | 58.6 | 340 100 | 39.2 | 14.9 |
| Dunedin | 29 712 | 48 420 | 2.6 | 24.5 | 5.3 | 21 113 | 5.0 | 3 495 | 16 100 | 67.7 | 184 800 | 27.6 | 16.5 |
| Fort Lauderdale | 36 220 | 50 648 | 6.9 | 25.7 | 13.9 | 93 159 | 15.3 | 18 373 | 71 491 | 57.0 | 291 600 | 33.7 | 17.6 |
| Fort Myers | 22 657 | 37 347 | 4.0 | 33.5 | 18.4 | 35 138 | 60.9 | 10 170 | 22 872 | 46.7 | 164 000 | 29.9 | 12.9 |
| Fort Pierce | 16 782 | 30 869 | 1.2 | 42.3 | 24.0 | 21 357 | 24.1 | 5 507 | 15 170 | 49.7 | 120 300 | 34.1 | 18.5 |
| Gainesville | 19 100 | 30 952 | 2.3 | 43.0 | 16.0 | 57 576 | 43.5 | 6 547 | 48 385 | 38.5 | 164 500 | 25.5 | 11.6 |
| Greenacres | 21 959 | 42 787 | 1.3 | 29.2 | 11.9 | 17 249 | 21.0 | 2 865 | 14 081 | 68.6 | 156 100 | 32.0 | 16.8 |
| Hallandale Beach | 25 168 | 34 645 | 1.9 | 36.8 | 14.3 | 27 057 | 7.8 | 8 756 | 17 782 | 60.8 | 171 200 | 41.5 | 23.7 |
| Hialeah | 14 820 | 31 096 | 0.6 | 40.4 | 18.8 | 74 067 | 2.6 | 2 862 | 72 603 | 51.9 | 197 800 | 40.1 | 17.3 |
| Hollywood | 26 676 | 45 611 | 3.4 | 25.7 | 10.0 | 71 070 | 3.9 | 12 632 | 56 727 | 62.7 | 222 800 | 32.9 | 18.5 |
| Homestead | 16 899 | 38 724 | 1.1 | 32.7 | 25.3 | 23 419 | 111.0 | 4 423 | 17 977 | 42.8 | 169 600 | 32.1 | 17.0 |
| Jacksonville | 25 716 | 49 192 | 2.7 | 24.0 | 11.3 | 366 273 | 18.6 | 43 167 | 311 932 | 63.3 | 166 400 | 26.4 | 12.1 |
| Jupiter | 43 336 | 66 370 | 9.8 | 17.9 | 5.6 | 29 825 | 41.7 | 5 905 | 22 905 | 72.9 | 293 400 | 31.8 | 13.7 |
| Kissimmee | 17 633 | 38 158 | 0.8 | 29.2 | 17.5 | 26 275 | 33.6 | 5 549 | 21 808 | 44.6 | 151 300 | 32.1 | 12.0 |
| Lakeland | 24 306 | 40 650 | 2.3 | 29.5 | 11.9 | 48 218 | 23.3 | 7 460 | 40 448 | 56.8 | 136 300 | 25.2 | 13.8 |
| Lake Worth | 18 661 | 37 288 | 1.3 | 34.0 | 26.1 | 16 473 | 3.6 | 3 515 | 12 240 | 51.6 | 161 700 | 34.5 | 15.9 |
| Largo | 25 470 | 40 493 | 1.3 | 28.8 | 8.6 | 46 859 | 16.4 | 8 837 | 36 029 | 61.4 | 114 900 | 28.9 | 15.4 |
| Lauderdale Lakes | 18 071 | 35 080 | 0.7 | 34.0 | 17.4 | 15 000 | 4.5 | 3 109 | 12 293 | 64.6 | 112 300 | 38.3 | 19.3 |
| Lauderhill | 19 337 | 38 585 | 1.0 | 32.0 | 19.2 | 29 519 | 15.0 | 4 693 | 23 763 | 62.6 | 147 500 | 33.5 | 20.9 |
| Margate | 23 966 | 45 674 | 1.4 | 26.9 | 9.7 | 24 863 | 0.5 | 3 380 | 21 134 | 77.1 | 151 400 | 32.6 | 17.6 |
| Melbourne | 25 152 | 42 089 | 2.0 | 28.5 | 8.8 | 38 955 | 15.7 | 4 915 | 33 354 | 62.7 | 153 400 | 27.3 | 12.7 |
| Miami | 20 732 | 30 270 | 3.2 | 42.8 | 22.8 | 183 994 | 23.9 | 25 677 | 149 648 | 34.7 | 257 500 | 39.6 | 19.3 |
| Miami Beach | 42 079 | 42 411 | 8.1 | 30.8 | 10.1 | 67 499 | 13.0 | 20 331 | 43 907 | 40.6 | 349 400 | 35.1 | 22.9 |
| Miami Gardens | 16 692 | 44 215 | 0.6 | 26.9 | 16.1 | 34 284 | NA | 2 065 | 30 863 | 68.5 | 183 800 | 36.1 | 13.8 |
| Miami Lakes | 29 670 | 63 794 | 5.7 | 15.6 | 5.1 | 10 698 | 18.8 | 445 | 9 837 | 66.7 | 340 000 | 35.9 | 14.9 |
| Miramar | 24 977 | 64 767 | 4.0 | 13.7 | 7.3 | 40 294 | 55.6 | 2 874 | 35 306 | 76.2 | 267 500 | 36.1 | 17.8 |
| North Lauderdale | 16 667 | 42 541 | 0.3 | 26.1 | 17.8 | 14 709 | 28.1 | 1 732 | 12 307 | 60.3 | 158 700 | 36.5 | 20.2 |
| North Miami | 17 908 | 37 792 | 1.5 | 32.4 | 20.1 | 22 110 | -0.7 | 2 835 | 18 120 | 53.2 | 196 600 | 41.7 | 16.4 |
| North Miami Beach | 18 097 | 41 489 | 0.8 | 27.8 | 16.8 | 16 402 | 7.1 | 1 990 | 13 605 | 57.4 | 206 200 | 39.4 | 18.2 |
| North Port | 23 163 | 49 026 | 1.4 | 20.0 | 7.0 | 27 986 | 170.2 | 5 555 | 20 856 | 78.2 | 152 500 | 29.8 | 13.8 |
| Oakland Park | 25 374 | 44 470 | 1.2 | 24.1 | 11.6 | 20 076 | 38.1 | 2 577 | 17 489 | 60.7 | 182 900 | 33.4 | 13.7 |
| Ocala | 22 567 | 36 706 | 3.2 | 35.0 | 16.9 | 26 764 | 29.8 | 3 661 | 22 178 | 54.3 | 140 700 | 27.2 | 14.6 |
| Ocoee | 26 604 | 61 653 | 3.4 | 14.9 | 8.1 | 12 802 | 53.8 | 1 010 | 11 677 | 76.6 | 213 000 | 28.8 | 11.8 |
| Orlando | 25 864 | 42 755 | 3.2 | 27.2 | 14.0 | 121 254 | 36.8 | 18 733 | 98 067 | 40.6 | 199 600 | 30.2 | 13.7 |
| Ormond Beach | 30 697 | 48 427 | 5.0 | 23.3 | 6.6 | 19 576 | 12.8 | 2 514 | 15 997 | 81.4 | 201 300 | 28.8 | 16.3 |
| Oviedo | 28 794 | 83 742 | 5.3 | 9.9 | 4.5 | 11 720 | 28.9 | 595 | 9 879 | 81.8 | 253 100 | 25.4 | 10.0 |
| Palm Bay | 20 932 | 44 768 | 1.0 | 23.8 | 9.5 | 45 220 | 37.3 | 5 738 | 36 733 | 77.0 | 138 600 | 29.6 | 12.2 |
| Palm Beach Gardens | 56 119 | 71 349 | 13.1 | 13.3 | 2.8 | 27 663 | 52.6 | 4 859 | 21 777 | 74.6 | 323 200 | 29.7 | 13.4 |
| Palm Coast | 22 929 | 48 594 | 1.8 | 22.8 | 9.3 | 35 058 | 132.0 | 5 253 | 27 677 | 79.5 | 197 000 | 31.9 | 13.8 |
| Panama City | 22 613 | 41 067 | 1.4 | 29.3 | 13.2 | 17 438 | 5.5 | 2 646 | 15 399 | 54.2 | 151 200 | 26.2 | 13.4 |
| Pembroke Pines | 28 456 | 61 873 | 3.8 | 19.1 | 5.3 | 61 703 | 11.6 | 4 830 | 55 474 | 75.8 | 249 500 | 31.0 | 21.2 |
| Pensacola | 30 556 | 44 628 | 4.7 | 27.7 | 12.0 | 26 848 | -0.3 | 3 256 | 23 600 | 63.5 | 165 800 | 25.7 | 12.4 |
| Pinellas Park | 22 433 | 43 132 | 0.9 | 26.7 | 9.7 | 23 458 | 7.5 | 2 835 | 20 370 | 71.8 | 132 600 | 29.0 | 16.0 |
| Plantation | 35 909 | 66 740 | 6.9 | 14.3 | 6.1 | 37 587 | 7.1 | 3 397 | 33 635 | 71.7 | 284 500 | 29.4 | 14.4 |
| Plant City | 22 271 | 47 565 | 1.7 | 24.6 | 13.8 | 13 732 | 16.5 | 1 493 | 11 955 | 61.8 | 162 700 | 28.4 | 14.2 |
| Pompano Beach | 26 109 | 39 943 | 3.1 | 32.2 | 15.9 | 55 885 | 25.9 | 13 703 | 41 641 | 60.3 | 193 300 | 34.1 | 17.7 |
| Port Orange | 27 242 | 47 763 | 2.6 | 24.1 | 5.7 | 27 972 | 34.2 | 3 131 | 23 016 | 77.6 | 171 200 | 27.3 | 15.2 |
| Port St. Lucie | 22 557 | 49 310 | 1.5 | 19.9 | 9.6 | 70 877 | 92.0 | 9 975 | 57 006 | 78.0 | 167 600 | 34.2 | 16.6 |
| Riviera Beach | 22 399 | 37 555 | 2.7 | 34.6 | 19.7 | 17 124 | 19.4 | 4 744 | 12 227 | 60.0 | 174 600 | 35.5 | 17.4 |
| Royal Palm Beach | 26 661 | 66 403 | 2.9 | 12.7 | 6.1 | 12 854 | 58.1 | 1 298 | 10 741 | 82.7 | 233 600 | 33.2 | 13.7 |
| St. Cloud | 21 512 | 50 740 | 1.2 | 21.9 | 9.0 | 14 544 | 68.6 | 1 979 | 12 519 | 70.2 | 160 500 | 31.9 | 13.9 |
| St. Petersburg | 27 400 | 44 510 | 3.0 | 26.5 | 10.4 | 129 401 | 3.9 | 20 586 | 104 491 | 63.2 | 167 800 | 29.8 | 15.2 |
| Sanford | 20 346 | 43 520 | 1.3 | 28.4 | 13.9 | 23 061 | 49.0 | 2 943 | 18 774 | 56.2 | 156 300 | 29.2 | 12.2 |
| Sarasota | 32 329 | 41 973 | 5.4 | 30.2 | 14.1 | 29 151 | 8.2 | 6 009 | 22 460 | 59.4 | 205 800 | 35.6 | 16.5 |
| Sunrise | 23 633 | 49 659 | 0.9 | 22.4 | 7.6 | 37 609 | 5.5 | 5 116 | 31 064 | 74.6 | 176 500 | 33.5 | 20.8 |
| Tallahassee | 24 195 | 38 972 | 2.9 | 34.9 | 15.6 | 84 248 | 23.2 | 9 433 | 73 558 | 42.6 | 191 400 | 24.8 | 12.2 |
| Tamarac | 25 520 | 41 837 | 1.0 | 28.2 | 7.7 | 32 794 | 10.3 | 4 379 | 27 681 | 78.8 | 155 500 | 34.2 | 22.7 |
| Tampa | 28 863 | 43 957 | 5.4 | 29.1 | 15.4 | 157 130 | 15.8 | 21 175 | 134 125 | 53.4 | 189 400 | 28.5 | 14.1 |
| Titusville | 24 478 | 44 148 | 1.8 | 24.6 | 10.5 | 22 729 | 18.2 | 3 712 | 17 755 | 69.7 | 140 700 | 27.0 | 11.2 |
| Wellington | 35 368 | 78 268 | 10.5 | 12.0 | 6.4 | 22 685 | 54.2 | 3 026 | 17 919 | 79.3 | 334 000 | 29.8 | 15.2 |
| Weston | 41 941 | 94 084 | 16.4 | 9.4 | 3.7 | 24 394 | 28.9 | 3 174 | 20 564 | 74.4 | 421 300 | 30.0 | 15.6 |
| West Palm Beach | 30 584 | 45 806 | 4.3 | 26.7 | 14.3 | 54 179 | 34.1 | 11 267 | 40 974 | 52.9 | 220 900 | 32.3 | 17.3 |
| Winter Garden | 25 762 | 65 424 | 3.8 | 15.6 | 5.7 | 13 260 | 128.8 | 1 385 | 10 453 | 70.7 | 247 600 | 28.1 | 12.4 |
| Winter Haven | 21 107 | 36 895 | 1.4 | 34.5 | 16.8 | 17 037 | 22.3 | 2 714 | 13 798 | 60.1 | 125 000 | 29.1 | 14.7 |
| Winter Park | 46 566 | 57 432 | 12.3 | 20.0 | 7.8 | 13 626 | 18.2 | 1 398 | 11 877 | 63.6 | 363 500 | 25.7 | 13.4 |
| Winter Springs | 33 163 | 69 542 | 6.7 | 12.0 | 4.6 | 14 052 | 14.3 | 951 | 11 945 | 78.7 | 231 500 | 25.2 | 10.0 |

1. Based on population estimated by the American Community Survey.    2. Includes units rented or sold but not occupied.    3. Specified owner-occupied units; $1,000,000 represents $1,000,000 or more    4. 50.0 represents 50 percent or more.    5. 10.0 represents 10 percent or less.

# Table D. Cities — Housing, Labor Force, and Employment

| City | Occupied housing units, 2007–2011 (cont.) | | | | Migration, 2007–2011 | | Civilian labor force, 2012 | | | | Civilian employment[4], 2007–2011 | | | |
|---|---|---|---|---|---|---|---|---|---|---|---|---|---|---|
| | | | | | | | | | Unemployment | | | Percent | | |
| | Percent renter occupied | Median gross rent[1] | Median rent as a percent of income[2] | Percent with no vehicle available | Percent who lived in the same house one year ago | Percent who lived outside this city one year ago | Total | Percent change, 2011–2012 | Total | Rate[3] | Population age 16 and older | In labor force | Full-year full-time worker | Households with no workers (percent) |
| | 55 | 56 | 57 | 58 | 59 | 60 | 61 | 62 | 63 | 64 | 65 | 66 | 67 | 68 |
| FLORIDA—Cont'd | | | | | | | | | | | | | | |
| Deerfield Beach | 32.2 | 1 139 | 37.8 | 10.5 | 82.1 | 14.1 | 40 356 | 2.8 | 2 742 | 6.8 | 63 804 | 62.9 | 37.4 | 34.5 |
| DeLand | 39.4 | 840 | 43.5 | 14.4 | 77.2 | 19.7 | 12 038 | 3.0 | 1 134 | 9.4 | 21 305 | 52.7 | 32.3 | 41.9 |
| Delray Beach | 33.9 | 1 273 | 35.6 | 6.6 | 82.1 | 12.8 | 28 826 | 1.6 | 2 469 | 8.6 | 52 005 | 61.8 | 37.1 | 37.5 |
| Deltona | 15.2 | 1 105 | 33.3 | 3.5 | 89.2 | 7.9 | 46 279 | 1.9 | 4 299 | 9.3 | 66 687 | 62.8 | 39.8 | 25.5 |
| Doral | 41.4 | 1 721 | 33.7 | 2.9 | 75.0 | 19.2 | 26 903 | 3.8 | 1 551 | 5.8 | 31 458 | 69.7 | 52.4 | 9.1 |
| Dunedin | 32.3 | 901 | 32.4 | 8.2 | 83.0 | 13.1 | 16 479 | 2.8 | 1 354 | 8.2 | 30 531 | 59.6 | 36.3 | 36.6 |
| Fort Lauderdale | 43.0 | 1 038 | 33.9 | 8.7 | 79.0 | 11.4 | 97 092 | 3.3 | 6 666 | 6.9 | 140 029 | 65.3 | 39.5 | 28.1 |
| Fort Myers | 53.3 | 869 | 37.0 | 12.2 | 71.9 | 14.9 | 28 760 | 2.1 | 2 455 | 8.5 | 50 137 | 59.1 | 33.2 | 33.0 |
| Fort Pierce | 50.3 | 857 | 41.4 | 13.3 | 81.3 | 11.1 | 17 989 | 3.4 | 2 546 | 14.2 | 32 364 | 59.3 | 29.2 | 36.6 |
| Gainesville | 61.5 | 838 | 42.5 | 10.9 | 64.1 | 18.7 | 64 993 | 2.4 | 4 415 | 6.8 | 110 327 | 56.3 | 28.5 | 29.3 |
| Greenacres | 31.4 | 1 110 | 44.5 | 5.9 | 82.2 | 15.7 | 17 683 | 2.7 | 1 341 | 7.6 | 29 469 | 67.3 | 41.2 | 30.8 |
| Hallandale Beach | 39.2 | 1 013 | 38.7 | 14.3 | 79.1 | 14.9 | 18 223 | 3.3 | 1 634 | 9.0 | 31 493 | 57.7 | 34.1 | 40.0 |
| Hialeah | 48.1 | 967 | 44.4 | 13.6 | 92.1 | 3.9 | 106 425 | 1.9 | 12 418 | 11.7 | 189 661 | 58.7 | 39.1 | 28.9 |
| Hollywood | 37.3 | 1 003 | 37.2 | 8.1 | 83.0 | 10.4 | 82 214 | 3.4 | 6 362 | 7.7 | 114 956 | 67.2 | 39.5 | 26.3 |
| Homestead | 57.2 | 1 025 | 39.0 | 12.5 | 78.3 | 12.5 | 29 818 | 4.1 | 2 448 | 8.2 | 39 738 | 69.0 | 45.9 | 21.4 |
| Jacksonville | 36.7 | 910 | 32.1 | 7.8 | 80.5 | 6.4 | 421 439 | 2.4 | 36 365 | 8.6 | 642 931 | 68.1 | 42.1 | 23.9 |
| Jupiter | 27.1 | 1 321 | 35.1 | 4.6 | 86.7 | 8.5 | 29 259 | 2.8 | 1 848 | 6.3 | 44 197 | 61.7 | 40.0 | 32.4 |
| Kissimmee | 55.4 | 969 | 39.1 | 10.5 | 81.0 | 13.1 | 33 122 | 3.2 | 2 967 | 9.0 | 45 989 | 69.2 | 42.6 | 20.4 |
| Lakeland | 43.2 | 875 | 32.5 | 8.7 | 77.8 | 13.7 | 43 027 | 0.4 | 3 948 | 9.2 | 80 553 | 57.4 | 34.8 | 35.3 |
| Lake Worth | 48.4 | 925 | 35.7 | 15.0 | 76.7 | 12.0 | 17 901 | 2.2 | 1 420 | 7.9 | 28 541 | 69.1 | 38.3 | 28.8 |
| Largo | 38.6 | 910 | 31.1 | 9.7 | 82.5 | 13.5 | 35 592 | 2.8 | 2 936 | 8.2 | 67 352 | 56.0 | 35.7 | 40.5 |
| Lauderdale Lakes | 35.4 | 998 | 38.1 | 12.8 | 88.6 | 10.3 | 15 924 | 2.6 | 1 483 | 9.3 | 26 184 | 69.1 | 38.2 | 28.9 |
| Lauderhill | 37.4 | 1 027 | 43.6 | 11.3 | 82.8 | 13.1 | 36 099 | 3.5 | 2 863 | 7.9 | 51 799 | 68.1 | 39.9 | 25.1 |
| Margate | 22.9 | 1 200 | 37.6 | 8.2 | 86.9 | 11.2 | 30 364 | 2.6 | 2 339 | 7.7 | 44 220 | 66.5 | 41.0 | 29.2 |
| Melbourne | 37.3 | 864 | 33.7 | 6.9 | 83.2 | 11.3 | 38 991 | 2.0 | 3 356 | 8.6 | 64 980 | 58.8 | 34.2 | 36.4 |
| Miami | 65.3 | 910 | 39.4 | 19.7 | 81.5 | 8.1 | 183 783 | 2.5 | 18 843 | 10.3 | 329 295 | 60.7 | 37.8 | 30.5 |
| Miami Beach | 59.4 | 1 063 | 34.7 | 25.8 | 76.0 | 14.1 | 50 419 | 3.0 | 3 576 | 7.1 | 75 238 | 68.3 | 46.7 | 27.6 |
| Miami Gardens | 31.5 | 1 032 | 42.4 | 8.1 | 90.9 | 6.9 | 55 397 | 2.6 | 6 861 | 12.4 | 81 525 | 64.4 | 41.2 | 22.3 |
| Miami Lakes | 33.3 | 1 380 | 34.3 | 2.9 | 91.7 | 7.5 | NA | NA | NA | NA | 22 771 | 66.2 | 47.3 | 18.3 |
| Miramar | 23.8 | 1 443 | 37.3 | 2.8 | 87.3 | 9.5 | 70 184 | 4.0 | 5 115 | 7.3 | 87 467 | 74.7 | 49.3 | 10.8 |
| North Lauderdale | 39.7 | 1 194 | 43.0 | 7.1 | 84.7 | 13.3 | 24 346 | 3.7 | 1 681 | 6.9 | 30 544 | 73.7 | 44.7 | 14.6 |
| North Miami | 46.8 | 975 | 43.0 | 9.9 | 82.8 | 12.9 | 29 871 | 3.5 | 3 244 | 10.9 | 46 516 | 67.4 | 41.9 | 19.2 |
| North Miami Beach | 42.6 | 974 | 37.7 | 8.6 | 86.7 | 11.0 | 20 951 | 3.2 | 2 132 | 10.2 | 33 201 | 67.3 | 43.7 | 18.9 |
| North Port | 21.8 | 983 | 33.0 | 4.2 | 82.5 | 12.0 | 25 297 | 2.9 | 2 305 | 9.1 | 42 868 | 61.5 | 37.5 | 34.3 |
| Oakland Park | 39.3 | 1 028 | 38.0 | 6.7 | 78.4 | 18.3 | 27 439 | 3.6 | 1 584 | 5.8 | 34 440 | 75.7 | 44.2 | 21.2 |
| Ocala | 45.7 | 840 | 35.4 | 9.3 | 74.9 | 13.4 | 24 338 | 0.0 | 2 241 | 9.2 | 44 337 | 57.9 | 33.9 | 34.2 |
| Ocoee | 23.4 | 1 202 | 31.7 | 3.8 | 86.8 | 10.9 | 20 515 | 3.2 | 1 348 | 6.6 | 26 946 | 74.4 | 48.7 | 15.6 |
| Orlando | 59.4 | 975 | 34.2 | 8.7 | 70.9 | 14.8 | 137 830 | 3.4 | 11 470 | 8.3 | 190 239 | 73.7 | 45.3 | 20.5 |
| Ormond Beach | 18.6 | 982 | 37.7 | 4.7 | 90.2 | 7.8 | 19 408 | 2.5 | 1 439 | 7.4 | 32 924 | 52.3 | 30.0 | 40.1 |
| Oviedo | 18.2 | 1 262 | 35.7 | 2.3 | 88.7 | 9.2 | 19 215 | 4.1 | 1 221 | 6.4 | 24 283 | 70.9 | 46.2 | 14.6 |
| Palm Bay | 23.0 | 947 | 35.3 | 3.8 | 84.2 | 9.3 | 52 983 | 2.1 | 4 996 | 9.4 | 81 400 | 62.3 | 36.4 | 29.3 |
| Palm Beach Gardens | 25.4 | 1 349 | 35.0 | 4.4 | 84.5 | 11.8 | 25 241 | 3.3 | 1 479 | 5.9 | 40 643 | 60.5 | 39.7 | 32.1 |
| Palm Coast | 20.5 | 1 085 | 34.2 | 3.7 | 86.7 | 8.6 | 27 831 | 3.2 | 3 174 | 11.4 | 59 814 | 52.4 | 30.5 | 40.7 |
| Panama City | 45.8 | 843 | 32.0 | 9.7 | 75.5 | 15.5 | 18 120 | 3.7 | 1 618 | 8.9 | 29 438 | 62.4 | 36.2 | 29.4 |
| Pembroke Pines | 24.2 | 1 372 | 37.8 | 7.0 | 85.9 | 10.0 | 90 680 | 3.3 | 6 236 | 6.9 | 122 867 | 66.4 | 42.9 | 25.3 |
| Pensacola | 36.5 | 819 | 34.0 | 10.7 | 82.5 | 10.8 | 25 840 | 2.1 | 1 920 | 7.4 | 43 811 | 65.4 | 38.6 | 32.0 |
| Pinellas Park | 28.2 | 937 | 32.3 | 8.2 | 88.0 | 9.3 | 23 532 | 1.7 | 1 699 | 7.2 | 41 053 | 59.2 | 37.8 | 35.1 |
| Plantation | 28.3 | 1 338 | 32.8 | 4.0 | 84.0 | 12.7 | 54 859 | 3.8 | 3 341 | 6.1 | 68 476 | 71.6 | 47.1 | 18.2 |
| Plant City | 38.2 | 846 | 33.3 | 6.0 | 83.0 | 8.2 | 16 072 | 2.8 | 1 465 | 9.1 | 25 848 | 64.3 | 42.1 | 25.1 |
| Pompano Beach | 39.7 | 1 063 | 41.4 | 11.1 | 80.2 | 13.2 | 52 411 | 3.5 | 3 851 | 7.3 | 84 448 | 59.2 | 35.1 | 36.0 |
| Port Orange | 22.4 | 929 | 29.7 | 4.1 | 86.7 | 9.7 | 30 152 | 2.3 | 2 134 | 7.1 | 47 318 | 57.4 | 35.9 | 36.5 |
| Port St. Lucie | 22.0 | 1 206 | 34.8 | 3.3 | 82.4 | 9.6 | 78 848 | 0.1 | 7 523 | 9.5 | 124 458 | 64.1 | 38.1 | 29.6 |
| Riviera Beach | 40.0 | 968 | 41.0 | 10.6 | 85.9 | 9.4 | 14 419 | 2.4 | 1 507 | 10.5 | 25 072 | 63.7 | 37.3 | 32.7 |
| Royal Palm Beach | 17.3 | 1 383 | 38.6 | 3.2 | 87.0 | 9.5 | 19 135 | 2.9 | 1 332 | 7.0 | 25 106 | 71.3 | 44.2 | 16.8 |
| St. Cloud | 29.8 | 1 043 | 32.5 | 4.2 | 83.5 | 10.1 | 17 045 | 3.3 | 1 338 | 7.8 | 26 495 | 66.7 | 41.6 | 24.4 |
| St. Petersburg | 36.8 | 898 | 33.0 | 10.0 | 83.7 | 7.4 | 121 354 | 2.7 | 10 370 | 8.5 | 201 380 | 65.6 | 42.4 | 28.7 |
| Sanford | 43.8 | 926 | 34.7 | 7.4 | 80.2 | 13.9 | 26 353 | 3.5 | 2 441 | 9.3 | 40 368 | 67.0 | 43.4 | 25.2 |
| Sarasota | 40.6 | 934 | 31.3 | 11.4 | 77.2 | 13.3 | 23 710 | 2.9 | 2 035 | 8.6 | 44 565 | 57.9 | 32.6 | 37.8 |
| Sunrise | 25.4 | 1 262 | 34.9 | 6.8 | 86.7 | 10.4 | 49 050 | 3.0 | 3 703 | 7.5 | 67 931 | 70.5 | 46.0 | 23.8 |
| Tallahassee | 57.4 | 907 | 40.0 | 8.1 | 64.2 | 15.1 | 95 023 | -0.5 | 7 034 | 7.4 | 153 154 | 65.9 | 35.4 | 23.5 |
| Tamarac | 21.2 | 1 195 | 37.1 | 7.4 | 84.6 | 12.7 | 30 982 | 2.6 | 2 716 | 8.8 | 51 101 | 61.4 | 37.4 | 39.2 |
| Tampa | 46.6 | 923 | 33.3 | 10.9 | 77.8 | 10.9 | 162 972 | 3.0 | 14 960 | 9.2 | 267 154 | 66.4 | 40.8 | 25.6 |
| Titusville | 30.3 | 837 | 32.7 | 6.0 | 79.0 | 12.1 | 20 903 | 0.1 | 2 010 | 9.6 | 35 848 | 57.2 | 36.0 | 35.2 |
| Wellington | 20.7 | 1 489 | 36.5 | 2.6 | 86.1 | 10.8 | 30 099 | 3.5 | 2 095 | 7.0 | 41 262 | 69.0 | 44.7 | 18.7 |
| Weston | 25.6 | 1 807 | 32.3 | 2.3 | 84.7 | 9.7 | 36 710 | 3.8 | 2 113 | 5.8 | 47 049 | 69.0 | 43.9 | 13.6 |
| West Palm Beach | 47.1 | 1 038 | 33.8 | 10.2 | 79.9 | 12.3 | 51 230 | 2.9 | 4 381 | 8.6 | 81 691 | 65.4 | 40.4 | 29.6 |
| Winter Garden | 29.3 | 970 | 29.7 | 4.8 | 80.0 | 16.3 | 18 141 | 4.0 | 1 260 | 6.9 | 24 228 | 71.9 | 46.9 | 15.0 |
| Winter Haven | 39.9 | 796 | 36.5 | 11.2 | 78.8 | 14.4 | 13 521 | 1.3 | 1 286 | 9.5 | 26 792 | 53.7 | 33.1 | 39.2 |
| Winter Park | 36.4 | 1 027 | 30.5 | 7.8 | 81.6 | 14.7 | 13 842 | 4.0 | 933 | 6.7 | 23 331 | 58.6 | 36.0 | 31.8 |
| Winter Springs | 21.3 | 1 165 | 28.4 | 2.8 | 87.7 | 10.5 | 18 542 | 3.7 | 1 373 | 7.4 | 26 514 | 68.5 | 43.4 | 21.6 |

1. $2,000 represents $2,000 or more.   2. 50.0 represents 50 percent or more.   3. Percent of civilian labor force.   4. Persons 16 years old and over.

| City | Value of residential construction authorized by building permits, 2011 | | | Wholesale trade,[1] 2007 | | | | Retail trade,[2] 2007 | | | |
|---|---|---|---|---|---|---|---|---|---|---|---|
| | New construction ($1,000) | Number of housing units | Percent single family | Number of establish-ments | Number of employees | Sales (mil dol) | Annual payroll (mil dol) | Number of establish-ments | Number of employees | Sales (mil dol) | Annual payroll (mil dol) |
| | 69 | 70 | 71 | 72 | 73 | 74 | 75 | 76 | 77 | 78 | 79 |
| FLORIDA—Cont'd | | | | | | | | | | | |
| Deerfield Beach............ | 2 299 | 7 | 100.0 | 204 | 3 698 | 10 610.9 | 210.4 | 327 | 4 122 | 1 145.9 | 110.3 |
| DeLand...................... | 25 488 | 90 | 100.0 | 34 | 258 | 99.5 | 10.8 | 177 | 2 821 | 674.8 | 66.9 |
| Delray Beach................ | 23 625 | 84 | 67.9 | 118 | 994 | 477.9 | 44.3 | 395 | 4 993 | 1 568.8 | 143.5 |
| Deltona...................... | 5 919 | 19 | 100.0 | 14 | 47 | 7.6 | 1.2 | 95 | 1 461 | 294.3 | 27.0 |
| Doral........................ | 14 053 | 116 | 92.2 | 1 277 | 13 811 | 17 259.1 | 597.7 | 571 | 8 569 | 2 282.9 | 212.7 |
| Dunedin..................... | 902 | 5 | 100.0 | 29 | 197 | 81.4 | 9.3 | 126 | 1 218 | 225.0 | 24.9 |
| Fort Lauderdale............ | 23 827 | 46 | 91.3 | 612 | 6 433 | 3 213.9 | 288.4 | 1 216 | 13 480 | 4 715.7 | 406.5 |
| Fort Myers.................. | 90 089 | 408 | 82.6 | 156 | 2 381 | 1 049.5 | 100.8 | 624 | 9 748 | 2 577.7 | 245.9 |
| Fort Pierce................. | 2 535 | 26 | 19.2 | 52 | 263 | 130.1 | 11.3 | 239 | 3 260 | 966.7 | 78.8 |
| Gainesville................. | 13 975 | 191 | 22.5 | 131 | 1 691 | 1 089.2 | 63.6 | 639 | 9 918 | 2 168.4 | 211.8 |
| Greenacres.................. | 2 891 | 21 | 100.0 | 15 | 70 | 23.0 | 3.1 | 101 | 1 584 | 473.2 | 44.2 |
| Hallandale Beach ......... | 1 521 | 7 | 71.4 | 78 | 348 | 208.4 | 15.1 | 132 | 1 537 | 360.9 | 36.2 |
| Hialeah...................... | 2 394 | 17 | 100.0 | 512 | 3 463 | 1 438.1 | 116.2 | 1 055 | 11 206 | 2 449.7 | 244.0 |
| Hollywood................... | 0 | 0 | 0.0 | 309 | 1 940 | 1 278.6 | 98.4 | 594 | 6 753 | 1 781.7 | 162.8 |
| Homestead................... | 13 411 | 96 | 66.7 | 46 | 321 | 155.4 | 9.8 | 143 | 2 043 | 512.7 | 45.7 |
| Jacksonville................ | 217 803 | 1 515 | 63.2 | 1 116 | 19 604 | 17 104.0 | 953.9 | 3 169 | 49 068 | 12 749.7 | 1 165.2 |
| Jupiter...................... | 70 922 | 198 | 99.0 | 89 | 769 | 401.6 | 42.4 | 291 | 3 544 | 828.5 | 85.0 |
| Kissimmee................... | 17 239 | 105 | 100.0 | 46 | D | D | D | 297 | 4 262 | 1 003.2 | 96.7 |
| Lakeland.................... | 26 381 | 121 | 100.0 | 150 | 2 848 | 10 346.8 | 138.5 | 598 | 9 096 | 2 250.1 | 209.6 |
| Lake Worth.................. | 8 765 | 70 | 7.1 | 61 | 698 | 364.4 | 37.2 | 172 | 1 290 | 312.1 | 33.4 |
| Largo........................ | 3 161 | 14 | 100.0 | 83 | D | D | D | 354 | 5 197 | 1 308.0 | 128.2 |
| Lauderdale Lakes........ | 550 | 10 | 0.0 | 25 | 176 | 52.0 | 4.3 | 81 | 1 090 | 243.7 | 23.7 |
| Lauderhill.................. | 0 | 0 | 0.0 | 32 | 161 | 104.6 | 4.8 | 200 | 1 800 | 355.9 | 39.9 |
| Margate...................... | 0 | 0 | 0.0 | 59 | 345 | 163.9 | 12.5 | 194 | 3 041 | 1 071.4 | 88.3 |
| Melbourne .................. | 24 688 | 88 | 100.0 | 125 | 1 276 | 675.7 | 61.0 | 479 | 7 029 | 1 695.4 | 162.2 |
| Miami........................ | 33 487 | 287 | 7.3 | 1 438 | 9 237 | 11 188.2 | 420.8 | 2 362 | 20 112 | 5 622.5 | 498.8 |
| Miami Beach................ | 18 209 | 17 | 41.2 | 136 | 487 | 409.6 | 27.9 | 528 | 5 232 | 1 102.3 | 119.7 |
| Miami Gardens............. | 3 928 | 37 | 100.0 | 187 | 3 917 | 1 820.1 | 207.2 | 277 | 4 364 | 1 592.6 | 124.8 |
| Miami Lakes................ | 0 | 0 | 0.0 | 111 | 1 656 | 974.4 | 74.0 | 94 | 1 186 | 376.7 | 33.7 |
| Miramar..................... | 42 384 | 676 | 43.2 | 154 | 2 920 | 2 158.9 | 169.3 | 184 | 4 052 | 1 881.9 | 123.9 |
| North Lauderdale ........ | 0 | 0 | 0.0 | 21 | 65 | 10.2 | 1.3 | 71 | 1 012 | 226.1 | 22.1 |
| North Miami................ | 610 | 1 | 100.0 | 94 | 522 | 292.2 | 22.1 | 204 | 1 833 | 434.1 | 44.9 |
| North Miami Beach ...... | 3 803 | 27 | 100.0 | 83 | 287 | 148.9 | 10.5 | 234 | 2 483 | 731.1 | 64.1 |
| North Port.................. | 23 521 | 94 | 100.0 | 21 | 161 | 32.3 | 4.1 | 61 | 1 256 | 257.9 | 26.2 |
| Oakland Park .............. | 2 209 | 40 | 100.0 | 158 | 880 | 430.4 | 43.7 | 270 | 2 444 | 594.3 | 59.9 |
| Ocala........................ | 8 471 | 32 | 100.0 | 170 | 2 228 | 1 071.6 | 86.4 | 597 | 9 774 | 2 529.6 | 233.5 |
| Ocoee........................ | 60 885 | 209 | 100.0 | 27 | 837 | 551.6 | 44.4 | 191 | 3 505 | 573.7 | 61.4 |
| Orlando...................... | 123 356 | 945 | 32.6 | 589 | 9 294 | 5 439.6 | 450.3 | 1 552 | 23 831 | 7 481.2 | 580.2 |
| Ormond Beach............. | 12 700 | 43 | 100.0 | 49 | 931 | 393.7 | 32.2 | 188 | 2 433 | 525.7 | 50.7 |
| Oviedo....................... | 47 908 | 261 | 100.0 | 40 | 180 | 107.6 | 10.8 | 147 | 1 979 | 310.3 | 34.4 |
| Palm Bay.................... | 30 117 | 125 | 100.0 | 41 | 241 | 122.1 | 11.4 | 189 | 2 945 | 719.1 | 63.6 |
| Palm Beach Gardens.... | 61 449 | 111 | 100.0 | 52 | 230 | 185.8 | 11.8 | 342 | 6 687 | 1 380.2 | 151.5 |
| Palm Coast................. | 21 642 | 80 | 100.0 | 34 | 96 | 37.1 | 4.1 | 121 | 2 154 | 532.5 | 50.2 |
| Panama City................ | NA | NA | NA | 67 | 539 | 275.1 | 25.0 | 381 | 5 211 | 1 327.8 | 116.7 |
| Pembroke Pines........... | 8 034 | 44 | 100.0 | 163 | 563 | 320.5 | 24.5 | 597 | 11 008 | 3 020.6 | 265.1 |
| Pensacola................... | 8 077 | 27 | 100.0 | 73 | 957 | 472.3 | 39.0 | 437 | 5 921 | 1 160.4 | 115.9 |
| Pinellas Park.............. | 9 543 | 55 | 100.0 | 180 | 2 550 | 1 030.5 | 93.9 | 304 | 6 201 | 2 770.0 | 185.3 |
| Plantation ................. | 4 323 | 12 | 100.0 | 127 | 567 | 332.8 | 21.6 | 364 | 6 326 | 1 343.9 | 130.7 |
| Plant City.................. | 13 320 | 117 | 59.0 | 89 | 1 508 | 860.6 | 52.9 | 155 | 2 615 | 711.7 | 68.4 |
| Pompano Beach............ | 5 534 | 46 | 100.0 | 515 | 7 335 | 4 374.9 | 332.9 | 654 | 9 001 | 3 788.0 | 274.4 |
| Port Orange............... | 24 010 | 91 | 100.0 | 41 | 346 | 383.8 | 15.6 | 166 | 2 603 | 519.0 | 51.3 |
| Port St. Lucie ............. | 20 006 | 181 | 84.5 | 99 | 309 | 108.9 | 12.2 | 302 | 8 458 | 2 177.3 | 210.4 |
| Riviera Beach............. | 0 | 0 | 0.0 | 112 | 2 816 | 1 383.4 | 140.1 | 129 | 1 328 | 474.8 | 41.6 |
| Royal Palm Beach ....... | 20 465 | 67 | 100.0 | 23 | 54 | 15.4 | 1.7 | 123 | 2 632 | 592.6 | 59.9 |
| St. Cloud................... | 45 168 | 208 | 100.0 | 14 | D | D | D | 103 | 1 727 | 411.6 | 37.9 |
| St. Petersburg ............. | 16 702 | 114 | 87.7 | 205 | 1 976 | 806.3 | 83.4 | 970 | 13 597 | 3 261.7 | 298.0 |
| Sanford...................... | 30 323 | 172 | 98.8 | 88 | 1 581 | 570.5 | 61.5 | 364 | 5 966 | 1 462.3 | 126.2 |
| Sarasota..................... | 23 869 | 44 | 100.0 | 87 | 629 | 308.4 | 27.4 | 491 | 5 483 | 1 117.6 | 127.8 |
| Sunrise...................... | 61 508 | 555 | 52.6 | 250 | 2 908 | 1 828.5 | 156.3 | 500 | 8 288 | 2 125.2 | 186.2 |
| Tallahassee ................ | 64 860 | 612 | 43.8 | 162 | 1 641 | 533.7 | 65.3 | 890 | 14 333 | 2 927.8 | 286.2 |
| Tamarac...................... | 0 | 0 | 0.0 | 71 | 1 015 | 955.1 | 45.2 | 149 | 2 977 | 546.6 | 88.7 |
| Tampa........................ | 224 404 | 694 | 85.0 | 634 | 8 805 | 6 460.5 | 423.1 | 1 726 | 24 672 | 6 572.1 | 620.1 |
| Titusville................... | 6 477 | 22 | 100.0 | 25 | 320 | 108.6 | 11.3 | 164 | 2 698 | 613.1 | 59.9 |
| Wellington................. | 67 522 | 173 | 100.0 | 90 | 285 | 195.5 | 13.5 | 250 | 3 310 | 558.6 | 66.6 |
| Weston ...................... | 0 | 0 | 0.0 | 224 | 1 914 | 1 577.3 | 107.4 | 154 | 1 952 | 404.9 | 48.7 |
| West Palm Beach ........ | 5 413 | 15 | 100.0 | 167 | 1 712 | 1 068.0 | 79.0 | 578 | 9 352 | 3 028.8 | 260.9 |
| Winter Garden............. | 39 238 | 219 | 70.3 | 37 | 434 | 303.3 | 17.1 | 119 | 1 005 | 298.0 | 28.5 |
| Winter Haven .............. | 13 195 | 83 | 100.0 | 41 | 464 | 205.7 | 16.4 | 213 | 3 007 | 667.5 | 66.4 |
| Winter Park ................ | 16 849 | 30 | 100.0 | 54 | 382 | 230.9 | 20.8 | 253 | 2 997 | 785.4 | 73.4 |
| Winter Springs............. | 1 443 | 7 | 100.0 | 23 | 105 | 30.8 | 3.7 | 51 | 323 | 84.2 | 7.6 |

1. Merchant wholesalers except manufacturers' sales branches and offices.  2. Establishments with payroll.

# Table D. Cities — Real Estate, Professional Services, and Manufacturing

| City | Real estate and rental and leasing, 2007 | | | | Professional, scientific, and technical services,[1] 2007 | | | | Manufacturing, 2007 | | | |
|---|---|---|---|---|---|---|---|---|---|---|---|---|
| | Number of establishments | Number of employees | Receipts (mil dol) | Annual payroll (mil dol) | Number of establishments | Number of employees | Receipts (mil dol) | Annual payroll (mil dol) | Number of establishments | Number of employees | Receipts (mil dol) | Annual payroll (mil dol) |
| | 80 | 81 | 82 | 83 | 84 | 85 | 86 | 87 | 88 | 89 | 90 | 91 |
| **FLORIDA—Cont'd** | | | | | | | | | | | | |
| Deerfield Beach | 147 | 905 | 142.8 | 35.2 | 384 | 2 273 | 312.7 | 101.5 | 119 | 2 642 | 496.9 | 104.6 |
| DeLand | 77 | 342 | 36.3 | 7.3 | 132 | 726 | 69.6 | 27.0 | 52 | 2 269 | 403.1 | 90.8 |
| Delray Beach | 156 | 555 | 111.3 | 21.0 | 434 | 1 938 | 238.3 | 94.1 | 64 | 652 | 152.3 | 22.5 |
| Deltona | 44 | 98 | 11.0 | 2.6 | 78 | 237 | 19.4 | 6.4 | NA | NA | NA | NA |
| Doral | 206 | 686 | 249.7 | 30.1 | 503 | D | D | D | 131 | 3 187 | 632.3 | 130.3 |
| Dunedin | 49 | 140 | 26.2 | 3.0 | 176 | 3 115 | 98.2 | 49.1 | NA | NA | NA | NA |
| Fort Lauderdale | 729 | 3 653 | 742.5 | 147.6 | 2 323 | D | D | D | 324 | 4 977 | 1 068.8 | 208.2 |
| Fort Myers | 226 | 1 469 | 277.1 | 45.1 | 469 | D | D | D | 93 | 2 002 | 367.8 | 73.9 |
| Fort Pierce | 72 | 252 | 47.0 | 7.4 | 142 | D | D | D | 35 | 681 | 145.8 | 24.6 |
| Gainesville | 255 | 1 350 | 235.1 | 40.0 | 495 | D | D | D | 88 | 2 132 | 589.2 | 96.6 |
| Greenacres | 28 | 120 | 27.4 | 4.5 | 68 | 335 | 29.8 | 13.1 | NA | NA | NA | NA |
| Hallandale Beach | 94 | 188 | 36.5 | 5.9 | 146 | 429 | 63.1 | 19.8 | NA | NA | NA | NA |
| Hialeah | 271 | 768 | 188.7 | 20.3 | 364 | 1 289 | 127.6 | 37.1 | 468 | 6 542 | 917.0 | 205.4 |
| Hollywood | 334 | 1 128 | 201.7 | 35.7 | 885 | D | D | D | 121 | 2 181 | 401.3 | 76.8 |
| Homestead | 43 | 138 | 21.2 | 3.8 | 98 | 395 | 32.9 | 13.7 | NA | NA | NA | NA |
| Jacksonville | 1 257 | 7 869 | 1 955.8 | 347.0 | 2 820 | D | D | D | 624 | 25 890 | 11 145.3 | 1 233.1 |
| Jupiter | 159 | 697 | 90.0 | 25.0 | 390 | D | D | D | 57 | 1 127 | 515.7 | 62.5 |
| Kissimmee | 176 | 797 | 134.3 | 30.0 | 171 | 687 | 70.5 | 28.6 | NA | NA | NA | NA |
| Lakeland | 204 | 1 197 | 189.0 | 33.7 | 385 | D | D | D | 84 | 3 540 | 1 001.5 | 138.5 |
| Lake Worth | 59 | 143 | 26.0 | 3.8 | 149 | D | D | D | 58 | 547 | 146.2 | 20.9 |
| Largo | 139 | 1 562 | 236.0 | 80.6 | 252 | D | D | D | 92 | 3 512 | 640.9 | 144.3 |
| Lauderdale Lakes | 19 | 211 | 20.0 | 5.6 | 38 | 107 | 8.8 | 3.8 | NA | NA | NA | NA |
| Lauderhill | 57 | 493 | 76.8 | 15.7 | 99 | 375 | 35.8 | 11.9 | NA | NA | NA | NA |
| Margate | 84 | 392 | 66.4 | 11.3 | 147 | 656 | 68.9 | 23.4 | NA | NA | NA | NA |
| Melbourne | 183 | 929 | 146.7 | 26.4 | 396 | 3 372 | 590.4 | 196.8 | 114 | 6 354 | 2 784.6 | 339.8 |
| Miami | 1 115 | 4 189 | 1 317.6 | 197.2 | 3 235 | 23 525 | 4 436.8 | 1 906.4 | 396 | 4 176 | 1 079.4 | 139.1 |
| Miami Beach | 458 | 2 249 | 602.3 | 162.0 | 559 | D | D | D | NA | NA | NA | NA |
| Miami Gardens | 66 | 279 | 85.3 | 9.7 | 98 | 476 | 44.7 | 18.3 | 73 | 2 716 | 547.6 | 98.4 |
| Miami Lakes | 116 | 700 | 156.2 | 32.8 | 266 | 1 306 | 215.2 | 59.3 | 27 | 3 455 | D | 216.5 |
| Miramar | 83 | 224 | 69.6 | 7.8 | 229 | 1 191 | 175.7 | 69.4 | 41 | 1 157 | 203.9 | 64.3 |
| North Lauderdale | 24 | 111 | 19.0 | 2.6 | 56 | D | D | D | NA | NA | NA | NA |
| North Miami | 108 | 265 | 45.2 | 8.3 | 163 | 847 | 83.7 | 39.7 | 33 | 613 | 114.9 | 20.5 |
| North Miami Beach | 91 | 534 | 74.4 | 11.4 | 216 | D | D | D | NA | NA | NA | NA |
| North Port | 33 | 79 | 10.5 | 2.0 | 48 | 191 | 13.9 | 6.6 | NA | NA | NA | NA |
| Oakland Park | 119 | 555 | 73.3 | 17.3 | 263 | D | D | D | 131 | 1 338 | 246.7 | 49.6 |
| Ocala | 222 | 990 | 139.3 | 25.5 | 389 | 2 171 | 240.8 | 94.0 | 112 | 6 586 | 1 297.9 | 236.9 |
| Ocoee | 32 | 1 133 | 37.4 | 29.6 | 93 | 449 | 36.8 | 14.7 | NA | NA | NA | NA |
| Orlando | 779 | 8 239 | 2 231.9 | 363.2 | 1 835 | D | D | D | 281 | 12 806 | 5 742.1 | 707.5 |
| Ormond Beach | 97 | 453 | 62.4 | 11.6 | 176 | 989 | 98.3 | 34.8 | 48 | 951 | 152.8 | 35.3 |
| Oviedo | 75 | 171 | 48.8 | 5.4 | 154 | D | D | D | NA | NA | NA | NA |
| Palm Bay | 79 | 219 | 33.2 | 5.1 | 120 | D | D | D | 52 | 10 509 | 2 894.8 | D |
| Palm Beach Gardens | 131 | 591 | 117.9 | 30.4 | 458 | D | D | D | 20 | 605 | 135.5 | 39.8 |
| Palm Coast | 133 | 316 | 40.5 | 8.7 | 133 | 429 | 79.3 | 37.4 | 23 | 768 | D | D |
| Panama City | 107 | 426 | 66.9 | 12.2 | 206 | D | D | D | 45 | 1 622 | 862.4 | 72.1 |
| Pembroke Pines | 213 | 698 | 180.7 | 19.6 | 564 | 1 763 | 193.4 | 68.5 | NA | NA | NA | NA |
| Pensacola | 136 | 543 | 122.3 | 15.3 | 444 | 4 210 | 477.8 | 215.6 | 48 | 934 | 300.5 | 41.8 |
| Pinellas Park | 71 | 305 | 54.2 | 8.9 | 164 | D | D | D | 256 | 10 171 | 2 230.7 | 419.3 |
| Plantation | 229 | 1 417 | 210.3 | 56.8 | 676 | D | D | D | 39 | 1 023 | D | 61.8 |
| Plant City | 53 | 235 | 39.4 | 5.5 | 80 | D | D | D | 63 | 3 846 | 1 215.6 | 140.0 |
| Pompano Beach | 260 | 1 585 | 285.9 | 57.7 | 505 | 2 028 | 354.2 | 93.2 | 307 | 7 410 | 1 562.8 | 273.5 |
| Port Orange | 95 | 394 | 52.7 | 10.5 | 123 | 483 | 49.9 | 18.3 | NA | NA | NA | NA |
| Port St. Lucie | 169 | 500 | 80.6 | 13.7 | 260 | 1 248 | 115.6 | 45.3 | 44 | 854 | 408.4 | 40.9 |
| Riviera Beach | 47 | 219 | 60.6 | 8.6 | 68 | 369 | 47.7 | 16.7 | 90 | 1 499 | 1 199.7 | 61.2 |
| Royal Palm Beach | 32 | 94 | 12.1 | 2.2 | 85 | 314 | 37.9 | 11.2 | NA | NA | NA | NA |
| St. Cloud | 56 | 123 | 16.2 | 2.6 | 54 | 221 | 19.9 | 9.3 | NA | NA | NA | NA |
| St. Petersburg | 388 | 1 905 | 304.1 | 66.7 | 1 132 | D | D | D | 157 | 4 557 | 1 601.2 | 213.3 |
| Sanford | 89 | 557 | 148.5 | 16.6 | 134 | D | D | D | 72 | 2 405 | 701.6 | 86.5 |
| Sarasota | 271 | 932 | 206.0 | 31.7 | 656 | D | D | D | 60 | 672 | 93.6 | 31.4 |
| Sunrise | 120 | 532 | 249.6 | 19.7 | 367 | 2 420 | 297.8 | 115.6 | 65 | 787 | 211.0 | 35.3 |
| Tallahassee | 373 | 2 141 | 330.0 | 61.1 | 1 183 | 9 322 | 1 822.7 | 629.6 | 83 | 1 976 | 574.2 | 84.9 |
| Tamarac | 80 | 379 | 52.8 | 11.4 | 150 | 744 | 68.3 | 23.7 | 28 | 634 | 86.8 | 21.6 |
| Tampa | 845 | 5 600 | 1 167.2 | 254.0 | 2 497 | 23 091 | 3 950.6 | 1 662.3 | 371 | 9 239 | 2 836.5 | 380.4 |
| Titusville | 48 | 231 | 26.7 | 4.7 | 89 | 561 | 59.7 | 26.3 | NA | NA | NA | NA |
| Wellington | 128 | 549 | 76.1 | 25.2 | 277 | 823 | 109.9 | 40.6 | NA | NA | NA | NA |
| Weston | 187 | 346 | 84.2 | 11.1 | 461 | 1 342 | 196.5 | 94.3 | 20 | 534 | 55.6 | 18.5 |
| West Palm Beach | 288 | 1 547 | 284.8 | 64.8 | 1 013 | 7 964 | 1 374.6 | 608.4 | 114 | 2 482 | 473.6 | 123.1 |
| Winter Garden | 63 | 179 | 28.8 | 7.0 | 81 | 313 | 30.5 | 12.4 | 25 | 527 | 212.4 | 18.1 |
| Winter Haven | 81 | 383 | 62.3 | 12.2 | 130 | 584 | 58.4 | 25.4 | 27 | 567 | 279.2 | 25.5 |
| Winter Park | 181 | 586 | 82.5 | 23.5 | 482 | 3 471 | 560.2 | 239.7 | NA | NA | NA | NA |
| Winter Springs | 39 | 48 | 8.6 | 1.3 | 102 | 238 | 21.0 | 8.6 | NA | NA | NA | NA |

1. Establishments subject to federal tax.

# Accommodation and Food Services, Arts, Entertainment, and Recreation, and Health Care and Social Assistance

| City | Accommodation and food services, 2007 | | | | Arts, entertainment, and recreation,[1] 2007 | | | | Health care and social assistance,[1] 2007 | | | |
|---|---|---|---|---|---|---|---|---|---|---|---|---|
| | Number of establish-ments | Number of employees | Sales (mil dol) | Annual payroll (mil dol) | Number of establish-ments | Number of employees | Receipts (mil dol) | Annual payroll (mil dol) | Number of establish-ments | Number of employees | Receipts (mil dol) | Annual payroll (mil dol) |
| | 92 | 93 | 94 | 95 | 96 | 97 | 98 | 99 | 100 | 101 | 102 | 103 |
| FLORIDA—Cont'd | | | | | | | | | | | | |
| Deerfield Beach............ | 162 | 3 235 | 184.3 | 48.3 | 28 | 299 | 50.5 | 6.6 | 186 | D | D | D |
| DeLand...................... | 84 | 1 539 | 57.7 | 17.0 | 11 | D | D | D | 109 | 1 643 | 204.0 | 60.4 |
| Delray Beach................ | 204 | 3 683 | 218.4 | 59.5 | 45 | 308 | 23.5 | 7.2 | 335 | 3 854 | 570.6 | 185.0 |
| Deltona...................... | 46 | 694 | 27.2 | 6.6 | 12 | D | D | D | 68 | 550 | 46.6 | 18.0 |
| Doral........................ | 186 | 4 503 | 308.8 | 80.3 | 37 | D | D | D | 151 | 2 539 | 315.9 | 114.9 |
| Dunedin..................... | 88 | 1 151 | 48.7 | 13.1 | 15 | D | D | D | 109 | D | D | D |
| Fort Lauderdale............ | 679 | 18 389 | 1 356.2 | 363.0 | 153 | 1 105 | 131.9 | 32.0 | 773 | 11 439 | 1 196.1 | 481.1 |
| Fort Myers.................. | 257 | 4 685 | 260.1 | 66.8 | 33 | 988 | 52.3 | 19.6 | 340 | 4 660 | 591.5 | 230.9 |
| Fort Pierce.................. | 118 | 2 217 | 97.7 | 28.0 | 9 | 152 | 14.4 | 3.0 | 178 | 2 792 | 353.2 | 115.8 |
| Gainesville................. | 359 | 7 338 | 315.0 | 84.8 | 36 | 751 | 32.4 | 10.2 | 397 | 6 146 | 697.1 | 259.7 |
| Greenacres.................. | 58 | 987 | 41.6 | 11.5 | 7 | 19 | 0.8 | 0.2 | 70 | 662 | 56.6 | 20.1 |
| Hallandale Beach.......... | 77 | 2 145 | 98.2 | 35.4 | 22 | D | D | D | 140 | D | D | D |
| Hialeah...................... | 312 | 4 015 | 232.2 | 55.9 | 38 | D | D | D | 811 | 8 639 | 1 067.7 | 323.6 |
| Hollywood................... | 332 | 5 433 | 395.1 | 119.8 | 92 | 425 | 49.0 | 7.3 | 509 | D | D | D |
| Homestead.................. | 74 | 1 428 | 65.6 | 17.6 | 11 | 139 | 37.6 | 3.6 | 132 | 989 | 101.9 | 33.9 |
| Jacksonville................ | 1 655 | 31 715 | 1 568.2 | 441.2 | 213 | 3 762 | 396.7 | 143.1 | 1 804 | 25 425 | 2 813.3 | 1 141.4 |
| Jupiter...................... | 138 | 2 925 | 132.0 | 39.0 | 41 | 1 019 | 63.0 | 25.5 | 260 | D | D | D |
| Kissimmee.................. | 124 | 3 419 | 291.5 | 77.6 | 26 | D | D | D | 232 | 3 496 | 499.7 | 169.4 |
| Lakeland.................... | 234 | 6 154 | 261.1 | 76.1 | 33 | 512 | 24.9 | 8.2 | 308 | 5 434 | 665.2 | 208.7 |
| Lake Worth.................. | 88 | 1 056 | 47.1 | 14.7 | 18 | D | D | D | 80 | 1 035 | 74.8 | 32.9 |
| Largo........................ | 175 | 2 843 | 127.7 | 38.3 | 22 | D | D | D | 310 | 6 535 | 626.9 | 242.5 |
| Lauderdale Lakes.......... | 36 | 411 | 22.9 | 5.8 | 2 | D | D | D | 99 | D | D | D |
| Lauderhill................... | 86 | 1 010 | 48.7 | 12.3 | 17 | D | D | D | 117 | 1 317 | 97.2 | 29.8 |
| Margate .................... | 101 | 1 403 | 73.3 | 18.9 | 17 | D | D | D | 177 | D | D | D |
| Melbourne .................. | 202 | 3 872 | 165.8 | 50.0 | 36 | 483 | 20.2 | 6.2 | 354 | 5 573 | 705.7 | 288.4 |
| Miami....................... | 994 | 19 303 | 1 337.8 | 355.2 | 191 | 2 853 | 385.2 | 158.4 | 1 797 | 13 565 | 1 659.3 | 539.5 |
| Miami Beach................ | 549 | 16 909 | 1 345.6 | 386.9 | 112 | 1 411 | 140.1 | 39.2 | 370 | 2 520 | 297.6 | 113.2 |
| Miami Gardens............. | 90 | 1 372 | 76.5 | 18.6 | 18 | D | D | D | 119 | 1 121 | 86.6 | 29.2 |
| Miami Lakes................ | 60 | 1 556 | 84.7 | 25.4 | 17 | D | D | D | 145 | D | D | D |
| Miramar .................... | 95 | 1 470 | 69.4 | 18.9 | 26 | D | D | D | 165 | D | D | D |
| North Lauderdale ......... | 34 | 508 | 26.9 | 6.4 | 4 | D | D | D | 35 | D | D | D |
| North Miami................ | 94 | 1 550 | 78.8 | 20.1 | 17 | D | D | D | 126 | 1 110 | 95.8 | 32.0 |
| North Miami Beach ....... | 104 | 1 592 | 90.3 | 22.7 | 18 | 264 | 13.6 | 2.8 | 232 | 2 466 | 274.8 | 89.3 |
| North Port.................. | 29 | 524 | 20.2 | 6.1 | 4 | 54 | 2.0 | 1.0 | 47 | 581 | 39.0 | 15.7 |
| Oakland Park .............. | 109 | 1 648 | 82.7 | 21.7 | 20 | D | D | D | 135 | 1 853 | 207.7 | 70.4 |
| Ocala........................ | 242 | 5 391 | 245.6 | 70.9 | 28 | D | D | D | 497 | 7 844 | 969.9 | 337.6 |
| Ocoee....................... | 74 | 1 081 | 54.9 | 14.7 | 21 | D | D | D | 99 | 1 135 | 130.9 | 50.6 |
| Orlando...................... | 851 | 22 678 | 1 514.5 | 373.8 | 133 | 15 577 | 1 613.8 | 418.3 | 793 | 8 550 | 1 133.7 | 503.3 |
| Ormond Beach............. | 117 | 2 473 | 105.8 | 32.0 | 23 | D | D | D | 223 | D | D | D |
| Oviedo...................... | 64 | 1 126 | 41.1 | 11.3 | 14 | 224 | 8.0 | 2.0 | 116 | D | D | D |
| Palm Bay.................... | 99 | 1 701 | 70.4 | 19.4 | 9 | D | D | D | 126 | 1 605 | 123.6 | 56.4 |
| Palm Beach Gardens.... | 150 | 5 178 | 277.7 | 86.8 | 37 | D | D | D | 329 | 3 630 | 513.3 | 163.3 |
| Palm Coast................. | 76 | 1 776 | 88.4 | 24.8 | 15 | 213 | 12.2 | 4.2 | 104 | D | D | D |
| Panama City................ | 166 | 2 987 | 133.7 | 38.5 | 16 | D | D | D | 300 | 4 517 | 570.2 | 198.4 |
| Pembroke Pines............ | 284 | 5 793 | 271.3 | 76.0 | 54 | D | D | D | 501 | D | D | D |
| Pensacola................... | 187 | 4 497 | 208.6 | 59.4 | 22 | D | D | D | 338 | 6 369 | 827.5 | 329.5 |
| Pinellas Park ............... | 119 | 1 878 | 128.8 | 34.9 | 14 | 144 | 6.9 | 2.3 | 126 | 1 592 | 140.5 | 56.1 |
| Plantation .................. | 186 | 3 569 | 194.4 | 51.9 | 39 | D | D | D | 534 | 5 622 | 787.1 | 245.9 |
| Plant City................... | 80 | 1 597 | 77.5 | 19.1 | 5 | D | D | D | 98 | D | D | D |
| Pompano Beach........... | 266 | 3 739 | 197.7 | 50.2 | 62 | D | D | D | 269 | 2 650 | 282.6 | 93.3 |
| Port Orange................ | 88 | 1 785 | 70.6 | 20.1 | 20 | D | D | D | 117 | D | D | D |
| Port St. Lucie .............. | 158 | 3 292 | 127.5 | 35.9 | 30 | D | D | D | 284 | 4 051 | 486.2 | 153.0 |
| Riviera Beach.............. | 39 | 950 | 44.9 | 10.4 | 14 | 685 | 53.1 | 19.4 | 36 | 190 | 14.5 | 5.7 |
| Royal Palm Beach ....... | 83 | 1 436 | 61.1 | 17.8 | 13 | 106 | 6.4 | 1.8 | 116 | 1 857 | 248.6 | 75.8 |
| St. Cloud ................... | 63 | 1 340 | 57.3 | 16.0 | 8 | D | D | D | 43 | D | D | D |
| St. Petersburg ............. | 465 | 8 782 | 451.1 | 126.6 | 56 | 1 412 | 200.1 | 90.3 | 774 | 9 186 | 1 214.4 | 427.9 |
| Sanford...................... | 129 | 2 932 | 123.8 | 36.1 | 14 | D | D | D | 103 | 1 765 | 226.8 | 73.8 |
| Sarasota..................... | 258 | 5 897 | 350.1 | 103.6 | 37 | 684 | 39.9 | 11.1 | 464 | 5 185 | 676.8 | 241.0 |
| Sunrise...................... | 186 | 3 596 | 181.7 | 48.8 | 36 | D | D | D | 244 | 3 991 | 497.3 | 225.0 |
| Tallahassee................. | 538 | 12 939 | 514.5 | 142.2 | 52 | 998 | 112.0 | 15.7 | 504 | 8 075 | 801.3 | 353.6 |
| Tamarac..................... | 86 | 1 310 | 64.5 | 15.1 | 15 | D | D | D | 203 | 2 744 | 305.0 | 106.8 |
| Tampa....................... | 956 | 23 982 | 1 376.2 | 377.7 | 126 | 6 136 | 659.7 | 287.3 | 1 197 | 14 681 | 2 066.7 | 719.4 |
| Titusville.................... | 97 | 1 986 | 89.2 | 23.1 | 11 | 113 | 5.6 | 1.6 | 137 | D | D | D |
| Wellington.................. | 101 | 2 125 | 92.5 | 27.5 | 54 | 260 | 18.2 | 3.8 | 176 | D | D | D |
| Weston ..................... | 98 | 2 203 | 120.6 | 31.9 | 30 | D | D | D | 195 | D | D | D |
| West Palm Beach ......... | 295 | 6 038 | 326.6 | 91.0 | 60 | 608 | 88.5 | 26.0 | 509 | 7 574 | 1 095.9 | 366.0 |
| Winter Garden ............. | 48 | 547 | 25.7 | 6.7 | 8 | D | D | D | 43 | 515 | 41.7 | 18.2 |
| Winter Haven .............. | 106 | 1 625 | 70.0 | 18.9 | 5 | D | D | D | 168 | D | D | D |
| Winter Park ................ | 128 | 3 271 | 152.0 | 46.2 | 31 | D | D | D | 272 | 3 373 | 441.9 | 165.4 |
| Winter Springs............. | 26 | 257 | 9.6 | 2.5 | 14 | D | D | D | 29 | D | D | D |

1. Establishments subject to federal tax.

# Table D. Cities — Other Services and Federal Funds

| City | Other services[1], 2007 | | | | Selected federal funds, 2009–2010 (mil dol) | | | | | | | | |
| | | | | | Procurement contracts | | Grants | | | | | | |
| | Number of establish-ments | Number of employees | Receipts (mil dol) | Annual payroll (mil dol) | Defense | Other | Total[2] | Medicaid and other health related | Nutrition and family welfare | Energy and envi-ronment | Disasters and emergency prepared-ness | Housing and community develop-ment | Employment and training |
| | 104 | 105 | 106 | 107 | 108 | 109 | 110 | 111 | 112 | 113 | 114 | 115 | 116 |
| **FLORIDA—Cont'd** | | | | | | | | | | | | | |
| Deerfield Beach | 161 | 879 | 64.9 | 21.3 | 5.7 | 5.4 | 5.3 | 0.0 | 0.0 | 0.0 | 0.0 | 5.3 | 0.0 |
| DeLand | 71 | 371 | 24.4 | 8.4 | 0.1 | 0.3 | 16.6 | 0.0 | 0.0 | 2.4 | 0.0 | 12.5 | 0.0 |
| Delray Beach | 181 | 743 | 63.7 | 15.9 | 23.4 | 0.5 | 13.9 | 0.0 | 0.0 | 0.1 | 0.0 | 13.3 | 0.0 |
| Deltona | 44 | 165 | 7.4 | 2.4 | 0.0 | 0.0 | 1.2 | 0.0 | 0.0 | 0.7 | 0.0 | 0.5 | 0.0 |
| Doral | 130 | 1 131 | 134.6 | 30.2 | 3.2 | 8.1 | 0.8 | 0.0 | 0.0 | 0.0 | 0.0 | 0.0 | 0.0 |
| Dunedin | 79 | 260 | 29.3 | 5.7 | 0.2 | 0.1 | 2.1 | 0.0 | 0.0 | 0.2 | 0.0 | 0.0 | 0.0 |
| Fort Lauderdale | 559 | 3 246 | 314.4 | 91.4 | 44.8 | 43.1 | 145.6 | 27.4 | 0.2 | 3.0 | 0.6 | 47.4 | 4.3 |
| Fort Myers | 238 | 1 417 | 131.8 | 36.0 | 1.0 | 7.0 | 57.1 | 7.3 | 5.5 | 5.1 | 0.1 | 21.1 | 0.0 |
| Fort Pierce | 91 | 372 | 28.7 | 9.5 | 0.1 | 3.0 | 20.8 | 0.5 | 0.1 | 3.7 | 0.0 | 9.3 | 0.0 |
| Gainesville | 207 | 1 182 | 84.0 | 26.0 | 10.0 | 125.8 | 407.9 | 224.6 | 4.8 | 17.0 | 0.0 | 21.7 | 0.4 |
| Greenacres | 48 | 125 | 7.7 | 2.5 | 0.0 | 0.1 | 0.0 | 0.0 | 0.0 | 0.0 | 0.0 | 0.0 | 0.0 |
| Hallandale Beach | 88 | 471 | 34.9 | 11.6 | NA | NA | NA | NA | NA | NA | NA | NA | NA |
| Hialeah | 478 | 1 814 | 146.7 | 38.5 | 42.2 | 2.7 | 42.6 | 0.4 | 0.0 | 2.4 | 0.0 | 38.7 | 0.0 |
| Hollywood | 264 | 1 888 | 138.5 | 45.5 | 2.2 | 1.4 | 15.3 | 0.9 | 0.0 | 0.7 | 0.0 | 9.1 | 0.0 |
| Homestead | 58 | 216 | 15.6 | 4.1 | 51.9 | 2.2 | 20.5 | 0.3 | 0.0 | 0.5 | 0.0 | 18.5 | 0.0 |
| Jacksonville | 1 368 | D | D | D | 845.0 | 213.6 | 346.7 | 38.6 | 32.1 | 117.8 | 0.0 | 78.3 | 5.9 |
| Jupiter | 143 | 665 | 46.7 | 15.8 | 10.9 | 1.3 | 11.4 | 0.4 | 0.0 | 1.4 | 0.0 | 0.0 | 0.0 |
| Kissimmee | 111 | 407 | 32.7 | 9.3 | 4.9 | 0.5 | 11.4 | 1.0 | 0.0 | 0.0 | 0.0 | 2.1 | 0.0 |
| Lakeland | 156 | 875 | 61.7 | 20.2 | 2.0 | 1.5 | 34.6 | 0.4 | 0.0 | 15.8 | 0.0 | 13.0 | 0.3 |
| Lake Worth | 98 | 347 | 24.7 | 7.8 | 3.4 | 0.0 | 27.1 | 0.0 | 0.0 | 0.3 | 0.0 | 23.7 | 0.3 |
| Largo | 160 | 676 | 50.2 | 16.1 | 29.9 | 3.9 | 19.2 | 0.4 | 0.0 | 0.0 | 0.0 | 1.6 | 0.0 |
| Lauderdale Lakes | 31 | 83 | 7.5 | 2.2 | 0.0 | 0.1 | 74.6 | 0.3 | 0.0 | 0.0 | 0.0 | 74.2 | 0.0 |
| Lauderhill | 83 | 341 | 24.1 | 6.7 | 0.0 | 0.0 | 2.6 | 0.0 | 0.0 | 0.6 | 0.0 | 2.0 | 0.0 |
| Margate | 107 | 399 | 35.5 | 8.0 | 0.2 | 0.6 | 0.9 | 0.0 | 0.0 | 0.5 | 0.0 | 0.4 | 0.0 |
| Melbourne | 167 | 802 | 54.4 | 18.7 | 1 040.8 | 231.8 | 20.5 | 0.9 | 0.0 | 1.0 | 0.2 | 12.5 | 0.0 |
| Miami | 879 | 4 795 | 360.0 | 97.3 | 200.6 | 216.9 | 1 039.2 | 92.5 | 54.1 | 217.8 | 70.6 | 337.3 | 0.2 |
| Miami Beach | 176 | 1 483 | 112.6 | 24.6 | 0.5 | 7.8 | 41.1 | 10.9 | 0.0 | 0.8 | 0.0 | 28.6 | 0.0 |
| Miami Gardens | 51 | 1 605 | 44.1 | 20.0 | 0.0 | 0.0 | 2.3 | 0.1 | 0.0 | 0.0 | 0.0 | 1.4 | 0.0 |
| Miami Lakes | 30 | 92 | 7.0 | 2.1 | 0.3 | 0.5 | 0.0 | 0.0 | 0.0 | 0.0 | 0.0 | 0.0 | 0.0 |
| Miramar | 92 | 395 | 33.4 | 10.4 | 10.2 | 10.4 | 4.0 | 2.4 | 0.0 | 0.8 | 0.0 | 0.8 | 0.0 |
| North Lauderdale | 45 | 221 | 23.8 | 7.1 | 0.0 | 0.0 | 0.5 | 0.0 | 0.5 | 0.0 | 0.0 | 0.0 | 0.0 |
| North Miami | 99 | 392 | 26.3 | 6.0 | 1.1 | 0.6 | 2.4 | 0.0 | 0.0 | 0.5 | 0.0 | 1.8 | 0.0 |
| North Miami Beach | 103 | 394 | 28.3 | 8.0 | 0.0 | 0.0 | 0.1 | 0.0 | 0.0 | 0.0 | 0.0 | 0.0 | 0.0 |
| North Port | 38 | 118 | 8.7 | 2.8 | 0.0 | 0.0 | 0.0 | 0.0 | 0.0 | 0.0 | 0.0 | 0.0 | 0.0 |
| Oakland Park | 185 | 584 | 51.7 | 14.1 | 0.0 | 0.0 | 0.3 | 0.0 | 0.0 | 0.0 | 0.0 | 0.0 | 0.0 |
| Ocala | 181 | 1 059 | 79.9 | 23.2 | 15.3 | 5.4 | 26.0 | 0.0 | 0.1 | 4.0 | 0.0 | 11.4 | 4.4 |
| Ocoee | 53 | D | D | D | 3.2 | 0.1 | 0.8 | 0.0 | 0.0 | 0.0 | 0.0 | 0.0 | 0.0 |
| Orlando | 501 | 4 728 | 334.7 | 100.1 | 3 058.4 | 472.0 | 290.7 | 36.2 | 16.3 | 70.1 | 0.3 | 62.7 | 1.1 |
| Ormond Beach | 74 | 308 | 18.3 | 5.6 | 1.3 | 0.4 | 1.7 | 0.0 | 0.0 | 0.0 | -0.1 | 1.5 | 0.0 |
| Oviedo | 58 | 300 | 19.0 | 5.7 | 13.6 | 0.8 | 2.8 | 0.0 | 0.0 | 0.3 | 0.0 | 2.5 | 0.0 |
| Palm Bay | 96 | 326 | 27.5 | 8.5 | 393.8 | 48.2 | 15.5 | 1.3 | 0.0 | 3.4 | 0.0 | 0.6 | 0.0 |
| Palm Beach Gardens | 95 | 498 | 38.8 | 13.8 | 15.9 | 146.4 | 0.1 | 0.0 | 0.0 | 0.1 | 0.0 | 0.0 | 0.0 |
| Palm Coast | 58 | 213 | 11.7 | 3.6 | 0.4 | 0.0 | 1.3 | 0.0 | 0.8 | 0.0 | 0.0 | 0.0 | 0.0 |
| Panama City | 92 | 624 | 40.1 | 12.3 | 274.6 | 46.4 | 13.7 | 1.3 | 5.1 | 0.2 | 0.0 | 3.5 | 0.0 |
| Pembroke Pines | 196 | 1 128 | 78.6 | 21.7 | 1.5 | 1.3 | 4.1 | 0.0 | 0.0 | 1.5 | 0.0 | 0.9 | 0.0 |
| Pensacola | 111 | 820 | 58.4 | 17.0 | 340.2 | 129.7 | 62.3 | 1.9 | 6.9 | 4.4 | 0.0 | 20.7 | 0.3 |
| Pinellas Park | 147 | 869 | 84.5 | 25.5 | 20.5 | 0.7 | 5.7 | 3.3 | 1.4 | 0.0 | 0.0 | 0.1 | 0.0 |
| Plantation | 154 | 858 | 52.5 | 24.3 | 8.6 | 5.1 | 1.4 | 0.0 | 0.0 | 0.8 | 0.0 | 0.5 | 0.0 |
| Plant City | 51 | 269 | 20.8 | 6.6 | 7.8 | 0.4 | 1.8 | 0.0 | 0.0 | 0.2 | 0.0 | 1.5 | 0.0 |
| Pompano Beach | 297 | 1 607 | 157.0 | 40.4 | 31.9 | 44.3 | 103.6 | 1.9 | 0.0 | 0.0 | 0.0 | 10.9 | 0.0 |
| Port Orange | 82 | 413 | 21.6 | 6.5 | 0.1 | 0.6 | 0.8 | 0.0 | 0.5 | 0.0 | 0.0 | 0.3 | 0.0 |
| Port St. Lucie | 125 | 424 | 31.4 | 9.4 | 1.4 | 1.5 | 3.6 | 1.5 | 0.0 | 1.3 | 0.0 | 0.7 | 0.0 |
| Riviera Beach | 67 | 355 | 48.2 | 12.4 | 0.0 | 22.0 | 0.3 | 0.0 | 0.0 | 0.0 | 0.0 | 0.2 | 0.0 |
| Royal Palm Beach | 57 | 275 | 19.2 | 5.6 | 0.0 | 0.3 | 0.0 | 0.0 | 0.0 | 0.0 | 0.0 | 0.0 | 0.0 |
| St. Cloud | 41 | D | D | D | 0.3 | 0.0 | 0.1 | 0.0 | 0.0 | 0.0 | 0.0 | 0.0 | 0.0 |
| St. Petersburg | 418 | 1 877 | 120.7 | 40.4 | 424.5 | 190.7 | 82.1 | 3.4 | 13.4 | 16.2 | 0.0 | 33.6 | 2.6 |
| Sanford | 113 | 647 | 54.1 | 18.0 | 22.2 | 1.6 | 28.9 | 4.0 | 0.0 | 3.2 | 0.0 | 9.8 | 0.3 |
| Sarasota | 164 | 1 171 | 72.1 | 23.3 | 1.7 | 1.5 | 62.4 | 4.7 | 3.2 | 1.4 | 0.0 | 39.0 | 0.0 |
| Sunrise | 127 | 521 | 41.1 | 11.9 | 64.8 | 7.6 | 17.9 | 0.6 | 13.5 | 1.4 | 0.0 | 2.3 | 0.0 |
| Tallahassee | 312 | 1 966 | 132.7 | 45.5 | 27.1 | 21.6 | 4 447.5 | 527.5 | 582.2 | 176.8 | 32.3 | 155.3 | 356.7 |
| Tamarac | 63 | 278 | 15.6 | 4.7 | 0.3 | 4.5 | 2.2 | 0.0 | 0.0 | 1.3 | 0.0 | 0.4 | 0.0 |
| Tampa | 769 | 7 266 | 431.8 | 130.5 | 998.2 | 342.0 | 496.2 | 200.1 | 24.7 | 10.2 | 1.4 | 197.1 | 1.8 |
| Titusville | 73 | 528 | 45.1 | 20.9 | 27.0 | 13.8 | 4.5 | 0.0 | 0.0 | 0.0 | 0.0 | 3.8 | 0.0 |
| Wellington | 94 | 527 | 38.8 | 13.1 | 137.8 | 1.9 | 0.5 | 0.0 | 0.0 | 0.5 | 0.0 | 0.0 | 0.0 |
| Weston | 84 | 496 | 30.4 | 11.1 | 0.8 | 4.9 | 1.1 | 1.0 | 0.0 | 0.1 | 0.0 | 0.0 | 0.0 |
| West Palm Beach | 203 | 1 198 | 85.8 | 28.0 | 55.5 | 11.5 | 189.6 | 19.6 | 15.0 | 1.9 | 0.4 | 122.2 | 0.0 |
| Winter Garden | 41 | 193 | 15.4 | 4.1 | 0.0 | 0.7 | 0.2 | 0.0 | 0.0 | 0.2 | 0.0 | 0.0 | 0.0 |
| Winter Haven | 60 | 228 | 18.9 | 5.7 | 0.4 | 1.0 | 11.8 | 0.0 | 5.6 | 0.0 | 0.0 | 1.3 | 2.9 |
| Winter Park | 107 | 506 | 35.4 | 11.8 | 21.5 | 0.6 | 7.7 | 0.9 | 1.3 | 0.0 | 0.0 | 0.3 | 0.0 |
| Winter Springs | 28 | 65 | 5.5 | 1.4 | 6.1 | 0.0 | 2.4 | 0.0 | 0.0 | 0.0 | 0.0 | 0.0 | 0.0 |

1. Establishments subject to federal tax.  2. Includes program categories not shown separately. State totals include additional categories not allocated by city.

# Table D. Cities — **City Government Finances**

| City | General revenue Total (mil dol) | Intergovernmental Total (mil dol) | Intergovernmental Percent from state government | Taxes Total (mil dol) | Taxes Per capita[1] (dollars) Total | Taxes Per capita[1] (dollars) Property | Taxes Per capita[1] (dollars) Sales and gross receipts | General expenditure Total (mil dol) | General expenditure Per capita[1] (dollars) Total | General expenditure Per capita[1] (dollars) Capital outlays |
|---|---|---|---|---|---|---|---|---|---|---|
| | 117 | 118 | 119 | 120 | 121 | 122 | 123 | 124 | 125 | 126 |
| **FLORIDA—Cont'd** | | | | | | | | | | |
| Deerfield Beach | 116.2 | 23.8 | 94.7 | 51.4 | 690 | 478 | 212 | 110.0 | 1 475 | 128 |
| DeLand | 35.6 | 3.6 | 70.8 | 18.6 | 691 | 281 | 410 | 37.0 | 1 377 | 431 |
| Delray Beach | 142.5 | 18.1 | 48.4 | 80.8 | 1 261 | 952 | 232 | 158.4 | 2 471 | 719 |
| Deltona | 57.0 | 10.8 | 84.6 | 27.5 | 324 | 116 | 208 | 42.3 | 498 | 70 |
| Doral | 52.8 | 3.5 | 82.8 | 34.6 | 1 510 | 750 | 760 | 45.8 | 1 996 | 1 140 |
| Dunedin | 47.3 | 4.5 | 90.1 | 21.7 | 598 | 244 | 354 | 54.8 | 1 511 | 391 |
| Fort Lauderdale | 447.7 | 128.1 | 18.3 | 193.6 | 1 054 | 685 | 370 | 394.6 | 2 149 | 188 |
| Fort Myers | 171.9 | 24.9 | 39.9 | 74.6 | 1 161 | 459 | 702 | 141.1 | 2 196 | 183 |
| Fort Pierce | 105.4 | 50.4 | 21.4 | 23.3 | 580 | 302 | 278 | 81.1 | 2 018 | 432 |
| Gainesville | 176.1 | 15.9 | 60.1 | 48.5 | 424 | 193 | 232 | 195.2 | 1 707 | 339 |
| Greenacres | 27.4 | 6.0 | 100.0 | 15.6 | 482 | 258 | 224 | 22.3 | 690 | 140 |
| Hallandale Beach | 63.7 | 8.5 | 55.0 | 31.7 | 820 | 512 | 307 | 66.1 | 1 712 | 212 |
| Hialeah | 215.3 | 53.2 | 54.0 | 109.5 | 516 | 256 | 260 | 223.8 | 1 054 | 139 |
| Hollywood | 277.5 | 57.3 | 48.3 | 122.4 | 859 | 559 | 300 | 272.8 | 1 915 | 234 |
| Homestead | 80.0 | 14.7 | 91.9 | 34.1 | 603 | 189 | 414 | 76.6 | 1 354 | 183 |
| Jacksonville | 1 810.6 | 262.0 | 73.8 | 745.0 | 925 | 511 | 413 | 1 627.8 | 2 021 | 369 |
| Jupiter | 66.7 | 9.8 | 63.1 | 36.6 | 750 | 410 | 340 | 61.0 | 1 250 | 269 |
| Kissimmee | 79.9 | 28.3 | 40.5 | 30.7 | 497 | 234 | 262 | 78.1 | 1 264 | 249 |
| Lakeland | 161.4 | 29.3 | 61.1 | 54.1 | 583 | 226 | 358 | 173.7 | 1 872 | 201 |
| Lake Worth | 74.4 | 28.5 | 23.1 | 24.2 | 681 | 398 | 283 | 67.8 | 1 906 | 249 |
| Largo | 105.8 | 12.6 | 81.8 | 41.3 | 564 | 204 | 360 | 99.5 | 1 358 | 180 |
| Lauderdale Lakes | 39.7 | 9.9 | 64.8 | 16.3 | 522 | 219 | 304 | 34.8 | 1 112 | 252 |
| Lauderhill | 61.3 | 16.4 | 46.6 | 29.7 | 440 | 208 | 232 | 64.4 | 953 | 0 |
| Margate | 72.4 | 18.1 | 90.5 | 30.3 | 554 | 376 | 178 | 69.4 | 1 271 | 28 |
| Melbourne | 116.9 | 18.6 | 59.5 | 45.9 | 591 | 224 | 367 | 102.9 | 1 324 | 135 |
| Miami | 683.7 | 168.6 | 36.4 | 345.6 | 844 | 609 | 234 | 734.5 | 1 793 | 273 |
| Miami Beach | 409.0 | 74.8 | 14.9 | 208.3 | 2 450 | 1 407 | 1 043 | 335.2 | 3 942 | 364 |
| Miami Gardens | 52.0 | 19.4 | 63.9 | 30.4 | 312 | 120 | 192 | 54.0 | 555 | 43 |
| Miami Lakes | 25.4 | 9.5 | 38.5 | 14.4 | 661 | 324 | 337 | 24.5 | 1 126 | 100 |
| Miramar | 162.6 | 34.1 | 37.1 | 74.9 | 692 | 400 | 292 | 134.3 | 1 241 | 149 |
| North Lauderdale | 37.7 | 11.2 | 45.0 | 15.3 | 365 | 176 | 178 | 37.8 | 904 | 26 |
| North Miami | 76.3 | 17.2 | 41.8 | 33.6 | 598 | 336 | 261 | 75.0 | 1 336 | 27 |
| North Miami Beach | 75.6 | 17.0 | 33.1 | 27.6 | 723 | 414 | 309 | 66.8 | 1 748 | 217 |
| North Port | 107.7 | 19.2 | 24.2 | 52.7 | 971 | 259 | 708 | 66.3 | 1 221 | 232 |
| Oakland Park | 61.3 | 8.1 | 22.3 | 28.7 | 681 | 350 | 331 | 86.5 | 2 053 | 131 |
| Ocala | 92.4 | 12.3 | 78.5 | 33.5 | 627 | 333 | 294 | 93.4 | 1 747 | 173 |
| Ocoee | 40.4 | 11.0 | 72.6 | 15.0 | 472 | 240 | 231 | 35.8 | 1 122 | 325 |
| Orlando | 542.4 | 124.2 | 42.4 | 205.3 | 901 | 413 | 488 | 504.5 | 2 214 | 129 |
| Ormond Beach | 51.9 | 8.4 | 44.4 | 25.1 | 653 | 309 | 344 | 48.3 | 1 257 | 168 |
| Oviedo | 33.0 | 7.5 | 73.9 | 16.6 | 538 | 302 | 236 | 37.8 | 1 226 | 338 |
| Palm Bay | 92.6 | 15.6 | 78.0 | 50.2 | 502 | 233 | 269 | 80.4 | 803 | 83 |
| Palm Beach Gardens | 76.1 | 9.6 | 100.0 | 50.7 | 1 036 | 837 | 199 | 69.6 | 1 423 | 152 |
| Palm Coast | 52.7 | 7.0 | 98.8 | 25.0 | 350 | 206 | 143 | 63.8 | 893 | 346 |
| Panama City | 58.3 | 8.7 | 88.6 | 28.8 | 783 | 272 | 511 | 50.8 | 1 380 | 146 |
| Pembroke Pines | 204.7 | 48.3 | 34.2 | 88.0 | 600 | 290 | 310 | 242.2 | 1 650 | 110 |
| Pensacola | 132.4 | 49.6 | 27.4 | 45.0 | 830 | 280 | 550 | 129.7 | 2 390 | 687 |
| Pinellas Park | 74.5 | 11.7 | 69.4 | 32.9 | 693 | 298 | 396 | 75.6 | 1 593 | 43 |
| Plantation | 129.0 | 38.2 | 34.9 | 58.3 | 691 | 365 | 326 | 130.5 | 1 547 | 139 |
| Plant City | 59.2 | 15.2 | 81.5 | 21.8 | 675 | 252 | 422 | 45.6 | 1 410 | 112 |
| Pompano Beach | 166.6 | 25.8 | 38.0 | 89.8 | 874 | 479 | 395 | 145.4 | 1 415 | 120 |
| Port Orange | 69.5 | 8.7 | 75.6 | 23.8 | 433 | 224 | 210 | 52.9 | 964 | 135 |
| Port St. Lucie | 258.4 | 20.1 | 61.8 | 88.6 | 585 | 250 | 335 | 239.7 | 1 583 | 632 |
| Riviera Beach | 75.1 | 3.8 | 78.2 | 39.8 | 1 087 | 747 | 340 | 70.0 | 1 914 | 140 |
| Royal Palm Beach | 30.7 | 4.6 | 70.7 | 15.3 | 504 | 175 | 329 | 22.8 | 750 | 94 |
| St. Cloud | 80.4 | 17.0 | 30.2 | 27.5 | 1 004 | 157 | 847 | 72.4 | 2 644 | 198 |
| St. Petersburg | 400.9 | 83.6 | 39.9 | 158.5 | 643 | 374 | 269 | 341.7 | 1 387 | 194 |
| Sanford | 87.4 | 24.8 | 24.2 | 31.5 | 624 | 263 | 361 | 69.8 | 1 384 | 334 |
| Sarasota | 135.3 | 28.0 | 56.5 | 51.6 | 982 | 425 | 558 | 114.0 | 2 173 | 160 |
| Sunrise | 179.1 | 22.2 | 55.2 | 67.7 | 754 | 375 | 379 | 137.7 | 1 534 | 138 |
| Tallahassee | 283.5 | 54.0 | 67.8 | 97.3 | 576 | 188 | 388 | 314.3 | 1 860 | 74 |
| Tamarac | 87.6 | 18.7 | 9.3 | 32.5 | 545 | 332 | 212 | 72.3 | 1 212 | 170 |
| Tampa | 659.9 | 123.2 | 58.6 | 286.7 | 851 | 419 | 433 | 566.8 | 1 683 | 229 |
| Titusville | 40.4 | 7.3 | 92.6 | 19.9 | 452 | 228 | 225 | 41.7 | 950 | 110 |
| Wellington | 76.0 | 14.7 | 47.8 | 33.4 | 614 | 268 | 346 | 62.2 | 1 141 | 250 |
| Weston | 73.3 | 14.2 | 100.0 | 25.5 | 398 | 151 | 247 | 63.5 | 989 | 106 |
| West Palm Beach | 245.0 | 44.6 | 27.3 | 119.3 | 1 200 | 773 | 427 | 220.5 | 2 219 | 305 |
| Winter Garden | 54.5 | 5.9 | 91.9 | 10.7 | 373 | 202 | 172 | 39.5 | 1 377 | 523 |
| Winter Haven | 53.4 | 5.9 | 72.7 | 22.2 | 680 | 308 | 372 | 49.6 | 1 522 | 369 |
| Winter Park | 62.1 | 9.1 | 87.8 | 29.0 | 1 038 | 645 | 393 | 60.9 | 2 180 | 271 |
| Winter Springs | 35.2 | 4.4 | 95.8 | 19.2 | 582 | 231 | 351 | 28.0 | 849 | 140 |

1. Based on population estimated as of July 1 of the year shown.

# Table D. Cities — **City Government Finances**

| City | City government finances, 2006 (cont.) | | | | | | | | | |
|------|---|---|---|---|---|---|---|---|---|---|
| | General expenditure (cont.) | | | | | | | | | |
| | Percent of total for: | | | | | | | | | |
| | Public welfare | Highways | Parking facilities | Education | Health and hospitals | Police protection | Sewerage and sanitation | Parks and recreation | Housing and community development | Interest on debt |
| | 127 | 128 | 129 | 130 | 131 | 132 | 133 | 134 | 135 | 136 |
| FLORIDA—Cont'd | | | | | | | | | | |
| Deerfield Beach............ | 13.5 | 1.9 | 0.1 | 0.0 | 0.0 | 13.3 | 20.3 | 6.7 | 1.0 | 1.7 |
| DeLand....................... | 0.0 | 3.7 | 0.0 | 0.0 | 0.0 | 17.0 | 13.3 | 9.3 | 2.4 | 1.9 |
| Delray Beach............... | 0.0 | 1.6 | 12.2 | 0.0 | 0.0 | 16.5 | 5.7 | 14.8 | 9.1 | 1.6 |
| Deltona...................... | 0.0 | 12.2 | 0.0 | 0.0 | 0.0 | 17.0 | 20.1 | 6.9 | 5.4 | 0.0 |
| Doral.......................... | 0.0 | 2.1 | 0.0 | 0.0 | 0.0 | 24.4 | 0.0 | 58.4 | 0.0 | 1.0 |
| Dunedin..................... | 0.0 | 4.0 | 0.0 | 0.0 | 0.0 | 8.4 | 22.1 | 27.6 | 0.0 | 0.8 |
| Fort Lauderdale............ | 0.0 | 2.4 | 2.2 | 0.0 | 0.0 | 22.4 | 4.4 | 12.4 | 9.5 | 1.1 |
| Fort Myers.................... | 0.0 | 6.9 | 0.5 | 0.0 | 0.0 | 16.5 | 23.7 | 12.5 | 6.1 | 3.8 |
| Fort Pierce.................. | 0.0 | 4.8 | 0.0 | 0.0 | 0.0 | 17.2 | 18.1 | 10.2 | 11.9 | 1.7 |
| Gainesville.................. | 0.5 | 5.4 | 0.2 | 0.0 | 0.0 | 18.1 | 24.6 | 5.6 | 2.6 | 6.9 |
| Greenacres.................. | 0.0 | 11.9 | 0.0 | 0.0 | 0.0 | 28.0 | 3.9 | 7.6 | 0.0 | 1.1 |
| Hallandale Beach......... | 2.0 | 1.5 | 0.0 | 0.0 | 0.0 | 22.0 | 18.4 | 3.4 | 9.8 | 0.5 |
| Hialeah ...................... | 0.0 | 10.7 | 0.0 | 0.0 | 0.1 | 17.7 | 17.0 | 6.2 | 3.1 | 2.4 |
| Hollywood................... | 0.0 | 3.1 | 1.6 | 0.0 | 0.0 | 24.1 | 15.7 | 7.9 | 1.7 | 3.3 |
| Homestead.................. | 0.0 | 5.3 | 0.0 | 0.0 | 0.0 | 32.2 | 17.1 | 8.8 | 9.1 | 1.2 |
| Jacksonville................ | 5.1 | 4.9 | 0.1 | 0.0 | 1.3 | 10.7 | 11.8 | 4.5 | 1.5 | 20.7 |
| Jupiter....................... | 0.0 | 10.1 | 0.0 | 0.0 | 0.0 | 26.7 | 6.5 | 6.8 | 0.0 | 2.9 |
| Kissimmee.................. | 0.0 | 17.9 | 0.0 | 0.0 | 0.0 | 21.3 | 7.9 | 9.2 | 0.0 | 4.1 |
| Lakeland..................... | 0.0 | 7.8 | 0.5 | 0.0 | 0.0 | 16.7 | 15.2 | 16.4 | 1.8 | 2.0 |
| Lake Worth................. | 0.0 | 5.2 | 0.1 | 0.0 | 0.0 | 20.1 | 28.0 | 8.6 | 0.0 | 1.0 |
| Largo......................... | 0.0 | 1.4 | 0.0 | 0.0 | 0.0 | 16.6 | 26.4 | 9.2 | 10.1 | 1.5 |
| Lauderdale Lakes......... | 1.5 | 9.4 | 0.0 | 0.0 | 0.0 | 19.1 | 6.5 | 19.7 | 1.2 | 3.8 |
| Lauderhill................... | 0.0 | 14.5 | 0.0 | 0.0 | 7.0 | 19.7 | 2.3 | 9.1 | 1.1 | 4.4 |
| Margate ..................... | 0.0 | 2.3 | 0.0 | 0.0 | 0.0 | 26.0 | 7.4 | 5.7 | 2.7 | 0.2 |
| Melbourne .................. | 0.0 | 15.0 | 0.0 | 0.0 | 0.0 | 16.1 | 14.3 | 9.7 | 2.4 | 2.4 |
| Miami......................... | 0.0 | 7.0 | 3.6 | 0.0 | 0.0 | 17.2 | 4.1 | 8.2 | 7.1 | 2.9 |
| Miami Beach................ | 0.0 | 3.2 | 6.3 | 0.0 | 3.9 | 20.7 | 12.9 | 19.9 | 0.9 | 4.5 |
| Miami Gardens............. | 0.0 | 16.4 | 0.0 | 0.0 | 0.0 | 50.7 | 0.0 | 7.3 | 0.0 | 0.6 |
| Miami Lakes................ | 0.0 | 30.8 | 0.0 | 0.0 | 0.0 | 25.2 | 0.0 | 13.0 | 0.0 | 0.0 |
| Miramar ..................... | 0.0 | 2.2 | 0.0 | 0.0 | 0.0 | 21.2 | 5.5 | 10.8 | 0.9 | 3.8 |
| North Lauderdale ......... | 0.0 | 3.2 | 0.0 | 8.5 | 0.0 | 19.3 | 12.7 | 10.7 | 1.1 | 1.8 |
| North Miami................ | 0.0 | 4.6 | 0.0 | 0.0 | 0.0 | 18.4 | 28.1 | 7.0 | 4.8 | 2.0 |
| North Miami Beach ....... | 0.0 | 1.6 | 0.0 | 0.0 | 0.0 | 30.7 | 19.2 | 5.4 | 0.4 | 3.1 |
| North Port................... | 0.0 | 22.4 | 0.0 | 0.0 | 0.0 | 13.7 | 21.0 | 4.6 | 0.0 | 0.4 |
| Oakland Park .............. | 0.0 | 2.3 | 0.0 | 0.0 | 0.0 | 11.7 | 24.7 | 6.2 | 0.0 | 0.6 |
| Ocala......................... | 0.2 | 14.6 | 0.1 | 0.0 | 1.1 | 21.9 | 22.5 | 5.5 | 1.0 | 2.0 |
| Ocoee........................ | 0.0 | 20.0 | 0.0 | 0.0 | 0.0 | 20.1 | 8.9 | 8.8 | 0.0 | 4.4 |
| Orlando...................... | 0.0 | 7.0 | 2.4 | 0.0 | 0.0 | 21.1 | 14.8 | 11.1 | 2.4 | 3.5 |
| Ormond Beach............. | 0.0 | 9.1 | 0.0 | 0.0 | 0.0 | 15.2 | 22.1 | 10.6 | 0.0 | 0.9 |
| Oviedo....................... | 0.0 | 25.0 | 0.0 | 0.0 | 0.0 | 14.2 | 5.7 | 19.8 | 0.0 | 2.8 |
| Palm Bay.................... | 0.0 | 17.0 | 0.0 | 0.0 | 0.0 | 23.8 | 13.2 | 6.4 | 5.2 | 1.6 |
| Palm Beach Gardens.... | 0.0 | 1.0 | 0.0 | 0.0 | 0.0 | 29.6 | 0.0 | 21.5 | 0.0 | 2.1 |
| Palm Coast................. | 0.0 | 13.2 | 0.0 | 0.0 | 0.0 | 2.8 | 36.7 | 7.7 | 0.0 | 3.8 |
| Panama City................ | 0.1 | 12.8 | 0.0 | 0.0 | 0.4 | 17.0 | 9.6 | 12.7 | 0.8 | 1.1 |
| Pembroke Pines........... | 1.1 | 3.1 | 0.0 | 0.0 | 0.0 | 10.3 | 14.8 | 6.5 | 2.6 | 8.3 |
| Pensacola................... | 0.0 | 4.2 | 0.0 | 0.0 | 0.0 | 13.1 | 4.8 | 4.6 | 6.6 | 3.5 |
| Pinellas Park .............. | 0.0 | 5.6 | 0.0 | 0.0 | 2.5 | 16.4 | 23.9 | 5.1 | 0.5 | 0.9 |
| Plantation .................. | 0.0 | 4.8 | 0.0 | 0.0 | 4.3 | 24.8 | 7.9 | 10.4 | 2.0 | 1.9 |
| Plant City................... | 0.0 | 5.8 | 0.0 | 0.0 | 0.5 | 15.4 | 34.7 | 10.5 | 6.1 | 2.0 |
| Pompano Beach........... | 0.0 | 3.0 | 0.0 | 0.0 | 7.5 | 26.8 | 11.0 | 11.5 | 2.2 | 0.4 |
| Port Orange................ | 0.0 | 9.0 | 0.0 | 0.0 | 0.0 | 19.4 | 24.6 | 13.5 | 1.6 | 2.8 |
| Port St. Lucie .............. | 0.0 | 45.9 | 0.0 | 0.0 | 0.6 | 12.8 | 4.6 | 5.0 | 0.8 | 5.6 |
| Riviera Beach.............. | 0.1 | 0.9 | 0.0 | 0.0 | 0.0 | 19.3 | 11.9 | 7.5 | 3.6 | 0.4 |
| Royal Palm Beach ........ | 0.0 | 14.5 | 0.0 | 0.0 | 0.0 | 24.9 | 10.8 | 18.1 | 0.0 | 0.7 |
| St. Cloud ................... | 0.0 | 10.1 | 0.0 | 0.0 | 1.7 | 10.2 | 17.2 | 13.5 | 0.0 | 2.7 |
| St. Petersburg.............. | 0.0 | 5.2 | 1.1 | 0.0 | 2.8 | 24.0 | 13.1 | 20.5 | 2.3 | 2.4 |
| Sanford...................... | 0.0 | 10.1 | 0.0 | 0.0 | 0.6 | 15.9 | 29.6 | 7.4 | 0.6 | 0.2 |
| Sarasota..................... | 0.0 | 8.5 | 0.4 | 0.0 | 0.0 | 23.4 | 18.1 | 16.2 | 11.7 | 1.0 |
| Sunrise...................... | 0.0 | 3.4 | 0.0 | 0.0 | 0.0 | 18.0 | 29.0 | 8.2 | 0.8 | 1.8 |
| Tallahassee................. | 0.0 | 24.6 | 0.1 | 0.0 | 0.0 | 13.3 | 15.9 | 8.7 | 1.9 | 2.6 |
| Tamarac..................... | 0.0 | 6.7 | 0.0 | 0.0 | 0.0 | 13.0 | 11.6 | 9.1 | 2.9 | 3.5 |
| Tampa ....................... | 0.0 | 10.3 | 2.6 | 0.0 | 0.0 | 21.0 | 25.5 | 12.0 | 4.8 | 5.7 |
| Titusville.................... | 0.0 | 4.4 | 0.0 | 0.0 | 0.0 | 21.8 | 16.7 | 9.5 | 10.1 | 0.6 |
| Wellington................... | 0.0 | 7.3 | 0.0 | 0.0 | 0.0 | 8.4 | 16.8 | 14.1 | 0.0 | 1.7 |
| Weston ...................... | 0.0 | 0.0 | 0.0 | 0.0 | 0.0 | 11.9 | 4.8 | 9.0 | 2.4 | 0.4 |
| West Palm Beach ......... | 0.0 | 6.6 | 1.5 | 0.0 | 1.5 | 19.8 | 11.9 | 6.4 | 6.5 | 2.8 |
| Winter Garden............. | 0.1 | 18.5 | 0.0 | 0.0 | 0.0 | 12.6 | 24.1 | 5.9 | 1.9 | 2.1 |
| Winter Haven .............. | 0.0 | 4.7 | 0.0 | 0.0 | 0.0 | 16.9 | 26.0 | 11.8 | 0.0 | 2.1 |
| Winter Park ................ | 0.0 | 4.1 | 0.0 | 0.0 | 0.0 | 16.9 | 18.6 | 10.5 | 0.8 | 1.8 |
| Winter Springs............. | 0.0 | 11.2 | 0.0 | 0.0 | 0.0 | 20.3 | 14.1 | 7.6 | 0.1 | 4.3 |

# Table D. Cities — City Government Finances, City Government Employment, and Climate

| City | City government finances, 2007 (cont.) Debt outstanding Total (mil dol) | Per capita[1] (dollars) | Debt issued during year | City government employment, 2011 | Climate[2] Average daily temperature (degrees Fahrenheit) Mean January | July | Limits January[3] | July[4] | Annual precipitation (inches) | Heating degree days | Cooling degree days |
|---|---|---|---|---|---|---|---|---|---|---|---|
| | 137 | 138 | 139 | 140 | 141 | 142 | 143 | 144 | 145 | 146 | 147 |
| **FLORIDA—Cont'd** | | | | | | | | | | | |
| Deerfield Beach.......... | 63.4 | 850 | 6.2 | 612 | 67.2 | 83.3 | 57.8 | 91.8 | 57.27 | 219 | 4 241 |
| DeLand..................... | 38.7 | 1 440 | 13.3 | NA | NA | NA | NA | NA | NA | NA | NA |
| Delray Beach............. | 93.6 | 1 459 | 7.9 | 774 | 66.2 | 82.5 | 57.3 | 90.1 | 61.39 | 246 | 3 999 |
| Deltona.................... | 99.1 | 1 166 | 18.6 | 306 | 57.1 | 81.2 | 44.5 | 91.2 | 57.03 | 954 | 2 819 |
| Doral...................... | 21.3 | 927 | 21.3 | NA | NA | NA | NA | NA | NA | NA | NA |
| Dunedin................... | 36.3 | 1 002 | 3.2 | 338 | 60.9 | 82.5 | 50.2 | 91.3 | 52.42 | 623 | 3 414 |
| Fort Lauderdale........... | 218.8 | 1 192 | 16.9 | 2 505 | 67.5 | 82.6 | 59.2 | 89.8 | 64.19 | 167 | 4 120 |
| Fort Myers................. | 247.9 | 3 858 | 40.7 | 902 | 64.9 | 83.0 | 54.5 | 91.7 | 54.19 | 302 | 3 957 |
| Fort Pierce................ | 153.7 | 3 823 | 20.2 | 643 | 62.6 | 81.7 | 50.7 | 91.5 | 53.50 | 477 | 3 430 |
| Gainesville................ | 783.8 | 6 853 | 394.0 | 2 068 | 54.4 | 81.1 | 41.8 | 92.4 | 49.56 | 1 249 | 2 608 |
| Greenacres................ | 6.1 | 189 | 0.0 | NA | 66.2 | 82.5 | 57.3 | 90.1 | 61.39 | 246 | 3 999 |
| Hallandale Beach......... | 14.2 | 368 | 0.0 | 431 | 68.1 | 83.7 | 59.6 | 90.9 | 58.53 | 149 | 4 361 |
| Hialeah ................... | 145.1 | 684 | 10.1 | 1 658 | 67.9 | 82.7 | 62.6 | 87.0 | 46.60 | 141 | 4 090 |
| Hollywood................. | 347.2 | 2 437 | 31.2 | 1 389 | 67.5 | 82.6 | 59.2 | 89.8 | 64.19 | 167 | 4 120 |
| Homestead................ | 29.5 | 521 | 1.2 | 376 | 67.0 | 81.8 | 56.2 | 90.6 | 55.55 | 238 | 3 923 |
| Jacksonville.............. | 10 924.0 | 13 560 | 1 203.5 | 9 368 | 54.5 | 82.5 | 42.6 | 92.7 | 51.88 | 1 222 | 2 810 |
| Jupiter..................... | 85.6 | 1 755 | 0.0 | 376 | 66.2 | 82.5 | 57.3 | 90.1 | 61.39 | 246 | 3 999 |
| Kissimmee................. | 408.5 | 6 613 | 10.6 | 894 | 59.7 | 81.8 | 47.7 | 91.6 | 48.01 | 694 | 3 111 |
| Lakeland.................. | 940.7 | 10 137 | 189.0 | 2 161 | 62.5 | 84.0 | 51.1 | 94.6 | 49.13 | 487 | 3 886 |
| Lake Worth................ | 94.7 | 2 663 | 12.9 | 333 | 65.1 | 81.1 | 52.5 | 91.3 | 58.44 | 273 | 3 438 |
| Largo..................... | 30.1 | 410 | 0.0 | 850 | 61.3 | 82.5 | 52.4 | 89.7 | 44.77 | 591 | 3 482 |
| Lauderdale Lakes.......... | 16.1 | 514 | 1.5 | NA | 67.2 | 83.3 | 57.8 | 91.8 | 57.27 | 219 | 4 241 |
| Lauderhill................. | 82.3 | 1 218 | 0.0 | 407 | 67.5 | 82.6 | 59.2 | 89.8 | 64.19 | 167 | 4 120 |
| Margate ................... | 24.7 | 453 | 0.0 | 493 | 67.2 | 83.3 | 57.8 | 91.8 | 57.27 | 219 | 4 241 |
| Melbourne ................ | 120.2 | 1 548 | 7.3 | 872 | 60.9 | 81.2 | 50.0 | 90.5 | 48.29 | 595 | 3 186 |
| Miami..................... | 544.0 | 1 328 | 43.0 | 3 923 | 68.1 | 83.7 | 59.6 | 90.9 | 58.53 | 149 | 4 361 |
| Miami Beach.............. | 471.4 | 5 544 | 62.6 | 1 883 | 68.1 | 83.7 | 59.6 | 90.9 | 58.53 | 149 | 4 361 |
| Miami Gardens............ | 11.0 | 113 | 0.0 | 553 | NA | NA | NA | NA | NA | NA | NA |
| Miami Lakes............... | 0.0 | 0 | 0.0 | NA | NA | NA | NA | NA | NA | NA | NA |
| Miramar................... | 132.6 | 1 225 | 6.7 | 820 | 68.1 | 83.7 | 59.6 | 90.9 | 58.53 | 149 | 4 361 |
| North Lauderdale ......... | 14.2 | 339 | 0.0 | NA | 67.5 | 82.6 | 59.2 | 89.8 | 64.19 | 167 | 4 120 |
| North Miami............... | 22.2 | 395 | 1.2 | 456 | 68.1 | 83.7 | 59.6 | 90.9 | 58.53 | 149 | 4 361 |
| North Miami Beach ....... | 108.7 | 2 845 | 0.0 | 551 | 68.1 | 83.7 | 59.6 | 90.9 | 58.53 | 149 | 4 361 |
| North Port................. | 44.1 | 812 | 6.2 | 517 | NA | NA | NA | NA | NA | NA | NA |
| Oakland Park ............. | 23.0 | 545 | 0.0 | NA | 67.5 | 82.6 | 59.2 | 89.8 | 64.19 | 167 | 4 120 |
| Ocala...................... | 186.6 | 3 488 | 7.6 | 978 | 58.1 | 81.7 | 45.7 | 92.2 | 49.68 | 902 | 2 971 |
| Ocoee..................... | 60.1 | 1 885 | 5.6 | NA | NA | NA | NA | NA | NA | NA | NA |
| Orlando.................... | 480.8 | 2 110 | 85.1 | 2 799 | 60.9 | 82.4 | 49.9 | 92.2 | 48.35 | 580 | 3 428 |
| Ormond Beach............ | 34.0 | 884 | 8.3 | 335 | 60.9 | 82.4 | 49.9 | 92.2 | 48.35 | 580 | 3 428 |
| Oviedo.................... | 40.2 | 1 304 | 0.1 | 283 | 58.7 | 81.5 | 47.0 | 91.9 | 51.31 | 799 | 3 017 |
| Palm Bay.................. | 140.7 | 1 405 | 47.4 | 746 | 60.9 | 81.2 | 50.0 | 90.5 | 48.29 | 595 | 3 186 |
| Palm Beach Gardens.... | 36.2 | 739 | 6.1 | 456 | 66.2 | 82.5 | 57.3 | 90.1 | 61.39 | 246 | 3 999 |
| Palm Coast................ | 114.1 | 1 598 | 10.9 | NA | 57.4 | 82.8 | 46.4 | 92.0 | 49.79 | 909 | 3 193 |
| Panama City.............. | 42.5 | 1 155 | 0.0 | 557 | 50.3 | 80.0 | 38.7 | 89.0 | 64.76 | 1 810 | 2 174 |
| Pembroke Pines........... | 308.0 | 2 098 | 0.0 | 872 | 67.5 | 82.6 | 59.2 | 89.8 | 64.19 | 167 | 4 120 |
| Pensacola................. | 91.3 | 1 681 | 0.0 | 854 | 52.0 | 82.6 | 42.7 | 90.7 | 64.28 | 1 498 | 2 650 |
| Pinellas Park.............. | 42.8 | 903 | 0.0 | 512 | 61.7 | 83.4 | 54.0 | 90.2 | 49.58 | 548 | 3 718 |
| Plantation................. | 67.1 | 795 | 0.0 | 813 | 67.5 | 82.6 | 59.2 | 89.8 | 64.19 | 167 | 4 120 |
| Plant City................. | 35.5 | 1 098 | 2.2 | NA | 61.1 | 81.5 | 49.8 | 90.8 | 51.17 | 625 | 3 261 |
| Pompano Beach........... | 62.6 | 609 | 49.4 | 771 | 67.2 | 83.3 | 57.8 | 91.8 | 57.27 | 219 | 4 241 |
| Port Orange............... | 159.2 | 2 899 | 38.8 | NA | 57.1 | 81.2 | 44.5 | 91.2 | 57.03 | 954 | 2 819 |
| Port St. Lucie ............. | 774.4 | 5 115 | 174.8 | 1 002 | 64.5 | 81.8 | 54.7 | 89.5 | 59.53 | 315 | 3 600 |
| Riviera Beach............. | 49.1 | 1 343 | 7.4 | 481 | 66.2 | 82.5 | 57.3 | 90.1 | 61.39 | 246 | 3 999 |
| Royal Palm Beach ....... | 4.6 | 152 | 0.0 | NA | NA | NA | NA | NA | NA | NA | NA |
| St. Cloud ................. | 48.1 | 1 757 | 9.5 | NA | NA | NA | NA | NA | NA | NA | NA |
| St. Petersburg............. | 573.0 | 2 325 | 66.4 | 2 943 | 61.7 | 83.4 | 54.0 | 90.2 | 49.58 | 548 | 3 718 |
| Sanford................... | 50.0 | 991 | 11.5 | 580 | 58.7 | 81.5 | 47.0 | 91.9 | 51.31 | 799 | 3 017 |
| Sarasota.................. | 86.1 | 1 640 | 0.8 | 659 | 61.7 | 83.4 | 54.0 | 90.2 | 49.58 | 548 | 3 718 |
| Sunrise................... | 300.0 | 3 341 | 3.6 | 917 | 67.5 | 82.6 | 59.2 | 89.8 | 64.19 | 167 | 4 120 |
| Tallahassee............... | 675.5 | 3 998 | 146.0 | 3 006 | 51.8 | 82.4 | 39.7 | 92.0 | 63.21 | 1 604 | 2 551 |
| Tamarac................... | 53.4 | 895 | 20.6 | NA | 67.2 | 83.3 | 57.8 | 91.8 | 57.27 | 219 | 4 241 |
| Tampa.................... | 1 533.7 | 4 553 | 36.3 | 4 244 | 61.3 | 82.5 | 52.4 | 89.7 | 44.77 | 591 | 3 482 |
| Titusville.................. | 64.9 | 1 478 | 0.0 | 465 | 59.9 | 82.4 | 49.5 | 91.4 | 52.79 | 677 | 3 300 |
| Wellington................ | 40.9 | 750 | 0.0 | NA | 66.2 | 82.5 | 57.3 | 90.1 | 61.39 | 246 | 3 999 |
| Weston.................... | 6.8 | 106 | 0.0 | NA | 67.5 | 82.6 | 59.2 | 89.8 | 64.19 | 167 | 4 120 |
| West Palm Beach ........ | 272.5 | 2 742 | 42.9 | 1 499 | 66.2 | 82.5 | 57.3 | 90.1 | 61.39 | 246 | 3 999 |
| Winter Garden............ | 30.6 | 1 066 | 12.0 | NA | NA | NA | NA | NA | NA | NA | NA |
| Winter Haven ............. | 85.4 | 2 622 | 0.0 | 473 | 62.3 | 82.3 | 51.0 | 92.5 | 50.22 | 538 | 3 551 |
| Winter Park............... | 147.2 | 5 268 | 9.1 | NA | NA | NA | NA | NA | NA | NA | NA |
| Winter Springs............ | 43.3 | 1 314 | 0.4 | NA | 60.9 | 82.4 | 49.9 | 92.2 | 48.35 | 580 | 3 428 |

1. Based on the population estimated as of July 1 of the year shown.   2. Represents normal values based on the 30-year period, 1971–2000.   3. Average daily minimum.   4. Average daily maximum.

# Table D. Cities — **Land Area and Population**

| STATE Place code | City | Land area,[1] 2010 (sq km) | Population, 2012 Total persons | Rank | Per square kilometer | Race alone or in combination, not of Hispanic origin (percent), 2010 — White | Black | American Indian, Alaska Native | Asian | Hawaiian Pacific Islander | Percent Hispanic or Latino[2], 2010 | Percent Foreign born 2007–2011 |
|---|---|---|---|---|---|---|---|---|---|---|---|---|
| | | 1 | 2 | 3 | 4 | 5 | 6 | 7 | 8 | 9 | 10 | 11 |
| 13 00000 | GEORGIA............... | 148 959.2 | 9 919 945 | X | 66.6 | 57.1 | 30.9 | 0.7 | 3.7 | 0.1 | 8.8 | 9.7 |
| 13 01052 | Albany ...................... | 142.8 | 77 431 | 418 | 542.2 | 25.2 | 72.0 | 0.5 | 1.0 | 0.1 | 2.1 | 2.3 |
| 13 01696 | Alpharetta................. | 69.7 | 61 981 | 558 | 889.3 | 66.5 | 11.4 | 0.5 | 14.5 | 0.2 | 8.5 | 21.9 |
| 13 03436 | Athens-Clarke County ... | 308.7 | 118 999 | 221 | 394.8 | 58.5 | 27.1 | 0.5 | 4.8 | 0.1 | 10.4 | 11.2 |
| 13 04000 | Atlanta...................... | 344.9 | 443 775 | 40 | 1 286.7 | 37.4 | 54.4 | 0.7 | 3.7 | 0.1 | 5.2 | 7.6 |
| 13 04200 | Augusta-Richmond County | 840.0 | 197 872 | 117 | 252.6 | 39.7 | 54.9 | 0.8 | 2.2 | 0.3 | 4.1 | 3.6 |
| 13 19000 | Columbus .................. | 560.4 | 198 413 | 116 | 354.1 | 45.4 | 46.3 | 0.8 | 2.8 | 0.3 | 6.4 | 5.0 |
| 13 21380 | Dalton....................... | 53.2 | 33 413 | 1 092 | 628.1 | 43.4 | 6.6 | 0.3 | 2.5 | 0.1 | 48.0 | 26.9 |
| 13 23900 | Douglasville.............. | 58.2 | 31 269 | 1 158 | 537.3 | 35.0 | 56.5 | 0.7 | 2.1 | 0.2 | 7.2 | 7.9 |
| 13 24600 | Duluth....................... | 25.9 | 27 926 | 1 293 | 1 078.2 | 43.1 | 20.7 | 0.7 | 23.3 | 0.1 | 14.0 | 29.4 |
| 13 24768 | Dunwoody.................. | 33.5 | 47 224 | 782 | 1 409.7 | 65.3 | 13.0 | 0.6 | 12.1 | 0.1 | 10.3 | 22.5 |
| 13 25720 | East Point.................. | 38.0 | 35 584 | 1 029 | 936.4 | 12.7 | 75.2 | 0.8 | 1.1 | 0.1 | 11.5 | 8.5 |
| 13 31908 | Gainesville................ | 82.7 | 34 786 | 1 051 | 420.6 | 40.1 | 15.4 | 0.5 | 3.5 | 0.1 | 41.6 | 29.4 |
| 13 38964 | Hinesville.................. | 52.8 | 34 751 | 1 053 | 658.2 | 38.1 | 48.4 | 1.1 | 3.6 | 1.1 | 11.5 | 8.6 |
| 13 42425 | Johns Creek .............. | 79.6 | 82 306 | 381 | 1 034.0 | 61.6 | 9.8 | 0.4 | 24.6 | 0.1 | 5.2 | 25.0 |
| 13 43192 | Kennesaw .................. | 24.5 | 30 990 | 1 176 | 1 264.9 | 60.8 | 23.1 | 0.7 | 6.1 | 0.1 | 10.8 | 16.3 |
| 13 44340 | LaGrange .................. | 102.3 | 30 478 | 1 194 | 297.9 | 44.4 | 48.8 | 0.5 | 2.7 | 0.1 | 4.7 | 5.6 |
| 13 45488 | Lawrenceville............ | 34.7 | 29 481 | 1 236 | 849.6 | 39.8 | 32.4 | 0.6 | 6.3 | 0.1 | 22.3 | 26.8 |
| 13 49000 | Macon ...................... | 144.3 | 91 234 | 330 | 632.3 | 28.5 | 68.5 | 0.5 | 1.0 | 0.1 | 2.5 | 2.7 |
| 13 49756 | Marietta ................... | 59.8 | 58 359 | 606 | 975.9 | 44.4 | 32.0 | 0.6 | 3.4 | 0.2 | 20.6 | 23.7 |
| 13 51670 | Milton ...................... | 99.8 | 35 015 | 1 042 | 350.9 | 73.9 | 9.5 | 0.5 | 11.3 | 0.1 | 6.0 | 16.1 |
| 13 55020 | Newnan ..................... | 47.4 | 34 174 | 1 070 | 721.0 | 56.0 | 30.9 | 0.7 | 3.2 | 0.2 | 11.0 | 9.5 |
| 13 59724 | Peachtree City........... | 63.6 | 34 662 | 1 056 | 545.0 | 79.6 | 8.1 | 0.6 | 6.2 | 0.2 | 7.1 | 10.5 |
| 13 66668 | Rome........................ | 80.1 | 36 159 | 1 011 | 451.4 | 53.7 | 28.6 | 0.6 | 2.2 | 0.1 | 16.2 | 11.1 |
| 13 67284 | Roswell..................... | 105.5 | 93 692 | 317 | 888.1 | 67.1 | 12.2 | 0.5 | 4.8 | 0.1 | 16.6 | 18.9 |
| 13 68516 | Sandy Springs............ | 97.5 | 99 419 | 293 | 1 019.7 | 60.2 | 20.3 | 0.6 | 5.7 | 0.1 | 14.2 | 20.3 |
| 13 69000 | Savannah .................. | 267.2 | 142 022 | 180 | 531.5 | 37.6 | 56.0 | 0.7 | 2.5 | 0.2 | 4.7 | 6.0 |
| 13 71492 | Smyrna ..................... | 39.8 | 52 650 | 686 | 1 322.9 | 48.3 | 32.2 | 0.8 | 5.6 | 0.1 | 14.9 | 16.7 |
| 13 73256 | Statesboro ................ | 35.0 | 29 779 | 1 224 | 850.8 | 54.5 | 40.7 | 0.5 | 2.4 | 0.2 | 3.0 | 3.9 |
| 13 73704 | Stockbridge .............. | 34.5 | 26 281 | 1 382 | 761.8 | 26.9 | 56.5 | 0.9 | 8.3 | 0.2 | 9.5 | 15.2 |
| 13 78800 | Valdosta ................... | 92.8 | 57 597 | 616 | 620.7 | 42.7 | 51.6 | 0.6 | 2.1 | 0.2 | 4.0 | 4.5 |
| 13 80508 | Warner Robins ............ | 90.8 | 70 712 | 467 | 778.8 | 52.2 | 38.1 | 0.9 | 3.6 | 0.2 | 7.6 | 5.8 |
| 15 00000 | HAWAII..................... | 16 634.5 | 1 392 313 | X | 83.7 | 36.5 | 2.5 | 1.7 | 53.4 | 22.9 | 8.9 | 17.8 |
| 15 06290 | East Honolulu CDP ...... | 59.6 | NA | NA | NA | 40.6 | 1.1 | 1.2 | 63.8 | 12.2 | 4.1 | 15.0 |
| 15 14650 | Hilo CDP.................... | 138.3 | NA | NA | NA | 34.5 | 1.2 | 2.1 | 55.1 | 33.0 | 10.4 | 8.1 |
| 15 22700 | Kahului CDP................ | 37.4 | NA | NA | NA | 19.1 | 1.0 | 1.2 | 66.5 | 25.4 | 9.4 | 27.1 |
| 15 23150 | Kailua CDP (Honolulu County) ... | 20.1 | NA | NA | NA | 62.1 | 1.5 | 1.9 | 38.5 | 22.8 | 6.5 | 8.0 |
| 15 28250 | Kaneohe CDP.............. | 16.9 | NA | NA | NA | 39.1 | 1.2 | 1.9 | 58.9 | 29.0 | 8.4 | 8.0 |
| 15 51050 | Mililani Town CDP........ | 10.4 | NA | NA | NA | 33.1 | 3.2 | 1.6 | 65.4 | 19.0 | 9.3 | 12.5 |
| 15 62600 | Pearl City CDP............ | 23.6 | NA | NA | NA | 26.5 | 3.7 | 1.2 | 67.2 | 16.4 | 8.2 | 13.1 |
| 15 71550 | Urban Honolulu CDP .... | 156.8 | 345 610 | 54 | 2 204.1 | 26.5 | 2.3 | 1.2 | 65.9 | 16.7 | 5.4 | 28.3 |
| 15 79700 | Waipahu CDP .............. | 7.2 | NA | NA | NA | 9.5 | 1.5 | 0.6 | 75.5 | 21.5 | 5.8 | 37.0 |
| 16 00000 | IDAHO...................... | 214 044.7 | 1 595 728 | X | 7.5 | 85.6 | 0.9 | 1.9 | 1.8 | 0.3 | 11.2 | 5.9 |
| 16 08830 | Boise City ................. | 205.6 | 212 303 | 99 | 1 032.6 | 87.3 | 1.9 | 1.2 | 4.2 | 0.4 | 7.1 | 7.5 |
| 16 12250 | Caldwell.................... | 57.1 | 47 668 | 778 | 834.8 | 62.4 | 0.8 | 1.3 | 1.5 | 0.3 | 35.4 | 12.0 |
| 16 16750 | Coeur d'Alene............ | 40.3 | 45 579 | 808 | 1 131.0 | 93.2 | 0.8 | 2.2 | 1.4 | 0.3 | 4.3 | 2.6 |
| 16 39700 | Idaho Falls................ | 57.9 | 57 899 | 612 | 1 000.0 | 84.5 | 1.0 | 1.3 | 1.5 | 0.2 | 12.9 | 5.6 |
| 16 46540 | Lewiston ................... | 44.6 | 32 051 | 1 138 | 718.6 | 94.2 | 0.6 | 2.8 | 1.3 | 0.2 | 2.8 | 1.7 |
| 16 52120 | Meridian.................... | 69.4 | 80 386 | 400 | 1 158.3 | 90.1 | 1.2 | 0.9 | 2.7 | 0.3 | 6.8 | 4.5 |
| 16 56260 | Nampa....................... | 80.8 | 83 930 | 371 | 1 038.7 | 74.5 | 1.0 | 1.5 | 1.4 | 0.5 | 22.9 | 8.7 |
| 16 64090 | Pocatello................... | 83.5 | 54 777 | 659 | 656.0 | 88.6 | 1.4 | 2.1 | 2.2 | 0.4 | 7.2 | 2.9 |
| 16 64810 | Post Falls ................. | 36.5 | 28 651 | 1 268 | 785.0 | 93.2 | 0.7 | 1.9 | 1.4 | 0.2 | 4.6 | 1.8 |
| 16 67420 | Rexburg .................... | 25.3 | 25 732 | 1 403 | 1 017.1 | 92.0 | 0.8 | 0.5 | 1.9 | 0.4 | 5.6 | 2.6 |
| 16 82810 | Twin Falls ................. | 46.9 | 45 158 | 813 | 962.9 | 83.7 | 0.8 | 1.2 | 2.4 | 0.2 | 13.1 | 9.5 |
| 17 00000 | ILLINOIS.................. | 143 793.4 | 12 875 255 | X | 89.5 | 64.9 | 15.0 | 0.5 | 5.1 | 0.1 | 15.8 | 13.7 |
| 17 00243 | Addison ..................... | 25.3 | 37 287 | 973 | 1 473.8 | 48.3 | 4.0 | 0.3 | 8.0 | 0.1 | 40.1 | 35.8 |
| 17 00685 | Algonquin .................. | 31.7 | 30 004 | 1 213 | 946.5 | 83.8 | 2.0 | 0.4 | 8.1 | 0.1 | 6.8 | 13.3 |
| 17 01114 | Alton ........................ | 40.1 | 27 415 | 1 325 | 683.7 | 70.5 | 29.1 | 1.0 | 0.8 | 0.1 | 1.9 | 1.3 |
| 17 02154 | Arlington Heights.......... | 43.0 | 75 777 | 434 | 1 762.3 | 85.6 | 1.4 | 0.2 | 7.9 | 0.1 | 5.7 | 18.1 |
| 17 03012 | Aurora...................... | 116.4 | 199 932 | 112 | 1 717.6 | 41.2 | 11.1 | 0.4 | 7.3 | 0.1 | 41.3 | 24.8 |
| 17 04013 | Bartlett .................... | 40.5 | 41 618 | 874 | 1 027.6 | 74.3 | 2.6 | 0.4 | 15.2 | 0.1 | 8.6 | 16.7 |
| 17 04078 | Batavia ..................... | 25.0 | 26 318 | 1 379 | 1 052.7 | 88.7 | 2.8 | 0.3 | 2.3 | 0.0 | 6.8 | 4.6 |
| 17 04845 | Belleville .................. | 58.9 | 43 765 | 835 | 743.0 | 70.5 | 26.8 | 0.8 | 1.6 | 0.2 | 2.6 | 2.1 |
| 17 05092 | Belvidere .................. | 31.3 | 25 371 | 1 426 | 810.6 | 65.8 | 3.0 | 0.5 | 1.3 | 0.1 | 30.6 | 16.7 |
| 17 05573 | Berwyn ..................... | 10.1 | 56 800 | 631 | 5 623.8 | 31.8 | 6.3 | 0.4 | 2.8 | 0.1 | 59.4 | 25.3 |
| 17 06613 | Bloomington .............. | 70.5 | 77 733 | 416 | 1 102.6 | 76.8 | 11.5 | 0.6 | 7.6 | 0.1 | 5.6 | 8.3 |
| 17 07133 | Bolingbrook .............. | 62.3 | 74 039 | 443 | 1 188.4 | 43.4 | 21.2 | 0.5 | 12.2 | 0.1 | 24.5 | 23.1 |
| 17 09447 | Buffalo Grove ............ | 24.6 | 41 715 | 872 | 1 695.7 | 77.6 | 1.2 | 0.2 | 16.9 | 0.1 | 4.9 | 25.7 |

1. Dry land or land partially or temporarily covered by water.  2. May be of any race.

# Table D. Cities — Population

| City | Age of population (percent), 2010 | | | | | | | | | | | Population | | | |
|---|---|---|---|---|---|---|---|---|---|---|---|---|---|---|---|
| | | | | | | | | | | | | Census counts | | Percent change | |
| | Under 5 years | 5 to 17 years | 18 to 24 years | 25 to 34 years | 35 to 44 years | 45 to 54 years | 55 to 64 years | 65 to 74 years | 75 years and over | Median age | Percent female | 2000 | 2010 | 2000–2010 | 2010–2012 |
| | 12 | 13 | 14 | 15 | 16 | 17 | 18 | 19 | 20 | 21 | 22 | 23 | 24 | 25 | 26 |
| GEORGIA | 7.1 | 18.6 | 10.0 | 13.8 | 14.4 | 14.4 | 11.0 | 6.3 | 4.4 | 35.3 | 51.2 | 8 186 453 | 9 687 663 | 18.3 | 2.4 |
| Albany | 7.9 | 18.4 | 14.2 | 14.0 | 11.4 | 12.2 | 10.6 | 5.9 | 5.4 | 31.4 | 53.9 | 76 939 | 77 434 | 0.6 | 0.0 |
| Alpharetta | 6.5 | 22.3 | 6.0 | 12.6 | 17.7 | 18.0 | 9.5 | 4.0 | 3.4 | 36.8 | 51.3 | 34 854 | 57 500 | 65.1 | 7.8 |
| Athens-Clarke County | 6.0 | 11.5 | 30.4 | 16.8 | 10.1 | 8.9 | 7.9 | 4.6 | 3.9 | 25.9 | 52.5 | 101 489 | 115 453 | 15.0 | 3.1 |
| Atlanta | 6.4 | 13.0 | 14.3 | 19.8 | 14.8 | 12.3 | 9.6 | 5.5 | 4.4 | 32.9 | 50.2 | 416 474 | 420 279 | 0.8 | 5.6 |
| Augusta-Richmond County | 7.4 | 17.2 | 12.5 | 15.1 | 11.6 | 13.7 | 11.2 | 6.3 | 5.0 | 33.2 | 51.6 | 199 775 | 195 844 | 0.4 | 1.0 |
| Columbus | 7.4 | 18.1 | 11.4 | 14.9 | 12.3 | 13.5 | 10.6 | 6.0 | 5.6 | 33.5 | 52.1 | 186 291 | 189 885 | 1.9 | 4.5 |
| Dalton | 9.1 | 20.4 | 10.8 | 14.8 | 14.0 | 11.4 | 8.7 | 5.6 | 5.1 | 31.3 | 50.7 | 27 912 | 33 133 | 18.7 | 0.8 |
| Douglasville | 8.2 | 20.1 | 9.5 | 15.9 | 17.3 | 13.2 | 8.9 | 4.3 | 2.5 | 32.7 | 53.2 | 20 065 | 30 956 | 54.3 | 1.0 |
| Duluth | 7.3 | 17.1 | 8.2 | 17.0 | 16.8 | 15.7 | 10.6 | 4.4 | 2.8 | 35.2 | 52.2 | 22 122 | 26 600 | 20.2 | 5.0 |
| Dunwoody | 7.3 | 16.1 | 6.6 | 18.7 | 16.8 | 12.6 | 9.6 | 6.9 | 5.5 | 35.7 | 51.9 | 32 808 | 46 267 | 41.0 | 2.1 |
| East Point | 7.9 | 18.0 | 10.8 | 16.3 | 13.8 | 13.4 | 11.1 | 5.4 | 3.3 | 33.1 | 52.6 | 39 595 | 33 712 | -14.9 | 5.6 |
| Gainesville | 10.1 | 20.3 | 13.1 | 16.7 | 12.5 | 9.1 | 7.6 | 4.8 | 5.8 | 28.5 | 52.2 | 25 578 | 33 809 | 32.2 | 2.9 |
| Hinesville | 10.3 | 20.4 | 12.9 | 17.2 | 12.2 | 13.3 | 8.5 | 3.7 | 1.7 | 28.2 | 52.7 | 30 392 | 33 439 | 10.0 | 3.9 |
| Johns Creek | 6.0 | 24.8 | 5.7 | 8.5 | 17.9 | 19.8 | 10.6 | 4.0 | 2.7 | 38.4 | 51.4 | NA | 76 727 | NA | 7.3 |
| Kennesaw | 7.4 | 19.5 | 10.6 | 16.4 | 16.8 | 13.6 | 8.2 | 4.0 | 3.3 | 32.3 | 52.7 | 21 675 | 30 052 | 37.4 | 3.1 |
| LaGrange | 8.3 | 19.2 | 11.6 | 13.1 | 12.4 | 12.5 | 10.1 | 6.0 | 6.8 | 33.0 | 53.8 | 25 998 | 29 617 | 13.8 | 2.9 |
| Lawrenceville | 8.8 | 21.0 | 9.1 | 15.1 | 14.9 | 12.7 | 9.1 | 4.4 | 4.8 | 32.4 | 52.2 | 22 397 | 28 391 | 27.5 | 3.8 |
| Macon | 8.1 | 18.5 | 12.1 | 13.2 | 11.3 | 13.2 | 11.1 | 6.3 | 6.0 | 33.3 | 53.9 | 97 255 | 91 348 | -6.1 | -0.1 |
| Marietta | 8.2 | 15.2 | 11.6 | 18.8 | 14.5 | 12.2 | 9.3 | 4.9 | 5.1 | 32.6 | 51.1 | 58 748 | 56 537 | -3.7 | 3.2 |
| Milton | 6.3 | 24.6 | 5.7 | 11.1 | 17.9 | 18.9 | 9.3 | 3.9 | 2.3 | 36.7 | 51.1 | NA | 32 712 | NA | 7.0 |
| Newnan | 9.5 | 19.0 | 8.7 | 17.4 | 15.7 | 11.6 | 8.9 | 5.2 | 4.0 | 32.3 | 52.5 | 16 242 | 33 188 | 103.4 | 3.0 |
| Peachtree City | 4.7 | 22.8 | 6.0 | 7.8 | 14.0 | 19.0 | 13.7 | 6.8 | 5.2 | 41.7 | 51.7 | 31 580 | 34 364 | 8.8 | 0.9 |
| Rome | 8.2 | 17.5 | 10.0 | 14.2 | 12.3 | 12.7 | 11.0 | 6.8 | 7.4 | 35.1 | 52.4 | 34 980 | 36 303 | 3.8 | -0.4 |
| Roswell | 7.4 | 18.2 | 6.7 | 13.7 | 15.7 | 15.5 | 12.4 | 5.9 | 4.5 | 37.6 | 50.7 | 79 334 | 88 347 | 11.4 | 6.1 |
| Sandy Springs | 6.8 | 14.4 | 8.6 | 20.3 | 15.0 | 13.1 | 10.9 | 5.5 | 5.2 | 34.9 | 51.8 | 85 781 | 93 853 | 9.4 | 5.9 |
| Savannah | 7.1 | 15.2 | 16.1 | 16.2 | 11.1 | 12.2 | 10.3 | 5.9 | 5.7 | 31.3 | 52.1 | 131 510 | 136 322 | 3.6 | 4.2 |
| Smyrna | 9.1 | 13.5 | 8.1 | 22.1 | 18.4 | 12.6 | 8.5 | 4.1 | 3.7 | 33.7 | 52.0 | 40 999 | 51 265 | 25.1 | 2.7 |
| Statesboro | 4.9 | 8.8 | 50.7 | 11.8 | 5.8 | 6.2 | 5.1 | 3.3 | 3.5 | 22.0 | 50.7 | 22 698 | 28 414 | 25.2 | 4.8 |
| Stockbridge | 7.8 | 22.7 | 8.8 | 14.9 | 18.3 | 13.3 | 7.9 | 3.8 | 2.4 | 32.4 | 53.6 | 9 853 | 25 637 | 160.2 | 2.5 |
| Valdosta | 7.7 | 15.1 | 23.3 | 15.1 | 9.8 | 10.2 | 8.7 | 5.3 | 4.8 | 26.9 | 53.1 | 43 724 | 54 764 | 24.7 | 5.2 |
| Warner Robins | 8.4 | 19.6 | 10.4 | 16.9 | 13.4 | 13.2 | 8.7 | 5.1 | 4.3 | 31.2 | 52.2 | 48 804 | 67 619 | 36.4 | 4.6 |
| HAWAII | 6.4 | 15.9 | 9.6 | 13.6 | 13.0 | 14.2 | 12.9 | 7.4 | 7.0 | 38.6 | 49.9 | 1 211 537 | 1 360 301 | 12.3 | 2.4 |
| East Honolulu CDP | 4.6 | 14.7 | 5.5 | 8.8 | 12.7 | 16.3 | 16.2 | 10.8 | 10.2 | 47.2 | 51.1 | NA | NA | NA | NA |
| Hilo CDP | 6.0 | 15.3 | 11.3 | 11.5 | 10.6 | 13.4 | 13.8 | 8.5 | 9.5 | 40.5 | 51.2 | 40 759 | 43 263 | 6.1 | NA |
| Kahului CDP | 7.0 | 17.9 | 8.9 | 13.3 | 13.8 | 13.3 | 9.9 | 7.3 | 8.5 | 37.2 | 50.7 | 20 146 | 26 337 | 30.7 | NA |
| Kailua CDP (Honolulu County) | 5.4 | 15.1 | 7.8 | 12.0 | 12.7 | 15.6 | 15.0 | 8.3 | 8.1 | 42.8 | 50.7 | 36 513 | 38 635 | 5.8 | NA |
| Kaneohe CDP | 5.8 | 15.0 | 8.8 | 12.5 | 11.8 | 15.5 | 12.9 | 8.2 | 9.6 | 41.9 | 51.4 | 34 970 | 34 597 | -1.1 | NA |
| Mililani Town CDP | 5.7 | 16.0 | 9.2 | 12.6 | 11.9 | 14.4 | 16.7 | 8.5 | 5.0 | 40.3 | 50.2 | 28 608 | 27 629 | -3.4 | NA |
| Pearl City CDP | 5.8 | 13.5 | 11.1 | 13.6 | 12.2 | 12.1 | 12.3 | 10.2 | 9.2 | 39.9 | 47.4 | 30 976 | 47 698 | 54.0 | NA |
| Urban Honolulu CDP | 4.9 | 12.5 | 9.7 | 14.5 | 13.2 | 14.2 | 13.2 | 8.1 | 9.8 | 41.3 | 50.6 | NA | 337 256 | NA | 2.5 |
| Waipahu CDP | 7.1 | 17.7 | 10.0 | 12.8 | 12.5 | 12.8 | 11.2 | 8.0 | 7.9 | 37.0 | 50.5 | 33 108 | 38 216 | 15.4 | NA |
| IDAHO | 7.8 | 19.6 | 9.9 | 13.3 | 12.2 | 13.3 | 11.5 | 7.0 | 5.4 | 34.6 | 49.9 | 1 293 953 | 1 567 652 | 21.1 | 1.8 |
| Boise City | 6.4 | 16.3 | 11.2 | 15.6 | 13.2 | 14.4 | 11.8 | 5.9 | 5.2 | 35.3 | 50.6 | 185 787 | 206 099 | 10.7 | 3.0 |
| Caldwell | 10.7 | 22.4 | 11.5 | 16.4 | 12.0 | 10.3 | 7.8 | 5.0 | 3.9 | 28.2 | 50.6 | 25 967 | 46 294 | 78.1 | 3.0 |
| Coeur d'Alene | 6.7 | 16.1 | 11.8 | 14.8 | 11.9 | 12.7 | 11.3 | 7.0 | 7.6 | 35.4 | 51.4 | 34 514 | 44 137 | 27.9 | 3.3 |
| Idaho Falls | 9.2 | 20.1 | 9.2 | 15.1 | 11.2 | 12.8 | 10.5 | 5.9 | 5.8 | 32.2 | 50.5 | 50 730 | 56 887 | 12.0 | 1.8 |
| Lewiston | 5.7 | 15.8 | 10.8 | 12.2 | 11.6 | 13.6 | 12.0 | 8.3 | 9.9 | 39.9 | 50.8 | 30 904 | 31 894 | 3.2 | 0.5 |
| Meridian | 9.3 | 24.1 | 6.5 | 14.1 | 16.4 | 12.1 | 8.6 | 5.0 | 3.9 | 32.5 | 51.0 | 34 919 | 75 100 | 115.0 | 7.0 |
| Nampa | 9.8 | 22.5 | 9.9 | 15.5 | 13.1 | 10.6 | 8.3 | 5.4 | 4.9 | 30.1 | 51.0 | 51 867 | 81 725 | 57.2 | 2.7 |
| Pocatello | 8.3 | 17.5 | 14.4 | 16.6 | 10.8 | 11.4 | 10.4 | 5.6 | 5.1 | 30.2 | 50.1 | 51 466 | 54 224 | 5.4 | 1.0 |
| Post Falls | 8.6 | 20.5 | 8.7 | 15.0 | 13.6 | 12.5 | 10.0 | 6.8 | 4.5 | 33.0 | 51.2 | 17 247 | 27 574 | 59.9 | 3.9 |
| Rexburg | 9.6 | 10.8 | 49.2 | 15.6 | 4.3 | 3.9 | 2.9 | 1.8 | 1.9 | 22.3 | 52.7 | 17 257 | 25 484 | 47.7 | 1.0 |
| Twin Falls | 8.8 | 18.1 | 11.8 | 15.4 | 11.1 | 11.5 | 9.8 | 6.7 | 6.7 | 31.9 | 51.3 | 34 469 | 44 308 | 28.0 | 1.9 |
| ILLINOIS | 6.5 | 17.9 | 9.7 | 13.8 | 13.5 | 14.6 | 11.5 | 6.6 | 5.9 | 36.6 | 51.0 | 12 419 293 | 12 830 632 | 3.3 | 0.3 |
| Addison | 7.7 | 18.6 | 9.8 | 15.9 | 13.3 | 13.5 | 10.7 | 6.3 | 4.1 | 33.7 | 49.8 | 35 914 | 36 966 | 2.9 | 0.9 |
| Algonquin | 6.6 | 22.4 | 6.5 | 10.0 | 17.3 | 18.4 | 10.8 | 4.9 | 3.2 | 38.3 | 50.7 | 23 276 | 30 046 | 29.1 | -0.1 |
| Alton | 7.3 | 16.8 | 9.8 | 14.9 | 11.8 | 14.3 | 11.3 | 6.8 | 7.1 | 36.0 | 52.2 | 30 496 | 27 865 | -8.6 | -1.6 |
| Arlington Heights | 5.5 | 16.6 | 6.3 | 11.3 | 13.6 | 16.4 | 13.1 | 8.0 | 9.2 | 42.7 | 52.0 | 76 031 | 75 101 | -1.2 | 0.9 |
| Aurora | 9.1 | 22.4 | 9.1 | 16.8 | 16.1 | 12.3 | 7.8 | 3.7 | 2.8 | 30.7 | 50.4 | 142 990 | 197 850 | 38.4 | 1.1 |
| Bartlett | 6.8 | 20.5 | 6.9 | 11.6 | 16.7 | 17.5 | 11.7 | 4.8 | 3.6 | 38.0 | 51.0 | 36 706 | 41 226 | 12.3 | 1.0 |
| Batavia | 5.7 | 21.8 | 7.2 | 8.7 | 14.0 | 18.6 | 12.7 | 5.1 | 6.2 | 40.4 | 51.3 | 23 866 | 26 045 | 9.1 | 1.0 |
| Belleville | 6.7 | 16.6 | 9.3 | 15.5 | 13.0 | 15.0 | 10.9 | 5.9 | 7.1 | 36.5 | 52.5 | 41 410 | 44 490 | 7.4 | -1.6 |
| Belvidere | 7.8 | 22.3 | 9.0 | 12.8 | 14.7 | 12.8 | 8.7 | 6.3 | 5.6 | 33.6 | 50.6 | 20 820 | 25 585 | 22.9 | -0.8 |
| Berwyn | 8.0 | 19.8 | 9.9 | 15.5 | 15.0 | 12.8 | 9.5 | 4.9 | 4.5 | 32.9 | 50.5 | 54 016 | 56 657 | 4.9 | 0.3 |
| Bloomington | 7.0 | 17.5 | 10.3 | 16.4 | 13.8 | 14.3 | 10.6 | 5.1 | 5.0 | 34.1 | 51.3 | 64 808 | 76 608 | 18.2 | 1.5 |
| Bolingbrook | 8.0 | 22.7 | 8.7 | 13.5 | 17.0 | 14.2 | 9.6 | 4.2 | 2.1 | 33.1 | 50.4 | 56 321 | 73 366 | 30.3 | 0.9 |
| Buffalo Grove | 4.8 | 18.8 | 6.4 | 10.1 | 14.6 | 19.3 | 14.1 | 6.2 | 5.7 | 41.9 | 51.6 | 42 909 | 41 491 | -3.3 | 0.5 |

| City | Households, 2010 | | | | Persons in group quarters, 2010 | | | | Serious crimes known to police,[2] 2011 | | | | Educational attainment, 2007–2011 | | |
|---|---|---|---|---|---|---|---|---|---|---|---|---|---|---|---|
| | | | Percent | | | Institutional | | | Total | | Rate[3] | | | Attainment[4] (percent) | |
| | Number | Persons per house-hold | Female family house-holder[1] | One-person | Total | Total | Persons in nursing facilities | Non-institu-tional | Number | Rate[3] | Violent | Property | Population age 25 and older | High school graduate or less | Bachelor's degree or more |
| | 27 | 28 | 29 | 30 | 31 | 32 | 33 | 34 | 35 | 36 | 37 | 38 | 39 | 40 | 41 |
| GEORGIA.................. | 3 585 584 | 2.63 | 15.8 | 25.4 | 253 199 | 144 545 | 34 738 | 108 654 | 392 586 | 4 000 | 373 | 3 627 | 6 152 481 | 45.4 | 27.5 |
| Albany....................... | 29 781 | 2.46 | 27.7 | 31.8 | 4 288 | 1 421 | 400 | 2 867 | 5 359 | 6 831 | 816 | 6 015 | 46 029 | 50.2 | 17.8 |
| Alpharetta................. | 21 742 | 2.64 | 9.3 | 25.6 | 69 | 57 | 19 | 12 | 1 496 | 2 566 | 99 | 2 466 | 36 705 | 17.0 | 62.7 |
| Athens-Clarke County...... | 45 414 | 2.37 | 13.4 | 30.6 | 9 183 | 779 | 348 | 8 404 | 5 290 | 4 517 | 356 | 4 161 | 59 582 | 37.4 | 40.7 |
| Atlanta..................... | 185 142 | 2.11 | 16.5 | 44.0 | 29 484 | 6 756 | 1 626 | 22 728 | 36 241 | 8 517 | 1 433 | 7 084 | 276 974 | 34.0 | 46.1 |
| Augusta-Richmond County......................... | 76 924 | 2.47 | 22.6 | 30.4 | 10 508 | 3 907 | 1 137 | 6 601 | 14 326 | 7 220 | 499 | 6 721 | 124 671 | 49.9 | 19.7 |
| Columbus.................. | 74 081 | 2.47 | 21.3 | 29.9 | 7 017 | 3 486 | 898 | 3 531 | 13 383 | 6 956 | 485 | 6 471 | 116 945 | 44.7 | 21.7 |
| Dalton...................... | 11 337 | 2.84 | 15.2 | 27.3 | 904 | 754 | 340 | 150 | 1 394 | 4 153 | 268 | 3 885 | 19 786 | 60.2 | 20.4 |
| Douglasville.............. | 11 627 | 2.58 | 21.7 | 28.3 | 937 | 826 | 0 | 111 | 2 078 | 6 624 | 571 | 6 054 | 19 009 | 39.3 | 28.9 |
| Duluth...................... | 10 555 | 2.52 | 14.1 | 28.4 | 34 | 0 | 0 | 34 | 599 | 2 223 | 208 | 2 015 | 17 551 | 26.6 | 46.2 |
| Dunwoody................. | 19 944 | 2.31 | 8.1 | 33.7 | 154 | 0 | 0 | 154 | 1 771 | 3 778 | 205 | 3 573 | 31 244 | 15.1 | 66.5 |
| East Point................ | 13 333 | 2.50 | 26.1 | 33.5 | 420 | 44 | 27 | 376 | 3 931 | 11 509 | 1 154 | 10 355 | 22 148 | 48.2 | 25.2 |
| Gainesville............... | 11 273 | 2.85 | 18.2 | 28.9 | 1 713 | 649 | 434 | 1 064 | 1 698 | 4 958 | 339 | 4 619 | 18 602 | 59.0 | 21.8 |
| Hinesville................. | 12 324 | 2.69 | 22.7 | 21.7 | 310 | 263 | 0 | 47 | 1 768 | 5 219 | 466 | 4 752 | 18 689 | 41.8 | 18.0 |
| Johns Creek.............. | 26 266 | 2.92 | 9.0 | 16.2 | 0 | 0 | 0 | 0 | 609 | 783 | 45 | 738 | 47 704 | 14.4 | 63.5 |
| Kennesaw................. | 11 413 | 2.59 | 15.2 | 26.8 | 244 | 244 | 99 | 0 | 592 | 1 962 | 70 | 1 892 | 18 117 | 29.8 | 39.9 |
| LaGrange.................. | 11 243 | 2.52 | 26.1 | 30.2 | 1 242 | 627 | 381 | 615 | 1 869 | 6 235 | 454 | 5 781 | 17 570 | 55.9 | 21.8 |
| Lawrenceville............ | 9 973 | 2.84 | 19.3 | 25.6 | 268 | 238 | 238 | 30 | 1 171 | 4 049 | 294 | 3 755 | 16 610 | 50.8 | 20.7 |
| Macon...................... | 35 603 | 2.45 | 27.8 | 33.8 | 4 292 | 2 026 | 680 | 2 266 | 8 375 | 9 049 | 612 | 8 437 | 55 662 | 58.1 | 16.9 |
| Marietta................... | 23 065 | 2.38 | 15.6 | 34.1 | 1 769 | 758 | 730 | 1 011 | 3 010 | 5 251 | 673 | 4 577 | 37 523 | 37.2 | 37.1 |
| Milton...................... | 11 659 | 2.80 | 8.6 | 20.2 | 4 | 0 | 0 | 4 | 341 | 1 030 | 42 | 988 | 19 486 | 12.0 | 66.4 |
| Newnan.................... | 12 439 | 2.61 | 18.7 | 27.1 | 518 | 518 | 135 | 0 | 1 279 | 3 821 | 481 | 3 340 | 19 969 | 43.1 | 31.2 |
| Peachtree City........... | 12 726 | 2.69 | 9.5 | 19.9 | 118 | 118 | 118 | 0 | 460 | 1 321 | 23 | 1 298 | 22 575 | 19.0 | 51.1 |
| Rome....................... | 13 885 | 2.50 | 19.2 | 32.1 | 1 606 | 1 409 | 447 | 197 | 2 429 | 6 604 | 617 | 5 987 | 22 974 | 55.0 | 22.4 |
| Roswell.................... | 33 945 | 2.59 | 10.5 | 24.8 | 516 | 356 | 305 | 160 | 1 799 | 2 010 | 80 | 1 929 | 59 098 | 23.5 | 53.4 |
| Sandy Springs............ | 42 334 | 2.21 | 9.5 | 37.1 | 327 | 205 | 205 | 122 | 2 628 | 2 764 | 161 | 2 603 | 65 090 | 20.0 | 58.9 |
| Savannah.................. | 52 545 | 2.40 | 22.4 | 32.7 | 10 014 | 4 499 | 584 | 5 515 | 10 468 | 4 623 | 393 | 4 231 | 83 747 | 47.9 | 24.4 |
| Smyrna.................... | 23 002 | 2.22 | 12.4 | 38.3 | 279 | 269 | 112 | 10 | 1 559 | 3 001 | 304 | 2 697 | 35 243 | 24.8 | 50.9 |
| Statesboro................ | 10 207 | 2.36 | 15.0 | 31.0 | 4 290 | 266 | 266 | 4 024 | 1 339 | 4 650 | 347 | 4 303 | 9 855 | 44.8 | 27.1 |
| Stockbridge.............. | 9 499 | 2.70 | 22.0 | 26.6 | 8 | 0 | 0 | 8 | NA | NA | NA | NA | 14 497 | 34.9 | 32.7 |
| Valdosta................... | 20 471 | 2.46 | 20.4 | 28.9 | 4 122 | 1 147 | 444 | 2 975 | 2 768 | 5 011 | 485 | 4 526 | 28 271 | 49.2 | 23.5 |
| Warner Robins............ | 26 136 | 2.53 | 19.6 | 28.2 | 338 | 223 | 208 | 115 | 4 448 | 6 593 | 517 | 6 076 | 40 335 | 43.3 | 21.2 |
| HAWAII...................... | 455 338 | 2.89 | 12.6 | 23.3 | 42 880 | 11 306 | 5 198 | 31 574 | 49 838 | 3 625 | 287 | 3 338 | 915 429 | 38.5 | 29.5 |
| East Honolulu CDP......... | 17 684 | 2.81 | 9.4 | 16.0 | 235 | 160 | 160 | 75 | NA | NA | NA | NA | 37 492 | 20.8 | 52.7 |
| Hilo CDP.................... | 15 483 | 2.69 | 14.7 | 25.8 | 1 648 | 605 | 575 | 1 043 | NA | NA | NA | NA | 31 291 | 37.3 | 30.0 |
| Kahului CDP................ | 7 111 | 3.46 | 16.6 | 19.5 | 1 740 | 1 296 | 564 | 444 | NA | NA | NA | NA | 16 684 | 57.2 | 17.5 |
| Kailua CDP (Honolulu County)...................... | 12 921 | 2.98 | 11.5 | 17.1 | 119 | 30 | 8 | 89 | NA | NA | NA | NA | 27 793 | 28.4 | 44.3 |
| Kaneohe CDP.............. | 11 138 | 3.05 | 14.4 | 18.0 | 643 | 411 | 411 | 232 | NA | NA | NA | NA | 23 800 | 36.8 | 31.9 |
| Mililani Town CDP.......... | 9 038 | 3.06 | 11.4 | 13.2 | 0 | 0 | 0 | 0 | NA | NA | NA | NA | 19 957 | 30.9 | 33.6 |
| Pearl City CDP............ | 14 268 | 3.08 | 13.1 | 16.5 | 3 694 | 165 | 156 | 3 529 | NA | NA | NA | NA | 32 417 | 36.5 | 28.3 |
| Urban Honolulu CDP....... | 129 408 | 2.51 | 12.1 | 32.9 | 13 052 | 4 247 | 1 823 | 8 805 | NA | NA | NA | NA | 243 089 | 38.6 | 33.6 |
| Waipahu CDP.............. | 8 383 | 4.45 | 19.3 | 12.9 | 910 | 390 | 369 | 520 | NA | NA | NA | NA | 26 138 | 56.9 | 15.2 |
| IDAHO ....................... | 579 408 | 2.66 | 9.6 | 23.8 | 28 951 | 17 076 | 4 820 | 11 875 | 35 971 | 2 269 | 201 | 2 069 | 970 727 | 39.9 | 24.6 |
| Boise City................. | 85 704 | 2.36 | 10.3 | 30.6 | 3 717 | 1 762 | 548 | 1 955 | 5 947 | 2 860 | 248 | 2 612 | 136 653 | 28.7 | 36.9 |
| Caldwell.................... | 14 895 | 3.00 | 15.5 | 21.7 | 1 532 | 913 | 149 | 619 | 1 526 | 3 264 | 323 | 2 941 | 25 624 | 57.4 | 12.5 |
| Coeur d'Alene............ | 18 395 | 2.33 | 11.6 | 31.4 | 1 215 | 813 | 428 | 402 | 1 907 | 4 273 | 513 | 3 760 | 28 609 | 38.6 | 23.2 |
| Idaho Falls................ | 21 203 | 2.63 | 11.3 | 26.5 | 1 011 | 477 | 72 | 534 | 1 732 | 3 012 | 259 | 2 752 | 34 876 | 35.8 | 27.5 |
| Lewiston................... | 13 324 | 2.32 | 10.3 | 30.2 | 966 | 594 | 385 | 372 | 1 428 | 4 428 | 158 | 4 270 | 21 715 | 45.7 | 19.7 |
| Meridian................... | 25 302 | 2.96 | 10.4 | 16.6 | 307 | 126 | 103 | 181 | 1 174 | 1 546 | 144 | 1 403 | 43 796 | 28.9 | 33.4 |
| Nampa...................... | 27 729 | 2.88 | 13.5 | 22.0 | 1 751 | 540 | 360 | 1 211 | 2 698 | 3 272 | 270 | 3 001 | 45 483 | 46.7 | 16.8 |
| Pocatello.................. | 20 832 | 2.53 | 11.3 | 27.5 | 1 519 | 630 | 307 | 889 | 1 944 | 3 544 | 244 | 3 300 | 31 438 | 34.0 | 30.0 |
| Post Falls................. | 10 263 | 2.68 | 12.7 | 21.9 | 84 | 42 | 42 | 42 | 790 | 2 834 | 176 | 2 658 | 16 418 | 35.9 | 18.9 |
| Rexburg.................... | 7 179 | 3.41 | 4.4 | 9.2 | 1 027 | 127 | 44 | 900 | 216 | 838 | 47 | 792 | 7 534 | 14.3 | 36.1 |
| Twin Falls................. | 16 744 | 2.58 | 12.2 | 26.6 | 897 | 592 | 314 | 305 | 1 607 | 3 602 | 269 | 3 333 | 26 234 | 43.7 | 17.8 |
| ILLINOIS.................... | 4 836 972 | 2.59 | 12.9 | 27.8 | 301 773 | 159 989 | 81 516 | 141 784 | 401 272 | 3 118 | 429 | 2 689 | 8 405 202 | 41.0 | 30.7 |
| Addison.................... | 11 940 | 3.08 | 12.8 | 17.7 | 112 | 46 | 0 | 66 | 800 | 2 159 | 143 | 2 016 | 24 094 | 52.1 | 21.1 |
| Algonquin.................. | 10 247 | 2.93 | 7.4 | 16.4 | 0 | 0 | 0 | 0 | 538 | 1 785 | 146 | 1 639 | 19 271 | 25.5 | 43.8 |
| Alton....................... | 11 734 | 2.33 | 19.2 | 34.4 | 518 | 356 | 202 | 162 | 1 540 | 5 510 | 540 | 4 970 | 18 358 | 44.5 | 18.2 |
| Arlington Heights.......... | 30 919 | 2.41 | 7.1 | 30.1 | 723 | 545 | 538 | 178 | 1 131 | 1 501 | 64 | 1 438 | 53 502 | 25.0 | 51.6 |
| Aurora...................... | 62 564 | 3.12 | 13.7 | 20.0 | 2 477 | 751 | 577 | 1 726 | 4 457 | 2 245 | 320 | 1 925 | 115 726 | 44.9 | 31.2 |
| Bartlett.................... | 14 073 | 2.92 | 7.5 | 17.5 | 58 | 58 | 58 | 0 | 304 | 736 | 39 | 697 | 26 057 | 26.4 | 43.1 |
| Batavia.................... | 9 554 | 2.71 | 8.8 | 23.1 | 157 | 148 | 148 | 9 | 450 | 1 723 | 96 | 1 627 | 16 291 | 21.6 | 49.0 |
| Belleville.................. | 18 795 | 2.30 | 16.4 | 34.4 | 1 246 | 1 167 | 740 | 79 | 2 092 | 4 689 | 448 | 4 241 | 29 654 | 36.5 | 23.2 |
| Belvidere.................. | 8 803 | 2.88 | 13.7 | 24.4 | 230 | 221 | 150 | 9 | 477 | 1 859 | 187 | 1 672 | 15 329 | 62.8 | 14.1 |
| Berwyn..................... | 18 910 | 2.99 | 16.5 | 24.6 | 52 | 17 | 14 | 35 | 1 514 | 2 664 | 236 | 2 428 | 35 049 | 54.6 | 18.6 |
| Bloomington............... | 31 663 | 2.35 | 10.7 | 32.6 | 2 234 | 566 | 280 | 1 668 | 2 103 | 2 737 | 470 | 2 267 | 48 288 | 29.7 | 45.1 |
| Bolingbrook............... | 22 212 | 3.29 | 12.5 | 14.2 | 279 | 279 | 279 | 0 | 1 382 | 1 878 | 219 | 1 659 | 44 400 | 38.0 | 32.9 |
| Buffalo Grove............. | 16 206 | 2.55 | 7.5 | 24.7 | 118 | 112 | 112 | 6 | 441 | 1 060 | 22 | 1 038 | 29 338 | 19.0 | 60.1 |

1. No spouse present. 2. Data for serious crimes have not been adjusted for underreporting. This may affect comparability between geographic areas and over time. 3. Per 100,000 population estimated by the FBI. 4. Persons 25 years old and over.

| City | Money income, 2007–2011 Households | | | | | Housing units, 2010 | | | Occupied Housing units 2007–2011 | | | Median owner costs as a percent of income | |
|---|---|---|---|---|---|---|---|---|---|---|---|---|---|
| | Per capita income[1] (dollars) | Median income | Percent with income of $200,000 or more | Percent with income of less than $25,000 | Families with income below poverty (percent) | Total | Percent change, 2000–2010 | Vacant units for sale or rent[2] | Total | Owner-occupied Percent | Median value[3] (dollars) | With a mortgage[4] | Without a mortgage[5] |
| | 42 | 43 | 44 | 45 | 46 | 47 | 48 | 49 | 50 | 51 | 52 | 53 | 54 |
| GEORGIA | 25 383 | 49 736 | 3.8 | 25.1 | 12.6 | 4 088 801 | 24.6 | 503 217 | 3 490 754 | 66.8 | 160 200 | 24.4 | 11.7 |
| Albany | 17 424 | 30 155 | 1.5 | 42.8 | 26.4 | 33 436 | 3.9 | 3 655 | 29 351 | 41.5 | 98 200 | 24.3 | 13.8 |
| Alpharetta | 45 190 | 92 149 | 13.0 | 8.8 | 2.9 | 23 029 | 57.2 | 1 287 | 21 126 | 65.1 | 326 400 | 22.1 | 10.7 |
| Athens-Clarke County | 19 596 | 34 151 | 2.5 | 40.2 | 18.0 | 51 068 | 21.2 | 5 654 | 41 349 | 45.6 | 161 100 | 24.4 | 11.5 |
| Atlanta | 35 884 | 45 946 | 8.2 | 30.9 | 19.5 | 224 573 | 20.1 | 39 431 | 179 089 | 47.0 | 228 000 | 26.4 | 15.1 |
| Augusta-Richmond County | 20 393 | 39 090 | 1.5 | 33.0 | 19.5 | 86 331 | 4.9 | 9 407 | 73 214 | 57.0 | 101 700 | 24.1 | 12.5 |
| Columbus | 22 726 | 41 088 | 2.4 | 30.6 | 15.2 | 82 690 | 8.5 | 8 609 | 72 087 | 54.9 | 134 900 | 23.7 | 11.2 |
| Dalton | 21 430 | 38 231 | 3.4 | 33.1 | 22.9 | 13 378 | 29.8 | 2 041 | 11 602 | 50.3 | 141 100 | 22.9 | 10.7 |
| Douglasville | 26 033 | 49 079 | 3.6 | 22.6 | 15.3 | 13 163 | 66.4 | 1 536 | 11 453 | 49.3 | 163 800 | 26.5 | 10.0 |
| Duluth | 28 852 | 56 826 | 3.3 | 18.0 | 11.2 | 11 313 | 23.6 | 758 | 10 293 | 57.0 | 191 000 | 25.7 | 11.5 |
| Dunwoody | 44 137 | 74 411 | 11.7 | 14.1 | 7.7 | 21 671 | 48.4 | 1 727 | 18 973 | 56.8 | 376 600 | 23.3 | 12.1 |
| East Point | 21 696 | 41 622 | 1.4 | 28.3 | 17.8 | 17 225 | 11.1 | 3 892 | 13 317 | 47.6 | 136 100 | 26.1 | 12.9 |
| Gainesville | 19 595 | 38 205 | 3.5 | 30.6 | 21.3 | 12 967 | 45.5 | 1 694 | 11 064 | 38.5 | 174 000 | 25.6 | 14.2 |
| Hinesville | 20 586 | 45 233 | 1.6 | 24.0 | 13.7 | 14 653 | 24.4 | 2 329 | 12 779 | 51.7 | 126 500 | 23.7 | 10.5 |
| Johns Creek | 46 875 | 110 648 | 18.8 | 8.0 | 3.8 | 27 744 | NA | 1 478 | 25 072 | 83.5 | 340 300 | 22.8 | 10.7 |
| Kennesaw | 28 080 | 60 288 | 2.5 | 15.1 | 7.7 | 12 328 | 40.7 | 915 | 11 092 | 68.9 | 173 200 | 24.3 | 11.9 |
| LaGrange | 18 715 | 31 885 | 2.2 | 38.7 | 23.6 | 12 846 | 16.7 | 1 603 | 10 930 | 45.4 | 124 800 | 23.8 | 11.7 |
| Lawrenceville | 19 600 | 46 941 | 2.2 | 27.0 | 18.0 | 11 187 | 45.8 | 1 214 | 9 407 | 55.2 | 147 900 | 24.9 | 12.8 |
| Macon | 16 860 | 26 545 | 1.7 | 47.5 | 27.4 | 42 794 | -3.8 | 7 191 | 34 040 | 46.8 | 90 300 | 26.2 | 13.5 |
| Marietta | 27 488 | 44 046 | 4.0 | 26.1 | 15.3 | 26 918 | 6.0 | 3 853 | 23 565 | 42.9 | 221 300 | 24.9 | 11.7 |
| Milton | 54 903 | 119 250 | 25.9 | 7.1 | 5.2 | 12 328 | NA | 669 | 10 826 | 75.2 | 463 600 | 22.3 | 10.0 |
| Newnan | 25 087 | 50 112 | 3.0 | 24.7 | 14.8 | 13 860 | 108.6 | 1 421 | 12 036 | 52.0 | 188 800 | 25.4 | 10.5 |
| Peachtree City | 39 551 | 91 045 | 10.3 | 10.0 | 4.3 | 13 538 | 17.8 | 812 | 12 510 | 76.6 | 279 400 | 23.1 | 10.0 |
| Rome | 20 434 | 33 719 | 3.1 | 39.4 | 19.5 | 15 797 | 9.3 | 1 912 | 13 424 | 53.4 | 127 300 | 25.4 | 15.6 |
| Roswell | 40 915 | 77 173 | 11.8 | 11.9 | 4.5 | 36 344 | 15.8 | 2 399 | 33 223 | 69.2 | 300 400 | 22.8 | 12.1 |
| Sandy Springs | 52 959 | 66 837 | 15.7 | 17.2 | 6.0 | 46 955 | 9.9 | 4 621 | 40 832 | 49.9 | 438 900 | 22.7 | 11.5 |
| Savannah | 20 322 | 35 623 | 1.4 | 36.2 | 18.6 | 61 883 | 7.6 | 9 338 | 52 088 | 47.4 | 145 400 | 27.1 | 13.4 |
| Smyrna | 37 260 | 55 989 | 6.6 | 18.0 | 9.2 | 25 745 | 30.6 | 2 743 | 22 934 | 55.8 | 221 600 | 22.8 | 10.0 |
| Statesboro | 11 520 | 19 544 | 0.3 | 58.2 | 24.4 | 11 602 | 25.3 | 1 395 | 9 836 | 27.2 | 119 400 | 24.1 | 12.6 |
| Stockbridge | 23 653 | 55 474 | 1.3 | 13.1 | 9.1 | 10 312 | NA | 813 | 8 898 | 63.9 | 160 600 | 30.4 | 10.6 |
| Valdosta | 17 792 | 31 215 | 1.7 | 40.0 | 22.2 | 22 709 | 19.5 | 2 238 | 19 640 | 43.6 | 124 000 | 25.6 | 12.4 |
| Warner Robins | 22 092 | 45 183 | 1.0 | 24.4 | 14.1 | 29 084 | 33.2 | 2 948 | 25 248 | 58.1 | 113 000 | 21.1 | 10.3 |
| HAWAII | 29 203 | 67 116 | 5.5 | 16.5 | 7.1 | 519 508 | 12.8 | 64 170 | 445 513 | 58.7 | 529 500 | 29.5 | 10.0 |
| East Honolulu CDP | 48 893 | 110 451 | 17.2 | 6.9 | 2.4 | 18 774 | NA | 1 090 | 17 577 | 82.6 | 781 400 | 28.2 | 10.1 |
| Hilo CDP | 24 968 | 53 058 | 3.5 | 26.4 | 10.6 | 16 905 | 5.5 | 1 422 | 16 261 | 64.0 | 317 000 | 23.8 | 10.0 |
| Kahului CDP | 21 758 | 58 214 | 3.2 | 19.3 | 8.3 | 7 773 | 28.6 | 662 | 6 782 | 56.1 | 579 500 | 33.6 | 10.0 |
| Kailua CDP (Honolulu County) | 39 659 | 93 539 | 13.4 | 9.2 | 5.0 | 13 650 | 6.9 | 729 | 12 877 | 73.8 | 782 400 | 29.7 | 10.9 |
| Kaneohe CDP | 32 561 | 82 686 | 6.7 | 11.6 | 4.2 | 11 553 | 0.7 | 415 | 11 006 | 70.7 | 616 800 | 28.0 | 10.1 |
| Mililani Town CDP | 34 643 | 93 161 | 6.4 | 5.0 | 2.4 | 9 272 | 0.0 | 234 | 9 353 | 78.9 | 553 500 | 27.5 | 10.0 |
| Pearl City CDP | 31 383 | 84 029 | 6.3 | 10.1 | 5.0 | 14 622 | 60.5 | 354 | 14 159 | 71.2 | 572 100 | 24.6 | 10.0 |
| Urban Honolulu CDP | 30 269 | 56 939 | 5.1 | 20.4 | 7.5 | 143 173 | NA | 13 765 | 127 727 | 44.8 | 545 700 | 28.8 | 11.0 |
| Waipahu CDP | 20 222 | 67 436 | 6.8 | 18.4 | 11.3 | 8 850 | 10.2 | 467 | 8 400 | 58.5 | 513 800 | 26.8 | 10.0 |
| IDAHO | 22 788 | 46 890 | 2.2 | 24.1 | 10.2 | 667 796 | 26.5 | 88 388 | 575 497 | 70.6 | 171 300 | 24.5 | 10.5 |
| Boise City | 28 084 | 49 516 | 3.3 | 22.6 | 9.3 | 92 700 | 18.9 | 6 996 | 85 481 | 61.5 | 197 900 | 23.5 | 10.8 |
| Caldwell | 15 913 | 38 604 | 1.2 | 28.9 | 16.6 | 16 323 | 68.4 | 1 428 | 15 254 | 66.3 | 117 000 | 28.1 | 11.1 |
| Coeur d'Alene | 22 993 | 40 132 | 1.6 | 28.7 | 11.4 | 20 219 | 36.8 | 1 824 | 18 938 | 55.9 | 192 700 | 26.8 | 12.7 |
| Idaho Falls | 24 020 | 45 990 | 2.8 | 24.0 | 10.6 | 22 977 | 15.9 | 1 774 | 20 962 | 66.4 | 146 900 | 21.9 | 10.0 |
| Lewiston | 24 590 | 43 927 | 1.3 | 28.3 | 7.0 | 14 057 | 5.0 | 733 | 13 378 | 65.6 | 163 700 | 22.1 | 12.6 |
| Meridian | 26 662 | 63 388 | 2.5 | 14.1 | 4.4 | 26 674 | 117.1 | 1 372 | 25 260 | 76.3 | 208 200 | 24.5 | 10.0 |
| Nampa | 17 131 | 42 111 | 0.8 | 26.7 | 14.7 | 30 507 | 56.2 | 2 778 | 26 814 | 67.0 | 136 800 | 26.5 | 12.4 |
| Pocatello | 21 232 | 42 402 | 1.5 | 30.1 | 12.1 | 22 404 | 8.3 | 1 572 | 20 589 | 66.1 | 129 900 | 22.7 | 10.8 |
| Post Falls | 22 036 | 48 689 | 1.0 | 22.0 | 10.8 | 11 150 | 66.7 | 887 | 10 371 | 67.8 | 187 400 | 25.0 | 13.2 |
| Rexburg | 12 423 | 25 869 | 1.8 | 48.5 | 31.3 | 7 617 | 69.2 | 438 | 6 675 | 33.8 | 176 200 | 22.7 | 10.0 |
| Twin Falls | 18 981 | 41 124 | 1.0 | 26.3 | 12.7 | 18 033 | 27.4 | 1 289 | 15 915 | 59.6 | 143 200 | 23.8 | 10.3 |
| ILLINOIS | 29 376 | 56 576 | 5.0 | 21.6 | 9.6 | 5 296 715 | 8.4 | 459 743 | 4 773 002 | 68.7 | 198 500 | 25.6 | 13.7 |
| Addison | 25 542 | 61 281 | 3.2 | 18.6 | 9.8 | 12 581 | 7.3 | 641 | 12 050 | 71.7 | 274 500 | 28.5 | 18.7 |
| Algonquin | 38 390 | 98 092 | 10.0 | 6.2 | 2.7 | 10 727 | 33.4 | 480 | 10 192 | 89.0 | 274 700 | 24.8 | 12.8 |
| Alton | 19 433 | 36 272 | 1.0 | 37.3 | 16.8 | 13 266 | -4.5 | 1 532 | 11 627 | 61.9 | 84 900 | 22.5 | 13.2 |
| Arlington Heights | 41 654 | 78 494 | 10.8 | 12.5 | 2.6 | 32 795 | 3.4 | 1 876 | 30 057 | 77.0 | 358 100 | 25.7 | 14.4 |
| Aurora | 26 400 | 62 358 | 5.0 | 15.3 | 10.2 | 67 273 | 37.5 | 4 709 | 62 546 | 70.0 | 203 400 | 27.9 | 14.9 |
| Bartlett | 36 135 | 94 568 | 7.1 | 9.4 | 3.8 | 14 509 | 17.4 | 436 | 13 631 | 89.5 | 309 400 | 28.0 | 14.5 |
| Batavia | 38 679 | 88 529 | 11.4 | 15.8 | 8.7 | 10 042 | 13.9 | 488 | 9 253 | 77.7 | 297 900 | 25.9 | 12.2 |
| Belleville | 25 322 | 48 463 | 1.3 | 26.7 | 10.4 | 21 099 | 9.4 | 2 304 | 18 083 | 63.0 | 110 500 | 22.7 | 13.3 |
| Belvidere | 20 115 | 49 721 | 1.6 | 23.2 | 12.4 | 9 565 | 20.5 | 762 | 8 578 | 73.1 | 132 100 | 27.4 | 14.3 |
| Berwyn | 20 698 | 50 361 | 1.3 | 21.2 | 11.7 | 20 719 | 0.1 | 1 809 | 18 605 | 60.4 | 233 500 | 31.2 | 17.3 |
| Bloomington | 32 672 | 58 662 | 5.5 | 19.3 | 5.7 | 34 339 | 20.4 | 2 676 | 30 454 | 64.9 | 157 300 | 21.2 | 13.1 |
| Bolingbrook | 28 097 | 81 713 | 5.4 | 10.7 | 6.5 | 23 141 | 29.2 | 929 | 22 048 | 85.2 | 237 200 | 27.8 | 13.9 |
| Buffalo Grove | 45 071 | 91 634 | 11.8 | 9.3 | 1.9 | 17 034 | 6.9 | 828 | 16 347 | 82.5 | 331 700 | 27.1 | 17.2 |

1. Based on population estimated by the American Community Survey.    2. Includes units rented or sold but not occupied.    3. Specified owner-occupied units; $1,000,000 represents $1,000,000 or more    4. 50.0 represents 50 percent or more.    5. 10.0 represents 10 percent or less.

## Table D. Cities — Housing, Labor Force, and Employment

| City | Occupied housing units, 2007–2011 (cont.) | | | | Migration, 2007–2011 | | Civilian labor force, 2012 | | | | Civilian employment[4], 2007–2011 | | | |
|---|---|---|---|---|---|---|---|---|---|---|---|---|---|---|
| | | | | | | | | | Unemployment | | | Percent | | |
| | Percent renter occupied | Median gross rent[1] | Median rent as a percent of income[2] | Percent with no vehicle available | Percent who lived in the same house one year ago | Percent who lived outside this city one year ago | Total | Percent change, 2011–2012 | Total | Rate[3] | Population age 16 and older | In labor force | Full-year full-time worker | Households with no workers (percent) |
| | 55 | 56 | 57 | 58 | 59 | 60 | 61 | 62 | 63 | 64 | 65 | 66 | 67 | 68 |
| GEORGIA | 33.2 | 835 | 31.3 | 6.7 | 83.0 | 13.7 | 4 806 103 | 1.5 | 434 495 | 9.0 | 7 402 545 | 65.0 | 40.8 | 24.5 |
| Albany | 58.5 | 647 | 33.8 | 13.5 | 76.9 | 9.3 | 34 411 | -0.4 | 3 790 | 11.0 | 58 957 | 58.7 | 33.7 | 33.7 |
| Alpharetta | 34.9 | 1 099 | 23.4 | 3.5 | 82.8 | 13.3 | 31 626 | 3.0 | 2 056 | 6.5 | 41 245 | 73.2 | 54.7 | 14.2 |
| Athens-Clarke County | 54.4 | 744 | 36.2 | 8.4 | 74.0 | 13.5 | 68 767 | 3.5 | 4 831 | 7.0 | 97 696 | 57.1 | 30.2 | 28.4 |
| Atlanta | 53.0 | 910 | 31.3 | 17.8 | 75.9 | 12.1 | 194 778 | 1.9 | 21 893 | 11.2 | 345 964 | 65.4 | 40.3 | 26.8 |
| Augusta-Richmond County | 43.0 | 724 | 31.0 | 9.1 | 78.1 | 10.6 | 89 272 | 0.4 | 9 242 | 10.4 | 155 442 | 61.6 | 33.9 | 30.2 |
| Columbus | 45.1 | 758 | 31.4 | 10.3 | 74.5 | 12.6 | 85 897 | 1.2 | 7 843 | 9.1 | 145 578 | 63.7 | 35.7 | 28.8 |
| Dalton | 49.7 | 658 | 29.7 | 9.7 | 75.9 | 12.7 | 13 041 | -3.7 | 1 581 | 12.1 | 24 116 | 65.1 | 40.4 | 25.6 |
| Douglasville | 50.7 | 907 | 28.7 | 4.7 | 72.8 | 20.0 | 15 137 | 1.5 | 1 542 | 10.2 | 22 419 | 69.3 | 45.4 | 21.0 |
| Duluth | 43.0 | 1 024 | 30.1 | 1.5 | 82.6 | 14.5 | 16 620 | 2.4 | 1 269 | 7.6 | 19 960 | 73.4 | 51.5 | 17.6 |
| Dunwoody | 43.2 | 1 144 | 27.9 | 5.2 | 82.0 | 14.8 | NA | NA | NA | NA | 35 015 | 69.0 | 48.4 | 21.1 |
| East Point | 52.4 | 854 | 34.3 | 16.7 | 78.8 | 16.2 | 15 991 | 0.5 | 2 155 | 13.5 | 27 085 | 68.0 | 41.9 | 25.7 |
| Gainesville | 61.5 | 806 | 30.8 | 13.9 | 77.5 | 12.7 | 15 556 | 3.9 | 1 299 | 8.4 | 24 094 | 65.3 | 41.7 | 24.4 |
| Hinesville | 48.3 | 788 | 27.7 | 6.2 | 73.1 | 20.7 | 15 301 | -0.6 | 1 331 | 8.7 | 24 465 | 70.4 | 35.5 | 15.0 |
| Johns Creek | 16.5 | 1 167 | 25.3 | 1.5 | 88.8 | 9.7 | 37 281 | 3.3 | 2 749 | 7.4 | 54 354 | 71.8 | 52.0 | 12.2 |
| Kennesaw | 31.1 | 1 064 | 29.3 | 2.7 | 79.6 | 16.5 | 16 810 | 0.6 | 1 593 | 9.5 | 22 133 | 77.5 | 49.4 | 15.5 |
| LaGrange | 54.6 | 670 | 32.8 | 16.0 | 72.6 | 13.9 | 14 759 | 5.2 | 1 607 | 10.9 | 22 247 | 60.4 | 35.9 | 33.8 |
| Lawrenceville | 44.8 | 890 | 34.5 | 5.7 | 76.9 | 15.8 | 14 608 | 2.0 | 1 640 | 11.2 | 20 512 | 70.5 | 42.8 | 19.5 |
| Macon | 53.2 | 657 | 38.1 | 17.3 | 78.1 | 8.4 | 40 605 | 1.1 | 4 656 | 11.5 | 69 722 | 54.6 | 29.7 | 37.3 |
| Marietta | 57.1 | 866 | 30.5 | 9.4 | 72.4 | 19.5 | 31 727 | 2.9 | 2 925 | 9.2 | 45 584 | 75.6 | 44.2 | 18.2 |
| Milton | 24.8 | 1 120 | 24.2 | 1.3 | 85.8 | 12.9 | NA | NA | NA | NA | 22 248 | 72.2 | 50.1 | 9.8 |
| Newnan | 48.0 | 897 | 29.3 | 7.2 | 73.4 | 18.7 | 15 087 | 2.7 | 1 407 | 9.3 | 23 384 | 63.5 | 42.7 | 26.1 |
| Peachtree City | 23.4 | 1 126 | 27.7 | 1.6 | 86.5 | 9.4 | 16 940 | 4.0 | 1 225 | 7.2 | 26 349 | 66.5 | 41.9 | 20.7 |
| Rome | 46.6 | 674 | 33.8 | 15.0 | 81.4 | 9.9 | 17 279 | 0.5 | 1 991 | 11.5 | 28 199 | 57.8 | 33.4 | 36.7 |
| Roswell | 30.8 | 1 003 | 31.1 | 4.2 | 85.4 | 10.3 | 49 992 | 2.7 | 3 317 | 6.6 | 67 274 | 74.2 | 51.4 | 16.5 |
| Sandy Springs | 50.1 | 988 | 27.8 | 6.4 | 76.1 | 19.0 | 57 258 | 2.9 | 3 880 | 6.8 | 75 196 | 73.3 | 50.3 | 18.6 |
| Savannah | 52.6 | 861 | 34.4 | 13.2 | 85.3 | 8.3 | 65 910 | 3.0 | 6 486 | 9.8 | 108 602 | 59.4 | 36.6 | 29.8 |
| Smyrna | 44.2 | 944 | 30.0 | 3.4 | 74.0 | 20.6 | 29 933 | 2.0 | 2 612 | 8.7 | 40 566 | 77.5 | 51.5 | 16.1 |
| Statesboro | 72.8 | 603 | 48.0 | 8.8 | 61.3 | 29.2 | 12 642 | 1.1 | 1 649 | 13.0 | 24 861 | 50.1 | 20.1 | 27.5 |
| Stockbridge | 36.1 | 1 030 | 29.2 | 2.7 | 84.3 | 13.9 | 13 225 | 2.2 | 1 462 | 11.1 | 17 762 | 69.5 | 46.6 | 17.3 |
| Valdosta | 56.4 | 740 | 34.1 | 9.1 | 73.7 | 13.6 | 27 502 | 1.2 | 2 424 | 8.8 | 42 429 | 62.5 | 30.4 | 31.1 |
| Warner Robins | 41.9 | 780 | 29.6 | 6.2 | 78.8 | 12.7 | 33 432 | 1.1 | 2 772 | 8.3 | 49 475 | 67.5 | 38.0 | 23.1 |
| HAWAII | 41.3 | 1 313 | 33.1 | 8.8 | 84.9 | 11.3 | 651 586 | -0.6 | 37 918 | 5.8 | 1 079 024 | 66.5 | 40.6 | 22.2 |
| East Honolulu CDP | 17.4 | 2 000 | 33.2 | 3.9 | 90.9 | 7.4 | NA | NA | NA | NA | 41 142 | 66.6 | 45.9 | 21.9 |
| Hilo CDP | 36.0 | 872 | 33.8 | 8.9 | 85.2 | 8.0 | NA | NA | NA | NA | 38 090 | 60.7 | 36.2 | 31.0 |
| Kahului CDP | 43.9 | 1 031 | 29.6 | 8.7 | 80.6 | 9.2 | NA | NA | NA | NA | 19 734 | 63.0 | 39.8 | 25.4 |
| Kailua CDP (Honolulu County) | 26.2 | 1 941 | 31.3 | 4.5 | 88.3 | 8.1 | NA | NA | NA | NA | 31 784 | 68.0 | 41.5 | 19.2 |
| Kaneohe CDP | 29.3 | 1 682 | 31.9 | 5.6 | 86.9 | 8.6 | NA | NA | NA | NA | 27 938 | 66.7 | 43.7 | 20.6 |
| Mililani Town CDP | 21.1 | 1 815 | 34.5 | 2.3 | 89.6 | 8.9 | NA | NA | NA | NA | 23 035 | 68.7 | 45.8 | 15.9 |
| Pearl City CDP | 28.8 | 1 723 | 32.4 | 4.3 | 86.9 | 12.1 | NA | NA | NA | NA | 38 024 | 65.6 | 39.2 | 21.3 |
| Urban Honolulu CDP | 55.2 | 1 185 | 32.4 | 18.0 | 84.6 | 8.3 | NA | NA | NA | NA | 283 256 | 63.9 | 40.5 | 24.6 |
| Waipahu CDP | 41.5 | 1 099 | 32.1 | 10.8 | 88.1 | 7.6 | NA | NA | NA | NA | 31 701 | 62.0 | 38.6 | 21.3 |
| IDAHO | 29.4 | 709 | 29.1 | 4.1 | 82.0 | 12.0 | 773 300 | 2.1 | 54 621 | 7.1 | 1 172 324 | 65.1 | 37.9 | 25.7 |
| Boise City | 38.5 | 761 | 29.5 | 5.7 | 78.3 | 10.2 | 111 075 | 3.2 | 7 081 | 6.4 | 166 033 | 70.4 | 41.5 | 22.1 |
| Caldwell | 33.7 | 688 | 30.1 | 6.0 | 81.0 | 11.1 | 20 773 | 1.5 | 1 817 | 8.7 | 32 329 | 66.3 | 34.9 | 25.5 |
| Coeur d'Alene | 44.1 | 762 | 33.1 | 5.8 | 76.7 | 14.8 | 23 048 | 1.2 | 1 886 | 8.2 | 35 032 | 65.4 | 35.8 | 29.1 |
| Idaho Falls | 33.6 | 674 | 30.7 | 6.3 | 79.8 | 11.3 | 28 250 | 2.2 | 1 811 | 6.4 | 41 852 | 67.1 | 40.4 | 24.3 |
| Lewiston | 34.4 | 611 | 28.0 | 7.4 | 82.7 | 8.2 | 15 617 | 0.1 | 917 | 5.9 | 25 922 | 63.3 | 37.2 | 33.7 |
| Meridian | 23.7 | 1 004 | 28.4 | 3.4 | 82.9 | 12.4 | 37 836 | 3.1 | 2 222 | 5.9 | 50 507 | 72.2 | 47.3 | 18.9 |
| Nampa | 33.0 | 748 | 30.6 | 5.0 | 76.3 | 13.8 | 37 466 | 1.7 | 3 070 | 8.2 | 55 880 | 65.5 | 35.3 | 26.7 |
| Pocatello | 33.9 | 593 | 30.0 | 5.9 | 75.3 | 13.2 | 27 419 | 1.1 | 1 892 | 6.9 | 41 331 | 67.9 | 37.4 | 25.0 |
| Post Falls | 32.2 | 798 | 27.6 | 1.9 | 82.3 | 8.5 | 13 867 | 0.7 | 1 226 | 8.8 | 19 238 | 72.9 | 42.1 | 24.5 |
| Rexburg | 66.2 | 625 | 43.4 | 3.3 | 43.0 | 29.7 | 11 544 | 8.0 | 630 | 5.5 | 20 318 | 62.6 | 19.6 | 16.3 |
| Twin Falls | 40.4 | 664 | 28.0 | 5.5 | 80.5 | 10.4 | 22 161 | 2.0 | 1 518 | 6.8 | 32 811 | 64.0 | 40.6 | 23.2 |
| ILLINOIS | 31.3 | 860 | 30.7 | 10.5 | 86.7 | 8.0 | 6 592 992 | 1.2 | 585 039 | 8.9 | 10 029 404 | 66.7 | 40.9 | 25.2 |
| Addison | 28.3 | 897 | 33.6 | 4.6 | 87.6 | 7.5 | 20 139 | 1.6 | 1 818 | 9.0 | 28 294 | 72.1 | 43.1 | 17.8 |
| Algonquin | 11.0 | 1 591 | 29.1 | 1.9 | 93.9 | 4.6 | 16 913 | 2.8 | 1 322 | 7.8 | 22 632 | 74.7 | 48.9 | 13.4 |
| Alton | 38.1 | 730 | 34.2 | 9.5 | 83.8 | 10.3 | 12 958 | 0.0 | 1 504 | 11.6 | 21 841 | 59.7 | 34.6 | 34.2 |
| Arlington Heights | 23.0 | 1 101 | 26.3 | 5.6 | 90.0 | 7.5 | 42 487 | 3.5 | 2 804 | 6.6 | 60 154 | 66.7 | 42.3 | 24.7 |
| Aurora | 30.0 | 981 | 32.5 | 6.2 | 86.0 | 8.0 | 107 951 | 2.5 | 9 374 | 8.7 | 139 618 | 74.7 | 47.1 | 15.7 |
| Bartlett | 10.5 | 1 177 | 38.0 | 3.6 | 91.8 | 6.6 | 23 952 | 2.5 | 1 788 | 7.5 | 30 565 | 74.6 | 49.0 | 12.3 |
| Batavia | 22.3 | 1 030 | 28.6 | 4.4 | 89.1 | 9.6 | 14 605 | 2.6 | 1 124 | 7.7 | 19 038 | 74.0 | 43.2 | 20.1 |
| Belleville | 37.0 | 727 | 31.3 | 7.6 | 85.4 | 9.8 | 22 606 | 0.2 | 2 261 | 10.0 | 34 874 | 68.3 | 42.9 | 26.3 |
| Belvidere | 26.9 | 678 | 30.2 | 8.4 | 88.1 | 5.1 | 12 224 | -2.0 | 1 637 | 13.4 | 18 567 | 65.1 | 36.7 | 27.8 |
| Berwyn | 39.6 | 884 | 31.2 | 11.0 | 87.5 | 7.5 | 28 985 | 2.4 | 2 777 | 9.6 | 42 318 | 68.6 | 39.7 | 23.0 |
| Bloomington | 35.1 | 720 | 24.9 | 7.7 | 81.5 | 9.0 | 42 223 | 0.4 | 2 959 | 7.0 | 59 314 | 71.4 | 45.7 | 21.3 |
| Bolingbrook | 14.8 | 981 | 33.6 | 3.8 | 91.8 | 6.6 | 41 966 | 2.6 | 3 552 | 8.5 | 53 878 | 76.9 | 50.1 | 12.6 |
| Buffalo Grove | 17.5 | 1 217 | 26.4 | 4.6 | 91.1 | 8.1 | 23 372 | 3.4 | 1 664 | 7.1 | 32 880 | 73.5 | 49.2 | 17.2 |

1. $2,000 represents $2,000 or more.  2. 50.0 represents 50 percent or more.  3. Percent of civilian labor force.  4. Persons 16 years old and over.

| City | Value of residential construction authorized by building permits, 2011 | | | Wholesale trade,[1] 2007 | | | | Retail trade,[2] 2007 | | | |
|---|---|---|---|---|---|---|---|---|---|---|---|
| | New construction ($1,000) | Number of housing units | Percent single family | Number of establishments | Number of employees | Sales (mil dol) | Annual payroll (mil dol) | Number of establishments | Number of employees | Sales (mil dol) | Annual payroll (mil dol) |
| | 69 | 70 | 71 | 72 | 73 | 74 | 75 | 76 | 77 | 78 | 79 |
| GEORGIA................. | 2 760 775 | 18 493 | 74.7 | 11 545 | 166 619 | 141 962.4 | 8 246.5 | 36 218 | 475 344 | 117 516.9 | 10 760.2 |
| Albany ...................... | 4 899 | 54 | 55.6 | 137 | 1 857 | 1 108.6 | 73.6 | 495 | 6 561 | 1 428.5 | 129.1 |
| Alpharetta ................ | 72 253 | 434 | 21.7 | 167 | 4 459 | 18 722.2 | 338.4 | 404 | 8 233 | 1 941.3 | 185.8 |
| Athens-Clarke County ... | 20 420 | 171 | 49.1 | 106 | 1 994 | 1 782.5 | 84.1 | 553 | 7 752 | 1 669.1 | 161.5 |
| Atlanta ..................... | 68 332 | 737 | 30.8 | 706 | 9 721 | 7 523.6 | 501.2 | 1 943 | 26 962 | 5 594.1 | 643.9 |
| Augusta-Richmond County .................. | 46 227 | 266 | 100.0 | 196 | 2 249 | 916.4 | 94.3 | 895 | 11 084 | 2 505.1 | 233.6 |
| Columbus ................. | 33 828 | 369 | 58.8 | 173 | 1 906 | 1 173.6 | 81.2 | 845 | 12 642 | 2 889.2 | 260.7 |
| Dalton ...................... | 0 | 0 | 0.0 | 132 | 2 689 | 977.8 | 103.3 | 312 | 3 304 | 828.4 | 73.2 |
| Douglasville ............. | 3 512 | 11 | 100.0 | 25 | 175 | 57.5 | 8.4 | 270 | 5 181 | 1 034.5 | 100.4 |
| Duluth ...................... | 16 684 | 46 | 100.0 | 129 | 2 692 | 2 034.2 | 226.5 | 263 | 4 656 | 1 766.7 | 166.3 |
| Dunwoody ................ | 1 716 | 5 | 100.0 | 57 | D | D | D | 286 | 6 132 | 1 016.3 | 126.8 |
| East Point ................ | 2 318 | 19 | 100.0 | 32 | 591 | 437.9 | 29.6 | 103 | 1 325 | 271.2 | 26.4 |
| Gainesville .............. | 7 086 | 45 | 100.0 | 107 | 1 554 | 3 411.9 | 65.1 | 341 | 4 748 | 1 138.6 | 115.1 |
| Hinesville ................ | 31 496 | 142 | 100.0 | 2 | D | D | D | 137 | 1 585 | 379.8 | 33.6 |
| Johns Creek ............ | 37 532 | 271 | 47.2 | 70 | 316 | 327.8 | 20.3 | 161 | 2 240 | 409.2 | 47.3 |
| Kennesaw ................ | 22 641 | 141 | 19.1 | 97 | 1 790 | 971.6 | 91.6 | 169 | 2 587 | 665.6 | 64.7 |
| LaGrange ................. | 9 335 | 62 | 100.0 | 30 | 577 | 365.5 | 23.9 | 212 | 2 831 | 670.2 | 60.6 |
| Lawrenceville........... | 1 042 | 11 | 100.0 | 116 | 1 348 | 1 083.1 | 63.6 | 381 | 4 681 | 1 074.3 | 112.8 |
| Macon ...................... | 1 675 | 20 | 100.0 | 142 | 2 113 | 1 085.4 | 91.3 | 677 | 9 114 | 1 838.5 | 186.0 |
| Marietta .................. | 24 737 | 109 | 100.0 | 300 | 4 304 | 2 585.3 | 213.1 | 463 | 7 449 | 2 465.7 | 223.1 |
| Milton...................... | 19 830 | 105 | 100.0 | 17 | 81 | 76.8 | 11.2 | 30 | 351 | 61.4 | 7.7 |
| Newnan .................... | 23 238 | 103 | 100.0 | 28 | 562 | 345.8 | 23.7 | 201 | 3 320 | 736.0 | 71.5 |
| Peachtree City.......... | 3 189 | 15 | 100.0 | 91 | 985 | 620.1 | 50.1 | 159 | 2 667 | 533.2 | 53.9 |
| Rome....................... | NA | NA | NA | 72 | 1 028 | 510.7 | 37.4 | 315 | 4 049 | 897.2 | 81.9 |
| Roswell .................... | 39 597 | 128 | 100.0 | 191 | 1 892 | 1 568.3 | 135.3 | 386 | 5 589 | 1 761.7 | 162.0 |
| Sandy Springs........... | 12 914 | 64 | 100.0 | 150 | 3 211 | 6 167.9 | 285.4 | 270 | 3 899 | 1 176.9 | 121.0 |
| Savannah ................. | 36 665 | 447 | 44.1 | 183 | 2 113 | 1 633.9 | 106.6 | 941 | 11 511 | 2 521.2 | 250.3 |
| Smyrna .................... | 22 177 | 142 | 98.6 | 87 | 2 677 | 2 088.3 | 139.8 | 213 | 2 981 | 1 069.5 | 83.1 |
| Statesboro ............... | 28 933 | 395 | 4.6 | 22 | 119 | 60.3 | 3.9 | 227 | 3 163 | 636.9 | 62.6 |
| Stockbridge ............. | NA | NA | NA | 9 | D | D | D | 95 | 1 827 | 391.9 | 41.2 |
| Valdosta .................. | 17 898 | 338 | 19.8 | 90 | 828 | 565.8 | 33.9 | 393 | 5 343 | 1 220.8 | 109.1 |
| Warner Robins ........... | 44 988 | 335 | 78.5 | 23 | 222 | 59.9 | 8.3 | 295 | 4 669 | 1 080.6 | 104.3 |
| HAWAII................ | 653 884 | 2 743 | 59.5 | 1 629 | 17 707 | 8 894.7 | 699.1 | 5 012 | 70 661 | 17 611.9 | 1 766.4 |
| East Honolulu CDP ....... | NA | NA | NA | NA | NA | NA | NA | NA | NA | NA | NA |
| Hilo CDP ................... | NA | NA | NA | 77 | 950 | 428.4 | 30.2 | 258 | 4 178 | 1 156.3 | 108.9 |
| Kahului CDP.............. | NA | NA | NA | 52 | 652 | 356.3 | 32.8 | 213 | 4 591 | 1 329.0 | 133.1 |
| Kailua CDP (Honolulu County)..................... | NA | NA | NA | 23 | 74 | 21.8 | 3.5 | 103 | 1 578 | 350.9 | 38.2 |
| Kaneohe CDP ............. | NA | NA | NA | 19 | 39 | 15.1 | 1.6 | 129 | 2 113 | 555.3 | 51.6 |
| Mililani Town CDP........ | NA | NA | NA | 7 | 10 | 2.2 | 0.3 | 36 | 1 106 | 248.1 | 26.0 |
| Pearl City CDP............ | NA | NA | NA | 32 | 378 | 228.8 | 15.2 | 50 | 1 666 | 474.2 | 39.1 |
| Urban Honolulu CDP .... | NA | NA | NA | NA | NA | NA | NA | NA | NA | NA | NA |
| Waipahu CDP ............. | NA | NA | NA | 51 | 904 | 302.9 | 34.2 | 104 | 2 560 | 858.3 | 80.1 |
| IDAHO .................... | 732 769 | 3 815 | 82.9 | 1 846 | 21 844 | 14 286.7 | 900.0 | 6 300 | 80 447 | 20 526.6 | 1 833.6 |
| Boise City ................ | 87 915 | 418 | 85.9 | 354 | 5 159 | 4 925.8 | 259.2 | 1 002 | 16 168 | 3 893.1 | 366.1 |
| Caldwell................... | 4 763 | 37 | 100.0 | 35 | 240 | 83.4 | 9.5 | 132 | 2 148 | 611.8 | 54.1 |
| Coeur d'Alene .............. | 30 873 | 275 | 42.2 | 46 | 713 | 379.1 | 28.0 | 333 | 4 317 | 1 234.6 | 110.5 |
| Idaho Falls ............... | 5 707 | 64 | 93.8 | 96 | 1 192 | 1 151.1 | 47.5 | 389 | 5 750 | 1 453.1 | 121.4 |
| Lewiston .................. | 5 634 | 28 | 85.7 | 41 | 490 | 434.9 | 19.6 | 202 | 2 700 | 680.5 | 67.0 |
| Meridian................... | 134 530 | 595 | 90.6 | 85 | 1 463 | 683.9 | 76.2 | 204 | 3 967 | 1 329.0 | 112.5 |
| Nampa ..................... | 20 971 | 218 | 33.9 | 94 | 1 148 | 709.7 | 54.2 | 311 | 5 342 | 1 483.9 | 134.9 |
| Pocatello.................. | 4 255 | 34 | 100.0 | 65 | 579 | 383.1 | 20.8 | 250 | 3 246 | 762.6 | 67.8 |
| Post Falls ................. | 18 978 | 130 | 66.9 | 21 | 318 | 181.8 | 16.8 | 108 | 1 598 | 519.9 | 41.4 |
| Rexburg ................... | 5 815 | 47 | 27.7 | 27 | 342 | 139.5 | 8.5 | 102 | 1 586 | 386.3 | 35.3 |
| Twin Falls ................ | 14 425 | 93 | 100.0 | 75 | 897 | 330.6 | 29.4 | 354 | 4 897 | 1 150.3 | 108.6 |
| ILLINOIS.................. | 2 118 058 | 11 809 | 57.9 | 16 704 | 259 758 | 231 082.8 | 14 319.6 | 43 055 | 639 147 | 165 450.5 | 14 895.5 |
| Addison ................... | 0 | 0 | 0.0 | 205 | 3 703 | 1 899.4 | 203.5 | 112 | 2 793 | 1 090.5 | 95.3 |
| Algonquin ................ | 0 | 0 | 0.0 | 24 | 79 | 38.7 | 4.6 | 155 | 3 105 | 635.4 | 55.6 |
| Alton ....................... | 0 | 0 | 0.0 | 26 | 268 | 189.2 | 10.9 | 181 | 2 774 | 601.0 | 62.0 |
| Arlington Heights.......... | 29 275 | 82 | 90.2 | 202 | 1 856 | 1 395.4 | 119.5 | 256 | 4 269 | 978.0 | 98.5 |
| Aurora...................... | 17 488 | 67 | 100.0 | 138 | 2 866 | 7 694.2 | 151.8 | 597 | 10 131 | 2 148.1 | 204.5 |
| Bartlett .................... | 1 170 | 8 | 25.0 | 51 | 548 | 318.2 | 26.1 | 49 | 744 | 150.8 | 16.2 |
| Batavia .................... | 2 103 | 6 | 100.0 | 81 | 1 533 | 2 074.0 | 81.6 | 89 | 2 032 | 470.8 | 42.2 |
| Belleville .................. | 6 012 | 44 | 100.0 | 38 | 424 | 207.0 | 18.4 | 203 | 2 498 | 616.4 | 66.2 |
| Belvidere ................. | 469 | 4 | 100.0 | 11 | 119 | 78.2 | 5.8 | 79 | 1 366 | 365.2 | 30.9 |
| Berwyn .................... | 85 | 1 | 100.0 | 10 | 54 | 7.0 | 1.2 | 127 | 1 378 | 328.8 | 36.9 |
| Bloomington ............. | 26 112 | 261 | 55.9 | 75 | 1 344 | 3 984.1 | 73.8 | 382 | 5 581 | 1 298.3 | 118.7 |
| Bolingbrook ............. | 8 978 | 53 | 100.0 | 86 | 5 309 | 4 024.5 | 250.8 | 204 | 4 916 | 1 046.4 | 102.9 |
| Buffalo Grove ........... | 3 301 | 12 | 100.0 | 119 | 2 491 | 2 170.3 | 157.3 | 128 | 1 703 | 491.8 | 46.7 |

1. Merchant wholesalers except manufacturers' sales branches and offices.  2. Establishments with payroll.

| City | Real estate and rental and leasing, 2007 | | | | Professional, scientific, and technical services,[1] 2007 | | | | Manufacturing, 2007 | | | |
|---|---|---|---|---|---|---|---|---|---|---|---|---|
| | Number of establishments | Number of employees | Receipts (mil dol) | Annual payroll (mil dol) | Number of establishments | Number of employees | Receipts (mil dol) | Annual payroll (mil dol) | Number of establishments | Number of employees | Receipts (mil dol) | Annual payroll (mil dol) |
| | 80 | 81 | 82 | 83 | 84 | 85 | 86 | 87 | 88 | 89 | 90 | 91 |
| GEORGIA | 12 620 | 65 875 | 14 021.9 | 2 903.2 | 27 668 | 213 419 | 34 966.0 | 12 689.5 | 8 699 | 411 158 | 144 280.8 | 16 128.1 |
| Albany | 129 | 564 | 78.6 | 14.9 | 192 | D | D | D | 70 | 4 975 | 3 263.0 | 246.5 |
| Alpharetta | 219 | 1 135 | 305.0 | 62.5 | 870 | D | D | D | NA | NA | NA | NA |
| Athens-Clarke County | 224 | 839 | 128.3 | 24.3 | 283 | D | D | D | 91 | 6 632 | 1 971.2 | 255.2 |
| Atlanta | 1 231 | 12 285 | 2 727.8 | 752.2 | 3 250 | 42 668 | 9 456.3 | 3 651.7 | 346 | 12 257 | 5 304.3 | 504.2 |
| Augusta-Richmond County | 233 | 1 449 | 220.1 | 38.5 | 437 | 3 181 | 397.2 | 144.3 | 129 | 9 055 | 5 256.3 | 452.0 |
| Columbus | 259 | 1 549 | 292.8 | 54.0 | 348 | D | D | D | 141 | 7 055 | 2 111.4 | 266.7 |
| Dalton | 66 | 281 | 41.4 | 7.7 | 117 | D | D | D | 191 | 16 869 | 6 207.2 | 531.4 |
| Douglasville | 60 | 225 | 33.0 | 6.7 | 130 | 587 | 51.9 | 21.6 | NA | NA | NA | NA |
| Duluth | 138 | 711 | 179.8 | 29.7 | 302 | 2 440 | 300.7 | 129.8 | 49 | 1 176 | 389.7 | 69.5 |
| Dunwoody | 147 | 1 016 | 551.9 | 122.8 | 505 | 5 866 | 921.7 | 381.2 | 16 | D | D | D |
| East Point | 36 | 620 | 92.7 | 14.1 | 71 | D | D | D | 31 | 854 | 295.9 | 36.5 |
| Gainesville | 97 | 300 | 76.0 | 10.5 | 201 | D | D | D | 111 | 8 629 | 2 533.2 | 308.6 |
| Hinesville | 42 | 182 | 26.8 | 4.6 | 34 | 194 | 16.1 | 4.6 | NA | NA | NA | NA |
| Johns Creek | 107 | 475 | 67.5 | 17.1 | 446 | 1 699 | 257.3 | 95.1 | 11 | D | D | D |
| Kennesaw | 65 | 268 | 46.7 | 8.1 | 166 | 645 | 73.7 | 27.6 | 58 | 1 380 | 326.3 | 58.5 |
| LaGrange | 50 | 406 | 34.8 | 8.0 | 62 | 325 | 29.8 | 13.6 | 47 | 4 325 | 1 613.2 | 184.0 |
| Lawrenceville | 89 | 438 | 73.4 | 16.0 | 251 | D | D | D | 74 | 2 976 | 933.7 | 133.5 |
| Macon | 147 | 838 | 163.1 | 23.3 | 311 | D | D | D | 91 | 2 482 | 644.5 | 113.5 |
| Marietta | 193 | 1 326 | 228.6 | 48.6 | 635 | D | D | D | 148 | 11 727 | 3 782.9 | 695.1 |
| Milton | 37 | 103 | 13.0 | 2.9 | 122 | D | D | D | NA | NA | NA | NA |
| Newnan | 66 | 233 | 40.8 | 7.4 | 87 | 420 | 54.3 | 19.5 | 34 | 1 378 | 344.6 | 47.7 |
| Peachtree City | 84 | 182 | 30.6 | 6.2 | 156 | D | D | D | 43 | 3 037 | 1 622.7 | 150.5 |
| Rome | 66 | 303 | 51.7 | 8.9 | 135 | 617 | 71.1 | 21.9 | 71 | 5 141 | 2 006.6 | 188.0 |
| Roswell | 214 | 839 | 193.5 | 37.1 | 792 | 7 311 | 811.2 | 307.9 | 57 | 694 | 107.3 | 27.5 |
| Sandy Springs | 368 | D | D | D | 976 | 10 482 | 2 097.8 | 754.7 | NA | NA | NA | NA |
| Savannah | 253 | 1 422 | 231.4 | 43.1 | 506 | D | D | D | 107 | 4 136 | 2 160.5 | 183.4 |
| Smyrna | 115 | 674 | 144.6 | 37.0 | 281 | 3 256 | 1 102.5 | 227.9 | 43 | 781 | 144.6 | 31.0 |
| Statesboro | 64 | 278 | 38.2 | 5.8 | 82 | 555 | 55.3 | 18.2 | 31 | 1 649 | 472.5 | 55.3 |
| Stockbridge | 36 | 100 | 18.4 | 2.8 | 77 | 487 | 60.2 | 20.4 | NA | NA | NA | NA |
| Valdosta | 94 | 675 | 64.1 | 16.7 | 168 | D | D | D | 71 | 3 570 | 1 918.8 | 124.4 |
| Warner Robins | 83 | 377 | 51.5 | 9.3 | 168 | D | D | D | 31 | 668 | 181.9 | 29.9 |
| HAWAII | 2 084 | 16 759 | 3 974.0 | 653.8 | 3 254 | 21 772 | 3 068.3 | 1 193.5 | 984 | 14 127 | 8 799.3 | 511.5 |
| East Honolulu CDP | NA | NA | NA | NA | NA | NA | NA | NA | NA | NA | NA | NA |
| Hilo CDP | 88 | 442 | 76.5 | 10.0 | 116 | D | D | D | 55 | 544 | 110.6 | 19.3 |
| Kahului CDP | 51 | 718 | 180.7 | 23.1 | 43 | 243 | 24.0 | 8.2 | NA | NA | NA | NA |
| Kailua CDP (Honolulu County) | 44 | 186 | 33.8 | 6.7 | 102 | 490 | 90.0 | 27.7 | NA | NA | NA | NA |
| Kaneohe CDP | 24 | 96 | 16.6 | 3.0 | 51 | D | D | D | NA | NA | NA | NA |
| Mililani Town CDP | 13 | 48 | 5.4 | 1.2 | 21 | 79 | 6.0 | 1.7 | NA | NA | NA | NA |
| Pearl City CDP | 12 | 53 | 6.1 | 1.3 | 16 | 90 | 8.5 | 4.0 | NA | NA | NA | NA |
| Urban Honolulu CDP | NA | NA | NA | NA | NA | NA | NA | NA | NA | NA | NA | NA |
| Waipahu CDP | 30 | 156 | 20.9 | 4.6 | 14 | 156 | 9.8 | 3.9 | NA | NA | NA | NA |
| IDAHO | 2 530 | 8 371 | 1 241.7 | 233.5 | 4 189 | D | D | D | 1 942 | 64 778 | 18 011.0 | 2 829.4 |
| Boise City | 545 | 2 533 | 396.3 | 88.0 | 1 173 | D | D | D | 223 | 18 120 | 4 442.3 | 1 138.1 |
| Caldwell | 51 | 220 | 20.1 | 4.4 | 50 | D | D | D | 69 | 2 147 | D | 66.6 |
| Coeur d'Alene | 122 | 580 | 117.6 | 20.1 | 250 | D | D | D | 67 | 1 211 | 388.1 | 45.5 |
| Idaho Falls | 119 | 451 | 74.6 | 10.4 | 308 | D | D | D | 76 | 1 302 | 376.8 | 48.0 |
| Lewiston | 37 | D | D | D | 74 | D | D | D | 29 | D | D | 45.2 |
| Meridian | 155 | 530 | 69.0 | 18.7 | 171 | 860 | 131.3 | 38.1 | 51 | 1 342 | 225.3 | 47.3 |
| Nampa | 121 | 323 | 39.7 | 6.5 | 137 | 762 | 68.0 | 27.7 | 97 | 4 996 | 1 412.6 | 184.2 |
| Pocatello | 81 | 263 | 43.4 | 5.8 | 136 | D | D | D | 45 | D | 634.8 | D |
| Post Falls | 44 | 123 | 15.0 | 2.9 | 52 | 668 | 61.3 | 25.8 | 47 | 1 266 | 217.0 | 45.4 |
| Rexburg | 47 | 145 | 19.6 | 2.6 | 52 | 873 | 34.0 | 9.7 | 18 | D | D | D |
| Twin Falls | 90 | 307 | 45.5 | 7.5 | 174 | D | D | D | 62 | 1 803 | 614.1 | 59.1 |
| ILLINOIS | 13 899 | 87 468 | 21 725.0 | 3 985.2 | 38 797 | 363 231 | 61 896.1 | 24 197.9 | 15 704 | 663 586 | 257 760.7 | 31 715.9 |
| Addison | 44 | 278 | 76.3 | 16.3 | 97 | 501 | 91.7 | 27.9 | 346 | 7 508 | 1 286.6 | 317.5 |
| Algonquin | 34 | D | D | D | 105 | 336 | 32.3 | 12.1 | 35 | 715 | 111.9 | 29.7 |
| Alton | 35 | 142 | 21.3 | 3.8 | 61 | D | D | D | 26 | 848 | D | 36.5 |
| Arlington Heights | 128 | 802 | 144.5 | 31.5 | 529 | D | D | D | 93 | 2 322 | 768.7 | 122.6 |
| Aurora | 132 | 818 | 127.6 | 20.2 | 413 | 2 269 | 297.6 | 115.6 | 157 | 9 917 | 4 331.0 | 506.8 |
| Bartlett | 27 | 75 | 13.4 | 2.6 | 125 | 285 | 48.5 | 14.8 | 26 | 1 102 | 274.2 | 49.6 |
| Batavia | 27 | 132 | 18.3 | 3.7 | 129 | D | D | D | 96 | 3 688 | 1 066.4 | 162.8 |
| Belleville | 64 | 239 | 32.7 | 6.3 | 171 | 1 118 | 132.1 | 64.3 | 49 | 1 856 | 435.7 | 73.7 |
| Belvidere | 18 | 57 | 6.9 | 1.1 | 41 | D | D | D | 35 | 5 701 | 5 359.5 | 348.1 |
| Berwyn | 45 | 127 | 18.0 | 2.6 | 77 | 312 | 27.7 | 11.1 | 14 | 503 | D | D |
| Bloomington | 103 | 565 | 90.9 | 14.4 | 224 | D | D | D | 60 | 2 753 | 821.0 | 129.9 |
| Bolingbrook | 45 | 172 | 31.3 | 4.5 | 149 | 932 | 99.8 | 37.7 | 52 | 3 218 | 1 362.4 | 131.7 |
| Buffalo Grove | 57 | 432 | 57.6 | 20.3 | 316 | 3 424 | 477.2 | 199.6 | 64 | 4 219 | 1 160.8 | 188.6 |

1. Establishments subject to federal tax.

# Table D. Cities — Accommodation and Food Services, Arts, Entertainment, and Recreation, and Health Care and Social Assistance

| City | Accommodation and food services, 2007 | | | | Arts, entertainment, and recreation,[1] 2007 | | | | Health care and social assistance,[1] 2007 | | | |
|---|---|---|---|---|---|---|---|---|---|---|---|---|
| | Number of establishments | Number of employees | Sales (mil dol) | Annual payroll (mil dol) | Number of establishments | Number of employees | Receipts (mil dol) | Annual payroll (mil dol) | Number of establishments | Number of employees | Receipts (mil dol) | Annual payroll (mil dol) |
| | 92 | 93 | 94 | 95 | 96 | 97 | 98 | 99 | 100 | 101 | 102 | 103 |
| GEORGIA | 18 640 | 355 423 | 16 976.2 | 4 704.4 | 2 319 | 31 121 | 2 527.7 | 836.4 | 18 379 | 229 101 | 23 274.0 | 9 144.8 |
| Albany | 208 | 4 015 | 165.6 | 41.3 | 18 | D | D | D | 237 | D | D | D |
| Alpharetta | 318 | 7 164 | 377.1 | 108.6 | 33 | D | D | D | 298 | 3 491 | 395.5 | 162.1 |
| Athens-Clarke County | 331 | 7 062 | 293.4 | 80.3 | 36 | 408 | 28.6 | 6.3 | 355 | D | D | D |
| Atlanta | 1 528 | 41 275 | 2 743.7 | 770.6 | 224 | 2 961 | 589.0 | 243.9 | 1 203 | 14 437 | 1 982.7 | 753.8 |
| Augusta-Richmond County | 431 | 9 726 | 395.4 | 108.6 | 32 | D | D | D | 548 | 7 955 | 964.8 | 347.7 |
| Columbus | 418 | 9 898 | 428.2 | 120.7 | 37 | D | D | D | 484 | 6 110 | 635.8 | 246.8 |
| Dalton | 143 | 2 775 | 117.2 | 31.6 | 8 | D | D | D | 132 | D | D | D |
| Douglasville | 137 | 3 446 | 145.2 | 40.0 | 9 | 210 | 10.0 | 2.4 | 108 | D | D | D |
| Duluth | 158 | 1 969 | 81.9 | 26.2 | 24 | 298 | 39.6 | 5.8 | 155 | D | D | D |
| Dunwoody | 119 | 3 326 | 198.3 | 59.0 | 13 | D | D | D | 180 | 2 292 | 259.8 | 98.3 |
| East Point | 74 | 1 889 | 119.7 | 34.9 | 13 | 31 | 11.6 | 2.8 | 82 | D | D | D |
| Gainesville | 156 | 2 562 | 116.4 | 30.6 | 16 | D | D | D | 245 | D | D | D |
| Hinesville | 70 | 1 294 | 50.2 | 12.0 | 1 | D | D | D | 42 | 461 | 28.2 | 11.9 |
| Johns Creek | 112 | 2 087 | 85.3 | 26.6 | 21 | 210 | 26.1 | 12.2 | 121 | D | D | D |
| Kennesaw | 100 | 1 760 | 76.1 | 21.7 | 19 | D | D | D | 74 | D | D | D |
| LaGrange | 92 | 1 878 | 71.7 | 19.3 | 6 | D | D | D | 86 | D | D | D |
| Lawrenceville | 137 | 2 044 | 106.7 | 27.6 | 20 | D | D | D | 231 | D | D | D |
| Macon | 261 | 4 791 | 184.4 | 49.9 | 14 | D | D | D | 393 | D | D | D |
| Marietta | 271 | 4 116 | 207.5 | 55.5 | 27 | D | D | D | 339 | D | D | D |
| Milton | 25 | 191 | 13.7 | 3.3 | 10 | 212 | 14.6 | 4.6 | 16 | D | D | D |
| Newnan | 104 | 2 566 | 104.0 | 30.4 | 7 | D | D | D | 72 | D | D | D |
| Peachtree City | 87 | 2 101 | 83.4 | 25.0 | 20 | D | D | D | 95 | D | D | D |
| Rome | 156 | 2 981 | 125.6 | 33.0 | 9 | D | D | D | 203 | 4 802 | 537.4 | 196.3 |
| Roswell | 239 | 3 862 | 181.7 | 52.9 | 44 | 441 | 30.7 | 9.2 | 340 | 5 303 | 459.1 | 183.0 |
| Sandy Springs | 264 | 4 087 | 250.2 | 65.2 | 44 | 574 | 38.7 | 12.4 | 598 | 7 763 | 1 218.0 | 497.0 |
| Savannah | 521 | 12 365 | 663.2 | 180.9 | 51 | 543 | 36.8 | 8.9 | 457 | 7 158 | 895.1 | 364.6 |
| Smyrna | 163 | 2 993 | 147.2 | 40.2 | 27 | D | D | D | 186 | D | D | D |
| Statesboro | 124 | D | D | D | 7 | D | D | D | 136 | D | D | D |
| Stockbridge | 68 | 957 | 39.7 | 9.4 | 11 | D | D | D | 131 | D | D | D |
| Valdosta | 171 | 4 114 | 159.6 | 41.9 | 9 | 76 | 4.3 | 1.1 | 244 | D | D | D |
| Warner Robins | 143 | 3 217 | 121.4 | 32.9 | 8 | D | D | D | 153 | D | D | D |
| HAWAII | 3 528 | 98 353 | 8 042.2 | 2 209.8 | 397 | 7 676 | 563.7 | 163.1 | 2 778 | 29 023 | 2 978.6 | 1 244.1 |
| East Honolulu CDP | NA | NA | NA | NA | NA | NA | NA | NA | NA | NA | NA | NA |
| Hilo CDP | 149 | 2 616 | 132.0 | 36.3 | 6 | 79 | 4.2 | 1.0 | 178 | 2 407 | 194.8 | 82.5 |
| Kahului CDP | 94 | D | D | D | 10 | D | D | D | 76 | 669 | 85.9 | 36.0 |
| Kailua CDP (Honolulu County) | 95 | 1 510 | 69.9 | 19.3 | 10 | 76 | 5.3 | 2.0 | 110 | 863 | 74.7 | 35.2 |
| Kaneohe CDP | 78 | 1 135 | 59.5 | 14.5 | 14 | D | D | D | 78 | 744 | 74.2 | 29.0 |
| Mililani Town CDP | 39 | 1 055 | 47.2 | 12.2 | 4 | 118 | 7.9 | 2.0 | 25 | D | D | D |
| Pearl City CDP | 43 | 716 | 36.8 | 9.7 | 1 | D | D | D | 32 | 409 | 45.1 | 19.3 |
| Urban Honolulu CDP | NA | NA | NA | NA | NA | NA | NA | NA | NA | NA | NA | NA |
| Waipahu CDP | 69 | 1 033 | 56.4 | 14.5 | 1 | D | D | D | 70 | 581 | 57.8 | 19.9 |
| IDAHO | 3 482 | 56 662 | 2 416.0 | 662.7 | 590 | 7 065 | 310.3 | 97.3 | 3 974 | 44 499 | 3 510.2 | 1 422.7 |
| Boise City | 606 | 13 055 | 593.2 | 163.9 | 67 | 1 514 | 56.5 | 16.7 | 832 | 9 567 | 901.7 | 402.3 |
| Caldwell | 63 | 971 | 36.8 | 10.3 | 6 | D | D | D | 90 | 1 327 | 118.2 | 44.3 |
| Coeur d'Alene | 192 | 3 801 | 180.7 | 50.1 | 29 | D | D | D | 246 | D | D | D |
| Idaho Falls | 166 | 3 070 | 124.0 | 33.5 | 21 | D | D | D | 382 | 4 361 | 379.9 | 147.3 |
| Lewiston | 91 | 1 664 | 63.9 | 20.0 | 10 | D | D | D | 125 | D | D | D |
| Meridian | 149 | 2 876 | 117.5 | 34.1 | 13 | D | D | D | 192 | 2 448 | 187.7 | 71.5 |
| Nampa | 145 | 2 698 | 97.0 | 25.9 | 15 | 426 | 7.3 | 2.5 | 175 | D | D | D |
| Pocatello | 130 | 2 350 | 92.7 | 25.1 | 14 | D | D | D | 225 | D | D | D |
| Post Falls | 62 | 1 034 | 39.1 | 12.1 | 8 | D | D | D | 80 | D | D | D |
| Rexburg | 46 | 1 028 | 29.5 | 8.3 | 7 | 111 | 4.2 | 1.0 | 74 | D | D | D |
| Twin Falls | 143 | 2 606 | 104.5 | 27.2 | 17 | D | D | D | 234 | D | D | D |
| ILLINOIS | 26 774 | 468 827 | 25 469.0 | 6 894.3 | 3 666 | 51 012 | 5 306.0 | 1 579.8 | 25 651 | 325 085 | 32 056.1 | 13 445.1 |
| Addison | 77 | 1 491 | 83.8 | 22.5 | 10 | 76 | 4.5 | 1.5 | 59 | 882 | 63.1 | 34.2 |
| Algonquin | 81 | 1 665 | 67.6 | 22.3 | 13 | D | D | D | 74 | D | D | D |
| Alton | 96 | 1 697 | 73.6 | 20.6 | 10 | D | D | D | 113 | 1 376 | 127.4 | 55.8 |
| Arlington Heights | 181 | 3 120 | 177.7 | 48.5 | 23 | 121 | 6.7 | 1.8 | 363 | D | D | D |
| Aurora | 267 | 4 486 | 211.9 | 57.6 | 31 | 1 781 | 475.8 | 43.6 | 277 | 4 139 | 491.5 | 190.6 |
| Bartlett | 50 | 615 | 33.3 | 7.7 | 8 | 139 | 4.0 | 1.5 | 54 | D | D | D |
| Batavia | 70 | 1 043 | 47.8 | 14.5 | 8 | D | D | D | 53 | D | D | D |
| Belleville | 145 | 1 964 | 87.4 | 23.0 | 14 | D | D | D | 203 | 3 418 | 332.9 | 166.7 |
| Belvidere | 51 | 754 | 35.3 | 9.3 | 6 | 49 | 2.3 | 0.5 | 39 | D | D | D |
| Berwyn | 94 | 1 184 | 61.5 | 15.4 | 9 | 76 | 5.3 | 1.7 | 138 | 3 191 | 343.6 | 156.5 |
| Bloomington | 233 | 5 530 | 221.2 | 65.5 | 24 | 355 | 11.8 | 3.7 | 184 | 2 680 | 306.2 | 138.0 |
| Bolingbrook | 139 | 2 787 | 143.5 | 41.2 | 14 | 257 | 10.1 | 4.7 | 100 | 907 | 72.3 | 33.0 |
| Buffalo Grove | 97 | 1 742 | 85.7 | 23.2 | 18 | D | D | D | 143 | 1 049 | 124.7 | 48.4 |

1. Establishments subject to federal tax.

# Table D. Cities — Other Services and Federal Funds

| | Other services[1], 2007 | | | | Selected federal funds, 2009–2010 (mil dol) | | | | | | | | |
| | | | | | Procurement contracts | | Grants | | | | | | |
| City | Number of establishments | Number of employees | Receipts (mil dol) | Annual payroll (mil dol) | Defense | Other | Total[2] | Medicaid and other health related | Nutrition and family welfare | Energy and environment | Disasters and emergency preparedness | Housing and community development | Employment and training |
|---|---|---|---|---|---|---|---|---|---|---|---|---|---|
| | 104 | 105 | 106 | 107 | 108 | 109 | 110 | 111 | 112 | 113 | 114 | 115 | 116 |
| GEORGIA.................. | 12 420 | 81 240 | 6 485.3 | 2 183.1 | 8 377.5 | 4 083.2 | 16 750.6 | 8 036.6 | 2 202.4 | 368.4 | 99.5 | 936.8 | 217.3 |
| Albany ......................... | 136 | D | D | D | 78.2 | 29.9 | 29.4 | 4.9 | 0.5 | 0.8 | 0.0 | 4.5 | 0.0 |
| Alpharetta.................... | 150 | D | D | D | 60.4 | 14.9 | 34.8 | 0.2 | 0.0 | 34.5 | 0.0 | 0.0 | 0.0 |
| Athens-Clarke County ... | 160 | D | D | D | 0.0 | 0.0 | 4.4 | 0.0 | 0.0 | 0.8 | 0.0 | 0.2 | 0.0 |
| Atlanta ........................ | 904 | 8 419 | 671.6 | 204.2 | 702.4 | 1 859.6 | 4 102.9 | 1 051.6 | 413.0 | 229.3 | 33.7 | 251.1 | 206.9 |
| Augusta-Richmond County ...................... | 226 | 1 628 | 125.0 | 41.6 | NA | NA | NA | NA | NA | NA | NA | NA | NA |
| Columbus .................... | 277 | 1 862 | 122.7 | 42.3 | 24.6 | 2.5 | 43.6 | 3.3 | 6.2 | 1.9 | 0.0 | 22.8 | 0.0 |
| Dalton ......................... | 79 | 404 | 37.7 | 11.6 | 1.6 | 1.5 | 1.3 | 0.6 | 0.0 | 0.0 | 0.0 | 0.5 | 0.0 |
| Douglasville ................. | 91 | D | D | D | 0.5 | 0.6 | 1.0 | 0.0 | 0.0 | 0.0 | 0.0 | 0.3 | 0.0 |
| Duluth.......................... | 163 | 1 111 | 93.4 | 41.0 | 8.5 | 2.2 | 0.7 | 0.7 | 0.0 | 0.0 | 0.0 | 0.0 | 0.0 |
| Dunwoody .................... | 73 | 436 | 26.3 | 9.1 | NA | NA | NA | NA | NA | NA | NA | NA | NA |
| East Point ................... | 43 | D | D | D | 1.2 | 2.9 | 4.8 | 0.4 | 0.0 | 0.0 | 0.0 | 4.1 | 0.0 |
| Gainesville .................. | 110 | D | D | D | 263.9 | 34.8 | 24.0 | 0.1 | 20.6 | 0.6 | 0.0 | 1.5 | 0.0 |
| Hinesville .................... | 44 | D | D | D | 33.9 | 0.0 | 11.5 | 0.0 | 0.0 | 0.0 | 0.0 | 0.5 | 0.0 |
| Johns Creek................ | 91 | D | D | D | NA | NA | NA | NA | NA | NA | NA | NA | NA |
| Kennesaw .................... | 105 | D | D | D | 3.5 | 20.8 | 6.6 | 0.7 | 0.0 | 0.0 | 0.0 | 0.0 | 0.0 |
| LaGrange .................... | 55 | D | D | D | 1.0 | 0.5 | 3.4 | 0.7 | 0.0 | 0.0 | 0.0 | 0.8 | 0.0 |
| Lawrenceville............... | 138 | 990 | 96.7 | 33.0 | 28.4 | 6.1 | 15.9 | 0.9 | 0.0 | 0.0 | 0.0 | 6.6 | 0.0 |
| Macon ......................... | 176 | 943 | 81.6 | 24.8 | 11.7 | 29.2 | 45.8 | 6.3 | 5.4 | 0.9 | 0.0 | 24.6 | 0.0 |
| Marietta ...................... | 232 | 1 399 | 153.9 | 46.5 | 3 485.4 | 183.6 | 68.7 | 4.5 | 3.1 | 18.1 | 0.0 | 28.0 | 0.1 |
| Milton .......................... | 19 | D | D | D | NA | NA | NA | NA | NA | NA | NA | NA | NA |
| Newnan ....................... | 69 | 235 | 21.7 | 5.5 | 1.0 | 2.3 | 1.6 | 0.0 | 0.0 | 0.0 | 0.0 | 1.5 | 0.0 |
| Peachtree City............. | 79 | D | D | D | 11.6 | 1.2 | 0.1 | 0.0 | 0.0 | 0.0 | 0.0 | 0.0 | 0.0 |
| Rome........................... | 67 | D | D | D | 0.0 | 6.1 | 5.6 | 0.7 | 0.0 | 0.0 | 0.0 | 3.8 | 0.0 |
| Roswell ....................... | 205 | D | D | D | 1.7 | 1.1 | 1.3 | 0.0 | 0.0 | 1.1 | 0.0 | 0.2 | 0.0 |
| Sandy Springs.............. | 155 | D | D | D | 4.6 | 10.0 | 1.5 | 0.0 | 0.0 | 0.0 | 0.0 | 1.5 | 0.0 |
| Savannah .................... | 227 | 1 505 | 124.1 | 38.6 | 255.1 | 8.8 | 71.6 | 6.1 | 6.7 | 4.3 | -1.7 | 32.9 | 0.3 |
| Smyrna ....................... | 99 | 434 | 41.8 | 12.0 | 2.9 | 5.1 | 2.9 | 1.3 | 0.0 | 0.0 | 1.4 | 0.0 | 0.0 |
| Statesboro .................. | 60 | 298 | 21.9 | 5.6 | 1.3 | 0.3 | 6.3 | 1.0 | 0.0 | 0.3 | 0.0 | 0.5 | 0.0 |
| Stockbridge ................. | 44 | D | D | D | 0.4 | 0.4 | 0.0 | 0.0 | 0.0 | 0.0 | 0.0 | 0.0 | 0.0 |
| Valdosta ..................... | 96 | 432 | 28.0 | 8.4 | 29.0 | 0.4 | 18.8 | 0.8 | 6.6 | 0.0 | 0.0 | 2.2 | 3.4 |
| Warner Robins ............. | 84 | D | D | D | 318.1 | 3.3 | 9.3 | 0.0 | 7.3 | 0.0 | 0.0 | 1.3 | 0.0 |
| HAWAII....................... | 1 615 | 11 669 | 908.6 | 279.4 | 2 350.8 | 394.0 | 3 025.6 | 1 232.7 | 331.2 | 141.4 | 6.0 | 170.3 | 50.2 |
| East Honolulu CDP ....... | NA | NA | NA | NA | NA | NA | NA | NA | NA | NA | NA | NA | NA |
| Hilo CDP ..................... | 72 | 470 | 39.1 | 10.8 | NA | NA | NA | NA | NA | NA | NA | NA | NA |
| Kahului CDP ................ | 60 | 577 | 46.3 | 13.9 | NA | NA | NA | NA | NA | NA | NA | NA | NA |
| Kailua CDP (Honolulu County)..................... | 39 | 193 | 14.4 | 4.9 | NA | NA | NA | NA | NA | NA | NA | NA | NA |
| Kaneohe CDP .............. | 43 | 363 | 22.0 | 7.9 | NA | NA | NA | NA | NA | NA | NA | NA | NA |
| Mililani Town CDP........ | 10 | 58 | 4.1 | 1.1 | NA | NA | NA | NA | NA | NA | NA | NA | NA |
| Pearl City CDP............. | 30 | 177 | 16.6 | 5.1 | NA | NA | NA | NA | NA | NA | NA | NA | NA |
| Urban Honolulu CDP .... | NA | NA | NA | NA | NA | NA | NA | NA | NA | NA | NA | NA | NA |
| Waipahu CDP .............. | 52 | 258 | 22.0 | 6.5 | NA | NA | NA | NA | NA | NA | NA | NA | NA |
| IDAHO ........................ | 2 114 | 11 031 | 837.1 | 249.3 | 264.9 | 2 368.4 | 2 979.5 | 1 473.1 | 282.9 | 199.2 | 8.6 | 71.0 | 68.1 |
| Boise City .................... | 368 | 2 413 | 175.6 | 62.7 | 28.0 | 112.7 | 583.7 | 44.4 | 44.6 | 142.0 | 4.9 | 53.5 | 66.7 |
| Caldwell ...................... | 46 | 307 | 24.9 | 7.8 | 0.4 | 1.1 | 12.3 | 0.7 | 7.5 | 0.0 | 0.0 | 0.0 | 1.1 |
| Coeur d'Alene ............. | 91 | 579 | 37.6 | 11.4 | 0.1 | 602.7 | 3.7 | 1.1 | 0.0 | 0.5 | 0.0 | 0.6 | 0.0 |
| Idaho Falls .................. | 92 | D | D | D | 64.8 | 1 344.4 | 16.5 | 10.8 | 1.9 | 1.0 | 0.0 | 0.7 | 0.0 |
| Lewiston...................... | 68 | D | D | D | 0.4 | 13.8 | 7.8 | 0.1 | 3.4 | 0.4 | 0.0 | 0.5 | 0.0 |
| Meridian....................... | 89 | 508 | 29.0 | 8.9 | 1.3 | 0.6 | 18.9 | 0.1 | 0.0 | 0.8 | 0.0 | 0.2 | 0.0 |
| Nampa......................... | 105 | 598 | 42.2 | 12.1 | -0.3 | 7.0 | 12.8 | 4.9 | 0.0 | 0.1 | 0.0 | 6.7 | 0.0 |
| Pocatello...................... | 81 | D | D | D | 0.4 | 4.8 | 20.4 | 4.1 | 1.5 | 2.0 | 0.0 | 3.5 | 0.2 |
| Post Falls .................... | 47 | 294 | 19.0 | 5.5 | 0.0 | 0.3 | 0.2 | 0.0 | 0.0 | 0.0 | 0.0 | 0.0 | 0.0 |
| Rexburg ...................... | 21 | D | D | D | 0.3 | 0.0 | 3.0 | 2.3 | 0.0 | 0.1 | 0.0 | 0.0 | 0.0 |
| Twin Falls ................... | 94 | 722 | 48.0 | 15.2 | 0.1 | 3.2 | 9.9 | 2.4 | 4.6 | 0.7 | 0.0 | 0.3 | 0.0 |
| ILLINOIS................. | 18 732 | 122 938 | 10 459.8 | 3 264.5 | 7 118.7 | 4 481.8 | 24 060.1 | 12 147.7 | 2 913.9 | 769.9 | 259.9 | 1 735.3 | 405.0 |
| Addison ....................... | 115 | 615 | 72.1 | 23.3 | 9.0 | 2.4 | 0.1 | 0.0 | 0.0 | 0.0 | 0.0 | 0.1 | 0.0 |
| Algonquin .................... | 49 | 275 | 15.4 | 5.1 | 0.0 | 0.0 | 0.0 | 0.0 | 0.0 | 0.0 | 0.0 | 0.0 | 0.0 |
| Alton ........................... | 50 | 250 | 18.3 | 6.1 | 1.5 | 0.6 | 9.9 | 0.4 | 7.0 | 0.0 | 0.0 | 0.9 | 0.0 |
| Arlington Heights........... | 157 | 1 033 | 91.8 | 29.1 | 0.3 | 3.7 | 36.1 | 0.0 | 0.0 | 0.8 | 0.0 | 0.5 | 0.0 |
| Aurora ......................... | 184 | 1 136 | 102.6 | 25.8 | 20.1 | 0.7 | 16.0 | 1.9 | 0.0 | 1.6 | 0.0 | 11.4 | 0.4 |
| Bartlett........................ | 46 | D | D | D | 0.0 | 0.0 | 0.0 | 0.0 | 0.0 | 0.0 | 0.0 | 0.0 | 0.0 |
| Batavia ....................... | 52 | 479 | 51.5 | 18.1 | 0.3 | 440.2 | 11.8 | 0.0 | 0.0 | 7.6 | 3.4 | 0.0 | 0.0 |
| Belleville ...................... | 112 | 661 | 47.6 | 17.4 | 26.9 | 0.2 | 24.1 | 0.0 | 1.6 | 2.1 | 0.4 | 16.8 | 0.0 |
| Belvidere ..................... | 33 | D | D | D | 0.2 | 0.0 | 1.0 | 0.0 | 0.0 | 0.0 | 0.0 | 1.0 | 0.0 |
| Berwyn ........................ | 61 | 195 | 19.3 | 4.7 | 0.0 | 0.1 | 2.2 | 0.0 | 0.0 | 0.4 | 0.0 | 1.4 | 0.0 |
| Bloomington ................. | 120 | 956 | 66.5 | 22.1 | 0.3 | 8.5 | 24.4 | 6.7 | 3.3 | 0.7 | 0.0 | 7.7 | 0.1 |
| Bolingbrook .................. | 80 | 444 | 44.2 | 13.7 | 5.8 | 1.7 | 2.8 | 0.0 | 0.0 | 2.5 | 0.0 | 0.3 | 0.0 |
| Buffalo Grove .............. | 71 | 572 | 34.7 | 13.4 | 9.2 | 30.3 | 0.0 | 0.0 | 0.0 | 0.0 | 0.0 | 0.0 | 0.0 |

1. Establishments subject to federal tax.   2. Includes program categories not shown separately. State totals include additional categories not allocated by city.

# Table D. Cities — City Government Finances

| City | General revenue Total (mil dol) | Intergovernmental Total (mil dol) | Intergovernmental Percent from state government | Taxes Total (mil dol) | Taxes Per capita (dollars) Total | Taxes Per capita (dollars) Property | Taxes Per capita (dollars) Sales and gross receipts | General expenditure Total (mil dol) | General expenditure Per capita (dollars) Total | General expenditure Per capita (dollars) Capital outlays |
|---|---|---|---|---|---|---|---|---|---|---|
| | 117 | 118 | 119 | 120 | 121 | 122 | 123 | 124 | 125 | 126 |
| GEORGIA.................. | X | X | X | X | X | X | X | X | X | X |
| Albany ....................... | 108.5 | 43.4 | 8.5 | 25.4 | 335 | 196 | 140 | 95.5 | 1 260 | 223 |
| Alpharetta ................. | 64.2 | 10.4 | 2.1 | 38.6 | 778 | 465 | 313 | 58.9 | 1 185 | 290 |
| Athens-Clarke County ... | 190.0 | 63.2 | 22.3 | 61.6 | 540 | 355 | 183 | 172.6 | 1 513 | 347 |
| Atlanta ...................... | 1 600.8 | 206.1 | 30.5 | 413.5 | 796 | 403 | 392 | 1 851.5 | 3 566 | 1 521 |
| Augusta-Richmond County ..................... | 306.1 | 99.9 | 22.1 | 87.9 | 457 | 258 | 197 | 269.7 | 1 403 | 252 |
| Columbus .................. | 328.9 | 123.5 | 38.9 | 120.0 | 641 | 453 | 186 | 265.7 | 1 420 | 199 |
| Dalton ....................... | 76.8 | 9.4 | 4.2 | 16.9 | 507 | 366 | 141 | 93.7 | 2 804 | 1 064 |
| Douglasville.............. | 29.1 | 10.9 | 10.3 | 12.1 | 401 | 140 | 261 | 30.3 | 1 007 | 370 |
| Duluth ....................... | 27.0 | 10.0 | 10.3 | 10.7 | 414 | 219 | 195 | 23.8 | 915 | 422 |
| Dunwoody ................. | NA | NA | NA | NA | NA | NA | NA | NA | NA | NA |
| East Point.................. | 40.3 | 11.2 | 1.0 | 14.2 | 330 | 200 | 130 | 46.5 | 1 084 | 91 |
| Gainesville................ | 103.0 | 20.5 | 11.1 | 18.8 | 540 | 268 | 272 | 106.2 | 3 050 | 1 159 |
| Hinesville................... | 23.2 | 5.9 | 13.9 | 9.5 | 310 | 182 | 128 | 23.3 | 764 | 100 |
| Johns Creek............... | 51.0 | 13.0 | 13.9 | 20.8 | 349 | 205 | 144 | 51.2 | 860 | 113 |
| Kennesaw.................. | 12.5 | 1.0 | 13.5 | 5.4 | 170 | 47 | 123 | 17.7 | 561 | 48 |
| LaGrange .................. | 31.8 | 5.2 | 11.8 | 4.5 | 161 | 2 | 159 | 47.5 | 1 697 | 488 |
| Lawrenceville............. | 20.1 | 5.5 | 2.8 | 6.2 | 214 | 78 | 130 | 24.9 | 859 | 226 |
| Macon....................... | 96.1 | 40.6 | 3.3 | 36.5 | 392 | 203 | 190 | 92.0 | 988 | 52 |
| Marietta .................... | 87.5 | 22.0 | 1.6 | 30.8 | 459 | 184 | 268 | 85.4 | 1 274 | 168 |
| Milton ....................... | 24.8 | 10.4 | 5.4 | 7.5 | 494 | 243 | 251 | 23.8 | 1 578 | 372 |
| Newnan..................... | 22.6 | 8.3 | 8.7 | 9.7 | 337 | 138 | 200 | 19.7 | 682 | 190 |
| Peachtree City............ | 38.1 | 12.4 | 4.9 | 15.9 | 461 | 260 | 201 | 35.0 | 1 013 | 173 |
| Rome........................ | 60.4 | 18.0 | 7.3 | 18.6 | 510 | 251 | 212 | 52.4 | 1 437 | 337 |
| Roswell..................... | 88.7 | 23.1 | 0.4 | 40.1 | 459 | 288 | 171 | 73.6 | 843 | 73 |
| Sandy Springs............. | 77.4 | 23.1 | 1.5 | 50.3 | 604 | 316 | 287 | 59.3 | 713 | 46 |
| Savannah.................. | 353.0 | 108.1 | 6.8 | 92.1 | 707 | 381 | 309 | 341.5 | 2 620 | 596 |
| Smyrna...................... | 47.2 | 8.3 | 11.0 | 22.3 | 449 | 348 | 100 | 51.0 | 1 030 | 188 |
| Statesboro................. | 27.6 | 4.8 | 4.3 | 7.8 | 293 | 130 | 163 | 33.0 | 1 242 | 274 |
| Stockbridge ............... | 13.8 | 6.3 | 7.1 | 3.1 | 217 | 7 | 210 | 12.6 | 892 | 341 |
| Valdosta ................... | 56.5 | 23.7 | 5.4 | 17.0 | 357 | 176 | 181 | 54.2 | 1 139 | 269 |
| Warner Robins ............ | 44.5 | 3.5 | 6.3 | 22.5 | 373 | 210 | 162 | 50.8 | 840 | 117 |
| HAWAII................... | X | X | X | X | X | X | X | X | X | X |
| East Honolulu CDP ...... | NA | NA | NA | NA | NA | NA | NA | NA | NA | NA |
| Hilo CDP ................... | NA | NA | NA | NA | NA | NA | NA | NA | NA | NA |
| Kahului CDP............... | NA | NA | NA | NA | NA | NA | NA | NA | NA | NA |
| Kailua CDP (Honolulu County) .................... | NA | NA | NA | NA | NA | NA | NA | NA | NA | NA |
| Kaneohe CDP............. | NA | NA | NA | NA | NA | NA | NA | NA | NA | NA |
| Mililani Town CDP........ | NA | NA | NA | NA | NA | NA | NA | NA | NA | NA |
| Pearl City CDP............. | NA | NA | NA | NA | NA | NA | NA | NA | NA | NA |
| Urban Honolulu CDP .... | NA | NA | NA | NA | NA | NA | NA | NA | NA | NA |
| Waipahu CDP .............. | NA | NA | NA | NA | NA | NA | NA | NA | NA | NA |
| IDAHO ................... | X | X | X | X | X | X | X | X | X | X |
| Boise City.................. | 243.6 | 36.4 | 43.9 | 99.1 | 489 | 412 | 76 | 202.6 | 999 | 120 |
| Caldwell..................... | 37.4 | 5.7 | 66.5 | 15.8 | 395 | 314 | 82 | 37.6 | 942 | 294 |
| Coeur d'Alene ............. | 42.8 | 6.9 | 61.9 | 19.4 | 459 | 308 | 151 | 45.9 | 1 085 | 342 |
| Idaho Falls................. | 70.7 | 17.3 | 48.9 | 22.0 | 412 | 386 | 27 | 69.1 | 1 297 | 409 |
| Lewiston .................... | 39.5 | 10.1 | 80.1 | 14.2 | 448 | 415 | 33 | 33.6 | 1 057 | 107 |
| Meridian .................... | 38.5 | 4.3 | 73.0 | 13.5 | 209 | 168 | 41 | 34.0 | 526 | 176 |
| Nampa...................... | 74.3 | 10.3 | 84.0 | 29.3 | 370 | 282 | 89 | 89.2 | 1 126 | 437 |
| Pocatello................... | 61.1 | 15.7 | 45.3 | 21.0 | 385 | 342 | 42 | 56.1 | 1 028 | 316 |
| Post Falls .................. | 27.4 | 2.9 | 100.0 | 14.2 | 558 | 251 | 307 | 35.4 | 1 395 | 865 |
| Rexburg..................... | 16.7 | 5.4 | 77.3 | 4.3 | 157 | 99 | 59 | 16.6 | 602 | 213 |
| Twin Falls.................. | 33.7 | 6.4 | 80.9 | 13.2 | 318 | 288 | 30 | 30.9 | 743 | 172 |
| ILLINOIS.................. | X | X | X | X | X | X | X | X | X | X |
| Addison ..................... | 40.3 | 12.8 | 99.4 | 18.7 | 507 | 252 | 237 | 41.9 | 1 135 | 230 |
| Algonquin .................. | 26.9 | 10.3 | 100.0 | 10.5 | 348 | 156 | 192 | 26.8 | 884 | 290 |
| Alton ........................ | 40.2 | 19.7 | 100.0 | 9.9 | 337 | 174 | 163 | 46.6 | 1 584 | 254 |
| Arlington Heights........... | 97.1 | 21.4 | 97.1 | 62.3 | 845 | 576 | 269 | 104.9 | 1 423 | 436 |
| Aurora....................... | 211.2 | 67.8 | 89.5 | 118.9 | 696 | 431 | 235 | 215.7 | 1 263 | 185 |
| Bartlett ..................... | 31.0 | 7.4 | 97.5 | 14.1 | 342 | 232 | 88 | 31.2 | 755 | 139 |
| Batavia ..................... | 33.3 | 10.7 | 83.8 | 11.2 | 409 | 218 | 190 | 28.9 | 1 057 | 128 |
| Belleville ................... | 49.0 | 14.0 | 99.2 | 20.4 | 497 | 339 | 158 | 46.1 | 1 122 | 256 |
| Belvidere ................... | 22.1 | 7.4 | 96.1 | 5.2 | 200 | 170 | 30 | 20.3 | 775 | 171 |
| Berwyn ..................... | 59.4 | 13.8 | 87.8 | 33.8 | 671 | 436 | 178 | 56.4 | 1 121 | 67 |
| Bloomington ............... | 98.3 | 28.7 | 95.4 | 41.9 | 578 | 235 | 344 | 109.8 | 1 516 | 331 |
| Bolingbrook ................ | 92.4 | 21.8 | 90.2 | 41.9 | 594 | 193 | 402 | 83.1 | 1 179 | 92 |
| Buffalo Grove .............. | 42.3 | 11.0 | 98.6 | 18.2 | 422 | 245 | 177 | 39.5 | 916 | 0 |

1. Based on population estimated as of July 1 of the year shown.

# Table D. Cities — **City Government Finances**

| City | City government finances, 2006 (cont.) | | | | | | | | | |
|---|---|---|---|---|---|---|---|---|---|---|
| | General expenditure (cont.) | | | | | | | | | |
| | Percent of total for: | | | | | | | | | |
| | Public welfare | Highways | Parking facilities | Education | Health and hospitals | Police protection | Sewerage and sanitation | Parks and recreation | Housing and community development | Interest on debt |
| | 127 | 128 | 129 | 130 | 131 | 132 | 133 | 134 | 135 | 136 |
| GEORGIA................. | X | X | X | X | X | X | X | X | X | X |
| Albany ..................... | 0.0 | 6.6 | 0.0 | 0.0 | 0.0 | 13.4 | 23.6 | 8.2 | 6.8 | 0.4 |
| Alpharetta ............... | 0.0 | 28.6 | 0.0 | 0.2 | 0.0 | 14.0 | 4.3 | 13.0 | 0.1 | 4.8 |
| Athens-Clarke County ... | 0.3 | 7.0 | 0.5 | 0.0 | 6.1 | 13.0 | 14.7 | 6.0 | 3.4 | 0.2 |
| Atlanta .................... | 0.0 | 3.2 | 0.0 | 0.0 | 0.0 | 11.3 | 19.7 | 6.6 | 1.1 | 7.4 |
| Augusta-Richmond County ................... | 0.3 | 6.5 | 0.1 | 0.0 | 7.8 | 11.9 | 22.3 | 5.8 | 6.8 | 0.6 |
| Columbus ................ | 0.1 | 8.8 | 0.0 | 0.0 | 6.1 | 12.6 | 14.0 | 5.7 | 2.6 | 4.0 |
| Dalton ..................... | 0.0 | 8.1 | 0.0 | 0.0 | 0.0 | 7.8 | 32.4 | 5.0 | 0.0 | 1.4 |
| Douglasville ............. | 0.1 | 35.0 | 0.0 | 0.0 | 0.0 | 23.6 | 12.9 | 5.7 | 2.6 | 1.9 |
| Duluth ..................... | 0.0 | 14.5 | 0.0 | 0.0 | 0.0 | 23.3 | 0.3 | 7.5 | 4.5 | 0.0 |
| Dunwoody ............... | NA | NA | NA | NA | NA | NA | NA | NA | NA | NA |
| East Point ............... | 0.0 | 3.5 | 0.0 | 0.0 | 0.0 | 22.7 | 11.8 | 2.3 | 0.8 | 6.4 |
| Gainesville .............. | 2.9 | 2.9 | 0.0 | 0.0 | 0.0 | 7.2 | 38.8 | 3.3 | 1.0 | 16.7 |
| Hinesville ................ | 0.0 | 14.3 | 0.0 | 0.0 | 0.0 | 23.5 | 24.7 | 1.9 | 4.5 | 0.0 |
| Johns Creek ............ | 0.0 | 14.3 | 0.0 | 0.0 | 0.0 | 23.5 | 24.7 | 1.9 | 4.5 | 0.0 |
| Kennesaw................ | 0.0 | 12.1 | 0.0 | 0.0 | 0.0 | 21.0 | 11.5 | 10.3 | 1.6 | 5.6 |
| LaGrange ................ | 0.0 | 8.2 | 0.0 | 0.0 | 0.4 | 15.4 | 31.7 | 1.8 | 2.8 | 3.6 |
| Lawrenceville .......... | 0.0 | 16.3 | 0.0 | 0.0 | 0.0 | 26.1 | 13.9 | 4.3 | 0.8 | 0.4 |
| Macon..................... | 0.0 | 4.2 | 0.1 | 0.0 | 0.3 | 17.5 | 9.0 | 5.4 | 2.9 | 1.6 |
| Marietta .................. | 6.6 | 8.6 | 0.0 | 0.0 | 0.0 | 15.2 | 15.8 | 2.0 | 5.1 | 5.2 |
| Milton ..................... | 0.0 | 13.8 | 0.0 | 0.0 | 0.0 | 19.8 | 21.0 | 8.8 | 0.9 | 0.3 |
| Newnan ................... | 0.0 | 17.5 | 0.0 | 0.0 | 0.3 | 26.3 | 0.0 | 11.8 | 1.7 | 0.0 |
| Peachtree City.......... | 0.4 | 18.4 | 0.0 | 0.0 | 0.6 | 15.6 | 1.5 | 12.1 | 0.0 | 2.0 |
| Rome....................... | 0.0 | 8.8 | 0.1 | 0.0 | 0.0 | 14.9 | 31.4 | 1.8 | 2.3 | 1.1 |
| Roswell.................... | 0.0 | 11.1 | 0.0 | 0.0 | 0.0 | 21.3 | 12.5 | 14.2 | 5.3 | 3.0 |
| Sandy Springs.......... | 0.0 | 16.3 | 0.0 | 0.0 | 0.0 | 19.4 | 0.0 | 1.5 | 8.5 | 0.6 |
| Savannah ................ | 0.3 | 3.7 | 1.3 | 0.0 | 0.0 | 15.5 | 29.4 | 6.6 | 6.0 | 1.6 |
| Smyrna ................... | 0.0 | 15.6 | 0.0 | 0.0 | 0.0 | 18.3 | 19.2 | 12.2 | 0.0 | 4.1 |
| Statesboro .............. | 0.0 | 9.3 | 0.0 | 0.0 | 0.2 | 26.1 | 27.1 | 3.5 | 1.2 | 0.3 |
| Stockbridge ............. | 0.0 | 22.0 | 0.0 | 0.0 | 0.0 | 1.0 | 18.6 | 1.5 | 19.4 | 2.7 |
| Valdosta ................. | 0.0 | 13.8 | 0.0 | 0.0 | 0.0 | 19.8 | 21.0 | 8.8 | 0.9 | 0.3 |
| Warner Robins .......... | 0.1 | 18.2 | 0.0 | 0.0 | 0.7 | 20.9 | 22.5 | 5.0 | 5.1 | 0.0 |
| HAWAII .................... | X | X | X | X | X | X | X | X | X | X |
| East Honolulu CDP ....... | NA | NA | NA | NA | NA | NA | NA | NA | NA | NA |
| Hilo CDP.................. | NA | NA | NA | NA | NA | NA | NA | NA | NA | NA |
| Kahului CDP............... | NA | NA | NA | NA | NA | NA | NA | NA | NA | NA |
| Kailua CDP (Honolulu County)................... | NA | NA | NA | NA | NA | NA | NA | NA | NA | NA |
| Kaneohe CDP............. | NA | NA | NA | NA | NA | NA | NA | NA | NA | NA |
| Mililani Town CDP........ | NA | NA | NA | NA | NA | NA | NA | NA | NA | NA |
| Pearl City CDP............ | NA | NA | NA | NA | NA | NA | NA | NA | NA | NA |
| Urban Honolulu CDP .... | NA | NA | NA | NA | NA | NA | NA | NA | NA | NA |
| Waipahu CDP ............. | NA | NA | NA | NA | NA | NA | NA | NA | NA | NA |
| IDAHO ..................... | X | X | X | X | X | X | X | X | X | X |
| Boise City................ | 0.0 | 1.2 | 0.3 | 0.0 | 0.0 | 15.6 | 24.4 | 8.3 | 0.9 | 2.8 |
| Caldwell................... | 0.0 | 12.0 | 0.0 | 0.0 | 0.0 | 15.3 | 24.8 | 5.4 | 5.9 | 2.4 |
| Coeur d'Alene .............. | 0.0 | 10.2 | 0.1 | 0.0 | 0.0 | 16.1 | 35.7 | 6.2 | 0.0 | 1.0 |
| Idaho Falls .............. | 0.0 | 10.1 | 0.0 | 0.0 | 3.7 | 12.8 | 22.9 | 9.5 | 0.0 | 0.5 |
| Lewiston ................. | 0.0 | 11.0 | 0.0 | 0.0 | 0.0 | 17.4 | 22.0 | 8.9 | 3.1 | 0.0 |
| Meridian .................. | 0.0 | 0.0 | 0.0 | 0.0 | 0.0 | 19.6 | 28.9 | 10.4 | 0.0 | 0.3 |
| Nampa .................... | 0.0 | 7.5 | 0.0 | 0.0 | 0.0 | 13.3 | 17.4 | 12.9 | 1.9 | 2.9 |
| Pocatello................. | 0.0 | 26.0 | 0.0 | 0.0 | 4.3 | 15.6 | 17.5 | 5.1 | 1.9 | 1.4 |
| Post Falls ................ | 0.0 | 13.1 | 0.0 | 0.0 | 0.2 | 9.2 | 50.2 | 3.4 | 0.0 | 1.5 |
| Rexburg................... | 0.0 | 18.1 | 0.0 | 0.0 | 6.0 | 9.5 | 19.3 | 14.0 | 0.0 | 1.3 |
| Twin Falls ................ | 0.0 | 10.6 | 0.1 | 0.0 | 0.6 | 19.2 | 17.1 | 5.9 | 0.0 | 1.4 |
| ILLINOIS................... | X | X | X | X | X | X | X | X | X | X |
| Addison ................... | 0.0 | 16.2 | 0.0 | 0.0 | 0.0 | 27.3 | 5.0 | 0.0 | 6.2 | 6.7 |
| Algonquin ................ | 0.0 | 14.1 | 0.0 | 0.0 | 0.0 | 23.6 | 32.5 | 10.6 | 0.0 | 3.3 |
| Alton ...................... | 0.0 | 14.5 | 0.0 | 0.0 | 0.4 | 18.3 | 9.7 | 12.5 | 0.0 | 2.1 |
| Arlington Heights.......... | 0.3 | 10.2 | 1.1 | 0.0 | 1.3 | 17.5 | 1.5 | 0.3 | 0.5 | 2.4 |
| Aurora..................... | 0.0 | 15.7 | 1.4 | 0.0 | 0.4 | 27.2 | 1.0 | 5.1 | 2.2 | 5.9 |
| Bartlett ................... | 0.0 | 25.6 | 0.3 | 0.0 | 0.0 | 29.7 | 7.9 | 7.1 | 0.0 | 5.7 |
| Batavia ................... | 0.0 | 20.9 | 0.0 | 0.0 | 0.0 | 22.4 | 8.8 | 0.0 | 0.0 | 0.8 |
| Belleville ................. | 0.0 | 21.8 | 0.2 | 0.0 | 0.0 | 16.5 | 14.9 | 3.3 | 0.0 | 2.7 |
| Belvidere ................ | 0.0 | 12.4 | 0.0 | 0.0 | 0.1 | 17.3 | 13.1 | 0.0 | 0.0 | 1.6 |
| Berwyn ................... | 0.0 | 6.9 | 0.0 | 0.0 | 0.0 | 33.4 | 7.6 | 2.1 | 2.0 | 5.5 |
| Bloomington ............ | 0.0 | 6.1 | 0.7 | 0.0 | 0.0 | 15.0 | 15.5 | 25.3 | 3.9 | 3.5 |
| Bolingbrook ............. | 0.0 | 16.1 | 0.0 | 0.0 | 0.0 | 19.1 | 8.1 | 12.9 | 0.4 | 10.4 |
| Buffalo Grove ............. | 0.0 | 11.5 | 0.4 | 0.0 | 0.0 | 25.6 | 10.6 | 8.0 | 0.0 | 1.3 |

| City | Debt outstanding Total (mil dol) [137] | Per capita[1] (dollars) [138] | Debt issued during year [139] | City government employment, 2011 [140] | Climate[2] Mean January [141] | Mean July [142] | Limits January[3] [143] | Limits July[4] [144] | Annual precipitation (inches) [145] | Heating degree days [146] | Cooling degree days [147] |
|---|---|---|---|---|---|---|---|---|---|---|---|
| GEORGIA.................. | X | X | X | X | X | X | X | X | X | X | X |
| Albany...................... | 88.4 | 1 166 | 6.6 | 1 277 | 47.5 | 81.4 | 35.1 | 92.5 | 53.40 | 2 106 | 2 264 |
| Alpharetta................. | 89.3 | 1 797 | 21.8 | 441 | 39.5 | 77.2 | 29.1 | 87.5 | 51.82 | 3 490 | 1 327 |
| Athens-Clarke County ... | 35.0 | 307 | 0.0 | 1 713 | 42.2 | 79.8 | 32.9 | 90.2 | 47.83 | 2 861 | 1 785 |
| Atlanta..................... | 7 062.5 | 13 604 | 271.3 | 8 091 | 41.7 | 79.5 | 31.3 | 90.6 | 49.10 | 3 004 | 1 679 |
| Augusta-Richmond County ................. | 651.3 | 3 390 | 63.6 | 2 643 | 44.8 | 80.8 | 33.1 | 92.0 | 44.58 | 2 525 | 1 986 |
| Columbus ................. | 353.5 | 1 890 | 50.4 | 3 108 | 46.8 | 82.0 | 36.6 | 91.7 | 48.57 | 2 154 | 2 296 |
| Dalton..................... | 128.6 | 3 849 | 14.5 | 682 | 39.4 | 78.0 | 28.8 | 89.8 | 53.64 | 3 534 | 1 393 |
| Douglasville ............. | 11.3 | 376 | 0.0 | 208 | NA | NA | NA | NA | NA | NA | NA |
| Duluth...................... | 0.0 | 0 | 0.0 | NA | NA | NA | NA | NA | NA | NA | NA |
| Dunwoody ................ | NA | NA | NA | NA | NA | NA | NA | NA | NA | NA | NA |
| East Point................ | 134.7 | 3 137 | 19.6 | 524 | 42.7 | 80.0 | 33.5 | 89.4 | 50.20 | 2 827 | 1 810 |
| Gainesville............... | 653.7 | 18 776 | 133.9 | 669 | 36.0 | 72.9 | 24.7 | 84.0 | 58.19 | 4 421 | 752 |
| Hinesville................. | 8.9 | 293 | 0.0 | 196 | 51.6 | 82.6 | 40.7 | 93.3 | 48.32 | 1 551 | 2 539 |
| Johns Creek.............. | 19.7 | 330 | 0.0 | NA | NA | NA | NA | NA | NA | NA | NA |
| Kennesaw................. | 23.6 | 746 | 0.0 | 212 | NA | NA | NA | NA | NA | NA | NA |
| LaGrange................. | 82.4 | 2 946 | 7.7 | 419 | 42.2 | 78.7 | 31.3 | 89.3 | 53.38 | 3 078 | 1 551 |
| Lawrenceville............ | 5.2 | 181 | 0.0 | 244 | NA | NA | NA | NA | NA | NA | NA |
| Macon..................... | 35.6 | 382 | 0.1 | 1 277 | 45.5 | 81.1 | 34.5 | 91.8 | 45.00 | 2 364 | 2 115 |
| Marietta................... | 156.4 | 2 333 | 0.0 | 743 | 39.4 | 77.9 | 28.5 | 89.3 | 54.43 | 3 505 | 1 403 |
| Milton...................... | 4.8 | 316 | 0.0 | NA | NA | NA | NA | NA | NA | NA | NA |
| Newnan.................... | 0.0 | 0 | 0.0 | 239 | NA | NA | NA | NA | NA | NA | NA |
| Peachtree City........... | 16.0 | 464 | 1.1 | 270 | 42.6 | 79.4 | 31.8 | 90.5 | 50.10 | 2 958 | 1 679 |
| Rome....................... | 82.7 | 2 269 | 0.0 | 581 | 39.4 | 77.5 | 29.1 | 87.7 | 56.16 | 3 510 | 1 360 |
| Roswell.................... | 45.0 | 516 | 0.0 | 747 | 39.5 | 77.2 | 29.1 | 87.5 | 51.82 | 3 490 | 1 327 |
| Sandy Springs........... | 0.0 | 0 | 0.0 | 260 | NA | NA | NA | NA | NA | NA | NA |
| Savannah................. | 203.1 | 1 559 | 0.0 | 2 424 | 49.2 | 82.1 | 38.0 | 92.3 | 49.58 | 1 799 | 2 454 |
| Smyrna.................... | 44.0 | 888 | 0.0 | 388 | 42.7 | 80.0 | 33.5 | 89.4 | 50.20 | 2 827 | 1 810 |
| Statesboro................ | 10.2 | 384 | 0.0 | 276 | NA | NA | NA | NA | NA | NA | NA |
| Stockbridge.............. | 23.2 | 1 641 | 9.8 | NA | NA | NA | NA | NA | NA | NA | NA |
| Valdosta .................. | 10.9 | 228 | 0.2 | 787 | 50.0 | 80.9 | 38.0 | 92.0 | 53.06 | 1 782 | 2 319 |
| Warner Robins .......... | 18.7 | 309 | 0.0 | 544 | 45.5 | 81.1 | 34.5 | 91.8 | 45.00 | 2 364 | 2 115 |
| HAWAII.................... | X | X | X | X | X | X | X | X | X | X | X |
| East Honolulu CDP ...... | NA | NA | NA | NA | NA | NA | NA | NA | NA | NA | NA |
| Hilo CDP .................. | NA | NA | NA | NA | NA | NA | NA | NA | NA | NA | NA |
| Kahului CDP............. | NA | NA | NA | NA | NA | NA | NA | NA | NA | NA | NA |
| Kailua CDP (Honolulu County).................. | NA | NA | NA | NA | NA | NA | NA | NA | NA | NA | NA |
| Kaneohe CDP............ | NA | NA | NA | NA | NA | NA | NA | NA | NA | NA | NA |
| Mililani Town CDP........ | NA | NA | NA | NA | NA | NA | NA | NA | NA | NA | NA |
| Pearl City CDP........... | NA | NA | NA | NA | NA | NA | NA | NA | NA | NA | NA |
| Urban Honolulu CDP .... | NA | NA | NA | NA | NA | NA | NA | NA | NA | NA | NA |
| Waipahu CDP ............ | NA | NA | NA | NA | NA | NA | NA | NA | NA | NA | NA |
| IDAHO..................... | X | X | X | X | X | X | X | X | X | X | X |
| Boise City................. | 201.6 | 994 | 0.8 | 1 616 | 30.2 | 74.7 | 23.6 | 89.2 | 12.19 | 5 727 | 807 |
| Caldwell................... | 24.3 | 609 | 0.2 | 237 | 29.3 | 68.8 | 19.6 | 85.7 | 10.90 | 6 749 | 410 |
| Coeur d'Alene ............ | 26.6 | 629 | 17.8 | 352 | 28.4 | 68.7 | 22.1 | 82.6 | 26.07 | 6 540 | 426 |
| Idaho Falls................ | 52.3 | 982 | 7.7 | 655 | 19.3 | 68.4 | 11.1 | 85.9 | 11.02 | 7 917 | 322 |
| Lewiston .................. | 0.0 | 0 | 0.0 | 290 | 33.7 | 73.5 | 28.0 | 87.6 | 12.74 | 5 220 | 792 |
| Meridian................... | 2.2 | 34 | 0.0 | 303 | 29.4 | 71.8 | 22.1 | 89.2 | 9.94 | 5 752 | 579 |
| Nampa..................... | 43.1 | 544 | 0.0 | 573 | 28.9 | 73.3 | 20.8 | 90.5 | 11.37 | 5 873 | 692 |
| Pocatello.................. | 37.1 | 681 | 0.6 | 561 | 24.4 | 69.2 | 16.3 | 87.5 | 12.58 | 7 109 | 387 |
| Post Falls................. | 15.4 | 607 | 0.0 | 183 | NA | NA | NA | NA | NA | NA | NA |
| Rexburg................... | 2.3 | 82 | 0.0 | 120 | NA | NA | NA | NA | NA | NA | NA |
| Twin Falls................. | 42.5 | 1 023 | 34.7 | 267 | 28.2 | 72.2 | 19.7 | 87.9 | 9.42 | 6 300 | 587 |
| ILLINOIS.................. | X | X | X | X | X | X | X | X | X | X | X |
| Addison ................... | 77.8 | 2 105 | 18.5 | 253 | 22.0 | 73.3 | 14.3 | 83.5 | 36.27 | 6 498 | 830 |
| Algonquin ................. | 20.5 | 676 | 0.1 | NA | NA | NA | NA | NA | NA | NA | NA |
| Alton....................... | 27.2 | 924 | 2.2 | 241 | 27.7 | 78.4 | 19.4 | 88.1 | 38.54 | 5 149 | 1 354 |
| Arlington Heights.......... | 78.3 | 1 062 | 36.5 | 575 | 22.0 | 73.3 | 14.3 | 83.5 | 36.27 | 6 498 | 830 |
| Aurora..................... | 362.5 | 2 122 | 69.4 | 1 411 | 20.0 | 72.4 | 10.5 | 84.2 | 38.39 | 6 859 | 661 |
| Bartlett.................... | 31.9 | 772 | 0.0 | 176 | 19.3 | 72.6 | 10.9 | 83.0 | 37.22 | 6 975 | 679 |
| Batavia ................... | 69.5 | 2 545 | 41.9 | NA | NA | NA | NA | NA | NA | NA | NA |
| Belleville.................. | 30.8 | 751 | 1.4 | 363 | 30.9 | 78.1 | 22.1 | 89.6 | 39.37 | 4 612 | 1 339 |
| Belvidere ................. | 8.1 | 309 | 0.0 | NA | NA | NA | NA | NA | NA | NA | NA |
| Berwyn .................... | 65.5 | 1 301 | 8.9 | 329 | 25.8 | 75.3 | 17.3 | 86.2 | 40.96 | 5 555 | 1 027 |
| Bloomington ............. | 82.9 | 1 145 | 0.3 | 622 | 22.4 | 75.2 | 13.7 | 85.6 | 37.45 | 6 190 | 998 |
| Bolingbrook .............. | 272.1 | 3 861 | 63.5 | 391 | 23.1 | 74.8 | 14.2 | 86.8 | 37.94 | 6 053 | 942 |
| Buffalo Grove ............ | 10.4 | 241 | 0.0 | 257 | 18.4 | 72.1 | 9.6 | 82.3 | 36.56 | 7 149 | 624 |

1. Based on the population estimated as of July 1 of the year shown.    2. Represents normal values based on the 30-year period, 1971–2000.    3. Average daily minimum.    4. Average daily maximum.

# Table D. Cities — **Land Area and Population**

| STATE Place code | City | Land area,[1] 2010 (sq km) | Total persons | Rank | Per square kilometer | White | Black | American Indian, Alaska Native | Asian | Hawaiian Pacific Islander | Percent Hispanic or Latino[2], 2010 | Percent Foreign born 2007–2011 |
|---|---|---|---|---|---|---|---|---|---|---|---|---|
| | | | Population, 2012 | | | Race alone or in combination, not of Hispanic origin (percent), 2010 | | | | | | |
| | | 1 | 2 | 3 | 4 | 5 | 6 | 7 | 8 | 9 | 10 | 11 |
| | **ILLINOIS—Cont'd** | | | | | | | | | | | |
| 17 09642 | Burbank | 10.8 | 29 124 | 1 250 | 2 696.7 | 69.0 | 1.8 | 0.3 | 3.1 | 0.1 | 26.6 | 31.9 |
| 17 10487 | Calumet City | 18.6 | 37 232 | 976 | 2 001.7 | 14.0 | 71.0 | 0.6 | 0.5 | 0.1 | 15.0 | 8.1 |
| 17 11163 | Carbondale | 44.3 | 26 241 | 1 385 | 592.3 | 62.5 | 26.8 | 1.1 | 6.7 | 0.2 | 5.4 | 9.3 |
| 17 11332 | Carol Stream | 23.6 | 40 222 | 907 | 1 704.3 | 64.5 | 6.3 | 0.3 | 15.8 | 0.1 | 14.2 | 21.0 |
| 17 11358 | Carpentersville | 20.5 | 38 196 | 958 | 1 863.2 | 37.7 | 6.9 | 0.4 | 5.9 | 0.0 | 50.1 | 31.1 |
| 17 12385 | Champaign | 58.1 | 82 517 | 379 | 1 420.3 | 67.0 | 16.7 | 0.6 | 11.6 | 0.2 | 6.3 | 12.8 |
| 17 14000 | Chicago | 589.6 | 2 714 856 | 3 | 4 604.6 | 32.7 | 33.0 | 0.5 | 6.0 | 0.1 | 28.9 | 21.0 |
| 17 14026 | Chicago Heights | 26.1 | 30 392 | 1 200 | 1 164.4 | 24.3 | 42.0 | 0.5 | 0.5 | 0.1 | 33.9 | 13.6 |
| 17 14351 | Cicero | 15.2 | 84 137 | 370 | 5 535.3 | 9.4 | 3.3 | 0.1 | 0.7 | 0.0 | 86.6 | 43.6 |
| 17 15599 | Collinsville | 38.0 | 25 240 | 1 430 | 664.2 | 84.5 | 11.0 | 0.7 | 1.1 | 0.1 | 4.3 | 2.2 |
| 17 17887 | Crystal Lake | 47.5 | 40 480 | 894 | 852.2 | 84.6 | 1.4 | 0.5 | 3.1 | 0.0 | 11.7 | 11.0 |
| 17 18563 | Danville | 46.3 | 32 649 | 1 113 | 705.2 | 62.0 | 31.9 | 0.8 | 1.5 | 0.1 | 6.5 | 3.4 |
| 17 18823 | Decatur | 109.4 | 75 407 | 438 | 689.3 | 73.2 | 25.3 | 0.7 | 1.1 | 0.1 | 2.2 | 2.0 |
| 17 19161 | DeKalb | 38.0 | 43 842 | 830 | 1 153.7 | 70.4 | 13.4 | 0.5 | 4.7 | 0.1 | 12.5 | 10.1 |
| 17 19642 | Des Plaines | 37.0 | 58 840 | 599 | 1 590.3 | 69.1 | 2.0 | 0.3 | 12.2 | 0.1 | 17.2 | 28.4 |
| 17 20591 | Downers Grove | 37.1 | 49 399 | 743 | 1 331.5 | 86.1 | 3.3 | 0.3 | 6.3 | 0.1 | 5.2 | 8.5 |
| 17 22255 | East St. Louis | 36.2 | 26 708 | 1 364 | 737.8 | 1.2 | 98.4 | 0.5 | 0.2 | 0.1 | 0.5 | 0.1 |
| 17 23074 | Elgin | 96.3 | 109 927 | 242 | 1 141.5 | 43.8 | 7.7 | 0.4 | 5.8 | 0.1 | 43.6 | 26.2 |
| 17 23256 | Elk Grove Village | 29.4 | 33 350 | 1 096 | 1 134.4 | 78.5 | 1.7 | 0.3 | 11.0 | 0.1 | 9.5 | 19.2 |
| 17 23620 | Elmhurst | 26.6 | 45 171 | 812 | 1 698.2 | 86.2 | 2.2 | 0.2 | 5.9 | 0.0 | 6.6 | 9.6 |
| 17 24582 | Evanston | 20.2 | 75 430 | 437 | 3 734.2 | 63.8 | 19.2 | 0.7 | 10.0 | 0.1 | 9.0 | 17.0 |
| 17 27884 | Freeport | 30.5 | 25 185 | 1 434 | 825.7 | 78.5 | 18.6 | 0.7 | 1.1 | 0.1 | 4.1 | 3.3 |
| 17 28326 | Galesburg | 46.0 | 31 745 | 1 144 | 690.1 | 80.5 | 13.2 | 0.7 | 1.1 | 0.1 | 6.9 | 3.2 |
| 17 29730 | Glendale Heights | 13.9 | 34 535 | 1 060 | 2 484.5 | 40.5 | 6.2 | 0.5 | 23.2 | 0.1 | 30.7 | 35.1 |
| 17 29756 | Glen Ellyn | 17.1 | 27 650 | 1 312 | 1 617.0 | 83.8 | 3.1 | 0.3 | 7.3 | 0.1 | 6.6 | 9.4 |
| 17 29938 | Glenview | 36.1 | 45 029 | 814 | 1 247.3 | 80.5 | 1.2 | 0.2 | 13.4 | 0.1 | 5.8 | 20.7 |
| 17 30926 | Granite City | 50.0 | 29 545 | 1 233 | 590.9 | 88.6 | 6.3 | 0.8 | 0.8 | 0.1 | 5.0 | 2.3 |
| 17 32018 | Gurnee | 35.0 | 31 273 | 1 157 | 893.5 | 68.5 | 8.3 | 0.6 | 12.7 | 0.2 | 11.7 | 15.6 |
| 17 32746 | Hanover Park | 16.4 | 38 373 | 952 | 2 339.8 | 39.2 | 7.3 | 0.5 | 16.0 | 0.1 | 38.3 | 35.7 |
| 17 33383 | Harvey | 16.3 | 25 381 | 1 424 | 1 557.1 | 4.3 | 76.3 | 0.5 | 0.9 | 0.1 | 19.0 | 9.5 |
| 17 34722 | Highland Park | 31.6 | 29 914 | 1 218 | 946.6 | 87.9 | 2.0 | 0.2 | 3.5 | 0.1 | 7.3 | 11.4 |
| 17 35411 | Hoffman Estates | 53.9 | 52 305 | 690 | 970.4 | 57.8 | 5.1 | 0.4 | 24.0 | 0.1 | 14.1 | 31.2 |
| 17 38570 | Joliet | 160.9 | 148 268 | 164 | 921.5 | 54.3 | 16.5 | 0.4 | 2.3 | 0.0 | 27.8 | 14.5 |
| 17 38934 | Kankakee | 36.6 | 27 349 | 1 330 | 747.2 | 39.9 | 42.2 | 0.6 | 0.8 | 0.0 | 18.5 | 9.2 |
| 17 41183 | Lake in the Hills | 26.9 | 29 098 | 1 254 | 1 081.7 | 81.0 | 2.3 | 0.4 | 6.0 | 0.1 | 11.6 | 12.5 |
| 17 42028 | Lansing | 17.6 | 28 479 | 1 276 | 1 618.1 | 52.9 | 32.1 | 0.5 | 1.1 | 0.1 | 14.5 | 7.0 |
| 17 44407 | Lombard | 26.6 | 43 773 | 834 | 1 645.6 | 77.2 | 5.0 | 0.3 | 10.6 | 0.1 | 8.1 | 12.8 |
| 17 45694 | McHenry | 38.2 | 26 825 | 1 358 | 702.2 | 84.8 | 0.9 | 0.4 | 1.8 | 0.1 | 12.8 | 9.3 |
| 17 48242 | Melrose Park | 11.0 | 25 527 | 1 417 | 2 320.6 | 23.1 | 5.5 | 0.2 | 1.9 | 0.0 | 69.6 | 39.4 |
| 17 49867 | Moline | 42.6 | 43 259 | 842 | 1 015.5 | 76.7 | 6.1 | 0.5 | 2.7 | 0.1 | 15.6 | 10.7 |
| 17 51089 | Mount Prospect | 26.8 | 54 505 | 664 | 2 033.8 | 70.0 | 2.6 | 0.3 | 12.5 | 0.1 | 15.5 | 32.3 |
| 17 51349 | Mundelein | 24.8 | 31 249 | 1 161 | 1 260.0 | 59.4 | 1.6 | 0.3 | 9.5 | 0.1 | 30.1 | 29.3 |
| 17 51622 | Naperville | 100.4 | 143 684 | 176 | 1 431.1 | 74.6 | 5.1 | 0.4 | 16.1 | 0.1 | 5.3 | 16.4 |
| 17 53000 | Niles | 15.1 | 29 962 | 1 216 | 1 984.2 | 72.7 | 1.6 | 0.2 | 17.9 | 0.1 | 8.7 | 44.4 |
| 17 53234 | Normal | 47.5 | 53 837 | 672 | 1 133.4 | 84.3 | 9.1 | 0.4 | 3.8 | 0.1 | 4.1 | 4.8 |
| 17 53481 | Northbrook | 34.2 | 33 477 | 1 089 | 978.9 | 85.0 | 0.8 | 0.1 | 12.5 | 0.0 | 2.5 | 19.2 |
| 17 53559 | North Chicago | 20.5 | 29 667 | 1 227 | 1 447.2 | 38.5 | 30.5 | 1.0 | 4.9 | 0.6 | 27.2 | 19.1 |
| 17 54638 | Oak Forest | 15.4 | 28 155 | 1 286 | 1 828.2 | 77.8 | 4.9 | 0.4 | 4.5 | 0.1 | 13.4 | 7.7 |
| 17 54820 | Oak Lawn | 22.3 | 56 995 | 625 | 2 555.8 | 78.1 | 5.4 | 0.3 | 2.7 | 0.1 | 14.3 | 15.1 |
| 17 54885 | Oak Park | 12.2 | 52 015 | 695 | 4 263.5 | 66.3 | 22.9 | 0.6 | 6.1 | 0.1 | 6.8 | 10.2 |
| 17 55249 | O'Fallon | 37.2 | 29 193 | 1 246 | 784.8 | 77.6 | 16.8 | 0.8 | 3.9 | 0.2 | 3.5 | 3.8 |
| 17 56640 | Orland Park | 56.7 | 57 392 | 619 | 1 012.2 | 87.0 | 1.8 | 0.2 | 5.6 | 0.1 | 6.2 | 13.6 |
| 17 56887 | Oswego | 40.2 | 31 672 | 1 147 | 787.9 | 79.6 | 5.5 | 0.3 | 4.2 | 0.1 | 11.7 | 6.3 |
| 17 57225 | Palatine | 35.3 | 69 144 | 484 | 1 958.8 | 68.6 | 3.0 | 0.3 | 11.1 | 0.1 | 18.0 | 23.1 |
| 17 57875 | Park Ridge | 18.4 | 37 721 | 966 | 2 050.1 | 91.0 | 0.6 | 0.2 | 4.3 | 0.0 | 4.7 | 16.4 |
| 17 58447 | Pekin | 37.7 | 34 084 | 1 072 | 904.1 | 94.4 | 2.5 | 0.8 | 0.9 | 0.1 | 2.4 | 1.0 |
| 17 59000 | Peoria | 124.3 | 115 687 | 230 | 930.7 | 63.2 | 29.0 | 0.7 | 5.1 | 0.1 | 4.9 | 6.1 |
| 17 60287 | Plainfield | 60.2 | 40 466 | 895 | 672.2 | 75.7 | 6.0 | 0.3 | 8.5 | 0.1 | 10.7 | 11.5 |
| 17 62367 | Quincy | 41.2 | 40 798 | 888 | 990.2 | 91.9 | 6.8 | 0.6 | 1.1 | 0.1 | 1.4 | 1.5 |
| 17 65000 | Rockford | 158.2 | 150 843 | 160 | 953.5 | 60.7 | 21.8 | 0.7 | 3.3 | 0.1 | 15.8 | 10.3 |
| 17 65078 | Rock Island | 43.6 | 38 920 | 941 | 892.7 | 70.3 | 19.9 | 0.8 | 2.2 | 0.1 | 9.4 | 5.4 |
| 17 65442 | Romeoville | 47.8 | 39 752 | 915 | 831.6 | 51.7 | 12.2 | 0.6 | 7.0 | 0.1 | 29.9 | 21.1 |
| 17 66040 | Round Lake Beach | 13.1 | 28 116 | 1 287 | 2 146.3 | 44.7 | 4.5 | 0.5 | 3.5 | 0.1 | 48.0 | 29.0 |
| 17 66703 | St. Charles | 37.8 | 33 327 | 1 097 | 881.7 | 84.0 | 2.7 | 0.3 | 3.6 | 0.1 | 10.2 | 10.5 |
| 17 68003 | Schaumburg | 49.8 | 74 781 | 442 | 1 501.6 | 66.5 | 4.5 | 0.4 | 21.0 | 0.1 | 8.8 | 24.2 |
| 17 70122 | Skokie | 26.1 | 65 074 | 524 | 2 493.3 | 57.6 | 7.8 | 0.4 | 27.4 | 0.2 | 8.8 | 39.8 |
| 17 72000 | Springfield | 154.1 | 117 126 | 227 | 760.1 | 76.9 | 20.1 | 0.7 | 2.6 | 0.1 | 2.0 | 3.9 |
| 17 73157 | Streamwood | 20.2 | 40 238 | 906 | 1 992.0 | 52.1 | 4.6 | 0.4 | 16.0 | 0.1 | 28.2 | 31.4 |
| 17 75484 | Tinley Park | 41.5 | 57 144 | 622 | 1 377.0 | 85.3 | 3.8 | 0.3 | 4.5 | 0.1 | 6.9 | 8.2 |
| 17 77005 | Urbana | 30.2 | 41 581 | 875 | 1 376.9 | 60.0 | 17.2 | 0.5 | 19.0 | 0.2 | 5.2 | 19.4 |
| 17 77694 | Vernon Hills | 20.0 | 25 678 | 1 407 | 1 283.9 | 66.8 | 2.4 | 0.2 | 20.4 | 0.1 | 11.4 | 26.8 |

1. Dry land or land partially or temporarily covered by water.   2. May be of any race.

# Table D. Cities — **Population**

| City | Age of population (percent), 2010 | | | | | | | | | | | Population | | | |
|---|---|---|---|---|---|---|---|---|---|---|---|---|---|---|---|
| | | | | | | | | | | | | Census counts | | Percent change | |
| | Under 5 years | 5 to 17 years | 18 to 24 years | 25 to 34 years | 35 to 44 years | 45 to 54 years | 55 to 64 years | 65 to 74 years | 75 years and over | Median age | Percent female | 2000 | 2010 | 2000–2010 | 2010–2012 |
| | 12 | 13 | 14 | 15 | 16 | 17 | 18 | 19 | 20 | 21 | 22 | 23 | 24 | 25 | 26 |
| ILLINOIS—Cont'd | | | | | | | | | | | | | | | |
| Burbank | 6.2 | 18.3 | 10.5 | 12.8 | 12.5 | 15.0 | 11.4 | 7.0 | 6.3 | 36.8 | 50.5 | 27 902 | 28 925 | 3.7 | 0.7 |
| Calumet City | 7.0 | 21.2 | 9.7 | 11.9 | 13.8 | 14.0 | 10.6 | 6.1 | 5.7 | 35.1 | 54.0 | 39 071 | 37 042 | -5.2 | 0.5 |
| Carbondale | 4.0 | 8.3 | 44.4 | 16.1 | 7.2 | 6.4 | 6.0 | 3.3 | 4.2 | 23.5 | 46.9 | 20 681 | 26 125 | 25.2 | 0.4 |
| Carol Stream | 6.5 | 18.8 | 10.0 | 14.1 | 13.5 | 17.5 | 11.0 | 4.3 | 4.3 | 35.5 | 51.1 | 40 438 | 39 716 | -1.8 | 1.3 |
| Carpentersville | 10.1 | 23.8 | 9.1 | 17.1 | 16.2 | 11.5 | 6.8 | 3.2 | 2.0 | 29.4 | 49.6 | 30 586 | 37 691 | 23.2 | 1.3 |
| Champaign | 5.4 | 11.9 | 31.2 | 16.0 | 9.8 | 9.8 | 8.2 | 3.9 | 3.7 | 25.7 | 49.1 | 67 518 | 81 070 | 20.0 | 1.8 |
| Chicago | 6.9 | 16.2 | 11.2 | 19.1 | 14.0 | 12.6 | 9.8 | 5.6 | 4.7 | 32.9 | 51.5 | 2 896 016 | 2 695 598 | -6.9 | 0.7 |
| Chicago Heights | 8.7 | 22.0 | 10.6 | 13.9 | 12.4 | 12.4 | 9.4 | 5.4 | 5.2 | 31.2 | 51.1 | 32 776 | 30 276 | -7.6 | 0.4 |
| Cicero | 9.8 | 24.0 | 11.6 | 16.4 | 14.5 | 10.7 | 7.0 | 3.3 | 2.7 | 27.8 | 49.1 | 85 616 | 83 891 | -2.0 | 0.3 |
| Collinsville | 6.9 | 15.1 | 9.6 | 16.5 | 12.5 | 14.6 | 11.8 | 6.6 | 6.5 | 36.4 | 51.1 | 24 707 | 25 576 | 3.5 | -1.3 |
| Crystal Lake | 6.1 | 22.0 | 8.0 | 11.5 | 14.7 | 17.5 | 10.2 | 5.2 | 4.8 | 37.0 | 50.6 | 38 000 | 40 739 | 7.2 | -0.6 |
| Danville | 7.7 | 18.0 | 9.1 | 14.0 | 11.4 | 13.3 | 11.6 | 7.2 | 7.7 | 36.1 | 50.0 | 33 904 | 33 027 | -2.6 | -1.1 |
| Decatur | 6.7 | 15.4 | 10.8 | 12.7 | 10.7 | 13.9 | 12.9 | 7.9 | 9.0 | 39.1 | 53.2 | 81 860 | 76 114 | -7.0 | -0.9 |
| DeKalb | 6.0 | 11.6 | 37.3 | 14.4 | 8.2 | 8.3 | 6.7 | 3.5 | 4.0 | 23.6 | 49.7 | 39 018 | 44 101 | 12.4 | -0.6 |
| Des Plaines | 5.4 | 14.8 | 7.7 | 13.0 | 12.9 | 15.8 | 13.4 | 8.0 | 9.2 | 42.2 | 51.3 | 58 720 | 58 364 | -0.6 | 0.8 |
| Downers Grove | 5.5 | 17.2 | 7.2 | 10.6 | 12.8 | 17.0 | 14.5 | 7.6 | 7.7 | 42.6 | 51.8 | 48 724 | 48 860 | -1.8 | 1.1 |
| East St. Louis | 8.4 | 20.9 | 10.4 | 11.8 | 11.3 | 12.6 | 11.3 | 7.3 | 6.0 | 33.6 | 54.6 | 31 542 | 27 006 | -14.4 | -1.1 |
| Elgin | 8.8 | 19.7 | 9.6 | 16.0 | 14.8 | 12.9 | 9.6 | 4.8 | 3.9 | 32.5 | 50.2 | 94 487 | 108 190 | 14.5 | 1.6 |
| Elk Grove Village | 4.9 | 15.7 | 8.0 | 12.3 | 12.8 | 17.7 | 13.8 | 7.6 | 7.2 | 42.4 | 51.8 | 34 727 | 33 127 | -4.6 | 0.7 |
| Elmhurst | 6.1 | 20.4 | 9.2 | 7.9 | 14.0 | 16.6 | 11.4 | 6.7 | 7.7 | 40.1 | 51.8 | 42 762 | 44 140 | 3.2 | 2.3 |
| Evanston | 5.8 | 13.5 | 16.7 | 14.8 | 13.0 | 12.8 | 11.2 | 6.1 | 6.1 | 34.3 | 52.4 | 74 239 | 74 486 | 0.3 | 1.3 |
| Freeport | 6.7 | 16.5 | 8.4 | 11.5 | 11.2 | 14.4 | 12.2 | 8.3 | 10.8 | 41.3 | 53.2 | 26 443 | 25 637 | -3.0 | -1.8 |
| Galesburg | 5.5 | 14.2 | 12.4 | 12.7 | 11.3 | 13.3 | 12.5 | 8.2 | 9.9 | 39.7 | 49.5 | 33 706 | 32 185 | -4.5 | -1.4 |
| Glendale Heights | 7.7 | 18.6 | 10.6 | 18.1 | 14.6 | 13.1 | 10.1 | 4.9 | 2.4 | 32.0 | 49.1 | 31 765 | 34 212 | 7.7 | 0.9 |
| Glen Ellyn | 6.4 | 21.4 | 6.3 | 9.3 | 13.6 | 17.1 | 12.7 | 6.3 | 6.8 | 40.3 | 51.6 | 26 999 | 27 365 | 1.7 | 1.0 |
| Glenview | 5.2 | 19.4 | 5.4 | 6.6 | 12.7 | 16.4 | 14.6 | 9.2 | 10.6 | 45.5 | 52.6 | 41 847 | 44 692 | 6.8 | 0.8 |
| Granite City | 6.4 | 16.5 | 9.3 | 13.7 | 12.5 | 15.0 | 11.6 | 7.0 | 7.9 | 38.2 | 51.5 | 31 301 | 29 849 | -4.6 | -1.0 |
| Gurnee | 6.3 | 21.9 | 6.9 | 11.0 | 15.8 | 18.1 | 11.2 | 4.9 | 3.9 | 37.9 | 52.2 | 28 834 | 31 298 | 8.5 | -0.1 |
| Hanover Park | 7.9 | 21.5 | 10.5 | 15.6 | 14.8 | 13.9 | 9.7 | 4.1 | 2.0 | 31.5 | 49.5 | 38 278 | 37 958 | -0.8 | 1.1 |
| Harvey | 8.3 | 23.2 | 11.0 | 13.0 | 12.4 | 11.9 | 9.7 | 6.4 | 4.1 | 30.8 | 51.3 | 30 000 | 25 282 | -15.7 | 0.4 |
| Highland Park | 5.3 | 20.6 | 4.5 | 6.1 | 12.7 | 16.2 | 15.3 | 9.9 | 9.5 | 45.4 | 51.6 | 31 365 | 29 791 | -5.1 | 0.4 |
| Hoffman Estates | 6.6 | 18.4 | 8.2 | 14.0 | 14.8 | 16.2 | 12.5 | 5.5 | 3.9 | 37.0 | 50.7 | 49 495 | 51 895 | 4.8 | 0.8 |
| Joliet | 8.9 | 22.0 | 9.1 | 15.5 | 16.1 | 12.2 | 7.9 | 4.2 | 4.1 | 31.7 | 50.6 | 106 221 | 147 463 | 38.8 | 0.5 |
| Kankakee | 8.8 | 19.5 | 10.2 | 15.1 | 12.1 | 12.6 | 9.8 | 5.4 | 6.4 | 32.2 | 51.1 | 27 491 | 27 537 | 0.2 | -0.7 |
| Lake in the Hills | 8.1 | 23.4 | 6.7 | 13.4 | 19.9 | 15.2 | 8.0 | 3.5 | 1.7 | 33.9 | 50.3 | 23 152 | 28 965 | 25.1 | 0.5 |
| Lansing | 5.9 | 19.0 | 8.3 | 12.6 | 12.9 | 15.7 | 12.0 | 6.6 | 6.9 | 38.3 | 52.8 | 28 332 | 28 331 | 0.0 | 0.5 |
| Lombard | 6.0 | 15.5 | 8.4 | 14.9 | 13.6 | 15.8 | 11.5 | 6.5 | 7.7 | 39.1 | 51.8 | 42 322 | 43 395 | 2.0 | 0.9 |
| McHenry | 6.7 | 19.2 | 7.9 | 13.2 | 15.0 | 15.7 | 10.8 | 5.9 | 5.6 | 37.2 | 51.5 | 21 501 | 26 987 | 25.5 | -0.6 |
| Melrose Park | 9.5 | 20.5 | 10.1 | 16.3 | 14.3 | 11.3 | 8.2 | 4.9 | 4.8 | 30.9 | 49.9 | 23 171 | 25 414 | 9.7 | 0.4 |
| Moline | 6.5 | 16.3 | 8.5 | 13.7 | 12.1 | 13.9 | 12.9 | 7.9 | 8.3 | 39.2 | 51.7 | 43 768 | 43 490 | -0.7 | -0.5 |
| Mount Prospect | 6.3 | 16.6 | 7.2 | 13.3 | 14.0 | 15.1 | 11.6 | 7.8 | 8.1 | 39.7 | 50.7 | 56 265 | 54 167 | -3.7 | 0.6 |
| Mundelein | 7.5 | 19.5 | 8.4 | 14.5 | 14.6 | 16.2 | 10.9 | 5.0 | 3.5 | 35.1 | 49.9 | 30 935 | 31 064 | 0.4 | 0.6 |
| Naperville | 5.8 | 22.9 | 7.4 | 10.4 | 15.3 | 18.2 | 11.4 | 4.8 | 3.9 | 37.9 | 51.4 | 128 358 | 141 845 | 10.5 | 1.3 |
| Niles | 4.1 | 12.6 | 7.2 | 10.3 | 11.3 | 14.7 | 14.1 | 10.1 | 15.6 | 48.2 | 52.8 | 30 068 | 29 803 | -0.9 | 0.5 |
| Normal | 5.2 | 12.6 | 35.7 | 12.4 | 9.3 | 9.4 | 7.2 | 3.9 | 4.4 | 23.5 | 52.9 | 45 386 | 52 533 | 15.7 | 2.5 |
| Northbrook | 4.5 | 19.1 | 4.9 | 5.4 | 11.6 | 16.5 | 15.7 | 10.6 | 11.8 | 48.0 | 52.2 | 33 435 | 33 168 | -0.8 | 0.9 |
| North Chicago | 6.7 | 13.4 | 38.4 | 18.1 | 7.9 | 6.5 | 4.7 | 2.4 | 1.9 | 22.8 | 39.5 | 35 918 | 32 572 | -9.3 | -8.9 |
| Oak Forest | 6.1 | 18.2 | 9.0 | 13.3 | 13.6 | 16.1 | 12.4 | 6.7 | 4.5 | 37.7 | 50.6 | 28 051 | 27 962 | -0.3 | 0.7 |
| Oak Lawn | 5.6 | 16.2 | 8.5 | 12.5 | 11.8 | 15.0 | 12.3 | 8.0 | 10.0 | 41.2 | 52.4 | 55 245 | 56 687 | 2.6 | 0.5 |
| Oak Park | 6.5 | 17.7 | 6.2 | 13.8 | 15.8 | 15.6 | 13.7 | 6.1 | 4.6 | 38.9 | 53.6 | 52 524 | 51 878 | -1.2 | 0.3 |
| O'Fallon | 6.3 | 21.1 | 8.1 | 12.5 | 15.4 | 16.5 | 11.0 | 5.3 | 3.8 | 36.4 | 51.5 | 21 910 | 28 575 | 29.1 | 2.2 |
| Orland Park | 4.5 | 17.1 | 7.5 | 9.3 | 11.0 | 16.5 | 15.0 | 9.3 | 9.8 | 45.4 | 52.4 | 51 077 | 56 767 | 11.1 | 1.1 |
| Oswego | 8.4 | 24.2 | 6.3 | 12.9 | 19.4 | 13.8 | 8.2 | 4.2 | 2.6 | 33.9 | 50.9 | 13 326 | 30 353 | 127.8 | 4.3 |
| Palatine | 6.6 | 17.3 | 7.6 | 15.8 | 14.9 | 15.8 | 11.5 | 5.9 | 4.6 | 36.8 | 50.6 | 65 479 | 68 557 | 4.7 | 0.9 |
| Park Ridge | 5.0 | 19.4 | 6.5 | 7.1 | 12.3 | 17.7 | 13.7 | 8.3 | 10.0 | 44.8 | 52.1 | 37 775 | 37 480 | -0.8 | 0.6 |
| Pekin | 6.4 | 15.5 | 8.4 | 14.5 | 13.1 | 14.4 | 11.8 | 7.4 | 8.5 | 38.9 | 50.9 | 33 857 | 34 094 | 0.7 | 0.0 |
| Peoria | 7.5 | 17.1 | 12.0 | 14.7 | 11.9 | 12.5 | 11.3 | 6.3 | 6.8 | 34.0 | 52.4 | 112 936 | 115 021 | 1.8 | 0.6 |
| Plainfield | 8.8 | 26.4 | 6.0 | 10.7 | 21.1 | 14.1 | 7.6 | 3.2 | 2.0 | 33.8 | 50.4 | 13 038 | 39 836 | 203.6 | 1.6 |
| Quincy | 6.6 | 15.7 | 10.2 | 12.7 | 11.2 | 13.6 | 11.7 | 7.9 | 10.4 | 39.4 | 52.1 | 40 366 | 40 630 | 0.7 | 0.4 |
| Rockford | 7.6 | 18.2 | 9.3 | 13.8 | 12.7 | 13.4 | 11.1 | 6.5 | 7.4 | 35.8 | 51.7 | 150 115 | 152 891 | 1.8 | -1.3 |
| Rock Island | 6.7 | 15.7 | 12.7 | 12.7 | 11.0 | 13.5 | 12.3 | 7.2 | 8.2 | 37.0 | 52.0 | 39 684 | 39 006 | -1.7 | -0.2 |
| Romeoville | 8.1 | 22.4 | 10.8 | 14.7 | 17.5 | 12.0 | 7.1 | 4.7 | 2.5 | 31.3 | 50.6 | 21 153 | 39 613 | 87.6 | 0.4 |
| Round Lake Beach | 8.8 | 24.1 | 9.5 | 15.3 | 16.2 | 12.9 | 7.6 | 3.5 | 2.0 | 30.2 | 49.6 | 25 859 | 28 175 | 9.0 | -0.2 |
| St. Charles | 5.5 | 19.4 | 7.6 | 11.9 | 13.9 | 16.0 | 13.2 | 6.4 | 6.0 | 39.4 | 49.8 | 27 896 | 32 974 | 18.2 | 1.1 |
| Schaumburg | 6.1 | 14.3 | 7.7 | 17.7 | 14.5 | 14.9 | 12.6 | 6.7 | 5.6 | 37.8 | 51.7 | 75 386 | 74 227 | -1.5 | 0.7 |
| Skokie | 5.3 | 16.5 | 7.9 | 11.3 | 12.1 | 15.0 | 14.5 | 8.2 | 9.2 | 42.6 | 52.6 | 63 348 | 64 784 | 2.3 | 0.4 |
| Springfield | 6.5 | 16.4 | 9.5 | 14.0 | 11.9 | 14.4 | 13.0 | 7.1 | 7.1 | 38.2 | 52.8 | 111 454 | 116 249 | 4.3 | 0.8 |
| Streamwood | 7.9 | 18.4 | 8.1 | 16.0 | 15.9 | 14.7 | 10.9 | 5.1 | 2.9 | 34.7 | 50.4 | 36 407 | 39 858 | 9.5 | 1.0 |
| Tinley Park | 5.8 | 17.6 | 8.0 | 12.6 | 12.6 | 16.9 | 13.3 | 7.0 | 6.3 | 40.0 | 52.0 | 48 401 | 56 701 | 17.2 | 0.8 |
| Urbana | 4.5 | 8.2 | 38.0 | 18.1 | 7.7 | 7.8 | 7.1 | 3.8 | 4.9 | 24.8 | 49.9 | 36 395 | 41 440 | 13.3 | 0.3 |
| Vernon Hills | 6.6 | 20.3 | 6.2 | 11.4 | 17.0 | 17.7 | 11.6 | 4.5 | 4.8 | 38.5 | 52.0 | 20 120 | 25 107 | 24.8 | 2.3 |

# Table D. Cities — Households, Group Quarters, Crime, and Education

| City | Households, 2010 Number | Persons per house-hold | Percent Female family house-holder[1] | Percent One-person | Persons in group quarters, 2010 Total | Institutional Total | Persons in nursing facilities | Non-institu-tional | Serious crimes known to police[2] 2011 Total Number | Rate[3] | Rate[3] Violent | Property | Educational attainment, 2007–2011 Population age 25 and older | Attainment[4] (percent) High school graduate or less | Bachelor's degree or more |
|---|---|---|---|---|---|---|---|---|---|---|---|---|---|---|---|
| | 27 | 28 | 29 | 30 | 31 | 32 | 33 | 34 | 35 | 36 | 37 | 38 | 39 | 40 | 41 |
| **ILLINOIS—Cont'd** | | | | | | | | | | | | | | | |
| Burbank | 9 287 | 3.09 | 12.8 | 18.6 | 242 | 186 | 186 | 56 | 589 | 2 030 | 179 | 1 851 | 18 613 | 64.1 | 11.4 |
| Calumet City | 13 978 | 2.65 | 27.3 | 31.4 | 24 | 4 | 0 | 20 | NA | NA | NA | NA | 22 818 | 47.2 | 15.7 |
| Carbondale | 11 035 | 2.02 | 9.2 | 42.7 | 3 600 | 359 | 193 | 3 241 | 1 388 | 5 343 | 1 047 | 4 296 | 10 618 | 21.5 | 52.1 |
| Carol Stream | 14 264 | 2.78 | 11.6 | 23.1 | 44 | 44 | 44 | 0 | 544 | 1 733 | 113 | 1 253 | 25 714 | 34.7 | 34.9 |
| Carpentersville | 10 852 | 3.47 | 14.4 | 15.5 | 5 | 0 | 0 | 5 | 655 | 1 733 | 103 | 1 629 | 21 383 | 55.9 | 21.6 |
| Champaign | 32 207 | 2.25 | 10.0 | 35.9 | 8 514 | 392 | 341 | 8 122 | 3 013 | 3 706 | 900 | 2 806 | 40 871 | 24.2 | 49.8 |
| Chicago | 1 045 560 | 2.52 | 17.7 | 35.0 | 60 246 | 27 250 | 14 382 | 32 996 | 145 053 | 5 365 | 992 | 4 373 | 1 772 555 | 43.6 | 32.9 |
| Chicago Heights | 9 587 | 3.09 | 26.0 | 22.1 | 644 | 507 | 502 | 137 | 1 464 | 4 821 | 771 | 4 050 | 17 554 | 55.8 | 13.6 |
| Cicero | 22 101 | 3.79 | 17.6 | 15.5 | 196 | 173 | 173 | 23 | 2 314 | 2 750 | 396 | 2 354 | 46 078 | 72.2 | 7.7 |
| Collinsville | 10 927 | 2.33 | 13.2 | 30.4 | 65 | 59 | 59 | 6 | 825 | 3 216 | 222 | 2 993 | 17 389 | 42.4 | 23.3 |
| Crystal Lake | 14 421 | 2.81 | 10.1 | 22.1 | 267 | 163 | 163 | 104 | 718 | 1 757 | 164 | 1 593 | 25 987 | 28.0 | 40.0 |
| Danville | 12 843 | 2.38 | 19.7 | 34.5 | 2 422 | 2 243 | 159 | 179 | 2 541 | 7 671 | 1 011 | 6 659 | 21 078 | 53.7 | 15.7 |
| Decatur | 32 344 | 2.23 | 16.9 | 35.2 | 3 918 | 1 908 | 1 005 | 2 010 | 3 316 | 4 343 | 630 | 3 713 | 51 073 | 49.5 | 19.4 |
| DeKalb | 15 386 | 2.44 | 11.2 | 29.7 | 6 292 | 363 | 363 | 5 929 | 1 615 | 3 671 | 468 | 3 203 | 19 177 | 33.5 | 33.9 |
| Des Plaines | 22 700 | 2.53 | 8.8 | 29.8 | 888 | 822 | 702 | 66 | 832 | 1 421 | 104 | 1 317 | 41 579 | 41.5 | 30.3 |
| Downers Grove | 19 187 | 2.46 | 8.0 | 29.1 | 548 | 176 | 153 | 372 | 880 | 1 834 | 52 | 1 782 | 33 228 | 22.1 | 51.5 |
| East St. Louis | 10 119 | 2.63 | 40.0 | 33.4 | 433 | 109 | 90 | 324 | 3 803 | 14 040 | 6 007 | 8 033 | 16 647 | 55.7 | 10.0 |
| Elgin | 35 094 | 3.03 | 13.3 | 22.4 | 1 953 | 1 041 | 699 | 912 | 2 355 | 2 170 | 264 | 1 906 | 67 166 | 48.9 | 23.6 |
| Elk Grove Village | 13 307 | 2.48 | 9.6 | 28.4 | 132 | 96 | 96 | 36 | 834 | 2 510 | 51 | 2 459 | 23 293 | 33.2 | 34.0 |
| Elmhurst | 15 765 | 2.72 | 8.1 | 24.0 | 1 298 | 373 | 373 | 925 | 639 | 1 444 | 32 | 1 412 | 28 191 | 21.5 | 54.3 |
| Evanston | 30 047 | 2.25 | 9.7 | 37.5 | 7 024 | 1 297 | 1 150 | 5 727 | 2 304 | 3 084 | 238 | 2 846 | 48 028 | 18.2 | 65.4 |
| Freeport | 11 032 | 2.26 | 14.8 | 36.4 | 754 | 613 | 468 | 141 | 1 028 | 3 998 | 198 | 3 799 | 18 079 | 48.0 | 17.7 |
| Galesburg | 13 008 | 2.19 | 14.0 | 37.9 | 3 771 | 2 468 | 485 | 1 303 | 1 315 | 4 072 | 362 | 3 710 | 21 838 | 55.5 | 15.2 |
| Glendale Heights | 11 257 | 3.04 | 12.3 | 20.4 | 1 | 0 | 0 | 1 | 594 | 1 731 | 111 | 1 620 | 21 198 | 43.2 | 27.9 |
| Glen Ellyn | 10 424 | 2.63 | 8.0 | 26.0 | 5 | 0 | 0 | 5 | 413 | 1 500 | 69 | 1 431 | 18 081 | 17.5 | 61.9 |
| Glenview | 16 783 | 2.62 | 7.0 | 24.3 | 642 | 606 | 606 | 36 | 667 | 1 488 | 98 | 1 390 | 30 939 | 19.1 | 60.7 |
| Granite City | 12 214 | 2.42 | 15.4 | 30.4 | 256 | 158 | 158 | 98 | 1 037 | 3 464 | 578 | 2 886 | 20 841 | 58.5 | 11.3 |
| Gurnee | 11 536 | 2.71 | 10.5 | 24.4 | 89 | 61 | 61 | 28 | 1 334 | 4 250 | 105 | 4 145 | 20 114 | 23.3 | 47.8 |
| Hanover Park | 10 921 | 3.48 | 13.7 | 13.2 | 0 | 0 | 0 | 0 | 497 | 1 305 | 100 | 1 205 | 22 252 | 48.5 | 24.4 |
| Harvey | 7 947 | 3.15 | 32.2 | 24.1 | 252 | 192 | 192 | 60 | 2 180 | 8 597 | 1 696 | 6 901 | 14 295 | 61.0 | 10.0 |
| Highland Park | 11 410 | 2.59 | 6.9 | 22.3 | 255 | 183 | 173 | 72 | 375 | 1 256 | 84 | 1 172 | 20 726 | 13.1 | 66.9 |
| Hoffman Estates | 18 132 | 2.84 | 10.1 | 19.6 | 435 | 172 | 172 | 263 | 750 | 1 441 | 131 | 1 310 | 34 577 | 29.1 | 44.2 |
| Joliet | 48 019 | 3.01 | 14.0 | 22.1 | 2 945 | 2 185 | 1 189 | 760 | 4 378 | 2 961 | 350 | 2 611 | 87 879 | 47.6 | 22.3 |
| Kankakee | 9 646 | 2.67 | 23.7 | 31.5 | 1 810 | 921 | 305 | 889 | 1 556 | 5 634 | 916 | 4 718 | 16 536 | 57.5 | 11.8 |
| Lake in the Hills | 9 544 | 3.03 | 8.6 | 16.0 | 0 | 0 | 0 | 0 | 260 | 895 | 114 | 781 | 17 779 | 34.6 | 29.6 |
| Lansing | 10 957 | 2.58 | 17.9 | 27.7 | 91 | 83 | 83 | 8 | 1 478 | 5 201 | 355 | 4 846 | 19 428 | 44.5 | 21.3 |
| Lombard | 17 405 | 2.45 | 9.5 | 30.7 | 502 | 288 | 288 | 214 | 1 125 | 2 585 | 133 | 2 451 | 30 242 | 28.1 | 43.4 |
| McHenry | 10 075 | 2.66 | 10.4 | 25.3 | 194 | 186 | 186 | 8 | 635 | 2 346 | 151 | 2 194 | 17 701 | 43.2 | 24.6 |
| Melrose Park | 7 958 | 3.19 | 15.4 | 23.5 | 52 | 0 | 0 | 52 | 612 | 2 401 | 208 | 2 193 | 14 672 | 67.1 | 10.5 |
| Moline | 18 573 | 2.32 | 12.1 | 33.2 | 322 | 280 | 280 | 42 | 1 798 | 4 123 | 484 | 3 639 | 29 530 | 43.0 | 26.6 |
| Mount Prospect | 20 564 | 2.63 | 8.6 | 24.9 | 121 | 0 | 0 | 121 | 710 | 1 307 | 63 | 1 244 | 38 136 | 34.9 | 39.7 |
| Mundelein | 10 507 | 2.94 | 9.2 | 19.6 | 203 | 0 | 0 | 203 | 396 | 1 271 | 55 | 1 216 | 20 371 | 35.8 | 41.1 |
| Naperville | 50 009 | 2.79 | 7.9 | 20.5 | 2 489 | 1 188 | 1 108 | 1 301 | 2 222 | 1 562 | 79 | 1 483 | 88 946 | 14.7 | 65.4 |
| Niles | 11 906 | 2.41 | 9.4 | 32.4 | 1 118 | 1 100 | 1 100 | 18 | 727 | 2 432 | 74 | 2 358 | 22 780 | 46.3 | 29.0 |
| Normal | 17 993 | 2.45 | 9.7 | 27.0 | 8 332 | 391 | 377 | 7 941 | 1 405 | 2 668 | 201 | 2 467 | 24 805 | 27.9 | 46.5 |
| Northbrook | 12 642 | 2.57 | 6.1 | 22.5 | 678 | 611 | 611 | 67 | 477 | 1 434 | 36 | 1 398 | 23 044 | 15.0 | 65.7 |
| North Chicago | 6 620 | 3.00 | 20.3 | 27.8 | 12 741 | 196 | 0 | 12 545 | NA | NA | NA | NA | 15 269 | 49.4 | 17.1 |
| Oak Forest | 10 208 | 2.74 | 11.5 | 23.3 | 43 | 5 | 5 | 38 | 431 | 1 537 | 89 | 1 448 | 18 032 | 42.4 | 21.6 |
| Oak Lawn | 22 361 | 2.51 | 11.8 | 31.4 | 493 | 479 | 479 | 14 | 1 280 | 2 251 | 113 | 2 139 | 38 803 | 46.6 | 25.1 |
| Oak Park | 22 670 | 2.27 | 12.2 | 36.2 | 383 | 255 | 224 | 128 | 1 833 | 3 523 | 271 | 3 252 | 35 559 | 12.0 | 67.5 |
| O'Fallon | 10 747 | 2.63 | 12.5 | 22.9 | 0 | 0 | 0 | 0 | 652 | 2 299 | 102 | 2 196 | 17 166 | 20.8 | 46.4 |
| Orland Park | 21 639 | 2.60 | 8.6 | 24.7 | 464 | 451 | 451 | 13 | 1 634 | 2 870 | 32 | 2 838 | 39 605 | 35.2 | 36.5 |
| Oswego | 9 935 | 3.05 | 8.5 | 15.3 | 52 | 47 | 47 | 5 | 484 | 1 590 | 76 | 1 514 | 17 681 | 23.8 | 42.7 |
| Palatine | 26 876 | 2.54 | 9.0 | 27.8 | 168 | 134 | 134 | 34 | 870 | 1 265 | 52 | 1 213 | 45 426 | 28.7 | 48.1 |
| Park Ridge | 14 118 | 2.62 | 8.7 | 24.8 | 492 | 434 | 399 | 58 | 505 | 1 343 | 61 | 1 282 | 25 634 | 24.0 | 51.4 |
| Pekin | 13 820 | 2.32 | 13.8 | 31.6 | 2 042 | 1 933 | 281 | 109 | 915 | 2 676 | 398 | 2 278 | 23 500 | 51.6 | 15.5 |
| Peoria | 47 152 | 2.36 | 16.5 | 34.4 | 3 832 | 1 313 | 1 109 | 2 519 | 6 252 | 5 420 | 706 | 4 714 | 71 547 | 38.3 | 32.2 |
| Plainfield | 11 920 | 3.31 | 7.9 | 11.5 | 109 | 109 | 109 | 0 | 515 | 1 297 | 55 | 1 242 | 22 328 | 24.8 | 47.8 |
| Quincy | 17 151 | 2.25 | 12.6 | 35.6 | 2 087 | 1 378 | 1 015 | 709 | 1 467 | 3 600 | 474 | 3 126 | 26 938 | 49.1 | 21.5 |
| Rockford | 59 973 | 2.48 | 17.7 | 31.9 | 4 179 | 2 881 | 1 728 | 1 298 | 9 268 | 6 044 | 1 377 | 4 667 | 99 419 | 51.7 | 21.1 |
| Rock Island | 15 930 | 2.30 | 15.3 | 35.1 | 2 441 | 685 | 452 | 1 756 | 1 527 | 3 902 | 741 | 3 161 | 25 159 | 45.1 | 22.5 |
| Romeoville | 11 987 | 3.21 | 12.8 | 16.1 | 1 188 | 0 | 0 | 1 188 | 786 | 1 975 | 55 | 1 920 | 23 019 | 47.0 | 21.8 |
| Round Lake Beach | 8 055 | 3.48 | 12.2 | 16.8 | 139 | 139 | 139 | 0 | 743 | 2 629 | 152 | 2 477 | 15 498 | 56.3 | 16.5 |
| St. Charles | 12 424 | 2.56 | 8.8 | 25.5 | 1 211 | 1 121 | 161 | 90 | 616 | 1 863 | 100 | 1 763 | 22 097 | 26.8 | 47.1 |
| Schaumburg | 31 539 | 2.34 | 9.3 | 32.4 | 414 | 374 | 374 | 40 | 2 421 | 3 252 | 85 | 3 167 | 52 579 | 28.8 | 42.7 |
| Skokie | 23 531 | 2.72 | 12.0 | 23.9 | 706 | 494 | 475 | 212 | 1 864 | 2 869 | 217 | 2 652 | 45 579 | 28.6 | 46.6 |
| Springfield | 50 714 | 2.23 | 14.8 | 36.7 | 3 396 | 1 489 | 831 | 1 907 | 8 434 | 7 233 | 1 079 | 6 154 | 78 118 | 36.1 | 32.5 |
| Streamwood | 13 034 | 3.04 | 10.6 | 18.7 | 288 | 268 | 160 | 20 | 659 | 1 648 | 98 | 1 551 | 25 741 | 40.4 | 32.2 |
| Tinley Park | 21 666 | 2.62 | 9.5 | 26.1 | 45 | 0 | 0 | 45 | 936 | 1 646 | 62 | 1 584 | 38 236 | 35.0 | 32.2 |
| Urbana | 16 961 | 2.02 | 8.2 | 42.5 | 7 050 | 781 | 339 | 6 269 | 1 661 | 4 015 | 476 | 3 538 | 18 927 | 22.3 | 55.4 |
| Vernon Hills | 9 517 | 2.63 | 8.4 | 25.9 | 43 | 43 | 43 | 0 | 605 | 2 402 | 67 | 2 334 | 16 254 | 20.4 | 58.0 |

1. No spouse present.   2. Data for serious crimes have not been adjusted for underreporting. This may affect comparability between geographic areas and over time.   3. Per 100,000 population estimated by the FBI.   4. Persons 25 years old and over.

# Table D. Cities — Income, Poverty, and Housing

| City | Per capita income[1] (dollars) | Median income | Percent with income of $200,000 or more | Percent with income of less than $25,000 | Families with income below poverty (percent) | Total | Percent change, 2000-2010 | Vacant units for sale or rent[2] | Total | Percent | Median value[3] (dollars) | With a mortgage[4] | Without a mortgage[5] |
|---|---|---|---|---|---|---|---|---|---|---|---|---|---|
| | 42 | 43 | 44 | 45 | 46 | 47 | 48 | 49 | 50 | 51 | 52 | 53 | 54 |
| **ILLINOIS—Cont'd** | | | | | | | | | | | | | |
| Burbank | 21 324 | 55 927 | 1.9 | 19.6 | 9.0 | 9 721 | 2.0 | 434 | 8 928 | 82.1 | 226 100 | 31.0 | 14.2 |
| Calumet City | 20 650 | 41 978 | 1.0 | 26.9 | 16.1 | 15 646 | -1.8 | 1 668 | 14 290 | 58.6 | 134 800 | 29.5 | 15.2 |
| Carbondale | 14 978 | 18 813 | 1.9 | 57.7 | 31.1 | 12 419 | 12.7 | 1 384 | 9 435 | 29.3 | 107 700 | 21.9 | 11.0 |
| Carol Stream | 29 578 | 72 757 | 4.0 | 14.0 | 6.8 | 15 050 | 6.2 | 786 | 14 194 | 69.3 | 259 100 | 25.7 | 14.8 |
| Carpentersville | 21 347 | 55 653 | 3.5 | 18.1 | 12.0 | 11 583 | 29.6 | 731 | 11 178 | 76.0 | 174 000 | 32.1 | 15.9 |
| Champaign | 24 200 | 38 348 | 3.4 | 35.7 | 12.2 | 34 434 | 20.4 | 2 227 | 31 788 | 47.1 | 152 400 | 22.1 | 10.9 |
| Chicago | 27 940 | 47 371 | 4.9 | 28.6 | 17.6 | 1 194 337 | 3.6 | 148 777 | 1 030 746 | 47.0 | 260 800 | 29.6 | 15.2 |
| Chicago Heights | 17 539 | 43 097 | 1.2 | 31.1 | 22.5 | 11 060 | -3.7 | 1 473 | 9 637 | 61.8 | 133 100 | 28.0 | 13.5 |
| Cicero | 14 677 | 45 101 | 0.5 | 23.7 | 16.8 | 24 329 | -1.3 | 2 228 | 21 486 | 52.7 | 199 500 | 36.7 | 16.2 |
| Collinsville | 27 090 | 47 210 | 1.8 | 26.0 | 13.5 | 11 891 | 7.1 | 964 | 11 271 | 62.2 | 124 300 | 21.8 | 13.6 |
| Crystal Lake | 31 133 | 77 550 | 4.8 | 12.9 | 3.7 | 15 176 | 13.6 | 755 | 14 383 | 78.4 | 235 800 | 25.9 | 17.3 |
| Danville | 19 658 | 34 148 | 1.2 | 39.3 | 26.5 | 14 719 | -1.0 | 1 876 | 13 349 | 57.2 | 66 000 | 20.4 | 12.3 |
| Decatur | 23 050 | 39 697 | 2.1 | 31.0 | 13.0 | 36 134 | -3.0 | 3 790 | 31 436 | 63.4 | 79 700 | 19.9 | 11.9 |
| DeKalb | 19 120 | 40 003 | 2.8 | 35.8 | 15.9 | 16 436 | 21.4 | 1 050 | 15 059 | 44.3 | 176 800 | 26.0 | 14.2 |
| Des Plaines | 30 453 | 63 528 | 3.7 | 15.0 | 4.2 | 24 075 | 4.9 | 1 375 | 21 883 | 80.5 | 269 400 | 28.5 | 16.2 |
| Downers Grove | 43 462 | 80 314 | 11.2 | 12.4 | 2.6 | 20 478 | 4.9 | 1 291 | 18 534 | 81.6 | 348 900 | 24.4 | 13.9 |
| East St. Louis | 11 907 | 19 934 | 0.1 | 60.4 | 38.9 | 12 055 | -6.6 | 1 936 | 11 065 | 49.6 | 61 700 | 39.4 | 17.7 |
| Elgin | 23 682 | 59 032 | 2.2 | 17.1 | 9.3 | 37 848 | 15.7 | 2 754 | 35 837 | 71.6 | 203 400 | 29.7 | 15.7 |
| Elk Grove Village | 33 482 | 68 972 | 4.9 | 12.4 | 2.7 | 13 905 | 3.3 | 598 | 12 944 | 77.6 | 286 800 | 27.0 | 13.4 |
| Elmhurst | 42 877 | 87 935 | 13.5 | 12.0 | 2.0 | 16 590 | 2.1 | 825 | 15 692 | 81.7 | 383 000 | 26.3 | 13.9 |
| Evanston | 42 651 | 68 292 | 13.2 | 19.4 | 5.6 | 33 181 | 7.7 | 3 134 | 29 055 | 58.2 | 383 100 | 26.3 | 14.7 |
| Freeport | 22 136 | 37 909 | 0.9 | 35.3 | 15.5 | 12 396 | -0.7 | 1 364 | 11 039 | 63.8 | 82 000 | 21.3 | 14.8 |
| Galesburg | 19 056 | 33 299 | 1.0 | 39.6 | 17.1 | 14 280 | 1.2 | 1 272 | 13 040 | 59.3 | 73 800 | 21.7 | 13.1 |
| Glendale Heights | 24 982 | 64 458 | 2.8 | 12.8 | 7.8 | 11 864 | 7.3 | 607 | 11 345 | 73.4 | 212 700 | 30.5 | 14.7 |
| Glen Ellyn | 49 973 | 89 302 | 18.4 | 15.3 | 3.6 | 11 051 | 4.3 | 627 | 10 538 | 75.8 | 416 800 | 25.0 | 14.4 |
| Glenview | 51 953 | 103 080 | 19.5 | 10.5 | 2.3 | 17 746 | 12.2 | 963 | 16 157 | 84.8 | 530 000 | 26.7 | 14.8 |
| Granite City | 21 040 | 40 583 | 0.8 | 31.2 | 15.1 | 13 578 | -3.9 | 1 364 | 12 741 | 72.8 | 83 400 | 22.2 | 13.7 |
| Gurnee | 36 950 | 84 931 | 10.2 | 12.8 | 3.9 | 12 031 | 11.2 | 495 | 11 370 | 74.5 | 282 800 | 24.6 | 15.4 |
| Hanover Park | 21 900 | 66 036 | 4.2 | 13.6 | 10.5 | 11 483 | 0.7 | 562 | 10 801 | 80.5 | 213 600 | 30.5 | 12.8 |
| Harvey | 13 998 | 30 983 | 0.5 | 42.6 | 27.3 | 9 805 | -3.6 | 1 858 | 7 607 | 52.7 | 101 500 | 33.5 | 17.4 |
| Highland Park | 68 004 | 114 600 | 25.6 | 9.5 | 3.7 | 12 256 | 2.8 | 846 | 11 568 | 84.2 | 568 500 | 27.9 | 15.3 |
| Hoffman Estates | 33 663 | 78 274 | 6.7 | 9.6 | 4.1 | 18 970 | 8.5 | 838 | 18 052 | 76.6 | 284 400 | 25.9 | 13.1 |
| Joliet | 22 826 | 60 528 | 1.3 | 18.0 | 9.7 | 51 285 | 34.3 | 3 266 | 46 831 | 74.0 | 188 700 | 27.9 | 14.1 |
| Kankakee | 15 673 | 32 458 | 0.5 | 38.8 | 25.4 | 10 935 | -0.1 | 1 289 | 9 640 | 50.5 | 103 000 | 26.7 | 14.3 |
| Lake in the Hills | 31 366 | 82 818 | 4.9 | 10.0 | 5.9 | 9 885 | 25.8 | 341 | 9 665 | 92.8 | 236 200 | 28.7 | 16.2 |
| Lansing | 25 445 | 51 083 | 0.6 | 21.4 | 7.5 | 11 741 | 0.1 | 784 | 11 550 | 72.8 | 150 500 | 27.7 | 13.7 |
| Lombard | 34 327 | 72 706 | 4.3 | 14.0 | 2.0 | 18 454 | 8.9 | 1 049 | 17 592 | 73.7 | 263 600 | 27.2 | 13.7 |
| McHenry | 30 533 | 67 317 | 3.7 | 18.6 | 6.9 | 10 741 | 32.1 | 666 | 9 922 | 78.8 | 216 200 | 25.9 | 15.3 |
| Melrose Park | 17 077 | 43 863 | 0.5 | 24.6 | 12.9 | 8 525 | 7.2 | 567 | 7 528 | 54.1 | 244 100 | 36.6 | 15.1 |
| Moline | 27 512 | 48 529 | 3.2 | 22.4 | 7.8 | 19 856 | 1.9 | 1 283 | 18 115 | 69.1 | 112 300 | 21.5 | 11.6 |
| Mount Prospect | 34 002 | 69 048 | 5.2 | 12.3 | 4.0 | 21 836 | -1.1 | 1 272 | 20 579 | 72.3 | 329 000 | 27.5 | 15.2 |
| Mundelein | 35 105 | 83 612 | 9.1 | 7.4 | 3.9 | 10 992 | 8.3 | 485 | 10 567 | 79.8 | 250 000 | 26.5 | 14.3 |
| Naperville | 46 108 | 105 585 | 17.8 | 7.6 | 2.7 | 52 270 | 14.7 | 2 261 | 48 415 | 77.8 | 394 300 | 24.5 | 11.8 |
| Niles | 27 520 | 47 495 | 2.9 | 22.1 | 5.8 | 12 572 | 1.9 | 666 | 11 455 | 77.4 | 311 700 | 32.5 | 17.7 |
| Normal | 23 252 | 50 465 | 1.3 | 29.9 | 9.8 | 18 816 | 20.3 | 823 | 17 907 | 57.2 | 157 900 | 21.4 | 10.6 |
| Northbrook | 54 601 | 110 902 | 22.1 | 10.4 | 3.3 | 13 434 | 7.6 | 792 | 12 054 | 90.0 | 546 700 | 26.6 | 14.2 |
| North Chicago | 17 125 | 43 499 | 1.1 | 26.6 | 17.3 | 7 745 | -7.3 | 1 125 | 7 205 | 40.3 | 141 900 | 37.7 | 18.6 |
| Oak Forest | 26 639 | 70 711 | 1.5 | 15.5 | 8.0 | 10 672 | 6.8 | 464 | 9 498 | 80.1 | 219 500 | 26.5 | 14.5 |
| Oak Lawn | 28 924 | 58 769 | 2.5 | 18.2 | 5.6 | 23 517 | 2.6 | 1 156 | 21 824 | 83.4 | 225 800 | 27.5 | 16.3 |
| Oak Park | 45 990 | 74 141 | 13.0 | 15.6 | 5.3 | 24 519 | 3.4 | 1 849 | 21 910 | 63.1 | 381 100 | 25.8 | 14.2 |
| O'Fallon | 33 181 | 77 348 | 4.6 | 16.3 | 7.5 | 11 414 | 32.7 | 667 | 10 127 | 68.4 | 198 200 | 22.5 | 13.1 |
| Orland Park | 37 386 | 80 328 | 8.1 | 11.7 | 3.3 | 22 443 | 17.6 | 804 | 21 163 | 89.9 | 306 100 | 26.7 | 15.8 |
| Oswego | 33 606 | 93 588 | 5.8 | 6.4 | 2.5 | 10 388 | 125.0 | 453 | 9 493 | 88.3 | 258 400 | 26.6 | 12.5 |
| Palatine | 35 701 | 72 882 | 7.0 | 13.2 | 6.7 | 28 621 | 9.2 | 1 745 | 25 861 | 71.8 | 300 400 | 26.7 | 15.6 |
| Park Ridge | 43 766 | 90 177 | 14.1 | 9.6 | 2.3 | 15 030 | 2.8 | 912 | 13 852 | 86.0 | 445 600 | 28.1 | 15.1 |
| Pekin | 23 912 | 44 113 | 1.5 | 25.7 | 9.7 | 14 714 | 5.1 | 894 | 13 916 | 73.0 | 99 400 | 20.2 | 12.4 |
| Peoria | 28 688 | 46 030 | 4.5 | 28.9 | 15.8 | 52 621 | 7.3 | 5 469 | 46 936 | 59.2 | 120 700 | 21.0 | 12.2 |
| Plainfield | 34 402 | 108 239 | 9.1 | 7.0 | 2.5 | 12 532 | 174.2 | 612 | 11 135 | 90.4 | 309 800 | 27.1 | 13.2 |
| Quincy | 24 105 | 41 647 | 2.1 | 30.5 | 11.5 | 18 655 | 3.7 | 1 504 | 16 598 | 66.8 | 93 900 | 20.8 | 10.9 |
| Rockford | 21 895 | 38 864 | 2.3 | 33.7 | 19.2 | 66 700 | 4.9 | 6 727 | 59 606 | 59.2 | 109 500 | 24.7 | 14.3 |
| Rock Island | 23 101 | 41 915 | 2.1 | 31.1 | 13.1 | 17 422 | -0.5 | 1 492 | 15 660 | 69.0 | 97 900 | 21.5 | 12.8 |
| Romeoville | 22 630 | 66 859 | 1.2 | 11.1 | 6.2 | 12 623 | 71.3 | 636 | 11 625 | 87.6 | 198 500 | 30.9 | 15.1 |
| Round Lake Beach | 19 579 | 60 456 | 1.5 | 17.9 | 13.5 | 8 587 | 13.5 | 532 | 7 885 | 81.9 | 167 800 | 30.5 | 10.9 |
| St. Charles | 39 974 | 77 011 | 11.3 | 10.9 | 3.6 | 13 157 | 18.9 | 733 | 12 201 | 71.2 | 299 300 | 26.4 | 14.6 |
| Schaumburg | 35 830 | 67 426 | 4.4 | 12.9 | 4.8 | 33 610 | 1.6 | 2 071 | 31 316 | 67.1 | 257 600 | 27.0 | 13.5 |
| Skokie | 32 555 | 66 642 | 6.9 | 17.6 | 6.1 | 25 066 | 5.8 | 1 535 | 23 035 | 74.6 | 337 600 | 30.5 | 15.8 |
| Springfield | 29 061 | 48 022 | 3.3 | 25.9 | 12.8 | 55 729 | 3.4 | 5 015 | 50 498 | 64.3 | 114 100 | 21.0 | 11.7 |
| Streamwood | 28 346 | 71 602 | 4.2 | 10.4 | 3.4 | 13 629 | 10.0 | 595 | 12 819 | 88.8 | 221 900 | 29.0 | 13.4 |
| Tinley Park | 32 986 | 77 097 | 4.5 | 11.2 | 3.4 | 22 491 | 24.7 | 825 | 20 728 | 86.5 | 249 100 | 26.0 | 15.7 |
| Urbana | 19 587 | 32 808 | 2.4 | 41.1 | 13.5 | 19 090 | 25.2 | 2 129 | 15 818 | 34.9 | 149 500 | 21.2 | 10.0 |
| Vernon Hills | 42 205 | 90 301 | 13.7 | 8.9 | 2.7 | 9 956 | 25.2 | 439 | 9 266 | 74.5 | 348 900 | 26.4 | 17.1 |

1. Based on population estimated by the American Community Survey.    2. Includes units rented or sold but not occupied.    3. Specified owner-occupied units; $1,000,000 represents $1,000,000 or more    4. 50.0 represents 50 percent or more.    5. 10.0 represents 10 percent or less.

# Table D. Cities — Housing, Labor Force, and Employment

| City | Occupied housing units, 2007–2011 (cont.) | | | | Migration, 2007–2011 | | Civilian labor force, 2012 | | | | Civilian employment[4], 2007–2011 | | | |
|---|---|---|---|---|---|---|---|---|---|---|---|---|---|---|
| | | | | | | | | | Unemployment | | | Percent | | |
| | Percent renter occupied | Median gross rent[1] | Median rent as a percent of income[2] | Percent with no vehicle available | Percent who lived in the same house one year ago | Percent who lived outside this city one year ago | Total | Percent change, 2011–2012 | Total | Rate[3] | Population age 16 and older | In labor force | Full-year full-time worker | Households with no workers (percent) |
| | 55 | 56 | 57 | 58 | 59 | 60 | 61 | 62 | 63 | 64 | 65 | 66 | 67 | 68 |
| ILLINOIS—Cont'd | | | | | | | | | | | | | | |
| Burbank | 17.9 | 983 | 30.9 | 6.8 | 92.2 | 6.2 | 15 275 | 2.4 | 1 351 | 8.8 | 22 532 | 64.5 | 39.4 | 24.9 |
| Calumet City | 41.4 | 842 | 31.1 | 12.8 | 85.6 | 12.5 | 18 422 | 2.1 | 2 189 | 11.9 | 28 059 | 63.4 | 38.0 | 32.7 |
| Carbondale | 70.7 | 635 | 47.5 | 15.8 | 57.5 | 27.6 | 13 593 | -1.7 | 1 042 | 7.7 | 23 050 | 53.3 | 18.3 | 35.3 |
| Carol Stream | 30.7 | 983 | 31.5 | 5.1 | 88.6 | 8.6 | 23 328 | 3.2 | 1 875 | 8.0 | 31 254 | 76.6 | 47.3 | 17.2 |
| Carpentersville | 24.0 | 978 | 31.4 | 5.0 | 88.1 | 7.7 | 19 086 | -1.3 | 2 115 | 11.1 | 26 045 | 75.3 | 47.2 | 12.6 |
| Champaign | 52.9 | 794 | 39.9 | 12.3 | 66.1 | 19.2 | 40 212 | -0.8 | 3 234 | 8.0 | 67 801 | 63.5 | 31.6 | 24.2 |
| Chicago | 53.0 | 916 | 32.1 | 26.4 | 83.4 | 4.9 | 1 273 805 | 2.5 | 128 909 | 10.1 | 2 141 619 | 66.1 | 40.5 | 26.0 |
| Chicago Heights | 38.2 | 862 | 38.6 | 13.8 | 86.5 | 9.7 | 13 402 | -0.8 | 1 834 | 13.7 | 22 026 | 60.8 | 33.6 | 31.2 |
| Cicero | 47.3 | 809 | 31.2 | 10.3 | 85.1 | 7.6 | 34 042 | 0.9 | 3 865 | 11.4 | 57 265 | 69.9 | 41.2 | 18.2 |
| Collinsville | 37.8 | 745 | 31.0 | 6.7 | 87.6 | 7.7 | 13 729 | 0.1 | 1 161 | 8.5 | 20 288 | 65.0 | 39.8 | 29.9 |
| Crystal Lake | 21.6 | 1 115 | 29.1 | 4.1 | 90.3 | 6.2 | 22 115 | 2.1 | 1 856 | 8.4 | 31 083 | 72.2 | 44.5 | 17.9 |
| Danville | 42.8 | 595 | 33.1 | 17.1 | 81.9 | 8.5 | 13 134 | 0.5 | 1 373 | 10.5 | 25 451 | 58.0 | 33.4 | 38.3 |
| Decatur | 36.6 | 626 | 29.6 | 11.9 | 81.4 | 6.7 | 35 519 | 0.7 | 4 236 | 11.9 | 61 338 | 58.8 | 35.7 | 35.0 |
| DeKalb | 55.7 | 785 | 39.1 | 10.0 | 65.0 | 20.2 | 23 807 | 3.4 | 1 848 | 7.8 | 37 027 | 67.1 | 27.9 | 24.6 |
| Des Plaines | 19.5 | 998 | 32.0 | 7.5 | 91.5 | 5.5 | 31 326 | 2.2 | 2 627 | 8.4 | 47 416 | 66.8 | 41.8 | 26.6 |
| Downers Grove | 18.4 | 980 | 27.1 | 5.6 | 91.0 | 7.7 | 27 001 | 3.4 | 1 840 | 6.8 | 38 396 | 67.9 | 43.6 | 22.8 |
| East St. Louis | 50.4 | 518 | 34.8 | 25.7 | 85.3 | 7.8 | 9 069 | -0.4 | 1 441 | 15.9 | 20 342 | 49.1 | 25.1 | 48.2 |
| Elgin | 28.4 | 890 | 32.1 | 5.2 | 85.5 | 6.4 | 60 040 | 0.3 | 6 309 | 10.5 | 80 294 | 71.8 | 45.5 | 18.2 |
| Elk Grove Village | 22.4 | 955 | 29.1 | 5.5 | 91.2 | 7.9 | 20 196 | 3.4 | 1 488 | 7.4 | 27 006 | 70.9 | 46.8 | 21.7 |
| Elmhurst | 18.3 | 1 149 | 29.7 | 5.4 | 91.5 | 6.6 | 24 338 | 3.4 | 1 612 | 6.6 | 33 515 | 66.2 | 41.1 | 23.1 |
| Evanston | 41.8 | 1 113 | 32.3 | 14.5 | 79.9 | 13.3 | 41 458 | 2.9 | 2 807 | 6.8 | 61 271 | 64.9 | 38.0 | 25.1 |
| Freeport | 36.2 | 587 | 35.1 | 12.1 | 83.9 | 6.7 | 12 185 | -1.9 | 1 291 | 10.6 | 20 611 | 62.3 | 35.5 | 37.0 |
| Galesburg | 40.7 | 568 | 33.1 | 12.7 | 86.6 | 7.6 | 14 532 | -1.8 | 1 256 | 8.6 | 26 598 | 52.3 | 29.4 | 40.1 |
| Glendale Heights | 26.6 | 1 015 | 31.5 | 3.4 | 87.9 | 8.6 | 20 553 | 3.0 | 1 692 | 8.2 | 25 098 | 78.5 | 50.0 | 11.7 |
| Glen Ellyn | 24.2 | 907 | 28.7 | 4.6 | 89.2 | 8.3 | 14 907 | 3.4 | 947 | 6.4 | 20 600 | 65.6 | 41.5 | 25.1 |
| Glenview | 15.2 | 1 544 | 31.9 | 4.5 | 92.8 | 5.3 | 23 537 | 3.5 | 1 453 | 6.2 | 34 884 | 61.7 | 40.1 | 26.0 |
| Granite City | 27.2 | 641 | 34.7 | 7.5 | 87.5 | 5.4 | 14 285 | 0.5 | 1 435 | 10.0 | 24 325 | 61.6 | 37.0 | 34.7 |
| Gurnee | 25.5 | 1 054 | 31.9 | 3.8 | 88.6 | 9.0 | 17 134 | 2.7 | 1 321 | 7.7 | 23 495 | 75.0 | 48.3 | 16.9 |
| Hanover Park | 19.5 | 992 | 29.5 | 3.9 | 91.1 | 7.3 | 21 796 | 0.4 | 2 069 | 9.5 | 27 442 | 75.8 | 47.9 | 12.2 |
| Harvey | 47.3 | 912 | 37.2 | 18.4 | 83.2 | 12.2 | 10 134 | 2.8 | 1 462 | 14.4 | 17 658 | 57.2 | 28.3 | 37.2 |
| Highland Park | 15.8 | 1 291 | 31.6 | 2.9 | 91.0 | 6.6 | 15 258 | 3.0 | 917 | 6.0 | 23 237 | 66.1 | 39.8 | 23.1 |
| Hoffman Estates | 23.4 | 1 047 | 25.3 | 4.0 | 88.6 | 8.8 | 30 315 | 2.6 | 2 058 | 6.8 | 40 564 | 73.8 | 49.6 | 13.6 |
| Joliet | 26.0 | 833 | 33.9 | 6.9 | 87.2 | 7.4 | 74 386 | 1.1 | 8 526 | 11.5 | 106 141 | 70.6 | 42.3 | 20.7 |
| Kankakee | 49.5 | 680 | 38.8 | 16.6 | 80.5 | 7.8 | 11 908 | 0.7 | 1 730 | 14.5 | 20 301 | 62.6 | 34.0 | 32.8 |
| Lake in the Hills | 7.2 | 1 128 | 32.8 | 0.9 | 92.5 | 6.5 | 16 960 | 2.6 | 1 396 | 8.2 | 20 625 | 76.7 | 51.6 | 12.4 |
| Lansing | 27.2 | 915 | 31.5 | 5.6 | 92.2 | 6.7 | 15 278 | 2.6 | 1 451 | 9.5 | 22 302 | 67.6 | 42.6 | 28.3 |
| Lombard | 26.3 | 1 114 | 27.8 | 5.3 | 87.0 | 10.4 | 24 943 | 2.8 | 1 870 | 7.5 | 35 217 | 71.7 | 45.0 | 23.0 |
| McHenry | 21.2 | 964 | 34.5 | 7.0 | 90.8 | 7.5 | 15 419 | 1.4 | 1 336 | 8.7 | 20 642 | 71.2 | 40.9 | 24.9 |
| Melrose Park | 45.9 | 845 | 31.0 | 9.6 | 89.4 | 8.0 | 12 556 | 1.5 | 1 233 | 9.8 | 18 125 | 68.7 | 41.4 | 20.0 |
| Moline | 30.9 | 663 | 26.3 | 6.7 | 86.4 | 8.3 | 23 316 | 0.6 | 1 738 | 7.5 | 34 743 | 66.5 | 40.6 | 28.2 |
| Mount Prospect | 27.7 | 939 | 26.5 | 6.1 | 90.3 | 7.3 | 30 788 | 2.8 | 2 040 | 6.6 | 43 607 | 67.8 | 44.8 | 22.7 |
| Mundelein | 20.2 | 1 067 | 24.1 | 2.4 | 89.3 | 6.2 | 16 504 | 0.5 | 1 494 | 9.1 | 24 155 | 78.6 | 49.5 | 13.4 |
| Naperville | 22.2 | 1 193 | 25.7 | 3.0 | 87.9 | 8.9 | 77 138 | 3.5 | 5 264 | 6.8 | 105 118 | 70.6 | 46.0 | 13.9 |
| Niles | 22.6 | 936 | 37.2 | 11.9 | 93.0 | 5.3 | 14 817 | 3.7 | 1 095 | 7.4 | 25 382 | 54.9 | 35.4 | 37.2 |
| Normal | 42.8 | 709 | 40.8 | 6.2 | 66.2 | 21.7 | 27 416 | 1.1 | 1 942 | 7.1 | 43 818 | 67.2 | 32.5 | 21.5 |
| Northbrook | 18.2 | 1 715 | 38.1 | 3.7 | 91.3 | 6.0 | 16 985 | 3.6 | 1 045 | 6.2 | 26 213 | 60.3 | 37.8 | 25.8 |
| North Chicago | 59.7 | 1 030 | 31.3 | 8.2 | 58.8 | 36.8 | 8 583 | -1.5 | 1 326 | 15.4 | 26 325 | 78.0 | 21.4 | 25.1 |
| Oak Forest | 19.9 | 927 | 28.9 | 3.5 | 89.9 | 8.1 | 16 167 | 2.5 | 1 410 | 8.7 | 21 767 | 71.8 | 39.0 | 19.3 |
| Oak Lawn | 16.6 | 914 | 30.7 | 7.4 | 92.0 | 6.5 | 28 408 | 2.2 | 2 497 | 8.8 | 45 457 | 64.1 | 38.8 | 29.2 |
| Oak Park | 36.9 | 963 | 30.1 | 13.2 | 86.7 | 9.6 | 31 970 | 3.6 | 2 111 | 6.6 | 40 049 | 74.9 | 50.7 | 18.7 |
| O'Fallon | 31.6 | 958 | 28.0 | 5.2 | 84.0 | 12.9 | 14 045 | 0.0 | 1 054 | 7.5 | 20 571 | 71.5 | 42.4 | 18.7 |
| Orland Park | 10.1 | 984 | 28.9 | 3.9 | 94.0 | 4.9 | 29 899 | 2.6 | 2 178 | 7.3 | 45 989 | 63.4 | 37.9 | 28.7 |
| Oswego | 11.7 | 1 380 | 32.1 | 1.6 | 91.1 | 7.5 | 17 358 | 3.2 | 1 337 | 7.7 | 20 402 | 76.5 | 50.3 | 13.2 |
| Palatine | 28.2 | 1 074 | 28.5 | 3.1 | 86.1 | 9.8 | 41 865 | 2.0 | 2 898 | 6.9 | 53 075 | 73.0 | 48.3 | 17.0 |
| Park Ridge | 14.0 | 1 136 | 26.1 | 4.1 | 94.1 | 3.7 | 19 725 | 3.5 | 1 343 | 6.8 | 29 478 | 65.3 | 41.5 | 25.1 |
| Pekin | 27.0 | 596 | 28.2 | 7.4 | 83.2 | 8.6 | 17 691 | 1.0 | 1 586 | 9.0 | 27 241 | 61.6 | 38.9 | 29.6 |
| Peoria | 40.8 | 687 | 30.6 | 12.9 | 80.2 | 9.3 | 57 334 | 1.7 | 5 129 | 8.9 | 88 920 | 63.6 | 37.4 | 29.5 |
| Plainfield | 9.6 | 1 368 | 23.6 | 2.3 | 88.9 | 9.5 | 21 480 | 2.2 | 1 594 | 7.4 | 25 921 | 73.6 | 51.1 | 10.7 |
| Quincy | 33.2 | 588 | 28.9 | 8.8 | 83.8 | 5.8 | 21 654 | -2.0 | 1 440 | 6.7 | 32 294 | 64.9 | 41.0 | 30.3 |
| Rockford | 40.8 | 690 | 34.7 | 11.3 | 85.4 | 5.7 | 68 615 | 0.7 | 8 838 | 12.9 | 117 259 | 61.9 | 34.3 | 33.8 |
| Rock Island | 31.0 | 611 | 30.1 | 14.2 | 81.8 | 10.4 | 19 764 | 1.3 | 1 656 | 8.4 | 31 045 | 63.1 | 34.9 | 33.1 |
| Romeoville | 12.4 | 1 298 | 35.1 | 3.2 | 89.3 | 8.3 | 23 590 | 1.8 | 2 118 | 9.0 | 27 900 | 69.7 | 45.2 | 18.5 |
| Round Lake Beach | 18.1 | 1 021 | 36.9 | 2.7 | 88.7 | 7.3 | 14 915 | -3.8 | 1 853 | 12.4 | 19 331 | 76.6 | 45.3 | 11.2 |
| St. Charles | 28.8 | 1 062 | 28.7 | 4.6 | 86.9 | 8.7 | 19 557 | 2.6 | 1 374 | 7.0 | 25 486 | 71.2 | 47.0 | 18.7 |
| Schaumburg | 32.9 | 1 186 | 27.7 | 5.5 | 86.0 | 10.9 | 46 825 | 3.1 | 3 156 | 6.7 | 60 884 | 74.3 | 49.7 | 18.8 |
| Skokie | 25.4 | 1 068 | 31.9 | 8.9 | 89.3 | 7.5 | 33 482 | 3.4 | 2 470 | 7.4 | 52 810 | 64.2 | 38.9 | 25.6 |
| Springfield | 35.7 | 697 | 30.7 | 9.4 | 80.8 | 9.7 | 62 933 | 0.6 | 4 965 | 7.9 | 92 266 | 67.2 | 42.4 | 28.1 |
| Streamwood | 11.2 | 1 432 | 34.8 | 0.9 | 91.6 | 7.3 | 23 868 | 1.6 | 2 011 | 8.4 | 30 434 | 76.2 | 49.7 | 12.7 |
| Tinley Park | 13.5 | 961 | 29.4 | 3.6 | 92.7 | 6.0 | 31 692 | 2.0 | 2 429 | 7.7 | 43 826 | 70.1 | 44.2 | 21.6 |
| Urbana | 65.1 | 754 | 38.6 | 18.1 | 59.2 | 26.4 | 19 791 | -0.5 | 1 762 | 8.9 | 36 790 | 58.0 | 23.2 | 30.5 |
| Vernon Hills | 25.5 | 1 248 | 34.0 | 7.8 | 89.2 | 9.1 | 14 666 | -3.3 | 963 | 6.6 | 18 878 | 74.5 | 50.5 | 16.2 |

1. $2,000 represents $2,000 or more.   2. 50.0 represents 50 percent or more.   3. Percent of civilian labor force.   4. Persons 16 years old and over.

| City | Value of residential construction authorized by building permits, 2011 | | | Wholesale trade,[1] 2007 | | | | Retail trade,[2] 2007 | | | |
|---|---|---|---|---|---|---|---|---|---|---|---|
| | New construction ($1,000) | Number of housing units | Percent single family | Number of establish- ments | Number of employees | Sales (mil dol) | Annual payroll (mil dol) | Number of establish- ments | Number of employees | Sales (mil dol) | Annual payroll (mil dol) |
| | 69 | 70 | 71 | 72 | 73 | 74 | 75 | 76 | 77 | 78 | 79 |
| ILLINOIS—Cont'd | | | | | | | | | | | |
| Burbank | 1 290 | 9 | 100.0 | 5 | 17 | 6.6 | 0.5 | 96 | 1 592 | 367.9 | 30.0 |
| Calumet City | 85 | 1 | 100.0 | 10 | 96 | 35.0 | 6.0 | 186 | 3 191 | 529.7 | 64.5 |
| Carbondale | 4 534 | 81 | 14.8 | 9 | 134 | 29.9 | 4.5 | 175 | 3 185 | 557.1 | 55.4 |
| Carol Stream | 3 532 | 33 | 100.0 | 117 | 3 082 | 6 930.4 | 180.9 | 93 | 1 557 | 385.2 | 35.6 |
| Carpentersville | 1 736 | 9 | 100.0 | 12 | 95 | 29.3 | 5.2 | 57 | 876 | 239.0 | 19.4 |
| Champaign | 33 698 | 346 | 15.6 | 61 | 1 644 | 922.4 | 61.0 | 405 | 7 172 | 1 354.4 | 126.8 |
| Chicago | 361 386 | 2 606 | 8.2 | 2 449 | 34 677 | 28 519.3 | 1 827.9 | 7 544 | 89 349 | 19 842.7 | 2 114.8 |
| Chicago Heights | 0 | 0 | 0.0 | 33 | 311 | 353.2 | 16.2 | 79 | 845 | 167.2 | 18.7 |
| Cicero | 0 | 0 | 0.0 | 46 | 635 | 479.6 | 29.8 | 135 | 1 996 | 536.7 | 43.1 |
| Collinsville | 4 421 | 25 | 28.0 | 33 | 334 | 208.9 | 16.5 | 103 | 1 581 | 473.0 | 39.8 |
| Crystal Lake | 1 704 | 10 | 100.0 | 82 | 712 | 485.2 | 37.7 | 223 | 4 188 | 1 077.4 | 101.0 |
| Danville | 1 062 | 4 | 100.0 | 44 | D | D | D | 168 | 2 405 | 512.3 | 48.6 |
| Decatur | 1 307 | 16 | 100.0 | 83 | 992 | 491.9 | 46.1 | 316 | 4 449 | 1 120.4 | 101.9 |
| DeKalb | 0 | 0 | 0.0 | 18 | 178 | 44.9 | 6.8 | 152 | 3 008 | 618.0 | 56.4 |
| Des Plaines | 7 025 | 40 | 100.0 | 138 | 3 148 | 2 063.7 | 200.8 | 197 | 2 520 | 740.9 | 65.1 |
| Downers Grove | 15 951 | 43 | 100.0 | 131 | 2 098 | 3 132.4 | 151.2 | 264 | 5 066 | 1 526.6 | 126.1 |
| East St. Louis | 11 341 | 97 | 3.1 | 17 | 239 | 351.1 | 8.5 | 65 | 516 | 80.6 | 10.4 |
| Elgin | 21 009 | 133 | 100.0 | 196 | 3 454 | 3 304.3 | 212.6 | 223 | 3 337 | 1 099.2 | 97.6 |
| Elk Grove Village | 0 | 0 | 0.0 | 499 | 7 758 | 4 987.2 | 429.0 | 124 | 2 844 | 815.0 | 88.0 |
| Elmhurst | 27 940 | 63 | 100.0 | 139 | 3 424 | 1 709.5 | 264.4 | 155 | 2 185 | 812.3 | 66.6 |
| Evanston | 14 756 | 174 | 6.3 | 53 | 552 | 395.3 | 26.9 | 250 | 4 311 | 1 010.6 | 108.0 |
| Freeport | 0 | 0 | 0.0 | 26 | 165 | 62.8 | 4.9 | 114 | 1 715 | 377.6 | 35.6 |
| Galesburg | 424 | 3 | 100.0 | 23 | 230 | 109.7 | 6.9 | 171 | 3 358 | 618.3 | 62.8 |
| Glendale Heights | 0 | 0 | 0.0 | 67 | 1 673 | 1 111.6 | 100.4 | 59 | 1 403 | 392.6 | 35.5 |
| Glen Ellyn | 7 749 | 21 | 100.0 | 34 | 280 | 276.9 | 14.7 | 111 | 1 443 | 359.8 | 33.6 |
| Glenview | 12 114 | 21 | 100.0 | 110 | 1 645 | 1 127.2 | 105.9 | 215 | 4 002 | 1 456.7 | 162.6 |
| Granite City | 1 165 | 13 | 53.8 | 29 | 360 | 363.2 | 19.0 | 86 | 1 270 | 297.8 | 29.6 |
| Gurnee | 1 021 | 3 | 100.0 | 73 | 1 072 | 777.1 | 68.7 | 273 | 5 486 | 1 116.7 | 102.0 |
| Hanover Park | 1 673 | 16 | 100.0 | 39 | 1 395 | 1 052.6 | 69.9 | 72 | 995 | 186.4 | 19.5 |
| Harvey | 0 | 0 | 0.0 | 26 | 297 | 108.6 | 14.2 | 67 | 531 | 175.7 | 15.2 |
| Highland Park | 11 394 | 57 | 21.1 | 67 | 198 | 591.3 | 18.2 | 204 | 3 007 | 1 003.3 | 86.1 |
| Hoffman Estates | 723 | 2 | 100.0 | 69 | 725 | 798.8 | 62.9 | 133 | 2 411 | 930.5 | 76.5 |
| Joliet | 14 464 | 102 | 90.2 | 98 | 1 099 | 511.8 | 51.9 | 420 | 8 658 | 1 985.3 | 185.5 |
| Kankakee | 454 | 4 | 100.0 | 22 | 207 | 134.5 | 10.4 | 89 | 1 057 | 246.3 | 23.5 |
| Lake in the Hills | 12 547 | 105 | 12.4 | 21 | 194 | 207.2 | 8.5 | 49 | 733 | 195.1 | 18.2 |
| Lansing | 0 | 0 | 0.0 | 25 | 301 | 109.2 | 18.7 | 122 | 2 282 | 479.0 | 48.4 |
| Lombard | 2 865 | 13 | 100.0 | 122 | 1 332 | 1 141.5 | 68.8 | 249 | 4 758 | 920.4 | 94.4 |
| McHenry | 746 | 6 | 100.0 | 46 | 2 056 | 789.1 | 118.8 | 148 | 2 636 | 607.7 | 57.3 |
| Melrose Park | 425 | 5 | 100.0 | 63 | 2 330 | 942.2 | 80.1 | 94 | 2 167 | 537.3 | 45.6 |
| Moline | 1 471 | 10 | 100.0 | 38 | 439 | 224.9 | 19.1 | 284 | 4 919 | 994.8 | 100.1 |
| Mount Prospect | 897 | 3 | 100.0 | 91 | 1 951 | 1 887.6 | 125.3 | 168 | 3 688 | 3 841.8 | 100.5 |
| Mundelein | 5 312 | 36 | 100.0 | 68 | 1 130 | 791.1 | 87.4 | 107 | 1 519 | 305.3 | 33.8 |
| Naperville | 50 878 | 186 | 100.0 | 217 | 4 725 | 3 000.6 | 391.0 | 495 | 9 752 | 3 362.0 | 262.2 |
| Niles | 519 | 1 | 100.0 | 89 | 1 459 | 610.0 | 80.3 | 276 | 6 189 | 1 618.3 | 147.0 |
| Normal | 25 921 | 311 | 16.4 | 23 | 711 | 372.6 | 39.8 | 134 | 2 868 | 636.4 | 56.4 |
| Northbrook | 13 022 | 20 | 100.0 | 212 | 2 524 | 2 692.6 | 169.5 | 257 | 4 273 | 1 038.9 | 117.9 |
| North Chicago | 0 | 0 | 0.0 | 16 | 451 | 333.7 | 29.7 | 34 | 207 | 71.4 | 5.1 |
| Oak Forest | 146 | 1 | 100.0 | 21 | 124 | 72.8 | 5.8 | 54 | 780 | 241.7 | 18.6 |
| Oak Lawn | 460 | 2 | 100.0 | 25 | 96 | 36.3 | 3.3 | 184 | 3 814 | 1 106.2 | 101.1 |
| Oak Park | 0 | 0 | 0.0 | 20 | 35 | 13.3 | 2.0 | 187 | 1 743 | 315.3 | 36.1 |
| O'Fallon | 27 091 | 95 | 100.0 | 17 | 74 | 23.5 | 3.2 | 109 | 2 493 | 812.5 | 64.8 |
| Orland Park | 10 551 | 34 | 100.0 | 50 | 345 | 100.6 | 13.0 | 398 | 8 924 | 1 900.6 | 187.3 |
| Oswego | 16 930 | 112 | 100.0 | 20 | 110 | 34.4 | 4.8 | 91 | 1 908 | 403.2 | 39.9 |
| Palatine | 9 833 | 34 | 91.2 | 89 | 486 | 450.0 | 26.7 | 191 | 3 270 | 831.7 | 74.4 |
| Park Ridge | 6 830 | 23 | 100.0 | 49 | 236 | 237.4 | 14.5 | 100 | 1 180 | 389.5 | 35.1 |
| Pekin | 4 206 | 20 | 100.0 | 16 | 210 | 128.5 | 6.9 | 151 | 2 363 | 561.9 | 53.1 |
| Peoria | 36 037 | 161 | 88.8 | 173 | 2 397 | 1 188.0 | 113.9 | 585 | 9 177 | 1 895.2 | 190.9 |
| Plainfield | 21 378 | 88 | 100.0 | 34 | 303 | 230.6 | 23.0 | 115 | 2 166 | 471.5 | 43.5 |
| Quincy | 7 777 | 49 | 95.9 | 68 | 1 276 | 563.7 | 45.8 | 281 | 4 382 | 838.5 | 81.4 |
| Rockford | 11 144 | 58 | 22.4 | 204 | 3 253 | 1 871.7 | 134.9 | 544 | 9 578 | 2 276.6 | 216.3 |
| Rock Island | 651 | 4 | 100.0 | 63 | 1 634 | 828.0 | 74.6 | 97 | 1 055 | 213.7 | 22.4 |
| Romeoville | 1 220 | 6 | 100.0 | 55 | 1 127 | 890.7 | 56.9 | 65 | 841 | 224.4 | 20.3 |
| Round Lake Beach | 0 | 0 | 0.0 | 5 | 9 | 2.9 | 0.5 | 65 | 1 537 | 313.6 | 29.8 |
| St. Charles | 2 868 | 11 | 100.0 | 113 | 1 209 | 1 240.5 | 64.2 | 210 | 4 171 | 996.5 | 97.4 |
| Schaumburg | 250 | 1 | 100.0 | 277 | 4 190 | 3 955.1 | 299.1 | 551 | 13 348 | 3 290.2 | 320.6 |
| Skokie | 670 | 2 | 100.0 | 147 | D | D | D | 367 | 6 024 | 1 224.5 | 134.4 |
| Springfield | 37 446 | 207 | 49.8 | 120 | 2 176 | 1 396.8 | 84.6 | 608 | 10 676 | 2 366.9 | 215.1 |
| Streamwood | 1 736 | 14 | 100.0 | 24 | 175 | 59.0 | 8.6 | 69 | 1 632 | 300.9 | 32.8 |
| Tinley Park | 1 829 | 9 | 100.0 | 59 | 702 | 429.5 | 37.3 | 167 | 3 799 | 1 134.9 | 94.2 |
| Urbana | 2 351 | 15 | 100.0 | 25 | 692 | 773.0 | 26.1 | 89 | 1 616 | 446.7 | 40.0 |
| Vernon Hills | 1 200 | 6 | 100.0 | 67 | 2 832 | 1 637.7 | 156.1 | 227 | 6 239 | 2 720.0 | 182.3 |

1. Merchant wholesalers except manufacturers' sales branches and offices.    2. Establishments with payroll.

## Table D. Cities — Real Estate, Professional Services, and Manufacturing

| City | Real estate and rental and leasing, 2007 | | | | Professional, scientific, and technical services,[1] 2007 | | | | Manufacturing, 2007 | | | |
|---|---|---|---|---|---|---|---|---|---|---|---|---|
| | Number of establish-ments | Number of employees | Receipts (mil dol) | Annual payroll (mil dol) | Number of establish-ments | Number of employees | Receipts (mil dol) | Annual payroll (mil dol) | Number of establish-ments | Number of employees | Receipts (mil dol) | Annual payroll (mil dol) |
| | 80 | 81 | 82 | 83 | 84 | 85 | 86 | 87 | 88 | 89 | 90 | 91 |
| ILLINOIS—Cont'd | | | | | | | | | | | | |
| Burbank | 14 | 63 | 11.4 | 2.0 | 28 | 92 | 7.0 | 2.2 | NA | NA | NA | NA |
| Calumet City | 19 | 79 | 32.1 | 1.6 | 29 | D | D | D | NA | NA | NA | NA |
| Carbondale | 48 | 282 | 31.6 | 5.0 | 64 | D | D | D | NA | NA | NA | NA |
| Carol Stream | 49 | 284 | 44.9 | 9.8 | 97 | D | D | D | 101 | 5 322 | 1 527.9 | 259.4 |
| Carpentersville | 20 | 100 | 19.0 | 3.2 | 36 | 126 | 18.0 | 6.7 | 28 | 1 968 | 535.8 | 86.1 |
| Champaign | 116 | 1 040 | 242.6 | 32.3 | 263 | D | D | D | 56 | 1 898 | 897.7 | 74.7 |
| Chicago | 3 479 | 28 882 | 8 128.6 | 1 706.8 | 9 751 | 139 501 | 30 057.1 | 11 723.3 | 2 185 | 73 447 | 22 115.6 | 3 113.1 |
| Chicago Heights | 20 | 153 | 13.2 | 2.8 | 34 | 340 | 18.6 | 8.9 | 60 | 3 317 | 1 757.4 | 163.6 |
| Cicero | 24 | 101 | 17.0 | 2.9 | 38 | 293 | 13.3 | 4.3 | 93 | 3 371 | 1 051.5 | 157.2 |
| Collinsville | 27 | 170 | 26.6 | 5.7 | 68 | 471 | 54.5 | 19.7 | NA | NA | NA | NA |
| Crystal Lake | 59 | 373 | 61.6 | 13.6 | 214 | 863 | 160.2 | 40.1 | 90 | 3 406 | 751.9 | 164.9 |
| Danville | 41 | 183 | 25.1 | 3.8 | 62 | 307 | 37.5 | 10.5 | 52 | 4 183 | 1 805.3 | 185.3 |
| Decatur | 80 | 416 | 59.1 | 11.2 | 139 | 1 019 | 106.4 | 43.9 | 85 | 7 555 | D | 353.6 |
| DeKalb | 40 | 457 | 41.3 | 9.3 | 56 | D | D | D | 43 | 1 502 | 375.6 | 68.3 |
| Des Plaines | 94 | 1 405 | 1 224.9 | 68.6 | 259 | D | D | D | 125 | 9 476 | 2 294.5 | 446.1 |
| Downers Grove | 109 | 488 | 102.1 | 21.8 | 376 | D | D | D | 81 | 3 524 | 736.9 | 185.8 |
| East St. Louis | 15 | 65 | 7.9 | 1.7 | 14 | D | D | D | NA | NA | NA | NA |
| Elgin | 96 | 545 | 94.4 | 18.7 | 249 | 1 647 | 245.6 | 89.1 | 201 | 8 938 | 2 142.4 | 424.1 |
| Elk Grove Village | 66 | 531 | 134.4 | 28.0 | 172 | 2 318 | 373.0 | 107.1 | 477 | 18 094 | 4 638.5 | 821.2 |
| Elmhurst | 82 | 532 | 118.8 | 29.3 | 248 | 1 220 | 166.6 | 67.0 | 82 | 2 125 | 401.8 | 97.0 |
| Evanston | 109 | 629 | 86.4 | 19.5 | 438 | D | D | D | 61 | 1 347 | 315.9 | 69.6 |
| Freeport | 24 | 76 | 9.1 | 1.8 | 58 | 364 | 30.9 | 12.7 | 35 | 2 342 | 439.9 | D |
| Galesburg | 27 | 129 | 16.6 | 2.4 | 54 | D | D | D | 33 | D | 364.0 | 29.0 |
| Glendale Heights | 20 | 99 | 59.4 | 3.6 | 58 | 291 | 30.8 | 12.0 | 53 | 3 209 | 711.1 | 140.6 |
| Glen Ellyn | 44 | 165 | 33.5 | 7.8 | 196 | 821 | 122.8 | 48.9 | NA | NA | NA | NA |
| Glenview | 100 | 566 | 411.8 | 30.7 | 280 | 1 510 | 146.9 | 121.5 | 51 | 809 | 200.3 | 38.2 |
| Granite City | 29 | 213 | 24.2 | 5.2 | 51 | D | D | D | 33 | 4 851 | 2 388.4 | 276.4 |
| Gurnee | 49 | 276 | 61.7 | 12.6 | 133 | 367 | 70.8 | 19.9 | 76 | 2 157 | 664.5 | 101.1 |
| Hanover Park | 12 | 23 | 3.6 | 0.6 | 49 | 7 | 21.7 | 6.6 | 12 | 536 | D | 26.7 |
| Harvey | 10 | 75 | 27.3 | 3.6 | 7 | 46 | 2.7 | 1.2 | 32 | 1 939 | 697.4 | 88.0 |
| Highland Park | 68 | 203 | 87.2 | 11.0 | 245 | 547 | 109.4 | 39.6 | 28 | 898 | 234.8 | 30.5 |
| Hoffman Estates | 47 | 243 | 45.1 | 10.0 | 231 | 2 663 | 413.1 | 210.1 | 24 | 822 | 266.2 | 76.8 |
| Joliet | 101 | 478 | 77.1 | 14.7 | 233 | D | D | D | 84 | 3 672 | 1 596.7 | 201.9 |
| Kankakee | 27 | 93 | 14.2 | 2.5 | 58 | D | D | D | 31 | 1 912 | 969.7 | 106.2 |
| Lake in the Hills | 20 | 86 | 8.4 | 1.9 | 64 | 131 | 36.9 | 5.1 | NA | NA | NA | NA |
| Lansing | 33 | 121 | 28.6 | 3.8 | 75 | 281 | 26.4 | 11.0 | 33 | 1 565 | 289.0 | 65.4 |
| Lombard | 72 | 2 245 | 503.1 | 91.0 | 237 | 2 437 | 802.7 | 167.5 | 80 | 1 747 | 505.5 | 80.3 |
| McHenry | 37 | 249 | 24.2 | 6.3 | 81 | 505 | 60.1 | 28.9 | 66 | 1 940 | 336.9 | 76.2 |
| Melrose Park | 21 | 126 | 23.9 | 4.5 | 22 | 208 | 12.4 | 12.4 | 116 | 6 001 | 2 323.9 | 312.3 |
| Moline | 56 | 302 | 52.0 | 6.6 | 127 | 1 116 | 169.2 | 37.4 | 47 | 2 367 | 781.5 | 115.6 |
| Mount Prospect | 63 | 267 | 79.9 | 11.0 | 188 | 1 449 | 346.5 | 112.0 | 48 | 1 622 | 438.1 | 84.0 |
| Mundelein | 22 | 64 | 8.6 | 1.3 | 105 | 500 | 78.2 | 21.9 | 68 | 2 418 | 569.5 | 116.2 |
| Naperville | 227 | 842 | 253.1 | 34.5 | 1 002 | D | D | D | 99 | 2 472 | 579.3 | 119.8 |
| Niles | 54 | 410 | 81.4 | 14.6 | 94 | 467 | 69.3 | 20.6 | 81 | 3 541 | 1 048.1 | 171.4 |
| Normal | 37 | 337 | 44.2 | 9.5 | 71 | D | D | D | 28 | 2 342 | D | 125.3 |
| Northbrook | 137 | 614 | 143.1 | 38.0 | 610 | 19 892 | 1 308.5 | 715.2 | 89 | 3 140 | 696.9 | 151.4 |
| North Chicago | 10 | 68 | 12.5 | 6.3 | 11 | D | D | D | 19 | 1 365 | 355.9 | D |
| Oak Forest | 22 | 109 | 10.8 | 4.4 | 58 | 185 | 23.3 | 7.5 | NA | NA | NA | NA |
| Oak Lawn | 68 | 313 | 41.8 | 8.0 | 111 | D | D | D | NA | NA | NA | NA |
| Oak Park | 97 | 401 | 57.4 | 12.1 | 314 | 1 178 | 135.0 | 58.7 | NA | NA | NA | NA |
| O'Fallon | 48 | D | D | D | 81 | D | D | D | NA | NA | NA | NA |
| Orland Park | 92 | 311 | 80.9 | 7.6 | 241 | 1 078 | 124.8 | 48.0 | 41 | 1 477 | 496.7 | 90.9 |
| Oswego | 26 | 75 | 11.3 | 1.9 | 65 | D | D | D | 24 | 500 | D | 22.2 |
| Palatine | 90 | 308 | 52.1 | 9.9 | 330 | 1 481 | 206.3 | 75.6 | 41 | 1 786 | 670.0 | 81.0 |
| Park Ridge | 85 | 486 | 75.9 | 14.8 | 247 | 1 774 | 205.6 | 84.7 | NA | NA | NA | NA |
| Pekin | 25 | 89 | 11.8 | 2.5 | 50 | 294 | 22.2 | 9.5 | 30 | 1 224 | D | 55.7 |
| Peoria | 175 | 926 | 147.4 | 26.1 | 350 | D | D | D | 95 | 4 217 | D | 174.5 |
| Plainfield | 36 | 108 | 15.1 | 2.8 | 114 | 209 | 31.4 | 9.9 | 19 | 1 002 | 178.5 | 37.5 |
| Quincy | 53 | 249 | 28.4 | 6.0 | 121 | 749 | 61.6 | 22.3 | 55 | D | D | D |
| Rockford | 164 | 1 313 | 170.9 | 39.1 | 454 | D | D | D | 390 | 17 157 | 5 349.8 | 884.6 |
| Rock Island | 33 | 151 | 18.4 | 3.9 | 102 | D | D | D | 50 | 2 170 | 397.6 | 72.5 |
| Romeoville | 18 | 143 | 36.4 | 6.9 | 31 | 226 | 26.2 | 8.2 | 56 | 1 884 | 439.1 | 83.0 |
| Round Lake Beach | 12 | 46 | 7.3 | 1.0 | 22 | D | D | D | NA | NA | NA | NA |
| St. Charles | 92 | 339 | 99.9 | 15.4 | 265 | 1 700 | 249.5 | 111.1 | 105 | 5 588 | 1 559.1 | 259.1 |
| Schaumburg | 168 | 1 303 | 294.3 | 62.2 | 589 | D | D | D | 160 | 5 593 | 3 074.4 | 254.4 |
| Skokie | 115 | 1 199 | 188.0 | 42.7 | 398 | 2 529 | 552.1 | 197.9 | 154 | 6 021 | 1 355.1 | 289.8 |
| Springfield | 167 | 819 | 136.9 | 21.3 | 452 | 4 033 | 513.6 | 205.7 | 71 | 2 373 | 545.5 | 107.6 |
| Streamwood | 17 | 50 | 7.6 | 1.4 | 75 | 261 | 22.8 | 7.9 | 37 | 922 | 216.7 | 40.4 |
| Tinley Park | 52 | 175 | 27.0 | 4.3 | 148 | 1 273 | 156.8 | 45.6 | 43 | 1 421 | 358.8 | 65.8 |
| Urbana | 42 | 204 | 61.4 | 10.0 | 79 | D | D | D | 25 | D | D | D |
| Vernon Hills | 24 | 260 | 58.3 | 7.4 | 149 | 1 465 | 248.1 | 101.7 | 29 | 1 982 | 519.3 | 123.5 |

1. Establishments subject to federal tax.

# Accommodation and Food Services, Arts, Entertainment, and Recreation, and Health Care and Social Assistance

| City | Accommodation and food services, 2007 | | | | Arts, entertainment, and recreation,[1] 2007 | | | | Health care and social assistance,[1] 2007 | | | |
|---|---|---|---|---|---|---|---|---|---|---|---|---|
| | Number of establish-ments | Number of employees | Sales (mil dol) | Annual payroll (mil dol) | Number of establish-ments | Number of employees | Receipts (mil dol) | Annual payroll (mil dol) | Number of establish-ments | Number of employees | Receipts (mil dol) | Annual payroll (mil dol) |
| | 92 | 93 | 94 | 95 | 96 | 97 | 98 | 99 | 100 | 101 | 102 | 103 |
| ILLINOIS—Cont'd | | | | | | | | | | | | |
| Burbank | 62 | 751 | 38.7 | 9.3 | 3 | D | D | D | 38 | D | D | D |
| Calumet City | 88 | 1 285 | 54.7 | 14.7 | 8 | 85 | 4.9 | 1.3 | 65 | 1 957 | 69.0 | 37.1 |
| Carbondale | 106 | 2 217 | 80.2 | 22.4 | 3 | D | D | D | 86 | 1 562 | 131.8 | 51.0 |
| Carol Stream | 66 | 992 | 55.2 | 12.6 | 9 | 206 | 4.4 | 1.3 | 59 | 563 | 49.5 | 22.5 |
| Carpentersville | 40 | 961 | 33.7 | 10.1 | 3 | D | D | D | 18 | 65 | 5.7 | 2.3 |
| Champaign | 288 | 6 348 | 241.5 | 68.8 | 21 | 283 | 9.2 | 3.5 | 151 | 2 550 | 293.0 | 111.9 |
| Chicago | 5 572 | 105 396 | 7 663.3 | 2 049.8 | 676 | D | D | D | 4 725 | 57 699 | 5 867.6 | 2 193.0 |
| Chicago Heights | 45 | 641 | 27.0 | 6.9 | 5 | 17 | 1.5 | 0.3 | 56 | 1 194 | 120.9 | 57.1 |
| Cicero | 84 | 978 | 57.6 | 13.8 | 12 | D | D | D | 52 | 677 | 49.2 | 19.3 |
| Collinsville | 80 | 1 597 | 64.9 | 18.7 | 10 | D | D | D | 50 | 374 | 25.9 | 10.3 |
| Crystal Lake | 107 | 2 373 | 99.0 | 29.9 | 21 | 216 | 7.1 | 1.7 | 182 | 1 890 | 185.2 | 85.4 |
| Danville | 99 | 1 764 | 64.0 | 19.4 | 9 | D | D | D | 82 | D | D | D |
| Decatur | 178 | 3 751 | 138.2 | 41.2 | 16 | D | D | D | 208 | 2 696 | 313.4 | 133.2 |
| DeKalb | 98 | 1 808 | 69.6 | 17.7 | 3 | D | D | D | 38 | 726 | 63.1 | 28.9 |
| Des Plaines | 166 | 2 446 | 134.6 | 34.1 | 13 | D | D | D | 185 | 2 611 | 264.7 | 96.0 |
| Downers Grove | 147 | 3 069 | 165.4 | 46.7 | 15 | D | D | D | 194 | D | D | D |
| East St. Louis | 37 | D | D | D | 1 | D | D | D | 31 | 471 | 25.0 | 12.5 |
| Elgin | 159 | 2 270 | 106.3 | 29.3 | 19 | D | D | D | 215 | 2 893 | 279.3 | 132.2 |
| Elk Grove Village | 85 | 1 384 | 85.5 | 21.7 | 16 | D | D | D | 118 | D | D | D |
| Elmhurst | 119 | 1 986 | 99.4 | 27.0 | 15 | 24 | 1.9 | 0.3 | 203 | D | D | D |
| Evanston | 212 | 3 654 | 210.3 | 56.0 | 44 | 322 | 29.1 | 9.3 | 269 | 3 216 | 501.8 | 268.6 |
| Freeport | 71 | 1 050 | 39.7 | 12.4 | 8 | D | D | D | 61 | D | D | D |
| Galesburg | 102 | 1 547 | 60.2 | 16.9 | 9 | D | D | D | 81 | D | D | D |
| Glendale Heights | 49 | 741 | 37.0 | 9.6 | 9 | 99 | 5.8 | 1.6 | 32 | D | D | D |
| Glen Ellyn | 60 | 866 | 42.6 | 11.3 | 8 | 211 | 6.7 | 2.5 | 80 | 972 | 99.4 | 42.1 |
| Glenview | 202 | 5 145 | 266.4 | 79.1 | 40 | 272 | 23.6 | 8.3 | 212 | 2 977 | 291.5 | 116.0 |
| Granite City | 63 | 1 176 | 42.9 | 12.9 | 10 | D | D | D | 61 | 1 567 | 156.0 | 60.6 |
| Gurnee | 121 | 2 985 | 141.0 | 40.8 | 13 | D | D | D | 146 | 1 163 | 152.7 | 60.8 |
| Hanover Park | 47 | 585 | 27.3 | 6.8 | 3 | D | D | D | 26 | D | D | D |
| Harvey | 43 | 411 | 22.2 | 5.1 | 1 | D | D | D | 48 | D | D | D |
| Highland Park | 73 | 1 294 | 68.1 | 20.9 | 25 | 228 | 10.6 | 4.4 | 164 | D | D | D |
| Hoffman Estates | 110 | 2 236 | 129.8 | 39.5 | 21 | D | D | D | 196 | D | D | D |
| Joliet | 229 | 6 100 | 564.3 | 107.9 | 24 | 520 | 72.5 | 11.0 | 285 | 3 936 | 475.4 | 210.1 |
| Kankakee | 62 | 756 | 28.4 | 6.9 | 6 | D | D | D | 72 | D | D | D |
| Lake in the Hills | 26 | 490 | 20.9 | 5.8 | 8 | 86 | 6.7 | 2.3 | 39 | 281 | 30.2 | 10.1 |
| Lansing | 60 | 1 220 | 53.4 | 15.5 | 8 | D | D | D | 48 | 364 | 24.4 | 9.6 |
| Lombard | 128 | 2 936 | 161.3 | 48.0 | 15 | D | D | D | 119 | 1 558 | 193.9 | 73.9 |
| McHenry | 78 | 1 301 | 59.4 | 15.6 | 9 | 69 | 5.8 | 1.4 | 86 | D | D | D |
| Melrose Park | 69 | 1 042 | 55.9 | 13.7 | 9 | D | D | D | 104 | D | D | D |
| Moline | 157 | 3 155 | 122.2 | 35.4 | 11 | D | D | D | 157 | D | D | D |
| Mount Prospect | 105 | 1 408 | 70.4 | 18.4 | 11 | D | D | D | 97 | 739 | 62.7 | 31.9 |
| Mundelein | 68 | 934 | 48.1 | 13.3 | 15 | 128 | 9.5 | 3.1 | 47 | 326 | 26.6 | 10.7 |
| Naperville | 311 | 6 770 | 335.2 | 100.8 | 48 | 600 | 28.6 | 9.5 | 508 | D | D | D |
| Niles | 128 | 1 851 | 102.2 | 26.5 | 3 | D | D | D | 140 | 2 499 | 189.7 | 72.5 |
| Normal | 93 | 2 468 | 91.4 | 27.4 | 5 | D | D | D | 61 | D | D | D |
| Northbrook | 103 | 2 029 | 158.2 | 50.3 | 30 | D | D | D | 254 | 2 408 | 242.9 | 103.9 |
| North Chicago | 39 | 595 | 27.5 | 7.1 | 1 | D | D | D | 9 | D | D | D |
| Oak Forest | 34 | 542 | 24.2 | 6.3 | 8 | D | D | D | 53 | D | D | D |
| Oak Lawn | 103 | 2 349 | 116.4 | 31.5 | 13 | D | D | D | 252 | D | D | D |
| Oak Park | 96 | 1 486 | 71.5 | 21.4 | 21 | 122 | 14.9 | 3.9 | 249 | 2 503 | 205.8 | 91.2 |
| O'Fallon | 69 | 1 460 | 54.1 | 15.9 | 11 | D | D | D | 49 | 809 | 65.3 | 21.7 |
| Orland Park | 156 | 4 138 | 176.5 | 53.1 | 31 | D | D | D | 262 | D | D | D |
| Oswego | 59 | 952 | 46.9 | 12.8 | 11 | D | D | D | 48 | D | D | D |
| Palatine | 126 | 1 841 | 85.9 | 23.4 | 21 | D | D | D | 123 | 985 | 78.8 | 34.1 |
| Park Ridge | 63 | 725 | 35.2 | 9.5 | 11 | D | D | D | 188 | D | D | D |
| Pekin | 89 | 1 342 | 53.1 | 15.0 | 9 | D | D | D | 75 | 902 | 64.4 | 30.7 |
| Peoria | 332 | 6 428 | 272.5 | 78.9 | 32 | D | D | D | 343 | 6 072 | 707.3 | 349.4 |
| Plainfield | 65 | 1 543 | 58.8 | 16.6 | 15 | D | D | D | 91 | D | D | D |
| Quincy | 122 | 2 280 | 79.4 | 22.7 | 15 | D | D | D | 103 | 1 682 | 244.7 | 80.3 |
| Rockford | 356 | 7 378 | 320.1 | 88.4 | 30 | 362 | 20.7 | 5.9 | 371 | 5 860 | 647.8 | 305.7 |
| Rock Island | 78 | 1 253 | 44.2 | 13.7 | 10 | D | D | D | 72 | 822 | 58.5 | 25.2 |
| Romeoville | 59 | 1 105 | 52.1 | 13.9 | 8 | 494 | 22.4 | 6.2 | 28 | D | D | D |
| Round Lake Beach | 39 | 706 | 43.1 | 8.5 | 5 | D | D | D | 26 | D | D | D |
| St. Charles | 139 | 3 102 | 156.4 | 48.6 | 15 | 212 | 14.9 | 4.2 | 148 | 1 483 | 165.1 | 72.4 |
| Schaumburg | 273 | 8 038 | 458.0 | 133.8 | 23 | D | D | D | 228 | 2 276 | 205.1 | 79.2 |
| Skokie | 150 | 3 055 | 172.3 | 47.6 | 24 | 362 | 26.8 | 7.1 | 332 | 3 530 | 339.9 | 141.3 |
| Springfield | 379 | 7 782 | 311.8 | 95.5 | 34 | 505 | 68.3 | 6.4 | 295 | D | D | D |
| Streamwood | 57 | 786 | 42.0 | 11.0 | 5 | D | D | D | 42 | D | D | D |
| Tinley Park | 111 | 2 632 | 124.2 | 32.4 | 19 | D | D | D | 145 | 1 754 | 157.1 | 51.8 |
| Urbana | 97 | 1 949 | 78.5 | 20.9 | 9 | 68 | 2.9 | 1.3 | 43 | 2 715 | 322.6 | 172.9 |
| Vernon Hills | 85 | 1 804 | 97.0 | 30.0 | 15 | D | D | D | 92 | 899 | 105.0 | 41.0 |

1. Establishments subject to federal tax.

# Table D. Cities — Other Services and Federal Funds

| City | Other services[1], 2007 | | | | Selected federal funds, 2009–2010 (mil dol) | | | | | | | | |
|---|---|---|---|---|---|---|---|---|---|---|---|---|---|
| | | | | | Procurement contracts | | Grants | | | | | | |
| | Number of establish-ments | Number of employees | Receipts (mil dol) | Annual payroll (mil dol) | Defense | Other | Total[2] | Medicaid and other health related | Nutrition and family welfare | Energy and envi-ronment | Disasters and emergency prepared-ness | Housing and community develop-ment | Employment and training |
| | 104 | 105 | 106 | 107 | 108 | 109 | 110 | 111 | 112 | 113 | 114 | 115 | 116 |

ILLINOIS—Cont'd

| City | 104 | 105 | 106 | 107 | 108 | 109 | 110 | 111 | 112 | 113 | 114 | 115 | 116 |
|---|---|---|---|---|---|---|---|---|---|---|---|---|---|
| Burbank | 30 | D | D | D | 0.0 | 0.0 | 0.2 | 0.0 | 0.0 | 0.0 | 0.0 | 0.2 | 0.0 |
| Calumet City | 41 | 179 | 14.4 | 4.5 | 0.0 | 0.0 | 0.1 | 0.0 | 0.0 | 0.1 | 0.0 | 0.0 | 0.0 |
| Carbondale | 44 | D | D | D | 0.8 | 3.2 | 44.9 | 20.8 | 3.2 | 0.9 | 0.0 | 0.0 | 0.0 |
| Carol Stream | 63 | 407 | 40.1 | 12.2 | 9.0 | 0.3 | 0.2 | 0.0 | 0.0 | 0.2 | 0.0 | 0.0 | 0.0 |
| Carpentersville | 24 | 107 | 5.5 | 1.6 | 0.5 | 0.0 | 0.0 | 0.0 | 0.0 | 0.0 | 0.0 | 0.0 | 0.0 |
| Champaign | 106 | 727 | 45.2 | 15.0 | 14.5 | 5.8 | 445.2 | 159.8 | 0.3 | 45.4 | -0.3 | 14.7 | 0.0 |
| Chicago | 3 320 | 23 822 | 2 101.5 | 609.9 | 543.6 | 726.4 | 4 225.5 | 1 110.6 | 389.1 | 95.3 | 6.5 | 1 297.2 | 377.7 |
| Chicago Heights | 44 | 313 | 19.6 | 6.4 | 13.7 | 4.1 | 13.2 | 11.0 | 0.2 | 0.0 | 0.0 | 0.0 | 0.0 |
| Cicero | 66 | 242 | 22.6 | 6.3 | 0.1 | 0.2 | 3.4 | 0.0 | 0.0 | 0.5 | 0.0 | 2.7 | 0.0 |
| Collinsville | 44 | 263 | 20.9 | 5.6 | 0.1 | 0.2 | 8.1 | 0.0 | 0.0 | 0.0 | 0.0 | 8.0 | 0.0 |
| Crystal Lake | 96 | 690 | 50.8 | 15.9 | 2.2 | 0.1 | 0.0 | 0.0 | 0.0 | 0.0 | 0.0 | 0.0 | 0.0 |
| Danville | 55 | 443 | 25.0 | 7.3 | 14.7 | 65.5 | 13.3 | 0.2 | 3.8 | 0.4 | 0.0 | 4.3 | 0.0 |
| Decatur | 114 | D | D | D | 1.9 | 12.1 | 188.4 | 5.9 | 2.7 | 165.9 | 0.0 | 10.6 | 0.0 |
| DeKalb | 47 | 275 | 17.3 | 5.1 | 0.0 | 0.2 | 62.6 | 0.0 | 0.0 | 1.9 | 0.0 | 6.0 | 0.0 |
| Des Plaines | 148 | 806 | 100.3 | 28.7 | 11.8 | 21.5 | 39.9 | 3.7 | 0.0 | 33.2 | 0.0 | 1.4 | 0.0 |
| Downers Grove | 115 | 1 075 | 154.0 | 49.0 | 13.6 | 3.8 | 0.7 | 0.4 | 0.0 | 0.2 | 0.0 | 0.0 | 0.0 |
| East St. Louis | 17 | 122 | 6.9 | 2.3 | 0.0 | 0.1 | 26.4 | 11.2 | 0.0 | 0.0 | 0.0 | 12.5 | 0.4 |
| Elgin | 145 | 1 449 | 136.5 | 47.6 | 10.4 | 5.3 | 16.8 | 2.6 | 0.0 | 1.0 | 0.0 | 11.0 | 0.0 |
| Elk Grove Village | 99 | 1 163 | 124.9 | 40.6 | 22.1 | 1.2 | 6.1 | 5.3 | 0.0 | 0.5 | 0.0 | 0.0 | 0.0 |
| Elmhurst | 98 | 810 | 72.7 | 27.1 | 0.9 | 6.7 | 0.2 | 0.0 | 0.0 | 0.0 | 0.0 | 0.0 | 0.0 |
| Evanston | 114 | 820 | 49.7 | 18.8 | 17.9 | 15.9 | 527.2 | 411.0 | 1.0 | 20.5 | 0.0 | 21.1 | 0.0 |
| Freeport | 51 | D | D | D | 0.6 | 0.3 | 3.6 | 0.0 | 1.2 | 0.0 | 0.0 | 1.2 | 0.0 |
| Galesburg | 49 | D | D | D | 0.0 | 0.3 | 5.4 | 0.5 | 0.0 | 0.0 | 0.0 | 2.1 | 0.0 |
| Glendale Heights | 34 | D | D | D | 0.1 | 0.2 | 0.0 | 0.0 | 0.0 | 0.0 | 0.0 | 0.0 | 0.0 |
| Glen Ellyn | 51 | 298 | 16.5 | 7.1 | 0.0 | 0.0 | 0.9 | 0.7 | 0.0 | 0.0 | 0.0 | 0.0 | 0.0 |
| Glenview | 109 | 699 | 54.4 | 19.6 | 43.2 | 0.3 | 0.0 | 0.0 | 0.0 | 0.0 | 0.0 | 0.0 | 0.0 |
| Granite City | 47 | 349 | 39.4 | 10.0 | 31.8 | 0.6 | 10.8 | 0.1 | 1.8 | 0.0 | 0.0 | 1.5 | 0.0 |
| Gurnee | 54 | 479 | 39.0 | 10.5 | 0.6 | 0.7 | 0.6 | 0.0 | 0.0 | 0.0 | 0.0 | 0.6 | 0.0 |
| Hanover Park | 36 | D | D | D | 1.0 | 1.0 | 0.0 | 0.0 | 0.0 | 0.0 | 0.0 | 0.0 | 0.0 |
| Harvey | 16 | D | D | D | 1.1 | 0.3 | 2.4 | 0.7 | 0.0 | 0.0 | 0.0 | 0.0 | 0.0 |
| Highland Park | 80 | 531 | 41.3 | 14.9 | 0.3 | 0.0 | 0.7 | 0.0 | 0.0 | 0.5 | 0.0 | 0.0 | 0.0 |
| Hoffman Estates | 50 | 371 | 21.2 | 11.6 | 0.1 | 0.1 | 0.4 | 0.0 | 0.0 | 0.1 | 0.0 | 0.3 | 0.0 |
| Joliet | 164 | 1 266 | 96.0 | 28.0 | 13.2 | 11.4 | 35.0 | 1.7 | 6.0 | 2.8 | 1.2 | 21.3 | 0.0 |
| Kankakee | 56 | 370 | 30.3 | 9.3 | 0.0 | 0.0 | 13.1 | 0.0 | 2.7 | 0.0 | 0.0 | 7.8 | 0.0 |
| Lake in the Hills | 30 | D | D | D | 0.0 | 0.0 | 0.0 | 0.0 | 0.0 | 0.0 | 0.0 | 0.0 | 0.0 |
| Lansing | 48 | 411 | 27.9 | 9.2 | 0.1 | 0.0 | 0.0 | 0.0 | 0.0 | 0.0 | 0.0 | 0.0 | 0.0 |
| Lombard | 106 | 826 | 63.6 | 22.8 | 1.8 | 3.1 | 0.4 | 0.4 | 0.0 | 0.0 | 0.0 | 0.0 | 0.0 |
| McHenry | 56 | D | D | D | 0.1 | 0.2 | 0.2 | 0.0 | 0.0 | 0.0 | 0.0 | 0.2 | 0.0 |
| Melrose Park | 43 | D | D | D | 15.4 | 0.1 | 0.3 | 0.0 | 0.0 | 0.0 | 0.0 | 0.0 | 0.0 |
| Moline | 84 | 600 | 43.9 | 13.8 | 71.6 | 6.9 | 8.2 | 0.0 | 0.0 | 0.0 | 0.0 | 3.5 | 0.0 |
| Mount Prospect | 83 | 515 | 40.6 | 12.0 | 0.1 | 1.2 | 0.6 | 0.0 | 0.0 | 0.2 | 0.0 | 0.4 | 0.0 |
| Mundelein | 56 | D | D | D | 2.2 | 9.3 | 0.4 | 0.0 | 0.0 | 0.0 | 0.0 | 0.0 | 0.0 |
| Naperville | 236 | 1 832 | 126.3 | 42.6 | 18.2 | 19.4 | 25.6 | 0.0 | 0.4 | 14.5 | 0.0 | 0.7 | 0.0 |
| Niles | 71 | 306 | 25.2 | 6.9 | 3.8 | 0.5 | 2.2 | 0.0 | 0.0 | 2.2 | 0.0 | 0.4 | 0.0 |
| Normal | 50 | 475 | 26.6 | 10.0 | 0.0 | 0.1 | 11.7 | 1.7 | 0.0 | 1.3 | 0.0 | 0.4 | 0.0 |
| Northbrook | 74 | 535 | 39.7 | 13.3 | 8.8 | 1.4 | 1.7 | 0.1 | 0.0 | 0.0 | 0.0 | 0.0 | 0.0 |
| North Chicago | 18 | 148 | 17.7 | 4.9 | 38.1 | 50.6 | 28.2 | 13.8 | 0.0 | 0.0 | 0.0 | 4.9 | 0.5 |
| Oak Forest | 38 | 164 | 18.2 | 4.8 | 0.0 | 0.0 | 0.0 | 0.0 | 0.0 | 0.0 | 0.0 | 0.0 | 0.0 |
| Oak Lawn | 99 | 734 | 52.7 | 17.0 | 0.0 | 0.1 | 0.4 | 0.0 | 0.0 | 0.0 | 0.0 | 0.3 | 0.0 |
| Oak Park | 87 | 536 | 33.3 | 11.4 | 0.0 | 2.4 | 10.0 | 3.5 | 0.0 | 0.3 | 0.0 | 6.1 | 0.0 |
| O'Fallon | 49 | 298 | 18.2 | 5.8 | 1.1 | 0.1 | 0.5 | 0.0 | 0.0 | 0.0 | 0.0 | 0.0 | 0.0 |
| Orland Park | 113 | 961 | 80.3 | 25.3 | 0.0 | 2.2 | 0.1 | 0.0 | 0.0 | 0.0 | 0.0 | 0.0 | 0.0 |
| Oswego | 51 | 362 | 24.7 | 7.8 | 0.6 | 0.8 | 0.0 | 0.0 | 0.0 | 0.0 | 0.0 | 0.0 | 0.0 |
| Palatine | 134 | 922 | 64.7 | 20.4 | 4.8 | 5.9 | 1.5 | 0.0 | 0.0 | 0.6 | 0.0 | 0.9 | 0.0 |
| Park Ridge | 59 | 303 | 20.0 | 7.1 | 33.3 | 2.0 | 0.4 | 0.0 | 0.4 | 0.0 | 0.0 | 0.0 | 0.0 |
| Pekin | 53 | 281 | 18.2 | 4.9 | 3.2 | 3.9 | 0.9 | 0.0 | 0.0 | 0.0 | 0.0 | 0.7 | 0.0 |
| Peoria | 178 | 2 909 | 254.2 | 120.5 | 10.3 | 21.3 | 59.4 | 2.8 | 5.4 | 8.4 | 0.0 | 16.1 | 0.5 |
| Plainfield | 54 | D | D | D | 1.1 | 0.1 | 0.0 | 0.0 | 0.0 | 0.0 | 0.0 | 0.0 | 0.0 |
| Quincy | 95 | 549 | 45.5 | 12.9 | 5.3 | 0.8 | 11.4 | 0.7 | 1.7 | 0.5 | 0.0 | 1.9 | 0.0 |
| Rockford | 247 | 2 058 | 164.3 | 51.5 | 117.7 | 6.5 | 43.5 | 5.0 | 0.1 | 1.5 | 0.0 | 27.7 | 0.5 |
| Rock Island | 50 | 402 | 34.7 | 11.2 | 7.8 | 0.7 | 30.2 | 0.0 | 4.8 | 0.5 | 0.0 | 22.6 | 0.0 |
| Romeoville | 38 | 480 | 60.2 | 16.5 | 0.3 | 0.0 | 1.2 | 0.1 | 0.0 | 0.1 | 0.0 | 0.0 | 0.0 |
| Round Lake Beach | 27 | D | D | D | 0.0 | 0.0 | 0.0 | 0.0 | 0.0 | 0.0 | 0.0 | 0.0 | 0.0 |
| St. Charles | 80 | 535 | 42.1 | 14.0 | 4.4 | 0.1 | 0.2 | 0.0 | 0.0 | 0.0 | 0.0 | 0.0 | 0.0 |
| Schaumburg | 204 | 1 621 | 135.5 | 45.7 | 7.7 | 19.5 | 52.6 | 1.5 | 0.0 | 0.0 | 0.0 | 0.5 | 0.0 |
| Skokie | 154 | 1 085 | 95.8 | 30.8 | 1.1 | 4.5 | 1.7 | 0.0 | 0.0 | 0.4 | 0.0 | 0.6 | 0.0 |
| Springfield | 190 | 1 536 | 104.6 | 35.6 | 25.0 | 15.8 | 2 100.1 | 121.1 | 367.8 | 256.9 | 227.3 | 15.6 | 15.9 |
| Streamwood | 47 | 307 | 19.0 | 6.6 | 0.1 | 0.0 | 0.0 | 0.0 | 0.0 | 0.0 | 0.0 | 0.0 | 0.0 |
| Tinley Park | 64 | 560 | 34.1 | 12.6 | 4.2 | 0.0 | 1.5 | 0.0 | 0.0 | 0.4 | 0.0 | 1.1 | 0.0 |
| Urbana | 44 | D | D | D | 8.2 | 7.1 | 110.4 | 1.8 | 4.1 | 12.9 | 0.0 | 2.5 | 0.0 |
| Vernon Hills | 34 | 406 | 25.6 | 9.1 | 141.3 | 134.5 | 0.3 | 0.0 | 0.0 | 0.0 | 0.0 | 0.0 | 0.0 |

1. Establishments subject to federal tax.   2. Includes program categories not shown separately. State totals include additional categories not allocated by city.

# Table D. Cities — City Government Finances

| | City government finances, 2007 | | | | | | | | | |
|---|---|---|---|---|---|---|---|---|---|---|
| | General revenue | | | | | | | General expenditure | | |
| | | Intergovernmental | | Taxes | | | | | Per capita[1] (dollars) | |
| | | | | | Per capita[1] (dollars) | | | | | |
| City | Total (mil dol) | Total (mil dol) | Percent from state government | Total (mil dol) | Total | Property | Sales and gross receipts | Total (mil dol) | Total | Capital outlays |
| | 117 | 118 | 119 | 120 | 121 | 122 | 123 | 124 | 125 | 126 |
| ILLINOIS—Cont'd | | | | | | | | | | |
| Burbank | 21.3 | 6.9 | 100.0 | 12.9 | 465 | 252 | 214 | 20.6 | 746 | 104 |
| Calumet City | 44.2 | 12.8 | 98.9 | 27.0 | 729 | 454 | 270 | 45.0 | 1 214 | 97 |
| Carbondale | 28.6 | 12.5 | 80.5 | 8.9 | 339 | 28 | 311 | 27.8 | 1 055 | 96 |
| Carol Stream | 30.0 | 11.0 | 100.0 | 9.5 | 239 | 13 | 203 | 25.9 | 651 | 49 |
| Carpentersville | 28.9 | 11.2 | 98.8 | 10.1 | 269 | 181 | 88 | 29.1 | 775 | 56 |
| Champaign | 83.7 | 26.1 | 98.0 | 43.6 | 578 | 241 | 337 | 77.3 | 1 023 | 252 |
| Chicago | 5 612.0 | 1 465.4 | 57.9 | 2 038.7 | 719 | 128 | 497 | 6 914.2 | 2 437 | 526 |
| Chicago Heights | 34.4 | 9.7 | 84.5 | 18.4 | 596 | 414 | 182 | 30.3 | 983 | 33 |
| Cicero | 100.1 | 16.1 | 96.6 | 61.2 | 756 | 508 | 248 | 86.8 | 1 072 | 208 |
| Collinsville | 25.1 | 11.1 | 98.1 | 6.1 | 237 | 137 | 100 | 23.1 | 893 | 158 |
| Crystal Lake | 44.6 | 16.7 | 98.8 | 15.8 | 380 | 298 | 82 | 41.7 | 1 001 | 178 |
| Danville | 37.4 | 14.9 | 88.5 | 14.4 | 442 | 198 | 244 | 30.8 | 949 | 0 |
| Decatur | 69.7 | 30.9 | 81.4 | 31.6 | 412 | 155 | 256 | 72.4 | 944 | 103 |
| DeKalb | 43.1 | 15.1 | 72.1 | 22.5 | 514 | 226 | 288 | 44.8 | 1 025 | 285 |
| Des Plaines | 81.1 | 18.4 | 97.3 | 46.5 | 815 | 487 | 307 | 82.3 | 1 444 | 225 |
| Downers Grove | 58.7 | 21.3 | 98.1 | 29.5 | 601 | 309 | 292 | 51.2 | 1 045 | 145 |
| East St. Louis | 36.5 | 20.2 | 88.0 | 14.7 | 507 | 334 | 173 | 39.8 | 1 373 | 209 |
| Elgin | 140.1 | 51.3 | 97.1 | 51.6 | 495 | 390 | 105 | 123.3 | 1 183 | 266 |
| Elk Grove Village | 58.1 | 15.8 | 81.2 | 33.3 | 994 | 476 | 472 | 52.7 | 1 570 | 139 |
| Elmhurst | 58.6 | 16.9 | 99.9 | 26.7 | 588 | 314 | 259 | 59.3 | 1 307 | 78 |
| Evanston | 148.6 | 31.8 | 91.3 | 74.8 | 986 | 542 | 384 | 142.6 | 1 879 | 375 |
| Freeport | 23.5 | 9.8 | 85.8 | 7.2 | 291 | 146 | 145 | 22.5 | 909 | 43 |
| Galesburg | 29.7 | 12.0 | 87.0 | 11.5 | 368 | 222 | 146 | 26.1 | 838 | 18 |
| Glendale Heights | 32.0 | 10.3 | 96.7 | 13.2 | 412 | 234 | 155 | 26.8 | 839 | 33 |
| Glen Ellyn | 34.2 | 6.9 | 96.0 | 12.4 | 457 | 296 | 130 | 29.7 | 1 091 | 223 |
| Glenview | 103.2 | 24.0 | 76.0 | 49.4 | 1 066 | 785 | 280 | 85.0 | 1 834 | 324 |
| Granite City | 38.0 | 16.9 | 93.3 | 11.9 | 389 | 241 | 148 | 35.8 | 1 166 | 158 |
| Gurnee | 35.1 | 23.2 | 89.4 | 7.0 | 230 | 15 | 215 | 31.2 | 1 021 | 53 |
| Hanover Park | 31.0 | 7.1 | 97.7 | 16.2 | 438 | 279 | 154 | 28.7 | 778 | 89 |
| Harvey | 23.3 | 7.3 | 94.0 | 12.4 | 439 | 295 | 144 | 24.7 | 876 | 39 |
| Highland Park | 56.9 | 12.5 | 96.6 | 31.0 | 984 | 411 | 484 | 53.3 | 1 694 | 259 |
| Hoffman Estates | 103.1 | 13.3 | 96.4 | 55.8 | 1 050 | 790 | 239 | 103.9 | 1 955 | 1 011 |
| Joliet | 192.4 | 80.0 | 95.7 | 64.7 | 448 | 209 | 213 | 168.5 | 1 168 | 95 |
| Kankakee | 41.1 | 14.3 | 86.3 | 15.0 | 563 | 416 | 147 | 39.2 | 1 472 | 117 |
| Lake in the Hills | 16.9 | 5.9 | 96.5 | 8.5 | 286 | 180 | 107 | 22.3 | 752 | 253 |
| Lansing | 36.1 | 9.1 | 100.0 | 19.9 | 740 | 591 | 148 | 25.2 | 940 | 41 |
| Lombard | 58.8 | 18.7 | 89.5 | 20.8 | 486 | 166 | 320 | 113.5 | 2 648 | 1 678 |
| McHenry | 23.2 | 10.0 | 99.4 | 5.1 | 194 | 167 | 27 | 24.3 | 919 | 192 |
| Melrose Park | 35.2 | 9.9 | 100.0 | 19.2 | 871 | 637 | 234 | 39.9 | 1 811 | 13 |
| Moline | 62.5 | 19.6 | 89.7 | 27.9 | 647 | 366 | 282 | 68.2 | 1 586 | 332 |
| Mount Prospect | 62.8 | 16.7 | 97.0 | 37.9 | 707 | 448 | 239 | 58.7 | 1 092 | 63 |
| Mundelein | 38.0 | 9.0 | 100.0 | 17.9 | 547 | 279 | 268 | 32.2 | 983 | 179 |
| Naperville | 153.3 | 49.4 | 93.7 | 71.2 | 500 | 290 | 168 | 155.4 | 1 091 | 173 |
| Niles | 47.1 | 17.5 | 97.8 | 22.8 | 791 | 211 | 558 | 41.5 | 1 439 | 81 |
| Normal | 54.0 | 15.4 | 90.0 | 23.6 | 456 | 144 | 312 | 61.9 | 1 196 | 152 |
| Northbrook | 51.2 | 14.3 | 100.0 | 26.0 | 764 | 416 | 348 | 52.2 | 1 532 | 211 |
| North Chicago | 22.5 | 9.8 | 87.3 | 9.5 | 288 | 156 | 121 | 27.5 | 837 | 261 |
| Oak Forest | 21.3 | 6.2 | 100.0 | 11.7 | 420 | 336 | 83 | 23.9 | 856 | 181 |
| Oak Lawn | 58.0 | 20.1 | 97.4 | 26.1 | 488 | 335 | 153 | 53.8 | 1 008 | 28 |
| Oak Park | 79.2 | 14.6 | 81.3 | 45.7 | 917 | 637 | 184 | 96.4 | 1 933 | 563 |
| O'Fallon | 28.1 | 12.9 | 97.6 | 7.9 | 294 | 171 | 123 | 31.6 | 1 168 | 464 |
| Orland Park | 91.4 | 36.4 | 82.1 | 35.2 | 633 | 377 | 256 | 80.4 | 1 445 | 329 |
| Oswego | 16.2 | 5.4 | 98.2 | 4.7 | 163 | 35 | 128 | 20.8 | 718 | 230 |
| Palatine | 71.2 | 18.1 | 92.9 | 41.6 | 618 | 430 | 188 | 63.6 | 945 | 180 |
| Park Ridge | 40.6 | 8.9 | 98.9 | 27.3 | 741 | 409 | 312 | 46.5 | 1 261 | 162 |
| Pekin | 35.0 | 12.9 | 97.5 | 10.9 | 325 | 167 | 158 | 32.2 | 964 | 133 |
| Peoria | 160.6 | 60.0 | 92.7 | 67.9 | 598 | 232 | 366 | 179.7 | 1 583 | 488 |
| Plainfield | 30.2 | 7.9 | 99.6 | 10.8 | 306 | 121 | 184 | 46.5 | 1 315 | 665 |
| Quincy | 41.2 | 19.5 | 93.0 | 12.2 | 304 | 83 | 221 | 36.3 | 906 | 185 |
| Rockford | 174.1 | 85.1 | 83.0 | 66.8 | 427 | 322 | 105 | 169.8 | 1 084 | 110 |
| Rock Island | 52.7 | 16.1 | 86.5 | 19.8 | 518 | 329 | 188 | 48.9 | 1 279 | 74 |
| Romeoville | 54.2 | 8.8 | 98.3 | 22.4 | 604 | 316 | 266 | 53.0 | 1 428 | 499 |
| Round Lake Beach | 18.5 | 7.5 | 99.8 | 8.7 | 312 | 178 | 134 | 21.3 | 763 | 383 |
| St. Charles | 52.3 | 14.9 | 96.5 | 23.8 | 726 | 350 | 376 | 62.3 | 1 902 | 557 |
| Schaumburg | 123.4 | 42.6 | 95.9 | 48.8 | 676 | 33 | 643 | 167.4 | 2 320 | 935 |
| Skokie | 82.8 | 25.9 | 92.6 | 46.7 | 700 | 410 | 277 | 74.5 | 1 117 | 118 |
| Springfield | 139.7 | 62.8 | 65.0 | 54.4 | 465 | 194 | 270 | 119.2 | 1 018 | 2 |
| Streamwood | 30.4 | 9.0 | 94.8 | 13.7 | 368 | 189 | 154 | 31.8 | 851 | 281 |
| Tinley Park | 54.4 | 20.2 | 95.3 | 24.7 | 418 | 347 | 72 | 45.8 | 775 | 151 |
| Urbana | 36.0 | 12.2 | 85.1 | 15.2 | 386 | 163 | 223 | 35.5 | 898 | 151 |
| Vernon Hills | 23.9 | 13.3 | 95.9 | 5.6 | 232 | 0 | 232 | 25.8 | 1 071 | 315 |

1. Based on population estimated as of July 1 of the year shown.

# Table D. Cities — City Government Finances

| City | Public welfare | Highways | Parking facilities | Education | Health and hospitals | Police protection | Sewerage and sanitation | Parks and recreation | Housing and community development | Interest on debt |
|---|---|---|---|---|---|---|---|---|---|---|
| | 127 | 128 | 129 | 130 | 131 | 132 | 133 | 134 | 135 | 136 |
| **ILLINOIS—Cont'd** | | | | | | | | | | |
| Burbank | 0.0 | 33.1 | 0.0 | 0.0 | 0.0 | 34.1 | 0.0 | 0.0 | 0.0 | 2.4 |
| Calumet City | 0.0 | 16.1 | 0.0 | 0.0 | 0.5 | 21.5 | 5.2 | 0.0 | 0.0 | 4.0 |
| Carbondale | 0.0 | 22.2 | 0.5 | 0.0 | 0.0 | 25.0 | 9.1 | 0.6 | 2.3 | 3.3 |
| Carol Stream | 0.0 | 25.9 | 0.0 | 0.0 | 0.0 | 41.4 | 8.9 | 0.0 | 0.0 | 4.2 |
| Carpentersville | 0.0 | 22.3 | 0.0 | 0.0 | 0.0 | 28.7 | 7.9 | 0.2 | 0.0 | 3.3 |
| Champaign | 2.5 | 10.3 | 1.4 | 0.0 | 0.0 | 20.6 | 2.9 | 0.0 | 1.7 | 2.5 |
| Chicago | 3.7 | 7.2 | 0.1 | 0.0 | 2.9 | 18.0 | 4.5 | 0.7 | 1.7 | 10.5 |
| Chicago Heights | 0.0 | 6.7 | 0.0 | 0.0 | 0.0 | 27.0 | 10.7 | 0.5 | 0.2 | 6.7 |
| Cicero | 0.3 | 17.6 | 0.0 | 0.0 | 0.7 | 22.1 | 5.8 | 0.2 | 2.0 | 7.2 |
| Collinsville | 0.5 | 9.7 | 0.0 | 0.0 | 0.6 | 20.7 | 20.7 | 0.0 | 0.0 | 3.4 |
| Crystal Lake | 0.0 | 12.1 | 0.0 | 0.0 | 0.3 | 20.3 | 5.9 | 0.0 | 0.0 | 2.7 |
| Danville | 0.0 | 14.0 | 0.6 | 0.0 | 0.0 | 25.3 | 12.6 | 7.3 | 2.8 | 1.5 |
| Decatur | 0.0 | 24.0 | 0.7 | 0.0 | 0.0 | 23.8 | 1.7 | 0.1 | 2.7 | 4.1 |
| DeKalb | 0.0 | 14.6 | 0.0 | 0.0 | 0.0 | 18.9 | 3.7 | 0.0 | 4.0 | 2.9 |
| Des Plaines | 0.6 | 18.3 | 0.3 | 0.0 | 0.0 | 20.7 | 4.7 | 0.0 | 0.3 | 6.0 |
| Downers Grove | 0.0 | 13.3 | 1.8 | 0.0 | 0.0 | 24.7 | 0.0 | 0.0 | 0.0 | 3.9 |
| East St. Louis | 0.0 | 21.5 | 0.0 | 0.0 | 0.0 | 16.6 | 0.9 | 0.0 | 5.3 | 2.3 |
| Elgin | 0.0 | 7.0 | 0.0 | 0.0 | 0.0 | 23.4 | 10.5 | 11.7 | 0.6 | 3.0 |
| Elk Grove Village | 0.0 | 22.1 | 0.0 | 0.0 | 1.2 | 28.1 | 3.7 | 0.4 | 0.0 | 2.0 |
| Elmhurst | 0.2 | 16.0 | 0.8 | 0.0 | 0.7 | 20.7 | 10.7 | 2.4 | 0.0 | 5.5 |
| Evanston | 1.4 | 10.4 | 2.9 | 0.0 | 2.7 | 13.7 | 11.3 | 9.6 | 5.4 | 8.1 |
| Freeport | 0.0 | 4.9 | 0.0 | 0.0 | 0.2 | 16.7 | 21.1 | 1.2 | 0.4 | 5.4 |
| Galesburg | 0.0 | 11.5 | 0.0 | 0.0 | 0.0 | 19.9 | 5.3 | 7.9 | 0.0 | 2.1 |
| Glendale Heights | 0.0 | 25.2 | 0.0 | 0.0 | 0.0 | 24.1 | 10.1 | 15.7 | 0.0 | 1.9 |
| Glen Ellyn | 0.0 | 15.2 | 0.7 | 0.0 | 0.0 | 18.7 | 15.5 | 9.8 | 0.0 | 2.7 |
| Glenview | 0.0 | 14.0 | 0.5 | 0.0 | 0.0 | 16.5 | 4.8 | 0.0 | 0.0 | 7.3 |
| Granite City | 0.0 | 25.4 | 0.0 | 0.0 | 0.0 | 19.4 | 15.0 | 0.0 | 1.1 | 0.0 |
| Gurnee | 0.0 | 15.5 | 0.0 | 0.0 | 0.0 | 31.4 | 3.3 | 0.0 | 0.0 | 1.5 |
| Hanover Park | 0.0 | 10.1 | 1.0 | 0.0 | 0.0 | 32.2 | 8.7 | 0.0 | 0.0 | 3.2 |
| Harvey | 0.0 | 12.9 | 1.1 | 0.0 | 0.0 | 20.9 | 6.8 | 0.0 | 0.3 | 2.0 |
| Highland Park | 0.0 | 18.4 | 1.8 | 0.0 | 0.0 | 25.8 | 0.0 | 5.3 | 0.0 | 3.6 |
| Hoffman Estates | 0.0 | 8.3 | 0.0 | 0.0 | 0.6 | 13.3 | 2.4 | 0.2 | 0.0 | 5.9 |
| Joliet | 0.0 | 14.8 | 0.6 | 0.0 | 0.1 | 20.6 | 8.4 | 5.0 | 1.8 | 1.9 |
| Kankakee | 0.0 | 15.1 | 0.0 | 0.0 | 0.0 | 18.8 | 18.3 | 0.2 | 3.1 | 6.0 |
| Lake in the Hills | 0.0 | 25.4 | 2.8 | 0.0 | 0.0 | 26.5 | 0.0 | 9.6 | 0.0 | 0.5 |
| Lansing | 0.0 | 6.7 | 0.0 | 0.0 | 0.0 | 31.8 | 8.8 | 0.1 | 0.0 | 3.9 |
| Lombard | 0.0 | 3.4 | 0.1 | 0.0 | 0.0 | 9.5 | 3.9 | 0.0 | 0.0 | 4.7 |
| McHenry | 0.0 | 22.2 | 0.0 | 0.0 | 0.0 | 29.4 | 7.4 | 14.9 | 0.0 | 3.1 |
| Melrose Park | 0.0 | 5.9 | 0.0 | 0.0 | 3.4 | 26.1 | 1.4 | 9.3 | 0.0 | 12.6 |
| Moline | 0.0 | 14.1 | 0.2 | 0.0 | 0.0 | 15.8 | 8.0 | 5.3 | 1.0 | 7.0 |
| Mount Prospect | 1.8 | 15.3 | 0.7 | 0.0 | 0.2 | 22.2 | 11.0 | 0.6 | 0.5 | 2.2 |
| Mundelein | 0.0 | 20.0 | 0.1 | 0.0 | 0.0 | 25.8 | 11.8 | 0.0 | 0.0 | 2.9 |
| Naperville | 0.1 | 23.4 | 0.5 | 0.0 | 0.0 | 21.9 | 8.5 | 5.4 | 0.0 | 1.9 |
| Niles | 0.0 | 18.4 | 0.0 | 0.0 | 0.0 | 26.7 | 3.8 | 4.0 | 0.0 | 4.4 |
| Normal | 0.0 | 8.4 | 0.0 | 0.0 | 0.0 | 14.0 | 6.8 | 12.4 | 0.0 | 3.8 |
| Northbrook | 0.0 | 23.0 | 0.4 | 0.0 | 0.0 | 22.8 | 2.1 | 0.0 | 2.3 | 3.3 |
| North Chicago | 0.0 | 5.9 | 0.0 | 0.0 | 0.0 | 25.3 | 7.3 | 0.0 | 1.0 | 2.3 |
| Oak Forest | 0.0 | 16.0 | 0.9 | 0.0 | 0.0 | 26.5 | 3.4 | 0.0 | 0.0 | 3.1 |
| Oak Lawn | 0.0 | 10.3 | 0.2 | 0.0 | 0.6 | 19.6 | 8.6 | 0.5 | 0.5 | 4.0 |
| Oak Park | 0.0 | 16.4 | 11.7 | 0.0 | 1.8 | 15.7 | 6.0 | 0.0 | 1.1 | 2.4 |
| O'Fallon | 0.5 | 9.2 | 0.0 | 0.0 | 3.6 | 13.4 | 7.8 | 3.8 | 0.0 | 3.9 |
| Orland Park | 0.0 | 11.1 | 0.2 | 0.0 | 0.0 | 27.3 | 4.8 | 13.2 | 0.0 | 3.9 |
| Oswego | 0.0 | 27.7 | 0.0 | 0.0 | 0.0 | 28.8 | 9.8 | 0.0 | 0.0 | 4.1 |
| Palatine | 0.0 | 7.3 | 1.0 | 0.0 | 0.0 | 24.4 | 8.4 | 0.0 | 0.5 | 5.5 |
| Park Ridge | 0.0 | 7.5 | 0.7 | 0.0 | 0.4 | 17.6 | 7.9 | 1.6 | 0.0 | 4.0 |
| Pekin | 0.0 | 12.0 | 0.0 | 0.0 | 0.0 | 21.6 | 10.7 | 0.2 | 0.1 | 6.4 |
| Peoria | 0.0 | 13.3 | 1.6 | 0.0 | 0.0 | 17.4 | 3.0 | 1.5 | 1.5 | 4.5 |
| Plainfield | 0.0 | 27.2 | 0.0 | 0.0 | 0.0 | 31.0 | 12.1 | 0.0 | 0.0 | 4.0 |
| Quincy | 0.0 | 22.2 | 0.0 | 0.0 | 0.0 | 20.4 | 9.2 | 0.2 | 4.0 | 2.2 |
| Rockford | 9.7 | 14.6 | 0.8 | 0.0 | 0.1 | 24.0 | 4.6 | 0.1 | 7.6 | 3.6 |
| Rock Island | 0.0 | 12.1 | 0.5 | 0.0 | 0.0 | 19.7 | 11.3 | 10.6 | 1.1 | 0.9 |
| Romeoville | 0.0 | 19.0 | 0.0 | 0.0 | 0.0 | 18.4 | 9.1 | 6.8 | 0.0 | 4.3 |
| Round Lake Beach | 0.0 | 10.8 | 0.0 | 0.0 | 0.0 | 24.9 | 0.0 | 0.2 | 0.0 | 4.4 |
| St. Charles | 0.0 | 29.7 | 0.0 | 0.0 | 1.1 | 15.5 | 8.1 | 0.0 | 0.0 | 6.8 |
| Schaumburg | 0.0 | 12.2 | 0.3 | 0.0 | 0.3 | 15.5 | 1.0 | 1.4 | 0.2 | 5.5 |
| Skokie | 0.0 | 11.4 | 0.0 | 0.0 | 2.3 | 17.5 | 5.5 | 2.7 | 0.7 | 3.5 |
| Springfield | 0.0 | 14.4 | 0.6 | 0.0 | 0.0 | 24.4 | 2.9 | 2.4 | 2.7 | 10.5 |
| Streamwood | 0.0 | 6.7 | 0.0 | 0.0 | 0.0 | 23.4 | 6.3 | 1.0 | 0.5 | 2.2 |
| Tinley Park | 0.0 | 12.1 | 1.3 | 0.0 | 0.0 | 29.1 | 9.9 | 0.0 | 0.0 | 3.2 |
| Urbana | 0.5 | 23.9 | 1.0 | 0.0 | 0.0 | 16.7 | 4.7 | 0.0 | 8.6 | 2.2 |
| Vernon Hills | 0.0 | 13.2 | 0.0 | 0.0 | 0.0 | 27.4 | 0.0 | 3.3 | 0.0 | 1.7 |

| City | City government finances, 2007 (cont.) | | | | Climate[2] | | | | | | |
|---|---|---|---|---|---|---|---|---|---|---|---|
| | Debt outstanding | | | | Average daily temperature (degrees Fahrenheit) | | | | | | |
| | | | | | Mean | | Limits | | | | |
| | Total (mil dol) | Per capita[1] (dollars) | Debt issued during year | City government employment, 2011 | January | July | January[3] | July[4] | Annual precipitation (inches) | Heating degree days | Cooling degree days |
| | 137 | 138 | 139 | 140 | 141 | 142 | 143 | 144 | 145 | 146 | 147 |
| ILLINOIS—Cont'd | | | | | | | | | | | |
| Burbank | 10.2 | 369 | 0.4 | 147 | 23.5 | 75.5 | 16.2 | 84.7 | 38.35 | 6 083 | 1 001 |
| Calumet City | 52.5 | 1 415 | 4.8 | 299 | 22.0 | 74.2 | 14.8 | 83.7 | 38.65 | 6 355 | 866 |
| Carbondale | 38.3 | 1 454 | 6.7 | 236 | NA | NA | NA | NA | NA | NA | NA |
| Carol Stream | 28.1 | 707 | 0.0 | 178 | 23.1 | 74.8 | 14.2 | 86.8 | 37.94 | 6 053 | 942 |
| Carpentersville | 29.1 | 776 | 10.0 | 198 | 19.3 | 72.6 | 10.9 | 83.0 | 37.22 | 6 975 | 679 |
| Champaign | 44.6 | 591 | 0.0 | 616 | 33.7 | 79.0 | 25.0 | 89.5 | 47.93 | 4 183 | 1 501 |
| Chicago | 16 150.0 | 5 693 | 933.7 | 34 226 | 25.3 | 75.4 | 18.3 | 84.4 | 38.01 | 5 787 | 994 |
| Chicago Heights | 57.8 | 1 875 | 0.0 | 293 | 22.0 | 74.2 | 14.8 | 83.7 | 38.65 | 6 355 | 866 |
| Cicero | 148.7 | 1 836 | 3.6 | 649 | 22.0 | 73.3 | 14.3 | 83.5 | 36.27 | 6 498 | 830 |
| Collinsville | 22.2 | 857 | 20.0 | NA | NA | NA | NA | NA | NA | NA | NA |
| Crystal Lake | 34.9 | 839 | 8.4 | 312 | 28.6 | 76.3 | 19.0 | 87.2 | 46.96 | 5 168 | 1 112 |
| Danville | 17.2 | 530 | 4.0 | 299 | 25.8 | 75.3 | 17.3 | 86.2 | 40.96 | 5 555 | 1 027 |
| Decatur | 62.3 | 813 | 5.0 | 549 | 25.8 | 76.2 | 17.1 | 87.8 | 39.74 | 5 458 | 1 142 |
| DeKalb | 31.8 | 727 | 0.0 | 203 | 18.5 | 73.1 | 10.3 | 83.6 | 37.38 | 6 979 | 736 |
| Des Plaines | 122.9 | 2 156 | 0.0 | 480 | 22.0 | 73.3 | 14.3 | 83.5 | 36.27 | 6 498 | 830 |
| Downers Grove | 124.2 | 2 535 | 44.7 | 395 | 23.1 | 74.8 | 14.2 | 86.8 | 37.94 | 6 053 | 942 |
| East St. Louis | 21.1 | 728 | 0.2 | 190 | 29.1 | 78.6 | 20.0 | 88.7 | 40.33 | 4 826 | 1 378 |
| Elgin | 133.4 | 1 279 | 13.8 | 711 | 19.3 | 72.6 | 10.9 | 83.0 | 37.22 | 6 975 | 679 |
| Elk Grove Village | 19.1 | 568 | 0.8 | 305 | 22.0 | 73.3 | 14.3 | 83.5 | 36.27 | 6 498 | 830 |
| Elmhurst | 68.2 | 1 504 | 17.9 | 590 | 23.1 | 74.8 | 14.2 | 86.8 | 37.94 | 6 053 | 942 |
| Evanston | 293.5 | 3 867 | 29.2 | 823 | 22.0 | 72.9 | 13.7 | 83.2 | 36.80 | 6 630 | 702 |
| Freeport | 28.9 | 1 166 | 10.0 | 199 | 17.2 | 71.9 | 9.0 | 82.0 | 34.79 | 7 317 | 611 |
| Galesburg | 13.9 | 448 | 0.0 | 288 | 21.3 | 74.9 | 13.5 | 84.5 | 37.22 | 6 347 | 941 |
| Glendale Heights | 14.7 | 461 | 3.0 | 235 | 22.0 | 73.3 | 14.3 | 83.5 | 36.27 | 6 498 | 830 |
| Glen Ellyn | 26.2 | 966 | 1.0 | NA | 21.7 | 74.4 | 12.2 | 85.7 | 38.58 | 6 359 | 888 |
| Glenview | 156.3 | 3 374 | 37.9 | 352 | 22.0 | 73.3 | 14.3 | 83.5 | 36.27 | 6 498 | 830 |
| Granite City | 0.0 | 0 | 0.0 | 229 | 27.7 | 78.4 | 19.4 | 88.1 | 38.54 | 5 149 | 1 354 |
| Gurnee | 11.4 | 372 | 0.0 | 204 | 19.9 | 72.2 | 12.1 | 82.2 | 35.50 | 6 955 | 634 |
| Hanover Park | 20.7 | 559 | 0.0 | 211 | 18.4 | 72.1 | 9.6 | 82.3 | 36.56 | 7 149 | 624 |
| Harvey | 16.5 | 585 | 0.0 | 200 | 22.0 | 74.2 | 14.8 | 83.7 | 38.65 | 6 355 | 866 |
| Highland Park | 50.9 | 1 619 | 0.0 | 259 | 22.0 | 72.9 | 13.7 | 83.2 | 36.80 | 6 630 | 702 |
| Hoffman Estates | 150.3 | 2 827 | 2.0 | 343 | 18.4 | 72.1 | 9.6 | 82.3 | 36.56 | 7 149 | 624 |
| Joliet | 80.4 | 557 | 6.3 | 944 | 21.7 | 73.7 | 13.5 | 84.6 | 36.96 | 6 464 | 809 |
| Kankakee | 59.5 | 2 237 | 9.6 | 291 | 21.7 | 74.4 | 12.2 | 85.7 | 38.58 | 6 359 | 888 |
| Lake in the Hills | 6.5 | 219 | 5.6 | NA | NA | NA | NA | NA | NA | NA | NA |
| Lansing | 19.9 | 742 | 0.0 | 212 | 21.7 | 74.4 | 12.2 | 85.7 | 38.58 | 6 359 | 888 |
| Lombard | 212.7 | 4 964 | 5.3 | 303 | 23.1 | 74.8 | 14.2 | 86.8 | 37.94 | 6 053 | 942 |
| McHenry | 18.5 | 700 | 3.0 | NA | NA | NA | NA | NA | NA | NA | NA |
| Melrose Park | 103.9 | 4 717 | 14.9 | 282 | NA | NA | NA | NA | NA | NA | NA |
| Moline | 86.0 | 1 999 | 0.0 | 396 | 21.8 | 76.4 | 13.3 | 85.1 | 35.10 | 6 179 | 1 100 |
| Mount Prospect | 42.8 | 797 | 10.0 | 445 | 22.0 | 73.3 | 14.3 | 83.5 | 36.27 | 6 498 | 830 |
| Mundelein | 19.9 | 607 | 0.0 | NA | 18.4 | 72.1 | 9.6 | 82.3 | 36.56 | 7 149 | 624 |
| Naperville | 126.0 | 885 | 0.0 | 1 134 | 23.1 | 74.8 | 14.2 | 86.8 | 37.94 | 6 053 | 942 |
| Niles | 41.2 | 1 428 | 0.0 | 282 | 22.0 | 73.3 | 14.3 | 83.5 | 36.27 | 6 498 | 830 |
| Normal | 72.6 | 1 404 | 34.7 | 402 | 25.8 | 76.2 | 17.1 | 87.8 | 39.74 | 5 458 | 1 142 |
| Northbrook | 63.0 | 1 852 | 13.1 | 272 | 22.0 | 72.9 | 13.7 | 83.2 | 36.80 | 6 630 | 702 |
| North Chicago | 16.2 | 492 | 0.0 | 184 | 20.3 | 71.5 | 12.0 | 81.7 | 34.09 | 7 031 | 613 |
| Oak Forest | 16.6 | 596 | 0.0 | NA | 22.0 | 74.2 | 14.8 | 83.7 | 38.65 | 6 355 | 866 |
| Oak Lawn | 62.0 | 1 161 | 7.5 | 441 | 23.5 | 75.5 | 16.2 | 84.7 | 38.35 | 6 083 | 1 001 |
| Oak Park | 117.8 | 2 362 | 40.2 | 450 | 22.0 | 73.3 | 14.3 | 83.5 | 36.27 | 6 498 | 830 |
| O'Fallon | 42.7 | 1 577 | 24.0 | NA | NA | NA | NA | NA | NA | NA | NA |
| Orland Park | 80.8 | 1 452 | 12.0 | 409 | 23.5 | 75.5 | 16.2 | 84.7 | 38.35 | 6 083 | 1 001 |
| Oswego | 25.2 | 868 | 11.6 | NA | NA | NA | NA | NA | NA | NA | NA |
| Palatine | 93.0 | 1 382 | 4.3 | 354 | 18.4 | 72.1 | 9.6 | 82.3 | 36.56 | 7 149 | 624 |
| Park Ridge | 48.5 | 1 317 | 20.6 | 258 | 22.0 | 73.3 | 14.3 | 83.5 | 36.27 | 6 498 | 830 |
| Pekin | 50.2 | 1 501 | 0.0 | 244 | 24.4 | 75.8 | 15.7 | 87.4 | 35.71 | 5 695 | 1 088 |
| Peoria | 183.9 | 1 620 | 9.8 | 833 | 22.5 | 75.1 | 14.3 | 85.7 | 36.03 | 6 097 | 998 |
| Plainfield | 42.6 | 1 205 | 0.0 | 127 | NA | NA | NA | NA | NA | NA | NA |
| Quincy | 20.1 | 500 | 1.3 | 377 | 24.9 | 76.8 | 16.0 | 88.0 | 35.63 | 5 707 | 1 117 |
| Rockford | 129.8 | 829 | 17.5 | 1 074 | 19.0 | 72.9 | 10.8 | 83.1 | 36.63 | 6 933 | 768 |
| Rock Island | 19.9 | 520 | 4.9 | 377 | 21.8 | 76.4 | 13.3 | 85.1 | 35.10 | 6 179 | 1 100 |
| Romeoville | 46.1 | 1 242 | 0.0 | 292 | NA | NA | NA | NA | NA | NA | NA |
| Round Lake Beach | 28.9 | 1 032 | 3.9 | NA | 19.9 | 72.2 | 12.1 | 82.2 | 35.50 | 6 955 | 634 |
| St. Charles | 97.7 | 2 981 | 16.5 | 276 | 19.3 | 72.6 | 10.9 | 83.0 | 37.22 | 6 975 | 679 |
| Schaumburg | 318.4 | 4 413 | 4.7 | 541 | 18.4 | 72.1 | 9.6 | 82.3 | 36.56 | 7 149 | 624 |
| Skokie | 56.9 | 853 | 0.0 | 610 | 22.0 | 73.3 | 14.3 | 83.5 | 36.27 | 6 498 | 830 |
| Springfield | 513.9 | 4 389 | 0.0 | 1 626 | 25.1 | 76.3 | 17.1 | 86.5 | 35.56 | 5 596 | 1 165 |
| Streamwood | 15.7 | 422 | 0.0 | 187 | 19.3 | 72.6 | 10.9 | 83.0 | 37.22 | 6 975 | 679 |
| Tinley Park | 34.7 | 587 | 0.0 | 338 | 21.8 | 76.4 | 13.3 | 85.1 | 35.10 | 6 179 | 1 100 |
| Urbana | 18.4 | 467 | 0.0 | 305 | 20.7 | 73.2 | 12.4 | 83.7 | 34.47 | 6 606 | 774 |
| Vernon Hills | 15.5 | 642 | 5.1 | 104 | NA | NA | NA | NA | NA | NA | NA |

1. Based on the population estimated as of July 1 of the year shown.   2. Represents normal values based on the 30-year period, 1971–2000.   3. Average daily minimum.   4. Average daily maximum.

# Table D. Cities — Land Area and Population

| STATE Place code | City | Land area,[1] 2010 (sq km) | Population, 2012 Total persons | Rank | Per square kilometer | Race alone or in combination, not of Hispanic origin (percent), 2010 — White | Black | American Indian, Alaska Native | Asian | Hawaiian Pacific Islander | Percent Hispanic or Latino[2], 2010 | Percent Foreign born 2007–2011 |
|---|---|---|---|---|---|---|---|---|---|---|---|---|
| | | 1 | 2 | 3 | 4 | 5 | 6 | 7 | 8 | 9 | 10 | 11 |
| | **ILLINOIS—Cont'd** | | | | | | | | | | | |
| 17 79293 | Waukegan | 61.3 | 88 862 | 341 | 1 449.6 | 22.9 | 19.2 | 0.5 | 4.6 | 0.1 | 53.4 | 31.6 |
| 17 80060 | West Chicago | 38.3 | 27 576 | 1 316 | 720.0 | 40.6 | 2.4 | 0.3 | 6.4 | 0.1 | 51.1 | 33.9 |
| 17 81048 | Wheaton | 29.1 | 53 469 | 674 | 1 837.4 | 85.2 | 4.8 | 0.4 | 6.2 | 0.1 | 4.9 | 11.1 |
| 17 81087 | Wheeling | 22.5 | 37 946 | 964 | 1 686.5 | 53.3 | 2.4 | 0.4 | 13.5 | 0.0 | 31.2 | 40.6 |
| 17 82075 | Wilmette | 14.0 | 27 294 | 1 333 | 1 949.6 | 84.7 | 1.0 | 0.2 | 12.3 | 0.1 | 3.3 | 15.2 |
| 17 83245 | Woodridge | 24.4 | 33 305 | 1 098 | 1 365.0 | 64.8 | 9.4 | 0.4 | 13.3 | 0.1 | 13.4 | 20.9 |
| 18 00000 | **INDIANA** | 92 789.2 | 6 537 334 | X | 70.5 | 82.9 | 9.8 | 0.6 | 1.9 | 0.1 | 6.0 | 4.5 |
| 18 01468 | Anderson | 107.2 | 55 554 | 646 | 518.2 | 79.0 | 16.7 | 0.8 | 0.7 | 0.1 | 4.8 | 2.7 |
| 18 05860 | Bloomington | 60.0 | 81 963 | 387 | 1 366.1 | 83.5 | 5.5 | 0.7 | 9.1 | 0.1 | 3.5 | 10.8 |
| 18 10342 | Carmel | 122.9 | 83 565 | 373 | 679.9 | 85.2 | 3.4 | 0.4 | 9.8 | 0.1 | 2.5 | 10.7 |
| 18 14734 | Columbus | 71.2 | 45 429 | 810 | 638.0 | 85.5 | 3.5 | 0.5 | 5.9 | 0.2 | 5.8 | 8.4 |
| 18 16138 | Crown Point | 45.9 | 28 171 | 1 285 | 613.7 | 83.7 | 6.6 | 0.3 | 2.1 | 0.0 | 8.1 | 7.2 |
| 18 19486 | East Chicago | 36.5 | 29 476 | 1 237 | 807.6 | 7.7 | 41.5 | 0.4 | 0.1 | 0.1 | 50.9 | 14.1 |
| 18 20728 | Elkhart | 60.7 | 51 152 | 712 | 842.7 | 60.8 | 17.4 | 0.9 | 1.2 | 0.1 | 22.5 | 14.2 |
| 18 22000 | Evansville | 114.4 | 120 235 | 218 | 1 051.0 | 83.3 | 14.4 | 0.7 | 1.3 | 0.1 | 2.6 | 2.2 |
| 18 23278 | Fishers | 87.0 | 81 833 | 389 | 940.6 | 85.0 | 6.3 | 0.3 | 6.4 | 0.1 | 3.4 | 6.9 |
| 18 25000 | Fort Wayne | 286.5 | 254 555 | 74 | 888.5 | 72.8 | 17.1 | 0.9 | 3.8 | 0.1 | 8.0 | 6.6 |
| 18 27000 | Gary | 129.2 | 79 170 | 404 | 612.8 | 9.9 | 85.2 | 0.8 | 0.4 | 0.0 | 5.1 | 1.5 |
| 18 28386 | Goshen | 42.0 | 32 064 | 1 137 | 763.4 | 68.0 | 3.1 | 0.6 | 1.5 | 0.1 | 28.1 | 15.2 |
| 18 29898 | Greenwood | 55.0 | 52 652 | 685 | 957.3 | 89.0 | 2.4 | 0.6 | 4.3 | 0.1 | 5.0 | 5.2 |
| 18 31000 | Hammond | 59.0 | 79 686 | 402 | 1 350.6 | 42.7 | 22.7 | 0.6 | 1.2 | 0.1 | 34.1 | 12.6 |
| 18 34114 | Hobart | 68.2 | 28 735 | 1 265 | 421.3 | 78.0 | 7.3 | 0.7 | 1.3 | 0.0 | 13.9 | 4.1 |
| 18 36000 | Indianapolis | 949.1 | 834 852 | 13 | 891.8 | 60.7 | 28.6 | 0.7 | 2.5 | 0.1 | 9.4 | 8.3 |
| 18 38358 | Jeffersonville | 88.2 | 45 677 | 806 | 517.9 | 81.0 | 15.0 | 0.8 | 1.5 | 0.2 | 4.1 | 3.0 |
| 18 40392 | Kokomo | 47.9 | 56 866 | 629 | 1 187.2 | 84.5 | 12.5 | 1.0 | 1.3 | 0.1 | 3.3 | 2.0 |
| 18 40788 | Lafayette | 71.9 | 67 925 | 492 | 944.7 | 80.1 | 7.1 | 0.8 | 1.7 | 0.1 | 12.1 | 7.4 |
| 18 42426 | Lawrence | 52.1 | 46 756 | 791 | 897.4 | 61.0 | 27.5 | 0.8 | 2.1 | 0.2 | 11.2 | 7.6 |
| 18 46908 | Marion | 40.7 | 29 639 | 1 229 | 728.2 | 78.6 | 16.7 | 0.8 | 1.1 | 0.1 | 5.5 | 1.8 |
| 18 48528 | Merrillville | 86.0 | 35 631 | 1 028 | 414.3 | 41.6 | 45.1 | 0.5 | 1.6 | 0.1 | 12.9 | 4.6 |
| 18 48798 | Michigan City | 50.7 | 31 150 | 1 168 | 614.4 | 65.0 | 30.1 | 0.9 | 1.0 | 0.1 | 5.9 | 3.3 |
| 18 49932 | Mishawaka | 44.0 | 48 031 | 772 | 1 091.6 | 86.1 | 8.2 | 1.0 | 2.3 | 0.2 | 4.5 | 5.2 |
| 18 51876 | Muncie | 70.4 | 70 087 | 476 | 995.6 | 85.0 | 12.4 | 0.8 | 1.6 | 0.2 | 2.3 | 2.6 |
| 18 52326 | New Albany | 38.7 | 36 462 | 1 001 | 942.2 | 86.5 | 10.4 | 0.8 | 1.0 | 0.1 | 3.7 | 2.5 |
| 18 54180 | Noblesville | 81.3 | 55 075 | 651 | 677.4 | 90.0 | 4.2 | 0.5 | 2.2 | 0.1 | 4.3 | 4.4 |
| 18 60246 | Plainfield | 57.7 | 29 154 | 1 248 | 505.3 | 84.4 | 8.6 | 0.5 | 3.8 | 0.1 | 4.0 | 4.9 |
| 18 61092 | Portage | 66.4 | 36 860 | 990 | 555.1 | 75.3 | 7.6 | 0.8 | 1.2 | 0.1 | 16.4 | 3.7 |
| 18 64260 | Richmond | 61.9 | 36 599 | 1 000 | 591.3 | 85.5 | 11.1 | 1.1 | 1.5 | 0.3 | 4.1 | 3.4 |
| 18 68220 | Schererville | 38.1 | 29 101 | 1 253 | 763.8 | 80.9 | 5.7 | 0.3 | 3.2 | 0.1 | 10.6 | 10.0 |
| 18 71000 | South Bend | 107.4 | 100 800 | 287 | 938.5 | 58.6 | 28.6 | 1.0 | 1.7 | 0.2 | 13.0 | 7.1 |
| 18 75428 | Terre Haute | 89.5 | 61 112 | 567 | 682.8 | 83.8 | 12.7 | 1.0 | 1.8 | 0.1 | 3.1 | 3.2 |
| 18 78326 | Valparaiso | 40.2 | 32 014 | 1 139 | 796.4 | 87.1 | 3.8 | 0.6 | 2.7 | 0.1 | 7.1 | 4.9 |
| 18 82700 | Westfield | 69.5 | 32 070 | 1 136 | 461.4 | 89.1 | 2.6 | 0.4 | 3.0 | 0.0 | 5.8 | 4.9 |
| 18 82862 | West Lafayette | 19.7 | 30 419 | 1 197 | 1 544.1 | 75.9 | 3.2 | 0.4 | 18.5 | 0.2 | 3.6 | 21.6 |
| 19 00000 | **IOWA** | 144 669.3 | 3 074 186 | X | 21.2 | 89.9 | 3.6 | 0.7 | 2.1 | 0.1 | 5.0 | 4.2 |
| 19 01855 | Ames | 62.7 | 60 634 | 576 | 967.0 | 84.0 | 4.0 | 0.5 | 9.6 | 0.1 | 3.4 | 11.2 |
| 19 02305 | Ankeny | 76.0 | 49 080 | 750 | 645.8 | 94.3 | 1.6 | 0.4 | 2.4 | 0.1 | 2.3 | 2.9 |
| 19 06355 | Bettendorf | 55.0 | 34 255 | 1 067 | 622.8 | 90.6 | 2.9 | 0.5 | 3.6 | 0.1 | 3.6 | 3.4 |
| 19 09550 | Burlington | 37.5 | 25 665 | 1 409 | 684.4 | 88.7 | 8.8 | 0.8 | 1.1 | 0.1 | 3.1 | 1.8 |
| 19 11755 | Cedar Falls | 74.5 | 39 993 | 913 | 536.8 | 93.6 | 2.7 | 0.4 | 2.8 | 0.1 | 2.0 | 3.2 |
| 19 12000 | Cedar Rapids | 183.4 | 128 119 | 197 | 698.6 | 88.4 | 7.1 | 0.8 | 2.7 | 0.2 | 3.3 | 3.3 |
| 19 14430 | Clinton | 91.1 | 26 647 | 1 368 | 292.5 | 91.3 | 5.6 | 0.9 | 1.0 | 0.0 | 3.3 | 2.1 |
| 19 16860 | Council Bluffs | 106.1 | 62 115 | 554 | 585.4 | 88.4 | 2.6 | 1.0 | 1.0 | 0.1 | 8.5 | 4.0 |
| 19 19000 | Davenport | 163.0 | 101 363 | 284 | 621.9 | 79.4 | 12.7 | 1.0 | 2.6 | 0.1 | 7.3 | 4.3 |
| 19 21000 | Des Moines | 209.5 | 206 688 | 104 | 986.6 | 72.7 | 11.7 | 0.8 | 5.0 | 0.1 | 12.0 | 10.6 |
| 19 22395 | Dubuque | 77.6 | 58 155 | 609 | 749.4 | 91.7 | 4.8 | 0.6 | 1.5 | 0.5 | 2.4 | 2.4 |
| 19 28515 | Fort Dodge | 41.6 | 24 751 | 1 460 | 595.0 | 88.3 | 6.6 | 0.6 | 1.1 | 0.1 | 5.0 | 2.9 |
| 19 38595 | Iowa City | 64.8 | 70 133 | 473 | 1 082.3 | 81.6 | 6.5 | 0.6 | 7.7 | 0.1 | 5.3 | 10.0 |
| 19 49485 | Marion | 41.6 | 35 843 | 1 019 | 861.6 | 94.1 | 2.9 | 0.6 | 1.9 | 0.1 | 2.0 | 3.5 |
| 19 49755 | Marshalltown | 49.9 | 27 683 | 1 309 | 554.8 | 71.5 | 2.8 | 0.6 | 2.1 | 0.2 | 24.1 | 14.1 |
| 19 50160 | Mason City | 72.0 | 27 823 | 1 299 | 386.4 | 92.1 | 2.6 | 0.6 | 1.1 | 0.1 | 5.1 | 2.6 |
| 19 60465 | Ottumwa | 41.1 | 24 806 | 1 458 | 603.6 | 85.5 | 2.4 | 0.7 | 1.1 | 0.2 | 11.3 | 7.0 |
| 19 73335 | Sioux City | 148.5 | 82 719 | 378 | 557.0 | 75.6 | 4.1 | 2.9 | 3.2 | 0.2 | 16.4 | 9.5 |
| 19 79950 | Urbandale | 56.8 | 41 020 | 883 | 722.2 | 90.3 | 3.4 | 0.3 | 4.1 | 0.1 | 3.1 | 7.4 |
| 19 82425 | Waterloo | 159.0 | 68 297 | 490 | 429.5 | 77.3 | 17.2 | 0.7 | 1.4 | 0.3 | 5.6 | 6.5 |
| 19 83910 | West Des Moines | 99.9 | 59 296 | 593 | 593.6 | 86.4 | 4.0 | 0.4 | 5.4 | 0.1 | 5.2 | 10.6 |

1. Dry land or land partially or temporarily covered by water.   2. May be of any race.

# Table D. Cities — **Population**

| City | Age of population (percent), 2010 | | | | | | | | | | | Population | | | |
|---|---|---|---|---|---|---|---|---|---|---|---|---|---|---|---|
| | | | | | | | | | | | | Census counts | | Percent change | |
| | Under 5 years | 5 to 17 years | 18 to 24 years | 25 to 34 years | 35 to 44 years | 45 to 54 years | 55 to 64 years | 65 to 74 years | 75 years and over | Median age | Percent female | 2000 | 2010 | 2000–2010 | 2010–2012 |
| | 12 | 13 | 14 | 15 | 16 | 17 | 18 | 19 | 20 | 21 | 22 | 23 | 24 | 25 | 26 |
| **ILLINOIS—Cont'd** | | | | | | | | | | | | | | | |
| Waukegan | 9.2 | 21.3 | 10.5 | 16.0 | 14.1 | 12.8 | 8.6 | 4.1 | 3.3 | 30.5 | 49.6 | 87 901 | 89 078 | 1.3 | -0.2 |
| West Chicago | 9.3 | 23.1 | 9.8 | 14.8 | 15.2 | 13.2 | 8.3 | 3.9 | 2.3 | 30.1 | 48.6 | 23 469 | 27 298 | 15.4 | 1.0 |
| Wheaton | 5.5 | 18.3 | 11.5 | 11.0 | 12.3 | 16.2 | 12.9 | 6.2 | 6.0 | 38.4 | 51.2 | 55 416 | 52 978 | -4.6 | 0.9 |
| Wheeling | 7.0 | 15.0 | 8.2 | 18.1 | 13.9 | 13.9 | 11.7 | 6.2 | 6.0 | 36.1 | 50.8 | 34 496 | 37 648 | 9.1 | 0.8 |
| Wilmette | 5.4 | 24.0 | 4.7 | 4.1 | 12.2 | 18.1 | 14.8 | 8.3 | 8.5 | 44.8 | 52.0 | 27 651 | 27 087 | -2.0 | 0.8 |
| Woodridge | 6.8 | 17.2 | 8.6 | 15.9 | 14.7 | 16.2 | 12.4 | 5.6 | 2.7 | 36.1 | 50.8 | 30 934 | 32 971 | 6.6 | 1.0 |
| **INDIANA** | 6.7 | 18.1 | 10.0 | 12.8 | 13.0 | 14.6 | 11.9 | 7.0 | 6.0 | 37.0 | 50.8 | 6 080 485 | 6 483 800 | 6.6 | 0.8 |
| Anderson | 6.7 | 15.7 | 11.6 | 12.7 | 12.1 | 13.3 | 11.6 | 7.9 | 8.4 | 37.8 | 52.1 | 59 734 | 56 129 | -6.0 | -1.0 |
| Bloomington | 3.9 | 7.5 | 44.4 | 15.6 | 7.4 | 6.9 | 6.3 | 3.6 | 4.3 | 23.3 | 49.7 | 69 291 | 80 307 | 16.0 | 2.1 |
| Carmel | 6.5 | 22.9 | 5.3 | 9.4 | 15.9 | 17.7 | 11.9 | 5.9 | 4.4 | 39.2 | 51.3 | 37 733 | 79 191 | 109.9 | 5.5 |
| Columbus | 7.1 | 18.1 | 8.2 | 13.7 | 13.6 | 13.4 | 11.4 | 7.3 | 7.1 | 37.1 | 51.6 | 39 059 | 44 062 | 12.8 | 3.1 |
| Crown Point | 5.7 | 15.5 | 8.0 | 14.5 | 13.2 | 14.2 | 12.8 | 7.9 | 8.2 | 39.6 | 50.0 | 19 806 | 27 827 | 37.9 | 1.2 |
| East Chicago | 9.6 | 21.8 | 9.7 | 14.0 | 11.4 | 12.4 | 9.8 | 5.7 | 5.6 | 30.9 | 53.2 | 32 414 | 29 698 | -8.4 | -0.7 |
| Elkhart | 9.5 | 19.6 | 9.4 | 14.5 | 13.0 | 12.7 | 9.8 | 5.8 | 5.8 | 32.7 | 51.8 | 51 874 | 50 923 | -1.8 | 0.4 |
| Evansville | 6.8 | 15.3 | 11.6 | 14.6 | 11.5 | 14.2 | 11.6 | 6.8 | 7.5 | 36.5 | 51.9 | 121 582 | 120 081 | -3.4 | 0.1 |
| Fishers | 8.9 | 24.1 | 4.9 | 15.2 | 19.3 | 14.4 | 7.7 | 3.4 | 2.1 | 33.2 | 51.4 | 37 835 | 76 946 | 103.0 | 6.4 |
| Fort Wayne | 7.6 | 18.8 | 10.2 | 14.1 | 12.5 | 13.6 | 11.3 | 6.0 | 6.0 | 34.5 | 51.6 | 205 727 | 253 691 | 23.3 | 0.3 |
| Gary | 7.8 | 20.3 | 8.7 | 11.4 | 10.3 | 14.0 | 13.0 | 7.8 | 6.7 | 36.7 | 54.0 | 102 746 | 80 294 | -21.9 | -1.4 |
| Goshen | 8.9 | 18.5 | 11.4 | 14.3 | 11.8 | 11.2 | 8.9 | 6.4 | 8.6 | 32.4 | 51.1 | 29 383 | 31 700 | 8.0 | 1.1 |
| Greenwood | 7.9 | 18.7 | 9.0 | 15.9 | 13.9 | 12.9 | 10.1 | 6.1 | 5.5 | 34.0 | 51.6 | 36 037 | 50 997 | 38.2 | 3.2 |
| Hammond | 7.7 | 19.9 | 10.2 | 14.5 | 12.8 | 13.8 | 10.4 | 5.4 | 5.3 | 33.3 | 51.0 | 83 048 | 80 830 | -2.7 | -1.4 |
| Hobart | 6.3 | 16.7 | 8.0 | 14.7 | 13.3 | 14.6 | 12.0 | 7.4 | 7.0 | 38.0 | 51.5 | 25 363 | 29 059 | 14.6 | -1.1 |
| Indianapolis | 7.6 | 17.4 | 10.6 | 16.1 | 13.1 | 14.0 | 10.6 | 5.6 | 5.0 | 33.7 | 51.7 | 791 926 | 820 442 | 4.8 | 1.8 |
| Jeffersonville | 7.0 | 16.3 | 8.0 | 15.6 | 13.7 | 14.8 | 12.8 | 6.7 | 5.2 | 37.3 | 51.2 | 27 362 | 45 036 | 64.3 | 1.4 |
| Kokomo | 7.4 | 16.6 | 8.8 | 13.4 | 11.9 | 14.1 | 12.1 | 8.0 | 7.8 | 38.2 | 53.2 | 46 113 | 56 842 | -1.4 | 0.0 |
| Lafayette | 8.0 | 15.9 | 13.0 | 17.7 | 12.0 | 12.1 | 10.1 | 5.8 | 5.5 | 31.9 | 51.3 | 56 397 | 67 191 | 19.0 | 1.1 |
| Lawrence | 7.7 | 20.4 | 8.1 | 14.9 | 14.4 | 14.9 | 10.0 | 4.9 | 4.6 | 34.2 | 52.5 | 38 915 | 46 001 | 18.2 | 1.6 |
| Marion | 6.4 | 14.6 | 16.3 | 11.3 | 10.7 | 13.2 | 11.4 | 7.7 | 8.3 | 36.2 | 53.0 | 31 320 | 29 948 | -4.4 | -1.0 |
| Merrillville | 6.4 | 19.2 | 8.6 | 13.6 | 13.2 | 13.8 | 11.6 | 6.3 | 7.3 | 36.7 | 53.0 | 30 560 | 35 246 | 15.3 | 1.1 |
| Michigan City | 6.9 | 16.6 | 9.0 | 15.0 | 12.8 | 14.7 | 11.5 | 6.8 | 6.8 | 37.1 | 48.6 | 32 900 | 31 479 | -4.3 | -1.0 |
| Mishawaka | 6.8 | 16.2 | 11.5 | 15.8 | 12.5 | 12.9 | 10.7 | 6.2 | 7.4 | 34.7 | 52.9 | 46 557 | 48 262 | 3.6 | -0.5 |
| Muncie | 5.5 | 12.2 | 27.6 | 11.9 | 9.5 | 10.7 | 9.6 | 6.5 | 6.5 | 28.1 | 52.5 | 67 430 | 70 199 | 3.9 | -0.2 |
| New Albany | 7.0 | 15.9 | 10.0 | 14.6 | 12.3 | 14.2 | 12.0 | 6.9 | 7.0 | 37.1 | 52.5 | 37 603 | 36 372 | -3.3 | 0.2 |
| Noblesville | 9.3 | 20.9 | 6.6 | 16.6 | 16.3 | 12.6 | 9.0 | 5.0 | 3.8 | 33.0 | 51.6 | 28 590 | 51 965 | 81.8 | 6.0 |
| Plainfield | 6.6 | 18.0 | 8.9 | 15.7 | 15.1 | 14.1 | 10.3 | 5.9 | 5.4 | 35.5 | 47.2 | 18 396 | 27 634 | 50.2 | 5.5 |
| Portage | 6.6 | 19.1 | 8.6 | 13.7 | 13.7 | 14.5 | 11.7 | 6.6 | 5.5 | 36.4 | 51.6 | 33 496 | 36 828 | 9.9 | 0.1 |
| Richmond | 7.0 | 15.2 | 11.4 | 12.8 | 11.6 | 13.8 | 11.8 | 7.9 | 8.5 | 38.4 | 52.1 | 39 124 | 36 812 | -5.9 | -0.6 |
| Schererville | 5.5 | 16.6 | 7.8 | 12.3 | 13.7 | 15.9 | 14.3 | 7.8 | 6.2 | 40.9 | 51.5 | 24 851 | 29 243 | 17.7 | -0.5 |
| South Bend | 8.2 | 19.1 | 10.0 | 15.0 | 12.0 | 12.6 | 10.5 | 5.5 | 7.0 | 33.3 | 51.6 | 107 789 | 101 124 | -6.1 | -0.3 |
| Terre Haute | 6.0 | 14.0 | 18.2 | 14.6 | 11.8 | 12.4 | 10.3 | 6.0 | 6.6 | 32.7 | 48.4 | 59 614 | 60 785 | 2.0 | 0.5 |
| Valparaiso | 5.9 | 15.4 | 15.9 | 14.9 | 12.0 | 12.2 | 10.6 | 5.7 | 7.4 | 33.4 | 51.4 | 27 428 | 31 733 | 15.7 | 0.9 |
| Westfield | 8.8 | 23.0 | 6.0 | 14.2 | 17.4 | 14.8 | 8.9 | 4.1 | 2.8 | 33.7 | 51.1 | 9 293 | 30 079 | 223.6 | 6.6 |
| West Lafayette | 3.5 | 8.3 | 49.5 | 11.8 | 6.6 | 6.4 | 5.2 | 3.2 | 5.5 | 22.8 | 45.8 | 28 778 | 29 596 | 2.8 | 2.8 |
| **IOWA** | 6.6 | 17.3 | 10.0 | 12.6 | 12.0 | 14.4 | 12.2 | 7.4 | 7.5 | 38.1 | 50.5 | 2 926 324 | 3 046 857 | 4.1 | 0.9 |
| Ames | 4.5 | 8.9 | 40.6 | 15.4 | 7.5 | 7.6 | 7.4 | 4.1 | 4.0 | 23.8 | 47.0 | 50 731 | 58 965 | 16.2 | 2.8 |
| Ankeny | 9.2 | 18.5 | 9.1 | 18.4 | 15.3 | 11.8 | 9.3 | 4.9 | 3.5 | 31.9 | 51.0 | 27 117 | 45 580 | 68.1 | 7.7 |
| Bettendorf | 6.0 | 19.5 | 5.8 | 11.4 | 13.2 | 15.6 | 13.7 | 7.6 | 7.1 | 40.7 | 51.4 | 31 275 | 33 217 | 6.2 | 3.1 |
| Burlington | 6.9 | 16.8 | 7.8 | 13.0 | 11.6 | 13.9 | 12.5 | 8.1 | 9.3 | 39.7 | 51.9 | 26 839 | 25 669 | -4.4 | 0.0 |
| Cedar Falls | 5.0 | 12.3 | 29.8 | 11.9 | 8.6 | 10.0 | 10.1 | 5.6 | 6.8 | 26.8 | 51.9 | 36 145 | 39 260 | 8.6 | 1.9 |
| Cedar Rapids | 6.7 | 16.8 | 11.2 | 14.9 | 12.5 | 13.7 | 11.1 | 6.4 | 6.8 | 35.3 | 50.9 | 120 758 | 126 326 | 4.6 | 1.4 |
| Clinton | 6.6 | 16.5 | 9.3 | 11.7 | 11.1 | 15.3 | 12.4 | 8.2 | 8.9 | 40.4 | 51.5 | 27 772 | 26 885 | -3.2 | -0.9 |
| Council Bluffs | 7.3 | 16.8 | 10.8 | 14.0 | 12.0 | 14.1 | 11.5 | 6.8 | 6.7 | 35.9 | 51.3 | 58 268 | 62 228 | 6.8 | -0.2 |
| Davenport | 7.3 | 16.7 | 10.8 | 14.9 | 12.3 | 13.8 | 11.6 | 6.3 | 6.2 | 35.3 | 51.3 | 98 359 | 99 685 | 1.3 | 1.7 |
| Des Moines | 7.9 | 16.9 | 10.9 | 16.3 | 13.0 | 13.4 | 10.6 | 5.6 | 5.4 | 33.5 | 51.1 | 198 682 | 204 184 | 2.4 | 1.2 |
| Dubuque | 6.2 | 15.3 | 13.0 | 12.8 | 10.5 | 13.8 | 12.0 | 7.4 | 9.1 | 38.0 | 51.6 | 57 686 | 57 637 | -0.1 | 0.9 |
| Fort Dodge | 6.1 | 15.6 | 13.3 | 13.1 | 10.3 | 13.3 | 12.1 | 7.2 | 9.0 | 36.8 | 48.7 | 25 136 | 25 206 | 0.3 | -1.8 |
| Iowa City | 4.7 | 10.2 | 33.5 | 16.5 | 9.3 | 9.1 | 8.7 | 4.1 | 4.0 | 25.6 | 50.3 | 62 220 | 67 894 | 9.1 | 3.3 |
| Marion | 7.5 | 19.0 | 7.0 | 14.9 | 14.4 | 13.6 | 10.6 | 7.0 | 6.1 | 36.1 | 51.7 | 26 294 | 34 768 | 32.2 | 3.1 |
| Marshalltown | 7.8 | 18.3 | 9.3 | 12.3 | 10.8 | 12.8 | 12.1 | 7.5 | 9.2 | 37.3 | 50.2 | 26 009 | 27 552 | 5.9 | 0.5 |
| Mason City | 6.2 | 15.7 | 9.7 | 11.9 | 11.2 | 14.9 | 13.2 | 7.7 | 9.4 | 40.9 | 51.8 | 29 172 | 28 079 | -3.7 | -0.9 |
| Ottumwa | 7.2 | 16.1 | 10.8 | 13.1 | 11.7 | 13.4 | 11.6 | 7.1 | 8.9 | 37.4 | 51.6 | 24 998 | 25 023 | 0.1 | -0.9 |
| Sioux City | 8.1 | 18.5 | 11.5 | 13.5 | 12.0 | 12.9 | 11.1 | 6.2 | 6.2 | 33.7 | 50.8 | 85 013 | 82 695 | -2.7 | 0.0 |
| Urbandale | 7.0 | 19.0 | 6.3 | 13.5 | 15.4 | 15.0 | 11.9 | 6.2 | 5.6 | 37.8 | 51.6 | 29 072 | 39 463 | 35.7 | 3.9 |
| Waterloo | 7.5 | 16.2 | 10.3 | 14.9 | 11.5 | 13.2 | 12.3 | 6.9 | 7.1 | 35.9 | 51.6 | 68 747 | 68 406 | -0.5 | -0.2 |
| West Des Moines | 7.1 | 17.0 | 9.2 | 18.7 | 13.9 | 13.3 | 10.1 | 5.7 | 5.0 | 33.5 | 51.7 | 46 403 | 56 701 | 22.0 | 4.6 |

| City | Households, 2010 | | | | Persons in group quarters, 2010 | | | | Serious crimes known to police,[2] 2011 | | | | Educational attainment, 2007–2011 | | |
|---|---|---|---|---|---|---|---|---|---|---|---|---|---|---|---|
| | | | Percent | | | Institutional | | | Total | | Rate[3] | | | Attainment[4] (percent) | |
| | Number | Persons per house-hold | Female family house-holder[1] | One-person | Total | Total | Persons in nursing facilities | Non-institu-tional | Number | Rate[3] | Violent | Property | Population age 25 and older | High school graduate or less | Bachelor's degree or more |
| | 27 | 28 | 29 | 30 | 31 | 32 | 33 | 34 | 35 | 36 | 37 | 38 | 39 | 40 | 41 |
| ILLINOIS—Cont'd | | | | | | | | | | | | | | | |
| Waukegan | 28 079 | 3.10 | 18.0 | 23.4 | 2 077 | 1 586 | 842 | 491 | 3 437 | 3 847 | 492 | 3 354 | 52 468 | 59.4 | 16.6 |
| West Chicago | 7 330 | 3.65 | 10.4 | 12.4 | 333 | 325 | 325 | 8 | 368 | 1 355 | 85 | 1 270 | 14 980 | 50.3 | 25.7 |
| Wheaton | 19 191 | 2.58 | 8.2 | 25.7 | 3 379 | 1 395 | 578 | 1 984 | 772 | 1 455 | 43 | 1 412 | 34 445 | 16.4 | 59.5 |
| Wheeling | 14 461 | 2.57 | 9.7 | 29.2 | 465 | 461 | 461 | 4 | 584 | 1 547 | 87 | 1 459 | 25 773 | 39.1 | 37.2 |
| Wilmette | 9 742 | 2.77 | 7.1 | 20.8 | 126 | 69 | 69 | 57 | 423 | 1 557 | 33 | 1 524 | 17 689 | 7.0 | 78.7 |
| Woodridge | 12 646 | 2.60 | 11.3 | 25.2 | 88 | 86 | 0 | 2 | 544 | 1 645 | 115 | 1 530 | 22 069 | 24.9 | 45.2 |
| INDIANA | 2 502 154 | 2.52 | 12.4 | 26.9 | 186 923 | 95 336 | 41 158 | 91 587 | 227 681 | 3 494 | 332 | 3 162 | 4 199 481 | 49.2 | 22.7 |
| Anderson | 23 560 | 2.28 | 17.1 | 34.5 | 2 401 | 910 | 527 | 1 491 | 3 152 | 5 587 | 360 | 5 227 | 36 976 | 57.7 | 14.5 |
| Bloomington | 31 425 | 2.09 | 7.5 | 38.2 | 14 669 | 543 | 282 | 14 126 | 3 316 | 4 103 | 302 | 3 801 | 35 266 | 23.4 | 54.8 |
| Carmel | 28 997 | 2.71 | 6.3 | 20.8 | 600 | 579 | 470 | 21 | 848 | 1 065 | 21 | 1 044 | 50 398 | 13.4 | 66.7 |
| Columbus | 17 787 | 2.43 | 11.7 | 29.7 | 870 | 704 | 450 | 166 | 2 678 | 6 047 | 196 | 5 851 | 29 380 | 40.2 | 31.8 |
| Crown Point | 10 394 | 2.45 | 10.0 | 27.5 | 1 863 | 1 839 | 338 | 24 | 492 | 1 792 | 62 | 1 730 | 18 762 | 42.1 | 30.3 |
| East Chicago | 10 724 | 2.75 | 31.4 | 29.0 | 178 | 98 | 92 | 80 | 2 196 | 7 357 | 854 | 6 503 | 17 224 | 63.4 | 8.3 |
| Elkhart | 19 261 | 2.60 | 18.5 | 30.8 | 915 | 611 | 611 | 304 | 177 | 346 | 18 | 328 | 31 261 | 61.0 | 14.0 |
| Evansville | 50 588 | 2.23 | 15.6 | 36.5 | 4 727 | 2 103 | 1 194 | 2 624 | 5 947 | 5 039 | 416 | 4 623 | 78 191 | 51.1 | 18.5 |
| Fishers | 27 218 | 2.82 | 7.9 | 19.8 | 27 | 27 | 27 | 0 | 711 | 921 | 14 | 907 | 46 442 | 13.9 | 61.6 |
| Fort Wayne | 101 585 | 2.44 | 14.8 | 31.2 | 5 356 | 2 680 | 1 643 | 2 676 | 9 821 | 3 852 | 308 | 3 544 | 160 932 | 42.4 | 25.5 |
| Gary | 31 380 | 2.54 | 30.9 | 32.8 | 708 | 261 | 237 | 447 | 5 977 | 7 406 | 792 | 6 614 | 52 897 | 55.3 | 12.6 |
| Goshen | 11 344 | 2.67 | 13.1 | 27.4 | 1 467 | 808 | 411 | 659 | 1 166 | 3 657 | 113 | 3 544 | 19 049 | 58.3 | 19.2 |
| Greenwood | 19 615 | 2.51 | 11.6 | 27.8 | 481 | 456 | 405 | 25 | 1 954 | 3 904 | 354 | 3 551 | 32 261 | 42.0 | 26.8 |
| Hammond | 29 949 | 2.67 | 19.7 | 30.3 | 975 | 82 | 71 | 893 | 4 366 | 5 374 | 673 | 4 701 | 50 635 | 60.8 | 12.2 |
| Hobart | 11 650 | 2.48 | 12.1 | 28.2 | 144 | 1 | 0 | 143 | 1 544 | 5 286 | 223 | 5 064 | 19 578 | 51.5 | 16.0 |
| Indianapolis | 336 186 | 2.42 | 17.2 | 32.1 | 16 040 | 8 750 | 4 382 | 7 290 | 56 137 | 6 739 | 1 101 | 5 638 | 532 270 | 45.6 | 27.2 |
| Jeffersonville | 18 580 | 2.37 | 13.9 | 30.5 | 878 | 535 | 109 | 343 | 2 712 | 6 002 | 1 005 | 4 997 | 29 836 | 47.0 | 20.8 |
| Kokomo | 19 848 | 2.25 | 16.6 | 35.4 | 722 | 532 | 426 | 190 | 2 742 | 6 000 | 403 | 5 597 | 30 546 | 54.1 | 15.6 |
| Lafayette | 28 545 | 2.30 | 13.7 | 34.9 | 1 433 | 1 058 | 477 | 375 | 3 408 | 5 050 | 605 | 4 446 | 41 719 | 45.9 | 26.3 |
| Lawrence | 17 864 | 2.56 | 17.5 | 27.6 | 333 | 289 | 223 | 44 | NA | NA | NA | NA | 28 704 | 41.3 | 30.9 |
| Marion | 11 828 | 2.25 | 17.0 | 36.7 | 3 364 | 797 | 481 | 2 567 | 1 490 | 4 950 | 206 | 4 744 | 19 172 | 61.4 | 15.2 |
| Merrillville | 13 696 | 2.54 | 17.9 | 29.7 | 455 | 366 | 362 | 89 | 1 492 | 4 212 | 316 | 3 895 | 22 962 | 47.4 | 18.9 |
| Michigan City | 12 136 | 2.37 | 19.0 | 34.3 | 2 670 | 2 506 | 234 | 164 | 1 936 | 6 154 | 305 | 5 849 | 21 287 | 54.4 | 14.2 |
| Mishawaka | 21 343 | 2.21 | 14.4 | 37.4 | 1 013 | 212 | 83 | 801 | 3 041 | 6 270 | 301 | 5 969 | 31 890 | 49.5 | 24.1 |
| Muncie | 27 722 | 2.22 | 14.1 | 35.2 | 8 508 | 1 267 | 744 | 7 241 | 2 946 | 4 182 | 728 | 3 454 | 38 330 | 52.6 | 21.3 |
| New Albany | 15 575 | 2.27 | 18.2 | 33.7 | 1 008 | 724 | 429 | 284 | 2 322 | 6 352 | 306 | 6 045 | 24 342 | 55.3 | 16.8 |
| Noblesville | 19 080 | 2.69 | 10.8 | 21.6 | 661 | 632 | 316 | 29 | 1 005 | 1 924 | 115 | 1 809 | 31 973 | 24.3 | 46.4 |
| Plainfield | 9 747 | 2.57 | 12.3 | 25.7 | 2 615 | 2 595 | 145 | 20 | 759 | 2 733 | 155 | 2 578 | 18 294 | 44.3 | 25.8 |
| Portage | 13 992 | 2.61 | 14.6 | 24.3 | 255 | 233 | 233 | 22 | 1 290 | 3 485 | 300 | 3 185 | 24 454 | 54.5 | 14.4 |
| Richmond | 15 098 | 2.29 | 16.3 | 34.2 | 2 292 | 1 198 | 561 | 1 094 | 2 092 | 5 654 | 527 | 5 127 | 24 221 | 57.2 | 16.9 |
| Schererville | 11 883 | 2.45 | 9.7 | 27.7 | 120 | 63 | 0 | 57 | 792 | 2 695 | 44 | 2 650 | 20 497 | 39.5 | 31.3 |
| South Bend | 39 760 | 2.48 | 18.9 | 33.3 | 2 692 | 1 697 | 773 | 995 | 6 840 | 6 727 | 732 | 5 995 | 64 119 | 49.6 | 21.7 |
| Terre Haute | 22 645 | 2.29 | 15.7 | 34.9 | 8 875 | 4 173 | 589 | 4 702 | 4 090 | 6 447 | 247 | 6 447 | 37 244 | 50.9 | 19.0 |
| Valparaiso | 12 610 | 2.28 | 10.9 | 34.5 | 2 936 | 1 070 | 546 | 1 866 | 990 | 3 104 | 100 | 3 004 | 19 359 | 36.5 | 33.7 |
| Westfield | 10 490 | 2.85 | 9.3 | 18.0 | 139 | 99 | 99 | 40 | 517 | 1 711 | 69 | 1 641 | 17 709 | 22.0 | 53.2 |
| West Lafayette | 11 945 | 2.22 | 4.4 | 34.2 | 3 069 | 155 | 155 | 2 914 | 512 | 1 721 | 178 | 1 543 | 11 282 | 12.5 | 74.7 |
| IOWA | 1 221 576 | 2.41 | 9.3 | 28.4 | 98 112 | 43 282 | 26 871 | 54 830 | 79 187 | 2 586 | 256 | 2 330 | 1 999 820 | 43.5 | 24.9 |
| Ames | 22 759 | 2.25 | 5.4 | 30.5 | 7 767 | 294 | 181 | 7 473 | 1 848 | 3 118 | 300 | 2 817 | 26 278 | 15.2 | 60.8 |
| Ankeny | 17 433 | 2.58 | 7.2 | 22.6 | 663 | 174 | 146 | 489 | 728 | 1 589 | 105 | 1 484 | 27 891 | 20.4 | 47.9 |
| Bettendorf | 13 681 | 2.42 | 8.4 | 28.2 | 176 | 172 | 158 | 4 | 591 | 1 770 | 174 | 1 596 | 22 366 | 24.4 | 45.0 |
| Burlington | 10 938 | 2.30 | 14.2 | 32.5 | 495 | 367 | 235 | 128 | 1 270 | 4 923 | 558 | 4 365 | 17 497 | 46.3 | 18.3 |
| Cedar Falls | 14 608 | 2.37 | 7.2 | 28.0 | 4 574 | 354 | 354 | 4 220 | 680 | 1 723 | 182 | 1 541 | 20 360 | 28.4 | 44.4 |
| Cedar Rapids | 53 236 | 2.31 | 11.0 | 32.5 | 3 518 | 1 561 | 769 | 1 957 | 5 266 | 4 147 | 283 | 3 863 | 82 429 | 35.4 | 29.6 |
| Clinton | 11 246 | 2.33 | 12.7 | 32.1 | 713 | 379 | 347 | 334 | 1 435 | 5 310 | 500 | 4 810 | 18 083 | 51.2 | 14.9 |
| Council Bluffs | 24 354 | 2.43 | 15.0 | 30.0 | 1 908 | 964 | 440 | 944 | 4 929 | 7 879 | 1 053 | 6 826 | 40 245 | 51.6 | 15.5 |
| Davenport | 40 620 | 2.38 | 14.3 | 31.5 | 3 111 | 1 247 | 751 | 1 864 | 5 560 | 5 549 | 651 | 4 898 | 64 229 | 40.7 | 25.9 |
| Des Moines | 81 369 | 2.43 | 14.2 | 32.5 | 6 104 | 1 641 | 1 005 | 4 463 | 11 832 | 5 786 | 524 | 5 262 | 131 471 | 46.3 | 24.0 |
| Dubuque | 23 506 | 2.28 | 11.1 | 33.7 | 4 027 | 1 133 | 806 | 2 894 | 1 836 | 3 169 | 233 | 2 936 | 38 053 | 46.1 | 27.1 |
| Fort Dodge | 10 275 | 2.21 | 13.0 | 36.8 | 2 509 | 1 651 | 345 | 858 | 1 313 | 5 182 | 560 | 4 622 | 16 392 | 48.0 | 19.1 |
| Iowa City | 27 657 | 2.22 | 7.2 | 34.3 | 6 585 | 296 | 168 | 6 289 | 1 784 | 2 615 | 242 | 2 373 | 33 689 | 18.0 | 58.2 |
| Marion | 14 108 | 2.44 | 9.8 | 28.4 | 292 | 214 | 210 | 78 | 493 | 1 411 | 129 | 1 282 | 22 559 | 30.6 | 33.3 |
| Marshalltown | 10 335 | 2.55 | 11.9 | 29.8 | 1 190 | 1 040 | 985 | 150 | 1 119 | 4 040 | 531 | 3 510 | 17 722 | 52.4 | 19.4 |
| Mason City | 12 366 | 2.20 | 10.8 | 35.0 | 856 | 448 | 344 | 408 | 1 345 | 4 765 | 152 | 4 613 | 19 153 | 40.0 | 20.3 |
| Ottumwa | 10 251 | 2.36 | 12.9 | 32.9 | 826 | 371 | 248 | 455 | 964 | 3 832 | 290 | 3 542 | 16 561 | 54.0 | 15.1 |
| Sioux City | 31 571 | 2.54 | 13.8 | 29.4 | 2 565 | 743 | 437 | 1 822 | 3 874 | 4 661 | 410 | 4 251 | 51 242 | 50.1 | 19.8 |
| Urbandale | 15 596 | 2.52 | 7.2 | 25.0 | 234 | 230 | 222 | 4 | 719 | 1 812 | 159 | 1 654 | 26 272 | 22.6 | 48.1 |
| Waterloo | 28 607 | 2.35 | 14.9 | 31.6 | 1 165 | 687 | 515 | 478 | 2 516 | 3 659 | 519 | 3 140 | 44 414 | 49.5 | 18.5 |
| West Des Moines | 24 311 | 2.32 | 8.6 | 31.2 | 273 | 262 | 262 | 11 | 1 956 | 3 437 | 202 | 3 235 | 37 016 | 22.0 | 50.1 |

1. No spouse present.  2. Data for serious crimes have not been adjusted for underreporting. This may affect comparability between geographic areas and over time.  3. Per 100,000 population estimated by the FBI.  4. Persons 25 years old and over.

# Table D. Cities — Income, Poverty, and Housing

| City | Money income, 2007–2011 Households | | | | | Housing units, 2010 | | | Occupied Housing units 2007–2011 | | | | |
|---|---|---|---|---|---|---|---|---|---|---|---|---|---|
| | Per capita income[1] (dollars) | Median income | Percent with income of $200,000 or more | Percent with income of less than $25,000 | Families with income below poverty (percent) | Total | Percent change, 2000–2010 | Vacant units for sale or rent[2] | Owner-occupied Total | Percent | Median value[3] (dollars) | Median owner costs as a percent of income With a mortgage[4] | Without a mortgage[5] |
| | 42 | 43 | 44 | 45 | 46 | 47 | 48 | 49 | 50 | 51 | 52 | 53 | 54 |
| ILLINOIS—Cont'd | | | | | | | | | | | | | |
| Waukegan | 20 401 | 46 656 | 2.1 | 23.9 | 14.2 | 30 746 | 5.1 | 2 667 | 29 110 | 56.1 | 161 400 | 29.6 | 16.7 |
| West Chicago | 25 436 | 63 377 | 4.7 | 13.8 | 10.3 | 7 763 | 15.2 | 433 | 7 666 | 67.2 | 251 100 | 29.1 | 14.4 |
| Wheaton | 42 179 | 84 980 | 12.6 | 11.9 | 4.2 | 20 112 | 1.1 | 921 | 18 995 | 73.4 | 354 000 | 24.9 | 12.1 |
| Wheeling | 27 502 | 59 026 | 3.0 | 19.5 | 8.6 | 15 397 | 12.5 | 936 | 14 296 | 66.2 | 229 700 | 30.2 | 15.4 |
| Wilmette | 71 480 | 130 260 | 32.0 | 7.5 | 1.5 | 10 290 | -0.4 | 548 | 9 537 | 86.7 | 665 600 | 25.3 | 13.6 |
| Woodridge | 35 000 | 72 873 | 6.1 | 11.2 | 4.0 | 13 392 | 14.6 | 746 | 12 625 | 67.1 | 265 700 | 27.7 | 13.5 |
| INDIANA | 24 497 | 48 393 | 2.4 | 24.1 | 10.1 | 2 795 541 | 10.4 | 293 387 | 2 472 870 | 71.1 | 123 300 | 21.7 | 11.5 |
| Anderson | 18 835 | 35 330 | 0.6 | 34.9 | 19.6 | 27 953 | 1.3 | 4 393 | 22 964 | 61.4 | 74 900 | 23.2 | 13.4 |
| Bloomington | 18 071 | 26 516 | 2.5 | 47.9 | 18.0 | 33 239 | 17.2 | 1 814 | 30 063 | 33.6 | 166 300 | 21.4 | 10.8 |
| Carmel | 51 354 | 106 071 | 18.3 | 8.2 | 2.9 | 30 738 | 117.0 | 1 741 | 28 487 | 78.5 | 291 100 | 19.3 | 10.0 |
| Columbus | 28 453 | 51 955 | 3.3 | 23.0 | 9.9 | 19 700 | 14.9 | 1 913 | 17 852 | 64.4 | 143 500 | 19.3 | 11.3 |
| Crown Point | 31 919 | 64 227 | 4.7 | 14.8 | 4.2 | 10 976 | 36.0 | 582 | 9 879 | 79.0 | 175 800 | 22.6 | 12.1 |
| East Chicago | 14 082 | 28 185 | 0.4 | 44.7 | 33.3 | 12 958 | -2.3 | 2 234 | 9 866 | 44.8 | 86 800 | 26.9 | 14.5 |
| Elkhart | 17 650 | 33 851 | 0.9 | 36.9 | 23.3 | 22 699 | 4.9 | 3 438 | 19 369 | 55.0 | 90 200 | 23.6 | 14.5 |
| Evansville | 21 257 | 36 143 | 1.1 | 33.8 | 14.7 | 57 799 | 1.2 | 7 211 | 50 647 | 56.0 | 89 900 | 21.6 | 12.6 |
| Fishers | 39 616 | 92 347 | 9.3 | 5.6 | 2.1 | 28 511 | 82.0 | 1 293 | 26 712 | 83.0 | 210 400 | 20.9 | 10.0 |
| Fort Wayne | 23 300 | 44 597 | 1.8 | 25.6 | 12.3 | 113 541 | 24.9 | 11 956 | 101 118 | 64.6 | 100 500 | 20.3 | 10.2 |
| Gary | 16 300 | 27 701 | 0.6 | 46.4 | 30.4 | 39 531 | -9.4 | 8 151 | 32 093 | 54.8 | 69 500 | 26.2 | 16.7 |
| Goshen | 18 795 | 39 987 | 1.2 | 27.2 | 13.7 | 12 631 | 12.2 | 1 287 | 11 414 | 66.0 | 104 500 | 23.1 | 14.2 |
| Greenwood | 27 405 | 54 947 | 1.8 | 18.8 | 8.1 | 21 339 | 33.6 | 1 724 | 19 713 | 63.0 | 132 300 | 20.7 | 10.9 |
| Hammond | 17 746 | 38 396 | 0.6 | 32.0 | 18.0 | 32 945 | -3.5 | 2 996 | 29 316 | 64.8 | 96 900 | 25.0 | 14.1 |
| Hobart | 24 727 | 54 880 | 1.0 | 18.3 | 5.4 | 12 399 | 20.6 | 749 | 11 090 | 75.0 | 133 200 | 22.2 | 17.7 |
| Indianapolis | 24 580 | 42 772 | 2.5 | 28.1 | 14.7 | 384 414 | 7.6 | 48 228 | 328 693 | 57.2 | 120 900 | 22.4 | 12.0 |
| Jeffersonville | 24 819 | 48 968 | 1.6 | 23.5 | 7.3 | 19 991 | 60.9 | 1 411 | 17 603 | 66.4 | 125 300 | 20.9 | 11.8 |
| Kokomo | 20 332 | 35 211 | 0.6 | 34.5 | 16.9 | 23 010 | 3.0 | 3 162 | 19 797 | 60.3 | 83 800 | 20.2 | 12.1 |
| Lafayette | 21 712 | 38 556 | 1.2 | 32.1 | 14.9 | 31 260 | 22.4 | 2 715 | 28 739 | 50.8 | 102 500 | 21.3 | 10.0 |
| Lawrence | 25 873 | 54 254 | 2.6 | 20.1 | 8.5 | 19 515 | 19.9 | 1 651 | 16 870 | 74.4 | 129 500 | 22.3 | 13.2 |
| Marion | 17 055 | 30 342 | 0.5 | 41.5 | 19.7 | 13 715 | -0.6 | 1 887 | 12 229 | 56.8 | 65 300 | 21.8 | 13.3 |
| Merrillville | 23 583 | 51 768 | 0.6 | 22.6 | 7.0 | 14 842 | 19.8 | 1 146 | 13 164 | 69.5 | 131 900 | 25.0 | 13.1 |
| Michigan City | 18 847 | 35 011 | 0.9 | 35.3 | 17.6 | 14 435 | 1.5 | 2 299 | 12 411 | 59.6 | 93 300 | 23.6 | 13.9 |
| Mishawaka | 21 825 | 37 620 | 1.0 | 33.6 | 13.8 | 24 088 | 11.4 | 2 745 | 20 947 | 52.8 | 94 900 | 22.2 | 13.0 |
| Muncie | 16 782 | 30 200 | 0.9 | 41.6 | 19.7 | 31 958 | 5.8 | 4 236 | 27 975 | 53.5 | 74 800 | 22.4 | 13.2 |
| New Albany | 21 006 | 38 640 | 0.7 | 30.9 | 16.1 | 17 315 | 1.5 | 1 740 | 15 550 | 57.3 | 114 700 | 23.7 | 11.6 |
| Noblesville | 30 792 | 70 484 | 4.6 | 11.3 | 5.2 | 21 121 | 86.3 | 2 041 | 18 634 | 74.8 | 169 500 | 22.2 | 10.0 |
| Plainfield | 25 555 | 55 280 | 2.8 | 15.7 | 7.4 | 10 386 | 38.3 | 639 | 9 868 | 73.4 | 147 200 | 22.7 | 13.1 |
| Portage | 23 517 | 49 590 | 0.9 | 22.4 | 10.2 | 14 807 | 11.1 | 815 | 14 132 | 70.1 | 137 500 | 20.6 | 15.9 |
| Richmond | 20 251 | 35 040 | 1.4 | 37.4 | 21.5 | 17 649 | -0.4 | 2 551 | 15 333 | 58.2 | 85 900 | 21.4 | 12.0 |
| Schererville | 33 105 | 67 756 | 4.9 | 14.3 | 4.8 | 12 393 | 24.0 | 510 | 11 547 | 76.1 | 202 900 | 22.6 | 10.0 |
| South Bend | 19 058 | 34 749 | 1.3 | 34.0 | 21.3 | 46 324 | 0.2 | 6 564 | 39 791 | 61.3 | 86 600 | 23.0 | 12.6 |
| Terre Haute | 17 429 | 31 838 | 1.2 | 38.7 | 17.9 | 25 518 | -0.3 | 2 873 | 22 064 | 57.6 | 75 300 | 20.3 | 13.2 |
| Valparaiso | 25 482 | 50 549 | 2.5 | 25.5 | 8.3 | 13 506 | 15.8 | 896 | 12 223 | 59.9 | 166 000 | 21.6 | 11.8 |
| Westfield | 35 545 | 86 054 | 7.4 | 9.6 | 4.6 | 11 209 | NA | 719 | 10 308 | 84.4 | 201 300 | 21.7 | 11.1 |
| West Lafayette | 22 315 | 29 014 | 3.8 | 46.4 | 8.8 | 12 591 | 16.5 | 646 | 12 221 | 33.4 | 171 200 | 19.2 | 10.0 |
| IOWA | 26 110 | 50 451 | 2.5 | 23.0 | 7.6 | 1 336 417 | 8.4 | 114 841 | 1 219 137 | 73.0 | 121 300 | 21.1 | 11.8 |
| Ames | 24 171 | 42 062 | 2.8 | 31.5 | 7.9 | 23 876 | 27.6 | 1 117 | 22 567 | 42.5 | 170 700 | 20.5 | 10.0 |
| Ankeny | 32 102 | 72 703 | 2.4 | 11.0 | 2.1 | 18 339 | 69.8 | 906 | 16 988 | 79.3 | 173 500 | 21.6 | 11.5 |
| Bettendorf | 36 055 | 69 239 | 7.1 | 14.4 | 3.6 | 14 437 | 10.6 | 756 | 13 229 | 78.3 | 166 600 | 19.7 | 10.0 |
| Burlington | 23 609 | 39 527 | 1.2 | 32.0 | 12.1 | 11 899 | -1.0 | 961 | 10 927 | 68.9 | 83 200 | 21.3 | 12.7 |
| Cedar Falls | 24 042 | 47 974 | 2.4 | 26.7 | 8.4 | 15 477 | 16.4 | 869 | 14 114 | 64.6 | 155 200 | 19.6 | 10.0 |
| Cedar Rapids | 28 008 | 51 108 | 2.9 | 22.4 | 7.9 | 57 217 | 9.7 | 3 981 | 53 227 | 69.7 | 129 200 | 20.8 | 12.5 |
| Clinton | 22 380 | 41 699 | 1.2 | 28.6 | 10.7 | 12 202 | -1.8 | 956 | 11 032 | 68.6 | 91 800 | 20.9 | 13.0 |
| Council Bluffs | 21 731 | 42 844 | 0.8 | 26.6 | 12.0 | 26 594 | 9.1 | 1 801 | 24 533 | 63.8 | 112 200 | 22.2 | 13.2 |
| Davenport | 23 963 | 42 983 | 1.7 | 28.7 | 13.1 | 44 087 | 6.6 | 3 467 | 40 694 | 63.7 | 118 000 | 22.2 | 12.4 |
| Des Moines | 24 006 | 44 997 | 1.6 | 26.6 | 12.4 | 88 729 | 4.3 | 7 360 | 82 600 | 63.5 | 118 100 | 23.2 | 13.6 |
| Dubuque | 24 147 | 43 362 | 1.8 | 24.6 | 8.2 | 25 029 | 5.1 | 1 523 | 23 719 | 67.0 | 124 700 | 21.2 | 12.5 |
| Fort Dodge | 22 257 | 38 015 | 1.1 | 33.4 | 11.2 | 11 215 | 0.1 | 940 | 10 653 | 61.4 | 81 800 | 19.1 | 11.4 |
| Iowa City | 25 189 | 41 956 | 3.3 | 35.3 | 10.0 | 29 270 | 12.4 | 1 613 | 26 820 | 48.8 | 179 300 | 22.4 | 10.6 |
| Marion | 30 042 | 58 551 | 2.7 | 17.2 | 3.2 | 15 064 | 37.2 | 956 | 14 021 | 73.1 | 143 100 | 20.5 | 12.0 |
| Marshalltown | 21 924 | 44 970 | 1.3 | 24.1 | 11.2 | 11 171 | 2.9 | 836 | 10 348 | 69.4 | 95 400 | 21.8 | 11.8 |
| Mason City | 25 580 | 41 561 | 2.2 | 30.6 | 11.5 | 13 352 | 2.3 | 986 | 12 889 | 67.8 | 97 500 | 20.6 | 11.9 |
| Ottumwa | 21 301 | 36 574 | 1.2 | 33.6 | 15.1 | 11 257 | 2.6 | 1 006 | 10 483 | 71.2 | 69 900 | 20.7 | 13.4 |
| Sioux City | 21 573 | 43 158 | 1.4 | 27.9 | 13.0 | 33 425 | -1.1 | 1 854 | 31 285 | 64.3 | 91 900 | 20.7 | 12.1 |
| Urbandale | 39 484 | 83 401 | 8.1 | 8.6 | 2.5 | 16 319 | 37.7 | 723 | 15 461 | 79.8 | 193 100 | 20.4 | 10.0 |
| Waterloo | 22 017 | 40 238 | 1.5 | 30.1 | 14.2 | 30 723 | 4.2 | 2 116 | 28 657 | 65.6 | 102 700 | 21.4 | 12.5 |
| West Des Moines | 37 646 | 67 179 | 5.9 | 13.1 | 4.7 | 26 219 | 26.2 | 1 908 | 23 604 | 64.0 | 183 000 | 21.1 | 11.0 |

1. Based on population estimated by the American Community Survey.   2. Includes units rented or sold but not occupied.   3. Specified owner-occupied units; $1,000,000 represents $1,000,000 or more   4. 50.0 represents 50 percent or more.   5. 10.0 represents 10 percent or less.

# Table D. Cities — Housing, Labor Force, and Employment

| City | Occupied housing units, 2007–2011 (cont.) | | | | Migration, 2007–2011 | | Civilian labor force, 2012 | | | | Civilian employment[4], 2007–2011 | | | |
|---|---|---|---|---|---|---|---|---|---|---|---|---|---|---|
| | | | | | | | | | Unemployment | | | Percent | | |
| | Percent renter occupied | Median gross rent[1] | Median rent as a percent of income[2] | Percent with no vehicle available | Percent who lived in the same house one year ago | Percent who lived outside this city one year ago | Total | Percent change, 2011–2012 | Total | Rate[3] | Population age 16 and older | In labor force | Full-year full-time worker | Households with no workers (percent) |
| | 55 | 56 | 57 | 58 | 59 | 60 | 61 | 62 | 63 | 64 | 65 | 66 | 67 | 68 |
| **ILLINOIS—Cont'd** | | | | | | | | | | | | | | |
| Waukegan | 43.9 | 842 | 30.7 | 12.3 | 84.7 | 7.2 | 42 532 | -1.5 | 4 928 | 11.6 | 65 455 | 70.1 | 41.3 | 21.8 |
| West Chicago | 32.8 | 867 | 29.8 | 2.8 | 85.9 | 8.0 | 15 036 | 0.9 | 1 379 | 9.2 | 18 943 | 76.6 | 45.8 | 13.2 |
| Wheaton | 26.6 | 1 136 | 29.0 | 4.8 | 84.7 | 10.5 | 29 004 | 3.4 | 1 873 | 6.5 | 42 337 | 67.3 | 40.8 | 21.0 |
| Wheeling | 33.8 | 984 | 29.2 | 6.3 | 86.8 | 9.1 | 22 943 | 2.3 | 1 676 | 7.3 | 29 819 | 72.5 | 47.0 | 19.4 |
| Wilmette | 13.3 | 1 435 | 24.5 | 4.1 | 91.9 | 5.5 | 13 146 | 3.6 | 759 | 5.8 | 20 322 | 62.1 | 39.5 | 23.4 |
| Woodridge | 32.9 | 1 046 | 26.5 | 3.8 | 87.6 | 10.5 | 19 904 | 2.9 | 1 540 | 7.7 | 26 108 | 76.3 | 48.0 | 15.4 |
| **INDIANA** | 28.9 | 704 | 29.7 | 6.4 | 84.4 | 9.7 | 3 149 743 | 0.9 | 263 993 | 8.4 | 5 035 313 | 65.2 | 39.6 | 26.8 |
| Anderson | 38.6 | 652 | 33.5 | 11.9 | 79.2 | 7.3 | 25 378 | 0.6 | 2 779 | 11.0 | 44 626 | 58.7 | 31.9 | 39.0 |
| Bloomington | 66.4 | 743 | 49.2 | 12.4 | 52.2 | 26.8 | 39 367 | 0.3 | 2 566 | 6.5 | 71 680 | 53.2 | 20.9 | 32.6 |
| Carmel | 21.5 | 1 006 | 25.7 | 2.2 | 86.0 | 10.7 | 39 613 | 4.4 | 2 116 | 5.3 | 57 285 | 70.9 | 47.5 | 16.9 |
| Columbus | 35.6 | 764 | 27.6 | 6.0 | 80.0 | 9.9 | 22 910 | 8.6 | 1 481 | 6.5 | 33 744 | 66.8 | 42.5 | 27.1 |
| Crown Point | 21.0 | 955 | 27.5 | 3.5 | 84.7 | 12.9 | 13 239 | 1.2 | 1 086 | 8.2 | 21 484 | 62.5 | 40.8 | 23.1 |
| East Chicago | 55.2 | 687 | 35.5 | 20.5 | 81.0 | 12.2 | 9 863 | 2.5 | 1 329 | 13.5 | 20 991 | 54.0 | 30.1 | 38.1 |
| Elkhart | 45.0 | 666 | 32.5 | 11.8 | 76.1 | 10.4 | 22 805 | 3.6 | 2 660 | 11.7 | 37 468 | 66.5 | 35.4 | 29.1 |
| Evansville | 44.0 | 671 | 31.6 | 11.8 | 80.0 | 7.8 | 57 860 | 0.3 | 4 855 | 8.4 | 94 328 | 63.9 | 40.1 | 30.7 |
| Fishers | 17.0 | 1 026 | 23.3 | 1.0 | 87.5 | 9.7 | 44 242 | 3.9 | 2 246 | 5.1 | 52 845 | 77.0 | 53.6 | 9.7 |
| Fort Wayne | 35.4 | 638 | 26.9 | 7.8 | 85.4 | 5.1 | 122 252 | -0.6 | 10 713 | 8.8 | 194 028 | 66.1 | 41.3 | 26.6 |
| Gary | 45.2 | 686 | 39.4 | 17.4 | 83.7 | 7.0 | 28 988 | 4.6 | 3 910 | 13.5 | 62 866 | 53.2 | 26.9 | 44.2 |
| Goshen | 34.0 | 740 | 34.0 | 9.7 | 78.6 | 11.1 | 14 301 | 2.4 | 1 290 | 9.0 | 23 654 | 64.5 | 33.7 | 27.3 |
| Greenwood | 37.0 | 795 | 27.4 | 5.2 | 82.4 | 12.6 | 27 491 | 3.0 | 1 973 | 7.2 | 38 064 | 70.4 | 46.2 | 22.4 |
| Hammond | 35.2 | 754 | 32.5 | 11.3 | 87.5 | 8.4 | 33 407 | 1.7 | 3 308 | 9.9 | 61 328 | 61.5 | 35.7 | 30.9 |
| Hobart | 25.0 | 801 | 27.9 | 4.8 | 88.6 | 8.1 | 13 990 | 1.2 | 1 408 | 10.1 | 22 690 | 65.9 | 37.7 | 26.1 |
| Indianapolis | 42.8 | 737 | 31.5 | 8.7 | 80.2 | 6.5 | 424 190 | 3.2 | 37 256 | 8.8 | 641 096 | 68.4 | 41.2 | 25.5 |
| Jeffersonville | 33.6 | 718 | 28.1 | 6.2 | 87.0 | 7.9 | 22 032 | 1.0 | 1 465 | 6.6 | 34 590 | 70.0 | 45.5 | 23.7 |
| Kokomo | 39.7 | 624 | 32.3 | 11.8 | 78.7 | 8.1 | 19 280 | 1.3 | 1 976 | 10.2 | 35 731 | 59.3 | 32.8 | 38.2 |
| Lafayette | 49.2 | 707 | 31.2 | 8.5 | 74.4 | 12.2 | 34 542 | 1.5 | 2 789 | 8.1 | 52 602 | 70.6 | 41.7 | 24.6 |
| Lawrence | 25.6 | 766 | 30.1 | 3.3 | 88.8 | 9.3 | 24 531 | 3.6 | 1 932 | 7.9 | 34 035 | 73.9 | 46.5 | 19.8 |
| Marion | 43.2 | 571 | 29.8 | 11.3 | 80.5 | 9.2 | 12 588 | -2.2 | 1 450 | 11.5 | 24 451 | 53.9 | 27.1 | 42.8 |
| Merrillville | 30.5 | 918 | 33.8 | 7.1 | 86.2 | 10.4 | 17 369 | 2.5 | 1 605 | 9.2 | 26 979 | 65.8 | 40.5 | 26.5 |
| Michigan City | 40.4 | 668 | 32.4 | 10.1 | 78.6 | 10.6 | 13 322 | 0.7 | 1 517 | 11.4 | 25 420 | 58.9 | 32.2 | 31.5 |
| Mishawaka | 47.2 | 683 | 28.4 | 8.4 | 79.0 | 14.7 | 24 412 | 0.5 | 2 402 | 9.8 | 38 217 | 67.9 | 39.0 | 26.8 |
| Muncie | 46.5 | 640 | 37.8 | 10.8 | 63.0 | 15.0 | 31 350 | 2.8 | 3 044 | 9.7 | 59 005 | 58.5 | 24.8 | 36.7 |
| New Albany | 42.7 | 682 | 28.8 | 11.0 | 80.4 | 10.9 | 17 105 | 0.1 | 1 502 | 8.8 | 28 675 | 65.1 | 40.9 | 30.8 |
| Noblesville | 25.2 | 837 | 26.3 | 3.0 | 83.3 | 11.2 | 27 296 | 2.9 | 1 818 | 6.7 | 36 817 | 75.8 | 50.9 | 13.4 |
| Plainfield | 26.6 | 866 | 24.0 | 3.2 | 80.2 | 15.9 | 13 849 | 3.1 | 994 | 7.2 | 21 222 | 61.6 | 41.8 | 23.0 |
| Portage | 29.9 | 776 | 28.9 | 2.9 | 87.1 | 8.4 | 17 957 | 1.6 | 1 675 | 9.3 | 28 249 | 63.8 | 39.2 | 27.2 |
| Richmond | 41.8 | 578 | 30.6 | 14.5 | 75.2 | 9.7 | 15 251 | -2.7 | 1 646 | 10.8 | 29 379 | 58.3 | 32.8 | 36.2 |
| Schererville | 23.9 | 784 | 26.9 | 3.8 | 90.7 | 7.1 | 15 314 | 1.5 | 1 058 | 6.9 | 23 461 | 70.5 | 46.6 | 21.7 |
| South Bend | 38.7 | 687 | 32.5 | 11.4 | 78.9 | 9.4 | 43 724 | 0.3 | 4 963 | 11.4 | 77 133 | 64.5 | 35.1 | 32.0 |
| Terre Haute | 42.4 | 613 | 32.5 | 10.5 | 81.3 | 11.2 | 26 759 | 0.8 | 2 847 | 10.6 | 49 852 | 53.9 | 28.4 | 37.0 |
| Valparaiso | 40.1 | 804 | 28.7 | 8.3 | 78.5 | 12.2 | 15 948 | 2.5 | 1 192 | 7.5 | 25 279 | 63.4 | 35.7 | 28.0 |
| Westfield | 15.6 | 803 | 24.0 | 2.5 | 87.7 | 9.4 | 15 052 | 3.8 | 806 | 5.4 | 20 350 | 77.5 | 54.8 | 10.8 |
| West Lafayette | 66.6 | 787 | 50.0 | 12.3 | 59.2 | 23.9 | 13 339 | 3.0 | 706 | 5.3 | 26 539 | 54.3 | 21.4 | 34.8 |
| **IOWA** | 27.0 | 637 | 27.6 | 5.8 | 84.3 | 9.5 | 1 638 542 | -1.0 | 85 724 | 5.2 | 2 392 818 | 68.8 | 43.8 | 25.1 |
| Ames | 57.5 | 731 | 35.2 | 7.6 | 59.8 | 22.1 | 32 195 | 0.7 | 1 158 | 3.6 | 51 017 | 68.4 | 29.7 | 19.3 |
| Ankeny | 20.7 | 728 | 25.4 | 3.0 | 82.6 | 11.6 | 26 461 | 0.8 | 928 | 3.5 | 33 127 | 78.8 | 54.9 | 14.2 |
| Bettendorf | 21.7 | 732 | 25.1 | 4.1 | 87.1 | 8.7 | 17 776 | -0.8 | 864 | 4.9 | 25 495 | 67.9 | 46.9 | 22.4 |
| Burlington | 31.1 | 588 | 30.3 | 10.2 | 82.7 | 8.9 | 12 592 | -1.3 | 850 | 6.8 | 20 364 | 62.4 | 36.9 | 33.1 |
| Cedar Falls | 35.4 | 691 | 40.1 | 5.4 | 72.8 | 16.1 | 24 342 | 1.9 | 914 | 3.8 | 33 072 | 66.9 | 33.5 | 25.3 |
| Cedar Rapids | 30.3 | 641 | 27.6 | 7.7 | 80.1 | 8.9 | 71 034 | -0.8 | 3 854 | 5.4 | 99 744 | 70.9 | 45.4 | 23.8 |
| Clinton | 31.4 | 560 | 28.8 | 10.8 | 83.6 | 6.2 | 13 629 | -4.0 | 880 | 6.5 | 21 249 | 63.9 | 38.1 | 33.0 |
| Council Bluffs | 36.2 | 711 | 30.0 | 7.3 | 79.7 | 8.3 | 30 594 | -0.7 | 1 409 | 4.6 | 48 252 | 68.9 | 44.9 | 26.2 |
| Davenport | 36.3 | 644 | 29.7 | 7.3 | 83.1 | 7.9 | 51 360 | -1.3 | 3 517 | 6.8 | 77 589 | 66.1 | 40.6 | 26.6 |
| Des Moines | 36.5 | 698 | 30.7 | 9.7 | 78.7 | 8.9 | 105 919 | -0.4 | 6 710 | 6.3 | 157 782 | 71.0 | 45.3 | 24.0 |
| Dubuque | 33.0 | 614 | 27.4 | 9.5 | 81.8 | 8.2 | 32 014 | 0.8 | 1 494 | 4.7 | 46 791 | 68.8 | 40.1 | 26.4 |
| Fort Dodge | 38.6 | 527 | 26.0 | 10.1 | 84.0 | 9.0 | 12 134 | -2.3 | 833 | 6.9 | 20 214 | 65.6 | 37.0 | 30.2 |
| Iowa City | 51.2 | 778 | 44.1 | 9.3 | 61.6 | 20.5 | 41 781 | 0.7 | 1 460 | 3.5 | 58 710 | 69.1 | 31.5 | 21.9 |
| Marion | 26.9 | 592 | 26.9 | 5.3 | 83.2 | 11.3 | 20 627 | -0.4 | 839 | 4.1 | 26 112 | 72.4 | 50.1 | 20.3 |
| Marshalltown | 30.6 | 573 | 27.9 | 9.2 | 86.1 | 5.9 | 12 959 | -2.1 | 912 | 7.0 | 20 906 | 62.4 | 39.0 | 29.6 |
| Mason City | 32.2 | 568 | 29.6 | 7.0 | 83.2 | 8.0 | 15 011 | -1.8 | 856 | 5.7 | 22 505 | 69.4 | 42.4 | 27.8 |
| Ottumwa | 28.8 | 570 | 28.9 | 9.1 | 81.6 | 6.3 | 11 988 | -1.4 | 921 | 7.7 | 19 935 | 64.2 | 37.3 | 30.5 |
| Sioux City | 35.7 | 615 | 30.2 | 8.9 | 81.8 | 7.8 | 42 803 | -1.5 | 2 266 | 5.3 | 62 954 | 69.2 | 43.1 | 25.0 |
| Urbandale | 20.2 | 783 | 24.6 | 2.7 | 86.4 | 10.5 | 23 046 | 0.6 | 896 | 3.9 | 29 449 | 77.6 | 55.3 | 15.2 |
| Waterloo | 34.4 | 625 | 31.3 | 9.2 | 79.3 | 9.1 | 36 301 | 0.4 | 2 342 | 6.5 | 53 540 | 66.1 | 39.6 | 29.1 |
| West Des Moines | 36.0 | 828 | 23.8 | 2.9 | 79.0 | 16.5 | 33 418 | 0.9 | 1 275 | 3.8 | 43 745 | 76.6 | 53.5 | 17.4 |

1. $2,000 represents $2,000 or more.　2. 50.0 represents 50 percent or more.　3. Percent of civilian labor force.　4. Persons 16 years old and over.

| City | Value of residential construction authorized by building permits, 2011 | | | Wholesale trade,[1] 2007 | | | | Retail trade,[2] 2007 | | | |
|---|---|---|---|---|---|---|---|---|---|---|---|
| | New construction ($1,000) | Number of housing units | Percent single family | Number of establishments | Number of employees | Sales (mil dol) | Annual payroll (mil dol) | Number of establishments | Number of employees | Sales (mil dol) | Annual payroll (mil dol) |
| | 69 | 70 | 71 | 72 | 73 | 74 | 75 | 76 | 77 | 78 | 79 |
| ILLINOIS—Cont'd | | | | | | | | | | | |
| Waukegan | 3 461 | 22 | 72.7 | 67 | 1 398 | 1 285.6 | 76.0 | 236 | 4 515 | 1 112.9 | 139.7 |
| West Chicago | 1 180 | 7 | 100.0 | 80 | 1 592 | 946.9 | 84.1 | 93 | 1 241 | 372.0 | 35.8 |
| Wheaton | 6 114 | 14 | 100.0 | 58 | 253 | 168.7 | 17.4 | 191 | 3 068 | 603.8 | 61.6 |
| Wheeling | 492 | 3 | 100.0 | 137 | 2 218 | 1 125.9 | 127.3 | 108 | 1 271 | 334.2 | 35.6 |
| Wilmette | 15 200 | 17 | 100.0 | 28 | 75 | 102.3 | 4.2 | 129 | 1 398 | 297.8 | 38.1 |
| Woodridge | 1 492 | 5 | 100.0 | 55 | 1 904 | 1 509.1 | 115.2 | 92 | 1 702 | 428.3 | 40.9 |
| INDIANA | 1 975 556 | 12 618 | 73.9 | 6 756 | 97 219 | 67 634.9 | 4 295.6 | 23 692 | 333 172 | 78 745.6 | 7 123.1 |
| Anderson | 4 736 | 20 | 90.0 | 38 | 707 | 212.3 | 26.2 | 269 | 4 063 | 863.0 | 79.4 |
| Bloomington | NA | NA | NA | 49 | 628 | 450.6 | 27.5 | 394 | 6 324 | 1 267.8 | 122.0 |
| Carmel | 102 506 | 596 | 43.0 | 100 | 985 | 1 276.5 | 67.1 | 249 | 3 602 | 786.3 | 82.5 |
| Columbus | NA | NA | NA | 55 | 885 | 677.7 | 47.0 | 236 | 3 787 | 822.0 | 81.1 |
| Crown Point | 31 086 | 134 | 97.0 | 25 | 259 | 244.0 | 11.7 | 88 | 1 239 | 257.1 | 25.0 |
| East Chicago | 4 876 | 59 | 3.4 | 33 | 507 | 380.8 | 20.0 | 53 | 450 | 130.2 | 11.4 |
| Elkhart | 160 | 2 | 100.0 | 143 | 2 152 | 1 330.5 | 91.1 | 283 | 4 492 | 1 121.6 | 100.3 |
| Evansville | 4 857 | 46 | 95.7 | 194 | 4 327 | 2 395.3 | 230.9 | 728 | 11 399 | 2 450.3 | 245.5 |
| Fishers | 91 718 | 504 | 91.1 | 86 | 1 493 | 761.3 | 90.6 | 171 | 3 367 | 910.0 | 83.7 |
| Fort Wayne | 0 | 0 | 0.0 | 422 | 6 310 | 4 927.4 | 242.8 | 1 157 | 19 477 | 4 392.0 | 402.2 |
| Gary | 202 | 1 | 100.0 | 55 | 1 323 | 802.3 | 75.6 | 198 | 1 522 | 548.1 | 29.8 |
| Goshen | 2 599 | 15 | 100.0 | 26 | 461 | 220.4 | 17.9 | 172 | 3 175 | 737.3 | 72.5 |
| Greenwood | 33 906 | 223 | 97.3 | 41 | 742 | 456.0 | 32.5 | 310 | 5 811 | 1 216.2 | 122.9 |
| Hammond | 0 | 0 | 0.0 | 64 | 1 067 | 512.8 | 53.8 | 236 | 3 116 | 1 031.8 | 70.3 |
| Hobart | 1 480 | 6 | 100.0 | 26 | 223 | 316.1 | 10.5 | 267 | 5 547 | 1 073.4 | 99.4 |
| Indianapolis | 134 832 | 1 124 | 46.0 | 1 264 | 24 462 | 15 103.1 | 1 201.6 | 3 036 | 49 297 | 12 140.2 | 1 192.8 |
| Jeffersonville | 10 468 | 91 | 100.0 | 41 | 761 | 629.0 | 33.3 | 106 | 1 435 | 330.7 | 32.8 |
| Kokomo | 425 | 6 | 100.0 | 46 | 388 | 237.2 | 18.0 | 328 | 4 829 | 1 078.4 | 97.3 |
| Lafayette | 8 441 | 69 | 100.0 | 74 | 859 | 285.3 | 37.8 | 431 | 7 594 | 1 596.7 | 150.1 |
| Lawrence | 7 403 | 59 | 100.0 | 37 | 281 | 205.1 | 12.9 | 123 | 2 004 | 408.3 | 43.3 |
| Marion | NA | NA | NA | 27 | 249 | 95.0 | 9.7 | 203 | 2 684 | 607.0 | 55.3 |
| Merrillville | 6 934 | 109 | 15.6 | 30 | 323 | 195.8 | 15.2 | 199 | 3 869 | 1 071.2 | 90.4 |
| Michigan City | 3 060 | 21 | 100.0 | 38 | 559 | 332.9 | 22.3 | 262 | 3 721 | 730.1 | 68.0 |
| Mishawaka | 7 728 | 69 | 27.5 | 65 | 890 | 991.9 | 52.7 | 385 | 7 739 | 1 766.8 | 152.1 |
| Muncie | 5 014 | 50 | 80.0 | 63 | 801 | 320.7 | 25.3 | 379 | 5 143 | 1 044.6 | 99.6 |
| New Albany | 2 762 | 19 | 100.0 | 57 | 802 | 1 390.8 | 30.4 | 154 | 2 463 | 515.3 | 53.0 |
| Noblesville | 71 067 | 420 | 100.0 | 69 | 442 | 147.5 | 20.9 | 165 | 3 199 | 727.9 | 73.5 |
| Plainfield | 27 024 | 301 | 31.6 | 28 | 2 020 | 2 337.3 | 84.5 | 137 | 2 849 | 715.6 | 60.8 |
| Portage | 967 | 6 | 100.0 | 29 | 637 | 472.4 | 31.3 | 103 | 1 886 | 454.0 | 41.3 |
| Richmond | 2 133 | 14 | 100.0 | 43 | 427 | 248.2 | 16.5 | 220 | 3 612 | 902.5 | 76.6 |
| Schererville | 4 755 | 16 | 100.0 | 26 | 173 | 68.0 | 8.0 | 131 | 2 499 | 625.9 | 60.1 |
| South Bend | NA | NA | NA | 168 | 3 485 | 1 880.0 | 142.8 | 336 | 6 510 | 1 425.2 | 148.7 |
| Terre Haute | 13 395 | 234 | 13.2 | 83 | 1 001 | 432.7 | 36.2 | 362 | 5 627 | 1 174.3 | 112.5 |
| Valparaiso | 14 735 | 57 | 75.4 | 37 | 308 | 206.5 | 25.8 | 204 | 3 626 | 852.1 | 79.1 |
| Westfield | 67 895 | 328 | 78.0 | 29 | 433 | 180.9 | 20.2 | 100 | 2 268 | 492.6 | 47.0 |
| West Lafayette | 34 483 | 238 | 38.7 | 10 | 107 | 22.9 | 3.2 | 85 | 1 504 | 268.7 | 26.9 |
| IOWA | 1 245 724 | 7 526 | 78.1 | 4 361 | 55 874 | 41 068.3 | 2 276.7 | 13 203 | 177 156 | 39 234.6 | 3 561.1 |
| Ames | 36 100 | 414 | 14.0 | 42 | 270 | 150.6 | 12.0 | 224 | 3 950 | 836.1 | 80.0 |
| Ankeny | 112 939 | 570 | 100.0 | 56 | 1 262 | 1 118.3 | 54.9 | 122 | 2 988 | 755.5 | 65.2 |
| Bettendorf | 33 446 | 147 | 89.1 | 40 | 462 | 503.9 | 22.2 | 108 | 1 586 | 306.9 | 34.2 |
| Burlington | 1 576 | 7 | 100.0 | 24 | 308 | 331.5 | 10.2 | 121 | 1 633 | 261.0 | 29.8 |
| Cedar Falls | 37 956 | 244 | 75.4 | 42 | 776 | 416.1 | 29.4 | 161 | 2 767 | 611.0 | 57.3 |
| Cedar Rapids | 27 864 | 326 | 76.4 | 211 | 3 637 | 1 974.4 | 173.6 | 562 | 11 148 | 2 774.6 | 236.6 |
| Clinton | 2 118 | 12 | 83.3 | 25 | 177 | 66.2 | 5.7 | 142 | 2 145 | 470.9 | 42.5 |
| Council Bluffs | 20 151 | 100 | 100.0 | 59 | 1 115 | 1 984.8 | 50.9 | 253 | 5 378 | 1 294.8 | 106.1 |
| Davenport | 28 426 | 155 | 80.6 | 184 | 2 949 | 2 268.3 | 128.2 | 523 | 9 471 | 2 168.1 | 200.0 |
| Des Moines | 31 036 | 224 | 51.3 | 278 | 4 779 | 2 667.7 | 221.4 | 718 | 10 528 | 2 240.8 | 229.1 |
| Dubuque | 20 406 | 226 | 49.6 | 85 | 1 156 | 1 079.9 | 46.0 | 355 | 5 778 | 1 156.7 | 110.8 |
| Fort Dodge | 840 | 6 | 100.0 | 43 | 429 | 189.7 | 19.6 | 164 | 2 555 | 531.7 | 49.4 |
| Iowa City | 43 296 | 225 | 56.0 | 32 | 507 | 208.4 | 18.9 | 276 | 4 064 | 889.5 | 88.7 |
| Marion | 20 299 | 201 | 63.7 | 29 | 346 | 242.1 | 15.1 | 116 | 1 714 | 384.2 | 38.0 |
| Marshalltown | 2 663 | 12 | 83.3 | 23 | 289 | 186.7 | 13.5 | 145 | 1 984 | 373.0 | 39.1 |
| Mason City | 2 594 | 16 | 75.0 | 49 | 497 | 323.8 | 19.6 | 192 | 3 470 | 719.0 | 67.3 |
| Ottumwa | 723 | 6 | 100.0 | 21 | 223 | 123.4 | 7.8 | 140 | 2 323 | 458.8 | 43.3 |
| Sioux City | 8 256 | 43 | 67.4 | 137 | 2 298 | 1 492.6 | 97.6 | 418 | 7 017 | 1 425.6 | 136.0 |
| Urbandale | 46 689 | 182 | 100.0 | 103 | 1 440 | 817.5 | 72.1 | 164 | 2 938 | 961.1 | 93.5 |
| Waterloo | 6 983 | 61 | 93.4 | 82 | 1 411 | 641.8 | 51.6 | 320 | 5 346 | 1 134.5 | 108.0 |
| West Des Moines | 61 614 | 309 | 80.6 | 47 | 589 | 275.1 | 28.5 | 408 | 8 702 | 1 228.5 | 144.6 |

1. Merchant wholesalers except manufacturers' sales branches and offices.    2. Establishments with payroll.

# Table D. Cities — **Real Estate, Professional Services, and Manufacturing**

| City | Real estate and rental and leasing, 2007 | | | | Professional, scientific, and technical services,[1] 2007 | | | | Manufacturing, 2007 | | | |
|---|---|---|---|---|---|---|---|---|---|---|---|---|
| | Number of establish-ments | Number of employees | Receipts (mil dol) | Annual payroll (mil dol) | Number of establish-ments | Number of employees | Receipts (mil dol) | Annual payroll (mil dol) | Number of establish-ments | Number of employees | Receipts (mil dol) | Annual payroll (mil dol) |
| | 80 | 81 | 82 | 83 | 84 | 85 | 86 | 87 | 88 | 89 | 90 | 91 |
| ILLINOIS—Cont'd | | | | | | | | | | | | |
| Waukegan | 55 | 304 | 53.8 | 8.6 | 158 | D | D | D | 86 | 5 521 | 1 601.4 | 287.8 |
| West Chicago | 32 | 226 | 52.2 | 10.4 | 82 | D | D | D | 107 | 5 323 | 2 130.7 | 224.2 |
| Wheaton | 67 | 306 | 46.2 | 11.3 | 401 | D | D | D | NA | NA | NA | NA |
| Wheeling | 34 | 119 | 60.0 | 4.7 | 126 | 966 | 125.9 | 58.8 | 166 | 9 448 | 2 714.0 | 421.2 |
| Wilmette | 64 | 297 | 72.9 | 11.8 | 182 | 415 | 74.5 | 27.4 | NA | NA | NA | NA |
| Woodridge | 33 | 273 | 36.6 | 9.1 | 89 | 875 | 211.6 | 68.0 | 32 | 1 682 | 365.4 | 71.9 |
| INDIANA | 6 389 | 34 272 | 5 448.1 | 1 061.6 | 12 959 | 95 701 | 12 128.9 | 4 785.9 | 9 015 | 536 907 | 221 877.8 | 24 474.7 |
| Anderson | 64 | 276 | 41.4 | 6.4 | 123 | D | D | D | 56 | 1 984 | D | 77.5 |
| Bloomington | 145 | 854 | 113.8 | 20.9 | 222 | D | D | D | 52 | D | D | 85.7 |
| Carmel | 141 | 2 014 | 385.4 | 102.8 | 442 | 3 251 | 501.2 | 197.6 | 51 | 783 | 459.4 | 31.5 |
| Columbus | 63 | 244 | 36.2 | 7.6 | 133 | D | D | D | 103 | 10 953 | 4 714.6 | 475.1 |
| Crown Point | 32 | 101 | 17.6 | 2.7 | 84 | D | D | D | 35 | 948 | 221.2 | 35.4 |
| East Chicago | 13 | 106 | 27.2 | 5.5 | 18 | 116 | 9.7 | 3.2 | 51 | 9 604 | 6 191.5 | 568.5 |
| Elkhart | 76 | 391 | 68.9 | 11.5 | 135 | D | D | D | 323 | 18 896 | 4 281.5 | 696.3 |
| Evansville | 171 | 1 105 | 153.9 | 28.0 | 358 | D | D | D | 184 | 10 577 | 5 534.5 | 454.6 |
| Fishers | 82 | 343 | 94.4 | 11.3 | 242 | 1 457 | 206.9 | 65.9 | 24 | 659 | 138.2 | 30.4 |
| Fort Wayne | 340 | 1 736 | 288.4 | 48.7 | 751 | 6 416 | 676.9 | 320.1 | 413 | 19 604 | D | 927.7 |
| Gary | 51 | 326 | 40.2 | 7.1 | 55 | D | D | D | 37 | 5 998 | D | 336.6 |
| Goshen | 42 | 166 | 20.4 | 4.3 | 74 | D | D | D | 116 | 13 960 | 3 666.5 | 587.1 |
| Greenwood | 84 | 370 | 69.6 | 9.6 | 129 | 791 | 66.6 | 23.8 | 45 | D | D | D |
| Hammond | 56 | 376 | 42.9 | 11.8 | 105 | D | D | D | 76 | 3 563 | 1 779.6 | 193.8 |
| Hobart | 28 | 131 | 24.8 | 3.6 | 48 | D | D | D | 22 | 546 | 87.3 | 17.8 |
| Indianapolis | 1 236 | 10 076 | 1 891.2 | 381.8 | 2 671 | D | D | D | 928 | 48 817 | 21 317.5 | 2 715.6 |
| Jeffersonville | 47 | 345 | 53.6 | 9.4 | 95 | 450 | 51.4 | 17.1 | 89 | 5 104 | 1 364.8 | 213.1 |
| Kokomo | 73 | 296 | 44.6 | 7.0 | 109 | D | D | D | 63 | 11 686 | D | 865.5 |
| Lafayette | 125 | 730 | 138.0 | 25.7 | 181 | D | D | D | 83 | 8 459 | 5 253.9 | 390.9 |
| Lawrence | 30 | 182 | 23.3 | 5.2 | 83 | D | D | D | NA | NA | NA | NA |
| Marion | 37 | 146 | 18.2 | 3.3 | 62 | D | D | D | 46 | 3 349 | 1 171.8 | 213.1 |
| Merrillville | 73 | 560 | 73.8 | 15.7 | 185 | 1 476 | 137.0 | 58.5 | 33 | 660 | 122.0 | 27.3 |
| Michigan City | 39 | 185 | 32.8 | 3.8 | 63 | 380 | 38.0 | 13.5 | 60 | 3 439 | 1 107.2 | 143.5 |
| Mishawaka | 67 | 465 | 79.9 | 13.7 | 106 | 873 | 73.7 | 29.3 | 106 | 3 665 | 1 542.7 | 156.5 |
| Muncie | 87 | 383 | 63.5 | 9.9 | 118 | D | D | D | 84 | 3 684 | 950.3 | 171.8 |
| New Albany | 52 | 254 | 27.3 | 5.3 | 115 | D | D | D | 89 | D | D | 227.0 |
| Noblesville | 59 | 190 | 28.4 | 4.7 | 151 | D | D | D | 55 | 2 173 | 568.1 | 85.0 |
| Plainfield | 27 | 105 | 14.8 | 2.2 | 42 | 648 | 60.3 | 25.3 | 24 | 580 | 125.1 | D |
| Portage | 37 | 221 | 31.4 | 5.8 | 47 | 331 | 43.2 | 13.0 | 23 | 1 874 | D | 113.2 |
| Richmond | 47 | 241 | 26.5 | 6.1 | 64 | 333 | 27.9 | 10.7 | 93 | 5 978 | 2 178.1 | 233.2 |
| Schererville | 40 | 167 | 35.4 | 4.0 | 85 | D | D | D | 20 | 729 | 201.3 | 37.2 |
| South Bend | 104 | 740 | 99.5 | 22.4 | 305 | D | D | D | 186 | 7 811 | 2 210.1 | 353.3 |
| Terre Haute | 78 | 498 | 60.1 | 14.5 | 171 | 1 067 | 99.1 | 33.5 | 85 | 6 902 | D | 309.9 |
| Valparaiso | 67 | 348 | 39.8 | 7.8 | 129 | 898 | 96.1 | 34.6 | 55 | 2 053 | 1 004.8 | 108.9 |
| Westfield | 26 | 81 | 12.7 | 2.1 | 67 | D | D | D | 28 | 1 547 | 267.5 | 59.6 |
| West Lafayette | 45 | 284 | 35.8 | 7.1 | 64 | D | D | D | NA | NA | NA | NA |
| IOWA | 2 969 | 14 667 | 2 556.0 | 473.0 | 6 181 | 42 118 | 5 015.6 | 1 883.8 | 3 802 | 223 049 | 97 592.1 | 9 525.7 |
| Ames | 71 | 290 | 29.5 | 7.5 | 127 | 744 | 65.5 | 31.6 | 40 | 2 586 | 1 418.7 | 140.2 |
| Ankeny | 60 | 174 | 36.4 | 5.3 | 81 | 472 | 46.2 | 21.1 | 28 | 2 392 | 1 178.1 | 135.0 |
| Bettendorf | 45 | 175 | 46.0 | 4.9 | 94 | D | D | D | 29 | 3 255 | 1 350.6 | 180.6 |
| Burlington | 28 | 593 | 94.2 | 22.8 | 41 | 266 | 23.9 | 11.2 | 36 | D | 920.8 | D |
| Cedar Falls | 48 | 199 | 51.5 | 6.5 | 93 | 1 446 | 107.7 | 90.3 | 41 | 1 254 | D | 47.5 |
| Cedar Rapids | 179 | 1 488 | 330.4 | 86.6 | 374 | 3 720 | 474.6 | 203.5 | 144 | 15 137 | 6 894.3 | 1 004.4 |
| Clinton | 34 | 104 | 16.2 | 3.0 | 50 | 318 | 26.9 | 11.9 | 28 | 3 097 | 3 532.8 | 149.0 |
| Council Bluffs | 79 | 384 | 62.7 | 9.7 | 114 | D | D | D | 46 | 4 342 | D | 156.9 |
| Davenport | 123 | 1 577 | 212.1 | 40.0 | 266 | D | D | D | 107 | 7 431 | 4 016.5 | 345.2 |
| Des Moines | 213 | 1 670 | 281.7 | 57.9 | 523 | D | D | D | 189 | 6 405 | 3 552.9 | 274.8 |
| Dubuque | 80 | 416 | 70.1 | 16.0 | 131 | D | D | D | 89 | 4 912 | 1 059.9 | 186.5 |
| Fort Dodge | 38 | 114 | 17.7 | 2.8 | 66 | D | D | D | 37 | 1 572 | D | 77.2 |
| Iowa City | 86 | 443 | 75.3 | 13.0 | 140 | D | D | D | 46 | 3 319 | D | 137.5 |
| Marion | 33 | 138 | 13.6 | 2.9 | 55 | 433 | 51.1 | 23.2 | 42 | 719 | 121.7 | 27.2 |
| Marshalltown | 35 | 344 | 43.2 | 10.1 | 46 | 329 | 48.9 | 11.8 | 39 | D | D | D |
| Mason City | 44 | 134 | 19.9 | 3.4 | 63 | D | D | D | 37 | 3 214 | 1 210.3 | 133.4 |
| Ottumwa | 25 | 78 | 12.8 | 2.0 | 43 | D | D | D | 21 | D | D | D |
| Sioux City | 90 | 554 | 83.7 | 14.1 | 165 | D | D | D | 82 | 4 396 | 2 288.0 | 177.8 |
| Urbandale | 52 | 197 | 32.7 | 5.6 | 176 | 1 444 | 182.6 | 80.2 | 31 | 1 411 | 556.9 | 60.1 |
| Waterloo | 92 | 481 | 61.4 | 12.2 | 124 | D | D | D | 92 | 8 328 | 4 506.4 | 396.9 |
| West Des Moines | 114 | 807 | 225.7 | 38.4 | 321 | 2 946 | 448.4 | 153.8 | 32 | 1 117 | 257.3 | 56.0 |

1. Establishments subject to federal tax.

# Table D. Cities — Accommodation and Food Services, Arts, Entertainment, and Recreation, and Health Care and Social Assistance

| City | Accommodation and food services, 2007 | | | | Arts, entertainment, and recreation,[1] 2007 | | | | Health care and social assistance,[1] 2007 | | | |
|---|---|---|---|---|---|---|---|---|---|---|---|---|
| | Number of establish-ments | Number of employees | Sales (mil dol) | Annual payroll (mil dol) | Number of establish-ments | Number of employees | Receipts (mil dol) | Annual payroll (mil dol) | Number of establish-ments | Number of employees | Receipts (mil dol) | Annual payroll (mil dol) |
| | 92 | 93 | 94 | 95 | 96 | 97 | 98 | 99 | 100 | 101 | 102 | 103 |
| ILLINOIS—Cont'd | | | | | | | | | | | | |
| Waukegan | 148 | 2 162 | 110.9 | 28.4 | 10 | 126 | 8.3 | 1.9 | 105 | 2 413 | 282.4 | 103.8 |
| West Chicago | 58 | 736 | 31.5 | 8.7 | 6 | 73 | 5.5 | 1.8 | 21 | 361 | 23.6 | 10.1 |
| Wheaton | 106 | 1 973 | 89.0 | 26.4 | 17 | 336 | 14.6 | 5.3 | 168 | 1 721 | 152.2 | 74.7 |
| Wheeling | 68 | 1 920 | 110.9 | 36.2 | 7 | D | D | D | 62 | D | D | D |
| Wilmette | 45 | D | D | D | 21 | D | D | D | 102 | 675 | 57.9 | 25.7 |
| Woodridge | 39 | 800 | 37.4 | 10.7 | 6 | D | D | D | 79 | 461 | 44.9 | 16.4 |
| INDIANA | 12 932 | 254 293 | 11 669.8 | 3 175.2 | 1 687 | 25 762 | 2 558.3 | 769.6 | 11 919 | 181 493 | 17 014.6 | 6 813.4 |
| Anderson | 156 | 3 285 | 117.0 | 33.2 | 21 | D | D | D | 151 | D | D | D |
| Bloomington | 298 | 6 769 | 268.0 | 73.3 | 19 | 183 | 10.3 | 2.3 | 214 | 3 369 | 311.6 | 140.4 |
| Carmel | 140 | 2 845 | 134.9 | 40.3 | 36 | 368 | 17.0 | 6.3 | 276 | 5 761 | 657.7 | 235.8 |
| Columbus | 126 | 2 581 | 105.4 | 30.7 | 11 | D | D | D | 161 | 2 037 | 177.3 | 76.4 |
| Crown Point | 58 | 924 | 33.9 | 9.0 | 12 | D | D | D | 63 | 883 | 77.6 | 37.7 |
| East Chicago | 41 | D | D | D | 1 | D | D | D | 32 | 305 | 25.3 | 9.5 |
| Elkhart | 192 | 3 695 | 133.4 | 37.9 | 16 | D | D | D | 121 | 1 892 | 268.9 | 92.1 |
| Evansville | 366 | 9 033 | 426.8 | 118.6 | 35 | D | D | D | 388 | D | D | D |
| Fishers | 138 | 2 961 | 125.8 | 34.9 | 20 | D | D | D | 160 | D | D | D |
| Fort Wayne | 614 | 14 155 | 506.1 | 156.1 | 78 | D | D | D | 750 | 17 070 | 1 801.5 | 707.4 |
| Gary | 105 | 1 744 | 168.4 | 31.1 | 9 | D | D | D | 94 | 1 519 | 92.6 | 39.9 |
| Goshen | 91 | 2 019 | 71.4 | 19.4 | 6 | D | D | D | 71 | 935 | 84.5 | 35.7 |
| Greenwood | 148 | 3 414 | 134.2 | 41.0 | 19 | 317 | 11.7 | 4.0 | 111 | D | D | D |
| Hammond | 156 | D | D | D | 6 | D | D | D | 67 | D | D | D |
| Hobart | 92 | D | D | D | 8 | 135 | 3.7 | 1.2 | 53 | D | D | D |
| Indianapolis | 1 957 | 43 393 | 2 138.2 | 632.9 | 248 | D | D | D | 1 865 | 31 197 | 3 338.9 | 1 377.5 |
| Jeffersonville | 75 | 1 643 | 66.1 | 20.2 | 7 | D | D | D | 108 | 1 544 | 167.7 | 70.5 |
| Kokomo | 165 | 3 728 | 143.5 | 42.3 | 13 | D | D | D | 168 | D | D | D |
| Lafayette | 223 | 5 259 | 194.9 | 60.2 | 17 | 228 | 7.4 | 2.3 | 187 | 3 658 | 441.0 | 178.9 |
| Lawrence | 85 | 1 332 | 57.3 | 15.9 | 19 | D | D | D | 40 | D | D | D |
| Marion | 98 | 1 924 | 68.6 | 18.9 | 10 | D | D | D | 116 | D | D | D |
| Merrillville | 127 | 3 190 | 141.2 | 38.9 | 10 | 275 | 9.9 | 2.8 | 240 | D | D | D |
| Michigan City | 104 | 3 383 | 313.9 | 60.6 | 4 | D | D | D | 78 | D | D | D |
| Mishawaka | 181 | 4 692 | 179.5 | 53.3 | 20 | D | D | D | 130 | D | D | D |
| Muncie | 170 | 4 336 | 139.9 | 42.0 | 22 | D | D | D | 204 | 4 250 | 391.1 | 174.2 |
| New Albany | 73 | 1 358 | 57.0 | 15.9 | 10 | D | D | D | 140 | 2 025 | 161.4 | 66.7 |
| Noblesville | 96 | 1 830 | 75.5 | 21.6 | 20 | D | D | D | 120 | D | D | D |
| Plainfield | 77 | 1 933 | 82.7 | 23.3 | 6 | D | D | D | 40 | D | D | D |
| Portage | 72 | 1 310 | 53.5 | 14.6 | 7 | D | D | D | 55 | 915 | 76.5 | 29.2 |
| Richmond | 100 | 2 445 | 85.2 | 25.1 | 10 | 73 | 2.2 | 0.6 | 91 | D | D | D |
| Schererville | 88 | D | D | D | 6 | 114 | 3.3 | 1.1 | 76 | D | D | D |
| South Bend | 252 | 4 667 | 188.2 | 52.4 | 16 | 163 | 31.2 | 3.6 | 246 | 4 390 | 638.2 | 228.0 |
| Terre Haute | 206 | 4 053 | 171.6 | 47.9 | 15 | 151 | 26.1 | 3.0 | 229 | D | D | D |
| Valparaiso | 113 | 2 433 | 93.8 | 26.5 | 7 | 104 | 4.6 | 1.3 | 159 | 1 955 | 208.2 | 85.5 |
| Westfield | 58 | 1 441 | 58.4 | 17.6 | 13 | D | D | D | 40 | D | D | D |
| West Lafayette | 125 | 2 508 | 97.1 | 26.5 | 6 | D | D | D | 41 | D | D | D |
| IOWA | 7 014 | 116 838 | 4 737.7 | 1 276.0 | 978 | 13 748 | 1 216.6 | 259.1 | 5 399 | 70 263 | 5 853.9 | 2 731.9 |
| Ames | 182 | 3 872 | 136.2 | 39.4 | 13 | 189 | 6.6 | 2.3 | 88 | 1 719 | 174.9 | 79.5 |
| Ankeny | 95 | 1 926 | 70.2 | 20.8 | 18 | D | D | D | 71 | 761 | 54.4 | 22.8 |
| Bettendorf | 64 | 2 150 | 153.6 | 33.1 | 11 | D | D | D | 86 | D | D | D |
| Burlington | 83 | 1 811 | 63.4 | 19.0 | 9 | D | D | D | 64 | 563 | 35.0 | 13.4 |
| Cedar Falls | 99 | 2 785 | 81.2 | 25.1 | 7 | 25 | 1.1 | 0.3 | 58 | D | D | D |
| Cedar Rapids | 382 | 7 800 | 299.1 | 86.9 | 30 | 829 | 29.0 | 9.6 | 291 | 4 089 | 463.7 | 201.1 |
| Clinton | 79 | 1 173 | 45.5 | 12.3 | 7 | D | D | D | 79 | 1 069 | 84.5 | 33.0 |
| Council Bluffs | 153 | 5 312 | 431.9 | 92.4 | 14 | D | D | D | 132 | 1 692 | 148.2 | 68.6 |
| Davenport | 296 | 6 211 | 239.8 | 70.9 | 30 | 754 | 94.3 | 14.0 | 252 | 2 797 | 309.9 | 142.8 |
| Des Moines | 497 | 8 479 | 378.1 | 110.5 | 50 | 544 | 34.0 | 9.7 | 364 | 6 110 | 788.0 | 383.9 |
| Dubuque | 193 | 3 815 | 125.2 | 37.6 | 25 | D | D | D | 134 | 2 711 | 272.8 | 141.7 |
| Fort Dodge | 70 | 1 321 | 58.7 | 14.9 | 9 | D | D | D | 75 | D | D | D |
| Iowa City | 177 | 3 671 | 125.1 | 36.0 | 11 | 314 | 6.6 | 2.0 | 140 | 1 606 | 147.3 | 60.3 |
| Marion | 44 | 815 | 28.9 | 9.1 | 5 | D | D | D | 50 | 641 | 38.1 | 15.1 |
| Marshalltown | 75 | 1 143 | 39.3 | 10.9 | 8 | D | D | D | 41 | D | D | D |
| Mason City | 96 | 1 575 | 55.4 | 15.9 | 10 | D | D | D | 64 | D | D | D |
| Ottumwa | 69 | 1 085 | 40.9 | 11.2 | 6 | D | D | D | 70 | D | D | D |
| Sioux City | 225 | 4 384 | 149.4 | 44.6 | 21 | 715 | 66.5 | 13.4 | 198 | 2 175 | 246.1 | 102.2 |
| Urbandale | 81 | 1 752 | 71.9 | 20.1 | 15 | D | D | D | 63 | 727 | 50.5 | 20.9 |
| Waterloo | 159 | 3 077 | 101.8 | 31.8 | 22 | D | D | D | 140 | 1 818 | 188.6 | 95.2 |
| West Des Moines | 185 | 4 429 | 186.5 | 58.1 | 24 | D | D | D | 212 | 2 859 | 337.4 | 160.9 |

1. Establishments subject to federal tax.

| City | Other services[1], 2007 | | | | Procurement contracts | | Selected federal funds, 2009–2010 (mil dol) Grants | | | | | | |
| | Number of establishments | Number of employees | Receipts (mil dol) | Annual payroll (mil dol) | Defense | Other | Total[2] | Medicaid and other health related | Nutrition and family welfare | Energy and environment | Disasters and emergency preparedness | Housing and community development | Employment and training |
| | 104 | 105 | 106 | 107 | 108 | 109 | 110 | 111 | 112 | 113 | 114 | 115 | 116 |
| **ILLINOIS—Cont'd** | | | | | | | | | | | | | |
| Waukegan | 100 | 500 | 43.9 | 13.0 | 235.0 | 35.0 | 28.2 | 3.1 | 5.7 | 0.8 | 0.0 | 15.4 | 0.1 |
| West Chicago | 46 | 231 | 23.1 | 6.3 | 4.4 | 0.9 | 1.7 | 0.0 | 0.0 | 0.1 | 0.0 | 0.0 | 0.0 |
| Wheaton | 95 | 682 | 35.9 | 13.6 | 0.0 | 0.0 | 45.5 | 2.1 | 0.0 | 6.2 | 0.0 | 34.9 | 0.0 |
| Wheeling | 62 | 735 | 75.3 | 20.5 | 4.5 | 3.9 | 1.0 | 0.2 | 0.0 | 0.8 | 0.0 | 0.0 | 0.0 |
| Wilmette | 56 | 381 | 31.6 | 10.3 | 0.0 | 0.4 | 0.4 | 0.2 | 0.0 | 0.0 | 0.0 | 0.2 | 0.0 |
| Woodridge | 34 | 339 | 13.9 | 10.5 | 2.6 | 0.1 | 0.0 | 0.0 | 0.0 | 0.0 | 0.0 | 0.0 | 0.0 |
| **INDIANA** | 8 961 | 56 731 | 4 531.3 | 1 397.9 | 4 369.9 | 1 128.5 | 11 964.8 | 6 228.9 | 1 304.6 | 611.2 | 24.8 | 633.7 | 226.3 |
| Anderson | 94 | 664 | 44.1 | 14.7 | 4.5 | 0.4 | 35.4 | 1.3 | 2.6 | 0.0 | 0.0 | 9.4 | 0.0 |
| Bloomington | 109 | D | D | D | 4.6 | 7.3 | 419.2 | 319.5 | 2.6 | 8.4 | 0.0 | 10.9 | 0.0 |
| Carmel | 107 | 650 | 44.6 | 15.5 | 0.4 | 24.5 | 26.1 | 3.4 | 0.0 | 22.3 | 0.0 | 0.0 | 0.0 |
| Columbus | 80 | 652 | 48.4 | 15.6 | 19.4 | 0.6 | 54.0 | 1.4 | 2.6 | 43.6 | 0.0 | 4.3 | 0.0 |
| Crown Point | 65 | 514 | 45.0 | 11.4 | 0.7 | 0.1 | 9.4 | 0.8 | 0.0 | 3.0 | 0.0 | 4.2 | 0.0 |
| East Chicago | 25 | 155 | 15.5 | 3.9 | 5.8 | 0.0 | 40.3 | 1.1 | 0.0 | 31.6 | 0.0 | 7.6 | 0.0 |
| Elkhart | 129 | 931 | 77.9 | 26.3 | 7.2 | -2.4 | 9.7 | 0.7 | 0.0 | 0.6 | 0.0 | 7.0 | 0.0 |
| Evansville | 214 | 1 736 | 131.6 | 43.8 | 128.3 | 2.4 | 42.4 | 2.7 | 5.0 | 3.1 | 0.0 | 16.2 | 0.4 |
| Fishers | 83 | 666 | 29.6 | 12.4 | 2.1 | 0.1 | 0.7 | 0.0 | 0.0 | 0.6 | 0.0 | 0.0 | 0.0 |
| Fort Wayne | 469 | 3 671 | 264.3 | 93.8 | 822.0 | 54.2 | 56.6 | 1.9 | 5.2 | 10.4 | 0.0 | 21.8 | 0.4 |
| Gary | 71 | 500 | 41.4 | 12.8 | 1.3 | 1.0 | 30.4 | 0.7 | 0.2 | 0.6 | 0.0 | 21.3 | 0.0 |
| Goshen | 60 | 434 | 33.3 | 11.8 | 7.5 | 0.1 | 4.8 | 0.0 | 0.1 | 1.8 | 0.0 | 2.4 | 0.0 |
| Greenwood | 93 | 831 | 64.3 | 21.3 | 1.0 | 0.2 | 0.3 | 0.0 | 0.0 | 0.0 | 0.0 | 0.0 | 0.0 |
| Hammond | 120 | 880 | 88.1 | 27.6 | 9.5 | 0.3 | 11.4 | 0.3 | 0.0 | 1.0 | 0.0 | 10.0 | 0.0 |
| Hobart | 48 | 296 | 16.3 | 5.9 | 0.1 | 0.0 | 0.4 | 0.0 | 0.0 | 0.0 | 0.0 | 0.0 | 0.0 |
| Indianapolis | 1 133 | 9 402 | 830.9 | 258.2 | 1 289.4 | 356.9 | 2 170.3 | 163.9 | 298.5 | 360.4 | 7.4 | 415.4 | 219.2 |
| Jeffersonville | 61 | 542 | 40.9 | 13.8 | 2.3 | 30.7 | 6.3 | 0.5 | 2.4 | 0.4 | 0.0 | 2.7 | 0.0 |
| Kokomo | 89 | D | D | D | 0.5 | 0.5 | 12.9 | 0.0 | 2.7 | 0.9 | 0.0 | 5.4 | 0.0 |
| Lafayette | 145 | D | D | D | 1.4 | 4.6 | 32.1 | 1.3 | 3.5 | 1.5 | 0.0 | 8.4 | 0.0 |
| Lawrence | 64 | 307 | 24.7 | 7.0 | 0.0 | 0.0 | 0.0 | 0.0 | 0.0 | 0.0 | 0.0 | 0.0 | 0.0 |
| Marion | 46 | 237 | 12.9 | 4.1 | 0.1 | 30.2 | 6.4 | 0.1 | 2.0 | 0.0 | 0.0 | 2.5 | 0.0 |
| Merrillville | 69 | 458 | 37.2 | 12.1 | 1.4 | 2.5 | 16.2 | 0.6 | 9.9 | 0.0 | 0.0 | 0.0 | 4.7 |
| Michigan City | 53 | 265 | 17.7 | 5.7 | 0.0 | 0.0 | 5.9 | 0.0 | 2.0 | 0.2 | 0.0 | 3.1 | 0.0 |
| Mishawaka | 106 | 672 | 46.1 | 15.9 | 240.9 | 2.3 | 3.6 | 0.4 | 0.2 | 0.0 | 0.0 | 2.6 | 0.0 |
| Muncie | 123 | 804 | 57.3 | 17.8 | 0.0 | 14.1 | 29.9 | 2.2 | 1.5 | 5.7 | 0.0 | 10.5 | 0.0 |
| New Albany | 70 | 388 | 23.3 | 7.8 | 3.4 | 1.4 | 7.2 | 0.0 | 1.8 | 0.2 | 0.0 | 5.2 | 0.0 |
| Noblesville | 80 | 421 | 27.4 | 8.4 | 0.6 | 0.3 | 4.3 | 0.0 | 0.3 | 0.0 | 0.0 | 2.0 | 0.0 |
| Plainfield | 42 | 226 | 19.7 | 5.9 | 0.9 | 40.5 | 0.0 | 0.0 | 0.0 | 0.0 | 0.0 | 0.0 | 0.0 |
| Portage | 56 | 368 | 30.8 | 9.7 | 1.4 | 0.0 | 8.4 | 2.0 | 0.0 | 0.2 | 0.0 | 0.0 | 0.1 |
| Richmond | 58 | 250 | 20.6 | 6.4 | 2.2 | 1.2 | 7.6 | 0.4 | 1.8 | 0.0 | 0.0 | 1.8 | 0.0 |
| Schererville | 65 | 539 | 45.3 | 12.9 | 0.0 | 0.0 | 0.0 | 0.0 | 0.0 | 0.0 | 0.0 | 0.0 | 0.0 |
| South Bend | 197 | 1 845 | 164.8 | 49.8 | 876.9 | 9.2 | 42.3 | 1.5 | 5.9 | 1.3 | 0.0 | 22.1 | 0.3 |
| Terre Haute | 103 | 945 | 55.7 | 18.7 | 4.3 | 48.6 | 23.3 | 1.2 | 2.3 | 1.6 | 0.0 | 8.0 | 0.0 |
| Valparaiso | 89 | 681 | 48.7 | 17.7 | 3.7 | 5.0 | 4.3 | 1.8 | 0.0 | 0.2 | 0.5 | 0.2 | 0.0 |
| Westfield | 36 | D | D | D | 0.3 | 0.1 | 0.0 | 0.0 | 0.0 | 0.0 | 0.0 | 0.0 | 0.0 |
| West Lafayette | 29 | D | D | D | 8.4 | 1.1 | 292.8 | 77.1 | 0.0 | 31.5 | 2.4 | 0.5 | 0.0 |
| **IOWA** | 4 878 | 24 331 | 1 856.5 | 544.9 | 1 556.7 | 815.9 | 6 394.4 | 2 962.1 | 661.9 | 100.1 | 245.4 | 698.1 | 92.1 |
| Ames | 67 | D | D | D | 15.0 | 59.4 | 189.0 | 38.9 | 0.4 | 21.2 | 0.4 | 2.5 | 0.0 |
| Ankeny | 68 | 481 | 38.7 | 10.5 | 1.3 | 0.1 | 7.6 | 0.1 | 0.0 | 5.1 | 0.0 | 0.0 | 0.9 |
| Bettendorf | 59 | D | D | D | 1.1 | 0.2 | 3.2 | 0.0 | 0.0 | 0.0 | 0.0 | 0.5 | 0.0 |
| Burlington | 52 | 241 | 19.8 | 4.9 | 0.7 | 0.1 | 7.0 | 0.0 | 3.3 | 0.0 | 0.0 | 2.6 | 0.0 |
| Cedar Falls | 41 | 306 | 27.2 | 8.0 | 0.2 | 0.1 | 12.8 | 0.0 | 0.2 | 1.3 | 0.0 | 1.5 | 0.0 |
| Cedar Rapids | 230 | 1 605 | 108.0 | 36.4 | 1 097.7 | 233.2 | 39.0 | 1.8 | 0.3 | 1.4 | 0.0 | 7.7 | 0.0 |
| Clinton | 54 | 281 | 13.1 | 8.5 | 0.2 | 0.0 | 7.5 | 0.3 | 0.0 | 0.0 | 0.0 | 1.8 | 0.0 |
| Council Bluffs | 101 | 505 | 37.5 | 11.0 | 0.6 | 0.8 | 15.4 | 1.4 | 0.1 | 0.6 | 0.0 | 5.7 | 0.0 |
| Davenport | 180 | 1 258 | 87.2 | 29.3 | 49.2 | 2.4 | 40.2 | 9.7 | 4.1 | 1.4 | 0.0 | 6.5 | 0.0 |
| Des Moines | 297 | 2 100 | 146.3 | 48.2 | 19.6 | 44.4 | 1 314.5 | 89.2 | 133.7 | 52.4 | 54.2 | 588.6 | 83.9 |
| Dubuque | 126 | 1 038 | 63.9 | 19.6 | 3.4 | 1.1 | 31.6 | 0.8 | 1.7 | 0.7 | 0.0 | 10.9 | 2.1 |
| Fort Dodge | 48 | D | D | D | 3.0 | 0.2 | 10.3 | 1.2 | 1.8 | 0.8 | 0.0 | 4.6 | 0.0 |
| Iowa City | 102 | 646 | 42.5 | 14.6 | 11.7 | 59.9 | 421.8 | 370.2 | 1.9 | 4.4 | 0.0 | 8.8 | 0.2 |
| Marion | 45 | 198 | 15.9 | 5.1 | 0.2 | -0.2 | 0.3 | 0.0 | 0.0 | 0.0 | 0.0 | 0.0 | 0.0 |
| Marshalltown | 50 | D | D | D | 0.0 | 1.9 | 26.2 | 0.1 | 3.5 | 0.0 | 0.0 | 2.6 | 0.0 |
| Mason City | 64 | 348 | 23.5 | 7.7 | 0.0 | 0.1 | 9.1 | 0.5 | 2.4 | 0.0 | 0.0 | 3.3 | 0.0 |
| Ottumwa | 41 | 176 | 11.8 | 3.7 | 0.2 | 1.1 | 8.1 | 1.7 | 2.0 | 0.7 | 0.0 | 1.3 | 0.0 |
| Sioux City | 133 | D | D | D | 4.3 | 4.7 | 28.1 | 2.6 | 3.1 | 1.3 | 0.0 | 10.3 | 4.5 |
| Urbandale | 64 | 407 | 33.5 | 11.0 | 0.1 | 0.9 | 0.1 | 0.0 | 0.0 | 0.0 | 0.0 | 0.0 | 0.0 |
| Waterloo | 101 | 786 | 54.9 | 18.3 | -0.1 | 21.1 | 39.3 | 4.1 | 5.0 | 1.4 | 0.0 | 10.4 | 0.2 |
| West Des Moines | 82 | 487 | 28.2 | 12.1 | 18.4 | 40.2 | 2.2 | 0.5 | 0.5 | 0.6 | 0.0 | 0.3 | 0.0 |

1. Establishments subject to federal tax.　2. Includes program categories not shown separately. State totals include additional categories not allocated by city.

# Table D. Cities — **City Government Finances**

| City | City government finances, 2007 | | | | | | | | | |
|---|---|---|---|---|---|---|---|---|---|---|
| | General revenue | | | | | | | General expenditure | | |
| | | Intergovernmental | | Taxes | | | | | Per capita[1] (dollars) | |
| | | | | | Per capita[1] (dollars) | | | | | |
| | Total (mil dol) | Total (mil dol) | Percent from state government | Total (mil dol) | Total | Property | Sales and gross receipts | Total (mil dol) | Total | Capital outlays |
| | 117 | 118 | 119 | 120 | 121 | 122 | 123 | 124 | 125 | 126 |
| ILLINOIS—Cont'd | | | | | | | | | | |
| Waukegan | 84.8 | 30.6 | 90.3 | 38.0 | 417 | 243 | 150 | 91.3 | 1 002 | 186 |
| West Chicago | 26.2 | 7.0 | 95.8 | 8.1 | 305 | 142 | 163 | 24.4 | 920 | 153 |
| Wheaton | 49.5 | 14.0 | 97.5 | 25.6 | 469 | 319 | 132 | 56.2 | 1 031 | 169 |
| Wheeling | 44.3 | 12.2 | 98.4 | 23.3 | 644 | 377 | 267 | 43.1 | 1 192 | 266 |
| Wilmette | 34.8 | 7.1 | 96.8 | 19.9 | 748 | 408 | 288 | 32.6 | 1 228 | 179 |
| Woodridge | 28.0 | 9.0 | 93.0 | 12.7 | 371 | 181 | 166 | 21.1 | 618 | 7 |
| INDIANA | X | X | X | X | X | X | X | X | X | X |
| Anderson | 68.6 | 24.7 | 38.1 | 16.2 | 283 | 267 | 15 | 85.5 | 1 492 | 276 |
| Bloomington | 76.3 | 28.9 | 65.2 | 22.6 | 313 | 303 | 10 | 62.8 | 869 | 93 |
| Carmel | 79.6 | 32.1 | 35.7 | 28.1 | 437 | 381 | 55 | 145.4 | 2 258 | 236 |
| Columbus | 50.9 | 19.7 | 61.6 | 15.2 | 383 | 375 | 8 | 57.1 | 1 435 | 151 |
| Crown Point | 14.2 | 4.9 | 75.2 | 6.6 | 278 | 237 | 41 | 14.5 | 606 | 43 |
| East Chicago | 79.5 | 18.1 | 85.4 | 44.2 | 1 465 | 1 459 | 6 | 145.7 | 4 833 | 391 |
| Elkhart | 76.4 | 34.8 | 72.0 | 25.9 | 492 | 407 | 26 | 63.0 | 1 196 | 64 |
| Evansville | 196.3 | 52.7 | 55.9 | 45.5 | 391 | 308 | 22 | 227.2 | 1 954 | 107 |
| Fishers | 45.6 | 18.3 | 33.5 | 15.0 | 227 | 153 | 75 | 77.9 | 1 178 | 128 |
| Fort Wayne | 292.7 | 44.0 | 71.1 | 123.1 | 490 | 285 | 18 | 265.0 | 1 055 | 101 |
| Gary | 156.0 | 36.3 | 97.8 | 76.1 | 789 | 774 | 14 | 157.8 | 1 637 | 101 |
| Goshen | 35.2 | 12.7 | 70.4 | 11.3 | 354 | 276 | 25 | 104.2 | 3 266 | 282 |
| Greenwood | 45.1 | 11.3 | 53.1 | 10.8 | 233 | 227 | 6 | 41.4 | 892 | 168 |
| Hammond | 128.2 | 66.4 | 86.6 | 48.1 | 623 | 522 | 23 | 144.7 | 1 875 | 138 |
| Hobart | 34.3 | 5.2 | 87.5 | 14.1 | 508 | 473 | 31 | 20.0 | 719 | 114 |
| Indianapolis | 2 229.6 | 490.8 | 83.8 | 931.1 | 1 170 | 902 | 119 | 2 369.9 | 2 979 | 832 |
| Jeffersonville | 42.5 | 12.2 | 52.8 | 11.5 | 388 | 275 | 53 | 40.9 | 1 380 | 95 |
| Kokomo | 61.0 | 18.6 | 58.3 | 22.3 | 486 | 456 | 5 | 59.8 | 1 303 | 38 |
| Lafayette | 65.2 | 19.6 | 54.5 | 23.8 | 373 | 289 | 8 | 87.0 | 1 366 | 388 |
| Lawrence | 24.1 | 9.4 | 52.4 | 11.0 | 257 | 227 | 29 | 26.5 | 619 | 43 |
| Marion | 28.3 | 10.6 | 60.7 | 11.1 | 366 | 359 | 8 | 32.1 | 1 057 | 58 |
| Merrillville | 17.8 | 6.8 | 67.5 | 7.8 | 242 | 215 | 15 | 24.5 | 763 | 52 |
| Michigan City | 49.3 | 22.2 | 87.9 | 16.7 | 524 | 356 | 24 | 14.7 | 462 | 144 |
| Mishawaka | 64.6 | 21.7 | 80.5 | 29.0 | 587 | 529 | 29 | 69.6 | 1 408 | 266 |
| Muncie | 55.3 | 19.7 | 63.4 | 21.3 | 326 | 298 | 3 | 65.9 | 1 008 | 38 |
| New Albany | 30.5 | 11.8 | 53.8 | 11.7 | 316 | 179 | 12 | 30.8 | 832 | 41 |
| Noblesville | 62.7 | 16.4 | 36.8 | 20.1 | 484 | 361 | 36 | 97.4 | 2 344 | 509 |
| Plainfield | 28.0 | 5.6 | 95.1 | 11.3 | 439 | 328 | 54 | 30.5 | 1 186 | 182 |
| Portage | 34.2 | 13.2 | 39.3 | 10.4 | 284 | 261 | 23 | 31.9 | 873 | 327 |
| Richmond | 40.4 | 14.6 | 69.2 | 12.5 | 338 | 304 | 13 | 45.4 | 1 227 | 191 |
| Schererville | 41.0 | 4.7 | 82.5 | 9.6 | 334 | 297 | 29 | 44.6 | 1 550 | 164 |
| South Bend | 150.1 | 28.3 | 100.0 | 57.3 | 551 | 523 | 28 | 135.7 | 1 304 | 142 |
| Terre Haute | 77.8 | 16.7 | 67.1 | 29.4 | 498 | 401 | 17 | 89.8 | 1 523 | 289 |
| Valparaiso | 51.0 | 10.9 | 78.4 | 10.8 | 360 | 322 | 23 | 57.5 | 1 919 | 95 |
| Westfield | 18.2 | 5.6 | 24.8 | 3.7 | 179 | 130 | 30 | 30.6 | 1 494 | 158 |
| West Lafayette | 35.5 | 8.7 | 72.8 | 9.1 | 292 | 236 | 3 | 36.7 | 1 181 | 185 |
| IOWA | X | X | X | X | X | X | X | X | X | X |
| Ames | 219.5 | 18.5 | 82.4 | 24.0 | 438 | 351 | 87 | 187.0 | 3 416 | 410 |
| Ankeny | 36.8 | 3.8 | 83.2 | 21.1 | 520 | 463 | 57 | 57.8 | 1 424 | 778 |
| Bettendorf | 42.0 | 8.2 | 65.3 | 24.3 | 748 | 543 | 205 | 40.7 | 1 255 | 298 |
| Burlington | 28.5 | 6.7 | 78.2 | 12.7 | 501 | 378 | 123 | 32.3 | 1 273 | 358 |
| Cedar Falls | 58.3 | 7.1 | 57.0 | 24.6 | 654 | 503 | 151 | 52.8 | 1 406 | 533 |
| Cedar Rapids | 221.3 | 37.9 | 34.7 | 86.3 | 683 | 607 | 76 | 184.8 | 1 462 | 253 |
| Clinton | 35.7 | 8.7 | 64.2 | 16.6 | 625 | 449 | 176 | 31.2 | 1 171 | 340 |
| Council Bluffs | 87.9 | 17.8 | 65.8 | 46.9 | 783 | 530 | 254 | 80.9 | 1 351 | 369 |
| Davenport | 130.1 | 28.2 | 67.0 | 66.1 | 668 | 560 | 107 | 137.4 | 1 388 | 315 |
| Des Moines | 353.8 | 53.5 | 38.4 | 139.6 | 708 | 578 | 130 | 360.7 | 1 831 | 449 |
| Dubuque | 92.0 | 19.2 | 39.9 | 34.3 | 598 | 364 | 235 | 85.1 | 1 485 | 391 |
| Fort Dodge | 27.5 | 6.2 | 45.0 | 13.0 | 514 | 399 | 114 | 27.7 | 1 099 | 241 |
| Iowa City | 103.5 | 20.3 | 36.3 | 44.3 | 660 | 617 | 43 | 91.7 | 1 368 | 264 |
| Marion | 23.5 | 3.0 | 92.1 | 13.9 | 431 | 399 | 32 | 25.0 | 778 | 142 |
| Marshalltown | 27.8 | 6.5 | 47.1 | 14.0 | 543 | 360 | 183 | 22.8 | 882 | 126 |
| Mason City | 34.6 | 8.6 | 39.6 | 16.3 | 591 | 405 | 186 | 36.1 | 1 314 | 426 |
| Ottumwa | 39.1 | 11.9 | 37.8 | 14.8 | 603 | 439 | 164 | 40.3 | 1 641 | 701 |
| Sioux City | 126.6 | 30.1 | 47.6 | 61.8 | 747 | 530 | 217 | 125.5 | 1 518 | 419 |
| Urbandale | 32.5 | 4.7 | 87.5 | 22.6 | 594 | 522 | 73 | 29.9 | 785 | 185 |
| Waterloo | 100.6 | 22.3 | 31.8 | 49.8 | 750 | 552 | 198 | 104.2 | 1 570 | 455 |
| West Des Moines | 83.7 | 9.5 | 61.3 | 53.2 | 971 | 899 | 72 | 66.3 | 1 212 | 232 |

1. Based on population estimated as of July 1 of the year shown.

# Table D. Cities — **City Government Finances**

| City | Public welfare | Highways | Parking facilities | Education | Health and hospitals | Police protection | Sewerage and sanitation | Parks and recreation | Housing and community development | Interest on debt |
|---|---|---|---|---|---|---|---|---|---|---|
| | 127 | 128 | 129 | 130 | 131 | 132 | 133 | 134 | 135 | 136 |
| **ILLINOIS—Cont'd** | | | | | | | | | | |
| Waukegan | 0.0 | 11.3 | 0.4 | 0.0 | 0.0 | 28.6 | 7.2 | 6.9 | 1.5 | 5.6 |
| West Chicago | 0.0 | 9.9 | 0.5 | 0.0 | 0.0 | 30.8 | 14.4 | 2.1 | 0.0 | 9.6 |
| Wheaton | 0.2 | 13.2 | 0.9 | 0.0 | 0.0 | 21.2 | 4.1 | 1.5 | 0.0 | 4.0 |
| Wheeling | 0.0 | 9.7 | 0.1 | 0.0 | 0.0 | 24.7 | 4.9 | 0.0 | 0.0 | 6.0 |
| Wilmette | 0.0 | 22.3 | 0.8 | 0.0 | 0.6 | 24.3 | 13.9 | 0.3 | 0.2 | 4.6 |
| Woodridge | 0.0 | 13.4 | 0.0 | 0.0 | 0.0 | 40.2 | 2.7 | 0.0 | 0.0 | 2.9 |
| **INDIANA** | X | X | X | X | X | X | X | X | X | X |
| Anderson | 0.2 | 5.6 | 0.1 | 0.0 | 0.7 | 12.1 | 28.9 | 4.7 | 2.4 | 3.2 |
| Bloomington | 0.0 | 7.8 | 3.0 | 0.0 | 1.6 | 13.7 | 19.4 | 11.0 | 6.8 | 7.0 |
| Carmel | 0.0 | 11.3 | 0.0 | 0.0 | 0.6 | 8.0 | 4.7 | 1.1 | 0.0 | 5.7 |
| Columbus | 0.0 | 5.6 | 0.0 | 0.0 | 0.6 | 11.8 | 11.8 | 12.2 | 1.3 | 0.1 |
| Crown Point | 0.0 | 11.3 | 0.0 | 0.0 | 0.0 | 23.6 | 0.4 | 5.4 | 0.0 | 1.8 |
| East Chicago | 0.0 | 1.9 | 0.0 | 0.0 | 3.3 | 7.2 | 22.7 | 5.2 | 0.6 | 0.5 |
| Elkhart | 0.0 | 5.2 | 2.1 | 0.0 | 0.0 | 12.9 | 11.8 | 8.2 | 1.1 | 0.8 |
| Evansville | 0.1 | 3.1 | 0.4 | 0.0 | 2.1 | 12.8 | 12.4 | 5.9 | 1.4 | 2.6 |
| Fishers | 0.0 | 5.7 | 0.0 | 0.0 | 0.0 | 10.3 | 8.4 | 2.4 | 0.1 | 3.5 |
| Fort Wayne | 0.0 | 7.2 | 0.6 | 0.0 | 0.8 | 15.5 | 21.1 | 5.2 | 3.4 | 2.6 |
| Gary | 0.8 | 2.9 | 0.0 | 0.0 | 2.3 | 14.2 | 17.9 | 12.8 | 2.9 | 1.6 |
| Goshen | 0.0 | 2.9 | 0.0 | 0.0 | 0.0 | 3.4 | 4.1 | 1.4 | 1.8 | 8.2 |
| Greenwood | 0.0 | 3.5 | 0.0 | 0.0 | 0.0 | 12.5 | 33.8 | 5.1 | 0.0 | 2.0 |
| Hammond | 0.0 | 2.6 | 0.0 | 0.0 | 0.6 | 46.3 | 3.3 | 4.0 | 2.0 | 1.3 |
| Hobart | 0.0 | 8.2 | 0.0 | 0.0 | 0.2 | 18.8 | 8.6 | 11.9 | 0.0 | 3.5 |
| Indianapolis | 4.4 | 1.7 | 0.1 | 0.0 | 26.5 | 7.1 | 5.8 | 11.6 | 3.8 | 8.6 |
| Jeffersonville | 0.0 | 3.3 | 0.0 | 0.0 | 0.3 | 7.6 | 24.6 | 3.4 | 1.2 | 2.6 |
| Kokomo | 0.4 | 10.4 | 0.0 | 0.0 | 0.0 | 21.1 | 16.3 | 4.7 | 1.5 | 2.6 |
| Lafayette | 0.0 | 14.8 | 0.3 | 0.0 | 0.0 | 0.7 | 7.4 | 6.7 | 1.0 | 7.5 |
| Lawrence | 0.0 | 11.4 | 0.0 | 0.0 | 3.3 | 19.5 | 5.5 | 3.9 | 0.0 | 3.9 |
| Marion | 0.0 | 9.8 | 0.0 | 0.0 | 0.0 | 18.0 | 11.6 | 5.0 | 0.5 | 2.4 |
| Merrillville | 0.0 | 11.1 | 0.0 | 0.0 | 3.8 | 19.0 | 0.0 | 1.2 | 12.7 | 12.0 |
| Michigan City | 0.0 | 9.4 | 0.0 | 0.0 | 0.0 | 0.2 | 0.0 | 15.2 | 0.0 | 11.4 |
| Mishawaka | 0.0 | 4.6 | 0.0 | 0.0 | 1.6 | 9.5 | 25.0 | 4.3 | 0.9 | 2.3 |
| Muncie | 0.0 | 4.9 | 0.0 | 0.0 | 0.5 | 16.1 | 34.4 | 2.2 | 2.6 | 1.2 |
| New Albany | 0.0 | 5.8 | 0.2 | 0.0 | 3.3 | 19.8 | 9.7 | 5.1 | 0.1 | 11.2 |
| Noblesville | 0.0 | 18.5 | 0.0 | 0.0 | 0.0 | 6.8 | 8.8 | 4.4 | 0.5 | 5.0 |
| Plainfield | 0.0 | 3.8 | 0.0 | 0.0 | 0.0 | 13.9 | 12.7 | 9.5 | 0.0 | 0.0 |
| Portage | 0.0 | 11.3 | 0.0 | 0.0 | 0.3 | 0.2 | 4.0 | 10.2 | 0.0 | 0.0 |
| Richmond | 0.0 | 6.5 | 0.2 | 0.0 | 1.1 | 15.3 | 23.1 | 7.8 | 0.0 | 2.0 |
| Schererville | 0.0 | 13.6 | 0.0 | 0.0 | 0.2 | 11.1 | 37.9 | 3.5 | 0.9 | 1.8 |
| South Bend | 0.0 | 1.5 | 0.4 | 0.0 | 1.2 | 19.5 | 15.9 | 3.0 | 0.1 | 2.2 |
| Terre Haute | 0.0 | 5.2 | 0.1 | 0.0 | 1.6 | 8.3 | 17.5 | 3.4 | 4.2 | 4.6 |
| Valparaiso | 0.0 | 3.3 | 0.0 | 0.0 | 0.0 | 5.3 | 12.9 | 5.6 | 0.0 | 2.5 |
| Westfield | 0.0 | 6.0 | 0.0 | 0.0 | 0.3 | 10.7 | 28.6 | 5.7 | 1.3 | 5.5 |
| West Lafayette | 0.0 | 12.2 | 0.0 | 0.0 | 0.0 | 11.6 | 34.5 | 3.1 | 5.4 | 4.6 |
| **IOWA** | X | X | X | X | X | X | X | X | X | X |
| Ames | 0.5 | 1.9 | 0.4 | 0.0 | 75.1 | 3.4 | 4.2 | 1.5 | 0.9 | 1.5 |
| Ankeny | 0.1 | 18.9 | 0.0 | 0.0 | 2.5 | 8.4 | 9.9 | 10.7 | 1.7 | 3.5 |
| Bettendorf | 0.0 | 21.7 | 0.0 | 0.0 | 0.0 | 14.1 | 12.3 | 13.7 | 1.1 | 6.5 |
| Burlington | 0.0 | 13.7 | 0.3 | 0.0 | 1.7 | 13.6 | 14.0 | 12.8 | 0.0 | 5.3 |
| Cedar Falls | 0.0 | 15.8 | 0.4 | 0.0 | 1.6 | 7.2 | 15.4 | 8.1 | 3.1 | 2.2 |
| Cedar Rapids | 0.0 | 13.1 | 1.4 | 0.0 | 0.4 | 12.8 | 19.9 | 4.2 | 4.4 | 7.0 |
| Clinton | 0.0 | 11.8 | 0.3 | 0.0 | 3.0 | 18.0 | 21.7 | 17.0 | 1.4 | 3.8 |
| Council Bluffs | 0.0 | 5.7 | 0.1 | 0.0 | 1.0 | 15.8 | 9.9 | 5.9 | 1.0 | 3.4 |
| Davenport | 0.0 | 8.6 | 0.8 | 0.0 | 0.0 | 15.9 | 10.3 | 6.3 | 4.5 | 9.4 |
| Des Moines | 0.3 | 13.4 | 2.7 | 0.0 | 0.0 | 13.5 | 15.5 | 6.6 | 5.8 | 6.1 |
| Dubuque | 0.6 | 14.3 | 2.6 | 0.0 | 1.9 | 12.3 | 11.9 | 10.6 | 6.3 | 2.3 |
| Fort Dodge | 3.1 | 7.8 | 0.3 | 0.0 | 0.2 | 10.9 | 10.4 | 7.4 | 3.5 | 4.6 |
| Iowa City | 0.0 | 7.0 | 3.4 | 0.0 | 0.6 | 10.0 | 12.0 | 6.1 | 9.9 | 9.6 |
| Marion | 0.0 | 10.6 | 0.0 | 0.0 | 0.1 | 17.6 | 11.4 | 5.4 | 2.0 | 2.2 |
| Marshalltown | 0.2 | 9.2 | 0.2 | 0.0 | 6.0 | 20.5 | 13.7 | 7.4 | 6.5 | 5.0 |
| Mason City | 1.8 | 11.3 | 0.2 | 0.0 | 3.7 | 14.4 | 14.8 | 7.4 | 0.5 | 2.5 |
| Ottumwa | 0.2 | 11.1 | 0.0 | 0.0 | 1.1 | 8.0 | 31.4 | 21.1 | 0.0 | 3.1 |
| Sioux City | 0.0 | 19.0 | 1.2 | 0.0 | 0.2 | 13.7 | 19.9 | 9.4 | 5.0 | 4.1 |
| Urbandale | 0.0 | 12.6 | 0.0 | 0.0 | 3.0 | 17.4 | 5.0 | 10.9 | 1.6 | 6.1 |
| Waterloo | 0.3 | 20.3 | 0.3 | 0.0 | 1.5 | 12.2 | 12.6 | 7.1 | 6.6 | 9.4 |
| West Des Moines | 1.5 | 9.0 | 0.0 | 0.0 | 3.6 | 11.7 | 11.6 | 5.8 | 0.9 | 8.9 |

| City | City government finances, 2007 (cont.) Debt outstanding Total (mil dol) | Per capita[1] (dollars) | Debt issued during year | City government employment, 2011 | Climate[2] Average daily temperature (degrees Fahrenheit) Mean January | Mean July | Limits January[3] | Limits July[4] | Annual precipitation (inches) | Heating degree days | Cooling degree days |
|---|---|---|---|---|---|---|---|---|---|---|---|
| | 137 | 138 | 139 | 140 | 141 | 142 | 143 | 144 | 145 | 146 | 147 |
| **ILLINOIS—Cont'd** | | | | | | | | | | | |
| Waukegan | 116.1 | 1 274 | 10.4 | 530 | 20.3 | 71.5 | 12.0 | 81.7 | 34.09 | 7 031 | 613 |
| West Chicago | 55.4 | 2 087 | 0.0 | NA | NA | NA | NA | NA | NA | NA | NA |
| Wheaton | 50.1 | 919 | 0.0 | 440 | 23.1 | 74.8 | 14.2 | 86.8 | 37.94 | 6 053 | 942 |
| Wheeling | 59.4 | 1 645 | 0.0 | 233 | 18.4 | 72.1 | 9.6 | 82.3 | 36.56 | 7 149 | 624 |
| Wilmette | 57.9 | 2 181 | 0.0 | 211 | 22.0 | 73.3 | 14.3 | 83.5 | 36.27 | 6 498 | 830 |
| Woodridge | 13.0 | 381 | 0.0 | 173 | 23.1 | 74.8 | 14.2 | 86.8 | 37.94 | 6 053 | 942 |
| **INDIANA** | X | X | X | X | X | X | X | X | X | X | X |
| Anderson | 70.6 | 1 233 | 0.0 | 705 | 25.7 | 74.0 | 18.4 | 83.8 | 39.82 | 5 807 | 872 |
| Bloomington | 116.6 | 1 614 | 16.6 | 806 | 27.9 | 75.4 | 19.3 | 86.0 | 44.91 | 5 348 | 1 017 |
| Carmel | 338.8 | 5 261 | 157.2 | 460 | 25.3 | 74.2 | 17.0 | 84.5 | 42.85 | 5 901 | 873 |
| Columbus | 4.5 | 112 | 1.0 | 482 | 27.9 | 75.9 | 19.1 | 86.4 | 41.94 | 5 367 | 1 059 |
| Crown Point | 17.5 | 734 | 4.7 | 178 | NA | NA | NA | NA | NA | NA | NA |
| East Chicago | 61.5 | 2 041 | 33.2 | 689 | 23.7 | 74.0 | 15.3 | 84.8 | 38.13 | 6 055 | 887 |
| Elkhart | 20.5 | 390 | 6.1 | 597 | 22.8 | 72.1 | 14.3 | 83.3 | 38.56 | 6 487 | 663 |
| Evansville | 191.4 | 1 646 | 6.3 | 1 286 | 33.2 | 79.6 | 24.8 | 90.5 | 45.76 | 4 140 | 1 616 |
| Fishers | 65.0 | 984 | 13.2 | 360 | 25.3 | 74.2 | 17.0 | 84.5 | 42.85 | 5 901 | 873 |
| Fort Wayne | 298.6 | 1 189 | 69.7 | 1 968 | 23.6 | 73.4 | 16.1 | 84.3 | 36.55 | 6 205 | 830 |
| Gary | 84.4 | 876 | 9.6 | 1 134 | 22.2 | 73.5 | 13.9 | 83.9 | 38.02 | 6 497 | 776 |
| Goshen | 268.9 | 8 432 | 3.4 | 244 | 24.3 | 73.7 | 17.0 | 84.5 | 36.59 | 6 075 | 826 |
| Greenwood | 22.7 | 488 | 1.5 | 284 | 25.7 | 74.7 | 18.0 | 84.0 | 40.24 | 5 783 | 942 |
| Hammond | 50.6 | 655 | 14.2 | 856 | 22.2 | 73.5 | 13.9 | 83.9 | 38.02 | 6 497 | 776 |
| Hobart | 11.9 | 428 | 12.0 | 265 | 22.2 | 73.5 | 13.9 | 83.9 | 38.02 | 6 497 | 776 |
| Indianapolis | 4 518.8 | 5 681 | 652.8 | 12 433 | 26.5 | 75.4 | 18.5 | 85.6 | 40.95 | 5 521 | 1 042 |
| Jeffersonville | 27.8 | 939 | 1.6 | 270 | 31.3 | 75.8 | 21.4 | 88.5 | 45.47 | 4 829 | 1 079 |
| Kokomo | 42.2 | 919 | 0.3 | 476 | 22.8 | 73.0 | 15.0 | 84.1 | 41.54 | 6 368 | 771 |
| Lafayette | 186.4 | 2 927 | 56.9 | 755 | 23.0 | 73.5 | 14.3 | 84.5 | 36.90 | 6 206 | 842 |
| Lawrence | 21.9 | 511 | 9.6 | 306 | 25.7 | 74.7 | 18.0 | 84.0 | 40.24 | 5 783 | 942 |
| Marion | 20.3 | 667 | 0.0 | 252 | 24.2 | 73.8 | 16.3 | 84.5 | 39.01 | 6 143 | 819 |
| Merrillville | 70.1 | 2 180 | 0.0 | 128 | 21.1 | 72.7 | 12.1 | 83.6 | 40.04 | 6 642 | 734 |
| Michigan City | 34.2 | 1 073 | 0.0 | 370 | 23.4 | 73.0 | 15.7 | 83.1 | 39.70 | 6 294 | 812 |
| Mishawaka | 97.2 | 1 967 | 10.0 | 501 | 24.3 | 73.7 | 17.0 | 84.5 | 36.59 | 6 075 | 826 |
| Muncie | 25.4 | 388 | 6.2 | 500 | 24.4 | 72.5 | 15.9 | 83.9 | 41.23 | 6 215 | 717 |
| New Albany | 74.6 | 2 014 | 12.1 | 266 | 31.3 | 75.8 | 21.4 | 88.5 | 45.47 | 4 829 | 1 079 |
| Noblesville | 162.4 | 3 909 | 80.6 | 381 | 25.3 | 74.2 | 17.0 | 84.5 | 42.85 | 5 901 | 873 |
| Plainfield | 0.0 | 0 | 0.0 | 235 | NA | NA | NA | NA | NA | NA | NA |
| Portage | 0.0 | 0 | 0.0 | 256 | 22.9 | 73.0 | 15.5 | 83.1 | 40.06 | 6 270 | 745 |
| Richmond | 25.1 | 679 | 4.0 | 520 | 25.7 | 73.1 | 17.2 | 84.6 | 39.55 | 5 942 | 769 |
| Schererville | 21.7 | 752 | 0.0 | 183 | NA | NA | NA | NA | NA | NA | NA |
| South Bend | 174.3 | 1 675 | 22.2 | 1 298 | 23.4 | 73.0 | 15.7 | 83.1 | 39.70 | 6 294 | 812 |
| Terre Haute | 74.2 | 1 259 | 0.0 | 576 | 26.5 | 76.2 | 17.7 | 87.3 | 42.47 | 5 433 | 1 107 |
| Valparaiso | 44.7 | 1 494 | 16.3 | 290 | 22.9 | 73.0 | 15.5 | 83.1 | 40.06 | 6 270 | 745 |
| Westfield | 45.3 | 2 213 | 7.2 | 177 | NA | NA | NA | NA | NA | NA | NA |
| West Lafayette | 45.2 | 1 453 | 0.8 | 222 | 25.2 | 75.5 | 17.2 | 86.3 | 36.32 | 5 732 | 1 024 |
| **IOWA** | X | X | X | X | X | X | X | X | X | X | X |
| Ames | 61.4 | 1 121 | 5.3 | 654 | 18.5 | 73.8 | 9.6 | 84.3 | 34.07 | 6 791 | 830 |
| Ankeny | 110.9 | 2 732 | 17.4 | 247 | 18.2 | 74.8 | 8.7 | 85.8 | 33.38 | 6 961 | 881 |
| Bettendorf | 60.7 | 1 870 | 14.6 | 250 | 21.1 | 76.2 | 13.2 | 85.4 | 34.11 | 6 246 | 1 072 |
| Burlington | 44.3 | 1 744 | 11.0 | 233 | 22.8 | 76.3 | 15.1 | 85.4 | 37.94 | 5 948 | 1 095 |
| Cedar Falls | 67.7 | 1 802 | 0.0 | 448 | 16.1 | 73.6 | 6.3 | 85.0 | 33.15 | 7 348 | 758 |
| Cedar Rapids | 337.6 | 2 671 | 87.9 | 1 292 | 19.9 | 74.8 | 11.5 | 85.3 | 36.62 | 6 488 | 910 |
| Clinton | 23.8 | 895 | 2.3 | 230 | 20.4 | 74.7 | 12.5 | 85.0 | 35.68 | 6 416 | 915 |
| Council Bluffs | 95.4 | 1 592 | 14.1 | 471 | 21.1 | 76.2 | 10.4 | 87.7 | 33.25 | 6 323 | 1 057 |
| Davenport | 248.6 | 2 512 | 25.7 | 905 | 21.1 | 76.2 | 13.2 | 85.4 | 34.11 | 6 246 | 1 072 |
| Des Moines | 613.7 | 3 115 | 226.5 | 2 011 | 20.4 | 76.1 | 11.7 | 86.0 | 34.72 | 6 436 | 1 052 |
| Dubuque | 39.9 | 696 | 0.7 | 633 | 17.8 | 75.1 | 8.7 | 85.4 | 33.96 | 6 891 | 908 |
| Fort Dodge | 39.8 | 1 576 | 3.2 | 189 | 15.4 | 73.1 | 5.8 | 84.3 | 34.39 | 7 513 | 746 |
| Iowa City | 215.9 | 3 219 | 12.2 | 810 | 21.7 | 76.9 | 13.4 | 87.5 | 37.27 | 6 052 | 1 134 |
| Marion | 11.5 | 357 | 0.3 | 184 | 16.8 | 73.9 | 7.1 | 84.4 | 36.40 | 7 191 | 787 |
| Marshalltown | 26.4 | 1 022 | 0.0 | 212 | 16.8 | 73.9 | 7.1 | 84.4 | 36.40 | 7 191 | 787 |
| Mason City | 35.4 | 1 287 | 6.3 | 295 | 13.9 | 72.4 | 5.1 | 83.3 | 34.48 | 7 765 | 655 |
| Ottumwa | 30.9 | 1 261 | 7.5 | 243 | NA | NA | NA | NA | NA | NA | NA |
| Sioux City | 136.7 | 1 653 | 20.1 | 801 | 18.6 | 74.6 | 8.5 | 86.2 | 25.99 | 6 900 | 914 |
| Urbandale | 46.6 | 1 224 | 6.4 | 216 | 20.4 | 76.1 | 11.7 | 86.0 | 34.72 | 6 436 | 1 052 |
| Waterloo | 127.0 | 1 913 | 27.7 | 578 | 16.1 | 73.6 | 6.3 | 85.0 | 33.15 | 7 348 | 758 |
| West Des Moines | 160.5 | 2 934 | 4.1 | 432 | 20.4 | 76.1 | 11.7 | 86.0 | 34.72 | 6 436 | 1 052 |

1. Based on the population estimated as of July 1 of the year shown. 2. Represents normal values based on the 30-year period, 1971–2000. 3. Average daily minimum. 4. Average daily maximum.

# Table D. Cities — Land Area and Population

| STATE Place code | City | Land area,[1] 2010 (sq km) | Population, 2012 Total persons | Rank | Per square kilometer | Race alone or in combination, not of Hispanic origin (percent), 2010 — White | Black | American Indian, Alaska Native | Asian | Hawaiian Pacific Islander | Percent Hispanic or Latino[2], 2010 | Percent Foreign born 2007–2011 |
|---|---|---|---|---|---|---|---|---|---|---|---|---|
| | | 1 | 2 | 3 | 4 | 5 | 6 | 7 | 8 | 9 | 10 | 11 |
| 20 00000 | KANSAS | 211 754.1 | 2 885 905 | X | 13.6 | 80.3 | 6.7 | 1.7 | 2.9 | 0.1 | 10.5 | 6.5 |
| 20 18250 | Dodge City | 37.4 | 28 075 | 1 288 | 750.7 | 38.2 | 2.6 | 0.7 | 1.8 | 0.2 | 57.5 | 28.5 |
| 20 25325 | Garden City | 22.8 | 26 985 | 1 344 | 1 183.6 | 44.0 | 2.9 | 0.7 | 4.5 | 0.1 | 48.6 | 20.9 |
| 20 33625 | Hutchinson | 58.8 | 41 962 | 869 | 713.6 | 84.0 | 5.4 | 1.3 | 0.8 | 0.0 | 10.6 | 2.7 |
| 20 36000 | Kansas City | 323.3 | 147 268 | 166 | 455.5 | 42.1 | 27.9 | 1.4 | 2.9 | 0.2 | 27.8 | 15.0 |
| 20 38900 | Lawrence | 86.9 | 89 512 | 338 | 1 030.1 | 82.0 | 6.0 | 4.1 | 5.5 | 0.2 | 5.7 | 7.9 |
| 20 39000 | Leavenworth | 62.3 | 35 816 | 1 021 | 574.9 | 73.8 | 16.8 | 1.7 | 2.8 | 0.5 | 8.1 | 4.4 |
| 20 39075 | Leawood | 39.0 | 32 539 | 1 119 | 834.3 | 91.8 | 2.2 | 0.4 | 4.5 | 0.1 | 2.2 | 5.2 |
| 20 39350 | Lenexa | 88.3 | 49 398 | 744 | 559.4 | 82.4 | 6.6 | 0.9 | 4.5 | 0.2 | 7.3 | 8.8 |
| 20 44250 | Manhattan | 48.6 | 56 069 | 640 | 1 153.7 | 82.8 | 6.6 | 1.1 | 6.2 | 0.3 | 5.8 | 7.8 |
| 20 52575 | Olathe | 154.5 | 130 045 | 193 | 841.7 | 79.8 | 6.3 | 0.9 | 4.8 | 0.1 | 10.2 | 9.7 |
| 20 53775 | Overland Park | 193.8 | 178 919 | 133 | 923.2 | 82.5 | 5.0 | 0.8 | 7.0 | 0.1 | 6.3 | 9.4 |
| 20 62700 | Salina | 65.0 | 48 045 | 771 | 739.2 | 82.7 | 5.1 | 1.1 | 2.9 | 0.1 | 10.7 | 5.9 |
| 20 64500 | Shawnee | 108.4 | 63 622 | 538 | 586.9 | 83.6 | 6.1 | 0.9 | 3.8 | 0.2 | 7.5 | 8.0 |
| 20 71000 | Topeka | 155.8 | 127 939 | 198 | 821.2 | 72.9 | 13.0 | 2.4 | 1.8 | 0.1 | 13.4 | 5.5 |
| 20 79000 | Wichita | 412.6 | 385 577 | 49 | 934.5 | 67.3 | 12.8 | 2.1 | 5.5 | 0.2 | 15.3 | 9.5 |
| 21 00000 | KENTUCKY | 102 269.1 | 4 380 415 | X | 42.8 | 87.7 | 8.5 | 0.6 | 1.4 | 0.1 | 3.1 | 3.1 |
| 21 08902 | Bowling Green | 97.9 | 60 600 | 578 | 619.0 | 74.9 | 15.1 | 0.6 | 4.6 | 0.2 | 6.5 | 10.9 |
| 21 17848 | Covington | 34.2 | 40 713 | 890 | 1 190.4 | 83.4 | 13.8 | 0.9 | 0.7 | 0.2 | 3.6 | 2.6 |
| 21 24274 | Elizabethtown | 65.7 | 29 335 | 1 242 | 446.5 | 80.8 | 13.2 | 0.9 | 3.5 | 0.4 | 4.3 | 4.8 |
| 21 27982 | Florence | 26.7 | 31 088 | 1 172 | 1 164.3 | 86.4 | 5.5 | 0.6 | 3.5 | 0.2 | 5.5 | 6.1 |
| 21 28900 | Frankfort | 37.1 | 27 590 | 1 315 | 743.7 | 78.0 | 18.3 | 0.8 | 1.6 | 0.1 | 3.8 | 3.5 |
| 21 30700 | Georgetown | 41.0 | 30 271 | 1 207 | 738.3 | 87.1 | 8.1 | 0.5 | 1.5 | 0.1 | 4.3 | 2.9 |
| 21 35866 | Henderson | 39.6 | 28 911 | 1 261 | 730.1 | 85.2 | 13.0 | 0.5 | 0.7 | 0.1 | 2.3 | 1.3 |
| 21 37918 | Hopkinsville | 79.4 | 32 966 | 1 104 | 415.2 | 62.9 | 33.2 | 0.8 | 1.4 | 0.3 | 3.5 | 3.0 |
| 21 40222 | Jeffersontown | 25.7 | 26 923 | 1 350 | 1 047.6 | 81.7 | 12.3 | 0.6 | 2.2 | 0.2 | 5.0 | 8.8 |
| 21 46027 | Lexington-Fayette | 734.7 | 305 489 | 62 | 415.8 | 74.9 | 15.6 | 0.6 | 3.8 | 0.1 | 6.9 | 8.5 |
| 21 48003 | Louisville/Jefferson County | 985.3 | 605 110 | 27 | 718.3 | 72.2 | 21.8 | 0.7 | 2.6 | 0.1 | 4.4 | 6.0 |
| 21 56136 | Nicholasville | 33.7 | 28 400 | 1 278 | 842.7 | 91.3 | 5.4 | 0.8 | 0.9 | 0.1 | 3.5 | 2.6 |
| 21 58620 | Owensboro | 49.5 | 58 083 | 610 | 1 173.4 | 88.2 | 9.0 | 0.4 | 1.1 | 0.1 | 3.2 | 2.5 |
| 21 58836 | Paducah | 51.5 | 25 048 | 1 443 | 486.4 | 72.3 | 25.7 | 0.9 | 1.2 | 0.1 | 2.7 | 2.3 |
| 21 65226 | Richmond | 59.1 | 32 112 | 1 134 | 543.4 | 87.6 | 9.3 | 0.9 | 1.6 | 0.1 | 2.7 | 3.0 |
| 22 00000 | LOUISIANA | 111 897.6 | 4 601 893 | X | 41.1 | 61.4 | 32.5 | 1.1 | 1.8 | 0.1 | 4.2 | 3.7 |
| 22 00975 | Alexandria | 73.6 | 48 367 | 765 | 657.2 | 38.5 | 58.0 | 0.9 | 2.2 | 0.0 | 1.8 | 2.2 |
| 22 05000 | Baton Rouge | 199.3 | 230 058 | 90 | 1 154.3 | 38.6 | 54.9 | 0.5 | 3.6 | 0.1 | 3.3 | 5.4 |
| 22 08920 | Bossier City | 109.7 | 64 655 | 528 | 589.4 | 63.5 | 26.5 | 0.9 | 2.8 | 0.3 | 8.1 | 4.3 |
| 22 13960 | Central | 161.2 | 27 548 | 1 318 | 170.9 | 89.1 | 8.6 | 0.8 | 0.7 | 0.0 | 1.6 | 1.0 |
| 22 36255 | Houma | 37.3 | 33 707 | 1 084 | 903.7 | 65.5 | 25.1 | 4.8 | 1.1 | 0.1 | 4.8 | 2.9 |
| 22 39475 | Kenner | 38.5 | 66 820 | 503 | 1 735.6 | 49.8 | 24.0 | 0.5 | 4.1 | 0.1 | 22.4 | 16.8 |
| 22 40735 | Lafayette | 127.5 | 122 761 | 214 | 962.8 | 62.9 | 31.6 | 0.7 | 2.1 | 0.1 | 3.8 | 5.1 |
| 22 41155 | Lake Charles | 108.9 | 73 474 | 446 | 674.7 | 46.8 | 48.6 | 0.9 | 1.9 | 0.1 | 2.9 | 3.3 |
| 22 51410 | Monroe | 75.7 | 49 156 | 749 | 649.4 | 33.6 | 64.3 | 0.5 | 1.3 | 0.1 | 1.1 | 1.8 |
| 22 54035 | New Iberia | 28.9 | 30 846 | 1 181 | 1 067.3 | 52.3 | 42.1 | 0.5 | 3.0 | 0.1 | 3.1 | 3.7 |
| 22 55000 | New Orleans | 438.8 | 369 250 | 51 | 841.5 | 31.4 | 60.4 | 0.6 | 3.2 | 0.1 | 5.2 | 5.8 |
| 22 70000 | Shreveport | 272.9 | 201 867 | 109 | 739.7 | 40.9 | 55.2 | 0.8 | 1.6 | 0.1 | 2.5 | 2.4 |
| 22 70805 | Slidell | 38.4 | 27 369 | 1 328 | 712.7 | 74.2 | 17.8 | 0.9 | 2.0 | 0.1 | 6.3 | 4.5 |
| 23 00000 | MAINE | 79 882.8 | 1 329 192 | X | 16.6 | 95.8 | 1.6 | 1.3 | 1.4 | 0.1 | 1.3 | 3.3 |
| 23 02795 | Bangor | 88.7 | 32 817 | 1 110 | 370.0 | 93.9 | 2.2 | 2.1 | 2.0 | 0.1 | 1.5 | 3.7 |
| 23 38740 | Lewiston | 88.4 | 36 460 | 1 002 | 412.4 | 87.6 | 9.8 | 1.1 | 1.5 | 0.1 | 2.0 | 5.3 |
| 23 60545 | Portland | 55.2 | 66 214 | 510 | 1 199.5 | 85.7 | 7.9 | 1.0 | 4.3 | 0.1 | 3.0 | 10.7 |
| 23 71990 | South Portland | 31.0 | 25 088 | 1 438 | 809.3 | 91.7 | 2.6 | 0.7 | 4.4 | 0.1 | 2.2 | 8.1 |
| 24 00000 | MARYLAND | 25 141.6 | 5 884 563 | X | 234.1 | 56.4 | 30.2 | 0.8 | 6.3 | 0.1 | 8.2 | 13.5 |
| 24 01600 | Annapolis | 18.6 | 38 620 | 947 | 2 076.3 | 54.9 | 26.7 | 0.6 | 2.5 | 0.1 | 16.8 | 15.1 |
| 24 04000 | Baltimore | 209.6 | 621 342 | 26 | 2 964.4 | 29.2 | 64.4 | 0.9 | 2.8 | 0.1 | 4.2 | 7.2 |
| 24 08775 | Bowie | 47.7 | 56 129 | 638 | 1 176.7 | 41.1 | 50.0 | 1.1 | 5.1 | 0.1 | 5.6 | 13.6 |
| 24 18750 | College Park | 14.6 | 31 208 | 1 165 | 2 137.5 | 60.5 | 14.9 | 0.6 | 14.2 | 0.1 | 11.9 | 18.2 |
| 24 30325 | Frederick | 57.0 | 66 382 | 507 | 1 164.6 | 60.6 | 19.9 | 0.8 | 6.8 | 0.2 | 14.4 | 16.4 |
| 24 31175 | Gaithersburg | 26.4 | 62 794 | 547 | 2 378.6 | 42.2 | 16.7 | 0.7 | 18.4 | 0.2 | 24.2 | 38.1 |
| 24 36075 | Hagerstown | 30.5 | 40 638 | 891 | 1 332.4 | 77.4 | 18.3 | 0.8 | 1.7 | 0.2 | 5.6 | 7.3 |
| 24 45900 | Laurel | 11.1 | 25 554 | 1 415 | 2 302.2 | 26.1 | 49.7 | 0.9 | 9.9 | 0.1 | 15.5 | 29.5 |
| 24 67675 | Rockville | 35.0 | 63 244 | 544 | 1 807.0 | 55.0 | 10.0 | 0.5 | 22.2 | 0.2 | 14.3 | 34.5 |
| 24 69925 | Salisbury | 34.7 | 31 243 | 1 162 | 900.4 | 55.0 | 35.7 | 0.7 | 3.8 | 0.1 | 7.0 | 12.4 |
| 25 00000 | MASSACHUSETTS | 20 202.1 | 6 646 144 | X | 329.0 | 77.6 | 6.8 | 0.5 | 5.9 | 0.1 | 9.6 | 14.7 |
| 25 00840 | Agawam Town | 60.4 | 28 608 | 1 273 | 473.6 | 93.3 | 1.7 | 0.4 | 2.1 | 0.1 | 3.3 | 6.0 |
| 25 02690 | Attleboro | 69.4 | 43 837 | 831 | 631.7 | 85.4 | 3.6 | 0.6 | 5.1 | 0.1 | 6.3 | 10.5 |
| 25 03690 | Barnstable Town | 154.9 | 44 824 | 816 | 289.4 | 89.7 | 4.1 | 1.3 | 1.6 | 0.1 | 3.1 | 9.7 |

1. Dry land or land partially or temporarily covered by water.    2. May be of any race.

| City | Age of population (percent), 2010 | | | | | | | | | | | Population | | | |
|---|---|---|---|---|---|---|---|---|---|---|---|---|---|---|---|
| | | | | | | | | | | | | Census counts | | Percent change | |
| | Under 5 years | 5 to 17 years | 18 to 24 years | 25 to 34 years | 35 to 44 years | 45 to 54 years | 55 to 64 years | 65 to 74 years | 75 years and over | Median age | Percent female | 2000 | 2010 | 2000–2010 | 2010–2012 |
| | 12 | 13 | 14 | 15 | 16 | 17 | 18 | 19 | 20 | 21 | 22 | 23 | 24 | 25 | 26 |
| KANSAS | 7.2 | 18.3 | 10.1 | 13.2 | 12.2 | 14.2 | 11.6 | 6.7 | 6.5 | 36.0 | 50.4 | 2 688 418 | 2 853 116 | 6.1 | 1.1 |
| Dodge City | 10.3 | 21.5 | 11.8 | 15.5 | 12.5 | 11.5 | 8.1 | 4.3 | 4.6 | 28.9 | 48.6 | 25 176 | 27 340 | 8.6 | 2.7 |
| Garden City | 9.6 | 21.6 | 11.6 | 13.7 | 12.2 | 13.1 | 9.2 | 4.7 | 4.3 | 29.9 | 50.2 | 28 451 | 26 666 | -6.3 | 1.2 |
| Hutchinson | 6.8 | 16.2 | 10.6 | 13.3 | 11.1 | 13.7 | 11.6 | 7.7 | 8.9 | 37.8 | 49.7 | 40 787 | 42 080 | 3.2 | -0.3 |
| Kansas City | 8.8 | 19.6 | 9.7 | 15.2 | 12.5 | 13.4 | 10.3 | 5.6 | 4.9 | 32.5 | 50.6 | 146 866 | 145 786 | -0.7 | 1.0 |
| Lawrence | 5.5 | 12.0 | 28.6 | 17.1 | 10.4 | 9.9 | 8.5 | 4.0 | 4.0 | 26.7 | 49.8 | 80 098 | 87 643 | 9.4 | 2.1 |
| Leavenworth | 8.1 | 17.9 | 8.5 | 15.9 | 15.8 | 13.7 | 10.2 | 5.4 | 4.6 | 34.8 | 46.1 | 35 420 | 35 251 | -0.5 | 1.6 |
| Leawood | 5.5 | 22.6 | 4.2 | 5.3 | 12.9 | 18.1 | 16.3 | 8.2 | 7.1 | 44.7 | 51.5 | 27 656 | 31 867 | 15.2 | 2.1 |
| Lenexa | 7.1 | 17.6 | 8.2 | 14.9 | 13.3 | 15.2 | 13.3 | 5.3 | 5.0 | 36.6 | 51.3 | 40 238 | 48 190 | 19.8 | 2.5 |
| Manhattan | 5.6 | 9.8 | 39.0 | 16.5 | 7.5 | 7.5 | 6.7 | 3.5 | 4.0 | 23.8 | 49.1 | 44 831 | 52 279 | 16.6 | 7.2 |
| Olathe | 8.9 | 21.1 | 7.5 | 15.9 | 16.2 | 13.8 | 9.4 | 4.0 | 3.2 | 32.9 | 50.5 | 92 962 | 125 872 | 35.4 | 3.3 |
| Overland Park | 6.4 | 18.4 | 7.3 | 14.4 | 13.7 | 15.5 | 12.0 | 6.2 | 6.2 | 37.8 | 51.7 | 149 080 | 173 362 | 16.3 | 3.2 |
| Salina | 7.6 | 17.5 | 10.0 | 13.4 | 11.9 | 13.8 | 11.5 | 7.0 | 7.3 | 36.4 | 50.6 | 45 679 | 47 707 | 4.4 | 0.7 |
| Shawnee | 7.5 | 20.2 | 6.9 | 13.4 | 15.4 | 15.3 | 11.3 | 5.7 | 4.4 | 36.4 | 51.1 | 47 996 | 62 209 | 29.6 | 2.3 |
| Topeka | 7.5 | 16.9 | 9.8 | 14.6 | 11.5 | 13.4 | 12.0 | 6.9 | 7.4 | 36.0 | 52.2 | 122 377 | 127 473 | 4.2 | 0.4 |
| Wichita | 8.0 | 18.5 | 10.2 | 14.7 | 12.3 | 13.8 | 11.0 | 5.8 | 5.7 | 33.9 | 50.7 | 344 284 | 382 373 | 11.1 | 0.8 |
| KENTUCKY | 6.5 | 17.1 | 9.5 | 13.0 | 13.3 | 14.8 | 12.4 | 7.5 | 5.8 | 38.1 | 50.8 | 4 041 769 | 4 339 357 | 7.4 | 0.9 |
| Bowling Green | 6.1 | 14.0 | 24.9 | 15.2 | 10.4 | 10.5 | 8.2 | 5.3 | 5.4 | 27.6 | 51.7 | 49 296 | 58 887 | 17.8 | 2.9 |
| Covington | 7.9 | 15.4 | 9.7 | 17.5 | 13.5 | 14.8 | 10.7 | 5.3 | 5.2 | 34.6 | 49.9 | 43 370 | 40 563 | -6.3 | 0.4 |
| Elizabethtown | 7.6 | 17.5 | 9.8 | 14.6 | 12.9 | 13.9 | 10.5 | 6.5 | 6.8 | 35.4 | 52.1 | 22 542 | 28 541 | 26.6 | 2.8 |
| Florence | 8.2 | 16.4 | 9.5 | 15.7 | 13.6 | 12.7 | 10.8 | 6.9 | 6.2 | 35.2 | 52.0 | 23 551 | 29 953 | 27.2 | 3.8 |
| Frankfort | 6.4 | 14.4 | 13.1 | 14.0 | 12.6 | 13.6 | 11.9 | 7.1 | 7.0 | 36.7 | 51.9 | 27 741 | 27 269 | -8.0 | 1.2 |
| Georgetown | 8.6 | 19.3 | 11.3 | 16.5 | 15.5 | 12.0 | 8.5 | 4.7 | 3.6 | 31.7 | 51.8 | 18 080 | 29 117 | 60.9 | 4.0 |
| Henderson | 7.3 | 16.0 | 8.7 | 13.9 | 12.6 | 14.2 | 12.6 | 7.3 | 7.4 | 38.3 | 53.0 | 27 373 | 28 757 | 5.1 | 0.5 |
| Hopkinsville | 7.7 | 17.3 | 9.8 | 13.7 | 12.1 | 13.4 | 11.4 | 7.1 | 7.5 | 36.1 | 52.9 | 30 089 | 32 035 | 4.9 | 2.9 |
| Jeffersontown | 6.1 | 16.6 | 8.2 | 14.6 | 13.2 | 14.5 | 13.0 | 7.5 | 6.2 | 38.4 | 52.0 | 26 633 | 26 595 | -0.1 | 1.2 |
| Lexington-Fayette | 6.5 | 14.7 | 14.1 | 16.6 | 13.3 | 13.5 | 10.8 | 5.7 | 4.8 | 33.7 | 50.8 | 260 512 | 295 803 | 13.5 | 3.3 |
| Louisville/Jefferson County | 6.6 | 16.6 | 9.2 | 14.1 | 12.9 | 14.9 | 12.3 | 6.9 | 6.5 | 37.9 | 51.7 | 693 604 | 597 336 | 6.8 | 1.3 |
| Nicholasville | 8.8 | 19.2 | 8.8 | 16.1 | 14.6 | 13.3 | 9.5 | 5.4 | 4.3 | 33.1 | 52.3 | 19 680 | 28 035 | 42.4 | 1.3 |
| Owensboro | 7.4 | 16.3 | 9.5 | 13.4 | 11.7 | 13.7 | 11.8 | 7.9 | 8.3 | 38.1 | 52.9 | 54 067 | 57 380 | 5.9 | 1.2 |
| Paducah | 6.3 | 15.4 | 8.0 | 13.0 | 11.4 | 14.5 | 13.2 | 8.5 | 9.7 | 41.4 | 54.0 | 26 307 | 25 024 | -4.9 | 0.1 |
| Richmond | 6.0 | 11.8 | 28.8 | 16.3 | 10.7 | 9.7 | 7.3 | 4.6 | 4.7 | 26.6 | 52.1 | 27 152 | 31 364 | 15.5 | 2.4 |
| LOUISIANA | 6.9 | 17.7 | 10.5 | 13.9 | 12.5 | 14.4 | 11.8 | 6.9 | 5.4 | 35.8 | 51.0 | 4 468 976 | 4 533 372 | 1.4 | 1.5 |
| Alexandria | 7.2 | 19.4 | 8.9 | 13.4 | 11.6 | 14.1 | 11.4 | 7.0 | 7.0 | 36.0 | 53.1 | 46 342 | 47 946 | 3.0 | 0.9 |
| Baton Rouge | 6.5 | 15.9 | 17.4 | 15.6 | 10.7 | 12.2 | 10.4 | 5.8 | 5.4 | 30.7 | 51.9 | 227 818 | 229 495 | 0.7 | 0.2 |
| Bossier City | 8.1 | 18.0 | 11.0 | 16.1 | 12.2 | 12.7 | 9.6 | 6.3 | 5.9 | 32.6 | 51.1 | 56 461 | 61 630 | 8.6 | 4.9 |
| Central | 6.0 | 17.1 | 8.6 | 12.1 | 12.0 | 16.3 | 14.0 | 8.5 | 5.3 | 40.6 | 51.0 | NA | 26 867 | NA | 2.5 |
| Houma | 7.3 | 18.4 | 9.2 | 13.7 | 12.5 | 14.8 | 11.6 | 6.6 | 6.0 | 36.2 | 50.9 | 32 393 | 33 695 | 4.1 | 0.0 |
| Kenner | 6.7 | 16.3 | 9.6 | 14.4 | 12.2 | 14.8 | 13.4 | 7.1 | 5.4 | 37.4 | 51.2 | 70 517 | 66 705 | -5.4 | 0.2 |
| Lafayette | 6.1 | 15.7 | 15.4 | 14.9 | 11.2 | 13.7 | 11.2 | 6.1 | 5.6 | 33.2 | 51.4 | 110 257 | 120 658 | 9.4 | 1.7 |
| Lake Charles | 7.0 | 16.5 | 12.2 | 14.3 | 10.8 | 13.6 | 11.7 | 7.0 | 7.0 | 35.0 | 51.7 | 71 757 | 71 992 | 0.3 | 2.1 |
| Monroe | 7.8 | 19.3 | 14.1 | 13.0 | 10.5 | 12.1 | 10.6 | 5.9 | 6.7 | 31.4 | 54.1 | 53 107 | 48 820 | -8.1 | 0.7 |
| New Iberia | 7.9 | 19.3 | 9.3 | 13.0 | 11.1 | 14.1 | 11.5 | 7.1 | 6.6 | 35.4 | 52.3 | 32 623 | 30 617 | -6.1 | 0.7 |
| New Orleans | 6.4 | 14.9 | 12.8 | 16.4 | 12.4 | 14.2 | 12.0 | 6.1 | 4.9 | 34.6 | 51.6 | 484 674 | 343 829 | -29.1 | 7.4 |
| Shreveport | 7.3 | 17.7 | 10.8 | 14.6 | 11.5 | 13.2 | 11.6 | 6.5 | 6.6 | 34.6 | 53.2 | 200 145 | 200 410 | -0.4 | 0.7 |
| Slidell | 7.1 | 18.4 | 8.5 | 13.2 | 12.7 | 14.2 | 11.9 | 7.2 | 6.8 | 37.3 | 51.5 | 25 695 | 27 068 | 5.3 | 1.1 |
| MAINE | 5.2 | 15.4 | 8.7 | 10.9 | 12.9 | 16.5 | 14.5 | 8.5 | 7.4 | 42.7 | 51.1 | 1 274 923 | 1 328 361 | 4.2 | 0.1 |
| Bangor | 5.5 | 12.3 | 16.1 | 14.4 | 11.6 | 13.7 | 12.1 | 6.6 | 7.8 | 36.7 | 51.8 | 31 473 | 33 037 | 5.0 | -0.7 |
| Lewiston | 7.2 | 14.9 | 12.9 | 12.4 | 11.8 | 13.7 | 11.6 | 7.4 | 8.1 | 37.4 | 51.9 | 35 690 | 36 592 | 2.5 | -0.4 |
| Portland | 5.4 | 11.7 | 11.4 | 19.2 | 13.9 | 14.3 | 11.5 | 5.9 | 6.7 | 36.7 | 51.2 | 64 249 | 66 194 | 3.0 | 0.0 |
| South Portland | 5.9 | 14.5 | 9.7 | 13.9 | 14.5 | 15.1 | 12.8 | 7.0 | 6.7 | 39.4 | 52.3 | 23 324 | 25 002 | 7.2 | 0.3 |
| MARYLAND | 6.3 | 17.1 | 9.7 | 13.2 | 13.8 | 15.6 | 12.1 | 6.7 | 5.6 | 38.0 | 51.6 | 5 296 486 | 5 773 552 | 9.0 | 1.9 |
| Annapolis | 7.5 | 13.4 | 9.9 | 17.8 | 13.2 | 12.9 | 12.5 | 7.1 | 5.9 | 36.0 | 52.2 | 35 838 | 38 394 | 7.1 | 0.6 |
| Baltimore | 6.6 | 14.9 | 12.6 | 16.7 | 12.3 | 14.1 | 11.1 | 6.2 | 5.5 | 34.4 | 52.9 | 651 154 | 620 961 | -4.6 | 0.1 |
| Bowie | 5.9 | 18.6 | 7.5 | 10.8 | 15.4 | 18.3 | 11.9 | 6.4 | 5.1 | 40.1 | 53.1 | 50 269 | 54 930 | 8.9 | 2.2 |
| College Park | 2.4 | 5.3 | 60.6 | 10.0 | 5.6 | 6.2 | 4.8 | 2.8 | 2.4 | 21.3 | 46.9 | 24 657 | 30 413 | 23.3 | 2.6 |
| Frederick | 7.7 | 16.0 | 9.8 | 17.0 | 14.9 | 13.8 | 9.9 | 5.0 | 5.8 | 34.6 | 51.8 | 52 767 | 65 239 | 23.6 | 1.8 |
| Gaithersburg | 8.3 | 15.9 | 7.9 | 17.8 | 16.0 | 14.3 | 10.3 | 4.8 | 4.7 | 35.1 | 51.4 | 52 613 | 59 880 | 13.9 | 4.9 |
| Hagerstown | 8.7 | 17.2 | 9.3 | 15.4 | 13.1 | 13.5 | 10.4 | 6.1 | 6.3 | 34.5 | 52.7 | 36 687 | 39 739 | 8.1 | 2.3 |
| Laurel | 8.0 | 14.7 | 9.4 | 20.4 | 16.8 | 14.4 | 9.4 | 4.2 | 2.8 | 33.7 | 52.3 | 19 960 | 25 115 | 25.8 | 1.7 |
| Rockville | 6.5 | 14.9 | 7.2 | 15.4 | 15.6 | 14.7 | 11.6 | 6.8 | 7.1 | 38.7 | 52.1 | 47 388 | 61 285 | 29.2 | 3.2 |
| Salisbury | 7.3 | 14.4 | 22.8 | 14.8 | 10.7 | 10.6 | 8.3 | 5.1 | 6.0 | 28.1 | 53.7 | 23 743 | 30 340 | 27.8 | 3.0 |
| MASSACHUSETTS | 5.6 | 16.1 | 10.4 | 12.9 | 13.5 | 15.5 | 12.3 | 7.0 | 6.8 | 39.1 | 51.6 | 6 349 097 | 6 547 629 | 3.1 | 1.5 |
| Agawam Town | 4.7 | 15.6 | 7.3 | 10.3 | 13.1 | 16.7 | 14.3 | 8.2 | 9.9 | 44.4 | 52.2 | 28 144 | 28 438 | 1.0 | 0.6 |
| Attleboro | 6.4 | 16.3 | 7.9 | 12.9 | 15.6 | 16.5 | 11.5 | 6.5 | 6.4 | 39.5 | 51.2 | 42 068 | 43 593 | 3.6 | 0.6 |
| Barnstable Town | 4.6 | 13.7 | 6.9 | 9.7 | 11.3 | 17.0 | 15.7 | 10.5 | 10.5 | 47.3 | 51.8 | 47 821 | 45 193 | -5.5 | -0.8 |

# Table D. Cities — Households, Group Quarters, Crime, and Education

| City | Households, 2010 | | | | Persons in group quarters, 2010 | | | | Serious crimes known to police,[2] 2011 | | | | Educational attainment, 2007–2011 | | |
|---|---|---|---|---|---|---|---|---|---|---|---|---|---|---|---|
| | | | Percent | | | Institutional | | | Total | | Rate[3] | | | Attainment[4] (percent) | |
| | Number | Persons per house-hold | Female family house-holder[1] | One-person | Total | Total | Persons in nursing facilities | Non-institu-tional | Number | Rate[3] | Violent | Property | Population age 25 and older | High school graduate or less | Bachelor's degree or more |
| | 27 | 28 | 29 | 30 | 31 | 32 | 33 | 34 | 35 | 36 | 37 | 38 | 39 | 40 | 41 |
| KANSAS | 1 112 096 | 2.49 | 10.4 | 27.8 | 79 074 | 41 393 | 20 672 | 37 681 | 98 600 | 3 434 | 354 | 3 080 | 1 822 400 | 38.9 | 29.7 |
| Dodge City | 8 777 | 3.05 | 13.0 | 22.7 | 596 | 363 | 207 | 233 | 1 039 | 3 776 | 425 | 3 351 | 15 419 | 58.4 | 17.3 |
| Garden City | 9 071 | 2.88 | 13.9 | 24.0 | 548 | 231 | 96 | 317 | 951 | 3 545 | 362 | 3 183 | 14 852 | 55.5 | 17.9 |
| Hutchinson | 16 981 | 2.31 | 12.3 | 33.2 | 2 850 | 2 402 | 447 | 448 | 2 983 | 7 044 | 553 | 6 492 | 27 788 | 41.0 | 19.8 |
| Kansas City | 53 925 | 2.68 | 18.9 | 28.8 | 1 109 | 815 | 421 | 294 | 8 830 | 6 019 | 645 | 5 373 | 89 566 | 57.9 | 14.5 |
| Lawrence | 34 970 | 2.28 | 8.8 | 32.0 | 7 984 | 430 | 270 | 7 554 | 4 187 | 4 747 | 392 | 4 355 | 45 577 | 21.8 | 52.8 |
| Leavenworth | 12 256 | 2.55 | 13.2 | 28.7 | 4 031 | 3 352 | 72 | 679 | 1 300 | 3 665 | 665 | 2 999 | 23 151 | 40.7 | 29.6 |
| Leawood | 11 781 | 2.70 | 4.8 | 18.1 | 11 | 0 | 0 | 11 | 464 | 1 447 | 56 | 1 391 | 21 261 | 8.6 | 74.7 |
| Lenexa | 19 288 | 2.48 | 9.0 | 25.2 | 348 | 327 | 325 | 21 | 1 155 | 2 382 | 142 | 2 239 | 31 922 | 20.0 | 51.6 |
| Manhattan | 20 008 | 2.30 | 8.2 | 30.3 | 6 227 | 401 | 306 | 5 826 | NA | NA | NA | NA | 23 703 | 20.0 | 51.6 |
| Olathe | 44 507 | 2.80 | 9.6 | 20.0 | 1 418 | 789 | 661 | 629 | 2 430 | 1 918 | 178 | 1 740 | 77 085 | 24.0 | 44.7 |
| Overland Park | 71 443 | 2.41 | 8.4 | 29.8 | 1 343 | 1 215 | 1 040 | 128 | 4 304 | 2 467 | 166 | 2 301 | 117 049 | 17.0 | 56.6 |
| Salina | 19 391 | 2.39 | 11.8 | 31.6 | 1 435 | 545 | 377 | 890 | 2 441 | 5 084 | 348 | 4 737 | 30 884 | 43.8 | 23.6 |
| Shawnee | 23 651 | 2.61 | 9.8 | 23.1 | 406 | 384 | 384 | 22 | 1 347 | 2 152 | 173 | 1 979 | 39 801 | 28.0 | 41.7 |
| Topeka | 53 943 | 2.29 | 14.2 | 35.9 | 4 083 | 2 648 | 1 246 | 1 435 | 8 226 | 6 412 | 543 | 5 869 | 82 499 | 42.8 | 27.7 |
| Wichita | 151 818 | 2.48 | 13.1 | 31.1 | 6 420 | 3 555 | 1 666 | 2 865 | 22 503 | 5 848 | 770 | 5 078 | 239 282 | 40.7 | 27.9 |
| KENTUCKY | 1 719 965 | 2.45 | 12.7 | 27.5 | 125 870 | 70 779 | 26 044 | 55 091 | 128 764 | 2 947 | 238 | 2 709 | 2 881 383 | 52.6 | 20.6 |
| Bowling Green | 22 735 | 2.28 | 14.1 | 35.4 | 6 147 | 1 173 | 492 | 4 974 | 2 890 | 4 943 | 287 | 4 656 | 31 177 | 46.2 | 28.6 |
| Covington | 17 033 | 2.30 | 17.2 | 37.3 | 1 406 | 946 | 420 | 460 | 2 709 | 6 620 | 748 | 5 872 | 27 057 | 54.6 | 17.8 |
| Elizabethtown | 11 711 | 2.34 | 15.1 | 32.1 | 1 075 | 995 | 284 | 80 | 1 067 | 3 714 | 150 | 3 564 | 18 096 | 43.0 | 26.1 |
| Florence | 12 493 | 2.38 | 13.8 | 32.5 | 268 | 265 | 265 | 3 | 1 707 | 5 660 | 225 | 5 435 | 19 539 | 47.0 | 21.4 |
| Frankfort | 11 140 | 2.14 | 16.7 | 38.3 | 1 109 | 648 | 188 | 996 | 1 444 | 5 618 | 405 | 5 213 | 17 259 | 50.4 | 26.0 |
| Georgetown | 10 733 | 2.59 | 14.9 | 24.9 | 1 284 | 211 | 136 | 1 073 | 1 224 | 4 178 | 413 | 3 765 | 17 670 | 45.0 | 23.0 |
| Henderson | 12 091 | 2.28 | 16.2 | 33.7 | 1 162 | 806 | 262 | 356 | 985 | 3 402 | 211 | 3 191 | 19 643 | 54.7 | 16.9 |
| Hopkinsville | 12 854 | 2.35 | 19.8 | 32.4 | 1 425 | 1 204 | 348 | 221 | 1 427 | 4 488 | 355 | 4 133 | 20 155 | 52.4 | 15.3 |
| Jeffersontown | 11 065 | 2.37 | 12.3 | 29.4 | 351 | 351 | 351 | 0 | 664 | 2 480 | 172 | 2 308 | 17 829 | 36.0 | 32.7 |
| Lexington-Fayette | 123 043 | 2.30 | 12.3 | 32.7 | 12 804 | 3 996 | 1 092 | 8 808 | 13 825 | 4 642 | 457 | 4 185 | 188 392 | 32.7 | 39.3 |
| Louisville/Jefferson County | 309 175 | 2.35 | 15.4 | 32.0 | 14 153 | 8 529 | 4 831 | 5 624 | 36 035 | 5 418 | 614 | 4 803 | 498 002 | 41.5 | 29.2 |
| Nicholasville | 10 492 | 2.64 | 16.7 | 22.3 | 312 | 269 | 80 | 43 | 1 476 | 5 232 | 280 | 4 952 | 17 233 | 50.1 | 17.8 |
| Owensboro | 24 215 | 2.29 | 15.5 | 34.0 | 1 817 | 1 025 | 806 | 792 | 2 478 | 4 298 | 251 | 4 046 | 38 027 | 53.2 | 17.9 |
| Paducah | 11 462 | 2.09 | 16.4 | 41.5 | 1 090 | 1 024 | 510 | 66 | 1 235 | 4 901 | 325 | 4 576 | 17 917 | 44.5 | 19.5 |
| Richmond | 12 435 | 2.17 | 13.8 | 35.6 | 4 344 | 480 | 207 | 3 864 | 1 976 | 6 257 | 361 | 5 896 | 16 587 | 45.7 | 26.7 |
| LOUISIANA | 1 728 360 | 2.55 | 17.2 | 26.9 | 127 427 | 88 104 | 24 524 | 39 323 | 194 150 | 4 244 | 555 | 3 689 | 2 899 261 | 53.0 | 21.1 |
| Alexandria | 18 272 | 2.48 | 24.5 | 31.2 | 2 356 | 1 611 | 531 | 745 | 4 211 | 8 744 | 1 352 | 7 392 | 30 498 | 50.9 | 22.0 |
| Baton Rouge | 91 474 | 2.40 | 20.6 | 32.7 | 9 554 | 3 531 | 1 129 | 6 023 | 15 134 | 6 535 | 1 066 | 5 469 | 134 015 | 40.8 | 32.4 |
| Bossier City | 23 866 | 2.50 | 16.9 | 28.4 | 1 614 | 811 | 671 | 803 | 2 724 | 4 402 | 596 | 3 806 | 38 413 | 44.6 | 23.4 |
| Central | 10 179 | 2.63 | 11.9 | 18.8 | 59 | 0 | 0 | 59 | NA | NA | NA | NA | 18 392 | 48.0 | 20.3 |
| Houma | 12 751 | 2.63 | 17.4 | 26.1 | 212 | 134 | 114 | 78 | 1 762 | 5 177 | 623 | 4 554 | 22 142 | 59.4 | 17.5 |
| Kenner | 24 844 | 2.67 | 17.2 | 25.6 | 422 | 319 | 303 | 103 | 2 765 | 4 108 | 239 | 3 869 | 45 048 | 49.1 | 21.5 |
| Lafayette | 49 444 | 2.35 | 15.5 | 31.9 | 4 509 | 1 775 | 613 | 2 734 | 7 354 | 6 041 | 693 | 5 349 | 75 668 | 39.2 | 33.0 |
| Lake Charles | 28 940 | 2.38 | 19.4 | 32.4 | 3 149 | 2 018 | 596 | 1 131 | 2 637 | 3 630 | 476 | 3 153 | 45 692 | 49.6 | 22.5 |
| Monroe | 18 445 | 2.47 | 27.6 | 33.5 | 3 273 | 1 229 | 663 | 2 044 | 4 744 | 9 630 | 1 693 | 7 937 | 29 023 | 49.6 | 25.8 |
| New Iberia | 11 706 | 2.58 | 21.9 | 28.8 | 433 | 367 | 367 | 66 | NA | NA | NA | NA | 19 176 | 64.4 | 13.3 |
| New Orleans | 142 158 | 2.33 | 20.9 | 35.9 | 13 165 | 5 509 | 1 509 | 7 656 | 16 761 | 4 831 | 792 | 4 039 | 212 143 | 41.9 | 32.3 |
| Shreveport | 80 651 | 2.40 | 23.0 | 32.6 | 5 574 | 3 588 | 1 975 | 1 986 | 11 128 | 5 533 | 768 | 4 765 | 127 069 | 47.2 | 24.1 |
| Slidell | 10 050 | 2.66 | 16.2 | 23.4 | 315 | 286 | 286 | 29 | 1 644 | 6 018 | 450 | 5 568 | 18 135 | 43.4 | 21.7 |
| MAINE | 557 219 | 2.32 | 10.0 | 28.6 | 35 545 | 12 409 | 7 878 | 23 136 | 35 445 | 2 669 | 123 | 2 545 | 934 144 | 44.2 | 27.1 |
| Bangor | 14 475 | 2.10 | 12.6 | 37.9 | 2 690 | 854 | 561 | 1 836 | 1 741 | 5 270 | 209 | 5 061 | 21 767 | 40.1 | 28.1 |
| Lewiston | 15 267 | 2.26 | 13.7 | 34.4 | 2 117 | 365 | 344 | 1 752 | 1 429 | 3 906 | 210 | 3 695 | 24 005 | 56.0 | 14.6 |
| Portland | 30 725 | 2.07 | 10.1 | 40.5 | 2 613 | 1 065 | 592 | 1 548 | 2 829 | 4 274 | 287 | 3 987 | 47 127 | 30.2 | 44.2 |
| South Portland | 10 877 | 2.24 | 12.0 | 31.9 | 636 | 195 | 73 | 441 | 923 | 3 692 | 240 | 3 452 | 17 438 | 30.6 | 38.7 |
| MARYLAND | 2 156 411 | 2.61 | 14.6 | 26.1 | 138 375 | 66 838 | 28 001 | 71 537 | 195 496 | 3 354 | 494 | 2 860 | 3 828 550 | 38.1 | 36.1 |
| Annapolis | 16 136 | 2.34 | 14.9 | 35.0 | 603 | 143 | 143 | 460 | 1 210 | 3 122 | 454 | 2 668 | 27 124 | 34.0 | 43.9 |
| Baltimore | 249 903 | 2.38 | 23.8 | 36.1 | 25 199 | 9 951 | 3 793 | 15 248 | 38 710 | 6 175 | 1 418 | 4 758 | 407 022 | 51.0 | 25.8 |
| Bowie | 19 950 | 2.73 | 14.0 | 23.4 | 255 | 148 | 145 | 107 | 912 | 1 651 | 143 | 1 508 | 35 895 | 24.8 | 46.2 |
| College Park | 6 757 | 2.79 | 7.9 | 24.8 | 11 535 | 0 | 0 | 11 535 | NA | NA | NA | NA | 10 076 | 30.5 | 48.4 |
| Frederick | 25 352 | 2.50 | 12.8 | 30.7 | 1 785 | 803 | 803 | 982 | 2 093 | 3 178 | 465 | 2 713 | 42 823 | 35.1 | 35.8 |
| Gaithersburg | 22 000 | 2.70 | 12.7 | 26.7 | 547 | 372 | 366 | 175 | NA | NA | NA | NA | 40 442 | 25.2 | 52.3 |
| Hagerstown | 16 449 | 2.36 | 18.4 | 34.5 | 806 | 546 | 508 | 260 | 1 698 | 4 241 | 470 | 3 771 | 26 429 | 55.6 | 15.2 |
| Laurel | 10 498 | 2.37 | 15.7 | 37.6 | 183 | 0 | 0 | 183 | 1 066 | 4 205 | 698 | 3 506 | 16 906 | 34.5 | 36.9 |
| Rockville | 23 686 | 2.54 | 9.9 | 27.0 | 1 103 | 833 | 665 | 270 | NA | NA | NA | NA | 42 960 | 21.4 | 59.8 |
| Salisbury | 11 983 | 2.42 | 19.1 | 32.5 | 1 391 | 155 | 135 | 1 236 | 2 201 | 7 186 | 1 205 | 5 981 | 16 967 | 46.5 | 25.7 |
| MASSACHUSETTS | 2 547 075 | 2.48 | 12.5 | 28.7 | 238 882 | 74 667 | 43 833 | 164 215 | 177 009 | 2 687 | 428 | 2 259 | 4 419 291 | 37.4 | 38.7 |
| Agawam Town | 11 664 | 2.38 | 10.3 | 30.0 | 677 | 669 | 669 | 8 | 241 | 842 | 147 | 696 | 20 456 | 40.8 | 25.4 |
| Attleboro | 16 884 | 2.55 | 11.3 | 26.4 | 564 | 451 | 429 | 113 | 1 095 | 2 497 | 383 | 2 114 | 29 907 | 44.3 | 29.4 |
| Barnstable Town | 19 225 | 2.33 | 10.6 | 29.0 | 363 | 106 | 79 | 257 | 1 584 | 3 484 | 669 | 2 815 | 33 962 | 31.2 | 36.7 |

1. No spouse present.   2. Data for serious crimes have not been adjusted for underreporting. This may affect comparability between geographic areas and over time.   3. Per 100,000 population estimated by the FBI.   4. Persons 25 years old and over.

# Table D. Cities — Income, Poverty, and Housing

| City | Money income, 2007–2011 | | | | | Housing units, 2010 | | | Occupied Housing units 2007–2011 | | | | |
|---|---|---|---|---|---|---|---|---|---|---|---|---|---|
| | Households | | | | Families with income below poverty (percent) | | | | Owner-occupied | | | Median owner costs as a percent of income | |
| | Per capita income[1] (dollars) | Median income | Percent with income of $200,000 or more | Percent with income of less than $25,000 | | Total | Percent change, 2000–2010 | Vacant units for sale or rent[2] | Total | Percent | Median value[3] (dollars) | With a mortgage[4] | Without a mortgage[5] |
| | 42 | 43 | 44 | 45 | 46 | 47 | 48 | 49 | 50 | 51 | 52 | 53 | 54 |
| KANSAS.............. | 26 545 | 50 594 | 3.2 | 22.8 | 8.6 | 1 233 215 | 9.0 | 121 119 | 1 104 479 | 69.0 | 125 500 | 21.6 | 11.9 |
| Dodge City............. | 19 198 | 47 588 | 2.0 | 23.4 | 14.7 | 9 378 | 4.3 | 601 | 8 754 | 63.9 | 85 900 | 22.3 | 13.3 |
| Garden City.............. | 20 969 | 48 855 | 2.5 | 18.1 | 9.5 | 9 656 | -1.7 | 585 | 8 827 | 64.9 | 102 300 | 23.7 | 11.3 |
| Hutchinson .............. | 21 500 | 40 004 | 1.3 | 28.9 | 11.7 | 18 580 | 5.1 | 1 599 | 17 212 | 64.5 | 86 500 | 22.0 | 13.6 |
| Kansas City.............. | 18 755 | 38 564 | 0.7 | 31.6 | 18.2 | 61 969 | 0.8 | 8 044 | 52 823 | 62.1 | 93 300 | 25.6 | 15.1 |
| Lawrence................. | 24 614 | 42 761 | 2.9 | 31.4 | 9.3 | 37 502 | 14.4 | 2 532 | 34 714 | 45.9 | 177 300 | 23.3 | 12.4 |
| Leavenworth ........... | 24 100 | 51 587 | 2.0 | 23.4 | 10.2 | 13 670 | 5.9 | 1 414 | 12 288 | 50.3 | 123 100 | 21.9 | 12.8 |
| Leawood .................. | 66 507 | 129 104 | 28.3 | 7.7 | 1.6 | 12 384 | 22.2 | 603 | 11 918 | 94.0 | 388 400 | 21.3 | 10.4 |
| Lenexa.................... | 37 605 | 76 131 | 7.0 | 12.7 | 4.7 | 20 832 | 27.4 | 1 544 | 18 889 | 64.6 | 216 900 | 20.9 | 10.0 |
| Manhattan .............. | 20 872 | 38 599 | 2.1 | 35.8 | 9.9 | 21 619 | 22.1 | 1 611 | 19 927 | 40.5 | 171 600 | 21.9 | 10.1 |
| Olathe .................... | 31 580 | 76 528 | 5.0 | 11.0 | 3.5 | 46 851 | 40.6 | 2 344 | 43 774 | 74.0 | 194 600 | 21.9 | 10.0 |
| Overland Park .......... | 39 476 | 71 612 | 8.1 | 12.9 | 4.0 | 76 280 | 21.7 | 4 837 | 72 234 | 65.7 | 224 200 | 21.6 | 10.9 |
| Salina .................... | 23 825 | 42 410 | 1.9 | 26.3 | 10.7 | 20 803 | 6.1 | 1 412 | 19 279 | 64.3 | 112 200 | 21.6 | 11.6 |
| Shawnee ................. | 32 946 | 72 516 | 4.4 | 11.9 | 3.3 | 24 954 | 30.6 | 1 303 | 23 116 | 72.4 | 200 200 | 22.3 | 12.1 |
| Topeka ................... | 23 803 | 40 362 | 1.9 | 29.1 | 14.6 | 59 582 | 5.5 | 5 639 | 54 409 | 58.5 | 95 600 | 21.9 | 12.4 |
| Wichita .................. | 25 139 | 45 625 | 2.7 | 25.9 | 12.1 | 167 310 | 10.0 | 15 492 | 150 581 | 62.6 | 114 800 | 21.1 | 11.4 |
| KENTUCKY .............. | 23 033 | 42 248 | 2.3 | 30.5 | 13.7 | 1 927 164 | 10.1 | 207 199 | 1 681 085 | 69.5 | 118 700 | 21.8 | 10.9 |
| Bowling Green............. | 19 845 | 33 072 | 1.7 | 37.5 | 19.6 | 24 712 | 16.6 | 1 977 | 22 224 | 42.4 | 127 400 | 23.4 | 10.4 |
| Covington ............... | 20 452 | 37 175 | 1.5 | 36.0 | 21.6 | 20 053 | -1.9 | 3 020 | 16 885 | 50.2 | 108 300 | 23.9 | 11.3 |
| Elizabethtown............. | 25 269 | 43 235 | 3.0 | 28.3 | 12.1 | 12 664 | 26.3 | 953 | 11 103 | 54.9 | 154 300 | 20.0 | 10.0 |
| Florence ................. | 23 815 | 49 244 | 0.9 | 23.2 | 8.4 | 13 447 | 31.2 | 954 | 11 973 | 54.9 | 139 700 | 22.6 | 10.0 |
| Frankfort ................ | 22 969 | 39 524 | 1.1 | 29.9 | 18.0 | 12 938 | -3.4 | 1 798 | 11 514 | 49.8 | 124 200 | 22.1 | 10.2 |
| Georgetown ............. | 24 376 | 51 692 | 1.3 | 22.6 | 11.6 | 11 957 | 66.8 | 1 224 | 11 033 | 63.5 | 144 400 | 19.4 | 10.0 |
| Henderson .............. | 20 901 | 34 412 | 1.0 | 35.2 | 14.9 | 13 171 | 4.0 | 1 080 | 12 365 | 60.3 | 96 900 | 23.2 | 10.0 |
| Hopkinsville ............. | 19 232 | 36 078 | 1.5 | 36.1 | 20.8 | 14 318 | 7.8 | 1 464 | 12 723 | 54.2 | 101 400 | 21.9 | 10.6 |
| Jeffersontown ........... | 27 182 | 59 319 | 2.3 | 16.0 | 4.7 | 11 800 | 5.5 | 735 | 10 187 | 67.3 | 162 100 | 21.7 | 10.2 |
| Lexington-Fayette......... | 29 125 | 48 306 | 4.1 | 26.7 | 11.8 | 135 160 | 16.3 | 12 117 | 122 075 | 56.9 | 161 100 | 21.6 | 10.0 |
| Louisville/Jefferson County ... | 27 301 | 46 298 | 3.6 | 26.6 | 12.0 | 337 616 | NA | 28 441 | 301 312 | 64.3 | 147 900 | 22.3 | 11.3 |
| Nicholasville ............. | 19 526 | 43 453 | 0.9 | 28.8 | 14.3 | 11 405 | 47.0 | 913 | 10 333 | 59.5 | 138 100 | 23.1 | 10.7 |
| Owensboro .............. | 21 183 | 37 289 | 1.3 | 34.5 | 14.8 | 26 072 | 7.0 | 1 857 | 23 380 | 60.3 | 98 700 | 21.1 | 10.8 |
| Paducah ................. | 21 027 | 30 549 | 1.2 | 41.9 | 20.1 | 12 851 | -2.5 | 1 389 | 11 223 | 50.0 | 95 600 | 20.4 | 12.4 |
| Richmond ............... | 17 275 | 30 693 | 0.8 | 42.5 | 20.7 | 13 788 | 16.5 | 1 353 | 12 024 | 39.2 | 135 200 | 22.3 | 11.4 |
| LOUISIANA .............. | 23 853 | 44 086 | 2.9 | 29.7 | 14.1 | 1 964 981 | 6.4 | 236 621 | 1 675 097 | 67.9 | 135 400 | 21.5 | 10.1 |
| Alexandria ............... | 21 397 | 35 810 | 2.1 | 36.9 | 20.0 | 20 366 | 2.4 | 2 094 | 17 237 | 55.4 | 117 400 | 23.1 | 11.5 |
| Baton Rouge ............. | 23 565 | 37 381 | 3.2 | 35.4 | 17.7 | 100 801 | 3.6 | 9 327 | 88 063 | 51.7 | 151 900 | 22.9 | 10.7 |
| Bossier City.............. | 25 091 | 46 518 | 2.9 | 26.0 | 13.7 | 25 579 | 11.7 | 1 713 | 23 864 | 58.4 | 135 300 | 21.4 | 10.0 |
| Central ................... | 29 458 | 62 616 | 3.4 | 14.8 | 4.4 | 10 574 | NA | 395 | 10 233 | 85.5 | 165 300 | 20.9 | 10.0 |
| Houma ................... | 23 895 | 44 204 | 2.2 | 30.3 | 14.2 | 13 924 | 12.1 | 1 173 | 12 625 | 67.4 | 146 000 | 20.9 | 10.1 |
| Kenner................... | 25 574 | 49 689 | 3.8 | 23.3 | 11.1 | 28 076 | 2.5 | 3 232 | 24 041 | 61.9 | 183 100 | 24.0 | 11.0 |
| Lafayette ................ | 28 030 | 44 688 | 4.9 | 29.8 | 12.6 | 53 356 | 13.9 | 3 912 | 48 405 | 57.3 | 165 100 | 21.9 | 10.9 |
| Lake Charles................ | 22 908 | 35 996 | 2.4 | 34.6 | 17.8 | 32 469 | 3.7 | 3 529 | 28 513 | 57.2 | 117 800 | 22.2 | 10.3 |
| Monroe .................. | 20 766 | 29 051 | 3.3 | 44.5 | 30.4 | 20 570 | -3.5 | 2 125 | 18 067 | 47.1 | 111 900 | 22.6 | 11.8 |
| New Iberia ............... | 18 622 | 36 025 | 1.2 | 36.5 | 20.8 | 13 059 | 1.1 | 1 353 | 11 687 | 61.7 | 102 600 | 23.8 | 11.5 |
| New Orleans ............. | 25 668 | 37 325 | 4.0 | 36.6 | 20.5 | 189 896 | -11.7 | 47 738 | 134 342 | 48.3 | 183 500 | 27.9 | 14.3 |
| Shreveport............... | 23 135 | 36 803 | 3.0 | 34.5 | 17.0 | 88 253 | 1.5 | 7 602 | 77 470 | 56.9 | 118 500 | 22.3 | 10.9 |
| Slidell ................... | 22 930 | 49 031 | 2.4 | 22.3 | 13.4 | 11 155 | 10.4 | 1 105 | 10 035 | 72.6 | 160 500 | 24.7 | 12.1 |
| MAINE .................... | 26 195 | 47 898 | 2.4 | 25.4 | 8.5 | 721 830 | 10.7 | 164 611 | 551 601 | 72.7 | 176 600 | 24.6 | 14.1 |
| Bangor.................... | 24 945 | 37 707 | 2.8 | 33.7 | 13.3 | 15 674 | 7.5 | 1 199 | 14 377 | 48.7 | 149 400 | 22.6 | 15.8 |
| Lewiston ................. | 20 942 | 37 941 | 0.8 | 35.3 | 15.5 | 16 731 | 1.6 | 1 464 | 15 046 | 50.5 | 152 600 | 25.2 | 19.6 |
| Portland ................. | 29 200 | 45 153 | 3.0 | 29.4 | 12.2 | 33 836 | 6.2 | 3 111 | 31 126 | 44.5 | 244 200 | 26.7 | 14.2 |
| South Portland ........... | 28 728 | 52 907 | 2.3 | 20.3 | 7.6 | 11 484 | 11.0 | 607 | 10 696 | 63.1 | 224 800 | 27.1 | 17.3 |
| MARYLAND ............. | 35 751 | 72 419 | 8.1 | 15.1 | 6.1 | 2 378 814 | 10.9 | 222 403 | 2 128 377 | 68.7 | 319 800 | 25.5 | 12.6 |
| Annapolis................. | 42 901 | 70 908 | 10.1 | 16.6 | 8.7 | 17 845 | 10.2 | 1 709 | 16 466 | 53.0 | 408 000 | 24.2 | 11.0 |
| Baltimore ................ | 23 853 | 40 100 | 2.7 | 32.8 | 17.7 | 296 685 | -1.3 | 46 782 | 238 959 | 49.5 | 163 700 | 26.3 | 15.9 |
| Bowie.................... | 41 650 | 103 114 | 10.8 | 5.6 | 1.7 | 20 687 | 11.1 | 737 | 19 470 | 86.0 | 344 500 | 26.6 | 11.7 |
| College Park.............. | 18 244 | 63 724 | 5.9 | 29.6 | 3.3 | 8 212 | 31.4 | 1 455 | 6 469 | 51.3 | 336 800 | 26.7 | 10.6 |
| Frederick ................ | 32 830 | 66 161 | 4.2 | 13.7 | 6.1 | 27 559 | 25.0 | 2 207 | 25 643 | 57.0 | 280 900 | 26.1 | 15.0 |
| Gaithersburg............. | 39 591 | 81 118 | 8.6 | 11.9 | 5.6 | 23 337 | 13.5 | 1 337 | 22 684 | 56.5 | 376 900 | 25.1 | 10.0 |
| Hagerstown ............. | 20 684 | 36 806 | 0.9 | 34.9 | 19.8 | 18 682 | 9.5 | 2 233 | 16 446 | 42.6 | 174 300 | 27.6 | 14.7 |
| Laurel ................... | 33 574 | 66 998 | 3.4 | 11.1 | 4.7 | 11 397 | 19.4 | 899 | 9 678 | 53.7 | 292 500 | 31.4 | 12.7 |
| Rockville ................ | 47 571 | 92 288 | 13.7 | 8.6 | 2.3 | 25 199 | 41.6 | 1 513 | 23 593 | 61.0 | 489 300 | 25.0 | 10.7 |
| Salisbury................. | 21 359 | 40 590 | 1.8 | 29.3 | 14.2 | 13 401 | 37.2 | 1 418 | 11 432 | 37.5 | 172 300 | 27.9 | 13.3 |
| MASSACHUSETTS ... | 35 051 | 65 981 | 7.2 | 20.0 | 7.6 | 2 808 254 | 7.1 | 261 179 | 2 522 409 | 63.6 | 343 500 | 26.4 | 15.5 |
| Agawam Town ............. | 29 914 | 65 339 | 1.3 | 17.8 | 6.2 | 12 139 | 4.1 | 475 | 11 506 | 78.5 | 230 700 | 24.2 | 16.2 |
| Attleboro ................ | 30 398 | 65 298 | 3.0 | 16.6 | 4.1 | 18 022 | 8.9 | 1 138 | 16 393 | 68.2 | 293 500 | 27.8 | 15.1 |
| Barnstable Town ......... | 36 121 | 62 191 | 5.3 | 18.7 | 5.4 | 26 343 | 5.3 | 7 118 | 20 119 | 76.7 | 370 200 | 30.7 | 17.7 |

1. Based on population estimated by the American Community Survey.   2. Includes units rented or sold but not occupied.   3. Specified owner-occupied units; $1,000,000 represents $1,000,000 or more.   4. 50.0 represents 50 percent or more.   5. 10.0 represents 10 percent or less.

# Table D. Cities — Housing, Labor Force, and Employment

| City | Occupied housing units, 2007–2011 (cont.) | | | | Migration, 2007–2011 | | Civilian labor force, 2012 | | Unemployment | | Civilian employment[4], 2007–2011 | | | |
|---|---|---|---|---|---|---|---|---|---|---|---|---|---|---|
| | | | | | | | | | | | | | Percent | |
| | Percent renter occupied | Median gross rent[1] | Median rent as a percent of income[2] | Percent with no vehicle available | Percent who lived in the same house one year ago | Percent who lived outside this city one year ago | Total | Percent change, 2011–2012 | Total | Rate[3] | Population age 16 and older | In labor force | Full-year full-time worker | Households with no workers (percent) |
| | 55 | 56 | 57 | 58 | 59 | 60 | 61 | 62 | 63 | 64 | 65 | 66 | 67 | 68 |
| KANSAS | 31.0 | 699 | 27.7 | 5.2 | 82.7 | 10.0 | 1 489 320 | -0.6 | 85 454 | 5.7 | 2 192 495 | 68.7 | 43.8 | 23.5 |
| Dodge City | 36.1 | 599 | 24.5 | 8.5 | 81.8 | 9.0 | 15 509 | 3.2 | 631 | 4.1 | 19 338 | 69.8 | 46.3 | 20.7 |
| Garden City | 35.1 | 645 | 22.9 | 5.6 | 81.9 | 9.6 | 14 011 | -3.4 | 674 | 4.8 | 18 918 | 73.8 | 51.1 | 14.2 |
| Hutchinson | 35.5 | 603 | 26.2 | 6.4 | 80.0 | 10.2 | 20 625 | -1.1 | 1 323 | 6.4 | 33 329 | 62.4 | 40.8 | 28.7 |
| Kansas City | 37.9 | 714 | 32.5 | 10.0 | 80.8 | 8.5 | 65 254 | -0.4 | 5 803 | 8.9 | 108 175 | 66.3 | 38.5 | 29.5 |
| Lawrence | 54.1 | 809 | 36.0 | 4.9 | 66.9 | 13.8 | 49 748 | 0.7 | 2 799 | 5.6 | 73 513 | 71.1 | 35.9 | 18.1 |
| Leavenworth | 49.7 | 789 | 26.9 | 7.9 | 67.4 | 25.8 | 15 047 | -1.6 | 1 357 | 9.0 | 27 036 | 59.0 | 31.2 | 25.0 |
| Leawood | 6.0 | 1 850 | 41.3 | 3.1 | 90.3 | 7.9 | 15 969 | 1.2 | 567 | 3.6 | 23 617 | 67.6 | 43.7 | 21.0 |
| Lenexa | 35.4 | 898 | 26.4 | 4.0 | 81.6 | 15.6 | 28 530 | 0.5 | 1 593 | 5.6 | 36 991 | 77.0 | 52.1 | 14.8 |
| Manhattan | 59.5 | 777 | 36.4 | 5.5 | 71.0 | 18.6 | 28 207 | 0.5 | 1 222 | 4.3 | 44 495 | 65.6 | 29.6 | 20.8 |
| Olathe | 26.0 | 844 | 27.1 | 2.8 | 85.0 | 9.8 | 62 704 | 0.7 | 3 214 | 5.1 | 90 498 | 77.7 | 52.1 | 13.5 |
| Overland Park | 34.3 | 911 | 25.7 | 3.7 | 83.6 | 10.8 | 98 583 | 0.7 | 5 023 | 5.1 | 134 708 | 73.9 | 50.3 | 18.9 |
| Salina | 35.7 | 626 | 28.7 | 5.8 | 81.1 | 7.9 | 25 808 | -0.1 | 1 567 | 6.1 | 36 699 | 71.1 | 44.4 | 24.2 |
| Shawnee | 27.6 | 791 | 26.1 | 2.6 | 86.6 | 9.6 | 32 876 | 1.0 | 1 377 | 4.2 | 46 318 | 75.9 | 50.9 | 14.6 |
| Topeka | 41.5 | 659 | 29.2 | 9.1 | 79.5 | 7.2 | 65 220 | -1.2 | 4 780 | 7.3 | 98 878 | 66.8 | 42.0 | 28.4 |
| Wichita | 37.4 | 650 | 29.1 | 7.0 | 80.5 | 5.9 | 185 369 | -2.5 | 13 829 | 7.5 | 288 236 | 69.6 | 43.5 | 24.1 |
| KENTUCKY | 30.5 | 623 | 29.0 | 7.9 | 84.7 | 10.6 | 2 074 806 | 0.9 | 170 926 | 8.2 | 3 412 180 | 60.5 | 37.2 | 31.8 |
| Bowling Green | 57.6 | 623 | 32.5 | 10.4 | 66.4 | 18.7 | 29 933 | 3.4 | 2 113 | 7.1 | 47 070 | 64.2 | 31.3 | 28.0 |
| Covington | 49.8 | 653 | 33.7 | 19.7 | 78.0 | 12.1 | 19 302 | 1.1 | 1 617 | 8.4 | 32 275 | 63.1 | 38.5 | 30.0 |
| Elizabethtown | 45.1 | 626 | 27.4 | 6.4 | 82.1 | 11.8 | 14 118 | 0.6 | 945 | 6.7 | 21 563 | 60.2 | 37.9 | 27.3 |
| Florence | 45.1 | 771 | 27.1 | 10.6 | 82.3 | 13.1 | 16 630 | 2.7 | 1 099 | 6.6 | 23 115 | 67.3 | 41.7 | 25.0 |
| Frankfort | 50.2 | 618 | 29.4 | 8.9 | 75.8 | 11.3 | 12 038 | 0.0 | 867 | 7.2 | 20 978 | 62.8 | 36.9 | 31.1 |
| Georgetown | 36.5 | 701 | 26.3 | 7.9 | 73.0 | 16.3 | 14 493 | 1.6 | 928 | 6.4 | 21 535 | 69.2 | 44.8 | 25.9 |
| Henderson | 39.7 | 560 | 31.0 | 10.9 | 81.3 | 8.3 | 14 011 | -0.1 | 1 027 | 7.3 | 22 717 | 61.4 | 38.6 | 34.1 |
| Hopkinsville | 45.8 | 577 | 27.9 | 10.3 | 81.4 | 10.2 | 13 653 | 5.1 | 1 294 | 9.5 | 23 912 | 58.7 | 33.4 | 36.4 |
| Jeffersontown | 32.7 | 819 | 26.5 | 2.5 | 83.9 | 13.0 | 14 302 | 2.0 | 1 002 | 7.0 | 20 717 | 72.0 | 46.3 | 18.8 |
| Lexington-Fayette | 43.1 | 722 | 29.4 | 8.1 | 74.6 | 9.7 | 156 246 | 2.3 | 9 884 | 6.3 | 237 217 | 69.5 | 42.4 | 22.0 |
| Louisville/Jefferson County | 35.7 | 689 | 29.0 | 10.2 | 85.2 | 7.2 | 365 294 | 1.7 | 31 260 | 8.6 | 583 467 | 66.2 | 40.5 | 28.5 |
| Nicholasville | 40.5 | 719 | 32.2 | 5.6 | 76.8 | 11.6 | 13 524 | 2.1 | 970 | 7.2 | 20 904 | 68.9 | 42.2 | 22.4 |
| Owensboro | 39.7 | 580 | 27.8 | 9.8 | 82.4 | 6.8 | 28 806 | 2.9 | 1 911 | 6.6 | 44 643 | 58.0 | 37.5 | 36.0 |
| Paducah | 50.0 | 522 | 28.2 | 12.8 | 74.8 | 13.8 | 10 646 | -0.1 | 922 | 8.7 | 20 446 | 55.6 | 33.7 | 39.1 |
| Richmond | 60.8 | 543 | 30.9 | 9.7 | 64.2 | 19.8 | 17 266 | 2.8 | 1 188 | 6.9 | 25 956 | 63.2 | 27.2 | 30.8 |
| LOUISIANA | 32.1 | 745 | 31.7 | 8.5 | 85.1 | 10.5 | 2 083 710 | 1.7 | 134 361 | 6.4 | 3 503 250 | 61.7 | 39.4 | 27.7 |
| Alexandria | 44.6 | 756 | 38.5 | 12.0 | 82.8 | 7.1 | 19 650 | -0.8 | 1 419 | 7.2 | 35 629 | 58.1 | 38.9 | 30.9 |
| Baton Rouge | 48.3 | 757 | 35.2 | 10.7 | 78.3 | 9.4 | 109 261 | 2.5 | 8 008 | 7.3 | 183 031 | 65.0 | 36.7 | 26.3 |
| Bossier City | 41.6 | 746 | 29.5 | 7.6 | 79.2 | 12.6 | 28 115 | 0.7 | 1 606 | 5.7 | 46 813 | 68.1 | 40.3 | 24.9 |
| Central | 14.5 | 719 | 30.6 | 3.0 | 91.0 | 6.3 | 13 981 | 3.3 | 675 | 4.8 | 21 560 | 68.7 | 47.0 | 22.6 |
| Houma | 32.6 | 690 | 32.8 | 11.9 | 84.9 | 7.7 | 16 265 | 4.3 | 765 | 4.7 | 26 149 | 59.6 | 38.8 | 28.9 |
| Kenner | 38.1 | 938 | 31.8 | 6.9 | 86.6 | 8.9 | 32 825 | 1.9 | 1 911 | 5.8 | 53 102 | 68.2 | 43.8 | 23.0 |
| Lafayette | 42.7 | 745 | 30.0 | 9.3 | 82.3 | 9.1 | 63 978 | 4.9 | 3 084 | 4.8 | 97 245 | 65.9 | 39.4 | 23.8 |
| Lake Charles | 42.8 | 706 | 31.0 | 10.1 | 76.6 | 10.9 | 33 628 | 2.7 | 2 159 | 6.4 | 56 467 | 61.5 | 34.6 | 29.4 |
| Monroe | 52.9 | 599 | 35.7 | 14.7 | 84.1 | 7.2 | 20 269 | 1.3 | 1 801 | 8.9 | 37 165 | 57.1 | 33.4 | 33.7 |
| New Iberia | 38.3 | 653 | 29.4 | 12.9 | 83.9 | 7.3 | 13 603 | 5.0 | 887 | 6.5 | 23 097 | 58.9 | 34.4 | 32.0 |
| New Orleans | 51.7 | 924 | 39.2 | 18.4 | 77.7 | 11.4 | 151 058 | 1.5 | 11 846 | 7.8 | 260 172 | 62.6 | 37.7 | 30.3 |
| Shreveport | 43.1 | 711 | 31.7 | 11.7 | 82.5 | 6.4 | 90 921 | 0.4 | 6 343 | 7.0 | 154 387 | 63.1 | 39.3 | 29.5 |
| Slidell | 27.4 | 1 053 | 36.5 | 4.3 | 82.9 | 11.7 | 12 681 | 1.4 | 899 | 7.1 | 21 116 | 60.7 | 37.2 | 28.0 |
| MAINE | 27.3 | 736 | 30.3 | 7.0 | 86.2 | 11.0 | 706 097 | 1.8 | 51 596 | 7.3 | 1 086 610 | 65.1 | 38.9 | 29.7 |
| Bangor | 51.3 | 714 | 31.8 | 12.8 | 74.7 | 16.2 | 17 384 | 1.6 | 1 202 | 6.9 | 27 610 | 64.9 | 35.0 | 30.5 |
| Lewiston | 49.5 | 656 | 30.3 | 15.6 | 80.5 | 10.7 | 18 554 | 0.7 | 1 429 | 7.7 | 29 698 | 62.2 | 36.9 | 34.8 |
| Portland | 55.5 | 873 | 31.1 | 17.4 | 75.0 | 14.1 | 39 814 | 3.7 | 2 329 | 5.8 | 56 374 | 70.2 | 41.4 | 27.8 |
| South Portland | 36.9 | 925 | 28.1 | 6.5 | 84.4 | 11.3 | 14 915 | 3.4 | 851 | 5.7 | 19 955 | 72.1 | 47.3 | 23.7 |
| MARYLAND | 31.3 | 1 139 | 30.7 | 9.3 | 86.4 | 10.5 | 3 122 629 | 1.9 | 213 058 | 6.8 | 4 547 457 | 69.6 | 45.8 | 21.1 |
| Annapolis | 47.0 | 1 285 | 30.3 | 11.3 | 83.0 | 12.1 | 22 970 | 2.2 | 1 362 | 5.9 | 31 327 | 72.0 | 47.3 | 22.2 |
| Baltimore | 50.5 | 889 | 33.7 | 29.6 | 82.7 | 6.4 | 279 416 | 2.1 | 28 598 | 10.2 | 500 442 | 62.4 | 37.9 | 31.5 |
| Bowie | 14.0 | 1 756 | 29.9 | 2.8 | 91.3 | 7.2 | 31 819 | 1.6 | 1 730 | 5.4 | 41 978 | 76.5 | 53.9 | 14.4 |
| College Park | 48.7 | 1 321 | 43.2 | 7.9 | 65.5 | 28.1 | 15 953 | 2.3 | 1 167 | 7.3 | 27 714 | 51.3 | 20.8 | 26.1 |
| Frederick | 43.0 | 1 141 | 28.8 | 7.6 | 78.4 | 12.3 | 36 022 | 0.3 | 2 236 | 6.2 | 50 460 | 73.7 | 48.9 | 18.0 |
| Gaithersburg | 43.5 | 1 381 | 29.4 | 7.6 | 83.5 | 13.0 | 34 110 | 1.2 | 1 791 | 5.3 | 46 486 | 76.8 | 52.6 | 14.9 |
| Hagerstown | 57.4 | 765 | 32.5 | 16.5 | 77.4 | 10.5 | 19 699 | 1.1 | 1 945 | 9.9 | 31 019 | 65.7 | 37.5 | 32.7 |
| Laurel | 46.3 | 1 214 | 28.4 | 8.0 | 80.7 | 14.1 | NA | NA | NA | NA | 19 739 | 78.7 | 54.5 | 13.2 |
| Rockville | 39.0 | 1 657 | 29.2 | 9.4 | 83.3 | 13.1 | 32 546 | 1.2 | 1 635 | 5.0 | 48 231 | 72.5 | 48.9 | 17.7 |
| Salisbury | 62.5 | 982 | 35.1 | 14.5 | 69.2 | 18.0 | 15 756 | 1.5 | 1 476 | 9.4 | 24 215 | 64.1 | 35.1 | 29.0 |
| MASSACHUSETTS | 36.4 | 1 037 | 30.2 | 12.4 | 86.5 | 9.0 | 3 475 446 | 0.8 | 233 684 | 6.7 | 5 267 692 | 67.8 | 40.8 | 25.7 |
| Agawam Town | 21.5 | 830 | 30.4 | 5.6 | 91.5 | 5.1 | 15 399 | -1.1 | 990 | 6.4 | 23 390 | 69.4 | 42.3 | 24.7 |
| Attleboro | 31.8 | 941 | 27.6 | 5.5 | 87.7 | 7.2 | 24 804 | 1.2 | 2 220 | 8.9 | 34 727 | 72.9 | 46.1 | 22.4 |
| Barnstable Town | 23.3 | 1 118 | 32.7 | 6.7 | 89.7 | 6.8 | 26 327 | 7.5 | 1 748 | 6.6 | 38 285 | 63.4 | 37.0 | 30.3 |

1. $2,000 represents $2,000 or more.   2. 50.0 represents 50 percent or more.   3. Percent of civilian labor force.   4. Persons 16 years old and over.

| City | Value of residential construction authorized by building permits, 2011 | | | Wholesale trade,[1] 2007 | | | | Retail trade,[2] 2007 | | | |
|---|---|---|---|---|---|---|---|---|---|---|---|
| | New construction ($1,000) | Number of housing units | Percent single family | Number of establish-ments | Number of employees | Sales (mil dol) | Annual payroll (mil dol) | Number of establish-ments | Number of employees | Sales (mil dol) | Annual payroll (mil dol) |
| | 69 | 70 | 71 | 72 | 73 | 74 | 75 | 76 | 77 | 78 | 79 |
| KANSAS................ | 860 729 | 5 386 | 64.4 | 3 747 | 47 285 | 45 863.9 | 2 150.4 | 11 463 | 149 672 | 34 538.3 | 3 133.7 |
| Dodge City ................. | 5 512 | 71 | 23.9 | 40 | 433 | 333.3 | 17.6 | 124 | 1 571 | 380.1 | 33.2 |
| Garden City ............... | 4 879 | 45 | 22.2 | 14 | 132 | 132.4 | 5.3 | 152 | 2 248 | 461.2 | 43.5 |
| Hutchinson ................ | 2 778 | 15 | 86.7 | 36 | 473 | 464.1 | 17.1 | 241 | 3 264 | 720.4 | 68.9 |
| Kansas City .............. | 9 863 | 62 | 85.5 | 214 | 5 328 | 3 855.9 | 265.1 | 422 | 6 267 | 1 556.3 | 158.6 |
| Lawrence ................... | 54 054 | 465 | 21.9 | 63 | 641 | 354.9 | 24.8 | 363 | 5 823 | 1 130.5 | 105.7 |
| Leavenworth .............. | 8 209 | 35 | 100.0 | 7 | 19 | 5.4 | 0.7 | 121 | 1 529 | 353.2 | 32.0 |
| Leawood .................... | 12 504 | 31 | 100.0 | 38 | 355 | 203.3 | 23.7 | 136 | 2 403 | 334.1 | 40.0 |
| Lenexa...................... | 26 235 | 89 | 100.0 | 285 | 5 111 | 2 182.2 | 256.3 | 185 | 3 734 | 1 849.1 | 107.4 |
| Manhattan ................. | 62 940 | 481 | 41.0 | 34 | 567 | 126.0 | 18.4 | 260 | 4 688 | 837.1 | 80.8 |
| Olathe ...................... | 91 057 | 335 | 94.6 | 136 | 2 873 | 1 426.9 | 140.5 | 408 | 7 408 | 2 090.1 | 176.5 |
| Overland Park ............ | 113 961 | 736 | 37.2 | 272 | 2 390 | 9 823.7 | 196.8 | 772 | 15 086 | 2 809.9 | 324.8 |
| Salina ...................... | 8 802 | 82 | 56.1 | 66 | 909 | 505.5 | 35.8 | 267 | 4 131 | 1 047.1 | 84.6 |
| Shawnee ................... | 19 366 | 77 | 75.3 | 49 | 829 | 632.8 | 42.7 | 194 | 3 595 | 726.3 | 78.9 |
| Topeka ..................... | 14 249 | 84 | 92.9 | 124 | 1 454 | 571.4 | 60.7 | 674 | 9 716 | 2 136.6 | 201.2 |
| Wichita..................... | 73 028 | 543 | 75.3 | 519 | 7 491 | 11 827.5 | 349.6 | 1 518 | 23 854 | 5 765.6 | 519.7 |
| KENTUCKY .............. | 915 114 | 7 782 | 61.6 | 3 794 | 59 854 | 74 680.8 | 2 869.5 | 16 404 | 214 782 | 50 405.9 | 4 502.2 |
| Bowling Green.............. | 33 537 | 581 | 14.3 | 120 | 1 638 | 2 071.9 | 68.7 | 482 | 7 172 | 1 609.8 | 144.8 |
| Covington .................. | 2 323 | 16 | 68.8 | 26 | 744 | 158.1 | 19.1 | 139 | 2 025 | 417.8 | 42.4 |
| Elizabethtown ............ | 19 183 | 333 | 15.9 | 34 | 365 | 220.2 | 12.7 | 280 | 4 192 | 973.0 | 93.9 |
| Florence ................... | NA | NA | NA | 40 | 697 | 814.2 | 37.1 | 325 | 6 780 | 1 579.0 | 140.1 |
| Frankfort ................... | 380 | 3 | 100.0 | 14 | 215 | 205.3 | 9.2 | 140 | 1 998 | 402.8 | 40.0 |
| Georgetown................ | NA | NA | NA | 14 | D | D | D | 109 | 1 581 | 440.7 | 31.9 |
| Henderson ................. | 3 089 | 38 | 31.6 | 26 | 351 | 419.3 | 16.8 | 168 | 2 315 | 581.3 | 48.7 |
| Hopkinsville ............... | 12 281 | 126 | 49.2 | 50 | 856 | 776.5 | 31.8 | 197 | 2 427 | 584.7 | 54.4 |
| Jeffersontown ............. | 1 618 | 8 | 100.0 | 155 | 2 419 | 1 186.1 | 122.6 | 150 | 3 074 | 866.8 | 74.2 |
| Lexington-Fayette........ | 83 346 | 739 | 69.4 | 375 | 8 540 | 4 442.4 | 568.5 | 1 249 | 22 335 | 4 778.5 | 510.4 |
| Louisville/Jefferson County | 138 324 | 998 | 62.7 | 1 026 | 16 413 | 13 000.6 | 763.2 | 2 775 | 43 687 | 10 002.4 | 978.5 |
| Nicholasville ............. | 5 088 | 50 | 100.0 | 27 | D | D | D | 118 | 1 759 | 621.0 | 47.0 |
| Owensboro ................ | 19 851 | 269 | 78.4 | 69 | 861 | 568.8 | 34.9 | 361 | 4 763 | 1 071.4 | 100.4 |
| Paducah ................... | 14 212 | 86 | 41.9 | 72 | 1 503 | 3 423.6 | 61.2 | 373 | 5 842 | 1 408.6 | 121.2 |
| Richmond .................. | 7 722 | 110 | 61.8 | 25 | 208 | 131.8 | 7.7 | 206 | 3 012 | 662.9 | 58.8 |
| LOUISIANA .............. | 1 918 793 | 12 173 | 81.8 | 4 839 | 63 911 | 51 415.6 | 2 808.3 | 17 135 | 231 365 | 56 543.2 | 5 096.1 |
| Alexandria ................. | 22 557 | 188 | 51.1 | 80 | 981 | 442.6 | 40.4 | 398 | 5 762 | 1 415.2 | 125.7 |
| Baton Rouge .............. | 74 778 | 528 | 24.8 | 346 | 4 642 | 5 407.5 | 204.8 | 1 173 | 16 258 | 3 830.3 | 374.8 |
| Bossier City ............... | 62 551 | 644 | 59.0 | 60 | 1 307 | 926.2 | 60.8 | 389 | 5 610 | 1 559.3 | 127.3 |
| Central...................... | NA | NA | NA | NA | NA | NA | NA | NA | NA | NA | NA |
| Houma ...................... | NA | NA | NA | 60 | 684 | 374.2 | 31.1 | 186 | 2 432 | 505.2 | 52.2 |
| Kenner...................... | 4 649 | 17 | 100.0 | 124 | 1 009 | 518.1 | 42.9 | 369 | 6 512 | 1 875.1 | 164.1 |
| Lafayette ................... | NA | NA | NA | 257 | 3 482 | 1 389.2 | 147.8 | 829 | 13 436 | 3 273.0 | 293.3 |
| Lake Charles .............. | 82 557 | 808 | 32.4 | 75 | 937 | 411.1 | 34.1 | 505 | 6 847 | 1 507.5 | 142.2 |
| Monroe ..................... | 18 854 | 111 | 76.6 | 80 | 1 184 | 1 184.4 | 46.2 | 395 | 6 299 | 1 352.3 | 125.7 |
| New Iberia ................. | 5 741 | 38 | 84.2 | 40 | 773 | 256.6 | 37.2 | 210 | 2 982 | 736.6 | 65.2 |
| New Orleans .............. | 156 896 | 1 094 | 65.5 | 253 | 3 030 | 1 938.4 | 145.6 | 1 155 | 11 877 | 2 718.0 | 305.5 |
| Shreveport ................. | 76 363 | 293 | 100.0 | 274 | D | D | D | 909 | 13 397 | 3 240.4 | 304.8 |
| Slidell ...................... | 1 829 | 16 | 75.0 | 36 | 328 | 253.1 | 12.3 | 288 | 5 190 | 1 143.6 | 109.3 |
| MAINE...................... | 435 668 | 2 744 | 83.1 | 1 439 | 16 939 | 8 823.7 | 686.4 | 6 911 | 83 279 | 20 444.0 | 1 893.7 |
| Bangor...................... | 4 820 | 22 | 90.9 | 71 | 1 272 | 854.1 | 50.6 | 332 | 6 123 | 1 824.0 | 136.5 |
| Lewiston .................... | 3 433 | 20 | 100.0 | 46 | 689 | 252.8 | 28.5 | 169 | 2 029 | 561.0 | 45.2 |
| Portland .................... | 4 635 | 31 | 93.5 | 172 | 2 475 | 1 124.5 | 105.2 | 416 | 5 116 | 1 321.8 | 131.0 |
| South Portland ............ | 2 986 | 17 | 100.0 | 57 | 1 269 | 1 108.4 | 50.3 | 252 | 5 393 | 1 069.6 | 116.5 |
| MARYLAND .............. | 2 204 630 | 13 481 | 62.0 | 5 020 | 79 868 | 51 276.8 | 4 158.4 | 19 601 | 294 806 | 75 664.2 | 7 290.8 |
| Annapolis................... | 6 016 | 26 | 100.0 | 58 | 495 | 812.5 | 30.2 | 311 | 3 368 | 973.6 | 95.9 |
| Baltimore ................... | 85 745 | 989 | 7.6 | 534 | 9 046 | 4 843.4 | 468.9 | 1 950 | 16 682 | 4 348.8 | 401.5 |
| Bowie........................ | NA | NA | NA | 12 | 47 | 16.6 | 2.1 | 167 | 4 136 | 854.4 | 85.5 |
| College Park............... | NA | NA | NA | 16 | 56 | 15.3 | 3.1 | 87 | 2 001 | 543.6 | 54.0 |
| Frederick ................... | 23 324 | 121 | 100.0 | 78 | 1 101 | 487.0 | 59.8 | 356 | 5 491 | 1 398.0 | 141.1 |
| Gaithersburg............... | 51 740 | 432 | 13.0 | 73 | 858 | 499.1 | 55.4 | 371 | 7 650 | 2 068.4 | 202.1 |
| Hagerstown ............... | 4 733 | 43 | 95.3 | 53 | 466 | 141.5 | 16.4 | 225 | 4 104 | 1 059.1 | 95.8 |
| Laurel ...................... | 316 | 1 | 100.0 | 12 | 139 | 33.9 | 7.0 | 154 | 2 280 | 460.1 | 47.8 |
| Rockville.................... | 40 732 | 291 | 5.2 | 89 | 1 959 | 3 282.8 | 151.2 | 316 | 4 343 | 1 245.3 | 125.7 |
| Salisbury.................... | 1 756 | 13 | 100.0 | 69 | 813 | 416.1 | 31.5 | 298 | 5 181 | 1 104.6 | 106.3 |
| MASSACHUSETTS ... | 1 761 071 | 7 725 | 63.4 | 7 284 | 123 267 | 95 275.7 | 7 644.3 | 25 469 | 360 218 | 88 083.0 | 8 916.5 |
| Agawam Town ............ | 5 345 | 19 | 100.0 | NA | NA | NA | NA | NA | NA | NA | NA |
| Attleboro ................... | 6 732 | 53 | 86.8 | 38 | 619 | 260.1 | 31.5 | 158 | 2 716 | 664.8 | 58.7 |
| Barnstable Town .......... | 18 629 | 25 | 100.0 | 41 | 425 | 148.9 | 19.6 | 434 | 5 635 | 1 395.5 | 143.3 |

1. Merchant wholesalers except manufacturers' sales branches and offices.   2. Establishments with payroll.

# Table D. Cities — Real Estate, Professional Services, and Manufacturing

| City | Real estate and rental and leasing, 2007 | | | | Professional, scientific, and technical services,[1] 2007 | | | | Manufacturing, 2007 | | | |
|---|---|---|---|---|---|---|---|---|---|---|---|---|
| | Number of establishments | Number of employees | Receipts (mil dol) | Annual payroll (mil dol) | Number of establishments | Number of employees | Receipts (mil dol) | Annual payroll (mil dol) | Number of establishments | Number of employees | Receipts (mil dol) | Annual payroll (mil dol) |
| | 80 | 81 | 82 | 83 | 84 | 85 | 86 | 87 | 88 | 89 | 90 | 91 |
| KANSAS | 3 314 | 15 160 | 2 428.8 | 439.7 | 7 042 | 55 922 | 7 781.4 | 2 736.5 | 3 170 | 177 659 | 76 751.8 | 7 983.4 |
| Dodge City | 26 | D | D | D | 45 | D | D | D | 21 | D | D | D |
| Garden City | 29 | 100 | 13.8 | 2.4 | 53 | D | D | D | NA | NA | NA | NA |
| Hutchinson | 54 | D | D | D | 92 | D | D | D | 45 | 1 413 | 315.2 | 55.8 |
| Kansas City | 127 | 730 | 126.2 | 21.2 | 140 | D | D | D | 204 | 10 394 | 7 369.7 | 604.1 |
| Lawrence | 151 | 685 | 90.1 | 16.9 | 247 | D | D | D | 66 | 3 447 | 820.1 | 123.8 |
| Leavenworth | 32 | 175 | 20.7 | 4.4 | 68 | D | D | D | 14 | 535 | 94.7 | 19.0 |
| Leawood | 109 | 300 | 86.3 | 12.9 | 211 | 1 435 | 240.4 | 98.2 | NA | NA | NA | NA |
| Lenexa | 118 | 771 | 139.0 | 27.9 | 307 | D | D | D | 150 | 7 287 | 2 087.7 | 320.3 |
| Manhattan | 101 | 496 | 53.0 | 10.5 | 138 | D | D | D | 29 | 1 162 | 184.0 | 36.3 |
| Olathe | 148 | 577 | 108.3 | 18.5 | 358 | D | D | D | 110 | 5 447 | 3 245.9 | 279.9 |
| Overland Park | 397 | 2 043 | 438.2 | 80.8 | 1 155 | D | D | D | 97 | 1 358 | 238.1 | 57.3 |
| Salina | 69 | 277 | 44.9 | 6.3 | 115 | D | D | D | 58 | 3 765 | 1 026.9 | 145.9 |
| Shawnee | 74 | 313 | 58.8 | 6.9 | 191 | 1 372 | 144.1 | 47.0 | 48 | 1 759 | 758.1 | 106.0 |
| Topeka | 207 | 931 | 144.0 | 28.1 | 408 | D | D | D | 94 | 3 965 | 1 658.1 | 145.1 |
| Wichita | 520 | 3 170 | 467.8 | 87.1 | 983 | D | D | D | 478 | 33 140 | 14 213.2 | 1 655.3 |
| KENTUCKY | 3 898 | 20 146 | 3 894.3 | 593.4 | 8 075 | 61 428 | 7 872.2 | 2 831.6 | 4 165 | 247 096 | 119 105.4 | 10 773.2 |
| Bowling Green | 114 | 1 046 | 107.5 | 27.1 | 175 | D | D | D | 98 | 9 133 | 4 473.8 | 404.8 |
| Covington | 39 | 287 | 73.1 | 9.6 | 135 | D | D | D | 31 | 1 052 | 278.7 | 41.9 |
| Elizabethtown | 58 | 235 | 38.8 | 5.5 | 90 | D | D | D | 57 | 4 359 | D | 185.6 |
| Florence | 71 | 288 | 79.3 | 8.6 | 111 | 586 | 66.6 | 22.2 | 41 | 870 | D | D |
| Frankfort | 37 | 123 | 17.9 | 2.9 | 96 | 616 | 78.2 | 27.5 | 13 | 870 | D | 36.6 |
| Georgetown | 42 | 140 | 24.2 | 3.4 | 47 | 382 | 30.1 | 12.9 | 22 | 9 060 | D | D |
| Henderson | 35 | 203 | 15.8 | 4.4 | 73 | 385 | 32.4 | 10.6 | 59 | 4 336 | D | 152.0 |
| Hopkinsville | 51 | 179 | 22.0 | 3.2 | 61 | 346 | 30.1 | 11.4 | 54 | D | D | 197.5 |
| Jeffersontown | 75 | 713 | 194.4 | 22.9 | 156 | D | D | D | 101 | 4 718 | 865.7 | 173.1 |
| Lexington-Fayette | 476 | 2 268 | 391.2 | 68.2 | 1 053 | D | D | D | 255 | 9 602 | 3 061.2 | 401.7 |
| Louisville/Jefferson County | 991 | 6 888 | 1 995.1 | 263.3 | 2 266 | 15 049 | 2 652.2 | 793.2 | 797 | 45 142 | 25 695.4 | 2 233.8 |
| Nicholasville | 34 | 145 | 25.1 | 4.5 | 37 | 152 | 12.5 | 4.3 | 55 | 2 584 | D | D |
| Owensboro | 63 | 432 | 37.9 | 9.4 | 140 | D | D | D | 82 | 4 930 | 2 092.4 | 194.4 |
| Paducah | 69 | 336 | 53.6 | 8.8 | 139 | D | D | D | 32 | 1 274 | 345.2 | D |
| Richmond | 53 | 198 | 33.3 | 4.5 | 72 | D | D | D | 32 | 2 192 | D | 83.8 |
| LOUISIANA | 4 625 | 30 922 | 6 014.9 | 1 194.9 | 11 128 | 84 666 | 11 856.6 | 4 234.6 | 3 442 | 148 080 | 205 054.7 | 7 564.5 |
| Alexandria | 107 | 590 | 69.0 | 14.7 | 195 | 1 268 | 134.5 | 49.9 | 34 | 1 165 | D | 29.7 |
| Baton Rouge | 353 | 1 827 | 316.6 | 58.1 | 1 148 | 13 858 | 2 088.3 | 722.9 | 197 | 4 423 | 2 443.5 | 198.7 |
| Bossier City | 86 | 457 | 81.2 | 12.3 | 96 | 610 | 54.2 | 18.2 | 52 | 1 671 | D | 59.2 |
| Central | NA | NA | NA | NA | NA | NA | NA | NA | NA | NA | NA | NA |
| Houma | 79 | 602 | 110.2 | 25.4 | 168 | D | D | D | 37 | 812 | 138.2 | 36.3 |
| Kenner | 80 | 1 057 | 199.7 | 31.4 | 165 | 920 | 117.8 | 48.5 | 55 | 1 062 | 150.7 | 40.7 |
| Lafayette | 306 | 2 156 | 571.5 | 107.1 | 928 | D | D | D | 128 | 5 125 | 1 055.5 | 187.8 |
| Lake Charles | 121 | 440 | 77.4 | 12.8 | 304 | D | D | D | 40 | 2 358 | D | 184.8 |
| Monroe | 122 | 582 | 103.8 | 19.6 | 308 | D | D | D | 45 | 1 546 | 413.6 | 63.2 |
| New Iberia | 58 | 654 | 147.6 | 33.1 | 120 | 549 | 65.7 | 17.8 | 57 | 2 978 | D | 117.5 |
| New Orleans | 362 | 1 764 | 354.4 | 61.8 | 1 290 | D | D | D | 141 | 7 607 | 3 088.9 | 402.0 |
| Shreveport | 290 | 1 839 | 258.8 | 49.0 | 568 | 4 053 | 474.9 | 170.2 | 162 | 6 383 | D | 256.0 |
| Slidell | 40 | 171 | 31.4 | 4.1 | 138 | D | D | D | NA | NA | NA | NA |
| MAINE | 1 771 | 6 942 | 1 054.0 | 209.4 | 3 444 | 20 504 | 2 686.1 | 1 004.9 | 1 825 | 58 938 | 16 363.2 | 2 524.5 |
| Bangor | 96 | 482 | 92.3 | 15.1 | 163 | D | D | D | 45 | 1 022 | 225.3 | 41.7 |
| Lewiston | 46 | 285 | 34.0 | 6.5 | 71 | D | D | D | 70 | 2 240 | 537.5 | 90.2 |
| Portland | 248 | 1 376 | 261.2 | 48.8 | 570 | D | D | D | 105 | 3 198 | 886.7 | 124.6 |
| South Portland | 54 | 414 | 83.5 | 16.7 | 98 | 838 | 99.4 | 41.8 | 31 | 1 595 | 298.0 | 95.4 |
| MARYLAND | 6 768 | 49 766 | 12 391.9 | 2 262.6 | 19 345 | D | D | D | 3 680 | 127 780 | 41 456.1 | 6 453.7 |
| Annapolis | 104 | 618 | 106.3 | 25.6 | 387 | D | D | D | 47 | 618 | 127.6 | 26.6 |
| Baltimore | 647 | 4 677 | 837.5 | 214.9 | 1 506 | D | D | D | 479 | 16 253 | 5 730.9 | 726.5 |
| Bowie | 54 | 195 | 32.8 | 6.7 | 164 | D | D | D | NA | NA | NA | NA |
| College Park | 20 | 73 | 7.9 | 2.1 | 61 | D | D | D | 6 | D | D | D |
| Frederick | 105 | 765 | 120.1 | 27.2 | 368 | D | D | D | 55 | 2 317 | 1 614.3 | 121.4 |
| Gaithersburg | 117 | 756 | 207.7 | 44.4 | 425 | D | D | D | 40 | 1 996 | 559.5 | 137.1 |
| Hagerstown | 58 | 250 | 35.4 | 6.7 | 113 | 1 251 | 74.4 | 30.0 | 64 | 3 878 | 1 434.9 | 214.8 |
| Laurel | 36 | 593 | 62.3 | 19.7 | 91 | D | D | D | NA | NA | NA | NA |
| Rockville | 139 | 2 575 | 592.3 | 128.4 | 871 | 16 740 | 2 715.0 | 1 166.8 | 65 | 1 301 | 199.9 | 58.1 |
| Salisbury | 93 | 578 | 81.6 | 18.5 | 162 | D | D | D | 47 | 3 260 | 811.6 | 109.6 |
| MASSACHUSETTS | 7 053 | 48 576 | 14 029.8 | 2 287.6 | 21 773 | 243 374 | 49 085.7 | 20 652.0 | 7 737 | 289 256 | 86 429.0 | 15 712.0 |
| Agawam Town | NA | NA | NA | NA | NA | NA | NA | NA | NA | NA | NA | NA |
| Attleboro | 34 | 121 | 16.7 | 5.1 | 76 | 352 | 40.9 | 16.0 | 109 | 5 721 | 1 711.3 | 289.0 |
| Barnstable Town | 76 | 262 | 66.1 | 8.6 | 201 | D | D | D | 41 | 562 | D | 27.5 |

1. Establishments subject to federal tax.

Table D. Cities — **Accommodation and Food Services, Arts, Entertainment, and Recreation, and Health Care and Social Assistance**

| City | Accommodation and food services, 2007 | | | | Arts, entertainment, and recreation,[1] 2007 | | | | Health care and social assistance,[1] 2007 | | | |
|---|---|---|---|---|---|---|---|---|---|---|---|---|
| | Number of establish-ments | Number of employees | Sales (mil dol) | Annual payroll (mil dol) | Number of establish-ments | Number of employees | Receipts (mil dol) | Annual payroll (mil dol) | Number of establish-ments | Number of employees | Receipts (mil dol) | Annual payroll (mil dol) |
| | 92 | 93 | 94 | 95 | 96 | 97 | 98 | 99 | 100 | 101 | 102 | 103 |
| KANSAS | 5 866 | 104 795 | 4 192.3 | 1 173.7 | 769 | 10 017 | 546.6 | 146.7 | 5 778 | 83 531 | 7 948.2 | 3 175.8 |
| Dodge City | 66 | 938 | 39.6 | 9.9 | 6 | D | D | D | 52 | D | D | D |
| Garden City | 65 | 1 107 | 48.4 | 12.3 | 4 | D | D | D | 64 | D | D | D |
| Hutchinson | 100 | 1 984 | 75.3 | 20.3 | 5 | D | D | D | 121 | 1 942 | 224.1 | 97.6 |
| Kansas City | 216 | 4 494 | 220.7 | 61.7 | 24 | D | D | D | 216 | 3 372 | 280.0 | 129.9 |
| Lawrence | 262 | 5 634 | 203.0 | 57.6 | 27 | D | D | D | 196 | 1 940 | 159.3 | 74.5 |
| Leavenworth | 56 | 933 | 35.0 | 9.7 | 4 | D | D | D | 57 | 519 | 39.3 | 18.5 |
| Leawood | 52 | D | D | D | 13 | 95 | 5.8 | 3.1 | 141 | D | D | D |
| Lenexa | 105 | 1 778 | 80.7 | 24.1 | 19 | 275 | 13.1 | 4.1 | 118 | 3 962 | 342.7 | 141.6 |
| Manhattan | 152 | 3 466 | 125.8 | 33.4 | 15 | 188 | 8.9 | 2.3 | 116 | D | D | D |
| Olathe | 225 | 5 329 | 203.2 | 61.8 | 27 | 603 | 21.6 | 6.9 | 225 | 2 689 | 272.7 | 110.4 |
| Overland Park | 438 | 10 877 | 525.9 | 158.3 | 75 | 1 669 | 79.3 | 25.0 | 561 | 10 621 | 1 331.7 | 510.3 |
| Salina | 120 | 2 509 | 94.0 | 26.2 | 13 | D | D | D | 136 | 1 767 | 189.1 | 73.0 |
| Shawnee | 108 | 1 966 | 82.2 | 23.1 | 15 | D | D | D | 105 | D | D | D |
| Topeka | 342 | D | D | D | 29 | D | D | D | 359 | D | D | D |
| Wichita | 937 | 18 895 | 758.6 | 222.1 | 86 | 1 813 | 81.0 | 23.8 | 905 | 17 563 | 2 125.6 | 749.3 |
| KENTUCKY | 7 309 | 151 551 | 6 300.9 | 1 787.4 | 1 021 | 12 434 | 893.9 | 260.1 | 8 686 | 115 673 | 10 089.6 | 4 218.4 |
| Bowling Green | 200 | 5 185 | 223.1 | 61.7 | 16 | D | D | D | 246 | D | D | D |
| Covington | 135 | 2 503 | 124.9 | 35.3 | 8 | D | D | D | 40 | D | D | D |
| Elizabethtown | 111 | 2 954 | 109.0 | 31.5 | 10 | D | D | D | 184 | D | D | D |
| Florence | 159 | 4 275 | 185.1 | 53.7 | 22 | 433 | 24.5 | 7.7 | 121 | 1 718 | 136.0 | 59.4 |
| Frankfort | 83 | 1 910 | 70.2 | 22.1 | 5 | D | D | D | 106 | 1 833 | 178.4 | 62.8 |
| Georgetown | 67 | 1 572 | 65.2 | 18.0 | 3 | D | D | D | 62 | D | D | D |
| Henderson | 81 | 1 298 | 52.9 | 14.6 | 8 | D | D | D | 108 | D | D | D |
| Hopkinsville | 79 | 1 568 | 56.8 | 15.1 | 7 | D | D | D | 140 | 1 482 | 125.5 | 43.4 |
| Jeffersontown | 108 | 2 904 | 131.1 | 40.9 | 15 | D | D | D | 89 | 2 394 | 201.8 | 69.6 |
| Lexington-Fayette | 704 | 17 027 | 785.7 | 230.3 | 102 | 1 609 | 114.8 | 40.9 | 821 | 11 213 | 1 149.2 | 526.2 |
| Louisville/Jefferson County | 1 561 | 35 897 | 1 629.2 | 480.6 | 243 | 3 741 | 291.3 | 95.9 | 1 909 | 27 997 | 2 708.5 | 1 159.0 |
| Nicholasville | 47 | 1 025 | 39.8 | 11.1 | 6 | D | D | D | 43 | 436 | 27.5 | 13.2 |
| Owensboro | 134 | 3 322 | 120.2 | 37.5 | 13 | D | D | D | 221 | 2 935 | 245.9 | 104.8 |
| Paducah | 169 | 4 156 | 158.9 | 46.4 | 9 | D | D | D | 184 | D | D | D |
| Richmond | 95 | 2 528 | 90.7 | 25.5 | 8 | 87 | 2.5 | 0.7 | 108 | D | D | D |
| LOUISIANA | 8 169 | 180 289 | 9 729.9 | 2 579.0 | 1 062 | 20 064 | 2 468.3 | 578.3 | 9 725 | 145 174 | 13 178.8 | 4 934.9 |
| Alexandria | 158 | 3 256 | 129.3 | 33.1 | 12 | D | D | D | 270 | 5 309 | 582.5 | 210.6 |
| Baton Rouge | 599 | 15 567 | 716.7 | 197.5 | 56 | 2 070 | 262.5 | 37.2 | 725 | 11 500 | 1 084.6 | 417.0 |
| Bossier City | 198 | 9 254 | 694.5 | 170.3 | 28 | 1 560 | 155.4 | 24.8 | 138 | D | D | D |
| Central | NA | NA | NA | NA | NA | NA | NA | NA | NA | NA | NA | NA |
| Houma | 105 | 1 662 | 90.6 | 26.2 | 15 | 122 | 6.4 | 2.2 | 147 | D | D | D |
| Kenner | 190 | 3 710 | 193.4 | 52.5 | 24 | 1 288 | 452.3 | 176.8 | 149 | 2 094 | 217.3 | 76.8 |
| Lafayette | 421 | 11 003 | 516.5 | 138.8 | 34 | D | D | D | 715 | 12 024 | 1 274.8 | 467.0 |
| Lake Charles | 189 | 6 553 | 563.8 | 116.2 | 29 | D | D | D | 317 | 4 658 | 482.8 | 168.7 |
| Monroe | 170 | 3 817 | 142.9 | 37.7 | 19 | D | D | D | 320 | 3 918 | 385.7 | 139.4 |
| New Iberia | 76 | 1 636 | 62.9 | 15.6 | 7 | 108 | 6.3 | 1.1 | 160 | D | D | D |
| New Orleans | 1 058 | 28 356 | 2 148.2 | 602.4 | 109 | 2 551 | 284.1 | 109.0 | 594 | 6 413 | 847.2 | 277.8 |
| Shreveport | 409 | 11 967 | 661.4 | 171.8 | 58 | D | D | D | 653 | D | D | D |
| Slidell | 172 | 3 029 | 133.0 | 36.1 | 13 | D | D | D | 197 | 2 356 | 283.8 | 108.1 |
| MAINE | 3 938 | 49 363 | 2 515.8 | 747.7 | 635 | 5 204 | 361.3 | 85.0 | 3 203 | 39 757 | 3 015.8 | 1 397.3 |
| Bangor | 140 | 2 886 | 136.1 | 40.7 | 12 | D | D | D | 220 | 3 696 | 310.0 | 151.0 |
| Lewiston | 83 | 1 250 | 52.0 | 14.8 | 14 | 114 | 5.7 | 2.0 | 127 | 1 589 | 132.3 | 58.4 |
| Portland | 287 | 5 067 | 246.0 | 78.4 | 40 | 354 | 29.1 | 6.1 | 312 | 4 231 | 397.4 | 186.2 |
| South Portland | 127 | 3 046 | 137.6 | 45.7 | 9 | D | D | D | 101 | 1 261 | 124.4 | 60.2 |
| MARYLAND | 10 802 | 192 619 | 10 758.4 | 2 915.9 | 1 735 | 26 548 | 2 140.5 | 743.0 | 12 542 | 143 677 | 15 363.7 | 6 218.0 |
| Annapolis | 170 | 4 132 | 230.4 | 70.9 | 32 | 560 | 40.1 | 11.3 | 136 | D | D | D |
| Baltimore | 1 481 | 21 456 | 1 434.7 | 372.1 | 104 | 2 595 | 312.5 | 164.3 | 1 065 | 13 768 | 1 480.1 | 622.9 |
| Bowie | 75 | D | D | D | 13 | D | D | D | 172 | 1 381 | 130.2 | 48.7 |
| College Park | 105 | 1 820 | 103.4 | 25.6 | 5 | 56 | 3.0 | 1.1 | 33 | D | D | D |
| Frederick | 197 | 3 508 | 168.4 | 50.9 | 23 | 238 | 11.9 | 3.3 | 300 | 3 880 | 422.6 | 181.0 |
| Gaithersburg | 238 | 4 085 | 265.9 | 69.0 | 21 | D | D | D | 160 | 1 968 | 174.0 | 73.2 |
| Hagerstown | 129 | 2 543 | 113.9 | 32.7 | 12 | 107 | 3.8 | 0.9 | 124 | 1 347 | 156.6 | 63.8 |
| Laurel | 83 | 1 956 | 106.8 | 32.0 | 19 | D | D | D | 95 | 1 256 | 133.1 | 57.9 |
| Rockville | 237 | 3 440 | 242.4 | 63.6 | 32 | 331 | 16.1 | 4.0 | 263 | 3 503 | 492.4 | 202.8 |
| Salisbury | 149 | 3 313 | 151.4 | 40.6 | 11 | D | D | D | 169 | D | D | D |
| MASSACHUSETTS | 16 039 | 257 302 | 14 917.2 | 4 339.7 | 2 261 | 34 183 | 3 137.0 | 1 122.2 | 12 828 | 202 678 | 21 341.6 | 9 279.6 |
| Agawam Town | NA | NA | NA | NA | NA | NA | NA | NA | NA | NA | NA | NA |
| Attleboro | 89 | 2 009 | 83.9 | 27.5 | 10 | D | D | D | 92 | 1 579 | 148.1 | 58.4 |
| Barnstable Town | 193 | 3 066 | 185.2 | 57.0 | 28 | 197 | 17.2 | 5.0 | 152 | 2 027 | 223.5 | 104.8 |

1. Establishments subject to federal tax.

# Table D. Cities — Other Services and Federal Funds

| City | Other services[1], 2007 | | | | Selected federal funds, 2009–2010 (mil dol) | | | | | | | | |
|---|---|---|---|---|---|---|---|---|---|---|---|---|---|
| | | | | | Procurement contracts | | Grants | | | | | | |
| | Number of establishments | Number of employees | Receipts (mil dol) | Annual payroll (mil dol) | Defense | Other | Total[2] | Medicaid and other health related | Nutrition and family welfare | Energy and environment | Disasters and emergency preparedness | Housing and community development | Employment and training |
| | 104 | 105 | 106 | 107 | 108 | 109 | 110 | 111 | 112 | 113 | 114 | 115 | 116 |
| KANSAS | 4 281 | 24 265 | 1 825.9 | 572.9 | 1 940.8 | 1 118.9 | 4 736.3 | 2 241.5 | 600.2 | 156.7 | 123.0 | 133.5 | 62.6 |
| Dodge City | 39 | D | D | D | 0.5 | 0.6 | 7.1 | 0.0 | 1.7 | 0.0 | 0.0 | 2.3 | 0.0 |
| Garden City | 39 | D | D | D | 0.0 | 0.5 | 4.8 | 1.0 | 0.0 | 0.0 | 0.0 | 0.1 | 0.0 |
| Hutchinson | 73 | D | D | D | 0.0 | 0.0 | 5.6 | 0.7 | 2.2 | 0.0 | 0.0 | 0.6 | 0.1 |
| Kansas City | 177 | D | D | D | 18.1 | 38.9 | 149.5 | 111.1 | 7.5 | 5.4 | 0.2 | 18.8 | 0.0 |
| Lawrence | 118 | 731 | 45.0 | 14.3 | 12.5 | 15.3 | 181.6 | 75.9 | 2.6 | 17.5 | 0.0 | 6.6 | 0.1 |
| Leavenworth | 43 | 269 | 17.3 | 5.2 | 88.8 | 487.8 | 2.6 | 0.0 | 0.0 | 0.0 | 0.0 | 1.9 | 0.0 |
| Leawood | 42 | 588 | 49.8 | 11.7 | 8.8 | 11.3 | 1.0 | 0.2 | 0.0 | 0.0 | 0.0 | 0.5 | 0.0 |
| Lenexa | 84 | 660 | 65.7 | 21.6 | 7.0 | 12.7 | 0.5 | 0.0 | 0.0 | 0.0 | 0.0 | 0.0 | 0.0 |
| Manhattan | 81 | D | D | D | 9.2 | 16.7 | 104.8 | 19.8 | 1.6 | 12.0 | 2.0 | 3.2 | 0.0 |
| Olathe | 165 | 1 018 | 89.9 | 27.3 | 13.5 | 0.9 | 14.2 | 0.5 | 1.4 | 0.6 | 0.5 | 2.8 | 0.0 |
| Overland Park | 289 | 1 737 | 118.7 | 39.0 | 6.7 | 18.6 | 4.3 | 0.9 | 1.3 | 0.8 | 0.0 | 0.7 | 0.0 |
| Salina | 91 | D | D | D | 3.5 | 1.7 | 7.7 | 0.8 | 3.8 | 0.1 | 0.0 | 1.5 | 0.0 |
| Shawnee | 90 | 1 682 | 64.7 | 32.0 | 0.9 | 0.5 | 0.9 | 0.0 | 0.0 | 0.5 | 0.0 | 0.4 | 0.0 |
| Topeka | 217 | 1 409 | 102.5 | 31.7 | 20.5 | 12.7 | 673.4 | 78.5 | 110.0 | 70.3 | 6.7 | 39.2 | 57.4 |
| Wichita | 605 | 4 760 | 301.7 | 127.2 | 988.4 | 68.1 | 78.2 | 6.9 | 12.1 | 6.9 | 0.0 | 25.6 | 3.2 |
| KENTUCKY | 5 037 | 33 941 | 2 777.7 | 801.2 | 5 180.5 | 2 305.6 | 9 502.2 | 5 482.6 | 1 065.1 | 161.0 | 78.3 | 357.8 | 137.3 |
| Bowling Green | 114 | 911 | 64.5 | 18.8 | 0.1 | 5.1 | 71.5 | 1.0 | 6.0 | 5.5 | 0.0 | 4.9 | 1.2 |
| Covington | 68 | 481 | 32.8 | 10.9 | 0.4 | 9.3 | 38.8 | 2.0 | 4.6 | 0.0 | 0.0 | 29.0 | 0.0 |
| Elizabethtown | 69 | 542 | 38.4 | 12.1 | 4.8 | 0.8 | 2.3 | 0.1 | 0.0 | 0.1 | 0.0 | 0.3 | 0.0 |
| Florence | 76 | 592 | 33.2 | 11.3 | 90.0 | 6.5 | 0.5 | 0.0 | 0.0 | 0.2 | 0.0 | 0.0 | 0.3 |
| Frankfort | 51 | 226 | 14.7 | 4.5 | 0.8 | 1.5 | 1 068.1 | 98.9 | 210.0 | 74.0 | 38.0 | 87.2 | 99.1 |
| Georgetown | 36 | D | D | D | 0.6 | 0.0 | 3.0 | 0.1 | 0.0 | 0.0 | 0.0 | 2.7 | 0.0 |
| Henderson | 45 | D | D | D | 0.9 | 0.2 | 5.2 | 0.5 | 0.0 | 0.0 | 0.0 | 3.8 | 0.0 |
| Hopkinsville | 55 | D | D | D | 4.3 | 1.9 | 5.6 | 0.5 | 0.0 | 0.0 | 0.0 | 3.0 | 0.0 |
| Jeffersontown | 78 | 845 | 118.0 | 28.8 | 6.1 | 1.1 | 0.2 | 0.0 | 0.0 | 0.0 | 0.0 | 0.0 | 0.0 |
| Lexington-Fayette | 429 | 3 634 | 248.1 | 92.9 | 442.7 | 230.9 | 350.0 | 196.7 | 14.3 | 18.1 | 0.1 | 23.4 | 0.0 |
| Louisville/Jefferson County | 1 108 | 10 083 | 928.2 | 244.7 | NA | NA | NA | NA | NA | NA | NA | NA | NA |
| Nicholasville | 50 | D | D | D | 0.6 | 5.9 | -2.2 | 0.0 | 0.0 | -3.0 | 0.0 | 0.1 | 0.0 |
| Owensboro | 101 | 755 | 50.5 | 17.2 | 2.2 | 3.0 | 39.6 | 0.1 | 12.1 | 1.0 | 0.0 | 4.1 | 0.2 |
| Paducah | 80 | 632 | 69.9 | 14.4 | 0.5 | 66.2 | 10.5 | 0.7 | 1.8 | 0.0 | -0.2 | 4.3 | 0.0 |
| Richmond | 48 | 241 | 14.1 | 4.2 | 312.8 | 1.0 | 12.9 | 2.7 | 5.4 | 0.0 | -0.5 | 4.2 | 0.0 |
| LOUISIANA | 5 446 | 35 039 | 3 464.7 | 965.6 | 5 841.7 | 1 448.9 | 15 087.6 | 6 250.9 | 1 238.6 | 213.4 | 2 909.7 | 1 731.7 | 117.0 |
| Alexandria | 100 | 662 | 52.2 | 14.4 | 1.4 | 43.5 | 29.1 | 1.8 | 6.4 | 0.0 | 0.0 | 8.1 | 0.3 |
| Baton Rouge | 423 | 3 042 | 248.2 | 81.5 | 172.6 | -20.0 | 2 574.9 | 115.6 | 214.2 | 110.0 | 55.5 | 1 264.8 | 104.6 |
| Bossier City | 99 | 765 | 47.4 | 13.8 | 34.4 | 0.2 | 15.1 | 0.0 | 3.0 | 0.7 | 0.0 | 5.7 | 0.0 |
| Central | NA | NA | NA | NA | NA | NA | NA | NA | NA | NA | NA | NA | NA |
| Houma | 58 | 598 | 104.1 | 34.7 | 2.9 | 0.0 | 0.0 | 0.0 | 0.0 | 0.0 | 0.0 | 0.0 | 0.0 |
| Kenner | 129 | 851 | 97.4 | 24.9 | 105.3 | 0.5 | 9.5 | 0.0 | 0.0 | 0.0 | 0.0 | 9.4 | 0.0 |
| Lafayette | 261 | 1 993 | 151.3 | 47.3 | 3.5 | 15.3 | 55.8 | 5.5 | 9.5 | 1.6 | 0.0 | 14.5 | 4.9 |
| Lake Charles | 117 | 759 | 65.4 | 19.8 | 28.2 | 64.0 | 30.9 | 0.0 | 3.8 | 8.9 | 0.0 | 10.1 | 0.0 |
| Monroe | 74 | 628 | 47.6 | 14.8 | 4.7 | 1.6 | 51.9 | 3.5 | 5.1 | 0.6 | 0.0 | 16.9 | 0.0 |
| New Iberia | 72 | D | D | D | -0.1 | 0.0 | 5.0 | 1.8 | 0.1 | 0.7 | 0.0 | 2.1 | 0.0 |
| New Orleans | 408 | 2 514 | 196.4 | 55.7 | 2 386.5 | 481.2 | 772.0 | 300.3 | 24.1 | 17.6 | 1.0 | 259.5 | 0.8 |
| Shreveport | 308 | D | D | D | 4.9 | 35.0 | 100.1 | 32.7 | 11.2 | 1.7 | 0.0 | 20.8 | 4.3 |
| Slidell | 94 | 487 | 33.9 | 10.5 | 30.3 | 0.5 | 4.1 | 0.0 | 0.0 | 0.0 | 0.0 | 3.9 | 0.0 |
| MAINE | 2 124 | 9 136 | 812.9 | 218.9 | 1 336.2 | 399.5 | 3 787.4 | 2 186.8 | 340.3 | 250.6 | 6.3 | 151.8 | 58.3 |
| Bangor | 75 | 504 | 57.3 | 12.4 | 50.2 | 55.8 | 22.6 | 2.8 | 5.4 | 0.1 | 0.1 | 4.4 | 2.6 |
| Lewiston | 58 | 305 | 18.8 | 6.7 | 0.0 | 0.0 | 16.1 | 0.1 | 2.8 | 0.1 | 0.0 | 9.9 | 0.3 |
| Portland | 182 | 1 100 | 93.9 | 26.4 | 243.3 | 44.1 | 122.7 | 22.4 | 6.7 | 6.5 | 0.0 | 32.8 | 0.4 |
| South Portland | 69 | 526 | 31.2 | 9.6 | 6.0 | 2.5 | 8.9 | 2.3 | 0.0 | 0.0 | 0.0 | 4.8 | 0.0 |
| MARYLAND | 8 270 | 57 508 | 4 832.5 | 1 602.5 | 12 017.6 | 14 504.9 | 14 441.4 | 7 701.5 | 1 138.0 | 631.3 | 53.1 | 710.2 | 256.3 |
| Annapolis | 153 | 1 034 | 92.1 | 32.2 | 658.8 | 40.0 | 608.0 | 0.5 | 6.7 | 22.3 | 0.1 | 7.5 | 0.0 |
| Baltimore | 728 | 6 191 | 559.3 | 160.9 | 383.4 | 688.6 | 4 036.3 | 1 903.0 | 257.1 | 314.4 | 0.4 | 221.5 | 147.5 |
| Bowie | 53 | 377 | 25.4 | 7.6 | 6.3 | 28.9 | 7.6 | 0.0 | 0.2 | 0.7 | 0.0 | 0.2 | 0.0 |
| College Park | 43 | D | D | D | 4.6 | 153.7 | 336.4 | 76.5 | 0.1 | 15.8 | 2.6 | 0.7 | 0.0 |
| Frederick | 144 | 1 016 | 70.8 | 24.9 | 291.4 | 275.4 | 24.7 | 10.0 | 2.2 | 0.4 | 0.0 | 8.3 | 1.8 |
| Gaithersburg | 129 | 1 057 | 81.0 | 33.3 | 298.1 | 548.3 | 45.8 | 29.2 | 0.9 | 0.7 | 0.0 | 6.1 | 0.0 |
| Hagerstown | 79 | 445 | 37.1 | 10.0 | 15.5 | 15.3 | 28.6 | 1.4 | 3.5 | 2.8 | 0.0 | 12.6 | 1.8 |
| Laurel | 47 | 467 | 29.6 | 8.8 | 7.1 | 73.5 | 1.6 | 0.0 | 0.0 | 0.6 | 0.0 | 0.6 | 0.0 |
| Rockville | 182 | 1 047 | 106.8 | 33.2 | 306.1 | 2 072.2 | 444.3 | 283.2 | 6.2 | 13.7 | -1.3 | 23.6 | 24.9 |
| Salisbury | 89 | 790 | 60.0 | 20.7 | 9.8 | 0.8 | 20.6 | 0.1 | 7.8 | 0.0 | 0.0 | 2.4 | 0.0 |
| MASSACHUSETTS | 10 744 | 66 722 | 6 164.8 | 1 906.5 | 12 673.5 | 3 313.8 | 22 351.8 | 14 088.0 | 1 526.5 | 867.2 | 87.3 | 1 328.9 | 215.3 |
| Agawam Town | NA | NA | NA | NA | NA | NA | NA | NA | NA | NA | NA | NA | NA |
| Attleboro | 60 | 267 | 21.3 | 5.8 | 2.0 | 122.0 | 1.5 | 0.0 | 0.0 | 0.2 | 0.0 | 1.3 | 0.0 |
| Barnstable Town | 127 | 747 | 60.4 | 21.5 | NA | NA | NA | NA | NA | NA | NA | NA | NA |

1. Establishments subject to federal tax.    2. Includes program categories not shown separately. State totals include additional categories not allocated by city.

# Table D. Cities — **City Government Finances**

| City | City government finances, 2007 | | | | | | | | | |
|---|---|---|---|---|---|---|---|---|---|---|
| | General revenue | | | | | | | General expenditure | | |
| | | Intergovernmental | | Taxes | | | | | Per capita[1] (dollars) | |
| | | | | | Per capita[1] (dollars) | | | | | |
| | Total (mil dol) | Total (mil dol) | Percent from state government | Total (mil dol) | Total | Property | Sales and gross receipts | Total (mil dol) | Total | Capital outlays |
| | 117 | 118 | 119 | 120 | 121 | 122 | 123 | 124 | 125 | 126 |
| KANSAS................. | X | X | X | X | X | X | X | X | X | X |
| Dodge City ................. | 37.7 | 11.9 | 30.3 | 12.6 | 488 | 247 | 241 | 34.2 | 1 328 | 402 |
| Garden City ................ | 25.0 | 5.2 | 20.6 | 10.9 | 409 | 190 | 219 | 29.1 | 1 094 | 227 |
| Hutchinson ................ | 39.7 | 6.6 | 21.9 | 21.3 | 524 | 267 | 257 | 27.1 | 666 | 86 |
| Kansas City ............... | 362.8 | 38.8 | 89.1 | 170.4 | 1 197 | 659 | 538 | 387.2 | 2 721 | 469 |
| Lawrence.................... | 223.6 | 14.7 | 33.5 | 41.4 | 460 | 249 | 211 | 193.8 | 2 157 | 154 |
| Leavenworth .............. | 35.8 | 6.9 | 16.4 | 18.3 | 527 | 306 | 222 | 33.8 | 972 | 207 |
| Leawood .................... | 45.7 | 7.9 | 20.7 | 29.0 | 935 | 546 | 389 | 32.1 | 1 035 | 380 |
| Lenexa...................... | 81.8 | 19.2 | 72.4 | 51.2 | 1 121 | 597 | 524 | 104.2 | 2 280 | 1 154 |
| Manhattan ................. | 52.5 | 7.9 | 35.5 | 29.7 | 575 | 321 | 254 | 40.6 | 784 | 30 |
| Olathe....................... | 168.9 | 16.5 | 31.7 | 69.7 | 590 | 278 | 312 | 170.0 | 1 440 | 392 |
| Overland Park ............. | 170.2 | 47.9 | 60.5 | 98.3 | 580 | 150 | 430 | 170.0 | 1 004 | 417 |
| Salina ....................... | 53.9 | 10.7 | 33.6 | 22.0 | 474 | 214 | 260 | 55.0 | 1 185 | 311 |
| Shawnee.................... | 50.5 | 8.2 | 30.1 | 34.8 | 580 | 261 | 319 | 54.9 | 916 | 157 |
| Topeka...................... | 159.8 | 20.2 | 23.1 | 83.7 | 682 | 285 | 398 | 167.6 | 1 367 | 11 |
| Wichita...................... | 377.7 | 108.8 | 25.3 | 163.1 | 451 | 330 | 122 | 329.4 | 911 | 73 |
| KENTUCKY .............. | X | X | X | X | X | X | X | X | X | X |
| Bowling Green.............. | 78.2 | 12.1 | 61.3 | 52.3 | 963 | 178 | 96 | 73.4 | 1 354 | 190 |
| Covington .................. | 65.8 | 11.2 | 20.8 | 38.2 | 886 | 141 | 174 | 46.9 | 1 089 | 76 |
| Elizabethtown ............. | 31.7 | 2.1 | 92.8 | 17.2 | 722 | 117 | 202 | 20.5 | 864 | 46 |
| Florence .................... | 23.5 | 1.2 | 96.0 | 16.3 | 596 | 221 | 91 | 25.4 | 930 | 246 |
| Frankfort ................... | 58.2 | 3.4 | 59.8 | 23.5 | 865 | 112 | 139 | 58.8 | 2 169 | 719 |
| Georgetown ............... | 63.4 | 11.6 | 19.1 | 17.9 | 849 | 61 | 130 | 40.8 | 1 935 | 656 |
| Henderson ................. | 36.0 | 9.2 | 18.5 | 15.0 | 541 | 176 | 179 | 31.3 | 1 127 | 123 |
| Hopkinsville ............... | 30.4 | 5.9 | 30.4 | 15.3 | 483 | 114 | 27 | 32.9 | 1 040 | 105 |
| Jeffersontown ............. | 15.0 | 0.2 | 91.8 | 14.7 | 563 | 138 | 42 | 12.6 | 482 | 46 |
| Lexington-Fayette......... | 380.1 | 44.8 | 16.6 | 254.3 | 911 | 145 | 144 | 345.5 | 1 238 | 27 |
| Louisville/Jefferson County | NA | NA | NA | NA | NA | NA | NA | NA | NA | NA |
| Nicholasville .............. | 18.7 | 1.6 | 98.8 | 11.4 | 440 | 116 | 126 | 14.6 | 564 | 138 |
| Owensboro ................ | 88.7 | 24.3 | 10.2 | 28.4 | 512 | 150 | 79 | 87.0 | 1 571 | 504 |
| Paducah .................... | 51.0 | 9.9 | 40.1 | 27.2 | 1 066 | 209 | 193 | 35.6 | 1 395 | 226 |
| Richmond ................... | 29.8 | 3.0 | 69.8 | 17.8 | 550 | 62 | 159 | 30.2 | 935 | 251 |
| LOUISIANA .............. | X | X | X | X | X | X | X | X | X | X |
| Alexandria ................. | 80.5 | 20.1 | 44.4 | 42.9 | 935 | 135 | 800 | 70.8 | 1 545 | 238 |
| Baton Rouge............... | 881.2 | 154.4 | 54.3 | 428.2 | 1 886 | 551 | 1 334 | 753.6 | 3 319 | 379 |
| Bossier City ............... | 107.8 | 10.3 | 74.2 | 66.1 | 1 070 | 154 | 915 | 85.8 | 1 389 | 286 |
| Central...................... | NA | NA | NA | NA | NA | NA | NA | NA | NA | NA |
| Houma...................... | 347.4 | 64.8 | 79.2 | 97.2 | 2 980 | 1 074 | 1 906 | 312.1 | 9 568 | 1 120 |
| Kenner ...................... | 87.7 | 45.8 | 14.0 | 21.1 | 324 | 115 | 208 | 77.1 | 1 183 | 226 |
| Lafayette................... | 322.8 | 59.3 | 66.3 | 161.9 | 1 426 | 582 | 843 | 301.2 | 2 653 | 587 |
| Lake Charles.............. | 123.1 | 30.0 | 10.6 | 65.7 | 935 | 85 | 850 | 112.1 | 1 595 | 511 |
| Monroe ..................... | 122.0 | 24.7 | 8.5 | 71.9 | 1 404 | 211 | 1 193 | 103.1 | 2 014 | 539 |
| New Iberia ................. | 33.1 | 4.4 | 28.9 | 21.4 | 650 | 108 | 542 | 28.0 | 851 | 162 |
| New Orleans .............. | 1 157.0 | 361.6 | 22.8 | 391.1 | 1 636 | 784 | 832 | 992.2 | 4 149 | 537 |
| Shreveport................. | 321.6 | 54.4 | 43.4 | 191.3 | 959 | 271 | 688 | 301.1 | 1 509 | 404 |
| Slidell ....................... | 48.0 | 9.5 | 1.9 | 31.2 | 1 148 | 171 | 977 | 39.5 | 1 453 | 135 |
| MAINE ...................... | X | X | X | X | X | X | X | X | X | X |
| Bangor...................... | 109.9 | 35.5 | 84.9 | 46.2 | 1 452 | 1 395 | 57 | 113.2 | 3 555 | 560 |
| Lewiston .................... | 101.9 | 44.0 | 100.0 | 42.7 | 1 211 | 1 199 | 12 | 112.3 | 3 186 | 538 |
| Portland .................... | 265.4 | 55.6 | 76.6 | 128.1 | 2 039 | 1 976 | 63 | 271.4 | 4 320 | 366 |
| South Portland ............ | 79.3 | 12.5 | 95.2 | 55.7 | 2 346 | 2 295 | 51 | 72.9 | 3 068 | 177 |
| MARYLAND .............. | X | X | X | X | X | X | X | X | X | X |
| Annapolis................... | 63.8 | 15.7 | 39.8 | 29.5 | 807 | 698 | 107 | 66.2 | 1 808 | 194 |
| Baltimore ................... | 3 088.2 | 1 530.1 | 83.0 | 1 071.2 | 1 680 | 940 | 183 | 2 814.1 | 4 415 | 517 |
| Bowie........................ | 43.6 | 10.6 | 34.9 | 19.4 | 364 | 328 | 36 | 32.5 | 610 | 76 |
| College Park................ | 10.8 | 2.3 | 47.8 | 6.4 | 240 | 181 | 59 | 13.1 | 491 | 120 |
| Frederick ................... | 75.6 | 14.6 | 33.1 | 38.5 | 651 | 592 | 53 | 71.7 | 1 210 | 31 |
| Gaithersburg............... | 42.8 | 15.3 | 20.6 | 19.9 | 345 | 287 | 58 | 37.8 | 655 | 38 |
| Hagerstown ............... | 67.0 | 9.7 | 44.8 | 22.6 | 570 | 459 | 94 | 56.4 | 1 423 | 5 |
| Laurel....................... | 21.8 | 4.4 | 38.5 | 15.7 | 726 | 630 | 96 | 21.0 | 972 | 204 |
| Rockville.................... | 98.4 | 28.0 | 28.1 | 35.0 | 597 | 531 | 59 | 106.3 | 1 811 | 471 |
| Salisbury.................... | 46.1 | 15.2 | 75.9 | 17.8 | 641 | 576 | 65 | 38.8 | 1 393 | 171 |
| MASSACHUSETTS ... | X | X | X | X | X | X | X | X | X | X |
| Agawam Town ............. | NA | NA | NA | NA | NA | NA | NA | NA | NA | NA |
| Attleboro ................... | 119.4 | 51.5 | 98.2 | 52.0 | 1 207 | 1 170 | 37 | 111.1 | 2 578 | 247 |
| Barnstable Town .......... | 151.3 | 29.3 | 95.9 | 93.2 | 1 995 | 1 924 | 71 | 147.0 | 3 146 | 197 |

1. Based on population estimated as of July 1 of the year shown.

# Table D. Cities — **City Government Finances**

| City | City government finances, 2006 (cont.) | | | | | | | | | |
|---|---|---|---|---|---|---|---|---|---|---|
| | General expenditure (cont.) | | | | | | | | | |
| | Percent of total for: | | | | | | | | | |
| | Public welfare | Highways | Parking facilities | Education | Health and hospitals | Police protection | Sewerage and sanitation | Parks and recreation | Housing and community development | Interest on debt |
| | 127 | 128 | 129 | 130 | 131 | 132 | 133 | 134 | 135 | 136 |
| KANSAS | X | X | X | X | X | X | X | X | X | X |
| Dodge City | 0.1 | 16.5 | 0.0 | 0.0 | 0.9 | 12.2 | 11.1 | 13.0 | 0.0 | 4.6 |
| Garden City | 0.0 | 4.4 | 0.0 | 0.0 | 0.0 | 14.3 | 11.8 | 10.2 | 0.9 | 6.3 |
| Hutchinson | 0.5 | 9.1 | 0.1 | 0.0 | 0.0 | 20.9 | 25.3 | 9.1 | 0.0 | 4.4 |
| Kansas City | 0.0 | 7.7 | 0.0 | 0.0 | 4.4 | 12.6 | 5.9 | 1.9 | 1.9 | 27.2 |
| Lawrence | 0.2 | 3.5 | 0.4 | 0.0 | 58.7 | 6.7 | 9.4 | 4.2 | 0.8 | 3.6 |
| Leavenworth | 0.0 | 2.1 | 0.0 | 0.0 | 0.6 | 16.8 | 16.4 | 7.7 | 7.0 | 4.7 |
| Leawood | 0.0 | 8.7 | 0.0 | 0.0 | 0.0 | 40.1 | 0.0 | 9.6 | 0.0 | 6.1 |
| Lenexa | 0.0 | 41.4 | 0.0 | 0.0 | 0.0 | 12.1 | 11.9 | 4.7 | 0.0 | 5.0 |
| Manhattan | 0.0 | 6.7 | 0.0 | 0.0 | 1.4 | 21.0 | 9.9 | 12.6 | 1.3 | 7.0 |
| Olathe | 0.0 | 5.1 | 0.0 | 0.0 | 0.0 | 11.6 | 11.0 | 0.9 | 0.0 | 20.6 |
| Overland Park | 0.0 | 7.0 | 0.0 | 0.0 | 0.0 | 16.8 | 1.6 | 5.8 | 0.0 | 1.8 |
| Salina | 0.0 | 5.3 | 0.0 | 0.0 | 1.9 | 10.4 | 10.3 | 10.2 | 3.3 | 2.1 |
| Shawnee | 0.0 | 16.5 | 0.0 | 0.0 | 0.0 | 15.9 | 6.2 | 13.3 | 0.0 | 16.1 |
| Topeka | 1.4 | 5.3 | 1.1 | 0.0 | 0.0 | 16.3 | 8.5 | 7.0 | 1.5 | 8.7 |
| Wichita | 0.4 | 7.6 | 0.0 | 0.0 | 1.0 | 18.6 | 12.3 | 6.9 | 7.1 | 7.5 |
| KENTUCKY | X | X | X | X | X | X | X | X | X | X |
| Bowling Green | 0.0 | 11.6 | 0.0 | 0.0 | 0.0 | 16.2 | 6.6 | 25.1 | 7.2 | 5.4 |
| Covington | 0.0 | 12.5 | 1.7 | 0.0 | 0.0 | 21.3 | 0.3 | 4.0 | 19.0 | 15.4 |
| Elizabethtown | 0.0 | 14.8 | 0.1 | 0.0 | 0.0 | 15.2 | 13.7 | 5.2 | 3.5 | 9.5 |
| Florence | 0.0 | 22.6 | 0.0 | 0.0 | 0.0 | 20.1 | 0.0 | 7.0 | 0.0 | 14.7 |
| Frankfort | 0.0 | 7.7 | 0.0 | 0.0 | 4.9 | 7.3 | 17.5 | 5.1 | 0.0 | 3.1 |
| Georgetown | 19.0 | 3.6 | 0.0 | 1.2 | 0.0 | 9.4 | 22.0 | 0.6 | 0.7 | 23.5 |
| Henderson | 0.0 | 7.3 | 0.0 | 0.0 | 0.0 | 12.5 | 22.2 | 2.9 | 17.9 | 0.9 |
| Hopkinsville | 0.0 | 4.6 | 0.0 | 0.0 | 0.0 | 15.0 | 16.5 | 0.0 | 23.5 | 14.3 |
| Jeffersontown | 0.0 | 0.6 | 0.0 | 0.0 | 0.0 | 45.8 | 10.2 | 1.0 | 0.0 | 33.0 |
| Lexington-Fayette | 3.1 | 1.1 | 0.1 | 0.0 | 6.6 | 14.5 | 10.9 | 5.1 | 0.0 | 7.7 |
| Louisville/Jefferson County | NA | NA | NA | NA | NA | NA | NA | NA | NA | NA |
| Nicholasville | 0.0 | 12.6 | 0.0 | 0.0 | 0.0 | 24.0 | 26.2 | 0.0 | 0.1 | 1.0 |
| Owensboro | 0.0 | 6.6 | 0.1 | 0.0 | 0.0 | 11.9 | 28.9 | 6.2 | 8.5 | 0.6 |
| Paducah | 0.0 | 18.8 | 0.0 | 0.0 | 0.0 | 15.6 | 13.9 | 3.0 | 17.3 | 3.5 |
| Richmond | 0.0 | 4.1 | 0.0 | 0.0 | 2.1 | 14.1 | 21.5 | 20.1 | 3.4 | 4.5 |
| LOUISIANA | X | X | X | X | X | X | X | X | X | X |
| Alexandria | 0.0 | 13.6 | 0.0 | 0.0 | 0.0 | 21.5 | 16.9 | 8.2 | 8.4 | 1.0 |
| Baton Rouge | 0.4 | 8.2 | 0.1 | 1.7 | 9.9 | 12.4 | 17.7 | 2.9 | 5.4 | 4.6 |
| Bossier City | 0.0 | 13.6 | 0.0 | 0.0 | 4.8 | 19.6 | 9.0 | 9.0 | 7.8 | 4.1 |
| Central | NA | NA | NA | NA | NA | NA | NA | NA | NA | NA |
| Houma | 0.5 | 1.8 | 0.0 | 0.0 | 49.0 | 5.8 | 6.0 | 2.5 | 3.0 | 2.1 |
| Kenner | 0.3 | 12.4 | 0.0 | 0.0 | 0.3 | 22.4 | 17.9 | 8.6 | 4.8 | 3.3 |
| Lafayette | 0.0 | 10.7 | 0.1 | 0.0 | 1.1 | 12.6 | 9.1 | 7.2 | 4.7 | 8.0 |
| Lake Charles | 0.0 | 16.1 | 0.0 | 0.0 | 0.5 | 12.5 | 19.7 | 8.3 | 9.4 | 1.1 |
| Monroe | 0.0 | 9.7 | 0.0 | 0.0 | 0.0 | 11.0 | 14.2 | 9.6 | 15.7 | 6.5 |
| New Iberia | 0.0 | 9.4 | 0.0 | 0.0 | 0.0 | 16.3 | 33.3 | 6.3 | 11.2 | 4.0 |
| New Orleans | 0.0 | 2.1 | 0.0 | 0.0 | 1.5 | 13.9 | 14.0 | 4.5 | 9.8 | 11.1 |
| Shreveport | 0.0 | 6.6 | 0.3 | 0.0 | 0.0 | 16.6 | 11.5 | 7.6 | 10.4 | 1.4 |
| Slidell | 0.0 | 8.1 | 0.0 | 0.0 | 1.0 | 16.1 | 16.5 | 3.3 | 2.3 | 1.9 |
| MAINE | X | X | X | X | X | X | X | X | X | X |
| Bangor | 1.2 | 0.0 | 0.6 | 35.1 | 1.2 | 5.8 | 0.0 | 4.2 | 2.0 | 3.0 |
| Lewiston | 0.5 | 3.0 | 0.4 | 44.8 | 0.0 | 4.4 | 6.5 | 1.9 | 0.7 | 6.9 |
| Portland | 8.1 | 4.2 | 0.6 | 32.5 | 3.0 | 5.0 | 9.1 | 3.0 | 1.1 | 4.7 |
| South Portland | 0.4 | 3.4 | 0.0 | 49.8 | 0.1 | 5.5 | 7.0 | 4.1 | 0.0 | 2.0 |
| MARYLAND | X | X | X | X | X | X | X | X | X | X |
| Annapolis | 0.0 | 9.4 | 3.2 | 0.0 | 0.0 | 25.0 | 12.9 | 4.9 | 1.0 | 2.5 |
| Baltimore | 0.1 | 6.5 | 0.7 | 42.2 | 4.5 | 12.6 | 7.8 | 3.5 | 3.5 | 1.7 |
| Bowie | 0.0 | 13.7 | 0.0 | 0.0 | 0.5 | 6.8 | 25.1 | 17.1 | 0.8 | 0.3 |
| College Park | 0.0 | 21.6 | 13.8 | 0.0 | 0.7 | 2.9 | 19.5 | 8.1 | 0.7 | 0.2 |
| Frederick | 0.0 | 7.8 | 4.0 | 0.0 | 0.0 | 27.9 | 13.6 | 12.2 | 1.2 | 5.5 |
| Gaithersburg | 0.0 | 10.4 | 0.0 | 0.0 | 0.9 | 16.5 | 6.0 | 23.7 | 5.0 | 0.0 |
| Hagerstown | 0.0 | 7.2 | 0.8 | 0.0 | 0.0 | 19.3 | 21.2 | 5.3 | 3.5 | 2.5 |
| Laurel | 0.0 | 17.7 | 0.0 | 0.0 | 0.0 | 33.2 | 5.7 | 6.1 | 0.0 | 2.2 |
| Rockville | 0.0 | 9.9 | 0.3 | 0.0 | 0.3 | 6.7 | 8.9 | 19.1 | 1.9 | 3.1 |
| Salisbury | 0.0 | 11.1 | 1.4 | 0.0 | 0.5 | 22.0 | 19.7 | 7.0 | 2.4 | 2.3 |
| MASSACHUSETTS | X | X | X | X | X | X | X | X | X | X |
| Agawam Town | NA | NA | NA | NA | NA | NA | NA | NA | NA | NA |
| Attleboro | 0.5 | 3.1 | 0.0 | 59.8 | 0.3 | 5.3 | 13.1 | 1.5 | 0.7 | 3.8 |
| Barnstable Town | 0.2 | 3.4 | 0.0 | 53.3 | 0.6 | 7.4 | 3.2 | 2.3 | 0.4 | 3.6 |

# Table D. Cities — City Government Finances, City Government Employment, and Climate

| City | City government finances, 2007 (cont.) Debt outstanding Total (mil dol) | Per capita[1] (dollars) | Debt issued during year | City government employment, 2011 | Climate[2] Average daily temperature (degrees Fahrenheit) Mean January | July | Limits January[3] | July[4] | Annual precipitation (inches) | Heating degree days | Cooling degree days |
|---|---|---|---|---|---|---|---|---|---|---|---|
| | 137 | 138 | 139 | 140 | 141 | 142 | 143 | 144 | 145 | 146 | 147 |
| KANSAS | X | X | X | X | X | X | X | X | X | X | X |
| Dodge City | 40.0 | 1 554 | 1.1 | 246 | 30.1 | 79.8 | 18.7 | 92.8 | 22.35 | 5 037 | 1 481 |
| Garden City | 51.3 | 1 926 | 8.9 | 315 | 28.6 | 77.8 | 14.7 | 92.1 | 18.77 | 5 423 | 1 191 |
| Hutchinson | 35.9 | 884 | 2.6 | 396 | 28.5 | 79.9 | 17.0 | 92.7 | 30.32 | 5 146 | 1 454 |
| Kansas City | 2 963.9 | 20 826 | 68.5 | 2 578 | 29.1 | 79.0 | 19.9 | 89.4 | 40.17 | 4 847 | 1 406 |
| Lawrence | 259.5 | 2 888 | 69.2 | 1 944 | 29.9 | 80.2 | 20.5 | 90.6 | 39.78 | 4 685 | 1 582 |
| Leavenworth | 34.3 | 987 | 1.3 | 262 | 26.6 | 79.1 | 16.4 | 89.8 | 40.94 | 5 331 | 1 356 |
| Leawood | 52.7 | 1 698 | 13.1 | 258 | 29.1 | 79.0 | 19.9 | 89.4 | 40.17 | 4 847 | 1 406 |
| Lenexa | 277.3 | 6 070 | 16.4 | 401 | 29.1 | 79.0 | 19.9 | 89.4 | 40.17 | 4 847 | 1 406 |
| Manhattan | 86.4 | 1 670 | 59.1 | 365 | 27.8 | 79.9 | 16.1 | 92.5 | 34.80 | 5 120 | 1 465 |
| Olathe | 621.3 | 5 263 | 53.2 | 834 | 29.1 | 79.0 | 19.9 | 89.4 | 40.17 | 4 847 | 1 406 |
| Overland Park | 144.6 | 853 | 79.6 | 914 | 29.1 | 79.0 | 19.9 | 89.4 | 40.17 | 4 847 | 1 406 |
| Salina | 47.4 | 1 020 | 2.2 | 516 | 29.0 | 81.3 | 18.8 | 93.3 | 32.19 | 4 952 | 1 600 |
| Shawnee | 197.1 | 3 287 | 7.6 | 283 | 29.1 | 79.0 | 19.9 | 89.4 | 40.17 | 4 847 | 1 406 |
| Topeka | 520.6 | 4 245 | 135.9 | 1 330 | 27.2 | 78.4 | 17.2 | 89.1 | 35.64 | 5 225 | 1 357 |
| Wichita | 819.6 | 2 268 | 88.7 | 3 165 | 30.2 | 81.0 | 20.3 | 92.9 | 30.38 | 4 765 | 1 658 |
| KENTUCKY | X | X | X | X | X | X | X | X | X | X | X |
| Bowling Green | 265.4 | 4 892 | 14.9 | 725 | 34.2 | 78.5 | 25.4 | 89.2 | 51.63 | 4 243 | 1 413 |
| Covington | 168.6 | 3 914 | 9.1 | 416 | 32.0 | 76.1 | 24.1 | 85.9 | 45.91 | 4 713 | 1 154 |
| Elizabethtown | 46.4 | 1 953 | 0.0 | 277 | NA | NA | NA | NA | NA | NA | NA |
| Florence | 84.2 | 3 086 | 0.0 | 200 | NA | NA | NA | NA | NA | NA | NA |
| Frankfort | 55.7 | 2 055 | 11.8 | 576 | 30.3 | 75.2 | 20.8 | 86.9 | 43.56 | 5 129 | 994 |
| Georgetown | 585.6 | 27 788 | 7.2 | 172 | NA | NA | NA | NA | NA | NA | NA |
| Henderson | 33.4 | 1 204 | 10.0 | 476 | 32.6 | 77.6 | 23.6 | 88.4 | 44.77 | 4 374 | 1 344 |
| Hopkinsville | 158.0 | 4 993 | 9.5 | 416 | 33.2 | 78.2 | 24.4 | 88.5 | 50.92 | 4 298 | 1 433 |
| Jeffersontown | 171.0 | 6 538 | 0.0 | 112 | 33.0 | 78.4 | 24.9 | 87.0 | 44.54 | 4 352 | 1 443 |
| Lexington-Fayette | 764.3 | 2 739 | 139.6 | 3 800 | 31.6 | 75.9 | 22.5 | 86.3 | 46.39 | 4 769 | 1 094 |
| Louisville/Jefferson County | NA | NA | NA | NA | NA | NA | NA | NA | NA | NA | NA |
| Nicholasville | 23.3 | 903 | 6.6 | 219 | NA | NA | NA | NA | NA | NA | NA |
| Owensboro | 385.8 | 6 963 | 0.0 | 781 | 33.5 | 79.2 | 24.4 | 90.7 | 46.53 | 4 159 | 1 565 |
| Paducah | 36.4 | 1 424 | 6.0 | 530 | 35.2 | 79.9 | 27.2 | 90.8 | 46.04 | 3 893 | 1 635 |
| Richmond | 134.8 | 4 169 | 6.5 | 278 | 34.7 | 75.8 | 25.6 | 87.0 | 47.33 | 4 231 | 1 150 |
| LOUISIANA | X | X | X | X | X | X | X | X | X | X | X |
| Alexandria | 82.2 | 1 792 | 0.0 | 868 | 48.1 | 83.3 | 38.0 | 92.8 | 61.44 | 1 908 | 2 602 |
| Baton Rouge | 1 018.7 | 4 486 | 329.5 | 7 566 | 50.1 | 81.7 | 40.2 | 90.7 | 63.08 | 1 689 | 2 628 |
| Bossier City | 110.9 | 1 795 | 37.4 | 744 | 48.3 | 81.0 | 37.4 | 91.0 | 61.06 | 1 981 | 2 220 |
| Central | NA | NA | NA | NA | NA | NA | NA | NA | NA | NA | NA |
| Houma | 166.0 | 5 088 | 4.5 | 2 620 | 53.1 | 82.5 | 43.4 | 90.7 | 63.67 | 1 346 | 2 804 |
| Kenner | 59.7 | 916 | 0.0 | 657 | 52.6 | 82.7 | 43.4 | 91.1 | 64.16 | 1 417 | 2 773 |
| Lafayette | 745.2 | 6 563 | 26.9 | 3 083 | 51.3 | 82.2 | 41.6 | 91.2 | 60.54 | 1 531 | 2 671 |
| Lake Charles | 37.6 | 536 | 0.7 | 991 | 50.9 | 82.6 | 41.2 | 91.0 | 57.19 | 1 546 | 2 705 |
| Monroe | 147.1 | 2 873 | 6.1 | 1 139 | 44.6 | 83.0 | 33.5 | 94.1 | 58.04 | 2 399 | 2 311 |
| New Iberia | 25.0 | 760 | 3.0 | NA | 51.3 | 82.3 | 41.4 | 91.1 | 60.89 | 1 544 | 2 680 |
| New Orleans | 1 934.1 | 8 088 | 281.2 | 6 593 | 52.7 | 82.2 | 43.3 | 90.9 | 65.15 | 1 416 | 2 686 |
| Shreveport | 632.9 | 3 171 | 2.2 | 2 824 | 46.4 | 83.4 | 36.5 | 93.3 | 51.30 | 2 251 | 2 405 |
| Slidell | 27.9 | 1 027 | 0.3 | NA | 50.7 | 82.1 | 40.2 | 91.1 | 62.66 | 1 652 | 2 548 |
| MAINE | X | X | X | X | X | X | X | X | X | X | X |
| Bangor | 81.6 | 2 561 | 3.6 | 1 203 | 18.0 | 69.2 | 8.3 | 79.6 | 39.57 | 7 676 | 313 |
| Lewiston | 120.7 | 3 425 | 16.6 | 1 246 | 20.5 | 71.4 | 11.5 | 81.5 | 45.79 | 7 107 | 465 |
| Portland | 310.8 | 4 948 | 26.1 | 2 613 | 21.7 | 68.7 | 12.5 | 78.8 | 45.83 | 7 318 | 347 |
| South Portland | 29.8 | 1 254 | 2.1 | 941 | NA | NA | NA | NA | NA | NA | NA |
| MARYLAND | X | X | X | X | X | X | X | X | X | X | X |
| Annapolis | 44.8 | 1 223 | 0.0 | 597 | 32.8 | 77.5 | 23.8 | 87.7 | 44.78 | 4 695 | 1 162 |
| Baltimore | 2 446.9 | 3 839 | 358.6 | 26 541 | 36.8 | 81.7 | 29.4 | 90.6 | 43.59 | 4 720 | 1 147 |
| Bowie | 2.9 | 55 | 0.0 | NA | 31.8 | 75.2 | 21.2 | 87.1 | 44.66 | 4 970 | 917 |
| College Park | 0.3 | 13 | 0.0 | NA | NA | NA | NA | NA | NA | NA | NA |
| Frederick | 134.9 | 2 278 | 0.0 | 512 | 33.3 | 77.9 | 25.1 | 88.9 | 40.64 | 4 430 | 1 272 |
| Gaithersburg | 44.0 | 763 | 0.0 | 312 | 31.8 | 75.3 | 23.8 | 85.4 | 43.08 | 4 990 | 983 |
| Hagerstown | 39.3 | 991 | 11.2 | 441 | 29.3 | 75.2 | 20.8 | 86.1 | 39.45 | 5 249 | 902 |
| Laurel | 12.7 | 587 | 3.6 | 197 | NA | NA | NA | NA | NA | NA | NA |
| Rockville | 98.8 | 1 684 | 0.3 | 682 | 31.8 | 75.3 | 23.8 | 85.4 | 43.08 | 4 990 | 983 |
| Salisbury | 54.5 | 1 959 | 27.4 | 376 | NA | NA | NA | NA | NA | NA | NA |
| MASSACHUSETTS | X | X | X | X | X | X | X | X | X | X | X |
| Agawam Town | NA | NA | NA | NA | NA | NA | NA | NA | NA | NA | NA |
| Attleboro | 116.4 | 2 699 | 5.0 | 1 339 | 27.4 | 72.2 | 17.8 | 83.0 | 48.34 | 6 012 | 558 |
| Barnstable Town | 143.5 | 3 069 | 74.0 | NA | 29.2 | 70.5 | 21.2 | 77.8 | 43.03 | 6 026 | 413 |

1. Based on the population estimated as of July 1 of the year shown.   2. Represents normal values based on the 30-year period, 1971–2000.   3. Average daily minimum.   4. Average daily maximum.

# Table D. Cities — Land Area and Population

| STATE Place code | City | Land area,[1] 2010 (sq km) | Population, 2012 | | | Race alone or in combination, not of Hispanic origin (percent), 2010 | | | | | Percent Hispanic or Latino,[2] 2010 | Percent Foreign born 2007–2011 |
| | | | Total persons | Rank | Per square kilometer | White | Black | American Indian, Alaska Native | Asian | Hawaiian Pacific Islander | | |
| | | 1 | 2 | 3 | 4 | 5 | 6 | 7 | 8 | 9 | 10 | 11 |
| | **MASSACHUSETTS— Cont'd** | | | | | | | | | | | |
| 25 05595 | Beverly | 39.1 | 40 286 | 902 | 1 030.3 | 92.6 | 2.1 | 0.5 | 2.1 | 0.1 | 3.5 | 6.1 |
| 25 07000 | Boston | 125.0 | 636 479 | 21 | 5 091.8 | 48.5 | 23.8 | 0.7 | 9.7 | 0.2 | 17.5 | 27.1 |
| 25 07740 | Braintree Town | 35.6 | 36 249 | 1 007 | 1 018.2 | 86.3 | 3.2 | 0.4 | 8.0 | 0.1 | 2.5 | 11.2 |
| 25 09000 | Brockton | 55.2 | 94 094 | 315 | 1 704.6 | 45.1 | 34.5 | 0.9 | 2.7 | 0.5 | 10.0 | 24.3 |
| 25 11000 | Cambridge | 16.5 | 106 471 | 263 | 6 452.8 | 65.1 | 12.4 | 0.7 | 17.1 | 0.2 | 7.6 | 27.4 |
| 25 13205 | Chelsea | 5.7 | 36 828 | 994 | 6 461.1 | 26.5 | 7.5 | 0.4 | 3.5 | 0.1 | 62.1 | 44.1 |
| 25 13660 | Chicopee | 59.1 | 55 490 | 647 | 938.9 | 80.6 | 3.4 | 0.5 | 1.6 | 0.1 | 14.8 | 8.9 |
| 25 21990 | Everett | 8.9 | 42 567 | 859 | 4 782.8 | 55.5 | 14.6 | 0.5 | 5.1 | 0.2 | 21.1 | 36.0 |
| 25 23000 | Fall River | 85.8 | 88 945 | 340 | 1 036.7 | 85.3 | 4.6 | 0.7 | 2.9 | 0.1 | 7.4 | 19.1 |
| 25 23875 | Fitchburg | 72.1 | 40 411 | 897 | 560.5 | 70.2 | 5.3 | 0.6 | 4.1 | 0.1 | 21.6 | 10.9 |
| 25 25172 | Franklin Town | 69.0 | 32 374 | 1 123 | 469.2 | 92.6 | 1.7 | 0.3 | 4.5 | 0.1 | 2.0 | 6.9 |
| 25 26150 | Gloucester | 67.9 | 29 191 | 1 247 | 429.9 | 95.1 | 1.1 | 0.4 | 1.2 | 0.1 | 2.7 | 7.5 |
| 25 29405 | Haverhill | 85.4 | 61 797 | 562 | 723.6 | 80.9 | 3.2 | 0.5 | 2.0 | 0.1 | 14.5 | 10.0 |
| 25 30840 | Holyoke | 55.1 | 40 135 | 909 | 728.4 | 47.8 | 3.0 | 0.5 | 1.3 | 0.0 | 48.4 | 5.4 |
| 25 34550 | Lawrence | 17.9 | 77 326 | 421 | 4 319.9 | 21.0 | 2.6 | 0.3 | 2.5 | 0.0 | 73.8 | 36.1 |
| 25 35075 | Leominster | 74.6 | 40 989 | 884 | 549.5 | 77.1 | 5.4 | 0.5 | 3.3 | 0.1 | 14.5 | 13.6 |
| 25 37000 | Lowell | 35.2 | 108 522 | 252 | 3 083.0 | 54.6 | 6.7 | 0.4 | 21.1 | 0.2 | 17.3 | 24.4 |
| 25 37490 | Lynn | 27.8 | 91 253 | 329 | 3 282.5 | 49.4 | 11.9 | 0.6 | 7.4 | 0.1 | 32.1 | 29.6 |
| 25 37875 | Malden | 13.1 | 60 374 | 580 | 4 608.7 | 54.6 | 15.4 | 0.5 | 20.8 | 0.2 | 8.4 | 39.5 |
| 25 38715 | Marlborough | 54.0 | 39 204 | 929 | 726.0 | 77.6 | 3.4 | 0.5 | 5.6 | 0.1 | 10.8 | 18.6 |
| 25 39835 | Medford | 21.0 | 57 033 | 624 | 2 715.9 | 78.1 | 9.5 | 0.5 | 7.6 | 0.1 | 4.4 | 21.2 |
| 25 40115 | Melrose | 12.1 | 27 435 | 1 323 | 2 267.4 | 90.9 | 2.8 | 0.3 | 4.5 | 0.0 | 2.5 | 13.7 |
| 25 40710 | Methuen Town | 57.6 | 48 009 | 773 | 833.5 | 75.8 | 2.3 | 0.3 | 4.2 | 0.1 | 18.1 | 14.9 |
| 25 45000 | New Bedford | 51.8 | 94 929 | 314 | 1 832.6 | 70.5 | 7.9 | 1.2 | 1.2 | 0.3 | 16.7 | 19.7 |
| 25 45560 | Newton | 46.2 | 86 307 | 356 | 1 868.1 | 81.5 | 2.9 | 0.3 | 12.8 | 0.1 | 4.1 | 20.4 |
| 25 46330 | Northampton | 88.7 | 28 592 | 1 274 | 322.3 | 86.0 | 3.2 | 0.7 | 5.0 | 0.1 | 6.8 | 9.0 |
| 25 52490 | Peabody | 42.0 | 51 867 | 699 | 1 234.9 | 88.7 | 2.4 | 0.3 | 2.1 | 0.1 | 6.3 | 13.6 |
| 25 53960 | Pittsfield | 104.8 | 44 168 | 824 | 421.5 | 88.3 | 6.8 | 0.6 | 1.6 | 0.1 | 5.0 | 5.1 |
| 25 55745 | Quincy | 42.9 | 93 027 | 320 | 2 168.5 | 66.9 | 5.1 | 0.5 | 24.8 | 0.1 | 3.3 | 27.3 |
| 25 56585 | Revere | 14.7 | 53 179 | 677 | 3 617.6 | 63.9 | 5.2 | 0.4 | 5.9 | 0.1 | 24.4 | 30.5 |
| 25 59105 | Salem | 21.4 | 42 219 | 865 | 1 972.9 | 77.5 | 4.4 | 0.5 | 3.1 | 0.1 | 15.6 | 16.8 |
| 25 62535 | Somerville | 10.7 | 77 104 | 425 | 7 206.0 | 71.5 | 7.4 | 0.5 | 9.8 | 0.2 | 10.6 | 26.0 |
| 25 67000 | Springfield | 82.5 | 153 552 | 158 | 1 861.2 | 38.4 | 21.1 | 0.8 | 2.7 | 0.2 | 38.8 | 10.3 |
| 25 69170 | Taunton | 121.0 | 56 055 | 641 | 463.3 | 86.5 | 6.1 | 0.7 | 1.3 | 0.2 | 5.5 | 11.0 |
| 25 72600 | Waltham | 33.0 | 61 918 | 560 | 1 876.3 | 70.1 | 6.3 | 0.3 | 10.5 | 0.1 | 13.7 | 27.6 |
| 25 73440 | Watertown Town | 10.3 | 32 863 | 1 107 | 3 190.6 | 83.7 | 3.5 | 0.3 | 8.3 | 0.1 | 5.3 | 25.9 |
| 25 76030 | Westfield | 120.0 | 41 399 | 877 | 345.0 | 89.6 | 1.8 | 0.6 | 1.6 | 0.1 | 7.5 | 6.8 |
| 25 77890 | West Springfield Town | 43.3 | 28 574 | 1 275 | 659.9 | 83.5 | 3.5 | 0.5 | 5.0 | 0.1 | 8.7 | 16.4 |
| 25 78972 | Weymouth Town | 43.5 | 54 906 | 656 | 1 262.2 | 89.5 | 3.5 | 0.5 | 3.6 | 0.1 | 2.6 | 8.9 |
| 25 81035 | Woburn | 32.7 | 38 949 | 940 | 1 191.1 | 82.9 | 4.5 | 0.3 | 7.8 | 0.0 | 4.5 | 15.4 |
| 25 82000 | Worcester | 96.8 | 182 669 | 127 | 1 887.1 | 61.5 | 11.5 | 0.8 | 6.6 | 0.1 | 20.9 | 20.6 |
| 26 00000 | **MICHIGAN** | 146 435.1 | 9 883 360 | X | 67.5 | 78.3 | 14.9 | 1.2 | 2.9 | 0.1 | 4.4 | 6.0 |
| 26 01380 | Allen Park | 18.1 | 27 732 | 1 304 | 1 532.2 | 88.5 | 2.5 | 0.9 | 1.1 | 0.1 | 8.1 | 5.7 |
| 26 03000 | Ann Arbor | 72.1 | 116 121 | 228 | 1 610.6 | 73.2 | 8.8 | 0.8 | 16.0 | 0.1 | 4.1 | 17.7 |
| 26 05920 | Battle Creek | 110.4 | 51 911 | 696 | 470.2 | 72.0 | 20.5 | 1.5 | 2.8 | 0.1 | 6.7 | 6.2 |
| 26 06020 | Bay City | 26.3 | 34 521 | 1 061 | 1 312.6 | 87.2 | 4.9 | 1.4 | 0.7 | 0.0 | 8.5 | 1.0 |
| 26 12060 | Burton | 60.5 | 29 432 | 1 238 | 486.5 | 88.3 | 8.3 | 1.5 | 1.0 | 0.1 | 3.1 | 1.3 |
| 26 21000 | Dearborn | 62.7 | 96 474 | 301 | 1 538.7 | 90.4 | 4.4 | 0.5 | 4.6 | 0.2 | 3.4 | 25.5 |
| 26 21020 | Dearborn Heights | 30.4 | 56 838 | 630 | 1 869.7 | 85.2 | 8.5 | 0.8 | 2.9 | 0.1 | 4.7 | 15.0 |
| 26 22000 | Detroit | 359.4 | 701 475 | 18 | 1 951.8 | 8.9 | 83.6 | 1.0 | 1.3 | 0.1 | 6.8 | 5.1 |
| 26 24120 | East Lansing | 35.2 | 48 518 | 761 | 1 378.4 | 80.6 | 7.7 | 0.7 | 11.8 | 0.1 | 3.4 | 14.2 |
| 26 24290 | Eastpointe | 13.3 | 32 411 | 1 122 | 2 436.9 | 66.7 | 30.8 | 1.4 | 1.5 | 0.1 | 2.1 | 3.1 |
| 26 27440 | Farmington Hills | 86.2 | 80 756 | 396 | 936.8 | 80.9 | 18.1 | 0.6 | 11.1 | 0.1 | 1.9 | 17.6 |
| 26 29000 | Flint | 86.6 | 100 515 | 288 | 1 160.7 | 38.4 | 58.7 | 1.7 | 0.7 | 0.1 | 3.9 | 1.6 |
| 26 31420 | Garden City | 15.2 | 27 235 | 1 337 | 1 791.8 | 91.9 | 4.1 | 1.1 | 1.2 | 0.1 | 3.3 | 2.7 |
| 26 34000 | Grand Rapids | 115.0 | 190 411 | 123 | 1 655.7 | 61.5 | 22.2 | 1.2 | 2.3 | 0.1 | 15.6 | 10.3 |
| 26 38640 | Holland | 43.0 | 33 279 | 1 099 | 773.9 | 70.6 | 4.1 | 0.7 | 3.4 | 0.2 | 22.7 | 11.1 |
| 26 40680 | Inkster | 16.2 | 24 962 | 1 449 | 1 540.9 | 21.9 | 75.3 | 1.4 | 2.0 | 0.1 | 2.6 | 3.6 |
| 26 41420 | Jackson | 28.1 | 33 411 | 1 093 | 1 189.0 | 73.1 | 24.0 | 1.4 | 0.9 | 0.1 | 5.3 | 1.8 |
| 26 42160 | Kalamazoo | 63.9 | 75 092 | 441 | 1 175.1 | 69.2 | 24.6 | 1.5 | 2.3 | 0.1 | 6.4 | 5.9 |
| 26 42820 | Kentwood | 54.1 | 49 694 | 734 | 918.6 | 69.0 | 17.0 | 1.1 | 7.3 | 0.1 | 8.5 | 13.5 |
| 26 46000 | Lansing | 93.4 | 113 996 | 235 | 1 220.5 | 59.6 | 26.3 | 1.8 | 4.3 | 0.1 | 12.5 | 8.3 |
| 26 47800 | Lincoln Park | 15.3 | 37 478 | 971 | 2 449.5 | 78.2 | 6.8 | 1.3 | 0.7 | 0.1 | 14.9 | 5.4 |
| 26 49000 | Livonia | 92.5 | 95 586 | 306 | 1 033.4 | 91.3 | 3.7 | 0.6 | 3.1 | 0.1 | 2.5 | 7.7 |
| 26 50560 | Madison Heights | 18.4 | 29 985 | 1 214 | 1 629.6 | 84.6 | 7.3 | 1.0 | 6.8 | 0.2 | 2.5 | 17.8 |
| 26 53780 | Midland | 87.3 | 42 020 | 867 | 481.3 | 91.7 | 2.6 | 0.7 | 3.7 | 0.1 | 2.4 | 5.7 |
| 26 56020 | Mount Pleasant | 20.1 | 26 183 | 1 389 | 1 302.6 | 87.7 | 4.9 | 2.7 | 3.6 | 0.1 | 3.3 | 5.0 |
| 26 56320 | Muskegon | 36.8 | 37 046 | 983 | 1 006.7 | 56.1 | 36.6 | 2.0 | 0.6 | 0.0 | 8.2 | 3.1 |
| 26 59440 | Novi | 78.4 | 56 912 | 627 | 725.9 | 72.6 | 8.7 | 0.5 | 16.9 | 0.1 | 3.0 | 18.0 |

1. Dry land or land partially or temporarily covered by water.    2. May be of any race.

# Table D. Cities — **Population**

| City | Age of population (percent), 2010 | | | | | | | | | Median age | Percent female | Population | | | |
|---|---|---|---|---|---|---|---|---|---|---|---|---|---|---|---|
| | | | | | | | | | | | | Census counts | | Percent change | |
| | Under 5 years | 5 to 17 years | 18 to 24 years | 25 to 34 years | 35 to 44 years | 45 to 54 years | 55 to 64 years | 65 to 74 years | 75 years and over | | | 2000 | 2010 | 2000–2010 | 2010–2012 |
| | 12 | 13 | 14 | 15 | 16 | 17 | 18 | 19 | 20 | 21 | 22 | 23 | 24 | 25 | 26 |
| **MASSACHUSETTS—Cont'd** | | | | | | | | | | | | | | | |
| Beverly | 5.3 | 14.1 | 12.2 | 12.2 | 12.7 | 15.7 | 13.2 | 6.9 | 7.7 | 40.1 | 52.6 | 39 862 | 39 502 | -0.9 | 2.0 |
| Boston | 5.2 | 11.5 | 19.4 | 20.7 | 12.5 | 11.4 | 9.1 | 5.3 | 4.7 | 30.8 | 52.1 | 589 141 | 617 594 | 4.8 | 3.1 |
| Braintree Town | 5.8 | 17.0 | 6.5 | 11.7 | 14.1 | 15.8 | 12.0 | 7.9 | 9.0 | 41.6 | 52.8 | 33 698 | 35 744 | 6.1 | 1.4 |
| Brockton | 7.3 | 18.4 | 9.8 | 13.3 | 13.6 | 14.5 | 11.1 | 6.4 | 5.5 | 35.9 | 51.9 | 94 304 | 93 810 | -0.5 | 0.3 |
| Cambridge | 4.3 | 7.1 | 20.8 | 28.7 | 11.9 | 8.9 | 8.8 | 5.2 | 4.3 | 30.2 | 51.4 | 101 355 | 105 162 | 3.8 | 1.2 |
| Chelsea | 8.7 | 16.6 | 11.2 | 19.4 | 15.4 | 11.9 | 8.0 | 4.4 | 4.4 | 31.8 | 49.1 | 35 080 | 35 177 | 0.3 | 4.7 |
| Chicopee | 5.6 | 15.1 | 9.9 | 13.4 | 12.2 | 14.8 | 12.9 | 7.7 | 8.3 | 40.1 | 52.2 | 54 653 | 55 298 | 1.2 | 0.3 |
| Everett | 6.9 | 15.9 | 9.8 | 16.9 | 15.5 | 13.9 | 9.7 | 5.6 | 5.8 | 35.3 | 50.9 | 38 037 | 41 667 | 9.5 | 2.2 |
| Fall River | 6.5 | 15.0 | 9.7 | 14.9 | 13.6 | 13.9 | 11.3 | 7.1 | 8.0 | 38.0 | 52.5 | 91 938 | 88 857 | -3.4 | 0.1 |
| Fitchburg | 6.7 | 16.1 | 14.1 | 13.3 | 12.6 | 14.1 | 10.5 | 6.0 | 6.4 | 34.7 | 51.4 | 39 102 | 40 318 | 3.1 | 0.2 |
| Franklin Town | 6.1 | 22.4 | 8.1 | 8.7 | 16.0 | 18.7 | 10.6 | 5.0 | 4.4 | 38.7 | 51.0 | 29 560 | 31 635 | 7.0 | 2.3 |
| Gloucester | 4.5 | 14.1 | 7.1 | 9.8 | 12.2 | 17.6 | 17.0 | 9.2 | 8.5 | 46.4 | 51.9 | 30 273 | 28 789 | -4.9 | 1.4 |
| Haverhill | 7.0 | 16.1 | 8.6 | 13.7 | 14.6 | 16.1 | 11.9 | 6.0 | 6.1 | 38.5 | 52.0 | 58 969 | 60 879 | 3.2 | 1.5 |
| Holyoke | 7.7 | 18.6 | 10.2 | 13.4 | 12.1 | 13.1 | 10.7 | 6.3 | 7.8 | 35.0 | 53.1 | 39 838 | 39 880 | 0.1 | 0.6 |
| Lawrence | 8.4 | 20.7 | 12.2 | 15.0 | 13.6 | 12.6 | 8.9 | 4.6 | 4.0 | 30.5 | 51.9 | 72 043 | 76 377 | 6.0 | 1.2 |
| Leominster | 5.9 | 16.8 | 8.2 | 12.4 | 13.8 | 16.4 | 12.2 | 6.9 | 7.3 | 40.0 | 51.5 | 41 303 | 40 759 | -1.3 | 0.6 |
| Lowell | 7.3 | 16.4 | 13.5 | 16.1 | 13.3 | 13.6 | 9.7 | 5.2 | 4.9 | 32.6 | 50.4 | 105 167 | 106 519 | 1.3 | 1.9 |
| Lynn | 7.4 | 17.5 | 10.8 | 14.8 | 13.6 | 14.0 | 10.5 | 5.9 | 5.5 | 34.7 | 51.0 | 89 050 | 90 329 | 1.4 | 1.0 |
| Malden | 6.3 | 13.3 | 9.5 | 18.9 | 15.2 | 14.4 | 10.7 | 6.0 | 5.7 | 36.2 | 51.6 | 56 340 | 59 450 | 5.5 | 1.6 |
| Marlborough | 6.6 | 15.0 | 7.8 | 15.4 | 15.3 | 16.2 | 11.1 | 6.2 | 6.4 | 38.5 | 50.5 | 36 255 | 38 499 | 6.2 | 1.8 |
| Medford | 5.2 | 11.4 | 11.5 | 18.0 | 13.7 | 13.7 | 11.2 | 6.8 | 8.4 | 37.7 | 52.2 | 55 765 | 56 253 | 0.7 | 1.4 |
| Melrose | 5.9 | 16.1 | 5.5 | 12.1 | 15.4 | 15.9 | 13.3 | 7.7 | 8.1 | 41.9 | 53.0 | 27 134 | 26 983 | -0.6 | 1.7 |
| Methuen Town | 6.1 | 17.8 | 8.3 | 12.0 | 14.1 | 15.8 | 12.0 | 6.6 | 7.2 | 39.3 | 52.4 | 43 789 | 47 255 | 7.9 | 1.6 |
| New Bedford | 6.9 | 16.3 | 10.1 | 14.6 | 12.8 | 13.7 | 11.0 | 6.7 | 7.9 | 36.6 | 52.0 | 93 768 | 95 072 | 1.4 | -0.2 |
| Newton | 5.3 | 16.3 | 12.1 | 9.7 | 12.6 | 14.8 | 13.8 | 7.3 | 8.0 | 40.5 | 53.2 | 83 829 | 85 146 | 1.6 | 1.4 |
| Northampton | 3.8 | 12.4 | 14.4 | 13.7 | 11.9 | 15.4 | 14.9 | 6.7 | 6.9 | 40.0 | 56.9 | 28 978 | 28 549 | -1.5 | 0.2 |
| Peabody | 4.9 | 14.2 | 7.3 | 11.3 | 12.8 | 15.9 | 13.0 | 8.6 | 11.9 | 44.6 | 52.5 | 48 129 | 51 251 | 6.5 | 1.2 |
| Pittsfield | 5.7 | 15.5 | 8.0 | 11.9 | 12.3 | 15.9 | 13.2 | 8.0 | 9.5 | 42.5 | 52.0 | 45 793 | 44 737 | -2.3 | -1.3 |
| Quincy | 5.4 | 11.2 | 8.7 | 18.6 | 14.2 | 14.8 | 12.0 | 7.2 | 7.9 | 39.2 | 52.1 | 88 025 | 92 271 | 4.8 | 0.8 |
| Revere | 6.2 | 14.1 | 9.3 | 16.1 | 14.7 | 14.2 | 10.8 | 7.0 | 7.5 | 37.9 | 51.0 | 47 283 | 51 755 | 9.5 | 2.8 |
| Salem | 5.6 | 13.1 | 12.8 | 15.0 | 13.5 | 14.7 | 12.3 | 6.5 | 6.5 | 37.6 | 53.5 | 40 407 | 41 340 | 2.3 | 2.1 |
| Somerville | 4.6 | 7.4 | 15.0 | 31.4 | 14.2 | 10.3 | 8.0 | 4.7 | 4.5 | 31.4 | 50.9 | 77 478 | 75 674 | -2.2 | 1.9 |
| Springfield | 7.3 | 19.7 | 13.1 | 13.4 | 12.4 | 12.9 | 10.3 | 5.6 | 5.4 | 32.2 | 52.6 | 152 082 | 153 060 | 0.6 | 0.3 |
| Taunton | 6.3 | 16.3 | 8.3 | 13.4 | 14.4 | 16.3 | 11.6 | 6.9 | 6.7 | 39.3 | 52.1 | 55 976 | 55 874 | -0.2 | 0.3 |
| Waltham | 5.3 | 9.3 | 18.4 | 18.8 | 12.8 | 12.5 | 10.7 | 6.1 | 6.2 | 33.9 | 50.2 | 59 226 | 60 632 | 2.4 | 2.1 |
| Watertown Town | 5.7 | 9.8 | 7.0 | 21.7 | 15.2 | 13.8 | 11.9 | 7.0 | 7.9 | 38.3 | 53.1 | 32 986 | 31 915 | -3.2 | 3.0 |
| Westfield | 5.3 | 16.1 | 14.7 | 10.4 | 12.3 | 14.9 | 12.5 | 6.9 | 6.7 | 38.3 | 51.1 | 40 072 | 41 094 | 2.6 | 0.7 |
| West Springfield Town | 5.9 | 15.2 | 9.1 | 13.3 | 12.6 | 15.6 | 13.2 | 7.3 | 7.8 | 40.4 | 51.2 | 27 899 | 28 391 | 1.8 | 0.6 |
| Weymouth Town | 5.9 | 14.8 | 7.3 | 12.9 | 14.2 | 16.6 | 13.2 | 7.7 | 7.5 | 41.7 | 52.6 | 53 988 | 53 743 | -0.5 | 2.2 |
| Woburn | 5.9 | 13.8 | 7.4 | 15.2 | 14.2 | 15.7 | 11.8 | 7.2 | 8.7 | 40.5 | 51.6 | 37 258 | 38 126 | 2.3 | 2.2 |
| Worcester | 6.6 | 15.5 | 15.3 | 14.7 | 13.0 | 13.3 | 10.0 | 5.5 | 6.2 | 33.4 | 51.3 | 172 648 | 181 045 | 4.9 | 0.9 |
| **MICHIGAN** | 6.0 | 17.7 | 9.9 | 11.8 | 12.9 | 15.3 | 12.7 | 7.3 | 6.4 | 38.9 | 50.9 | 9 938 444 | 9 883 635 | -0.6 | 0.0 |
| Allen Park | 5.0 | 16.6 | 7.9 | 11.8 | 13.0 | 15.9 | 12.6 | 6.9 | 10.3 | 41.7 | 51.9 | 29 376 | 28 210 | -4.0 | -1.7 |
| Ann Arbor | 4.3 | 10.1 | 29.4 | 17.8 | 10.0 | 9.9 | 9.2 | 4.8 | 4.5 | 27.8 | 50.7 | 114 024 | 113 939 | -0.1 | 1.9 |
| Battle Creek | 7.7 | 18.4 | 9.1 | 13.2 | 12.6 | 14.0 | 11.6 | 6.5 | 6.9 | 36.3 | 52.1 | 53 364 | 52 347 | -1.9 | -0.8 |
| Bay City | 7.3 | 17.5 | 9.8 | 14.4 | 12.8 | 14.3 | 11.5 | 6.3 | 5.9 | 35.8 | 51.3 | 36 817 | 34 932 | -5.1 | -1.2 |
| Burton | 6.1 | 17.9 | 8.8 | 12.4 | 13.6 | 15.8 | 12.1 | 7.0 | 6.2 | 38.6 | 51.2 | 30 308 | 29 999 | -1.0 | -1.9 |
| Dearborn | 8.0 | 21.7 | 10.0 | 12.8 | 12.7 | 12.8 | 10.1 | 5.5 | 6.5 | 33.0 | 50.6 | 97 775 | 98 153 | 0.4 | -1.7 |
| Dearborn Heights | 6.6 | 18.4 | 8.6 | 12.4 | 12.9 | 14.4 | 10.8 | 7.2 | 8.8 | 38.3 | 51.6 | 58 264 | 57 774 | -0.8 | -1.6 |
| Detroit | 7.0 | 19.6 | 11.5 | 12.1 | 13.0 | 13.7 | 11.6 | 6.1 | 5.4 | 34.8 | 52.7 | 951 270 | 713 777 | -25.0 | -1.7 |
| East Lansing | 2.4 | 5.2 | 62.3 | 10.1 | 4.5 | 4.3 | 4.9 | 2.8 | 3.5 | 21.6 | 51.5 | 46 525 | 48 557 | 4.4 | -0.1 |
| Eastpointe | 6.6 | 19.2 | 8.8 | 13.6 | 14.9 | 14.8 | 10.9 | 4.8 | 6.5 | 36.3 | 51.6 | 34 077 | 32 442 | -4.8 | -0.1 |
| Farmington Hills | 5.1 | 16.5 | 7.1 | 12.1 | 13.1 | 16.4 | 13.8 | 7.6 | 8.3 | 42.1 | 52.9 | 82 111 | 79 740 | -2.9 | 1.3 |
| Flint | 8.0 | 19.3 | 11.3 | 13.1 | 12.5 | 14.3 | 10.9 | 5.7 | 5.0 | 33.6 | 52.0 | 124 943 | 102 434 | -18.0 | -1.9 |
| Garden City | 5.3 | 17.0 | 8.6 | 12.4 | 14.1 | 16.7 | 11.8 | 6.8 | 7.2 | 39.9 | 50.9 | 30 047 | 27 692 | -7.8 | -1.7 |
| Grand Rapids | 8.0 | 16.7 | 14.4 | 17.1 | 11.6 | 11.8 | 9.4 | 4.8 | 6.3 | 30.8 | 51.3 | 197 800 | 188 040 | -4.9 | 1.3 |
| Holland | 7.4 | 16.5 | 16.7 | 13.3 | 11.3 | 11.7 | 9.3 | 5.3 | 8.4 | 31.7 | 52.5 | 35 048 | 33 051 | -5.7 | 0.7 |
| Inkster | 7.3 | 20.6 | 10.6 | 12.5 | 12.9 | 13.5 | 11.2 | 6.4 | 4.9 | 34.2 | 53.2 | 30 115 | 25 369 | -15.8 | -1.6 |
| Jackson | 9.0 | 19.6 | 10.5 | 14.7 | 13.0 | 12.9 | 10.1 | 5.1 | 5.1 | 32.2 | 52.3 | 36 316 | 33 534 | -7.7 | -0.4 |
| Kalamazoo | 6.4 | 14.0 | 27.0 | 15.0 | 9.9 | 10.0 | 8.2 | 4.3 | 5.1 | 26.2 | 50.7 | 77 145 | 74 262 | -3.7 | 1.1 |
| Kentwood | 7.3 | 18.0 | 9.9 | 15.6 | 13.3 | 13.8 | 10.5 | 5.4 | 6.1 | 34.3 | 52.0 | 45 255 | 48 707 | 7.6 | 2.0 |
| Lansing | 7.7 | 16.6 | 12.2 | 17.8 | 12.4 | 13.0 | 10.8 | 5.1 | 4.5 | 32.2 | 51.6 | 119 128 | 114 297 | -4.1 | -0.3 |
| Lincoln Park | 6.7 | 18.2 | 8.6 | 14.2 | 14.5 | 14.8 | 11.5 | 5.6 | 5.9 | 36.7 | 51.0 | 40 008 | 38 144 | -4.7 | -1.7 |
| Livonia | 4.5 | 16.3 | 7.8 | 10.0 | 12.2 | 17.6 | 13.9 | 7.8 | 9.9 | 44.5 | 51.7 | 100 545 | 96 942 | -3.6 | -1.4 |
| Madison Heights | 6.1 | 14.3 | 8.8 | 16.3 | 14.0 | 15.3 | 11.3 | 6.8 | 7.1 | 38.3 | 50.9 | 31 101 | 29 694 | -4.5 | 1.0 |
| Midland | 6.0 | 17.4 | 11.0 | 11.9 | 11.8 | 14.8 | 11.4 | 6.9 | 8.7 | 38.3 | 51.9 | 41 685 | 41 863 | 0.4 | 0.4 |
| Mount Pleasant | 3.6 | 7.4 | 53.1 | 11.0 | 5.8 | 6.4 | 5.5 | 3.1 | 4.1 | 22.0 | 52.6 | 25 946 | 26 016 | 0.3 | 0.6 |
| Muskegon | 7.1 | 16.2 | 12.2 | 15.7 | 13.1 | 13.6 | 10.5 | 5.3 | 6.3 | 34.1 | 47.9 | 40 105 | 38 401 | -4.2 | -3.5 |
| Novi | 5.8 | 19.7 | 6.6 | 12.2 | 15.8 | 17.3 | 11.3 | 5.2 | 6.1 | 39.1 | 51.6 | 47 386 | 55 224 | 16.5 | 3.1 |

# Table D. Cities — **Households, Group Quarters, Crime, and Education**

| City | Households, 2010 Number | Persons per house-hold | Percent Female family householder[1] | Percent One-person | Persons in group quarters, 2010 Total | Institutional Total | Persons in nursing facilities | Non-institu-tional | Serious crimes known to police,[2] 2011 Number | Rate[3] | Rate[3] Violent | Rate[3] Property | Population age 25 and older | High school graduate or less | Bachelor's degree or more |
|---|---|---|---|---|---|---|---|---|---|---|---|---|---|---|---|
| | 27 | 28 | 29 | 30 | 31 | 32 | 33 | 34 | 35 | 36 | 37 | 38 | 39 | 40 | 41 |
| **MASSACHUSETTS— Cont'd** | | | | | | | | | | | | | | | |
| Beverly | 15 850 | 2.33 | 10.5 | 31.3 | 2 514 | 533 | 369 | 1 981 | 836 | 2 104 | 234 | 1 870 | 27 019 | 30.3 | 42.3 |
| Boston | 252 699 | 2.26 | 16.3 | 37.1 | 46 214 | 6 697 | 3 280 | 39 517 | 24 697 | 3 975 | 845 | 3 129 | 389 917 | 38.7 | 42.8 |
| Braintree Town | 13 736 | 2.56 | 12.0 | 27.4 | 545 | 524 | 514 | 21 | 907 | 2 522 | 192 | 2 330 | 24 757 | 34.4 | 35.6 |
| Brockton | 33 303 | 2.76 | 22.3 | 26.9 | 1 768 | 1 088 | 790 | 680 | 4 359 | 4 619 | 1 231 | 3 387 | 60 164 | 52.8 | 18.2 |
| Cambridge | 44 032 | 2.00 | 8.4 | 40.7 | 17 102 | 324 | 277 | 16 778 | 3 615 | 3 417 | 430 | 2 987 | 72 507 | 16.8 | 73.1 |
| Chelsea | 11 831 | 2.92 | 21.8 | 29.3 | 682 | 570 | 570 | 112 | 1 974 | 5 578 | 1 749 | 3 829 | 22 548 | 68.9 | 14.5 |
| Chicopee | 23 799 | 2.28 | 15.6 | 34.3 | 1 155 | 341 | 231 | 814 | 1 885 | 3 388 | 462 | 2 926 | 38 135 | 55.1 | 16.1 |
| Everett | 15 543 | 2.67 | 17.8 | 27.7 | 191 | 150 | 150 | 41 | 1 251 | 2 984 | 465 | 2 519 | 28 542 | 58.2 | 16.5 |
| Fall River | 38 457 | 2.27 | 18.0 | 34.9 | 1 735 | 1 071 | 994 | 664 | 4 277 | 4 784 | 1 218 | 3 566 | 61 561 | 62.1 | 14.1 |
| Fitchburg | 15 165 | 2.49 | 16.2 | 29.8 | 2 538 | 669 | 356 | 1 869 | 1 728 | 4 260 | 749 | 3 511 | 25 531 | 51.5 | 20.2 |
| Franklin Town | 10 995 | 2.80 | 8.5 | 20.8 | 875 | 79 | 72 | 796 | 119 | 374 | 16 | 358 | 19 626 | 26.7 | 48.0 |
| Gloucester | 12 486 | 2.27 | 10.7 | 32.8 | 450 | 230 | 216 | 220 | 575 | 1 985 | 76 | 1 909 | 21 629 | 40.9 | 33.0 |
| Haverhill | 24 150 | 2.47 | 14.4 | 29.6 | 1 300 | 671 | 618 | 629 | 1 823 | 2 976 | 591 | 2 385 | 41 723 | 40.7 | 30.1 |
| Holyoke | 15 361 | 2.51 | 24.9 | 32.0 | 1 385 | 1 086 | 934 | 299 | 2 825 | 7 041 | 1 007 | 6 034 | 25 898 | 53.0 | 20.4 |
| Lawrence | 25 181 | 3.00 | 30.0 | 24.5 | 902 | 542 | 310 | 360 | 3 245 | 4 223 | 994 | 3 229 | 44 799 | 65.3 | 11.7 |
| Leominster | 16 767 | 2.41 | 13.5 | 30.0 | 327 | 251 | 224 | 76 | 1 508 | 3 677 | 605 | 3 073 | 28 149 | 47.2 | 23.2 |
| Lowell | 38 470 | 2.66 | 18.9 | 29.4 | 4 346 | 1 112 | 1 101 | 3 234 | 3 906 | 3 645 | 743 | 2 902 | 68 335 | 53.6 | 23.3 |
| Lynn | 33 310 | 2.69 | 19.3 | 30.6 | 835 | 284 | 263 | 551 | 3 424 | 3 768 | 885 | 2 883 | 58 246 | 57.8 | 17.2 |
| Malden | 23 673 | 2.50 | 13.9 | 30.0 | 373 | 116 | 116 | 257 | 1 557 | 2 603 | 418 | 2 185 | 41 155 | 46.1 | 30.2 |
| Marlborough | 15 395 | 2.46 | 10.3 | 28.7 | 661 | 286 | 253 | 375 | 957 | 2 471 | 472 | 1 998 | 27 519 | 40.6 | 38.1 |
| Medford | 22 810 | 2.38 | 11.4 | 29.6 | 1 959 | 479 | 465 | 1 480 | NA | NA | NA | NA | 40 495 | 35.9 | 41.7 |
| Melrose | 11 213 | 2.38 | 9.1 | 31.3 | 267 | 229 | 223 | 38 | 352 | 1 297 | 169 | 1 127 | 19 300 | 24.9 | 50.6 |
| Methuen Town | 17 529 | 2.67 | 14.4 | 24.9 | 420 | 277 | 232 | 143 | 1 080 | 2 272 | 183 | 2 089 | 31 685 | 43.7 | 27.8 |
| New Bedford | 38 761 | 2.40 | 20.0 | 32.4 | 1 966 | 1 415 | 1 196 | 551 | 4 425 | 4 626 | 1 144 | 3 483 | 63 370 | 64.4 | 14.6 |
| Newton | 31 168 | 2.50 | 8.4 | 25.6 | 7 103 | 483 | 474 | 6 620 | 1 261 | 1 472 | 93 | 1 379 | 55 127 | 14.9 | 74.1 |
| Northampton | 12 000 | 2.12 | 11.3 | 37.2 | 3 156 | 846 | 527 | 2 310 | 886 | 3 085 | 355 | 2 730 | 19 055 | 27.3 | 51.9 |
| Peabody | 21 313 | 2.38 | 10.7 | 31.4 | 520 | 397 | 389 | 123 | 1 417 | 2 748 | 240 | 2 508 | 36 829 | 41.9 | 30.0 |
| Pittsfield | 19 653 | 2.22 | 14.4 | 35.3 | 1 184 | 894 | 501 | 290 | 1 535 | 3 410 | 598 | 2 813 | 31 813 | 44.4 | 26.5 |
| Quincy | 40 658 | 2.24 | 10.6 | 37.7 | 1 400 | 729 | 698 | 671 | 2 170 | 2 338 | 424 | 1 913 | 68 227 | 38.6 | 37.6 |
| Revere | 20 454 | 2.52 | 14.9 | 32.0 | 280 | 228 | 228 | 52 | 1 521 | 2 921 | 348 | 2 573 | 36 167 | 60.1 | 18.5 |
| Salem | 17 842 | 2.22 | 14.4 | 35.3 | 1 770 | 167 | 156 | 1 603 | 1 105 | 2 657 | 286 | 2 371 | 28 028 | 36.9 | 37.6 |
| Somerville | 32 105 | 2.29 | 8.9 | 32.0 | 2 269 | 37 | 22 | 2 232 | 2 024 | 2 656 | 370 | 2 286 | 52 867 | 32.0 | 52.8 |
| Springfield | 56 752 | 2.60 | 27.2 | 30.0 | 5 677 | 954 | 553 | 4 723 | 8 924 | 5 795 | 1 027 | 4 768 | 91 157 | 57.2 | 17.2 |
| Taunton | 22 332 | 2.47 | 15.2 | 28.9 | 784 | 574 | 406 | 210 | 1 309 | 2 329 | 532 | 1 797 | 38 209 | 52.6 | 19.6 |
| Waltham | 23 690 | 2.28 | 9.1 | 34.9 | 6 686 | 308 | 287 | 6 378 | 1 042 | 1 708 | 285 | 1 423 | 40 864 | 36.9 | 45.5 |
| Watertown Town | 14 709 | 2.15 | 8.3 | 35.8 | 234 | 104 | 0 | 130 | 546 | 1 700 | 159 | 1 542 | 23 994 | 28.9 | 54.6 |
| Westfield | 15 335 | 2.49 | 11.4 | 27.5 | 2 976 | 359 | 294 | 2 617 | 796 | 1 925 | 225 | 1 700 | 26 285 | 45.8 | 25.9 |
| West Springfield Town | 12 124 | 2.33 | 12.2 | 34.3 | 170 | 120 | 120 | 50 | 1 509 | 5 283 | 634 | 4 649 | 19 350 | 45.9 | 26.0 |
| Weymouth Town | 22 435 | 2.37 | 12.0 | 32.3 | 460 | 373 | 373 | 87 | 1 132 | 2 094 | 342 | 1 751 | 38 854 | 37.7 | 32.7 |
| Woburn | 15 524 | 2.43 | 11.3 | 29.9 | 323 | 238 | 238 | 85 | 821 | 2 141 | 214 | 1 927 | 27 632 | 42.1 | 31.7 |
| Worcester | 68 613 | 2.46 | 17.6 | 31.8 | 12 152 | 2 093 | 1 845 | 10 059 | 7 896 | 4 335 | 994 | 3 341 | 114 917 | 44.3 | 30.1 |
| **MICHIGAN** | 3 872 508 | 2.49 | 13.2 | 27.9 | 229 068 | 109 867 | 42 473 | 119 201 | 301 962 | 3 057 | 445 | 2 612 | 6 566 864 | 42.7 | 25.3 |
| Allen Park | 11 580 | 2.42 | 11.6 | 30.1 | 171 | 138 | 132 | 33 | 613 | 2 175 | 135 | 2 040 | 19 571 | 43.2 | 22.2 |
| Ann Arbor | 47 060 | 2.17 | 7.1 | 37.4 | 11 840 | 78 | 61 | 11 762 | 2 819 | 2 476 | 234 | 2 242 | 62 382 | 12.0 | 70.9 |
| Battle Creek | 21 118 | 2.41 | 18.5 | 32.6 | 1 399 | 862 | 228 | 537 | 3 656 | 5 929 | 920 | 5 010 | 33 692 | 46.4 | 19.5 |
| Bay City | 14 436 | 2.38 | 16.6 | 33.7 | 515 | 180 | 0 | 335 | 966 | 2 767 | 490 | 2 278 | 22 772 | 50.5 | 16.8 |
| Burton | 11 964 | 2.50 | 16.3 | 27.0 | 111 | 0 | 0 | 111 | 1 574 | 5 251 | 570 | 4 680 | 20 429 | 49.5 | 14.0 |
| Dearborn | 34 342 | 2.85 | 11.9 | 29.6 | 226 | 195 | 180 | 31 | 4 117 | 4 198 | 368 | 3 830 | 60 332 | 41.7 | 30.3 |
| Dearborn Heights | 22 266 | 2.57 | 13.9 | 30.1 | 602 | 504 | 344 | 98 | 1 897 | 3 286 | 364 | 2 922 | 38 730 | 50.5 | 18.0 |
| Detroit | 269 445 | 2.59 | 31.4 | 34.0 | 14 759 | 6 541 | 3 365 | 8 218 | 59 013 | 8 274 | 2 139 | 6 135 | 455 297 | 56.3 | 12.2 |
| East Lansing | 14 774 | 2.23 | 5.6 | 33.3 | 15 701 | 193 | 193 | 15 508 | 1 120 | 2 307 | 171 | 2 136 | 14 320 | 12.1 | 69.9 |
| Eastpointe | 12 557 | 2.58 | 19.5 | 28.7 | 21 | 0 | 0 | 21 | 1 282 | 3 955 | 725 | 3 230 | 21 076 | 49.9 | 11.9 |
| Farmington Hills | 33 559 | 2.36 | 9.9 | 31.5 | 693 | 319 | 251 | 374 | 1 367 | 1 716 | 129 | 1 586 | 56 821 | 23.9 | 50.9 |
| Flint | 40 472 | 2.45 | 29.0 | 33.9 | 3 193 | 988 | 85 | 2 205 | 9 014 | 8 806 | 2 341 | 6 466 | 65 224 | 56.4 | 11.5 |
| Garden City | 10 894 | 2.54 | 13.6 | 26.8 | 54 | 0 | 0 | 54 | 763 | 2 757 | 271 | 2 486 | 18 828 | 52.2 | 12.6 |
| Grand Rapids | 72 126 | 2.49 | 16.4 | 32.3 | 8 260 | 3 298 | 2 011 | 4 962 | 7 569 | 4 028 | 742 | 3 286 | 115 696 | 43.0 | 27.6 |
| Holland | 12 021 | 2.52 | 11.9 | 29.8 | 2 723 | 283 | 273 | 2 440 | 1 200 | 3 634 | 357 | 3 276 | 19 011 | 44.5 | 30.8 |
| Inkster | 9 821 | 2.56 | 30.0 | 31.6 | 230 | 18 | 3 | 212 | 1 455 | 5 740 | 1 811 | 3 929 | 15 533 | 53.8 | 10.4 |
| Jackson | 13 294 | 2.46 | 22.4 | 33.9 | 773 | 468 | 263 | 305 | 1 886 | 5 628 | 1 137 | 4 491 | 21 343 | 47.4 | 13.4 |
| Kalamazoo | 29 141 | 2.29 | 15.6 | 36.8 | 7 462 | 1 126 | 489 | 6 336 | 3 908 | 5 266 | 822 | 4 444 | 38 152 | 34.5 | 32.3 |
| Kentwood | 19 741 | 2.45 | 13.1 | 30.9 | 395 | 246 | 114 | 149 | 1 550 | 3 185 | 368 | 2 817 | 31 233 | 35.8 | 32.6 |
| Lansing | 48 450 | 2.33 | 17.9 | 35.0 | 1 181 | 273 | 120 | 908 | 5 483 | 4 801 | 1 024 | 3 777 | 72 341 | 40.3 | 24.5 |
| Lincoln Park | 14 924 | 2.55 | 16.9 | 29.0 | 64 | 13 | 0 | 51 | 1 831 | 4 804 | 554 | 4 250 | 25 582 | 61.3 | 9.1 |
| Livonia | 38 714 | 2.47 | 9.7 | 26.7 | 1 366 | 791 | 764 | 575 | 2 282 | 2 356 | 173 | 2 182 | 69 029 | 33.8 | 34.1 |
| Madison Heights | 12 712 | 2.32 | 12.9 | 34.1 | 156 | 149 | 149 | 7 | 1 046 | 3 525 | 303 | 3 222 | 21 428 | 48.4 | 22.3 |
| Midland | 17 506 | 2.33 | 9.8 | 31.8 | 1 159 | 489 | 352 | 670 | 541 | 1 293 | 124 | 1 169 | 27 583 | 28.3 | 42.4 |
| Mount Pleasant | 8 376 | 2.35 | 9.3 | 31.6 | 6 365 | 442 | 286 | 5 923 | 487 | 1 873 | 158 | 1 716 | 9 718 | 28.8 | 41.8 |
| Muskegon | 13 967 | 2.38 | 22.9 | 36.0 | 5 199 | 4 459 | 426 | 740 | 2 524 | 6 578 | 949 | 5 629 | 25 342 | 57.9 | 11.3 |
| Novi | 22 258 | 2.46 | 8.6 | 29.5 | 360 | 316 | 316 | 44 | 1 010 | 1 830 | 78 | 1 752 | 36 868 | 19.4 | 54.6 |

1. No spouse present.  2. Data for serious crimes have not been adjusted for underreporting. This may affect comparability between geographic areas and over time.  3. Per 100,000 population estimated by the FBI.  4. Persons 25 years old and over.

# Table D. Cities — Income, Poverty, and Housing

| City | Money income, 2007–2011 | | | | | Housing units, 2010 | | | Occupied Housing units 2007–2011 | | | | |
|---|---|---|---|---|---|---|---|---|---|---|---|---|---|
| | | Households | | | Families with income below poverty (percent) | | | | Owner-occupied | | | Median owner costs as a percent of income | |
| | Per capita income[1] (dollars) | Median income | Percent with income of $200,000 or more | Percent with income of less than $25,000 | | Total | Percent change, 2000–2010 | Vacant units for sale or rent[2] | Total | Percent | Median value[3] (dollars) | With a mortgage[4] | Without a mortgage[5] |
| | 42 | 43 | 44 | 45 | 46 | 47 | 48 | 49 | 50 | 51 | 52 | 53 | 54 |
| **MASSACHUSETTS—Cont'd** | | | | | | | | | | | | | |
| Beverly | 36 889 | 67 733 | 8.2 | 19.3 | 7.1 | 16 641 | 2.2 | 791 | 15 278 | 63.2 | 368 400 | 26.0 | 15.1 |
| Boston | 33 158 | 51 739 | 6.6 | 29.3 | 16.0 | 272 481 | 8.2 | 19 782 | 247 621 | 34.6 | 381 900 | 27.5 | 14.9 |
| Braintree Town | 37 317 | 83 710 | 8.0 | 12.9 | 4.7 | 14 302 | 10.7 | 566 | 13 267 | 74.6 | 372 900 | 25.4 | 16.3 |
| Brockton | 22 312 | 49 848 | 1.8 | 25.0 | 12.7 | 35 552 | 2.1 | 2 249 | 33 238 | 57.9 | 254 300 | 31.3 | 17.8 |
| Cambridge | 46 242 | 69 017 | 10.8 | 21.7 | 10.1 | 47 291 | 5.7 | 3 259 | 45 386 | 35.6 | 546 900 | 24.3 | 12.0 |
| Chelsea | 20 214 | 43 155 | 1.2 | 30.7 | 20.3 | 12 621 | 2.3 | 790 | 12 035 | 31.8 | 301 900 | 32.1 | 24.7 |
| Chicopee | 23 703 | 45 763 | 0.9 | 28.2 | 9.8 | 25 140 | 2.9 | 1 401 | 23 136 | 58.8 | 182 500 | 25.7 | 16.7 |
| Everett | 24 575 | 48 319 | 2.0 | 24.7 | 9.5 | 16 715 | 5.1 | 1 172 | 15 681 | 40.3 | 340 000 | 36.1 | 18.3 |
| Fall River | 21 118 | 34 789 | 1.0 | 37.9 | 18.5 | 42 750 | 2.1 | 4 293 | 38 245 | 37.5 | 252 900 | 29.6 | 18.2 |
| Fitchburg | 24 061 | 48 064 | 1.5 | 28.3 | 13.5 | 17 117 | 7.0 | 1 952 | 14 741 | 57.5 | 213 900 | 25.8 | 17.9 |
| Franklin Town | 39 043 | 92 066 | 9.7 | 9.9 | 2.6 | 11 394 | 10.3 | 399 | 10 866 | 79.8 | 396 600 | 24.9 | 15.9 |
| Gloucester | 35 080 | 59 061 | 6.3 | 20.3 | 6.0 | 14 557 | 4.3 | 2 071 | 12 310 | 64.9 | 376 400 | 30.2 | 17.6 |
| Haverhill | 30 574 | 60 611 | 3.6 | 21.2 | 9.9 | 25 657 | 8.1 | 1 507 | 24 334 | 63.7 | 276 400 | 26.5 | 15.1 |
| Holyoke | 20 370 | 33 915 | 1.6 | 42.2 | 27.0 | 16 384 | 1.1 | 1 023 | 16 012 | 41.0 | 189 400 | 26.1 | 14.7 |
| Lawrence | 17 068 | 31 478 | 1.2 | 40.3 | 26.9 | 27 137 | 6.0 | 1 956 | 27 048 | 32.5 | 241 700 | 39.7 | 18.0 |
| Leominster | 28 445 | 58 585 | 2.5 | 22.4 | 8.0 | 17 873 | 5.3 | 1 106 | 16 095 | 61.6 | 250 600 | 25.7 | 14.6 |
| Lowell | 23 600 | 51 471 | 1.6 | 26.6 | 15.5 | 41 431 | 5.0 | 2 961 | 39 399 | 48.9 | 242 600 | 28.2 | 14.8 |
| Lynn | 22 190 | 44 367 | 1.6 | 29.6 | 15.4 | 35 776 | 3.1 | 2 466 | 34 018 | 48.0 | 268 300 | 31.5 | 17.6 |
| Malden | 26 893 | 52 842 | 2.1 | 25.2 | 11.3 | 25 161 | 6.5 | 1 488 | 23 422 | 43.8 | 343 900 | 33.4 | 15.3 |
| Marlborough | 37 314 | 72 853 | 6.8 | 15.1 | 3.7 | 16 416 | 10.2 | 1 021 | 15 856 | 60.2 | 328 300 | 25.8 | 15.6 |
| Medford | 34 615 | 72 033 | 4.4 | 16.3 | 5.4 | 24 046 | 6.0 | 1 236 | 22 461 | 59.9 | 392 600 | 27.6 | 18.5 |
| Melrose | 39 873 | 84 599 | 7.9 | 15.8 | 2.9 | 11 751 | 4.5 | 538 | 10 963 | 66.0 | 428 900 | 24.9 | 14.5 |
| Methuen Town | 29 778 | 65 799 | 3.6 | 18.2 | 5.1 | 18 340 | 8.6 | 811 | 17 508 | 73.5 | 295 100 | 26.9 | 16.9 |
| New Bedford | 21 558 | 37 493 | 1.1 | 37.3 | 18.7 | 42 933 | 3.4 | 4 172 | 38 869 | 44.2 | 239 900 | 30.0 | 19.7 |
| Newton | 60 323 | 109 724 | 25.7 | 12.5 | 4.4 | 32 648 | 1.7 | 1 480 | 30 735 | 69.5 | 689 600 | 24.6 | 13.9 |
| Northampton | 33 175 | 54 413 | 5.5 | 22.5 | 9.1 | 12 728 | 2.6 | 728 | 11 853 | 57.2 | 278 600 | 25.5 | 12.9 |
| Peabody | 32 442 | 65 471 | 3.4 | 18.2 | 4.0 | 22 220 | 17.6 | 907 | 20 890 | 65.5 | 350 400 | 27.0 | 13.9 |
| Pittsfield | 26 767 | 44 513 | 1.9 | 29.5 | 12.8 | 21 487 | 0.6 | 1 834 | 19 966 | 60.9 | 175 800 | 25.4 | 15.5 |
| Quincy | 32 911 | 60 947 | 3.8 | 21.2 | 7.9 | 42 838 | 6.8 | 2 180 | 39 965 | 49.6 | 352 600 | 29.3 | 16.7 |
| Revere | 25 085 | 50 592 | 1.4 | 26.6 | 14.9 | 22 100 | 9.5 | 1 646 | 19 425 | 50.0 | 327 800 | 33.6 | 21.0 |
| Salem | 30 961 | 56 203 | 3.5 | 23.4 | 9.2 | 19 130 | 5.3 | 1 288 | 17 690 | 51.7 | 320 400 | 28.3 | 19.2 |
| Somerville | 32 785 | 64 480 | 4.3 | 20.0 | 9.2 | 33 720 | 3.8 | 1 615 | 31 476 | 33.3 | 447 000 | 28.2 | 18.4 |
| Springfield | 18 483 | 35 603 | 1.1 | 37.9 | 21.8 | 61 706 | 0.9 | 4 954 | 56 211 | 50.7 | 156 200 | 27.4 | 18.1 |
| Taunton | 26 309 | 53 401 | 1.7 | 22.1 | 9.2 | 23 896 | 4.3 | 1 564 | 21 799 | 62.5 | 275 100 | 27.6 | 15.3 |
| Waltham | 33 717 | 68 326 | 6.3 | 19.9 | 6.4 | 24 926 | 4.4 | 1 236 | 23 520 | 48.1 | 414 700 | 27.5 | 15.4 |
| Watertown Town | 41 090 | 76 718 | 6.0 | 14.6 | 3.2 | 15 584 | 3.8 | 875 | 14 042 | 53.4 | 417 900 | 29.6 | 19.3 |
| Westfield | 26 605 | 53 772 | 3.6 | 24.8 | 5.4 | 16 075 | 4.1 | 740 | 15 207 | 67.0 | 225 300 | 23.9 | 15.3 |
| West Springfield Town | 27 946 | 54 251 | 2.7 | 24.2 | 9.3 | 12 697 | 3.6 | 573 | 11 571 | 61.7 | 210 000 | 23.9 | 16.4 |
| Weymouth Town | 35 939 | 68 594 | 4.8 | 17.2 | 5.9 | 23 480 | 4.0 | 1 045 | 22 543 | 69.0 | 329 700 | 26.9 | 17.4 |
| Woburn | 33 725 | 72 540 | 3.7 | 14.1 | 4.0 | 16 309 | 6.0 | 785 | 15 357 | 61.6 | 372 000 | 27.2 | 15.2 |
| Worcester | 24 544 | 45 846 | 2.4 | 29.8 | 15.4 | 74 645 | 5.5 | 6 032 | 70 248 | 46.6 | 234 400 | 27.4 | 17.4 |
| **MICHIGAN** | 25 482 | 48 669 | 2.9 | 25.2 | 11.1 | 4 532 233 | 7.0 | 659 725 | 3 825 182 | 73.5 | 137 300 | 24.5 | 13.8 |
| Allen Park | 26 769 | 55 553 | 2.1 | 20.1 | 5.6 | 12 206 | -0.4 | 626 | 11 007 | 89.4 | 129 100 | 22.9 | 14.8 |
| Ann Arbor | 32 734 | 53 377 | 6.6 | 25.3 | 6.1 | 49 789 | 5.5 | 2 729 | 45 457 | 46.4 | 234 900 | 23.5 | 12.7 |
| Battle Creek | 21 457 | 38 760 | 1.9 | 33.6 | 17.7 | 24 277 | 3.1 | 3 159 | 20 564 | 62.6 | 91 800 | 23.7 | 14.3 |
| Bay City | 18 411 | 36 113 | 0.5 | 34.7 | 14.9 | 15 923 | -2.1 | 1 487 | 14 332 | 70.9 | 78 000 | 24.3 | 15.9 |
| Burton | 21 685 | 44 253 | 1.1 | 26.0 | 11.1 | 13 075 | 5.9 | 1 111 | 11 716 | 75.4 | 89 000 | 24.1 | 12.9 |
| Dearborn | 22 816 | 46 685 | 2.7 | 29.0 | 20.2 | 37 871 | -2.8 | 3 529 | 33 574 | 70.5 | 130 400 | 27.0 | 14.9 |
| Dearborn Heights | 22 293 | 47 241 | 1.3 | 24.4 | 9.4 | 24 068 | 0.6 | 1 802 | 21 658 | 79.3 | 112 200 | 26.5 | 14.6 |
| Detroit | 15 261 | 27 862 | 0.7 | 45.5 | 31.1 | 349 170 | -6.9 | 79 725 | 264 209 | 53.8 | 71 100 | 31.5 | 18.1 |
| East Lansing | 17 642 | 31 694 | 4.9 | 43.1 | 8.3 | 15 787 | 3.1 | 1 013 | 13 189 | 37.5 | 186 200 | 22.4 | 10.7 |
| Eastpointe | 20 136 | 44 802 | 0.2 | 26.1 | 12.9 | 13 796 | -1.2 | 1 239 | 12 674 | 78.0 | 93 900 | 27.3 | 17.1 |
| Farmington Hills | 39 331 | 70 828 | 8.0 | 15.2 | 4.2 | 36 178 | 3.8 | 2 619 | 33 349 | 65.6 | 221 700 | 23.4 | 14.6 |
| Flint | 14 682 | 26 621 | 0.3 | 47.9 | 33.3 | 51 321 | -7.5 | 10 849 | 41 175 | 55.9 | 57 200 | 26.6 | 15.4 |
| Garden City | 24 358 | 54 094 | 0.3 | 16.5 | 5.7 | 11 616 | -0.9 | 722 | 10 384 | 83.2 | 111 600 | 25.4 | 14.1 |
| Grand Rapids | 20 281 | 38 731 | 1.2 | 32.8 | 19.5 | 80 619 | 3.4 | 8 493 | 73 089 | 57.5 | 118 000 | 23.9 | 13.5 |
| Holland | 19 373 | 41 334 | 1.3 | 26.2 | 11.9 | 13 212 | 5.2 | 1 191 | 11 778 | 67.1 | 127 800 | 25.0 | 14.8 |
| Inkster | 15 157 | 29 076 | 0.3 | 44.6 | 29.6 | 11 647 | -3.0 | 1 826 | 9 789 | 52.4 | 78 400 | 28.7 | 17.7 |
| Jackson | 16 377 | 29 589 | 0.6 | 42.8 | 24.9 | 15 457 | 1.4 | 2 163 | 13 642 | 56.6 | 82 100 | 24.2 | 14.5 |
| Kalamazoo | 18 348 | 31 291 | 1.6 | 40.1 | 23.1 | 32 433 | 2.0 | 3 292 | 28 524 | 46.3 | 105 200 | 24.9 | 14.6 |
| Kentwood | 24 922 | 50 799 | 1.8 | 24.9 | 11.2 | 21 584 | 10.7 | 1 843 | 19 589 | 63.4 | 137 700 | 23.7 | 14.6 |
| Lansing | 19 766 | 37 528 | 0.7 | 33.8 | 19.9 | 54 181 | 1.8 | 5 731 | 48 218 | 55.3 | 97 400 | 24.7 | 14.1 |
| Lincoln Park | 19 650 | 41 945 | 0.5 | 28.3 | 14.5 | 16 530 | -1.7 | 1 606 | 14 617 | 74.7 | 88 200 | 25.7 | 15.1 |
| Livonia | 31 959 | 69 887 | 3.3 | 14.0 | 3.5 | 40 401 | 4.5 | 1 687 | 37 309 | 87.5 | 171 000 | 22.9 | 12.7 |
| Madison Heights | 23 011 | 42 294 | 0.8 | 28.4 | 13.8 | 13 685 | 0.5 | 973 | 12 615 | 65.7 | 113 800 | 24.3 | 16.1 |
| Midland | 32 185 | 50 203 | 6.6 | 25.0 | 7.6 | 18 578 | 4.7 | 1 072 | 17 814 | 66.8 | 140 100 | 20.5 | 11.9 |
| Mount Pleasant | 15 792 | 28 020 | 2.0 | 46.7 | 20.0 | 8 981 | 0.8 | 605 | 8 325 | 36.7 | 130 600 | 22.2 | 11.1 |
| Muskegon | 14 690 | 25 863 | 0.4 | 48.7 | 27.8 | 16 105 | 0.5 | 2 138 | 14 643 | 50.0 | 74 000 | 25.1 | 13.6 |
| Novi | 42 666 | 76 561 | 10.9 | 12.5 | 4.6 | 24 226 | 23.2 | 1 968 | 22 445 | 66.3 | 250 200 | 23.3 | 14.1 |

1. Based on population estimated by the American Community Survey.   2. Includes units rented or sold but not occupied.   3. Specified owner-occupied units; $1,000,000 represents $1,000,000 or more   4. 50.0 represents 50 percent or more.   5. 10.0 represents 10 percent or less.

| City | Occupied housing units, 2007–2011 (cont.) | | | | Migration, 2007–2011 | | Civilian labor force, 2012 | | | | Civilian employment[4], 2007–2011 | | | |
|---|---|---|---|---|---|---|---|---|---|---|---|---|---|---|
| | | | | | | | | | Unemployment | | | Percent | | |
| | Percent renter occupied | Median gross rent[1] | Median rent as a percent of income[2] | Percent with no vehicle available | Percent who lived in the same house one year ago | Percent who lived outside this city one year ago | Total | Percent change, 2011–2012 | Total | Rate[3] | Population age 16 and older | In labor force | Full-year full-time worker | Households with no workers (percent) |
| | 55 | 56 | 57 | 58 | 59 | 60 | 61 | 62 | 63 | 64 | 65 | 66 | 67 | 68 |
| **MASSACHUSETTS—Cont'd** | | | | | | | | | | | | | | |
| Beverly | 36.8 | 1 030 | 29.8 | 9.6 | 86.6 | 9.2 | 21 580 | 0.8 | 1 255 | 5.8 | 32 931 | 67.8 | 41.0 | 26.7 |
| Boston | 65.4 | 1 238 | 31.2 | 36.1 | 75.9 | 11.6 | 320 246 | 1.3 | 20 626 | 6.4 | 518 562 | 68.6 | 39.4 | 27.2 |
| Braintree Town | 25.4 | 1 223 | 29.9 | 6.9 | 89.9 | 7.0 | 19 223 | 1.1 | 1 160 | 6.0 | 28 552 | 68.8 | 42.4 | 23.1 |
| Brockton | 42.1 | 1 010 | 34.6 | 14.2 | 84.6 | 7.0 | 45 531 | 0.0 | 4 115 | 9.0 | 72 709 | 68.8 | 39.0 | 28.3 |
| Cambridge | 64.4 | 1 529 | 29.8 | 32.7 | 72.9 | 20.5 | 60 666 | 1.7 | 2 540 | 4.2 | 92 054 | 68.5 | 40.5 | 24.6 |
| Chelsea | 68.2 | 1 089 | 33.4 | 30.9 | 83.9 | 8.3 | 14 487 | -0.4 | 1 262 | 8.7 | 26 877 | 67.6 | 40.6 | 28.7 |
| Chicopee | 41.2 | 750 | 29.2 | 11.3 | 86.2 | 9.2 | 27 251 | -0.7 | 2 214 | 8.1 | 45 041 | 63.1 | 37.6 | 33.8 |
| Everett | 59.7 | 1 115 | 31.9 | 18.2 | 84.2 | 11.3 | 21 409 | 0.8 | 1 475 | 6.9 | 33 087 | 71.8 | 42.8 | 25.5 |
| Fall River | 62.5 | 679 | 29.4 | 18.2 | 83.6 | 6.9 | 43 522 | -1.4 | 5 641 | 13.0 | 72 690 | 60.5 | 33.6 | 37.8 |
| Fitchburg | 42.5 | 829 | 32.8 | 14.3 | 83.7 | 9.6 | 18 465 | -2.1 | 1 851 | 10.0 | 32 422 | 65.1 | 35.3 | 29.0 |
| Franklin Town | 20.2 | 1 122 | 26.4 | 3.7 | 90.0 | 7.2 | 16 929 | 0.6 | 954 | 5.6 | 23 272 | 73.4 | 45.6 | 17.0 |
| Gloucester | 35.1 | 956 | 29.5 | 8.3 | 91.0 | 5.1 | 15 731 | -1.0 | 1 232 | 7.8 | 24 021 | 65.5 | 36.7 | 29.1 |
| Haverhill | 36.3 | 974 | 32.3 | 10.9 | 86.1 | 7.6 | 32 029 | 0.8 | 2 328 | 7.3 | 47 799 | 70.0 | 43.4 | 26.2 |
| Holyoke | 59.0 | 703 | 33.4 | 23.1 | 84.9 | 6.8 | 15 885 | 0.3 | 1 631 | 10.3 | 30 876 | 57.5 | 30.6 | 42.4 |
| Lawrence | 67.5 | 950 | 36.2 | 23.7 | 81.8 | 5.9 | 32 201 | -1.2 | 4 646 | 14.4 | 56 639 | 59.8 | 35.2 | 31.0 |
| Leominster | 38.4 | 857 | 30.6 | 10.7 | 87.9 | 6.3 | 20 108 | -1.8 | 1 769 | 8.8 | 32 597 | 68.3 | 40.9 | 29.1 |
| Lowell | 51.1 | 939 | 29.6 | 15.3 | 82.8 | 7.3 | 52 820 | 0.8 | 4 610 | 8.7 | 84 739 | 66.5 | 39.7 | 27.8 |
| Lynn | 52.0 | 924 | 33.1 | 20.5 | 84.1 | 5.5 | 43 532 | 0.8 | 3 438 | 7.9 | 70 977 | 66.5 | 40.1 | 29.6 |
| Malden | 56.2 | 1 178 | 29.9 | 19.2 | 81.8 | 14.7 | 33 481 | 0.8 | 1 985 | 5.9 | 48 726 | 71.4 | 41.2 | 24.0 |
| Marlborough | 39.8 | 1 064 | 26.7 | 9.6 | 87.4 | 7.6 | 22 826 | 1.0 | 1 233 | 5.4 | 31 443 | 74.9 | 50.1 | 19.8 |
| Medford | 40.1 | 1 328 | 28.1 | 10.3 | 82.0 | 13.5 | 30 910 | 1.2 | 1 738 | 5.6 | 48 023 | 69.8 | 43.2 | 23.7 |
| Melrose | 34.0 | 1 116 | 25.6 | 10.9 | 90.0 | 7.9 | 15 333 | 1.0 | 742 | 4.8 | 21 610 | 70.3 | 44.2 | 24.1 |
| Methuen Town | 26.5 | 941 | 31.7 | 7.6 | 88.7 | 7.1 | 24 740 | 1.4 | 2 091 | 8.5 | 36 655 | 68.6 | 42.3 | 26.4 |
| New Bedford | 55.8 | 758 | 31.2 | 18.4 | 84.7 | 5.9 | 43 961 | 0.3 | 5 492 | 12.5 | 74 996 | 62.5 | 34.5 | 35.3 |
| Newton | 30.5 | 1 609 | 27.4 | 6.4 | 84.2 | 12.1 | 47 617 | 1.5 | 2 023 | 4.2 | 68 403 | 66.0 | 41.7 | 22.1 |
| Northampton | 42.8 | 876 | 30.9 | 10.9 | 81.8 | 13.5 | 16 170 | 0.6 | 814 | 5.0 | 24 530 | 67.6 | 34.4 | 25.3 |
| Peabody | 34.5 | 1 163 | 33.0 | 10.9 | 90.6 | 5.6 | 27 880 | 1.0 | 1 774 | 6.4 | 41 941 | 65.6 | 41.4 | 31.4 |
| Pittsfield | 39.1 | 743 | 29.9 | 13.6 | 86.4 | 5.5 | 23 334 | -1.1 | 1 749 | 7.5 | 36 260 | 63.8 | 35.4 | 33.6 |
| Quincy | 50.4 | 1 153 | 28.6 | 16.7 | 81.9 | 11.6 | 53 181 | 0.8 | 3 226 | 6.1 | 78 138 | 70.0 | 44.3 | 26.4 |
| Revere | 50.0 | 1 147 | 34.9 | 18.9 | 83.8 | 10.7 | 25 102 | 0.5 | 1 884 | 7.5 | 41 475 | 67.1 | 40.1 | 29.4 |
| Salem | 48.3 | 1 050 | 30.4 | 15.1 | 81.0 | 11.3 | 23 914 | 0.1 | 1 575 | 6.6 | 34 222 | 71.7 | 42.4 | 26.2 |
| Somerville | 66.7 | 1 355 | 27.7 | 23.7 | 76.6 | 16.2 | 46 982 | 1.2 | 2 135 | 4.5 | 67 040 | 75.2 | 46.6 | 19.6 |
| Springfield | 49.3 | 756 | 34.5 | 21.5 | 83.4 | 7.1 | 65 735 | -1.9 | 7 200 | 11.0 | 117 197 | 57.7 | 32.0 | 36.1 |
| Taunton | 37.5 | 881 | 30.9 | 7.6 | 88.5 | 5.9 | 30 793 | -1.9 | 2 378 | 7.7 | 44 806 | 70.6 | 41.7 | 25.2 |
| Waltham | 51.9 | 1 321 | 29.7 | 8.5 | 79.0 | 16.0 | 35 773 | 0.8 | 1 801 | 5.0 | 53 017 | 67.8 | 41.7 | 21.1 |
| Watertown Town | 46.6 | 1 370 | 22.9 | 10.0 | 85.5 | 11.9 | 13 091 | 0.7 | 766 | 5.9 | 27 801 | 72.0 | 48.2 | 19.8 |
| Westfield | 33.0 | 823 | 33.9 | 8.4 | 88.5 | 6.5 | 15 840 | 2.8 | 884 | 5.6 | 33 420 | 60.8 | 37.1 | 30.8 |
| West Springfield Town | 38.3 | 784 | 28.2 | 8.0 | 86.3 | 10.1 | 14 427 | -0.9 | 1 092 | 7.6 | 22 850 | 67.3 | 41.0 | 27.6 |
| Weymouth Town | 31.0 | 1 123 | 30.7 | 7.1 | 90.8 | 7.1 | 30 041 | 0.4 | 1 918 | 6.4 | 43 479 | 71.2 | 43.8 | 24.8 |
| Woburn | 38.4 | 1 194 | 27.1 | 6.3 | 87.4 | 8.1 | 21 988 | 0.9 | 1 268 | 5.8 | 31 247 | 71.9 | 44.2 | 22.6 |
| Worcester | 53.4 | 886 | 30.5 | 16.2 | 83.9 | 7.3 | 84 637 | -0.6 | 7 073 | 8.4 | 146 128 | 63.6 | 37.6 | 30.0 |
| **MICHIGAN** | 26.5 | 742 | 32.7 | 7.4 | 85.4 | 10.8 | 4 657 459 | 0.6 | 425 953 | 9.1 | 7 840 553 | 62.7 | 34.7 | 31.4 |
| Allen Park | 10.6 | 795 | 32.8 | 5.3 | 93.0 | 5.1 | 12 088 | 1.4 | 610 | 5.0 | 22 854 | 61.9 | 34.2 | 35.9 |
| Ann Arbor | 53.6 | 959 | 33.2 | 10.9 | 64.1 | 20.8 | 62 782 | 1.1 | 3 804 | 6.1 | 100 465 | 61.0 | 30.7 | 26.9 |
| Battle Creek | 37.4 | 685 | 35.8 | 11.5 | 79.5 | 8.7 | 23 851 | -0.9 | 2 059 | 8.6 | 40 094 | 60.5 | 32.3 | 34.3 |
| Bay City | 29.1 | 513 | 32.4 | 12.8 | 83.2 | 7.7 | 16 862 | -0.3 | 1 542 | 9.1 | 27 064 | 62.4 | 32.7 | 34.7 |
| Burton | 24.6 | 704 | 34.5 | 7.0 | 89.5 | 7.5 | 12 823 | -0.2 | 946 | 7.4 | 23 921 | 60.9 | 33.3 | 35.9 |
| Dearborn | 29.5 | 967 | 36.5 | 8.5 | 86.8 | 6.1 | 35 564 | 0.9 | 2 641 | 7.4 | 72 455 | 56.5 | 30.5 | 35.2 |
| Dearborn Heights | 20.7 | 955 | 35.6 | 6.6 | 87.4 | 8.9 | 23 675 | 1.0 | 1 619 | 6.8 | 44 956 | 57.8 | 31.7 | 34.7 |
| Detroit | 46.2 | 761 | 43.7 | 22.4 | 83.6 | 3.8 | 343 856 | -1.1 | 63 896 | 18.6 | 563 055 | 54.3 | 24.5 | 44.4 |
| East Lansing | 62.5 | 808 | 50.0 | 10.2 | 47.4 | 32.1 | 19 138 | -1.7 | 1 681 | 8.8 | 45 095 | 51.2 | 15.0 | 28.1 |
| Eastpointe | 22.0 | 1 004 | 40.6 | 6.2 | 82.7 | 15.7 | 16 990 | 1.3 | 1 806 | 10.6 | 24 989 | 67.2 | 37.0 | 30.9 |
| Farmington Hills | 34.4 | 954 | 28.1 | 4.7 | 84.6 | 12.1 | 39 720 | 2.2 | 3 023 | 7.6 | 65 104 | 66.2 | 40.9 | 25.1 |
| Flint | 44.1 | 647 | 45.6 | 16.8 | 79.8 | 6.7 | 47 378 | -3.4 | 7 853 | 16.6 | 79 788 | 49.8 | 21.9 | 49.4 |
| Garden City | 16.8 | 952 | 29.8 | 5.2 | 89.1 | 9.1 | 13 310 | 1.1 | 897 | 6.7 | 22 125 | 67.0 | 37.1 | 30.5 |
| Grand Rapids | 42.5 | 736 | 35.4 | 12.6 | 77.6 | 11.0 | 100 375 | 2.3 | 9 161 | 9.1 | 147 124 | 67.2 | 35.4 | 29.0 |
| Holland | 32.9 | 699 | 32.9 | 7.9 | 73.9 | 16.6 | 17 518 | 1.5 | 1 560 | 8.9 | 26 067 | 63.1 | 33.2 | 28.0 |
| Inkster | 47.6 | 712 | 42.2 | 15.2 | 81.8 | 13.0 | 11 600 | -0.1 | 1 532 | 13.2 | 19 453 | 54.0 | 26.4 | 45.2 |
| Jackson | 43.4 | 624 | 36.8 | 19.5 | 76.3 | 10.4 | 15 990 | -2.3 | 1 973 | 12.3 | 25 644 | 57.9 | 30.3 | 39.6 |
| Kalamazoo | 53.7 | 685 | 38.1 | 14.1 | 64.3 | 19.4 | 37 738 | -1.2 | 3 652 | 9.7 | 61 051 | 64.5 | 28.9 | 31.6 |
| Kentwood | 36.6 | 723 | 27.2 | 8.2 | 82.4 | 14.6 | 26 302 | 3.6 | 1 554 | 5.9 | 38 249 | 72.7 | 43.2 | 22.6 |
| Lansing | 44.7 | 689 | 34.6 | 12.3 | 78.5 | 11.3 | 61 799 | -2.1 | 6 449 | 10.4 | 90 566 | 67.5 | 36.6 | 30.1 |
| Lincoln Park | 25.3 | 720 | 35.7 | 8.4 | 85.9 | 9.5 | 17 284 | 0.7 | 1 507 | 8.7 | 29 891 | 60.9 | 33.4 | 33.8 |
| Livonia | 12.5 | 863 | 29.3 | 4.0 | 91.9 | 5.5 | 44 109 | 1.5 | 1 968 | 4.5 | 79 442 | 64.5 | 38.1 | 29.1 |
| Madison Heights | 34.3 | 733 | 30.0 | 9.6 | 84.8 | 12.2 | 15 203 | 1.6 | 1 536 | 10.1 | 24 640 | 67.5 | 38.4 | 30.0 |
| Midland | 33.2 | 650 | 30.4 | 7.1 | 82.1 | 10.1 | 20 755 | 1.6 | 1 133 | 5.5 | 33 366 | 61.8 | 36.4 | 31.6 |
| Mount Pleasant | 63.3 | 670 | 41.1 | 15.0 | 48.3 | 30.5 | 13 679 | 1.0 | 973 | 7.1 | 23 621 | 60.2 | 18.0 | 29.3 |
| Muskegon | 50.0 | 589 | 38.5 | 17.2 | 74.1 | 15.1 | 16 811 | 1.0 | 1 917 | 11.4 | 30 829 | 52.7 | 23.3 | 41.8 |
| Novi | 33.7 | 972 | 26.5 | 4.6 | 85.0 | 12.5 | 24 030 | 2.6 | 1 392 | 5.8 | 42 514 | 69.9 | 45.6 | 21.7 |

1. $2,000 represents $2,000 or more.  2. 50.0 represents 50 percent or more.  3. Percent of civilian labor force.  4. Persons 16 years old and over.

# Table D. Cities — **Construction, Wholesale Trade, and Retail Trade**

| City | Value of residential construction authorized by building permits, 2011 | | | Wholesale trade,[1] 2007 | | | | Retail trade,[2] 2007 | | | |
|---|---|---|---|---|---|---|---|---|---|---|---|
| | New construction ($1,000) | Number of housing units | Percent single family | Number of establish- ments | Number of employees | Sales (mil dol) | Annual payroll (mil dol) | Number of establish- ments | Number of employees | Sales (mil dol) | Annual payroll (mil dol) |
| | 69 | 70 | 71 | 72 | 73 | 74 | 75 | 76 | 77 | 78 | 79 |
| **MASSACHUSETTS— Cont'd** | | | | | | | | | | | |
| Beverly | 5 392 | 37 | 16.2 | 51 | 368 | 184.1 | 21.6 | 155 | 2 608 | 852.3 | 70.1 |
| Boston | 171 603 | 785 | 4.2 | 565 | 10 156 | 6 225.7 | 583.8 | 2 157 | 27 909 | 6 808.8 | 725.3 |
| Braintree Town | 7 502 | 63 | 20.6 | NA | NA | NA | NA | NA | NA | NA | NA |
| Brockton | 3 024 | 24 | 87.5 | 65 | 1 062 | 757.7 | 54.6 | 329 | 5 208 | 1 263.5 | 138.6 |
| Cambridge | 20 216 | 34 | 41.2 | 90 | 1 693 | 2 066.4 | 189.9 | 474 | 6 627 | 1 287.7 | 150.6 |
| Chelsea | 7 493 | 113 | 0.0 | 90 | 1 606 | 2 447.5 | 94.2 | 78 | 1 334 | 348.2 | 36.1 |
| Chicopee | 2 324 | 15 | 86.7 | 36 | 922 | 725.5 | 42.4 | 167 | 2 582 | 721.3 | 62.9 |
| Everett | 6 376 | 68 | 20.6 | 61 | 1 566 | 1 050.6 | 84.6 | 120 | 1 811 | 496.7 | 45.7 |
| Fall River | 4 650 | 45 | 86.7 | 76 | 1 642 | 727.8 | 63.9 | 298 | 3 488 | 931.2 | 91.4 |
| Fitchburg | 2 186 | 18 | 100.0 | 32 | 249 | 105.8 | 11.8 | 144 | 1 876 | 489.5 | 42.8 |
| Franklin Town | 5 112 | 21 | 100.0 | NA | NA | NA | NA | NA | NA | NA | NA |
| Gloucester | 8 207 | 29 | 89.7 | 56 | 417 | 491.5 | 21.3 | 117 | 1 146 | 253.7 | 29.2 |
| Haverhill | 4 895 | 29 | 93.1 | 51 | 722 | 266.2 | 39.3 | 143 | 2 230 | 648.0 | 60.2 |
| Holyoke | 1 256 | 13 | 23.1 | 29 | 421 | 125.3 | 16.3 | 261 | 4 373 | 712.6 | 77.6 |
| Lawrence | 1 636 | 18 | 11.1 | 66 | 1 204 | 538.2 | 58.1 | 173 | 1 579 | 429.6 | 45.9 |
| Leominster | 7 581 | 30 | 100.0 | 48 | 730 | 429.0 | 37.3 | 221 | 3 896 | 766.0 | 76.7 |
| Lowell | 10 081 | 90 | 48.9 | 65 | 964 | 523.4 | 51.0 | 224 | 2 331 | 573.9 | 54.1 |
| Lynn | 829 | 5 | 100.0 | 41 | 526 | 430.8 | 26.7 | 215 | 2 276 | 623.8 | 57.1 |
| Malden | 828 | 9 | 55.6 | 32 | 515 | 229.9 | 26.2 | 131 | 1 397 | 456.9 | 35.0 |
| Marlborough | 2 481 | 19 | 100.0 | 80 | 1 973 | 1 051.3 | 184.0 | 225 | 3 543 | 758.0 | 69.4 |
| Medford | 140 | 2 | 0.0 | 47 | 809 | 413.0 | 40.0 | 160 | 2 312 | 596.3 | 59.9 |
| Melrose | 1 917 | 8 | 75.0 | 11 | 73 | 24.6 | 4.2 | 61 | 768 | 173.1 | 19.1 |
| Methuen Town | 9 476 | 38 | 100.0 | 33 | 735 | 1 721.2 | 46.0 | 107 | 2 157 | 486.0 | 49.9 |
| New Bedford | 2 096 | 17 | 100.0 | 100 | 1 746 | 919.5 | 79.4 | 305 | 3 061 | 727.0 | 71.9 |
| Newton | 33 476 | 74 | 100.0 | 116 | 2 246 | 4 040.0 | 126.8 | 378 | 5 680 | 1 153.6 | 156.1 |
| Northampton | 4 442 | 20 | 85.0 | 28 | 217 | 65.1 | 7.6 | 185 | 2 140 | 468.9 | 50.7 |
| Peabody | 3 704 | 22 | 81.8 | 76 | 2 037 | 4 327.3 | 141.1 | 273 | 5 071 | 1 219.5 | 132.5 |
| Pittsfield | 2 644 | 16 | 87.5 | 43 | 561 | 217.9 | 22.5 | 209 | 3 205 | 747.8 | 77.3 |
| Quincy | 9 127 | 80 | 11.3 | 58 | 739 | 530.4 | 36.6 | 245 | 4 032 | 1 142.2 | 105.0 |
| Revere | 877 | 4 | 50.0 | 26 | D | D | D | 115 | 1 665 | 360.4 | 34.3 |
| Salem | 768 | 5 | 100.0 | 39 | 314 | 166.3 | 17.0 | 173 | 2 680 | 544.2 | 64.4 |
| Somerville | 0 | 0 | 0.0 | 46 | 560 | 291.2 | 33.4 | 172 | 2 962 | 761.5 | 69.1 |
| Springfield | 8 057 | 57 | 96.5 | 123 | 1 892 | 1 097.0 | 94.4 | 485 | 6 592 | 1 521.3 | 150.5 |
| Taunton | 4 061 | 31 | 93.5 | 57 | 1 932 | 1 393.0 | 105.4 | 242 | 4 868 | 1 085.1 | 107.3 |
| Waltham | 13 521 | 49 | 83.7 | 115 | 2 961 | 8 050.6 | 283.0 | 224 | 2 932 | 811.3 | 85.6 |
| Watertown Town | 26 932 | 220 | 0.0 | 39 | 506 | 193.4 | 26.5 | 171 | 3 392 | 889.4 | 97.8 |
| Westfield | 2 995 | 21 | 57.1 | 38 | 1 109 | 1 826.1 | 45.0 | 144 | 2 198 | 530.8 | 51.0 |
| West Springfield Town | 4 560 | 29 | 93.1 | NA | NA | NA | NA | NA | NA | NA | NA |
| Weymouth Town | 36 744 | 276 | 16.7 | NA | NA | NA | NA | NA | NA | NA | NA |
| Woburn | 8 189 | 28 | 100.0 | 224 | 3 716 | 2 178.4 | 215.0 | 192 | 3 601 | 1 010.7 | 111.9 |
| Worcester | 9 464 | 79 | 81.0 | 209 | 2 968 | 1 321.9 | 139.0 | 593 | 8 591 | 1 923.3 | 205.4 |
| **MICHIGAN** | 1 688 198 | 9 341 | 85.0 | 9 892 | 137 315 | 107 109.3 | 7 016.1 | 37 619 | 470 794 | 109 102.6 | 10 001.5 |
| Allen Park | 0 | 0 | 0.0 | 17 | 209 | 132.8 | 11.5 | 111 | 1 680 | 297.0 | 31.2 |
| Ann Arbor | 21 744 | 291 | 4.8 | 73 | 641 | 364.1 | 39.4 | 518 | 7 836 | 1 467.2 | 165.7 |
| Battle Creek | 1 660 | 10 | 100.0 | 39 | 490 | 344.6 | 21.9 | 261 | 3 920 | 757.6 | 72.7 |
| Bay City | 189 | 2 | 100.0 | 46 | 571 | 217.1 | 26.9 | 156 | 1 338 | 274.8 | 29.1 |
| Burton | 314 | 2 | 100.0 | 25 | 244 | 68.9 | 10.5 | 180 | 2 799 | 538.9 | 55.0 |
| Dearborn | 2 288 | 4 | 100.0 | 134 | 1 549 | 1 733.8 | 78.5 | 556 | 6 001 | 1 181.6 | 110.7 |
| Dearborn Heights | 924 | 12 | 100.0 | 42 | 152 | 69.4 | 6.3 | 193 | 1 781 | 377.8 | 35.0 |
| Detroit | 28 259 | 245 | 7.3 | 450 | 7 278 | 7 112.1 | 381.1 | 2 157 | 12 933 | 3 271.8 | 265.3 |
| East Lansing | 601 | 5 | 100.0 | 15 | 68 | 55.6 | 3.9 | 76 | 1 488 | 278.3 | 24.2 |
| Eastpointe | 0 | 0 | 0.0 | 19 | 56 | 13.3 | 2.0 | 137 | 1 404 | 342.7 | 37.7 |
| Farmington Hills | 5 381 | 18 | 100.0 | 212 | 2 920 | 2 236.2 | 188.5 | 267 | 4 095 | 1 151.2 | 103.6 |
| Flint | 524 | 4 | 100.0 | 71 | 1 557 | 757.6 | 95.5 | 432 | 4 597 | 876.5 | 89.6 |
| Garden City | 0 | 0 | 0.0 | 12 | 50 | 10.5 | 1.1 | 115 | 1 126 | 404.4 | 32.9 |
| Grand Rapids | 5 478 | 59 | 39.0 | 222 | 5 471 | 3 319.6 | 280.7 | 613 | 6 933 | 1 500.4 | 154.5 |
| Holland | 1 456 | 6 | 100.0 | 47 | 767 | 440.8 | 43.1 | 177 | 2 248 | 509.1 | 46.5 |
| Inkster | 0 | 0 | 0.0 | 9 | 152 | 76.7 | 11.9 | 51 | 278 | 72.3 | 5.5 |
| Jackson | 120 | 2 | 100.0 | 61 | 972 | 733.7 | 48.6 | 191 | 1 868 | 398.1 | 40.7 |
| Kalamazoo | 5 844 | 29 | 100.0 | 102 | 1 503 | 611.6 | 61.9 | 301 | 3 160 | 637.3 | 68.7 |
| Kentwood | 4 249 | 51 | 100.0 | 127 | 2 549 | 1 395.8 | 122.3 | 303 | 4 914 | 898.6 | 95.4 |
| Lansing | 8 309 | 50 | 74.0 | 125 | 1 949 | 1 657.6 | 88.9 | 451 | 6 709 | 1 552.2 | 149.7 |
| Lincoln Park | 0 | 0 | 0.0 | 14 | 165 | 75.4 | 7.1 | 140 | 1 637 | 347.3 | 32.9 |
| Livonia | 5 004 | 19 | 100.0 | 279 | 4 608 | 4 355.0 | 224.4 | 506 | 7 560 | 2 683.7 | 159.0 |
| Madison Heights | 175 | 3 | 100.0 | 111 | 1 943 | 965.8 | 102.6 | 175 | 3 589 | 891.5 | 84.4 |
| Midland | 10 578 | 86 | 83.7 | 32 | D | D | D | 244 | 3 910 | 746.7 | 71.1 |
| Mount Pleasant | 2 158 | 43 | 11.6 | 27 | 526 | 197.5 | 12.6 | 132 | 2 661 | 496.1 | 47.7 |
| Muskegon | 1 417 | 9 | 100.0 | 37 | 961 | 394.7 | 48.8 | 145 | 2 121 | 407.5 | 43.5 |
| Novi | 40 081 | 275 | 100.0 | 151 | 2 259 | 3 321.6 | 139.4 | 359 | 6 845 | 1 361.1 | 143.7 |

1. Merchant wholesalers except manufacturers' sales branches and offices.   2. Establishments with payroll.

| City | Real estate and rental and leasing, 2007 | | | | Professional, scientific, and technical services,[1] 2007 | | | | Manufacturing, 2007 | | | |
|---|---|---|---|---|---|---|---|---|---|---|---|---|
| | Number of establishments | Number of employees | Receipts (mil dol) | Annual payroll (mil dol) | Number of establishments | Number of employees | Receipts (mil dol) | Annual payroll (mil dol) | Number of establishments | Number of employees | Receipts (mil dol) | Annual payroll (mil dol) |
| | 80 | 81 | 82 | 83 | 84 | 85 | 86 | 87 | 88 | 89 | 90 | 91 |
| **MASSACHUSETTS— Cont'd** | | | | | | | | | | | | |
| Beverly | 43 | 193 | 31.8 | 6.8 | 164 | D | D | D | 57 | 3 090 | 722.2 | 208.3 |
| Boston | 1 022 | 11 955 | 5 544.2 | 846.9 | 2 971 | 52 195 | 13 235.0 | 5 456.7 | 319 | 9 922 | 3 193.3 | 580.7 |
| Braintree Town | NA | NA | NA | NA | NA | NA | NA | NA | NA | NA | NA | NA |
| Brockton | 56 | 317 | 49.2 | 10.0 | 150 | D | D | D | 91 | 2 702 | 443.3 | 104.2 |
| Cambridge | 160 | 937 | 332.5 | 44.6 | 824 | D | D | D | 75 | 2 906 | 800.2 | 184.4 |
| Chelsea | 25 | 137 | 15.4 | 4.3 | 37 | 385 | 45.1 | 20.2 | 43 | 2 102 | 367.8 | 73.0 |
| Chicopee | 44 | 161 | 31.2 | 4.9 | 48 | 220 | 21.0 | 8.4 | 85 | 4 401 | 1 118.3 | 192.7 |
| Everett | 18 | 92 | 17.0 | 4.2 | 36 | 145 | 12.1 | 4.2 | 49 | 811 | 145.8 | 37.5 |
| Fall River | 87 | 339 | 61.8 | 9.8 | 169 | D | D | D | 164 | 6 067 | 1 060.1 | 215.2 |
| Fitchburg | 35 | 142 | 18.3 | 3.5 | 63 | 314 | 28.3 | 10.6 | 74 | 2 271 | 464.4 | 102.7 |
| Franklin Town | NA | NA | NA | NA | NA | NA | NA | NA | NA | NA | NA | NA |
| Gloucester | 28 | 92 | 11.1 | 2.4 | 99 | D | D | D | 53 | 2 941 | 1 218.7 | 211.9 |
| Haverhill | 49 | 238 | 40.7 | 8.9 | 114 | 739 | 80.6 | 33.3 | 97 | 2 658 | 601.2 | 109.7 |
| Holyoke | 48 | 422 | 74.9 | 11.2 | 59 | D | D | D | 82 | 2 233 | 451.8 | 98.6 |
| Lawrence | 42 | 242 | 38.5 | 7.6 | 84 | D | D | D | 100 | 4 491 | 851.2 | 174.4 |
| Leominster | 44 | 295 | 46.7 | 12.8 | 99 | D | D | D | 97 | 3 225 | 1 024.3 | 142.3 |
| Lowell | 81 | 543 | 77.0 | 13.5 | 143 | D | D | D | 77 | 3 905 | 762.9 | 209.9 |
| Lynn | 54 | 275 | 53.5 | 8.1 | 86 | D | D | D | 43 | 4 887 | D | D |
| Malden | 62 | 318 | 111.3 | 13.5 | 77 | 528 | 37.2 | 14.7 | 48 | 1 694 | 372.3 | 71.0 |
| Marlborough | 51 | 242 | 70.3 | 8.9 | 176 | D | D | D | 73 | 6 934 | 2 661.5 | 638.8 |
| Medford | 37 | 189 | 43.3 | 7.0 | 115 | D | D | D | 39 | 506 | 79.9 | 23.5 |
| Melrose | 22 | 63 | 16.1 | 2.1 | 76 | 261 | 32.3 | 12.4 | NA | NA | NA | NA |
| Methuen Town | 39 | 136 | 22.5 | 4.5 | 85 | 369 | 47.4 | 19.4 | 42 | 1 641 | 543.5 | 90.4 |
| New Bedford | 81 | 400 | 53.6 | 12.4 | 181 | D | D | D | 129 | 7 611 | 1 995.0 | 292.4 |
| Newton | 166 | 1 677 | 1 370.8 | 83.8 | 599 | D | D | D | 48 | 787 | 284.9 | 43.4 |
| Northampton | 39 | 122 | 21.0 | 3.1 | 123 | D | D | D | 38 | 1 381 | 466.0 | 73.0 |
| Peabody | 46 | 318 | 76.0 | 10.4 | 112 | 854 | 113.1 | 43.4 | 74 | 2 784 | 708.4 | 165.4 |
| Pittsfield | 44 | 283 | 32.0 | 7.4 | 134 | D | D | D | 52 | 2 787 | 552.3 | 152.9 |
| Quincy | 96 | 706 | 106.2 | 27.8 | 294 | D | D | D | 47 | 613 | 246.1 | 35.3 |
| Revere | 23 | 332 | 31.2 | 7.5 | 44 | 237 | 17.8 | 7.4 | 16 | D | D | D |
| Salem | 39 | 205 | 40.2 | 7.4 | 171 | D | D | D | 49 | 789 | 157.9 | 39.4 |
| Somerville | 67 | 263 | 61.1 | 10.4 | 173 | D | D | D | 67 | 1 523 | 269.2 | 78.3 |
| Springfield | 117 | 772 | 119.9 | 27.9 | 354 | D | D | D | 123 | 4 822 | 1 158.3 | 226.4 |
| Taunton | 39 | 135 | 38.4 | 3.8 | 107 | 2 335 | 576.0 | 152.1 | 71 | 5 292 | 1 388.5 | 386.6 |
| Waltham | 97 | 906 | 196.2 | 40.6 | 404 | D | D | D | 117 | 4 172 | 1 017.4 | 231.3 |
| Watertown Town | 39 | 526 | 122.6 | 38.3 | 120 | D | D | D | 50 | 1 692 | 392.7 | 108.3 |
| Westfield | 37 | 162 | 25.0 | 4.1 | 62 | 499 | 75.0 | 28.1 | 97 | 3 323 | 783.4 | 153.3 |
| West Springfield Town | NA | NA | NA | NA | NA | NA | NA | NA | NA | NA | NA | NA |
| Weymouth Town | NA | NA | NA | NA | NA | NA | NA | NA | NA | NA | NA | NA |
| Woburn | 72 | 806 | 139.7 | 43.8 | 298 | D | D | D | 153 | 4 869 | 1 596.7 | 312.3 |
| Worcester | 169 | 1 526 | 295.0 | 51.7 | 451 | D | D | D | 212 | 8 673 | 2 116.0 | 454.6 |
| **MICHIGAN** | 8 862 | 54 874 | 12 858.6 | 1 685.7 | 22 552 | 249 864 | 29 536.8 | 15 304.5 | 13 675 | 581 739 | 234 455.8 | 29 910.3 |
| Allen Park | 27 | D | D | D | 57 | 1 813 | 113.7 | 80.5 | NA | NA | NA | NA |
| Ann Arbor | 175 | 1 685 | 405.9 | 58.0 | 602 | 7 037 | 799.1 | 455.3 | 64 | 1 400 | | 62.0 |
| Battle Creek | 52 | 337 | 48.1 | 9.2 | 101 | D | D | D | 78 | 8 084 | 3 825.1 | 392.8 |
| Bay City | 31 | 136 | 13.1 | 2.5 | 97 | 754 | 56.3 | 33.0 | 52 | 2 103 | 613.3 | 127.0 |
| Burton | 19 | 107 | 16.2 | 4.7 | 40 | 220 | 20.8 | 6.1 | NA | NA | NA | NA |
| Dearborn | 102 | D | D | D | 284 | D | D | D | 96 | 10 493 | D | 759.2 |
| Dearborn Heights | 40 | D | D | D | 70 | 361 | 32.7 | 15.2 | NA | NA | NA | NA |
| Detroit | 321 | D | D | D | 685 | 13 636 | 2 451.1 | 929.0 | 472 | 22 962 | 20 216.1 | 1 486.3 |
| East Lansing | 58 | 687 | 61.7 | 20.5 | 126 | D | D | D | NA | NA | NA | NA |
| Eastpointe | 16 | 75 | 9.1 | 2.1 | 40 | 221 | 14.5 | 6.7 | NA | NA | NA | NA |
| Farmington Hills | 200 | 4 754 | 548.4 | 179.2 | 743 | 10 597 | 1 570.9 | 759.6 | 104 | 2 250 | 645.3 | 115.9 |
| Flint | 81 | 519 | 67.7 | 12.5 | 171 | D | D | D | 76 | 9 791 | D | D |
| Garden City | 13 | D | D | D | 17 | 75 | 7.4 | 3.1 | NA | NA | NA | NA |
| Grand Rapids | 188 | 1 136 | 145.9 | 27.9 | 615 | D | D | D | 315 | 19 627 | 5 497.9 | 1 068.9 |
| Holland | 39 | 204 | 35.3 | 5.9 | 98 | D | D | D | 99 | 8 901 | 2 669.1 | 367.1 |
| Inkster | 23 | D | D | D | 9 | 25 | 1.7 | 0.7 | NA | NA | NA | NA |
| Jackson | 45 | 201 | 26.3 | 4.0 | 102 | D | D | D | 101 | 2 578 | 660.6 | 107.7 |
| Kalamazoo | 98 | 807 | 83.3 | 18.3 | 236 | D | D | D | 116 | 4 462 | 1 347.5 | 210.5 |
| Kentwood | 56 | 417 | 82.1 | 10.5 | 132 | 1 418 | 173.3 | 68.9 | 130 | 8 624 | 1 838.1 | 357.2 |
| Lansing | 101 | 924 | 119.8 | 23.2 | 247 | D | D | D | 95 | 5 096 | D | 327.4 |
| Lincoln Park | 18 | D | D | D | 29 | D | D | D | NA | NA | NA | NA |
| Livonia | 139 | 1 077 | 150.9 | 28.1 | 394 | D | D | D | 280 | 11 265 | 3 195.9 | 604.9 |
| Madison Heights | 43 | 396 | 82.4 | 24.9 | 122 | 1 523 | 173.7 | 76.0 | 163 | 4 288 | 872.8 | 200.8 |
| Midland | 67 | D | D | D | 124 | D | D | D | 36 | 4 487 | D | 344.4 |
| Mount Pleasant | 33 | D | D | D | 81 | 1 141 | 48.8 | 26.7 | 26 | D | D | D |
| Muskegon | 19 | 100 | 12.4 | 2.6 | 86 | D | D | D | 79 | 3 806 | 991.6 | 173.4 |
| Novi | 78 | 497 | 94.0 | 19.0 | 274 | 4 007 | 589.0 | 259.7 | 80 | 2 211 | D | 109.7 |

1. Establishments subject to federal tax.

# Table D. Cities — Accommodation and Food Services, Arts, Entertainment, and Recreation, and Health Care and Social Assistance

| City | Accommodation and food services, 2007 | | | | Arts, entertainment, and recreation,[1] 2007 | | | | Health care and social assistance,[1] 2007 | | | |
|---|---|---|---|---|---|---|---|---|---|---|---|---|
| | Number of establishments | Number of employees | Sales (mil dol) | Annual payroll (mil dol) | Number of establishments | Number of employees | Receipts (mil dol) | Annual payroll (mil dol) | Number of establishments | Number of employees | Receipts (mil dol) | Annual payroll (mil dol) |
| | 92 | 93 | 94 | 95 | 96 | 97 | 98 | 99 | 100 | 101 | 102 | 103 |
| **MASSACHUSETTS— Cont'd** | | | | | | | | | | | | |
| Beverly | 117 | 1 354 | 72.7 | 21.3 | 19 | D | D | D | 119 | D | D | D |
| Boston | 2 073 | 46 895 | 3 661.7 | 1 057.5 | 182 | D | D | D | 899 | 18 698 | 3 110.4 | 1 379.7 |
| Braintree Town | NA | NA | NA | NA | NA | NA | NA | NA | NA | NA | NA | NA |
| Brockton | 155 | 2 812 | 122.8 | 40.9 | 14 | 248 | 11.7 | 3.5 | 198 | 3 585 | 364.3 | 180.0 |
| Cambridge | 398 | 8 044 | 594.9 | 172.8 | 50 | 651 | 133.4 | 20.7 | 214 | 3 195 | 510.3 | 195.3 |
| Chelsea | 56 | 556 | 33.4 | 8.6 | NA | NA | NA | NA | 30 | 635 | 47.6 | 20.4 |
| Chicopee | 118 | 1 575 | 68.7 | 19.7 | 3 | D | D | D | 48 | 942 | 62.7 | 27.5 |
| Everett | 77 | D | D | D | 5 | D | D | D | 43 | D | D | D |
| Fall River | 181 | 2 574 | 105.5 | 29.9 | 13 | D | D | D | 200 | 3 976 | 351.5 | 167.6 |
| Fitchburg | 89 | 1 145 | 53.6 | 15.4 | 6 | D | D | D | 80 | 1 299 | 106.6 | 45.4 |
| Franklin Town | NA | NA | NA | NA | NA | NA | NA | NA | NA | NA | NA | NA |
| Gloucester | 119 | 1 031 | 61.1 | 17.9 | 15 | 111 | 11.5 | 3.8 | 55 | 488 | 49.8 | 22.7 |
| Haverhill | 124 | 1 695 | 84.0 | 23.3 | 24 | D | D | D | 98 | 2 404 | 254.5 | 98.1 |
| Holyoke | 96 | D | D | D | 9 | 81 | 5.5 | 1.5 | 82 | 1 262 | 107.0 | 52.4 |
| Lawrence | 91 | 858 | 42.1 | 11.1 | 5 | 39 | 2.3 | 0.4 | 67 | 1 017 | 136.9 | 56.1 |
| Leominster | 97 | 1 874 | 79.6 | 25.2 | 16 | D | D | D | 97 | 1 554 | 132.5 | 61.1 |
| Lowell | 183 | 2 207 | 107.9 | 28.8 | 17 | 388 | 14.1 | 5.0 | 145 | 2 819 | 252.6 | 125.8 |
| Lynn | 140 | 1 169 | 63.4 | 16.4 | 9 | 129 | 9.1 | 2.2 | 103 | 1 459 | 119.2 | 55.0 |
| Malden | 96 | 1 033 | 52.4 | 15.4 | 10 | 69 | 5.1 | 1.6 | 75 | 917 | 96.9 | 31.1 |
| Marlborough | 140 | 2 462 | 127.8 | 38.2 | 14 | 278 | 14.6 | 3.8 | 70 | 1 054 | 91.4 | 38.3 |
| Medford | 92 | 1 300 | 82.6 | 19.2 | 10 | D | D | D | 91 | D | D | D |
| Melrose | 36 | 377 | 20.4 | 5.9 | 2 | D | D | D | 67 | D | D | D |
| Methuen Town | 97 | 1 485 | 76.3 | 22.5 | 10 | 310 | 12.7 | 3.4 | 90 | 864 | 82.9 | 40.1 |
| New Bedford | 211 | 2 496 | 101.3 | 27.1 | 19 | D | D | D | 137 | 2 700 | 234.0 | 105.8 |
| Newton | 177 | D | D | D | 44 | 359 | 87.3 | 22.7 | 388 | 5 190 | 587.1 | 271.2 |
| Northampton | 101 | 1 874 | 81.7 | 25.5 | 18 | 113 | 7.6 | 2.0 | 108 | 1 603 | 153.7 | 78.0 |
| Peabody | 125 | 2 468 | 137.5 | 40.2 | 7 | D | D | D | 112 | 2 291 | 281.7 | 119.9 |
| Pittsfield | 131 | 2 142 | 92.6 | 28.1 | 18 | 214 | 10.9 | 3.2 | 146 | 1 679 | 182.7 | 86.8 |
| Quincy | 234 | 3 264 | 188.7 | 52.0 | 20 | D | D | D | 196 | 3 878 | 383.1 | 155.8 |
| Revere | 101 | 1 340 | 90.1 | 22.2 | 5 | D | D | D | 49 | D | D | D |
| Salem | 122 | 1 710 | 98.5 | 29.0 | 20 | 234 | 12.5 | 3.9 | 115 | D | D | D |
| Somerville | 181 | D | D | D | 16 | D | D | D | 59 | 1 026 | 117.1 | 44.7 |
| Springfield | 294 | 4 867 | 222.5 | 65.5 | 16 | 119 | 7.8 | 2.2 | 291 | 5 910 | 618.5 | 305.1 |
| Taunton | 111 | 2 130 | 90.8 | 27.4 | 6 | D | D | D | 86 | 1 045 | 125.8 | 50.7 |
| Waltham | 272 | 3 647 | 252.9 | 70.5 | 33 | 477 | 29.6 | 8.0 | 137 | 2 360 | 249.4 | 102.4 |
| Watertown Town | 90 | 1 117 | 64.0 | 17.4 | 10 | 303 | 16.7 | 5.0 | 88 | 1 340 | 170.9 | 62.4 |
| Westfield | 76 | 1 039 | 43.7 | 12.8 | 10 | D | D | D | 79 | 722 | 64.5 | 29.7 |
| West Springfield Town | NA | NA | NA | NA | NA | NA | NA | NA | NA | NA | NA | NA |
| Weymouth Town | NA | NA | NA | NA | NA | NA | NA | NA | NA | NA | NA | NA |
| Woburn | 100 | 1 855 | 115.7 | 31.1 | 15 | D | D | D | 107 | 1 936 | 279.3 | 96.5 |
| Worcester | 430 | 5 843 | 302.0 | 85.9 | 28 | 1 087 | 26.5 | 7.8 | 401 | 9 043 | 1 084.4 | 439.7 |
| **MICHIGAN** | 19 678 | 339 181 | 14 536.6 | 4 207.3 | 2 975 | 41 065 | 3 940.6 | 1 170.2 | 21 150 | 228 681 | 21 054.9 | 9 168.6 |
| Allen Park | 77 | 1 537 | 61.6 | 18.7 | 11 | D | D | D | 83 | 1 087 | 87.5 | 38.4 |
| Ann Arbor | 338 | 7 686 | 372.7 | 108.3 | 38 | 230 | 13.0 | 3.9 | 316 | D | D | D |
| Battle Creek | 145 | 2 830 | 110.2 | 33.6 | 14 | 252 | 8.4 | 3.7 | 159 | 2 051 | 192.8 | 77.3 |
| Bay City | 104 | 1 601 | 48.4 | 15.1 | 12 | D | D | D | 111 | D | D | D |
| Burton | 65 | 1 158 | 44.9 | 12.6 | 9 | 104 | 1.7 | 0.5 | 81 | D | D | D |
| Dearborn | 281 | 5 031 | 255.0 | 76.8 | 20 | D | D | D | 358 | D | D | D |
| Dearborn Heights | 99 | 1 718 | 64.6 | 18.5 | 9 | D | D | D | 91 | 926 | 80.7 | 34.3 |
| Detroit | 958 | 16 550 | 1 253.9 | 333.3 | 65 | 8 209 | 1 388.0 | 389.9 | 719 | 9 945 | 822.9 | 356.1 |
| East Lansing | 109 | 2 602 | 104.8 | 28.7 | 6 | D | D | D | 110 | 1 757 | 178.2 | 95.8 |
| Eastpointe | 51 | 749 | 28.0 | 8.5 | 5 | D | D | D | 94 | D | D | D |
| Farmington Hills | 172 | 2 758 | 131.9 | 37.5 | 32 | D | D | D | 417 | 4 287 | 432.5 | 191.1 |
| Flint | 183 | 2 152 | 87.2 | 22.5 | 5 | D | D | D | 182 | 1 638 | 224.9 | 77.5 |
| Garden City | 46 | 725 | 28.2 | 7.1 | 8 | D | D | D | 70 | D | D | D |
| Grand Rapids | 396 | 8 765 | 331.7 | 105.3 | 46 | 647 | 33.0 | 10.0 | 379 | 5 548 | 597.9 | 242.7 |
| Holland | 91 | 1 965 | 68.3 | 24.3 | 6 | 81 | 2.4 | 1.0 | 95 | 1 585 | 132.5 | 62.2 |
| Inkster | 23 | 187 | 10.5 | 2.6 | 1 | D | D | D | 17 | 118 | 6.3 | 2.3 |
| Jackson | 107 | 1 749 | 66.4 | 18.5 | 9 | 115 | 5.0 | 1.4 | 146 | 1 779 | 202.9 | 98.0 |
| Kalamazoo | 199 | 4 543 | 167.0 | 54.1 | 25 | 411 | 16.3 | 5.3 | 168 | 3 061 | 257.0 | 134.3 |
| Kentwood | 105 | 2 278 | 94.9 | 28.2 | 10 | D | D | D | 100 | 1 537 | 163.1 | 69.1 |
| Lansing | 227 | 3 774 | 152.7 | 44.4 | 19 | 398 | 63.1 | 8.9 | 233 | D | D | D |
| Lincoln Park | 66 | 944 | 39.7 | 9.5 | 5 | D | D | D | 64 | 638 | 57.1 | 26.0 |
| Livonia | 243 | 5 634 | 246.2 | 71.4 | 26 | D | D | D | 420 | 4 576 | 394.7 | 173.4 |
| Madison Heights | 104 | 1 861 | 79.7 | 22.3 | 10 | 116 | 8.8 | 2.4 | 99 | D | D | D |
| Midland | 102 | 2 267 | 97.1 | 27.8 | 10 | D | D | D | 155 | D | D | D |
| Mount Pleasant | 89 | 2 564 | 87.1 | 24.4 | 6 | D | D | D | 116 | 1 075 | 76.7 | 35.4 |
| Muskegon | 80 | 1 357 | 53.8 | 15.1 | 9 | D | D | D | 124 | 1 904 | 225.4 | 121.9 |
| Novi | 151 | 3 825 | 178.7 | 53.1 | 16 | D | D | D | 200 | D | D | D |

1. Establishments subject to federal tax.

| City | Other services[1], 2007 | | | | Selected federal funds, 2009–2010 (mil dol) | | | | | | | | |
|---|---|---|---|---|---|---|---|---|---|---|---|---|---|
| | | | | | Procurement contracts | | Grants | | | | | | |
| | Number of establishments | Number of employees | Receipts (mil dol) | Annual payroll (mil dol) | Defense | Other | Total[2] | Medicaid and other health related | Nutrition and family welfare | Energy and environment | Disasters and emergency preparedness | Housing and community development | Employment and training |
| | 104 | 105 | 106 | 107 | 108 | 109 | 110 | 111 | 112 | 113 | 114 | 115 | 116 |
| MASSACHUSETTS— Cont'd | | | | | | | | | | | | | |
| Beverly | 66 | 650 | 32.8 | 13.5 | 12.4 | 1.5 | 21.0 | 10.8 | 2.2 | 1.5 | 1.5 | 3.6 | 0.0 |
| Boston | 1 041 | 8 143 | 704.5 | 200.9 | 186.5 | 614.8 | 6 428.2 | 3 771.0 | 282.9 | 183.6 | 58.7 | 703.2 | 198.5 |
| Braintree Town | NA | NA | NA | NA | NA | NA | NA | NA | NA | NA | NA | NA | NA |
| Brockton | 136 | 928 | 68.9 | 23.1 | 12.2 | 38.5 | 29.4 | 3.6 | 0.0 | 1.1 | 0.0 | 18.6 | 0.9 |
| Cambridge | 147 | 1 114 | 104.0 | 29.4 | 660.7 | 435.6 | 1 398.8 | 693.7 | 0.3 | 113.8 | 0.0 | 49.4 | 0.0 |
| Chelsea | 33 | D | D | D | 10.0 | 2.7 | 20.3 | 0.3 | 2.2 | 0.2 | 1.5 | 6.6 | 2.5 |
| Chicopee | 86 | 414 | 31.4 | 9.5 | 40.2 | 21.0 | 4.5 | 0.0 | 0.0 | 0.0 | 0.0 | 3.3 | 0.0 |
| Everett | 66 | 468 | 38.4 | 14.0 | 0.0 | 0.5 | 4.4 | 0.0 | 0.0 | 0.0 | 0.0 | 4.3 | 0.0 |
| Fall River | 148 | 745 | 52.9 | 15.5 | 23.9 | 0.5 | 36.9 | 2.8 | 4.0 | 2.2 | -0.4 | 25.2 | 0.0 |
| Fitchburg | 55 | 227 | 21.3 | 7.0 | 0.0 | 0.2 | 20.6 | 4.2 | 5.0 | 0.0 | 0.0 | 3.9 | 0.0 |
| Franklin Town | NA | NA | NA | NA | NA | NA | NA | NA | NA | NA | NA | NA | NA |
| Gloucester | 56 | 239 | 17.5 | 5.6 | 8.5 | 7.0 | 12.7 | 0.0 | 1.3 | 2.1 | 0.0 | 8.9 | 0.0 |
| Haverhill | 80 | D | D | D | 1.0 | 1.9 | 22.0 | 0.0 | 1.7 | 0.5 | 0.0 | 5.1 | 0.0 |
| Holyoke | 50 | 238 | 16.9 | 4.9 | 0.2 | 1.7 | 46.1 | 4.6 | 11.1 | 8.5 | 0.0 | 13.4 | 0.0 |
| Lawrence | 82 | 519 | 43.1 | 14.7 | 14.7 | 5.3 | 28.0 | 4.8 | 4.9 | 1.0 | 0.0 | 15.9 | 0.0 |
| Leominster | 59 | 239 | 21.7 | 5.7 | 0.0 | 0.1 | 2.8 | 0.0 | 0.0 | 0.0 | 0.0 | 2.7 | 0.0 |
| Lowell | 142 | 695 | 56.9 | 18.6 | 31.2 | 24.3 | 81.9 | 12.1 | 5.8 | 15.7 | -0.1 | 21.4 | 0.1 |
| Lynn | 105 | 547 | 49.3 | 14.1 | 1 384.5 | 0.6 | 36.1 | 2.7 | 2.9 | 0.0 | 0.0 | 30.3 | 0.0 |
| Malden | 98 | 472 | 45.2 | 13.8 | 2.0 | 0.4 | 250.3 | 2.7 | 1.6 | 1.7 | 0.0 | 18.1 | 0.0 |
| Marlborough | 64 | 439 | 71.0 | 12.5 | 392.6 | 121.4 | 13.7 | 5.1 | 0.0 | 3.5 | 0.0 | 1.7 | 0.0 |
| Medford | 102 | 592 | 53.8 | 17.1 | 0.8 | 0.2 | 42.5 | 1.2 | 0.0 | 8.0 | 0.0 | 13.0 | 0.0 |
| Melrose | 34 | 177 | 19.0 | 5.8 | 0.2 | 0.0 | 2.9 | 0.1 | 0.0 | 0.0 | 0.0 | 2.8 | 0.0 |
| Methuen Town | 62 | D | D | D | 0.6 | 2.8 | 6.7 | 0.0 | 0.0 | 0.2 | 0.0 | 5.3 | 0.0 |
| New Bedford | 150 | 855 | 87.6 | 24.4 | 145.1 | 6.9 | 45.7 | 1.9 | 2.7 | 4.0 | 0.0 | 24.7 | 0.0 |
| Newton | 177 | 1 125 | 97.4 | 34.2 | 13.3 | 17.8 | 171.4 | 43.9 | 0.0 | 8.1 | 0.0 | 12.4 | 0.0 |
| Northampton | 69 | 335 | 22.6 | 7.7 | 26.1 | 32.7 | 12.9 | 3.4 | 0.0 | 0.1 | -0.1 | 6.2 | 0.0 |
| Peabody | 100 | 562 | 55.0 | 13.9 | 3.8 | 12.0 | 7.2 | 0.2 | 0.0 | 0.7 | 0.0 | 6.2 | 0.0 |
| Pittsfield | 83 | 483 | 34.3 | 12.3 | 110.1 | 18.9 | 17.1 | 0.1 | 2.5 | 1.0 | 0.0 | 7.1 | 0.0 |
| Quincy | 179 | 869 | 86.4 | 26.2 | 45.7 | 1.2 | 83.7 | 1.0 | 3.2 | 55.4 | 0.0 | 18.7 | 0.0 |
| Revere | 74 | 316 | 33.4 | 9.0 | 0.2 | 0.0 | 10.4 | 0.0 | 0.0 | 0.0 | 0.0 | 10.2 | 0.0 |
| Salem | 87 | 366 | 35.9 | 10.4 | 0.7 | 0.5 | 18.1 | 0.9 | 0.0 | 0.6 | 0.0 | 12.5 | 0.2 |
| Somerville | 99 | 1 295 | 99.2 | 35.3 | 2.5 | 7.7 | 173.4 | 124.6 | 4.8 | 2.1 | 0.0 | 16.6 | 10.5 |
| Springfield | 197 | 1 636 | 119.8 | 40.5 | 4.0 | 5.3 | 69.1 | 11.3 | 1.1 | 4.7 | 0.0 | 30.9 | 0.8 |
| Taunton | 78 | 352 | 26.6 | 8.2 | 1 386.7 | 6.8 | 25.1 | 0.8 | 2.5 | 0.2 | 0.0 | 13.2 | 0.0 |
| Waltham | 128 | 826 | 127.5 | 32.9 | 171.3 | 4.6 | 64.7 | 37.6 | 0.0 | 4.3 | 0.0 | 7.5 | 0.0 |
| Watertown Town | 65 | 842 | 90.1 | 43.2 | 2.8 | 29.9 | 393.3 | 90.3 | 0.0 | 257.8 | 0.0 | 1.9 | 0.0 |
| Westfield | 62 | 346 | 30.7 | 10.9 | 8.9 | 1.7 | 7.5 | 0.0 | 1.4 | 0.0 | 0.0 | 2.3 | 0.0 |
| West Springfield Town | NA | NA | NA | NA | NA | NA | NA | NA | NA | NA | NA | NA | NA |
| Weymouth Town | NA | NA | NA | NA | NA | NA | NA | NA | NA | NA | NA | NA | NA |
| Woburn | 95 | D | D | D | 654.8 | 70.3 | 25.7 | 9.8 | 0.0 | 7.1 | 0.0 | 3.8 | 0.0 |
| Worcester | 259 | 1 801 | 166.9 | 50.2 | 49.8 | 14.2 | 452.3 | 358.5 | 8.9 | 5.8 | 0.0 | 44.2 | 0.7 |
| MICHIGAN | 13 953 | 79 193 | 6 221.1 | 1 956.5 | 4 080.3 | 2 386.4 | 20 577.3 | 11 165.6 | 2 752.7 | 1 031.9 | 7.1 | 937.6 | 542.1 |
| Allen Park | 41 | 250 | 16.4 | 5.8 | 0.0 | 0.0 | 0.1 | 0.0 | 0.0 | 0.0 | 0.0 | 0.1 | 0.0 |
| Ann Arbor | 147 | 953 | 62.6 | 22.3 | 74.4 | 179.7 | 1 384.4 | 1 004.1 | 5.0 | 43.8 | 0.3 | 17.5 | 0.0 |
| Battle Creek | 87 | D | D | D | 115.8 | 8.5 | 20.8 | 4.3 | 6.9 | 0.5 | 0.0 | 6.0 | 0.3 |
| Bay City | 63 | 441 | 33.4 | 10.3 | 1.5 | 9.7 | 7.5 | 0.4 | 0.1 | 1.1 | 0.0 | 3.1 | 0.0 |
| Burton | 66 | 298 | 25.0 | 7.8 | 0.0 | 0.0 | 0.5 | 0.0 | 0.0 | 0.0 | 0.0 | 0.0 | 0.0 |
| Dearborn | 189 | 875 | 70.7 | 21.6 | 0.8 | 198.6 | 12.5 | 0.0 | 0.3 | 6.3 | 0.0 | 4.1 | 0.0 |
| Dearborn Heights | 93 | 434 | 32.5 | 10.0 | 0.0 | 0.0 | 3.9 | 0.0 | 0.0 | 0.0 | 0.0 | 3.7 | 0.0 |
| Detroit | 698 | 4 200 | 321.6 | 107.5 | 29.2 | 428.2 | 653.1 | 182.6 | 54.8 | 116.4 | 0.4 | 130.8 | 13.4 |
| East Lansing | 26 | 229 | 9.6 | 2.7 | 2.7 | 5.6 | 333.0 | 98.3 | 0.6 | 35.6 | 0.0 | 0.8 | 0.4 |
| Eastpointe | 57 | 230 | 21.3 | 6.6 | 0.0 | 0.0 | 1.4 | 0.0 | 0.0 | 0.0 | 0.0 | 1.4 | 0.0 |
| Farmington Hills | 149 | 943 | 82.9 | 25.9 | 5.3 | 17.3 | 1.5 | 0.0 | 0.0 | 0.0 | 0.0 | 1.5 | 0.0 |
| Flint | 129 | 923 | 54.4 | 30.7 | 1.0 | 13.9 | 69.1 | 5.0 | 17.4 | 3.2 | 0.0 | 19.0 | 4.5 |
| Garden City | 46 | 197 | 13.7 | 4.2 | 0.0 | 0.0 | 0.1 | 0.0 | 0.1 | 0.0 | 0.0 | 0.0 | 0.0 |
| Grand Rapids | 237 | 1 707 | 123.8 | 42.5 | 8.6 | 40.3 | 125.5 | 22.8 | 11.8 | 6.5 | 0.0 | 41.5 | 4.0 |
| Holland | 58 | 515 | 32.9 | 13.6 | 22.9 | 20.7 | 10.1 | 0.1 | 3.3 | 0.0 | 0.1 | 0.8 | 0.0 |
| Inkster | 19 | D | D | D | 0.0 | 0.3 | 6.7 | 0.0 | 0.7 | 0.0 | 0.0 | 5.6 | 0.0 |
| Jackson | 63 | 524 | 47.0 | 15.3 | 17.2 | 0.7 | 20.6 | 3.1 | 7.0 | 0.0 | 0.0 | 7.1 | 0.3 |
| Kalamazoo | 132 | 1 188 | 97.4 | 31.5 | 11.7 | 4.8 | 46.2 | 13.7 | 4.9 | 1.8 | 0.0 | 5.0 | 0.4 |
| Kentwood | 72 | 596 | 41.1 | 13.0 | 4.1 | 0.1 | 0.0 | 0.0 | 0.0 | 0.0 | 0.0 | 0.0 | 0.0 |
| Lansing | 150 | 1 314 | 86.5 | 28.7 | 508.2 | 96.8 | 2 770.2 | 223.3 | 454.2 | 144.8 | -2.3 | 483.5 | 469.5 |
| Lincoln Park | 68 | 336 | 25.6 | 8.0 | 0.0 | 0.0 | 3.1 | 0.0 | 0.0 | 0.0 | 0.0 | 3.1 | 0.0 |
| Livonia | 224 | 1 544 | 173.2 | 46.0 | 23.6 | 1.8 | 9.1 | 0.6 | 0.0 | 0.7 | 0.0 | 6.9 | 0.0 |
| Madison Heights | 76 | 761 | 79.8 | 25.4 | 8.1 | 0.4 | 2.3 | 0.1 | 0.0 | 0.0 | 0.0 | 2.2 | 0.0 |
| Midland | 76 | 616 | 47.5 | 13.4 | 0.2 | 1.3 | 11.5 | 0.1 | 0.0 | 8.6 | 0.0 | 1.5 | 0.0 |
| Mount Pleasant | 51 | 314 | 16.4 | 5.0 | 0.0 | 1.9 | 6.2 | 0.3 | 0.3 | 2.8 | 0.0 | 1.6 | 0.0 |
| Muskegon | 49 | 314 | 21.0 | 6.8 | 32.8 | 0.8 | 18.7 | 0.3 | 6.4 | 2.2 | 0.0 | 2.7 | 0.0 |
| Novi | 90 | 832 | 57.3 | 24.2 | 4.7 | 0.6 | 4.2 | 1.1 | 0.0 | 0.9 | 0.0 | 0.0 | 0.0 |

1. Establishments subject to federal tax.   2. Includes program categories not shown separately. State totals include additional categories not allocated by city.

| | City government finances, 2007 | | | | | | | | | |
|---|---|---|---|---|---|---|---|---|---|---|
| | General revenue | | | | | | | General expenditure | | |
| | | Intergovernmental | | | Taxes | | | | Per capita[1] (dollars) | |
| | | | | | | Per capita[1] (dollars) | | | | | |
| City | Total (mil dol) | Total (mil dol) | Percent from state government | Total (mil dol) | Total | Property | Sales and gross receipts | Total (mil dol) | Total | Capital outlays |
| | 117 | 118 | 119 | 120 | 121 | 122 | 123 | 124 | 125 | 126 |

| City | | | | | | | | | | |
|---|---|---|---|---|---|---|---|---|---|---|
| **MASSACHUSETTS—Cont'd** | | | | | | | | | | |
| Beverly | 111.6 | 23.9 | 94.6 | 69.9 | 1 784 | 1 753 | 31 | 105.6 | 2 695 | 106 |
| Boston | 3 016.3 | 1 196.8 | 92.2 | 1 299.2 | 2 168 | 2 022 | 145 | 2 815.5 | 4 698 | 424 |
| Braintree Town | NA | NA | NA | NA | NA | NA | NA | NA | NA | NA |
| Brockton | 334.1 | 204.7 | 98.2 | 98.3 | 1 056 | 1 028 | 28 | 325.8 | 3 500 | 438 |
| Cambridge | 1 129.4 | 311.5 | 74.7 | 258.5 | 2 550 | 2 459 | 91 | 1 105.8 | 10 907 | 759 |
| Chelsea | 128.6 | 79.6 | 93.4 | 33.9 | 887 | 829 | 58 | 133.0 | 3 480 | 154 |
| Chicopee | 219.4 | 144.8 | 97.8 | 59.5 | 1 105 | 1 080 | 24 | 169.2 | 3 141 | 587 |
| Everett | 145.5 | 69.5 | 98.9 | 69.4 | 1 863 | 1 843 | 20 | 161.8 | 4 341 | 1 125 |
| Fall River | 260.5 | 167.7 | 92.8 | 66.8 | 735 | 711 | 23 | 307.8 | 3 386 | 592 |
| Fitchburg | 120.0 | 68.2 | 97.7 | 37.5 | 942 | 904 | 38 | 125.9 | 3 160 | 159 |
| Franklin Town | NA | NA | NA | NA | NA | NA | NA | NA | NA | NA |
| Gloucester | 88.6 | 18.8 | 92.2 | 52.8 | 1 743 | 1 695 | 48 | 98.6 | 3 252 | 456 |
| Haverhill | 174.9 | 79.6 | 95.8 | 75.8 | 1 266 | 1 215 | 51 | 176.1 | 2 940 | 265 |
| Holyoke | 168.7 | 106.8 | 98.0 | 43.4 | 1 092 | 1 070 | 22 | 182.6 | 4 596 | 532 |
| Lawrence | 289.1 | 216.1 | 91.9 | 44.4 | 634 | 610 | 23 | 270.2 | 3 857 | 277 |
| Leominster | 107.0 | 52.2 | 98.3 | 47.3 | 1 150 | 1 126 | 24 | 110.9 | 2 695 | 318 |
| Lowell | 364.4 | 240.8 | 94.7 | 94.0 | 908 | 881 | 27 | 343.5 | 3 318 | 309 |
| Lynn | 263.5 | 163.9 | 97.9 | 88.4 | 1 014 | 990 | 24 | 262.3 | 3 010 | 150 |
| Malden | 161.9 | 72.9 | 95.5 | 61.0 | 1 094 | 1 053 | 41 | 180.3 | 3 237 | 48 |
| Marlborough | 119.1 | 24.2 | 98.6 | 85.2 | 2 238 | 2 174 | 64 | 107.8 | 2 833 | 27 |
| Medford | 134.6 | 38.7 | 92.7 | 79.1 | 1 423 | 1 379 | 44 | 136.3 | 2 453 | 66 |
| Melrose | 93.2 | 40.2 | 98.6 | 43.4 | 1 621 | 1 619 | 2 | 94.6 | 3 532 | 1 014 |
| Methuen Town | 118.9 | 48.9 | 99.6 | 58.9 | 1 339 | 1 300 | 39 | 117.1 | 2 663 | 77 |
| New Bedford | 348.5 | 216.0 | 93.6 | 92.7 | 1 009 | 941 | 68 | 294.9 | 3 211 | 238 |
| Newton | 316.1 | 55.5 | 87.3 | 225.5 | 2 707 | 2 629 | 78 | 297.4 | 3 571 | 194 |
| Northampton | 78.8 | 22.3 | 88.9 | 37.7 | 1 329 | 1 280 | 48 | 77.9 | 2 741 | 244 |
| Peabody | 155.7 | 54.1 | 92.9 | 79.9 | 1 552 | 1 487 | 65 | 148.9 | 2 895 | 52 |
| Pittsfield | 135.4 | 64.4 | 90.3 | 58.4 | 1 360 | 1 332 | 28 | 131.4 | 3 061 | 182 |
| Quincy | 267.1 | 64.2 | 88.2 | 152.6 | 1 666 | 1 626 | 40 | 282.7 | 3 086 | 247 |
| Revere | 132.3 | 64.9 | 97.4 | 59.9 | 1 082 | 1 047 | 35 | 125.5 | 2 267 | 158 |
| Salem | 158.5 | 77.5 | 94.2 | 65.3 | 1 595 | 1 575 | 20 | 155.6 | 3 804 | 866 |
| Somerville | 215.6 | 93.8 | 95.2 | 88.4 | 1 189 | 1 149 | 40 | 224.5 | 3 017 | 347 |
| Springfield | 573.3 | 398.4 | 91.9 | 147.9 | 986 | 958 | 29 | 563.8 | 3 760 | 152 |
| Taunton | 159.0 | 76.6 | 97.6 | 63.5 | 1 139 | 1 096 | 43 | 188.6 | 3 381 | 796 |
| Waltham | 207.7 | 59.5 | 98.5 | 127.3 | 2 130 | 2 019 | 111 | 200.9 | 3 362 | 187 |
| Watertown Town | 98.3 | 19.8 | 99.7 | 65.2 | 2 005 | 1 997 | 8 | 99.4 | 3 057 | 172 |
| Westfield | 131.8 | 65.1 | 92.0 | 52.2 | 1 299 | 1 276 | 24 | 122.4 | 3 047 | 185 |
| West Springfield Town | NA | NA | NA | NA | NA | NA | NA | NA | NA | NA |
| Weymouth Town | NA | NA | NA | NA | NA | NA | NA | NA | NA | NA |
| Woburn | 171.4 | 75.5 | 99.9 | 79.5 | 2 145 | 2 089 | 56 | 134.8 | 3 638 | 438 |
| Worcester | 610.5 | 353.7 | 91.9 | 197.3 | 1 134 | 1 097 | 37 | 661.2 | 3 801 | 318 |
| **MICHIGAN** | X | X | X | X | X | X | X | X | X | X |
| Allen Park | 38.1 | 7.6 | 81.3 | 16.8 | 628 | 579 | 49 | 31.0 | 1 154 | 56 |
| Ann Arbor | 181.4 | 35.6 | 54.0 | 72.5 | 630 | 619 | 11 | 199.0 | 1 729 | 376 |
| Battle Creek | 106.5 | 28.6 | 58.4 | 46.7 | 895 | 602 | 21 | 100.1 | 1 917 | 100 |
| Bay City | 59.7 | 16.2 | 62.1 | 14.4 | 422 | 406 | 16 | 57.0 | 1 674 | 170 |
| Burton | 18.8 | 5.6 | 92.3 | 5.0 | 165 | 153 | 13 | 17.2 | 569 | 115 |
| Dearborn | 166.3 | 25.2 | 80.1 | 81.2 | 910 | 883 | 26 | 188.7 | 2 115 | 552 |
| Dearborn Heights | 60.9 | 14.6 | 65.1 | 29.5 | 551 | 531 | 20 | 52.1 | 972 | 18 |
| Detroit | 2 511.7 | 773.0 | 76.8 | 869.2 | 948 | 350 | 292 | 2 338.6 | 2 550 | 301 |
| East Lansing | 59.6 | 13.2 | 77.5 | 19.6 | 424 | 396 | 28 | 61.3 | 1 325 | 171 |
| Eastpointe | 40.9 | 7.5 | 76.9 | 20.7 | 636 | 614 | 21 | 33.3 | 1 020 | 69 |
| Farmington Hills | 88.7 | 14.5 | 86.8 | 45.0 | 570 | 559 | 11 | 87.1 | 1 103 | 47 |
| Flint | 492.5 | 109.3 | 81.1 | 46.8 | 408 | 226 | 19 | 509.3 | 4 442 | 213 |
| Garden City | 27.6 | 6.1 | 93.7 | 13.5 | 490 | 474 | 16 | 25.5 | 924 | 38 |
| Grand Rapids | 291.9 | 71.8 | 53.1 | 108.3 | 559 | 236 | 21 | 330.6 | 1 707 | 335 |
| Holland | 53.0 | 13.0 | 60.9 | 17.9 | 528 | 511 | 16 | 50.2 | 1 475 | 223 |
| Inkster | 38.1 | 15.6 | 47.0 | 11.8 | 430 | 416 | 14 | 39.2 | 1 428 | 255 |
| Jackson | 50.6 | 17.6 | 47.0 | 20.3 | 597 | 361 | 7 | 52.0 | 1 528 | 176 |
| Kalamazoo | 130.3 | 33.9 | 72.0 | 42.7 | 588 | 562 | 27 | 117.6 | 1 619 | 237 |
| Kentwood | 37.1 | 7.5 | 83.7 | 17.9 | 377 | 345 | 32 | 38.0 | 804 | 105 |
| Lansing | 232.9 | 46.3 | 66.0 | 73.5 | 639 | 384 | 10 | 235.5 | 2 049 | 408 |
| Lincoln Park | 37.2 | 11.6 | 66.3 | 16.2 | 445 | 429 | 16 | 36.7 | 1 007 | 45 |
| Livonia | 122.2 | 24.6 | 64.1 | 58.3 | 621 | 594 | 26 | 112.6 | 1 198 | 33 |
| Madison Heights | 42.2 | 7.8 | 72.4 | 22.6 | 763 | 737 | 26 | 41.0 | 1 382 | 220 |
| Midland | 70.2 | 9.6 | 89.9 | 34.7 | 845 | 831 | 15 | 58.7 | 1 429 | 240 |
| Mount Pleasant | 19.7 | 5.5 | 86.4 | 7.2 | 270 | 256 | 15 | 17.9 | 675 | 29 |
| Muskegon | 45.9 | 17.3 | 62.4 | 16.5 | 419 | 205 | 26 | 47.3 | 1 201 | 190 |
| Novi | 73.1 | 6.8 | 97.2 | 37.3 | 689 | 646 | 43 | 55.6 | 1 028 | 48 |

1. Based on population estimated as of July 1 of the year shown.

# Table D. Cities — **City Government Finances**

| City | City government finances, 2006 (cont.) | | | | | | | | | |
|---|---|---|---|---|---|---|---|---|---|---|
| | General expenditure (cont.) | | | | | | | | | |
| | Percent of total for: | | | | | | | | | |
| | Public welfare | Highways | Parking facilities | Education | Health and hospitals | Police protection | Sewerage and sanitation | Parks and recreation | Housing and community development | Interest on debt |
| | 127 | 128 | 129 | 130 | 131 | 132 | 133 | 134 | 135 | 136 |
| MASSACHUSETTS— Cont'd | | | | | | | | | | |
| Beverly | 0.2 | 3.7 | 0.0 | 50.7 | 0.4 | 5.5 | 9.3 | 1.8 | 0.5 | 2.9 |
| Boston | 3.2 | 1.7 | 0.1 | 34.7 | 6.0 | 10.8 | 8.7 | 1.4 | 3.1 | 1.9 |
| Braintree Town | NA | NA | NA | NA | NA | NA | NA | NA | NA | NA |
| Brockton | 0.1 | 2.3 | 0.1 | 62.7 | 0.3 | 5.3 | 12.1 | 0.4 | 0.6 | 3.3 |
| Cambridge | 0.0 | 1.0 | 0.1 | 13.9 | 63.3 | 2.9 | 1.1 | 1.2 | 0.3 | 0.8 |
| Chelsea | 0.2 | 1.5 | 0.0 | 53.2 | 0.1 | 5.4 | 2.3 | 0.1 | 3.1 | 2.8 |
| Chicopee | 0.5 | 2.2 | 0.0 | 67.4 | 0.2 | 4.9 | 4.9 | 1.2 | 0.8 | 0.8 |
| Everett | 0.2 | 3.3 | 0.0 | 62.5 | 0.9 | 5.2 | 1.8 | 0.1 | 0.2 | 1.4 |
| Fall River | 0.5 | 3.0 | 0.1 | 62.9 | 0.9 | 6.5 | 3.4 | 0.4 | 2.0 | 2.3 |
| Fitchburg | 0.0 | 3.0 | 0.1 | 55.4 | 0.5 | 6.0 | 8.6 | 0.5 | 1.4 | 2.3 |
| Franklin Town | NA | NA | NA | NA | NA | NA | NA | NA | NA | NA |
| Gloucester | 0.1 | 2.5 | 0.0 | 45.0 | 0.4 | 5.3 | 17.5 | 0.0 | 0.0 | 2.9 |
| Haverhill | 0.2 | 2.5 | 0.0 | 59.2 | 0.7 | 4.8 | 7.8 | 0.2 | 0.9 | 2.8 |
| Holyoke | 3.8 | 2.3 | 0.1 | 55.8 | 0.3 | 6.2 | 14.0 | 0.6 | 1.3 | 0.9 |
| Lawrence | 0.2 | 1.2 | 0.3 | 67.1 | 0.1 | 5.4 | 4.0 | 0.3 | 0.8 | 2.1 |
| Leominster | 0.3 | 4.0 | 0.0 | 62.5 | 0.4 | 5.5 | 5.5 | 1.9 | 0.7 | 1.2 |
| Lowell | 0.2 | 1.8 | 0.7 | 54.9 | 0.6 | 6.4 | 8.1 | 1.3 | 2.5 | 2.4 |
| Lynn | 0.1 | 2.3 | 0.3 | 65.9 | 0.3 | 7.0 | 1.6 | 0.4 | 1.1 | 2.1 |
| Malden | 1.5 | 1.8 | 0.0 | 47.0 | 0.4 | 4.8 | 1.9 | 0.3 | 4.2 | 2.8 |
| Marlborough | 0.1 | 4.6 | 0.0 | 61.1 | 0.3 | 5.8 | 5.7 | 0.3 | 0.1 | 2.0 |
| Medford | 0.2 | 2.9 | 0.0 | 51.5 | 0.3 | 8.5 | 5.1 | 0.6 | 1.7 | 2.0 |
| Melrose | 0.1 | 1.3 | 0.0 | 56.6 | 0.5 | 3.5 | 2.9 | 2.0 | 0.1 | 2.2 |
| Methuen Town | 0.4 | 5.5 | 0.0 | 62.8 | 0.7 | 6.6 | 6.2 | 0.1 | 0.8 | 2.3 |
| New Bedford | 0.4 | 1.5 | 0.1 | 58.8 | 1.0 | 7.5 | 6.8 | 0.4 | 2.4 | 2.8 |
| Newton | 0.1 | 2.8 | 0.0 | 59.4 | 0.7 | 4.7 | 3.4 | 1.5 | 1.3 | 0.9 |
| Northampton | 0.4 | 4.0 | 0.8 | 44.5 | 0.6 | 5.5 | 5.3 | 0.3 | 3.1 | 3.0 |
| Peabody | 0.1 | 2.4 | 0.0 | 53.1 | 0.7 | 5.9 | 2.9 | 2.0 | 2.7 | 1.4 |
| Pittsfield | 0.1 | 3.8 | 0.0 | 58.8 | 0.5 | 5.1 | 5.4 | 1.0 | 1.8 | 1.7 |
| Quincy | 0.3 | 3.0 | 0.0 | 45.0 | 0.7 | 7.0 | 4.1 | 1.0 | 1.7 | 1.3 |
| Revere | 0.5 | 4.7 | 0.1 | 55.6 | 0.2 | 5.8 | 0.5 | 0.2 | 0.9 | 1.7 |
| Salem | 0.1 | 2.0 | 0.4 | 61.7 | 0.3 | 4.5 | 3.0 | 0.7 | 1.0 | 1.9 |
| Somerville | 0.1 | 2.5 | 0.0 | 46.7 | 0.5 | 4.8 | 3.2 | 0.3 | 1.7 | 1.5 |
| Springfield | 0.1 | 2.2 | 0.0 | 64.2 | 0.2 | 6.3 | 1.9 | 1.5 | 1.0 | 2.7 |
| Taunton | 3.6 | 3.1 | 0.0 | 65.0 | 0.1 | 5.6 | 3.0 | 0.6 | 1.1 | 1.3 |
| Waltham | 0.2 | 3.6 | 0.1 | 44.0 | 0.3 | 6.1 | 4.4 | 0.6 | 0.5 | 1.6 |
| Watertown Town | 0.1 | 2.5 | 0.2 | 43.5 | 0.4 | 6.6 | 3.6 | 0.5 | 0.3 | 2.3 |
| Westfield | 0.4 | 4.4 | 0.0 | 62.1 | 1.7 | 4.9 | 4.9 | 0.6 | 0.6 | 2.8 |
| West Springfield Town | NA | NA | NA | NA | NA | NA | NA | NA | NA | NA |
| Weymouth Town | NA | NA | NA | NA | NA | NA | NA | NA | NA | NA |
| Woburn | 0.1 | 1.4 | 0.0 | 56.5 | 0.4 | 5.8 | 2.3 | 0.6 | 0.0 | 1.7 |
| Worcester | 0.0 | 2.5 | 0.1 | 52.8 | 0.5 | 5.9 | 5.2 | 0.6 | 1.3 | 4.5 |
| MICHIGAN | X | X | X | X | X | X | X | X | X | X |
| Allen Park | 0.0 | 10.4 | 0.0 | 0.0 | 0.0 | 20.3 | 18.7 | 4.9 | 0.8 | 2.1 |
| Ann Arbor | 0.0 | 7.6 | 8.0 | 0.0 | 0.0 | 13.4 | 15.1 | 5.4 | 8.3 | 2.6 |
| Battle Creek | 0.0 | 11.9 | 0.8 | 0.0 | 0.0 | 14.9 | 12.7 | 6.5 | 4.8 | 3.5 |
| Bay City | 0.0 | 11.7 | 0.0 | 0.0 | 0.0 | 13.1 | 17.4 | 1.8 | 11.0 | 3.0 |
| Burton | 0.0 | 26.5 | 0.0 | 0.0 | 0.0 | 25.2 | 24.7 | 0.5 | 0.0 | 3.0 |
| Dearborn | 0.0 | 10.9 | 0.7 | 0.0 | 0.5 | 14.6 | 34.5 | 7.6 | 3.2 | 1.0 |
| Dearborn Heights | 0.0 | 12.3 | 0.0 | 0.0 | 0.0 | 23.3 | 21.2 | 1.9 | 1.9 | 3.2 |
| Detroit | 1.4 | 4.7 | 0.3 | 2.6 | 2.8 | 15.2 | 25.3 | 3.0 | 3.4 | 13.2 |
| East Lansing | 0.0 | 11.9 | 4.4 | 0.0 | 0.2 | 13.0 | 14.1 | 10.3 | 0.7 | 4.0 |
| Eastpointe | 0.0 | 8.7 | 0.0 | 0.0 | 0.0 | 24.8 | 19.2 | 4.9 | 4.3 | 0.5 |
| Farmington Hills | 0.0 | 11.8 | 0.0 | 0.0 | 0.0 | 22.5 | 17.5 | 10.4 | 0.5 | 1.7 |
| Flint | 0.0 | 3.2 | 0.0 | 0.0 | 68.6 | 6.1 | 7.2 | 1.4 | 2.9 | 1.0 |
| Garden City | 0.0 | 11.8 | 0.0 | 0.0 | 0.0 | 17.5 | 20.3 | 3.0 | 0.7 | 3.3 |
| Grand Rapids | 0.0 | 7.9 | 3.8 | 0.0 | 0.0 | 13.7 | 20.4 | 2.5 | 14.8 | 5.7 |
| Holland | 0.3 | 28.0 | 0.3 | 0.0 | 0.8 | 14.9 | 15.2 | 11.2 | 1.6 | 3.0 |
| Inkster | 0.0 | 20.1 | 0.0 | 0.0 | 0.0 | 15.0 | 10.5 | 2.7 | 12.1 | 1.3 |
| Jackson | 0.0 | 17.7 | 0.3 | 0.0 | 0.3 | 17.3 | 9.3 | 6.6 | 14.2 | 4.0 |
| Kalamazoo | 0.0 | 8.6 | 1.7 | 0.0 | 0.0 | 25.4 | 19.9 | 3.6 | 2.1 | 13.6 |
| Kentwood | 0.0 | 27.2 | 0.0 | 0.0 | 0.0 | 25.9 | 5.7 | 3.1 | 0.0 | 2.1 |
| Lansing | 0.0 | 7.6 | 1.9 | 0.0 | 0.0 | 13.3 | 18.7 | 5.8 | 7.2 | 4.7 |
| Lincoln Park | 0.0 | 8.7 | 0.0 | 0.0 | 0.0 | 21.0 | 15.2 | 4.7 | 11.3 | 1.3 |
| Livonia | 0.0 | 13.6 | 0.0 | 0.0 | 0.0 | 19.2 | 20.6 | 9.9 | 8.2 | 1.6 |
| Madison Heights | 0.0 | 16.7 | 0.0 | 0.0 | 0.0 | 14.6 | 14.5 | 3.5 | 3.9 | 0.4 |
| Midland | 0.0 | 18.7 | 0.2 | 0.0 | 0.0 | 9.9 | 17.0 | 10.5 | 6.1 | 1.7 |
| Mount Pleasant | 0.0 | 12.7 | 0.0 | 0.0 | 0.0 | 22.6 | 14.7 | 8.2 | 3.2 | 2.2 |
| Muskegon | 0.0 | 18.1 | 0.0 | 0.0 | 0.0 | 18.3 | 13.6 | 5.9 | 8.0 | 0.5 |
| Novi | 0.0 | 14.4 | 0.0 | 0.0 | 0.0 | 20.0 | 12.8 | 8.5 | 1.3 | 6.6 |

| City | City government finances, 2007 (cont.) | | | | Climate[2] | | | | | | |
|---|---|---|---|---|---|---|---|---|---|---|---|
| | Debt outstanding | | | | Average daily temperature (degrees Fahrenheit) | | | | | | |
| | | | | | Mean | | Limits | | | | |
| | Total (mil dol) | Per capita[1] (dollars) | Debt issued during year | City government employment, 2011 | January | July | January[3] | July[4] | Annual precipitation (inches) | Heating degree days | Cooling degree days |
| | 137 | 138 | 139 | 140 | 141 | 142 | 143 | 144 | 145 | 146 | 147 |
| MASSACHUSETTS— Cont'd | | | | | | | | | | | |
| Beverly | 70.3 | 1 794 | 0.0 | NA | 28.8 | 72.6 | 20.4 | 82.1 | 45.51 | 5 704 | 582 |
| Boston | 1 440.6 | 2 404 | 187.6 | 19 160 | 29.3 | 73.9 | 22.1 | 82.2 | 42.53 | 5 630 | 777 |
| Braintree Town | NA | NA | NA | NA | NA | NA | NA | NA | NA | NA | NA |
| Brockton | 248.6 | 2 671 | 37.0 | 2 951 | 27.9 | 72.1 | 17.8 | 83.2 | 48.25 | 6 008 | 529 |
| Cambridge | 280.1 | 2 763 | 67.9 | 5 699 | 29.3 | 73.9 | 22.1 | 82.2 | 42.53 | 5 630 | 777 |
| Chelsea | 72.7 | 1 902 | 3.2 | NA | 29.3 | 73.9 | 22.1 | 82.2 | 42.53 | 5 630 | 777 |
| Chicopee | 36.2 | 673 | 0.0 | 1 879 | 21.5 | 68.9 | 10.4 | 81.7 | 48.07 | 7 312 | 287 |
| Everett | 82.1 | 2 204 | 20.4 | 1 117 | 29.3 | 73.9 | 22.1 | 82.2 | 42.53 | 5 630 | 777 |
| Fall River | 253.4 | 2 788 | 38.0 | 2 425 | 28.5 | 74.2 | 20.0 | 83.1 | 50.77 | 5 734 | 740 |
| Fitchburg | 87.1 | 2 187 | 7.6 | NA | 24.2 | 71.9 | 15.2 | 81.0 | 49.13 | 6 576 | 548 |
| Franklin Town | NA | NA | NA | NA | NA | NA | NA | NA | NA | NA | NA |
| Gloucester | 122.5 | 4 040 | 34.9 | NA | 28.8 | 72.6 | 20.4 | 82.1 | 45.51 | 5 704 | 582 |
| Haverhill | 120.4 | 2 011 | 8.2 | 1 710 | 25.3 | 72.2 | 15.6 | 83.5 | 46.88 | 6 435 | 550 |
| Holyoke | 66.0 | 1 660 | 13.4 | 1 913 | 21.5 | 68.9 | 10.4 | 81.7 | 48.07 | 7 312 | 287 |
| Lawrence | 154.7 | 2 208 | 56.4 | 2 540 | 24.5 | 71.8 | 14.5 | 82.9 | 44.09 | 6 539 | 510 |
| Leominster | 36.9 | 897 | 0.0 | NA | 24.2 | 71.9 | 15.2 | 81.0 | 49.13 | 6 576 | 548 |
| Lowell | 219.0 | 2 115 | 47.1 | 3 101 | 23.6 | 72.4 | 14.1 | 84.5 | 43.14 | 6 575 | 532 |
| Lynn | 96.4 | 1 106 | 6.7 | 2 854 | 29.3 | 73.9 | 22.1 | 82.2 | 42.53 | 5 630 | 777 |
| Malden | 116.2 | 2 085 | 12.5 | 1 389 | 29.3 | 73.9 | 22.1 | 82.2 | 42.53 | 5 630 | 777 |
| Marlborough | 57.4 | 1 507 | 0.5 | 1 218 | 25.9 | 73.4 | 16.2 | 84.0 | 45.87 | 6 060 | 651 |
| Medford | 64.5 | 1 160 | 4.2 | 1 138 | 29.3 | 73.9 | 22.1 | 82.2 | 42.53 | 5 630 | 777 |
| Melrose | 50.4 | 1 883 | 4.6 | NA | 29.3 | 73.9 | 22.1 | 82.2 | 42.53 | 5 630 | 777 |
| Methuen Town | 74.5 | 1 693 | 1.1 | 1 061 | 24.5 | 71.8 | 14.5 | 82.9 | 44.09 | 6 539 | 510 |
| New Bedford | 259.8 | 2 828 | 16.9 | 2 743 | 28.5 | 74.2 | 20.0 | 83.1 | 50.77 | 5 734 | 740 |
| Newton | 76.9 | 923 | 17.2 | 2 905 | 25.9 | 73.4 | 16.2 | 84.0 | 45.87 | 6 060 | 651 |
| Northampton | 53.8 | 1 893 | 9.4 | 1 329 | 22.3 | 71.2 | 11.2 | 83.2 | 45.57 | 6 856 | 452 |
| Peabody | 56.2 | 1 093 | 9.0 | 1 419 | 28.8 | 72.6 | 20.4 | 82.1 | 45.51 | 5 704 | 582 |
| Pittsfield | 70.8 | 1 650 | 0.0 | NA | 19.9 | 67.6 | 11.2 | 77.5 | 48.71 | 7 689 | 222 |
| Quincy | 122.5 | 1 338 | 30.1 | 1 965 | 26.0 | 71.6 | 18.1 | 81.2 | 51.19 | 6 371 | 558 |
| Revere | 33.1 | 597 | 12.0 | 1 162 | 29.3 | 73.9 | 22.1 | 82.2 | 42.53 | 5 630 | 777 |
| Salem | 69.4 | 1 696 | 2.3 | 1 195 | 28.8 | 72.6 | 20.4 | 82.1 | 45.51 | 5 704 | 582 |
| Somerville | 83.3 | 1 120 | 37.1 | 1 608 | 29.3 | 73.9 | 22.1 | 82.2 | 42.53 | 5 630 | 777 |
| Springfield | 347.9 | 2 320 | 55.6 | 6 343 | 25.7 | 73.7 | 17.2 | 84.9 | 46.16 | 6 104 | 759 |
| Taunton | 79.5 | 1 425 | 8.8 | 1 538 | 27.4 | 72.2 | 17.8 | 83.0 | 48.34 | 6 012 | 558 |
| Waltham | 77.4 | 1 294 | 26.1 | 1 492 | 25.4 | 71.5 | 15.7 | 82.7 | 46.95 | 6 370 | 485 |
| Watertown Town | 40.3 | 1 240 | 3.5 | NA | 29.3 | 73.9 | 22.1 | 82.2 | 42.53 | 5 630 | 777 |
| Westfield | 83.6 | 2 083 | 0.1 | 1 472 | 21.5 | 68.9 | 10.4 | 81.7 | 48.07 | 7 312 | 287 |
| West Springfield Town | NA | NA | NA | NA | NA | NA | NA | NA | NA | NA | NA |
| Weymouth Town | NA | NA | NA | NA | NA | NA | NA | NA | NA | NA | NA |
| Woburn | 58.0 | 1 565 | 1.1 | NA | 25.5 | 71.5 | 15.7 | 82.5 | 48.31 | 6 401 | 472 |
| Worcester | 658.1 | 3 783 | 51.5 | 5 413 | 23.6 | 70.1 | 15.8 | 79.3 | 49.05 | 6 831 | 371 |
| MICHIGAN | X | X | X | X | X | X | X | X | X | X | X |
| Allen Park | 40.2 | 1 499 | 0.0 | 150 | 24.5 | 73.5 | 17.8 | 83.4 | 32.89 | 6 422 | 736 |
| Ann Arbor | 158.4 | 1 377 | 7.5 | 949 | 23.4 | 72.6 | 16.6 | 83.0 | 35.35 | 6 503 | 691 |
| Battle Creek | 110.6 | 2 118 | 0.0 | 534 | 23.1 | 71.0 | 15.3 | 82.5 | 35.15 | 6 742 | 559 |
| Bay City | 105.9 | 3 113 | 2.6 | 314 | 21.0 | 71.5 | 13.8 | 81.5 | 31.25 | 7 106 | 545 |
| Burton | 13.8 | 454 | 0.0 | 90 | 21.3 | 70.6 | 13.3 | 82.0 | 31.61 | 7 005 | 555 |
| Dearborn | 206.0 | 2 308 | 43.7 | 1 360 | 24.7 | 73.7 | 16.1 | 85.7 | 33.58 | 6 224 | 788 |
| Dearborn Heights | 69.7 | 1 301 | 20.6 | 309 | 24.7 | 73.7 | 16.1 | 85.7 | 33.58 | 6 224 | 788 |
| Detroit | 7 711.2 | 8 410 | 1 553.8 | 11 645 | 24.7 | 73.7 | 16.1 | 85.7 | 33.58 | 6 224 | 788 |
| East Lansing | 81.6 | 1 764 | 13.6 | 392 | 21.6 | 70.3 | 13.9 | 82.1 | 31.53 | 7 098 | 558 |
| Eastpointe | 14.2 | 434 | 0.0 | 179 | 25.3 | 73.6 | 18.8 | 83.3 | 33.97 | 6 160 | 757 |
| Farmington Hills | 34.4 | 436 | 6.6 | 439 | 24.7 | 73.7 | 16.1 | 85.7 | 33.58 | 6 224 | 788 |
| Flint | 135.6 | 1 182 | 0.0 | 3 242 | 21.3 | 70.6 | 13.3 | 82.0 | 31.61 | 7 005 | 555 |
| Garden City | 68.2 | 2 474 | 0.0 | 137 | 24.7 | 73.7 | 16.1 | 85.7 | 33.58 | 6 224 | 788 |
| Grand Rapids | 541.6 | 2 797 | 33.5 | 1 707 | 22.4 | 71.4 | 15.6 | 82.3 | 37.13 | 6 896 | 613 |
| Holland | 55.7 | 1 638 | 0.0 | 464 | 24.4 | 71.4 | 17.6 | 82.5 | 36.25 | 6 589 | 611 |
| Inkster | 34.8 | 1 269 | 12.4 | 215 | 24.5 | 73.5 | 17.8 | 83.4 | 32.89 | 6 422 | 736 |
| Jackson | 51.9 | 1 526 | 0.0 | 322 | 22.5 | 71.3 | 14.7 | 82.7 | 30.67 | 6 873 | 570 |
| Kalamazoo | 395.6 | 5 446 | 11.8 | 760 | 24.3 | 73.2 | 17.0 | 84.2 | 37.41 | 6 235 | 773 |
| Kentwood | 19.7 | 417 | 0.0 | 223 | 22.4 | 71.4 | 15.6 | 82.3 | 37.13 | 6 896 | 613 |
| Lansing | 446.0 | 3 880 | 36.7 | 1 664 | 21.6 | 70.3 | 13.9 | 82.1 | 31.53 | 7 098 | 558 |
| Lincoln Park | 12.3 | 339 | 0.0 | 188 | 24.5 | 73.5 | 17.8 | 83.4 | 32.89 | 6 422 | 736 |
| Livonia | 67.2 | 715 | 13.5 | 701 | 24.7 | 73.7 | 16.1 | 85.7 | 33.58 | 6 224 | 788 |
| Madison Heights | 16.2 | 546 | 1.5 | 172 | 24.7 | 73.7 | 16.1 | 85.7 | 33.58 | 6 224 | 788 |
| Midland | 24.8 | 603 | 0.0 | 403 | 22.9 | 72.7 | 16.2 | 83.8 | 30.69 | 6 645 | 679 |
| Mount Pleasant | 15.8 | 595 | 0.0 | 146 | 20.7 | 70.6 | 13.5 | 82.2 | 31.57 | 7 329 | 492 |
| Muskegon | 46.5 | 1 180 | 9.4 | 255 | 23.5 | 69.9 | 17.1 | 80.0 | 32.88 | 6 943 | 487 |
| Novi | 76.7 | 1 417 | 0.0 | 291 | 22.1 | 71.0 | 14.3 | 81.7 | 29.28 | 6 989 | 550 |

1. Based on the population estimated as of July 1 of the year shown.   2. Represents normal values based on the 30-year period, 1971–2000.   3. Average daily minimum.   4. Average daily maximum.

# Table D. Cities — Land Area and Population

| STATE Place code | City | Land area,[1] 2010 (sq km) | Population, 2012 | | | Race alone or in combination, not of Hispanic origin (percent), 2010 | | | | | Percent Hispanic or Latino,[2] 2010 | Percent Foreign born 2007–2011 |
|---|---|---|---|---|---|---|---|---|---|---|---|---|
| | | | | | | Race alone or in combination | | | | | | |
| | | | Total persons | Rank | Per square kilometer | White | Black | American Indian, Alaska Native | Asian | Hawaiian Pacific Islander | | |
| | | 1 | 2 | 3 | 4 | 5 | 6 | 7 | 8 | 9 | 10 | 11 |
| | **MICHIGAN—Cont'd** | | | | | | | | | | | |
| 26 59920 | Oak Park ..................... | 13.4 | 29 594 | 1 231 | 2 208.5 | 39.0 | 59.1 | 1.0 | 2.2 | 0.1 | 1.4 | 10.0 |
| 26 65440 | Pontiac ..................... | 51.7 | 60 175 | 582 | 1 163.9 | 29.1 | 53.6 | 1.3 | 2.6 | 0.1 | 16.5 | 7.2 |
| 26 65560 | Portage ..................... | 83.5 | 47 126 | 785 | 564.4 | 87.6 | 6.1 | 1.0 | 4.7 | 0.1 | 3.1 | 5.6 |
| 26 65820 | Port Huron ................. | 20.9 | 29 684 | 1 226 | 1 420.3 | 84.4 | 11.2 | 1.7 | 0.8 | 0.1 | 5.4 | 3.3 |
| 26 69035 | Rochester Hills ............. | 85.0 | 72 283 | 459 | 850.4 | 81.5 | 5.0 | 0.5 | 11.4 | 0.0 | 3.1 | 15.9 |
| 26 69800 | Roseville .................... | 25.5 | 47 321 | 781 | 1 855.7 | 84.0 | 13.0 | 1.3 | 2.0 | 0.1 | 2.0 | 4.7 |
| 26 70040 | Royal Oak ................... | 30.5 | 58 410 | 604 | 1 915.1 | 90.6 | 4.9 | 0.7 | 3.0 | 0.1 | 2.3 | 7.0 |
| 26 70520 | Saginaw ..................... | 44.9 | 50 790 | 717 | 1 131.2 | 39.7 | 47.0 | 1.0 | 0.5 | 0.1 | 14.3 | 1.5 |
| 26 70760 | St. Clair Shores ........... | 30.1 | 59 749 | 587 | 1 985.0 | 92.9 | 4.5 | 0.9 | 1.5 | 0.1 | 1.7 | 5.2 |
| 26 74900 | Southfield .................. | 68.1 | 72 507 | 457 | 1 064.7 | 25.9 | 71.7 | 0.9 | 2.2 | 0.1 | 1.3 | 9.0 |
| 26 74960 | Southgate .................. | 17.7 | 29 585 | 1 232 | 1 671.5 | 85.8 | 6.1 | 0.9 | 2.0 | 0.1 | 6.5 | 6.6 |
| 26 76460 | Sterling Heights ........... | 94.6 | 130 410 | 192 | 1 378.5 | 85.7 | 5.6 | 0.6 | 7.9 | 0.2 | 1.9 | 22.8 |
| 26 79000 | Taylor ....................... | 61.1 | 62 114 | 555 | 1 016.6 | 76.7 | 16.9 | 1.3 | 2.0 | 0.1 | 5.1 | 4.7 |
| 26 80700 | Troy ......................... | 86.7 | 82 212 | 383 | 948.2 | 74.2 | 4.4 | 0.5 | 20.2 | 0.1 | 2.1 | 24.4 |
| 26 84000 | Warren ...................... | 89.1 | 134 141 | 188 | 1 505.5 | 79.2 | 14.5 | 1.1 | 5.4 | 0.1 | 2.1 | 10.8 |
| 26 86000 | Westland .................... | 52.9 | 82 883 | 376 | 1 566.8 | 75.3 | 18.2 | 1.1 | 3.5 | 0.1 | 3.8 | 7.5 |
| 26 88900 | Wyandotte .................. | 13.7 | 25 485 | 1 420 | 1 860.2 | 92.4 | 1.8 | 1.3 | 0.7 | 0.1 | 5.1 | 2.2 |
| 26 88940 | Wyoming .................... | 63.8 | 73 371 | 448 | 1 150.0 | 70.5 | 8.1 | 1.1 | 3.2 | 0.1 | 19.4 | 9.8 |
| 27 00000 | **MINNESOTA** ............ | 206 232.3 | 5 379 139 | X | 26.1 | 84.8 | 6.0 | 1.7 | 4.6 | 0.1 | 4.7 | 7.1 |
| 27 01486 | Andover ..................... | 87.7 | 31 200 | 1 166 | 355.8 | 93.6 | 2.2 | 0.8 | 2.9 | 0.1 | 2.0 | 3.5 |
| 27 01900 | Apple Valley ................ | 43.7 | 49 978 | 727 | 1 143.7 | 83.6 | 6.7 | 0.7 | 6.2 | 0.2 | 4.9 | 9.2 |
| 27 06382 | Blaine ....................... | 87.7 | 59 412 | 589 | 677.4 | 84.5 | 4.5 | 1.2 | 8.7 | 0.1 | 3.2 | 8.2 |
| 27 06616 | Bloomington ................ | 89.8 | 86 033 | 359 | 958.1 | 79.5 | 8.5 | 1.0 | 6.6 | 0.1 | 6.8 | 11.7 |
| 27 07948 | Brooklyn Center ........... | 20.6 | 30 643 | 1 187 | 1 487.5 | 49.1 | 28.3 | 1.4 | 15.1 | 0.1 | 9.6 | 22.9 |
| 27 07966 | Brooklyn Park ............. | 67.5 | 77 752 | 415 | 1 151.9 | 52.7 | 26.3 | 1.1 | 16.4 | 0.2 | 6.4 | 20.4 |
| 27 08794 | Burnsville .................. | 64.5 | 61 130 | 566 | 947.8 | 76.4 | 11.4 | 1.0 | 5.9 | 0.2 | 7.9 | 12.2 |
| 27 13114 | Coon Rapids ............... | 58.6 | 61 931 | 559 | 1 056.8 | 86.9 | 6.7 | 1.5 | 4.2 | 0.1 | 3.2 | 7.4 |
| 27 13456 | Cottage Grove ............. | 87.1 | 35 181 | 1 039 | 403.9 | 85.4 | 4.7 | 1.0 | 5.9 | 0.1 | 4.8 | 5.7 |
| 27 17000 | Duluth ....................... | 175.6 | 86 211 | 357 | 491.0 | 92.1 | 3.4 | 3.8 | 2.0 | 0.1 | 1.5 | 3.0 |
| 27 17288 | Eagan ....................... | 80.6 | 64 854 | 526 | 804.6 | 81.4 | 6.6 | 0.8 | 8.8 | 0.1 | 4.5 | 10.6 |
| 27 18116 | Eden Prairie ............... | 84.0 | 62 258 | 553 | 741.2 | 81.7 | 6.3 | 0.5 | 10.1 | 0.1 | 3.0 | 14.7 |
| 27 18188 | Edina ........................ | 40.0 | 49 050 | 753 | 1 226.3 | 88.1 | 3.5 | 0.5 | 7.0 | 0.1 | 2.3 | 9.4 |
| 27 22814 | Fridley ...................... | 26.3 | 27 639 | 1 313 | 1 050.9 | 75.3 | 13.1 | 2.1 | 5.7 | 0.1 | 7.3 | 13.4 |
| 27 31076 | Inver Grove Heights ...... | 71.9 | 34 198 | 1 069 | 475.6 | 83.4 | 4.8 | 0.9 | 4.0 | 0.2 | 8.9 | 6.3 |
| 27 35180 | Lakeville .................... | 93.4 | 57 342 | 620 | 613.9 | 89.2 | 3.4 | 0.7 | 4.9 | 0.1 | 3.5 | 6.1 |
| 27 39878 | Mankato ..................... | 46.4 | 40 119 | 910 | 864.6 | 89.7 | 4.9 | 0.7 | 3.4 | 0.1 | 2.9 | 5.4 |
| 27 40166 | Maple Grove ............... | 84.5 | 64 420 | 533 | 762.4 | 86.6 | 5.0 | 0.6 | 7.0 | 0.1 | 2.5 | 9.1 |
| 27 40382 | Maplewood ................. | 44.0 | 39 337 | 925 | 894.0 | 74.7 | 9.3 | 1.0 | 11.1 | 0.1 | 6.2 | 10.3 |
| 27 43000 | Minneapolis ................ | 139.8 | 392 880 | 47 | 2 810.3 | 63.1 | 20.4 | 2.8 | 6.5 | 0.2 | 10.5 | 14.9 |
| 27 43252 | Minnetonka ................. | 69.7 | 51 123 | 713 | 733.5 | 90.3 | 4.5 | 0.6 | 4.0 | 0.1 | 2.4 | 6.6 |
| 27 43864 | Moorhead ................... | 51.3 | 39 039 | 935 | 761.0 | 90.2 | 2.7 | 2.3 | 2.6 | 0.1 | 4.1 | 3.8 |
| 27 47680 | Oakdale ..................... | 28.4 | 27 726 | 1 305 | 976.3 | 81.0 | 7.1 | 0.9 | 8.8 | 0.1 | 4.3 | 8.9 |
| 27 49300 | Owatonna ................... | 37.6 | 25 421 | 1 421 | 676.1 | 87.7 | 4.4 | 0.4 | 1.2 | 0.0 | 7.3 | 4.3 |
| 27 51730 | Plymouth .................... | 84.7 | 72 928 | 454 | 861.0 | 84.3 | 6.1 | 0.7 | 7.7 | 0.1 | 3.0 | 10.8 |
| 27 54214 | Richfield .................... | 17.8 | 36 087 | 1 014 | 2 027.4 | 65.2 | 10.4 | 1.3 | 6.8 | 0.1 | 18.3 | 19.5 |
| 27 54880 | Rochester ................... | 141.4 | 108 992 | 249 | 770.8 | 81.1 | 7.2 | 0.6 | 7.7 | 0.1 | 5.2 | 11.9 |
| 27 55852 | Roseville .................... | 33.7 | 34 666 | 1 055 | 1 028.7 | 81.3 | 7.1 | 1.0 | 8.1 | 0.1 | 4.6 | 11.5 |
| 27 56896 | St. Cloud ................... | 103.7 | 65 986 | 513 | 636.3 | 85.3 | 8.9 | 1.2 | 4.2 | 0.1 | 2.4 | 5.8 |
| 27 57220 | St. Louis Park.............. | 27.6 | 46 362 | 796 | 1 679.8 | 83.5 | 8.7 | 1.0 | 4.7 | 0.2 | 4.3 | 9.8 |
| 27 58000 | St. Paul ..................... | 134.6 | 290 770 | 66 | 2 160.3 | 58.6 | 17.3 | 1.9 | 15.8 | 0.2 | 9.6 | 17.5 |
| 27 58738 | Savage ...................... | 40.5 | 27 959 | 1 291 | 690.3 | 82.8 | 5.2 | 0.9 | 9.2 | 0.4 | 3.4 | 10.5 |
| 27 59350 | Shakopee ................... | 72.5 | 38 744 | 945 | 534.4 | 76.2 | 5.1 | 1.6 | 11.2 | 0.1 | 7.8 | 15.4 |
| 27 59998 | Shoreview .................. | 27.9 | 25 628 | 1 411 | 918.6 | 87.9 | 2.9 | 0.7 | 8.1 | 0.1 | 2.2 | 7.3 |
| 27 71032 | Winona ...................... | 48.8 | 27 944 | 1 292 | 572.6 | 93.1 | 2.4 | 0.5 | 3.2 | 0.1 | 1.7 | 3.1 |
| 27 71428 | Woodbury ................... | 90.0 | 64 496 | 531 | 716.6 | 81.1 | 6.4 | 0.6 | 10.1 | 0.1 | 3.8 | 9.9 |
| 28 00000 | **MISSISSIPPI**.............. | 121 530.7 | 2 984 926 | X | 24.6 | 58.8 | 37.4 | 0.8 | 1.1 | 0.1 | 2.7 | 2.2 |
| 28 06220 | Biloxi ........................ | 99.0 | 44 578 | 820 | 450.3 | 66.6 | 20.4 | 1.0 | 5.3 | 0.4 | 8.7 | 8.1 |
| 28 14420 | Clinton ...................... | 108.3 | 25 752 | 1 401 | 237.8 | 60.1 | 34.4 | 0.5 | 4.3 | 0.1 | 1.5 | 4.7 |
| 28 29180 | Greenville .................. | 69.7 | 33 418 | 1 091 | 479.5 | 20.3 | 78.1 | 0.3 | 0.8 | 0.0 | 0.9 | 1.6 |
| 28 29700 | Gulfport ..................... | 144.0 | 70 113 | 474 | 486.9 | 56.5 | 37.0 | 0.9 | 2.3 | 0.2 | 5.2 | 4.4 |
| 28 31020 | Hattiesburg ................. | 138.3 | 47 169 | 783 | 341.1 | 41.3 | 53.6 | 0.5 | 1.1 | 0.1 | 4.3 | 3.7 |
| 28 33700 | Horn Lake .................. | 41.5 | 26 529 | 1 372 | 639.3 | 57.7 | 33.7 | 0.7 | 1.3 | 0.1 | 8.0 | 4.3 |
| 28 36000 | Jackson ..................... | 287.6 | 175 437 | 135 | 610.0 | 18.5 | 79.7 | 0.4 | 0.5 | 0.1 | 1.6 | 1.6 |
| 28 46640 | Meridian..................... | 139.2 | 40 832 | 887 | 293.3 | 35.5 | 61.8 | 0.4 | 1.1 | 0.1 | 1.7 | 2.1 |
| 28 54040 | Olive Branch ............... | 95.1 | 34 512 | 1 063 | 362.9 | 71.1 | 23.6 | 0.4 | 1.6 | 0.1 | 4.2 | 5.2 |
| 28 55760 | Pearl ........................ | 61.1 | 26 154 | 1 391 | 428.1 | 69.3 | 23.6 | 0.6 | 1.1 | 0.3 | 6.4 | 2.9 |
| 28 69280 | Southaven .................. | 106.8 | 50 374 | 722 | 471.7 | 70.6 | 22.8 | 0.6 | 2.1 | 0.1 | 5.0 | 3.2 |
| 28 74840 | Tupelo ....................... | 132.5 | 35 490 | 1 031 | 267.8 | 58.7 | 37.4 | 0.3 | 1.2 | 0.0 | 3.5 | 2.7 |

1. Dry land or land partially or temporarily covered by water.    2. May be of any race.

# Table D. Cities — **Population**

| City | Age of population (percent), 2010 | | | | | | | | | | | Population | | | |
|---|---|---|---|---|---|---|---|---|---|---|---|---|---|---|---|
| | | | | | | | | | | | | Census counts | | Percent change | |
| | Under 5 years | 5 to 17 years | 18 to 24 years | 25 to 34 years | 35 to 44 years | 45 to 54 years | 55 to 64 years | 65 to 74 years | 75 years and over | Median age | Percent female | 2000 | 2010 | 2000–2010 | 2010–2012 |
| | 12 | 13 | 14 | 15 | 16 | 17 | 18 | 19 | 20 | 21 | 22 | 23 | 24 | 25 | 26 |
| MICHIGAN—Cont'd | | | | | | | | | | | | | | | |
| Oak Park | 6.3 | 18.5 | 9.7 | 12.2 | 13.5 | 14.0 | 12.8 | 6.4 | 6.5 | 37.5 | 54.9 | 29 793 | 29 319 | -1.6 | 0.9 |
| Pontiac | 8.5 | 18.8 | 11.2 | 13.8 | 14.4 | 13.6 | 10.5 | 5.2 | 4.1 | 33.4 | 50.9 | 66 337 | 59 515 | -10.3 | 1.1 |
| Portage | 6.7 | 18.1 | 7.9 | 13.4 | 13.4 | 14.6 | 12.3 | 7.0 | 6.6 | 38.1 | 52.1 | 44 897 | 46 292 | 3.1 | 1.8 |
| Port Huron | 7.9 | 17.7 | 9.8 | 13.7 | 12.6 | 13.8 | 11.4 | 6.2 | 6.9 | 35.8 | 52.2 | 32 338 | 30 184 | -6.7 | -1.7 |
| Rochester Hills | 5.7 | 18.0 | 7.6 | 10.8 | 13.8 | 16.4 | 14.0 | 7.2 | 6.5 | 40.9 | 51.6 | 68 825 | 70 995 | 3.2 | 1.8 |
| Roseville | 6.3 | 16.7 | 9.0 | 13.9 | 14.3 | 15.6 | 11.1 | 6.0 | 7.1 | 37.9 | 51.6 | 48 129 | 47 299 | -1.7 | 0.0 |
| Royal Oak | 5.8 | 10.9 | 7.5 | 21.4 | 14.5 | 14.6 | 12.2 | 5.9 | 7.1 | 37.8 | 51.0 | 60 062 | 57 236 | -4.7 | 2.1 |
| Saginaw | 8.2 | 20.2 | 10.5 | 13.0 | 12.0 | 13.8 | 11.3 | 5.3 | 5.6 | 33.5 | 52.9 | 61 799 | 51 508 | -16.7 | -1.4 |
| St. Clair Shores | 5.0 | 14.1 | 7.0 | 12.3 | 12.7 | 16.4 | 13.4 | 8.1 | 11.1 | 44.2 | 52.2 | 63 096 | 59 730 | -5.4 | 0.0 |
| Southfield | 4.8 | 15.7 | 8.6 | 11.7 | 13.1 | 14.4 | 14.8 | 8.1 | 8.8 | 42.0 | 55.3 | 78 296 | 71 739 | -8.4 | 1.1 |
| Southgate | 4.9 | 15.4 | 9.1 | 12.9 | 13.3 | 15.2 | 12.9 | 7.8 | 8.5 | 40.8 | 52.2 | 30 136 | 30 047 | -0.3 | -1.5 |
| Sterling Heights | 5.5 | 16.2 | 8.7 | 12.5 | 13.4 | 15.3 | 13.2 | 8.3 | 6.9 | 40.4 | 51.5 | 124 471 | 129 699 | 4.2 | 0.5 |
| Taylor | 7.1 | 17.7 | 10.0 | 13.0 | 13.4 | 14.8 | 11.3 | 6.9 | 5.9 | 36.9 | 52.1 | 65 868 | 63 131 | -4.2 | -1.6 |
| Troy | 5.2 | 18.7 | 6.7 | 10.5 | 13.5 | 17.2 | 14.5 | 7.8 | 6.0 | 41.8 | 50.7 | 80 959 | 80 980 | 0.0 | 1.5 |
| Warren | 6.1 | 16.6 | 9.0 | 12.6 | 13.6 | 15.1 | 10.9 | 7.3 | 8.8 | 39.4 | 51.6 | 138 247 | 134 056 | -3.0 | 0.1 |
| Westland | 6.3 | 15.8 | 9.5 | 13.9 | 13.8 | 15.3 | 11.4 | 6.7 | 7.3 | 38.3 | 52.5 | 86 602 | 84 094 | -2.9 | -1.4 |
| Wyandotte | 5.4 | 16.0 | 8.5 | 12.6 | 13.8 | 16.9 | 13.0 | 6.4 | 7.4 | 40.4 | 51.1 | 28 006 | 25 883 | -7.6 | -1.5 |
| Wyoming | 8.3 | 18.8 | 10.6 | 16.4 | 13.3 | 13.8 | 9.7 | 4.7 | 4.4 | 32.1 | 50.7 | 69 368 | 72 125 | 4.0 | 1.7 |
| MINNESOTA | 6.7 | 17.5 | 9.5 | 13.5 | 12.8 | 15.2 | 11.9 | 6.7 | 6.2 | 37.4 | 50.4 | 4 919 479 | 5 303 925 | 7.8 | 1.4 |
| Andover | 5.7 | 24.7 | 7.5 | 9.4 | 16.1 | 19.4 | 10.4 | 4.6 | 2.1 | 37.3 | 49.3 | 26 588 | 30 598 | 15.1 | 2.0 |
| Apple Valley | 6.5 | 18.9 | 7.4 | 13.4 | 14.1 | 17.0 | 13.1 | 6.0 | 3.6 | 37.9 | 51.5 | 45 527 | 49 084 | 7.8 | 1.8 |
| Blaine | 7.9 | 18.6 | 7.4 | 15.1 | 15.5 | 15.5 | 11.5 | 5.6 | 2.9 | 35.6 | 50.9 | 44 942 | 57 181 | 27.2 | 3.9 |
| Bloomington | 5.4 | 14.3 | 7.8 | 13.6 | 11.5 | 15.4 | 13.5 | 9.1 | 9.3 | 42.7 | 51.6 | 85 172 | 82 893 | -2.7 | 3.8 |
| Brooklyn Center | 8.9 | 18.7 | 10.2 | 15.8 | 12.2 | 12.7 | 9.4 | 5.5 | 6.7 | 32.6 | 51.3 | 29 172 | 30 104 | 3.2 | 1.8 |
| Brooklyn Park | 8.7 | 20.3 | 9.6 | 15.0 | 14.0 | 14.1 | 10.5 | 4.7 | 3.2 | 32.5 | 51.1 | 67 388 | 75 781 | 12.5 | 2.6 |
| Burnsville | 7.4 | 16.7 | 9.0 | 15.7 | 13.0 | 14.9 | 11.6 | 6.7 | 5.0 | 35.9 | 51.3 | 60 220 | 60 307 | 0.1 | 1.4 |
| Coon Rapids | 6.9 | 17.6 | 8.9 | 14.3 | 13.2 | 16.0 | 11.8 | 6.5 | 4.8 | 36.9 | 51.6 | 61 607 | 61 476 | -0.2 | 0.7 |
| Cottage Grove | 7.3 | 21.6 | 7.8 | 13.3 | 15.7 | 15.4 | 10.6 | 5.1 | 3.2 | 35.0 | 50.1 | 30 582 | 34 589 | 13.1 | 1.7 |
| Duluth | 5.6 | 12.9 | 19.6 | 13.4 | 10.1 | 12.9 | 11.9 | 6.3 | 7.4 | 33.6 | 51.0 | 86 918 | 86 265 | -0.8 | -0.1 |
| Eagan | 6.4 | 19.1 | 8.0 | 14.2 | 13.9 | 19.0 | 11.8 | 4.6 | 3.0 | 36.8 | 50.9 | 63 557 | 64 205 | 1.0 | 1.0 |
| Eden Prairie | 6.6 | 19.9 | 6.5 | 13.8 | 13.9 | 18.2 | 12.6 | 4.9 | 3.7 | 37.6 | 51.5 | 54 901 | 60 797 | 10.7 | 2.4 |
| Edina | 5.4 | 18.8 | 4.6 | 8.9 | 12.1 | 15.8 | 13.8 | 8.6 | 12.0 | 45.2 | 53.4 | 47 425 | 47 941 | 1.1 | 2.3 |
| Fridley | 7.2 | 16.3 | 8.7 | 15.1 | 12.8 | 14.3 | 11.4 | 7.9 | 6.3 | 37.1 | 50.5 | 27 449 | 27 208 | -0.9 | 1.6 |
| Inver Grove Heights | 6.4 | 18.1 | 8.4 | 13.0 | 13.3 | 16.9 | 12.1 | 5.9 | 5.9 | 38.4 | 52.0 | 29 751 | 33 882 | 13.9 | 0.9 |
| Lakeville | 7.4 | 24.4 | 6.7 | 11.7 | 17.0 | 17.9 | 9.1 | 4.0 | 1.8 | 34.8 | 49.9 | 43 128 | 55 954 | 29.7 | 2.5 |
| Mankato | 5.6 | 10.7 | 32.7 | 15.1 | 8.7 | 8.6 | 8.0 | 4.6 | 6.0 | 25.4 | 50.0 | 32 427 | 39 349 | 21.2 | 2.0 |
| Maple Grove | 7.1 | 19.8 | 6.4 | 13.1 | 15.6 | 17.9 | 12.7 | 4.8 | 2.5 | 37.6 | 51.2 | 50 365 | 61 567 | 22.2 | 4.6 |
| Maplewood | 6.4 | 16.5 | 9.0 | 13.3 | 11.8 | 15.6 | 12.1 | 6.9 | 8.3 | 39.3 | 52.0 | 34 947 | 38 018 | 8.8 | 3.5 |
| Minneapolis | 6.9 | 13.3 | 15.2 | 21.0 | 13.7 | 12.2 | 9.7 | 4.3 | 3.7 | 31.4 | 49.7 | 382 618 | 382 578 | 0.0 | 2.7 |
| Minnetonka | 4.9 | 15.9 | 5.9 | 11.9 | 11.3 | 17.0 | 16.4 | 8.2 | 8.5 | 45.0 | 52.5 | 51 301 | 49 734 | -3.1 | 2.8 |
| Moorhead | 6.5 | 14.4 | 23.7 | 13.9 | 9.6 | 11.3 | 9.2 | 5.1 | 6.4 | 28.3 | 51.6 | 32 177 | 38 065 | 18.3 | 2.6 |
| Oakdale | 6.2 | 17.9 | 9.5 | 13.2 | 12.8 | 17.3 | 11.9 | 6.1 | 5.1 | 37.9 | 52.1 | 26 653 | 27 378 | 2.7 | 1.3 |
| Owatonna | 7.8 | 19.1 | 7.4 | 13.1 | 13.2 | 14.3 | 11.3 | 6.5 | 7.3 | 37.2 | 51.2 | 22 434 | 25 599 | 14.1 | -0.7 |
| Plymouth | 6.0 | 18.0 | 6.9 | 13.6 | 13.5 | 16.9 | 13.2 | 7.0 | 5.1 | 39.5 | 51.6 | 65 894 | 70 576 | 7.1 | 3.3 |
| Richfield | 7.5 | 13.8 | 8.5 | 18.6 | 12.8 | 13.6 | 11.1 | 6.0 | 8.2 | 36.2 | 50.8 | 34 439 | 35 228 | 2.3 | 2.4 |
| Rochester | 7.9 | 16.9 | 8.3 | 16.9 | 12.6 | 14.1 | 10.5 | 6.3 | 6.4 | 35.0 | 51.6 | 85 806 | 106 748 | 24.4 | 2.1 |
| Roseville | 5.2 | 13.4 | 10.8 | 13.3 | 10.5 | 14.1 | 12.6 | 8.8 | 11.3 | 42.1 | 52.9 | 33 690 | 33 660 | -0.1 | 3.0 |
| St. Cloud | 5.9 | 12.9 | 23.9 | 15.5 | 9.9 | 11.8 | 9.6 | 5.0 | 5.3 | 28.8 | 48.5 | 59 107 | 66 003 | 11.4 | 0.0 |
| St. Louis Park | 6.5 | 12.0 | 8.0 | 22.9 | 13.6 | 13.0 | 11.0 | 5.7 | 7.3 | 35.4 | 52.2 | 44 126 | 45 250 | 2.5 | 2.5 |
| St. Paul | 7.8 | 17.3 | 13.8 | 17.0 | 12.5 | 12.5 | 10.0 | 4.6 | 4.4 | 30.9 | 51.1 | 287 151 | 285 068 | -0.7 | 2.0 |
| Savage | 7.7 | 23.8 | 6.1 | 13.0 | 17.8 | 17.6 | 8.4 | 3.8 | 1.7 | 34.6 | 49.9 | 21 115 | 26 911 | 27.4 | 3.9 |
| Shakopee | 10.0 | 20.2 | 6.6 | 18.8 | 18.4 | 12.2 | 7.0 | 3.8 | 3.0 | 32.2 | 51.2 | 20 568 | 37 076 | 80.3 | 4.5 |
| Shoreview | 5.0 | 16.6 | 7.1 | 10.3 | 11.5 | 18.5 | 16.6 | 8.1 | 6.3 | 44.6 | 52.1 | 25 924 | 25 043 | -3.4 | 2.3 |
| Winona | 3.9 | 10.6 | 33.2 | 10.5 | 8.0 | 10.5 | 10.0 | 6.1 | 7.3 | 26.7 | 52.7 | 27 069 | 27 595 | 1.9 | 1.3 |
| Woodbury | 7.5 | 22.1 | 6.2 | 13.4 | 16.1 | 16.1 | 10.3 | 4.8 | 3.5 | 35.6 | 51.8 | 46 463 | 61 961 | 33.4 | 4.1 |
| MISSISSIPPI | 7.1 | 18.4 | 10.3 | 13.1 | 12.6 | 14.1 | 11.7 | 7.2 | 5.6 | 36.0 | 51.4 | 2 844 658 | 2 967 299 | 4.3 | 0.6 |
| Biloxi | 7.1 | 14.8 | 14.9 | 15.0 | 11.7 | 13.7 | 10.6 | 6.4 | 5.7 | 33.5 | 48.6 | 50 644 | 44 054 | -13.0 | 1.2 |
| Clinton | 6.4 | 18.2 | 9.9 | 13.4 | 12.8 | 14.1 | 11.6 | 7.0 | 6.7 | 36.7 | 53.8 | 23 347 | 25 215 | 8.0 | 2.1 |
| Greenville | 7.8 | 21.1 | 9.4 | 12.3 | 11.3 | 13.6 | 12.3 | 6.7 | 5.6 | 34.5 | 54.3 | 41 633 | 34 402 | -17.4 | -2.9 |
| Gulfport | 8.0 | 17.0 | 10.7 | 15.3 | 12.6 | 13.9 | 11.0 | 6.5 | 5.1 | 34.3 | 51.0 | 71 127 | 67 793 | -4.7 | 3.4 |
| Hattiesburg | 7.4 | 13.7 | 22.3 | 17.6 | 10.0 | 10.0 | 8.2 | 5.1 | 5.6 | 27.8 | 52.6 | 44 779 | 45 988 | 2.7 | 2.6 |
| Horn Lake | 8.4 | 22.5 | 9.9 | 16.6 | 15.2 | 12.6 | 8.4 | 4.1 | 2.3 | 30.7 | 51.5 | 14 099 | 26 066 | 84.9 | 1.8 |
| Jackson | 7.8 | 19.6 | 12.8 | 14.8 | 11.7 | 13.1 | 10.3 | 5.4 | 4.6 | 31.2 | 53.5 | 184 256 | 173 513 | -5.8 | 1.1 |
| Meridian | 8.0 | 18.6 | 10.2 | 13.2 | 11.9 | 13.0 | 11.2 | 6.6 | 7.2 | 34.9 | 53.8 | 39 968 | 41 148 | 3.0 | -0.8 |
| Olive Branch | 6.7 | 21.6 | 7.4 | 12.6 | 16.1 | 14.5 | 10.5 | 6.1 | 4.5 | 36.0 | 51.7 | 21 054 | 33 484 | 59.0 | 3.1 |
| Pearl | 7.9 | 18.4 | 9.5 | 15.8 | 12.8 | 13.4 | 10.3 | 7.1 | 4.8 | 33.9 | 52.5 | 21 961 | 25 700 | 14.3 | 1.8 |
| Southaven | 7.7 | 20.5 | 8.6 | 15.2 | 15.0 | 13.0 | 9.6 | 6.2 | 4.2 | 33.7 | 51.9 | 28 977 | 48 982 | 69.0 | 2.8 |
| Tupelo | 7.5 | 19.6 | 8.1 | 13.9 | 12.7 | 13.2 | 10.7 | 7.1 | 7.1 | 35.7 | 53.1 | 34 211 | 34 546 | 1.0 | 2.7 |

# Table D. Cities — Households, Group Quarters, Crime, and Education

| City | Households, 2010 | | | | Persons in group quarters, 2010 | | | | Serious crimes known to police,[2] 2011 | | | | Educational attainment, 2007–2011 | | |
| | | | Percent | | | Institutional | | | Total | | Rate[3] | | | Attainment[4] (percent) | |
| | Number | Persons per house-hold | Female family householder[1] | One-person | Total | Total | Persons in nursing facilities | Non-institu-tional | Number | Rate[3] | Violent | Property | Population age 25 and older | High school graduate or less | Bachelor's degree or more |
| | 27 | 28 | 29 | 30 | 31 | 32 | 33 | 34 | 35 | 36 | 37 | 38 | 39 | 40 | 41 |
| **MICHIGAN—Cont'd** | | | | | | | | | | | | | | | |
| Oak Park | 11 719 | 2.50 | 23.9 | 30.9 | 58 | 0 | 0 | 58 | 1 003 | 3 424 | 509 | 2 915 | 19 403 | 32.8 | 29.4 |
| Pontiac | 22 220 | 2.56 | 27.0 | 33.1 | 2 563 | 1 586 | 102 | 977 | NA | NA | NA | NA | 36 698 | 57.3 | 11.6 |
| Portage | 19 199 | 2.40 | 10.9 | 29.1 | 156 | 111 | 111 | 45 | 1 745 | 3 772 | 184 | 3 589 | 30 548 | 27.6 | 39.0 |
| Port Huron | 12 177 | 2.42 | 19.9 | 33.0 | 761 | 235 | 228 | 526 | 1 281 | 4 247 | 637 | 3 611 | 20 316 | 52.6 | 13.8 |
| Rochester Hills | 27 578 | 2.53 | 8.1 | 25.7 | 1 181 | 507 | 507 | 674 | NA | NA | NA | NA | 49 354 | 21.8 | 50.2 |
| Roseville | 19 553 | 2.41 | 17.4 | 31.7 | 245 | 148 | 148 | 97 | 2 313 | 4 894 | 383 | 4 511 | 32 509 | 55.3 | 10.6 |
| Royal Oak | 28 063 | 2.03 | 8.1 | 41.4 | 404 | 249 | 225 | 155 | 1 147 | 2 005 | 142 | 1 864 | 44 194 | 24.6 | 49.4 |
| Saginaw | 19 799 | 2.52 | 28.7 | 32.1 | 1 693 | 876 | 346 | 817 | 3 054 | 5 934 | 2 267 | 3 666 | 31 953 | 59.2 | 10.7 |
| St. Clair Shores | 26 585 | 2.24 | 11.9 | 35.1 | 277 | 248 | 248 | 29 | 1 215 | 2 036 | 213 | 1 823 | 44 465 | 40.9 | 23.5 |
| Southfield | 31 778 | 2.22 | 19.4 | 37.9 | 1 189 | 453 | 451 | 736 | 3 068 | 4 280 | 530 | 3 750 | 51 318 | 27.7 | 38.1 |
| Southgate | 13 062 | 2.29 | 12.3 | 33.9 | 117 | 88 | 88 | 29 | 1 192 | 3 970 | 236 | 3 734 | 20 835 | 49.7 | 16.2 |
| Sterling Heights | 49 451 | 2.61 | 10.5 | 26.5 | 772 | 566 | 554 | 206 | 2 873 | 2 217 | 157 | 2 060 | 89 681 | 42.4 | 26.5 |
| Taylor | 24 370 | 2.56 | 20.4 | 25.5 | 673 | 540 | 512 | 133 | 2 820 | 4 470 | 507 | 3 963 | 41 600 | 57.8 | 9.2 |
| Troy | 30 703 | 2.63 | 7.3 | 23.4 | 310 | 117 | 117 | 193 | 1 851 | 2 287 | 89 | 2 198 | 55 083 | 21.1 | 56.5 |
| Warren | 53 442 | 2.49 | 15.9 | 30.4 | 1 248 | 945 | 945 | 303 | 4 556 | 3 401 | 532 | 2 869 | 92 868 | 53.3 | 15.9 |
| Westland | 35 886 | 2.31 | 16.4 | 34.3 | 1 034 | 779 | 548 | 255 | 2 730 | 3 249 | 419 | 2 830 | 57 384 | 49.6 | 17.8 |
| Wyandotte | 10 991 | 2.35 | 13.2 | 33.0 | 88 | 0 | 0 | 88 | 770 | 2 977 | 217 | 2 761 | 18 379 | 52.5 | 15.4 |
| Wyoming | 26 970 | 2.66 | 14.4 | 25.6 | 358 | 149 | 149 | 209 | 1 854 | 2 572 | 365 | 2 208 | 44 842 | 49.2 | 18.8 |
| **MINNESOTA** | 2 087 227 | 2.48 | 9.5 | 28.0 | 135 395 | 56 308 | 32 989 | 79 087 | 148 089 | 2 771 | 221 | 2 549 | 3 490 475 | 35.9 | 31.8 |
| Andover | 9 811 | 3.11 | 7.1 | 10.6 | 39 | 0 | 0 | 39 | NA | NA | NA | NA | 18 590 | 29.8 | 31.5 |
| Apple Valley | 18 875 | 2.58 | 10.2 | 23.6 | 316 | 198 | 189 | 118 | 1 232 | 2 491 | 83 | 2 408 | 32 250 | 23.4 | 44.5 |
| Blaine | 21 077 | 2.71 | 10.8 | 20.7 | 147 | 71 | 31 | 76 | 2 011 | 3 490 | 89 | 3 401 | 36 782 | 33.7 | 29.8 |
| Bloomington | 35 905 | 2.28 | 9.7 | 32.2 | 991 | 489 | 481 | 502 | 3 287 | 3 935 | 163 | 3 772 | 59 342 | 30.8 | 38.5 |
| Brooklyn Center | 10 756 | 2.78 | 18.1 | 27.7 | 182 | 93 | 86 | 89 | 1 681 | 5 541 | 481 | 5 060 | 18 509 | 48.3 | 18.4 |
| Brooklyn Park | 26 229 | 2.88 | 15.0 | 22.3 | 209 | 17 | 8 | 192 | 3 098 | 4 057 | 333 | 3 724 | 45 135 | 36.0 | 29.5 |
| Burnsville | 24 283 | 2.47 | 11.5 | 27.6 | 443 | 294 | 287 | 149 | 1 809 | 2 977 | 214 | 2 763 | 40 319 | 29.0 | 35.4 |
| Coon Rapids | 23 532 | 2.60 | 13.0 | 23.8 | 359 | 205 | 201 | 154 | 2 784 | 4 494 | 181 | 4 313 | 41 029 | 38.1 | 23.1 |
| Cottage Grove | 11 719 | 2.95 | 9.3 | 14.9 | 64 | 13 | 7 | 51 | 590 | 1 693 | 34 | 1 658 | 21 387 | 31.9 | 31.8 |
| Duluth | 35 705 | 2.23 | 11.2 | 35.1 | 6 640 | 1 416 | 924 | 5 224 | 4 631 | 5 327 | 328 | 4 999 | 52 241 | 34.0 | 31.2 |
| Eagan | 25 249 | 2.54 | 9.0 | 25.9 | 197 | 61 | 61 | 136 | 1 557 | 2 406 | 70 | 2 337 | 42 606 | 19.6 | 50.3 |
| Eden Prairie | 23 930 | 2.53 | 8.0 | 25.1 | 208 | 127 | 112 | 81 | 993 | 1 621 | 54 | 1 567 | 39 402 | 14.6 | 60.5 |
| Edina | 20 672 | 2.31 | 6.4 | 33.1 | 190 | 112 | 100 | 78 | 787 | 1 629 | 41 | 1 588 | 33 660 | 14.4 | 64.0 |
| Fridley | 11 110 | 2.44 | 14.1 | 28.8 | 131 | 48 | 48 | 83 | 1 368 | 4 989 | 357 | 4 632 | 18 617 | 41.4 | 27.4 |
| Inver Grove Heights | 13 476 | 2.50 | 11.4 | 26.2 | 193 | 154 | 140 | 39 | 711 | 2 083 | 255 | 1 828 | 22 151 | 34.7 | 30.8 |
| Lakeville | 18 683 | 2.99 | 9.2 | 14.0 | 46 | 14 | 6 | 32 | 803 | 1 424 | 57 | 1 367 | 33 978 | 23.2 | 45.0 |
| Mankato | 14 851 | 2.35 | 9.0 | 30.9 | 4 347 | 324 | 239 | 4 023 | 1 952 | 4 928 | 235 | 4 693 | 19 871 | 30.6 | 33.0 |
| Maple Grove | 22 867 | 2.69 | 8.3 | 19.3 | 50 | 4 | 4 | 46 | 1 239 | 1 997 | 60 | 1 937 | 39 735 | 19.2 | 49.8 |
| Maplewood | 14 882 | 2.48 | 12.1 | 29.1 | 1 131 | 800 | 362 | 331 | 2 308 | 6 024 | 183 | 5 842 | 25 591 | 36.9 | 31.0 |
| Minneapolis | 163 540 | 2.23 | 11.7 | 40.3 | 18 066 | 3 896 | 2 814 | 14 170 | 22 912 | 5 943 | 965 | 4 978 | 250 683 | 30.4 | 44.7 |
| Minnetonka | 21 901 | 2.25 | 7.3 | 31.1 | 380 | 292 | 209 | 88 | 941 | 1 878 | 62 | 1 816 | 36 226 | 18.3 | 52.7 |
| Moorhead | 14 304 | 2.41 | 10.6 | 29.2 | 3 650 | 344 | 263 | 3 306 | 869 | 2 265 | 117 | 2 148 | 20 858 | 33.4 | 34.1 |
| Oakdale | 10 948 | 2.48 | 12.7 | 28.4 | 177 | 7 | 2 | 170 | 1 163 | 4 215 | 167 | 4 049 | 17 957 | 34.9 | 27.1 |
| Owatonna | 10 068 | 2.49 | 10.0 | 27.9 | 531 | 321 | 203 | 210 | 530 | 2 055 | 151 | 1 903 | 16 748 | 43.1 | 26.3 |
| Plymouth | 28 663 | 2.42 | 8.5 | 26.4 | 1 128 | 730 | 229 | 398 | 1 270 | 1 786 | 82 | 1 704 | 47 776 | 17.4 | 55.7 |
| Richfield | 14 818 | 2.35 | 10.8 | 34.3 | 347 | 112 | 110 | 235 | 955 | 2 690 | 242 | 2 448 | 24 457 | 37.6 | 32.1 |
| Rochester | 43 025 | 2.42 | 9.5 | 30.1 | 2 615 | 1 760 | 646 | 855 | 2 540 | 2 361 | 202 | 2 159 | 70 597 | 27.9 | 42.7 |
| Roseville | 14 623 | 2.20 | 8.4 | 35.3 | 1 426 | 342 | 292 | 1 084 | 1 573 | 4 637 | 195 | 4 443 | 23 653 | 28.2 | 45.2 |
| St. Cloud | 25 439 | 2.37 | 10.4 | 30.8 | 5 615 | 1 690 | 448 | 3 925 | 2 808 | 4 232 | 347 | 3 885 | 37 228 | 36.2 | 28.1 |
| St. Louis Park | 21 743 | 2.05 | 9.1 | 40.1 | 755 | 633 | 630 | 122 | 1 470 | 3 224 | 143 | 3 081 | 32 287 | 19.2 | 53.0 |
| St. Paul | 111 001 | 2.47 | 14.8 | 35.8 | 11 438 | 2 351 | 1 608 | 9 087 | 13 817 | 4 803 | 655 | 4 148 | 173 418 | 37.2 | 37.2 |
| Savage | 9 116 | 2.95 | 8.2 | 14.8 | 6 | 4 | 0 | 2 | 653 | 2 408 | 81 | 2 327 | 16 388 | 23.6 | 43.9 |
| Shakopee | 12 772 | 2.83 | 10.5 | 20.4 | 884 | 843 | 167 | 41 | 1 102 | 2 950 | 203 | 2 746 | 23 082 | 33.0 | 36.3 |
| Shoreview | 10 402 | 2.39 | 7.9 | 27.3 | 204 | 9 | 0 | 195 | 303 | 1 201 | 48 | 1 153 | 17 863 | 20.9 | 51.2 |
| Winona | 10 449 | 2.24 | 8.5 | 35.6 | 4 223 | 376 | 324 | 3 847 | 503 | 1 809 | 169 | 1 640 | 14 861 | 39.0 | 29.1 |
| Woodbury | 22 594 | 2.73 | 8.7 | 20.4 | 286 | 161 | 161 | 125 | 1 326 | 2 124 | 42 | 2 082 | 39 063 | 17.0 | 55.8 |
| **MISSISSIPPI** | 1 115 768 | 2.58 | 18.5 | 26.3 | 91 964 | 55 135 | 16 496 | 36 829 | 98 151 | 3 295 | 270 | 3 026 | 1 892 687 | 50.3 | 19.7 |
| Biloxi | 17 104 | 2.40 | 16.2 | 31.2 | 3 065 | 209 | 158 | 2 856 | 2 545 | 5 755 | 461 | 5 294 | 27 948 | 40.8 | 22.8 |
| Clinton | 9 766 | 2.54 | 15.7 | 25.4 | 397 | 265 | 265 | 132 | 414 | 1 636 | 55 | 1 580 | 15 728 | 25.7 | 43.7 |
| Greenville | 12 678 | 2.68 | 30.9 | 27.1 | 432 | 370 | 254 | 62 | 2 443 | 7 075 | 232 | 6 843 | 21 464 | 53.5 | 19.6 |
| Gulfport | 26 307 | 2.50 | 21.0 | 28.3 | 1 984 | 1 222 | 278 | 762 | 3 806 | 5 593 | 282 | 5 311 | 43 448 | 47.0 | 19.9 |
| Hattiesburg | 18 501 | 2.30 | 21.0 | 35.7 | 3 529 | 832 | 468 | 2 697 | 1 723 | 3 732 | 171 | 3 561 | 25 228 | 39.0 | 32.1 |
| Horn Lake | 9 052 | 2.87 | 21.3 | 20.9 | 56 | 56 | 56 | 0 | 641 | 2 450 | 92 | 2 358 | 15 619 | 51.6 | 11.2 |
| Jackson | 64 523 | 2.60 | 29.1 | 30.2 | 6 035 | 1 419 | 998 | 4 616 | 14 431 | 8 286 | 930 | 7 355 | 104 615 | 43.6 | 26.8 |
| Meridian | 16 509 | 2.39 | 25.6 | 34.2 | 1 678 | 1 161 | 268 | 517 | 2 689 | 6 510 | 571 | 5 939 | 26 206 | 48.0 | 20.0 |
| Olive Branch | 12 078 | 2.77 | 14.4 | 19.1 | 0 | 0 | 0 | 0 | 1 071 | 3 186 | 274 | 2 913 | 21 382 | 41.1 | 26.8 |
| Pearl | 9 792 | 2.56 | 18.9 | 26.5 | 70 | 57 | 57 | 13 | 730 | 2 898 | 226 | 2 672 | 16 490 | 48.3 | 18.8 |
| Southaven | 17 969 | 2.71 | 16.6 | 21.9 | 264 | 264 | 264 | 0 | 1 682 | 3 421 | 285 | 3 136 | 30 508 | 42.4 | 20.8 |
| Tupelo | 13 602 | 2.47 | 19.2 | 30.1 | 895 | 834 | 471 | 61 | NA | NA | NA | NA | 22 446 | 41.2 | 27.0 |

1. No spouse present.  2. Data for serious crimes have not been adjusted for underreporting. This may affect comparability between geographic areas and over time.  3. Per 100,000 population estimated by the FBI.  4. Persons 25 years old and over.

# Table D. Cities — Income, Poverty, and Housing

| City | Money income, 2007–2011 | | | | | Housing units, 2010 | | | Occupied Housing units 2007–2011 | | | | |
|---|---|---|---|---|---|---|---|---|---|---|---|---|---|
| | | Households | | | Families with income below poverty (percent) | | | | Owner-occupied | | | Median owner costs as a percent of income | |
| | Per capita income[1] (dollars) | Median income | Percent with income of $200,000 or more | Percent with income of less than $25,000 | | Total | Percent change, 2000–2010 | Vacant units for sale or rent[2] | Total | Percent | Median value[3] (dollars) | With a mortgage[4] | Without a mortgage[5] |
| | 42 | 43 | 44 | 45 | 46 | 47 | 48 | 49 | 50 | 51 | 52 | 53 | 54 |
| **MICHIGAN—Cont'd** | | | | | | | | | | | | | |
| Oak Park | 23 084 | 44 901 | 1.4 | 27.5 | 15.1 | 12 782 | 12.4 | 1 063 | 11 838 | 63.2 | 117 500 | 27.6 | 18.3 |
| Pontiac | 15 991 | 29 189 | 0.3 | 44.6 | 29.5 | 27 084 | 2.8 | 4 864 | 23 345 | 50.9 | 82 400 | 27.8 | 17.7 |
| Portage | 29 971 | 56 330 | 3.5 | 19.5 | 7.4 | 20 559 | 8.9 | 1 360 | 18 987 | 70.2 | 155 900 | 22.0 | 12.5 |
| Port Huron | 18 931 | 33 460 | 1.1 | 38.6 | 22.6 | 13 871 | -0.9 | 1 694 | 12 526 | 57.7 | 93 900 | 26.5 | 15.1 |
| Rochester Hills | 39 041 | 79 009 | 9.0 | 15.2 | 4.7 | 29 494 | 8.1 | 1 916 | 27 518 | 76.4 | 226 400 | 23.1 | 13.2 |
| Roseville | 20 651 | 40 681 | 0.5 | 29.5 | 12.1 | 21 260 | 3.6 | 1 707 | 19 768 | 71.3 | 95 300 | 26.6 | 15.4 |
| Royal Oak | 38 205 | 62 495 | 3.5 | 16.3 | 3.2 | 30 207 | 0.9 | 2 144 | 28 356 | 70.3 | 167 000 | 22.7 | 13.8 |
| Saginaw | 14 520 | 27 445 | 0.8 | 46.7 | 32.7 | 23 574 | -8.1 | 3 775 | 19 403 | 62.0 | 59 300 | 27.1 | 15.9 |
| St. Clair Shores | 28 774 | 52 775 | 1.7 | 21.7 | 7.1 | 28 467 | 0.9 | 1 882 | 26 977 | 82.2 | 125 400 | 24.1 | 14.8 |
| Southfield | 29 228 | 50 747 | 2.5 | 20.8 | 9.8 | 35 986 | 0.8 | 4 208 | 31 808 | 53.8 | 147 900 | 27.2 | 16.7 |
| Southgate | 24 361 | 45 882 | 0.8 | 24.9 | 5.6 | 13 933 | 4.3 | 871 | 12 773 | 67.8 | 116 300 | 24.8 | 16.6 |
| Sterling Heights | 26 544 | 57 272 | 1.9 | 18.3 | 8.5 | 52 190 | 9.8 | 2 739 | 49 155 | 77.5 | 163 800 | 24.4 | 13.8 |
| Taylor | 20 227 | 42 373 | 0.9 | 28.2 | 17.2 | 26 422 | 2.0 | 2 052 | 23 544 | 67.0 | 99 700 | 25.1 | 14.6 |
| Troy | 41 192 | 85 946 | 11.3 | 12.9 | 4.2 | 32 907 | 6.6 | 2 204 | 30 149 | 76.6 | 237 000 | 22.8 | 12.2 |
| Warren | 22 311 | 45 434 | 0.8 | 25.7 | 12.1 | 57 938 | 1.2 | 4 496 | 54 084 | 76.0 | 113 400 | 24.9 | 15.7 |
| Westland | 23 652 | 44 466 | 0.6 | 26.8 | 12.2 | 39 201 | 3.0 | 3 315 | 34 960 | 63.5 | 116 800 | 25.0 | 14.7 |
| Wyandotte | 25 706 | 50 009 | 1.5 | 24.5 | 9.5 | 12 081 | -1.8 | 1 090 | 10 710 | 76.0 | 110 400 | 23.5 | 14.9 |
| Wyoming | 20 521 | 45 246 | 0.8 | 23.0 | 11.6 | 28 983 | 5.4 | 2 013 | 27 068 | 68.4 | 114 400 | 24.4 | 11.9 |
| **MINNESOTA** | 30 310 | 58 476 | 4.2 | 19.6 | 7.1 | 2 347 201 | 13.6 | 259 974 | 2 094 265 | 73.6 | 201 400 | 24.2 | 12.0 |
| Andover | 32 615 | 89 803 | 5.0 | 6.1 | 3.1 | 10 091 | 23.0 | 280 | 9 651 | 93.2 | 256 000 | 24.5 | 10.0 |
| Apple Valley | 36 728 | 78 767 | 6.4 | 10.5 | 3.6 | 19 600 | 18.5 | 725 | 19 040 | 83.1 | 232 900 | 23.3 | 10.9 |
| Blaine | 30 976 | 71 954 | 3.4 | 10.1 | 3.3 | 21 921 | 35.6 | 844 | 20 656 | 88.6 | 208 700 | 24.7 | 13.5 |
| Bloomington | 35 732 | 60 150 | 5.0 | 15.6 | 4.9 | 37 641 | 1.5 | 1 736 | 35 736 | 70.0 | 234 700 | 24.6 | 11.8 |
| Brooklyn Center | 21 371 | 48 083 | 1.0 | 22.5 | 14.3 | 11 640 | 0.4 | 884 | 10 603 | 63.6 | 166 600 | 27.6 | 14.4 |
| Brooklyn Park | 25 818 | 61 537 | 3.4 | 16.4 | 10.1 | 27 841 | 12.1 | 1 612 | 25 500 | 72.7 | 214 400 | 26.1 | 12.3 |
| Burnsville | 32 164 | 63 688 | 4.0 | 14.9 | 5.9 | 25 759 | 6.2 | 1 476 | 24 476 | 68.2 | 230 100 | 24.2 | 12.2 |
| Coon Rapids | 29 070 | 63 615 | 2.6 | 14.4 | 5.3 | 24 462 | 7.3 | 930 | 23 578 | 77.9 | 193 900 | 25.0 | 12.1 |
| Cottage Grove | 30 530 | 82 469 | 3.1 | 8.9 | 3.7 | 12 102 | 20.8 | 383 | 11 566 | 90.2 | 224 300 | 24.2 | 11.2 |
| Duluth | 24 174 | 41 116 | 2.2 | 30.7 | 12.0 | 38 208 | 3.3 | 2 503 | 36 325 | 59.2 | 151 200 | 22.3 | 12.8 |
| Eagan | 40 213 | 80 243 | 8.9 | 9.4 | 3.6 | 26 414 | 8.3 | 1 165 | 25 340 | 73.8 | 257 700 | 22.5 | 10.0 |
| Eden Prairie | 49 375 | 91 711 | 15.1 | 9.0 | 3.9 | 25 075 | 19.3 | 1 145 | 22 954 | 73.9 | 321 300 | 22.6 | 10.0 |
| Edina | 57 055 | 80 652 | 16.7 | 14.1 | 1.5 | 22 560 | 4.2 | 1 888 | 20 586 | 74.4 | 391 700 | 23.5 | 13.3 |
| Fridley | 26 831 | 52 024 | 1.2 | 17.2 | 7.9 | 11 760 | 2.2 | 650 | 11 577 | 65.1 | 198 100 | 26.0 | 13.2 |
| Inver Grove Heights | 34 317 | 64 640 | 5.4 | 11.1 | 2.9 | 14 062 | 22.8 | 586 | 13 354 | 74.6 | 226 800 | 25.6 | 11.6 |
| Lakeville | 36 572 | 95 646 | 8.2 | 7.4 | 2.6 | 19 456 | 41.0 | 773 | 18 344 | 91.2 | 267 500 | 23.2 | 10.0 |
| Mankato | 20 909 | 40 560 | 1.4 | 32.0 | 10.7 | 15 784 | 24.0 | 933 | 14 622 | 54.8 | 154 300 | 24.2 | 12.4 |
| Maple Grove | 41 994 | 94 199 | 11.3 | 6.1 | 2.2 | 23 626 | 33.2 | 759 | 22 316 | 88.0 | 260 200 | 22.1 | 10.0 |
| Maplewood | 28 932 | 57 594 | 2.6 | 17.4 | 7.1 | 15 561 | 11.1 | 679 | 14 651 | 73.1 | 216 300 | 25.8 | 12.6 |
| Minneapolis | 30 693 | 47 478 | 4.4 | 28.5 | 15.8 | 178 287 | 5.7 | 14 747 | 168 273 | 50.4 | 223 400 | 25.7 | 14.1 |
| Minnetonka | 48 225 | 81 588 | 11.9 | 10.4 | 2.5 | 23 294 | 4.8 | 1 393 | 21 591 | 74.7 | 309 300 | 23.0 | 12.6 |
| Moorhead | 22 051 | 46 794 | 1.5 | 28.0 | 9.1 | 15 274 | 25.5 | 970 | 13 969 | 62.9 | 147 000 | 22.5 | 12.0 |
| Oakdale | 30 864 | 66 971 | 3.0 | 15.5 | 5.6 | 11 388 | 9.5 | 440 | 10 704 | 77.8 | 208 700 | 24.4 | 10.4 |
| Owatonna | 26 330 | 55 764 | 2.3 | 21.1 | 6.2 | 10 724 | 20.0 | 656 | 9 950 | 73.4 | 156 900 | 23.8 | 10.7 |
| Plymouth | 46 766 | 86 466 | 13.5 | 11.3 | 3.6 | 29 982 | 18.7 | 1 319 | 27 879 | 73.0 | 309 600 | 21.8 | 10.0 |
| Richfield | 27 532 | 52 131 | 2.0 | 21.6 | 8.6 | 15 735 | 2.5 | 917 | 14 816 | 64.7 | 212 800 | 24.4 | 14.2 |
| Rochester | 32 948 | 63 428 | 5.1 | 17.1 | 5.5 | 45 683 | 29.7 | 2 658 | 42 613 | 72.0 | 165 800 | 21.9 | 10.0 |
| Roseville | 34 095 | 56 941 | 4.2 | 18.8 | 5.1 | 15 490 | 3.8 | 867 | 14 770 | 66.2 | 232 200 | 23.6 | 11.8 |
| St. Cloud | 22 871 | 40 687 | 2.1 | 31.0 | 13.1 | 27 338 | 17.8 | 1 899 | 25 950 | 53.6 | 155 000 | 24.1 | 11.6 |
| St. Louis Park | 38 337 | 62 694 | 4.9 | 15.2 | 6.2 | 23 285 | 10.2 | 1 542 | 21 357 | 61.2 | 240 400 | 24.2 | 13.4 |
| St. Paul | 25 576 | 45 939 | 3.5 | 28.0 | 17.0 | 120 795 | 4.4 | 9 794 | 111 882 | 52.2 | 198 100 | 25.1 | 12.0 |
| Savage | 35 086 | 91 361 | 7.9 | 4.6 | 1.8 | 9 429 | 34.5 | 313 | 8 897 | 88.1 | 270 700 | 24.4 | 10.0 |
| Shakopee | 31 628 | 78 028 | 4.2 | 11.1 | 3.6 | 13 339 | 71.2 | 567 | 12 848 | 79.0 | 228 400 | 24.4 | 10.3 |
| Shoreview | 43 328 | 82 908 | 9.3 | 10.0 | 1.8 | 10 826 | 5.2 | 424 | 10 641 | 84.4 | 258 200 | 22.0 | 12.0 |
| Winona | 20 194 | 35 964 | 1.2 | 39.1 | 9.5 | 10 989 | 3.1 | 540 | 10 643 | 60.8 | 147 100 | 24.3 | 10.9 |
| Woodbury | 42 226 | 92 780 | 11.0 | 7.2 | 2.4 | 23 568 | 34.4 | 974 | 22 277 | 82.4 | 281 100 | 23.1 | 10.0 |
| **MISSISSIPPI** | 20 521 | 38 718 | 2.0 | 33.9 | 17.0 | 1 274 719 | 9.7 | 158 951 | 1 085 062 | 70.6 | 99 200 | 23.1 | 12.2 |
| Biloxi | 25 503 | 42 529 | 2.5 | 30.5 | 15.2 | 21 278 | -3.9 | 4 174 | 17 498 | 54.0 | 158 400 | 24.0 | 10.6 |
| Clinton | 26 593 | 59 000 | 2.9 | 20.0 | 5.2 | 10 359 | 16.2 | 593 | 9 294 | 74.2 | 146 700 | 21.1 | 10.0 |
| Greenville | 17 263 | 30 040 | 1.8 | 44.6 | 27.9 | 14 561 | -10.5 | 1 883 | 12 472 | 53.1 | 76 100 | 23.3 | 13.0 |
| Gulfport | 20 845 | 39 246 | 1.6 | 31.8 | 17.2 | 31 602 | 6.8 | 5 295 | 25 015 | 58.9 | 130 300 | 26.0 | 13.2 |
| Hattiesburg | 19 227 | 25 934 | 2.4 | 48.4 | 27.4 | 21 381 | 11.5 | 2 880 | 18 235 | 38.2 | 106 900 | 24.9 | 13.4 |
| Horn Lake | 18 726 | 48 084 | 0.3 | 24.1 | 11.4 | 9 705 | 90.4 | 653 | 9 064 | 70.4 | 99 000 | 22.8 | 11.2 |
| Jackson | 19 301 | 34 567 | 2.7 | 36.7 | 22.6 | 74 537 | -1.5 | 10 014 | 62 192 | 53.5 | 89 600 | 23.9 | 12.3 |
| Meridian | 19 585 | 30 186 | 2.8 | 43.7 | 27.9 | 18 591 | 3.6 | 2 082 | 16 159 | 54.3 | 82 800 | 26.1 | 12.4 |
| Olive Branch | 27 328 | 68 287 | 2.1 | 13.1 | 3.7 | 12 942 | 60.6 | 864 | 11 843 | 81.4 | 166 000 | 23.8 | 10.0 |
| Pearl | 21 540 | 43 384 | 0.5 | 25.3 | 9.7 | 10 396 | 14.6 | 604 | 10 201 | 65.4 | 108 200 | 21.6 | 10.0 |
| Southaven | 24 556 | 56 105 | 1.5 | 18.6 | 8.8 | 19 101 | 66.3 | 1 132 | 18 047 | 68.6 | 141 000 | 22.3 | 10.0 |
| Tupelo | 24 806 | 39 415 | 4.7 | 34.3 | 19.3 | 15 371 | 5.0 | 1 769 | 13 583 | 61.1 | 117 500 | 23.2 | 11.6 |

1. Based on population estimated by the American Community Survey.　2. Includes units rented or sold but not occupied.　3. Specified owner-occupied units; $1,000,000 represents $1,000,000 or more.　4. 50.0 represents 50 percent or more.　5. 10.0 represents 10 percent or less.

| City | Occupied housing units, 2007–2011 (cont.) | | | | Migration, 2007–2011 | | Civilian labor force, 2012 | | | | Civilian employment[4], 2007–2011 | | | |
|---|---|---|---|---|---|---|---|---|---|---|---|---|---|---|
| | | | | | | | | | Unemployment | | | Percent | | |
| | Percent renter occupied | Median gross rent[1] | Median rent as a percent of income[2] | Percent with no vehicle available | Percent who lived in the same house one year ago | Percent who lived outside this city one year ago | Total | Percent change, 2011–2012 | Total | Rate[3] | Population age 16 and older | In labor force | Full-year full-time worker | Households with no workers (percent) |
| | 55 | 56 | 57 | 58 | 59 | 60 | 61 | 62 | 63 | 64 | 65 | 66 | 67 | 68 |
| MICHIGAN—Cont'd | | | | | | | | | | | | | | |
| Oak Park | 36.8 | 1 007 | 34.5 | 9.6 | 83.7 | 14.1 | 13 620 | 0.8 | 1 847 | 13.6 | 23 295 | 63.7 | 34.2 | 29.9 |
| Pontiac | 49.1 | 719 | 38.2 | 16.9 | 74.8 | 10.0 | 29 864 | -1.3 | 6 790 | 22.7 | 45 607 | 61.0 | 28.2 | 39.0 |
| Portage | 29.8 | 687 | 30.5 | 4.7 | 84.5 | 10.6 | 24 435 | 0.1 | 1 318 | 5.4 | 36 047 | 69.6 | 42.0 | 25.7 |
| Port Huron | 42.3 | 681 | 34.0 | 14.3 | 79.4 | 8.6 | 14 765 | -1.9 | 2 510 | 17.0 | 23 746 | 62.4 | 32.3 | 37.9 |
| Rochester Hills | 23.6 | 1 048 | 29.4 | 4.2 | 87.0 | 11.0 | 33 020 | 2.7 | 1 751 | 5.3 | 56 215 | 67.9 | 40.9 | 24.7 |
| Roseville | 28.7 | 773 | 35.6 | 9.3 | 88.2 | 7.8 | 24 900 | 0.4 | 3 611 | 14.5 | 37 795 | 64.3 | 33.4 | 34.8 |
| Royal Oak | 29.7 | 835 | 23.9 | 4.8 | 84.4 | 11.4 | 32 774 | 2.6 | 1 847 | 5.6 | 49 592 | 73.7 | 48.5 | 22.8 |
| Saginaw | 38.0 | 660 | 45.1 | 17.2 | 82.4 | 7.4 | 23 992 | -1.8 | 3 521 | 14.7 | 39 309 | 55.0 | 25.5 | 43.1 |
| St. Clair Shores | 17.8 | 784 | 30.4 | 5.4 | 91.3 | 5.9 | 30 791 | 1.2 | 3 379 | 11.0 | 49 994 | 65.4 | 37.1 | 32.3 |
| Southfield | 46.2 | 954 | 32.7 | 8.3 | 79.7 | 14.4 | 38 958 | 1.2 | 4 486 | 11.5 | 58 906 | 62.8 | 37.8 | 32.2 |
| Southgate | 32.2 | 749 | 28.0 | 7.2 | 85.5 | 10.9 | 13 318 | 1.0 | 922 | 6.9 | 24 500 | 61.3 | 35.5 | 35.7 |
| Sterling Heights | 22.5 | 827 | 29.2 | 5.7 | 89.1 | 7.6 | 64 181 | 2.0 | 5 133 | 8.0 | 104 609 | 64.6 | 37.6 | 27.7 |
| Taylor | 33.0 | 774 | 32.7 | 7.1 | 82.5 | 12.9 | 27 543 | 0.6 | 2 479 | 9.0 | 50 152 | 62.6 | 30.7 | 33.7 |
| Troy | 23.4 | 1 006 | 24.0 | 4.6 | 89.3 | 8.6 | 39 805 | 2.1 | 3 143 | 7.9 | 63 819 | 66.4 | 41.5 | 22.4 |
| Warren | 24.0 | 763 | 31.2 | 7.9 | 87.0 | 8.6 | 66 983 | 1.0 | 8 100 | 12.1 | 108 222 | 62.2 | 34.7 | 33.8 |
| Westland | 36.5 | 761 | 31.7 | 8.8 | 83.3 | 11.6 | 39 712 | 1.1 | 2 541 | 6.4 | 68 022 | 65.0 | 37.3 | 32.8 |
| Wyandotte | 24.0 | 688 | 32.4 | 8.2 | 87.1 | 9.9 | 12 669 | 0.8 | 1 046 | 8.3 | 21 208 | 64.5 | 38.3 | 33.0 |
| Wyoming | 31.6 | 692 | 29.9 | 6.0 | 81.2 | 13.8 | 39 791 | 3.2 | 2 735 | 6.9 | 55 094 | 72.3 | 39.8 | 22.8 |
| MINNESOTA | 26.4 | 783 | 29.7 | 7.1 | 85.6 | 10.0 | 2 969 367 | 1.0 | 167 696 | 5.6 | 4 147 665 | 70.9 | 43.1 | 23.5 |
| Andover | 6.8 | 1 162 | 37.7 | 3.0 | 92.8 | 6.3 | 17 236 | 1.6 | 946 | 5.5 | 22 234 | 77.6 | 49.0 | 12.7 |
| Apple Valley | 16.9 | 1 084 | 31.3 | 3.5 | 86.9 | 9.7 | 29 512 | 1.8 | 1 447 | 4.9 | 37 634 | 77.7 | 49.3 | 16.6 |
| Blaine | 11.4 | 1 075 | 30.9 | 2.7 | 87.7 | 9.6 | 34 046 | 1.8 | 1 844 | 5.4 | 42 983 | 76.8 | 50.2 | 16.3 |
| Bloomington | 30.0 | 917 | 30.4 | 6.6 | 86.7 | 9.7 | 48 219 | 2.1 | 2 492 | 5.2 | 68 421 | 69.3 | 43.1 | 26.4 |
| Brooklyn Center | 36.4 | 895 | 36.0 | 12.0 | 80.5 | 18.3 | 16 308 | 2.3 | 1 132 | 6.9 | 22 349 | 69.3 | 42.4 | 24.7 |
| Brooklyn Park | 27.3 | 821 | 34.6 | 7.7 | 85.1 | 11.7 | 44 629 | 1.9 | 2 578 | 5.8 | 54 270 | 76.0 | 48.1 | 15.8 |
| Burnsville | 31.8 | 922 | 28.5 | 5.5 | 81.0 | 12.1 | 36 998 | 1.8 | 1 894 | 5.1 | 48 112 | 75.2 | 46.6 | 20.3 |
| Coon Rapids | 22.1 | 921 | 31.8 | 4.9 | 86.9 | 9.1 | 35 773 | 1.5 | 2 003 | 5.6 | 48 972 | 76.0 | 47.2 | 19.1 |
| Cottage Grove | 9.8 | 1 087 | 28.9 | 1.5 | 93.0 | 4.7 | 19 788 | 2.3 | 1 082 | 5.5 | 25 530 | 77.4 | 48.3 | 15.4 |
| Duluth | 40.8 | 685 | 34.4 | 12.7 | 76.0 | 10.3 | 45 788 | 0.7 | 2 868 | 6.3 | 71 835 | 65.1 | 33.2 | 29.0 |
| Eagan | 26.2 | 937 | 25.9 | 4.2 | 85.7 | 10.3 | 38 873 | 2.2 | 1 839 | 4.7 | 49 504 | 79.8 | 53.5 | 14.5 |
| Eden Prairie | 26.1 | 1 078 | 24.4 | 3.3 | 85.7 | 11.5 | 35 251 | 2.6 | 1 611 | 4.6 | 45 732 | 75.8 | 49.9 | 13.5 |
| Edina | 25.6 | 1 106 | 27.0 | 5.8 | 86.4 | 10.1 | 23 844 | 2.9 | 1 085 | 4.6 | 37 585 | 63.8 | 39.4 | 31.3 |
| Fridley | 34.9 | 851 | 27.4 | 6.2 | 81.7 | 14.1 | 15 971 | 1.9 | 925 | 5.8 | 21 783 | 69.6 | 44.2 | 24.7 |
| Inver Grove Heights | 25.4 | 972 | 27.5 | 3.2 | 86.9 | 10.2 | 20 274 | 1.6 | 1 071 | 5.3 | 26 575 | 74.1 | 47.3 | 18.9 |
| Lakeville | 8.8 | 1 131 | 31.6 | 1.2 | 91.9 | 6.7 | 31 213 | 1.9 | 1 515 | 4.9 | 39 329 | 80.2 | 53.3 | 11.9 |
| Mankato | 45.2 | 691 | 36.3 | 8.6 | 71.2 | 15.1 | 24 150 | 0.1 | 1 263 | 5.2 | 33 082 | 73.1 | 33.7 | 23.7 |
| Maple Grove | 12.0 | 1 207 | 27.0 | 2.0 | 91.2 | 7.4 | 37 808 | 2.4 | 1 719 | 4.5 | 45 280 | 79.3 | 55.5 | 12.2 |
| Maplewood | 26.9 | 863 | 32.7 | 8.5 | 86.4 | 12.1 | 20 799 | 2.4 | 1 198 | 5.8 | 29 853 | 65.0 | 40.6 | 27.0 |
| Minneapolis | 49.6 | 793 | 31.1 | 19.0 | 74.5 | 12.3 | 216 047 | 2.4 | 11 921 | 5.5 | 313 687 | 73.0 | 41.3 | 23.4 |
| Minnetonka | 25.3 | 1 045 | 26.0 | 3.8 | 87.1 | 11.1 | 29 337 | 2.5 | 1 339 | 4.6 | 40 582 | 70.0 | 45.8 | 22.2 |
| Moorhead | 37.1 | 656 | 34.8 | 7.9 | 77.4 | 13.6 | 22 567 | 5.5 | 825 | 3.7 | 30 040 | 71.0 | 36.7 | 24.0 |
| Oakdale | 22.2 | 845 | 29.7 | 4.9 | 89.6 | 8.8 | 15 746 | 1.8 | 922 | 5.9 | 21 643 | 73.6 | 45.0 | 22.2 |
| Owatonna | 26.6 | 678 | 31.0 | 8.3 | 83.4 | 8.0 | 14 936 | 1.7 | 858 | 5.7 | 19 505 | 72.5 | 46.2 | 25.0 |
| Plymouth | 27.0 | 1 057 | 27.7 | 3.2 | 85.6 | 12.2 | 41 224 | 2.6 | 1 951 | 4.7 | 55 033 | 72.9 | 47.6 | 17.9 |
| Richfield | 35.3 | 764 | 31.8 | 9.6 | 83.4 | 11.9 | 20 587 | 2.0 | 1 040 | 5.1 | 28 362 | 73.7 | 45.3 | 25.2 |
| Rochester | 28.0 | 770 | 27.9 | 6.7 | 85.1 | 7.3 | 59 801 | 2.2 | 2 695 | 4.5 | 81 892 | 72.2 | 47.6 | 19.9 |
| Roseville | 33.8 | 848 | 27.9 | 9.3 | 84.5 | 13.3 | 18 621 | 2.3 | 895 | 4.8 | 28 091 | 64.1 | 39.4 | 30.8 |
| St. Cloud | 46.4 | 687 | 35.1 | 9.0 | 69.0 | 18.0 | 38 472 | 1.0 | 2 233 | 5.8 | 55 352 | 68.7 | 33.0 | 25.2 |
| St. Louis Park | 38.8 | 920 | 26.7 | 7.6 | 79.4 | 17.2 | 28 147 | 2.3 | 1 288 | 4.6 | 37 343 | 76.5 | 51.0 | 18.7 |
| St. Paul | 47.8 | 778 | 31.8 | 15.2 | 77.9 | 11.0 | 147 105 | 2.2 | 9 057 | 6.2 | 220 898 | 70.1 | 39.5 | 24.4 |
| Savage | 11.9 | 1 041 | 28.5 | 2.6 | 90.8 | 8.3 | 15 630 | 1.9 | 797 | 5.1 | 19 355 | 81.8 | 51.2 | 8.8 |
| Shakopee | 21.0 | 921 | 27.1 | 3.8 | 87.0 | 8.9 | 22 127 | 1.6 | 1 134 | 5.1 | 26 398 | 80.4 | 56.1 | 12.7 |
| Shoreview | 15.6 | 913 | 31.4 | 3.1 | 89.8 | 8.7 | 14 863 | 2.4 | 680 | 4.6 | 20 375 | 71.1 | 45.4 | 23.0 |
| Winona | 39.2 | 568 | 34.8 | 10.5 | 75.4 | 13.6 | 15 551 | 1.7 | 897 | 5.8 | 24 288 | 69.4 | 30.0 | 27.6 |
| Woodbury | 17.6 | 1 224 | 25.6 | 2.1 | 90.0 | 7.7 | 35 233 | 2.8 | 1 619 | 4.6 | 44 532 | 76.3 | 53.3 | 14.6 |
| MISSISSIPPI | 29.4 | 680 | 32.0 | 6.9 | 85.2 | 10.7 | 1 333 046 | 1.0 | 122 060 | 9.2 | 2 287 478 | 59.4 | 37.3 | 30.7 |
| Biloxi | 46.0 | 844 | 31.4 | 7.3 | 78.9 | 15.9 | 19 576 | 0.3 | 1 981 | 10.1 | 35 585 | 69.5 | 38.7 | 25.4 |
| Clinton | 25.8 | 885 | 33.5 | 3.6 | 85.3 | 9.2 | 14 109 | 2.3 | 819 | 5.8 | 19 827 | 66.7 | 44.6 | 23.2 |
| Greenville | 46.9 | 594 | 34.8 | 14.4 | 79.9 | 7.5 | 14 184 | -3.4 | 2 024 | 14.3 | 25 845 | 58.8 | 33.2 | 35.0 |
| Gulfport | 41.1 | 834 | 35.6 | 6.1 | 76.1 | 14.3 | 31 780 | 0.6 | 3 229 | 10.2 | 52 665 | 64.1 | 36.8 | 26.8 |
| Hattiesburg | 61.8 | 657 | 35.5 | 9.7 | 71.9 | 15.7 | 22 733 | 0.0 | 2 472 | 10.9 | 37 436 | 63.9 | 33.3 | 27.7 |
| Horn Lake | 29.6 | 888 | 31.3 | 4.2 | 81.6 | 14.0 | 13 089 | 4.6 | 884 | 6.8 | 18 891 | 71.4 | 48.2 | 17.7 |
| Jackson | 46.5 | 757 | 36.4 | 9.8 | 80.4 | 6.2 | 82 744 | 1.4 | 7 494 | 9.1 | 131 390 | 62.7 | 39.6 | 27.8 |
| Meridian | 45.7 | 600 | 31.0 | 12.5 | 81.6 | 8.8 | 17 064 | 2.1 | 2 156 | 12.6 | 31 486 | 59.1 | 32.6 | 33.5 |
| Olive Branch | 18.6 | 973 | 25.8 | 1.9 | 87.6 | 9.3 | 17 210 | 3.7 | 1 177 | 6.8 | 25 031 | 71.6 | 49.6 | 17.6 |
| Pearl | 34.6 | 784 | 33.0 | 5.1 | 79.1 | 15.0 | 13 811 | 1.7 | 814 | 5.9 | 19 875 | 65.0 | 47.7 | 23.9 |
| Southaven | 31.4 | 904 | 28.1 | 2.1 | 82.8 | 11.4 | 25 399 | 4.2 | 1 558 | 6.1 | 35 255 | 71.4 | 49.2 | 18.7 |
| Tupelo | 38.9 | 606 | 31.1 | 7.1 | 81.8 | 9.8 | 17 041 | 3.9 | 1 692 | 9.9 | 26 143 | 61.8 | 40.3 | 25.8 |

1. $2,000 represents $2,000 or more.  2. 50.0 represents 50 percent or more.  3. Percent of civilian labor force.  4. Persons 16 years old and over.

# Table D. Cities — **Construction, Wholesale Trade, and Retail Trade**

| City | Value of residential construction authorized by building permits, 2011 | | | Wholesale trade,[1] 2007 | | | | Retail trade,[2] 2007 | | | |
|---|---|---|---|---|---|---|---|---|---|---|---|
| | New construction ($1,000) | Number of housing units | Percent single family | Number of establishments | Number of employees | Sales (mil dol) | Annual payroll (mil dol) | Number of establishments | Number of employees | Sales (mil dol) | Annual payroll (mil dol) |
| | 69 | 70 | 71 | 72 | 73 | 74 | 75 | 76 | 77 | 78 | 79 |
| MICHIGAN—Cont'd | | | | | | | | | | | |
| Oak Park | 0 | 0 | 0.0 | 62 | 634 | 281.9 | 34.0 | 131 | 1 030 | 221.3 | 26.1 |
| Pontiac | 2 511 | 26 | 100.0 | 54 | 1 202 | 788.0 | 83.6 | 196 | 1 566 | 377.1 | 35.4 |
| Portage | 10 608 | 44 | 68.2 | 49 | 560 | 215.6 | 33.5 | 318 | 6 241 | 1 136.8 | 109.3 |
| Port Huron | 667 | 3 | 100.0 | 18 | 189 | 140.1 | 8.9 | 130 | 1 457 | 237.5 | 26.3 |
| Rochester Hills | 43 582 | 119 | 100.0 | 79 | 946 | 450.6 | 56.5 | 255 | 5 071 | 1 183.2 | 123.0 |
| Roseville | 0 | 0 | 0.0 | 64 | 747 | 380.2 | 36.0 | 264 | 5 045 | 1 178.8 | 106.9 |
| Royal Oak | 4 867 | 29 | 100.0 | 52 | 549 | 794.4 | 34.6 | 239 | 2 884 | 632.5 | 69.1 |
| Saginaw | 75 | 1 | 100.0 | 41 | 765 | 241.9 | 26.1 | 164 | 1 340 | 233.3 | 25.9 |
| St. Clair Shores | 489 | 2 | 100.0 | 48 | 214 | 95.2 | 8.2 | 189 | 2 125 | 518.0 | 52.0 |
| Southfield | 0 | 0 | 0.0 | 193 | 3 194 | 3 250.9 | 198.4 | 434 | 6 216 | 2 165.7 | 167.2 |
| Southgate | 537 | 4 | 100.0 | 10 | 47 | 8.9 | 1.4 | 136 | 2 547 | 791.5 | 58.1 |
| Sterling Heights | 16 271 | 75 | 100.0 | 149 | 1 781 | 774.7 | 88.5 | 494 | 8 239 | 1 628.0 | 170.5 |
| Taylor | 0 | 0 | 0.0 | 91 | 1 198 | 1 205.7 | 59.4 | 319 | 5 453 | 1 189.1 | 110.7 |
| Troy | 13 596 | 55 | 100.0 | 317 | 4 196 | 2 727.4 | 237.4 | 601 | 12 596 | 2 615.6 | 298.1 |
| Warren | 381 | 3 | 100.0 | 191 | 3 524 | 1 900.1 | 170.6 | 489 | 6 337 | 1 517.6 | 150.6 |
| Westland | 1 798 | 17 | 88.2 | 55 | 547 | 171.7 | 22.3 | 349 | 5 681 | 1 119.9 | 108.0 |
| Wyandotte | 2 998 | 20 | 100.0 | 13 | 50 | 18.5 | 1.3 | 83 | 532 | 141.1 | 12.8 |
| Wyoming | 9 008 | 55 | 92.7 | 173 | 6 179 | 3 358.9 | 346.0 | 278 | 4 402 | 978.3 | 101.0 |
| MINNESOTA | 1 763 836 | 8 890 | 75.7 | 6 913 | 110 487 | 82 878.1 | 6 417.8 | 20 777 | 307 034 | 71 384.1 | 6 685.6 |
| Andover | 11 803 | 58 | 100.0 | 11 | D | D | D | 41 | 704 | 145.8 | 13.0 |
| Apple Valley | 7 929 | 31 | 100.0 | 33 | 170 | 106.5 | 8.0 | 136 | 3 726 | 839.3 | 77.4 |
| Blaine | 79 870 | 336 | 100.0 | 68 | 934 | 563.0 | 48.2 | 261 | 4 357 | 766.7 | 85.3 |
| Bloomington | 3 439 | 17 | 100.0 | 243 | 5 523 | 4 442.9 | 409.7 | 547 | 13 463 | 2 847.6 | 375.0 |
| Brooklyn Center | 0 | 0 | 0.0 | 26 | 303 | 99.2 | 10.0 | 94 | 2 331 | 672.9 | 60.7 |
| Brooklyn Park | 17 066 | 77 | 100.0 | 94 | 1 505 | 1 101.7 | 84.7 | 161 | 3 018 | 851.6 | 77.4 |
| Burnsville | 2 446 | 10 | 100.0 | 155 | 2 140 | 775.6 | 109.0 | 354 | 6 030 | 1 357.5 | 138.6 |
| Coon Rapids | 4 442 | 18 | 100.0 | 29 | 295 | 152.1 | 19.0 | 207 | 5 303 | 1 133.2 | 117.9 |
| Cottage Grove | 14 251 | 49 | 100.0 | 11 | D | D | D | 59 | 1 168 | 226.3 | 22.7 |
| Duluth | 12 838 | 102 | 29.4 | 82 | 947 | 590.9 | 40.3 | 476 | 7 090 | 1 294.7 | 136.6 |
| Eagan | 20 913 | 73 | 100.0 | 155 | 3 978 | 1 729.2 | 234.8 | 176 | 3 625 | 906.9 | 82.0 |
| Eden Prairie | 9 766 | 32 | 100.0 | 207 | 3 428 | 7 152.9 | 218.9 | 232 | 6 651 | 2 684.2 | 203.7 |
| Edina | 29 380 | 57 | 100.0 | 123 | 1 032 | 707.8 | 67.9 | 317 | 5 655 | 984.1 | 121.5 |
| Fridley | 164 | 1 | 100.0 | 74 | D | D | D | 91 | 2 346 | 598.6 | 60.4 |
| Inver Grove Heights | 8 420 | 23 | 100.0 | 20 | D | D | D | 68 | 1 467 | 413.7 | 35.3 |
| Lakeville | 40 241 | 221 | 57.9 | 52 | 594 | 255.1 | 26.4 | 110 | 2 048 | 536.9 | 45.1 |
| Mankato | 21 642 | 161 | 60.2 | 49 | 837 | 970.1 | 38.5 | 281 | 5 875 | 1 128.1 | 103.4 |
| Maple Grove | 50 208 | 245 | 90.2 | 94 | 1 501 | 1 119.7 | 121.0 | 238 | 5 145 | 886.6 | 94.5 |
| Maplewood | 2 833 | 16 | 100.0 | 34 | 314 | 175.2 | 15.2 | 247 | 5 272 | 1 130.3 | 111.5 |
| Minneapolis | 89 412 | 616 | 8.0 | 518 | 7 683 | 5 518.6 | 391.2 | 1 164 | 14 740 | 3 867.0 | 386.8 |
| Minnetonka | 16 482 | 40 | 100.0 | 152 | 2 435 | 2 873.4 | 167.9 | 324 | 7 218 | 1 581.0 | 153.1 |
| Moorhead | 23 075 | 165 | 50.9 | 30 | 349 | 261.5 | 17.0 | 127 | 2 153 | 478.1 | 42.0 |
| Oakdale | 3 722 | 18 | 100.0 | 36 | 310 | 159.2 | 17.1 | 79 | 1 513 | 358.8 | 37.1 |
| Owatonna | 6 180 | 54 | 25.9 | 18 | 288 | 176.3 | 15.1 | 123 | 2 340 | 437.7 | 43.9 |
| Plymouth | 83 796 | 288 | 76.7 | 222 | 5 164 | 3 515.5 | 309.1 | 210 | 4 234 | 1 903.3 | 133.8 |
| Richfield | 141 | 1 | 100.0 | 17 | 307 | 78.9 | 17.5 | 126 | 2 400 | 1 768.0 | 70.7 |
| Rochester | 44 352 | 219 | 89.0 | 78 | 853 | 607.7 | 39.7 | 503 | 9 700 | 1 932.1 | 204.6 |
| Roseville | 27 331 | 186 | 4.3 | 83 | 1 436 | 823.4 | 68.4 | 314 | 7 056 | 1 335.0 | 137.9 |
| St. Cloud | 12 839 | 126 | 20.6 | 77 | 2 835 | 1 125.7 | 133.3 | 370 | 7 350 | 1 481.0 | 144.5 |
| St. Louis Park | 1 609 | 5 | 100.0 | 134 | 2 016 | 1 337.4 | 115.0 | 178 | 3 976 | 1 086.9 | 106.5 |
| St. Paul | 12 174 | 75 | 41.3 | 296 | 5 321 | 3 129.2 | 290.8 | 752 | 10 077 | 1 794.1 | 209.9 |
| Savage | 27 343 | 103 | 100.0 | 36 | 802 | 732.9 | 47.7 | 74 | 1 082 | 274.1 | 24.6 |
| Shakopee | 32 161 | 119 | 100.0 | 36 | 519 | 421.2 | 30.7 | 121 | 2 226 | 544.4 | 49.3 |
| Shoreview | 3 889 | 11 | 100.0 | 29 | 2 287 | 912.6 | 140.0 | 52 | 1 073 | 193.6 | 19.3 |
| Winona | 9 230 | 100 | 13.0 | 39 | 341 | 231.0 | 13.7 | 140 | 2 560 | 461.2 | 48.2 |
| Woodbury | 75 669 | 286 | 95.1 | 40 | 270 | 119.9 | 12.1 | 224 | 4 677 | 922.4 | 85.0 |
| MISSISSIPPI | 724 061 | 5 273 | 81.0 | 2 556 | 32 382 | 23 003.6 | 1 276.0 | 12 452 | 141 426 | 33 751.4 | 2 910.9 |
| Biloxi | 26 299 | 144 | 94.4 | 38 | 408 | 160.6 | 12.7 | 227 | 2 532 | 573.4 | 52.8 |
| Clinton | 7 173 | 51 | 100.0 | 15 | 97 | 27.1 | 4.7 | 93 | 906 | 194.5 | 17.1 |
| Greenville | 519 | 3 | 100.0 | 39 | 363 | 555.9 | 20.9 | 217 | 2 295 | 418.6 | 42.1 |
| Gulfport | 56 952 | 533 | 47.7 | 86 | 961 | 604.2 | 48.8 | 409 | 6 087 | 1 641.2 | 144.9 |
| Hattiesburg | 4 371 | 37 | 67.6 | 72 | 824 | 419.9 | 29.6 | 496 | 7 567 | 2 701.3 | 159.4 |
| Horn Lake | 795 | 8 | 100.0 | 11 | 57 | 17.8 | 1.9 | 69 | 1 164 | 288.2 | 24.7 |
| Jackson | 38 399 | 301 | 49.2 | 257 | 3 995 | 1 931.9 | 179.3 | 788 | 10 919 | 2 660.1 | 255.5 |
| Meridian | 6 086 | 41 | 100.0 | 61 | 1 261 | 889.7 | 50.9 | 381 | 4 875 | 1 100.4 | 103.8 |
| Olive Branch | 9 804 | 83 | 100.0 | 47 | 846 | 615.7 | 37.8 | 115 | 1 885 | 565.8 | 46.6 |
| Pearl | 3 733 | 27 | 100.0 | 61 | 1 173 | 743.3 | 62.1 | 118 | 1 818 | 423.1 | 39.4 |
| Southaven | 11 997 | 121 | 91.7 | 28 | 1 100 | 986.0 | 36.3 | 208 | 4 015 | 1 005.8 | 88.9 |
| Tupelo | 9 663 | 63 | 100.0 | 118 | 1 446 | 690.0 | 52.0 | 410 | 5 709 | 1 212.0 | 117.6 |

1. Merchant wholesalers except manufacturers' sales branches and offices.    2. Establishments with payroll.

# Table D. Cities — Real Estate, Professional Services, and Manufacturing

| City | Real estate and rental and leasing, 2007 | | | | Professional, scientific, and technical services,[1] 2007 | | | | Manufacturing, 2007 | | | |
|---|---|---|---|---|---|---|---|---|---|---|---|---|
| | Number of establish-ments | Number of employees | Receipts (mil dol) | Annual payroll (mil dol) | Number of establish-ments | Number of employees | Receipts (mil dol) | Annual payroll (mil dol) | Number of establish-ments | Number of employees | Receipts (mil dol) | Annual payroll (mil dol) |
| | 80 | 81 | 82 | 83 | 84 | 85 | 86 | 87 | 88 | 89 | 90 | 91 |
| **MICHIGAN—Cont'd** | | | | | | | | | | | | |
| Oak Park | 36 | 485 | 26.9 | 14.7 | 40 | 203 | 25.5 | 9.6 | 61 | 1 099 | 189.1 | 45.8 |
| Pontiac | 36 | 137 | 21.0 | 4.1 | 57 | D | D | D | 52 | 4 423 | D | 416.6 |
| Portage | 52 | 1 232 | 79.8 | 35.8 | 133 | D | D | D | 64 | 7 052 | 4 511.5 | 439.1 |
| Port Huron | 31 | 134 | 16.1 | 3.3 | 75 | D | D | D | 62 | 4 210 | 1 619.5 | 184.4 |
| Rochester Hills | 47 | 217 | 33.4 | 5.6 | 253 | 3 209 | 553.3 | 188.2 | 104 | 3 147 | 868.3 | 167.7 |
| Roseville | 54 | 264 | 58.8 | 6.8 | 52 | 424 | 26.7 | 15.2 | 145 | 4 445 | 748.9 | 195.9 |
| Royal Oak | 69 | 440 | 48.5 | 14.0 | 255 | 1 957 | 184.9 | 123.2 | 73 | 1 982 | 394.6 | 59.3 |
| Saginaw | 28 | 100 | 13.3 | 2.3 | 95 | 1 114 | 92.1 | 43.0 | 62 | 3 783 | 1 543.3 | 232.1 |
| St. Clair Shores | 53 | 231 | 26.8 | 7.6 | 156 | 602 | 76.1 | 27.9 | 44 | 1 341 | D | 53.5 |
| Southfield | 252 | 3 264 | 661.7 | 129.5 | 818 | D | D | D | 89 | 3 013 | 1 041.3 | 161.4 |
| Southgate | 23 | D | D | D | 44 | 330 | 22.0 | 10.7 | NA | NA | NA | NA |
| Sterling Heights | 100 | 466 | 115.7 | 14.7 | 284 | D | D | D | 272 | 14 955 | 7 662.4 | 1 018.5 |
| Taylor | 48 | D | D | D | 86 | D | D | D | 91 | 4 058 | 1 251.1 | 171.4 |
| Troy | 147 | 1 390 | 263.6 | 51.5 | 925 | 16 536 | 2 697.5 | 1 115.9 | 270 | 8 351 | 1 590.5 | 356.0 |
| Warren | 93 | 655 | 127.0 | 21.3 | 203 | D | D | D | 381 | 16 381 | 7 570.1 | 873.5 |
| Westland | 63 | D | D | D | 66 | 432 | 35.5 | 12.1 | 71 | 1 546 | 335.1 | 70.0 |
| Wyandotte | 19 | D | D | D | 43 | D | D | D | 34 | 1 390 | 599.2 | 101.6 |
| Wyoming | 74 | 696 | 107.8 | 23.3 | 101 | D | D | D | 174 | 8 535 | 2 542.0 | 443.5 |
| **MINNESOTA** | 6 889 | 39 430 | 9 208.0 | 1 317.4 | 16 595 | 140 786 | 20 473.1 | 8 425.3 | 7 951 | 340 514 | 107 563.1 | 15 999.2 |
| Andover | 40 | 182 | 15.3 | 3.4 | 78 | 331 | 20.8 | 9.3 | NA | NA | NA | NA |
| Apple Valley | 65 | 278 | 43.5 | 6.0 | 155 | D | D | D | 16 | 551 | D | 27.6 |
| Blaine | 68 | 251 | 63.0 | 6.7 | 110 | D | D | D | 152 | 3 511 | 477.2 | 155.4 |
| Bloomington | 208 | 3 531 | 636.9 | 184.3 | 618 | D | D | D | 145 | 8 561 | 1 444.5 | 478.0 |
| Brooklyn Center | 30 | D | D | D | 67 | 412 | 51.1 | 22.0 | 33 | 2 076 | 346.3 | 98.7 |
| Brooklyn Park | 57 | 298 | 43.3 | 10.2 | 144 | 813 | 155.4 | 45.3 | 117 | 5 704 | 1 325.6 | 320.7 |
| Burnsville | 119 | 564 | 87.3 | 21.8 | 301 | D | D | D | 109 | 3 522 | 824.3 | 162.6 |
| Coon Rapids | 78 | 227 | 31.9 | 5.5 | 131 | 780 | 94.4 | 37.5 | 67 | 3 318 | 866.4 | 178.9 |
| Cottage Grove | 28 | 69 | 10.5 | 1.2 | 44 | 99 | 9.7 | 3.3 | 14 | 1 580 | 719.9 | 93.3 |
| Duluth | 125 | 692 | 102.7 | 15.2 | 249 | D | D | D | 91 | 3 111 | 1 081.1 | 139.8 |
| Eagan | 113 | 535 | 108.3 | 19.1 | 340 | D | D | D | 93 | 3 607 | 1 196.9 | 176.5 |
| Eden Prairie | 147 | 1 478 | 485.3 | 57.4 | 450 | 11 071 | 1 396.2 | 500.1 | 109 | 9 043 | 1 956.4 | 516.0 |
| Edina | 229 | 1 990 | 338.3 | 73.1 | 518 | D | D | D | 73 | 1 847 | 578.8 | 91.8 |
| Fridley | 34 | 274 | 83.6 | 5.5 | 82 | 446 | 58.3 | 27.2 | 130 | 7 953 | 2 612.6 | 447.6 |
| Inver Grove Heights | 30 | 77 | 14.5 | 2.5 | 108 | 678 | 46.3 | 50.6 | 29 | 856 | 284.9 | 44.9 |
| Lakeville | 87 | 228 | 33.3 | 6.5 | 162 | 396 | 54.2 | 21.6 | 74 | 3 057 | 714.3 | 132.5 |
| Mankato | 71 | 620 | 72.7 | 13.1 | 109 | D | D | D | 51 | 2 838 | 2 349.3 | 116.0 |
| Maple Grove | 93 | 269 | 41.3 | 9.9 | 291 | 1 120 | 141.5 | 74.2 | 105 | 7 124 | 2 443.1 | 436.8 |
| Maplewood | 60 | 235 | 43.6 | 4.3 | 90 | 580 | 123.3 | 28.5 | 26 | 562 | 165.0 | 23.7 |
| Minneapolis | 651 | 4 429 | 3 014.6 | 159.5 | 2 305 | D | D | D | 499 | 15 783 | 4 107.5 | 778.0 |
| Minnetonka | 157 | 1 087 | 344.2 | 73.9 | 485 | 4 586 | 698.7 | 323.6 | 86 | 4 543 | 1 393.9 | 263.1 |
| Moorhead | 31 | 167 | 16.0 | 3.0 | 44 | D | D | D | 29 | D | D | D |
| Oakdale | 24 | 90 | 16.5 | 2.8 | 87 | 596 | 82.4 | 28.7 | 40 | 997 | 275.7 | 46.8 |
| Owatonna | 24 | 241 | 12.4 | 4.2 | 45 | 142 | 14.7 | 4.7 | 43 | 5 287 | 1 309.6 | 244.8 |
| Plymouth | 168 | 758 | 827.3 | 38.2 | 468 | 5 079 | 1 119.4 | 310.9 | 194 | 11 757 | 3 583.4 | 662.4 |
| Richfield | 26 | D | D | D | 96 | 373 | 42.5 | 17.8 | NA | NA | NA | NA |
| Rochester | 136 | 735 | 108.7 | 19.6 | 231 | D | D | D | 62 | 8 002 | 2 798.6 | 535.3 |
| Roseville | 74 | 702 | 137.2 | 28.4 | 210 | D | D | D | 66 | 2 435 | 568.5 | 111.6 |
| St. Cloud | 106 | 802 | 91.9 | 20.3 | 172 | D | D | D | 71 | 7 544 | 1 926.4 | 302.6 |
| St. Louis Park | 135 | 1 867 | 191.1 | 54.0 | 359 | D | D | D | 78 | 3 302 | 720.0 | 158.0 |
| St. Paul | 362 | 3 273 | 474.6 | 126.4 | 968 | D | D | D | 263 | 9 382 | 3 509.0 | 527.8 |
| Savage | 45 | 105 | 22.2 | 3.2 | 109 | 254 | 39.0 | 11.2 | 39 | 1 270 | 486.9 | 60.9 |
| Shakopee | 44 | 124 | 17.6 | 3.1 | 90 | D | D | D | 41 | 3 413 | 1 194.9 | 227.1 |
| Shoreview | 36 | 120 | 19.2 | 3.0 | 124 | 429 | 52.6 | 22.0 | 30 | 1 157 | 295.2 | 62.1 |
| Winona | 39 | 108 | 14.4 | 2.0 | 60 | D | D | D | 68 | 3 313 | D | 133.5 |
| Woodbury | 99 | 288 | 63.3 | 7.8 | 248 | 901 | 141.8 | 44.0 | 20 | 918 | 202.6 | 44.5 |
| **MISSISSIPPI** | 2 517 | 10 169 | 1 734.6 | 283.7 | 4 751 | 30 855 | 3 971.9 | 1 350.3 | 2 598 | 159 235 | 59 869.5 | 5 756.6 |
| Biloxi | 82 | 326 | 58.5 | 9.3 | 147 | D | D | D | NA | NA | NA | NA |
| Clinton | 27 | 74 | 10.4 | 1.4 | 52 | 206 | 20.4 | 7.3 | 14 | D | D | 46.8 |
| Greenville | 49 | 245 | 27.8 | 7.5 | 72 | D | D | D | 32 | 1 435 | 652.9 | 55.6 |
| Gulfport | 118 | 448 | 85.5 | 15.5 | 189 | D | D | D | 56 | 1 809 | 346.6 | 65.4 |
| Hattiesburg | 111 | 442 | 65.4 | 12.5 | 201 | D | D | D | 60 | 3 846 | 788.4 | 117.6 |
| Horn Lake | 16 | 57 | 13.2 | 1.3 | 14 | 56 | 3.8 | 1.1 | 15 | 640 | 187.7 | 32.5 |
| Jackson | 241 | 1 605 | 402.4 | 58.9 | 613 | D | D | D | 122 | 3 732 | 893.3 | 157.6 |
| Meridian | 65 | 262 | 35.7 | 5.5 | 105 | D | D | D | 48 | 1 662 | 330.1 | 50.6 |
| Olive Branch | 35 | 164 | 26.2 | 4.9 | 34 | 127 | 10.8 | 3.4 | 71 | 2 903 | 1 139.9 | 129.4 |
| Pearl | 33 | 180 | 30.2 | 5.4 | 24 | 135 | 26.7 | 5.4 | 28 | 582 | 407.0 | 25.7 |
| Southaven | 37 | 144 | 42.1 | 4.2 | 75 | 509 | 37.3 | 14.0 | NA | NA | NA | NA |
| Tupelo | 80 | 365 | 69.8 | 10.3 | 163 | D | D | D | 89 | 5 055 | 1 348.5 | 188.8 |

1. Establishments subject to federal tax.

# Accommodation and Food Services, Arts, Entertainment, and Recreation, and Health Care and Social Assistance

| City | Accommodation and food services, 2007 | | | | Arts, entertainment, and recreation,[1] 2007 | | | | Health care and social assistance,[1] 2007 | | | |
|---|---|---|---|---|---|---|---|---|---|---|---|---|
| | Number of establish-ments | Number of employees | Sales (mil dol) | Annual payroll (mil dol) | Number of establish-ments | Number of employees | Receipts (mil dol) | Annual payroll (mil dol) | Number of establish-ments | Number of employees | Receipts (mil dol) | Annual payroll (mil dol) |
| | 92 | 93 | 94 | 95 | 96 | 97 | 98 | 99 | 100 | 101 | 102 | 103 |
| **MICHIGAN—Cont'd** | | | | | | | | | | | | |
| Oak Park | 39 | 454 | 19.6 | 5.5 | 3 | 3 | 0.1 | 0.0 | 69 | 604 | 39.3 | 14.9 |
| Pontiac | 116 | 1 491 | 82.8 | 21.7 | 14 | D | D | D | 112 | 1 117 | 138.3 | 61.8 |
| Portage | 133 | 3 641 | 121.4 | 37.7 | 13 | D | D | D | 161 | 1 836 | 152.3 | 69.7 |
| Port Huron | 69 | 1 059 | 43.2 | 12.5 | 15 | D | D | D | 133 | 1 244 | 156.8 | 78.8 |
| Rochester Hills | 121 | D | D | D | 15 | D | D | D | 264 | 3 063 | 268.1 | 123.7 |
| Roseville | 107 | 2 900 | 116.2 | 36.1 | 9 | 106 | 5.0 | 1.2 | 101 | 1 071 | 81.4 | 37.8 |
| Royal Oak | 142 | 2 966 | 135.0 | 39.6 | 20 | D | D | D | 165 | D | D | D |
| Saginaw | 92 | 1 172 | 42.2 | 11.5 | 3 | D | D | D | 118 | 1 715 | 167.8 | 73.4 |
| St. Clair Shores | 116 | 1 995 | 80.8 | 23.1 | 26 | D | D | D | 193 | 1 934 | 200.9 | 94.2 |
| Southfield | 254 | 4 114 | 213.8 | 59.4 | 27 | 486 | 24.2 | 8.8 | 682 | 9 139 | 988.0 | 396.1 |
| Southgate | 86 | 2 234 | 98.5 | 28.7 | 2 | D | D | D | 98 | 718 | 90.9 | 31.6 |
| Sterling Heights | 232 | 5 096 | 207.6 | 66.9 | 30 | 345 | 28.5 | 7.9 | 292 | 3 412 | 282.9 | 122.9 |
| Taylor | 138 | 2 486 | 97.9 | 28.2 | 11 | D | D | D | 111 | 1 632 | 138.1 | 54.5 |
| Troy | 277 | 6 365 | 325.4 | 96.9 | 33 | D | D | D | 432 | D | D | D |
| Warren | 309 | 4 992 | 216.1 | 60.1 | 21 | 309 | 14.8 | 4.1 | 334 | D | D | D |
| Westland | 143 | 2 825 | 114.1 | 32.2 | 14 | D | D | D | 139 | 1 694 | 129.0 | 57.2 |
| Wyandotte | 58 | 668 | 27.7 | 7.4 | 5 | D | D | D | 45 | D | D | D |
| Wyoming | 124 | 2 182 | 87.9 | 23.8 | 16 | D | D | D | 86 | 1 035 | 88.2 | 38.1 |
| **MINNESOTA** | 11 340 | 221 081 | 10 423.7 | 2 978.4 | 1 990 | 28 038 | 2 185.6 | 796.1 | 10 263 | 157 035 | 13 229.6 | 6 021.1 |
| Andover | 23 | 424 | 15.7 | 4.5 | 6 | D | D | D | 27 | D | D | D |
| Apple Valley | 69 | 1 736 | 77.6 | 23.4 | 12 | 116 | 9.5 | 1.4 | 105 | 993 | 104.0 | 36.4 |
| Blaine | 97 | 2 430 | 93.3 | 29.3 | 12 | D | D | D | 69 | D | D | D |
| Bloomington | 258 | 7 752 | 459.7 | 137.3 | 35 | 684 | 31.0 | 9.2 | 181 | 3 061 | 249.3 | 111.4 |
| Brooklyn Center | 50 | 976 | 50.5 | 14.2 | 5 | 65 | 2.5 | 0.9 | 79 | 1 174 | 91.5 | 36.6 |
| Brooklyn Park | 79 | 1 745 | 75.5 | 23.0 | 12 | D | D | D | 103 | 1 411 | 81.8 | 34.2 |
| Burnsville | 128 | 3 128 | 126.2 | 39.4 | 25 | 760 | 16.8 | 4.7 | 188 | D | D | D |
| Coon Rapids | 106 | 2 918 | 110.1 | 33.8 | 19 | D | D | D | 130 | D | D | D |
| Cottage Grove | 38 | 693 | 25.9 | 7.2 | 6 | 84 | 3.3 | 1.0 | 37 | 453 | 44.9 | 15.0 |
| Duluth | 230 | 5 249 | 211.0 | 61.8 | 31 | 193 | 9.6 | 2.4 | 264 | 4 379 | 380.4 | 174.5 |
| Eagan | 128 | 3 250 | 155.2 | 45.4 | 13 | D | D | D | 138 | 2 553 | 211.5 | 85.6 |
| Eden Prairie | 139 | 3 182 | 154.2 | 51.5 | 34 | D | D | D | 119 | 1 914 | 229.2 | 94.8 |
| Edina | 100 | 2 950 | 161.0 | 48.2 | 23 | 98 | 7.1 | 2.2 | 340 | D | D | D |
| Fridley | 47 | 680 | 34.8 | 9.8 | 7 | D | D | D | 66 | D | D | D |
| Inver Grove Heights | 50 | 944 | 41.1 | 11.9 | 11 | D | D | D | 56 | 526 | 43.4 | 19.8 |
| Lakeville | 59 | 1 682 | 54.4 | 18.0 | 19 | 224 | 15.0 | 4.9 | 77 | 795 | 60.7 | 23.1 |
| Mankato | 144 | 3 813 | 132.8 | 39.4 | 14 | 110 | 10.2 | 1.8 | 112 | D | D | D |
| Maple Grove | 103 | 3 326 | 147.6 | 45.5 | 18 | D | D | D | 118 | 2 183 | 192.1 | 80.1 |
| Maplewood | 92 | 2 367 | 97.5 | 29.1 | 16 | D | D | D | 132 | 1 808 | 301.0 | 98.4 |
| Minneapolis | 1 095 | 24 428 | 1 333.5 | 421.5 | 167 | 2 758 | 502.7 | 235.6 | 746 | 13 034 | 1 258.1 | 627.4 |
| Minnetonka | 108 | 2 708 | 142.2 | 43.9 | 24 | 356 | 22.3 | 8.0 | 124 | 1 749 | 211.0 | 84.2 |
| Moorhead | 63 | 1 354 | 50.0 | 14.6 | 7 | D | D | D | 65 | 639 | 39.1 | 17.2 |
| Oakdale | 39 | 992 | 66.0 | 15.6 | 9 | D | D | D | 40 | 248 | 24.5 | 7.3 |
| Owatonna | 72 | 1 373 | 62.7 | 15.6 | 7 | D | D | D | 69 | D | D | D |
| Plymouth | 128 | 2 771 | 122.3 | 37.5 | 25 | 346 | 25.0 | 5.9 | 190 | 1 995 | 262.5 | 131.3 |
| Richfield | 64 | 1 254 | 68.6 | 18.2 | 6 | D | D | D | 72 | 1 414 | 101.2 | 42.8 |
| Rochester | 278 | 6 882 | 312.8 | 89.6 | 23 | D | D | D | 197 | D | D | D |
| Roseville | 124 | 3 672 | 151.0 | 51.6 | 18 | D | D | D | 129 | 3 307 | 285.6 | 119.5 |
| St. Cloud | 160 | 4 467 | 164.2 | 47.3 | 24 | 242 | 19.9 | 4.1 | 178 | 3 917 | 360.2 | 212.9 |
| St. Louis Park | 93 | 2 341 | 106.0 | 34.6 | 19 | D | D | D | 178 | D | D | D |
| St. Paul | 598 | 10 672 | 499.5 | 148.0 | 82 | 2 225 | 153.2 | 70.7 | 643 | 12 304 | 992.8 | 472.5 |
| Savage | 38 | D | D | D | 9 | 236 | 10.0 | 2.8 | 38 | D | D | D |
| Shakopee | 72 | 1 520 | 69.0 | 21.3 | 18 | D | D | D | 67 | 611 | 56.2 | 25.0 |
| Shoreview | 29 | 569 | 26.2 | 7.3 | 4 | D | D | D | 55 | 556 | 48.7 | 21.0 |
| Winona | 78 | 1 654 | 58.7 | 14.8 | 16 | D | D | D | 53 | D | D | D |
| Woodbury | 97 | 2 512 | 96.2 | 30.0 | 14 | D | D | D | 141 | D | D | D |
| **MISSISSIPPI** | 4 817 | 119 626 | 7 045.1 | 1 812.3 | 506 | 5 960 | 425.4 | 112.4 | 4 858 | 72 601 | 7 228.8 | 2 752.9 |
| Biloxi | 104 | 11 235 | 1 247.1 | 331.2 | 15 | D | D | D | 126 | 2 213 | 256.7 | 86.9 |
| Clinton | 54 | 1 168 | 45.1 | 11.2 | 5 | D | D | D | 46 | 782 | 47.3 | 17.5 |
| Greenville | 75 | 1 462 | 91.0 | 19.7 | 9 | D | D | D | 113 | 951 | 71.5 | 28.4 |
| Gulfport | 162 | 5 009 | 304.1 | 84.3 | 16 | 161 | 10.7 | 3.8 | 208 | D | D | D |
| Hattiesburg | 213 | 5 429 | 217.0 | 60.2 | 16 | D | D | D | 180 | D | D | D |
| Horn Lake | 46 | 1 176 | 50.9 | 13.1 | 5 | 42 | 1.4 | 0.4 | 11 | D | D | D |
| Jackson | 363 | 7 472 | 335.7 | 90.3 | 24 | 524 | 47.3 | 10.2 | 505 | 8 491 | 1 066.8 | 406.5 |
| Meridian | 140 | 3 511 | 131.8 | 36.9 | 10 | D | D | D | 155 | D | D | D |
| Olive Branch | 66 | 1 609 | 64.5 | 17.6 | 9 | D | D | D | 44 | 250 | 29.4 | 9.9 |
| Pearl | 62 | 1 455 | 61.2 | 16.6 | 6 | D | D | D | 26 | 250 | 29.4 | 9.9 |
| Southaven | 118 | 2 967 | 124.6 | 31.9 | 13 | D | D | D | 106 | D | D | D |
| Tupelo | 164 | 3 657 | 131.9 | 37.0 | 8 | D | D | D | 166 | D | D | D |

1. Establishments subject to federal tax.

# Table D. Cities — Other Services and Federal Funds

| City | Other services¹, 2007 | | | | Selected federal funds, 2009–2010 (mil dol) | | | | | | | | |
| | | | | | Procurement contracts | | Grants | | | | | | |
| | Number of establishments | Number of employees | Receipts (mil dol) | Annual payroll (mil dol) | Defense | Other | Total² | Medicaid and other health related | Nutrition and family welfare | Energy and environment | Disasters and emergency preparedness | Housing and community development | Employment and training |
| | 104 | 105 | 106 | 107 | 108 | 109 | 110 | 111 | 112 | 113 | 114 | 115 | 116 |
| **MICHIGAN—Cont'd** | | | | | | | | | | | | | |
| Oak Park | 34 | 139 | 12.3 | 4.4 | 0.1 | 3.2 | 7.9 | 0.0 | 0.0 | 0.0 | 0.0 | 7.7 | 0.0 |
| Pontiac | 65 | 476 | 43.0 | 13.7 | 3.9 | 6.2 | 142.1 | 2.4 | 0.0 | 122.0 | 0.0 | 13.2 | 0.7 |
| Portage | 91 | D | D | D | 0.8 | 3.0 | 10.4 | 0.0 | 0.0 | 0.0 | 0.0 | 0.2 | 0.0 |
| Port Huron | 40 | 228 | 14.0 | 4.7 | 26.6 | 2.8 | 17.2 | 0.2 | 2.9 | 3.4 | 0.0 | 5.7 | 0.0 |
| Rochester Hills | 95 | 606 | 40.1 | 13.4 | 1.5 | 0.1 | 1.4 | 0.0 | 0.0 | 0.0 | 0.0 | 0.0 | 0.0 |
| Roseville | 86 | 464 | 34.9 | 10.8 | 7.2 | 0.3 | 2.9 | 0.0 | 0.0 | 0.0 | 0.0 | 2.8 | 0.0 |
| Royal Oak | 110 | 687 | 48.8 | 16.2 | 0.5 | 0.4 | 7.5 | 3.5 | 0.0 | 0.5 | 0.0 | 2.8 | 0.0 |
| Saginaw | 57 | 243 | 16.9 | 4.8 | 15.9 | 17.5 | 29.2 | 4.5 | 7.2 | 1.4 | 0.0 | 12.0 | 0.0 |
| St. Clair Shores | 97 | 497 | 28.1 | 8.9 | 0.2 | 0.7 | 2.6 | 0.0 | 0.0 | 0.5 | 0.0 | 1.9 | 0.0 |
| Southfield | 142 | 808 | 65.8 | 21.5 | 81.5 | 22.9 | 30.1 | 4.5 | 2.6 | 15.0 | 0.0 | 5.3 | 0.0 |
| Southgate | 54 | 506 | 79.9 | 19.3 | 0.1 | 0.0 | 3.0 | 0.0 | 0.0 | 1.2 | 0.0 | 0.1 | 0.0 |
| Sterling Heights | 158 | 809 | 62.6 | 20.5 | 2 108.9 | 35.8 | 7.1 | 0.5 | 0.0 | 1.2 | 0.0 | 1.4 | 0.0 |
| Taylor | 112 | 1 122 | 99.2 | 39.2 | 0.7 | 0.2 | 13.8 | 0.0 | 0.0 | 0.0 | 0.0 | 12.3 | 0.0 |
| Troy | 198 | 1 515 | 117.1 | 40.1 | 41.2 | 138.0 | 267.8 | 0.7 | 9.5 | 251.9 | 0.0 | 2.4 | 0.4 |
| Warren | 222 | 1 615 | 168.9 | 56.0 | 157.2 | 17.9 | 56.2 | 0.3 | 0.0 | 44.3 | 0.0 | 1.8 | 5.0 |
| Westland | 118 | 741 | 67.2 | 20.8 | 1.0 | 0.2 | 34.8 | 0.7 | 24.1 | 0.7 | 0.0 | 8.8 | 0.0 |
| Wyandotte | 55 | 237 | 20.5 | 5.3 | 0.2 | 1.8 | 3.8 | 0.0 | 0.0 | 3.8 | 0.0 | 0.0 | 0.0 |
| Wyoming | 124 | 790 | 67.5 | 23.6 | 0.5 | 0.3 | 10.6 | 0.0 | 0.0 | 0.0 | 0.0 | 9.4 | 0.0 |
| **MINNESOTA** | 8 519 | 52 215 | 4 106.5 | 1 281.6 | 1 520.3 | 1 430.1 | 10 527.8 | 6 006.5 | 1 249.2 | 223.7 | 26.4 | 437.2 | 187.0 |
| Andover | 36 | D | D | D | 0.0 | 0.0 | 0.0 | 0.0 | 0.0 | 0.0 | 0.0 | 0.0 | 0.0 |
| Apple Valley | 61 | 422 | 31.8 | 11.4 | 0.1 | 0.2 | 0.5 | 0.0 | 0.0 | 0.5 | 0.0 | 0.0 | 0.0 |
| Blaine | 113 | D | D | D | 0.1 | 0.0 | 4.2 | 0.0 | 0.0 | 4.2 | 0.0 | 0.0 | 0.0 |
| Bloomington | 166 | 1 575 | 101.7 | 41.3 | 11.7 | 21.6 | 8.2 | 1.6 | 0.0 | 0.0 | 0.0 | 6.3 | 0.0 |
| Brooklyn Center | 23 | 146 | 6.8 | 2.5 | 0.1 | 0.5 | 0.1 | 0.0 | 0.0 | 0.1 | 0.0 | 0.0 | 0.0 |
| Brooklyn Park | 86 | 613 | 46.2 | 16.4 | 2.5 | 3.6 | 2.7 | 0.0 | 0.0 | 0.0 | 0.0 | 0.0 | 2.6 |
| Burnsville | 106 | 819 | 58.8 | 20.6 | 29.7 | 3.2 | 2.0 | 0.0 | 0.0 | 0.4 | 0.0 | 0.0 | 0.0 |
| Coon Rapids | 77 | D | D | D | 0.0 | 0.5 | 0.5 | 0.0 | 0.0 | 0.4 | 0.0 | 0.0 | 0.0 |
| Cottage Grove | 28 | D | D | D | 0.3 | 0.1 | 0.1 | 0.0 | 0.0 | 0.0 | 0.0 | 0.0 | 0.0 |
| Duluth | 137 | 942 | 54.3 | 19.5 | 22.5 | 22.0 | 49.7 | 4.4 | 3.7 | 2.8 | 0.0 | 15.1 | 0.0 |
| Eagan | 112 | 1 216 | 117.9 | 37.0 | 160.5 | 7.1 | 23.6 | 0.0 | 0.0 | 1.5 | 0.0 | 21.9 | 0.0 |
| Eden Prairie | 114 | 947 | 70.7 | 24.8 | 15.2 | 70.7 | 6.6 | 5.4 | 0.0 | 0.6 | 0.0 | 0.3 | 0.0 |
| Edina | 81 | 997 | 75.1 | 26.5 | 2.4 | 26.3 | 0.7 | 0.7 | 0.0 | 0.0 | 0.0 | 0.0 | 0.0 |
| Fridley | 54 | D | D | D | 0.4 | 3.8 | 0.0 | 0.0 | 0.0 | 0.0 | 0.0 | 0.0 | 0.0 |
| Inver Grove Heights | 50 | 291 | 19.4 | 6.9 | 0.2 | 9.8 | -0.1 | 0.0 | 0.0 | 0.0 | 0.0 | 0.0 | 0.0 |
| Lakeville | 79 | 506 | 45.2 | 15.6 | 0.1 | 0.1 | 0.0 | 0.0 | 0.0 | 0.0 | 0.0 | 0.0 | 0.0 |
| Mankato | 87 | D | D | D | 0.0 | 0.5 | 12.5 | 0.1 | 2.9 | 0.7 | 0.0 | 6.8 | 0.0 |
| Maple Grove | 87 | 841 | 59.3 | 20.9 | 4.1 | 1.9 | 9.2 | 8.8 | 0.0 | 0.0 | 0.0 | 0.0 | 0.0 |
| Maplewood | 82 | D | D | D | 0.0 | 0.0 | 3.0 | 0.0 | 0.0 | 0.6 | 0.0 | 0.0 | 0.0 |
| Minneapolis | 685 | 5 055 | 426.7 | 130.5 | 516.9 | 296.3 | 1 161.7 | 601.3 | 22.0 | 27.5 | 3.8 | 104.4 | 15.2 |
| Minnetonka | 85 | 703 | 38.2 | 14.8 | 2.1 | 0.8 | 0.9 | 0.7 | 0.0 | 0.0 | 0.0 | 0.2 | 0.0 |
| Moorhead | 62 | D | D | D | 50.7 | 0.0 | 6.3 | 2.3 | 1.8 | 0.0 | 0.0 | 1.1 | 0.0 |
| Oakdale | 34 | 114 | 10.3 | 3.3 | 1.7 | 1.9 | 0.6 | 0.1 | 0.0 | 0.4 | 0.0 | 0.1 | 0.0 |
| Owatonna | 49 | D | D | D | 1.6 | 0.1 | 1.1 | 0.1 | 0.0 | 0.0 | 0.0 | 0.6 | 0.0 |
| Plymouth | 89 | 593 | 42.6 | 14.7 | 1.2 | 6.4 | 7.6 | 0.0 | 0.0 | 3.9 | 0.0 | 3.3 | 0.0 |
| Richfield | 56 | 337 | 24.7 | 9.2 | 0.1 | 0.5 | 1.6 | 0.1 | 0.0 | 0.0 | 0.0 | 1.6 | 0.0 |
| Rochester | 147 | D | D | D | 3.2 | 5.0 | 22.1 | 0.8 | 2.1 | 0.0 | 0.0 | 4.2 | 0.0 |
| Roseville | 83 | 940 | 73.5 | 25.1 | 0.0 | 0.0 | 3.3 | 0.0 | 0.0 | 0.0 | 0.0 | 0.0 | 0.0 |
| St. Cloud | 119 | 916 | 76.5 | 24.6 | 0.2 | 36.5 | 15.5 | 0.2 | 3.2 | 0.0 | 0.0 | 6.5 | 0.0 |
| St. Louis Park | 97 | 501 | 36.4 | 11.3 | 0.1 | 1.2 | 8.8 | 5.9 | 0.0 | 0.0 | 0.0 | 2.9 | 0.0 |
| St. Paul | 398 | 2 848 | 216.0 | 71.5 | 80.6 | 78.2 | 1 309.5 | 137.2 | 183.7 | 155.6 | 0.4 | 168.7 | 148.5 |
| Savage | 50 | D | D | D | 0.4 | 0.0 | 0.0 | 0.0 | 0.0 | 0.0 | 0.0 | 0.0 | 0.0 |
| Shakopee | 56 | D | D | D | 0.0 | 0.4 | 5.4 | 0.0 | 2.2 | 0.0 | 0.0 | 3.1 | 0.0 |
| Shoreview | 25 | D | D | D | 0.0 | 0.0 | 0.0 | 0.0 | 0.0 | 0.0 | 0.0 | 0.0 | 0.0 |
| Winona | 46 | D | D | D | 2.9 | 0.3 | 5.1 | 0.1 | 0.0 | 1.5 | 0.0 | 1.3 | 0.1 |
| Woodbury | 73 | 663 | 38.4 | 14.7 | 0.1 | 0.0 | 0.2 | 0.0 | 0.0 | 0.0 | 0.0 | 0.2 | 0.0 |
| **MISSISSIPPI** | 3 076 | 16 201 | 1 295.3 | 373.2 | 1 634.0 | 1 031.9 | 7 871.1 | 4 459.9 | 856.9 | 259.2 | 185.7 | 233.4 | 95.6 |
| Biloxi | 48 | 331 | 28.7 | 8.7 | 168.6 | 34.9 | 42.5 | 5.5 | 0.5 | 25.6 | 0.0 | 5.7 | 0.1 |
| Clinton | 24 | 142 | 10.8 | 3.9 | 0.0 | 0.1 | 0.3 | 0.0 | 0.0 | 0.0 | 0.0 | 0.0 | 0.0 |
| Greenville | 55 | D | D | D | 1.0 | 2.6 | 12.7 | 0.3 | 7.3 | 0.2 | 0.0 | 0.0 | 0.3 |
| Gulfport | 119 | 720 | 74.6 | 20.5 | 90.0 | 34.7 | 68.7 | 0.9 | 9.3 | -1.6 | 0.0 | 50.8 | 0.0 |
| Hattiesburg | 89 | 644 | 37.1 | 12.0 | 31.5 | 5.3 | 99.8 | 16.8 | 5.9 | 35.1 | 0.0 | 2.5 | 0.4 |
| Horn Lake | 24 | D | D | D | 0.0 | 0.3 | 0.0 | 0.0 | 0.0 | 0.0 | 0.0 | 0.0 | 0.0 |
| Jackson | 239 | 1 797 | 108.9 | 36.2 | 31.0 | 102.6 | 1 183.5 | 171.9 | 175.3 | 68.4 | 101.1 | 99.2 | 86.3 |
| Meridian | 95 | D | D | D | 12.9 | 1.3 | 15.4 | 2.8 | 0.0 | 0.0 | 0.0 | 3.7 | 4.5 |
| Olive Branch | 38 | D | D | D | 0.1 | 1.5 | 0.0 | 0.0 | 0.0 | 0.0 | 0.0 | 0.0 | 0.0 |
| Pearl | 50 | 233 | 20.9 | 6.1 | 0.2 | 0.4 | 5.5 | 4.5 | 0.0 | 0.0 | 0.0 | 0.0 | 0.0 |
| Southaven | 57 | 385 | 29.8 | 9.9 | 0.6 | 0.1 | 0.2 | 0.0 | 0.0 | 0.2 | 0.0 | 0.0 | 0.0 |
| Tupelo | 87 | D | D | D | 0.6 | 21.0 | 2.2 | 0.0 | 0.0 | 0.0 | 0.0 | 0.7 | 0.0 |

1. Establishments subject to federal tax.   2. Includes program categories not shown separately. State totals include additional categories not allocated by city.

# Table D. Cities — City Government Finances

| City | City government finances, 2007 | | | | | | | | | |
|------|------|------|------|------|------|------|------|------|------|------|
| | General revenue | | | | | | | General expenditure | | |
| | | Intergovernmental | | Taxes | | | | | Per capita[1] (dollars) | |
| | | | | | Per capita[1] (dollars) | | | | | |
| | Total (mil dol) | Total (mil dol) | Percent from state government | Total (mil dol) | Total | Property | Sales and gross receipts | Total (mil dol) | Total | Capital outlays |
| | 117 | 118 | 119 | 120 | 121 | 122 | 123 | 124 | 125 | 126 |
| MICHIGAN—Cont'd | | | | | | | | | | |
| Oak Park | 34.3 | 4.6 | 95.9 | 17.4 | 567 | 554 | 13 | 39.5 | 1 285 | 232 |
| Pontiac | 107.6 | 31.6 | 60.3 | 47.0 | 707 | 465 | 38 | 114.0 | 1 714 | 136 |
| Portage | 40.5 | 8.0 | 94.0 | 22.4 | 487 | 462 | 25 | 41.5 | 900 | 143 |
| Port Huron | 58.3 | 13.3 | 63.7 | 23.9 | 770 | 540 | 24 | 59.3 | 1 907 | 335 |
| Rochester Hills | 74.4 | 16.4 | 59.3 | 33.0 | 475 | 445 | 30 | 63.4 | 914 | 68 |
| Roseville | 58.8 | 12.0 | 68.9 | 29.7 | 632 | 623 | 9 | 52.8 | 1 124 | 67 |
| Royal Oak | 75.7 | 15.6 | 64.0 | 31.7 | 552 | 505 | 47 | 72.2 | 1 257 | 136 |
| Saginaw | 88.7 | 28.1 | 55.7 | 27.0 | 480 | 208 | 31 | 82.2 | 1 461 | 116 |
| St. Clair Shores | 75.9 | 17.9 | 61.0 | 37.5 | 619 | 598 | 21 | 65.3 | 1 076 | 136 |
| Southfield | 102.6 | 21.1 | 55.6 | 62.2 | 826 | 794 | 31 | 110.2 | 1 461 | 102 |
| Southgate | 34.5 | 5.2 | 96.9 | 18.9 | 662 | 643 | 19 | 33.5 | 1 176 | 29 |
| Sterling Heights | 115.7 | 23.3 | 85.5 | 57.4 | 451 | 437 | 14 | 114.8 | 901 | 117 |
| Taylor | 128.7 | 31.4 | 39.3 | 53.9 | 864 | 821 | 42 | 107.6 | 1 726 | 8 |
| Troy | 102.8 | 14.0 | 84.5 | 56.8 | 705 | 687 | 19 | 96.0 | 1 191 | 171 |
| Warren | 157.1 | 27.9 | 90.4 | 87.3 | 650 | 633 | 17 | 175.4 | 1 306 | 224 |
| Westland | 90.0 | 28.4 | 58.0 | 33.7 | 414 | 399 | 15 | 82.0 | 1 009 | 27 |
| Wyandotte | 45.2 | 8.0 | 64.2 | 18.4 | 717 | 696 | 21 | 55.2 | 2 154 | 330 |
| Wyoming | 85.3 | 21.7 | 50.3 | 26.7 | 379 | 344 | 35 | 101.7 | 1 443 | 488 |
| MINNESOTA | X | X | X | X | X | X | X | X | X | X |
| Andover | 20.8 | 2.7 | 95.4 | 10.2 | 337 | 317 | 20 | 19.1 | 632 | 236 |
| Apple Valley | 38.0 | 1.1 | 97.5 | 21.7 | 433 | 399 | 34 | 41.9 | 838 | 175 |
| Blaine | 41.3 | 3.0 | 76.9 | 21.0 | 379 | 326 | 52 | 47.4 | 856 | 348 |
| Bloomington | 100.6 | 12.6 | 79.6 | 52.9 | 650 | 459 | 191 | 101.1 | 1 242 | 280 |
| Brooklyn Center | 38.4 | 2.4 | 89.8 | 16.3 | 593 | 516 | 53 | 38.9 | 1 415 | 304 |
| Brooklyn Park | 67.9 | 10.2 | 84.9 | 32.2 | 451 | 406 | 45 | 53.6 | 750 | 191 |
| Burnsville | 53.5 | 6.3 | 54.0 | 30.1 | 509 | 450 | 59 | 52.2 | 883 | 237 |
| Coon Rapids | 43.4 | 4.3 | 100.0 | 21.6 | 350 | 276 | 74 | 46.3 | 749 | 228 |
| Cottage Grove | 38.9 | 4.1 | 84.3 | 12.8 | 386 | 340 | 45 | 32.7 | 988 | 409 |
| Duluth | 183.4 | 75.5 | 60.8 | 37.5 | 445 | 210 | 234 | 180.3 | 2 137 | 707 |
| Eagan | 49.5 | 2.4 | 96.5 | 22.7 | 357 | 327 | 30 | 47.9 | 752 | 175 |
| Eden Prairie | 67.4 | 4.3 | 85.7 | 34.4 | 558 | 501 | 57 | 60.1 | 974 | 205 |
| Edina | 57.3 | 2.9 | 89.3 | 31.6 | 689 | 602 | 87 | 53.0 | 1 154 | 196 |
| Fridley | 25.0 | 2.6 | 94.8 | 9.1 | 351 | 317 | 34 | 30.7 | 1 183 | 120 |
| Inver Grove Heights | 25.6 | 1.7 | 86.0 | 13.0 | 388 | 354 | 0 | 29.4 | 877 | 178 |
| Lakeville | 39.3 | 2.4 | 95.2 | 20.6 | 380 | 331 | 49 | 35.2 | 651 | 200 |
| Mankato | 69.0 | 15.8 | 74.8 | 16.0 | 445 | 284 | 161 | 69.5 | 1 937 | 703 |
| Maple Grove | 81.3 | 5.0 | 100.0 | 27.9 | 452 | 385 | 66 | 80.6 | 1 303 | 729 |
| Maplewood | 38.4 | 1.8 | 96.2 | 15.7 | 434 | 391 | 43 | 39.0 | 1 080 | 306 |
| Minneapolis | 956.7 | 230.0 | 75.6 | 380.8 | 1 009 | 713 | 296 | 844.3 | 2 237 | 235 |
| Minnetonka | 48.9 | 2.5 | 88.3 | 30.3 | 603 | 525 | 78 | 44.5 | 883 | 211 |
| Moorhead | 63.9 | 20.2 | 79.4 | 5.0 | 141 | 89 | 52 | 76.6 | 2 169 | 1 097 |
| Oakdale | 21.7 | 2.3 | 74.9 | 10.2 | 376 | 314 | 35 | 20.3 | 752 | 164 |
| Owatonna | 25.7 | 8.1 | 76.7 | 7.6 | 307 | 261 | 35 | 24.8 | 1 002 | 260 |
| Plymouth | 52.6 | 8.0 | 94.5 | 26.4 | 372 | 328 | 44 | 51.7 | 727 | 162 |
| Richfield | 41.9 | 11.0 | 97.3 | 17.4 | 520 | 445 | 32 | 38.6 | 1 157 | 137 |
| Rochester | 169.1 | 22.6 | 96.6 | 50.8 | 513 | 342 | 170 | 201.5 | 2 033 | 941 |
| Roseville | 29.6 | 2.5 | 100.0 | 16.4 | 506 | 408 | 98 | 25.6 | 788 | 158 |
| St. Cloud | 82.3 | 21.4 | 83.5 | 29.3 | 441 | 247 | 194 | 90.0 | 1 353 | 546 |
| St. Louis Park | 58.7 | 13.4 | 85.3 | 27.9 | 634 | 563 | 71 | 58.7 | 1 333 | 113 |
| St. Paul | 482.0 | 165.9 | 55.7 | 126.8 | 457 | 275 | 182 | 461.3 | 1 664 | 201 |
| Savage | 33.0 | 3.0 | 99.2 | 14.9 | 540 | 486 | 55 | 34.9 | 1 263 | 660 |
| Shakopee | 31.5 | 3.8 | 66.2 | 13.5 | 403 | 317 | 80 | 31.2 | 933 | 350 |
| Shoreview | 21.4 | 1.0 | 76.1 | 9.4 | 349 | 330 | 19 | 22.3 | 825 | 131 |
| Winona | 30.8 | 16.7 | 98.2 | 6.4 | 239 | 177 | 62 | 35.4 | 1 326 | 545 |
| Woodbury | 66.6 | 3.3 | 89.0 | 24.3 | 438 | 366 | 71 | 48.1 | 868 | 326 |
| MISSISSIPPI | X | X | X | X | X | X | X | X | X | X |
| Biloxi | 140.4 | 74.9 | 44.9 | 21.3 | 480 | 380 | 100 | 122.0 | 2 754 | 292 |
| Clinton | 21.5 | 9.7 | 96.4 | 7.4 | 280 | 237 | 43 | 24.9 | 942 | 401 |
| Greenville | 29.1 | 8.2 | 83.6 | 13.4 | 371 | 288 | 83 | 25.5 | 706 | 90 |
| Gulfport | 429.2 | 111.2 | 31.6 | 28.5 | 430 | 334 | 96 | 404.8 | 6 108 | 641 |
| Hattiesburg | 65.2 | 36.7 | 67.9 | 19.6 | 390 | 245 | 144 | 52.6 | 1 047 | 250 |
| Horn Lake | 13.0 | 4.2 | 95.6 | 6.2 | 257 | 232 | 25 | 12.6 | 520 | 35 |
| Jackson | 232.6 | 78.9 | 62.9 | 72.0 | 410 | 343 | 67 | 243.0 | 1 383 | 496 |
| Meridian | 42.4 | 16.6 | 100.0 | 13.8 | 360 | 290 | 70 | 31.6 | 826 | 37 |
| Olive Branch | 28.0 | 8.8 | 100.0 | 9.6 | 315 | 277 | 38 | 26.4 | 860 | 158 |
| Pearl | 17.8 | 8.6 | 81.0 | 4.0 | 165 | 157 | 7 | 18.2 | 754 | 97 |
| Southaven | 39.1 | 12.0 | 100.0 | 18.0 | 422 | 348 | 74 | 46.5 | 1 093 | 382 |
| Tupelo | 61.0 | 32.1 | 86.8 | 11.6 | 321 | 298 | 23 | 55.4 | 1 535 | 485 |

1. Based on population estimated as of July 1 of the year shown.

# Table D. Cities — City Government Finances

| City | City government finances, 2006 (cont.) | | | | | | | | | |
|---|---|---|---|---|---|---|---|---|---|---|
| | General expenditure (cont.) | | | | | | | | | |
| | Percent of total for: | | | | | | | | | |
| | Public welfare | Highways | Parking facilities | Education | Health and hospitals | Police protection | Sewerage and sanitation | Parks and recreation | Housing and community development | Interest on debt |
| | 127 | 128 | 129 | 130 | 131 | 132 | 133 | 134 | 135 | 136 |
| MICHIGAN—Cont'd | | | | | | | | | | |
| Oak Park ..................... | 0.0 | 22.9 | 0.0 | 0.0 | 0.0 | 26.4 | 18.4 | 2.9 | 0.4 | 4.2 |
| Pontiac ......................... | 0.0 | 8.3 | 1.4 | 0.0 | 0.0 | 13.7 | 12.7 | 5.0 | 10.2 | 4.6 |
| Portage ........................ | 0.3 | 16.9 | 0.0 | 0.0 | 0.0 | 16.7 | 15.6 | 5.4 | 1.0 | 7.3 |
| Port Huron .................. | 0.0 | 12.8 | 0.3 | 0.0 | 0.0 | 13.5 | 26.5 | 10.3 | 9.1 | 3.8 |
| Rochester Hills .............. | 0.0 | 22.2 | 0.0 | 0.0 | 0.3 | 11.9 | 14.8 | 17.5 | 0.2 | 3.7 |
| Roseville ...................... | 0.0 | 8.8 | 0.0 | 0.0 | 0.0 | 20.5 | 17.8 | 3.3 | 6.9 | 1.7 |
| Royal Oak .................... | 0.0 | 13.1 | 1.8 | 0.0 | 0.6 | 15.6 | 19.9 | 4.3 | 5.5 | 1.6 |
| Saginaw........................ | 0.0 | 8.0 | 0.4 | 0.0 | 0.0 | 16.0 | 22.4 | 0.2 | 16.8 | 4.1 |
| St. Clair Shores............ | 0.0 | 10.3 | 0.0 | 0.0 | 0.0 | 18.7 | 22.7 | 7.2 | 2.9 | 4.1 |
| Southfield ..................... | 0.0 | 18.1 | 0.0 | 0.0 | 0.0 | 19.1 | 2.7 | 7.8 | 1.9 | 2.2 |
| Southgate ..................... | 0.0 | 10.7 | 0.0 | 0.0 | 0.0 | 18.2 | 12.2 | 5.5 | 0.5 | 4.1 |
| Sterling Heights............ | 0.0 | 16.4 | 0.0 | 0.0 | 0.0 | 25.1 | 15.2 | 3.5 | 1.8 | 2.0 |
| Taylor .......................... | 0.0 | 11.5 | 0.0 | 0.0 | 0.0 | 12.8 | 5.0 | 6.4 | 15.3 | 5.0 |
| Troy ............................. | 0.0 | 17.6 | 0.0 | 0.0 | 0.0 | 24.6 | 15.7 | 14.3 | 0.1 | 3.7 |
| Warren.......................... | 0.0 | 8.6 | 0.0 | 0.0 | 0.0 | 21.9 | 15.7 | 4.4 | 2.2 | 3.5 |
| Westland ...................... | 0.0 | 10.0 | 0.0 | 0.0 | 0.0 | 19.0 | 17.1 | 5.7 | 10.6 | 0.6 |
| Wyandotte .................... | 0.0 | 17.8 | 0.0 | 0.0 | 0.0 | 10.1 | 19.8 | 7.6 | 0.0 | 1.3 |
| Wyoming ...................... | 0.0 | 10.3 | 0.0 | 0.0 | 0.3 | 12.0 | 37.7 | 3.9 | 8.4 | 4.0 |
| MINNESOTA ............ | X | X | X | X | X | X | X | X | X | X |
| Andover........................ | 0.0 | 30.8 | 0.0 | 0.0 | 0.1 | 9.7 | 12.0 | 14.9 | 3.8 | 10.1 |
| Apple Valley ................. | 0.0 | 23.0 | 0.0 | 0.0 | 0.0 | 16.0 | 8.9 | 15.1 | 0.0 | 4.8 |
| Blaine .......................... | 0.0 | 4.7 | 0.0 | 0.0 | 0.0 | 27.2 | 14.1 | 5.7 | 7.6 | 2.7 |
| Bloomington ................. | 0.0 | 22.7 | 0.0 | 0.0 | 6.1 | 18.0 | 12.9 | 11.8 | 0.8 | 2.0 |
| Brooklyn Center ........... | 0.0 | 13.4 | 0.0 | 0.0 | 0.0 | 15.7 | 12.5 | 7.0 | 11.0 | 3.2 |
| Brooklyn Park............... | 0.0 | 17.8 | 0.0 | 0.0 | 0.0 | 19.9 | 11.1 | 13.3 | 9.9 | 5.9 |
| Burnsville..................... | 0.0 | 23.9 | 0.0 | 0.0 | 0.0 | 19.7 | 8.5 | 11.7 | 0.0 | 2.8 |
| Coon Rapids ................ | 0.0 | 8.3 | 0.0 | 0.0 | 0.5 | 12.9 | 14.9 | 9.1 | 2.7 | 2.0 |
| Cottage Grove............... | 0.0 | 12.2 | 0.0 | 0.0 | 3.4 | 13.4 | 9.7 | 11.8 | 2.4 | 5.3 |
| Duluth.......................... | 0.0 | 7.3 | 0.0 | 0.0 | 5.6 | 9.4 | 11.8 | 10.4 | 0.2 | 3.1 |
| Eagan........................... | 0.0 | 11.3 | 0.0 | 0.0 | 0.0 | 19.2 | 11.0 | 14.1 | 3.7 | 9.8 |
| Eden Prairie ................. | 1.1 | 13.8 | 0.0 | 0.0 | 0.2 | 14.3 | 10.7 | 11.2 | 5.0 | 14.5 |
| Edina........................... | 0.0 | 16.4 | 0.0 | 0.0 | 0.8 | 15.1 | 13.4 | 30.1 | 2.6 | 4.3 |
| Fridley.......................... | 0.0 | 10.6 | 0.0 | 0.0 | 0.0 | 15.2 | 14.0 | 14.6 | 14.5 | 6.4 |
| Inver Grove Heights...... | 0.0 | 21.1 | 0.0 | 0.0 | 0.0 | 13.8 | 7.5 | 24.9 | 0.0 | 4.7 |
| Lakeville ...................... | 0.0 | 14.1 | 0.0 | 0.0 | 0.1 | 20.7 | 14.3 | 19.9 | 0.0 | 8.4 |
| Mankato........................ | 0.0 | 26.7 | 0.7 | 0.0 | 0.0 | 9.6 | 11.5 | 5.2 | 20.8 | 4.9 |
| Maple Grove................. | 0.6 | 11.0 | 0.0 | 0.0 | 0.0 | 8.3 | 5.5 | 9.1 | 1.1 | 1.7 |
| Maplewood................... | 0.0 | 5.7 | 0.0 | 0.0 | 4.4 | 17.0 | 11.9 | 12.1 | 3.4 | 5.5 |
| Minneapolis ................. | 0.0 | 9.4 | 4.8 | 0.0 | 1.7 | 15.3 | 10.9 | 10.1 | 14.9 | 10.4 |
| Minnetonka .................. | 0.0 | 19.5 | 0.0 | 0.0 | 0.6 | 17.0 | 18.4 | 15.2 | 3.3 | 0.8 |
| Moorhead ..................... | 0.0 | 6.2 | 0.0 | 0.0 | 1.1 | 7.4 | 10.5 | 5.0 | 3.5 | 6.6 |
| Oakdale........................ | 0.0 | 6.2 | 0.0 | 0.0 | 0.0 | 17.4 | 11.5 | 11.5 | 0.0 | 1.6 |
| Owatonna ..................... | 0.0 | 27.2 | 0.0 | 0.0 | 0.0 | 13.5 | 4.7 | 15.9 | 7.5 | 3.9 |
| Plymouth ...................... | 6.9 | 24.2 | 0.0 | 0.0 | 0.0 | 18.6 | 11.1 | 15.4 | 0.7 | 2.5 |
| Richfield....................... | 0.0 | 4.1 | 0.0 | 0.0 | 0.2 | 15.0 | 8.7 | 10.2 | 28.0 | 2.8 |
| Rochester ..................... | 0.0 | 2.8 | 1.6 | 0.0 | 0.1 | 7.6 | 21.2 | 5.6 | 0.2 | 15.7 |
| Roseville....................... | 0.0 | 12.6 | 0.0 | 0.0 | 0.0 | 16.6 | 13.9 | 14.0 | 4.2 | 2.1 |
| St. Cloud ...................... | 0.0 | 28.9 | 1.6 | 0.0 | 0.7 | 14.0 | 13.8 | 7.3 | 1.2 | 3.4 |
| St. Louis Park............... | 0.0 | 12.4 | 0.0 | 0.0 | 0.3 | 10.6 | 11.9 | 10.4 | 20.6 | 14.3 |
| St. Paul........................ | 0.0 | 6.0 | 2.5 | 0.0 | 0.8 | 17.0 | 6.9 | 9.6 | 14.8 | 8.1 |
| Savage ......................... | 0.0 | 33.9 | 0.0 | 0.0 | 0.0 | 28.1 | 5.9 | 6.8 | 2.9 | 10.0 |
| Shakopee ..................... | 0.0 | 28.8 | 0.0 | 0.0 | 0.0 | 15.6 | 11.1 | 21.2 | 1.4 | 2.8 |
| Shoreview..................... | 0.0 | 16.5 | 0.0 | 0.0 | 0.2 | 11.6 | 20.0 | 26.5 | 0.0 | 8.9 |
| Winona ......................... | 0.0 | 40.2 | 0.0 | 0.0 | 0.2 | 11.3 | 8.5 | 10.8 | 1.0 | 1.3 |
| Woodbury ..................... | 0.0 | 14.1 | 0.0 | 0.0 | 2.5 | 14.0 | 9.6 | 14.8 | 2.4 | 6.0 |
| MISSISSIPPI............ | X | X | X | X | X | X | X | X | X | X |
| Biloxi............................ | 0.4 | 13.4 | 0.0 | 0.0 | 0.1 | 11.3 | 42.9 | 3.8 | 0.5 | 2.4 |
| Clinton ......................... | 0.0 | 27.2 | 0.0 | 0.0 | 0.0 | 14.5 | 21.0 | 13.8 | 0.0 | 2.7 |
| Greenville ..................... | 1.0 | 14.3 | 0.0 | 0.0 | 0.1 | 22.2 | 13.3 | 3.2 | 0.0 | 1.4 |
| Gulfport........................ | 0.0 | 2.9 | 0.0 | 0.0 | 63.5 | 4.8 | 4.8 | 1.1 | 0.4 | 2.4 |
| Hattiesburg................... | 0.0 | 18.7 | 0.4 | 0.0 | 1.4 | 18.4 | 12.7 | 8.5 | 1.3 | 2.6 |
| Horn Lake ..................... | 0.0 | 13.4 | 0.0 | 0.0 | 5.5 | 30.0 | 11.7 | 2.9 | 0.0 | 8.0 |
| Jackson ........................ | 1.1 | 12.2 | 0.0 | 0.0 | 0.4 | 13.8 | 24.0 | 3.4 | 2.5 | 2.7 |
| Meridian........................ | 0.0 | 13.3 | 0.5 | 0.0 | 0.0 | 20.8 | 18.3 | 6.3 | 3.5 | 4.3 |
| Olive Branch................. | 0.0 | 8.9 | 0.0 | 0.0 | 3.2 | 17.3 | 17.1 | 4.6 | 0.0 | 9.0 |
| Pearl............................ | 0.0 | 12.3 | 0.0 | 0.0 | 1.7 | 13.3 | 17.6 | 6.9 | 2.3 | 4.6 |
| Southaven ..................... | 0.0 | 4.4 | 0.0 | 0.0 | 0.4 | 14.0 | 6.8 | 13.0 | 0.0 | 5.1 |
| Tupelo .......................... | 0.0 | 22.2 | 0.0 | 0.0 | 0.0 | 16.3 | 20.7 | 7.7 | 0.0 | 3.2 |

| City | City government finances, 2007 (cont.) | | | Climate[2] | | | | | | | |
| | Debt outstanding | | | | Average daily temperature (degrees Fahrenheit) | | | | | | |
| | | | | | Mean | | Limits | | | | |
| | Total (mil dol) | Per capita[1] (dollars) | Debt issued during year | City government employment, 2011 | January | July | January[3] | July[4] | Annual precipitation (inches) | Heating degree days | Cooling degree days |
| | 137 | 138 | 139 | 140 | 141 | 142 | 143 | 144 | 145 | 146 | 147 |
| **MICHIGAN—Cont'd** | | | | | | | | | | | |
| Oak Park | 43.6 | 1 418 | 0.1 | 189 | 24.7 | 73.7 | 16.1 | 85.7 | 33.58 | 6 224 | 788 |
| Pontiac | 146.0 | 2 195 | 0.0 | 441 | 22.9 | 71.9 | 15.9 | 82.3 | 30.03 | 6 680 | 626 |
| Portage | 95.7 | 2 078 | 0.8 | 230 | 24.3 | 73.2 | 17.0 | 84.2 | 37.41 | 6 235 | 773 |
| Port Huron | 103.7 | 3 337 | 18.8 | 266 | 22.8 | 72.2 | 15.1 | 81.9 | 31.39 | 6 845 | 626 |
| Rochester Hills | 52.2 | 753 | 0.0 | 264 | 22.0 | 70.6 | 13.7 | 82.7 | 35.74 | 7 046 | 523 |
| Roseville | 18.2 | 387 | 4.9 | 268 | 25.3 | 73.6 | 18.8 | 83.3 | 33.97 | 6 160 | 757 |
| Royal Oak | 134.6 | 2 345 | 1.1 | 336 | 24.7 | 73.7 | 16.1 | 85.7 | 33.58 | 6 224 | 788 |
| Saginaw | 110.5 | 1 963 | 1.5 | 421 | 21.4 | 71.2 | 14.9 | 81.9 | 31.61 | 7 099 | 548 |
| St. Clair Shores | 59.5 | 982 | 3.8 | 288 | 25.3 | 73.6 | 18.8 | 83.3 | 33.97 | 6 160 | 757 |
| Southfield | 86.6 | 1 148 | 0.0 | 728 | 24.7 | 73.7 | 16.1 | 85.7 | 33.58 | 6 224 | 788 |
| Southgate | 25.8 | 903 | 0.0 | 173 | 24.5 | 73.5 | 17.8 | 83.4 | 32.89 | 6 422 | 736 |
| Sterling Heights | 49.5 | 389 | 7.9 | 603 | 24.4 | 71.9 | 18.0 | 81.8 | 32.24 | 6 620 | 597 |
| Taylor | 189.9 | 3 045 | 0.3 | 374 | 24.5 | 73.5 | 17.8 | 83.4 | 32.89 | 6 422 | 736 |
| Troy | 79.4 | 986 | 4.3 | 513 | 22.9 | 71.9 | 15.9 | 82.3 | 30.03 | 6 680 | 626 |
| Warren | 177.7 | 1 324 | 11.8 | 417 | 24.7 | 73.7 | 16.1 | 85.7 | 33.58 | 6 224 | 788 |
| Westland | 18.1 | 223 | 0.0 | 344 | 24.6 | 73.9 | 17.6 | 84.7 | 32.80 | 6 167 | 828 |
| Wyandotte | 78.1 | 3 048 | 10.6 | 267 | 24.5 | 73.5 | 17.8 | 83.4 | 32.89 | 6 422 | 736 |
| Wyoming | 141.6 | 2 010 | 32.0 | 311 | 22.4 | 71.4 | 15.6 | 82.3 | 37.13 | 6 896 | 613 |
| **MINNESOTA** | X | X | X | X | X | X | X | X | X | X | X |
| Andover | 59.7 | 1 972 | 12.9 | 91 | 10.9 | 70.4 | 1.8 | 80.5 | 31.36 | 8 367 | 500 |
| Apple Valley | 42.4 | 847 | 6.6 | 212 | 9.2 | 69.4 | -1.1 | 80.5 | 29.19 | 8 805 | 416 |
| Blaine | 47.5 | 857 | 5.2 | 197 | 10.9 | 70.4 | 1.8 | 80.5 | 31.36 | 8 367 | 500 |
| Bloomington | 117.9 | 1 448 | 31.4 | 580 | 13.1 | 73.2 | 4.3 | 83.3 | 29.41 | 7 876 | 699 |
| Brooklyn Center | 59.2 | 2 153 | 1.5 | 180 | 13.0 | 71.4 | 2.8 | 82.8 | 30.50 | 7 983 | 587 |
| Brooklyn Park | 83.1 | 1 164 | 1.3 | 438 | 13.0 | 71.4 | 2.8 | 82.8 | 30.50 | 7 983 | 587 |
| Burnsville | 55.5 | 939 | 12.8 | 296 | 13.8 | 74.0 | 3.4 | 85.8 | 30.44 | 7 549 | 803 |
| Coon Rapids | 59.2 | 959 | 0.0 | 275 | 13.0 | 71.4 | 2.8 | 82.8 | 30.50 | 7 983 | 587 |
| Cottage Grove | 58.0 | 1 752 | 29.2 | 142 | 12.0 | 72.1 | 2.5 | 82.6 | 29.95 | 8 032 | 617 |
| Duluth | 437.1 | 5 179 | 28.5 | 1 013 | 8.4 | 65.5 | -1.2 | 76.3 | 31.00 | 9 724 | 189 |
| Eagan | 91.6 | 1 437 | 0.0 | 271 | 13.1 | 73.2 | 4.3 | 83.3 | 29.41 | 7 876 | 699 |
| Eden Prairie | 263.2 | 4 268 | 13.5 | 318 | 10.2 | 71.4 | -0.3 | 82.2 | 28.82 | 8 429 | 567 |
| Edina | 79.2 | 1 724 | 0.0 | 281 | 13.8 | 74.0 | 3.4 | 85.8 | 30.44 | 7 549 | 803 |
| Fridley | 8.4 | 322 | 2.5 | 157 | 10.9 | 70.4 | 1.8 | 80.5 | 31.36 | 8 367 | 500 |
| Inver Grove Heights | 44.7 | 1 334 | 10.1 | 170 | 10.1 | 71.0 | 0.0 | 81.3 | 34.60 | 8 345 | 533 |
| Lakeville | 85.1 | 1 573 | 10.8 | 208 | 13.1 | 72.2 | 3.8 | 83.6 | 31.43 | 7 773 | 658 |
| Mankato | 113.4 | 3 159 | 14.1 | 258 | 12.5 | 72.1 | 2.4 | 83.4 | 33.42 | 8 029 | 650 |
| Maple Grove | 216.2 | 3 494 | 45.5 | 296 | 13.0 | 71.4 | 2.8 | 82.8 | 30.50 | 7 983 | 587 |
| Maplewood | 154.9 | 4 285 | 6.4 | 169 | 14.5 | 73.0 | 6.2 | 83.2 | 32.59 | 7 606 | 715 |
| Minneapolis | 2 975.0 | 7 883 | 64.7 | 5 111 | 13.1 | 73.2 | 4.3 | 83.3 | 29.41 | 7 876 | 699 |
| Minnetonka | 19.0 | 378 | 0.0 | 270 | 13.1 | 73.2 | 4.3 | 83.3 | 29.41 | 7 876 | 699 |
| Moorhead | 202.5 | 5 731 | 45.4 | 321 | 3.8 | 69.8 | -7.1 | 81.5 | 21.56 | 9 628 | 478 |
| Oakdale | 23.2 | 859 | 5.0 | 112 | 14.5 | 73.0 | 6.2 | 83.2 | 32.59 | 7 606 | 715 |
| Owatonna | 26.1 | 1 054 | 2.8 | 209 | NA | NA | NA | NA | NA | NA | NA |
| Plymouth | 161.1 | 2 267 | 0.0 | 284 | 13.0 | 71.4 | 2.8 | 82.8 | 30.50 | 7 983 | 587 |
| Richfield | 68.8 | 2 061 | 8.6 | 151 | 13.1 | 73.2 | 4.3 | 83.3 | 29.41 | 7 876 | 699 |
| Rochester | 1 284.8 | 12 962 | 40.6 | 906 | 9.8 | 70.0 | 0.0 | 80.9 | 29.10 | 8 703 | 474 |
| Roseville | 21.7 | 667 | 9.6 | 191 | 14.5 | 73.0 | 6.2 | 83.2 | 32.59 | 7 606 | 715 |
| St. Cloud | 364.2 | 5 476 | 50.5 | 475 | 8.8 | 69.8 | -1.2 | 81.7 | 27.13 | 8 815 | 443 |
| St. Louis Park | 177.3 | 4 028 | 0.0 | 271 | 13.0 | 71.4 | 2.8 | 82.8 | 30.50 | 7 983 | 587 |
| St. Paul | 874.5 | 3 154 | 35.6 | 2 959 | 14.5 | 73.0 | 6.2 | 83.2 | 32.59 | 7 606 | 715 |
| Savage | 96.5 | 3 492 | 20.6 | 117 | NA | NA | NA | NA | NA | NA | NA |
| Shakopee | 116.1 | 3 470 | 14.0 | 199 | NA | NA | NA | NA | NA | NA | NA |
| Shoreview | 43.0 | 1 588 | 3.5 | 97 | 14.5 | 73.0 | 6.2 | 83.2 | 32.59 | 7 606 | 715 |
| Winona | 20.5 | 768 | 2.3 | 182 | 17.6 | 75.8 | 9.2 | 85.3 | 34.20 | 6 839 | 990 |
| Woodbury | 120.0 | 2 164 | 24.3 | 208 | 11.5 | 72.1 | 1.9 | 81.9 | 29.92 | 8 104 | 621 |
| **MISSISSIPPI** | X | X | X | X | X | X | X | X | X | X | X |
| Biloxi | 71.3 | 1 609 | 8.0 | 632 | 50.7 | 81.7 | 43.5 | 88.5 | 64.84 | 1 645 | 2 517 |
| Clinton | 33.3 | 1 262 | 6.5 | 196 | NA | NA | NA | NA | NA | NA | NA |
| Greenville | 18.4 | 510 | 0.0 | 436 | 42.3 | 82.6 | 33.0 | 92.6 | 54.20 | 2 715 | 2 216 |
| Gulfport | 235.1 | 3 547 | 33.6 | 3 055 | 51.6 | 82.6 | 42.6 | 91.3 | 65.20 | 1 514 | 2 679 |
| Hattiesburg | 94.3 | 1 877 | 32.2 | 709 | 47.9 | 81.7 | 36.0 | 92.1 | 62.47 | 2 024 | 2 327 |
| Horn Lake | 24.4 | 1 011 | 1.2 | 205 | NA | NA | NA | NA | NA | NA | NA |
| Jackson | 360.8 | 2 053 | 4.5 | 1 858 | 45.0 | 81.4 | 35.0 | 91.4 | 55.95 | 2 401 | 2 264 |
| Meridian | 63.4 | 1 656 | 11.2 | 524 | 46.1 | 81.7 | 34.7 | 92.9 | 58.65 | 2 352 | 2 173 |
| Olive Branch | 57.4 | 1 875 | 4.3 | 338 | NA | NA | NA | NA | NA | NA | NA |
| Pearl | 18.9 | 786 | 2.8 | 218 | NA | NA | NA | NA | NA | NA | NA |
| Southaven | 83.1 | 1 952 | 28.6 | 373 | 37.9 | 80.4 | 27.8 | 90.3 | 55.06 | 3 442 | 1 749 |
| Tupelo | 81.7 | 2 264 | 14.3 | 502 | 40.4 | 80.6 | 30.5 | 91.4 | 55.86 | 3 086 | 1 884 |

1. Based on the population estimated as of July 1 of the year shown.   2. Represents normal values based on the 30-year period, 1971–2000.   3. Average daily minimum.   4. Average daily maximum.

# Table D. Cities — Land Area and Population

| STATE Place code | City | Land area,[1] 2010 (sq km) | Population, 2012 | | | Race alone or in combination, not of Hispanic origin (percent), 2010 | | | | | | |
|---|---|---|---|---|---|---|---|---|---|---|---|---|
| | | | | | | Race alone or in combination | | | | | Percent Hispanic or Latino[2], 2010 | Percent Foreign born 2007-2011 |
| | | Land area,[1] 2010 (sq km) | Total persons | Rank | Per square kilometer | White | Black | American Indian, Alaska Native | Asian | Hawaiian Pacific Islander | | |
| | | 1 | 2 | 3 | 4 | 5 | 6 | 7 | 8 | 9 | 10 | 11 |
| 29 00000 | MISSOURI.................. | 178 039.7 | 6 021 988 | X | 33.8 | 82.6 | 12.3 | 1.1 | 2.0 | 0.2 | 3.5 | 3.8 |
| 29 03160 | Ballwin....................... | 23.3 | 30 443 | 1 196 | 1 306.6 | 89.1 | 3.0 | 0.5 | 6.3 | 0.0 | 2.4 | 7.6 |
| 29 06652 | Blue Springs............... | 57.7 | 53 014 | 680 | 918.8 | 86.9 | 7.4 | 1.1 | 1.8 | 0.3 | 5.0 | 2.4 |
| 29 11242 | Cape Girardeau........... | 73.6 | 38 544 | 949 | 523.7 | 82.2 | 14.1 | 0.7 | 2.2 | 0.1 | 2.8 | 3.1 |
| 29 13600 | Chesterfield............... | 82.3 | 47 684 | 777 | 579.4 | 85.6 | 2.9 | 0.4 | 9.3 | 0.1 | 2.8 | 10.3 |
| 29 15670 | Columbia..................... | 163.4 | 113 225 | 236 | 692.9 | 79.5 | 12.6 | 0.9 | 6.0 | 0.1 | 3.4 | 8.3 |
| 29 24778 | Florissant................... | 32.5 | 52 252 | 693 | 1 607.8 | 70.0 | 28.0 | 0.7 | 1.2 | 0.1 | 2.0 | 2.4 |
| 29 27190 | Gladstone................... | 20.9 | 25 931 | 1 394 | 1 240.7 | 84.5 | 6.3 | 1.4 | 2.4 | 0.7 | 7.3 | 4.6 |
| 29 31276 | Hazelwood.................. | 41.5 | 25 677 | 1 408 | 618.7 | 64.5 | 31.8 | 0.8 | 1.8 | 0.1 | 3.0 | 4.4 |
| 29 35000 | Independence.............. | 200.9 | 117 270 | 226 | 583.7 | 84.6 | 6.6 | 1.4 | 1.3 | 0.9 | 7.7 | 4.4 |
| 29 37000 | Jefferson City............. | 93.1 | 43 183 | 843 | 463.8 | 78.4 | 17.9 | 0.8 | 2.2 | 0.1 | 2.6 | 3.4 |
| 29 37592 | Joplin........................... | 92.1 | 49 526 | 738 | 537.7 | 88.5 | 4.6 | 3.2 | 2.0 | 0.4 | 4.5 | 2.6 |
| 29 38000 | Kansas City................. | 815.7 | 464 310 | 37 | 569.2 | 56.8 | 31.0 | 1.2 | 3.0 | 0.3 | 10.0 | 7.7 |
| 29 39044 | Kirkwood..................... | 23.7 | 27 553 | 1 317 | 1 162.6 | 89.4 | 7.6 | 0.5 | 1.9 | 0.1 | 1.8 | 3.4 |
| 29 41348 | Lee's Summit .............. | 164.1 | 92 468 | 323 | 563.5 | 85.6 | 9.2 | 0.8 | 2.3 | 0.2 | 3.9 | 3.3 |
| 29 42032 | Liberty........................ | 75.2 | 29 811 | 1 222 | 396.4 | 90.7 | 4.5 | 1.2 | 1.5 | 0.2 | 4.1 | 2.2 |
| 29 46586 | Maryland Heights ........ | 56.5 | 27 446 | 1 322 | 485.8 | 73.1 | 12.8 | 0.6 | 10.7 | 0.1 | 4.5 | 16.8 |
| 29 54074 | O'Fallon ..................... | 75.6 | 81 979 | 386 | 1 084.4 | 89.7 | 4.6 | 0.6 | 3.7 | 0.1 | 2.7 | 3.7 |
| 29 60788 | Raytown...................... | 25.7 | 29 513 | 1 234 | 1 148.4 | 67.9 | 26.8 | 1.4 | 1.5 | 0.4 | 5.1 | 5.0 |
| 29 64082 | St. Charles.................. | 61.3 | 66 463 | 506 | 1 084.2 | 86.9 | 6.8 | 0.7 | 3.0 | 0.1 | 4.2 | 4.3 |
| 29 64550 | St. Joseph .................. | 113.9 | 77 176 | 423 | 677.6 | 86.8 | 7.2 | 1.0 | 1.2 | 0.3 | 5.7 | 3.3 |
| 29 65000 | St. Louis..................... | 160.3 | 318 172 | 58 | 1 984.9 | 50.3 | 43.8 | 0.9 | 3.4 | 0.1 | 3.5 | 6.9 |
| 29 65126 | St. Peters.................... | 57.9 | 54 078 | 670 | 934.0 | 91.6 | 4.3 | 0.6 | 2.4 | 0.1 | 2.5 | 3.5 |
| 29 70000 | Springfield.................. | 211.7 | 162 191 | 146 | 766.1 | 89.4 | 5.3 | 1.8 | 2.4 | 0.3 | 3.7 | 3.3 |
| 29 75220 | University City ............ | 15.3 | 35 228 | 1 037 | 2 302.5 | 51.2 | 42.4 | 0.9 | 5.0 | 0.1 | 2.8 | 9.1 |
| 29 78442 | Wentzville................... | 51.7 | 31 216 | 1 164 | 603.8 | 89.7 | 7.0 | 0.5 | 1.5 | 0.1 | 2.7 | 1.3 |
| 29 79820 | Wildwood..................... | 172.0 | 35 698 | 1 027 | 207.5 | 91.7 | 2.0 | 0.5 | 4.8 | 0.1 | 2.3 | 4.6 |
| 30 00000 | MONTANA ............... | 376 961.9 | 1 005 141 | X | 2.7 | 89.9 | 0.7 | 7.5 | 1.0 | 0.2 | 2.9 | 2.0 |
| 30 06550 | Billings....................... | 112.4 | 106 954 | 258 | 951.5 | 89.0 | 1.3 | 5.3 | 1.2 | 0.2 | 5.2 | 1.8 |
| 30 08950 | Bozeman..................... | 49.5 | 38 695 | 946 | 781.7 | 93.4 | 0.8 | 1.8 | 2.6 | 0.2 | 2.9 | 4.0 |
| 30 11390 | Butte-Silver Bow......... | 1 860.9 | 33 730 | 1 083 | 18.2 | 93.7 | 0.5 | 2.8 | 0.7 | 0.1 | 3.7 | 2.0 |
| 30 32800 | Great Falls.................. | 56.4 | 58 893 | 597 | 1 044.2 | 89.7 | 1.7 | 6.8 | 1.5 | 0.2 | 3.4 | 2.2 |
| 30 35600 | Helena......................... | 42.3 | 29 134 | 1 249 | 688.7 | 93.8 | 0.7 | 3.6 | 1.1 | 0.1 | 2.8 | 1.6 |
| 30 50200 | Missoula...................... | 71.3 | 68 394 | 489 | 959.2 | 92.6 | 1.0 | 3.8 | 1.9 | 0.2 | 2.9 | 2.7 |
| 31 00000 | NEBRASKA............... | 198 973.7 | 1 855 525 | X | 9.3 | 83.5 | 5.2 | 1.3 | 2.2 | 0.1 | 9.2 | 6.0 |
| 31 03950 | Bellevue...................... | 41.1 | 52 604 | 687 | 1 279.9 | 78.7 | 7.4 | 1.2 | 3.3 | 0.3 | 11.9 | 9.2 |
| 31 17670 | Fremont ...................... | 22.8 | 26 167 | 1 390 | 1 147.7 | 86.2 | 1.0 | 0.7 | 0.8 | 0.2 | 11.9 | 6.5 |
| 31 19595 | Grand Island............... | 73.6 | 49 989 | 726 | 679.2 | 69.5 | 2.3 | 0.8 | 1.5 | 0.1 | 26.7 | 13.5 |
| 31 25055 | Kearney....................... | 33.1 | 31 790 | 1 142 | 960.4 | 89.6 | 1.4 | 0.5 | 2.0 | 0.0 | 7.3 | 4.5 |
| 31 28000 | Lincoln........................ | 230.8 | 265 404 | 72 | 1 149.9 | 85.3 | 5.0 | 1.2 | 4.4 | 0.1 | 6.3 | 7.4 |
| 31 37000 | Omaha......................... | 329.2 | 421 570 | 43 | 1 280.6 | 69.8 | 14.9 | 1.2 | 2.9 | 0.2 | 13.1 | 9.2 |
| 32 00000 | NEVADA.................... | 284 331.9 | 2 758 931 | X | 9.7 | 56.6 | 8.7 | 1.5 | 8.5 | 1.1 | 26.5 | 19.2 |
| 32 09700 | Carson City................. | 374.7 | 54 838 | 658 | 146.4 | 72.4 | 2.2 | 2.8 | 2.7 | 0.4 | 21.3 | 11.5 |
| 32 31900 | Henderson................... | 279.0 | 265 679 | 71 | 952.3 | 71.6 | 5.9 | 1.1 | 8.9 | 1.1 | 14.9 | 11.7 |
| 32 40000 | Las Vegas................... | 351.8 | 596 424 | 31 | 1 695.3 | 50.2 | 11.8 | 1.0 | 7.3 | 1.0 | 31.5 | 21.8 |
| 32 51800 | North Las Vegas .......... | 262.5 | 223 491 | 95 | 851.4 | 33.8 | 20.8 | 1.0 | 7.8 | 1.4 | 38.8 | 23.0 |
| 32 60600 | Reno........................... | 266.8 | 231 027 | 89 | 865.9 | 64.8 | 3.4 | 1.6 | 7.5 | 1.0 | 24.3 | 17.1 |
| 32 68400 | Sparks......................... | 92.6 | 92 183 | 324 | 995.5 | 63.6 | 3.2 | 1.6 | 7.0 | 1.0 | 26.3 | 16.3 |
| 33 00000 | NEW HAMPSHIRE..... | 23 187.3 | 1 320 718 | X | 57.0 | 93.6 | 1.5 | 0.7 | 2.6 | 0.1 | 2.8 | 5.2 |
| 33 14200 | Concord....................... | 166.4 | 42 630 | 857 | 256.2 | 91.9 | 2.7 | 0.9 | 3.9 | 0.1 | 2.1 | 4.7 |
| 33 18820 | Dover.......................... | 69.2 | 30 220 | 1 209 | 436.7 | 91.2 | 2.4 | 0.7 | 5.3 | 0.2 | 2.2 | 6.6 |
| 33 45140 | Manchester.................. | 85.7 | 110 209 | 241 | 1 286.0 | 83.9 | 4.6 | 0.7 | 4.2 | 0.1 | 8.1 | 11.8 |
| 33 50260 | Nashua........................ | 79.9 | 86 933 | 353 | 1 088.0 | 80.5 | 2.9 | 0.6 | 7.1 | 0.1 | 9.8 | 12.7 |
| 33 65140 | Rochester.................... | 117.6 | 29 823 | 1 221 | 253.6 | 95.7 | 1.4 | 0.8 | 1.6 | 0.1 | 1.8 | 2.1 |
| 34 00000 | NEW JERSEY............ | 19 047.3 | 8 864 590 | X | 465.4 | 60.5 | 13.5 | 0.5 | 8.9 | 0.1 | 17.7 | 20.6 |
| 34 02080 | Atlantic City................ | 27.8 | 39 504 | 919 | 1 421.0 | 17.1 | 36.8 | 0.9 | 16.4 | 0.1 | 30.4 | 28.1 |
| 34 03580 | Bayonne...................... | 15.0 | 64 416 | 534 | 4 294.4 | 58.2 | 8.4 | 0.4 | 8.2 | 0.2 | 25.8 | 26.1 |
| 34 05170 | Bergenfield.................. | 7.5 | 27 017 | 1 342 | 3 602.3 | 40.5 | 7.1 | 0.4 | 26.6 | 0.1 | 26.5 | 37.1 |
| 34 07600 | Bridgeton..................... | 16.0 | 25 290 | 1 427 | 1 580.6 | 20.4 | 35.4 | 1.5 | 0.7 | 0.0 | 43.6 | 24.1 |
| 34 10000 | Camden....................... | 23.1 | 77 250 | 422 | 3 344.2 | 5.6 | 45.4 | 0.7 | 2.3 | 0.1 | 47.0 | 13.2 |
| 34 13690 | Clifton......................... | 29.2 | 84 722 | 366 | 2 901.4 | 54.6 | 4.2 | 0.3 | 9.8 | 0.1 | 31.9 | 35.6 |
| 34 19390 | East Orange................. | 10.2 | 64 268 | 536 | 6 300.8 | 2.8 | 88.2 | 0.9 | 0.9 | 0.2 | 7.9 | 23.2 |
| 34 21000 | Elizabeth..................... | 31.9 | 126 458 | 201 | 3 964.2 | 18.9 | 19.1 | 0.3 | 2.3 | 0.1 | 59.5 | 46.5 |
| 34 21480 | Englewood................... | 12.7 | 27 605 | 1 314 | 2 173.6 | 32.2 | 32.1 | 0.8 | 8.6 | 0.1 | 27.5 | 31.2 |
| 34 22470 | Fair Lawn .................... | 13.3 | 32 847 | 1 108 | 2 469.7 | 78.3 | 1.7 | 0.2 | 10.3 | 0.0 | 10.2 | 28.2 |
| 34 24420 | Fort Lee....................... | 6.6 | 35 732 | 1 026 | 5 413.9 | 47.8 | 2.6 | 0.2 | 39.3 | 0.1 | 11.0 | 49.3 |

1. Dry land or land partially or temporarily covered by water.   2. May be of any race.

| City | Age of population (percent), 2010 | | | | | | | | | Median age | Percent female | Population | | | |
|---|---|---|---|---|---|---|---|---|---|---|---|---|---|---|---|
| | | | | | | | | | | | | Census counts | | Percent change | |
| | Under 5 years | 5 to 17 years | 18 to 24 years | 25 to 34 years | 35 to 44 years | 45 to 54 years | 55 to 64 years | 65 to 74 years | 75 years and over | | | 2000 | 2010 | 2000–2010 | 2010–2012 |
| | 12 | 13 | 14 | 15 | 16 | 17 | 18 | 19 | 20 | 21 | 22 | 23 | 24 | 25 | 26 |
| MISSOURI.............. | 6.5 | 17.3 | 9.8 | 12.9 | 12.5 | 14.8 | 12.1 | 7.5 | 6.5 | 37.9 | 51.0 | 5 595 211 | 5 988 924 | 7.0 | 0.6 |
| Ballwin.................... | 5.9 | 19.0 | 6.8 | 10.3 | 13.5 | 16.5 | 12.9 | 8.0 | 7.1 | 41.2 | 51.8 | 31 283 | 30 404 | -2.8 | 0.1 |
| Blue Springs................ | 7.2 | 20.7 | 8.5 | 14.0 | 13.8 | 14.6 | 11.8 | 5.7 | 3.6 | 34.7 | 51.5 | 48 080 | 52 580 | 9.3 | 0.8 |
| Cape Girardeau........... | 6.1 | 13.2 | 20.2 | 13.6 | 9.9 | 11.7 | 10.6 | 6.4 | 8.3 | 32.1 | 52.6 | 35 349 | 37 943 | 7.3 | 1.6 |
| Chesterfield ............... | 4.3 | 17.9 | 5.7 | 8.2 | 11.2 | 16.8 | 15.7 | 10.1 | 10.0 | 46.6 | 52.2 | 46 802 | 47 484 | 1.5 | 0.4 |
| Columbia .................. | 6.0 | 12.9 | 27.2 | 16.3 | 10.5 | 10.4 | 8.4 | 4.2 | 4.3 | 26.8 | 51.7 | 84 531 | 108 841 | 28.4 | 4.0 |
| Florissant.................. | 6.4 | 17.5 | 8.6 | 14.1 | 12.1 | 14.7 | 11.2 | 6.7 | 8.8 | 38.0 | 53.2 | 50 497 | 52 158 | 3.3 | 0.2 |
| Gladstone.................. | 6.4 | 14.9 | 7.8 | 12.7 | 11.8 | 14.8 | 13.9 | 8.9 | 8.7 | 41.7 | 52.1 | 26 365 | 25 410 | -3.6 | 2.1 |
| Hazelwood................. | 6.2 | 17.0 | 10.0 | 14.6 | 12.5 | 16.0 | 11.3 | 6.6 | 5.8 | 36.8 | 53.0 | 26 206 | 25 703 | -1.9 | -0.1 |
| Independence............. | 6.8 | 16.2 | 8.7 | 13.2 | 11.7 | 15.0 | 12.3 | 8.0 | 8.1 | 39.4 | 52.0 | 113 288 | 116 830 | 3.1 | 0.4 |
| Jefferson City ............ | 6.5 | 14.4 | 10.4 | 15.5 | 13.0 | 14.5 | 12.3 | 6.3 | 7.1 | 37.5 | 48.8 | 39 636 | 43 088 | 8.7 | 0.2 |
| Joplin...................... | 7.3 | 15.3 | 12.8 | 14.5 | 11.7 | 12.7 | 10.9 | 7.2 | 7.6 | 35.0 | 52.1 | 45 504 | 50 150 | 10.2 | -1.2 |
| Kansas City................ | 7.5 | 16.6 | 10.0 | 16.4 | 13.3 | 14.1 | 11.0 | 5.8 | 5.2 | 34.6 | 51.5 | 441 545 | 459 787 | 4.1 | 1.0 |
| Kirkwood................... | 5.9 | 17.3 | 6.1 | 11.3 | 12.4 | 15.6 | 14.3 | 8.0 | 9.1 | 42.6 | 54.0 | 27 324 | 27 540 | 0.8 | 0.0 |
| Lee's Summit ............. | 6.9 | 21.2 | 7.0 | 12.0 | 14.8 | 15.7 | 10.9 | 6.0 | 5.5 | 37.2 | 52.1 | 70 700 | 91 391 | 29.2 | 1.2 |
| Liberty..................... | 6.7 | 19.9 | 9.7 | 11.9 | 14.1 | 15.3 | 11.3 | 5.9 | 5.2 | 36.4 | 51.3 | 26 232 | 29 167 | 11.1 | 2.2 |
| Maryland Heights ......... | 6.0 | 14.2 | 10.8 | 19.0 | 12.9 | 14.4 | 10.4 | 6.6 | 5.6 | 35.0 | 51.3 | 25 756 | 27 472 | 6.7 | -0.1 |
| O'Fallon .................. | 8.0 | 22.0 | 7.1 | 14.0 | 16.9 | 14.8 | 8.4 | 5.0 | 4.0 | 34.3 | 51.2 | 46 169 | 79 585 | 71.8 | 3.0 |
| Raytown ................... | 6.1 | 17.0 | 8.0 | 12.4 | 12.5 | 15.7 | 12.1 | 7.1 | 9.1 | 40.3 | 52.7 | 30 388 | 29 526 | -2.8 | 0.0 |
| St. Charles ............... | 5.9 | 13.8 | 13.8 | 14.7 | 11.3 | 14.9 | 11.7 | 7.1 | 6.9 | 36.6 | 51.0 | 60 321 | 65 806 | 9.1 | 1.0 |
| St. Joseph ................ | 7.1 | 16.6 | 11.6 | 14.0 | 12.0 | 13.9 | 11.0 | 6.7 | 7.1 | 35.6 | 50.2 | 73 990 | 76 803 | 3.8 | 0.5 |
| St. Louis .................. | 6.6 | 14.5 | 12.3 | 18.1 | 12.6 | 14.0 | 10.8 | 5.5 | 5.5 | 33.9 | 51.7 | 348 189 | 319 294 | -8.3 | -0.4 |
| St. Peters ................. | 5.7 | 17.5 | 8.4 | 13.7 | 13.2 | 17.3 | 12.8 | 5.9 | 5.5 | 38.8 | 51.8 | 51 381 | 52 627 | 2.3 | 2.8 |
| Springfield ................ | 6.0 | 12.3 | 18.4 | 15.3 | 10.7 | 12.3 | 10.5 | 6.8 | 7.7 | 33.2 | 51.5 | 151 580 | 159 495 | 5.2 | 1.7 |
| University City ............ | 6.0 | 13.5 | 11.3 | 16.3 | 12.2 | 12.3 | 12.3 | 8.1 | 7.9 | 37.4 | 53.4 | 37 428 | 35 371 | -5.5 | -0.4 |
| Wentzville................. | 10.6 | 23.2 | 6.1 | 17.4 | 16.3 | 11.4 | 7.7 | 4.7 | 2.8 | 31.2 | 51.5 | 6 896 | 29 219 | 321.5 | 6.8 |
| Wildwood................... | 5.0 | 25.3 | 5.8 | 5.6 | 14.7 | 20.6 | 14.0 | 5.6 | 3.3 | 41.5 | 50.5 | 32 884 | 35 517 | 8.0 | 0.5 |
| MONTANA ............... | 6.3 | 16.3 | 9.6 | 12.4 | 11.4 | 15.1 | 14.0 | 8.2 | 6.7 | 39.8 | 49.8 | 902 195 | 989 417 | 9.7 | 1.6 |
| Billings.................... | 7.0 | 15.6 | 9.8 | 14.7 | 11.5 | 14.2 | 12.1 | 7.2 | 7.8 | 37.5 | 51.7 | 89 847 | 104 167 | 15.9 | 2.7 |
| Bozeman................... | 5.5 | 10.2 | 28.2 | 20.7 | 10.7 | 9.0 | 7.7 | 3.5 | 4.6 | 27.2 | 47.4 | 27 509 | 37 285 | 35.5 | 3.8 |
| Butte-Silver Bow........... | 5.8 | 15.2 | 10.8 | 11.3 | 11.3 | 15.5 | 13.7 | 8.7 | 7.7 | 41.3 | 49.5 | 34 606 | 33 525 | -1.2 | 0.6 |
| Great Falls................. | 6.7 | 15.8 | 9.9 | 13.4 | 11.2 | 14.4 | 12.0 | 8.2 | 8.4 | 39.0 | 51.1 | 56 690 | 58 604 | 3.2 | 0.5 |
| Helena..................... | 5.9 | 14.2 | 11.6 | 12.9 | 10.5 | 14.5 | 14.9 | 7.5 | 8.1 | 40.3 | 52.0 | 25 780 | 28 198 | 9.3 | 3.3 |
| Missoula................... | 5.7 | 12.2 | 19.8 | 18.7 | 10.9 | 11.5 | 10.6 | 5.2 | 5.4 | 30.9 | 50.1 | 57 053 | 66 861 | 17.1 | 2.3 |
| NEBRASKA............... | 7.2 | 17.9 | 10.0 | 13.4 | 12.1 | 14.2 | 11.7 | 6.7 | 6.8 | 36.2 | 50.4 | 1 711 263 | 1 826 341 | 6.7 | 1.6 |
| Bellevue................... | 7.3 | 19.1 | 9.8 | 14.0 | 12.6 | 14.8 | 10.8 | 6.8 | 4.7 | 34.8 | 50.8 | 44 382 | 51 026 | 13.0 | 3.1 |
| Fremont.................... | 7.3 | 17.0 | 9.7 | 12.8 | 11.2 | 13.6 | 11.2 | 7.6 | 9.6 | 38.0 | 51.5 | 25 174 | 26 397 | 4.9 | -0.9 |
| Grand Island .............. | 8.4 | 19.2 | 8.7 | 14.1 | 12.6 | 13.3 | 10.7 | 6.0 | 6.9 | 34.7 | 50.2 | 42 940 | 48 520 | 13.0 | 3.0 |
| Kearney.................... | 7.5 | 14.7 | 20.4 | 15.4 | 10.2 | 11.0 | 9.6 | 5.3 | 5.8 | 29.0 | 51.1 | 27 431 | 30 802 | 12.2 | 3.2 |
| Lincoln..................... | 7.2 | 15.5 | 15.6 | 16.0 | 11.9 | 12.4 | 10.5 | 5.4 | 5.3 | 31.8 | 50.0 | 225 581 | 258 381 | 14.5 | 2.7 |
| Omaha..................... | 7.5 | 17.6 | 11.3 | 15.5 | 12.3 | 13.5 | 10.9 | 5.8 | 5.6 | 33.5 | 50.8 | 390 007 | 409 853 | 4.9 | 2.9 |
| NEVADA................... | 6.9 | 17.7 | 9.2 | 14.3 | 14.2 | 13.9 | 11.7 | 7.3 | 4.7 | 36.3 | 49.5 | 1 998 257 | 2 700 552 | 35.1 | 2.2 |
| Carson City ............... | 5.8 | 15.5 | 8.5 | 12.0 | 12.6 | 15.2 | 13.8 | 8.7 | 7.8 | 41.7 | 48.1 | 52 457 | 55 274 | 5.4 | -0.8 |
| Henderson................. | 5.9 | 16.8 | 7.8 | 13.0 | 14.5 | 14.3 | 13.5 | 9.0 | 5.2 | 39.6 | 50.8 | 175 381 | 257 583 | 47.0 | 3.1 |
| Las Vegas ................. | 7.2 | 18.4 | 8.9 | 14.2 | 14.7 | 13.8 | 10.8 | 7.0 | 5.0 | 35.9 | 49.6 | 478 434 | 583 787 | 22.0 | 2.2 |
| North Las Vegas .......... | 9.0 | 22.5 | 9.7 | 15.9 | 15.3 | 12.0 | 8.4 | 4.7 | 2.4 | 30.6 | 50.2 | 115 488 | 216 940 | 87.9 | 3.0 |
| Reno....................... | 7.0 | 15.8 | 12.5 | 15.2 | 13.0 | 13.4 | 11.4 | 6.6 | 5.0 | 34.6 | 49.2 | 180 480 | 225 986 | 24.8 | 2.2 |
| Sparks..................... | 7.2 | 18.6 | 9.7 | 13.7 | 13.9 | 14.2 | 11.4 | 6.5 | 4.8 | 35.5 | 50.6 | 66 346 | 90 264 | 36.1 | 2.1 |
| NEW HAMPSHIRE..... | 5.3 | 16.5 | 9.4 | 11.0 | 13.6 | 17.2 | 13.5 | 7.4 | 6.2 | 41.1 | 50.7 | 1 235 786 | 1 316 469 | 6.5 | 0.3 |
| Concord.................... | 5.5 | 15.2 | 9.3 | 14.2 | 13.9 | 15.9 | 12.3 | 6.1 | 7.7 | 39.4 | 50.4 | 40 687 | 42 695 | 4.9 | -0.2 |
| Dover...................... | 6.0 | 14.2 | 11.1 | 16.4 | 14.1 | 14.5 | 10.5 | 6.0 | 7.0 | 36.7 | 51.0 | 26 884 | 29 983 | 11.5 | 0.8 |
| Manchester................ | 6.7 | 14.9 | 10.2 | 16.8 | 13.6 | 14.8 | 11.2 | 5.7 | 6.1 | 36.0 | 50.4 | 107 006 | 109 565 | 2.4 | 0.6 |
| Nashua .................... | 6.3 | 15.8 | 9.3 | 13.8 | 14.3 | 15.9 | 11.9 | 6.5 | 6.2 | 38.5 | 50.7 | 86 605 | 86 494 | -0.1 | 0.5 |
| Rochester.................. | 6.0 | 16.0 | 7.7 | 12.7 | 13.5 | 16.3 | 12.9 | 7.8 | 6.9 | 40.7 | 51.7 | 28 461 | 29 752 | 4.5 | 0.2 |
| NEW JERSEY........... | 6.2 | 17.3 | 8.7 | 12.6 | 14.1 | 15.7 | 11.9 | 7.0 | 6.5 | 39.0 | 51.3 | 8 414 350 | 8 791 898 | 4.5 | 0.8 |
| Atlantic City ............... | 7.8 | 16.8 | 10.2 | 13.6 | 13.2 | 14.5 | 11.2 | 6.9 | 5.8 | 36.3 | 51.0 | 40 517 | 39 558 | -2.4 | -0.1 |
| Bayonne ................... | 6.1 | 16.4 | 8.9 | 14.2 | 13.9 | 15.1 | 12.3 | 6.6 | 6.6 | 38.4 | 52.2 | 61 842 | 63 024 | 1.9 | 2.2 |
| Bergenfield ................ | 6.5 | 17.4 | 8.6 | 12.3 | 13.8 | 15.7 | 12.6 | 6.9 | 6.2 | 39.0 | 52.2 | 26 247 | 26 764 | 2.0 | 0.9 |
| Bridgeton .................. | 9.9 | 18.0 | 12.2 | 20.0 | 14.6 | 11.7 | 6.5 | 3.8 | 3.4 | 29.7 | 42.5 | 22 771 | 25 349 | 11.3 | -0.2 |
| Camden .................... | 9.2 | 21.8 | 13.1 | 15.6 | 12.4 | 12.0 | 8.2 | 4.6 | 3.0 | 28.5 | 51.4 | 79 904 | 77 346 | -3.2 | -0.1 |
| Clifton ..................... | 6.1 | 15.9 | 8.8 | 14.5 | 13.8 | 14.8 | 12.2 | 6.6 | 7.3 | 38.4 | 51.8 | 78 672 | 84 136 | 6.9 | 0.7 |
| East Orange ............... | 7.2 | 18.4 | 10.2 | 14.2 | 13.6 | 14.1 | 10.5 | 6.6 | 5.2 | 35.0 | 55.2 | 69 824 | 64 094 | -8.0 | 0.3 |
| Elizabeth................... | 8.0 | 17.7 | 10.6 | 16.5 | 14.8 | 13.8 | 9.5 | 5.2 | 4.0 | 33.2 | 50.4 | 120 568 | 124 969 | 3.7 | 1.2 |
| Englewood................. | 6.6 | 15.6 | 7.7 | 14.4 | 14.5 | 14.5 | 12.5 | 7.8 | 6.4 | 38.9 | 52.6 | 26 203 | 27 147 | 3.6 | 1.7 |
| Fair Lawn .................. | 5.2 | 16.8 | 6.8 | 10.3 | 13.7 | 16.4 | 14.4 | 7.4 | 8.9 | 43.1 | 52.0 | 31 637 | 32 457 | 2.6 | 1.2 |
| Fort Lee.................... | 5.1 | 11.8 | 5.3 | 12.7 | 15.5 | 14.3 | 13.5 | 10.6 | 11.2 | 44.7 | 53.5 | 35 461 | 35 345 | -0.3 | 1.1 |

## Table D. Cities — Households, Group Quarters, Crime, and Education

| City | Households, 2010 Number | Persons per household | Percent Female family householder[1] | Percent One-person | Persons in group quarters, 2010 Total | Institutional Total | Persons in nursing facilities | Non-institutional | Serious crimes known to police[2] 2011 Total Number | Rate[3] | Rate[3] Violent | Rate[3] Property | Population age 25 and older | Attainment[4] (percent) High school graduate or less | Bachelor's degree or more |
|---|---|---|---|---|---|---|---|---|---|---|---|---|---|---|---|
| | 27 | 28 | 29 | 30 | 31 | 32 | 33 | 34 | 35 | 36 | 37 | 38 | 39 | 40 | 41 |
| MISSOURI | 2 375 611 | 2.45 | 12.3 | 28.3 | 174 142 | 93 274 | 44 866 | 80 868 | 225 771 | 3 756 | 447 | 3 309 | 3 943 728 | 45.3 | 25.4 |
| Ballwin | 11 874 | 2.56 | 8.8 | 23.1 | 2 | 0 | 0 | 2 | 360 | 1 180 | 29 | 1 150 | 20 966 | 17.9 | 52.4 |
| Blue Springs | 19 522 | 2.68 | 13.7 | 20.4 | 218 | 182 | 182 | 36 | 1 636 | 3 100 | 220 | 2 881 | 33 225 | 34.7 | 30.0 |
| Cape Girardeau | 15 205 | 2.27 | 12.8 | 33.6 | 3 466 | 789 | 712 | 2 677 | 2 725 | 7 156 | 662 | 6 494 | 23 200 | 42.3 | 31.1 |
| Chesterfield | 19 224 | 2.42 | 5.9 | 26.1 | 934 | 925 | 925 | 9 | 778 | 1 632 | 69 | 1 563 | 33 475 | 14.5 | 64.3 |
| Columbia | 43 065 | 2.32 | 10.6 | 32.0 | 8 804 | 1 146 | 624 | 7 658 | 4 845 | 4 449 | 534 | 3 915 | 57 177 | 25.5 | 52.2 |
| Florissant | 21 247 | 2.42 | 17.5 | 29.9 | 788 | 668 | 542 | 120 | 1 217 | 2 325 | 191 | 2 134 | 35 301 | 42.3 | 20.0 |
| Gladstone | 11 182 | 2.27 | 12.3 | 32.4 | 42 | 36 | 36 | 6 | 815 | 3 196 | 267 | 2 929 | 17 091 | 38.9 | 28.2 |
| Hazelwood | 10 933 | 2.34 | 17.3 | 33.7 | 140 | 0 | 0 | 140 | 1 087 | 4 214 | 295 | 3 919 | 17 481 | 40.6 | 24.3 |
| Independence | 48 742 | 2.37 | 13.9 | 31.7 | 1 225 | 1 048 | 982 | 177 | 7 190 | 6 132 | 426 | 5 706 | 78 641 | 51.3 | 18.1 |
| Jefferson City | 17 278 | 2.21 | 12.4 | 36.2 | 4 964 | 3 990 | 456 | 974 | 1 858 | 4 297 | 567 | 3 731 | 28 929 | 39.0 | 33.5 |
| Joplin | 20 860 | 2.31 | 13.5 | 33.3 | 1 988 | 743 | 653 | 1 245 | 3 804 | 7 558 | 503 | 7 055 | 32 366 | 46.2 | 21.0 |
| Kansas City | 192 406 | 2.34 | 16.1 | 34.7 | 8 812 | 4 192 | 2 499 | 4 620 | 31 269 | 6 776 | 1 204 | 5 572 | 302 860 | 39.8 | 30.1 |
| Kirkwood | 11 894 | 2.29 | 9.9 | 33.6 | 257 | 223 | 218 | 34 | 792 | 2 865 | 123 | 2 742 | 19 577 | 16.3 | 59.1 |
| Lee's Summit | 34 429 | 2.63 | 10.9 | 22.8 | 714 | 626 | 573 | 88 | 2 223 | 2 424 | 117 | 2 308 | 57 773 | 25.7 | 42.6 |
| Liberty | 10 582 | 2.63 | 11.0 | 23.4 | 1 358 | 585 | 277 | 773 | 532 | 1 818 | 191 | 1 627 | 18 446 | 33.9 | 36.8 |
| Maryland Heights | 12 180 | 2.21 | 11.4 | 35.2 | 559 | 522 | 473 | 37 | 758 | 2 749 | 145 | 2 604 | 19 501 | 34.0 | 36.7 |
| O'Fallon | 28 234 | 2.80 | 10.0 | 19.3 | 294 | 254 | 247 | 40 | 1 296 | 1 628 | 89 | 1 539 | 46 661 | 30.8 | 39.1 |
| Raytown | 12 104 | 2.39 | 16.9 | 30.7 | 559 | 401 | 395 | 158 | 1 320 | 4 454 | 297 | 4 158 | 20 017 | 43.1 | 22.2 |
| St. Charles | 26 715 | 2.29 | 10.8 | 31.9 | 4 623 | 917 | 508 | 3 706 | 2 155 | 3 264 | 232 | 3 032 | 43 448 | 39.6 | 31.6 |
| St. Joseph | 29 727 | 2.43 | 14.5 | 30.7 | 4 493 | 3 104 | 673 | 1 389 | 4 337 | 5 628 | 365 | 5 263 | 50 010 | 52.7 | 19.4 |
| St. Louis | 142 057 | 2.16 | 19.4 | 42.6 | 11 978 | 4 822 | 2 060 | 7 156 | 31 619 | 9 867 | 1 857 | 8 010 | 210 822 | 44.5 | 27.7 |
| St. Peters | 20 861 | 2.51 | 10.0 | 26.3 | 203 | 184 | 184 | 19 | 1 589 | 3 011 | 269 | 2 742 | 35 900 | 31.9 | 32.8 |
| Springfield | 69 754 | 2.13 | 11.8 | 37.3 | 10 739 | 3 302 | 1 443 | 7 437 | 15 724 | 9 823 | 816 | 9 007 | 100 627 | 42.1 | 25.7 |
| University City | 16 154 | 2.18 | 15.0 | 36.5 | 232 | 200 | 169 | 32 | 1 650 | 4 648 | 546 | 4 101 | 25 018 | 23.7 | 52.7 |
| Wentzville | 9 767 | 2.96 | 11.1 | 15.6 | 137 | 133 | 133 | 4 | 587 | 2 012 | 110 | 1 902 | 16 889 | 30.3 | 31.9 |
| Wildwood | 12 112 | 2.93 | 6.0 | 13.6 | 66 | 62 | 40 | 4 | NA | NA | NA | NA | 21 975 | 12.9 | 63.4 |
| MONTANA | 409 607 | 2.35 | 9.0 | 29.7 | 28 849 | 11 929 | 5 200 | 16 920 | 25 825 | 2 587 | 267 | 2 320 | 663 484 | 39.4 | 28.2 |
| Billings | 43 945 | 2.29 | 11.3 | 32.6 | 3 351 | 1 750 | 753 | 1 601 | 5 009 | 4 766 | 299 | 4 467 | 69 435 | 37.3 | 31.1 |
| Bozeman | 15 775 | 2.17 | 7.0 | 33.5 | 3 030 | 199 | 145 | 2 831 | 1 245 | 3 310 | 239 | 3 071 | 20 352 | 16.5 | 52.3 |
| Butte-Silver Bow | 14 932 | 2.22 | 10.6 | 35.1 | 998 | 610 | 276 | 388 | 1 136 | 3 292 | 293 | 3 000 | 23 254 | 46.9 | 22.5 |
| Great Falls | 25 301 | 2.26 | 11.5 | 33.5 | 1 263 | 798 | 482 | 465 | 2 877 | 4 874 | 300 | 4 574 | 39 131 | 40.0 | 23.1 |
| Helena | 12 780 | 2.07 | 10.6 | 39.8 | 1 682 | 432 | 191 | 1 250 | 1 078 | 3 790 | 489 | 3 302 | 19 383 | 23.8 | 46.2 |
| Missoula | 29 081 | 2.18 | 9.6 | 35.0 | 3 519 | 766 | 374 | 2 753 | 2 859 | 4 243 | 297 | 3 946 | 41 139 | 28.1 | 41.4 |
| NEBRASKA | 721 130 | 2.46 | 9.8 | 28.7 | 51 165 | 23 633 | 13 519 | 27 532 | 55 391 | 3 006 | 253 | 2 753 | 1 173 189 | 38.9 | 27.8 |
| Bellevue | 19 142 | 2.62 | 13.0 | 24.3 | 74 | 31 | 15 | 43 | 1 287 | 2 544 | 97 | 2 447 | 32 335 | 36.3 | 26.9 |
| Fremont | 10 725 | 2.38 | 11.2 | 30.2 | 832 | 468 | 386 | 364 | 767 | 2 880 | 165 | 2 715 | 17 421 | 51.3 | 18.3 |
| Grand Island | 18 326 | 2.59 | 12.0 | 29.1 | 1 058 | 781 | 546 | 277 | 2 597 | 5 305 | 304 | 5 001 | 30 120 | 51.3 | 15.9 |
| Kearney | 12 201 | 2.36 | 9.9 | 30.4 | 2 002 | 390 | 284 | 1 612 | 921 | 2 965 | 145 | 2 820 | 17 361 | 34.3 | 35.5 |
| Lincoln | 103 540 | 2.36 | 10.2 | 31.3 | 13 579 | 4 236 | 1 001 | 9 343 | 11 155 | 4 279 | 371 | 3 909 | 156 428 | 30.2 | 36.0 |
| Omaha | 162 627 | 2.45 | 13.7 | 32.3 | 11 183 | 4 676 | 2 002 | 6 507 | 21 073 | 5 107 | 560 | 4 548 | 260 977 | 36.9 | 32.1 |
| NEVADA | 1 006 250 | 2.65 | 12.7 | 25.7 | 36 154 | 25 835 | 5 005 | 10 319 | 85 040 | 3 123 | 562 | 2 561 | 1 764 861 | 44.9 | 22.2 |
| Carson City | 21 427 | 2.41 | 12.0 | 30.4 | 3 625 | 3 560 | 313 | 65 | 1 423 | 2 553 | 266 | 2 287 | 38 633 | 45.1 | 21.0 |
| Henderson | 101 314 | 2.53 | 11.0 | 24.2 | 1 104 | 787 | 585 | 317 | 5 348 | 2 058 | 220 | 1 838 | 178 116 | 34.4 | 30.4 |
| Las Vegas | 211 689 | 2.71 | 14.1 | 26.0 | 9 482 | 6 514 | 1 628 | 2 968 | 52 239 | 3 582 | 741 | 2 840 | 381 426 | 47.3 | 21.5 |
| North Las Vegas | 66 499 | 3.23 | 16.8 | 16.7 | 2 441 | 2 167 | 683 | 274 | 3 678 | 1 681 | 357 | 1 324 | 122 343 | 53.3 | 14.8 |
| Reno | 90 924 | 2.43 | 11.8 | 32.1 | 4 583 | 1 679 | 323 | 2 904 | 7 658 | 3 372 | 488 | 2 884 | 142 588 | 38.4 | 28.4 |
| Sparks | 33 502 | 2.68 | 13.0 | 24.3 | 321 | 256 | 256 | 65 | 2 732 | 3 001 | 313 | 2 688 | 59 044 | 42.9 | 21.0 |
| NEW HAMPSHIRE | 518 973 | 2.46 | 9.7 | 25.6 | 40 104 | 13 113 | 7 767 | 26 991 | 32 584 | 2 472 | 188 | 2 284 | 901 420 | 38.3 | 33.1 |
| Concord | 17 592 | 2.26 | 11.6 | 33.6 | 2 903 | 2 282 | 454 | 621 | 1 420 | 3 322 | 285 | 3 036 | 30 409 | 32.9 | 36.5 |
| Dover | 12 827 | 2.27 | 10.3 | 31.8 | 896 | 789 | 358 | 107 | 619 | 2 062 | 103 | 1 958 | 19 757 | 32.5 | 37.8 |
| Manchester | 45 766 | 2.34 | 13.1 | 32.4 | 2 578 | 1 547 | 662 | 1 031 | 4 810 | 4 384 | 563 | 3 821 | 74 135 | 46.9 | 25.8 |
| Nashua | 35 044 | 2.42 | 11.6 | 29.4 | 1 685 | 546 | 505 | 1 139 | 2 360 | 2 725 | 248 | 2 477 | 59 761 | 37.1 | 34.8 |
| Rochester | 12 378 | 2.38 | 12.2 | 27.8 | 240 | 192 | 181 | 48 | 1 114 | 3 739 | 352 | 3 387 | 20 844 | 49.7 | 18.7 |
| NEW JERSEY | 3 214 360 | 2.68 | 13.3 | 25.2 | 186 876 | 100 621 | 45 512 | 86 255 | 216 922 | 2 459 | 308 | 2 151 | 5 926 262 | 41.9 | 35.0 |
| Atlantic City | 15 504 | 2.50 | 22.2 | 37.5 | 802 | 186 | 186 | 616 | 3 679 | 9 269 | 1 867 | 7 402 | 26 377 | 63.4 | 15.6 |
| Bayonne | 25 237 | 2.49 | 16.8 | 31.6 | 276 | 0 | 0 | 276 | 955 | 1 510 | 234 | 1 276 | 44 239 | 50.9 | 29.0 |
| Bergenfield | 8 852 | 3.02 | 13.7 | 19.4 | 38 | 0 | 0 | 38 | 177 | 659 | 67 | 592 | 18 252 | 38.5 | 38.7 |
| Bridgeton | 6 265 | 3.36 | 27.7 | 25.8 | 4 276 | 4 257 | 0 | 19 | 1 370 | 5 387 | 1 207 | 4 180 | 15 202 | 75.1 | 7.5 |
| Camden | 24 475 | 3.02 | 37.9 | 24.8 | 3 321 | 2 229 | 290 | 1 092 | 6 614 | 8 523 | 2 773 | 5 750 | 43 078 | 73.0 | 7.2 |
| Clifton | 30 661 | 2.74 | 13.0 | 26.0 | 254 | 192 | 182 | 62 | 1 853 | 2 195 | 255 | 1 940 | 57 932 | 46.9 | 30.8 |
| East Orange | 24 945 | 2.53 | 29.0 | 35.8 | 1 235 | 780 | 716 | 455 | 1 655 | 2 567 | 651 | 1 915 | 42 029 | 53.4 | 17.2 |
| Elizabeth | 41 596 | 2.94 | 22.0 | 23.5 | 2 545 | 1 833 | 398 | 712 | 6 414 | 5 115 | 1 049 | 4 067 | 77 891 | 67.5 | 12.4 |
| Englewood | 10 057 | 2.68 | 17.1 | 27.3 | 164 | 136 | 136 | 28 | 397 | 1 458 | 250 | 1 208 | 18 581 | 37.0 | 44.0 |
| Fair Lawn | 11 930 | 2.70 | 9.1 | 21.3 | 187 | 152 | 152 | 35 | 407 | 1 250 | 83 | 1 167 | 22 697 | 28.6 | 49.5 |
| Fort Lee | 16 371 | 2.16 | 8.5 | 38.4 | 7 | 0 | 0 | 7 | 350 | 987 | 54 | 933 | 27 313 | 27.6 | 53.9 |

1. No spouse present.   2. Data for serious crimes have not been adjusted for underreporting. This may affect comparability between geographic areas and over time.   3. Per 100,000 population estimated by the FBI.   4. Persons 25 years old and over.

| City | Money income, 2007–2011 | | | | | Housing units, 2010 | | | Occupied Housing units 2007–2011 | | | | |
|---|---|---|---|---|---|---|---|---|---|---|---|---|---|
| | | Households | | | Families with income below poverty (percent) | | | | | Owner-occupied | | Median owner costs as a percent of income | |
| | Per capita income[1] (dollars) | Median income | Percent with income of $200,000 or more | Percent with income of less than $25,000 | | Total | Percent change, 2000–2010 | Vacant units for sale or rent[2] | Total | Percent | Median value[3] (dollars) | With a mortgage[4] | Without a mortgage[5] |
| | 42 | 43 | 44 | 45 | 46 | 47 | 48 | 49 | 50 | 51 | 52 | 53 | 54 |
| MISSOURI.............. | 25 371 | 47 202 | 2.7 | 25.6 | 10.3 | 2 712 729 | 11.1 | 337 118 | 2 354 104 | 69.5 | 138 900 | 22.4 | 11.6 |
| Ballwin...................... | 38 073 | 81 388 | 6.3 | 10.9 | 3.1 | 12 435 | 3.2 | 561 | 11 747 | 81.5 | 233 500 | 21.3 | 10.8 |
| Blue Springs............ | 28 502 | 66 573 | 3.9 | 14.5 | 6.6 | 20 643 | 16.0 | 1 121 | 18 963 | 72.8 | 149 800 | 22.2 | 10.9 |
| Cape Girardeau......... | 22 140 | 39 837 | 2.6 | 30.1 | 14.7 | 16 760 | 6.0 | 1 555 | 14 923 | 55.0 | 130 900 | 21.1 | 11.2 |
| Chesterfield ............. | 51 725 | 95 006 | 16.8 | 12.9 | 1.7 | 20 393 | 8.5 | 1 169 | 19 045 | 80.3 | 339 200 | 20.7 | 12.6 |
| Columbia .................. | 24 726 | 43 102 | 2.8 | 30.7 | 10.4 | 46 758 | 30.0 | 3 693 | 42 388 | 48.6 | 167 300 | 21.2 | 10.1 |
| Florissant ................. | 25 215 | 51 673 | 0.6 | 18.6 | 4.5 | 22 632 | 8.0 | 1 385 | 21 577 | 74.3 | 115 000 | 23.5 | 12.0 |
| Gladstone ................. | 27 052 | 51 478 | 2.4 | 20.0 | 6.6 | 12 148 | 1.8 | 966 | 10 799 | 68.1 | 138 600 | 23.5 | 12.9 |
| Hazelwood ................ | 24 910 | 47 218 | 0.7 | 20.9 | 10.0 | 11 730 | 2.9 | 797 | 11 020 | 60.5 | 127 700 | 22.6 | 11.7 |
| Independence ........... | 23 013 | 44 050 | 0.9 | 27.0 | 11.6 | 53 834 | 7.3 | 5 092 | 47 659 | 66.0 | 107 700 | 22.8 | 12.9 |
| Jefferson City .......... | 26 494 | 48 545 | 2.0 | 23.8 | 9.1 | 18 852 | 10.9 | 1 574 | 17 445 | 58.7 | 134 200 | 18.2 | 10.0 |
| Joplin....................... | 22 458 | 37 587 | 2.2 | 31.9 | 14.3 | 23 322 | 9.2 | 2 462 | 20 552 | 56.2 | 95 300 | 21.9 | 12.1 |
| Kansas City.............. | 26 372 | 45 246 | 2.8 | 27.5 | 13.8 | 221 860 | 9.7 | 29 454 | 192 271 | 57.3 | 136 900 | 23.2 | 13.3 |
| Kirkwood .................. | 45 994 | 74 088 | 10.4 | 15.1 | 3.0 | 12 895 | 4.6 | 1 001 | 11 842 | 78.2 | 232 900 | 21.4 | 12.4 |
| Lee's Summit ........... | 33 973 | 75 534 | 5.3 | 12.2 | 4.9 | 36 679 | 33.9 | 2 250 | 33 222 | 76.1 | 186 800 | 21.7 | 11.8 |
| Liberty ..................... | 29 953 | 63 921 | 4.1 | 13.8 | 6.3 | 11 284 | 14.5 | 702 | 10 610 | 75.8 | 165 000 | 23.1 | 11.7 |
| Maryland Heights ..... | 29 529 | 54 643 | 1.9 | 17.8 | 7.2 | 13 092 | 10.7 | 912 | 12 542 | 56.9 | 159 200 | 22.9 | 11.4 |
| O'Fallon................... | 29 755 | 77 739 | 3.1 | 9.9 | 2.7 | 29 376 | 84.8 | 1 142 | 26 876 | 84.3 | 205 700 | 22.5 | 11.9 |
| Raytown................... | 23 742 | 49 348 | 0.5 | 22.2 | 7.1 | 13 276 | -0.2 | 1 172 | 11 985 | 73.0 | 107 600 | 23.1 | 12.7 |
| St. Charles .............. | 29 158 | 56 929 | 2.8 | 18.6 | 7.2 | 28 590 | 13.4 | 1 875 | 26 585 | 67.3 | 180 200 | 21.4 | 12.2 |
| St. Joseph............... | 21 699 | 40 962 | 1.5 | 29.1 | 11.6 | 33 189 | 4.7 | 3 462 | 29 209 | 64.1 | 99 400 | 20.6 | 11.4 |
| St. Louis.................. | 22 050 | 34 402 | 1.5 | 38.0 | 21.0 | 176 002 | -0.2 | 33 945 | 139 693 | 46.4 | 123 300 | 24.3 | 13.8 |
| St. Peters................ | 31 524 | 70 774 | 2.4 | 11.5 | 1.7 | 21 717 | 15.5 | 856 | 20 839 | 82.3 | 171 700 | 21.7 | 10.7 |
| Springfield ............... | 21 233 | 33 771 | 1.6 | 37.1 | 16.3 | 77 620 | 11.1 | 7 866 | 70 077 | 49.6 | 105 900 | 21.7 | 10.1 |
| University City .......... | 36 770 | 53 807 | 8.4 | 23.7 | 9.3 | 18 021 | 3.0 | 1 867 | 16 042 | 57.4 | 192 400 | 22.2 | 13.2 |
| Wentzville................ | 27 930 | 70 642 | 2.2 | 9.7 | 2.7 | 10 305 | NA | 538 | 9 402 | 86.6 | 203 200 | 25.2 | 11.8 |
| Wildwood ................. | 50 849 | 118 019 | 23.1 | 6.3 | 2.3 | 12 604 | 11.5 | 492 | 11 901 | 91.0 | 351 000 | 21.2 | 10.0 |
| MONTANA ............... | 24 640 | 45 324 | 2.1 | 26.6 | 9.7 | 482 825 | 17.0 | 73 218 | 403 495 | 68.9 | 179 900 | 24.0 | 11.6 |
| Billings .................... | 27 582 | 47 869 | 3.0 | 24.1 | 8.6 | 46 317 | 18.3 | 2 372 | 43 724 | 65.1 | 172 900 | 22.5 | 11.0 |
| Bozeman .................. | 25 699 | 44 412 | 2.6 | 27.2 | 10.1 | 17 464 | 50.0 | 1 689 | 15 396 | 45.4 | 269 000 | 25.3 | 11.2 |
| Butte-Silver Bow........... | 22 249 | 40 030 | 0.7 | 31.7 | 11.1 | 16 717 | 3.3 | 1 785 | 14 981 | 65.5 | 120 700 | 20.9 | 12.2 |
| Great Falls............... | 22 894 | 42 540 | 1.2 | 28.2 | 12.9 | 26 854 | 6.3 | 1 553 | 24 566 | 64.4 | 149 900 | 23.3 | 11.3 |
| Helena ..................... | 28 856 | 47 749 | 2.5 | 25.1 | 7.2 | 13 457 | 11.0 | 677 | 13 083 | 56.9 | 192 500 | 22.8 | 11.1 |
| Missoula .................. | 23 847 | 37 316 | 2.0 | 34.5 | 10.4 | 30 682 | 22.3 | 1 601 | 28 920 | 49.3 | 238 100 | 26.1 | 12.0 |
| NEBRASKA.............. | 26 113 | 50 695 | 2.8 | 22.9 | 8.1 | 796 793 | 10.3 | 75 663 | 715 703 | 68.3 | 125 400 | 21.8 | 12.6 |
| Bellevue................... | 25 665 | 58 053 | 1.3 | 16.1 | 7.9 | 20 591 | 18.0 | 1 449 | 19 264 | 66.4 | 137 700 | 22.0 | 11.4 |
| Fremont.................... | 21 815 | 44 154 | 0.9 | 27.3 | 10.0 | 11 427 | 8.0 | 702 | 10 741 | 62.8 | 115 000 | 21.4 | 13.5 |
| Grand Island............ | 22 166 | 45 095 | 1.5 | 25.6 | 9.3 | 19 426 | 11.7 | 1 100 | 18 119 | 63.0 | 106 300 | 21.1 | 13.4 |
| Kearney ................... | 23 861 | 47 399 | 2.1 | 24.9 | 9.9 | 12 738 | 15.7 | 537 | 11 661 | 59.0 | 134 200 | 21.3 | 10.0 |
| Lincoln .................... | 25 765 | 49 114 | 2.6 | 24.3 | 9.1 | 110 546 | 16.1 | 7 000 | 102 976 | 59.2 | 141 200 | 22.3 | 11.3 |
| Omaha..................... | 26 842 | 46 978 | 3.5 | 25.4 | 11.4 | 177 518 | 7.1 | 14 891 | 162 607 | 59.8 | 132 700 | 22.6 | 13.3 |
| NEVADA.................. | 27 625 | 55 553 | 3.6 | 19.6 | 9.5 | 1 173 814 | 41.9 | 167 564 | 986 741 | 59.1 | 225 400 | 28.7 | 11.8 |
| Carson City ............. | 27 704 | 54 235 | 2.8 | 22.5 | 9.9 | 23 534 | 10.6 | 2 107 | 21 289 | 61.0 | 244 600 | 25.8 | 11.8 |
| Henderson................ | 35 155 | 67 934 | 6.3 | 14.4 | 5.5 | 113 586 | 59.0 | 12 272 | 99 459 | 67.0 | 275 800 | 28.2 | 10.8 |
| Las Vegas ............... | 26 755 | 54 174 | 3.9 | 20.9 | 11.0 | 243 701 | 27.7 | 32 012 | 211 684 | 55.9 | 222 000 | 28.7 | 12.1 |
| North Las Vegas ......... | 21 603 | 57 425 | 1.8 | 16.1 | 10.5 | 76 073 | 107.9 | 9 574 | 63 952 | 60.6 | 199 300 | 30.7 | 10.0 |
| Reno ....................... | 27 782 | 49 700 | 3.6 | 24.4 | 11.6 | 102 582 | 28.9 | 11 658 | 88 788 | 48.5 | 256 800 | 28.2 | 12.2 |
| Sparks..................... | 26 025 | 56 637 | 1.8 | 19.0 | 9.4 | 36 455 | 39.8 | 2 953 | 33 342 | 60.9 | 229 600 | 28.5 | 14.0 |
| NEW HAMPSHIRE..... | 32 357 | 64 664 | 5.0 | 16.7 | 5.2 | 614 754 | 12.4 | 95 781 | 514 869 | 72.5 | 250 000 | 26.8 | 16.5 |
| Concord ................... | 30 037 | 54 163 | 3.3 | 20.5 | 6.6 | 18 852 | 11.7 | 1 260 | 18 007 | 55.4 | 227 400 | 26.2 | 20.0 |
| Dover....................... | 31 795 | 57 521 | 3.9 | 18.8 | 7.0 | 13 685 | 14.8 | 858 | 12 429 | 54.8 | 242 800 | 26.8 | 16.6 |
| Manchester............... | 27 467 | 53 278 | 2.3 | 22.9 | 10.2 | 49 288 | 7.4 | 3 522 | 45 130 | 49.9 | 231 200 | 27.9 | 16.9 |
| Nashua..................... | 33 032 | 66 074 | 4.2 | 18.8 | 5.4 | 37 168 | 5.0 | 2 124 | 35 220 | 58.9 | 253 900 | 25.5 | 17.0 |
| Rochester................. | 27 902 | 52 536 | 1.9 | 18.5 | 9.0 | 13 372 | 13.0 | 994 | 12 357 | 70.4 | 189 700 | 26.7 | 18.8 |
| NEW JERSEY........... | 35 678 | 71 180 | 8.8 | 16.9 | 7.0 | 3 553 562 | 7.3 | 339 202 | 3 180 854 | 66.6 | 349 100 | 28.7 | 18.8 |
| Atlantic City ............. | 19 840 | 28 526 | 1.6 | 43.9 | 28.1 | 20 013 | -1.0 | 4 509 | 16 300 | 33.7 | 223 900 | 36.0 | 22.9 |
| Bayonne................... | 29 548 | 55 714 | 3.8 | 21.2 | 10.2 | 27 799 | 3.6 | 2 562 | 25 227 | 41.7 | 350 800 | 31.9 | 19.8 |
| Bergenfield............... | 35 233 | 86 191 | 9.8 | 14.3 | 4.4 | 9 200 | 0.6 | 348 | 8 985 | 71.9 | 374 700 | 31.2 | 19.2 |
| Bridgeton.................. | 13 174 | 35 084 | 1.2 | 37.6 | 26.8 | 6 782 | -0.2 | 517 | 6 160 | 42.9 | 127 600 | 27.6 | 20.8 |
| Camden.................... | 12 590 | 26 347 | 0.3 | 47.3 | 35.3 | 28 358 | -4.7 | 3 883 | 24 904 | 40.0 | 89 400 | 32.6 | 18.0 |
| Clifton ..................... | 30 378 | 63 106 | 4.9 | 17.8 | 6.9 | 31 946 | 2.9 | 1 285 | 29 333 | 61.9 | 361 000 | 33.6 | 23.0 |
| East Orange.............. | 21 352 | 40 348 | 1.0 | 33.2 | 16.8 | 28 803 | 1.1 | 3 858 | 24 785 | 26.4 | 253 800 | 36.0 | 25.1 |
| Elizabeth.................. | 19 613 | 44 678 | 1.7 | 26.5 | 15.5 | 45 516 | 6.3 | 3 920 | 39 375 | 27.3 | 333 300 | 38.9 | 25.1 |
| Englewood................ | 43 565 | 68 524 | 12.1 | 20.7 | 8.9 | 10 695 | 11.2 | 638 | 10 184 | 56.8 | 423 200 | 35.2 | 23.3 |
| Fair Lawn................. | 41 117 | 95 725 | 11.1 | 12.6 | 2.9 | 12 266 | 2.2 | 336 | 11 814 | 76.7 | 419 500 | 27.8 | 18.9 |
| Fort Lee................... | 45 157 | 69 911 | 9.6 | 18.4 | 7.0 | 17 818 | 2.1 | 1 447 | 16 404 | 60.8 | 357 800 | 28.7 | 17.2 |

1. Based on population estimated by the American Community Survey.  2. Includes units rented or sold but not occupied.  3. Specified owner-occupied units; $1,000,000 represents $1,000,000 or more  4. 50.0 represents 50 percent or more.  5. 10.0 represents 10 percent or less.

# Table D. Cities — Housing, Labor Force, and Employment

| City | Occupied housing units, 2007–2011 (cont.) | | | | Migration, 2007–2011 | | Civilian labor force, 2012 | | | | Civilian employment[4], 2007–2011 | | | |
|---|---|---|---|---|---|---|---|---|---|---|---|---|---|---|
| | | | | | | | | | Unemployment | | | Percent | | |
| | Percent renter occupied | Median gross rent[1] | Median rent as a percent of income[2] | Percent with no vehicle available | Percent who lived in the same house one year ago | Percent who lived outside this city one year ago | Total | Percent change, 2011–2012 | Total | Rate[3] | Population age 16 and older | In labor force | Full-year full-time worker | Households with no workers (percent) |
| | 55 | 56 | 57 | 58 | 59 | 60 | 61 | 62 | 63 | 64 | 65 | 66 | 67 | 68 |
| MISSOURI................ | 30.5 | 693 | 29.1 | 7.1 | 83.5 | 11.4 | 2 992 858 | -0.5 | 207 391 | 6.9 | 4 700 400 | 65.0 | 40.6 | 27.6 |
| Ballwin........................ | 18.5 | 924 | 27.6 | 1.1 | 86.9 | 10.9 | 16 060 | 0.1 | 793 | 4.9 | 24 016 | 70.1 | 45.4 | 21.3 |
| Blue Springs.............. | 27.2 | 855 | 27.5 | 1.9 | 87.8 | 7.8 | 28 652 | 1.1 | 1 679 | 5.9 | 39 540 | 73.1 | 49.1 | 18.3 |
| Cape Girardeau.......... | 45.0 | 629 | 29.1 | 8.2 | 72.5 | 14.4 | 19 027 | -0.7 | 1 154 | 6.1 | 30 944 | 63.9 | 36.1 | 28.7 |
| Chesterfield................ | 19.7 | 972 | 29.7 | 3.5 | 89.2 | 8.6 | 24 204 | 0.2 | 1 093 | 4.5 | 38 060 | 62.6 | 40.3 | 26.8 |
| Columbia.................... | 51.4 | 766 | 33.0 | 7.7 | 66.1 | 17.2 | 61 489 | 5.9 | 2 700 | 4.4 | 89 063 | 67.7 | 36.5 | 21.9 |
| Florissant.................. | 25.7 | 793 | 28.9 | 5.6 | 86.6 | 10.9 | 26 680 | -0.6 | 1 893 | 7.1 | 41 509 | 69.2 | 45.4 | 26.5 |
| Gladstone.................. | 31.9 | 713 | 27.4 | 5.4 | 80.7 | 16.5 | 13 923 | -0.3 | 882 | 6.3 | 20 174 | 66.8 | 43.0 | 27.8 |
| Hazelwood................ | 39.5 | 768 | 28.5 | 6.5 | 85.6 | 12.1 | 14 539 | -1.1 | 1 012 | 7.0 | 20 296 | 70.7 | 47.8 | 24.8 |
| Independence.............. | 34.0 | 717 | 29.4 | 6.8 | 85.6 | 7.3 | 57 715 | 0.7 | 4 101 | 7.1 | 91 753 | 63.6 | 39.6 | 30.1 |
| Jefferson City.............. | 41.3 | 551 | 23.7 | 8.6 | 78.5 | 11.8 | 21 211 | -0.9 | 1 119 | 5.3 | 34 511 | 63.7 | 44.3 | 26.5 |
| Joplin........................ | 43.8 | 659 | 29.6 | 9.5 | 76.6 | 11.7 | 24 516 | -0.6 | 1 421 | 5.8 | 40 223 | 65.0 | 38.9 | 29.6 |
| Kansas City................ | 42.7 | 752 | 30.2 | 11.1 | 79.6 | 8.6 | 228 878 | 0.6 | 17 014 | 7.4 | 358 241 | 69.1 | 44.4 | 25.4 |
| Kirkwood.................... | 21.8 | 944 | 24.8 | 5.0 | 88.0 | 9.0 | 14 510 | 0.2 | 688 | 4.7 | 22 106 | 69.0 | 45.3 | 23.9 |
| Lee's Summit.............. | 23.9 | 956 | 29.9 | 4.3 | 87.3 | 8.1 | 47 774 | 1.8 | 2 510 | 5.3 | 66 574 | 73.2 | 49.6 | 19.7 |
| Liberty...................... | 24.2 | 764 | 28.2 | 3.8 | 83.3 | 12.1 | 15 319 | 1.8 | 972 | 6.3 | 22 174 | 67.4 | 44.4 | 22.0 |
| Maryland Heights........ | 43.1 | 797 | 22.9 | 3.7 | 79.5 | 17.8 | 16 432 | -0.1 | 886 | 5.4 | 23 009 | 70.9 | 47.5 | 20.3 |
| O'Fallon.................... | 15.7 | 907 | 26.9 | 2.6 | 87.8 | 9.6 | 42 511 | -0.5 | 2 170 | 5.1 | 55 375 | 77.3 | 52.4 | 14.9 |
| Raytown.................... | 27.0 | 792 | 29.4 | 6.9 | 84.1 | 12.3 | 14 722 | 1.1 | 1 156 | 7.9 | 23 249 | 66.9 | 45.2 | 26.9 |
| St. Charles................ | 32.7 | 780 | 26.8 | 5.5 | 83.7 | 11.9 | 36 529 | -0.7 | 2 167 | 5.9 | 53 753 | 68.8 | 43.1 | 25.0 |
| St. Joseph................ | 35.9 | 636 | 29.3 | 9.7 | 77.6 | 9.7 | 43 383 | 1.6 | 2 447 | 5.6 | 60 554 | 63.6 | 38.3 | 28.1 |
| St. Louis.................... | 53.6 | 690 | 32.5 | 21.6 | 77.9 | 9.5 | 139 923 | -1.5 | 13 015 | 9.3 | 257 027 | 66.2 | 38.9 | 31.2 |
| St. Peters.................. | 17.7 | 816 | 23.7 | 2.7 | 91.5 | 7.3 | 30 370 | -0.6 | 1 721 | 5.7 | 42 461 | 74.9 | 50.8 | 18.2 |
| Springfield.................. | 50.4 | 634 | 30.5 | 8.9 | 71.5 | 14.2 | 81 209 | 0.6 | 5 022 | 6.2 | 134 492 | 63.4 | 35.2 | 29.8 |
| University City.............. | 42.6 | 844 | 29.0 | 12.9 | 79.6 | 16.9 | 18 696 | -0.3 | 1 134 | 6.1 | 29 528 | 66.7 | 41.5 | 28.1 |
| Wentzville.................. | 13.4 | 732 | 31.4 | 3.0 | 90.2 | 7.8 | 14 299 | -0.7 | 762 | 5.3 | 19 153 | 75.8 | 52.9 | 14.9 |
| Wildwood.................. | 9.0 | 1 012 | 26.1 | 2.0 | 92.3 | 6.4 | 18 186 | -0.1 | 874 | 4.8 | 25 599 | 70.0 | 46.9 | 14.9 |
| MONTANA................ | 31.1 | 649 | 27.8 | 5.1 | 83.7 | 10.9 | 507 565 | 3.4 | 30 515 | 6.0 | 786 732 | 65.2 | 38.5 | 27.3 |
| Billings...................... | 34.9 | 680 | 28.0 | 6.4 | 82.4 | 8.0 | 58 837 | 5.2 | 2 574 | 4.4 | 81 919 | 69.1 | 42.7 | 23.8 |
| Bozeman.................... | 54.6 | 826 | 31.6 | 4.9 | 60.9 | 23.0 | 21 562 | 5.0 | 1 044 | 4.8 | 31 931 | 71.1 | 37.4 | 19.2 |
| Butte-Silver Bow.......... | 34.5 | 552 | 29.1 | 9.1 | 81.7 | 8.3 | 18 007 | 2.5 | 1 048 | 5.8 | 27 690 | 61.8 | 38.1 | 31.8 |
| Great Falls................ | 35.6 | 555 | 25.5 | 9.1 | 80.9 | 8.7 | 29 423 | 1.5 | 1 580 | 5.4 | 46 486 | 64.3 | 37.6 | 30.1 |
| Helena...................... | 43.1 | 665 | 28.3 | 8.7 | 76.5 | 14.0 | 15 550 | 2.4 | 738 | 4.7 | 23 364 | 67.2 | 41.6 | 26.6 |
| Missoula.................... | 50.7 | 698 | 34.4 | 7.6 | 74.7 | 12.6 | 36 243 | 4.2 | 2 008 | 5.5 | 55 625 | 69.1 | 36.0 | 26.2 |
| NEBRASKA................ | 31.7 | 672 | 26.9 | 5.7 | 82.9 | 9.2 | 1 020 913 | 3.1 | 40 245 | 3.9 | 1 409 203 | 71.0 | 46.3 | 22.7 |
| Bellevue.................... | 33.6 | 775 | 26.8 | 3.5 | 82.0 | 11.8 | 27 059 | 2.7 | 1 165 | 4.3 | 38 817 | 73.4 | 46.8 | 19.0 |
| Fremont.................... | 37.2 | 641 | 25.3 | 6.5 | 82.2 | 7.6 | 14 545 | 2.5 | 601 | 4.1 | 20 647 | 68.0 | 43.7 | 26.8 |
| Grand Island.............. | 37.0 | 612 | 24.9 | 6.8 | 79.6 | 8.2 | 27 459 | 3.9 | 1 031 | 3.8 | 35 573 | 74.0 | 49.6 | 22.7 |
| Kearney.................... | 41.0 | 648 | 27.2 | 4.3 | 74.6 | 13.2 | 19 898 | 3.5 | 555 | 2.8 | 24 563 | 73.8 | 44.7 | 18.1 |
| Lincoln...................... | 40.8 | 689 | 28.8 | 6.5 | 76.4 | 8.7 | 151 005 | 4.2 | 5 194 | 3.4 | 203 871 | 72.9 | 44.3 | 20.8 |
| Omaha...................... | 40.2 | 735 | 29.5 | 9.5 | 80.3 | 7.0 | 219 088 | 2.6 | 10 059 | 4.6 | 317 259 | 71.3 | 44.3 | 24.0 |
| NEVADA.................... | 40.9 | 1 011 | 30.8 | 7.2 | 78.2 | 13.9 | 1 378 876 | -0.9 | 152 468 | 11.1 | 2 086 005 | 67.2 | 41.9 | 23.8 |
| Carson City................ | 39.0 | 926 | 30.6 | 5.6 | 80.7 | 9.1 | 45 902 | -1.0 | 5 064 | 11.0 | 45 040 | 63.1 | 35.7 | 33.9 |
| Henderson.................. | 33.0 | 1 193 | 29.2 | 3.5 | 82.4 | 10.2 | 142 881 | 0.0 | 15 009 | 10.5 | 204 494 | 67.3 | 43.6 | 23.5 |
| Las Vegas.................. | 44.1 | 1 016 | 31.8 | 9.5 | 76.6 | 11.1 | 288 753 | -0.3 | 33 561 | 11.6 | 450 396 | 66.3 | 41.5 | 24.7 |
| North Las Vegas.......... | 39.4 | 1 140 | 33.0 | 5.8 | 73.8 | 16.2 | 96 767 | -1.1 | 12 906 | 13.3 | 149 891 | 69.3 | 43.9 | 17.1 |
| Reno........................ | 51.5 | 879 | 31.1 | 9.9 | 73.9 | 11.1 | 117 802 | -0.1 | 13 004 | 11.0 | 176 278 | 68.8 | 40.4 | 24.9 |
| Sparks...................... | 39.1 | 982 | 31.4 | 6.6 | 76.5 | 14.1 | 48 388 | -0.3 | 5 347 | 11.1 | 69 036 | 69.9 | 42.8 | 22.5 |
| NEW HAMPSHIRE..... | 27.5 | 956 | 29.5 | 5.0 | 86.6 | 10.1 | 742 448 | 1.1 | 41 133 | 5.5 | 1 063 324 | 69.9 | 43.5 | 22.6 |
| Concord.................... | 44.6 | 938 | 29.5 | 10.1 | 81.3 | 10.7 | 22 488 | 1.1 | 1 091 | 4.9 | 35 198 | 66.7 | 43.3 | 24.1 |
| Dover........................ | 45.2 | 922 | 29.7 | 8.1 | 79.1 | 14.9 | 18 074 | 3.4 | 856 | 4.7 | 24 827 | 73.4 | 44.2 | 22.1 |
| Manchester................ | 50.1 | 963 | 30.3 | 9.1 | 78.7 | 9.1 | 62 393 | 0.1 | 3 798 | 6.1 | 88 087 | 70.3 | 45.1 | 24.1 |
| Nashua...................... | 41.1 | 1 060 | 29.5 | 7.5 | 83.9 | 7.8 | 49 766 | 0.4 | 3 075 | 6.2 | 69 503 | 72.5 | 46.1 | 23.3 |
| Rochester.................. | 29.6 | 952 | 35.0 | 7.4 | 83.5 | 9.3 | 16 512 | 3.4 | 1 000 | 6.1 | 24 399 | 68.6 | 43.7 | 24.4 |
| NEW JERSEY............ | 33.4 | 1 131 | 31.5 | 11.7 | 89.7 | 7.9 | 4 595 460 | 2.0 | 436 174 | 9.5 | 6 935 191 | 66.8 | 42.6 | 24.0 |
| Atlantic City................ | 66.3 | 801 | 34.7 | 43.6 | 85.9 | 7.6 | 16 951 | 2.9 | 3 018 | 17.8 | 30 575 | 62.9 | 33.7 | 39.9 |
| Bayonne.................... | 58.3 | 1 026 | 27.9 | 24.2 | 92.8 | 4.1 | 31 503 | 1.8 | 3 602 | 11.4 | 50 920 | 64.7 | 44.6 | 26.8 |
| Bergenfield................ | 28.1 | 1 162 | 30.0 | 10.3 | 92.8 | 5.9 | 14 578 | 2.1 | 1 128 | 7.7 | 21 290 | 68.7 | 48.5 | 19.1 |
| Bridgeton.................. | 57.1 | 950 | 41.3 | 20.8 | 81.7 | 11.9 | 8 377 | -3.3 | 1 276 | 15.2 | 18 683 | 49.5 | 25.9 | 34.4 |
| Camden.................... | 60.0 | 820 | 43.2 | 34.8 | 82.2 | 5.9 | 27 407 | -0.4 | 5 064 | 18.5 | 55 836 | 57.4 | 29.7 | 39.8 |
| Clifton...................... | 38.1 | 1 166 | 33.2 | 11.0 | 92.1 | 5.3 | 43 805 | 1.7 | 4 407 | 10.1 | 67 342 | 67.2 | 46.6 | 24.1 |
| East Orange.............. | 73.6 | 931 | 30.8 | 34.4 | 80.5 | 11.0 | 29 080 | 2.2 | 3 887 | 13.4 | 50 651 | 67.4 | 38.3 | 33.4 |
| Elizabeth.................... | 72.7 | 995 | 31.7 | 24.5 | 83.9 | 6.9 | 56 894 | 1.6 | 7 319 | 12.9 | 93 371 | 69.9 | 46.1 | 22.4 |
| Englewood.................. | 43.2 | 1 282 | 31.5 | 14.0 | 89.4 | 7.6 | 14 233 | 2.0 | 1 337 | 9.4 | 21 606 | 68.0 | 44.6 | 22.0 |
| Fair Lawn.................. | 23.3 | 1 286 | 28.3 | 6.2 | 93.3 | 5.7 | 17 539 | 2.3 | 1 466 | 8.4 | 26 042 | 68.4 | 46.4 | 20.6 |
| Fort Lee.................... | 39.2 | 1 501 | 30.7 | 11.5 | 90.8 | 6.5 | 18 250 | 2.9 | 1 165 | 6.4 | 30 313 | 62.9 | 43.8 | 28.1 |

1. $2,000 represents $2,000 or more.   2. 50.0 represents 50 percent or more.   3. Percent of civilian labor force.   4. Persons 16 years old and over.

| City | Value of residential construction authorized by building permits, 2011 | | | Wholesale trade,[1] 2007 | | | | Retail trade,[2] 2007 | | | |
|---|---|---|---|---|---|---|---|---|---|---|---|
| | New construction ($1,000) | Number of housing units | Percent single family | Number of establish-ments | Number of employees | Sales (mil dol) | Annual payroll (mil dol) | Number of establish-ments | Number of employees | Sales (mil dol) | Annual payroll (mil dol) |
| | 69 | 70 | 71 | 72 | 73 | 74 | 75 | 76 | 77 | 78 | 79 |
| MISSOURI | 1 425 673 | 9 242 | 65.6 | 6 903 | 96 451 | 81 032.9 | 4 533.6 | 23 360 | 317 318 | 76 575.2 | 7 155.3 |
| Ballwin | 2 925 | 9 | 100.0 | 17 | 55 | 44.9 | 2.7 | 101 | 1 905 | 523.1 | 45.9 |
| Blue Springs | 7 188 | 80 | 60.0 | 43 | 278 | 236.6 | 13.5 | 182 | 2 854 | 788.5 | 67.0 |
| Cape Girardeau | 10 270 | 65 | 75.4 | 84 | 1 611 | 1 625.5 | 63.3 | 313 | 4 809 | 1 018.2 | 93.6 |
| Chesterfield | NA | NA | NA | 144 | 1 712 | 1 194.1 | 122.5 | 340 | 5 576 | 1 047.6 | 112.3 |
| Columbia | 99 660 | 866 | 36.5 | 96 | 1 170 | 508.3 | 46.3 | 542 | 10 194 | 2 672.8 | 214.8 |
| Florissant | 245 | 2 | 100.0 | 24 | 126 | 29.7 | 3.6 | 190 | 3 586 | 737.2 | 83.9 |
| Gladstone | 0 | 0 | 0.0 | 17 | 59 | 19.5 | 2.2 | 84 | 1 873 | 436.2 | 43.4 |
| Hazelwood | 625 | 4 | 100.0 | 61 | 1 472 | 870.0 | 75.6 | 149 | 2 975 | 978.0 | 83.2 |
| Independence | 19 674 | 197 | 42.6 | 81 | 578 | 176.3 | 20.9 | 490 | 9 020 | 1 878.5 | 186.1 |
| Jefferson City | 11 245 | 72 | 91.7 | 53 | 2 277 | 620.8 | 67.1 | 306 | 5 229 | 1 134.4 | 110.0 |
| Joplin | 11 189 | 99 | 53.5 | 88 | 1 199 | 487.1 | 46.8 | 426 | 6 272 | 1 543.5 | 126.5 |
| Kansas City | 90 736 | 509 | 77.4 | 627 | 12 675 | 15 540.1 | 691.5 | 1 558 | 25 485 | 6 713.0 | 592.7 |
| Kirkwood | 9 156 | 28 | 100.0 | 38 | 237 | 94.2 | 13.3 | 134 | 2 394 | 649.0 | 63.3 |
| Lee's Summit | 46 125 | 165 | 100.0 | 94 | 1 304 | 589.6 | 60.6 | 253 | 4 732 | 1 092.0 | 105.7 |
| Liberty | 4 113 | 17 | 100.0 | 20 | 282 | 279.6 | 15.0 | 97 | 1 847 | 411.9 | 40.9 |
| Maryland Heights | 0 | 0 | 0.0 | 232 | 5 738 | 3 732.8 | 322.9 | 131 | 3 697 | 987.0 | 312.5 |
| O'Fallon | 32 004 | 284 | 82.7 | 73 | 724 | 705.6 | 37.5 | 202 | 3 285 | 776.7 | 75.2 |
| Raytown | 160 | 2 | 100.0 | 31 | 233 | 78.3 | 10.2 | 99 | 1 519 | 367.1 | 36.7 |
| St. Charles | 41 473 | 109 | 100.0 | 80 | 1 449 | 3 807.1 | 74.0 | 295 | 4 714 | 1 093.7 | 104.8 |
| St. Joseph | 13 323 | 85 | 62.4 | 92 | 1 358 | 1 001.8 | 54.0 | 358 | 5 847 | 1 419.1 | 126.9 |
| St. Louis | 26 740 | 218 | 18.8 | 522 | 9 422 | 5 042.1 | 462.3 | 1 028 | 11 368 | 2 496.7 | 263.5 |
| St. Peters | 26 908 | 223 | 82.1 | 76 | D | D | D | 334 | 5 810 | 1 545.1 | 138.2 |
| Springfield | 36 391 | 563 | 17.4 | 373 | 6 953 | 4 816.0 | 293.0 | 1 064 | 17 200 | 4 176.4 | 379.3 |
| University City | 346 | 1 | 100.0 | 29 | 284 | 147.9 | 20.5 | 94 | 987 | 183.4 | 22.8 |
| Wentzville | 48 519 | 218 | 83.5 | 33 | D | D | D | 89 | 1 678 | 468.7 | 46.7 |
| Wildwood | NA | NA | NA | 41 | 131 | 51.9 | 6.0 | 37 | 474 | 93.6 | 11.5 |
| MONTANA | 285 875 | 1 914 | 63.1 | 1 254 | 12 849 | 8 202.8 | 503.4 | 5 258 | 58 883 | 14 686.9 | 1 317.8 |
| Billings | 45 894 | 253 | 96.0 | 235 | 3 630 | 2 226.0 | 157.6 | 645 | 8 951 | 2 406.3 | 219.8 |
| Bozeman | 43 528 | 197 | 83.2 | 57 | 722 | 253.2 | 27.1 | 371 | 5 400 | 1 210.2 | 128.6 |
| Butte-Silver Bow | 4 925 | 51 | 84.3 | 31 | D | D | D | 189 | 2 183 | 504.7 | 44.3 |
| Great Falls | 12 159 | 82 | 53.7 | 94 | 942 | 597.0 | 37.8 | 346 | 5 153 | 1 226.0 | 114.3 |
| Helena | 24 249 | 156 | 53.2 | 32 | 335 | 167.3 | 12.9 | 251 | 3 597 | 775.5 | 79.5 |
| Missoula | 28 591 | 498 | 16.7 | 118 | 1 371 | 688.1 | 54.3 | 485 | 7 019 | 1 718.6 | 158.6 |
| NEBRASKA | 726 319 | 5 203 | 69.1 | 2 668 | 32 329 | 24 019.9 | 1 323.5 | 7 888 | 108 209 | 26 486.6 | 2 230.5 |
| Bellevue | 23 089 | 104 | 100.0 | 13 | 39 | 9.0 | 1.3 | 99 | 2 080 | 573.1 | 49.1 |
| Fremont | 3 146 | 26 | 46.2 | 33 | 396 | 363.0 | 15.2 | 142 | 2 060 | 580.6 | 47.3 |
| Grand Island | 15 793 | 115 | 60.9 | 81 | 899 | 553.4 | 39.0 | 306 | 4 795 | 962.9 | 94.1 |
| Kearney | 18 287 | 112 | 95.5 | 32 | 558 | 473.3 | 25.7 | 209 | 3 197 | 593.4 | 59.5 |
| Lincoln | 112 151 | 923 | 58.9 | 239 | 3 562 | 2 557.8 | 157.1 | 996 | 16 660 | 3 526.9 | 333.6 |
| Omaha | 202 221 | 1 834 | 63.2 | 675 | 9 809 | 5 606.0 | 460.7 | 1 707 | 34 372 | 7 495.1 | 759.5 |
| NEVADA | 789 438 | 6 163 | 76.0 | 2 614 | 36 052 | 19 255.9 | 1 698.5 | 8 492 | 139 829 | 37 434.0 | 3 691.7 |
| Carson City | 2 424 | 13 | 69.2 | 92 | D | D | D | 262 | 3 698 | 991.5 | 99.5 |
| Henderson | 121 813 | 1 120 | 67.1 | 183 | 1 292 | 566.3 | 57.1 | 704 | 15 060 | 4 803.0 | 404.1 |
| Las Vegas | 106 483 | 928 | 87.7 | 410 | 3 578 | 1 566.6 | 157.5 | 1 791 | 32 904 | 9 178.9 | 892.6 |
| North Las Vegas | 107 565 | 646 | 78.9 | 179 | 5 661 | 2 698.7 | 269.5 | 276 | 5 885 | 1 443.4 | 137.6 |
| Reno | 73 638 | 341 | 93.5 | 294 | 5 486 | 3 017.5 | 234.7 | 1 087 | 18 504 | 5 014.9 | 503.1 |
| Sparks | 31 824 | 130 | 100.0 | 247 | 4 534 | 2 998.8 | 208.4 | 323 | 5 092 | 1 166.4 | 128.6 |
| NEW HAMPSHIRE | 432 254 | 2 346 | 68.5 | 1 561 | 21 457 | 14 564.5 | 1 196.3 | 6 603 | 98 333 | 25 353.9 | 2 380.5 |
| Concord | 1 770 | 12 | 66.7 | 49 | 1 232 | 778.0 | 63.9 | 318 | 6 020 | 1 412.6 | 133.9 |
| Dover | 10 039 | 67 | 80.6 | 37 | 480 | 216.3 | 30.8 | 113 | 1 482 | 381.5 | 41.8 |
| Manchester | 30 904 | 300 | 30.3 | 171 | 2 531 | 1 350.6 | 126.6 | 489 | 8 057 | 2 132.5 | 196.9 |
| Nashua | 12 397 | 95 | 62.1 | 112 | 1 566 | 1 250.1 | 121.2 | 492 | 10 041 | 2 925.2 | 244.1 |
| Rochester | 2 912 | 21 | 100.0 | 13 | D | D | D | 144 | 2 419 | 651.6 | 65.8 |
| NEW JERSEY | 2 043 169 | 12 952 | 50.0 | 14 033 | 221 729 | 233 413.0 | 13 266.6 | 34 482 | 460 843 | 124 813.6 | 12 050.0 |
| Atlantic City | 2 261 | 25 | 100.0 | 13 | 355 | 70.9 | 8.7 | 316 | 2 692 | 554.0 | 59.5 |
| Bayonne | 5 527 | 46 | 52.2 | 46 | 1 380 | 622.0 | 76.0 | 216 | 1 605 | 369.8 | 36.5 |
| Bergenfield | 578 | 2 | 100.0 | 39 | 239 | 150.0 | 10.9 | 102 | 955 | 206.9 | 23.1 |
| Bridgeton | 1 235 | 16 | 100.0 | 14 | D | D | D | 112 | 908 | 241.8 | 22.4 |
| Camden | 5 559 | 52 | 17.3 | 64 | 1 222 | 849.4 | 58.5 | 192 | 1 256 | 270.5 | 28.0 |
| Clifton | 10 110 | 78 | 62.8 | 175 | 2 801 | 1 178.8 | 132.3 | 306 | 4 611 | 1 263.4 | 119.5 |
| East Orange | 2 | 0 | 0.0 | 15 | 148 | 143.5 | 6.8 | 137 | 896 | 237.2 | 21.9 |
| Elizabeth | 6 344 | 78 | 2.6 | 113 | 3 926 | 3 548.4 | 231.2 | 556 | 5 925 | 1 304.0 | 112.8 |
| Englewood | 10 175 | 47 | 21.3 | 113 | 1 476 | 933.8 | 84.4 | 165 | 2 048 | 1 004.5 | 92.0 |
| Fair Lawn | 3 569 | 17 | 41.2 | 57 | 739 | 801.1 | 32.1 | 112 | 1 374 | 440.5 | 55.4 |
| Fort Lee | 6 251 | 29 | 41.4 | 167 | 2 065 | 3 797.2 | 181.2 | 148 | 1 126 | 311.8 | 28.0 |

1. Merchant wholesalers except manufacturers' sales branches and offices.   2. Establishments with payroll.

# Table D. Cities — **Real Estate, Professional Services, and Manufacturing**

| City | Real estate and rental and leasing, 2007 | | | | Professional, scientific, and technical services,[1] 2007 | | | | Manufacturing, 2007 | | | |
|---|---|---|---|---|---|---|---|---|---|---|---|---|
| | Number of establish-ments | Number of employees | Receipts (mil dol) | Annual payroll (mil dol) | Number of establish-ments | Number of employees | Receipts (mil dol) | Annual payroll (mil dol) | Number of establish-ments | Number of employees | Receipts (mil dol) | Annual payroll (mil dol) |
| | 80 | 81 | 82 | 83 | 84 | 85 | 86 | 87 | 88 | 89 | 90 | 91 |
| MISSOURI | 7 003 | 39 625 | 7 186.3 | 1 248.8 | 13 524 | 130 786 | 19 749.8 | 7 454.7 | 6 886 | 295 313 | 110 907.6 | 12 996.5 |
| Ballwin | 29 | 94 | 11.5 | 1.8 | 85 | 187 | 23.6 | 8.5 | NA | NA | NA | NA |
| Blue Springs | 78 | 250 | 43.1 | 6.1 | 132 | D | D | D | 34 | 1 037 | D | 48.0 |
| Cape Girardeau | 88 | 312 | 51.9 | 6.9 | 106 | D | D | D | 39 | 2 650 | 2 605.4 | 134.8 |
| Chesterfield | 146 | 895 | 186.9 | 37.2 | 370 | 9 133 | 1 567.9 | 614.1 | 48 | 1 858 | 479.1 | 92.4 |
| Columbia | 202 | 903 | 136.4 | 23.4 | 325 | D | D | D | 63 | 3 354 | 1 259.9 | 129.9 |
| Florissant | 43 | 223 | 29.7 | 6.2 | 67 | 466 | 22.5 | 10.1 | NA | NA | NA | NA |
| Gladstone | 44 | 206 | 30.1 | 8.0 | 75 | D | D | D | NA | NA | NA | NA |
| Hazelwood | 38 | 384 | 60.1 | 15.5 | 40 | 1 940 | 526.5 | 152.4 | 39 | 3 413 | 1 112.2 | 202.9 |
| Independence | 121 | 569 | 137.7 | 13.8 | 237 | D | D | D | 97 | 4 394 | 1 039.4 | 201.1 |
| Jefferson City | 59 | 207 | 36.3 | 5.0 | 200 | 1 312 | 161.2 | 59.8 | 43 | 3 117 | D | 134.9 |
| Joplin | 92 | 489 | 53.9 | 13.2 | 148 | D | D | D | 91 | 5 843 | 1 902.5 | 218.0 |
| Kansas City | 622 | 5 816 | 1 381.0 | 213.3 | 1 543 | D | D | D | 434 | 19 070 | 7 789.3 | 897.7 |
| Kirkwood | 51 | 180 | 26.5 | 5.2 | 136 | 675 | 85.1 | 31.4 | 32 | 591 | 123.0 | 27.5 |
| Lee's Summit | 136 | 499 | 73.0 | 14.0 | 291 | 1 539 | 256.9 | 83.6 | 76 | 2 143 | 421.7 | 89.5 |
| Liberty | 41 | 185 | 28.1 | 4.9 | 102 | D | D | D | 20 | 1 311 | D | 62.4 |
| Maryland Heights | 67 | 345 | 97.0 | 16.4 | 179 | 2 947 | 620.4 | 234.6 | 111 | 3 673 | 1 082.3 | 173.5 |
| O'Fallon | 73 | 310 | 46.3 | 7.7 | 116 | 737 | 74.0 | 27.7 | 62 | 5 519 | 1 132.9 | 224.8 |
| Raytown | 22 | 124 | 13.5 | 2.8 | 76 | 499 | 37.9 | 17.2 | NA | NA | NA | NA |
| St. Charles | 120 | 666 | 256.7 | 24.7 | 265 | 4 800 | 287.1 | 121.1 | 77 | 2 392 | D | 121.9 |
| St. Joseph | 99 | 449 | 48.8 | 9.4 | 169 | D | D | D | 93 | D | D | D |
| St. Louis | 418 | 2 633 | 606.6 | 94.7 | 1 005 | D | D | D | 543 | 21 432 | 10 920.6 | 998.2 |
| St. Peters | 68 | 302 | 57.6 | 8.0 | 132 | 768 | 80.4 | 25.7 | 53 | 1 825 | 695.2 | D |
| Springfield | 375 | 2 593 | 322.7 | 63.7 | 675 | D | D | D | 273 | 13 588 | 3 554.2 | 520.0 |
| University City | 50 | 589 | 67.5 | 14.0 | 91 | 352 | 39.2 | 13.7 | NA | NA | NA | NA |
| Wentzville | 15 | 63 | 9.5 | 1.5 | 46 | 205 | 18.2 | 6.4 | 23 | 3 095 | D | D |
| Wildwood | 34 | 58 | 13.2 | 2.5 | 97 | 226 | 38.2 | 14.6 | NA | NA | NA | NA |
| MONTANA | 1 892 | 6 410 | 848.3 | 153.3 | 3 403 | 16 547 | 1 770.9 | 670.6 | 1 324 | 19 525 | 10 638.1 | 808.2 |
| Billings | 226 | 805 | 121.9 | 23.7 | 489 | D | D | D | 126 | 2 484 | D | 128.1 |
| Bozeman | 169 | 518 | 86.8 | 13.7 | 394 | 1 859 | 229.8 | 86.8 | 71 | 985 | 228.0 | 35.9 |
| Butte-Silver Bow | 45 | 144 | 14.9 | 3.0 | 107 | D | D | D | NA | NA | NA | NA |
| Great Falls | 119 | 349 | 53.9 | 7.8 | 177 | D | D | D | 53 | 938 | 640.2 | 39.5 |
| Helena | 80 | 603 | 75.0 | 13.0 | 206 | 1 625 | 198.6 | 81.4 | NA | NA | NA | NA |
| Missoula | 174 | 843 | 105.3 | 18.9 | 378 | D | D | D | 67 | D | D | 21.0 |
| NEBRASKA | 2 032 | 9 974 | 1 645.5 | 292.0 | 4 205 | 40 692 | 4 836.4 | 2 011.0 | 1 984 | 99 547 | 40 158.0 | 3 788.6 |
| Bellevue | 46 | 193 | 26.8 | 3.2 | 75 | 1 757 | 324.3 | 119.9 | 13 | 608 | 123.7 | 23.3 |
| Fremont | 43 | D | D | D | 43 | 189 | 15.4 | 5.5 | 33 | 929 | 395.7 | 36.8 |
| Grand Island | 64 | 256 | 44.4 | 7.2 | 91 | D | D | D | 63 | 6 524 | D | 240.2 |
| Kearney | 48 | 161 | 26.9 | 4.1 | 66 | 442 | 36.3 | 16.2 | 23 | 538 | D | D |
| Lincoln | 343 | 1 536 | 247.5 | 42.6 | 727 | 7 989 | 1 082.1 | 373.8 | 223 | 11 908 | 3 932.9 | 486.9 |
| Omaha | 599 | 5 226 | 775.7 | 168.3 | 1 385 | D | D | D | 448 | 20 354 | 8 853.9 | 817.4 |
| NEVADA | 4 613 | 31 603 | 6 187.3 | 1 106.5 | 7 895 | 57 357 | 8 881.4 | 3 241.1 | 2 035 | 51 958 | 15 735.8 | 2 290.8 |
| Carson City | 147 | 569 | 73.4 | 16.0 | 381 | D | D | D | 143 | 3 528 | 621.6 | 141.7 |
| Henderson | 431 | 1 532 | 361.9 | 58.5 | 678 | D | D | D | 128 | 5 086 | 1 634.7 | 197.1 |
| Las Vegas | 1 099 | 5 391 | 1 048.7 | 209.8 | 2 220 | 14 869 | 2 496.1 | 865.1 | 233 | 3 744 | 872.9 | 137.2 |
| North Las Vegas | 139 | 3 182 | 318.0 | 97.1 | 136 | D | D | D | 137 | 5 728 | 1 311.6 | 213.5 |
| Reno | 505 | 2 847 | 509.0 | 91.0 | 1 236 | D | D | D | 249 | 9 355 | 3 875.0 | 496.6 |
| Sparks | 126 | 795 | 134.7 | 25.8 | 157 | D | D | D | 196 | 4 760 | 1 522.3 | 210.7 |
| NEW HAMPSHIRE | 1 534 | 7 266 | 1 371.8 | 248.2 | 3 961 | 29 160 | 3 730.8 | 1 570.2 | 2 104 | 81 592 | 18 592.4 | 4 196.2 |
| Concord | 78 | 447 | 83.9 | 14.2 | 241 | 1 820 | 254.3 | 113.7 | 66 | 2 606 | 567.4 | 112.2 |
| Dover | 42 | 189 | 31.5 | 4.9 | 91 | D | D | D | 45 | 1 215 | 167.1 | 48.9 |
| Manchester | 141 | 1 161 | 234.3 | 38.9 | 398 | D | D | D | 153 | 6 970 | 1 493.4 | 309.1 |
| Nashua | 121 | 520 | 118.5 | 21.6 | 336 | D | D | D | 134 | 9 964 | 2 693.5 | 924.0 |
| Rochester | 30 | 113 | 15.3 | 2.4 | 45 | 302 | 25.5 | 10.7 | 42 | 1 531 | 281.0 | 60.3 |
| NEW JERSEY | 9 618 | 64 021 | 16 347.6 | 2 939.1 | 31 040 | 330 133 | 52 442.8 | 23 639.9 | 9 250 | 310 606 | 116 608.1 | 16 399.3 |
| Atlantic City | 63 | 739 | 139.4 | 20.7 | 69 | D | D | D | NA | NA | NA | NA |
| Bayonne | 52 | 243 | 48.6 | 9.0 | 79 | 290 | 27.7 | 10.0 | 39 | 1 208 | 470.9 | 58.1 |
| Bergenfield | 19 | 44 | 6.4 | 1.1 | 59 | 146 | 26.1 | 6.4 | NA | NA | NA | NA |
| Bridgeton | 10 | 90 | 10.5 | 2.0 | 40 | D | D | D | 15 | 659 | 254.8 | 29.0 |
| Camden | 35 | 196 | 32.8 | 5.4 | 54 | D | D | D | 56 | 2 851 | 641.1 | 192.0 |
| Clifton | 99 | 733 | 107.0 | 29.5 | 263 | 3 746 | 472.3 | 198.9 | 176 | 5 671 | 1 429.0 | 295.7 |
| East Orange | 70 | 385 | 66.9 | 10.4 | 56 | D | D | D | NA | NA | NA | NA |
| Elizabeth | 110 | 358 | 140.0 | 12.1 | 114 | D | D | D | 81 | 3 314 | 808.7 | 154.7 |
| Englewood | 74 | 250 | 59.0 | 11.4 | 125 | 791 | 154.8 | 50.3 | 61 | 1 582 | 468.2 | 67.2 |
| Fair Lawn | 34 | 100 | 36.4 | 2.9 | 218 | 1 037 | 257.2 | 71.3 | 40 | 2 031 | 634.7 | 97.5 |
| Fort Lee | 120 | 574 | 142.7 | 22.7 | 257 | 1 127 | 255.0 | 73.6 | NA | NA | NA | NA |

1. Establishments subject to federal tax.

Table D. Cities — **Accommodation and Food Services, Arts, Entertainment, and Recreation, and Health Care and Social Assistance**

| City | Accommodation and food services, 2007 | | | | Arts, entertainment, and recreation,[1] 2007 | | | | Health care and social assistance,[1] 2007 | | | |
|---|---|---|---|---|---|---|---|---|---|---|---|---|
| | Number of establish-ments | Number of employees | Sales (mil dol) | Annual payroll (mil dol) | Number of establish-ments | Number of employees | Receipts (mil dol) | Annual payroll (mil dol) | Number of establish-ments | Number of employees | Receipts (mil dol) | Annual payroll (mil dol) |
| | 92 | 93 | 94 | 95 | 96 | 97 | 98 | 99 | 100 | 101 | 102 | 103 |
| MISSOURI | 12 261 | 241 438 | 11 070.6 | 3 109.1 | 1 696 | 25 744 | 2 735.9 | 1 026.2 | 12 881 | 159 529 | 14 101.7 | 5 911.6 |
| Ballwin | 37 | 787 | 27.1 | 8.4 | 10 | D | D | D | 38 | D | D | D |
| Blue Springs | 107 | 2 203 | 83.7 | 22.7 | 18 | D | D | D | 113 | D | D | D |
| Cape Girardeau | 126 | 3 284 | 119.7 | 35.1 | 14 | 136 | 7.9 | 2.6 | 194 | D | D | D |
| Chesterfield | 161 | 4 566 | 191.9 | 61.2 | 32 | 286 | 17.2 | 4.4 | 223 | 3 750 | 389.8 | 176.4 |
| Columbia | 362 | 7 659 | 286.3 | 83.7 | 33 | 546 | 17.9 | 6.8 | 387 | 4 126 | 423.1 | 177.8 |
| Florissant | 123 | 2 577 | 96.4 | 28.7 | 9 | D | D | D | 146 | 1 867 | 146.9 | 64.1 |
| Gladstone | 37 | 824 | 33.3 | 10.1 | 5 | D | D | D | 82 | 806 | 65.6 | 27.2 |
| Hazelwood | 66 | 1 148 | 59.2 | 17.4 | 6 | D | D | D | 47 | 378 | 41.0 | 14.2 |
| Independence | 217 | 5 267 | 216.8 | 67.9 | 17 | D | D | D | 224 | 3 795 | 432.7 | 165.1 |
| Jefferson City | 140 | 2 963 | 118.9 | 35.2 | 16 | D | D | D | 163 | D | D | D |
| Joplin | 190 | 4 200 | 168.3 | 48.5 | 9 | D | D | D | 263 | 2 508 | 233.5 | 113.7 |
| Kansas City | 1 110 | 26 835 | 1 668.7 | 426.6 | 104 | 2 464 | 503.4 | 281.6 | 886 | 13 090 | 1 483.9 | 645.2 |
| Kirkwood | 59 | 1 585 | 58.5 | 17.8 | 12 | 116 | 7.3 | 2.2 | 111 | 832 | 114.5 | 40.6 |
| Lee's Summit | 153 | 3 172 | 119.9 | 37.5 | 36 | D | D | D | 195 | 3 005 | 334.7 | 127.1 |
| Liberty | 55 | 1 020 | 42.7 | 13.0 | 5 | 74 | 2.6 | 0.8 | 85 | D | D | D |
| Maryland Heights | 93 | 4 251 | 438.0 | 98.4 | 9 | D | D | D | 64 | 2 747 | 329.8 | 103.7 |
| O'Fallon | 143 | 3 286 | 113.2 | 35.3 | 25 | 322 | 18.1 | 6.7 | 133 | D | D | D |
| Raytown | 43 | 693 | 28.7 | 8.4 | 8 | D | D | D | 50 | D | D | D |
| St. Charles | 196 | 4 467 | 178.1 | 52.2 | 23 | D | D | D | 158 | 1 753 | 181.9 | 69.3 |
| St. Joseph | 189 | 4 084 | 151.7 | 44.8 | 14 | D | D | D | 229 | D | D | D |
| St. Louis | 934 | 20 372 | 1 059.3 | 311.4 | 62 | 2 672 | 450.0 | 226.8 | 722 | 11 401 | 1 052.1 | 365.9 |
| St. Peters | 190 | 3 702 | 135.2 | 41.2 | 24 | D | D | D | 191 | 1 766 | 179.9 | 74.3 |
| Springfield | 598 | 13 951 | 540.5 | 160.7 | 54 | 470 | 28.7 | 7.4 | 506 | D | D | D |
| University City | 77 | 1 250 | 52.6 | 16.3 | 9 | 81 | 2.8 | 0.8 | 74 | 1 240 | 59.2 | 23.5 |
| Wentzville | 62 | 1 374 | 45.7 | 14.4 | 6 | D | D | D | 59 | 551 | 52.2 | 18.1 |
| Wildwood | 24 | D | D | D | 11 | 125 | 5.6 | 1.4 | 40 | 395 | 24.7 | 11.8 |
| MONTANA | 3 360 | 46 137 | 2 079.4 | 554.2 | 881 | 8 207 | 589.4 | 110.3 | 2 438 | 21 763 | 1 944.6 | 801.7 |
| Billings | 312 | 7 102 | 335.8 | 91.1 | 82 | 792 | 68.6 | 10.2 | 368 | D | D | D |
| Bozeman | 153 | 3 297 | 141.0 | 38.0 | 44 | 318 | 31.9 | 5.2 | 206 | 1 608 | 150.6 | 60.2 |
| Butte-Silver Bow | 133 | 1 946 | 78.3 | 22.7 | 34 | 276 | 33.0 | 3.9 | 113 | 1 458 | 85.9 | 36.9 |
| Great Falls | 209 | 3 588 | 157.7 | 44.4 | 54 | D | D | D | 197 | D | D | D |
| Helena | 145 | 2 729 | 106.9 | 30.3 | 25 | 337 | 14.4 | 3.0 | 172 | 1 531 | 134.3 | 56.3 |
| Missoula | 260 | 5 473 | 233.1 | 60.8 | 61 | 695 | 53.0 | 8.9 | 319 | D | D | D |
| NEBRASKA | 4 241 | 69 142 | 2 685.6 | 749.1 | 573 | 6 394 | 396.8 | 92.8 | 3 830 | 49 338 | 4 447.4 | 1 888.7 |
| Bellevue | 91 | 1 808 | 70.8 | 20.3 | 9 | D | D | D | 61 | 977 | 59.7 | 25.7 |
| Fremont | 77 | 1 233 | 47.5 | 12.4 | 4 | D | D | D | 79 | D | D | D |
| Grand Island | 122 | 2 330 | 86.2 | 25.1 | 13 | 230 | 9.3 | 2.6 | 129 | D | D | D |
| Kearney | 118 | 2 480 | 98.4 | 27.2 | 15 | D | D | D | 91 | 1 133 | 132.1 | 63.8 |
| Lincoln | 619 | 11 603 | 457.9 | 128.2 | 80 | 1 447 | 54.4 | 16.8 | 677 | D | D | D |
| Omaha | 1 123 | 23 858 | 1 041.5 | 298.0 | 129 | 1 976 | 119.2 | 29.4 | 1 156 | 17 234 | 1 853.5 | 787.1 |
| NEVADA | 5 570 | 325 544 | 28 815.5 | 8 594.6 | 1 153 | 28 815 | 3 275.5 | 752.7 | 5 269 | 72 716 | 9 225.8 | 3 345.0 |
| Carson City | 167 | 2 664 | 127.7 | 37.8 | 48 | 1 762 | 138.4 | 39.5 | 192 | 2 048 | 278.5 | 101.3 |
| Henderson | 463 | 15 786 | 1 145.5 | 333.9 | 128 | D | D | D | 612 | D | D | D |
| Las Vegas | 1 128 | 42 712 | 3 134.0 | 924.7 | 226 | 4 369 | 521.9 | 120.4 | 1 593 | 28 718 | 4 019.0 | 1 373.4 |
| North Las Vegas | 199 | 6 458 | 476.1 | 127.8 | 33 | 1 554 | 107.8 | 28.5 | 141 | D | D | D |
| Reno | 702 | 27 677 | 1 918.0 | 580.7 | 103 | 1 816 | 161.5 | 39.0 | 757 | 9 418 | 1 226.5 | 542.7 |
| Sparks | 202 | 5 809 | 340.3 | 105.4 | 24 | D | D | D | 167 | 2 083 | 168.3 | 68.1 |
| NEW HAMPSHIRE | 3 508 | 55 268 | 2 631.0 | 799.8 | 548 | 9 606 | 659.1 | 205.7 | 2 655 | 32 711 | 3 095.7 | 1 386.1 |
| Concord | 135 | 2 769 | 132.4 | 41.1 | 13 | 217 | 6.9 | 2.2 | 158 | 2 267 | 248.0 | 124.6 |
| Dover | 79 | 1 364 | 58.7 | 18.8 | 8 | D | D | D | 116 | 1 286 | 129.6 | 64.0 |
| Manchester | 294 | 5 777 | 265.3 | 82.3 | 30 | 858 | 73.4 | 34.4 | 236 | 3 281 | 322.1 | 157.8 |
| Nashua | 228 | 4 574 | 231.7 | 70.4 | 25 | 428 | 28.1 | 8.0 | 248 | 3 236 | 353.7 | 151.0 |
| Rochester | 66 | 1 048 | 43.1 | 12.0 | 3 | D | D | D | 66 | 662 | 68.3 | 31.6 |
| NEW JERSEY | 19 526 | 291 327 | 19 993.6 | 5 232.4 | 2 939 | 35 241 | 2 958.6 | 921.7 | 22 056 | 253 078 | 26 415.5 | 10 529.7 |
| Atlantic City | 238 | 47 392 | 5 602.5 | 1 369.0 | 16 | 131 | 15.8 | 4.0 | 48 | 490 | 39.5 | 16.7 |
| Bayonne | 112 | 983 | 49.5 | 12.4 | 8 | D | D | D | 152 | 1 042 | 119.0 | 44.3 |
| Bergenfield | 44 | 342 | 22.3 | 5.3 | 4 | D | D | D | 52 | 302 | 37.3 | 11.1 |
| Bridgeton | 35 | 441 | 21.2 | 5.2 | 1 | D | D | D | 31 | D | D | D |
| Camden | 93 | 600 | 42.2 | 9.7 | 7 | 84 | 27.9 | 3.8 | 76 | 1 342 | 126.6 | 66.0 |
| Clifton | 157 | D | D | D | 17 | D | D | D | 330 | 2 687 | 294.0 | 110.7 |
| East Orange | 47 | 703 | 33.6 | 8.3 | 2 | D | D | D | 130 | 2 371 | 139.0 | 61.0 |
| Elizabeth | 253 | 2 627 | 192.0 | 49.1 | 6 | D | D | D | 188 | 1 860 | 175.7 | 68.7 |
| Englewood | 54 | 744 | 43.8 | 10.2 | 14 | D | D | D | 216 | D | D | D |
| Fair Lawn | 69 | 751 | 44.2 | 11.2 | 12 | D | D | D | 198 | 1 872 | 216.1 | 88.4 |
| Fort Lee | 107 | 1 209 | 80.6 | 18.6 | 25 | D | D | D | 190 | D | D | D |

1. Establishments subject to federal tax.

| City | Other services[1], 2007 | | | | Selected federal funds, 2009–2010 (mil dol) | | | | | | | | |
|---|---|---|---|---|---|---|---|---|---|---|---|---|---|
| | | | | | Procurement contracts | | Grants | | | | | | |
| | Number of establish-ments | Number of employees | Receipts (mil dol) | Annual payroll (mil dol) | Defense | Other | Total[2] | Medicaid and other health related | Nutrition and family welfare | Energy and envi-ronment | Disasters and emergency prepared-ness | Housing and community develop-ment | Employment and training |
| | 104 | 105 | 106 | 107 | 108 | 109 | 110 | 111 | 112 | 113 | 114 | 115 | 116 |
| MISSOURI................. | 9 114 | 53 749 | 4 220.1 | 1 361.4 | 10 334.5 | 2 667.9 | 14 002.5 | 7 868.9 | 1 212.9 | 968.8 | 87.3 | 519.6 | 199.3 |
| Ballwin........................ | 41 | 233 | 14.6 | 5.6 | 1.0 | 0.0 | 0.0 | 0.0 | 0.0 | 0.0 | 0.0 | 0.0 | 0.0 |
| Blue Springs............... | 86 | 418 | 30.4 | 9.7 | 0.2 | 0.2 | 1.0 | 0.0 | 0.0 | 0.5 | 0.0 | 0.5 | 0.0 |
| Cape Girardeau............ | 87 | 433 | 29.7 | 9.8 | 5.7 | 1.8 | 30.8 | 1.6 | 0.0 | 0.3 | 0.1 | 0.2 | 0.0 |
| Chesterfield ................. | 85 | 876 | 48.8 | 16.0 | 22.9 | 9.9 | 73.6 | 1.0 | 0.0 | 71.8 | 0.0 | 0.0 | 0.0 |
| Columbia .................... | 203 | 1 451 | 108.9 | 31.6 | 4.8 | 38.6 | 263.1 | 98.6 | 5.7 | 10.9 | -2.1 | 11.1 | 0.4 |
| Florissant ................... | 94 | 597 | 46.2 | 14.8 | 0.1 | 0.0 | 2.2 | 0.0 | 0.0 | 0.5 | 0.0 | 0.2 | 0.0 |
| Gladstone ................... | 46 | 275 | 20.1 | 6.3 | 0.0 | 0.2 | 0.1 | 0.0 | 0.0 | 0.1 | 0.0 | 0.0 | 0.0 |
| Hazelwood.................. | 38 | 271 | 22.1 | 7.1 | 3.4 | 2.0 | 3.4 | 0.0 | 0.0 | 0.0 | 0.0 | 0.0 | 3.2 |
| Independence............... | 174 | 833 | 64.7 | 19.5 | 793.9 | 2.7 | 12.7 | 0.0 | 0.0 | 0.4 | 0.0 | 11.7 | 0.0 |
| Jefferson City .............. | 98 | D | D | D | 1.9 | 3.6 | 1 371.9 | 139.7 | 236.9 | 93.4 | 12.0 | 150.1 | 165.7 |
| Joplin ........................ | 133 | 716 | 44.3 | 13.5 | 15.6 | 10.8 | 21.4 | 0.1 | 6.3 | 7.2 | 0.0 | 5.4 | 0.0 |
| Kansas City ................ | 734 | 5 132 | 416.6 | 131.9 | 101.9 | 1 268.1 | 306.4 | 87.8 | 21.9 | 64.5 | 2.0 | 77.7 | 0.5 |
| Kirkwood.................... | 52 | 403 | 26.7 | 9.8 | 0.1 | 0.5 | 0.2 | 0.0 | 0.0 | 0.0 | 0.0 | 0.1 | 0.0 |
| Lee's Summit .............. | 112 | 668 | 46.0 | 14.7 | 2.4 | 5.0 | 10.8 | 0.1 | 0.0 | 0.8 | 0.0 | 5.1 | 0.0 |
| Liberty ...................... | 44 | 259 | 17.6 | 6.3 | 3.3 | 2.1 | 3.3 | 0.0 | 0.0 | 0.4 | 0.0 | 2.2 | 0.0 |
| Maryland Heights ......... | 59 | 549 | 52.7 | 19.9 | 230.9 | 95.0 | 0.0 | 0.0 | 0.0 | 0.0 | 0.0 | 0.0 | 0.0 |
| O'Fallon ..................... | 122 | 862 | 54.5 | 18.8 | 56.2 | 0.3 | 1.0 | 0.0 | 0.0 | 0.7 | 0.0 | 0.3 | 0.0 |
| Raytown .................... | 65 | 470 | 26.5 | 13.5 | 0.1 | 2.0 | 0.2 | 0.0 | 0.0 | 0.0 | 0.0 | 0.1 | 0.0 |
| St. Charles ................. | 127 | 884 | 67.0 | 21.9 | 273.8 | 0.2 | 7.7 | 0.0 | 0.0 | 0.7 | 0.0 | 6.8 | 0.0 |
| St. Joseph .................. | 150 | D | D | D | 14.6 | 4.9 | 9.4 | 0.0 | 0.0 | 0.0 | 0.0 | 6.9 | 0.0 |
| St. Louis .................... | 517 | 3 996 | 306.0 | 106.8 | 3 022.3 | 201.9 | 1 828.5 | 850.7 | 36.6 | 643.1 | 1.1 | 101.5 | 14.1 |
| St. Peters ................... | 144 | 1 123 | 74.1 | 26.2 | 28.0 | 0.5 | 0.3 | 0.0 | 0.0 | 0.0 | 0.0 | 0.3 | 0.0 |
| Springfield .................. | 449 | D | D | D | 8.0 | 23.0 | 57.1 | 6.5 | 11.4 | 1.5 | 0.0 | 9.5 | 0.0 |
| University City ............. | 56 | 408 | 34.1 | 11.7 | 0.1 | 0.9 | 2.9 | 0.0 | 0.0 | 0.1 | 2.6 | 0.2 | 0.0 |
| Wentzville................... | 46 | D | D | D | 1.0 | 0.0 | 0.8 | 0.4 | 0.0 | 0.0 | 0.0 | 0.0 | 0.0 |
| Wildwood ................... | 17 | 97 | 5.1 | 1.5 | 7.0 | 0.0 | 0.0 | 0.0 | 0.0 | 0.0 | 0.0 | 0.0 | 0.0 |
| MONTANA ............. | 1 619 | 7 260 | 647.7 | 164.8 | 312.7 | 506.7 | 2 939.4 | 1 080.2 | 271.7 | 254.3 | 6.6 | 95.5 | 54.0 |
| Billings....................... | 241 | 1 418 | 117.5 | 34.1 | 2.1 | 75.9 | 37.5 | 16.8 | 4.7 | 1.1 | 0.0 | 6.4 | 0.3 |
| Bozeman .................... | 80 | 396 | 28.2 | 9.1 | 17.2 | 14.5 | 90.9 | 33.6 | 1.2 | 12.8 | -0.1 | 0.0 | 0.0 |
| Butte-Silver Bow............ | 51 | 240 | 19.7 | 4.8 | 0.0 | 0.0 | 16.1 | 3.7 | 1.4 | 3.3 | 0.0 | 0.8 | 0.0 |
| Great Falls .................. | 102 | D | D | D | 17.4 | 4.6 | 22.6 | 6.9 | 2.6 | 1.1 | -1.7 | 4.4 | 0.0 |
| Helena ...................... | 70 | 427 | 32.7 | 9.4 | 5.8 | 18.0 | 458.1 | 44.9 | 47.2 | 104.2 | 4.9 | 39.5 | 49.1 |
| Missoula .................... | 161 | 955 | 71.4 | 21.2 | 4.1 | 36.2 | 86.0 | 22.3 | 3.1 | 8.9 | 0.0 | 10.0 | 0.0 |
| NEBRASKA............. | 3 226 | 17 286 | 1 299.7 | 406.5 | 793.2 | 513.6 | 3 507.0 | 1 703.0 | 411.7 | 131.7 | 37.6 | 119.9 | 51.0 |
| Bellevue..................... | 60 | 403 | 31.3 | 10.5 | 32.2 | 2.3 | 13.1 | 0.0 | 0.0 | 0.2 | 0.0 | 1.4 | 0.0 |
| Fremont ..................... | 49 | D | D | D | 0.5 | 0.2 | 6.8 | 0.0 | 0.7 | 0.0 | 0.0 | 1.2 | 0.0 |
| Grand Island................ | 115 | 567 | 45.6 | 11.3 | 0.0 | 3.9 | 9.0 | 0.3 | 0.0 | 0.0 | 0.0 | 2.2 | 0.0 |
| Kearney ..................... | 59 | 281 | 20.2 | 5.6 | 0.0 | 0.4 | 7.7 | 0.0 | 4.5 | 0.0 | 0.0 | 1.1 | 0.1 |
| Lincoln ...................... | 425 | 2 627 | 154.9 | 57.2 | 13.7 | 63.3 | 697.7 | 91.9 | 83.4 | 70.0 | 14.6 | 40.1 | 46.3 |
| Omaha ...................... | 782 | 6 236 | 425.1 | 161.9 | 226.6 | 217.4 | 310.3 | 152.2 | 8.9 | 27.3 | 0.1 | 50.2 | 2.4 |
| NEVADA.................. | 2 989 | 22 756 | 1 750.6 | 564.6 | 1 315.0 | 1 092.1 | 3 701.8 | 1 312.3 | 423.8 | 446.2 | 4.3 | 225.1 | 92.0 |
| Carson City ................ | 117 | 820 | 57.8 | 20.1 | 13.0 | 7.9 | 550.5 | 32.1 | 100.6 | 57.0 | 0.9 | 21.3 | 86.6 |
| Henderson .................. | 271 | 1 908 | 155.8 | 49.7 | 2.4 | 15.9 | 6.5 | 1.4 | 0.0 | 1.6 | 0.0 | 1.8 | 0.0 |
| Las Vegas .................. | 665 | 4 876 | 370.4 | 119.6 | 77.9 | 696.6 | 470.5 | 18.9 | 5.7 | 196.0 | 0.2 | 134.1 | 4.6 |
| North Las Vegas .......... | 131 | 2 797 | 198.0 | 70.6 | 0.8 | 21.6 | 20.7 | 0.0 | 0.0 | 13.8 | 0.0 | 0.4 | 0.5 |
| Reno ......................... | 365 | 2 887 | 183.0 | 67.5 | 28.8 | 54.0 | 351.7 | 38.4 | 13.6 | 115.6 | 0.3 | 47.7 | 0.0 |
| Sparks ...................... | 178 | 1 227 | 126.6 | 36.1 | 633.3 | 3.3 | 6.7 | 2.0 | 0.0 | 2.4 | 0.0 | 0.7 | 0.3 |
| NEW HAMPSHIRE..... | 2 281 | 12 269 | 1 117.9 | 346.5 | 1 091.9 | 343.5 | 2 311.1 | 1 132.7 | 209.8 | 102.2 | 14.3 | 120.8 | 43.3 |
| Concord...................... | 105 | 549 | 48.0 | 16.0 | 11.1 | 18.3 | 368.3 | 39.2 | 48.4 | 43.6 | 4.3 | 20.6 | 40.2 |
| Dover......................... | 50 | 300 | 22.4 | 6.9 | 3.3 | 1.0 | 8.2 | 1.1 | 0.0 | 0.1 | 0.0 | 4.0 | 0.0 |
| Manchester.................. | 227 | 1 570 | 130.1 | 43.3 | 15.0 | 19.6 | 78.4 | 3.1 | 4.2 | 2.6 | 0.3 | 56.1 | 0.0 |
| Nashua....................... | 151 | 1 172 | 109.7 | 36.7 | 583.6 | 8.8 | 25.5 | 1.5 | 0.0 | 2.2 | 0.0 | 12.1 | 0.2 |
| Rochester.................... | 51 | 327 | 26.2 | 8.3 | 2.3 | 0.7 | 2.8 | 0.1 | 0.0 | 0.0 | 0.0 | 2.4 | 0.0 |
| NEW JERSEY............ | 16 350 | 85 202 | 7 212.2 | 2 257.6 | 7 857.5 | 2 378.8 | 15 456.8 | 8 131.6 | 1 857.8 | 572.3 | 130.5 | 1 041.9 | 272.7 |
| Atlantic City ................ | 55 | 665 | 45.1 | 14.8 | 0.7 | 4.7 | 20.0 | 0.2 | 6.8 | 0.0 | 0.0 | 12.0 | 0.0 |
| Bayonne..................... | 110 | 410 | 30.8 | 8.3 | 27.7 | 2.6 | 16.1 | 0.0 | 1.5 | 0.5 | 3.6 | 7.0 | 0.0 |
| Bergenfield.................. | 62 | 178 | 15.9 | 3.9 | 0.5 | 0.0 | 0.3 | 0.0 | 0.0 | 0.0 | 0.0 | 0.0 | 0.0 |
| Bridgeton.................... | 26 | 117 | 9.6 | 2.5 | 0.1 | 0.1 | 15.7 | 3.2 | 8.9 | 0.0 | 0.0 | 2.5 | 0.0 |
| Camden...................... | 56 | 323 | 28.2 | 8.4 | 131.1 | 9.9 | 88.4 | 4.7 | 3.1 | 6.4 | 0.0 | 51.5 | 0.4 |
| Clifton........................ | 184 | 747 | 64.8 | 20.7 | 269.2 | 1.3 | 5.0 | 0.0 | 0.0 | 0.7 | 0.0 | 4.1 | 0.0 |
| East Orange ................ | 49 | D | D | D | 0.0 | 44.7 | 23.1 | 3.1 | 4.3 | 0.6 | 0.0 | 14.9 | 0.0 |
| Elizabeth..................... | 191 | 917 | 90.6 | 23.5 | 24.6 | 7.0 | 35.1 | 2.2 | 0.2 | 2.4 | 0.0 | 29.1 | 0.0 |
| Englewood................... | 85 | 381 | 31.1 | 9.7 | 3.2 | 3.9 | 52.5 | 1.9 | 0.0 | 0.5 | 0.0 | 48.4 | 0.0 |
| Fair Lawn ................... | 76 | 342 | 32.6 | 10.3 | 1.5 | 0.1 | 0.0 | 0.0 | 0.0 | 0.0 | 0.0 | 0.0 | 0.0 |
| Fort Lee..................... | 103 | 381 | 33.3 | 10.2 | 41.3 | 6.1 | 7.4 | 1.6 | 0.0 | 0.0 | 0.0 | 5.8 | 0.0 |

1. Establishments subject to federal tax.    2. Includes program categories not shown separately. State totals include additional categories not allocated by city.

| City | City government finances, 2007 | | | | | | | | | |
|---|---|---|---|---|---|---|---|---|---|---|
| | General revenue | | | | | | | General expenditure | | |
| | | Intergovernmental | | Taxes | | | | | Per capita[1] (dollars) | |
| | | | | | Per capita[1] (dollars) | | | | | |
| | Total (mil dol) | Total (mil dol) | Percent from state government | Total (mil dol) | Total | Property | Sales and gross receipts | Total (mil dol) | Total | Capital outlays |
| | 117 | 118 | 119 | 120 | 121 | 122 | 123 | 124 | 125 | 126 |
| MISSOURI | X | X | X | X | X | X | X | X | X | X |
| Ballwin | 19.5 | 1.6 | 57.3 | 12.8 | 426 | 0 | 416 | 15.9 | 529 | 66 |
| Blue Springs | 35.7 | 7.4 | 18.5 | 19.1 | 348 | 90 | 257 | 30.2 | 548 | 23 |
| Cape Girardeau | 44.9 | 3.7 | 100.0 | 28.6 | 770 | 48 | 723 | 39.3 | 1 059 | 241 |
| Chesterfield | 54.7 | 26.8 | 15.1 | 22.3 | 482 | 331 | 151 | 39.0 | 842 | 206 |
| Columbia | 132.1 | 20.1 | 23.6 | 57.6 | 581 | 97 | 484 | 138.3 | 1 395 | 191 |
| Florissant | 24.2 | 12.8 | 18.6 | 7.8 | 152 | 0 | 102 | 30.0 | 589 | 60 |
| Gladstone | 21.3 | 2.2 | 55.9 | 13.3 | 477 | 116 | 361 | 31.7 | 1 135 | 528 |
| Hazelwood | 39.8 | 12.5 | 13.4 | 23.5 | 924 | 398 | 208 | 38.8 | 1 521 | 365 |
| Independence | 126.0 | 15.8 | 32.4 | 79.4 | 717 | 102 | 615 | 158.5 | 1 431 | 664 |
| Jefferson City | 52.0 | 3.0 | 100.0 | 32.1 | 792 | 105 | 687 | 46.5 | 1 146 | 245 |
| Joplin | 62.5 | 9.0 | 35.0 | 36.0 | 734 | 37 | 697 | 60.1 | 1 223 | 439 |
| Kansas City | 1 317.7 | 136.2 | 15.0 | 672.4 | 1 493 | 320 | 813 | 1 359.8 | 3 019 | 579 |
| Kirkwood | 29.4 | 7.8 | 24.2 | 15.6 | 581 | 304 | 253 | 19.4 | 722 | 10 |
| Lee's Summit | 135.2 | 18.7 | 12.4 | 65.2 | 788 | 300 | 488 | 123.8 | 1 494 | 556 |
| Liberty | 40.2 | 1.6 | 57.2 | 16.1 | 535 | 149 | 387 | 50.4 | 1 680 | 502 |
| Maryland Heights | 42.2 | 15.8 | 19.5 | 19.1 | 730 | 69 | 661 | 31.5 | 1 207 | 275 |
| O'Fallon | 63.4 | 4.8 | 51.0 | 34.2 | 456 | 149 | 306 | 45.7 | 609 | 59 |
| Raytown | 19.1 | 2.2 | 100.0 | 9.3 | 327 | 59 | 268 | 16.7 | 588 | 0 |
| St. Charles | 80.1 | 10.2 | 84.5 | 53.9 | 847 | 159 | 688 | 83.2 | 1 307 | 434 |
| St. Joseph | 105.3 | 12.8 | 96.1 | 45.5 | 615 | 263 | 351 | 102.5 | 1 387 | 331 |
| St. Louis | 877.5 | 208.9 | 59.3 | 451.5 | 1 287 | 215 | 581 | 840.8 | 2 397 | 152 |
| St. Peters | 90.4 | 6.5 | 95.9 | 37.5 | 681 | 201 | 480 | 62.4 | 1 132 | 161 |
| Springfield | 282.6 | 43.9 | 19.5 | 120.7 | 780 | 145 | 635 | 239.9 | 1 550 | 319 |
| University City | 34.1 | 11.8 | 13.7 | 10.8 | 295 | 89 | 206 | 28.7 | 786 | 0 |
| Wentzville | 27.7 | 5.0 | 25.1 | 15.9 | 709 | 231 | 479 | 38.0 | 1 693 | 824 |
| Wildwood | 13.8 | 7.7 | 17.9 | 3.5 | 101 | 26 | 75 | 11.2 | 327 | 41 |
| MONTANA | X | X | X | X | X | X | X | X | X | X |
| Billings | 144.1 | 27.9 | 66.0 | 29.3 | 287 | 229 | 36 | 130.6 | 1 282 | 294 |
| Bozeman | 51.0 | 11.3 | 92.1 | 17.7 | 466 | 315 | 151 | 57.3 | 1 509 | 486 |
| Butte-Silver Bow | 48.3 | 12.9 | 73.5 | 20.0 | 611 | 586 | 25 | 48.0 | 1 469 | 119 |
| Great Falls | 51.3 | 11.3 | 78.1 | 14.8 | 252 | 220 | 32 | 44.7 | 760 | 24 |
| Helena | 34.0 | 6.9 | 71.7 | 7.4 | 256 | 236 | 20 | 31.5 | 1 095 | 172 |
| Missoula | 55.8 | 13.0 | 90.3 | 24.3 | 362 | 317 | 45 | 56.7 | 845 | 174 |
| NEBRASKA | X | X | X | X | X | X | X | X | X | X |
| Bellevue | 35.2 | 4.6 | 71.0 | 22.3 | 460 | 246 | 170 | 36.2 | 749 | 144 |
| Fremont | 22.5 | 5.1 | 57.9 | 9.1 | 360 | 148 | 212 | 19.9 | 787 | 151 |
| Grand Island | 55.5 | 6.7 | 100.0 | 20.7 | 463 | 124 | 339 | 55.4 | 1 236 | 172 |
| Kearney | 32.4 | 5.9 | 100.0 | 10.6 | 352 | 63 | 289 | 32.6 | 1 083 | 239 |
| Lincoln | 279.7 | 68.7 | 64.1 | 140.8 | 566 | 190 | 376 | 309.0 | 1 242 | 404 |
| Omaha | 427.2 | 33.3 | 95.6 | 280.0 | 660 | 224 | 436 | 448.5 | 1 057 | 142 |
| NEVADA | X | X | X | X | X | X | X | X | X | X |
| Carson City | 112.3 | 36.1 | 89.8 | 34.0 | 619 | 301 | 318 | 118.9 | 2 164 | 466 |
| Henderson | 389.2 | 114.6 | 91.3 | 147.9 | 593 | 340 | 254 | 252.9 | 1 014 | 50 |
| Las Vegas | 1 041.9 | 394.0 | 69.5 | 251.5 | 450 | 246 | 204 | 834.0 | 1 492 | 260 |
| North Las Vegas | 352.5 | 106.0 | 51.9 | 108.9 | 514 | 337 | 177 | 334.0 | 1 574 | 295 |
| Reno | 294.7 | 90.7 | 65.2 | 123.1 | 573 | 277 | 296 | 290.2 | 1 351 | 216 |
| Sparks | 128.1 | 35.0 | 82.6 | 55.5 | 637 | 293 | 344 | 96.8 | 1 111 | 27 |
| NEW HAMPSHIRE | X | X | X | X | X | X | X | X | X | X |
| Concord | 62.7 | 6.1 | 60.6 | 35.9 | 846 | 815 | 31 | 74.9 | 1 767 | 573 |
| Dover | 93.8 | 29.4 | 63.9 | 50.9 | 1 768 | 1 741 | 27 | 102.8 | 3 572 | 706 |
| Manchester | 406.7 | 142.7 | 78.6 | 154.5 | 1 420 | 1 290 | 130 | 401.0 | 3 684 | 581 |
| Nashua | 246.4 | 81.4 | 90.5 | 135.4 | 1 559 | 1 534 | 25 | 225.8 | 2 601 | 268 |
| Rochester | 77.0 | 36.0 | 91.0 | 34.1 | 1 116 | 1 000 | 117 | 90.1 | 2 952 | 524 |
| NEW JERSEY | X | X | X | X | X | X | X | X | X | X |
| Atlantic City | 213.7 | 34.6 | 37.5 | 159.4 | 4 017 | 3 846 | 171 | 188.5 | 4 749 | 178 |
| Bayonne | 196.5 | 68.6 | 98.3 | 107.3 | 1 853 | 1 836 | 18 | 316.4 | 5 467 | 1 727 |
| Bergenfield | 73.5 | 3.3 | 99.6 | 68.0 | 2 631 | 2 605 | 27 | 61.8 | 2 392 | 199 |
| Bridgeton | 31.4 | 13.9 | 63.9 | 8.8 | 358 | 327 | 31 | 29.7 | 1 207 | 231 |
| Camden | 188.1 | 143.2 | 79.4 | 27.8 | 353 | 294 | 59 | 185.8 | 2 361 | 229 |
| Clifton | 85.5 | 19.6 | 77.6 | 59.9 | 763 | 734 | 29 | 84.4 | 1 074 | 126 |
| East Orange | 379.3 | 278.0 | 95.7 | 81.1 | 1 230 | 1 211 | 19 | 384.1 | 5 824 | 739 |
| Elizabeth | 219.6 | 59.0 | 70.5 | 111.6 | 894 | 813 | 81 | 218.0 | 1 746 | 188 |
| Englewood | 118.5 | 31.8 | 79.9 | 82.5 | 2 944 | 2 910 | 34 | 116.9 | 4 172 | 505 |
| Fair Lawn | 41.1 | 6.0 | 97.7 | 33.3 | 1 081 | 1 042 | 39 | 36.0 | 1 171 | 125 |
| Fort Lee | 63.0 | 9.3 | 32.9 | 50.7 | 1 388 | 1 336 | 52 | 59.1 | 1 619 | 116 |

1. Based on population estimated as of July 1 of the year shown.

| City | City government finances, 2006 (cont.) | | | | | | | | | |
|---|---|---|---|---|---|---|---|---|---|---|
| | General expenditure (cont.) | | | | | | | | | |
| | Percent of total for: | | | | | | | | | |
| | Public welfare | Highways | Parking facilities | Education | Health and hospitals | Police protection | Sewerage and sanitation | Parks and recreation | Housing and community development | Interest on debt |
| | 127 | 128 | 129 | 130 | 131 | 132 | 133 | 134 | 135 | 136 |
| MISSOURI.................. | X | X | X | X | X | X | X | X | X | X |
| Ballwin........................ | 0.0 | 16.0 | 0.0 | 0.0 | 0.0 | 31.1 | 3.8 | 24.2 | 0.0 | 10.4 |
| Blue Springs................. | 0.0 | 5.9 | 2.6 | 0.0 | 0.0 | 27.4 | 16.2 | 16.6 | 0.0 | 8.5 |
| Cape Girardeau............. | 0.0 | 21.3 | 0.0 | 0.0 | 0.7 | 15.0 | 15.5 | 10.2 | 0.5 | 2.1 |
| Chesterfield.................. | 0.0 | 31.3 | 0.0 | 0.0 | 0.0 | 18.6 | 0.0 | 18.1 | 0.4 | 13.6 |
| Columbia...................... | 0.7 | 4.5 | 0.9 | 0.0 | 3.5 | 10.1 | 15.5 | 10.5 | 1.0 | 1.7 |
| Florissant.................... | 0.0 | 0.0 | 0.0 | 0.0 | 2.3 | 28.0 | 2.3 | 20.4 | 0.8 | 1.6 |
| Gladstone.................... | 0.0 | 7.2 | 0.0 | 0.0 | 0.0 | 13.8 | 9.1 | 43.6 | 0.0 | 2.6 |
| Hazelwood.................... | 0.0 | 19.9 | 0.0 | 0.0 | 0.0 | 16.9 | 0.3 | 6.2 | 0.0 | 3.3 |
| Independence............... | 0.0 | 7.6 | 0.0 | 0.0 | 1.9 | 21.4 | 19.5 | 8.1 | 0.4 | 5.1 |
| Jefferson City.............. | 0.0 | 9.6 | 1.6 | 0.0 | 1.1 | 16.9 | 16.5 | 12.2 | 0.7 | 5.8 |
| Joplin.......................... | 0.4 | 14.3 | 0.1 | 0.0 | 4.2 | 14.4 | 16.8 | 5.6 | 1.2 | 1.6 |
| Kansas City.................. | 0.5 | 4.9 | 0.3 | 0.0 | 4.8 | 13.0 | 7.3 | 3.9 | 0.7 | 4.9 |
| Kirkwood..................... | 0.0 | 5.6 | 0.0 | 0.0 | 0.0 | 23.3 | 10.6 | 13.0 | 0.0 | 8.1 |
| Lee's Summit............... | 0.0 | 24.1 | 0.0 | 0.0 | 0.0 | 12.6 | 9.7 | 9.1 | 1.1 | 2.9 |
| Liberty........................ | 0.0 | 13.2 | 0.0 | 0.0 | 0.0 | 8.6 | 36.3 | 10.4 | 3.6 | 3.3 |
| Maryland Heights ......... | 0.9 | 26.6 | 0.0 | 0.0 | 0.0 | 27.2 | 6.8 | 11.1 | 4.0 | 5.1 |
| O'Fallon...................... | 0.0 | 12.9 | 0.0 | 0.0 | 0.0 | 21.7 | 15.8 | 12.6 | 0.6 | 12.8 |
| Raytown...................... | 0.0 | 11.4 | 0.0 | 0.0 | 11.5 | 31.6 | 19.6 | 7.8 | 2.6 | 3.3 |
| St. Charles .................. | 0.0 | 21.6 | 0.4 | 0.0 | 0.0 | 19.5 | 18.2 | 7.4 | 0.4 | 5.6 |
| St. Joseph ................... | 0.0 | 9.1 | 0.3 | 0.0 | 2.9 | 11.1 | 11.0 | 5.0 | 2.8 | 21.7 |
| St. Louis ..................... | 0.0 | 1.9 | 1.2 | 0.0 | 5.2 | 19.7 | 1.8 | 3.0 | 9.5 | 8.5 |
| St. Peters ................... | 0.0 | 20.6 | 0.0 | 0.0 | 1.1 | 15.4 | 19.5 | 16.6 | 3.5 | 3.3 |
| Springfield .................. | 0.0 | 25.2 | 0.0 | 0.0 | 3.5 | 21.8 | 7.0 | 13.9 | 3.7 | 3.7 |
| University City ............. | 0.0 | 12.5 | 0.8 | 0.0 | 0.0 | 25.9 | 8.4 | 12.3 | 0.0 | 3.5 |
| Wentzville.................... | 0.0 | 28.1 | 0.0 | 0.0 | 0.0 | 12.6 | 34.8 | 4.9 | 0.0 | 5.0 |
| Wildwood..................... | 0.0 | 28.2 | 0.0 | 0.0 | 0.0 | 22.0 | 0.0 | 3.9 | 0.0 | 0.9 |
| MONTANA ................ | X | X | X | X | X | X | X | X | X | X |
| Billings........................ | 0.0 | 15.4 | 5.4 | 0.0 | 0.4 | 12.8 | 14.2 | 4.1 | 2.3 | 2.1 |
| Bozeman...................... | 6.8 | 4.9 | 0.3 | 0.0 | 0.0 | 11.2 | 11.5 | 0.0 | 2.8 | 0.9 |
| Butte-Silver Bow........... | 0.3 | 6.1 | 0.4 | 0.0 | 8.6 | 11.3 | 11.1 | 4.8 | 7.7 | 5.1 |
| Great Falls................... | 0.0 | 8.7 | 1.7 | 0.0 | 0.6 | 20.8 | 20.2 | 9.4 | 3.1 | 3.6 |
| Helena........................ | 0.0 | 11.6 | 3.0 | 0.0 | 0.4 | 17.5 | 25.6 | 10.9 | 0.3 | 2.7 |
| Missoula ..................... | 0.2 | 13.9 | 0.0 | 0.0 | 2.2 | 16.7 | 10.7 | 6.5 | 5.6 | 1.2 |
| NEBRASKA.............. | X | X | X | X | X | X | X | X | X | X |
| Bellevue...................... | 1.1 | 17.8 | 0.0 | 0.0 | 0.0 | 17.4 | 6.1 | 9.4 | 0.6 | 4.6 |
| Fremont....................... | 0.0 | 20.9 | 0.0 | 0.0 | 0.0 | 16.2 | 26.5 | 15.2 | 2.3 | 1.3 |
| Grand Island................ | 0.0 | 15.4 | 0.1 | 0.0 | 0.0 | 13.6 | 20.2 | 7.7 | 0.4 | 1.5 |
| Kearney...................... | 0.0 | 18.8 | 0.2 | 0.0 | 0.0 | 16.5 | 20.9 | 11.0 | 4.0 | 2.0 |
| Lincoln........................ | 0.0 | 21.0 | 1.5 | 0.0 | 8.0 | 11.0 | 18.0 | 6.4 | 6.4 | 2.1 |
| Omaha........................ | 0.0 | 12.1 | 0.5 | 0.0 | 0.0 | 19.3 | 11.7 | 5.2 | 1.5 | 6.8 |
| NEVADA.................. | X | X | X | X | X | X | X | X | X | X |
| Carson City ................. | 1.7 | 9.6 | 0.0 | 0.0 | 5.4 | 19.4 | 5.3 | 7.6 | 1.5 | 3.9 |
| Henderson................... | 0.0 | 4.2 | 0.0 | 0.0 | 0.0 | 24.7 | 9.4 | 15.4 | 5.1 | 3.8 |
| Las Vegas ................... | 0.1 | 9.2 | 0.5 | 0.0 | 0.3 | 16.1 | 6.0 | 15.0 | 3.0 | 2.3 |
| North Las Vegas ........... | 0.0 | 19.0 | 0.0 | 0.0 | 0.3 | 18.2 | 5.2 | 7.7 | 2.2 | 2.7 |
| Reno........................... | 0.0 | 5.0 | 0.0 | 0.0 | 0.0 | 20.4 | 21.6 | 7.4 | 1.9 | 6.1 |
| Sparks........................ | 0.0 | 8.8 | 0.0 | 0.0 | 0.0 | 22.2 | 12.3 | 8.7 | 2.7 | 3.6 |
| NEW HAMPSHIRE..... | X | X | X | X | X | X | X | X | X | X |
| Concord....................... | 1.5 | 9.1 | 1.0 | 0.0 | 0.4 | 10.5 | 12.0 | 4.7 | 0.0 | 1.8 |
| Dover.......................... | 0.6 | 6.1 | 0.0 | 44.8 | 0.0 | 6.6 | 5.4 | 2.9 | 0.9 | 3.2 |
| Manchester.................. | 0.3 | 5.1 | 0.5 | 38.4 | 1.1 | 6.3 | 5.8 | 3.3 | 0.9 | 5.1 |
| Nashua........................ | 0.6 | 3.2 | 0.0 | 51.7 | 0.7 | 7.3 | 10.3 | 1.3 | 0.8 | 5.1 |
| Rochester.................... | 0.8 | 7.5 | 0.0 | 58.7 | 0.1 | 5.3 | 3.8 | 1.2 | 0.2 | 3.3 |
| NEW JERSEY ............ | X | X | X | X | X | X | X | X | X | X |
| Atlantic City ............... | 2.3 | 0.7 | 0.0 | 0.0 | 2.4 | 21.5 | 1.7 | 2.6 | 13.4 | 3.0 |
| Bayonne...................... | 0.0 | 3.2 | 0.3 | 41.4 | 0.6 | 7.3 | 3.3 | 1.3 | 7.4 | 2.7 |
| Bergenfield.................. | 0.0 | 0.0 | 0.0 | 64.5 | 0.6 | 9.7 | 7.9 | 1.1 | 0.0 | 1.4 |
| Bridgeton..................... | 0.0 | 5.4 | 0.0 | 0.0 | 0.0 | 18.0 | 19.5 | 1.9 | 18.4 | 0.5 |
| Camden....................... | 0.0 | 3.2 | 0.0 | 0.0 | 0.6 | 21.1 | 6.6 | 2.0 | 17.4 | 1.8 |
| Clifton ........................ | 0.1 | 4.5 | 0.0 | 0.0 | 1.2 | 20.1 | 8.4 | 1.9 | 2.8 | 3.0 |
| East Orange................. | 0.0 | 0.6 | 0.1 | 65.3 | 1.9 | 6.8 | 2.9 | 1.1 | 4.0 | 0.8 |
| Elizabeth..................... | 0.0 | 2.8 | 0.9 | 0.0 | 2.6 | 18.7 | 9.6 | 5.0 | 14.3 | 1.6 |
| Englewood.................... | 0.2 | 5.1 | 0.7 | 54.6 | 0.9 | 8.9 | 2.5 | 0.9 | 4.2 | 0.9 |
| Fair Lawn .................... | 0.4 | 4.9 | 0.0 | 0.0 | 1.5 | 19.1 | 14.5 | 6.0 | 0.0 | 4.8 |
| Fort Lee...................... | 0.2 | 3.2 | 0.0 | 0.0 | 1.8 | 24.9 | 10.9 | 2.6 | 8.8 | 4.2 |

| | City government finances, 2007 (cont.) | | | | Climate[2] | | | | | | |
| | Debt outstanding | | | | Average daily temperature (degrees Fahrenheit) | | | | | | |
| | | | | | Mean | | Limits | | | | |
| City | Total (mil dol) | Per capita[1] (dollars) | Debt issued during year | City government employment, 2011 | January | July | January[3] | July[4] | Annual precipitation (inches) | Heating degree days | Cooling degree days |
| | 137 | 138 | 139 | 140 | 141 | 142 | 143 | 144 | 145 | 146 | 147 |
| MISSOURI................ | X | X | X | X | X | X | X | X | X | X | X |
| Ballwin...................... | 30.2 | 1 004 | 0.0 | 158 | 27.5 | 78.1 | 17.3 | 89.2 | 38.00 | 5 199 | 1 293 |
| Blue Springs................ | 91.0 | 1 653 | 11.4 | 262 | 24.6 | 76.6 | 14.9 | 87.2 | 41.18 | 5 623 | 1 137 |
| Cape Girardeau............ | 68.2 | 1 836 | 0.0 | 413 | 32.4 | 79.5 | 24.0 | 90.1 | 46.54 | 4 344 | 1 515 |
| Chesterfield................. | 114.5 | 2 475 | 0.3 | 193 | 27.5 | 78.1 | 17.3 | 89.2 | 38.00 | 5 199 | 1 293 |
| Columbia .................... | 143.2 | 1 444 | 60.6 | 1 467 | 27.8 | 77.4 | 18.2 | 88.6 | 40.28 | 5 177 | 1 246 |
| Florissant ................... | 14.2 | 278 | 3.6 | 357 | 29.6 | 80.2 | 21.2 | 89.8 | 38.75 | 4 758 | 1 561 |
| Gladstone ................... | 44.9 | 1 605 | 28.3 | 214 | 29.3 | 81.3 | 20.7 | 90.5 | 35.51 | 4 734 | 1 676 |
| Hazelwood................... | 30.7 | 1 206 | 6.3 | 193 | 29.6 | 80.2 | 21.2 | 89.8 | 38.75 | 4 758 | 1 561 |
| Independence............... | 203.7 | 1 840 | 64.1 | 1 139 | 26.6 | 77.1 | 17.1 | 87.5 | 43.14 | 5 373 | 1 176 |
| Jefferson City .............. | 50.6 | 1 247 | 10.1 | 438 | 28.2 | 77.9 | 17.7 | 89.4 | 39.59 | 5 158 | 1 261 |
| Joplin........................ | 18.4 | 375 | 0.0 | 514 | 33.1 | 79.9 | 23.7 | 90.4 | 46.07 | 4 253 | 1 555 |
| Kansas City ................. | 2 467.0 | 5 478 | 374.6 | 6 646 | 29.3 | 81.3 | 20.7 | 90.5 | 35.51 | 4 734 | 1 676 |
| Kirkwood..................... | 33.7 | 1 258 | 0.3 | 247 | 29.6 | 80.2 | 21.2 | 89.8 | 38.75 | 4 758 | 1 561 |
| Lee's Summit ............... | 112.4 | 1 357 | 17.1 | 662 | 24.6 | 76.6 | 14.9 | 87.2 | 41.18 | 5 623 | 1 137 |
| Liberty....................... | 49.9 | 1 665 | 0.0 | 217 | 26.6 | 77.1 | 17.1 | 87.5 | 43.14 | 5 373 | 1 176 |
| Maryland Heights ......... | 29.9 | 1 144 | 0.6 | 214 | 29.5 | 80.7 | 21.2 | 90.5 | 38.84 | 4 650 | 1 633 |
| O'Fallon ..................... | 343.2 | 4 577 | 15.8 | 410 | 28.3 | 79.0 | 19.0 | 90.2 | 38.28 | 5 020 | 1 399 |
| Raytown ..................... | 13.2 | 464 | 7.6 | 163 | 24.6 | 76.6 | 14.9 | 87.2 | 41.18 | 5 623 | 1 137 |
| St. Charles ................. | 154.8 | 2 432 | 11.1 | 447 | 27.5 | 78.1 | 17.3 | 89.2 | 38.00 | 5 199 | 1 293 |
| St. Joseph .................. | 375.0 | 5 073 | 0.0 | 655 | 26.4 | 78.7 | 15.9 | 89.9 | 35.24 | 5 345 | 1 339 |
| St. Louis .................... | 1 653.9 | 4 715 | 492.2 | 6 335 | 29.5 | 80.7 | 21.2 | 90.5 | 38.84 | 4 650 | 1 633 |
| St. Peters ................... | 61.1 | 1 108 | 0.1 | 495 | 28.3 | 79.0 | 19.0 | 90.2 | 38.28 | 5 020 | 1 399 |
| Springfield .................. | 484.9 | 3 133 | 137.4 | 2 675 | 31.7 | 78.5 | 21.8 | 89.9 | 44.97 | 4 602 | 1 366 |
| University City ............. | 23.2 | 636 | 0.0 | 298 | 29.5 | 80.7 | 21.2 | 90.5 | 38.84 | 4 650 | 1 633 |
| Wentzville................... | 47.5 | 2 113 | 4.2 | 191 | NA | NA | NA | NA | NA | NA | NA |
| Wildwood.................... | 2.6 | 75 | 0.0 | NA | 27.5 | 78.1 | 17.3 | 89.2 | 38.00 | 5 199 | 1 293 |
| MONTANA ................ | X | X | X | X | X | X | X | X | X | X | X |
| Billings...................... | 101.4 | 996 | 27.6 | 877 | 24.0 | 72.0 | 15.1 | 85.8 | 14.77 | 7 006 | 583 |
| Bozeman..................... | 15.2 | 400 | 2.2 | 340 | 22.6 | 65.3 | 12.0 | 81.8 | 16.45 | 7 984 | 216 |
| Butte-Silver Bow............ | 48.1 | 1 474 | 0.0 | 435 | 17.6 | 62.7 | 5.4 | 79.8 | 12.78 | 9 399 | 127 |
| Great Falls.................. | 54.0 | 918 | 3.6 | 489 | 21.7 | 66.2 | 11.3 | 82.0 | 14.89 | 7 828 | 288 |
| Helena ...................... | 41.9 | 1 460 | 0.8 | 300 | 20.2 | 67.8 | 9.9 | 83.4 | 11.32 | 7 975 | 277 |
| Missoula .................... | 68.8 | 1 025 | 21.2 | 460 | 23.5 | 66.9 | 16.2 | 83.6 | 13.82 | 7 622 | 256 |
| NEBRASKA............... | X | X | X | X | X | X | X | X | X | X | X |
| Bellevue..................... | 39.2 | 810 | 0.0 | 256 | 21.7 | 76.7 | 11.6 | 87.4 | 30.22 | 6 311 | 1 095 |
| Fremont...................... | 46.7 | 1 843 | 9.9 | 279 | 21.1 | 76.2 | 10.4 | 87.7 | 29.80 | 6 444 | 1 004 |
| Grand Island ............... | 85.0 | 1 897 | 15.0 | 580 | 22.4 | 75.8 | 12.2 | 87.1 | 25.89 | 6 385 | 1 027 |
| Kearney...................... | 38.5 | 1 279 | 5.6 | 262 | 22.4 | 74.7 | 11.0 | 85.7 | 25.20 | 6 652 | 852 |
| Lincoln....................... | 907.8 | 3 649 | 139.0 | 2 612 | 22.4 | 77.8 | 11.5 | 89.6 | 28.37 | 6 242 | 1 154 |
| Omaha....................... | 823.8 | 1 941 | 97.7 | 2 834 | 21.7 | 76.7 | 11.6 | 87.4 | 30.22 | 6 311 | 1 095 |
| NEVADA.................... | X | X | X | X | X | X | X | X | X | X | X |
| Carson City ................. | 141.2 | 2 571 | 12.4 | 596 | 33.7 | 70.0 | 21.7 | 89.2 | 10.36 | 5 661 | 419 |
| Henderson................... | 404.6 | 1 622 | 2.1 | 2 218 | 47.0 | 91.2 | 36.8 | 104.1 | 4.49 | 2 239 | 3 214 |
| Las Vegas .................. | 352.8 | 631 | 34.2 | 2 594 | 47.0 | 91.2 | 36.8 | 104.1 | 4.49 | 2 239 | 3 214 |
| North Las Vegas ......... | 378.6 | 1 785 | 154.9 | 1 565 | 47.0 | 91.2 | 36.8 | 104.1 | 4.49 | 2 239 | 3 214 |
| Reno......................... | 751.0 | 3 495 | 45.0 | 1 230 | 33.6 | 71.3 | 21.8 | 91.2 | 7.48 | 5 600 | 493 |
| Sparks ...................... | 108.6 | 1 247 | 32.0 | 518 | 33.6 | 71.3 | 21.8 | 91.2 | 7.48 | 5 600 | 493 |
| NEW HAMPSHIRE..... | X | X | X | X | X | X | X | X | X | X | X |
| Concord...................... | 68.5 | 1 615 | 13.3 | 507 | 20.1 | 70.0 | 9.7 | 82.9 | 37.60 | 7 478 | 442 |
| Dover........................ | 108.4 | 3 768 | 20.6 | 898 | 23.3 | 70.7 | 13.1 | 83.2 | 42.80 | 6 748 | 427 |
| Manchester.................. | 555.2 | 5 099 | 0.0 | 3 462 | 18.8 | 68.4 | 5.2 | 82.1 | 39.82 | 7 742 | 263 |
| Nashua...................... | 165.6 | 1 907 | 12.9 | 2 746 | 22.8 | 70.8 | 12.1 | 82.5 | 45.43 | 6 834 | 445 |
| Rochester.................... | 66.3 | 2 173 | 0.0 | 1 042 | 23.3 | 70.7 | 13.1 | 83.2 | 42.80 | 6 748 | 427 |
| NEW JERSEY.......... | X | X | X | X | X | X | X | X | X | X | X |
| Atlantic City ................ | 169.9 | 4 281 | 2.5 | 1 505 | 35.2 | 75.2 | 29.0 | 80.6 | 38.37 | 4 480 | 951 |
| Bayonne ..................... | 393.2 | 6 793 | 17.4 | 2 099 | 31.3 | 77.2 | 24.4 | 85.2 | 46.25 | 4 843 | 1 220 |
| Bergenfield .................. | 20.7 | 802 | 5.0 | NA | 28.6 | 75.0 | 19.5 | 85.5 | 51.50 | 5 522 | 824 |
| Bridgeton.................... | 5.7 | 232 | 0.0 | 232 | NA | NA | NA | NA | NA | NA | NA |
| Camden...................... | 124.7 | 1 585 | 3.9 | 892 | 32.3 | 76.3 | 23.2 | 87.8 | 48.25 | 4 801 | 1 054 |
| Clifton ....................... | 69.4 | 883 | 15.8 | 592 | 28.6 | 75.0 | 19.5 | 85.5 | 51.50 | 5 522 | 824 |
| East Orange ................ | 109.2 | 1 655 | 23.0 | 2 871 | 31.3 | 77.2 | 24.4 | 85.2 | 46.25 | 4 843 | 1 220 |
| Elizabeth..................... | 137.6 | 1 102 | 22.1 | 1 374 | 29.6 | 74.5 | 19.8 | 85.7 | 50.94 | 5 450 | 787 |
| Englewood................... | 35.7 | 1 274 | 0.0 | 911 | 29.6 | 75.3 | 22.7 | 82.5 | 46.33 | 5 367 | 882 |
| Fair Lawn ................... | 29.9 | 971 | 0.0 | 251 | 28.6 | 75.0 | 19.5 | 85.5 | 51.50 | 5 522 | 824 |
| Fort Lee..................... | 69.6 | 1 907 | 0.0 | 344 | 29.6 | 75.3 | 22.7 | 82.5 | 46.33 | 5 367 | 882 |

1. Based on the population estimated as of July 1 of the year shown.   2. Represents normal values based on the 30-year period, 1971–2000.   3. Average daily minimum.   4. Average daily maximum.

# Table D. Cities — Land Area and Population

| STATE Place code | City | Land area,[1] 2010 (sq km) | Total persons | Rank | Per square kilometer | White | Black | American Indian, Alaska Native | Asian | Hawaiian Pacific Islander | Percent Hispanic or Latino,[2] 2010 | Percent Foreign born 2007–2011 |
|---|---|---|---|---|---|---|---|---|---|---|---|---|
| | | Population, 2012 | | | | Race alone or in combination, not of Hispanic origin (percent), 2010 | | | | | | |
| | | | | | | Race alone or in combination | | | | | | |
| | | 1 | 2 | 3 | 4 | 5 | 6 | 7 | 8 | 9 | 10 | 11 |
| | **NEW JERSEY—** Cont'd | | | | | | | | | | | |
| 34 25770 | Garfield...................... | 5.4 | 30 872 | 1 179 | 5 717.0 | 59.8 | 5.7 | 0.2 | 2.6 | 0.1 | 32.2 | 42.0 |
| 34 28680 | Hackensack................ | 10.8 | 43 845 | 829 | 4 059.7 | 30.8 | 23.3 | 0.5 | 10.9 | 0.1 | 35.3 | 39.1 |
| 34 32250 | Hoboken..................... | 3.3 | 52 034 | 694 | 15 767.9 | 74.7 | 3.0 | 0.2 | 8.2 | 0.1 | 15.2 | 14.8 |
| 34 36000 | Jersey City ................ | 38.3 | 254 441 | 75 | 6 643.4 | 22.7 | 24.9 | 0.7 | 24.8 | 0.2 | 27.6 | 38.2 |
| 34 36510 | Kearny ...................... | 22.7 | 41 389 | 878 | 1 823.3 | 49.8 | 4.6 | 0.2 | 4.7 | 0.2 | 39.9 | 40.9 |
| 34 40350 | Linden ...................... | 27.7 | 40 880 | 885 | 1 475.8 | 45.7 | 26.6 | 0.6 | 3.0 | 0.1 | 24.9 | 32.0 |
| 34 41310 | Long Branch............... | 13.7 | 30 646 | 1 186 | 2 236.9 | 54.0 | 14.1 | 0.5 | 2.5 | 0.1 | 28.1 | 31.1 |
| 34 46680 | Millville...................... | 108.8 | 28 619 | 1 271 | 263.0 | 64.2 | 20.1 | 1.6 | 1.5 | 0.1 | 14.9 | 4.1 |
| 34 51000 | Newark ...................... | 62.6 | 277 727 | 68 | 4 436.5 | 12.5 | 50.6 | 0.6 | 1.8 | 0.1 | 33.8 | 26.6 |
| 34 51210 | New Brunswick............ | 13.5 | 56 160 | 637 | 4 160.0 | 27.7 | 14.7 | 0.4 | 8.0 | 0.1 | 49.9 | 36.8 |
| 34 55950 | Paramus .................... | 27.1 | 26 532 | 1 371 | 979.0 | 68.1 | 1.5 | 0.2 | 23.9 | 0.5 | 7.3 | 26.8 |
| 34 56550 | Passaic ..................... | 8.2 | 70 218 | 471 | 8 563.2 | 16.5 | 7.8 | 0.2 | 4.6 | 0.0 | 71.0 | 46.3 |
| 34 57000 | Paterson .................... | 21.8 | 145 219 | 174 | 6 661.4 | 10.0 | 29.0 | 0.4 | 3.7 | 0.1 | 57.6 | 29.3 |
| 34 58200 | Perth Amboy ............... | 12.2 | 51 744 | 700 | 4 241.3 | 12.4 | 7.7 | 0.2 | 1.7 | 0.0 | 78.1 | 36.2 |
| 34 59190 | Plainfield ................... | 15.6 | 50 244 | 723 | 3 220.8 | 9.1 | 49.6 | 0.7 | 1.2 | 0.1 | 40.4 | 34.8 |
| 34 61530 | Rahway ..................... | 10.1 | 27 785 | 1 301 | 2 751.0 | 41.5 | 30.9 | 0.8 | 4.7 | 0.1 | 23.5 | 21.3 |
| 34 65790 | Sayreville .................. | 41.0 | 43 761 | 836 | 1 067.3 | 60.4 | 10.6 | 0.3 | 16.9 | 0.1 | 12.3 | 24.7 |
| 34 74000 | Trenton ..................... | 19.8 | 84 477 | 368 | 4 266.5 | 14.4 | 51.1 | 0.7 | 1.3 | 0.1 | 33.7 | 23.1 |
| 34 74630 | Union City .................. | 3.3 | 67 744 | 495 | 20 528.5 | 11.0 | 1.8 | 0.1 | 2.4 | 0.0 | 84.7 | 57.6 |
| 34 76070 | Vineland .................... | 177.2 | 60 854 | 571 | 343.4 | 47.4 | 13.2 | 0.8 | 2.0 | 0.1 | 38.0 | 11.4 |
| 34 79040 | Westfield ................... | 17.4 | 30 639 | 1 188 | 1 760.9 | 86.0 | 3.5 | 0.2 | 6.7 | 0.1 | 4.9 | 12.3 |
| 34 79610 | West New York ........... | 2.6 | 51 464 | 705 | 19 793.8 | 13.8 | 2.0 | 0.2 | 6.3 | 0.0 | 78.1 | 59.9 |
| 35 00000 | **NEW MEXICO**........... | 314 160.8 | 2 085 538 | X | 6.6 | 41.7 | 2.2 | 9.2 | 1.7 | 0.1 | 46.3 | 9.8 |
| 35 01780 | Alamogordo................ | 55.5 | 31 500 | 1 151 | 567.6 | 61.2 | 6.1 | 1.8 | 2.6 | 0.5 | 30.5 | 8.5 |
| 35 02000 | Albuquerque............... | 486.2 | 555 417 | 32 | 1 142.4 | 43.7 | 3.3 | 4.5 | 3.2 | 0.2 | 46.7 | 10.7 |
| 35 12150 | Carlsbad ................... | 74.9 | 26 697 | 1 366 | 356.4 | 54.1 | 1.9 | 1.2 | 1.2 | 0.1 | 42.5 | 3.0 |
| 35 16420 | Clovis ....................... | 58.8 | 39 197 | 930 | 666.6 | 49.6 | 7.2 | 1.2 | 1.9 | 0.1 | 41.8 | 9.4 |
| 35 25800 | Farmington ................ | 81.6 | 45 854 | 803 | 561.9 | 54.4 | 1.3 | 23.0 | 0.9 | 0.1 | 22.4 | 5.2 |
| 35 32520 | Hobbs ....................... | 62.0 | 35 007 | 1 043 | 564.6 | 39.1 | 6.1 | 1.2 | 0.7 | 0.1 | 53.7 | 12.1 |
| 35 39380 | Las Cruces ................ | 198.1 | 101 047 | 285 | 510.1 | 38.6 | 2.4 | 1.3 | 1.9 | 0.2 | 56.8 | 12.2 |
| 35 63460 | Rio Rancho ................ | 267.7 | 90 818 | 331 | 339.3 | 55.8 | 3.3 | 3.4 | 2.4 | 0.3 | 36.7 | 5.6 |
| 35 64930 | Roswell ..................... | 77.3 | 48 477 | 762 | 627.1 | 42.9 | 2.3 | 1.1 | 0.9 | 0.1 | 53.4 | 12.5 |
| 35 70500 | Santa Fe ................... | 119.1 | 69 204 | 482 | 581.1 | 47.4 | 1.1 | 1.9 | 1.8 | 0.1 | 48.7 | 13.5 |
| 36 00000 | **NEW YORK**.............. | 122 056.8 | 19 570 261 | X | 160.3 | 59.5 | 15.2 | 0.7 | 8.0 | 0.1 | 17.6 | 21.8 |
| 36 01000 | Albany ...................... | 55.4 | 97 904 | 297 | 1 767.2 | 56.3 | 31.0 | 0.9 | 5.6 | 0.2 | 8.6 | 11.4 |
| 36 03078 | Auburn ...................... | 21.6 | 27 365 | 1 329 | 1 266.9 | 87.1 | 10.1 | 0.9 | 0.8 | 0.1 | 3.6 | 3.2 |
| 36 06607 | Binghamton ................ | 27.2 | 46 551 | 793 | 1 711.4 | 78.2 | 12.9 | 1.0 | 4.8 | 0.2 | 6.4 | 9.8 |
| 36 11000 | Buffalo ...................... | 104.6 | 259 384 | 73 | 2 479.8 | 47.7 | 39.0 | 1.2 | 3.6 | 0.1 | 10.5 | 7.4 |
| 36 24229 | Elmira ....................... | 18.8 | 28 987 | 1 258 | 1 541.9 | 80.6 | 17.4 | 1.2 | 0.9 | 0.1 | 4.3 | 2.6 |
| 36 27485 | Freeport..................... | 12.0 | 43 138 | 844 | 3 594.8 | 24.6 | 32.2 | 0.7 | 2.0 | 0.1 | 41.7 | 35.8 |
| 36 29113 | Glen Cove .................. | 17.2 | 27 100 | 1 341 | 1 575.6 | 60.4 | 7.1 | 0.4 | 5.1 | 0.2 | 27.9 | 30.8 |
| 36 32402 | Harrison .................... | 43.4 | 27 785 | 1 301 | 640.2 | 78.3 | 2.6 | 0.3 | 8.3 | 0.1 | 11.7 | 21.9 |
| 36 33139 | Hempstead ................ | 9.5 | 54 883 | 657 | 5 777.2 | 7.2 | 47.1 | 0.7 | 1.6 | 0.1 | 44.2 | 39.2 |
| 36 38077 | Ithaca ....................... | 14.0 | 30 331 | 1 202 | 2 166.5 | 69.8 | 7.5 | 1.0 | 17.9 | 0.2 | 6.9 | 18.2 |
| 36 38264 | Jamestown ................. | 23.1 | 30 767 | 1 182 | 1 331.9 | 86.6 | 5.9 | 1.3 | 0.6 | 0.1 | 8.8 | 1.8 |
| 36 42654 | Lindenhurst ................ | 9.7 | 27 256 | 1 336 | 2 809.9 | 86.7 | 1.6 | 0.3 | 2.4 | 0.0 | 9.7 | 11.2 |
| 36 43335 | Long Beach ................ | 5.7 | 33 480 | 1 088 | 5 873.7 | 76.4 | 6.5 | 0.3 | 3.2 | 0.1 | 14.1 | 15.6 |
| 36 47042 | Middletown ................ | 13.2 | 27 886 | 1 296 | 2 112.6 | 39.3 | 20.2 | 1.1 | 2.2 | 0.1 | 39.7 | 20.8 |
| 36 49121 | Mount Vernon ............. | 11.4 | 67 896 | 493 | 5 955.8 | 19.8 | 63.0 | 0.9 | 2.4 | 0.2 | 14.3 | 32.2 |
| 36 50034 | Newburgh ................... | 9.9 | 28 651 | 1 268 | 2 894.0 | 22.2 | 30.0 | 1.0 | 1.1 | 0.1 | 47.9 | 26.0 |
| 36 50617 | New Rochelle ............. | 26.8 | 78 388 | 408 | 2 924.9 | 49.0 | 19.0 | 0.4 | 4.7 | 0.1 | 27.8 | 27.4 |
| 36 51000 | New York ................... | 783.8 | 8 336 697 | 1 | 10 636.3 | 34.3 | 23.6 | 0.5 | 13.6 | 0.2 | 28.6 | 36.8 |
| 36 51055 | Niagara Falls .............. | 36.5 | 49 722 | 733 | 1 362.2 | 72.2 | 23.7 | 3.0 | 1.5 | 0.1 | 3.0 | 4.7 |
| 36 53682 | North Tonawanda ......... | 26.2 | 31 269 | 1 158 | 1 193.5 | 96.4 | 1.2 | 0.8 | 1.0 | 0.1 | 1.7 | 3.0 |
| 36 55530 | Ossining .................... | 8.2 | 25 266 | 1 428 | 3 081.2 | 38.0 | 16.2 | 0.2 | 4.7 | 0.1 | 41.4 | 35.9 |
| 36 59223 | Port Chester ............... | 6.0 | 29 247 | 1 245 | 4 874.5 | 32.3 | 5.7 | 0.3 | 2.2 | 0.0 | 59.4 | 45.0 |
| 36 59641 | Poughkeepsie ............. | 13.3 | 30 847 | 1 180 | 2 319.3 | 46.0 | 34.3 | 0.8 | 2.0 | 0.1 | 19.5 | 22.3 |
| 36 63000 | Rochester .................. | 92.7 | 210 532 | 101 | 2 271.1 | 39.9 | 41.8 | 1.1 | 3.5 | 0.1 | 16.4 | 8.6 |
| 36 63418 | Rome ........................ | 193.7 | 32 840 | 1 109 | 169.5 | 86.5 | 8.1 | 0.7 | 1.4 | 0.1 | 5.3 | 4.3 |
| 36 65255 | Saratoga Springs ......... | 72.7 | 26 960 | 1 346 | 370.8 | 92.1 | 3.4 | 0.6 | 2.6 | 0.1 | 3.2 | 4.7 |
| 36 65508 | Schenectady ............... | 27.9 | 66 078 | 511 | 2 368.4 | 61.4 | 22.0 | 1.7 | 5.1 | 0.4 | 10.5 | 12.4 |
| 36 70420 | Spring Valley .............. | 5.2 | 32 082 | 1 135 | 6 169.6 | 28.9 | 36.6 | 0.6 | 4.2 | 0.3 | 30.6 | 48.5 |
| 36 73000 | Syracuse ................... | 64.9 | 144 170 | 175 | 2 221.4 | 56.3 | 31.1 | 2.1 | 6.1 | 0.2 | 8.3 | 10.5 |
| 36 75484 | Troy ......................... | 26.8 | 49 946 | 729 | 1 863.7 | 72.7 | 17.5 | 0.8 | 4.0 | 0.1 | 7.9 | 9.1 |
| 36 76540 | Utica ........................ | 43.4 | 61 822 | 561 | 1 424.5 | 67.1 | 16.3 | 0.7 | 7.9 | 0.2 | 10.5 | 15.9 |
| 36 76705 | Valley Stream ............. | 9.0 | 37 646 | 967 | 4 182.9 | 46.9 | 18.4 | 0.3 | 12.3 | 0.2 | 22.2 | 33.2 |
| 36 78608 | Watertown .................. | 23.4 | 27 900 | 1 295 | 1 192.3 | 85.9 | 7.6 | 1.2 | 2.5 | 0.4 | 5.6 | 4.7 |
| 36 81677 | White Plains ............... | 25.3 | 57 403 | 618 | 2 268.9 | 50.0 | 13.9 | 0.3 | 7.0 | 0.1 | 29.6 | 31.2 |

1. Dry land or land partially or temporarily covered by water.  2. May be of any race.

| City | Age of population (percent), 2010 | | | | | | | | | | | Population | | | |
|---|---|---|---|---|---|---|---|---|---|---|---|---|---|---|---|
| | | | | | | | | | | | | Census counts | | Percent change | |
| | Under 5 years | 5 to 17 years | 18 to 24 years | 25 to 34 years | 35 to 44 years | 45 to 54 years | 55 to 64 years | 65 to 74 years | 75 years and over | Median age | Percent female | 2000 | 2010 | 2000– 2010 | 2010– 2012 |
| | 12 | 13 | 14 | 15 | 16 | 17 | 18 | 19 | 20 | 21 | 22 | 23 | 24 | 25 | 26 |
| NEW JERSEY— Cont'd | | | | | | | | | | | | | | | |
| Garfield | 6.9 | 16.5 | 9.2 | 16.7 | 14.2 | 14.1 | 11.3 | 5.5 | 5.8 | 35.5 | 52.3 | 29 786 | 30 487 | 2.4 | 1.3 |
| Hackensack | 6.4 | 12.2 | 8.3 | 19.0 | 15.6 | 14.4 | 11.6 | 6.5 | 5.9 | 37.5 | 50.5 | 42 677 | 43 010 | 0.8 | 1.9 |
| Hoboken | 6.8 | 5.4 | 12.1 | 38.3 | 17.5 | 8.0 | 5.5 | 3.3 | 3.0 | 31.2 | 49.5 | 38 577 | 50 005 | 29.6 | 4.1 |
| Jersey City | 7.1 | 14.1 | 10.0 | 22.4 | 15.2 | 12.5 | 9.6 | 5.3 | 3.7 | 33.2 | 50.6 | 240 055 | 247 597 | 3.1 | 2.8 |
| Kearny | 5.5 | 15.2 | 11.0 | 16.2 | 15.0 | 15.3 | 11.1 | 5.9 | 4.8 | 36.4 | 48.5 | 40 513 | 40 684 | 0.4 | 1.7 |
| Linden | 5.5 | 16.3 | 9.2 | 13.9 | 14.1 | 15.4 | 12.2 | 6.6 | 6.8 | 38.8 | 52.3 | 39 394 | 40 499 | 2.8 | 0.9 |
| Long Branch | 7.2 | 14.5 | 12.2 | 17.8 | 13.3 | 13.1 | 10.7 | 5.7 | 5.6 | 33.8 | 49.9 | 31 340 | 30 719 | -2.0 | -0.2 |
| Millville | 7.0 | 18.9 | 9.9 | 12.3 | 12.8 | 14.0 | 11.9 | 7.3 | 6.0 | 36.6 | 52.6 | 26 847 | 28 400 | 5.8 | 0.8 |
| Newark | 7.5 | 18.0 | 11.9 | 16.8 | 15.0 | 13.2 | 8.9 | 5.1 | 3.5 | 32.3 | 50.5 | 273 546 | 277 138 | 1.3 | 0.2 |
| New Brunswick | 7.2 | 13.9 | 33.2 | 17.7 | 10.7 | 7.3 | 4.9 | 2.7 | 2.5 | 23.3 | 48.8 | 48 573 | 55 181 | 13.6 | 1.8 |
| Paramus | 4.0 | 17.5 | 7.1 | 7.4 | 11.8 | 17.0 | 13.3 | 9.1 | 12.8 | 46.3 | 51.3 | 25 737 | 26 342 | 2.4 | 0.7 |
| Passaic | 9.9 | 21.6 | 11.4 | 16.4 | 13.3 | 11.4 | 8.2 | 4.4 | 3.4 | 29.2 | 49.8 | 67 861 | 69 781 | 2.8 | 0.6 |
| Paterson | 8.0 | 19.9 | 11.4 | 14.8 | 14.1 | 13.3 | 9.5 | 5.4 | 3.5 | 32.1 | 51.7 | 149 222 | 146 199 | -2.0 | -0.7 |
| Perth Amboy | 7.9 | 19.4 | 11.0 | 15.7 | 14.4 | 13.2 | 9.1 | 5.0 | 4.3 | 32.4 | 50.7 | 47 303 | 50 814 | 7.4 | 1.8 |
| Plainfield | 8.3 | 17.5 | 10.5 | 16.1 | 14.6 | 14.0 | 9.5 | 5.5 | 4.0 | 33.3 | 49.7 | 47 829 | 49 808 | 4.1 | 0.9 |
| Rahway | 5.9 | 15.9 | 8.5 | 14.4 | 14.3 | 15.6 | 11.9 | 6.6 | 6.9 | 38.8 | 52.3 | 26 500 | 27 346 | 3.2 | 1.6 |
| Sayreville | 6.6 | 16.0 | 8.0 | 14.3 | 14.7 | 16.2 | 12.1 | 6.4 | 5.7 | 38.6 | 51.2 | 40 377 | 42 702 | 5.8 | 2.5 |
| Trenton | 7.9 | 17.1 | 11.0 | 17.7 | 14.9 | 13.2 | 9.3 | 4.8 | 4.0 | 32.6 | 48.4 | 85 403 | 84 913 | -0.6 | -0.5 |
| Union City | 7.3 | 16.4 | 10.6 | 17.4 | 15.0 | 13.6 | 9.1 | 5.7 | 4.8 | 33.9 | 49.9 | 67 088 | 66 455 | -0.9 | 1.9 |
| Vineland | 7.0 | 17.5 | 9.4 | 12.8 | 13.4 | 14.2 | 11.8 | 7.2 | 6.8 | 37.7 | 52.0 | 56 271 | 60 724 | 7.9 | 0.2 |
| Westfield | 6.6 | 23.4 | 4.7 | 6.8 | 15.8 | 17.7 | 12.0 | 6.3 | 6.8 | 41.0 | 51.9 | 29 644 | 30 316 | 2.3 | 1.1 |
| West New York | 7.4 | 13.6 | 9.7 | 19.6 | 15.8 | 12.7 | 9.2 | 6.1 | 5.8 | 34.8 | 50.4 | 45 768 | 49 708 | 8.6 | 3.5 |
| NEW MEXICO | 7.0 | 18.1 | 9.9 | 13.0 | 12.1 | 14.2 | 12.5 | 7.5 | 5.8 | 36.7 | 50.6 | 1 819 046 | 2 059 180 | 13.2 | 1.3 |
| Alamogordo | 7.5 | 16.1 | 9.6 | 14.2 | 11.1 | 13.5 | 11.3 | 8.8 | 8.0 | 37.4 | 50.9 | 35 582 | 30 403 | -14.6 | 3.6 |
| Albuquerque | 7.0 | 17.0 | 10.7 | 15.2 | 12.8 | 13.8 | 11.5 | 6.4 | 5.7 | 35.1 | 51.4 | 448 607 | 546 537 | 21.7 | 1.6 |
| Carlsbad | 7.3 | 18.3 | 9.0 | 12.6 | 11.1 | 13.6 | 12.5 | 7.6 | 8.0 | 37.6 | 50.9 | 25 625 | 26 138 | 2.0 | 2.1 |
| Clovis | 8.8 | 19.8 | 10.4 | 15.1 | 12.0 | 12.5 | 9.6 | 6.1 | 5.6 | 31.8 | 50.4 | 32 667 | 37 778 | 15.6 | 3.8 |
| Farmington | 8.6 | 19.3 | 10.0 | 15.1 | 11.7 | 13.3 | 10.9 | 5.5 | 5.6 | 32.7 | 50.7 | 37 844 | 45 895 | 21.2 | -0.1 |
| Hobbs | 9.6 | 20.2 | 10.7 | 15.6 | 12.0 | 12.6 | 9.1 | 5.3 | 4.7 | 30.8 | 48.6 | 28 657 | 34 126 | 19.1 | 2.6 |
| Las Cruces | 7.1 | 17.2 | 13.7 | 15.1 | 11.0 | 11.9 | 10.3 | 7.3 | 6.4 | 32.4 | 51.3 | 74 267 | 97 621 | 31.4 | 3.5 |
| Rio Rancho | 7.2 | 20.9 | 7.8 | 12.9 | 14.3 | 14.9 | 11.2 | 6.0 | 4.8 | 35.9 | 51.3 | 51 765 | 87 396 | 69.1 | 3.9 |
| Roswell | 8.4 | 19.8 | 10.7 | 12.5 | 10.8 | 12.4 | 10.8 | 7.0 | 7.5 | 33.5 | 51.3 | 45 293 | 48 401 | 6.8 | 0.2 |
| Santa Fe | 5.5 | 13.3 | 7.5 | 12.3 | 12.6 | 14.6 | 16.6 | 9.8 | 7.7 | 44.0 | 52.6 | 62 203 | 67 981 | 9.2 | 1.8 |
| NEW YORK | 6.0 | 16.4 | 10.2 | 13.7 | 13.5 | 14.9 | 11.9 | 7.0 | 6.5 | 38.0 | 51.6 | 18 976 457 | 19 378 104 | 2.1 | 1.0 |
| Albany | 5.5 | 12.4 | 21.5 | 17.0 | 10.9 | 11.6 | 10.0 | 5.3 | 5.9 | 30.3 | 51.6 | 95 658 | 97 856 | 2.3 | 0.0 |
| Auburn | 6.2 | 14.7 | 9.2 | 14.9 | 12.7 | 14.4 | 11.5 | 6.6 | 9.7 | 39.1 | 49.3 | 28 574 | 27 688 | -3.1 | -1.2 |
| Binghamton | 6.2 | 13.8 | 15.0 | 14.2 | 10.5 | 13.4 | 11.6 | 6.9 | 8.5 | 35.8 | 51.0 | 47 380 | 47 376 | 0.0 | -1.7 |
| Buffalo | 6.7 | 16.9 | 13.9 | 14.6 | 11.7 | 14.0 | 10.9 | 5.9 | 5.5 | 33.2 | 52.1 | 292 648 | 261 310 | -10.7 | -0.7 |
| Elmira | 7.2 | 16.5 | 13.1 | 14.5 | 11.9 | 14.3 | 10.7 | 5.4 | 6.4 | 33.9 | 49.4 | 30 940 | 29 200 | -5.6 | -0.7 |
| Freeport | 6.4 | 17.0 | 10.1 | 13.6 | 14.2 | 15.0 | 11.8 | 6.5 | 5.5 | 37.2 | 51.3 | 43 783 | 42 860 | -2.1 | 0.6 |
| Glen Cove | 5.8 | 14.8 | 8.7 | 13.5 | 13.5 | 14.7 | 12.4 | 7.6 | 9.0 | 40.6 | 51.3 | 26 622 | 26 964 | 1.3 | 0.5 |
| Harrison | 4.8 | 17.9 | 19.2 | 8.6 | 12.5 | 14.2 | 10.0 | 6.2 | 6.6 | 34.6 | 53.1 | 24 154 | 27 472 | 13.7 | 1.1 |
| Hempstead | 8.5 | 17.2 | 11.2 | 17.1 | 14.6 | 12.8 | 9.2 | 5.5 | 4.0 | 32.5 | 50.7 | 56 554 | 53 891 | -4.7 | 1.8 |
| Ithaca | 2.3 | 5.9 | 52.5 | 15.2 | 6.3 | 6.1 | 5.8 | 2.7 | 3.2 | 22.4 | 49.6 | 29 287 | 30 014 | 2.5 | 1.1 |
| Jamestown | 7.3 | 17.3 | 10.1 | 13.2 | 11.7 | 14.0 | 11.7 | 6.6 | 8.0 | 36.9 | 51.4 | 31 730 | 31 146 | -1.8 | -1.2 |
| Lindenhurst | 5.0 | 17.5 | 9.1 | 11.3 | 14.8 | 18.4 | 11.8 | 6.3 | 5.8 | 40.3 | 51.4 | 27 819 | 27 253 | -2.0 | 0.0 |
| Long Beach | 4.6 | 11.7 | 7.1 | 16.2 | 14.1 | 16.1 | 14.2 | 7.5 | 8.5 | 42.5 | 51.7 | 35 462 | 33 275 | -6.2 | 0.6 |
| Middletown | 8.1 | 19.1 | 9.8 | 14.9 | 14.1 | 13.5 | 9.8 | 5.5 | 5.1 | 33.7 | 51.1 | 25 388 | 28 086 | 10.6 | -0.7 |
| Mount Vernon | 6.6 | 16.3 | 9.2 | 13.3 | 14.2 | 15.1 | 11.4 | 7.3 | 6.6 | 38.4 | 54.6 | 68 381 | 67 290 | -1.6 | 0.9 |
| Newburgh | 9.4 | 21.3 | 14.0 | 15.8 | 13.0 | 11.0 | 7.8 | 4.5 | 3.3 | 28.2 | 51.4 | 28 259 | 28 866 | 2.1 | -0.7 |
| New Rochelle | 6.1 | 16.6 | 10.5 | 12.6 | 13.1 | 14.2 | 11.7 | 7.1 | 8.0 | 38.4 | 52.0 | 72 182 | 77 062 | 6.8 | 1.7 |
| New York | 6.3 | 15.3 | 10.6 | 17.0 | 14.1 | 13.5 | 10.9 | 6.5 | 5.6 | 35.5 | 52.5 | 8 008 278 | 8 175 136 | 2.1 | 2.0 |
| Niagara Falls | 6.1 | 15.9 | 10.1 | 12.6 | 11.6 | 15.7 | 12.5 | 6.9 | 8.6 | 39.8 | 52.3 | 55 593 | 50 193 | -9.7 | -0.9 |
| North Tonawanda | 5.1 | 14.3 | 9.3 | 12.7 | 12.2 | 16.4 | 14.3 | 7.3 | 8.4 | 42.4 | 51.2 | 33 262 | 31 568 | -5.1 | -0.9 |
| Ossining | 6.4 | 14.9 | 8.2 | 17.7 | 16.8 | 15.0 | 10.5 | 5.4 | 5.1 | 36.6 | 46.9 | 24 010 | 25 091 | 4.4 | 0.7 |
| Port Chester | 6.9 | 15.7 | 10.0 | 18.4 | 15.7 | 13.2 | 9.5 | 5.0 | 5.6 | 34.4 | 47.6 | 27 867 | 28 967 | 3.9 | 1.0 |
| Poughkeepsie | 7.2 | 15.0 | 15.8 | 15.4 | 11.5 | 12.1 | 10.0 | 6.1 | 6.9 | 32.4 | 52.0 | 29 871 | 31 045 | 9.6 | -0.6 |
| Rochester | 7.5 | 17.3 | 14.2 | 16.8 | 12.5 | 12.8 | 9.9 | 5.0 | 4.0 | 30.8 | 51.7 | 219 773 | 210 512 | -4.2 | 0.0 |
| Rome | 6.1 | 14.7 | 9.1 | 13.8 | 12.4 | 14.8 | 12.6 | 7.7 | 8.7 | 40.2 | 48.6 | 34 950 | 33 725 | -3.5 | -2.6 |
| Saratoga Springs | 4.1 | 12.9 | 15.5 | 12.2 | 12.1 | 13.8 | 13.7 | 7.8 | 7.9 | 39.8 | 51.7 | 26 186 | 26 586 | 1.5 | 1.4 |
| Schenectady | 7.5 | 16.9 | 12.9 | 14.8 | 12.4 | 14.0 | 10.1 | 5.3 | 6.1 | 33.4 | 51.6 | 61 821 | 66 135 | 7.0 | -0.1 |
| Spring Valley | 10.9 | 20.4 | 11.3 | 18.3 | 13.1 | 10.8 | 8.1 | 4.3 | 2.8 | 28.8 | 49.2 | 25 464 | 31 347 | 23.1 | 2.3 |
| Syracuse | 7.0 | 16.0 | 19.1 | 14.8 | 10.7 | 12.1 | 9.7 | 4.9 | 5.6 | 29.6 | 52.3 | 147 306 | 145 170 | -1.5 | -0.7 |
| Troy | 6.4 | 13.8 | 20.8 | 15.5 | 10.7 | 12.0 | 9.9 | 5.4 | 5.5 | 30.2 | 49.5 | 49 170 | 50 129 | 2.0 | -0.4 |
| Utica | 7.5 | 17.2 | 12.4 | 13.1 | 11.5 | 12.7 | 10.7 | 6.5 | 8.3 | 34.8 | 51.9 | 60 651 | 62 235 | 2.6 | -0.7 |
| Valley Stream | 5.6 | 17.5 | 9.2 | 11.7 | 13.8 | 16.6 | 12.4 | 6.0 | 7.3 | 39.7 | 51.9 | 36 368 | 37 511 | 3.1 | 0.4 |
| Watertown | 9.0 | 15.5 | 12.1 | 17.2 | 11.7 | 12.0 | 9.3 | 5.7 | 7.5 | 32.1 | 52.2 | 26 705 | 27 023 | 1.2 | 3.2 |
| White Plains | 5.9 | 14.2 | 7.6 | 15.9 | 14.7 | 14.1 | 12.2 | 7.7 | 7.6 | 39.2 | 51.9 | 53 077 | 56 853 | 7.1 | 1.0 |

# Table D. Cities — Households, Group Quarters, Crime, and Education

| City | Households, 2010 | | | | Persons in group quarters, 2010 | | | | Serious crimes known to police,[2] 2011 | | | | Educational attainment, 2007–2011 | | |
|---|---|---|---|---|---|---|---|---|---|---|---|---|---|---|---|
| | | | Percent | | | Institutional | | | Total | | Rate[3] | | | Attainment[4] (percent) | |
| | Number | Persons per house-hold | Female family house-holder[1] | One-person | Total | Total | Persons in nursing facilities | Non-institu-tional | Number | Rate[3] | Violent | Property | Population age 25 and older | High school graduate or less | Bachelor's degree or more |
| | 27 | 28 | 29 | 30 | 31 | 32 | 33 | 34 | 35 | 36 | 37 | 38 | 39 | 40 | 41 |
| **NEW JERSEY—Cont'd** | | | | | | | | | | | | | | | |
| Garfield | 11 073 | 2.75 | 17.8 | 24.7 | 32 | 0 | 0 | 32 | 592 | 1 935 | 265 | 1 671 | 20 645 | 57.9 | 18.9 |
| Hackensack | 18 142 | 2.30 | 13.9 | 39.3 | 1 301 | 985 | 172 | 316 | 984 | 2 280 | 218 | 2 062 | 31 612 | 43.1 | 34.5 |
| Hoboken | 25 041 | 1.93 | 6.9 | 39.7 | 1 574 | 0 | 0 | 1 574 | 1 096 | 2 185 | 389 | 1 796 | 37 037 | 18.6 | 72.4 |
| Jersey City | 96 859 | 2.53 | 18.2 | 30.2 | 2 843 | 984 | 914 | 1 859 | 7 607 | 3 062 | 767 | 2 295 | 168 719 | 40.2 | 40.6 |
| Kearny | 13 462 | 2.83 | 15.6 | 21.0 | 2 570 | 2 501 | 167 | 69 | 1 207 | 2 957 | 211 | 2 746 | 27 311 | 59.2 | 18.8 |
| Linden | 14 909 | 2.70 | 17.6 | 26.2 | 245 | 242 | 214 | 3 | 1 431 | 3 522 | 276 | 3 246 | 28 267 | 57.5 | 17.9 |
| Long Branch | 11 753 | 2.60 | 15.6 | 31.0 | 184 | 75 | 70 | 109 | 803 | 2 605 | 425 | 2 180 | 20 843 | 55.3 | 23.5 |
| Millville | 10 648 | 2.65 | 20.0 | 26.6 | 212 | 117 | 117 | 95 | 1 929 | 6 770 | 786 | 5 984 | 17 891 | 62.8 | 13.5 |
| Newark | 94 542 | 2.76 | 28.9 | 27.9 | 16 367 | 8 545 | 1 015 | 7 822 | 13 259 | 4 768 | 1 166 | 3 602 | 172 195 | 65.8 | 12.5 |
| New Brunswick | 14 119 | 3.36 | 17.5 | 25.8 | 7 745 | 182 | 147 | 7 563 | 2 088 | 3 771 | 865 | 2 906 | 25 521 | 65.2 | 20.3 |
| Paramus | 8 630 | 2.92 | 9.1 | 17.8 | 1 165 | 1 110 | 521 | 55 | 1 729 | 6 542 | 231 | 6 311 | 18 801 | 33.7 | 46.8 |
| Passaic | 19 411 | 3.57 | 23.7 | 19.5 | 458 | 232 | 224 | 226 | 2 164 | 3 091 | 843 | 2 248 | 39 072 | 70.1 | 14.8 |
| Paterson | 44 329 | 3.24 | 29.5 | 21.0 | 2 628 | 1 353 | 212 | 1 275 | 6 222 | 4 242 | 1 016 | 3 226 | 88 155 | 70.1 | 9.9 |
| Perth Amboy | 15 419 | 3.25 | 24.6 | 20.3 | 667 | 445 | 445 | 222 | 1 416 | 2 777 | 443 | 2 334 | 31 682 | 65.3 | 15.0 |
| Plainfield | 15 180 | 3.23 | 24.1 | 21.3 | 732 | 342 | 327 | 390 | 2 153 | 4 308 | 934 | 3 374 | 32 147 | 57.0 | 20.9 |
| Rahway | 10 533 | 2.58 | 16.8 | 29.5 | 124 | 109 | 109 | 15 | 625 | 2 278 | 310 | 1 968 | 18 603 | 50.1 | 22.6 |
| Sayreville | 15 636 | 2.72 | 12.4 | 22.4 | 200 | 193 | 193 | 7 | 659 | 1 538 | 117 | 1 421 | 29 603 | 44.8 | 30.8 |
| Trenton | 28 578 | 2.79 | 28.1 | 30.8 | 5 123 | 4 250 | 1 166 | 873 | 3 778 | 4 434 | 1 418 | 3 017 | 54 277 | 66.1 | 10.9 |
| Union City | 22 814 | 2.88 | 21.8 | 23.8 | 649 | 342 | 341 | 307 | 1 569 | 2 353 | 405 | 1 948 | 43 269 | 64.1 | 16.2 |
| Vineland | 21 450 | 2.76 | 18.2 | 23.3 | 1 491 | 897 | 593 | 594 | 1 640 | 2 692 | 271 | 2 421 | 39 662 | 57.9 | 16.8 |
| Westfield | 10 566 | 2.85 | 7.5 | 19.2 | 220 | 204 | 204 | 16 | 344 | 1 131 | 33 | 1 098 | 19 608 | 18.5 | 65.4 |
| West New York | 18 852 | 2.64 | 16.8 | 29.5 | 14 | 0 | 0 | 14 | 788 | 1 580 | 371 | 1 209 | 33 502 | 57.5 | 25.3 |
| **NEW MEXICO** | 791 395 | 2.55 | 14.0 | 28.0 | 42 629 | 25 266 | 5 567 | 17 363 | 85 351 | 4 099 | 568 | 3 532 | 1 316 741 | 43.6 | 25.4 |
| Alamogordo | 12 763 | 2.33 | 12.6 | 30.9 | 611 | 515 | 278 | 96 | 1 091 | 3 549 | 361 | 3 188 | 20 560 | 42.6 | 18.4 |
| Albuquerque | 224 330 | 2.40 | 14.3 | 31.9 | 7 659 | 2 897 | 1 712 | 4 762 | 32 186 | 5 831 | 763 | 5 068 | 353 279 | 36.0 | 32.2 |
| Carlsbad | 10 257 | 2.50 | 14.0 | 28.1 | 533 | 470 | 217 | 63 | 1 254 | 4 744 | 726 | 4 018 | 17 154 | 47.9 | 16.9 |
| Clovis | 14 288 | 2.60 | 15.5 | 27.8 | 597 | 503 | 188 | 94 | 2 372 | 6 210 | 547 | 5 663 | 22 481 | 44.5 | 20.1 |
| Farmington | 16 446 | 2.70 | 13.6 | 23.7 | 1 465 | 979 | 164 | 486 | 2 132 | 4 596 | 1 086 | 3 509 | 27 723 | 43.8 | 20.1 |
| Hobbs | 11 629 | 2.81 | 15.5 | 24.1 | 1 494 | 1 316 | 146 | 178 | 1 622 | 4 701 | 472 | 4 228 | 20 522 | 56.9 | 15.5 |
| Las Cruces | 39 433 | 2.43 | 15.7 | 29.6 | 1 610 | 1 186 | 251 | 424 | 4 970 | 5 035 | 430 | 4 605 | 58 717 | 36.3 | 30.1 |
| Rio Rancho | 31 892 | 2.74 | 12.0 | 21.5 | 197 | 141 | 141 | 56 | 1 799 | 2 033 | 203 | 1 829 | 53 743 | 33.4 | 27.2 |
| Roswell | 17 654 | 2.66 | 16.4 | 26.8 | 1 489 | 452 | 216 | 1 037 | 2 986 | 6 105 | 613 | 5 492 | 29 394 | 49.1 | 16.8 |
| Santa Fe | 31 895 | 2.10 | 11.7 | 40.6 | 1 119 | 270 | 247 | 849 | 4 054 | 5 900 | 444 | 5 457 | 49 365 | 31.0 | 43.4 |
| **NEW YORK** | 7 317 755 | 2.57 | 14.9 | 29.1 | 585 678 | 231 163 | 116 558 | 354 515 | 449 745 | 2 311 | 398 | 1 912 | 12 999 473 | 43.1 | 32.5 |
| Albany | 41 157 | 2.13 | 16.0 | 41.3 | 10 248 | 1 452 | 941 | 8 796 | 5 550 | 5 646 | 955 | 4 691 | 58 257 | 39.0 | 36.6 |
| Auburn | 11 691 | 2.17 | 15.9 | 39.4 | 2 328 | 2 139 | 370 | 189 | 1 047 | 3 765 | 467 | 3 297 | 19 742 | 51.5 | 17.4 |
| Binghamton | 21 150 | 2.18 | 15.6 | 40.5 | 1 262 | 846 | 458 | 416 | 2 552 | 5 363 | 563 | 4 799 | 30 666 | 49.7 | 23.3 |
| Buffalo | 112 536 | 2.24 | 22.0 | 39.7 | 9 371 | 2 530 | 1 201 | 6 841 | 17 555 | 6 688 | 1 238 | 5 450 | 166 163 | 48.1 | 22.5 |
| Elmira | 10 991 | 2.34 | 19.5 | 36.1 | 3 458 | 2 380 | 296 | 1 078 | 1 211 | 4 129 | 239 | 3 890 | 18 219 | 58.6 | 12.8 |
| Freeport | 13 279 | 3.18 | 20.3 | 22.2 | 574 | 354 | 346 | 220 | 1 088 | 2 527 | 404 | 2 123 | 28 841 | 50.9 | 24.8 |
| Glen Cove | 9 764 | 2.69 | 14.1 | 26.4 | 723 | 404 | 396 | 319 | 231 | 853 | 66 | 786 | 18 972 | 44.3 | 36.1 |
| Harrison | 8 375 | 2.77 | 9.7 | 21.2 | 4 285 | 0 | 0 | 4 285 | 136 | 493 | 40 | 453 | 16 935 | 31.0 | 50.0 |
| Hempstead | 15 234 | 3.45 | 27.8 | 22.1 | 1 306 | 686 | 678 | 620 | 1 488 | 2 749 | 811 | 1 938 | 34 563 | 60.5 | 16.5 |
| Ithaca | 10 408 | 2.14 | 7.0 | 43.0 | 7 701 | 179 | 172 | 7 522 | 1 002 | 3 323 | 113 | 3 211 | 10 803 | 22.1 | 62.4 |
| Jamestown | 13 122 | 2.29 | 16.8 | 35.7 | 1 134 | 399 | 353 | 735 | 1 327 | 4 242 | 649 | 3 593 | 20 163 | 51.3 | 17.2 |
| Lindenhurst | 9 316 | 2.92 | 12.2 | 19.3 | 29 | 0 | 0 | 29 | NA | NA | NA | NA | 18 365 | 51.1 | 20.9 |
| Long Beach | 14 809 | 2.17 | 10.5 | 38.8 | 1 094 | 920 | 822 | 174 | 315 | 942 | 120 | 823 | 25 240 | 29.7 | 46.6 |
| Middletown | 9 976 | 2.77 | 19.0 | 28.7 | 489 | 190 | 181 | 299 | 1 110 | 3 934 | 578 | 3 357 | 17 147 | 54.1 | 18.5 |
| Mount Vernon | 26 260 | 2.53 | 24.4 | 32.8 | 833 | 429 | 418 | 404 | 2 117 | 3 132 | 973 | 2 158 | 44 855 | 48.7 | 24.4 |
| Newburgh | 9 030 | 3.09 | 26.6 | 25.9 | 945 | 24 | 0 | 921 | 1 770 | 6 104 | 1 817 | 4 287 | 16 042 | 66.6 | 13.1 |
| New Rochelle | 27 953 | 2.64 | 12.9 | 29.9 | 3 277 | 1 256 | 999 | 2 021 | 1 557 | 2 011 | 276 | 1 735 | 50 949 | 41.4 | 39.3 |
| New York | 3 109 784 | 2.57 | 18.7 | 32.0 | 185 530 | 70 041 | 45 516 | 115 489 | 191 666 | 2 334 | 624 | 1 710 | 5 505 880 | 45.9 | 33.7 |
| Niagara Falls | 22 603 | 2.20 | 19.7 | 38.1 | 376 | 159 | 157 | 217 | 3 522 | 6 985 | 1 152 | 5 833 | 34 471 | 55.4 | 14.1 |
| North Tonawanda | 14 004 | 2.24 | 11.3 | 34.1 | 142 | 74 | 70 | 68 | 654 | 2 062 | 148 | 1 914 | 22 686 | 45.0 | 21.5 |
| Ossining | 8 344 | 2.78 | 14.0 | 26.7 | 1 858 | 1 830 | 102 | 28 | 278 | 1 104 | 175 | 930 | 17 918 | 49.3 | 32.2 |
| Port Chester | 9 240 | 3.08 | 14.3 | 24.2 | 465 | 154 | 154 | 311 | 959 | 3 296 | 265 | 3 031 | 19 395 | 59.4 | 22.3 |
| Poughkeepsie | 12 400 | 2.41 | 20.0 | 36.1 | 2 904 | 921 | 540 | 1 983 | 1 355 | 4 121 | 991 | 3 129 | 21 445 | 49.7 | 22.1 |
| Rochester | 87 027 | 2.30 | 24.1 | 38.5 | 10 200 | 3 657 | 1 960 | 6 543 | 12 963 | 6 129 | 959 | 5 169 | 128 922 | 48.8 | 24.3 |
| Rome | 13 526 | 2.28 | 15.2 | 34.9 | 2 882 | 2 581 | 462 | 301 | 467 | 1 379 | 77 | 1 302 | 23 636 | 51.9 | 17.4 |
| Saratoga Springs | 11 312 | 2.13 | 7.9 | 36.7 | 2 510 | 445 | 352 | 2 065 | 628 | 2 352 | 75 | 2 277 | 18 794 | 27.6 | 48.3 |
| Schenectady | 26 633 | 2.35 | 19.7 | 35.9 | 3 470 | 677 | 296 | 2 793 | 3 731 | 5 616 | 953 | 4 663 | 41 766 | 53.3 | 18.1 |
| Spring Valley | 8 755 | 3.56 | 19.9 | 20.8 | 216 | 0 | 0 | 216 | 637 | 2 023 | 508 | 1 515 | 17 619 | 52.9 | 22.6 |
| Syracuse | 57 355 | 2.31 | 20.8 | 38.4 | 12 782 | 2 332 | 1 523 | 10 450 | 6 577 | 4 510 | 893 | 3 617 | 83 281 | 48.1 | 25.9 |
| Troy | 20 505 | 2.22 | 18.0 | 37.1 | 4 508 | 493 | 202 | 4 015 | 2 689 | 5 340 | 737 | 4 603 | 29 957 | 48.0 | 22.8 |
| Utica | 24 905 | 2.38 | 19.0 | 36.5 | 3 076 | 1 171 | 983 | 1 905 | 2 883 | 4 612 | 611 | 4 001 | 39 333 | 53.8 | 15.5 |
| Valley Stream | 12 189 | 3.07 | 14.4 | 18.4 | 41 | 0 | 0 | 41 | NA | NA | NA | NA | 25 453 | 41.8 | 32.4 |
| Watertown | 11 409 | 2.29 | 15.9 | 35.4 | 905 | 667 | 473 | 238 | 1 208 | 4 450 | 328 | 4 122 | 16 724 | 46.5 | 22.3 |
| White Plains | 22 910 | 2.40 | 10.7 | 35.3 | 1 755 | 704 | 460 | 1 051 | 1 352 | 2 367 | 152 | 2 215 | 40 831 | 35.4 | 46.0 |

1. No spouse present.   2. Data for serious crimes have not been adjusted for underreporting. This may affect comparability between geographic areas and over time.   3. Per 100,000 population estimated by the FBI.   4. Persons 25 years old and over.

| City | Money income, 2007–2011 | | | | | Housing units, 2010 | | | Occupied Housing units 2007–2011 | | | | |
|---|---|---|---|---|---|---|---|---|---|---|---|---|---|
| | Per capita income[1] (dollars) | Households | | | Families with income below poverty (percent) | Total | Percent change, 2000–2010 | Vacant units for sale or rent[2] | Owner-occupied | | | Median owner costs as a percent of income | |
| | | Median income | Percent with income of $200,000 or more | Percent with income of less than $25,000 | | | | | Total | Percent | Median value[3] (dollars) | With a mortgage[4] | Without a mortgage[5] |
| | 42 | 43 | 44 | 45 | 46 | 47 | 48 | 49 | 50 | 51 | 52 | 53 | 54 |
| NEW JERSEY—Cont'd | | | | | | | | | | | | | |
| Garfield | 24 748 | 51 233 | 3.3 | 21.7 | 7.6 | 11 788 | 0.8 | 715 | 11 264 | 40.5 | 357 200 | 39.3 | 23.9 |
| Hackensack | 32 078 | 57 820 | 3.9 | 21.0 | 10.2 | 19 375 | 2.3 | 1 233 | 18 484 | 35.3 | 337 100 | 33.6 | 20.4 |
| Hoboken | 71 026 | 104 789 | 20.5 | 14.0 | 8.9 | 26 855 | 34.3 | 1 814 | 23 555 | 32.8 | 567 700 | 22.7 | 19.8 |
| Jersey City | 32 120 | 57 520 | 6.9 | 23.9 | 13.9 | 108 720 | 16.1 | 11 861 | 94 599 | 31.8 | 353 000 | 32.1 | 19.2 |
| Kearny | 25 582 | 61 343 | 2.9 | 16.3 | 8.4 | 14 180 | 2.2 | 718 | 13 535 | 46.9 | 358 400 | 33.3 | 19.7 |
| Linden | 27 432 | 58 603 | 3.3 | 19.3 | 5.7 | 15 872 | 2.0 | 963 | 14 704 | 58.0 | 324 800 | 33.0 | 21.7 |
| Long Branch | 30 433 | 52 266 | 6.3 | 22.4 | 11.4 | 14 170 | 1.3 | 2 417 | 11 753 | 42.3 | 373 100 | 35.6 | 18.5 |
| Millville | 23 222 | 50 022 | 1.7 | 27.6 | 15.4 | 11 435 | 7.4 | 787 | 10 036 | 63.8 | 177 700 | 28.5 | 15.0 |
| Newark | 17 617 | 35 696 | 1.2 | 36.5 | 23.5 | 109 520 | 9.4 | 14 978 | 91 712 | 24.9 | 282 400 | 39.1 | 22.1 |
| New Brunswick | 16 157 | 40 528 | 2.3 | 30.9 | 15.8 | 15 053 | 8.3 | 934 | 14 833 | 24.7 | 260 000 | 30.0 | 20.7 |
| Paramus | 40 098 | 104 105 | 14.4 | 8.5 | 1.6 | 8 915 | 8.6 | 285 | 8 322 | 88.6 | 578 500 | 28.6 | 15.4 |
| Passaic | 14 606 | 30 363 | 1.4 | 40.2 | 27.1 | 20 432 | 1.2 | 1 021 | 20 357 | 27.5 | 345 400 | 41.3 | 23.1 |
| Paterson | 15 498 | 34 302 | 0.9 | 37.6 | 24.6 | 47 946 | 1.6 | 3 617 | 43 640 | 29.8 | 318 700 | 49.0 | 21.3 |
| Perth Amboy | 20 744 | 45 369 | 2.0 | 28.0 | 16.5 | 16 556 | 8.7 | 1 137 | 16 597 | 36.8 | 292 200 | 33.5 | 21.4 |
| Plainfield | 23 955 | 51 803 | 4.1 | 25.3 | 14.3 | 16 621 | 2.7 | 1 441 | 15 743 | 51.3 | 290 300 | 33.7 | 22.1 |
| Rahway | 28 484 | 58 142 | 2.4 | 20.1 | 7.9 | 11 300 | 8.9 | 767 | 10 293 | 59.1 | 328 300 | 33.4 | 22.8 |
| Sayreville | 33 857 | 73 937 | 4.9 | 13.0 | 4.1 | 16 393 | 7.6 | 757 | 15 483 | 68.8 | 338 900 | 27.0 | 20.0 |
| Trenton | 17 902 | 37 219 | 1.6 | 36.2 | 22.6 | 33 035 | -2.6 | 4 457 | 28 285 | 42.1 | 126 400 | 25.3 | 18.1 |
| Union City | 18 542 | 40 108 | 1.5 | 31.1 | 19.0 | 24 931 | 5.0 | 2 117 | 22 408 | 19.7 | 359 300 | 40.9 | 24.5 |
| Vineland | 25 744 | 54 978 | 3.6 | 23.0 | 10.4 | 22 661 | 8.1 | 1 211 | 20 944 | 69.1 | 184 400 | 26.5 | 16.7 |
| Westfield | 63 735 | 127 658 | 30.7 | 7.7 | 1.0 | 10 950 | 1.2 | 384 | 10 090 | 81.0 | 649 800 | 24.7 | 19.2 |
| West New York | 24 662 | 44 640 | 4.3 | 28.8 | 16.6 | 20 018 | 15.3 | 1 166 | 18 331 | 21.2 | 363 300 | 39.1 | 21.3 |
| NEW MEXICO | 23 537 | 44 631 | 2.7 | 28.3 | 14.4 | 901 388 | 15.5 | 109 993 | 762 002 | 69.6 | 161 800 | 23.6 | 10.0 |
| Alamogordo | 22 820 | 41 017 | 1.8 | 27.3 | 11.4 | 14 052 | -11.2 | 1 289 | 12 642 | 62.1 | 107 600 | 19.9 | 10.0 |
| Albuquerque | 26 436 | 47 333 | 2.8 | 25.7 | 12.5 | 239 166 | 20.4 | 14 836 | 220 060 | 61.2 | 191 300 | 24.2 | 10.1 |
| Carlsbad | 24 177 | 44 985 | 1.5 | 27.7 | 9.4 | 11 243 | -2.4 | 986 | 9 909 | 71.7 | 90 700 | 18.4 | 10.0 |
| Clovis | 20 584 | 39 732 | 1.3 | 32.6 | 17.2 | 15 573 | 8.9 | 1 285 | 13 920 | 64.2 | 110 400 | 21.3 | 10.6 |
| Farmington | 26 029 | 52 980 | 3.7 | 20.8 | 12.0 | 17 548 | 16.6 | 1 102 | 15 966 | 67.7 | 174 100 | 22.1 | 10.0 |
| Hobbs | 20 526 | 45 121 | 2.2 | 26.0 | 15.4 | 12 900 | 7.5 | 1 271 | 11 257 | 66.3 | 97 500 | 19.4 | 10.0 |
| Las Cruces | 20 684 | 38 701 | 1.0 | 34.4 | 16.0 | 42 370 | 33.9 | 2 937 | 37 355 | 57.4 | 154 000 | 23.6 | 10.4 |
| Rio Rancho | 26 916 | 58 649 | 3.0 | 16.2 | 7.2 | 33 964 | 68.3 | 2 072 | 30 856 | 79.2 | 182 300 | 26.0 | 10.0 |
| Roswell | 18 523 | 35 723 | 1.0 | 32.4 | 16.5 | 19 743 | 2.4 | 2 089 | 17 810 | 65.9 | 86 000 | 21.3 | 10.0 |
| Santa Fe | 34 443 | 50 610 | 5.3 | 26.1 | 11.8 | 37 200 | 22.0 | 5 305 | 31 266 | 61.2 | 310 900 | 28.8 | 10.2 |
| NEW YORK | 31 796 | 56 951 | 6.5 | 23.0 | 11.0 | 8 108 103 | 5.6 | 790 348 | 7 215 687 | 54.8 | 301 000 | 26.3 | 15.4 |
| Albany | 23 235 | 38 394 | 1.7 | 34.6 | 17.4 | 46 362 | 2.4 | 5 205 | 40 250 | 39.5 | 179 600 | 24.0 | 14.0 |
| Auburn | 21 424 | 37 973 | 0.5 | 34.8 | 13.0 | 12 639 | 0.0 | 948 | 12 008 | 49.6 | 93 700 | 20.4 | 15.8 |
| Binghamton | 20 951 | 30 267 | 1.7 | 43.6 | 21.4 | 23 842 | -0.5 | 2 692 | 20 622 | 46.4 | 83 700 | 23.3 | 15.8 |
| Buffalo | 20 072 | 30 230 | 1.5 | 43.2 | 26.1 | 133 444 | -8.3 | 20 908 | 113 359 | 42.6 | 66 200 | 22.3 | 14.3 |
| Elmira | 16 830 | 29 488 | 1.5 | 42.5 | 26.4 | 12 313 | -4.5 | 1 322 | 10 982 | 46.9 | 65 300 | 19.1 | 15.1 |
| Freeport | 29 476 | 71 041 | 6.7 | 18.9 | 10.4 | 13 865 | 0.3 | 586 | 13 840 | 66.8 | 372 400 | 34.6 | 19.7 |
| Glen Cove | 36 463 | 69 093 | 10.5 | 17.1 | 8.2 | 10 352 | 6.3 | 588 | 9 677 | 59.5 | 542 100 | 32.6 | 23.4 |
| Harrison | 65 966 | 109 005 | 25.9 | 11.9 | 4.0 | 8 956 | 3.5 | 581 | 8 679 | 66.4 | 834 100 | 28.7 | 18.0 |
| Hempstead | 21 521 | 55 433 | 3.2 | 23.2 | 13.0 | 16 034 | 3.0 | 800 | 16 171 | 43.9 | 353 300 | 36.7 | 20.7 |
| Ithaca | 16 246 | 28 940 | 2.1 | 45.2 | 11.9 | 10 950 | 2.2 | 542 | 10 175 | 26.1 | 174 100 | 25.5 | 13.5 |
| Jamestown | 18 773 | 31 657 | 0.4 | 40.0 | 21.8 | 14 738 | -1.9 | 1 616 | 13 595 | 48.6 | 63 400 | 20.8 | 14.2 |
| Lindenhurst | 33 210 | 89 044 | 6.7 | 9.6 | 2.2 | 9 665 | 4.1 | 349 | 8 819 | 83.2 | 377 600 | 29.8 | 20.8 |
| Long Beach | 44 781 | 79 546 | 8.9 | 16.8 | 6.7 | 16 450 | 2.0 | 1 641 | 14 756 | 57.6 | 517 000 | 30.5 | 18.7 |
| Middletown | 23 387 | 55 251 | 2.7 | 23.7 | 14.0 | 10 866 | 7.1 | 890 | 9 500 | 51.3 | 225 200 | 29.9 | 16.1 |
| Mount Vernon | 27 392 | 49 346 | 4.0 | 23.1 | 10.2 | 28 990 | 7.2 | 2 730 | 26 207 | 37.1 | 418 900 | 31.9 | 21.5 |
| Newburgh | 16 502 | 37 671 | 0.8 | 33.8 | 24.2 | 10 505 | 0.2 | 1 475 | 9 162 | 35.1 | 210 400 | 29.5 | 20.0 |
| New Rochelle | 41 496 | 65 549 | 12.6 | 20.3 | 7.9 | 29 586 | 9.6 | 1 633 | 28 732 | 50.1 | 591 900 | 28.7 | 20.3 |
| New York | 31 417 | 51 270 | 6.7 | 27.3 | 16.4 | 3 371 062 | 5.3 | 261 278 | 3 049 978 | 32.6 | 514 900 | 30.4 | 14.4 |
| Niagara Falls | 20 409 | 32 617 | 0.9 | 39.3 | 16.3 | 26 220 | -5.8 | 3 617 | 22 328 | 56.7 | 66 500 | 21.1 | 16.0 |
| North Tonawanda | 26 010 | 46 203 | 1.0 | 26.9 | 6.7 | 14 757 | 2.3 | 753 | 14 096 | 66.2 | 98 100 | 22.3 | 14.6 |
| Ossining | 30 685 | 70 872 | 9.6 | 17.7 | 13.7 | 8 862 | 4.1 | 518 | 8 313 | 54.1 | 424 300 | 31.1 | 17.6 |
| Port Chester | 27 076 | 54 658 | 4.3 | 20.0 | 11.6 | 10 046 | 2.8 | 806 | 10 008 | 45.0 | 462 600 | 33.6 | 22.8 |
| Poughkeepsie | 23 373 | 39 061 | 2.5 | 36.2 | 21.8 | 13 984 | 6.3 | 1 584 | 13 044 | 39.5 | 253 200 | 28.7 | 20.2 |
| Rochester | 18 267 | 30 367 | 1.1 | 41.9 | 27.6 | 97 158 | -2.7 | 10 131 | 86 009 | 40.6 | 74 000 | 24.0 | 15.4 |
| Rome | 22 265 | 44 209 | 1.4 | 28.3 | 10.4 | 14 893 | -8.6 | 1 367 | 13 418 | 58.2 | 88 000 | 20.8 | 14.9 |
| Saratoga Springs | 36 148 | 63 145 | 5.5 | 21.6 | 3.2 | 12 936 | 11.7 | 1 624 | 11 665 | 60.4 | 291 800 | 24.3 | 13.5 |
| Schenectady | 20 149 | 37 436 | 1.2 | 33.2 | 18.1 | 30 095 | -0.8 | 3 462 | 24 455 | 49.9 | 114 300 | 27.3 | 16.6 |
| Spring Valley | 18 056 | 48 371 | 3.5 | 24.0 | 17.0 | 9 374 | 20.2 | 619 | 8 632 | 28.7 | 277 200 | 36.7 | 22.2 |
| Syracuse | 18 617 | 31 689 | 1.4 | 41.2 | 26.0 | 64 356 | -5.6 | 7 001 | 55 768 | 40.7 | 84 600 | 22.3 | 14.4 |
| Troy | 21 663 | 36 514 | 1.1 | 34.0 | 22.5 | 23 474 | 1.6 | 2 969 | 20 013 | 40.3 | 143 000 | 23.2 | 14.9 |
| Utica | 18 152 | 32 050 | 1.0 | 39.8 | 23.5 | 28 166 | -3.4 | 3 261 | 24 386 | 49.1 | 87 200 | 22.1 | 14.9 |
| Valley Stream | 30 891 | 84 981 | 5.8 | 10.4 | 4.1 | 12 625 | -0.6 | 436 | 11 498 | 82.5 | 419 000 | 32.7 | 21.3 |
| Watertown | 21 814 | 37 514 | 1.9 | 34.5 | 18.5 | 12 562 | 0.9 | 1 153 | 11 585 | 43.0 | 116 700 | 22.6 | 13.3 |
| White Plains | 44 473 | 76 164 | 14.4 | 17.1 | 6.9 | 24 382 | 13.0 | 1 472 | 22 797 | 53.4 | 518 500 | 26.5 | 17.8 |

1. Based on population estimated by the American Community Survey.   2. Includes units rented or sold but not occupied.   3. Specified owner-occupied units; $1,000,000 represents $1,000,000 or more   4. 50.0 represents 50 percent or more.   5. 10.0 represents 10 percent or less.

# Table D. Cities — Housing, Labor Force, and Employment

| City | Occupied housing units, 2007–2011 (cont.) | | | | Migration, 2007–2011 | | Civilian labor force, 2012 | | | | Civilian employment[4], 2007–2011 | | | |
|---|---|---|---|---|---|---|---|---|---|---|---|---|---|---|
| | | | | | | | | | Unemployment | | | Percent | | |
| | Percent renter occupied | Median gross rent[1] | Median rent as a percent of income[2] | Percent with no vehicle available | Percent who lived in the same house one year ago | Percent who lived outside this city one year ago | Total | Percent change, 2011–2012 | Total | Rate[3] | Population age 16 and older | In labor force | Full-year full-time worker | Households with no workers (percent) |
| | 55 | 56 | 57 | 58 | 59 | 60 | 61 | 62 | 63 | 64 | 65 | 66 | 67 | 68 |
| **NEW JERSEY— Cont'd** | | | | | | | | | | | | | | |
| Garfield | 59.5 | 1 156 | 32.3 | 14.3 | 94.5 | 3.5 | 16 944 | 1.8 | 2 248 | 13.3 | 24 571 | 68.8 | 48.7 | 22.1 |
| Hackensack | 64.7 | 1 217 | 29.1 | 16.4 | 86.4 | 8.8 | 24 336 | 1.2 | 2 299 | 9.4 | 36 189 | 68.9 | 50.6 | 21.6 |
| Hoboken | 67.2 | 1 714 | 23.4 | 35.6 | 75.8 | 15.0 | 34 775 | 2.5 | 1 748 | 5.0 | 42 675 | 77.8 | 61.9 | 15.0 |
| Jersey City | 68.2 | 1 127 | 28.0 | 38.5 | 83.6 | 7.8 | 118 892 | 2.2 | 12 927 | 10.9 | 200 436 | 69.6 | 45.9 | 20.7 |
| Kearny | 53.1 | 1 129 | 28.7 | 15.4 | 89.0 | 7.6 | 19 965 | 0.1 | 2 281 | 11.4 | 32 308 | 67.6 | 45.6 | 19.6 |
| Linden | 42.0 | 1 105 | 29.7 | 10.5 | 90.8 | 6.3 | 21 650 | 1.3 | 2 287 | 10.6 | 33 011 | 69.0 | 45.6 | 26.6 |
| Long Branch | 57.7 | 1 199 | 31.2 | 16.1 | 80.4 | 9.8 | 15 802 | 2.0 | 1 679 | 10.6 | 25 202 | 72.8 | 40.4 | 23.8 |
| Millville | 36.2 | 789 | 34.9 | 11.2 | 86.5 | 6.9 | 13 762 | -0.5 | 1 962 | 14.3 | 21 555 | 64.3 | 36.3 | 32.2 |
| Newark | 75.1 | 941 | 33.0 | 38.4 | 85.4 | 6.6 | 108 176 | 0.5 | 16 265 | 15.0 | 212 619 | 62.0 | 36.2 | 30.7 |
| New Brunswick | 75.3 | 1 277 | 38.4 | 30.1 | 70.4 | 15.0 | 29 840 | 3.9 | 2 297 | 7.7 | 44 249 | 62.6 | 34.5 | 22.1 |
| Paramus | 11.4 | 1 654 | 36.6 | 4.5 | 93.6 | 5.1 | 12 992 | 1.7 | 971 | 7.5 | 21 295 | 60.4 | 38.3 | 23.8 |
| Passaic | 72.5 | 1 021 | 42.8 | 41.5 | 95.9 | 2.4 | 30 000 | 2.0 | 3 973 | 13.2 | 49 317 | 60.8 | 33.7 | 23.1 |
| Paterson | 70.2 | 1 060 | 40.0 | 28.6 | 89.4 | 3.3 | 60 839 | 0.7 | 10 018 | 16.5 | 110 025 | 57.2 | 39.9 | 30.6 |
| Perth Amboy | 63.2 | 1 103 | 34.5 | 23.3 | 89.8 | 5.4 | 24 197 | 3.6 | 3 748 | 15.5 | 38 763 | 62.3 | 45.2 | 23.0 |
| Plainfield | 48.7 | 1 104 | 37.7 | 16.2 | 86.7 | 5.7 | 27 273 | -1.1 | 3 244 | 11.9 | 39 011 | 74.4 | 44.6 | 24.1 |
| Rahway | 40.9 | 1 128 | 32.1 | 11.2 | 90.7 | 4.8 | 14 607 | 2.1 | 1 555 | 10.6 | 21 807 | 66.0 | 43.2 | 26.8 |
| Sayreville | 31.2 | 1 087 | 25.0 | 6.4 | 94.0 | 4.5 | 23 554 | 3.7 | 2 101 | 8.9 | 34 228 | 68.1 | 46.0 | 20.7 |
| Trenton | 57.9 | 962 | 35.7 | 31.5 | 82.4 | 8.2 | 40 827 | 0.8 | 5 127 | 12.6 | 65 652 | 63.3 | 37.2 | 34.3 |
| Union City | 80.3 | 1 004 | 32.8 | 44.8 | 87.2 | 6.6 | 29 372 | 1.4 | 3 919 | 13.3 | 51 717 | 69.6 | 44.0 | 21.0 |
| Vineland | 30.9 | 940 | 32.6 | 10.8 | 87.2 | 4.7 | 29 184 | -1.0 | 4 041 | 13.8 | 47 582 | 66.9 | 39.4 | 28.4 |
| Westfield | 19.0 | 1 425 | 27.6 | 4.0 | 92.6 | 5.4 | 15 840 | 2.8 | 884 | 5.6 | 22 155 | 67.1 | 42.3 | 18.9 |
| West New York | 78.8 | 1 071 | 31.4 | 38.9 | 82.2 | 11.5 | 22 453 | 1.7 | 2 650 | 11.8 | 39 311 | 71.6 | 43.7 | 22.4 |
| **NEW MEXICO** | 30.4 | 713 | 29.5 | 5.6 | 84.6 | 9.1 | 935 890 | 1.4 | 64 591 | 6.9 | 1 581 130 | 61.6 | 38.0 | 27.9 |
| Alamogordo | 37.9 | 617 | 26.8 | 3.7 | 77.6 | 12.2 | 12 340 | 0.2 | 716 | 5.8 | 24 321 | 60.1 | 35.0 | 31.8 |
| Albuquerque | 38.8 | 738 | 29.8 | 6.7 | 82.1 | 7.0 | 255 580 | 0.5 | 17 321 | 6.8 | 424 445 | 66.7 | 41.8 | 25.0 |
| Carlsbad | 28.3 | 660 | 24.5 | 4.0 | 84.1 | 6.6 | 14 416 | 4.2 | 603 | 4.2 | 20 017 | 62.8 | 40.0 | 28.8 |
| Clovis | 35.8 | 557 | 29.6 | 6.8 | 79.1 | 8.1 | 17 366 | 0.7 | 806 | 4.6 | 27 443 | 65.6 | 37.4 | 25.2 |
| Farmington | 32.3 | 729 | 25.5 | 4.2 | 82.6 | 10.7 | 22 081 | 3.8 | 1 113 | 5.0 | 33 227 | 63.5 | 41.9 | 20.7 |
| Hobbs | 33.7 | 748 | 25.6 | 5.5 | 80.9 | 12.0 | 15 589 | 9.5 | 693 | 4.4 | 24 741 | 59.1 | 37.5 | 23.1 |
| Las Cruces | 42.6 | 691 | 34.1 | 6.8 | 74.9 | 10.7 | 47 085 | 3.5 | 2 712 | 5.8 | 74 620 | 62.1 | 35.5 | 29.0 |
| Rio Rancho | 20.8 | 969 | 29.8 | 3.2 | 83.7 | 10.8 | 39 944 | 0.9 | 2 865 | 7.2 | 62 818 | 67.3 | 44.2 | 22.0 |
| Roswell | 34.1 | 591 | 30.0 | 6.4 | 78.8 | 9.2 | 18 948 | -1.5 | 1 274 | 6.7 | 35 598 | 61.0 | 37.3 | 28.9 |
| Santa Fe | 38.8 | 903 | 33.7 | 6.6 | 80.7 | 10.0 | 36 982 | 2.5 | 1 921 | 5.2 | 56 627 | 66.4 | 39.0 | 30.2 |
| **NEW YORK** | 45.2 | 1 025 | 31.3 | 28.8 | 88.5 | 6.4 | 9 587 184 | 1.0 | 814 645 | 8.5 | 15 494 360 | 63.8 | 40.6 | 26.8 |
| Albany | 60.5 | 835 | 33.4 | 25.3 | 76.4 | 12.2 | 47 064 | 1.8 | 4 076 | 8.7 | 82 281 | 61.8 | 35.2 | 30.6 |
| Auburn | 50.4 | 627 | 27.6 | 18.4 | 77.0 | 12.2 | 13 097 | 1.1 | 1 190 | 9.1 | 22 933 | 59.7 | 36.0 | 33.2 |
| Binghamton | 53.6 | 609 | 37.0 | 23.1 | 85.0 | 8.2 | 20 326 | -2.0 | 1 874 | 9.2 | 39 118 | 56.2 | 29.6 | 38.4 |
| Buffalo | 57.4 | 666 | 35.5 | 29.7 | 81.1 | 7.0 | 115 688 | 0.6 | 12 650 | 10.9 | 208 462 | 59.9 | 31.7 | 37.0 |
| Elmira | 53.1 | 595 | 32.4 | 23.3 | 77.4 | 11.5 | 11 653 | -1.1 | 1 245 | 10.7 | 22 991 | 52.7 | 28.8 | 37.6 |
| Freeport | 33.2 | 1 237 | 37.6 | 14.6 | 89.5 | 7.0 | 22 450 | 1.8 | 2 036 | 9.1 | 33 954 | 71.2 | 44.1 | 21.9 |
| Glen Cove | 40.5 | 1 498 | 34.0 | 11.7 | 91.9 | 5.3 | 13 403 | 0.1 | 974 | 7.3 | 22 052 | 62.6 | 42.1 | 22.7 |
| Harrison | 33.6 | 1 724 | 30.9 | 6.7 | 89.1 | 6.8 | 13 384 | 1.4 | 994 | 7.4 | 21 576 | 63.0 | 37.3 | 19.7 |
| Hempstead | 56.1 | 1 261 | 35.3 | 26.7 | 87.2 | 8.2 | 26 249 | 0.7 | 2 469 | 9.4 | 41 400 | 70.5 | 45.5 | 21.3 |
| Ithaca | 73.9 | 865 | 41.1 | 31.0 | 54.0 | 26.9 | 15 691 | 3.7 | 986 | 6.3 | 27 727 | 55.5 | 18.1 | 33.7 |
| Jamestown | 51.4 | 564 | 32.7 | 21.0 | 80.1 | 10.0 | 14 238 | 0.2 | 1 328 | 9.3 | 24 338 | 61.9 | 32.9 | 36.6 |
| Lindenhurst | 16.8 | 1 500 | 31.6 | 5.1 | 93.8 | 4.7 | 14 614 | 2.1 | 1 259 | 8.6 | 21 868 | 68.8 | 41.2 | 19.8 |
| Long Beach | 42.4 | 1 600 | 29.7 | 12.0 | 89.4 | 6.1 | 18 548 | 2.2 | 1 439 | 7.8 | 28 514 | 67.0 | 49.1 | 23.4 |
| Middletown | 48.7 | 1 073 | 36.9 | 18.9 | 82.9 | 9.9 | 12 787 | 0.7 | 1 178 | 9.2 | 21 359 | 69.1 | 41.3 | 25.9 |
| Mount Vernon | 62.9 | 1 130 | 35.2 | 27.1 | 89.8 | 4.4 | 33 345 | 0.7 | 3 199 | 9.6 | 53 235 | 68.3 | 44.4 | 24.7 |
| Newburgh | 64.9 | 968 | 34.7 | 32.5 | 78.9 | 5.1 | 11 714 | 1.2 | 1 297 | 11.1 | 20 761 | 62.8 | 40.4 | 28.7 |
| New Rochelle | 49.9 | 1 243 | 33.5 | 17.9 | 87.6 | 6.3 | 38 825 | -0.4 | 3 196 | 8.2 | 61 396 | 64.1 | 42.4 | 24.4 |
| New York | 67.4 | 1 125 | 31.1 | 55.1 | 88.6 | 3.3 | 4 002 506 | 1.7 | 369 998 | 9.2 | 6 564 212 | 63.3 | 41.3 | 26.7 |
| Niagara Falls | 43.3 | 609 | 35.4 | 20.2 | 89.7 | 4.1 | 22 964 | -0.9 | 2 623 | 11.4 | 41 342 | 58.3 | 33.4 | 39.1 |
| North Tonawanda | 33.8 | 621 | 29.3 | 7.5 | 89.6 | 5.5 | 17 313 | 0.0 | 1 377 | 8.0 | 26 102 | 63.8 | 39.4 | 34.7 |
| Ossining | 45.9 | 1 303 | 34.2 | 12.3 | 86.9 | 7.1 | 18 738 | 1.0 | 1 327 | 7.1 | 20 515 | 67.8 | 41.8 | 19.9 |
| Port Chester | 55.0 | 1 364 | 35.6 | 20.7 | 84.3 | 5.6 | 14 769 | 0.0 | 942 | 6.4 | 23 149 | 72.8 | 41.4 | 18.4 |
| Poughkeepsie | 60.5 | 961 | 39.5 | 26.5 | 79.1 | 8.0 | 14 450 | 0.4 | 1 306 | 9.0 | 25 617 | 63.4 | 37.3 | 33.7 |
| Rochester | 59.4 | 733 | 38.1 | 25.7 | 76.2 | 8.0 | 93 842 | 1.0 | 10 178 | 10.8 | 165 018 | 60.5 | 33.5 | 34.3 |
| Rome | 41.8 | 641 | 26.3 | 14.5 | 81.7 | 9.9 | 14 044 | -0.9 | 1 275 | 9.1 | 27 871 | 54.0 | 33.7 | 33.5 |
| Saratoga Springs | 39.6 | 873 | 32.9 | 11.0 | 83.2 | 12.5 | 14 367 | 1.5 | 989 | 6.9 | 22 463 | 65.5 | 38.7 | 29.0 |
| Schenectady | 50.1 | 797 | 31.2 | 18.9 | 86.2 | 7.1 | 30 965 | 1.9 | 2 942 | 9.5 | 51 498 | 62.5 | 38.5 | 31.5 |
| Spring Valley | 71.3 | 1 146 | 33.6 | 21.0 | 87.0 | 6.0 | 14 645 | 1.2 | 1 006 | 6.9 | 21 854 | 70.8 | 39.7 | 20.6 |
| Syracuse | 59.3 | 693 | 34.7 | 27.1 | 72.4 | 12.2 | 62 994 | 0.5 | 6 322 | 10.0 | 115 056 | 57.6 | 31.1 | 35.6 |
| Troy | 59.7 | 769 | 31.7 | 23.5 | 76.8 | 12.3 | 23 859 | 1.2 | 2 343 | 9.8 | 40 731 | 63.3 | 34.0 | 31.5 |
| Utica | 50.9 | 623 | 32.6 | 22.0 | 80.6 | 8.3 | 26 216 | -1.0 | 2 592 | 9.9 | 47 904 | 58.3 | 32.4 | 39.6 |
| Valley Stream | 17.5 | 1 349 | 32.4 | 6.2 | 94.0 | 4.7 | 19 867 | 2.5 | 1 508 | 7.6 | 30 119 | 68.6 | 43.3 | 20.7 |
| Watertown | 57.0 | 722 | 30.5 | 18.0 | 74.3 | 16.2 | 11 428 | -1.5 | 1 054 | 9.2 | 21 062 | 65.5 | 34.1 | 29.4 |
| White Plains | 46.6 | 1 344 | 31.7 | 17.3 | 86.7 | 7.5 | 29 892 | 0.9 | 1 938 | 6.5 | 45 940 | 69.0 | 45.6 | 22.9 |

1. $2,000 represents $2,000 or more.  2. 50.0 represents 50 percent or more.  3. Percent of civilian labor force.  4. Persons 16 years old and over.

| City | Value of residential construction authorized by building permits, 2011 | | | Wholesale trade,[1] 2007 | | | | Retail trade,[2] 2007 | | | |
|---|---|---|---|---|---|---|---|---|---|---|---|
| | New construction ($1,000) | Number of housing units | Percent single family | Number of establishments | Number of employees | Sales (mil dol) | Annual payroll (mil dol) | Number of establishments | Number of employees | Sales (mil dol) | Annual payroll (mil dol) |
| | 69 | 70 | 71 | 72 | 73 | 74 | 75 | 76 | 77 | 78 | 79 |
| **NEW JERSEY—** Cont'd | | | | | | | | | | | |
| Garfield | 2 852 | 32 | 0.0 | 51 | 755 | 236.7 | 23.4 | 76 | 531 | 152.0 | 15.6 |
| Hackensack | 26 457 | 228 | 0.0 | 223 | 2 147 | 1 699.4 | 131.2 | 278 | 4 052 | 1 144.3 | 108.5 |
| Hoboken | 82 685 | 309 | 0.6 | 36 | 245 | 575.9 | 16.6 | 153 | 1 351 | 312.4 | 31.4 |
| Jersey City | 83 036 | 548 | 0.0 | 210 | 4 366 | 3 264.5 | 227.9 | 818 | 8 754 | 2 210.1 | 201.6 |
| Kearny | 5 | 0 | 0.0 | 85 | 1 623 | 1 154.2 | 86.6 | 129 | 1 789 | 443.4 | 46.2 |
| Linden | 1 955 | 18 | 88.9 | 119 | 1 629 | 1 957.5 | 84.0 | 192 | 2 864 | 725.3 | 67.6 |
| Long Branch | 5 157 | 28 | 100.0 | 27 | D | D | D | 93 | 1 066 | 248.4 | 32.3 |
| Millville | 3 354 | 34 | 100.0 | 28 | D | D | D | 98 | 2 075 | 484.9 | 51.5 |
| Newark | 16 121 | 114 | 0.9 | 324 | 4 954 | 3 119.2 | 245.3 | 935 | 6 467 | 1 637.2 | 147.8 |
| New Brunswick | 10 361 | 110 | 17.3 | 65 | 843 | 623.7 | 45.7 | 135 | 958 | 201.5 | 20.3 |
| Paramus | 6 877 | 17 | 100.0 | 112 | 932 | 1 641.0 | 67.7 | 611 | 15 080 | 3 621.1 | 359.8 |
| Passaic | 2 222 | 57 | 8.8 | 93 | 814 | 422.7 | 32.9 | 274 | 1 874 | 415.4 | 42.2 |
| Paterson | 2 611 | 19 | 89.5 | 190 | 2 064 | 852.2 | 99.2 | 492 | 2 700 | 642.1 | 61.6 |
| Perth Amboy | 5 579 | 35 | 8.6 | 50 | 582 | 361.4 | 27.1 | 189 | 1 336 | 340.7 | 32.1 |
| Plainfield | 104 | 3 | 100.0 | 26 | 155 | 41.4 | 4.8 | 125 | 685 | 169.3 | 17.3 |
| Rahway | 914 | 9 | 33.3 | 61 | 767 | 961.2 | 45.1 | 87 | 798 | 265.7 | 26.1 |
| Sayreville | 6 098 | 108 | 19.4 | 53 | 420 | 547.5 | 23.3 | 98 | 1 221 | 328.7 | 30.1 |
| Trenton | 0 | 0 | 0.0 | 60 | 854 | 663.7 | 45.3 | 234 | 1 470 | 402.3 | 36.4 |
| Union City | 15 | 2 | 0.0 | 59 | 289 | 110.8 | 10.2 | 297 | 1 367 | 341.7 | 28.9 |
| Vineland | 7 107 | 79 | 100.0 | 86 | 1 357 | 980.4 | 55.3 | 281 | 3 885 | 1 052.0 | 94.5 |
| Westfield | 9 222 | 31 | 90.3 | 19 | 99 | 27.1 | 3.3 | 138 | 1 546 | 323.5 | 33.9 |
| West New York | 26 811 | 261 | 0.0 | 43 | 163 | 48.6 | 4.1 | 241 | 1 284 | 270.2 | 27.0 |
| **NEW MEXICO** | 677 704 | 4 067 | 83.6 | 1 763 | 19 891 | 10 589.3 | 805.8 | 7 208 | 97 385 | 24 470.0 | 2 250.8 |
| Alamogordo | NA | NA | NA | 15 | 62 | 27.2 | 2.0 | 146 | 2 128 | 491.4 | 42.4 |
| Albuquerque | 156 058 | 1 024 | 73.6 | 735 | 10 490 | 5 165.6 | 433.3 | 2 030 | 34 923 | 8 951.7 | 859.0 |
| Carlsbad | 24 084 | 272 | 17.6 | 26 | 182 | 66.2 | 6.6 | 125 | 1 512 | 361.4 | 34.7 |
| Clovis | 37 335 | 191 | 66.0 | 40 | 196 | 144.6 | 6.5 | 186 | 2 425 | 562.4 | 50.1 |
| Farmington | 20 235 | 143 | 58.0 | 107 | 1 111 | 606.3 | 54.9 | 346 | 5 296 | 1 368.3 | 123.4 |
| Hobbs | 4 454 | 28 | 71.4 | 67 | 631 | 285.1 | 29.6 | 142 | 2 189 | 628.5 | 53.4 |
| Las Cruces | 82 055 | 457 | 96.1 | 83 | 812 | 272.0 | 25.7 | 425 | 7 046 | 1 723.8 | 144.4 |
| Rio Rancho | 83 349 | 463 | 97.8 | 22 | 111 | 57.6 | 6.4 | 108 | 2 501 | 905.3 | 64.1 |
| Roswell | 705 | 4 | 100.0 | 38 | 350 | 237.6 | 10.8 | 233 | 3 102 | 788.3 | 66.3 |
| Santa Fe | 12 536 | 94 | 100.0 | 98 | 1 010 | 512.6 | 51.2 | 763 | 8 769 | 2 183.9 | 236.2 |
| **NEW YORK** | 3 355 501 | 22 575 | 37.2 | 30 863 | 357 459 | 313 461.9 | 19 609.0 | 76 637 | 892 863 | 230 718.1 | 22 336.7 |
| Albany | 2 190 | 23 | 73.9 | 130 | 1 777 | 1 352.9 | 95.4 | 381 | 5 687 | 1 362.3 | 134.1 |
| Auburn | 120 | 2 | 100.0 | 26 | 396 | 188.9 | 17.7 | 161 | 2 699 | 583.4 | 57.0 |
| Binghamton | 0 | 0 | 0.0 | 51 | 622 | 191.9 | 22.0 | 191 | 2 280 | 471.7 | 46.2 |
| Buffalo | 4 274 | 32 | 18.8 | 281 | 4 538 | 2 037.3 | 182.5 | 795 | 8 315 | 1 449.6 | 159.4 |
| Elmira | 0 | 0 | 0.0 | 33 | 404 | 151.7 | 16.5 | 101 | 1 367 | 308.3 | 30.2 |
| Freeport | 570 | 3 | 33.3 | 87 | 793 | 310.0 | 32.0 | 185 | 1 734 | 665.9 | 57.4 |
| Glen Cove | 1 538 | 2 | 100.0 | 49 | 192 | 130.8 | 8.8 | 131 | 1 337 | 581.8 | 45.0 |
| Harrison | 13 378 | 18 | 100.0 | 71 | 2 150 | 5 874.5 | 176.7 | 70 | 310 | 92.9 | 10.4 |
| Hempstead | 17 889 | 233 | 0.4 | 46 | 461 | 177.8 | 22.4 | 197 | 2 166 | 839.8 | 63.5 |
| Ithaca | 4 579 | 39 | 10.3 | 21 | 158 | 40.6 | 5.1 | 187 | 2 879 | 610.4 | 63.3 |
| Jamestown | 5 900 | 36 | 2.8 | 37 | D | D | D | 127 | 1 511 | 359.2 | 34.1 |
| Lindenhurst | 443 | 3 | 100.0 | 39 | D | D | D | 88 | 720 | 243.0 | 23.4 |
| Long Beach | 1 800 | 9 | 100.0 | 25 | 34 | 17.9 | 1.5 | 87 | 624 | 178.3 | 18.1 |
| Middletown | 1 207 | 16 | 100.0 | 33 | 361 | 128.5 | 12.4 | 131 | 1 394 | 457.1 | 37.5 |
| Mount Vernon | 627 | 6 | 66.7 | 100 | 1 185 | 541.4 | 51.8 | 222 | 2 491 | 583.8 | 64.6 |
| Newburgh | 300 | 2 | 100.0 | 57 | 768 | 1 365.4 | 34.9 | 117 | 1 397 | 359.9 | 31.6 |
| New Rochelle | 42 000 | 221 | 9.0 | 88 | 1 020 | 865.4 | 79.4 | 267 | 2 886 | 1 031.5 | 88.5 |
| New York | 104 708 | 1 116 | 0.1 | 16 230 | 164 336 | 147 228.0 | 9 512.3 | 31 459 | 287 574 | 78 206.5 | 8 041.7 |
| Niagara Falls | 7 828 | 60 | 13.3 | 35 | 362 | 160.6 | 14.7 | 182 | 2 429 | 513.0 | 46.5 |
| North Tonawanda | 2 227 | 13 | 100.0 | 36 | 1 071 | 220.0 | 51.6 | 74 | 741 | 137.2 | 15.7 |
| Ossining | 0 | 0 | 0.0 | 22 | 92 | 33.5 | 4.0 | 73 | 546 | 171.3 | 13.7 |
| Port Chester | 498 | 3 | 33.3 | 47 | 477 | 174.2 | 25.9 | 152 | 2 037 | 613.2 | 56.8 |
| Poughkeepsie | 1 610 | 16 | 25.0 | 34 | 340 | 160.1 | 16.3 | 153 | 1 599 | 405.5 | 39.3 |
| Rochester | 19 186 | 206 | 22.3 | 301 | 4 041 | 1 647.9 | 177.9 | 695 | 6 232 | 1 181.7 | 128.0 |
| Rome | 3 903 | 20 | 10.0 | 16 | 81 | 57.0 | 4.1 | 137 | 2 150 | 461.0 | 49.0 |
| Saratoga Springs | 59 227 | 241 | 11.2 | 22 | 121 | 113.6 | 6.3 | 169 | 2 419 | 614.0 | 53.8 |
| Schenectady | 625 | 7 | 100.0 | 47 | 588 | 340.6 | 21.9 | 183 | 1 712 | 441.7 | 42.4 |
| Spring Valley | 1 800 | 11 | 9.1 | 42 | 264 | 233.3 | 12.8 | 114 | 1 310 | 460.2 | 34.1 |
| Syracuse | 21 536 | 336 | 18.2 | 161 | 3 049 | 1 109.2 | 139.7 | 601 | 7 597 | 1 654.5 | 162.4 |
| Troy | 368 | 4 | 100.0 | 41 | 457 | 908.6 | 16.8 | 130 | 1 544 | 380.1 | 40.1 |
| Utica | 1 750 | 10 | 100.0 | 59 | 989 | 524.7 | 38.6 | 179 | 2 604 | 580.1 | 55.7 |
| Valley Stream | 233 | 1 | 100.0 | 72 | 418 | 317.2 | 22.3 | 209 | 2 558 | 697.9 | 58.7 |
| Watertown | 13 873 | 107 | 100.0 | 32 | 583 | 182.9 | 19.1 | 222 | 3 738 | 905.9 | 79.7 |
| White Plains | 3 475 | 13 | 69.2 | 111 | 1 426 | 3 327.6 | 109.3 | 471 | 8 610 | 2 004.6 | 221.0 |

1. Merchant wholesalers except manufacturers' sales branches and offices.  2. Establishments with payroll.

# Table D. Cities — Real Estate, Professional Services, and Manufacturing

| City | Real estate and rental and leasing, 2007 | | | | Professional, scientific, and technical services,[1] 2007 | | | | Manufacturing, 2007 | | | |
|---|---|---|---|---|---|---|---|---|---|---|---|---|
| | Number of establish-ments | Number of employees | Receipts (mil dol) | Annual payroll (mil dol) | Number of establish-ments | Number of employees | Receipts (mil dol) | Annual payroll (mil dol) | Number of establish-ments | Number of employees | Receipts (mil dol) | Annual payroll (mil dol) |
| | 80 | 81 | 82 | 83 | 84 | 85 | 86 | 87 | 88 | 89 | 90 | 91 |
| **NEW JERSEY— Cont'd** | | | | | | | | | | | | |
| Garfield | 13 | 63 | 9.2 | 1.5 | 29 | 194 | 11.7 | 4.1 | 71 | 1 136 | 205.2 | 46.8 |
| Hackensack | 143 | 727 | 203.5 | 35.2 | 475 | 2 896 | 528.2 | 210.3 | 105 | 1 503 | 269.3 | 64.0 |
| Hoboken | 106 | 673 | 136.9 | 26.9 | 210 | 1 310 | 307.2 | 96.0 | NA | NA | NA | NA |
| Jersey City | 241 | 1 328 | 543.9 | 48.4 | 534 | D | D | D | 105 | 2 649 | 745.3 | 97.2 |
| Kearny | 43 | 368 | 103.6 | 19.2 | 58 | 213 | 27.7 | 8.1 | 62 | 1 850 | 552.9 | 82.0 |
| Linden | 41 | 295 | 46.0 | 8.7 | 57 | 914 | 88.3 | 58.2 | 112 | 3 886 | D | 236.8 |
| Long Branch | 30 | 79 | 21.1 | 2.2 | 49 | D | D | D | NA | NA | NA | NA |
| Millville | 18 | 78 | 10.9 | 2.0 | 49 | 264 | 29.4 | 8.7 | 48 | 3 201 | 829.8 | 122.5 |
| Newark | 222 | 2 181 | 533.1 | 76.1 | 413 | 8 444 | 1 706.2 | 660.1 | 309 | 9 590 | 3 209.2 | 413.2 |
| New Brunswick | 41 | 201 | 61.2 | 8.9 | 153 | D | D | D | 59 | 1 726 | 518.5 | 81.0 |
| Paramus | 65 | 609 | 355.3 | 36.9 | 227 | D | D | D | NA | NA | NA | NA |
| Passaic | 61 | 217 | 42.8 | 5.6 | 55 | 212 | 25.0 | 8.5 | 119 | 1 886 | 313.7 | 61.3 |
| Paterson | 73 | 353 | 63.4 | 11.0 | 101 | 517 | 53.2 | 18.0 | 278 | 5 473 | 1 153.7 | 226.4 |
| Perth Amboy | 29 | 109 | 34.2 | 4.4 | 45 | D | D | D | 49 | 2 139 | 938.5 | 87.4 |
| Plainfield | 30 | 95 | 24.9 | 2.4 | 44 | 220 | 22.0 | 10.7 | 23 | 600 | 82.0 | 20.7 |
| Rahway | 21 | 174 | 22.9 | 9.4 | 28 | 299 | 27.6 | 13.8 | 37 | 4 650 | D | D |
| Sayreville | 21 | 111 | 25.8 | 3.7 | 103 | 640 | 82.1 | 40.7 | 44 | 1 867 | 1 093.5 | 106.9 |
| Trenton | 50 | 352 | 51.9 | 10.9 | 117 | D | D | D | 67 | 1 609 | 333.8 | 68.7 |
| Union City | 67 | 178 | 27.3 | 4.1 | 87 | 270 | 28.8 | 8.9 | 55 | 505 | 77.2 | 14.1 |
| Vineland | 79 | 332 | 60.9 | 11.1 | 125 | 705 | 68.3 | 27.7 | 90 | 4 456 | 1 149.4 | 156.4 |
| Westfield | 33 | 117 | 50.8 | 4.7 | 170 | 1 160 | 215.4 | 82.2 | NA | NA | NA | NA |
| West New York | 69 | 690 | 171.2 | 25.4 | 67 | 174 | 26.1 | 8.2 | NA | NA | NA | NA |
| **NEW MEXICO** | 2 525 | 11 678 | 1 954.7 | 355.6 | 4 789 | 43 001 | 5 975.8 | 2 516.7 | 1 574 | 35 409 | 17 122.7 | 1 560.5 |
| Alamogordo | 50 | 224 | 23.5 | 3.7 | 55 | 264 | 16.4 | 6.6 | NA | NA | NA | NA |
| Albuquerque | 886 | 4 949 | 848.5 | 144.4 | 2 023 | D | D | D | 559 | 14 761 | 3 779.2 | 653.3 |
| Carlsbad | 24 | 149 | 15.6 | 4.2 | 44 | D | D | D | NA | NA | NA | NA |
| Clovis | 48 | D | D | D | 65 | 320 | 22.4 | 8.6 | NA | NA | NA | NA |
| Farmington | 88 | 686 | 168.5 | 37.2 | 173 | D | D | D | 50 | 660 | 74.6 | 22.1 |
| Hobbs | 44 | 397 | 100.5 | 23.3 | 50 | 418 | 46.8 | 21.2 | NA | NA | NA | NA |
| Las Cruces | 175 | 789 | 116.6 | 17.8 | 239 | D | D | D | 69 | 747 | 262.4 | 23.1 |
| Rio Rancho | 49 | 183 | 27.7 | 4.4 | 95 | 503 | 47.0 | 19.1 | 29 | 5 323 | D | 307.4 |
| Roswell | 78 | 240 | 35.7 | 6.2 | 97 | 745 | 102.6 | 33.4 | 30 | 520 | D | 15.3 |
| Santa Fe | 241 | 934 | 183.5 | 36.3 | 547 | D | D | D | 117 | 736 | 106.4 | 26.6 |
| **NEW YORK** | 32 588 | 171 601 | 49 867.2 | 7 941.7 | 58 087 | 539 635 | 112 045.6 | 41 604.5 | 18 629 | 533 835 | 162 720.2 | 24 268.0 |
| Albany | 164 | 1 181 | 249.5 | 32.7 | 434 | D | D | D | 71 | 1 791 | 544.3 | 76.7 |
| Auburn | 44 | 148 | 23.8 | 3.3 | 64 | 446 | 32.8 | 14.7 | 56 | 2 151 | 789.1 | 100.0 |
| Binghamton | 59 | 378 | 34.9 | 8.3 | 141 | D | D | D | 63 | 2 080 | 589.3 | 64.3 |
| Buffalo | 253 | 1 884 | 281.4 | 48.4 | 655 | D | D | D | 360 | 12 848 | 4 499.8 | 614.4 |
| Elmira | 38 | 212 | 39.1 | 5.6 | 55 | D | D | D | 27 | 2 156 | 403.0 | 86.0 |
| Freeport | 46 | 164 | 25.7 | 5.7 | 114 | 344 | 49.7 | 16.3 | 90 | 2 505 | 569.2 | 109.9 |
| Glen Cove | 29 | 101 | 19.9 | 3.7 | 88 | 367 | 56.3 | 17.4 | NA | NA | NA | NA |
| Harrison | 98 | 642 | 117.5 | 33.6 | 184 | D | D | D | NA | NA | NA | NA |
| Hempstead | 68 | 341 | 50.3 | 10.8 | 94 | D | D | D | NA | NA | NA | NA |
| Ithaca | 51 | 339 | 60.0 | 8.1 | 121 | D | D | D | 38 | 1 462 | D | 62.1 |
| Jamestown | 27 | 109 | 14.0 | 2.3 | 73 | D | D | D | 61 | 1 872 | 262.4 | 71.1 |
| Lindenhurst | 15 | 31 | 3.6 | 0.9 | 62 | D | D | D | 51 | 530 | 93.2 | 21.5 |
| Long Beach | 54 | 163 | 43.9 | 5.4 | 93 | 200 | 25.1 | 8.1 | NA | NA | NA | NA |
| Middletown | 31 | 100 | 22.4 | 2.4 | 64 | 342 | 31.8 | 13.4 | 36 | 1 005 | 198.2 | 38.2 |
| Mount Vernon | 172 | 511 | 102.3 | 17.3 | 99 | 319 | 53.7 | 12.2 | 112 | 2 784 | 548.7 | 115.6 |
| Newburgh | 47 | 176 | 17.3 | 4.6 | 62 | D | D | D | 43 | 753 | 122.4 | 25.3 |
| New Rochelle | 165 | 556 | 123.2 | 22.4 | 252 | 1 843 | 112.0 | 42.0 | 57 | 896 | 182.4 | 38.5 |
| New York | 18 972 | 106 396 | 36 279.1 | 5 588.3 | 24 909 | 300 564 | 76 850.6 | 27 940.7 | 6 626 | 101 310 | 20 411.6 | 3 818.4 |
| Niagara Falls | 37 | 248 | 27.3 | 6.9 | 93 | D | D | D | 51 | 1 877 | 1 073.3 | 114.9 |
| North Tonawanda | 11 | 30 | 2.6 | 0.6 | 41 | 283 | 15.5 | 6.9 | 58 | 1 468 | 416.2 | 60.5 |
| Ossining | 29 | 129 | 23.5 | 3.0 | 62 | 574 | 54.1 | 29.4 | NA | NA | NA | NA |
| Port Chester | 39 | D | D | D | 69 | 204 | 29.6 | 8.5 | 34 | 1 085 | 148.8 | 41.9 |
| Poughkeepsie | 83 | 412 | 71.9 | 11.3 | 143 | D | D | D | 39 | 6 649 | D | D |
| Rochester | 257 | 1 792 | 249.3 | 55.8 | 679 | D | D | D | 463 | 29 362 | 9 084.3 | 1 317.6 |
| Rome | 44 | 183 | 31.8 | 4.4 | 71 | D | D | D | 40 | 1 377 | 754.7 | 63.3 |
| Saratoga Springs | 42 | 244 | 50.1 | 7.0 | 156 | D | D | D | 24 | 1 696 | 540.3 | 75.4 |
| Schenectady | 57 | 281 | 35.1 | 8.3 | 142 | 1 173 | 140.5 | 65.5 | 60 | 2 171 | 1 096.5 | 112.7 |
| Spring Valley | 50 | 135 | 27.5 | 3.6 | 45 | 119 | 12.6 | 3.9 | NA | NA | NA | NA |
| Syracuse | 260 | 1 523 | 294.1 | 62.3 | 487 | D | D | D | 131 | 5 249 | 1 558.7 | 270.4 |
| Troy | 39 | 220 | 30.5 | 4.7 | 116 | D | D | D | 38 | 729 | 103.6 | 26.8 |
| Utica | 71 | 268 | 38.7 | 5.1 | 137 | D | D | D | 83 | 2 200 | 543.0 | 83.5 |
| Valley Stream | 59 | 202 | 45.2 | 7.6 | 151 | 962 | 99.5 | 39.4 | NA | NA | NA | NA |
| Watertown | 54 | 268 | 50.3 | 6.3 | 56 | 468 | 45.4 | 18.5 | 24 | 1 218 | 393.0 | 56.7 |
| White Plains | 198 | 1 206 | 425.2 | 71.3 | 676 | D | D | D | NA | NA | NA | NA |

1. Establishments subject to federal tax.

**Accommodation and Food Services, Arts, Entertainment, and Recreation, and Health Care and Social Assistance**

| City | Accommodation and food services, 2007 | | | | Arts, entertainment, and recreation,[1] 2007 | | | | Health care and social assistance,[1] 2007 | | | |
|---|---|---|---|---|---|---|---|---|---|---|---|---|
| | Number of establishments | Number of employees | Sales (mil dol) | Annual payroll (mil dol) | Number of establishments | Number of employees | Receipts (mil dol) | Annual payroll (mil dol) | Number of establishments | Number of employees | Receipts (mil dol) | Annual payroll (mil dol) |
| | 92 | 93 | 94 | 95 | 96 | 97 | 98 | 99 | 100 | 101 | 102 | 103 |
| NEW JERSEY— Cont'd | | | | | | | | | | | | |
| Garfield | 51 | 345 | 22.9 | 5.7 | 4 | D | D | D | 29 | D | D | D |
| Hackensack | 120 | 2 033 | 134.7 | 38.3 | 13 | 229 | 13.5 | 4.7 | 317 | D | D | D |
| Hoboken | 200 | 1 894 | 121.9 | 31.2 | 21 | D | D | D | 98 | D | D | D |
| Jersey City | 433 | 4 265 | 324.8 | 75.4 | 38 | D | D | D | 404 | 4 546 | 371.8 | 145.0 |
| Kearny | 67 | 538 | 34.8 | 9.1 | 3 | D | D | D | 71 | 523 | 52.7 | 17.7 |
| Linden | 98 | 793 | 45.6 | 11.5 | 6 | 62 | 3.6 | 1.0 | 65 | 956 | 66.8 | 28.2 |
| Long Branch | 96 | D | D | D | 6 | D | D | D | 93 | D | D | D |
| Millville | 59 | 691 | 32.0 | 8.7 | 2 | D | D | D | 55 | 761 | 53.5 | 24.0 |
| Newark | 542 | 6 939 | 552.6 | 135.8 | 25 | 344 | 118.4 | 85.5 | 289 | 3 577 | 376.9 | 138.4 |
| New Brunswick | 152 | 1 992 | 114.7 | 36.1 | 6 | D | D | D | 77 | 787 | 93.7 | 40.6 |
| Paramus | 122 | 2 686 | 151.5 | 41.4 | 16 | D | D | D | 199 | 2 216 | 253.3 | 89.2 |
| Passaic | 88 | D | D | D | 8 | D | D | D | 91 | D | D | D |
| Paterson | 198 | D | D | D | 5 | D | D | D | 147 | 1 298 | 137.4 | 58.6 |
| Perth Amboy | 97 | 512 | 32.5 | 7.3 | 4 | 14 | 1.0 | 0.3 | 68 | D | D | D |
| Plainfield | 70 | 595 | 29.6 | 8.0 | 4 | D | D | D | 68 | 790 | 70.3 | 29.5 |
| Rahway | 66 | 592 | 32.6 | 8.2 | 3 | 72 | 4.0 | 1.1 | 42 | D | D | D |
| Sayreville | 86 | 811 | 40.0 | 11.0 | 13 | 283 | 18.3 | 4.4 | 55 | 531 | 47.3 | 18.0 |
| Trenton | 157 | 1 107 | 66.2 | 16.7 | 3 | D | D | D | 104 | 1 367 | 150.2 | 69.1 |
| Union City | 130 | 910 | 47.7 | 11.1 | 4 | 27 | 2.9 | 0.6 | 152 | 1 766 | 102.4 | 45.1 |
| Vineland | 124 | 1 769 | 88.9 | 22.2 | 11 | 76 | 7.8 | 2.0 | 156 | 2 111 | 245.5 | 94.8 |
| Westfield | 64 | 719 | 42.1 | 11.5 | 12 | 205 | 7.4 | 2.8 | 154 | 1 599 | 174.2 | 74.3 |
| West New York | 84 | D | D | D | 7 | 22 | 1.8 | 0.7 | 96 | D | D | D |
| NEW MEXICO | 4 090 | 80 415 | 3 734.3 | 1 054.8 | 516 | 12 527 | 1 335.5 | 258.5 | 3 713 | 57 423 | 4 854.5 | 1 958.2 |
| Alamogordo | 79 | 1 293 | 48.5 | 13.6 | 6 | D | D | D | 75 | D | D | D |
| Albuquerque | 1 222 | 28 156 | 1 321.6 | 386.8 | 148 | 2 889 | 468.1 | 49.9 | 1 296 | 21 688 | 2 043.3 | 846.3 |
| Carlsbad | 73 | 1 081 | 51.3 | 13.1 | 4 | D | D | D | 60 | 1 145 | 137.7 | 47.7 |
| Clovis | 82 | 1 925 | 68.0 | 17.7 | 7 | D | D | D | 79 | D | D | D |
| Farmington | 126 | 3 003 | 127.8 | 33.9 | 9 | D | D | D | 192 | D | D | D |
| Hobbs | 80 | 1 493 | 69.1 | 16.8 | 9 | D | D | D | 72 | D | D | D |
| Las Cruces | 247 | 5 276 | 211.6 | 57.6 | 13 | D | D | D | 361 | 7 504 | 637.2 | 249.4 |
| Rio Rancho | 75 | 1 582 | 62.9 | 18.4 | 14 | 326 | 9.9 | 3.8 | 93 | D | D | D |
| Roswell | 108 | 2 235 | 88.9 | 24.3 | 2 | D | D | D | 138 | D | D | D |
| Santa Fe | 333 | 7 985 | 480.8 | 144.0 | 60 | 282 | 26.3 | 8.6 | 367 | 3 684 | 374.4 | 152.8 |
| NEW YORK | 43 791 | 591 653 | 39 813.5 | 10 956.3 | 9 289 | 101 381 | 15 566.1 | 4 656.2 | 41 201 | 459 964 | 46 577.9 | 18 427.7 |
| Albany | 413 | 5 321 | 309.7 | 76.8 | 26 | 811 | 14.3 | 5.3 | 241 | 3 540 | 468.7 | 175.5 |
| Auburn | 93 | 1 392 | 53.0 | 13.0 | 12 | D | D | D | 115 | 1 259 | 101.5 | 43.0 |
| Binghamton | 146 | 2 387 | 104.7 | 27.9 | 12 | 122 | 9.5 | 2.3 | 108 | 1 295 | 152.1 | 59.2 |
| Buffalo | 600 | 9 962 | 414.7 | 121.0 | 42 | 578 | 114.2 | 63.3 | 403 | 6 236 | 565.7 | 263.0 |
| Elmira | 66 | 955 | 33.3 | 9.5 | 4 | 104 | 2.2 | 0.8 | 82 | 849 | 103.7 | 41.3 |
| Freeport | 80 | 591 | 38.9 | 10.1 | 19 | 111 | 18.1 | 3.4 | 98 | D | D | D |
| Glen Cove | 72 | 660 | 36.5 | 12.1 | 16 | D | D | D | 110 | D | D | D |
| Harrison | 72 | 977 | 88.1 | 23.4 | 20 | D | D | D | 52 | D | D | D |
| Hempstead | 94 | 802 | 53.3 | 14.3 | 4 | D | D | D | 118 | 1 756 | 177.3 | 63.6 |
| Ithaca | 194 | 2 448 | 118.8 | 35.7 | 13 | 76 | 4.9 | 1.2 | 63 | 650 | 50.6 | 19.1 |
| Jamestown | 74 | 854 | 31.4 | 9.2 | 9 | D | D | D | 81 | D | D | D |
| Lindenhurst | 64 | 721 | 37.2 | 9.5 | 7 | 48 | 2.2 | 0.5 | 35 | D | D | D |
| Long Beach | 82 | 733 | 39.1 | 9.5 | 16 | 153 | 10.1 | 3.5 | 111 | 1 050 | 128.4 | 43.2 |
| Middletown | 88 | 1 654 | 77.3 | 22.0 | 5 | D | D | D | 83 | 974 | 116.1 | 63.5 |
| Mount Vernon | 97 | 649 | 40.8 | 10.4 | 14 | D | D | D | 115 | 1 524 | 85.8 | 36.7 |
| Newburgh | 90 | 1 042 | 54.0 | 15.3 | 9 | D | D | D | 86 | 738 | 77.4 | 30.4 |
| New Rochelle | 156 | 1 997 | 132.3 | 36.1 | 41 | D | D | D | 252 | 1 940 | 236.9 | 83.9 |
| New York | 17 494 | 249 519 | 22 095.1 | 6 009.6 | 4 574 | 49 339 | 10 570.7 | 3 162.4 | 16 239 | 185 098 | 18 567.4 | 7 309.4 |
| Niagara Falls | 154 | 5 174 | 520.9 | 110.8 | 12 | D | D | D | 82 | 980 | 62.7 | 27.5 |
| North Tonawanda | 56 | 624 | 24.6 | 6.6 | 9 | 22 | 2.9 | 0.5 | 52 | 398 | 27.2 | 11.4 |
| Ossining | 42 | 427 | 21.7 | 8.1 | 6 | D | D | D | 44 | 309 | 25.3 | 10.2 |
| Port Chester | 86 | 757 | 55.0 | 14.2 | 8 | D | D | D | 41 | 397 | 46.3 | 17.6 |
| Poughkeepsie | 104 | 1 518 | 81.7 | 22.6 | 9 | 174 | 8.3 | 2.3 | 118 | 1 886 | 233.4 | 105.3 |
| Rochester | 529 | 6 870 | 324.0 | 90.5 | 61 | 1 005 | 49.0 | 16.4 | 281 | 4 375 | 402.6 | 170.2 |
| Rome | 81 | 942 | 39.5 | 11.5 | 10 | 58 | 2.4 | 1.0 | 88 | 1 219 | 84.1 | 34.8 |
| Saratoga Springs | 163 | 2 358 | 131.5 | 40.5 | 28 | D | D | D | 102 | 1 081 | 113.0 | 41.7 |
| Schenectady | 156 | 1 452 | 72.5 | 18.9 | 11 | D | D | D | 155 | 1 652 | 163.2 | 72.0 |
| Spring Valley | 41 | 186 | 15.3 | 3.4 | 1 | D | D | D | 38 | 381 | 32.1 | 10.3 |
| Syracuse | 392 | 5 488 | 251.0 | 75.8 | 22 | 143 | 11.3 | 3.0 | 328 | 4 611 | 592.5 | 230.9 |
| Troy | 120 | 1 535 | 66.8 | 18.6 | 9 | 69 | 5.4 | 1.4 | 124 | 1 487 | 158.9 | 67.7 |
| Utica | 140 | 1 875 | 85.9 | 24.8 | 9 | 48 | 2.9 | 0.6 | 160 | 1 647 | 193.7 | 73.3 |
| Valley Stream | 76 | 923 | 48.7 | 12.7 | 20 | D | D | D | 121 | D | D | D |
| Watertown | 111 | 2 076 | 97.3 | 27.0 | 11 | 48 | 2.9 | 0.8 | 102 | 1 263 | 123.2 | 59.3 |
| White Plains | 194 | 2 668 | 177.9 | 50.8 | 23 | 465 | 26.9 | 9.1 | 362 | 5 152 | 566.8 | 266.4 |

1. Establishments subject to federal tax.

# Table D. Cities — Other Services and Federal Funds

| City | Other services[1], 2007 | | | | Selected federal funds, 2009–2010 (mil dol) | | | | | | | | |
|---|---|---|---|---|---|---|---|---|---|---|---|---|---|
| | | | | | Procurement contracts | | Grants | | | | | | |
| | Number of establish-ments | Number of employees | Receipts (mil dol) | Annual payroll (mil dol) | Defense | Other | Total[2] | Medicaid and other health related | Nutrition and family welfare | Energy and envi-ronment | Disasters and emergency prepared-ness | Housing and community develop-ment | Employment and training |
| | 104 | 105 | 106 | 107 | 108 | 109 | 110 | 111 | 112 | 113 | 114 | 115 | 116 |
| NEW JERSEY—Cont'd | | | | | | | | | | | | | |
| Garfield | 63 | D | D | D | 0.4 | 0.0 | 1.0 | 0.0 | 0.0 | 0.0 | 0.0 | 0.7 | 0.0 |
| Hackensack | 129 | 749 | 63.5 | 20.2 | 4.9 | 1.0 | 23.6 | 4.6 | 3.8 | 8.3 | 0.0 | 3.1 | 0.0 |
| Hoboken | 105 | D | D | D | 3.4 | 2.1 | 24.0 | 1.3 | 4.2 | 0.3 | 0.0 | 4.3 | 0.0 |
| Jersey City | 341 | 1 286 | 119.1 | 30.3 | 78.7 | 5.7 | 101.5 | 3.6 | 8.4 | 4.1 | 0.9 | 75.1 | 0.0 |
| Kearny | 69 | D | D | D | 0.0 | 0.1 | 0.2 | 0.0 | 0.0 | 0.2 | 0.0 | 0.0 | 0.0 |
| Linden | 105 | 529 | 50.3 | 17.0 | 0.2 | 0.3 | 5.4 | 0.0 | 0.0 | 0.0 | 0.0 | 4.2 | 0.0 |
| Long Branch | 60 | 238 | 19.0 | 5.6 | 0.1 | 0.2 | 13.0 | 0.5 | 0.0 | 0.0 | 0.0 | 10.6 | 0.0 |
| Millville | 35 | 163 | 12.3 | 3.8 | 4.9 | 0.0 | 3.5 | 0.0 | 0.0 | 0.0 | 0.0 | 2.7 | 0.0 |
| Newark | 476 | 3 232 | 346.3 | 112.8 | 15.9 | 203.8 | 1 054.9 | 105.2 | 30.4 | 15.2 | 0.0 | 138.9 | 2.5 |
| New Brunswick | 72 | 305 | 25.7 | 8.5 | 6.4 | 7.6 | 328.7 | 192.4 | 0.0 | 7.3 | 2.5 | 19.5 | 1.2 |
| Paramus | 66 | 525 | 45.6 | 15.8 | 16.3 | 2.7 | 7.4 | 0.5 | 0.0 | 0.0 | 0.0 | 0.0 | 0.0 |
| Passaic | 94 | 346 | 26.4 | 8.5 | 1.9 | 0.3 | 23.7 | 0.9 | 2.1 | 0.0 | 0.0 | 19.4 | 0.0 |
| Paterson | 193 | 1 211 | 100.1 | 30.8 | 11.9 | 2.0 | 64.7 | 10.8 | 7.8 | 1.5 | 0.0 | 37.1 | 4.9 |
| Perth Amboy | 85 | D | D | D | 0.0 | 0.0 | 14.1 | 0.9 | 0.0 | 0.0 | 0.0 | 12.9 | 0.0 |
| Plainfield | 75 | 269 | 22.3 | 6.8 | 35.5 | 0.0 | 11.6 | 2.6 | 0.0 | 0.0 | 0.0 | 8.7 | 0.0 |
| Rahway | 45 | 232 | 22.0 | 7.0 | 1.7 | 0.0 | 2.3 | 0.0 | 0.0 | 0.0 | 0.0 | 2.3 | 0.0 |
| Sayreville | 82 | D | D | D | 0.9 | 0.2 | 2.2 | 0.0 | 0.0 | 0.0 | 0.0 | 2.2 | 0.0 |
| Trenton | 92 | 286 | 26.5 | 7.5 | 45.5 | 15.1 | 1 913.7 | 214.7 | 291.8 | 159.0 | 28.3 | 272.2 | 262.3 |
| Union City | 94 | 253 | 18.0 | 4.6 | 0.0 | 0.0 | 9.4 | 1.4 | 0.0 | 0.5 | 0.0 | 6.7 | 0.0 |
| Vineland | 137 | 636 | 47.0 | 14.3 | 33.1 | 3.8 | 12.5 | 0.4 | 0.0 | 0.3 | 0.0 | 4.9 | 0.7 |
| Westfield | 76 | 427 | 39.0 | 12.4 | 0.0 | 0.2 | 0.0 | 0.0 | 0.0 | 0.0 | 0.0 | 0.0 | 0.0 |
| West New York | 80 | D | D | D | 0.0 | 0.0 | 12.1 | 2.2 | 4.0 | 0.0 | 0.0 | 5.7 | 0.0 |
| NEW MEXICO | 2 202 | 13 461 | 1 108.3 | 324.9 | 1 519.7 | 5 979.2 | 6 720.2 | 3 712.9 | 585.8 | 251.0 | 3.9 | 159.9 | 60.1 |
| Alamogordo | 42 | D | D | D | 14.5 | 2.4 | 1.4 | 0.0 | 0.0 | 0.1 | 0.0 | 0.0 | 0.0 |
| Albuquerque | 739 | 5 676 | 410.1 | 138.9 | 398.5 | 2 752.9 | 522.2 | 212.9 | 19.2 | 28.1 | 0.0 | 61.2 | 57.7 |
| Carlsbad | 39 | 212 | 17.3 | 4.7 | 0.6 | 177.7 | 21.1 | 0.1 | 5.3 | 12.9 | 0.0 | 3.2 | 0.0 |
| Clovis | 58 | D | D | D | 2.1 | 0.5 | 40.3 | 0.0 | 0.0 | 0.8 | 0.0 | 3.2 | 0.0 |
| Farmington | 101 | 838 | 115.1 | 22.8 | 0.0 | 0.3 | 9.2 | 0.6 | 0.3 | 1.1 | 0.0 | 1.6 | 0.0 |
| Hobbs | 61 | D | D | D | 0.0 | 0.2 | 4.0 | 0.0 | 2.3 | 0.0 | 0.0 | 0.0 | 0.0 |
| Las Cruces | 127 | 767 | 45.9 | 14.6 | 47.2 | 40.6 | 84.2 | 23.1 | 5.5 | 10.3 | 0.0 | 11.7 | 0.0 |
| Rio Rancho | 56 | 350 | 30.6 | 8.3 | 0.2 | 0.5 | 3.4 | 0.5 | 0.0 | 0.4 | 0.0 | 0.4 | 0.0 |
| Roswell | 52 | D | D | D | 3.2 | 15.9 | 13.7 | 0.0 | 0.0 | 2.4 | 0.0 | 6.8 | 0.0 |
| Santa Fe | 175 | 891 | 67.8 | 21.5 | 15.8 | 28.2 | 598.5 | 78.8 | 104.5 | 104.2 | 0.0 | 32.8 | 1.3 |
| NEW YORK | 32 231 | 155 249 | 13 318.0 | 3 874.0 | 8 809.8 | 5 073.4 | 63 103.6 | 39 959.0 | 6 704.4 | 1 201.8 | 144.2 | 3 570.2 | 553.2 |
| Albany | 132 | 778 | 60.6 | 18.7 | 12.5 | 132.0 | 4 416.7 | 255.0 | 83.2 | 409.7 | 1.1 | 541.9 | 463.3 |
| Auburn | 56 | 255 | 19.8 | 5.2 | 2.1 | 2.7 | 6.9 | 0.1 | 2.5 | 0.9 | 0.0 | 2.3 | 0.0 |
| Binghamton | 78 | 469 | 33.8 | 11.3 | 3.3 | 7.4 | 77.8 | 10.1 | 5.2 | 29.9 | 0.0 | 8.0 | 0.0 |
| Buffalo | 307 | 1 649 | 144.2 | 43.6 | 98.2 | 146.0 | 316.7 | 96.7 | 22.1 | 10.6 | 0.2 | 95.4 | 0.7 |
| Elmira | 32 | 211 | 14.8 | 4.3 | 1.2 | 0.2 | 19.7 | 0.0 | 3.0 | 0.0 | 0.0 | 3.1 | 0.0 |
| Freeport | 107 | 349 | 34.3 | 8.7 | 9.3 | 6.5 | 4.0 | 0.0 | 0.0 | 0.0 | 0.0 | 3.6 | 0.0 |
| Glen Cove | 74 | 204 | 16.5 | 4.2 | 0.1 | 0.0 | 9.2 | 0.1 | 1.4 | 0.0 | 0.0 | 5.1 | 0.0 |
| Harrison | 43 | D | D | D | 14.2 | 1.0 | 0.0 | 0.0 | 0.0 | 0.0 | 0.0 | 0.0 | 0.0 |
| Hempstead | 92 | 751 | 59.3 | 18.9 | 0.0 | 0.3 | 24.3 | 1.1 | 7.4 | 0.0 | 0.0 | 14.0 | 0.0 |
| Ithaca | 42 | 279 | 19.7 | 6.0 | 17.9 | 12.0 | 412.4 | 147.5 | 3.1 | 32.3 | 1.2 | 8.3 | 1.6 |
| Jamestown | 38 | 192 | 15.5 | 4.6 | 63.1 | 0.3 | 6.0 | 0.2 | 0.0 | 0.0 | 0.1 | 5.2 | 0.0 |
| Lindenhurst | 76 | 276 | 26.1 | 6.6 | 7.0 | 0.1 | 2.0 | 0.0 | 0.0 | 0.0 | 0.0 | 0.0 | 0.0 |
| Long Beach | 54 | 169 | 8.9 | 2.5 | 0.0 | 0.0 | 5.7 | 0.2 | 0.0 | 0.0 | 0.0 | 5.5 | 0.0 |
| Middletown | 75 | 613 | 118.5 | 18.5 | 0.5 | 1.8 | 3.8 | 0.8 | 1.9 | 0.0 | 0.0 | 0.9 | 0.0 |
| Mount Vernon | 125 | 697 | 82.7 | 22.5 | 11.5 | 0.2 | 9.9 | 6.6 | 0.0 | 0.6 | 0.0 | 2.1 | 0.0 |
| Newburgh | 57 | 232 | 19.7 | 5.4 | 20.3 | 8.8 | 9.0 | 1.4 | 2.2 | 0.0 | 0.0 | 4.9 | 0.0 |
| New Rochelle | 146 | 651 | 56.6 | 15.0 | -0.5 | 0.7 | 25.1 | 0.6 | 0.0 | 1.7 | 0.0 | 17.2 | 0.0 |
| New York | 13 086 | 60 996 | 5 070.5 | 1 503.3 | 611.4 | 2 225.2 | 34 534.2 | 25 615.8 | 2 238.1 | 249.6 | 5.4 | 2 298.3 | 42.8 |
| Niagara Falls | 66 | 285 | 21.8 | 6.9 | 37.1 | 4.9 | 15.2 | 0.0 | 3.7 | 0.6 | 0.0 | 8.4 | 0.0 |
| North Tonawanda | 60 | 194 | 13.1 | 4.1 | 6.4 | 0.5 | 2.8 | 0.0 | 0.0 | 0.0 | 0.0 | 1.8 | 0.0 |
| Ossining | 37 | 110 | 9.4 | 2.8 | 0.0 | 0.0 | 7.6 | 4.3 | 0.0 | 0.0 | 0.0 | 3.0 | 0.0 |
| Port Chester | 72 | 260 | 33.4 | 8.6 | 0.0 | 0.0 | 4.2 | 0.6 | 2.1 | 0.0 | 0.0 | 1.2 | 0.0 |
| Poughkeepsie | 88 | 373 | 28.2 | 8.2 | 0.4 | 4.2 | 27.5 | 0.0 | 0.3 | -0.2 | 0.0 | 12.0 | 0.3 |
| Rochester | 307 | 1 973 | 180.9 | 55.1 | 1 754.9 | 50.9 | 797.7 | 428.2 | 16.7 | 80.1 | 0.2 | 78.1 | 16.6 |
| Rome | 48 | 189 | 19.1 | 4.9 | 129.0 | 2.4 | 14.1 | 0.2 | 7.6 | 0.0 | 0.0 | 5.2 | 0.0 |
| Saratoga Springs | 41 | 267 | 17.5 | 5.5 | 2.9 | 1.3 | 3.8 | 0.9 | 0.0 | 0.0 | 0.0 | 1.9 | 0.0 |
| Schenectady | 96 | 815 | 69.2 | 17.9 | 278.1 | 0.4 | 98.0 | 12.6 | 4.4 | 39.8 | 0.0 | 26.5 | 6.4 |
| Spring Valley | 35 | 89 | 10.7 | 2.1 | 0.2 | 0.5 | 9.6 | 1.0 | 0.0 | 0.0 | 0.0 | 8.4 | 0.0 |
| Syracuse | 206 | 1 374 | 110.7 | 34.9 | 66.1 | 134.4 | 198.7 | 50.2 | 10.5 | 10.5 | 0.6 | 52.2 | 4.5 |
| Troy | 58 | 284 | 27.1 | 7.8 | 5.7 | 3.5 | 176.5 | 18.1 | 5.2 | 98.7 | 0.4 | 12.0 | 3.8 |
| Utica | 87 | 513 | 33.4 | 9.7 | 20.6 | 2.7 | 31.3 | 0.0 | 0.1 | 0.8 | 0.0 | 11.3 | 5.9 |
| Valley Stream | 123 | D | D | D | 0.0 | 0.0 | 0.0 | 0.0 | 0.0 | 0.0 | 0.0 | 0.0 | 0.0 |
| Watertown | 56 | 330 | 27.4 | 7.7 | 26.0 | 0.7 | 12.6 | 0.0 | 2.2 | 0.5 | 0.0 | 2.4 | 0.0 |
| White Plains | 141 | 969 | 77.4 | 22.9 | 14.0 | 12.2 | 53.6 | 9.9 | 0.5 | 6.0 | 0.0 | 18.2 | 0.0 |

1. Establishments subject to federal tax.   2. Includes program categories not shown separately. State totals include additional categories not allocated by city.

| City | General revenue — Total (mil dol) 117 | Intergovernmental — Total (mil dol) 118 | Intergovernmental — Percent from state government 119 | Taxes — Total (mil dol) 120 | Taxes Per capita (dollars) — Total 121 | Taxes Per capita (dollars) — Property 122 | Taxes Per capita (dollars) — Sales and gross receipts 123 | General expenditure — Total (mil dol) 124 | General expenditure Per capita (dollars) — Total 125 | General expenditure Per capita (dollars) — Capital outlays 126 |
|---|---|---|---|---|---|---|---|---|---|---|
| **NEW JERSEY— Cont'd** | | | | | | | | | | |
| Garfield | 29.0 | 6.8 | 72.0 | 18.4 | 632 | 613 | 19 | 29.2 | 1 000 | 78 |
| Hackensack | 68.9 | 8.5 | 64.4 | 54.6 | 1 268 | 1 246 | 22 | 57.8 | 1 342 | 120 |
| Hoboken | 92.7 | 29.8 | 56.2 | 32.5 | 801 | 711 | 90 | 88.2 | 2 174 | 55 |
| Jersey City | 548.0 | 192.3 | 63.9 | 165.9 | 684 | 614 | 70 | 541.6 | 2 234 | 145 |
| Kearny | 65.1 | 32.7 | 99.5 | 30.2 | 810 | 781 | 29 | 69.0 | 1 851 | 210 |
| Linden | 79.1 | 28.2 | 88.7 | 38.5 | 977 | 891 | 87 | 74.5 | 1 892 | 220 |
| Long Branch | 60.6 | 21.6 | 30.7 | 28.3 | 876 | 826 | 49 | 56.4 | 1 743 | 115 |
| Millville | 42.9 | 14.7 | 89.4 | 18.5 | 649 | 600 | 50 | 37.2 | 1 306 | 75 |
| Newark | 843.1 | 494.2 | 37.5 | 242.7 | 866 | 636 | 111 | 758.4 | 2 707 | 171 |
| New Brunswick | 236.3 | 145.4 | 90.6 | 53.6 | 1 061 | 1 007 | 54 | 245.8 | 4 864 | 112 |
| Paramus | 49.5 | 6.3 | 98.6 | 37.1 | 1 413 | 1 295 | 118 | 52.7 | 2 007 | 135 |
| Passaic | 104.1 | 44.1 | 59.2 | 46.0 | 686 | 668 | 18 | 99.0 | 1 475 | 15 |
| Paterson | 237.4 | 97.2 | 73.1 | 93.7 | 639 | 624 | 15 | 222.9 | 1 521 | 114 |
| Perth Amboy | 88.0 | 25.6 | 50.1 | 42.3 | 865 | 850 | 15 | 119.0 | 2 434 | 776 |
| Plainfield | 95.0 | 27.2 | 59.7 | 44.5 | 957 | 939 | 18 | 88.2 | 1 897 | 108 |
| Rahway | 46.5 | 9.5 | 60.4 | 32.1 | 1 140 | 1 022 | 118 | 48.4 | 1 718 | 192 |
| Sayreville | 47.9 | 19.8 | 67.2 | 21.2 | 500 | 476 | 24 | 45.6 | 1 077 | 155 |
| Trenton | 491.6 | 384.4 | 97.0 | 73.4 | 886 | 858 | 28 | 525.0 | 6 340 | 590 |
| Union City | 241.4 | 187.5 | 96.2 | 44.3 | 707 | 694 | 13 | 258.5 | 4 121 | 159 |
| Vineland | 52.5 | 11.6 | 85.9 | 24.8 | 424 | 403 | 21 | 76.5 | 1 308 | 59 |
| Westfield | 33.3 | 5.1 | 89.2 | 23.8 | 807 | 752 | 54 | 32.7 | 1 105 | 85 |
| West New York | 172.4 | 112.3 | 92.7 | 39.2 | 845 | 819 | 26 | 185.9 | 4 004 | 159 |
| **NEW MEXICO** | X | X | X | X | X | X | X | X | X | X |
| Alamogordo | 42.8 | 16.3 | 91.3 | 15.5 | 436 | 80 | 356 | 36.5 | 1 024 | 235 |
| Albuquerque | 939.6 | 298.1 | 84.2 | 352.4 | 680 | 210 | 469 | 769.8 | 1 485 | 420 |
| Carlsbad | 40.2 | 9.7 | 34.4 | 21.1 | 844 | 66 | 778 | 37.2 | 1 486 | 418 |
| Clovis | 43.6 | 5.9 | 60.1 | 23.5 | 707 | 37 | 671 | 38.3 | 1 154 | 281 |
| Farmington | 85.3 | 35.1 | 96.5 | 27.2 | 640 | 29 | 611 | 95.5 | 2 252 | 243 |
| Hobbs | 65.0 | 25.2 | 100.0 | 25.1 | 846 | 45 | 802 | 52.8 | 1 783 | 574 |
| Las Cruces | 174.6 | 43.4 | 88.9 | 78.0 | 870 | 104 | 734 | 157.2 | 1 752 | 328 |
| Rio Rancho | 116.2 | 12.9 | 49.5 | 52.3 | 688 | 128 | 523 | 134.3 | 1 768 | 1 029 |
| Roswell | 51.8 | 32.0 | 90.8 | 6.6 | 145 | 80 | 65 | 56.0 | 1 228 | 360 |
| Santa Fe | 175.1 | 72.5 | 81.3 | 51.9 | 708 | 26 | 682 | 157.3 | 2 148 | 352 |
| **NEW YORK** | X | X | X | X | X | X | X | X | X | X |
| Albany | 217.9 | 75.8 | 27.8 | 57.0 | 605 | 518 | 88 | 208.7 | 2 216 | 183 |
| Auburn | 42.3 | 16.0 | 45.1 | 11.7 | 427 | 376 | 51 | 38.6 | 1 414 | 137 |
| Binghamton | 70.6 | 30.9 | 36.1 | 27.9 | 619 | 581 | 38 | 85.0 | 1 888 | 526 |
| Buffalo | 1 339.3 | 1 028.6 | 82.2 | 163.5 | 600 | 524 | 76 | 1 301.4 | 4 773 | 716 |
| Elmira | 31.2 | 14.9 | 34.9 | 10.0 | 341 | 303 | 38 | 31.3 | 1 062 | 120 |
| Freeport | 60.7 | 8.4 | 36.9 | 36.9 | 870 | 811 | 56 | 66.1 | 1 557 | 226 |
| Glen Cove | 45.1 | 18.1 | 63.8 | 21.2 | 813 | 697 | 116 | 55.0 | 2 112 | 509 |
| Harrison | 14.4 | 5.9 | 100.0 | 7.6 | 285 | 202 | 81 | 14.4 | 544 | 269 |
| Hempstead | 63.0 | 4.3 | 22.2 | 49.0 | 946 | 898 | 48 | 57.8 | 1 116 | 38 |
| Ithaca | 55.1 | 14.0 | 59.6 | 26.9 | 898 | 509 | 389 | 55.4 | 1 849 | 370 |
| Jamestown | 62.0 | 24.9 | 74.1 | 13.3 | 449 | 419 | 29 | 71.3 | 2 411 | 220 |
| Lindenhurst | 10.5 | 1.4 | 66.0 | 5.9 | 215 | 151 | 64 | 11.1 | 402 | 79 |
| Long Beach | 108.6 | 9.1 | 58.4 | 40.4 | 1 168 | 974 | 194 | 102.4 | 2 961 | 1 288 |
| Middletown | 36.2 | 11.6 | 26.9 | 14.8 | 574 | 477 | 97 | 33.9 | 1 311 | 88 |
| Mount Vernon | 94.5 | 15.7 | 62.1 | 66.2 | 975 | 602 | 373 | 91.2 | 1 344 | 96 |
| Newburgh | 48.0 | 16.3 | 41.2 | 16.9 | 598 | 474 | 124 | 50.7 | 1 796 | 185 |
| New Rochelle | 124.3 | 25.1 | 45.5 | 74.8 | 1 021 | 568 | 453 | 124.4 | 1 699 | 247 |
| New York | 76 228.4 | 27 704.3 | 83.8 | 38 153.1 | 4 611 | 1 595 | 795 | 68 299.1 | 8 254 | 1 110 |
| Niagara Falls | 105.2 | 55.8 | 57.7 | 38.6 | 747 | 551 | 196 | 89.3 | 1 728 | 116 |
| North Tonawanda | 42.2 | 18.6 | 32.9 | 16.1 | 512 | 450 | 62 | 40.2 | 1 281 | 91 |
| Ossining | 28.6 | 7.1 | 8.0 | 15.1 | 631 | 569 | 62 | 30.4 | 1 269 | 218 |
| Port Chester | 41.6 | 9.8 | 6.8 | 22.5 | 797 | 733 | 63 | 39.0 | 1 382 | 231 |
| Poughkeepsie | 53.3 | 26.1 | 22.6 | 17.7 | 597 | 521 | 76 | 62.9 | 2 122 | 417 |
| Rochester | 1 011.7 | 723.4 | 78.7 | 194.3 | 940 | 858 | 81 | 997.5 | 4 824 | 362 |
| Rome | 43.7 | 13.5 | 82.0 | 23.1 | 681 | 397 | 284 | 48.9 | 1 444 | 224 |
| Saratoga Springs | 43.0 | 4.6 | 55.8 | 29.2 | 1 015 | 588 | 426 | 45.6 | 1 583 | 140 |
| Schenectady | 90.5 | 29.5 | 41.4 | 35.3 | 574 | 508 | 65 | 85.9 | 1 396 | 174 |
| Spring Valley | 32.0 | 12.2 | 10.0 | 18.1 | 688 | 648 | 39 | 31.8 | 1 211 | 66 |
| Syracuse | 659.1 | 477.0 | 77.1 | 87.8 | 631 | 576 | 56 | 634.1 | 4 559 | 188 |
| Troy | 81.1 | 33.4 | 42.2 | 21.3 | 447 | 383 | 64 | 75.5 | 1 582 | 111 |
| Utica | 74.3 | 27.8 | 66.9 | 32.1 | 550 | 305 | 243 | 77.9 | 1 332 | 177 |
| Valley Stream | 30.9 | 2.1 | 55.1 | 24.3 | 698 | 619 | 80 | 30.6 | 878 | 105 |
| Watertown | 44.4 | 27.0 | 26.8 | 9.7 | 352 | 306 | 46 | 51.4 | 1 872 | 416 |
| White Plains | 153.4 | 12.9 | 55.1 | 96.1 | 1 674 | 689 | 985 | 169.2 | 2 948 | 208 |

1. Based on population estimated as of July 1 of the year shown.

| City | Public welfare | Highways | Parking facilities | Education | Health and hospitals | Police protection | Sewerage and sanitation | Parks and recreation | Housing and community development | Interest on debt |
|---|---|---|---|---|---|---|---|---|---|---|
| | | | | | | City government finances, 2006 (cont.) | | | | |
| | | | | | | General expenditure (cont.) | | | | |
| | | | | | | Percent of total for: | | | | |
| | 127 | 128 | 129 | 130 | 131 | 132 | 133 | 134 | 135 | 136 |
| NEW JERSEY—Cont'd | | | | | | | | | | |
| Garfield | 0.0 | 11.0 | 0.0 | 0.0 | 1.3 | 25.3 | 12.8 | 3.0 | 12.0 | 2.1 |
| Hackensack | 0.4 | 5.4 | 1.1 | 0.0 | 1.3 | 22.1 | 8.7 | 3.3 | 9.7 | 1.6 |
| Hoboken | 0.0 | 1.7 | 9.2 | 0.0 | 0.7 | 15.8 | 5.3 | 2.2 | 16.4 | 3.1 |
| Jersey City | 0.0 | 2.0 | 1.3 | 0.0 | 1.8 | 16.7 | 12.3 | 2.2 | 14.8 | 5.1 |
| Kearny | 0.0 | 7.8 | 0.0 | 0.0 | 1.0 | 22.0 | 14.5 | 1.6 | 0.0 | 2.5 |
| Linden | 0.5 | 3.5 | 0.1 | 0.0 | 1.4 | 17.2 | 9.9 | 4.1 | 1.8 | 2.1 |
| Long Branch | 0.0 | 2.7 | 0.0 | 0.0 | 1.2 | 16.7 | 11.7 | 3.0 | 25.7 | 4.1 |
| Millville | 0.0 | 4.6 | 0.0 | 0.0 | 0.3 | 15.8 | 12.3 | 1.9 | 7.5 | 1.7 |
| Newark | 0.7 | 0.9 | 0.1 | 0.0 | 4.7 | 19.6 | 10.4 | 2.0 | 20.0 | 1.8 |
| New Brunswick | 0.0 | 0.8 | 2.5 | 58.4 | 0.3 | 5.9 | 3.1 | 0.8 | 8.7 | 3.9 |
| Paramus | 0.1 | 3.3 | 0.0 | 0.0 | 1.8 | 22.0 | 8.9 | 4.9 | 0.0 | 3.0 |
| Passaic | 0.0 | 2.6 | 0.2 | 0.0 | 2.2 | 16.8 | 10.0 | 1.2 | 21.2 | 1.1 |
| Paterson | 0.0 | 2.1 | 5.9 | 0.0 | 3.5 | 17.7 | 10.4 | 2.0 | 10.5 | 1.8 |
| Perth Amboy | 0.0 | 12.9 | 0.4 | 0.0 | 1.4 | 11.3 | 6.1 | 1.7 | 11.1 | 3.1 |
| Plainfield | 0.7 | 4.0 | 0.0 | 0.0 | 1.7 | 15.7 | 21.2 | 1.3 | 12.0 | 2.7 |
| Rahway | 0.0 | 11.4 | 0.0 | 0.0 | 1.7 | 17.5 | 11.0 | 2.9 | 9.2 | 3.0 |
| Sayreville | 0.0 | 6.0 | 0.0 | 0.0 | 0.7 | 22.6 | 14.8 | 3.5 | 10.0 | 2.1 |
| Trenton | 0.1 | 0.7 | 0.3 | 61.0 | 0.8 | 7.1 | 3.6 | 0.8 | 3.7 | 1.8 |
| Union City | 0.0 | 1.4 | 0.8 | 62.5 | 0.7 | 7.2 | 2.7 | 1.3 | 4.6 | 1.3 |
| Vineland | 0.0 | 4.0 | 0.0 | 0.0 | 5.6 | 14.9 | 10.6 | 0.8 | 6.9 | 2.3 |
| Westfield | 0.3 | 16.7 | 0.7 | 0.0 | 2.6 | 19.1 | 6.2 | 3.4 | 0.0 | 1.4 |
| West New York | 0.0 | 1.8 | 1.3 | 59.3 | 0.4 | 5.9 | 1.9 | 1.8 | 6.4 | 0.8 |
| NEW MEXICO | X | X | X | X | X | X | X | X | X | X |
| Alamogordo | 6.0 | 11.1 | 0.0 | 0.0 | 0.0 | 17.6 | 13.8 | 15.8 | 1.5 | 2.2 |
| Albuquerque | 3.0 | 12.3 | 0.4 | 0.0 | 1.8 | 19.8 | 10.4 | 12.1 | 5.1 | 4.3 |
| Carlsbad | 0.0 | 13.6 | 0.0 | 0.0 | 0.6 | 16.3 | 14.7 | 13.0 | 0.2 | 0.5 |
| Clovis | 0.0 | 17.3 | 0.0 | 0.0 | 0.2 | 18.1 | 17.8 | 6.2 | 0.0 | 1.1 |
| Farmington | 0.0 | 11.9 | 0.0 | 0.0 | 1.0 | 14.4 | 7.7 | 13.8 | 0.0 | 11.5 |
| Hobbs | 0.0 | 16.3 | 0.0 | 0.0 | 0.0 | 18.6 | 19.9 | 8.2 | 0.2 | 0.0 |
| Las Cruces | 2.6 | 7.4 | 0.0 | 0.0 | 5.7 | 14.3 | 17.0 | 7.7 | 2.1 | 2.6 |
| Rio Rancho | 0.9 | 19.7 | 0.0 | 0.0 | 0.0 | 10.8 | 8.5 | 9.2 | 0.5 | 2.5 |
| Roswell | 0.0 | 8.4 | 0.0 | 0.0 | 0.8 | 13.7 | 23.6 | 10.3 | 0.6 | 1.8 |
| Santa Fe | 3.4 | 10.3 | 2.6 | 0.0 | 0.0 | 14.7 | 9.7 | 12.0 | 5.5 | 9.5 |
| NEW YORK | X | X | X | X | X | X | X | X | X | X |
| Albany | 0.0 | 4.3 | 0.0 | 0.0 | 0.2 | 20.8 | 5.5 | 3.2 | 16.4 | 13.7 |
| Auburn | 0.0 | 8.6 | 0.7 | 0.0 | 0.1 | 13.7 | 17.6 | 3.7 | 3.9 | 6.0 |
| Binghamton | 0.0 | 9.8 | 0.7 | 0.0 | 0.2 | 12.1 | 24.1 | 3.7 | 7.5 | 4.0 |
| Buffalo | 0.0 | 3.4 | 0.1 | 60.6 | 0.1 | 5.4 | 4.3 | 0.2 | 4.1 | 2.4 |
| Elmira | 0.0 | 10.1 | 1.0 | 0.0 | 0.5 | 20.0 | 3.6 | 3.4 | 3.5 | 3.8 |
| Freeport | 0.0 | 15.7 | 0.1 | 0.0 | 0.0 | 19.3 | 8.1 | 6.0 | 1.6 | 3.8 |
| Glen Cove | 0.0 | 19.5 | 0.0 | 0.0 | 0.3 | 20.5 | 13.1 | 6.5 | 8.1 | 6.2 |
| Harrison | 0.0 | 6.4 | 0.0 | 0.0 | 0.0 | 3.1 | 25.9 | 12.0 | 0.0 | 11.8 |
| Hempstead | 0.0 | 5.1 | 0.5 | 0.0 | 0.0 | 31.2 | 4.8 | 3.7 | 3.7 | 4.0 |
| Ithaca | 0.0 | 20.7 | 2.7 | 0.0 | 0.1 | 12.4 | 13.2 | 7.8 | 3.7 | 4.3 |
| Jamestown | 0.0 | 5.6 | 0.1 | 50.0 | 0.1 | 7.1 | 7.7 | 2.3 | 0.0 | 1.1 |
| Lindenhurst | 0.0 | 28.4 | 0.3 | 0.0 | 0.0 | 0.0 | 5.8 | 8.6 | 1.9 | 1.9 |
| Long Beach | 0.0 | 2.0 | 0.0 | 0.0 | 0.1 | 10.7 | 8.8 | 5.6 | 0.0 | 1.5 |
| Middletown | 0.0 | 7.1 | 0.0 | 0.0 | 0.0 | 19.3 | 14.2 | 4.6 | 6.0 | 5.2 |
| Mount Vernon | 0.0 | 3.4 | 0.0 | 0.0 | 0.4 | 19.2 | 6.7 | 3.8 | 6.4 | 3.0 |
| Newburgh | 0.0 | 5.1 | 0.2 | 0.0 | 0.2 | 25.5 | 10.3 | 4.4 | 1.1 | 7.2 |
| New Rochelle | 0.0 | 7.1 | 1.1 | 0.0 | 0.5 | 22.0 | 6.0 | 2.6 | 12.2 | 5.6 |
| New York | 15.7 | 1.4 | 0.0 | 27.5 | 10.1 | 5.7 | 5.1 | 1.3 | 5.4 | 4.9 |
| Niagara Falls | 0.0 | 6.2 | 0.6 | 0.0 | 0.1 | 17.7 | 3.6 | 2.3 | 9.6 | 1.4 |
| North Tonawanda | 0.0 | 10.6 | 0.0 | 0.0 | 0.1 | 11.4 | 12.9 | 4.6 | 0.9 | 1.4 |
| Ossining | 0.0 | 7.1 | 0.1 | 0.0 | 0.3 | 22.6 | 6.5 | 18.1 | 6.8 | 3.5 |
| Port Chester | 0.0 | 4.2 | 0.0 | 0.0 | 0.6 | 17.0 | 6.0 | 5.9 | 8.0 | 5.7 |
| Poughkeepsie | 0.0 | 5.2 | 0.9 | 0.0 | 0.3 | 18.2 | 12.2 | 1.4 | 7.2 | 4.8 |
| Rochester | 0.0 | 2.0 | 0.2 | 58.9 | 0.1 | 6.9 | 2.3 | 1.9 | 1.3 | 1.8 |
| Rome | 0.0 | 20.3 | 0.7 | 0.0 | 0.2 | 14.0 | 8.0 | 2.8 | 2.2 | 3.1 |
| Saratoga Springs | 0.0 | 9.1 | 0.3 | 0.0 | 0.0 | 14.0 | 8.6 | 20.8 | 0.6 | 1.9 |
| Schenectady | 0.0 | 5.6 | 0.7 | 0.0 | 0.1 | 18.1 | 14.6 | 2.2 | 4.4 | 7.0 |
| Spring Valley | 0.0 | 3.7 | 0.1 | 0.0 | 0.2 | 23.0 | 0.2 | 1.8 | 28.4 | 2.4 |
| Syracuse | 0.0 | 3.3 | 0.0 | 56.8 | 0.1 | 6.8 | 1.6 | 1.2 | 1.1 | 4.5 |
| Troy | 0.0 | 5.0 | 0.0 | 0.0 | 0.2 | 18.3 | 6.6 | 3.4 | 4.1 | 21.2 |
| Utica | 0.0 | 8.1 | 0.6 | 0.0 | 0.1 | 16.6 | 4.2 | 5.0 | 10.3 | 8.9 |
| Valley Stream | 0.0 | 18.3 | 0.7 | 0.0 | 0.6 | 0.7 | 13.7 | 10.5 | 0.0 | 3.8 |
| Watertown | 0.0 | 24.2 | 0.1 | 0.0 | 0.2 | 12.7 | 8.3 | 3.1 | 2.1 | 4.2 |
| White Plains | 0.0 | 9.3 | 9.8 | 0.0 | 0.0 | 17.1 | 5.2 | 4.9 | 4.0 | 2.1 |

| | City government finances, 2007 (cont.) | | | | Climate[2] | | | | | | |
|---|---|---|---|---|---|---|---|---|---|---|---|
| | Debt outstanding | | | | Average daily temperature (degrees Fahrenheit) | | | | | | |
| | | | | | Mean | | Limits | | | | |
| City | Total (mil dol) | Per capita[1] (dollars) | Debt issued during year | City government employment, 2011 | January | July | January[3] | July[4] | Annual precipitation (inches) | Heating degree days | Cooling degree days |
| | 137 | 138 | 139 | 140 | 141 | 142 | 143 | 144 | 145 | 146 | 147 |
| **NEW JERSEY— Cont'd** | | | | | | | | | | | |
| Garfield | 20.8 | 712 | 1.0 | 182 | 28.6 | 75.0 | 19.5 | 85.5 | 51.50 | 5 522 | 824 |
| Hackensack | 23.6 | 548 | 0.0 | 458 | 28.6 | 75.0 | 19.5 | 85.5 | 51.50 | 5 522 | 824 |
| Hoboken | 93.3 | 2 301 | 0.0 | 760 | 29.6 | 75.3 | 22.7 | 82.5 | 46.33 | 5 367 | 882 |
| Jersey City | 716.2 | 2 955 | 105.5 | 3 287 | 29.6 | 75.3 | 22.7 | 82.5 | 46.33 | 5 367 | 882 |
| Kearny | 59.5 | 1 595 | 12.6 | NA | 31.3 | 77.2 | 24.4 | 85.2 | 46.25 | 4 843 | 1 220 |
| Linden | 28.3 | 718 | 9.5 | 625 | 28.5 | 74.0 | 18.2 | 85.8 | 51.61 | 5 595 | 757 |
| Long Branch | 66.0 | 2 041 | 24.3 | NA | 31.7 | 74.1 | 22.8 | 82.6 | 48.63 | 5 168 | 750 |
| Millville | 29.8 | 1 047 | 0.0 | 271 | 32.7 | 76.3 | 24.1 | 85.9 | 43.20 | 4 835 | 1 009 |
| Newark | 469.8 | 1 677 | 0.7 | 3 803 | 31.3 | 77.2 | 24.4 | 85.2 | 46.25 | 4 843 | 1 220 |
| New Brunswick | 236.9 | 4 688 | 24.2 | 1 970 | 29.7 | 74.8 | 21.1 | 85.4 | 48.78 | 5 346 | 816 |
| Paramus | 44.8 | 1 706 | 0.0 | NA | 28.6 | 75.0 | 19.5 | 85.5 | 51.50 | 5 522 | 824 |
| Passaic | 26.3 | 391 | 0.0 | 596 | 28.6 | 75.0 | 19.5 | 85.5 | 51.50 | 5 522 | 824 |
| Paterson | 97.6 | 666 | 0.0 | 1 779 | 28.6 | 75.0 | 19.5 | 85.5 | 51.50 | 5 522 | 824 |
| Perth Amboy | 134.8 | 2 758 | 49.9 | 393 | 29.7 | 74.8 | 21.1 | 85.4 | 48.78 | 5 346 | 816 |
| Plainfield | 40.9 | 879 | 0.4 | 587 | 30.0 | 74.9 | 21.5 | 86.6 | 49.63 | 5 266 | 854 |
| Rahway | 48.6 | 1 726 | 8.8 | 294 | 29.6 | 74.5 | 19.8 | 85.7 | 50.94 | 5 450 | 787 |
| Sayreville | 29.8 | 703 | 5.0 | 255 | 29.7 | 74.8 | 21.1 | 85.4 | 48.78 | 5 346 | 816 |
| Trenton | 365.0 | 4 408 | 52.6 | 2 835 | 30.4 | 75.2 | 21.3 | 86.9 | 48.83 | 5 262 | 903 |
| Union City | 77.1 | 1 230 | 33.6 | 2 217 | 29.6 | 75.3 | 22.7 | 82.5 | 46.33 | 5 367 | 882 |
| Vineland | 86.3 | 1 475 | 23.4 | 690 | 26.7 | 70.4 | 16.8 | 81.7 | 53.28 | 6 281 | 438 |
| Westfield | 16.9 | 571 | 0.0 | NA | 30.0 | 74.9 | 21.5 | 86.6 | 49.63 | 5 266 | 854 |
| West New York | 54.3 | 1 170 | 31.1 | 1 373 | 29.6 | 75.3 | 22.7 | 82.5 | 46.33 | 5 367 | 882 |
| **NEW MEXICO** | X | X | X | X | X | X | X | X | X | X | X |
| Alamogordo | 29.7 | 834 | 1.5 | 327 | 42.2 | 79.7 | 28.9 | 93.0 | 13.20 | 31 | 1 715 |
| Albuquerque | 952.1 | 1 837 | 162.5 | 6 502 | 35.7 | 78.5 | 23.8 | 92.3 | 9.47 | 4 281 | 1 290 |
| Carlsbad | 21.7 | 865 | 0.0 | 383 | 42.5 | 81.7 | 27.5 | 95.8 | 14.15 | 2 823 | 2 029 |
| Clovis | 17.4 | 524 | 0.0 | 380 | 37.9 | 77.5 | 25.0 | 91.0 | 18.50 | 3 955 | 1 305 |
| Farmington | 688.8 | 16 235 | 0.0 | 896 | 29.8 | 74.9 | 17.9 | 90.7 | 8.39 | 5 508 | 805 |
| Hobbs | 15.9 | 536 | 0.1 | 417 | 42.9 | 80.1 | 29.1 | 93.5 | 18.15 | 2 849 | 1 842 |
| Las Cruces | 166.1 | 1 851 | 30.5 | 1 234 | 39.0 | 78.7 | 21.1 | 94.9 | 11.44 | 3 818 | 1 364 |
| Rio Rancho | 211.4 | 2 783 | 35.6 | 637 | 33.8 | 73.9 | 19.7 | 90.0 | 9.28 | 4 981 | 773 |
| Roswell | 60.5 | 1 327 | 0.4 | 539 | 40.0 | 80.8 | 24.4 | 94.8 | 13.34 | 3 332 | 1 814 |
| Santa Fe | 294.9 | 4 029 | 83.3 | 1 503 | 29.3 | 69.8 | 15.5 | 85.6 | 14.22 | 6 073 | 414 |
| **NEW YORK** | X | X | X | X | X | X | X | X | X | X | X |
| Albany | 470.7 | 4 999 | 31.6 | 1 430 | 22.2 | 71.1 | 13.3 | 82.2 | 38.60 | 6 860 | 544 |
| Auburn | 65.3 | 2 390 | 0.0 | 313 | 23.7 | 71.2 | 16.0 | 81.5 | 36.98 | 6 694 | 528 |
| Binghamton | 114.4 | 2 541 | 0.0 | 579 | 21.7 | 68.7 | 15.0 | 78.1 | 38.65 | 7 237 | 396 |
| Buffalo | 666.0 | 2 443 | 70.6 | 9 158 | 24.5 | 70.8 | 17.8 | 79.6 | 40.54 | 6 692 | 548 |
| Elmira | 48.3 | 1 641 | 5.2 | 315 | 23.9 | 70.3 | 15.0 | 82.3 | 34.95 | 6 806 | 446 |
| Freeport | 146.6 | 3 457 | 1.0 | 385 | 30.7 | 73.8 | 24.2 | 81.0 | 42.97 | 5 504 | 779 |
| Glen Cove | 81.1 | 3 112 | 0.0 | NA | 31.9 | 74.2 | 25.4 | 82.8 | 46.36 | 5 231 | 839 |
| Harrison | 53.4 | 2 016 | 8.9 | NA | NA | NA | NA | NA | NA | NA | NA |
| Hempstead | 45.3 | 875 | 13.9 | 458 | 31.9 | 74.2 | 25.4 | 82.8 | 46.36 | 5 231 | 839 |
| Ithaca | 64.7 | 2 158 | 0.0 | 441 | 22.6 | 68.7 | 13.9 | 80.1 | 36.71 | 7 182 | 312 |
| Jamestown | 42.8 | 1 449 | 24.7 | 622 | 22.3 | 69.2 | 14.1 | 80.1 | 45.68 | 7 048 | 389 |
| Lindenhurst | 6.6 | 239 | 1.9 | NA | 30.7 | 73.8 | 24.2 | 81.0 | 42.97 | 5 504 | 779 |
| Long Beach | 41.8 | 1 207 | 5.6 | 475 | 31.8 | 74.8 | 24.7 | 82.9 | 42.46 | 4 947 | 949 |
| Middletown | 48.3 | 1 869 | 3.7 | NA | 26.5 | 73.0 | 17.5 | 84.0 | 44.00 | 5 820 | 674 |
| Mount Vernon | 49.5 | 729 | 0.0 | 830 | 29.7 | 74.2 | 20.1 | 86.0 | 46.46 | 5 400 | 770 |
| Newburgh | 76.2 | 2 702 | 0.0 | NA | 26.6 | 74.3 | 17.1 | 84.9 | 45.79 | 5 813 | 790 |
| New Rochelle | 157.0 | 2 143 | 19.0 | 645 | 29.7 | 74.2 | 20.1 | 86.0 | 46.46 | 5 400 | 770 |
| New York | 90 693.9 | 10 961 | 12 027.4 | 399 928 | 32.1 | 76.5 | 26.2 | 84.2 | 49.69 | 4 754 | 1 151 |
| Niagara Falls | 33.4 | 647 | 9.4 | 821 | 24.2 | 71.4 | 16.8 | 81.8 | 33.93 | 6 752 | 508 |
| North Tonawanda | 16.7 | 533 | 5.3 | NA | 24.2 | 71.4 | 16.8 | 81.8 | 33.93 | 6 752 | 508 |
| Ossining | 26.9 | 1 124 | 0.0 | NA | NA | NA | NA | NA | NA | NA | NA |
| Port Chester | 45.4 | 1 611 | 3.1 | NA | 28.4 | 73.8 | 21.0 | 82.5 | 50.45 | 5 660 | 716 |
| Poughkeepsie | 77.1 | 2 600 | 4.8 | 455 | 24.5 | 71.9 | 14.7 | 83.6 | 44.12 | 6 438 | 550 |
| Rochester | 355.2 | 1 718 | 0.0 | 9 592 | 23.9 | 70.7 | 16.6 | 81.4 | 33.98 | 6 728 | 576 |
| Rome | 50.6 | 1 495 | 7.5 | 370 | 20.8 | 70.2 | 11.9 | 81.3 | 46.27 | 7 146 | 416 |
| Saratoga Springs | 25.0 | 869 | 8.5 | NA | 20.9 | 71.2 | 11.6 | 83.0 | 43.31 | 6 904 | 477 |
| Schenectady | 143.5 | 2 332 | 31.7 | 627 | 22.2 | 71.1 | 13.3 | 82.2 | 38.60 | 6 860 | 544 |
| Spring Valley | 16.0 | 607 | 0.9 | NA | 27.3 | 73.1 | 18.2 | 83.8 | 51.01 | 5 809 | 642 |
| Syracuse | 654.6 | 4 707 | 20.8 | 8 711 | 22.7 | 70.9 | 14.0 | 81.7 | 40.05 | 6 803 | 551 |
| Troy | 290.0 | 6 074 | 0.0 | 592 | 22.2 | 71.1 | 13.3 | 82.2 | 38.60 | 6 860 | 544 |
| Utica | 133.1 | 2 277 | 22.4 | 620 | 22.2 | 70.5 | 12.6 | 83.2 | 41.90 | 6 855 | 441 |
| Valley Stream | 29.7 | 851 | 0.0 | NA | 22.2 | 70.5 | 12.6 | 83.2 | 41.90 | 6 855 | 441 |
| Watertown | 36.2 | 1 319 | 0.0 | NA | 18.6 | 70.2 | 9.1 | 79.4 | 42.57 | 7 517 | 421 |
| White Plains | 77.4 | 1 348 | 24.0 | 972 | 29.7 | 74.2 | 20.1 | 86.0 | 46.46 | 5 400 | 770 |

1. Based on the population estimated as of July 1 of the year shown.    2. Represents normal values based on the 30-year period, 1971–2000.    3. Average daily minimum.    4. Average daily maximum.

# Table D. Cities — Land Area and Population

| STATE Place code | City | Land area,[1] 2010 (sq km) | Population, 2012 | | | Race alone or in combination, not of Hispanic origin (percent), 2010 | | | | | Percent Hispanic or Latino[2], 2010 | Percent Foreign born 2007–2011 |
|---|---|---|---|---|---|---|---|---|---|---|---|---|
| | | | Total persons | Rank | Per square kilometer | White | Black | American Indian, Alaska Native | Asian | Hawaiian Pacific Islander | | |
| | | 1 | 2 | 3 | 4 | 5 | 6 | 7 | 8 | 9 | 10 | 11 |
| 37 00000 | NORTH CAROLINA... | 125 919.8 | 9 752 073 | X | 77.4 | 66.6 | 22.1 | 1.7 | 2.6 | 0.1 | 8.4 | 7.4 |
| 37 01520 | Apex | 39.8 | 40 420 | 896 | 1 015.6 | 77.7 | 8.2 | 0.7 | 8.1 | 0.1 | 7.1 | 12.2 |
| 37 02080 | Asheboro | 48.0 | 25 559 | 1 414 | 532.5 | 59.5 | 12.7 | 0.8 | 1.5 | 0.1 | 26.9 | 16.2 |
| 37 02140 | Asheville | 116.4 | 85 712 | 360 | 736.4 | 78.1 | 14.4 | 1.0 | 1.8 | 0.2 | 6.5 | 7.3 |
| 37 09060 | Burlington | 65.2 | 51 306 | 710 | 786.9 | 53.5 | 28.8 | 0.8 | 2.3 | 0.1 | 16.0 | 9.9 |
| 37 10740 | Cary | 140.8 | 145 693 | 171 | 1 034.8 | 70.7 | 8.5 | 0.7 | 14.2 | 0.1 | 7.7 | 18.4 |
| 37 11800 | Chapel Hill | 54.7 | 58 424 | 603 | 1 068.1 | 71.5 | 10.3 | 0.7 | 13.1 | 0.1 | 6.4 | 16.8 |
| 37 12000 | Charlotte | 771.0 | 775 202 | 17 | 1 005.5 | 46.4 | 35.6 | 0.8 | 5.5 | 0.1 | 13.1 | 14.7 |
| 37 14100 | Concord | 156.1 | 81 981 | 385 | 525.2 | 67.0 | 18.4 | 0.7 | 3.0 | 0.1 | 12.3 | 10.0 |
| 37 19000 | Durham | 278.1 | 239 358 | 83 | 860.7 | 39.2 | 41.6 | 0.8 | 5.6 | 0.1 | 14.2 | 14.6 |
| 37 22920 | Fayetteville | 377.7 | 202 103 | 107 | 535.1 | 44.1 | 43.1 | 2.1 | 3.7 | 0.7 | 10.1 | 6.4 |
| 37 25480 | Garner | 38.2 | 26 732 | 1 362 | 699.8 | 55.0 | 33.5 | 0.9 | 2.2 | 0.1 | 9.9 | 6.3 |
| 37 25580 | Gastonia | 130.8 | 72 723 | 455 | 556.0 | 60.9 | 28.6 | 0.8 | 1.6 | 0.1 | 9.6 | 8.1 |
| 37 26880 | Goldsboro | 72.9 | 37 051 | 982 | 508.2 | 39.1 | 55.2 | 0.8 | 2.6 | 0.2 | 4.3 | 3.2 |
| 37 28000 | Greensboro | 327.7 | 277 080 | 69 | 845.5 | 47.1 | 41.6 | 1.1 | 4.5 | 0.1 | 7.5 | 10.0 |
| 37 28080 | Greenville | 89.6 | 87 242 | 350 | 973.7 | 56.3 | 37.8 | 0.8 | 3.0 | 0.1 | 3.8 | 4.5 |
| 37 31060 | Hickory | 76.9 | 40 093 | 911 | 521.4 | 70.9 | 15.3 | 0.5 | 3.5 | 0.1 | 11.4 | 9.8 |
| 37 31400 | High Point | 139.4 | 106 586 | 260 | 764.6 | 51.8 | 33.7 | 0.9 | 6.5 | 0.1 | 8.5 | 11.9 |
| 37 33120 | Huntersville | 102.6 | 49 344 | 745 | 480.9 | 80.2 | 10.0 | 0.7 | 3.3 | 0.1 | 7.4 | 7.5 |
| 37 33560 | Indian Trail | 56.2 | 34 800 | 1 050 | 619.2 | 76.7 | 10.5 | 0.9 | 2.2 | 0.1 | 10.9 | 10.1 |
| 37 34200 | Jacksonville | 120.5 | 69 220 | 481 | 574.4 | 63.9 | 21.2 | 1.3 | 3.6 | 0.5 | 13.0 | 4.9 |
| 37 35200 | Kannapolis | 82.7 | 43 782 | 832 | 529.4 | 66.2 | 21.1 | 0.8 | 1.4 | 0.0 | 12.1 | 6.6 |
| 37 41960 | Matthews | 44.3 | 28 699 | 1 266 | 647.8 | 79.8 | 10.2 | 0.6 | 4.8 | 0.1 | 5.8 | 8.3 |
| 37 43920 | Monroe | 77.1 | 33 641 | 1 085 | 436.3 | 44.2 | 25.8 | 0.6 | 1.1 | 0.0 | 29.4 | 18.3 |
| 37 44220 | Mooresville | 54.2 | 33 451 | 1 090 | 617.2 | 78.4 | 11.8 | 0.9 | 3.8 | 0.1 | 6.9 | 5.1 |
| 37 46340 | New Bern | 73.1 | 30 316 | 1 204 | 414.7 | 57.1 | 33.8 | 0.8 | 4.2 | 0.2 | 5.8 | 4.5 |
| 37 55000 | Raleigh | 370.1 | 423 179 | 42 | 1 143.4 | 54.8 | 29.8 | 0.7 | 5.0 | 0.1 | 11.4 | 14.2 |
| 37 57500 | Rocky Mount | 113.4 | 57 136 | 623 | 503.8 | 33.3 | 61.9 | 1.1 | 1.2 | 0.1 | 3.7 | 3.7 |
| 37 58860 | Salisbury | 57.4 | 33 622 | 1 086 | 585.7 | 49.8 | 38.3 | 0.8 | 1.8 | 0.1 | 10.6 | 7.6 |
| 37 59280 | Sanford | 69.4 | 29 064 | 1 256 | 418.8 | 45.3 | 28.0 | 0.8 | 1.4 | 0.1 | 25.6 | 16.1 |
| 37 67240 | Thomasville | 43.4 | 26 841 | 1 357 | 618.5 | 64.4 | 20.2 | 1.0 | 1.3 | 0.0 | 14.4 | 10.3 |
| 37 70540 | Wake Forest | 39.1 | 32 936 | 1 105 | 842.4 | 75.7 | 16.0 | 0.9 | 3.6 | 0.1 | 5.6 | 8.9 |
| 37 74440 | Wilmington | 133.4 | 109 922 | 243 | 824.0 | 72.3 | 20.5 | 1.0 | 1.7 | 0.1 | 6.1 | 6.0 |
| 37 74540 | Wilson | 74.5 | 49 610 | 737 | 665.9 | 41.3 | 48.4 | 0.5 | 1.4 | 0.1 | 9.4 | 7.7 |
| 37 75000 | Winston-Salem | 343.0 | 234 349 | 85 | 683.2 | 48.4 | 35.1 | 0.8 | 2.4 | 0.1 | 14.7 | 11.0 |
| 38 00000 | NORTH DAKOTA...... | 178 711.2 | 699 628 | X | 3.9 | 90.3 | 1.6 | 6.2 | 1.3 | 0.1 | 2.0 | 2.5 |
| 38 07200 | Bismarck | 79.9 | 64 751 | 527 | 810.4 | 92.9 | 1.0 | 5.2 | 0.8 | 0.1 | 1.3 | 1.3 |
| 38 25700 | Fargo | 126.5 | 109 779 | 245 | 867.8 | 90.6 | 3.3 | 2.0 | 3.5 | 0.1 | 2.2 | 6.0 |
| 38 32060 | Grand Forks | 51.6 | 53 456 | 675 | 1 036.0 | 90.1 | 2.6 | 3.8 | 2.8 | 0.1 | 2.8 | 3.8 |
| 38 53380 | Minot | 45.1 | 43 746 | 837 | 970.0 | 90.9 | 3.0 | 4.2 | 1.4 | 0.2 | 2.7 | 2.9 |
| 38 84780 | West Fargo | 37.4 | 27 478 | 1 320 | 734.7 | 93.7 | 2.4 | 1.6 | 1.8 | 0.1 | 1.8 | 4.0 |
| 39 00000 | OHIO ...... | 105 828.7 | 11 544 225 | X | 109.1 | 82.7 | 13.1 | 0.7 | 2.0 | 0.1 | 3.1 | 3.9 |
| 39 01000 | Akron | 160.7 | 198 549 | 114 | 1 235.5 | 63.7 | 33.3 | 1.0 | 2.5 | 0.1 | 2.1 | 4.2 |
| 39 03828 | Barberton | 23.4 | 26 316 | 1 380 | 1 124.6 | 92.1 | 7.2 | 0.9 | 0.5 | 0.1 | 1.4 | 2.1 |
| 39 04720 | Beavercreek | 68.4 | 45 780 | 804 | 669.3 | 88.5 | 3.0 | 0.7 | 6.9 | 0.1 | 2.6 | 7.1 |
| 39 07972 | Bowling Green | 32.5 | 31 384 | 1 153 | 965.7 | 86.4 | 7.1 | 0.7 | 2.6 | 0.1 | 4.8 | 4.7 |
| 39 09680 | Brunswick | 33.5 | 34 364 | 1 066 | 1 025.8 | 95.0 | 1.6 | 0.5 | 1.5 | 0.1 | 2.3 | 3.7 |
| 39 12000 | Canton | 66.0 | 72 683 | 456 | 1 101.3 | 72.0 | 27.5 | 1.5 | 0.6 | 0.1 | 2.6 | 2.2 |
| 39 15000 | Cincinnati | 201.9 | 296 550 | 65 | 1 468.8 | 50.0 | 46.2 | 0.8 | 2.3 | 0.1 | 2.8 | 4.9 |
| 39 16000 | Cleveland | 201.2 | 390 928 | 48 | 1 943.0 | 34.9 | 53.9 | 0.8 | 2.1 | 0.1 | 10.0 | 4.7 |
| 39 16014 | Cleveland Heights | 21.0 | 45 475 | 809 | 2 165.5 | 50.9 | 43.9 | 0.8 | 4.8 | 0.1 | 2.0 | 8.8 |
| 39 18000 | Columbus | 562.5 | 809 798 | 15 | 1 439.6 | 61.7 | 29.6 | 0.9 | 4.7 | 0.1 | 5.6 | 10.3 |
| 39 19778 | Cuyahoga Falls | 66.4 | 49 245 | 747 | 741.6 | 93.9 | 4.0 | 0.7 | 1.6 | 0.0 | 1.4 | 2.7 |
| 39 21000 | Dayton | 144.1 | 141 359 | 181 | 981.0 | 52.7 | 44.5 | 1.0 | 1.3 | 0.1 | 3.0 | 3.1 |
| 39 21434 | Delaware | 49.1 | 35 925 | 1 017 | 731.7 | 91.2 | 5.8 | 0.7 | 1.7 | 0.1 | 2.5 | 3.2 |
| 39 22694 | Dublin | 63.3 | 42 906 | 850 | 677.8 | 80.7 | 2.1 | 0.3 | 16.4 | 0.1 | 1.8 | 15.1 |
| 39 25256 | Elyria | 53.3 | 54 086 | 669 | 1 014.7 | 78.8 | 17.6 | 1.0 | 1.1 | 0.1 | 4.9 | 1.5 |
| 39 25704 | Euclid | 27.5 | 48 281 | 767 | 1 755.7 | 44.8 | 53.9 | 0.7 | 1.1 | 0.0 | 1.6 | 3.9 |
| 39 25914 | Fairborn | 34.1 | 32 599 | 1 115 | 956.0 | 86.0 | 9.1 | 1.0 | 4.0 | 0.2 | 2.4 | 4.4 |
| 39 25970 | Fairfield | 54.2 | 42 647 | 855 | 786.8 | 78.8 | 13.8 | 0.6 | 2.9 | 0.1 | 5.5 | 8.2 |
| 39 27048 | Findlay | 49.6 | 41 526 | 876 | 837.2 | 89.4 | 2.9 | 0.6 | 2.8 | 0.0 | 5.7 | 4.3 |
| 39 29106 | Gahanna | 32.2 | 33 828 | 1 079 | 1 050.6 | 82.6 | 12.2 | 0.8 | 3.7 | 0.1 | 2.6 | 4.6 |
| 39 29428 | Garfield Heights | 18.7 | 28 454 | 1 277 | 1 521.6 | 60.4 | 36.7 | 0.6 | 1.7 | 0.1 | 2.3 | 3.9 |
| 39 31860 | Green | 83.0 | 25 789 | 1 399 | 310.7 | 95.2 | 2.2 | 0.5 | 1.9 | 0.0 | 1.2 | 3.0 |
| 39 32592 | Grove City | 42.0 | 36 832 | 993 | 877.0 | 93.0 | 3.7 | 0.8 | 1.8 | 0.1 | 2.6 | 2.1 |
| 39 33012 | Hamilton | 55.9 | 62 295 | 552 | 1 114.4 | 84.2 | 10.0 | 0.7 | 0.9 | 0.1 | 6.4 | 4.5 |
| 39 35476 | Hilliard | 34.1 | 30 564 | 1 192 | 896.3 | 88.8 | 3.7 | 0.4 | 6.3 | 0.1 | 2.3 | 5.4 |
| 39 36610 | Huber Heights | 57.7 | 38 129 | 962 | 660.8 | 80.7 | 14.9 | 0.8 | 3.4 | 0.2 | 3.1 | 5.3 |
| 39 39872 | Kent | 23.8 | 29 807 | 1 223 | 1 252.4 | 84.0 | 11.2 | 0.8 | 4.3 | 0.1 | 2.2 | 5.3 |

1. Dry land or land partially or temporarily covered by water.   2. May be of any race.

# Table D. Cities — **Population**

| City | Age of population (percent), 2010 | | | | | | | | | Median age | Percent female | Population — Census counts | | Percent change | |
|---|---|---|---|---|---|---|---|---|---|---|---|---|---|---|---|
| | Under 5 years | 5 to 17 years | 18 to 24 years | 25 to 34 years | 35 to 44 years | 45 to 54 years | 55 to 64 years | 65 to 74 years | 75 years and over | | | 2000 | 2010 | 2000–2010 | 2010–2012 |
| | 12 | 13 | 14 | 15 | 16 | 17 | 18 | 19 | 20 | 21 | 22 | 23 | 24 | 25 | 26 |
| NORTH CAROLINA... | 6.6 | 17.3 | 9.8 | 13.1 | 13.9 | 14.4 | 11.9 | 7.3 | 5.6 | 37.4 | 51.3 | 8 049 313 | 9 535 471 | 18.5 | 2.3 |
| Apex | 8.5 | 24.5 | 5.2 | 12.9 | 20.9 | 15.5 | 6.9 | 3.3 | 2.3 | 34.3 | 51.4 | 20 212 | 37 486 | 85.4 | 7.8 |
| Asheboro | 8.6 | 18.5 | 9.6 | 14.7 | 13.7 | 11.7 | 9.4 | 6.8 | 7.1 | 34.0 | 52.4 | 21 672 | 25 184 | 15.4 | 1.5 |
| Asheville | 5.7 | 12.8 | 10.6 | 16.5 | 13.1 | 12.7 | 12.2 | 7.5 | 8.9 | 38.2 | 52.8 | 68 889 | 83 433 | 21.1 | 2.7 |
| Burlington | 7.1 | 17.1 | 8.9 | 12.9 | 13.1 | 13.7 | 11.5 | 7.2 | 8.5 | 38.3 | 53.2 | 44 917 | 50 883 | 11.2 | 0.8 |
| Cary | 7.0 | 20.8 | 6.3 | 13.4 | 17.1 | 16.7 | 10.1 | 5.1 | 3.5 | 36.6 | 51.3 | 94 536 | 135 260 | 43.1 | 7.7 |
| Chapel Hill | 4.2 | 13.2 | 31.5 | 13.1 | 10.5 | 10.4 | 8.0 | 4.6 | 4.6 | 25.6 | 53.4 | 48 715 | 57 233 | 17.5 | 2.1 |
| Charlotte | 7.6 | 17.7 | 10.1 | 17.6 | 15.7 | 13.4 | 9.5 | 4.7 | 3.8 | 33.2 | 51.7 | 540 828 | 735 780 | 35.2 | 5.4 |
| Concord | 8.0 | 20.4 | 7.6 | 14.1 | 16.2 | 13.5 | 9.4 | 5.8 | 4.8 | 34.9 | 51.8 | 55 977 | 79 067 | 41.2 | 3.7 |
| Durham | 7.7 | 15.0 | 13.0 | 19.4 | 14.2 | 12.1 | 9.6 | 4.6 | 4.2 | 32.1 | 52.5 | 187 035 | 228 386 | 22.1 | 4.8 |
| Fayetteville | 8.5 | 17.2 | 14.5 | 16.9 | 11.6 | 12.2 | 9.3 | 5.5 | 4.2 | 29.9 | 51.6 | 121 015 | 200 574 | 65.7 | 0.8 |
| Garner | 7.1 | 17.3 | 7.7 | 14.8 | 15.6 | 14.5 | 11.1 | 6.4 | 5.3 | 37.1 | 52.5 | 17 757 | 25 757 | 45.0 | 3.8 |
| Gastonia | 7.0 | 17.7 | 8.9 | 12.5 | 14.1 | 14.4 | 11.8 | 7.1 | 6.6 | 38.0 | 52.7 | 66 277 | 71 741 | 8.2 | 1.4 |
| Goldsboro | 7.3 | 15.7 | 11.9 | 13.9 | 10.9 | 13.7 | 11.5 | 7.6 | 7.3 | 36.1 | 51.5 | 39 043 | 36 446 | -6.7 | 1.7 |
| Greensboro | 6.5 | 16.2 | 14.5 | 14.9 | 13.2 | 12.8 | 10.5 | 5.9 | 5.6 | 33.4 | 53.0 | 223 891 | 269 668 | 20.4 | 2.7 |
| Greenville | 6.1 | 12.6 | 28.8 | 16.2 | 10.4 | 9.6 | 7.9 | 4.1 | 4.2 | 26.0 | 54.2 | 60 476 | 84 581 | 39.8 | 3.1 |
| Hickory | 6.8 | 16.8 | 10.1 | 12.7 | 13.7 | 13.9 | 11.7 | 7.3 | 7.1 | 37.7 | 52.3 | 37 222 | 40 065 | 7.5 | 0.1 |
| High Point | 7.1 | 18.2 | 10.3 | 13.3 | 14.2 | 14.1 | 10.9 | 6.1 | 5.8 | 35.8 | 53.1 | 85 839 | 104 372 | 21.6 | 2.1 |
| Huntersville | 8.4 | 20.5 | 5.8 | 15.0 | 19.2 | 15.1 | 9.3 | 4.3 | 2.6 | 35.2 | 51.0 | 24 960 | 46 781 | 87.4 | 5.5 |
| Indian Trail | 8.6 | 24.1 | 6.3 | 13.3 | 19.3 | 13.5 | 8.0 | 4.7 | 2.3 | 33.7 | 50.9 | 11 905 | 33 521 | 181.5 | 3.8 |
| Jacksonville | 9.7 | 13.6 | 35.8 | 15.9 | 8.0 | 6.8 | 4.7 | 2.7 | 2.7 | 22.9 | 41.2 | 66 715 | 70 145 | 5.1 | -1.3 |
| Kannapolis | 8.1 | 18.6 | 8.3 | 14.1 | 13.9 | 13.4 | 10.4 | 6.9 | 6.2 | 35.6 | 52.1 | 36 910 | 42 612 | 15.5 | 2.7 |
| Matthews | 5.4 | 19.5 | 7.2 | 10.5 | 14.5 | 17.2 | 12.4 | 6.5 | 6.8 | 40.3 | 51.9 | 22 127 | 27 198 | 22.9 | 5.5 |
| Monroe | 9.2 | 20.4 | 9.4 | 14.8 | 14.5 | 11.7 | 9.0 | 6.0 | 5.1 | 32.5 | 50.8 | 26 228 | 32 797 | 25.0 | 2.6 |
| Mooresville | 6.9 | 21.5 | 9.0 | 13.8 | 16.5 | 14.0 | 8.5 | 5.1 | 4.7 | 34.2 | 51.5 | 18 823 | 32 711 | 73.8 | 2.3 |
| New Bern | 7.5 | 15.3 | 9.5 | 13.6 | 10.7 | 12.9 | 12.5 | 9.0 | 9.0 | 38.8 | 53.3 | 23 128 | 29 554 | 27.7 | 2.6 |
| Raleigh | 7.2 | 15.9 | 13.9 | 18.4 | 15.2 | 12.4 | 8.8 | 4.4 | 3.8 | 31.9 | 51.7 | 276 093 | 403 947 | 46.3 | 4.8 |
| Rocky Mount | 6.7 | 17.9 | 9.3 | 11.9 | 12.2 | 14.8 | 13.1 | 7.6 | 6.6 | 38.7 | 54.2 | 55 893 | 57 471 | 2.8 | -0.6 |
| Salisbury | 7.0 | 15.7 | 12.1 | 13.9 | 11.6 | 12.6 | 11.2 | 7.3 | 8.6 | 36.2 | 50.5 | 26 462 | 33 624 | 27.2 | 0.0 |
| Sanford | 8.5 | 19.5 | 9.4 | 15.0 | 13.5 | 12.6 | 9.8 | 5.8 | 5.9 | 33.3 | 51.5 | 23 220 | 28 093 | 21.0 | 3.5 |
| Thomasville | 7.6 | 18.9 | 8.5 | 13.4 | 14.2 | 13.3 | 10.2 | 6.9 | 7.0 | 36.2 | 52.3 | 19 788 | 26 757 | 35.2 | 0.3 |
| Wake Forest | 9.2 | 23.3 | 6.0 | 13.0 | 19.1 | 13.3 | 8.1 | 4.8 | 3.4 | 34.2 | 51.9 | 12 588 | 30 096 | 139.3 | 9.4 |
| Wilmington | 5.6 | 12.9 | 16.9 | 15.1 | 11.8 | 12.3 | 11.5 | 7.1 | 6.8 | 34.7 | 52.2 | 75 838 | 106 476 | 40.4 | 3.2 |
| Wilson | 7.2 | 18.1 | 9.4 | 12.7 | 12.7 | 13.5 | 12.3 | 7.3 | 6.8 | 37.2 | 53.4 | 44 405 | 49 169 | 10.7 | 0.9 |
| Winston-Salem | 7.3 | 17.2 | 11.9 | 14.0 | 13.0 | 13.3 | 10.8 | 6.3 | 6.2 | 34.6 | 53.0 | 185 776 | 229 626 | 23.6 | 2.1 |
| NORTH DAKOTA | 6.6 | 15.7 | 12.0 | 13.5 | 11.2 | 14.4 | 12.2 | 7.0 | 7.5 | 37.0 | 49.5 | 642 200 | 672 591 | 4.7 | 4.0 |
| Bismarck | 6.4 | 14.4 | 11.0 | 14.9 | 11.2 | 14.5 | 12.3 | 7.2 | 8.1 | 38.0 | 51.4 | 55 532 | 61 290 | 10.3 | 5.6 |
| Fargo | 6.4 | 12.9 | 19.8 | 17.9 | 11.1 | 11.8 | 9.9 | 4.7 | 5.5 | 30.2 | 49.6 | 90 599 | 105 549 | 16.5 | 4.0 |
| Grand Forks | 6.1 | 12.3 | 24.7 | 15.4 | 9.7 | 11.8 | 9.9 | 5.0 | 5.1 | 28.4 | 48.8 | 49 321 | 52 838 | 7.1 | 1.2 |
| Minot | 7.1 | 14.0 | 14.1 | 16.2 | 10.5 | 12.4 | 10.8 | 6.7 | 8.3 | 33.8 | 50.7 | 36 567 | 40 890 | 11.8 | 7.0 |
| West Fargo | 8.7 | 18.2 | 9.3 | 18.0 | 14.9 | 12.9 | 10.1 | 4.5 | 3.3 | 32.6 | 50.4 | 14 940 | 25 830 | 72.9 | 6.4 |
| OHIO | 6.2 | 17.4 | 9.5 | 12.2 | 12.8 | 15.1 | 12.6 | 7.4 | 6.7 | 38.8 | 51.2 | 11 353 140 | 11 536 502 | 1.6 | 0.1 |
| Akron | 6.7 | 16.1 | 12.5 | 13.8 | 12.3 | 14.0 | 11.9 | 6.2 | 6.4 | 35.7 | 51.7 | 217 074 | 199 110 | -8.3 | -0.3 |
| Barberton | 6.6 | 16.9 | 8.2 | 12.5 | 12.2 | 14.2 | 12.8 | 7.5 | 9.0 | 39.8 | 52.1 | 27 899 | 26 554 | -4.8 | -0.9 |
| Beavercreek | 5.3 | 17.4 | 8.6 | 12.4 | 12.4 | 15.7 | 13.9 | 8.1 | 6.2 | 40.4 | 50.1 | 37 984 | 45 193 | 19.0 | 1.3 |
| Bowling Green | 4.1 | 8.7 | 43.2 | 12.2 | 7.2 | 8.0 | 7.7 | 4.2 | 4.7 | 23.2 | 52.0 | 29 636 | 30 043 | 1.3 | 4.5 |
| Brunswick | 5.9 | 19.4 | 7.5 | 11.6 | 15.4 | 15.8 | 12.5 | 7.3 | 4.6 | 39.1 | 50.9 | 33 388 | 34 255 | 2.6 | 0.3 |
| Canton | 7.9 | 17.2 | 10.8 | 13.4 | 12.2 | 14.1 | 11.7 | 6.3 | 6.5 | 35.6 | 52.6 | 80 806 | 73 014 | -9.7 | -0.5 |
| Cincinnati | 7.4 | 14.8 | 14.6 | 16.6 | 11.9 | 13.4 | 10.7 | 5.4 | 5.4 | 32.5 | 52.0 | 331 285 | 296 950 | -10.4 | -0.1 |
| Cleveland | 7.1 | 17.5 | 11.0 | 13.6 | 12.5 | 15.1 | 11.3 | 6.2 | 5.8 | 35.7 | 52.0 | 478 403 | 396 814 | -17.1 | -1.5 |
| Cleveland Heights | 6.1 | 16.2 | 10.5 | 16.0 | 11.8 | 12.6 | 13.2 | 7.4 | 6.1 | 35.8 | 53.4 | 49 958 | 46 121 | -7.7 | -1.4 |
| Columbus | 7.6 | 15.6 | 14.1 | 18.9 | 13.4 | 12.5 | 9.3 | 4.7 | 3.9 | 31.2 | 51.2 | 711 470 | 788 577 | 10.6 | 2.7 |
| Cuyahoga Falls | 5.8 | 15.1 | 8.5 | 15.1 | 12.8 | 14.8 | 12.7 | 7.1 | 8.2 | 39.4 | 52.7 | 49 374 | 49 608 | 0.6 | -0.7 |
| Dayton | 6.9 | 16.0 | 14.2 | 13.5 | 11.8 | 14.2 | 11.5 | 6.2 | 5.6 | 34.4 | 51.3 | 166 179 | 141 762 | -14.8 | -0.3 |
| Delaware | 8.2 | 17.3 | 11.9 | 15.5 | 15.0 | 11.8 | 9.2 | 5.6 | 5.4 | 33.2 | 52.0 | 25 243 | 34 753 | 37.7 | 3.4 |
| Dublin | 6.8 | 23.5 | 4.9 | 9.7 | 17.5 | 17.9 | 11.7 | 4.5 | 3.3 | 38.3 | 50.6 | 31 392 | 41 375 | 33.0 | 3.7 |
| Elyria | 6.9 | 17.3 | 9.0 | 13.0 | 12.7 | 14.4 | 12.3 | 7.1 | 7.2 | 38.1 | 52.2 | 55 953 | 54 533 | -2.5 | -0.8 |
| Euclid | 5.8 | 17.1 | 7.8 | 11.6 | 12.7 | 15.9 | 13.1 | 7.4 | 8.6 | 41.0 | 55.2 | 52 717 | 48 920 | -7.2 | -1.3 |
| Fairborn | 7.0 | 13.5 | 16.7 | 15.8 | 10.5 | 12.7 | 10.7 | 6.9 | 6.3 | 32.4 | 51.1 | 32 052 | 32 352 | 0.9 | 0.8 |
| Fairfield | 6.4 | 16.7 | 8.7 | 14.0 | 13.2 | 15.2 | 12.7 | 7.0 | 6.0 | 38.3 | 51.8 | 42 097 | 42 506 | 1.0 | 0.3 |
| Findlay | 6.7 | 15.5 | 12.9 | 13.8 | 11.6 | 13.4 | 11.5 | 7.2 | 7.3 | 35.9 | 52.4 | 38 967 | 41 193 | 5.7 | 0.8 |
| Gahanna | 5.6 | 19.8 | 7.1 | 12.0 | 13.4 | 17.2 | 13.2 | 6.6 | 5.2 | 39.4 | 52.1 | 32 636 | 33 243 | 1.9 | 1.8 |
| Garfield Heights | 6.2 | 18.8 | 8.5 | 12.1 | 13.0 | 14.5 | 11.5 | 6.6 | 8.9 | 38.5 | 54.0 | 30 734 | 28 849 | -6.1 | -1.4 |
| Green | 5.4 | 18.7 | 7.5 | 9.7 | 13.4 | 16.8 | 13.9 | 7.7 | 6.9 | 41.8 | 51.3 | 22 817 | 25 744 | 12.6 | 0.2 |
| Grove City | 6.2 | 19.2 | 8.4 | 12.4 | 15.0 | 14.9 | 11.8 | 6.4 | 5.8 | 37.8 | 51.7 | 27 075 | 35 577 | 31.4 | 3.5 |
| Hamilton | 8.1 | 16.7 | 9.5 | 15.3 | 12.3 | 13.7 | 11.2 | 6.3 | 6.9 | 35.3 | 51.2 | 60 690 | 62 327 | 2.9 | -0.1 |
| Hilliard | 7.0 | 23.1 | 6.3 | 12.2 | 16.5 | 17.0 | 9.3 | 4.5 | 4.1 | 35.9 | 51.2 | 24 230 | 28 234 | 17.4 | 8.3 |
| Huber Heights | 6.8 | 18.6 | 8.3 | 13.3 | 13.0 | 14.4 | 12.7 | 7.7 | 5.2 | 37.4 | 51.7 | 38 212 | 38 101 | -0.3 | 0.1 |
| Kent | 4.2 | 9.9 | 44.0 | 11.6 | 7.6 | 7.9 | 7.4 | 3.5 | 3.9 | 22.7 | 53.7 | 27 906 | 28 906 | 3.6 | 3.1 |

| City | Households, 2010 Number | Persons per house-hold | Percent Female family house-holder[1] | Percent One-person | Persons in group quarters, 2010 Total | Institutional Total | Persons in nursing facilities | Non-institutional | Serious crimes known to police,[2] 2011 Total Number | Total Rate[3] | Rate[3] Violent | Rate[3] Property | Population age 25 and older | Attainment[4] (percent) High school graduate or less | Attainment[4] (percent) Bachelor's degree or more |
|---|---|---|---|---|---|---|---|---|---|---|---|---|---|---|---|
| | 27 | 28 | 29 | 30 | 31 | 32 | 33 | 34 | 35 | 36 | 37 | 38 | 39 | 40 | 41 |
| NORTH CAROLINA ...... | 3 745 155 | 2.48 | 13.7 | 27.0 | 257 246 | 113 296 | 46 638 | 143 950 | 374 336 | 3 877 | 350 | 3 527 | 6 229 136 | 43.6 | 26.5 |
| Apex.......................... | 13 225 | 2.82 | 9.7 | 20.0 | 121 | 98 | 97 | 23 | 616 | 1 623 | 63 | 1 560 | 22 032 | 13.1 | 61.8 |
| Asheboro.................. | 9 880 | 2.46 | 16.0 | 33.0 | 665 | 565 | 357 | 100 | 1 865 | 7 363 | 288 | 7 075 | 15 798 | 57.7 | 17.4 |
| Asheville.................. | 37 380 | 2.12 | 12.2 | 38.0 | 4 249 | 2 292 | 1 047 | 1 957 | 4 393 | 5 202 | 526 | 4 676 | 57 776 | 31.5 | 39.5 |
| Burlington................ | 20 632 | 2.38 | 17.5 | 33.0 | 906 | 464 | 445 | 442 | 4 074 | 8 052 | 800 | 7 251 | 33 243 | 45.6 | 24.4 |
| Cary........................ | 51 791 | 2.61 | 7.9 | 23.9 | 260 | 211 | 193 | 49 | 2 201 | 1 607 | 79 | 1 528 | 86 735 | 16.1 | 61.6 |
| Chapel Hill.............. | 20 564 | 2.35 | 8.2 | 30.6 | 9 003 | 258 | 227 | 8 745 | 1 629 | 2 811 | 183 | 2 628 | 27 835 | 14.0 | 73.2 |
| Charlotte.................. | 289 860 | 2.48 | 15.6 | 30.3 | 13 369 | 5 104 | 2 595 | 8 265 | 36 795 | 4 661 | 606 | 4 054 | 467 711 | 32.3 | 39.6 |
| Concord................... | 29 137 | 2.68 | 13.5 | 23.5 | 893 | 797 | 431 | 96 | 3 204 | 4 002 | 116 | 3 885 | 49 586 | 40.3 | 26.3 |
| Durham.................... | 93 441 | 2.34 | 15.5 | 33.7 | 9 936 | 1 962 | 1 136 | 7 974 | 12 977 | 5 612 | 738 | 4 874 | 144 225 | 30.3 | 46.3 |
| Fayetteville.............. | 78 274 | 2.45 | 19.5 | 28.7 | 8 841 | 1 253 | 689 | 7 588 | 14 022 | 6 904 | 517 | 6 387 | 118 426 | 35.2 | 23.9 |
| Garner..................... | 10 207 | 2.49 | 14.7 | 27.0 | 284 | 243 | 232 | 41 | 1 240 | 4 756 | 219 | 4 538 | 16 898 | 32.3 | 35.0 |
| Gastonia.................. | 27 770 | 2.52 | 19.0 | 27.1 | 1 745 | 1 149 | 691 | 596 | 4 829 | 6 647 | 641 | 6 005 | 46 592 | 47.3 | 21.7 |
| Goldsboro ............... | 14 965 | 2.27 | 21.7 | 35.5 | 2 422 | 1 606 | 394 | 816 | 2 998 | 8 125 | 930 | 7 195 | 23 957 | 46.6 | 18.2 |
| Greensboro.............. | 111 731 | 2.31 | 16.5 | 33.8 | 11 389 | 2 110 | 1 407 | 9 279 | 13 844 | 5 069 | 523 | 4 547 | 168 926 | 37.0 | 35.0 |
| Greenville................ | 36 071 | 2.18 | 15.5 | 36.6 | 5 858 | 760 | 734 | 5 098 | NA | NA | NA | NA | 43 049 | 32.0 | 35.6 |
| Hickory................... | 16 614 | 2.33 | 14.4 | 33.7 | 1 351 | 312 | 312 | 1 039 | 2 738 | 6 758 | 587 | 6 170 | 26 945 | 42.1 | 29.0 |
| High Point............... | 40 912 | 2.46 | 17.6 | 29.8 | 3 577 | 940 | 599 | 2 637 | 5 657 | 5 352 | 568 | 4 785 | 65 472 | 41.7 | 30.1 |
| Huntersville............. | 17 423 | 2.67 | 8.6 | 21.6 | 268 | 260 | 260 | 8 | 1 085 | 2 291 | 144 | 2 147 | 29 514 | 19.4 | 52.4 |
| Indian Trail.............. | 11 121 | 3.01 | 10.9 | 14.8 | 0 | 0 | 0 | 0 | NA | NA | NA | NA | 18 963 | 34.3 | 33.5 |
| Jacksonville............. | 19 985 | 2.69 | 14.3 | 20.2 | 16 413 | 825 | 379 | 15 588 | 2 205 | 3 104 | 241 | 2 863 | 29 194 | 33.1 | 23.1 |
| Kannapolis............... | 16 375 | 2.58 | 17.0 | 26.3 | 330 | 303 | 278 | 27 | 1 333 | 3 088 | 215 | 2 873 | 27 409 | 52.6 | 16.3 |
| Matthews................. | 10 526 | 2.56 | 9.5 | 23.5 | 269 | 259 | 254 | 10 | 813 | 2 952 | 131 | 2 821 | 17 717 | 20.7 | 47.1 |
| Monroe.................... | 11 120 | 2.92 | 17.4 | 23.7 | 379 | 273 | 248 | 106 | NA | NA | NA | NA | 20 167 | 56.6 | 14.5 |
| Mooresville.............. | 12 374 | 2.61 | 13.6 | 25.2 | 372 | 252 | 252 | 120 | 1 561 | 4 712 | 254 | 4 459 | 19 936 | 34.7 | 25.9 |
| New Bern................. | 12 770 | 2.25 | 16.0 | 34.4 | 753 | 618 | 433 | 135 | 1 982 | 6 629 | 585 | 6 044 | 19 378 | 40.9 | 23.0 |
| Raleigh.................... | 162 999 | 2.36 | 13.5 | 32.8 | 19 526 | 5 387 | 1 443 | 14 139 | 14 966 | 3 659 | 422 | 3 238 | 247 716 | 26.1 | 47.3 |
| Rocky Mount............ | 23 097 | 2.42 | 22.9 | 31.4 | 1 597 | 906 | 377 | 691 | 4 485 | 7 705 | 978 | 6 728 | 38 016 | 52.5 | 19.4 |
| Salisbury................. | 12 567 | 2.38 | 19.7 | 32.6 | 3 775 | 2 057 | 622 | 1 718 | 2 487 | 7 296 | 654 | 6 641 | 21 587 | 48.5 | 24.0 |
| Sanford................... | 10 458 | 2.60 | 19.3 | 28.7 | 858 | 684 | 289 | 174 | 1 042 | 3 663 | 288 | 3 374 | 17 089 | 50.4 | 22.2 |
| Thomasville............. | 10 537 | 2.50 | 18.3 | 28.3 | 390 | 315 | 275 | 75 | 1 396 | 5 152 | 480 | 4 672 | 16 972 | 60.0 | 14.3 |
| Wake Forest ............ | 10 521 | 2.83 | 10.4 | 18.9 | 303 | 138 | 138 | 165 | 770 | 2 525 | 148 | 2 377 | 17 143 | 21.5 | 50.9 |
| Wilmington .............. | 46 948 | 2.16 | 13.4 | 36.0 | 5 118 | 430 | 382 | 4 688 | 6 370 | 5 908 | 614 | 5 294 | 68 094 | 33.6 | 37.1 |
| Wilson ..................... | 19 585 | 2.43 | 20.8 | 30.8 | 1 534 | 1 003 | 756 | 531 | 2 456 | 4 933 | 490 | 4 443 | 31 337 | 49.4 | 23.4 |
| Winston-Salem.......... | 92 337 | 2.38 | 17.3 | 33.1 | 9 431 | 2 480 | 1 268 | 6 951 | 15 439 | 6 640 | 673 | 5 967 | 144 750 | 41.0 | 31.7 |
| NORTH DAKOTA......... | 281 192 | 2.30 | 8.2 | 31.5 | 25 056 | 9 675 | 6 433 | 15 381 | 14 935 | 2 184 | 247 | 1 937 | 435 706 | 37.4 | 26.5 |
| Bismarck.................. | 27 263 | 2.18 | 9.6 | 34.8 | 1 815 | 1 371 | 534 | 444 | 2 003 | 3 215 | 266 | 2 948 | 41 124 | 31.5 | 32.3 |
| Fargo....................... | 46 791 | 2.15 | 8.6 | 36.6 | 4 924 | 1 011 | 678 | 3 913 | 3 073 | 2 863 | 359 | 2 504 | 62 749 | 26.1 | 38.6 |
| Grand Forks............. | 22 260 | 2.21 | 9.7 | 34.8 | 3 754 | 478 | 285 | 3 276 | 1 702 | 3 168 | 253 | 2 915 | 29 039 | 30.3 | 35.5 |
| Minot...................... | 17 863 | 2.20 | 9.6 | 34.9 | 1 524 | 527 | 421 | 997 | 890 | 2 141 | 281 | 1 859 | 25 432 | 35.5 | 27.6 |
| West Fargo............... | 10 348 | 2.49 | 9.1 | 26.4 | 51 | 0 | 0 | 51 | 485 | 1 846 | 202 | 1 645 | 15 916 | 29.2 | 32.2 |
| OHIO........................ | 4 603 435 | 2.44 | 13.1 | 28.9 | 306 266 | 166 042 | 83 019 | 140 224 | 422 781 | 3 662 | 307 | 3 355 | 7 688 501 | 47.5 | 24.5 |
| Akron...................... | 83 712 | 2.31 | 19.5 | 34.8 | 6 133 | 1 981 | 878 | 4 152 | 12 713 | 6 380 | 896 | 5 484 | 129 514 | 50.7 | 20.0 |
| Barberton ................ | 11 054 | 2.37 | 16.3 | 32.2 | 371 | 259 | 259 | 112 | 1 343 | 5 055 | 252 | 4 803 | 18 471 | 61.7 | 12.8 |
| Beavercreek............. | 18 195 | 2.47 | 6.8 | 24.9 | 278 | 257 | 257 | 21 | 1 098 | 2 428 | 60 | 2 368 | 30 433 | 24.8 | 47.8 |
| Bowling Green.......... | 11 288 | 2.16 | 7.5 | 35.8 | 5 632 | 503 | 278 | 5 129 | 831 | 2 765 | 180 | 2 586 | 12 566 | 28.4 | 48.1 |
| Brunswick................ | 12 967 | 2.63 | 10.6 | 21.9 | 200 | 147 | 147 | 53 | 480 | 1 400 | 315 | 1 085 | 22 883 | 46.9 | 20.7 |
| Canton..................... | 29 705 | 2.35 | 21.1 | 35.4 | 3 102 | 1 256 | 701 | 1 846 | 5 597 | 7 661 | 1 109 | 6 552 | 47 585 | 58.8 | 13.0 |
| Cincinnati................ | 133 420 | 2.12 | 19.1 | 43.4 | 14 443 | 4 531 | 2 199 | 9 912 | 23 625 | 7 950 | 1 035 | 6 915 | 190 919 | 43.0 | 31.0 |
| Cleveland................. | 167 490 | 2.29 | 25.3 | 39.5 | 13 742 | 6 258 | 3 062 | 7 484 | 30 849 | 7 768 | 1 368 | 6 401 | 262 301 | 57.9 | 13.8 |
| Cleveland Heights...... | 19 957 | 2.27 | 15.2 | 36.1 | 738 | 118 | 118 | 620 | 1 161 | 2 515 | 310 | 2 206 | 30 683 | 24.8 | 49.9 |
| Columbus................. | 331 602 | 2.31 | 15.9 | 35.1 | 21 099 | 6 086 | 3 236 | 15 013 | 54 721 | 6 948 | 664 | 6 284 | 492 273 | 39.2 | 32.3 |
| Cuyahoga Falls.......... | 22 250 | 2.21 | 11.4 | 35.6 | 530 | 345 | 345 | 185 | 1 423 | 2 864 | 121 | 2 743 | 34 594 | 40.4 | 29.2 |
| Dayton..................... | 58 404 | 2.26 | 21.4 | 38.8 | 9 365 | 2 099 | 773 | 7 266 | 9 850 | 6 955 | 967 | 5 987 | 87 702 | 51.0 | 15.0 |
| Delaware.................. | 13 253 | 2.47 | 11.7 | 28.4 | 2 041 | 572 | 377 | 1 469 | 1 094 | 3 146 | 213 | 2 933 | 21 062 | 36.5 | 32.1 |
| Dublin..................... | 14 984 | 2.78 | 5.9 | 18.4 | 127 | 127 | 127 | 0 | 549 | 1 314 | 38 | 1 276 | 26 096 | 8.4 | 71.3 |
| Elyria...................... | 22 400 | 2.39 | 17.8 | 30.5 | 1 040 | 881 | 430 | 159 | 2 444 | 4 478 | 352 | 4 127 | 36 117 | 53.8 | 14.0 |
| Euclid...................... | 22 685 | 2.13 | 20.9 | 41.4 | 675 | 489 | 391 | 186 | 516 | 1 054 | 90 | 964 | 33 420 | 45.9 | 19.7 |
| Fairborn................... | 14 306 | 2.24 | 14.4 | 32.7 | 275 | 229 | 229 | 46 | 1 155 | 3 567 | 232 | 3 336 | 19 440 | 44.4 | 25.0 |
| Fairfield................... | 17 415 | 2.41 | 13.1 | 28.7 | 506 | 404 | 384 | 102 | 1 395 | 3 279 | 263 | 3 016 | 29 228 | 44.7 | 24.6 |
| Findlay.................... | 17 354 | 2.29 | 11.8 | 32.6 | 1 506 | 504 | 383 | 1 002 | 2 073 | 5 028 | 194 | 4 834 | 27 023 | 44.9 | 25.4 |
| Gahanna.................. | 13 037 | 2.54 | 11.5 | 24.4 | 171 | 166 | 158 | 5 | 848 | 2 549 | 54 | 2 495 | 22 015 | 27.2 | 45.8 |
| Garfield Heights........ | 11 691 | 2.43 | 21.3 | 31.8 | 391 | 308 | 265 | 83 | 353 | 1 223 | 118 | 1 105 | 19 439 | 57.1 | 12.9 |
| Green...................... | 10 070 | 2.54 | 10.0 | 23.9 | 141 | 133 | 130 | 8 | NA | NA | NA | NA | 17 779 | 38.1 | 34.3 |
| Grove City................ | 13 946 | 2.53 | 11.8 | 25.6 | 282 | 248 | 165 | 34 | 1 269 | 3 565 | 104 | 3 461 | 23 244 | 41.5 | 26.5 |
| Hamilton.................. | 24 658 | 2.47 | 17.3 | 30.6 | 1 663 | 1 354 | 436 | 309 | 4 748 | 7 594 | 573 | 7 021 | 41 410 | 61.5 | 15.0 |
| Hilliard.................... | 10 198 | 2.77 | 9.2 | 21.2 | 155 | 155 | 155 | 0 | 771 | 2 709 | 63 | 2 646 | 17 846 | 26.8 | 46.4 |
| Huber Heights........... | 14 720 | 2.58 | 14.9 | 22.8 | 184 | 64 | 64 | 120 | 1 462 | 3 834 | 215 | 3 619 | 25 593 | 41.4 | 20.7 |
| Kent........................ | 10 288 | 2.22 | 12.5 | 33.4 | 6 067 | 81 | 81 | 5 986 | 708 | 2 448 | 201 | 2 247 | 12 574 | 31.7 | 41.2 |

1. No spouse present.    2. Data for serious crimes have not been adjusted for underreporting. This may affect comparability between geographic areas and over time.    3. Per 100,000 population estimated by the FBI.    4. Persons 25 years old and over.

# Table D. Cities — Income, Poverty, and Housing

| | Money income, 2007–2011 | | | | Housing units, 2010 | | | Occupied Housing units 2007–2011 | | | | |
| | | Households | | | | | | | Owner-occupied | | Median owner costs as a percent of income | |
| City | Per capita income[1] (dollars) | Median income | Percent with income of $200,000 or more | Percent with income of less than $25,000 | Families with income below poverty (percent) | Total | Percent change, 2000–2010 | Vacant units for sale or rent[2] | Total | Percent | Median value[3] (dollars) | With a mortgage[4] | Without a mortgage[5] |
| | 42 | 43 | 44 | 45 | 46 | 47 | 48 | 49 | 50 | 51 | 52 | 53 | 54 |
| NORTH CAROLINA... | 25 256 | 46 291 | 3.1 | 26.5 | 11.8 | 4 327 528 | 22.8 | 582 373 | 3 664 119 | 67.8 | 152 700 | 23.4 | 11.9 |
| Apex | 33 172 | 86 782 | 4.5 | 6.9 | 1.5 | 13 922 | 72.9 | 697 | 12 346 | 76.7 | 254 200 | 20.8 | 10.0 |
| Asheboro | 17 764 | 30 840 | 1.2 | 40.6 | 25.4 | 11 158 | 16.7 | 1 278 | 10 207 | 52.1 | 116 500 | 24.1 | 15.8 |
| Asheville | 26 664 | 40 863 | 2.9 | 30.8 | 14.1 | 41 626 | 23.9 | 4 246 | 37 558 | 52.1 | 195 300 | 25.5 | 13.7 |
| Burlington | 23 465 | 42 097 | 2.5 | 29.4 | 15.9 | 23 414 | 19.9 | 2 782 | 20 991 | 58.1 | 124 300 | 23.8 | 11.9 |
| Cary | 42 344 | 91 997 | 12.2 | 9.5 | 3.0 | 55 303 | 50.1 | 3 512 | 48 560 | 71.8 | 301 900 | 20.2 | 10.0 |
| Chapel Hill | 34 483 | 58 415 | 12.7 | 26.1 | 8.7 | 22 254 | 16.6 | 1 690 | 19 970 | 49.1 | 368 200 | 22.5 | 10.0 |
| Charlotte | 31 667 | 53 146 | 5.6 | 21.3 | 11.3 | 319 918 | 38.8 | 30 058 | 287 302 | 58.7 | 174 100 | 23.6 | 11.5 |
| Concord | 26 350 | 52 549 | 3.7 | 21.1 | 9.3 | 32 130 | 43.1 | 2 993 | 28 684 | 68.1 | 170 700 | 23.1 | 11.6 |
| Durham | 27 156 | 47 394 | 3.5 | 25.9 | 13.1 | 103 221 | 27.6 | 9 780 | 92 455 | 50.9 | 178 700 | 23.4 | 11.4 |
| Fayetteville | 23 163 | 44 266 | 2.0 | 25.8 | 14.4 | 87 005 | 62.7 | 8 731 | 75 149 | 52.9 | 121 100 | 23.8 | 12.7 |
| Garner | 28 515 | 60 894 | 2.0 | 15.6 | 4.9 | 10 993 | 51.9 | 786 | 10 021 | 66.2 | 167 400 | 22.4 | 11.5 |
| Gastonia | 22 048 | 39 427 | 2.5 | 32.2 | 17.2 | 31 238 | 12.2 | 3 468 | 27 431 | 57.9 | 133 800 | 24.9 | 13.7 |
| Goldsboro | 20 628 | 35 384 | 1.3 | 36.1 | 20.0 | 16 824 | 2.3 | 1 859 | 14 850 | 44.1 | 118 400 | 24.2 | 13.1 |
| Greensboro | 25 824 | 41 973 | 3.4 | 28.8 | 12.8 | 124 074 | 25.2 | 12 343 | 108 905 | 55.2 | 147 800 | 23.8 | 11.7 |
| Greenville | 22 506 | 34 134 | 3.2 | 39.1 | 20.6 | 40 564 | 43.5 | 4 493 | 33 786 | 38.1 | 147 600 | 23.1 | 13.2 |
| Hickory | 26 324 | 37 939 | 3.8 | 31.3 | 13.3 | 18 719 | 12.0 | 2 105 | 16 526 | 53.7 | 151 600 | 21.4 | 12.7 |
| High Point | 23 107 | 44 020 | 2.4 | 28.6 | 16.1 | 46 677 | 29.9 | 5 765 | 39 553 | 59.1 | 146 800 | 24.9 | 13.6 |
| Huntersville | 37 799 | 83 360 | 8.9 | 11.8 | 3.9 | 18 477 | 87.2 | 1 054 | 16 950 | 76.0 | 248 300 | 20.9 | 12.0 |
| Indian Trail | 25 892 | 63 619 | 3.2 | 9.9 | 4.4 | 11 700 | 166.4 | 579 | 10 452 | 85.6 | 182 000 | 24.3 | 11.7 |
| Jacksonville | 21 047 | 42 369 | 1.1 | 23.7 | 10.5 | 21 135 | 15.2 | 1 150 | 19 658 | 38.9 | 147 000 | 25.3 | 11.2 |
| Kannapolis | 21 352 | 41 645 | 1.8 | 30.5 | 13.0 | 18 645 | 17.4 | 2 270 | 16 342 | 63.5 | 129 600 | 24.1 | 14.7 |
| Matthews | 33 976 | 69 577 | 7.9 | 13.7 | 6.1 | 11 021 | 33.2 | 495 | 10 239 | 74.6 | 224 600 | 20.3 | 10.1 |
| Monroe | 18 969 | 43 787 | 0.7 | 27.4 | 18.4 | 12 375 | 27.4 | 1 255 | 11 223 | 57.8 | 151 800 | 23.7 | 13.5 |
| Mooresville | 26 066 | 53 177 | 2.0 | 24.1 | 7.7 | 13 655 | 74.1 | 1 281 | 11 752 | 66.4 | 189 600 | 24.7 | 11.6 |
| New Bern | 24 220 | 35 334 | 1.5 | 35.1 | 18.7 | 14 471 | 31.0 | 1 701 | 12 832 | 53.4 | 155 300 | 25.6 | 16.9 |
| Raleigh | 30 377 | 52 819 | 4.7 | 20.7 | 10.7 | 176 124 | 45.9 | 13 125 | 158 354 | 54.8 | 205 200 | 23.1 | 10.4 |
| Rocky Mount | 21 910 | 38 080 | 2.3 | 34.8 | 15.9 | 26 953 | 11.1 | 3 856 | 23 393 | 54.8 | 108 300 | 24.5 | 14.7 |
| Salisbury | 20 041 | 35 845 | 2.4 | 36.5 | 18.9 | 14 626 | 28.5 | 2 059 | 12 362 | 53.3 | 126 100 | 24.0 | 13.3 |
| Sanford | 20 014 | 41 096 | 1.7 | 31.6 | 19.6 | 11 411 | 23.1 | 953 | 9 792 | 55.4 | 136 000 | 22.2 | 13.1 |
| Thomasville | 17 637 | 34 796 | 0.3 | 40.1 | 24.0 | 11 870 | 39.2 | 1 333 | 10 804 | 58.7 | 103 800 | 24.2 | 13.3 |
| Wake Forest | 32 304 | 72 155 | 6.2 | 12.7 | 7.3 | 11 370 | 123.8 | 849 | 9 673 | 76.1 | 246 500 | 22.5 | 10.9 |
| Wilmington | 28 217 | 39 764 | 3.8 | 33.1 | 14.0 | 53 400 | 38.3 | 6 452 | 46 341 | 47.6 | 236 100 | 26.0 | 13.3 |
| Wilson | 20 903 | 36 539 | 1.7 | 34.9 | 19.1 | 21 870 | 17.1 | 2 285 | 19 365 | 50.6 | 135 700 | 25.9 | 17.3 |
| Winston-Salem | 24 728 | 41 228 | 3.5 | 29.8 | 15.7 | 103 974 | 25.8 | 11 637 | 90 245 | 58.7 | 141 700 | 23.6 | 11.3 |
| NORTH DAKOTA...... | 27 305 | 49 415 | 2.7 | 24.4 | 7.3 | 317 498 | 9.6 | 36 306 | 278 669 | 66.5 | 118 200 | 19.9 | 10.6 |
| Bismarck | 29 503 | 50 062 | 2.2 | 24.1 | 7.2 | 28 648 | 18.6 | 1 385 | 26 974 | 65.5 | 151 400 | 21.2 | 12.4 |
| Fargo | 28 191 | 42 710 | 3.5 | 28.0 | 7.6 | 49 956 | 21.0 | 3 165 | 46 851 | 45.4 | 148 500 | 21.9 | 11.7 |
| Grand Forks | 25 454 | 41 661 | 2.9 | 31.5 | 8.3 | 23 449 | 12.6 | 1 189 | 21 672 | 49.9 | 148 400 | 21.6 | 12.4 |
| Minot | 26 148 | 46 687 | 1.8 | 22.8 | 9.9 | 18 744 | 13.7 | 881 | 17 275 | 62.3 | 124 800 | 21.2 | 11.1 |
| West Fargo | 29 481 | 62 555 | 2.2 | 15.7 | 5.2 | 10 760 | 83.8 | 412 | 10 227 | 68.9 | 149 300 | 21.9 | 12.5 |
| OHIO | 25 618 | 48 071 | 2.8 | 25.5 | 10.8 | 5 127 508 | 7.2 | 524 073 | 4 554 007 | 68.7 | 135 600 | 23.2 | 13.1 |
| Akron | 19 935 | 34 190 | 1.3 | 37.8 | 19.9 | 96 288 | -1.0 | 12 576 | 84 080 | 55.8 | 89 800 | 24.0 | 15.0 |
| Barberton | 19 221 | 35 985 | 0.5 | 37.1 | 16.7 | 12 191 | 0.2 | 1 137 | 11 210 | 65.3 | 94 900 | 24.5 | 13.8 |
| Beavercreek | 37 003 | 73 357 | 5.3 | 9.4 | 2.8 | 19 449 | 31.1 | 1 254 | 17 907 | 75.2 | 176 800 | 21.5 | 12.1 |
| Bowling Green | 20 149 | 34 961 | 2.2 | 38.0 | 10.3 | 12 301 | 15.9 | 1 013 | 10 767 | 40.7 | 170 100 | 19.7 | 10.0 |
| Brunswick | 26 513 | 61 046 | 1.3 | 14.8 | 5.1 | 13 600 | 10.9 | 633 | 12 967 | 77.7 | 161 400 | 23.0 | 12.2 |
| Canton | 17 191 | 30 264 | 1.2 | 41.7 | 23.1 | 34 571 | -2.6 | 4 866 | 29 962 | 55.2 | 80 000 | 23.9 | 12.6 |
| Cincinnati | 24 509 | 34 104 | 2.7 | 39.4 | 21.8 | 161 095 | -2.9 | 27 675 | 131 892 | 41.4 | 129 100 | 24.3 | 14.3 |
| Cleveland | 16 665 | 27 470 | 0.5 | 46.3 | 27.9 | 207 536 | -3.8 | 40 046 | 169 665 | 46.3 | 84 300 | 27.4 | 15.9 |
| Cleveland Heights | 28 597 | 47 966 | 4.0 | 28.3 | 13.4 | 22 465 | 2.9 | 2 508 | 19 522 | 57.9 | 140 900 | 26.2 | 15.4 |
| Columbus | 23 618 | 43 348 | 1.7 | 28.9 | 16.6 | 370 965 | 13.3 | 39 363 | 319 741 | 48.6 | 137 400 | 24.0 | 13.4 |
| Cuyahoga Falls | 25 399 | 46 450 | 0.9 | 23.6 | 8.2 | 23 859 | 4.9 | 1 609 | 22 109 | 64.2 | 124 300 | 23.1 | 13.3 |
| Dayton | 16 424 | 28 843 | 0.6 | 44.1 | 26.5 | 74 065 | -4.2 | 15 661 | 57 843 | 48.7 | 76 000 | 24.2 | 14.8 |
| Delaware | 25 789 | 57 201 | 2.0 | 20.0 | 7.8 | 14 192 | 37.9 | 939 | 13 220 | 62.7 | 166 400 | 22.9 | 13.3 |
| Dublin | 51 177 | 113 361 | 18.9 | 6.1 | 2.6 | 15 779 | 31.1 | 795 | 14 735 | 80.9 | 328 100 | 21.9 | 10.9 |
| Elyria | 21 062 | 42 383 | 0.6 | 26.8 | 13.3 | 25 085 | 5.2 | 2 685 | 22 260 | 62.8 | 107 400 | 24.2 | 13.8 |
| Euclid | 22 620 | 37 600 | 0.9 | 32.3 | 12.8 | 26 037 | -0.3 | 3 352 | 22 344 | 52.8 | 105 100 | 25.0 | 15.8 |
| Fairborn | 22 914 | 40 981 | 0.6 | 33.4 | 15.7 | 15 893 | 10.3 | 1 587 | 13 949 | 50.4 | 112 400 | 21.6 | 10.6 |
| Fairfield | 28 940 | 54 581 | 1.8 | 15.2 | 6.9 | 18 803 | 5.7 | 1 388 | 17 113 | 66.0 | 150 000 | 22.2 | 11.9 |
| Findlay | 24 633 | 43 827 | 2.1 | 29.1 | 12.5 | 19 318 | 12.5 | 1 964 | 17 561 | 61.6 | 123 100 | 22.4 | 11.7 |
| Gahanna | 36 765 | 75 641 | 6.4 | 12.0 | 1.8 | 13 577 | 9.9 | 540 | 12 930 | 75.0 | 187 700 | 21.9 | 13.5 |
| Garfield Heights | 20 704 | 43 807 | 0.5 | 27.7 | 9.5 | 13 125 | 1.6 | 1 434 | 11 445 | 73.1 | 95 900 | 24.6 | 16.9 |
| Green | 32 103 | 61 559 | 5.4 | 16.5 | 4.4 | 10 858 | 18.3 | 788 | 10 039 | 79.6 | 176 300 | 22.1 | 12.4 |
| Grove City | 29 873 | 65 287 | 2.4 | 15.0 | 5.4 | 14 720 | 38.2 | 774 | 13 298 | 71.7 | 164 100 | 23.0 | 14.1 |
| Hamilton | 19 842 | 38 628 | 0.6 | 32.8 | 16.3 | 27 878 | 7.5 | 3 220 | 25 234 | 56.6 | 107 600 | 23.7 | 13.6 |
| Hilliard | 34 190 | 84 543 | 6.9 | 11.0 | 3.0 | 10 637 | 19.6 | 439 | 9 817 | 76.2 | 206 800 | 22.4 | 13.3 |
| Huber Heights | 25 823 | 54 897 | 2.2 | 16.9 | 6.3 | 15 875 | 6.2 | 1 155 | 14 791 | 71.8 | 113 300 | 22.9 | 13.0 |
| Kent | 19 129 | 26 923 | 1.5 | 46.2 | 18.5 | 11 174 | 6.8 | 886 | 10 718 | 37.5 | 142 900 | 22.6 | 12.6 |

1. Based on population estimated by the American Community Survey.   2. Includes units rented or sold but not occupied.   3. Specified owner-occupied units; $1,000,000 represents $1,000,000 or more   4. 50.0 represents 50 percent or more.   5. 10.0 represents 10 percent or less.

| City | Occupied housing units, 2007–2011 (cont.) | | | | Migration, 2007–2011 | | Civilian labor force, 2012 | | | | Civilian employment[4], 2007–2011 | | | |
|---|---|---|---|---|---|---|---|---|---|---|---|---|---|---|
| | | | | | | | | | Unemployment | | | Percent | | |
| | Percent renter occupied | Median gross rent[1] | Median rent as a percent of income[2] | Percent with no vehicle available | Percent who lived in the same house one year ago | Percent who lived outside this city one year ago | Total | Percent change, 2011–2012 | Total | Rate[3] | Population age 16 and older | In labor force | Full-year full-time worker | Households with no workers (percent) |
| | 55 | 56 | 57 | 58 | 59 | 60 | 61 | 62 | 63 | 64 | 65 | 66 | 67 | 68 |
| NORTH CAROLINA... | 32.2 | 744 | 30.1 | 6.5 | 83.9 | 11.4 | 4 723 379 | 2.5 | 447 930 | 9.5 | 7 411 079 | 64.6 | 39.0 | 27.4 |
| Apex | 23.3 | 948 | 23.6 | 1.7 | 83.6 | 12.9 | 19 970 | 5.0 | 1 153 | 5.8 | 24 702 | 78.0 | 52.9 | 10.8 |
| Asheboro | 47.9 | 618 | 32.5 | 8.6 | 78.2 | 12.7 | 12 054 | 0.5 | 1 090 | 9.0 | 18 740 | 60.9 | 34.6 | 34.3 |
| Asheville | 47.9 | 791 | 29.2 | 10.7 | 77.2 | 14.6 | 42 964 | 3.9 | 2 921 | 6.8 | 68 199 | 65.2 | 36.8 | 31.1 |
| Burlington | 41.9 | 748 | 30.0 | 8.2 | 79.7 | 12.7 | 23 471 | 3.3 | 2 265 | 9.7 | 39 161 | 65.4 | 39.8 | 30.1 |
| Cary | 28.2 | 918 | 25.3 | 2.4 | 83.9 | 12.1 | 72 658 | 4.7 | 4 244 | 5.8 | 99 551 | 73.2 | 50.5 | 14.1 |
| Chapel Hill | 50.9 | 877 | 35.8 | 9.7 | 63.4 | 24.0 | 29 978 | 4.4 | 1 623 | 5.4 | 48 062 | 57.4 | 28.9 | 25.2 |
| Charlotte | 41.3 | 850 | 29.3 | 7.6 | 77.7 | 8.7 | 390 311 | 5.0 | 31 946 | 8.2 | 558 734 | 72.6 | 45.6 | 19.3 |
| Concord | 31.9 | 767 | 29.1 | 4.9 | 84.7 | 9.0 | 39 104 | 4.1 | 2 519 | 6.4 | 58 671 | 70.2 | 44.1 | 22.1 |
| Durham | 49.1 | 809 | 30.8 | 9.4 | 74.6 | 12.5 | 123 092 | 3.7 | 8 652 | 7.0 | 177 845 | 69.3 | 42.8 | 22.6 |
| Fayetteville | 47.1 | 838 | 28.7 | 6.8 | 71.8 | 17.2 | 88 886 | 1.6 | 6 672 | 7.5 | 153 365 | 67.7 | 30.8 | 24.7 |
| Garner | 33.8 | 883 | 28.6 | 3.8 | 85.6 | 13.5 | 13 734 | 4.2 | 1 019 | 7.4 | 19 322 | 73.7 | 50.9 | 19.7 |
| Gastonia | 42.1 | 738 | 32.2 | 8.3 | 81.7 | 8.2 | 32 961 | 4.5 | 3 328 | 10.1 | 55 721 | 62.9 | 37.0 | 28.8 |
| Goldsboro | 55.9 | 640 | 29.6 | 15.6 | 75.3 | 15.3 | 13 013 | 3.3 | 1 430 | 11.0 | 29 177 | 56.9 | 29.3 | 35.7 |
| Greensboro | 44.8 | 722 | 30.2 | 8.7 | 81.5 | 8.3 | 139 775 | 1.8 | 12 668 | 9.1 | 212 983 | 67.3 | 39.6 | 25.3 |
| Greenville | 61.9 | 696 | 35.5 | 10.6 | 64.7 | 19.1 | 46 020 | 4.4 | 3 740 | 8.1 | 68 400 | 66.1 | 33.0 | 25.4 |
| Hickory | 46.3 | 629 | 28.7 | 9.3 | 80.7 | 10.0 | 18 294 | -0.1 | 1 780 | 9.7 | 32 237 | 62.8 | 39.7 | 29.4 |
| High Point | 40.9 | 756 | 31.0 | 9.5 | 83.7 | 8.3 | 52 496 | 1.9 | 5 077 | 9.7 | 79 015 | 66.6 | 39.7 | 25.8 |
| Huntersville | 24.0 | 909 | 26.5 | 2.4 | 85.1 | 12.1 | 25 081 | 5.0 | 1 544 | 6.2 | 33 169 | 78.6 | 54.2 | 13.8 |
| Indian Trail | 14.4 | 1 066 | 27.7 | 0.9 | 86.9 | 10.2 | 17 866 | 4.8 | 992 | 5.6 | 22 313 | 73.8 | 48.9 | 14.6 |
| Jacksonville | 61.1 | 937 | 30.7 | 6.0 | 61.5 | 31.5 | 19 327 | 2.8 | 2 009 | 10.4 | 54 324 | 77.1 | 21.2 | 18.9 |
| Kannapolis | 36.5 | 754 | 31.1 | 8.8 | 85.4 | 9.9 | 20 973 | 3.1 | 1 947 | 9.3 | 31 937 | 65.8 | 42.4 | 29.2 |
| Matthews | 25.4 | 883 | 33.6 | 5.1 | 86.6 | 11.4 | 14 479 | 4.7 | 986 | 6.8 | 20 544 | 69.8 | 42.4 | 21.7 |
| Monroe | 42.2 | 767 | 32.6 | 8.4 | 86.0 | 9.6 | 15 442 | 3.6 | 1 352 | 8.8 | 23 698 | 67.8 | 42.9 | 21.7 |
| Mooresville | 33.6 | 844 | 30.8 | 3.7 | 81.1 | 11.5 | 16 359 | 3.5 | 1 351 | 8.3 | 24 153 | 70.2 | 43.2 | 22.6 |
| New Bern | 46.6 | 731 | 32.7 | 15.5 | 80.7 | 11.6 | 12 885 | 3.4 | 1 098 | 8.5 | 23 179 | 58.5 | 30.4 | 38.1 |
| Raleigh | 45.2 | 855 | 30.0 | 6.8 | 76.6 | 12.1 | 222 174 | 4.5 | 15 427 | 6.9 | 312 653 | 71.4 | 45.6 | 18.3 |
| Rocky Mount | 45.2 | 718 | 31.6 | 12.6 | 82.3 | 7.7 | 25 544 | 0.0 | 3 348 | 13.1 | 45 222 | 60.8 | 36.4 | 34.9 |
| Salisbury | 46.7 | 682 | 30.3 | 9.8 | 79.4 | 14.4 | 14 913 | 2.7 | 1 445 | 9.7 | 26 344 | 51.8 | 30.7 | 35.9 |
| Sanford | 44.6 | 671 | 28.0 | 13.1 | 82.9 | 7.5 | 12 564 | 1.4 | 1 404 | 11.2 | 20 515 | 65.9 | 39.7 | 29.5 |
| Thomasville | 41.3 | 617 | 30.3 | 10.0 | 83.4 | 8.6 | 12 031 | 2.4 | 1 198 | 10.0 | 20 054 | 64.7 | 36.5 | 31.7 |
| Wake Forest | 23.9 | 936 | 28.5 | 4.1 | 81.2 | 15.9 | NA | NA | NA | NA | 19 640 | 71.1 | 45.0 | 18.5 |
| Wilmington | 52.4 | 822 | 33.8 | 9.8 | 73.4 | 13.5 | 53 833 | 4.3 | 4 484 | 8.3 | 87 885 | 64.8 | 34.3 | 29.7 |
| Wilson | 49.4 | 745 | 32.6 | 12.3 | 78.9 | 8.6 | 23 627 | 2.0 | 2 823 | 11.9 | 37 599 | 61.7 | 37.2 | 33.1 |
| Winston-Salem | 41.3 | 685 | 31.7 | 9.4 | 83.1 | 6.6 | 112 387 | 2.9 | 9 711 | 8.6 | 177 672 | 63.1 | 38.2 | 28.6 |
| NORTH DAKOTA | 33.5 | 584 | 25.6 | 5.4 | 83.1 | 10.3 | 392 064 | 5.7 | 12 236 | 3.1 | 536 039 | 70.3 | 44.5 | 23.1 |
| Bismarck | 34.5 | 601 | 24.5 | 5.1 | 82.5 | 8.4 | 35 171 | -0.7 | 947 | 2.7 | 49 430 | 71.4 | 48.3 | 22.3 |
| Fargo | 54.6 | 629 | 28.0 | 8.1 | 72.4 | 13.6 | 60 869 | -0.2 | 1 963 | 3.2 | 85 304 | 76.4 | 45.6 | 19.0 |
| Grand Forks | 50.1 | 651 | 31.1 | 7.7 | 73.1 | 13.2 | 30 121 | -2.5 | 1 013 | 3.4 | 43 940 | 72.1 | 38.8 | 21.6 |
| Minot | 37.7 | 610 | 24.8 | 6.8 | 77.5 | 12.2 | 22 491 | 6.2 | 573 | 2.5 | 32 435 | 72.3 | 42.4 | 22.3 |
| West Fargo | 31.1 | 653 | 25.1 | 2.7 | 84.0 | 12.7 | 14 499 | -0.3 | 465 | 3.2 | 19 467 | 80.4 | 55.8 | 14.0 |
| OHIO | 31.3 | 697 | 30.1 | 8.1 | 85.3 | 9.6 | 5 747 885 | 0.0 | 413 023 | 7.2 | 9 110 226 | 64.6 | 39.0 | 28.9 |
| Akron | 44.2 | 669 | 34.8 | 14.4 | 84.0 | 6.1 | 98 010 | 0.0 | 7 420 | 7.6 | 159 033 | 64.3 | 36.2 | 34.0 |
| Barberton | 34.7 | 622 | 30.1 | 12.2 | 91.1 | 5.1 | 12 849 | -1.2 | 1 032 | 8.0 | 21 184 | 62.8 | 36.9 | 36.2 |
| Beavercreek | 24.8 | 1 055 | 25.0 | 2.3 | 87.8 | 9.5 | 22 522 | 0.0 | 1 353 | 6.0 | 36 091 | 65.4 | 41.2 | 23.2 |
| Bowling Green | 59.3 | 624 | 35.2 | 8.4 | 52.7 | 26.2 | 15 842 | 2.6 | 966 | 6.1 | 27 111 | 65.9 | 24.4 | 22.9 |
| Brunswick | 22.3 | 786 | 30.9 | 3.2 | 89.1 | 7.1 | 19 329 | 1.1 | 1 209 | 6.3 | 26 909 | 73.1 | 43.9 | 20.4 |
| Canton | 44.8 | 556 | 32.6 | 16.1 | 80.4 | 8.9 | 32 477 | 0.1 | 2 851 | 8.8 | 56 795 | 62.3 | 32.9 | 35.5 |
| Cincinnati | 58.6 | 617 | 31.5 | 22.0 | 74.8 | 9.4 | 141 099 | 0.3 | 10 830 | 7.7 | 239 277 | 64.1 | 37.2 | 32.1 |
| Cleveland | 53.7 | 646 | 34.8 | 24.3 | 80.8 | 6.5 | 162 742 | 0.8 | 15 404 | 9.5 | 316 049 | 59.9 | 31.7 | 39.2 |
| Cleveland Heights | 42.1 | 818 | 32.3 | 12.2 | 82.5 | 12.5 | 25 632 | 2.0 | 1 462 | 5.7 | 37 001 | 67.4 | 40.5 | 27.4 |
| Columbus | 51.4 | 776 | 30.2 | 10.3 | 76.6 | 9.8 | 427 956 | 2.4 | 26 377 | 6.2 | 615 679 | 70.2 | 43.3 | 24.0 |
| Cuyahoga Falls | 35.8 | 713 | 27.6 | 7.4 | 92.4 | 5.1 | 27 297 | 0.0 | 1 772 | 6.5 | 40 065 | 67.4 | 44.0 | 27.2 |
| Dayton | 51.3 | 629 | 38.1 | 19.6 | 72.6 | 11.8 | 59 716 | -1.7 | 5 414 | 9.1 | 115 907 | 58.7 | 27.5 | 40.1 |
| Delaware | 37.3 | 767 | 29.1 | 4.8 | 78.3 | 14.1 | 17 879 | 2.6 | 1 051 | 5.9 | 26 119 | 70.7 | 46.3 | 20.7 |
| Dublin | 19.1 | 1 100 | 23.5 | 2.0 | 88.1 | 9.1 | 20 309 | 3.5 | 959 | 4.7 | 29 356 | 72.6 | 51.5 | 12.8 |
| Elyria | 37.2 | 688 | 29.2 | 9.0 | 84.0 | 8.0 | 28 491 | 1.4 | 2 261 | 7.9 | 43 190 | 66.9 | 39.8 | 28.9 |
| Euclid | 47.2 | 713 | 33.5 | 15.4 | 81.5 | 11.2 | 24 744 | 1.6 | 1 947 | 7.9 | 39 050 | 64.8 | 39.3 | 31.1 |
| Fairborn | 49.6 | 743 | 36.5 | 6.7 | 79.6 | 13.6 | 15 737 | -1.6 | 1 181 | 7.5 | 26 068 | 66.6 | 35.8 | 26.7 |
| Fairfield | 34.0 | 857 | 27.2 | 3.0 | 84.4 | 10.9 | 24 166 | 0.4 | 1 594 | 6.6 | 33 970 | 72.6 | 46.9 | 19.8 |
| Findlay | 38.4 | 636 | 28.4 | 7.4 | 78.2 | 10.6 | 22 116 | -0.5 | 1 324 | 6.0 | 33 179 | 66.0 | 40.2 | 29.4 |
| Gahanna | 25.0 | 892 | 25.5 | 4.3 | 88.2 | 9.6 | 18 090 | 2.7 | 959 | 5.3 | 26 723 | 73.8 | 50.0 | 17.4 |
| Garfield Heights | 26.9 | 745 | 36.0 | 10.8 | 88.5 | 9.1 | 14 383 | 0.8 | 1 140 | 7.9 | 22 582 | 65.6 | 40.8 | 29.2 |
| Green | 20.4 | 836 | 28.5 | 2.8 | 91.6 | 7.0 | 13 978 | 0.1 | 863 | 6.2 | 20 362 | 68.0 | 43.9 | 26.5 |
| Grove City | 28.3 | 827 | 27.7 | 3.6 | 84.4 | 10.2 | 18 888 | 2.2 | 1 045 | 5.5 | 26 586 | 71.8 | 48.1 | 22.9 |
| Hamilton | 43.4 | 689 | 32.9 | 11.7 | 81.3 | 8.6 | 29 418 | -0.1 | 2 389 | 8.1 | 48 509 | 62.9 | 38.0 | 31.8 |
| Hilliard | 23.8 | 931 | 28.9 | 5.3 | 87.9 | 10.6 | 15 557 | 2.6 | 801 | 5.1 | 20 526 | 75.2 | 51.4 | 18.1 |
| Huber Heights | 28.2 | 834 | 29.6 | 4.2 | 86.9 | 9.6 | 18 923 | -1.4 | 1 438 | 7.6 | 29 708 | 64.8 | 40.0 | 24.9 |
| Kent | 62.5 | 696 | 41.3 | 9.4 | 59.8 | 27.1 | 17 180 | 1.7 | 986 | 5.7 | 24 932 | 67.7 | 26.6 | 25.5 |

1. $2,000 represents $2,000 or more.  2. 50.0 represents 50 percent or more.  3. Percent of civilian labor force.  4. Persons 16 years old and over.

| City | Value of residential construction authorized by building permits, 2011 | | | Wholesale trade,[1] 2007 | | | | Retail trade,[2] 2007 | | | |
|---|---|---|---|---|---|---|---|---|---|---|---|
| | New construction ($1,000) | Number of housing units | Percent single family | Number of establishments | Number of employees | Sales (mil dol) | Annual payroll (mil dol) | Number of establishments | Number of employees | Sales (mil dol) | Annual payroll (mil dol) |
| | 69 | 70 | 71 | 72 | 73 | 74 | 75 | 76 | 77 | 78 | 79 |
| NORTH CAROLINA... | 5 053 273 | 32 804 | 75.8 | 10 049 | 142 342 | 88 795.9 | 6 969.2 | 36 592 | 466 577 | 114 578.2 | 10 342.7 |
| Apex | 57 663 | 453 | 53.6 | 43 | 469 | 320.3 | 26.9 | 108 | 1 908 | 439.9 | 41.9 |
| Asheboro | 3 148 | 81 | 11.1 | 35 | 339 | 154.0 | 14.9 | 215 | 2 503 | 570.9 | 52.9 |
| Asheville | 33 745 | 164 | 100.0 | 134 | 1 508 | 785.3 | 67.0 | 804 | 11 457 | 2 616.9 | 254.2 |
| Burlington | 13 241 | 98 | 100.0 | 67 | 934 | 318.7 | 35.2 | 415 | 5 832 | 1 216.9 | 117.0 |
| Cary | 168 099 | 970 | 100.0 | 127 | 1 999 | 2 236.7 | 152.1 | 524 | 9 274 | 2 293.0 | 209.5 |
| Chapel Hill | 12 587 | 47 | 100.0 | 23 | 398 | 403.0 | 35.9 | 196 | 2 888 | 569.5 | 62.7 |
| Charlotte | NA | NA | NA | 1 552 | 24 881 | 15 551.6 | 1 369.3 | 2 544 | 38 969 | 10 101.4 | 970.9 |
| Concord | NA | NA | NA | 100 | 2 237 | 1 145.9 | 103.8 | 478 | 7 685 | 1 995.1 | 167.7 |
| Durham | 164 743 | 1 243 | 71.0 | 183 | 2 669 | 2 648.8 | 169.1 | 868 | 13 805 | 2 978.1 | 297.3 |
| Fayetteville | 180 914 | 1 736 | 29.8 | 111 | 1 243 | 552.7 | 54.6 | 843 | 13 255 | 3 298.5 | 291.0 |
| Garner | 9 671 | 49 | 100.0 | 58 | 1 009 | 801.5 | 50.7 | 124 | 2 120 | 541.1 | 48.3 |
| Gastonia | 52 080 | 362 | 24.9 | 81 | 692 | 559.5 | 28.2 | 397 | 6 645 | 1 391.5 | 132.2 |
| Goldsboro | 7 183 | 60 | 100.0 | 57 | 1 365 | 862.8 | 53.7 | 347 | 4 309 | 1 027.1 | 85.8 |
| Greensboro | 83 827 | 1 215 | 24.2 | 567 | 8 524 | 7 790.2 | 412.6 | 1 293 | 21 155 | 5 080.7 | 502.1 |
| Greenville | 23 740 | 211 | 81.0 | 67 | 905 | 463.2 | 40.1 | 457 | 6 652 | 1 503.2 | 140.0 |
| Hickory | NA | NA | NA | 140 | 4 304 | 2 975.0 | 181.3 | 511 | 7 297 | 1 807.2 | 162.9 |
| High Point | 32 892 | 169 | 100.0 | 320 | 4 722 | 2 663.4 | 222.5 | 467 | 5 734 | 1 343.0 | 131.2 |
| Huntersville | NA | NA | NA | 51 | 517 | 224.5 | 28.5 | 156 | 2 832 | 823.7 | 66.5 |
| Indian Trail | NA | NA | NA | 86 | 826 | 321.2 | 36.0 | 97 | 1 552 | 462.8 | 42.0 |
| Jacksonville | 35 737 | 346 | 71.1 | 16 | 103 | 36.3 | 5.4 | 332 | 5 647 | 1 473.9 | 121.2 |
| Kannapolis | NA | NA | NA | 19 | 158 | 71.2 | 6.3 | 191 | 2 419 | 596.5 | 52.5 |
| Matthews | NA | NA | NA | 54 | 605 | 264.1 | 39.6 | 188 | 3 373 | 853.6 | 77.0 |
| Monroe | 13 632 | 49 | 100.0 | 73 | 1 298 | 653.5 | 51.5 | 246 | 3 583 | 884.0 | 76.2 |
| Mooresville | NA | NA | NA | 67 | 694 | 313.6 | 33.8 | 242 | 3 659 | 1 054.3 | 87.3 |
| New Bern | 19 368 | 135 | 100.0 | 35 | 473 | 698.7 | 18.3 | 249 | 3 150 | 728.8 | 67.8 |
| Raleigh | 341 665 | 2 307 | 42.8 | 589 | 8 369 | 4 243.2 | 447.4 | 1 761 | 28 116 | 7 066.4 | 672.2 |
| Rocky Mount | 1 973 | 28 | 100.0 | 66 | 1 408 | 975.5 | 55.7 | 392 | 4 811 | 1 045.6 | 96.1 |
| Salisbury | NA | NA | NA | 48 | 887 | 442.7 | 35.0 | 223 | 3 161 | 782.6 | 68.1 |
| Sanford | 5 576 | 45 | 100.0 | 35 | 673 | 572.9 | 26.2 | 201 | 2 340 | 583.0 | 50.6 |
| Thomasville | 5 817 | 36 | 100.0 | 36 | 577 | 230.7 | 22.6 | 139 | 1 716 | 419.6 | 37.6 |
| Wake Forest | 65 114 | 364 | 100.0 | 16 | 101 | 42.3 | 5.1 | 80 | 1 593 | 454.6 | 38.7 |
| Wilmington | NA | NA | NA | 150 | 1 293 | 744.6 | 53.7 | 845 | 12 145 | 3 076.1 | 284.9 |
| Wilson | 11 499 | 50 | 92.0 | 74 | 842 | 654.7 | 42.1 | 309 | 3 695 | 953.7 | 81.3 |
| Winston-Salem | 80 065 | 921 | 54.4 | 268 | 5 166 | 2 841.7 | 217.1 | 1 081 | 16 204 | 3 886.0 | 357.7 |
| NORTH DAKOTA | 783 616 | 6 201 | 47.0 | 1 332 | 14 866 | 13 099.3 | 627.1 | 3 361 | 44 054 | 10 527.3 | 891.4 |
| Bismarck | 81 289 | 511 | 86.5 | 118 | 1 531 | 845.9 | 68.8 | 375 | 6 653 | 1 377.0 | 133.6 |
| Fargo | 88 874 | 966 | 29.3 | 249 | 4 419 | 3 067.3 | 208.5 | 545 | 10 379 | 2 552.5 | 224.8 |
| Grand Forks | 41 001 | 326 | 24.2 | 61 | 841 | 528.9 | 36.9 | 297 | 5 634 | 1 181.5 | 110.5 |
| Minot | 126 011 | 1 071 | 42.0 | 56 | 825 | 943.8 | 35.9 | 252 | 4 392 | 1 005.7 | 89.4 |
| West Fargo | 41 538 | 296 | 53.4 | 38 | 464 | 165.1 | 20.0 | 80 | 1 405 | 269.1 | 27.9 |
| OHIO | 2 259 867 | 13 762 | 67.7 | 12 591 | 192 403 | 135 575.3 | 8 914.0 | 40 075 | 591 237 | 138 816.0 | 12 729.5 |
| Akron | 5 014 | 84 | 39.3 | 236 | 3 404 | 1 540.3 | 158.8 | 676 | 8 221 | 1 720.2 | 174.3 |
| Barberton | 540 | 4 | 100.0 | 30 | 1 501 | 177.8 | 37.0 | 68 | 781 | 170.5 | 16.3 |
| Beavercreek | NA | NA | NA | 23 | D | D | D | 232 | 5 106 | 887.4 | 84.4 |
| Bowling Green | NA | NA | NA | 15 | 130 | 34.0 | 3.5 | 111 | 1 839 | 394.7 | 33.9 |
| Brunswick | 5 620 | 33 | 100.0 | 56 | 654 | 268.9 | 30.2 | 115 | 1 553 | 594.4 | 41.6 |
| Canton | 1 554 | 13 | 100.0 | 100 | 1 407 | 612.4 | 62.0 | 232 | 3 215 | 725.7 | 71.0 |
| Cincinnati | 23 908 | 254 | 33.1 | 390 | 6 264 | 5 749.5 | 324.4 | 1 016 | 13 048 | 3 310.5 | 320.4 |
| Cleveland | 12 471 | 129 | 66.7 | 606 | 9 806 | 4 912.5 | 506.4 | 1 314 | 10 259 | 2 298.1 | 232.5 |
| Cleveland Heights | 1 739 | 6 | 100.0 | 6 | D | D | D | 123 | 1 748 | 378.8 | 40.2 |
| Columbus | 184 188 | 2 309 | 28.9 | 825 | 16 326 | 11 029.4 | 769.7 | 2 641 | 48 684 | 12 077.0 | 1 132.2 |
| Cuyahoga Falls | 0 | 0 | 0.0 | 46 | 527 | 184.1 | 22.2 | 184 | 3 674 | 986.5 | 81.3 |
| Dayton | 9 916 | 96 | 93.8 | 187 | 3 202 | 1 370.4 | 145.3 | 422 | 4 514 | 961.3 | 107.4 |
| Delaware | 18 836 | 98 | 100.0 | 24 | 174 | 63.5 | 7.5 | 115 | 1 606 | 419.7 | 37.1 |
| Dublin | 42 491 | 205 | 33.7 | 83 | 3 809 | 2 043.4 | 203.1 | 130 | 4 095 | 1 435.3 | 133.8 |
| Elyria | 1 939 | 20 | 100.0 | 57 | 527 | 401.3 | 24.0 | 257 | 4 814 | 930.8 | 90.6 |
| Euclid | 0 | 0 | 0.0 | 36 | 511 | 336.0 | 27.3 | 104 | 1 178 | 337.1 | 31.7 |
| Fairborn | 17 062 | 64 | 100.0 | 9 | 308 | 316.1 | 18.3 | 82 | 1 114 | 269.0 | 25.4 |
| Fairfield | 3 232 | 19 | 89.5 | 77 | 1 495 | 825.4 | 67.5 | 172 | 4 303 | 1 518.4 | 127.1 |
| Findlay | 7 302 | 24 | 100.0 | 42 | D | D | D | 245 | 3 701 | 819.3 | 74.4 |
| Gahanna | 1 896 | 9 | 100.0 | 43 | 520 | 406.0 | 21.6 | 90 | 1 861 | 587.2 | 50.1 |
| Garfield Heights | 0 | 0 | 0.0 | 28 | 347 | 137.2 | 12.8 | 83 | 1 359 | 256.1 | 24.0 |
| Green | NA | NA | NA | 34 | 744 | 501.9 | 44.7 | 64 | 1 416 | 639.9 | 43.2 |
| Grove City | 23 282 | 110 | 83.6 | 33 | 980 | 1 745.0 | 35.8 | 115 | 2 554 | 557.0 | 58.7 |
| Hamilton | 1 850 | 17 | 76.5 | 39 | 585 | 496.6 | 32.5 | 217 | 3 416 | 694.0 | 66.1 |
| Hilliard | 23 125 | 261 | 14.6 | 46 | 782 | 331.4 | 37.8 | 84 | 1 376 | 360.5 | 35.6 |
| Huber Heights | NA | NA | NA | 23 | 516 | 233.1 | 25.1 | 99 | 1 893 | 377.3 | 35.6 |
| Kent | 25 455 | 448 | 3.1 | 17 | 209 | 130.3 | 11.5 | 81 | 916 | 318.7 | 27.1 |

1. Merchant wholesalers except manufacturers' sales branches and offices.  2. Establishments with payroll.

| City | Real estate and rental and leasing, 2007 | | | | Professional, scientific, and technical services,[1] 2007 | | | | Manufacturing, 2007 | | | |
|---|---|---|---|---|---|---|---|---|---|---|---|---|
| | Number of establish-ments | Number of employees | Receipts (mil dol) | Annual payroll (mil dol) | Number of establish-ments | Number of employees | Receipts (mil dol) | Annual payroll (mil dol) | Number of establish-ments | Number of employees | Receipts (mil dol) | Annual payroll (mil dol) |
| | 80 | 81 | 82 | 83 | 84 | 85 | 86 | 87 | 88 | 89 | 90 | 91 |
| NORTH CAROLINA... | 11 258 | 53 563 | 11 175.1 | 1 881.4 | 22 385 | 182 224 | 26 003.8 | 10 698.3 | 10 150 | 506 013 | 205 867.3 | 19 589.8 |
| Apex | 34 | 88 | 14.9 | 2.6 | 167 | 419 | 52.1 | 19.8 | 33 | 1 181 | D | 61.1 |
| Asheboro | 37 | 173 | 31.6 | 4.3 | 73 | 376 | 33.6 | 11.0 | 80 | 8 766 | 2 758.2 | 283.2 |
| Asheville | 245 | 900 | 186.6 | 33.3 | 556 | D | D | D | 115 | 3 100 | D | 112.6 |
| Burlington | 79 | 307 | 51.0 | 8.1 | 114 | D | D | D | 100 | 5 331 | 1 001.0 | 182.3 |
| Cary | 213 | 880 | 207.0 | 38.7 | 806 | D | D | D | 75 | 1 808 | 606.9 | 86.4 |
| Chapel Hill | 88 | D | D | D | 286 | 3 208 | 317.4 | 126.3 | NA | NA | NA | NA |
| Charlotte | 1 460 | 10 841 | 2 676.3 | 513.2 | 3 009 | D | D | D | 716 | 24 523 | 8 996.3 | 1 103.9 |
| Concord | 127 | 459 | 69.4 | 13.7 | 208 | D | D | D | 84 | 5 967 | D | 319.3 |
| Durham | 289 | 1 832 | 351.7 | 71.0 | 838 | D | D | D | 147 | 8 554 | D | 514.2 |
| Fayetteville | 261 | 1 238 | 191.1 | 33.5 | 375 | D | D | D | 62 | D | D | D |
| Garner | 34 | 94 | 21.3 | 2.9 | 76 | 413 | 40.3 | 14.8 | 22 | 1 263 | 606.5 | 60.5 |
| Gastonia | 99 | 877 | 143.1 | 24.6 | 166 | D | D | D | 129 | 6 225 | 1 805.4 | 226.1 |
| Goldsboro | 57 | 244 | 29.8 | 5.6 | 109 | 736 | 59.4 | 21.0 | 46 | 2 489 | 399.9 | 86.3 |
| Greensboro | 465 | 3 336 | 1 225.1 | 108.5 | 992 | D | D | D | 350 | 18 969 | 19 687.6 | 925.5 |
| Greenville | 147 | 644 | 90.5 | 17.0 | 221 | 1 223 | 139.8 | 53.6 | 39 | 2 412 | D | 118.5 |
| Hickory | 111 | 404 | 96.4 | 12.1 | 210 | 1 360 | 146.1 | 51.9 | 188 | 10 207 | 1 770.4 | 351.5 |
| High Point | 119 | 790 | 168.5 | 26.4 | 306 | 2 445 | 343.1 | 131.1 | 284 | 15 048 | 3 380.2 | 540.7 |
| Huntersville | 69 | 139 | 33.1 | 4.9 | 152 | 660 | 92.4 | 37.0 | 29 | 1 065 | 228.7 | 48.1 |
| Indian Trail | 29 | 104 | 21.8 | 4.1 | 45 | 207 | 20.2 | 8.2 | 61 | 1 354 | D | 49.0 |
| Jacksonville | 99 | 468 | 79.9 | 11.6 | 127 | D | D | D | NA | NA | NA | NA |
| Kannapolis | 44 | 173 | 21.7 | 4.6 | 54 | 392 | 40.9 | 11.4 | 31 | 596 | D | 16.9 |
| Matthews | 52 | 189 | 24.5 | 6.2 | 138 | 642 | 98.3 | 37.4 | 40 | 990 | 277.7 | 38.6 |
| Monroe | 57 | 241 | 55.0 | 8.2 | 100 | 538 | 51.2 | 19.6 | 91 | 7 591 | 2 721.0 | 319.0 |
| Mooresville | 88 | 273 | 60.6 | 10.8 | 149 | 1 900 | 188.9 | 75.3 | 62 | 1 999 | 655.5 | 80.9 |
| New Bern | 60 | 220 | 33.8 | 6.5 | 127 | D | D | D | 35 | 3 110 | 911.8 | 133.7 |
| Raleigh | 787 | 4 794 | 1 356.2 | 235.6 | 2 132 | D | D | D | 294 | 6 235 | 2 285.7 | 280.8 |
| Rocky Mount | 81 | 413 | 75.4 | 11.4 | 141 | 883 | 95.5 | 35.8 | 56 | 5 697 | 1 481.0 | 223.9 |
| Salisbury | 57 | 190 | 37.1 | 6.0 | 109 | 907 | 70.1 | 28.9 | 68 | 2 995 | D | D |
| Sanford | 49 | 175 | 29.1 | 5.4 | 68 | D | D | D | 49 | 4 633 | 1 089.8 | 150.6 |
| Thomasville | 26 | 78 | 9.7 | 1.5 | 51 | 191 | 20.3 | 5.2 | 82 | 3 166 | D | 114.9 |
| Wake Forest | 35 | 68 | 14.4 | 2.6 | 95 | 326 | 35.6 | 13.7 | NA | NA | NA | NA |
| Wilmington | 289 | 1 318 | 239.5 | 43.4 | 647 | D | D | D | 102 | 4 009 | 1 725.8 | 224.2 |
| Wilson | 63 | 173 | 28.2 | 4.1 | 105 | D | D | D | 65 | 6 950 | 8 024.2 | 281.4 |
| Winston-Salem | 341 | D | D | D | 711 | D | D | D | 232 | 11 806 | 9 391.1 | 529.9 |
| NORTH DAKOTA | 770 | 3 748 | 668.8 | 96.0 | 1 432 | 9 707 | 1 110.7 | 416.9 | 767 | 26 361 | 11 349.8 | 991.4 |
| Bismarck | 105 | 358 | 53.3 | 8.2 | 249 | D | D | D | 65 | 1 991 | D | 81.7 |
| Fargo | 223 | 1 526 | 215.9 | 43.8 | 349 | D | D | D | 136 | 6 055 | 1 805.1 | 226.1 |
| Grand Forks | 53 | 386 | 54.7 | 8.8 | 107 | 912 | 88.7 | 45.4 | 43 | 2 512 | D | 78.5 |
| Minot | 64 | 433 | 142.3 | 10.2 | 85 | D | D | D | NA | NA | NA | NA |
| West Fargo | 25 | 73 | 6.3 | 1.4 | 33 | D | D | D | 47 | 1 842 | D | 71.8 |
| OHIO | 10 973 | 67 048 | 15 011.3 | 2 339.2 | 24 963 | 224 265 | 32 285.4 | 12 304.2 | 16 237 | 760 267 | 295 890.9 | 35 485.5 |
| Akron | 168 | 1 083 | 154.9 | 33.3 | 536 | D | D | D | 306 | 8 736 | 2 379.8 | 404.7 |
| Barberton | 7 | 50 | 5.0 | 0.7 | 43 | D | D | D | 65 | 2 292 | 679.3 | 88.3 |
| Beavercreek | 44 | 203 | 49.6 | 4.8 | 173 | D | D | D | NA | NA | NA | NA |
| Bowling Green | 40 | 193 | 20.0 | 4.4 | 56 | D | D | D | 39 | 2 637 | 910.1 | 112.4 |
| Brunswick | 27 | 105 | 12.9 | 1.8 | 71 | 371 | 32.6 | 13.2 | 48 | 938 | 178.3 | 40.1 |
| Canton | 75 | 282 | 48.0 | 7.3 | 175 | 861 | 101.5 | 32.0 | 146 | 9 975 | 3 526.9 | 467.2 |
| Cincinnati | 450 | 2 423 | 505.9 | 102.3 | 1 157 | 20 569 | 3 124.8 | 1 408.7 | 428 | 18 795 | 6 446.6 | 877.5 |
| Cleveland | 361 | 5 548 | 1 866.6 | 287.2 | 1 260 | D | D | D | 922 | 26 961 | 7 497.0 | 1 271.1 |
| Cleveland Heights | 51 | 183 | 24.8 | 3.7 | 113 | 229 | 30.8 | 10.6 | NA | NA | NA | NA |
| Columbus | 993 | 8 129 | 1 767.2 | 325.0 | 2 122 | D | D | D | 600 | 24 027 | 11 317.9 | 1 102.5 |
| Cuyahoga Falls | 53 | 282 | 33.6 | 8.3 | 116 | 699 | 71.0 | 29.9 | 81 | 4 091 | 1 170.2 | 165.4 |
| Dayton | 138 | 918 | 129.3 | 26.4 | 358 | D | D | D | 303 | 12 820 | 3 197.1 | 571.1 |
| Delaware | 44 | 131 | 18.6 | 3.6 | 53 | 233 | 25.7 | 9.8 | 34 | 2 728 | 1 584.5 | 142.1 |
| Dublin | 82 | 540 | 134.9 | 24.7 | 341 | 3 427 | 499.9 | 200.8 | 29 | 1 978 | 437.2 | 86.6 |
| Elyria | 54 | 334 | 41.9 | 8.6 | 77 | D | D | D | 108 | 5 650 | 1 538.0 | 260.8 |
| Euclid | 51 | 319 | 37.0 | 8.7 | 49 | D | D | D | 80 | 5 429 | 1 671.5 | 290.5 |
| Fairborn | 30 | 141 | 14.0 | 3.3 | 77 | D | D | D | 12 | 572 | D | 23.5 |
| Fairfield | 49 | 319 | 132.9 | 10.9 | 84 | 512 | 50.0 | 21.2 | 90 | 4 636 | 1 155.8 | 173.9 |
| Findlay | 55 | 436 | 46.2 | 11.5 | 106 | 861 | 74.3 | 31.0 | 63 | 6 513 | 1 769.5 | 300.0 |
| Gahanna | 41 | 154 | 39.4 | 5.7 | 146 | 892 | 107.1 | 42.9 | 34 | 1 107 | 238.8 | 42.3 |
| Garfield Heights | 18 | 73 | 17.6 | 2.7 | 52 | 376 | 39.6 | 19.0 | 38 | 1 223 | 233.3 | 51.9 |
| Green | 26 | 224 | 39.0 | 4.8 | 63 | 968 | 75.5 | 50.9 | 44 | 1 529 | 403.3 | 57.6 |
| Grove City | 36 | 145 | 19.6 | 4.2 | 54 | 321 | 28.2 | 10.2 | 30 | 1 714 | 379.7 | 74.1 |
| Hamilton | 47 | 248 | 36.8 | 6.6 | 112 | D | D | D | 79 | 2 827 | 1 034.2 | 125.6 |
| Hilliard | 49 | 154 | 20.0 | 4.2 | 76 | 404 | 48.6 | 23.0 | 31 | 1 514 | 355.4 | 65.5 |
| Huber Heights | 24 | 126 | 20.4 | 5.8 | 34 | 330 | 26.9 | 10.0 | 34 | 1 348 | 432.8 | 73.7 |
| Kent | 24 | 89 | 12.5 | 2.3 | 50 | 321 | 36.4 | 13.5 | 63 | 1 855 | D | 74.3 |

1. Establishments subject to federal tax.

# Table D. Cities — Accommodation and Food Services, Arts, Entertainment, and Recreation, and Health Care and Social Assistance

| City | Accommodation and food services, 2007 | | | | Arts, entertainment, and recreation,[1] 2007 | | | | Health care and social assistance,[1] 2007 | | | |
|---|---|---|---|---|---|---|---|---|---|---|---|---|
| | Number of establishments | Number of employees | Sales (mil dol) | Annual payroll (mil dol) | Number of establishments | Number of employees | Receipts (mil dol) | Annual payroll (mil dol) | Number of establishments | Number of employees | Receipts (mil dol) | Annual payroll (mil dol) |
| | 92 | 93 | 94 | 95 | 96 | 97 | 98 | 99 | 100 | 101 | 102 | 103 |
| NORTH CAROLINA ... | 18 268 | 343 235 | 16 126.9 | 4 395.1 | 2 676 | 37 489 | 3 588.0 | 1 148.8 | 17 964 | 286 998 | 22 794.8 | 10 132.8 |
| Apex | 75 | 1 237 | 57.1 | 15.8 | 10 | D | D | D | 87 | 762 | 51.7 | 23.1 |
| Asheboro | 88 | 1 649 | 67.5 | 18.5 | 6 | D | D | D | 122 | 1 552 | 125.2 | 58.2 |
| Asheville | 478 | 11 166 | 560.1 | 167.5 | 51 | 480 | 23.7 | 7.9 | 464 | 6 999 | 776.0 | 339.8 |
| Burlington | 183 | 3 616 | 151.8 | 44.4 | 17 | D | D | D | 174 | 2 696 | 214.0 | 103.9 |
| Cary | 322 | 6 654 | 317.5 | 88.6 | 46 | 821 | 48.1 | 15.5 | 395 | 4 388 | 438.8 | 180.7 |
| Chapel Hill | 222 | 4 683 | 219.7 | 64.8 | 21 | 229 | 7.1 | 3.2 | 191 | D | D | D |
| Charlotte | 1 803 | 37 995 | 2 107.7 | 578.3 | 211 | 5 136 | 559.0 | 265.3 | 1 542 | 24 083 | 2 463.3 | 1 129.8 |
| Concord | 206 | 4 796 | 239.3 | 67.8 | 36 | 1 593 | 497.4 | 129.2 | 196 | 3 580 | 288.6 | 142.9 |
| Durham | 550 | 11 809 | 652.1 | 179.5 | 56 | D | D | D | 560 | D | D | D |
| Fayetteville | 453 | 10 088 | 408.1 | 108.3 | 36 | D | D | D | 571 | D | D | D |
| Garner | 71 | 1 637 | 69.7 | 18.9 | 7 | D | D | D | 69 | 1 222 | 78.6 | 34.7 |
| Gastonia | 179 | 4 008 | 182.2 | 49.8 | 24 | 186 | 10.5 | 2.4 | 265 | D | D | D |
| Goldsboro | 150 | 2 791 | 110.0 | 29.7 | 15 | D | D | D | 190 | 3 116 | 244.8 | 102.6 |
| Greensboro | 759 | 16 581 | 769.6 | 218.6 | 80 | D | D | D | 700 | 11 476 | 1 044.9 | 496.8 |
| Greenville | 252 | 6 365 | 265.1 | 71.8 | 25 | 305 | 13.7 | 4.1 | 267 | D | D | D |
| Hickory | 232 | 4 776 | 196.6 | 56.6 | 15 | 173 | 15.6 | 3.6 | 226 | 5 072 | 585.7 | 231.6 |
| High Point | 249 | 4 994 | 206.3 | 59.1 | 24 | D | D | D | 229 | 4 335 | 486.7 | 194.2 |
| Huntersville | 86 | 2 164 | 103.9 | 27.7 | 30 | 706 | 129.9 | 44.3 | 113 | 1 380 | 141.3 | 55.3 |
| Indian Trail | 51 | 568 | 29.0 | 7.1 | 9 | 87 | 6.3 | 1.2 | 21 | D | D | D |
| Jacksonville | 174 | 4 352 | 183.7 | 47.4 | 17 | 456 | 16.0 | 5.3 | 170 | D | D | D |
| Kannapolis | 81 | 1 275 | 55.2 | 15.3 | 8 | D | D | D | 58 | 838 | 57.8 | 25.5 |
| Matthews | 90 | 1 940 | 89.1 | 23.5 | 18 | D | D | D | 109 | D | D | D |
| Monroe | 105 | 2 151 | 99.7 | 23.1 | 5 | D | D | D | 106 | 1 726 | 142.5 | 64.0 |
| Mooresville | 150 | 2 908 | 126.7 | 35.1 | 51 | D | D | D | 132 | D | D | D |
| New Bern | 103 | 2 352 | 91.2 | 23.8 | 11 | D | D | D | 163 | D | D | D |
| Raleigh | 980 | 20 611 | 999.7 | 280.6 | 131 | 3 172 | 275.0 | 90.1 | 1 111 | 16 932 | 1 652.4 | 771.8 |
| Rocky Mount | 155 | 3 695 | 150.3 | 41.0 | 19 | D | D | D | 201 | 3 504 | 268.0 | 117.1 |
| Salisbury | 128 | 2 500 | 103.7 | 29.1 | 18 | D | D | D | 131 | 2 223 | 177.0 | 82.5 |
| Sanford | 85 | 1 643 | 61.2 | 15.9 | 7 | D | D | D | 127 | 2 277 | 168.7 | 68.6 |
| Thomasville | 60 | 995 | 36.8 | 10.6 | 4 | D | D | D | 37 | 687 | 43.7 | 20.7 |
| Wake Forest | 52 | 771 | 34.5 | 10.0 | 18 | D | D | D | 68 | D | D | D |
| Wilmington | 418 | 8 924 | 373.2 | 107.0 | 55 | 701 | 33.7 | 9.7 | 506 | D | D | D |
| Wilson | 117 | 2 394 | 105.2 | 27.0 | 13 | D | D | D | 138 | D | D | D |
| Winston-Salem | 527 | 10 856 | 508.1 | 142.4 | 63 | 557 | 26.6 | 7.3 | 541 | D | D | D |
| NORTH DAKOTA | 1 840 | 30 307 | 1 214.2 | 337.8 | 267 | 2 539 | 131.1 | 35.4 | 1 176 | 14 135 | 1 426.8 | 570.7 |
| Bismarck | 162 | 4 332 | 166.9 | 49.6 | 20 | D | D | D | 178 | D | D | D |
| Fargo | 296 | 7 976 | 314.2 | 93.5 | 45 | 608 | 44.4 | 8.2 | 285 | 5 745 | 785.3 | 304.6 |
| Grand Forks | 162 | 3 980 | 135.4 | 39.7 | 20 | 170 | 7.9 | 2.2 | 93 | D | D | D |
| Minot | 124 | 2 687 | 100.2 | 28.3 | 17 | D | D | D | 101 | D | D | D |
| West Fargo | 32 | 528 | 19.8 | 5.7 | 1 | D | D | D | 36 | D | D | D |
| OHIO | 23 959 | 436 598 | 17 779.9 | 5 078.5 | 3 122 | 40 269 | 4 067.9 | 1 360.1 | 22 693 | 346 386 | 28 636.8 | 12 631.1 |
| Akron | 443 | 6 065 | 247.8 | 67.8 | 40 | 570 | 49.7 | 13.2 | 367 | 6 681 | 617.6 | 304.4 |
| Barberton | 46 | 703 | 23.2 | 6.3 | 4 | D | D | D | 80 | 1 893 | 204.9 | 82.4 |
| Beavercreek | 100 | D | D | D | 4 | 48 | 3.3 | 0.8 | 108 | D | D | D |
| Bowling Green | 96 | 2 026 | 62.4 | 18.8 | 13 | D | D | D | 72 | 870 | 72.4 | 32.4 |
| Brunswick | 73 | 1 093 | 41.0 | 10.8 | 8 | D | D | D | 53 | 666 | 40.9 | 17.9 |
| Canton | 160 | 2 224 | 79.9 | 21.8 | 11 | 208 | 5.9 | 2.1 | 159 | 3 037 | 316.4 | 150.4 |
| Cincinnati | 730 | 13 938 | 712.8 | 207.1 | 83 | 1 379 | 389.9 | 257.8 | 698 | 15 502 | 1 549.1 | 811.2 |
| Cleveland | 995 | 16 038 | 868.1 | 235.2 | 97 | 3 115 | 589.0 | 298.8 | 447 | 7 487 | 492.6 | 220.4 |
| Cleveland Heights | 86 | 1 162 | 50.8 | 14.6 | 12 | 61 | 3.4 | 0.9 | 96 | 1 245 | 80.4 | 35.3 |
| Columbus | 1 852 | 41 282 | 1 944.8 | 553.4 | 145 | 3 364 | 254.2 | 101.1 | 1 457 | 24 611 | 2 450.4 | 1 105.0 |
| Cuyahoga Falls | 117 | 2 514 | 106.8 | 31.5 | 6 | D | D | D | 134 | D | D | D |
| Dayton | 294 | 4 483 | 190.9 | 54.7 | 20 | 270 | 21.4 | 5.5 | 332 | 5 790 | 632.4 | 315.1 |
| Delaware | 85 | 1 401 | 55.0 | 14.2 | 9 | 48 | 4.7 | 1.2 | 75 | 930 | 68.0 | 28.9 |
| Dublin | 114 | 3 032 | 147.4 | 45.6 | 26 | D | D | D | 167 | D | D | D |
| Elyria | 139 | 2 501 | 89.3 | 25.9 | 10 | D | D | D | 116 | 1 509 | 137.7 | 57.4 |
| Euclid | 78 | 683 | 26.1 | 6.8 | 7 | D | D | D | 90 | D | D | D |
| Fairborn | 84 | 1 573 | 64.7 | 18.2 | 4 | 64 | 1.5 | 0.4 | 35 | 388 | 25.3 | 10.1 |
| Fairfield | 95 | 2 099 | 94.6 | 25.2 | 12 | D | D | D | 152 | D | D | D |
| Findlay | 135 | 2 981 | 108.5 | 31.8 | 8 | D | D | D | 127 | D | D | D |
| Gahanna | 95 | 1 907 | 78.2 | 21.0 | 10 | D | D | D | 114 | 1 989 | 137.6 | 67.9 |
| Garfield Heights | 55 | 712 | 27.5 | 7.3 | 3 | 9 | 0.5 | 0.2 | 66 | 1 086 | 153.8 | 45.0 |
| Green | 58 | 1 195 | 46.5 | 13.1 | 12 | 140 | 10.5 | 3.0 | 66 | D | D | D |
| Grove City | 113 | 2 551 | 104.6 | 32.2 | 14 | D | D | D | 85 | D | D | D |
| Hamilton | 119 | 2 341 | 88.6 | 26.2 | 7 | D | D | D | 113 | 1 409 | 143.4 | 55.7 |
| Hilliard | 57 | 1 514 | 58.1 | 17.7 | 18 | 257 | 26.4 | 9.2 | 77 | 783 | 62.6 | 23.0 |
| Huber Heights | 69 | 1 389 | 55.6 | 16.0 | 8 | D | D | D | 68 | D | D | D |
| Kent | 74 | 1 308 | 54.4 | 13.4 | 5 | D | D | D | 40 | 520 | 36.6 | 16.1 |

1. Establishments subject to federal tax.

| City | Other services[1], 2007 | | | | Selected federal funds, 2009–2010 (mil dol) | | | | | | | | |
|---|---|---|---|---|---|---|---|---|---|---|---|---|---|
| | | | | | Procurement contracts | | Grants | | | | | | |
| | Number of establish-ments | Number of employees | Receipts (mil dol) | Annual payroll (mil dol) | Defense | Other | Total[2] | Medicaid and other health related | Nutrition and family welfare | Energy and envi-ronment | Disasters and emergency prepared-ness | Housing and community develop-ment | Employment and training |
| | 104 | 105 | 106 | 107 | 108 | 109 | 110 | 111 | 112 | 113 | 114 | 115 | 116 |
| NORTH CAROLINA... | 11 846 | 67 498 | 5 307.6 | 1 628.9 | 3 626.5 | 2 464.0 | 20 098.9 | 11 594.5 | 2 009.1 | 976.2 | 25.2 | 644.5 | 302.8 |
| Apex | 51 | D | D | D | 0.9 | 26.9 | 0.1 | 0.0 | 0.0 | 0.0 | 0.0 | 0.0 | 0.0 |
| Asheboro | 45 | D | D | D | 15.6 | 3.3 | 11.3 | 0.6 | 3.1 | 0.3 | 0.3 | 5.3 | 0.0 |
| Asheville | 200 | 1 206 | 80.4 | 27.3 | 19.4 | 71.6 | 34.6 | 2.3 | 7.0 | 1.6 | 0.0 | 14.4 | 0.5 |
| Burlington | 90 | 528 | 31.1 | 10.5 | 5.0 | 2.6 | 6.3 | 2.7 | 0.4 | 0.2 | 0.0 | 1.5 | 0.0 |
| Cary | 194 | 1 823 | 134.4 | 48.3 | 15.1 | 16.7 | 15.5 | 4.5 | 0.0 | 7.9 | 0.0 | 0.5 | 0.0 |
| Chapel Hill | 61 | 558 | 34.0 | 12.6 | 3.1 | 64.3 | 914.9 | 749.9 | 7.9 | 8.4 | 0.2 | 2.2 | 3.8 |
| Charlotte | 1 090 | 8 624 | 685.8 | 231.6 | 85.9 | 270.5 | 462.1 | 16.6 | 7.5 | 288.3 | -0.4 | 87.4 | 0.1 |
| Concord | 116 | 700 | 46.1 | 14.0 | 1.0 | 3.0 | 10.0 | 0.7 | 1.2 | 0.0 | 1.3 | 6.7 | 0.0 |
| Durham | 309 | 2 641 | 282.8 | 77.1 | 70.5 | 279.9 | 1 372.5 | 821.2 | 3.4 | 205.8 | 0.0 | 40.7 | 0.0 |
| Fayetteville | 252 | 1 824 | 116.4 | 39.3 | 57.2 | 30.0 | 62.8 | 0.6 | 6.2 | 2.2 | 0.0 | 18.3 | 0.1 |
| Garner | 52 | 314 | 26.0 | 8.1 | 0.7 | 0.3 | 0.0 | 0.0 | 0.0 | 0.0 | 0.0 | 0.0 | 0.0 |
| Gastonia | 122 | 759 | 45.7 | 14.7 | 0.3 | 1.1 | 22.9 | 2.5 | 4.2 | 0.0 | 0.0 | 11.6 | 0.0 |
| Goldsboro | 83 | D | D | D | 14.1 | 0.5 | 18.7 | 0.0 | 5.0 | 0.4 | 0.0 | 5.6 | 0.0 |
| Greensboro | 425 | 2 632 | 213.4 | 68.6 | 48.3 | 30.9 | 150.9 | 16.5 | 8.6 | 7.6 | 0.3 | 24.5 | 0.1 |
| Greenville | 109 | 707 | 49.7 | 13.3 | 9.9 | 3.1 | 36.2 | 21.6 | 0.1 | 0.1 | 0.0 | 7.1 | 0.0 |
| Hickory | 114 | D | D | D | 0.7 | 3.3 | 9.6 | 0.4 | 0.0 | 0.0 | 0.0 | 8.7 | 0.3 |
| High Point | 171 | 1 165 | 91.8 | 28.1 | 21.2 | 79.3 | 14.3 | -1.1 | 0.0 | 0.8 | 0.0 | 12.4 | 0.0 |
| Huntersville | 65 | 387 | 23.4 | 7.7 | 0.3 | 0.3 | 0.1 | 0.0 | 0.0 | 0.0 | 0.0 | 0.1 | 0.0 |
| Indian Trail | 56 | D | D | D | 0.3 | 0.1 | 0.0 | 0.0 | 0.0 | 0.0 | 0.0 | 0.0 | 0.0 |
| Jacksonville | 117 | 758 | 42.2 | 14.2 | 33.8 | 0.2 | 27.3 | 0.2 | 1.8 | 0.6 | 0.0 | 4.5 | 0.0 |
| Kannapolis | 58 | D | D | D | 0.0 | 0.0 | 2.5 | 0.0 | 1.3 | 0.2 | 0.0 | 0.4 | 0.0 |
| Matthews | 56 | 292 | 22.1 | 6.8 | 0.1 | 0.3 | 0.2 | 0.0 | 0.0 | 0.0 | 0.0 | 0.0 | 0.0 |
| Monroe | 94 | 518 | 43.4 | 13.5 | 12.7 | 6.1 | 9.0 | 0.0 | 4.1 | 0.7 | 0.0 | 3.0 | 0.0 |
| Mooresville | 89 | 436 | 34.1 | 10.2 | 6.5 | 0.1 | 0.3 | 0.0 | 0.0 | 0.0 | 0.0 | 0.2 | 0.0 |
| New Bern | 64 | 309 | 19.4 | 5.4 | 1.3 | 4.9 | 8.8 | 0.0 | 0.0 | 0.1 | 0.0 | 5.9 | 0.0 |
| Raleigh | 693 | 5 015 | 345.4 | 118.8 | 64.9 | 66.0 | 2 880.8 | 252.1 | 450.7 | 362.4 | 0.7 | 118.3 | 296.1 |
| Rocky Mount | 102 | D | D | D | 11.6 | 0.6 | 14.6 | 0.0 | 4.6 | 0.6 | 0.0 | 8.0 | 0.0 |
| Salisbury | 49 | 286 | 20.0 | 6.7 | 0.5 | 50.7 | 20.8 | 0.0 | 7.1 | 0.0 | 0.0 | 6.2 | 0.0 |
| Sanford | 57 | 326 | 21.0 | 7.1 | 0.3 | 0.6 | 3.2 | 0.0 | 0.0 | 0.0 | 0.0 | 3.1 | 0.0 |
| Thomasville | 56 | D | D | D | 3.4 | 1.3 | 1.0 | 0.0 | 0.0 | 0.0 | 0.0 | 1.0 | 0.0 |
| Wake Forest | 43 | 246 | 24.3 | 7.6 | 0.8 | 0.0 | 0.0 | 0.0 | 0.0 | 0.0 | 0.0 | 0.0 | 0.0 |
| Wilmington | 272 | 1 638 | 120.7 | 36.7 | 25.5 | 27.2 | 99.4 | 32.1 | 2.1 | 29.8 | 0.0 | 18.5 | 0.3 |
| Wilson | 74 | D | D | D | 13.4 | 1.3 | 9.8 | 4.1 | 0.0 | 0.2 | 0.0 | 4.3 | 0.0 |
| Winston-Salem | 330 | 2 049 | 137.4 | 52.4 | 20.5 | 10.5 | 333.3 | 241.6 | 4.3 | 2.7 | 2.0 | 42.5 | 0.0 |
| NORTH DAKOTA | 1 241 | 6 059 | 487.1 | 140.7 | 288.2 | 397.1 | 2 237.3 | 630.3 | 202.8 | 279.8 | 141.1 | 75.4 | 23.8 |
| Bismarck | 140 | D | D | D | 3.8 | 29.5 | 290.6 | 28.5 | 36.4 | 42.5 | 10.3 | 18.0 | 22.0 |
| Fargo | 225 | 1 703 | 112.8 | 44.1 | 20.6 | 179.9 | 117.0 | 19.3 | 4.0 | 15.6 | 0.0 | 9.0 | 0.0 |
| Grand Forks | 103 | 672 | 46.2 | 13.9 | 10.3 | 15.6 | 110.1 | 20.4 | 2.3 | 44.5 | 0.0 | 7.7 | 0.0 |
| Minot | 86 | 505 | 36.8 | 10.7 | 18.9 | 16.8 | 29.2 | 2.1 | 3.9 | 0.2 | 0.0 | 4.4 | 0.0 |
| West Fargo | 38 | 239 | 23.1 | 7.2 | 1.1 | 0.9 | 3.9 | 0.0 | 0.0 | 0.1 | 0.0 | 2.5 | 0.0 |
| OHIO | 16 338 | 106 072 | 8 483.2 | 2 613.6 | 6 064.3 | 2 765.1 | 24 399.0 | 13 659.6 | 3 021.0 | 847.8 | 15.8 | 1 215.5 | 404.6 |
| Akron | 313 | 2 040 | 166.1 | 49.7 | 307.0 | 8.5 | 173.0 | 13.3 | 11.0 | 64.3 | 0.0 | 59.3 | 7.2 |
| Barberton | 46 | 250 | 19.2 | 6.3 | 0.5 | 0.0 | 2.2 | 0.0 | 0.0 | 0.9 | 0.0 | 0.8 | 0.0 |
| Beavercreek | 48 | D | D | D | 7.9 | 3.8 | 0.7 | 0.4 | 0.0 | 0.2 | 0.0 | 0.0 | 0.0 |
| Bowling Green | 47 | 222 | 14.5 | 4.4 | 0.1 | 0.1 | 12.5 | 1.9 | 0.0 | 1.6 | 0.0 | 0.8 | 0.0 |
| Brunswick | 55 | 368 | 29.0 | 8.1 | 1.3 | 0.6 | 0.0 | 0.0 | 0.0 | 0.0 | 0.0 | 0.0 | 0.0 |
| Canton | 132 | 670 | 43.7 | 13.4 | 5.4 | 2.0 | 43.2 | 1.7 | 6.0 | 8.4 | 0.0 | 20.1 | 0.4 |
| Cincinnati | 418 | 2 971 | 238.8 | 78.3 | 1 784.8 | 302.2 | 699.6 | 400.1 | 29.2 | 29.3 | 0.0 | 152.3 | 11.6 |
| Cleveland | 624 | 3 972 | 355.6 | 93.2 | 65.4 | 355.4 | 1 129.0 | 570.0 | 35.5 | 14.5 | 0.2 | 245.2 | 0.8 |
| Cleveland Heights | 53 | 321 | 27.3 | 8.5 | 0.0 | 0.7 | 4.3 | 0.6 | 0.0 | 0.0 | 0.0 | 3.7 | 0.0 |
| Columbus | 1 150 | 9 379 | 673.5 | 215.0 | 535.1 | 262.5 | 3 619.3 | 645.9 | 651.1 | 532.3 | 7.4 | 252.5 | 339.4 |
| Cuyahoga Falls | 95 | 550 | 39.6 | 13.2 | 3.7 | 0.1 | 3.2 | 0.0 | 0.0 | 0.4 | 0.0 | 2.4 | 0.0 |
| Dayton | 195 | 1 702 | 150.5 | 52.6 | 343.3 | 118.3 | 202.9 | 15.1 | 20.1 | 12.2 | 0.0 | 85.7 | 1.0 |
| Delaware | 34 | 169 | 13.9 | 4.7 | 0.3 | 0.5 | 4.5 | 0.1 | 0.0 | 0.0 | 0.0 | 2.6 | 0.0 |
| Dublin | 40 | 524 | 42.5 | 15.1 | 538.7 | 3.7 | 1.6 | 0.8 | 0.0 | 0.1 | 0.0 | 0.0 | 0.0 |
| Elyria | 76 | 583 | 67.9 | 17.2 | 5.9 | 1.0 | 5.4 | 0.0 | 0.0 | 0.9 | 0.0 | 1.3 | 0.0 |
| Euclid | 63 | 289 | 20.6 | 10.8 | 3.0 | 0.2 | 4.7 | 0.0 | 0.0 | 2.7 | 0.0 | 1.2 | 0.0 |
| Fairborn | 40 | 187 | 11.3 | 3.7 | 67.0 | 1.1 | 0.6 | 0.0 | 0.0 | 0.0 | 0.0 | 0.3 | 0.0 |
| Fairfield | 96 | 594 | 48.3 | 15.6 | 74.2 | 12.6 | 4.6 | 0.1 | 4.4 | 0.0 | 0.0 | 0.0 | 0.0 |
| Findlay | 85 | 542 | 45.8 | 14.8 | 0.2 | 0.4 | 6.7 | 0.0 | 2.6 | 1.0 | 0.0 | 2.9 | 0.0 |
| Gahanna | 56 | 663 | 46.2 | 15.6 | 0.3 | 0.8 | 0.3 | 0.0 | 0.0 | 0.0 | 0.0 | 0.1 | 0.0 |
| Garfield Heights | 42 | 230 | 11.6 | 3.7 | 0.0 | 0.0 | 0.0 | 0.0 | 0.0 | 0.0 | 0.0 | 0.0 | 0.0 |
| Green | 37 | D | D | D | 0.0 | 0.4 | 0.0 | 0.0 | 0.0 | 0.0 | 0.0 | 0.0 | 0.0 |
| Grove City | 63 | 522 | 38.7 | 18.1 | 14.2 | 0.1 | 0.3 | 0.0 | 0.0 | 0.0 | 0.0 | 0.0 | 0.0 |
| Hamilton | 78 | 380 | 35.4 | 10.7 | 0.1 | 0.2 | 17.1 | 0.2 | 0.0 | 0.7 | 0.0 | 14.0 | 0.0 |
| Hilliard | 43 | 269 | 26.1 | 7.3 | 1.8 | 0.0 | 0.2 | 0.0 | 0.0 | 0.0 | 0.0 | 0.1 | 0.0 |
| Huber Heights | 52 | 226 | 15.1 | 6.1 | 0.0 | 0.0 | 0.2 | 0.0 | 0.0 | 0.2 | 0.0 | 0.0 | 0.0 |
| Kent | 45 | 237 | 11.7 | 4.6 | 0.9 | 0.2 | 26.8 | 8.7 | 0.0 | 1.4 | 0.0 | 0.6 | 0.0 |

1. Establishments subject to federal tax.   2. Includes program categories not shown separately. State totals include additional categories not allocated by city.

# Table D. Cities — City Government Finances

<table>
<tr><td rowspan="8">City</td><td colspan="9">City government finances, 2007</td></tr>
<tr><td colspan="6">General revenue</td><td colspan="3">General expenditure</td></tr>
<tr><td colspan="3">Intergovernmental</td><td colspan="3">Taxes</td><td></td><td colspan="2">Per capita[1] (dollars)</td></tr>
<tr><td></td><td></td><td></td><td></td><td colspan="3">Per capita[1] (dollars)</td><td></td><td></td></tr>
<tr><td rowspan="4">Total (mil dol)</td><td rowspan="4">Total (mil dol)</td><td rowspan="4">Percent from state government</td><td rowspan="4">Total (mil dol)</td><td></td><td></td><td></td><td rowspan="4">Total (mil dol)</td><td rowspan="4">Total</td><td rowspan="4">Capital outlays</td></tr>
<tr><td rowspan="3">Total</td><td rowspan="3">Property</td><td rowspan="3">Sales and gross receipts</td></tr>
<tr></tr>
<tr></tr>
<tr><td>117</td><td>118</td><td>119</td><td>120</td><td>121</td><td>122</td><td>123</td><td>124</td><td>125</td><td>126</td></tr>
<tr><td>NORTH CAROLINA...</td><td>X</td><td>X</td><td>X</td><td>X</td><td>X</td><td>X</td><td>X</td><td>X</td><td>X</td><td>X</td></tr>
<tr><td>Apex</td><td>37.5</td><td>8.1</td><td>27.5</td><td>13.0</td><td>412</td><td>366</td><td>46</td><td>32.6</td><td>1 030</td><td>310</td></tr>
<tr><td>Asheboro</td><td>27.0</td><td>7.2</td><td>37.7</td><td>10.8</td><td>447</td><td>419</td><td>28</td><td>24.0</td><td>991</td><td>62</td></tr>
<tr><td>Asheville</td><td>122.1</td><td>36.8</td><td>26.8</td><td>49.4</td><td>669</td><td>560</td><td>110</td><td>100.1</td><td>1 356</td><td>157</td></tr>
<tr><td>Burlington</td><td>63.0</td><td>16.7</td><td>38.2</td><td>24.8</td><td>499</td><td>444</td><td>55</td><td>54.6</td><td>1 101</td><td>176</td></tr>
<tr><td>Cary</td><td>197.2</td><td>35.2</td><td>28.8</td><td>64.6</td><td>530</td><td>446</td><td>84</td><td>159.7</td><td>1 312</td><td>483</td></tr>
<tr><td>Chapel Hill</td><td>79.9</td><td>38.3</td><td>25.3</td><td>32.0</td><td>621</td><td>557</td><td>64</td><td>64.3</td><td>1 247</td><td>320</td></tr>
<tr><td>Charlotte</td><td>1 458.3</td><td>406.3</td><td>25.3</td><td>412.2</td><td>614</td><td>467</td><td>147</td><td>1 187.2</td><td>1 768</td><td>491</td></tr>
<tr><td>Concord</td><td>105.4</td><td>27.6</td><td>27.0</td><td>36.8</td><td>569</td><td>529</td><td>40</td><td>87.9</td><td>1 360</td><td>200</td></tr>
<tr><td>Durham</td><td>293.7</td><td>82.8</td><td>24.4</td><td>117.6</td><td>540</td><td>465</td><td>75</td><td>259.4</td><td>1 191</td><td>157</td></tr>
<tr><td>Fayetteville</td><td>196.5</td><td>57.5</td><td>29.3</td><td>64.7</td><td>377</td><td>341</td><td>36</td><td>168.7</td><td>982</td><td>188</td></tr>
<tr><td>Garner</td><td>23.1</td><td>7.2</td><td>27.8</td><td>14.4</td><td>570</td><td>482</td><td>88</td><td>20.3</td><td>801</td><td>101</td></tr>
<tr><td>Gastonia</td><td>78.8</td><td>22.8</td><td>29.3</td><td>28.2</td><td>397</td><td>343</td><td>54</td><td>70.5</td><td>992</td><td>82</td></tr>
<tr><td>Goldsboro</td><td>40.8</td><td>12.7</td><td>32.0</td><td>14.1</td><td>374</td><td>332</td><td>43</td><td>37.4</td><td>994</td><td>132</td></tr>
<tr><td>Greensboro</td><td>361.7</td><td>90.9</td><td>29.4</td><td>148.4</td><td>601</td><td>542</td><td>59</td><td>370.3</td><td>1 498</td><td>229</td></tr>
<tr><td>Greenville</td><td>94.1</td><td>25.4</td><td>33.4</td><td>27.8</td><td>366</td><td>306</td><td>60</td><td>90.2</td><td>1 186</td><td>151</td></tr>
<tr><td>Hickory</td><td>63.2</td><td>18.8</td><td>28.7</td><td>24.4</td><td>596</td><td>537</td><td>58</td><td>51.7</td><td>1 261</td><td>98</td></tr>
<tr><td>High Point</td><td>156.3</td><td>37.0</td><td>46.3</td><td>59.7</td><td>595</td><td>520</td><td>75</td><td>143.7</td><td>1 431</td><td>314</td></tr>
<tr><td>Huntersville</td><td>25.9</td><td>8.0</td><td>48.9</td><td>13.3</td><td>312</td><td>280</td><td>32</td><td>24.6</td><td>579</td><td>133</td></tr>
<tr><td>Indian Trail</td><td>5.2</td><td>2.0</td><td>68.2</td><td>2.6</td><td>144</td><td>123</td><td>21</td><td>5.2</td><td>288</td><td>45</td></tr>
<tr><td>Jacksonville</td><td>52.5</td><td>20.1</td><td>29.6</td><td>15.5</td><td>207</td><td>180</td><td>27</td><td>52.9</td><td>709</td><td>168</td></tr>
<tr><td>Kannapolis</td><td>38.4</td><td>9.2</td><td>36.7</td><td>13.0</td><td>313</td><td>292</td><td>21</td><td>35.2</td><td>847</td><td>177</td></tr>
<tr><td>Matthews</td><td>21.8</td><td>5.2</td><td>43.0</td><td>10.0</td><td>375</td><td>318</td><td>57</td><td>16.6</td><td>621</td><td>89</td></tr>
<tr><td>Monroe</td><td>53.3</td><td>10.3</td><td>31.1</td><td>16.0</td><td>506</td><td>432</td><td>73</td><td>39.8</td><td>1 258</td><td>133</td></tr>
<tr><td>Mooresville</td><td>44.8</td><td>9.7</td><td>24.8</td><td>20.0</td><td>923</td><td>895</td><td>28</td><td>47.7</td><td>2 198</td><td>890</td></tr>
<tr><td>New Bern</td><td>37.9</td><td>9.7</td><td>43.2</td><td>11.2</td><td>396</td><td>355</td><td>41</td><td>41.6</td><td>1 475</td><td>157</td></tr>
<tr><td>Raleigh</td><td>485.3</td><td>128.8</td><td>28.8</td><td>177.6</td><td>473</td><td>383</td><td>89</td><td>564.0</td><td>1 501</td><td>512</td></tr>
<tr><td>Rocky Mount</td><td>66.7</td><td>20.8</td><td>29.3</td><td>19.5</td><td>344</td><td>308</td><td>35</td><td>65.4</td><td>1 151</td><td>156</td></tr>
<tr><td>Salisbury</td><td>43.7</td><td>9.3</td><td>37.6</td><td>15.7</td><td>545</td><td>520</td><td>25</td><td>39.0</td><td>1 358</td><td>166</td></tr>
<tr><td>Sanford</td><td>33.0</td><td>7.9</td><td>36.0</td><td>11.6</td><td>404</td><td>376</td><td>29</td><td>26.5</td><td>925</td><td>77</td></tr>
<tr><td>Thomasville</td><td>23.9</td><td>7.4</td><td>28.3</td><td>9.7</td><td>369</td><td>343</td><td>26</td><td>30.4</td><td>1 158</td><td>400</td></tr>
<tr><td>Wake Forest</td><td>24.3</td><td>6.6</td><td>26.5</td><td>13.2</td><td>520</td><td>431</td><td>89</td><td>22.2</td><td>878</td><td>224</td></tr>
<tr><td>Wilmington</td><td>149.4</td><td>50.2</td><td>21.8</td><td>48.4</td><td>486</td><td>424</td><td>62</td><td>159.8</td><td>1 604</td><td>588</td></tr>
<tr><td>Wilson</td><td>56.6</td><td>13.5</td><td>46.0</td><td>17.6</td><td>368</td><td>337</td><td>31</td><td>54.5</td><td>1 141</td><td>132</td></tr>
<tr><td>Winston-Salem</td><td>274.5</td><td>66.4</td><td>36.3</td><td>98.9</td><td>459</td><td>398</td><td>62</td><td>289.9</td><td>1 346</td><td>318</td></tr>
<tr><td>NORTH DAKOTA......</td><td>X</td><td>X</td><td>X</td><td>X</td><td>X</td><td>X</td><td>X</td><td>X</td><td>X</td><td>X</td></tr>
<tr><td>Bismarck</td><td>82.3</td><td>15.0</td><td>53.0</td><td>29.1</td><td>488</td><td>232</td><td>256</td><td>89.4</td><td>1 502</td><td>564</td></tr>
<tr><td>Fargo</td><td>148.4</td><td>23.6</td><td>53.4</td><td>49.1</td><td>530</td><td>163</td><td>347</td><td>140.8</td><td>1 520</td><td>672</td></tr>
<tr><td>Grand Forks</td><td>82.7</td><td>13.6</td><td>53.5</td><td>30.3</td><td>586</td><td>191</td><td>395</td><td>53.5</td><td>1 034</td><td>81</td></tr>
<tr><td>Minot</td><td>38.8</td><td>5.0</td><td>78.0</td><td>22.4</td><td>635</td><td>265</td><td>370</td><td>25.1</td><td>711</td><td>107</td></tr>
<tr><td>West Fargo</td><td>12.1</td><td>1.2</td><td>92.3</td><td>6.8</td><td>296</td><td>178</td><td>118</td><td>13.6</td><td>591</td><td>43</td></tr>
<tr><td>OHIO</td><td>X</td><td>X</td><td>X</td><td>X</td><td>X</td><td>X</td><td>X</td><td>X</td><td>X</td><td>X</td></tr>
<tr><td>Akron</td><td>323.9</td><td>74.6</td><td>57.7</td><td>145.4</td><td>699</td><td>157</td><td>4</td><td>407.5</td><td>1 960</td><td>320</td></tr>
<tr><td>Barberton</td><td>32.7</td><td>5.4</td><td>76.4</td><td>13.4</td><td>500</td><td>62</td><td>8</td><td>32.7</td><td>1 222</td><td>227</td></tr>
<tr><td>Beavercreek</td><td>20.7</td><td>5.0</td><td>93.4</td><td>11.9</td><td>299</td><td>269</td><td>29</td><td>20.4</td><td>513</td><td>35</td></tr>
<tr><td>Bowling Green</td><td>38.0</td><td>4.6</td><td>100.0</td><td>21.4</td><td>717</td><td>133</td><td>3</td><td>30.9</td><td>1 035</td><td>41</td></tr>
<tr><td>Brunswick</td><td>21.9</td><td>4.2</td><td>98.8</td><td>12.6</td><td>361</td><td>61</td><td>33</td><td>26.0</td><td>747</td><td>127</td></tr>
<tr><td>Canton</td><td>102.9</td><td>23.4</td><td>75.1</td><td>48.1</td><td>614</td><td>46</td><td>16</td><td>103.6</td><td>1 323</td><td>170</td></tr>
<tr><td>Cincinnati</td><td>841.2</td><td>286.2</td><td>15.9</td><td>423.8</td><td>1 275</td><td>210</td><td>88</td><td>815.7</td><td>2 454</td><td>690</td></tr>
<tr><td>Cleveland</td><td>970.0</td><td>239.7</td><td>62.6</td><td>424.1</td><td>968</td><td>152</td><td>110</td><td>967.7</td><td>2 209</td><td>367</td></tr>
<tr><td>Cleveland Heights</td><td>63.3</td><td>14.0</td><td>88.3</td><td>35.0</td><td>755</td><td>243</td><td>27</td><td>57.1</td><td>1 232</td><td>44</td></tr>
<tr><td>Columbus</td><td>1 140.2</td><td>197.5</td><td>52.8</td><td>591.1</td><td>790</td><td>63</td><td>42</td><td>1 097.7</td><td>1 468</td><td>298</td></tr>
<tr><td>Cuyahoga Falls</td><td>65.8</td><td>8.3</td><td>91.3</td><td>29.4</td><td>576</td><td>213</td><td>14</td><td>64.0</td><td>1 254</td><td>203</td></tr>
<tr><td>Dayton</td><td>311.3</td><td>46.2</td><td>54.3</td><td>139.7</td><td>899</td><td>156</td><td>11</td><td>276.2</td><td>1 777</td><td>109</td></tr>
<tr><td>Delaware</td><td>40.4</td><td>9.5</td><td>95.4</td><td>14.2</td><td>431</td><td>43</td><td>28</td><td>65.2</td><td>1 976</td><td>1 121</td></tr>
<tr><td>Dublin</td><td>98.1</td><td>6.6</td><td>39.4</td><td>76.3</td><td>2 009</td><td>210</td><td>103</td><td>81.6</td><td>2 151</td><td>668</td></tr>
<tr><td>Elyria</td><td>57.0</td><td>8.9</td><td>89.6</td><td>28.3</td><td>514</td><td>71</td><td>32</td><td>58.7</td><td>1 065</td><td>147</td></tr>
<tr><td>Euclid</td><td>62.5</td><td>11.6</td><td>91.0</td><td>30.9</td><td>646</td><td>144</td><td>3</td><td>59.8</td><td>1 248</td><td>135</td></tr>
<tr><td>Fairborn</td><td>34.9</td><td>5.3</td><td>100.0</td><td>14.2</td><td>440</td><td>141</td><td>13</td><td>42.8</td><td>1 322</td><td>425</td></tr>
<tr><td>Fairfield</td><td>51.9</td><td>7.3</td><td>95.5</td><td>28.9</td><td>683</td><td>128</td><td>14</td><td>57.6</td><td>1 363</td><td>490</td></tr>
<tr><td>Findlay</td><td>47.0</td><td>8.7</td><td>97.8</td><td>21.4</td><td>572</td><td>69</td><td>9</td><td>45.0</td><td>1 200</td><td>325</td></tr>
<tr><td>Gahanna</td><td>41.1</td><td>8.1</td><td>95.7</td><td>18.4</td><td>545</td><td>59</td><td>23</td><td>58.9</td><td>1 749</td><td>847</td></tr>
<tr><td>Garfield Heights</td><td>30.2</td><td>3.5</td><td>95.5</td><td>19.9</td><td>709</td><td>337</td><td>10</td><td>29.5</td><td>1 053</td><td>32</td></tr>
<tr><td>Green</td><td>24.9</td><td>5.2</td><td>34.3</td><td>18.2</td><td>775</td><td>66</td><td>19</td><td>31.7</td><td>1 352</td><td>501</td></tr>
<tr><td>Grove City</td><td>30.9</td><td>4.5</td><td>74.6</td><td>21.3</td><td>644</td><td>72</td><td>41</td><td>34.3</td><td>1 036</td><td>466</td></tr>
<tr><td>Hamilton</td><td>66.4</td><td>8.7</td><td>84.9</td><td>29.8</td><td>478</td><td>45</td><td>61</td><td>68.9</td><td>1 106</td><td>90</td></tr>
<tr><td>Hilliard</td><td>26.8</td><td>4.4</td><td>65.5</td><td>18.3</td><td>667</td><td>50</td><td>63</td><td>33.6</td><td>1 222</td><td>131</td></tr>
<tr><td>Huber Heights</td><td>30.7</td><td>2.9</td><td>63.7</td><td>18.8</td><td>502</td><td>92</td><td>27</td><td>28.9</td><td>773</td><td>160</td></tr>
<tr><td>Kent</td><td>28.9</td><td>4.9</td><td>73.8</td><td>14.1</td><td>498</td><td>103</td><td>18</td><td>26.5</td><td>937</td><td>104</td></tr>
</table>

1. Based on population estimated as of July 1 of the year shown.

| City | City government finances, 2006 (cont.) | | | | | | | | | |
|---|---|---|---|---|---|---|---|---|---|---|
| | General expenditure (cont.) | | | | | | | | | |
| | Percent of total for: | | | | | | | | | |
| | Public welfare | Highways | Parking facilities | Education | Health and hospitals | Police protection | Sewerage and sanitation | Parks and recreation | Housing and community development | Interest on debt |
| | 127 | 128 | 129 | 130 | 131 | 132 | 133 | 134 | 135 | 136 |
| NORTH CAROLINA... | X | X | X | X | X | X | X | X | X | X |
| Apex | 0.0 | 12.3 | 0.0 | 0.0 | 0.2 | 17.0 | 24.8 | 10.5 | 0.0 | 1.6 |
| Asheboro | 0.0 | 7.6 | 0.0 | 0.0 | 0.0 | 22.0 | 24.4 | 11.5 | 0.0 | 1.7 |
| Asheville | 0.0 | 8.6 | 1.0 | 0.0 | 0.2 | 17.0 | 16.3 | 13.5 | 3.6 | 3.0 |
| Burlington | 0.0 | 16.3 | 0.0 | 0.0 | 1.1 | 18.0 | 22.9 | 10.4 | 1.1 | 3.0 |
| Cary | 0.0 | 15.9 | 0.0 | 0.0 | 0.0 | 9.4 | 25.8 | 9.9 | 0.5 | 4.7 |
| Chapel Hill | 0.0 | 6.8 | 1.8 | 0.0 | 0.0 | 16.9 | 6.2 | 8.6 | 3.8 | 3.0 |
| Charlotte | 0.0 | 8.1 | 0.1 | 0.0 | 0.4 | 13.7 | 27.8 | 3.1 | 4.2 | 10.3 |
| Concord | 0.0 | 7.4 | 0.0 | 0.0 | 0.0 | 15.0 | 23.8 | 4.8 | 1.1 | 4.2 |
| Durham | 0.0 | 10.4 | 0.9 | 0.0 | 0.0 | 17.1 | 17.2 | 9.8 | 4.2 | 3.5 |
| Fayetteville | 0.0 | 7.9 | 0.1 | 0.0 | 0.0 | 21.5 | 24.9 | 10.1 | 2.0 | 3.5 |
| Garner | 0.0 | 10.0 | 0.0 | 0.0 | 0.9 | 27.5 | 6.5 | 16.3 | 0.0 | 1.9 |
| Gastonia | 0.0 | 5.8 | 0.0 | 0.0 | 0.0 | 19.1 | 30.1 | 6.4 | 5.0 | 3.5 |
| Goldsboro | 0.0 | 7.7 | 0.0 | 0.0 | 0.2 | 17.7 | 24.8 | 8.3 | 3.4 | 2.3 |
| Greensboro | 0.0 | 7.5 | 0.3 | 0.0 | 0.1 | 17.7 | 30.0 | 10.1 | 3.2 | 3.4 |
| Greenville | 0.0 | 5.3 | 0.0 | 0.0 | 0.0 | 18.6 | 23.8 | 7.7 | 3.3 | 4.1 |
| Hickory | 0.0 | 9.5 | 0.0 | 0.0 | 0.2 | 16.5 | 20.1 | 6.7 | 1.3 | 2.1 |
| High Point | 0.0 | 15.3 | 0.6 | 0.0 | 1.0 | 15.0 | 23.2 | 7.2 | 1.7 | 4.6 |
| Huntersville | 0.0 | 17.2 | 0.0 | 0.0 | 0.9 | 25.3 | 0.0 | 31.0 | 0.0 | 2.9 |
| Indian Trail | 0.0 | 17.5 | 0.0 | 0.0 | 0.0 | 8.6 | 32.7 | 0.9 | 0.0 | 0.0 |
| Jacksonville | 0.0 | 4.9 | 0.0 | 0.0 | 0.0 | 18.4 | 32.0 | 12.9 | 1.0 | 1.6 |
| Kannapolis | 0.0 | 21.4 | 0.0 | 0.0 | 0.0 | 19.1 | 20.8 | 5.2 | 2.6 | 4.0 |
| Matthews | 0.0 | 12.8 | 0.0 | 0.0 | 2.6 | 32.8 | 9.2 | 11.2 | 0.0 | 3.7 |
| Monroe | 0.0 | 6.3 | 0.0 | 0.0 | 0.1 | 18.2 | 18.6 | 16.1 | 2.9 | 1.9 |
| Mooresville | 0.0 | 6.4 | 0.0 | 0.0 | 0.0 | 9.5 | 31.7 | 4.3 | 0.4 | 2.9 |
| New Bern | 0.0 | 6.4 | 0.0 | 0.0 | 0.3 | 18.2 | 28.7 | 5.7 | 0.9 | 2.3 |
| Raleigh | 0.1 | 8.1 | 5.3 | 0.0 | 0.0 | 12.5 | 21.5 | 23.4 | 2.7 | 5.3 |
| Rocky Mount | 0.0 | 5.5 | 0.0 | 0.0 | 0.0 | 16.3 | 33.6 | 11.7 | 3.2 | 1.3 |
| Salisbury | 0.0 | 11.3 | 0.0 | 0.0 | 0.1 | 18.2 | 22.4 | 6.6 | 2.1 | 2.9 |
| Sanford | 0.0 | 9.6 | 0.0 | 0.0 | 0.1 | 26.4 | 26.5 | 2.3 | 2.9 | 1.6 |
| Thomasville | 0.0 | 5.8 | 0.0 | 0.0 | 0.0 | 13.7 | 47.2 | 4.7 | 1.1 | 1.8 |
| Wake Forest | 0.0 | 9.3 | 0.0 | 0.0 | 0.0 | 19.2 | 8.4 | 15.9 | 0.0 | 2.0 |
| Wilmington | 0.0 | 7.8 | 0.6 | 0.0 | 0.0 | 16.6 | 38.7 | 7.2 | 1.4 | 3.7 |
| Wilson | 0.0 | 6.1 | 0.3 | 0.0 | 0.0 | 18.0 | 26.8 | 8.5 | 2.8 | 3.1 |
| Winston-Salem | 0.0 | 7.1 | 0.5 | 0.0 | 0.0 | 16.9 | 31.4 | 7.4 | 3.8 | 6.5 |
| NORTH DAKOTA | X | X | X | X | X | X | X | X | X | X |
| Bismarck | 0.0 | 16.3 | 1.2 | 0.0 | 2.1 | 9.5 | 17.6 | 3.9 | 0.5 | 1.5 |
| Fargo | 0.2 | 27.7 | 0.9 | 0.0 | 4.7 | 8.0 | 21.3 | 7.3 | 3.8 | 7.9 |
| Grand Forks | 0.0 | 7.3 | 0.6 | 0.0 | 2.4 | 12.5 | 18.8 | 2.8 | 11.3 | 18.7 |
| Minot | 0.0 | 16.9 | 0.4 | 0.0 | 0.0 | 19.5 | 12.5 | 4.3 | 0.0 | 3.2 |
| West Fargo | 0.3 | 5.8 | 0.0 | 0.0 | 0.0 | 21.4 | 22.7 | 0.0 | 0.0 | 30.4 |
| OHIO | X | X | X | X | X | X | X | X | X | X |
| Akron | 0.0 | 13.9 | 1.0 | 0.0 | 7.2 | 13.4 | 8.0 | 5.9 | 1.5 | 4.6 |
| Barberton | 10.7 | 6.4 | 0.0 | 0.0 | 7.2 | 17.3 | 18.9 | 4.5 | 4.8 | 1.8 |
| Beavercreek | 0.0 | 24.5 | 0.0 | 0.0 | 1.3 | 31.8 | 0.0 | 15.5 | 2.6 | 5.9 |
| Bowling Green | 0.0 | 14.3 | 0.0 | 0.0 | 0.7 | 15.8 | 19.0 | 5.3 | 0.0 | 4.1 |
| Brunswick | 0.6 | 16.7 | 0.0 | 0.5 | 0.7 | 23.6 | 10.9 | 9.4 | 0.4 | 2.2 |
| Canton | 0.0 | 10.8 | 0.3 | 0.0 | 5.4 | 18.1 | 14.9 | 3.0 | 10.9 | 1.3 |
| Cincinnati | 0.0 | 2.7 | 0.8 | 0.6 | 4.6 | 13.8 | 24.3 | 5.1 | 5.2 | 2.3 |
| Cleveland | 0.4 | 3.4 | 0.4 | 0.0 | 4.7 | 17.9 | 6.3 | 6.0 | 10.4 | 9.3 |
| Cleveland Heights | 0.0 | 10.2 | 1.5 | 0.0 | 1.8 | 16.5 | 7.5 | 7.2 | 11.9 | 3.2 |
| Columbus | 0.0 | 8.7 | 0.3 | 0.0 | 3.2 | 20.5 | 23.2 | 6.2 | 0.7 | 10.1 |
| Cuyahoga Falls | 0.0 | 6.2 | 0.0 | 0.0 | 0.0 | 17.1 | 14.0 | 12.2 | 2.2 | 3.1 |
| Dayton | 0.0 | 13.1 | 0.0 | 0.0 | 0.0 | 18.2 | 8.8 | 4.5 | 4.9 | 2.9 |
| Delaware | 0.0 | 7.2 | 0.1 | 0.0 | 0.2 | 7.0 | 48.1 | 6.4 | 0.3 | 2.4 |
| Dublin | 0.0 | 24.3 | 0.0 | 0.0 | 0.2 | 11.3 | 4.7 | 16.8 | 0.0 | 4.0 |
| Elyria | 0.0 | 10.8 | 0.0 | 0.0 | 3.6 | 18.3 | 18.7 | 5.1 | 1.5 | 3.8 |
| Euclid | 0.0 | 3.5 | 0.0 | 0.0 | 0.5 | 17.6 | 22.4 | 5.2 | 1.8 | 4.1 |
| Fairborn | 0.0 | 7.9 | 0.0 | 0.0 | 0.0 | 33.8 | 14.8 | 0.7 | 2.5 | 2.7 |
| Fairfield | 0.0 | 22.1 | 0.0 | 0.0 | 0.1 | 13.5 | 9.1 | 6.5 | 2.1 | 3.4 |
| Findlay | 0.0 | 14.5 | 0.3 | 0.0 | 3.4 | 17.2 | 10.3 | 8.6 | 0.0 | 4.3 |
| Gahanna | 0.0 | 10.0 | 0.0 | 0.0 | 0.3 | 12.2 | 11.8 | 3.6 | 7.6 | 5.6 |
| Garfield Heights | 0.0 | 8.7 | 0.0 | 0.0 | 0.3 | 21.3 | 7.2 | 3.5 | 0.1 | 5.8 |
| Green | 0.0 | 11.2 | 0.0 | 0.0 | 0.7 | 4.5 | 0.0 | 10.2 | 0.0 | 2.6 |
| Grove City | 0.1 | 14.2 | 0.8 | 0.0 | 0.6 | 24.1 | 2.4 | 8.6 | 3.3 | 5.0 |
| Hamilton | 0.0 | 7.4 | 0.9 | 0.0 | 2.3 | 19.7 | 19.6 | 3.9 | 2.9 | 2.9 |
| Hilliard | 0.0 | 22.3 | 0.0 | 0.0 | 0.8 | 21.3 | 2.4 | 10.8 | 0.0 | 4.9 |
| Huber Heights | 0.0 | 15.8 | 0.0 | 0.0 | 0.0 | 18.8 | 10.4 | 0.9 | 0.0 | 7.1 |
| Kent | 0.0 | 6.6 | 0.0 | 0.0 | 1.7 | 24.8 | 14.8 | 6.0 | 10.4 | 8.1 |

| City | City government finances, 2007 (cont.) Debt outstanding — Total (mil dol) | Per capita[1] (dollars) | Debt issued during year | City government employment, 2011 | Climate[2] — Mean January | July | Limits January[3] | July[4] | Annual precipitation (inches) | Heating degree days | Cooling degree days |
|---|---|---|---|---|---|---|---|---|---|---|---|
| | 137 | 138 | 139 | 140 | 141 | 142 | 143 | 144 | 145 | 146 | 147 |
| NORTH CAROLINA... | X | X | X | X | X | X | X | X | X | X | X |
| Apex | 13.2 | 418 | 0.0 | 323 | NA | NA | NA | NA | NA | NA | NA |
| Asheboro | 12.9 | 532 | 0.0 | 336 | NA | NA | NA | NA | NA | NA | NA |
| Asheville | 74.2 | 1 004 | 0.0 | 1 051 | 36.4 | 73.9 | 26.6 | 84.3 | 37.32 | 4 237 | 877 |
| Burlington | 36.5 | 736 | 9.3 | 649 | 38.7 | 79.3 | 27.6 | 90.6 | 45.08 | 3 588 | 1 489 |
| Cary | 263.2 | 2 161 | 86.9 | 1 209 | 39.5 | 78.7 | 30.1 | 87.9 | 46.49 | 3 431 | 1 456 |
| Chapel Hill | 56.2 | 1 091 | 8.1 | 817 | 38.5 | 79.4 | 27.8 | 88.6 | 48.04 | 3 650 | 1 491 |
| Charlotte | 3 431.9 | 5 110 | 839.8 | 7 075 | 41.7 | 80.3 | 32.1 | 90.1 | 43.51 | 3 162 | 1 681 |
| Concord | 151.1 | 2 337 | 0.0 | 849 | 39.4 | 79.2 | 27.9 | 90.3 | 47.30 | 3 463 | 1 540 |
| Durham | 392.9 | 1 804 | 102.9 | 2 378 | 39.7 | 78.8 | 29.6 | 89.1 | 43.05 | 3 465 | 1 521 |
| Fayetteville | 282.7 | 1 645 | 4.5 | 1 962 | 41.7 | 80.4 | 31.1 | 90.4 | 46.78 | 3 097 | 1 721 |
| Garner | 7.9 | 313 | 0.0 | NA | NA | NA | NA | NA | NA | NA | NA |
| Gastonia | 83.9 | 1 180 | 0.0 | 981 | 42.0 | 79.9 | 31.7 | 89.9 | 49.19 | 3 009 | 1 701 |
| Goldsboro | 49.6 | 1 319 | 5.6 | 471 | 43.4 | 81.2 | 33.0 | 91.4 | 49.84 | 2 771 | 1 922 |
| Greensboro | 445.9 | 1 804 | 104.8 | 3 086 | 39.7 | 78.6 | 29.0 | 88.9 | 42.89 | 3 443 | 1 438 |
| Greenville | 144.6 | 1 901 | 24.6 | 1 227 | 42.0 | 78.8 | 31.9 | 88.4 | 49.30 | 3 113 | 1 516 |
| Hickory | 38.9 | 948 | 0.0 | 634 | 39.0 | 77.7 | 29.2 | 87.8 | 48.98 | 3 608 | 1 333 |
| High Point | 199.2 | 1 984 | 0.1 | 1 436 | 39.7 | 78.2 | 29.6 | 89.0 | 46.19 | 3 399 | 1 424 |
| Huntersville | 15.3 | 359 | 0.0 | 161 | NA | NA | NA | NA | NA | NA | NA |
| Indian Trail | 0.0 | 0 | 0.0 | NA | NA | NA | NA | NA | NA | NA | NA |
| Jacksonville | 38.5 | 515 | 10.9 | 538 | 44.7 | 80.2 | 33.9 | 89.5 | 54.07 | 2 656 | 1 832 |
| Kannapolis | 44.3 | 1 067 | 5.1 | 283 | 39.4 | 79.2 | 27.9 | 90.3 | 47.30 | 3 463 | 1 540 |
| Matthews | 12.5 | 469 | 0.0 | NA | NA | NA | NA | NA | NA | NA | NA |
| Monroe | 24.9 | 786 | 0.0 | 525 | 41.5 | 79.0 | 31.0 | 89.7 | 48.73 | 3 125 | 1 538 |
| Mooresville | 84.1 | 3 874 | 7.8 | 444 | NA | NA | NA | NA | NA | NA | NA |
| New Bern | 42.5 | 1 507 | 0.9 | 457 | NA | NA | NA | NA | NA | NA | NA |
| Raleigh | 975.6 | 2 596 | 307.4 | 3 855 | 39.1 | 79.4 | 28.1 | 89.9 | 45.70 | 3 514 | 1 550 |
| Rocky Mount | 23.4 | 412 | 0.0 | 959 | 41.1 | 79.2 | 30.8 | 89.7 | 46.51 | 3 215 | 1 518 |
| Salisbury | 53.6 | 1 865 | 6.0 | 480 | 40.2 | 78.7 | 29.5 | 89.5 | 42.86 | 3 356 | 1 466 |
| Sanford | 25.7 | 897 | 3.0 | 346 | NA | NA | NA | NA | NA | NA | NA |
| Thomasville | 27.5 | 1 047 | 0.0 | NA | NA | NA | NA | NA | NA | NA | NA |
| Wake Forest | 20.3 | 803 | 11.5 | NA | NA | NA | NA | NA | NA | NA | NA |
| Wilmington | 194.3 | 1 950 | 0.0 | 976 | 44.8 | 80.1 | 33.3 | 90.0 | 58.44 | 2 606 | 1 791 |
| Wilson | 99.2 | 2 076 | 55.3 | 761 | 40.4 | 79.2 | 29.5 | 90.2 | 47.18 | 3 328 | 1 575 |
| Winston-Salem | 553.0 | 2 568 | 128.3 | 2 486 | 39.7 | 78.2 | 29.6 | 89.0 | 46.19 | 3 399 | 1 424 |
| NORTH DAKOTA...... | X | X | X | X | X | X | X | X | X | X | X |
| Bismarck | 62.7 | 1 054 | 20.7 | 620 | 10.2 | 70.4 | -0.6 | 84.5 | 16.84 | 8 802 | 471 |
| Fargo | 463.8 | 5 005 | 33.7 | 827 | 6.8 | 70.6 | -2.3 | 82.2 | 21.19 | 9 092 | 533 |
| Grand Forks | 238.1 | 4 601 | 22.6 | 451 | 5.3 | 69.4 | -4.3 | 81.9 | 19.60 | 9 489 | 420 |
| Minot | 28.7 | 812 | 6.8 | 349 | 7.5 | 68.4 | -1.8 | 80.4 | 18.65 | 9 479 | 422 |
| West Fargo | 103.5 | 4 484 | 10.0 | 103 | NA | NA | NA | NA | NA | NA | NA |
| OHIO ...... | X | X | X | X | X | X | X | X | X | X | X |
| Akron | 700.6 | 3 370 | 59.2 | 2 225 | 27.2 | 74.1 | 20.1 | 83.9 | 36.07 | 5 752 | 856 |
| Barberton | 14.7 | 550 | 0.0 | 256 | 29.1 | 73.6 | 20.3 | 85.0 | 39.16 | 5 348 | 813 |
| Beavercreek | 19.8 | 499 | 0.3 | 147 | 27.6 | 73.1 | 19.5 | 83.5 | 40.06 | 5 531 | 768 |
| Bowling Green | 38.1 | 1 274 | 0.5 | 298 | 23.1 | 72.9 | 15.2 | 84.2 | 33.18 | 6 492 | 690 |
| Brunswick | 12.2 | 351 | 0.5 | 158 | 25.7 | 71.9 | 18.8 | 81.4 | 38.71 | 6 121 | 702 |
| Canton | 50.2 | 641 | 23.2 | 927 | 25.2 | 71.8 | 17.4 | 82.3 | 38.47 | 6 154 | 678 |
| Cincinnati | 725.2 | 2 181 | 76.5 | 5 644 | 30.6 | 76.8 | 22.7 | 86.8 | 39.57 | 4 841 | 1 210 |
| Cleveland | 2 617.6 | 5 976 | 453.2 | 7 791 | 25.7 | 71.9 | 18.8 | 81.4 | 38.71 | 6 121 | 702 |
| Cleveland Heights | 20.5 | 442 | 0.0 | 463 | 25.7 | 71.9 | 18.8 | 81.4 | 38.71 | 6 121 | 702 |
| Columbus | 1 828.4 | 2 445 | 416.9 | 7 945 | 28.3 | 74.7 | 20.2 | 85.6 | 40.03 | 5 349 | 935 |
| Cuyahoga Falls | 63.1 | 1 238 | 0.0 | 494 | 29.1 | 73.6 | 20.3 | 85.0 | 39.16 | 5 348 | 813 |
| Dayton | 235.4 | 1 514 | 6.7 | 2 033 | 26.3 | 74.3 | 19.0 | 84.2 | 39.58 | 5 690 | 935 |
| Delaware | 47.2 | 1 431 | 8.7 | 213 | 25.1 | 73.0 | 16.6 | 84.6 | 37.58 | 6 178 | 739 |
| Dublin | 66.5 | 1 753 | 0.0 | 431 | 28.3 | 74.7 | 20.2 | 85.6 | 40.03 | 5 349 | 935 |
| Elyria | 65.3 | 1 186 | 15.2 | 537 | 27.1 | 73.8 | 19.3 | 85.0 | 38.02 | 5 731 | 818 |
| Euclid | 49.6 | 1 034 | 6.8 | 454 | 23.0 | 68.8 | 14.3 | 80.0 | 47.33 | 6 956 | 372 |
| Fairborn | 21.3 | 658 | 0.5 | 237 | 27.9 | 77.0 | 20.6 | 87.2 | 39.41 | 5 343 | 1 214 |
| Fairfield | 42.5 | 1 004 | 7.5 | 342 | 28.7 | 76.6 | 19.9 | 88.1 | 43.36 | 5 261 | 1 135 |
| Findlay | 28.9 | 771 | 0.0 | 328 | 24.5 | 73.6 | 17.4 | 83.5 | 36.91 | 6 194 | 809 |
| Gahanna | 52.5 | 1 557 | 37.4 | 171 | 28.3 | 75.1 | 20.3 | 85.3 | 38.52 | 5 492 | 951 |
| Garfield Heights | 33.9 | 1 209 | 8.0 | 216 | 25.7 | 71.9 | 18.8 | 81.4 | 38.71 | 6 121 | 702 |
| Green | 36.0 | 1 535 | 0.0 | NA | NA | NA | NA | NA | NA | NA | NA |
| Grove City | 29.1 | 880 | 25.0 | 167 | 28.3 | 74.7 | 20.2 | 85.6 | 40.03 | 5 349 | 935 |
| Hamilton | 296.8 | 4 765 | 48.2 | 658 | 28.7 | 76.6 | 19.9 | 88.1 | 43.36 | 5 261 | 1 135 |
| Hilliard | 47.3 | 1 718 | 1.9 | 138 | NA | NA | NA | NA | NA | NA | NA |
| Huber Heights | 60.3 | 1 612 | 9.8 | 177 | 27.9 | 77.0 | 20.6 | 87.2 | 39.41 | 5 343 | 1 214 |
| Kent | 18.8 | 666 | 0.0 | 199 | 27.2 | 74.1 | 20.1 | 83.9 | 36.07 | 5 752 | 856 |

1. Based on the population estimated as of July 1 of the year shown.   2. Represents normal values based on the 30-year period, 1971–2000.   3. Average daily minimum.   4. Average daily maximum.

# Table D. Cities — **Land Area and Population**

| STATE Place code | City | Land area,[1] 2010 (sq km) | Population, 2012 Total persons | Rank | Per square kilometer | Race alone or in combination, not of Hispanic origin (percent), 2010 White | Black | American Indian, Alaska Native | Asian | Hawaiian Pacific Islander | Percent Hispanic or Latino[2], 2010 | Percent Foreign born 2007–2011 |
|---|---|---|---|---|---|---|---|---|---|---|---|---|
| | | 1 | 2 | 3 | 4 | 5 | 6 | 7 | 8 | 9 | 10 | 11 |
| | **OHIO—Cont'd** | | | | | | | | | | | |
| 39 40040 | Kettering | 48.4 | 55 990 | 643 | 1 156.8 | 92.9 | 4.1 | 0.7 | 1.9 | 0.1 | 2.1 | 2.5 |
| 39 41664 | Lakewood | 14.3 | 51 385 | 707 | 3 593.4 | 87.1 | 7.4 | 0.8 | 2.5 | 0.1 | 4.1 | 7.9 |
| 39 41720 | Lancaster | 48.8 | 38 880 | 943 | 796.7 | 96.5 | 1.8 | 0.8 | 0.7 | 0.1 | 1.6 | 1.3 |
| 39 43554 | Lima | 35.1 | 38 339 | 955 | 1 092.3 | 68.8 | 29.4 | 0.9 | 0.7 | 0.1 | 3.7 | 2.1 |
| 39 44856 | Lorain | 61.3 | 63 707 | 537 | 1 039.3 | 57.8 | 18.4 | 1.0 | 0.5 | 0.0 | 25.2 | 3.0 |
| 39 47138 | Mansfield | 80.0 | 47 052 | 788 | 588.2 | 74.8 | 23.9 | 0.9 | 1.0 | 0.1 | 1.9 | 2.0 |
| 39 47754 | Marion | 30.4 | 36 904 | 987 | 1 213.9 | 86.8 | 10.7 | 0.7 | 0.5 | 0.1 | 3.0 | 1.1 |
| 39 48188 | Mason | 48.3 | 31 091 | 1 170 | 643.7 | 84.0 | 3.6 | 0.3 | 9.9 | 0.2 | 3.2 | 8.4 |
| 39 48244 | Massillon | 48.1 | 32 156 | 1 130 | 668.5 | 88.4 | 10.5 | 0.7 | 0.5 | 0.1 | 2.0 | 0.9 |
| 39 48790 | Medina | 30.0 | 26 533 | 1 370 | 884.4 | 94.1 | 4.2 | 0.5 | 1.3 | 0.0 | 1.8 | 2.8 |
| 39 49056 | Mentor | 69.0 | 47 023 | 790 | 681.5 | 96.2 | 1.3 | 0.2 | 1.7 | 0.1 | 1.3 | 4.6 |
| 39 49840 | Middletown | 67.8 | 48 702 | 760 | 718.3 | 83.8 | 13.3 | 0.7 | 0.7 | 0.1 | 3.8 | 2.2 |
| 39 54040 | Newark | 54.1 | 47 688 | 776 | 881.5 | 94.4 | 4.9 | 0.9 | 0.8 | 0.1 | 1.2 | 1.1 |
| 39 56882 | North Olmsted | 30.2 | 32 354 | 1 126 | 1 071.3 | 91.6 | 2.4 | 0.4 | 3.2 | 0.1 | 3.5 | 8.3 |
| 39 56966 | North Ridgeville | 60.7 | 30 571 | 1 191 | 503.6 | 93.8 | 1.9 | 0.6 | 1.6 | 0.0 | 3.3 | 6.0 |
| 39 57008 | North Royalton | 55.2 | 30 325 | 1 203 | 549.4 | 94.4 | 1.4 | 0.3 | 3.2 | 0.0 | 1.6 | 9.5 |
| 39 61000 | Parma | 51.9 | 80 597 | 397 | 1 552.9 | 92.0 | 2.7 | 0.5 | 2.3 | 0.1 | 3.6 | 9.8 |
| 39 66390 | Reynoldsburg | 28.9 | 36 347 | 1 004 | 1 257.7 | 70.9 | 25.3 | 1.0 | 2.3 | 0.1 | 3.4 | 7.2 |
| 39 67468 | Riverside | 25.2 | 25 145 | 1 435 | 997.8 | 87.7 | 7.7 | 0.9 | 2.6 | 0.1 | 3.3 | 3.0 |
| 39 70380 | Sandusky | 25.2 | 25 493 | 1 419 | 1 011.6 | 72.0 | 25.7 | 1.0 | 0.7 | 0.0 | 4.9 | 1.6 |
| 39 71682 | Shaker Heights | 16.3 | 28 039 | 1 289 | 1 720.2 | 55.7 | 38.2 | 0.7 | 5.5 | 0.1 | 2.2 | 7.8 |
| 39 74118 | Springfield | 65.5 | 60 147 | 583 | 918.3 | 77.4 | 20.8 | 1.1 | 1.0 | 0.1 | 3.0 | 2.3 |
| 39 74944 | Stow | 44.3 | 34 674 | 1 054 | 782.7 | 93.3 | 3.2 | 0.4 | 2.9 | 0.1 | 1.5 | 3.7 |
| 39 75098 | Strongsville | 63.8 | 44 620 | 819 | 699.4 | 91.8 | 2.1 | 0.4 | 4.8 | 0.1 | 2.0 | 9.1 |
| 39 77000 | Toledo | 209.0 | 284 012 | 67 | 1 358.9 | 64.0 | 28.9 | 0.9 | 1.5 | 0.1 | 7.4 | 3.4 |
| 39 77588 | Troy | 30.4 | 25 374 | 1 425 | 834.7 | 91.2 | 5.6 | 0.6 | 2.8 | 0.0 | 1.8 | 3.4 |
| 39 79002 | Upper Arlington | 25.5 | 34 203 | 1 068 | 1 341.3 | 92.3 | 1.1 | 0.4 | 5.7 | 0.0 | 1.6 | 7.7 |
| 39 80892 | Warren | 41.8 | 40 723 | 889 | 974.2 | 69.5 | 29.9 | 1.0 | 0.6 | 0.0 | 1.9 | 1.6 |
| 39 83342 | Westerville | 32.3 | 37 073 | 979 | 1 147.8 | 89.1 | 7.2 | 0.6 | 2.9 | 0.0 | 1.9 | 5.2 |
| 39 83622 | Westlake | 41.3 | 32 487 | 1 121 | 786.6 | 90.8 | 1.9 | 0.2 | 5.8 | 0.1 | 2.5 | 11.9 |
| 39 86548 | Wooster | 42.2 | 26 375 | 1 378 | 625.0 | 92.0 | 4.9 | 0.7 | 2.2 | 0.1 | 2.2 | 3.3 |
| 39 86772 | Xenia | 34.4 | 25 944 | 1 393 | 754.2 | 83.8 | 15.4 | 1.1 | 0.8 | 0.2 | 1.7 | 1.6 |
| 39 88000 | Youngstown | 87.9 | 65 405 | 520 | 744.1 | 45.4 | 46.2 | 1.1 | 0.7 | 0.1 | 9.3 | 4.2 |
| 39 88084 | Zanesville | 30.5 | 25 411 | 1 423 | 833.1 | 87.9 | 13.3 | 1.6 | 0.6 | 0.1 | 1.2 | 1.2 |
| 40 00000 | **OKLAHOMA** | 177 660.9 | 3 814 820 | X | 21.5 | 73.3 | 8.4 | 12.2 | 2.2 | 0.2 | 8.9 | 5.4 |
| 40 04450 | Bartlesville | 58.9 | 36 245 | 1 008 | 615.4 | 80.7 | 4.2 | 12.4 | 1.8 | 0.1 | 5.9 | 4.2 |
| 40 09050 | Broken Arrow | 159.5 | 102 019 | 277 | 639.6 | 80.3 | 5.2 | 8.4 | 4.3 | 0.1 | 6.5 | 5.4 |
| 40 23200 | Edmond | 219.4 | 84 885 | 364 | 386.9 | 83.3 | 6.3 | 4.8 | 3.9 | 0.2 | 5.1 | 5.7 |
| 40 23950 | Enid | 190.8 | 49 854 | 731 | 261.3 | 80.6 | 4.5 | 3.9 | 1.5 | 2.3 | 10.3 | 7.0 |
| 40 41850 | Lawton | 209.9 | 98 376 | 296 | 468.7 | 58.6 | 23.3 | 6.2 | 3.9 | 0.9 | 12.6 | 6.3 |
| 40 48350 | Midwest City | 63.2 | 56 080 | 639 | 887.3 | 66.6 | 24.0 | 6.9 | 2.5 | 0.3 | 5.6 | 3.6 |
| 40 49200 | Moore | 56.5 | 57 810 | 614 | 1 023.2 | 79.8 | 5.9 | 7.7 | 3.1 | 0.2 | 8.9 | 4.0 |
| 40 50050 | Muskogee | 109.8 | 38 981 | 939 | 355.0 | 59.9 | 18.4 | 21.2 | 1.0 | 0.1 | 7.1 | 4.2 |
| 40 52500 | Norman | 463.0 | 115 562 | 231 | 249.6 | 80.6 | 5.5 | 7.6 | 4.7 | 0.2 | 6.4 | 6.7 |
| 40 55000 | Oklahoma City | 1 570.6 | 599 199 | 29 | 381.5 | 60.0 | 16.4 | 5.6 | 4.6 | 0.2 | 17.2 | 11.9 |
| 40 56650 | Owasso | 42.2 | 31 453 | 1 152 | 745.3 | 81.7 | 3.4 | 10.9 | 2.4 | 0.3 | 6.7 | 4.2 |
| 40 59850 | Ponca City | 47.6 | 24 974 | 1 446 | 524.7 | 80.5 | 4.0 | 12.0 | 1.0 | 0.1 | 7.2 | 3.7 |
| 40 66800 | Shawnee | 114.3 | 30 649 | 1 185 | 268.1 | 75.9 | 5.5 | 18.0 | 1.2 | 0.1 | 5.1 | 2.1 |
| 40 70300 | Stillwater | 76.5 | 46 560 | 792 | 608.6 | 81.3 | 5.8 | 6.7 | 6.3 | 0.1 | 4.3 | 8.7 |
| 40 75000 | Tulsa | 509.6 | 393 987 | 46 | 773.1 | 62.0 | 17.4 | 8.5 | 2.8 | 0.1 | 14.1 | 9.6 |
| 41 00000 | **OREGON** | 248 607.8 | 3 899 353 | X | 15.7 | 81.1 | 2.3 | 2.3 | 4.7 | 0.6 | 11.7 | 9.8 |
| 41 01000 | Albany | 45.4 | 51 322 | 709 | 1 130.4 | 85.4 | 1.0 | 2.2 | 2.2 | 0.4 | 11.4 | 6.5 |
| 41 05350 | Beaverton | 48.5 | 92 680 | 322 | 1 910.9 | 69.4 | 3.4 | 1.3 | 12.3 | 0.8 | 16.3 | 21.8 |
| 41 05800 | Bend | 85.5 | 79 109 | 405 | 925.3 | 89.3 | 0.8 | 1.4 | 2.0 | 0.3 | 8.2 | 4.9 |
| 41 15800 | Corvallis | 36.6 | 54 998 | 655 | 1 502.7 | 83.0 | 1.7 | 1.5 | 9.1 | 0.7 | 7.4 | 11.3 |
| 41 23850 | Eugene | 113.2 | 157 986 | 154 | 1 395.6 | 85.5 | 2.2 | 2.3 | 5.5 | 0.6 | 7.8 | 7.8 |
| 41 30550 | Grants Pass | 28.2 | 34 805 | 1 049 | 1 234.2 | 88.7 | 0.8 | 2.6 | 1.7 | 0.5 | 8.5 | 3.2 |
| 41 31250 | Gresham | 60.1 | 108 956 | 250 | 1 812.9 | 71.6 | 4.5 | 1.8 | 5.4 | 1.0 | 18.9 | 17.2 |
| 41 34100 | Hillsboro | 61.9 | 95 327 | 311 | 1 540.0 | 65.6 | 2.5 | 1.4 | 10.3 | 0.9 | 22.6 | 19.5 |
| 41 38500 | Keizer | 18.4 | 36 907 | 986 | 2 005.8 | 77.5 | 1.2 | 2.1 | 2.5 | 1.0 | 18.3 | 8.5 |
| 41 40550 | Lake Oswego | 27.7 | 37 243 | 975 | 1 344.5 | 89.3 | 1.1 | 0.9 | 7.2 | 0.4 | 3.7 | 10.1 |
| 41 45000 | McMinnville | 27.4 | 32 535 | 1 120 | 1 187.4 | 75.8 | 0.9 | 2.2 | 2.3 | 0.4 | 20.6 | 11.1 |
| 41 47000 | Medford | 66.7 | 76 462 | 429 | 1 146.4 | 82.4 | 1.4 | 2.3 | 2.2 | 0.7 | 13.8 | 6.8 |
| 41 55200 | Oregon City | 23.5 | 32 755 | 1 111 | 1 393.8 | 89.3 | 1.1 | 1.7 | 2.6 | 0.5 | 7.3 | 5.6 |
| 41 59000 | Portland | 345.6 | 603 106 | 28 | 1 745.1 | 75.5 | 7.4 | 1.9 | 8.7 | 0.8 | 9.4 | 13.7 |
| 41 61200 | Redmond | 43.5 | 26 924 | 1 349 | 618.9 | 85.0 | 0.8 | 2.2 | 1.2 | 0.5 | 12.5 | 5.2 |
| 41 64900 | Salem | 124.1 | 157 429 | 155 | 1 268.6 | 73.3 | 2.0 | 2.3 | 3.7 | 1.3 | 20.3 | 12.4 |
| 41 69600 | Springfield | 40.8 | 59 869 | 586 | 1 467.4 | 83.9 | 1.9 | 3.1 | 2.1 | 0.5 | 12.1 | 5.3 |

1. Dry land or land partially or temporarily covered by water.    2. May be of any race.

# Table D. Cities — **Population**

| City | Age of population (percent), 2010 | | | | | | | | | Median age | Percent female | Population Census counts | | Percent change | |
|---|---|---|---|---|---|---|---|---|---|---|---|---|---|---|---|
| | Under 5 years | 5 to 17 years | 18 to 24 years | 25 to 34 years | 35 to 44 years | 45 to 54 years | 55 to 64 years | 65 to 74 years | 75 years and over | | | 2000 | 2010 | 2000–2010 | 2010–2012 |
| | 12 | 13 | 14 | 15 | 16 | 17 | 18 | 19 | 20 | 21 | 22 | 23 | 24 | 25 | 26 |
| OHIO—Cont'd | | | | | | | | | | | | | | | |
| Kettering | 5.8 | 15.2 | 8.4 | 13.7 | 11.9 | 14.6 | 12.5 | 8.3 | 9.7 | 40.9 | 52.3 | 57 502 | 56 163 | -2.3 | -0.3 |
| Lakewood | 5.8 | 13.8 | 9.5 | 20.1 | 14.1 | 14.3 | 11.4 | 5.5 | 5.5 | 35.4 | 50.9 | 56 646 | 52 131 | -8.0 | -1.4 |
| Lancaster | 7.5 | 16.6 | 8.6 | 14.3 | 12.7 | 13.2 | 11.4 | 7.7 | 8.0 | 37.5 | 52.0 | 35 335 | 38 783 | 9.7 | 0.3 |
| Lima | 7.5 | 17.3 | 13.3 | 14.6 | 12.3 | 13.1 | 10.5 | 5.8 | 5.6 | 32.9 | 47.2 | 40 081 | 38 765 | -3.3 | -1.1 |
| Lorain | 7.3 | 19.4 | 8.8 | 12.4 | 12.3 | 14.0 | 12.0 | 6.8 | 7.1 | 36.8 | 52.5 | 68 652 | 64 097 | -6.6 | -0.6 |
| Mansfield | 6.2 | 14.0 | 10.1 | 15.0 | 12.9 | 14.1 | 11.9 | 7.3 | 8.4 | 38.5 | 47.0 | 49 346 | 47 821 | -3.1 | -1.6 |
| Marion | 6.6 | 15.6 | 9.9 | 14.9 | 13.8 | 15.0 | 11.5 | 6.3 | 6.3 | 37.3 | 45.1 | 35 318 | 36 837 | 4.3 | 0.2 |
| Mason | 5.7 | 25.1 | 5.7 | 8.6 | 17.5 | 18.1 | 9.3 | 5.2 | 4.8 | 38.4 | 51.5 | 22 016 | 30 712 | 39.5 | 1.2 |
| Massillon | 6.4 | 16.6 | 8.2 | 12.7 | 12.2 | 14.6 | 12.5 | 8.2 | 8.6 | 40.1 | 51.5 | 31 325 | 32 141 | 2.6 | 0.0 |
| Medina | 7.3 | 21.0 | 7.4 | 12.3 | 15.2 | 14.9 | 10.4 | 5.5 | 6.1 | 36.4 | 51.9 | 25 139 | 26 678 | 6.1 | -0.5 |
| Mentor | 4.6 | 16.6 | 6.8 | 9.6 | 12.7 | 17.7 | 15.5 | 8.9 | 7.6 | 44.8 | 51.6 | 50 278 | 47 159 | -6.2 | -0.3 |
| Middletown | 7.5 | 16.7 | 9.0 | 13.0 | 11.7 | 14.8 | 12.3 | 7.4 | 7.5 | 38.3 | 52.5 | 51 605 | 48 694 | -5.6 | 0.0 |
| Newark | 7.4 | 16.6 | 9.8 | 13.6 | 12.1 | 14.3 | 11.7 | 7.3 | 7.1 | 37.3 | 52.2 | 46 279 | 47 573 | 2.8 | 0.2 |
| North Olmsted | 5.0 | 15.6 | 7.7 | 11.6 | 12.0 | 15.9 | 14.4 | 9.2 | 8.7 | 43.5 | 51.7 | 34 113 | 32 718 | -4.1 | -1.1 |
| North Ridgeville | 6.7 | 16.4 | 5.9 | 12.2 | 14.9 | 14.7 | 14.2 | 9.1 | 6.0 | 40.7 | 50.9 | 22 338 | 29 466 | 31.9 | 3.8 |
| North Royalton | 4.2 | 15.9 | 7.6 | 12.5 | 11.8 | 18.0 | 14.7 | 7.7 | 7.4 | 43.5 | 51.2 | 28 648 | 30 444 | 6.3 | -0.4 |
| Parma | 5.5 | 14.9 | 8.5 | 13.0 | 12.7 | 15.2 | 12.5 | 7.8 | 9.8 | 41.5 | 51.9 | 85 655 | 81 601 | -4.7 | -1.2 |
| Reynoldsburg | 6.7 | 19.6 | 8.0 | 12.8 | 14.0 | 15.3 | 12.1 | 6.4 | 5.2 | 37.3 | 52.6 | 32 069 | 35 930 | 11.9 | 1.2 |
| Riverside | 7.5 | 17.2 | 10.9 | 14.6 | 12.1 | 13.1 | 10.7 | 7.1 | 6.7 | 34.8 | 51.5 | 23 545 | 25 201 | 7.0 | -0.2 |
| Sandusky | 7.3 | 16.6 | 9.2 | 13.1 | 11.1 | 14.9 | 12.8 | 7.2 | 7.8 | 38.5 | 52.4 | 27 844 | 25 793 | -7.4 | -1.2 |
| Shaker Heights | 6.1 | 20.6 | 5.8 | 9.9 | 13.2 | 15.2 | 13.7 | 7.5 | 8.0 | 40.9 | 54.8 | 29 405 | 28 448 | -3.3 | -1.4 |
| Springfield | 7.6 | 16.8 | 11.5 | 12.9 | 11.3 | 12.8 | 11.8 | 7.2 | 8.1 | 36.0 | 52.4 | 65 358 | 60 608 | -7.3 | -0.8 |
| Stow | 5.5 | 17.2 | 8.1 | 13.3 | 13.5 | 15.8 | 12.8 | 6.8 | 7.0 | 39.7 | 51.8 | 32 139 | 34 837 | 8.4 | -0.5 |
| Strongsville | 4.7 | 18.6 | 6.5 | 9.0 | 12.6 | 17.5 | 15.1 | 8.5 | 7.5 | 44.2 | 51.4 | 43 858 | 44 750 | 2.0 | -0.3 |
| Toledo | 7.4 | 16.7 | 12.8 | 14.2 | 12.1 | 13.6 | 11.2 | 6.1 | 6.0 | 34.2 | 51.6 | 313 619 | 287 208 | -8.4 | -1.1 |
| Troy | 7.3 | 17.9 | 7.9 | 14.4 | 13.7 | 13.9 | 11.9 | 6.8 | 6.3 | 36.9 | 51.3 | 21 999 | 25 236 | 13.9 | 0.5 |
| Upper Arlington | 5.8 | 19.3 | 5.1 | 9.4 | 13.5 | 16.3 | 13.9 | 7.7 | 9.0 | 42.8 | 52.2 | 33 686 | 33 682 | 0.3 | 1.5 |
| Warren | 7.0 | 16.8 | 9.2 | 13.2 | 11.9 | 14.2 | 11.7 | 7.6 | 8.4 | 38.3 | 51.9 | 46 832 | 41 557 | -11.3 | -2.0 |
| Westerville | 5.2 | 17.2 | 10.1 | 10.0 | 12.2 | 15.8 | 15.3 | 7.5 | 6.7 | 41.2 | 53.0 | 35 318 | 36 121 | 2.3 | 2.6 |
| Westlake | 4.5 | 17.0 | 5.7 | 10.3 | 12.4 | 16.2 | 14.9 | 8.4 | 10.6 | 45.0 | 52.6 | 31 719 | 32 729 | 3.2 | -0.7 |
| Wooster | 6.1 | 14.2 | 14.8 | 12.3 | 10.8 | 12.8 | 12.4 | 7.9 | 8.8 | 37.3 | 52.4 | 24 811 | 26 119 | 5.3 | 1.0 |
| Xenia | 7.0 | 17.8 | 9.2 | 13.5 | 11.9 | 13.5 | 11.4 | 7.6 | 8.1 | 37.1 | 52.8 | 24 164 | 25 657 | 6.4 | 1.1 |
| Youngstown | 6.4 | 16.4 | 10.9 | 12.7 | 11.7 | 13.8 | 12.3 | 6.9 | 8.9 | 38.0 | 50.8 | 82 026 | 66 982 | -18.3 | -2.4 |
| Zanesville | 7.7 | 17.4 | 9.7 | 13.5 | 12.1 | 12.9 | 11.5 | 7.0 | 8.2 | 36.3 | 53.4 | 25 586 | 25 484 | -0.4 | -0.3 |
| OKLAHOMA | 7.0 | 17.7 | 10.2 | 13.5 | 12.3 | 14.0 | 11.7 | 7.5 | 6.0 | 36.2 | 50.5 | 3 450 654 | 3 751 354 | 8.7 | 1.7 |
| Bartlesville | 6.7 | 16.9 | 8.7 | 12.0 | 11.3 | 14.3 | 12.5 | 8.4 | 9.3 | 39.9 | 52.2 | 34 748 | 35 750 | 2.9 | 1.4 |
| Broken Arrow | 7.2 | 20.2 | 7.9 | 13.8 | 14.2 | 14.7 | 11.7 | 6.1 | 4.4 | 35.7 | 51.4 | 74 859 | 98 835 | 32.0 | 3.2 |
| Edmond | 6.3 | 18.5 | 12.9 | 12.5 | 12.0 | 14.7 | 11.9 | 6.4 | 4.7 | 34.8 | 51.6 | 68 315 | 81 403 | 19.2 | 4.3 |
| Enid | 8.0 | 16.8 | 9.6 | 14.4 | 11.1 | 13.6 | 11.2 | 7.3 | 7.8 | 36.0 | 51.0 | 47 045 | 49 379 | 5.0 | 1.0 |
| Lawton | 8.0 | 16.9 | 15.3 | 18.1 | 12.0 | 11.9 | 8.4 | 5.0 | 4.4 | 29.7 | 48.1 | 92 757 | 96 867 | 4.4 | 1.6 |
| Midwest City | 7.6 | 17.6 | 9.9 | 14.6 | 11.7 | 13.8 | 11.5 | 6.8 | 6.5 | 35.2 | 52.6 | 54 088 | 54 371 | 0.5 | 3.1 |
| Moore | 8.6 | 19.3 | 9.2 | 18.5 | 13.5 | 12.7 | 9.6 | 5.4 | 3.2 | 31.5 | 51.2 | 41 138 | 55 081 | 33.9 | 5.0 |
| Muskogee | 7.7 | 17.7 | 10.2 | 13.4 | 11.0 | 13.4 | 11.8 | 7.3 | 7.7 | 36.0 | 52.3 | 38 310 | 39 223 | 2.4 | -0.6 |
| Norman | 5.8 | 14.0 | 21.8 | 15.6 | 10.9 | 11.8 | 10.0 | 5.5 | 4.5 | 29.6 | 50.3 | 95 694 | 110 925 | 15.9 | 4.2 |
| Oklahoma City | 7.9 | 17.5 | 10.1 | 15.8 | 12.8 | 13.6 | 10.9 | 6.1 | 5.2 | 34.0 | 50.8 | 506 132 | 580 003 | 14.6 | 3.3 |
| Owasso | 8.0 | 21.6 | 8.9 | 15.0 | 14.9 | 13.7 | 8.5 | 4.8 | 4.5 | 32.7 | 51.7 | 18 502 | 29 748 | 56.3 | 5.7 |
| Ponca City | 7.7 | 17.7 | 8.3 | 13.1 | 10.5 | 13.2 | 12.6 | 8.0 | 8.9 | 38.1 | 51.1 | 25 919 | 25 401 | -2.1 | -1.7 |
| Shawnee | 7.6 | 16.8 | 13.7 | 13.0 | 10.9 | 12.8 | 10.6 | 7.5 | 7.0 | 33.9 | 52.7 | 28 692 | 29 857 | 4.1 | 2.7 |
| Stillwater | 5.0 | 9.8 | 39.0 | 15.7 | 7.8 | 7.9 | 6.7 | 4.1 | 4.1 | 23.9 | 49.4 | 39 065 | 45 688 | 17.0 | 1.9 |
| Tulsa | 7.5 | 17.0 | 10.8 | 15.1 | 12.3 | 13.4 | 11.4 | 6.3 | 6.1 | 34.7 | 51.3 | 393 049 | 391 890 | -0.3 | 0.5 |
| OREGON | 6.2 | 16.4 | 9.4 | 13.7 | 13.0 | 14.1 | 13.3 | 7.6 | 6.4 | 38.4 | 50.5 | 3 421 399 | 3 831 073 | 12.0 | 1.8 |
| Albany | 7.1 | 17.8 | 9.7 | 14.4 | 13.0 | 12.8 | 11.9 | 7.0 | 6.2 | 35.6 | 51.2 | 40 852 | 50 158 | 22.8 | 2.3 |
| Beaverton | 6.8 | 16.1 | 9.2 | 18.3 | 14.7 | 13.7 | 10.8 | 5.3 | 5.2 | 34.7 | 51.4 | 76 129 | 89 757 | 18.0 | 3.3 |
| Bend | 6.9 | 16.8 | 8.7 | 15.4 | 14.7 | 13.3 | 11.8 | 6.6 | 5.9 | 36.6 | 51.0 | 52 029 | 76 639 | 47.3 | 3.2 |
| Corvallis | 4.3 | 10.6 | 32.4 | 13.8 | 9.0 | 10.0 | 9.3 | 4.8 | 5.7 | 26.4 | 49.7 | 49 322 | 54 461 | 10.4 | 1.0 |
| Eugene | 4.9 | 13.3 | 18.7 | 14.6 | 11.5 | 12.0 | 12.4 | 6.2 | 6.4 | 33.8 | 51.1 | 137 893 | 156 342 | 13.3 | 1.1 |
| Grants Pass | 6.8 | 17.5 | 8.5 | 12.4 | 11.3 | 12.9 | 12.1 | 8.2 | 10.4 | 39.3 | 52.7 | 23 003 | 34 544 | 50.1 | 0.8 |
| Gresham | 7.8 | 18.7 | 10.2 | 15.3 | 12.9 | 13.5 | 11.0 | 5.7 | 5.0 | 33.6 | 51.0 | 90 205 | 105 594 | 17.1 | 3.2 |
| Hillsboro | 8.4 | 18.4 | 9.3 | 19.5 | 15.7 | 12.0 | 8.8 | 4.3 | 3.5 | 32.0 | 49.8 | 70 186 | 92 105 | 30.5 | 3.5 |
| Keizer | 7.1 | 20.2 | 8.1 | 13.6 | 12.9 | 13.2 | 11.5 | 6.8 | 6.6 | 35.7 | 52.0 | 32 203 | 36 478 | 13.3 | 1.2 |
| Lake Oswego | 4.1 | 18.0 | 5.7 | 8.7 | 12.4 | 17.9 | 17.2 | 8.5 | 7.5 | 45.8 | 52.7 | 35 278 | 36 625 | 3.8 | 1.7 |
| McMinnville | 7.4 | 18.4 | 12.7 | 12.7 | 12.0 | 11.5 | 10.7 | 6.9 | 7.7 | 34.0 | 51.8 | 26 499 | 32 187 | 21.5 | 1.1 |
| Medford | 7.2 | 16.9 | 9.1 | 13.5 | 12.0 | 13.3 | 12.0 | 7.2 | 9.0 | 37.9 | 51.6 | 63 154 | 74 907 | 18.6 | 2.1 |
| Oregon City | 6.7 | 18.8 | 8.9 | 13.8 | 14.9 | 13.9 | 11.8 | 5.9 | 5.3 | 36.3 | 50.7 | 25 754 | 31 859 | 23.7 | 2.8 |
| Portland | 6.0 | 13.1 | 9.7 | 19.6 | 15.9 | 13.3 | 11.9 | 5.4 | 5.0 | 35.8 | 50.5 | 529 121 | 583 778 | 10.3 | 3.3 |
| Redmond | 8.1 | 19.8 | 8.7 | 15.0 | 13.8 | 11.9 | 9.9 | 6.5 | 6.2 | 33.9 | 51.7 | 13 481 | 26 215 | 94.5 | 2.7 |
| Salem | 7.4 | 17.8 | 10.7 | 14.7 | 13.0 | 13.0 | 11.4 | 6.0 | 5.9 | 34.5 | 50.1 | 136 924 | 154 650 | 12.9 | 1.8 |
| Springfield | 7.3 | 16.9 | 10.2 | 16.2 | 12.8 | 13.6 | 11.4 | 6.1 | 5.4 | 34.5 | 51.0 | 52 864 | 59 374 | 12.4 | 0.8 |

# Table D. Cities — Households, Group Quarters, Crime, and Education

| City | Households, 2010 Number | Persons per house-hold | Female family house-holder[1] Percent | One-person Percent | Persons in group quarters, 2010 Total | Institutional Total | Persons in nursing facilities | Non-institutional | Serious crimes known to police,[2] 2011 Total Number | Rate[3] | Violent | Property | Population age 25 and older | High school graduate or less | Bachelor's degree or more |
|---|---|---|---|---|---|---|---|---|---|---|---|---|---|---|---|
| | 27 | 28 | 29 | 30 | 31 | 32 | 33 | 34 | 35 | 36 | 37 | 38 | 39 | 40 | 41 |
| **OHIO—Cont'd** | | | | | | | | | | | | | | | |
| Kettering | 25 427 | 2.19 | 11.3 | 34.9 | 427 | 304 | 304 | 123 | 1 330 | 2 366 | 114 | 2 253 | 40 093 | 33.0 | 31.0 |
| Lakewood | 25 274 | 2.05 | 10.8 | 44.8 | 370 | 304 | 303 | 66 | 1 210 | 2 319 | 142 | 2 178 | 36 615 | 33.2 | 39.0 |
| Lancaster | 16 048 | 2.36 | 14.2 | 31.7 | 871 | 692 | 383 | 179 | 2 465 | 6 352 | 301 | 6 050 | 26 186 | 55.6 | 15.5 |
| Lima | 14 221 | 2.42 | 22.1 | 33.5 | 4 300 | 3 401 | 279 | 899 | 2 666 | 6 871 | 1 041 | 5 830 | 23 811 | 60.4 | 9.8 |
| Lorain | 25 529 | 2.48 | 21.0 | 30.8 | 662 | 444 | 423 | 218 | 3 528 | 5 500 | 499 | 5 001 | 41 742 | 58.0 | 11.8 |
| Mansfield | 18 696 | 2.21 | 16.6 | 37.1 | 6 594 | 5 881 | 519 | 713 | 3 245 | 6 781 | 359 | 6 421 | 34 198 | 58.0 | 13.5 |
| Marion | 12 868 | 2.45 | 17.1 | 30.4 | 5 267 | 5 112 | 363 | 155 | 2 612 | 7 086 | 269 | 6 817 | 24 855 | 63.0 | 9.9 |
| Mason | 11 016 | 2.77 | 8.4 | 22.4 | 186 | 76 | 76 | 110 | 452 | 1 471 | 36 | 1 435 | 19 015 | 25.4 | 51.6 |
| Massillon | 13 140 | 2.37 | 14.9 | 31.1 | 951 | 683 | 348 | 268 | 1 299 | 4 038 | 270 | 3 767 | 22 591 | 59.8 | 14.2 |
| Medina | 10 382 | 2.53 | 12.0 | 27.8 | 361 | 345 | 186 | 16 | NA | NA | NA | NA | 16 754 | 37.5 | 34.2 |
| Mentor | 19 166 | 2.44 | 9.4 | 25.7 | 403 | 381 | 381 | 22 | 1 171 | 2 481 | 93 | 2 388 | 34 130 | 38.9 | 28.7 |
| Middletown | 20 238 | 2.38 | 18.1 | 31.5 | 573 | 472 | 399 | 101 | 4 733 | 9 713 | 747 | 8 966 | 32 180 | 61.0 | 13.8 |
| Newark | 19 840 | 2.35 | 14.8 | 31.9 | 1 011 | 750 | 486 | 261 | 2 162 | 4 541 | 179 | 4 363 | 32 073 | 54.9 | 16.7 |
| North Olmsted | 13 645 | 2.37 | 9.6 | 30.1 | 323 | 264 | 264 | 59 | 581 | 1 774 | 55 | 1 720 | 23 775 | 34.6 | 30.4 |
| North Ridgeville | 11 500 | 2.54 | 8.6 | 21.9 | 225 | 213 | 213 | 12 | 278 | 943 | 44 | 899 | 20 657 | 41.9 | 22.4 |
| North Royalton | 12 944 | 2.33 | 7.9 | 31.0 | 247 | 226 | 226 | 21 | NA | NA | NA | NA | 21 234 | 36.7 | 32.9 |
| Parma | 34 489 | 2.34 | 12.4 | 31.8 | 1 063 | 897 | 792 | 166 | 287 | 351 | 47 | 305 | 57 999 | 49.2 | 19.6 |
| Reynoldsburg | 14 387 | 2.49 | 15.9 | 28.0 | 25 | 0 | 0 | 25 | 1 132 | 3 152 | 217 | 2 934 | 23 255 | 38.7 | 29.2 |
| Riverside | 10 284 | 2.45 | 15.0 | 28.9 | 0 | 0 | 0 | 0 | 723 | 2 867 | 214 | 2 653 | 17 219 | 52.3 | 15.2 |
| Sandusky | 11 082 | 2.28 | 19.7 | 35.1 | 579 | 305 | 240 | 274 | 1 486 | 5 757 | 465 | 5 292 | 17 516 | 60.7 | 12.8 |
| Shaker Heights | 11 840 | 2.39 | 15.3 | 31.1 | 156 | 119 | 44 | 37 | 666 | 2 339 | 119 | 2 220 | 19 135 | 13.8 | 64.5 |
| Springfield | 24 459 | 2.38 | 18.6 | 34.1 | 2 497 | 1 128 | 854 | 1 369 | 5 020 | 8 277 | 643 | 7 634 | 38 716 | 57.4 | 14.4 |
| Stow | 14 226 | 2.42 | 9.0 | 27.2 | 454 | 405 | 405 | 49 | 755 | 2 166 | 66 | 2 100 | 23 508 | 30.5 | 40.6 |
| Strongsville | 17 659 | 2.52 | 7.4 | 24.9 | 304 | 277 | 264 | 27 | 958 | 2 139 | 58 | 2 081 | 30 732 | 31.2 | 41.6 |
| Toledo | 119 730 | 2.33 | 19.9 | 34.8 | 8 475 | 2 987 | 1 239 | 5 488 | 12 699 | 4 418 | 998 | 3 420 | 182 946 | 50.5 | 17.3 |
| Troy | 10 353 | 2.38 | 12.9 | 30.5 | 420 | 263 | 163 | 157 | 904 | 3 605 | 68 | 3 537 | 17 280 | 47.9 | 21.9 |
| Upper Arlington | 13 754 | 2.44 | 7.3 | 26.9 | 254 | 254 | 254 | 0 | 500 | 1 479 | 41 | 1 438 | 23 486 | 11.5 | 71.5 |
| Warren | 17 003 | 2.30 | 21.3 | 35.6 | 2 517 | 2 302 | 525 | 215 | 2 406 | 5 785 | 623 | 5 163 | 27 400 | 63.3 | 11.3 |
| Westerville | 13 859 | 2.48 | 9.1 | 24.4 | 1 685 | 454 | 454 | 1 231 | 406 | 1 123 | 44 | 1 079 | 24 105 | 23.1 | 50.7 |
| Westlake | 13 870 | 2.30 | 6.9 | 34.2 | 871 | 830 | 830 | 41 | 1 | 3 | 0 | 3 | 23 712 | 25.8 | 50.1 |
| Wooster | 10 733 | 2.21 | 11.3 | 35.4 | 2 381 | 387 | 230 | 1 994 | 976 | 3 734 | 275 | 3 459 | 16 645 | 50.1 | 26.0 |
| Xenia | 10 390 | 2.39 | 16.3 | 31.0 | 925 | 700 | 312 | 225 | 1 160 | 4 507 | 198 | 4 309 | 16 739 | 49.6 | 18.7 |
| Youngstown | 26 839 | 2.28 | 24.8 | 37.8 | 5 831 | 3 929 | 644 | 1 902 | 4 603 | 6 867 | 925 | 5 942 | 45 838 | 63.9 | 10.9 |
| Zanesville | 10 864 | 2.29 | 19.1 | 36.2 | 582 | 514 | 290 | 68 | 1 991 | 7 806 | 435 | 7 371 | 16 823 | 62.1 | 11.9 |
| **OKLAHOMA** | 1 460 450 | 2.49 | 12.3 | 27.5 | 112 017 | 64 411 | 21 678 | 47 606 | 144 495 | 3 811 | 455 | 3 356 | 2 411 080 | 46.2 | 23.0 |
| Bartlesville | 14 977 | 2.34 | 11.8 | 30.7 | 658 | 256 | 145 | 402 | 1 178 | 3 260 | 296 | 2 964 | 23 945 | 41.8 | 30.1 |
| Broken Arrow | 36 141 | 2.72 | 10.3 | 19.2 | 468 | 466 | 466 | 2 | 2 431 | 2 433 | 144 | 2 289 | 62 208 | 31.3 | 30.3 |
| Edmond | 31 475 | 2.54 | 9.6 | 23.2 | 1 586 | 313 | 268 | 1 273 | 1 704 | 2 071 | 70 | 2 001 | 49 974 | 20.5 | 51.0 |
| Enid | 19 726 | 2.41 | 11.9 | 30.5 | 1 824 | 1 005 | 593 | 819 | 2 065 | 4 138 | 445 | 3 693 | 31 696 | 50.1 | 22.6 |
| Lawton | 34 901 | 2.48 | 15.8 | 29.4 | 10 143 | 3 772 | 523 | 6 371 | 6 360 | 6 496 | 847 | 5 649 | 56 787 | 45.5 | 19.9 |
| Midwest City | 22 726 | 2.38 | 17.5 | 31.3 | 285 | 260 | 235 | 25 | 2 938 | 5 346 | 480 | 4 866 | 36 041 | 41.0 | 20.1 |
| Moore | 20 446 | 2.68 | 14.1 | 21.1 | 309 | 179 | 179 | 130 | 2 537 | 4 557 | 214 | 4 343 | 34 565 | 43.1 | 21.4 |
| Muskogee | 15 704 | 2.41 | 17.3 | 32.7 | 1 353 | 834 | 430 | 519 | 1 237 | 3 120 | 583 | 2 538 | 25 489 | 48.5 | 17.6 |
| Norman | 44 661 | 2.33 | 10.1 | 30.7 | 6 757 | 1 124 | 566 | 5 633 | 3 671 | 3 274 | 170 | 3 104 | 63 925 | 27.4 | 43.1 |
| Oklahoma City | 230 233 | 2.47 | 13.9 | 30.5 | 12 144 | 6 609 | 2 521 | 5 535 | 39 221 | 6 691 | 871 | 5 819 | 368 727 | 41.1 | 27.9 |
| Owasso | 10 689 | 2.68 | 11.6 | 22.5 | 242 | 214 | 173 | 28 | 803 | 2 748 | 287 | 2 460 | 17 341 | 30.6 | 30.8 |
| Ponca City | 10 395 | 2.37 | 12.3 | 31.8 | 700 | 433 | 245 | 267 | 1 233 | 4 805 | 507 | 4 299 | 16 732 | 47.1 | 21.1 |
| Shawnee | 11 619 | 2.43 | 16.0 | 30.7 | 1 670 | 468 | 249 | 1 202 | 2 112 | 6 999 | 858 | 6 140 | 18 333 | 49.2 | 20.4 |
| Stillwater | 17 941 | 2.16 | 8.3 | 35.0 | 6 945 | 367 | 180 | 6 578 | 1 481 | 3 207 | 219 | 2 989 | 20 438 | 23.4 | 47.9 |
| Tulsa | 163 975 | 2.34 | 14.6 | 34.5 | 8 386 | 4 284 | 2 033 | 4 102 | 25 883 | 6 534 | 1 000 | 5 535 | 252 639 | 40.1 | 29.5 |
| **OREGON** | 1 518 938 | 2.47 | 10.5 | 27.4 | 86 642 | 36 612 | 11 491 | 50 030 | 130 180 | 3 362 | 248 | 3 115 | 2 579 164 | 36.3 | 29.0 |
| Albany | 19 705 | 2.50 | 12.4 | 26.7 | 824 | 560 | 256 | 264 | 1 483 | 2 926 | 87 | 2 839 | 31 809 | 39.2 | 21.9 |
| Beaverton | 37 213 | 2.39 | 10.6 | 30.9 | 945 | 460 | 393 | 485 | 1 945 | 2 143 | 183 | 1 960 | 59 711 | 25.9 | 42.8 |
| Bend | 31 790 | 2.39 | 9.9 | 27.1 | 578 | 183 | 157 | 395 | 2 630 | 3 396 | 265 | 3 131 | 52 752 | 25.0 | 36.5 |
| Corvallis | 22 283 | 2.22 | 7.0 | 33.2 | 4 899 | 116 | 74 | 4 783 | 1 844 | 3 350 | 142 | 3 208 | 27 839 | 19.2 | 51.9 |
| Eugene | 66 419 | 2.24 | 10.0 | 33.2 | 7 249 | 1 131 | 585 | 6 118 | 8 338 | 5 282 | 291 | 4 991 | 97 382 | 26.1 | 40.4 |
| Grants Pass | 14 313 | 2.34 | 14.5 | 32.8 | 1 051 | 627 | 355 | 424 | 2 098 | 6 011 | 312 | 5 699 | 22 675 | 43.7 | 14.7 |
| Gresham | 38 704 | 2.69 | 14.3 | 25.2 | 1 514 | 553 | 491 | 961 | 4 823 | 4 519 | 392 | 4 128 | 66 150 | 45.7 | 18.4 |
| Hillsboro | 33 289 | 2.71 | 11.0 | 24.0 | 1 528 | 989 | 220 | 539 | 2 211 | 2 388 | 158 | 2 230 | 56 647 | 32.9 | 34.2 |
| Keizer | 13 703 | 2.64 | 13.3 | 24.2 | 364 | 190 | 190 | 174 | 838 | 2 273 | 174 | 2 099 | 22 986 | 38.1 | 22.4 |
| Lake Oswego | 15 893 | 2.29 | 7.4 | 30.1 | 222 | 187 | 148 | 35 | 521 | 1 408 | 51 | 1 356 | 25 966 | 11.3 | 66.5 |
| McMinnville | 11 674 | 2.61 | 13.0 | 26.4 | 1 716 | 396 | 183 | 1 320 | 1 183 | 3 637 | 188 | 3 449 | 19 938 | 46.4 | 21.2 |
| Medford | 30 079 | 2.44 | 13.1 | 28.9 | 1 553 | 691 | 450 | 862 | 4 319 | 5 705 | 515 | 5 190 | 49 984 | 40.5 | 22.0 |
| Oregon City | 11 973 | 2.61 | 12.4 | 23.5 | 650 | 555 | 157 | 95 | 833 | 2 587 | 106 | 2 482 | 20 102 | 36.8 | 21.2 |
| Portland | 248 546 | 2.28 | 10.1 | 34.5 | 17 754 | 4 821 | 2 160 | 12 933 | 33 059 | 5 603 | 515 | 5 089 | 409 486 | 29.0 | 42.0 |
| Redmond | 9 947 | 2.61 | 13.9 | 24.0 | 300 | 181 | 181 | 119 | 1 533 | 5 786 | 306 | 5 480 | 15 574 | 42.8 | 16.3 |
| Salem | 57 290 | 2.55 | 13.0 | 28.8 | 8 635 | 5 610 | 639 | 3 025 | 6 516 | 4 169 | 334 | 3 835 | 98 629 | 39.6 | 25.9 |
| Springfield | 23 665 | 2.49 | 15.2 | 27.9 | 587 | 181 | 140 | 406 | 2 586 | 4 307 | 248 | 4 059 | 38 357 | 46.5 | 14.9 |

1. No spouse present.  2. Data for serious crimes have not been adjusted for underreporting. This may affect comparability between geographic areas and over time.  3. Per 100,000 population estimated by the FBI.  4. Persons 25 years old and over.

# Table D. Cities — Income, Poverty, and Housing

| City | Money income, 2007–2011 | | | | | Housing units, 2010 | | | Occupied Housing units 2007–2011 | | | | |
|---|---|---|---|---|---|---|---|---|---|---|---|---|---|
| | | Households | | | | | | | | Owner-occupied | | Median owner costs as a percent of income | |
| | Per capita income[1] (dollars) | Median income | Percent with income of $200,000 or more | Percent with income of less than $25,000 | Families with income below poverty (percent) | Total | Percent change, 2000–2010 | Vacant units for sale or rent[2] | Total | Percent | Median value[3] (dollars) | With a mortgage[4] | Without a mortgage[5] |
| | 42 | 43 | 44 | 45 | 46 | 47 | 48 | 49 | 50 | 51 | 52 | 53 | 54 |
| OHIO—Cont'd | | | | | | | | | | | | | |
| Kettering | 31 087 | 50 797 | 3.0 | 22.0 | 6.4 | 27 602 | 2.5 | 2 175 | 25 559 | 65.6 | 135 000 | 22.6 | 12.6 |
| Lakewood | 27 365 | 43 139 | 2.0 | 30.0 | 13.5 | 28 498 | 0.3 | 3 224 | 24 615 | 42.2 | 136 500 | 23.9 | 15.1 |
| Lancaster | 21 887 | 38 869 | 1.0 | 31.1 | 12.6 | 17 685 | 11.6 | 1 637 | 16 505 | 56.7 | 121 600 | 23.7 | 11.1 |
| Lima | 15 225 | 28 641 | 0.1 | 45.0 | 27.4 | 16 784 | -5.0 | 2 563 | 14 537 | 51.8 | 73 000 | 22.2 | 13.7 |
| Lorain | 18 494 | 34 769 | 0.6 | 37.8 | 25.4 | 29 144 | 3.3 | 3 615 | 26 126 | 57.3 | 101 700 | 23.7 | 13.3 |
| Mansfield | 18 357 | 33 482 | 1.2 | 35.9 | 15.3 | 22 022 | -1.4 | 3 326 | 19 082 | 56.6 | 83 700 | 23.6 | 13.1 |
| Marion | 15 746 | 32 431 | 0.8 | 39.7 | 22.9 | 15 066 | 2.3 | 2 198 | 13 030 | 59.3 | 79 000 | 22.6 | 14.7 |
| Mason | 36 523 | 83 695 | 11.3 | 10.3 | 3.4 | 11 471 | 41.1 | 455 | 10 698 | 84.4 | 217 400 | 22.9 | 15.0 |
| Massillon | 20 546 | 38 376 | 0.6 | 33.3 | 11.9 | 14 497 | 7.1 | 1 357 | 13 582 | 68.3 | 98 500 | 23.5 | 13.4 |
| Medina | 27 291 | 56 389 | 3.9 | 23.2 | 11.6 | 11 152 | 13.9 | 770 | 10 204 | 66.7 | 168 600 | 23.1 | 11.4 |
| Mentor | 31 503 | 65 044 | 3.2 | 12.7 | 4.7 | 20 218 | 4.8 | 1 052 | 18 907 | 86.8 | 172 500 | 23.1 | 12.5 |
| Middletown | 19 716 | 36 546 | 0.9 | 34.7 | 18.4 | 23 296 | 0.5 | 3 058 | 19 922 | 57.6 | 108 100 | 25.0 | 15.1 |
| Newark | 21 951 | 37 927 | 1.2 | 32.9 | 15.2 | 21 976 | 6.3 | 2 136 | 20 328 | 57.4 | 114 800 | 21.8 | 11.0 |
| North Olmsted | 29 293 | 57 668 | 2.1 | 16.4 | 3.8 | 14 500 | 3.1 | 855 | 13 599 | 79.0 | 154 600 | 25.0 | 15.3 |
| North Ridgeville | 29 310 | 64 963 | 1.5 | 12.3 | 3.3 | 12 109 | 41.0 | 609 | 11 427 | 88.8 | 164 500 | 24.0 | 13.6 |
| North Royalton | 32 291 | 62 763 | 4.6 | 15.0 | 3.3 | 13 710 | 16.6 | 766 | 12 249 | 72.8 | 195 800 | 23.9 | 15.3 |
| Parma | 24 970 | 49 939 | 0.9 | 21.3 | 6.3 | 36 608 | 0.5 | 2 119 | 33 247 | 75.3 | 127 200 | 22.8 | 14.6 |
| Reynoldsburg | 27 928 | 56 034 | 1.9 | 19.4 | 10.0 | 15 611 | 15.9 | 1 224 | 14 114 | 63.0 | 151 600 | 22.9 | 12.8 |
| Riverside | 21 717 | 38 774 | 0.1 | 26.4 | 12.1 | 11 304 | 8.8 | 1 020 | 10 704 | 57.8 | 97 400 | 23.1 | 13.9 |
| Sandusky | 20 363 | 34 967 | 1.3 | 37.3 | 17.7 | 13 386 | 0.4 | 2 304 | 11 230 | 56.9 | 87 600 | 23.5 | 13.5 |
| Shaker Heights | 49 293 | 76 989 | 16.1 | 17.3 | 6.1 | 13 318 | 2.5 | 1 478 | 11 432 | 62.9 | 233 900 | 22.6 | 15.0 |
| Springfield | 18 285 | 33 819 | 1.0 | 38.9 | 21.0 | 28 437 | -2.9 | 3 978 | 24 144 | 56.5 | 84 600 | 22.4 | 13.6 |
| Stow | 30 968 | 64 577 | 2.9 | 13.5 | 4.6 | 15 141 | 17.8 | 915 | 13 683 | 69.2 | 167 100 | 21.7 | 12.6 |
| Strongsville | 36 621 | 77 087 | 6.3 | 13.3 | 3.5 | 18 476 | 9.6 | 817 | 16 973 | 81.5 | 202 600 | 22.6 | 13.9 |
| Toledo | 18 809 | 34 170 | 0.7 | 37.4 | 20.7 | 138 039 | -1.3 | 18 309 | 119 359 | 57.2 | 93 300 | 24.0 | 14.5 |
| Troy | 23 869 | 48 450 | 0.6 | 24.9 | 12.1 | 11 166 | 17.1 | 813 | 10 570 | 60.1 | 130 100 | 21.3 | 12.5 |
| Upper Arlington | 52 591 | 96 810 | 16.9 | 8.9 | 2.0 | 14 544 | 0.8 | 790 | 13 424 | 82.7 | 309 600 | 22.4 | 13.7 |
| Warren | 16 442 | 29 231 | 0.6 | 43.4 | 28.7 | 20 384 | -4.5 | 3 381 | 16 719 | 58.0 | 69 400 | 23.7 | 14.9 |
| Westerville | 37 143 | 83 234 | 7.5 | 12.5 | 3.7 | 14 467 | 10.1 | 608 | 13 426 | 75.3 | 214 600 | 20.9 | 10.0 |
| Westlake | 42 392 | 71 974 | 9.5 | 11.9 | 2.7 | 14 843 | 8.4 | 973 | 13 152 | 73.2 | 231 300 | 22.5 | 12.2 |
| Wooster | 23 871 | 40 604 | 2.2 | 28.0 | 12.9 | 11 822 | 10.0 | 1 089 | 10 574 | 62.5 | 127 000 | 23.4 | 12.8 |
| Xenia | 19 846 | 39 691 | 0.2 | 30.2 | 17.0 | 11 424 | 15.4 | 1 034 | 10 475 | 63.5 | 99 900 | 23.3 | 12.0 |
| Youngstown | 14 996 | 24 880 | 0.3 | 50.2 | 28.6 | 33 123 | -10.9 | 6 284 | 27 937 | 60.1 | 49 900 | 23.9 | 15.6 |
| Zanesville | 17 762 | 27 676 | 1.0 | 46.5 | 26.1 | 12 385 | 5.4 | 1 521 | 10 978 | 46.2 | 80 200 | 23.6 | 14.8 |
| OKLAHOMA | 23 770 | 44 287 | 2.5 | 27.5 | 12.0 | 1 664 378 | 9.9 | 203 928 | 1 432 735 | 67.8 | 108 400 | 21.3 | 10.9 |
| Bartlesville | 28 294 | 46 665 | 3.8 | 26.1 | 12.0 | 16 768 | 4.1 | 1 791 | 15 091 | 69.0 | 105 300 | 19.8 | 11.2 |
| Broken Arrow | 29 141 | 65 385 | 3.2 | 12.4 | 4.6 | 38 013 | 40.2 | 1 872 | 35 007 | 79.8 | 147 000 | 21.5 | 10.8 |
| Edmond | 37 467 | 69 843 | 9.5 | 17.6 | 4.9 | 33 178 | 25.8 | 1 703 | 30 136 | 69.9 | 194 100 | 21.3 | 10.0 |
| Enid | 23 217 | 39 343 | 1.9 | 28.7 | 13.4 | 21 936 | 3.2 | 2 210 | 19 660 | 64.1 | 83 700 | 20.5 | 10.8 |
| Lawton | 21 097 | 43 633 | 1.9 | 27.7 | 15.0 | 39 409 | 8.2 | 4 508 | 34 511 | 50.6 | 100 900 | 20.5 | 10.0 |
| Midwest City | 23 430 | 43 956 | 1.0 | 26.6 | 11.1 | 24 723 | 3.9 | 1 997 | 22 996 | 62.7 | 95 100 | 21.4 | 10.2 |
| Moore | 24 936 | 56 601 | 1.4 | 16.1 | 6.7 | 21 444 | 34.8 | 998 | 19 882 | 75.2 | 115 500 | 21.6 | 11.5 |
| Muskogee | 19 147 | 33 196 | 1.1 | 37.0 | 21.5 | 18 055 | 2.8 | 2 351 | 16 071 | 59.8 | 81 900 | 22.3 | 11.3 |
| Norman | 27 343 | 46 595 | 3.4 | 26.4 | 9.2 | 47 965 | 15.5 | 3 304 | 43 009 | 57.8 | 147 100 | 21.0 | 10.8 |
| Oklahoma City | 25 450 | 44 973 | 3.0 | 26.6 | 13.3 | 256 930 | 12.6 | 26 697 | 224 986 | 60.6 | 129 300 | 22.3 | 11.4 |
| Owasso | 27 634 | 66 572 | 2.7 | 12.7 | 5.4 | 11 346 | 64.9 | 657 | 10 125 | 71.3 | 149 700 | 20.9 | 10.5 |
| Ponca City | 22 229 | 39 711 | 1.7 | 32.4 | 13.1 | 11 950 | 0.5 | 1 555 | 10 212 | 66.0 | 83 200 | 19.0 | 11.8 |
| Shawnee | 19 626 | 35 871 | 1.6 | 37.0 | 18.5 | 13 205 | 4.0 | 1 586 | 11 266 | 60.8 | 89 500 | 20.6 | 11.7 |
| Stillwater | 19 159 | 30 133 | 2.1 | 43.7 | 12.6 | 19 753 | 17.5 | 1 812 | 17 851 | 37.4 | 150 300 | 22.7 | 10.0 |
| Tulsa | 26 727 | 40 268 | 3.8 | 30.2 | 15.1 | 185 127 | 3.1 | 21 152 | 164 535 | 54.4 | 118 700 | 22.3 | 12.0 |
| OREGON | 26 561 | 49 850 | 3.1 | 24.1 | 10.2 | 1 675 562 | 15.3 | 156 624 | 1 509 554 | 63.1 | 252 600 | 26.9 | 12.8 |
| Albany | 22 249 | 45 980 | 1.0 | 27.1 | 14.3 | 20 979 | 20.6 | 1 274 | 19 362 | 59.8 | 179 400 | 25.7 | 12.0 |
| Beaverton | 30 225 | 55 115 | 3.9 | 19.2 | 9.6 | 39 500 | 21.5 | 2 287 | 36 458 | 49.7 | 297 600 | 25.8 | 13.0 |
| Bend | 30 203 | 52 596 | 3.8 | 20.5 | 7.5 | 36 110 | 60.5 | 4 320 | 32 413 | 58.3 | 296 100 | 28.2 | 12.2 |
| Corvallis | 22 870 | 36 328 | 3.1 | 37.6 | 12.0 | 23 423 | 12.1 | 1 140 | 21 318 | 43.3 | 253 300 | 24.0 | 11.3 |
| Eugene | 25 222 | 41 326 | 2.9 | 32.2 | 10.4 | 69 951 | 14.1 | 3 532 | 65 631 | 50.1 | 248 100 | 26.2 | 13.5 |
| Grants Pass | 20 845 | 33 710 | 1.9 | 35.9 | 16.9 | 15 561 | 57.8 | 1 248 | 14 283 | 51.7 | 221 300 | 29.1 | 13.6 |
| Gresham | 21 748 | 47 852 | 1.2 | 24.4 | 13.5 | 41 015 | 16.2 | 2 311 | 38 000 | 54.8 | 236 200 | 27.8 | 14.3 |
| Hillsboro | 27 034 | 64 197 | 2.8 | 15.5 | 7.9 | 35 487 | 30.5 | 2 198 | 32 177 | 56.3 | 262 800 | 26.1 | 11.6 |
| Keizer | 23 857 | 50 902 | 2.1 | 19.9 | 11.7 | 14 445 | 13.1 | 742 | 13 477 | 59.5 | 216 700 | 26.5 | 13.1 |
| Lake Oswego | 50 572 | 81 669 | 14.7 | 11.2 | 4.4 | 16 995 | 8.5 | 1 102 | 15 641 | 71.1 | 507 800 | 25.8 | 12.8 |
| McMinnville | 22 505 | 41 782 | 2.6 | 29.0 | 12.5 | 12 389 | 26.0 | 715 | 11 594 | 59.3 | 214 200 | 26.0 | 14.0 |
| Medford | 23 568 | 41 969 | 2.0 | 28.7 | 13.6 | 32 430 | 23.3 | 2 351 | 30 743 | 51.1 | 243 300 | 29.2 | 13.5 |
| Oregon City | 25 905 | 57 618 | 1.6 | 20.3 | 9.8 | 12 900 | 26.9 | 927 | 11 898 | 63.3 | 284 200 | 27.8 | 12.9 |
| Portland | 30 631 | 50 177 | 4.3 | 25.5 | 11.7 | 265 439 | 11.9 | 16 893 | 247 711 | 54.2 | 292 800 | 27.4 | 14.7 |
| Redmond | 19 222 | 42 433 | 0.6 | 27.7 | 13.2 | 10 965 | 92.8 | 1 018 | 9 695 | 58.6 | 200 400 | 32.9 | 14.6 |
| Salem | 23 162 | 44 226 | 2.0 | 26.3 | 13.4 | 61 276 | 14.0 | 3 986 | 58 206 | 56.6 | 199 500 | 26.7 | 13.9 |
| Springfield | 19 701 | 37 255 | 0.8 | 32.1 | 15.2 | 24 809 | 15.0 | 1 144 | 23 906 | 53.0 | 179 200 | 27.1 | 14.4 |

1. Based on population estimated by the American Community Survey.    2. Includes units rented or sold but not occupied.    3. Specified owner-occupied units; $1,000,000 represents $1,000,000 or more    4. 50.0 represents 50 percent or more.    5. 10.0 represents 10 percent or less.

# Table D. Cities — Housing, Labor Force, and Employment

| City | Occupied housing units, 2007–2011 (cont.) | | | | Migration, 2007–2011 | | Civilian labor force, 2012 | | Unemployment | | Civilian employment[4], 2007–2011 | | | |
|---|---|---|---|---|---|---|---|---|---|---|---|---|---|---|
| | Percent renter occupied | Median gross rent[1] | Median rent as a percent of income[2] | Percent with no vehicle available | Percent who lived in the same house one year ago | Percent who lived outside this city one year ago | Total | Percent change, 2011–2012 | Total | Rate[3] | Population age 16 and older | In labor force | Full-year full-time worker | Households with no workers (percent) |
| | 55 | 56 | 57 | 58 | 59 | 60 | 61 | 62 | 63 | 64 | 65 | 66 | 67 | 68 |
| **OHIO—Cont'd** | | | | | | | | | | | | | | |
| Kettering | 34.4 | 712 | 28.3 | 6.0 | 85.3 | 10.5 | 28 167 | -0.6 | 1 950 | 6.9 | 45 614 | 67.3 | 42.1 | 28.3 |
| Lakewood | 57.8 | 691 | 28.7 | 14.8 | 78.1 | 14.2 | 30 801 | 1.2 | 1 801 | 5.8 | 43 423 | 73.4 | 44.7 | 25.2 |
| Lancaster | 43.3 | 690 | 30.2 | 9.2 | 80.2 | 9.3 | 18 919 | 1.9 | 1 302 | 6.9 | 30 623 | 62.3 | 36.6 | 33.7 |
| Lima | 48.2 | 595 | 35.4 | 17.2 | 78.3 | 9.4 | 16 171 | -1.5 | 1 454 | 9.0 | 30 060 | 57.8 | 27.4 | 39.4 |
| Lorain | 42.7 | 619 | 34.3 | 12.8 | 80.4 | 7.2 | 29 874 | 1.4 | 2 867 | 9.6 | 48 858 | 61.0 | 32.6 | 37.3 |
| Mansfield | 43.4 | 603 | 29.0 | 13.1 | 79.1 | 10.8 | 20 661 | -3.1 | 1 704 | 8.2 | 39 674 | 53.5 | 28.9 | 35.3 |
| Marion | 40.7 | 646 | 36.0 | 11.0 | 74.7 | 13.9 | 15 951 | -3.5 | 1 248 | 7.8 | 29 525 | 51.5 | 30.0 | 34.7 |
| Mason | 15.6 | 1 020 | 31.3 | 2.1 | 89.4 | 6.9 | 16 003 | 1.0 | 894 | 5.6 | 21 970 | 72.4 | 46.8 | 15.8 |
| Massillon | 31.7 | 613 | 33.5 | 7.6 | 84.7 | 9.2 | 15 451 | -0.3 | 1 188 | 7.7 | 26 188 | 61.4 | 35.0 | 35.8 |
| Medina | 33.3 | 770 | 33.4 | 7.7 | 84.5 | 9.3 | 14 194 | 0.7 | 845 | 6.0 | 19 984 | 69.1 | 42.2 | 24.3 |
| Mentor | 13.2 | 871 | 32.0 | 4.0 | 91.8 | 6.2 | 27 338 | 1.0 | 1 566 | 5.7 | 38 660 | 69.0 | 44.7 | 22.5 |
| Middletown | 42.4 | 694 | 33.4 | 11.1 | 80.5 | 8.3 | 23 874 | -0.4 | 1 999 | 8.4 | 38 352 | 59.9 | 34.7 | 37.5 |
| Newark | 42.6 | 624 | 30.3 | 11.8 | 80.8 | 9.4 | 22 776 | 1.2 | 1 580 | 6.9 | 37 474 | 63.8 | 38.4 | 33.4 |
| North Olmsted | 21.0 | 752 | 27.3 | 3.8 | 90.8 | 7.1 | 18 015 | 1.0 | 1 086 | 6.0 | 26 943 | 67.8 | 41.0 | 27.1 |
| North Ridgeville | 11.2 | 723 | 33.1 | 2.5 | 91.3 | 6.2 | 17 304 | 0.8 | 1 006 | 5.8 | 23 068 | 68.8 | 44.8 | 24.1 |
| North Royalton | 27.2 | 764 | 21.8 | 3.9 | 91.7 | 6.7 | 17 545 | 1.1 | 1 039 | 5.9 | 24 795 | 69.1 | 44.4 | 24.3 |
| Parma | 24.7 | 715 | 29.7 | 6.2 | 88.7 | 7.6 | 41 780 | 0.6 | 2 920 | 7.0 | 66 985 | 66.4 | 39.3 | 28.8 |
| Reynoldsburg | 37.0 | 811 | 29.2 | 4.9 | 80.5 | 13.1 | 19 364 | 2.3 | 1 131 | 5.8 | 27 177 | 71.3 | 48.3 | 22.6 |
| Riverside | 42.2 | 725 | 27.4 | 6.4 | 82.8 | 14.4 | 11 560 | -0.7 | 947 | 8.2 | 19 836 | 63.4 | 34.7 | 32.5 |
| Sandusky | 43.1 | 595 | 30.8 | 11.9 | 82.5 | 5.4 | 13 415 | 1.6 | 1 020 | 7.6 | 20 615 | 61.7 | 32.7 | 34.8 |
| Shaker Heights | 37.1 | 931 | 32.2 | 7.1 | 88.3 | 8.7 | 14 936 | 2.0 | 833 | 5.6 | 21 880 | 67.7 | 42.5 | 22.9 |
| Springfield | 43.5 | 622 | 33.7 | 13.2 | 80.1 | 8.2 | 27 311 | -1.6 | 2 073 | 7.6 | 47 911 | 57.2 | 32.1 | 37.4 |
| Stow | 30.8 | 858 | 24.1 | 4.3 | 90.1 | 7.7 | 19 349 | 0.5 | 1 102 | 5.7 | 27 822 | 69.0 | 45.4 | 22.4 |
| Strongsville | 18.5 | 785 | 26.3 | 4.1 | 92.2 | 6.6 | 24 827 | 1.7 | 1 422 | 5.7 | 35 208 | 69.3 | 43.4 | 23.5 |
| Toledo | 42.8 | 629 | 33.4 | 13.3 | 81.1 | 5.8 | 130 715 | 0.3 | 11 302 | 8.6 | 226 925 | 64.4 | 33.1 | 34.6 |
| Troy | 39.9 | 673 | 26.8 | 8.6 | 80.0 | 11.0 | 12 676 | -1.6 | 863 | 6.8 | 19 496 | 67.0 | 44.3 | 27.0 |
| Upper Arlington | 17.3 | 1 027 | 26.9 | 3.8 | 91.7 | 5.8 | 17 016 | 3.7 | 832 | 4.9 | 26 572 | 66.1 | 44.4 | 22.9 |
| Warren | 42.0 | 599 | 33.6 | 12.7 | 84.7 | 6.5 | 17 615 | 0.3 | 1 623 | 9.2 | 32 204 | 50.1 | 28.3 | 42.0 |
| Westerville | 24.7 | 892 | 29.1 | 5.0 | 85.9 | 10.9 | 19 546 | 3.0 | 1 060 | 5.4 | 28 782 | 68.9 | 43.5 | 19.8 |
| Westlake | 26.8 | 983 | 24.1 | 5.6 | 89.3 | 8.7 | 16 929 | 1.5 | 956 | 5.6 | 26 573 | 63.6 | 41.7 | 25.2 |
| Wooster | 37.5 | 618 | 27.8 | 8.6 | 78.5 | 11.5 | 13 331 | 1.1 | 769 | 5.8 | 21 312 | 61.1 | 36.0 | 29.8 |
| Xenia | 36.5 | 665 | 36.9 | 9.6 | 86.1 | 7.6 | 11 780 | -1.7 | 970 | 8.2 | 19 689 | 61.5 | 38.5 | 31.4 |
| Youngstown | 39.9 | 562 | 39.2 | 18.0 | 83.8 | 8.2 | 25 399 | -1.0 | 2 467 | 9.7 | 55 245 | 51.8 | 23.0 | 45.6 |
| Zanesville | 53.8 | 575 | 33.5 | 17.3 | 78.4 | 8.7 | 9 957 | -1.3 | 1 010 | 10.1 | 19 832 | 57.8 | 30.6 | 42.6 |
| **OKLAHOMA** | 32.2 | 659 | 28.5 | 5.7 | 81.6 | 11.0 | 1 802 639 | 2.3 | 93 842 | 5.2 | 2 897 182 | 63.0 | 40.8 | 27.5 |
| Bartlesville | 31.0 | 617 | 25.5 | 6.7 | 82.0 | 8.5 | 19 763 | 2.6 | 769 | 3.9 | 27 959 | 61.1 | 42.3 | 32.5 |
| Broken Arrow | 20.2 | 828 | 27.4 | 2.3 | 86.1 | 9.3 | 50 472 | 2.0 | 2 141 | 4.2 | 73 392 | 72.9 | 51.3 | 15.9 |
| Edmond | 30.1 | 845 | 29.8 | 3.1 | 78.9 | 13.0 | 41 189 | 4.2 | 1 470 | 3.6 | 63 069 | 68.3 | 44.3 | 20.3 |
| Enid | 35.9 | 619 | 25.1 | 5.2 | 79.1 | 8.2 | 26 908 | 3.0 | 943 | 3.5 | 37 800 | 65.2 | 40.4 | 26.4 |
| Lawton | 49.4 | 713 | 27.8 | 7.2 | 67.2 | 18.4 | 34 980 | -1.3 | 2 325 | 6.6 | 73 738 | 67.4 | 34.0 | 22.6 |
| Midwest City | 37.3 | 694 | 28.2 | 5.4 | 81.8 | 12.2 | 24 294 | 3.2 | 1 337 | 5.5 | 42 132 | 66.5 | 43.0 | 26.9 |
| Moore | 24.8 | 868 | 27.5 | 2.3 | 82.4 | 12.0 | 26 990 | 4.0 | 1 195 | 4.4 | 41 016 | 72.1 | 48.0 | 18.6 |
| Muskogee | 40.2 | 577 | 32.1 | 12.8 | 85.4 | 6.7 | 17 175 | 1.2 | 1 027 | 6.0 | 30 591 | 56.4 | 35.8 | 37.1 |
| Norman | 42.2 | 714 | 31.9 | 5.3 | 72.1 | 13.7 | 56 996 | 4.1 | 2 296 | 4.0 | 90 646 | 66.2 | 38.7 | 22.2 |
| Oklahoma City | 39.4 | 699 | 29.9 | 6.8 | 78.5 | 9.4 | 271 650 | 3.7 | 13 035 | 4.8 | 441 972 | 67.6 | 43.5 | 24.1 |
| Owasso | 28.7 | 796 | 26.2 | 3.5 | 81.1 | 13.7 | 12 900 | 1.9 | 556 | 4.3 | 20 499 | 74.5 | 51.5 | 14.8 |
| Ponca City | 34.0 | 636 | 27.8 | 6.3 | 79.2 | 8.5 | 12 029 | -1.4 | 746 | 6.2 | 19 796 | 61.1 | 39.4 | 31.6 |
| Shawnee | 39.2 | 615 | 29.3 | 9.0 | 79.6 | 11.6 | 15 034 | 3.6 | 672 | 4.5 | 23 110 | 60.7 | 36.3 | 30.6 |
| Stillwater | 62.6 | 639 | 38.6 | 6.1 | 59.9 | 20.3 | 22 705 | 4.2 | 952 | 4.2 | 39 148 | 64.3 | 28.1 | 23.6 |
| Tulsa | 45.6 | 697 | 29.9 | 8.4 | 78.2 | 8.5 | 189 538 | 1.6 | 9 991 | 5.3 | 305 377 | 66.0 | 42.2 | 27.0 |
| **OREGON** | 36.9 | 830 | 31.3 | 7.7 | 81.9 | 12.0 | 1 962 908 | 0.1 | 171 178 | 8.7 | 3 039 160 | 64.1 | 36.2 | 29.0 |
| Albany | 40.2 | 744 | 31.1 | 8.0 | 81.7 | 10.7 | 24 572 | -1.4 | 2 331 | 9.5 | 37 695 | 61.7 | 36.2 | 32.2 |
| Beaverton | 50.3 | 913 | 29.1 | 7.9 | 79.3 | 15.3 | 51 031 | 1.6 | 3 525 | 6.9 | 70 649 | 71.1 | 43.3 | 20.8 |
| Bend | 41.7 | 904 | 29.4 | 5.6 | 81.2 | 8.8 | 39 248 | -0.9 | 3 812 | 9.7 | 60 206 | 68.8 | 38.8 | 27.5 |
| Corvallis | 56.7 | 752 | 41.8 | 10.9 | 68.4 | 19.2 | 27 848 | 0.3 | 1 676 | 6.0 | 46 591 | 59.8 | 25.6 | 30.0 |
| Eugene | 49.9 | 803 | 35.9 | 11.5 | 72.5 | 13.3 | 80 780 | -1.3 | 6 071 | 7.5 | 129 920 | 61.6 | 30.2 | 31.4 |
| Grants Pass | 48.3 | 737 | 36.9 | 10.6 | 82.5 | 8.2 | 14 459 | -1.3 | 1 570 | 10.9 | 26 763 | 56.2 | 30.6 | 40.7 |
| Gresham | 45.2 | 842 | 33.2 | 8.8 | 80.7 | 12.7 | 55 118 | 0.5 | 4 527 | 8.2 | 80 212 | 67.2 | 38.1 | 27.0 |
| Hillsboro | 43.7 | 985 | 28.3 | 5.8 | 77.9 | 14.4 | 50 222 | 0.9 | 3 437 | 6.8 | 67 768 | 73.3 | 44.5 | 16.8 |
| Keizer | 40.5 | 773 | 28.5 | 6.5 | 79.5 | 15.9 | 19 108 | 0.7 | 1 652 | 8.6 | 27 208 | 66.2 | 40.1 | 26.3 |
| Lake Oswego | 28.9 | 1 157 | 29.2 | 4.4 | 85.2 | 10.6 | 19 755 | 2.0 | 1 185 | 6.0 | 29 446 | 66.0 | 40.0 | 24.9 |
| McMinnville | 40.7 | 765 | 32.5 | 9.3 | 78.5 | 11.2 | 14 767 | 0.1 | 1 244 | 8.4 | 24 603 | 63.0 | 33.9 | 31.8 |
| Medford | 48.9 | 831 | 34.9 | 10.0 | 78.0 | 11.3 | 36 775 | 0.1 | 3 905 | 10.6 | 58 820 | 62.6 | 33.9 | 33.9 |
| Oregon City | 36.7 | 914 | 33.5 | 8.4 | 79.6 | 13.5 | 16 897 | 0.2 | 1 421 | 8.4 | 24 543 | 68.1 | 37.4 | 25.0 |
| Portland | 45.8 | 855 | 31.9 | 15.0 | 79.7 | 9.5 | 323 608 | 0.7 | 24 652 | 7.6 | 476 556 | 69.9 | 39.6 | 24.8 |
| Redmond | 41.4 | 857 | 33.5 | 4.5 | 80.7 | 10.8 | 12 576 | 0.1 | 1 191 | 9.5 | 19 312 | 65.0 | 35.2 | 33.4 |
| Salem | 43.4 | 741 | 32.0 | 9.0 | 79.2 | 10.7 | 75 560 | 0.6 | 7 065 | 9.4 | 118 643 | 62.3 | 36.1 | 29.4 |
| Springfield | 47.0 | 751 | 32.3 | 9.4 | 76.9 | 13.1 | 29 495 | -2.4 | 2 828 | 9.6 | 46 616 | 66.1 | 35.1 | 28.2 |

1. $2,000 represents $2,000 or more.  2. 50.0 represents 50 percent or more.  3. Percent of civilian labor force.  4. Persons 16 years old and over.

| City | Value of residential construction authorized by building permits, 2011 | | | Wholesale trade,[1] 2007 | | | | Retail trade,[2] 2007 | | | |
|---|---|---|---|---|---|---|---|---|---|---|---|
| | New construction ($1,000) | Number of housing units | Percent single family | Number of establish-ments | Number of employees | Sales (mil dol) | Annual payroll (mil dol) | Number of establish-ments | Number of employees | Sales (mil dol) | Annual payroll (mil dol) |
| | 69 | 70 | 71 | 72 | 73 | 74 | 75 | 76 | 77 | 78 | 79 |
| **OHIO—Cont'd** | | | | | | | | | | | |
| Kettering | 6 817 | 31 | 100.0 | 32 | 255 | 116.5 | 11.7 | 170 | 3 629 | 1 550.1 | 81.4 |
| Lakewood | 0 | 0 | 0.0 | 32 | D | D | D | 124 | 1 273 | 238.5 | 25.4 |
| Lancaster | 3 519 | 23 | 30.4 | 32 | 231 | 81.9 | 7.5 | 238 | 3 172 | 576.4 | 59.3 |
| Lima | 1 115 | 16 | 0.0 | 48 | 725 | 401.2 | 29.5 | 129 | 1 423 | 289.0 | 29.6 |
| Lorain | 2 835 | 31 | 100.0 | 35 | 488 | 233.7 | 21.3 | 123 | 1 662 | 319.1 | 30.5 |
| Mansfield | 1 961 | 10 | 100.0 | 74 | 1 215 | 630.1 | 48.7 | 196 | 2 510 | 531.3 | 56.9 |
| Marion | 2 383 | 28 | 78.6 | 24 | 401 | 277.3 | 14.9 | 86 | 893 | 206.5 | 20.0 |
| Mason | 13 478 | 42 | 100.0 | 45 | 1 409 | 634.4 | 80.6 | 84 | 1 168 | 226.1 | 23.7 |
| Massillon | 3 259 | 37 | 43.2 | 33 | 474 | 318.4 | 20.7 | 124 | 2 536 | 574.1 | 54.8 |
| Medina | 180 | 2 | 100.0 | 46 | 550 | 349.8 | 23.3 | 115 | 1 894 | 334.8 | 32.4 |
| Mentor | 6 655 | 31 | 100.0 | 116 | 1 431 | 631.3 | 65.7 | 325 | 6 577 | 1 478.8 | 139.4 |
| Middletown | 1 949 | 19 | 100.0 | 40 | 838 | 482.0 | 40.0 | 173 | 3 252 | 852.3 | 70.6 |
| Newark | 5 306 | 27 | 100.0 | 42 | 569 | 495.1 | 22.6 | 162 | 2 071 | 496.3 | 43.0 |
| North Olmsted | 371 | 2 | 100.0 | 22 | 129 | 144.8 | 8.6 | 283 | 5 132 | 1 130.5 | 102.4 |
| North Ridgeville | 26 926 | 257 | 70.0 | 33 | 182 | 79.2 | 7.8 | 64 | 885 | 195.1 | 20.3 |
| North Royalton | 7 243 | 36 | 100.0 | 58 | 408 | 247.5 | 18.2 | 69 | 715 | 147.9 | 14.9 |
| Parma | 499 | 3 | 100.0 | 61 | 735 | 199.2 | 34.6 | 301 | 4 662 | 963.1 | 86.1 |
| Reynoldsburg | 1 019 | 5 | 100.0 | 17 | 67 | 43.8 | 2.8 | 113 | 1 938 | 416.2 | 41.2 |
| Riverside | NA | NA | NA | 12 | 115 | 49.5 | 3.7 | 57 | 506 | 130.4 | 10.9 |
| Sandusky | 1 387 | 8 | 100.0 | 28 | 272 | 105.5 | 11.6 | 121 | 1 424 | 283.4 | 27.8 |
| Shaker Heights | 0 | 0 | 0.0 | 9 | 17 | 6.7 | 1.0 | 62 | 698 | 134.7 | 13.9 |
| Springfield | 6 825 | 101 | 10.9 | 51 | 1 482 | 1 706.1 | 55.5 | 242 | 4 072 | 914.8 | 84.6 |
| Stow | 4 552 | 18 | 100.0 | 40 | 801 | 625.0 | 47.5 | 106 | 2 302 | 481.4 | 43.7 |
| Strongsville | 16 237 | 64 | 100.0 | 72 | 1 741 | 950.5 | 88.4 | 246 | 4 691 | 831.5 | 87.7 |
| Toledo | 5 034 | 38 | 86.8 | 302 | 4 740 | 2 924.2 | 206.8 | 1 065 | 14 799 | 2 831.8 | 292.7 |
| Troy | NA | NA | NA | 17 | D | D | D | 104 | 1 786 | 413.7 | 38.1 |
| Upper Arlington | 14 864 | 32 | 100.0 | 16 | 47 | 13.6 | 1.9 | 90 | 1 040 | 159.9 | 19.0 |
| Warren | 62 | 1 | 100.0 | 41 | 551 | 1 168.1 | 21.1 | 168 | 2 240 | 589.2 | 50.1 |
| Westerville | 10 425 | 40 | 95.0 | 49 | 860 | 379.7 | 40.6 | 134 | 2 286 | 442.6 | 49.7 |
| Westlake | 8 174 | 26 | 100.0 | 105 | 1 567 | 915.2 | 87.2 | 159 | 2 544 | 481.6 | 48.9 |
| Wooster | 5 118 | 33 | 39.4 | 35 | 530 | 579.1 | 20.0 | 182 | 2 890 | 608.7 | 59.4 |
| Xenia | NA | NA | NA | 13 | D | D | D | 83 | 1 398 | 307.1 | 32.4 |
| Youngstown | 0 | 0 | 0.0 | 104 | 2 226 | 872.0 | 81.8 | 230 | 2 075 | 365.4 | 41.3 |
| Zanesville | 114 | 1 | 100.0 | 27 | D | D | D | 232 | 3 437 | 726.1 | 62.4 |
| **OKLAHOMA** | 1 285 644 | 8 782 | 73.4 | 3 917 | 52 262 | 48 074.7 | 2 312.2 | 13 554 | 170 984 | 43 095.4 | 3 610.4 |
| Bartlesville | 15 599 | 111 | 85.6 | 22 | D | D | D | 172 | 2 369 | 588.9 | 50.8 |
| Broken Arrow | 83 444 | 764 | 50.5 | 126 | 1 625 | 713.9 | 82.7 | 237 | 4 185 | 1 164.6 | 96.9 |
| Edmond | 111 293 | 388 | 99.5 | 88 | D | D | D | 341 | 4 480 | 999.1 | 91.8 |
| Enid | 4 675 | 21 | 90.5 | 62 | 637 | 763.9 | 28.7 | 242 | 3 211 | 716.7 | 66.5 |
| Lawton | 29 168 | 179 | 88.8 | 46 | 366 | 117.2 | 9.5 | 375 | 5 143 | 1 152.2 | 103.1 |
| Midwest City | 12 740 | 95 | 100.0 | 16 | 413 | 94.7 | 10.9 | 174 | 3 585 | 1 011.5 | 87.5 |
| Moore | 43 552 | 252 | 100.0 | 40 | 524 | 159.8 | 18.4 | 122 | 2 117 | 440.7 | 43.1 |
| Muskogee | 2 983 | 20 | 100.0 | 53 | 864 | 498.9 | 46.3 | 232 | 3 029 | 763.8 | 63.2 |
| Norman | 68 641 | 389 | 90.0 | 58 | 957 | 442.9 | 39.5 | 437 | 6 907 | 1 768.0 | 147.1 |
| Oklahoma City | 200 573 | 1 404 | 92.1 | 1 008 | D | D | D | 2 223 | 32 456 | 8 430.8 | 751.0 |
| Owasso | 22 151 | 179 | 100.0 | 15 | 111 | 28.8 | 3.7 | 102 | 2 258 | 490.6 | 43.7 |
| Ponca City | 300 | 3 | 100.0 | 26 | 127 | 45.7 | 4.7 | 141 | 1 812 | 391.5 | 35.6 |
| Shawnee | 19 739 | 202 | 26.2 | 23 | 205 | 70.8 | 6.8 | 199 | 2 598 | 631.8 | 52.3 |
| Stillwater | 27 126 | 281 | 22.4 | 22 | 291 | 387.0 | 14.0 | 213 | 3 137 | 632.9 | 59.8 |
| Tulsa | 135 894 | 1 107 | 28.8 | 806 | 13 655 | 8 307.1 | 712.7 | 1 800 | 28 095 | 7 081.7 | 626.9 |
| **OREGON** | 1 407 354 | 7 663 | 63.3 | 4 806 | 67 040 | 51 910.8 | 3 215.5 | 14 991 | 204 793 | 50 370.9 | 4 916.3 |
| Albany | 13 733 | 75 | 97.3 | 40 | 377 | 225.6 | 13.2 | 188 | 2 997 | 770.9 | 70.3 |
| Beaverton | 20 742 | 133 | 74.4 | 215 | 2 525 | 2 952.0 | 172.3 | 425 | 7 793 | 2 594.3 | 215.3 |
| Bend | 61 989 | 292 | 99.3 | 145 | 1 590 | 1 001.4 | 73.7 | 572 | 7 977 | 2 087.9 | 201.0 |
| Corvallis | 38 974 | 328 | 9.1 | 26 | 416 | 323.4 | 16.2 | 224 | 3 185 | 633.6 | 67.1 |
| Eugene | 47 561 | 427 | 26.2 | 278 | 3 362 | 1 569.6 | 154.5 | 780 | 12 435 | 2 582.5 | 279.3 |
| Grants Pass | 4 056 | 20 | 90.0 | 31 | 328 | 270.9 | 9.7 | 264 | 3 713 | 862.5 | 93.2 |
| Gresham | 9 051 | 42 | 100.0 | 60 | 1 182 | 1 428.5 | 55.3 | 290 | 4 468 | 1 256.9 | 111.0 |
| Hillsboro | 75 485 | 545 | 23.1 | 102 | 2 073 | 1 072.3 | 130.8 | 330 | 6 609 | 1 902.9 | 152.0 |
| Keizer | 3 567 | 15 | 100.0 | 15 | 63 | 34.3 | 1.5 | 75 | 1 053 | 198.4 | 21.7 |
| Lake Oswego | 22 516 | 69 | 97.1 | 84 | 1 115 | 764.0 | 66.5 | 161 | 1 540 | 322.4 | 35.5 |
| McMinnville | 11 312 | 73 | 50.7 | 24 | 305 | 160.7 | 14.0 | 125 | 1 928 | 518.7 | 46.9 |
| Medford | 27 359 | 194 | 44.3 | 122 | 1 478 | 711.7 | 58.3 | 547 | 7 889 | 2 045.7 | 189.1 |
| Oregon City | 29 201 | 137 | 100.0 | 17 | 296 | 109.5 | 12.3 | 117 | 1 799 | 395.8 | 39.3 |
| Portland | 194 049 | 1 364 | 33.1 | 1 176 | 21 291 | 20 566.4 | 1 053.0 | 2 562 | 33 811 | 8 174.1 | 888.5 |
| Redmond | 4 853 | 31 | 100.0 | 43 | 268 | 131.7 | 10.4 | 143 | 1 587 | 438.0 | 45.0 |
| Salem | 44 641 | 270 | 59.3 | 165 | 1 753 | 2 260.8 | 75.0 | 642 | 10 742 | 2 617.1 | 262.9 |
| Springfield | 12 033 | 67 | 97.0 | 52 | 1 101 | 499.1 | 47.0 | 227 | 3 650 | 755.6 | 75.1 |

1. Merchant wholesalers except manufacturers' sales branches and offices.  2. Establishments with payroll.

# Table D. Cities — **Real Estate, Professional Services, and Manufacturing**

| City | Real estate and rental and leasing, 2007 | | | | Professional, scientific, and technical services,[1] 2007 | | | | Manufacturing, 2007 | | | |
|---|---|---|---|---|---|---|---|---|---|---|---|---|
| | Number of establishments | Number of employees | Receipts (mil dol) | Annual payroll (mil dol) | Number of establishments | Number of employees | Receipts (mil dol) | Annual payroll (mil dol) | Number of establishments | Number of employees | Receipts (mil dol) | Annual payroll (mil dol) |
| | 80 | 81 | 82 | 83 | 84 | 85 | 86 | 87 | 88 | 89 | 90 | 91 |
| **OHIO—Cont'd** | | | | | | | | | | | | |
| Kettering | 57 | 339 | 62.2 | 9.9 | 132 | D | D | D | 47 | 2 164 | 530.9 | 100.9 |
| Lakewood | 56 | 189 | 32.5 | 4.6 | 116 | 424 | 45.8 | 18.8 | 35 | 535 | 106.1 | 24.5 |
| Lancaster | 58 | 206 | 23.4 | 4.2 | 77 | D | D | D | 58 | 2 919 | 669.0 | 131.1 |
| Lima | 41 | 244 | 23.0 | 6.6 | 83 | D | D | D | 38 | 2 845 | 7 330.7 | D |
| Lorain | 48 | 166 | 19.2 | 4.1 | 76 | D | D | D | 52 | 2 517 | 1 744.2 | 165.6 |
| Mansfield | 59 | 306 | 24.0 | 6.3 | 123 | 704 | 65.6 | 27.0 | 118 | 6 538 | 2 130.7 | 281.7 |
| Marion | 37 | 132 | 18.5 | 3.7 | 45 | D | D | D | 35 | 2 030 | 1 159.2 | 86.5 |
| Mason | 32 | 132 | 18.2 | 3.8 | 110 | 1 112 | 106.8 | 107.4 | 40 | 4 128 | 1 148.1 | 182.7 |
| Massillon | 28 | 126 | 15.1 | 2.7 | 52 | 301 | 20.7 | 10.7 | 65 | 3 810 | 1 199.6 | 155.3 |
| Medina | 34 | 107 | 18.7 | 2.7 | 110 | 504 | 55.5 | 20.6 | 60 | 3 216 | 1 031.3 | 138.9 |
| Mentor | 68 | 576 | 95.1 | 15.5 | 173 | 868 | 103.9 | 33.8 | 232 | 7 497 | 1 944.1 | 326.7 |
| Middletown | 60 | 233 | 36.5 | 6.6 | 74 | 538 | 54.6 | 23.8 | 58 | 3 834 | 4 793.1 | 239.5 |
| Newark | 42 | 239 | 22.2 | 5.4 | 86 | D | D | D | 45 | 3 198 | 927.0 | 128.5 |
| North Olmsted | 36 | 160 | 42.3 | 5.1 | 83 | 366 | 30.6 | 11.6 | NA | NA | NA | NA |
| North Ridgeville | 16 | 52 | 6.9 | 0.8 | 44 | 224 | 24.5 | 12.0 | 41 | 1 325 | 253.5 | 49.2 |
| North Royalton | 23 | D | D | D | 86 | 287 | 27.3 | 11.0 | 77 | 862 | 131.5 | 36.4 |
| Parma | 67 | 364 | 50.1 | 9.7 | 116 | D | D | D | 51 | 2 492 | 890.4 | 184.3 |
| Reynoldsburg | 39 | 131 | 14.7 | 2.4 | 80 | 444 | 42.0 | 14.3 | NA | NA | NA | NA |
| Riverside | 26 | 101 | 22.7 | 2.7 | 42 | D | D | D | NA | NA | NA | NA |
| Sandusky | 33 | 132 | 19.6 | 3.9 | 54 | D | D | D | 47 | 1 805 | 473.5 | 86.6 |
| Shaker Heights | 38 | 122 | 20.0 | 3.8 | 101 | 438 | 83.2 | 30.3 | NA | NA | NA | NA |
| Springfield | 62 | 313 | 38.1 | 7.2 | 103 | D | D | D | 94 | 3 997 | 967.5 | 164.5 |
| Stow | 35 | 165 | 23.0 | 3.7 | 95 | 593 | 60.0 | 25.1 | 52 | 1 695 | 320.0 | 87.2 |
| Strongsville | 50 | 231 | 51.8 | 5.1 | 127 | 495 | 62.6 | 19.7 | 75 | 2 988 | 659.1 | 132.5 |
| Toledo | 276 | 2 022 | 745.1 | 76.3 | 510 | D | D | D | 365 | 15 647 | 10 634.8 | 908.7 |
| Troy | 33 | 157 | 29.4 | 4.1 | 60 | 326 | 33.7 | 14.5 | 64 | 4 033 | 1 431.6 | 187.6 |
| Upper Arlington | 53 | 196 | 37.4 | 6.4 | 136 | D | D | D | NA | NA | NA | NA |
| Warren | 33 | 150 | 18.5 | 3.4 | 107 | 449 | 38.1 | 13.2 | 55 | 7 339 | 1 882.4 | 445.7 |
| Westerville | 66 | 362 | 39.1 | 10.7 | 216 | D | D | D | 38 | 1 384 | 297.4 | 48.7 |
| Westlake | 67 | 925 | 124.1 | 26.7 | 221 | 1 618 | 154.4 | 102.5 | 52 | 1 764 | 426.8 | 73.0 |
| Wooster | 43 | 131 | 15.6 | 3.4 | 75 | 461 | 49.1 | 16.0 | 35 | 3 887 | 1 245.0 | 177.8 |
| Xenia | 27 | 95 | 9.6 | 1.7 | 38 | 175 | 12.8 | 3.5 | 34 | 699 | 133.5 | D |
| Youngstown | 60 | 283 | 30.7 | 6.5 | 106 | D | D | D | 115 | 3 210 | 1 147.8 | 143.6 |
| Zanesville | 41 | 205 | 29.1 | 5.1 | 67 | D | D | D | 39 | 1 582 | 537.6 | 76.1 |
| **OKLAHOMA** | 4 003 | 24 887 | 3 852.3 | 806.2 | 9 128 | D | D | D | 3 964 | 142 351 | 60 681.4 | 5 971.2 |
| Bartlesville | 45 | 213 | 28.3 | 5.1 | 80 | D | D | D | 37 | 978 | 293.6 | 42.8 |
| Broken Arrow | 95 | D | D | D | 237 | 1 159 | 132.2 | 52.9 | 132 | 4 754 | 1 504.2 | 223.6 |
| Edmond | 158 | 2 132 | 237.5 | 58.2 | 378 | D | D | D | NA | NA | NA | NA |
| Enid | 68 | 324 | 39.0 | 8.1 | 119 | 544 | 56.0 | 19.6 | 56 | 2 120 | D | 64.3 |
| Lawton | 128 | D | D | D | 146 | D | D | D | 42 | 3 395 | D | D |
| Midwest City | 72 | 290 | 47.8 | 6.3 | 87 | D | D | D | NA | NA | NA | NA |
| Moore | 35 | 136 | 29.8 | 4.5 | 49 | 346 | 26.5 | 12.4 | NA | NA | NA | NA |
| Muskogee | 56 | 533 | 43.5 | 10.1 | 88 | D | D | D | 50 | 2 857 | 972.6 | 129.2 |
| Norman | 197 | 884 | 162.6 | 27.7 | 426 | D | D | D | 80 | 2 255 | 931.0 | 95.5 |
| Oklahoma City | 879 | 5 974 | 996.7 | 238.7 | 2 253 | D | D | D | 702 | 23 758 | 7 711.8 | 954.0 |
| Owasso | 39 | 109 | 22.8 | 2.9 | 61 | 214 | 21.1 | 7.6 | 23 | 786 | 191.9 | 29.0 |
| Ponca City | 31 | D | D | D | 68 | 381 | 35.8 | 13.9 | 37 | 2 093 | D | 66.8 |
| Shawnee | 36 | 168 | 19.1 | 3.6 | 83 | D | D | D | 41 | 2 624 | 864.3 | 113.1 |
| Stillwater | 56 | 193 | 27.5 | 4.0 | 114 | D | D | D | 36 | 1 900 | 984.6 | 71.3 |
| Tulsa | 744 | 5 083 | 871.9 | 170.6 | 1 958 | 14 698 | 2 170.9 | 811.8 | 725 | 24 382 | 8 815.2 | 1 108.2 |
| **OREGON** | 6 391 | 30 978 | 5 077.2 | 950.3 | 11 363 | 83 190 | 9 750.4 | 4 869.5 | 5 717 | 183 953 | 66 880.7 | 8 138.9 |
| Albany | 65 | 254 | 32.3 | 5.7 | 101 | D | D | D | 69 | 2 289 | 714.5 | 100.4 |
| Beaverton | 249 | 1 173 | 221.0 | 40.5 | 446 | D | D | D | 123 | 6 822 | 1 855.8 | 406.1 |
| Bend | 284 | 872 | 138.6 | 25.9 | 445 | D | D | D | 171 | 3 198 | 529.7 | 122.9 |
| Corvallis | 98 | 495 | 53.6 | 10.0 | 210 | D | D | D | 54 | 3 506 | 408.6 | 178.5 |
| Eugene | 323 | 1 547 | 257.1 | 39.1 | 714 | D | D | D | 305 | 9 542 | 2 276.1 | 400.3 |
| Grants Pass | 78 | 355 | 39.3 | 8.3 | 95 | D | D | D | 79 | 2 170 | 340.1 | 70.3 |
| Gresham | 136 | 476 | 62.7 | 11.2 | 128 | 425 | 33.7 | 13.8 | 71 | 6 000 | 1 939.5 | 319.4 |
| Hillsboro | 103 | 656 | 172.4 | 21.4 | 214 | D | D | D | 164 | 8 924 | 9 152.2 | 500.0 |
| Keizer | 46 | 147 | 19.1 | 2.9 | 55 | 188 | 20.2 | 5.9 | NA | NA | NA | NA |
| Lake Oswego | 151 | 612 | 210.2 | 40.1 | 314 | D | D | D | 43 | 993 | D | 52.4 |
| McMinnville | 39 | 122 | 17.4 | 3.1 | 85 | D | D | D | 54 | 2 304 | 868.8 | 93.6 |
| Medford | 183 | 947 | 135.6 | 24.9 | 255 | D | D | D | 101 | 1 756 | 375.9 | 63.7 |
| Oregon City | 46 | 129 | 27.0 | 3.4 | 104 | D | D | D | 44 | 923 | 243.5 | 41.2 |
| Portland | 1 307 | 9 115 | 1 676.4 | 350.8 | 3 116 | D | D | D | 1 035 | 30 694 | 8 434.6 | 1 315.5 |
| Redmond | 59 | 267 | 34.2 | 7.0 | 39 | 201 | 18.5 | 6.2 | 63 | 1 228 | 217.6 | 44.3 |
| Salem | 303 | 1 658 | 240.3 | 48.2 | 520 | D | D | D | 188 | 5 541 | 1 294.1 | 191.4 |
| Springfield | 79 | 342 | 57.6 | 8.2 | 86 | 510 | 39.6 | 15.6 | 86 | 2 164 | 1 029.2 | 94.6 |

1. Establishments subject to federal tax.

# Accommodation and Food Services, Arts, Entertainment, and Recreation, and Health Care and Social Assistance

| City | Accommodation and food services, 2007 | | | | Arts, entertainment, and recreation,[1] 2007 | | | | Health care and social assistance,[1] 2007 | | | |
|---|---|---|---|---|---|---|---|---|---|---|---|---|
| | Number of establishments | Number of employees | Sales (mil dol) | Annual payroll (mil dol) | Number of establishments | Number of employees | Receipts (mil dol) | Annual payroll (mil dol) | Number of establishments | Number of employees | Receipts (mil dol) | Annual payroll (mil dol) |
| | 92 | 93 | 94 | 95 | 96 | 97 | 98 | 99 | 100 | 101 | 102 | 103 |
| **OHIO—Cont'd** | | | | | | | | | | | | |
| Kettering | 109 | 2 389 | 88.9 | 26.9 | 12 | D | D | D | 181 | D | D | D |
| Lakewood | 114 | 1 420 | 61.1 | 16.6 | 13 | 85 | 5.0 | 1.3 | 117 | 1 145 | 87.1 | 38.2 |
| Lancaster | 110 | 2 550 | 90.9 | 26.2 | 8 | D | D | D | 148 | D | D | D |
| Lima | 78 | 1 161 | 47.1 | 12.4 | 5 | D | D | D | 170 | D | D | D |
| Lorain | 84 | 1 044 | 40.4 | 10.2 | 14 | 122 | 7.5 | 1.8 | 105 | 1 493 | 149.1 | 68.4 |
| Mansfield | 132 | 2 036 | 73.8 | 21.6 | 11 | D | D | D | 211 | D | D | D |
| Marion | 50 | 830 | 30.6 | 8.8 | 5 | D | D | D | 107 | D | D | D |
| Mason | 66 | 2 038 | 87.6 | 25.3 | 18 | 330 | 24.9 | 7.8 | 90 | 1 251 | 97.1 | 42.4 |
| Massillon | 84 | 1 330 | 51.7 | 13.7 | 3 | 9 | 0.2 | 0.1 | 55 | 1 636 | 81.3 | 34.5 |
| Medina | 66 | 1 245 | 43.8 | 12.4 | 6 | D | D | D | 103 | 1 396 | 106.7 | 48.5 |
| Mentor | 168 | 3 812 | 157.8 | 43.4 | 13 | D | D | D | 138 | D | D | D |
| Middletown | 107 | 2 584 | 97.0 | 29.0 | 8 | 103 | 2.8 | 1.0 | 116 | D | D | D |
| Newark | 107 | 2 198 | 84.2 | 23.1 | 12 | D | D | D | 115 | 2 879 | 189.7 | 102.0 |
| North Olmsted | 124 | 2 467 | 103.5 | 28.7 | 8 | 84 | 2.8 | 0.9 | 74 | 1 055 | 73.8 | 28.6 |
| North Ridgeville | 40 | 548 | 20.6 | 5.1 | 8 | 74 | 3.2 | 1.0 | 31 | D | D | D |
| North Royalton | 41 | 475 | 18.3 | 4.8 | 1 | D | D | D | 57 | D | D | D |
| Parma | 190 | 2 915 | 103.2 | 29.3 | 14 | D | D | D | 194 | 2 895 | 266.8 | 119.2 |
| Reynoldsburg | 71 | 1 175 | 51.2 | 14.8 | 7 | 44 | 1.8 | 0.5 | 85 | 1 158 | 58.0 | 27.2 |
| Riverside | 52 | 847 | 33.6 | 9.4 | 4 | D | D | D | 35 | D | D | D |
| Sandusky | 82 | 1 116 | 70.9 | 14.2 | 16 | D | D | D | 62 | D | D | D |
| Shaker Heights | 37 | 540 | 19.1 | 5.4 | 6 | 140 | 6.4 | 2.6 | 61 | 742 | 44.0 | 21.0 |
| Springfield | 162 | 3 379 | 129.4 | 36.8 | 10 | 94 | 4.2 | 1.4 | 202 | 2 889 | 237.9 | 104.5 |
| Stow | 76 | 1 795 | 62.3 | 18.3 | 10 | D | D | D | 69 | D | D | D |
| Strongsville | 114 | 2 769 | 104.4 | 28.1 | 12 | 151 | 4.1 | 1.2 | 93 | 971 | 102.9 | 39.0 |
| Toledo | 624 | 11 505 | 428.7 | 120.7 | 64 | 893 | 39.2 | 10.6 | 592 | 9 105 | 801.1 | 411.8 |
| Troy | 69 | 1 555 | 62.0 | 17.9 | 6 | D | D | D | 72 | D | D | D |
| Upper Arlington | 60 | D | D | D | 6 | D | D | D | 79 | 1 010 | 94.8 | 51.1 |
| Warren | 97 | 1 207 | 45.1 | 12.6 | 11 | 83 | 2.3 | 0.8 | 161 | 2 126 | 144.1 | 65.0 |
| Westerville | 96 | 2 085 | 86.8 | 22.5 | 13 | D | D | D | 203 | D | D | D |
| Westlake | 101 | 2 665 | 124.4 | 35.2 | 7 | D | D | D | 228 | 3 251 | 287.4 | 129.5 |
| Wooster | 71 | 1 798 | 61.1 | 19.0 | 5 | D | D | D | 77 | 1 327 | 118.1 | 53.4 |
| Xenia | 50 | 894 | 35.6 | 10.1 | 5 | D | D | D | 61 | 486 | 51.1 | 16.7 |
| Youngstown | 111 | 1 191 | 47.2 | 12.5 | 10 | D | D | D | 141 | 2 528 | 198.3 | 90.5 |
| Zanesville | 109 | 2 213 | 83.7 | 23.7 | 5 | D | D | D | 126 | D | D | D |
| **OKLAHOMA** | 6 900 | 129 159 | 5 106.6 | 1 401.3 | 862 | 22 167 | 2 330.9 | 412.6 | 8 577 | 121 175 | 10 860.0 | 4 171.7 |
| Bartlesville | 100 | 1 740 | 67.7 | 16.8 | 11 | D | D | D | 124 | D | D | D |
| Broken Arrow | 151 | 3 392 | 125.5 | 35.9 | 28 | D | D | D | 170 | D | D | D |
| Edmond | 189 | 4 635 | 155.0 | 46.0 | 28 | 424 | 23.1 | 8.2 | 346 | 3 152 | 320.9 | 117.6 |
| Enid | 108 | D | D | D | 10 | 49 | 3.7 | 0.7 | 180 | D | D | D |
| Lawton | 179 | 3 665 | 131.4 | 34.6 | 15 | D | D | D | 216 | 2 748 | 230.5 | 78.0 |
| Midwest City | 114 | 2 485 | 99.3 | 26.6 | 12 | D | D | D | 174 | 3 258 | 409.5 | 128.7 |
| Moore | 83 | 1 963 | 74.3 | 20.3 | 9 | D | D | D | 66 | D | D | D |
| Muskogee | 109 | 2 203 | 80.6 | 21.0 | 12 | 71 | 2.0 | 0.5 | 156 | D | D | D |
| Norman | 285 | 7 112 | 281.6 | 79.0 | 40 | 1 059 | 92.4 | 19.3 | 358 | D | D | D |
| Oklahoma City | 1 239 | 27 218 | 1 163.9 | 325.0 | 136 | 2 409 | 190.8 | 49.5 | 1 883 | 31 441 | 3 405.0 | 1 278.7 |
| Owasso | 79 | 1 748 | 67.0 | 17.9 | 6 | 44 | 1.7 | 0.5 | 68 | D | D | D |
| Ponca City | 67 | 1 217 | 43.6 | 10.9 | 4 | D | D | D | 92 | D | D | D |
| Shawnee | 105 | 2 393 | 90.7 | 24.1 | 5 | D | D | D | 89 | 1 283 | 95.5 | 39.1 |
| Stillwater | 120 | 2 746 | 98.2 | 26.3 | 9 | D | D | D | 104 | D | D | D |
| Tulsa | 1 051 | 21 344 | 929.0 | 264.5 | 110 | 2 142 | 232.5 | 42.9 | 1 415 | 21 613 | 2 657.9 | 1 049.8 |
| **OREGON** | 10 241 | 150 538 | 7 555.8 | 2 152.9 | 1 211 | 17 801 | 1 105.7 | 408.0 | 9 011 | 91 816 | 9 444.8 | 3 751.5 |
| Albany | 116 | 1 783 | 86.3 | 22.6 | 15 | D | D | D | 96 | 1 060 | 86.6 | 34.3 |
| Beaverton | 275 | 4 565 | 226.6 | 69.2 | 41 | 605 | 63.5 | 9.5 | 277 | 3 488 | 322.9 | 119.8 |
| Bend | 302 | 4 742 | 231.3 | 67.7 | 49 | 1 493 | 60.4 | 19.4 | 341 | D | D | D |
| Corvallis | 179 | 2 966 | 120.3 | 34.3 | 19 | D | D | D | 148 | D | D | D |
| Eugene | 508 | 8 243 | 369.8 | 107.5 | 43 | 656 | 22.9 | 7.5 | 503 | 6 188 | 737.8 | 256.7 |
| Grants Pass | 149 | 2 034 | 92.1 | 27.7 | 15 | D | D | D | 189 | 2 364 | 205.8 | 71.5 |
| Gresham | 223 | 3 640 | 166.2 | 50.3 | 22 | D | D | D | 266 | 2 517 | 229.1 | 89.8 |
| Hillsboro | 230 | 3 770 | 194.3 | 54.5 | 18 | 235 | 13.0 | 3.3 | 217 | 2 137 | 212.0 | 81.9 |
| Keizer | 47 | 1 014 | 42.0 | 11.3 | 12 | 159 | 7.2 | 3.1 | 52 | 583 | 45.4 | 16.5 |
| Lake Oswego | 102 | 1 742 | 85.7 | 26.7 | 16 | 79 | 5.2 | 1.4 | 161 | D | D | D |
| McMinnville | 82 | 1 212 | 52.5 | 15.3 | 6 | D | D | D | 107 | 1 735 | 167.1 | 66.6 |
| Medford | 263 | 4 248 | 202.0 | 58.7 | 28 | 437 | 21.8 | 6.6 | 294 | D | D | D |
| Oregon City | 71 | 1 085 | 57.3 | 16.0 | 8 | 100 | 5.1 | 1.6 | 102 | D | D | D |
| Portland | 2 205 | 34 188 | 1 842.4 | 539.5 | 227 | 2 730 | 311.5 | 166.5 | 1 725 | 16 888 | 2 022.3 | 822.3 |
| Redmond | 89 | 1 355 | 57.3 | 15.8 | 6 | D | D | D | 73 | D | D | D |
| Salem | 393 | 6 630 | 309.5 | 86.5 | 34 | 605 | 37.8 | 13.4 | 509 | 6 251 | 587.2 | 248.5 |
| Springfield | 157 | 2 502 | 120.7 | 33.2 | 20 | D | D | D | 126 | 2 539 | 312.7 | 126.3 |

1. Establishments subject to federal tax.

# Table D. Cities — **Other Services and Federal Funds**

| City | Other services[1], 2007 | | | | Selected federal funds, 2009–2010 (mil dol) | | | | | | | | |
| | | | | | Procurement contracts | | Grants | | | | | | |
| | Number of establishments | Number of employees | Receipts (mil dol) | Annual payroll (mil dol) | Defense | Other | Total[2] | Medicaid and other health related | Nutrition and family welfare | Energy and environment | Disasters and emergency preparedness | Housing and community development | Employment and training |
| | 104 | 105 | 106 | 107 | 108 | 109 | 110 | 111 | 112 | 113 | 114 | 115 | 116 |
| **OHIO—Cont'd** | | | | | | | | | | | | | |
| Kettering | 87 | 560 | 30.7 | 10.6 | 0.0 | 0.0 | 1.1 | 0.3 | 0.0 | 0.0 | 0.0 | 0.8 | 0.0 |
| Lakewood | 50 | 295 | 18.5 | 6.2 | 0.0 | 0.8 | 2.9 | 0.0 | 0.0 | 0.0 | 0.0 | 2.9 | 0.0 |
| Lancaster | 68 | D | D | D | 0.2 | 1.4 | 10.1 | 0.0 | 1.7 | 0.0 | 0.0 | 7.1 | 0.0 |
| Lima | 58 | 376 | 28.9 | 7.6 | 87.2 | 2.4 | 10.0 | 1.3 | 0.0 | 0.0 | 0.0 | 7.6 | 0.0 |
| Lorain | 70 | 515 | 30.7 | 9.9 | 0.9 | 0.3 | 38.1 | 2.8 | 6.8 | 1.0 | 0.0 | 24.1 | 0.0 |
| Mansfield | 91 | 829 | 52.0 | 15.6 | 6.8 | 0.3 | 26.2 | 1.5 | 0.5 | 0.0 | 0.0 | 19.4 | 0.0 |
| Marion | 39 | 228 | 15.1 | 4.9 | 0.1 | 0.2 | 8.8 | 1.2 | 5.8 | 0.0 | 0.0 | 0.1 | 0.0 |
| Mason | 39 | 287 | 13.2 | 5.5 | 12.8 | 4.2 | 0.0 | 0.0 | 0.0 | 0.0 | 0.0 | 0.0 | 0.0 |
| Massillon | 56 | 389 | 40.0 | 12.9 | 0.3 | 0.0 | 1.0 | 0.0 | 0.0 | 0.1 | 0.0 | 0.9 | 0.0 |
| Medina | 60 | 457 | 30.7 | 10.4 | 3.3 | 0.6 | 3.4 | 0.0 | 0.0 | 0.0 | 0.0 | 3.4 | 0.0 |
| Mentor | 135 | 1 109 | 90.6 | 29.1 | 24.5 | 3.3 | 1.5 | 0.4 | 0.7 | 0.0 | 0.0 | 0.3 | 0.0 |
| Middletown | 58 | 288 | 21.8 | 6.7 | 0.1 | 0.1 | 16.6 | 1.4 | 0.0 | 0.9 | 0.0 | 11.8 | 0.0 |
| Newark | 63 | 469 | 32.6 | 11.6 | 14.6 | 0.8 | 15.4 | 0.3 | 3.3 | 0.0 | 0.0 | 10.4 | 0.0 |
| North Olmsted | 93 | 557 | 33.8 | 12.1 | 0.1 | 1.2 | 0.0 | 0.0 | 0.0 | 0.0 | 0.0 | 0.0 | 0.0 |
| North Ridgeville | 44 | 168 | 11.3 | 3.4 | 0.5 | 0.1 | 0.0 | 0.0 | 0.0 | 0.0 | 0.0 | 0.0 | 0.0 |
| North Royalton | 59 | 279 | 26.5 | 8.3 | 13.1 | 0.9 | 0.0 | 0.0 | 0.0 | 0.0 | 0.0 | 0.0 | 0.0 |
| Parma | 136 | 1 003 | 90.2 | 30.1 | 0.1 | 0.2 | 7.2 | 0.0 | 0.0 | 1.0 | 0.0 | 6.2 | 0.0 |
| Reynoldsburg | 47 | 253 | 19.4 | 6.2 | 1.8 | 1.4 | 5.0 | 1.4 | 0.0 | 3.1 | 0.3 | 0.0 | 0.0 |
| Riverside | 17 | 78 | 6.2 | 2.2 | 0.0 | 0.0 | 0.0 | 0.0 | 0.0 | 0.0 | 0.0 | 0.0 | 0.0 |
| Sandusky | 35 | 190 | 11.9 | 3.4 | 24.9 | 32.5 | 22.8 | 0.0 | 2.0 | 0.0 | 0.0 | 8.2 | 0.0 |
| Shaker Heights | 23 | 131 | 6.8 | 2.2 | 0.1 | 0.2 | 1.0 | 0.4 | 0.4 | 0.0 | 0.0 | 0.2 | 0.0 |
| Springfield | 101 | 694 | 115.6 | 19.7 | 19.6 | 0.7 | 30.0 | 0.5 | 0.0 | 0.6 | 0.0 | 20.1 | 0.0 |
| Stow | 51 | 448 | 26.4 | 8.7 | 5.9 | 0.0 | 0.0 | 0.0 | 0.0 | 0.0 | 0.0 | 0.0 | 0.0 |
| Strongsville | 62 | 716 | 54.5 | 19.2 | 1.8 | 0.5 | 0.0 | 0.0 | 0.0 | 0.0 | 0.0 | 0.0 | 0.0 |
| Toledo | 415 | 2 866 | 240.0 | 67.9 | 5.3 | 11.4 | 167.5 | 38.4 | 14.0 | 23.1 | 3.0 | 55.7 | 0.2 |
| Troy | 44 | 358 | 17.0 | 5.9 | 52.0 | 0.3 | 6.6 | 0.4 | 0.0 | 0.0 | 0.0 | 5.5 | 0.0 |
| Upper Arlington | 31 | 266 | 13.9 | 4.8 | 2.7 | 0.2 | 5.2 | 0.8 | 0.0 | 0.0 | 0.0 | 4.4 | 0.0 |
| Warren | 65 | 329 | 22.5 | 6.2 | 2.0 | 0.3 | 20.3 | 0.0 | 4.7 | 0.0 | 0.0 | 10.5 | 0.3 |
| Westerville | 64 | D | D | D | 17.9 | -3.8 | 3.1 | 0.0 | 0.0 | 0.4 | 0.0 | 0.1 | 0.0 |
| Westlake | 65 | 592 | 29.5 | 11.6 | 6.4 | 2.7 | 0.5 | 0.5 | 0.0 | 0.0 | 0.0 | 0.0 | 0.0 |
| Wooster | 46 | 328 | 19.8 | 7.1 | 2.6 | 0.3 | 18.7 | 0.2 | 4.6 | 0.1 | 0.0 | 5.2 | 0.0 |
| Xenia | 35 | 182 | 12.6 | 4.2 | 7.7 | 0.5 | 12.3 | 1.0 | 0.1 | 0.0 | 0.0 | 8.9 | 0.0 |
| Youngstown | 83 | D | D | D | 7.3 | 3.4 | 49.4 | 2.6 | 7.3 | 6.3 | 0.0 | 21.9 | 0.6 |
| Zanesville | 78 | 702 | 44.4 | 14.2 | 0.4 | 6.0 | 11.8 | 0.0 | 1.9 | 0.4 | 0.0 | 5.8 | 3.0 |
| **OKLAHOMA** | 4 462 | 25 063 | 1 975.4 | 564.4 | 2 409.9 | 964.9 | 7 854.8 | 3 961.4 | 1 023.5 | 301.8 | 117.8 | 352.7 | 90.7 |
| Bartlesville | 51 | D | D | D | 0.1 | 2.2 | 1.7 | 0.0 | 0.0 | 0.2 | 0.0 | 0.0 | 0.0 |
| Broken Arrow | 125 | 922 | 70.7 | 25.1 | 39.1 | 0.2 | 0.5 | 0.0 | 0.0 | 0.0 | 0.0 | 0.0 | 0.0 |
| Edmond | 140 | 844 | 52.4 | 17.4 | 3.0 | 3.0 | 8.4 | 1.8 | 2.7 | 0.8 | 0.0 | 0.5 | 0.0 |
| Enid | 94 | 487 | 39.9 | 10.4 | 78.2 | 0.3 | 2.5 | 0.2 | 0.1 | 0.2 | 0.0 | 0.7 | 0.3 |
| Lawton | 122 | 628 | 37.5 | 11.2 | 76.8 | 19.3 | 33.2 | 2.2 | 0.6 | 1.0 | 0.0 | 7.3 | 0.4 |
| Midwest City | 60 | 439 | 26.7 | 8.3 | 1.2 | 0.4 | 1.3 | 0.1 | 0.0 | 0.5 | 0.0 | 0.6 | 0.0 |
| Moore | 52 | D | D | D | 0.0 | 1.0 | 0.4 | 0.0 | 0.0 | 0.4 | 0.0 | 0.0 | 0.0 |
| Muskogee | 58 | 422 | 26.4 | 8.0 | 6.8 | 32.1 | 8.8 | 0.0 | 2.8 | 0.6 | 0.0 | 3.9 | 0.0 |
| Norman | 117 | D | D | D | 4.0 | 31.2 | 80.4 | 1.9 | 7.3 | 10.1 | 0.0 | 8.8 | 0.6 |
| Oklahoma City | 838 | 6 390 | 516.6 | 151.1 | 921.8 | 257.6 | 1 360.0 | 252.9 | 184.7 | 229.1 | 0.2 | 143.7 | 85.3 |
| Owasso | 34 | D | D | D | 0.2 | 0.0 | 0.3 | 0.0 | 0.0 | 0.0 | 0.0 | 0.0 | 0.0 |
| Ponca City | 41 | 198 | 16.2 | 4.3 | 185.5 | 0.9 | 4.4 | 0.4 | 0.5 | 0.2 | 0.0 | 1.7 | 0.1 |
| Shawnee | 43 | D | D | D | 4.2 | 0.2 | 27.9 | 1.7 | 3.7 | 0.5 | 0.0 | 12.6 | 0.1 |
| Stillwater | 59 | 360 | 20.0 | 5.6 | 20.3 | 12.7 | 80.2 | 10.0 | 0.1 | 2.1 | 0.0 | 3.9 | 0.0 |
| Tulsa | 717 | 4 694 | 374.5 | 115.4 | 46.6 | 108.4 | 136.6 | 13.2 | 11.4 | 9.8 | 0.2 | 43.6 | 0.4 |
| **OREGON** | 5 333 | 29 509 | 2 595.4 | 799.5 | 891.5 | 1 155.6 | 8 694.5 | 4 360.1 | 926.3 | 456.7 | 49.4 | 345.9 | 206.8 |
| Albany | 66 | D | D | D | 1.3 | 5.1 | 17.8 | 0.1 | 0.0 | 0.1 | 0.0 | 15.3 | 0.0 |
| Beaverton | 160 | 1 240 | 105.3 | 33.0 | 14.7 | 6.7 | 14.1 | 0.3 | 0.0 | 2.2 | 0.0 | 0.7 | 5.0 |
| Bend | 157 | 895 | 73.5 | 23.1 | 4.6 | 17.0 | 20.2 | 1.2 | 0.3 | 11.0 | 0.0 | 0.4 | 0.4 |
| Corvallis | 63 | 384 | 21.2 | 8.2 | 47.7 | 40.4 | 169.5 | 41.6 | 0.9 | 18.3 | -0.3 | 1.2 | 0.4 |
| Eugene | 284 | 1 930 | 158.6 | 51.6 | 7.0 | 14.1 | 252.1 | 130.4 | 1.4 | 9.2 | 0.0 | 22.0 | 0.2 |
| Grants Pass | 76 | 328 | 24.6 | 7.0 | 2.3 | 4.5 | 11.2 | 2.8 | 0.0 | 0.9 | 0.0 | 4.0 | 0.0 |
| Gresham | 117 | 569 | 45.9 | 13.1 | 0.2 | 0.3 | 8.0 | 0.1 | 5.2 | 1.2 | 0.0 | 1.0 | 0.0 |
| Hillsboro | 135 | 926 | 110.5 | 42.3 | 4.0 | 10.2 | 41.0 | 0.5 | 4.4 | 3.6 | 0.0 | 27.3 | 0.0 |
| Keizer | 36 | 174 | 10.4 | 3.4 | 0.0 | 0.0 | 0.4 | 0.1 | 0.0 | 0.2 | 0.0 | 0.0 | 0.0 |
| Lake Oswego | 71 | 292 | 25.7 | 7.7 | 20.9 | 3.0 | 1.2 | 1.2 | 0.0 | 0.0 | 0.0 | 9.8 | 0.0 |
| McMinnville | 36 | 170 | 12.5 | 4.2 | 0.7 | 0.5 | 14.8 | 0.1 | 1.8 | 0.1 | 0.0 | 9.8 | 0.0 |
| Medford | 151 | 1 154 | 96.6 | 35.5 | 1.0 | 12.7 | 24.3 | 3.9 | 0.3 | 1.3 | 0.0 | 12.0 | 0.4 |
| Oregon City | 47 | 222 | 19.3 | 6.3 | 1.0 | 0.7 | 30.8 | 1.5 | 2.1 | 0.1 | 0.0 | 17.1 | 0.9 |
| Portland | 1 164 | 7 975 | 784.9 | 231.9 | 309.9 | 408.9 | 1 443.6 | 519.5 | 16.3 | 171.3 | 0.2 | 104.4 | 12.6 |
| Redmond | 35 | D | D | D | 0.0 | 0.1 | 14.6 | 0.0 | 1.4 | 0.3 | 0.0 | 7.8 | 0.0 |
| Salem | 233 | 1 204 | 93.1 | 29.9 | 13.3 | 9.6 | 1 226.4 | 51.9 | 216.6 | 40.1 | 7.9 | 64.0 | 186.4 |
| Springfield | 83 | 437 | 34.9 | 11.0 | 2.5 | 5.1 | 8.4 | 0.0 | 5.4 | 0.4 | 0.0 | 0.7 | 0.0 |

1. Establishments subject to federal tax.   2. Includes program categories not shown separately. State totals include additional categories not allocated by city.

| City | City government finances, 2007 | | | | | | | | | |
|---|---|---|---|---|---|---|---|---|---|---|
| | General revenue | | | | | | | General expenditure | | |
| | | Intergovernmental | | Taxes | | | | | Per capita[1] (dollars) | |
| | | | | | Per capita[1] (dollars) | | | | | |
| | Total (mil dol) | Total (mil dol) | Percent from state government | Total (mil dol) | Total | Property | Sales and gross receipts | Total (mil dol) | Total | Capital outlays |
| | 117 | 118 | 119 | 120 | 121 | 122 | 123 | 124 | 125 | 126 |
| OHIO—Cont'd | | | | | | | | | | |
| Kettering | 66.6 | 11.2 | 86.0 | 41.2 | 761 | 174 | 10 | 61.5 | 1 137 | 160 |
| Lakewood | 65.9 | 13.7 | 79.6 | 34.9 | 681 | 271 | 43 | 77.2 | 1 505 | 304 |
| Lancaster | 48.6 | 7.3 | 86.7 | 18.0 | 487 | 114 | 1 | 49.6 | 1 342 | 235 |
| Lima | 45.7 | 9.1 | 83.4 | 18.4 | 484 | 35 | 27 | 46.1 | 1 214 | 68 |
| Lorain | 66.2 | 18.3 | 100.0 | 26.4 | 376 | 64 | 24 | 67.4 | 961 | 138 |
| Mansfield | 66.3 | 11.8 | 88.1 | 38.0 | 765 | 166 | 163 | 70.6 | 1 422 | 145 |
| Marion | 39.2 | 8.2 | 88.3 | 16.7 | 467 | 54 | 13 | 38.4 | 1 076 | 95 |
| Mason | 56.5 | 7.6 | 100.0 | 30.9 | 1 046 | 992 | 54 | 68.9 | 2 331 | 866 |
| Massillon | 37.3 | 7.0 | 85.1 | 15.4 | 476 | 58 | 12 | 38.5 | 1 188 | 159 |
| Medina | 32.6 | 5.7 | 100.0 | 17.9 | 685 | 120 | 10 | 25.5 | 972 | 149 |
| Mentor | 57.3 | 10.5 | 95.6 | 36.8 | 711 | 112 | 32 | 63.2 | 1 222 | 208 |
| Middletown | 76.2 | 22.2 | 92.7 | 24.4 | 476 | 115 | 12 | 67.7 | 1 320 | 107 |
| Newark | 46.8 | 9.8 | 92.6 | 25.1 | 532 | 70 | 33 | 44.6 | 945 | 84 |
| North Olmsted | 44.2 | 6.8 | 95.7 | 25.0 | 792 | 330 | 40 | 44.3 | 1 402 | 259 |
| North Ridgeville | 30.4 | 3.5 | 94.3 | 13.8 | 501 | 188 | 42 | 30.0 | 1 087 | 295 |
| North Royalton | 25.9 | 4.0 | 100.0 | 13.6 | 462 | 154 | 13 | 25.0 | 850 | 60 |
| Parma | 65.2 | 13.2 | 86.3 | 43.0 | 546 | 89 | 18 | 61.9 | 785 | 105 |
| Reynoldsburg | 28.1 | 4.9 | 100.0 | 11.9 | 354 | 106 | 16 | 32.4 | 965 | 326 |
| Riverside | 11.9 | 2.4 | 100.0 | 7.0 | 275 | 92 | 2 | 11.6 | 456 | 100 |
| Sandusky | 32.8 | 5.1 | 58.7 | 15.9 | 614 | 91 | 218 | 32.3 | 1 249 | 207 |
| Shaker Heights | 62.2 | 20.4 | 100.0 | 28.8 | 1 076 | 287 | 34 | 52.8 | 1 972 | 256 |
| Springfield | 85.6 | 21.2 | 94.7 | 32.6 | 523 | 39 | 34 | 79.6 | 1 276 | 364 |
| Stow | 33.8 | 6.9 | 96.6 | 20.9 | 612 | 231 | 27 | 44.0 | 1 294 | 526 |
| Strongsville | 62.1 | 5.8 | 100.0 | 37.8 | 882 | 210 | 0 | 57.3 | 1 337 | 167 |
| Toledo | 387.2 | 64.3 | 46.0 | 205.8 | 698 | 59 | 65 | 474.2 | 1 607 | 432 |
| Troy | 32.9 | 4.1 | 100.0 | 15.3 | 694 | 90 | 4 | 32.4 | 1 470 | 295 |
| Upper Arlington | 38.8 | 5.2 | 100.0 | 23.9 | 752 | 220 | 23 | 69.9 | 2 203 | 237 |
| Warren | 62.4 | 10.0 | 62.2 | 24.3 | 548 | 31 | 64 | 61.4 | 1 387 | 143 |
| Westerville | 61.8 | 10.9 | 98.6 | 33.9 | 948 | 314 | 32 | 61.1 | 1 710 | 344 |
| Westlake | 51.9 | 7.6 | 99.6 | 32.1 | 1 045 | 393 | 30 | 53.7 | 1 749 | 607 |
| Wooster | 124.7 | 15.9 | 97.7 | 12.9 | 494 | 108 | 28 | 124.6 | 4 789 | 1 156 |
| Xenia | 27.0 | 6.1 | 97.3 | 11.6 | 491 | 75 | 54 | 24.7 | 1 043 | 166 |
| Youngstown | 94.9 | 18.3 | 77.1 | 50.9 | 689 | 28 | 16 | 102.5 | 1 389 | 260 |
| Zanesville | 32.6 | 7.8 | 100.0 | 16.1 | 639 | 50 | 22 | 29.4 | 1 170 | 41 |
| OKLAHOMA | X | X | X | X | X | X | X | X | X | X |
| Bartlesville | 35.6 | 2.1 | 15.6 | 20.7 | 584 | 79 | 484 | 34.0 | 961 | 208 |
| Broken Arrow | 71.0 | 2.5 | 76.5 | 43.2 | 476 | 89 | 367 | 81.2 | 895 | 347 |
| Edmond | 87.5 | 12.4 | 36.9 | 45.4 | 580 | 1 | 544 | 89.5 | 1 144 | 248 |
| Enid | 49.4 | 6.2 | 35.0 | 30.1 | 640 | 12 | 601 | 36.6 | 778 | 170 |
| Lawton | 73.4 | 5.2 | 24.5 | 43.7 | 477 | 40 | 420 | 73.2 | 800 | 159 |
| Midwest City | 51.0 | 2.0 | 17.9 | 29.2 | 522 | 43 | 466 | 50.3 | 898 | 33 |
| Moore | 37.7 | 2.6 | 17.9 | 21.5 | 421 | 40 | 365 | 36.7 | 719 | 78 |
| Muskogee | 132.5 | 3.7 | 63.1 | 30.6 | 764 | 9 | 697 | 138.2 | 3 454 | 231 |
| Norman | 331.2 | 7.5 | 29.8 | 57.4 | 538 | 21 | 500 | 387.3 | 3 630 | 1 015 |
| Oklahoma City | 1 013.0 | 85.6 | 45.1 | 479.2 | 876 | 102 | 711 | 986.9 | 1 803 | 637 |
| Owasso | 26.1 | 0.5 | 62.6 | 17.7 | 672 | 0 | 642 | 23.5 | 893 | 213 |
| Ponca City | 30.4 | 1.1 | 21.2 | 14.5 | 590 | 15 | 547 | 39.6 | 1 612 | 349 |
| Shawnee | 28.6 | 2.0 | 60.9 | 17.9 | 591 | 4 | 567 | 25.8 | 854 | 62 |
| Stillwater | 41.8 | 0.8 | 100.0 | 25.9 | 552 | 28 | 498 | 47.3 | 1 007 | 51 |
| Tulsa | 601.7 | 74.1 | 18.0 | 261.6 | 681 | 69 | 613 | 462.3 | 1 204 | 149 |
| OREGON | X | X | X | X | X | X | X | X | X | X |
| Albany | 58.5 | 7.7 | 58.2 | 33.4 | 708 | 454 | 254 | 80.3 | 1 701 | 779 |
| Beaverton | 72.8 | 12.7 | 67.7 | 41.4 | 457 | 296 | 160 | 59.3 | 654 | 83 |
| Bend | 82.8 | 13.7 | 51.0 | 44.7 | 599 | 276 | 324 | 83.6 | 1 121 | 306 |
| Corvallis | 64.6 | 9.3 | 53.1 | 26.4 | 517 | 372 | 145 | 55.8 | 1 092 | 105 |
| Eugene | 267.9 | 47.4 | 23.8 | 107.2 | 720 | 593 | 126 | 229.9 | 1 543 | 209 |
| Grants Pass | 35.1 | 4.3 | 54.4 | 20.9 | 630 | 374 | 256 | 34.4 | 1 038 | 196 |
| Gresham | 102.1 | 32.1 | 71.8 | 39.1 | 392 | 217 | 175 | 102.4 | 1 026 | 175 |
| Hillsboro | 99.7 | 9.6 | 99.2 | 55.1 | 602 | 384 | 218 | 87.7 | 959 | 126 |
| Keizer | 19.4 | 3.1 | 99.6 | 9.0 | 256 | 175 | 81 | 20.8 | 589 | 193 |
| Lake Oswego | 59.6 | 3.7 | 71.5 | 35.6 | 971 | 759 | 212 | 75.3 | 2 053 | 816 |
| McMinnville | 42.6 | 3.7 | 78.8 | 14.8 | 480 | 315 | 165 | 27.2 | 881 | 115 |
| Medford | 82.9 | 9.2 | 61.6 | 49.8 | 690 | 344 | 346 | 71.0 | 984 | 227 |
| Oregon City | 41.4 | 5.8 | 98.2 | 22.5 | 723 | 368 | 355 | 37.4 | 1 202 | 380 |
| Portland | 1 048.5 | 193.7 | 39.6 | 451.5 | 820 | 493 | 327 | 1 208.8 | 2 196 | 599 |
| Redmond | 53.0 | 13.7 | 66.9 | 19.5 | 818 | 360 | 458 | 47.0 | 1 977 | 739 |
| Salem | 206.8 | 40.9 | 53.9 | 87.9 | 578 | 390 | 189 | 206.7 | 1 361 | 197 |
| Springfield | 99.9 | 10.8 | 99.3 | 27.7 | 489 | 341 | 148 | 81.7 | 1 442 | 262 |

1. Based on population estimated as of July 1 of the year shown.

# Table D. Cities — **City Government Finances**

| | City government finances, 2006 (cont.) | | | | | | | | | |
| | General expenditure (cont.) | | | | | | | | | |
| | Percent of total for: | | | | | | | | | |
| City | Public welfare | Highways | Parking facilities | Education | Health and hospitals | Police protection | Sewerage and sanitation | Parks and recreation | Housing and community development | Interest on debt |
| | 127 | 128 | 129 | 130 | 131 | 132 | 133 | 134 | 135 | 136 |
| **OHIO—Cont'd** | | | | | | | | | | |
| Kettering | 0.0 | 21.4 | 0.0 | 0.0 | 0.3 | 21.0 | 0.0 | 17.5 | 2.9 | 1.9 |
| Lakewood | 0.7 | 2.8 | 1.5 | 0.0 | 5.3 | 14.1 | 25.1 | 1.3 | 6.1 | 6.6 |
| Lancaster | 0.0 | 7.2 | 0.0 | 0.0 | 0.6 | 14.6 | 29.9 | 3.9 | 2.1 | 2.9 |
| Lima | 0.0 | 6.4 | 0.0 | 0.0 | 0.0 | 18.2 | 28.9 | 2.4 | 6.5 | 3.8 |
| Lorain | 6.3 | 3.9 | 2.3 | 0.0 | 2.6 | 16.5 | 18.7 | 1.5 | 13.7 | 2.1 |
| Mansfield | 0.0 | 14.9 | 0.0 | 0.0 | 0.2 | 18.9 | 18.9 | 1.3 | 6.3 | 0.5 |
| Marion | 0.0 | 10.2 | 0.0 | 0.0 | 2.7 | 16.1 | 29.3 | 3.5 | 1.9 | 7.6 |
| Mason | 0.0 | 10.2 | 0.0 | 0.0 | 0.0 | 4.0 | 12.8 | 15.0 | 0.0 | 8.8 |
| Massillon | 0.0 | 9.2 | 0.0 | 0.0 | 1.7 | 11.2 | 23.0 | 8.1 | 0.5 | 3.7 |
| Medina | 0.0 | 14.5 | 0.0 | 0.0 | 0.5 | 25.8 | 11.3 | 12.1 | 3.7 | 7.6 |
| Mentor | 0.0 | 29.7 | 0.0 | 0.0 | 0.0 | 17.7 | 1.1 | 12.8 | 2.2 | 3.5 |
| Middletown | 0.0 | 10.4 | 0.2 | 0.0 | 2.8 | 13.7 | 11.7 | 3.7 | 16.0 | 12.4 |
| Newark | 0.0 | 7.3 | 0.0 | 0.0 | 4.1 | 20.7 | 11.2 | 1.6 | 3.9 | 4.1 |
| North Olmsted | 1.2 | 17.9 | 0.0 | 0.0 | 0.1 | 16.2 | 15.5 | 7.3 | 0.0 | 7.5 |
| North Ridgeville | 0.0 | 9.4 | 0.0 | 0.0 | 3.8 | 15.8 | 34.2 | 1.2 | 4.0 | 2.2 |
| North Royalton | 1.2 | 7.0 | 0.0 | 0.0 | 0.3 | 25.4 | 18.2 | 1.6 | 3.7 | 4.9 |
| Parma | 0.0 | 12.3 | 0.0 | 0.0 | 0.5 | 18.3 | 8.2 | 5.4 | 4.0 | 2.4 |
| Reynoldsburg | 0.0 | 3.9 | 0.0 | 0.0 | 0.5 | 20.5 | 21.1 | 3.0 | 0.0 | 3.9 |
| Riverside | 0.0 | 14.8 | 0.0 | 0.0 | 0.0 | 31.4 | 0.0 | 0.5 | 0.0 | 1.4 |
| Sandusky | 0.0 | 10.8 | 0.1 | 0.0 | 0.0 | 17.4 | 19.4 | 7.2 | 12.7 | 4.0 |
| Shaker Heights | 0.0 | 6.7 | 0.0 | 0.0 | 1.1 | 24.0 | 8.8 | 9.9 | 8.9 | 2.1 |
| Springfield | 1.1 | 4.2 | 0.0 | 0.0 | 11.9 | 16.1 | 9.6 | 3.8 | 3.6 | 2.0 |
| Stow | 0.0 | 7.2 | 0.0 | 0.0 | 1.2 | 8.1 | 3.0 | 31.0 | 3.4 | 1.5 |
| Strongsville | 0.6 | 13.8 | 0.0 | 0.0 | 0.6 | 10.4 | 15.8 | 7.8 | 0.0 | 3.8 |
| Toledo | 0.0 | 12.6 | 0.1 | 0.0 | 0.4 | 16.7 | 30.8 | 2.7 | 2.7 | 3.5 |
| Troy | 0.0 | 6.5 | 0.1 | 0.0 | 0.0 | 13.6 | 11.7 | 9.7 | 19.6 | 2.9 |
| Upper Arlington | 0.0 | 8.1 | 0.0 | 0.0 | 0.2 | 9.2 | 4.5 | 51.2 | 0.0 | 1.7 |
| Warren | 0.0 | 7.4 | 0.2 | 0.0 | 1.5 | 13.0 | 23.5 | 2.9 | 7.7 | 1.9 |
| Westerville | 0.0 | 6.5 | 0.0 | 0.0 | 0.0 | 17.0 | 12.9 | 14.4 | 0.0 | 2.2 |
| Westlake | 0.0 | 2.9 | 0.0 | 0.0 | 1.3 | 12.5 | 5.2 | 8.0 | 0.1 | 6.2 |
| Wooster | 0.0 | 3.9 | 0.0 | 0.0 | 67.0 | 3.8 | 14.3 | 1.5 | 0.6 | 1.0 |
| Xenia | 0.0 | 6.8 | 0.3 | 0.0 | 0.3 | 20.2 | 17.0 | 1.5 | 0.9 | 1.2 |
| Youngstown | 0.0 | 6.6 | 0.0 | 0.0 | 2.3 | 19.5 | 15.5 | 3.2 | 5.1 | 2.0 |
| Zanesville | 0.0 | 4.2 | 0.0 | 0.0 | 0.5 | 34.2 | 21.9 | 3.9 | 0.0 | 0.5 |
| **OKLAHOMA** | X | X | X | X | X | X | X | X | X | X |
| Bartlesville | 0.0 | 12.6 | 0.0 | 0.0 | 0.0 | 12.4 | 19.1 | 8.5 | 2.4 | 1.7 |
| Broken Arrow | 0.0 | 11.3 | 0.0 | 0.0 | 0.4 | 17.3 | 23.8 | 10.1 | 0.7 | 3.9 |
| Edmond | 1.4 | 18.1 | 0.0 | 0.0 | 0.0 | 17.8 | 10.2 | 11.1 | 0.9 | 4.7 |
| Enid | 0.5 | 19.5 | 0.0 | 0.0 | 0.0 | 19.5 | 11.4 | 5.8 | 0.7 | 0.0 |
| Lawton | 0.0 | 9.3 | 0.0 | 0.0 | 0.0 | 19.8 | 13.0 | 9.9 | 2.7 | 1.2 |
| Midwest City | 0.0 | 5.7 | 0.0 | 0.0 | 1.5 | 19.9 | 16.9 | 6.1 | 4.0 | 4.5 |
| Moore | 0.0 | 9.6 | 0.0 | 0.0 | 0.0 | 18.6 | 6.1 | 4.3 | 1.5 | 2.0 |
| Muskogee | 0.1 | 2.2 | 0.0 | 0.0 | 66.7 | 5.4 | 5.4 | 3.8 | 0.4 | 1.5 |
| Norman | 0.0 | 5.2 | 0.0 | 0.0 | 65.2 | 4.8 | 12.7 | 1.5 | 1.3 | 1.6 |
| Oklahoma City | 0.0 | 9.1 | 0.0 | 0.0 | 0.0 | 13.9 | 18.2 | 9.3 | 1.0 | 3.0 |
| Owasso | 0.0 | 4.2 | 0.0 | 0.0 | 3.4 | 19.6 | 10.9 | 9.1 | 2.0 | 5.9 |
| Ponca City | 0.0 | 10.2 | 0.0 | 0.0 | 1.8 | 14.3 | 14.0 | 9.6 | 3.1 | 1.5 |
| Shawnee | 0.0 | 6.8 | 0.0 | 0.0 | 0.0 | 22.6 | 12.2 | 2.0 | 3.3 | 4.4 |
| Stillwater | 0.6 | 11.1 | 0.0 | 0.0 | 0.8 | 18.7 | 11.5 | 8.0 | 0.0 | 2.9 |
| Tulsa | 5.3 | 6.0 | 0.8 | 0.0 | 8.2 | 16.4 | 21.9 | 5.2 | 1.7 | 5.7 |
| **OREGON** | X | X | X | X | X | X | X | X | X | X |
| Albany | 0.0 | 6.8 | 0.0 | 0.0 | 2.6 | 13.2 | 49.5 | 6.1 | 0.0 | 1.6 |
| Beaverton | 0.0 | 6.8 | 0.0 | 0.0 | 0.0 | 31.0 | 12.5 | 0.0 | 0.8 | 1.2 |
| Bend | 0.0 | 14.6 | 0.5 | 0.0 | 0.0 | 16.2 | 9.5 | 0.0 | 1.9 | 4.2 |
| Corvallis | 0.0 | 7.2 | 0.3 | 0.0 | 0.0 | 18.3 | 15.0 | 11.2 | 7.2 | 6.3 |
| Eugene | 0.0 | 1.8 | 1.4 | 0.0 | 0.0 | 18.2 | 11.3 | 10.3 | 4.7 | 1.2 |
| Grants Pass | 0.0 | 5.4 | 0.0 | 0.0 | 0.0 | 19.3 | 19.2 | 8.1 | 3.5 | 1.6 |
| Gresham | 0.0 | 15.5 | 0.0 | 0.0 | 0.0 | 19.3 | 20.6 | 1.6 | 3.1 | 3.7 |
| Hillsboro | 0.0 | 9.4 | 0.0 | 0.0 | 0.0 | 23.1 | 21.0 | 17.7 | 0.0 | 0.0 |
| Keizer | 0.0 | 13.6 | 0.0 | 0.0 | 0.0 | 24.6 | 20.0 | 1.5 | 6.5 | 4.7 |
| Lake Oswego | 0.0 | 5.6 | 0.0 | 0.0 | 0.0 | 11.1 | 11.9 | 8.3 | 1.8 | 3.5 |
| McMinnville | 0.0 | 6.0 | 0.0 | 0.0 | 10.6 | 20.4 | 12.1 | 10.3 | 0.2 | 5.0 |
| Medford | 0.0 | 17.5 | 0.5 | 0.0 | 0.0 | 23.7 | 12.5 | 9.6 | 0.9 | 3.7 |
| Oregon City | 0.0 | 12.8 | 0.7 | 0.0 | 0.0 | 12.9 | 26.5 | 7.6 | 8.4 | 3.9 |
| Portland | 0.0 | 14.8 | 0.4 | 0.0 | 0.0 | 11.8 | 19.8 | 8.7 | 3.8 | 9.8 |
| Redmond | 0.0 | 23.4 | 0.0 | 0.0 | 0.0 | 11.6 | 15.4 | 9.3 | 3.5 | 3.3 |
| Salem | 0.0 | 9.1 | 0.6 | 0.0 | 1.0 | 13.9 | 24.5 | 5.2 | 10.7 | 6.5 |
| Springfield | 0.0 | 9.6 | 0.0 | 0.0 | 6.0 | 18.8 | 26.7 | 0.0 | 5.4 | 0.7 |

| | City government finances, 2007 (cont.) | | | | Climate[2] | | | | | | |
| | Debt outstanding | | | | Average daily temperature (degrees Fahrenheit) | | | | | | |
| | | | | | Mean | | Limits | | | | |
| City | Total (mil dol) | Per capita[1] (dollars) | Debt issued during year | City government employment, 2011 | January | July | January[3] | July[4] | Annual precipitation (inches) | Heating degree days | Cooling degree days |
| | 137 | 138 | 139 | 140 | 141 | 142 | 143 | 144 | 145 | 146 | 147 |
| **OHIO—Cont'd** | | | | | | | | | | | |
| Kettering | 11.1 | 205 | 0.0 | 495 | 27.9 | 77.0 | 20.6 | 87.2 | 39.41 | 5 343 | 1 214 |
| Lakewood | 120.9 | 2 357 | 24.6 | 472 | 25.7 | 71.9 | 18.8 | 81.4 | 38.71 | 6 121 | 702 |
| Lancaster | 34.6 | 937 | 0.0 | 426 | 26.5 | 73.1 | 17.8 | 84.4 | 36.55 | 5 887 | 764 |
| Lima | 28.6 | 753 | 4.5 | 379 | 25.5 | 73.6 | 18.1 | 84.0 | 37.20 | 5 932 | 835 |
| Lorain | 43.0 | 613 | 0.0 | 469 | 27.1 | 73.8 | 19.3 | 85.0 | 38.02 | 5 731 | 818 |
| Mansfield | 9.0 | 182 | 0.0 | 439 | 24.3 | 71.0 | 16.2 | 81.8 | 43.24 | 6 364 | 653 |
| Marion | 40.7 | 1 141 | 24.5 | 288 | 24.5 | 72.7 | 16.0 | 83.7 | 38.35 | 6 300 | 703 |
| Mason | 111.3 | 3 766 | 0.0 | 268 | NA | NA | NA | NA | NA | NA | NA |
| Massillon | 31.9 | 985 | 0.0 | 302 | 25.2 | 71.8 | 17.4 | 82.3 | 38.47 | 6 154 | 678 |
| Medina | 42.8 | 1 633 | 0.0 | 222 | 23.7 | 71.3 | 16.2 | 82.0 | 38.34 | 6 525 | 558 |
| Mentor | 35.1 | 679 | 0.0 | 441 | 23.0 | 68.8 | 14.3 | 80.0 | 47.33 | 6 956 | 372 |
| Middletown | 131.4 | 2 561 | 80.2 | 407 | 27.5 | 74.2 | 18.3 | 86.3 | 39.54 | 5 609 | 879 |
| Newark | 27.3 | 579 | 4.8 | 389 | 25.8 | 72.7 | 17.3 | 83.8 | 41.62 | 6 084 | 687 |
| North Olmsted | 60.9 | 1 925 | 38.7 | 257 | 25.7 | 71.9 | 18.8 | 81.4 | 38.71 | 6 121 | 702 |
| North Ridgeville | 24.9 | 901 | 13.8 | 198 | NA | NA | NA | NA | NA | NA | NA |
| North Royalton | 7.7 | 263 | 0.0 | 183 | 25.7 | 71.9 | 18.8 | 81.4 | 38.71 | 6 121 | 702 |
| Parma | 82.4 | 1 045 | 10.8 | 471 | 25.7 | 71.9 | 18.8 | 81.4 | 38.71 | 6 121 | 702 |
| Reynoldsburg | 31.3 | 932 | 9.7 | 137 | 28.3 | 75.1 | 20.3 | 85.3 | 38.52 | 5 492 | 951 |
| Riverside | 3.8 | 148 | 0.0 | NA | NA | NA | NA | NA | NA | NA | NA |
| Sandusky | 31.3 | 1 209 | 0.1 | 226 | 25.6 | 73.8 | 18.9 | 81.8 | 34.46 | 6 065 | 785 |
| Shaker Heights | 27.5 | 1 026 | 2.8 | 379 | 25.7 | 71.9 | 18.8 | 81.4 | 38.71 | 6 121 | 702 |
| Springfield | 41.6 | 666 | 3.8 | 602 | 26.1 | 73.5 | 18.2 | 83.8 | 37.70 | 5 921 | 796 |
| Stow | 24.8 | 728 | 0.0 | 285 | 27.2 | 74.1 | 20.1 | 83.9 | 36.07 | 5 752 | 856 |
| Strongsville | 43.8 | 1 023 | 11.7 | 381 | 25.7 | 71.9 | 18.8 | 81.4 | 38.71 | 6 121 | 702 |
| Toledo | 359.7 | 1 219 | 74.8 | 2 176 | 27.5 | 77.6 | 21.7 | 87.1 | 33.52 | 5 464 | 1 257 |
| Troy | 29.0 | 1 316 | 0.0 | 193 | NA | NA | NA | NA | NA | NA | NA |
| Upper Arlington | 25.8 | 814 | 4.0 | 254 | 28.3 | 75.1 | 20.3 | 85.3 | 38.52 | 5 492 | 951 |
| Warren | 26.7 | 604 | 1.7 | 381 | 24.0 | 70.2 | 15.3 | 82.4 | 37.80 | 6 678 | 458 |
| Westerville | 35.4 | 991 | 0.0 | 489 | 27.7 | 74.4 | 19.7 | 85.4 | 39.35 | 5 434 | 924 |
| Westlake | 48.4 | 1 575 | 0.0 | 319 | 27.1 | 73.8 | 19.3 | 85.0 | 38.02 | 5 731 | 818 |
| Wooster | 122.7 | 4 719 | 0.0 | 897 | NA | NA | NA | NA | NA | NA | NA |
| Xenia | 9.7 | 409 | 2.1 | 213 | NA | NA | NA | NA | NA | NA | NA |
| Youngstown | 43.4 | 588 | 8.4 | 759 | 24.9 | 69.9 | 17.4 | 81.0 | 38.02 | 6 451 | 552 |
| Zanesville | 7.5 | 298 | 0.0 | 307 | 24.3 | 68.4 | 16.3 | 78.7 | 36.91 | 6 639 | 373 |
| **OKLAHOMA** | X | X | X | X | X | X | X | X | X | X | X |
| Bartlesville | 58.8 | 1 660 | 8.1 | 344 | 35.4 | 82.2 | 23.7 | 94.5 | 38.99 | 3 743 | 1 894 |
| Broken Arrow | 121.0 | 1 334 | 20.5 | 599 | 34.8 | 81.3 | 23.5 | 92.9 | 40.46 | 3 917 | 1 746 |
| Edmond | 170.2 | 2 175 | 3.8 | 694 | 36.7 | 82.0 | 26.2 | 93.1 | 35.85 | 3 663 | 1 907 |
| Enid | 44.6 | 948 | 0.3 | 475 | 33.1 | 82.6 | 21.9 | 94.4 | 34.25 | 4 269 | 1 852 |
| Lawton | 63.4 | 693 | 0.0 | 891 | 38.2 | 84.2 | 26.4 | 95.7 | 31.64 | 3 326 | 2 199 |
| Midwest City | 46.3 | 828 | 0.0 | 492 | 36.7 | 82.0 | 26.2 | 93.1 | 35.85 | 3 663 | 1 907 |
| Moore | 16.3 | 319 | 0.4 | 276 | 36.7 | 82.0 | 26.2 | 93.1 | 35.85 | 3 663 | 1 907 |
| Muskogee | 68.4 | 1 711 | 24.3 | 476 | 36.1 | 82.1 | 25.2 | 93.1 | 43.77 | 3 667 | 1 858 |
| Norman | 298.5 | 2 798 | 127.8 | 3 065 | 35.8 | 82.1 | 23.2 | 93.9 | 41.65 | 3 713 | 1 906 |
| Oklahoma City | 1 083.8 | 1 980 | 178.5 | 4 307 | 36.7 | 82.0 | 26.2 | 93.1 | 35.85 | 3 663 | 1 907 |
| Owasso | 35.7 | 1 353 | 8.5 | 198 | NA | NA | NA | NA | NA | NA | NA |
| Ponca City | 27.0 | 1 099 | 16.0 | 404 | 33.8 | 82.9 | 23.8 | 94.1 | 36.41 | 4 053 | 1 964 |
| Shawnee | 37.9 | 1 253 | 13.7 | 260 | 37.3 | 83.0 | 25.5 | 94.5 | 40.87 | 3 460 | 2 024 |
| Stillwater | 42.2 | 899 | 0.2 | 1 308 | 34.5 | 82.3 | 21.9 | 93.6 | 36.71 | 3 899 | 1 881 |
| Tulsa | 1 412.5 | 3 678 | 174.9 | 3 856 | 37.4 | 81.9 | 27.1 | 92.2 | 45.10 | 3 413 | 1 905 |
| **OREGON** | X | X | X | X | X | X | X | X | X | X | X |
| Albany | 93.2 | 1 973 | 37.6 | 400 | 40.3 | 66.5 | 33.6 | 81.2 | 43.66 | 4 715 | 247 |
| Beaverton | 41.6 | 459 | 1.0 | 491 | 40.0 | 66.8 | 33.8 | 79.2 | 39.95 | 4 723 | 287 |
| Bend | 82.5 | 1 107 | 5.8 | 443 | 31.2 | 63.5 | 22.6 | 80.7 | 11.73 | 7 042 | 147 |
| Corvallis | 78.4 | 1 533 | 0.0 | 442 | 38.1 | 63.8 | 31.6 | 77.4 | 67.76 | 5 501 | 139 |
| Eugene | 351.5 | 2 359 | 12.9 | 1 888 | 39.8 | 66.2 | 33.0 | 81.5 | 50.90 | 4 786 | 242 |
| Grants Pass | 24.6 | 740 | 9.8 | 216 | NA | NA | NA | NA | NA | NA | NA |
| Gresham | 79.7 | 800 | 3.8 | 530 | 40.0 | 68.3 | 33.5 | 81.5 | 45.70 | 4 491 | 450 |
| Hillsboro | 51.8 | 566 | 0.0 | 744 | 40.5 | 67.6 | 35.1 | 80.4 | 38.19 | 4 532 | 323 |
| Keizer | 27.8 | 787 | 4.2 | 94 | 40.3 | 66.8 | 33.5 | 81.5 | 40.00 | 4 784 | 257 |
| Lake Oswego | 76.7 | 2 090 | 26.7 | 339 | 41.8 | 69.3 | 35.7 | 82.6 | 46.05 | 4 132 | 475 |
| McMinnville | 40.6 | 1 313 | 13.1 | 259 | 39.6 | 66.6 | 33.0 | 81.9 | 41.66 | 4 815 | 288 |
| Medford | 84.9 | 1 176 | 19.0 | 468 | 39.1 | 72.7 | 30.9 | 90.2 | 18.37 | 4 539 | 711 |
| Oregon City | 30.6 | 983 | 3.1 | 169 | 41.8 | 69.3 | 35.7 | 82.6 | 46.05 | 4 132 | 475 |
| Portland | 2 572.7 | 4 674 | 411.3 | 5 680 | 41.8 | 69.3 | 35.7 | 82.6 | 46.05 | 4 132 | 475 |
| Redmond | 52.1 | 2 192 | 1.9 | 197 | NA | NA | NA | NA | NA | NA | NA |
| Salem | 520.8 | 3 429 | 72.8 | 1 235 | 40.3 | 66.8 | 33.5 | 81.5 | 40.00 | 4 784 | 257 |
| Springfield | 52.4 | 925 | 31.8 | 556 | 39.8 | 66.2 | 33.0 | 81.5 | 50.90 | 4 786 | 242 |

1. Based on the population estimated as of July 1 of the year shown.     2. Represents normal values based on the 30-year period, 1971–2000.     3. Average daily minimum.     4. Average daily maximum.

# Table D. Cities — **Land Area and Population**

| STATE Place code | City | Land area,[1] 2010 (sq km) | Total persons | Rank | Per square kilometer | White | Black | American Indian, Alaska Native | Asian | Hawaiian Pacific Islander | Percent Hispanic or Latino[2], 2010 | Percent Foreign born 2007–2011 |
|---|---|---|---|---|---|---|---|---|---|---|---|---|
| | | 1 | 2 | 3 | 4 | 5 | 6 | 7 | 8 | 9 | 10 | 11 |
| | **OREGON—Cont'd** | | | | | | | | | | | |
| 41 73650 | Tigard | 30.6 | 49 774 | 732 | 1 626.6 | 76.7 | 2.3 | 1.4 | 8.8 | 1.3 | 12.7 | 14.3 |
| 41 74950 | Tualatin | 21.3 | 26 716 | 1 363 | 1 254.3 | 76.4 | 1.7 | 1.2 | 5.2 | 1.3 | 17.3 | 15.1 |
| 41 80150 | West Linn | 19.1 | 25 600 | 1 412 | 1 340.3 | 90.6 | 1.1 | 1.0 | 5.5 | 0.4 | 4.0 | 8.2 |
| 42 00000 | **PENNSYLVANIA** | 115 883.1 | 12 763 536 | X | 110.1 | 80.7 | 11.3 | 0.5 | 3.1 | 0.1 | 5.7 | 5.7 |
| 42 02000 | Allentown | 45.4 | 118 974 | 222 | 2 620.6 | 45.0 | 11.0 | 0.5 | 2.5 | 0.1 | 42.8 | 14.6 |
| 42 02184 | Altoona | 25.7 | 46 148 | 799 | 1 795.6 | 94.8 | 4.5 | 0.4 | 0.6 | 0.1 | 1.3 | 1.4 |
| 42 06064 | Bethel Park | 30.2 | 32 374 | 1 123 | 1 072.0 | 96.2 | 1.6 | 0.2 | 1.8 | 0.1 | 1.0 | 2.7 |
| 42 06088 | Bethlehem | 49.5 | 75 103 | 440 | 1 517.2 | 66.9 | 6.4 | 0.4 | 3.2 | 0.1 | 24.4 | 7.2 |
| 42 13208 | Chester | 12.5 | 34 031 | 1 075 | 2 722.5 | 16.4 | 74.8 | 1.0 | 0.9 | 0.1 | 9.0 | 3.7 |
| 42 21648 | Easton | 10.6 | 26 951 | 1 347 | 2 542.5 | 61.6 | 17.8 | 0.9 | 2.8 | 0.1 | 19.9 | 10.8 |
| 42 24000 | Erie | 49.4 | 101 047 | 285 | 2 045.5 | 74.7 | 18.7 | 0.7 | 1.9 | 0.1 | 6.9 | 5.9 |
| 42 32800 | Harrisburg | 21.1 | 49 279 | 746 | 2 335.5 | 27.5 | 52.8 | 1.0 | 3.8 | 0.1 | 18.0 | 7.4 |
| 42 33408 | Hazleton | 15.6 | 25 224 | 1 431 | 1 616.9 | 59.7 | 2.3 | 0.3 | 0.9 | 0.0 | 37.3 | 20.8 |
| 42 41216 | Lancaster | 18.7 | 59 360 | 591 | 3 174.3 | 43.7 | 15.5 | 0.8 | 3.3 | 0.1 | 39.3 | 10.1 |
| 42 42168 | Lebanon | 10.8 | 25 554 | 1 415 | 2 366.1 | 62.7 | 4.6 | 0.5 | 1.2 | 0.1 | 32.1 | 4.5 |
| 42 50528 | Monroeville | 51.1 | 28 386 | 1 279 | 555.5 | 80.4 | 12.9 | 0.5 | 6.5 | 0.1 | 1.5 | 7.6 |
| 42 54656 | Norristown | 9.1 | 34 427 | 1 065 | 3 783.2 | 34.0 | 37.2 | 0.8 | 2.4 | 0.1 | 28.3 | 20.3 |
| 42 60000 | Philadelphia | 347.3 | 1 547 607 | 5 | 4 456.1 | 38.1 | 43.4 | 0.7 | 6.9 | 0.1 | 12.3 | 11.6 |
| 42 61000 | Pittsburgh | 143.4 | 306 211 | 61 | 2 135.4 | 66.7 | 27.3 | 0.7 | 5.0 | 0.1 | 2.3 | 7.1 |
| 42 61536 | Plum | 74.0 | 27 395 | 1 326 | 370.2 | 94.1 | 4.1 | 0.3 | 1.4 | 0.1 | 0.9 | 2.7 |
| 42 63624 | Reading | 25.6 | 88 102 | 345 | 3 441.5 | 30.2 | 11.4 | 0.5 | 1.2 | 0.1 | 58.2 | 17.0 |
| 42 69000 | Scranton | 65.6 | 75 809 | 433 | 1 155.6 | 81.8 | 5.9 | 0.5 | 3.4 | 0.1 | 9.9 | 6.6 |
| 42 73808 | State College | 11.8 | 41 983 | 868 | 3 557.9 | 82.3 | 4.2 | 0.4 | 10.8 | 0.1 | 3.9 | 11.0 |
| 42 85152 | Wilkes-Barre | 18.1 | 41 243 | 880 | 2 278.6 | 76.8 | 11.8 | 0.5 | 1.6 | 0.0 | 11.3 | 5.3 |
| 42 85312 | Williamsport | 22.6 | 29 497 | 1 235 | 1 305.2 | 83.0 | 16.1 | 0.9 | 1.0 | 0.0 | 2.6 | 1.8 |
| 42 87048 | York | 13.7 | 43 550 | 839 | 3 178.8 | 44.5 | 28.5 | 1.0 | 1.5 | 0.0 | 28.5 | 9.0 |
| 44 00000 | **RHODE ISLAND** | 2 677.6 | 1 050 292 | X | 392.3 | 78.0 | 6.2 | 1.0 | 3.4 | 0.1 | 12.4 | 12.9 |
| 44 19180 | Cranston | 73.4 | 80 529 | 398 | 1 097.1 | 78.6 | 5.5 | 0.7 | 5.6 | 0.1 | 10.8 | 11.9 |
| 44 22960 | East Providence | 34.3 | 47 096 | 786 | 1 373.1 | 84.6 | 7.8 | 1.4 | 1.9 | 0.2 | 4.1 | 15.2 |
| 44 54640 | Pawtucket | 22.5 | 71 170 | 464 | 3 163.1 | 59.0 | 15.4 | 0.9 | 1.9 | 0.4 | 19.7 | 25.6 |
| 44 59000 | Providence | 47.7 | 178 432 | 134 | 3 740.7 | 39.6 | 15.2 | 1.7 | 7.0 | 0.2 | 38.1 | 29.4 |
| 44 74300 | Warwick | 90.8 | 81 873 | 388 | 901.7 | 92.1 | 2.2 | 0.8 | 2.7 | 0.1 | 3.4 | 5.9 |
| 44 80780 | Woonsocket | 20.0 | 41 032 | 882 | 2 051.6 | 74.1 | 7.2 | 1.1 | 6.2 | 0.1 | 14.2 | 9.1 |
| 45 00000 | **SOUTH CAROLINA** | 77 856.8 | 4 723 723 | X | 60.7 | 65.2 | 28.5 | 0.8 | 1.6 | 0.1 | 5.1 | 4.8 |
| 45 00550 | Aiken | 53.6 | 29 884 | 1 219 | 557.5 | 66.5 | 29.0 | 0.7 | 2.3 | 0.1 | 2.6 | 5.6 |
| 45 01360 | Anderson | 37.8 | 26 708 | 1 364 | 706.6 | 61.2 | 34.6 | 0.7 | 1.1 | 0.1 | 4.1 | 4.7 |
| 45 13330 | Charleston | 282.3 | 125 583 | 205 | 444.9 | 69.7 | 25.8 | 0.6 | 2.1 | 0.2 | 2.9 | 4.5 |
| 45 16000 | Columbia | 342.4 | 131 686 | 190 | 384.6 | 50.8 | 42.7 | 0.7 | 2.8 | 0.2 | 4.3 | 4.8 |
| 45 25810 | Florence | 54.1 | 37 498 | 970 | 693.1 | 50.2 | 46.6 | 0.6 | 2.1 | 0.1 | 1.5 | 2.4 |
| 45 29815 | Goose Creek | 103.8 | 38 579 | 948 | 371.7 | 70.8 | 19.2 | 1.1 | 5.0 | 0.3 | 6.1 | 6.0 |
| 45 30850 | Greenville | 74.3 | 60 709 | 574 | 817.1 | 62.4 | 30.6 | 0.6 | 1.7 | 0.1 | 5.9 | 6.6 |
| 45 30985 | Greer | 53.5 | 26 645 | 1 369 | 498.0 | 65.7 | 18.0 | 0.5 | 2.5 | 0.1 | 14.5 | 11.8 |
| 45 34045 | Hilton Head Island | 107.1 | 38 366 | 953 | 358.2 | 75.8 | 7.6 | 0.3 | 1.1 | 0.0 | 15.8 | 14.6 |
| 45 48535 | Mount Pleasant | 116.8 | 71 875 | 460 | 615.4 | 90.2 | 5.4 | 0.4 | 2.0 | 0.1 | 2.7 | 4.3 |
| 45 49075 | Myrtle Beach | 60.4 | 28 292 | 1 282 | 468.4 | 69.8 | 14.7 | 1.0 | 2.3 | 0.3 | 13.7 | 17.1 |
| 45 50875 | North Charleston | 189.6 | 101 989 | 278 | 537.9 | 39.5 | 47.9 | 0.8 | 2.5 | 0.2 | 10.9 | 9.8 |
| 45 61405 | Rock Hill | 92.5 | 68 094 | 491 | 736.2 | 53.7 | 39.2 | 0.9 | 2.0 | 0.1 | 5.7 | 4.8 |
| 45 68290 | Spartanburg | 51.2 | 37 401 | 972 | 730.5 | 45.1 | 50.1 | 0.6 | 2.1 | 0.1 | 3.4 | 4.0 |
| 45 70270 | Summerville | 46.7 | 44 719 | 818 | 957.6 | 71.5 | 22.4 | 1.0 | 2.2 | 0.2 | 5.0 | 3.8 |
| 45 70405 | Sumter | 83.1 | 40 836 | 886 | 491.4 | 45.2 | 49.7 | 0.7 | 2.2 | 0.2 | 3.6 | 4.2 |
| 46 00000 | **SOUTH DAKOTA** | 196 349.6 | 833 354 | X | 4.2 | 86.4 | 1.7 | 9.7 | 1.2 | 0.1 | 2.7 | 2.4 |
| 46 00100 | Aberdeen | 40.2 | 26 791 | 1 359 | 666.4 | 92.7 | 1.1 | 4.5 | 1.5 | 0.2 | 1.6 | 1.0 |
| 46 52980 | Rapid City | 143.5 | 69 854 | 478 | 486.8 | 81.6 | 1.9 | 13.9 | 1.8 | 0.2 | 4.1 | 2.2 |
| 46 59020 | Sioux Falls | 189.0 | 159 908 | 149 | 846.1 | 86.8 | 5.2 | 3.3 | 2.2 | 0.1 | 4.4 | 6.3 |
| 47 00000 | **TENNESSEE** | 106 797.9 | 6 456 243 | X | 60.5 | 76.9 | 17.2 | 0.8 | 1.7 | 0.1 | 4.6 | 4.5 |
| 47 03440 | Bartlett | 69.0 | 55 945 | 644 | 810.8 | 78.3 | 16.5 | 0.5 | 3.1 | 0.1 | 2.7 | 3.6 |
| 47 08280 | Brentwood | 106.7 | 39 012 | 937 | 365.6 | 89.6 | 3.2 | 0.5 | 5.9 | 0.1 | 2.1 | 6.6 |
| 47 08540 | Bristol | 83.7 | 26 675 | 1 367 | 318.7 | 93.6 | 3.9 | 0.8 | 1.0 | 0.1 | 1.9 | 2.0 |
| 47 14000 | Chattanooga | 355.2 | 171 279 | 138 | 482.2 | 57.2 | 35.7 | 0.7 | 2.2 | 0.1 | 5.5 | 5.9 |
| 47 15160 | Clarksville | 252.8 | 142 519 | 179 | 563.8 | 64.4 | 24.7 | 1.4 | 3.5 | 0.7 | 9.3 | 6.0 |
| 47 15400 | Cleveland | 69.7 | 42 386 | 861 | 608.1 | 83.2 | 8.3 | 0.9 | 1.7 | 0.1 | 7.5 | 6.9 |
| 47 16420 | Collierville | 75.9 | 46 462 | 794 | 612.1 | 79.0 | 11.1 | 0.5 | 7.7 | 0.1 | 2.6 | 6.7 |
| 47 16540 | Columbia | 81.7 | 34 901 | 1 046 | 427.2 | 71.1 | 22.0 | 0.7 | 1.0 | 0.0 | 7.0 | 4.5 |
| 47 16920 | Cookeville | 84.6 | 31 010 | 1 173 | 366.5 | 87.1 | 4.1 | 0.9 | 2.4 | 0.1 | 7.0 | 5.2 |

1. Dry land or land partially or temporarily covered by water. 2. May be of any race.

# Table D. Cities — **Population**

| City | Under 5 years | 5 to 17 years | 18 to 24 years | 25 to 34 years | 35 to 44 years | 45 to 54 years | 55 to 64 years | 65 to 74 years | 75 years and over | Median age | Percent female | 2000 | 2010 | 2000–2010 | 2010–2012 |
|---|---|---|---|---|---|---|---|---|---|---|---|---|---|---|---|
| | 12 | 13 | 14 | 15 | 16 | 17 | 18 | 19 | 20 | 21 | 22 | 23 | 24 | 25 | 26 |
| **OREGON—Cont'd** | | | | | | | | | | | | | | | |
| Tigard | 6.8 | 17.4 | 8.0 | 14.6 | 14.6 | 15.2 | 12.2 | 5.9 | 5.4 | 37.4 | 51.0 | 41 223 | 48 085 | 16.5 | 3.5 |
| Tualatin | 7.3 | 19.6 | 8.4 | 15.3 | 15.7 | 15.2 | 11.5 | 4.1 | 2.9 | 34.6 | 50.9 | 22 791 | 26 049 | 14.3 | 2.6 |
| West Linn | 5.7 | 20.6 | 6.0 | 8.8 | 14.5 | 17.9 | 15.5 | 6.8 | 4.3 | 41.5 | 51.3 | 22 261 | 25 107 | 12.8 | 2.0 |
| **PENNSYLVANIA** | 5.7 | 16.2 | 9.9 | 11.9 | 12.7 | 15.3 | 12.8 | 7.7 | 7.7 | 40.1 | 51.3 | 12 281 054 | 12 702 379 | 3.4 | 0.5 |
| Allentown | 7.9 | 18.3 | 12.3 | 14.5 | 12.4 | 13.0 | 9.7 | 5.5 | 6.4 | 32.7 | 51.8 | 106 632 | 118 032 | 10.7 | 0.8 |
| Altoona | 6.4 | 16.2 | 10.4 | 12.4 | 12.2 | 14.0 | 12.6 | 7.8 | 7.8 | 38.9 | 52.0 | 49 523 | 46 321 | -6.5 | -0.4 |
| Bethel Park | 4.6 | 16.1 | 5.8 | 9.7 | 12.1 | 16.9 | 14.6 | 9.5 | 10.7 | 46.1 | 52.3 | 33 556 | 32 313 | -3.7 | 0.2 |
| Bethlehem | 5.6 | 14.3 | 15.6 | 13.7 | 11.1 | 12.4 | 11.0 | 6.8 | 9.4 | 35.7 | 51.9 | 71 329 | 74 982 | 5.1 | 0.2 |
| Chester | 8.1 | 19.1 | 16.0 | 12.8 | 11.0 | 12.5 | 10.1 | 5.3 | 5.1 | 29.9 | 52.8 | 36 854 | 33 972 | -7.8 | 0.2 |
| Easton | 6.8 | 15.7 | 17.6 | 14.1 | 12.7 | 13.3 | 9.5 | 5.1 | 5.1 | 31.9 | 49.6 | 26 263 | 26 800 | 2.0 | 0.6 |
| Erie | 7.5 | 16.4 | 14.1 | 14.1 | 11.4 | 12.9 | 10.6 | 5.9 | 7.0 | 33.2 | 51.7 | 103 717 | 101 786 | -1.9 | -0.7 |
| Harrisburg | 8.9 | 17.9 | 11.0 | 15.7 | 12.6 | 13.7 | 11.1 | 5.1 | 3.9 | 32.2 | 51.9 | 48 950 | 49 528 | 1.2 | -0.5 |
| Hazleton | 7.1 | 18.2 | 10.3 | 11.6 | 12.6 | 13.4 | 10.8 | 7.6 | 8.5 | 37.6 | 51.7 | 23 329 | 25 340 | 8.6 | -0.5 |
| Lancaster | 8.0 | 17.6 | 14.5 | 16.6 | 12.9 | 12.6 | 9.2 | 4.9 | 3.7 | 30.5 | 50.3 | 56 348 | 59 322 | 5.3 | 0.1 |
| Lebanon | 8.0 | 18.0 | 9.3 | 14.1 | 12.5 | 13.3 | 11.1 | 6.7 | 7.0 | 35.6 | 51.6 | 24 461 | 25 477 | 4.2 | 0.3 |
| Monroeville | 4.9 | 13.7 | 7.1 | 12.0 | 11.1 | 15.2 | 14.6 | 9.2 | 12.2 | 45.9 | 52.8 | 29 349 | 28 336 | -3.3 | 0.2 |
| Norristown | 8.9 | 17.3 | 11.3 | 18.6 | 13.5 | 12.3 | 8.9 | 4.8 | 4.3 | 31.2 | 50.2 | 31 282 | 34 324 | 9.7 | 0.3 |
| Philadelphia | 6.6 | 15.9 | 13.3 | 16.1 | 12.3 | 13.0 | 10.5 | 6.2 | 5.9 | 33.5 | 52.8 | 1 517 550 | 1 526 006 | 0.6 | 1.4 |
| Pittsburgh | 4.9 | 11.3 | 18.9 | 16.9 | 10.5 | 12.4 | 11.2 | 6.4 | 7.3 | 33.2 | 51.6 | 334 563 | 305 702 | -8.6 | 0.2 |
| Plum | 5.3 | 16.9 | 7.1 | 11.1 | 13.2 | 16.5 | 13.1 | 8.9 | 7.9 | 42.6 | 51.2 | 26 940 | 27 126 | 0.7 | 1.0 |
| Reading | 9.5 | 21.5 | 13.1 | 14.0 | 12.4 | 11.7 | 8.5 | 4.7 | 4.6 | 28.9 | 51.5 | 81 207 | 88 080 | 8.5 | 0.0 |
| Scranton | 6.1 | 14.4 | 13.9 | 12.7 | 11.3 | 13.3 | 12.0 | 7.2 | 9.2 | 37.9 | 51.8 | 76 415 | 76 089 | -0.4 | -0.4 |
| State College | 1.8 | 3.2 | 70.6 | 9.4 | 3.7 | 3.3 | 3.2 | 2.0 | 2.7 | 21.5 | 46.0 | 38 420 | 42 034 | 9.4 | -0.1 |
| Wilkes-Barre | 5.7 | 14.5 | 15.7 | 12.5 | 11.4 | 13.1 | 10.8 | 6.9 | 9.3 | 36.5 | 51.1 | 43 123 | 41 498 | -3.8 | -0.6 |
| Williamsport | 6.5 | 14.2 | 22.4 | 12.9 | 10.2 | 12.3 | 10.1 | 5.4 | 6.0 | 29.7 | 48.9 | 30 706 | 29 381 | -4.3 | 0.4 |
| York | 9.2 | 19.5 | 13.2 | 14.7 | 12.4 | 12.5 | 9.5 | 5.0 | 4.0 | 30.1 | 51.8 | 40 862 | 43 718 | 7.0 | -0.4 |
| **RHODE ISLAND** | 5.5 | 15.8 | 11.4 | 12.1 | 13.0 | 15.4 | 12.4 | 7.0 | 7.4 | 39.4 | 51.7 | 1 048 319 | 1 052 567 | 0.4 | -0.2 |
| Cranston | 5.0 | 15.4 | 9.1 | 12.7 | 13.9 | 16.0 | 12.5 | 6.8 | 8.5 | 40.8 | 50.6 | 79 269 | 80 387 | 1.4 | 0.2 |
| East Providence | 5.4 | 14.1 | 7.9 | 13.1 | 12.8 | 15.5 | 12.9 | 8.1 | 10.2 | 42.6 | 53.2 | 48 688 | 47 037 | -3.4 | 0.1 |
| Pawtucket | 7.0 | 16.3 | 9.9 | 14.5 | 14.0 | 14.9 | 10.7 | 6.2 | 6.4 | 36.7 | 52.1 | 72 958 | 71 148 | -2.5 | 0.0 |
| Providence | 6.9 | 16.4 | 20.3 | 16.2 | 12.2 | 11.0 | 8.3 | 4.3 | 4.4 | 28.5 | 51.8 | 173 618 | 178 036 | 2.5 | 0.2 |
| Warwick | 4.7 | 14.4 | 7.6 | 11.8 | 13.4 | 16.8 | 14.1 | 8.0 | 9.1 | 43.7 | 52.2 | 85 808 | 82 672 | -3.7 | -1.0 |
| Woonsocket | 7.6 | 16.4 | 9.3 | 14.5 | 13.1 | 14.5 | 11.4 | 6.1 | 7.1 | 36.8 | 51.6 | 43 224 | 41 186 | -4.7 | -0.4 |
| **SOUTH CAROLINA** | 6.5 | 16.8 | 10.3 | 12.8 | 13.0 | 14.3 | 12.6 | 8.0 | 5.7 | 37.9 | 51.4 | 4 012 012 | 4 625 364 | 15.3 | 2.1 |
| Aiken | 5.2 | 14.5 | 10.3 | 10.3 | 9.9 | 13.0 | 14.8 | 11.7 | 10.2 | 44.8 | 54.0 | 25 337 | 29 555 | 16.5 | 1.1 |
| Anderson | 7.7 | 15.7 | 12.1 | 12.3 | 11.5 | 12.0 | 10.7 | 7.5 | 10.4 | 36.8 | 55.5 | 25 514 | 26 367 | 4.6 | 1.3 |
| Charleston | 6.3 | 11.7 | 17.3 | 18.1 | 11.6 | 11.7 | 11.0 | 6.4 | 5.8 | 32.5 | 52.7 | 96 650 | 120 422 | 24.2 | 4.3 |
| Columbia | 5.4 | 11.5 | 26.1 | 17.5 | 10.9 | 11.0 | 8.9 | 4.4 | 4.3 | 28.1 | 48.5 | 116 278 | 129 765 | 11.2 | 1.5 |
| Florence | 7.3 | 17.2 | 8.8 | 13.5 | 13.4 | 13.4 | 12.4 | 7.5 | 6.5 | 37.4 | 54.5 | 30 248 | 37 114 | 22.5 | 1.0 |
| Goose Creek | 7.4 | 17.5 | 16.5 | 15.0 | 13.0 | 13.6 | 9.6 | 5.0 | 2.4 | 30.2 | 48.4 | 29 208 | 35 948 | 23.0 | 7.3 |
| Greenville | 6.5 | 12.9 | 14.0 | 17.3 | 13.1 | 12.7 | 10.8 | 6.2 | 6.6 | 34.6 | 51.9 | 56 002 | 59 140 | 4.3 | 2.7 |
| Greer | 8.5 | 18.1 | 8.6 | 16.3 | 15.0 | 13.0 | 9.5 | 5.9 | 5.1 | 33.9 | 52.5 | 16 843 | 25 646 | 51.5 | 3.9 |
| Hilton Head Island | 4.6 | 12.0 | 5.9 | 10.0 | 10.3 | 12.3 | 16.0 | 15.5 | 13.4 | 50.9 | 50.9 | 33 862 | 37 099 | 9.6 | 3.4 |
| Mount Pleasant | 6.0 | 18.2 | 6.2 | 13.5 | 16.0 | 15.4 | 12.6 | 6.7 | 5.6 | 39.1 | 51.9 | 47 609 | 67 866 | 42.5 | 5.9 |
| Myrtle Beach | 5.8 | 12.8 | 9.8 | 16.1 | 13.4 | 14.5 | 12.5 | 8.5 | 6.7 | 39.2 | 49.2 | 22 759 | 27 109 | 19.1 | 4.4 |
| North Charleston | 8.8 | 16.7 | 13.2 | 18.1 | 12.7 | 12.9 | 9.2 | 4.8 | 3.7 | 30.6 | 50.4 | 79 641 | 97 662 | 22.4 | 4.4 |
| Rock Hill | 7.4 | 17.0 | 14.7 | 15.1 | 13.4 | 12.3 | 9.7 | 5.4 | 5.0 | 31.9 | 54.0 | 49 765 | 66 520 | 32.9 | 2.4 |
| Spartanburg | 7.6 | 16.0 | 13.9 | 12.0 | 11.3 | 13.0 | 11.6 | 7.2 | 7.4 | 35.5 | 55.9 | 39 673 | 37 007 | -6.7 | 1.1 |
| Summerville | 7.4 | 19.6 | 8.8 | 14.6 | 14.4 | 13.8 | 10.9 | 5.7 | 4.8 | 34.7 | 52.8 | 27 752 | 43 023 | 56.4 | 3.9 |
| Sumter | 8.3 | 17.6 | 13.1 | 13.8 | 11.1 | 11.9 | 10.1 | 6.9 | 7.0 | 32.5 | 52.9 | 39 643 | 40 524 | 2.2 | 0.8 |
| **SOUTH DAKOTA** | 7.3 | 17.6 | 10.0 | 12.9 | 11.4 | 14.4 | 12.0 | 7.1 | 7.2 | 36.9 | 50.0 | 754 844 | 814 180 | 7.9 | 2.4 |
| Aberdeen | 7.0 | 15.2 | 12.8 | 13.5 | 10.6 | 13.2 | 11.2 | 6.8 | 9.6 | 36.4 | 52.4 | 24 658 | 26 091 | 5.8 | 2.7 |
| Rapid City | 7.5 | 16.4 | 10.7 | 14.7 | 11.1 | 13.6 | 11.6 | 7.1 | 7.4 | 35.6 | 50.5 | 59 607 | 67 969 | 14.0 | 2.8 |
| Sioux Falls | 8.0 | 16.6 | 10.6 | 16.8 | 12.9 | 13.6 | 10.5 | 5.4 | 5.5 | 33.6 | 50.4 | 123 975 | 153 890 | 24.1 | 3.9 |
| **TENNESSEE** | 6.4 | 17.1 | 9.6 | 13.0 | 13.5 | 14.6 | 12.4 | 7.7 | 5.8 | 38.0 | 51.3 | 5 689 283 | 6 346 113 | 11.5 | 1.7 |
| Bartlett | 5.3 | 20.0 | 7.5 | 10.0 | 14.2 | 16.7 | 13.8 | 7.1 | 5.4 | 40.4 | 51.7 | 40 543 | 54 614 | 34.7 | 2.4 |
| Brentwood | 5.3 | 25.7 | 4.8 | 4.8 | 14.8 | 19.8 | 13.9 | 6.7 | 4.3 | 41.9 | 50.9 | 23 445 | 37 060 | 58.1 | 5.3 |
| Bristol | 5.4 | 15.2 | 8.7 | 11.3 | 13.1 | 14.7 | 13.5 | 9.0 | 9.1 | 42.3 | 52.4 | 24 821 | 26 711 | 7.6 | -0.1 |
| Chattanooga | 6.4 | 14.5 | 12.0 | 14.4 | 12.0 | 13.7 | 12.4 | 7.3 | 7.3 | 37.3 | 52.4 | 155 554 | 167 971 | 7.8 | 2.0 |
| Clarksville | 9.6 | 18.9 | 13.7 | 18.8 | 13.0 | 11.3 | 7.5 | 4.2 | 3.0 | 28.6 | 51.3 | 103 455 | 132 957 | 28.5 | 7.2 |
| Cleveland | 6.5 | 15.4 | 15.2 | 13.2 | 12.0 | 12.4 | 10.6 | 7.6 | 7.2 | 34.8 | 52.4 | 37 192 | 41 285 | 11.0 | 2.7 |
| Collierville | 5.7 | 23.2 | 6.5 | 8.9 | 15.8 | 18.8 | 12.1 | 5.4 | 3.6 | 39.2 | 51.2 | 31 872 | 45 604 | 37.9 | 1.9 |
| Columbia | 7.6 | 17.1 | 9.7 | 14.3 | 11.7 | 13.7 | 11.6 | 6.8 | 7.5 | 36.0 | 53.2 | 33 055 | 34 681 | 4.9 | 0.6 |
| Cookeville | 5.8 | 12.8 | 23.9 | 13.5 | 10.1 | 10.5 | 9.8 | 6.8 | 6.8 | 29.7 | 50.1 | 23 923 | 30 435 | 27.2 | 1.9 |

# Table D. Cities — **Households, Group Quarters, Crime, and Education**

| City | Households, 2010 | | | | Persons in group quarters, 2010 | | | | Serious crimes known to police,[2] 2011 | | | | Educational attainment, 2007–2011 | | |
|---|---|---|---|---|---|---|---|---|---|---|---|---|---|---|---|
| | | | Percent | | | Institutional | | | Total | | Rate[3] | | | Attainment[4] (percent) | |
| | Number | Persons per house-hold | Female family house-holder[1] | One-person | Total | Total | Persons in nursing facilities | Non-institu-tional | Number | Rate[3] | Violent | Property | Population age 25 and older | High school graduate or less | Bachelor's degree or more |
| | 27 | 28 | 29 | 30 | 31 | 32 | 33 | 34 | 35 | 36 | 37 | 38 | 39 | 40 | 41 |
| **OREGON—Cont'd** | | | | | | | | | | | | | | | |
| Tigard | 19 157 | 2.49 | 10.0 | 26.9 | 347 | 111 | 78 | 236 | 1 779 | 3 665 | 113 | 3 551 | 32 669 | 26.6 | 39.9 |
| Tualatin | 10 000 | 2.60 | 11.4 | 24.6 | 87 | 45 | 45 | 42 | 744 | 2 826 | 163 | 2 662 | 16 721 | 27.9 | 42.6 |
| West Linn | 9 523 | 2.62 | 9.0 | 20.6 | 127 | 63 | 60 | 64 | 278 | 1 096 | 39 | 1 056 | 17 341 | 12.6 | 56.2 |
| **PENNSYLVANIA** | 5 018 904 | 2.45 | 12.2 | 28.6 | 426 113 | 197 112 | 87 775 | 229 001 | 328 419 | 2 577 | 355 | 2 222 | 8 611 136 | 49.7 | 26.7 |
| Allentown | 42 804 | 2.64 | 20.6 | 29.9 | 5 070 | 2 089 | 885 | 2 981 | 5 222 | 4 410 | 546 | 3 864 | 71 448 | 59.6 | 16.4 |
| Altoona | 19 301 | 2.34 | 15.2 | 32.8 | 1 189 | 452 | 443 | 737 | 1 233 | 2 653 | 308 | 2 346 | 31 309 | 59.3 | 15.2 |
| Bethel Park | 13 659 | 2.35 | 7.6 | 29.0 | 217 | 184 | 184 | 33 | 353 | 1 089 | 80 | 1 009 | 23 021 | 32.3 | 43.4 |
| Bethlehem | 29 365 | 2.34 | 15.3 | 33.0 | 6 265 | 955 | 882 | 5 310 | 2 081 | 2 767 | 291 | 2 475 | 47 582 | 48.1 | 27.1 |
| Chester | 11 662 | 2.64 | 35.6 | 31.2 | 3 151 | 1 328 | 143 | 1 823 | 2 395 | 7 028 | 3 148 | 3 879 | 19 940 | 68.3 | 9.4 |
| Easton | 9 307 | 2.55 | 18.8 | 30.9 | 3 087 | 1 093 | 311 | 1 994 | 928 | 3 452 | 357 | 3 095 | 16 435 | 58.1 | 18.5 |
| Erie | 40 913 | 2.36 | 18.5 | 34.9 | 5 244 | 1 578 | 715 | 3 666 | 4 169 | 4 083 | 422 | 3 661 | 63 591 | 57.2 | 20.1 |
| Harrisburg | 20 605 | 2.36 | 25.6 | 39.4 | 987 | 265 | 89 | 722 | 3 212 | 6 465 | 1 403 | 5 062 | 31 281 | 59.7 | 17.6 |
| Hazleton | 9 798 | 2.54 | 19.8 | 31.9 | 410 | 384 | 218 | 26 | 568 | 2 234 | 460 | 1 774 | 16 406 | 66.6 | 12.2 |
| Lancaster | 21 793 | 2.58 | 21.4 | 31.6 | 3 189 | 1 214 | 121 | 1 975 | 3 518 | 5 912 | 847 | 5 065 | 34 974 | 63.8 | 16.1 |
| Lebanon | 10 358 | 2.42 | 17.9 | 34.8 | 364 | 106 | 102 | 258 | 730 | 2 856 | 340 | 2 516 | 16 472 | 73.2 | 9.8 |
| Monroeville | 12 612 | 2.21 | 10.5 | 33.8 | 520 | 457 | 457 | 63 | 396 | 1 391 | 190 | 1 201 | 21 264 | 33.6 | 39.2 |
| Norristown | 11 963 | 2.79 | 23.0 | 29.5 | 947 | 224 | 224 | 723 | 1 364 | 3 961 | 1 066 | 2 895 | 22 013 | 62.5 | 16.8 |
| Philadelphia | 599 736 | 2.45 | 22.5 | 34.1 | 57 383 | 19 376 | 7 877 | 38 007 | 77 885 | 5 088 | 1 193 | 3 894 | 973 241 | 55.2 | 22.6 |
| Pittsburgh | 136 217 | 2.07 | 14.9 | 41.7 | 24 329 | 6 967 | 2 242 | 17 362 | 12 539 | 4 063 | 802 | 3 261 | 201 032 | 41.8 | 34.4 |
| Plum | 10 886 | 2.48 | 9.4 | 24.5 | 132 | 132 | 122 | 0 | 318 | 1 169 | 360 | 808 | 18 931 | 38.9 | 32.4 |
| Reading | 29 979 | 2.85 | 26.3 | 28.6 | 2 545 | 485 | 265 | 2 060 | 4 059 | 4 594 | 858 | 3 736 | 49 770 | 71.3 | 9.4 |
| Scranton | 30 069 | 2.35 | 15.2 | 35.3 | 5 472 | 2 380 | 1 444 | 3 092 | 2 782 | 3 645 | 296 | 3 349 | 49 649 | 57.0 | 19.2 |
| State College | 12 610 | 2.30 | 3.8 | 33.6 | 13 071 | 194 | 155 | 12 877 | 950 | 1 678 | 101 | 1 578 | 9 838 | 18.6 | 64.7 |
| Wilkes-Barre | 16 874 | 2.28 | 16.5 | 38.3 | 3 065 | 1 115 | 420 | 1 950 | 1 696 | 4 074 | 512 | 3 562 | 26 386 | 58.2 | 14.8 |
| Williamsport | 11 646 | 2.27 | 16.4 | 35.8 | 2 896 | 408 | 143 | 2 488 | 1 354 | 4 594 | 339 | 4 254 | 17 190 | 55.0 | 18.0 |
| York | 16 253 | 2.62 | 25.3 | 32.5 | 1 121 | 113 | 0 | 1 008 | 2 452 | 5 591 | 1 644 | 3 947 | 25 495 | 71.5 | 10.1 |
| **RHODE ISLAND** | 413 600 | 2.44 | 13.5 | 29.6 | 42 663 | 12 932 | 8 420 | 29 731 | 30 743 | 2 924 | 248 | 2 677 | 708 587 | 43.4 | 30.6 |
| Cranston | 31 012 | 2.45 | 13.6 | 29.6 | 4 523 | 4 004 | 224 | 519 | 2 148 | 2 675 | 130 | 2 546 | 56 384 | 45.1 | 29.2 |
| East Providence | 20 201 | 2.29 | 13.6 | 33.2 | 800 | 759 | 680 | 41 | 912 | 1 941 | 138 | 1 803 | 34 823 | 51.0 | 23.5 |
| Pawtucket | 29 022 | 2.43 | 18.9 | 31.7 | 524 | 357 | 335 | 167 | 2 601 | 3 660 | 391 | 3 269 | 48 573 | 56.6 | 17.7 |
| Providence | 62 718 | 2.60 | 20.8 | 31.7 | 15 086 | 1 200 | 1 152 | 13 886 | 9 582 | 5 388 | 640 | 4 748 | 99 968 | 50.0 | 29.1 |
| Warwick | 35 234 | 2.33 | 10.9 | 31.8 | 660 | 502 | 494 | 158 | 2 279 | 2 760 | 102 | 2 658 | 61 205 | 42.0 | 28.6 |
| Woonsocket | 17 062 | 2.37 | 17.8 | 33.4 | 802 | 568 | 568 | 234 | 1 505 | 3 659 | 423 | 3 236 | 27 439 | 59.6 | 13.8 |
| **SOUTH CAROLINA** | 1 801 181 | 2.49 | 15.6 | 26.5 | 139 154 | 63 765 | 19 020 | 75 389 | 209 445 | 4 476 | 572 | 3 904 | 3 031 432 | 47.3 | 24.2 |
| Aiken | 12 773 | 2.20 | 13.2 | 32.7 | 1 382 | 469 | 427 | 913 | 1 413 | 4 731 | 388 | 4 342 | 20 133 | 28.3 | 44.5 |
| Anderson | 11 080 | 2.25 | 20.8 | 36.3 | 1 751 | 716 | 577 | 1 035 | 2 247 | 8 323 | 785 | 7 538 | 17 516 | 53.7 | 19.7 |
| Charleston | 52 341 | 2.18 | 13.1 | 34.6 | 5 770 | 300 | 291 | 5 470 | 4 162 | 3 426 | 329 | 3 097 | 76 538 | 27.6 | 46.7 |
| Columbia | 45 666 | 2.18 | 17.1 | 38.0 | 29 919 | 7 777 | 920 | 22 142 | 8 710 | 6 660 | 820 | 5 840 | 74 670 | 34.6 | 38.6 |
| Florence | 14 979 | 2.43 | 21.2 | 29.6 | 654 | 389 | 384 | 265 | 3 585 | 9 563 | 939 | 8 624 | 23 930 | 43.1 | 29.2 |
| Goose Creek | 12 356 | 2.72 | 14.0 | 18.5 | 2 322 | 0 | 0 | 2 322 | 951 | 2 616 | 256 | 2 360 | 20 497 | 38.8 | 25.8 |
| Greenville | 25 599 | 2.08 | 14.7 | 41.7 | 5 129 | 1 393 | 208 | 3 736 | 3 973 | 6 724 | 817 | 5 906 | 38 612 | 36.6 | 39.2 |
| Greer | 10 012 | 2.52 | 16.3 | 27.9 | 272 | 130 | 130 | 142 | 876 | 3 394 | 391 | 3 002 | 16 626 | 47.5 | 25.7 |
| Hilton Head Island | 16 535 | 2.23 | 6.8 | 28.3 | 202 | 202 | 202 | 0 | NA | NA | NA | NA | 29 348 | 26.0 | 50.4 |
| Mount Pleasant | 27 742 | 2.43 | 8.1 | 26.5 | 568 | 544 | 544 | 24 | 1 404 | 2 046 | 233 | 1 813 | 45 106 | 15.4 | 59.4 |
| Myrtle Beach | 12 113 | 2.22 | 12.8 | 35.8 | 217 | 22 | 22 | 195 | 4 634 | 16 897 | 1 615 | 15 282 | 18 741 | 46.1 | 27.0 |
| North Charleston | 36 915 | 2.54 | 21.7 | 28.8 | 3 859 | 2 139 | 283 | 1 720 | 6 409 | 6 500 | 688 | 5 812 | 59 064 | 52.2 | 17.1 |
| Rock Hill | 25 966 | 2.43 | 18.8 | 30.3 | 3 005 | 612 | 442 | 2 393 | 3 416 | 5 104 | 622 | 4 483 | 39 027 | 42.3 | 28.1 |
| Spartanburg | 15 184 | 2.27 | 24.3 | 35.9 | 2 489 | 302 | 175 | 2 187 | 3 521 | 9 403 | 1 757 | 7 646 | 23 548 | 44.5 | 28.3 |
| Summerville | 16 866 | 2.55 | 15.4 | 25.3 | 318 | 251 | 160 | 67 | 1 531 | 3 488 | 271 | 3 217 | 27 589 | 35.2 | 28.9 |
| Sumter | 15 633 | 2.48 | 21.1 | 30.9 | 1 790 | 364 | 330 | 1 426 | 2 699 | 6 584 | 837 | 5 747 | 24 772 | 43.2 | 25.8 |
| **SOUTH DAKOTA** | 322 282 | 2.42 | 9.7 | 29.4 | 34 050 | 14 797 | 7 005 | 19 253 | 17 073 | 2 072 | 254 | 1 818 | 525 090 | 42.3 | 25.8 |
| Aberdeen | 11 418 | 2.18 | 9.5 | 36.9 | 1 191 | 433 | 351 | 758 | 558 | 2 113 | 269 | 1 844 | 16 806 | 42.9 | 24.3 |
| Rapid City | 28 586 | 2.29 | 13.1 | 32.9 | 2 471 | 1 331 | 491 | 1 140 | 3 417 | 4 968 | 640 | 4 328 | 43 805 | 35.8 | 29.7 |
| Sioux Falls | 61 707 | 2.40 | 10.9 | 30.6 | 6 085 | 3 336 | 982 | 2 749 | 5 173 | 3 321 | 285 | 3 036 | 98 072 | 36.3 | 32.3 |
| **TENNESSEE** | 2 493 552 | 2.48 | 13.9 | 26.9 | 153 472 | 84 371 | 33 041 | 69 101 | 269 205 | 4 204 | 608 | 3 596 | 4 205 976 | 50.1 | 23.0 |
| Bartlett | 19 456 | 2.77 | 10.8 | 17.3 | 703 | 688 | 244 | 15 | 917 | 1 664 | 196 | 1 468 | 35 639 | 31.6 | 33.0 |
| Brentwood | 12 170 | 3.02 | 5.4 | 11.0 | 349 | 312 | 275 | 37 | 392 | 1 048 | 48 | 1 000 | 23 224 | 11.7 | 67.8 |
| Bristol | 11 456 | 2.26 | 12.9 | 32.8 | 833 | 226 | 218 | 607 | 1 305 | 4 844 | 423 | 4 420 | 18 796 | 50.5 | 19.7 |
| Chattanooga | 70 749 | 2.26 | 17.3 | 35.3 | 7 562 | 3 067 | 1 212 | 4 495 | 12 158 | 7 186 | 874 | 6 313 | 112 083 | 46.2 | 25.6 |
| Clarksville | 49 439 | 2.63 | 16.3 | 23.7 | 2 921 | 904 | 419 | 2 017 | 5 114 | 3 813 | 659 | 3 154 | 75 401 | 40.6 | 22.9 |
| Cleveland | 16 107 | 2.40 | 14.3 | 30.0 | 2 703 | 786 | 430 | 1 917 | 2 705 | 6 494 | 1 049 | 5 444 | 25 403 | 44.8 | 24.4 |
| Collierville | 15 179 | 2.89 | 9.1 | 14.8 | 62 | 62 | 62 | 0 | 745 | 1 679 | 104 | 1 576 | 27 097 | 21.9 | 50.7 |
| Columbia | 14 012 | 2.41 | 18.8 | 30.0 | 863 | 795 | 462 | 68 | 1 712 | 4 892 | 869 | 4 024 | 22 460 | 56.3 | 15.3 |
| Cookeville | 12 471 | 2.25 | 12.0 | 33.9 | 2 410 | 431 | 201 | 1 979 | 1 853 | 6 034 | 570 | 5 464 | 17 615 | 47.4 | 28.1 |

1. No spouse present.  2. Data for serious crimes have not been adjusted for underreporting. This may affect comparability between geographic areas and over time.  3. Per 100,000 population estimated by the FBI.  4. Persons 25 years old and over.

**1116 OR(Tigard)—TN(Cookeville)**                                                                 Items 27—41

| City | Money income, 2007-2011 | | | | | Housing units, 2010 | | | Occupied Housing units 2007-2011 | | | | |
|---|---|---|---|---|---|---|---|---|---|---|---|---|---|
| | | Households | | | | | | | | Owner-occupied | | Median owner costs as a percent of income | |
| | Per capita income[1] (dollars) | Median income | Percent with income of $200,000 or more | Percent with income of less than $25,000 | Families with income below poverty (percent) | Total | Percent change, 2000-2010 | Vacant units for sale or rent[2] | Total | Percent | Median value[3] (dollars) | With a mortgage[4] | Without a mortgage[5] |
| | 42 | 43 | 44 | 45 | 46 | 47 | 48 | 49 | 50 | 51 | 52 | 53 | 54 |
| OREGON—Cont'd | | | | | | | | | | | | | |
| Tigard | 33 749 | 62 521 | 6.1 | 17.1 | 5.5 | 20 068 | 15.4 | 911 | 19 081 | 62.1 | 324 000 | 26.3 | 12.4 |
| Tualatin | 29 987 | 60 818 | 4.2 | 17.0 | 8.6 | 10 528 | 14.2 | 528 | 9 886 | 55.2 | 335 800 | 25.2 | 10.0 |
| West Linn | 43 350 | 92 342 | 10.2 | 9.6 | 3.0 | 10 035 | 14.8 | 512 | 9 779 | 80.8 | 406 700 | 26.9 | 12.9 |
| PENNSYLVANIA | 27 824 | 51 651 | 3.8 | 23.8 | 8.8 | 5 567 315 | 6.0 | 548 411 | 4 952 566 | 70.6 | 163 200 | 23.7 | 13.8 |
| Allentown | 17 663 | 35 737 | 0.9 | 36.7 | 21.6 | 46 921 | 2.1 | 4 117 | 43 089 | 48.2 | 143 800 | 26.9 | 16.0 |
| Altoona | 19 449 | 35 052 | 0.9 | 36.0 | 15.2 | 21 179 | -2.3 | 1 878 | 19 275 | 66.2 | 81 900 | 21.3 | 12.8 |
| Bethel Park | 32 371 | 65 797 | 3.4 | 11.9 | 1.7 | 14 311 | 3.2 | 652 | 12 917 | 79.7 | 152 700 | 21.8 | 12.9 |
| Bethlehem | 23 442 | 45 631 | 1.9 | 28.6 | 13.6 | 31 221 | 5.4 | 1 856 | 29 326 | 54.2 | 178 500 | 25.0 | 14.6 |
| Chester | 14 646 | 27 661 | 0.8 | 45.4 | 28.0 | 13 745 | -8.2 | 2 083 | 11 917 | 40.1 | 71 700 | 25.6 | 14.7 |
| Easton | 19 812 | 39 488 | 1.7 | 32.8 | 20.7 | 10 356 | -1.8 | 1 049 | 9 403 | 51.4 | 141 400 | 28.0 | 20.9 |
| Erie | 18 525 | 32 445 | 1.2 | 39.5 | 20.0 | 44 790 | -0.4 | 3 877 | 40 377 | 54.8 | 82 800 | 23.8 | 14.3 |
| Harrisburg | 19 061 | 32 949 | 0.4 | 40.9 | 28.5 | 24 269 | -0.3 | 3 664 | 21 542 | 39.8 | 83 800 | 24.5 | 15.0 |
| Hazleton | 18 642 | 33 964 | 1.1 | 35.8 | 16.4 | 11 409 | -1.0 | 1 611 | 9 848 | 57.1 | 94 200 | 25.3 | 15.8 |
| Lancaster | 16 212 | 33 115 | 0.6 | 39.7 | 25.5 | 23 377 | 1.5 | 1 584 | 22 173 | 44.4 | 98 500 | 25.4 | 13.7 |
| Lebanon | 17 983 | 33 120 | 0.5 | 39.9 | 23.6 | 11 278 | 0.5 | 920 | 10 810 | 47.4 | 88 900 | 20.2 | 13.0 |
| Monroeville | 31 327 | 59 023 | 3.3 | 19.5 | 4.1 | 13 496 | 2.6 | 884 | 12 291 | 69.5 | 126 400 | 21.3 | 11.9 |
| Norristown | 21 435 | 43 309 | 1.0 | 27.8 | 14.4 | 13 420 | -0.8 | 1 457 | 12 886 | 43.1 | 154 600 | 27.2 | 17.4 |
| Philadelphia | 21 671 | 36 957 | 2.1 | 36.6 | 20.5 | 670 171 | 1.2 | 70 435 | 578 125 | 54.9 | 140 700 | 25.9 | 15.6 |
| Pittsburgh | 25 619 | 37 161 | 3.3 | 36.3 | 15.4 | 156 165 | -4.4 | 19 948 | 134 001 | 50.6 | 87 800 | 21.4 | 14.8 |
| Plum | 30 474 | 66 680 | 3.6 | 14.2 | 3.8 | 11 494 | 8.2 | 608 | 10 528 | 81.2 | 137 200 | 22.0 | 11.6 |
| Reading | 13 350 | 27 416 | 0.2 | 45.5 | 33.8 | 34 208 | -0.3 | 4 229 | 31 304 | 44.7 | 68 800 | 27.8 | 15.2 |
| Scranton | 19 681 | 36 968 | 0.9 | 34.4 | 15.3 | 33 853 | -4.2 | 3 784 | 29 898 | 54.2 | 108 200 | 23.6 | 17.2 |
| State College | 13 775 | 23 355 | 2.4 | 52.0 | 12.3 | 13 007 | 4.2 | 397 | 12 289 | 18.9 | 255 100 | 21.4 | 10.0 |
| Wilkes-Barre | 17 444 | 30 348 | 0.3 | 42.5 | 18.9 | 19 595 | -3.4 | 2 721 | 16 697 | 50.4 | 78 700 | 23.8 | 16.0 |
| Williamsport | 17 849 | 30 662 | 1.1 | 43.5 | 20.5 | 12 864 | -4.9 | 1 218 | 11 630 | 41.6 | 94 500 | 23.6 | 14.3 |
| York | 14 669 | 29 814 | 0.6 | 42.2 | 32.6 | 18 496 | -0.2 | 2 243 | 16 023 | 44.0 | 83 800 | 27.1 | 16.9 |
| RHODE ISLAND | 29 685 | 55 975 | 4.3 | 23.4 | 8.9 | 463 388 | 5.4 | 49 788 | 410 475 | 62.1 | 270 600 | 27.3 | 16.0 |
| Cranston | 28 496 | 58 442 | 4.0 | 21.1 | 6.5 | 33 117 | 3.3 | 2 105 | 30 296 | 66.7 | 249 300 | 27.9 | 18.7 |
| East Providence | 28 813 | 49 408 | 2.9 | 27.1 | 6.8 | 21 440 | 0.6 | 1 239 | 20 560 | 58.4 | 239 000 | 27.8 | 15.8 |
| Pawtucket | 21 753 | 39 628 | 1.3 | 33.1 | 15.8 | 32 055 | 0.7 | 3 033 | 29 063 | 46.1 | 217 400 | 30.1 | 18.3 |
| Providence | 21 628 | 38 922 | 3.6 | 35.8 | 22.6 | 71 530 | 5.3 | 8 812 | 61 797 | 36.7 | 230 500 | 31.3 | 16.0 |
| Warwick | 31 596 | 59 973 | 2.8 | 19.1 | 4.8 | 37 730 | 1.7 | 2 496 | 35 351 | 74.0 | 228 500 | 26.9 | 16.9 |
| Woonsocket | 21 316 | 39 329 | 0.9 | 34.2 | 18.2 | 19 214 | 2.4 | 2 152 | 16 659 | 42.0 | 214 500 | 29.5 | 15.9 |
| SOUTH CAROLINA | 23 854 | 44 587 | 2.5 | 28.3 | 12.7 | 2 137 683 | 21.9 | 336 502 | 1 758 732 | 69.8 | 137 000 | 23.2 | 11.4 |
| Aiken | 33 578 | 52 487 | 5.3 | 23.4 | 11.9 | 14 162 | 25.3 | 1 389 | 12 476 | 67.8 | 173 300 | 20.4 | 10.0 |
| Anderson | 19 194 | 30 166 | 1.3 | 44.3 | 23.7 | 12 938 | 7.3 | 1 858 | 10 952 | 50.0 | 129 500 | 24.0 | 11.5 |
| Charleston | 31 287 | 50 938 | 5.2 | 26.5 | 12.3 | 59 522 | 34.8 | 7 181 | 49 741 | 53.4 | 259 700 | 26.0 | 13.4 |
| Columbia | 24 603 | 38 995 | 4.2 | 33.4 | 16.1 | 52 471 | 13.9 | 6 805 | 46 496 | 47.5 | 161 100 | 22.9 | 11.0 |
| Florence | 26 270 | 42 719 | 2.9 | 30.1 | 14.9 | 16 665 | 27.5 | 1 686 | 14 526 | 59.8 | 148 300 | 20.9 | 10.0 |
| Goose Creek | 23 697 | 61 524 | 1.0 | 13.4 | 6.4 | 13 484 | 42.4 | 1 128 | 11 495 | 67.9 | 172 200 | 24.0 | 10.0 |
| Greenville | 29 835 | 40 925 | 5.1 | 32.3 | 15.3 | 29 418 | 7.5 | 3 819 | 25 173 | 46.0 | 188 200 | 22.1 | 11.2 |
| Greer | 23 591 | 42 454 | 0.7 | 30.4 | 11.7 | 11 127 | 48.5 | 1 115 | 10 191 | 62.0 | 138 600 | 23.3 | 12.4 |
| Hilton Head Island | 47 611 | 71 005 | 11.2 | 14.8 | 3.6 | 33 306 | 35.0 | 16 771 | 17 106 | 76.4 | 485 100 | 31.9 | 11.9 |
| Mount Pleasant | 40 808 | 76 688 | 9.4 | 13.2 | 4.3 | 30 674 | 52.4 | 2 932 | 26 008 | 74.3 | 355 200 | 25.9 | 11.1 |
| Myrtle Beach | 26 393 | 36 963 | 4.0 | 34.2 | 19.7 | 23 262 | 59.2 | 11 149 | 11 748 | 54.3 | 175 000 | 28.6 | 12.4 |
| North Charleston | 19 454 | 39 182 | 1.1 | 31.7 | 18.0 | 42 219 | 25.5 | 5 304 | 35 316 | 48.7 | 145 300 | 26.6 | 13.6 |
| Rock Hill | 22 610 | 42 629 | 2.0 | 29.9 | 13.5 | 29 159 | 42.4 | 3 193 | 25 057 | 54.9 | 135 300 | 23.7 | 12.5 |
| Spartanburg | 21 304 | 33 375 | 2.7 | 42.1 | 21.4 | 17 516 | -1.1 | 2 332 | 15 042 | 52.9 | 119 200 | 22.0 | 11.5 |
| Summerville | 26 822 | 54 843 | 2.9 | 19.2 | 9.6 | 18 557 | 64.9 | 1 691 | 16 093 | 65.9 | 186 100 | 23.1 | 12.2 |
| Sumter | 21 764 | 37 409 | 2.4 | 32.1 | 16.2 | 18 150 | 12.6 | 2 517 | 15 584 | 53.3 | 123 900 | 22.0 | 13.0 |
| SOUTH DAKOTA | 24 925 | 48 010 | 2.4 | 24.2 | 8.8 | 363 438 | 12.4 | 41 156 | 318 466 | 68.7 | 127 000 | 22.0 | 11.2 |
| Aberdeen | 23 365 | 43 479 | 1.8 | 29.4 | 5.5 | 12 158 | 8.1 | 740 | 11 024 | 63.9 | 123 600 | 21.4 | 13.7 |
| Rapid City | 25 893 | 44 740 | 2.9 | 24.4 | 11.0 | 30 254 | 20.4 | 1 668 | 27 741 | 57.8 | 151 500 | 23.7 | 11.8 |
| Sioux Falls | 27 997 | 51 831 | 3.3 | 21.2 | 8.5 | 66 283 | 28.1 | 4 576 | 60 891 | 62.1 | 149 600 | 21.7 | 10.0 |
| TENNESSEE | 24 197 | 43 989 | 2.8 | 28.3 | 12.7 | 2 812 133 | 15.3 | 318 581 | 2 457 997 | 69.0 | 137 200 | 23.4 | 11.1 |
| Bartlett | 30 429 | 75 988 | 3.3 | 7.5 | 3.6 | 20 143 | 43.9 | 687 | 18 513 | 87.2 | 174 200 | 22.7 | 11.6 |
| Brentwood | 56 358 | 127 596 | 28.6 | 3.9 | 1.5 | 12 577 | 58.5 | 407 | 11 987 | 93.5 | 483 700 | 21.3 | 10.0 |
| Bristol | 22 141 | 35 320 | 2.5 | 36.5 | 12.7 | 12 773 | 10.9 | 1 317 | 11 706 | 67.8 | 100 900 | 25.0 | 12.5 |
| Chattanooga | 23 491 | 36 689 | 2.6 | 34.5 | 18.0 | 79 607 | 10.4 | 8 858 | 69 947 | 54.8 | 134 700 | 23.9 | 12.2 |
| Clarksville | 21 527 | 47 483 | 1.0 | 23.9 | 12.0 | 54 815 | 36.9 | 5 376 | 47 736 | 58.1 | 129 400 | 22.5 | 10.0 |
| Cleveland | 21 825 | 37 502 | 2.8 | 35.2 | 16.2 | 17 841 | 8.4 | 1 734 | 15 701 | 49.3 | 151 300 | 23.2 | 12.2 |
| Collierville | 39 788 | 102 298 | 13.4 | 8.1 | 3.5 | 15 781 | 46.7 | 602 | 14 064 | 83.6 | 277 100 | 22.9 | 10.3 |
| Columbia | 20 306 | 37 685 | 1.6 | 34.1 | 15.2 | 15 906 | 10.7 | 1 894 | 14 176 | 60.0 | 116 000 | 23.8 | 13.3 |
| Cookeville | 19 405 | 29 616 | 2.1 | 43.9 | 18.5 | 13 706 | 26.9 | 1 235 | 12 130 | 46.1 | 154 600 | 23.5 | 10.8 |

1. Based on population estimated by the American Community Survey.    2. Includes units rented or sold but not occupied.    3. Specified owner-occupied units; $1,000,000 represents $1,000,000 or more.    4. 50.0 represents 50 percent or more.    5. 10.0 represents 10 percent or less.

# Table D. Cities — Housing, Labor Force, and Employment

| City | Percent renter occupied | Median gross rent[1] | Median rent as a percent of income[2] | Percent with no vehicle available | Percent who lived in the same house one year ago | Percent who lived outside this city one year ago | Civilian labor force, 2012 Total | Percent change, 2011–2012 | Unemployment Total | Rate[3] | Population age 16 and older | In labor force | Full-year full-time worker | Households with no workers (percent) |
|---|---|---|---|---|---|---|---|---|---|---|---|---|---|---|
| | 55 | 56 | 57 | 58 | 59 | 60 | 61 | 62 | 63 | 64 | 65 | 66 | 67 | 68 |
| **OREGON—Cont'd** | | | | | | | | | | | | | | |
| Tigard | 37.9 | 872 | 29.8 | 6.3 | 82.4 | 14.3 | 26 946 | 1.3 | 1 839 | 6.8 | 37 920 | 71.6 | 43.8 | 20.6 |
| Tualatin | 44.8 | 924 | 30.2 | 6.1 | 84.4 | 12.3 | 15 080 | 1.6 | 977 | 6.5 | 19 894 | 72.3 | 45.3 | 16.9 |
| West Linn | 19.2 | 1 068 | 28.5 | 2.6 | 87.6 | 8.3 | 13 499 | 1.3 | 866 | 6.4 | 19 703 | 70.0 | 43.1 | 19.0 |
| **PENNSYLVANIA** | 29.4 | 770 | 29.7 | 11.5 | 87.7 | 9.1 | 6 486 578 | 1.8 | 513 171 | 7.9 | 10 209 810 | 63.2 | 39.4 | 28.9 |
| Allentown | 51.8 | 820 | 36.3 | 20.9 | 76.6 | 9.7 | 58 012 | 3.3 | 6 696 | 11.5 | 89 317 | 61.5 | 34.6 | 32.6 |
| Altoona | 33.8 | 530 | 31.0 | 13.5 | 85.3 | 7.1 | 22 869 | 1.2 | 1 842 | 8.1 | 37 003 | 58.7 | 35.1 | 37.1 |
| Bethel Park | 20.3 | 846 | 26.4 | 4.4 | 92.0 | 6.5 | 18 074 | 3.2 | 1 003 | 5.5 | 26 124 | 65.8 | 42.1 | 26.2 |
| Bethlehem | 45.8 | 865 | 30.8 | 14.6 | 77.3 | 12.2 | 36 638 | 2.8 | 3 477 | 9.5 | 61 857 | 59.4 | 34.0 | 31.5 |
| Chester | 59.9 | 781 | 35.3 | 37.5 | 80.9 | 10.9 | 14 069 | 1.9 | 1 948 | 13.8 | 26 469 | 53.2 | 27.3 | 38.3 |
| Easton | 48.6 | 841 | 29.9 | 19.5 | 70.4 | 16.6 | 13 151 | 2.7 | 1 279 | 9.7 | 22 005 | 57.2 | 31.2 | 27.7 |
| Erie | 45.2 | 609 | 32.0 | 19.3 | 80.1 | 7.0 | 48 488 | 1.8 | 4 267 | 8.8 | 79 728 | 61.4 | 33.2 | 33.2 |
| Harrisburg | 60.2 | 731 | 32.9 | 26.6 | 76.3 | 11.1 | 23 351 | 2.0 | 2 500 | 10.7 | 37 728 | 64.7 | 39.4 | 33.5 |
| Hazleton | 42.9 | 611 | 30.2 | 18.4 | 83.8 | 8.2 | 12 419 | 3.7 | 1 791 | 14.4 | 19 681 | 58.4 | 35.0 | 36.8 |
| Lancaster | 55.6 | 696 | 34.8 | 24.2 | 79.5 | 12.2 | 27 832 | 1.7 | 2 695 | 9.7 | 45 401 | 61.9 | 35.0 | 30.1 |
| Lebanon | 52.6 | 601 | 33.1 | 22.8 | 82.3 | 8.3 | 13 204 | 1.7 | 1 157 | 8.8 | 19 745 | 65.3 | 36.9 | 37.2 |
| Monroeville | 30.5 | 861 | 27.7 | 7.5 | 90.8 | 7.5 | 16 016 | 3.3 | 1 021 | 6.4 | 23 800 | 63.0 | 41.3 | 29.7 |
| Norristown | 56.9 | 953 | 32.7 | 21.8 | 87.1 | 6.6 | 17 753 | 1.3 | 1 520 | 8.6 | 26 756 | 72.8 | 44.8 | 23.9 |
| Philadelphia | 45.1 | 850 | 34.1 | 33.7 | 85.9 | 4.4 | 656 173 | 2.0 | 70 795 | 10.8 | 1 210 107 | 59.2 | 34.7 | 35.0 |
| Pittsburgh | 49.4 | 724 | 31.1 | 26.0 | 79.4 | 11.1 | 156 038 | 3.4 | 11 808 | 7.6 | 261 481 | 61.1 | 35.5 | 33.0 |
| Plum | 18.8 | 823 | 24.7 | 3.8 | 92.3 | 6.3 | 15 601 | 2.7 | 1 028 | 6.6 | 21 773 | 69.4 | 44.8 | 22.5 |
| Reading | 55.3 | 681 | 35.9 | 27.3 | 75.3 | 9.7 | 36 459 | 1.8 | 4 178 | 11.5 | 64 046 | 60.3 | 31.3 | 36.7 |
| Scranton | 45.8 | 637 | 29.1 | 15.9 | 83.4 | 8.8 | 36 601 | 0.9 | 3 461 | 9.5 | 62 540 | 58.7 | 34.7 | 33.4 |
| State College | 81.1 | 848 | 50.0 | 21.7 | 38.8 | 41.9 | 18 861 | 4.3 | 1 160 | 6.2 | 40 638 | 42.7 | 13.5 | 33.0 |
| Wilkes-Barre | 49.6 | 612 | 31.1 | 22.9 | 78.1 | 13.8 | 19 534 | 1.8 | 2 121 | 10.9 | 34 068 | 56.7 | 31.9 | 37.7 |
| Williamsport | 58.4 | 604 | 33.6 | 19.4 | 77.5 | 13.6 | 15 305 | 5.9 | 1 362 | 8.9 | 23 823 | 60.4 | 30.0 | 34.3 |
| York | 56.0 | 662 | 33.7 | 25.5 | 73.3 | 12.1 | 20 572 | 3.0 | 2 656 | 12.9 | 32 666 | 62.1 | 30.7 | 36.5 |
| **RHODE ISLAND** | 37.9 | 901 | 30.5 | 9.4 | 86.6 | 9.3 | 560 381 | -1.1 | 58 293 | 10.4 | 855 960 | 66.3 | 38.7 | 28.1 |
| Cranston | 33.3 | 967 | 33.1 | 5.7 | 88.0 | 8.7 | 42 060 | -0.2 | 4 417 | 10.5 | 65 941 | 62.6 | 37.9 | 27.3 |
| East Providence | 41.6 | 823 | 28.4 | 9.1 | 88.3 | 5.3 | 25 169 | -1.1 | 2 853 | 11.3 | 38 880 | 66.5 | 40.7 | 31.9 |
| Pawtucket | 53.9 | 807 | 31.4 | 16.3 | 86.2 | 7.3 | 36 897 | 0.4 | 4 552 | 12.3 | 56 589 | 67.7 | 39.3 | 31.0 |
| Providence | 63.3 | 913 | 32.7 | 19.4 | 75.2 | 12.2 | 81 406 | -0.4 | 10 117 | 12.4 | 141 276 | 64.9 | 33.4 | 30.2 |
| Warwick | 26.0 | 990 | 30.1 | 6.1 | 91.2 | 5.2 | 46 655 | -0.7 | 4 402 | 9.4 | 69 333 | 68.1 | 41.6 | 27.5 |
| Woonsocket | 58.0 | 763 | 29.5 | 15.3 | 87.0 | 5.0 | 20 968 | -0.8 | 2 578 | 12.3 | 32 568 | 61.3 | 37.6 | 34.2 |
| **SOUTH CAROLINA** | 30.2 | 728 | 30.3 | 7.1 | 84.7 | 12.9 | 2 167 195 | 1.4 | 197 083 | 9.1 | 3 624 311 | 62.4 | 38.2 | 29.4 |
| Aiken | 32.2 | 756 | 29.0 | 8.9 | 83.4 | 12.0 | 13 754 | -0.5 | 1 073 | 7.8 | 24 406 | 53.1 | 33.4 | 36.5 |
| Anderson | 50.0 | 637 | 36.0 | 15.0 | 73.5 | 15.1 | 10 424 | 0.4 | 1 080 | 10.4 | 21 507 | 56.9 | 30.1 | 40.3 |
| Charleston | 46.6 | 918 | 33.0 | 11.3 | 77.4 | 14.6 | 62 456 | 3.3 | 4 181 | 6.7 | 97 927 | 66.8 | 42.8 | 25.3 |
| Columbia | 52.5 | 769 | 33.7 | 12.5 | 64.4 | 25.6 | 54 426 | 2.8 | 5 039 | 9.3 | 110 422 | 65.0 | 31.6 | 26.2 |
| Florence | 40.2 | 637 | 32.2 | 12.3 | 83.6 | 8.9 | 16 677 | 1.7 | 1 425 | 8.5 | 28 447 | 64.5 | 40.6 | 28.2 |
| Goose Creek | 32.1 | 1 009 | 29.2 | 2.0 | 75.2 | 21.9 | 15 375 | 4.4 | 1 181 | 7.7 | 26 959 | 73.4 | 40.3 | 14.6 |
| Greenville | 54.0 | 697 | 28.8 | 11.1 | 75.1 | 17.1 | 30 365 | 2.1 | 2 085 | 6.9 | 48 261 | 65.8 | 39.4 | 27.9 |
| Greer | 38.0 | 696 | 30.2 | 7.7 | 82.3 | 11.2 | 11 999 | 3.6 | 880 | 7.3 | 19 152 | 67.3 | 42.7 | 27.3 |
| Hilton Head Island | 23.6 | 1 136 | 31.1 | 5.6 | 88.6 | 7.4 | 16 288 | 6.7 | 913 | 5.6 | 32 297 | 55.9 | 32.9 | 39.3 |
| Mount Pleasant | 25.7 | 1 214 | 31.1 | 3.7 | 80.8 | 10.9 | 37 976 | 4.3 | 1 864 | 4.9 | 50 810 | 70.8 | 47.7 | 19.7 |
| Myrtle Beach | 45.7 | 809 | 36.8 | 11.3 | 82.6 | 12.4 | 14 532 | 5.9 | 1 447 | 10.0 | 22 011 | 67.5 | 36.7 | 29.0 |
| North Charleston | 51.3 | 808 | 32.4 | 12.1 | 77.9 | 15.5 | 45 228 | 2.8 | 4 013 | 8.9 | 73 865 | 68.1 | 40.2 | 23.2 |
| Rock Hill | 45.1 | 748 | 30.6 | 8.4 | 76.2 | 12.7 | 32 735 | -2.6 | 4 246 | 13.0 | 50 468 | 70.2 | 42.2 | 24.2 |
| Spartanburg | 47.1 | 624 | 33.0 | 16.0 | 79.9 | 11.4 | 15 755 | 3.1 | 1 663 | 10.6 | 29 795 | 58.0 | 30.4 | 38.1 |
| Summerville | 34.1 | 909 | 29.1 | 4.5 | 80.7 | 16.5 | 22 690 | 4.0 | 1 416 | 6.2 | 32 505 | 66.6 | 41.3 | 25.3 |
| Sumter | 46.7 | 676 | 27.0 | 13.3 | 85.6 | 9.7 | 15 256 | -0.2 | 1 482 | 9.7 | 31 068 | 61.1 | 33.6 | 31.6 |
| **SOUTH DAKOTA** | 31.3 | 595 | 26.1 | 5.5 | 84.2 | 9.3 | 445 728 | 2.5 | 19 628 | 4.4 | 630 184 | 69.5 | 45.6 | 23.9 |
| Aberdeen | 36.1 | 488 | 22.6 | 9.5 | 85.7 | 7.1 | 15 306 | 2.6 | 575 | 3.8 | 20 655 | 70.3 | 46.2 | 26.3 |
| Rapid City | 42.2 | 711 | 28.5 | 6.6 | 75.4 | 11.1 | 36 621 | 3.0 | 1 793 | 4.9 | 52 649 | 69.0 | 40.3 | 25.7 |
| Sioux Falls | 37.9 | 685 | 27.0 | 6.5 | 81.2 | 6.9 | 90 060 | 2.2 | 3 835 | 4.3 | 117 875 | 75.0 | 51.4 | 19.7 |
| **TENNESSEE** | 31.0 | 707 | 30.2 | 6.2 | 84.1 | 10.2 | 3 113 562 | 0.8 | 249 400 | 8.0 | 4 978 954 | 62.7 | 39.0 | 28.9 |
| Bartlett | 12.8 | 1 176 | 30.9 | 1.5 | 92.4 | 6.4 | 28 651 | -0.8 | 1 849 | 6.5 | 41 747 | 70.4 | 48.1 | 17.0 |
| Brentwood | 6.5 | 1 867 | 24.6 | 0.9 | 91.9 | 5.8 | 18 700 | 4.2 | 978 | 5.2 | 26 303 | 64.3 | 41.7 | 15.3 |
| Bristol | 32.2 | 574 | 29.8 | 7.8 | 81.2 | 10.3 | 13 030 | -0.5 | 866 | 6.6 | 21 894 | 54.6 | 34.8 | 36.7 |
| Chattanooga | 45.2 | 676 | 30.0 | 12.4 | 79.7 | 9.0 | 78 533 | 1.2 | 6 635 | 8.4 | 135 047 | 63.5 | 37.1 | 32.3 |
| Clarksville | 41.9 | 772 | 28.1 | 4.3 | 70.7 | 18.4 | 57 980 | 2.5 | 4 598 | 7.9 | 96 829 | 68.5 | 34.6 | 21.5 |
| Cleveland | 50.7 | 655 | 30.8 | 7.1 | 74.5 | 12.5 | 20 243 | 6.9 | 1 613 | 8.0 | 32 841 | 61.4 | 33.2 | 29.9 |
| Collierville | 16.4 | 991 | 28.4 | 1.7 | 87.9 | 9.4 | 21 763 | 0.6 | 1 384 | 6.4 | 31 534 | 70.7 | 46.9 | 13.4 |
| Columbia | 40.0 | 657 | 31.0 | 7.8 | 80.1 | 10.9 | 14 964 | -1.8 | 1 502 | 10.0 | 26 505 | 63.1 | 39.1 | 30.3 |
| Cookeville | 53.9 | 580 | 32.1 | 5.1 | 75.9 | 13.0 | 15 442 | -1.0 | 1 141 | 7.4 | 25 260 | 54.6 | 28.7 | 37.0 |

1. $2,000 represents $2,000 or more.    2. 50.0 represents 50 percent or more.    3. Percent of civilian labor force.    4. Persons 16 years old and over.

## Table D. Cities — Construction, Wholesale Trade, and Retail Trade

| City | Value of residential construction authorized by building permits, 2011 | | | Wholesale trade,[1] 2007 | | | | Retail trade,[2] 2007 | | | |
|---|---|---|---|---|---|---|---|---|---|---|---|
| | New construction ($1,000) | Number of housing units | Percent single family | Number of establishments | Number of employees | Sales (mil dol) | Annual payroll (mil dol) | Number of establishments | Number of employees | Sales (mil dol) | Annual payroll (mil dol) |
| | 69 | 70 | 71 | 72 | 73 | 74 | 75 | 76 | 77 | 78 | 79 |
| **OREGON—Cont'd** | | | | | | | | | | | |
| Tigard | 24 797 | 88 | 100.0 | 177 | 2 928 | 2 572.7 | 187.6 | 345 | 7 479 | 1 807.4 | 188.2 |
| Tualatin | 5 070 | 19 | 100.0 | 110 | 2 197 | 971.4 | 109.5 | 124 | 2 241 | 483.3 | 55.0 |
| West Linn | 18 031 | 59 | 100.0 | 24 | 78 | 106.6 | 4.1 | 50 | 550 | 113.6 | 11.9 |
| **PENNSYLVANIA** | 2 545 786 | 14 967 | 78.8 | 13 161 | 200 151 | 142 859.2 | 10 100.7 | 46 532 | 672 042 | 166 842.8 | 14 862.3 |
| Allentown | 5 358 | 31 | 100.0 | 150 | 2 980 | 1 576.9 | 218.5 | 368 | 5 329 | 1 299.7 | 126.0 |
| Altoona | 560 | 4 | 100.0 | 46 | 682 | 272.0 | 22.6 | 217 | 4 426 | 917.1 | 84.1 |
| Bethel Park | 2 374 | 8 | 100.0 | 37 | 357 | 123.7 | 13.4 | 168 | 3 786 | 684.6 | 69.9 |
| Bethlehem | 2 325 | 20 | 90.0 | 64 | D | D | D | 215 | 3 236 | 696.9 | 71.6 |
| Chester | 180 | 2 | 100.0 | 22 | 232 | 114.3 | 10.5 | 55 | 345 | 94.5 | 9.4 |
| Easton | 5 049 | 58 | 74.1 | 22 | 478 | 238.9 | 24.5 | 94 | 1 098 | 268.4 | 26.6 |
| Erie | 2 395 | 15 | 40.0 | 108 | 1 541 | 646.0 | 65.3 | 336 | 4 931 | 945.9 | 100.3 |
| Harrisburg | 2 644 | 12 | 100.0 | 52 | 2 143 | 2 551.3 | 93.5 | 214 | 2 871 | 560.9 | 57.1 |
| Hazleton | 0 | 0 | 0.0 | 32 | 477 | 199.0 | 21.0 | 145 | 1 748 | 540.3 | 38.5 |
| Lancaster | 902 | 8 | 100.0 | 64 | 868 | 412.4 | 31.5 | 339 | 5 062 | 950.9 | 101.1 |
| Lebanon | 220 | 1 | 100.0 | 19 | 232 | 95.0 | 7.2 | 120 | 1 263 | 232.6 | 26.2 |
| Monroeville | 2 040 | 8 | 100.0 | 50 | 542 | 242.5 | 24.4 | 314 | 6 621 | 1 497.4 | 127.2 |
| Norristown | 190 | 6 | 0.0 | 50 | 755 | 399.5 | 42.5 | 80 | 601 | 168.5 | 18.8 |
| Philadelphia | 192 715 | 1 552 | 28.7 | 1 067 | 18 338 | 11 566.1 | 956.3 | 4 420 | 50 225 | 11 167.8 | 1 158.1 |
| Pittsburgh | 62 579 | 284 | 100.0 | 396 | 6 948 | 7 097.2 | 353.4 | 1 161 | 16 455 | 3 413.0 | 367.6 |
| Plum | 6 893 | 40 | 100.0 | 32 | 350 | 178.0 | 14.2 | 52 | 558 | 121.2 | 14.1 |
| Reading | 0 | 0 | 0.0 | 60 | 1 233 | 569.3 | 60.1 | 225 | 2 954 | 733.6 | 69.0 |
| Scranton | 2 420 | 14 | 100.0 | 100 | 1 973 | 844.5 | 73.2 | 341 | 4 370 | 957.6 | 94.5 |
| State College | 20 | 0 | 0.0 | 9 | 17 | 10.8 | 1.0 | 164 | 2 560 | 363.1 | 39.7 |
| Wilkes-Barre | 275 | 1 | 100.0 | 51 | 581 | 230.2 | 24.4 | 249 | 5 134 | 1 878.7 | 113.6 |
| Williamsport | 200 | 10 | 0.0 | 40 | 795 | 363.6 | 26.3 | 114 | 1 524 | 270.6 | 29.4 |
| York | 680 | 5 | 100.0 | 70 | 911 | 786.0 | 45.1 | 134 | 1 624 | 328.9 | 38.0 |
| **RHODE ISLAND** | 129 276 | 700 | 81.6 | 1 277 | 18 128 | 9 182.8 | 914.9 | 4 080 | 50 865 | 12 286.5 | 1 215.4 |
| Cranston | 3 462 | 27 | 100.0 | 142 | 2 191 | 1 223.1 | 110.7 | 314 | 4 726 | 1 050.9 | 109.2 |
| East Providence | 581 | 8 | 62.5 | 87 | 1 474 | 885.4 | 75.7 | 147 | 2 058 | 554.2 | 53.7 |
| Pawtucket | 1 362 | 8 | 50.0 | 70 | 753 | 291.6 | 31.2 | 194 | 1 765 | 468.1 | 45.2 |
| Providence | 1 820 | 20 | 60.0 | 195 | 1 785 | 1 001.7 | 89.1 | 660 | 7 461 | 1 474.0 | 156.0 |
| Warwick | 1 808 | 17 | 100.0 | 161 | 1 720 | 774.5 | 84.1 | 484 | 8 503 | 2 153.7 | 211.9 |
| Woonsocket | 369 | 3 | 100.0 | 42 | 480 | 192.8 | 23.4 | 148 | 1 885 | 441.9 | 43.0 |
| **SOUTH CAROLINA** | 2 760 219 | 15 542 | 82.7 | 4 323 | 58 524 | 40 498.0 | 2 599.4 | 18 886 | 231 685 | 54 298.4 | 4 878.1 |
| Aiken | 9 297 | 83 | 100.0 | 23 | D | D | D | 229 | 2 711 | 529.5 | 49.6 |
| Anderson | 2 666 | 39 | 84.6 | 44 | 478 | 178.0 | 14.9 | 315 | 4 231 | 761.9 | 78.4 |
| Charleston | 73 441 | 615 | 63.7 | 106 | 1 362 | 856.2 | 67.2 | 796 | 10 386 | 2 183.7 | 228.3 |
| Columbia | 40 928 | 251 | 79.3 | 173 | 2 737 | 1 449.0 | 124.0 | 723 | 12 683 | 2 720.2 | 265.8 |
| Florence | NA | NA | NA | 49 | 946 | 366.4 | 40.1 | 364 | 5 512 | 1 173.1 | 106.2 |
| Goose Creek | 26 418 | 199 | 100.0 | 12 | 447 | 201.4 | 22.4 | 84 | 1 439 | 336.5 | 30.3 |
| Greenville | 17 641 | 78 | 84.6 | 178 | 3 685 | 4 957.4 | 197.9 | 713 | 10 133 | 2 356.7 | 221.1 |
| Greer | 12 632 | 112 | 100.0 | 42 | 335 | 145.1 | 16.3 | 152 | 2 450 | 737.4 | 59.3 |
| Hilton Head Island | 25 853 | 69 | 59.4 | 57 | 227 | 95.9 | 12.3 | 326 | 3 375 | 736.0 | 82.4 |
| Mount Pleasant | 119 477 | 822 | 32.7 | 66 | 260 | 121.2 | 13.0 | 366 | 5 072 | 1 016.2 | 106.7 |
| Myrtle Beach | 47 154 | 193 | 96.9 | 81 | 591 | 234.9 | 22.3 | 606 | 7 762 | 1 773.1 | 171.9 |
| North Charleston | 48 810 | 612 | 49.0 | 215 | 4 229 | 2 186.1 | 198.8 | 599 | 9 752 | 2 321.2 | 222.8 |
| Rock Hill | 28 112 | 147 | 67.3 | 58 | 718 | 425.8 | 33.8 | 320 | 4 361 | 1 059.8 | 89.4 |
| Spartanburg | 2 837 | 12 | 100.0 | 67 | 749 | 640.5 | 28.2 | 372 | 5 963 | 1 251.1 | 117.5 |
| Summerville | 33 373 | 150 | 100.0 | 43 | 358 | 133.4 | 15.5 | 206 | 3 142 | 751.9 | 63.4 |
| Sumter | NA | NA | NA | 33 | 347 | 120.8 | 13.9 | 313 | 4 079 | 826.3 | 74.9 |
| **SOUTH DAKOTA** | 391 886 | 2 813 | 69.7 | 1 248 | 13 402 | 11 400.5 | 550.8 | 4 172 | 50 842 | 12 266.2 | 1 045.3 |
| Aberdeen | 13 310 | 174 | 54.0 | 42 | 600 | 1 121.6 | 25.4 | 176 | 2 761 | 622.7 | 59.9 |
| Rapid City | 33 672 | 212 | 51.9 | 137 | 1 725 | 889.4 | 67.1 | 496 | 7 339 | 1 855.7 | 167.8 |
| Sioux Falls | 101 637 | 824 | 62.5 | 282 | 4 460 | 2 681.5 | 207.3 | 775 | 14 756 | 3 875.9 | 334.2 |
| **TENNESSEE** | 2 353 489 | 14 977 | 76.9 | 6 282 | 99 238 | 80 116.5 | 4 593.4 | 24 234 | 320 739 | 77 547.3 | 7 244.6 |
| Bartlett | 31 252 | 231 | 37.7 | 60 | 1 035 | 472.6 | 57.6 | 151 | 3 196 | 986.7 | 88.2 |
| Brentwood | 86 803 | 232 | 100.0 | 61 | 848 | 505.7 | 49.3 | 172 | 2 949 | 931.0 | 84.3 |
| Bristol | 1 481 | 17 | 47.1 | 48 | 741 | 455.7 | 45.9 | 140 | 2 079 | 610.6 | 51.7 |
| Chattanooga | 35 735 | 285 | 70.9 | 416 | 5 506 | 2 799.8 | 251.2 | 1 188 | 17 322 | 4 054.0 | 395.5 |
| Clarksville | 136 818 | 1 506 | 66.1 | 62 | 562 | 320.1 | 24.2 | 478 | 7 524 | 1 753.2 | 170.7 |
| Cleveland | 10 228 | 103 | 46.6 | 35 | D | D | D | 320 | 3 756 | 977.7 | 90.1 |
| Collierville | 34 843 | 103 | 100.0 | 53 | 734 | 510.9 | 40.3 | 186 | 3 698 | 800.2 | 88.5 |
| Columbia | 3 594 | 32 | 100.0 | 39 | 515 | 194.3 | 24.1 | 246 | 3 073 | 743.0 | 67.0 |
| Cookeville | 23 092 | 186 | 38.7 | 55 | 472 | 300.4 | 16.7 | 295 | 3 940 | 979.2 | 89.8 |

1. Merchant wholesalers except manufacturers' sales branches and offices.  2. Establishments with payroll.

# Table D. Cities — **Real Estate, Professional Services, and Manufacturing**

| City | Real estate and rental and leasing, 2007 | | | | Professional, scientific, and technical services,[1] 2007 | | | | Manufacturing, 2007 | | | |
|---|---|---|---|---|---|---|---|---|---|---|---|---|
| | Number of establish-ments | Number of employees | Receipts (mil dol) | Annual payroll (mil dol) | Number of establish-ments | Number of employees | Receipts (mil dol) | Annual payroll (mil dol) | Number of establish-ments | Number of employees | Receipts (mil dol) | Annual payroll (mil dol) |
| | 80 | 81 | 82 | 83 | 84 | 85 | 86 | 87 | 88 | 89 | 90 | 91 |
| OREGON—Cont'd | | | | | | | | | | | | |
| Tigard | 144 | 799 | 287.7 | 34.9 | 365 | 4 087 | 445.4 | 216.6 | 108 | 2 596 | D | 129.7 |
| Tualatin | 41 | 773 | 123.1 | 26.7 | 92 | D | D | D | 128 | 7 068 | 2 007.1 | 331.1 |
| West Linn | 46 | 103 | 20.9 | 3.1 | 125 | 365 | 38.1 | 15.2 | NA | NA | NA | NA |
| PENNSYLVANIA | 9 904 | 68 954 | 13 602.6 | 2 611.8 | 29 534 | 292 791 | 45 888.3 | 18 184.2 | 15 406 | 650 804 | 234 840.4 | 29 433.0 |
| Allentown | 98 | 603 | 95.1 | 17.0 | 223 | D | D | D | 184 | 3 350 | 779.3 | 135.5 |
| Altoona | 37 | 213 | 40.8 | 5.3 | 101 | 924 | 78.2 | 32.7 | 51 | 1 060 | 227.6 | 35.1 |
| Bethel Park | 31 | 153 | 55.5 | 3.6 | 96 | 374 | 48.6 | 17.1 | 41 | 522 | 79.6 | 16.7 |
| Bethlehem | 55 | 286 | 50.0 | 7.5 | 187 | 1 196 | 185.2 | 71.1 | 65 | 5 383 | 1 509.9 | 286.6 |
| Chester | 11 | 54 | 8.4 | 1.2 | 19 | D | D | D | 29 | 1 625 | D | 108.5 |
| Easton | 19 | 71 | 14.1 | 1.6 | 79 | 329 | 34.4 | 12.1 | 26 | 1 076 | 299.7 | 50.5 |
| Erie | 64 | 406 | 45.2 | 12.1 | 194 | D | D | D | 158 | 6 486 | 1 595.3 | 284.4 |
| Harrisburg | 36 | 238 | 210.7 | 13.4 | 282 | 3 327 | 641.9 | 216.3 | 43 | 1 269 | 348.0 | 48.5 |
| Hazleton | 27 | 340 | 64.7 | 6.7 | 54 | 257 | 21.4 | 8.8 | 53 | 2 977 | 1 063.3 | 113.2 |
| Lancaster | 52 | 278 | 77.5 | 9.2 | 230 | D | D | D | 95 | 5 270 | 1 517.8 | 234.6 |
| Lebanon | 29 | 169 | 25.3 | 4.7 | 52 | D | D | D | 50 | 1 749 | 381.8 | 55.9 |
| Monroeville | 47 | 309 | 55.0 | 10.3 | 114 | 3 036 | 662.6 | 199.5 | 18 | 622 | 119.1 | 31.4 |
| Norristown | 26 | 125 | 23.2 | 4.0 | 94 | D | D | D | 31 | 827 | 185.5 | 28.2 |
| Philadelphia | 1 088 | 9 813 | 1 956.1 | 433.9 | 2 703 | 44 302 | 9 243.3 | 3 533.1 | 946 | 32 672 | 18 069.4 | 1 396.7 |
| Pittsburgh | 433 | 3 813 | 681.0 | 170.9 | 1 539 | D | D | D | 341 | 8 408 | 2 535.0 | 362.8 |
| Plum | 16 | 76 | 5.5 | 2.3 | 39 | 329 | 49.5 | 24.1 | 33 | 546 | 137.0 | 20.4 |
| Reading | 53 | 360 | 46.7 | 10.5 | 137 | D | D | D | 116 | 8 043 | 2 783.0 | 424.7 |
| Scranton | 49 | 347 | 32.4 | 9.1 | 210 | D | D | D | 89 | 3 023 | 662.4 | 110.9 |
| State College | 58 | 486 | 78.4 | 13.3 | 112 | 714 | 86.6 | 35.9 | NA | NA | NA | NA |
| Wilkes-Barre | 28 | 214 | 47.7 | 7.5 | 132 | D | D | D | 35 | 1 440 | 315.1 | 58.4 |
| Williamsport | 26 | 81 | 10.3 | 1.8 | 81 | 769 | 54.6 | 22.8 | 55 | 4 329 | 1 418.0 | 178.5 |
| York | 33 | 257 | 32.9 | 8.3 | 164 | D | D | D | 89 | 5 749 | 2 800.8 | 284.6 |
| RHODE ISLAND | 1 233 | 6 493 | 1 462.8 | 227.2 | 3 096 | 22 732 | 2 777.8 | 1 173.9 | 1 831 | 53 718 | 12 061.5 | 2 374.8 |
| Cranston | 96 | 616 | 90.1 | 17.8 | 238 | 1 598 | 181.8 | 68.1 | 192 | 4 815 | 1 606.7 | 214.0 |
| East Providence | 68 | 383 | 462.5 | 17.7 | 148 | 1 408 | 163.5 | 61.0 | 101 | 3 128 | 740.2 | 126.8 |
| Pawtucket | 55 | 263 | 33.7 | 8.8 | 114 | D | D | D | 163 | 4 805 | 912.4 | 204.9 |
| Providence | 218 | 1 458 | 244.9 | 53.6 | 799 | 7 799 | 1 057.1 | 512.3 | 303 | 5 828 | 1 050.5 | 214.2 |
| Warwick | 128 | 1 219 | 213.8 | 44.9 | 346 | 1 958 | 252.8 | 92.5 | 174 | 4 581 | 1 414.1 | 185.5 |
| Woonsocket | 39 | 161 | 20.4 | 4.0 | 48 | 260 | 40.3 | 11.9 | 59 | 1 306 | 192.6 | 45.2 |
| SOUTH CAROLINA | 5 473 | 30 417 | 5 194.1 | 989.8 | 9 459 | 74 372 | 9 343.3 | 3 622.6 | 4 335 | 242 153 | 93 977.5 | 10 061.5 |
| Aiken | 67 | 266 | 37.3 | 6.5 | 117 | D | D | D | 23 | D | D | D |
| Anderson | 60 | 240 | 44.5 | 7.3 | 143 | D | D | D | 59 | 3 230 | 860.3 | 126.8 |
| Charleston | 297 | 1 593 | 263.2 | 57.6 | 608 | 4 331 | 688.8 | 265.4 | 61 | 1 024 | 409.9 | 43.7 |
| Columbia | 262 | 2 385 | 616.0 | 92.9 | 865 | D | D | D | 93 | 3 888 | D | 203.4 |
| Florence | 76 | 439 | 61.8 | 10.2 | 127 | D | D | D | 21 | D | D | D |
| Goose Creek | 32 | 434 | 51.2 | 9.3 | 62 | 699 | 107.1 | 26.8 | 14 | 1 025 | 666.6 | 62.4 |
| Greenville | 245 | 1 822 | 429.6 | 73.8 | 728 | 6 866 | 1 376.5 | 450.7 | 107 | 4 053 | 978.4 | 162.0 |
| Greer | 37 | 191 | 27.9 | 4.4 | 70 | 273 | 24.2 | 9.6 | 37 | 5 333 | D | D |
| Hilton Head Island | 250 | 2 482 | 306.3 | 98.3 | 263 | 1 287 | 193.2 | 91.3 | NA | NA | NA | NA |
| Mount Pleasant | 187 | 507 | 136.1 | 18.7 | 354 | D | D | D | NA | NA | NA | NA |
| Myrtle Beach | 256 | 2 495 | 441.3 | 81.8 | 227 | 1 281 | 162.3 | 62.9 | 47 | 1 561 | D | 71.1 |
| North Charleston | 152 | 1 278 | 221.9 | 37.0 | 292 | D | D | D | 138 | 7 832 | 3 944.9 | 369.0 |
| Rock Hill | 87 | 459 | 66.8 | 12.4 | 168 | D | D | D | 57 | 3 000 | 1 145.1 | 139.1 |
| Spartanburg | 103 | 532 | 79.8 | 22.3 | 217 | D | D | D | 42 | D | D | D |
| Summerville | 78 | 214 | 40.2 | 5.8 | 106 | 503 | 41.3 | 15.7 | 27 | D | D | D |
| Sumter | 62 | 240 | 28.5 | 5.5 | 110 | 520 | 43.2 | 12.7 | 35 | 1 661 | 345.6 | 60.3 |
| SOUTH DAKOTA | 888 | 3 844 | 523.9 | 90.3 | 1 735 | 10 073 | 1 093.4 | 385.9 | 1 052 | 40 961 | 13 051.1 | 1 539.3 |
| Aberdeen | 53 | D | D | D | 70 | 364 | 34.4 | 13.5 | 32 | D | D | D |
| Rapid City | 134 | 637 | 106.0 | 15.5 | 258 | D | D | D | 100 | 2 575 | 623.6 | 90.9 |
| Sioux Falls | 202 | 1 288 | 214.6 | 38.7 | 460 | D | D | D | 160 | 10 329 | 3 113.0 | 428.1 |
| TENNESSEE | 6 087 | 37 737 | 6 950.4 | 1 243.0 | 11 278 | D | D | D | 6 752 | 369 165 | 140 447.8 | 15 165.6 |
| Bartlett | 44 | 242 | 96.6 | 5.5 | 110 | 741 | 104.5 | 37.4 | 33 | 937 | 299.3 | 39.4 |
| Brentwood | 115 | 739 | 121.1 | 25.6 | 344 | 3 706 | 627.9 | 274.2 | NA | NA | NA | NA |
| Bristol | 38 | 151 | 27.7 | 4.1 | 66 | 491 | 44.0 | 21.1 | 51 | D | 1 445.1 | 110.2 |
| Chattanooga | 314 | 2 049 | 326.2 | 93.6 | 620 | D | D | D | 370 | 18 580 | 6 159.7 | 798.8 |
| Clarksville | 139 | 559 | 109.1 | 14.9 | 150 | D | D | D | 53 | 3 604 | 1 827.2 | 145.7 |
| Cleveland | 68 | 378 | 82.1 | 10.7 | 131 | D | D | D | 92 | D | 4 222.7 | D |
| Collierville | 49 | 211 | 36.0 | 5.1 | 100 | 385 | 42.0 | 16.0 | 32 | 3 466 | 1 582.4 | 130.3 |
| Columbia | 67 | 241 | 38.9 | 5.9 | 80 | D | D | D | 39 | D | D | D |
| Cookeville | 60 | 204 | 36.9 | 4.8 | 121 | D | D | D | 91 | 4 100 | D | 153.4 |

1. Establishments subject to federal tax.

Table D. Cities — **Accommodation and Food Services, Arts, Entertainment, and Recreation, and Health Care and Social Assistance**

| City | Accommodation and food services, 2007 | | | | Arts, entertainment, and recreation,[1] 2007 | | | | Health care and social assistance,[1] 2007 | | | |
|---|---|---|---|---|---|---|---|---|---|---|---|---|
| | Number of establish-ments | Number of employees | Sales (mil dol) | Annual payroll (mil dol) | Number of establish-ments | Number of employees | Receipts (mil dol) | Annual payroll (mil dol) | Number of establish-ments | Number of employees | Receipts (mil dol) | Annual payroll (mil dol) |
| | 92 | 93 | 94 | 95 | 96 | 97 | 98 | 99 | 100 | 101 | 102 | 103 |
| OREGON—Cont'd | | | | | | | | | | | | |
| Tigard | 165 | 2 940 | 147.0 | 43.0 | 13 | D | D | D | 175 | 1 904 | 183.6 | 72.0 |
| Tualatin | 82 | 1 487 | 75.4 | 23.4 | 11 | D | D | D | 126 | D | D | D |
| West Linn | 43 | 707 | 29.9 | 8.8 | 12 | D | D | D | 81 | 546 | 44.8 | 18.9 |
| PENNSYLVANIA | 26 910 | 420 209 | 19 625.4 | 5 454.0 | 3 420 | 53 939 | 4 743.5 | 1 682.1 | 27 138 | 368 531 | 35 089.4 | 15 093.0 |
| Allentown | 258 | 3 250 | 150.3 | 42.5 | 25 | 425 | 17.4 | 5.8 | 296 | 3 821 | 400.4 | 169.8 |
| Altoona | 113 | 1 750 | 64.1 | 17.1 | 10 | D | D | D | 151 | D | D | D |
| Bethel Park | 73 | 1 621 | 61.4 | 17.2 | 13 | D | D | D | 98 | 1 201 | 109.0 | 49.0 |
| Bethlehem | 213 | 2 815 | 141.4 | 39.5 | 10 | 157 | 5.0 | 1.3 | 195 | 2 197 | 223.0 | 105.6 |
| Chester | 39 | 295 | 16.2 | 4.0 | NA | NA | NA | NA | 45 | 1 401 | 197.0 | 90.8 |
| Easton | 87 | 1 117 | 50.1 | 12.3 | 1 | D | D | D | 44 | 1 657 | 226.4 | 67.7 |
| Erie | 220 | 3 227 | 122.7 | 32.5 | 26 | D | D | D | 351 | 5 218 | 481.3 | 257.4 |
| Harrisburg | 183 | 2 657 | 137.7 | 39.1 | 18 | 158 | 8.8 | 2.2 | 103 | 1 513 | 157.7 | 71.1 |
| Hazleton | 84 | 944 | 38.2 | 10.8 | 4 | D | D | D | 107 | 955 | 108.4 | 36.3 |
| Lancaster | 145 | 2 614 | 127.4 | 38.8 | 14 | 61 | 4.9 | 1.6 | 149 | 3 072 | 349.5 | 151.9 |
| Lebanon | 64 | 547 | 25.2 | 5.9 | 4 | D | D | D | 77 | 850 | 71.9 | 36.8 |
| Monroeville | 121 | 3 138 | 144.2 | 39.6 | 11 | 221 | 6.1 | 2.2 | 171 | 2 784 | 241.5 | 107.6 |
| Norristown | 55 | 410 | 21.7 | 4.8 | 3 | D | D | D | 72 | 1 391 | 148.1 | 74.6 |
| Philadelphia | 3 396 | 48 552 | 3 051.4 | 837.9 | 214 | 7 245 | 1 000.8 | 595.0 | 2 382 | 38 459 | 4 274.2 | 1 818.6 |
| Pittsburgh | 1 144 | 20 474 | 1 042.9 | 310.8 | 102 | 2 542 | 563.1 | 278.1 | 885 | 18 910 | 2 173.7 | 1 068.3 |
| Plum | 34 | 602 | 17.1 | 4.8 | 12 | 76 | 3.5 | 1.0 | 22 | 133 | 7.3 | 3.2 |
| Reading | 137 | D | D | D | 13 | 332 | 20.5 | 6.1 | 100 | 1 522 | 110.2 | 44.3 |
| Scranton | 195 | 3 044 | 128.2 | 34.7 | 15 | D | D | D | 212 | 2 712 | 286.2 | 138.6 |
| State College | 125 | 2 827 | 100.0 | 28.9 | 8 | 44 | 4.8 | 1.2 | 85 | 1 179 | 118.2 | 55.1 |
| Wilkes-Barre | 122 | 2 044 | 91.1 | 23.9 | 7 | D | D | D | 115 | 1 147 | 116.7 | 48.6 |
| Williamsport | 81 | 1 105 | 47.2 | 12.3 | 3 | D | D | D | 96 | 1 712 | 145.6 | 78.5 |
| York | 92 | 1 492 | 65.3 | 17.5 | 4 | 49 | 1.3 | 0.4 | 56 | 848 | 75.9 | 37.8 |
| RHODE ISLAND | 2 926 | 44 426 | 2 148.7 | 622.1 | 395 | 6 863 | 526.8 | 143.4 | 2 502 | 34 762 | 3 015.1 | 1 309.5 |
| Cranston | 188 | 3 227 | 144.4 | 40.7 | 20 | D | D | D | 231 | 3 318 | 230.5 | 109.8 |
| East Providence | 113 | 1 600 | 68.6 | 17.9 | 16 | D | D | D | 129 | 2 288 | 231.3 | 112.0 |
| Pawtucket | 144 | 1 668 | 65.2 | 18.1 | 10 | 74 | 14.8 | 6.3 | 139 | 2 060 | 153.7 | 72.5 |
| Providence | 517 | 9 156 | 472.0 | 138.1 | 37 | 1 596 | 44.6 | 14.0 | 447 | 5 447 | 639.0 | 294.3 |
| Warwick | 249 | 5 817 | 264.4 | 77.6 | 39 | D | D | D | 307 | 4 301 | 359.8 | 156.2 |
| Woonsocket | 95 | 1 249 | 53.9 | 14.5 | 6 | D | D | D | 82 | 1 394 | 105.0 | 49.9 |
| SOUTH CAROLINA | 9 291 | 182 899 | 8 383.5 | 2 311.0 | 1 271 | 19 444 | 1 105.6 | 316.1 | 7 883 | 115 669 | 11 213.4 | 4 523.3 |
| Aiken | 108 | 2 160 | 80.4 | 21.7 | 24 | 423 | 25.2 | 7.2 | 140 | 3 129 | 300.1 | 103.3 |
| Anderson | 155 | 3 447 | 126.8 | 35.1 | 12 | 140 | 5.8 | 2.3 | 195 | D | D | D |
| Charleston | 435 | 10 992 | 641.3 | 173.6 | 61 | 1 169 | 89.2 | 29.5 | 419 | 4 511 | 626.3 | 260.7 |
| Columbia | 491 | 10 913 | 496.0 | 140.7 | 41 | D | D | D | 472 | 7 864 | 863.7 | 373.3 |
| Florence | 140 | 3 211 | 135.7 | 37.1 | 12 | D | D | D | 217 | D | D | D |
| Goose Creek | 63 | 1 014 | 43.7 | 11.2 | 3 | D | D | D | 42 | D | D | D |
| Greenville | 367 | 8 250 | 385.6 | 112.2 | 41 | 851 | 36.1 | 12.6 | 298 | 4 660 | 537.5 | 241.2 |
| Greer | 82 | 1 307 | 53.0 | 13.7 | 8 | D | D | D | 71 | D | D | D |
| Hilton Head Island | 218 | 5 313 | 321.6 | 120.9 | 53 | D | D | D | 148 | D | D | D |
| Mount Pleasant | 196 | 3 810 | 181.1 | 54.1 | 43 | D | D | D | 269 | D | D | D |
| Myrtle Beach | 532 | 13 682 | 797.8 | 218.5 | 69 | 1 893 | 128.3 | 29.2 | 210 | D | D | D |
| North Charleston | 275 | 6 474 | 306.8 | 78.2 | 17 | 681 | 22.6 | 7.3 | 253 | 5 838 | 741.3 | 228.4 |
| Rock Hill | 170 | 3 829 | 157.9 | 43.5 | 15 | D | D | D | 183 | 4 639 | 563.8 | 202.6 |
| Spartanburg | 202 | 4 322 | 176.3 | 51.1 | 16 | 92 | 5.7 | 1.7 | 178 | D | D | D |
| Summerville | 114 | 3 049 | 116.1 | 32.4 | 8 | D | D | D | 125 | D | D | D |
| Sumter | 118 | 2 837 | 96.4 | 26.6 | 10 | 48 | 1.9 | 0.4 | 139 | 2 065 | 178.6 | 74.4 |
| SOUTH DAKOTA | 2 426 | 36 710 | 1 622.8 | 436.2 | 535 | 4 868 | 399.3 | 75.8 | 1 535 | 17 404 | 1 697.4 | 666.9 |
| Aberdeen | 97 | 1 858 | 70.5 | 18.9 | 21 | D | D | D | 116 | D | D | D |
| Rapid City | 229 | 5 384 | 231.9 | 67.8 | 60 | 467 | 36.1 | 6.7 | 259 | D | D | D |
| Sioux Falls | 391 | 9 548 | 387.3 | 118.4 | 96 | 1 475 | 118.7 | 19.6 | 343 | 4 728 | 612.1 | 266.5 |
| TENNESSEE | 11 592 | 239 379 | 10 626.8 | 3 009.2 | 2 006 | 21 937 | 2 873.8 | 885.3 | 11 720 | 185 582 | 19 249.5 | 7 599.6 |
| Bartlett | 87 | 1 956 | 75.8 | 21.0 | 8 | 153 | 4.8 | 1.6 | 98 | D | D | D |
| Brentwood | 83 | 2 193 | 107.9 | 30.2 | 64 | D | D | D | 273 | D | D | D |
| Bristol | 85 | 1 725 | 61.2 | 16.0 | 10 | D | D | D | 118 | D | D | D |
| Chattanooga | 586 | 12 921 | 554.8 | 164.9 | 65 | 1 169 | 49.9 | 14.6 | 699 | 11 422 | 1 395.6 | 547.2 |
| Clarksville | 279 | 5 871 | 235.5 | 61.4 | 19 | D | D | D | 222 | D | D | D |
| Cleveland | 143 | D | D | D | 14 | D | D | D | 159 | D | D | D |
| Collierville | 81 | 1 605 | 66.1 | 19.4 | 13 | D | D | D | 61 | D | D | D |
| Columbia | 105 | 2 321 | 81.8 | 23.6 | 8 | 51 | 1.7 | 0.7 | 134 | D | D | D |
| Cookeville | 132 | 3 106 | 128.5 | 36.2 | 10 | D | D | D | 162 | 1 720 | 164.3 | 59.8 |

1. Establishments subject to federal tax.

Items 92—103

| City | Number of establish-ments | Number of employees | Receipts (mil dol) | Annual payroll (mil dol) | Defense | Other | Total[2] | Medicaid and other health related | Nutrition and family welfare | Energy and envi-ronment | Disasters and emergency prepared-ness | Housing and community develop-ment | Employment and training |
|---|---|---|---|---|---|---|---|---|---|---|---|---|---|
| | 104 | 105 | 106 | 107 | 108 | 109 | 110 | 111 | 112 | 113 | 114 | 115 | 116 |
| **OREGON—Cont'd** | | | | | | | | | | | | | |
| Tigard | 119 | 780 | 68.6 | 22.1 | 5.5 | 1.1 | 6.1 | 3.5 | 0.0 | 0.0 | 0.0 | 0.0 | 0.0 |
| Tualatin | 65 | 490 | 49.8 | 15.3 | 2.4 | 1.7 | 1.4 | 1.2 | 0.0 | 0.1 | 0.0 | 0.0 | 0.0 |
| West Linn | 31 | 139 | 7.8 | 2.9 | 2.3 | 0.2 | 0.0 | 0.0 | 0.0 | 0.0 | 0.0 | 0.0 | 0.0 |
| **PENNSYLVANIA** | 20 165 | 113 790 | 9 502.5 | 2 798.3 | 11 900.9 | 7 451.5 | 29 411.2 | 16 147.3 | 2 976.8 | 1 336.9 | 32.0 | 1 242.1 | 427.4 |
| Allentown | 200 | 1 202 | 95.1 | 28.6 | 44.6 | 6.5 | 495.3 | 2.2 | 8.9 | 436.0 | 0.0 | 18.9 | 0.0 |
| Altoona | 112 | 582 | 38.8 | 11.9 | 1.3 | 55.0 | 18.4 | 0.4 | 3.1 | 0.0 | 0.0 | 8.3 | 0.0 |
| Bethel Park | 80 | 552 | 31.8 | 11.4 | 0.0 | 0.0 | 0.3 | 0.3 | 0.0 | 0.0 | 0.0 | 0.0 | 0.0 |
| Bethlehem | 102 | 788 | 80.6 | 27.9 | 10.8 | 1.1 | 233.2 | 4.1 | 0.0 | 5.7 | 0.0 | 9.4 | 197.0 |
| Chester | 32 | 275 | 17.8 | 5.7 | 5.1 | 1.2 | 22.6 | 2.8 | 0.0 | 0.0 | 0.0 | 18.5 | 0.0 |
| Easton | 44 | 246 | 19.1 | 6.8 | 1.8 | 10.4 | 13.8 | 0.3 | 0.0 | 2.5 | 0.0 | 10.2 | 0.0 |
| Erie | 165 | 744 | 53.6 | 16.4 | 39.7 | 29.0 | 45.7 | 2.5 | 6.3 | 2.2 | 0.0 | 19.8 | 0.0 |
| Harrisburg | 71 | 355 | 33.8 | 10.5 | 522.5 | 21.6 | 4 756.8 | 231.4 | 590.5 | 338.6 | 0.8 | 107.5 | 163.0 |
| Hazleton | 55 | 209 | 14.1 | 4.3 | 0.4 | 0.2 | 4.4 | 0.0 | 0.0 | 0.0 | 0.0 | 3.0 | 0.0 |
| Lancaster | 99 | 566 | 37.6 | 12.8 | 20.4 | 3.1 | 55.4 | 0.8 | 6.7 | 5.4 | 0.0 | 22.4 | 0.0 |
| Lebanon | 51 | 215 | 14.7 | 4.6 | 3.8 | 74.7 | 7.5 | 0.0 | 0.0 | 0.0 | 0.0 | 4.8 | 0.0 |
| Monroeville | 89 | 594 | 31.3 | 10.9 | 523.5 | 0.7 | -0.2 | 0.0 | 0.0 | 0.0 | -0.2 | 0.0 | 0.0 |
| Norristown | 41 | 237 | 18.0 | 4.4 | 2.2 | 0.8 | 76.8 | 2.6 | 3.4 | 35.9 | 0.0 | 32.5 | 0.4 |
| Philadelphia | 1 903 | 10 803 | 836.4 | 252.6 | 421.6 | 882.3 | 2 976.3 | 1 657.1 | 52.6 | 247.2 | 0.0 | 431.0 | 46.7 |
| Pittsburgh | 574 | 3 536 | 265.6 | 81.6 | 224.3 | 225.0 | 1 697.2 | 1 039.3 | 32.1 | 84.6 | 0.3 | 170.9 | 2.5 |
| Plum | 34 | 178 | 16.7 | 3.6 | 0.1 | 0.2 | 0.0 | 0.0 | 0.0 | 0.0 | 0.0 | 0.0 | 0.0 |
| Reading | 97 | 823 | 63.8 | 24.0 | 54.8 | 8.0 | 48.2 | 1.1 | 4.6 | 3.8 | 0.0 | 23.9 | 0.4 |
| Scranton | 138 | 794 | 62.7 | 17.7 | 119.8 | 11.2 | 32.0 | 4.5 | 5.6 | 0.9 | 0.0 | 13.1 | 0.0 |
| State College | 41 | 257 | 15.3 | 5.0 | 23.7 | 1.9 | 309.3 | 120.4 | 0.3 | 29.6 | 0.0 | 1.7 | 0.0 |
| Wilkes-Barre | 74 | 329 | 22.2 | 5.7 | 2.4 | 3.8 | 38.0 | 2.6 | 6.8 | 2.6 | 0.0 | 18.5 | 0.0 |
| Williamsport | 51 | 364 | 37.1 | 9.5 | 17.7 | 8.5 | 23.4 | 0.1 | 3.6 | 0.9 | 0.0 | 5.7 | 0.4 |
| York | 46 | 338 | 34.5 | 9.9 | 1 207.2 | 14.2 | 38.0 | 3.1 | 3.3 | 5.6 | 0.1 | 16.6 | 0.4 |
| **RHODE ISLAND** | 1 929 | 10 073 | 820.0 | 264.1 | 776.9 | 224.5 | 3 152.0 | 1 752.5 | 292.4 | 57.9 | 53.3 | 144.4 | 55.0 |
| Cranston | 180 | 1 110 | 79.0 | 28.9 | 13.5 | 0.8 | 80.8 | 9.7 | 24.4 | 1.6 | 0.0 | 4.1 | 34.2 |
| East Providence | 97 | 482 | 50.8 | 15.2 | 1.4 | 1.1 | 12.4 | 5.8 | 0.0 | 0.0 | 2.4 | 3.7 | 0.0 |
| Pawtucket | 120 | 706 | 67.6 | 19.1 | 0.1 | 5.8 | 18.7 | 6.5 | 0.0 | 0.2 | 0.0 | 10.1 | 0.0 |
| Providence | 269 | 2 010 | 151.1 | 51.7 | 14.1 | 49.5 | 881.9 | 317.5 | 40.8 | 45.9 | 35.2 | 68.8 | 17.9 |
| Warwick | 184 | 983 | 83.6 | 25.8 | 5.8 | 15.0 | 37.4 | 1.2 | 4.1 | 2.8 | 0.1 | 5.1 | 2.8 |
| Woonsocket | 65 | 312 | 29.5 | 8.6 | 13.3 | 1.2 | 21.5 | 3.8 | 1.9 | 0.0 | 0.0 | 15.1 | 0.0 |
| **SOUTH CAROLINA** | 5 842 | 35 233 | 2 710.9 | 846.7 | 4 496.7 | 3 674.6 | 8 210.5 | 4 833.3 | 853.8 | 157.2 | 7.8 | 250.2 | 144.0 |
| Aiken | 61 | 526 | 24.0 | 8.0 | 6.1 | 2 319.8 | 11.7 | 0.0 | 2.6 | 0.7 | 0.0 | 5.8 | 0.0 |
| Anderson | 77 | D | D | D | 12.1 | 0.9 | 16.6 | 9.9 | 0.4 | 0.4 | 0.0 | 4.8 | 0.0 |
| Charleston | 182 | 1 296 | 73.1 | 25.9 | 175.3 | 505.0 | 297.9 | 208.8 | 0.1 | 3.8 | 0.0 | 29.2 | 0.0 |
| Columbia | 234 | 1 828 | 120.5 | 42.0 | 475.4 | 113.9 | 1 115.1 | 208.2 | 151.0 | 48.9 | 0.3 | 83.6 | 128.2 |
| Florence | 57 | 576 | 36.0 | 10.8 | 4.7 | 6.5 | 29.0 | 2.3 | 5.9 | 0.0 | 0.0 | 6.4 | 4.3 |
| Goose Creek | 40 | 165 | 10.5 | 3.0 | 54.6 | 1.3 | 0.0 | 0.0 | 0.0 | 0.0 | 0.0 | 0.0 | 0.0 |
| Greenville | 186 | 1 133 | 69.3 | 24.3 | 252.0 | 4.6 | 62.7 | 6.6 | 12.9 | 3.0 | 0.0 | 24.5 | 0.0 |
| Greer | 58 | D | D | D | 49.6 | 1.0 | 1.7 | 0.0 | 0.0 | 0.0 | 0.0 | 1.7 | 0.0 |
| Hilton Head Island | 95 | 399 | 32.7 | 10.3 | 4.6 | 0.0 | 0.0 | 0.0 | 0.0 | 0.0 | 0.0 | 0.0 | 0.0 |
| Mount Pleasant | 142 | 963 | 64.6 | 23.8 | 18.1 | 1.4 | 0.6 | 0.0 | 0.0 | 0.5 | 0.0 | 0.0 | 0.0 |
| Myrtle Beach | 125 | 653 | 47.7 | 12.9 | 5.1 | 1.0 | 14.7 | 0.0 | 0.0 | 0.0 | 0.0 | 4.6 | 0.0 |
| North Charleston | 192 | 1 863 | 193.6 | 62.9 | 235.3 | 176.6 | 21.9 | 0.0 | 0.0 | 0.0 | 0.0 | 15.1 | 0.0 |
| Rock Hill | 103 | 858 | 60.5 | 19.8 | 2.2 | 1.6 | 25.3 | 3.8 | 6.9 | 0.7 | 0.0 | 5.8 | 0.2 |
| Spartanburg | 101 | 784 | 57.5 | 14.8 | 0.6 | 1.8 | 34.3 | 6.5 | 4.9 | 0.1 | 0.0 | 17.8 | 0.4 |
| Summerville | 89 | 449 | 34.5 | 10.7 | 16.9 | 0.2 | 1.2 | 0.4 | 0.0 | 0.0 | 0.0 | 0.2 | 0.0 |
| Sumter | 84 | 564 | 38.1 | 11.6 | 30.9 | 4.8 | 27.8 | 1.2 | 7.2 | 3.1 | 0.0 | 6.5 | 0.5 |
| **SOUTH DAKOTA** | 1 359 | 6 196 | 465.7 | 129.1 | 560.7 | 352.2 | 2 250.2 | 761.9 | 216.0 | 233.4 | 56.2 | 89.0 | 34.2 |
| Aberdeen | 52 | D | D | D | 57.4 | 8.1 | 6.9 | 0.2 | 2.7 | 0.1 | 0.0 | 1.9 | 0.0 |
| Rapid City | 166 | 988 | 71.6 | 22.2 | 76.7 | 13.7 | 81.3 | 13.9 | 8.1 | 11.1 | 0.0 | 9.5 | 0.1 |
| Sioux Falls | 262 | 1 905 | 128.4 | 40.0 | 36.3 | 40.5 | 145.9 | 18.2 | 4.7 | 75.4 | 0.0 | 14.9 | 0.0 |
| **TENNESSEE** | 7 153 | 50 425 | 3 847.7 | 1 234.7 | 3 100.9 | 7 039.8 | 14 094.4 | 8 035.9 | 1 360.7 | 285.7 | 199.5 | 545.3 | 149.9 |
| Bartlett | 78 | 582 | 45.0 | 14.4 | 5.0 | 5.1 | 0.0 | 0.0 | 0.0 | 0.0 | 0.0 | 0.0 | 0.0 |
| Brentwood | 67 | 623 | 46.9 | 15.6 | 3.3 | 28.9 | 0.0 | 0.0 | 0.0 | 0.0 | 0.0 | 0.0 | 0.0 |
| Bristol | 57 | 761 | 71.3 | 20.9 | 0.1 | 3.5 | 3.4 | 0.0 | 0.0 | 0.0 | 0.0 | 3.0 | 0.0 |
| Chattanooga | 369 | 3 439 | 222.7 | 82.0 | 31.7 | 483.1 | 183.0 | 6.2 | 7.6 | 114.9 | 0.0 | 28.2 | 0.0 |
| Clarksville | 165 | 946 | 62.8 | 18.6 | 20.4 | 1.3 | 13.8 | 0.0 | 1.5 | 1.0 | 0.0 | 2.4 | 0.0 |
| Cleveland | 76 | D | D | D | 0.1 | 2.3 | 17.0 | 0.1 | 11.8 | 0.0 | 0.0 | 2.0 | 0.0 |
| Collierville | 50 | D | D | D | 4.3 | 0.0 | 0.2 | 0.0 | 0.0 | 0.2 | 0.0 | 0.0 | 0.0 |
| Columbia | 57 | D | D | D | 0.5 | 3.3 | 1.2 | 0.0 | 0.0 | 0.0 | 0.0 | 0.5 | 0.0 |
| Cookeville | 81 | D | D | D | 1.8 | 56.7 | 19.9 | 0.3 | 9.3 | 0.9 | 0.0 | 1.2 | 0.0 |

1. Establishments subject to federal tax.    2. Includes program categories not shown separately. State totals include additional categories not allocated by city.

# Table D. Cities — **City Government Finances**

| City | General revenue Total (mil dol) | Intergovernmental Total (mil dol) | Intergovernmental Percent from state government | Taxes Total (mil dol) | Taxes Per capita¹ (dollars) Total | Taxes Per capita¹ (dollars) Property | Taxes Sales and gross receipts | General expenditure Total (mil dol) | General expenditure Per capita¹ (dollars) Total | General expenditure Per capita¹ (dollars) Capital outlays |
|---|---|---|---|---|---|---|---|---|---|---|
| | 117 | 118 | 119 | 120 | 121 | 122 | 123 | 124 | 125 | 126 |
| **OREGON—Cont'd** | | | | | | | | | | |
| Tigard | 33.5 | 5.1 | 60.9 | 21.1 | 425 | 233 | 192 | 32.1 | 646 | 112 |
| Tualatin | 30.3 | 2.7 | 66.0 | 16.5 | 626 | 419 | 206 | 31.2 | 1 186 | 329 |
| West Linn | 61.4 | 4.1 | 98.3 | 40.4 | 1 618 | 832 | 786 | 62.3 | 2 496 | 959 |
| **PENNSYLVANIA** | X | X | X | X | X | X | X | X | X | X |
| Allentown | 116.2 | 14.3 | 41.4 | 50.3 | 469 | 278 | 100 | 115.1 | 1 075 | 79 |
| Altoona | 25.7 | 7.1 | 35.6 | 14.5 | 312 | 180 | 75 | 28.5 | 613 | 37 |
| Bethel Park | 21.4 | 2.7 | 54.2 | 11.9 | 375 | 117 | 31 | 21.8 | 688 | 47 |
| Bethlehem | 69.1 | 15.3 | 82.9 | 31.8 | 438 | 260 | 74 | 70.4 | 970 | 0 |
| Chester | 35.9 | 4.7 | 71.5 | 19.2 | 524 | 199 | 109 | 33.7 | 919 | 13 |
| Easton | 36.8 | 5.9 | 61.7 | 10.6 | 406 | 254 | 65 | 39.4 | 1 511 | 33 |
| Erie | 103.0 | 25.7 | 29.8 | 39.4 | 380 | 263 | 52 | 89.6 | 865 | 32 |
| Harrisburg | 86.8 | 8.8 | 55.3 | 25.4 | 538 | 273 | 174 | 85.0 | 1 801 | 88 |
| Hazleton | 19.3 | 8.2 | 38.3 | 6.7 | 307 | 80 | 70 | 15.9 | 729 | 110 |
| Lancaster | 56.4 | 11.1 | 59.7 | 23.6 | 432 | 283 | 73 | 60.3 | 1 102 | 74 |
| Lebanon | 14.2 | 1.1 | 98.3 | 9.5 | 396 | 115 | 8 | 12.9 | 536 | 41 |
| Monroeville | 25.1 | 1.7 | 95.5 | 20.5 | 741 | 153 | 325 | 27.8 | 1 003 | 107 |
| Norristown | 25.8 | 3.1 | 42.7 | 19.2 | 618 | 315 | 93 | 26.9 | 866 | 98 |
| Philadelphia | 6 421.1 | 2 606.1 | 73.2 | 2 857.5 | 1 971 | 273 | 185 | 5 767.3 | 3 978 | 275 |
| Pittsburgh | 619.0 | 219.1 | 77.3 | 331.1 | 1 064 | 418 | 297 | 476.3 | 1 530 | 91 |
| Plum | 10.2 | 1.2 | 86.4 | 7.5 | 287 | 146 | 29 | 9.9 | 378 | 0 |
| Reading | 94.3 | 14.6 | 99.0 | 39.8 | 492 | 186 | 114 | 96.2 | 1 191 | 36 |
| Scranton | 74.0 | 16.3 | 49.3 | 41.2 | 568 | 167 | 81 | 73.5 | 1 014 | 1 |
| State College | 27.1 | 3.3 | 33.6 | 10.1 | 252 | 106 | 38 | 33.4 | 837 | 167 |
| Wilkes-Barre | 55.5 | 24.4 | 73.0 | 21.4 | 522 | 155 | 87 | 58.1 | 1 415 | 245 |
| Williamsport | 28.4 | 11.8 | 48.7 | 14.1 | 478 | 294 | 117 | 20.7 | 700 | 116 |
| York | 57.6 | 9.0 | 37.7 | 20.5 | 509 | 323 | 130 | 53.2 | 1 323 | 34 |
| **RHODE ISLAND** | X | X | X | X | X | X | X | X | X | X |
| Cranston | 263.1 | 76.1 | 97.9 | 147.2 | 1 830 | 1 830 | 0 | 281.0 | 3 492 | 158 |
| East Providence | 132.9 | 42.6 | 98.5 | 74.2 | 1 521 | 1 491 | 30 | 129.5 | 2 654 | 48 |
| Pawtucket | 198.7 | 110.2 | 84.0 | 75.8 | 1 048 | 1 037 | 11 | 193.0 | 2 668 | 95 |
| Providence | 750.5 | 343.4 | 95.6 | 290.6 | 1 685 | 1 632 | 53 | 731.4 | 4 241 | 385 |
| Warwick | 293.3 | 61.9 | 97.4 | 196.4 | 2 308 | 2 246 | 62 | 298.2 | 3 504 | 112 |
| Woonsocket | 144.0 | 82.8 | 99.2 | 43.9 | 1 007 | 949 | 58 | 143.9 | 3 300 | 58 |
| **SOUTH CAROLINA** | X | X | X | X | X | X | X | X | X | X |
| Aiken | 37.3 | 2.6 | 57.0 | 20.0 | 684 | 279 | 405 | 34.3 | 1 175 | 172 |
| Anderson | 33.1 | 3.5 | 63.4 | 17.9 | 677 | 391 | 285 | 35.3 | 1 336 | 110 |
| Charleston | 174.8 | 23.0 | 32.3 | 70.3 | 639 | 409 | 230 | 188.0 | 1 709 | 64 |
| Columbia | 129.2 | 9.6 | 35.9 | 71.7 | 574 | 324 | 250 | 128.1 | 1 027 | 90 |
| Florence | 36.9 | 2.8 | 51.6 | 19.6 | 622 | 253 | 369 | 29.8 | 948 | 59 |
| Goose Creek | 16.7 | 3.2 | 31.0 | 9.9 | 272 | 96 | 176 | 13.8 | 377 | 0 |
| Greenville | 86.1 | 8.0 | 100.0 | 59.8 | 1 017 | 422 | 596 | 81.4 | 1 385 | 0 |
| Greer | 23.8 | 1.5 | 62.6 | 15.1 | 644 | 308 | 315 | 29.0 | 1 239 | 145 |
| Hilton Head Island | 59.7 | 6.8 | 98.6 | 41.7 | 1 227 | 450 | 777 | 51.9 | 1 526 | 442 |
| Mount Pleasant | 65.3 | 5.8 | 95.6 | 41.0 | 634 | 311 | 323 | 68.4 | 1 057 | 170 |
| Myrtle Beach | 123.6 | 14.4 | 92.0 | 56.5 | 1 884 | 692 | 1 192 | 119.0 | 3 970 | 658 |
| North Charleston | 103.1 | 16.6 | 31.1 | 63.5 | 695 | 376 | 289 | 93.8 | 1 026 | 209 |
| Rock Hill | 79.9 | 7.5 | 28.9 | 35.8 | 552 | 353 | 199 | 74.7 | 1 151 | 210 |
| Spartanburg | 40.3 | 5.9 | 1.9 | 28.2 | 726 | 393 | 333 | 35.5 | 915 | 0 |
| Summerville | 25.3 | 2.1 | 69.0 | 19.2 | 436 | 157 | 279 | 19.1 | 434 | 52 |
| Sumter | 41.7 | 8.0 | 29.1 | 21.1 | 545 | 179 | 366 | 39.2 | 1 012 | 213 |
| **SOUTH DAKOTA** | X | X | X | X | X | X | X | X | X | X |
| Aberdeen | 32.7 | 5.0 | 18.0 | 18.9 | 773 | 219 | 554 | 44.4 | 1 819 | 798 |
| Rapid City | 99.9 | 14.1 | 9.9 | 54.4 | 851 | 188 | 663 | 93.8 | 1 465 | 415 |
| Sioux Falls | 179.8 | 9.6 | 29.0 | 128.4 | 847 | 231 | 616 | 203.0 | 1 340 | 541 |
| **TENNESSEE** | X | X | X | X | X | X | X | X | X | X |
| Bartlett | 52.9 | 6.0 | 94.9 | 31.6 | 665 | 299 | 366 | 47.5 | 999 | 136 |
| Brentwood | 44.7 | 6.4 | 100.0 | 25.3 | 721 | 265 | 455 | 33.0 | 941 | 218 |
| Bristol | 73.6 | 33.2 | 57.2 | 22.9 | 901 | 746 | 132 | 69.6 | 2 730 | 254 |
| Chattanooga | 337.9 | 105.9 | 35.5 | 110.3 | 649 | 529 | 121 | 308.0 | 1 813 | 189 |
| Clarksville | 93.2 | 36.2 | 39.0 | 30.6 | 256 | 187 | 69 | 100.8 | 845 | 205 |
| Cleveland | 84.1 | 37.5 | 65.8 | 27.1 | 692 | 398 | 295 | 83.7 | 2 135 | 229 |
| Collierville | 54.2 | 15.2 | 42.2 | 21.2 | 540 | 412 | 129 | 48.2 | 1 230 | 283 |
| Columbia | 33.5 | 4.3 | 100.0 | 13.3 | 392 | 201 | 186 | 37.5 | 1 104 | 285 |
| Cookeville | 184.4 | 3.6 | 90.0 | 7.0 | 241 | 175 | 66 | 181.5 | 6 280 | 1 237 |

1. Based on population estimated as of July 1 of the year shown.

# Table D. Cities — **City Government Finances**

| City | Public welfare | Highways | Parking facilities | Education | Health and hospitals | Police protection | Sewerage and sanitation | Parks and recreation | Housing and community development | Interest on debt |
|---|---|---|---|---|---|---|---|---|---|---|
| | 127 | 128 | 129 | 130 | 131 | 132 | 133 | 134 | 135 | 136 |
| **OREGON—Cont'd** | | | | | | | | | | |
| Tigard | 0.5 | 12.1 | 0.0 | 0.0 | 0.0 | 28.7 | 9.1 | 4.5 | 0.0 | 1.8 |
| Tualatin | 0.0 | 6.6 | 0.0 | 0.0 | 0.0 | 12.1 | 20.6 | 7.0 | 9.0 | 1.5 |
| West Linn | 0.0 | 10.2 | 0.0 | 0.0 | 0.0 | 12.5 | 27.8 | 7.4 | 5.5 | 3.9 |
| **PENNSYLVANIA** | X | X | X | X | X | X | X | X | X | X |
| Allentown | 0.0 | 9.9 | 0.0 | 0.0 | 5.9 | 19.1 | 17.9 | 2.7 | 4.6 | 3.4 |
| Altoona | 0.0 | 19.0 | 0.0 | 0.0 | 0.0 | 14.9 | 0.0 | 1.0 | 8.9 | 3.2 |
| Bethel Park | 0.0 | 32.5 | 0.0 | 0.0 | 0.0 | 23.0 | 23.6 | 4.8 | 0.5 | 0.8 |
| Bethlehem | 0.0 | 9.1 | 0.0 | 0.0 | 4.8 | 14.2 | 13.8 | 4.8 | 6.1 | 10.4 |
| Chester | 0.0 | 6.2 | 0.0 | 0.0 | 1.3 | 32.2 | 3.6 | 2.0 | 4.7 | 3.0 |
| Easton | 0.0 | 4.0 | 0.8 | 0.0 | 0.3 | 18.8 | 19.7 | 6.3 | 2.4 | 6.5 |
| Erie | 0.0 | 8.6 | 0.0 | 0.0 | 0.0 | 14.1 | 15.2 | 4.5 | 8.1 | 5.6 |
| Harrisburg | 0.0 | 6.8 | 0.0 | 0.0 | 0.2 | 21.2 | 31.1 | 3.4 | 8.9 | 3.5 |
| Hazleton | 0.0 | 17.3 | 0.0 | 0.0 | 0.7 | 19.1 | 10.9 | 1.9 | 9.8 | 2.5 |
| Lancaster | 0.0 | 4.5 | 0.0 | 0.0 | 0.7 | 24.5 | 16.4 | 2.5 | 4.8 | 5.0 |
| Lebanon | 0.0 | 20.9 | 0.0 | 0.0 | 0.0 | 20.0 | 4.4 | 18.7 | 0.0 | 7.0 |
| Monroeville | 0.0 | 19.7 | 0.0 | 0.0 | 0.3 | 30.8 | 4.6 | 13.2 | 1.6 | 2.8 |
| Norristown | 0.0 | 16.3 | 0.0 | 0.0 | 1.5 | 23.6 | 5.4 | 2.0 | 0.0 | 5.5 |
| Philadelphia | 8.7 | 1.5 | 0.0 | 0.4 | 23.0 | 9.2 | 5.4 | 1.5 | 3.7 | 2.6 |
| Pittsburgh | 0.0 | 2.7 | 0.0 | 0.0 | 2.8 | 13.1 | 5.1 | 2.3 | 12.5 | 8.7 |
| Plum | 0.0 | 33.6 | 0.0 | 0.0 | 0.0 | 31.5 | 11.7 | 0.4 | 0.0 | 1.6 |
| Reading | 0.0 | 6.9 | 0.0 | 0.0 | 3.1 | 26.2 | 18.0 | 2.1 | 13.7 | 3.1 |
| Scranton | 0.0 | 4.8 | 0.0 | 0.0 | 0.6 | 19.0 | 4.7 | 2.0 | 9.0 | 4.5 |
| State College | 0.0 | 13.1 | 15.8 | 0.0 | 0.8 | 20.8 | 21.7 | 2.9 | 4.3 | 3.9 |
| Wilkes-Barre | 0.0 | 32.1 | 0.5 | 0.0 | 3.1 | 14.0 | 3.5 | 1.3 | 15.1 | 2.3 |
| Williamsport | 0.0 | 19.9 | 0.0 | 0.0 | 0.0 | 27.8 | 0.2 | 7.5 | 4.7 | 0.8 |
| York | 0.0 | 5.3 | 1.0 | 0.0 | 3.2 | 14.6 | 20.1 | 4.2 | 8.8 | 7.0 |
| **RHODE ISLAND** | X | X | X | X | X | X | X | X | X | X |
| Cranston | 0.0 | 5.3 | 0.0 | 54.0 | 1.1 | 10.8 | 5.5 | 1.4 | 0.9 | 1.4 |
| East Providence | 0.0 | 2.6 | 0.0 | 56.9 | 0.3 | 8.4 | 6.0 | 2.3 | 0.8 | 1.5 |
| Pawtucket | 0.0 | 1.3 | 0.0 | 59.7 | 0.0 | 8.4 | 1.8 | 1.4 | 2.4 | 1.4 |
| Providence | 0.0 | 0.7 | 0.0 | 51.8 | 0.0 | 7.3 | 1.2 | 2.5 | 0.0 | 2.4 |
| Warwick | 0.7 | 2.0 | 0.0 | 56.1 | 0.5 | 8.5 | 2.8 | 0.9 | 0.5 | 2.8 |
| Woonsocket | 0.2 | 1.3 | 0.0 | 55.6 | 0.0 | 5.5 | 9.6 | 0.9 | 2.2 | 5.3 |
| **SOUTH CAROLINA** | X | X | X | X | X | X | X | X | X | X |
| Aiken | 0.0 | 8.6 | 0.0 | 0.0 | 0.0 | 23.5 | 16.9 | 14.4 | 5.2 | 0.3 |
| Anderson | 0.0 | 0.0 | 0.0 | 0.0 | 0.0 | 15.8 | 22.7 | 10.3 | 4.8 | 2.7 |
| Charleston | 0.4 | 5.3 | 3.9 | 0.0 | 0.0 | 16.5 | 15.2 | 11.4 | 2.3 | 19.0 |
| Columbia | 0.0 | 3.0 | 1.6 | 0.0 | 0.8 | 18.5 | 8.3 | 6.8 | 2.8 | 3.6 |
| Florence | 0.0 | 6.7 | 0.0 | 0.0 | 0.1 | 24.4 | 20.2 | 10.8 | 3.3 | 0.6 |
| Goose Creek | 0.0 | 4.1 | 1.6 | 0.0 | 4.7 | 34.1 | 8.2 | 10.1 | 0.0 | 4.1 |
| Greenville | 0.0 | 11.2 | 2.9 | 0.0 | 0.0 | 19.2 | 5.8 | 20.0 | 4.3 | 5.5 |
| Greer | 0.0 | 11.2 | 0.0 | 0.0 | 0.0 | 14.1 | 25.9 | 5.1 | 0.0 | 13.5 |
| Hilton Head Island | 0.0 | 0.0 | 3.9 | 0.0 | 0.0 | 4.9 | 1.6 | 7.2 | 0.0 | 8.9 |
| Mount Pleasant | 0.0 | 6.8 | 0.0 | 0.0 | 0.0 | 12.2 | 23.1 | 5.7 | 0.0 | 1.9 |
| Myrtle Beach | 0.1 | 5.2 | 0.6 | 0.0 | 0.0 | 14.9 | 13.6 | 19.3 | 3.7 | 7.3 |
| North Charleston | 0.0 | 0.0 | 9.6 | 0.0 | 0.0 | 25.1 | 11.0 | 5.2 | 4.2 | 4.7 |
| Rock Hill | 0.0 | 10.3 | 0.0 | 0.0 | 0.0 | 15.2 | 20.0 | 9.6 | 5.1 | 2.7 |
| Spartanburg | 0.0 | 9.9 | 0.2 | 0.0 | 0.0 | 18.6 | 11.3 | 4.9 | 2.4 | 5.5 |
| Summerville | 0.0 | 1.6 | 0.0 | 0.0 | 0.0 | 29.9 | 16.6 | 11.6 | 0.0 | 0.1 |
| Sumter | 0.0 | 0.9 | 0.0 | 0.0 | 0.2 | 22.4 | 20.2 | 7.7 | 4.5 | 1.0 |
| **SOUTH DAKOTA** | X | X | X | X | X | X | X | X | X | X |
| Aberdeen | 0.0 | 13.6 | 0.0 | 0.0 | 1.6 | 6.4 | 19.5 | 24.7 | 0.0 | 0.3 |
| Rapid City | 0.1 | 12.2 | 0.4 | 0.0 | 3.2 | 14.4 | 12.6 | 11.9 | 3.3 | 4.5 |
| Sioux Falls | 0.0 | 10.4 | 1.0 | 0.0 | 4.7 | 11.6 | 32.8 | 13.9 | 5.9 | 1.7 |
| **TENNESSEE** | X | X | X | X | X | X | X | X | X | X |
| Bartlett | 0.0 | 10.9 | 0.0 | 0.0 | 0.0 | 23.6 | 13.9 | 12.0 | 0.0 | 1.6 |
| Brentwood | 0.0 | 11.6 | 0.0 | 0.7 | 0.2 | 15.8 | 6.3 | 4.5 | 0.0 | 3.3 |
| Bristol | 0.2 | 6.5 | 0.0 | 50.8 | 0.0 | 9.5 | 10.8 | 6.1 | 1.7 | 0.9 |
| Chattanooga | 4.5 | 7.4 | 0.2 | 0.0 | 0.5 | 14.2 | 17.0 | 6.2 | 3.4 | 6.9 |
| Clarksville | 0.0 | 8.7 | 0.1 | 0.0 | 0.0 | 18.8 | 37.1 | 4.4 | 2.0 | 6.9 |
| Cleveland | 0.0 | 7.5 | 0.0 | 44.5 | 0.6 | 12.3 | 11.4 | 2.5 | 0.7 | 3.5 |
| Collierville | 0.0 | 12.9 | 0.0 | 0.0 | 0.9 | 18.3 | 25.8 | 9.0 | 0.0 | 3.9 |
| Columbia | 0.0 | 7.8 | 0.0 | 0.0 | 0.0 | 15.7 | 34.2 | 3.7 | 0.0 | 2.0 |
| Cookeville | 0.0 | 0.5 | 0.0 | 0.0 | 87.5 | 3.7 | 1.3 | 1.0 | 0.0 | 2.1 |

# Table D. Cities — City Government Finances, City Government Employment, and Climate

| | City government finances, 2007 (cont.) | | | | Climate[2] | | | | | | |
|---|---|---|---|---|---|---|---|---|---|---|---|
| | Debt outstanding | | | | Average daily temperature (degrees Fahrenheit) | | | | | | |
| | | | | | Mean | | Limits | | | | |
| City | Total (mil dol) | Per capita[1] (dollars) | Debt issued during year | City government employment, 2011 | January | July | January[3] | July[4] | Annual precipitation (inches) | Heating degree days | Cooling degree days |
| | 137 | 138 | 139 | 140 | 141 | 142 | 143 | 144 | 145 | 146 | 147 |
| OREGON—Cont'd | | | | | | | | | | | |
| Tigard | 13.7 | 275 | 0.0 | 283 | 40.0 | 66.8 | 33.8 | 79.2 | 39.95 | 4 723 | 287 |
| Tualatin | 22.0 | 835 | 4.2 | NA | NA | NA | NA | NA | NA | NA | NA |
| West Linn | 60.7 | 2 433 | 0.0 | NA | NA | NA | NA | NA | NA | NA | NA |
| PENNSYLVANIA | X | X | X | X | X | X | X | X | X | X | X |
| Allentown | 130.6 | 1 219 | 15.3 | 881 | 27.1 | 73.3 | 19.1 | 83.9 | 45.17 | 5 830 | 787 |
| Altoona | 30.8 | 663 | 0.0 | 256 | 26.5 | 71.1 | 18.2 | 81.9 | 42.69 | 6 055 | 546 |
| Bethel Park | 3.0 | 94 | 0.0 | NA | 28.6 | 73.1 | 19.8 | 84.5 | 37.78 | 5 727 | 709 |
| Bethlehem | 192.2 | 2 650 | 0.0 | 683 | 27.1 | 73.3 | 19.1 | 83.9 | 45.17 | 5 830 | 787 |
| Chester | 21.7 | 590 | 12.5 | 312 | 33.7 | 78.7 | 27.9 | 87.5 | 40.66 | 4 469 | 1 333 |
| Easton | 35.7 | 1 367 | 0.8 | 236 | 27.1 | 73.3 | 19.1 | 83.9 | 45.17 | 5 830 | 787 |
| Erie | 198.7 | 1 917 | 6.1 | 664 | 26.9 | 72.1 | 20.3 | 80.4 | 42.77 | 6 243 | 620 |
| Harrisburg | 161.2 | 3 415 | 17.9 | 537 | 30.3 | 75.9 | 23.1 | 85.7 | 41.45 | 5 201 | 955 |
| Hazleton | 8.4 | 384 | 0.0 | NA | NA | NA | NA | NA | NA | NA | NA |
| Lancaster | 77.3 | 1 415 | 16.3 | 530 | 29.1 | 74.4 | 20.7 | 84.7 | 43.47 | 5 448 | 809 |
| Lebanon | 22.5 | 934 | 0.0 | 153 | NA | NA | NA | NA | NA | NA | NA |
| Monroeville | 22.9 | 826 | 0.0 | 149 | 28.6 | 73.1 | 19.8 | 84.5 | 37.78 | 5 727 | 709 |
| Norristown | 42.2 | 1 355 | 0.0 | 176 | 30.2 | 75.1 | 20.4 | 86.6 | 43.87 | 5 174 | 884 |
| Philadelphia | 6 788.3 | 4 683 | 687.0 | 29 607 | 32.3 | 77.6 | 25.5 | 85.5 | 42.05 | 4 759 | 1 235 |
| Pittsburgh | 1 015.6 | 3 263 | 241.8 | 3 251 | 27.5 | 72.6 | 19.9 | 82.7 | 37.85 | 5 829 | 726 |
| Plum | 2.8 | 109 | 0.0 | NA | 28.6 | 73.1 | 19.8 | 84.5 | 37.78 | 5 727 | 709 |
| Reading | 172.4 | 2 135 | 75.5 | 649 | 27.1 | 73.6 | 19.1 | 83.8 | 45.28 | 5 876 | 723 |
| Scranton | 73.5 | 1 014 | 0.0 | 551 | 26.3 | 72.1 | 18.5 | 82.6 | 37.56 | 6 234 | 611 |
| State College | 33.7 | 845 | 0.0 | 166 | 25.4 | 71.2 | 18.3 | 80.7 | 39.76 | 6 345 | 538 |
| Wilkes-Barre | 60.1 | 1 465 | 9.1 | 280 | 21.5 | 67.7 | 13.2 | 77.4 | 47.89 | 7 466 | 234 |
| Williamsport | 0.0 | 2 | 0.0 | 200 | 25.5 | 72.4 | 17.9 | 83.2 | 41.59 | 6 063 | 709 |
| York | 89.9 | 2 235 | 0.0 | 386 | 30.0 | 74.6 | 20.9 | 86.5 | 43.00 | 5 233 | 862 |
| RHODE ISLAND | X | X | X | X | X | X | X | X | X | X | X |
| Cranston | 90.0 | 1 119 | 0.0 | 2 072 | 28.7 | 73.3 | 20.3 | 82.6 | 46.45 | 5 754 | 714 |
| East Providence | 34.8 | 713 | 0.0 | 1 352 | 28.7 | 73.3 | 20.3 | 82.6 | 46.45 | 5 754 | 714 |
| Pawtucket | 154.9 | 2 141 | 0.0 | 1 791 | 28.7 | 73.3 | 20.3 | 82.6 | 46.45 | 5 754 | 714 |
| Providence | 478.9 | 2 777 | 89.9 | 5 270 | 28.7 | 73.3 | 20.3 | 82.6 | 46.45 | 5 754 | 714 |
| Warwick | 214.9 | 2 526 | 9.5 | 2 540 | 28.7 | 73.3 | 20.3 | 82.6 | 46.45 | 5 754 | 714 |
| Woonsocket | 137.7 | 3 158 | 1.2 | 1 364 | 25.4 | 72.3 | 13.3 | 84.3 | 48.75 | 6 302 | 534 |
| SOUTH CAROLINA | X | X | X | X | X | X | X | X | X | X | X |
| Aiken | 6.5 | 222 | 0.0 | 357 | 45.6 | 81.7 | 33.4 | 93.7 | 52.43 | 2 413 | 2 081 |
| Anderson | 89.8 | 3 401 | 6.9 | 439 | 41.7 | 79.7 | 31.3 | 90.5 | 46.67 | 3 087 | 1 700 |
| Charleston | 1 031.5 | 9 376 | 170.3 | 2 033 | 49.8 | 82.8 | 42.4 | 88.5 | 46.39 | 1 755 | 2 473 |
| Columbia | 177.8 | 1 424 | 0.0 | 2 441 | 47.3 | 83.6 | 36.5 | 95.2 | 47.14 | 2 044 | 2 475 |
| Florence | 37.1 | 1 180 | 0.0 | 479 | 45.0 | 81.2 | 35.2 | 90.7 | 44.76 | 2 523 | 2 029 |
| Goose Creek | 8.2 | 226 | 0.0 | 260 | 47.9 | 81.7 | 36.9 | 90.9 | 51.53 | 2 005 | 2 306 |
| Greenville | 114.1 | 1 943 | 8.1 | 1 138 | 40.8 | 78.8 | 31.4 | 88.8 | 50.24 | 3 272 | 1 526 |
| Greer | 89.1 | 3 810 | 10.5 | NA | NA | NA | NA | NA | NA | NA | NA |
| Hilton Head Island | 108.0 | 3 176 | 0.0 | 247 | 47.9 | 80.5 | 37.3 | 88.2 | 52.52 | 2 128 | 2 012 |
| Mount Pleasant | 101.8 | 1 573 | 0.0 | 572 | 47.1 | 81.1 | 37.5 | 88.5 | 49.38 | 2 260 | 2 124 |
| Myrtle Beach | 192.6 | 6 427 | 35.3 | 909 | NA | NA | NA | NA | NA | NA | NA |
| North Charleston | 122.3 | 1 337 | 11.6 | 1 006 | 47.9 | 81.7 | 36.9 | 90.9 | 51.53 | 2 005 | 2 306 |
| Rock Hill | 151.9 | 2 342 | 14.1 | 835 | 42.2 | 80.1 | 32.5 | 90.1 | 48.32 | 2 934 | 1 721 |
| Spartanburg | 138.8 | 3 573 | 0.0 | 627 | 42.1 | 79.3 | 30.1 | 91.1 | 49.95 | 3 080 | 1 591 |
| Summerville | 5.8 | 131 | 5.7 | 366 | 49.1 | 81.8 | 38.0 | 91.8 | 48.24 | 1 907 | 2 251 |
| Sumter | 52.4 | 1 350 | 32.7 | 549 | 44.9 | 80.7 | 33.6 | 91.8 | 48.65 | 2 577 | 1 913 |
| SOUTH DAKOTA | X | X | X | X | X | X | X | X | X | X | X |
| Aberdeen | 37.8 | 1 547 | 9.7 | 297 | NA | NA | NA | NA | NA | NA | NA |
| Rapid City | 89.1 | 1 393 | 2.1 | 874 | 22.3 | 70.2 | 10.3 | 82.7 | 18.45 | 7 623 | 480 |
| Sioux Falls | 178.6 | 1 179 | 48.4 | 1 152 | 14.0 | 73.0 | 2.9 | 85.6 | 24.69 | 7 812 | 747 |
| TENNESSEE | X | X | X | X | X | X | X | X | X | X | X |
| Bartlett | 40.7 | 856 | 5.0 | 496 | 37.3 | 79.6 | 27.3 | 89.9 | 55.09 | 3 665 | 1 635 |
| Brentwood | 33.3 | 949 | 0.0 | NA | NA | NA | NA | NA | NA | NA | NA |
| Bristol | 17.3 | 678 | 0.0 | 911 | NA | NA | NA | NA | NA | NA | NA |
| Chattanooga | 675.3 | 3 975 | 176.7 | 3 048 | 39.4 | 79.6 | 29.9 | 89.8 | 54.52 | 3 427 | 1 608 |
| Clarksville | 828.5 | 6 946 | 119.1 | 1 075 | 35.2 | 79.0 | 25.0 | 90.4 | 51.78 | 4 058 | 1 512 |
| Cleveland | 124.1 | 3 166 | 24.5 | 1 021 | 38.0 | 77.5 | 27.7 | 88.5 | 55.42 | 3 782 | 1 333 |
| Collierville | 69.8 | 1 782 | 1.6 | 458 | 37.9 | 81.1 | 28.2 | 91.1 | 53.63 | 3 491 | 1 838 |
| Columbia | 49.0 | 1 442 | 8.5 | 494 | 35.6 | 77.2 | 25.0 | 88.5 | 56.13 | 4 183 | 1 267 |
| Cookeville | 124.2 | 4 297 | 7.0 | 2 266 | NA | NA | NA | NA | NA | NA | NA |

1. Based on the population estimated as of July 1 of the year shown.    2. Represents normal values based on the 30-year period, 1971–2000.    3. Average daily minimum.    4. Average daily maximum.

# Table D. Cities — Land Area and Population

| STATE Place code | City | Land area,[1] 2010 (sq km) | Population, 2012 | | | Race alone or in combination, not of Hispanic origin (percent), 2010 | | | | | | |
|---|---|---|---|---|---|---|---|---|---|---|---|---|
| | | | | | | Race alone or in combination | | | | | | |
| | | | Total persons | Rank | Per square kilometer | White | Black | American Indian, Alaska Native | Asian | Hawaiian Pacific Islander | Percent Hispanic or Latino[2], 2010 | Percent Foreign born 2007–2011 |
| | | 1 | 2 | 3 | 4 | 5 | 6 | 7 | 8 | 9 | 10 | 11 |
| | **TENNESSEE— Cont'd** | | | | | | | | | | | |
| 47 27740 | Franklin | 106.8 | 66 280 | 509 | 620.6 | 81.5 | 7.2 | 0.6 | 4.3 | 0.1 | 7.6 | 9.6 |
| 47 28540 | Gallatin | 80.8 | 31 603 | 1 148 | 391.1 | 75.9 | 15.6 | 0.7 | 1.0 | 0.1 | 8.0 | 6.0 |
| 47 28960 | Germantown | 51.7 | 39 446 | 923 | 763.0 | 88.9 | 3.8 | 0.4 | 5.7 | 0.1 | 1.9 | 8.1 |
| 47 33280 | Hendersonville | 81.3 | 53 080 | 679 | 652.9 | 88.0 | 6.9 | 0.8 | 2.0 | 0.1 | 3.6 | 4.6 |
| 47 37640 | Jackson | 139.2 | 67 265 | 500 | 483.2 | 48.9 | 46.4 | 0.4 | 1.4 | 0.1 | 4.0 | 4.3 |
| 47 38320 | Johnson City | 111.2 | 64 528 | 530 | 580.3 | 86.8 | 7.6 | 0.8 | 2.3 | 0.1 | 4.2 | 5.0 |
| 47 39560 | Kingsport | 129.0 | 51 501 | 703 | 399.2 | 92.4 | 4.9 | 0.8 | 1.2 | 0.1 | 2.1 | 1.9 |
| 47 40000 | Knoxville | 255.2 | 182 200 | 128 | 713.9 | 76.1 | 18.3 | 0.9 | 2.0 | 0.2 | 4.6 | 4.6 |
| 47 41200 | La Vergne | 64.6 | 33 777 | 1 080 | 522.9 | 60.4 | 24.2 | 0.6 | 3.8 | 0.2 | 13.0 | 11.1 |
| 47 41520 | Lebanon | 100.1 | 27 710 | 1 306 | 276.8 | 80.0 | 13.1 | 0.8 | 1.5 | 0.1 | 6.2 | 6.6 |
| 47 46380 | Maryville | 43.5 | 27 914 | 1 294 | 641.7 | 91.6 | 3.9 | 0.8 | 1.9 | 0.1 | 3.2 | 4.2 |
| 47 48000 | Memphis | 816.0 | 655 155 | 20 | 802.9 | 28.3 | 63.8 | 0.5 | 1.8 | 0.1 | 6.5 | 6.2 |
| 47 50280 | Morristown | 72.3 | 29 269 | 1 244 | 404.8 | 72.6 | 7.7 | 0.7 | 1.0 | 0.2 | 19.7 | 12.6 |
| 47 51560 | Murfreesboro | 143.4 | 114 038 | 234 | 795.2 | 75.0 | 16.3 | 0.8 | 4.0 | 0.1 | 5.9 | 6.7 |
| 47 52004 | Nashville-Davidson | 1 305.4 | 624 496 | 25 | 507.5 | 59.0 | 28.5 | 0.7 | 3.6 | 0.1 | 9.8 | 11.7 |
| 47 55120 | Oak Ridge | 220.8 | 29 320 | 1 243 | 132.8 | 84.3 | 9.5 | 1.2 | 3.0 | 0.1 | 4.6 | 5.7 |
| 47 69420 | Smyrna | 76.7 | 41 705 | 873 | 543.7 | 73.3 | 12.3 | 0.8 | 4.8 | 0.1 | 10.7 | 7.2 |
| 47 70580 | Spring Hill | 70.1 | 31 140 | 1 169 | 444.2 | 86.9 | 6.1 | 0.6 | 2.1 | 0.3 | 5.6 | 3.2 |
| 48 00000 | **TEXAS** | 676 587.0 | 26 059 203 | X | 38.5 | 46.4 | 12.0 | 0.7 | 4.2 | 0.1 | 37.6 | 16.2 |
| 48 01000 | Abilene | 276.6 | 118 887 | 223 | 429.8 | 64.1 | 10.0 | 0.9 | 2.1 | 0.2 | 24.5 | 5.8 |
| 48 01924 | Allen | 68.1 | 89 640 | 336 | 1 316.3 | 66.8 | 8.8 | 1.0 | 14.0 | 0.1 | 11.2 | 15.4 |
| 48 03000 | Amarillo | 257.6 | 195 250 | 119 | 758.0 | 61.1 | 7.0 | 1.0 | 3.4 | 0.1 | 28.8 | 10.4 |
| 48 04000 | Arlington | 248.3 | 375 600 | 50 | 1 512.7 | 46.5 | 19.3 | 0.9 | 7.4 | 0.2 | 27.4 | 19.9 |
| 48 05000 | Austin | 771.6 | 842 592 | 11 | 1 092.0 | 50.3 | 8.3 | 0.7 | 7.1 | 0.1 | 35.1 | 19.3 |
| 48 06128 | Baytown | 91.8 | 73 238 | 449 | 797.8 | 39.5 | 15.6 | 0.5 | 1.6 | 0.1 | 43.4 | 17.7 |
| 48 07000 | Beaumont | 214.5 | 118 228 | 224 | 551.2 | 35.7 | 47.7 | 0.7 | 3.5 | 0.1 | 13.4 | 9.0 |
| 48 07132 | Bedford | 25.9 | 48 150 | 769 | 1 859.1 | 75.1 | 7.5 | 1.1 | 5.1 | 0.5 | 12.5 | 9.8 |
| 48 08236 | Big Spring | 49.5 | 27 546 | 1 319 | 556.5 | 47.6 | 7.9 | 0.9 | 1.1 | 0.1 | 43.1 | 18.8 |
| 48 10768 | Brownsville | 342.7 | 180 097 | 131 | 525.5 | 5.9 | 0.2 | 0.1 | 0.7 | 0.0 | 93.2 | 30.2 |
| 48 10912 | Bryan | 115.0 | 78 061 | 412 | 678.8 | 44.0 | 18.2 | 0.6 | 2.0 | 0.1 | 36.2 | 12.4 |
| 48 11428 | Burleson | 67.4 | 38 983 | 938 | 578.4 | 84.6 | 2.7 | 1.0 | 1.4 | 0.1 | 11.5 | 3.1 |
| 48 13024 | Carrollton | 94.0 | 125 409 | 206 | 1 334.1 | 47.6 | 8.7 | 0.7 | 14.3 | 0.1 | 30.0 | 24.6 |
| 48 13492 | Cedar Hill | 92.8 | 46 461 | 795 | 500.7 | 27.1 | 52.5 | 0.9 | 2.4 | 0.1 | 18.7 | 7.7 |
| 48 13552 | Cedar Park | 59.2 | 57 957 | 611 | 979.0 | 71.3 | 4.8 | 0.9 | 6.0 | 0.2 | 19.0 | 8.9 |
| 48 15364 | Cleburne | 76.6 | 29 344 | 1 241 | 383.1 | 67.2 | 4.8 | 0.7 | 0.7 | 0.4 | 27.1 | 11.1 |
| 48 15976 | College Station | 128.1 | 97 801 | 298 | 763.5 | 69.7 | 7.0 | 0.6 | 10.0 | 0.2 | 14.0 | 14.2 |
| 48 16432 | Conroe | 136.5 | 61 533 | 564 | 450.8 | 49.3 | 10.4 | 0.7 | 2.0 | 0.1 | 38.5 | 23.8 |
| 48 16612 | Coppell | 37.3 | 40 022 | 912 | 1 073.0 | 67.7 | 4.8 | 0.8 | 17.0 | 0.2 | 11.3 | 18.8 |
| 48 16624 | Copperas Cove | 46.7 | 33 374 | 1 095 | 714.6 | 62.5 | 20.0 | 1.7 | 4.4 | 1.5 | 15.0 | 7.5 |
| 48 17000 | Corpus Christi | 416.0 | 312 195 | 60 | 750.5 | 34.1 | 4.2 | 0.5 | 2.1 | 0.1 | 59.7 | 7.6 |
| 48 19000 | Dallas | 881.9 | 1 241 162 | 9 | 1 407.4 | 29.6 | 25.1 | 0.6 | 3.2 | 0.1 | 42.4 | 24.6 |
| 48 19624 | Deer Park | 27.1 | 32 995 | 1 103 | 1 217.5 | 70.4 | 1.6 | 0.7 | 1.7 | 0.2 | 26.3 | 7.2 |
| 48 19792 | Del Rio | 52.2 | 35 543 | 1 030 | 680.9 | 14.0 | 1.2 | 0.3 | 0.5 | 0.1 | 84.1 | 23.3 |
| 48 19972 | Denton | 227.8 | 121 123 | 216 | 531.7 | 63.7 | 10.9 | 1.2 | 4.8 | 0.2 | 21.2 | 13.3 |
| 48 20092 | DeSoto | 56.0 | 51 102 | 714 | 912.5 | 18.3 | 69.0 | 0.6 | 1.1 | 0.1 | 12.1 | 5.0 |
| 48 21628 | Duncanville | 29.1 | 39 501 | 920 | 1 357.4 | 33.3 | 30.1 | 0.7 | 1.9 | 0.0 | 35.0 | 14.2 |
| 48 21892 | Eagle Pass | 24.8 | 27 283 | 1 335 | 1 100.1 | 3.7 | 0.2 | 0.2 | 0.5 | 0.0 | 95.5 | 35.9 |
| 48 22660 | Edinburg | 97.5 | 81 029 | 393 | 831.1 | 8.2 | 1.4 | 0.1 | 2.2 | 0.0 | 88.2 | 20.6 |
| 48 24000 | El Paso | 661.1 | 672 538 | 19 | 1 017.3 | 14.9 | 3.1 | 0.4 | 1.4 | 0.2 | 80.7 | 25.5 |
| 48 24768 | Euless | 42.0 | 52 780 | 683 | 1 256.7 | 57.2 | 11.4 | 1.1 | 11.1 | 2.3 | 19.0 | 17.5 |
| 48 25452 | Farmers Branch | 30.6 | 29 368 | 1 240 | 959.7 | 45.2 | 4.9 | 0.7 | 4.8 | 0.0 | 45.4 | 23.4 |
| 48 26232 | Flower Mound | 107.2 | 67 825 | 494 | 632.7 | 79.1 | 3.5 | 0.9 | 9.4 | 0.2 | 8.4 | 8.9 |
| 48 27000 | Fort Worth | 880.1 | 777 992 | 16 | 884.0 | 43.0 | 19.2 | 0.8 | 4.2 | 0.2 | 34.1 | 17.5 |
| 48 27648 | Friendswood | 53.7 | 36 898 | 988 | 687.1 | 78.8 | 3.7 | 0.7 | 5.4 | 0.1 | 12.5 | 8.1 |
| 48 27684 | Frisco | 160.1 | 128 176 | 196 | 800.6 | 69.2 | 8.6 | 0.9 | 11.2 | 0.1 | 12.1 | 14.5 |
| 48 28068 | Galveston | 106.8 | 47 762 | 774 | 447.2 | 46.3 | 19.2 | 1.0 | 3.5 | 0.1 | 31.3 | 12.8 |
| 48 29000 | Garland | 147.9 | 233 564 | 86 | 1 579.2 | 37.8 | 14.8 | 0.8 | 9.9 | 0.1 | 37.8 | 27.0 |
| 48 29336 | Georgetown | 124.0 | 52 303 | 691 | 421.8 | 73.3 | 3.9 | 0.7 | 1.4 | 0.1 | 21.8 | 10.1 |
| 48 30464 | Grand Prairie | 186.8 | 181 824 | 129 | 973.4 | 30.3 | 20.5 | 0.8 | 6.9 | 0.1 | 42.7 | 20.9 |
| 48 30644 | Grapevine | 82.7 | 48 447 | 763 | 585.8 | 73.5 | 3.6 | 0.9 | 5.1 | 0.3 | 18.0 | 9.9 |
| 48 30920 | Greenville | 84.5 | 25 834 | 1 397 | 305.7 | 59.0 | 17.2 | 1.2 | 1.2 | 0.3 | 22.4 | 10.2 |
| 48 31928 | Haltom City | 32.0 | 43 376 | 840 | 1 355.5 | 48.3 | 4.4 | 0.9 | 8.4 | 0.3 | 38.9 | 24.6 |
| 48 32312 | Harker Heights | 39.3 | 27 826 | 1 297 | 708.0 | 56.5 | 21.3 | 1.4 | 5.5 | 1.3 | 18.4 | 8.7 |
| 48 32372 | Harlingen | 103.1 | 65 679 | 517 | 637.0 | 18.3 | 0.7 | 0.2 | 1.4 | 0.1 | 79.5 | 17.2 |
| 48 35000 | Houston | 1 552.9 | 2 160 821 | 4 | 1 391.5 | 26.4 | 23.6 | 0.4 | 6.5 | 0.1 | 43.8 | 28.4 |
| 48 35528 | Huntsville | 92.9 | 39 666 | 917 | 427.0 | 54.3 | 25.8 | 0.6 | 1.6 | 0.1 | 18.7 | 7.9 |
| 48 35576 | Hurst | 25.7 | 38 194 | 959 | 1 486.1 | 71.0 | 6.1 | 1.2 | 2.8 | 0.5 | 20.1 | 12.7 |
| 48 37000 | Irving | 173.6 | 225 427 | 93 | 1 298.5 | 32.0 | 12.5 | 0.8 | 14.7 | 0.2 | 41.1 | 33.1 |
| 48 38632 | Keller | 47.8 | 41 923 | 870 | 877.1 | 85.8 | 2.6 | 0.9 | 4.6 | 0.2 | 7.4 | 6.7 |

1. Dry land or land partially or temporarily covered by water.  2. May be of any race.

# Table D. Cities — **Population**

| City | Age of population (percent), 2010 | | | | | | | | | | | Population | | | |
|---|---|---|---|---|---|---|---|---|---|---|---|---|---|---|---|
| | | | | | | | | | | | | Census counts | | Percent change | |
| | Under 5 years | 5 to 17 years | 18 to 24 years | 25 to 34 years | 35 to 44 years | 45 to 54 years | 55 to 64 years | 65 to 74 years | 75 years and over | Median age | Percent female | 2000 | 2010 | 2000– 2010 | 2010– 2012 |
| | 12 | 13 | 14 | 15 | 16 | 17 | 18 | 19 | 20 | 21 | 22 | 23 | 24 | 25 | 26 |
| TENNESSEE— Cont'd | | | | | | | | | | | | | | | |
| Franklin | 7.4 | 20.0 | 6.6 | 13.3 | 16.8 | 15.5 | 10.4 | 5.3 | 4.8 | 36.8 | 52.2 | 41 842 | 62 608 | 49.3 | 5.9 |
| Gallatin | 7.5 | 16.7 | 9.0 | 14.7 | 13.2 | 13.8 | 11.5 | 7.5 | 6.1 | 36.6 | 52.0 | 23 230 | 30 382 | 30.3 | 4.0 |
| Germantown | 4.9 | 19.2 | 5.6 | 7.2 | 12.1 | 17.5 | 17.5 | 9.5 | 6.6 | 45.7 | 51.6 | 37 348 | 38 844 | 4.0 | 1.5 |
| Hendersonville | 6.4 | 19.4 | 7.3 | 11.9 | 15.3 | 15.1 | 11.8 | 7.5 | 5.3 | 38.5 | 51.7 | 40 620 | 51 328 | 26.5 | 3.4 |
| Jackson | 7.4 | 17.3 | 13.4 | 13.4 | 12.0 | 13.1 | 10.6 | 6.4 | 6.3 | 33.8 | 53.8 | 59 643 | 66 929 | 9.3 | 0.5 |
| Johnson City | 5.3 | 13.8 | 15.7 | 13.1 | 11.8 | 13.2 | 11.8 | 7.7 | 7.6 | 36.9 | 51.9 | 55 469 | 63 166 | 13.9 | 2.2 |
| Kingsport | 5.8 | 15.3 | 7.3 | 10.5 | 12.4 | 14.4 | 13.5 | 10.3 | 10.5 | 44.0 | 53.6 | 44 905 | 51 519 | 7.3 | 0.0 |
| Knoxville | 6.2 | 12.9 | 17.7 | 16.0 | 11.8 | 12.3 | 10.5 | 6.0 | 6.6 | 32.7 | 52.0 | 173 890 | 178 874 | 2.9 | 1.9 |
| La Vergne | 8.7 | 23.1 | 7.8 | 17.4 | 17.0 | 13.0 | 7.7 | 3.6 | 1.6 | 31.2 | 50.9 | 18 687 | 32 588 | 74.4 | 3.6 |
| Lebanon | 7.5 | 16.9 | 10.3 | 13.5 | 13.1 | 13.3 | 10.9 | 7.7 | 6.7 | 36.3 | 52.3 | 20 235 | 26 146 | 29.4 | 6.0 |
| Maryville | 5.3 | 19.0 | 10.1 | 10.4 | 13.8 | 13.8 | 10.6 | 7.6 | 9.5 | 39.1 | 53.4 | 23 120 | 27 601 | 18.8 | 1.1 |
| Memphis | 7.6 | 18.3 | 11.4 | 15.2 | 12.6 | 13.5 | 11.0 | 5.5 | 4.9 | 33.0 | 52.5 | 650 100 | 646 889 | -0.5 | 1.3 |
| Morristown | 8.1 | 16.7 | 9.5 | 14.1 | 12.5 | 12.1 | 11.0 | 7.8 | 8.2 | 36.2 | 52.1 | 24 965 | 29 150 | 16.7 | 0.4 |
| Murfreesboro | 7.1 | 16.4 | 18.7 | 17.0 | 13.1 | 11.4 | 8.2 | 4.5 | 3.7 | 29.0 | 50.9 | 68 816 | 109 048 | 58.0 | 4.6 |
| Nashville-Davidson | 7.1 | 14.6 | 11.7 | 18.1 | 13.7 | 13.6 | 10.7 | 5.6 | 4.9 | 33.9 | 51.6 | 569 891 | 603 527 | 10.0 | 3.5 |
| Oak Ridge | 5.5 | 16.5 | 7.1 | 11.0 | 11.7 | 15.0 | 13.9 | 8.4 | 10.9 | 43.5 | 52.8 | 27 387 | 29 330 | 7.1 | 0.0 |
| Smyrna | 8.6 | 19.3 | 9.0 | 16.3 | 15.3 | 13.8 | 9.1 | 5.2 | 3.4 | 33.0 | 51.3 | 25 569 | 39 974 | 56.3 | 4.3 |
| Spring Hill | 10.6 | 23.3 | 5.3 | 17.1 | 19.0 | 12.5 | 7.3 | 3.3 | 1.7 | 31.9 | 51.5 | 7 715 | 29 036 | 276.4 | 7.2 |
| TEXAS | 7.7 | 19.6 | 10.2 | 14.4 | 13.8 | 13.7 | 10.3 | 5.9 | 4.5 | 33.6 | 50.4 | 20 851 820 | 25 145 561 | 20.6 | 3.6 |
| Abilene | 7.5 | 15.9 | 15.5 | 15.1 | 11.2 | 12.5 | 9.6 | 6.2 | 6.3 | 31.7 | 49.5 | 115 930 | 117 063 | 1.0 | 1.6 |
| Allen | 8.2 | 24.3 | 6.1 | 11.9 | 19.6 | 16.2 | 8.2 | 3.6 | 2.0 | 34.7 | 50.9 | 43 554 | 84 246 | 93.4 | 6.4 |
| Amarillo | 8.3 | 19.1 | 9.8 | 14.7 | 12.2 | 13.2 | 10.7 | 6.2 | 5.8 | 33.4 | 51.5 | 173 627 | 190 695 | 9.8 | 2.4 |
| Arlington | 7.8 | 20.1 | 11.1 | 15.2 | 14.4 | 13.7 | 9.5 | 4.8 | 3.4 | 32.1 | 50.9 | 332 969 | 365 372 | 9.8 | 2.8 |
| Austin | 7.3 | 14.9 | 14.5 | 20.7 | 14.8 | 12.1 | 8.7 | 3.9 | 3.1 | 31.0 | 49.4 | 656 562 | 790 637 | 20.4 | 6.6 |
| Baytown | 8.6 | 20.6 | 10.5 | 14.3 | 13.0 | 12.4 | 10.4 | 5.4 | 4.7 | 32.1 | 51.2 | 66 430 | 71 690 | 8.1 | 2.2 |
| Beaumont | 7.3 | 17.5 | 12.0 | 14.0 | 11.8 | 14.0 | 11.3 | 6.1 | 6.1 | 34.4 | 51.3 | 113 866 | 118 296 | 3.9 | -0.1 |
| Bedford | 5.3 | 14.6 | 8.7 | 14.8 | 13.2 | 15.7 | 14.0 | 7.7 | 6.1 | 40.3 | 52.5 | 47 152 | 46 979 | -0.4 | 2.5 |
| Big Spring | 6.7 | 15.6 | 11.5 | 14.6 | 11.9 | 17.6 | 10.3 | 6.0 | 5.9 | 36.5 | 42.0 | 25 233 | 27 282 | 8.1 | 1.0 |
| Brownsville | 9.0 | 25.1 | 10.0 | 13.4 | 13.2 | 10.8 | 8.7 | 5.4 | 4.5 | 29.5 | 52.8 | 139 722 | 175 026 | 25.3 | 2.9 |
| Bryan | 8.3 | 17.3 | 17.4 | 17.1 | 11.7 | 11.2 | 8.0 | 4.6 | 4.5 | 28.5 | 49.8 | 65 660 | 76 220 | 16.1 | 2.4 |
| Burleson | 8.4 | 21.8 | 7.8 | 15.1 | 14.9 | 13.0 | 9.4 | 5.8 | 4.0 | 32.9 | 51.3 | 20 976 | 36 690 | 74.9 | 6.2 |
| Carrollton | 6.7 | 19.3 | 8.5 | 14.6 | 15.2 | 16.5 | 11.2 | 5.1 | 2.9 | 35.6 | 51.1 | 109 576 | 119 097 | 8.7 | 5.3 |
| Cedar Hill | 7.3 | 22.8 | 8.4 | 12.8 | 15.9 | 15.4 | 10.3 | 4.2 | 2.9 | 34.1 | 53.3 | 32 093 | 45 028 | 40.3 | 3.2 |
| Cedar Park | 8.6 | 21.9 | 7.3 | 15.2 | 18.5 | 13.9 | 7.9 | 3.8 | 2.9 | 33.4 | 51.4 | 26 049 | 51 739 | 87.9 | 12.0 |
| Cleburne | 8.4 | 19.5 | 9.6 | 13.8 | 13.2 | 12.0 | 10.5 | 6.8 | 6.3 | 33.9 | 51.0 | 26 005 | 29 380 | 12.8 | -0.1 |
| College Station | 4.8 | 9.9 | 47.3 | 14.8 | 7.6 | 6.2 | 4.7 | 2.7 | 2.0 | 22.3 | 49.2 | 67 890 | 94 063 | 38.2 | 4.0 |
| Conroe | 8.9 | 17.7 | 11.4 | 17.5 | 13.1 | 11.2 | 9.3 | 5.8 | 5.1 | 31.5 | 49.5 | 36 811 | 57 126 | 52.7 | 7.7 |
| Coppell | 6.0 | 24.4 | 6.1 | 10.0 | 16.4 | 21.7 | 10.2 | 3.2 | 2.1 | 37.7 | 50.9 | 35 958 | 38 659 | 7.5 | 3.5 |
| Copperas Cove | 9.7 | 19.6 | 12.4 | 17.7 | 12.7 | 11.9 | 8.2 | 5.2 | 2.6 | 29.0 | 51.5 | 29 592 | 32 032 | 8.2 | 4.2 |
| Corpus Christi | 7.1 | 18.7 | 10.4 | 13.9 | 12.2 | 14.2 | 11.6 | 6.3 | 5.6 | 34.8 | 51.0 | 277 454 | 305 215 | 10.0 | 2.3 |
| Dallas | 8.6 | 17.9 | 10.5 | 18.4 | 14.2 | 12.5 | 9.1 | 4.8 | 4.1 | 31.8 | 50.0 | 1 188 580 | 1 197 833 | 0.8 | 3.6 |
| Deer Park | 6.9 | 20.3 | 8.9 | 13.5 | 13.6 | 14.6 | 11.9 | 6.1 | 4.2 | 35.3 | 50.7 | 28 520 | 32 010 | 12.2 | 3.1 |
| Del Rio | 8.2 | 21.2 | 9.6 | 13.1 | 13.1 | 11.8 | 9.9 | 7.2 | 6.0 | 33.4 | 50.3 | 33 867 | 35 593 | 5.1 | -0.1 |
| Denton | 6.1 | 14.3 | 25.0 | 16.2 | 11.4 | 10.1 | 7.9 | 5.1 | 3.8 | 27.1 | 51.2 | 80 537 | 114 252 | 40.8 | 6.0 |
| DeSoto | 6.5 | 20.4 | 7.9 | 11.2 | 14.8 | 15.4 | 13.1 | 6.4 | 4.4 | 37.8 | 54.2 | 37 646 | 49 047 | 30.3 | 4.2 |
| Duncanville | 7.4 | 20.5 | 9.0 | 12.6 | 13.0 | 13.7 | 12.0 | 6.9 | 4.9 | 35.4 | 52.5 | 36 081 | 38 524 | 6.8 | 2.5 |
| Eagle Pass | 8.2 | 23.6 | 8.8 | 11.7 | 12.9 | 11.2 | 10.3 | 7.1 | 6.2 | 33.1 | 52.4 | 22 413 | 26 248 | 17.1 | 3.9 |
| Edinburg | 8.9 | 22.0 | 13.9 | 16.4 | 13.9 | 10.3 | 7.2 | 4.1 | 3.2 | 28.0 | 50.3 | 48 465 | 76 952 | 59.1 | 5.3 |
| El Paso | 7.9 | 21.3 | 10.8 | 13.2 | 13.0 | 12.9 | 9.7 | 5.9 | 5.3 | 32.5 | 52.0 | 563 662 | 649 138 | 15.2 | 3.6 |
| Euless | 7.1 | 16.9 | 9.2 | 17.8 | 16.0 | 15.3 | 10.1 | 5.0 | 2.7 | 34.4 | 51.0 | 46 005 | 51 277 | 11.5 | 2.9 |
| Farmers Branch | 6.6 | 17.3 | 9.5 | 15.7 | 13.4 | 13.9 | 10.3 | 7.2 | 6.1 | 35.6 | 50.8 | 27 508 | 28 616 | 4.0 | 2.6 |
| Flower Mound | 6.0 | 26.7 | 5.6 | 7.3 | 18.8 | 20.5 | 9.6 | 3.7 | 1.9 | 38.1 | 50.4 | 50 702 | 64 685 | 27.5 | 4.9 |
| Fort Worth | 9.0 | 20.3 | 10.2 | 16.4 | 14.6 | 12.5 | 8.8 | 4.5 | 3.7 | 31.2 | 50.9 | 534 694 | 742 066 | 38.6 | 4.8 |
| Friendswood | 5.2 | 22.3 | 7.2 | 8.9 | 13.8 | 18.2 | 12.7 | 6.7 | 5.0 | 40.2 | 51.5 | 29 037 | 35 803 | 23.3 | 3.1 |
| Frisco | 9.6 | 23.7 | 4.9 | 13.9 | 22.5 | 13.0 | 7.0 | 3.7 | 1.7 | 33.9 | 51.1 | 33 714 | 117 003 | 247.0 | 9.5 |
| Galveston | 5.9 | 13.5 | 13.1 | 13.6 | 11.1 | 15.8 | 13.5 | 7.6 | 6.0 | 38.8 | 48.9 | 57 247 | 47 743 | -16.6 | 0.0 |
| Garland | 7.6 | 20.9 | 9.6 | 13.7 | 14.4 | 14.2 | 10.5 | 5.5 | 3.7 | 33.7 | 51.0 | 215 768 | 226 876 | 5.1 | 2.9 |
| Georgetown | 5.7 | 15.4 | 8.8 | 10.3 | 10.8 | 10.8 | 12.5 | 14.7 | 11.0 | 44.0 | 51.8 | 28 339 | 47 416 | 67.3 | 10.3 |
| Grand Prairie | 8.5 | 22.4 | 9.7 | 15.2 | 15.5 | 13.4 | 8.8 | 4.1 | 2.5 | 31.3 | 51.1 | 127 427 | 175 462 | 37.6 | 3.6 |
| Grapevine | 5.7 | 19.4 | 8.0 | 13.3 | 15.2 | 18.7 | 11.8 | 4.6 | 3.2 | 37.5 | 50.5 | 42 059 | 46 334 | 10.2 | 4.6 |
| Greenville | 8.5 | 17.9 | 10.1 | 14.7 | 11.9 | 12.8 | 9.7 | 7.2 | 7.2 | 34.0 | 51.3 | 23 960 | 25 557 | 6.7 | 1.1 |
| Haltom City | 8.8 | 19.1 | 11.0 | 15.9 | 13.6 | 12.9 | 9.1 | 5.3 | 4.3 | 31.7 | 49.7 | 39 018 | 42 409 | 8.7 | 2.3 |
| Harker Heights | 8.0 | 22.5 | 9.4 | 14.7 | 16.2 | 13.6 | 8.3 | 4.3 | 2.9 | 31.6 | 50.6 | 17 308 | 26 718 | 54.3 | 4.1 |
| Harlingen | 8.6 | 21.8 | 9.4 | 12.9 | 12.2 | 11.5 | 10.0 | 6.6 | 7.0 | 32.8 | 52.2 | 57 564 | 64 898 | 12.7 | 1.2 |
| Houston | 8.1 | 17.7 | 11.0 | 17.8 | 13.9 | 12.8 | 9.7 | 5.1 | 4.0 | 32.1 | 49.8 | 1 953 631 | 2 097 217 | 7.5 | 3.0 |
| Huntsville | 4.7 | 9.3 | 29.3 | 15.4 | 12.2 | 12.4 | 8.3 | 4.5 | 4.0 | 28.6 | 40.9 | 35 078 | 38 548 | 9.9 | 2.9 |
| Hurst | 6.9 | 17.2 | 7.9 | 13.1 | 13.2 | 15.0 | 11.8 | 8.0 | 6.9 | 38.8 | 51.7 | 36 273 | 37 337 | 2.9 | 2.3 |
| Irving | 8.6 | 17.9 | 10.5 | 20.1 | 15.7 | 12.4 | 7.9 | 4.1 | 2.9 | 31.3 | 50.0 | 191 615 | 216 290 | 12.9 | 4.2 |
| Keller | 5.5 | 24.9 | 5.8 | 7.0 | 16.6 | 20.3 | 11.3 | 4.8 | 3.8 | 39.9 | 51.2 | 27 345 | 39 633 | 44.9 | 5.8 |

# Table D. Cities — Households, Group Quarters, Crime, and Education

| City | Households, 2010 | | | | Persons in group quarters, 2010 | | | | Serious crimes known to police,[2] 2011 | | | | Educational attainment, 2007–2011 | | |
|---|---|---|---|---|---|---|---|---|---|---|---|---|---|---|---|
| | | | Percent | | | Institutional | | | Total | | Rate[3] | | | Attainment[4] (percent) | |
| | Number | Persons per household | Female family householder[1] | One-person | Total | Total | Persons in nursing facilities | Non-institutional | Number | Rate[3] | Violent | Property | Population age 25 and older | High school graduate or less | Bachelor's degree or more |
| | 27 | 28 | 29 | 30 | 31 | 32 | 33 | 34 | 35 | 36 | 37 | 38 | 39 | 40 | 41 |
| TENNESSEE—Cont'd | | | | | | | | | | | | | | | |
| Franklin | 24 040 | 2.57 | 10.0 | 25.5 | 795 | 792 | 491 | 3 | 1 129 | 1 791 | 165 | 1 626 | 40 474 | 23.1 | 53.0 |
| Gallatin | 11 871 | 2.48 | 15.7 | 27.9 | 890 | 870 | 308 | 20 | 715 | 2 340 | 281 | 2 059 | 19 817 | 49.8 | 17.8 |
| Germantown | 14 910 | 2.60 | 6.4 | 19.7 | 43 | 43 | 43 | 0 | 506 | 1 291 | 71 | 1 220 | 27 056 | 12.2 | 63.0 |
| Hendersonville | 20 111 | 2.55 | 11.2 | 24.4 | 139 | 128 | 128 | 11 | 1 032 | 1 991 | 233 | 1 757 | 33 260 | 36.1 | 33.0 |
| Jackson | 25 191 | 2.42 | 21.4 | 30.8 | 4 297 | 1 456 | 557 | 2 841 | 4 425 | 6 725 | 1 014 | 5 711 | 40 058 | 47.4 | 25.9 |
| Johnson City | 27 017 | 2.19 | 11.8 | 35.4 | 3 936 | 750 | 626 | 3 186 | 3 243 | 5 089 | 436 | 4 653 | 40 804 | 36.6 | 35.3 |
| Kingsport | 21 289 | 2.22 | 13.5 | 33.9 | 887 | 744 | 660 | 143 | 3 619 | 7 440 | 767 | 6 674 | 34 472 | 48.8 | 25.1 |
| Knoxville | 78 048 | 2.16 | 14.6 | 38.3 | 10 048 | 1 723 | 1 287 | 8 325 | 14 622 | 8 101 | 945 | 7 157 | 113 383 | 42.6 | 29.7 |
| La Vergne | 10 916 | 2.98 | 16.9 | 17.2 | 5 | 0 | 0 | 5 | 957 | 2 910 | 401 | 2 509 | 18 381 | 49.0 | 17.1 |
| Lebanon | 10 130 | 2.48 | 16.2 | 28.0 | 1 101 | 609 | 375 | 492 | 1 270 | 4 806 | 681 | 4 125 | 16 784 | 54.4 | 20.7 |
| Maryville | 10 712 | 2.41 | 12.8 | 30.4 | 1 644 | 886 | 529 | 758 | 931 | 3 359 | 274 | 3 085 | 18 025 | 39.4 | 32.2 |
| Memphis | 250 344 | 2.52 | 25.3 | 32.2 | 16 536 | 10 165 | 2 710 | 6 371 | 52 739 | 8 080 | 1 584 | 6 496 | 408 405 | 48.1 | 23.1 |
| Morristown | 11 412 | 2.47 | 16.0 | 31.0 | 903 | 763 | 487 | 140 | 2 169 | 7 378 | 663 | 6 714 | 19 412 | 60.8 | 15.4 |
| Murfreesboro | 41 940 | 2.49 | 13.1 | 27.3 | 4 434 | 1 348 | 458 | 3 086 | 5 526 | 5 036 | 601 | 4 434 | 62 798 | 32.2 | 35.5 |
| Nashville-Davidson | 259 499 | 2.32 | 14.7 | 34.5 | 25 870 | 9 226 | 2 169 | 16 644 | 36 597 | 5 972 | 1 184 | 4 789 | 412 924 | 39.6 | 34.4 |
| Oak Ridge | 12 772 | 2.26 | 12.9 | 33.3 | 483 | 226 | 218 | 257 | 1 299 | 4 389 | 476 | 3 913 | 20 211 | 35.1 | 38.3 |
| Smyrna | 14 807 | 2.68 | 15.0 | 23.0 | 365 | 353 | 215 | 12 | 859 | 2 130 | 181 | 1 949 | 24 670 | 44.4 | 21.7 |
| Spring Hill | 9 861 | 2.94 | 9.9 | 16.5 | 47 | 30 | 0 | 17 | 392 | 1 338 | 119 | 1 219 | 16 699 | 27.8 | 38.3 |
| TEXAS | 8 922 933 | 2.75 | 14.1 | 24.2 | 581 139 | 375 392 | 94 278 | 205 747 | 996 372 | 3 881 | 408 | 3 472 | 15 443 904 | 45.2 | 26.1 |
| Abilene | 43 612 | 2.46 | 13.7 | 28.7 | 9 592 | 5 306 | 816 | 4 286 | 4 812 | 4 026 | 358 | 3 668 | 71 756 | 46.7 | 22.5 |
| Allen | 27 870 | 3.02 | 9.9 | 14.8 | 171 | 171 | 164 | 0 | 1 606 | 1 867 | 86 | 1 781 | 50 090 | 18.4 | 49.9 |
| Amarillo | 73 918 | 2.55 | 14.1 | 27.9 | 1 881 | 1 419 | 1 019 | 462 | 10 614 | 5 451 | 629 | 4 822 | 118 730 | 42.6 | 22.3 |
| Arlington | 133 072 | 2.72 | 15.0 | 24.9 | 3 132 | 1 061 | 1 053 | 2 071 | 19 082 | 5 114 | 502 | 4 612 | 221 019 | 39.4 | 28.9 |
| Austin | 324 892 | 2.37 | 11.0 | 34.0 | 20 261 | 4 199 | 1 869 | 16 062 | 45 720 | 5 665 | 430 | 5 235 | 496 404 | 30.8 | 44.5 |
| Baytown | 24 955 | 2.85 | 16.3 | 24.1 | 601 | 507 | 507 | 94 | 3 767 | 5 138 | 289 | 4 849 | 43 288 | 52.7 | 14.4 |
| Beaumont | 45 648 | 2.48 | 19.2 | 30.7 | 5 133 | 2 634 | 513 | 2 499 | 7 725 | 6 396 | 885 | 5 511 | 74 113 | 46.8 | 23.0 |
| Bedford | 21 016 | 2.22 | 10.8 | 34.0 | 331 | 325 | 287 | 6 | 1 690 | 3 523 | 354 | 3 169 | 33 439 | 26.5 | 34.5 |
| Big Spring | 8 267 | 2.56 | 16.7 | 28.8 | 6 080 | 5 768 | 280 | 312 | 1 225 | 4 398 | 682 | 3 716 | 18 403 | 57.9 | 10.3 |
| Brownsville | 49 871 | 3.48 | 22.9 | 15.2 | 1 637 | 963 | 671 | 674 | 8 687 | 4 861 | 280 | 4 581 | 94 512 | 61.7 | 15.0 |
| Bryan | 27 725 | 2.64 | 15.4 | 28.1 | 3 097 | 2 822 | 361 | 275 | 3 330 | 4 280 | 545 | 3 735 | 40 765 | 50.8 | 25.3 |
| Burleson | 12 888 | 2.84 | 12.7 | 18.3 | 108 | 108 | 108 | 0 | 1 205 | 3 217 | 211 | 3 006 | 22 454 | 38.7 | 24.4 |
| Carrollton | 43 299 | 2.74 | 12.4 | 22.5 | 376 | 350 | 350 | 26 | 3 528 | 2 901 | 169 | 2 732 | 78 896 | 34.5 | 36.7 |
| Cedar Hill | 15 506 | 2.89 | 19.3 | 20.3 | 293 | 171 | 171 | 122 | 1 720 | 3 741 | 235 | 3 506 | 26 760 | 29.4 | 31.7 |
| Cedar Park | 17 817 | 2.74 | 11.7 | 21.4 | 137 | 107 | 107 | 30 | 762 | 1 525 | 140 | 1 385 | 28 746 | 22.6 | 41.7 |
| Cleburne | 10 439 | 2.73 | 14.1 | 25.0 | 876 | 794 | 316 | 82 | 1 588 | 5 301 | 534 | 4 767 | 18 314 | 59.6 | 12.6 |
| College Station | 35 037 | 2.38 | 7.7 | 27.5 | 10 347 | 201 | 201 | 10 146 | 3 281 | 3 424 | 301 | 3 123 | 34 383 | 20.0 | 57.5 |
| Conroe | 20 017 | 2.69 | 14.5 | 27.9 | 2 263 | 2 088 | 291 | 175 | 2 298 | 4 004 | 340 | 3 664 | 34 071 | 53.0 | 19.2 |
| Coppell | 13 806 | 2.80 | 9.3 | 18.7 | 3 | 0 | 0 | 3 | 677 | 1 715 | 84 | 1 632 | 24 523 | 13.1 | 64.3 |
| Copperas Cove | 11 858 | 2.68 | 15.8 | 21.9 | 284 | 174 | 174 | 110 | 1 032 | 3 155 | 373 | 2 782 | 19 419 | 37.9 | 17.1 |
| Corpus Christi | 112 795 | 2.66 | 16.6 | 25.6 | 5 640 | 3 199 | 1 344 | 2 441 | 16 884 | 5 418 | 638 | 4 780 | 190 998 | 46.3 | 21.2 |
| Dallas | 458 057 | 2.57 | 16.0 | 33.9 | 18 725 | 12 739 | 3 693 | 5 986 | 70 189 | 5 739 | 681 | 5 058 | 752 118 | 48.6 | 28.8 |
| Deer Park | 11 133 | 2.87 | 12.3 | 17.9 | 109 | 87 | 87 | 22 | 875 | 2 677 | 119 | 2 558 | 20 198 | 43.0 | 20.4 |
| Del Rio | 11 599 | 2.95 | 17.8 | 22.0 | 1 373 | 1 347 | 203 | 26 | 913 | 2 512 | 250 | 2 262 | 21 515 | 61.9 | 15.5 |
| Denton | 42 635 | 2.45 | 10.2 | 29.5 | 8 976 | 1 646 | 391 | 7 330 | 3 663 | 3 164 | 259 | 2 905 | 60 661 | 32.7 | 36.5 |
| DeSoto | 18 210 | 2.68 | 19.6 | 25.7 | 304 | 275 | 275 | 29 | 1 804 | 3 602 | 300 | 3 303 | 31 522 | 32.6 | 28.5 |
| Duncanville | 13 280 | 2.89 | 19.2 | 20.4 | 176 | 165 | 165 | 11 | 1 716 | 4 363 | 315 | 4 047 | 24 293 | 43.5 | 26.6 |
| Eagle Pass | 8 272 | 3.13 | 20.1 | 19.6 | 342 | 311 | 59 | 31 | 929 | 3 466 | 209 | 3 257 | 15 788 | 59.6 | 19.1 |
| Edinburg | 23 099 | 3.16 | 20.4 | 17.3 | 4 072 | 3 008 | 169 | 1 064 | 4 934 | 6 268 | 358 | 5 909 | 40 730 | 48.0 | 23.0 |
| El Paso | 216 894 | 2.95 | 20.7 | 21.5 | 9 414 | 5 777 | 1 482 | 3 637 | 19 170 | 2 892 | 431 | 2 461 | 383 149 | 49.3 | 21.9 |
| Euless | 21 531 | 2.38 | 13.5 | 32.4 | 109 | 99 | 99 | 10 | 1 879 | 3 589 | 244 | 3 344 | 33 729 | 35.7 | 30.8 |
| Farmers Branch | 10 797 | 2.64 | 11.5 | 28.6 | 103 | 0 | 0 | 103 | 1 064 | 3 642 | 127 | 3 515 | 18 717 | 44.6 | 30.4 |
| Flower Mound | 21 011 | 3.07 | 7.8 | 11.4 | 159 | 155 | 110 | 4 | 688 | 1 042 | 79 | 963 | 39 242 | 13.6 | 56.1 |
| Fort Worth | 262 660 | 2.77 | 15.3 | 26.5 | 13 977 | 8 117 | 2 410 | 5 860 | 39 751 | 5 252 | 605 | 4 647 | 439 442 | 45.7 | 25.9 |
| Friendswood | 12 726 | 2.80 | 9.5 | 18.7 | 207 | 201 | 201 | 6 | 343 | 938 | 33 | 905 | 23 047 | 19.9 | 46.3 |
| Frisco | 39 901 | 2.93 | 8.1 | 17.5 | 225 | 225 | 225 | 0 | 2 589 | 2 167 | 102 | 2 065 | 67 560 | 14.3 | 58.2 |
| Galveston | 19 943 | 2.27 | 14.7 | 36.7 | 2 477 | 1 261 | 86 | 1 216 | 2 593 | 5 319 | 620 | 4 700 | 33 046 | 45.8 | 26.4 |
| Garland | 75 696 | 2.99 | 16.1 | 20.8 | 567 | 478 | 463 | 89 | 9 213 | 3 977 | 229 | 3 748 | 138 310 | 48.6 | 21.4 |
| Georgetown | 18 830 | 2.38 | 9.4 | 25.0 | 2 499 | 1 436 | 389 | 1 063 | 861 | 1 779 | 134 | 1 645 | 31 998 | 30.4 | 39.5 |
| Grand Prairie | 58 171 | 3.01 | 16.3 | 21.0 | 257 | 188 | 188 | 69 | 7 547 | 4 214 | 330 | 3 884 | 102 061 | 49.4 | 21.2 |
| Grapevine | 18 502 | 2.49 | 10.5 | 27.1 | 242 | 226 | 226 | 16 | 1 579 | 3 338 | 192 | 3 145 | 30 557 | 24.7 | 45.6 |
| Greenville | 9 716 | 2.56 | 15.8 | 29.1 | 678 | 604 | 316 | 74 | 1 245 | 4 771 | 694 | 4 077 | 15 991 | 51.6 | 18.5 |
| Haltom City | 15 269 | 2.77 | 14.5 | 26.8 | 96 | 96 | 96 | 0 | 1 838 | 4 245 | 275 | 3 970 | 26 314 | 61.7 | 12.9 |
| Harker Heights | 9 488 | 2.80 | 14.7 | 19.3 | 166 | 166 | 166 | 0 | 1 074 | 3 940 | 260 | 3 679 | 14 727 | 33.3 | 26.5 |
| Harlingen | 21 645 | 2.95 | 19.7 | 21.2 | 1 070 | 457 | 415 | 613 | 4 415 | 6 668 | 509 | 6 159 | 40 162 | 53.7 | 19.5 |
| Houston | 782 643 | 2.64 | 16.2 | 31.0 | 37 071 | 18 243 | 4 778 | 18 828 | 129 228 | 6 028 | 975 | 5 054 | 1 321 370 | 48.5 | 28.4 |
| Huntsville | 11 791 | 2.32 | 12.8 | 31.9 | 11 239 | 8 489 | 190 | 2 750 | 1 233 | 3 133 | 478 | 2 655 | 22 587 | 51.5 | 18.4 |
| Hurst | 14 652 | 2.53 | 12.7 | 25.3 | 245 | 239 | 224 | 6 | 2 082 | 5 461 | 464 | 4 997 | 25 022 | 37.9 | 28.7 |
| Irving | 82 538 | 2.61 | 13.6 | 30.1 | 873 | 393 | 393 | 480 | 7 308 | 3 309 | 233 | 3 076 | 134 929 | 42.0 | 33.3 |
| Keller | 13 514 | 2.91 | 7.3 | 14.6 | 251 | 251 | 251 | 0 | 525 | 1 298 | 59 | 1 238 | 24 165 | 18.0 | 52.3 |

1. No spouse present.    2. Data for serious crimes have not been adjusted for underreporting. This may affect comparability between geographic areas and over time.    3. Per 100,000 population estimated by the FBI.    4. Persons 25 years old and over.

| City | Money income, 2007–2011 | | | | | Housing units, 2010 | | | Occupied Housing units 2007–2011 | | | | |
|---|---|---|---|---|---|---|---|---|---|---|---|---|---|
| | | Households | | | | | | | | Owner-occupied | | Median owner costs as a percent of income | |
| | Per capita income[1] (dollars) | Median income | Percent with income of $200,000 or more | Percent with income of less than $25,000 | Families with income below poverty (percent) | Total | Percent change, 2000–2010 | Vacant units for sale or rent[2] | Total | Percent | Median value[3] (dollars) | With a mortgage[4] | Without a mortgage[5] |
| | 42 | 43 | 44 | 45 | 46 | 47 | 48 | 49 | 50 | 51 | 52 | 53 | 54 |
| **TENNESSEE—** Cont'd | | | | | | | | | | | | | |
| Franklin | 37 519 | 77 118 | 7.7 | 12.7 | 5.9 | 25 586 | 48.6 | 1 546 | 23 757 | 68.9 | 309 400 | 23.5 | 10.0 |
| Gallatin | 24 788 | 45 941 | 1.9 | 25.1 | 11.9 | 13 093 | 35.8 | 1 222 | 11 924 | 57.2 | 155 700 | 24.0 | 12.0 |
| Germantown | 54 157 | 112 979 | 18.7 | 6.2 | 1.9 | 15 536 | 13.4 | 626 | 14 397 | 88.8 | 286 100 | 21.4 | 10.0 |
| Hendersonville | 32 119 | 63 719 | 5.4 | 17.8 | 7.0 | 21 543 | 30.6 | 1 432 | 19 235 | 70.5 | 198 200 | 23.2 | 10.0 |
| Jackson | 21 848 | 35 433 | 3.0 | 35.9 | 18.4 | 28 052 | 9.8 | 2 861 | 24 042 | 58.2 | 109 900 | 24.2 | 13.2 |
| Johnson City | 26 100 | 37 284 | 4.9 | 34.6 | 16.1 | 30 583 | 19.5 | 3 566 | 26 761 | 55.7 | 153 000 | 21.9 | 10.8 |
| Kingsport | 24 739 | 39 901 | 2.4 | 32.8 | 13.7 | 23 784 | 9.0 | 2 495 | 21 293 | 66.4 | 120 400 | 21.2 | 10.0 |
| Knoxville | 22 655 | 33 467 | 1.9 | 37.3 | 16.2 | 88 009 | 3.7 | 9 961 | 82 829 | 51.0 | 114 500 | 24.0 | 12.9 |
| La Vergne | 21 689 | 55 998 | 1.3 | 14.5 | 10.4 | 11 612 | 66.3 | 696 | 10 290 | 76.9 | 136 600 | 24.2 | 10.0 |
| Lebanon | 24 080 | 45 186 | 2.8 | 27.0 | 10.5 | 11 030 | 26.1 | 900 | 10 052 | 61.5 | 171 600 | 24.1 | 11.7 |
| Maryville | 26 961 | 51 366 | 3.2 | 23.8 | 8.1 | 11 629 | 19.1 | 917 | 10 661 | 64.9 | 184 000 | 22.5 | 11.2 |
| Memphis | 21 397 | 37 072 | 2.6 | 34.5 | 21.3 | 291 883 | 7.4 | 41 539 | 244 431 | 52.7 | 99 000 | 26.1 | 14.3 |
| Morristown | 18 140 | 32 838 | 1.2 | 39.3 | 19.4 | 12 705 | 15.2 | 1 293 | 11 502 | 55.1 | 102 500 | 23.1 | 14.6 |
| Murfreesboro | 25 667 | 48 766 | 2.8 | 23.7 | 10.8 | 45 500 | 57.2 | 3 560 | 40 518 | 55.3 | 173 400 | 23.0 | 10.0 |
| Nashville-Davidson | 28 526 | 46 737 | 4.1 | 25.5 | 13.5 | 283 978 | 12.3 | 24 479 | 254 111 | 56.8 | 166 300 | 25.1 | 11.2 |
| Oak Ridge | 31 446 | 53 419 | 3.9 | 24.3 | 11.1 | 14 494 | 8.0 | 1 722 | 12 445 | 65.6 | 142 100 | 19.5 | 10.0 |
| Smyrna | 24 273 | 51 059 | 1.4 | 18.5 | 8.8 | 15 787 | 57.9 | 980 | 15 062 | 67.3 | 151 700 | 23.2 | 10.1 |
| Spring Hill | 28 189 | 75 728 | 2.4 | 7.6 | 2.8 | 10 569 | NA | 708 | 9 202 | 83.4 | 197 700 | 22.7 | 10.0 |
| **TEXAS** | 25 548 | 50 920 | 4.4 | 24.1 | 13.2 | 9 977 436 | 22.3 | 1 054 503 | 8 667 807 | 64.5 | 126 400 | 23.1 | 12.4 |
| Abilene | 20 825 | 40 430 | 1.8 | 28.9 | 13.1 | 47 783 | 4.8 | 4 171 | 42 290 | 58.6 | 88 600 | 21.6 | 12.4 |
| Allen | 37 068 | 98 745 | 10.2 | 8.3 | 3.6 | 28 877 | 89.4 | 1 007 | 26 959 | 80.8 | 194 700 | 22.0 | 10.0 |
| Amarillo | 23 752 | 44 769 | 2.6 | 26.9 | 13.0 | 80 298 | 11.0 | 6 380 | 71 024 | 62.4 | 108 800 | 21.7 | 11.2 |
| Arlington | 25 317 | 52 699 | 3.1 | 20.5 | 12.1 | 144 805 | 10.7 | 11 733 | 132 182 | 58.5 | 131 800 | 23.5 | 12.0 |
| Austin | 31 170 | 51 596 | 5.4 | 22.9 | 13.0 | 354 241 | 28.1 | 29 349 | 322 979 | 45.5 | 209 900 | 23.9 | 12.5 |
| Baytown | 21 383 | 48 062 | 2.0 | 24.2 | 16.3 | 28 998 | 10.2 | 4 043 | 23 770 | 61.5 | 98 800 | 22.6 | 12.9 |
| Beaumont | 23 674 | 40 283 | 3.3 | 32.4 | 17.9 | 50 689 | 3.8 | 5 041 | 45 073 | 57.6 | 97 300 | 21.7 | 13.2 |
| Bedford | 34 926 | 61 584 | 4.2 | 14.1 | 6.0 | 22 301 | 5.5 | 1 285 | 20 501 | 55.2 | 156 000 | 21.3 | 11.6 |
| Big Spring | 15 861 | 38 666 | 1.1 | 31.7 | 17.8 | 9 640 | -2.4 | 1 373 | 7 962 | 60.7 | 58 800 | 20.1 | 11.5 |
| Brownsville | 12 900 | 31 371 | 1.3 | 41.2 | 31.5 | 53 936 | 28.8 | 4 065 | 47 193 | 62.8 | 80 300 | 26.7 | 14.4 |
| Bryan | 19 015 | 35 881 | 2.1 | 37.8 | 20.3 | 30 582 | 18.6 | 2 857 | 27 041 | 49.2 | 108 800 | 23.1 | 12.7 |
| Burleson | 28 492 | 66 374 | 2.8 | 9.3 | 3.3 | 13 591 | 74.5 | 703 | 12 841 | 78.2 | 121 100 | 21.6 | 11.5 |
| Carrollton | 31 563 | 69 401 | 5.0 | 11.8 | 7.3 | 45 508 | 12.3 | 2 209 | 42 722 | 65.0 | 165 400 | 23.0 | 11.4 |
| Cedar Hill | 28 514 | 64 662 | 4.8 | 12.4 | 6.3 | 16 338 | 47.0 | 832 | 14 788 | 75.4 | 132 100 | 25.4 | 11.4 |
| Cedar Park | 30 692 | 74 030 | 2.8 | 9.4 | 5.5 | 18 726 | 108.8 | 909 | 16 626 | 71.4 | 182 900 | 24.4 | 13.1 |
| Cleburne | 20 626 | 45 543 | 1.8 | 23.9 | 12.9 | 11 418 | 14.5 | 979 | 10 160 | 59.4 | 95 200 | 22.3 | 14.1 |
| College Station | 19 994 | 31 332 | 3.8 | 43.6 | 15.7 | 37 226 | 43.1 | 2 189 | 31 832 | 33.7 | 174 300 | 21.6 | 11.0 |
| Conroe | 22 192 | 46 213 | 3.5 | 26.2 | 17.4 | 22 215 | 54.5 | 2 198 | 19 382 | 51.3 | 129 600 | 24.1 | 12.4 |
| Coppell | 46 259 | 106 981 | 17.0 | 6.6 | 2.3 | 14 343 | 14.2 | 537 | 13 641 | 72.8 | 265 700 | 21.6 | 10.0 |
| Copperas Cove | 22 357 | 51 850 | 1.1 | 19.0 | 13.1 | 13 094 | 16.7 | 1 236 | 10 339 | 63.0 | 99 800 | 22.7 | 10.5 |
| Corpus Christi | 23 870 | 45 267 | 2.6 | 27.3 | 14.5 | 125 469 | 16.3 | 12 674 | 109 849 | 59.5 | 111 300 | 23.7 | 13.5 |
| Dallas | 27 251 | 42 259 | 5.7 | 28.6 | 19.6 | 516 639 | 6.7 | 58 582 | 452 487 | 45.2 | 129 600 | 25.7 | 13.8 |
| Deer Park | 29 932 | 75 557 | 4.1 | 10.9 | 5.4 | 11 742 | 18.6 | 609 | 10 731 | 79.1 | 130 200 | 19.9 | 10.9 |
| Del Rio | 16 528 | 36 979 | 0.8 | 35.0 | 18.3 | 12 958 | 9.5 | 1 359 | 11 085 | 65.1 | 85 200 | 22.3 | 14.5 |
| Denton | 23 484 | 46 151 | 2.8 | 28.0 | 9.6 | 46 211 | 41.1 | 3 576 | 39 919 | 47.5 | 147 400 | 23.7 | 12.9 |
| DeSoto | 27 559 | 61 018 | 2.4 | 18.9 | 6.9 | 19 488 | 38.1 | 1 278 | 17 620 | 70.0 | 144 900 | 27.2 | 14.5 |
| Duncanville | 24 532 | 53 996 | 2.3 | 18.2 | 10.0 | 14 011 | 5.6 | 731 | 13 447 | 69.6 | 113 000 | 24.5 | 11.8 |
| Eagle Pass | 16 341 | 33 418 | 2.5 | 40.1 | 23.4 | 9 019 | 17.6 | 747 | 7 714 | 63.3 | 97 500 | 26.3 | 13.8 |
| Edinburg | 16 414 | 39 232 | 1.6 | 34.8 | 24.7 | 25 167 | 57.8 | 2 068 | 22 541 | 56.9 | 95 000 | 23.0 | 14.0 |
| El Paso | 18 781 | 39 442 | 2.1 | 32.7 | 20.1 | 227 605 | 17.5 | 10 711 | 210 348 | 61.0 | 114 200 | 23.7 | 11.6 |
| Euless | 29 674 | 53 968 | 2.3 | 15.6 | 7.1 | 23 447 | 16.8 | 1 916 | 21 334 | 45.7 | 139 900 | 22.3 | 12.3 |
| Farmers Branch | 30 579 | 60 638 | 4.6 | 16.3 | 8.0 | 11 549 | 13.0 | 752 | 10 618 | 64.9 | 142 400 | 22.8 | 12.3 |
| Flower Mound | 44 526 | 118 143 | 17.3 | 4.2 | 1.9 | 21 570 | 27.1 | 559 | 20 424 | 92.1 | 253 700 | 21.4 | 10.0 |
| Fort Worth | 24 270 | 50 456 | 3.2 | 24.3 | 14.5 | 291 086 | 37.8 | 28 434 | 257 484 | 59.8 | 121 900 | 23.9 | 13.7 |
| Friendswood | 42 087 | 104 216 | 14.6 | 8.2 | 3.5 | 13 254 | 28.3 | 528 | 12 141 | 82.1 | 215 900 | 21.3 | 11.8 |
| Frisco | 42 358 | 105 647 | 13.3 | 6.1 | 3.4 | 42 306 | 209.0 | 2 405 | 37 454 | 79.1 | 248 000 | 22.5 | 12.3 |
| Galveston | 25 526 | 37 368 | 3.4 | 34.9 | 16.4 | 32 368 | 8.0 | 12 425 | 21 111 | 48.6 | 128 300 | 23.8 | 13.7 |
| Garland | 21 977 | 52 441 | 2.4 | 18.5 | 11.1 | 80 834 | 7.4 | 5 138 | 72 531 | 65.3 | 118 200 | 25.3 | 12.7 |
| Georgetown | 31 231 | 61 636 | 3.7 | 15.0 | 6.0 | 20 037 | 81.6 | 1 207 | 18 246 | 73.0 | 183 900 | 24.3 | 12.0 |
| Grand Prairie | 22 193 | 51 692 | 1.9 | 20.7 | 13.0 | 62 424 | 34.9 | 4 253 | 57 316 | 61.2 | 123 600 | 25.0 | 12.5 |
| Grapevine | 38 304 | 76 040 | 8.4 | 11.5 | 5.2 | 19 685 | 19.2 | 1 183 | 18 223 | 61.0 | 217 800 | 21.2 | 12.9 |
| Greenville | 20 346 | 38 709 | 1.7 | 33.4 | 21.4 | 10 838 | 9.3 | 1 122 | 9 208 | 54.9 | 81 900 | 22.4 | 12.6 |
| Haltom City | 19 766 | 43 676 | 0.5 | 24.0 | 13.1 | 16 626 | 5.0 | 1 357 | 15 329 | 57.3 | 88 200 | 24.0 | 14.0 |
| Harker Heights | 24 419 | 62 104 | 2.3 | 18.4 | 11.2 | 10 347 | 51.2 | 859 | 8 427 | 60.3 | 171 000 | 25.2 | 11.2 |
| Harlingen | 17 462 | 35 267 | 2.1 | 37.9 | 24.8 | 25 585 | 10.1 | 3 940 | 21 140 | 60.9 | 77 900 | 23.4 | 13.5 |
| Houston | 26 849 | 44 124 | 5.3 | 28.2 | 18.2 | 892 646 | 14.1 | 110 003 | 769 867 | 46.6 | 124 400 | 24.0 | 12.8 |
| Huntsville | 12 318 | 29 465 | 1.1 | 44.3 | 19.8 | 12 853 | 12.7 | 1 062 | 10 695 | 36.3 | 129 600 | 24.0 | 13.5 |
| Hurst | 27 878 | 51 168 | 3.5 | 21.3 | 9.2 | 15 761 | 6.8 | 1 109 | 14 612 | 66.7 | 138 100 | 22.2 | 14.6 |
| Irving | 26 754 | 48 005 | 4.0 | 21.6 | 13.3 | 91 128 | 13.5 | 8 590 | 81 676 | 40.3 | 138 100 | 25.9 | 12.7 |
| Keller | 43 898 | 115 228 | 15.3 | 7.2 | 2.4 | 14 051 | 52.9 | 537 | 12 873 | 86.9 | 267 500 | 22.2 | 13.0 |

1. Based on population estimated by the American Community Survey.    2. Includes units rented or sold but not occupied.    3. Specified owner-occupied units; $1,000,000 represents $1,000,000 or more    4. 50.0 represents 50 percent or more.    5. 10.0 represents 10 percent or less.

| City | Occupied housing units, 2007–2011 (cont.) | | | | Migration, 2007–2011 | | Civilian labor force, 2012 | | | | Civilian employment[4], 2007–2011 | | | |
|---|---|---|---|---|---|---|---|---|---|---|---|---|---|---|
| | | | | | | | | | Unemployment | | | Percent | | |
| | Percent renter occupied | Median gross rent[1] | Median rent as a percent of income[2] | Percent with no vehicle available | Percent who lived in the same house one year ago | Percent who lived outside this city one year ago | Total | Percent change, 2011–2012 | Total | Rate[3] | Population age 16 and older | In labor force | Full-year full-time worker | Households with no workers (percent) |
| | 55 | 56 | 57 | 58 | 59 | 60 | 61 | 62 | 63 | 64 | 65 | 66 | 67 | 68 |
| **TENNESSEE— Cont'd** | | | | | | | | | | | | | | |
| Franklin........................ | 31.1 | 1 058 | 26.4 | 3.4 | 79.6 | 14.0 | 34 936 | 4.2 | 1 880 | 5.4 | 46 696 | 70.9 | 46.7 | 18.5 |
| Gallatin........................ | 42.8 | 751 | 25.8 | 7.5 | 75.0 | 16.1 | 14 354 | 2.0 | 1 131 | 7.9 | 23 251 | 64.2 | 40.7 | 27.1 |
| Germantown.................. | 11.2 | 1 142 | 23.6 | 1.5 | 89.4 | 8.4 | 19 510 | 0.2 | 1 106 | 5.7 | 30 722 | 65.2 | 43.7 | 21.1 |
| Hendersonville.............. | 29.5 | 844 | 29.1 | 4.3 | 82.3 | 12.5 | 28 564 | 3.0 | 1 767 | 6.2 | 38 812 | 69.4 | 46.8 | 21.8 |
| Jackson........................ | 41.8 | 728 | 37.5 | 9.5 | 81.4 | 9.4 | 31 488 | 1.3 | 2 784 | 8.8 | 50 234 | 62.8 | 35.6 | 32.6 |
| Johnson City ................ | 44.3 | 617 | 30.9 | 7.5 | 78.2 | 12.4 | 32 557 | -0.4 | 2 191 | 6.7 | 51 813 | 58.5 | 36.0 | 32.2 |
| Kingsport...................... | 33.6 | 523 | 27.3 | 8.5 | 83.4 | 8.9 | 20 965 | -0.6 | 1 598 | 7.6 | 39 512 | 56.2 | 35.0 | 38.3 |
| Knoxville....................... | 49.0 | 688 | 31.8 | 9.3 | 80.9 | 8.5 | 91 325 | -0.4 | 6 765 | 7.4 | 149 127 | 61.4 | 36.2 | 31.7 |
| La Vergne..................... | 23.1 | 1 009 | 28.4 | 2.6 | 84.1 | 12.0 | 19 288 | 2.4 | 1 310 | 6.8 | 21 989 | 73.8 | 51.1 | 14.5 |
| Lebanon ....................... | 38.5 | 728 | 30.0 | 7.4 | 79.5 | 12.3 | 13 443 | 1.8 | 1 007 | 7.5 | 20 328 | 61.7 | 38.2 | 27.9 |
| Maryville....................... | 35.1 | 646 | 28.2 | 6.8 | 79.6 | 13.6 | 13 186 | -0.8 | 919 | 7.0 | 21 599 | 62.4 | 36.7 | 30.6 |
| Memphis........................ | 47.3 | 786 | 34.7 | 12.5 | 79.2 | 5.4 | 289 719 | -0.5 | 29 533 | 10.2 | 501 619 | 64.5 | 38.5 | 28.0 |
| Morristown..................... | 44.9 | 628 | 29.1 | 10.2 | 78.6 | 11.2 | 12 989 | 0.0 | 1 287 | 9.9 | 22 796 | 56.5 | 33.7 | 40.2 |
| Murfreesboro................. | 44.7 | 809 | 31.3 | 4.3 | 73.0 | 15.3 | 59 939 | 3.1 | 4 002 | 6.7 | 84 489 | 69.7 | 40.7 | 21.6 |
| Nashville-Davidson........ | 43.2 | 798 | 30.5 | 7.6 | 79.3 | 8.3 | 335 020 | 3.1 | 22 259 | 6.6 | 498 409 | 68.9 | 43.6 | 22.6 |
| Oak Ridge ..................... | 34.4 | 686 | 26.0 | 7.4 | 82.0 | 10.9 | 14 264 | 0.0 | 1 055 | 7.4 | 23 268 | 60.8 | 39.8 | 32.9 |
| Smyrna......................... | 32.7 | 792 | 27.9 | 3.9 | 79.8 | 15.6 | 22 772 | 2.3 | 1 570 | 6.9 | 29 401 | 72.4 | 49.7 | 19.9 |
| Spring Hill..................... | 16.6 | 1 035 | 27.1 | 1.1 | 85.3 | 12.3 | 15 576 | 3.8 | 977 | 6.3 | 18 479 | 76.2 | 52.0 | 12.6 |
| **TEXAS**...................... | 35.5 | 814 | 29.6 | 6.0 | 82.1 | 10.7 | 12 597 465 | 1.9 | 854 865 | 6.8 | 18 747 892 | 65.5 | 43.0 | 21.6 |
| Abilene ........................ | 41.4 | 730 | 31.0 | 6.1 | 75.6 | 11.7 | 58 306 | -0.5 | 3 179 | 5.5 | 93 531 | 61.3 | 35.7 | 24.5 |
| Allen ............................ | 19.2 | 1 164 | 30.3 | 1.7 | 83.6 | 12.4 | 46 956 | 2.3 | 2 707 | 5.8 | 56 998 | 77.2 | 54.4 | 9.4 |
| Amarillo........................ | 37.6 | 692 | 29.9 | 6.8 | 80.5 | 6.5 | 102 754 | -0.1 | 4 949 | 4.8 | 143 314 | 68.5 | 46.5 | 22.2 |
| Arlington....................... | 41.5 | 823 | 30.6 | 4.5 | 78.5 | 9.7 | 206 042 | 2.7 | 13 098 | 6.4 | 273 401 | 73.0 | 47.3 | 16.9 |
| Austin........................... | 54.5 | 920 | 30.5 | 7.2 | 73.0 | 10.7 | 460 166 | 3.7 | 24 728 | 5.4 | 625 830 | 73.7 | 47.5 | 17.2 |
| Baytown........................ | 38.5 | 794 | 29.4 | 6.3 | 79.8 | 10.6 | 34 506 | 0.9 | 3 524 | 10.2 | 52 334 | 62.0 | 39.8 | 24.5 |
| Beaumont...................... | 42.4 | 734 | 31.2 | 10.1 | 81.0 | 7.0 | 58 781 | 0.6 | 5 319 | 9.0 | 90 934 | 61.3 | 37.3 | 30.1 |
| Bedford......................... | 44.8 | 884 | 27.1 | 4.0 | 79.8 | 16.4 | 31 540 | 3.1 | 1 918 | 6.1 | 38 147 | 73.7 | 52.2 | 18.2 |
| Big Spring...................... | 39.3 | 637 | 29.3 | 10.0 | 75.1 | 13.7 | 10 480 | 0.9 | 673 | 6.4 | 21 503 | 44.8 | 26.6 | 34.0 |
| Brownsville.................... | 37.2 | 590 | 33.0 | 10.9 | 86.5 | 4.5 | 68 341 | -1.1 | 7 370 | 10.8 | 118 931 | 58.0 | 34.2 | 24.7 |
| Bryan............................ | 50.8 | 744 | 35.8 | 8.8 | 71.3 | 19.1 | 38 258 | -0.7 | 2 143 | 5.6 | 57 782 | 66.2 | 37.1 | 23.4 |
| Burleson........................ | 21.8 | 994 | 26.7 | 3.1 | 87.5 | 8.7 | 19 602 | 3.0 | 1 088 | 5.6 | 25 870 | 73.0 | 51.8 | 18.9 |
| Carrollton...................... | 35.0 | 948 | 27.2 | 2.7 | 82.9 | 10.9 | 70 591 | 1.8 | 4 251 | 6.0 | 92 267 | 76.8 | 52.3 | 12.5 |
| Cedar Hill ..................... | 24.6 | 1 104 | 32.6 | 4.4 | 89.4 | 8.9 | 24 694 | 1.6 | 1 821 | 7.4 | 32 003 | 73.6 | 53.3 | 17.1 |
| Cedar Park .................... | 28.6 | 1 016 | 30.5 | 1.7 | 82.5 | 13.7 | 27 408 | 3.9 | 1 522 | 5.6 | 33 871 | 75.4 | 52.4 | 12.7 |
| Cleburne....................... | 40.6 | 822 | 29.4 | 4.4 | 79.3 | 12.3 | 13 527 | 2.9 | 881 | 6.5 | 21 982 | 62.5 | 41.2 | 25.2 |
| College Station.............. | 66.3 | 830 | 50.0 | 6.2 | 56.5 | 26.3 | 47 273 | -0.4 | 2 603 | 5.5 | 78 779 | 58.1 | 26.0 | 24.9 |
| Conroe.......................... | 48.7 | 800 | 29.9 | 7.0 | 73.9 | 15.4 | 28 771 | 3.7 | 1 575 | 5.5 | 41 763 | 67.3 | 40.9 | 20.7 |
| Coppell.......................... | 27.2 | 1 133 | 24.7 | 1.7 | 86.1 | 10.7 | 20 897 | 2.6 | 1 253 | 6.0 | 28 383 | 74.8 | 52.2 | 9.8 |
| Copperas Cove .............. | 37.0 | 850 | 27.5 | 3.8 | 80.2 | 15.6 | 13 470 | -0.2 | 1 019 | 7.6 | 23 504 | 65.2 | 37.9 | 23.8 |
| Corpus Christi ............... | 40.5 | 823 | 32.2 | 8.5 | 79.3 | 7.1 | 160 642 | 3.4 | 9 576 | 6.0 | 231 974 | 65.1 | 40.5 | 23.9 |
| Dallas........................... | 54.8 | 811 | 29.4 | 10.0 | 79.8 | 8.1 | 581 653 | 1.8 | 42 612 | 7.3 | 910 265 | 67.7 | 45.5 | 21.2 |
| Deer Park...................... | 20.9 | 934 | 28.1 | 3.4 | 85.3 | 11.2 | 17 892 | 2.6 | 1 181 | 6.6 | 24 123 | 69.7 | 48.8 | 16.0 |
| Del Rio.......................... | 34.9 | 543 | 28.9 | 7.2 | 85.5 | 7.2 | 15 625 | -2.8 | 1 151 | 7.4 | 25 985 | 60.2 | 35.6 | 28.8 |
| Denton.......................... | 52.5 | 810 | 36.6 | 5.4 | 67.2 | 19.8 | 64 191 | 2.3 | 3 487 | 5.4 | 91 419 | 68.1 | 35.5 | 20.8 |
| DeSoto.......................... | 30.0 | 875 | 33.2 | 5.4 | 88.1 | 9.5 | 26 874 | 1.5 | 2 032 | 7.6 | 36 998 | 66.7 | 48.0 | 20.8 |
| Duncanville.................... | 30.4 | 979 | 30.4 | 4.2 | 88.5 | 9.0 | 20 227 | 2.4 | 1 574 | 7.8 | 29 116 | 67.6 | 46.2 | 22.0 |
| Eagle Pass.................... | 36.7 | 518 | 27.2 | 10.7 | 86.9 | 5.9 | 12 955 | -6.5 | 1 705 | 13.2 | 18 633 | 58.2 | 34.6 | 29.0 |
| Edinburg....................... | 43.1 | 642 | 31.8 | 6.4 | 78.1 | 12.6 | 34 725 | -0.1 | 2 713 | 7.8 | 53 918 | 64.2 | 37.7 | 21.1 |
| El Paso......................... | 39.0 | 661 | 30.8 | 8.8 | 83.7 | 6.1 | 272 540 | -0.5 | 23 470 | 8.6 | 474 875 | 60.5 | 37.1 | 23.8 |
| Euless.......................... | 54.3 | 914 | 25.2 | 3.3 | 78.4 | 16.3 | 31 540 | 3.1 | 1 918 | 6.1 | 40 115 | 76.6 | 52.2 | 13.8 |
| Farmers Branch ............ | 35.1 | 987 | 26.2 | 2.9 | 83.1 | 12.3 | 15 504 | 2.7 | 1 003 | 6.5 | 22 366 | 70.9 | 45.3 | 19.9 |
| Flower Mound ............... | 7.9 | 1 463 | 29.0 | 1.0 | 89.7 | 7.1 | 35 860 | 2.3 | 1 998 | 5.6 | 45 283 | 74.5 | 53.4 | 9.8 |
| Fort Worth .................... | 40.2 | 827 | 30.7 | 6.7 | 81.1 | 9.5 | 357 963 | 2.8 | 24 097 | 6.7 | 532 425 | 68.4 | 45.8 | 20.3 |
| Friendswood.................. | 17.9 | 1 117 | 29.4 | 1.7 | 86.1 | 11.5 | 19 285 | 3.8 | 1 154 | 6.0 | 27 023 | 68.4 | 48.0 | 17.0 |
| Frisco........................... | 20.9 | 1 170 | 27.0 | 1.7 | 83.0 | 12.1 | 64 386 | 2.1 | 3 362 | 5.2 | 76 287 | 78.4 | 57.0 | 9.3 |
| Galveston ..................... | 51.4 | 778 | 34.6 | 13.5 | 72.6 | 14.7 | 22 412 | 2.6 | 1 800 | 8.0 | 41 239 | 61.1 | 36.7 | 30.5 |
| Garland......................... | 34.7 | 923 | 30.5 | 4.5 | 83.8 | 8.7 | 116 201 | 1.8 | 7 902 | 6.8 | 168 416 | 71.5 | 47.1 | 16.4 |
| Georgetown................... | 27.0 | 947 | 29.2 | 4.4 | 82.6 | 12.0 | 22 770 | 3.4 | 1 338 | 5.9 | 36 561 | 51.7 | 33.9 | 41.7 |
| Grand Prairie................. | 38.8 | 875 | 30.9 | 4.4 | 81.1 | 12.8 | 90 047 | 2.0 | 6 090 | 6.8 | 123 660 | 72.2 | 50.4 | 16.2 |
| Grapevine...................... | 39.0 | 1 028 | 26.3 | 2.7 | 80.5 | 13.3 | 27 666 | 2.7 | 1 493 | 5.4 | 36 011 | 76.1 | 51.0 | 14.0 |
| Greenville...................... | 45.1 | 730 | 34.9 | 7.7 | 74.3 | 13.5 | 11 727 | 3.7 | 1 021 | 8.7 | 18 863 | 58.3 | 36.9 | 29.1 |
| Haltom City.................... | 42.7 | 779 | 27.7 | 3.5 | 82.0 | 12.5 | 22 583 | 2.5 | 1 435 | 6.4 | 31 788 | 71.6 | 48.0 | 19.1 |
| Harker Heights.............. | 39.7 | 799 | 27.5 | 2.5 | 69.9 | 24.0 | 12 117 | 0.2 | 831 | 6.9 | 18 345 | 68.1 | 40.0 | 17.7 |
| Harlingen...................... | 39.1 | 680 | 29.3 | 9.8 | 90.3 | 5.6 | 27 084 | 0.9 | 2 420 | 8.9 | 47 509 | 49.7 | 36.0 | 34.3 |
| Houston........................ | 53.4 | 820 | 29.9 | 9.9 | 79.4 | 7.4 | 1 032 595 | 3.1 | 71 253 | 6.9 | 1 605 215 | 68.1 | 44.6 | 19.9 |
| Huntsville...................... | 63.7 | 691 | 37.3 | 7.5 | 72.1 | 22.1 | 15 575 | -0.5 | 1 063 | 6.8 | 34 089 | 35.0 | 19.7 | 28.8 |
| Hurst............................ | 33.3 | 794 | 30.4 | 2.5 | 81.9 | 13.8 | 20 699 | 2.4 | 1 270 | 6.1 | 29 490 | 67.9 | 46.4 | 22.8 |
| Irving............................ | 59.7 | 869 | 27.4 | 5.5 | 75.6 | 12.9 | 121 940 | 2.2 | 7 549 | 6.2 | 161 310 | 73.5 | 49.7 | 14.6 |
| Keller............................ | 13.1 | 1 204 | 28.6 | 1.0 | 89.3 | 9.4 | 21 282 | 3.4 | 1 169 | 5.5 | 28 120 | 71.7 | 51.1 | 13.3 |

1. $2,000 represents $2,000 or more.  2. 50.0 represents 50 percent or more.  3. Percent of civilian labor force.  4. Persons 16 years old and over.

| City | Value of residential construction authorized by building permits, 2011 | | | Wholesale trade,[1] 2007 | | | | Retail trade,[2] 2007 | | | |
|---|---|---|---|---|---|---|---|---|---|---|---|
| | New construction ($1,000) | Number of housing units | Percent single family | Number of establish-ments | Number of employees | Sales (mil dol) | Annual payroll (mil dol) | Number of establish-ments | Number of employees | Sales (mil dol) | Annual payroll (mil dol) |
| | 69 | 70 | 71 | 72 | 73 | 74 | 75 | 76 | 77 | 78 | 79 |
| **TENNESSEE— Cont'd** | | | | | | | | | | | |
| Franklin.................... | 137 829 | 624 | 50.3 | 115 | 1 321 | 2 156.7 | 94.0 | 483 | 8 846 | 2 024.0 | 198.1 |
| Gallatin.................... | 29 288 | 157 | 100.0 | 46 | 669 | 470.3 | 25.4 | 146 | 1 904 | 477.8 | 45.9 |
| Germantown............. | NA | NA | NA | 42 | 467 | 265.5 | 20.0 | 176 | 2 293 | 365.0 | 44.0 |
| Hendersonville.......... | 17 812 | 121 | 100.0 | 49 | D | D | D | 168 | 2 571 | 621.0 | 58.0 |
| Jackson.................... | 24 632 | 130 | 100.0 | 125 | 1 774 | 988.5 | 72.9 | 459 | 6 786 | 1 553.8 | 146.2 |
| Johnson City ............. | 26 297 | 190 | 85.8 | 106 | 1 737 | 1 025.2 | 60.6 | 442 | 7 266 | 1 674.9 | 150.2 |
| Kingsport................. | 13 159 | 75 | 88.0 | 80 | 966 | 379.4 | 35.6 | 373 | 5 355 | 1 260.8 | 117.2 |
| Knoxville.................. | 19 131 | 167 | 100.0 | 452 | 6 580 | 3 106.5 | 318.3 | 1 452 | 27 067 | 6 470.5 | 648.3 |
| La Vergne................. | 4 881 | 25 | 100.0 | 71 | 3 466 | 5 145.4 | 166.3 | 50 | 550 | 159.8 | 14.2 |
| Lebanon................... | 18 427 | 164 | 73.8 | 39 | 1 056 | 862.5 | 52.8 | 231 | 2 778 | 767.8 | 63.6 |
| Maryville.................. | 6 698 | 53 | 100.0 | 26 | 205 | 527.4 | 9.1 | 184 | 2 788 | 543.8 | 53.6 |
| Memphis.................. | NA | NA | NA | 1 048 | 22 822 | 25 485.6 | 1 173.2 | 2 571 | 36 773 | 8 975.2 | 880.5 |
| Morristown............... | 3 791 | 39 | 100.0 | 49 | D | D | D | 277 | 4 011 | 1 018.2 | 87.9 |
| Murfreesboro............ | 66 799 | 408 | 98.0 | 102 | 898 | 526.1 | 42.9 | 538 | 8 282 | 2 008.1 | 184.7 |
| Nashville-Davidson....... | 310 495 | 1 932 | 55.8 | 1 009 | 20 028 | 11 942.6 | 983.6 | 2 795 | 42 241 | 10 581.8 | 1 046.2 |
| Oak Ridge................ | 2 945 | 11 | 100.0 | 18 | 118 | 94.0 | 6.1 | 129 | 2 055 | 477.1 | 44.3 |
| Smyrna.................... | 10 978 | 97 | 100.0 | 34 | 996 | 526.0 | 43.0 | 107 | 1 949 | 467.8 | 41.9 |
| Spring Hill................. | 51 828 | 307 | 95.1 | 7 | 77 | 45.3 | 3.8 | 46 | 734 | 159.2 | 14.4 |
| **TEXAS.................... ** | 14 736 206 | 97 450 | 67.2 | 27 066 | 386 370 | 424 238.2 | 20 260.6 | 78 795 | 1 138 440 | 311 334.8 | 26 395.2 |
| Abilene ................... | 27 339 | 154 | 96.1 | 125 | 1 372 | 988.0 | 50.3 | 547 | 8 023 | 1 897.2 | 176.4 |
| Allen ...................... | 121 770 | 420 | 100.0 | 43 | 543 | 213.7 | 37.7 | 217 | 3 179 | 647.1 | 61.0 |
| Amarillo .................. | 146 067 | 648 | 93.4 | 227 | 3 368 | 2 351.2 | 142.7 | 859 | 12 913 | 3 720.1 | 288.8 |
| Arlington ................. | 51 058 | 360 | 64.4 | 357 | 5 707 | 4 470.0 | 280.8 | 1 091 | 18 017 | 4 890.4 | 421.7 |
| Austin ..................... | 415 619 | 4 178 | 41.0 | 918 | 17 256 | 12 730.5 | 1 254.5 | 3 094 | 51 460 | 13 493.5 | 1 300.7 |
| Baytown................... | 11 512 | 87 | 100.0 | 42 | 385 | 186.5 | 14.8 | 270 | 4 221 | 1 242.1 | 94.0 |
| Beaumont................. | 37 377 | 414 | 63.8 | 180 | 3 112 | 2 269.7 | 148.2 | 660 | 9 983 | 2 474.6 | 228.6 |
| Bedford................... | 2 817 | 19 | 100.0 | 35 | 233 | 470.6 | 14.2 | 127 | 1 957 | 618.8 | 56.0 |
| Big Spring................. | 541 | 5 | 100.0 | 16 | 98 | 48.3 | 4.1 | 103 | 1 202 | 320.4 | 26.4 |
| Brownsville............... | 58 684 | 613 | 99.7 | 193 | 1 618 | 783.0 | 41.2 | 617 | 9 329 | 2 024.3 | 177.7 |
| Bryan...................... | 38 297 | 409 | 33.0 | 74 | 1 102 | 520.1 | 39.3 | 294 | 3 600 | 991.3 | 87.5 |
| Burleson .................. | 29 170 | 188 | 100.0 | 18 | 109 | 42.5 | 3.8 | 146 | 2 738 | 674.7 | 61.2 |
| Carrollton................. | 72 433 | 646 | 24.0 | 376 | 7 000 | 4 226.5 | 346.5 | 361 | 5 154 | 1 808.8 | 163.4 |
| Cedar Hill ................ | 7 403 | 31 | 100.0 | 13 | 164 | 97.9 | 7.3 | 105 | 2 466 | 478.1 | 46.8 |
| Cedar Park............... | 94 208 | 564 | 89.7 | 34 | 283 | 95.6 | 11.6 | 135 | 1 927 | 484.0 | 44.0 |
| Cleburne.................. | 2 084 | 19 | 100.0 | 35 | 411 | 242.8 | 17.6 | 155 | 2 364 | 639.5 | 58.4 |
| College Station........... | 109 375 | 1 017 | 45.8 | 20 | 212 | 173.7 | 8.5 | 323 | 5 380 | 1 092.6 | 99.4 |
| Conroe.................... | 83 600 | 829 | 23.4 | 114 | 1 420 | 4 002.7 | 61.2 | 367 | 6 146 | 1 921.9 | 154.1 |
| Coppell ................... | 27 139 | 44 | 100.0 | 67 | 2 208 | 1 881.7 | 125.1 | 57 | 1 079 | 413.1 | 35.7 |
| Copperas Cove .......... | 21 739 | 151 | 93.4 | 5 | 5 | 1.3 | 0.1 | 74 | 1 012 | 249.2 | 21.4 |
| Corpus Christi ........... | 116 859 | 867 | 72.8 | 358 | 4 002 | 2 682.6 | 184.2 | 1 081 | 16 200 | 4 133.8 | 350.2 |
| Dallas ..................... | 487 837 | 4 250 | 19.0 | 2 101 | 31 471 | 19 169.4 | 1 546.6 | 4 209 | 60 028 | 16 256.5 | 1 563.1 |
| Deer Park................. | 11 794 | 69 | 100.0 | 35 | 713 | 406.9 | 45.3 | 60 | 1 067 | 258.1 | 24.2 |
| Del Rio ................... | 802 | 53 | 88.7 | 23 | 127 | 39.3 | 3.7 | 163 | 2 136 | 512.8 | 40.8 |
| Denton.................... | 155 975 | 960 | 27.0 | 83 | 1 685 | 1 266.8 | 59.5 | 408 | 6 516 | 1 695.3 | 140.9 |
| DeSoto.................... | 27 812 | 143 | 100.0 | 34 | 535 | 256.8 | 26.9 | 82 | 1 363 | 345.8 | 32.1 |
| Duncanville............... | 5 052 | 17 | 100.0 | 23 | 237 | 67.0 | 11.7 | 133 | 1 482 | 462.3 | 37.7 |
| Eagle Pass................ | 7 726 | 136 | 48.5 | 29 | 161 | 94.7 | 7.1 | 171 | 2 263 | 493.5 | 40.6 |
| Edinburg.................. | 42 831 | 397 | 89.4 | 68 | 1 320 | 524.1 | 40.1 | 199 | 3 256 | 890.2 | 64.5 |
| El Paso.................... | 544 478 | 3 837 | 77.3 | 846 | 8 016 | 4 793.1 | 290.2 | 2 131 | 32 240 | 7 892.9 | 653.3 |
| Euless..................... | 15 430 | 50 | 100.0 | 45 | 401 | 279.7 | 25.2 | 96 | 1 167 | 366.1 | 27.8 |
| Farmers Branch .......... | 6 518 | 36 | 100.0 | 227 | 6 362 | 3 631.9 | 385.4 | 167 | 2 217 | 619.9 | 66.2 |
| Flower Mound ........... | 58 411 | 400 | 23.3 | 54 | 515 | 251.2 | 25.6 | 144 | 2 799 | 547.5 | 49.4 |
| Fort Worth ............... | 445 056 | 3 570 | 68.0 | 689 | 14 729 | 11 371.3 | 782.4 | 1 956 | 30 304 | 9 586.1 | 816.1 |
| Friendswood.............. | 52 895 | 163 | 100.0 | 22 | 82 | 34.4 | 3.0 | 86 | 1 084 | 330.9 | 23.9 |
| Frisco..................... | 346 608 | 1 309 | 100.0 | 83 | 1 047 | 2 266.8 | 75.5 | 421 | 7 750 | 1 918.3 | 175.4 |
| Galveston ................ | 19 745 | 89 | 100.0 | 31 | 502 | 1 084.7 | 17.4 | 238 | 2 786 | 558.4 | 57.3 |
| Garland ................... | 41 388 | 294 | 50.3 | 183 | 2 941 | 1 470.5 | 140.6 | 626 | 9 531 | 2 320.0 | 225.2 |
| Georgetown............... | 134 906 | 531 | 100.0 | 41 | 336 | 188.6 | 17.7 | 195 | 3 307 | 1 084.1 | 89.3 |
| Grand Prairie............. | 62 577 | 346 | 100.0 | 258 | 5 486 | 3 794.6 | 249.8 | 299 | 4 954 | 1 470.6 | 129.9 |
| Grapevine................. | 29 840 | 342 | 8.8 | 87 | 1 813 | 3 263.3 | 93.2 | 365 | 5 623 | 1 611.4 | 133.0 |
| Greenville................. | 3 815 | 21 | 100.0 | 21 | 198 | 101.5 | 5.1 | 138 | 2 265 | 600.8 | 60.2 |
| Haltom City............... | 2 182 | 19 | 100.0 | 87 | 1 034 | 381.5 | 44.8 | 164 | 1 611 | 496.6 | 43.6 |
| Harker Heights ........... | 28 424 | 143 | 98.6 | 2 | D | D | D | 55 | 1 064 | 279.4 | 25.0 |
| Harlingen.................. | 14 032 | 107 | 100.0 | 75 | 866 | 374.3 | 25.3 | 329 | 5 074 | 1 149.5 | 102.4 |
| Houston................... | 770 405 | 7 735 | 33.3 | 4 409 | 78 172 | 189 998.4 | 4 899.1 | 8 646 | 130 578 | 36 570.2 | 3 266.0 |
| Huntsville................. | 7 938 | 46 | 100.0 | 27 | 233 | 152.6 | 8.7 | 130 | 2 171 | 589.1 | 45.2 |
| Hurst...................... | 589 | 3 | 100.0 | 29 | 187 | 151.9 | 8.0 | 292 | 5 835 | 1 227.8 | 117.2 |
| Irving...................... | 181 890 | 1 266 | 26.9 | 380 | 9 717 | 13 529.5 | 643.1 | 645 | 14 897 | 4 784.6 | 376.6 |
| Keller...................... | 62 526 | 211 | 100.0 | 26 | 185 | 43.9 | 4.8 | 91 | 1 417 | 355.5 | 30.1 |

1. Merchant wholesalers except manufacturers' sales branches and offices.   2. Establishments with payroll.

# Table D. Cities — Real Estate, Professional Services, and Manufacturing

| City | Real estate and rental and leasing, 2007 | | | | Professional, scientific, and technical services,[1] 2007 | | | | Manufacturing, 2007 | | | |
|---|---|---|---|---|---|---|---|---|---|---|---|---|
| | Number of establish-ments | Number of employees | Receipts (mil dol) | Annual payroll (mil dol) | Number of establish-ments | Number of employees | Receipts (mil dol) | Annual payroll (mil dol) | Number of establish-ments | Number of employees | Receipts (mil dol) | Annual payroll (mil dol) |
| | 80 | 81 | 82 | 83 | 84 | 85 | 86 | 87 | 88 | 89 | 90 | 91 |
| TENNESSEE— Cont'd | | | | | | | | | | | | |
| Franklin | 125 | 1 838 | 273.5 | 56.7 | 324 | D | D | D | 81 | 2 501 | 848.9 | 93.6 |
| Gallatin | 45 | 400 | 121.9 | 19.3 | 54 | D | D | D | 74 | 3 000 | 860.8 | 111.7 |
| Germantown | 64 | D | D | D | 107 | 478 | 71.6 | 23.6 | NA | NA | NA | NA |
| Hendersonville | 73 | 297 | 49.5 | 8.8 | 117 | 601 | 72.1 | 36.3 | 62 | 852 | 139.3 | 32.6 |
| Jackson | 98 | 728 | 97.0 | 17.4 | 178 | D | D | D | 89 | 8 828 | 4 012.9 | 389.3 |
| Johnson City | 112 | 911 | 107.7 | 16.9 | 192 | D | D | D | 101 | 5 611 | 1 433.3 | 194.7 |
| Kingsport | 70 | 305 | 54.4 | 8.1 | 133 | 877 | 135.2 | 35.6 | 45 | 11 452 | D | D |
| Knoxville | 385 | 2 497 | 477.4 | 79.9 | 831 | D | D | D | 270 | D | D | D |
| La Vergne | 16 | 144 | 41.9 | 4.9 | 12 | D | D | D | 52 | 4 422 | 1 401.8 | 221.1 |
| Lebanon | 61 | 271 | 57.4 | 8.1 | 89 | D | D | D | 54 | 5 236 | D | 233.9 |
| Maryville | 33 | 138 | 25.1 | 3.6 | 99 | D | D | D | 35 | 3 628 | D | 176.8 |
| Memphis | 818 | 7 093 | 1 240.3 | 274.1 | 1 467 | 14 364 | 1 936.2 | 802.6 | 569 | 23 906 | 14 709.6 | 1 174.0 |
| Morristown | 54 | 265 | 41.0 | 6.3 | 70 | D | D | D | 88 | 12 463 | 3 142.6 | 438.5 |
| Murfreesboro | 150 | 800 | 297.6 | 20.2 | 234 | D | D | D | 93 | 5 328 | 2 273.3 | 223.4 |
| Nashville-Davidson | 934 | 6 617 | 1 588.0 | 252.2 | 1 912 | 23 798 | 2 943.3 | 1 285.4 | 633 | 23 715 | 7 347.2 | 999.0 |
| Oak Ridge | 47 | 246 | 36.0 | 6.0 | 159 | D | D | D | 52 | 5 916 | 1 006.6 | 395.2 |
| Smyrna | 39 | 145 | 35.5 | 3.9 | 51 | 353 | 38.9 | 16.8 | 33 | 7 897 | D | 428.2 |
| Spring Hill | 20 | 110 | 18.0 | 3.9 | 21 | D | D | D | 5 | D | D | D |
| TEXAS | 26 593 | 173 745 | 36 399.2 | 7 067.2 | 57 373 | 534 386 | 90 668.7 | 35 376.4 | 21 115 | 893 842 | 593 541.5 | 42 835.7 |
| Abilene | 156 | 628 | 132.2 | 19.1 | 260 | D | D | D | 88 | 2 282 | D | D |
| Allen | 61 | 285 | 54.2 | 9.4 | 218 | 1 252 | 174.5 | 69.1 | 20 | 1 545 | 440.6 | D |
| Amarillo | 256 | 1 199 | 203.0 | 35.0 | 429 | D | D | D | 164 | 6 376 | D | 235.2 |
| Arlington | 380 | 1 742 | 326.4 | 56.7 | 774 | D | D | D | 261 | 12 392 | 12 265.1 | 616.6 |
| Austin | 1 537 | 11 708 | 2 286.4 | 471.0 | 4 095 | 45 252 | 6 926.2 | 3 401.9 | 590 | 31 091 | 27 028.0 | 1 615.5 |
| Baytown | 84 | 483 | 102.5 | 13.7 | 117 | 1 482 | 85.4 | 114.3 | 48 | 4 833 | D | 464.1 |
| Beaumont | 194 | 988 | 175.9 | 34.5 | 386 | D | D | D | 116 | 6 480 | D | 396.9 |
| Bedford | 71 | 302 | 66.9 | 12.5 | 155 | 981 | 172.9 | 55.1 | NA | NA | NA | NA |
| Big Spring | 35 | 178 | 36.0 | 3.4 | 42 | 183 | 13.9 | 4.9 | 16 | 572 | D | 25.2 |
| Brownsville | 141 | 604 | 60.9 | 12.4 | 252 | D | D | D | 102 | 2 889 | 928.6 | 108.0 |
| Bryan | 95 | 487 | 80.8 | 14.6 | 164 | D | D | D | 73 | 3 948 | 788.6 | 129.6 |
| Burleson | 31 | 130 | 25.9 | 5.1 | 68 | 310 | 25.5 | 8.6 | 38 | 1 078 | 192.0 | 38.4 |
| Carrollton | 140 | 985 | 211.8 | 50.3 | 411 | D | D | D | 199 | 11 698 | 3 090.8 | 554.4 |
| Cedar Hill | 16 | 31 | 7.7 | 0.8 | 44 | 118 | 13.4 | 4.2 | 26 | 1 318 | 160.5 | 38.4 |
| Cedar Park | 58 | 318 | 35.3 | 14.0 | 110 | 460 | 60.5 | 22.5 | 25 | 981 | 419.8 | 50.0 |
| Cleburne | 39 | 119 | 26.7 | 3.6 | 72 | 356 | 42.1 | 13.3 | 37 | 1 725 | 698.9 | 83.7 |
| College Station | 115 | 566 | 83.2 | 14.3 | 177 | D | D | D | 21 | 613 | D | 24.5 |
| Conroe | 78 | 357 | 89.7 | 12.8 | 185 | 1 087 | 102.6 | 38.3 | 97 | 3 278 | D | 148.3 |
| Coppell | 56 | 504 | 52.8 | 14.3 | 155 | 921 | 145.7 | 53.2 | 22 | 1 203 | 297.2 | 38.3 |
| Copperas Cove | 43 | 136 | 15.9 | 2.6 | 29 | 247 | 34.5 | 17.6 | NA | NA | NA | NA |
| Corpus Christi | 394 | 2 413 | 384.7 | 73.2 | 757 | D | D | D | 191 | 5 961 | D | 310.6 |
| Dallas | 2 179 | 23 891 | 5 259.0 | 1 361.5 | 5 402 | D | D | D | 1 318 | 71 657 | 21 239.9 | 3 722.1 |
| Deer Park | 30 | 295 | 135.6 | 18.0 | 54 | 982 | 89.1 | 55.4 | 37 | 3 892 | 14 234.2 | 327.2 |
| Del Rio | 26 | 92 | 11.3 | 2.1 | 39 | D | D | D | NA | NA | NA | NA |
| Denton | 143 | 661 | 113.3 | 19.9 | 233 | D | D | D | 85 | 4 346 | 2 411.0 | 211.0 |
| DeSoto | 33 | 129 | 17.9 | 3.5 | 64 | 194 | 18.1 | 6.3 | 29 | 1 314 | 459.1 | 64.3 |
| Duncanville | 32 | 181 | 26.6 | 4.6 | 54 | 199 | 21.1 | 6.7 | 26 | 1 154 | 186.1 | 37.4 |
| Eagle Pass | 34 | 84 | 15.1 | 1.9 | 39 | D | D | D | NA | NA | NA | NA |
| Edinburg | 63 | 225 | 36.8 | 6.5 | 154 | D | D | D | 39 | 970 | 276.0 | 32.2 |
| El Paso | 635 | 3 439 | 612.6 | 104.3 | 1 109 | D | D | D | 513 | 14 792 | 14 103.1 | 577.0 |
| Euless | 47 | 308 | 68.0 | 8.8 | 84 | 316 | 41.4 | 14.4 | 39 | 983 | 148.6 | 40.5 |
| Farmers Branch | 98 | 1 008 | 222.4 | 45.6 | 283 | 3 421 | 518.7 | 208.5 | 110 | 5 769 | 1 417.5 | 267.6 |
| Flower Mound | 72 | 314 | 51.5 | 10.6 | 247 | D | D | D | 17 | 547 | 125.0 | D |
| Fort Worth | 656 | 3 915 | 1 555.2 | 175.9 | 1 534 | 15 959 | 2 246.6 | 1 113.6 | 731 | 65 224 | 24 367.5 | 3 606.7 |
| Friendswood | 33 | 126 | 16.0 | 3.1 | 115 | 336 | 41.7 | 15.9 | NA | NA | NA | NA |
| Frisco | 104 | 492 | 153.6 | 22.4 | 323 | D | D | D | 28 | 551 | 253.6 | D |
| Galveston | 75 | 388 | 57.6 | 10.1 | 113 | 480 | 83.4 | 30.7 | NA | NA | NA | NA |
| Garland | 183 | 1 137 | 197.3 | 31.7 | 301 | 3 291 | 757.9 | 278.3 | 297 | 10 604 | 4 338.5 | 445.1 |
| Georgetown | 65 | 246 | 77.1 | 10.7 | 144 | 513 | 59.2 | 22.3 | 45 | 943 | 227.6 | 42.5 |
| Grand Prairie | 116 | 2 146 | 333.5 | 90.0 | 183 | 1 128 | 124.6 | 44.4 | 210 | 14 061 | 3 733.7 | 736.5 |
| Grapevine | 72 | 580 | 184.1 | 25.5 | 190 | 1 141 | 135.7 | 43.5 | 47 | 1 533 | 427.7 | 56.9 |
| Greenville | 46 | 206 | 28.9 | 5.1 | 61 | D | D | D | 43 | 13 016 | 2 784.1 | D |
| Haltom City | 45 | 251 | 57.0 | 8.1 | 55 | 275 | 24.7 | 9.0 | 113 | 2 884 | 614.7 | 96.0 |
| Harker Heights | 37 | 149 | 17.9 | 3.8 | 26 | D | D | D | NA | NA | NA | NA |
| Harlingen | 107 | 559 | 71.7 | 10.2 | 144 | D | D | D | 62 | 1 246 | 229.8 | 35.1 |
| Houston | 3 576 | 31 940 | 7 873.4 | 1 462.7 | 8 915 | D | D | D | 2 582 | 97 035 | 49 122.0 | 4 774.3 |
| Huntsville | 44 | D | D | D | 68 | 354 | 23.8 | 6.9 | 22 | 585 | D | 25.1 |
| Hurst | 63 | 279 | 79.1 | 9.0 | 167 | 749 | 97.7 | 37.5 | NA | NA | NA | NA |
| Irving | 351 | 4 341 | 1 571.2 | 242.7 | 844 | D | D | D | 187 | 9 661 | 3 441.1 | 465.2 |
| Keller | 34 | 189 | 44.8 | 6.4 | 148 | 476 | 69.8 | 20.1 | NA | NA | NA | NA |

1. Establishments subject to federal tax.

## Table D. Cities — Accommodation and Food Services, Arts, Entertainment, and Recreation, and Health Care and Social Assistance

| City | Accommodation and food services, 2007 | | | | Arts, entertainment, and recreation,[1] 2007 | | | | Health care and social assistance,[1] 2007 | | | |
|---|---|---|---|---|---|---|---|---|---|---|---|---|
| | Number of establish-ments | Number of employees | Sales (mil dol) | Annual payroll (mil dol) | Number of establish-ments | Number of employees | Receipts (mil dol) | Annual payroll (mil dol) | Number of establish-ments | Number of employees | Receipts (mil dol) | Annual payroll (mil dol) |
| | 92 | 93 | 94 | 95 | 96 | 97 | 98 | 99 | 100 | 101 | 102 | 103 |
| TENNESSEE—Cont'd | | | | | | | | | | | | |
| Franklin....................... | 220 | 4 926 | 229.4 | 65.9 | 80 | 567 | 70.9 | 15.2 | 220 | 3 880 | 434.2 | 221.3 |
| Gallatin .................... | 75 | 1 073 | 45.6 | 11.5 | 7 | D | D | D | 76 | D | D | D |
| Germantown .............. | 73 | 1 638 | 70.7 | 20.4 | 13 | D | D | D | 149 | D | D | D |
| Hendersonville.............. | 97 | 2 018 | 78.0 | 23.8 | 26 | D | D | D | 131 | D | D | D |
| Jackson ...................... | 206 | 5 457 | 203.7 | 54.9 | 19 | D | D | D | 240 | D | D | D |
| Johnson City ............... | 212 | 5 577 | 220.3 | 66.6 | 19 | 207 | 11.4 | 2.8 | 245 | D | D | D |
| Kingsport .................... | 186 | 4 302 | 172.0 | 47.6 | 20 | D | D | D | 223 | D | D | D |
| Knoxville .................... | 696 | 18 112 | 780.3 | 233.8 | 58 | 998 | 45.6 | 13.2 | 746 | 10 784 | 1 375.2 | 604.9 |
| La Vergne................... | 30 | 399 | 18.0 | 4.5 | 3 | D | D | D | 16 | D | D | D |
| Lebanon .................... | 105 | 2 138 | 90.8 | 26.8 | 10 | D | D | D | 132 | 2 661 | 236.9 | 91.6 |
| Maryville .................... | 90 | 1 877 | 73.1 | 22.3 | 8 | D | D | D | 134 | D | D | D |
| Memphis..................... | 1 345 | 31 224 | 1 463.1 | 407.8 | 96 | 2 244 | 231.5 | 123.8 | 1 424 | 22 942 | 2 471.7 | 997.2 |
| Morristown.................. | 100 | D | D | D | 11 | 38 | 2.0 | 0.7 | 134 | D | D | D |
| Murfreesboro .............. | 266 | 6 483 | 257.7 | 73.3 | 18 | 159 | 9.5 | 2.0 | 277 | D | D | D |
| Nashville-Davidson........ | 1 605 | 38 979 | 2 203.0 | 626.4 | 622 | 5 305 | 1 557.7 | 484.8 | 1 504 | 29 785 | 3 704.3 | 1 365.8 |
| Oak Ridge .................. | 72 | 1 756 | 79.4 | 22.4 | 4 | D | D | D | 101 | 1 385 | 152.5 | 72.4 |
| Smyrna...................... | 92 | 1 884 | 76.0 | 22.0 | 5 | D | D | D | 88 | D | D | D |
| Spring Hill................... | 36 | 578 | 19.1 | 5.8 | 6 | 56 | 2.0 | 0.6 | 23 | D | D | D |
| TEXAS...................... | 43 509 | 866 189 | 42 054.6 | 11 502.3 | 5 002 | 79 475 | 6 731.7 | 2 220.8 | 48 875 | 780 459 | 71 221.3 | 27 771.8 |
| Abilene ...................... | 268 | D | D | D | 39 | 272 | 16.9 | 3.4 | 301 | D | D | D |
| Allen ......................... | 109 | 2 152 | 99.5 | 26.7 | 13 | D | D | D | 194 | D | D | D |
| Amarillo ..................... | 462 | 9 616 | 428.3 | 113.5 | 43 | 521 | 28.6 | 6.5 | 569 | 8 906 | 1 017.5 | 349.2 |
| Arlington .................... | 625 | 13 989 | 647.1 | 176.3 | 76 | 2 190 | 419.7 | 247.2 | 806 | 11 518 | 1 402.2 | 495.8 |
| Austin ....................... | 2 121 | 49 569 | 2 655.7 | 745.4 | 255 | 4 457 | 388.8 | 115.8 | 2 005 | 31 869 | 3 705.7 | 1 457.1 |
| Baytown...................... | 139 | 2 846 | 133.0 | 34.4 | 12 | D | D | D | 190 | D | D | D |
| Beaumont ................... | 261 | 6 190 | 258.4 | 75.4 | 37 | D | D | D | 503 | 6 944 | 570.7 | 228.2 |
| Bedford...................... | 89 | 2 232 | 102.3 | 27.1 | 17 | D | D | D | 219 | D | D | D |
| Big Spring................... | 68 | D | D | D | 2 | D | D | D | 66 | D | D | D |
| Brownsville ................. | 280 | 4 870 | 200.9 | 51.3 | 24 | 288 | 11.1 | 3.5 | 388 | 10 497 | 575.3 | 236.2 |
| Bryan ........................ | 130 | 2 153 | 89.6 | 23.3 | 16 | 385 | 17.6 | 7.9 | 217 | 2 468 | 279.7 | 104.9 |
| Burleson .................... | 93 | 2 061 | 83.8 | 24.2 | 8 | 28 | 1.1 | 0.3 | 63 | 1 591 | 79.3 | 37.3 |
| Carrollton................... | 197 | 2 857 | 147.9 | 38.4 | 33 | D | D | D | 297 | 3 531 | 324.6 | 125.3 |
| Cedar Hill................... | 72 | D | D | D | 10 | 89 | 4.9 | 1.7 | 58 | 706 | 41.1 | 18.9 |
| Cedar Park.................. | 82 | 1 424 | 65.6 | 16.8 | 15 | D | D | D | 103 | D | D | D |
| Cleburne.................... | 70 | 1 338 | 54.1 | 14.2 | 8 | 61 | 2.5 | 0.6 | 87 | D | D | D |
| College Station............. | 230 | 6 283 | 248.7 | 67.8 | 16 | D | D | D | 114 | 2 192 | 268.9 | 87.7 |
| Conroe ...................... | 145 | 3 242 | 148.2 | 40.3 | 19 | 190 | 9.8 | 2.5 | 169 | 3 820 | 597.1 | 167.9 |
| Coppell ...................... | 66 | D | D | D | 10 | D | D | D | 80 | D | D | D |
| Copperas Cove ............ | 48 | 921 | 32.1 | 8.4 | 5 | 37 | 1.2 | 0.3 | 28 | 311 | 14.9 | 5.9 |
| Corpus Christi ............. | 717 | 14 005 | 607.1 | 170.7 | 59 | 1 304 | 68.2 | 19.4 | 890 | D | D | D |
| Dallas ....................... | 2 647 | 57 958 | 3 378.6 | 954.1 | 301 | 5 043 | 547.3 | 200.0 | 3 180 | 45 235 | 6 245.5 | 2 727.9 |
| Deer Park................... | 42 | 736 | 32.9 | 8.0 | 3 | 7 | 0.3 | 0.1 | 50 | D | D | D |
| Del Rio...................... | 80 | 1 415 | 57.8 | 15.2 | 8 | D | D | D | 71 | 2 335 | 75.1 | 34.0 |
| Denton....................... | 229 | 4 995 | 207.5 | 56.8 | 22 | 231 | 11.7 | 3.0 | 339 | 5 726 | 722.4 | 243.6 |
| DeSoto ...................... | 60 | 1 235 | 46.0 | 14.9 | 6 | 106 | 7.9 | 2.2 | 144 | D | D | D |
| Duncanville.................. | 57 | 1 491 | 66.3 | 17.5 | 6 | D | D | D | 103 | 1 137 | 79.1 | 30.3 |
| Eagle Pass ................. | 60 | D | D | D | 6 | D | D | D | 72 | D | D | D |
| Edinburg .................... | 108 | 2 037 | 80.3 | 21.5 | 12 | D | D | D | 256 | 8 284 | 476.9 | 224.0 |
| El Paso...................... | 1 194 | 23 499 | 990.6 | 258.0 | 82 | 1 288 | 134.0 | 22.5 | 1 137 | D | D | D |
| Euless....................... | 83 | 2 182 | 131.5 | 39.2 | 8 | 140 | 7.6 | 2.1 | 69 | 747 | 75.4 | 26.8 |
| Farmers Branch .......... | 93 | 1 321 | 76.8 | 21.8 | 13 | 370 | 19.2 | 7.6 | 136 | D | D | D |
| Flower Mound ............. | 100 | 2 056 | 79.9 | 24.4 | 24 | D | D | D | 140 | D | D | D |
| Fort Worth.................. | 1 103 | 23 998 | 1 246.1 | 339.1 | 128 | 2 245 | 243.5 | 50.1 | 1 325 | 19 388 | 2 197.9 | 856.8 |
| Friendswood................ | 74 | D | D | D | 11 | 159 | 9.7 | 3.2 | 94 | D | D | D |
| Frisco........................ | 178 | 4 689 | 257.7 | 74.7 | 29 | D | D | D | 225 | D | D | D |
| Galveston ................... | 203 | 5 316 | 275.9 | 76.6 | 19 | D | D | D | 84 | D | D | D |
| Garland ..................... | 299 | 5 150 | 227.9 | 62.9 | 31 | 681 | 41.9 | 10.4 | 378 | D | D | D |
| Georgetown................ | 96 | 1 727 | 77.5 | 21.3 | 12 | D | D | D | 126 | 2 146 | 170.6 | 75.7 |
| Grand Prairie.............. | 190 | 3 784 | 191.2 | 49.2 | 26 | D | D | D | 185 | 2 236 | 138.7 | 58.4 |
| Grapevine................... | 221 | 9 432 | 697.9 | 195.5 | 19 | 449 | 19.1 | 5.8 | 184 | D | D | D |
| Greenville................... | 64 | 1 319 | 55.0 | 16.2 | 6 | 66 | 1.7 | 0.5 | 100 | 1 165 | 107.6 | 45.2 |
| Haltom City................. | 67 | 889 | 33.8 | 8.8 | 6 | 106 | 4.5 | 1.5 | 33 | D | D | D |
| Harker Heights ............ | 48 | 583 | 24.5 | 5.6 | 10 | 60 | 5.0 | 0.6 | 28 | D | D | D |
| Harlingen ................... | 155 | 3 136 | 129.6 | 33.6 | 15 | 268 | 9.1 | 2.7 | 311 | D | D | D |
| Houston ..................... | 5 177 | 111 291 | 6 263.9 | 1 660.1 | 464 | 8 787 | 1 445.8 | 509.2 | 5 956 | 85 100 | 8 718.9 | 3 273.8 |
| Huntsville.................... | 84 | 1 740 | 63.8 | 16.7 | 4 | D | D | D | 83 | D | D | D |
| Hurst......................... | 97 | 2 035 | 100.4 | 25.7 | 12 | D | D | D | 104 | 1 196 | 109.7 | 42.4 |
| Irving......................... | 489 | 12 088 | 722.7 | 199.5 | 49 | D | D | D | 450 | D | D | D |
| Keller......................... | 69 | 1 042 | 48.9 | 13.5 | 9 | 188 | 8.4 | 2.0 | 105 | 939 | 86.9 | 32.9 |

1. Establishments subject to federal tax.

Items 92—103

# Table D. Cities — Other Services and Federal Funds

| City | Other services[1], 2007 | | | | Selected federal funds, 2009–2010 (mil dol) | | | | | | | | |
| | | | | | Procurement contracts | | Grants | | | | | | |
| | Number of establishments | Number of employees | Receipts (mil dol) | Annual payroll (mil dol) | Defense | Other | Total[2] | Medicaid and other health related | Nutrition and family welfare | Energy and environment | Disasters and emergency preparedness | Housing and community development | Employment and training |
| | 104 | 105 | 106 | 107 | 108 | 109 | 110 | 111 | 112 | 113 | 114 | 115 | 116 |
| **TENNESSEE— Cont'd** | | | | | | | | | | | | | |
| Franklin | 130 | 998 | 77.1 | 23.4 | 24.8 | 1.6 | 3.5 | 1.8 | 0.1 | 0.1 | 0.0 | 1.1 | 0.0 |
| Gallatin | 50 | 324 | 17.6 | 5.4 | 0.0 | 0.2 | 2.6 | 0.0 | 0.0 | 0.4 | 0.0 | 0.7 | 0.0 |
| Germantown | 51 | 512 | 23.3 | 10.1 | 0.0 | 3.8 | 0.3 | 0.0 | 0.0 | 0.0 | 0.0 | 0.3 | 0.0 |
| Hendersonville | 84 | 522 | 38.9 | 11.2 | 1.8 | 0.1 | 0.1 | 0.0 | 0.0 | 0.0 | 0.0 | 0.0 | 0.0 |
| Jackson | 106 | 772 | 57.4 | 20.9 | 0.1 | 3.7 | 18.1 | 0.0 | 0.0 | 0.0 | 0.0 | 12.2 | 0.0 |
| Johnson City | 128 | 756 | 51.2 | 16.2 | 10.4 | 1.7 | 27.1 | 11.1 | 0.3 | 0.0 | 0.0 | 5.1 | 0.0 |
| Kingsport | 94 | 730 | 47.4 | 14.6 | 204.8 | 2.8 | 19.2 | 0.0 | 7.8 | 1.9 | 0.0 | 8.6 | 0.0 |
| Knoxville | 429 | 3 172 | 228.3 | 77.7 | 71.5 | 372.9 | 210.1 | 28.8 | 8.2 | 30.2 | 0.0 | 39.4 | 0.0 |
| La Vergne | 27 | 674 | 88.8 | 26.4 | 1.0 | 0.0 | 0.0 | 0.0 | 0.0 | 0.0 | 0.0 | 0.0 | 0.0 |
| Lebanon | 52 | 305 | 26.1 | 7.0 | 1.4 | 7.8 | 9.1 | 0.1 | 6.9 | 0.4 | 0.0 | 0.6 | 0.0 |
| Maryville | 65 | D | D | D | 5.8 | 0.6 | 5.6 | 1.0 | 0.3 | 0.0 | 0.0 | 2.4 | 0.0 |
| Memphis | 857 | 7 640 | 632.5 | 192.5 | 1 513.6 | 495.9 | 587.3 | 225.3 | 90.7 | 7.0 | -1.3 | 110.0 | 3.1 |
| Morristown | 52 | 263 | 17.8 | 5.3 | 24.6 | 0.5 | 14.0 | 0.0 | 7.3 | 0.0 | 0.0 | 3.7 | 0.3 |
| Murfreesboro | 162 | 927 | 70.6 | 23.5 | 3.5 | 429.3 | 17.0 | 0.8 | 0.0 | 1.6 | 0.0 | 5.5 | 0.0 |
| Nashville-Davidson | 981 | 10 214 | 724.8 | 273.9 | 16.0 | 438.7 | 2 476.4 | 907.1 | 275.9 | 113.3 | 160.3 | 277.1 | 142.4 |
| Oak Ridge | 46 | D | D | D | 65.4 | 3 380.3 | 53.0 | 38.2 | 0.0 | 7.9 | 0.0 | 2.0 | 0.0 |
| Smyrna | 41 | D | D | D | 1.7 | 7.0 | 1.0 | 0.0 | 0.0 | 0.0 | 0.0 | 0.0 | 0.9 |
| Spring Hill | 21 | D | D | D | 0.0 | 0.0 | 0.0 | 0.0 | 0.0 | 0.0 | 0.0 | 0.0 | 0.0 |
| **TEXAS** | 28 404 | 209 702 | 17 917.8 | 5 592.5 | 30 331.5 | 10 263.0 | 44 624.1 | 23 603.8 | 5 505.0 | 1 098.2 | 533.5 | 3 383.1 | 492.2 |
| Abilene | 176 | 1 144 | 82.2 | 23.3 | 19.1 | 0.9 | 21.0 | 0.0 | 3.0 | 0.4 | 0.0 | 8.1 | 0.0 |
| Allen | 67 | 499 | 28.6 | 11.1 | 2.8 | 2.1 | 2.8 | 0.0 | 0.0 | 0.7 | 1.8 | 0.3 | 0.0 |
| Amarillo | 302 | 2 230 | 169.5 | 46.6 | 2 394.6 | 537.6 | 65.5 | 0.0 | 10.1 | 17.3 | 0.0 | 20.4 | 0.0 |
| Arlington | 406 | 3 093 | 225.6 | 71.3 | 415.0 | 2.1 | 97.3 | 8.5 | 1.8 | 23.2 | 0.0 | 30.0 | 3.0 |
| Austin | 1 246 | 11 182 | 899.4 | 315.4 | 446.7 | 418.7 | 7 296.9 | 674.6 | 990.0 | 484.9 | 42.3 | 1 957.2 | 407.2 |
| Baytown | 105 | D | D | D | 124.7 | 0.0 | 8.6 | 0.0 | 0.0 | 0.0 | 0.0 | 7.1 | 0.0 |
| Beaumont | 191 | 1 680 | 141.1 | 43.6 | 12.7 | 15.5 | 27.6 | 0.9 | 3.0 | 0.0 | 0.0 | 15.0 | 0.0 |
| Bedford | 51 | 329 | 21.0 | 7.6 | 8.4 | 0.7 | 0.4 | 0.0 | 0.0 | 0.0 | 0.0 | 0.0 | 0.0 |
| Big Spring | 38 | D | D | D | 0.6 | 12.6 | 4.1 | 0.0 | 0.0 | 0.0 | 0.0 | 1.5 | 0.0 |
| Brownsville | 126 | 570 | 33.7 | 8.6 | 14.4 | 27.0 | 54.2 | 9.3 | 0.0 | 0.6 | 0.0 | 22.5 | 0.0 |
| Bryan | 119 | D | D | D | 11.6 | 2.3 | 33.9 | 2.1 | 4.3 | 0.5 | 0.0 | 12.6 | 0.0 |
| Burleson | 50 | D | D | D | 0.0 | 0.0 | 0.7 | 0.4 | 0.0 | 0.0 | 0.3 | 0.0 | 0.0 |
| Carrollton | 166 | 1 685 | 192.9 | 64.0 | 3.2 | 18.4 | 1.7 | 0.0 | 0.0 | 0.0 | 0.0 | 1.7 | 0.0 |
| Cedar Hill | 39 | D | D | D | 0.0 | 0.0 | 0.3 | 0.0 | 0.0 | 0.0 | 0.0 | 0.0 | 0.0 |
| Cedar Park | 72 | D | D | D | 1.7 | 0.6 | 0.0 | 0.0 | 0.0 | 0.0 | 0.0 | 0.0 | 0.0 |
| Cleburne | 56 | 375 | 29.4 | 8.6 | 0.0 | 11.7 | 2.4 | 0.0 | 0.0 | 0.0 | 0.0 | 1.8 | 0.0 |
| College Station | 67 | 458 | 23.2 | 7.5 | 34.5 | 18.9 | 305.9 | 95.9 | 1.8 | 29.7 | 1.3 | 1.9 | 0.2 |
| Conroe | 111 | 758 | 73.6 | 19.7 | 0.3 | 0.0 | 10.7 | 0.7 | 0.4 | 3.8 | 0.0 | 5.5 | 0.0 |
| Coppell | 46 | D | D | D | 0.0 | 2.1 | 0.9 | 0.0 | 0.0 | 0.9 | 0.0 | 0.0 | 0.0 |
| Copperas Cove | 43 | 336 | 39.8 | 10.7 | 0.0 | 0.3 | 14.7 | 0.0 | 0.0 | 0.0 | 0.0 | 0.1 | 0.0 |
| Corpus Christi | 408 | 3 133 | 308.9 | 98.3 | 271.1 | 53.7 | 59.5 | 4.0 | 9.3 | 9.1 | 0.0 | 18.6 | 0.4 |
| Dallas | 1 567 | 12 760 | 1 252.6 | 351.6 | 195.3 | 425.0 | 991.8 | 410.0 | 36.6 | 15.9 | 1.3 | 260.5 | 0.9 |
| Deer Park | 67 | D | D | D | 952.9 | 0.0 | 0.0 | 0.0 | 0.0 | 0.0 | 0.0 | 0.0 | 0.0 |
| Del Rio | 30 | D | D | D | 18.7 | 11.5 | 6.0 | 0.0 | 2.1 | 0.0 | 0.0 | 3.4 | 0.0 |
| Denton | 139 | 766 | 57.5 | 17.6 | 7.3 | 19.9 | 38.7 | 2.4 | 1.3 | 2.6 | 0.0 | 13.8 | 0.0 |
| DeSoto | 37 | 156 | 16.2 | 4.1 | 2.5 | 0.4 | 0.0 | 0.0 | 0.0 | 0.0 | 0.0 | 0.0 | 0.0 |
| Duncanville | 70 | 376 | 31.2 | 9.4 | 0.0 | 0.4 | 0.0 | 0.0 | 0.0 | 0.0 | 0.0 | 0.0 | 0.0 |
| Eagle Pass | 26 | D | D | D | 0.6 | 0.2 | 10.8 | 4.1 | 0.7 | 0.1 | 0.0 | 3.1 | 0.0 |
| Edinburg | 77 | 253 | 18.6 | 4.9 | 0.1 | 1.5 | 64.1 | 2.3 | 24.2 | 4.5 | 0.0 | 5.8 | 0.0 |
| El Paso | 705 | 4 510 | 278.2 | 84.6 | 446.8 | 206.7 | 245.5 | 32.6 | 29.4 | 12.0 | 1.8 | 55.8 | 1.3 |
| Euless | 52 | D | D | D | 16.1 | 0.8 | 0.8 | 0.4 | 0.0 | 0.5 | 0.0 | 0.0 | 0.0 |
| Farmers Branch | 74 | 1 254 | 71.1 | 31.3 | 1.8 | 4.4 | 0.0 | 0.0 | 0.0 | 0.0 | 0.0 | 0.0 | 0.0 |
| Flower Mound | 79 | 696 | 29.9 | 14.5 | 0.1 | 1.1 | 0.9 | 0.0 | 0.0 | 0.6 | 0.0 | 0.2 | 0.0 |
| Fort Worth | 699 | 6 713 | 548.7 | 177.5 | 7 742.9 | 221.8 | 199.1 | 40.3 | 22.5 | 0.5 | 0.0 | 81.8 | 0.0 |
| Friendswood | 54 | D | D | D | 0.0 | 0.1 | 0.0 | 0.0 | 0.0 | 0.0 | 0.0 | 0.0 | 0.0 |
| Frisco | 115 | 935 | 58.5 | 20.2 | 0.4 | 1.5 | 0.2 | 0.0 | 0.0 | 0.0 | 0.2 | 0.0 | 0.0 |
| Galveston | 73 | 422 | 27.9 | 8.5 | 171.0 | 42.5 | 245.1 | 181.8 | 7.0 | 1.1 | 0.0 | 17.2 | 4.7 |
| Garland | 256 | 1 263 | 107.1 | 33.9 | 196.3 | 5.4 | 17.2 | 0.0 | 0.0 | 2.0 | 0.0 | 15.2 | 0.0 |
| Georgetown | 71 | 475 | 30.2 | 9.5 | 0.4 | 0.2 | 11.0 | 0.7 | 5.4 | 1.5 | 0.0 | 2.2 | 0.0 |
| Grand Prairie | 122 | 1 761 | 110.1 | 43.4 | 2 252.0 | 106.7 | 28.3 | 0.0 | 0.0 | 0.0 | 0.0 | 22.9 | 0.0 |
| Grapevine | 78 | 866 | 76.3 | 20.1 | 0.3 | 2.2 | 1.4 | 0.0 | 0.0 | 0.5 | 0.0 | 0.6 | 0.0 |
| Greenville | 45 | 202 | 15.7 | 4.6 | 1 345.3 | 0.3 | 8.5 | 2.9 | 1.1 | 0.4 | 0.0 | 3.7 | 0.0 |
| Haltom City | 67 | 728 | 72.3 | 16.5 | 0.2 | 0.0 | 0.2 | 0.0 | 0.0 | 0.0 | 0.0 | 0.2 | 0.0 |
| Harker Heights | 22 | 83 | 6.6 | 1.6 | 0.3 | 0.6 | 0.8 | 0.0 | 0.0 | 0.0 | 0.0 | 0.8 | 0.0 |
| Harlingen | 91 | 570 | 36.2 | 10.2 | 0.8 | 13.9 | 25.8 | 9.0 | 0.0 | 1.0 | 0.0 | 6.5 | 0.0 |
| Houston | 3 343 | 32 243 | 2 860.5 | 952.6 | 1 530.1 | 4 174.0 | 2 135.2 | 1 103.7 | 50.7 | 330.0 | 0.9 | 248.1 | 6.1 |
| Huntsville | 47 | 298 | 19.2 | 5.1 | 10.2 | 0.0 | 8.2 | 0.7 | 0.0 | 0.0 | 0.1 | 1.5 | 0.0 |
| Hurst | 73 | D | D | D | 976.0 | 15.9 | 3.9 | 0.0 | 0.0 | 0.0 | 0.0 | 0.0 | 0.0 |
| Irving | 248 | 2 866 | 292.5 | 89.9 | 44.2 | 12.8 | 48.0 | 0.0 | 0.0 | 2.2 | 0.0 | 3.5 | 36.6 |
| Keller | 46 | D | D | D | 0.9 | 0.0 | 0.0 | 0.0 | 0.0 | 0.0 | 0.0 | 0.0 | 0.0 |

1. Establishments subject to federal tax.   2. Includes program categories not shown separately. State totals include additional categories not allocated by city.

| | City government finances, 2007 | | | | | | | | | |
|---|---|---|---|---|---|---|---|---|---|---|
| | General revenue | | | | | | | General expenditure | | |
| | | Intergovernmental | | Taxes | | | | | Per capita[1] (dollars) | |
| | | | | | Per capita[1] (dollars) | | | | | |
| City | Total (mil dol) | Total (mil dol) | Percent from state government | Total (mil dol) | Total | Property | Sales and gross receipts | Total (mil dol) | Total | Capital outlays |
| | 117 | 118 | 119 | 120 | 121 | 122 | 123 | 124 | 125 | 126 |
| **TENNESSEE— Cont'd** | | | | | | | | | | |
| Franklin | 83.3 | 10.3 | 82.6 | 50.5 | 880 | 171 | 709 | 81.9 | 1 428 | 479 |
| Gallatin | 32.0 | 8.7 | 42.3 | 10.0 | 348 | 269 | 79 | 27.5 | 956 | 188 |
| Germantown | 54.0 | 14.3 | 61.2 | 22.6 | 606 | 537 | 70 | 45.3 | 1 214 | 133 |
| Hendersonville | 28.4 | 14.0 | 38.6 | 10.3 | 218 | 149 | 69 | 27.9 | 593 | 51 |
| Jackson | 85.3 | 10.6 | 77.9 | 56.5 | 895 | 445 | 430 | 81.3 | 1 287 | 81 |
| Johnson City | 134.5 | 38.5 | 97.6 | 54.1 | 886 | 479 | 406 | 129.7 | 2 125 | 24 |
| Kingsport | 146.1 | 69.4 | 47.5 | 50.3 | 1 133 | 963 | 170 | 116.9 | 2 631 | 141 |
| Knoxville | 327.2 | 77.2 | 50.2 | 154.5 | 842 | 520 | 322 | 291.1 | 1 586 | 474 |
| La Vergne | 17.0 | 2.8 | 26.1 | 8.7 | 298 | 111 | 188 | 14.0 | 482 | 59 |
| Lebanon | 25.1 | 2.5 | 91.1 | 14.3 | 595 | 109 | 486 | 30.2 | 1 251 | 120 |
| Maryville | 90.2 | 43.5 | 100.0 | 34.5 | 1 290 | 1 277 | 14 | 74.7 | 2 790 | 95 |
| Memphis | 2 055.1 | 1 097.3 | 60.5 | 626.5 | 930 | 703 | 225 | 1 902.6 | 2 823 | 173 |
| Morristown | 18.5 | 1.1 | 76.9 | 6.2 | 226 | 0 | 225 | 21.2 | 773 | 219 |
| Murfreesboro | 161.7 | 84.7 | 46.7 | 42.7 | 434 | 303 | 131 | 178.5 | 1 814 | 435 |
| Nashville-Davidson | 2 125.7 | 470.0 | 98.1 | 1 161.6 | 1 966 | 1 290 | 674 | 2 104.6 | 3 562 | 494 |
| Oak Ridge | 118.7 | 73.6 | 30.6 | 31.6 | 1 150 | 684 | 446 | 115.8 | 4 209 | 49 |
| Smyrna | 44.0 | 6.8 | 58.2 | 16.1 | 439 | 175 | 264 | 45.5 | 1 243 | 328 |
| Spring Hill | 14.2 | 3.9 | 17.4 | 1.7 | 73 | 0 | 73 | 15.9 | 668 | 194 |
| **TEXAS** | X | X | X | X | X | X | X | X | X | X |
| Abilene | 117.7 | 18.3 | 39.2 | 65.3 | 562 | 208 | 354 | 119.0 | 1 024 | 235 |
| Allen | 83.7 | 2.0 | 100.0 | 56.2 | 724 | 378 | 346 | 78.0 | 1 005 | 188 |
| Amarillo | 195.3 | 20.5 | 29.3 | 95.7 | 514 | 133 | 381 | 218.2 | 1 173 | 252 |
| Arlington | 514.4 | 55.8 | 9.1 | 224.1 | 604 | 283 | 321 | 473.0 | 1 275 | 421 |
| Austin | 1 198.0 | 154.8 | 13.7 | 471.1 | 634 | 316 | 318 | 1 165.8 | 1 569 | 299 |
| Baytown | 86.6 | 9.5 | 77.1 | 35.3 | 503 | 227 | 276 | 75.1 | 1 071 | 173 |
| Beaumont | 142.5 | 16.2 | 43.8 | 79.1 | 722 | 299 | 423 | 125.8 | 1 148 | 132 |
| Bedford | 36.0 | 1.1 | 12.6 | 25.6 | 522 | 255 | 267 | 32.5 | 663 | 5 |
| Big Spring | 79.4 | 58.5 | 4.0 | 11.7 | 487 | 129 | 359 | 77.5 | 3 221 | 25 |
| Brownsville | 144.5 | 10.7 | 25.8 | 65.2 | 377 | 164 | 214 | 158.1 | 915 | 144 |
| Bryan | 76.4 | 3.2 | 19.8 | 37.6 | 522 | 239 | 283 | 75.7 | 1 051 | 235 |
| Burleson | 37.4 | 0.5 | 79.2 | 21.5 | 645 | 261 | 384 | 43.1 | 1 291 | 453 |
| Carrollton | 128.9 | 6.5 | 87.5 | 83.4 | 674 | 413 | 260 | 88.8 | 717 | 6 |
| Cedar Hill | 48.1 | 2.6 | 60.7 | 32.3 | 727 | 385 | 342 | 46.7 | 1 052 | 294 |
| Cedar Park | 50.7 | 0.5 | 100.0 | 35.2 | 605 | 221 | 384 | 39.0 | 672 | 195 |
| Cleburne | 33.8 | 0.0 | 100.0 | 19.1 | 645 | 327 | 318 | 30.0 | 1 015 | 0 |
| College Station | 72.3 | 3.5 | 28.0 | 39.1 | 487 | 207 | 280 | 86.2 | 1 074 | 211 |
| Conroe | 57.8 | 3.1 | 78.7 | 43.1 | 821 | 187 | 634 | 55.9 | 1 065 | 257 |
| Coppell | 60.6 | 0.5 | 11.2 | 42.5 | 1 085 | 670 | 415 | 52.9 | 1 350 | 291 |
| Copperas Cove | 20.6 | 0.2 | 6.0 | 9.8 | 327 | 200 | 126 | 17.6 | 587 | 42 |
| Corpus Christi | 313.1 | 24.0 | 29.4 | 162.5 | 569 | 249 | 320 | 343.0 | 1 202 | 304 |
| Dallas | 2 386.1 | 171.5 | 24.6 | 938.7 | 757 | 428 | 329 | 2 523.6 | 2 034 | 603 |
| Deer Park | 34.4 | 1.4 | 0.0 | 14.9 | 485 | 295 | 191 | 26.3 | 860 | 0 |
| Del Rio | 31.6 | 5.3 | 32.7 | 12.0 | 327 | 125 | 202 | 26.8 | 733 | 103 |
| Denton | 138.3 | 5.2 | 67.2 | 75.0 | 649 | 260 | 389 | 117.7 | 1 019 | 125 |
| DeSoto | 49.9 | 1.7 | 77.3 | 29.7 | 633 | 391 | 243 | 50.8 | 1 085 | 240 |
| Duncanville | 36.0 | 1.4 | 100.0 | 23.0 | 636 | 337 | 299 | 33.7 | 930 | 46 |
| Eagle Pass | 39.6 | 15.4 | 100.0 | 7.9 | 299 | 99 | 200 | 38.2 | 1 455 | 513 |
| Edinburg | 52.6 | 3.6 | 65.0 | 27.1 | 395 | 212 | 183 | 46.1 | 671 | 46 |
| El Paso | 611.5 | 101.6 | 38.3 | 297.1 | 490 | 247 | 243 | 531.6 | 876 | 231 |
| Euless | 64.3 | 0.9 | 28.5 | 41.0 | 783 | 215 | 568 | 63.0 | 1 203 | 191 |
| Farmers Branch | 56.3 | 3.5 | 53.6 | 36.9 | 1 395 | 629 | 766 | 59.8 | 2 260 | 372 |
| Flower Mound | 48.8 | 0.9 | 9.7 | 37.3 | 546 | 355 | 191 | 53.7 | 786 | 210 |
| Fort Worth | 818.1 | 56.4 | 100.0 | 490.1 | 719 | 386 | 333 | 829.7 | 1 217 | 335 |
| Friendswood | 25.0 | 0.5 | 18.4 | 16.7 | 500 | 337 | 162 | 24.7 | 738 | 153 |
| Frisco | 176.8 | 30.0 | 60.9 | 103.0 | 1 163 | 453 | 710 | 211.8 | 2 393 | 1 195 |
| Galveston | 114.0 | 10.0 | 17.4 | 50.7 | 890 | 283 | 607 | 86.7 | 1 522 | 159 |
| Garland | 212.8 | 17.6 | 13.8 | 100.1 | 458 | 305 | 153 | 268.8 | 1 228 | 361 |
| Georgetown | 46.0 | 0.5 | 5.8 | 23.9 | 509 | 190 | 319 | 38.7 | 825 | 0 |
| Grand Prairie | 257.7 | 31.3 | 24.1 | 115.9 | 731 | 344 | 388 | 217.2 | 1 371 | 349 |
| Grapevine | 95.4 | 1.0 | 100.0 | 63.0 | 1 257 | 525 | 732 | 80.2 | 1 600 | 136 |
| Greenville | 48.0 | 2.2 | 52.2 | 16.1 | 627 | 301 | 325 | 44.9 | 1 749 | 616 |
| Haltom City | 22.7 | 0.5 | 0.0 | 13.8 | 345 | 135 | 210 | 30.0 | 748 | 196 |
| Harker Heights | 13.9 | 0.6 | 15.6 | 8.9 | 364 | 193 | 172 | 15.0 | 610 | 26 |
| Harlingen | 73.0 | 8.5 | 5.7 | 35.8 | 558 | 200 | 357 | 64.0 | 997 | 21 |
| Houston | 3 112.6 | 299.0 | 22.0 | 1 607.1 | 728 | 380 | 347 | 3 338.9 | 1 512 | 300 |
| Huntsville | 28.1 | 1.3 | 100.0 | 12.3 | 326 | 105 | 221 | 28.2 | 747 | 138 |
| Hurst | 46.9 | 2.0 | 67.5 | 31.9 | 830 | 276 | 554 | 44.2 | 1 150 | 23 |
| Irving | 236.3 | 11.1 | 34.4 | 160.4 | 804 | 383 | 421 | 230.0 | 1 153 | 130 |
| Keller | 47.8 | 1.0 | 100.0 | 28.2 | 739 | 390 | 350 | 37.3 | 980 | 129 |

1. Based on population estimated as of July 1 of the year shown.

| City | Public welfare | Highways | Parking facilities | Education | Health and hospitals | Police protection | Sewerage and sanitation | Parks and recreation | Housing and community development | Interest on debt |
|---|---|---|---|---|---|---|---|---|---|---|
| | 127 | 128 | 129 | 130 | 131 | 132 | 133 | 134 | 135 | 136 |
| **TENNESSEE—** Cont'd | | | | | | | | | | |
| Franklin | 0.7 | 17.8 | 0.0 | 0.0 | 0.0 | 17.0 | 19.2 | 5.6 | 0.0 | 4.6 |
| Gallatin | 0.0 | 10.3 | 0.0 | 0.0 | 0.2 | 19.7 | 21.1 | 13.0 | 0.0 | 0.0 |
| Germantown | 0.0 | 10.4 | 0.0 | 0.0 | 0.5 | 18.6 | 12.6 | 15.9 | 3.4 | 2.5 |
| Hendersonville | 0.5 | 6.1 | 0.0 | 0.1 | 0.0 | 20.7 | 9.5 | 5.9 | 0.0 | 1.8 |
| Jackson | 0.0 | 4.4 | 0.0 | 11.6 | 5.0 | 17.6 | 10.8 | 8.3 | 0.1 | 3.9 |
| Johnson City | 1.1 | 5.0 | 0.0 | 45.6 | 0.0 | 8.1 | 9.5 | 2.7 | 0.1 | 10.7 |
| Kingsport | 0.0 | 3.7 | 0.0 | 49.4 | 0.0 | 8.3 | 7.1 | 3.9 | 0.4 | 2.5 |
| Knoxville | 0.0 | 3.1 | 0.2 | 0.0 | 0.0 | 14.6 | 37.7 | 2.1 | 2.3 | 6.3 |
| La Vergne | 0.0 | 3.5 | 0.0 | 0.0 | 0.6 | 29.2 | 16.9 | 4.9 | 0.0 | 3.2 |
| Lebanon | 0.0 | 11.6 | 0.0 | 0.0 | 0.0 | 24.1 | 21.8 | 7.2 | 0.0 | 3.1 |
| Maryville | 0.0 | 4.1 | 3.4 | 59.6 | 0.4 | 6.6 | 4.8 | 2.3 | 0.3 | 2.2 |
| Memphis | 0.0 | 3.3 | 0.0 | 56.7 | 0.6 | 8.9 | 4.2 | 2.8 | 2.6 | 3.6 |
| Morristown | 0.0 | 3.1 | 0.0 | 0.0 | 0.0 | 15.5 | 36.8 | 3.1 | 0.0 | 2.2 |
| Murfreesboro | 0.1 | 16.8 | 0.1 | 31.5 | 0.0 | 10.1 | 10.9 | 6.4 | 0.2 | 3.5 |
| Nashville-Davidson | 1.4 | 2.4 | 0.0 | 32.6 | 8.6 | 8.2 | 6.6 | 4.3 | 0.0 | 7.2 |
| Oak Ridge | 0.0 | 1.3 | 0.0 | 41.0 | 0.0 | 4.8 | 1.6 | 3.3 | 0.5 | 2.5 |
| Smyrna | 0.6 | 14.1 | 0.0 | 0.0 | 0.0 | 17.4 | 4.6 | 15.2 | 0.6 | 3.4 |
| Spring Hill | 0.0 | 3.2 | 0.0 | 0.0 | 0.0 | 15.9 | 37.7 | 3.1 | 0.0 | 0.0 |
| **TEXAS** | X | X | X | X | X | X | X | X | X | X |
| Abilene | 0.0 | 6.5 | 0.0 | 0.0 | 5.7 | 15.8 | 14.1 | 5.0 | 2.1 | 1.9 |
| Allen | 0.0 | 5.7 | 0.0 | 0.0 | 0.0 | 14.4 | 13.5 | 16.0 | 3.2 | 7.2 |
| Amarillo | 0.1 | 8.7 | 0.0 | 0.0 | 8.6 | 13.4 | 14.7 | 5.9 | 4.7 | 0.2 |
| Arlington | 0.1 | 9.6 | 0.0 | 0.0 | 0.4 | 14.2 | 9.6 | 30.3 | 0.9 | 15.6 |
| Austin | 0.0 | 5.4 | 0.0 | 0.0 | 10.8 | 16.2 | 15.4 | 7.8 | 2.9 | 6.4 |
| Baytown | 0.0 | 9.2 | 0.0 | 0.0 | 4.2 | 20.0 | 16.6 | 6.2 | 1.4 | 6.9 |
| Beaumont | 0.0 | 11.6 | 0.0 | 0.0 | 5.8 | 20.9 | 11.3 | 4.6 | 2.8 | 4.1 |
| Bedford | 0.0 | 7.9 | 0.0 | 0.0 | 1.1 | 25.8 | 13.2 | 7.2 | 0.0 | 7.4 |
| Big Spring | 0.0 | 2.4 | 0.0 | 0.0 | 2.0 | 5.1 | 5.2 | 1.6 | 0.0 | 0.1 |
| Brownsville | 0.0 | 5.1 | 0.3 | 0.0 | 1.0 | 16.2 | 13.6 | 4.5 | 1.4 | 15.9 |
| Bryan | 0.0 | 8.2 | 0.0 | 0.0 | 0.0 | 15.9 | 16.8 | 5.8 | 3.3 | 7.7 |
| Burleson | 0.0 | 30.5 | 0.0 | 0.0 | 1.1 | 11.9 | 16.9 | 7.1 | 0.0 | 4.6 |
| Carrollton | 0.0 | 5.9 | 0.0 | 0.0 | 2.4 | 20.7 | 13.5 | 9.4 | 0.6 | 7.1 |
| Cedar Hill | 0.0 | 25.1 | 0.0 | 0.0 | 0.0 | 13.8 | 10.5 | 5.1 | 0.3 | 5.2 |
| Cedar Park | 0.0 | 21.7 | 0.0 | 0.0 | 0.3 | 12.8 | 19.6 | 4.9 | 1.6 | 8.2 |
| Cleburne | 0.0 | 6.4 | 0.0 | 0.0 | 1.4 | 17.9 | 22.7 | 9.2 | 0.0 | 5.9 |
| College Station | 0.0 | 11.0 | 0.6 | 0.0 | 0.0 | 11.7 | 17.3 | 14.3 | 2.1 | 6.6 |
| Conroe | 0.0 | 12.3 | 0.0 | 0.0 | 0.0 | 17.2 | 17.7 | 7.1 | 1.2 | 5.5 |
| Coppell | 0.0 | 18.1 | 0.0 | 0.0 | 0.4 | 15.7 | 3.1 | 12.9 | 0.0 | 6.2 |
| Copperas Cove | 0.0 | 9.2 | 0.0 | 0.0 | 0.0 | 21.8 | 18.7 | 10.3 | 0.0 | 4.4 |
| Corpus Christi | 0.0 | 6.2 | 0.1 | 0.0 | 3.8 | 17.3 | 23.4 | 11.2 | 1.2 | 5.7 |
| Dallas | 0.4 | 12.7 | 0.1 | 0.0 | 1.2 | 13.0 | 9.8 | 5.3 | 2.4 | 15.8 |
| Deer Park | 0.0 | 2.5 | 0.0 | 0.0 | 0.6 | 17.0 | 18.3 | 6.5 | 0.0 | 5.2 |
| Del Rio | 1.7 | 16.2 | 0.0 | 0.0 | 1.7 | 18.1 | 16.6 | 4.6 | 0.0 | 5.8 |
| Denton | 0.0 | 4.2 | 0.0 | 0.0 | 0.2 | 16.0 | 25.1 | 8.4 | 1.7 | 6.8 |
| DeSoto | 0.0 | 9.0 | 0.0 | 0.0 | 0.6 | 12.2 | 19.6 | 8.1 | 0.0 | 9.9 |
| Duncanville | 0.0 | 11.4 | 0.0 | 0.0 | 2.5 | 18.5 | 18.3 | 4.8 | 0.0 | 4.6 |
| Eagle Pass | 0.0 | 5.2 | 0.0 | 0.0 | 0.1 | 11.8 | 31.9 | 17.1 | 0.9 | 5.4 |
| Edinburg | 0.0 | 7.2 | 0.0 | 0.0 | 2.9 | 18.8 | 23.2 | 13.8 | 1.7 | 3.0 |
| El Paso | 0.0 | 9.2 | 0.0 | 0.0 | 4.6 | 17.4 | 12.5 | 11.1 | 5.4 | 6.2 |
| Euless | 0.0 | 10.9 | 0.0 | 0.0 | 0.5 | 13.2 | 3.3 | 11.8 | 0.0 | 4.8 |
| Farmers Branch | 0.0 | 17.3 | 0.0 | 0.0 | 0.0 | 27.2 | 13.4 | 11.8 | 0.0 | 1.4 |
| Flower Mound | 0.0 | 21.9 | 0.0 | 0.0 | 1.8 | 16.8 | 8.5 | 12.9 | 0.0 | 5.9 |
| Fort Worth | 0.0 | 11.7 | 0.0 | 0.0 | 1.7 | 20.6 | 16.2 | 6.9 | 1.2 | 2.7 |
| Friendswood | 0.0 | 6.0 | 0.0 | 0.0 | 0.7 | 21.7 | 8.9 | 7.5 | 1.1 | 3.0 |
| Frisco | 0.0 | 15.2 | 0.0 | 4.4 | 0.1 | 6.3 | 6.7 | 3.0 | 0.0 | 10.1 |
| Galveston | 0.0 | 7.6 | 0.5 | 0.0 | 0.5 | 16.0 | 10.7 | 17.8 | 5.3 | 9.7 |
| Garland | 1.4 | 8.1 | 0.0 | 0.0 | 1.1 | 14.4 | 17.6 | 4.1 | 6.4 | 5.8 |
| Georgetown | 0.7 | 4.5 | 0.0 | 0.0 | 0.0 | 17.0 | 22.1 | 8.3 | 0.0 | 6.5 |
| Grand Prairie | 0.0 | 14.7 | 0.0 | 0.0 | 0.8 | 12.6 | 13.8 | 11.2 | 11.3 | 8.2 |
| Grapevine | 0.0 | 8.8 | 0.0 | 0.0 | 0.0 | 12.7 | 7.7 | 12.1 | 0.1 | 8.5 |
| Greenville | 0.0 | 4.0 | 0.0 | 0.0 | 0.3 | 15.5 | 18.2 | 3.3 | 1.7 | 4.7 |
| Haltom City | 0.0 | 11.9 | 0.0 | 0.0 | 0.8 | 21.6 | 17.6 | 3.2 | 0.2 | 3.6 |
| Harker Heights | 0.0 | 4.8 | 0.0 | 0.0 | 0.0 | 20.9 | 13.9 | 6.5 | 0.0 | 4.3 |
| Harlingen | 0.0 | 5.7 | 0.0 | 0.0 | 5.6 | 15.4 | 17.3 | 8.6 | 1.8 | 1.8 |
| Houston | 0.0 | 7.4 | 0.1 | 0.0 | 3.0 | 15.1 | 10.4 | 5.2 | 2.3 | 13.3 |
| Huntsville | 0.0 | 5.7 | 0.0 | 0.0 | 0.7 | 13.8 | 43.4 | 3.6 | 0.0 | 3.8 |
| Hurst | 0.0 | 8.1 | 0.0 | 0.0 | 2.2 | 28.0 | 14.6 | 14.5 | 0.0 | 0.7 |
| Irving | 0.0 | 9.9 | 0.0 | 0.0 | 0.7 | 17.7 | 15.7 | 8.9 | 2.3 | 3.4 |
| Keller | 0.0 | 7.0 | 0.0 | 0.0 | 0.3 | 14.5 | 8.5 | 15.0 | 3.3 | 16.8 |

| | City government finances, 2007 (cont.) | | | | Climate[2] | | | | | | |
|---|---|---|---|---|---|---|---|---|---|---|---|
| | Debt outstanding | | | | Average daily temperature (degrees Fahrenheit) | | | | | | |
| | | | | | Mean | | Limits | | | | |
| City | Total (mil dol) | Per capita[1] (dollars) | Debt issued during year | City government employment, 2011 | January | July | January[3] | July[4] | Annual precipitation (inches) | Heating degree days | Cooling degree days |
| | 137 | 138 | 139 | 140 | 141 | 142 | 143 | 144 | 145 | 146 | 147 |
| **TENNESSEE—Cont'd** | | | | | | | | | | | |
| Franklin | 103.3 | 1 800 | 20.3 | 630 | 35.1 | 77.4 | 25.2 | 88.9 | 54.33 | 4 199 | 1 294 |
| Gallatin | 18.0 | 628 | 7.5 | 418 | NA | NA | NA | NA | NA | NA | NA |
| Germantown | 28.5 | 763 | 9.8 | 343 | 37.9 | 81.1 | 28.2 | 91.1 | 53.63 | 3 491 | 1 838 |
| Hendersonville | 14.3 | 305 | 7.7 | NA | 36.8 | 79.1 | 27.9 | 88.7 | 48.11 | 3 677 | 1 652 |
| Jackson | 121.8 | 1 927 | 0.0 | 731 | 37.1 | 79.6 | 28.2 | 89.4 | 54.86 | 3 649 | 1 648 |
| Johnson City | 496.3 | 8 133 | 62.6 | 2 022 | 34.2 | 74.2 | 24.3 | 84.8 | 41.33 | 4 445 | 956 |
| Kingsport | 129.1 | 2 905 | 37.1 | 2 033 | 35.6 | 76.2 | 26.2 | 86.9 | 44.44 | 4 178 | 1 139 |
| Knoxville | 652.5 | 3 555 | 0.0 | 2 517 | 38.5 | 78.7 | 30.3 | 88.2 | 48.22 | 3 531 | 1 527 |
| La Vergne | 31.0 | 1 069 | 0.0 | NA | NA | NA | NA | NA | NA | NA | NA |
| Lebanon | 31.2 | 1 292 | 2.7 | 334 | NA | NA | NA | NA | NA | NA | NA |
| Maryville | 82.8 | 3 095 | 31.0 | 935 | NA | NA | NA | NA | NA | NA | NA |
| Memphis | 2 952.3 | 4 380 | 292.0 | 22 613 | 39.9 | 82.5 | 31.3 | 92.1 | 54.65 | 3 041 | 2 187 |
| Morristown | 12.9 | 470 | 1.1 | 415 | NA | NA | NA | NA | NA | NA | NA |
| Murfreesboro | 288.3 | 2 930 | 69.8 | 2 135 | 35.4 | 78.1 | 25.3 | 89.1 | 54.98 | 4 107 | 1 388 |
| Nashville-Davidson | 3 858.6 | 6 531 | 254.9 | 21 583 | 36.8 | 79.1 | 27.9 | 88.7 | 48.11 | 3 677 | 1 652 |
| Oak Ridge | 154.8 | 5 628 | 26.0 | 1 080 | 36.6 | 77.3 | 27.2 | 88.1 | 55.05 | 3 993 | 1 301 |
| Smyrna | 41.9 | 1 146 | 10.8 | 425 | 36.8 | 79.1 | 27.9 | 88.7 | 48.11 | 3 677 | 1 652 |
| Spring Hill | 8.5 | 357 | 0.0 | NA | NA | NA | NA | NA | NA | NA | NA |
| **TEXAS** | X | X | X | X | X | X | X | X | X | X | X |
| Abilene | 122.7 | 1 055 | 25.7 | 1 109 | 43.5 | 83.5 | 31.8 | 94.8 | 23.78 | 2 659 | 2 386 |
| Allen | 109.6 | 1 412 | 7.1 | NA | 41.8 | 82.4 | 31.1 | 92.7 | 41.01 | 2 843 | 2 060 |
| Amarillo | 161.4 | 867 | 20.9 | 2 064 | 35.8 | 78.2 | 22.6 | 91.0 | 19.71 | 4 318 | 1 344 |
| Arlington | 1 943.9 | 5 239 | 479.6 | 2 512 | 44.1 | 85.0 | 34.0 | 95.4 | 34.73 | 2 370 | 2 568 |
| Austin | 4 644.7 | 6 251 | 635.7 | 12 445 | 50.2 | 84.2 | 40.0 | 95.0 | 33.65 | 1 648 | 2 974 |
| Baytown | 158.9 | 2 266 | 38.0 | 741 | 51.6 | 83.6 | 41.9 | 91.6 | 53.75 | 1 471 | 2 841 |
| Beaumont | 225.6 | 2 059 | 28.8 | 1 373 | 51.1 | 83.1 | 41.1 | 92.7 | 57.38 | 1 548 | 2 734 |
| Bedford | 61.5 | 1 256 | 0.0 | NA | 44.1 | 85.0 | 34.0 | 95.4 | 34.73 | 2 370 | 2 568 |
| Big Spring | 10.0 | 414 | 5.6 | 282 | 42.7 | 82.7 | 29.6 | 94.3 | 20.12 | 2 724 | 2 243 |
| Brownsville | 506.6 | 2 932 | 20.7 | 1 660 | 59.6 | 83.9 | 50.5 | 92.4 | 27.55 | 644 | 3 874 |
| Bryan | 174.3 | 2 420 | 54.4 | 921 | 50.2 | 84.6 | 39.8 | 95.6 | 39.67 | 1 616 | 2 938 |
| Burleson | 72.0 | 2 158 | 9.0 | NA | NA | NA | NA | NA | NA | NA | NA |
| Carrollton | 176.0 | 1 422 | 24.8 | 612 | 44.1 | 85.0 | 34.0 | 95.4 | 34.73 | 2 370 | 2 568 |
| Cedar Hill | 85.0 | 1 914 | 19.6 | NA | 43.7 | 84.3 | 33.2 | 94.9 | 34.54 | 2 437 | 2 508 |
| Cedar Park | 126.9 | 2 184 | 2.8 | 363 | 47.2 | 83.8 | 35.1 | 95.7 | 36.42 | 1 998 | 2 584 |
| Cleburne | 99.3 | 3 359 | 12.9 | NA | 45.9 | 84.5 | 34.0 | 97.0 | 36.25 | 2 158 | 2 604 |
| College Station | 188.8 | 2 350 | 32.7 | 858 | 50.2 | 84.6 | 39.8 | 95.6 | 39.67 | 1 616 | 2 938 |
| Conroe | 76.6 | 1 458 | 15.0 | 508 | 50.3 | 83.7 | 40.0 | 94.3 | 49.32 | 1 647 | 2 793 |
| Coppell | 72.6 | 1 851 | 8.2 | NA | 44.1 | 85.0 | 34.0 | 95.4 | 34.73 | 2 370 | 2 568 |
| Copperas Cove | 44.2 | 1 471 | 9.3 | NA | 46.0 | 83.5 | 34.0 | 95.3 | 32.88 | 2 190 | 2 477 |
| Corpus Christi | 869.9 | 3 047 | 89.8 | 2 731 | 56.1 | 83.8 | 46.2 | 93.2 | 32.26 | 950 | 3 497 |
| Dallas | 8 852.4 | 7 136 | 852.6 | 14 494 | 45.9 | 86.5 | 36.4 | 96.1 | 37.05 | 2 219 | 2 878 |
| Deer Park | 44.3 | 1 445 | 0.0 | 354 | 54.3 | 84.5 | 45.2 | 93.6 | 53.96 | 1 174 | 3 179 |
| Del Rio | 71.3 | 1 950 | 0.7 | 471 | 51.3 | 85.3 | 39.7 | 96.2 | 18.80 | 1 417 | 3 226 |
| Denton | 401.6 | 3 477 | 24.9 | 1 234 | 42.7 | 83.6 | 32.0 | 94.1 | 37.79 | 2 650 | 2 269 |
| DeSoto | 105.4 | 2 248 | 8.9 | NA | 46.0 | 84.6 | 35.0 | 96.0 | 38.81 | 2 130 | 2 608 |
| Duncanville | 34.4 | 951 | 4.7 | NA | 45.9 | 86.5 | 36.4 | 96.1 | 37.05 | 2 219 | 2 878 |
| Eagle Pass | 58.6 | 2 229 | 11.7 | NA | NA | NA | NA | NA | NA | NA | NA |
| Edinburg | 56.2 | 818 | 27.4 | NA | 58.7 | 85.1 | 48.2 | 95.5 | 22.61 | 719 | 3 898 |
| El Paso | 1 100.0 | 1 812 | 173.6 | 5 990 | 45.1 | 83.3 | 32.9 | 94.5 | 9.43 | 2 543 | 2 254 |
| Euless | 76.3 | 1 457 | 9.7 | NA | 44.1 | 85.0 | 34.0 | 95.4 | 34.73 | 2 370 | 2 568 |
| Farmers Branch | 19.2 | 723 | 0.0 | NA | 45.9 | 86.5 | 36.4 | 96.1 | 37.05 | 2 219 | 2 878 |
| Flower Mound | 119.0 | 1 741 | 15.6 | NA | 44.1 | 85.0 | 34.0 | 95.4 | 34.73 | 2 370 | 2 568 |
| Fort Worth | 1 183.0 | 1 735 | 46.1 | 6 386 | 43.3 | 84.5 | 31.4 | 96.6 | 34.01 | 2 509 | 2 466 |
| Friendswood | 51.0 | 1 522 | 24.3 | 209 | 54.3 | 84.5 | 45.2 | 93.6 | 53.96 | 1 174 | 3 179 |
| Frisco | 641.0 | 7 240 | 95.3 | 591 | 41.8 | 82.4 | 31.1 | 92.7 | 41.01 | 2 843 | 2 060 |
| Galveston | 309.5 | 5 436 | 47.8 | 826 | 55.8 | 84.3 | 49.7 | 88.7 | 43.84 | 1 008 | 3 268 |
| Garland | 659.6 | 3 015 | 88.2 | 1 495 | 45.9 | 86.5 | 36.4 | 96.1 | 37.05 | 2 219 | 2 878 |
| Georgetown | 107.1 | 2 284 | 33.1 | NA | 47.2 | 83.8 | 35.1 | 95.7 | 36.42 | 1 998 | 2 584 |
| Grand Prairie | 358.8 | 2 265 | 18.2 | 1 165 | 44.1 | 85.0 | 34.0 | 95.4 | 34.73 | 2 370 | 2 568 |
| Grapevine | 230.2 | 4 594 | 11.4 | 576 | 42.4 | 84.0 | 30.8 | 95.5 | 34.66 | 2 649 | 2 340 |
| Greenville | 69.7 | 2 713 | 4.9 | NA | NA | NA | NA | NA | NA | NA | NA |
| Haltom City | 51.9 | 1 294 | 3.4 | 292 | 43.0 | 84.1 | 31.4 | 95.7 | 34.12 | 2 608 | 2 358 |
| Harker Heights | 36.3 | 1 477 | 17.3 | NA | NA | NA | NA | NA | NA | NA | NA |
| Harlingen | 48.6 | 756 | 8.6 | NA | 58.6 | 84.4 | 48.4 | 94.5 | 28.13 | 737 | 3 736 |
| Houston | 12 167.5 | 5 510 | 1 370.0 | 22 059 | 54.3 | 84.5 | 45.2 | 93.6 | 53.96 | 1 174 | 3 179 |
| Huntsville | 49.2 | 1 303 | 1.1 | NA | 48.5 | 83.2 | 39.0 | 93.8 | 48.51 | 1 835 | 2 600 |
| Hurst | 46.2 | 1 202 | 8.1 | NA | 44.1 | 85.0 | 34.0 | 95.4 | 34.73 | 2 370 | 2 568 |
| Irving | 368.1 | 1 845 | 91.2 | 1 814 | 45.9 | 86.5 | 36.4 | 96.1 | 37.05 | 2 219 | 2 878 |
| Keller | 152.0 | 3 991 | 5.4 | NA | 43.0 | 84.1 | 31.4 | 95.7 | 34.12 | 2 608 | 2 358 |

1. Based on the population estimated as of July 1 of the year shown.   2. Represents normal values based on the 30-year period, 1971–2000.   3. Average daily minimum.   4. Average daily maximum.

# Table D. Cities — **Land Area and Population**

| STATE Place code | City | Land area,[1] 2010 (sq km) | Total persons | Rank | Per square kilometer | White | Black | American Indian, Alaska Native | Asian | Hawaiian Pacific Islander | Percent Hispanic or Latino[2], 2010 | Percent Foreign born 2007–2011 |
|---|---|---|---|---|---|---|---|---|---|---|---|---|
| | | | Population, 2012 | | | Race alone or in combination, not of Hispanic origin (percent), 2010 | | | | | | |
| | | | | | | Race alone or in combination | | | | | | |
| | | 1 | 2 | 3 | 4 | 5 | 6 | 7 | 8 | 9 | 10 | 11 |
| | TEXAS—Cont'd | | | | | | | | | | | |
| 48 39148 | Killeen | 138.8 | 134 654 | 187 | 970.1 | 38.0 | 35.1 | 1.3 | 5.4 | 1.7 | 22.9 | 10.1 |
| 48 39352 | Kingsville | 35.8 | 26 206 | 1 387 | 732.0 | 21.6 | 4.2 | 0.3 | 2.8 | 0.1 | 71.4 | 7.0 |
| 48 39952 | Kyle | 49.4 | 30 875 | 1 178 | 625.0 | 46.8 | 5.8 | 0.7 | 1.5 | 0.2 | 46.3 | 6.1 |
| 48 40588 | Lake Jackson | 50.4 | 27 166 | 1 338 | 539.0 | 70.9 | 5.4 | 0.8 | 3.4 | 0.1 | 20.5 | 7.3 |
| 48 41212 | Lancaster | 78.4 | 37 845 | 965 | 482.7 | 13.8 | 69.4 | 0.6 | 0.5 | 0.1 | 17.0 | 7.7 |
| 48 41440 | La Porte | 48.3 | 34 469 | 1 064 | 713.6 | 62.8 | 6.5 | 0.9 | 1.5 | 0.1 | 29.4 | 10.0 |
| 48 41464 | Laredo | 230.3 | 244 731 | 81 | 1 062.7 | 3.5 | 0.2 | 0.1 | 0.6 | 0.0 | 95.6 | 29.5 |
| 48 41980 | League City | 132.8 | 88 188 | 344 | 664.1 | 69.8 | 7.5 | 0.7 | 6.2 | 0.1 | 17.3 | 10.5 |
| 48 42016 | Leander | 59.2 | 29 620 | 1 230 | 500.3 | 68.0 | 5.2 | 1.1 | 3.1 | 0.2 | 24.5 | 9.0 |
| 48 42508 | Lewisville | 94.3 | 99 453 | 292 | 1 054.6 | 51.3 | 11.8 | 0.9 | 8.4 | 0.1 | 29.2 | 20.8 |
| 48 43012 | Little Elm | 37.7 | 28 966 | 1 259 | 768.3 | 57.4 | 15.2 | 1.2 | 4.2 | 0.2 | 24.0 | 15.8 |
| 48 43888 | Longview | 144.2 | 81 092 | 391 | 562.4 | 57.4 | 23.4 | 0.8 | 1.6 | 0.1 | 18.0 | 9.6 |
| 48 45000 | Lubbock | 317.0 | 236 065 | 84 | 744.7 | 56.7 | 8.6 | 0.7 | 2.7 | 0.1 | 32.1 | 5.9 |
| 48 45072 | Lufkin | 86.4 | 36 009 | 1 016 | 416.8 | 46.7 | 27.7 | 0.5 | 1.8 | 0.0 | 24.1 | 10.9 |
| 48 45384 | McAllen | 125.2 | 134 719 | 186 | 1 076.0 | 12.0 | 0.7 | 0.2 | 2.7 | 0.0 | 84.6 | 28.6 |
| 48 45744 | McKinney | 161.1 | 143 223 | 177 | 889.0 | 66.2 | 11.1 | 1.0 | 4.8 | 0.1 | 18.6 | 12.9 |
| 48 46452 | Mansfield | 94.2 | 59 317 | 592 | 629.7 | 66.1 | 14.8 | 0.9 | 4.5 | 0.2 | 15.4 | 11.1 |
| 48 47892 | Mesquite | 119.2 | 143 195 | 178 | 1 201.3 | 43.0 | 22.3 | 0.8 | 3.6 | 0.1 | 31.6 | 14.7 |
| 48 48072 | Midland | 186.7 | 119 385 | 219 | 639.4 | 52.8 | 8.0 | 0.8 | 1.5 | 0.1 | 37.6 | 8.7 |
| 48 48768 | Mission | 88.0 | 80 452 | 399 | 914.2 | 12.5 | 0.5 | 0.2 | 1.6 | 0.0 | 85.4 | 25.5 |
| 48 48804 | Missouri City | 73.6 | 69 020 | 486 | 937.8 | 26.2 | 42.2 | 0.7 | 17.1 | 0.1 | 15.3 | 23.1 |
| 48 50256 | Nacogdoches | 70.1 | 34 047 | 1 074 | 485.7 | 52.4 | 29.3 | 0.7 | 2.1 | 0.1 | 16.8 | 9.4 |
| 48 50820 | New Braunfels | 113.6 | 60 761 | 572 | 534.9 | 61.8 | 2.0 | 0.6 | 1.3 | 0.1 | 35.0 | 6.8 |
| 48 52356 | North Richland Hills | 47.1 | 65 290 | 522 | 1 386.2 | 76.2 | 5.1 | 1.1 | 3.3 | 0.2 | 15.6 | 8.1 |
| 48 53388 | Odessa | 108.7 | 106 102 | 265 | 976.1 | 42.3 | 5.7 | 0.8 | 1.2 | 0.1 | 50.6 | 11.4 |
| 48 55080 | Paris | 94.5 | 25 082 | 1 440 | 265.4 | 66.2 | 24.4 | 2.8 | 1.1 | 0.1 | 8.2 | 3.6 |
| 48 56000 | Pasadena | 110.8 | 152 272 | 159 | 1 374.3 | 33.3 | 2.2 | 0.4 | 2.3 | 0.1 | 62.2 | 25.9 |
| 48 56348 | Pearland | 121.8 | 96 294 | 303 | 790.6 | 50.2 | 16.9 | 0.7 | 13.2 | 0.1 | 20.5 | 15.3 |
| 48 57176 | Pflugerville | 57.8 | 51 894 | 697 | 897.8 | 49.3 | 16.0 | 0.7 | 8.1 | 0.2 | 27.7 | 13.3 |
| 48 57200 | Pharr | 60.7 | 73 138 | 451 | 1 204.9 | 6.1 | 0.2 | 0.1 | 0.5 | 0.0 | 93.0 | 33.1 |
| 48 58016 | Plano | 185.4 | 272 068 | 70 | 1 467.5 | 60.2 | 8.0 | 0.8 | 18.1 | 0.2 | 14.7 | 22.8 |
| 48 58820 | Port Arthur | 199.2 | 54 010 | 671 | 271.1 | 23.5 | 41.0 | 0.6 | 6.1 | 0.1 | 29.6 | 18.5 |
| 48 61796 | Richardson | 74.0 | 103 297 | 275 | 1 395.9 | 59.8 | 8.9 | 0.8 | 16.2 | 0.1 | 16.0 | 22.4 |
| 48 62828 | Rockwall | 71.7 | 39 957 | 914 | 557.3 | 74.0 | 6.2 | 0.9 | 3.5 | 0.1 | 16.6 | 10.9 |
| 48 63284 | Rosenberg | 58.2 | 31 734 | 1 145 | 545.3 | 25.6 | 13.2 | 0.3 | 1.1 | 0.1 | 60.3 | 18.3 |
| 48 63500 | Round Rock | 88.4 | 106 573 | 261 | 1 205.6 | 55.8 | 10.2 | 0.8 | 6.0 | 0.2 | 29.0 | 12.3 |
| 48 63572 | Rowlett | 51.5 | 57 703 | 615 | 1 120.4 | 63.0 | 13.8 | 1.0 | 7.2 | 0.1 | 16.5 | 10.6 |
| 48 64472 | San Angelo | 147.3 | 95 887 | 305 | 651.0 | 55.6 | 4.7 | 0.8 | 1.5 | 0.2 | 38.5 | 7.1 |
| 48 65000 | San Antonio | 1 193.8 | 1 382 951 | 7 | 1 158.4 | 27.6 | 6.8 | 0.5 | 2.8 | 0.2 | 63.2 | 13.7 |
| 48 65516 | San Juan | 29.7 | 35 204 | 1 038 | 1 185.3 | 3.0 | 0.1 | 0.0 | 0.1 | 0.0 | 96.7 | 32.7 |
| 48 65600 | San Marcos | 78.3 | 50 001 | 725 | 638.6 | 55.1 | 5.6 | 0.8 | 2.0 | 0.2 | 37.8 | 5.7 |
| 48 66128 | Schertz | 73.6 | 34 883 | 1 047 | 474.0 | 62.7 | 9.3 | 1.0 | 3.5 | 0.3 | 25.7 | 6.5 |
| 48 66644 | Seguin | 89.3 | 26 272 | 1 383 | 294.2 | 36.1 | 7.7 | 0.4 | 0.9 | 0.0 | 55.4 | 9.1 |
| 48 67496 | Sherman | 107.2 | 39 122 | 933 | 364.9 | 65.5 | 11.9 | 2.3 | 2.0 | 0.1 | 20.5 | 10.4 |
| 48 68636 | Socorro | 57.1 | 32 693 | 1 112 | 572.6 | 2.2 | 0.2 | 0.9 | 0.1 | 0.0 | 96.7 | 33.2 |
| 48 69032 | Southlake | 56.7 | 27 706 | 1 308 | 488.6 | 85.7 | 2.4 | 0.7 | 7.2 | 0.1 | 5.5 | 8.1 |
| 48 70808 | Sugar Land | 83.9 | 82 480 | 380 | 983.1 | 46.0 | 7.6 | 0.5 | 36.8 | 0.1 | 10.6 | 34.0 |
| 48 72176 | Temple | 178.7 | 69 148 | 483 | 387.0 | 57.1 | 17.4 | 0.8 | 2.5 | 0.2 | 23.7 | 8.5 |
| 48 72368 | Texarkana | 75.2 | 37 217 | 977 | 494.9 | 54.6 | 37.9 | 1.1 | 1.6 | 0.1 | 6.4 | 3.7 |
| 48 72392 | Texas City | 165.3 | 45 671 | 807 | 276.3 | 42.1 | 29.9 | 0.8 | 1.2 | 0.1 | 27.0 | 7.2 |
| 48 72530 | The Colony | 36.3 | 39 030 | 936 | 1 075.2 | 64.1 | 8.8 | 1.3 | 6.6 | 0.2 | 21.2 | 15.5 |
| 48 74144 | Tyler | 139.5 | 99 323 | 294 | 712.0 | 51.9 | 25.2 | 0.7 | 2.2 | 0.1 | 21.2 | 11.5 |
| 48 75428 | Victoria | 91.9 | 64 376 | 535 | 700.5 | 42.7 | 7.8 | 0.5 | 1.5 | 0.0 | 48.3 | 6.0 |
| 48 76000 | Waco | 230.4 | 127 018 | 200 | 551.3 | 47.1 | 21.8 | 0.6 | 2.1 | 0.1 | 29.6 | 11.1 |
| 48 76816 | Waxahachie | 123.4 | 31 091 | 1 170 | 252.0 | 63.1 | 13.0 | 1.0 | 0.7 | 0.2 | 23.2 | 7.1 |
| 48 76864 | Weatherford | 64.4 | 26 385 | 1 377 | 409.7 | 82.5 | 2.8 | 1.3 | 1.1 | 0.1 | 13.6 | 7.5 |
| 48 77272 | Weslaco | 38.1 | 36 846 | 991 | 967.1 | 13.5 | 0.3 | 0.2 | 1.2 | 0.0 | 85.0 | 20.8 |
| 48 79000 | Wichita Falls | 186.8 | 104 552 | 270 | 559.7 | 65.4 | 13.2 | 1.4 | 2.9 | 0.2 | 18.9 | 7.9 |
| 48 80356 | Wylie | 54.5 | 44 267 | 823 | 812.2 | 63.5 | 13.0 | 1.0 | 6.3 | 0.2 | 17.9 | 12.2 |
| 49 00000 | UTAH | 212 818.3 | 2 855 287 | X | 13.4 | 82.0 | 1.3 | 1.4 | 2.7 | 1.3 | 13.0 | 8.2 |
| 49 01310 | American Fork | 23.8 | 27 147 | 1 339 | 1 140.6 | 90.4 | 0.6 | 0.8 | 1.5 | 1.1 | 7.4 | 4.2 |
| 49 07690 | Bountiful | 34.8 | 42 898 | 851 | 1 232.7 | 91.9 | 0.8 | 0.5 | 2.0 | 1.2 | 4.9 | 4.2 |
| 49 11320 | Cedar City | 95.4 | 29 118 | 1 251 | 305.2 | 87.7 | 1.0 | 3.0 | 1.5 | 0.7 | 7.9 | 3.9 |
| 49 13850 | Clearfield | 19.7 | 30 376 | 1 201 | 1 541.9 | 76.7 | 3.9 | 1.3 | 3.8 | 1.1 | 16.1 | 8.2 |
| 49 16270 | Cottonwood Heights | 22.9 | 34 017 | 1 076 | 1 485.5 | 90.0 | 1.3 | 0.6 | 4.2 | 0.7 | 5.1 | 6.5 |
| 49 20120 | Draper | 77.9 | 44 103 | 825 | 566.1 | 88.0 | 1.6 | 0.8 | 3.7 | 1.0 | 7.0 | 6.9 |
| 49 36070 | Holladay | 20.5 | 26 936 | 1 348 | 1 314.0 | 90.8 | 1.2 | 0.6 | 3.5 | 0.6 | 4.7 | 6.6 |
| 49 40360 | Kaysville | 27.1 | 28 283 | 1 283 | 1 043.7 | 93.7 | 0.7 | 0.4 | 1.4 | 0.4 | 4.5 | 3.2 |
| 49 43660 | Layton | 57.0 | 68 677 | 488 | 1 204.9 | 84.0 | 2.2 | 0.8 | 3.1 | 0.8 | 11.2 | 4.8 |

1. Dry land or land partially or temporarily covered by water.  2. May be of any race.

# Table D. Cities — **Population**

| City | Age of population (percent), 2010 | | | | | | | | | | | Population | | | |
|---|---|---|---|---|---|---|---|---|---|---|---|---|---|---|---|
| | | | | | | | | | | | | Census counts | | Percent change | |
| | Under 5 years | 5 to 17 years | 18 to 24 years | 25 to 34 years | 35 to 44 years | 45 to 54 years | 55 to 64 years | 65 to 74 years | 75 years and over | Median age | Percent female | 2000 | 2010 | 2000–2010 | 2010–2012 |
| | 12 | 13 | 14 | 15 | 16 | 17 | 18 | 19 | 20 | 21 | 22 | 23 | 24 | 25 | 26 |
| **TEXAS—Cont'd** | | | | | | | | | | | | | | | |
| Killeen | 10.6 | 19.9 | 14.1 | 20.7 | 12.8 | 10.5 | 6.4 | 3.2 | 2.0 | 27.1 | 51.0 | 86 911 | 127 911 | 47.2 | 5.3 |
| Kingsville | 8.0 | 16.8 | 20.1 | 14.3 | 10.4 | 10.2 | 9.1 | 6.1 | 5.0 | 27.6 | 49.2 | 25 575 | 26 213 | 2.5 | 0.0 |
| Kyle | 10.3 | 23.5 | 7.3 | 19.2 | 17.9 | 11.1 | 6.5 | 2.9 | 1.3 | 30.2 | 50.2 | 5 314 | 28 016 | 427.2 | 10.2 |
| Lake Jackson | 6.6 | 19.8 | 8.5 | 12.5 | 12.9 | 16.0 | 11.8 | 6.1 | 5.8 | 37.1 | 51.0 | 26 386 | 26 849 | 1.8 | 1.2 |
| Lancaster | 8.2 | 23.0 | 8.9 | 13.8 | 15.6 | 13.9 | 9.4 | 4.3 | 3.0 | 32.3 | 54.2 | 25 894 | 36 655 | 40.4 | 3.2 |
| La Porte | 7.3 | 20.1 | 9.4 | 13.9 | 14.1 | 15.0 | 11.6 | 5.3 | 3.3 | 34.5 | 50.4 | 31 880 | 33 800 | 6.0 | 2.0 |
| Laredo | 9.7 | 25.3 | 10.9 | 14.1 | 13.8 | 10.8 | 7.4 | 4.4 | 3.5 | 27.9 | 51.6 | 176 576 | 236 100 | 33.7 | 3.7 |
| League City | 7.8 | 20.7 | 7.3 | 15.1 | 16.5 | 15.4 | 9.9 | 4.6 | 2.7 | 34.5 | 50.9 | 45 444 | 83 560 | 83.9 | 5.5 |
| Leander | 9.5 | 24.6 | 6.5 | 16.1 | 18.6 | 12.2 | 7.6 | 3.2 | 1.7 | 31.4 | 50.7 | 7 596 | 26 310 | 249.1 | 12.6 |
| Lewisville | 8.3 | 17.4 | 11.2 | 20.5 | 15.3 | 12.9 | 7.9 | 3.8 | 2.7 | 30.9 | 50.6 | 77 737 | 95 290 | 22.6 | 4.4 |
| Little Elm | 11.1 | 23.8 | 5.9 | 18.9 | 20.4 | 10.1 | 5.8 | 2.7 | 1.3 | 30.8 | 50.9 | 3 646 | 25 898 | 610.3 | 11.8 |
| Longview | 7.7 | 17.7 | 10.9 | 14.4 | 12.1 | 13.3 | 10.5 | 6.5 | 6.9 | 34.4 | 51.2 | 73 344 | 80 455 | 9.7 | 0.8 |
| Lubbock | 7.3 | 16.2 | 19.0 | 15.3 | 10.6 | 11.6 | 9.3 | 5.5 | 5.2 | 29.2 | 50.9 | 199 564 | 229 555 | 15.0 | 2.8 |
| Lufkin | 8.3 | 18.6 | 10.6 | 13.7 | 11.6 | 12.5 | 10.3 | 6.9 | 7.5 | 34.0 | 52.9 | 32 709 | 35 066 | 7.2 | 2.7 |
| McAllen | 8.1 | 21.9 | 9.6 | 14.3 | 13.8 | 11.8 | 9.5 | 5.8 | 5.1 | 32.2 | 52.2 | 106 414 | 129 875 | 22.0 | 3.7 |
| McKinney | 8.9 | 23.0 | 7.0 | 15.0 | 18.5 | 12.7 | 7.8 | 4.2 | 2.8 | 32.7 | 50.9 | 54 369 | 131 103 | 141.2 | 9.2 |
| Mansfield | 7.2 | 24.6 | 7.6 | 12.1 | 17.9 | 15.3 | 8.8 | 4.1 | 2.4 | 34.0 | 50.9 | 28 031 | 56 368 | 101.1 | 5.2 |
| Mesquite | 7.8 | 22.0 | 10.1 | 13.8 | 14.1 | 14.6 | 9.1 | 4.7 | 3.8 | 32.3 | 52.3 | 124 523 | 139 629 | 12.3 | 2.6 |
| Midland | 8.2 | 19.1 | 10.4 | 14.8 | 11.6 | 14.0 | 10.6 | 5.5 | 5.8 | 33.0 | 51.3 | 94 996 | 111 147 | 17.0 | 7.4 |
| Mission | 8.9 | 24.7 | 9.5 | 13.2 | 13.9 | 10.7 | 7.9 | 6.0 | 5.4 | 30.4 | 51.9 | 45 408 | 77 358 | 69.7 | 4.0 |
| Missouri City | 5.9 | 20.3 | 8.3 | 10.9 | 14.3 | 17.2 | 14.2 | 5.8 | 3.2 | 38.5 | 52.3 | 52 913 | 67 255 | 27.3 | 2.6 |
| Nacogdoches | 6.5 | 13.7 | 31.0 | 12.7 | 8.6 | 9.2 | 8.2 | 4.8 | 5.3 | 24.5 | 54.3 | 29 914 | 32 929 | 10.3 | 3.4 |
| New Braunfels | 7.5 | 19.7 | 7.8 | 14.1 | 14.0 | 12.7 | 10.5 | 6.8 | 6.9 | 35.6 | 52.0 | 36 494 | 57 742 | 58.2 | 5.2 |
| North Richland Hills | 6.5 | 17.7 | 8.7 | 13.0 | 13.6 | 15.7 | 12.4 | 6.5 | 5.9 | 38.3 | 51.5 | 55 635 | 63 343 | 13.9 | 3.1 |
| Odessa | 8.6 | 19.6 | 11.5 | 14.7 | 11.9 | 13.0 | 9.9 | 5.6 | 5.1 | 31.6 | 51.0 | 90 943 | 99 940 | 9.9 | 6.2 |
| Paris | 7.3 | 17.7 | 10.5 | 12.1 | 12.1 | 12.9 | 10.9 | 8.3 | 8.3 | 37.1 | 53.4 | 25 898 | 25 171 | -2.8 | -0.4 |
| Pasadena | 8.7 | 22.0 | 10.9 | 14.5 | 13.4 | 13.2 | 9.0 | 4.6 | 3.7 | 30.7 | 50.3 | 141 674 | 149 293 | 5.2 | 2.0 |
| Pearland | 9.1 | 20.5 | 6.8 | 15.3 | 17.3 | 14.0 | 9.4 | 4.6 | 3.1 | 34.1 | 51.4 | 37 640 | 89 882 | 142.4 | 7.1 |
| Pflugerville | 7.8 | 22.8 | 6.9 | 14.5 | 17.9 | 15.5 | 8.6 | 3.6 | 2.4 | 33.8 | 51.6 | 16 335 | 48 368 | 187.3 | 7.3 |
| Pharr | 10.1 | 25.3 | 10.2 | 14.7 | 12.9 | 9.3 | 7.5 | 5.4 | 4.6 | 28.0 | 52.0 | 46 660 | 70 492 | 50.9 | 3.8 |
| Plano | 6.3 | 19.6 | 7.5 | 13.5 | 15.8 | 16.9 | 11.6 | 5.5 | 3.3 | 37.2 | 51.1 | 222 030 | 259 841 | 17.0 | 4.7 |
| Port Arthur | 8.0 | 19.0 | 9.8 | 13.0 | 11.8 | 14.1 | 11.1 | 6.4 | 6.9 | 35.3 | 50.8 | 57 755 | 53 822 | -6.8 | 0.3 |
| Richardson | 6.3 | 16.9 | 10.2 | 14.2 | 13.9 | 14.6 | 11.4 | 6.8 | 5.8 | 36.8 | 50.8 | 91 802 | 99 223 | 8.1 | 4.1 |
| Rockwall | 7.2 | 22.1 | 6.5 | 12.1 | 16.1 | 14.7 | 10.6 | 6.3 | 4.3 | 36.4 | 51.1 | 17 976 | 37 611 | 108.6 | 6.2 |
| Rosenberg | 8.8 | 21.8 | 10.4 | 15.3 | 13.5 | 11.9 | 8.8 | 5.4 | 4.1 | 30.7 | 51.5 | 24 043 | 30 615 | 27.3 | 3.7 |
| Round Rock | 8.8 | 22.3 | 8.0 | 16.4 | 17.6 | 13.4 | 8.1 | 3.3 | 2.1 | 32.0 | 50.8 | 61 136 | 99 994 | 63.4 | 6.6 |
| Rowlett | 6.3 | 22.7 | 7.4 | 11.1 | 16.5 | 17.7 | 10.7 | 4.5 | 3.1 | 36.7 | 51.0 | 44 503 | 56 199 | 26.3 | 2.7 |
| San Angelo | 7.3 | 16.1 | 15.0 | 14.1 | 10.7 | 12.4 | 10.7 | 6.9 | 6.9 | 32.8 | 51.3 | 88 439 | 93 232 | 5.4 | 2.8 |
| San Antonio | 7.6 | 19.2 | 11.4 | 14.9 | 13.2 | 13.2 | 10.1 | 5.6 | 4.8 | 32.7 | 51.2 | 1 144 646 | 1 327 816 | 16.0 | 4.2 |
| San Juan | 9.9 | 25.3 | 10.8 | 14.9 | 13.1 | 10.2 | 8.1 | 4.4 | 3.4 | 27.7 | 51.6 | 26 229 | 33 861 | 29.1 | 4.0 |
| San Marcos | 4.4 | 9.8 | 44.8 | 15.2 | 7.3 | 6.3 | 5.5 | 3.2 | 3.5 | 23.1 | 50.3 | 34 733 | 44 894 | 29.3 | 11.4 |
| Schertz | 6.3 | 20.8 | 7.5 | 11.7 | 15.3 | 16.2 | 10.6 | 6.9 | 4.6 | 37.8 | 51.7 | 18 694 | 31 790 | 68.3 | 9.7 |
| Seguin | 7.4 | 18.0 | 12.4 | 11.9 | 11.1 | 12.0 | 11.2 | 7.5 | 8.5 | 35.3 | 51.7 | 22 011 | 25 158 | 14.4 | 4.4 |
| Sherman | 7.9 | 17.3 | 13.1 | 13.9 | 11.9 | 12.6 | 10.1 | 6.4 | 6.8 | 33.2 | 52.2 | 35 082 | 38 315 | 9.8 | 2.1 |
| Socorro | 8.3 | 24.2 | 11.4 | 12.9 | 12.5 | 12.3 | 9.7 | 5.3 | 3.4 | 29.5 | 51.8 | 27 152 | 32 015 | 17.9 | 2.1 |
| Southlake | 5.2 | 29.0 | 4.8 | 3.6 | 15.2 | 23.9 | 12.4 | 3.8 | 2.0 | 40.9 | 49.9 | 21 519 | 26 575 | 23.5 | 4.3 |
| Sugar Land | 5.3 | 19.3 | 7.5 | 9.9 | 13.5 | 18.6 | 15.4 | 6.1 | 4.3 | 41.2 | 50.4 | 63 328 | 79 113 | 24.5 | 4.3 |
| Temple | 8.4 | 18.0 | 9.2 | 14.9 | 11.7 | 13.2 | 10.8 | 6.4 | 7.4 | 34.6 | 52.2 | 54 514 | 66 312 | 21.3 | 4.3 |
| Texarkana | 7.1 | 18.7 | 9.6 | 13.3 | 12.5 | 13.4 | 10.9 | 6.7 | 7.8 | 36.0 | 52.5 | 34 782 | 36 409 | 4.7 | 2.2 |
| Texas City | 7.5 | 18.8 | 8.9 | 13.7 | 12.2 | 13.9 | 12.2 | 6.4 | 6.4 | 35.9 | 52.1 | 41 521 | 45 081 | 8.6 | 1.3 |
| The Colony | 7.3 | 19.7 | 8.9 | 17.2 | 16.7 | 15.9 | 9.2 | 3.4 | 1.6 | 33.1 | 50.1 | 26 531 | 36 328 | 36.9 | 7.4 |
| Tyler | 7.2 | 17.1 | 14.3 | 13.9 | 11.3 | 11.7 | 10.0 | 6.7 | 7.7 | 32.8 | 52.8 | 83 650 | 96 908 | 15.8 | 2.5 |
| Victoria | 7.9 | 19.1 | 9.5 | 13.6 | 11.5 | 13.5 | 11.4 | 6.9 | 6.6 | 34.9 | 52.0 | 60 603 | 62 592 | 3.3 | 2.9 |
| Waco | 7.7 | 17.0 | 19.8 | 14.3 | 10.4 | 10.9 | 8.7 | 5.2 | 6.0 | 28.2 | 52.1 | 113 726 | 124 799 | 9.7 | 1.8 |
| Waxahachie | 9.0 | 19.2 | 11.2 | 15.2 | 12.4 | 11.7 | 10.0 | 6.0 | 5.4 | 31.7 | 51.5 | 21 426 | 29 616 | 38.2 | 5.0 |
| Weatherford | 7.5 | 17.4 | 10.6 | 13.7 | 12.1 | 12.7 | 10.8 | 7.5 | 7.7 | 35.7 | 51.9 | 19 000 | 25 250 | 32.9 | 4.5 |
| Weslaco | 9.0 | 22.4 | 9.2 | 12.8 | 12.2 | 10.0 | 8.9 | 7.3 | 8.2 | 32.5 | 52.6 | 26 935 | 35 471 | 32.4 | 3.9 |
| Wichita Falls | 7.0 | 15.7 | 15.8 | 14.7 | 11.3 | 12.9 | 10.1 | 6.1 | 6.2 | 32.4 | 48.2 | 104 197 | 104 554 | 0.3 | 0.0 |
| Wylie | 9.7 | 24.0 | 6.9 | 16.1 | 19.2 | 12.4 | 6.8 | 3.2 | 1.9 | 31.7 | 51.3 | 15 132 | 41 425 | 173.8 | 6.9 |
| UTAH | 9.5 | 22.0 | 11.5 | 16.1 | 12.0 | 11.1 | 8.7 | 5.0 | 4.0 | 29.2 | 49.8 | 2 233 169 | 2 763 885 | 23.8 | 3.3 |
| American Fork | 10.6 | 27.1 | 8.7 | 14.9 | 12.3 | 10.4 | 7.3 | 4.6 | 4.1 | 27.6 | 49.9 | 21 941 | 26 263 | 19.7 | 3.4 |
| Bountiful | 8.3 | 20.4 | 8.9 | 13.3 | 10.5 | 12.4 | 10.0 | 7.7 | 8.6 | 34.2 | 51.2 | 41 301 | 42 561 | 3.0 | 0.8 |
| Cedar City | 9.5 | 18.7 | 22.4 | 15.8 | 9.2 | 8.8 | 7.0 | 4.9 | 3.7 | 24.8 | 50.9 | 20 527 | 28 857 | 40.6 | 0.9 |
| Clearfield | 12.0 | 22.7 | 13.6 | 19.7 | 11.7 | 8.9 | 5.9 | 3.0 | 2.5 | 25.8 | 49.3 | 25 974 | 30 112 | 15.9 | 0.9 |
| Cottonwood Heights | 6.1 | 16.9 | 9.7 | 14.9 | 12.0 | 14.0 | 13.1 | 8.3 | 5.0 | 36.9 | 50.2 | 27 569 | 33 433 | 21.3 | 1.7 |
| Draper | 8.6 | 24.4 | 8.5 | 15.7 | 17.1 | 12.9 | 7.4 | 3.4 | 2.0 | 30.7 | 46.4 | 25 220 | 42 274 | 67.6 | 4.3 |
| Holladay | 6.8 | 18.3 | 8.1 | 12.9 | 11.3 | 13.0 | 12.3 | 8.3 | 9.1 | 38.5 | 51.6 | 14 561 | 26 472 | 81.8 | 1.8 |
| Kaysville | 10.4 | 28.9 | 8.0 | 12.4 | 13.0 | 12.4 | 7.6 | 3.9 | 3.3 | 27.6 | 49.9 | 20 351 | 27 300 | 34.1 | 3.6 |
| Layton | 9.9 | 23.6 | 9.9 | 15.6 | 12.8 | 12.2 | 9.0 | 4.2 | 2.9 | 29.4 | 49.9 | 58 474 | 67 311 | 15.1 | 2.0 |

# Table D. Cities — **Households, Group Quarters, Crime, and Education**

| City | Households, 2010 | | | | Persons in group quarters, 2010 | | | | Serious crimes known to police,[2] 2011 | | | | Educational attainment, 2007–2011 | | |
|---|---|---|---|---|---|---|---|---|---|---|---|---|---|---|---|
| | | | Percent | | | Institutional | | | Total | | Rate[3] | | | Attainment[4] (percent) | |
| | Number | Persons per house-hold | Female family house-holder[1] | One-person | Total | Total | Persons in nursing facilities | Non-institu-tional | Number | Rate[3] | Violent | Property | Population age 25 and older | High school graduate or less | Bachelor's degree or more |
| | 27 | 28 | 29 | 30 | 31 | 32 | 33 | 34 | 35 | 36 | 37 | 38 | 39 | 40 | 41 |
| TEXAS—Cont'd | | | | | | | | | | | | | | | |
| Killeen | 48 052 | 2.66 | 17.2 | 24.4 | 179 | 97 | 60 | 82 | 6 025 | 4 613 | 624 | 3 989 | 68 537 | 38.2 | 16.8 |
| Kingsville | 9 095 | 2.69 | 17.5 | 24.7 | 1 791 | 293 | 173 | 1 498 | 1 247 | 4 659 | 867 | 3 792 | 14 333 | 48.9 | 22.6 |
| Kyle | 8 759 | 3.15 | 13.7 | 14.5 | 391 | 388 | 0 | 3 | 486 | 1 699 | 283 | 1 416 | 15 119 | 36.1 | 24.4 |
| Lake Jackson | 10 319 | 2.60 | 10.1 | 23.9 | 57 | 56 | 56 | 1 | 599 | 2 185 | 146 | 2 039 | 17 264 | 25.9 | 32.4 |
| Lancaster | 12 520 | 2.88 | 27.1 | 22.3 | 360 | 359 | 359 | 1 | 1 392 | 3 749 | 304 | 3 445 | 21 639 | 47.1 | 18.1 |
| La Porte | 11 890 | 2.84 | 13.1 | 20.3 | 64 | 46 | 46 | 18 | 688 | 1 994 | 133 | 1 860 | 21 240 | 50.9 | 16.4 |
| Laredo | 63 545 | 3.66 | 21.1 | 13.5 | 3 479 | 2 014 | 367 | 1 465 | 11 539 | 4 787 | 465 | 4 322 | 125 097 | 56.5 | 17.7 |
| League City | 30 192 | 2.75 | 10.2 | 20.3 | 471 | 471 | 368 | 0 | 1 979 | 2 320 | 110 | 2 209 | 51 465 | 24.8 | 42.1 |
| Leander | 8 557 | 3.10 | 12.6 | 14.0 | 0 | 0 | 0 | 0 | 370 | 1 366 | 74 | 1 293 | 14 337 | 32.1 | 30.7 |
| Lewisville | 37 496 | 2.53 | 12.5 | 30.1 | 399 | 286 | 0 | 113 | 3 297 | 3 389 | 190 | 3 199 | 60 181 | 36.3 | 29.7 |
| Little Elm | 8 160 | 3.17 | 11.5 | 14.3 | 0 | 0 | 0 | 0 | 238 | 900 | 53 | 847 | 14 160 | 31.1 | 31.2 |
| Longview | 30 562 | 2.51 | 15.4 | 29.1 | 3 690 | 1 913 | 767 | 1 777 | 4 229 | 5 148 | 491 | 4 657 | 50 680 | 46.6 | 20.8 |
| Lubbock | 88 506 | 2.48 | 14.0 | 28.8 | 9 933 | 2 400 | 1 214 | 7 533 | 13 878 | 5 921 | 768 | 5 153 | 129 532 | 40.2 | 29.4 |
| Lufkin | 12 928 | 2.62 | 18.6 | 27.8 | 1 239 | 823 | 536 | 416 | 2 075 | 5 795 | 539 | 5 256 | 22 451 | 51.0 | 18.6 |
| McAllen | 41 573 | 3.10 | 19.0 | 19.1 | 1 110 | 899 | 890 | 211 | 6 121 | 4 616 | 186 | 4 430 | 76 174 | 48.0 | 27.8 |
| McKinney | 44 353 | 2.91 | 10.9 | 18.7 | 2 192 | 1 454 | 439 | 738 | 3 069 | 2 292 | 182 | 2 111 | 75 304 | 25.9 | 45.1 |
| Mansfield | 18 305 | 3.06 | 11.4 | 14.4 | 363 | 355 | 159 | 8 | 1 017 | 1 767 | 108 | 1 659 | 31 758 | 28.7 | 38.5 |
| Mesquite | 48 390 | 2.88 | 18.9 | 22.4 | 663 | 644 | 644 | 19 | 6 939 | 4 860 | 278 | 4 582 | 83 604 | 47.7 | 19.1 |
| Midland | 41 887 | 2.62 | 13.5 | 26.0 | 1 567 | 684 | 362 | 883 | 3 621 | 3 191 | 294 | 2 896 | 67 712 | 41.6 | 25.3 |
| Mission | 23 117 | 3.33 | 17.1 | 14.9 | 179 | 162 | 162 | 17 | 2 851 | 3 624 | 127 | 3 496 | 41 981 | 54.9 | 21.2 |
| Missouri City | 22 376 | 3.00 | 15.2 | 15.8 | 180 | 138 | 138 | 42 | 1 262 | 1 835 | 131 | 1 704 | 41 873 | 24.9 | 40.1 |
| Nacogdoches | 12 142 | 2.30 | 15.7 | 35.2 | 5 025 | 632 | 428 | 4 393 | 1 367 | 4 058 | 309 | 3 749 | 15 619 | 44.8 | 27.7 |
| New Braunfels | 21 259 | 2.67 | 12.5 | 23.7 | 940 | 666 | 411 | 274 | 2 062 | 3 498 | 202 | 3 296 | 36 757 | 39.6 | 28.2 |
| North Richland Hills | 24 854 | 2.54 | 11.9 | 24.8 | 294 | 267 | 267 | 27 | 2 089 | 3 230 | 286 | 2 944 | 42 030 | 33.3 | 30.7 |
| Odessa | 36 608 | 2.67 | 16.1 | 26.3 | 2 143 | 1 285 | 437 | 858 | 3 882 | 3 804 | 733 | 3 071 | 59 489 | 53.6 | 16.1 |
| Paris | 10 306 | 2.38 | 19.6 | 32.8 | 614 | 406 | 258 | 208 | 1 569 | 6 105 | 646 | 5 459 | 16 470 | 53.0 | 16.6 |
| Pasadena | 48 471 | 3.06 | 15.1 | 21.4 | 884 | 737 | 547 | 147 | 5 832 | 3 832 | 372 | 3 460 | 86 347 | 61.2 | 13.5 |
| Pearland | 31 222 | 2.91 | 11.2 | 17.1 | 318 | 312 | 299 | 6 | 1 868 | 2 005 | 136 | 1 869 | 53 882 | 25.9 | 45.3 |
| Pflugerville | 15 789 | 2.96 | 13.4 | 17.0 | 183 | 131 | 131 | 52 | 938 | 1 957 | 131 | 1 826 | 27 552 | 28.0 | 34.1 |
| Pharr | 19 699 | 3.57 | 20.8 | 13.7 | 19 | 15 | 0 | 4 | 2 708 | 3 767 | 356 | 3 411 | 37 541 | 69.2 | 12.9 |
| Plano | 99 131 | 2.61 | 9.7 | 24.4 | 859 | 791 | 733 | 68 | 7 216 | 2 720 | 164 | 2 556 | 172 548 | 20.7 | 54.0 |
| Port Arthur | 20 183 | 2.63 | 19.8 | 30.1 | 687 | 515 | 501 | 172 | 3 287 | 5 982 | 790 | 5 192 | 33 706 | 59.3 | 10.3 |
| Richardson | 38 714 | 2.54 | 10.1 | 26.8 | 931 | 517 | 501 | 414 | 2 981 | 2 942 | 171 | 2 772 | 66 121 | 24.9 | 50.5 |
| Rockwall | 13 212 | 2.81 | 10.0 | 20.0 | 325 | 325 | 158 | 0 | 1 095 | 2 861 | 128 | 2 733 | 23 311 | 30.2 | 37.5 |
| Rosenberg | 10 163 | 3.00 | 19.8 | 21.1 | 134 | 129 | 129 | 5 | 700 | 2 239 | 218 | 2 022 | 17 650 | 65.2 | 11.6 |
| Round Rock | 35 050 | 2.84 | 12.5 | 20.8 | 454 | 398 | 251 | 56 | 2 561 | 2 511 | 113 | 2 398 | 60 019 | 28.7 | 37.0 |
| Rowlett | 18 371 | 3.04 | 11.4 | 12.6 | 335 | 335 | 334 | 0 | 1 049 | 1 828 | 113 | 1 715 | 34 016 | 32.8 | 32.2 |
| San Angelo | 36 117 | 2.45 | 14.2 | 29.8 | 4 858 | 788 | 365 | 4 070 | 3 926 | 4 126 | 264 | 3 862 | 56 626 | 48.8 | 22.3 |
| San Antonio | 479 642 | 2.71 | 17.6 | 26.9 | 27 800 | 11 979 | 5 617 | 15 821 | 87 906 | 6 486 | 519 | 5 967 | 811 201 | 45.9 | 23.9 |
| San Juan | 8 882 | 3.80 | 19.2 | 9.9 | 121 | 112 | 112 | 9 | 1 645 | 4 759 | 735 | 4 024 | 17 511 | 76.7 | 8.0 |
| San Marcos | 17 031 | 2.27 | 10.2 | 33.1 | 6 202 | 729 | 300 | 5 473 | 1 727 | 3 768 | 347 | 3 421 | 18 154 | 40.9 | 30.4 |
| Schertz | 11 379 | 2.75 | 11.8 | 18.6 | 188 | 188 | 188 | 0 | 710 | 2 210 | 261 | 1 949 | 19 745 | 30.9 | 31.6 |
| Seguin | 8 794 | 2.68 | 17.9 | 27.3 | 1 644 | 881 | 396 | 763 | 1 339 | 5 209 | 331 | 4 878 | 15 342 | 60.9 | 14.8 |
| Sherman | 14 805 | 2.51 | 14.7 | 29.8 | 1 368 | 509 | 285 | 859 | 1 707 | 4 340 | 402 | 3 938 | 24 246 | 47.9 | 20.9 |
| Socorro | 8 792 | 3.64 | 19.1 | 10.9 | 25 | 0 | 0 | 25 | 568 | 1 738 | 174 | 1 563 | 17 047 | 71.4 | 7.4 |
| Southlake | 8 193 | 3.24 | 3.9 | 7.5 | 0 | 0 | 0 | 0 | 470 | 1 732 | 29 | 1 703 | 15 913 | 10.3 | 68.6 |
| Sugar Land | 26 709 | 2.90 | 8.6 | 15.6 | 1 413 | 1 245 | 313 | 168 | 1 525 | 1 895 | 119 | 1 776 | 51 988 | 20.5 | 54.6 |
| Temple | 26 113 | 2.47 | 14.9 | 31.0 | 1 613 | 989 | 908 | 624 | 2 253 | 3 338 | 276 | 3 063 | 43 845 | 45.7 | 24.7 |
| Texarkana | 14 422 | 2.41 | 20.4 | 32.4 | 1 641 | 1 469 | 554 | 172 | 2 944 | 7 919 | 1 256 | 6 663 | 23 826 | 43.5 | 23.6 |
| Texas City | 16 628 | 2.66 | 20.3 | 26.2 | 937 | 916 | 470 | 21 | 1 718 | 3 731 | 330 | 3 401 | 29 897 | 50.4 | 12.7 |
| The Colony | 13 168 | 2.76 | 11.5 | 21.5 | 0 | 0 | 0 | 0 | 622 | 1 677 | 137 | 1 539 | 23 195 | 26.7 | 35.3 |
| Tyler | 37 896 | 2.46 | 15.2 | 31.2 | 3 647 | 1 709 | 893 | 1 938 | 4 924 | 4 977 | 500 | 4 476 | 59 512 | 39.0 | 29.1 |
| Victoria | 23 421 | 2.62 | 16.6 | 26.3 | 1 324 | 1 053 | 478 | 271 | 3 640 | 5 696 | 604 | 5 092 | 39 135 | 48.8 | 17.4 |
| Waco | 46 402 | 2.52 | 17.4 | 31.0 | 8 019 | 3 026 | 1 488 | 4 993 | 7 188 | 5 641 | 601 | 5 040 | 67 690 | 49.5 | 21.5 |
| Waxahachie | 10 457 | 2.72 | 15.7 | 23.3 | 1 209 | 715 | 232 | 494 | 1 197 | 3 958 | 241 | 3 716 | 17 393 | 44.3 | 24.2 |
| Weatherford | 9 770 | 2.47 | 12.7 | 28.3 | 1 077 | 845 | 450 | 232 | 750 | 2 909 | 151 | 2 758 | 15 673 | 39.0 | 23.7 |
| Weslaco | 11 212 | 3.12 | 19.4 | 18.6 | 637 | 590 | 488 | 47 | 2 369 | 6 504 | 423 | 6 082 | 20 851 | 59.7 | 17.4 |
| Wichita Falls | 38 454 | 2.41 | 14.3 | 31.0 | 11 889 | 5 334 | 1 072 | 6 555 | 5 335 | 4 998 | 430 | 4 568 | 64 054 | 49.4 | 20.9 |
| Wylie | 13 237 | 3.12 | 12.1 | 14.0 | 155 | 155 | 155 | 0 | 719 | 1 700 | 85 | 1 615 | 23 599 | 29.5 | 32.1 |
| UTAH | 877 692 | 3.10 | 9.7 | 18.7 | 46 152 | 22 161 | 5 854 | 23 991 | 89 252 | 3 168 | 195 | 2 973 | 1 542 258 | 33.9 | 29.6 |
| American Fork | 7 274 | 3.57 | 9.5 | 13.6 | 283 | 72 | 62 | 211 | 963 | 2 620 | 63 | 2 557 | 13 727 | 25.8 | 34.2 |
| Bountiful | 14 504 | 2.91 | 8.8 | 20.4 | 330 | 318 | 318 | 12 | 862 | 1 987 | 95 | 1 893 | 26 437 | 23.0 | 40.8 |
| Cedar City | 9 469 | 2.94 | 10.0 | 18.5 | 986 | 259 | 83 | 727 | 951 | 3 233 | 177 | 3 056 | 14 191 | 30.5 | 31.6 |
| Clearfield | 9 361 | 3.08 | 15.0 | 18.9 | 1 263 | 144 | 96 | 1 119 | 805 | 2 623 | 179 | 2 444 | 16 292 | 39.2 | 20.4 |
| Cottonwood Heights | 12 459 | 2.68 | 9.4 | 21.2 | 14 | 0 | 0 | 14 | 1 006 | 2 952 | 132 | 2 820 | 22 049 | 21.5 | 45.9 |
| Draper | 11 544 | 3.32 | 7.7 | 13.4 | 3 960 | 3 960 | 71 | 0 | 956 | 2 219 | 109 | 2 110 | 24 012 | 24.4 | 36.0 |
| Holladay | 9 927 | 2.65 | 9.7 | 24.3 | 166 | 160 | 160 | 6 | NA | NA | NA | NA | 17 876 | 17.3 | 50.2 |
| Kaysville | 7 524 | 3.63 | 7.5 | 11.7 | 24 | 0 | 0 | 24 | 373 | 1 340 | 57 | 1 283 | 13 915 | 19.3 | 43.3 |
| Layton | 21 375 | 3.15 | 11.1 | 16.5 | 44 | 26 | 0 | 18 | 2 081 | 3 033 | 131 | 2 902 | 37 508 | 28.3 | 32.7 |

1. No spouse present.  2. Data for serious crimes have not been adjusted for underreporting. This may affect comparability between geographic areas and over time.  3. Per 100,000 population estimated by the FBI.  4. Persons 25 years old and over.

# Table D. Cities — Income, Poverty, and Housing

| | Money income, 2007–2011 | | | | | Housing units, 2010 | | | Occupied Housing units 2007–2011 | | | | |
| | Households | | | | Families with income below poverty (percent) | | | | Owner-occupied | | | Median owner costs as a percent of income | |
| City | Per capita income[1] (dollars) | Median income | Percent with income of $200,000 or more | Percent with income of less than $25,000 | | Total | Percent change, 2000–2010 | Vacant units for sale or rent[2] | Total | Percent | Median value[3] (dollars) | With a mortgage[4] | Without a mortgage[5] |
|---|---|---|---|---|---|---|---|---|---|---|---|---|---|
| | 42 | 43 | 44 | 45 | 46 | 47 | 48 | 49 | 50 | 51 | 52 | 53 | 54 |
| **TEXAS—Cont'd** | | | | | | | | | | | | | |
| Killeen | 20 081 | 44 787 | 0.7 | 23.4 | 13.8 | 53 913 | 52.8 | 5 861 | 43 321 | 50.8 | 107 600 | 24.8 | 11.1 |
| Kingsville | 18 271 | 33 785 | 3.0 | 39.0 | 20.0 | 10 354 | -0.6 | 1 259 | 9 103 | 51.0 | 69 500 | 25.6 | 10.3 |
| Kyle | 23 285 | 73 790 | 1.2 | 10.2 | 7.2 | 9 226 | NA | 467 | 7 717 | 80.0 | 146 100 | 23.2 | 14.0 |
| Lake Jackson | 31 235 | 74 381 | 4.3 | 11.4 | 4.8 | 11 149 | 6.3 | 830 | 9 931 | 70.7 | 138 800 | 19.5 | 10.0 |
| Lancaster | 21 408 | 52 561 | 0.7 | 22.4 | 11.0 | 13 622 | 41.7 | 1 102 | 12 513 | 67.4 | 108 200 | 27.7 | 14.6 |
| La Porte | 26 172 | 66 848 | 1.6 | 16.3 | 7.9 | 12 875 | 10.2 | 985 | 11 343 | 76.2 | 118 500 | 20.6 | 12.2 |
| Laredo | 14 769 | 38 495 | 1.5 | 32.9 | 25.2 | 68 610 | 36.2 | 5 065 | 62 392 | 63.2 | 110 700 | 28.3 | 15.2 |
| League City | 36 667 | 88 240 | 7.4 | 8.3 | 3.6 | 32 119 | 86.3 | 1 927 | 28 460 | 77.0 | 178 400 | 22.7 | 11.8 |
| Leander | 26 291 | 71 042 | 3.8 | 9.5 | 4.1 | 8 949 | NA | 392 | 7 815 | 78.3 | 154 200 | 23.7 | 13.2 |
| Lewisville | 28 144 | 56 811 | 2.4 | 15.2 | 6.8 | 39 967 | 26.0 | 2 471 | 36 984 | 46.6 | 150 600 | 22.7 | 12.6 |
| Little Elm | 25 504 | 79 179 | 1.5 | 8.5 | 4.6 | 8 581 | NA | 421 | 7 454 | 83.8 | 147 500 | 25.3 | 11.9 |
| Longview | 22 857 | 43 414 | 2.4 | 28.2 | 12.7 | 32 751 | 6.8 | 2 189 | 30 065 | 56.5 | 121 100 | 21.5 | 11.7 |
| Lubbock | 23 364 | 42 925 | 2.8 | 30.7 | 12.8 | 95 926 | 14.2 | 7 420 | 86 605 | 56.2 | 108 700 | 21.8 | 11.8 |
| Lufkin | 22 664 | 35 565 | 2.2 | 32.6 | 15.7 | 14 183 | 5.9 | 1 255 | 13 339 | 57.4 | 92 600 | 20.8 | 13.4 |
| McAllen | 20 199 | 39 193 | 3.2 | 34.6 | 24.6 | 45 862 | 21.0 | 4 289 | 41 116 | 62.2 | 105 300 | 23.7 | 13.9 |
| McKinney | 32 528 | 80 855 | 7.3 | 12.6 | 6.6 | 47 915 | 146.7 | 3 562 | 41 584 | 72.3 | 185 600 | 23.6 | 13.7 |
| Mansfield | 34 103 | 93 906 | 7.2 | 10.0 | 5.3 | 19 106 | 103.0 | 801 | 17 001 | 81.7 | 183 500 | 22.9 | 11.7 |
| Mesquite | 22 320 | 52 034 | 1.5 | 19.1 | 10.2 | 51 952 | 11.9 | 3 562 | 47 461 | 63.1 | 112 700 | 24.5 | 11.7 |
| Midland | 32 672 | 57 399 | 7.7 | 19.8 | 9.8 | 44 708 | 12.3 | 2 821 | 40 562 | 67.1 | 139 400 | 20.1 | 11.4 |
| Mission | 17 225 | 41 339 | 3.0 | 31.8 | 21.4 | 27 291 | 54.0 | 4 174 | 21 545 | 73.9 | 93 200 | 25.1 | 12.5 |
| Missouri City | 31 356 | 82 634 | 7.5 | 10.1 | 5.9 | 23 374 | 34.0 | 998 | 20 977 | 88.1 | 156 800 | 24.5 | 12.4 |
| Nacogdoches | 16 497 | 26 928 | 1.6 | 46.9 | 25.1 | 13 655 | 10.3 | 1 493 | 11 711 | 40.4 | 98 700 | 22.1 | 13.1 |
| New Braunfels | 26 713 | 57 071 | 3.4 | 19.7 | 7.4 | 23 381 | 55.7 | 2 122 | 20 890 | 66.3 | 154 100 | 21.6 | 13.2 |
| North Richland Hills | 31 063 | 63 287 | 4.0 | 14.9 | 6.3 | 26 395 | 22.8 | 1 541 | 24 175 | 65.5 | 146 700 | 22.4 | 13.0 |
| Odessa | 25 597 | 50 813 | 3.5 | 24.5 | 12.8 | 39 806 | 4.8 | 3 198 | 36 408 | 62.7 | 94 800 | 18.9 | 11.3 |
| Paris | 18 574 | 32 137 | 0.7 | 37.5 | 20.2 | 11 883 | 1.0 | 1 577 | 9 934 | 55.6 | 75 900 | 18.9 | 14.6 |
| Pasadena | 20 383 | 46 998 | 2.6 | 26.1 | 17.6 | 53 899 | 6.9 | 5 428 | 47 477 | 56.3 | 104 500 | 23.5 | 11.4 |
| Pearland | 35 329 | 89 898 | 6.8 | 8.4 | 3.3 | 33 169 | 138.7 | 1 947 | 29 831 | 81.2 | 177 800 | 23.4 | 11.7 |
| Pflugerville | 29 643 | 75 558 | 4.4 | 9.7 | 6.1 | 16 418 | 209.9 | 629 | 14 885 | 76.2 | 163 000 | 23.1 | 12.0 |
| Pharr | 12 328 | 30 486 | 0.3 | 42.4 | 33.6 | 22 796 | 37.4 | 3 097 | 19 059 | 63.9 | 68 700 | 29.2 | 13.4 |
| Plano | 40 960 | 82 901 | 11.3 | 10.8 | 5.1 | 103 672 | 20.4 | 4 541 | 97 462 | 65.5 | 214 700 | 22.0 | 10.3 |
| Port Arthur | 17 874 | 32 178 | 1.2 | 39.4 | 23.6 | 23 577 | -4.6 | 3 394 | 20 066 | 61.2 | 62 600 | 23.1 | 13.0 |
| Richardson | 35 144 | 70 228 | 6.8 | 15.3 | 5.7 | 40 630 | 11.7 | 1 916 | 37 702 | 62.8 | 179 500 | 22.4 | 12.5 |
| Rockwall | 31 348 | 77 637 | 3.7 | 10.3 | 4.1 | 13 957 | 96.1 | 745 | 12 743 | 75.6 | 194 700 | 23.5 | 15.4 |
| Rosenberg | 19 166 | 42 690 | 2.3 | 26.7 | 15.7 | 11 162 | 32.2 | 999 | 9 969 | 53.5 | 103 000 | 24.8 | 13.2 |
| Round Rock | 30 674 | 72 108 | 4.9 | 9.7 | 4.8 | 37 223 | 71.9 | 2 173 | 34 311 | 61.2 | 168 300 | 22.5 | 10.4 |
| Rowlett | 30 412 | 82 155 | 5.1 | 7.6 | 3.4 | 18 969 | 30.1 | 598 | 17 578 | 87.6 | 161 300 | 24.3 | 13.4 |
| San Angelo | 22 249 | 41 057 | 2.1 | 30.0 | 13.6 | 39 548 | 4.8 | 3 431 | 35 289 | 63.4 | 89 300 | 21.6 | 12.3 |
| San Antonio | 22 333 | 43 961 | 2.7 | 28.1 | 15.1 | 524 246 | 21.0 | 44 604 | 468 498 | 57.5 | 111 900 | 23.2 | 12.0 |
| San Juan | 11 195 | 31 672 | 0.4 | 36.1 | 27.0 | 9 740 | 25.8 | 858 | 8 560 | 73.8 | 78 000 | 28.2 | 14.6 |
| San Marcos | 15 060 | 27 597 | 0.2 | 45.8 | 15.8 | 18 179 | 36.8 | 1 148 | 16 269 | 27.8 | 121 300 | 24.6 | 15.3 |
| Schertz | 30 650 | 71 842 | 4.2 | 11.7 | 4.7 | 12 047 | 74.5 | 668 | 10 916 | 78.2 | 161 000 | 20.9 | 10.5 |
| Seguin | 18 271 | 40 616 | 0.9 | 32.8 | 17.0 | 9 714 | 18.7 | 920 | 8 683 | 58.4 | 90 700 | 21.4 | 11.3 |
| Sherman | 21 738 | 42 116 | 2.3 | 27.2 | 12.9 | 16 404 | 10.0 | 1 599 | 14 762 | 55.6 | 96 800 | 25.0 | 12.9 |
| Socorro | 11 581 | 31 091 | 0.4 | 39.2 | 27.7 | 9 313 | 28.0 | 521 | 8 396 | 81.3 | 77 800 | 31.0 | 13.4 |
| Southlake | 67 942 | 183 441 | 45.7 | 5.6 | 2.6 | 8 494 | 28.7 | 301 | 7 928 | 95.6 | 491 700 | 23.1 | 12.1 |
| Sugar Land | 43 529 | 103 265 | 17.0 | 8.5 | 4.1 | 27 727 | 31.0 | 1 018 | 25 746 | 80.7 | 241 000 | 22.4 | 10.0 |
| Temple | 26 310 | 47 955 | 3.7 | 25.2 | 9.5 | 28 422 | 21.2 | 2 309 | 23 944 | 59.9 | 110 900 | 20.3 | 11.0 |
| Texarkana | 23 326 | 39 237 | 3.1 | 33.6 | 15.6 | 16 115 | 6.5 | 1 693 | 13 649 | 54.9 | 97 100 | 21.8 | 11.6 |
| Texas City | 22 580 | 46 618 | 1.5 | 29.5 | 13.8 | 18 773 | 12.6 | 2 145 | 16 978 | 58.8 | 96 600 | 22.1 | 12.0 |
| The Colony | 33 603 | 76 663 | 5.0 | 6.9 | 1.9 | 14 052 | 59.0 | 884 | 13 376 | 70.9 | 143 700 | 21.5 | 11.4 |
| Tyler | 27 608 | 42 279 | 5.1 | 29.9 | 14.7 | 41 742 | 17.4 | 3 846 | 37 936 | 55.5 | 126 100 | 22.5 | 11.8 |
| Victoria | 23 791 | 44 803 | 2.3 | 27.3 | 15.0 | 25 660 | 6.1 | 2 239 | 23 508 | 60.1 | 103 500 | 21.9 | 13.0 |
| Waco | 18 185 | 31 971 | 1.7 | 40.3 | 22.2 | 51 452 | 12.2 | 5 050 | 45 062 | 46.3 | 89 000 | 24.0 | 13.8 |
| Waxahachie | 22 351 | 52 673 | 2.7 | 22.4 | 12.0 | 11 554 | 47.0 | 1 097 | 9 996 | 62.5 | 129 500 | 23.6 | 15.0 |
| Weatherford | 24 740 | 46 718 | 2.6 | 26.0 | 9.6 | 10 853 | 31.3 | 1 083 | 9 924 | 63.6 | 131 700 | 24.8 | 13.0 |
| Weslaco | 15 662 | 36 424 | 2.1 | 37.6 | 26.7 | 14 394 | 41.0 | 3 182 | 10 865 | 65.5 | 69 200 | 22.9 | 13.1 |
| Wichita Falls | 22 426 | 42 559 | 2.6 | 27.1 | 11.2 | 43 632 | 4.3 | 5 178 | 37 623 | 60.9 | 90 500 | 22.4 | 13.1 |
| Wylie | 27 484 | 75 070 | 1.4 | 7.8 | 3.1 | 13 840 | 162.5 | 603 | 13 004 | 86.8 | 156 600 | 24.8 | 14.7 |
| **UTAH** | 23 650 | 57 783 | 3.3 | 17.6 | 8.3 | 979 709 | 27.5 | 102 017 | 871 358 | 70.7 | 221 300 | 24.6 | 10.0 |
| American Fork | 21 136 | 68 725 | 2.2 | 15.0 | 7.3 | 7 598 | 24.2 | 324 | 7 374 | 78.2 | 223 200 | 24.9 | 10.0 |
| Bountiful | 30 349 | 67 615 | 5.4 | 13.4 | 4.6 | 15 193 | 10.1 | 689 | 14 271 | 76.3 | 243 100 | 22.4 | 10.0 |
| Cedar City | 17 885 | 40 737 | 1.1 | 31.5 | 18.5 | 10 860 | 52.2 | 1 391 | 9 922 | 52.2 | 201 000 | 26.8 | 10.6 |
| Clearfield | 18 205 | 45 723 | 0.6 | 21.2 | 14.0 | 10 062 | 19.7 | 701 | 9 702 | 52.6 | 153 800 | 25.0 | 10.0 |
| Cottonwood Heights | 36 127 | 72 492 | 8.9 | 10.7 | 3.6 | 13 194 | 33.2 | 735 | 12 111 | 71.7 | 308 000 | 22.5 | 10.0 |
| Draper | 30 627 | 89 935 | 9.1 | 7.8 | 3.7 | 12 125 | 84.3 | 581 | 11 102 | 79.4 | 391 400 | 26.0 | 10.0 |
| Holladay | 37 930 | 66 383 | 8.2 | 16.5 | 5.2 | 10 537 | 99.0 | 610 | 10 028 | 72.6 | 355 000 | 25.1 | 10.0 |
| Kaysville | 26 367 | 82 292 | 6.0 | 11.1 | 4.6 | 7 700 | 35.3 | 176 | 7 341 | 87.7 | 268 800 | 23.2 | 10.0 |
| Layton | 25 156 | 64 705 | 3.3 | 12.8 | 5.9 | 22 356 | 16.8 | 981 | 21 641 | 75.9 | 208 100 | 23.5 | 10.0 |

1. Based on population estimated by the American Community Survey.   2. Includes units rented or sold but not occupied.   3. Specified owner-occupied units; $1,000,000 represents $1,000,000 or more   4. 50.0 represents 50 percent or more.   5. 10.0 represents 10 percent or less.

# Table D. Cities — Housing, Labor Force, and Employment

| City | Occupied housing units, 2007–2011 (cont.) | | | | Migration, 2007–2011 | | Civilian labor force, 2012 | | Unemployment | | Civilian employment[4], 2007–2011 | Percent | | |
|---|---|---|---|---|---|---|---|---|---|---|---|---|---|---|
| | Percent renter occupied | Median gross rent[1] | Median rent as a percent of income[2] | Percent with no vehicle available | Percent who lived in the same house one year ago | Percent who lived outside this city one year ago | Total | Percent change, 2011–2012 | Total | Rate[3] | Population age 16 and older | In labor force | Full-year full-time worker | Households with no workers (percent) |
| | 55 | 56 | 57 | 58 | 59 | 60 | 61 | 62 | 63 | 64 | 65 | 66 | 67 | 68 |
| TEXAS—Cont'd | | | | | | | | | | | | | | |
| Killeen | 49.2 | 845 | 28.4 | 5.0 | 66.3 | 21.3 | 51 326 | -0.1 | 4 192 | 8.2 | 89 019 | 72.6 | 35.3 | 17.6 |
| Kingsville | 49.0 | 646 | 29.8 | 9.3 | 76.8 | 11.9 | 14 453 | 2.2 | 827 | 5.7 | 19 987 | 58.5 | 31.0 | 32.0 |
| Kyle | 20.0 | 1 219 | 27.4 | 1.8 | 81.5 | 16.0 | 13 857 | 4.0 | 655 | 4.7 | 17 527 | 75.8 | 54.6 | 8.2 |
| Lake Jackson | 29.3 | 845 | 25.7 | 2.7 | 80.6 | 12.8 | 13 610 | 2.0 | 892 | 6.6 | 20 742 | 68.0 | 47.6 | 20.3 |
| Lancaster | 32.6 | 893 | 32.9 | 4.8 | 89.2 | 8.0 | 17 805 | 2.1 | 1 603 | 9.0 | 25 662 | 70.5 | 50.3 | 19.9 |
| La Porte | 23.8 | 1 015 | 26.4 | 2.8 | 84.7 | 11.5 | 18 748 | 2.3 | 1 405 | 7.5 | 25 689 | 70.2 | 48.5 | 16.3 |
| Laredo | 36.8 | 727 | 34.0 | 8.3 | 82.1 | 3.7 | 95 816 | 1.3 | 6 425 | 6.7 | 158 802 | 63.0 | 39.5 | 17.4 |
| League City | 23.0 | 1 021 | 27.2 | 2.3 | 84.7 | 10.8 | 46 476 | 3.1 | 2 746 | 5.9 | 59 182 | 74.7 | 54.2 | 11.8 |
| Leander | 21.7 | 1 281 | 32.2 | 2.3 | 77.6 | 15.3 | 14 013 | 4.0 | 644 | 4.6 | 16 800 | 77.6 | 51.4 | 9.5 |
| Lewisville | 53.4 | 921 | 27.0 | 3.3 | 72.8 | 15.5 | 58 974 | 2.1 | 3 334 | 5.7 | 72 299 | 79.7 | 55.9 | 12.1 |
| Little Elm | 16.2 | 1 293 | 26.6 | 1.0 | 84.1 | 13.0 | 14 329 | 2.9 | 629 | 4.4 | 15 891 | 80.6 | 56.4 | 10.5 |
| Longview | 43.5 | 721 | 27.9 | 8.6 | 78.2 | 10.8 | 44 141 | 2.7 | 2 539 | 5.8 | 61 579 | 63.6 | 39.8 | 27.1 |
| Lubbock | 43.8 | 760 | 33.6 | 5.6 | 72.7 | 11.6 | 119 317 | -0.5 | 6 469 | 5.4 | 179 169 | 66.8 | 40.3 | 22.6 |
| Lufkin | 42.6 | 701 | 30.1 | 8.5 | 79.1 | 10.1 | 16 126 | -0.9 | 1 082 | 6.7 | 27 198 | 61.2 | 38.8 | 28.3 |
| McAllen | 37.8 | 702 | 32.3 | 7.0 | 84.5 | 8.2 | 61 419 | 0.2 | 4 556 | 7.4 | 94 390 | 61.3 | 39.1 | 23.2 |
| McKinney | 27.7 | 992 | 29.8 | 3.2 | 83.4 | 11.2 | 68 526 | 2.9 | 4 399 | 6.4 | 89 069 | 70.7 | 50.8 | 13.2 |
| Mansfield | 18.3 | 1 116 | 30.7 | 2.5 | 85.5 | 11.8 | 30 834 | 3.1 | 1 735 | 5.6 | 38 355 | 73.5 | 52.3 | 12.7 |
| Mesquite | 36.9 | 932 | 30.9 | 4.4 | 85.4 | 9.3 | 75 316 | 1.6 | 5 138 | 6.8 | 101 833 | 71.6 | 52.2 | 15.8 |
| Midland | 32.9 | 873 | 28.7 | 5.2 | 80.5 | 8.4 | 73 657 | 10.9 | 2 540 | 3.4 | 82 511 | 68.7 | 48.0 | 19.0 |
| Mission | 26.1 | 680 | 34.9 | 5.2 | 87.3 | 7.9 | 31 639 | -0.1 | 2 729 | 8.6 | 51 684 | 57.4 | 35.6 | 25.1 |
| Missouri City | 11.9 | 1 379 | 27.4 | 1.2 | 90.2 | 8.5 | 38 991 | 3.5 | 2 580 | 6.6 | 49 910 | 70.1 | 49.7 | 13.0 |
| Nacogdoches | 59.6 | 678 | 37.7 | 8.8 | 67.8 | 18.1 | 16 234 | -4.3 | 1 068 | 6.6 | 26 432 | 58.3 | 31.5 | 28.6 |
| New Braunfels | 33.7 | 907 | 30.5 | 5.1 | 78.9 | 12.8 | 29 571 | 2.1 | 1 568 | 5.3 | 42 184 | 66.4 | 44.0 | 23.2 |
| North Richland Hills | 34.5 | 896 | 29.4 | 4.1 | 83.6 | 12.8 | 36 499 | 2.6 | 2 156 | 5.9 | 49 444 | 71.3 | 50.0 | 18.6 |
| Odessa | 37.3 | 705 | 24.5 | 6.0 | 80.7 | 8.9 | 61 097 | 10.2 | 2 546 | 4.2 | 74 269 | 67.3 | 45.6 | 20.8 |
| Paris | 44.4 | 606 | 29.9 | 13.2 | 76.4 | 9.5 | 11 185 | -2.4 | 1 126 | 10.1 | 19 955 | 58.0 | 34.6 | 35.8 |
| Pasadena | 43.7 | 760 | 29.7 | 6.1 | 81.0 | 9.1 | 69 762 | 1.9 | 5 714 | 8.2 | 107 738 | 64.8 | 42.0 | 21.4 |
| Pearland | 18.8 | 1 077 | 25.8 | 2.1 | 87.5 | 9.7 | 50 470 | 3.4 | 2 652 | 5.3 | 63 035 | 74.0 | 54.5 | 12.7 |
| Pflugerville | 23.8 | 1 135 | 34.3 | 2.9 | 84.8 | 12.6 | 27 228 | 4.3 | 1 361 | 5.0 | 31 990 | 77.4 | 55.7 | 11.6 |
| Pharr | 36.1 | 652 | 33.5 | 8.5 | 84.7 | 9.3 | 27 698 | -0.6 | 2 582 | 9.3 | 46 719 | 58.1 | 33.2 | 26.3 |
| Plano | 34.5 | 1 012 | 27.0 | 3.4 | 86.2 | 9.1 | 150 574 | 2.3 | 9 026 | 6.0 | 199 710 | 72.9 | 51.9 | 13.6 |
| Port Arthur | 38.8 | 634 | 29.0 | 12.4 | 85.6 | 7.0 | 23 786 | -0.9 | 3 898 | 16.4 | 41 168 | 56.7 | 33.3 | 35.7 |
| Richardson | 37.2 | 1 050 | 27.0 | 3.5 | 82.7 | 12.3 | 55 973 | 2.4 | 3 316 | 5.9 | 78 800 | 70.2 | 48.6 | 17.9 |
| Rockwall | 24.4 | 1 135 | 27.6 | 1.9 | 84.7 | 11.4 | 20 693 | 2.3 | 1 147 | 5.5 | 26 759 | 70.4 | 49.2 | 17.9 |
| Rosenberg | 46.5 | 799 | 29.8 | 8.0 | 76.7 | 14.8 | 15 176 | 1.4 | 919 | 6.1 | 21 998 | 65.3 | 48.1 | 21.4 |
| Round Rock | 38.8 | 1 004 | 27.0 | 3.2 | 77.4 | 17.8 | 55 619 | 3.6 | 3 103 | 5.6 | 70 492 | 76.8 | 52.3 | 10.7 |
| Rowlett | 12.4 | 1 329 | 29.3 | 1.1 | 90.6 | 6.9 | 30 430 | 2.3 | 2 082 | 6.8 | 41 252 | 72.2 | 51.9 | 11.4 |
| San Angelo | 36.6 | 678 | 29.9 | 6.7 | 74.4 | 13.8 | 46 243 | 1.3 | 2 477 | 5.4 | 72 951 | 65.9 | 38.0 | 26.9 |
| San Antonio | 42.5 | 775 | 29.9 | 9.5 | 80.3 | 6.1 | 628 882 | 2.2 | 40 592 | 6.5 | 1 000 941 | 64.7 | 41.1 | 24.0 |
| San Juan | 26.2 | 548 | 34.4 | 7.7 | 87.5 | 7.7 | 13 414 | -1.7 | 1 514 | 11.3 | 22 298 | 61.2 | 34.7 | 23.1 |
| San Marcos | 72.2 | 834 | 43.6 | 5.9 | 57.6 | 25.5 | 25 882 | 3.8 | 1 356 | 5.2 | 38 259 | 59.3 | 26.7 | 23.3 |
| Schertz | 21.8 | 862 | 24.5 | 2.1 | 87.5 | 11.6 | 16 078 | 2.2 | 863 | 5.4 | 22 813 | 67.1 | 42.8 | 22.3 |
| Seguin | 41.6 | 723 | 30.6 | 10.0 | 82.1 | 10.0 | 11 406 | 2.2 | 713 | 6.3 | 19 333 | 60.7 | 37.3 | 26.4 |
| Sherman | 44.4 | 750 | 26.8 | 6.6 | 73.3 | 11.7 | 17 763 | 1.0 | 1 298 | 7.3 | 29 951 | 62.6 | 40.0 | 27.8 |
| Socorro | 18.7 | 590 | 35.3 | 6.3 | 92.4 | 6.7 | 11 682 | -1.4 | 1 239 | 10.6 | 22 557 | 60.2 | 32.7 | 20.4 |
| Southlake | 4.4 | 1 652 | 23.0 | 0.8 | 92.7 | 6.4 | 12 774 | 3.0 | 727 | 5.7 | 18 589 | 67.5 | 46.8 | 9.4 |
| Sugar Land | 19.3 | 1 345 | 28.0 | 2.1 | 90.1 | 8.0 | 43 000 | 3.8 | 2 143 | 5.0 | 60 971 | 66.6 | 48.2 | 13.1 |
| Temple | 40.1 | 751 | 29.9 | 8.0 | 84.1 | 9.3 | 32 997 | -0.5 | 1 910 | 5.8 | 50 963 | 61.5 | 43.6 | 27.9 |
| Texarkana | 45.1 | 666 | 29.8 | 11.7 | 83.1 | 10.8 | 17 044 | -1.9 | 1 207 | 7.1 | 28 390 | 60.6 | 35.7 | 32.6 |
| Texas City | 41.2 | 815 | 33.1 | 7.0 | 80.1 | 11.6 | 21 101 | 3.0 | 2 034 | 9.6 | 35 268 | 61.8 | 40.5 | 27.7 |
| The Colony | 29.1 | 1 135 | 24.5 | 1.1 | 83.7 | 12.9 | 21 234 | 2.0 | 1 427 | 6.7 | 27 765 | 82.3 | 59.5 | 10.1 |
| Tyler | 44.5 | 780 | 32.9 | 8.6 | 75.7 | 12.4 | 47 779 | -0.2 | 3 355 | 7.0 | 75 006 | 63.3 | 39.0 | 28.1 |
| Victoria | 39.9 | 708 | 30.3 | 7.3 | 75.6 | 9.2 | 34 109 | 1.4 | 1 820 | 5.3 | 46 947 | 64.9 | 42.8 | 26.5 |
| Waco | 53.7 | 736 | 35.6 | 9.2 | 74.0 | 12.5 | 56 722 | 0.6 | 4 110 | 7.2 | 95 420 | 60.1 | 34.2 | 29.1 |
| Waxahachie | 37.5 | 885 | 32.8 | 5.1 | 77.3 | 11.6 | 14 366 | 2.4 | 948 | 6.6 | 21 442 | 67.2 | 44.9 | 21.3 |
| Weatherford | 36.4 | 844 | 29.5 | 9.3 | 79.3 | 12.8 | 12 102 | 2.8 | 732 | 6.0 | 19 086 | 60.4 | 41.0 | 29.6 |
| Weslaco | 34.5 | 605 | 32.4 | 8.2 | 87.0 | 7.6 | 14 769 | -0.7 | 1 621 | 11.0 | 25 412 | 54.9 | 32.5 | 35.8 |
| Wichita Falls | 39.1 | 701 | 29.1 | 7.0 | 74.9 | 13.4 | 46 930 | -2.0 | 3 052 | 6.5 | 82 669 | 62.6 | 35.9 | 26.5 |
| Wylie | 13.2 | 1 059 | 28.6 | 1.6 | 87.2 | 9.8 | 22 800 | 2.7 | 1 349 | 5.9 | 27 017 | 77.6 | 57.6 | 9.5 |
| UTAH | 29.3 | 813 | 28.7 | 4.4 | 82.3 | 12.9 | 1 353 597 | 0.5 | 77 348 | 5.7 | 1 948 759 | 69.1 | 41.1 | 19.1 |
| American Fork | 21.8 | 848 | 30.0 | 2.5 | 88.5 | 9.2 | 10 806 | 0.8 | 663 | 6.1 | 17 064 | 64.4 | 38.5 | 17.5 |
| Bountiful | 23.7 | 797 | 25.2 | 3.7 | 87.0 | 9.5 | 20 461 | 1.0 | 1 070 | 5.2 | 32 184 | 62.4 | 37.8 | 24.2 |
| Cedar City | 47.8 | 626 | 28.3 | 5.7 | 73.6 | 12.8 | 12 827 | -3.6 | 928 | 7.2 | 21 452 | 65.5 | 31.5 | 22.2 |
| Clearfield | 47.4 | 902 | 30.8 | 3.8 | 74.8 | 21.2 | 12 890 | -0.2 | 891 | 6.9 | 19 964 | 73.7 | 44.3 | 17.0 |
| Cottonwood Heights | 28.3 | 941 | 26.1 | 2.6 | 84.8 | 13.7 | 19 828 | 0.4 | 1 011 | 5.1 | 26 433 | 69.6 | 43.1 | 19.4 |
| Draper | 20.6 | 1 156 | 28.7 | 1.2 | 84.6 | 13.4 | 18 853 | 0.4 | 914 | 4.8 | 28 588 | 63.1 | 40.9 | 10.2 |
| Holladay | 27.4 | 912 | 25.3 | 2.9 | 88.8 | 10.4 | 14 016 | 0.7 | 710 | 5.1 | 20 678 | 64.0 | 39.0 | 26.3 |
| Kaysville | 12.3 | 688 | 26.2 | 2.2 | 88.0 | 8.9 | 11 686 | 0.8 | 530 | 4.5 | 16 974 | 70.0 | 41.0 | 14.4 |
| Layton | 24.1 | 825 | 27.8 | 3.4 | 82.4 | 13.8 | 33 083 | 0.9 | 1 876 | 5.7 | 46 884 | 70.5 | 43.1 | 16.2 |

1. $2,000 represents $2,000 or more.   2. 50.0 represents 50 percent or more.   3. Percent of civilian labor force.   4. Persons 16 years old and over.

# Table D. Cities — Construction, Wholesale Trade, and Retail Trade

| City | Value of residential construction authorized by building permits, 2011 | | | Wholesale trade,[1] 2007 | | | | Retail trade,[2] 2007 | | | |
|---|---|---|---|---|---|---|---|---|---|---|---|
| | New construction ($1,000) | Number of housing units | Percent single family | Number of establishments | Number of employees | Sales (mil dol) | Annual payroll (mil dol) | Number of establishments | Number of employees | Sales (mil dol) | Annual payroll (mil dol) |
| | 69 | 70 | 71 | 72 | 73 | 74 | 75 | 76 | 77 | 78 | 79 |
| **TEXAS—Cont'd** | | | | | | | | | | | |
| Killeen | 142 007 | 1 107 | 89.3 | 21 | 153 | 72.5 | 9.5 | 384 | 5 886 | 1 525.1 | 129.7 |
| Kingsville | 5 882 | 41 | 43.9 | 3 | D | D | D | 102 | 1 868 | 624.2 | 46.3 |
| Kyle | 38 605 | 592 | 33.1 | 7 | 111 | 51.8 | 3.7 | 27 | 273 | 112.7 | 12.0 |
| Lake Jackson | 2 804 | 11 | 100.0 | 11 | 48 | 16.1 | 2.1 | 120 | 2 683 | 582.4 | 52.6 |
| Lancaster | 9 752 | 48 | 100.0 | 14 | 264 | 97.6 | 11.2 | 60 | 1 004 | 227.1 | 23.6 |
| La Porte | 3 152 | 18 | 100.0 | 33 | 407 | 211.3 | 26.9 | 72 | 752 | 259.6 | 19.1 |
| Laredo | 115 842 | 956 | 66.9 | 348 | 2 501 | 1 468.1 | 78.8 | 811 | 12 789 | 2 900.5 | 234.5 |
| League City | 127 732 | 643 | 95.3 | 38 | 339 | 100.9 | 12.9 | 154 | 2 159 | 728.9 | 62.0 |
| Leander | 74 561 | 325 | 100.0 | 8 | 47 | 44.7 | 1.7 | 30 | 698 | 112.1 | 12.1 |
| Lewisville | 35 486 | 479 | 24.2 | 105 | 2 012 | 1 233.9 | 106.7 | 446 | 8 523 | 2 488.5 | 209.8 |
| Little Elm | 107 248 | 343 | 100.0 | 3 | D | D | D | 22 | 280 | 65.0 | 5.6 |
| Longview | 34 182 | 242 | 78.5 | 162 | 2 394 | 1 051.7 | 99.3 | 551 | 7 414 | 1 855.9 | 176.3 |
| Lubbock | 165 687 | 1 444 | 43.6 | 321 | 4 431 | 3 536.4 | 197.3 | 946 | 16 033 | 3 715.9 | 329.8 |
| Lufkin | 25 319 | 403 | 28.5 | 50 | 595 | 276.0 | 22.3 | 293 | 4 327 | 1 018.7 | 93.4 |
| McAllen | 77 269 | 475 | 83.6 | 255 | 2 504 | 1 828.8 | 86.8 | 893 | 15 462 | 3 599.1 | 303.1 |
| McKinney | 425 104 | 1 538 | 76.2 | 92 | 910 | 730.6 | 46.6 | 300 | 6 504 | 2 002.3 | 165.3 |
| Mansfield | 44 935 | 226 | 100.0 | 62 | 1 129 | 408.0 | 48.5 | 115 | 2 134 | 574.7 | 46.3 |
| Mesquite | 4 570 | 35 | 94.3 | 66 | 968 | 782.6 | 48.8 | 455 | 7 872 | 1 871.5 | 165.7 |
| Midland | 96 880 | 539 | 100.0 | 147 | 1 525 | 1 562.3 | 73.8 | 501 | 7 285 | 2 137.6 | 169.5 |
| Mission | 47 032 | 326 | 100.0 | 54 | 312 | 140.0 | 8.8 | 205 | 3 440 | 845.8 | 69.6 |
| Missouri City | 26 588 | 142 | 100.0 | 48 | 167 | 108.5 | 7.1 | 132 | 2 544 | 696.9 | 51.9 |
| Nacogdoches | 9 600 | 64 | 78.1 | 33 | 449 | 265.6 | 15.1 | 212 | 2 652 | 640.7 | 57.1 |
| New Braunfels | 39 004 | 490 | 100.0 | 46 | 451 | 712.2 | 20.3 | 285 | 4 089 | 1 284.6 | 105.3 |
| North Richland Hills | 28 296 | 122 | 100.0 | 35 | 325 | 91.6 | 15.1 | 190 | 4 220 | 1 376.9 | 116.7 |
| Odessa | 90 369 | 740 | 45.4 | 180 | 2 138 | 1 052.8 | 106.4 | 417 | 6 188 | 1 903.7 | 157.5 |
| Paris | 809 | 14 | 35.7 | 37 | 290 | 115.2 | 10.9 | 205 | 2 467 | 596.4 | 52.4 |
| Pasadena | 8 347 | 40 | 100.0 | 110 | 1 134 | 549.5 | 56.2 | 410 | 6 236 | 1 479.8 | 134.9 |
| Pearland | 142 922 | 1 070 | 64.6 | 47 | 646 | 334.8 | 32.1 | 181 | 3 135 | 779.6 | 71.3 |
| Pflugerville | 24 585 | 213 | 98.1 | 13 | 146 | 62.8 | 6.8 | 61 | 807 | 218.6 | 20.5 |
| Pharr | 19 971 | 290 | 100.0 | 105 | 1 221 | 622.4 | 44.1 | 183 | 2 416 | 613.2 | 51.4 |
| Plano | 108 207 | 1 022 | 34.1 | 372 | 5 651 | 4 512.4 | 422.8 | 1 086 | 22 006 | 7 210.4 | 585.7 |
| Port Arthur | 14 565 | 161 | 100.0 | 26 | 297 | 165.1 | 12.5 | 197 | 3 366 | 1 078.3 | 73.9 |
| Richardson | 20 962 | 253 | 21.7 | 270 | 9 924 | 12 498.2 | 900.6 | 353 | 5 001 | 1 910.8 | 165.3 |
| Rockwall | 36 785 | 188 | 100.0 | 41 | 173 | 63.9 | 7.8 | 168 | 2 790 | 787.0 | 64.6 |
| Rosenberg | 23 892 | 147 | 100.0 | 18 | 372 | 187.8 | 14.5 | 159 | 2 827 | 814.8 | 75.4 |
| Round Rock | 38 252 | 259 | 100.0 | 106 | 1 450 | 817.4 | 86.1 | 366 | 8 635 | 6 550.1 | 226.0 |
| Rowlett | 6 079 | 26 | 100.0 | 33 | 186 | 80.2 | 8.5 | 91 | 1 407 | 364.5 | 31.7 |
| San Angelo | 24 414 | 145 | 100.0 | 105 | 791 | 280.3 | 29.8 | 426 | 5 873 | 1 511.3 | 128.3 |
| San Antonio | 456 039 | 4 070 | 39.2 | 1 284 | 20 806 | 11 116.9 | 946.1 | 4 104 | 71 703 | 20 252.1 | 1 669.4 |
| San Juan | 8 390 | 119 | 93.3 | 10 | 93 | 53.9 | 3.3 | 57 | 666 | 156.6 | 12.6 |
| San Marcos | 90 920 | 1 229 | 12.0 | 31 | 353 | 208.8 | 14.2 | 379 | 6 463 | 1 331.8 | 112.8 |
| Schertz | 74 697 | 474 | 62.9 | 31 | 1 199 | 706.3 | 61.8 | 54 | 1 254 | 392.5 | 28.9 |
| Seguin | 10 162 | 77 | 100.0 | 32 | 414 | 143.8 | 11.4 | 144 | 1 744 | 433.7 | 39.5 |
| Sherman | 5 269 | 37 | 78.4 | 44 | 471 | 444.4 | 14.9 | 244 | 4 147 | 1 014.8 | 90.3 |
| Socorro | 9 592 | 103 | 98.1 | 15 | 67 | 24.5 | 1.4 | 61 | 334 | 69.0 | 5.6 |
| Southlake | 64 480 | 92 | 100.0 | 61 | 639 | 656.5 | 35.9 | 207 | 4 324 | 1 219.6 | 112.9 |
| Sugar Land | 102 709 | 371 | 100.0 | 152 | 2 248 | 3 573.1 | 110.8 | 410 | 7 114 | 1 719.9 | 154.9 |
| Temple | 73 493 | 567 | 64.7 | 62 | 2 387 | 3 972.4 | 103.4 | 302 | 4 084 | 1 133.8 | 98.0 |
| Texarkana | 16 620 | 283 | 11.0 | 75 | 874 | 1 459.9 | 31.9 | 368 | 5 330 | 1 241.0 | 118.0 |
| Texas City | 13 209 | 144 | 100.0 | 30 | 222 | 149.9 | 11.9 | 155 | 1 978 | 499.7 | 43.2 |
| The Colony | 69 489 | 618 | 9.7 | 11 | 146 | 121.5 | 10.3 | 53 | 808 | 204.6 | 18.2 |
| Tyler | 23 001 | 187 | 58.8 | 150 | 1 455 | 608.4 | 65.8 | 650 | 10 390 | 2 653.4 | 246.5 |
| Victoria | 14 783 | 83 | 100.0 | 79 | 1 046 | 461.9 | 45.0 | 371 | 5 694 | 1 346.2 | 123.6 |
| Waco | 56 472 | 373 | 79.6 | 137 | 2 251 | 4 248.8 | 90.8 | 601 | 8 393 | 1 970.7 | 176.8 |
| Waxahachie | 30 455 | 359 | 36.5 | 31 | 267 | 116.9 | 11.4 | 145 | 2 102 | 537.2 | 48.6 |
| Weatherford | 27 169 | 224 | 100.0 | 25 | 339 | 317.3 | 12.0 | 166 | 2 770 | 1 032.0 | 74.5 |
| Weslaco | 9 495 | 109 | 90.8 | 33 | 481 | 215.9 | 13.3 | 160 | 2 502 | 671.3 | 48.5 |
| Wichita Falls | 27 125 | 126 | 71.4 | 120 | 1 197 | 429.1 | 44.9 | 468 | 7 054 | 1 597.3 | 148.0 |
| Wylie | 40 730 | 217 | 100.0 | 21 | 434 | 80.9 | 7.3 | 43 | 999 | 221.5 | 24.5 |
| **UTAH** | 1 759 629 | 9 983 | 68.7 | 3 043 | 43 900 | 25 417.4 | 2 012.0 | 8 984 | 142 266 | 36 574.2 | 3 240.7 |
| American Fork | 13 253 | 55 | 100.0 | 29 | 322 | 160.0 | 15.2 | 132 | 2 605 | 724.2 | 57.9 |
| Bountiful | 8 332 | 40 | 30.0 | 25 | 137 | 19.7 | 2.8 | 138 | 2 165 | 594.5 | 52.5 |
| Cedar City | 6 879 | 35 | 82.9 | 28 | 338 | 250.6 | 12.7 | 163 | 2 016 | 558.5 | 43.0 |
| Clearfield | 3 286 | 23 | 100.0 | 26 | 492 | 349.9 | 22.4 | 57 | 629 | 123.9 | 9.7 |
| Cottonwood Heights | 4 854 | 17 | 100.0 | 32 | 349 | 357.4 | 25.4 | 69 | 1 641 | 1 048.5 | 65.4 |
| Draper | 20 350 | 199 | 53.3 | 49 | 481 | 165.4 | 26.6 | 157 | 2 957 | 820.7 | 78.6 |
| Holladay | 9 135 | 22 | 100.0 | 24 | 148 | 42.7 | 5.7 | 105 | 1 010 | 142.6 | 17.9 |
| Kaysville | 27 414 | 91 | 100.0 | 22 | 289 | 112.1 | 11.7 | 51 | 676 | 149.9 | 15.8 |
| Layton | 33 565 | 163 | 97.5 | 47 | 414 | 188.9 | 14.7 | 300 | 5 530 | 1 225.3 | 108.9 |

1. Merchant wholesalers except manufacturers' sales branches and offices.  2. Establishments with payroll.

# Table D. Cities — Real Estate, Professional Services, and Manufacturing

| City | Real estate and rental and leasing, 2007 | | | | Professional, scientific, and technical services,[1] 2007 | | | | Manufacturing, 2007 | | | |
|---|---|---|---|---|---|---|---|---|---|---|---|---|
| | Number of establish-ments | Number of employees | Receipts (mil dol) | Annual payroll (mil dol) | Number of establish-ments | Number of employees | Receipts (mil dol) | Annual payroll (mil dol) | Number of establish-ments | Number of employees | Receipts (mil dol) | Annual payroll (mil dol) |
| | 80 | 81 | 82 | 83 | 84 | 85 | 86 | 87 | 88 | 89 | 90 | 91 |
| TEXAS—Cont'd | | | | | | | | | | | | |
| Killeen | 147 | 754 | 100.0 | 17.1 | 112 | 1 247 | 119.2 | 47.4 | NA | NA | NA | NA |
| Kingsville | 30 | D | D | D | 33 | 151 | 10.4 | 3.2 | NA | NA | NA | NA |
| Kyle | 5 | 17 | 1.2 | 0.4 | 17 | 46 | 12.6 | 2.2 | NA | NA | NA | NA |
| Lake Jackson | 35 | 326 | 59.6 | 11.0 | 46 | D | D | D | NA | NA | NA | NA |
| Lancaster | 20 | 87 | 12.4 | 2.2 | 18 | 107 | 7.6 | 3.3 | 30 | 1 351 | 259.8 | 48.3 |
| La Porte | 34 | 378 | 81.1 | 18.7 | 50 | 2 420 | 238.0 | 123.0 | 28 | 1 463 | D | 108.1 |
| Laredo | 201 | D | D | D | 309 | D | D | D | 89 | 914 | 242.4 | 30.7 |
| League City | 47 | 215 | 33.5 | 5.9 | 135 | 627 | 95.8 | 37.8 | NA | NA | NA | NA |
| Leander | 13 | 30 | 7.1 | 1.2 | 27 | 131 | 9.5 | 3.5 | NA | NA | NA | NA |
| Lewisville | 108 | 496 | 126.8 | 16.1 | 215 | D | D | D | 99 | 2 834 | 597.6 | 103.7 |
| Little Elm | 9 | 16 | 2.5 | 0.3 | 14 | 52 | 4.4 | 2.0 | NA | NA | NA | NA |
| Longview | 137 | 653 | 131.0 | 22.7 | 289 | D | D | D | 131 | 8 125 | 3 834.7 | 339.5 |
| Lubbock | 352 | 2 182 | 227.8 | 49.3 | 545 | 3 289 | 357.0 | 122.4 | 200 | 4 544 | 1 256.7 | 164.5 |
| Lufkin | 67 | 318 | 39.4 | 8.3 | 139 | 634 | 77.1 | 27.4 | 42 | 4 309 | 760.8 | 148.0 |
| McAllen | 234 | 959 | 202.2 | 26.8 | 427 | D | D | D | 95 | 2 197 | 605.0 | 70.0 |
| McKinney | 113 | 430 | 77.9 | 14.4 | 302 | D | D | D | 65 | 6 134 | 3 171.6 | 320.2 |
| Mansfield | 35 | 121 | 15.5 | 2.8 | 92 | 508 | 45.0 | 18.4 | 80 | 3 452 | 964.6 | 141.2 |
| Mesquite | 92 | 426 | 103.8 | 11.9 | 126 | 965 | 87.7 | 31.4 | 83 | 2 849 | 987.5 | 135.6 |
| Midland | 194 | 920 | 176.6 | 33.5 | 407 | D | D | D | 83 | 1 271 | D | 42.6 |
| Mission | 50 | 181 | 25.4 | 4.2 | 48 | 190 | 19.1 | 7.0 | 30 | 543 | 117.8 | 14.6 |
| Missouri City | 36 | 114 | 19.9 | 4.0 | 123 | 309 | 32.5 | 12.2 | NA | NA | NA | NA |
| Nacogdoches | 39 | 130 | 18.2 | 2.7 | 83 | D | D | D | 46 | 3 801 | 1 374.7 | 119.7 |
| New Braunfels | 95 | 380 | 63.0 | 10.1 | 131 | 458 | 44.8 | 15.6 | 64 | 2 516 | 655.8 | 89.8 |
| North Richland Hills | 61 | 403 | 43.6 | 10.1 | 111 | D | D | D | 22 | 832 | 385.5 | 35.9 |
| Odessa | 130 | 673 | 149.8 | 22.8 | 184 | D | D | D | 116 | 1 542 | 366.8 | 69.7 |
| Paris | 42 | D | D | D | 55 | D | D | D | 39 | 3 734 | 2 232.2 | 164.5 |
| Pasadena | 130 | 764 | 133.8 | 23.1 | 160 | D | D | D | 112 | 5 184 | 10 066.1 | 304.5 |
| Pearland | 66 | 430 | 123.7 | 15.2 | 137 | 512 | 53.7 | 22.4 | 65 | 2 462 | 450.0 | 101.3 |
| Pflugerville | 19 | 77 | 12.2 | 1.9 | 35 | 211 | 17.1 | 7.8 | NA | NA | NA | NA |
| Pharr | 40 | 321 | 36.0 | 6.3 | 54 | 584 | 30.6 | 10.4 | NA | NA | NA | NA |
| Plano | 394 | 3 094 | 533.4 | 133.4 | 1 281 | D | D | D | 164 | 4 870 | 1 072.4 | 282.7 |
| Port Arthur | 40 | 212 | 49.1 | 6.3 | 54 | 300 | 31.9 | 12.3 | 35 | 5 297 | 26 687.7 | 362.3 |
| Richardson | 166 | 799 | 134.4 | 31.8 | 667 | D | D | D | 146 | 6 824 | 1 883.9 | 429.3 |
| Rockwall | 36 | D | D | D | 138 | D | D | D | 50 | D | 247.8 | D |
| Rosenberg | 37 | 132 | 21.8 | 3.5 | 34 | 176 | 12.3 | 4.5 | 35 | 1 171 | D | 42.3 |
| Round Rock | 127 | 585 | 123.1 | 17.6 | 239 | 1 521 | 212.7 | 92.9 | 71 | 3 203 | 1 038.1 | 185.6 |
| Rowlett | 28 | 65 | 11.0 | 1.7 | 80 | 195 | 27.3 | 8.4 | 47 | 585 | 67.6 | D |
| San Angelo | 132 | 620 | 74.4 | 15.6 | 170 | D | D | D | 104 | 2 500 | 791.6 | 98.0 |
| San Antonio | 1 555 | 10 279 | 1 917.9 | 364.3 | 3 143 | D | D | D | 865 | 33 695 | 11 971.4 | 1 298.5 |
| San Juan | 6 | 40 | 2.3 | 0.4 | 11 | D | D | D | NA | NA | NA | NA |
| San Marcos | 78 | 306 | 56.3 | 7.6 | 76 | 1 226 | 58.4 | 24.6 | 38 | 2 060 | 532.4 | 84.8 |
| Schertz | 20 | 125 | 18.6 | 3.8 | 24 | 77 | 8.3 | 3.0 | NA | NA | NA | NA |
| Seguin | 35 | 215 | 24.7 | 5.5 | 48 | 184 | 13.3 | 5.4 | 49 | 4 371 | 1 145.3 | 176.0 |
| Sherman | 57 | 274 | 43.7 | 6.7 | 124 | 500 | 49.4 | 18.1 | 53 | 3 429 | 1 669.4 | 193.2 |
| Socorro | 7 | 29 | 2.3 | 0.4 | 4 | 30 | 1.2 | 0.4 | NA | NA | NA | NA |
| Southlake | 84 | 360 | 52.7 | 15.5 | 188 | D | D | D | NA | NA | NA | NA |
| Sugar Land | 154 | 652 | 175.5 | 27.8 | 408 | 2 930 | 486.4 | 182.1 | 63 | 4 819 | 1 577.9 | 227.7 |
| Temple | 82 | 400 | 64.5 | 11.1 | 100 | D | D | D | 62 | 5 283 | 1 604.2 | 191.9 |
| Texarkana | 79 | 376 | 49.5 | 9.8 | 133 | D | D | D | 37 | D | D | D |
| Texas City | 45 | 244 | 77.4 | 9.2 | 47 | 401 | 49.0 | 19.3 | 29 | 4 412 | 23 145.7 | 449.7 |
| The Colony | 17 | 109 | 29.6 | 3.7 | 35 | 135 | 7.5 | 2.7 | NA | NA | NA | NA |
| Tyler | 170 | 1 055 | 145.5 | 30.7 | 435 | D | D | D | 120 | 7 320 | 4 644.6 | 351.6 |
| Victoria | 107 | 697 | 112.6 | 26.9 | 138 | D | D | D | 56 | D | D | D |
| Waco | 146 | 1 150 | 246.9 | 47.4 | 268 | D | D | D | 153 | 11 568 | 5 303.2 | 463.8 |
| Waxahachie | 48 | 142 | 27.0 | 4.4 | 69 | D | D | D | 57 | 3 951 | 1 276.4 | 161.1 |
| Weatherford | 48 | 199 | 29.0 | 5.7 | 82 | D | D | D | 43 | 1 008 | 211.4 | 36.2 |
| Weslaco | 37 | 216 | 19.5 | 3.4 | 47 | D | D | D | NA | NA | NA | NA |
| Wichita Falls | 163 | 798 | 95.2 | 18.6 | 207 | D | D | D | 104 | 3 904 | 932.1 | 170.8 |
| Wylie | 20 | 84 | 10.9 | 1.7 | 39 | D | D | D | 38 | 1 963 | 608.9 | 85.1 |
| UTAH | 4 886 | 20 413 | 3 390.8 | 617.4 | 8 203 | 67 426 | 8 197.7 | 3 157.3 | 3 368 | 123 249 | 42 431.7 | 5 508.5 |
| American Fork | 65 | 193 | 16.8 | 6.7 | 106 | 2 245 | 133.1 | 64.1 | 24 | 687 | 202.2 | 38.3 |
| Bountiful | 78 | 200 | 22.7 | 5.1 | 180 | D | D | D | NA | NA | NA | NA |
| Cedar City | 75 | 160 | 26.9 | 3.5 | 95 | D | D | D | 63 | D | 729.3 | 57.8 |
| Clearfield | 33 | 117 | 38.1 | 3.6 | 49 | 1 225 | 285.8 | 97.7 | 45 | 5 091 | 1 388.6 | 209.8 |
| Cottonwood Heights | 176 | 785 | 146.4 | 33.9 | 208 | 1 630 | 289.3 | 121.4 | 27 | 834 | 120.1 | 36.0 |
| Draper | 105 | 277 | 55.7 | 9.1 | 200 | 1 172 | 170.2 | 58.1 | 45 | 1 259 | 299.9 | 50.3 |
| Holladay | 107 | 290 | 57.9 | 11.2 | 159 | D | D | D | NA | NA | NA | NA |
| Kaysville | 33 | D | D | D | 88 | 591 | 52.4 | 20.9 | NA | NA | NA | NA |
| Layton | 118 | 293 | 38.4 | 6.9 | 179 | D | D | D | 40 | 985 | 332.0 | 34.8 |

1. Establishments subject to federal tax.

# Table D. Cities — Accommodation and Food Services, Arts, Entertainment, and Recreation, and Health Care and Social Assistance

| City | Accommodation and food services, 2007 | | | | Arts, entertainment, and recreation,[1] 2007 | | | | Health care and social assistance,[1] 2007 | | | |
|---|---|---|---|---|---|---|---|---|---|---|---|---|
| | Number of establishments | Number of employees | Sales (mil dol) | Annual payroll (mil dol) | Number of establishments | Number of employees | Receipts (mil dol) | Annual payroll (mil dol) | Number of establishments | Number of employees | Receipts (mil dol) | Annual payroll (mil dol) |
| | 92 | 93 | 94 | 95 | 96 | 97 | 98 | 99 | 100 | 101 | 102 | 103 |
| **TEXAS—Cont'd** | | | | | | | | | | | | |
| Killeen | 215 | 4 508 | 191.3 | 49.9 | 22 | D | D | D | 156 | 1 651 | 125.0 | 50.8 |
| Kingsville | 62 | 1 087 | 39.5 | 11.1 | 6 | D | D | D | 50 | D | D | D |
| Kyle | 19 | 227 | 11.4 | 2.3 | 3 | D | D | D | 12 | D | D | D |
| Lake Jackson | 53 | 1 227 | 56.3 | 14.7 | 6 | 146 | 4.8 | 1.8 | 126 | D | D | D |
| Lancaster | 34 | 497 | 22.3 | 5.6 | 6 | 26 | 1.7 | 0.5 | 40 | D | D | D |
| La Porte | 48 | 934 | 42.4 | 11.5 | 3 | D | D | D | 46 | D | D | D |
| Laredo | 358 | D | D | D | 29 | D | D | D | 399 | 11 210 | 654.6 | 258.7 |
| League City | 85 | 1 565 | 74.8 | 19.9 | 21 | D | D | D | 114 | D | D | D |
| Leander | 12 | 142 | 5.3 | 1.5 | 3 | D | D | D | 22 | D | D | D |
| Lewisville | 217 | 4 751 | 240.8 | 65.3 | 23 | 418 | 19.6 | 5.4 | 235 | 3 693 | 401.0 | 150.7 |
| Little Elm | 28 | 361 | 12.7 | 3.2 | 3 | D | D | D | 8 | 64 | 5.5 | 1.9 |
| Longview | 219 | 4 860 | 199.7 | 58.8 | 19 | D | D | D | 335 | D | D | D |
| Lubbock | 544 | 12 781 | 522.9 | 139.0 | 53 | D | D | D | 664 | D | D | D |
| Lufkin | 116 | 2 561 | 105.6 | 29.8 | 13 | 90 | 4.2 | 0.9 | 203 | 4 695 | 309.7 | 131.4 |
| McAllen | 335 | 7 776 | 357.5 | 91.1 | 22 | 348 | 20.7 | 4.4 | 627 | 13 300 | 1 031.1 | 402.2 |
| McKinney | 180 | 3 937 | 178.3 | 49.7 | 25 | 607 | 28.3 | 10.3 | 240 | 3 278 | 410.5 | 142.9 |
| Mansfield | 81 | 1 828 | 75.9 | 20.7 | 19 | 197 | 12.0 | 3.5 | 117 | D | D | D |
| Mesquite | 206 | 5 128 | 219.7 | 63.4 | 23 | D | D | D | 294 | 5 276 | 379.9 | 157.3 |
| Midland | 242 | 5 162 | 246.7 | 66.0 | 30 | D | D | D | 294 | D | D | D |
| Mission | 123 | 1 885 | 80.8 | 18.7 | 12 | D | D | D | 212 | D | D | D |
| Missouri City | 74 | 1 253 | 53.2 | 14.6 | 13 | D | D | D | 128 | D | D | D |
| Nacogdoches | 101 | 2 220 | 86.9 | 23.0 | 6 | D | D | D | 166 | D | D | D |
| New Braunfels | 173 | 3 494 | 151.3 | 41.0 | 24 | 520 | 34.4 | 12.6 | 196 | 1 913 | 185.9 | 69.9 |
| North Richland Hills | 110 | 2 639 | 106.3 | 31.2 | 14 | D | D | D | 126 | D | D | D |
| Odessa | 214 | 4 986 | 219.5 | 57.3 | 22 | 377 | 11.3 | 2.9 | 265 | D | D | D |
| Paris | 77 | 1 326 | 56.5 | 15.7 | 6 | D | D | D | 156 | D | D | D |
| Pasadena | 194 | 4 157 | 176.7 | 45.3 | 10 | 124 | 8.9 | 2.3 | 298 | 4 418 | 580.8 | 191.3 |
| Pearland | 115 | 2 679 | 99.3 | 29.0 | 16 | D | D | D | 144 | 1 206 | 96.7 | 39.5 |
| Pflugerville | 49 | 923 | 36.6 | 10.1 | 6 | 46 | 2.9 | 0.5 | 29 | D | D | D |
| Pharr | 83 | 1 588 | 76.1 | 16.1 | 9 | 114 | 4.2 | 1.3 | 116 | 4 821 | 106.5 | 53.6 |
| Plano | 596 | 13 066 | 655.3 | 188.1 | 64 | 1 364 | 80.9 | 21.8 | 1 099 | D | D | D |
| Port Arthur | 82 | 1 651 | 73.6 | 20.7 | 9 | 102 | 4.7 | 1.6 | 123 | 2 001 | 231.3 | 74.5 |
| Richardson | 263 | 4 515 | 254.4 | 68.3 | 30 | D | D | D | 438 | D | D | D |
| Rockwall | 89 | 1 918 | 81.4 | 24.3 | 17 | 231 | 9.8 | 3.2 | 117 | D | D | D |
| Rosenberg | 80 | 1 511 | 66.6 | 19.6 | 2 | D | D | D | 41 | 576 | 37.5 | 13.6 |
| Round Rock | 229 | 5 138 | 271.2 | 70.8 | 33 | D | D | D | 229 | 3 061 | 396.4 | 151.2 |
| Rowlett | 65 | 977 | 44.8 | 11.7 | 11 | D | D | D | 76 | D | D | D |
| San Angelo | 202 | 4 150 | 174.1 | 47.7 | 21 | 228 | 11.9 | 3.7 | 215 | D | D | D |
| San Antonio | 2 872 | 68 118 | 3 545.9 | 985.1 | 272 | 7 854 | 618.7 | 208.5 | 3 221 | 64 987 | 6 306.5 | 2 305.7 |
| San Juan | 23 | D | D | D | 3 | D | D | D | 36 | D | D | D |
| San Marcos | 178 | 3 896 | 158.7 | 43.7 | 12 | D | D | D | 125 | D | D | D |
| Schertz | 47 | 980 | 42.7 | 11.6 | 2 | D | D | D | 23 | D | D | D |
| Seguin | 77 | 1 306 | 56.1 | 15.6 | 10 | D | D | D | 94 | D | D | D |
| Sherman | 101 | 2 304 | 102.2 | 28.8 | 10 | D | D | D | 202 | D | D | D |
| Socorro | 14 | 183 | 8.5 | 1.9 | 3 | D | D | D | 5 | D | D | D |
| Southlake | 83 | 2 199 | 108.6 | 31.0 | 21 | 389 | 21.3 | 6.1 | 115 | D | D | D |
| Sugar Land | 239 | 5 017 | 244.4 | 67.7 | 23 | D | D | D | 398 | D | D | D |
| Temple | 150 | 2 943 | 133.0 | 34.8 | 15 | 241 | 8.7 | 2.5 | 155 | D | D | D |
| Texarkana | 118 | 2 975 | 139.3 | 42.4 | 16 | 176 | 7.0 | 2.3 | 228 | D | D | D |
| Texas City | 75 | 1 495 | 60.3 | 16.2 | 7 | D | D | D | 98 | D | D | D |
| The Colony | 40 | 733 | 33.3 | 8.7 | 9 | 144 | 8.3 | 2.2 | 28 | 222 | 15.4 | 6.5 |
| Tyler | 260 | 6 187 | 273.9 | 74.6 | 31 | D | D | D | 454 | 8 564 | 858.2 | 390.5 |
| Victoria | 160 | 3 119 | 128.4 | 34.8 | 22 | 255 | 12.0 | 3.2 | 283 | 4 405 | 425.6 | 167.1 |
| Waco | 320 | 7 206 | 287.0 | 80.4 | 34 | D | D | D | 337 | 6 716 | 458.5 | 211.6 |
| Waxahachie | 75 | 1 351 | 58.7 | 16.8 | 10 | D | D | D | 67 | 1 039 | 70.2 | 28.0 |
| Weatherford | 90 | 1 426 | 63.9 | 17.1 | 7 | D | D | D | 107 | D | D | D |
| Weslaco | 83 | 1 745 | 70.1 | 18.3 | 8 | D | D | D | 150 | D | D | D |
| Wichita Falls | 248 | 6 052 | 231.0 | 72.1 | 25 | 310 | 14.4 | 3.7 | 282 | 4 632 | 391.5 | 145.4 |
| Wylie | 34 | 573 | 27.1 | 7.5 | 5 | 46 | 2.7 | 0.6 | 36 | D | D | D |
| **UTAH** | 4 541 | 91 808 | 3 980.6 | 1 148.6 | 727 | 16 419 | 807.9 | 282.7 | 5 731 | 67 064 | 6 411.4 | 2 364.8 |
| American Fork | 53 | 1 253 | 48.1 | 13.4 | 5 | D | D | D | 117 | D | D | D |
| Bountiful | 69 | D | D | D | 11 | D | D | D | 173 | 2 362 | 208.4 | 77.9 |
| Cedar City | 92 | 1 517 | 56.6 | 15.9 | 7 | D | D | D | 91 | D | D | D |
| Clearfield | 34 | 711 | 23.6 | 6.1 | 6 | 78 | 1.5 | 0.4 | 40 | D | D | D |
| Cottonwood Heights | 41 | 605 | 31.7 | 9.4 | 12 | D | D | D | 108 | D | D | D |
| Draper | 69 | 1 049 | 49.9 | 13.2 | 8 | D | D | D | 91 | D | D | D |
| Holladay | 52 | 784 | 35.5 | 9.9 | 9 | D | D | D | 101 | D | D | D |
| Kaysville | 23 | D | D | D | 10 | 38 | 1.0 | 0.3 | 40 | D | D | D |
| Layton | 126 | 2 945 | 112.9 | 33.2 | 15 | D | D | D | 139 | 2 196 | 241.7 | 83.3 |

1. Establishments subject to federal tax.

# Table D. Cities — Other Services and Federal Funds

| City | Other services[1], 2007 | | | | Procurement contracts | | Grants | | | | | | |
|---|---|---|---|---|---|---|---|---|---|---|---|---|---|
| | Number of establishments | Number of employees | Receipts (mil dol) | Annual payroll (mil dol) | Defense | Other | Total[2] | Medicaid and other health related | Nutrition and family welfare | Energy and environment | Disasters and emergency preparedness | Housing and community development | Employment and training |
| | 104 | 105 | 106 | 107 | 108 | 109 | 110 | 111 | 112 | 113 | 114 | 115 | 116 |
| **TEXAS—Cont'd** | | | | | | | | | | | | | |
| Killeen | 140 | 949 | 64.7 | 20.7 | 42.8 | 0.1 | 65.3 | 0.0 | 0.0 | 1.5 | 0.0 | 2.5 | 0.0 |
| Kingsville | 36 | D | D | D | 0.0 | 0.0 | 11.7 | 1.5 | 0.0 | 0.8 | 0.0 | 2.9 | 0.0 |
| Kyle | 12 | D | D | D | 2.0 | 0.0 | 0.3 | 0.0 | 0.0 | 0.0 | 0.0 | 0.1 | 0.0 |
| Lake Jackson | 28 | 148 | 8.5 | 2.6 | 0.1 | 0.0 | 1.3 | 0.0 | 0.0 | 0.2 | 0.0 | 0.0 | 0.0 |
| Lancaster | 24 | 230 | 33.8 | 8.9 | 0.8 | 206.2 | 9.1 | 0.0 | 0.0 | 0.0 | 0.0 | 8.3 | 0.0 |
| La Porte | 45 | 1 632 | 251.4 | 84.2 | 0.0 | 0.0 | 0.0 | 0.0 | 0.0 | 0.0 | 0.0 | 0.0 | 0.0 |
| Laredo | 223 | D | D | D | 2.7 | 35.6 | 132.1 | 9.4 | 76.7 | 2.1 | 0.0 | 14.9 | 0.0 |
| League City | 80 | 686 | 50.7 | 17.7 | 0.0 | 0.8 | 1.3 | 0.1 | 0.0 | 0.6 | 0.0 | 0.3 | 0.0 |
| Leander | 14 | 53 | 5.2 | 1.4 | 0.6 | 0.0 | 0.0 | 0.0 | 0.0 | 0.0 | 0.0 | 0.0 | 0.0 |
| Lewisville | 145 | 948 | 82.0 | 25.4 | 13.8 | 16.2 | 8.8 | 0.6 | 0.0 | 0.0 | 0.0 | 0.6 | 0.0 |
| Little Elm | 10 | 30 | 2.3 | 0.6 | 0.0 | 0.0 | 0.2 | 0.0 | 0.0 | 0.0 | 0.0 | 0.0 | 0.0 |
| Longview | 168 | 1 301 | 133.7 | 37.6 | 0.2 | 1.4 | 16.0 | 4.6 | 0.1 | 0.0 | 0.0 | 5.5 | 0.0 |
| Lubbock | 347 | 2 670 | 204.5 | 61.5 | 13.8 | 5.9 | 146.0 | 28.0 | 3.9 | 8.4 | 0.0 | 9.4 | 0.0 |
| Lufkin | 80 | D | D | D | 10.8 | 2.6 | 0.8 | 0.6 | 0.0 | 0.1 | 0.0 | 0.1 | 0.0 |
| McAllen | 155 | 1 103 | 83.2 | 24.8 | -35.7 | 20.9 | 20.3 | 0.0 | 0.0 | 1.3 | 0.0 | 8.3 | 0.0 |
| McKinney | 103 | 665 | 48.0 | 15.7 | 815.7 | 27.1 | 5.0 | 0.0 | 0.0 | 1.4 | 0.0 | 3.1 | 0.0 |
| Mansfield | 54 | 338 | 22.7 | 7.3 | 30.5 | 15.5 | 0.2 | 0.0 | 0.0 | 0.0 | 0.0 | 0.0 | 0.0 |
| Mesquite | 141 | 1 005 | 92.0 | 26.2 | 0.2 | 0.5 | 16.1 | 0.0 | 0.0 | 1.2 | 0.0 | 12.9 | 0.0 |
| Midland | 161 | D | D | D | 0.0 | 4.4 | 14.8 | 0.7 | 2.1 | 1.0 | 0.0 | 5.2 | 0.0 |
| Mission | 63 | 338 | 21.3 | 5.7 | 0.0 | 0.0 | 11.1 | 0.0 | 0.0 | 0.6 | 0.0 | 0.3 | 0.0 |
| Missouri City | 66 | D | D | D | 2.5 | 0.4 | 1.0 | 0.0 | 0.0 | 0.6 | 0.0 | 0.3 | 0.0 |
| Nacogdoches | 58 | 323 | 22.6 | 6.3 | 0.0 | 0.4 | 18.4 | 2.1 | 5.3 | 0.0 | 0.0 | 7.4 | 0.0 |
| New Braunfels | 90 | D | D | D | 253.4 | 1.1 | 5.4 | 0.2 | 0.3 | 0.5 | 0.0 | 2.2 | 0.0 |
| North Richland Hills | 76 | D | D | D | 0.6 | 0.1 | 0.6 | 0.0 | 0.0 | 0.6 | 0.0 | 0.0 | 0.0 |
| Odessa | 153 | D | D | D | 0.1 | 0.4 | 27.3 | 0.4 | 6.2 | 0.3 | 0.0 | 8.0 | 0.0 |
| Paris | 58 | D | D | D | 0.8 | 0.8 | 4.8 | 0.7 | 1.4 | 0.0 | 0.0 | 1.9 | 0.0 |
| Pasadena | 144 | 1 312 | 148.3 | 53.1 | 2.2 | 1.9 | 27.2 | 0.7 | 0.0 | 1.3 | 0.0 | 10.0 | 9.5 |
| Pearland | 103 | 687 | 74.1 | 24.6 | 1.1 | 0.0 | 4.1 | 3.1 | 0.0 | 0.7 | 0.0 | 0.3 | 0.0 |
| Pflugerville | 41 | 201 | 16.9 | 4.3 | 0.0 | 0.0 | 0.0 | 0.0 | 0.0 | 0.0 | 0.0 | 0.0 | 0.0 |
| Pharr | 41 | 241 | 23.5 | 4.7 | 0.0 | 0.2 | 28.1 | 7.6 | 0.0 | 0.6 | 0.0 | 17.9 | 0.0 |
| Plano | 354 | 2 884 | 226.2 | 72.2 | 102.8 | 125.3 | 14.1 | 2.0 | 1.2 | 1.1 | 0.0 | 8.2 | 0.0 |
| Port Arthur | 40 | 177 | 12.0 | 3.6 | 35.2 | 6.7 | 27.4 | 1.8 | 2.3 | 0.6 | -0.7 | 20.7 | 0.0 |
| Richardson | 151 | 1 623 | 151.0 | 56.8 | 204.3 | 51.9 | 43.9 | 16.0 | 7.6 | 3.0 | 0.0 | 0.0 | 0.0 |
| Rockwall | 49 | 377 | 20.9 | 7.4 | 54.0 | 0.4 | 0.3 | 0.0 | 0.0 | 0.0 | 0.0 | 0.2 | 0.0 |
| Rosenberg | 55 | D | D | D | 0.0 | 0.4 | 3.1 | 0.0 | 0.0 | 0.0 | 0.0 | 3.1 | 0.0 |
| Round Rock | 135 | 1 676 | 113.9 | 45.7 | 429.1 | 213.9 | 16.8 | 0.0 | 0.0 | 1.4 | 0.0 | 1.4 | 0.0 |
| Rowlett | 73 | D | D | D | 0.0 | 0.0 | 0.7 | 0.0 | 0.0 | 0.5 | 0.0 | 0.2 | 0.0 |
| San Angelo | 166 | D | D | D | 13.4 | 2.4 | 25.3 | 2.3 | 5.6 | 1.0 | 0.0 | 5.9 | 0.0 |
| San Antonio | 1 765 | 13 495 | 918.4 | 304.5 | 2 791.9 | 366.0 | 738.5 | 288.4 | 66.5 | 49.2 | 7.6 | 158.8 | 5.1 |
| San Juan | 21 | 55 | 3.7 | 0.7 | 0.0 | 0.0 | 1.7 | 0.0 | 0.0 | 0.0 | 0.5 | 0.9 | 0.0 |
| San Marcos | 69 | 487 | 32.2 | 11.2 | 4.0 | 54.5 | 25.7 | 7.5 | 4.6 | 0.4 | 0.0 | 2.7 | 0.0 |
| Schertz | 34 | 332 | 24.4 | 8.4 | 0.8 | 0.0 | 1.9 | 0.0 | 0.0 | 0.0 | 0.0 | 1.1 | 0.0 |
| Seguin | 51 | 304 | 19.1 | 6.3 | 0.0 | 0.1 | 4.1 | 0.0 | 2.2 | 0.0 | 0.0 | 1.8 | 0.0 |
| Sherman | 54 | 380 | 26.1 | 7.7 | 0.1 | 4.4 | 5.9 | 0.0 | 0.3 | 0.0 | 0.0 | 4.9 | 0.0 |
| Socorro | 23 | D | D | D | 0.0 | 0.0 | 0.0 | 0.0 | 0.0 | 0.0 | 0.0 | 0.0 | 0.0 |
| Southlake | 55 | 498 | 27.8 | 10.0 | 0.0 | 0.3 | 0.0 | 0.0 | 0.0 | 0.0 | 0.0 | 0.0 | 0.0 |
| Sugar Land | 120 | 813 | 58.7 | 20.8 | 42.9 | 36.2 | 6.2 | 0.0 | 0.3 | 5.3 | 0.0 | 0.3 | 0.0 |
| Temple | 115 | 584 | 43.1 | 13.2 | 59.2 | 72.9 | 16.0 | 3.5 | 0.8 | 4.8 | 0.0 | 1.2 | 0.0 |
| Texarkana | 95 | 714 | 57.3 | 16.4 | 87.1 | 1.2 | 15.9 | 0.0 | 0.5 | 0.7 | 0.0 | 10.6 | 0.0 |
| Texas City | 40 | 364 | 36.4 | 12.6 | 255.6 | 0.2 | 4.4 | 0.0 | 0.0 | 0.0 | 0.0 | 3.0 | 0.0 |
| The Colony | 28 | D | D | D | 2.0 | 0.7 | 0.0 | 0.0 | 0.0 | 0.0 | 0.0 | 0.0 | 0.0 |
| Tyler | 165 | 1 330 | 81.3 | 29.6 | 56.2 | 15.8 | 33.5 | 10.4 | 3.0 | 0.0 | 0.0 | 7.9 | 0.0 |
| Victoria | 124 | D | D | D | 0.2 | 1.2 | 10.9 | 0.0 | 4.4 | 1.1 | 0.0 | 2.6 | 0.0 |
| Waco | 184 | 1 288 | 90.7 | 28.8 | 231.1 | 18.2 | 49.3 | 3.2 | 6.5 | 1.6 | 0.0 | 19.1 | 0.0 |
| Waxahachie | 40 | 212 | 16.1 | 4.4 | 1.1 | 1.6 | 0.3 | 0.0 | 0.0 | 0.0 | 0.0 | 0.1 | 0.0 |
| Weatherford | 56 | 380 | 24.1 | 7.2 | 0.0 | 2.4 | 12.1 | 0.4 | 7.6 | 0.1 | 0.0 | 2.8 | 0.0 |
| Weslaco | 36 | 175 | 14.3 | 3.2 | 0.0 | 0.4 | 7.1 | 0.0 | 0.0 | 0.7 | 0.0 | 6.3 | 0.0 |
| Wichita Falls | 164 | 1 024 | 79.3 | 24.1 | 181.0 | 3.0 | 22.7 | 1.0 | 4.4 | 0.4 | 0.0 | 6.8 | 0.0 |
| Wylie | 29 | 142 | 10.9 | 3.5 | 2.7 | 0.0 | 0.1 | 0.0 | 0.0 | 0.0 | 0.0 | 0.0 | 0.0 |
| **UTAH** | 3 537 | 21 934 | 1 751.2 | 520.6 | 2 521.6 | 1 236.8 | 4 986.7 | 2 083.8 | 491.2 | 653.6 | 11.1 | 122.5 | 75.6 |
| American Fork | 46 | D | D | D | 1.2 | 0.0 | 0.1 | 0.0 | 0.0 | 0.0 | 0.0 | 0.0 | 0.0 |
| Bountiful | 57 | 282 | 21.1 | 5.5 | 3.6 | 0.5 | 0.1 | 0.0 | 0.0 | 0.0 | 0.0 | 0.1 | 0.0 |
| Cedar City | 45 | D | D | D | 3.1 | 12.6 | 10.5 | 0.8 | 3.0 | 1.5 | 1.0 | 2.4 | 0.0 |
| Clearfield | 37 | 188 | 10.0 | 3.2 | 493.4 | 0.1 | 10.0 | 0.0 | 0.0 | 0.3 | 0.0 | 0.6 | 0.0 |
| Cottonwood Heights | 24 | 132 | 5.9 | 2.1 | 0.0 | 0.1 | 0.1 | 0.0 | 0.0 | 0.0 | 0.0 | 0.0 | 0.0 |
| Draper | 65 | 459 | 31.7 | 8.9 | 4.3 | 1.3 | 23.4 | 0.0 | 0.0 | 1.1 | 0.0 | 0.0 | 0.0 |
| Holladay | 38 | D | D | D | 0.0 | 0.1 | 0.0 | 0.0 | 0.0 | 0.0 | 0.0 | 0.0 | 0.0 |
| Kaysville | 27 | D | D | D | 0.0 | 0.0 | 0.1 | 0.0 | 0.0 | 0.0 | 0.0 | 0.1 | 0.0 |
| Layton | 84 | 579 | 39.7 | 10.8 | 12.1 | 2.6 | 1.6 | 0.0 | 0.0 | 1.2 | 0.0 | 0.4 | 0.0 |

1. Establishments subject to federal tax.   2. Includes program categories not shown separately. State totals include additional categories not allocated by city.

# Table D. Cities — City Government Finances

| | City government finances, 2007 | | | | | | | | | |
| City | General revenue Total (mil dol) | Intergovernmental Total (mil dol) | Intergovernmental Percent from state government | Taxes Total (mil dol) | Taxes Per capita[1] (dollars) Total | Taxes Per capita[1] (dollars) Property | Taxes Per capita[1] (dollars) Sales and gross receipts | General expenditure Total (mil dol) | General expenditure Per capita[1] (dollars) Total | General expenditure Capital outlays |
|---|---|---|---|---|---|---|---|---|---|---|
| | 117 | 118 | 119 | 120 | 121 | 122 | 123 | 124 | 125 | 126 |
| **TEXAS—Cont'd** | | | | | | | | | | |
| Killeen | 99.2 | 12.5 | 2.8 | 47.3 | 420 | 184 | 237 | 109.2 | 971 | 356 |
| Kingsville | 18.1 | 0.2 | 100.0 | 9.4 | 385 | 169 | 216 | 14.9 | 610 | 70 |
| Kyle | 12.5 | 0.0 | 100.0 | 7.9 | 329 | 94 | 235 | 10.9 | 456 | 19 |
| Lake Jackson | 24.2 | 0.8 | 74.7 | 11.3 | 410 | 177 | 233 | 22.7 | 825 | 156 |
| Lancaster | 36.1 | 8.4 | 0.2 | 17.7 | 503 | 262 | 241 | 33.4 | 950 | 1 |
| La Porte | 39.1 | 1.1 | 100.0 | 18.8 | 550 | 355 | 195 | 37.1 | 1 083 | 178 |
| Laredo | 278.1 | 42.5 | 30.3 | 101.1 | 465 | 227 | 238 | 247.8 | 1 139 | 239 |
| League City | 50.7 | 0.7 | 100.0 | 35.3 | 518 | 339 | 178 | 46.1 | 676 | 58 |
| Leander | 15.9 | 0.5 | 16.2 | 8.0 | 342 | 201 | 141 | 17.7 | 752 | 271 |
| Lewisville | 95.7 | 5.1 | 79.4 | 57.1 | 582 | 261 | 322 | 97.8 | 997 | 281 |
| Little Elm | 19.8 | 0.6 | 100.0 | 8.4 | 353 | 165 | 188 | 19.2 | 802 | 303 |
| Longview | 86.8 | 8.5 | 45.8 | 53.4 | 695 | 260 | 435 | 78.7 | 1 025 | 114 |
| Lubbock | 213.8 | 32.9 | 4.9 | 108.4 | 499 | 197 | 302 | 216.9 | 998 | 214 |
| Lufkin | 41.8 | 0.9 | 12.0 | 23.1 | 679 | 261 | 419 | 35.5 | 1 043 | 36 |
| McAllen | 182.0 | 5.8 | 26.4 | 89.1 | 700 | 192 | 508 | 181.1 | 1 423 | 471 |
| McKinney | 123.4 | 2.7 | 6.3 | 87.6 | 758 | 374 | 384 | 134.8 | 1 166 | 379 |
| Mansfield | 61.5 | 0.1 | 100.0 | 42.0 | 953 | 499 | 455 | 69.1 | 1 568 | 568 |
| Mesquite | 130.4 | 13.2 | 1.3 | 81.2 | 616 | 269 | 348 | 123.4 | 937 | 122 |
| Midland | 109.9 | 9.4 | 18.0 | 64.7 | 623 | 248 | 375 | 106.1 | 1 022 | 169 |
| Mission | 42.2 | 4.6 | 11.9 | 24.0 | 368 | 192 | 176 | 41.0 | 628 | 113 |
| Missouri City | 39.8 | 1.2 | 16.5 | 32.8 | 443 | 272 | 171 | 45.7 | 617 | 181 |
| Nacogdoches | 34.8 | 4.5 | 32.8 | 14.3 | 447 | 206 | 241 | 31.7 | 992 | 185 |
| New Braunfels | 62.4 | 1.3 | 51.2 | 33.8 | 653 | 203 | 449 | 56.4 | 1 089 | 276 |
| North Richland Hills | 72.8 | 1.9 | 100.0 | 42.7 | 663 | 306 | 356 | 59.3 | 921 | 109 |
| Odessa | 74.5 | 4.2 | 15.5 | 39.4 | 407 | 170 | 236 | 76.9 | 794 | 85 |
| Paris | 30.7 | 1.9 | 94.0 | 17.6 | 675 | 291 | 384 | 28.3 | 1 083 | 176 |
| Pasadena | 131.7 | 14.1 | 10.3 | 65.4 | 446 | 186 | 261 | 123.1 | 840 | 148 |
| Pearland | 81.2 | 1.4 | 51.1 | 49.7 | 638 | 353 | 285 | 108.9 | 1 399 | 636 |
| Pflugerville | 27.5 | 0.3 | 4.0 | 16.4 | 477 | 262 | 214 | 44.3 | 1 286 | 715 |
| Pharr | 49.4 | 3.1 | 59.1 | 25.5 | 401 | 164 | 237 | 47.6 | 748 | 134 |
| Plano | 318.2 | 9.6 | 93.4 | 203.6 | 781 | 403 | 377 | 329.1 | 1 262 | 225 |
| Port Arthur | 81.1 | 16.8 | 46.5 | 27.1 | 490 | 220 | 269 | 72.0 | 1 301 | 37 |
| Richardson | 137.4 | 2.0 | 74.6 | 89.5 | 898 | 467 | 431 | 135.2 | 1 357 | 176 |
| Rockwall | 29.6 | 1.1 | 32.6 | 21.3 | 630 | 265 | 365 | 55.2 | 1 632 | 881 |
| Rosenberg | 24.6 | 1.9 | 24.4 | 15.2 | 462 | 152 | 310 | 21.6 | 653 | 32 |
| Round Rock | 139.1 | 1.1 | 64.0 | 104.0 | 1 072 | 222 | 850 | 126.3 | 1 302 | 467 |
| Rowlett | 58.8 | 0.5 | 16.5 | 34.1 | 614 | 404 | 210 | 61.6 | 1 108 | 244 |
| San Angelo | 81.5 | 11.2 | 7.4 | 46.7 | 516 | 251 | 264 | 79.7 | 880 | 176 |
| San Antonio | 1 515.8 | 191.1 | 62.8 | 612.3 | 461 | 220 | 239 | 1 503.3 | 1 131 | 220 |
| San Juan | 12.5 | 0.2 | 100.0 | 6.6 | 200 | 114 | 86 | 11.1 | 334 | 23 |
| San Marcos | 61.3 | 3.1 | 100.0 | 35.5 | 705 | 177 | 528 | 56.7 | 1 126 | 359 |
| Schertz | 22.0 | 0.0 | 100.0 | 9.3 | 317 | 147 | 170 | 19.2 | 653 | 5 |
| Seguin | 20.4 | 1.2 | 10.3 | 9.0 | 344 | 155 | 189 | 28.6 | 1 099 | 402 |
| Sherman | 41.3 | 0.7 | 41.3 | 21.6 | 573 | 189 | 384 | 40.1 | 1 064 | 207 |
| Socorro | 5.1 | 0.3 | 100.0 | 3.7 | 117 | 86 | 32 | 4.7 | 149 | 18 |
| Southlake | 55.2 | 0.0 | | 42.0 | 1 603 | 816 | 787 | 35.6 | 1 359 | 144 |
| Sugar Land | 108.2 | 10.9 | 5.1 | 64.6 | 810 | 272 | 539 | 114.6 | 1 438 | 576 |
| Temple | 74.5 | 4.3 | 92.9 | 38.2 | 654 | 294 | 360 | 70.8 | 1 215 | 203 |
| Texarkana | 42.6 | 1.8 | 75.2 | 25.4 | 704 | 274 | 430 | 35.5 | 983 | 53 |
| Texas City | 61.8 | 5.0 | 15.2 | 39.9 | 898 | 447 | 451 | 59.4 | 1 338 | 388 |
| The Colony | 31.8 | 0.3 | 28.5 | 21.6 | 521 | 312 | 209 | 27.2 | 656 | 105 |
| Tyler | 103.3 | 12.0 | 21.8 | 56.7 | 587 | 127 | 460 | 95.4 | 989 | 165 |
| Victoria | 51.9 | 2.4 | 28.5 | 29.5 | 474 | 175 | 300 | 51.8 | 832 | 60 |
| Waco | 701.4 | 216.2 | 3.7 | 79.3 | 649 | 298 | 351 | 702.5 | 5 748 | 174 |
| Waxahachie | 34.4 | 1.5 | 100.0 | 23.8 | 873 | 395 | 478 | 32.8 | 1 203 | 288 |
| Weatherford | 28.3 | 0.4 | 54.6 | 16.3 | 634 | 168 | 466 | 21.7 | 842 | 93 |
| Weslaco | 30.1 | 1.4 | 33.2 | 17.5 | 538 | 214 | 324 | 32.8 | 1 010 | 194 |
| Wichita Falls | 105.1 | 10.9 | 21.1 | 59.2 | 583 | 235 | 348 | 90.3 | 889 | 86 |
| Wylie | 34.6 | 5.6 | 100.0 | 17.7 | 507 | 352 | 155 | 30.9 | 885 | 216 |
| **UTAH** | X | X | X | X | X | X | X | X | X | X |
| American Fork | 26.7 | 1.3 | 66.7 | 12.3 | 464 | 159 | 305 | 23.9 | 904 | 153 |
| Bountiful | 28.3 | 3.7 | 97.7 | 13.5 | 309 | 74 | 235 | 28.4 | 648 | 237 |
| Cedar City | 31.9 | 4.7 | 21.4 | 13.2 | 474 | 169 | 305 | 24.9 | 895 | 96 |
| Clearfield | 21.9 | 1.7 | 47.7 | 11.3 | 412 | 166 | 246 | 21.7 | 792 | 72 |
| Cottonwood Heights | 15.6 | 1.3 | 98.2 | 13.3 | 377 | 196 | 181 | 13.1 | 371 | 53 |
| Draper | 32.9 | 1.6 | 99.8 | 18.7 | 484 | 167 | 317 | 28.8 | 747 | 248 |
| Holladay | 12.9 | 2.2 | 78.7 | 9.5 | 371 | 165 | 206 | 14.0 | 547 | 53 |
| Kaysville | 16.0 | 1.1 | 88.7 | 6.7 | 266 | 54 | 212 | 17.3 | 692 | 303 |
| Layton | 42.9 | 3.9 | 65.0 | 24.4 | 379 | 98 | 282 | 48.7 | 757 | 245 |

1. Based on population estimated as of July 1 of the year shown.

# Table D. Cities — **City Government Finances**

|  | City government finances, 2006 (cont.) | | | | | | | | | |
|--|--|--|--|--|--|--|--|--|--|--|
|  | General expenditure (cont.) | | | | | | | | | |
|  | Percent of total for: | | | | | | | | | |
| City | Public welfare | Highways | Parking facilities | Education | Health and hospitals | Police protection | Sewerage and sanitation | Parks and recreation | Housing and community development | Interest on debt |
|  | 127 | 128 | 129 | 130 | 131 | 132 | 133 | 134 | 135 | 136 |
| TEXAS—Cont'd |  |  |  |  |  |  |  |  |  |  |
| Killeen | 0.3 | 7.3 | 0.0 | 0.0 | 0.3 | 15.0 | 30.9 | 4.8 | 0.9 | 2.9 |
| Kingsville | 0.0 | 10.4 | 0.0 | 0.0 | 0.0 | 31.1 | 27.0 | 2.7 | 0.0 | 2.5 |
| Kyle | 0.0 | 0.6 | 0.0 | 0.0 | 0.6 | 15.0 | 24.5 | 11.6 | 0.0 | 10.1 |
| Lake Jackson | 0.0 | 21.3 | 0.0 | 0.0 | 3.0 | 16.5 | 17.6 | 20.3 | 0.9 | 5.4 |
| Lancaster | 0.0 | 3.1 | 0.0 | 0.0 | 0.0 | 15.5 | 12.8 | 5.8 | 22.9 | 2.0 |
| La Porte | 0.1 | 6.4 | 0.0 | 0.0 | 4.3 | 31.2 | 12.0 | 11.7 | 0.0 | 3.2 |
| Laredo | 0.2 | 1.6 | 0.5 | 0.0 | 4.2 | 17.3 | 10.7 | 3.0 | 5.7 | 4.9 |
| League City | 0.0 | 10.6 | 0.0 | 0.0 | 3.1 | 20.2 | 12.4 | 4.3 | 0.2 | 12.0 |
| Leander | 0.0 | 10.2 | 0.0 | 0.0 | 0.4 | 11.9 | 8.7 | 9.1 | 0.0 | 8.0 |
| Lewisville | 0.0 | 10.9 | 0.0 | 0.0 | 1.8 | 14.7 | 6.6 | 6.8 | 0.8 | 7.1 |
| Little Elm | 0.0 | 12.3 | 0.0 | 0.0 | 0.0 | 12.7 | 7.5 | 2.6 | 0.0 | 3.6 |
| Longview | 0.0 | 4.4 | 0.0 | 0.0 | 1.2 | 20.2 | 13.8 | 6.9 | 6.0 | 2.8 |
| Lubbock | 0.0 | 12.3 | 0.0 | 0.0 | 2.1 | 18.0 | 14.5 | 8.3 | 2.7 | 4.5 |
| Lufkin | 0.0 | 11.0 | 0.0 | 0.0 | 0.0 | 19.3 | 24.1 | 10.5 | 0.3 | 5.1 |
| McAllen | 1.4 | 8.0 | 0.5 | 0.0 | 0.5 | 14.8 | 10.3 | 25.7 | 1.2 | 2.9 |
| McKinney | 0.0 | 16.7 | 0.0 | 0.0 | 0.9 | 15.3 | 15.8 | 10.6 | 0.6 | 4.6 |
| Mansfield | 0.0 | 18.7 | 0.0 | 0.0 | 0.5 | 9.9 | 15.3 | 4.6 | 0.0 | 7.3 |
| Mesquite | 0.0 | 10.9 | 0.0 | 0.0 | 1.4 | 21.8 | 10.9 | 10.6 | 8.2 | 4.0 |
| Midland | 0.0 | 7.6 | 0.0 | 0.0 | 3.1 | 15.5 | 11.9 | 11.0 | 2.7 | 2.6 |
| Mission | 0.0 | 10.9 | 0.0 | 0.0 | 1.1 | 22.4 | 22.9 | 10.0 | 2.3 | 2.4 |
| Missouri City | 0.0 | 16.4 | 0.1 | 0.0 | 0.8 | 17.2 | 3.4 | 10.6 | 0.5 | 4.2 |
| Nacogdoches | 0.0 | 4.5 | 0.0 | 0.0 | 0.9 | 16.4 | 26.6 | 3.8 | 1.7 | 2.0 |
| New Braunfels | 0.0 | 15.1 | 0.0 | 0.0 | 0.6 | 15.0 | 20.9 | 7.1 | 0.9 | 5.4 |
| North Richland Hills | 0.0 | 8.3 | 0.0 | 0.0 | 1.3 | 24.0 | 12.4 | 20.1 | 0.0 | 4.5 |
| Odessa | 0.0 | 11.9 | 0.0 | 0.0 | 0.8 | 20.3 | 14.3 | 7.8 | 2.0 | 1.6 |
| Paris | 0.0 | 13.4 | 0.0 | 0.0 | 9.9 | 31.3 | 14.0 | 3.8 | 2.6 | 2.2 |
| Pasadena | 0.0 | 15.6 | 0.0 | 0.0 | 1.8 | 30.8 | 13.9 | 9.3 | 7.6 | 3.2 |
| Pearland | 0.0 | 36.7 | 0.0 | 0.0 | 2.3 | 8.5 | 19.8 | 3.0 | 0.0 | 7.4 |
| Pflugerville | 0.0 | 19.6 | 0.0 | 0.0 | 0.1 | 12.3 | 47.6 | 4.1 | 0.0 | 7.4 |
| Pharr | 0.0 | 5.3 | 0.0 | 0.0 | 0.4 | 19.6 | 14.3 | 7.9 | 2.7 | 3.6 |
| Plano | 0.0 | 7.0 | 0.0 | 0.0 | 0.6 | 14.5 | 14.6 | 11.4 | 0.0 | 4.0 |
| Port Arthur | 1.9 | 8.2 | 0.0 | 0.0 | 2.6 | 16.7 | 13.0 | 2.2 | 1.8 | 6.3 |
| Richardson | 0.0 | 9.6 | 0.0 | 0.0 | 1.3 | 15.6 | 17.1 | 9.9 | 0.0 | 6.1 |
| Rockwall | 0.0 | 24.4 | 0.0 | 0.0 | 1.4 | 11.5 | 6.8 | 32.8 | 0.0 | 3.5 |
| Rosenberg | 0.0 | 8.7 | 0.0 | 0.0 | 0.4 | 25.8 | 16.0 | 4.7 | 1.0 | 5.0 |
| Round Rock | 0.0 | 22.7 | 0.0 | 0.0 | 0.0 | 14.8 | 12.6 | 12.9 | 0.3 | 6.4 |
| Rowlett | 0.0 | 9.8 | 0.0 | 0.0 | 1.4 | 13.0 | 15.0 | 7.0 | 0.0 | 7.6 |
| San Angelo | 0.0 | 7.9 | 0.0 | 0.0 | 5.3 | 17.4 | 7.9 | 10.4 | 6.0 | 3.8 |
| San Antonio | 2.8 | 8.5 | 0.4 | 3.0 | 2.8 | 16.1 | 16.7 | 10.5 | 2.3 | 5.4 |
| San Juan | 0.0 | 13.3 | 0.0 | 0.0 | 0.0 | 20.4 | 24.6 | 10.0 | 0.0 | 5.1 |
| San Marcos | 0.0 | 3.5 | 0.0 | 0.0 | 2.1 | 15.6 | 24.4 | 3.9 | 1.0 | 3.6 |
| Schertz | 0.1 | 1.5 | 0.0 | 0.0 | 10.8 | 15.8 | 18.4 | 2.5 | 0.0 | 4.2 |
| Seguin | 0.0 | 20.8 | 0.0 | 0.0 | 0.5 | 21.1 | 15.3 | 5.1 | 0.0 | 3.4 |
| Sherman | 0.7 | 5.5 | 0.0 | 0.0 | 0.0 | 17.7 | 32.2 | 8.0 | 0.3 | 0.5 |
| Socorro | 0.0 | 14.7 | 0.0 | 0.0 | 5.2 | 25.9 | 0.0 | 0.0 | 0.0 | 3.6 |
| Southlake | 0.0 | 15.1 | 0.0 | 0.0 | 0.0 | 14.7 | 5.6 | 9.1 | 0.0 | 13.5 |
| Sugar Land | 0.0 | 4.7 | 0.0 | 0.0 | 0.5 | 10.4 | 12.3 | 2.2 | 0.3 | 6.7 |
| Temple | 0.0 | 4.4 | 0.0 | 0.0 | 3.5 | 16.2 | 21.5 | 9.3 | 1.3 | 3.3 |
| Texarkana | 0.0 | 10.2 | 0.0 | 0.0 | 5.0 | 21.4 | 26.7 | 4.3 | 1.4 | 5.8 |
| Texas City | 0.0 | 21.7 | 0.0 | 0.0 | 2.8 | 14.6 | 17.0 | 8.9 | 1.5 | 5.9 |
| The Colony | 0.0 | 16.3 | 0.0 | 0.0 | 0.0 | 17.8 | 5.3 | 9.5 | 0.0 | 4.0 |
| Tyler | 0.0 | 12.5 | 0.0 | 0.0 | 0.0 | 19.4 | 20.3 | 5.2 | 7.6 | 6.4 |
| Victoria | 0.0 | 10.6 | 0.0 | 0.0 | 1.0 | 18.7 | 17.9 | 5.2 | 2.2 | 5.2 |
| Waco | 0.0 | 1.1 | 0.0 | 0.0 | 0.9 | 4.0 | 3.9 | 2.1 | 0.4 | 81.6 |
| Waxahachie | 0.0 | 9.3 | 0.0 | 0.0 | 2.2 | 14.7 | 23.4 | 8.4 | 0.0 | 8.4 |
| Weatherford | 0.0 | 17.1 | 0.0 | 0.0 | 1.9 | 24.9 | 19.0 | 8.6 | 2.8 | 2.1 |
| Weslaco | 0.0 | 13.0 | 0.0 | 0.0 | 1.6 | 16.3 | 17.6 | 5.0 | 1.2 | 5.9 |
| Wichita Falls | 0.0 | 10.6 | 0.0 | 0.0 | 4.8 | 19.5 | 16.0 | 5.2 | 7.1 | 0.8 |
| Wylie | 0.0 | 12.1 | 0.0 | 0.0 | 2.2 | 14.9 | 26.2 | 4.9 | 0.0 | 4.2 |
| UTAH | X | X | X | X | X | X | X | X | X | X |
| American Fork | 0.0 | 6.9 | 0.0 | 0.0 | 0.0 | 15.5 | 12.1 | 21.2 | 0.5 | 5.9 |
| Bountiful | 0.0 | 18.5 | 0.0 | 0.0 | 0.0 | 19.1 | 20.1 | 12.9 | 11.1 | 1.5 |
| Cedar City | 0.0 | 17.0 | 0.0 | 0.0 | 0.0 | 14.9 | 11.3 | 15.9 | 0.1 | 4.0 |
| Clearfield | 0.0 | 10.7 | 0.0 | 0.0 | 0.0 | 15.2 | 11.2 | 11.7 | 0.0 | 8.8 |
| Cottonwood Heights | 0.0 | 23.9 | 0.0 | 0.0 | 0.0 | 30.3 | 5.6 | 2.3 | 0.0 | 0.0 |
| Draper | 0.0 | 20.4 | 0.0 | 0.0 | 1.4 | 11.7 | 10.2 | 11.5 | 6.6 | 4.0 |
| Holladay | 0.0 | 16.1 | 0.0 | 0.0 | 0.0 | 21.2 | 0.0 | 2.0 | 14.2 | 2.3 |
| Kaysville | 0.0 | 37.2 | 0.0 | 0.0 | 0.0 | 11.7 | 15.6 | 14.9 | 0.0 | 0.5 |
| Layton | 0.0 | 19.0 | 0.0 | 0.0 | 0.0 | 18.1 | 19.7 | 18.0 | 1.0 | 0.0 |

# Table D. Cities — City Government Finances, City Government Employment, and Climate

| City | City government finances, 2007 (cont.) | | | | Climate[2] | | | | | | |
|---|---|---|---|---|---|---|---|---|---|---|---|
| | Debt outstanding | | | | Average daily temperature (degrees Fahrenheit) | | | | | | |
| | | | | | Mean | | Limits | | | | |
| | Total (mil dol) | Per capita[1] (dollars) | Debt issued during year | City government employment, 2011 | January | July | January[3] | July[4] | Annual precipitation (inches) | Heating degree days | Cooling degree days |
| | 137 | 138 | 139 | 140 | 141 | 142 | 143 | 144 | 145 | 146 | 147 |
| TEXAS—Cont'd | | | | | | | | | | | |
| Killeen........................ | 146.0 | 1 299 | 54.8 | 1 108 | 46.0 | 83.5 | 34.0 | 95.3 | 32.88 | 2 190 | 2 477 |
| Kingsville..................... | 22.2 | 909 | 0.5 | 254 | 55.9 | 84.3 | 43.4 | 95.5 | 29.03 | 1 001 | 3 404 |
| Kyle........................... | 24.8 | 1 039 | 0.6 | NA | NA | NA | NA | NA | NA | NA | NA |
| Lake Jackson ............... | 40.9 | 1 488 | 0.0 | NA | 54.0 | 83.7 | 45.4 | 90.2 | 50.66 | 1 234 | 3 003 |
| Lancaster..................... | 17.1 | 486 | 0.0 | 245 | 44.4 | 84.0 | 33.3 | 95.7 | 38.69 | 2 380 | 2 452 |
| La Porte...................... | 40.6 | 1 184 | 7.0 | NA | 51.6 | 83.6 | 41.9 | 91.6 | 53.75 | 1 471 | 2 841 |
| Laredo........................ | 328.5 | 1 510 | 48.7 | 2 375 | 55.6 | 88.5 | 43.7 | 101.6 | 21.53 | 931 | 4 213 |
| League City.................. | 120.9 | 1 774 | 4.7 | 490 | 52.7 | 82.7 | 43.1 | 91.2 | 51.73 | 1 365 | 2 815 |
| Leander....................... | 55.6 | 2 363 | 7.2 | NA | NA | NA | NA | NA | NA | NA | NA |
| Lewisville.................... | 191.9 | 1 956 | 10.8 | 696 | 42.7 | 83.6 | 32.0 | 94.1 | 37.79 | 2 650 | 2 269 |
| Little Elm.................... | 38.1 | 1 594 | 12.2 | NA | NA | NA | NA | NA | NA | NA | NA |
| Longview..................... | 129.0 | 1 680 | 0.0 | 790 | 45.4 | 83.4 | 33.7 | 94.5 | 49.06 | 2 319 | 2 355 |
| Lubbock....................... | 576.9 | 2 654 | 188.8 | 2 061 | 38.1 | 79.8 | 24.4 | 91.9 | 18.69 | 3 508 | 1 769 |
| Lufkin......................... | 50.1 | 1 472 | 1.1 | NA | 48.6 | 82.6 | 37.9 | 93.5 | 46.62 | 1 900 | 2 480 |
| McAllen....................... | 138.7 | 1 090 | 0.0 | 1 661 | 58.7 | 85.1 | 48.2 | 95.5 | 22.61 | 719 | 3 898 |
| McKinney..................... | 215.7 | 1 865 | 94.7 | 817 | 41.8 | 82.4 | 31.1 | 92.7 | 41.01 | 2 843 | 2 060 |
| Mansfield..................... | 144.4 | 3 277 | 12.3 | 463 | 43.7 | 84.3 | 33.2 | 94.9 | 34.54 | 2 437 | 2 508 |
| Mesquite...................... | 224.5 | 1 704 | 63.1 | 1 106 | 45.9 | 86.5 | 36.4 | 96.1 | 37.05 | 2 219 | 2 878 |
| Midland....................... | 94.5 | 910 | 42.1 | 921 | 44.5 | 81.8 | 29.5 | 95.6 | 14.84 | 2 479 | 2 241 |
| Mission ....................... | 59.1 | 905 | 22.4 | NA | 58.8 | 86.3 | 47.5 | 97.7 | 22.13 | 740 | 4 128 |
| Missouri City................ | 55.2 | 746 | 16.5 | NA | 51.8 | 84.1 | 41.6 | 93.7 | 49.34 | 1 475 | 2 950 |
| Nacogdoches................. | 61.2 | 1 912 | 1.8 | NA | 46.5 | 83.9 | 36.4 | 93.5 | 48.36 | 2 150 | 2 555 |
| New Braunfels............... | 62.1 | 1 199 | 0.0 | NA | 48.6 | 82.7 | 35.5 | 94.7 | 35.74 | 1 840 | 2 545 |
| North Richland Hills ...... | 74.8 | 1 161 | 23.6 | NA | 44.1 | 85.0 | 34.0 | 95.4 | 34.73 | 2 370 | 2 568 |
| Odessa........................ | 76.0 | 785 | 5.4 | 871 | 43.2 | 81.7 | 29.6 | 94.3 | 14.80 | 2 716 | 2 139 |
| Paris.......................... | 43.7 | 1 676 | 0.0 | NA | 40.6 | 83.1 | 29.9 | 94.3 | 47.82 | 2 972 | 2 197 |
| Pasadena...................... | 148.9 | 1 016 | 0.0 | 949 | 54.3 | 84.5 | 45.2 | 93.6 | 53.96 | 1 174 | 3 179 |
| Pearland...................... | 271.4 | 3 486 | 84.0 | NA | 54.3 | 84.5 | 45.2 | 93.6 | 53.96 | 1 174 | 3 179 |
| Pflugerville.................. | 120.9 | 3 511 | 15.9 | 264 | NA | NA | NA | NA | NA | NA | NA |
| Pharr......................... | 50.1 | 787 | 1.5 | NA | 60.1 | 85.9 | 50.3 | 96.1 | 22.96 | 624 | 4 181 |
| Plano......................... | 318.5 | 1 221 | 46.4 | 2 325 | 44.1 | 85.0 | 34.0 | 95.4 | 34.73 | 2 370 | 2 568 |
| Port Arthur.................. | 97.1 | 1 756 | 0.0 | 667 | 52.2 | 82.7 | 42.9 | 91.6 | 59.89 | 1 447 | 2 823 |
| Richardson ................... | 262.3 | 2 632 | 87.6 | 950 | 45.9 | 86.5 | 36.4 | 96.1 | 37.05 | 2 219 | 2 878 |
| Rockwall...................... | 94.1 | 2 783 | 41.0 | 260 | NA | NA | NA | NA | NA | NA | NA |
| Rosenberg..................... | 28.7 | 871 | 0.0 | 216 | NA | NA | NA | NA | NA | NA | NA |
| Round Rock .................. | 158.1 | 1 630 | 6.2 | 790 | 47.2 | 83.8 | 35.1 | 95.7 | 36.42 | 1 998 | 2 584 |
| Rowlett....................... | 164.0 | 2 953 | 38.1 | NA | 42.1 | 82.8 | 30.8 | 94.2 | 40.06 | 2 710 | 2 212 |
| San Angelo................... | 81.4 | 900 | 19.8 | 912 | 44.9 | 82.4 | 31.8 | 94.4 | 20.91 | 2 396 | 2 383 |
| San Antonio.................. | 6 412.2 | 4 825 | 607.2 | 15 280 | 50.3 | 84.3 | 38.6 | 94.6 | 32.92 | 1 573 | 3 038 |
| San Juan...................... | 17.5 | 527 | 2.2 | NA | 60.1 | 85.9 | 50.3 | 96.1 | 22.96 | 624 | 4 181 |
| San Marcos................... | 136.0 | 2 700 | 20.8 | NA | 49.9 | 84.4 | 38.6 | 95.1 | 37.19 | 1 629 | 2 913 |
| Schertz ....................... | 78.2 | 2 666 | 0.0 | NA | NA | NA | NA | NA | NA | NA | NA |
| Seguin ........................ | 33.6 | 1 291 | 14.3 | 899 | NA | NA | NA | NA | NA | NA | NA |
| Sherman....................... | 4.9 | 129 | 1.6 | 395 | 41.5 | 82.8 | 32.2 | 92.7 | 42.04 | 2 850 | 2 137 |
| Socorro ....................... | 3.6 | 114 | 0.0 | 94 | 44.9 | 83.6 | 29.2 | 98.7 | 9.71 | 2 557 | 2 372 |
| Southlake .................... | 152.2 | 5 802 | 11.5 | 282 | NA | NA | NA | NA | NA | NA | NA |
| Sugar Land................... | 194.7 | 2 444 | 71.5 | 629 | 51.8 | 84.1 | 41.6 | 93.7 | 49.34 | 1 475 | 2 950 |
| Temple........................ | 91.6 | 1 571 | 3.8 | 717 | 46.1 | 83.7 | 34.9 | 95.0 | 35.81 | 2 191 | 2 551 |
| Texarkana.................... | 66.0 | 1 827 | 5.3 | NA | 41.6 | 82.6 | 30.7 | 93.1 | 51.24 | 2 893 | 2 138 |
| Texas City ................... | 84.9 | 1 912 | 0.0 | NA | 55.8 | 84.3 | 49.7 | 88.7 | 43.84 | 1 008 | 3 268 |
| The Colony................... | 85.5 | 2 063 | 27.1 | NA | 42.7 | 83.6 | 32.0 | 94.1 | 37.79 | 2 650 | 2 269 |
| Tyler.......................... | 200.0 | 2 074 | 0.0 | 773 | 47.5 | 83.4 | 37.7 | 93.6 | 45.27 | 1 958 | 2 521 |
| Victoria....................... | 143.5 | 2 306 | 9.9 | 581 | 53.2 | 84.2 | 43.6 | 93.4 | 40.10 | 1 248 | 3 203 |
| Waco.......................... | 10 174.6 | 83 247 | 2 578.0 | 1 515 | 46.1 | 85.4 | 35.1 | 96.7 | 33.34 | 2 164 | 2 840 |
| Waxahachie................... | 88.2 | 3 229 | 0.2 | NA | NA | NA | NA | NA | NA | NA | NA |
| Weatherford.................. | 63.9 | 2 483 | 24.0 | 373 | NA | NA | NA | NA | NA | NA | NA |
| Weslaco....................... | 60.9 | 1 874 | 1.3 | NA | 58.6 | 84.5 | 47.7 | 95.4 | 25.37 | 755 | 3 791 |
| Wichita Falls................ | 170.3 | 1 676 | 0.0 | 1 211 | 40.5 | 84.8 | 28.9 | 97.2 | 28.83 | 3 024 | 2 396 |
| Wylie.......................... | 70.9 | 2 029 | 38.0 | NA | NA | NA | NA | NA | NA | NA | NA |
| UTAH.......................... | X | X | X | X | X | X | X | X | X | X | X |
| American Fork.............. | 32.5 | 1 229 | 0.0 | 187 | NA | NA | NA | NA | NA | NA | NA |
| Bountiful .................... | 7.3 | 168 | 0.0 | 201 | 29.1 | 75.8 | 21.6 | 88.4 | 22.40 | 5 937 | 861 |
| Cedar City ................... | 25.0 | 898 | 0.0 | NA | NA | NA | NA | NA | NA | NA | NA |
| Clearfield.................... | 31.5 | 1 147 | 13.0 | 180 | 27.6 | 74.2 | 18.6 | 89.9 | 20.75 | 6 142 | 746 |
| Cottonwood Heights...... | 0.0 | 0 | 0.0 | NA | NA | NA | NA | NA | NA | NA | NA |
| Draper ....................... | 19.2 | 499 | 0.0 | 154 | 31.6 | 78.0 | 22.0 | 95.3 | 15.76 | 5 251 | 1 172 |
| Holladay ..................... | 12.9 | 507 | 6.0 | NA | NA | NA | NA | NA | NA | NA | NA |
| Kaysville ..................... | 0.8 | 31 | 0.0 | NA | NA | NA | NA | NA | NA | NA | NA |
| Layton........................ | 10.0 | 155 | 5.2 | 351 | 27.6 | 74.2 | 18.6 | 89.9 | 20.75 | 6 142 | 746 |

1. Based on the population estimated as of July 1 of the year shown.    2. Represents normal values based on the 30-year period, 1971–2000.    3. Average daily minimum.    4. Average daily maximum.

# Table D. Cities — Land Area and Population

| STATE Place code | City | Land area,[1] 2010 (sq km) | Population, 2012 | | | Race alone or in combination, not of Hispanic origin (percent), 2010 | | | | | Percent Hispanic or Latino,[2] 2010 | Percent Foreign born 2007–2011 |
|---|---|---|---|---|---|---|---|---|---|---|---|---|
| | | | Total persons | Rank | Per square kilometer | White | Black | American Indian, Alaska Native | Asian | Hawaiian Pacific Islander | | |
| | | 1 | 2 | 3 | 4 | 5 | 6 | 7 | 8 | 9 | 10 | 11 |
| | UTAH—Cont'd | | | | | | | | | | | |
| 49 44320 | Lehi | 68.2 | 51 173 | 711 | 750.3 | 90.6 | 0.7 | 0.7 | 2.2 | 1.3 | 6.4 | 4.3 |
| 49 45860 | Logan | 46.5 | 48 879 | 756 | 1 051.2 | 80.5 | 1.2 | 1.1 | 4.0 | 0.7 | 13.9 | 10.1 |
| 49 49710 | Midvale | 15.4 | 30 229 | 1 208 | 1 962.9 | 69.9 | 1.8 | 1.3 | 3.0 | 1.1 | 24.3 | 13.9 |
| 49 53230 | Murray | 31.8 | 48 263 | 768 | 1 517.7 | 85.7 | 2.1 | 1.0 | 3.3 | 0.7 | 9.1 | 7.2 |
| 49 55980 | Ogden | 70.2 | 83 793 | 372 | 1 193.6 | 65.3 | 2.5 | 1.5 | 1.9 | 0.6 | 30.1 | 13.0 |
| 49 57300 | Orem | 47.4 | 90 749 | 333 | 1 914.5 | 79.5 | 0.9 | 1.0 | 2.8 | 1.8 | 16.1 | 9.8 |
| 49 60930 | Pleasant Grove | 23.7 | 34 519 | 1 062 | 1 456.5 | 89.9 | 0.8 | 0.8 | 1.6 | 1.0 | 7.7 | 5.0 |
| 49 62470 | Provo | 107.9 | 115 919 | 229 | 1 074.3 | 79.6 | 0.9 | 1.1 | 3.6 | 1.9 | 15.2 | 12.0 |
| 49 64340 | Riverton | 32.7 | 40 398 | 899 | 1 235.4 | 91.6 | 0.7 | 0.6 | 1.7 | 1.0 | 5.7 | 3.1 |
| 49 65110 | Roy | 20.5 | 37 604 | 968 | 1 834.3 | 82.8 | 1.7 | 1.0 | 2.8 | 0.4 | 13.5 | 6.4 |
| 49 65330 | St. George | 182.3 | 75 561 | 436 | 414.5 | 83.5 | 1.0 | 1.7 | 1.4 | 1.5 | 12.8 | 7.9 |
| 49 67000 | Salt Lake City | 287.8 | 189 314 | 124 | 657.8 | 67.4 | 3.0 | 1.4 | 5.3 | 2.4 | 22.3 | 17.8 |
| 49 67400 | Sandy | 59.2 | 89 344 | 339 | 1 509.2 | 87.7 | 1.1 | 0.7 | 3.8 | 1.0 | 7.4 | 6.2 |
| 49 70850 | South Jordan | 57.1 | 55 934 | 645 | 979.6 | 89.7 | 1.0 | 0.3 | 3.4 | 1.3 | 6.0 | 4.9 |
| 49 71290 | Spanish Fork | 39.9 | 36 277 | 1 005 | 909.2 | 87.2 | 0.6 | 0.9 | 1.1 | 1.2 | 10.6 | 6.6 |
| 49 72280 | Springville | 37.3 | 30 621 | 1 189 | 820.9 | 86.0 | 0.7 | 0.9 | 1.2 | 1.1 | 11.8 | 6.5 |
| 49 75360 | Taylorsville | 28.1 | 60 227 | 581 | 2 143.3 | 72.5 | 2.3 | 1.0 | 4.5 | 2.6 | 18.6 | 13.4 |
| 49 76680 | Tooele | 55.6 | 32 115 | 1 133 | 577.6 | 84.3 | 1.2 | 1.5 | 1.0 | 0.7 | 12.9 | 2.6 |
| 49 82950 | West Jordan | 84.1 | 108 383 | 253 | 1 288.7 | 76.5 | 1.3 | 0.9 | 3.5 | 2.1 | 17.7 | 9.7 |
| 49 83470 | West Valley City | 92.1 | 132 434 | 189 | 1 437.9 | 55.3 | 2.3 | 1.3 | 5.5 | 4.2 | 33.1 | 21.1 |
| 50 00000 | VERMONT | 23 871.0 | 626 011 | X | 26.2 | 95.8 | 1.4 | 1.1 | 1.6 | 0.1 | 1.5 | 3.9 |
| 50 10675 | Burlington | 26.7 | 42 282 | 863 | 1 583.6 | 89.4 | 4.5 | 1.0 | 4.4 | 0.1 | 2.7 | 8.4 |
| 51 00000 | VIRGINIA | 102 278.9 | 8 185 867 | X | 80.0 | 66.8 | 20.1 | 0.8 | 6.4 | 0.2 | 7.9 | 11.0 |
| 51 01000 | Alexandria | 38.9 | 146 294 | 169 | 3 760.8 | 55.5 | 22.3 | 0.7 | 7.3 | 0.2 | 16.1 | 24.5 |
| 51 07784 | Blacksburg | 51.5 | 42 627 | 858 | 827.7 | 81.2 | 4.8 | 0.6 | 12.2 | 0.2 | 3.5 | 14.5 |
| 51 14968 | Charlottesville | 26.5 | 43 956 | 826 | 1 658.7 | 68.7 | 20.4 | 0.7 | 7.6 | 0.1 | 5.1 | 12.2 |
| 51 16000 | Chesapeake | 882.7 | 228 417 | 92 | 258.8 | 62.6 | 30.6 | 1.0 | 3.9 | 0.2 | 4.4 | 4.6 |
| 51 21344 | Danville | 111.2 | 42 996 | 848 | 386.7 | 47.6 | 48.9 | 0.5 | 1.1 | 0.1 | 2.9 | 3.2 |
| 51 35000 | Hampton | 133.2 | 136 836 | 185 | 1 027.3 | 43.1 | 50.8 | 1.4 | 3.1 | 0.2 | 4.5 | 5.3 |
| 51 35624 | Harrisonburg | 45.1 | 50 981 | 716 | 1 130.4 | 74.3 | 6.9 | 0.4 | 4.4 | 0.2 | 15.7 | 14.1 |
| 51 44984 | Leesburg | 32.1 | 45 936 | 800 | 1 431.0 | 65.6 | 10.5 | 0.7 | 8.5 | 0.1 | 17.4 | 19.5 |
| 51 47672 | Lynchburg | 127.2 | 77 113 | 424 | 606.2 | 64.6 | 30.5 | 0.8 | 2.8 | 0.1 | 3.0 | 4.5 |
| 51 48952 | Manassas | 25.6 | 40 605 | 892 | 1 586.1 | 49.7 | 14.5 | 0.7 | 5.7 | 0.2 | 31.4 | 24.5 |
| 51 56000 | Newport News | 178.0 | 180 726 | 130 | 1 015.3 | 48.6 | 41.9 | 1.3 | 3.8 | 0.3 | 7.5 | 7.0 |
| 51 57000 | Norfolk | 140.2 | 245 782 | 79 | 1 753.1 | 46.6 | 43.9 | 1.2 | 4.3 | 0.3 | 6.6 | 6.8 |
| 51 61832 | Petersburg | 59.4 | 31 973 | 1 140 | 538.3 | 16.2 | 79.7 | 0.8 | 1.0 | 0.1 | 3.8 | 3.4 |
| 51 64000 | Portsmouth | 87.2 | 96 470 | 302 | 1 106.3 | 42.1 | 54.2 | 1.2 | 1.6 | 0.2 | 3.1 | 2.9 |
| 51 67000 | Richmond | 154.9 | 210 309 | 102 | 1 357.7 | 40.4 | 51.2 | 0.8 | 2.9 | 0.1 | 6.3 | 7.1 |
| 51 68000 | Roanoke | 110.2 | 97 469 | 300 | 884.5 | 63.9 | 29.8 | 0.7 | 2.1 | 0.1 | 5.5 | 6.4 |
| 51 76432 | Suffolk | 1 036.4 | 85 181 | 363 | 82.2 | 52.4 | 43.5 | 0.8 | 2.2 | 0.1 | 2.9 | 2.7 |
| 51 82000 | Virginia Beach | 645.0 | 447 021 | 39 | 693.1 | 67.2 | 20.6 | 1.0 | 7.5 | 0.3 | 6.6 | 8.7 |
| 51 86720 | Winchester | 23.9 | 26 881 | 1 352 | 1 124.7 | 71.1 | 12.2 | 0.5 | 2.8 | 0.1 | 15.4 | 11.2 |
| 53 00000 | WASHINGTON | 172 119.0 | 6 897 012 | X | 40.1 | 75.8 | 4.5 | 2.5 | 8.7 | 1.0 | 11.2 | 12.8 |
| 53 03180 | Auburn | 76.7 | 73 505 | 445 | 958.3 | 69.1 | 6.3 | 3.3 | 10.7 | 2.2 | 12.9 | 19.0 |
| 53 05210 | Bellevue | 82.8 | 126 439 | 202 | 1 527.0 | 62.2 | 2.8 | 0.8 | 30.0 | 0.4 | 7.0 | 32.1 |
| 53 05280 | Bellingham | 70.1 | 82 234 | 382 | 1 173.1 | 84.7 | 2.1 | 2.3 | 6.8 | 0.5 | 7.0 | 10.4 |
| 53 07380 | Bothell | 31.4 | 34 651 | 1 057 | 1 103.5 | 78.6 | 2.3 | 1.3 | 12.2 | 0.5 | 8.7 | 14.2 |
| 53 07695 | Bremerton | 73.6 | 39 251 | 928 | 533.3 | 75.0 | 8.7 | 3.5 | 7.8 | 2.0 | 9.6 | 8.1 |
| 53 08850 | Burien | 19.2 | 49 410 | 742 | 2 573.4 | 60.4 | 6.9 | 2.2 | 11.7 | 2.3 | 20.7 | 21.7 |
| 53 17635 | Des Moines | 16.8 | 30 449 | 1 195 | 1 812.4 | 61.6 | 10.3 | 2.0 | 12.4 | 2.9 | 15.2 | 19.9 |
| 53 20750 | Edmonds | 23.1 | 40 400 | 898 | 1 748.9 | 83.6 | 3.4 | 1.6 | 8.9 | 0.7 | 5.3 | 12.6 |
| 53 22640 | Everett | 86.6 | 104 655 | 269 | 1 208.5 | 71.9 | 5.2 | 2.3 | 9.4 | 1.1 | 14.2 | 17.9 |
| 53 23515 | Federal Way | 57.7 | 91 933 | 326 | 1 593.1 | 55.9 | 11.6 | 2.0 | 16.4 | 3.4 | 16.2 | 24.6 |
| 53 33805 | Issaquah | 29.5 | 32 633 | 1 114 | 1 106.2 | 74.5 | 1.9 | 1.0 | 19.8 | 0.4 | 5.8 | 20.6 |
| 53 35275 | Kennewick | 69.8 | 75 971 | 432 | 1 088.4 | 70.9 | 2.2 | 1.4 | 3.1 | 0.3 | 24.2 | 11.9 |
| 53 35415 | Kent | 74.1 | 122 999 | 213 | 1 659.9 | 53.6 | 13.0 | 1.8 | 17.3 | 2.6 | 16.6 | 26.9 |
| 53 35940 | Kirkland | 27.9 | 50 697 | 719 | 1 817.1 | 79.4 | 2.5 | 1.0 | 13.7 | 0.6 | 6.3 | 19.2 |
| 53 36745 | Lacey | 41.6 | 43 860 | 828 | 1 054.3 | 74.3 | 7.1 | 2.1 | 10.6 | 2.5 | 9.2 | 10.8 |
| 53 37900 | Lake Stevens | 23.0 | 29 104 | 1 252 | 1 265.4 | 84.7 | 2.6 | 2.0 | 5.2 | 1.0 | 8.6 | 7.4 |
| 53 38038 | Lakewood | 44.5 | 58 852 | 598 | 1 322.5 | 59.8 | 14.5 | 2.7 | 11.9 | 3.4 | 15.3 | 16.0 |
| 53 40245 | Longview | 37.5 | 36 458 | 1 003 | 972.2 | 85.3 | 1.5 | 3.2 | 2.8 | 0.6 | 9.7 | 5.1 |
| 53 40840 | Lynnwood | 20.3 | 36 275 | 1 006 | 1 786.9 | 62.1 | 6.5 | 1.8 | 19.4 | 1.0 | 13.3 | 26.8 |
| 53 43955 | Marysville | 53.6 | 62 402 | 550 | 1 164.2 | 79.5 | 2.8 | 3.1 | 7.6 | 1.1 | 10.3 | 8.3 |
| 53 47560 | Mount Vernon | 31.9 | 32 287 | 1 129 | 1 012.1 | 61.6 | 1.3 | 1.8 | 3.3 | 0.4 | 33.7 | 18.5 |
| 53 51300 | Olympia | 46.2 | 47 698 | 775 | 1 032.4 | 84.2 | 3.2 | 2.3 | 7.6 | 0.8 | 6.3 | 8.0 |
| 53 53545 | Pasco | 79.0 | 65 398 | 521 | 827.8 | 40.1 | 2.2 | 0.8 | 2.4 | 0.2 | 55.7 | 28.9 |

1. Dry land or land partially or temporarily covered by water.    2. May be of any race.

# Table D. Cities — **Population**

| City | Age of population (percent), 2010 | | | | | | | | | Median age | Percent female | Population | | | |
|---|---|---|---|---|---|---|---|---|---|---|---|---|---|---|---|
| | | | | | | | | | | | | Census counts | | Percent change | |
| | Under 5 years | 5 to 17 years | 18 to 24 years | 25 to 34 years | 35 to 44 years | 45 to 54 years | 55 to 64 years | 65 to 74 years | 75 years and over | | | 2000 | 2010 | 2000–2010 | 2010–2012 |
| | 12 | 13 | 14 | 15 | 16 | 17 | 18 | 19 | 20 | 21 | 22 | 23 | 24 | 25 | 26 |
| **UTAH—Cont'd** | | | | | | | | | | | | | | | |
| Lehi | 15.8 | 27.5 | 6.8 | 20.6 | 13.1 | 6.9 | 4.7 | 2.7 | 1.8 | 24.9 | 49.8 | 19 028 | 47 460 | 149.1 | 7.8 |
| Logan | 10.2 | 14.4 | 28.6 | 20.7 | 7.8 | 6.7 | 5.2 | 2.9 | 3.5 | 24.2 | 50.7 | 42 670 | 48 174 | 12.9 | 1.5 |
| Midvale | 9.2 | 15.9 | 11.6 | 21.6 | 12.4 | 11.0 | 8.2 | 5.7 | 4.3 | 30.6 | 50.5 | 27 029 | 27 945 | 3.5 | 8.2 |
| Murray | 7.3 | 16.4 | 10.3 | 16.5 | 11.2 | 13.0 | 11.3 | 7.1 | 6.8 | 34.6 | 51.7 | 34 024 | 46 746 | 37.4 | 3.2 |
| Ogden | 9.7 | 18.5 | 12.8 | 17.5 | 11.6 | 11.5 | 8.8 | 4.7 | 4.7 | 29.6 | 49.2 | 77 226 | 82 825 | 7.3 | 1.2 |
| Orem | 10.2 | 20.7 | 16.2 | 18.0 | 9.5 | 9.3 | 7.7 | 4.3 | 4.0 | 26.2 | 50.1 | 84 324 | 88 328 | 4.7 | 2.7 |
| Pleasant Grove | 12.3 | 26.1 | 10.0 | 17.8 | 12.0 | 9.0 | 6.3 | 3.7 | 2.9 | 26.0 | 50.1 | 23 468 | 33 523 | 42.8 | 3.0 |
| Provo | 8.5 | 13.9 | 36.5 | 18.0 | 6.8 | 5.9 | 4.6 | 2.9 | 2.9 | 23.3 | 50.5 | 105 166 | 112 488 | 7.0 | 3.1 |
| Riverton | 10.6 | 27.3 | 8.6 | 15.0 | 14.7 | 11.7 | 7.0 | 3.2 | 1.9 | 27.9 | 49.8 | 25 011 | 38 753 | 54.9 | 4.2 |
| Roy | 9.5 | 22.0 | 9.7 | 17.0 | 12.4 | 11.6 | 8.5 | 4.8 | 4.4 | 30.0 | 50.3 | 32 885 | 36 884 | 12.2 | 2.0 |
| St. George | 8.7 | 19.4 | 11.3 | 13.5 | 9.6 | 9.1 | 9.4 | 9.4 | 9.5 | 32.5 | 51.1 | 49 663 | 72 903 | 46.8 | 3.6 |
| Salt Lake City | 7.8 | 14.8 | 14.0 | 20.9 | 12.9 | 11.2 | 9.2 | 4.7 | 4.7 | 30.9 | 48.7 | 181 743 | 186 443 | 2.6 | 1.5 |
| Sandy | 7.3 | 21.2 | 9.5 | 13.5 | 12.4 | 14.4 | 12.5 | 5.8 | 3.5 | 33.8 | 50.2 | 88 418 | 87 499 | -1.1 | 2.1 |
| South Jordan | 9.2 | 25.6 | 8.9 | 13.8 | 13.7 | 12.6 | 9.2 | 4.2 | 2.9 | 29.9 | 49.9 | 29 437 | 50 418 | 71.3 | 10.9 |
| Spanish Fork | 13.0 | 27.9 | 9.1 | 18.1 | 12.9 | 8.1 | 5.3 | 3.1 | 2.4 | 25.0 | 49.3 | 20 246 | 34 720 | 71.3 | 4.5 |
| Springville | 12.5 | 25.4 | 9.3 | 17.0 | 12.1 | 9.2 | 6.8 | 4.2 | 3.4 | 26.7 | 50.2 | 20 424 | 29 466 | 44.3 | 3.9 |
| Taylorsville | 8.6 | 18.8 | 11.3 | 16.9 | 11.8 | 12.5 | 11.1 | 5.4 | 3.6 | 31.4 | 50.5 | 57 439 | 58 652 | 2.1 | 2.7 |
| Tooele | 10.5 | 25.2 | 8.1 | 15.9 | 14.0 | 10.5 | 7.6 | 4.5 | 3.6 | 29.2 | 49.9 | 22 502 | 31 605 | 40.5 | 1.6 |
| West Jordan | 10.2 | 25.0 | 9.8 | 17.3 | 14.1 | 11.3 | 7.6 | 3.0 | 1.6 | 28.2 | 50.3 | 68 336 | 103 712 | 51.8 | 4.5 |
| West Valley City | 10.2 | 22.8 | 10.6 | 17.0 | 13.4 | 10.9 | 8.1 | 4.4 | 2.5 | 28.8 | 49.6 | 108 896 | 129 480 | 18.9 | 2.3 |
| **VERMONT** | 5.1 | 15.5 | 10.4 | 11.1 | 12.5 | 16.4 | 14.4 | 7.9 | 6.6 | 41.5 | 50.7 | 608 827 | 625 741 | 2.8 | 0.0 |
| Burlington | 4.1 | 9.4 | 33.2 | 15.7 | 9.7 | 10.0 | 8.5 | 4.6 | 4.8 | 26.5 | 51.4 | 38 889 | 42 417 | 9.1 | -0.3 |
| **VIRGINIA** | 6.4 | 16.8 | 10.0 | 13.6 | 13.9 | 15.2 | 11.9 | 6.9 | 5.3 | 37.5 | 50.9 | 7 078 515 | 8 001 031 | 13.0 | 2.3 |
| Alexandria | 7.1 | 10.0 | 7.2 | 24.4 | 17.7 | 13.4 | 11.0 | 5.2 | 3.9 | 35.6 | 51.9 | 128 283 | 139 966 | 9.1 | 4.5 |
| Blacksburg | 2.5 | 5.7 | 59.1 | 12.7 | 5.6 | 5.0 | 4.3 | 2.6 | 2.4 | 21.9 | 45.0 | 39 573 | 42 612 | 7.7 | 0.0 |
| Charlottesville | 5.3 | 9.6 | 28.1 | 18.7 | 10.2 | 10.0 | 8.8 | 4.9 | 4.4 | 27.8 | 52.3 | 45 049 | 43 475 | -3.5 | 1.1 |
| Chesapeake | 6.5 | 19.4 | 9.1 | 12.6 | 13.9 | 16.8 | 11.3 | 6.0 | 4.4 | 37.0 | 51.4 | 199 184 | 222 209 | 11.6 | 2.8 |
| Danville | 6.3 | 15.2 | 9.5 | 10.8 | 10.9 | 14.2 | 13.9 | 8.9 | 10.1 | 42.6 | 54.4 | 48 411 | 43 055 | -11.1 | -0.1 |
| Hampton | 6.5 | 16.3 | 12.8 | 13.9 | 11.7 | 15.2 | 11.4 | 6.8 | 5.4 | 35.5 | 52.2 | 146 437 | 137 520 | -6.1 | -0.5 |
| Harrisonburg | 5.0 | 10.1 | 41.8 | 12.7 | 8.2 | 7.8 | 6.2 | 3.7 | 4.5 | 22.7 | 53.4 | 40 468 | 48 915 | 20.9 | 4.2 |
| Leesburg | 9.1 | 21.6 | 7.1 | 15.2 | 17.7 | 15.3 | 8.1 | 3.4 | 2.6 | 33.3 | 51.1 | 28 311 | 42 616 | 50.5 | 7.8 |
| Lynchburg | 6.1 | 13.5 | 22.9 | 12.5 | 9.8 | 11.3 | 10.0 | 6.5 | 7.5 | 30.3 | 53.1 | 65 269 | 75 568 | 15.8 | 2.0 |
| Manassas | 8.4 | 20.0 | 9.6 | 16.5 | 14.5 | 14.4 | 9.6 | 4.1 | 2.8 | 32.1 | 49.9 | 35 135 | 37 821 | 7.6 | 7.4 |
| Newport News | 7.4 | 16.9 | 13.4 | 15.6 | 12.2 | 14.0 | 9.9 | 5.7 | 4.9 | 32.3 | 51.7 | 180 150 | 180 916 | 0.3 | -0.1 |
| Norfolk | 6.8 | 14.1 | 19.8 | 17.1 | 11.4 | 12.3 | 9.1 | 4.7 | 4.7 | 29.7 | 48.2 | 234 403 | 242 803 | 3.6 | 1.2 |
| Petersburg | 6.5 | 14.2 | 11.6 | 12.9 | 11.6 | 15.4 | 12.8 | 7.9 | 7.0 | 39.8 | 53.3 | 33 740 | 32 420 | -3.9 | -1.4 |
| Portsmouth | 7.4 | 16.3 | 10.4 | 15.0 | 12.0 | 14.1 | 11.6 | 6.7 | 6.6 | 35.7 | 51.9 | 100 565 | 95 535 | -5.0 | 1.0 |
| Richmond | 6.3 | 12.3 | 18.1 | 17.2 | 11.5 | 12.6 | 10.9 | 5.6 | 5.5 | 32.0 | 52.3 | 197 790 | 204 237 | 3.2 | 3.0 |
| Roanoke | 7.2 | 14.6 | 8.9 | 14.9 | 13.1 | 14.4 | 12.7 | 6.8 | 7.4 | 38.5 | 52.2 | 94 911 | 96 922 | 2.2 | 0.6 |
| Suffolk | 7.0 | 19.1 | 7.9 | 12.0 | 14.9 | 16.2 | 11.4 | 6.7 | 4.8 | 37.9 | 52.0 | 63 677 | 84 596 | 32.8 | 0.7 |
| Virginia Beach | 6.7 | 17.4 | 10.7 | 15.4 | 13.6 | 14.8 | 10.8 | 5.9 | 4.7 | 34.9 | 51.0 | 425 257 | 437 994 | 3.0 | 2.1 |
| Winchester | 6.8 | 15.4 | 12.9 | 14.8 | 11.8 | 13.4 | 10.9 | 6.7 | 7.3 | 35.1 | 50.8 | 23 585 | 26 203 | 11.1 | 2.6 |
| **WASHINGTON** | 6.5 | 17.0 | 9.7 | 13.9 | 13.5 | 14.7 | 12.4 | 6.8 | 5.5 | 37.3 | 50.2 | 5 894 121 | 6 724 543 | 14.1 | 2.6 |
| Auburn | 7.4 | 18.5 | 10.6 | 14.3 | 13.6 | 14.9 | 10.6 | 5.5 | 4.6 | 34.4 | 50.6 | 40 314 | 70 189 | 74.1 | 4.7 |
| Bellevue | 5.6 | 15.6 | 7.6 | 16.5 | 14.3 | 15.1 | 11.4 | 7.2 | 6.8 | 38.5 | 49.9 | 109 569 | 122 359 | 11.7 | 3.3 |
| Bellingham | 4.6 | 10.9 | 23.6 | 15.3 | 10.7 | 10.8 | 11.2 | 6.1 | 6.7 | 31.3 | 51.2 | 67 171 | 80 885 | 20.4 | 1.7 |
| Bothell | 6.3 | 16.1 | 8.1 | 14.8 | 14.5 | 15.7 | 12.4 | 6.0 | 6.1 | 38.3 | 51.2 | 30 150 | 33 505 | 11.1 | 3.4 |
| Bremerton | 7.0 | 12.5 | 17.0 | 17.8 | 11.3 | 12.4 | 10.1 | 5.7 | 6.2 | 31.9 | 46.9 | 37 259 | 37 728 | 1.3 | 4.0 |
| Burien | 6.8 | 15.6 | 8.4 | 14.1 | 14.0 | 15.4 | 12.9 | 6.9 | 5.9 | 38.5 | 49.7 | 31 881 | 48 072 | 4.5 | 2.8 |
| Des Moines | 6.5 | 15.7 | 8.6 | 13.5 | 13.4 | 15.2 | 12.3 | 6.6 | 8.2 | 39.4 | 51.3 | 29 267 | 29 673 | 1.4 | 2.6 |
| Edmonds | 4.4 | 14.2 | 7.0 | 10.4 | 12.1 | 16.7 | 16.2 | 9.7 | 9.5 | 46.3 | 52.7 | 39 515 | 39 698 | 0.5 | 1.8 |
| Everett | 7.2 | 15.5 | 11.3 | 16.9 | 13.8 | 14.5 | 10.6 | 5.3 | 5.0 | 34.4 | 49.1 | 91 488 | 103 022 | 12.6 | 1.6 |
| Federal Way | 7.1 | 18.5 | 10.2 | 14.3 | 13.4 | 15.0 | 11.2 | 5.8 | 4.5 | 34.9 | 51.0 | 83 259 | 89 306 | 7.3 | 2.9 |
| Issaquah | 8.4 | 15.3 | 5.4 | 17.3 | 18.2 | 13.2 | 9.5 | 5.2 | 7.5 | 36.8 | 52.3 | 11 212 | 30 434 | 171.4 | 7.2 |
| Kennewick | 8.5 | 19.7 | 10.3 | 14.6 | 12.1 | 13.0 | 10.9 | 5.8 | 5.1 | 32.6 | 50.1 | 54 693 | 73 917 | 35.1 | 2.8 |
| Kent | 8.0 | 18.2 | 10.1 | 16.6 | 14.0 | 14.4 | 9.9 | 5.0 | 3.8 | 33.0 | 50.1 | 79 524 | 118 588 | 16.2 | 3.7 |
| Kirkland | 6.0 | 12.7 | 8.2 | 19.0 | 16.1 | 15.1 | 11.9 | 5.8 | 5.1 | 37.5 | 51.3 | 45 054 | 48 787 | 8.3 | 3.9 |
| Lacey | 7.9 | 16.7 | 10.1 | 16.8 | 12.7 | 11.3 | 10.5 | 6.8 | 7.3 | 34.0 | 52.6 | 31 226 | 42 395 | 35.8 | 3.5 |
| Lake Stevens | 8.3 | 21.6 | 8.5 | 15.8 | 16.3 | 14.6 | 8.5 | 4.1 | 2.4 | 32.5 | 50.1 | 6 361 | 28 068 | 341.3 | 3.7 |
| Lakewood | 7.4 | 15.4 | 10.8 | 14.6 | 11.7 | 14.4 | 12.1 | 6.9 | 6.7 | 36.6 | 51.0 | 58 211 | 58 163 | -0.1 | 1.2 |
| Longview | 7.0 | 16.2 | 9.3 | 12.4 | 11.2 | 13.4 | 12.9 | 8.1 | 9.4 | 39.6 | 51.9 | 34 660 | 36 717 | 5.7 | -0.7 |
| Lynnwood | 6.3 | 15.4 | 10.6 | 14.8 | 13.3 | 14.5 | 11.7 | 6.6 | 6.8 | 37.3 | 51.0 | 33 847 | 35 845 | 5.9 | 1.2 |
| Marysville | 7.8 | 19.7 | 9.0 | 14.6 | 14.3 | 14.4 | 10.3 | 5.2 | 4.7 | 34.2 | 50.6 | 25 315 | 60 024 | 137.1 | 4.0 |
| Mount Vernon | 8.8 | 19.4 | 10.1 | 15.4 | 12.1 | 11.6 | 9.8 | 6.2 | 6.5 | 32.3 | 51.0 | 26 232 | 31 754 | 21.0 | 1.7 |
| Olympia | 5.4 | 14.1 | 11.2 | 15.4 | 13.2 | 13.6 | 13.2 | 6.6 | 7.3 | 38.0 | 52.7 | 42 514 | 46 476 | 9.3 | 2.6 |
| Pasco | 11.5 | 24.0 | 10.6 | 17.0 | 12.8 | 9.8 | 7.4 | 3.9 | 2.9 | 27.3 | 49.3 | 32 066 | 59 781 | 86.4 | 9.4 |

# Table D. Cities — Households, Group Quarters, Crime, and Education

| City | Households, 2010 Number | Persons per household | Percent Female family householder[1] | Percent One-person | Persons in group quarters, 2010 Total | Institutional Total | Persons in nursing facilities | Non-institutional | Serious crimes known to police,[2] 2011 Total Number | Total Rate[3] | Rate[3] Violent | Property | Population age 25 and older | Attainment[4] (percent) High school graduate or less | Bachelor's degree or more |
|---|---|---|---|---|---|---|---|---|---|---|---|---|---|---|---|
| | 27 | 28 | 29 | 30 | 31 | 32 | 33 | 34 | 35 | 36 | 37 | 38 | 39 | 40 | 41 |
| **UTAH—Cont'd** | | | | | | | | | | | | | | | |
| Lehi | 12 402 | 3.81 | 7.1 | 9.0 | 107 | 16 | 16 | 91 | 847 | 1 753 | 54 | 1 699 | 21 781 | 25.2 | 35.6 |
| Logan | 15 828 | 2.82 | 9.1 | 20.8 | 3 529 | 502 | 160 | 3 027 | 441 | 898 | 53 | 845 | 21 577 | 30.2 | 37.9 |
| Midvale | 10 913 | 2.55 | 13.9 | 29.0 | 85 | 10 | 0 | 75 | NA | NA | NA | NA | 17 880 | 45.7 | 20.9 |
| Murray | 18 226 | 2.56 | 12.6 | 26.6 | 175 | 124 | 97 | 51 | 3 299 | 6 924 | 422 | 6 502 | 31 705 | 31.5 | 30.3 |
| Ogden | 29 631 | 2.73 | 14.4 | 27.9 | 2 061 | 1 421 | 260 | 640 | 4 835 | 5 727 | 464 | 5 263 | 48 754 | 50.6 | 17.6 |
| Orem | 25 816 | 3.35 | 9.7 | 14.3 | 1 790 | 461 | 301 | 1 329 | 2 367 | 2 629 | 50 | 2 579 | 46 289 | 24.6 | 34.9 |
| Pleasant Grove | 9 381 | 3.57 | 9.2 | 12.6 | 51 | 42 | 42 | 9 | 614 | 1 798 | 50 | 1 748 | 16 839 | 22.7 | 36.6 |
| Provo | 31 524 | 3.24 | 8.2 | 12.8 | 10 353 | 1 037 | 223 | 9 316 | 3 061 | 2 670 | 136 | 2 534 | 44 803 | 24.7 | 39.5 |
| Riverton | 10 460 | 3.70 | 7.6 | 8.8 | 45 | 14 | 14 | 31 | NA | NA | NA | NA | 19 973 | 25.3 | 30.3 |
| Roy | 12 174 | 3.02 | 12.1 | 18.0 | 124 | 115 | 93 | 9 | 801 | 2 131 | 98 | 2 032 | 21 167 | 41.4 | 17.7 |
| St. George | 25 520 | 2.82 | 9.2 | 21.0 | 1 053 | 648 | 303 | 405 | 1 206 | 1 623 | 131 | 1 493 | 43 427 | 35.4 | 25.5 |
| Salt Lake City | 74 513 | 2.44 | 9.7 | 34.6 | 4 795 | 822 | 539 | 3 973 | 14 102 | 7 421 | 647 | 6 773 | 117 630 | 32.5 | 39.5 |
| Sandy | 28 296 | 3.08 | 9.5 | 15.8 | 365 | 287 | 287 | 78 | 2 759 | 3 095 | 138 | 2 957 | 53 922 | 26.1 | 37.0 |
| South Jordan | 14 333 | 3.52 | 6.6 | 11.0 | 7 | 7 | 7 | 0 | 992 | 1 930 | 53 | 1 878 | 26 486 | 23.4 | 37.2 |
| Spanish Fork | 9 069 | 3.73 | 8.4 | 11.3 | 832 | 813 | 27 | 19 | 583 | 1 649 | 28 | 1 620 | 16 605 | 30.3 | 25.5 |
| Springville | 8 531 | 3.44 | 9.5 | 13.9 | 119 | 119 | 55 | 0 | 920 | 3 063 | 133 | 2 930 | 14 941 | 28.7 | 34.4 |
| Taylorsville | 19 761 | 2.96 | 12.6 | 20.6 | 112 | 82 | 82 | 30 | 2 682 | 4 486 | 356 | 4 130 | 35 147 | 42.9 | 19.1 |
| Tooele | 9 959 | 3.15 | 11.9 | 18.3 | 243 | 237 | 103 | 6 | 1 390 | 4 315 | 211 | 4 104 | 17 626 | 41.0 | 17.0 |
| West Jordan | 29 849 | 3.46 | 12.0 | 12.7 | 502 | 394 | 162 | 108 | 3 176 | 3 004 | 203 | 2 801 | 55 291 | 38.4 | 23.2 |
| West Valley City | 37 139 | 3.48 | 14.1 | 15.1 | 193 | 158 | 77 | 35 | 5 992 | 4 540 | 453 | 4 087 | 73 667 | 55.6 | 13.0 |
| **VERMONT** | 256 442 | 2.34 | 9.6 | 28.2 | 25 329 | 5 571 | 3 588 | 19 758 | 15 311 | 2 444 | 135 | 2 309 | 429 206 | 40.7 | 33.8 |
| Burlington | 16 119 | 2.19 | 9.1 | 35.5 | 7 060 | 539 | 476 | 6 521 | 1 677 | 3 949 | 332 | 3 617 | 23 632 | 31.7 | 43.6 |
| **VIRGINIA** | 3 056 058 | 2.54 | 12.4 | 26.0 | 239 834 | 101 333 | 30 324 | 138 501 | 198 064 | 2 446 | 197 | 2 250 | 5 279 997 | 39.0 | 34.4 |
| Alexandria | 68 082 | 2.03 | 8.6 | 43.4 | 1 827 | 974 | 506 | 853 | 3 453 | 2 438 | 179 | 2 259 | 103 650 | 21.7 | 60.1 |
| Blacksburg | 14 455 | 2.35 | 4.6 | 26.8 | 8 718 | 150 | 134 | 8 568 | 619 | 1 435 | 56 | 1 380 | 13 569 | 13.8 | 69.8 |
| Charlottesville | 17 778 | 2.31 | 11.3 | 34.1 | 2 438 | 228 | 167 | 2 210 | 1 653 | 3 757 | 416 | 3 341 | 23 982 | 33.6 | 48.5 |
| Chesapeake | 79 574 | 2.75 | 15.6 | 19.8 | 3 721 | 3 258 | 650 | 463 | 8 110 | 3 607 | 398 | 3 208 | 142 953 | 37.5 | 28.1 |
| Danville | 18 831 | 2.21 | 21.4 | 36.5 | 1 483 | 987 | 558 | 496 | 2 260 | 5 187 | 381 | 4 806 | 29 884 | 52.5 | 16.9 |
| Hampton | 55 031 | 2.42 | 18.1 | 29.2 | 4 454 | 902 | 516 | 3 552 | 5 620 | 4 041 | 247 | 3 794 | 88 773 | 40.5 | 22.5 |
| Harrisonburg | 15 988 | 2.59 | 10.1 | 27.3 | 7 583 | 681 | 378 | 6 902 | 1 164 | 2 352 | 200 | 2 152 | 20 866 | 45.4 | 35.1 |
| Leesburg | 14 441 | 2.93 | 10.5 | 21.1 | 256 | 247 | 247 | 9 | 895 | 2 075 | 146 | 1 929 | 26 105 | 29.5 | 45.6 |
| Lynchburg | 28 476 | 2.30 | 16.3 | 33.3 | 10 198 | 1 534 | 863 | 8 664 | 2 763 | 3 613 | 366 | 3 247 | 43 227 | 42.9 | 30.1 |
| Manassas | 12 527 | 3.02 | 13.8 | 22.1 | 46 | 0 | 0 | 46 | 963 | 2 516 | 342 | 2 174 | 22 615 | 45.0 | 27.6 |
| Newport News | 70 664 | 2.45 | 18.9 | 29.1 | 7 499 | 1 555 | 633 | 5 944 | 6 910 | 3 778 | 464 | 3 314 | 112 195 | 39.9 | 23.5 |
| Norfolk | 86 485 | 2.43 | 19.3 | 31.1 | 32 780 | 2 746 | 924 | 30 034 | 13 733 | 5 589 | 581 | 5 008 | 142 878 | 44.0 | 24.7 |
| Petersburg | 13 634 | 2.30 | 25.9 | 36.0 | 1 058 | 587 | 273 | 471 | 1 630 | 4 968 | 479 | 4 490 | 21 676 | 62.6 | 13.9 |
| Portsmouth | 37 324 | 2.47 | 21.7 | 29.4 | 2 541 | 454 | 454 | 875 | 5 820 | 6 020 | 577 | 5 443 | 62 530 | 47.4 | 19.1 |
| Richmond | 87 151 | 2.20 | 18.9 | 37.9 | 12 725 | 2 884 | 1 312 | 9 841 | 10 105 | 4 890 | 692 | 4 197 | 128 776 | 43.5 | 32.9 |
| Roanoke | 42 712 | 2.22 | 17.3 | 37.1 | 2 126 | 1 083 | 517 | 1 043 | 5 245 | 5 342 | 604 | 4 738 | 66 771 | 48.7 | 22.4 |
| Suffolk | 30 868 | 2.70 | 16.2 | 20.9 | 1 128 | 1 029 | 267 | 99 | 2 669 | 3 118 | 307 | 2 811 | 54 887 | 44.1 | 25.3 |
| Virginia Beach | 165 089 | 2.60 | 13.9 | 23.3 | 9 253 | 2 961 | 1 520 | 6 292 | 12 997 | 2 932 | 177 | 2 755 | 283 791 | 31.0 | 32.3 |
| Winchester | 10 607 | 2.38 | 13.0 | 34.3 | 976 | 157 | 125 | 819 | 1 188 | 4 480 | 238 | 4 243 | 17 015 | 47.4 | 29.2 |
| **WASHINGTON** | 2 620 076 | 2.51 | 10.5 | 27.2 | 139 375 | 57 844 | 22 156 | 81 531 | 264 267 | 3 869 | 295 | 3 575 | 4 436 636 | 34.1 | 31.4 |
| Auburn | 26 058 | 2.67 | 13.0 | 25.6 | 668 | 289 | 228 | 379 | 4 076 | 5 718 | 391 | 5 327 | 44 251 | 40.3 | 21.9 |
| Bellevue | 50 355 | 2.41 | 7.6 | 28.1 | 1 110 | 154 | 154 | 956 | 3 679 | 2 960 | 113 | 2 848 | 86 119 | 16.4 | 60.7 |
| Bellingham | 34 671 | 2.18 | 8.9 | 35.3 | 5 172 | 1 065 | 570 | 4 107 | 3 956 | 4 815 | 243 | 4 572 | 47 702 | 25.7 | 38.6 |
| Bothell | 13 497 | 2.46 | 9.1 | 27.2 | 321 | 188 | 188 | 133 | 928 | 2 727 | 79 | 2 648 | 23 151 | 26.6 | 42.9 |
| Bremerton | 14 932 | 2.24 | 12.9 | 37.3 | 4 255 | 428 | 350 | 3 827 | 2 287 | 5 968 | 629 | 5 339 | 23 836 | 36.2 | 19.6 |
| Burien | 13 253 | 2.49 | 11.7 | 31.0 | 300 | 209 | 119 | 91 | NA | NA | NA | NA | 23 911 | 40.2 | 26.5 |
| Des Moines | 11 664 | 2.49 | 12.8 | 30.1 | 596 | 382 | 382 | 214 | 1 138 | 3 776 | 299 | 3 477 | 20 744 | 40.2 | 21.4 |
| Edmonds | 17 381 | 2.26 | 9.1 | 31.3 | 476 | 220 | 220 | 256 | 1 013 | 2 512 | 176 | 2 336 | 29 513 | 21.5 | 43.6 |
| Everett | 41 312 | 2.39 | 12.5 | 34.1 | 4 145 | 1 706 | 404 | 2 439 | 7 953 | 7 601 | 430 | 7 171 | 66 899 | 42.0 | 20.3 |
| Federal Way | 33 188 | 2.67 | 14.0 | 26.3 | 831 | 445 | 421 | 386 | 4 500 | 4 961 | 270 | 4 691 | 57 877 | 38.1 | 25.4 |
| Issaquah | 12 841 | 2.34 | 7.9 | 30.1 | 443 | 242 | 242 | 201 | 763 | 2 468 | 84 | 2 384 | 20 931 | 13.2 | 60.5 |
| Kennewick | 27 266 | 2.67 | 13.0 | 25.7 | 1 081 | 930 | 200 | 151 | 2 865 | 3 816 | 302 | 3 514 | 44 353 | 44.7 | 20.7 |
| Kent | 34 044 | 2.67 | 14.3 | 28.1 | 1 390 | 888 | 86 | 502 | 5 566 | 5 930 | 615 | 5 315 | 62 933 | 41.2 | 25.3 |
| Kirkland | 22 445 | 2.15 | 7.6 | 36.0 | 630 | 175 | 150 | 455 | 1 546 | 3 120 | 149 | 2 971 | 35 820 | 15.8 | 57.6 |
| Lacey | 16 949 | 2.44 | 12.9 | 28.3 | 998 | 207 | 204 | 791 | 1 476 | 3 428 | 221 | 3 207 | 27 691 | 30.5 | 30.8 |
| Lake Stevens | 9 810 | 2.86 | 11.9 | 19.1 | 29 | 5 | 5 | 24 | 558 | 1 957 | 123 | 1 835 | 17 225 | 36.6 | 24.4 |
| Lakewood | 24 069 | 2.36 | 15.1 | 32.3 | 1 268 | 992 | 152 | 276 | 3 257 | 5 513 | 860 | 4 653 | 38 622 | 41.6 | 21.5 |
| Longview | 15 281 | 2.34 | 13.4 | 33.6 | 962 | 769 | 389 | 193 | 2 170 | 5 830 | 435 | 5 395 | 25 050 | 42.5 | 15.9 |
| Lynnwood | 14 107 | 2.50 | 12.2 | 30.8 | 618 | 237 | 195 | 381 | 2 225 | 6 113 | 277 | 5 835 | 24 467 | 37.2 | 26.5 |
| Marysville | 21 219 | 2.80 | 12.5 | 20.9 | 600 | 225 | 191 | 375 | 1 938 | 3 179 | 154 | 3 025 | 37 204 | 41.4 | 17.6 |
| Mount Vernon | 11 342 | 2.74 | 12.2 | 26.8 | 639 | 399 | 173 | 240 | 1 913 | 5 933 | 319 | 5 614 | 19 209 | 43.8 | 20.1 |
| Olympia | 20 761 | 2.18 | 11.3 | 36.3 | 1 283 | 942 | 415 | 341 | 2 102 | 4 453 | 267 | 4 186 | 31 010 | 25.5 | 43.3 |
| Pasco | 17 983 | 3.30 | 14.9 | 17.0 | 385 | 276 | 98 | 109 | 1 806 | 2 974 | 344 | 2 630 | 31 162 | 58.3 | 14.9 |

1. No spouse present.   2. Data for serious crimes have not been adjusted for underreporting. This may affect comparability between geographic areas and over time.   3. Per 100,000 population estimated by the FBI.   4. Persons 25 years old and over.

# Table D. Cities — Income, Poverty, and Housing

| City | Money income, 2007–2011 | | | | | Housing units, 2010 | | | Occupied Housing units 2007–2011 | | | | |
|---|---|---|---|---|---|---|---|---|---|---|---|---|---|
| | | Households | | | Families with income below poverty (percent) | | | | Owner-occupied | | | Median owner costs as a percent of income | |
| | Per capita income[1] (dollars) | Median income | Percent with income of $200,000 or more | Percent with income of less than $25,000 | | Total | Percent change, 2000–2010 | Vacant units for sale or rent[2] | Total | Percent | Median value[3] (dollars) | With a mortgage[4] | Without a mortgage[5] |
| | 42 | 43 | 44 | 45 | 46 | 47 | 48 | 49 | 50 | 51 | 52 | 53 | 54 |
| **UTAH—Cont'd** | | | | | | | | | | | | | |
| Lehi | 21 657 | 70 383 | 3.4 | 9.8 | 4.8 | 13 064 | 146.5 | 662 | 11 689 | 83.3 | 250 300 | 26.3 | 10.0 |
| Logan | 17 916 | 36 018 | 1.4 | 33.5 | 17.5 | 16 790 | 14.0 | 962 | 16 151 | 41.1 | 164 700 | 25.1 | 10.0 |
| Midvale | 22 231 | 46 449 | 1.2 | 21.0 | 11.0 | 11 764 | 9.6 | 851 | 10 901 | 47.1 | 205 000 | 26.6 | 10.0 |
| Murray | 28 416 | 57 603 | 3.5 | 18.5 | 6.6 | 19 181 | 44.1 | 955 | 18 252 | 68.6 | 235 500 | 23.6 | 10.8 |
| Ogden | 20 028 | 42 029 | 1.5 | 28.3 | 16.4 | 32 482 | 9.1 | 2 851 | 30 060 | 55.4 | 136 100 | 24.2 | 10.0 |
| Orem | 20 971 | 52 703 | 2.9 | 19.3 | 10.3 | 26 970 | 11.6 | 1 154 | 26 299 | 63.1 | 216 800 | 23.9 | 10.0 |
| Pleasant Grove | 23 096 | 63 793 | 4.6 | 14.0 | 6.4 | 9 841 | 55.1 | 460 | 9 376 | 72.7 | 241 900 | 24.1 | 10.0 |
| Provo | 16 631 | 39 782 | 2.2 | 31.0 | 18.0 | 33 212 | 9.2 | 1 688 | 31 578 | 42.5 | 213 000 | 25.6 | 10.0 |
| Riverton | 24 650 | 80 939 | 2.9 | 5.7 | 3.3 | 10 810 | 63.9 | 350 | 10 093 | 86.8 | 285 000 | 25.4 | 10.0 |
| Roy | 22 052 | 57 749 | 0.7 | 13.2 | 6.8 | 12 599 | 14.3 | 425 | 12 323 | 83.2 | 160 000 | 23.4 | 10.0 |
| St. George | 21 457 | 48 510 | 2.3 | 21.6 | 8.5 | 32 089 | 52.2 | 6 569 | 25 142 | 65.2 | 240 700 | 28.6 | 10.0 |
| Salt Lake City | 26 700 | 44 501 | 3.9 | 27.7 | 12.2 | 80 724 | 4.8 | 6 211 | 74 801 | 48.6 | 244 400 | 24.5 | 10.1 |
| Sandy | 30 213 | 77 022 | 6.0 | 10.7 | 5.3 | 29 501 | 10.8 | 1 205 | 28 106 | 80.4 | 287 600 | 23.6 | 10.0 |
| South Jordan | 28 319 | 89 383 | 6.1 | 5.4 | 2.7 | 14 943 | 92.5 | 610 | 12 908 | 84.2 | 349 900 | 25.2 | 10.0 |
| Spanish Fork | 18 183 | 60 142 | 0.9 | 11.4 | 4.8 | 9 440 | 62.3 | 371 | 8 886 | 77.4 | 206 400 | 26.0 | 10.0 |
| Springville | 21 072 | 58 797 | 2.0 | 13.5 | 7.7 | 8 927 | 42.7 | 396 | 8 587 | 76.2 | 205 400 | 26.6 | 10.0 |
| Taylorsville | 22 399 | 57 587 | 2.0 | 18.3 | 8.8 | 20 671 | 7.8 | 910 | 19 196 | 71.1 | 195 700 | 23.6 | 10.0 |
| Tooele | 21 254 | 59 385 | 1.1 | 15.6 | 6.8 | 10 646 | 33.6 | 687 | 10 228 | 71.7 | 171 700 | 23.1 | 10.7 |
| West Jordan | 21 871 | 66 899 | 1.6 | 11.5 | 6.1 | 31 366 | 60.2 | 1 517 | 29 486 | 77.5 | 229 600 | 25.6 | 10.0 |
| West Valley City | 18 601 | 53 061 | 0.8 | 19.4 | 12.7 | 38 978 | 16.4 | 1 839 | 38 159 | 69.5 | 182 000 | 25.7 | 10.4 |
| **VERMONT** | 28 376 | 53 422 | 3.1 | 21.9 | 7.1 | 322 539 | 9.6 | 66 097 | 256 711 | 71.4 | 213 000 | 25.7 | 16.5 |
| Burlington | 24 856 | 41 024 | 2.9 | 30.5 | 12.7 | 16 897 | 3.1 | 778 | 16 773 | 41.5 | 258 600 | 28.0 | 16.5 |
| **VIRGINIA** | 33 040 | 63 302 | 7.0 | 18.3 | 7.5 | 3 364 939 | 15.9 | 308 881 | 2 991 025 | 68.4 | 254 600 | 24.5 | 11.0 |
| Alexandria | 54 892 | 82 899 | 12.5 | 11.1 | 5.7 | 72 376 | 12.6 | 4 294 | 64 217 | 45.0 | 480 300 | 23.7 | 11.6 |
| Blacksburg | 17 899 | 29 785 | 3.3 | 44.4 | 9.4 | 15 342 | 12.5 | 887 | 13 439 | 31.9 | 256 300 | 21.7 | 10.0 |
| Charlottesville | 25 464 | 43 980 | 3.5 | 30.9 | 8.2 | 19 189 | 9.1 | 1 411 | 17 387 | 41.3 | 283 800 | 24.7 | 13.6 |
| Chesapeake | 29 985 | 70 115 | 4.2 | 14.0 | 5.8 | 83 196 | 14.5 | 3 622 | 78 898 | 74.3 | 271 700 | 27.2 | 12.4 |
| Danville | 18 816 | 31 011 | 1.2 | 42.5 | 20.3 | 22 438 | -2.9 | 3 607 | 18 938 | 55.1 | 88 900 | 24.7 | 13.4 |
| Hampton | 24 715 | 51 083 | 1.2 | 21.9 | 10.4 | 59 566 | 3.9 | 4 535 | 52 667 | 61.1 | 197 500 | 26.1 | 14.2 |
| Harrisonburg | 16 992 | 37 850 | 1.7 | 33.9 | 11.5 | 17 444 | 27.4 | 1 456 | 15 179 | 37.3 | 218 400 | 22.6 | 10.0 |
| Leesburg | 38 315 | 99 040 | 12.1 | 8.4 | 4.9 | 15 119 | 41.7 | 678 | 13 775 | 71.2 | 415 900 | 26.5 | 10.0 |
| Lynchburg | 22 107 | 37 733 | 3.0 | 33.2 | 15.0 | 31 992 | 15.7 | 3 516 | 28 513 | 55.4 | 146 100 | 23.6 | 11.9 |
| Manassas | 28 781 | 73 091 | 5.1 | 13.6 | 10.8 | 13 123 | 8.3 | 596 | 11 872 | 66.4 | 278 900 | 24.6 | 14.6 |
| Newport News | 25 196 | 50 942 | 2.3 | 22.8 | 11.2 | 76 198 | 2.8 | 5 534 | 69 977 | 51.8 | 204 100 | 25.1 | 13.2 |
| Norfolk | 24 357 | 43 914 | 2.4 | 27.0 | 13.6 | 95 018 | 0.6 | 8 533 | 85 076 | 46.4 | 211 600 | 28.1 | 14.0 |
| Petersburg | 19 005 | 36 289 | 0.9 | 33.7 | 14.2 | 16 326 | 2.3 | 2 692 | 12 179 | 47.9 | 119 600 | 24.9 | 12.6 |
| Portsmouth | 23 108 | 46 340 | 1.4 | 26.0 | 13.5 | 40 806 | -1.9 | 3 482 | 36 899 | 61.0 | 184 700 | 28.5 | 14.5 |
| Richmond | 26 584 | 39 201 | 3.9 | 34.4 | 20.6 | 98 349 | 6.6 | 11 198 | 83 615 | 44.9 | 204 500 | 27.1 | 14.9 |
| Roanoke | 23 023 | 37 753 | 1.3 | 32.5 | 15.9 | 47 453 | 4.9 | 4 741 | 42 892 | 56.4 | 131 800 | 26.1 | 13.3 |
| Suffolk | 28 990 | 65 351 | 3.4 | 18.3 | 8.8 | 33 035 | 33.7 | 2 167 | 30 305 | 75.1 | 254 800 | 27.1 | 12.7 |
| Virginia Beach | 31 589 | 65 910 | 4.2 | 12.6 | 5.2 | 177 879 | 9.6 | 12 790 | 164 041 | 65.9 | 276 500 | 27.2 | 12.8 |
| Winchester | 26 343 | 46 065 | 3.7 | 25.5 | 12.4 | 11 872 | 12.1 | 1 265 | 10 147 | 49.8 | 255 000 | 26.8 | 13.4 |
| **WASHINGTON** | 30 481 | 58 890 | 4.5 | 19.3 | 8.4 | 2 885 677 | 17.7 | 265 601 | 2 602 568 | 64.4 | 283 200 | 26.6 | 12.1 |
| Auburn | 27 212 | 56 677 | 3.0 | 19.2 | 9.1 | 27 834 | 66.3 | 1 776 | 26 650 | 60.2 | 271 100 | 27.8 | 14.6 |
| Bellevue | 46 943 | 84 503 | 12.7 | 12.2 | 4.4 | 55 551 | 15.0 | 5 196 | 50 255 | 57.4 | 555 100 | 25.5 | 12.6 |
| Bellingham | 24 396 | 39 299 | 2.3 | 31.3 | 10.7 | 36 760 | 24.9 | 2 089 | 33 933 | 45.8 | 298 800 | 27.8 | 12.4 |
| Bothell | 36 877 | 70 935 | 6.5 | 11.8 | 4.3 | 14 255 | 15.3 | 758 | 13 569 | 64.4 | 374 200 | 25.8 | 15.3 |
| Bremerton | 22 251 | 39 380 | 1.1 | 30.2 | 14.4 | 17 273 | 3.9 | 2 341 | 15 110 | 40.2 | 214 800 | 26.8 | 11.9 |
| Burien | 30 983 | 51 858 | 3.7 | 22.0 | 9.9 | 14 322 | 2.1 | 1 069 | 14 148 | 52.9 | 329 100 | 27.3 | 13.0 |
| Des Moines | 30 364 | 60 762 | 3.7 | 16.5 | 9.0 | 12 588 | 6.2 | 924 | 11 470 | 65.1 | 295 800 | 28.2 | 14.0 |
| Edmonds | 42 204 | 72 452 | 7.5 | 13.9 | 4.3 | 18 378 | 4.9 | 997 | 17 193 | 71.9 | 420 600 | 28.4 | 13.1 |
| Everett | 25 580 | 48 410 | 2.0 | 23.0 | 12.2 | 44 609 | 15.6 | 3 297 | 40 743 | 45.8 | 272 700 | 28.7 | 14.8 |
| Federal Way | 26 514 | 55 846 | 2.5 | 21.0 | 11.2 | 35 444 | 8.8 | 2 256 | 34 328 | 57.2 | 280 300 | 28.6 | 13.2 |
| Issaquah | 47 351 | 87 038 | 11.1 | 11.5 | 1.0 | 13 914 | 173.6 | 1 073 | 12 461 | 65.2 | 447 700 | 27.1 | 14.9 |
| Kennewick | 23 214 | 49 299 | 2.1 | 24.7 | 11.4 | 28 507 | 29.3 | 1 241 | 26 323 | 62.4 | 161 900 | 21.4 | 10.3 |
| Kent | 26 180 | 58 622 | 2.8 | 19.2 | 12.7 | 36 424 | 12.0 | 2 380 | 36 726 | 54.6 | 300 500 | 27.8 | 12.4 |
| Kirkland | 53 792 | 88 756 | 12.2 | 9.9 | 3.7 | 24 345 | 11.0 | 1 900 | 22 624 | 59.3 | 478 800 | 26.2 | 14.6 |
| Lacey | 27 608 | 59 572 | 1.3 | 16.1 | 8.4 | 18 493 | 41.4 | 1 544 | 16 832 | 56.2 | 240 800 | 26.6 | 11.9 |
| Lake Stevens | 29 335 | 73 128 | 2.2 | 11.2 | 6.9 | 10 414 | NA | 604 | 9 550 | 78.2 | 280 600 | 29.6 | 17.0 |
| Lakewood | 26 316 | 42 273 | 3.4 | 27.5 | 13.3 | 26 548 | 4.7 | 2 479 | 24 404 | 44.4 | 246 700 | 26.4 | 12.6 |
| Longview | 23 159 | 40 226 | 1.8 | 32.0 | 16.6 | 16 380 | 7.7 | 1 099 | 15 233 | 56.9 | 181 500 | 24.7 | 11.7 |
| Lynnwood | 25 366 | 47 701 | 1.8 | 23.9 | 12.8 | 14 939 | 8.5 | 832 | 14 774 | 53.3 | 320 400 | 29.0 | 15.0 |
| Marysville | 25 903 | 65 736 | 1.5 | 16.1 | 7.8 | 22 363 | 130.6 | 1 144 | 20 990 | 68.7 | 264 600 | 28.6 | 13.6 |
| Mount Vernon | 22 487 | 48 429 | 1.3 | 24.0 | 11.5 | 12 058 | 24.0 | 716 | 11 520 | 56.2 | 240 400 | 30.5 | 12.7 |
| Olympia | 30 254 | 52 371 | 2.8 | 26.0 | 10.4 | 22 086 | 12.1 | 1 325 | 20 424 | 50.9 | 261 100 | 25.9 | 11.2 |
| Pasco | 17 281 | 47 252 | 1.3 | 25.4 | 19.3 | 18 782 | 81.7 | 799 | 16 691 | 64.9 | 146 800 | 24.2 | 10.4 |

1. Based on population estimated by the American Community Survey.  2. Includes units rented or sold but not occupied.  3. Specified owner-occupied units; $1,000,000 represents $1,000,000 or more  4. 50.0 represents 50 percent or more.  5. 10.0 represents 10 percent or less.

# Table D. Cities — Housing, Labor Force, and Employment

| City | Occupied housing units, 2007–2011 (cont.) | | | | Migration, 2007–2011 | | Civilian labor force, 2012 | | | | Civilian employment[4], 2007–2011 | | | |
|---|---|---|---|---|---|---|---|---|---|---|---|---|---|---|
| | | | | | | | | | Unemployment | | | Percent | | |
| | Percent renter occupied | Median gross rent[1] | Median rent as a percent of income[2] | Percent with no vehicle available | Percent who lived in the same house one year ago | Percent who lived outside this city one year ago | Total | Percent change, 2011–2012 | Total | Rate[3] | Population age 16 and older | In labor force | Full-year full-time worker | Households with no workers (percent) |
| | 55 | 56 | 57 | 58 | 59 | 60 | 61 | 62 | 63 | 64 | 65 | 66 | 67 | 68 |
| **UTAH—Cont'd** | | | | | | | | | | | | | | |
| Lehi | 16.7 | 999 | 29.2 | 1.4 | 86.7 | 11.0 | 20 281 | 2.5 | 1 027 | 5.1 | 26 569 | 70.0 | 44.4 | 13.0 |
| Logan | 58.9 | 642 | 29.4 | 5.3 | 62.1 | 23.6 | 27 757 | -1.3 | 1 225 | 4.4 | 37 129 | 72.0 | 31.4 | 14.5 |
| Midvale | 52.9 | 863 | 29.1 | 7.6 | 76.2 | 19.7 | 16 255 | -0.7 | 978 | 6.0 | 21 517 | 73.4 | 48.0 | 18.9 |
| Murray | 31.4 | 839 | 31.1 | 6.1 | 84.4 | 13.0 | 26 464 | -0.5 | 1 484 | 5.6 | 37 089 | 69.5 | 44.4 | 22.9 |
| Ogden | 44.6 | 695 | 28.4 | 9.4 | 78.3 | 12.5 | 38 174 | -0.5 | 2 924 | 7.7 | 60 839 | 66.1 | 37.7 | 25.7 |
| Orem | 36.9 | 825 | 29.2 | 3.4 | 81.3 | 12.1 | 39 488 | 2.3 | 2 231 | 5.6 | 63 858 | 68.5 | 37.8 | 17.0 |
| Pleasant Grove | 27.3 | 893 | 28.0 | 3.5 | 80.8 | 15.3 | 14 268 | 2.6 | 833 | 5.8 | 21 610 | 69.9 | 38.6 | 13.8 |
| Provo | 57.5 | 704 | 31.5 | 5.4 | 56.8 | 24.8 | 54 657 | 3.1 | 2 899 | 5.3 | 90 038 | 67.4 | 24.2 | 16.0 |
| Riverton | 13.2 | 997 | 26.8 | 1.4 | 88.3 | 10.5 | 19 069 | 0.0 | 960 | 5.0 | 24 792 | 75.7 | 48.0 | 9.7 |
| Roy | 16.8 | 826 | 24.8 | 1.9 | 87.7 | 10.0 | 18 425 | 0.4 | 1 211 | 6.6 | 25 719 | 70.4 | 45.8 | 18.4 |
| St. George | 34.8 | 881 | 30.0 | 4.4 | 79.7 | 12.0 | 31 332 | 3.6 | 2 090 | 6.7 | 54 125 | 58.2 | 31.9 | 34.1 |
| Salt Lake City | 51.4 | 745 | 29.4 | 11.8 | 75.0 | 14.4 | 102 496 | 0.0 | 5 538 | 5.4 | 148 077 | 71.2 | 41.6 | 21.8 |
| Sandy | 19.6 | 975 | 27.7 | 3.0 | 87.3 | 9.9 | 47 985 | 0.0 | 2 528 | 5.3 | 65 394 | 72.3 | 43.9 | 16.4 |
| South Jordan | 15.8 | 1 533 | 27.8 | 3.1 | 83.2 | 14.5 | 25 423 | 0.5 | 1 295 | 5.1 | 32 575 | 70.2 | 44.4 | 12.3 |
| Spanish Fork | 22.6 | 932 | 27.4 | 2.4 | 84.7 | 10.2 | 14 997 | 1.9 | 825 | 5.5 | 20 970 | 69.5 | 41.2 | 13.4 |
| Springville | 23.8 | 803 | 25.4 | 3.1 | 86.1 | 11.0 | 13 098 | 1.1 | 717 | 5.5 | 18 730 | 69.2 | 43.4 | 16.2 |
| Taylorsville | 28.9 | 874 | 32.1 | 4.1 | 82.7 | 14.5 | 33 965 | -0.5 | 1 924 | 5.7 | 43 397 | 73.3 | 46.1 | 16.8 |
| Tooele | 28.3 | 825 | 28.3 | 4.8 | 85.2 | 9.1 | 15 692 | -0.6 | 1 021 | 6.5 | 20 788 | 70.2 | 47.9 | 16.7 |
| West Jordan | 22.5 | 980 | 29.9 | 2.1 | 85.5 | 11.6 | 56 394 | -0.6 | 3 016 | 5.3 | 68 668 | 77.7 | 50.3 | 10.8 |
| West Valley City | 30.5 | 854 | 33.0 | 4.3 | 82.8 | 11.9 | 67 387 | -1.1 | 4 083 | 6.1 | 90 924 | 74.5 | 47.6 | 15.2 |
| **VERMONT** | 28.6 | 843 | 30.9 | 6.2 | 86.2 | 11.3 | 356 329 | -0.5 | 17 777 | 5.0 | 511 749 | 68.6 | 40.9 | 25.5 |
| Burlington | 58.5 | 965 | 36.7 | 14.7 | 67.4 | 17.7 | 25 081 | 2.3 | 1 009 | 4.0 | 37 097 | 66.3 | 32.0 | 27.1 |
| **VIRGINIA** | 31.6 | 1 024 | 29.6 | 6.2 | 84.3 | 12.0 | 4 209 532 | 1.6 | 247 036 | 5.9 | 6 295 555 | 67.2 | 43.6 | 22.7 |
| Alexandria | 55.0 | 1 395 | 27.1 | 9.6 | 78.0 | 15.7 | 90 927 | 2.1 | 4 214 | 4.6 | 115 699 | 78.4 | 57.7 | 13.9 |
| Blacksburg | 68.1 | 826 | 48.2 | 6.4 | 53.1 | 27.3 | 19 454 | 7.5 | 1 262 | 6.5 | 39 238 | 51.1 | 20.9 | 25.4 |
| Charlottesville | 58.7 | 967 | 33.8 | 10.6 | 67.3 | 20.4 | 22 105 | 2.3 | 1 310 | 5.9 | 37 248 | 60.2 | 33.4 | 27.9 |
| Chesapeake | 25.7 | 1 090 | 31.8 | 4.4 | 86.3 | 9.0 | 117 375 | 1.9 | 7 097 | 6.0 | 170 360 | 69.7 | 45.0 | 18.6 |
| Danville | 44.9 | 589 | 34.6 | 16.4 | 81.6 | 8.8 | 19 100 | -1.1 | 2 024 | 10.6 | 35 292 | 56.6 | 29.5 | 39.7 |
| Hampton | 38.9 | 963 | 32.1 | 6.9 | 85.2 | 7.8 | 63 959 | 1.3 | 4 988 | 7.8 | 110 084 | 65.8 | 40.1 | 24.0 |
| Harrisonburg | 62.7 | 815 | 32.9 | 8.1 | 67.0 | 26.0 | 25 277 | 0.9 | 1 726 | 6.8 | 41 930 | 52.2 | 27.6 | 25.2 |
| Leesburg | 28.8 | 1 309 | 31.5 | 2.8 | 84.7 | 9.6 | 25 610 | 2.1 | 970 | 3.8 | 30 436 | 78.3 | 54.0 | 9.3 |
| Lynchburg | 44.6 | 697 | 32.0 | 13.0 | 76.2 | 13.8 | 34 770 | -0.6 | 2 650 | 7.6 | 61 982 | 59.6 | 32.8 | 31.5 |
| Manassas | 33.6 | 1 226 | 35.5 | 7.9 | 81.8 | 13.7 | 21 906 | 1.1 | 1 374 | 6.3 | 27 416 | 75.0 | 52.0 | 14.0 |
| Newport News | 48.2 | 928 | 30.3 | 10.3 | 75.9 | 13.2 | 88 287 | 0.8 | 6 398 | 7.2 | 141 712 | 70.6 | 40.0 | 22.7 |
| Norfolk | 53.6 | 888 | 32.5 | 11.1 | 77.2 | 12.4 | 103 838 | 1.8 | 8 216 | 7.9 | 195 218 | 70.2 | 35.5 | 23.9 |
| Petersburg | 52.1 | 819 | 32.1 | 15.7 | 88.8 | 4.8 | 14 023 | 0.8 | 1 582 | 11.3 | 26 348 | 58.4 | 36.2 | 36.7 |
| Portsmouth | 39.0 | 919 | 33.0 | 10.6 | 82.0 | 9.3 | 43 818 | 1.9 | 3 616 | 8.3 | 75 801 | 65.3 | 37.1 | 26.5 |
| Richmond | 55.1 | 838 | 33.9 | 18.1 | 76.0 | 11.9 | 101 841 | 1.8 | 8 686 | 8.5 | 167 927 | 65.1 | 37.3 | 28.7 |
| Roanoke | 43.6 | 659 | 29.9 | 13.4 | 80.2 | 8.6 | 47 693 | 0.7 | 3 476 | 7.3 | 77 449 | 63.0 | 40.9 | 31.0 |
| Suffolk | 24.9 | 940 | 34.3 | 5.4 | 86.6 | 7.6 | 41 739 | 2.1 | 2 818 | 6.8 | 63 753 | 67.1 | 43.5 | 22.4 |
| Virginia Beach | 34.1 | 1 191 | 30.6 | 4.0 | 81.2 | 9.8 | 226 690 | 1.9 | 12 770 | 5.6 | 343 681 | 72.1 | 44.0 | 18.8 |
| Winchester | 50.2 | 906 | 29.1 | 9.0 | 72.6 | 20.0 | NA | NA | NA | NA | 21 087 | 67.1 | 39.9 | 28.5 |
| **WASHINGTON** | 35.6 | 923 | 29.8 | 6.6 | 82.3 | 12.6 | 3 481 463 | 0.2 | 284 170 | 8.2 | 5 269 197 | 65.9 | 38.9 | 25.4 |
| Auburn | 39.8 | 924 | 32.1 | 7.6 | 81.1 | 12.9 | 35 749 | 0.9 | 2 555 | 7.1 | 53 369 | 67.5 | 40.5 | 24.0 |
| Bellevue | 42.6 | 1 311 | 25.2 | 5.8 | 79.7 | 13.8 | 68 696 | 1.7 | 4 057 | 5.9 | 98 934 | 67.8 | 43.6 | 20.7 |
| Bellingham | 54.2 | 837 | 35.0 | 10.5 | 74.2 | 13.3 | 43 659 | -0.3 | 3 084 | 7.1 | 69 329 | 66.2 | 29.7 | 28.8 |
| Bothell | 35.6 | 1 218 | 29.2 | 5.2 | 84.8 | 12.7 | 19 519 | 0.5 | 1 245 | 6.4 | 26 021 | 70.8 | 45.1 | 21.8 |
| Bremerton | 59.8 | 834 | 34.1 | 14.2 | 71.4 | 18.1 | 15 986 | -2.1 | 1 444 | 9.0 | 31 096 | 65.2 | 29.7 | 33.7 |
| Burien | 47.1 | 900 | 31.5 | 8.7 | 80.5 | 15.5 | 18 076 | 1.0 | 1 330 | 7.4 | 27 032 | 69.3 | 42.2 | 24.6 |
| Des Moines | 34.9 | 966 | 29.4 | 5.8 | 82.6 | 12.5 | 15 731 | 0.5 | 1 312 | 8.3 | 23 873 | 64.1 | 40.4 | 25.6 |
| Edmonds | 28.1 | 964 | 29.4 | 3.3 | 87.0 | 10.3 | 21 793 | 0.7 | 1 495 | 6.9 | 32 896 | 66.3 | 40.5 | 25.9 |
| Everett | 54.2 | 923 | 30.8 | 10.0 | 74.7 | 15.7 | 52 312 | 0.4 | 4 468 | 8.5 | 81 487 | 68.8 | 38.9 | 24.4 |
| Federal Way | 42.8 | 972 | 33.6 | 8.1 | 79.9 | 12.3 | 49 369 | 0.9 | 3 743 | 7.6 | 69 267 | 68.4 | 41.6 | 22.6 |
| Issaquah | 34.8 | 1 394 | 27.8 | 5.5 | 81.3 | 15.4 | 18 284 | 1.9 | 835 | 4.6 | 22 989 | 70.3 | 47.3 | 23.6 |
| Kennewick | 37.6 | 733 | 29.8 | 5.7 | 78.9 | 14.1 | 40 172 | 1.5 | 3 160 | 7.9 | 53 108 | 66.0 | 41.2 | 24.0 |
| Kent | 45.4 | 984 | 31.8 | 7.6 | 80.4 | 13.4 | 65 043 | 1.4 | 4 443 | 6.8 | 77 561 | 70.3 | 43.7 | 20.4 |
| Kirkland | 40.7 | 1 345 | 24.6 | 4.3 | 79.5 | 15.3 | 31 847 | 1.4 | 1 879 | 5.9 | 40 847 | 74.6 | 50.8 | 17.5 |
| Lacey | 43.8 | 1 051 | 28.5 | 5.4 | 76.2 | 18.3 | 19 607 | -2.0 | 1 483 | 7.6 | 32 186 | 62.3 | 35.9 | 28.6 |
| Lake Stevens | 21.8 | 1 254 | 28.0 | 1.6 | 86.5 | 10.9 | 14 496 | 1.9 | 675 | 4.7 | 20 433 | 73.7 | 44.8 | 18.0 |
| Lakewood | 55.6 | 800 | 32.3 | 10.0 | 76.1 | 18.5 | 24 837 | -1.2 | 2 282 | 9.2 | 46 992 | 60.7 | 31.3 | 31.6 |
| Longview | 43.1 | 665 | 37.7 | 11.7 | 80.1 | 8.8 | 15 124 | -0.3 | 1 622 | 10.7 | 28 832 | 57.3 | 30.2 | 37.3 |
| Lynnwood | 46.7 | 951 | 34.9 | 9.7 | 81.8 | 12.7 | 19 617 | 0.4 | 1 484 | 7.6 | 29 328 | 66.4 | 38.9 | 27.4 |
| Marysville | 31.3 | 1 078 | 31.8 | 4.3 | 81.8 | 13.0 | 30 040 | 1.3 | 1 877 | 6.2 | 44 425 | 69.5 | 41.5 | 22.0 |
| Mount Vernon | 43.8 | 865 | 32.3 | 6.2 | 79.3 | 11.3 | 15 121 | -0.6 | 1 278 | 8.5 | 23 197 | 62.2 | 34.8 | 30.4 |
| Olympia | 49.1 | 880 | 31.2 | 9.6 | 75.9 | 15.8 | 24 470 | -2.0 | 1 706 | 7.0 | 37 733 | 68.5 | 39.6 | 26.6 |
| Pasco | 35.1 | 698 | 31.8 | 8.1 | 82.7 | 9.3 | 27 474 | -0.4 | 2 542 | 9.3 | 38 721 | 66.0 | 39.4 | 23.3 |

1. $2,000 represents $2,000 or more.  2. 50.0 represents 50 percent or more.  3. Percent of civilian labor force.  4. Persons 16 years old and over.

| City | Value of residential construction authorized by building permits, 2011 | | | Wholesale trade,[1] 2007 | | | | Retail trade,[2] 2007 | | | |
|---|---|---|---|---|---|---|---|---|---|---|---|
| | New construction ($1,000) | Number of housing units | Percent single family | Number of establishments | Number of employees | Sales (mil dol) | Annual payroll (mil dol) | Number of establishments | Number of employees | Sales (mil dol) | Annual payroll (mil dol) |
| | 69 | 70 | 71 | 72 | 73 | 74 | 75 | 76 | 77 | 78 | 79 |
| **UTAH—Cont'd** | | | | | | | | | | | |
| Lehi | 90 249 | 401 | 100.0 | 19 | 148 | 57.3 | 6.3 | 72 | 2 005 | 596.4 | 61.9 |
| Logan | 11 571 | 89 | 62.9 | 69 | 591 | 315.1 | 24.1 | 247 | 3 611 | 709.3 | 63.1 |
| Midvale | 49 687 | 602 | 23.6 | 56 | 664 | 287.1 | 29.3 | 146 | 2 108 | 629.0 | 47.3 |
| Murray | 46 323 | 309 | 13.3 | 114 | 1 184 | 449.2 | 53.5 | 351 | 6 832 | 2 046.1 | 187.2 |
| Ogden | 3 362 | 30 | 100.0 | 126 | 1 276 | 696.7 | 51.0 | 356 | 4 207 | 1 018.2 | 96.1 |
| Orem | 31 392 | 187 | 48.1 | 134 | 1 447 | 569.2 | 59.8 | 464 | 8 311 | 1 734.3 | 165.6 |
| Pleasant Grove | 17 982 | 61 | 83.6 | 21 | 71 | 32.9 | 2.8 | 50 | 855 | 215.6 | 16.9 |
| Provo | 21 710 | 103 | 72.8 | 66 | 1 478 | 619.5 | 87.6 | 316 | 5 033 | 1 202.5 | 103.6 |
| Riverton | 29 312 | 163 | 74.2 | 19 | 70 | 31.8 | 2.8 | 53 | 725 | 167.7 | 15.8 |
| Roy | 6 850 | 53 | 100.0 | 6 | D | D | D | 67 | 963 | 217.1 | 19.3 |
| St. George | 54 914 | 368 | 92.1 | 98 | 848 | 342.3 | 31.5 | 446 | 6 242 | 1 672.5 | 151.1 |
| Salt Lake City | 17 722 | 118 | 23.7 | 567 | 9 776 | 7 486.3 | 475.7 | 972 | 15 888 | 4 213.6 | 398.1 |
| Sandy | 19 848 | 92 | 93.5 | 138 | 1 487 | 428.8 | 54.9 | 380 | 6 843 | 2 042.0 | 169.2 |
| South Jordan | 137 510 | 651 | 100.0 | 39 | 707 | 577.2 | 53.8 | 85 | 2 045 | 543.5 | 46.7 |
| Spanish Fork | 18 981 | 82 | 100.0 | 19 | 692 | 232.4 | 17.2 | 76 | 998 | 202.7 | 16.3 |
| Springville | 11 575 | 66 | 75.8 | 27 | 684 | 213.2 | 30.7 | 71 | 1 213 | 303.6 | 25.4 |
| Taylorsville | 5 618 | 22 | 100.0 | 18 | D | D | D | 107 | 1 934 | 457.1 | 41.0 |
| Tooele | 3 193 | 22 | 100.0 | 8 | D | D | D | 75 | 1 391 | 366.6 | 31.6 |
| West Jordan | 47 025 | 319 | 49.5 | 61 | 1 351 | 824.0 | 63.4 | 203 | 4 672 | 931.6 | 83.8 |
| West Valley City | 16 362 | 171 | 52.0 | 154 | 3 351 | 2 250.8 | 191.7 | 299 | 5 823 | 1 563.7 | 145.7 |
| **VERMONT** | 221 336 | 1 299 | 62.0 | 762 | 9 852 | 5 121.7 | 424.8 | 3 852 | 40 416 | 9 310.1 | 938.7 |
| Burlington | 306 | 2 | 100.0 | 47 | 561 | 418.2 | 29.0 | 252 | 3 435 | 575.2 | 71.5 |
| **VIRGINIA** | 3 390 840 | 23 297 | 67.1 | 6 502 | 98 304 | 60 513.4 | 4 787.4 | 29 633 | 431 634 | 105 663.3 | 9 991.9 |
| Alexandria | 124 862 | 759 | 13.8 | 91 | 1 262 | 525.7 | 65.2 | 528 | 8 052 | 2 353.8 | 232.5 |
| Blacksburg | 8 267 | 36 | 100.0 | 12 | 71 | 20.7 | 4.2 | 109 | 1 271 | 212.4 | 19.8 |
| Charlottesville | 14 801 | 146 | 33.6 | 55 | 473 | 203.4 | 20.4 | 349 | 3 880 | 699.4 | 78.1 |
| Chesapeake | 184 508 | 1 044 | 62.5 | 239 | 3 428 | 2 123.3 | 156.1 | 869 | 16 523 | 3 977.8 | 345.5 |
| Danville | 2 716 | 24 | 100.0 | 55 | 462 | 204.1 | 18.8 | 330 | 4 395 | 892.2 | 81.8 |
| Hampton | 34 204 | 442 | 37.1 | 60 | 800 | 288.9 | 33.5 | 436 | 7 295 | 1 805.7 | 162.3 |
| Harrisonburg | 4 360 | 29 | 100.0 | 55 | 1 033 | 378.5 | 42.7 | 376 | 6 265 | 1 465.3 | 158.1 |
| Leesburg | NA | NA | NA | 21 | 128 | 55.4 | 8.4 | 266 | 4 750 | 1 238.4 | 112.5 |
| Lynchburg | 12 931 | 61 | 100.0 | 82 | 1 125 | 541.5 | 43.2 | 419 | 7 266 | 1 665.1 | 151.2 |
| Manassas | 4 776 | 44 | 100.0 | 44 | D | D | D | 187 | 2 635 | 921.2 | 85.3 |
| Newport News | 37 107 | 785 | 18.6 | 116 | 1 470 | 902.0 | 68.5 | 727 | 10 894 | 2 431.3 | 233.8 |
| Norfolk | 46 348 | 519 | 43.4 | 250 | 8 577 | 3 280.4 | 247.2 | 975 | 13 764 | 2 724.1 | 293.5 |
| Petersburg | 1 179 | 10 | 100.0 | 29 | 647 | 356.1 | 19.0 | 155 | 1 569 | 324.2 | 37.5 |
| Portsmouth | 26 995 | 153 | 100.0 | 48 | 611 | 173.6 | 27.4 | 296 | 3 428 | 682.1 | 75.7 |
| Richmond | 40 144 | 343 | 26.8 | 289 | 4 408 | 2 843.3 | 231.1 | 883 | 9 029 | 1 922.8 | 211.6 |
| Roanoke | 7 947 | 52 | 88.5 | 198 | 3 098 | 2 233.6 | 130.4 | 588 | 9 765 | 2 039.8 | 215.4 |
| Suffolk | 48 746 | 278 | 95.3 | 50 | 1 105 | 715.8 | 55.7 | 228 | 3 174 | 820.3 | 70.4 |
| Virginia Beach | 153 303 | 1 479 | 36.2 | 374 | 5 069 | 2 835.1 | 207.4 | 1 625 | 25 639 | 5 579.9 | 568.5 |
| Winchester | 7 220 | 32 | 81.3 | 30 | D | D | D | 307 | 4 695 | 998.7 | 101.1 |
| **WASHINGTON** | 4 036 365 | 20 864 | 63.1 | 8 181 | 111 294 | 76 791.0 | 5 557.6 | 23 075 | 328 053 | 92 968.5 | 8 585.3 |
| Auburn | 67 004 | 451 | 48.1 | 175 | 4 037 | 3 732.6 | 196.9 | 294 | 5 123 | 1 417.2 | 141.6 |
| Bellevue | 36 872 | 134 | 50.7 | 345 | 3 999 | 3 754.5 | 279.3 | 729 | 13 684 | 4 141.0 | 407.3 |
| Bellingham | 28 048 | 200 | 40.5 | 145 | 1 746 | 776.8 | 79.3 | 552 | 8 450 | 1 944.6 | 200.3 |
| Bothell | 37 436 | 110 | 95.5 | 76 | 1 391 | 1 148.6 | 115.3 | 107 | 1 602 | 505.5 | 43.1 |
| Bremerton | 11 742 | 100 | 29.0 | 25 | 281 | 177.4 | 10.9 | 153 | 2 230 | 696.4 | 67.9 |
| Burien | 15 049 | 55 | 100.0 | 20 | 88 | 15.5 | 3.6 | 154 | 2 070 | 586.8 | 57.8 |
| Des Moines | 2 651 | 9 | 100.0 | 12 | 131 | 113.0 | 21.8 | 52 | 730 | 177.5 | 19.1 |
| Edmonds | 14 715 | 104 | 14.4 | 38 | 140 | 197.7 | 7.7 | 143 | 1 636 | 484.2 | 53.9 |
| Everett | 25 781 | 232 | 17.7 | 139 | 2 039 | 1 436.1 | 114.8 | 481 | 7 619 | 2 079.9 | 215.7 |
| Federal Way | 15 999 | 57 | 100.0 | 59 | 562 | 421.7 | 37.2 | 285 | 4 774 | 1 261.5 | 118.2 |
| Issaquah | 32 764 | 131 | 96.2 | 51 | 361 | 299.7 | 21.7 | 167 | 3 547 | 2 352.3 | 106.2 |
| Kennewick | 64 309 | 271 | 98.5 | 60 | 594 | 344.3 | 26.5 | 364 | 5 973 | 1 404.0 | 136.7 |
| Kent | 64 412 | 263 | 96.2 | 419 | 9 140 | 7 016.4 | 463.9 | 362 | 5 401 | 1 504.4 | 155.7 |
| Kirkland | 37 991 | 117 | 82.9 | 126 | 1 106 | 645.8 | 70.1 | 241 | 5 069 | 1 591.5 | 151.5 |
| Lacey | 41 958 | 219 | 100.0 | 26 | 242 | 107.2 | 11.7 | 150 | 3 528 | 853.7 | 89.5 |
| Lake Stevens | 20 489 | 96 | 100.0 | 8 | 52 | 20.2 | 1.6 | 39 | 929 | 198.9 | 21.7 |
| Lakewood | 9 154 | 35 | 77.1 | 61 | 871 | 1 130.6 | 39.0 | 274 | 3 213 | 743.7 | 80.6 |
| Longview | 3 144 | 13 | 100.0 | 38 | 560 | 339.8 | 26.7 | 188 | 3 334 | 827.7 | 81.2 |
| Lynnwood | 2 628 | 10 | 100.0 | 87 | 921 | 332.5 | 41.0 | 445 | 8 594 | 2 053.2 | 212.8 |
| Marysville | 58 115 | 282 | 89.4 | 37 | 339 | 146.3 | 12.9 | 171 | 2 719 | 706.0 | 72.1 |
| Mount Vernon | 11 697 | 70 | 100.0 | 35 | 506 | 151.3 | 21.5 | 155 | 2 186 | 596.9 | 60.0 |
| Olympia | 36 349 | 211 | 42.7 | 46 | 351 | 209.5 | 17.3 | 387 | 5 524 | 1 335.0 | 138.6 |
| Pasco | 106 418 | 495 | 97.6 | 66 | 876 | 550.1 | 36.7 | 155 | 2 388 | 706.2 | 66.1 |

1. Merchant wholesalers except manufacturers' sales branches and offices.    2. Establishments with payroll.

| City | Real estate and rental and leasing, 2007 | | | | Professional, scientific, and technical services,[1] 2007 | | | | Manufacturing, 2007 | | | |
|---|---|---|---|---|---|---|---|---|---|---|---|---|
| | Number of establishments | Number of employees | Receipts (mil dol) | Annual payroll (mil dol) | Number of establishments | Number of employees | Receipts (mil dol) | Annual payroll (mil dol) | Number of establishments | Number of employees | Receipts (mil dol) | Annual payroll (mil dol) |
| | 80 | 81 | 82 | 83 | 84 | 85 | 86 | 87 | 88 | 89 | 90 | 91 |
| UTAH—Cont'd | | | | | | | | | | | | |
| Lehi | 50 | 53 | 10.7 | 2.0 | 110 | 1 606 | 99.6 | 56.9 | 35 | 1 720 | D | 102.1 |
| Logan | 107 | 415 | 48.3 | 10.9 | 171 | D | D | D | 109 | 6 969 | 2 130.6 | 284.5 |
| Midvale | 71 | 1 243 | 133.8 | 43.1 | 108 | 688 | 100.5 | 43.4 | 38 | 604 | 96.0 | 29.7 |
| Murray | 159 | 1 994 | 215.4 | 58.7 | 308 | 2 658 | 318.4 | 135.0 | 129 | 2 400 | 402.2 | 97.5 |
| Ogden | 133 | 499 | 59.2 | 9.6 | 258 | D | D | D | 146 | 9 325 | 2 752.7 | 374.6 |
| Orem | 210 | 555 | 103.3 | 14.2 | 385 | D | D | D | 113 | 3 629 | 780.6 | 153.3 |
| Pleasant Grove | 46 | 98 | 16.7 | 2.8 | 73 | 386 | 30.4 | 10.4 | NA | NA | NA | NA |
| Provo | 130 | 996 | 109.8 | 18.8 | 353 | D | D | D | 104 | 2 796 | 416.6 | 115.5 |
| Riverton | 62 | 148 | 10.2 | 2.7 | 77 | 243 | 13.9 | 5.3 | NA | NA | NA | NA |
| Roy | 17 | 65 | 5.8 | 1.0 | 38 | 390 | 57.7 | 20.8 | NA | NA | NA | NA |
| St. George | 271 | 675 | 99.0 | 15.3 | 315 | D | D | D | 93 | 2 305 | 465.9 | 83.5 |
| Salt Lake City | 536 | 3 371 | 920.2 | 123.1 | 1 336 | 14 855 | 2 364.4 | 1 010.1 | 480 | 24 868 | 9 175.7 | 1 203.5 |
| Sandy | 223 | 772 | 124.2 | 23.9 | 368 | 1 793 | 276.2 | 93.2 | 97 | 2 551 | 608.5 | 115.9 |
| South Jordan | 103 | 276 | 38.8 | 8.4 | 158 | 1 469 | 244.4 | 71.6 | 19 | D | D | D |
| Spanish Fork | 29 | 80 | 14.4 | 3.2 | 45 | 193 | 19.7 | 5.8 | 40 | 2 040 | 356.3 | 80.5 |
| Springville | 34 | 69 | 7.2 | 1.1 | 55 | 157 | 18.0 | 5.8 | 55 | 3 659 | 905.5 | 192.9 |
| Taylorsville | 50 | 190 | 20.9 | 4.5 | 80 | D | D | D | 19 | 699 | 114.5 | 31.7 |
| Tooele | 22 | 75 | 11.0 | 1.5 | 29 | D | D | D | 20 | 817 | D | 30.2 |
| West Jordan | 113 | 250 | 38.0 | 5.7 | 122 | D | D | D | 124 | 3 679 | 906.2 | 153.7 |
| West Valley City | 73 | 339 | 74.5 | 11.8 | 136 | D | D | D | 190 | 5 785 | 1 443.1 | 256.2 |
| VERMONT | 797 | 3 395 | 497.3 | 95.9 | 2 100 | 16 346 | 1 615.6 | 649.5 | 1 108 | 35 571 | 10 751.5 | 1 650.1 |
| Burlington | 72 | 464 | 75.5 | 13.4 | 249 | D | D | D | 33 | 1 264 | 224.3 | 65.4 |
| VIRGINIA | 9 475 | 60 502 | 12 636.8 | 2 408.7 | 27 078 | 376 172 | 66 543.7 | 26 936.8 | 5 777 | 277 456 | 92 417.8 | 12 169.6 |
| Alexandria | 229 | 2 484 | 811.8 | 127.1 | 1 166 | D | D | D | 88 | 1 483 | 284.5 | 56.3 |
| Blacksburg | 54 | 353 | 56.6 | 10.2 | 147 | D | D | D | 27 | 1 454 | D | 76.1 |
| Charlottesville | 98 | 557 | 86.5 | 19.7 | 290 | D | D | D | 51 | 1 589 | 677.1 | 79.1 |
| Chesapeake | 273 | 1 355 | 274.7 | 49.0 | 485 | D | D | D | 139 | 4 487 | 1 437.1 | 200.1 |
| Danville | 66 | 332 | 41.4 | 8.8 | 76 | D | D | D | 43 | 4 485 | 1 275.9 | 212.7 |
| Hampton | 115 | 873 | 113.9 | 24.2 | 280 | D | D | D | 77 | 2 790 | 522.4 | 122.0 |
| Harrisonburg | 80 | 346 | 68.3 | 8.8 | 150 | D | D | D | 47 | 2 824 | 746.3 | 103.1 |
| Leesburg | 54 | 240 | 66.9 | 9.5 | 262 | D | D | D | NA | NA | NA | NA |
| Lynchburg | 107 | 466 | 72.4 | 15.3 | 203 | D | D | D | 96 | 9 486 | 2 801.6 | 500.1 |
| Manassas | 59 | 230 | 41.7 | 8.3 | 218 | D | D | D | 41 | 4 038 | 1 408.7 | 340.5 |
| Newport News | 273 | 2 884 | 374.2 | 84.2 | 345 | D | D | D | 107 | 24 155 | 4 702.7 | 1 216.0 |
| Norfolk | 324 | 2 898 | 385.8 | 98.3 | 653 | D | D | D | 166 | 7 448 | 1 280.8 | 300.0 |
| Petersburg | 36 | 192 | 21.4 | 4.6 | 35 | D | D | D | 42 | 2 114 | 595.9 | 102.1 |
| Portsmouth | 93 | 383 | 48.6 | 8.5 | 144 | D | D | D | 63 | 2 360 | 652.9 | 105.2 |
| Richmond | 302 | 2 361 | 636.4 | 126.2 | 826 | 10 582 | 1 682.7 | 785.0 | 224 | 9 341 | 10 192.1 | 545.8 |
| Roanoke | 161 | 1 274 | 188.6 | 33.5 | 321 | D | D | D | 115 | 4 544 | 1 582.4 | 182.7 |
| Suffolk | 74 | 287 | 44.5 | 10.6 | 122 | D | D | D | 48 | 2 362 | 1 307.8 | 109.7 |
| Virginia Beach | 717 | 6 190 | 830.7 | 197.8 | 1 310 | D | D | D | 243 | 6 544 | 1 806.5 | 236.9 |
| Winchester | 76 | 329 | 63.3 | 12.0 | 147 | D | D | D | 30 | D | D | D |
| WASHINGTON | 10 480 | 51 196 | 10 467.3 | 1 818.7 | 19 242 | 150 367 | 23 394.7 | 9 778.0 | 7 650 | 269 851 | 112 053.3 | 13 274.5 |
| Auburn | 82 | 280 | 75.9 | 9.4 | 124 | 646 | 105.3 | 25.3 | 186 | 8 019 | 1 767.4 | 397.5 |
| Bellevue | 589 | 3 913 | 1 240.4 | 197.4 | 1 185 | 13 914 | 2 535.2 | 1 051.0 | 130 | 2 358 | 813.6 | 102.5 |
| Bellingham | 219 | 907 | 189.8 | 25.2 | 416 | 2 307 | 260.1 | 102.3 | 136 | 3 297 | 614.5 | 114.1 |
| Bothell | 89 | 326 | 91.0 | 10.7 | 187 | D | D | D | 37 | 2 063 | D | 127.7 |
| Bremerton | 70 | 250 | 34.0 | 6.5 | 74 | D | D | D | NA | NA | NA | NA |
| Burien | 72 | 329 | 119.3 | 10.7 | 90 | 553 | 41.6 | 15.9 | NA | NA | NA | NA |
| Des Moines | 29 | 86 | 17.0 | 2.6 | 29 | 91 | 7.7 | 2.6 | NA | NA | NA | NA |
| Edmonds | 98 | 311 | 65.3 | 12.2 | 176 | 721 | 103.5 | 39.9 | NA | NA | NA | NA |
| Everett | 191 | 926 | 134.1 | 30.1 | 291 | 3 107 | 403.0 | 164.3 | 136 | 29 991 | 18 143.4 | 1 933.6 |
| Federal Way | 125 | 636 | 238.7 | 22.8 | 185 | 1 829 | 147.1 | 87.5 | NA | NA | NA | NA |
| Issaquah | 77 | 361 | 92.7 | 16.4 | 169 | 3 278 | 1 038.9 | 251.3 | 24 | 1 277 | 510.4 | D |
| Kennewick | 119 | 734 | 158.3 | 22.9 | 176 | D | D | D | 42 | 612 | D | 26.6 |
| Kent | 149 | 890 | 180.4 | 28.8 | 203 | D | D | D | 264 | 19 431 | 6 922.6 | 1 279.1 |
| Kirkland | 191 | 1 074 | 337.0 | 42.6 | 403 | D | D | D | 63 | 877 | D | 40.3 |
| Lacey | 55 | 262 | 33.7 | 5.6 | 80 | 2 591 | 335.6 | 137.5 | NA | NA | NA | NA |
| Lake Stevens | 34 | 82 | 13.4 | 2.5 | 16 | 59 | 4.0 | 1.3 | NA | NA | NA | NA |
| Lakewood | 123 | 688 | 86.2 | 18.8 | 109 | 867 | 64.7 | 33.7 | 44 | 608 | 125.4 | 21.6 |
| Longview | 62 | 296 | 37.7 | 7.0 | 83 | D | D | D | 41 | 1 657 | 751.5 | 88.7 |
| Lynnwood | 106 | 448 | 138.6 | 17.8 | 142 | D | D | D | 62 | 686 | 91.1 | 23.5 |
| Marysville | 59 | 228 | 52.9 | 7.7 | 63 | 396 | 53.3 | 12.2 | 74 | 2 586 | 300.4 | 81.8 |
| Mount Vernon | 63 | 209 | 39.1 | 5.7 | 126 | 498 | 51.5 | 17.0 | 36 | 860 | 164.2 | 27.2 |
| Olympia | 117 | 477 | 127.3 | 12.4 | 297 | D | D | D | 35 | 672 | 237.5 | 29.0 |
| Pasco | 49 | 240 | 44.3 | 6.3 | 68 | D | D | D | 39 | D | D | D |

1. Establishments subject to federal tax.

Table D. Cities — **Accommodation and Food Services, Arts, Entertainment, and Recreation, and Health Care and Social Assistance**

| City | Accommodation and food services, 2007 | | | | Arts, entertainment, and recreation,[1] 2007 | | | | Health care and social assistance,[1] 2007 | | | |
|---|---|---|---|---|---|---|---|---|---|---|---|---|
| | Number of establish-ments | Number of employees | Sales (mil dol) | Annual payroll (mil dol) | Number of establish-ments | Number of employees | Receipts (mil dol) | Annual payroll (mil dol) | Number of establish-ments | Number of employees | Receipts (mil dol) | Annual payroll (mil dol) |
| | 92 | 93 | 94 | 95 | 96 | 97 | 98 | 99 | 100 | 101 | 102 | 103 |
| **UTAH—Cont'd** | | | | | | | | | | | | |
| Lehi | 33 | 551 | 24.9 | 6.3 | 8 | 18 | 1.1 | 0.2 | 47 | D | D | D |
| Logan | 94 | 2 018 | 71.6 | 22.0 | 14 | D | D | D | 163 | D | D | D |
| Midvale | 72 | 1 459 | 60.4 | 17.2 | 8 | 115 | 3.9 | 1.0 | 47 | D | D | D |
| Murray | 97 | 2 203 | 92.4 | 27.6 | 12 | D | D | D | 259 | D | D | D |
| Ogden | 195 | 3 097 | 120.8 | 33.2 | 14 | D | D | D | 270 | 3 051 | 308.1 | 118.7 |
| Orem | 127 | 3 081 | 123.7 | 36.6 | 33 | D | D | D | 214 | 3 522 | 265.7 | 102.4 |
| Pleasant Grove | 25 | 381 | 12.2 | 3.1 | 8 | 25 | 3.6 | 0.6 | 51 | D | D | D |
| Provo | 182 | 3 840 | 150.9 | 43.6 | 33 | D | D | D | 265 | D | D | D |
| Riverton | 26 | 565 | 20.7 | 6.1 | 6 | 6 | 0.4 | 0.2 | 52 | D | D | D |
| Roy | 40 | 672 | 28.0 | 6.9 | 3 | D | D | D | 50 | D | D | D |
| St. George | 193 | 4 211 | 187.2 | 55.5 | 26 | D | D | D | 302 | D | D | D |
| Salt Lake City | 669 | 16 676 | 880.8 | 264.5 | 76 | 2 059 | 203.9 | 96.3 | 594 | 6 808 | 820.0 | 267.9 |
| Sandy | 168 | 3 812 | 148.3 | 45.2 | 37 | 525 | 21.2 | 5.6 | 237 | D | D | D |
| South Jordan | 44 | 785 | 34.2 | 10.5 | 8 | D | D | D | 77 | 627 | 67.1 | 21.0 |
| Spanish Fork | 35 | D | D | D | 4 | D | D | D | 46 | D | D | D |
| Springville | 30 | 534 | 22.3 | 5.7 | 3 | D | D | D | 53 | D | D | D |
| Taylorsville | 93 | 1 691 | 71.3 | 18.6 | 7 | D | D | D | 80 | 833 | 65.9 | 23.9 |
| Tooele | 41 | 760 | 27.5 | 6.9 | 4 | D | D | D | 62 | D | D | D |
| West Jordan | 95 | D | D | D | 9 | D | D | D | 144 | 2 053 | 259.0 | 74.7 |
| West Valley City | 160 | 2 746 | 125.5 | 33.0 | 18 | D | D | D | 104 | D | D | D |
| **VERMONT** | 1 942 | 31 176 | 1 367.6 | 427.9 | 323 | 6 554 | 280.4 | 79.3 | 1 469 | 15 381 | 1 147.3 | 531.8 |
| Burlington | 138 | 2 343 | 108.6 | 34.3 | 12 | 94 | 4.1 | 1.4 | 106 | D | D | D |
| **VIRGINIA** | 15 765 | 302 446 | 15 340.5 | 4 273.0 | 2 011 | 32 788 | 2 621.1 | 713.5 | 14 942 | 203 981 | 19 704.5 | 8 418.1 |
| Alexandria | 355 | 6 961 | 471.7 | 135.1 | 32 | 574 | 41.5 | 15.6 | 335 | 2 688 | 318.7 | 134.3 |
| Blacksburg | 93 | 1 679 | 57.5 | 17.8 | 4 | D | D | D | 77 | D | D | D |
| Charlottesville | 261 | 5 617 | 303.6 | 85.8 | 23 | D | D | D | 142 | D | D | D |
| Chesapeake | 431 | 8 991 | 369.8 | 105.5 | 43 | D | D | D | 431 | D | D | D |
| Danville | 140 | 2 741 | 110.3 | 30.0 | 11 | D | D | D | 182 | D | D | D |
| Hampton | 233 | 5 888 | 233.6 | 69.2 | 27 | D | D | D | 206 | 2 377 | 206.4 | 95.9 |
| Harrisonburg | 175 | 4 284 | 168.6 | 46.7 | 10 | D | D | D | 128 | D | D | D |
| Leesburg | 106 | 2 300 | 124.6 | 43.0 | 13 | D | D | D | 119 | 1 231 | 107.0 | 45.1 |
| Lynchburg | 234 | 5 226 | 190.0 | 58.3 | 21 | 161 | 6.8 | 1.9 | 202 | D | D | D |
| Manassas | 101 | 1 307 | 75.6 | 19.0 | 8 | 42 | 4.5 | 2.6 | 160 | D | D | D |
| Newport News | 384 | 7 660 | 329.1 | 89.9 | 36 | 351 | 17.5 | 4.3 | 328 | 5 716 | 497.9 | 269.1 |
| Norfolk | 551 | 11 667 | 505.0 | 140.2 | 58 | 600 | 45.0 | 13.0 | 427 | 7 517 | 792.0 | 367.7 |
| Petersburg | 70 | 864 | 36.6 | 9.7 | 4 | 56 | 1.8 | 0.4 | 99 | D | D | D |
| Portsmouth | 169 | 2 513 | 106.2 | 28.8 | 15 | D | D | D | 174 | 3 121 | 238.8 | 108.2 |
| Richmond | 547 | 10 136 | 476.8 | 143.5 | 51 | 490 | 41.0 | 7.6 | 462 | 11 317 | 1 110.4 | 453.7 |
| Roanoke | 294 | 6 162 | 267.2 | 83.3 | 19 | 144 | 6.1 | 2.0 | 232 | 3 993 | 443.2 | 173.6 |
| Suffolk | 121 | 1 981 | 72.8 | 20.2 | 14 | 106 | 5.5 | 1.9 | 124 | D | D | D |
| Virginia Beach | 1 134 | 21 694 | 1 074.2 | 294.9 | 146 | 1 585 | 111.9 | 27.4 | 855 | 10 228 | 985.2 | 424.2 |
| Winchester | 123 | 2 343 | 104.6 | 29.5 | 12 | D | D | D | 200 | D | D | D |
| **WASHINGTON** | 15 893 | 233 235 | 12 389.4 | 3 618.1 | 2 021 | 45 093 | 4 116.5 | 1 255.9 | 15 513 | 172 010 | 16 738.9 | 6 870.8 |
| Auburn | 153 | 2 150 | 103.8 | 29.9 | 24 | D | D | D | 146 | 2 235 | 241.9 | 89.2 |
| Bellevue | 387 | 7 861 | 505.9 | 147.2 | 61 | 1 714 | 128.5 | 33.5 | 753 | 7 473 | 793.2 | 322.3 |
| Bellingham | 336 | 5 623 | 226.6 | 71.1 | 37 | 638 | 22.2 | 6.9 | 408 | D | D | D |
| Bothell | 110 | 1 457 | 82.7 | 21.4 | 5 | D | D | D | 126 | 1 156 | 93.4 | 39.1 |
| Bremerton | 121 | 1 498 | 64.9 | 19.6 | 10 | 305 | 9.7 | 3.8 | 115 | 1 864 | 182.4 | 70.8 |
| Burien | 90 | 1 165 | 57.0 | 17.3 | 8 | D | D | D | 157 | 1 217 | 142.8 | 53.0 |
| Des Moines | 43 | 788 | 38.8 | 12.6 | 3 | D | D | D | 50 | 852 | 58.3 | 25.2 |
| Edmonds | 121 | 1 482 | 75.4 | 23.8 | 8 | 264 | 16.0 | 4.2 | 186 | D | D | D |
| Everett | 332 | 4 661 | 249.5 | 71.7 | 27 | 422 | 19.5 | 6.4 | 344 | 4 847 | 537.8 | 247.3 |
| Federal Way | 235 | 3 505 | 172.1 | 47.6 | 22 | 519 | 35.5 | 10.1 | 310 | D | D | D |
| Issaquah | 113 | 1 793 | 91.1 | 26.5 | 9 | 136 | 4.2 | 1.4 | 143 | 1 635 | 184.1 | 62.0 |
| Kennewick | 174 | 2 835 | 127.8 | 35.7 | 21 | D | D | D | 217 | 2 526 | 223.3 | 78.0 |
| Kent | 259 | 3 331 | 170.9 | 47.9 | 23 | 240 | 33.0 | 6.2 | 215 | 2 101 | 153.7 | 57.4 |
| Kirkland | 187 | 3 354 | 176.9 | 58.0 | 22 | D | D | D | 286 | D | D | D |
| Lacey | 106 | 1 796 | 83.8 | 23.6 | 8 | 175 | 7.3 | 2.6 | 98 | 1 189 | 101.3 | 35.7 |
| Lake Stevens | 37 | 489 | 28.2 | 6.3 | 2 | D | D | D | 31 | D | D | D |
| Lakewood | 189 | 2 632 | 125.5 | 37.5 | 12 | D | D | D | 167 | 1 790 | 150.0 | 57.5 |
| Longview | 104 | 1 489 | 66.5 | 18.5 | 8 | D | D | D | 136 | 2 377 | 225.3 | 90.9 |
| Lynnwood | 199 | 3 384 | 200.3 | 52.1 | 11 | D | D | D | 177 | D | D | D |
| Marysville | 90 | 1 256 | 62.4 | 18.1 | 6 | D | D | D | 93 | 1 060 | 89.6 | 36.8 |
| Mount Vernon | 92 | 1 246 | 53.8 | 16.2 | 7 | D | D | D | 124 | 1 944 | 224.5 | 87.0 |
| Olympia | 212 | 3 628 | 165.4 | 52.3 | 15 | 195 | 13.1 | 3.5 | 350 | 3 914 | 444.9 | 166.7 |
| Pasco | 83 | 934 | 46.3 | 12.9 | 8 | D | D | D | 86 | 632 | 54.3 | 18.8 |

1. Establishments subject to federal tax.

# Table D. Cities — Other Services and Federal Funds

| City | Other services[1], 2007 | | | | Selected federal funds, 2009–2010 (mil dol) | | | | | | | | |
|---|---|---|---|---|---|---|---|---|---|---|---|---|---|
| | | | | | Procurement contracts | | Grants | | | | | | |
| | Number of establish-ments | Number of employees | Receipts (mil dol) | Annual payroll (mil dol) | Defense | Other | Total[2] | Medicaid and other health related | Nutrition and family welfare | Energy and envi-ronment | Disasters and emergency prepared-ness | Housing and community develop-ment | Employment and training |
| | 104 | 105 | 106 | 107 | 108 | 109 | 110 | 111 | 112 | 113 | 114 | 115 | 116 |
| UTAH—Cont'd | | | | | | | | | | | | | |
| Lehi | 25 | D | D | D | 0.0 | 0.3 | 0.2 | 0.0 | 0.0 | 0.0 | 0.0 | 0.0 | 0.0 |
| Logan | 75 | 469 | 37.0 | 9.1 | 3.6 | 6.9 | 103.4 | 8.2 | 5.0 | 9.7 | 0.0 | 3.1 | 0.0 |
| Midvale | 65 | 456 | 41.5 | 11.3 | 1.0 | 0.8 | 0.5 | 0.0 | 0.0 | 0.2 | 0.0 | 0.0 | 0.0 |
| Murray | 134 | 933 | 66.6 | 19.7 | 0.5 | 0.9 | 1.3 | 1.2 | 0.0 | 0.0 | 0.0 | 0.0 | 0.0 |
| Ogden | 140 | 1 010 | 77.6 | 24.7 | 58.2 | 26.8 | 30.5 | 3.7 | 5.7 | 1.0 | 0.0 | 10.1 | 0.3 |
| Orem | 142 | 851 | 60.2 | 18.6 | 0.6 | 1.6 | 92.1 | 0.3 | 0.6 | 83.3 | 0.0 | 0.2 | 0.0 |
| Pleasant Grove | 32 | 119 | 11.5 | 2.6 | 479.2 | 0.1 | 1.1 | 0.0 | 0.0 | 1.0 | 0.0 | 0.1 | 0.0 |
| Provo | 114 | 598 | 42.9 | 11.7 | 3.6 | 4.4 | 51.3 | 8.7 | 6.0 | 9.1 | 0.0 | 14.2 | 0.0 |
| Riverton | 35 | 148 | 11.1 | 2.9 | 0.0 | 0.0 | 0.0 | 0.0 | 0.0 | 0.0 | 0.0 | 0.0 | 0.0 |
| Roy | 37 | 213 | 14.3 | 4.0 | 3.6 | 0.1 | 0.0 | 0.0 | 0.0 | 0.0 | 0.0 | 0.0 | 0.0 |
| St. George | 132 | 702 | 63.5 | 17.5 | 0.2 | 1.2 | 20.7 | 1.0 | 0.6 | 1.1 | 0.0 | 1.9 | 0.0 |
| Salt Lake City | 465 | 3 690 | 278.8 | 85.8 | 529.1 | 104.3 | 1 688.1 | 391.1 | 103.5 | 483.1 | 10.2 | 46.2 | 71.8 |
| Sandy | 141 | 1 460 | 89.7 | 45.6 | 2.8 | 1.1 | 2.8 | 0.0 | 0.0 | 0.8 | 0.0 | 0.4 | 0.0 |
| South Jordan | 36 | 193 | 14.3 | 4.3 | 0.6 | 0.3 | 0.6 | 0.0 | 0.0 | 0.6 | 0.0 | 0.0 | 0.0 |
| Spanish Fork | 35 | D | D | D | 0.4 | 0.0 | 0.6 | 0.0 | 0.0 | 0.0 | 0.0 | 0.0 | 0.0 |
| Springville | 24 | D | D | D | 5.1 | 0.1 | 1.0 | 0.0 | 0.0 | 1.0 | 0.0 | 0.0 | 0.0 |
| Taylorsville | 42 | 178 | 13.5 | 4.2 | 0.0 | 0.3 | 3.8 | 0.0 | 0.0 | 0.5 | 0.0 | 0.4 | 2.8 |
| Tooele | 37 | D | D | D | 24.6 | 0.9 | 3.0 | 0.0 | 0.0 | 0.0 | 0.0 | 1.3 | 0.0 |
| West Jordan | 96 | 720 | 57.2 | 19.0 | 0.1 | 0.5 | 0.6 | 0.0 | 0.0 | 0.0 | 0.0 | 0.5 | 0.0 |
| West Valley City | 134 | 750 | 76.1 | 20.8 | 4.5 | 3.1 | 5.8 | -0.1 | 0.0 | 0.0 | 0.0 | 5.2 | 0.3 |
| VERMONT | 1 107 | 4 439 | 389.2 | 104.8 | 711.3 | 220.4 | 2 379.9 | 1 088.4 | 192.4 | 161.1 | 0.4 | 72.4 | 34.9 |
| Burlington | 64 | 323 | 20.9 | 7.6 | 433.8 | 10.0 | 196.5 | 127.4 | 3.6 | 3.1 | 0.0 | 17.9 | 0.8 |
| VIRGINIA | 11 978 | 76 121 | 6 677.6 | 2 125.9 | 40 377.7 | 17 960.0 | 12 227.5 | 5 483.9 | 1 142.6 | 427.2 | 277.1 | 592.7 | 273.7 |
| Alexandria | 254 | 2 071 | 181.2 | 63.9 | 834.3 | 721.1 | 348.5 | 17.6 | 2.8 | 22.7 | 200.3 | 27.8 | 5.0 |
| Blacksburg | 48 | D | D | D | 45.3 | 26.0 | 175.0 | 44.1 | 0.0 | 17.6 | 0.0 | 1.8 | 0.0 |
| Charlottesville | 113 | 929 | 66.5 | 23.2 | 46.9 | 25.3 | 338.4 | 236.9 | 0.2 | 13.5 | -0.5 | 8.0 | 0.0 |
| Chesapeake | 375 | 2 791 | 314.0 | 86.9 | 299.0 | 54.2 | 20.9 | 0.0 | 0.0 | 2.1 | 0.0 | 14.8 | 0.0 |
| Danville | 108 | D | D | D | 0.5 | 4.1 | 15.2 | 1.7 | 1.5 | 0.7 | 0.0 | 7.4 | 0.0 |
| Hampton | 165 | 1 046 | 76.5 | 25.7 | 482.7 | 252.2 | 132.1 | 1.6 | 0.2 | 1.1 | 0.0 | 25.1 | -0.1 |
| Harrisonburg | 107 | 590 | 49.3 | 15.6 | 21.3 | 2.4 | 16.9 | 0.6 | 0.1 | 1.6 | 0.0 | 5.4 | 5.0 |
| Leesburg | 81 | 483 | 37.6 | 11.8 | 1 640.9 | 28.7 | 23.2 | 0.9 | 0.0 | 2.1 | 0.0 | 10.1 | 0.0 |
| Lynchburg | 135 | 852 | 55.1 | 19.2 | 22.1 | 18.8 | 20.7 | 0.9 | 3.1 | 0.7 | 0.0 | 6.5 | 0.0 |
| Manassas | 114 | 698 | 58.5 | 18.1 | 746.3 | 46.6 | 37.3 | 22.2 | 2.2 | 7.2 | 0.0 | 0.0 | 0.0 |
| Newport News | 276 | 1 885 | 133.5 | 46.0 | 3 012.1 | 193.2 | 54.0 | 5.9 | 4.2 | 2.1 | 2.6 | 25.7 | 0.0 |
| Norfolk | 351 | 2 706 | 258.2 | 86.8 | 2 099.7 | 51.2 | 125.3 | 18.2 | 13.4 | 4.4 | 0.2 | 42.2 | 0.0 |
| Petersburg | 69 | 520 | 35.2 | 12.3 | 0.9 | 3.5 | 27.1 | 0.1 | 0.0 | 0.3 | 0.0 | 6.1 | 0.5 |
| Portsmouth | 154 | 1 437 | 105.2 | 39.0 | 168.1 | 90.2 | 29.0 | 1.5 | 0.0 | 0.0 | 0.0 | 22.4 | 0.0 |
| Richmond | 408 | 2 897 | 233.4 | 79.8 | 42.7 | 89.6 | 2 033.0 | 321.0 | 132.8 | 135.9 | 3.7 | 154.8 | 134.2 |
| Roanoke | 218 | 1 429 | 110.6 | 37.1 | 29.9 | 65.3 | 45.7 | 1.9 | 9.0 | 4.2 | 0.0 | 17.7 | 0.0 |
| Suffolk | 84 | D | D | D | 252.4 | 14.8 | 9.4 | 0.0 | 0.0 | 0.0 | 0.0 | 7.1 | 0.0 |
| Virginia Beach | 783 | 4 883 | 310.0 | 104.4 | 1 962.6 | 138.1 | 71.9 | 0.0 | 0.7 | 4.4 | 32.6 | 21.8 | 0.0 |
| Winchester | 73 | 491 | 35.0 | 12.3 | 2.0 | 14.2 | 5.8 | 0.8 | 0.0 | 0.0 | 0.0 | 2.3 | 0.1 |
| WASHINGTON | 9 809 | 54 544 | 4 643.2 | 1 461.8 | 5 150.5 | 4 890.3 | 14 725.4 | 7 161.4 | 1 608.2 | 1 129.9 | 45.7 | 656.3 | 259.1 |
| Auburn | 141 | 852 | 98.4 | 29.8 | 5.6 | 14.3 | 46.6 | 3.8 | 1.4 | 0.6 | 0.0 | 1.8 | 0.0 |
| Bellevue | 300 | 2 031 | 193.1 | 65.6 | 13.9 | 14.0 | 44.1 | 2.1 | 0.4 | 32.3 | 0.0 | 0.9 | 0.0 |
| Bellingham | 189 | 1 065 | 81.2 | 25.1 | 13.8 | 27.9 | 82.0 | 6.7 | 4.9 | 1.4 | -2.4 | 24.3 | 0.5 |
| Bothell | 52 | 330 | 38.0 | 10.3 | 7.0 | 3.1 | 2.3 | 2.3 | 0.0 | 0.0 | 0.0 | 0.0 | 0.0 |
| Bremerton | 56 | 294 | 24.6 | 7.6 | 70.5 | 0.5 | 26.5 | 0.9 | 5.5 | 2.6 | 0.0 | 13.5 | 0.0 |
| Burien | 81 | 494 | 36.8 | 12.2 | 0.1 | 0.1 | 0.5 | 0.1 | 0.0 | 0.0 | 0.0 | 0.4 | 0.0 |
| Des Moines | 29 | 104 | 9.7 | 3.2 | 0.0 | 1.9 | 0.7 | 0.0 | 0.0 | 0.0 | 0.0 | 0.0 | 0.0 |
| Edmonds | 56 | 261 | 19.0 | 7.1 | 0.3 | 3.4 | 0.0 | 0.0 | 0.0 | 0.0 | 0.0 | 0.0 | 0.0 |
| Everett | 197 | 1 496 | 126.6 | 48.7 | 34.8 | 6.4 | 128.9 | 2.2 | 0.6 | 27.9 | 0.0 | 64.6 | 5.1 |
| Federal Way | 128 | 661 | 47.7 | 15.3 | 0.9 | 1.3 | 60.9 | 0.0 | 0.0 | 1.2 | 0.0 | 0.0 | 0.0 |
| Issaquah | 72 | 364 | 30.3 | 9.5 | 2.6 | 2.5 | 3.0 | 0.0 | 0.0 | 0.5 | 0.0 | 0.0 | 0.0 |
| Kennewick | 118 | 652 | 47.6 | 14.7 | 0.1 | 0.4 | 14.1 | 0.0 | 0.0 | 6.0 | 0.2 | 7.5 | 0.0 |
| Kent | 193 | 1 418 | 126.4 | 37.5 | 1 475.2 | 10.0 | 2.1 | 0.1 | 0.0 | 0.8 | 0.0 | 0.9 | 0.0 |
| Kirkland | 176 | 884 | 70.9 | 22.5 | 3.4 | 4.3 | 1.7 | 0.5 | 0.0 | 0.0 | 0.0 | 0.0 | 0.0 |
| Lacey | 64 | 410 | 26.5 | 9.0 | 47.8 | 1.4 | 11.5 | 0.1 | 0.3 | 1.2 | 0.0 | 0.0 | 0.0 |
| Lake Stevens | 25 | D | D | D | 0.0 | 0.0 | 0.0 | 0.0 | 0.0 | 0.0 | 0.0 | 0.0 | 0.0 |
| Lakewood | 128 | 701 | 62.9 | 20.3 | 1.2 | 1.8 | 23.8 | 4.8 | 0.0 | 0.5 | 0.0 | 0.7 | 0.0 |
| Longview | 71 | 508 | 39.3 | 14.6 | 0.1 | 0.1 | 16.6 | 1.4 | 2.3 | 1.0 | 0.0 | 8.5 | 0.0 |
| Lynnwood | 122 | 956 | 87.5 | 26.8 | 1.0 | 1.9 | 23.4 | 0.0 | 5.7 | 0.0 | 0.0 | 0.0 | 0.0 |
| Marysville | 86 | D | D | D | -0.1 | 0.2 | 1.7 | 0.0 | 0.0 | 0.0 | 0.0 | 0.0 | 0.0 |
| Mount Vernon | 60 | 318 | 21.5 | 6.8 | 12.9 | 0.3 | 9.2 | 0.8 | 0.1 | 1.8 | 0.0 | 4.0 | 0.0 |
| Olympia | 122 | 598 | 50.7 | 16.2 | 2.0 | 9.3 | 1 715.6 | 151.2 | 303.6 | 184.3 | 7.8 | 44.3 | 226.8 |
| Pasco | 67 | D | D | D | 1.0 | 5.9 | 15.4 | 2.3 | 3.9 | 0.6 | 0.0 | 3.0 | 0.0 |

1. Establishments subject to federal tax.    2. Includes program categories not shown separately. State totals include additional categories not allocated by city.

# Table D. Cities — City Government Finances

| City | City government finances, 2007 | | | | | | | | | |
|---|---|---|---|---|---|---|---|---|---|---|
| | General revenue | | | | | | | General expenditure | | |
| | Intergovernmental | | | Taxes | | | | | Per capita[1] (dollars) | |
| | | | | | Per capita[1] (dollars) | | | | | |
| | Total (mil dol) | Total (mil dol) | Percent from state government | Total (mil dol) | Total | Property | Sales and gross receipts | Total (mil dol) | Total | Capital outlays |
| | 117 | 118 | 119 | 120 | 121 | 122 | 123 | 124 | 125 | 126 |
| **UTAH—Cont'd** | | | | | | | | | | |
| Lehi | 41.0 | 1.5 | 100.0 | 19.8 | 538 | 176 | 362 | 33.2 | 899 | 77 |
| Logan | 54.2 | 4.7 | 36.2 | 21.8 | 454 | 115 | 339 | 47.5 | 989 | 139 |
| Midvale | 19.2 | 1.9 | 61.0 | 12.3 | 443 | 118 | 325 | 19.6 | 704 | 42 |
| Murray | 50.4 | 2.2 | 78.6 | 28.8 | 629 | 195 | 434 | 63.5 | 1 390 | 90 |
| Ogden | 95.8 | 10.0 | 28.8 | 43.9 | 531 | 231 | 300 | 100.4 | 1 214 | 274 |
| Orem | 75.8 | 4.1 | 67.1 | 38.5 | 414 | 116 | 298 | 83.4 | 896 | 267 |
| Pleasant Grove | 24.1 | 7.0 | 14.4 | 8.7 | 277 | 82 | 195 | 39.9 | 1 266 | 776 |
| Provo | 89.8 | 10.7 | 41.7 | 39.5 | 336 | 109 | 227 | 88.5 | 752 | 192 |
| Riverton | 25.6 | 1.9 | 61.3 | 8.8 | 229 | 37 | 192 | 16.2 | 422 | 124 |
| Roy | 20.6 | 1.3 | 93.1 | 10.7 | 305 | 99 | 206 | 14.4 | 412 | 44 |
| St. George | 88.4 | 7.2 | 38.2 | 36.9 | 519 | 139 | 381 | 68.8 | 967 | 210 |
| Salt Lake City | 502.7 | 20.1 | 35.2 | 190.0 | 1 052 | 556 | 495 | 433.1 | 2 398 | 733 |
| Sandy | 69.5 | 5.6 | 68.3 | 42.1 | 438 | 138 | 300 | 58.8 | 613 | 78 |
| South Jordan | 45.1 | 3.6 | 98.8 | 22.1 | 459 | 187 | 272 | 35.2 | 733 | 175 |
| Spanish Fork | 26.0 | 2.5 | 36.5 | 9.0 | 316 | 66 | 250 | 17.5 | 611 | 32 |
| Springville | 29.1 | 1.2 | 97.0 | 9.5 | 354 | 85 | 239 | 19.5 | 726 | 159 |
| Taylorsville | 21.8 | 3.0 | 69.2 | 15.5 | 265 | 83 | 182 | 20.0 | 342 | 49 |
| Tooele | 24.8 | 2.0 | 79.9 | 10.7 | 365 | 124 | 226 | 19.9 | 676 | 103 |
| West Jordan | 63.5 | 4.2 | 81.6 | 33.4 | 326 | 116 | 210 | 61.8 | 603 | 89 |
| West Valley City | 98.6 | 6.4 | 58.8 | 60.1 | 491 | 220 | 271 | 103.3 | 844 | 82 |
| **VERMONT** | X | X | X | X | X | X | X | X | X | X |
| Burlington | 92.2 | 14.9 | 20.5 | 35.9 | 931 | 672 | 259 | 94.9 | 2 462 | 839 |
| **VIRGINIA** | X | X | X | X | X | X | X | X | X | X |
| Alexandria | 590.7 | 98.0 | 60.9 | 429.0 | 3 064 | 2 220 | 807 | 593.3 | 4 237 | 287 |
| Blacksburg | 32.3 | 8.9 | 53.8 | 13.6 | 329 | 105 | 216 | 33.8 | 819 | 262 |
| Charlottesville | 198.3 | 84.3 | 76.2 | 86.3 | 2 094 | 1 254 | 827 | 181.0 | 4 390 | 202 |
| Chesapeake | 905.2 | 384.0 | 94.6 | 418.2 | 1 908 | 1 343 | 565 | 804.0 | 3 669 | 295 |
| Danville | 163.2 | 83.7 | 91.6 | 47.9 | 1 066 | 577 | 481 | 153.6 | 3 417 | 124 |
| Hampton | 551.9 | 238.3 | 85.8 | 218.3 | 1 491 | 1 014 | 461 | 511.7 | 3 495 | 344 |
| Harrisonburg | 122.6 | 41.4 | 91.7 | 56.9 | 1 293 | 539 | 741 | 149.6 | 3 398 | 846 |
| Leesburg | 54.0 | 6.6 | 71.6 | 29.8 | 775 | 352 | 423 | 55.6 | 1 445 | 34 |
| Lynchburg | 265.4 | 106.2 | 94.0 | 103.9 | 1 457 | 803 | 654 | 246.1 | 3 452 | 446 |
| Manassas | 163.7 | 50.8 | 90.7 | 80.4 | 2 271 | 1 676 | 553 | 162.4 | 4 586 | 575 |
| Newport News | 800.5 | 364.4 | 88.0 | 301.9 | 1 685 | 1 162 | 523 | 724.8 | 4 046 | 330 |
| Norfolk | 1 108.7 | 503.7 | 73.4 | 396.5 | 1 682 | 1 005 | 677 | 1 147.4 | 4 867 | 704 |
| Petersburg | 121.9 | 73.7 | 86.0 | 40.3 | 1 227 | 806 | 410 | 120.5 | 3 663 | 255 |
| Portsmouth | 432.0 | 217.2 | 89.5 | 143.6 | 1 408 | 977 | 415 | 394.7 | 3 871 | 203 |
| Richmond | 985.7 | 408.8 | 78.4 | 395.9 | 1 978 | 1 311 | 667 | 977.7 | 4 885 | 281 |
| Roanoke | 415.2 | 193.1 | 88.2 | 166.5 | 1 798 | 1 008 | 790 | 406.2 | 4 387 | 635 |
| Suffolk | 310.6 | 138.5 | 85.4 | 141.0 | 1 733 | 1 324 | 383 | 298.4 | 3 669 | 416 |
| Virginia Beach | 1 696.9 | 649.4 | 83.9 | 844.0 | 1 941 | 1 349 | 568 | 1 578.8 | 3 632 | 489 |
| Winchester | 109.8 | 35.4 | 88.6 | 60.7 | 2 360 | 1 154 | 1 205 | 132.6 | 5 153 | 1 044 |
| **WASHINGTON** | X | X | X | X | X | X | X | X | X | X |
| Auburn | 88.9 | 6.8 | 58.4 | 44.7 | 898 | 293 | 536 | 75.6 | 1 518 | 226 |
| Bellevue | 258.2 | 26.9 | 35.4 | 153.2 | 1 263 | 228 | 921 | 243.3 | 2 005 | 571 |
| Bellingham | 102.9 | 11.9 | 44.5 | 53.9 | 695 | 169 | 477 | 114.4 | 1 476 | 389 |
| Bothell | 53.3 | 7.4 | 78.6 | 33.3 | 1 032 | 251 | 682 | 42.2 | 1 310 | 305 |
| Bremerton | 66.7 | 10.6 | 84.4 | 26.5 | 777 | 220 | 505 | 55.4 | 1 625 | 365 |
| Burien | 26.0 | 6.5 | 66.3 | 16.1 | 512 | 162 | 303 | 29.6 | 941 | 480 |
| Des Moines | 26.7 | 6.1 | 64.9 | 13.0 | 446 | 143 | 288 | 23.7 | 814 | 139 |
| Edmonds | 42.6 | 6.4 | 59.2 | 26.4 | 657 | 286 | 299 | 44.6 | 1 110 | 283 |
| Everett | 169.2 | 16.3 | 66.4 | 105.3 | 1 071 | 249 | 766 | 148.1 | 1 507 | 278 |
| Federal Way | 65.0 | 9.2 | 82.8 | 43.9 | 517 | 105 | 348 | 61.5 | 725 | 326 |
| Issaquah | 51.2 | 4.6 | 49.1 | 30.5 | 1 304 | 232 | 889 | 39.5 | 1 689 | 293 |
| Kennewick | 55.5 | 5.1 | 84.4 | 34.3 | 552 | 136 | 385 | 56.7 | 912 | 241 |
| Kent | 134.9 | 15.5 | 62.5 | 75.6 | 895 | 308 | 521 | 131.3 | 1 555 | 407 |
| Kirkland | 88.8 | 6.5 | 29.0 | 52.1 | 1 101 | 275 | 677 | 76.5 | 1 617 | 154 |
| Lacey | 78.0 | 6.2 | 66.0 | 30.7 | 806 | 194 | 535 | 43.2 | 1 133 | 220 |
| Lake Stevens | 6.2 | 0.5 | 91.4 | 3.4 | 252 | 81 | 142 | 6.2 | 458 | 48 |
| Lakewood | 43.6 | 6.5 | 75.4 | 27.4 | 479 | 96 | 348 | 38.3 | 669 | 111 |
| Longview | 47.1 | 5.5 | 48.5 | 22.7 | 618 | 197 | 401 | 43.1 | 1 176 | 132 |
| Lynnwood | 52.9 | 3.8 | 78.0 | 33.5 | 997 | 254 | 688 | 43.3 | 1 289 | 100 |
| Marysville | 49.6 | 4.7 | 69.6 | 18.3 | 543 | 197 | 286 | 46.0 | 1 369 | 385 |
| Mount Vernon | 37.8 | 3.2 | 77.8 | 19.0 | 620 | 193 | 375 | 32.0 | 1 043 | 216 |
| Olympia | 88.3 | 6.0 | 49.5 | 47.6 | 1 059 | 206 | 793 | 78.2 | 1 741 | 285 |
| Pasco | 52.7 | 10.8 | 33.2 | 25.2 | 478 | 101 | 359 | 46.8 | 888 | 363 |

1. Based on population estimated as of July 1 of the year shown.

| City | City government finances, 2006 (cont.) | | | | | | | | | |
|---|---|---|---|---|---|---|---|---|---|---|
| | General expenditure (cont.) | | | | | | | | | |
| | Percent of total for: | | | | | | | | | |
| | Public welfare | Highways | Parking facilities | Education | Health and hospitals | Police protection | Sewerage and sanitation | Parks and recreation | Housing and community development | Interest on debt |
| | 127 | 128 | 129 | 130 | 131 | 132 | 133 | 134 | 135 | 136 |
| **UTAH—Cont'd** | | | | | | | | | | |
| Lehi | 0.0 | 13.3 | 0.0 | 0.0 | 0.0 | 13.6 | 17.0 | 14.9 | 0.0 | 10.3 |
| Logan | 0.0 | 12.9 | 0.0 | 0.0 | 0.0 | 15.3 | 24.8 | 10.7 | 2.1 | 2.8 |
| Midvale | 0.0 | 11.4 | 0.0 | 0.0 | 2.7 | 25.6 | 10.9 | 2.4 | 3.5 | 1.0 |
| Murray | 0.0 | 6.6 | 0.0 | 0.0 | 0.0 | 14.8 | 6.2 | 10.2 | 0.3 | 1.1 |
| Ogden | 0.0 | 4.5 | 0.0 | 0.0 | 0.0 | 14.8 | 9.5 | 6.7 | 28.7 | 2.7 |
| Orem | 0.0 | 16.2 | 0.0 | 0.0 | 0.0 | 13.9 | 19.9 | 5.5 | 1.8 | 3.0 |
| Pleasant Grove | 0.0 | 6.1 | 0.0 | 0.0 | 0.0 | 9.0 | 18.8 | 5.6 | 45.9 | 1.6 |
| Provo | 0.0 | 6.5 | 0.0 | 0.0 | 0.0 | 14.7 | 9.6 | 8.3 | 9.8 | 2.3 |
| Riverton | 0.0 | 22.6 | 0.0 | 0.0 | 0.0 | 14.4 | 12.6 | 21.5 | 0.7 | 2.3 |
| Roy | 0.0 | 14.7 | 0.0 | 0.0 | 0.0 | 25.6 | 2.9 | 15.8 | 1.6 | 0.3 |
| St. George | 0.0 | 13.7 | 0.0 | 0.0 | 0.0 | 16.6 | 20.3 | 22.4 | 6.0 | 3.1 |
| Salt Lake City | 0.0 | 8.3 | 0.0 | 0.0 | 0.2 | 12.2 | 7.1 | 4.9 | 5.5 | 2.8 |
| Sandy | 0.0 | 8.7 | 0.0 | 0.0 | 0.0 | 18.4 | 14.3 | 12.3 | 1.4 | 3.6 |
| South Jordan | 0.0 | 30.4 | 0.0 | 0.0 | 0.0 | 11.9 | 5.7 | 5.6 | 2.4 | 6.4 |
| Spanish Fork | 0.0 | 18.0 | 0.0 | 0.0 | 0.0 | 17.5 | 15.0 | 22.5 | 0.0 | 0.1 |
| Springville | 0.0 | 7.7 | 0.0 | 0.0 | 1.0 | 17.2 | 21.5 | 18.0 | 0.0 | 4.1 |
| Taylorsville | 0.0 | 19.6 | 0.0 | 0.0 | 0.0 | 29.5 | 2.0 | 4.5 | 0.0 | 1.1 |
| Tooele | 0.0 | 9.6 | 0.0 | 0.0 | 0.0 | 15.7 | 17.1 | 12.9 | 11.1 | 5.4 |
| West Jordan | 0.0 | 19.5 | 0.0 | 0.0 | 0.0 | 20.3 | 16.8 | 4.4 | 5.5 | 3.3 |
| West Valley City | 0.0 | 8.0 | 0.0 | 0.0 | 0.0 | 18.4 | 7.3 | 12.0 | 9.7 | 5.1 |
| **VERMONT** | X | X | X | X | X | X | X | X | X | X |
| Burlington | 0.0 | 4.7 | 3.8 | 0.0 | 0.0 | 7.3 | 5.4 | 4.6 | 5.3 | 6.2 |
| **VIRGINIA** | X | X | X | X | X | X | X | X | X | X |
| Alexandria | 8.0 | 3.5 | 0.4 | 33.9 | 6.3 | 8.9 | 2.6 | 5.5 | 3.8 | 2.2 |
| Blacksburg | 0.0 | 25.6 | 0.0 | 0.0 | 1.3 | 16.5 | 11.9 | 5.5 | 2.3 | 1.9 |
| Charlottesville | 10.5 | 3.0 | 0.1 | 35.6 | 6.2 | 6.7 | 4.1 | 2.4 | 2.1 | 1.1 |
| Chesapeake | 2.8 | 5.5 | 0.0 | 55.9 | 3.1 | 5.1 | 2.7 | 1.8 | 0.3 | 2.9 |
| Danville | 5.4 | 4.8 | 0.0 | 45.9 | 0.5 | 5.9 | 6.1 | 4.1 | 5.6 | 1.5 |
| Hampton | 5.6 | 0.9 | 0.4 | 45.7 | 0.7 | 5.4 | 4.6 | 7.3 | 5.1 | 3.1 |
| Harrisonburg | 1.7 | 6.8 | 0.5 | 51.9 | 0.7 | 4.6 | 7.5 | 3.6 | 1.1 | 3.6 |
| Leesburg | 0.0 | 5.7 | 0.2 | 0.0 | 0.0 | 15.9 | 16.0 | 10.6 | 1.1 | 3.6 |
| Lynchburg | 3.2 | 4.7 | 0.0 | 38.6 | 6.1 | 7.4 | 8.5 | 3.6 | 2.3 | 1.0 |
| Manassas | 0.2 | 8.0 | 0.0 | 58.5 | 3.5 | 8.2 | 7.0 | 0.8 | 0.8 | 2.1 |
| Newport News | 6.7 | 4.2 | 0.0 | 45.3 | 10.6 | 5.9 | 2.8 | 4.2 | 4.0 | 0.6 |
| Norfolk | 7.0 | 4.1 | 1.2 | 33.1 | 2.8 | 5.5 | 5.2 | 5.9 | 10.2 | 3.1 |
| Petersburg | 6.7 | 3.6 | 0.0 | 47.1 | 0.9 | 12.5 | 1.2 | 1.7 | 1.4 | 1.1 |
| Portsmouth | 7.0 | 1.5 | 0.2 | 43.6 | 2.8 | 7.0 | 3.7 | 2.8 | 6.4 | 2.9 |
| Richmond | 7.7 | 4.0 | 0.0 | 32.7 | 4.3 | 11.5 | 6.3 | 1.9 | 7.1 | 1.1 |
| Roanoke | 9.3 | 3.4 | 0.8 | 40.8 | 0.5 | 5.0 | 4.3 | 2.0 | 6.4 | 2.8 |
| Suffolk | 3.5 | 4.9 | 0.0 | 48.6 | 0.4 | 4.5 | 4.7 | 3.1 | 0.8 | 6.3 |
| Virginia Beach | 2.6 | 3.8 | 0.0 | 52.8 | 3.8 | 5.4 | 5.1 | 7.0 | 1.8 | 0.3 |
| Winchester | 5.6 | 3.6 | 0.0 | 49.7 | 0.4 | 4.9 | 5.4 | 1.8 | 3.4 | 3.6 |
| **WASHINGTON** | X | X | X | X | X | X | X | X | X | X |
| Auburn | 0.0 | 11.9 | 0.0 | 0.0 | 0.7 | 15.7 | 29.5 | 7.5 | 0.6 | 0.6 |
| Bellevue | 0.0 | 15.2 | 0.0 | 0.0 | 5.1 | 9.5 | 14.8 | 11.0 | 4.2 | 3.3 |
| Bellingham | 0.0 | 9.1 | 0.7 | 0.0 | 4.3 | 10.9 | 17.4 | 18.8 | 4.4 | 2.1 |
| Bothell | 0.0 | 24.2 | 0.0 | 0.0 | 0.0 | 19.6 | 11.4 | 2.5 | 2.1 | 0.9 |
| Bremerton | 0.0 | 9.5 | 0.7 | 0.0 | 3.5 | 23.1 | 13.0 | 21.6 | 3.3 | 4.4 |
| Burien | 0.0 | 33.4 | 0.0 | 0.0 | 0.8 | 36.1 | 1.8 | 7.1 | 2.0 | 0.9 |
| Des Moines | 0.0 | 18.0 | 0.0 | 0.0 | 0.3 | 28.3 | 3.2 | 17.7 | 0.9 | 4.5 |
| Edmonds | 0.0 | 12.1 | 0.0 | 0.0 | 2.9 | 15.7 | 11.1 | 9.1 | 0.0 | 3.1 |
| Everett | 0.2 | 8.8 | 0.2 | 0.0 | 4.8 | 14.3 | 10.0 | 8.8 | 1.2 | 4.0 |
| Federal Way | 0.3 | 22.9 | 0.0 | 0.0 | 0.9 | 21.3 | 3.2 | 32.5 | 2.0 | 2.3 |
| Issaquah | 0.0 | 16.2 | 0.0 | 0.0 | 0.0 | 11.1 | 11.9 | 16.4 | 3.8 | 3.7 |
| Kennewick | 0.0 | 12.5 | 0.0 | 0.0 | 4.9 | 18.3 | 5.0 | 16.9 | 0.8 | 3.4 |
| Kent | 0.2 | 14.8 | 0.0 | 0.0 | 2.1 | 12.3 | 15.8 | 14.4 | 2.3 | 3.3 |
| Kirkland | 0.7 | 9.5 | 0.1 | 0.0 | 0.0 | 13.2 | 17.9 | 9.0 | 0.0 | 1.7 |
| Lacey | 0.0 | 20.5 | 0.0 | 0.0 | 0.0 | 14.5 | 20.8 | 11.6 | 0.1 | 1.0 |
| Lake Stevens | 0.2 | 12.2 | 0.0 | 0.0 | 0.0 | 29.4 | 27.0 | 2.6 | 2.0 | 2.8 |
| Lakewood | 1.0 | 20.5 | 0.0 | 0.0 | 0.6 | 41.7 | 4.4 | 4.5 | 3.4 | 0.2 |
| Longview | 0.3 | 8.5 | 0.0 | 0.0 | 0.0 | 16.8 | 26.5 | 8.5 | 4.7 | 1.4 |
| Lynnwood | 0.0 | 8.1 | 0.2 | 0.0 | 4.9 | 20.7 | 8.2 | 10.4 | 1.4 | 3.1 |
| Marysville | 0.0 | 24.2 | 0.0 | 0.0 | 3.0 | 12.1 | 14.7 | 5.8 | 0.0 | 8.3 |
| Mount Vernon | 0.0 | 9.7 | 0.0 | 0.0 | 0.2 | 15.3 | 32.5 | 5.8 | 1.2 | 1.5 |
| Olympia | 0.0 | 9.5 | 0.1 | 0.0 | 2.3 | 12.0 | 23.4 | 13.5 | 1.4 | 0.5 |
| Pasco | 0.0 | 21.3 | 0.0 | 0.0 | 3.9 | 12.5 | 15.9 | 10.1 | 0.3 | 4.6 |

# Table D. Cities — City Government Finances, City Government Employment, and Climate

| City | City government finances, 2007 (cont.) Debt outstanding Total (mil dol) | Per capita[1] (dollars) | Debt issued during year | City government employment, 2011 | Climate[2] Average daily temperature (degrees Fahrenheit) Mean January | July | Limits January[3] | July[4] | Annual precipitation (inches) | Heating degree days | Cooling degree days |
|---|---|---|---|---|---|---|---|---|---|---|---|
| | 137 | 138 | 139 | 140 | 141 | 142 | 143 | 144 | 145 | 146 | 147 |
| **UTAH—Cont'd** | | | | | | | | | | | |
| Lehi | 101.3 | 2 745 | 15.8 | 327 | NA | NA | NA | NA | NA | NA | NA |
| Logan | 45.6 | 951 | 10.9 | 474 | 21.8 | 71.6 | 12.7 | 88.3 | 17.86 | 7 174 | 522 |
| Midvale | 5.8 | 207 | 1.6 | 184 | 30.4 | 78.5 | 22.1 | 90.9 | 26.19 | 5 441 | 1 197 |
| Murray | 46.9 | 1 026 | 19.7 | 461 | 29.2 | 77.0 | 21.3 | 90.6 | 16.50 | 5 631 | 1 066 |
| Ogden | 92.5 | 1 119 | 9.3 | 674 | 28.1 | 76.6 | 20.1 | 90.0 | 23.67 | 5 868 | 980 |
| Orem | 68.7 | 738 | 5.0 | 516 | 28.6 | 76.5 | 20.3 | 92.3 | 12.84 | 5 564 | 1 016 |
| Pleasant Grove | 43.9 | 1 392 | 32.0 | NA | NA | NA | NA | NA | NA | NA | NA |
| Provo | 117.6 | 1 000 | 10.8 | 673 | 30.9 | 76.9 | 22.5 | 93.4 | 20.13 | 5 264 | 1 028 |
| Riverton | 43.3 | 1 126 | 15.4 | NA | 31.6 | 78.0 | 22.0 | 95.3 | 15.76 | 5 251 | 1 172 |
| Roy | 0.3 | 9 | 0.0 | 177 | 27.6 | 74.2 | 18.6 | 89.9 | 20.75 | 6 142 | 746 |
| St. George | 118.9 | 1 671 | 0.0 | 676 | 41.8 | 86.3 | 28.9 | 102.8 | 8.77 | 3 103 | 2 471 |
| Salt Lake City | 289.0 | 1 600 | 5.5 | 2 810 | 32.0 | 78.1 | 25.4 | 89.0 | 17.75 | 5 095 | 1 190 |
| Sandy | 69.0 | 719 | 0.5 | 541 | 30.4 | 78.5 | 22.1 | 90.9 | 26.19 | 5 441 | 1 197 |
| South Jordan | 66.1 | 1 376 | 30.5 | 340 | 31.6 | 78.0 | 22.0 | 95.3 | 15.76 | 5 251 | 1 172 |
| Spanish Fork | 37.3 | 1 300 | 22.0 | 192 | NA | NA | NA | NA | NA | NA | NA |
| Springville | 20.1 | 749 | 3.6 | 209 | NA | NA | NA | NA | NA | NA | NA |
| Taylorsville | 13.3 | 226 | 10.0 | 115 | 29.2 | 77.0 | 21.3 | 90.6 | 16.50 | 5 631 | 1 066 |
| Tooele | 38.3 | 1 301 | 0.0 | NA | NA | NA | NA | NA | NA | NA | NA |
| West Jordan | 42.9 | 419 | 7.5 | 440 | 30.4 | 78.5 | 22.1 | 90.9 | 26.19 | 5 441 | 1 197 |
| West Valley City | 115.3 | 942 | 104.2 | 697 | 29.2 | 77.0 | 21.3 | 90.6 | 16.50 | 5 631 | 1 066 |
| **VERMONT** | X | X | X | X | X | X | X | X | X | X | X |
| Burlington | 179.2 | 4 651 | 5.1 | 734 | 18.0 | 70.6 | 9.3 | 81.4 | 36.05 | 7 665 | 489 |
| **VIRGINIA** | X | X | X | X | X | X | X | X | X | X | X |
| Alexandria | 412.7 | 2 947 | 22.8 | 4 919 | 34.9 | 79.2 | 27.3 | 88.3 | 39.35 | 4 055 | 1 531 |
| Blacksburg | 26.4 | 640 | 4.9 | NA | 30.9 | 71.1 | 20.6 | 82.5 | 42.63 | 5 559 | 533 |
| Charlottesville | 75.2 | 1 825 | 16.0 | 1 839 | 35.5 | 76.9 | 26.2 | 88.0 | 48.87 | 4 103 | 1 212 |
| Chesapeake | 683.1 | 3 117 | 29.4 | 9 432 | 40.1 | 79.1 | 32.3 | 86.8 | 45.74 | 3 368 | 1 612 |
| Danville | 144.2 | 3 207 | 5.0 | 2 341 | 36.6 | 78.8 | 25.8 | 90.0 | 44.98 | 3 970 | 1 418 |
| Hampton | 332.9 | 2 273 | 0.0 | 5 664 | 39.4 | 78.5 | 32.0 | 85.2 | 47.90 | 3 535 | 1 432 |
| Harrisonburg | 354.6 | 8 051 | 50.0 | 1 483 | 30.5 | 73.5 | 20.4 | 85.3 | 36.12 | 5 333 | 758 |
| Leesburg | 91.4 | 2 377 | 20.2 | NA | 31.5 | 75.2 | 20.8 | 87.1 | 43.21 | 5 031 | 911 |
| Lynchburg | 60.6 | 850 | 7.0 | 2 817 | 34.5 | 75.1 | 24.5 | 86.4 | 43.31 | 4 354 | 1 075 |
| Manassas | 152.5 | 4 307 | 0.0 | 1 480 | 31.7 | 75.7 | 21.9 | 87.4 | 41.80 | 4 925 | 1 075 |
| Newport News | 872.0 | 4 867 | 136.9 | 9 054 | 41.2 | 80.3 | 33.8 | 87.9 | 43.53 | 3 179 | 1 682 |
| Norfolk | 1 484.8 | 6 298 | 163.1 | 11 907 | 40.1 | 79.1 | 32.3 | 86.8 | 45.74 | 3 368 | 1 612 |
| Petersburg | 45.7 | 1 388 | 12.8 | 1 553 | 39.7 | 79.6 | 29.2 | 91.0 | 45.26 | 3 334 | 1 619 |
| Portsmouth | 343.3 | 3 367 | 83.3 | 4 127 | 40.1 | 79.1 | 32.3 | 86.8 | 45.74 | 3 368 | 1 612 |
| Richmond | 1 196.4 | 5 978 | 373.2 | 10 124 | 36.4 | 77.9 | 27.6 | 87.5 | 43.91 | 3 919 | 1 435 |
| Roanoke | 377.1 | 4 073 | 13.0 | 3 845 | 35.8 | 76.2 | 26.6 | 87.5 | 42.49 | 4 284 | 1 134 |
| Suffolk | 388.0 | 4 770 | 137.5 | 3 568 | 39.6 | 78.5 | 30.3 | 88.1 | 48.71 | 3 467 | 1 427 |
| Virginia Beach | 1 359.9 | 3 128 | 181.9 | 18 337 | 40.7 | 78.8 | 32.2 | 86.9 | 44.50 | 3 336 | 1 482 |
| Winchester | 183.3 | 7 124 | 23.7 | 1 415 | NA | NA | NA | NA | NA | NA | NA |
| **WASHINGTON** | X | X | X | X | X | X | X | X | X | X | X |
| Auburn | 27.0 | 542 | 6.9 | 415 | 40.8 | 66.4 | 34.6 | 77.4 | 39.59 | 4 624 | 219 |
| Bellevue | 186.8 | 1 540 | 14.0 | 1 285 | 41.5 | 65.5 | 36.0 | 74.5 | 38.25 | 4 615 | 192 |
| Bellingham | 68.7 | 887 | 12.0 | 821 | 40.5 | 63.3 | 34.8 | 72.5 | 34.84 | 4 980 | 68 |
| Bothell | 7.9 | 244 | 0.0 | 291 | 40.8 | 65.2 | 35.2 | 75.0 | 35.96 | 4 756 | 174 |
| Bremerton | 69.9 | 2 051 | 1.4 | 365 | 40.1 | 64.6 | 34.7 | 75.2 | 53.96 | 4 994 | 158 |
| Burien | 15.3 | 488 | 9.8 | NA | 40.9 | 65.3 | 35.9 | 75.3 | 37.07 | 4 797 | 173 |
| Des Moines | 27.7 | 951 | 2.2 | NA | 40.9 | 65.3 | 35.9 | 75.3 | 37.07 | 4 797 | 173 |
| Edmonds | 34.2 | 853 | 0.8 | NA | 40.8 | 65.2 | 35.2 | 75.0 | 35.96 | 4 756 | 174 |
| Everett | 194.8 | 1 982 | 7.3 | 1 150 | 39.7 | 63.6 | 33.6 | 73.0 | 37.54 | 5 199 | 121 |
| Federal Way | 31.5 | 372 | 4.1 | 343 | 41.0 | 65.6 | 35.1 | 76.1 | 38.95 | 4 650 | 167 |
| Issaquah | 53.9 | 2 308 | 9.7 | 242 | NA | NA | NA | NA | NA | NA | NA |
| Kennewick | 61.2 | 985 | 13.8 | 361 | 34.2 | 75.2 | 28.0 | 89.3 | 8.01 | 4 731 | 909 |
| Kent | 138.6 | 1 641 | 19.8 | 634 | 40.8 | 66.4 | 34.6 | 77.4 | 39.59 | 4 624 | 219 |
| Kirkland | 31.4 | 664 | 0.3 | 481 | 40.8 | 65.2 | 35.2 | 75.0 | 35.96 | 4 756 | 174 |
| Lacey | 23.7 | 623 | 8.5 | NA | 38.1 | 62.8 | 31.8 | 76.1 | 50.79 | 5 531 | 97 |
| Lake Stevens | 6.6 | 491 | 1.4 | NA | NA | NA | NA | NA | NA | NA | NA |
| Lakewood | 5.5 | 96 | 3.8 | NA | 41.0 | 65.6 | 35.1 | 76.1 | 38.95 | 4 650 | 167 |
| Longview | 19.4 | 529 | 0.0 | 306 | 39.9 | 64.5 | 33.8 | 76.5 | 48.02 | 4 900 | 148 |
| Lynnwood | 21.6 | 642 | 0.0 | NA | 40.8 | 65.2 | 35.2 | 75.0 | 35.96 | 4 756 | 174 |
| Marysville | 99.3 | 2 956 | 2.6 | 258 | 39.7 | 63.6 | 33.6 | 73.0 | 37.54 | 5 199 | 121 |
| Mount Vernon | 14.9 | 486 | 1.6 | 200 | 39.9 | 62.3 | 34.1 | 73.0 | 32.70 | 5 197 | 47 |
| Olympia | 23.6 | 524 | 9.4 | NA | 38.1 | 62.8 | 31.8 | 76.1 | 50.79 | 5 531 | 97 |
| Pasco | 52.9 | 1 005 | 0.1 | NA | 34.2 | 75.2 | 28.0 | 89.3 | 8.01 | 4 731 | 909 |

1. Based on the population estimated as of July 1 of the year shown.   2. Represents normal values based on the 30-year period, 1971–2000.   3. Average daily minimum.   4. Average daily maximum.

# Table D. Cities — Land Area and Population

| STATE Place code | City | Land area,[1] 2010 (sq km) | Population, 2012 Total persons | Rank | Per square kilometer | Race alone or in combination, not of Hispanic origin (percent), 2010 — White | Black | American Indian, Alaska Native | Asian | Hawaiian Pacific Islander | Percent Hispanic or Latino[2], 2010 | Percent Foreign born 2007–2011 |
|---|---|---|---|---|---|---|---|---|---|---|---|---|
| | | 1 | 2 | 3 | 4 | 5 | 6 | 7 | 8 | 9 | 10 | 11 |
| | **WASHINGTON— Cont'd** | | | | | | | | | | | |
| 53 56625 | Pullman | 25.6 | 31 359 | 1 155 | 1 225.0 | 79.9 | 3.0 | 1.5 | 13.4 | 0.7 | 5.4 | 12.6 |
| 53 56695 | Puyallup | 36.1 | 38 147 | 961 | 1 056.7 | 85.0 | 3.3 | 2.5 | 5.8 | 1.2 | 6.9 | 6.2 |
| 53 57535 | Redmond | 42.2 | 56 561 | 633 | 1 340.3 | 64.0 | 2.2 | 0.8 | 27.6 | 0.3 | 7.8 | 30.3 |
| 53 57745 | Renton | 59.9 | 95 448 | 308 | 1 593.5 | 53.2 | 12.3 | 1.5 | 23.4 | 1.2 | 13.1 | 26.5 |
| 53 58235 | Richland | 92.5 | 51 440 | 706 | 556.1 | 85.1 | 1.9 | 1.5 | 5.6 | 0.2 | 7.8 | 7.8 |
| 53 61115 | Sammamish | 47.2 | 49 069 | 752 | 1 039.6 | 75.0 | 1.5 | 0.7 | 21.8 | 0.4 | 3.9 | 23.8 |
| 53 62288 | SeaTac | 26.0 | 27 667 | 1 310 | 1 064.1 | 42.9 | 18.2 | 2.4 | 16.5 | 4.1 | 20.3 | 33.0 |
| 53 63000 | Seattle | 217.4 | 634 535 | 22 | 2 918.7 | 70.1 | 9.1 | 1.7 | 16.3 | 0.7 | 6.6 | 17.5 |
| 53 63960 | Shoreline | 30.2 | 54 352 | 666 | 1 799.7 | 71.8 | 6.0 | 1.9 | 17.5 | 0.8 | 6.6 | 19.7 |
| 53 67000 | Spokane | 153.5 | 209 525 | 103 | 1 365.0 | 87.5 | 3.6 | 3.3 | 3.7 | 0.8 | 5.0 | 6.7 |
| 53 67167 | Spokane Valley | 97.8 | 90 641 | 334 | 926.8 | 91.0 | 2.0 | 2.2 | 2.5 | 0.4 | 4.6 | 4.8 |
| 53 70000 | Tacoma | 128.8 | 202 010 | 108 | 1 568.4 | 66.1 | 14.1 | 3.2 | 10.6 | 1.8 | 11.3 | 13.1 |
| 53 73465 | University Place | 21.8 | 31 562 | 1 149 | 1 447.8 | 73.8 | 11.2 | 2.1 | 12.2 | 1.5 | 6.7 | 13.1 |
| 53 74060 | Vancouver | 120.3 | 165 489 | 145 | 1 375.6 | 79.6 | 4.1 | 2.0 | 6.4 | 1.4 | 10.4 | 12.3 |
| 53 75775 | Walla Walla | 33.2 | 31 864 | 1 141 | 959.8 | 72.6 | 3.1 | 1.9 | 2.2 | 0.7 | 22.0 | 10.4 |
| 53 77105 | Wenatchee | 20.1 | 32 562 | 1 117 | 1 620.0 | 68.0 | 0.7 | 1.6 | 1.5 | 0.3 | 29.4 | 12.0 |
| 53 80010 | Yakima | 70.4 | 93 101 | 319 | 1 322.5 | 54.1 | 2.0 | 2.4 | 2.0 | 0.2 | 41.3 | 17.4 |
| 54 00000 | **WEST VIRGINIA** | 62 258.7 | 1 855 413 | X | 29.8 | 94.4 | 4.1 | 0.7 | 0.9 | 0.1 | 1.2 | 1.3 |
| 54 14600 | Charleston | 81.6 | 51 018 | 715 | 625.2 | 80.4 | 17.4 | 0.9 | 2.8 | 0.1 | 1.4 | 2.5 |
| 54 39460 | Huntington | 42.0 | 49 160 | 748 | 1 170.5 | 88.5 | 10.2 | 1.0 | 1.4 | 0.1 | 1.4 | 2.3 |
| 54 55756 | Morgantown | 26.3 | 31 000 | 1 174 | 1 178.7 | 89.6 | 4.9 | 0.5 | 4.0 | 0.1 | 2.6 | 4.6 |
| 54 62140 | Parkersburg | 30.6 | 31 261 | 1 160 | 1 021.6 | 96.0 | 3.0 | 0.9 | 0.7 | 0.1 | 1.2 | 0.7 |
| 54 86452 | Wheeling | 35.7 | 28 213 | 1 284 | 790.3 | 92.7 | 6.7 | 0.7 | 1.2 | 0.1 | 0.9 | 1.4 |
| 55 00000 | **WISCONSIN** | 140 268.1 | 5 726 398 | X | 40.8 | 84.6 | 6.8 | 1.3 | 2.6 | 0.1 | 5.9 | 4.6 |
| 55 02375 | Appleton | 63.0 | 73 016 | 453 | 1 159.0 | 86.7 | 2.4 | 1.0 | 6.4 | 0.1 | 5.0 | 6.4 |
| 55 06500 | Beloit | 45.0 | 36 842 | 992 | 818.7 | 66.4 | 16.9 | 1.0 | 1.6 | 0.1 | 17.1 | 9.2 |
| 55 10025 | Brookfield | 70.2 | 37 977 | 963 | 541.0 | 89.5 | 1.5 | 0.3 | 7.4 | 0.1 | 2.2 | 5.7 |
| 55 22300 | Eau Claire | 83.0 | 66 966 | 502 | 806.8 | 91.7 | 1.7 | 1.0 | 5.0 | 0.1 | 1.9 | 3.6 |
| 55 25950 | Fitchburg | 90.6 | 25 895 | 1 395 | 285.8 | 67.3 | 11.6 | 0.7 | 5.5 | 0.1 | 17.2 | 13.5 |
| 55 26275 | Fond du Lac | 48.8 | 43 045 | 847 | 882.1 | 88.8 | 3.2 | 1.0 | 2.0 | 0.1 | 6.4 | 4.5 |
| 55 27300 | Franklin | 89.6 | 36 083 | 1 015 | 402.7 | 84.8 | 5.2 | 0.6 | 6.0 | 0.1 | 4.5 | 8.6 |
| 55 31000 | Green Bay | 117.8 | 104 868 | 268 | 890.2 | 75.3 | 4.4 | 4.6 | 4.4 | 0.1 | 13.4 | 8.0 |
| 55 31175 | Greenfield | 29.8 | 37 072 | 980 | 1 244.0 | 84.7 | 2.8 | 1.1 | 4.4 | 0.1 | 8.4 | 6.4 |
| 55 37825 | Janesville | 87.7 | 63 588 | 539 | 725.1 | 90.4 | 3.4 | 0.6 | 1.7 | 0.1 | 5.4 | 3.9 |
| 55 39225 | Kenosha | 69.8 | 100 150 | 289 | 1 434.8 | 71.7 | 11.2 | 0.9 | 2.2 | 0.1 | 16.3 | 8.2 |
| 55 40775 | La Crosse | 53.1 | 51 647 | 702 | 972.6 | 90.3 | 3.1 | 1.0 | 5.4 | 0.1 | 2.0 | 4.1 |
| 55 48000 | Madison | 198.9 | 240 323 | 82 | 1 208.3 | 78.0 | 8.4 | 0.8 | 8.3 | 0.1 | 6.8 | 10.7 |
| 55 48500 | Manitowoc | 45.7 | 33 383 | 1 094 | 730.5 | 88.8 | 1.4 | 1.0 | 5.0 | 0.1 | 5.0 | 3.9 |
| 55 51000 | Menomonee Falls | 85.3 | 35 802 | 1 023 | 419.7 | 91.3 | 3.4 | 0.4 | 3.9 | 0.0 | 2.0 | 5.4 |
| 55 53000 | Milwaukee | 249.0 | 598 916 | 30 | 2 405.3 | 38.8 | 40.9 | 1.2 | 3.9 | 0.1 | 17.3 | 9.9 |
| 55 54875 | Mount Pleasant | 87.4 | 26 185 | 1 388 | 299.6 | 82.7 | 7.3 | 0.6 | 2.5 | 0.0 | 8.3 | 4.1 |
| 55 55750 | Neenah | 23.9 | 25 763 | 1 400 | 1 077.9 | 92.9 | 1.8 | 1.1 | 1.7 | 0.1 | 3.8 | 4.3 |
| 55 56375 | New Berlin | 94.4 | 39 703 | 916 | 420.6 | 92.5 | 1.0 | 0.5 | 4.2 | 0.1 | 2.6 | 5.2 |
| 55 58800 | Oak Creek | 73.7 | 34 908 | 1 045 | 473.6 | 84.5 | 3.3 | 1.1 | 5.2 | 0.1 | 7.5 | 7.1 |
| 55 60500 | Oshkosh | 66.3 | 66 653 | 505 | 1 005.3 | 90.2 | 3.6 | 1.1 | 3.6 | 0.1 | 2.7 | 3.6 |
| 55 66000 | Racine | 40.1 | 78 303 | 410 | 1 952.7 | 55.9 | 24.0 | 0.8 | 1.0 | 0.1 | 20.7 | 7.6 |
| 55 72975 | Sheboygan | 36.2 | 48 895 | 755 | 1 350.7 | 78.8 | 2.5 | 0.9 | 9.4 | 0.1 | 9.9 | 8.9 |
| 55 77200 | Stevens Point | 41.3 | 26 748 | 1 361 | 647.7 | 91.3 | 1.4 | 0.8 | 5.1 | 0.1 | 2.6 | 4.3 |
| 55 78600 | Sun Prairie | 31.7 | 30 403 | 1 198 | 959.1 | 85.3 | 7.6 | 0.7 | 4.4 | 0.1 | 4.3 | 4.2 |
| 55 78650 | Superior | 95.7 | 26 862 | 1 355 | 280.7 | 93.4 | 2.4 | 4.2 | 1.5 | 0.1 | 1.4 | 2.2 |
| 55 84250 | Waukesha | 64.3 | 70 920 | 466 | 1 103.0 | 81.8 | 3.0 | 0.6 | 4.0 | 0.1 | 12.1 | 6.7 |
| 55 84475 | Wausau | 48.6 | 39 160 | 932 | 805.8 | 83.6 | 2.1 | 1.3 | 11.8 | 0.1 | 2.9 | 7.6 |
| 55 84675 | Wauwatosa | 34.3 | 47 068 | 787 | 1 372.2 | 89.2 | 5.4 | 0.6 | 3.4 | 0.1 | 3.1 | 4.3 |
| 55 85300 | West Allis | 29.5 | 60 732 | 573 | 2 058.7 | 83.8 | 4.5 | 1.5 | 2.4 | 0.1 | 9.6 | 4.8 |
| 55 85350 | West Bend | 37.7 | 31 540 | 1 150 | 836.6 | 94.0 | 1.5 | 0.8 | 1.0 | 0.0 | 3.9 | 2.6 |
| 56 00000 | **WYOMING** | 251 470.1 | 576 412 | X | 2.3 | 87.3 | 1.1 | 2.8 | 1.1 | 0.2 | 8.9 | 3.1 |
| 56 13150 | Casper | 69.7 | 57 813 | 613 | 829.5 | 90.0 | 1.6 | 1.4 | 1.1 | 0.2 | 7.4 | 2.5 |
| 56 13900 | Cheyenne | 63.5 | 61 537 | 563 | 969.1 | 80.7 | 3.5 | 1.3 | 1.7 | 0.3 | 14.5 | 3.0 |
| 56 31855 | Gillette | 49.1 | 31 378 | 1 154 | 639.1 | 88.4 | 0.7 | 1.7 | 1.0 | 0.1 | 9.5 | 4.0 |
| 56 45050 | Laramie | 45.9 | 31 681 | 1 146 | 690.2 | 85.6 | 1.7 | 1.1 | 4.0 | 0.2 | 9.2 | 6.4 |

1. Dry land or land partially or temporarily covered by water.  2. May be of any race.

# Table D. Cities — **Population**

| City | Age of population (percent), 2010 | | | | | | | | | | | Population | | | |
|------|------|------|------|------|------|------|------|------|------|------|------|------|------|------|------|
| | | | | | | | | | | | | Census counts | | Percent change | |
| | Under 5 years | 5 to 17 years | 18 to 24 years | 25 to 34 years | 35 to 44 years | 45 to 54 years | 55 to 64 years | 65 to 74 years | 75 years and over | Median age | Percent female | 2000 | 2010 | 2000–2010 | 2010–2012 |
| | 12 | 13 | 14 | 15 | 16 | 17 | 18 | 19 | 20 | 21 | 22 | 23 | 24 | 25 | 26 |
| **WASHINGTON—Cont'd** | | | | | | | | | | | | | | | |
| Pullman | 3.9 | 7.4 | 51.8 | 15.1 | 6.6 | 5.8 | 4.7 | 2.2 | 2.5 | 22.3 | 48.7 | 24 675 | 29 799 | 20.8 | 5.2 |
| Puyallup | 6.5 | 17.1 | 10.2 | 14.1 | 12.8 | 15.4 | 11.4 | 6.1 | 6.4 | 36.8 | 52.0 | 33 011 | 37 022 | 12.2 | 3.0 |
| Redmond | 8.1 | 14.7 | 7.4 | 21.7 | 17.1 | 12.4 | 9.2 | 4.7 | 4.8 | 34.1 | 49.1 | 45 256 | 54 298 | 19.6 | 4.2 |
| Renton | 7.8 | 15.4 | 8.7 | 17.6 | 15.9 | 14.0 | 10.4 | 5.5 | 4.6 | 35.2 | 50.5 | 50 052 | 91 502 | 81.7 | 4.3 |
| Richland | 6.3 | 17.9 | 8.1 | 12.8 | 11.9 | 14.9 | 13.5 | 7.8 | 6.8 | 39.4 | 51.0 | 38 708 | 48 109 | 24.2 | 6.9 |
| Sammamish | 7.0 | 25.3 | 4.8 | 8.4 | 19.5 | 18.5 | 10.8 | 3.8 | 1.9 | 37.7 | 49.9 | 34 104 | 46 759 | 34.2 | 4.9 |
| SeaTac | 7.6 | 15.5 | 10.2 | 17.4 | 14.4 | 14.6 | 10.6 | 5.5 | 4.2 | 34.5 | 47.6 | 25 496 | 26 909 | 5.5 | 2.8 |
| Seattle | 5.3 | 10.1 | 11.8 | 20.8 | 16.4 | 13.2 | 11.6 | 5.4 | 5.3 | 36.1 | 50.0 | 563 374 | 608 660 | 8.0 | 4.3 |
| Shoreline | 4.9 | 14.2 | 8.1 | 12.9 | 13.8 | 16.3 | 14.6 | 7.1 | 8.0 | 42.1 | 51.3 | 53 025 | 53 007 | 0.0 | 2.5 |
| Spokane | 6.9 | 15.5 | 12.2 | 15.5 | 12.1 | 13.4 | 11.6 | 6.2 | 6.6 | 35.0 | 51.2 | 195 629 | 209 440 | 6.8 | 0.0 |
| Spokane Valley | 6.9 | 17.2 | 9.5 | 13.7 | 12.3 | 14.3 | 12.0 | 7.1 | 7.0 | 37.3 | 51.1 | NA | 89 745 | NA | 1.0 |
| Tacoma | 7.0 | 16.0 | 10.8 | 16.1 | 13.5 | 14.2 | 11.1 | 5.7 | 5.6 | 35.1 | 50.6 | 193 556 | 198 397 | 2.5 | 1.8 |
| University Place | 5.9 | 17.8 | 9.1 | 12.1 | 12.1 | 15.6 | 13.3 | 7.5 | 6.5 | 39.4 | 53.0 | 29 933 | 31 144 | 4.0 | 1.3 |
| Vancouver | 7.1 | 16.9 | 9.3 | 15.4 | 13.5 | 13.5 | 11.8 | 6.6 | 5.8 | 35.9 | 51.2 | 143 560 | 161 848 | 12.7 | 2.2 |
| Walla Walla | 6.2 | 15.8 | 14.5 | 14.2 | 12.0 | 12.4 | 10.7 | 6.0 | 8.0 | 34.4 | 48.1 | 29 686 | 31 731 | 6.9 | 0.4 |
| Wenatchee | 7.8 | 18.3 | 10.0 | 13.6 | 11.6 | 12.6 | 10.7 | 6.7 | 8.4 | 35.2 | 51.1 | 27 856 | 32 101 | 14.6 | 1.4 |
| Yakima | 8.6 | 19.7 | 10.4 | 14.3 | 11.9 | 11.8 | 10.1 | 6.3 | 6.8 | 32.7 | 50.7 | 71 845 | 91 276 | 26.8 | 2.0 |
| **WEST VIRGINIA** | 5.6 | 15.3 | 9.1 | 11.9 | 12.8 | 14.9 | 14.3 | 8.8 | 7.2 | 41.3 | 50.7 | 1 808 344 | 1 852 999 | 2.5 | 0.1 |
| Charleston | 5.8 | 14.3 | 9.0 | 12.9 | 12.0 | 15.2 | 14.6 | 8.0 | 8.2 | 41.7 | 52.4 | 53 421 | 51 349 | -3.8 | -0.6 |
| Huntington | 5.5 | 12.5 | 16.7 | 14.8 | 11.0 | 12.1 | 12.1 | 7.5 | 7.8 | 35.4 | 51.4 | 51 475 | 49 134 | -4.5 | 0.1 |
| Morgantown | 2.7 | 5.5 | 52.1 | 12.4 | 6.0 | 6.4 | 6.9 | 3.8 | 4.3 | 22.6 | 46.5 | 26 809 | 29 664 | 10.6 | 4.5 |
| Parkersburg | 6.4 | 14.9 | 8.2 | 12.8 | 12.2 | 14.7 | 12.8 | 8.9 | 9.1 | 41.2 | 52.5 | 33 099 | 31 425 | -4.9 | -0.5 |
| Wheeling | 5.1 | 13.4 | 9.4 | 11.2 | 10.6 | 14.8 | 14.8 | 9.1 | 11.5 | 45.2 | 53.1 | 31 419 | 28 479 | -9.3 | -0.9 |
| **WISCONSIN** | 6.3 | 17.3 | 9.7 | 12.7 | 12.8 | 15.4 | 12.3 | 7.0 | 6.6 | 38.5 | 50.4 | 5 363 675 | 5 686 986 | 6.0 | 0.7 |
| Appleton | 6.9 | 18.1 | 10.0 | 14.6 | 13.0 | 15.2 | 10.9 | 5.6 | 5.8 | 35.3 | 50.5 | 70 087 | 72 635 | 3.6 | 0.5 |
| Beloit | 7.7 | 19.4 | 12.0 | 13.3 | 12.4 | 12.9 | 10.2 | 5.8 | 6.1 | 33.1 | 52.1 | 35 775 | 36 967 | 3.3 | -0.3 |
| Brookfield | 4.5 | 19.0 | 5.3 | 7.2 | 11.2 | 18.2 | 14.8 | 9.3 | 10.6 | 46.7 | 51.5 | 38 649 | 37 920 | -1.9 | 0.2 |
| Eau Claire | 5.9 | 13.4 | 22.3 | 14.9 | 10.2 | 11.2 | 10.4 | 5.4 | 6.2 | 29.8 | 51.5 | 61 704 | 65 887 | 6.8 | 1.6 |
| Fitchburg | 8.0 | 16.5 | 9.5 | 19.5 | 13.5 | 13.7 | 11.6 | 4.6 | 3.0 | 32.9 | 48.4 | 20 501 | 25 170 | 23.2 | 2.9 |
| Fond du Lac | 6.7 | 15.9 | 10.1 | 15.1 | 12.3 | 13.6 | 11.6 | 6.4 | 8.3 | 36.9 | 52.3 | 42 203 | 43 021 | 1.9 | 0.1 |
| Franklin | 5.3 | 16.3 | 7.7 | 12.2 | 13.8 | 17.1 | 14.3 | 7.0 | 6.3 | 41.5 | 48.9 | 29 494 | 35 451 | 20.2 | 1.8 |
| Green Bay | 7.7 | 16.9 | 11.7 | 15.3 | 12.5 | 13.9 | 10.6 | 5.6 | 5.8 | 33.7 | 50.6 | 102 313 | 104 057 | 1.7 | 0.8 |
| Greenfield | 5.0 | 12.6 | 8.0 | 14.0 | 11.1 | 14.9 | 13.8 | 8.7 | 11.9 | 44.4 | 52.4 | 35 476 | 36 749 | 3.5 | 0.9 |
| Janesville | 6.7 | 18.1 | 8.4 | 14.0 | 13.8 | 14.2 | 10.9 | 7.2 | 6.7 | 37.1 | 51.1 | 59 498 | 63 589 | 6.9 | 0.0 |
| Kenosha | 7.6 | 19.2 | 10.9 | 14.4 | 13.8 | 13.8 | 9.4 | 5.3 | 5.6 | 33.5 | 50.9 | 90 352 | 99 226 | 9.8 | 0.9 |
| La Crosse | 5.0 | 11.2 | 26.5 | 14.1 | 9.0 | 11.4 | 9.6 | 5.5 | 7.6 | 29.2 | 52.1 | 51 818 | 51 323 | -1.0 | 0.6 |
| Madison | 5.8 | 11.7 | 19.5 | 19.6 | 11.9 | 11.5 | 10.4 | 4.9 | 4.7 | 30.9 | 50.8 | 208 054 | 233 337 | 12.1 | 3.0 |
| Manitowoc | 6.2 | 16.1 | 8.0 | 12.2 | 11.5 | 15.0 | 12.3 | 8.1 | 10.7 | 41.7 | 51.8 | 34 053 | 33 743 | -0.9 | -1.1 |
| Menomonee Falls | 5.7 | 17.3 | 6.0 | 10.5 | 13.0 | 17.5 | 12.1 | 8.1 | 9.8 | 43.3 | 51.8 | 32 647 | 35 626 | 9.1 | 0.5 |
| Milwaukee | 8.2 | 18.9 | 13.7 | 16.2 | 12.5 | 12.2 | 9.4 | 4.5 | 4.4 | 30.3 | 51.8 | 596 974 | 594 740 | -0.4 | 0.7 |
| Mount Pleasant | 5.4 | 15.2 | 6.4 | 10.0 | 12.1 | 16.0 | 15.2 | 9.4 | 10.4 | 45.8 | 52.1 | NA | 26 197 | NA | 0.0 |
| Neenah | 7.1 | 17.9 | 7.8 | 14.5 | 13.1 | 15.7 | 11.3 | 5.9 | 6.8 | 37.1 | 51.1 | 24 507 | 25 504 | 4.1 | 1.0 |
| New Berlin | 4.6 | 16.7 | 6.2 | 10.3 | 12.3 | 18.2 | 14.8 | 8.3 | 8.6 | 44.9 | 51.4 | 38 220 | 39 584 | 3.6 | 0.3 |
| Oak Creek | 6.5 | 17.1 | 8.2 | 14.9 | 15.0 | 15.9 | 11.4 | 6.0 | 5.0 | 37.4 | 50.9 | 28 456 | 34 452 | 21.1 | 1.3 |
| Oshkosh | 5.5 | 13.1 | 18.7 | 14.4 | 12.3 | 13.0 | 10.0 | 5.7 | 7.2 | 33.5 | 48.8 | 62 916 | 66 083 | 5.0 | 0.9 |
| Racine | 8.3 | 19.6 | 10.0 | 14.9 | 12.5 | 13.8 | 10.0 | 5.6 | 5.3 | 33.0 | 51.2 | 81 855 | 78 860 | -3.7 | -0.7 |
| Sheboygan | 7.5 | 17.8 | 8.8 | 14.5 | 12.7 | 14.0 | 10.7 | 6.4 | 7.5 | 36.2 | 50.5 | 50 792 | 49 289 | -3.0 | -0.8 |
| Stevens Point | 5.0 | 11.0 | 31.2 | 13.5 | 8.8 | 10.2 | 8.3 | 5.0 | 7.0 | 26.5 | 51.2 | 24 551 | 26 716 | 8.8 | 0.1 |
| Sun Prairie | 8.5 | 19.3 | 7.4 | 17.5 | 15.4 | 13.3 | 9.7 | 4.6 | 4.3 | 33.3 | 51.5 | 20 369 | 29 364 | 44.2 | 3.5 |
| Superior | 6.5 | 14.8 | 13.4 | 14.9 | 11.2 | 14.0 | 11.9 | 6.5 | 6.9 | 35.4 | 51.0 | 27 368 | 27 244 | -0.5 | -1.4 |
| Waukesha | 7.1 | 16.6 | 10.8 | 16.6 | 13.6 | 13.8 | 10.9 | 5.4 | 5.2 | 34.2 | 51.0 | 64 825 | 70 709 | 9.1 | 0.3 |
| Wausau | 7.3 | 16.2 | 10.0 | 14.5 | 11.5 | 13.5 | 11.3 | 6.6 | 9.2 | 36.8 | 50.9 | 38 426 | 39 114 | 1.8 | 0.1 |
| Wauwatosa | 6.3 | 15.6 | 5.9 | 15.8 | 13.0 | 14.6 | 12.2 | 6.0 | 10.6 | 39.8 | 53.4 | 47 271 | 46 446 | -1.9 | 1.3 |
| West Allis | 6.5 | 14.0 | 8.3 | 17.6 | 12.5 | 15.2 | 11.3 | 6.0 | 8.6 | 37.7 | 51.0 | 61 254 | 60 419 | -1.4 | 0.5 |
| West Bend | 7.3 | 17.4 | 7.5 | 15.1 | 13.7 | 13.5 | 10.9 | 6.6 | 8.0 | 37.0 | 51.7 | 28 152 | 31 155 | 10.4 | 1.2 |
| **WYOMING** | 7.1 | 16.9 | 10.0 | 13.8 | 11.9 | 14.8 | 13.0 | 7.0 | 5.4 | 36.8 | 49.0 | 493 782 | 563 626 | 14.1 | 2.3 |
| Casper | 7.2 | 16.7 | 10.1 | 14.7 | 12.0 | 14.5 | 12.0 | 6.1 | 6.8 | 36.0 | 50.3 | 49 644 | 55 316 | 11.4 | 4.5 |
| Cheyenne | 7.4 | 16.6 | 9.4 | 14.6 | 12.3 | 14.0 | 12.2 | 7.0 | 6.5 | 36.5 | 50.7 | 53 011 | 59 489 | 12.2 | 3.4 |
| Gillette | 9.2 | 18.8 | 11.0 | 18.1 | 12.5 | 14.9 | 9.7 | 3.4 | 2.4 | 30.6 | 47.7 | 19 646 | 29 775 | 48.1 | 5.4 |
| Laramie | 5.8 | 10.1 | 32.7 | 17.7 | 8.8 | 8.9 | 8.4 | 3.9 | 3.6 | 25.4 | 48.0 | 27 204 | 30 815 | 13.3 | 2.8 |

# Table D. Cities — Households, Group Quarters, Crime, and Education

| | Households, 2010 | | | | Persons in group quarters, 2010 | | | | Serious crimes known to police,[2] 2011 | | | | Educational attainment, 2007–2011 | | |
| | | | Percent | | | Institutional | | | Total | | Rate[3] | | | Attainment[4] (percent) | |
| City | Number | Persons per house-hold | Female family house-holder[1] | One-person | Total | Total | Persons in nursing facilities | Non-institu-tional | Number | Rate[3] | Violent | Property | Population age 25 and older | High school graduate or less | Bachelor's degree or more |
| | 27 | 28 | 29 | 30 | 31 | 32 | 33 | 34 | 35 | 36 | 37 | 38 | 39 | 40 | 41 |
| WASHINGTON—Cont'd | | | | | | | | | | | | | | | |
| Pullman | 11 029 | 2.18 | 4.7 | 34.5 | 5 788 | 18 | 18 | 5 770 | 516 | 1 705 | 93 | 1 612 | 10 441 | 13.1 | 67.4 |
| Puyallup | 14 950 | 2.43 | 12.8 | 28.5 | 710 | 443 | 403 | 267 | 2 757 | 7 332 | 287 | 7 045 | 24 184 | 40.8 | 22.4 |
| Redmond | 22 550 | 2.39 | 6.9 | 29.6 | 274 | 171 | 171 | 103 | 1 466 | 2 666 | 85 | 2 580 | 37 353 | 15.6 | 60.2 |
| Renton | 36 009 | 2.51 | 11.9 | 30.3 | 685 | 263 | 191 | 422 | 4 515 | 4 889 | 316 | 4 573 | 60 068 | 36.9 | 30.3 |
| Richland | 19 707 | 2.42 | 10.0 | 28.2 | 285 | 163 | 163 | 122 | 1 494 | 3 061 | 182 | 2 878 | 31 411 | 24.2 | 41.0 |
| Sammamish | 15 154 | 3.01 | 5.6 | 11.4 | 99 | 0 | 0 | 99 | 372 | 800 | 34 | 766 | 27 564 | 9.2 | 69.6 |
| SeaTac | 9 533 | 2.72 | 14.0 | 28.8 | 1 014 | 905 | 74 | 109 | 1 601 | 5 858 | 457 | 5 400 | 17 469 | 54.5 | 14.6 |
| Seattle | 283 510 | 2.06 | 7.3 | 41.3 | 24 925 | 4 904 | 2 588 | 20 021 | 35 456 | 5 735 | 593 | 5 143 | 438 782 | 19.7 | 55.8 |
| Shoreline | 21 561 | 2.39 | 10.3 | 29.7 | 1 415 | 581 | 578 | 834 | 1 776 | 3 299 | 156 | 3 143 | 37 585 | 26.3 | 43.0 |
| Spokane | 87 271 | 2.31 | 12.9 | 34.2 | 6 949 | 1 972 | 1 236 | 4 977 | 16 343 | 7 702 | 615 | 7 087 | 134 861 | 33.2 | 29.2 |
| Spokane Valley | 36 558 | 2.43 | 12.2 | 29.0 | 802 | 439 | 418 | 363 | 5 176 | 5 678 | 192 | 5 486 | 59 089 | 38.8 | 19.5 |
| Tacoma | 78 541 | 2.44 | 14.8 | 32.3 | 6 693 | 4 084 | 1 392 | 2 609 | 13 624 | 6 761 | 750 | 6 011 | 130 917 | 41.0 | 24.3 |
| University Place | 12 819 | 2.41 | 14.0 | 27.7 | 206 | 118 | 118 | 88 | 833 | 2 633 | 272 | 2 361 | 20 738 | 27.4 | 33.9 |
| Vancouver | 65 691 | 2.43 | 13.2 | 30.0 | 2 056 | 1 192 | 429 | 864 | 7 080 | 4 308 | 385 | 3 923 | 108 468 | 37.9 | 23.5 |
| Walla Walla | 11 537 | 2.43 | 12.0 | 33.4 | 3 651 | 2 600 | 190 | 1 051 | 1 513 | 4 695 | 403 | 4 291 | 20 016 | 38.7 | 21.2 |
| Wenatchee | 12 379 | 2.53 | 11.9 | 31.2 | 582 | 402 | 88 | 180 | 1 402 | 4 324 | 268 | 4 055 | 20 775 | 49.0 | 22.3 |
| Yakima | 33 074 | 2.68 | 15.7 | 28.7 | 2 448 | 1 841 | 650 | 607 | 5 612 | 6 067 | 520 | 5 547 | 55 973 | 52.2 | 18.3 |
| WEST VIRGINIA | 763 831 | 2.36 | 11.2 | 28.4 | 49 382 | 28 323 | 9 748 | 21 059 | 48 050 | 2 590 | 316 | 2 274 | 1 287 738 | 58.4 | 17.6 |
| Charleston | 23 453 | 2.11 | 14.1 | 39.4 | 1 940 | 675 | 220 | 1 265 | 3 524 | 6 847 | 991 | 5 856 | 37 571 | 37.5 | 37.8 |
| Huntington | 21 774 | 2.12 | 13.7 | 39.2 | 3 012 | 676 | 412 | 2 336 | 2 390 | 4 858 | 492 | 4 366 | 31 954 | 46.7 | 23.9 |
| Morgantown | 11 701 | 2.05 | 6.5 | 36.6 | 5 636 | 86 | 19 | 5 550 | 745 | 2 509 | 306 | 2 202 | 12 641 | 31.4 | 46.6 |
| Parkersburg | 13 807 | 2.24 | 14.3 | 35.0 | 547 | 341 | 326 | 206 | 1 510 | 4 789 | 818 | 3 971 | 22 379 | 52.4 | 15.2 |
| Wheeling | 12 816 | 2.11 | 12.7 | 40.4 | 1 436 | 523 | 413 | 913 | 977 | 3 425 | 782 | 2 644 | 20 455 | 46.1 | 25.7 |
| WISCONSIN | 2 279 768 | 2.43 | 10.3 | 28.2 | 150 214 | 74 295 | 33 808 | 75 919 | 152 481 | 2 670 | 237 | 2 433 | 3 771 680 | 43.8 | 26.0 |
| Appleton | 28 874 | 2.43 | 10.5 | 29.5 | 2 429 | 864 | 487 | 1 565 | 1 691 | 2 318 | 299 | 2 019 | 46 880 | 39.5 | 30.9 |
| Beloit | 13 781 | 2.57 | 18.3 | 29.4 | 1 553 | 242 | 242 | 1 311 | 1 489 | 4 011 | 420 | 3 590 | 22 136 | 60.2 | 13.9 |
| Brookfield | 14 576 | 2.57 | 5.4 | 21.4 | 513 | 460 | 460 | 53 | 1 046 | 2 746 | 66 | 2 681 | 26 885 | 22.6 | 53.9 |
| Eau Claire | 26 803 | 2.29 | 9.5 | 31.7 | 4 536 | 613 | 256 | 3 923 | 2 098 | 3 171 | 210 | 2 961 | 37 773 | 34.3 | 33.4 |
| Fitchburg | 9 955 | 2.45 | 10.5 | 27.3 | 822 | 815 | 0 | 7 | 752 | 2 964 | 233 | 2 732 | 16 632 | 29.8 | 44.2 |
| Fond du Lac | 17 942 | 2.28 | 11.1 | 34.4 | 2 087 | 1 481 | 480 | 606 | 1 215 | 2 812 | 338 | 2 474 | 28 892 | 49.9 | 18.3 |
| Franklin | 13 642 | 2.45 | 6.8 | 26.4 | 1 982 | 1 908 | 42 | 74 | 642 | 1 803 | 42 | 1 761 | 23 938 | 35.6 | 33.4 |
| Green Bay | 42 244 | 2.39 | 12.5 | 32.4 | 3 206 | 1 362 | 617 | 1 844 | 3 019 | 2 889 | 419 | 2 470 | 66 647 | 48.9 | 21.4 |
| Greenfield | 16 860 | 2.13 | 9.2 | 37.5 | 821 | 728 | 728 | 93 | 1 226 | 3 324 | 138 | 3 186 | 27 224 | 42.8 | 25.1 |
| Janesville | 25 828 | 2.43 | 12.7 | 28.2 | 930 | 756 | 309 | 174 | 2 568 | 4 022 | 265 | 3 757 | 41 948 | 47.4 | 21.6 |
| Kenosha | 37 376 | 2.56 | 15.9 | 28.8 | 3 488 | 1 620 | 736 | 1 868 | 3 310 | 3 322 | 280 | 3 042 | 61 560 | 46.5 | 22.6 |
| La Crosse | 21 428 | 2.18 | 9.7 | 37.7 | 4 681 | 827 | 540 | 3 854 | 2 017 | 3 913 | 320 | 3 593 | 29 724 | 39.4 | 26.5 |
| Madison | 102 516 | 2.17 | 8.4 | 36.2 | 10 740 | 2 171 | 1 173 | 8 569 | 8 762 | 3 741 | 350 | 3 391 | 142 866 | 22.3 | 52.9 |
| Manitowoc | 14 623 | 2.24 | 10.0 | 35.4 | 956 | 532 | 524 | 424 | 848 | 2 503 | 156 | 2 346 | 23 250 | 51.0 | 19.1 |
| Menomonee Falls | 14 567 | 2.43 | 6.9 | 26.8 | 217 | 202 | 202 | 15 | 469 | 1 311 | 25 | 1 286 | 25 186 | 34.5 | 38.6 |
| Milwaukee | 230 221 | 2.50 | 22.6 | 33.6 | 18 401 | 5 302 | 2 512 | 13 099 | 37 306 | 6 244 | 1 111 | 5 134 | 352 687 | 51.0 | 21.3 |
| Mount Pleasant | 11 136 | 2.33 | 8.5 | 29.2 | 290 | 268 | 265 | 22 | 713 | 2 710 | 87 | 2 622 | 18 644 | 40.7 | 26.7 |
| Neenah | 10 694 | 2.36 | 10.5 | 30.7 | 277 | 233 | 211 | 44 | 443 | 1 730 | 141 | 1 589 | 16 973 | 40.5 | 28.8 |
| New Berlin | 16 292 | 2.42 | 5.8 | 25.2 | 161 | 125 | 125 | 36 | NA | NA | NA | NA | 28 346 | 29.3 | 40.3 |
| Oak Creek | 14 064 | 2.44 | 8.2 | 28.6 | 125 | 0 | 0 | 125 | 1 173 | 3 390 | 87 | 3 303 | 22 873 | 39.5 | 27.2 |
| Oshkosh | 26 138 | 2.24 | 10.0 | 34.4 | 7 520 | 4 056 | 974 | 3 464 | 1 847 | 2 783 | 270 | 2 513 | 40 408 | 48.7 | 22.5 |
| Racine | 30 530 | 2.53 | 20.1 | 30.5 | 1 548 | 1 276 | 152 | 272 | 3 929 | 4 961 | 409 | 4 552 | 49 587 | 54.7 | 16.4 |
| Sheboygan | 20 308 | 2.38 | 11.7 | 33.4 | 953 | 766 | 472 | 187 | 1 577 | 3 186 | 265 | 2 921 | 32 190 | 52.4 | 18.5 |
| Stevens Point | 10 598 | 2.21 | 8.5 | 34.9 | 3 330 | 178 | 94 | 3 152 | 710 | 2 646 | 175 | 2 471 | 13 915 | 37.8 | 31.2 |
| Sun Prairie | 11 636 | 2.51 | 11.5 | 26.1 | 102 | 82 | 82 | 20 | 690 | 2 340 | 146 | 2 194 | 18 680 | 28.8 | 40.0 |
| Superior | 11 670 | 2.23 | 13.5 | 34.6 | 1 191 | 393 | 234 | 798 | 1 473 | 5 383 | 197 | 5 186 | 18 095 | 40.4 | 22.2 |
| Waukesha | 28 295 | 2.40 | 10.7 | 30.3 | 2 911 | 892 | 228 | 2 019 | 1 222 | 1 720 | 130 | 1 591 | 45 795 | 36.3 | 32.9 |
| Wausau | 16 487 | 2.31 | 11.5 | 35.4 | 1 100 | 820 | 526 | 280 | 1 301 | 3 312 | 313 | 2 999 | 26 107 | 46.4 | 23.8 |
| Wauwatosa | 20 435 | 2.23 | 8.2 | 34.3 | 871 | 732 | 615 | 139 | 1 902 | 4 082 | 215 | 3 867 | 32 882 | 21.4 | 51.7 |
| West Allis | 27 454 | 2.17 | 11.9 | 38.6 | 829 | 591 | 583 | 238 | 3 373 | 5 559 | 328 | 5 231 | 42 717 | 47.6 | 20.2 |
| West Bend | 12 769 | 2.39 | 10.0 | 29.2 | 530 | 429 | 215 | 101 | 774 | 2 480 | 93 | 2 387 | 21 273 | 40.7 | 23.3 |
| WYOMING | 226 879 | 2.42 | 8.9 | 28.0 | 13 712 | 6 701 | 2 450 | 7 011 | 14 123 | 2 486 | 219 | 2 266 | 364 833 | 38.6 | 24.2 |
| Casper | 22 794 | 2.38 | 11.2 | 30.3 | 1 125 | 548 | 483 | 577 | 2 160 | 3 874 | 185 | 3 689 | 36 001 | 35.7 | 24.1 |
| Cheyenne | 25 557 | 2.29 | 12.0 | 33.5 | 865 | 636 | 330 | 229 | 2 196 | 3 663 | 245 | 3 418 | 38 523 | 33.9 | 25.0 |
| Gillette | 10 975 | 2.61 | 10.3 | 24.3 | 422 | 260 | 123 | 162 | 921 | 3 141 | 126 | 3 015 | 17 012 | 42.8 | 19.4 |
| Laramie | 13 394 | 2.14 | 6.9 | 36.9 | 2 176 | 78 | 70 | 2 098 | 767 | 2 469 | 126 | 2 344 | 15 183 | 20.2 | 50.0 |

1. No spouse present.   2. Data for serious crimes have not been adjusted for underreporting. This may affect comparability between geographic areas and over time.   3. Per 100,000 population estimated by the FBI.   4. Persons 25 years old and over.

# Table D. Cities — Income, Poverty, and Housing

| City | Per capita income[1] (dollars) | Median income | Percent with income of $200,000 or more | Percent with income of less than $25,000 | Families with income below poverty (percent) | Total | Percent change, 2000–2010 | Vacant units for sale or rent[2] | Total | Percent | Median value[3] (dollars) | With a mortgage[4] | Without a mortgage[5] |
|---|---|---|---|---|---|---|---|---|---|---|---|---|---|
| | Money income, 2007–2011 Households | | | | | Housing units, 2010 | | | Occupied Housing units 2007–2011 Owner-occupied | | | Median owner costs as a percent of income | |
| | 42 | 43 | 44 | 45 | 46 | 47 | 48 | 49 | 50 | 51 | 52 | 53 | 54 |
| **WASHINGTON— Cont'd** | | | | | | | | | | | | | |
| Pullman | 17 263 | 24 321 | 2.8 | 50.9 | 15.6 | 11 966 | 27.4 | 937 | 9 994 | 31.5 | 229 700 | 21.4 | 10.0 |
| Puyallup | 29 912 | 61 099 | 2.3 | 17.0 | 5.8 | 16 171 | 20.8 | 1 221 | 14 769 | 53.8 | 284 200 | 26.8 | 11.8 |
| Redmond | 46 748 | 92 851 | 10.7 | 10.3 | 4.1 | 24 177 | 19.1 | 1 627 | 23 048 | 52.4 | 460 200 | 24.8 | 10.0 |
| Renton | 31 121 | 64 829 | 2.9 | 15.3 | 7.3 | 38 930 | 71.5 | 2 921 | 36 025 | 56.4 | 312 100 | 28.7 | 13.6 |
| Richland | 34 855 | 67 666 | 6.1 | 16.5 | 6.6 | 20 876 | 26.9 | 1 169 | 18 857 | 67.4 | 195 200 | 19.5 | 10.0 |
| Sammamish | 53 423 | 135 432 | 25.3 | 3.9 | 2.5 | 15 736 | 34.7 | 582 | 14 583 | 89.0 | 602 200 | 24.5 | 10.0 |
| SeaTac | 22 020 | 48 319 | 0.5 | 22.4 | 13.6 | 10 360 | 3.3 | 827 | 9 912 | 54.5 | 258 800 | 29.4 | 13.5 |
| Seattle | 41 695 | 61 856 | 8.0 | 20.4 | 6.8 | 308 516 | 14.0 | 25 006 | 282 480 | 48.0 | 453 000 | 26.2 | 13.2 |
| Shoreline | 34 884 | 66 774 | 5.4 | 16.8 | 4.4 | 22 787 | 6.8 | 1 226 | 21 405 | 65.7 | 364 200 | 28.3 | 13.5 |
| Spokane | 23 869 | 41 466 | 2.2 | 29.7 | 12.7 | 94 291 | 7.0 | 7 020 | 87 869 | 57.1 | 165 500 | 25.3 | 12.5 |
| Spokane Valley | 23 308 | 47 759 | 1.4 | 24.8 | 9.7 | 38 851 | NA | 2 293 | 36 348 | 63.4 | 183 200 | 25.4 | 11.0 |
| Tacoma | 26 096 | 49 232 | 2.3 | 24.3 | 12.9 | 85 786 | 5.9 | 7 245 | 79 430 | 53.7 | 239 200 | 28.6 | 14.1 |
| University Place | 31 168 | 59 544 | 3.9 | 17.2 | 6.4 | 13 573 | 6.8 | 754 | 12 706 | 56.6 | 317 800 | 25.5 | 14.2 |
| Vancouver | 25 821 | 50 387 | 2.0 | 22.4 | 11.9 | 70 005 | 16.6 | 4 314 | 66 066 | 51.5 | 228 500 | 27.3 | 11.9 |
| Walla Walla | 21 110 | 41 236 | 0.9 | 28.9 | 16.5 | 12 514 | 9.3 | 977 | 11 796 | 57.7 | 184 800 | 24.8 | 12.7 |
| Wenatchee | 23 777 | 44 879 | 2.4 | 24.5 | 9.7 | 13 175 | 14.6 | 796 | 12 219 | 58.4 | 218 300 | 26.8 | 10.6 |
| Yakima | 20 919 | 41 071 | 2.0 | 30.7 | 15.8 | 34 829 | 21.2 | 1 755 | 32 988 | 54.2 | 157 100 | 24.1 | 11.9 |
| **WEST VIRGINIA** | 22 010 | 39 550 | 1.7 | 32.8 | 12.8 | 881 917 | 4.4 | 118 086 | 740 080 | 74.3 | 96 500 | 19.9 | 10.0 |
| Charleston | 35 191 | 46 004 | 6.6 | 29.5 | 11.6 | 26 205 | -3.2 | 2 752 | 23 907 | 61.2 | 136 600 | 18.9 | 10.0 |
| Huntington | 20 011 | 28 483 | 2.2 | 45.6 | 23.0 | 25 146 | -3.0 | 3 372 | 21 396 | 52.7 | 84 200 | 21.1 | 11.0 |
| Morgantown | 18 648 | 25 948 | 2.7 | 49.7 | 9.2 | 12 664 | 7.2 | 963 | 10 082 | 40.5 | 166 100 | 17.3 | 10.0 |
| Parkersburg | 20 789 | 33 629 | 1.2 | 40.5 | 18.4 | 15 562 | -3.2 | 1 755 | 13 920 | 62.4 | 87 400 | 20.7 | 11.0 |
| Wheeling | 22 881 | 34 807 | 1.7 | 37.1 | 13.0 | 14 661 | -6.2 | 1 845 | 12 770 | 64.2 | 92 000 | 19.1 | 10.4 |
| **WISCONSIN** | 27 192 | 52 374 | 2.8 | 22.0 | 8.0 | 2 624 358 | 13.1 | 344 590 | 2 279 738 | 69.1 | 169 700 | 24.4 | 13.9 |
| Appleton | 27 179 | 52 183 | 3.0 | 21.2 | 8.2 | 30 348 | 9.7 | 1 474 | 28 678 | 70.1 | 139 100 | 23.1 | 13.7 |
| Beloit | 17 717 | 36 511 | 0.6 | 33.5 | 21.0 | 15 177 | 6.5 | 1 396 | 13 926 | 63.7 | 89 900 | 24.9 | 17.0 |
| Brookfield | 45 317 | 88 195 | 13.4 | 10.5 | 2.6 | 15 317 | 7.5 | 741 | 14 624 | 86.7 | 286 900 | 22.5 | 13.4 |
| Eau Claire | 23 759 | 42 226 | 1.8 | 30.8 | 9.4 | 28 134 | 13.7 | 1 331 | 26 557 | 56.8 | 137 500 | 22.8 | 13.2 |
| Fitchburg | 33 955 | 63 811 | 6.0 | 16.9 | 9.0 | 10 668 | 23.2 | 713 | 9 594 | 53.8 | 270 600 | 25.0 | 10.2 |
| Fond du Lac | 23 709 | 43 457 | 1.5 | 28.3 | 10.0 | 19 181 | 9.2 | 1 239 | 18 013 | 58.2 | 122 400 | 23.3 | 13.8 |
| Franklin | 34 494 | 77 654 | 5.3 | 12.4 | 3.6 | 14 356 | 31.0 | 714 | 12 391 | 79.2 | 239 200 | 23.2 | 14.1 |
| Green Bay | 23 389 | 42 484 | 1.7 | 28.1 | 12.4 | 45 241 | 4.8 | 2 997 | 42 815 | 58.8 | 132 100 | 23.9 | 13.0 |
| Greenfield | 29 225 | 50 577 | 2.0 | 20.6 | 3.9 | 17 790 | 9.9 | 930 | 16 412 | 60.7 | 185 400 | 24.4 | 17.7 |
| Janesville | 24 009 | 49 772 | 1.4 | 22.7 | 10.7 | 27 996 | 11.7 | 2 168 | 25 112 | 70.6 | 135 200 | 23.5 | 13.5 |
| Kenosha | 23 728 | 48 396 | 1.8 | 25.5 | 12.9 | 40 643 | 12.4 | 3 267 | 37 130 | 60.3 | 161 200 | 26.9 | 14.6 |
| La Crosse | 21 383 | 38 287 | 1.5 | 33.7 | 12.1 | 22 628 | 1.9 | 1 200 | 21 457 | 50.8 | 126 800 | 23.1 | 15.1 |
| Madison | 30 595 | 54 093 | 3.7 | 23.2 | 8.6 | 108 843 | 17.9 | 6 327 | 99 512 | 51.4 | 219 600 | 25.3 | 12.0 |
| Manitowoc | 24 687 | 42 417 | 1.8 | 26.3 | 7.1 | 15 955 | 6.4 | 1 332 | 14 703 | 66.1 | 108 400 | 22.6 | 13.6 |
| Menomonee Falls | 35 440 | 71 326 | 5.8 | 14.6 | 2.0 | 15 142 | 15.1 | 575 | 14 532 | 75.6 | 237 500 | 23.4 | 14.7 |
| Milwaukee | 19 111 | 35 851 | 1.0 | 35.4 | 22.6 | 255 569 | 2.5 | 25 348 | 230 153 | 45.5 | 139 000 | 28.1 | 17.8 |
| Mount Pleasant | 31 415 | 59 418 | 3.1 | 17.4 | 4.4 | 11 827 | NA | 691 | 10 867 | 78.5 | 198 400 | 24.6 | 15.4 |
| Neenah | 29 294 | 52 085 | 3.7 | 18.9 | 6.0 | 11 313 | 11.2 | 619 | 10 389 | 69.4 | 131 800 | 22.1 | 13.2 |
| New Berlin | 38 089 | 75 297 | 6.6 | 10.1 | 1.9 | 16 829 | 12.7 | 537 | 16 058 | 78.2 | 247 100 | 23.6 | 13.3 |
| Oak Creek | 30 235 | 67 384 | 1.8 | 15.1 | 3.8 | 14 754 | 24.0 | 690 | 13 378 | 61.5 | 220 400 | 23.0 | 13.9 |
| Oshkosh | 21 651 | 43 203 | 1.3 | 27.5 | 8.6 | 28 179 | 11.1 | 2 041 | 25 060 | 58.1 | 117 100 | 22.9 | 14.0 |
| Racine | 20 246 | 39 059 | 1.3 | 31.3 | 15.9 | 33 887 | 1.3 | 3 357 | 31 387 | 56.2 | 128 900 | 25.3 | 15.0 |
| Sheboygan | 21 759 | 43 203 | 0.7 | 25.6 | 8.9 | 22 339 | 2.4 | 2 031 | 20 301 | 63.8 | 118 000 | 22.9 | 14.3 |
| Stevens Point | 21 893 | 39 373 | 2.0 | 33.6 | 8.5 | 11 220 | 15.0 | 622 | 10 940 | 50.1 | 115 300 | 22.3 | 12.7 |
| Sun Prairie | 32 091 | 66 395 | 2.5 | 12.3 | 6.0 | 12 413 | 53.0 | 777 | 11 508 | 62.6 | 212 500 | 24.7 | 14.1 |
| Superior | 24 028 | 40 146 | 1.2 | 30.9 | 12.7 | 12 328 | 1.0 | 658 | 12 321 | 56.6 | 118 200 | 22.4 | 13.0 |
| Waukesha | 28 106 | 57 001 | 2.0 | 18.6 | 7.2 | 29 843 | 11.1 | 1 548 | 28 520 | 60.0 | 204 700 | 24.5 | 13.9 |
| Wausau | 23 785 | 41 168 | 1.7 | 28.5 | 11.2 | 18 154 | 8.8 | 1 667 | 16 600 | 59.0 | 114 700 | 22.1 | 13.5 |
| Wauwatosa | 36 775 | 67 133 | 4.9 | 14.9 | 2.7 | 21 520 | 2.9 | 1 085 | 19 791 | 66.4 | 229 300 | 22.9 | 13.5 |
| West Allis | 24 715 | 44 200 | 0.7 | 26.2 | 9.4 | 29 353 | 2.2 | 1 899 | 27 325 | 57.5 | 159 300 | 26.6 | 16.8 |
| West Bend | 27 164 | 53 164 | 2.0 | 21.5 | 6.6 | 13 546 | 13.7 | 777 | 13 224 | 64.5 | 179 300 | 24.5 | 15.3 |
| **WYOMING** | 28 952 | 56 380 | 2.9 | 19.1 | 6.5 | 261 868 | 17.0 | 34 989 | 219 628 | 70.5 | 181 900 | 21.6 | 10.0 |
| Casper | 30 603 | 53 064 | 3.8 | 18.7 | 5.5 | 24 536 | 11.6 | 1 742 | 22 340 | 67.2 | 180 800 | 21.0 | 10.0 |
| Cheyenne | 28 739 | 51 912 | 2.2 | 20.0 | 6.5 | 27 283 | 14.6 | 1 726 | 24 693 | 63.8 | 168 100 | 22.9 | 10.0 |
| Gillette | 32 370 | 74 404 | 3.5 | 12.3 | 7.3 | 12 153 | 52.3 | 1 178 | 10 469 | 70.5 | 194 300 | 20.1 | 10.0 |
| Laramie | 23 104 | 41 304 | 1.4 | 33.3 | 10.6 | 14 307 | 19.2 | 913 | 12 333 | 48.0 | 189 500 | 22.8 | 10.0 |

1. Based on population estimated by the American Community Survey.　2. Includes units rented or sold but not occupied.　3. Specified owner-occupied units; $1,000,000 represents $1,000,000 or more　4. 50.0 represents 50 percent or more.　5. 10.0 represents 10 percent or less.

# Table D. Cities — Housing, Labor Force, and Employment

| City | Occupied housing units, 2007–2011 (cont.) | | | | Migration, 2007–2011 | | Civilian labor force, 2012 | | Unemployment | | Civilian employment[4], 2007–2011 | | Percent | Households with no workers (percent) |
|---|---|---|---|---|---|---|---|---|---|---|---|---|---|---|
| | Percent renter occupied | Median gross rent[1] | Median rent as a percent of income[2] | Percent with no vehicle available | Percent who lived in the same house one year ago | Percent who lived outside this city one year ago | Total | Percent change, 2011–2012 | Total | Rate[3] | Population age 16 and older | In labor force | Full-year full-time worker | |
| | 55 | 56 | 57 | 58 | 59 | 60 | 61 | 62 | 63 | 64 | 65 | 66 | 67 | 68 |
| **WASHINGTON— Cont'd** | | | | | | | | | | | | | | |
| Pullman | 68.5 | 667 | 50.0 | 9.3 | 58.8 | 25.4 | 14 646 | -1.0 | 918 | 6.3 | 26 245 | 55.3 | 18.6 | 26.7 |
| Puyallup | 46.2 | 1 036 | 29.4 | 8.2 | 78.7 | 15.6 | 19 052 | -0.9 | 1 588 | 8.3 | 29 559 | 68.2 | 41.0 | 24.3 |
| Redmond | 47.6 | 1 356 | 22.7 | 6.1 | 76.4 | 16.9 | 33 225 | 1.3 | 1 728 | 5.2 | 42 422 | 72.6 | 49.2 | 15.8 |
| Renton | 43.6 | 1 045 | 28.0 | 6.3 | 79.0 | 14.6 | 53 719 | 1.8 | 3 220 | 6.0 | 70 232 | 73.9 | 49.3 | 20.0 |
| Richland | 32.6 | 823 | 27.3 | 5.7 | 83.1 | 11.5 | 26 322 | 2.8 | 2 126 | 8.1 | 36 751 | 65.2 | 42.1 | 24.6 |
| Sammamish | 11.0 | 1 550 | 25.2 | 1.0 | 89.7 | 7.9 | 24 942 | 2.5 | 1 339 | 5.4 | 31 627 | 70.5 | 48.3 | 10.0 |
| SeaTac | 45.5 | 891 | 31.8 | 8.2 | 79.3 | 17.1 | 14 754 | 0.7 | 1 240 | 8.4 | 21 259 | 64.9 | 42.2 | 22.6 |
| Seattle | 52.0 | 1 003 | 28.9 | 15.6 | 77.1 | 10.9 | 374 019 | 1.3 | 23 831 | 6.4 | 519 390 | 72.6 | 43.6 | 21.5 |
| Shoreline | 34.3 | 1 026 | 30.6 | 6.9 | 85.9 | 10.9 | 28 985 | 1.1 | 1 988 | 6.9 | 43 517 | 67.5 | 41.5 | 24.4 |
| Spokane | 42.9 | 704 | 32.1 | 10.0 | 78.7 | 9.3 | 101 694 | -1.5 | 8 976 | 8.8 | 165 693 | 63.8 | 35.4 | 30.7 |
| Spokane Valley | 36.6 | 738 | 29.9 | 6.9 | 81.9 | 12.2 | 46 374 | -2.1 | 3 971 | 8.6 | 70 168 | 65.9 | 38.2 | 28.4 |
| Tacoma | 46.3 | 861 | 31.5 | 9.7 | 78.3 | 12.0 | 96 226 | -0.9 | 8 962 | 9.3 | 159 307 | 65.0 | 37.3 | 27.9 |
| University Place | 43.4 | 889 | 30.9 | 4.3 | 81.7 | 14.7 | 16 592 | -0.5 | 1 131 | 6.8 | 24 740 | 69.6 | 42.7 | 25.1 |
| Vancouver | 48.5 | 865 | 30.0 | 7.6 | 80.4 | 10.5 | 80 250 | -2.2 | 8 602 | 10.7 | 127 107 | 65.6 | 37.7 | 27.9 |
| Walla Walla | 42.3 | 676 | 30.6 | 8.5 | 79.2 | 11.8 | 15 046 | 1.8 | 1 143 | 7.6 | 25 382 | 56.5 | 30.7 | 31.7 |
| Wenatchee | 41.6 | 734 | 28.4 | 8.7 | 83.5 | 9.3 | 17 362 | 8.8 | 1 362 | 7.8 | 24 747 | 61.6 | 39.5 | 32.6 |
| Yakima | 45.8 | 692 | 30.7 | 9.4 | 78.9 | 10.0 | 44 331 | 6.9 | 3 974 | 9.0 | 67 669 | 62.1 | 36.2 | 30.4 |
| **WEST VIRGINIA** | 25.7 | 574 | 29.1 | 8.8 | 87.7 | 10.1 | 804 917 | 1.3 | 59 075 | 7.3 | 1 504 751 | 54.9 | 35.1 | 36.1 |
| Charleston | 38.8 | 600 | 26.9 | 16.0 | 83.8 | 9.2 | 24 552 | 0.4 | 1 502 | 6.1 | 42 943 | 61.7 | 40.7 | 32.0 |
| Huntington | 47.3 | 579 | 35.2 | 18.6 | 78.2 | 11.3 | 21 385 | 1.1 | 1 544 | 7.2 | 41 034 | 53.7 | 30.6 | 39.2 |
| Morgantown | 59.5 | 619 | 45.6 | 10.8 | 62.5 | 26.3 | 15 810 | 4.8 | 836 | 5.3 | 27 329 | 52.1 | 21.7 | 34.1 |
| Parkersburg | 37.6 | 567 | 33.8 | 13.5 | 83.6 | 8.7 | 13 482 | 0.0 | 1 123 | 8.3 | 25 831 | 55.4 | 33.6 | 40.7 |
| Wheeling | 35.8 | 516 | 30.2 | 16.1 | 86.3 | 6.8 | 12 404 | 0.3 | 912 | 7.4 | 23 923 | 57.7 | 35.2 | 37.0 |
| **WISCONSIN** | 30.9 | 735 | 28.9 | 6.8 | 85.5 | 8.9 | 3 051 732 | 0.3 | 211 444 | 6.9 | 4 487 568 | 68.7 | 41.9 | 25.3 |
| Appleton | 29.9 | 636 | 27.1 | 6.6 | 86.5 | 7.7 | 39 937 | -0.4 | 3 277 | 8.2 | 56 193 | 69.5 | 43.2 | 22.9 |
| Beloit | 36.3 | 705 | 36.0 | 9.4 | 81.4 | 8.4 | 16 533 | -0.4 | 1 839 | 11.1 | 27 871 | 65.3 | 33.4 | 32.5 |
| Brookfield | 13.3 | 1 250 | 31.4 | 2.8 | 91.3 | 6.8 | 18 690 | 1.0 | 1 107 | 5.9 | 30 729 | 62.1 | 39.3 | 28.6 |
| Eau Claire | 43.2 | 680 | 31.8 | 6.8 | 75.1 | 11.1 | 39 102 | 3.5 | 2 492 | 6.4 | 54 003 | 71.1 | 36.1 | 23.9 |
| Fitchburg | 46.2 | 844 | 26.9 | 5.1 | 74.7 | 21.8 | 15 564 | 2.3 | 837 | 5.4 | 19 328 | 72.7 | 44.4 | 15.7 |
| Fond du Lac | 41.8 | 640 | 28.7 | 9.8 | 81.8 | 9.1 | 22 536 | 0.1 | 1 736 | 7.7 | 33 979 | 68.4 | 39.3 | 28.0 |
| Franklin | 20.8 | 909 | 25.0 | 3.6 | 84.6 | 15.0 | 19 203 | 0.5 | 1 102 | 5.7 | 27 696 | 65.4 | 42.3 | 21.7 |
| Green Bay | 41.2 | 621 | 29.4 | 8.2 | 83.1 | 7.5 | 59 330 | -0.4 | 5 366 | 9.0 | 81 567 | 68.5 | 41.2 | 25.7 |
| Greenfield | 39.3 | 809 | 28.2 | 6.7 | 86.9 | 10.8 | 20 170 | 0.2 | 1 322 | 6.6 | 30 727 | 64.2 | 43.0 | 32.0 |
| Janesville | 29.4 | 730 | 31.2 | 5.5 | 84.5 | 5.7 | 32 093 | 0.5 | 2 897 | 9.0 | 49 030 | 67.2 | 38.1 | 28.0 |
| Kenosha | 39.7 | 782 | 31.7 | 7.5 | 82.7 | 7.2 | 50 817 | 1.5 | 4 735 | 9.3 | 75 008 | 68.0 | 39.5 | 26.1 |
| La Crosse | 49.2 | 650 | 32.4 | 11.5 | 71.8 | 12.5 | 28 989 | 1.8 | 1 866 | 6.4 | 44 242 | 67.1 | 34.0 | 28.5 |
| Madison | 48.6 | 878 | 32.3 | 11.8 | 71.5 | 13.3 | 145 471 | 1.0 | 6 798 | 4.7 | 195 283 | 72.8 | 40.7 | 20.5 |
| Manitowoc | 33.9 | 586 | 26.0 | 7.1 | 88.5 | 4.8 | 17 330 | -1.4 | 1 506 | 8.7 | 27 100 | 65.6 | 38.7 | 31.8 |
| Menomonee Falls | 24.4 | 873 | 28.6 | 4.6 | 90.3 | 7.5 | 19 152 | 0.6 | 1 106 | 5.8 | 28 392 | 68.7 | 44.8 | 26.3 |
| Milwaukee | 54.5 | 754 | 34.2 | 17.5 | 78.1 | 5.8 | 271 204 | 0.4 | 27 519 | 10.1 | 449 434 | 66.4 | 37.4 | 27.9 |
| Mount Pleasant | 21.5 | 710 | 25.6 | 6.0 | 92.0 | 7.2 | 13 571 | 4.2 | 1 258 | 9.3 | 21 236 | 63.0 | 41.1 | 31.5 |
| Neenah | 30.6 | 631 | 25.2 | 6.3 | 87.2 | 7.5 | 14 426 | -0.9 | 1 251 | 8.7 | 19 544 | 71.3 | 46.0 | 23.8 |
| New Berlin | 21.8 | 1 020 | 26.9 | 3.9 | 90.0 | 8.1 | 22 054 | 0.8 | 1 291 | 5.9 | 31 929 | 68.3 | 44.8 | 25.2 |
| Oak Creek | 38.5 | 903 | 24.7 | 4.5 | 83.7 | 13.1 | 20 219 | 0.9 | 1 249 | 6.2 | 26 951 | 74.4 | 49.2 | 19.8 |
| Oshkosh | 41.9 | 627 | 27.6 | 8.4 | 78.6 | 11.1 | 36 445 | -0.5 | 2 584 | 7.1 | 54 509 | 62.9 | 36.9 | 25.2 |
| Racine | 43.8 | 700 | 33.4 | 13.1 | 84.8 | 5.0 | 36 878 | -1.5 | 4 326 | 11.7 | 59 542 | 66.2 | 39.5 | 29.8 |
| Sheboygan | 36.2 | 612 | 27.6 | 10.3 | 84.9 | 6.3 | 25 560 | -1.7 | 2 066 | 8.1 | 38 181 | 69.0 | 41.1 | 27.3 |
| Stevens Point | 49.9 | 631 | 32.3 | 7.6 | 66.5 | 18.7 | 15 621 | 0.3 | 1 264 | 8.1 | 22 542 | 67.0 | 31.6 | 26.5 |
| Sun Prairie | 37.4 | 915 | 25.6 | 3.2 | 84.6 | 10.9 | 17 414 | -0.1 | 999 | 5.7 | 21 779 | 78.7 | 52.6 | 15.7 |
| Superior | 43.4 | 616 | 29.4 | 10.4 | 81.8 | 9.0 | 14 230 | 1.2 | 892 | 6.3 | 22 178 | 69.3 | 39.1 | 27.2 |
| Waukesha | 40.0 | 801 | 27.7 | 7.4 | 83.1 | 10.0 | 40 280 | -0.2 | 3 066 | 7.6 | 55 352 | 73.8 | 46.3 | 21.9 |
| Wausau | 41.0 | 628 | 28.2 | 9.7 | 80.4 | 8.5 | 19 438 | -2.5 | 1 876 | 9.7 | 31 328 | 67.6 | 38.9 | 26.9 |
| Wauwatosa | 33.6 | 904 | 27.3 | 7.2 | 87.9 | 8.8 | 24 419 | 1.1 | 1 383 | 5.7 | 37 213 | 69.4 | 47.2 | 24.7 |
| West Allis | 42.5 | 735 | 29.3 | 11.8 | 86.2 | 9.8 | 32 442 | -0.1 | 2 460 | 7.6 | 48 934 | 69.1 | 43.9 | 27.9 |
| West Bend | 35.5 | 773 | 29.4 | 7.7 | 86.0 | 8.0 | 17 023 | -1.4 | 1 488 | 8.7 | 24 062 | 70.8 | 42.6 | 26.9 |
| **WYOMING** | 29.5 | 708 | 24.5 | 3.5 | 81.8 | 11.9 | 306 064 | 2.4 | 16 443 | 5.4 | 436 090 | 69.9 | 45.6 | 22.1 |
| Casper | 32.8 | 736 | 27.1 | 4.5 | 81.2 | 9.4 | 32 306 | 4.6 | 1 400 | 4.3 | 43 320 | 69.4 | 45.6 | 23.4 |
| Cheyenne | 36.2 | 689 | 24.9 | 5.3 | 79.7 | 10.7 | 29 937 | 2.4 | 1 716 | 5.7 | 45 665 | 70.2 | 45.9 | 22.7 |
| Gillette | 29.5 | 842 | 22.5 | 3.5 | 76.6 | 11.9 | 17 558 | -0.1 | 639 | 3.6 | 20 582 | 79.9 | 56.6 | 11.8 |
| Laramie | 52.0 | 687 | 34.3 | 4.6 | 67.4 | 19.5 | 17 212 | 3.6 | 687 | 4.0 | 25 848 | 68.0 | 36.7 | 21.5 |

1. $2,000 represents $2,000 or more.   2. 50.0 represents 50 percent or more.   3. Percent of civilian labor force.   4. Persons 16 years old and over.

Table D. Cities — **Construction, Wholesale Trade, and Retail Trade**

| City | Value of residential construction authorized by building permits, 2011 | | | Wholesale trade,[1] 2007 | | | | Retail trade,[2] 2007 | | | |
|---|---|---|---|---|---|---|---|---|---|---|---|
| | New construction ($1,000) | Number of housing units | Percent single family | Number of establish-ments | Number of employees | Sales (mil dol) | Annual payroll (mil dol) | Number of establish-ments | Number of employees | Sales (mil dol) | Annual payroll (mil dol) |
| | 69 | 70 | 71 | 72 | 73 | 74 | 75 | 76 | 77 | 78 | 79 |
| WASHINGTON— Cont'd | | | | | | | | | | | |
| Pullman | 12 965 | 83 | 30.1 | 11 | 85 | 55.7 | 3.8 | 49 | 878 | 187.8 | 15.7 |
| Puyallup | 33 509 | 234 | 28.2 | 54 | 683 | 356.3 | 30.5 | 254 | 5 473 | 1 436.9 | 142.3 |
| Redmond | 35 723 | 170 | 52.4 | 192 | 3 567 | 6 602.3 | 236.5 | 260 | 4 178 | 916.8 | 108.1 |
| Renton | 70 539 | 281 | 81.5 | 108 | 4 360 | 2 572.5 | 235.1 | 216 | 4 945 | 1 584.9 | 157.7 |
| Richland | 106 479 | 607 | 43.7 | 22 | 307 | 365.3 | 11.0 | 154 | 2 145 | 550.7 | 54.8 |
| Sammamish | 70 517 | 180 | 100.0 | 33 | 52 | 28.2 | 2.3 | 43 | 512 | 122.8 | 12.9 |
| SeaTac | 1 474 | 15 | 0.0 | 23 | 204 | 146.8 | 8.9 | 40 | 351 | 125.1 | 9.2 |
| Seattle | 448 401 | 3 173 | 10.0 | 1 188 | 17 272 | 11 531.4 | 1 072.6 | 2 674 | 34 791 | 15 968.8 | 989.9 |
| Shoreline | 5 172 | 19 | 100.0 | 39 | 151 | 68.9 | 6.4 | 147 | 2 769 | 851.9 | 79.5 |
| Spokane | 81 450 | 631 | 27.9 | 296 | 3 929 | 1 944.3 | 169.6 | 914 | 14 446 | 3 115.8 | 362.5 |
| Spokane Valley | 17 976 | 123 | 64.2 | 230 | 2 936 | 1 774.4 | 129.1 | 475 | 7 990 | 2 121.9 | 210.1 |
| Tacoma | 101 758 | 765 | 23.7 | 204 | 3 168 | 2 055.2 | 159.3 | 779 | 12 385 | 3 064.9 | 331.0 |
| University Place | 7 043 | 26 | 100.0 | 22 | 219 | 96.6 | 10.1 | 58 | 860 | 185.0 | 20.1 |
| Vancouver | 16 892 | 180 | 53.3 | 197 | 2 247 | 2 952.5 | 130.4 | 563 | 10 489 | 2 630.6 | 250.1 |
| Walla Walla | 11 343 | 132 | 9.1 | 35 | 340 | 158.2 | 12.0 | 170 | 1 917 | 400.3 | 45.8 |
| Wenatchee | 7 973 | 41 | 100.0 | 62 | 976 | 536.6 | 36.5 | 193 | 2 737 | 655.6 | 67.9 |
| Yakima | 23 972 | 180 | 36.7 | 114 | 2 201 | 998.8 | 79.9 | 395 | 5 553 | 1 387.3 | 139.6 |
| WEST VIRGINIA | 306 401 | 2 220 | 71.5 | 1 372 | 16 790 | 11 036.5 | 656.0 | 7 047 | 92 227 | 20 538.8 | 1 776.5 |
| Charleston | 3 081 | 14 | 100.0 | 112 | 1 705 | 782.8 | 74.3 | 353 | 5 292 | 1 006.1 | 95.8 |
| Huntington | 4 873 | 45 | 26.7 | 83 | 1 327 | 477.6 | 55.0 | 236 | 2 896 | 548.1 | 57.2 |
| Morgantown | 9 442 | 59 | 55.9 | 22 | 201 | 53.3 | 6.1 | 212 | 3 569 | 743.3 | 63.5 |
| Parkersburg | 954 | 14 | 100.0 | 47 | 407 | 178.0 | 13.4 | 237 | 3 588 | 820.9 | 74.2 |
| Wheeling | 3 380 | 20 | 70.0 | 63 | D | D | D | 167 | 1 846 | 402.1 | 39.2 |
| WISCONSIN | 1 605 963 | 9 939 | 65.4 | 6 215 | 99 773 | 59 996.2 | 4 639.0 | 21 205 | 320 140 | 72 283.3 | 6 778.3 |
| Appleton | 20 867 | 171 | 21.6 | 94 | 1 428 | 486.0 | 60.8 | 290 | 4 596 | 1 008.6 | 97.4 |
| Beloit | 0 | 0 | 0.0 | 15 | 323 | 297.9 | 19.4 | 113 | 1 826 | 467.1 | 38.8 |
| Brookfield | 11 169 | 17 | 100.0 | 112 | 1 767 | 736.3 | 107.4 | 327 | 6 851 | 1 216.2 | 132.1 |
| Eau Claire | 9 715 | 106 | 23.6 | 80 | 1 557 | 818.4 | 59.2 | 363 | 7 046 | 1 334.9 | 130.3 |
| Fitchburg | 5 524 | 47 | 42.6 | 33 | 991 | 597.4 | 44.1 | 64 | 821 | 221.0 | 25.2 |
| Fond du Lac | 8 682 | 68 | 30.9 | 45 | 824 | 511.0 | 42.0 | 251 | 4 291 | 903.2 | 81.9 |
| Franklin | 10 257 | 94 | 31.9 | 40 | 331 | 212.9 | 19.3 | 75 | 1 831 | 460.1 | 43.1 |
| Green Bay | 7 193 | 56 | 71.4 | 119 | 2 134 | 1 327.7 | 98.1 | 395 | 6 406 | 1 474.6 | 132.6 |
| Greenfield | 6 567 | 60 | 20.0 | 20 | 75 | 22.4 | 2.9 | 159 | 3 492 | 858.3 | 83.2 |
| Janesville | 5 703 | 31 | 87.1 | 55 | 1 883 | 1 642.3 | 97.0 | 323 | 6 243 | 1 630.6 | 150.1 |
| Kenosha | 13 713 | 143 | 25.2 | 58 | 922 | 465.7 | 47.3 | 327 | 5 059 | 1 276.4 | 115.5 |
| La Crosse | 4 993 | 64 | 50.0 | 75 | 1 774 | 2 645.1 | 73.0 | 269 | 5 174 | 1 015.3 | 97.1 |
| Madison | 80 742 | 621 | 28.5 | 272 | 5 005 | 2 321.3 | 243.4 | 1 024 | 19 133 | 4 103.6 | 397.4 |
| Manitowoc | 5 744 | 34 | 35.3 | 23 | 242 | 170.8 | 10.3 | 169 | 2 578 | 529.4 | 51.2 |
| Menomonee Falls | 12 437 | 33 | 100.0 | 108 | 1 864 | 884.2 | 114.4 | 133 | 2 916 | 573.5 | 67.7 |
| Milwaukee | 27 973 | 210 | 62.4 | 490 | 9 788 | 5 599.5 | 486.5 | 1 447 | 18 937 | 4 001.7 | 410.5 |
| Mount Pleasant | 5 452 | 29 | 100.0 | 19 | 295 | 113.4 | 11.2 | 76 | 1 472 | 393.1 | 35.3 |
| Neenah | 9 142 | 54 | 100.0 | 26 | 430 | 199.4 | 21.5 | 93 | 1 603 | 408.8 | 34.1 |
| New Berlin | 6 111 | 16 | 100.0 | 131 | 2 743 | 1 404.6 | 147.4 | 104 | 2 274 | 515.3 | 56.0 |
| Oak Creek | 9 762 | 48 | 100.0 | 34 | 1 003 | 794.4 | 47.1 | 83 | 2 316 | 588.6 | 53.3 |
| Oshkosh | 10 835 | 195 | 6.2 | 62 | 1 467 | 600.7 | 54.3 | 277 | 4 853 | 1 021.0 | 96.2 |
| Racine | 850 | 8 | 75.0 | 62 | 637 | 278.0 | 30.1 | 314 | 4 240 | 710.5 | 70.0 |
| Sheboygan | 879 | 6 | 100.0 | 45 | 632 | 273.4 | 24.4 | 201 | 3 217 | 714.8 | 68.1 |
| Stevens Point | 2 977 | 21 | 61.9 | 31 | 717 | 380.6 | 18.6 | 147 | 2 708 | 530.4 | 51.1 |
| Sun Prairie | 11 877 | 105 | 33.3 | 29 | 652 | 271.2 | 28.4 | 68 | 1 376 | 293.3 | 37.8 |
| Superior | 1 371 | 8 | 100.0 | 40 | D | D | D | 123 | 1 959 | 468.0 | 45.4 |
| Waukesha | 11 694 | 62 | 83.9 | 127 | 2 032 | 1 261.0 | 110.1 | 222 | 4 498 | 1 248.1 | 111.8 |
| Wausau | 10 098 | 93 | 18.3 | 49 | 968 | 434.4 | 42.7 | 209 | 4 752 | 969.1 | 94.1 |
| Wauwatosa | 21 595 | 235 | 1.3 | 81 | 2 306 | 1 481.9 | 93.9 | 295 | 5 552 | 1 018.7 | 104.8 |
| West Allis | 6 318 | 52 | 3.8 | 107 | 2 026 | 1 003.8 | 104.5 | 276 | 4 827 | 1 386.5 | 116.9 |
| West Bend | 7 459 | 74 | 17.6 | 27 | 353 | 102.6 | 12.1 | 141 | 3 173 | 633.8 | 59.8 |
| WYOMING | 425 156 | 2 114 | 68.7 | 705 | 6 347 | 6 352.9 | 306.6 | 2 951 | 32 033 | 8 957.6 | 758.1 |
| Casper | 42 429 | 317 | 53.9 | 87 | 787 | 2 387.1 | 38.3 | 351 | 4 679 | 1 200.0 | 115.0 |
| Cheyenne | 33 107 | 197 | 100.0 | 77 | 691 | 354.6 | 31.0 | 313 | 5 108 | 1 382.7 | 122.5 |
| Gillette | 73 507 | 194 | 100.0 | 54 | 902 | 665.8 | 51.8 | 164 | 2 178 | 693.4 | 55.7 |
| Laramie | 32 855 | 400 | 20.5 | 16 | 118 | 107.5 | 4.3 | 157 | 1 871 | 444.6 | 36.8 |

1. Merchant wholesalers except manufacturers' sales branches and offices.  2. Establishments with payroll.

# Table D. Cities — Real Estate, Professional Services, and Manufacturing

| City | Real estate and rental and leasing, 2007 | | | | Professional, scientific, and technical services,[1] 2007 | | | | Manufacturing, 2007 | | | |
|---|---|---|---|---|---|---|---|---|---|---|---|---|
| | Number of establishments | Number of employees | Receipts (mil dol) | Annual payroll (mil dol) | Number of establishments | Number of employees | Receipts (mil dol) | Annual payroll (mil dol) | Number of establishments | Number of employees | Receipts (mil dol) | Annual payroll (mil dol) |
| | 80 | 81 | 82 | 83 | 84 | 85 | 86 | 87 | 88 | 89 | 90 | 91 |
| **WASHINGTON— Cont'd** | | | | | | | | | | | | |
| Pullman | 35 | 185 | 18.2 | 3.2 | 36 | 144 | 14.7 | 5.5 | 12 | D | D | D |
| Puyallup | 113 | 595 | 87.0 | 15.4 | 117 | D | D | D | 41 | 678 | 148.9 | 28.7 |
| Redmond | 127 | 1 324 | 283.2 | 60.3 | 352 | D | D | D | 147 | 9 662 | 4 379.9 | 603.2 |
| Renton | 102 | 1 284 | 239.2 | 47.4 | 180 | 1 848 | 177.4 | 75.6 | 62 | 11 491 | D | 719.1 |
| Richland | 69 | 231 | 32.3 | 6.4 | 163 | 4 779 | 796.8 | 361.3 | 35 | 1 361 | 511.7 | 83.9 |
| Sammamish | 61 | 113 | 34.6 | 3.4 | 158 | 322 | 53.0 | 16.5 | NA | NA | NA | NA |
| SeaTac | 35 | 374 | 132.9 | 13.1 | 19 | 186 | 25.0 | 9.5 | NA | NA | NA | NA |
| Seattle | 1 622 | 10 440 | 2 279.7 | 472.8 | 4 328 | 47 828 | 8 836.0 | 3 877.4 | 970 | 28 376 | 7 076.2 | 1 226.4 |
| Shoreline | 95 | 340 | 92.2 | 12.9 | 96 | 311 | 31.2 | 12.0 | NA | NA | NA | NA |
| Spokane | 321 | 1 767 | 333.4 | 54.6 | 733 | 5 625 | 728.8 | 297.1 | 230 | 4 866 | 965.5 | 192.7 |
| Spokane Valley | 135 | 774 | 170.9 | 24.6 | 205 | 1 197 | 169.6 | 54.8 | 209 | 7 472 | 1 886.9 | 313.1 |
| Tacoma | 343 | 2 193 | 334.9 | 58.3 | 499 | D | D | D | 240 | 8 785 | 2 257.3 | 407.5 |
| University Place | 51 | D | D | D | 71 | 220 | 23.3 | 10.7 | NA | NA | NA | NA |
| Vancouver | 282 | 1 895 | 281.9 | 70.5 | 540 | D | D | D | 197 | 7 993 | 2 689.2 | 357.5 |
| Walla Walla | 52 | 155 | 22.1 | 4.4 | 83 | D | D | D | 75 | 884 | D | 41.9 |
| Wenatchee | 61 | 276 | 41.8 | 7.2 | 118 | D | D | D | 31 | 586 | D | D |
| Yakima | 153 | 660 | 110.8 | 17.1 | 217 | D | D | D | 111 | 3 122 | 680.1 | 119.1 |
| **WEST VIRGINIA** | 1 586 | 7 055 | 1 171.0 | 175.3 | 2 906 | 20 766 | 2 341.1 | 857.5 | 1 413 | 59 981 | 25 080.6 | 2 645.8 |
| Charleston | 160 | 806 | 188.2 | 24.0 | 397 | 3 541 | 515.4 | 164.4 | 39 | 694 | D | 25.5 |
| Huntington | 89 | 325 | 58.8 | 8.7 | 141 | D | D | D | 57 | 3 839 | 1 725.1 | 174.5 |
| Morgantown | 82 | 323 | 44.7 | 7.7 | 127 | D | D | D | NA | NA | NA | NA |
| Parkersburg | 54 | 331 | 52.3 | 8.3 | 93 | D | D | D | 33 | D | D | D |
| Wheeling | 57 | D | D | D | 129 | D | D | D | 51 | 908 | D | 30.5 |
| **WISCONSIN** | 5 119 | 27 226 | 4 043.5 | 788.9 | 11 255 | 97 445 | 12 797.3 | 4 999.0 | 9 659 | 487 573 | 163 563.2 | 21 850.3 |
| Appleton | 69 | 326 | 37.3 | 8.6 | 193 | 3 091 | 276.4 | 120.9 | 108 | 7 032 | 2 651.0 | 318.5 |
| Beloit | 22 | 98 | 47.0 | 2.8 | 37 | 148 | 12.7 | 5.6 | 57 | 3 310 | 1 522.9 | 137.7 |
| Brookfield | 110 | 1 064 | 102.3 | 32.5 | 309 | 3 601 | 579.3 | 225.9 | 72 | 2 033 | 429.7 | 99.4 |
| Eau Claire | 98 | 677 | 80.7 | 14.9 | 148 | 1 008 | 104.1 | 47.5 | 89 | 4 706 | 1 141.0 | 196.0 |
| Fitchburg | 38 | 240 | 36.6 | 7.8 | 86 | 815 | 266.7 | 63.8 | 33 | 3 596 | 1 207.8 | 194.1 |
| Fond du Lac | 50 | 215 | 27.1 | 4.2 | 90 | 1 019 | 73.5 | 56.5 | 76 | 4 365 | 1 535.4 | 205.4 |
| Franklin | 18 | 83 | 13.2 | 1.8 | 56 | 429 | 85.1 | 18.1 | 55 | 3 081 | 1 014.7 | 160.6 |
| Green Bay | 111 | 724 | 98.5 | 24.1 | 221 | D | D | D | 144 | 11 058 | 5 193.4 | 484.8 |
| Greenfield | 47 | 231 | 50.7 | 6.3 | 76 | 518 | 43.6 | 19.1 | NA | NA | NA | NA |
| Janesville | 67 | 269 | 37.9 | 6.0 | 108 | D | D | D | 97 | 8 225 | 10 171.3 | 497.5 |
| Kenosha | 97 | 440 | 57.3 | 8.8 | 119 | 617 | 60.3 | 25.8 | 123 | 3 838 | 1 584.3 | 190.3 |
| La Crosse | 75 | 452 | 59.4 | 11.3 | 151 | D | D | D | 94 | 4 355 | 1 438.6 | 165.8 |
| Madison | 393 | 3 012 | 436.9 | 100.6 | 934 | D | D | D | 207 | 9 145 | 2 418.3 | 450.2 |
| Manitowoc | 22 | 138 | 13.1 | 2.3 | 52 | 411 | 45.2 | 14.1 | 86 | 7 191 | 1 995.2 | 289.8 |
| Menomonee Falls | 34 | 319 | 44.1 | 17.0 | 111 | 907 | 100.3 | 42.9 | 187 | 9 018 | 2 070.6 | 420.6 |
| Milwaukee | 437 | 3 183 | 572.7 | 136.3 | 1 131 | 17 521 | 2 458.6 | 1 110.0 | 652 | 28 510 | 9 058.9 | 1 406.3 |
| Mount Pleasant | 29 | 105 | 13.0 | 2.9 | 54 | 305 | 32.1 | 15.8 | 33 | 2 626 | 4 040.6 | 180.0 |
| Neenah | 17 | 193 | 41.5 | 7.2 | 58 | 420 | 37.6 | 29.6 | 62 | 6 070 | 2 197.2 | 271.6 |
| New Berlin | 32 | 237 | 44.1 | 6.4 | 111 | D | D | D | 139 | 5 303 | 1 312.8 | 262.9 |
| Oak Creek | 35 | 429 | 92.4 | 14.6 | 36 | 258 | 20.9 | 8.0 | 64 | 6 439 | 2 478.6 | 312.6 |
| Oshkosh | 66 | 432 | 35.4 | 8.0 | 100 | D | D | D | 125 | 8 592 | 3 869.1 | 425.8 |
| Racine | 58 | 214 | 28.0 | 4.8 | 140 | D | D | D | 170 | 7 717 | 2 174.1 | 399.0 |
| Sheboygan | 39 | 260 | 61.3 | 10.0 | 85 | 632 | 146.3 | 34.8 | 97 | 7 776 | 2 059.1 | 323.1 |
| Stevens Point | 21 | 104 | 10.7 | 1.7 | 54 | 400 | 39.6 | 15.1 | 36 | 1 939 | 539.8 | 80.0 |
| Sun Prairie | 21 | 66 | 22.2 | 2.9 | 45 | 318 | 31.2 | 14.0 | 35 | 1 393 | 281.7 | 56.9 |
| Superior | 30 | D | D | D | 54 | 285 | 24.7 | 10.6 | 41 | D | D | D |
| Waukesha | 70 | 348 | 79.3 | 12.1 | 184 | 1 658 | 222.3 | 90.1 | 152 | 10 719 | 7 548.7 | 707.2 |
| Wausau | 46 | 188 | 24.4 | 4.3 | 131 | D | D | D | 73 | 6 401 | 1 579.0 | 238.1 |
| Wauwatosa | 49 | 225 | 86.1 | 8.7 | 267 | D | D | D | 46 | 4 017 | 1 286.4 | 322.7 |
| West Allis | 55 | 405 | 89.5 | 14.9 | 115 | 1 324 | 110.9 | 52.3 | 101 | 3 692 | 753.1 | 169.0 |
| West Bend | 27 | 127 | 16.1 | 2.3 | 61 | 320 | 30.4 | 12.0 | 55 | 2 299 | 522.8 | 93.7 |
| **WYOMING** | 1 121 | 4 651 | 991.6 | 159.7 | 1 890 | 8 711 | 1 079.3 | 387.5 | 596 | 11 904 | 8 834.8 | 573.7 |
| Casper | 135 | 610 | 158.4 | 23.6 | 231 | D | D | D | 43 | 603 | 135.0 | 25.8 |
| Cheyenne | 108 | 438 | 86.4 | 12.2 | 274 | 1 251 | 165.1 | 58.0 | 47 | 1 576 | 2 390.9 | 76.4 |
| Gillette | 62 | 341 | 72.1 | 9.7 | 89 | 498 | 50.8 | 19.5 | NA | NA | NA | NA |
| Laramie | 51 | D | D | D | 107 | D | D | D | NA | NA | NA | NA |

1. Establishments subject to federal tax.

## Table D. Cities — Accommodation and Food Services, Arts, Entertainment, and Recreation, and Health Care and Social Assistance

| City | Accommodation and food services, 2007 | | | | Arts, entertainment, and recreation,[1] 2007 | | | | Health care and social assistance,[1] 2007 | | | |
|---|---|---|---|---|---|---|---|---|---|---|---|---|
| | Number of establish-ments | Number of employees | Sales (mil dol) | Annual payroll (mil dol) | Number of establish-ments | Number of employees | Receipts (mil dol) | Annual payroll (mil dol) | Number of establish-ments | Number of employees | Receipts (mil dol) | Annual payroll (mil dol) |
| | 92 | 93 | 94 | 95 | 96 | 97 | 98 | 99 | 100 | 101 | 102 | 103 |
| WASHINGTON—Cont'd | | | | | | | | | | | | |
| Pullman | 88 | 1 165 | 42.4 | 11.6 | 2 | D | D | D | 46 | D | D | D |
| Puyallup | 159 | 2 945 | 125.4 | 38.5 | 13 | D | D | D | 182 | D | D | D |
| Redmond | 257 | 4 434 | 306.7 | 88.5 | 22 | D | D | D | 169 | 1 580 | 161.4 | 60.4 |
| Renton | 219 | 3 446 | 229.0 | 60.7 | 17 | D | D | D | 211 | 2 103 | 270.6 | 97.3 |
| Richland | 111 | 1 806 | 83.1 | 25.0 | 10 | D | D | D | 199 | D | D | D |
| Sammamish | 31 | 532 | 23.9 | 7.8 | 10 | 177 | 10.6 | 3.1 | 63 | 413 | 36.5 | 15.3 |
| SeaTac | 80 | 2 817 | 236.4 | 60.4 | 6 | D | D | D | 26 | 915 | 19.0 | 10.7 |
| Seattle | 2 569 | 42 686 | 2 730.8 | 822.4 | 307 | 4 686 | 615.7 | 313.3 | 1 859 | 21 038 | 2 746.2 | 1 193.7 |
| Shoreline | 92 | 1 017 | 44.9 | 13.3 | 18 | D | D | D | 156 | 1 658 | 127.3 | 53.5 |
| Spokane | 552 | 10 324 | 477.3 | 145.5 | 56 | 875 | 50.4 | 13.9 | 703 | 11 330 | 1 154.8 | 510.2 |
| Spokane Valley | 215 | 3 525 | 164.7 | 48.1 | 26 | 506 | 22.7 | 7.4 | 291 | 4 759 | 313.9 | 139.4 |
| Tacoma | 534 | 7 979 | 380.7 | 114.7 | 44 | 1 890 | 248.9 | 52.0 | 613 | 8 885 | 938.0 | 427.7 |
| University Place | 34 | 399 | 17.8 | 5.4 | 4 | D | D | D | 73 | D | D | D |
| Vancouver | 404 | 7 159 | 326.2 | 97.3 | 40 | 605 | 29.0 | 8.6 | 444 | 6 682 | 651.1 | 283.8 |
| Walla Walla | 99 | 1 556 | 70.4 | 21.4 | 12 | 47 | 3.4 | 0.8 | 100 | D | D | D |
| Wenatchee | 108 | 1 588 | 77.4 | 22.8 | 9 | 83 | 2.4 | 0.9 | 121 | D | D | D |
| Yakima | 221 | 3 320 | 150.8 | 45.5 | 23 | D | D | D | 273 | 4 411 | 490.0 | 188.5 |
| WEST VIRGINIA | 3 650 | 61 711 | 2 553.3 | 712.8 | 563 | 8 488 | 1 257.9 | 149.7 | 3 741 | 51 790 | 4 338.6 | 1 708.4 |
| Charleston | 215 | 4 144 | 190.8 | 54.8 | 24 | D | D | D | 344 | 4 939 | 591.0 | 231.6 |
| Huntington | 171 | 3 145 | 122.0 | 33.6 | 13 | 215 | 5.2 | 1.7 | 205 | D | D | D |
| Morgantown | 160 | 3 183 | 118.2 | 30.1 | 28 | 205 | 9.6 | 2.8 | 79 | D | D | D |
| Parkersburg | 139 | 2 266 | 87.1 | 24.5 | 15 | D | D | D | 176 | 3 218 | 326.6 | 119.5 |
| Wheeling | 105 | 1 699 | 76.5 | 20.5 | 17 | 703 | 127.4 | 13.5 | 167 | D | D | D |
| WISCONSIN | 14 439 | 227 475 | 9 247.3 | 2 535.2 | 2 075 | 27 979 | 2 362.6 | 748.6 | 11 149 | 165 008 | 15 006.0 | 6 808.4 |
| Appleton | 203 | 3 949 | 139.1 | 39.9 | 23 | 298 | 7.2 | 2.9 | 198 | 3 521 | 423.6 | 197.4 |
| Beloit | 95 | 1 387 | 53.6 | 14.8 | 5 | D | D | D | 43 | D | D | D |
| Brookfield | 125 | 3 025 | 124.0 | 37.3 | 21 | 390 | 16.0 | 5.4 | 257 | D | D | D |
| Eau Claire | 208 | 4 579 | 157.0 | 46.2 | 24 | 401 | 21.4 | 4.1 | 186 | 4 608 | 494.7 | 274.0 |
| Fitchburg | 40 | 814 | 34.8 | 9.7 | 9 | 166 | 5.6 | 1.8 | 30 | D | D | D |
| Fond du Lac | 125 | 2 531 | 87.5 | 25.5 | 14 | D | D | D | 124 | D | D | D |
| Franklin | 51 | 853 | 33.9 | 9.3 | 4 | D | D | D | 70 | 1 009 | 83.6 | 33.3 |
| Green Bay | 274 | 5 245 | 203.7 | 56.7 | 33 | D | D | D | 219 | 6 217 | 839.7 | 317.3 |
| Greenfield | 85 | D | D | D | 15 | D | D | D | 143 | D | D | D |
| Janesville | 178 | 3 239 | 121.1 | 34.3 | 18 | 372 | 11.0 | 3.1 | 107 | 2 259 | 245.3 | 98.6 |
| Kenosha | 236 | 3 787 | 147.8 | 41.1 | 30 | 435 | 29.1 | 6.9 | 279 | 3 483 | 301.3 | 135.3 |
| La Crosse | 214 | 3 882 | 142.9 | 42.4 | 22 | D | D | D | 101 | D | D | D |
| Madison | 698 | 14 968 | 595.3 | 177.7 | 65 | 1 067 | 89.2 | 16.3 | 414 | 8 994 | 1 242.7 | 529.7 |
| Manitowoc | 94 | 1 783 | 57.4 | 16.5 | 11 | 89 | 5.2 | 1.5 | 104 | D | D | D |
| Menomonee Falls | 61 | 1 122 | 39.5 | 10.6 | 9 | D | D | D | 67 | D | D | D |
| Milwaukee | 1 134 | 20 453 | 949.1 | 265.9 | 75 | 3 629 | 661.7 | 251.0 | 1 313 | 16 744 | 1 439.5 | 768.1 |
| Mount Pleasant | 55 | 1 411 | 56.9 | 16.1 | 4 | D | D | D | 67 | 534 | 48.6 | 18.6 |
| Neenah | 79 | 1 219 | 47.3 | 12.3 | 8 | 48 | 2.9 | 1.0 | 83 | 1 029 | 136.3 | 69.8 |
| New Berlin | 61 | 1 363 | 48.6 | 13.3 | 17 | D | D | D | 76 | 1 031 | 111.5 | 56.2 |
| Oak Creek | 59 | 1 302 | 50.3 | 13.2 | 8 | 76 | 4.8 | 1.3 | 47 | D | D | D |
| Oshkosh | 186 | 3 694 | 125.2 | 35.7 | 18 | D | D | D | 146 | 2 253 | 206.8 | 102.0 |
| Racine | 167 | D | D | D | 26 | 221 | 16.8 | 3.7 | 144 | 2 238 | 214.4 | 119.6 |
| Sheboygan | 138 | 2 133 | 85.6 | 23.4 | 9 | D | D | D | 155 | 3 189 | 239.3 | 135.3 |
| Stevens Point | 102 | 1 858 | 61.0 | 16.9 | 10 | D | D | D | 71 | D | D | D |
| Sun Prairie | 52 | 863 | 27.8 | 8.2 | 5 | D | D | D | 48 | 784 | 75.5 | 27.9 |
| Superior | 112 | 1 840 | 64.9 | 18.3 | 14 | D | D | D | 48 | 940 | 51.5 | 23.0 |
| Waukesha | 149 | 2 686 | 100.2 | 28.1 | 21 | 260 | 11.5 | 3.1 | 183 | 2 386 | 236.5 | 116.6 |
| Wausau | 133 | 2 132 | 82.1 | 22.7 | 14 | 139 | 6.4 | 2.3 | 160 | D | D | D |
| Wauwatosa | 130 | 3 189 | 133.3 | 38.7 | 10 | 299 | 9.7 | 2.7 | 393 | 6 044 | 515.1 | 252.9 |
| West Allis | 168 | D | D | D | 20 | 299 | 21.3 | 4.4 | 189 | 4 352 | 308.9 | 148.8 |
| West Bend | 80 | 1 364 | 50.2 | 13.6 | 12 | 101 | 5.0 | 1.2 | 90 | 1 052 | 62.7 | 27.9 |
| WYOMING | 1 768 | 26 992 | 1 469.0 | 411.9 | 325 | 3 211 | 173.3 | 54.2 | 1 297 | 11 680 | 1 139.3 | 469.9 |
| Casper | 142 | 3 298 | 142.7 | 43.4 | 18 | D | D | D | 220 | D | D | D |
| Cheyenne | 154 | 3 278 | 144.0 | 44.2 | 12 | D | D | D | 209 | 2 494 | 213.7 | 94.1 |
| Gillette | 68 | 1 632 | 82.6 | 22.1 | 3 | D | D | D | 66 | D | D | D |
| Laramie | 94 | 1 500 | 58.7 | 16.8 | 9 | 62 | 2.2 | 0.6 | 84 | D | D | D |

1. Establishments subject to federal tax.

# Table D. Cities — Other Services and Federal Funds

| City | Other services[1], 2007 | | | | Selected federal funds, 2009–2010 (mil dol) | | | | | | | | |
|---|---|---|---|---|---|---|---|---|---|---|---|---|---|
| | | | | | Procurement contracts | | Grants | | | | | | |
| | Number of establishments | Number of employees | Receipts (mil dol) | Annual payroll (mil dol) | Defense | Other | Total[2] | Medicaid and other health related | Nutrition and family welfare | Energy and environment | Disasters and emergency preparedness | Housing and community development | Employment and training |
| | 104 | 105 | 106 | 107 | 108 | 109 | 110 | 111 | 112 | 113 | 114 | 115 | 116 |
| WASHINGTON— Cont'd | | | | | | | | | | | | | |
| Pullman | 26 | D | D | D | 2.5 | 1.4 | 120.3 | 35.2 | 0.7 | 10.5 | 0.0 | 0.0 | 0.0 |
| Puyallup | 74 | 715 | 67.5 | 22.6 | 0.2 | 0.7 | 0.6 | 0.0 | 0.0 | 0.0 | 0.0 | 0.0 | 0.0 |
| Redmond | 125 | 950 | 83.7 | 28.6 | 57.6 | 26.6 | 12.2 | 1.5 | 2.7 | 0.6 | 0.0 | 0.1 | 0.0 |
| Renton | 127 | 832 | 78.5 | 26.9 | 8.7 | 9.7 | 8.5 | 3.3 | 0.1 | 0.3 | 0.0 | 4.4 | 0.0 |
| Richland | 59 | 424 | 32.9 | 11.4 | 6.3 | 3 100.3 | 133.4 | 32.3 | 0.0 | 93.0 | 0.0 | 0.6 | 0.0 |
| Sammamish | 29 | 134 | 11.4 | 3.1 | 1.3 | 0.1 | 0.0 | 0.0 | 0.0 | 0.0 | 0.0 | 0.0 | 0.0 |
| SeaTac | 47 | 697 | 62.5 | 16.7 | 0.7 | 3.7 | 0.3 | 0.0 | 0.0 | 0.0 | 0.0 | 0.0 | 0.0 |
| Seattle | 1 382 | 8 585 | 751.4 | 239.8 | 1 044.2 | 482.7 | 3 027.0 | 1 803.9 | 47.9 | 151.9 | 0.3 | 164.7 | 20.0 |
| Shoreline | 70 | 386 | 31.4 | 10.0 | 0.2 | 0.1 | 1.8 | 0.0 | 0.0 | 0.5 | 0.0 | 0.0 | 0.0 |
| Spokane | 385 | 2 352 | 182.5 | 56.9 | 11.8 | 82.8 | 136.1 | 7.1 | 0.0 | 22.9 | 0.0 | 47.7 | 1.0 |
| Spokane Valley | 170 | 1 438 | 154.2 | 34.4 | 0.0 | 0.0 | 11.3 | 0.0 | 0.0 | 11.3 | 0.0 | 0.0 | 0.0 |
| Tacoma | 333 | 2 491 | 202.0 | 72.2 | 72.0 | 80.7 | 261.3 | 8.0 | 6.8 | 16.1 | 7.8 | 54.7 | 1.2 |
| University Place | 39 | 299 | 19.5 | 6.6 | 0.0 | 0.1 | 0.0 | 0.0 | 0.0 | 0.0 | 0.0 | 0.0 | 0.0 |
| Vancouver | 277 | 1 299 | 99.7 | 31.4 | 19.7 | 47.9 | 53.7 | 1.1 | 6.7 | 7.2 | 0.0 | 23.0 | 0.0 |
| Walla Walla | 37 | D | D | D | 10.0 | 33.9 | 9.0 | 0.4 | 1.0 | 0.0 | 0.0 | 4.8 | 0.0 |
| Wenatchee | 69 | 271 | 20.1 | 5.9 | 0.0 | 0.9 | 44.5 | 3.3 | 2.7 | 1.6 | 0.0 | 2.8 | 0.0 |
| Yakima | 140 | 900 | 61.7 | 18.6 | 2.8 | 9.3 | 44.0 | 4.1 | 11.5 | 1.4 | 0.0 | 8.7 | 3.7 |
| WEST VIRGINIA | 2 211 | 12 382 | 1 024.3 | 298.5 | 344.6 | 1 437.9 | 4 970.2 | 2 463.2 | 510.8 | 422.2 | 32.0 | 131.6 | 53.4 |
| Charleston | 124 | 1 051 | 53.1 | 17.2 | 11.5 | 28.9 | 1 101.6 | 28.7 | 111.2 | 358.6 | 11.1 | 54.9 | 52.2 |
| Huntington | 89 | 579 | 44.7 | 13.3 | 2.6 | 26.9 | 71.6 | 17.2 | 6.2 | 5.1 | 0.0 | 13.0 | 0.3 |
| Morgantown | 63 | D | D | D | 17.2 | 321.4 | 132.6 | 46.9 | 1.9 | 18.9 | 0.0 | 1.1 | 0.5 |
| Parkersburg | 76 | 426 | 28.3 | 8.5 | 8.6 | 22.5 | 11.9 | 0.0 | 0.0 | 0.3 | 0.0 | 8.6 | 0.0 |
| Wheeling | 74 | 673 | 52.9 | 15.3 | 7.4 | 8.0 | 25.0 | 0.9 | 5.2 | 0.1 | 0.0 | 6.2 | 0.0 |
| WISCONSIN | 8 822 | 51 066 | 3 865.8 | 1 235.7 | 8 469.0 | 1 336.1 | 11 992.0 | 6 592.2 | 1 312.1 | 655.1 | 56.3 | 460.5 | 210.1 |
| Appleton | 141 | 1 081 | 66.9 | 22.0 | 16.4 | 13.9 | 20.8 | 0.1 | 0.0 | 1.0 | 0.0 | 4.1 | 0.0 |
| Beloit | 45 | 193 | 11.1 | 3.7 | 11.2 | 4.6 | 7.6 | 0.9 | 0.0 | 0.0 | 0.0 | 4.4 | 0.0 |
| Brookfield | 103 | 1 042 | 104.2 | 28.3 | 1.6 | 1.0 | 2.0 | 2.0 | 0.0 | 0.0 | 0.0 | 0.0 | 0.0 |
| Eau Claire | 135 | 1 009 | 69.6 | 24.3 | 16.1 | 2.5 | 11.0 | 0.3 | 0.0 | 0.7 | 0.0 | 3.8 | 0.0 |
| Fitchburg | 29 | 309 | 15.6 | 5.6 | 0.4 | 0.8 | 0.4 | 0.0 | 0.0 | 0.0 | 0.0 | 0.0 | 0.0 |
| Fond du Lac | 94 | 695 | 48.8 | 14.8 | 3.1 | 0.2 | 8.5 | 0.6 | 1.9 | 0.0 | 0.0 | 3.2 | 0.0 |
| Franklin | 48 | D | D | D | 0.5 | 0.2 | 0.0 | 0.0 | 0.0 | 0.0 | 0.0 | 0.0 | 0.0 |
| Green Bay | 146 | 1 055 | 72.0 | 21.3 | 47.8 | 45.4 | 39.8 | 3.8 | 5.2 | 6.9 | 0.0 | 16.7 | 0.2 |
| Greenfield | 67 | 532 | 36.1 | 12.9 | 0.1 | 0.3 | 0.2 | 0.1 | 0.0 | 0.0 | 0.0 | 0.0 | 0.0 |
| Janesville | 105 | 584 | 39.1 | 12.6 | 193.2 | 5.9 | 13.6 | 0.2 | 3.6 | 0.6 | 0.0 | 4.5 | 1.2 |
| Kenosha | 152 | 1 024 | 60.3 | 20.3 | 62.1 | 1.5 | 25.1 | 1.5 | 2.9 | 0.3 | 0.0 | 15.6 | 0.0 |
| La Crosse | 99 | 672 | 44.9 | 17.9 | 35.1 | 19.9 | 22.9 | 5.7 | 2.7 | 1.6 | 0.0 | 3.3 | 1.5 |
| Madison | 337 | 2 878 | 242.6 | 78.8 | 151.2 | 128.3 | 2 762.3 | 665.3 | 235.3 | 194.2 | 43.3 | 187.9 | 198.6 |
| Manitowoc | 57 | 331 | 21.4 | 6.4 | 0.1 | 5.9 | 1.3 | 0.1 | 0.0 | 0.5 | 0.0 | 0.1 | 0.0 |
| Menomonee Falls | 69 | 482 | 41.0 | 10.9 | 2.8 | 0.3 | 0.0 | 0.0 | 0.0 | 0.0 | 0.0 | 0.0 | 0.0 |
| Milwaukee | 711 | 4 559 | 381.3 | 122.9 | 121.5 | 166.2 | 819.7 | 251.5 | 32.1 | 322.3 | 0.2 | 122.2 | 5.5 |
| Mount Pleasant | 35 | 243 | 17.4 | 5.4 | 0.0 | 0.0 | 0.0 | 0.0 | 0.0 | 0.0 | 0.0 | 0.0 | 0.0 |
| Neenah | 53 | 415 | 29.5 | 9.8 | 73.0 | 0.8 | 2.6 | 0.5 | 0.0 | 0.0 | 1.2 | 0.2 | 0.0 |
| New Berlin | 64 | D | D | D | 15.0 | 1.9 | 0.3 | 0.3 | 0.0 | 0.0 | 0.0 | 0.0 | 0.0 |
| Oak Creek | 40 | D | D | D | 1.3 | 5.8 | 0.0 | 0.0 | 0.0 | 0.0 | 0.0 | 0.0 | 0.0 |
| Oshkosh | 97 | 723 | 42.9 | 14.1 | 7 026.8 | 1.7 | 12.7 | 0.6 | 4.1 | 1.5 | 0.0 | 3.4 | 0.2 |
| Racine | 114 | 831 | 56.6 | 19.4 | 46.2 | 1.4 | 21.4 | 0.1 | 4.3 | 2.5 | 0.0 | 10.0 | 0.4 |
| Sheboygan | 85 | 526 | 32.5 | 9.6 | 0.6 | 4.3 | 5.5 | 0.0 | 1.1 | 0.0 | 0.0 | 2.2 | 0.0 |
| Stevens Point | 49 | 319 | 22.2 | 6.6 | 0.1 | 0.5 | 11.4 | 0.4 | 2.8 | 0.0 | 0.0 | 1.6 | 0.3 |
| Sun Prairie | 42 | 207 | 12.7 | 4.0 | 0.6 | 0.2 | -0.1 | 0.0 | 0.0 | 0.0 | 0.0 | 0.0 | 0.0 |
| Superior | 55 | D | D | D | 0.5 | 1.4 | 14.2 | 0.0 | 3.7 | 1.7 | 0.0 | 3.6 | 0.0 |
| Waukesha | 130 | 865 | 82.4 | 23.9 | 88.9 | 26.4 | 41.4 | 0.2 | 2.4 | 26.4 | 0.0 | 9.8 | 0.0 |
| Wausau | 64 | 304 | 22.5 | 5.9 | 1.9 | 0.5 | 7.2 | 0.7 | 1.4 | 0.4 | 0.0 | 2.2 | 0.0 |
| Wauwatosa | 78 | 713 | 48.2 | 18.9 | 0.5 | 0.2 | 9.1 | 1.9 | 0.0 | 0.0 | 0.0 | 1.3 | 0.0 |
| West Allis | 135 | 745 | 62.0 | 19.1 | 0.4 | 0.3 | 5.7 | 1.8 | 0.0 | 0.5 | 0.0 | 2.8 | 0.0 |
| West Bend | 72 | 500 | 33.7 | 10.2 | 0.0 | 0.1 | 3.7 | 0.1 | 1.1 | 0.5 | 0.0 | 1.3 | 0.0 |
| WYOMING | 996 | 4 850 | 520.2 | 141.5 | 155.4 | 414.0 | 2 254.1 | 441.9 | 114.6 | 242.1 | 0.5 | 27.7 | 25.3 |
| Casper | 108 | D | D | D | 0.4 | 10.8 | 37.4 | 2.0 | 0.0 | 0.8 | 0.0 | 11.4 | 15.2 |
| Cheyenne | 87 | 521 | 39.9 | 13.3 | 32.2 | 49.6 | 372.3 | 29.9 | 21.8 | 180.4 | 0.1 | 10.8 | 9.4 |
| Gillette | 71 | D | D | D | 0.0 | 13.9 | 3.8 | 0.1 | 0.5 | 0.2 | 0.0 | 0.1 | 0.0 |
| Laramie | 54 | D | D | D | 2.5 | 0.1 | 76.9 | 16.9 | 1.6 | 21.9 | 0.0 | 0.1 | 0.0 |

1. Establishments subject to federal tax.   2. Includes program categories not shown separately. State totals include additional categories not allocated by city.

# Table D. Cities — **City Government Finances**

| City | General revenue | | | | | | | General expenditure | | |
|---|---|---|---|---|---|---|---|---|---|---|
| | | Intergovernmental | | Taxes | | | | | Per capita[1] (dollars) | |
| | | | | | Per capita[1] (dollars) | | | | | |
| | Total (mil dol) | Total (mil dol) | Percent from state government | Total (mil dol) | Total | Property | Sales and gross receipts | Total (mil dol) | Total | Capital outlays |
| | 117 | 118 | 119 | 120 | 121 | 122 | 123 | 124 | 125 | 126 |
| WASHINGTON— Cont'd | | | | | | | | | | |
| Pullman | 21.6 | 3.1 | 65.0 | 12.1 | 457 | 158 | 298 | 16.6 | 627 | 134 |
| Puyallup | 65.2 | 3.4 | 87.4 | 37.1 | 1 018 | 319 | 640 | 63.7 | 1 745 | 401 |
| Redmond | 112.1 | 15.1 | 27.5 | 63.3 | 1 281 | 255 | 877 | 94.2 | 1 906 | 538 |
| Renton | 116.1 | 10.0 | 78.0 | 65.8 | 1 091 | 393 | 609 | 108.8 | 1 804 | 346 |
| Richland | 64.3 | 7.2 | 83.8 | 27.5 | 614 | 238 | 332 | 55.8 | 1 246 | 272 |
| Sammamish | 38.9 | 1.8 | 92.7 | 30.3 | 859 | 521 | 209 | 44.7 | 1 268 | 748 |
| SeaTac | 57.8 | 18.1 | 10.3 | 32.7 | 1 272 | 396 | 838 | 40.5 | 1 574 | 563 |
| Seattle | 1 492.2 | 179.4 | 74.2 | 765.0 | 1 287 | 504 | 780 | 1 402.7 | 2 361 | 364 |
| Shoreline | 54.0 | 22.4 | 81.6 | 24.9 | 473 | 134 | 290 | 61.7 | 1 171 | 677 |
| Spokane | 307.2 | 26.2 | 72.4 | 127.3 | 633 | 261 | 340 | 264.0 | 1 314 | 317 |
| Spokane Valley | 45.9 | 5.3 | 91.7 | 35.5 | 417 | 112 | 275 | 33.0 | 389 | 80 |
| Tacoma | 400.5 | 42.9 | 70.6 | 161.9 | 824 | 271 | 505 | 395.4 | 2 012 | 564 |
| University Place | 17.8 | 1.6 | 83.0 | 12.0 | 393 | 114 | 237 | 23.5 | 773 | 344 |
| Vancouver | 199.1 | 30.0 | 67.7 | 110.8 | 686 | 216 | 424 | 160.3 | 993 | 266 |
| Walla Walla | 38.1 | 5.1 | 64.9 | 14.3 | 465 | 127 | 323 | 35.5 | 1 151 | 167 |
| Wenatchee | 36.9 | 6.9 | 81.3 | 19.2 | 644 | 163 | 446 | 32.0 | 1 074 | 240 |
| Yakima | 95.0 | 19.9 | 62.0 | 47.8 | 576 | 161 | 393 | 91.0 | 1 096 | 289 |
| WEST VIRGINIA | X | X | X | X | X | X | X | X | X | X |
| Charleston | 97.5 | 5.0 | 5.3 | 62.2 | 1 233 | 207 | 1 021 | 94.7 | 1 875 | 146 |
| Huntington | 60.5 | 5.2 | 31.5 | 24.6 | 501 | 92 | 410 | 59.6 | 1 217 | 12 |
| Morgantown | 52.1 | 11.4 | 78.0 | 18.7 | 636 | 118 | 519 | 48.7 | 1 660 | 241 |
| Parkersburg | 40.1 | 2.2 | 6.8 | 16.9 | 534 | 141 | 393 | 42.5 | 1 344 | 332 |
| Wheeling | 58.8 | 4.7 | 31.5 | 17.6 | 603 | 145 | 448 | 56.5 | 1 941 | 0 |
| WISCONSIN | X | X | X | X | X | X | X | X | X | X |
| Appleton | 98.1 | 31.4 | 70.8 | 36.7 | 524 | 487 | 30 | 88.5 | 1 264 | 203 |
| Beloit | 54.9 | 25.6 | 87.1 | 12.9 | 352 | 313 | 28 | 61.7 | 1 684 | 357 |
| Brookfield | 53.1 | 8.5 | 77.7 | 33.0 | 841 | 742 | 92 | 54.3 | 1 384 | 147 |
| Eau Claire | 73.7 | 23.6 | 73.2 | 28.5 | 439 | 388 | 45 | 75.6 | 1 163 | 217 |
| Fitchburg | 20.3 | 3.0 | 89.7 | 12.2 | 527 | 495 | 31 | 19.0 | 817 | 174 |
| Fond du Lac | 53.5 | 16.4 | 79.4 | 20.0 | 476 | 432 | 40 | 48.2 | 1 145 | 196 |
| Franklin | 37.6 | 5.3 | 84.1 | 24.2 | 691 | 539 | 151 | 38.5 | 1 100 | 259 |
| Green Bay | 119.0 | 40.5 | 79.3 | 44.2 | 439 | 410 | 23 | 120.5 | 1 196 | 194 |
| Greenfield | 31.8 | 5.6 | 88.5 | 17.5 | 485 | 453 | 32 | 39.3 | 1 088 | 322 |
| Janesville | 75.2 | 18.0 | 69.2 | 27.3 | 433 | 397 | 34 | 73.8 | 1 171 | 382 |
| Kenosha | 111.0 | 35.6 | 75.8 | 50.8 | 528 | 495 | 32 | 106.8 | 1 109 | 131 |
| La Crosse | 81.5 | 27.6 | 81.0 | 31.7 | 624 | 571 | 44 | 82.9 | 1 634 | 335 |
| Madison | 412.0 | 132.8 | 61.4 | 157.3 | 687 | 606 | 76 | 397.5 | 1 737 | 199 |
| Manitowoc | 47.7 | 14.3 | 85.3 | 12.6 | 381 | 340 | 36 | 56.6 | 1 713 | 243 |
| Menomonee Falls | 47.8 | 6.6 | 99.8 | 24.0 | 699 | 633 | 66 | 41.8 | 1 217 | 69 |
| Milwaukee | 871.6 | 390.8 | 80.3 | 246.8 | 410 | 387 | 23 | 942.6 | 1 565 | 245 |
| Mount Pleasant | 26.4 | 3.2 | 96.7 | 13.0 | 505 | 458 | 46 | 27.1 | 1 050 | 182 |
| Neenah | 29.8 | 7.7 | 81.3 | 14.5 | 581 | 549 | 30 | 35.0 | 1 404 | 291 |
| New Berlin | 42.5 | 4.6 | 97.2 | 20.9 | 536 | 493 | 42 | 37.9 | 972 | 61 |
| Oak Creek | 36.1 | 6.3 | 96.4 | 18.8 | 567 | 509 | 54 | 34.8 | 1 047 | 211 |
| Oshkosh | 88.1 | 26.4 | 81.1 | 29.6 | 458 | 411 | 42 | 89.0 | 1 378 | 351 |
| Racine | 130.9 | 55.1 | 81.4 | 43.3 | 549 | 522 | 26 | 128.3 | 1 628 | 163 |
| Sheboygan | 69.9 | 24.0 | 79.9 | 26.7 | 554 | 496 | 53 | 64.2 | 1 334 | 206 |
| Stevens Point | 30.3 | 11.4 | 81.4 | 11.5 | 461 | 410 | 48 | 27.3 | 1 097 | 196 |
| Sun Prairie | 32.2 | 5.2 | 88.2 | 17.8 | 642 | 580 | 53 | 44.9 | 1 616 | 661 |
| Superior | 41.6 | 18.5 | 89.5 | 12.1 | 455 | 368 | 80 | 39.4 | 1 481 | 283 |
| Waukesha | 83.2 | 18.9 | 77.4 | 43.2 | 646 | 603 | 40 | 79.8 | 1 195 | 208 |
| Wausau | 53.5 | 19.7 | 79.7 | 21.6 | 568 | 525 | 39 | 52.4 | 1 377 | 273 |
| Wauwatosa | 62.3 | 12.9 | 64.0 | 35.6 | 782 | 726 | 44 | 61.8 | 1 357 | 123 |
| West Allis | 82.9 | 25.4 | 68.8 | 36.2 | 606 | 568 | 25 | 77.3 | 1 294 | 208 |
| West Bend | 34.9 | 8.1 | 76.5 | 18.1 | 608 | 568 | 39 | 40.5 | 1 360 | 475 |
| WYOMING | X | X | X | X | X | X | X | X | X | X |
| Casper | 84.3 | 47.8 | 61.7 | 7.7 | 146 | 70 | 65 | 80.9 | 1 526 | 373 |
| Cheyenne | 88.6 | 39.9 | 59.6 | 11.8 | 211 | 84 | 118 | 84.5 | 1 518 | 413 |
| Gillette | 65.6 | 48.5 | 62.8 | 2.4 | 95 | 65 | 30 | 64.1 | 2 563 | 860 |
| Laramie | 41.0 | 23.4 | 72.3 | 3.9 | 144 | 64 | 80 | 36.6 | 1 343 | 219 |

1. Based on population estimated as of July 1 of the year shown.

# Table D. Cities — **City Government Finances**

| City | City government finances, 2006 (cont.) | | | | | | | | | |
|---|---|---|---|---|---|---|---|---|---|---|
| | General expenditure (cont.) | | | | | | | | | |
| | Percent of total for: | | | | | | | | | |
| | Public welfare | Highways | Parking facilities | Education | Health and hospitals | Police protection | Sewerage and sanitation | Parks and recreation | Housing and community development | Interest on debt |
| | 127 | 128 | 129 | 130 | 131 | 132 | 133 | 134 | 135 | 136 |
| WASHINGTON— Cont'd | | | | | | | | | | |
| Pullman | 0.0 | 11.1 | 0.0 | 0.0 | 5.9 | 19.8 | 22.2 | 11.0 | 0.0 | 0.3 |
| Puyallup | 0.0 | 18.1 | 0.0 | 0.0 | 3.0 | 15.7 | 8.1 | 8.2 | 1.0 | 3.3 |
| Redmond | 0.0 | 16.6 | 0.0 | 0.0 | 6.9 | 8.9 | 13.4 | 9.6 | 1.0 | 2.1 |
| Renton | 0.0 | 19.8 | 0.0 | 0.0 | 0.2 | 11.8 | 20.0 | 11.0 | 1.8 | 2.1 |
| Richland | 0.0 | 17.8 | 0.0 | 0.0 | 3.7 | 11.9 | 12.5 | 9.7 | 6.1 | 4.6 |
| Sammamish | 0.0 | 19.8 | 0.0 | 0.0 | 0.0 | 8.2 | 2.1 | 25.8 | 1.7 | 0.4 |
| SeaTac | 0.0 | 33.3 | 0.0 | 0.0 | 0.0 | 16.8 | 2.7 | 7.6 | 3.1 | 2.7 |
| Seattle | 5.3 | 6.4 | 0.3 | 0.1 | 1.1 | 13.0 | 25.8 | 12.4 | 1.9 | 3.8 |
| Shoreline | 0.0 | 37.8 | 0.0 | 0.0 | 0.0 | 12.9 | 1.6 | 23.2 | 2.2 | 0.3 |
| Spokane | 0.8 | 12.5 | 0.1 | 0.0 | 0.0 | 12.3 | 33.9 | 5.3 | 1.3 | 3.6 |
| Spokane Valley | 0.0 | 15.7 | 0.0 | 0.0 | 0.2 | 42.0 | 3.3 | 8.3 | 3.1 | 1.0 |
| Tacoma | 0.8 | 10.0 | 0.3 | 0.0 | 2.4 | 14.3 | 28.0 | 2.2 | 0.9 | 5.5 |
| University Place | 0.0 | 38.9 | 0.9 | 0.0 | 0.6 | 16.1 | 3.9 | 5.0 | 4.0 | 4.1 |
| Vancouver | 0.0 | 20.9 | 0.7 | 0.0 | 0.1 | 14.5 | 10.2 | 15.5 | 2.5 | 3.8 |
| Walla Walla | 0.0 | 8.4 | 0.0 | 0.0 | 9.2 | 14.3 | 21.9 | 6.9 | 0.0 | 2.4 |
| Wenatchee | 0.0 | 21.5 | 0.0 | 0.0 | 0.5 | 15.8 | 12.3 | 10.3 | 2.6 | 2.9 |
| Yakima | 0.0 | 14.7 | 0.0 | 0.0 | 0.5 | 17.1 | 18.4 | 5.7 | 2.8 | 2.3 |
| WEST VIRGINIA | X | X | X | X | X | X | X | X | X | X |
| Charleston | 0.0 | 14.2 | 3.3 | 0.0 | 0.0 | 17.4 | 18.6 | 10.1 | 4.8 | 2.1 |
| Huntington | 1.3 | 1.7 | 1.2 | 0.0 | 0.2 | 17.9 | 19.3 | 6.2 | 6.0 | 4.2 |
| Morgantown | 0.0 | 6.0 | 3.2 | 0.0 | 0.0 | 12.0 | 12.9 | 12.0 | 17.2 | 1.0 |
| Parkersburg | 0.3 | 10.4 | 0.5 | 0.0 | 4.5 | 13.7 | 30.4 | 1.8 | 0.4 | 3.5 |
| Wheeling | 0.1 | 10.0 | 0.8 | 0.0 | 0.0 | 12.3 | 9.3 | 42.3 | 1.2 | 1.6 |
| WISCONSIN | X | X | X | X | X | X | X | X | X | X |
| Appleton | 1.0 | 21.4 | 2.1 | 0.0 | 1.7 | 17.2 | 15.5 | 5.6 | 2.1 | 7.1 |
| Beloit | 0.0 | 16.7 | 3.4 | 0.0 | 2.2 | 17.4 | 15.4 | 5.6 | 0.9 | 6.6 |
| Brookfield | 0.0 | 16.8 | 0.0 | 0.0 | 5.0 | 14.7 | 27.3 | 4.7 | 0.0 | 6.4 |
| Eau Claire | 0.0 | 19.6 | 1.1 | 0.0 | 7.1 | 17.5 | 9.2 | 11.6 | 1.5 | 4.7 |
| Fitchburg | 0.1 | 17.6 | 0.0 | 0.0 | 2.4 | 25.8 | 12.1 | 6.9 | 0.0 | 3.1 |
| Fond du Lac | 0.0 | 13.7 | 0.9 | 0.0 | 7.6 | 16.5 | 14.8 | 6.3 | 4.1 | 9.2 |
| Franklin | 0.0 | 15.5 | 0.0 | 0.0 | 4.7 | 20.0 | 12.8 | 2.6 | 2.4 | 7.5 |
| Green Bay | 0.0 | 16.2 | 1.8 | 0.0 | 0.2 | 18.9 | 17.2 | 8.7 | 0.8 | 8.1 |
| Greenfield | 0.0 | 23.7 | 0.0 | 0.0 | 5.5 | 31.6 | 11.9 | 3.2 | 0.3 | 1.4 |
| Janesville | 0.2 | 20.2 | 0.1 | 0.0 | 3.5 | 15.8 | 15.5 | 5.0 | 4.5 | 3.8 |
| Kenosha | 0.0 | 7.2 | 0.0 | 0.0 | 8.4 | 20.8 | 13.3 | 10.5 | 6.9 | 6.4 |
| La Crosse | 0.3 | 15.9 | 3.7 | 0.1 | 0.3 | 14.0 | 9.4 | 9.9 | 3.1 | 5.0 |
| Madison | 0.0 | 9.4 | 1.9 | 0.0 | 3.0 | 13.2 | 9.0 | 27.6 | 4.8 | 3.1 |
| Manitowoc | 0.1 | 16.7 | 0.0 | 0.0 | 0.7 | 12.5 | 14.7 | 4.9 | 0.2 | 14.7 |
| Menomonee Falls | 0.0 | 19.1 | 0.0 | 0.0 | 0.4 | 19.5 | 22.3 | 2.4 | 0.1 | 10.6 |
| Milwaukee | 0.0 | 11.4 | 2.2 | 0.0 | 3.8 | 24.3 | 12.9 | 0.5 | 3.6 | 4.5 |
| Mount Pleasant | 0.0 | 19.9 | 0.0 | 0.0 | 15.2 | 16.4 | 28.6 | 0.7 | 0.0 | 5.7 |
| Neenah | 0.0 | 16.2 | 1.9 | 0.0 | 1.8 | 14.7 | 11.8 | 7.1 | 0.6 | 9.6 |
| New Berlin | 0.0 | 13.0 | 0.0 | 0.0 | 1.8 | 25.4 | 21.8 | 6.7 | 0.0 | 5.5 |
| Oak Creek | 0.0 | 20.6 | 0.0 | 0.0 | 13.2 | 24.2 | 10.4 | 3.9 | 0.0 | 1.7 |
| Oshkosh | 0.1 | 19.6 | 0.2 | 0.0 | 2.3 | 13.0 | 10.7 | 15.8 | 0.8 | 10.0 |
| Racine | 0.0 | 14.3 | 0.9 | 0.0 | 5.6 | 23.0 | 13.9 | 7.2 | 2.5 | 7.9 |
| Sheboygan | 0.0 | 16.0 | 0.6 | 0.0 | 0.2 | 17.5 | 13.9 | 6.3 | 8.4 | 4.5 |
| Stevens Point | 0.0 | 20.5 | 0.0 | 0.0 | 4.4 | 19.1 | 12.3 | 9.5 | 0.0 | 1.9 |
| Sun Prairie | 0.0 | 21.7 | 0.0 | 0.0 | 7.8 | 21.7 | 7.8 | 6.4 | 0.0 | 7.4 |
| Superior | 0.0 | 18.7 | 0.0 | 0.0 | 0.2 | 15.9 | 17.8 | 5.1 | 7.7 | 3.8 |
| Waukesha | 0.0 | 15.7 | 1.2 | 0.0 | 0.0 | 18.6 | 14.5 | 6.5 | 0.4 | 6.2 |
| Wausau | 0.0 | 22.2 | 4.8 | 0.0 | 3.7 | 13.9 | 10.9 | 4.7 | 10.4 | 5.1 |
| Wauwatosa | 0.0 | 12.3 | 0.1 | 0.0 | 8.8 | 23.2 | 10.8 | 2.1 | 2.6 | 5.8 |
| West Allis | 0.0 | 16.6 | 0.0 | 0.0 | 4.6 | 22.7 | 10.4 | 0.6 | 14.0 | 4.0 |
| West Bend | 0.0 | 21.1 | 0.2 | 0.0 | 1.2 | 16.3 | 13.2 | 6.6 | 0.8 | 10.3 |
| WYOMING | X | X | X | X | X | X | X | X | X | X |
| Casper | 1.3 | 10.4 | 0.1 | 0.0 | 2.4 | 11.9 | 25.6 | 16.2 | 0.9 | 0.2 |
| Cheyenne | 1.3 | 20.3 | 0.6 | 0.0 | 2.3 | 13.0 | 18.3 | 12.7 | 1.0 | 3.2 |
| Gillette | 0.0 | 33.3 | 0.0 | 0.0 | 0.5 | 11.0 | 18.9 | 3.1 | 1.3 | 1.1 |
| Laramie | 0.0 | 11.8 | 0.0 | 0.0 | 4.7 | 18.3 | 14.6 | 10.1 | 1.2 | 1.9 |

| | City government finances, 2007 (cont.) | | | | Climate[2] | | | | | | |
| | Debt outstanding | | | | Average daily temperature (degrees Fahrenheit) | | | | | | |
| | | | | | Mean | | Limits | | | | |
| City | Total (mil dol) | Per capita[1] (dollars) | Debt issued during year | City government employment, 2011 | January | July | January[3] | July[4] | Annual precipitation (inches) | Heating degree days | Cooling degree days |
| | 137 | 138 | 139 | 140 | 141 | 142 | 143 | 144 | 145 | 146 | 147 |

WASHINGTON—Cont'd

| City | 137 | 138 | 139 | 140 | 141 | 142 | 143 | 144 | 145 | 146 | 147 |
|---|---|---|---|---|---|---|---|---|---|---|---|
| Pullman | 2.8 | 105 | 0.4 | NA | NA | NA | NA | NA | NA | NA | NA |
| Puyallup | 56.3 | 1 543 | 0.0 | NA | 39.9 | 64.9 | 32.9 | 77.8 | 40.51 | 4 991 | 153 |
| Redmond | 42.2 | 854 | 0.3 | 676 | 25.1 | 55.0 | 20.0 | 65.0 | 82.86 | 9 630 | 12 |
| Renton | 90.1 | 1 494 | 18.0 | 759 | 40.9 | 65.3 | 35.9 | 75.3 | 37.07 | 4 797 | 173 |
| Richland | 131.3 | 2 935 | 6.3 | NA | 33.0 | 73.2 | 26.0 | 87.9 | 7.55 | 5 133 | 739 |
| Sammamish | 11.3 | 320 | 0.0 | NA | 40.8 | 65.2 | 35.2 | 75.0 | 35.96 | 4 756 | 174 |
| SeaTac | 13.4 | 520 | 0.0 | NA | 40.9 | 65.3 | 35.9 | 75.3 | 37.07 | 4 797 | 173 |
| Seattle | 3 487.3 | 5 869 | 341.6 | 10 702 | 41.5 | 65.5 | 36.0 | 74.5 | 38.25 | 4 615 | 192 |
| Shoreline | 23.7 | 450 | 18.8 | NA | 40.8 | 65.2 | 35.2 | 75.0 | 35.96 | 4 756 | 174 |
| Spokane | 195.4 | 972 | 2.6 | 2 286 | 27.3 | 68.6 | 21.7 | 82.5 | 16.67 | 6 820 | 394 |
| Spokane Valley | 8.8 | 103 | 0.0 | 91 | NA | NA | NA | NA | NA | NA | NA |
| Tacoma | 1 281.7 | 6 522 | 174.8 | 3 636 | 41.0 | 65.6 | 35.1 | 76.1 | 38.95 | 4 650 | 167 |
| University Place | 26.4 | 868 | 6.4 | NA | 41.0 | 65.6 | 35.1 | 76.1 | 38.95 | 4 650 | 167 |
| Vancouver | 223.7 | 1 386 | 17.5 | 1 036 | 39.0 | 65.4 | 32.4 | 77.3 | 41.92 | 4 990 | 197 |
| Walla Walla | 56.2 | 1 826 | 0.9 | 258 | 34.7 | 75.3 | 28.8 | 89.9 | 20.88 | 4 882 | 957 |
| Wenatchee | 26.2 | 878 | 0.0 | 191 | 29.2 | 74.4 | 23.2 | 87.8 | 9.12 | 5 533 | 832 |
| Yakima | 56.5 | 680 | 0.8 | 677 | 29.1 | 69.1 | 20.5 | 87.2 | 8.26 | 6 104 | 431 |
| WEST VIRGINIA | X | X | X | X | X | X | X | X | X | X | X |
| Charleston | 81.6 | 1 616 | 0.0 | 851 | 33.4 | 73.9 | 24.2 | 84.9 | 44.05 | 4 644 | 978 |
| Huntington | 53.8 | 1 098 | 3.9 | 386 | 32.1 | 76.3 | 23.5 | 87.1 | 41.74 | 4 737 | 1 128 |
| Morgantown | 29.0 | 987 | 0.0 | 454 | 30.8 | 73.5 | 22.3 | 83.4 | 43.30 | 5 174 | 815 |
| Parkersburg | 69.6 | 2 203 | 6.2 | 350 | 30.7 | 75.4 | 22.3 | 85.8 | 40.69 | 5 091 | 1 038 |
| Wheeling | 44.4 | 1 525 | 15.6 | 822 | 29.6 | 74.8 | 21.4 | 85.2 | 40.34 | 5 313 | 926 |
| WISCONSIN | X | X | X | X | X | X | X | X | X | X | X |
| Appleton | 143.8 | 2 053 | 16.4 | 670 | 16.0 | 71.6 | 7.8 | 81.4 | 30.16 | 7 721 | 572 |
| Beloit | 76.3 | 2 083 | 9.5 | 389 | 19.1 | 72.4 | 11.6 | 82.5 | 35.25 | 6 969 | 664 |
| Brookfield | 100.1 | 2 554 | 6.4 | 318 | 20.0 | 74.3 | 11.5 | 85.1 | 32.09 | 6 886 | 791 |
| Eau Claire | 74.4 | 1 146 | 5.1 | 579 | 11.9 | 71.4 | 2.5 | 82.6 | 32.12 | 8 196 | 554 |
| Fitchburg | 13.5 | 581 | 0.0 | 170 | NA | NA | NA | NA | NA | NA | NA |
| Fond du Lac | 97.6 | 2 321 | 8.7 | 348 | 16.6 | 71.8 | 9.1 | 81.1 | 30.15 | 7 534 | 586 |
| Franklin | 46.8 | 1 337 | 10.0 | 230 | 20.7 | 72.0 | 13.4 | 81.1 | 34.81 | 7 087 | 616 |
| Green Bay | 254.8 | 2 528 | 37.9 | 870 | 15.6 | 69.9 | 7.1 | 81.2 | 29.19 | 7 963 | 463 |
| Greenfield | 15.3 | 422 | 10.0 | 217 | 19.9 | 73.8 | 12.7 | 81.9 | 33.86 | 6 847 | 764 |
| Janesville | 86.1 | 1 366 | 21.2 | 492 | 17.7 | 72.1 | 8.6 | 83.8 | 32.78 | 7 238 | 629 |
| Kenosha | 190.4 | 1 977 | 5.5 | 827 | 20.8 | 71.3 | 13.2 | 78.7 | 34.74 | 6 999 | 549 |
| La Crosse | 90.6 | 1 786 | 9.4 | 601 | 15.9 | 74.0 | 6.3 | 85.2 | 32.36 | 7 340 | 775 |
| Madison | 311.0 | 1 359 | 51.6 | 3 101 | 17.3 | 71.6 | 9.3 | 82.1 | 32.95 | 7 493 | 582 |
| Manitowoc | 167.8 | 5 081 | 10.0 | 429 | 18.7 | 69.9 | 10.8 | 79.6 | 30.49 | 7 563 | 425 |
| Menomonee Falls | 89.3 | 2 597 | 4.5 | 256 | 16.5 | 69.3 | 8.1 | 80.2 | 33.45 | 7 832 | 407 |
| Milwaukee | 1 265.3 | 2 101 | 224.5 | 6 542 | 20.0 | 74.3 | 11.5 | 85.1 | 32.09 | 6 886 | 791 |
| Mount Pleasant | 18.2 | 705 | 9.0 | 210 | NA | NA | NA | NA | NA | NA | NA |
| Neenah | 80.7 | 3 233 | 22.1 | 271 | NA | NA | NA | NA | NA | NA | NA |
| New Berlin | 46.5 | 1 192 | 6.2 | 254 | 19.9 | 73.8 | 12.7 | 81.9 | 33.86 | 6 847 | 764 |
| Oak Creek | 95.7 | 2 882 | 1.3 | 282 | 20.7 | 72.0 | 13.4 | 81.1 | 34.81 | 7 087 | 616 |
| Oshkosh | 189.3 | 2 931 | 38.4 | 574 | 16.1 | 72.0 | 7.8 | 81.8 | 31.57 | 7 639 | 591 |
| Racine | 243.1 | 3 085 | 15.4 | 880 | 20.7 | 71.3 | 13.3 | 78.6 | 35.35 | 7 032 | 567 |
| Sheboygan | 107.2 | 2 227 | 30.9 | 457 | 20.9 | 71.4 | 13.2 | 81.4 | 31.90 | 7 056 | 559 |
| Stevens Point | 14.7 | 591 | 2.5 | 198 | NA | NA | NA | NA | NA | NA | NA |
| Sun Prairie | 70.1 | 2 526 | 12.7 | 227 | NA | NA | NA | NA | NA | NA | NA |
| Superior | 57.6 | 2 164 | 1.5 | 282 | 12.1 | 66.6 | 3.4 | 76.2 | 30.78 | 9 006 | 241 |
| Waukesha | 109.4 | 1 638 | 28.6 | 580 | 19.5 | 73.8 | 11.4 | 84.2 | 34.64 | 6 893 | 784 |
| Wausau | 58.6 | 1 541 | 5.8 | 313 | 13.0 | 70.1 | 3.6 | 80.8 | 33.36 | 8 237 | 464 |
| Wauwatosa | 89.0 | 1 956 | 4.0 | 422 | 20.0 | 74.3 | 11.5 | 85.1 | 32.09 | 6 886 | 791 |
| West Allis | 77.4 | 1 295 | 13.8 | 566 | 19.9 | 73.8 | 12.7 | 81.9 | 33.86 | 6 847 | 764 |
| West Bend | 88.5 | 2 971 | 14.5 | 271 | 18.4 | 70.6 | 10.7 | 81.3 | 32.85 | 7 371 | 502 |
| WYOMING | X | X | X | X | X | X | X | X | X | X | X |
| Casper | 14.8 | 280 | 5.8 | 621 | 22.3 | 70.0 | 12.2 | 86.8 | 13.03 | 7 571 | 428 |
| Cheyenne | 106.2 | 1 909 | 4.3 | 740 | 25.9 | 67.7 | 14.8 | 81.9 | 15.45 | 7 388 | 273 |
| Gillette | 18.2 | 727 | 6.3 | 293 | NA | NA | NA | NA | NA | NA | NA |
| Laramie | 26.3 | 967 | 0.1 | 288 | 20.3 | 62.9 | 7.8 | 79.4 | 11.19 | 9 233 | 75 |

1. Based on the population estimated as of July 1 of the year shown.   2. Represents normal values based on the 30-year period, 1971–2000.   3. Average daily minimum.   4. Average daily maximum.

PART E.

# Congressional Districts of the 113th Congress

(For explanation of symbols, see page viii)

Page

# Congressional District Highlights and Rankings

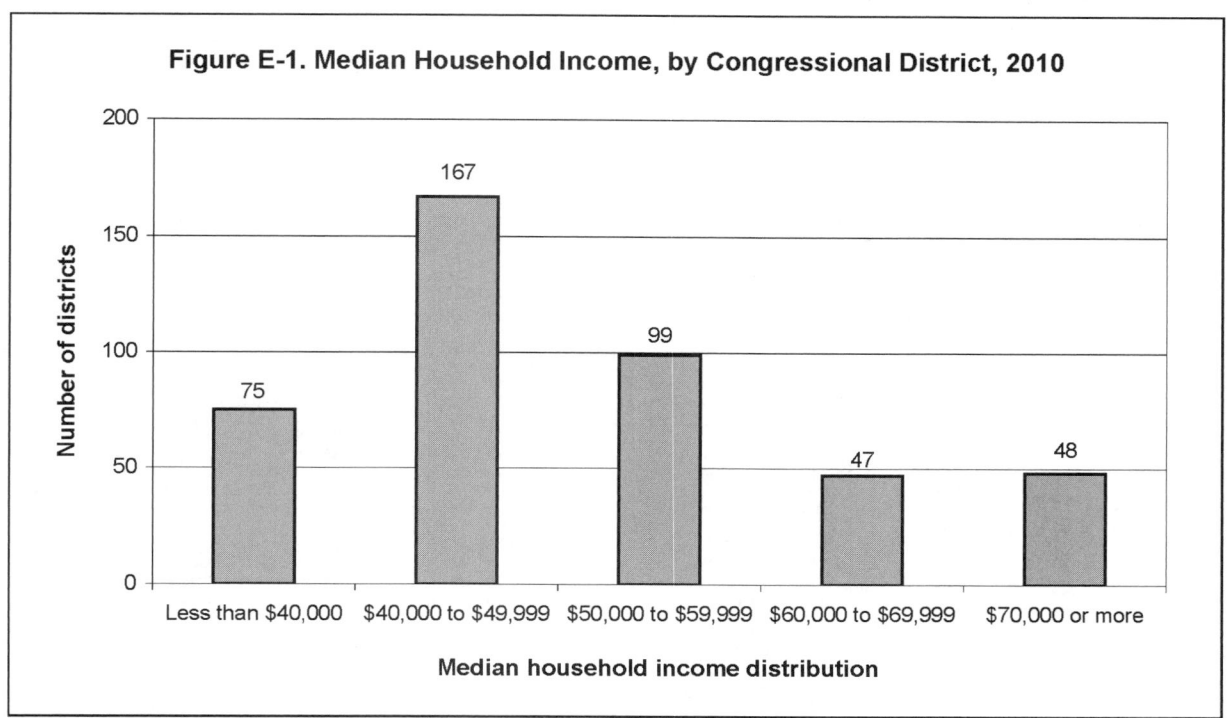

Figure E-1. Median Household Income, by Congressional District, 2010

Every 10 years, the Census Bureau conducts a count to reapportion the seats in the U.S. House of Representatives. The House's 435 seats are divided among the 50 states. (The District of Columbia has no representative in Congress, although it has a nonvoting delegate.) The seats are reapportioned according to the population measured on April 1 of the census year in order to account for population changes among the states over the previous decade. The number of districts within a state may change after each decennial census, and the districts' boundaries may change more than once during a decade. The 113th Congress, which convened in 2013, was the first to reflect the new boundaries based on the 2010 census. The data in Table E are for the boundaries of the 113th Congress.

As the state with the largest population, California had the most representatives with 53. Texas (36) and New York (27) were second and third largest, respectively. There were 7 states with just 1 representative: Alaska, Delaware, Montana, North Dakota, South Dakota, Vermont, and Wyoming. These states' representatives were considered 'At Large,' as they represented an entire state instead of a specific congressional district within the state.

Because the number of representatives is limited to 435, states with larger population growth add seats, while states with little or no growth lose seats. When the 113th Congress convened in January 2013, eight states had more representatives in congress and 10 states had fewer. Based on the 2010 census, Texas gained four seats, Florida gained two, while Washington, Nevada, Utah, Arizona, Georgia, and South

Carolina each gained one seat. New York and Ohio each lost two seats, while Massachusetts, New Jersey, Pennsylvania, Michigan, Illinois, Iowa, Missouri, and Louisiana each lost a seat.

While most of the congressional districts had about the same population size (average 715,000), they varied widely in other characteristics. In California's 33rd district, 95.9 percent of the residents were high school graduates, compared with just 50.9 percent in California's 40th district and 57.0 percent in California's 21st district. California's 40th district had the lowest proportion of college graduates, with only 8.2 percent of its residents holding a bachelor's degree, followed by Texas' 33rd district at 8.4 percent and California's 21st district at 8.9 percent. In New York's 12th district, 68.6 percent of residents were college graduates.

The highest unemployment rates were found in Michigan's 13th and 14th districts at 24.7 percent and 19.9 percent respectively. Four districts from California along with one district from New York, Illinois, Florida, and Ohio also ranked among the 10 highest. Ninety-one congressional districts had 20 percent or more of their populations living in poverty. New York's 15th district had the highest poverty rate in the nation at 39.4 percent and the lowest median household income at $23,894 in 2011. In Virginia's 10th district, the median household income was $109,505, the highest in the nation. Thirty-four congressional districts had median household incomes exceeding $75,000 per year, while 82 districts had median household incomes below $40,000.

**1177**

# Congressional Districts of the 113th Congress of the United States
## Selected Rankings

| Population, 2011 | | | Land area, 2010 | | | Population density, 2011 | | |
|---|---|---|---|---|---|---|---|---|
| Population rank | State congressional district Representative | Population [col 2] | Land area rank | State congressional district Representative | Land area (square kilometers) [col 1] | Density rank | State congressional district Representative | Population density (per square kilometer) [col 3] |
| 1 | MT At-Large Steve Daines (R) | 998 199 | 1 | AK At-Large: Don Young (R) | 1 477 953 | 1 | NY 13th Charles B. Rangel (D) | 27 824.3 |
| 2 | DE At-Large John C. Carney (D) | 907 135 | 2 | MT At-Large Steve Daines (R) | 376 962 | 2 | NY 15th: José E. Serrano (D) | 19 417.7 |
| 3 | SD At-Large Kristi Noem (R) | 824 082 | 3 | WYAt-Large Cynthia M. Lummis (R) | 251 470 | 3 | NY 10th: Jerrold Nadler (D) | 19 407.7 |
| 4 | ID 2nd: Michael K. Simpson (R) | 793 109 | 4 | SD At-Large Kristi Noem (R) | 196 350 | 4 | NY 12th: Carolyn B. Maloney (D) | 18 489.5 |
| 5 | ID 1st: Raul Labrador (R) | 791 876 | 5 | NM 2nd: Steve Pearce (R) | 185 804 | 5 | NY 9th: Yvette D. Clarke (D) | 18 369.6 |
| 6 | OR 1st: Earl Blumenauer (D) | 782 486 | 6 | OR 1st: Greg Walden (R) | 179 856 | 6 | NY 7th: Nydia M. Velázquez (D) | 17 319.1 |
| 7 | OR 1st: Suzanne Bonamici (D) | 775 806 | 7 | ND-At Large Kevin Cramer (R) | 178 711 | 7 | NY 14th: Joseph Crowley (D) | 9 716.7 |
| 8 | OR 1st: Kurt Schrader (D) | 772 980 | 8 | NE 3rd: Adrizan Smith (R) | 174 657 | 8 | NY 8th: Hakeem S. Jeffries (D) | 9 318.7 |
| 9 | IA 3rd: Tom Latham (R) | 770 819 | 9 | TX 23rd: Pete P. Gallego (D) | 150 373 | 9 | NY 6th: Grace Meng (D) | 9 173.5 |
| 10 | OR 1st: Greg Walden (R) | 770 403 | 10 | NV 2nd: Mark E. Amodei (R) | 144 598 | 10 | CA 12th: Nancy Pelosi (D) | 6 940.5 |
| 11 | OR 1st: Peter A. DeFazio (D) | 770 184 | 11 | AZ 1st: Ann Kirkpatrick (D) | 142 552 | 11 | CA 34th: Xavier Becerra (D) | 5 660.2 |
| 12 | LA 2nd: Cedric Richmond (D) | 767 984 | 12 | KS 1st Tim Huelskamp (R) | 136 084 | 12 | NY 5th: Gregory W. Meeks (D) | 5 509.6 |
| 13 | IA 2nd: David Loebsack (D) | 766 120 | 13 | NV 4th: Steven A. Horsford (D) | 132 084 | 13 | IL 4th: Luis V. Gutierrez (D) | 5 425.0 |
| 14 | OK 4th: Tom Cole (R) | 765 183 | 14 | CO 3rd: Scott R. Tipton (R) | 128 805 | 14 | NJ 8th: Albio Sires (D) | 5 269.8 |
| 15 | LA 5th: Rodney Alexander (R) | 765 180 | 15 | NM 3rd: Ben Ray Luján (D) | 116 442 | 15 | CA 37th: Karen Bass (D) | 5 023.6 |
| 16 | OK 1st: Jim Bridenstine (R) | 764 815 | 16 | ID 2nd: Michael K. Simpson (R) | 111 952 | 16 | CA 40th: Lucille Roybal-Allard (D) | 4 741.8 |
| 17 | IA 1st: Bruce L. Braley (D) | 763 903 | 17 | UT 2nd: Chris Stewart (R) | 103 568 | 17 | MA 7th: Michael E. Capuano (D) | 4 520.9 |
| 18 | LA 6th: Bill Cassidy (R) | 763 016 | 18 | ID 1st: Raul Labrador (R) | 102 092 | 18 | IL 7th: Danny K. Davis (D) | 4 341.8 |
| 19 | OK 5th: James Lankford (R) | 762 555 | 19 | TX 13th: Mac Thornberry (R) | 99 324 | 19 | NY 11th: Michael G. Grimm (R) | 4 248.6 |
| 20 | MO 3rd: Blaine Luetkemeyer (R) | 762 347 | 20 | CO 4th: Cory Gardner (R) | 98 685 | 20 | DC At-Large Eleanor Holmes Norton (D) . | 3 908.5 |
| 21 | IA 4th: Steve King (R) | 761 467 | 21 | OK 3rd: Frank D. Lucas (R) | 88 362 | 21 | CA 46th: Loretta Sanchez (D) | 3 827.5 |
| 22 | LA 3rd: Charles W. Boustany Jr. (R) | 760 696 | 22 | MN 7th: Collin C. Peterson (D) | 86 582 | 22 | PA 1st: Chaka Fattah (D) | 3 782.9 |
| 23 | LA 1st: Steve Scalise (R) | 759 507 | 23 | AZ 4th: Paul A. Gosar (R) | 85 986 | 23 | CA 43rd: Maxine Waters (D) | 3 768.1 |
| 24 | NC 4th: David E. Price (D) | 758 619 | 24 | CA 8th: Paul Cook (R) | 85 126 | 24 | NJ 10th: Donald M. Payne, Jr. (D) | 3 694.2 |
| 25 | LA 4th: John Fleming (R) | 758 453 | 25 | CA 1st: Doug LaMalfa (R) | 72 751 | 25 | NY 16th: Eliot L. Engel (D) | 3 552.0 |
| 26 | MO 4th: Vicky Hartzler (R) | 755 389 | 26 | MN 8th: Richard M. Nolan (D) | 72 282 | 26 | CA 44th: Janice Hahn (D) | 3 470.1 |
| 27 | MO 6th: Sam Graves (R) | 753 729 | 27 | TX 11th: K. Michael Conaway (R) | 72 085 | 27 | PA 1st: Robert A. Brady (D) | 3 363.8 |
| 28 | OK 2nd: Markwayne Mullin (R) | 753 014 | 28 | ME 2nd: Michael H. Michaud (D) | 71 373 | 28 | NJ 9th: Bill Pascrell, Jr. (D) | 3 006.8 |
| 29 | MO 2nd: Ann Wagner (R) | 752 403 | 29 | TX 19th: Randy Neugebauer (R) | 66 914 | 29 | CA 29th: Tony Cárdenas (D) | 2 882.5 |
| 30 | MO 7th: Bill Long (R) | 751 514 | 30 | MI 1st: Dan Benishek (R) | 64 822 | 30 | IL 5th: Michael Quigley (D) | 2 873.6 |
| 31 | VA 10th: Frank R. Wolf (R) | 750 886 | 31 | WI 1st: Sean P. Duffy (R) | 59 666 | 31 | CA 13th: Barbara Lee (D) | 2 840.7 |
| 32 | NC 9th: Robert Pittenger (R) | 750 582 | 32 | IA 4th: Steve King (R) | 58 940 | 32 | CA 38th: Linda T. Sánchez (D) | 2 717.5 |
| 33 | NC 8th: Richard Hudson (R) | 750 059 | 33 | AR 4th: Tom Cotton (R) | 57 855 | 33 | IL 9th: Janice D. Schakowsky (D) | 2 622.6 |
| 34 | NC 6th: Howard Coble (R) | 749 909 | 34 | OK 2nd: Markwayne Mullin (R) | 54 378 | 34 | FL 24th: Frederica S. Wilson (D) | 2 522.6 |
| 35 | NC 3rd: Walter B. Jones (R) | 749 823 | 35 | UT 3rd: Jason Chaffetz (R) | 51 982 | 35 | NY 4th: Carolyn McCarthy (D) | 2 494.0 |
| 36 | MS 4th: Steven Palazzo (R) | 749 289 | 36 | MO 8th: Jason T. Smith (R) | 51 544 | 36 | NV 1st: Dina Titus (D) | 2 438.4 |
| 37 | MO 8th: Jason T. Smith (R) | 747 756 | 37 | UT 1st: Rob Bishop (R) | 50 662 | 37 | CA 32nd: Grace F. Napolitano (D) | 2 155.9 |
| 38 | MO 5th: Emanuel Cleaver (D) | 747 573 | 38 | AR 1st Eric A. "Rick" Crawford (R) | 50 034 | 38 | WI 1st: Gwen Moore (D) | 2 153.6 |
| 39 | NJ 7th: Leonard Lance (R) | 747 216 | 39 | WA 4th: Doc Hastings (R) | 49 858 | 39 | CA 30th: Brad Sherman (D) | 2 063.3 |
| 40 | MD 8th: Chris Van Hollen (D) | 747 185 | 40 | MO 6th: Sam Graves (R) | 47 134 | 39 | CA 33rd: Susan A. Davis (D) | 2 063.3 |
| 41 | VA 11th: Gerald E. Connolly (D) | 746 993 | 41 | OR 1st: Peter A. DeFazio (D) | 44 740 | 41 | MN 5th: Keith Ellison (D) | 1 927.4 |
| 42 | NJ 8th: Albio Sires (D) | 746 415 | 42 | AZ 3rd: Raúl M. Grijalva (D) | 40 634 | 42 | VA 8th: James P. Moran (D) | 1 921.0 |
| 43 | OK 3rd: Frank D. Lucas (R) | 745 941 | 43 | MS 2nd: Bennie G. Thompson (D) | 40 278 | 43 | CA 48th: Dana Rohrabacher (R) | 1 889.7 |
| 44 | NC 7th: Mike McIntyre (D) | 745 559 | 44 | WA 5th: Cathy McMorris Rodgers (R) | 40 075 | 44 | WA 7th: Jim McDermott (D) | 1 830.0 |
| 45 | MS 3rd: Gregg Harper (R) | 745 254 | 45 | NY 21st: William L. Owens (D) | 39 147 | 45 | PA 1st: Allyson Y. Schwartz (D) | 1 813.6 |
| 46 | NC 2nd: Renee Ellmers (R) | 744 671 | 46 | IL 15th: John Shimkus (R) | 38 062 | 46 | TX 7th: John Abney Culberson (R) | 1 732.6 |
| 47 | CO 6th: Mike Coffman (R) | 744 526 | 47 | LA 5th: Rodney Alexander (R) | 37 433 | 47 | AZ 9th Kyrsten Sinema (D) | 1 693.7 |
| 48 | VA 3rd: Robert C. "Bobby" Scott (D) | 744 369 | 48 | MO 4th: Vicky Hartzler (R) | 37 299 | 48 | CA 35th: Gloria Negrete McLeod (D) | 1 624.8 |
| 49 | VA 1st: Robert J. Wittman (R) | 743 824 | 49 | KS 4th Mike Pompeo (R) | 37 077 | 49 | TX 9th: Al Green (D) | 1 611.8 |
| 50 | AZ 6th: David Schweikert (R) | 743 752 | 50 | KS 2nd Lynn Jenkins (R) | 36 631 | 50 | FL 23rd: Debbie Wasserman Schultz (D). | 1 606.5 |
| 51 | MS 2nd: Bennie G. Thompson (D) | 743 249 | 51 | CA 2nd: Jared Huffman (D) | 33 546 | 51 | CA 6th: Doris O. Matsui (D) | 1 574.0 |
| 52 | VA 8th: James P. Moran (D) | 742 531 | 52 | CA 4th: Tom McClintock (R) | 33 246 | 52 | FL 22nd: Lois Frankel (D) | 1 571.2 |
| 53 | NJ 9th: Bill Pascrell, Jr. (D) | 742 508 | 53 | MS 3rd: Gregg Harper (R) | 33 034 | 53 | VA 11th: Gerald E. Connolly (D) | 1 558.2 |
| 54 | FL 10th: Daniel Webster (R) | 741 792 | 54 | LA 4th: John Fleming (R) | 32 207 | 54 | NY 2nd: Peter T. King (R) | 1 535.9 |
| 55 | NC 10th: Patrick T. McHenry (R) | 740 773 | 55 | IA 2nd: David Loebsack (D) | 31 758 | 55 | CA 17th: Michael M. Honda (D) | 1 512.7 |
| 56 | MS 1st: Alan Nunnelee (R) | 740 720 | 56 | KY 1st: Ed Whitfield (R) | 31 286 | 56 | CO 1st: Diana DeGette (D) | 1 506.1 |
| 57 | NY 5th: Gregory W. Meeks (D) | 740 327 | 57 | IA 1st: Bruce L. Braley (D) | 31 206 | 57 | MI 9th: Sander M. Levin (D) | 1 498.5 |
| 58 | MO 1st: William Lacy Clay (D) | 739 977 | 58 | MN 1st: Timothy J. Walz (D) | 31 012 | 58 | TX 29th: Gene Green (D) | 1 482.7 |
| 59 | CO 1st: Diana DeGette (D) | 739 671 | 59 | KY 5th: Harold Rogers (R) | 29 099 | 59 | TX 32nd: Pete Sessions (R) | 1 480.2 |
| 60 | NC 1st: G. K. Butterfield (D) | 739 665 | 60 | WI 1st: Ron Kind (D) | 28 779 | 60 | MI 14th: Gary C. Peters (D) | 1 470.9 |
| 61 | NY 9th: Yvette D. Clarke (D) | 739 328 | 61 | PA 1st: Glenn Thompson (R) | 27 742 | 61 | MI 13th: John Conyers Jr. (D) | 1 460.5 |
| 62 | AR 2nd: Timothy Griffin (R) | 739 092 | 62 | MS 1st: Alan Nunnelee (R) | 27 383 | 62 | WA 9th: Adam Smith (D) | 1 460.0 |
| 63 | NY 13th Charles B. Rangel (D) | 738 943 | 63 | IL 18th: Aaron Schock (R) | 27 236 | 63 | FL 13th: C. W. Bill Young (R) | 1 442.3 |
| 64 | NJ 6th: Frank Pallone Jr. (D) | 738 756 | 64 | AL 7th: Terri A. Sewell (D) | 26 304 | 64 | TX 20th: Joaquin Castro (D) | 1 386.0 |
| 65 | MA 5th: Edward J. Markey (D) | 737 545 | 65 | AL 2nd: Martha Roby (R) | 26 267 | 65 | AZ 7th: Ed Pastor (D) | 1 365.1 |
| 66 | NC 12th: Melvin L. Watt (D) | 737 200 | 66 | TX 4th: Ralph M. Hall (R) | 26 218 | 66 | IL 8th: Tammy Duckworth (D) | 1 361.4 |
| 67 | IL 4th: Luis V. Gutierrez (D) | 737 025 | 67 | VA 5th: Robert Hurt (R) | 25 977 | 67 | CA 39th: Edward R. Royce (R) | 1 344.3 |
| 68 | VA 4th: J. Randy Forbes (R) | 736 977 | 68 | CA 23rd: Kevin McCarthy (R) | 25 636 | 68 | NJ 6th: Frank Pallone Jr. (D) | 1 323.3 |
| 69 | MD 4th: Donna F. Edwards (D) | 736 929 | 69 | OK 4th: Tom Cole (R) | 25 323 | 69 | FL 27th: Ileana Ros-Lehtinen (R) | 1 316.5 |
| 70 | MA 4th: Joseph P. Kennedy III (D) | 736 769 | 70 | WV 3rd: Nick J. Rahall II (D) | 25 240 | 70 | PA 1st: Michael F. Doyle (D) | 1 297.4 |
| 71 | NJ 2nd: Frank A. LoBiondo (R) | 736 397 | 71 | GA 2nd: Sanford D. Bishop Jr. (D) | 24 932 | 71 | TX 33rd: Marc A. Veasey (D) | 1 295.2 |
| 72 | AR 1st Tom Cotton (R) | 736 183 | 72 | TX 28th: Henry Cuellar (D) | 24 290 | 72 | CA 31st: Gary G. Miller (R) | 1 287.1 |
| 73 | NJ 4th: Christopher H. Smith (R) | 736 007 | 73 | VT At-large Peter Welch (D) | 23 871 | 73 | CA 47th: Alan S. Lowenthal (D) | 1 285.4 |
| 74 | VA 6th: Bob Goodlatte (R) | 734 204 | 74 | TN 7th: Marsha Blackburn (R) | 23 725 | 74 | HI 1st: Colleen Hanabusa (D) | 1 274.6 |
| 75 | VA 7th: Eric Cantor (R) | 733 911 | 75 | TX 27th: Blake Farenthold (R) | 23 642 | 75 | NY 26th Brian Higgins (D) | 1 268.4 |

# Congressional Districts of the 113th Congress of the United States
## Selected Rankings

| Percent Non-Hispanic White alone, 2011 | | | Percent Black alone, 2011 | | | Percent American Indian, Alaska Native alone, 2011 | | |
|---|---|---|---|---|---|---|---|---|
| Non-Hispanic White alone rank | State congressional district Representative | Percent white [col 11] | Black rank | State congressional district Representative | Percent black [col 5] | American indian Alaska Native rank | State congressional district Representative | Percent American Indian Alaska Native [col 6] |
| 1 | KY 5th: Harold Rogers (R) | 96.2 | 1 | MS 2nd: Bennie G. Thompson (D) | 65.2 | 1 | AZ 1st: Ann Kirkpatrick (D) | 23.2 |
| 2 | OH 6th: Bill Johnson (R) | 94.9 | 2 | AL 7th: Terri A. Sewell (D) | 64.1 | 2 | NM 3rd: Ben Ray Luján (D) | 17.2 |
| 3 | ME 2nd: Michael H. Michaud (D) | 94.7 | 3 | TN 9th: Steve Cohen (D) | 63.8 | 3 | AK At-Large: Don Young (R) | 14.2 |
| 4 | WV 1st: David McKinley (R) | 94.3 | 4 | LA 2nd: Cedric Richmond (D) | 62.9 | 4 | OK 2nd: Markwayne Mullin (R) | 13.2 |
| 5 | VT At-large Peter Welch (D) | 94.0 | 5 | PA 1st: Chaka Fattah (D) | 58.6 | 5 | SD At-Large Kristi Noem (R) | 8.7 |
| 6 | ME 1st: Chellie Pingree (D) | 93.8 | 6 | GA 5th: John Lewis (D) | 58.3 | 6 | NC 8th: Richard Hudson (R) | 7.1 |
| 6 | WV 3rd: Nick J. Rahall II (D) | 93.8 | 7 | MI 14th: Gary C. Peters (D) | 57.2 | 7 | MT At-Large Steve Daines (R) | 6.7 |
| 8 | PA 1st: Bill Shuster (R) | 93.3 | 7 | VA 3rd: Robert C. "Bobby" Scott (D) | 57.2 | 8 | NM 2nd: Steve Pearce (R) | 6.0 |
| 8 | PA 1st: Tim Murphy(R) | 93.3 | 9 | GA 4th: Henry C. "Hank" Johnson Jr. (D) | 56.9 | 9 | OK 1st: Jim Bridenstine (R) | 5.9 |
| 10 | PA 1st: Glenn Thompson (R) | 93.1 | 9 | SC 6th: James E. Clyburn (D) | 56.9 | 10 | ND-At Large Kevin Cramer (R) | 5.6 |
| 10 | PA 1st: Keith J. Rothfus (R) | 93.1 | 11 | MI 13th: John Conyers Jr. (D) | 56.5 | 11 | AZ 3rd: Raúl M. Grijalva (D) | 5.3 |
| 12 | WI 1st: Ron Kind (D) | 92.9 | 12 | FL 24th: Frederica S. Wilson (D) | 56.2 | 11 | OK 3rd: Frank D. Lucas (R) | 5.3 |
| 13 | MN 8th: Richard M. Nolan (D) | 92.8 | 13 | NY 8th: Hakeem S. Jeffries (D) | 56.0 | 11 | OK 4th: Tom Cole (R) | 5.3 |
| 14 | OH 16th: James B. Renacci (R) | 92.7 | 14 | IL 2nd: Robin L. Kelly (D) | 55.5 | 14 | OK 5th: James Lankford (R) | 4.7 |
| 15 | WI 1st: Sean P. Duffy (R) | 92.6 | 15 | MD 7th: Elijah E. Cummings (D) | 54.6 | 15 | NM 1st: Michelle Lujan Grisham (D) | 4.4 |
| 15 | IN 6th: Luke Messer (R) | 92.6 | 15 | IL 7th: Danny K. Davis (D) | 54.6 | 16 | MN 7th: Collin C. Peterson (D) | 2.9 |
| 17 | TN 1st: David P. Roe (R) | 92.1 | 17 | OH 11th: Marcia L. Fudge (D) | 54.2 | 17 | AZ 7th: Ed Pastor (D) | 2.7 |
| 17 | OH 7th Bob Gibbs (R) | 92.1 | 17 | GA 13th: David Scott (D) | 54.2 | 18 | MI 1st: Dan Benishek (R) | 2.6 |
| 17 | NH 1st: Carol Shea-Porter (D) | 92.1 | 17 | MD 4th: Donna F. Edwards (D) | 54.2 | 18 | MN 8th: Richard M. Nolan (D) | 2.6 |
| 17 | NY 27th: Chris Collins (R) | 92.1 | 20 | NJ 10th: Donald M. Payne, Jr. (D) | 53.4 | 20 | NV 2nd: Mark E. Amodei (R) | 2.5 |
| 21 | MI 4th: Dave Camp (R) | 92.0 | 21 | FL 20th: Alcee L. Hastings (D) | 52.9 | 21 | WA 6th: Derek Kilmer (D) | 2.3 |
| 22 | NH 2nd: Ann M. Kuster (D) | 91.9 | 22 | NY 9th: Yvette D. Clarke (D) | 52.7 | 21 | CA 2nd: Jared Huffman (D) | 2.3 |
| 23 | MI 1st: Dan Benishek (R) | 91.8 | 22 | FL 5th: Corrine Brown (D) | 52.7 | 21 | CO 3rd: Scott R. Tipton (R) | 2.3 |
| 24 | MO 3rd: Blaine Luetkemeyer (R) | 91.6 | 24 | NC 1st: G. K. Butterfield (D) | 52.1 | 24 | AZ 4th: Paul A. Gosar (R) | 2.2 |
| 25 | IN 8th: Larry Bucshon (R) | 91.4 | 25 | IL 1st: Bobby L. Rush (D) | 51.3 | 24 | WI 1st: Reid J. Ribble (R) | 2.2 |
| 26 | PA 1st: Mike Kelly (R) | 91.2 | 26 | NY 5th: Gregory W. Meeks (D) | 51.0 | 24 | WY At-Large Cynthia M. Lummis (R) | 2.2 |
| 26 | WV 2nd: Shelley Moore Capito (R) | 91.2 | 27 | GA 2nd: Sanford D. Bishop Jr. (D) | 50.2 | 27 | WI 1st: Sean P. Duffy (R) | 2.1 |
| 28 | MO 8th: Jason T. Smith (R) | 91.1 | 28 | DC At-Large Eleanor Holmes Norton (D) | 50.1 | 27 | WA 4th: Doc Hastings (R) | 2.1 |
| 28 | PA 1st: Tom Marino (R) | 91.1 | 29 | NC 12th: Melvin L. Watt (D) | 49.0 | 29 | AZ 9th: Kyrsten Sinema (D) | 2.0 |
| 30 | NY 21st: William L. Owens (D) | 91.0 | 30 | MO 1st: William Lacy Clay (D) | 48.9 | 30 | OR 1st: Greg Walden (R) | 1.9 |
| 30 | WI 1st: Thomas E. Petri (R) | 91.0 | 31 | TX 30th: Eddie Bernice Johnson (D) | 44.6 | 31 | WA 5th: Cathy McMorris Rodgers (R) | 1.8 |
| 32 | IL 15th: John Shimkus (R) | 90.9 | 32 | TX 18th: Sheila Jackson-Lee (D) | 38.6 | 32 | NC 7th: Mike McIntyre (D) | 1.7 |
| 32 | MI 10th: Candice S. Miller (R) | 90.9 | 32 | TX 9th: Al Green (D) | 38.6 | 32 | AZ 6th: David Schweikert (R) | 1.7 |
| 34 | OH 14th: David P. Joyce (R) | 90.8 | 34 | MD 5th: Steny H. Hoyer (D) | 37.3 | 32 | CA 1st: Doug LaMalfa (R) | 1.7 |
| 35 | KY 4th: Thomas Massie (R) | 90.6 | 35 | LA 5th: Rodney Alexander (R) | 35.9 | 32 | OR 1st: Peter A. DeFazio (D) | 1.7 |
| 35 | IN 9th: Todd C. Young (R) | 90.6 | 36 | MS 3rd: Gregg Harper (R) | 35.2 | 32 | CA 4th: Tom McClintock (R) | 1.7 |
| 35 | MN 6th: Michele Bachmann (R) | 90.6 | 37 | GA 12th: John Barrow (D) | 35.1 | 37 | UT 3rd: Jason Chaffetz (R) | 1.6 |
| 38 | OH 15th: Steve Stivers (R) | 90.4 | 38 | NY 15th: José E. Serrano (D) | 34.3 | 38 | CA 50th: Duncan Hunter (R) | 1.5 |
| 38 | OH 5th: Robert E. Latta (R) | 90.4 | 39 | LA 4th: John Fleming (R) | 33.9 | 38 | CA 6th: Doris O. Matsui (D) | 1.5 |
| 38 | Collin C. Peterson (D) | 90.4 | 40 | PA 1st: Robert A. Brady (D) | 33.7 | 38 | ID 1st: Raul Labrador (R) | 1.5 |
| 41 | IA 1st: Bruce L. Braley (D) | 90.3 | 40 | WI 1st: Gwen Moore (D) | 33.7 | 41 | NC 11th: Mark Meadows (D) | 1.4 |
| 42 | VA 9th: Morgan Griffith (R) | 90.0 | 42 | NC 4th: David E. Price (D) | 33.1 | 41 | CA 41st: Mark Takano (D) | 1.4 |
| 43 | IL 18th: Aaron Schock (R) | 89.8 | 43 | NY 16th: Eliot L. Engel (D) | 32.4 | 41 | WA 2nd: Rick Larsen (D) | 1.4 |
| 43 | TN 6th: Diane Black (R) | 89.8 | 44 | OH 3rd: Joyce Beatty (D) | 32.1 | 41 | CA 23rd: Kevin McCarthy (R) | 1.4 |
| 43 | WI 1st: F. James Sensenbrenner Jr. (R). | 89.8 | 45 | MD 2nd: C. A. Dutch Ruppersberger (D) | 31.8 | 41 | AZ 5th: Matt Salmon (R) | 1.4 |
| 46 | IA 4th: Steve King (R) | 89.7 | 46 | VA 4th: J. Randy Forbes (R) | 31.4 | 41 | CA 21st: David G. Valadao (R) | 1.4 |
| 46 | MO 7th: Bill Long (R) | 89.7 | 47 | NY 13th Charles B. Rangel (D) | 31.0 | 41 | NE 1st: Jeff Fortenberry (R) | 1.4 |
| 48 | NY 23rd: Tom Reed (R) | 89.4 | 47 | GA 8th: Austin Scott (R) | 31.0 | 48 | CA 3rd: John Garamendi (D) | 1.3 |
| 49 | MO 6th: Sam Graves (R) | 89.2 | 49 | AL 2nd: Martha Roby (R) | 29.7 | 48 | CA 8th: Paul Cook (R) | 1.3 |
| 50 | NY 22nd: Richard L. Hanna (R) | 89.0 | 50 | SC 7th: Tom Rice (R) | 29.6 | 48 | KS 2nd Lynn Jenkins (R) | 1.3 |
| 50 | MI 7th Tim Walberg (R) | 89.0 | 51 | GA 1st: Jack Kingston (R) | 29.0 | 48 | UT 2nd: Chris Stewart (R) | 1.3 |
| 52 | WI 1st: Reid J. Ribble (R) | 88.5 | 52 | IN 7th: André Carson (D) | 28.3 | 48 | WA 10th: Denny Heck (D) | 1.3 |
| 52 | ND-At Large Kevin Cramer (R) | 88.5 | 53 | AL 1st: Jo Bonner (R) | 28.1 | 53 | NV 4th: Steven A. Horsford (D) | 1.2 |
| 54 | MA 9th: William R. Keating (D) | 88.4 | 54 | SC 5th: Mick Mulvaney (R) | 27.9 | 53 | LA 1st: Steve Scalise (R) | 1.2 |
| 55 | OH 4th: Jim Jordan (R) | 88.3 | 55 | FL 14th: Kathy Castor (D) | 26.8 | 53 | TX 12th: Kay Granger (R) | 1.2 |
| 55 | KY 2nd: Brett Guthrie (R) | 88.3 | 56 | MA 7th: Michael E. Capuano (D) | 26.7 | 53 | CA 5th: Mike Thompson (D) | 1.2 |
| 57 | KY 1st: Ed Whitfield (R) | 88.2 | 57 | MS 1st: Alan Nunnelee (R) | 26.4 | 53 | CO 1st: Diana DeGette (D) | 1.2 |
| 58 | MO 2nd: Ann Wagner (R) | 88.1 | 58 | AL 3rd: Mike Rogers (R) | 25.9 | 53 | OR 1st: Suzanne Bonamici (D) | 1.2 |
| 59 | IA 2nd: David Loebsack (D) | 87.9 | 59 | LA 3rd: Charles W. Boustany Jr. (R) | 24.9 | 53 | MN 5th: Keith Ellison (D) | 1.2 |
| 59 | MN 1st: Timothy J. Walz (D) | 87.9 | 59 | SC 2nd: Joe Wilson (R) | 24.9 | 53 | AR 3rd: Steve Womack (R) | 1.2 |
| 59 | MO 4th: Vicky Hartzler (R) | 87.9 | 61 | TN 5th: Jim Cooper (D) | 24.8 | 61 | ID 2nd: Michael K. Simpson (R) | 1.1 |
| 62 | OH 12th: Patrick J. Tiberi (R) | 87.8 | 62 | GA 10th: Paul C. Broun (R) | 24.5 | 61 | CA 16th: Jim Costa (D) | 1.1 |
| 63 | NC 11th: Mark Meadows (D) | 87.5 | 62 | FL 2nd: Steve Southerland II (R) | 24.5 | 61 | CA 36th: Raul Ruiz (D) | 1.1 |
| 63 | IN 4th: Todd Rokita (R) | 87.5 | 64 | CA 37th: Karen Bass (D) | 24.3 | 64 | CA 51st: Juan Vargas (D) | 1.0 |
| 65 | OH 8th: John A. Boehner (R) | 87.4 | 65 | GA 3rd: Lynn A. Westmoreland (R) | 23.6 | 64 | OR 1st: Kurt Schrader (D) | 1.0 |
| 65 | MT At-Large Steve Daines (R) | 87.4 | 65 | CA 43rd: Maxine Waters (D) | 23.6 | 64 | WA 1st: Suzan K. DelBene (D) | 1.0 |
| 67 | PA 1st: Lou Barletta (R) | 87.2 | 67 | MS 4th: Steven Palazzo (R) | 23.1 | 64 | AL 1st: Jo Bonner (R) | 1.0 |
| 68 | TN 2nd: John J. Duncan Jr. (R) | 86.8 | 68 | LA 6th: Bill Cassidy (R) | 22.1 | 64 | CA 10th: Jeff Denham (R) | 1.0 |
| 68 | OH 2nd: Brad R. Wenstrup (R) | 86.8 | 69 | OH 1st: Steve Chabot (R) | 22.0 | 64 | CA 9th: Jerry McNerney (D) | 1.0 |
| 70 | PA 1st: Michael G. Fitzpatrick (R) | 86.7 | 69 | AR 2nd: Timothy Griffin (R) | 22.0 | 64 | WA 3rd: Jaime Herrera Beutler (R) | 1.0 |
| 71 | NE 3rd: Adrian Smith (R) | 86.6 | 71 | VA 2nd: Scott Rigell (R) | 21.9 | 64 | ME 2nd: Michael H. Michaud (D) | 1.0 |
| 72 | MA 4th: Joseph P. Kennedy III (D) | 86.5 | 72 | PA 1st: Michael F. Doyle (D) | 21.8 | 64 | KS 4th Mike Pompeo (R) | 1.0 |
| 73 | PA 1st: Patrick Meehan (R) | 85.9 | 73 | DE At-Large John C. Carney (D) | 21.4 | 64 | CA 31st: Gary G. Miller (R) | 1.0 |
| 74 | NY 19th: Christopher P. Gibson (R) | 85.8 | 74 | MO 5th: Emanuel Cleaver (D) | 21.3 | 74 | NE 3rd: Adrian Smith (R) | 0.9 |
| 75 | IA 3rd: Tom Latham (R) | 85.6 | 75 | VA 5th: Robert Hurt (R) | 21.0 | 74 | MS 3rd: Gregg Harper (R) | 0.9 |

# Congressional Districts of the 113th Congress of the United States
## Selected Rankings

| Percent Asian or Pacific Islander alone, 2011 | | | Percent Hispanic or Latino,[1] 2011 | | | Percent foreign born, 2011 | | |
|---|---|---|---|---|---|---|---|---|
| Asian or Pacific Islander rank | State congressional district Representative | Percent Asian or Pacific Islander [col 7] | Hispanic rank | State congressional district Representative | Percent Hispanic [col 10] | Foreign-born rank | State congressional district Representative | Percent foreign born [col 13] |
| 1 | HI 1st: Colleen Hanabusa (D) | 58.6 | 1 | CA 40th: Lucille Roybal-Allard (D) | 86.6 | 1 | FL 27th: Ileana Ros-Lehtinen (R) | 54.8 |
| 2 | CA 17th: Michael M. Honda (D) | 49.4 | 2 | TX 34th: Filemon Vela (D) | 82.6 | 2 | FL 25th: Mario Diaz-Balart (R) | 52.7 |
| 3 | CA 27th: Judy Chu (D) | 36.5 | 3 | TX 15th: Rubén Hinojosa (D) | 80.2 | 3 | NY 6th: Grace Meng (D) | 51.8 |
| 3 | NY 6th: Grace Meng (D) | 36.5 | 4 | TX 16th: Beto O'Rourke (D) | 79.3 | 4 | CA 34th: Xavier Becerra (D) | 49.9 |
| 5 | HI 2nd: Tulsi Gabbard (D) | 36.1 | 5 | TX 28th: Henry Cuellar (D) | 78.4 | 5 | NY 14th: Joseph Crowley (D) | 48.2 |
| 6 | CA 14th: Jackie Speier (D) | 32.8 | 6 | TX 29th: Gene Green (D) | 76.4 | 6 | FL 26th: Joe Garcia (D) | 48.0 |
| 7 | CA 12th: Nancy Pelosi (D) | 31.5 | 7 | FL 27th: Ileana Ros-Lehtinen (R) | 72.7 | 7 | CA 17th: Michael M. Honda (D) | 45.2 |
| 8 | CA 15th: Eric Swalwell (D) | 29.5 | 8 | CA 21st: David G. Valadao (R) | 72.1 | 8 | CA 29th: Tony Cárdenas (D) | 43.7 |
| 9 | CA 39th: Edward R. Royce (R) | 28.6 | 9 | IL 4th: Luis V. Gutierrez (D) | 71.8 | 9 | NJ 8th: Albio Sires (D) | 43.2 |
| 10 | CA 19th: Zoe Lofgren (D) | 26.2 | 10 | TX 23rd: Pete P. Gallego (D) | 70.8 | 10 | NY 5th: Gregory W. Meeks (D) | 43.1 |
| 11 | WA 9th: Adam Smith (D) | 22.4 | 11 | CA 44th: Janice Hahn (D) | 70.5 | 11 | CA 28th: Adam B. Schiff (D) | 42.6 |
| 12 | CA 13th: Barbara Lee (D) | 21.5 | 12 | FL 25th: Mario Diaz-Balart (R) | 70.4 | 12 | CA 46th: Loretta Sanchez (D) | 42.4 |
| 13 | CA 45th: John Campbell (R) | 21.3 | 13 | CA 35th: Gloria Negrete McLeod (D) | 70.0 | 13 | CA 40th: Lucille Roybal-Allard (D) | 41.9 |
| 14 | CA 47th: Alan S. Lowenthal (D) | 20.9 | 14 | FL 26th: Joe Garcia (D) | 69.5 | 14 | NY 9th: Yvette D. Clarke (D) | 40.9 |
| 15 | CA 18th: Anna G. Eshoo (D) | 20.2 | 15 | CA 51st: Juan Vargas (D) | 69.1 | 15 | FL 24th: Frederica S. Wilson (D) | 38.6 |
| 16 | CA 52nd: Scott H. Peters (D) | 19.7 | 16 | CA 29th: Tony Cárdenas (D) | 67.7 | 16 | CA 27th: Judy Chu (D) | 38.4 |
| 17 | CA 34th: Xavier Becerra (D) | 19.6 | 17 | CA 46th: Loretta Sanchez (D) | 67.4 | 17 | CA 14th: Jackie Speier (D) | 36.9 |
| 18 | CA 48th: Dana Rohrabacher (R) | 18.1 | 18 | CA 34th: Xavier Becerra (D) | 66.5 | 17 | NY 13th Charles B. Rangel (D) | 36.9 |
| 19 | CA 6th: Doris O. Matsui (D) | 17.7 | 19 | TX 20th: Joaquin Castro (D) | 66.3 | 19 | FL 23rd: Debbie Wasserman Schultz (D) | 36.7 |
| 19 | NY 7th: Nydia M. Velázquez (D) | 17.7 | 20 | NY 15th: José E. Serrano (D) | 66.1 | 20 | CA 32nd: Grace F. Napolitano (D) | 36.6 |
| 19 | VA 11th: Gerald E. Connolly (D) | 17.7 | 21 | AZ 7th: Ed Pastor (D) | 65.9 | 20 | NY 7th: Nydia M. Velázquez (D) | 36.6 |
| 22 | NJ 6th: Frank Pallone Jr. (D) | 17.4 | 22 | TX 33rd: Marc A. Veasey (D) | 65.0 | 22 | NJ 9th: Bill Pascrell, Jr. (D) | 36.4 |
| 23 | TX 22nd: Pete Olson (R) | 17.1 | 23 | TX 35th: Lloyd Doggett (D) | 64.0 | 22 | IL 4th: Luis V. Gutierrez (D) | 36.4 |
| 24 | NY 14th: Joseph Crowley (D) | 16.5 | 24 | CA 32nd: Grace F. Napolitano (D) | 61.9 | 24 | CA 19th: Zoe Lofgren (D) | 35.6 |
| 25 | CA 32nd: Grace F. Napolitano (D) | 16.4 | 25 | CA 38th: Linda T. Sánchez (D) | 61.2 | 25 | CA 12th: Nancy Pelosi (D) | 35.5 |
| 26 | NY 10th: Jerrold Nadler (D) | 16.3 | 26 | AZ 3rd: Raúl M. Grijalva (D) | 61.1 | 26 | CA 44th: Janice Hahn (D) | 34.7 |
| 27 | NJ 12th: Rush Holt (D) | 14.6 | 27 | CA 41st: Mark Takano (D) | 59.1 | 27 | NY 15th: José E. Serrano (D) | 34.6 |
| 28 | CA 38th: Linda T. Sánchez (D) | 14.4 | 28 | CA 16th: Jim Costa (D) | 58.1 | 27 | CA 51st: Juan Vargas (D) | 34.6 |
| 29 | CA 33rd: Henry A. Waxman (D) | 14.3 | 29 | NJ 8th: Albio Sires (D) | 54.4 | 29 | NY 8th: Hakeem S. Jeffries (D) | 33.4 |
| 30 | CA 9th: Jerry McNerney (D) | 13.7 | 30 | NY 13th Charles B. Rangel (D) | 52.5 | 30 | CA 30th: Brad Sherman (D) | 33.3 |
| 30 | CA 28th: Adam B. Schiff (D) | 13.7 | 31 | NM 2nd: Steve Pearce (R) | 52.1 | 31 | CA 37th: Karen Bass (D) | 33.2 |
| 30 | CA 43rd: Maxine Waters (D) | 13.7 | 32 | CA 20th: Sam Farr (D) | 51.5 | 32 | CA 39th: Edward R. Royce (R) | 33.1 |
| 30 | CA 53rd: Susan A. Davis (D) | 13.7 | 33 | TX 27th: Blake Farenthold (R) | 50.8 | 33 | TX 33rd: Marc A. Veasey (D) | 32.8 |
| 34 | CA 7th: Ami Bera (D) | 13.4 | 34 | CA 31st: Gary G. Miller (R) | 49.3 | 34 | CA 15th: Eric Swalwell (D) | 32.4 |
| 35 | CA 11th: George Miller (D) | 13.2 | 35 | NM 1st: Michelle Lujan Grisham (D) | 48.1 | 35 | TX 29th: Gene Green (D) | 32.1 |
| 36 | NY 5th: Gregory W. Meeks (D) | 13.1 | 36 | CA 36th: Raul Ruiz (D) | 47.9 | 36 | NV 1st: Dina Titus (D) | 31.9 |
| 37 | NJ 9th: Bill Pascrell, Jr. (D) | 13.0 | 37 | NY 14th: Joseph Crowley (D) | 46.9 | 37 | TX 9th: Al Green (D) | 31.5 |
| 37 | NJ 3rd: Steve Israel (D) | 13.0 | 38 | CA 43rd: Maxine Waters (D) | 45.9 | 38 | NY 10th: Jerrold Nadler (D) | 31.4 |
| 39 | CA 30th: Brad Sherman (D) | 12.9 | 38 | CA 22nd: Devin Nunes (R) | 45.9 | 39 | CA 38th: Linda T. Sánchez (D) | 31.3 |
| 40 | NY 11th: Michael G. Grimm (R) | 12.8 | 40 | FL 9th: Alan Grayson (D) | 45.7 | 40 | CA 43rd: Maxine Waters (D) | 31.2 |
| 41 | IL 8th: Tammy Duckworth (D) | 12.7 | 41 | NY 7th: Nydia M. Velázquez (D) | 43.8 | 41 | FL 20th: Alcee L. Hastings (D) | 31.1 |
| 41 | TX 3rd: Sam Johnson (R) | 12.7 | 42 | CA 26th: Julia Brownley (D) | 43.5 | 42 | CA 35th: Gloria Negrete McLeod (D) | 30.2 |
| 43 | NV 3rd: Joseph J. Heck (R) | 12.6 | 43 | NV 1st: Dina Titus (D) | 42.9 | 43 | MA 7th: Michael E. Capuano (D) | 30.1 |
| 44 | IL 9th: Janice D. Schakowsky (D) | 12.5 | 44 | CA 19th: Zoe Lofgren (D) | 41.3 | 44 | CA 21st: David G. Valadao (R) | 29.9 |
| 45 | GA 7th: Robert Woodall (R) | 11.8 | 45 | TX 18th: Sheila Jackson-Lee (D) | 41.0 | 45 | NJ 6th: Frank Pallone Jr. (D) | 29.0 |
| 45 | VA 10th: Frank R. Wolf (R) | 11.8 | 46 | CA 10th: Jeff Denham (R) | 40.0 | 46 | CA 47th: Alan S. Lowenthal (D) | 28.8 |
| 47 | NY 12th: Carolyn B. Maloney (D) | 11.6 | 47 | NM 3rd: Ben Ray Luján (D) | 39.8 | 47 | WA 9th: Adam Smith (D) | 28.6 |
| 48 | CA 46th: Loretta Sanchez (D) | 11.5 | 48 | CA 37th: Karen Bass (D) | 39.4 | 47 | NY 11th: Michael G. Grimm (R) | 28.6 |
| 49 | CA 5th: Mike Thompson (D) | 11.4 | 49 | CA 9th: Jerry McNerney (D) | 39.2 | 49 | NY 16th: Eliot L. Engel (D) | 28.5 |
| 50 | VA 8th: James P. Moran (D) | 11.1 | 50 | FL 23rd: Debbie Wasserman Schultz (D) | 38.1 | 50 | VA 8th: James P. Moran (D) | 28.3 |
| 51 | WA 7th: Jim McDermott (D) | 11.0 | 51 | CA 25th: Howard P. "Buck" McKeon (R) | 37.9 | 50 | IL 8th: Tammy Duckworth (D) | 28.3 |
| 52 | CA 3rd: John Garamendi (D) | 10.9 | 52 | TX 9th: Al Green (D) | 37.2 | 52 | VA 11th: Gerald E. Connolly (D) | 27.9 |
| 53 | MD 6th: John K. Delaney (D) | 10.5 | 53 | WA 4th: Doc Hastings (R) | 36.8 | 53 | NJ 10th: Donald M. Payne, Jr. (D) | 27.7 |
| 53 | MN 4th: Betty McCollum (D) | 10.5 | 54 | CA 8th: Paul Cook (R) | 35.9 | 54 | CA 45th: John Campbell (R) | 27.6 |
| 53 | TX 24th: Kenny Marchant (R) | 10.5 | 55 | TX 30th: Eddie Bernice Johnson (D) | 35.7 | 55 | CA 20th: Sam Farr (D) | 27.5 |
| 56 | MA 5th: Edward J. Markey (D) | 10.0 | 56 | CA 23rd: Kevin McCarthy (R) | 35.4 | 55 | TX 7th: John Abney Culberson (R) | 27.5 |
| 56 | MA 7th: Michael E. Capuano (D) | 10.0 | 57 | CA 47th: Alan S. Lowenthal (D) | 35.3 | 57 | AZ 7th: Ed Pastor (D) | 27.4 |
| 58 | TX 7th: John Abney Culberson (R) | 9.9 | 58 | TX 19th: Randy Neugebauer (R) | 34.7 | 58 | IL 9th: Janice D. Schakowsky (D) | 27.0 |
| 59 | CA 37th: Karen Bass (D) | 9.8 | 58 | CA 24th: Lois Capps (D) | 34.7 | 59 | CA 18th: Anna G. Eshoo (D) | 26.6 |
| 60 | CA 16th: Jim Costa (D) | 9.7 | 60 | CA 39th: Edward R. Royce (R) | 34.6 | 60 | CA 13th: Barbara Lee (D) | 26.4 |
| 61 | IL 10th: Bradley S. Schneider (D) | 9.6 | 61 | TX 11th: K. Michael Conaway (R) | 34.0 | 61 | CA 16th: Jim Costa (D) | 26.2 |
| 62 | GA 6th: Tom Price (R) | 9.5 | 62 | NJ 9th: Bill Pascrell, Jr. (D) | 33.6 | 61 | NY 12th: Carolyn B. Maloney (D) | 26.2 |
| 63 | CA 42nd: Ken Calvert (R) | 9.4 | 63 | CA 42nd: Ken Calvert (R) | 33.2 | 63 | NJ 12th: Rush Holt (D) | 26.0 |
| 63 | TX 9th: Al Green (D) | 9.4 | 64 | CA 53rd: Susan A. Davis (D) | 32.3 | 64 | TX 16th: Beto O'Rourke (D) | 25.2 |
| 65 | NV 1st: Dina Titus (D) | 9.2 | 65 | TX 7th: John Abney Culberson (R) | 31.5 | 65 | TX 15th: Rubén Hinojosa (D) | 24.7 |
| 65 | NJ 11th: Rodney P. Frelinghuysen (R) | 9.2 | 66 | CA 50th: Duncan Hunter (R) | 29.7 | 66 | FL 21st: Theodore E. Deutch (D) | 24.6 |
| 67 | WA 1st: Suzan K. DelBene (D) | 9.1 | 66 | NV 4th: Steven A. Horsford (D) | 29.7 | 66 | CA 11th: George Miller (D) | 24.6 |
| 68 | NJ 5th: Scott Garrett (R) | 8.5 | 68 | TX 2nd: Ted Poe (R) | 29.6 | 68 | CA 41st: Mark Takano (D) | 24.4 |
| 68 | NJ 7th: Leonard Lance (R) | 8.5 | 69 | FL 24th: Frederica S. Wilson (D) | 29.5 | 69 | CA 53rd: Susan A. Davis (D) | 24.2 |
| 70 | MD 8th: Chris Van Hollen (D) | 8.3 | 70 | IL 3rd: Daniel Lipinski (D) | 29.4 | 70 | CA 48th: Dana Rohrabacher (R) | 24.0 |
| 70 | PA 1st: Allyson Y. Schwartz (D) | 8.3 | 71 | CO 1st: Diana DeGette (D) | 29.0 | 71 | CA 6th: Doris O. Matsui (D) | 23.9 |
| 70 | WA 2nd: Rick Larsen (D) | 8.3 | 72 | CA 30th: Brad Sherman (D) | 28.8 | 72 | TX 22nd: Pete Olson (R) | 23.8 |
| 73 | CA 29th: Tony Cárdenas (D) | 8.2 | 72 | CA 3rd: John Garamendi (D) | 28.8 | 73 | IL 10th: Bradley S. Schneider (D) | 23.7 |
| 74 | CA 25th: Howard P. "Buck" McKeon (R) | 8.1 | 74 | CA 32nd: Pete Sessions (R) | 28.3 | 74 | CA 36th: Raul Ruiz (D) | 23.6 |
| 74 | WA 10th: Denny Heck (D) | 8.1 | 75 | TX 21st: Lamar Smith (R) | 27.7 | 75 | NY 17th: Nita M. Lowey (D) | 23.3 |

# Congressional Districts of the 113th Congress of the United States
## Selected Rankings

| Percent under 18 years old, 2011 | | | Percent 65 years old and over, 2011 | | | Percent college graduates (bachelor's degree or more), 2011 | | |
|---|---|---|---|---|---|---|---|---|
| Under 18 years old rank | State congressional district Representative | Percent under 18 years old [col 15 and 16] | 65 years old and over rank | State congressional district Representative | Percent 65 years old and over [col 22 and 23] | College graduates rank | State congressional district Representative | Percent college graduates [col 28] |
| 1 | TX 28th: Henry Cuellar (D) | 32.9 | 1 | FL 11th: Richard B. Nugent (R) | 30.6 | 1 | NY 12th: Carolyn B. Maloney (D) | 68.6 |
| 2 | TX 15th: Rubén Hinojosa (D) | 32.1 | 2 | FL 16th Vern Buchanan (R) | 28.3 | 2 | CA 33rd: Henry A. Waxman (D) | 62.4 |
| 2 | UT 1st: Rob Bishop (R) | 32.1 | 3 | FL 19th: Trey Radel (R) | 27.0 | 3 | VA 8th: James P. Moran (D) | 59.8 |
| 4 | CA 16th: Jim Costa (D) | 31.7 | 4 | FL 17th: Thomas J. Rooney (R) | 25.3 | 4 | CA 18th: Anna G. Eshoo (D) | 57.3 |
| 4 | UT 3rd: Jason Chaffetz (R) | 31.7 | 5 | FL 18th: Patrick Murphy (D) | 23.3 | 5 | NY 10th: Jerrold Nadler (D) | 57.2 |
| 6 | CA 21st: David G. Valadao (R) | 31.6 | 6 | AZ 4th: Paul A. Gosar (R) | 22.3 | 6 | GA 6th: Tom Price (R) | 56.3 |
| 6 | CA 40th: Lucille Roybal-Allard (D) | 31.6 | 7 | FL 13th: C. W. Bill Young (R) | 22.1 | 7 | WA 7th: Jim McDermott (D) | 54.8 |
| 6 | TX 29th: Gene Green (D) | 31.6 | 8 | FL 8th: Bill Posey (R) | 21.9 | 8 | CA 52nd: Scott H. Peters (D) | 54.6 |
| 9 | TX 33rd: Marc A. Veasey (D) | 31.5 | 8 | FL 21st: Theodore E. Deutch (D) | 21.9 | 9 | CA 12th: Nancy Pelosi (D) | 54.4 |
| 9 | UT 4th: Jim Matheson (D) | 31.5 | 10 | FL 6th: Ron DeSantis (R) | 20.8 | 10 | VA 11th: Gerald E. Connolly (D) | 53.7 |
| 11 | AZ 7th: Ed Pastor (D) | 31.0 | 11 | FL 12th: Gus M. Bilirakis (R) | 20.1 | 11 | MD 8th: Chris Van Hollen (D) | 52.8 |
| 11 | TX 34th: Filemon Vela (D) | 31.0 | 11 | FL 22nd: Lois Frankel (D) | 20.1 | 12 | DC At-Large Eleanor Holmes Norton (D) | 52.5 |
| 13 | CA 44th: Janice Hahn (D) | 30.3 | 13 | NC 11th: Mark Meadows (D) | 19.5 | 13 | MA 5th: Edward J. Markey (D) | 52.0 |
| 14 | CA 41st: Mark Takano (D) | 30.2 | 14 | MI 1st: Dan Benishek (R) | 19.0 | 14 | CO 2nd: Jared Polis (D) | 51.7 |
| 15 | TX 23rd: Pete P. Gallego (D) | 29.8 | 15 | AZ 8th: Trent Franks (R) | 18.9 | 14 | VA 10th: Frank R. Wolf (R) | 51.7 |
| 15 | UT 2nd: Chris Stewart (R) | 29.8 | 16 | CA 36th: Raul Ruiz (D) | 18.7 | 16 | TX 3rd: Sam Johnson (R) | 51.4 |
| 17 | NY 15th: José E. Serrano (D) | 29.4 | 17 | PA 1st: Keith J. Rothfus (R) | 18.4 | 17 | NY 3rd: Steve Israel (D) | 50.8 |
| 17 | WA 4th: Doc Hastings (R) | 29.4 | 18 | MA 9th: William R. Keating (D) | 18.3 | 18 | IL 5th: Michael Quigley (D) | 50.5 |
| 19 | AZ 3rd: Raúl M. Grijalva (D) | 29.2 | 19 | AZ 2nd: Ron Barber (D) | 17.7 | 19 | CA 17th: Michael M. Honda (D) | 50.3 |
| 20 | CA 22nd: Devin Nunes (R) | 29.1 | 19 | MN 7th: Collin C. Peterson (D) | 17.7 | 20 | IL 9th: Janice D. Schakowsky (D) | 50.2 |
| 20 | TX 26th: Michael C. Burgess (R) | 29.1 | 21 | CA 1st: Doug LaMalfa (R) | 17.6 | 20 | NJ 11th: Rodney P. Frelinghuysen (R) | 50.2 |
| 22 | CA 25th: Howard P. "Buck" McKeon (R) | 28.9 | 21 | PA 1st: Tim Murphy(R) | 17.6 | 22 | CA 45th: John Campbell (R) | 50.0 |
| 23 | CA 10th: Jeff Denham (R) | 28.8 | 23 | PA 1st: Bill Shuster (R) | 17.5 | 23 | IL 6th: Peter J. Roskam (R) | 49.7 |
| 23 | CA 35th: Gloria Negrete McLeod (D) | 28.8 | 24 | OR 1st: Greg Walden (R) | 17.4 | 24 | MA 4th: Joseph P. Kennedy III (D) | 48.8 |
| 23 | GA 7th: Robert Woodall (R) | 28.8 | 25 | NY 3rd: Steve Israel (D) | 17.3 | 25 | NJ 7th: Leonard Lance (R) | 47.7 |
| 26 | CA 8th: Paul Cook (R) | 28.7 | 26 | NE 3rd: Adrian Smith (R) | 17.2 | 26 | NC 9th: Robert Pittenger (R) | 47.5 |
| 26 | GA 13th: David Scott (D) | 28.7 | 26 | PA 1st: Tom Marino (R) | 17.2 | 27 | CT 4th: James A. Himes (D) | 46.5 |
| 28 | CA 31st: Gary G. Miller (R) | 28.6 | 26 | TN 1st: David P. Roe (R) | 17.2 | 28 | MO 2nd: Ann Wagner (R) | 46.0 |
| 28 | TX 22nd: Pete Olson (R) | 28.6 | 29 | NJ 3rd: Jon Runyan (R) | 17.1 | 29 | TX 7th: John Abney Culberson (R) | 45.7 |
| 30 | CA 9th: Jerry McNerney (D) | 28.5 | 29 | OR 1st: Peter A. DeFazio (D) | 17.1 | 30 | MN 3rd: Erik Paulsen (R) | 45.6 |
| 30 | TX 16th: Beto O'Rourke (D) | 28.5 | 31 | MN 8th: Richard M. Nolan (D) | 17.0 | 31 | CA 13th: Barbara Lee (D) | 45.0 |
| 32 | VA 10th: Frank R. Wolf (R) | 28.2 | 31 | PA 1st: Matt Cartwright (D) | 17.0 | 32 | MD 3rd: John P. Sarbanes (D) | 44.7 |
| 33 | CA 46th: Loretta Sanchez (D) | 28.1 | 33 | VA 9th: Morgan Griffith (R) | 16.9 | 33 | NJ 5th: Scott Garrett (R) | 44.3 |
| 34 | IL 4th: Luis V. Gutierrez (D) | 28.0 | 34 | IA 4th: Steve King (R) | 16.8 | 34 | MI 11th: Kerry L. Bentivolio (R) | 44.1 |
| 35 | IL 11th: Bill Foster (D) | 27.9 | 34 | OH 6th: Bill Johnson (R) | 16.8 | 35 | NY 17th: Nita M. Lowey (D) | 44.0 |
| 35 | IL 14th: Randy Hultgren (R) | 27.9 | 34 | WI 1st: Sean P. Duffy (R) | 16.8 | 36 | TX 21st: Lamar Smith (R) | 43.6 |
| 35 | TX 3rd: Sam Johnson (R) | 27.9 | 37 | ME 2nd: Michael H. Michaud (D) | 16.7 | 37 | KS 3rd Kevin Yoder (R) | 43.4 |
| 35 | TX 31st: John R. Carter (R) | 27.9 | 37 | VA 5th: Robert Hurt (R) | 16.7 | 38 | IN 5th:Susan W. Brooks (R) | 42.8 |
| 39 | AZ 5th: Matt Salmon (R) | 27.8 | 37 | WV 3rd: Nick J. Rahall II (D) | 16.7 | 39 | TX 24th: Kenny Marchant (R) | 42.7 |
| 39 | CO 6th: Mike Coffman (R) | 27.8 | 40 | AR 4th: Tom Cotton (R) | 16.6 | 40 | CO 1st: Diana DeGette (D) | 42.5 |
| 39 | TX 6th: Joe Barton (R) | 27.8 | 40 | OH 16th: James B. Renacci (R) | 16.6 | 41 | CA 48th: Dana Rohrabacher (R) | 42.4 |
| 42 | CA 51st: Juan Vargas (D) | 27.7 | 42 | CA 4th: Tom McClintock (R) | 16.5 | 41 | MN 5th: Keith Ellison (D) | 42.4 |
| 42 | TX 30th: Eddie Bernice Johnson (D) | 27.7 | 42 | NJ 4th: Christopher H. Smith (R) | 16.5 | 43 | CA 28th: Adam B. Schiff (D) | 42.1 |
| 44 | CA 23rd: Kevin McCarthy (R) | 27.6 | 44 | FL 27th: Ileana Ros-Lehtinen (R) | 16.4 | 44 | MA 8th: Stephen F. Lynch (D) | 41.7 |
| 45 | CA 42nd: Ken Calvert (R) | 27.5 | 44 | PA 1st: Mike Kelly (R) | 16.4 | 45 | NJ 12th: Rush Holt (D) | 41.6 |
| 45 | TX 18th: Sheila Jackson-Lee (D) | 27.5 | 46 | IL 15th: John Shimkus (R) | 16.3 | 46 | IL 10th: Bradley S. Schneider (D) | 41.5 |
| 47 | ID 2nd: Michael K. Simpson (R) | 27.4 | 46 | OK 2nd: Markwayne Mullin (R) | 16.3 | 47 | CA 11th: George Miller (D) | 41.0 |
| 48 | TX 5th: Jeb Hensarling (R) | 27.3 | 46 | PA 1st: Lou Barletta (R) | 16.3 | 48 | TX 26th: Michael C. Burgess (R) | 40.6 |
| 48 | TX 35th: Lloyd Doggett (D) | 27.3 | 46 | WV 1st: David McKinley (R) | 16.3 | 49 | PA 1st: Jim Gerlach (R) | 40.5 |
| 50 | NV 4th: Steven A. Horsford (D) | 27.1 | 50 | FL 10th: Daniel Webster (R) | 16.2 | 50 | MA 6th: John F. Tierney (D) | 40.3 |
| 50 | TX 9th: Al Green (D) | 27.1 | 50 | OH 14th: David P. Joyce (R) | 16.2 | 51 | CA 27th: Judy Chu (D) | 40.0 |
| 52 | GA 4th: Henry C. "Hank" Johnson Jr. (D) | 26.8 | 50 | PA 1st: Glenn Thompson (R) | 16.2 | 51 | CA 30th: Brad Sherman (D) | 40.0 |
| 52 | TX 20th: Joaquin Castro (D) | 26.8 | 50 | PA 1st: Michael F. Doyle (R) | 16.2 | 53 | TX 32nd: Pete Sessions (R) | 39.9 |
| 54 | MN 6th: Michele Bachmann (R) | 26.7 | 54 | HI 1st: Colleen Hanabusa (D) | 16.1 | 54 | CA 14th: Jackie Speier (D) | 39.8 |
| 55 | ID 1st: Raul Labrador (R) | 26.6 | 54 | IL 17th: Cheri Bustos (D) | 16.1 | 55 | MD 6th: John K. Delaney (D) | 39.5 |
| 55 | KS 3rd Kevin Yoder (R) | 26.6 | 54 | ME 1st: Chellie Pingree (D) | 16.1 | 55 | MA 7th: Michael E. Capuano (D) | 39.5 |
| 55 | NE 2nd: Lee Terry (R) | 26.6 | 54 | MO 8th: Jason T. Smith (R) | 16.1 | 57 | CA 39th: Edward R. Royce (R) | 39.4 |
| 55 | TX 36th: Steve Stockman (R) | 26.6 | 54 | SC 7th: Tom Rice (R) | 16.1 | 58 | AZ 6th: David Schweikert (R) | 39.3 |
| 59 | IL 2nd: Robin L. Kelly (D) | 26.5 | 54 | TN 3rd: Chuck Fleischmann (R) | 16.1 | 58 | TX 22nd: Pete Olson (R) | 39.3 |
| 59 | IN 3rd: Marlin Stutzman (R) | 26.5 | 54 | WA 6th: Derek Kilmer (D) | 16.1 | 60 | VA 7th: Eric Cantor (R) | 39.2 |
| 59 | NC 2nd: Renee Ellmers (R) | 26.5 | 61 | KY 1st: Ed Whitfield (R) | 16.0 | 61 | CO 6th: Mike Coffman (R) | 39.1 |
| 62 | IN 7th: André Carson (D) | 26.3 | 61 | NJ 11th: Rodney P. Frelinghuysen (R) | 16.0 | 62 | PA 1st: Patrick Meehan (R) | 38.9 |
| 62 | TX 10th: Michael T. McCaul (R) | 26.3 | 61 | NY 19th: Christopher P. Gibson (R) | 16.0 | 63 | CA 49th: Darrell E. Issa (R) | 38.8 |
| 62 | TX 32nd: Pete Sessions (R) | 26.3 | 64 | AL 4th: Robert B. Aderholt (R) | 15.9 | 63 | MN 4th: Betty McCollum (D) | 38.8 |
| 65 | CA 6th: Doris O. Matsui (D) | 26.2 | 64 | AR 1st Eric A. "Rick" Crawford (R) | 15.9 | 63 | WA 1st: Suzan K. DelBene (D) | 38.8 |
| 65 | KS 4th Mike Pompeo (R) | 26.2 | 64 | IL 9th: Janice D. Schakowsky (D) | 15.9 | 66 | NC 4th: David E. Price (D) | 38.7 |
| 65 | MN 2nd: John Kline (R) | 26.2 | 64 | IL 18th: Aaron Schock (R) | 15.9 | 67 | CA 15th: Eric Swalwell (D) | 38.6 |
| 65 | NC 9th: Robert Pittenger (R) | 26.2 | 64 | NY 22nd: Richard L. Hanna (R) | 15.9 | 68 | NY 4th: Carolyn McCarthy (D) | 38.4 |
| 69 | CO 4th: Cory Gardner (R) | 26.1 | 69 | MI 4th: Dave Camp (R) | 15.8 | 68 | NY 6th: Grace Meng (D) | 38.4 |
| 69 | IL 10th: Bradley S. Schneider (D) | 26.1 | 69 | MO 2nd: Ann Wagner (R) | 15.8 | 68 | TX 2nd: Ted Poe (R) | 38.4 |
| 71 | AK At-Large: Don Young (R) | 26.0 | 69 | NY 27th: Chris Collins(R) | 15.8 | 71 | GA 5th: John Lewis (D) | 38.1 |
| 71 | CA 43rd: Maxine Waters (D) | 26.0 | 69 | OH 11th: Tim Ryan (D) | 15.8 | 72 | CA 2nd: Jared Huffman (D) | 37.9 |
| 71 | GA 14th: Tom Graves (R) | 26.0 | 73 | CA 2nd: Jared Huffman (D) | 15.7 | 73 | GA 7th: Robert Woodall (R) | 37.8 |
| 71 | WI 1st: Gwen Moore (D) | 26.0 | 73 | PA 1st: Patrick Meehan (R) | 15.7 | 73 | GA 11th: Phil Gingrey (R) | 37.8 |
| 75 | MS 2nd: Bennie G. Thompson (D) | 25.9 | 73 | VA 6th: Bob Goodlatte (R) | 15.7 | 75 | WI 1st: Mark Pocan (D) | 37.6 |

# Congressional Districts of the 113th Congress of the United States
## Selected Rankings

| Median value of owner-occupied housing units, 2011 | | | Percent female-headed family households, 2011 | | | Percent of households with one person, 2011 | | |
|---|---|---|---|---|---|---|---|---|
| Median value rank | State congressional district Representative | Median value (dollars) [col 44] | Female house-holder rank | State congressional district Representative | Percent with female house holder [col 33] | One-person house-hold rank | State congressional district Representative | Percent one-person house-holds [col 34] |
| 1 | CA 33rd: Henry A. Waxman (D) | 907 800 | 1 | NY 15th: José E. Serrano (D) | 38.3 | 1 | NY 12th: Carolyn B. Maloney (D) | 49.5 |
| 2 | NY 12th: Carolyn B. Maloney (D) | 857 900 | 2 | NY 13th Charles B. Rangel (D) | 27.3 | 2 | DC At-Large Eleanor Holmes Norton (D) | 45.2 |
| 3 | CA 18th: Anna G. Eshoo (D) | 838 900 | 3 | NY 8th: Hakeem S. Jeffries (D) | 26.8 | 3 | NY 10th: Jerrold Nadler (D) | 42.9 |
| 4 | NY 10th: Jerrold Nadler (D) | 768 400 | 4 | LA 2nd: Cedric Richmond (D) | 25.2 | 4 | GA 5th: John Lewis (D) | 41.8 |
| 5 | CA 12th: Nancy Pelosi (D) | 730 200 | 5 | CA 44th: Janice Hahn (D) | 25.1 | 5 | PA 1st: Chaka Fattah (D) | 41.3 |
| 6 | CA 14th: Jackie Speier (D) | 668 800 | 5 | CA 40th: Lucille Roybal-Allard (D) | 25.1 | 6 | OH 11th: Marcia L. Fudge (D) | 41.0 |
| 7 | CA 28th: Adam B. Schiff (D) | 618 000 | 7 | TN 9th: Steve Cohen (D) | 24.7 | 7 | FL 22nd: Lois Frankel (D) | 40.8 |
| 8 | CA 17th: Michael M. Honda (D) | 611 800 | 8 | NY 5th: Gregory W. Meeks (D) | 24.5 | 8 | PA 1st: Michael F. Doyle (D) | 40.5 |
| 9 | CA 48th: Dana Rohrabacher (R) | 608 600 | 9 | MS 2nd: Bennie G. Thompson (D) | 24.3 | 9 | IL 7th: Danny K. Davis (D) | 40.0 |
| 10 | NY 7th: Nydia M. Velázquez (D) | 565 700 | 9 | MI 13th: John Conyers Jr. (D) | 24.3 | 9 | WA 7th: Jim McDermott (D) | 40.0 |
| 11 | CA 45th: John Campbell (R) | 562 900 | 11 | FL 5th: Corrine Brown (D) | 24.0 | 9 | CA 12th: Nancy Pelosi (D) | 40.0 |
| 12 | CA 27th: Judy Chu (D) | 553 700 | 12 | NJ 10th: Donald M. Payne, Jr. (D) | 23.9 | 12 | CO 1st: Diana DeGette (D) | 39.3 |
| 13 | HI 1st: Colleen Hanabusa (D) | 543 000 | 13 | IL 2nd: Robin L. Kelly (D) | 23.1 | 13 | FL 13th: C. W. Bill Young (R) | 39.1 |
| 14 | NY 3rd: Steve Israel (D) | 540 400 | 14 | IL 1st: Bobby L. Rush (D) | 23.0 | 14 | PA 1st: Robert A. Brady (D) | 39.0 |
| 15 | CA 52nd: Scott H. Peters (D) | 537 300 | 15 | CA 51st: Juan Vargas (D) | 22.8 | 15 | IL 5th: Michael Quigley (D) | 38.7 |
| 16 | NY 9th: Yvette D. Clarke (D) | 531 900 | 15 | FL 24th: Frederica S. Wilson (D) | 22.8 | 16 | MN 5th: Keith Ellison (D) | 38.4 |
| 17 | CA 49th: Darrell E. Issa (R) | 529 400 | 15 | AL 7th: Terri A. Sewell (D) | 22.8 | 17 | MO 1st: William Lacy Clay (D) | 37.4 |
| 18 | CA 37th: Karen Bass (D) | 509 400 | 18 | NY 9th: Yvette D. Clarke (D) | 22.7 | 18 | CA 28th: Adam B. Schiff (D) | 37.0 |
| 19 | CT 4th: James A. Himes (D) | 498 300 | 19 | NC 1st: G. K. Butterfield (D) | 22.6 | 19 | CA 33rd: Henry A. Waxman (D) | 36.7 |
| 20 | CA 15th: Eric Swalwell (D) | 494 600 | 20 | TX 18th: Sheila Jackson-Lee (D) | 22.2 | 20 | IL 9th: Janice D. Schakowsky (D) | 36.6 |
| 21 | NY 6th: Grace Meng (D) | 490 600 | 21 | MI 14th: Gary C. Peters (D) | 22.1 | 21 | MA 7th: Michael E. Capuano (D) | 36.3 |
| 22 | CA 39th: Edward R. Royce (R) | 488 600 | 21 | FL 20th: Alcee L. Hastings (D) | 22.1 | 21 | OH 3rd: Joyce Beatty (D) | 36.3 |
| 23 | CA 30th: Brad Sherman (D) | 484 500 | 23 | PA 1st: Chaka Fattah (D) | 21.8 | 23 | TN 9th: Steve Cohen (D) | 35.9 |
| 24 | CA 13th: Barbara Lee (D) | 480 700 | 24 | VA 3rd: Robert C. "Bobby" Scott (D) | 21.5 | 24 | NY 26th Brian Higgins (D) | 35.8 |
| 25 | NY 8th: Hakeem S. Jeffries (D) | 477 600 | 24 | GA 4th: Henry C. "Hank" Johnson Jr. (D) | 21.5 | 24 | WI 1st: Gwen Moore (D) | 35.8 |
| 26 | CA 19th: Zoe Lofgren (D) | 476 800 | 26 | GA 2nd: Sanford D. Bishop Jr. (D) | 21.4 | 24 | TN 5th: Jim Cooper (D) | 35.8 |
| 27 | VA 8th: James P. Moran (D) | 471 100 | 27 | TX 30th: Eddie Bernice Johnson (D) | 21.3 | 27 | MI 13th: John Conyers Jr. (D) | 35.5 |
| 28 | NY 11th: Michael G. Grimm (R) | 468 600 | 28 | IL 7th: Danny K. Davis (D) | 21.1 | 28 | VA 8th: James P. Moran (D) | 35.2 |
| 29 | NY 17th: Nita M. Lowey (D) | 460 800 | 29 | NC 12th: Melvin L. Watt (D) | 21.0 | 29 | MD 7th: Elijah E. Cummings (D) | 34.7 |
| 30 | CA 2nd: Jared Huffman (D) | 458 700 | 30 | CA 43rd: Maxine Waters (D) | 20.9 | 30 | OH 9th: Marcy Kaptur (D) | 34.3 |
| 31 | NY 16th: Eliot L. Engel (D) | 447 600 | 31 | OH 11th: Marcia L. Fudge (D) | 20.8 | 31 | CA 37th: Karen Bass (D) | 34.2 |
| 32 | CA 11th: George Miller (D) | 446 800 | 31 | SC 6th: James E. Clyburn (D) | 20.8 | 32 | NY 13th Charles B. Rangel (D) | 34.1 |
| 33 | CA 26th: Julia Brownley (D) | 437 900 | 33 | MO 1st: William Lacy Clay (D) | 20.5 | 33 | MI 14th: Gary C. Peters (D) | 34.0 |
| 34 | NY 4th: Carolyn McCarthy (D) | 436 500 | 34 | CA 16th: Jim Costa (D) | 20.4 | 34 | MI 9th: Sander M. Levin (D) | 33.8 |
| 35 | NY 14th: Joseph Crowley (D) | 436 000 | 35 | TX 9th: Al Green (D) | 20.3 | 35 | MO 5th: Emanuel Cleaver (D) | 33.6 |
| 36 | HI 2nd: Tulsi Gabbard (D) | 435 700 | 36 | MD 7th: Elijah E. Cummings (D) | 20.2 | 35 | OH 13th: Tim Ryan (D) | 33.6 |
| 37 | CA 47th: Alan S. Lowenthal (D) | 430 900 | 36 | GA 13th: David Scott (D) | 20.2 | 35 | AZ 2nd: Ron Barber (D) | 33.6 |
| 38 | NJ 11th: Rodney P. Frelinghuysen (R) | 426 300 | 36 | TX 33rd: Marc A. Veasey (D) | 20.2 | 38 | FL 14th: Kathy Castor (D) | 33.4 |
| 39 | NY 13th Charles B. Rangel (D) | 425 300 | 39 | FL 9th: Alan Grayson (D) | 20.0 | 39 | CA 13th: Barbara Lee (D) | 33.3 |
| 40 | CA 24th: Lois Capps (D) | 424 100 | 40 | PA 1st: Robert A. Brady (D) | 19.8 | 39 | NC 1st: G. K. Butterfield (D) | 33.3 |
| 41 | DC At-Large Eleanor Holmes Norton (D) | 422 400 | 41 | MD 4th: Donna F. Edwards (D) | 19.5 | 39 | LA 2nd: Cedric Richmond (D) | 33.3 |
| 42 | VA 10th: Frank R. Wolf (R) | 419 500 | 42 | WI 4th: Gwen Moore (D) | 19.4 | 42 | NV 1st: Dina Titus (D) | 33.2 |
| 43 | MA 5th: Edward J. Markey (D) | 418 100 | 42 | AZ 7th: Ed Pastor (D) | 19.4 | 42 | FL 23rd: Debbie Wasserman Schultz (D) | 33.2 |
| 44 | VA 11th: Gerald E. Connolly (D) | 409 600 | 44 | CA 35th: Gloria Negrete McLeod (D) | 19.3 | 44 | IN 7th: André Carson (D) | 33.1 |
| 45 | NJ 7th: Leonard Lance (R) | 409 300 | 44 | TX 16th: Beto O'Rourke (D) | 19.3 | 45 | KY 3rd: John A. Yarmuth (D) | 32.8 |
| 46 | NJ 5th: Scott Garrett (R) | 407 200 | 46 | TX 34th: Filemon Vela (D) | 19.2 | 45 | NY 20th: Paul Tonko (D) | 32.8 |
| 47 | MD 8th: Chris Van Hollen (D) | 405 300 | 46 | NY 7th: Nydia M. Velázquez (D) | 19.2 | 45 | NJ 10th: Donald M. Payne, Jr. (D) | 32.8 |
| 48 | NY 5th: Gregory W. Meeks (D) | 400 200 | 46 | CA 29th: Tony Cárdenas (D) | 19.2 | 48 | VA 3rd: Robert C. "Bobby" Scott (D) | 32.7 |
| 49 | WA 7th: Jim McDermott (D) | 397 700 | 46 | CA 38th: Linda T. Sánchez (D) | 19.2 | 49 | AZ 9th Kyrsten Sinema (D) | 32.4 |
| 50 | CA 20th: Sam Farr (D) | 383 900 | 50 | CA 21st: David G. Valadao (R) | 19.0 | 49 | AL 7th: Terri A. Sewell (D) | 32.4 |
| 51 | NY 1st: Timothy H. Bishop (D) | 378 100 | 51 | TX 35th: Lloyd Doggett (D) | 18.9 | 51 | NC 12th: Melvin L. Watt (D) | 32.3 |
| 52 | MA 4th: Joseph P. Kennedy III (D) | 376 000 | 51 | NY 16th: Eliot L. Engel (D) | 18.9 | 52 | OH 10th: Michael R. Turner (D) | 32.2 |
| 53 | CA 43rd: Maxine Waters (D) | 373 000 | 53 | TX 20th: Joaquin Castro (D) | 18.8 | 52 | NY 22nd: Richard L. Hanna (R) | 32.2 |
| 54 | NY 15th: José E. Serrano (D) | 369 900 | 53 | OH 3rd: Joyce Beatty (D) | 18.8 | 54 | TX 21st: Lamar Smith (R) | 32.1 |
| 55 | CA 38th: Linda T. Sánchez (D) | 368 400 | 55 | TX 28th: Henry Cuellar (D) | 18.7 | 55 | OR 1st: Earl Blumenauer (D) | 32.0 |
| 56 | CA 53rd: Susan A. Davis (D) | 367 900 | 56 | NJ 8th: Albio Sires (D) | 18.4 | 55 | NM 1st: Michelle Lujan Grisham (D) | 32.0 |
| 57 | NY 2nd: Peter T. King (R) | 366 400 | 57 | CA 41st: Mark Takano (D) | 18.3 | 55 | WV 1st: David McKinley (R) | 32.0 |
| 58 | MA 6th: John F. Tierney (D) | 365 100 | 58 | CA 46th: Loretta Sanchez (D) | 18.1 | 58 | FL 18th: Patrick Murphy (D) | 31.9 |
| 59 | NJ 9th: Bill Pascrell, Jr. (D) | 364 600 | 58 | MD 2nd: C. A. Dutch Ruppersberger (D) | 18.1 | 58 | NC 4th: David E. Price (D) | 31.9 |
| 60 | CA 34th: Xavier Becerra (D) | 359 000 | 60 | LA 5th: Rodney Alexander (R) | 18.0 | 58 | TX 24th: Kenny Marchant (R) | 31.9 |
| 61 | CA 46th: Loretta Sanchez (D) | 358 400 | 61 | MS 3rd: Gregg Harper (R) | 17.9 | 61 | IL 17th: Cheri Bustos (D) | 31.8 |
| 62 | CA 50th: Duncan Hunter (D) | 353 400 | 61 | GA 5th: John Lewis (D) | 17.9 | 61 | MD 3rd: John P. Sarbanes (D) | 31.8 |
| 63 | MA 8th: Stephen F. Lynch (D) | 350 500 | 61 | AZ 3rd: Raúl M. Grijalva (D) | 17.9 | 63 | CA 6th: Doris O. Matsui (D) | 31.7 |
| 64 | MA 7th: Michael E. Capuano (D) | 346 900 | 61 | TX 29th: Gene Green (D) | 17.9 | 63 | MI 12th: John D. Dingell (D) | 31.7 |
| 65 | CA 32nd: Grace F. Napolitano (D) | 346 600 | 65 | CA 32nd: Grace F. Napolitano (D) | 17.8 | 63 | MN 4th: Betty McCollum (D) | 31.7 |
| 66 | CA 25th: Howard P. "Buck" McKeon (R) | 340 400 | 65 | IN 7th: André Carson (D) | 17.8 | 66 | OK 5th: James Lankford (R) | 31.6 |
| 67 | NJ 4th: Christopher H. Smith (R) | 340 300 | 65 | IL 4th: Luis V. Gutierrez (D) | 17.8 | 66 | NY 25th: Louise McIntosh Slaughter (D) | 31.6 |
| 68 | WA 1st: Suzan K. DelBene (D) | 338 900 | 68 | MA 7th: Michael E. Capuano (D) | 17.7 | 66 | RI 1st: David Cicilline (D) | 31.6 |
| 69 | MA 9th: William R. Keating (D) | 336 400 | 69 | FL 14th: Kathy Castor (D) | 17.6 | 66 | SC 6th: James E. Clyburn (D) | 31.6 |
| 70 | CA 5th: Mike Thompson (D) | 335 000 | 70 | GA 12th: John Barrow (D) | 17.5 | 70 | FL 19th: Trey Radel (R) | 31.5 |
| 71 | NJ 12th: Rush Holt (D) | 332 100 | 70 | LA 4th: John Fleming (R) | 17.5 | 71 | IL 13th: Rodney Davis (R) | 31.4 |
| 72 | NJ 6th: Frank Pallone Jr. (D) | 331 300 | 72 | TX 15th: Rubén Hinojosa (D) | 17.3 | 72 | NY 9th: Yvette D. Clarke (D) | 31.3 |
| 73 | NJ 8th: Albio Sires (D) | 328 300 | 73 | FL 26th: Joe Garcia (D) | 17.2 | 73 | ND-At Large Kevin Cramer (R) | 31.1 |
| 74 | CA 29th: Tony Cárdenas (D) | 324 800 | 73 | FL 25th: Mario Diaz-Balart (R) | 17.2 | 73 | TN 2nd: John J. Duncan Jr. (R) | 31.1 |
| 75 | WA 9th: Adam Smith (D) | 322 800 | 73 | CA 34th: Xavier Becerra (D) | 17.2 | 75 | KY 6th: Garland "Andy" Barr (R) | 31.0 |

# Congressional Districts of the 113th Congress of the United States
## Selected Rankings

| Median household income, 2011 | | | Percent of persons below 65 years with no health insurance, 2011 | | | Percent of persons below the poverty level, 2011 | | |
|---|---|---|---|---|---|---|---|---|
| Median income rank | State congressional district Representative | Median income (dollars) [col 52] | No health insurance rank | State congressional district Representative | Percent withno health insurance [col 64] | Poverty rate rank | State congressional district Representative | Poverty rate [col 54] |
| 1 | VA 10th: Frank R. Wolf (R) | 109 505 | 1 | TX 33rd: Marc A. Veasey (D) | 41.1 | 1 | NY 15th: José E. Serrano (D) | 39.4 |
| 2 | VA 11th: Gerald E. Connolly (D) | 100 146 | 2 | TX 29th: Gene Green (D) | 38.7 | 2 | MI 13th: John Conyers Jr. (D) | 33.1 |
| 3 | CA 18th: Anna G. Eshoo (D) | 97 001 | 3 | CA 34th: Xavier Becerra (D) | 38.4 | 3 | TX 34th: Filemon Vela (D) | 33.0 |
| 4 | NY 3rd: Steve Israel (D) | 95 699 | 4 | FL 25th: Mario Diaz-Balart (R) | 37.0 | 4 | AZ 7th: Ed Pastor (D) | 32.9 |
| 5 | NJ 7th: Leonard Lance (R) | 95 189 | 5 | TX 15th: Rubén Hinojosa (D) | 36.9 | 5 | TX 15th: Rubén Hinojosa (D) | 32.5 |
| 6 | NJ 11th: Rodney P. Frelinghuysen (R) | 93 655 | 6 | TX 34th: Filemon Vela (D) | 35.4 | 6 | CA 16th: Jim Costa (D) | 31.2 |
| 7 | CA 17th: Michael M. Honda (D) | 92 030 | 7 | FL 24th: Frederica S. Wilson (D) | 35.2 | 7 | PA 1st: Chaka Fattah (D) | 30.7 |
| 8 | VA 8th: James P. Moran (D) | 91 027 | 8 | CA 40th: Lucille Roybal-Allard (D) | 34.9 | 7 | TX 33rd: Marc A. Veasey (D) | 30.7 |
| 9 | MD 8th: Chris Van Hollen (D) | 90 959 | 9 | NV 1st: Dina Titus (D) | 34.4 | 9 | CA 21st: David G. Valadao (R) | 30.6 |
| 10 | CA 45th: John Campbell (R) | 89 383 | 10 | TX 9th: Al Green (D) | 34.3 | 10 | TX 28th: Henry Cuellar (D) | 29.8 |
| 11 | CA 33rd: Henry A. Waxman (D) | 89 354 | 11 | TX 28th: Henry Cuellar (D) | 34.0 | 11 | MS 2nd: Bennie G. Thompson (D) | 29.7 |
| 12 | NY 4th: Carolyn McCarthy (D) | 87 860 | 12 | FL 20th: Alcee L. Hastings (D) | 33.9 | 12 | CA 34th: Xavier Becerra (D) | 29.4 |
| 13 | MD 5th: Steny H. Hoyer (D) | 87 457 | 13 | FL 27th: Ileana Ros-Lehtinen (R) | 33.8 | 13 | AL 7th: Terri A. Sewell (D) | 29.2 |
| 14 | NJ 5th: Scott Garrett (R) | 86 213 | 14 | TX 30th: Eddie Bernice Johnson (D) | 32.5 | 14 | CA 40th: Lucille Roybal-Allard (D) | 28.7 |
| 15 | IL 6th: Peter J. Roskam (R) | 85 655 | 15 | FL 26th: Joe Garcia (D) | 32.1 | 15 | IL 7th: Danny K. Davis (D) | 28.6 |
| 16 | NY 17th: Nita M. Lowey (D) | 84 664 | 16 | AZ 7th: Ed Pastor (D) | 31.6 | 16 | NY 7th: Nydia M. Velázquez (D) | 28.5 |
| 17 | TX 3rd: Sam Johnson (R) | 83 724 | 17 | CA 29th: Tony Cárdenas (D) | 31.2 | 17 | NY 13th: Charles B. Rangel (D) | 28.4 |
| 18 | NY 1st: Timothy H. Bishop (D) | 83 144 | 18 | TX 5th: Jeb Hensarling (R) | 31.1 | 18 | NC 1st: G. K. Butterfield (D) | 27.8 |
| 19 | NY 12th: Carolyn B. Maloney (D) | 82 360 | 19 | IL 4th: Luis V. Gutierrez (D) | 30.3 | 19 | TX 18th: Sheila Jackson-Lee (D) | 27.6 |
| 20 | NY 2nd: Peter T. King (R) | 82 197 | 20 | TX 18th: Sheila Jackson-Lee (D) | 29.8 | 20 | OH 11th: Marcia L. Fudge (D) | 27.4 |
| 21 | CA 15th: Eric Swalwell (D) | 82 179 | 21 | CA 46th: Loretta Sanchez (D) | 29.7 | 21 | FL 5th: Corrine Brown (D) | 27.2 |
| 22 | TX 22nd: Pete Olson (R) | 81 392 | 22 | CA 44th: Janice Hahn (D) | 29.3 | 21 | NC 12th: Melvin L. Watt (D) | 27.2 |
| 23 | MA 4th: Joseph P. Kennedy III (D) | 81 131 | 23 | TX 16th: Beto O'Rouke (D) | 28.8 | 21 | PA 1st: Robert A. Brady (D) | 27.2 |
| 24 | CA 14th: Jackie Speier (D) | 79 287 | 24 | TX 35th: Lloyd Doggett (D) | 28.5 | 24 | AZ 3rd: Raúl M. Grijalva (D) | 27.1 |
| 25 | CT 4th: James A. Himes (D) | 79 097 | 25 | CA 51st: Juan Vargas (D) | 28.2 | 24 | TX 29th: Gene Green (D) | 27.1 |
| 26 | IL 14th: Randy Hultgren (R) | 77 758 | 26 | CA 21st: David G. Valadao (R) | 28.0 | 26 | KY 5th: Harold Rogers (R) | 26.8 |
| 27 | CA 52nd: Scott H. Peters (D) | 77 409 | 27 | NJ 8th: Albio Sires (D) | 27.5 | 27 | GA 2nd: Sanford D. Bishop Jr. (D) | 26.7 |
| 28 | WA 1st: Suzan K. DelBene (D) | 77 382 | 28 | FL 17th: Thomas J. Rooney (R) | 27.4 | 28 | LA 5th: Rodney Alexander (R) | 26.6 |
| 29 | CA 39th: Edward R. Royce (R) | 76 748 | 29 | CA 35th: Gloria Negrete McLeod (D) | 27.3 | 29 | FL 24th: Frederica S. Wilson (D) | 26.5 |
| 30 | MA 6th: John F. Tierney (D) | 76 130 | 30 | TX 11th: K. Michael Conaway (R) | 27.2 | 29 | LA 2nd: Cedric Richmond (D) | 26.5 |
| 31 | CA 48th: Dana Rohrabacher (R) | 76 077 | 31 | FL 9th: Alan Grayson (D) | 26.9 | 29 | MI 14th: Gary C. Peters (D) | 26.5 |
| 32 | NJ 12th: Rush Holt (D) | 75 649 | 32 | CA 37th: Karen Bass (D) | 26.4 | 29 | SC 6th: James E. Clyburn (D) | 26.5 |
| 33 | MA 5th: Edward J. Markey (D) | 75 564 | 32 | CA 43rd: Maxine Waters (D) | 26.4 | 33 | TN 9th: Steve Cohen (D) | 26.4 |
| 34 | TX 26th: Michael C. Burgess (R) | 75 069 | 32 | FL 19th: Trey Radel (R) | 26.4 | 34 | GA 5th: John Lewis (D) | 26.2 |
| 35 | VA 1st: Robert J. Wittman (R) | 74 283 | 32 | OK 2nd: Markwayne Mullin (R) | 26.4 | 34 | WI 1st: Gwen Moore (D) | 26.2 |
| 36 | PA 1st: Patrick Meehan (R) | 73 638 | 36 | CA 41st: Mark Takano (D) | 25.9 | 36 | NY 8th: Hakeem S. Jeffries (D) | 25.7 |
| 37 | MN 3rd: Erik Paulsen (R) | 73 468 | 36 | FL 22nd: Lois Frankel (D) | 25.9 | 37 | OH 3rd: Joyce Beatty (D) | 25.6 |
| 38 | MD 3rd: John P. Sarbanes (D) | 73 053 | 38 | CA 36th: Raul Ruiz (D) | 25.8 | 38 | FL 20th: Alcee L. Hastings (D) | 25.5 |
| 39 | GA 6th: Tom Price (R) | 72 832 | 38 | TX 23rd: Pete P. Gallego (D) | 25.8 | 39 | TX 35th: Lloyd Doggett (D) | 25.1 |
| 40 | CA 26th: Julia Brownley (D) | 72 804 | 40 | GA 5th: John Lewis (D) | 25.7 | 40 | CA 51st: Juan Vargas (D) | 24.3 |
| 41 | CA 19th: Zoe Lofgren (D) | 71 479 | 41 | FL 5th: Corrine Brown (D) | 25.6 | 41 | IN 7th: André Carson (D) | 23.9 |
| 42 | PA 1st: Michael G. Fitzpatrick (R) | 71 404 | 41 | LA 5th: Rodney Alexander (R) | 25.6 | 42 | CA 6th: Doris O. Matsui (D) | 23.8 |
| 43 | NY 18th: Sean Patrick Maloney (D) | 71 399 | 43 | SC 7th: Tom Rice (R) | 25.5 | 43 | CA 43rd: Maxine Waters (D) | 23.6 |
| 44 | MO 2nd: Ann Wagner (R) | 71 239 | 44 | GA 4th: Henry C. "Hank" Johnson Jr. (D) | 25.3 | 44 | TX 30th: Eddie Bernice Johnson (D) | 23.4 |
| 45 | MD 4th: Donna F. Edwards (D) | 71 135 | 44 | TX 36th: Steve Stockman (R) | 25.3 | 45 | CA 44th: Janice Hahn (D) | 23.3 |
| 46 | NJ 4th: Christopher H. Smith (R) | 71 084 | 46 | FL 23rd: Debbie Wasserman Schultz(D) | 25.2 | 46 | GA 8th: Austin Scott (R) | 23.2 |
| 47 | CA 42nd: Ken Calvert (R) | 71 073 | 46 | NY 14th: Joseph Crowley (D) | 25.2 | 46 | NM 2nd: Steve Pearce (R) | 23.2 |
| 48 | NJ 6th: Frank Pallone Jr. (D) | 70 878 | 48 | TX 27th: Blake Farenthold (R) | 25.1 | 48 | AZ 1st: Ann Kirkpatrick (D) | 23.1 |
| 49 | MA 8th: Stephen F. Lynch (D) | 70 420 | 49 | TX 20th: Joaquin Castro (D) | 25.0 | 48 | IL 4th: Luis V. Gutierrez (D) | 23.1 |
| 50 | NY 10th: Jerrold Nadler (D) | 70 270 | 50 | NM 3rd: Ben Ray Luján (D) | 24.9 | 50 | CA 29th: Tony Cárdenas (D) | 22.9 |
| 51 | MN 2nd: John Kline (R) | 70 095 | 51 | FL 14th: Kathy Castor (D) | 24.8 | 50 | FL 14th: Kathy Castor (D) | 22.9 |
| 52 | CA 11th: George Miller (D) | 69 586 | 51 | NC 12th: Melvin L. Watt (D) | 24.8 | 50 | TX 17th: Bill Flores (R) | 22.9 |
| 53 | PA 1st: Jim Gerlach (R) | 69 570 | 53 | CA 32nd: Grace F. Napolitano (D) | 24.7 | 53 | SC 7th: Tom Rice (R) | 22.8 |
| 54 | MI 11th: Kerry L. Bentivolio (R) | 69 397 | 54 | CA 28th: Adam B. Schiff (D) | 24.5 | 54 | OH 9th: Marcy Kaptur (D) | 22.6 |
| 55 | TX 2nd: Ted Poe (R) | 69 181 | 54 | FL 16th: Vern Buchanan (R) | 24.5 | 55 | TX 16th: Beto O'Rourke (D) | 22.4 |
| 56 | CA 12th: Nancy Pelosi (D) | 69 046 | 54 | GA 9th: Doug Collins (R) | 24.5 | 56 | GA 12th: John Barrow (D) | 22.3 |
| 57 | CT 2nd: Joe Courtney (D) | 68 925 | 57 | FL 11th: Richard B. Nugent (R) | 24.4 | 57 | FL 27th: Ileana Ros-Lehtinen (R) | 22.1 |
| 58 | VA 7th: Eric Cantor (R) | 68 596 | 58 | CA 16th: Jim Costa (D) | 24.3 | 57 | MS 4th: Steven Palazzo (R) | 22.1 |
| 59 | CA 25th: Howard P. "Buck" McKeon (R) | 68 551 | 59 | MS 4th: Steven Palazzo (R) | 24.2 | 57 | MO 1st: William Lacy Clay (D) | 22.1 |
| 60 | MD 6th: John K. Delaney (D) | 68 361 | 60 | NV 2nd: Mark E. Amodei (R) | 24.1 | 57 | NV 1st: Dina Titus (D) | 22.1 |
| 61 | NJ 3rd: Jon Runyan (R) | 68 300 | 61 | FL 13th: C. W. Bill Young (R) | 24.0 | 61 | AR 1st Eric A. "Rick" Crawford (R) | 22.0 |
| 62 | CA 49th: Darrell E. Issa (R) | 68 129 | 62 | NV 4th: Steven A. Horsford (D) | 23.9 | 61 | VA 3rd: Robert C. "Bobby" Scott (D) | 22.0 |
| 63 | AK At-Large: Don Young (R) | 67 825 | 62 | TX 7th: John Abney Culberson (R) | 23.9 | 63 | MA 7th: Michael E. Capuano (D) | 21.9 |
| 64 | CA 30th: Brad Sherman (D) | 67 079 | 64 | OK 5th: James Lankford (R) | 23.7 | 64 | CA 37th: Karen Bass (D) | 21.8 |
| 65 | WA 8th: David G. Reichert (R) | 67 046 | 64 | SC 6th: James E. Clyburn (D) | 23.7 | 65 | CA 41st: Mark Takano (D) | 21.7 |
| 66 | IL 11th: Bill Foster (D) | 65 938 | 64 | TX 1st: Louie Gohmert (R) | 23.7 | 66 | TX 9th: Al Green (D) | 21.6 |
| 67 | IL 10th: Bradley S. Schneider (D) | 65 864 | 64 | TX 19th: Randy Neugebauer (R) | 23.7 | 67 | AR 4th: Tom Cotton (R) | 21.4 |
| 68 | NC 9th: Robert Pittenger (R) | 65 681 | 68 | TX 4th: Ralph M. Hall (R) | 23.6 | 67 | OR 1st: Peter A. DeFazio (D) | 21.4 |
| 69 | HI 1st: Colleen Hanabusa (D) | 65 602 | 69 | FL 18th: Patrick Murphy (D) | 23.5 | 69 | GA 10th: Paul C. Broun (R) | 21.2 |
| 70 | MN 6th: Michele Bachmann (R) | 65 461 | 69 | TX 32nd: Pete Sessions (R) | 23.5 | 70 | AL 3rd: Mike Rogers (R) | 20.8 |
| 71 | MD 1st: Andrew Harris (R) | 64 151 | 69 | WA 4th: Doc Hastings (R) | 23.5 | 70 | MS 3rd: Gregg Harper (R) | 20.8 |
| 72 | NH 1st: Carol Shea-Porter (D) | 63 587 | 72 | GA 1st: Jack Kingston (R) | 23.3 | 72 | NM 1st: Michelle Lujan Grisham (D) | 20.7 |
| 73 | CO 2nd: Jared Polis (D) | 63 571 | 73 | GA 8th: Austin Scott (R) | 23.2 | 72 | NM 3rd: Ben Ray Luján (D) | 20.7 |
| 74 | CA 27th: Judy Chu (D) | 63 561 | 73 | TX 8th: Kevin Brady (R) | 23.2 | 72 | NC 8th: Richard Hudson (R) | 20.7 |
| 75 | CO 6th: Mike Coffman (R) | 63 513 | 73 | TX 13th: Mac Thornberry (R) | 23.2 | 72 | OK 2nd: Markwayne Mullin (R) | 20.7 |

## Table E. Congressional Districts 113th Congress — **Land Area and Population Characteristics**

| STATE District | Representative, 113th Congress | Land area,[1] 2010 (sq km) | Population and population characteristics, 2011 | | | | | | | | | | | | |
|---|---|---|---|---|---|---|---|---|---|---|---|---|---|---|---|
| | | | | | Percent | | | | | | | | | | |
| | | | Total persons | Per square kilometer | Race alone | | | | | | | Hispanic or Latino[2] | Non-Hispanic White alone | Percent female | Percent foreign born | Percent born in state of residence |
| | | | | | White | Black | American Indian, Alaska Native | Asian and Pacific Islander | Some other race | Two or more races | | | | | |
| | | 1 | 2 | 3 | 4 | 5 | 6 | 7 | 8 | 9 | 10 | 11 | 12 | 13 | 14 |

1. Dry land or land partially or temporarily covered by water.   2. May be of any race.

## Table E. Congressional Districts 113th Congress — **Age and Education**

| STATE District | Population and population characteristics, 2011 (cont.) | | | | | | | | | | Education, 2011 | | |
|---|---|---|---|---|---|---|---|---|---|---|---|---|---|
| | Age (percent) | | | | | | | | | | Attainment[2] (percent) | | |
| | Under 5 years | 5 to 17 years | 18 to 24 years | 25 to 34 years | 35 to 44 years | 45 to 54 years | 55 to 64 years | 65 to 74 years | 75 years and over | Median age | Total Enrollment[1] | High school graduate or more | Bachelor's degree or more |
| | 15 | 16 | 17 | 18 | 19 | 20 | 21 | 22 | 23 | 24 | 25 | 26 | 27 |

1. All persons 3 years old and over enrolled in nursery school through college and graduate or professional school.   2. Persons 25 years old and over.

## Table E. Congressional Districts 113th Congress — **Households and Group Quarters**

| STATE District | Households, 2011 | | | | | | Group quarters, 2010 | | | | | |
|---|---|---|---|---|---|---|---|---|---|---|---|---|
| | Number | Persons per household | Family households (percent) | Married-couple family (percent) | Female family householder[1] | One person households (percent) | Total in group quarters | Percent 65 years and over | Persons in correctional institutions | Persons in nursing homes | Persons in college dormitories | Persons in military quarters |
| | 28 | 29 | 30 | 31 | 32 | 33 | 34 | 35 | 36 | 37 | 38 | 39 |

1. No spouse present.

## Table E. Congressional Districts 113th Congress — **Housing and Money Income**

| STATE District | Housing units, 2011 | | | | | | Money income, 2011 | | |
|---|---|---|---|---|---|---|---|---|---|
| | Total | Occupied units | | | | | Households | | |
| | | Percent Occupied | Owner-occupied | | | Renter-occupied | Per capita income (dollars) | Median income (dollars) | Percent with income of $100,000 or more |
| | | | Percent | Median value[1] (dollars) | Percent valued at $500,000 or more | Median rent[2] | | | |
| | 40 | 41 | 42 | 43 | 44 | 45 | 46 | 47 | 48 |

1. Specified owner-occupied units.   2. Specified renter-occupied units.

## Table E. Congressional Districts 113th Congress — **Poverty, Labor Force, Employment, and Social Security**

| STATE District | Poverty, 2011 (percent) | | | Civilian labor force, 2011 | | | Civilian employment,[2] 2011 | | | | | | Social Security beneficiaries, December 2012 | | |
|---|---|---|---|---|---|---|---|---|---|---|---|---|---|---|---|
| | | | | | Unemployment | | | Percent | | | | | | | |
| | Persons below poverty level | Families below poverty level | Households receiving food stamps in past 12 months | Total | Total | Rate[1] | Total | Manage-ment, profes-sional, and related occupations | Service, sales, and office | Con-struction and production | Persons under age 65 with no health insurance, 2010 (percent) | | Number | Rate[3] | Supple-mental Security Income recipients, December 2012 |
| | 49 | 50 | 51 | 52 | 53 | 54 | 55 | 56 | 57 | 58 | 59 | | 60 | 61 | 62 |

1. Percent of civilian labor force.    2. Persons 16 years old and over.    3. Per 1,000 resident population estimated in the 2011 American Community Survey.

# Table E. Congressional Districts 113th Congress — Land Area and Population Characteristics

| STATE District | Representative, 113th Congress | Land area,[1] 2010 (sq km) | Total persons | Per square kilometer | White | Black | American Indian, Alaska Native | Asian and Pacific Islander | Some other race | Two or more races | Hispanic or Latino[2] | Non-Hispanic White alone | Percent female | Percent foreign born | Percent born in state of residence |
|---|---|---|---|---|---|---|---|---|---|---|---|---|---|---|---|
| | | 1 | 2 | 3 | 4 | 5 | 6 | 7 | 8 | 9 | 10 | 11 | 12 | 13 | 14 |
| UNITED STATES | | 9 147 593 | 311 591 917 | 34.1 | 74.1 | 12.6 | 0.8 | 5.0 | 4.7 | 2.8 | 16.7 | 63.3 | 50.8 | 13.0 | 58.9 |
| ALABAMA | | 131 171 | 4 802 740 | 36.6 | 69.1 | 26.7 | 0.5 | 1.1 | 1.2 | 1.3 | 4.0 | 66.7 | 51.6 | 3.4 | 70.2 |
| District 1 | Jo Bonner (R) | 15 713 | 689 110 | 43.9 | 67.7 | 28.1 | 1.0 | 1.4 | 0.7 | 1.1 | 2.8 | 65.6 | 51.9 | 3.1 | 69.2 |
| District 2 | Martha Roby (R) | 26 267 | 678 860 | 25.8 | 66.3 | 29.7 | 0.4 | 1.0 | 0.7 | 1.9 | 3.3 | 63.8 | 51.5 | 2.6 | 69.1 |
| District 3 | Mike Rogers (R) | 19 539 | 683 095 | 35.0 | 70.7 | 25.9 | 0.3 | 1.3 | 0.6 | 1.3 | 2.5 | 69.3 | 51.0 | 2.7 | 65.9 |
| District 4 | Robert B. Aderholt (R) | 23 022 | 682 029 | 29.6 | 87.9 | 7.3 | 0.7 | 0.5 | 2.0 | 1.6 | 5.6 | 84.5 | 51.0 | 3.3 | 74.0 |
| District 5 | Mo Brooks (R) | 9 524 | 691 438 | 72.6 | 77.0 | 17.5 | 0.6 | 1.5 | 1.2 | 2.2 | 4.9 | 73.8 | 51.0 | 4.2 | 62.0 |
| District 6 | Spencer Bachus (R) | 10 802 | 687 709 | 63.7 | 80.8 | 13.9 | 0.4 | 1.8 | 2.6 | 0.6 | 5.5 | 78.0 | 51.2 | 5.1 | 70.7 |
| District 7 | Terri A. Sewell (D) | 26 304 | 690 499 | 26.3 | 33.6 | 64.1 | 0.1 | 0.8 | 0.8 | 0.6 | 2.5 | 32.0 | 53.7 | 2.7 | 80.6 |
| ALASKA | | 1 477 953 | 722 718 | 0.5 | 66.8 | 3.2 | 14.2 | 6.3 | 1.2 | 8.3 | 5.8 | 63.6 | 48.4 | 7.1 | 39.8 |
| At Large | Don Young (R) | 1 477 953 | 722 718 | 0.5 | 66.8 | 3.2 | 14.2 | 6.3 | 1.2 | 8.3 | 5.8 | 63.6 | 48.4 | 7.1 | 39.8 |
| ARIZONA | | 294 207 | 6 482 505 | 22.0 | 79.3 | 4.1 | 4.5 | 2.9 | 6.2 | 3.0 | 30.1 | 57.3 | 50.2 | 13.4 | 38.4 |
| District 1 | Ann Kirkpatrick (D) | 142 552 | 724 868 | 5.1 | 64.1 | 2.4 | 23.2 | 1.8 | 5.5 | 3.0 | 20.4 | 51.2 | 50.3 | 6.8 | 51.7 |
| District 2 | Ron Barber (D) | 20 301 | 722 918 | 35.6 | 81.8 | 4.1 | 0.9 | 3.3 | 5.9 | 4.0 | 26.5 | 63.8 | 50.8 | 10.7 | 35.9 |
| District 3 | Rául M. Grijalva (D) | 40 634 | 707 336 | 17.4 | 75.9 | 4.5 | 5.3 | 1.5 | 14.4 | 2.4 | 61.1 | 28.0 | 49.5 | 20.5 | 47.6 |
| District 4 | Paul A. Gosar (R) | 85 986 | 707 750 | 8.2 | 86.8 | 1.7 | 2.2 | 0.8 | 4.5 | 3.9 | 19.4 | 74.5 | 48.6 | 7.7 | 28.0 |
| District 5 | Matt Salmon (R) | 760 | 711 895 | 936.6 | 84.9 | 3.5 | 1.4 | 3.9 | 3.3 | 3.1 | 18.4 | 71.2 | 51.4 | 9.3 | 35.2 |
| District 6 | David Schweikert (R) | 1 619 | 743 752 | 459.4 | 86.6 | 2.4 | 1.7 | 4.3 | 2.7 | 2.3 | 15.1 | 74.9 | 51.1 | 13.5 | 30.5 |
| District 7 | Ed Pastor (D) | 531 | 725 197 | 1 365.1 | 69.5 | 9.1 | 2.7 | 2.7 | 14.3 | 1.9 | 65.9 | 19.9 | 48.3 | 27.4 | 46.9 |
| District 8 | Trent Franks (R) | 1 398 | 715 893 | 512.2 | 87.9 | 3.5 | 0.7 | 2.9 | 2.0 | 3.1 | 18.0 | 73.2 | 51.4 | 10.0 | 34.1 |
| District 9 | Kyrsten Sinema (D) | 427 | 722 896 | 1 693.7 | 80.4 | 5.9 | 2.0 | 4.9 | 3.5 | 3.3 | 26.3 | 58.6 | 50.3 | 15.0 | 35.6 |
| ARKANSAS | | 134 771 | 2 937 979 | 21.8 | 78.2 | 15.8 | 0.6 | 1.4 | 2.1 | 1.9 | 6.6 | 74.3 | 50.7 | 4.4 | 61.2 |
| District 1 | Eric A. "Rick" Crawford (R) | 50 034 | 729 510 | 14.6 | 78.7 | 18.4 | 0.3 | 0.6 | 0.6 | 1.4 | 2.8 | 76.8 | 50.5 | 1.6 | 67.1 |
| District 2 | Timothy Griffin (R) | 12 893 | 739 092 | 57.3 | 73.1 | 22.0 | 0.3 | 1.3 | 1.4 | 1.9 | 4.9 | 69.9 | 51.2 | 3.7 | 66.1 |
| District 3 | Steve Womack (R) | 13 988 | 733 194 | 52.4 | 85.2 | 3.0 | 1.2 | 3.2 | 4.2 | 3.1 | 12.7 | 77.6 | 50.2 | 9.4 | 47.2 |
| District 4 | Tom Cotton (R) | 57 855 | 736 183 | 12.7 | 75.6 | 19.7 | 0.5 | 0.6 | 2.2 | 1.4 | 5.5 | 72.8 | 51.0 | 2.9 | 64.6 |
| CALIFORNIA | | 403 466 | 37 691 912 | 93.4 | 62.9 | 6.0 | 0.8 | 13.6 | 12.6 | 4.2 | 38.1 | 39.6 | 50.3 | 27.0 | 54.3 |
| District 1 | Doug LaMalfa (R) | 72 751 | 699 301 | 9.6 | 85.9 | 1.4 | 1.7 | 2.8 | 3.2 | 5.0 | 12.4 | 78.4 | 50.1 | 6.4 | 68.4 |
| District 2 | Jared Huffman (D) | 33 546 | 707 530 | 21.1 | 80.8 | 1.8 | 2.3 | 3.9 | 6.7 | 4.4 | 17.0 | 72.1 | 50.3 | 12.6 | 60.2 |
| District 3 | John Garamendi (D) | 16 015 | 698 044 | 43.6 | 64.1 | 6.4 | 1.3 | 10.9 | 11.1 | 6.2 | 28.8 | 48.7 | 49.8 | 18.0 | 61.1 |
| District 4 | Tom McClintock (R) | 33 246 | 711 815 | 21.4 | 86.0 | 1.1 | 1.7 | 4.4 | 3.2 | 3.6 | 12.6 | 77.6 | 49.8 | 8.3 | 66.4 |
| District 5 | Mike Thompson (D) | 4 483 | 709 544 | 158.3 | 70.2 | 6.5 | 1.2 | 11.4 | 5.9 | 4.8 | 25.9 | 52.5 | 51.0 | 20.9 | 58.8 |
| District 6 | Doris O. Matsui (D) | 453 | 713 579 | 1 574.0 | 53.9 | 12.1 | 1.5 | 17.7 | 7.8 | 6.9 | 26.3 | 38.6 | 50.8 | 23.9 | 58.5 |
| District 7 | Ami Bera (D) | 1 421 | 710 607 | 500.1 | 66.0 | 7.8 | 0.6 | 13.4 | 5.7 | 6.3 | 17.2 | 56.8 | 51.3 | 17.5 | 60.4 |
| District 8 | Paul Cook (R) | 85 126 | 699 443 | 8.2 | 70.1 | 7.7 | 1.3 | 3.8 | 13.7 | 3.4 | 35.9 | 49.7 | 49.5 | 12.2 | 64.5 |
| District 9 | Jerry McNerney (D) | 3 225 | 707 132 | 219.2 | 61.2 | 8.3 | 1.0 | 13.7 | 9.8 | 5.9 | 39.2 | 35.6 | 50.3 | 21.5 | 63.2 |
| District 10 | Jeff Denham (R) | 4 711 | 713 912 | 151.6 | 75.2 | 3.9 | 1.0 | 7.0 | 7.9 | 4.9 | 40.0 | 46.2 | 49.7 | 20.3 | 64.0 |
| District 11 | George Miller (D) | 1 278 | 722 847 | 565.4 | 65.0 | 9.2 | 0.5 | 13.2 | 7.4 | 4.8 | 25.3 | 48.4 | 51.2 | 24.6 | 54.5 |
| District 12 | Nancy Pelosi (D) | 101 | 700 605 | 6 940.5 | 52.8 | 6.0 | 0.3 | 31.5 | 5.1 | 4.2 | 15.0 | 44.4 | 48.7 | 35.5 | 36.9 |
| District 13 | Barbara Lee (D) | 251 | 712 144 | 2 840.7 | 47.8 | 19.8 | 0.5 | 21.5 | 4.7 | 5.7 | 20.7 | 34.1 | 51.9 | 26.4 | 49.6 |
| District 14 | Jackie Speier (D) | 672 | 726 958 | 1 081.6 | 51.4 | 3.5 | 0.2 | 32.8 | 7.6 | 4.4 | 25.0 | 35.5 | 51.1 | 36.9 | 48.3 |
| District 15 | Eric Swalwell (D) | 1 553 | 708 580 | 456.4 | 50.0 | 6.4 | 0.4 | 29.5 | 8.5 | 5.3 | 24.2 | 36.5 | 50.4 | 32.4 | 51.0 |
| District 16 | Jim Costa (D) | 7 354 | 714 214 | 97.1 | 58.6 | 5.9 | 1.1 | 9.7 | 21.0 | 3.8 | 58.1 | 24.4 | 50.2 | 26.2 | 63.1 |
| District 17 | Michael M. Honda (D) | 479 | 724 244 | 1 512.7 | 36.1 | 2.6 | 0.5 | 49.4 | 6.9 | 4.5 | 19.2 | 25.7 | 49.6 | 45.2 | 41.2 |
| District 18 | Anna G. Eshoo (D) | 1 803 | 717 397 | 397.9 | 68.3 | 1.9 | 0.5 | 20.2 | 4.4 | 4.7 | 16.6 | 57.6 | 49.6 | 26.6 | 50.0 |
| District 19 | Zoe Lofgren (D) | 2 371 | 695 402 | 293.3 | 52.4 | 3.1 | 0.8 | 26.2 | 13.2 | 4.4 | 41.3 | 27.1 | 50.0 | 35.6 | 50.7 |
| District 20 | Sam Farr (D) | 12 624 | 712 087 | 56.4 | 75.8 | 2.4 | 0.6 | 5.7 | 12.3 | 3.3 | 51.5 | 38.4 | 49.5 | 27.5 | 54.7 |
| District 21 | David G. Valadao (R) | 17 430 | 714 164 | 41.0 | 69.5 | 4.0 | 1.4 | 3.1 | 19.1 | 2.9 | 72.1 | 19.2 | 46.5 | 29.9 | 59.4 |
| District 22 | Devin Nunes (R) | 3 018 | 711 709 | 235.8 | 71.6 | 3.1 | 0.8 | 7.4 | 13.1 | 4.0 | 45.9 | 41.9 | 50.9 | 18.6 | 67.3 |
| District 23 | Kevin McCarthy (R) | 25 636 | 707 345 | 27.6 | 75.8 | 6.8 | 1.4 | 5.3 | 6.4 | 4.4 | 35.4 | 49.7 | 48.8 | 14.0 | 66.7 |
| District 24 | Lois Capps (D) | 17 828 | 708 744 | 39.8 | 79.6 | 2.0 | 0.9 | 4.7 | 9.1 | 3.8 | 34.7 | 56.2 | 49.6 | 19.1 | 58.3 |
| District 25 | Howard P. "Buck" McKeon (R) | 4 378 | 714 313 | 163.1 | 63.7 | 7.7 | 0.5 | 8.1 | 14.3 | 5.7 | 37.9 | 43.1 | 49.3 | 20.5 | 61.4 |
| District 26 | Julia Brownley (D) | 2 432 | 708 300 | 291.2 | 75.9 | 2.1 | 0.6 | 6.9 | 10.3 | 4.1 | 43.5 | 45.8 | 50.4 | 22.5 | 56.3 |
| District 27 | Judy Chu (D) | 1 813 | 709 231 | 391.2 | 47.8 | 4.3 | 0.3 | 36.5 | 7.9 | 3.2 | 26.1 | 30.8 | 51.3 | 38.4 | 46.4 |
| District 28 | Adam B. Schiff (D) | 566 | 706 585 | 1 248.9 | 70.7 | 2.3 | 0.4 | 13.7 | 9.4 | 3.5 | 25.3 | 56.6 | 50.5 | 42.6 | 36.6 |
| District 29 | Tony Cárdenas (D) | 238 | 687 063 | 2 882.5 | 62.4 | 4.0 | 0.5 | 8.2 | 22.1 | 2.7 | 67.7 | 19.0 | 49.7 | 43.7 | 45.7 |
| District 30 | Brad Sherman (D) | 352 | 726 471 | 2 063.3 | 67.6 | 4.2 | 0.6 | 12.9 | 10.7 | 4.0 | 28.8 | 50.9 | 50.3 | 33.3 | 45.4 |
| District 31 | Gary G. Miller (R) | 565 | 727 523 | 1 287.1 | 57.0 | 9.9 | 1.0 | 7.9 | 18.5 | 5.7 | 49.3 | 29.0 | 50.2 | 22.2 | 63.4 |
| District 32 | Grace F. Napolitano (D) | 322 | 693 701 | 2 155.9 | 52.6 | 2.7 | 0.5 | 16.4 | 24.4 | 3.3 | 61.9 | 18.2 | 51.2 | 36.6 | 54.0 |
| District 33 | Henry A. Waxman (D) | 747 | 707 854 | 947.1 | 75.5 | 3.3 | 0.2 | 14.3 | 2.5 | 4.2 | 12.4 | 66.4 | 52.0 | 22.8 | 46.2 |
| District 34 | Xavier Becerra (D) | 123 | 698 741 | 5 660.2 | 38.2 | 4.0 | 0.5 | 19.6 | 35.1 | 2.6 | 66.5 | 9.2 | 48.4 | 49.9 | 40.5 |
| District 35 | Gloria Negrete McLeod (D) | 437 | 710 704 | 1 624.8 | 61.0 | 7.1 | 0.6 | 6.3 | 20.8 | 4.1 | 70.0 | 15.3 | 50.8 | 30.2 | 60.0 |
| District 36 | Raul Ruiz (D) | 15 314 | 713 166 | 46.6 | 68.2 | 3.8 | 1.1 | 3.8 | 20.4 | 2.7 | 47.9 | 42.6 | 50.0 | 23.6 | 52.2 |
| District 37 | Karen Bass (D) | 143 | 719 034 | 5 023.6 | 38.7 | 24.3 | 0.5 | 9.8 | 22.8 | 3.8 | 39.4 | 23.3 | 51.4 | 33.2 | 47.1 |

1. Dry land or land partially or temporarily covered by water.  2. May be of any race.

# Table E. Congressional Districts 113th Congress — **Age and Education**

| STATE District | Under 5 years | 5 to 17 years | 18 to 24 years | 25 to 34 years | 35 to 44 years | 45 to 54 years | 55 to 64 years | 65 to 74 years | 75 years and over | Median age | Total Enrollment[1] | High school graduate or more | Bachelor's degree or more |
|---|---|---|---|---|---|---|---|---|---|---|---|---|---|
| | 15 | 16 | 17 | 18 | 19 | 20 | 21 | 22 | 23 | 24 | 25 | 26 | 27 |
| UNITED STATES.............. | 6.4 | 17.3 | 10.0 | 13.4 | 13.1 | 14.3 | 12.2 | 7.2 | 6.1 | 37.3 | 83 131 910 | 85.9 | 28.5 |
| ALABAMA ........................ | 6.2 | 17.2 | 10.1 | 12.7 | 12.8 | 14.3 | 12.7 | 7.9 | 6.1 | 38.1 | 1 241 786 | 82.7 | 22.3 |
| District 1.............................. | 6.4 | 17.8 | 9.1 | 12.6 | 12.3 | 14.4 | 12.9 | 8.2 | 6.3 | 38.5 | 175 816 | 85.0 | 21.5 |
| District 2.............................. | 6.3 | 17.5 | 9.6 | 13.1 | 13.0 | 13.7 | 12.4 | 8.2 | 6.3 | 37.8 | 171 120 | 82.4 | 20.7 |
| District 3.............................. | 6.1 | 16.7 | 12.2 | 12.3 | 13.0 | 13.7 | 12.6 | 7.7 | 5.8 | 37.3 | 184 955 | 80.1 | 19.9 |
| District 4.............................. | 5.7 | 17.2 | 8.8 | 11.3 | 12.8 | 14.8 | 13.4 | 9.2 | 6.7 | 40.7 | 160 945 | 78.2 | 14.9 |
| District 5.............................. | 5.9 | 17.3 | 9.6 | 12.5 | 13.0 | 15.6 | 12.5 | 7.8 | 6.0 | 39.1 | 175 661 | 85.8 | 27.5 |
| District 6.............................. | 6.6 | 17.1 | 8.0 | 13.7 | 13.8 | 14.7 | 12.7 | 7.5 | 5.9 | 38.3 | 173 145 | 87.4 | 32.9 |
| District 7.............................. | 6.6 | 16.8 | 13.4 | 13.3 | 11.5 | 13.3 | 12.3 | 6.8 | 5.9 | 34.8 | 200 144 | 79.6 | 17.8 |
| ALASKA ........................... | 7.5 | 18.6 | 10.7 | 14.7 | 12.9 | 14.9 | 12.6 | 5.2 | 2.8 | 33.9 | 196 240 | 91.8 | 26.4 |
| At Large ............................. | 7.5 | 18.6 | 10.7 | 14.7 | 12.9 | 14.9 | 12.6 | 5.2 | 2.8 | 33.9 | 196 240 | 91.8 | 26.4 |
| ARIZONA .......................... | 6.9 | 18.2 | 10.0 | 13.4 | 12.7 | 12.9 | 11.7 | 8.0 | 6.2 | 36.2 | 1 751 916 | 85.7 | 26.6 |
| District 1.............................. | 7.0 | 18.5 | 11.0 | 11.6 | 12.0 | 12.8 | 12.8 | 8.8 | 5.7 | 37.1 | 192 331 | 85.3 | 23.5 |
| District 2.............................. | 5.8 | 14.9 | 9.7 | 13.0 | 11.3 | 13.6 | 14.1 | 9.6 | 8.1 | 40.9 | 183 979 | 90.1 | 30.3 |
| District 3.............................. | 8.3 | 20.9 | 12.7 | 14.7 | 12.8 | 11.5 | 9.5 | 5.9 | 3.7 | 30.6 | 215 050 | 73.3 | 15.8 |
| District 4.............................. | 6.1 | 16.1 | 7.3 | 10.8 | 10.8 | 12.3 | 14.3 | 13.1 | 9.1 | 44.0 | 158 240 | 86.9 | 17.7 |
| District 5.............................. | 6.7 | 21.1 | 7.4 | 12.5 | 14.2 | 13.2 | 10.2 | 8.1 | 6.6 | 36.8 | 210 621 | 92.5 | 33.1 |
| District 6.............................. | 6.1 | 16.8 | 7.7 | 13.1 | 14.5 | 14.1 | 13.1 | 8.5 | 6.1 | 39.4 | 178 301 | 91.3 | 39.3 |
| District 7.............................. | 9.5 | 21.5 | 13.3 | 15.5 | 13.3 | 12.0 | 8.0 | 4.2 | 2.7 | 28.2 | 211 659 | 66.3 | 13.1 |
| District 8.............................. | 5.9 | 17.7 | 7.4 | 12.8 | 11.9 | 13.2 | 12.1 | 9.5 | 9.4 | 40.3 | 186 930 | 92.0 | 27.9 |
| District 9.............................. | 6.9 | 15.9 | 13.3 | 16.3 | 13.7 | 13.8 | 10.9 | 5.1 | 4.1 | 33.4 | 214 805 | 88.4 | 34.4 |
| ARKANSAS...................... | 6.7 | 17.4 | 9.6 | 13.0 | 12.5 | 13.7 | 12.4 | 8.1 | 6.5 | 37.5 | 752 121 | 83.8 | 20.3 |
| District 1.............................. | 6.5 | 17.6 | 8.8 | 12.3 | 12.5 | 13.6 | 12.9 | 9.0 | 6.9 | 38.8 | 177 496 | 81.3 | 15.0 |
| District 2.............................. | 6.6 | 17.2 | 10.1 | 14.2 | 12.8 | 13.7 | 12.0 | 7.4 | 5.8 | 36.3 | 199 787 | 87.7 | 27.6 |
| District 3.............................. | 7.4 | 18.0 | 10.3 | 14.1 | 12.9 | 13.3 | 11.4 | 6.9 | 5.8 | 35.2 | 194 180 | 84.1 | 24.4 |
| District 4.............................. | 6.4 | 17.1 | 9.3 | 11.5 | 11.7 | 14.1 | 13.3 | 9.2 | 7.3 | 40.2 | 180 658 | 81.9 | 14.5 |
| CALIFORNIA.................... | 6.7 | 17.8 | 10.6 | 14.3 | 13.7 | 13.9 | 11.1 | 6.3 | 5.3 | 35.4 | 10 584 220 | 81.1 | 30.3 |
| District 1.............................. | 5.3 | 15.2 | 10.7 | 11.6 | 10.3 | 14.2 | 15.2 | 9.6 | 7.9 | 42.1 | 169 917 | 88.2 | 21.9 |
| District 2.............................. | 5.5 | 15.0 | 8.3 | 11.7 | 12.5 | 15.4 | 15.9 | 9.1 | 6.6 | 42.6 | 168 337 | 89.5 | 37.9 |
| District 3.............................. | 6.3 | 17.8 | 13.1 | 13.1 | 12.8 | 13.8 | 11.3 | 6.5 | 5.2 | 34.6 | 205 839 | 82.9 | 23.3 |
| District 4.............................. | 5.1 | 16.5 | 7.3 | 10.4 | 12.7 | 16.1 | 15.4 | 9.3 | 7.2 | 43.3 | 176 952 | 93.0 | 31.2 |
| District 5.............................. | 5.9 | 16.6 | 9.1 | 12.6 | 12.2 | 14.9 | 14.5 | 7.5 | 6.6 | 39.7 | 184 148 | 86.2 | 29.6 |
| District 6.............................. | 7.5 | 18.7 | 11.0 | 16.2 | 13.1 | 12.8 | 10.2 | 5.4 | 5.1 | 32.6 | 212 829 | 81.5 | 24.6 |
| District 7.............................. | 6.6 | 18.0 | 9.3 | 13.4 | 13.3 | 14.9 | 12.2 | 6.6 | 5.8 | 37.1 | 201 904 | 90.4 | 30.9 |
| District 8.............................. | 7.6 | 21.1 | 10.2 | 13.0 | 11.5 | 13.8 | 11.5 | 6.6 | 4.6 | 33.5 | 199 543 | 82.3 | 15.6 |
| District 9.............................. | 7.5 | 21.0 | 10.5 | 12.9 | 13.4 | 13.2 | 10.5 | 5.9 | 5.1 | 33.4 | 218 473 | 79.6 | 18.7 |
| District 10............................ | 7.5 | 21.3 | 10.2 | 13.3 | 13.1 | 13.9 | 10.4 | 5.7 | 4.6 | 33.0 | 211 540 | 77.4 | 17.6 |
| District 11............................ | 6.4 | 16.6 | 8.8 | 12.9 | 13.3 | 14.8 | 13.2 | 7.6 | 6.4 | 39.1 | 188 754 | 87.4 | 41.0 |
| District 12............................ | 4.4 | 8.5 | 8.3 | 22.8 | 16.9 | 13.8 | 11.8 | 6.5 | 6.9 | 38.1 | 141 826 | 86.6 | 54.4 |
| District 13............................ | 5.9 | 13.9 | 11.0 | 16.6 | 14.5 | 13.4 | 12.3 | 6.8 | 5.5 | 36.8 | 195 011 | 84.7 | 45.0 |
| District 14............................ | 6.1 | 14.8 | 8.7 | 13.8 | 15.1 | 14.5 | 13.1 | 7.3 | 6.4 | 39.3 | 190 415 | 86.7 | 39.8 |
| District 15............................ | 7.2 | 17.8 | 8.6 | 13.7 | 15.3 | 15.6 | 11.5 | 5.6 | 4.6 | 36.7 | 190 190 | 87.8 | 38.6 |
| District 16............................ | 8.9 | 22.8 | 12.4 | 14.4 | 12.3 | 11.8 | 8.5 | 4.9 | 4.1 | 28.9 | 224 698 | 63.9 | 10.9 |
| District 17............................ | 6.8 | 16.8 | 7.9 | 16.1 | 16.0 | 15.4 | 10.6 | 5.5 | 4.9 | 36.4 | 193 225 | 90.0 | 50.3 |
| District 18............................ | 5.9 | 17.3 | 8.0 | 13.1 | 14.3 | 15.6 | 12.2 | 7.3 | 6.2 | 39.2 | 196 829 | 93.6 | 57.3 |
| District 19............................ | 7.2 | 17.4 | 9.7 | 14.9 | 15.7 | 14.3 | 10.3 | 5.9 | 4.7 | 35.4 | 189 843 | 79.6 | 31.0 |
| District 20............................ | 7.3 | 18.0 | 12.6 | 14.2 | 12.8 | 12.8 | 11.3 | 5.8 | 5.1 | 33.3 | 205 498 | 73.1 | 26.3 |
| District 21............................ | 9.6 | 22.0 | 12.3 | 15.4 | 13.1 | 11.7 | 8.4 | 4.4 | 3.1 | 28.6 | 214 942 | 57.0 | 8.9 |
| District 22............................ | 8.2 | 21.0 | 10.7 | 13.8 | 12.6 | 12.4 | 10.6 | 5.7 | 5.0 | 32.3 | 218 777 | 78.7 | 22.4 |
| District 23............................ | 7.4 | 20.2 | 10.4 | 14.0 | 12.5 | 14.0 | 10.4 | 6.3 | 4.8 | 33.5 | 199 361 | 82.6 | 18.3 |
| District 24............................ | 5.8 | 15.1 | 15.8 | 12.6 | 11.3 | 13.2 | 12.2 | 7.2 | 6.9 | 35.6 | 210 143 | 83.4 | 31.7 |
| District 25............................ | 7.0 | 21.8 | 10.6 | 12.0 | 14.3 | 15.1 | 10.5 | 5.1 | 3.5 | 33.8 | 230 370 | 84.0 | 25.8 |
| District 26............................ | 6.7 | 18.7 | 10.0 | 12.9 | 12.9 | 14.6 | 11.6 | 6.8 | 5.8 | 36.4 | 201 470 | 81.9 | 31.6 |
| District 27............................ | 5.1 | 15.2 | 8.4 | 12.7 | 14.2 | 15.8 | 13.2 | 7.6 | 7.6 | 41.1 | 182 159 | 84.7 | 40.0 |
| District 28............................ | 4.5 | 11.8 | 8.9 | 17.9 | 15.4 | 15.0 | 12.4 | 7.4 | 6.7 | 39.3 | 157 253 | 85.6 | 42.1 |
| District 29............................ | 7.8 | 18.0 | 11.4 | 16.8 | 13.9 | 13.6 | 9.5 | 4.9 | 4.0 | 32.4 | 192 926 | 66.0 | 17.9 |
| District 30............................ | 5.6 | 14.8 | 9.4 | 15.6 | 14.8 | 14.7 | 11.6 | 7.1 | 6.5 | 38.1 | 185 953 | 88.0 | 40.0 |
| District 31............................ | 8.0 | 20.5 | 11.7 | 15.8 | 12.8 | 12.4 | 9.9 | 4.8 | 4.1 | 30.8 | 228 566 | 79.0 | 22.0 |
| District 32............................ | 6.4 | 18.4 | 11.5 | 13.9 | 13.4 | 14.1 | 10.8 | 6.4 | 5.1 | 34.9 | 204 471 | 73.2 | 19.7 |
| District 33............................ | 4.5 | 14.3 | 10.4 | 13.7 | 14.5 | 15.3 | 12.5 | 7.5 | 7.1 | 40.0 | 187 895 | 95.9 | 62.4 |
| District 34............................ | 6.4 | 16.0 | 11.3 | 17.3 | 15.5 | 13.0 | 10.3 | 5.3 | 4.8 | 34.2 | 181 654 | 61.3 | 19.5 |
| District 35............................ | 7.8 | 21.1 | 12.8 | 14.4 | 15.1 | 12.9 | 8.4 | 4.3 | 3.2 | 30.7 | 223 432 | 68.2 | 13.2 |
| District 36............................ | 6.5 | 18.7 | 8.3 | 12.3 | 12.0 | 12.4 | 11.1 | 9.5 | 9.1 | 38.4 | 176 913 | 78.0 | 19.4 |
| District 37............................ | 6.7 | 14.7 | 11.7 | 17.9 | 14.7 | 12.7 | 10.4 | 5.8 | 5.3 | 34.3 | 197 318 | 77.1 | 35.5 |

1. All persons 3 years old and over enrolled in nursery school through college and graduate or professional school.  2. Persons 25 years old and over.

# Table E. Congressional Districts 113th Congress — **Households and Group Quarters**

| STATE District | Households, 2011 | | | | | | Group quarters, 2010 | | | | | |
|---|---|---|---|---|---|---|---|---|---|---|---|---|
| | Number | Persons per household | Family households (percent) | Married-couple family (percent) | Female family householder[1] | One person households (percent) | Total in group quarters | Percent 65 years and over | Persons in correctional institutions | Persons in nursing homes | Persons in college dormitories | Persons in military quarters |
| | 28 | 29 | 30 | 31 | 32 | 33 | 34 | 35 | 36 | 37 | 38 | 39 |
| UNITED STATES.............. | 114 991 725 | 2.64 | 66.2 | 48.3 | 13.1 | 27.7 | 7 987 323 | 18.3 | 2 263 602 | 1 502 264 | 2 521 090 | 338 191 |
| ALABAMA ......................... | 1 844 546 | 2.54 | 67.9 | 48.2 | 15.3 | 28.2 | 115 816 | 18.7 | 41 177 | 22 995 | 36 341 | 2 152 |
| District 1 ............................. | 264 513 | 2.55 | 69.2 | 47.6 | 16.6 | 27.4 | 12 816 | 19.1 | 5 651 | 2 671 | 2 579 | 0 |
| District 2 ............................. | 257 657 | 2.56 | 67.4 | 47.2 | 16.3 | 28.4 | 22 477 | 15.4 | 13 081 | 3 727 | 3 107 | 1 274 |
| District 3 ............................. | 266 530 | 2.49 | 66.6 | 47.9 | 15.1 | 28.4 | 18 839 | 15.9 | 7 014 | 3 016 | 6 949 | 0 |
| District 4 ............................. | 265 226 | 2.54 | 71.5 | 53.4 | 13.2 | 25.8 | 8 631 | 39.0 | 2 922 | 3 652 | 791 | 0 |
| District 5 ............................. | 272 667 | 2.47 | 66.8 | 50.2 | 12.2 | 29.0 | 15 570 | 17.5 | 5 087 | 2 879 | 5 347 | 823 |
| District 6 ............................. | 260 763 | 2.59 | 70.4 | 55.8 | 11.3 | 26.2 | 11 242 | 23.8 | 4 884 | 2 733 | 2 830 | 0 |
| District 7 ............................. | 257 190 | 2.58 | 63.1 | 35.2 | 22.8 | 32.4 | 26 241 | 15.1 | 2 538 | 4 317 | 14 738 | 55 |
| ALASKA ............................. | 257 330 | 2.71 | 67.3 | 49.5 | 11.8 | 25.2 | 26 352 | 5.9 | 4 206 | 1 626 | 1 872 | 5 055 |
| At Large ............................. | 257 330 | 2.71 | 67.3 | 49.5 | 11.8 | 25.2 | 26 352 | 5.9 | 4 206 | 1 626 | 1 872 | 5 055 |
| ARIZONA ......................... | 2 356 055 | 2.69 | 65.5 | 47.1 | 13.0 | 27.6 | 139 384 | 12.2 | 67 767 | 13 819 | 27 987 | 5 172 |
| District 1 ............................. | 242 220 | 2.89 | 67.8 | 48.7 | 13.3 | 27.1 | 26 292 | 4.2 | 15 071 | 816 | 7 630 | 0 |
| District 2 ............................. | 293 717 | 2.39 | 59.4 | 42.7 | 12.4 | 33.6 | 17 245 | 19.9 | 7 538 | 2 914 | 118 | 3 352 |
| District 3 ............................. | 219 458 | 3.10 | 73.0 | 47.6 | 17.9 | 21.7 | 22 645 | 5.3 | 11 711 | 863 | 6 913 | 0 |
| District 4 ............................. | 268 113 | 2.54 | 66.7 | 53.1 | 10.0 | 27.1 | 25 777 | 6.9 | 19 869 | 1 431 | 1 213 | 1 164 |
| District 5 ............................. | 254 995 | 2.78 | 71.2 | 55.9 | 10.8 | 22.9 | 2 816 | 55.3 | 11 | 859 | 346 | 0 |
| District 6 ............................. | 297 654 | 2.48 | 64.3 | 48.5 | 11.2 | 28.8 | 3 987 | 53.4 | 10 | 1 594 | 274 | 0 |
| District 7 ............................. | 224 614 | 3.18 | 64.8 | 36.7 | 19.4 | 28.0 | 15 957 | 5.2 | 8 915 | 840 | 1 162 | 0 |
| District 8 ............................. | 271 460 | 2.60 | 70.4 | 54.7 | 11.1 | 24.6 | 10 620 | 30.5 | 4 624 | 2 809 | 861 | 656 |
| District 9 ............................. | 283 824 | 2.50 | 55.3 | 36.1 | 12.9 | 32.4 | 14 045 | 12.2 | 18 | 1 693 | 9 470 | 0 |
| ARKANSAS...................... | 1 127 621 | 2.54 | 67.2 | 49.3 | 13.6 | 28.1 | 78 931 | 21.7 | 25 844 | 18 532 | 24 144 | 619 |
| District 1 ............................. | 279 620 | 2.51 | 67.8 | 48.5 | 14.7 | 27.8 | 25 338 | 20.6 | 15 495 | 5 770 | 2 669 | 0 |
| District 2 ............................. | 287 000 | 2.52 | 65.1 | 47.2 | 14.0 | 29.3 | 17 297 | 20.1 | 3 461 | 3 521 | 6 184 | 616 |
| District 3 ............................. | 278 356 | 2.58 | 67.1 | 52.4 | 11.0 | 27.2 | 16 471 | 21.3 | 1 599 | 3 663 | 9 499 | 0 |
| District 4 ............................. | 282 645 | 2.53 | 68.6 | 49.2 | 14.6 | 28.0 | 19 825 | 24.7 | 5 289 | 5 578 | 5 792 | 3 |
| CALIFORNIA.................... | 12 468 743 | 2.96 | 68.3 | 48.6 | 13.7 | 24.5 | 819 816 | 15.4 | 256 807 | 111 884 | 172 843 | 57 628 |
| District 1 ............................. | 270 855 | 2.48 | 64.2 | 47.7 | 11.9 | 28.2 | 22 029 | 14.1 | 11 908 | 2 834 | 2 728 | 5 |
| District 2 ............................. | 271 340 | 2.52 | 62.8 | 47.9 | 11.0 | 29.7 | 22 791 | 13.5 | 9 975 | 2 246 | 2 645 | 393 |
| District 3 ............................. | 236 334 | 2.85 | 70.1 | 51.8 | 12.7 | 22.4 | 22 574 | 9.1 | 12 154 | 1 728 | 4 981 | 1 321 |
| District 4 ............................. | 269 605 | 2.59 | 68.9 | 56.6 | 8.9 | 24.7 | 14 528 | 15.3 | 8 633 | 1 677 | 458 | 0 |
| District 5 ............................. | 258 768 | 2.69 | 64.5 | 44.8 | 13.3 | 27.8 | 15 723 | 22.6 | 1 940 | 3 657 | 3 581 | 0 |
| District 6 ............................. | 256 749 | 2.74 | 59.8 | 36.9 | 16.3 | 31.7 | 9 832 | 19.4 | 2 254 | 1 789 | 1 493 | 0 |
| District 7 ............................. | 252 740 | 2.76 | 67.7 | 49.5 | 12.8 | 25.8 | 12 112 | 23.1 | 6 682 | 1 704 | 22 | 0 |
| District 8 ............................. | 225 740 | 3.03 | 72.9 | 50.4 | 15.5 | 22.4 | 14 962 | 10.8 | 6 717 | 1 325 | 117 | 4 748 |
| District 9 ............................. | 218 704 | 3.17 | 74.5 | 52.1 | 15.4 | 20.9 | 10 787 | 21.5 | 1 358 | 2 403 | 2 194 | 0 |
| District 10 ........................... | 225 443 | 3.12 | 74.4 | 52.3 | 15.3 | 19.9 | 10 988 | 24.1 | 4 848 | 2 580 | 584 | 0 |
| District 11 ........................... | 261 791 | 2.73 | 69.2 | 51.7 | 12.2 | 24.1 | 8 222 | 35.3 | 865 | 3 004 | 1 568 | 0 |
| District 12 ........................... | 308 905 | 2.21 | 43.1 | 30.4 | 8.5 | 40.0 | 21 551 | 18.3 | 1 573 | 2 810 | 5 993 | 0 |
| District 13 ........................... | 280 968 | 2.46 | 55.9 | 37.3 | 13.6 | 33.3 | 23 294 | 13.2 | 1 044 | 2 600 | 11 927 | 661 |
| District 14 ........................... | 249 447 | 2.87 | 68.3 | 52.3 | 11.1 | 24.8 | 9 485 | 29.2 | 1 090 | 1 939 | 2 487 | 0 |
| District 15 ........................... | 233 290 | 2.99 | 74.8 | 56.7 | 12.5 | 19.3 | 12 868 | 23.6 | 5 669 | 2 136 | 1 076 | 0 |
| District 16 ........................... | 196 279 | 3.53 | 76.9 | 48.2 | 20.4 | 18.3 | 20 070 | 11.0 | 12 113 | 2 113 | 1 443 | 0 |
| District 17 ........................... | 237 901 | 3.01 | 73.5 | 59.6 | 10.0 | 20.1 | 9 165 | 20.8 | 2 564 | 1 666 | 2 592 | 0 |
| District 18 ........................... | 267 814 | 2.63 | 67.8 | 55.1 | 8.6 | 24.8 | 12 929 | 24.9 | 4 | 2 889 | 6 712 | 5 |
| District 19 ........................... | 214 219 | 3.19 | 72.9 | 52.2 | 13.6 | 20.1 | 11 722 | 11.7 | 1 448 | 916 | 3 356 | 0 |
| District 20 ........................... | 219 586 | 3.08 | 69.4 | 50.4 | 12.4 | 23.3 | 29 930 | 8.9 | 11 516 | 2 072 | 8 411 | 2 504 |
| District 21 ........................... | 180 751 | 3.68 | 81.0 | 51.9 | 19.0 | 14.9 | 50 896 | 4.1 | 44 549 | 1 252 | 239 | 2 038 |
| District 22 ........................... | 229 515 | 3.06 | 72.3 | 50.4 | 14.5 | 22.1 | 6 647 | 28.5 | 1 349 | 1 709 | 1 566 | 0 |
| District 23 ........................... | 231 729 | 2.96 | 72.6 | 49.8 | 15.9 | 22.2 | 23 285 | 9.1 | 17 160 | 2 293 | 560 | 329 |
| District 24 ........................... | 246 667 | 2.75 | 63.5 | 48.3 | 10.7 | 26.7 | 35 008 | 7.2 | 11 387 | 1 805 | 15 714 | 475 |
| District 25 ........................... | 215 120 | 3.27 | 76.9 | 56.6 | 14.3 | 17.5 | 11 452 | 5.7 | 7 129 | 251 | 1 775 | 0 |
| District 26 ........................... | 225 158 | 3.10 | 72.7 | 54.6 | 12 | 21.4 | 9 971 | 18.2 | 1 535 | 1 644 | 2 316 | 1 349 |
| District 27 ........................... | 244 013 | 2.86 | 69.2 | 51.2 | 12.3 | 24.7 | 13 543 | 25.4 | 331 | 3 659 | 5 809 | 0 |
| District 28 ........................... | 294 002 | 2.37 | 52.2 | 37.0 | 10.7 | 37.0 | 9 845 | 32.8 | 183 | 3 356 | 647 | 0 |
| District 29 ........................... | 194 101 | 3.51 | 72.0 | 44.4 | 19.2 | 21.0 | 6 628 | 35.7 | 307 | 2 842 | 151 | 0 |
| District 30 ........................... | 264 706 | 2.71 | 62.0 | 45.4 | 10.9 | 29.2 | 8 697 | 41.0 | 20 | 2 996 | 2 746 | 0 |
| District 31 ........................... | 217 555 | 3.26 | 73.2 | 49.3 | 17.0 | 21.8 | 16 380 | 15.4 | 5 464 | 2 391 | 2 739 | 0 |
| District 32 ........................... | 192 566 | 3.55 | 79.1 | 53.2 | 17.8 | 16.7 | 8 443 | 29.1 | 74 | 2 895 | 3 298 | 0 |
| District 33 ........................... | 298 129 | 2.29 | 52.7 | 42.0 | 7.1 | 36.7 | 20 240 | 11.2 | 98 | 1 851 | 14 107 | 0 |
| District 34 ........................... | 227 834 | 2.97 | 61.6 | 35.9 | 17.2 | 29.9 | 26 056 | 11.7 | 8 722 | 3 270 | 2 438 | 0 |
| District 35 ........................... | 183 473 | 3.79 | 79.1 | 52.1 | 19.3 | 16.0 | 13 282 | 11.5 | 6 996 | 2 041 | 1 948 | 0 |
| District 36 ........................... | 255 400 | 2.73 | 65.3 | 46.7 | 12.5 | 27.9 | 14 355 | 16.9 | 9 107 | 1 504 | 70 | 0 |
| District 37 ........................... | 265 221 | 2.65 | 55.4 | 33.0 | 16.0 | 34.2 | 14 786 | 14.0 | 155 | 2 263 | 7 976 | 0 |

1. No spouse present.

# Table E. Congressional Districts 113th Congress — **Housing and Money Income**

| STATE District | Housing units, 2011 | | | | | | Money income, 2011 | | |
|---|---|---|---|---|---|---|---|---|---|
| | | Occupied units | | | | | | Households | |
| | | Owner-occupied | | | | Renter-occupied | | | |
| | Total | Percent Occupied | Percent | Median value[1] (dollars) | Percent valued at $500,000 or more | Median rent[2] | Per capita income (dollars) | Median income (dollars) | Percent with income of $100,000 or more |
| | 40 | 41 | 42 | 43 | 44 | 45 | 46 | 47 | 48 |
| UNITED STATES.............. | 132 316 248 | 86.9 | 64.6 | 179 900 | 9.9 | 871 | 26 708 | 50 502 | 20.8 |
| ALABAMA ...................... | 2 182 199 | 84.5 | 69.9 | 123 900 | 3.3 | 687 | 22 711 | 41 415 | 14.7 |
| District 1 .............................. | 325 408 | 81.3 | 69.9 | 129 700 | 3.6 | 757 | 22 830 | 43 258 | 14.6 |
| District 2 .............................. | 307 205 | 83.9 | 68.4 | 114 400 | 2.3 | 678 | 21 785 | 41 360 | 12.9 |
| District 3 .............................. | 317 964 | 83.8 | 68.0 | 116 800 | 2.7 | 654 | 20 805 | 39 261 | 12.0 |
| District 4 .............................. | 311 781 | 85.1 | 75.2 | 100 100 | 3.1 | 587 | 20 169 | 36 336 | 10.8 |
| District 5 .............................. | 305 418 | 89.3 | 71.7 | 139 800 | 3.2 | 646 | 26 344 | 46 886 | 19.9 |
| District 6 .............................. | 292 125 | 89.3 | 75.8 | 169 200 | 6.5 | 855 | 29 637 | 55 897 | 23.2 |
| District 7 .............................. | 322 298 | 79.8 | 60.1 | 91 500 | 1.4 | 663 | 17 365 | 30 327 | 8.4 |
| ALASKA ...................... | 311 182 | 82.7 | 63.1 | 238 300 | 6.7 | 1 049 | 31 405 | 67 825 | 28.9 |
| At Large .............................. | 311 182 | 82.7 | 63.1 | 238 300 | 6.7 | 1 049 | 31 405 | 67 825 | 28.9 |
| ARIZONA ...................... | 2 864 360 | 82.3 | 63.7 | 168 800 | 5.9 | 850 | 23 793 | 46 709 | 17.6 |
| District 1 .............................. | 329 406 | 73.5 | 70.6 | 135 300 | 5.7 | 826 | 20 193 | 43 377 | 14.1 |
| District 2 .............................. | 345 036 | 85.1 | 61.0 | 171 000 | 6.4 | 772 | 26 242 | 44 921 | 16.7 |
| District 3 .............................. | 262 341 | 83.7 | 64.1 | 110 500 | 1.9 | 761 | 16 205 | 37 771 | 11.5 |
| District 4 .............................. | 370 165 | 72.4 | 72.8 | 129 300 | 3.4 | 842 | 20 831 | 40 802 | 12.0 |
| District 5 .............................. | 295 248 | 86.4 | 71.8 | 171 200 | 3.8 | 1 034 | 28 076 | 60 624 | 26.1 |
| District 6 .............................. | 351 355 | 84.7 | 64.3 | 237 200 | 18.4 | 945 | 34 675 | 58 582 | 26.6 |
| District 7 .............................. | 262 952 | 85.4 | 48.1 | 87 200 | 2.1 | 734 | 14 071 | 31 611 | 7.9 |
| District 8 .............................. | 317 939 | 85.4 | 70.2 | 161 000 | 1.9 | 1 007 | 26 886 | 55 454 | 20.6 |
| District 9 .............................. | 329 918 | 86.0 | 50.1 | 168 900 | 7.5 | 842 | 26 554 | 48 033 | 18.7 |
| ARKANSAS...................... | 1 324 471 | 85.1 | 66.6 | 106 300 | 2.1 | 639 | 21 203 | 38 758 | 12.4 |
| District 1 .............................. | 332 471 | 84.1 | 66.8 | 87 800 | 1.6 | 584 | 18 737 | 34 704 | 8.5 |
| District 2 .............................. | 328 430 | 87.4 | 65.7 | 134 300 | 2.9 | 716 | 24 396 | 45 415 | 16.0 |
| District 3 .............................. | 318 843 | 87.3 | 63.6 | 127 100 | 2.6 | 651 | 22 602 | 41 109 | 15.6 |
| District 4 .............................. | 344 727 | 82.0 | 70.2 | 83 700 | 1.5 | 578 | 19 049 | 34 630 | 9.2 |
| CALIFORNIA.................... | 13 721 187 | 90.9 | 54.9 | 355 600 | 31.7 | 1 174 | 27 859 | 57 287 | 26.9 |
| District 1 .............................. | 320 323 | 84.6 | 64.5 | 227 700 | 9.9 | 855 | 22 736 | 41 709 | 15.3 |
| District 2 .............................. | 319 463 | 84.9 | 60.6 | 458 700 | 45.7 | 1 185 | 34 979 | 56 576 | 28.3 |
| District 3 .............................. | 261 456 | 90.4 | 60.0 | 235 400 | 11.3 | 1 026 | 25 137 | 53 602 | 22.4 |
| District 4 .............................. | 352 488 | 76.5 | 72.4 | 306 600 | 17.3 | 1 058 | 31 069 | 61 303 | 27.3 |
| District 5 .............................. | 284 404 | 91.0 | 58.5 | 335 000 | 23.2 | 1 186 | 29 929 | 58 942 | 26.8 |
| District 6 .............................. | 283 267 | 90.6 | 48.8 | 186 400 | 6.5 | 925 | 21 817 | 44 523 | 15.6 |
| District 7 .............................. | 271 789 | 93.0 | 62.4 | 239 200 | 9.3 | 1 072 | 28 290 | 60 537 | 25.7 |
| District 8 .............................. | 303 054 | 74.5 | 65.5 | 152 000 | 4.8 | 999 | 19 726 | 45 879 | 15.8 |
| District 9 .............................. | 240 036 | 91.1 | 60.5 | 202 600 | 7.7 | 969 | 22 155 | 52 209 | 23.5 |
| District 10 ............................ | 240 516 | 93.7 | 59.8 | 181 600 | 4.9 | 981 | 20 678 | 49 660 | 19.0 |
| District 11 ............................ | 281 496 | 93.0 | 63.2 | 446 800 | 44.9 | 1 238 | 37 228 | 69 586 | 35.9 |
| District 12 ............................ | 341 754 | 90.4 | 33.4 | 730 200 | 80.2 | 1 393 | 46 931 | 69 046 | 36.5 |
| District 13 ............................ | 308 249 | 91.1 | 45.0 | 480 700 | 47.4 | 1 139 | 34 295 | 56 906 | 28.3 |
| District 14 ............................ | 265 066 | 94.1 | 58.0 | 668 900 | 74.5 | 1 546 | 38 881 | 79 287 | 40.4 |
| District 15 ............................ | 244 584 | 95.4 | 62.9 | 494 600 | 49.2 | 1 374 | 35 430 | 82 179 | 41.3 |
| District 16 ............................ | 218 706 | 89.7 | 49.4 | 147 300 | 2.9 | 799 | 14 509 | 36 372 | 10.5 |
| District 17 ............................ | 246 663 | 96.4 | 54.6 | 611 900 | 64.1 | 1 590 | 38 017 | 92 030 | 46.4 |
| District 18 ............................ | 279 332 | 95.9 | 60.4 | 838 900 | 82.6 | 1 478 | 53 615 | 97 001 | 49.0 |
| District 19 ............................ | 225 925 | 94.8 | 58.7 | 476 800 | 45.9 | 1 354 | 30 096 | 71 479 | 34.7 |
| District 20 ............................ | 243 506 | 90.2 | 50.7 | 383 900 | 37.7 | 1 218 | 24 123 | 55 752 | 24.0 |
| District 21 ............................ | 196 031 | 92.2 | 50.4 | 134 600 | 3.1 | 779 | 13 734 | 37 228 | 10.5 |
| District 22 ............................ | 247 152 | 92.9 | 59.1 | 191 000 | 6.3 | 895 | 22 286 | 49 844 | 20.1 |
| District 23 ............................ | 264 805 | 87.5 | 61.5 | 173 600 | 3.5 | 884 | 22 529 | 51 232 | 20.8 |
| District 24 ............................ | 275 536 | 89.5 | 52.4 | 424 100 | 41.5 | 1 235 | 28 210 | 56 943 | 26.4 |
| District 25 ............................ | 231 242 | 93.0 | 68.3 | 340 400 | 21.9 | 1 324 | 26 703 | 68 551 | 32.5 |
| District 26 ............................ | 240 077 | 93.8 | 64.4 | 437 900 | 39.4 | 1 371 | 30 970 | 72 804 | 35.0 |
| District 27 ............................ | 261 161 | 93.4 | 54.7 | 553 700 | 57.2 | 1 247 | 32 323 | 63 561 | 30.6 |
| District 28 ............................ | 318 833 | 92.2 | 34.4 | 618 000 | 64.4 | 1 183 | 34 640 | 51 500 | 24.9 |
| District 29 ............................ | 207 656 | 93.5 | 41.6 | 324 800 | 10.1 | 1 077 | 17 273 | 43 780 | 15.0 |
| District 30 ............................ | 284 541 | 93.0 | 53.5 | 484 500 | 47.5 | 1 348 | 36 309 | 67 079 | 32.3 |
| District 31 ............................ | 232 814 | 93.4 | 56.3 | 240 000 | 6.4 | 1 043 | 21 169 | 50 882 | 21.4 |
| District 32 ............................ | 202 587 | 95.1 | 62.8 | 346 600 | 14.4 | 1 178 | 20 572 | 57 062 | 21.6 |
| District 33 ............................ | 326 902 | 91.2 | 48.8 | 907 800 | 84.1 | 1 643 | 60 865 | 89 354 | 46.1 |
| District 34 ............................ | 251 805 | 90.5 | 21.4 | 359 000 | 21.8 | 943 | 16 266 | 32 667 | 9.8 |
| District 35 ............................ | 194 579 | 94.3 | 60.8 | 236 600 | 3.7 | 1 097 | 17 230 | 51 699 | 16.8 |
| District 36 ............................ | 342 399 | 74.6 | 64.4 | 175 800 | 9.1 | 944 | 22 854 | 42 922 | 16.0 |
| District 37 ............................ | 287 951 | 92.1 | 34.4 | 509 400 | 50.9 | 1 183 | 27 714 | 46 081 | 20.8 |

1. Specified owner-occupied units.    2. Specified renter-occupied units.

# Table E. Congressional Districts 113th Congress — Poverty, Labor Force, Employment, and Social Security

| STATE District | Poverty, 2011 (percent) | | | Civilian labor force, 2011 | | | Civilian employment,[2] 2011 | | | | | Social Security beneficiaries, December 2012 | | Supplemental Security Income recipients, December 2012 |
|---|---|---|---|---|---|---|---|---|---|---|---|---|---|---|
| | | | | | Unemployment | | | Percent | | | | | | |
| | Persons below poverty level | Families below poverty level | Households receiving food stamps in past 12 months | Total | Total | Rate[1] | Total | Management, professional, and related occupations | Service, sales, and office | Construction and production | Persons under age 65 with no health insurance, 2010 (percent) | Number | Rate[3] | |
| | 49 | 50 | 51 | 52 | 53 | 54 | 55 | 56 | 57 | 58 | 59 | 60 | 61 | 62 |
| UNITED STATES | 15.9 | 11.7 | 13.0 | 156 460 172 | 16 060 624 | 10.3 | 140 399 548 | 36.0 | 42.8 | 21.2 | 17.3 | 55 289 100 | 177.4 | 8 261 836 |
| ALABAMA | 19.0 | 14.9 | 17.0 | 2 240 441 | 259 346 | 11.6 | 1 981 095 | 32.9 | 41.8 | 25.3 | 16.5 | 1 060 623 | 220.8 | 177 046 |
| District 1 | 18.6 | 15.1 | 16.1 | 319 166 | 36 209 | 11.3 | 282 957 | 32.3 | 44.8 | 22.9 | 18.4 | 153 975 | 223.4 | 22 448 |
| District 2 | 20.1 | 15.4 | 17.5 | 311 835 | 34 971 | 11.2 | 276 864 | 31.5 | 43.4 | 25.1 | 16.2 | 151 773 | 223.6 | 27 552 |
| District 3 | 20.8 | 15.9 | 18.7 | 316 375 | 41 742 | 13.2 | 274 633 | 31.3 | 40.0 | 28.7 | 16.9 | 154 881 | 226.7 | 25 188 |
| District 4 | 19.4 | 15.3 | 18.7 | 297 223 | 34 373 | 11.6 | 262 850 | 28.2 | 38.3 | 33.5 | 17.2 | 175 601 | 257.5 | 26 128 |
| District 5 | 14.9 | 11.1 | 12.9 | 345 178 | 33 271 | 9.6 | 311 907 | 34.8 | 41.2 | 24.0 | 16.6 | 138 153 | 199.8 | 16 981 |
| District 6 | 10.5 | 7.9 | 9.3 | 348 663 | 30 282 | 8.7 | 318 381 | 41.4 | 39.2 | 19.4 | 12.6 | 134 850 | 196.1 | 13 480 |
| District 7 | 29.2 | 24.5 | 26.1 | 302 001 | 48 498 | 16.1 | 253 503 | 28.5 | 46.2 | 25.3 | 17.8 | 151 390 | 219.2 | 45 269 |
| ALASKA | 10.5 | 6.9 | 10.4 | 377 710 | 33 367 | 8.8 | 344 343 | 36.0 | 40.5 | 23.6 | 21.7 | 84 875 | 117.4 | 12 944 |
| At Large | 10.5 | 6.9 | 10.4 | 377 710 | 33 367 | 8.8 | 344 343 | 36.0 | 40.5 | 23.6 | 21.7 | 84 875 | 117.4 | 12 944 |
| ARIZONA | 19.0 | 14.1 | 13.8 | 3 025 208 | 337 217 | 11.1 | 2 687 991 | 34.3 | 47.0 | 18.7 | 19.9 | 1 141 080 | 176.0 | 116 106 |
| District 1 | 23.1 | 16.5 | 16.7 | 308 654 | 43 777 | 14.2 | 264 877 | 31.4 | 46.6 | 22.0 | 21.1 | 132 827 | 183.2 | 19 543 |
| District 2 | 17.3 | 12.1 | 13.7 | 335 094 | 35 946 | 10.7 | 299 148 | 37.7 | 47.3 | 15.0 | 15.8 | 152 448 | 210.9 | 12 936 |
| District 3 | 27.1 | 22.1 | 22.9 | 307 615 | 45 430 | 14.8 | 262 185 | 26.3 | 47.6 | 26.1 | 23.1 | 97 379 | 137.7 | 18 156 |
| District 4 | 17.9 | 12.2 | 13.9 | 271 113 | 37 568 | 13.9 | 233 545 | 28.5 | 51.0 | 20.5 | 18.8 | 185 932 | 262.7 | 11 310 |
| District 5 | 10.1 | 7.5 | 8.5 | 343 992 | 26 092 | 7.6 | 317 900 | 40.8 | 44.6 | 14.6 | 14.0 | 116 216 | 163.2 | 5 427 |
| District 6 | 12.9 | 10.0 | 8.4 | 400 695 | 34 650 | 8.6 | 366 045 | 41.3 | 46.8 | 11.9 | 17.2 | 128 455 | 172.7 | 7 884 |
| District 7 | 32.9 | 29.2 | 26.7 | 326 627 | 44 292 | 13.6 | 282 335 | 20.6 | 48.3 | 31.0 | 31.6 | 75 233 | 103.7 | 23 190 |
| District 8 | 10.6 | 7.6 | 7.3 | 332 743 | 31 073 | 9.3 | 301 670 | 37.2 | 45.2 | 17.6 | 13.9 | 156 542 | 218.7 | 7 572 |
| District 9 | 19.5 | 14.4 | 11.1 | 398 675 | 38 389 | 9.6 | 360 286 | 38.2 | 46.8 | 14.9 | 21.3 | 96 048 | 132.9 | 10 088 |
| ARKANSAS | 19.5 | 14.9 | 15.3 | 1 363 235 | 337 217 | 9.4 | 1 235 755 | 31.1 | 42.1 | 26.9 | 19.9 | 657 841 | 223.9 | 112 119 |
| District 1 | 22.0 | 17.6 | 18.2 | 313 941 | 36 526 | 11.6 | 277 415 | 27.4 | 41.9 | 30.7 | 20.7 | 181 358 | 248.6 | 36 472 |
| District 2 | 16.1 | 11.0 | 13.4 | 368 681 | 32 392 | 8.8 | 336 289 | 37.5 | 42.5 | 20.0 | 17.8 | 149 804 | 202.7 | 26 583 |
| District 3 | 18.5 | 13.0 | 13.2 | 352 308 | 25 332 | 7.2 | 326 976 | 32.5 | 41.2 | 26.3 | 19.4 | 143 546 | 195.8 | 17 634 |
| District 4 | 21.4 | 17.7 | 16.4 | 328 305 | 33 230 | 10.1 | 295 075 | 25.6 | 42.6 | 31.8 | 21.9 | 183 133 | 248.8 | 31 430 |
| CALIFORNIA | 16.6 | 12.4 | 8.3 | 18 737 749 | 2 311 055 | 12.3 | 16 426 694 | 36.7 | 43.2 | 20.2 | 19.9 | 5 280 104 | 140.1 | 1 294 393 |
| District 1 | 19.7 | 13.3 | 10.0 | 303 373 | 43 107 | 14.2 | 260 266 | 35.2 | 45.3 | 19.5 | 20.3 | 174 726 | 249.9 | 33 362 |
| District 2 | 14.1 | 8.8 | 5.7 | 360 788 | 37 671 | 10.4 | 323 117 | 41.7 | 41.9 | 16.5 | 16.5 | 135 735 | 191.8 | 19 887 |
| District 3 | 16.6 | 11.8 | 10.3 | 334 335 | 47 691 | 14.3 | 286 644 | 32.9 | 43.7 | 23.4 | 16.2 | 118 983 | 170.5 | 25 897 |
| District 4 | 10.5 | 7.2 | 5.1 | 338 920 | 44 716 | 13.2 | 294 204 | 39.2 | 44.4 | 16.4 | 13.2 | 156 538 | 219.9 | 13 764 |
| District 5 | 14.1 | 9.2 | 7.2 | 368 300 | 41 527 | 11.3 | 326 773 | 36.7 | 43.6 | 19.7 | 16.9 | 134 226 | 189.2 | 19 864 |
| District 6 | 23.8 | 19.0 | 15.1 | 343 616 | 55 290 | 16.1 | 288 326 | 34.9 | 48.4 | 16.7 | 17.7 | 102 186 | 143.2 | 42 267 |
| District 7 | 12.4 | 8.6 | 8.5 | 363 392 | 50 169 | 13.8 | 313 223 | 41.0 | 44.6 | 14.4 | 13.5 | 104 084 | 146.5 | 21 787 |
| District 8 | 20.4 | 16.2 | 14.2 | 281 345 | 45 825 | 16.3 | 235 520 | 28.0 | 45.0 | 27.0 | 20.1 | 125 880 | 180.0 | 32 310 |
| District 9 | 18.4 | 14.4 | 12.6 | 332 338 | 56 991 | 17.1 | 275 347 | 29.2 | 44.1 | 26.7 | 18.1 | 115 378 | 163.2 | 32 629 |
| District 10 | 20.1 | 15.5 | 13.2 | 337 282 | 60 111 | 17.8 | 277 171 | 27.8 | 43.1 | 29.1 | 18.8 | 97 898 | 137.1 | 24 658 |
| District 11 | 13.9 | 10.0 | 6.8 | 368 699 | 44 497 | 12.1 | 324 202 | 43.6 | 41.2 | 15.3 | 15.2 | 111 819 | 154.7 | 16 579 |
| District 12 | 14.1 | 8.8 | 4.8 | 429 207 | 29 844 | 7.0 | 399 363 | 52.5 | 38.8 | 8.7 | 13.0 | 99 183 | 141.6 | 40 729 |
| District 13 | 17.6 | 13.1 | 8.1 | 382 251 | 42 066 | 11.0 | 340 185 | 47.1 | 38.9 | 14.0 | 15.8 | 90 099 | 126.5 | 32 221 |
| District 14 | 8.2 | 4.8 | 2.5 | 401 366 | 37 907 | 9.4 | 364 019 | 41.3 | 44.5 | 14.2 | 13.3 | 107 347 | 147.7 | 15 695 |
| District 15 | 9.2 | 6.9 | 5.7 | 374 151 | 37 768 | 10.1 | 336 383 | 42.3 | 40.1 | 17.6 | 12.5 | 94 817 | 133.8 | 18 193 |
| District 16 | 31.2 | 26.2 | 21.7 | 294 733 | 49 820 | 16.9 | 244 913 | 19.3 | 43.3 | 37.4 | 24.3 | 92 311 | 129.2 | 38 315 |
| District 17 | 7.9 | 5.1 | 3.9 | 380 099 | 34 000 | 8.9 | 346 099 | 54.0 | 31.6 | 14.4 | 11.7 | 62 967 | 86.9 | 14 220 |
| District 18 | 8.4 | 5.4 | 2.7 | 373 599 | 29 077 | 7.8 | 344 522 | 57.9 | 31.9 | 10.2 | 9.6 | 111 172 | 155.0 | 13 435 |
| District 19 | 13.6 | 9.5 | 8.0 | 368 098 | 44 139 | 12.0 | 323 959 | 35.3 | 43.7 | 21.0 | 16.2 | 90 155 | 129.6 | 27 620 |
| District 20 | 17.1 | 12.1 | 8.1 | 343 082 | 40 551 | 11.8 | 302 531 | 29.7 | 43.1 | 27.2 | 21.5 | 94 983 | 133.4 | 15 337 |
| District 21 | 30.6 | 25.9 | 21.5 | 293 154 | 49 351 | 16.8 | 243 803 | 16.3 | 37.7 | 46.0 | 28.0 | 80 331 | 112.5 | 33 148 |
| District 22 | 19.5 | 15.0 | 15.6 | 339 282 | 49 715 | 14.7 | 289 567 | 32.0 | 42.4 | 25.7 | 20.5 | 89 550 | 125.8 | 20 586 |
| District 23 | 19.4 | 15.4 | 12.3 | 319 733 | 45 614 | 14.3 | 274 119 | 30.5 | 43.2 | 26.3 | 18.7 | 106 552 | 150.6 | 26 500 |
| District 24 | 15.3 | 8.6 | 6.1 | 359 399 | 35 909 | 10.0 | 323 490 | 35.3 | 44.4 | 20.3 | 20.9 | 120 462 | 170.0 | 14 784 |
| District 25 | 13.0 | 10.0 | 7.4 | 345 464 | 42 796 | 12.4 | 302 668 | 36.3 | 43.6 | 20.1 | 15.9 | 82 377 | 115.3 | 16 613 |
| District 26 | 12.1 | 8.7 | 6.7 | 366 217 | 40 287 | 11.0 | 325 930 | 36.0 | 42.3 | 21.6 | 19.4 | 101 184 | 142.9 | 13 012 |
| District 27 | 11.4 | 8.2 | 3.4 | 367 323 | 35 110 | 9.6 | 332 213 | 45.8 | 41.8 | 12.5 | 19.2 | 123 444 | 174.1 | 38 008 |
| District 28 | 15.3 | 10.3 | 4.5 | 405 612 | 45 720 | 11.3 | 359 892 | 46.2 | 41.5 | 12.3 | 24.5 | 96 502 | 136.6 | 49 088 |
| District 29 | 22.9 | 19.6 | 10.8 | 351 784 | 48 123 | 13.7 | 303 661 | 25.5 | 48.0 | 26.5 | 31.2 | 58 026 | 84.5 | 27 865 |
| District 30 | 11.7 | 7.8 | 2.8 | 398 480 | 40 301 | 10.1 | 358 179 | 45.4 | 41.8 | 12.8 | 21.2 | 101 445 | 139.6 | 22 708 |
| District 31 | 19.3 | 14.9 | 13.4 | 345 065 | 52 913 | 15.3 | 292 152 | 32.7 | 44.6 | 22.7 | 21.9 | 73 765 | 101.4 | 22 430 |
| District 32 | 14.5 | 12.3 | 7.6 | 342 003 | 48 184 | 14.1 | 293 819 | 28.4 | 47.5 | 24.1 | 24.7 | 82 574 | 119.0 | 26 172 |
| District 33 | 9.1 | 5.1 | 1.5 | 398 335 | 34 099 | 8.6 | 364 236 | 61.0 | 33.1 | 5.9 | 10.4 | 111 217 | 157.1 | 12 492 |
| District 34 | 29.4 | 25.7 | 10.3 | 367 161 | 57 726 | 15.7 | 309 435 | 22.8 | 49.2 | 28.0 | 38.4 | 71 640 | 102.5 | 44 389 |
| District 35 | 20.2 | 16.4 | 12.5 | 343 483 | 58 731 | 17.1 | 284 752 | 21.7 | 46.4 | 31.8 | 27.3 | 69 774 | 98.2 | 23 020 |
| District 36 | 19.9 | 15.1 | 10.2 | 302 211 | 50 298 | 16.6 | 251 913 | 26.9 | 52.5 | 20.6 | 25.8 | 149 436 | 209.5 | 22 666 |
| District 37 | 21.8 | 18.1 | 9.0 | 381 054 | 45 505 | 11.9 | 335 549 | 39.8 | 44.2 | 16.0 | 26.4 | 81 843 | 113.8 | 31 088 |

1. Percent of civilian labor force.    2. Persons 16 years old and over.    3. Per 1,000 resident population estimated in the 2011 American Community Survey.

| STATE District | Representative, 113th Congress | Land area,[1] 2010 (sq km) | Total persons | Per square kilometer | Race alone — White | Black | American Indian, Alaska Native | Asian and Pacific Islander | Some other race | Two or more races | Hispanic or Latino[2] | Non-Hispanic White alone | Percent female | Percent foreign born | Percent born in state of residence |
|---|---|---|---|---|---|---|---|---|---|---|---|---|---|---|---|
| | | 1 | 2 | 3 | 4 | 5 | 6 | 7 | 8 | 9 | 10 | 11 | 12 | 13 | 14 |
| CALIFORNIA—Cont'd | | | | | | | | | | | | | | | |
| District 38 | Linda T. Sánchez (D) | 263 | 714 100 | 2 717.5 | 47.7 | 4.4 | 0.9 | 14.4 | 29.0 | 3.5 | 61.2 | 18.6 | 50.9 | 31.3 | 58.7 |
| District 39 | Edward R. Royce (R) | 529 | 711 645 | 1 344.3 | 55.1 | 2.4 | 0.4 | 28.6 | 9.8 | 3.7 | 34.6 | 32.3 | 50.3 | 33.1 | 53.0 |
| District 40 | Lucille Roybal-Allard (D) | 149 | 708 460 | 4 741.8 | 56.7 | 5.6 | 0.3 | 2.4 | 33.3 | 1.7 | 86.6 | 5.2 | 50.1 | 41.9 | 53.1 |
| District 41 | Mark Takano (D) | 820 | 722 665 | 881.5 | 62.1 | 9.8 | 1.4 | 5.5 | 17.6 | 3.5 | 59.1 | 23.8 | 50.5 | 24.4 | 62.6 |
| District 42 | Ken Calvert (R) | 2 424 | 717 412 | 295.9 | 69.2 | 6.1 | 0.6 | 9.4 | 10.6 | 4.2 | 33.2 | 48.8 | 49.9 | 18.3 | 60.9 |
| District 43 | Maxine Waters (D) | 187 | 702 983 | 3 768.1 | 40.3 | 23.6 | 0.3 | 13.7 | 18.1 | 4.0 | 45.9 | 15.2 | 52.6 | 31.2 | 53.4 |
| District 44 | Janice Hahn (D) | 206 | 713 249 | 3 470.1 | 49.0 | 15.1 | 0.4 | 5.2 | 25.5 | 4.7 | 70.5 | 7.2 | 51.6 | 34.7 | 56.1 |
| District 45 | John Campbell (R) | 856 | 721 016 | 842.6 | 66.9 | 1.4 | 0.3 | 21.3 | 6.8 | 3.4 | 18.7 | 55.7 | 51.1 | 27.6 | 50.4 |
| District 46 | Loretta Sanchez (D) | 186 | 710 948 | 3 827.5 | 57.3 | 2.3 | 0.5 | 11.5 | 26.0 | 2.4 | 67.4 | 18.0 | 49.5 | 42.4 | 48.0 |
| District 47 | Alan S. Lowenthal (D) | 560 | 719 805 | 1 285.4 | 54.2 | 8.1 | 0.4 | 20.9 | 11.1 | 5.2 | 35.3 | 32.6 | 51.2 | 28.8 | 53.9 |
| District 48 | Dana Rohrabacher (R) | 377 | 711 992 | 1 889.7 | 69.0 | 1.0 | 0.4 | 18.1 | 8.6 | 2.9 | 20.2 | 58.2 | 50.6 | 24.0 | 51.0 |
| District 49 | Darrell E. Issa (R) | 1 432 | 702 141 | 490.2 | 78.1 | 2.4 | 0.4 | 7.3 | 7.2 | 4.6 | 25.7 | 62.0 | 48.5 | 16.8 | 48.3 |
| District 50 | Duncan Hunter (R) | 7 219 | 724 472 | 100.4 | 81.4 | 2.2 | 1.5 | 5.8 | 4.8 | 4.2 | 29.7 | 58.1 | 51.2 | 18.9 | 54.1 |
| District 51 | Juan Vargas (D) | 12 410 | 717 894 | 57.8 | 62.3 | 8.3 | 1.0 | 7.6 | 17.0 | 3.8 | 69.1 | 13.8 | 49.8 | 34.6 | 51.0 |
| District 52 | Scott H. Peters (D) | 692 | 699 398 | 1 011.4 | 69.0 | 3.1 | 0.4 | 19.7 | 2.7 | 5.1 | 13.8 | 59.6 | 49.0 | 22.1 | 43.0 |
| District 53 | Susan A. Davis (D) | 351 | 723 699 | 2 063.3 | 66.6 | 7.4 | 0.6 | 13.7 | 5.8 | 5.9 | 32.3 | 43.0 | 50.3 | 24.2 | 47.9 |
| COLORADO | | 268 431 | 5 116 796 | 19.1 | 84.4 | 4.0 | 1.0 | 2.9 | 4.3 | 3.4 | 20.9 | 69.6 | 49.8 | 9.7 | 42.4 |
| District 1 | Diana DeGette (D) | 491 | 739 601 | 1 506.1 | 74.3 | 8.6 | 1.2 | 3.5 | 9.0 | 3.5 | 29.0 | 56.7 | 50.0 | 14.9 | 43.0 |
| District 2 | Jared Polis (D) | 19 516 | 727 317 | 37.3 | 91.2 | 0.9 | 0.5 | 2.6 | 2.2 | 2.7 | 9.8 | 84.4 | 49.8 | 6.9 | 36.1 |
| District 3 | Scott R. Tipton (R) | 128 805 | 719 526 | 5.6 | 88.2 | 0.9 | 2.3 | 0.8 | 5.1 | 2.8 | 24.3 | 71.4 | 49.5 | 6.0 | 47.4 |
| District 4 | Cory Gardner (R) | 98 685 | 722 690 | 7.3 | 90.7 | 1.3 | 0.9 | 2.1 | 2.8 | 2.3 | 21.8 | 72.9 | 49.2 | 8.4 | 47.5 |
| District 5 | Doug Lamborn (R) | 18 818 | 733 850 | 39.0 | 82.7 | 5.6 | 0.7 | 2.9 | 3.6 | 4.5 | 14.8 | 72.8 | 49.3 | 6.7 | 31.7 |
| District 6 | Mike Coffman (R) | 1 229 | 744 526 | 605.6 | 77.3 | 8.8 | 0.7 | 5.2 | 3.7 | 4.4 | 19.6 | 63.6 | 51.0 | 14.5 | 41.0 |
| District 7 | Ed Perlmutter (D) | 886 | 729 216 | 823.0 | 86.8 | 1.6 | 0.9 | 3.4 | 3.9 | 3.5 | 27.1 | 65.8 | 49.7 | 10.0 | 50.2 |
| CONNECTICUT | | 12 542 | 3 580 709 | 285.5 | 77.8 | 10.0 | 0.2 | 3.9 | 5.5 | 2.5 | 13.8 | 70.7 | 51.3 | 13.4 | 55.5 |
| District 1 | John B. Larson (D) | 1 749 | 715 378 | 408.9 | 72.5 | 14.2 | 0.2 | 5.1 | 5.3 | 2.7 | 15.4 | 64.5 | 52.0 | 15.9 | 58.9 |
| District 2 | Joe Courtney (D) | 5 148 | 711 006 | 138.1 | 87.5 | 4.3 | 0.2 | 2.9 | 2.1 | 3.1 | 6.9 | 83.6 | 49.9 | 6.6 | 56.2 |
| District 3 | Rosa L. DeLauro (D) | 1 218 | 718 549 | 589.9 | 76.0 | 13.1 | 0.1 | 4.0 | 4.8 | 2.0 | 13.2 | 68.4 | 52.0 | 12.2 | 62.5 |
| District 4 | James A. Himes (D) | 1 193 | 726 619 | 608.9 | 74.2 | 12.0 | 0.2 | 5.0 | 6.9 | 1.7 | 17.5 | 64.6 | 51.4 | 19.6 | 43.6 |
| District 5 | Elizabeth H. Esty (D) | 3 233 | 709 157 | 219.4 | 79.1 | 6.6 | 0.3 | 2.9 | 8.2 | 2.9 | 15.9 | 72.6 | 51.2 | 12.2 | 56.5 |
| DELAWARE | | 5 047 | 907 135 | 179.7 | 70.2 | 21.4 | 0.3 | 3.3 | 2.2 | 2.7 | 8.4 | 65.0 | 51.5 | 8.4 | 45.4 |
| At Large | John C. Carney (D) | 5 047 | 907 135 | 179.7 | 70.2 | 21.4 | 0.3 | 3.3 | 2.2 | 2.7 | 8.4 | 65.0 | 51.5 | 8.4 | 45.4 |
| DISTRICT OF COLUMBIA | | 158 | 617 996 | 3 908.5 | 39.9 | 50.1 | 0.3 | 3.6 | 4.0 | 2.1 | 9.5 | 35.2 | 52.7 | 13.5 | 38.2 |
| Delegate District (At Large) | Eleanor Holmes Norton (D) | 158 | 617 996 | 3 908.5 | 39.9 | 50.1 | 0.3 | 3.6 | 4.0 | 2.1 | 9.5 | 35.2 | 52.7 | 13.5 | 38.2 |
| FLORIDA | | 138 887 | 19 057 542 | 137.2 | 76.3 | 16.0 | 0.3 | 2.5 | 2.7 | 2.2 | 22.9 | 57.3 | 51.1 | 19.4 | 35.5 |
| District 1 | Jeff Miller (R) | 10 402 | 703 033 | 67.6 | 77.9 | 13.1 | 0.6 | 2.7 | 1.4 | 4.4 | 5.4 | 74.6 | 50.3 | 5.8 | 40.5 |
| District 2 | Steve Southerland II (R) | 22 309 | 701 463 | 31.4 | 69.3 | 24.5 | 0.4 | 1.8 | 1.2 | 2.7 | 5.5 | 65.6 | 49.8 | 5.5 | 54.9 |
| District 3 | Ted S. Yoho (R) | 18 923 | 700 008 | 37.0 | 79.7 | 13.4 | 0.4 | 2.9 | 1.3 | 2.3 | 8.1 | 73.7 | 49.7 | 7.6 | 49.2 |
| District 4 | Ander Crenshaw (R) | 4 859 | 700 499 | 144.2 | 77.3 | 13.5 | 0.3 | 4.6 | 1.1 | 3.2 | 8.0 | 71.6 | 50.6 | 9.7 | 45.1 |
| District 5 | Corrine Brown (D) | 3 510 | 701 732 | 200.0 | 38.8 | 52.7 | 0.4 | 2.3 | 3.4 | 2.4 | 12.3 | 31.1 | 51.9 | 13.6 | 53.0 |
| District 6 | Ron DeSantis (R) | 6 493 | 709 868 | 109.3 | 84.5 | 9.0 | 0.3 | 1.8 | 2.6 | 1.8 | 7.1 | 80.3 | 51.4 | 7.5 | 35.3 |
| District 7 | John L. Mica (R) | 1 330 | 702 203 | 527.9 | 79.7 | 9.9 | 0.3 | 3.7 | 3.6 | 2.8 | 19.2 | 66.0 | 50.4 | 11.4 | 35.7 |
| District 8 | Bill Posey (R) | 4 538 | 699 857 | 154.2 | 84.3 | 9.7 | 0.2 | 1.7 | 1.4 | 2.7 | 9.5 | 76.8 | 51.2 | 9.2 | 31.4 |
| District 9 | Alan Grayson (D) | 4 422 | 688 665 | 155.7 | 76.5 | 10.7 | 0.4 | 3.7 | 5.8 | 3.0 | 45.7 | 38.9 | 51.3 | 19.5 | 27.9 |
| District 10 | Daniel Webster (R) | 2 925 | 741 792 | 253.6 | 76.1 | 11.9 | 0.3 | 5.0 | 4.3 | 2.4 | 16.2 | 64.7 | 50.7 | 13.8 | 35.4 |
| District 11 | Richard B. Nugent (R) | 6 501 | 700 956 | 107.8 | 86.9 | 9.1 | 0.3 | 1.0 | 1.1 | 1.7 | 8.8 | 80.0 | 51.0 | 6.2 | 31.1 |
| District 12 | Gus M. Bilirakis (R) | 2 289 | 701 580 | 306.5 | 89.1 | 4.7 | 0.3 | 2.9 | 0.9 | 2.1 | 11.6 | 79.1 | 51.6 | 10.2 | 31.4 |
| District 13 | C. W. Bill Young (R) | 482 | 694 899 | 1 442.3 | 87.3 | 5.5 | 0.2 | 3.5 | 1.5 | 1.9 | 9.3 | 79.8 | 51.7 | 11.7 | 29.0 |
| District 14 | Kathy Castor (D) | 687 | 717 231 | 1 043.4 | 63.4 | 26.8 | 0.8 | 3.1 | 3.6 | 2.3 | 27.0 | 42.4 | 50.7 | 16.3 | 44.0 |
| District 15 | Dennis A. Ross (R) | 2 120 | 714 155 | 336.9 | 77.2 | 13.7 | 0.5 | 2.6 | 2.9 | 3.2 | 17.4 | 63.9 | 52.1 | 11.2 | 43.3 |
| District 16 | Vern Buchanan (R) | 2 267 | 702 795 | 310.0 | 87.0 | 6.7 | 0.2 | 1.4 | 3.1 | 1.5 | 11.2 | 79.3 | 52.1 | 12.8 | 25.9 |
| District 17 | Thomas J. Rooney (R) | 16 498 | 694 509 | 42.1 | 83.4 | 8.7 | 0.1 | 1.2 | 4.6 | 2.0 | 18.9 | 69.6 | 50.0 | 13.1 | 33.2 |
| District 18 | Patrick Murphy (D) | 3 917 | 687 549 | 175.5 | 81.3 | 11.6 | 0.2 | 1.9 | 2.8 | 2.2 | 14.1 | 70.6 | 51.3 | 12.6 | 31.2 |
| District 19 | Trey Radel (D) | 1 943 | 696 776 | 358.5 | 85.4 | 7.5 | 0.6 | 1.4 | 3.7 | 1.4 | 16.9 | 72.9 | 51.2 | 14.8 | 24.3 |
| District 20 | Alcee L. Hastings (D) | 6 287 | 713 165 | 113.4 | 39.9 | 52.9 | 0.4 | 1.9 | 2.9 | 2.0 | 20.9 | 23.6 | 51.3 | 31.1 | 41.9 |
| District 21 | Theodore E. Deutch (D) | 676 | 720 995 | 1 066.7 | 80.8 | 12.3 | 0.3 | 3.3 | 1.3 | 2.1 | 19.6 | 63.1 | 52.1 | 24.6 | 25.2 |
| District 22 | Lois Frankel (D) | 448 | 703 505 | 1 571.2 | 82.4 | 10.9 | 0.2 | 2.1 | 2.3 | 2.0 | 20.9 | 64.7 | 50.3 | 23.2 | 28.0 |
| District 23 | Debbie Wasserman Schultz (D) | 438 | 703 594 | 1 606.5 | 75.9 | 11.5 | 0.5 | 3.5 | 6.4 | 2.2 | 38.1 | 46.2 | 51.1 | 36.7 | 29.5 |
| District 24 | Frederica S. Wilson (D) | 275 | 693 086 | 2 522.6 | 37.7 | 56.2 | 0.1 | 1.9 | 2.0 | 2.1 | 29.5 | 13.8 | 52.5 | 38.6 | 42.8 |
| District 25 | Mario Diaz-Balart (R) | 8 373 | 723 113 | 86.4 | 85.2 | 7.6 | 0.2 | 2.1 | 3.4 | 1.5 | 70.4 | 20.6 | 51.6 | 52.7 | 28.2 |
| District 26 | Joe Garcia (D) | 5 435 | 728 285 | 134.0 | 85.7 | 9.8 | 0.3 | 1.5 | 1.6 | 1.1 | 69.5 | 19.7 | 51.0 | 48.0 | 33.1 |
| District 27 | Ileana Ros-Lehtinen (R) | 541 | 712 083 | 1 316.5 | 86.3 | 8.3 | 0.2 | 1.7 | 2.2 | 1.3 | 72.7 | 18.3 | 50.5 | 54.8 | 28.9 |

1. Dry land or land partially or temporarily covered by water.    2. May be of any race.

## Table E. Congressional Districts 113th Congress — **Age and Education**

| STATE District | Under 5 years | 5 to 17 years | 18 to 24 years | 25 to 34 years | 35 to 44 years | 45 to 54 years | 55 to 64 years | 65 to 74 years | 75 years and over | Median age | Total Enrollment[1] | High school graduate or more | Bachelor's degree or more |
|---|---|---|---|---|---|---|---|---|---|---|---|---|---|
| | 15 | 16 | 17 | 18 | 19 | 20 | 21 | 22 | 23 | 24 | 25 | 26 | 27 |
| **CALIFORNIA—Cont'd** | | | | | | | | | | | | | |
| District 38 | 6.6 | 18.9 | 11.3 | 14.3 | 14.0 | 13.0 | 10.5 | 5.7 | 5.6 | 34.2 | 213 211 | 76.6 | 20.9 |
| District 39 | 5.7 | 18.3 | 10.1 | 12.9 | 13.6 | 15.5 | 11.6 | 6.9 | 5.2 | 37.4 | 207 097 | 87.5 | 39.4 |
| District 40 | 8.4 | 23.3 | 11.8 | 14.9 | 15.2 | 11.7 | 8.2 | 3.7 | 2.9 | 29.1 | 224 054 | 50.9 | 8.2 |
| District 41 | 8.1 | 22.1 | 14.0 | 13.7 | 12.8 | 12.5 | 9.1 | 4.4 | 3.3 | 28.7 | 237 804 | 72.2 | 15.4 |
| District 42 | 7.4 | 20.1 | 9.8 | 13.4 | 14.8 | 14.6 | 9.9 | 5.9 | 4.2 | 34.5 | 208 813 | 86.1 | 25.1 |
| District 43 | 7.5 | 18.5 | 10.7 | 14.3 | 14.2 | 13.8 | 10.4 | 5.9 | 4.7 | 34.2 | 205 624 | 76.0 | 23.2 |
| District 44 | 8.7 | 21.6 | 12.0 | 14.9 | 12.8 | 12.8 | 8.8 | 5.0 | 3.5 | 29.9 | 222 983 | 60.6 | 10.8 |
| District 45 | 5.2 | 17.5 | 10.3 | 13.1 | 14.1 | 15.4 | 12.4 | 6.2 | 5.8 | 38.3 | 214 806 | 92.5 | 50.0 |
| District 46 | 8.3 | 19.8 | 12.4 | 16.4 | 14.2 | 12.3 | 8.4 | 4.5 | 3.6 | 30.6 | 212 889 | 64.6 | 16.4 |
| District 47 | 6.7 | 18.0 | 10.7 | 13.9 | 14.7 | 14.6 | 10.4 | 5.8 | 5.3 | 35.5 | 214 861 | 80.5 | 29.2 |
| District 48 | 5.2 | 15.2 | 8.5 | 13.5 | 14.4 | 15.9 | 12.2 | 8.5 | 6.5 | 40.7 | 172 488 | 89.9 | 42.4 |
| District 49 | 7.5 | 16.8 | 10.7 | 13.5 | 14.2 | 13.4 | 11.2 | 6.3 | 6.3 | 36.0 | 179 288 | 89.7 | 38.8 |
| District 50 | 6.4 | 18.8 | 9.2 | 13.1 | 12.8 | 15.0 | 12.6 | 6.4 | 5.8 | 37.1 | 192 673 | 83.6 | 23.7 |
| District 51 | 7.9 | 19.9 | 13.8 | 14.4 | 13.1 | 12.5 | 8.8 | 5.1 | 4.5 | 30.5 | 219 032 | 65.7 | 13.0 |
| District 52 | 5.3 | 14.8 | 12.0 | 16.7 | 13.6 | 14.3 | 11.4 | 6.5 | 5.2 | 35.7 | 195 294 | 94.5 | 54.6 |
| District 53 | 6.2 | 15.4 | 11.1 | 17.3 | 14.1 | 13.4 | 11.3 | 5.8 | 5.6 | 35.1 | 203 929 | 87.7 | 34.0 |
| **COLORADO** | 6.7 | 17.4 | 9.8 | 14.6 | 13.8 | 14.3 | 12.3 | 6.4 | 4.8 | 36.2 | 1 377 803 | 90.2 | 36.7 |
| District 1 | 6.9 | 15.0 | 9.3 | 19.5 | 15.2 | 12.5 | 10.8 | 5.8 | 4.9 | 34.5 | 185 617 | 87.0 | 42.5 |
| District 2 | 5.5 | 15.4 | 13.2 | 13.4 | 13.3 | 14.6 | 13.7 | 6.6 | 4.3 | 36.9 | 214 232 | 95.7 | 51.7 |
| District 3 | 6.4 | 16.9 | 8.9 | 12.8 | 12.5 | 14.5 | 13.9 | 8.1 | 6.0 | 39.0 | 181 286 | 88.7 | 29.9 |
| District 4 | 6.8 | 19.3 | 8.8 | 12.6 | 13.7 | 15.1 | 12.5 | 6.3 | 4.8 | 37.1 | 195 510 | 88.4 | 30.3 |
| District 5 | 6.7 | 17.8 | 10.5 | 14.1 | 13.1 | 14.6 | 12.1 | 6.5 | 4.6 | 35.8 | 206 215 | 93.1 | 33.9 |
| District 6 | 7.8 | 20.0 | 8.4 | 13.9 | 15.9 | 14.1 | 10.7 | 5.4 | 3.9 | 35.0 | 212 138 | 90.8 | 39.1 |
| District 7 | 6.6 | 16.9 | 9.4 | 15.5 | 13.4 | 14.4 | 12.2 | 6.3 | 5.2 | 36.2 | 182 805 | 88.0 | 29.3 |
| **CONNECTICUT** | 5.5 | 17.0 | 9.3 | 12.0 | 13.0 | 16.0 | 12.9 | 7.4 | 7.1 | 40.3 | 943 212 | 89.1 | 36.2 |
| District 1 | 5.9 | 15.9 | 8.8 | 12.7 | 12.9 | 15.3 | 13.2 | 7.4 | 8.0 | 40.6 | 178 011 | 87.5 | 33.9 |
| District 2 | 4.9 | 16.1 | 10.6 | 11.4 | 12.5 | 17.0 | 13.5 | 7.7 | 6.3 | 41.1 | 187 790 | 91.8 | 32.7 |
| District 3 | 5.2 | 16.0 | 10.5 | 13.0 | 12.8 | 15.1 | 12.4 | 7.5 | 7.5 | 39.2 | 190 081 | 89.6 | 33.6 |
| District 4 | 6.3 | 18.8 | 8.0 | 11.6 | 13.7 | 16.1 | 12.0 | 6.7 | 6.9 | 39.3 | 200 641 | 88.6 | 46.5 |
| District 5 | 5.1 | 18.0 | 8.6 | 11.1 | 13.3 | 16.5 | 13.4 | 7.6 | 6.5 | 40.9 | 186 689 | 87.9 | 34.3 |
| **DELAWARE** | 6.1 | 16.5 | 10.1 | 12.6 | 12.6 | 14.7 | 12.8 | 8.4 | 6.4 | 39.1 | 237 520 | 87.0 | 28.8 |
| At Large | 6.1 | 16.5 | 10.1 | 12.6 | 12.6 | 14.7 | 12.8 | 8.4 | 6.4 | 39.1 | 237 520 | 87.0 | 28.8 |
| **DISTRICT OF COLUMBIA** | 5.9 | 11.2 | 13.6 | 21.6 | 13.4 | 12.2 | 10.9 | 6.1 | 5.2 | 33.4 | 160 469 | 87.2 | 52.5 |
| Delegate District (At Large) | 5.9 | 11.2 | 13.6 | 21.6 | 13.4 | 12.2 | 10.9 | 6.1 | 5.2 | 33.4 | 160 469 | 87.2 | 52.5 |
| **FLORIDA** | 5.6 | 15.3 | 9.4 | 12.3 | 12.7 | 14.4 | 12.8 | 9.3 | 8.3 | 41.1 | 4 682 575 | 85.9 | 25.8 |
| District 1 | 6.3 | 15.6 | 10.9 | 12.9 | 12.0 | 15.0 | 12.9 | 8.1 | 6.3 | 38.7 | 177 416 | 89.1 | 25.5 |
| District 2 | 5.6 | 14.5 | 15.1 | 13.6 | 12.6 | 13.7 | 12.2 | 7.3 | 5.4 | 36.0 | 204 425 | 86.6 | 27.1 |
| District 3 | 5.6 | 14.8 | 14.4 | 12.2 | 12.1 | 13.2 | 12.7 | 8.6 | 6.4 | 38.0 | 194 921 | 86.1 | 23.2 |
| District 4 | 6.0 | 16.0 | 9.7 | 14.8 | 13.4 | 15.3 | 12.6 | 7.0 | 5.4 | 37.5 | 176 701 | 89.3 | 28.4 |
| District 5 | 7.6 | 18.1 | 10.9 | 14.9 | 13.3 | 13.1 | 11.3 | 6.2 | 4.6 | 33.9 | 193 742 | 80.9 | 15.8 |
| District 6 | 4.8 | 15.1 | 9.1 | 9.3 | 11.6 | 14.6 | 14.8 | 11.3 | 9.5 | 45.1 | 162 709 | 87.3 | 25.3 |
| District 7 | 5.6 | 15.8 | 12.1 | 13.4 | 12.4 | 14.9 | 12.5 | 7.2 | 6.2 | 37.7 | 213 908 | 91.3 | 32.6 |
| District 8 | 4.8 | 14.6 | 7.7 | 10.0 | 10.8 | 15.8 | 14.4 | 11.3 | 10.6 | 46.5 | 157 352 | 89.2 | 26.1 |
| District 9 | 6.1 | 18.6 | 10.6 | 14.9 | 14.3 | 14.1 | 10.5 | 6.4 | 4.5 | 34.8 | 196 803 | 85.1 | 21.6 |
| District 10 | 5.8 | 16.2 | 9.1 | 12.2 | 13.8 | 14.4 | 12.2 | 9.0 | 7.3 | 40.0 | 186 953 | 88.1 | 27.7 |
| District 11 | 4.3 | 12.7 | 6.3 | 8.6 | 9.6 | 12.8 | 15.2 | 16.9 | 13.7 | 51.9 | 125 431 | 85.8 | 16.7 |
| District 12 | 5.4 | 15.6 | 7.0 | 10.4 | 12.6 | 14.8 | 14.1 | 10.7 | 9.5 | 44.2 | 164 925 | 90.3 | 24.5 |
| District 13 | 4.4 | 12.3 | 7.1 | 11.6 | 11.9 | 15.6 | 15.0 | 10.8 | 11.3 | 46.8 | 130 767 | 88.7 | 26.0 |
| District 14 | 7.1 | 15.4 | 11.0 | 15.2 | 13.8 | 14.3 | 11.3 | 6.5 | 5.3 | 35.9 | 183 786 | 83.7 | 24.2 |
| District 15 | 6.1 | 17.9 | 10.4 | 12.8 | 13.0 | 14.3 | 12.1 | 7.3 | 6.1 | 37.1 | 199 144 | 85.8 | 24.1 |
| District 16 | 4.6 | 13.2 | 6.5 | 9.0 | 10.4 | 13.2 | 14.8 | 14.4 | 13.9 | 50.1 | 136 390 | 89.3 | 28.3 |
| District 17 | 5.1 | 14.1 | 8.1 | 9.8 | 10.6 | 12.9 | 14.1 | 13.5 | 11.8 | 46.6 | 142 588 | 81.8 | 18.0 |
| District 18 | 4.9 | 14.6 | 7.1 | 9.5 | 11.4 | 15.2 | 13.9 | 11.7 | 11.6 | 46.6 | 150 842 | 88.9 | 28.9 |
| District 19 | 5.0 | 13.6 | 6.9 | 9.8 | 10.3 | 12.8 | 14.6 | 14.7 | 12.3 | 48.6 | 143 830 | 89.5 | 29.1 |
| District 20 | 7.4 | 16.7 | 10.8 | 14.5 | 13.0 | 13.5 | 10.9 | 7.0 | 6.3 | 35.4 | 195 063 | 78.5 | 17.7 |
| District 21 | 4.8 | 16.9 | 7.5 | 9.6 | 13.2 | 14.2 | 11.9 | 9.9 | 11.9 | 43.6 | 181 637 | 90.9 | 33.5 |
| District 22 | 5.2 | 11.9 | 7.4 | 13.2 | 12.8 | 15.8 | 13.6 | 9.2 | 10.9 | 44.7 | 140 609 | 88.2 | 35.6 |
| District 23 | 5.6 | 15.8 | 7.7 | 13.3 | 14.9 | 15.8 | 11.9 | 7.6 | 7.4 | 40.3 | 179 888 | 89.3 | 37.0 |
| District 24 | 7.0 | 16.2 | 10.5 | 16.1 | 13.9 | 13.4 | 11.9 | 6.1 | 4.9 | 35.1 | 196 039 | 77.8 | 19.2 |
| District 25 | 6.4 | 16.1 | 10.1 | 12.7 | 14.9 | 14.6 | 10.7 | 7.3 | 7.0 | 38.6 | 181 369 | 80.4 | 25.3 |
| District 26 | 4.9 | 15.8 | 10.9 | 12.7 | 13.6 | 15.9 | 11.8 | 7.8 | 6.5 | 39.4 | 191 333 | 79.8 | 26.2 |
| District 27 | 5.6 | 15.5 | 9.0 | 12.9 | 14.8 | 14.9 | 10.9 | 8.6 | 7.8 | 39.8 | 174 004 | 75.7 | 27.5 |

1. All persons 3 years old and over enrolled in nursery school through college and graduate or professional school.   2. Persons 25 years old and over.

| STATE District | | Households, 2011 | | | | | Group quarters, 2010 | | | | | |
|---|---|---|---|---|---|---|---|---|---|---|---|---|
| | Number | Persons per household | Family households (percent) | Married-couple family (percent) | Female family householder[1] | One person households (percent) | Total in group quarters | Percent 65 years and over | Persons in correctional institutions | Persons in nursing homes | Persons in college dormitories | Persons in military quarters |
| | 28 | 29 | 30 | 31 | 32 | 33 | 34 | 35 | 36 | 37 | 38 | 39 |
| CALIFORNIA—Cont'd | | | | | | | | | | | | |
| District 38 | 202 653 | 3.48 | 79.9 | 52.8 | 19.2 | 16.4 | 9 032 | 26.5 | 156 | 2 794 | 3 305 | 0 |
| District 39 | 217 100 | 3.24 | 78.7 | 59.8 | 12.7 | 16.2 | 6 748 | 26.5 | 2 | 1 230 | 2 630 | 0 |
| District 40 | 174 117 | 4.05 | 82.7 | 46.2 | 25.1 | 13.3 | 3 676 | 37.5 | 7 | 1 571 | 5 | 0 |
| District 41 | 191 160 | 3.71 | 78.1 | 52.8 | 18.3 | 16.5 | 13 557 | 11.9 | 1 171 | 1 826 | 7 379 | 0 |
| District 42 | 210 843 | 3.37 | 78.8 | 63.2 | 10.5 | 16.3 | 7 838 | 10.4 | 5 652 | 440 | 161 | 0 |
| District 43 | 233 997 | 2.96 | 68.3 | 40.0 | 20.9 | 25.9 | 9 781 | 27.0 | 120 | 2 478 | 3 293 | 0 |
| District 44 | 177 733 | 3.97 | 80.6 | 46.3 | 25.1 | 15.5 | 9 346 | 16.1 | 2 843 | 1 687 | 587 | 20 |
| District 45 | 250 384 | 2.83 | 72.0 | 58.6 | 8.9 | 21.9 | 9 972 | 22.2 | 534 | 789 | 5 705 | 0 |
| District 46 | 181 677 | 3.82 | 77.0 | 50.1 | 18.1 | 17.4 | 14 720 | 19.0 | 4 906 | 2 887 | 1 967 | 0 |
| District 47 | 239 968 | 2.96 | 65.9 | 43.9 | 15.2 | 26.5 | 10 332 | 31.5 | 235 | 2 931 | 2 040 | 2 |
| District 48 | 269 109 | 2.63 | 62.7 | 48.0 | 10.1 | 27.9 | 6 462 | 30.5 | 13 | 1 555 | 1 249 | 14 |
| District 49 | 243 205 | 2.80 | 69.7 | 55.1 | 9.8 | 23.6 | 29 769 | 6.5 | 782 | 1 612 | 7 910 | 16 563 |
| District 50 | 237 038 | 3.02 | 74.2 | 55.8 | 12.8 | 19.1 | 7 634 | 26.3 | 889 | 1 975 | 757 | 0 |
| District 51 | 195 401 | 3.49 | 74.7 | 45.0 | 22.8 | 20.3 | 34 264 | 4.0 | 17 756 | 1 059 | 0 | 11 846 |
| District 52 | 262 849 | 2.56 | 58.3 | 47.5 | 7.4 | 30.5 | 30 029 | 8.6 | 2 774 | 1 881 | 4 151 | 15 213 |
| District 53 | 259 091 | 2.75 | 60.3 | 43.7 | 12.0 | 28.6 | 11 640 | 28.3 | 46 | 3 059 | 3 237 | 142 |
| COLORADO | 1 975 388 | 2.53 | 63.6 | 49.1 | 10.0 | 28.8 | 115 878 | 14.3 | 40 568 | 18 079 | 29 952 | 10 945 |
| District 1 | 316 220 | 2.29 | 49.4 | 35.2 | 10.4 | 39.3 | 16 543 | 12.3 | 3 960 | 2 592 | 4 940 | 0 |
| District 2 | 287 393 | 2.47 | 62.2 | 51.6 | 7.4 | 26.5 | 18 014 | 11.6 | 1 634 | 2 213 | 11 841 | 0 |
| District 3 | 287 348 | 2.44 | 64.3 | 50.8 | 9.3 | 29.1 | 15 327 | 20.4 | 3 982 | 3 460 | 5 041 | 0 |
| District 4 | 262 188 | 2.68 | 70.4 | 56.8 | 8.6 | 23.8 | 21 224 | 12.8 | 13 075 | 2 577 | 3 993 | 0 |
| District 5 | 274 957 | 2.56 | 67.8 | 53.6 | 10.3 | 26.5 | 29 493 | 6.9 | 12 094 | 2 245 | 2 580 | 10 678 |
| District 6 | 268 021 | 2.76 | 69.1 | 52.0 | 11.8 | 26.3 | 6 614 | 32.7 | 3 009 | 2 128 | 0 | 267 |
| District 7 | 279 261 | 2.58 | 64.8 | 46.2 | 12.4 | 28.4 | 8 663 | 28.1 | 2 814 | 2 864 | 1 557 | 0 |
| CONNECTICUT | 1 351 643 | 2.56 | 66.1 | 48.9 | 13.3 | 28.4 | 118 152 | 20.9 | 20 059 | 26 371 | 48 537 | 3 977 |
| District 1 | 283 353 | 2.46 | 64.5 | 45.7 | 14.6 | 30.6 | 18 545 | 33.0 | 1 335 | 6 778 | 5 649 | 0 |
| District 2 | 269 280 | 2.48 | 67.7 | 53.1 | 10.6 | 26.8 | 41 044 | 10.7 | 12 975 | 4 306 | 16 779 | 3 977 |
| District 3 | 273 877 | 2.52 | 64.8 | 44.9 | 15.5 | 29.0 | 26 693 | 17.9 | 902 | 5 257 | 16 566 | 0 |
| District 4 | 259 338 | 2.75 | 67.1 | 51.4 | 12.3 | 28.4 | 13 879 | 31.6 | 1 159 | 4 719 | 5 030 | 0 |
| District 5 | 265 795 | 2.60 | 66.4 | 49.6 | 13.2 | 27.2 | 17 991 | 28.1 | 3 688 | 5 311 | 4 513 | 0 |
| DELAWARE | 333 192 | 2.65 | 68.2 | 48.5 | 14.0 | 25.3 | 24 413 | 16.8 | 6 457 | 4 591 | 10 184 | 283 |
| At Large | 333 192 | 2.65 | 68.2 | 48.5 | 14.0 | 25.3 | 24 413 | 16.8 | 6 457 | 4 591 | 10 184 | 283 |
| DISTRICT OF COLUMBIA | 268 670 | 2.15 | 42.4 | 21.3 | 17.0 | 45.2 | 40 021 | 7.8 | 3 598 | 3 064 | 24 087 | 1 504 |
| Delegate District (At Large) | 268 670 | 2.15 | 42.4 | 21.3 | 17.0 | 45.2 | 40 021 | 7.8 | 3 598 | 3 064 | 24 087 | 1 504 |
| FLORIDA | 7 106 283 | 2.62 | 64.2 | 46.3 | 13.3 | 29.2 | 421 709 | 17.5 | 167 453 | 73 372 | 85 243 | 14 612 |
| District 1 | 262 458 | 2.57 | 66.2 | 49.6 | 12.5 | 28.4 | 29 238 | 8.8 | 10 881 | 2 652 | 4 832 | 8 580 |
| District 2 | 264 224 | 2.46 | 61.6 | 42.6 | 14.1 | 28.4 | 50 594 | 6.9 | 32 671 | 3 280 | 10 370 | 513 |
| District 3 | 256 694 | 2.58 | 64.4 | 47.6 | 12.8 | 27.0 | 36 561 | 9.3 | 21 156 | 3 439 | 9 235 | 0 |
| District 4 | 265 995 | 2.58 | 64.3 | 49.3 | 10.9 | 29.0 | 14 193 | 18.0 | 2 597 | 2 852 | 2 776 | 4 662 |
| District 5 | 248 939 | 2.75 | 63.4 | 33.6 | 24.0 | 29.6 | 21 011 | 10.6 | 10 195 | 2 281 | 1 357 | 0 |
| District 6 | 273 715 | 2.54 | 64.4 | 50.0 | 10.8 | 29.4 | 16 358 | 20.3 | 4 351 | 3 572 | 5 748 | 4 |
| District 7 | 245 241 | 2.78 | 64.2 | 48.6 | 12.2 | 27.8 | 18 305 | 15.3 | 757 | 3 056 | 13 306 | 0 |
| District 8 | 279 531 | 2.47 | 63.1 | 47.4 | 11.7 | 30.5 | 9 529 | 27.2 | 3 105 | 2 612 | 1 259 | 182 |
| District 9 | 240 165 | 2.83 | 72.0 | 46.8 | 20.0 | 21.7 | 6 844 | 24.1 | 3 819 | 1 838 | 245 | 0 |
| District 10 | 270 077 | 2.69 | 65.8 | 51.5 | 9.7 | 26.5 | 14 657 | 16.2 | 3 929 | 2 605 | 315 | 0 |
| District 11 | 293 719 | 2.30 | 66.0 | 52.8 | 9.7 | 28.3 | 21 369 | 15.3 | 16 221 | 2 953 | 312 | 0 |
| District 12 | 275 214 | 2.52 | 66.6 | 52.9 | 9.9 | 28.0 | 7 035 | 40.5 | 1 981 | 2 902 | 1 050 | 0 |
| District 13 | 301 358 | 2.26 | 53.6 | 39.3 | 10.3 | 39.1 | 15 037 | 35.3 | 3 506 | 5 478 | 1 751 | 0 |
| District 14 | 277 667 | 2.53 | 58.4 | 35.6 | 17.6 | 33.4 | 15 595 | 18.8 | 3 483 | 3 007 | 3 375 | 324 |
| District 15 | 249 408 | 2.81 | 68.0 | 50.0 | 14.0 | 25.5 | 14 102 | 15.6 | 854 | 2 303 | 7 847 | 0 |
| District 16 | 305 794 | 2.27 | 62.5 | 49.1 | 9.6 | 30.6 | 9 564 | 38.1 | 2 011 | 3 857 | 1 569 | 0 |
| District 17 | 259 028 | 2.59 | 68.2 | 53.8 | 10.3 | 26.6 | 21 009 | 15.9 | 12 761 | 3 312 | 606 | 0 |
| District 18 | 276 595 | 2.46 | 62.8 | 49.2 | 9.2 | 31.9 | 7 774 | 25.5 | 3 930 | 1 838 | 339 | 2 |
| District 19 | 274 250 | 2.50 | 62.5 | 50.4 | 8.2 | 31.5 | 10 530 | 26.8 | 2 727 | 2 860 | 2 688 | 9 |
| District 20 | 235 911 | 2.94 | 63.7 | 34.4 | 22.1 | 29.4 | 18 239 | 18.4 | 10 719 | 3 611 | 214 | 0 |
| District 21 | 275 503 | 2.61 | 67.1 | 51.2 | 11.9 | 27.8 | 3 161 | 52.8 | 619 | 1 396 | 19 | 0 |
| District 22 | 306 935 | 2.26 | 50.6 | 36.8 | 9.8 | 40.8 | 11 514 | 29.7 | 1 291 | 3 658 | 3 672 | 0 |
| District 23 | 276 867 | 2.52 | 60.4 | 43.9 | 12.1 | 33.2 | 5 037 | 23.7 | 938 | 1 239 | 1 463 | 59 |
| District 24 | 221 790 | 3.06 | 65.2 | 36.1 | 22.8 | 30.1 | 13 743 | 21.9 | 3 004 | 2 733 | 3 132 | 0 |
| District 25 | 215 119 | 3.33 | 76.9 | 53.1 | 17.2 | 17.8 | 9 430 | 12.7 | 5 752 | 717 | 596 | 0 |
| District 26 | 215 211 | 3.32 | 74.0 | 50.9 | 17.2 | 20.8 | 11 713 | 17.9 | 4 186 | 1 100 | 2 657 | 277 |
| District 27 | 238 875 | 2.94 | 66.3 | 44.4 | 15.4 | 28.0 | 9 567 | 24.6 | 9 | 2 221 | 4 510 | 0 |

1. No spouse present.

| STATE District | Housing units, 2011 | | | | | | Money income, 2011 | | |
|---|---|---|---|---|---|---|---|---|---|
| | Total | Percent Occupied | Occupied units | | | | Households | | |
| | | | Owner-occupied | | | Renter-occupied | | | |
| | | | Percent | Median value[1] (dollars) | Percent valued at $500,000 or more | Median rent[2] | Per capita income (dollars) | Median income (dollars) | Percent with income of $100,000 or more |
| | 40 | 41 | 42 | 43 | 44 | 45 | 46 | 47 | 48 |
| CALIFORNIA—Cont'd | | | | | | | | | |
| District 38 | 211 778 | 95.7 | 59.4 | 368 400 | 20.3 | 1 213 | 21 748 | 59 781 | 24.7 |
| District 39 | 227 468 | 95.4 | 68.8 | 488 600 | 47.9 | 1 355 | 31 265 | 76 748 | 37.3 |
| District 40 | 183 807 | 94.7 | 35.5 | 307 100 | 10.3 | 1 018 | 13 035 | 37 876 | 10.1 |
| District 41 | 208 286 | 91.8 | 61.1 | 193 500 | 3.4 | 1 084 | 18 016 | 49 887 | 18.3 |
| District 42 | 228 406 | 92.3 | 72.5 | 278 200 | 9.1 | 1 398 | 25 988 | 71 073 | 32.0 |
| District 43 | 252 411 | 92.7 | 42.3 | 373 000 | 28.1 | 1 097 | 21 139 | 44 230 | 16.8 |
| District 44 | 191 006 | 93.1 | 49.4 | 282 900 | 10.1 | 1 010 | 15 216 | 43 956 | 14.4 |
| District 45 | 263 748 | 94.9 | 66.7 | 562 500 | 58.7 | 1 671 | 39 686 | 89 383 | 45.7 |
| District 46 | 191 953 | 94.6 | 43.5 | 358 400 | 16.9 | 1 278 | 17 789 | 51 899 | 18.8 |
| District 47 | 256 780 | 93.5 | 48.0 | 430 900 | 34.4 | 1 151 | 26 612 | 55 590 | 25.4 |
| District 48 | 288 055 | 93.4 | 58.1 | 608 600 | 64.0 | 1 539 | 41 105 | 76 077 | 38.4 |
| District 49 | 269 086 | 90.4 | 58.5 | 529 400 | 53.1 | 1 473 | 34 718 | 68 129 | 33.4 |
| District 50 | 257 317 | 92.1 | 62.2 | 353 400 | 23.5 | 1 167 | 24 969 | 54 971 | 25.4 |
| District 51 | 217 318 | 89.9 | 43.4 | 218 800 | 4.5 | 919 | 15 761 | 38 528 | 11.8 |
| District 52 | 292 860 | 89.8 | 54.3 | 537 300 | 54.4 | 1 511 | 39 330 | 77 409 | 37.6 |
| District 53 | 282 760 | 91.6 | 50.7 | 367 900 | 21.0 | 1 183 | 28 155 | 59 959 | 25.2 |
| COLORADO | 2 224 661 | 88.8 | 64.4 | 233 700 | 11.2 | 900 | 29 804 | 55 387 | 23.8 |
| District 1 | 338 810 | 93.3 | 51.6 | 249 300 | 12.7 | 853 | 32 826 | 50 168 | 21.9 |
| District 2 | 351 806 | 81.7 | 67.4 | 307 700 | 22.8 | 1 033 | 34 531 | 63 571 | 29.2 |
| District 3 | 360 910 | 79.6 | 68.1 | 201 300 | 13.2 | 828 | 26 077 | 47 012 | 16.7 |
| District 4 | 286 190 | 91.6 | 70.8 | 220 900 | 8.7 | 840 | 28 698 | 57 836 | 26.6 |
| District 5 | 305 209 | 90.1 | 64.1 | 212 700 | 7.6 | 872 | 27 616 | 53 691 | 21.9 |
| District 6 | 285 841 | 93.8 | 67.0 | 243 200 | 7.8 | 989 | 31 367 | 63 513 | 29.6 |
| District 7 | 295 895 | 94.4 | 63.6 | 213 600 | 4.5 | 913 | 27 403 | 55 341 | 21.2 |
| CONNECTICUT | 1 494 042 | 90.5 | 67.4 | 278 700 | 16.8 | 1 021 | 35 932 | 65 753 | 31.3 |
| District 1 | 308 313 | 91.9 | 65.5 | 240 100 | 5.3 | 949 | 32 767 | 60 572 | 27.6 |
| District 2 | 301 315 | 89.4 | 73.4 | 250 700 | 9.3 | 963 | 32 960 | 68 925 | 30.7 |
| District 3 | 301 790 | 90.8 | 63.7 | 261 700 | 8.3 | 1 068 | 31 409 | 61 277 | 27.2 |
| District 4 | 283 596 | 91.4 | 66.1 | 498 300 | 49.8 | 1 235 | 48 487 | 79 097 | 40.9 |
| District 5 | 299 028 | 88.9 | 68.4 | 275 600 | 14.0 | 942 | 33 821 | 63 275 | 30.4 |
| DELAWARE | 409 779 | 81.3 | 71.6 | 236 900 | 6.4 | 960 | 29 123 | 58 814 | 24.7 |
| At Large | 409 779 | 81.3 | 71.6 | 236 900 | 6.4 | 960 | 29 123 | 58 814 | 24.7 |
| DISTRICT OF COLUMBIA | 298 908 | 89.9 | 41.2 | 422 400 | 41.1 | 1 216 | 44 578 | 63 124 | 33.0 |
| Delegate District (At Large) | 298 908 | 89.9 | 41.2 | 422 400 | 41.1 | 1 216 | 44 578 | 63 124 | 33.0 |
| FLORIDA | 9 027 271 | 78.7 | 66.7 | 151 000 | 6.3 | 949 | 24 905 | 44 299 | 16.3 |
| District 1 | 345 455 | 76.0 | 68.5 | 150 700 | 4.5 | 920 | 24 962 | 46 401 | 16.3 |
| District 2 | 339 431 | 77.8 | 62.2 | 150 200 | 3.7 | 868 | 22 507 | 42 107 | 14.7 |
| District 3 | 307 199 | 83.6 | 67.5 | 138 300 | 4.0 | 824 | 21 337 | 42 966 | 13.9 |
| District 4 | 309 578 | 85.9 | 67.5 | 163 800 | 5.0 | 979 | 28 000 | 53 036 | 20.7 |
| District 5 | 309 328 | 80.5 | 53.4 | 99 300 | 2.0 | 823 | 17 379 | 32 772 | 7.6 |
| District 6 | 362 870 | 75.4 | 73.1 | 159 300 | 6.8 | 915 | 26 427 | 43 375 | 16.0 |
| District 7 | 299 878 | 81.8 | 69.7 | 160 400 | 5.9 | 1 016 | 26 251 | 51 007 | 20.2 |
| District 8 | 353 229 | 79.1 | 73.8 | 139 200 | 5.0 | 840 | 26 692 | 45 366 | 16.7 |
| District 9 | 311 255 | 77.2 | 60.4 | 129 100 | 2.2 | 984 | 20 352 | 41 564 | 12.4 |
| District 10 | 336 217 | 80.3 | 68.1 | 154 300 | 6.3 | 984 | 25 561 | 48 832 | 17.2 |
| District 11 | 363 028 | 80.9 | 78.7 | 121 900 | 1.9 | 784 | 21 251 | 37 885 | 8.5 |
| District 12 | 338 647 | 81.3 | 76.5 | 142 100 | 3.8 | 924 | 26 753 | 46 766 | 18.6 |
| District 13 | 392 996 | 76.7 | 67.2 | 137 000 | 6.0 | 919 | 27 882 | 42 827 | 15.6 |
| District 14 | 329 935 | 84.2 | 49.5 | 124 100 | 5.8 | 888 | 23 004 | 38 036 | 13.2 |
| District 15 | 290 387 | 85.9 | 66.5 | 138 900 | 3.1 | 877 | 23 282 | 47 117 | 17.1 |
| District 16 | 400 829 | 76.3 | 71.7 | 159 700 | 8.3 | 917 | 27 928 | 45 622 | 16.3 |
| District 17 | 356 649 | 72.6 | 77.3 | 113 200 | 2.5 | 786 | 21 940 | 40 162 | 11.4 |
| District 18 | 362 378 | 76.3 | 75.3 | 163 100 | 9.3 | 1 004 | 30 041 | 47 516 | 19.2 |
| District 19 | 446 987 | 61.4 | 71.4 | 162 300 | 14.1 | 904 | 30 846 | 47 143 | 19.3 |
| District 20 | 293 051 | 80.5 | 56.1 | 105 600 | 0.9 | 984 | 17 264 | 35 941 | 9.4 |
| District 21 | 328 723 | 83.8 | 77.0 | 188 500 | 6.8 | 1 220 | 29 246 | 51 757 | 22.9 |
| District 22 | 402 325 | 76.3 | 62.3 | 210 400 | 15.7 | 1 121 | 36 639 | 51 227 | 23.2 |
| District 23 | 379 370 | 73.0 | 59.7 | 212 800 | 13.6 | 1 176 | 32 460 | 50 581 | 23.6 |
| District 24 | 271 731 | 81.6 | 52.8 | 131 400 | 4.1 | 960 | 17 842 | 36 062 | 11.2 |
| District 25 | 257 039 | 83.7 | 67.3 | 166 700 | 4.3 | 1 093 | 20 198 | 46 869 | 15.9 |
| District 26 | 261 584 | 82.3 | 69.0 | 197 600 | 6.6 | 1 151 | 21 374 | 48 899 | 18.8 |
| District 27 | 277 172 | 86.2 | 51.2 | 222 700 | 18.3 | 971 | 25 217 | 38 679 | 18.7 |

1. Specified owner-occupied units.   2. Specified renter-occupied units.

# Table E. Congressional Districts 113th Congress — Poverty, Labor Force, Employment, and Social Security

| STATE District | Poverty, 2011 (percent) Persons below poverty level | Families below poverty level | Households receiving food stamps in past 12 months | Civilian labor force, 2011 Total | Unemployment Total | Rate[1] | Civilian employment,[2] 2011 Total | Percent Management, professional, and related occupations | Service, sales, and office | Construction and production | Persons under age 65 with no health insurance, 2010 (percent) | Social Security beneficiaries, December 2012 Number | Rate[3] | Supplemental Security Income recipients, December 2012 |
|---|---|---|---|---|---|---|---|---|---|---|---|---|---|---|
| | 49 | 50 | 51 | 52 | 53 | 54 | 55 | 56 | 57 | 58 | 59 | 60 | 61 | 62 |
| **CALIFORNIA—Cont'd** | | | | | | | | | | | | | | |
| District 38 | 12.4 | 9.9 | 7.2 | 349 133 | 35 862 | 10.3 | 313 271 | 29.8 | 46.1 | 24.2 | 23.0 | 97 683 | 136.8 | 23 557 |
| District 39 | 11.1 | 8.0 | 4.2 | 367 247 | 35 283 | 9.6 | 331 964 | 40.8 | 43.9 | 15.3 | 18.6 | 96 087 | 135.0 | 16 607 |
| District 40 | 28.7 | 26.4 | 16.5 | 324 007 | 43 520 | 13.4 | 280 487 | 15.4 | 45.2 | 39.4 | 34.9 | 63 457 | 89.6 | 29 084 |
| District 41 | 21.7 | 18.0 | 14.9 | 329 472 | 57 566 | 17.5 | 271 906 | 25.2 | 45.6 | 29.2 | 25.9 | 69 973 | 96.8 | 21 152 |
| District 42 | 9.5 | 7.2 | 6.4 | 355 121 | 48 074 | 13.5 | 307 047 | 35.3 | 43.1 | 21.6 | 17.5 | 106 487 | 148.4 | 16 488 |
| District 43 | 23.6 | 19.1 | 10.4 | 341 214 | 38 431 | 11.3 | 302 783 | 29.6 | 46.8 | 23.6 | 26.4 | 85 929 | 122.2 | 32 091 |
| District 44 | 23.3 | 20.1 | 16.9 | 325 869 | 55 257 | 17.0 | 270 612 | 18.4 | 46.5 | 35.1 | 29.3 | 84 349 | 118.3 | 36 393 |
| District 45 | 8.7 | 4.9 | 1.9 | 383 394 | 28 994 | 7.6 | 354 400 | 51.2 | 38.5 | 10.3 | 12.3 | 101 432 | 140.7 | 11 097 |
| District 46 | 19.2 | 16.1 | 11.5 | 354 941 | 40 540 | 11.4 | 314 401 | 20.5 | 49.7 | 29.8 | 29.7 | 66 533 | 93.6 | 24 435 |
| District 47 | 17.2 | 13.1 | 9.4 | 370 355 | 42 710 | 11.5 | 327 645 | 35.8 | 46.0 | 18.2 | 20.4 | 88 150 | 122.5 | 32 001 |
| District 48 | 11.1 | 7.8 | 3.9 | 390 968 | 38 331 | 9.8 | 352 637 | 45.3 | 42.5 | 12.3 | 16.6 | 103 910 | 145.9 | 12 058 |
| District 49 | 12.7 | 9.5 | 3.4 | 330 170 | 30 479 | 9.2 | 299 691 | 42.9 | 44.3 | 12.8 | 16.3 | 101 574 | 144.7 | 8 235 |
| District 50 | 15.5 | 11.4 | 5.5 | 333 315 | 37 075 | 11.1 | 296 240 | 34.2 | 44.4 | 21.4 | 20.6 | 100 336 | 138.5 | 15 674 |
| District 51 | 24.3 | 21.4 | 15.3 | 313 339 | 54 702 | 17.5 | 258 637 | 20.7 | 53.9 | 25.4 | 28.2 | 108 523 | 151.2 | 39 791 |
| District 52 | 9.9 | 5.1 | 2.4 | 378 739 | 28 601 | 7.6 | 350 138 | 54.7 | 37.1 | 8.2 | 11.5 | 101 848 | 145.6 | 14 725 |
| District 53 | 14.3 | 9.7 | 5.5 | 385 171 | 42 481 | 11.0 | 342 690 | 40.4 | 43.8 | 15.9 | 19.5 | 83 224 | 115.0 | 17 667 |
| **COLORADO** | 13.5 | 9.1 | 8.3 | 2 747 663 | 255 244 | 9.3 | 2 492 419 | 40.1 | 41.4 | 18.5 | 16.9 | 748 595 | 146.3 | 70 743 |
| District 1 | 17.0 | 12.3 | 9.6 | 422 809 | 38 420 | 9.1 | 384 389 | 43.6 | 40.5 | 15.8 | 18.4 | 98 826 | 133.6 | 16 304 |
| District 2 | 13.0 | 6.0 | 5.3 | 418 292 | 33 744 | 8.1 | 384 548 | 48.4 | 37.7 | 13.9 | 12.4 | 102 848 | 141.4 | 4 957 |
| District 3 | 14.4 | 10.2 | 10.9 | 368 864 | 37 446 | 10.2 | 331 418 | 33.6 | 43.6 | 22.8 | 20.0 | 135 222 | 187.9 | 14 156 |
| District 4 | 12.7 | 8.9 | 8.0 | 372 600 | 28 506 | 7.7 | 344 094 | 38.4 | 40.1 | 21.5 | 15.8 | 80 437 | 111.3 | 7 549 |
| District 5 | 12.8 | 9.3 | 9.2 | 354 782 | 38 908 | 11.0 | 315 874 | 39.6 | 43.7 | 16.7 | 15.8 | 113 157 | 154.2 | 9 665 |
| District 6 | 11.0 | 8.3 | 7.2 | 406 948 | 37 394 | 9.2 | 369 554 | 41.7 | 41.6 | 16.7 | 16.9 | 109 267 | 146.8 | 8 775 |
| District 7 | 13.4 | 9.1 | 7.9 | 403 368 | 40 826 | 10.1 | 362 542 | 34.2 | 43.1 | 22.7 | 19.3 | 108 838 | 149.3 | 9 337 |
| **CONNECTICUT** | 10.9 | 7.9 | 11.3 | 1 949 486 | 206 992 | 10.6 | 1 742 494 | 40.9 | 42.0 | 17.1 | 10.1 | 640 424 | 178.9 | 61 361 |
| District 1 | 12.5 | 9.3 | 13.8 | 393 152 | 43 312 | 11.0 | 349 840 | 40.9 | 42.8 | 16.2 | 9.9 | 135 797 | 189.8 | 16 511 |
| District 2 | 8.3 | 5.6 | 9.5 | 383 135 | 34 533 | 9.0 | 348 602 | 39.6 | 41.8 | 18.6 | 7.6 | 131 707 | 185.2 | 7 840 |
| District 3 | 11.9 | 9.6 | 11.8 | 399 451 | 46 757 | 11.7 | 352 694 | 40.0 | 42.2 | 17.8 | 9.5 | 130 240 | 181.3 | 13 626 |
| District 4 | 9.7 | 6.5 | 9.2 | 384 642 | 41 623 | 10.8 | 343 019 | 44.8 | 41.6 | 13.6 | 12.3 | 112 594 | 155.0 | 10 086 |
| District 5 | 12.0 | 8.6 | 11.7 | 389 106 | 40 767 | 10.5 | 348 339 | 39.4 | 41.3 | 19.3 | 10.9 | 130 086 | 183.4 | 13 298 |
| **DELAWARE** | 11.9 | 8.0 | 11.9 | 461 640 | 41 275 | 8.9 | 420 365 | 37.6 | 41.9 | 20.5 | 10.9 | 182 065 | 200.7 | 16 494 |
| At Large | 11.9 | 8.0 | 11.9 | 461 640 | 41 275 | 8.9 | 420 365 | 37.6 | 41.9 | 20.5 | 10.9 | 182 065 | 200.7 | 16 494 |
| **DISTRICT OF COLUMBIA** | 18.7 | 15.4 | 14.4 | 350 483 | 39 876 | 11.4 | 310 607 | 60.8 | 31.8 | 7.4 | 7.7 | 77 277 | 125.0 | 26 597 |
| Delegate District (At Large) | 18.7 | 15.4 | 14.4 | 350 483 | 39 876 | 11.4 | 310 607 | 60.8 | 31.8 | 7.4 | 7.7 | 77 277 | 125.0 | 26 597 |
| **FLORIDA** | 17.0 | 12.4 | 14.2 | 9 249 754 | 1 147 856 | 12.4 | 8 101 898 | 33.1 | 49.0 | 18.0 | 25.0 | 4 004 631 | 210.1 | 528 321 |
| District 1 | 14.9 | 11.0 | 13.2 | 338 267 | 34 361 | 10.2 | 303 906 | 33.2 | 47.7 | 19.1 | 19.8 | 148 758 | 211.6 | 16 982 |
| District 2 | 20.0 | 13.7 | 14.9 | 342 220 | 40 733 | 11.9 | 301 487 | 36.3 | 45.6 | 18.1 | 19.2 | 128 290 | 182.9 | 19 986 |
| District 3 | 19.6 | 12.0 | 13.5 | 316 942 | 39 972 | 12.6 | 276 970 | 37.3 | 44.6 | 18.1 | 19.5 | 146 985 | 210.0 | 16 137 |
| District 4 | 12.3 | 8.7 | 10.2 | 371 335 | 41 452 | 11.2 | 329 883 | 37.5 | 45.1 | 17.4 | 18.8 | 123 103 | 175.7 | 12 420 |
| District 5 | 27.2 | 22.9 | 26.0 | 343 681 | 59 708 | 17.4 | 283 973 | 23.8 | 54.2 | 22.0 | 25.6 | 119 503 | 170.3 | 33 318 |
| District 6 | 16.9 | 11.4 | 13.1 | 318 803 | 35 623 | 11.2 | 283 180 | 33.4 | 48.7 | 17.9 | 20.8 | 190 923 | 269.0 | 13 751 |
| District 7 | 12.6 | 7.7 | 8.3 | 360 386 | 37 934 | 10.5 | 322 452 | 40.8 | 45.1 | 14.1 | 20.2 | 121 234 | 172.6 | 11 117 |
| District 8 | 13.9 | 9.0 | 12.2 | 326 264 | 42 837 | 13.1 | 283 427 | 34.2 | 47.9 | 18.0 | 22.2 | 188 763 | 269.7 | 13 549 |
| District 9 | 15.4 | 12.8 | 15.0 | 361 190 | 44 036 | 12.2 | 317 154 | 27.5 | 53.5 | 19.0 | 26.9 | 114 008 | 165.5 | 21 311 |
| District 10 | 15.5 | 11.2 | 11.8 | 372 836 | 41 365 | 11.1 | 331 471 | 34.7 | 49.9 | 15.3 | 20.6 | 148 708 | 200.5 | 14 639 |
| District 11 | 16.4 | 11.3 | 15.1 | 259 627 | 42 226 | 16.3 | 217 401 | 27.3 | 51.7 | 21.0 | 24.4 | 256 954 | 366.6 | 16 016 |
| District 12 | 13.5 | 8.9 | 11.2 | 320 137 | 36 926 | 11.5 | 283 211 | 39.2 | 46.3 | 14.5 | 17.2 | 171 525 | 244.5 | 12 818 |
| District 13 | 13.8 | 9.5 | 11.1 | 347 448 | 38 285 | 11.0 | 309 163 | 36.1 | 46.7 | 17.1 | 24.0 | 175 548 | 252.6 | 13 575 |
| District 14 | 22.9 | 18.6 | 22.2 | 369 053 | 48 385 | 13.1 | 320 668 | 31.8 | 51.0 | 17.2 | 24.8 | 119 745 | 167.0 | 32 793 |
| District 15 | 17.5 | 12.7 | 13.8 | 344 898 | 40 693 | 11.8 | 304 205 | 33.6 | 45.9 | 20.4 | 20.6 | 127 123 | 178.0 | 16 842 |
| District 16 | 13.1 | 8.9 | 8.9 | 312 873 | 36 764 | 11.8 | 276 109 | 33.2 | 50.2 | 16.7 | 24.5 | 205 130 | 291.9 | 9 810 |
| District 17 | 16.9 | 11.6 | 12.4 | 282 196 | 33 540 | 11.9 | 248 656 | 27.9 | 48.6 | 23.5 | 27.4 | 192 493 | 277.2 | 15 420 |
| District 18 | 14.8 | 10.1 | 8.5 | 324 159 | 40 197 | 12.4 | 283 962 | 34.8 | 48.7 | 16.5 | 23.5 | 172 038 | 250.2 | 10 248 |
| District 19 | 14.9 | 9.7 | 9.6 | 306 774 | 41 571 | 13.6 | 265 203 | 30.5 | 51.4 | 18.1 | 26.4 | 187 054 | 268.5 | 10 705 |
| District 20 | 25.5 | 20.7 | 21.7 | 364 405 | 62 278 | 17.1 | 302 127 | 23.3 | 55.8 | 20.9 | 33.9 | 113 976 | 159.8 | 26 398 |
| District 21 | 11.0 | 8.2 | 7.8 | 353 820 | 37 009 | 10.5 | 316 811 | 35.2 | 50.0 | 14.7 | 22.9 | 156 688 | 217.3 | 8 608 |
| District 22 | 16.2 | 12.0 | 9.6 | 375 469 | 43 500 | 11.6 | 331 969 | 38.6 | 45.6 | 15.8 | 25.9 | 148 220 | 210.7 | 10 706 |
| District 23 | 12.2 | 9.2 | 11.9 | 381 892 | 41 951 | 11.0 | 339 941 | 40.4 | 47.2 | 12.4 | 25.2 | 114 538 | 162.8 | 17 302 |
| District 24 | 26.5 | 21.8 | 25.0 | 349 405 | 56 040 | 16.0 | 293 365 | 26.0 | 54.4 | 19.6 | 35.2 | 99 435 | 143.5 | 41 189 |
| District 25 | 18.3 | 14.0 | 19.2 | 369 518 | 43 531 | 11.8 | 325 987 | 28.7 | 50.2 | 21.1 | 37.0 | 109 505 | 151.4 | 32 896 |
| District 26 | 15.6 | 13.0 | 19.3 | 375 562 | 39 916 | 10.6 | 335 646 | 30.4 | 51.3 | 18.3 | 32.1 | 108 426 | 148.9 | 32 645 |
| District 27 | 22.1 | 18.4 | 26.5 | 360 594 | 47 023 | 13.0 | 313 571 | 32.7 | 46.7 | 20.6 | 33.8 | 115 958 | 162.8 | 47 140 |

1. Percent of civilian labor force.    2. Persons 16 years old and over.    3. Per 1,000 resident population estimated in the 2011 American Community Survey.

# Table E. Congressional Districts 113th Congress — **Land Area and Population Characteristics**

| STATE District | Representative, 113th Congress | Land area,[1] 2010 (sq km) | Total persons | Per square kilometer | White | Black | American Indian, Alaska Native | Asian and Pacific Islander | Some other race | Two or more races | Hispanic or Latino[2] | Non-Hispanic White alone | Percent female | Percent foreign born | Percent born in state of residence |
|---|---|---|---|---|---|---|---|---|---|---|---|---|---|---|---|
| | | 1 | 2 | 3 | 4 | 5 | 6 | 7 | 8 | 9 | 10 | 11 | 12 | 13 | 14 |
| GEORGIA | | 148 959 | 9 815 210 | 65.9 | 60.7 | 30.8 | 0.3 | 3.4 | 2.9 | 1.9 | 9.1 | 55.4 | 51.0 | 9.6 | 55.8 |
| District 1 | Jack Kingston (R) | 20 675 | 703 020 | 34.0 | 65.2 | 29.0 | 0.2 | 2.0 | 2.0 | 1.6 | 6.4 | 61.1 | 50.8 | 6.1 | 55.7 |
| District 2 | Sanford D. Bishop Jr. (D) | 24 932 | 699 490 | 28.1 | 44.1 | 50.2 | 0.1 | 1.3 | 2.1 | 2.1 | 4.9 | 41.9 | 51.0 | 3.8 | 71.4 |
| District 3 | Lynn A. Westmoreland (R) | 9 941 | 687 745 | 69.2 | 71.8 | 23.6 | 0.1 | 1.5 | 0.9 | 2.1 | 5.6 | 67.5 | 51.4 | 5.1 | 61.6 |
| District 4 | Henry C. "Hank" Johnson Jr. (D) | 1 286 | 720 228 | 560.0 | 31.0 | 56.9 | 0.1 | 4.6 | 5.3 | 2.1 | 10.5 | 26.9 | 52.5 | 16.5 | 48.5 |
| District 5 | John Lewis (D) | 686 | 708 928 | 1 033.3 | 33.4 | 58.3 | 0.2 | 3.8 | 2.3 | 2.0 | 9.2 | 28.3 | 51.2 | 10.2 | 53.2 |
| District 6 | Tom Price (R) | 774 | 699 103 | 903.5 | 72.4 | 13.4 | 0.2 | 9.5 | 2.4 | 2.0 | 11.8 | 64.1 | 49.7 | 19.7 | 35.1 |
| District 7 | Robert Woodall (R) | 1 017 | 687 296 | 675.9 | 57.6 | 19.2 | 0.6 | 11.8 | 8.2 | 2.7 | 17.6 | 49.5 | 50.2 | 22.6 | 34.8 |
| District 8 | Austin Scott (R) | 22 563 | 693 640 | 30.7 | 63.0 | 31.0 | 0.1 | 1.3 | 2.9 | 1.8 | 5.7 | 60.4 | 51.1 | 4.5 | 69.2 |
| District 9 | Doug Collins (R) | 13 496 | 714 378 | 52.9 | 87.1 | 8.0 | 0.2 | 1.0 | 2.6 | 1.0 | 12.3 | 77.9 | 50.4 | 7.4 | 61.3 |
| District 10 | Paul C. Broun (R) | 18 379 | 694 613 | 37.8 | 69.1 | 24.5 | 0.3 | 2.2 | 1.6 | 2.4 | 5.2 | 66.1 | 50.7 | 5.9 | 65.4 |
| District 11 | Phil Gingrey (R) | 2 775 | 689 738 | 248.6 | 75.5 | 15.8 | 0.5 | 2.8 | 3.5 | 1.9 | 11.1 | 68.7 | 51.1 | 11.7 | 45.1 |
| District 12 | John Barrow (D) | 21 200 | 704 537 | 33.2 | 59.1 | 35.1 | 0.2 | 1.7 | 2.3 | 1.6 | 5.4 | 56.5 | 50.6 | 4.2 | 68.6 |
| District 13 | David Scott (D) | 1 852 | 718 096 | 387.8 | 37.7 | 54.2 | 0.3 | 2.9 | 2.6 | 2.3 | 9.8 | 31.1 | 52.6 | 10.6 | 52.3 |
| District 14 | Tom Graves (R) | 9 384 | 694 398 | 74.0 | 85.3 | 9.8 | 0.4 | 0.7 | 2.2 | 1.7 | 10.1 | 78.1 | 50.7 | 6.1 | 58.9 |
| HAWAII | | 16 635 | 1 374 810 | 82.6 | 25.0 | 1.9 | 0.3 | 47.4 | 1.3 | 24.1 | 9.2 | 22.9 | 49.9 | 17.9 | 54.6 |
| District 1 | Colleen Hanabusa (D) | 542 | 690 677 | 1 274.6 | 17.5 | 2.4 | 0.1 | 58.6 | 0.9 | 20.5 | 7.8 | 15.9 | 50.2 | 23.0 | 53.2 |
| District 2 | Tulsi Gabbard (D) | 16 093 | 684 133 | 42.5 | 32.5 | 1.4 | 0.4 | 36.1 | 1.7 | 27.8 | 10.6 | 29.9 | 49.6 | 12.7 | 56.0 |
| IDAHO | | 214 045 | 1 584 985 | 7.4 | 92.5 | 0.5 | 1.3 | 1.4 | 1.8 | 2.5 | 11.5 | 83.5 | 49.8 | 6.0 | 46.5 |
| District 1 | Raul Labrador (R) | 102 092 | 791 876 | 7.8 | 93.2 | 0.4 | 1.5 | 1.3 | 1.3 | 2.3 | 9.8 | 85.2 | 49.7 | 4.7 | 41.1 |
| District 2 | Michael K. Simpson (R) | 111 952 | 793 109 | 7.1 | 91.7 | 0.7 | 1.1 | 1.5 | 2.4 | 2.6 | 13.1 | 81.8 | 50.0 | 7.3 | 51.9 |
| ILLINOIS | | 143 793 | 12 869 257 | 89.5 | 72.5 | 14.5 | 0.2 | 4.7 | 6.1 | 2.0 | 16.2 | 63.1 | 51.0 | 14.0 | 67.0 |
| District 1 | Bobby L. Rush (D) | 669 | 711 982 | 1 063.9 | 40.6 | 51.3 | 0.3 | 2.0 | 4.4 | 1.4 | 9.8 | 35.8 | 53.5 | 6.9 | 76.5 |
| District 2 | Robin L. Kelly (D) | 2 799 | 718 507 | 256.7 | 36.7 | 55.5 | 0.1 | 0.8 | 4.4 | 2.4 | 13.3 | 28.9 | 52.7 | 6.7 | 74.8 |
| District 3 | Daniel Lipinski (D) | 614 | 713 092 | 1 160.8 | 78.8 | 3.8 | 0.3 | 3.3 | 11.7 | 2.0 | 29.4 | 62.4 | 50.4 | 21.1 | 69.6 |
| District 4 | Luis V. Gutierrez (D) | 136 | 737 025 | 5 425.0 | 57.9 | 3.9 | 0.2 | 2.4 | 33.1 | 2.5 | 71.8 | 21.1 | 49.6 | 36.4 | 51.6 |
| District 5 | Michael Quigley (D) | 248 | 712 292 | 2 873.6 | 81.8 | 2.4 | 0.2 | 6.9 | 6.6 | 2.1 | 17.9 | 71.1 | 49.9 | 21.9 | 54.5 |
| District 6 | Peter J. Roskam (R) | 981 | 712 712 | 726.5 | 85.1 | 2.8 | 0.1 | 7.9 | 2.1 | 2.0 | 7.9 | 79.7 | 51.2 | 16.6 | 66.1 |
| District 7 | Danny K. Davis (D) | 162 | 703 012 | 4 341.8 | 32.0 | 54.6 | 0.2 | 5.3 | 6.3 | 1.6 | 13.2 | 25.9 | 53.3 | 11.7 | 65.8 |
| District 8 | Tammy Duckworth (D) | 532 | 724 644 | 1 361.4 | 70.6 | 5.1 | 0.3 | 12.7 | 9.4 | 1.9 | 26.3 | 54.6 | 50.8 | 28.3 | 59.8 |
| District 9 | Janice D. Schakowsky (D) | 273 | 715 584 | 2 622.6 | 73.0 | 9.1 | 0.2 | 12.5 | 2.3 | 2.9 | 10.8 | 65.4 | 50.0 | 27.0 | 52.2 |
| District 10 | Bradley S. Schneider (D) | 776 | 705 564 | 908.7 | 76.6 | 7.0 | 0.1 | 9.6 | 4.4 | 2.3 | 21.6 | 60.5 | 50.3 | 23.7 | 56.3 |
| District 11 | Bill Foster (D) | 728 | 722 745 | 993.3 | 66.5 | 10.8 | 0.2 | 6.9 | 12.3 | 3.3 | 26.6 | 52.9 | 51.2 | 19.9 | 63.2 |
| District 12 | William L. Enyart (D) | 12 971 | 713 289 | 55.0 | 79.0 | 17.1 | 0.2 | 1.1 | 0.5 | 2.2 | 3.0 | 76.6 | 51.1 | 3.0 | 68.1 |
| District 13 | Rodney Davis (R) | 15 005 | 712 716 | 47.5 | 82.7 | 11.3 | 0.1 | 3.5 | 0.5 | 1.9 | 3.1 | 80.4 | 50.8 | 5.2 | 74.1 |
| District 14 | Randy Hultgren (R) | 4 138 | 718 232 | 173.6 | 85.8 | 2.9 | 0.2 | 3.8 | 5.4 | 1.9 | 12.2 | 79.4 | 49.8 | 11.0 | 68.2 |
| District 15 | John Shimkus (R) | 38 062 | 715 066 | 18.8 | 92.6 | 4.6 | 0.2 | 0.5 | 0.5 | 1.6 | 2.4 | 90.9 | 50.2 | 1.5 | 75.7 |
| District 16 | Adam Kinzinger (R) | 20 506 | 713 840 | 34.8 | 91.2 | 4.2 | 0.1 | 1.3 | 1.8 | 1.4 | 8.7 | 84.7 | 50.4 | 5.1 | 77.6 |
| District 17 | Cheri Bustos (D) | 17 957 | 711 719 | 39.6 | 82.9 | 11.5 | 0.4 | 1.0 | 2.1 | 2.1 | 8.0 | 77.6 | 50.9 | 4.4 | 74.0 |
| District 18 | Aaron Schock (R) | 27 236 | 707 238 | 26.0 | 91.4 | 3.9 | 0.2 | 2.4 | 0.6 | 1.4 | 2.3 | 89.8 | 50.6 | 3.8 | 77.8 |
| INDIANA | | 92 789 | 6 516 922 | 70.2 | 84.6 | 9.0 | 0.2 | 1.6 | 2.4 | 2.2 | 6.2 | 81.3 | 50.8 | 4.7 | 68.9 |
| District 1 | Peter J. Visclosky (D) | 2 997 | 722 224 | 241.0 | 70.4 | 19.8 | 0.4 | 1.0 | 6.0 | 2.4 | 14.1 | 63.8 | 50.9 | 6.1 | 59.6 |
| District 2 | Jackie Walorski (R) | 10 253 | 717 237 | 70.0 | 85.7 | 7.1 | 0.3 | 1.1 | 3.7 | 2.2 | 8.4 | 81.5 | 50.8 | 5.4 | 70.0 |
| District 3 | Marlin Stutzman (R) | 10 827 | 722 205 | 66.7 | 88.2 | 6.1 | 0.3 | 1.6 | 1.5 | 2.1 | 5.5 | 84.6 | 50.6 | 4.2 | 73.2 |
| District 4 | Todd Rokita (R) | 16 453 | 729 244 | 44.3 | 91.1 | 3.3 | 0.1 | 2.5 | 1.4 | 1.6 | 5.3 | 87.5 | 49.8 | 5.4 | 69.7 |
| District 5 | Susan W. Brooks (R) | 4 985 | 731 702 | 146.8 | 84.9 | 7.8 | 0.2 | 2.7 | 1.3 | 3.1 | 4.6 | 82.2 | 51.3 | 5.8 | 65.9 |
| District 6 | Luke Messer (R) | 16 076 | 720 186 | 44.8 | 93.8 | 2.1 | 0.1 | 1.0 | 0.8 | 2.1 | 2.3 | 92.6 | 50.6 | 1.9 | 70.8 |
| District 7 | André Carson (D) | 787 | 726 771 | 923.5 | 62.3 | 28.3 | 0.1 | 1.7 | 5.0 | 2.6 | 10.0 | 57.3 | 51.6 | 7.9 | 69.9 |
| District 8 | Larry Bucshon (R) | 18 791 | 720 783 | 38.4 | 92.7 | 3.9 | 0.1 | 1.0 | 0.7 | 1.7 | 2.0 | 91.4 | 50.6 | 2.1 | 76.7 |
| District 9 | Todd C. Young (D) | 11 621 | 726 570 | 62.5 | 92.1 | 2.8 | 0.1 | 1.7 | 1.3 | 2.0 | 2.9 | 90.6 | 50.8 | 3.6 | 64.7 |
| IOWA | | 144 669 | 3 062 309 | 21.2 | 91.5 | 2.9 | 0.4 | 1.8 | 1.4 | 2.0 | 5.2 | 88.4 | 50.6 | 4.4 | 72.5 |
| District 1 | Bruce L. Braley (D) | 31 206 | 763 903 | 24.5 | 92.1 | 3.2 | 0.6 | 1.2 | 1.0 | 2.0 | 3.2 | 90.3 | 50.5 | 2.7 | 77.0 |
| District 2 | David Loebsack (D) | 31 758 | 766 120 | 24.1 | 91.0 | 3.4 | 0.3 | 2.0 | 1.2 | 2.0 | 4.8 | 87.9 | 50.8 | 4.1 | 71.1 |
| District 3 | Tom Latham (R) | 22 765 | 770 819 | 33.9 | 89.9 | 3.7 | 0.3 | 2.6 | 1.4 | 2.1 | 6.3 | 85.6 | 50.8 | 6.2 | 67.8 |
| District 4 | Steve King (R) | 58 940 | 761 467 | 12.9 | 92.9 | 1.2 | 0.4 | 1.6 | 2.0 | 1.8 | 5.8 | 89.7 | 50.4 | 4.4 | 74.1 |
| KANSAS | | 211 754 | 2 871 238 | 13.6 | 85.1 | 5.8 | 0.8 | 2.4 | 2.5 | 3.4 | 10.8 | 77.7 | 50.4 | 6.9 | 59.0 |
| District 1 | Tim Huelskamp (R) | 136 084 | 718 350 | 5.3 | 88.4 | 3.2 | 0.6 | 1.6 | 3.5 | 2.7 | 14.1 | 78.8 | 49.7 | 7.4 | 63.9 |
| District 2 | Lynn Jenkins (R) | 36 631 | 714 459 | 19.5 | 87.7 | 5.1 | 1.3 | 1.4 | 0.9 | 3.6 | 5.9 | 83.5 | 50.3 | 3.6 | 62.6 |
| District 3 | Kevin Yoder (R) | 1 961 | 722 973 | 368.6 | 81.5 | 8.7 | 0.5 | 3.7 | 2.8 | 2.8 | 11.5 | 73.4 | 51.0 | 9.8 | 43.6 |
| District 4 | Mike Pompeo (R) | 37 077 | 715 456 | 19.3 | 82.8 | 6.3 | 1.0 | 2.8 | 2.7 | 4.4 | 11.2 | 75.2 | 50.7 | 6.9 | 66.2 |

1. Dry land or land partially or temporarily covered by water.   2. May be of any race.

# Table E. Congressional Districts 113th Congress — **Age and Education**

| | Population and population characteristics, 2011 (cont.) | | | | | | | | | | Education, 2011 | | |
|---|---|---|---|---|---|---|---|---|---|---|---|---|---|
| | Age (percent) | | | | | | | | | | | Attainment[2] (percent) | |
| STATE District | Under 5 years | 5 to 17 years | 18 to 24 years | 25 to 34 years | 35 to 44 years | 45 to 54 years | 55 to 64 years | 65 to 74 years | 75 years and over | Median age | Total Enrollment[1] | High school graduate or more | Bachelor's degree or more |
| | 15 | 16 | 17 | 18 | 19 | 20 | 21 | 22 | 23 | 24 | 25 | 26 | 27 |
| GEORGIA | 6.9 | 18.5 | 10.4 | 13.5 | 14.2 | 14.2 | 11.4 | 6.5 | 4.4 | 35.5 | 2 782 980 | 84.3 | 27.6 |
| District 1 | 7.1 | 17.5 | 11.5 | 14.3 | 12.9 | 12.9 | 11.6 | 6.9 | 5.2 | 34.6 | 189 203 | 85.1 | 22.8 |
| District 2 | 7.1 | 17.7 | 12.2 | 13.0 | 12.2 | 13.5 | 11.8 | 7.1 | 5.4 | 35.0 | 199 705 | 77.8 | 14.3 |
| District 3 | 6.4 | 19.2 | 9.5 | 11.6 | 13.5 | 15.0 | 12.4 | 7.4 | 5.0 | 37.7 | 193 894 | 84.2 | 24.3 |
| District 4 | 7.6 | 19.2 | 9.8 | 14.4 | 14.9 | 14.2 | 11.3 | 4.8 | 3.8 | 34.2 | 219 825 | 85.6 | 28.8 |
| District 5 | 7.3 | 13.8 | 13.2 | 19.1 | 15.6 | 12.2 | 9.8 | 5.1 | 3.8 | 32.9 | 198 943 | 85.7 | 38.1 |
| District 6 | 6.2 | 18.6 | 7.5 | 14.2 | 15.9 | 15.2 | 12.5 | 6.0 | 3.8 | 37.2 | 193 543 | 93.0 | 56.3 |
| District 7 | 7.8 | 21.1 | 8.7 | 13.4 | 15.4 | 15.4 | 10.1 | 5.3 | 2.8 | 34.3 | 204 816 | 87.2 | 37.8 |
| District 8 | 6.8 | 17.8 | 11.1 | 12.7 | 13.4 | 13.4 | 11.8 | 7.6 | 5.4 | 36.2 | 188 745 | 81.6 | 19.0 |
| District 9 | 6.2 | 18.8 | 9.0 | 11.4 | 13.7 | 14.2 | 11.7 | 9.1 | 5.9 | 38.4 | 187 635 | 79.5 | 19.0 |
| District 10 | 5.3 | 18.8 | 12.1 | 11.5 | 14.3 | 14.5 | 12.0 | 7.1 | 4.5 | 36.6 | 210 468 | 83.5 | 23.0 |
| District 11 | 6.6 | 18.5 | 9.6 | 14.9 | 15.7 | 15.1 | 10.1 | 5.9 | 3.6 | 35.4 | 189 793 | 89.6 | 37.8 |
| District 12 | 7.1 | 17.7 | 12.2 | 13.8 | 12.8 | 13.3 | 11.5 | 7.0 | 4.7 | 34.5 | 198 882 | 82.2 | 19.3 |
| District 13 | 7.8 | 20.9 | 9.7 | 12.7 | 15.0 | 15.1 | 10.7 | 5.0 | 3.1 | 34.3 | 223 168 | 86.1 | 27.3 |
| District 14 | 6.8 | 19.2 | 9.3 | 12.1 | 14.8 | 14.2 | 11.5 | 7.4 | 4.8 | 36.7 | 184 360 | 79.1 | 16.6 |
| HAWAII | 6.4 | 15.7 | 9.5 | 14.0 | 12.8 | 13.7 | 13.0 | 7.8 | 7.1 | 38.5 | 336 724 | 90.6 | 29.1 |
| District 1 | 6.2 | 14.5 | 9.7 | 14.6 | 13.3 | 13.4 | 12.3 | 7.9 | 8.2 | 38.9 | 172 569 | 90.0 | 32.2 |
| District 2 | 6.6 | 17.0 | 9.4 | 13.5 | 12.3 | 14.1 | 13.7 | 7.5 | 5.9 | 38.0 | 164 155 | 91.2 | 25.9 |
| IDAHO | 7.5 | 19.5 | 10.0 | 13.0 | 12.3 | 12.9 | 12.3 | 7.4 | 5.5 | 35.0 | 452 340 | 88.6 | 25.2 |
| District 1 | 7.0 | 19.6 | 8.8 | 12.5 | 12.6 | 13.3 | 12.5 | 8.0 | 5.8 | 36.6 | 215 467 | 88.6 | 24.3 |
| District 2 | 7.9 | 19.4 | 11.3 | 13.5 | 12.1 | 12.6 | 11.2 | 6.7 | 5.3 | 33.0 | 236 873 | 88.6 | 26.2 |
| ILLINOIS | 6.4 | 17.6 | 9.7 | 13.8 | 13.3 | 14.4 | 12.0 | 6.8 | 6.0 | 36.8 | 3 516 919 | 87.2 | 31.0 |
| District 1 | 6.5 | 17.5 | 10.7 | 12.6 | 12.7 | 14.4 | 12.1 | 6.7 | 6.7 | 37.1 | 207 104 | 86.7 | 25.6 |
| District 2 | 6.5 | 20.0 | 9.1 | 12.1 | 12.4 | 14.5 | 12.1 | 7.3 | 5.9 | 37.2 | 210 450 | 85.6 | 21.2 |
| District 3 | 6.3 | 18.7 | 9.1 | 13.5 | 13.3 | 14.5 | 11.9 | 6.1 | 6.5 | 36.9 | 200 661 | 83.6 | 24.9 |
| District 4 | 8.1 | 19.9 | 11.2 | 17.9 | 15.6 | 11.5 | 8.5 | 4.1 | 3.3 | 30.9 | 208 736 | 68.3 | 17.3 |
| District 5 | 5.9 | 12.3 | 9.5 | 23.3 | 14.6 | 12.5 | 10.6 | 6.0 | 5.4 | 34.4 | 165 180 | 89.7 | 50.5 |
| District 6 | 5.6 | 19.7 | 7.6 | 10.7 | 12.7 | 18.1 | 12.8 | 7.1 | 5.7 | 40.4 | 202 902 | 94.2 | 49.7 |
| District 7 | 6.6 | 16.5 | 11.7 | 18.8 | 12.9 | 12.7 | 10.2 | 6.2 | 4.2 | 32.7 | 194 535 | 83.3 | 37.1 |
| District 8 | 7.0 | 18.2 | 8.5 | 16.4 | 13.6 | 14.1 | 12.3 | 5.4 | 4.5 | 35.0 | 190 782 | 85.5 | 32.6 |
| District 9 | 5.9 | 13.9 | 8.6 | 13.9 | 13.4 | 15.1 | 13.3 | 8.2 | 7.7 | 40.8 | 177 389 | 90.0 | 50.2 |
| District 10 | 6.5 | 19.6 | 9.3 | 11.7 | 13.6 | 15.1 | 12.3 | 6.3 | 5.7 | 37.4 | 196 693 | 87.8 | 41.5 |
| District 11 | 7.8 | 20.1 | 9.2 | 14.4 | 15.3 | 13.5 | 10.2 | 5.4 | 4.2 | 33.9 | 214 868 | 86.0 | 34.5 |
| District 12 | 6.2 | 16.8 | 10.6 | 12.7 | 12.3 | 14.5 | 12.5 | 7.5 | 6.9 | 38.5 | 194 319 | 88.4 | 20.9 |
| District 13 | 6.0 | 14.7 | 16.0 | 12.7 | 11.3 | 13.2 | 12.1 | 7.2 | 6.6 | 35.4 | 218 754 | 89.8 | 28.0 |
| District 14 | 6.6 | 21.3 | 7.0 | 10.7 | 16.2 | 16.6 | 11.1 | 6.4 | 4.0 | 38.1 | 213 813 | 92.3 | 37.3 |
| District 15 | 6.0 | 16.7 | 9.2 | 11.6 | 12.2 | 14.9 | 13.1 | 8.5 | 7.8 | 40.4 | 174 200 | 88.1 | 17.5 |
| District 16 | 5.8 | 17.7 | 9.7 | 11.7 | 12.6 | 14.7 | 13.0 | 7.7 | 7.0 | 39.4 | 190 082 | 89.2 | 19.8 |
| District 17 | 6.6 | 16.8 | 9.4 | 12.2 | 11.8 | 14.1 | 13.0 | 8.4 | 7.7 | 39.5 | 175 151 | 86.2 | 16.7 |
| District 18 | 5.6 | 16.9 | 8.5 | 12.2 | 12.8 | 14.5 | 13.5 | 8.1 | 7.8 | 40.3 | 181 300 | 92.9 | 29.9 |
| INDIANA | 6.6 | 17.9 | 10.2 | 12.8 | 12.8 | 14.2 | 12.3 | 7.1 | 6.0 | 37.1 | 1 761 848 | 87.3 | 23.0 |
| District 1 | 6.3 | 18.2 | 8.8 | 13.0 | 12.8 | 14.6 | 13.0 | 7.1 | 6.2 | 37.8 | 193 901 | 87.7 | 21.2 |
| District 2 | 6.9 | 18.5 | 9.6 | 12.0 | 12.7 | 13.8 | 12.9 | 7.1 | 6.6 | 37.4 | 193 358 | 84.8 | 20.1 |
| District 3 | 7.0 | 19.5 | 9.2 | 12.3 | 12.5 | 14.2 | 12.2 | 7.0 | 6.1 | 36.5 | 195 664 | 87.3 | 21.0 |
| District 4 | 6.2 | 17.7 | 12.9 | 12.0 | 12.8 | 13.7 | 11.8 | 7.1 | 5.9 | 36.2 | 212 970 | 88.7 | 23.0 |
| District 5 | 6.3 | 18.7 | 8.5 | 13.1 | 13.9 | 14.9 | 12.2 | 6.7 | 5.8 | 37.7 | 197 805 | 92.4 | 42.8 |
| District 6 | 5.9 | 17.3 | 10.1 | 11.4 | 12.7 | 14.6 | 12.9 | 8.3 | 6.7 | 39.3 | 191 957 | 86.1 | 18.3 |
| District 7 | 8.3 | 18.0 | 10.3 | 16.1 | 13.3 | 13.6 | 10.4 | 5.5 | 4.5 | 33.2 | 196 730 | 82.6 | 19.4 |
| District 8 | 6.4 | 16.5 | 9.9 | 12.3 | 12.2 | 14.7 | 13.3 | 7.9 | 6.9 | 39.3 | 170 009 | 87.6 | 18.2 |
| District 9 | 5.9 | 17.1 | 12.5 | 12.5 | 12.4 | 14.3 | 12.3 | 7.2 | 5.8 | 37.0 | 209 454 | 87.9 | 22.5 |
| IOWA | 6.5 | 17.1 | 10.2 | 12.6 | 11.8 | 14.1 | 12.8 | 7.4 | 7.5 | 38.1 | 809 863 | 90.6 | 25.8 |
| District 1 | 6.1 | 17.0 | 10.4 | 12.0 | 11.9 | 14.2 | 12.8 | 7.7 | 7.8 | 39.0 | 201 607 | 91.1 | 24.9 |
| District 2 | 6.4 | 16.7 | 11.0 | 12.7 | 11.6 | 14.0 | 12.9 | 7.6 | 7.1 | 37.9 | 209 439 | 90.5 | 26.1 |
| District 3 | 7.1 | 17.9 | 8.4 | 14.3 | 13.1 | 14.1 | 12.2 | 6.7 | 6.1 | 36.6 | 195 369 | 91.5 | 31.1 |
| District 4 | 6.2 | 17.0 | 10.8 | 11.5 | 10.7 | 13.9 | 13.0 | 7.8 | 9.0 | 39.4 | 203 448 | 89.4 | 21.0 |
| KANSAS | 7.0 | 18.1 | 10.3 | 13.1 | 12.2 | 13.9 | 12.1 | 6.7 | 6.6 | 36.3 | 801 598 | 90.0 | 30.1 |
| District 1 | 7.1 | 17.7 | 12.1 | 12.3 | 11.3 | 13.2 | 11.8 | 7.0 | 7.5 | 35.7 | 199 586 | 87.1 | 23.2 |
| District 2 | 6.2 | 16.9 | 12.0 | 12.2 | 11.7 | 14.1 | 12.6 | 7.5 | 6.9 | 37.7 | 206 933 | 91.4 | 26.6 |
| District 3 | 7.4 | 19.2 | 7.8 | 14.5 | 13.8 | 14.4 | 11.7 | 5.9 | 5.2 | 35.8 | 198 771 | 92.4 | 43.4 |
| District 4 | 7.4 | 18.8 | 9.5 | 13.2 | 11.8 | 13.9 | 12.2 | 6.7 | 6.5 | 36.1 | 196 308 | 89.2 | 26.9 |

1. All persons 3 years old and over enrolled in nursery school through college and graduate or professional school.   2. Persons 25 years old and over.

| STATE District | Households, 2011 | | | | | | Group quarters, 2010 | | | | | |
|---|---|---|---|---|---|---|---|---|---|---|---|---|
| | Number | Persons per household | Family households (percent) | Married-couple family (percent) | Female family householder[1] | One person households (percent) | Total in group quarters | Percent 65 years and over | Persons in correctional institutions | Persons in nursing homes | Persons in college dormitories | Persons in military quarters |
| | 28 | 29 | 30 | 31 | 32 | 33 | 34 | 35 | 36 | 37 | 38 | 39 |
| GEORGIA | 3 494 542 | 2.74 | 68.0 | 47.7 | 15.5 | 26.6 | 253 199 | 12.5 | 104 012 | 34 738 | 72 288 | 16 072 |
| District 1 | 258 214 | 2.63 | 67.0 | 48.0 | 14.7 | 27.5 | 27 127 | 10.4 | 10 733 | 3 028 | 5 798 | 5 069 |
| District 2 | 249 069 | 2.64 | 66.2 | 39.9 | 21.4 | 29.5 | 36 912 | 8.4 | 17 145 | 3 559 | 7 343 | 5 167 |
| District 3 | 246 847 | 2.74 | 72.9 | 53.9 | 15.1 | 23.2 | 12 530 | 20.6 | 4 777 | 2 837 | 4 020 | 64 |
| District 4 | 241 904 | 2.94 | 68.6 | 41.6 | 21.5 | 26.6 | 7 638 | 17.9 | 4 367 | 1 472 | 653 | 0 |
| District 5 | 273 321 | 2.45 | 48.2 | 24.6 | 17.9 | 41.8 | 37 901 | 5.3 | 6 731 | 2 500 | 22 635 | 78 |
| District 6 | 269 180 | 2.59 | 64.5 | 52.8 | 8.6 | 29.6 | 2 582 | 49.0 | 89 | 1 109 | 620 | 0 |
| District 7 | 220 434 | 3.09 | 76.3 | 57.3 | 13.1 | 20.1 | 6 036 | 18.9 | 4 093 | 1 167 | 0 | 0 |
| District 8 | 252 063 | 2.66 | 67.2 | 47.4 | 15.3 | 28.9 | 25 169 | 13.4 | 13 355 | 4 044 | 5 390 | 401 |
| District 9 | 239 703 | 2.93 | 72.0 | 56.1 | 11.2 | 23.6 | 13 206 | 17.7 | 4 824 | 2 514 | 4 115 | 44 |
| District 10 | 243 380 | 2.76 | 71.6 | 53.0 | 15.0 | 21.3 | 24 558 | 12.0 | 10 678 | 2 840 | 9 699 | 74 |
| District 11 | 255 908 | 2.66 | 67.2 | 50.0 | 13.0 | 25.9 | 10 315 | 14.1 | 3 520 | 1 539 | 4 296 | 36 |
| District 12 | 249 796 | 2.69 | 68.5 | 45.3 | 17.5 | 26.4 | 31 500 | 10.7 | 15 029 | 3 980 | 5 294 | 5 139 |
| District 13 | 248 512 | 2.87 | 71.5 | 46.4 | 20.2 | 23.4 | 5 835 | 21.4 | 3 437 | 1 322 | 0 | 0 |
| District 14 | 246 211 | 2.77 | 73.9 | 55.2 | 13.4 | 22.1 | 11 890 | 21.5 | 5 234 | 2 827 | 2 425 | 0 |
| HAWAII | 448 563 | 2.97 | 69.5 | 51.2 | 12.6 | 24.1 | 42 880 | 12.2 | 5 673 | 5 198 | 7 540 | 12 551 |
| District 1 | 229 582 | 2.91 | 66.5 | 49.3 | 12.0 | 26.9 | 22 094 | 13.3 | 3 581 | 2 672 | 4 641 | 5 332 |
| District 2 | 218 981 | 3.03 | 72.7 | 53.2 | 13.1 | 21.1 | 20 786 | 10.9 | 2 092 | 2 526 | 2 899 | 7 219 |
| IDAHO | 580 193 | 2.68 | 68.7 | 55.0 | 9.3 | 24.8 | 28 951 | 16.9 | 11 275 | 4 820 | 7 223 | 466 |
| District 1 | 291 898 | 2.66 | 70.7 | 57.3 | 9.1 | 22.8 | 17 076 | 15.4 | 7 951 | 2 375 | 4 359 | 0 |
| District 2 | 288 295 | 2.70 | 66.7 | 52.8 | 9.6 | 26.9 | 11 875 | 19.2 | 3 324 | 2 445 | 2 864 | 466 |
| ILLINOIS | 4 737 208 | 2.65 | 65.4 | 47.9 | 13.0 | 29.0 | 301 773 | 22.6 | 70 828 | 81 516 | 92 960 | 12 483 |
| District 1 | 254 693 | 2.75 | 64.5 | 37.3 | 23.0 | 30.9 | 12 277 | 21.7 | 0 | 4 063 | 5 957 | 0 |
| District 2 | 256 882 | 2.75 | 65.5 | 36.7 | 23.1 | 30.5 | 11 056 | 31.1 | 685 | 5 037 | 2 054 | 0 |
| District 3 | 241 423 | 2.92 | 71.2 | 52.5 | 12.8 | 25.4 | 9 893 | 30.2 | 3 160 | 3 740 | 1 890 | 0 |
| District 4 | 220 555 | 3.33 | 69.7 | 42.4 | 17.8 | 22.9 | 3 134 | 34.4 | 1 | 1 268 | 285 | 0 |
| District 5 | 296 383 | 2.37 | 50.3 | 39.7 | 7.5 | 38.7 | 10 575 | 32.7 | 0 | 3 882 | 4 823 | 0 |
| District 6 | 255 337 | 2.76 | 74.8 | 62.8 | 8.7 | 21.9 | 8 897 | 36.8 | 786 | 4 034 | 3 517 | 0 |
| District 7 | 274 826 | 2.47 | 53.2 | 27.6 | 21.1 | 40.0 | 27 985 | 6.3 | 11 612 | 3 240 | 7 992 | 16 |
| District 8 | 254 508 | 2.83 | 68.7 | 52.5 | 11.3 | 26.4 | 4 890 | 45.7 | 0 | 2 564 | 744 | 0 |
| District 9 | 289 945 | 2.39 | 56.6 | 44.8 | 8.3 | 36.6 | 21 885 | 27.4 | 31 | 8 543 | 8 803 | 0 |
| District 10 | 241 721 | 2.83 | 72.9 | 56.7 | 11.4 | 23.8 | 22 648 | 19.5 | 704 | 5 665 | 2 088 | 12 155 |
| District 11 | 237 839 | 3.01 | 73.5 | 55.2 | 13.9 | 22.3 | 7 640 | 33.9 | 1 085 | 2 891 | 1 495 | 0 |
| District 12 | 275 440 | 2.52 | 64.1 | 45.6 | 14.2 | 30.6 | 22 538 | 22.6 | 10 700 | 5 209 | 3 332 | 307 |
| District 13 | 282 675 | 2.37 | 59.2 | 43.4 | 12.0 | 31.4 | 41 813 | 12.5 | 5 125 | 5 481 | 27 454 | 0 |
| District 14 | 246 322 | 2.90 | 76.8 | 64.1 | 8.5 | 19.2 | 4 671 | 33.0 | 1 364 | 1 562 | 158 | 0 |
| District 15 | 277 351 | 2.47 | 67.4 | 53.3 | 10.2 | 28.2 | 25 824 | 23.2 | 12 642 | 6 376 | 3 900 | 0 |
| District 16 | 268 488 | 2.57 | 67.2 | 52.5 | 10.7 | 26.8 | 20 149 | 26.0 | 6 821 | 5 619 | 6 178 | 0 |
| District 17 | 283 514 | 2.43 | 62.9 | 44.7 | 13.9 | 31.8 | 23 198 | 21.2 | 8 864 | 5 921 | 5 835 | 0 |
| District 18 | 279 306 | 2.44 | 66.4 | 54.4 | 8.5 | 28.1 | 22 700 | 27.7 | 7 248 | 6 421 | 6 455 | 5 |
| INDIANA | 2 467 111 | 2.57 | 66.5 | 49.3 | 12.7 | 27.9 | 186 923 | 20.5 | 48 694 | 41 158 | 75 434 | 228 |
| District 1 | 264 966 | 2.66 | 67.9 | 47.4 | 16.5 | 27.8 | 15 644 | 19.0 | 7 380 | 3 116 | 3 194 | 0 |
| District 2 | 267 937 | 2.60 | 68.7 | 51.9 | 12.1 | 26.5 | 22 238 | 20.0 | 5 936 | 4 482 | 8 659 | 0 |
| District 3 | 273 964 | 2.59 | 68.2 | 51.2 | 12.5 | 26.7 | 13 576 | 33.2 | 2 229 | 4 852 | 3 948 | 0 |
| District 4 | 272 135 | 2.57 | 67.5 | 52.4 | 10.4 | 25.7 | 29 932 | 15.3 | 7 233 | 4 934 | 15 651 | 0 |
| District 5 | 284 135 | 2.51 | 67.1 | 51.9 | 11.3 | 27.5 | 15 510 | 25.1 | 4 416 | 4 444 | 5 257 | 0 |
| District 6 | 276 431 | 2.53 | 66.9 | 49.9 | 11.9 | 27.5 | 21 817 | 23.8 | 5 096 | 5 532 | 8 541 | 178 |
| District 7 | 279 428 | 2.55 | 59.5 | 36.3 | 17.8 | 33.1 | 14 636 | 18.3 | 3 216 | 3 152 | 5 162 | 0 |
| District 8 | 273 779 | 2.52 | 67.2 | 51.6 | 11.5 | 28.6 | 30 174 | 19.4 | 10 561 | 5 980 | 10 509 | 50 |
| District 9 | 274 336 | 2.57 | 65.9 | 51.6 | 10.4 | 27 | 23 396 | 17.9 | 2 627 | 4 666 | 14 513 | 0 |
| IOWA | 1 216 765 | 2.44 | 64.5 | 51.4 | 9.2 | 29.5 | 98 112 | 26.1 | 13 309 | 26 871 | 44 574 | 3 |
| District 1 | 305 775 | 2.41 | 64.4 | 52.1 | 8.4 | 29.8 | 27 428 | 26.1 | 2 415 | 7 519 | 13 934 | 3 |
| District 2 | 304 896 | 2.43 | 62.5 | 48.9 | 10.4 | 30.3 | 25 370 | 21.8 | 5 185 | 5 702 | 11 804 | 0 |
| District 3 | 298 737 | 2.52 | 66.3 | 52.1 | 9.9 | 27.7 | 17 672 | 27.7 | 3 690 | 5 218 | 5 248 | 0 |
| District 4 | 307 357 | 2.39 | 64.8 | 52.4 | 8.3 | 30.0 | 27 642 | 29.1 | 2 019 | 8 432 | 13 588 | 0 |
| KANSAS | 1 101 701 | 2.53 | 65.5 | 50.6 | 10.7 | 28.4 | 79 074 | 24.4 | 18 009 | 20 672 | 27 754 | 3 943 |
| District 1 | 275 389 | 2.50 | 64.4 | 52.5 | 8.4 | 29.5 | 29 047 | 23.2 | 5 306 | 7 084 | 10 873 | 3 425 |
| District 2 | 276 162 | 2.48 | 64.8 | 50.0 | 10.2 | 27.9 | 28 892 | 17.4 | 7 436 | 5 478 | 12 652 | 192 |
| District 3 | 277 209 | 2.58 | 67.3 | 51.2 | 12.2 | 27.1 | 6 584 | 49.6 | 1 355 | 3 598 | 544 | 0 |
| District 4 | 272 941 | 2.57 | 65.6 | 48.7 | 12.0 | 29.1 | 14 551 | 29.4 | 3 912 | 4 512 | 3 685 | 326 |

1. No spouse present.

# Table E. Congressional Districts 113th Congress — **Housing and Money Income**

| STATE District | Housing units, 2011 | | | | | | Money income, 2011 | | |
|---|---|---|---|---|---|---|---|---|---|
| | | Occupied units | | | | | | Households | |
| | | | Owner-occupied | | | Renter-occupied | | | |
| | Total | Percent Occupied | Percent | Median value[1] (dollars) | Percent valued at $500,000 or more | Median rent[2] | Per capita income (dollars) | Median income (dollars) | Percent with income of $100,000 or more |
| | 40 | 41 | 42 | 43 | 44 | 45 | 46 | 47 | 48 |
| GEORGIA | 4 103 118 | 85.2 | 64.6 | 147 100 | 4.6 | 833 | 23 604 | 46 007 | 17.7 |
| District 1 | 310 575 | 83.1 | 63.7 | 147 200 | 4.9 | 846 | 21 847 | 43 077 | 13.6 |
| District 2 | 300 679 | 82.8 | 57.5 | 101 500 | 1.5 | 671 | 16 913 | 32 049 | 8.5 |
| District 3 | 278 921 | 88.5 | 69.3 | 155 000 | 4.0 | 831 | 23 569 | 50 155 | 18.2 |
| District 4 | 280 285 | 86.3 | 64.3 | 134 600 | 1.3 | 912 | 21 514 | 47 414 | 16.9 |
| District 5 | 340 752 | 80.2 | 46.8 | 150 200 | 10.7 | 886 | 26 087 | 40 708 | 16.9 |
| District 6 | 291 289 | 92.4 | 63.4 | 285 600 | 15.7 | 1 007 | 40 564 | 72 832 | 37.0 |
| District 7 | 251 725 | 87.6 | 67.3 | 189 300 | 3.9 | 995 | 26 554 | 59 843 | 27.6 |
| District 8 | 296 195 | 85.1 | 64.9 | 111 100 | 1.5 | 698 | 19 415 | 37 232 | 11.7 |
| District 9 | 321 736 | 74.5 | 74.3 | 154 400 | 4.6 | 741 | 19 877 | 41 786 | 14.1 |
| District 10 | 290 382 | 83.8 | 69.8 | 141 200 | 3.1 | 761 | 21 517 | 45 314 | 16.5 |
| District 11 | 285 729 | 89.6 | 63.6 | 185 900 | 8.2 | 884 | 31 423 | 55 813 | 25.6 |
| District 12 | 293 720 | 85.0 | 64.0 | 108 900 | 1.6 | 700 | 19 545 | 39 950 | 12.9 |
| District 13 | 281 294 | 88.3 | 67.3 | 128 600 | 1.6 | 895 | 22 214 | 47 004 | 16.3 |
| District 14 | 279 836 | 88.0 | 70.5 | 115 900 | 2.1 | 674 | 19 687 | 42 700 | 12.4 |
| HAWAII | 522 314 | 85.9 | 56.8 | 487 400 | 48.3 | 1 308 | 27 353 | 61 821 | 27.3 |
| District 1 | 251 523 | 91.3 | 54.1 | 543 000 | 55.7 | 1 341 | 29 320 | 65 602 | 30.9 |
| District 2 | 270 791 | 80.9 | 59.6 | 435 700 | 41.1 | 1 257 | 25 367 | 57 492 | 23.5 |
| IDAHO | 674 394 | 86.0 | 68.7 | 158 800 | 4.0 | 689 | 21 152 | 43 341 | 13.5 |
| District 1 | 341 938 | 85.4 | 71.9 | 164 100 | 4.0 | 722.0 | 21 327 | 45 103 | 13.3 |
| District 2 | 332 456 | 86.7 | 65.6 | 152 600 | 4.0 | 672 | 20 978 | 42 086 | 13.6 |
| ILLINOIS | 5 296 209 | 89.4 | 67.3 | 178 500 | 7.0 | 859 | 27 880 | 53 234 | 22.5 |
| District 1 | 295 248 | 86.3 | 61.4 | 179 600 | 3.4 | 867 | 22 862 | 46 458 | 17.8 |
| District 2 | 300 810 | 85.4 | 64.7 | 135 200 | 1.6 | 878 | 21 575 | 45 572 | 14.7 |
| District 3 | 261 528 | 92.3 | 75.7 | 214 200 | 6.2 | 891 | 25 022 | 56 579 | 21.8 |
| District 4 | 250 681 | 88.0 | 45.5 | 213 200 | 4.6 | 850 | 17 238 | 39 744 | 11.9 |
| District 5 | 327 028 | 90.6 | 53.6 | 313 000 | 21.0 | 1 016 | 40 759 | 62 632 | 30.1 |
| District 6 | 270 391 | 94.4 | 79.8 | 294 700 | 16.9 | 1 086 | 39 728 | 85 655 | 42.7 |
| District 7 | 336 357 | 81.7 | 40.4 | 242 900 | 15.7 | 968 | 28 888 | 44 535 | 20.6 |
| District 8 | 273 386 | 93.1 | 69.3 | 210 900 | 3.5 | 988 | 27 003 | 60 073 | 22.8 |
| District 9 | 317 822 | 91.2 | 62.3 | 309 500 | 19.5 | 938 | 36 736 | 59 321 | 28.4 |
| District 10 | 263 073 | 91.9 | 73.6 | 243 400 | 19.6 | 1 011 | 34 347 | 65 864 | 32.7 |
| District 11 | 259 052 | 91.8 | 73.7 | 204 300 | 5.2 | 996 | 29 519 | 65 938 | 28.6 |
| District 12 | 317 986 | 86.6 | 69.8 | 99 700 | 1.1 | 698 | 22 327 | 42 181 | 14.7 |
| District 13 | 317 038 | 89.2 | 64.5 | 118 000 | 1.4 | 723 | 24 014 | 44 915 | 15.9 |
| District 14 | 264 498 | 93.1 | 84.0 | 241 400 | 5.8 | 983 | 33 831 | 77 758 | 37.5 |
| District 15 | 314 424 | 88.2 | 76.6 | 92 000 | 1.2 | 619 | 22 983 | 45 122 | 14.2 |
| District 16 | 298 892 | 89.8 | 74.7 | 137 700 | 1.5 | 734 | 25 486 | 52 101 | 17.9 |
| District 17 | 321 421 | 88.2 | 68.7 | 96 000 | 1.3 | 622 | 21 711 | 41 194 | 11.5 |
| District 18 | 306 574 | 91.1 | 75.8 | 131 600 | 1.7 | 642 | 28 240 | 54 571 | 21.1 |
| INDIANA | 2 800 799 | 88.1 | 69.7 | 122 400 | 2.0 | 707 | 23 524 | 46 438 | 15.1 |
| District 1 | 301 363 | 87.9 | 70.5 | 141 600 | 2.3 | 761 | 24 073 | 50 669 | 18.1 |
| District 2 | 304 661 | 87.9 | 72.6 | 114 300 | 1.0 | 687 | 21 692 | 44 494 | 13.0 |
| District 3 | 311 225 | 88.0 | 73.8 | 113 700 | 1.8 | 627 | 22 760 | 46 504 | 12.9 |
| District 4 | 304 254 | 89.4 | 69.5 | 126 200 | 1.5 | 717 | 22 846 | 47 073 | 15.8 |
| District 5 | 308 667 | 92.1 | 71.6 | 161 900 | 5.2 | 779 | 32 817 | 58 115 | 25.9 |
| District 6 | 310 570 | 89.0 | 71.9 | 113 200 | 1.5 | 664 | 22 226 | 42 994 | 12.6 |
| District 7 | 333 679 | 83.7 | 54.3 | 103 000 | 1.3 | 719 | 19 357 | 36 565 | 9.0 |
| District 8 | 316 592 | 86.5 | 73.0 | 103 800 | 1.0 | 647 | 22 127 | 45 736 | 12.3 |
| District 9 | 309 788 | 88.6 | 70.6 | 134 800 | 1.9 | 730 | 23 706 | 48 522 | 16.2 |
| IOWA | 1 340 588 | 90.8 | 72.4 | 123 400 | 2.0 | 643 | 25 667 | 49 427 | 16.6 |
| District 1 | 333 159 | 91.8 | 74.8 | 131 200 | 1.8 | 604 | 25 986 | 50 125 | 16.8 |
| District 2 | 336 323 | 90.7 | 70.3 | 119 700 | 2.0 | 662 | 24 530 | 47 391 | 14.6 |
| District 3 | 326 855 | 91.4 | 71.8 | 142 800 | 2.3 | 723 | 27 658 | 54 641 | 20.7 |
| District 4 | 344 251 | 89.3 | 72.4 | 102 400 | 1.8 | 577 | 24 475 | 45 454 | 14.2 |
| KANSAS | 1 237 738 | 89.0 | 67.8 | 128 300 | 2.9 | 709 | 25 438 | 48 964 | 17.5 |
| District 1 | 315 226 | 87.4 | 66.9 | 95 900 | 1.4 | 631 | 22 346 | 43 340 | 12.5 |
| District 2 | 314 170 | 87.9 | 67.0 | 113 900 | 1.6 | 687 | 23 020 | 45 008 | 15.2 |
| District 3 | 299 850 | 92.4 | 69.1 | 188 400 | 6.2 | 841 | 32 525 | 61 380 | 27.2 |
| District 4 | 308 492 | 88.5 | 68.2 | 116 500 | 2.1 | 670 | 23 794 | 48 100 | 15.4 |

1. Specified owner-occupied units.  2. Specified renter-occupied units.

# Table E. Congressional Districts 113th Congress — Poverty, Labor Force, Employment, and Social Security

| STATE District | Poverty, 2011 (percent) | | | Civilian labor force, 2011 | | | Civilian employment,[2] 2011 | | | | Persons under age 65 with no health insurance, 2010 (percent) | Social Security beneficiaries, December 2012 | | Supplemental Security Income recipients, December 2012 |
|---|---|---|---|---|---|---|---|---|---|---|---|---|---|---|
| | | | | | Unemployment | | | Percent | | | | | | |
| | Persons below poverty level | Families below poverty level | Households receiving food stamps in past 12 months | Total | Total | Rate[1] | Total | Management, professional, and related occupations | Service, sales, and office | Construction and production | | Number | Rate[3] | |
| | 49 | 50 | 51 | 52 | 53 | 54 | 55 | 56 | 57 | 58 | 59 | 60 | 61 | 62 |
| GEORGIA | 19.1 | 14.7 | 15.1 | 4 774 331 | 580 555 | 12.2 | 4 193 776 | 35.2 | 42.2 | 22.6 | 21.8 | 1 582 151 | 161.2 | 247 965 |
| District 1 | 19.2 | 14.3 | 13.2 | 318 695 | 32 609 | 10.2 | 286 086 | 31.7 | 45.2 | 23.0 | 23.3 | 117 972 | 167.8 | 17 464 |
| District 2 | 26.7 | 21.8 | 24.9 | 294 298 | 43 062 | 14.6 | 251 236 | 28.4 | 44.4 | 27.2 | 23.0 | 129 361 | 184.9 | 30 938 |
| District 3 | 17.2 | 13.9 | 16.0 | 325 285 | 39 505 | 12.1 | 285 780 | 31.6 | 41.3 | 27.1 | 18.1 | 131 882 | 191.8 | 16 808 |
| District 4 | 19.0 | 15.2 | 17.1 | 369 413 | 57 743 | 15.6 | 311 670 | 33.8 | 44.2 | 22.1 | 25.3 | 101 697 | 141.2 | 18 590 |
| District 5 | 26.2 | 21.2 | 18.7 | 376 580 | 58 523 | 15.5 | 318 057 | 43.4 | 40.4 | 16.2 | 25.7 | 87 820 | 123.9 | 25 928 |
| District 6 | 10.1 | 7.1 | 4.6 | 394 768 | 33 616 | 8.5 | 361 152 | 51.2 | 37.7 | 11.1 | 17.5 | 84 226 | 120.5 | 6 076 |
| District 7 | 13.6 | 10.6 | 10.1 | 350 898 | 38 441 | 11.0 | 312 457 | 40.9 | 40.8 | 18.2 | 22.6 | 74 517 | 108.4 | 8 124 |
| District 8 | 23.2 | 18.1 | 18.6 | 308 391 | 35 701 | 11.6 | 272 690 | 31.6 | 42.3 | 26.1 | 23.2 | 132 838 | 191.5 | 24 729 |
| District 9 | 19.0 | 14.7 | 14.7 | 324 750 | 40 139 | 12.4 | 284 611 | 26.4 | 43.8 | 29.8 | 24.5 | 148 681 | 208.1 | 15 772 |
| District 10 | 21.2 | 14.2 | 14.3 | 323 219 | 35 801 | 11.1 | 287 418 | 34.7 | 42.6 | 22.7 | 17.3 | 126 905 | 182.7 | 17 795 |
| District 11 | 12.0 | 8.4 | 8.8 | 378 509 | 37 591 | 9.9 | 340 918 | 40.7 | 42.5 | 16.7 | 20.8 | 94 863 | 137.5 | 8 525 |
| District 12 | 22.3 | 17.0 | 16.8 | 308 535 | 30 370 | 9.8 | 278 165 | 30.5 | 42.3 | 27.2 | 21.6 | 127 336 | 180.7 | 24 571 |
| District 13 | 20.3 | 16.7 | 18.2 | 368 234 | 55 424 | 15.1 | 312 810 | 32.8 | 44.6 | 22.6 | 21.5 | 96 603 | 134.5 | 15 851 |
| District 14 | 18.4 | 14.4 | 16.1 | 332 756 | 42 030 | 12.6 | 290 726 | 28.1 | 40.1 | 31.8 | 21.0 | 127 450 | 183.5 | 16 794 |
| HAWAII | 12.0 | 8.6 | 10.8 | 681 799 | 52 276 | 7.7 | 629 523 | 34.0 | 47.5 | 18.5 | 8.2 | 240 456 | 174.9 | 25 299 |
| District 1 | 9.3 | 7.0 | 9.0 | 350 669 | 20 577 | 5.9 | 330 092 | 35.2 | 47.8 | 17.0 | 6.5 | 121 882 | 176.5 | 12 284 |
| District 2 | 14.9 | 10.1 | 12.7 | 331 130 | 31 699 | 9.6 | 299 431 | 32.6 | 47.3 | 20.1 | 9.8 | 118 574 | 173.3 | 13 015 |
| IDAHO | 16.5 | 11.6 | 13.5 | 760 733 | 75 817 | 10.0 | 684 916 | 33.8 | 42.0 | 24.2 | 18.9 | 288 294 | 181.9 | 29 440 |
| District 1 | 15.4 | 11.1 | 13.8 | 372 070 | 42 132 | 11.3 | 329 938 | 32.4 | 43.6 | 24.0 | 19.6 | 161 787 | 204.3 | 15 935 |
| District 2 | 17.5 | 12.1 | 13.3 | 388 663 | 33 685 | 8.7 | 354 978 | 35.1 | 40.5 | 24.4 | 18.3 | 126 507 | 159.5 | 13 505 |
| ILLINOIS | 15.0 | 11.0 | 12.1 | 6 661 181 | 734 332 | 11.0 | 5 926 849 | 36.0 | 42.5 | 21.4 | 14.8 | 2 102 954 | 163.4 | 278 013 |
| District 1 | 19.3 | 14.8 | 19.9 | 348 966 | 58 747 | 16.8 | 290 219 | 33.8 | 46.0 | 20.2 | 16.5 | 122 702 | 172.3 | 28 916 |
| District 2 | 20.1 | 16.0 | 20.0 | 338 854 | 60 683 | 17.9 | 278 171 | 30.6 | 44.7 | 24.7 | 18.0 | 131 646 | 183.2 | 28 321 |
| District 3 | 12.1 | 10.1 | 10.3 | 368 691 | 49 212 | 13.3 | 319 479 | 29.9 | 44.0 | 26.1 | 16.8 | 111 962 | 157.0 | 11 623 |
| District 4 | 23.1 | 20.9 | 19.1 | 380 392 | 53 829 | 14.2 | 326 563 | 20.1 | 47.6 | 32.3 | 30.3 | 83 687 | 113.5 | 23 149 |
| District 5 | 10.8 | 6.7 | 6.2 | 432 485 | 34 865 | 8.1 | 397 620 | 48.0 | 39.3 | 12.7 | 14.5 | 103 372 | 145.1 | 14 579 |
| District 6 | 6.3 | 4.7 | 4.5 | 385 367 | 29 804 | 7.7 | 355 563 | 48.1 | 39.2 | 12.7 | 7.1 | 100 354 | 140.8 | 5 108 |
| District 7 | 28.6 | 23.7 | 23.4 | 357 490 | 59 022 | 16.5 | 298 468 | 43.2 | 43.0 | 13.8 | 18.6 | 88 003 | 125.2 | 32 971 |
| District 8 | 11.1 | 8.2 | 8.7 | 406 142 | 39 800 | 9.8 | 366 342 | 33.3 | 44.4 | 22.3 | 16.4 | 92 516 | 127.7 | 7 841 |
| District 9 | 12.7 | 8.8 | 8.2 | 380 286 | 33 059 | 8.7 | 347 227 | 49.1 | 37.9 | 13.0 | 16.3 | 119 372 | 166.8 | 18 070 |
| District 10 | 11.6 | 8.6 | 9.0 | 361 091 | 36 274 | 10.0 | 324 817 | 39.9 | 42.7 | 17.4 | 14.8 | 97 001 | 137.5 | 8 779 |
| District 11 | 11.6 | 8.6 | 10.2 | 390 892 | 43 573 | 11.1 | 347 319 | 35.0 | 42.8 | 22.2 | 13.7 | 83 037 | 114.9 | 7 771 |
| District 12 | 20.3 | 14.6 | 15.8 | 333 396 | 32 401 | 9.7 | 300 995 | 30.7 | 45.4 | 24.0 | 13.1 | 135 263 | 189.6 | 19 763 |
| District 13 | 19.2 | 11.8 | 12.8 | 358 743 | 32 170 | 9.0 | 326 573 | 35.4 | 43.7 | 20.9 | 11.8 | 127 100 | 178.3 | 14 982 |
| District 14 | 7.5 | 5.1 | 4.7 | 385 510 | 34 496 | 8.9 | 351 014 | 40.8 | 38.6 | 20.6 | 8.2 | 110 500 | 153.9 | 4 787 |
| District 15 | 14.3 | 9.9 | 12.3 | 349 270 | 32 811 | 9.4 | 316 459 | 29.2 | 42.0 | 28.8 | 13.3 | 160 049 | 223.8 | 15 737 |
| District 16 | 11.6 | 8.3 | 10.4 | 370 396 | 39 599 | 10.7 | 330 797 | 29.4 | 43.3 | 27.3 | 11.5 | 147 284 | 206.3 | 10 490 |
| District 17 | 18.9 | 14.4 | 15.2 | 350 311 | 38 598 | 11.0 | 311 713 | 27.3 | 43.9 | 28.8 | 14.3 | 141 349 | 198.6 | 15 249 |
| District 18 | 10.6 | 6.8 | 8.1 | 362 899 | 25 389 | 7.0 | 337 510 | 38.0 | 39.9 | 22.1 | 8.6 | 147 757 | 208.9 | 9 877 |
| INDIANA | 16.0 | 11.7 | 12.5 | 3 260 792 | 326 292 | 10.0 | 2 934 500 | 31.9 | 41.2 | 26.9 | 16.5 | 1 244 654 | 191.0 | 125 090 |
| District 1 | 17.7 | 13.8 | 14.1 | 349 548 | 38 964 | 11.1 | 310 584 | 31.3 | 42.8 | 25.9 | 17.5 | 137 557 | 190.5 | 16 363 |
| District 2 | 17.9 | 13.9 | 14.2 | 357 375 | 39 534 | 11.1 | 317 841 | 28.5 | 39.6 | 31.9 | 19.0 | 139 328 | 194.3 | 12 948 |
| District 3 | 14.7 | 11.4 | 11.3 | 363 232 | 36 190 | 10.0 | 327 042 | 30.4 | 37.9 | 31.7 | 19.0 | 137 464 | 190.3 | 12 209 |
| District 4 | 14.4 | 8.8 | 10.5 | 358 896 | 30 402 | 8.5 | 328 494 | 31.8 | 39.6 | 28.7 | 14.3 | 136 600 | 187.3 | 9 606 |
| District 5 | 9.5 | 7.4 | 7.7 | 387 519 | 29 830 | 7.7 | 357 689 | 45.3 | 40.8 | 13.9 | 12.9 | 125 991 | 172.2 | 9 382 |
| District 6 | 16.3 | 11.9 | 13.0 | 351 198 | 39 273 | 11.2 | 311 925 | 29.6 | 41.4 | 29.1 | 16.5 | 158 904 | 220.6 | 14 525 |
| District 7 | 23.9 | 18.9 | 19.3 | 362 520 | 50 278 | 13.9 | 312 242 | 27.8 | 46.0 | 26.2 | 19.8 | 115 177 | 158.5 | 22 764 |
| District 8 | 14.5 | 9.9 | 11.3 | 357 536 | 28 239 | 7.9 | 329 297 | 28.0 | 41.2 | 30.9 | 15.5 | 151 742 | 210.5 | 15 061 |
| District 9 | 15.3 | 10.6 | 11.5 | 372 968 | 33 582 | 9.0 | 339 386 | 33.3 | 41.6 | 25.1 | 14.4 | 141 891 | 195.3 | 12 232 |
| IOWA | 12.8 | 8.1 | 10.8 | 1 637 404 | 98 648 | 6.0 | 1 538 756 | 33.8 | 41.2 | 25.0 | 10.4 | 600 700 | 196.2 | 49 751 |
| District 1 | 11.3 | 7.1 | 10.0 | 417 855 | 25 602 | 6.1 | 392 253 | 32.9 | 41.2 | 25.9 | 9.4 | 155 168 | 203.1 | 12 248 |
| District 2 | 15.0 | 9.5 | 11.2 | 399 106 | 25 682 | 6.4 | 373 424 | 32.6 | 40.3 | 27.0 | 11.8 | 150 499 | 196.4 | 14 746 |
| District 3 | 11.8 | 7.9 | 12.0 | 418 316 | 27 533 | 6.6 | 390 783 | 38.5 | 43.0 | 18.5 | 9.4 | 133 767 | 173.5 | 12 680 |
| District 4 | 13.1 | 8.0 | 10.1 | 402 127 | 19 831 | 4.9 | 382 296 | 31.1 | 40.0 | 28.9 | 10.8 | 161 266 | 211.8 | 10 077 |
| KANSAS | 13.8 | 9.2 | 9.7 | 1 500 639 | 111 601 | 7.4 | 1 389 038 | 36.3 | 40.4 | 23.3 | 14.3 | 507 526 | 176.8 | 48 488 |
| District 1 | 14.1 | 9.6 | 8.2 | 367 136 | 21 227 | 5.8 | 345 909 | 30.9 | 40.0 | 29.1 | 14.5 | 132 102 | 183.9 | 10 020 |
| District 2 | 15.3 | 9.5 | 11.0 | 368 279 | 28 421 | 7.7 | 339 858 | 35.1 | 41.4 | 23.5 | 14.0 | 143 826 | 201.3 | 15 229 |
| District 3 | 10.9 | 7.4 | 7.3 | 399 196 | 28 860 | 7.2 | 370 336 | 44.1 | 40.0 | 15.8 | 13.9 | 103 304 | 142.9 | 8 962 |
| District 4 | 14.9 | 10.6 | 12.4 | 366 028 | 33 093 | 9.0 | 332 935 | 34.4 | 40.3 | 25.3 | 15.0 | 128 294 | 179.3 | 14 277 |

1. Percent of civilian labor force.   2. Persons 16 years old and over.   3. Per 1,000 resident population estimated in the 2011 American Community Survey.

| STATE District | Representative, 113th Congress | Land area,[1] 2010 (sq km) | Total persons | Per square kilometer | White | Black | American Indian, Alaska Native | Asian and Pacific Islander | Some other race | Two or more races | Hispanic or Latino[2] | Non-Hispanic White alone | Percent female | Percent foreign born | Percent born in state of residence |
|---|---|---|---|---|---|---|---|---|---|---|---|---|---|---|---|
| | | 1 | 2 | 3 | 4 | 5 | 6 | 7 | 8 | 9 | 10 | 11 | 12 | 13 | 14 |
| KENTUCKY | | 102 269 | 4 369 356 | 42.7 | 87.8 | 8.0 | 0.2 | 1.2 | 1.0 | 1.8 | 3.2 | 86.1 | 50.9 | 3.2 | 70.1 |
| District 1 | Ed Whitfield (R) | 31 286 | 720 774 | 23.0 | 90.0 | 7.2 | 0.2 | 0.6 | 0.4 | 1.6 | 2.5 | 88.2 | 51.0 | 1.7 | 69.7 |
| District 2 | Brett Guthrie (R) | 18 589 | 733 610 | 39.5 | 89.9 | 5.6 | 0.3 | 1.0 | 0.9 | 2.2 | 3.0 | 88.3 | 50.7 | 2.9 | 71.6 |
| District 3 | John A. Yarmuth (D) | 827 | 726 812 | 878.8 | 72.8 | 20.8 | 0.2 | 2.3 | 1.2 | 2.7 | 4.6 | 70.0 | 51.8 | 6.5 | 69.6 |
| District 4 | Thomas Massie (R) | 11 350 | 731 100 | 64.4 | 92.1 | 3.7 | 0.4 | 1.1 | 1.5 | 1.3 | 3.0 | 90.6 | 50.3 | 3.1 | 62.4 |
| District 5 | Harold Rogers (R) | 29 099 | 723 855 | 24.9 | 96.7 | 1.4 | 0.1 | 0.3 | 0.3 | 1.2 | 0.9 | 96.2 | 50.3 | 0.6 | 78.4 |
| District 6 | Garland "Andy" Barr (R) | 11 118 | 733 205 | 65.9 | 85.4 | 9.2 | 0.2 | 1.7 | 1.4 | 2.1 | 4.0 | 83.2 | 51.5 | 4.3 | 69.2 |
| LOUISIANA | | 111 898 | 4 574 836 | 40.9 | 62.8 | 32.1 | 0.6 | 1.7 | 1.0 | 1.7 | 4.4 | 60.0 | 51.1 | 3.8 | 78.0 |
| District 1 | Steve Scalise (R) | 10 438 | 759 507 | 72.8 | 80.3 | 12.7 | 1.2 | 2.1 | 1.7 | 1.9 | 7.7 | 74.9 | 51.1 | 6.0 | 74.2 |
| District 2 | Cedric Richmond (D) | 3 285 | 767 984 | 233.8 | 30.6 | 62.9 | 0.3 | 2.8 | 1.7 | 1.7 | 5.9 | 27.3 | 52.3 | 5.8 | 80.3 |
| District 3 | Charles W. Boustany Jr. (R) | 18 087 | 760 696 | 42.1 | 70.6 | 24.9 | 0.7 | 1.5 | 0.6 | 1.7 | 3.0 | 68.7 | 51.1 | 3.0 | 82.2 |
| District 4 | John Fleming (R) | 32 207 | 758 453 | 23.5 | 61.0 | 33.9 | 0.9 | 0.8 | 1.4 | 2.0 | 3.3 | 59.4 | 51.0 | 2.1 | 72.3 |
| District 5 | Rodney Alexander (R) | 37 433 | 765 180 | 20.4 | 61.3 | 35.9 | 0.3 | 0.5 | 0.4 | 1.6 | 1.8 | 60.0 | 50.2 | 1.7 | 80.8 |
| District 6 | Bill Cassidy (R) | 10 448 | 763 016 | 73.0 | 73.6 | 22.1 | 0.4 | 2.2 | 0.5 | 1.3 | 4.2 | 69.8 | 50.9 | 4.3 | 77.9 |
| MAINE | | 79 883 | 1 328 188 | 16.6 | 95.2 | 1.0 | 0.6 | 1.0 | 0.2 | 1.9 | 1.4 | 94.3 | 51.0 | | 64.3 |
| District 1 | Chellie Pingree (D) | 8 509 | 668 146 | 78.5 | 94.9 | 1.4 | 0.3 | 1.4 | 0.2 | 1.8 | 1.6 | 93.8 | 51.3 | 4.0 | 58.4 |
| District 2 | Michael H. Michaud (D) | 71 373 | 660 042 | 9.2 | 95.5 | 0.6 | 1.0 | 0.6 | 0.2 | 2.0 | 1.1 | 94.7 | 50.6 | 2.4 | 70.4 |
| MARYLAND | | 25 142 | 5 828 289 | 231.8 | 58.6 | 29.6 | 0.2 | 5.7 | 3.3 | 2.6 | 8.4 | 54.2 | 51.6 | 13.9 | 48.0 |
| District 1 | Andrew Harris (R) | 10 301 | 722 628 | 70.2 | 82.6 | 12.4 | 0.1 | 2.0 | 0.9 | 2.0 | 3.3 | 80.5 | 51.0 | 4.8 | 63.3 |
| District 2 | C. A. Dutch Ruppersberger (D) | 904 | 727 061 | 804.6 | 58.3 | 31.8 | 0.3 | 4.8 | 2.0 | 2.8 | 6.5 | 54.8 | 53.2 | 10.7 | 62.8 |
| District 3 | John P. Sarbanes (D) | 788 | 721 896 | 916.5 | 65.8 | 20.9 | 0.2 | 7.8 | 2.7 | 2.6 | 6.8 | 62.0 | 51.9 | 14.6 | 49.6 |
| District 4 | Donna F. Edwards (D) | 771 | 736 929 | 955.4 | 32.2 | 54.2 | 0.2 | 3.3 | 7.9 | 2.2 | 15.6 | 26.0 | 51.9 | 19.0 | 29.7 |
| District 5 | Steny H. Hoyer (D) | 3 836 | 726 753 | 189.4 | 54.3 | 37.3 | 0.4 | 3.7 | 1.6 | 2.7 | 5.7 | 50.6 | 50.8 | 9.5 | 39.4 |
| District 6 | John K. Delaney (D) | 5 051 | 731 965 | 144.9 | 68.8 | 14.3 | 0.4 | 10.5 | 2.6 | 3.3 | 11.2 | 61.9 | 50.7 | 20.1 | 44.1 |
| District 7 | Elijah E. Cummings (D) | 1 264 | 713 872 | 564.8 | 36.1 | 54.6 | 0.3 | 4.9 | 1.3 | 2.8 | 3.5 | 34.5 | 52.3 | 9.0 | 63.1 |
| District 8 | Chris Van Hollen (D) | 2 227 | 747 185 | 335.5 | 70.3 | 11.8 | 0.1 | 8.3 | 6.8 | 2.6 | 14.2 | 63.5 | 51.2 | 23.3 | 33.0 |
| MASSACHUSETTS | | 20 202 | 6 587 536 | 326.1 | 80.5 | 6.8 | 0.2 | 5.6 | 4.3 | 2.6 | 9.9 | 75.8 | 51.6 | 14.9 | 62.9 |
| District 1 | Richard E. Neal (D) | 6 087 | 728 921 | 119.7 | 83.2 | 6.3 | 0.2 | 1.9 | 6.1 | 2.2 | 15.3 | 75.0 | 51.8 | 6.8 | 65.9 |
| District 2 | James P. McGovern (D) | 4 216 | 726 061 | 172.2 | 86.1 | 4.2 | 0.3 | 4.6 | 2.5 | 2.2 | 8.3 | 81.2 | 51.9 | 10.7 | 67.2 |
| District 3 | Niki Tsongas (D) | 1 963 | 732 090 | 373.0 | 78.0 | 2.9 | 0.2 | 6.4 | 9.8 | 2.7 | 16.0 | 72.8 | 49.9 | 15.8 | 63.6 |
| District 4 | Joseph P. Kennedy III (D) | 1 731 | 736 769 | 425.7 | 89.5 | 2.1 | 0.1 | 5.6 | 1.2 | 1.6 | 4.2 | 86.5 | 51.9 | 11.3 | 61.2 |
| District 5 | Edward J. Markey (D) | 687 | 737 545 | 1 074.3 | 79.9 | 4.7 | 0.1 | 10.0 | 2.1 | 3.1 | 7.4 | 75.6 | 51.9 | 22.9 | 54.4 |
| District 6 | John F. Tierney (D) | 1 364 | 731 681 | 536.3 | 87.2 | 2.8 | 0.2 | 3.7 | 4.0 | 2.1 | 8.1 | 84.1 | 51.7 | 11.6 | 71.6 |
| District 7 | Michael E. Capuano (D) | 162 | 733 814 | 4 520.9 | 51.2 | 26.7 | 0.2 | 10.0 | 6.8 | 5.1 | 19.9 | 42.5 | 52.4 | 30.1 | 44.0 |
| District 8 | Stephen F. Lynch (D) | 845 | 732 884 | 867.0 | 79.2 | 8.7 | 0.1 | 6.6 | 3.5 | 1.9 | 5.3 | 76.5 | 51.4 | 15.8 | 67.3 |
| District 9 | William R. Keating (D) | 3 146 | 727 771 | 231.3 | 90.8 | 3.1 | 0.3 | 1.3 | 2.6 | 2.0 | 4.2 | 88.4 | 51.7 | 9.1 | 70.9 |
| MICHIGAN | | 146 435 | 9 876 187 | 67.4 | 79.3 | 14.1 | 0.6 | 2.5 | 1.1 | 2.6 | 4.5 | 76.3 | 50.9 | 6.1 | 76.6 |
| District 1 | Dan Benishek (R) | 64 822 | 708 797 | 10.9 | 92.7 | 1.6 | 2.6 | 0.7 | 0.3 | 2.1 | 1.5 | 91.8 | 49.1 | 2.0 | 79.8 |
| District 2 | Bill Huizenga (R) | 8 498 | 709 073 | 83.4 | 85.9 | 6.3 | 0.4 | 2.1 | 2.4 | 2.9 | 8.7 | 80.8 | 50.3 | 5.8 | 78.7 |
| District 3 | Justin Amash (R) | 6 808 | 709 467 | 104.2 | 84.8 | 9.0 | 0.4 | 1.3 | 1.3 | 3.1 | 6.9 | 80.0 | 50.7 | 4.7 | 78.2 |
| District 4 | Dave Camp (R) | 21 906 | 703 259 | 32.1 | 93.8 | 2.0 | 0.8 | 0.9 | 0.5 | 1.9 | 2.8 | 92.0 | 49.9 | 2.2 | 85.0 |
| District 5 | Daniel T. Kildee (D) | 6 083 | 698 753 | 114.9 | 77.6 | 17.5 | 0.6 | 0.8 | 0.6 | 2.9 | 4.6 | 74.4 | 51.7 | 1.8 | 84.3 |
| District 6 | Fred Upton (R) | 9 186 | 707 375 | 77.0 | 85.2 | 8.7 | 0.4 | 1.4 | 1.7 | 2.7 | 5.5 | 81.8 | 50.9 | 4.7 | 69.2 |
| District 7 | Tim Walberg (R) | 10 950 | 701 436 | 64.1 | 91.8 | 4.1 | 0.5 | 0.8 | 0.8 | 2.0 | 4.0 | 89.0 | 49.8 | 2.3 | 73.4 |
| District 8 | Mike Rogers (R) | 3 893 | 706 826 | 181.6 | 86.4 | 5.6 | 0.2 | 3.9 | 1.0 | 3.0 | 4.6 | 83.4 | 50.6 | 7.0 | 75.6 |
| District 9 | Sander M. Levin (D) | 475 | 712 540 | 1 498.5 | 82.3 | 10.9 | 0.5 | 3.8 | 0.6 | 2.0 | 1.6 | 81.1 | 51.4 | 11.0 | 76.4 |
| District 10 | Candice S. Miller (R) | 10 724 | 701 831 | 65.4 | 93.1 | 2.5 | 0.2 | 1.5 | 0.9 | 1.7 | 3.5 | 90.9 | 50.7 | 5.3 | 84.5 |
| District 11 | Kerry L. Bentivolio (R) | 1 086 | 706 645 | 650.8 | 84.9 | 4.7 | 0.3 | 7.4 | 0.4 | 2.3 | 3.6 | 82.0 | 51.0 | 11.1 | 72.4 |
| District 12 | John D. Dingell (D) | 1 044 | 703 389 | 673.6 | 80.1 | 10.3 | 0.4 | 4.6 | 1.1 | 3.5 | 5.2 | 76.3 | 51.1 | 11.6 | 68.6 |
| District 13 | John Conyers Jr. (D) | 479 | 699 214 | 1 460.5 | 37.6 | 56.5 | 0.3 | 1.2 | 2.0 | 2.4 | 6.5 | 33.6 | 52.6 | 6.1 | 75.7 |
| District 14 | Gary C. Peters (D) | 481 | 707 582 | 1 470.9 | 33.6 | 57.2 | 0.2 | 4.3 | 1.3 | 3.4 | 4.6 | 30.9 | 53.0 | 9.9 | 70.9 |
| MINNESOTA | | 206 232 | 5 344 861 | 25.9 | 85.7 | 5.2 | 1.1 | 4.0 | 1.4 | 2.5 | 4.9 | 82.7 | 50.3 | 7.3 | 68.6 |
| District 1 | Timothy J. Walz (D) | 31 012 | 666 103 | 21.5 | 92.5 | 2.4 | 0.3 | 2.1 | 0.8 | 1.8 | 5.8 | 87.9 | 50.3 | 4.8 | 69.4 |
| District 2 | John Kline (R) | 6 314 | 668 891 | 105.9 | 87.2 | 3.7 | 0.5 | 4.0 | 1.6 | 2.9 | 5.2 | 84.2 | 50.5 | 7.6 | 67.8 |
| District 3 | Erik Paulsen (R) | 1 365 | 664 419 | 486.7 | 83.2 | 6.5 | 0.5 | 6.0 | 1.1 | 2.8 | 3.7 | 80.8 | 51.1 | 9.9 | 63.4 |
| District 4 | Betty McCollum (D) | 861 | 669 310 | 777.2 | 74.2 | 9.2 | 0.6 | 10.5 | 2.1 | 3.4 | 6.3 | 70.7 | 51.2 | 13.2 | 62.1 |
| District 5 | Keith Ellison (D) | 351 | 677 196 | 1 927.4 | 70.2 | 15.6 | 1.2 | 5.8 | 3.2 | 4.0 | 9.7 | 64.7 | 50.5 | 14.6 | 55.5 |
| District 6 | Michele Bachmann (R) | 7 465 | 675 415 | 90.5 | 91.9 | 2.2 | 0.5 | 2.3 | 1.2 | 1.9 | 2.5 | 90.6 | 49.8 | 3.7 | 78.3 |
| District 7 | Collin C. Peterson (D) | 86 582 | 661 532 | 7.6 | 92.7 | 0.8 | 2.9 | 1.0 | 0.9 | 1.7 | 3.8 | 90.4 | 49.6 | 2.4 | 73.6 |
| District 8 | Richard M. Nolan (D) | 72 282 | 661 995 | 9.2 | 93.7 | 1.1 | 2.6 | 0.7 | 0.2 | 1.8 | 1.3 | 92.8 | 49.3 | 1.9 | 78.9 |

1. Dry land or land partially or temporarily covered by water.    2. May be of any race.

# Table E. Congressional Districts 113th Congress — Age and Education

| STATE District | Population and population characteristics, 2011 (cont.) | | | | | | | | | | Education, 2011 | | |
| | Age (percent) | | | | | | | | | | | Attainment[2] (percent) | |
| | Under 5 years | 5 to 17 years | 18 to 24 years | 25 to 34 years | 35 to 44 years | 45 to 54 years | 55 to 64 years | 65 to 74 years | 75 years and over | Median age | Total Enrollment[1] | High school graduate or more | Bachelor's degree or more |
| | 15 | 16 | 17 | 18 | 19 | 20 | 21 | 22 | 23 | 24 | 25 | 26 | 27 |
| KENTUCKY | 6.4 | 17.1 | 9.7 | 12.9 | 13.0 | 14.6 | 12.7 | 7.7 | 5.9 | 38.2 | 1 127 708 | 83.1 | 21.1 |
| District 1 | 6.3 | 16.7 | 9.1 | 12.5 | 12.1 | 14.2 | 13.1 | 9.1 | 6.9 | 39.9 | 173 242 | 81.9 | 14.5 |
| District 2 | 6.4 | 18.0 | 10.1 | 12.3 | 12.6 | 14.8 | 12.5 | 7.6 | 5.7 | 37.5 | 195 226 | 83.7 | 17.7 |
| District 3 | 6.7 | 16.1 | 9.2 | 14.3 | 12.6 | 14.7 | 12.7 | 7.0 | 6.6 | 37.7 | 186 690 | 87.9 | 29.0 |
| District 4 | 6.5 | 18.8 | 8.4 | 12.6 | 13.8 | 15.3 | 12.5 | 7.1 | 5.0 | 38.2 | 200 516 | 87.0 | 24.9 |
| District 5 | 6.3 | 16.4 | 9.1 | 12.2 | 13.3 | 14.6 | 13.7 | 8.5 | 5.9 | 39.7 | 165 307 | 72.2 | 11.2 |
| District 6 | 6.2 | 16.4 | 12.1 | 13.7 | 13.5 | 14.0 | 12.0 | 6.8 | 5.3 | 36.1 | 206 727 | 85.8 | 29.3 |
| LOUISIANA | 6.8 | 17.7 | 10.6 | 13.8 | 12.4 | 14.0 | 12.3 | 7.0 | 5.4 | 35.9 | 1 213 228 | 82.5 | 21.1 |
| District 1 | 6.5 | 16.8 | 9.7 | 13.3 | 12.5 | 15.0 | 12.8 | 7.3 | 6.0 | 38.0 | 197 535 | 85.3 | 26.4 |
| District 2 | 6.9 | 16.8 | 11.0 | 14.9 | 12.3 | 14.2 | 12.6 | 6.5 | 4.6 | 35.2 | 206 120 | 79.8 | 20.0 |
| District 3 | 7.2 | 18.2 | 10.3 | 13.6 | 12.4 | 14.4 | 11.7 | 6.8 | 5.4 | 35.5 | 198 722 | 81.5 | 18.2 |
| District 4 | 6.9 | 18.0 | 10.3 | 13.2 | 12.4 | 13.3 | 12.3 | 7.5 | 6.0 | 36.2 | 192 710 | 83.6 | 19.7 |
| District 5 | 6.8 | 17.9 | 10.3 | 13.1 | 12.0 | 13.6 | 12.5 | 7.6 | 6.1 | 36.6 | 197 020 | 77.4 | 14.7 |
| District 6 | 6.8 | 17.9 | 11.6 | 14.8 | 13.1 | 13.3 | 11.5 | 6.3 | 4.7 | 34.3 | 221 121 | 87.4 | 27.6 |
| MAINE | 5.0 | 15.3 | 8.7 | 10.9 | 12.6 | 16.1 | 15.0 | 8.9 | 7.5 | 43.2 | 304 531 | 90.9 | 28.4 |
| District 1 | 5.0 | 15.5 | 8.2 | 11.1 | 13.1 | 16.3 | 14.7 | 8.5 | 7.5 | 42.9 | 151 585 | 92.8 | 35.1 |
| District 2 | 4.9 | 15.2 | 9.2 | 10.7 | 12.0 | 16.1 | 15.2 | 9.1 | 7.5 | 43.6 | 152 946 | 89.0 | 21.6 |
| MARYLAND | 6.2 | 16.9 | 9.7 | 13.3 | 13.4 | 15.4 | 12.4 | 6.9 | 5.7 | 38.0 | 1 577 839 | 88.9 | 36.9 |
| District 1 | 5.5 | 17.1 | 9.6 | 10.3 | 12.2 | 16.0 | 13.7 | 8.8 | 6.8 | 41.5 | 186 547 | 89.3 | 29.4 |
| District 2 | 6.5 | 16.1 | 10.0 | 14.8 | 13.7 | 14.9 | 12.4 | 5.9 | 5.7 | 36.8 | 191 798 | 86.8 | 27.6 |
| District 3 | 6.7 | 14.5 | 9.5 | 15.7 | 13.2 | 14.6 | 12.4 | 6.7 | 6.6 | 37.9 | 188 297 | 90.4 | 44.7 |
| District 4 | 6.8 | 17.8 | 9.3 | 14.9 | 14.5 | 14.8 | 11.7 | 6.3 | 3.9 | 35.7 | 202 763 | 85.5 | 31.7 |
| District 5 | 6.0 | 18.1 | 11.4 | 11.8 | 13.4 | 16.4 | 12.0 | 6.6 | 4.3 | 37.0 | 216 927 | 91.3 | 32.2 |
| District 6 | 6.1 | 17.7 | 8.4 | 13.3 | 13.8 | 15.9 | 12.4 | 7.0 | 5.4 | 38.5 | 195 185 | 89.8 | 39.5 |
| District 7 | 6.0 | 17.1 | 11.5 | 13.3 | 12.1 | 15.1 | 12.1 | 7.0 | 5.8 | 36.8 | 201 716 | 86.2 | 35.7 |
| District 8 | 6.2 | 16.6 | 8.1 | 12.8 | 14.0 | 15.8 | 12.8 | 7.0 | 6.6 | 40.0 | 194 606 | 91.4 | 52.8 |
| MASSACHUSETTS | 5.5 | 15.8 | 10.3 | 13.1 | 13.2 | 15.4 | 12.7 | 7.2 | 6.9 | 39.3 | 1 764 471 | 89.2 | 39.1 |
| District 1 | 5.5 | 16.4 | 9.9 | 11.9 | 12.1 | 15.3 | 13.8 | 7.6 | 7.6 | 41.0 | 185 959 | 86.3 | 26.9 |
| District 2 | 5.2 | 16.9 | 12.3 | 11.0 | 13.2 | 15.8 | 12.4 | 6.9 | 6.3 | 38.8 | 213 125 | 89.6 | 35.9 |
| District 3 | 6.0 | 17.4 | 8.9 | 12.0 | 13.8 | 16.7 | 13.0 | 6.1 | 6.1 | 39.6 | 189 429 | 87.3 | 34.7 |
| District 4 | 5.5 | 17.6 | 9.3 | 10.2 | 13.5 | 16.9 | 13.5 | 6.7 | 6.7 | 41.0 | 203 924 | 92.2 | 48.8 |
| District 5 | 6.0 | 14.7 | 8.7 | 14.4 | 14.3 | 15.1 | 12.3 | 7.3 | 7.1 | 39.2 | 193 009 | 92.1 | 52.0 |
| District 6 | 5.3 | 16.9 | 8.5 | 11.2 | 13.0 | 16.7 | 13.6 | 7.8 | 7.0 | 41.6 | 187 251 | 92.1 | 40.3 |
| District 7 | 5.7 | 11.8 | 18.0 | 22.2 | 12.7 | 11.0 | 8.9 | 5.2 | 4.5 | 30.8 | 239 183 | 83.1 | 39.5 |
| District 8 | 5.6 | 15.2 | 8.7 | 14.5 | 13.6 | 15.0 | 12.5 | 7.3 | 7.5 | 39.6 | 179 922 | 90.9 | 41.7 |
| District 9 | 4.7 | 15.5 | 8.5 | 10.4 | 12.2 | 15.8 | 14.5 | 10.0 | 8.3 | 43.9 | 172 669 | 88.9 | 32.0 |
| MICHIGAN | 5.9 | 17.3 | 10.1 | 11.8 | 12.6 | 15.0 | 13.3 | 7.5 | 6.5 | 39.2 | 2 695 641 | 88.8 | 25.6 |
| District 1 | 4.9 | 14.9 | 8.8 | 10.3 | 11.2 | 15.2 | 15.7 | 10.2 | 8.7 | 44.9 | 158 983 | 89.9 | 21.1 |
| District 2 | 6.6 | 18.0 | 11.0 | 12.7 | 11.9 | 14.3 | 12.7 | 6.8 | 5.9 | 36.5 | 198 049 | 88.3 | 23.4 |
| District 3 | 6.8 | 18.8 | 9.4 | 12.8 | 12.8 | 14.7 | 12.0 | 6.7 | 5.9 | 36.8 | 197 915 | 89.5 | 27.2 |
| District 4 | 5.4 | 16.2 | 11.9 | 10.9 | 11.3 | 14.8 | 13.5 | 8.8 | 7.0 | 40.0 | 194 226 | 89.6 | 20.2 |
| District 5 | 6.0 | 17.7 | 9.1 | 11.4 | 12.1 | 14.8 | 13.6 | 8.2 | 7.0 | 39.8 | 183 127 | 88.0 | 18.1 |
| District 6 | 6.2 | 17.4 | 10.9 | 11.6 | 12.0 | 14.4 | 13.2 | 7.7 | 6.5 | 38.7 | 198 837 | 88.9 | 24.6 |
| District 7 | 5.7 | 17.4 | 8.9 | 11.0 | 12.9 | 15.8 | 13.9 | 7.9 | 6.4 | 40.7 | 177 035 | 90.6 | 21.1 |
| District 8 | 5.3 | 17.6 | 12.3 | 11.7 | 12.6 | 15.5 | 13.0 | 6.9 | 5.0 | 37.8 | 221 727 | 92.2 | 36.5 |
| District 9 | 5.6 | 15.2 | 8.5 | 13.8 | 13.3 | 15.3 | 12.9 | 7.6 | 7.8 | 40.4 | 172 379 | 88.3 | 26.8 |
| District 10 | 5.5 | 18.3 | 7.8 | 10.8 | 13.5 | 16.4 | 13.5 | 7.8 | 6.4 | 41.0 | 183 845 | 90.2 | 21.2 |
| District 11 | 5.6 | 18.4 | 7.4 | 10.9 | 14.0 | 16.8 | 13.7 | 7.2 | 6.1 | 40.8 | 193 929 | 93.9 | 44.1 |
| District 12 | 5.6 | 16.0 | 14.1 | 13.5 | 13.1 | 13.8 | 12.1 | 6.0 | 5.7 | 35.6 | 220 591 | 88.2 | 32.3 |
| District 13 | 6.9 | 18.4 | 10.6 | 12.1 | 13.4 | 14.0 | 12.1 | 6.5 | 6.0 | 36.4 | 197 123 | 80.4 | 13.4 |
| District 14 | 6.6 | 18.0 | 10.1 | 12.2 | 12.1 | 14.2 | 13.1 | 7.2 | 6.6 | 38.1 | 197 875 | 84.6 | 28.6 |
| MINNESOTA | 6.6 | 17.3 | 9.5 | 13.5 | 12.5 | 15.0 | 12.4 | 6.9 | 6.3 | 37.6 | 1 423 499 | 92.0 | 32.4 |
| District 1 | 6.5 | 17.2 | 10.4 | 12.9 | 11.1 | 14.4 | 12.5 | 7.5 | 7.7 | 37.7 | 179 485 | 91.2 | 26.3 |
| District 2 | 6.7 | 19.4 | 8.1 | 13.1 | 14.3 | 16.3 | 11.6 | 5.8 | 4.7 | 37.0 | 188 242 | 94.7 | 36.2 |
| District 3 | 6.3 | 18.5 | 7.1 | 13.6 | 13.3 | 16.4 | 13.1 | 6.4 | 5.3 | 39.0 | 179 855 | 95.2 | 45.6 |
| District 4 | 6.8 | 17.0 | 10.8 | 14.5 | 12.1 | 14.6 | 12.3 | 6.2 | 5.6 | 35.7 | 186 552 | 90.6 | 38.8 |
| District 5 | 7.0 | 14.1 | 11.4 | 18.8 | 13.2 | 13.2 | 10.7 | 5.7 | 5.9 | 34.1 | 178 096 | 89.5 | 42.4 |
| District 6 | 7.2 | 19.5 | 9.9 | 12.7 | 14.1 | 15.5 | 11.4 | 5.6 | 4.0 | 35.5 | 195 425 | 93.1 | 28.1 |
| District 7 | 6.6 | 16.8 | 9.0 | 11.6 | 10.6 | 14.4 | 13.3 | 8.7 | 9.0 | 40.9 | 158 347 | 90.3 | 20.5 |
| District 8 | 5.6 | 16.0 | 8.9 | 11.3 | 11.3 | 15.3 | 14.5 | 9.2 | 7.8 | 42.2 | 157 497 | 91.7 | 20.9 |

1. All persons 3 years old and over enrolled in nursery school through college and graduate or professional school.　　2. Persons 25 years old and over.

# Table E. Congressional Districts 113th Congress — Households and Group Quarters

| STATE District | Households, 2011 | | | | | | Group quarters, 2010 | | | | | |
|---|---|---|---|---|---|---|---|---|---|---|---|---|
| | Number | Persons per household | Family households (percent) | Married-couple family (percent) | Female family householder[1] | One person households (percent) | Total in group quarters | Percent 65 years and over | Persons in correctional institutions | Persons in nursing homes | Persons in college dormitories | Persons in military quarters |
| | 28 | 29 | 30 | 31 | 32 | 33 | 34 | 35 | 36 | 37 | 38 | 39 |
| KENTUCKY | 1 672 134 | 2.54 | 67.0 | 49.5 | 13.0 | 28.2 | 125 870 | 19.2 | 41 122 | 26 044 | 36 340 | 5 856 |
| District 1 | 279 674 | 2.49 | 68.7 | 52.6 | 12.2 | 28.0 | 24 895 | 20.4 | 7 869 | 5 548 | 4 101 | 3 843 |
| District 2 | 270 511 | 2.63 | 70.2 | 53.2 | 12.5 | 25.4 | 20 479 | 21.3 | 4 501 | 4 378 | 7 527 | 2 013 |
| District 3 | 291 797 | 2.44 | 61.2 | 40.7 | 15.7 | 32.8 | 14 045 | 30.7 | 2 662 | 4 723 | 3 307 | 0 |
| District 4 | 265 151 | 2.69 | 70.5 | 54.3 | 11.2 | 24.8 | 16 978 | 21.9 | 9 255 | 3 657 | 1 768 | 0 |
| District 5 | 275 595 | 2.54 | 69.9 | 51.9 | 13.1 | 26.5 | 24 578 | 15.1 | 12 451 | 4 570 | 5 039 | 0 |
| District 6 | 289 406 | 2.45 | 62.2 | 45.1 | 12.9 | 31.0 | 24 895 | 12.1 | 4 384 | 3 168 | 14 598 | 0 |
| LOUISIANA | 1 702 030 | 2.61 | 65.7 | 43.7 | 17.1 | 28.9 | 127 427 | 16.7 | 60 804 | 24 524 | 24 891 | 2 861 |
| District 1 | 287 377 | 2.60 | 66.6 | 48.3 | 13.6 | 26.9 | 10 958 | 24.4 | 1 182 | 2 957 | 5 469 | 57 |
| District 2 | 289 152 | 2.59 | 61.5 | 30.3 | 25.2 | 33.3 | 22 900 | 12.0 | 11 687 | 3 058 | 4 007 | 138 |
| District 3 | 284 010 | 2.63 | 65.8 | 45.7 | 15.0 | 28.6 | 13 612 | 26.9 | 4 329 | 4 273 | 2 935 | 0 |
| District 4 | 282 509 | 2.60 | 65.5 | 43.5 | 17.5 | 30.0 | 25 561 | 18.4 | 13 410 | 5 425 | 2 390 | 2 524 |
| District 5 | 275 760 | 2.60 | 67.0 | 44.3 | 18.0 | 29.0 | 44 845 | 11.6 | 28 559 | 5 925 | 6 333 | 142 |
| District 6 | 283 222 | 2.66 | 67.9 | 50.0 | 13.0 | 25.7 | 9 551 | 23.4 | 1 637 | 2 886 | 3 757 | 0 |
| MAINE | 552 051 | 2.34 | 63.0 | 49.1 | 9.8 | 28.4 | 35 545 | 22.5 | 3 679 | 7 878 | 17 251 | 131 |
| District 1 | 275 709 | 2.36 | 62.0 | 48.5 | 9.4 | 29.7 | 17 895 | 24.5 | 2 708 | 4 128 | 7 433 | 119 |
| District 2 | 276 342 | 2.32 | 64.1 | 49.7 | 10.1 | 27.1 | 17 650 | 20.4 | 971 | 3 750 | 9 818 | 12 |
| MARYLAND | 2 134 517 | 2.67 | 66.3 | 46.6 | 14.9 | 27.8 | 138 375 | 19.4 | 35 832 | 28 001 | 48 141 | 7 534 |
| District 1 | 260 766 | 2.70 | 72.4 | 56.0 | 12.2 | 22.9 | 17 218 | 20.6 | 5 648 | 3 465 | 5 803 | 7 |
| District 2 | 275 614 | 2.57 | 63.9 | 40.9 | 18.1 | 28.3 | 18 966 | 17.1 | 7 411 | 3 533 | 3 971 | 2 113 |
| District 3 | 282 956 | 2.49 | 60.4 | 42.5 | 12.8 | 31.8 | 17 596 | 19.9 | 583 | 3 399 | 6 910 | 4 515 |
| District 4 | 261 098 | 2.80 | 67.2 | 41.5 | 19.5 | 26.9 | 5 755 | 42.2 | 1 149 | 2 597 | 410 | 115 |
| District 5 | 246 007 | 2.87 | 72.7 | 53.2 | 14.4 | 23.2 | 19 845 | 11.8 | 1 111 | 2 598 | 14 602 | 387 |
| District 6 | 266 717 | 2.66 | 68.1 | 51.5 | 13.0 | 26.7 | 21 617 | 17.6 | 12 569 | 3 716 | 2 766 | 93 |
| District 7 | 265 354 | 2.60 | 59.6 | 35.0 | 20.2 | 34.7 | 26 945 | 14.8 | 6 305 | 4 677 | 10 895 | 0 |
| District 8 | 276 005 | 2.67 | 67.3 | 53.3 | 9.6 | 27.2 | 10 433 | 37.8 | 1 056 | 4 016 | 2 784 | 304 |
| MASSACHUSETTS | 2 532 067 | 2.67 | 63.1 | 46.4 | 12.8 | 29.3 | 238 882 | 17.7 | 24 683 | 43 833 | 135 773 | 498 |
| District 1 | 285 484 | 2.47 | 64.3 | 43.7 | 15.6 | 29.7 | 24 496 | 20.9 | 1 897 | 5 855 | 13 226 | 0 |
| District 2 | 270 632 | 2.54 | 63.9 | 46.6 | 13.3 | 28.9 | 38 153 | 13.9 | 1 576 | 5 572 | 26 184 | 0 |
| District 3 | 273 736 | 2.61 | 68.4 | 49.6 | 13.8 | 26.3 | 19 120 | 19.7 | 6 829 | 3 823 | 4 944 | 0 |
| District 4 | 271 911 | 2.60 | 68.1 | 55.1 | 9.9 | 25.9 | 25 960 | 19.7 | 2 520 | 4 914 | 15 480 | 0 |
| District 5 | 290 558 | 2.45 | 61.4 | 49.4 | 9.3 | 30.7 | 27 384 | 16.5 | 771 | 4 440 | 18 907 | 25 |
| District 6 | 276 566 | 2.58 | 68.1 | 52.9 | 10.9 | 26.1 | 16 758 | 28.9 | 2 014 | 4 919 | 5 965 | 113 |
| District 7 | 286 438 | 2.38 | 49.2 | 27.5 | 17.7 | 36.3 | 53 188 | 4.7 | 1 895 | 2 728 | 42 309 | 73 |
| District 8 | 288 130 | 2.49 | 60.6 | 45.2 | 11.9 | 30.5 | 17 340 | 35.8 | 3 879 | 6 322 | 3 522 | 261 |
| District 9 | 288 612 | 2.46 | 64.6 | 48.2 | 12.7 | 29.2 | 16 483 | 30.2 | 3 302 | 5 260 | 5 236 | 26 |
| MICHIGAN | 3 772 433 | 2.56 | 65.6 | 48.2 | 12.8 | 29.0 | 229 068 | 19.8 | 62 083 | 42 473 | 78 033 | 214 |
| District 1 | 286 218 | 2.37 | 63.8 | 51.0 | 8.5 | 29.9 | 27 050 | 20.2 | 12 990 | 4 884 | 5 714 | 129 |
| District 2 | 260 298 | 2.64 | 69.0 | 53.7 | 10.7 | 26.0 | 17 676 | 17.4 | 5 021 | 2 948 | 6 414 | 0 |
| District 3 | 266 889 | 2.59 | 67.5 | 51.4 | 12.5 | 27.1 | 20 522 | 18.1 | 7 012 | 3 695 | 5 151 | 82 |
| District 4 | 268 889 | 2.51 | 67.6 | 53.4 | 9.5 | 25.6 | 28 516 | 13.6 | 9 024 | 3 606 | 13 524 | 0 |
| District 5 | 273 381 | 2.52 | 64.8 | 44.7 | 15.2 | 30.2 | 10 494 | 33.6 | 1 630 | 3 103 | 1 303 | 3 |
| District 6 | 264 347 | 2.61 | 67.5 | 50.8 | 12.0 | 26.7 | 14 916 | 22.3 | 1 476 | 3 141 | 6 864 | 0 |
| District 7 | 264 174 | 2.56 | 69.9 | 54.7 | 10.9 | 25.8 | 25 154 | 15 | 14 438 | 2 638 | 4 594 | 0 |
| District 8 | 264 552 | 2.59 | 65.5 | 51.5 | 9.5 | 27.7 | 21 845 | 10.0 | 988 | 1 873 | 16 015 | 0 |
| District 9 | 295 186 | 2.39 | 60.6 | 42.6 | 13.2 | 33.8 | 5 786 | 50.7 | 1 143 | 3 267 | 0 | 0 |
| District 10 | 260 527 | 2.66 | 71.9 | 58.3 | 10.1 | 23.7 | 8 383 | 36.3 | 3 120 | 2 375 | 0 | 0 |
| District 11 | 272 807 | 2.57 | 68.6 | 56.2 | 9.4 | 27.1 | 5 988 | 45.5 | 183 | 2 598 | 1 581 | 0 |
| District 12 | 270 082 | 2.54 | 60.2 | 43.7 | 11.6 | 31.7 | 18 415 | 11.9 | 387 | 2 155 | 13 873 | 0 |
| District 13 | 257 458 | 2.68 | 59.7 | 28.8 | 24.3 | 35.5 | 11 643 | 21.2 | 114 | 2 806 | 2 287 | 0 |
| District 14 | 267 625 | 2.60 | 62.0 | 34.0 | 22.1 | 34.0 | 12 680 | 23.4 | 4 557 | 3 384 | 713 | 0 |
| MINNESOTA | 2 096 477 | 2.48 | 64.7 | 50.9 | 9.5 | 28.6 | 135 395 | 24.9 | 20 397 | 32 989 | 50 444 | 0 |
| District 1 | 260 589 | 2.46 | 66.0 | 53.8 | 8.1 | 28.2 | 24 122 | 23.9 | 4 808 | 5 137 | 9 723 | 0 |
| District 2 | 248 707 | 2.64 | 70.1 | 56.6 | 9.6 | 24.4 | 10 052 | 25.8 | 1 042 | 2 781 | 4 486 | 0 |
| District 3 | 258 808 | 2.55 | 67.6 | 54.1 | 9.5 | 27.1 | 4 700 | 38.8 | 551 | 1 864 | 644 | 0 |
| District 4 | 261 574 | 2.49 | 61.2 | 45.5 | 10.9 | 31.7 | 21 600 | 16.8 | 3 286 | 3 540 | 9 958 | 0 |
| District 5 | 285 130 | 2.30 | 49.9 | 34.0 | 11.5 | 38.4 | 21 783 | 20.9 | 876 | 5 425 | 8 740 | 0 |
| District 6 | 242 751 | 2.72 | 73.0 | 59.4 | 9.4 | 20.4 | 14 779 | 19.1 | 3 328 | 2 246 | 5 885 | 0 |
| District 7 | 269 576 | 2.39 | 66.8 | 53.5 | 8.8 | 28.4 | 18 196 | 40.1 | 1 022 | 7 051 | 6 518 | 0 |
| District 8 | 269 342 | 2.38 | 65.1 | 52.5 | 8.3 | 28.8 | 20 163 | 25.9 | 5 484 | 4 945 | 4 490 | 0 |

1. No spouse present.

# Table E. Congressional Districts 113th Congress — Housing and Money Income

| STATE District | Housing units, 2011 | | | | | | Money income, 2011 | | |
| | Occupied units | | | | | | Households | | |
| | | | Owner-occupied | | | Renter-occupied | | | |
| | Total | Percent Occupied | Percent | Median value[1] (dollars) | Percent valued at $500,000 or more | Median rent[2] | Per capita income (dollars) | Median income (dollars) | Percent with income of $100,000 or more |
| | 40 | 41 | 42 | 43 | 44 | 45 | 46 | 47 | 48 |
|---|---|---|---|---|---|---|---|---|---|
| KENTUCKY | 1 932 731 | 86.5 | 68.9 | 120 600 | 2.7 | 626 | 22 300 | 41 141 | 13.8 |
| District 1 | 332 451 | 84.1 | 72.2 | 90 100 | 1.8 | 562 | 19 583 | 37 011 | 9.2 |
| District 2 | 313 390 | 86.3 | 70.8 | 119 600 | 2.3 | 616 | 21 617 | 41 857 | 12.6 |
| District 3 | 331 520 | 88.0 | 63.2 | 144 900 | 3.4 | 694 | 26 264 | 44 407 | 17.0 |
| District 4 | 301 857 | 87.8 | 73.6 | 148 000 | 3.5 | 688 | 25 192 | 51 881 | 20.4 |
| District 5 | 326 888 | 84.3 | 71.5 | 74 900 | 1.4 | 528 | 16 663 | 29 627 | 7.7 |
| District 6 | 326 625 | 88.6 | 62.8 | 146 100 | 4.0 | 658 | 24 408 | 43 399 | 16.3 |
| LOUISIANA | 1 978 974 | 86.0 | 66.4 | 139 400 | 3.0 | 747 | 22 882 | 41 734 | 16.3 |
| District 1 | 325 460 | 88.3 | 69.0 | 183 500 | 5.2 | 873 | 27 795 | 50 979.0 | 21.9 |
| District 2 | 355 256 | 81.4 | 54.8 | 141 500 | 2.7 | 826 | 19 965 | 34 603.0 | 12.2 |
| District 3 | 321 659 | 88.3 | 69.7 | 119 400 | 3.1 | 697 | 23 151 | 41 022.0 | 16.3 |
| District 4 | 335 009 | 84.3 | 66.7 | 109 200 | 2.1 | 674 | 22 201 | 40 569.0 | 14.3 |
| District 5 | 326 418 | 84.5 | 65.9 | 92 400 | 1.4 | 601 | 18 410 | 32 854.0 | 11.6 |
| District 6 | 315 172 | 89.9 | 72.8 | 164 600 | 3.5 | 821 | 25 819 | 54 406.0 | 21.1 |
| MAINE | 725 650 | 76.1 | 71.0 | 171 600 | 5.2 | 747 | 25 802 | 46 033 | 15.5 |
| District 1 | 348 735 | 79.1 | 70.2 | 216 900 | 7.9 | 850 | 29 408 | 52 323 | 19.5 |
| District 2 | 376 915 | 73.3 | 71.7 | 138 100 | 2.7 | 660 | 22 151 | 40 518 | 11.5 |
| MARYLAND | 2 391 508 | 89.3 | 67.3 | 287 100 | 17.3 | 1 153 | 34 500 | 70 004 | 33.4 |
| District 1 | 333 157 | 78.3 | 78.5 | 274 100 | 12.4 | 943 | 30 878 | 64 151 | 29.5 |
| District 2 | 301 066 | 91.5 | 62.1 | 225 900 | 5.8 | 1 056 | 28 537 | 58 345 | 23.4 |
| District 3 | 305 990 | 92.5 | 64.3 | 294 200 | 17.1 | 1 216 | 38 575 | 73 053 | 34.9 |
| District 4 | 284 187 | 91.9 | 63.4 | 279 200 | 12.7 | 1 183 | 33 156 | 71 135 | 32.3 |
| District 5 | 268 437 | 91.6 | 77.0 | 298 600 | 11.6 | 1 348 | 35 513 | 87 457 | 42.4 |
| District 6 | 290 927 | 91.7 | 70.0 | 282 100 | 21.4 | 1 151 | 34 626 | 68 361 | 34.1 |
| District 7 | 318 545 | 83.3 | 56.3 | 247 800 | 19.9 | 959 | 29 074 | 51 018 | 24.8 |
| District 8 | 289 199 | 95.4 | 68.2 | 405 300 | 36.6 | 1 480 | 45 271 | 90 959 | 46.3 |
| MASSACHUSETTS | 2 819 028 | 89.8 | 62.1 | 326 300 | 19.5 | 1 034 | 34 041 | 62 859 | 30.2 |
| District 1 | 320 399 | 89.1 | 65.4 | 213 500 | 4.8 | 752 | 26 415 | 49 270 | 19.5 |
| District 2 | 295 975 | 91.4 | 64.0 | 256 200 | 5.7 | 881 | 29 340 | 58 439 | 26.3 |
| District 3 | 295 316 | 92.7 | 64.4 | 289 800 | 15.2 | 932 | 32 350 | 63 270 | 29.6 |
| District 4 | 290 704 | 93.5 | 71.2 | 376 000 | 30.8 | 1 088 | 41 677 | 81 131 | 41.2 |
| District 5 | 305 981 | 95.0 | 60.0 | 418 100 | 35.5 | 1 250 | 41 531 | 75 564 | 37.3 |
| District 6 | 294 202 | 94.0 | 69.6 | 365 100 | 21.5 | 1 083 | 36 937 | 76 130 | 36.8 |
| District 7 | 308 404 | 92.9 | 33.0 | 346 900 | 20.6 | 1 235 | 28 407 | 48 034 | 21.3 |
| District 8 | 307 035 | 93.8 | 61.6 | 350 500 | 20.6 | 1 213 | 37 572 | 70 420 | 33.8 |
| District 9 | 401 012 | 72.0 | 70.9 | 336 400 | 20.9 | 895 | 31 960 | 57 517 | 26.6 |
| MICHIGAN | 4 525 654 | 83.4 | 71.7 | 118 100 | 2.6 | 739 | 24 409 | 45 981 | 16.9 |
| District 1 | 443 265 | 64.6 | 78.2 | 117 300 | 3.9 | 621 | 22 406 | 40 765 | 10.9 |
| District 2 | 310 465 | 83.8 | 73.9 | 121 800 | 2.0 | 694 | 21 610 | 45 712 | 14.0 |
| District 3 | 296 849 | 89.9 | 72.7 | 131 500 | 2.6 | 714 | 24 858 | 48 010 | 17.1 |
| District 4 | 344 660 | 78.0 | 77.8 | 109 000 | 1.7 | 673 | 22 199 | 42 586 | 13.0 |
| District 5 | 328 157 | 83.3 | 71.0 | 87 300 | 1.5 | 659 | 21 108 | 39 783 | 11.6 |
| District 6 | 325 869 | 81.1 | 74.2 | 126 500 | 3.3 | 669 | 22 822 | 44 376 | 14.5 |
| District 7 | 301 967 | 87.5 | 76.4 | 127 900 | 2.2 | 719 | 23 756 | 49 475 | 16.8 |
| District 8 | 291 206 | 90.8 | 72.1 | 164 400 | 3.6 | 785 | 28 978 | 57 241 | 24.8 |
| District 9 | 323 568 | 91.2 | 71.3 | 107 300 | 2.3 | 787 | 27 200 | 47 777 | 17.5 |
| District 10 | 298 535 | 87.3 | 79.2 | 138 500 | 2.0 | 780 | 25 066 | 53 121 | 20.2 |
| District 11 | 294 000 | 92.8 | 76.1 | 170 400 | 4.7 | 875 | 35 574 | 69 397 | 31.9 |
| District 12 | 297 054 | 90.9 | 65.0 | 113 400 | 2.4 | 804 | 26 512 | 48 575 | 19.5 |
| District 13 | 342 188 | 75.2 | 58.0 | 61 100 | 0.8 | 733 | 16 115 | 29 863 | 7.5 |
| District 14 | 327 871 | 81.6 | 57.9 | 87 000 | 2.8 | 839 | 23 395 | 38 315 | 16.0 |
| MINNESOTA | 2 354 075 | 89.1 | 72.8 | 183 500 | 5.4 | 787 | 29 404 | 56 954 | 22.7 |
| District 1 | 283 262 | 92.0 | 75.4 | 149 400 | 3.1 | 670 | 26 153 | 52 335 | 18.1 |
| District 2 | 263 837 | 94.3 | 79.2 | 212 900 | 4.9 | 858 | 31 943 | 70 095 | 30.6 |
| District 3 | 271 738 | 95.2 | 75.5 | 242 200 | 12.0 | 964 | 39 857 | 73 468 | 35.3 |
| District 4 | 275 983 | 94.8 | 63.7 | 203 900 | 6.0 | 829 | 30 071 | 57 791 | 23.8 |
| District 5 | 307 840 | 92.6 | 55.2 | 193 300 | 6.3 | 824 | 30 599 | 50 923 | 20.7 |
| District 6 | 258 076 | 94.1 | 80.2 | 193 600 | 3.4 | 825 | 27 789 | 65 461 | 25.9 |
| District 7 | 324 708 | 83.0 | 76.9 | 134 500 | 3.0 | 592 | 24 412 | 47 739 | 13.9 |
| District 8 | 368 631 | 73.1 | 78.1 | 159 500 | 4.5 | 646 | 24 360 | 46 692 | 14.5 |

1. Specified owner-occupied units.   2. Specified renter-occupied units.

## Table E. Congressional Districts 113th Congress — Poverty, Labor Force, Employment, and Social Security

| STATE District | Poverty, 2011 (percent) | | | Civilian labor force, 2011 | | | Civilian employment,[2] 2011 | | | | Persons under age 65 with no health insurance, 2010 (percent) | Social Security beneficiaries, December 2012 | | Supplemental Security Income recipients, December 2012 |
|---|---|---|---|---|---|---|---|---|---|---|---|---|---|---|
| | | | | | Unemployment | | | Percent | | | | | | |
| | Persons below poverty level | Families below poverty level | Households receiving food stamps in past 12 months | Total | Total | Rate[1] | Total | Management, professional, and related occupations | Service, sales, and office | Construction and production | | Number | Rate[3] | |
| | 49 | 50 | 51 | 52 | 53 | 54 | 55 | 56 | 57 | 58 | 59 | 60 | 61 | 62 |
| KENTUCKY | 19.1 | 14.7 | 17.4 | 2 052 108 | 213 707 | 10.4 | 1 838 401 | 32.9 | 41.1 | 26.0 | 16.6 | 930 222 | 212.9 | 192 587 |
| District 1 | 19.8 | 14.8 | 17.2 | 315 712 | 30 950 | 9.8 | 284 762 | 28.4 | 39.9 | 31.7 | 17.8 | 173 870 | 241.2 | 30 643 |
| District 2 | 17.6 | 14.4 | 16.5 | 355 272 | 38 164 | 10.7 | 317 108 | 29.1 | 40.4 | 30.6 | 14.6 | 151 603 | 206.7 | 24 864 |
| District 3 | 17.6 | 13.4 | 15.1 | 378 461 | 45 116 | 11.9 | 333 345 | 36.3 | 40.6 | 23.1 | 16.7 | 130 189 | 179.1 | 23 537 |
| District 4 | 14.0 | 10.2 | 12.5 | 363 447 | 29 954 | 8.2 | 333 493 | 35.7 | 41.9 | 22.5 | 14.2 | 146 288 | 200.1 | 20 636 |
| District 5 | 26.8 | 21.5 | 26.5 | 266 376 | 32 112 | 12.1 | 234 264 | 28.2 | 42.9 | 28.9 | 20.5 | 191 967 | 265.2 | 66 646 |
| District 6 | 19.2 | 13.3 | 16.3 | 372 840 | 37 411 | 10.0 | 335 429 | 37.8 | 41.2 | 20.9 | 16.0 | 136 305 | 185.9 | 26 261 |
| LOUISIANA | 20.4 | 16.1 | 16.4 | 2 175 279 | 201 340 | 9.3 | 1 973 939 | 31.1 | 44.3 | 24.6 | 19.9 | 826 350 | 180.6 | 180 936 |
| District 1 | 14.9 | 11.1 | 11.2 | 382 251 | 28 277 | 7.4 | 353 974 | 33.9 | 42.4 | 23.8 | 17.1 | 141 711 | 186.6 | 19 613 |
| District 2 | 26.5 | 22.2 | 22.5 | 376 144 | 47 129 | 12.5 | 329 015 | 27.9 | 49.3 | 22.7 | 22.2 | 128 146 | 166.9 | 42 485 |
| District 3 | 19.4 | 15.5 | 15.5 | 365 638 | 37 502 | 10.3 | 328 136 | 28.9 | 43.7 | 27.4 | 19.6 | 138 073 | 181.5 | 25 984 |
| District 4 | 20.5 | 16.5 | 17.0 | 335 321 | 24 190 | 7.2 | 311 131 | 30.2 | 43.8 | 25.9 | 20.8 | 145 868 | 192.3 | 34 170 |
| District 5 | 26.6 | 20.7 | 21.0 | 318 794 | 34 865 | 10.9 | 283 929 | 28.5 | 45.4 | 26.0 | 25.6 | 148 316 | 193.8 | 38 991 |
| District 6 | 15.0 | 11.0 | 11.6 | 397 131 | 29 377 | 7.4 | 367 754 | 36.2 | 41.8 | 22.0 | 14.6 | 124 236 | 162.8 | 19 693 |
| MAINE | 14.1 | 9.3 | 17.5 | 703 536 | 60 432 | 8.6 | 643 104 | 35.1 | 42.8 | 22.0 | 12.7 | 314 401 | 236.7 | 37 029 |
| District 1 | 11.4 | 7.3 | 13.8 | 366 864 | 26 435 | 7.2 | 340 429 | 38.7 | 41.9 | 19.5 | 11.4 | 149 207 | 223.3 | 14 366 |
| District 2 | 16.9 | 11.4 | 21.1 | 336 672 | 33 997 | 10.1 | 302 675 | 31.2 | 43.8 | 25.0 | 14.0 | 165 194 | 250.3 | 22 663 |
| MARYLAND | 10.1 | 7.1 | 9.9 | 3 177 062 | 282 496 | 8.9 | 2 894 566 | 43.7 | 40.5 | 15.8 | 11.7 | 895 352 | 153.6 | 115 100 |
| District 1 | 9.8 | 6.4 | 9.4 | 376 110 | 33 861 | 9.0 | 342 249 | 37.8 | 41.7 | 20.5 | 10.3 | 147 619 | 204.3 | 11 110 |
| District 2 | 13.1 | 10.9 | 13.1 | 394 005 | 42 349 | 10.7 | 351 656 | 38.8 | 43.0 | 18.2 | 11.5 | 118 114 | 162.5 | 17 811 |
| District 3 | 8.3 | 5.6 | 8.1 | 399 986 | 30 492 | 7.6 | 369 494 | 49.6 | 37.0 | 13.4 | 11.1 | 109 905 | 152.2 | 13 631 |
| District 4 | 8.3 | 6.6 | 8.8 | 424 352 | 40 300 | 9.5 | 384 052 | 36.3 | 46.0 | 17.6 | 16.0 | 91 527 | 124.2 | 10 924 |
| District 5 | 7.1 | 4.9 | 7.3 | 400 066 | 31 885 | 8.0 | 368 181 | 41.7 | 41.3 | 17.1 | 9.0 | 95 199 | 131.0 | 8 510 |
| District 6 | 8.7 | 5.5 | 10.0 | 392 391 | 29 242 | 7.5 | 363 149 | 45.8 | 39.2 | 15.0 | 12.0 | 108 541 | 148.3 | 12 915 |
| District 7 | 19.0 | 13.0 | 18.5 | 364 441 | 48 789 | 13.4 | 315 652 | 45.3 | 41.6 | 13.1 | 12.5 | 119 066 | 166.8 | 32 015 |
| District 8 | 6.5 | 4.4 | 4.2 | 425 711 | 25 578 | 6.0 | 400 133 | 53.6 | 34.6 | 11.8 | 11.3 | 105 381 | 141.0 | 8 184 |
| MASSACHUSETTS | 11.6 | 8.3 | 12.1 | 3 619 653 | 334 933 | 9.3 | 3 284 720 | 43.3 | 40.7 | 16.0 | 4.9 | 1 185 307 | 179.9 | 185 785 |
| District 1 | 14.7 | 10.9 | 18.3 | 381 688 | 40 712 | 10.7 | 340 976 | 33.5 | 45.9 | 20.5 | 4.9 | 157 865 | 216.6 | 36 253 |
| District 2 | 12.4 | 9.0 | 13.0 | 392 206 | 35 738 | 9.1 | 356 468 | 41.6 | 40.7 | 17.7 | 3.9 | 127 887 | 176.1 | 19 843 |
| District 3 | 11.3 | 9.0 | 13.8 | 393 402 | 37 970 | 9.7 | 355 432 | 42.2 | 37.7 | 20.1 | 5.7 | 120 728 | 164.9 | 23 230 |
| District 4 | 7.0 | 4.4 | 8.4 | 406 179 | 31 403 | 7.7 | 374 776 | 48.9 | 38.2 | 13.0 | 3.2 | 123 147 | 167.1 | 11 162 |
| District 5 | 8.8 | 6.3 | 7.1 | 418 540 | 31 118 | 7.4 | 387 422 | 52.2 | 36.8 | 11.0 | 4.6 | 117 559 | 159.4 | 11 543 |
| District 6 | 7.9 | 5.3 | 8.8 | 406 357 | 34 400 | 8.5 | 371 957 | 44.6 | 41.4 | 14.0 | 4.4 | 139 247 | 190.3 | 13 991 |
| District 7 | 21.9 | 16.5 | 18.9 | 418 018 | 48 188 | 11.5 | 369 830 | 44.7 | 42.7 | 12.6 | 6.9 | 91 028 | 124.0 | 35 055 |
| District 8 | 9.8 | 7.0 | 9.3 | 413 154 | 37 592 | 9.1 | 375 562 | 45.5 | 39.9 | 14.6 | 3.8 | 130 336 | 177.8 | 16 419 |
| District 9 | 11.0 | 8.0 | 11.7 | 390 109 | 37 812 | 9.7 | 352 297 | 34.5 | 44.1 | 21.4 | 6.3 | 177 510 | 243.9 | 18 289 |
| MICHIGAN | 17.5 | 12.5 | 18.1 | 4 821 613 | 629 735 | 13.1 | 4 191 878 | 34.6 | 42.6 | 22.9 | 13.6 | 2 061 941 | 208.8 | 271 777 |
| District 1 | 16.4 | 10.6 | 16.5 | 327 600 | 37 435 | 11.4 | 290 165 | 29.7 | 45.4 | 24.8 | 16.9 | 194 645 | 274.6 | 15 694 |
| District 2 | 15.2 | 10.5 | 17.1 | 355 689 | 39 758 | 11.2 | 315 931 | 31.4 | 39.3 | 29.2 | 12.8 | 142 866 | 201.5 | 16 341 |
| District 3 | 16.0 | 11.5 | 18.1 | 355 941 | 40 669 | 11.4 | 315 272 | 34.6 | 41.3 | 24.1 | 11.9 | 133 534 | 188.2 | 18 339 |
| District 4 | 18.3 | 11.9 | 17.9 | 325 475 | 39 167 | 12.0 | 286 308 | 30.7 | 44.4 | 24.9 | 13.8 | 166 877 | 237.3 | 16 807 |
| District 5 | 20.3 | 15.7 | 22.8 | 315 780 | 50 971 | 16.1 | 264 809 | 29.6 | 46.9 | 23.4 | 12.8 | 168 528 | 241.2 | 28 664 |
| District 6 | 17.9 | 12.5 | 17.6 | 351 585 | 41 209 | 11.7 | 310 376 | 32.5 | 40.3 | 27.2 | 13.9 | 148 582 | 210.0 | 17 533 |
| District 7 | 13.1 | 9.6 | 15.2 | 339 213 | 40 087 | 11.8 | 299 126 | 30.9 | 42.0 | 27.1 | 11.1 | 153 544 | 218.9 | 13 746 |
| District 8 | 13.5 | 7.7 | 13.3 | 364 297 | 33 523 | 9.2 | 330 774 | 41.9 | 39.8 | 18.3 | 10.1 | 122 386 | 173.1 | 11 134 |
| District 9 | 15.5 | 11.9 | 16.4 | 376 500 | 50 409 | 13.4 | 326 091 | 35.8 | 43.2 | 21.0 | 15.4 | 151 824 | 213.1 | 18 447 |
| District 10 | 12.5 | 9.5 | 14.0 | 349 741 | 41 084 | 11.7 | 308 657 | 34.0 | 40.7 | 25.3 | 12.2 | 149 127 | 212.5 | 11 563 |
| District 11 | 8.2 | 5.6 | 8.0 | 375 143 | 33 029 | 8.8 | 342 114 | 48.0 | 37.9 | 14.1 | 10.4 | 128 863 | 182.4 | 7 759 |
| District 12 | 19.0 | 12.8 | 16.6 | 356 817 | 42 986 | 12.0 | 313 831 | 37.7 | 42.8 | 19.5 | 12.0 | 127 961 | 181.9 | 16 217 |
| District 13 | 33.1 | 27.4 | 33.6 | 306 178 | 75 489 | 24.7 | 230 689 | 23.6 | 50.0 | 26.4 | 19.8 | 135 259 | 193.4 | 43 390 |
| District 14 | 26.5 | 21.4 | 27.3 | 321 654 | 63 919 | 19.9 | 257 735 | 37.7 | 47.0 | 15.4 | 17.6 | 137 945 | 195.0 | 36 143 |
| MINNESOTA | 11.9 | 7.6 | 8.6 | 2 955 217 | 226 336 | 7.7 | 2 728 881 | 38.7 | 40.4 | 20.8 | 10.1 | 927 508 | 173.5 | 91 559 |
| District 1 | 11.6 | 7.0 | 7.7 | 370 690 | 22 535 | 6.1 | 348 155 | 35.3 | 38.8 | 25.9 | 9.3 | 128 775 | 193.3 | 9 171 |
| District 2 | 6.9 | 4.3 | 5.0 | 384 817 | 26 529 | 6.9 | 358 288 | 40.4 | 40.7 | 19.0 | 8.5 | 95 974 | 143.5 | 6 299 |
| District 3 | 7.4 | 4.9 | 5.5 | 382 798 | 29 039 | 7.6 | 353 759 | 45.4 | 40.5 | 14.1 | 9.1 | 106 830 | 160.8 | 7 446 |
| District 4 | 14.7 | 9.8 | 10.0 | 365 642 | 29 670 | 8.1 | 335 972 | 42.9 | 41.5 | 15.6 | 10.9 | 104 787 | 156.6 | 17 499 |
| District 5 | 18.8 | 13.1 | 12.5 | 389 109 | 37 149 | 9.5 | 351 960 | 45.2 | 41.6 | 13.2 | 12.6 | 93 039 | 137.4 | 20 966 |
| District 6 | 9.1 | 5.6 | 6.9 | 376 683 | 27 948 | 7.4 | 348 735 | 35.9 | 39.2 | 24.9 | 8.5 | 95 574 | 141.5 | 6 346 |
| District 7 | 12.8 | 8.3 | 9.5 | 351 073 | 22 412 | 6.4 | 328 661 | 32.7 | 37.9 | 29.4 | 11.0 | 146 679 | 221.7 | 10 488 |
| District 8 | 14.0 | 8.8 | 10.5 | 334 405 | 31 054 | 9.3 | 303 351 | 30.6 | 43.3 | 26.1 | 11.0 | 155 850 | 235.4 | 13 344 |

1. Percent of civilian labor force.   2. Persons 16 years old and over.   3. Per 1,000 resident population estimated in the 2011 American Community Survey.

| STATE District | Representative, 113th Congress | Land area,[1] 2010 (sq km) | Total persons | Per square kilometer | White | Black | American Indian, Alaska Native | Asian and Pacific Islander | Some other race | Two or more races | Hispanic or Latino[2] | Non-Hispanic White alone | Percent female | Percent foreign born | Percent born in state of residence |
|---|---|---|---|---|---|---|---|---|---|---|---|---|---|---|---|
| | | 1 | 2 | 3 | 4 | 5 | 6 | 7 | 8 | 9 | 10 | 11 | 12 | 13 | 14 |
| MISSISSIPPI | | 121 531 | 2 978 512 | 24.5 | 59.4 | 37.4 | 0.4 | 0.9 | 0.6 | 1.2 | 2.9 | 57.7 | 51.4 | 2.2 | 71.5 |
| District 1 | Alan Nunnelee (R) | 27 383 | 740 720 | 27.0 | 70.5 | 26.4 | 0.2 | 0.5 | 0.8 | 1.5 | 3.0 | 68.9 | 52.1 | 1.6 | 62.3 |
| District 2 | Bennie G. Thompson (D) | 40 278 | 743 249 | 18.5 | 32.8 | 65.2 | 0.2 | 0.4 | 0.7 | 0.6 | 1.8 | 31.9 | 51.7 | 1.5 | 84.1 |
| District 3 | Gregg Harper (R) | 33 034 | 745 254 | 22.6 | 61.8 | 35.2 | 0.9 | 0.9 | 0.5 | 0.7 | 2.1 | 60.4 | 51.6 | 2.3 | 77.2 |
| District 4 | Steven Palazzo (R) | 20 835 | 749 289 | 36.0 | 72.5 | 23.1 | 0.2 | 1.9 | 0.6 | 1.7 | 4.0 | 69.5 | 50.3 | 3.3 | 62.4 |
| MISSOURI | | 178 040 | 6 010 688 | 33.8 | 83.0 | 11.5 | 0.4 | 1.7 | 1.0 | 2.4 | 3.7 | 80.8 | 51.0 | 4.0 | 66.2 |
| District 1 | William Lacy Clay (D) | 584 | 739 977 | 1 267.8 | 44.9 | 48.9 | 0.2 | 2.4 | 0.7 | 3.0 | 3.2 | 42.9 | 52.9 | 5.9 | 69.8 |
| District 2 | Ann Wagner (R) | 1 206 | 752 403 | 623.7 | 89.9 | 3.8 | 0.1 | 4.0 | 0.3 | 1.9 | 2.4 | 88.1 | 51.6 | 7.4 | 66.7 |
| District 3 | Blaine Luetkemeyer (R) | 17 745 | 762 347 | 43.0 | 92.8 | 3.2 | 0.3 | 0.9 | 0.9 | 1.9 | 2.3 | 91.6 | 50.2 | 2.6 | 73.7 |
| District 4 | Vicky Hartzler (R) | 37 299 | 755 389 | 20.3 | 90.0 | 5.0 | 0.4 | 1.4 | 0.9 | 2.3 | 3.3 | 87.9 | 50.0 | 2.9 | 62.4 |
| District 5 | Emanuel Cleaver (D) | 6 280 | 747 573 | 119.0 | 69.2 | 21.3 | 0.4 | 2.0 | 3.7 | 3.4 | 8.7 | 65.2 | 51.8 | 6.2 | 60.5 |
| District 6 | Sam Graves (R) | 47 134 | 753 729 | 16.0 | 91.3 | 4.0 | 0.4 | 1.3 | 0.8 | 2.1 | 3.1 | 89.2 | 50.2 | 3.0 | 65.1 |
| District 7 | Bill Long (R) | 16 247 | 751 514 | 46.3 | 92.9 | 1.6 | 0.8 | 1.1 | 0.7 | 3.0 | 4.2 | 89.7 | 51.0 | 3.1 | 57.2 |
| District 8 | Jason T. Smith (R) | 51 544 | 747 756 | 14.5 | 92.4 | 4.5 | 0.4 | 0.5 | 0.2 | 1.9 | 1.6 | 91.1 | 50.2 | 1.3 | 74.0 |
| MONTANA | | 376 962 | 998 199 | 2.6 | 89.3 | 0.4 | 6.7 | 0.7 | 0.5 | 2.4 | 2.9 | 87.4 | 49.9 | 2.0 | 55.5 |
| At Large | Steve Daines (R) | 376 962 | 998 199 | 2.6 | 89.3 | 0.4 | 6.7 | 0.7 | 0.5 | 2.4 | 2.9 | 87.4 | 49.9 | 2.0 | 55.5 |
| NEBRASKA | | 198 974 | 1 842 641 | 9.3 | 88.2 | 4.5 | 1.0 | 1.9 | 2.2 | 2.2 | 9.5 | 81.8 | 50.5 | 6.3 | 65.8 |
| District 1 | Jeff Fortenberry (R) | 22 997 | 616 728 | 26.8 | 90.5 | 2.6 | 1.4 | 2.2 | 0.7 | 2.5 | 7.9 | 84.3 | 50.1 | 6.4 | 66.9 |
| District 2 | Lee Terry (R) | 1 320 | 617 475 | 467.7 | 79.9 | 9.9 | 0.6 | 2.9 | 3.9 | 2.8 | 10.3 | 74.4 | 50.7 | 8.1 | 60.9 |
| District 3 | Adrian Smith (R) | 174 657 | 608 438 | 3.5 | 94.2 | 1.0 | 0.9 | 0.6 | 2.0 | 1.2 | 10.1 | 86.6 | 50.6 | 4.4 | 69.6 |
| NEVADA | | 284 332 | 2 723 322 | 9.6 | 71.5 | 8.2 | 1.2 | 7.7 | 7.4 | 3.9 | 27.1 | 53.5 | 49.6 | 19.2 | 25.3 |
| District 1 | Dina Titus (D) | 271 | 659 962 | 2 438.4 | 65.8 | 9.1 | 0.7 | 9.2 | 11.5 | 3.7 | 42.9 | 36.0 | 48.0 | 31.9 | 22.5 |
| District 2 | Mark E. Amodei (R) | 144 598 | 679 147 | 4.7 | 81.3 | 2.0 | 2.5 | 4.2 | 7.1 | 2.9 | 21.1 | 68.5 | 49.5 | 13.0 | 29.3 |
| District 3 | Joseph J. Heck (R) | 7 379 | 703 278 | 95.3 | 73.3 | 7.6 | 0.4 | 12.6 | 2.1 | 4.1 | 15.4 | 61.1 | 51.8 | 16.2 | 21.6 |
| District 4 | Steven A. Horsford (D) | 132 084 | 680 935 | 5.2 | 65.6 | 14.0 | 1.2 | 4.9 | 9.3 | 4.9 | 29.7 | 47.5 | 48.9 | 16.1 | 27.9 |
| NEW HAMPSHIRE | | 23 187 | 1 318 194 | 56.8 | 94.1 | 1.1 | 0.2 | 2.2 | 0.7 | 1.7 | 2.9 | 92.0 | 50.6 | 5.6 | 42.5 |
| District 1 | Carol Shea-Porter (D) | 6 381 | 660 761 | 103.6 | 94.3 | 1.2 | 0.2 | 2.0 | 0.8 | 1.4 | 3.1 | 92.1 | 50.5 | 5.8 | 42.7 |
| District 2 | Ann M. Kuster (D) | 16 806 | 657 433 | 39.1 | 93.9 | 1.0 | 0.1 | 2.4 | 0.5 | 2.0 | 2.7 | 91.9 | 50.7 | 5.4 | 42.4 |
| NEW JERSEY | | 19 047 | 8 821 155 | 463.1 | 69.2 | 13.4 | 0.2 | 8.5 | 6.2 | 2.5 | 18.1 | 58.6 | 51.3 | 21.5 | 52.1 |
| District 1 | Robert E. Andrews (D) | 907 | 727 496 | 802.5 | 69.8 | 16.0 | 0.2 | 5.1 | 5.9 | 3.0 | 11.6 | 65.7 | 51.6 | 9.4 | 53.2 |
| District 2 | Frank A. LoBiondo (R) | 5 419 | 736 397 | 135.9 | 74.2 | 13.8 | 0.8 | 3.6 | 5.2 | 2.5 | 15.0 | 67.0 | 50.9 | 10.4 | 58.3 |
| District 3 | Jon Runyan (R) | 2 330 | 732 131 | 314.2 | 81.4 | 10.7 | 0.1 | 3.5 | 1.8 | 2.5 | 7.5 | 76.3 | 51.5 | 8.8 | 58.8 |
| District 4 | Christopher H. Smith (R) | 1 792 | 736 007 | 410.7 | 85.0 | 6.8 | 0.2 | 4.0 | 2.0 | 2.1 | 9.3 | 78.7 | 51.8 | 11.2 | 59.5 |
| District 5 | Scott Garrett (R) | 2 567 | 731 055 | 284.7 | 80.3 | 4.7 | 0.1 | 8.5 | 4.8 | 1.7 | 12.6 | 72.8 | 51.5 | 19.8 | 51.8 |
| District 6 | Frank Pallone Jr. (D) | 558 | 738 756 | 1 323.3 | 67.2 | 9.5 | 0.3 | 17.4 | 2.8 | 2.8 | 20.8 | 50.8 | 50.8 | 29.0 | 49.6 |
| District 7 | Leonard Lance (R) | 2 513 | 747 216 | 297.4 | 81.1 | 4.5 | 0.1 | 8.5 | 4.5 | 1.4 | 11.7 | 74.1 | 50.8 | 17.8 | 56.9 |
| District 8 | Albio Sires (D) | 142 | 746 415 | 5 269.8 | 56.4 | 9.8 | 0.2 | 7.9 | 22.3 | 3.4 | 54.4 | 27.1 | 49.5 | 43.2 | 37.0 |
| District 9 | Bill Pascrell, Jr. (D) | 247 | 742 508 | 3 006.8 | 63.0 | 11.2 | 0.3 | 13.0 | 8.7 | 3.7 | 33.6 | 41.7 | 51.3 | 36.4 | 42.9 |
| District 10 | Donald M. Payne, Jr. (D) | 197 | 726 382 | 3 694.2 | 29.8 | 53.4 | 0.4 | 6.9 | 7.1 | 2.5 | 16.5 | 21.2 | 52.7 | 27.7 | 50.0 |
| District 11 | Rodney P. Frelinghuysen (R) | 1 308 | 724 761 | 554.2 | 84.0 | 3.6 | 0.0 | 9.2 | 1.2 | 1.9 | 8.8 | 76.8 | 51.9 | 17.3 | 59.8 |
| District 12 | Rush Holt (D) | 1 068 | 732 031 | 685.6 | 58.1 | 17.6 | 0.2 | 14.6 | 7.6 | 1.9 | 15.1 | 50.8 | 50.9 | 26.0 | 48.1 |
| NEW MEXICO | | 314 161 | 2 082 224 | 6.6 | 71.7 | 2.1 | 9.2 | 1.3 | 12.6 | 3.1 | 46.7 | 40.1 | 50.2 | 10.1 | 52.2 |
| District 1 | Michelle Lujan Grisham (D) | 11 914 | 698 441 | 58.6 | 68.2 | 2.8 | 4.4 | 1.9 | 18.9 | 3.8 | 48.1 | 41.8 | 50.8 | 10.7 | 50.2 |
| District 2 | Steve Pearce (R) | 185 804 | 702 936 | 3.8 | 80.7 | 1.6 | 6.0 | 0.7 | 8.9 | 2.0 | 52.1 | 39.4 | 49.7 | 11.9 | 51.0 |
| District 3 | Ben Ray Luján (D) | 116 442 | 680 847 | 5.8 | 65.9 | 2.0 | 17.2 | 1.3 | 10.1 | 3.4 | 39.8 | 38.9 | 50.1 | 7.7 | 55.6 |
| NEW YORK | | 122 057 | 19 465 197 | 159.5 | 65.3 | 15.6 | 0.3 | 7.4 | 8.6 | 2.7 | 18.0 | 57.8 | 51.5 | 22.2 | 63.6 |
| District 1 | Timothy H. Bishop (D) | 1 684 | 720 071 | 427.7 | 87.7 | 4.6 | 0.3 | 3.6 | 1.9 | 1.9 | 12.8 | 77.4 | 50.4 | 11.9 | 78.3 |
| District 2 | Peter T. King (R) | 471 | 724 053 | 1 535.9 | 74.9 | 10.0 | 0.2 | 3.1 | 9.5 | 2.4 | 22.6 | 63.5 | 51.5 | 16.4 | 76.0 |
| District 3 | Steve Israel (D) | 660 | 724 164 | 1 096.8 | 78.2 | 3.1 | 0.1 | 13.0 | 3.9 | 1.7 | 9.2 | 73.4 | 51.3 | 20.9 | 72.0 |
| District 4 | Carolyn McCarthy (D) | 287 | 716 038 | 2 494.0 | 68.9 | 14.6 | 0.3 | 6.0 | 7.5 | 2.8 | 17.7 | 60.5 | 51.7 | 21.5 | 70.6 |
| District 5 | Gregory W. Meeks (D) | 134 | 740 327 | 5 509.6 | 17.8 | 51.0 | 0.3 | 13.1 | 13.5 | 4.2 | 20.2 | 10.7 | 53.2 | 43.1 | 48.1 |
| District 6 | Grace Meng (D) | 77 | 707 630 | 9 173.5 | 49.4 | 3.8 | 0.4 | 36.5 | 6.9 | 3.1 | 17.5 | 39.6 | 52.1 | 51.8 | 42.3 |
| District 7 | Nydia M. Velázquez (D) | 42 | 724 899 | 17 319.1 | 47.0 | 10.2 | 0.7 | 17.7 | 21.3 | 3.1 | 43.8 | 28.0 | 50.8 | 36.6 | 46.7 |
| District 8 | Hakeem S. Jeffries (D) | 77 | 715 905 | 9 318.7 | 29.7 | 56.0 | 0.4 | 4.7 | 7.2 | 2.1 | 18.1 | 22.1 | 54.8 | 33.4 | 53.4 |
| District 9 | Yvette D. Clarke (D) | 40 | 739 328 | 18 369.6 | 32.6 | 52.7 | 0.1 | 6.6 | 6.2 | 1.7 | 11.9 | 29.4 | 54.2 | 45.9 | 47.1 |
| District 10 | Jerrold Nadler (D) | 37 | 716 172 | 19 407.7 | 72.6 | 3.7 | 0.1 | 16.3 | 4.7 | 2.6 | 13.0 | 65.7 | 50.7 | 31.4 | 44.7 |
| District 11 | Michael G. Grimm (R) | 171 | 724 434 | 4 248.6 | 73.3 | 8.2 | 0.1 | 12.8 | 4.1 | 1.6 | 16.1 | 62.6 | 51.6 | 28.6 | 64.2 |
| District 12 | Carolyn B. Maloney (D) | 38 | 708 096 | 18 489.5 | 75.8 | 4.9 | 0.3 | 11.6 | 4.9 | 2.5 | 13.9 | 67.8 | 53.1 | 26.2 | 41.3 |
| District 13 | Charles B. Rangel (D) | 27 | 738 943 | 27 824.3 | 24.6 | 31.0 | 0.4 | 4.8 | 33.0 | 6.1 | 52.5 | 13.2 | 52.5 | 36.9 | 46.8 |
| District 14 | Joseph Crowley (D) | 73 | 712 053 | 9 716.7 | 46.5 | 11.4 | 0.2 | 16.5 | 22.2 | 3.2 | 46.9 | 25.0 | 49.0 | 48.2 | 42.8 |

1. Dry land or land partially or temporarily covered by water.    2. May be of any race.

# Table E. Congressional Districts 113th Congress — **Age and Education**

| | Population and population characteristics, 2011 (cont.) | | | | | | | | | | Education, 2011 | | |
| | Age (percent) | | | | | | | | | | | Attainment[2] (percent) | |
| STATE District | Under 5 years | 5 to 17 years | 18 to 24 years | 25 to 34 years | 35 to 44 years | 45 to 54 years | 55 to 64 years | 65 to 74 years | 75 years and over | Median age | Total Enrollment[1] | High school graduate or more | Bachelor's degree or more |
| | 15 | 16 | 17 | 18 | 19 | 20 | 21 | 22 | 23 | 24 | 25 | 26 | 27 |
| MISSISSIPPI | 6.9 | 18.3 | 10.5 | 12.7 | 12.9 | 13.6 | 12.1 | 7.3 | 5.7 | 36.1 | 830 815 | 81.1 | 19.8 |
| District 1 | 6.6 | 18.7 | 10.2 | 12.0 | 13.4 | 13.6 | 12.0 | 7.7 | 5.8 | 37.0 | 198 346 | 81.2 | 17.3 |
| District 2 | 7.1 | 18.9 | 11.2 | 13.0 | 11.7 | 13.8 | 12.0 | 6.8 | 5.4 | 34.9 | 216 758 | 77.6 | 18.7 |
| District 3 | 6.9 | 18.0 | 10.4 | 12.3 | 13.3 | 13.3 | 12.4 | 7.5 | 5.9 | 36.6 | 210 155 | 82.7 | 23.7 |
| District 4 | 7.0 | 17.8 | 10.4 | 13.3 | 12.9 | 13.7 | 12.0 | 7.4 | 5.5 | 36.0 | 205 556 | 82.8 | 19.6 |
| MISSOURI | 6.3 | 17.2 | 9.8 | 13.1 | 12.3 | 14.5 | 12.6 | 7.6 | 6.5 | 38.0 | 1 569 557 | 87.6 | 26.1 |
| District 1 | 6.8 | 16.3 | 10.8 | 15.7 | 12.6 | 13.8 | 12.0 | 6.1 | 5.8 | 35.3 | 207 852 | 86.5 | 27.7 |
| District 2 | 5.5 | 17.3 | 7.5 | 12.0 | 12.0 | 16.3 | 13.5 | 8.0 | 7.8 | 41.6 | 193 628 | 94.3 | 46.0 |
| District 3 | 6.3 | 18.3 | 8.9 | 12.6 | 13.3 | 15.2 | 12.7 | 7.5 | 5.3 | 38.2 | 200 053 | 89.4 | 23.5 |
| District 4 | 6.4 | 16.9 | 12.6 | 13.0 | 11.3 | 13.4 | 12.2 | 7.7 | 6.5 | 35.9 | 206 016 | 87.7 | 23.2 |
| District 5 | 6.9 | 16.9 | 9.2 | 14.7 | 12.5 | 14.2 | 12.1 | 7.0 | 6.5 | 36.7 | 192 363 | 86.4 | 24.8 |
| District 6 | 6.5 | 17.6 | 9.4 | 12.3 | 13.0 | 14.8 | 12.4 | 7.6 | 6.4 | 38.2 | 194 676 | 89.2 | 25.2 |
| District 7 | 6.3 | 17.0 | 10.6 | 12.7 | 12.0 | 13.7 | 12.3 | 8.6 | 6.9 | 37.9 | 193 493 | 86.4 | 22.9 |
| District 8 | 6.0 | 17.0 | 9.2 | 11.7 | 11.8 | 14.6 | 13.6 | 8.9 | 7.2 | 40.4 | 181 476 | 80.4 | 14.4 |
| MONTANA | 6.1 | 16.3 | 9.9 | 12.5 | 11.1 | 14.5 | 14.6 | 8.4 | 6.7 | 39.7 | 242 981 | 92.3 | 28.2 |
| At Large | 6.1 | 16.3 | 9.9 | 12.5 | 11.1 | 14.5 | 14.6 | 8.4 | 6.7 | 39.7 | 242 981 | 92.3 | 28.2 |
| NEBRASKA | 7.1 | 17.9 | 10.1 | 13.3 | 11.9 | 13.9 | 12.2 | 6.8 | 6.6 | 36.3 | 515 647 | 91.0 | 27.9 |
| District 1 | 6.9 | 17.3 | 11.7 | 13.4 | 11.8 | 13.8 | 11.8 | 6.8 | 6.4 | 35.6 | 179 733 | 92.4 | 28.7 |
| District 2 | 7.9 | 18.7 | 9.7 | 15.7 | 13.3 | 13.4 | 11.1 | 5.4 | 4.8 | 33.6 | 179 758 | 91.3 | 35.7 |
| District 3 | 6.5 | 17.7 | 8.8 | 11.0 | 10.8 | 14.4 | 13.7 | 8.2 | 9.0 | 40.7 | 156 156 | 89.4 | 19.7 |
| NEVADA | 6.8 | 17.5 | 9.2 | 14.2 | 14.0 | 13.8 | 12.0 | 7.6 | 4.9 | 36.3 | 684 009 | 84.0 | 22.5 |
| District 1 | 6.8 | 16.7 | 10.4 | 15.0 | 13.4 | 14.6 | 11.2 | 7.3 | 4.6 | 35.7 | 151 502 | 75.7 | 15.0 |
| District 2 | 6.3 | 17.0 | 9.3 | 12.7 | 13.0 | 14.6 | 13.5 | 8.1 | 5.5 | 38.8 | 171 982 | 86.1 | 24.6 |
| District 3 | 6.1 | 17.3 | 7.7 | 15.1 | 15.4 | 13.2 | 12.4 | 7.8 | 4.8 | 37.4 | 179 675 | 90.7 | 31.8 |
| District 4 | 7.9 | 19.2 | 9.2 | 14.0 | 14.4 | 12.8 | 10.9 | 7.0 | 4.7 | 34.8 | 180 850 | 82.7 | 17.3 |
| NEW HAMPSHIRE | 5.1 | 16.1 | 9.4 | 11.1 | 13.2 | 16.9 | 14.1 | 7.7 | 6.3 | 41.3 | 324 586 | 91.4 | 33.4 |
| District 1 | 5.4 | 15.5 | 9.6 | 11.9 | 13.2 | 16.8 | 13.7 | 7.7 | 6.1 | 41.0 | 159 345 | 92.1 | 33.0 |
| District 2 | 4.9 | 16.7 | 9.3 | 10.2 | 13.2 | 17.1 | 14.5 | 7.7 | 6.4 | 41.9 | 165 241 | 90.7 | 33.8 |
| NEW JERSEY | 6.1 | 17.1 | 8.8 | 12.7 | 13.8 | 15.5 | 12.3 | 7.1 | 6.6 | 39.0 | 2 289 399 | 88.1 | 35.3 |
| District 1 | 6.0 | 17.4 | 9.4 | 13.1 | 13.2 | 15.2 | 12.4 | 6.9 | 6.4 | 38.4 | 193 188 | 88.1 | 28.0 |
| District 2 | 6.1 | 16.7 | 8.7 | 12.0 | 12.6 | 15.5 | 13.4 | 8.2 | 6.9 | 40.5 | 179 705 | 84.9 | 23.6 |
| District 3 | 5.1 | 16.1 | 8.0 | 10.9 | 13.2 | 16.3 | 13.3 | 8.6 | 8.5 | 42.8 | 174 338 | 90.9 | 30.1 |
| District 4 | 6.6 | 19.1 | 7.4 | 10.2 | 12.4 | 15.6 | 12.2 | 8.2 | 8.4 | 40.6 | 200 811 | 90.5 | 36.4 |
| District 5 | 5.2 | 18.5 | 7.5 | 9.8 | 14.0 | 17.0 | 13.4 | 7.5 | 7.1 | 41.9 | 194 808 | 92.3 | 44.3 |
| District 6 | 6.7 | 15.7 | 11.0 | 14.5 | 13.5 | 14.7 | 12.2 | 6.4 | 5.4 | 36.6 | 191 796 | 88.5 | 35.4 |
| District 7 | 5.2 | 19.2 | 7.0 | 9.5 | 14.3 | 18.5 | 13.2 | 6.9 | 6.2 | 41.8 | 201 697 | 93.3 | 47.7 |
| District 8 | 7.8 | 14.7 | 9.8 | 21.0 | 15.4 | 12.6 | 9.4 | 4.9 | 4.3 | 33.1 | 174 147 | 77.5 | 29.3 |
| District 9 | 6.7 | 16.4 | 9.1 | 14.4 | 14.4 | 14.6 | 11.5 | 6.9 | 6.0 | 37.4 | 191 153 | 83.9 | 30.7 |
| District 10 | 6.6 | 17.2 | 10.4 | 14.5 | 14.4 | 14.6 | 11.0 | 6.4 | 4.9 | 35.9 | 205 586 | 83.9 | 25.2 |
| District 11 | 5.0 | 16.8 | 7.8 | 10.0 | 13.6 | 16.9 | 14.0 | 7.9 | 8.1 | 43.2 | 185 247 | 94.0 | 50.2 |
| District 12 | 5.9 | 17.2 | 9.3 | 12.7 | 14.7 | 15.1 | 12.0 | 6.8 | 6.4 | 38.7 | 196 923 | 89.3 | 41.6 |
| NEW MEXICO | 6.9 | 17.9 | 10.1 | 13.2 | 11.8 | 13.6 | 12.8 | 7.8 | 5.8 | 36.7 | 571 157 | 83.2 | 25.6 |
| District 1 | 6.5 | 17.1 | 10.0 | 14.4 | 12.4 | 14.1 | 12.6 | 7.1 | 5.8 | 36.6 | 197 502 | 87.4 | 31.1 |
| District 2 | 7.2 | 18.3 | 10.7 | 12.9 | 10.9 | 13.0 | 12.5 | 8.3 | 6.2 | 35.7 | 191 973 | 78.5 | 19.7 |
| District 3 | 7.1 | 18.4 | 9.5 | 12.3 | 12.1 | 13.9 | 13.3 | 8.0 | 5.4 | 37.4 | 181 682 | 83.5 | 25.6 |
| NEW YORK | 5.9 | 16.1 | 10.2 | 13.9 | 13.2 | 14.8 | 12.3 | 7.2 | 6.5 | 38.0 | 5 020 940 | 85.0 | 32.9 |
| District 1 | 5.8 | 17.0 | 8.6 | 11.1 | 14.1 | 15.7 | 12.7 | 8.3 | 6.6 | 40.4 | 186 967 | 92.3 | 33.6 |
| District 2 | 5.4 | 17.8 | 8.9 | 12.4 | 13.4 | 16.9 | 12.2 | 6.3 | 6.7 | 39.4 | 187 706 | 87.2 | 26.7 |
| District 3 | 5.4 | 17.5 | 8.3 | 8.8 | 12.4 | 16.9 | 13.3 | 8.4 | 8.9 | 43.1 | 185 244 | 92.8 | 50.8 |
| District 4 | 5.7 | 17.3 | 9.0 | 11.5 | 13.2 | 16.1 | 12.8 | 7.2 | 7.2 | 40.2 | 192 039 | 88.9 | 38.4 |
| District 5 | 6.5 | 16.9 | 10.3 | 14.1 | 13.2 | 14.5 | 12.3 | 6.9 | 5.2 | 36.6 | 207 654 | 80.3 | 23.5 |
| District 6 | 5.5 | 13.4 | 7.6 | 15.6 | 14.4 | 15.0 | 13.0 | 8.1 | 7.4 | 40.3 | 160 950 | 84.2 | 38.4 |
| District 7 | 8.0 | 16.4 | 11.0 | 19.4 | 14.8 | 12.1 | 9.4 | 4.8 | 4.2 | 32.4 | 188 100 | 67.7 | 27.0 |
| District 8 | 6.4 | 15.9 | 11.1 | 15.3 | 13.3 | 13.8 | 11.5 | 7.0 | 5.7 | 35.8 | 187 177 | 81.3 | 26.5 |
| District 9 | 7.1 | 16.5 | 9.9 | 16.1 | 13.5 | 13.6 | 11.7 | 6.6 | 5.1 | 35.3 | 202 126 | 82.9 | 31.7 |
| District 10 | 7.0 | 12.6 | 9.4 | 21.3 | 14.0 | 11.1 | 11.8 | 6.4 | 6.5 | 34.9 | 169 618 | 86.8 | 57.2 |
| District 11 | 5.5 | 16.4 | 9.2 | 13.5 | 13.8 | 14.7 | 12.7 | 7.5 | 6.6 | 38.8 | 182 769 | 84.7 | 30.3 |
| District 12 | 4.1 | 7.5 | 10.2 | 25.9 | 15.4 | 11.8 | 10.9 | 7.7 | 6.5 | 36.3 | 131 116 | 92.3 | 68.6 |
| District 13 | 6.4 | 14.6 | 12.3 | 17.9 | 13.4 | 14.1 | 10.4 | 6.2 | 4.7 | 34.1 | 182 608 | 73.5 | 27.1 |
| District 14 | 6.1 | 14.5 | 10.0 | 18.4 | 15.8 | 13.5 | 10.3 | 5.9 | 5.6 | 35.5 | 170 116 | 74.7 | 24.6 |

1. All persons 3 years old and over enrolled in nursery school through college and graduate or professional school.   2. Persons 25 years old and over.

| STATE District | Number | Persons per household | Family households (percent) | Married-couple family (percent) | Female family householder[1] | One person households (percent) | Total in group quarters | Percent 65 years and over | Persons in correctional institutions | Persons in nursing homes | Persons in college dormitories | Persons in military quarters |
|---|---|---|---|---|---|---|---|---|---|---|---|---|
| | 28 | 29 | 30 | 31 | 32 | 33 | 34 | 35 | 36 | 37 | 38 | 39 |
| MISSISSIPPI | 1 080 991 | 2.67 | 68.5 | 45.1 | 18.8 | 27.6 | 91 964 | 16.0 | 34 273 | 16 496 | 26 472 | 3 938 |
| District 1 | 268 824 | 2.69 | 71.4 | 50.0 | 17.0 | 25.5 | 16 163 | 22.9 | 2 943 | 4 381 | 7 786 | 0 |
| District 2 | 256 590 | 2.78 | 66.7 | 36.7 | 24.3 | 29.8 | 31 417 | 11.7 | 14 994 | 4 226 | 8 476 | 8 |
| District 3 | 278 202 | 2.59 | 67.9 | 46.6 | 17.9 | 28.0 | 24 396 | 18.4 | 9 560 | 4 625 | 5 828 | 601 |
| District 4 | 277 375 | 2.63 | 68.1 | 46.6 | 16.4 | 27.1 | 19 988 | 14.6 | 6 776 | 3 264 | 4 382 | 3 329 |
| MISSOURI | 2 341 074 | 2.49 | 65.6 | 48.9 | 12.4 | 28.6 | 174 142 | 22.7 | 41 956 | 44 866 | 52 869 | 10 217 |
| District 1 | 308 606 | 2.33 | 55.6 | 30.2 | 20.5 | 37.4 | 20 470 | 17.6 | 1 344 | 4 741 | 9 050 | 0 |
| District 2 | 292 322 | 2.53 | 69.9 | 57.3 | 9.1 | 25.3 | 12 164 | 55.7 | 2 300 | 7 231 | 1 046 | 0 |
| District 3 | 288 714 | 2.58 | 70.6 | 55.0 | 11.2 | 24.9 | 17 473 | 19.1 | 6 107 | 3 662 | 5 666 | 0 |
| District 4 | 282 205 | 2.56 | 66.2 | 53.0 | 10.2 | 26.1 | 35 617 | 13.4 | 6 015 | 5 555 | 11 262 | 10 217 |
| District 5 | 301 753 | 2.43 | 59.7 | 39.4 | 15.4 | 33.6 | 13 581 | 31.8 | 1 420 | 5 172 | 2 626 | 0 |
| District 6 | 282 863 | 2.57 | 68.4 | 54.3 | 9.4 | 26.1 | 28 956 | 20.5 | 11 433 | 6 573 | 8 326 | 0 |
| District 7 | 295 679 | 2.48 | 66.5 | 51.6 | 10.1 | 27.4 | 19 749 | 22.7 | 2 358 | 4 919 | 9 841 | 0 |
| District 8 | 288 932 | 2.49 | 68.5 | 52.0 | 12.7 | 26.7 | 26 132 | 23.9 | 10 979 | 7 013 | 5 052 | 0 |
| MONTANA | 404 250 | 2.40 | 62.6 | 49.4 | 9.3 | 30.6 | 28 849 | 19.2 | 5 338 | 5 200 | 8 332 | 678 |
| At Large | 404 250 | 2.40 | 62.6 | 49.4 | 9.3 | 30.6 | 28 849 | 19.2 | 5 338 | 5 200 | 8 332 | 678 |
| NEBRASKA | 723 800 | 2.48 | 65.0 | 51.1 | 9.7 | 28.8 | 51 165 | 24.4 | 8 084 | 13 519 | 22 073 | 443 |
| District 1 | 243 614 | 2.45 | 66.5 | 52.4 | 9.6 | 26.5 | 20 411 | 19.1 | 3 362 | 4 124 | 10 719 | 443 |
| District 2 | 234 319 | 2.58 | 62.9 | 47.2 | 11.3 | 30.4 | 12 936 | 17.6 | 2 325 | 2 632 | 4 750 | 0 |
| District 3 | 245 867 | 2.40 | 65.6 | 53.6 | 8.3 | 29.5 | 17 818 | 35.5 | 2 397 | 6 763 | 6 604 | 0 |
| NEVADA | 982 352 | 2.74 | 64.8 | 45.8 | 12.8 | 27.7 | 36 154 | 15.2 | 19 891 | 5 005 | 3 336 | 1 022 |
| District 1 | 235 794 | 2.76 | 58.7 | 36.0 | 14.9 | 33.2 | 10 537 | 11.3 | 4 771 | 954 | 1 211 | 0 |
| District 2 | 255 894 | 2.60 | 65.2 | 49.7 | 10.2 | 27.8 | 12 184 | 12.8 | 6 685 | 1 334 | 2 125 | 166 |
| District 3 | 259 602 | 2.70 | 65.5 | 47.2 | 12.8 | 25.8 | 1 904 | 58.1 | 352 | 1 044 | 0 | 0 |
| District 4 | 231 062 | 2.90 | 70.1 | 49.9 | 13.4 | 23.9 | 11 529 | 14.2 | 8 083 | 1 673 | 0 | 856 |
| NEW HAMPSHIRE | 516 454 | 2.47 | 67.7 | 53.6 | 9.9 | 25.3 | 40 104 | 19.5 | 4 851 | 7 767 | 22 820 | 454 |
| District 1 | 261 331 | 2.46 | 67.2 | 52.5 | 10.4 | 25.3 | 17 989 | 21.5 | 1 640 | 3 963 | 10 357 | 454 |
| District 2 | 255 123 | 2.49 | 68.1 | 54.7 | 9.4 | 25.3 | 22 115 | 17.9 | 3 211 | 3 804 | 12 463 | 0 |
| NEW JERSEY | 3 167 629 | 2.73 | 69.2 | 50.7 | 13.6 | 26.2 | 186 876 | 23.7 | 44 468 | 45 512 | 55 483 | 1 452 |
| District 1 | 265 762 | 2.69 | 66.3 | 47.1 | 14.4 | 28.3 | 11 216 | 33.0 | 2 221 | 3 995 | 2 424 | 0 |
| District 2 | 267 845 | 2.65 | 67.4 | 48.1 | 14.7 | 27.6 | 23 031 | 17.9 | 11 704 | 4 360 | 2 376 | 768 |
| District 3 | 278 890 | 2.57 | 69.0 | 52.6 | 12.3 | 26.9 | 16 038 | 26.5 | 6 383 | 4 169 | 0 | 360 |
| District 4 | 265 071 | 2.74 | 70.1 | 55.2 | 10.7 | 26.2 | 9 086 | 50.3 | 1 319 | 4 614 | 1 306 | 254 |
| District 5 | 256 626 | 2.80 | 74.1 | 60.5 | 10.2 | 21.8 | 13 157 | 39.2 | 1 041 | 5 005 | 4 364 | 0 |
| District 6 | 251 459 | 2.84 | 72.2 | 53.7 | 12.5 | 23.2 | 23 661 | 12.3 | 2 976 | 3 169 | 15 266 | 70 |
| District 7 | 268 361 | 2.74 | 74.0 | 62.5 | 8.7 | 22.2 | 10 080 | 37.9 | 2 789 | 3 543 | 129 | 0 |
| District 8 | 266 426 | 2.77 | 62.7 | 37.0 | 18.4 | 27.8 | 10 356 | 22.0 | 3 043 | 2 492 | 1 409 | 0 |
| District 9 | 262 583 | 2.81 | 69.3 | 46.2 | 17.1 | 27.4 | 5 092 | 26.3 | 1 068 | 1 145 | 468 | 0 |
| District 10 | 260 395 | 2.71 | 63.1 | 32.5 | 23.9 | 32.8 | 23 316 | 11.0 | 7 245 | 2 896 | 6 771 | 0 |
| District 11 | 265 676 | 2.67 | 72.2 | 60.4 | 8.3 | 24.0 | 18 514 | 30.3 | 411 | 5 741 | 9 278 | 0 |
| District 12 | 258 535 | 2.74 | 70.0 | 53.1 | 12.3 | 25.8 | 23 329 | 16.9 | 4 268 | 4 383 | 11 692 | 0 |
| NEW MEXICO | 767 285 | 2.66 | 65.5 | 45.6 | 14.2 | 28.7 | 42 629 | 14.3 | 17 907 | 5 567 | 8 478 | 1 789 |
| District 1 | 274 963 | 2.50 | 61.0 | 40.1 | 14.0 | 32.0 | 13 070 | 15.9 | 4 489 | 1 768 | 2 750 | 530 |
| District 2 | 247 754 | 2.76 | 69.2 | 49.7 | 14.5 | 26.3 | 18 749 | 11.7 | 9 874 | 2 334 | 3 613 | 815 |
| District 3 | 244 568 | 2.73 | 66.8 | 47.6 | 14.0 | 27.4 | 10 810 | 17.2 | 3 544 | 1 465 | 2 115 | 444 |
| NEW YORK | 7 187 938 | 2.63 | 64.1 | 44.1 | 15.1 | 29.5 | 585 678 | 19.7 | 95 306 | 116 558 | 218 960 | 8 100 |
| District 1 | 249 021 | 2.81 | 74.6 | 59.1 | 10.8 | 20.6 | 20 075 | 20.6 | 1 648 | 4 504 | 9 203 | 6 |
| District 2 | 233 115 | 3.08 | 76.7 | 56.3 | 14.6 | 19.1 | 6 830 | 46.7 | 6 | 2 952 | 720 | 4 |
| District 3 | 249 016 | 2.86 | 76.8 | 63.7 | 9.7 | 20.4 | 13 657 | 41.2 | 10 | 5 607 | 3 982 | 4 |
| District 4 | 233 071 | 3.02 | 73.8 | 56.2 | 13.2 | 22.0 | 12 964 | 28.5 | 1 657 | 4 200 | 4 748 | 0 |
| District 5 | 217 116 | 3.35 | 76.3 | 43.9 | 24.5 | 20.5 | 14 214 | 30.2 | 234 | 5 713 | 2 367 | 0 |
| District 6 | 263 960 | 2.66 | 66.2 | 48.5 | 12.3 | 29.5 | 6 264 | 62.0 | 17 | 4 179 | 812 | 0 |
| District 7 | 242 142 | 2.94 | 64.6 | 38.2 | 19.2 | 25.7 | 12 793 | 12.2 | 3 636 | 1 600 | 1 803 | 0 |
| District 8 | 261 574 | 2.67 | 62.9 | 30.3 | 26.8 | 31.0 | 14 582 | 26.0 | 256 | 4 120 | 2 056 | 0 |
| District 9 | 270 311 | 2.70 | 62.0 | 33.7 | 22.7 | 31.3 | 8 107 | 27.0 | 0 | 2 585 | 611 | 0 |
| District 10 | 302 762 | 2.29 | 47.2 | 37.1 | 6.9 | 42.9 | 24 101 | 10.2 | 165 | 2 076 | 16 711 | 0 |
| District 11 | 256 117 | 2.79 | 71.0 | 53.5 | 13.1 | 26.1 | 9 226 | 36.4 | 924 | 3 540 | 1 457 | 60 |
| District 12 | 359 499 | 1.90 | 35.6 | 26.9 | 6.5 | 49.5 | 29 580 | 10.4 | 414 | 3 896 | 16 755 | 0 |
| District 13 | 264 008 | 2.74 | 57.7 | 23.2 | 27.3 | 34.1 | 17 253 | 29.6 | 334 | 5 101 | 1 924 | 0 |
| District 14 | 241 926 | 2.87 | 63.2 | 37.5 | 17.1 | 28.5 | 21 106 | 21.9 | 11 095 | 5 195 | 2 355 | 0 |

1. No spouse present.

| STATE District | Housing units, 2011 | | | | | | Money income, 2011 | | |
|---|---|---|---|---|---|---|---|---|---|
| | Total | Occupied units | | | | | Households | | |
| | | Percent Occupied | Owner-occupied | | | Renter-occupied | | | |
| | | | Percent | Median value[1] (dollars) | Percent valued at $500,000 or more | Median rent[2] | Per capita income (dollars) | Median income (dollars) | Percent with income of $100,000 or more |
| | 40 | 41 | 42 | 43 | 44 | 45 | 46 | 47 | 48 |
| MISSISSIPPI | 1 281 760 | 84.3 | 69.8 | 99 900 | 1.9 | 689 | 19 583 | 36 919 | 11.5 |
| District 1 | 319 893 | 84.0 | 74.0 | 99 100 | 1.7 | 663 | 19 960 | 39 353 | 11.5 |
| District 2 | 308 797 | 83.1 | 62.9 | 80 600 | 1.7 | 628 | 15 796 | 31 084 | 8.3 |
| District 3 | 321 991 | 86.4 | 73.8 | 104 300 | 2.2 | 702 | 21 547 | 38 630 | 14.0 |
| District 4 | 331 079 | 83.8 | 68.2 | 117 700 | 1.9 | 759 | 21 013 | 39 095 | 12.1 |
| MISSOURI | 2 723 449 | 86.0 | 68.0 | 136 900 | 3.3 | 708 | 24 634 | 45 247 | 15.9 |
| District 1 | 371 885 | 83.0 | 53.1 | 109 500 | 2.5 | 753 | 22 581 | 37 115.0 | 11.3 |
| District 2 | 310 583 | 94.1 | 79.1 | 208 000 | 9.7 | 871 | 38 744 | 71 239.0 | 34.0 |
| District 3 | 335 934 | 85.9 | 77.7 | 159 800 | 2.5 | 695 | 25 096 | 51 769.0 | 17.5 |
| District 4 | 341 732 | 82.6 | 68.7 | 127 900 | 2.5 | 699 | 21 605 | 42 910.0 | 12.4 |
| District 5 | 352 372 | 85.6 | 60.9 | 115 000 | 2.0 | 753 | 23 272 | 42 572.0 | 13.2 |
| District 6 | 325 889 | 86.8 | 71.6 | 141 200 | 2.6 | 694 | 25 143 | 49 367.0 | 18.9 |
| District 7 | 345 520 | 85.6 | 65.3 | 119 200 | 2.3 | 642 | 21 551 | 40 796.0 | 11.0 |
| District 8 | 339 534 | 85.1 | 69.4 | 97 800 | 1.5 | 558 | 19 007 | 35 965.0 | 8.9 |
| MONTANA | 489 183 | 82.6 | 67.9 | 184 100 | 7.7 | 650 | 23 893 | 44 222 | 13.1 |
| At Large | 489 183 | 82.6 | 67.9 | 184 100 | 7.7 | 650 | 23 893 | 44 222 | 13.1 |
| NEBRASKA | 801 182 | 90.3 | 66.9 | 127 400 | 2.0 | 673 | 26 243 | 50 296 | 17.6 |
| District 1 | 261 954 | 93.0 | 65.6 | 138 300 | 1.7 | 674 | 26 066 | 51 306 | 18.4 |
| District 2 | 256 328 | 91.4 | 64.4 | 147 500 | 2.7 | 753 | 28 946 | 55 114 | 22.2 |
| District 3 | 282 900 | 86.9 | 70.5 | 93 000 | 1.5 | 569 | 23 681 | 44 995 | 12.6 |
| NEVADA | 1 183 917 | 83.0 | 56.3 | 158 000 | 4.6 | 936 | 24 968 | 48 927 | 18.3 |
| District 1 | 296 856 | 79.4 | 43.5 | 105 300 | 2.7 | 820 | 19 037 | 36 447 | 9.4 |
| District 2 | 296 631 | 86.3 | 61.8 | 175 600 | 7.6 | 880 | 26 991 | 51 505 | 20.6 |
| District 3 | 312 933 | 83.0 | 59.2 | 190 000 | 5.5 | 1 146 | 30 949 | 61 286 | 26.2 |
| District 4 | 277 497 | 83.3 | 59.9 | 143 900 | 1.6 | 974 | 22 521 | 50 134 | 16.1 |
| NEW HAMPSHIRE | 617 702 | 83.6 | 71.5 | 237 500 | 5.8 | 939 | 31 871 | 62 647 | 27.2 |
| District 1 | 313 424 | 83.4 | 69.8 | 243 500 | 6.2 | 971 | 33 251 | 63 587 | 28.1 |
| District 2 | 304 278 | 83.8 | 73.1 | 231 500 | 5.5 | 898 | 30 483 | 61 832 | 26.4 |
| NEW JERSEY | 3 562 720 | 88.9 | 65.0 | 324 900 | 20.1 | 1 135 | 34 090 | 67 458 | 32.9 |
| District 1 | 291 163 | 91.3 | 70.2 | 214 600 | 3.8 | 938 | 29 307 | 61 225 | 27.2 |
| District 2 | 384 303 | 69.7 | 72.0 | 230 600 | 10.1 | 1 012 | 27 362 | 55 032 | 23.3 |
| District 3 | 315 074 | 88.5 | 80.4 | 258 600 | 9.1 | 1 193 | 33 593 | 68 300 | 31.6 |
| District 4 | 293 503 | 90.3 | 76.9 | 340 300 | 24.0 | 1 210 | 35 379 | 71 084 | 35.2 |
| District 5 | 273 356 | 93.9 | 77.0 | 407 200 | 33.6 | 1 219 | 40 796 | 86 213 | 43.0 |
| District 6 | 271 583 | 92.6 | 63.3 | 331 300 | 14.4 | 1 206 | 32 169 | 70 878 | 33.9 |
| District 7 | 284 167 | 94.4 | 79.3 | 409 300 | 33.7 | 1 299 | 46 765 | 95 189 | 47.8 |
| District 8 | 300 195 | 88.8 | 29.6 | 328 300 | 17.2 | 1 108 | 27 014 | 51 416 | 22.1 |
| District 9 | 286 725 | 91.6 | 47.6 | 364 600 | 21.3 | 1 176 | 30 282 | 55 907 | 26.3 |
| District 10 | 299 466 | 87.0 | 39.4 | 287 300 | 12.7 | 1 017 | 25 247 | 45 220 | 20.0 |
| District 11 | 280 826 | 94.6 | 76.8 | 426 300 | 35.8 | 1 357 | 45 011 | 93 655 | 47.0 |
| District 12 | 282 359 | 91.6 | 66.8 | 332 100 | 18.8 | 1 170 | 36 156 | 75 649 | 37.7 |
| NEW MEXICO | 908 168 | 84.5 | 68.2 | 159 000 | 5.7 | 729 | 22 829 | 41 963 | 15.8 |
| District 1 | 298 183 | 92.2 | 63.4 | 179 900 | 5.9 | 735 | 25 323 | 43 618 | 18.1 |
| District 2 | 301 699 | 82.1 | 70.7 | 116 100 | 2.8 | 643 | 20 060 | 37 252 | 11.7 |
| District 3 | 308 286 | 79.3 | 71.0 | 172 800 | 8.4 | 810 | 23 131 | 44 467 | 17.0 |
| NEW YORK | 8 119 804 | 88.5 | 53.6 | 285 300 | 23.0 | 1 058 | 30 679 | 55 246 | 25.5 |
| District 1 | 307 430 | 81.0 | 79.2 | 378 100 | 24.3 | 1 500 | 35 285 | 83 144.0 | 40.5 |
| District 2 | 245 952 | 94.8 | 79.0 | 366 400 | 14.0 | 1 376 | 32 030 | 82 197.0 | 39.8 |
| District 3 | 261 687 | 95.2 | 80.3 | 540 400 | 54.6 | 1 573 | 47 367 | 95 699.0 | 48.2 |
| District 4 | 248 700 | 93.7 | 76.5 | 436 500 | 33.2 | 1 398 | 36 501 | 87 860.0 | 43.3 |
| District 5 | 237 411 | 91.5 | 57.0 | 400 200 | 20.3 | 1 170 | 23 083 | 57 485.0 | 25.1 |
| District 6 | 285 176 | 92.6 | 45.0 | 490 600 | 48.7 | 1 315 | 27 552 | 55 043.0 | 24.3 |
| District 7 | 269 671 | 89.8 | 20.9 | 565 700 | 57.9 | 1 116 | 23 234 | 40 554.0 | 18.4 |
| District 8 | 298 933 | 87.5 | 32.3 | 477 600 | 45.0 | 1 033 | 22 008 | 39 912.0 | 16.5 |
| District 9 | 293 969 | 92.0 | 28.5 | 531 900 | 53.7 | 1 096 | 23 949 | 44 029.0 | 18.0 |
| District 10 | 348 383 | 86.9 | 27.6 | 768 400 | 76.7 | 1 550 | 54 393 | 70 270.0 | 37.3 |
| District 11 | 278 895 | 91.8 | 57.9 | 468 600 | 43.2 | 1 131 | 29 331 | 62 045.0 | 28.7 |
| District 12 | 425 426 | 84.5 | 26.8 | 857 900 | 80.8 | 1 702 | 75 700 | 82 360.0 | 43.3 |
| District 13 | 290 482 | 90.9 | 9.7 | 425 300 | 42.1 | 1 000 | 20 335 | 34 360.0 | 11.7 |
| District 14 | 264 850 | 91.3 | 28.4 | 436 000 | 38.1 | 1 244 | 22 164 | 46 990.0 | 18.4 |

1. Specified owner-occupied units.    2. Specified renter-occupied units.

| STATE District | Poverty, 2011 (percent) | | | Civilian labor force, 2011 | | | Civilian employment,[2] 2011 | | | | Persons under age 65 with no health insurance, 2010 (percent) | Social Security beneficiaries, December 2012 | | Supple-mental Security Income recipients, December 2012 |
|---|---|---|---|---|---|---|---|---|---|---|---|---|---|---|
| | | | | | Unemployment | | | Percent | | | | | | |
| | Persons below poverty level | Families below poverty level | Households receiving food stamps in past 12 months | Total | Total | Rate[1] | Total | Manage-ment, profes-sional, and related occupations | Service, sales, and office | Con-struction and production | | Number | Rate[3] | |
| | 49 | 50 | 51 | 52 | 53 | 54 | 55 | 56 | 57 | 58 | 59 | 60 | 61 | 62 |
| MISSISSIPPI | 22.6 | 17.4 | 17.3 | 1 332 465 | 151 170 | 11.3 | 1 181 295 | 31.1 | 40.8 | 28.1 | 20.3 | 622 029 | 208.8 | 126 650 |
| District 1 | 17.7 | 13.9 | 15.4 | 342 787 | 37 162 | 10.8 | 305 625 | 29.0 | 38.9 | 32.1 | 18.0 | 162 088 | 218.8 | 25 923 |
| District 2 | 29.7 | 23.6 | 23.8 | 311 911 | 44 969 | 14.4 | 266 942 | 29.4 | 43.5 | 27.2 | 20.8 | 154 807 | 208.3 | 48 119 |
| District 3 | 20.8 | 15.7 | 13.3 | 335 357 | 31 509 | 9.4 | 303 848 | 35.2 | 39.3 | 25.5 | 18.0 | 152 396 | 204.5 | 28 174 |
| District 4 | 22.1 | 16.9 | 17.1 | 342 410 | 37 530 | 11.0 | 304 880 | 30.6 | 41.9 | 27.5 | 24.2 | 152 738 | 203.8 | 24 434 |
| MISSOURI | 15.8 | 11.5 | 14.0 | 3 026 952 | 284 895 | 9.4 | 2 742 057 | 34.5 | 43.3 | 22.3 | 15.8 | 1 212 560 | 201.7 | 140 171 |
| District 1 | 22.1 | 17.5 | 21.2 | 388 612 | 57 158 | 14.7 | 331 454 | 35.2 | 48.2 | 16.6 | 19.3 | 133 587 | 180.5 | 30 184 |
| District 2 | 6.5 | 4.8 | 4.4 | 406 233 | 27 588 | 6.8 | 378 645 | 46.3 | 40.4 | 13.3 | 8.5 | 143 429 | 190.6 | 5 397 |
| District 3 | 11.3 | 8.6 | 10.8 | 400 640 | 30 675 | 7.7 | 369 965 | 32.5 | 42.9 | 24.6 | 11.7 | 145 887 | 191.4 | 10 201 |
| District 4 | 17.7 | 11.5 | 13.9 | 357 846 | 32 986 | 9.2 | 324 860 | 33.0 | 41.6 | 25.4 | 17.0 | 153 790 | 203.6 | 15 979 |
| District 5 | 18.7 | 14.5 | 15.9 | 386 589 | 41 252 | 10.7 | 345 337 | 33.9 | 45.2 | 20.8 | 19.3 | 142 013 | 190.0 | 18 937 |
| District 6 | 13.0 | 8.6 | 10.3 | 386 224 | 30 308 | 7.8 | 355 916 | 34.9 | 39.7 | 25.5 | 13.9 | 143 274 | 190.1 | 12 146 |
| District 7 | 16.9 | 11.9 | 15.1 | 369 103 | 31 719 | 8.6 | 337 384 | 30.9 | 46.0 | 23.0 | 19.9 | 163 385 | 217.4 | 17 290 |
| District 8 | 20.5 | 15.8 | 20.2 | 331 705 | 33 209 | 10.0 | 298 496 | 26.8 | 43.0 | 30.2 | 17.0 | 187 195 | 250.3 | 30 037 |
| MONTANA | 14.8 | 9.7 | 10.9 | 521 313 | 41 325 | 7.9 | 479 988 | 34.3 | 43.8 | 21.9 | 21.3 | 203 292 | 203.7 | 18 590 |
| At Large | 14.8 | 9.7 | 10.9 | 521 313 | 41 325 | 7.9 | 479 988 | 34.3 | 43.8 | 21.9 | 21.3 | 203 292 | 203.7 | 18 590 |
| NEBRASKA | 13.1 | 9.1 | 9.2 | 1 006 874 | 63 231 | 6.3 | 943 643 | 34.0 | 41.1 | 24.8 | 13.1 | 317 502 | 172.3 | 27 149 |
| District 1 | 13.0 | 8.8 | 8.6 | 343 160 | 21 481 | 6.3 | 321 679 | 34.0 | 42.0 | 24.0 | 12.3 | 102 319 | 165.9 | 8 271 |
| District 2 | 13.1 | 9.2 | 10.1 | 341 775 | 25 446 | 7.4 | 316 329 | 37.6 | 43.0 | 19.4 | 13.0 | 87 465 | 141.6 | 10 142 |
| District 3 | 13.3 | 9.3 | 8.9 | 321 939 | 16 304 | 5.1 | 305 635 | 30.4 | 38.3 | 31.3 | 14.0 | 127 718 | 209.9 | 8 736 |
| NEVADA | 15.9 | 11.9 | 10.7 | 1 379 559 | 174 677 | 12.7 | 1 204 882 | 27.2 | 54.4 | 18.4 | 24.7 | 442 298 | 162.4 | 46 318 |
| District 1 | 22.1 | 18.2 | 16.4 | 340 149 | 55 405 | 16.3 | 284 744 | 17.2 | 62.5 | 20.3 | 34.4 | 88 858 | 134.6 | 16 146 |
| District 2 | 13.0 | 9.2 | 8.8 | 348 564 | 39 170 | 11.2 | 309 394 | 31.1 | 46.9 | 22.0 | 24.1 | 124 797 | 183.8 | 9 735 |
| District 3 | 11.4 | 8.2 | 6.3 | 376 099 | 39 637 | 10.5 | 336 462 | 33.3 | 54.0 | 12.8 | 17.0 | 113 731 | 161.7 | 7 585 |
| District 4 | 17.5 | 13.1 | 12.2 | 314 747 | 40 465 | 12.9 | 274 282 | 25.7 | 55.2 | 19.1 | 23.9 | 114 912 | 168.8 | 12 852 |
| NEW HAMPSHIRE | 8.8 | 5.6 | 8.3 | 735 366 | 50 560 | 6.9 | 684 806 | 39.8 | 39.8 | 20.5 | 12.1 | 271 181 | 205.7 | 19 235 |
| District 1 | 8.9 | 6.0 | 7.9 | 376 689 | 24 070 | 6.4 | 352 619 | 38.5 | 41.2 | 20.3 | 12.6 | 133 902 | 202.6 | 9 596 |
| District 2 | 8.7 | 5.3 | 8.6 | 358 677 | 26 490 | 7.4 | 332 187 | 41.1 | 38.2 | 20.7 | 11.6 | 137 279 | 208.8 | 9 639 |
| NEW JERSEY | 10.4 | 7.8 | 8.0 | 4 662 195 | 509 682 | 10.9 | 4 152 513 | 40.4 | 42.2 | 17.5 | 14.8 | 1 525 574 | 172.9 | 177 344 |
| District 1 | 11.8 | 8.4 | 10.2 | 390 851 | 51 645 | 13.2 | 339 206 | 38.6 | 43.7 | 17.7 | 12.1 | 134 801 | 185.3 | 19 634 |
| District 2 | 12.4 | 9.3 | 10.4 | 373 932 | 49 486 | 13.2 | 324 446 | 32.1 | 47.9 | 20.0 | 15.4 | 156 079 | 211.9 | 17 356 |
| District 3 | 6.2 | 4.7 | 5.8 | 386 266 | 42 055 | 10.9 | 344 211 | 38.6 | 43.6 | 17.8 | 10.7 | 164 210 | 224.3 | 9 125 |
| District 4 | 9.2 | 6.5 | 5.8 | 361 498 | 35 056 | 9.7 | 326 442 | 42.3 | 42.6 | 15.1 | 10.2 | 152 380 | 207.0 | 8 635 |
| District 5 | 5.4 | 4.1 | 3.8 | 390 131 | 34 064 | 8.7 | 356 067 | 45.3 | 40.1 | 14.7 | 10.4 | 130 260 | 178.2 | 7 901 |
| District 6 | 10.4 | 7.4 | 6.4 | 392 372 | 38 768 | 9.9 | 353 604 | 40.0 | 40.8 | 19.2 | 16.6 | 109 889 | 148.7 | 13 074 |
| District 7 | 4.1 | 2.7 | 3.2 | 410 479 | 33 359 | 8.1 | 377 120 | 49.2 | 38.0 | 12.7 | 8.5 | 117 814 | 157.7 | 5 742 |
| District 8 | 18.9 | 16.8 | 14.3 | 422 558 | 51 523 | 12.2 | 371 035 | 31.9 | 43.4 | 24.6 | 27.5 | 89 368 | 119.7 | 27 238 |
| District 9 | 14.1 | 11.6 | 11.2 | 377 686 | 39 208 | 10.4 | 338 478 | 35.4 | 43.5 | 21.1 | 21.4 | 113 695 | 153.1 | 18 960 |
| District 10 | 18.2 | 15.3 | 16.1 | 368 422 | 57 746 | 15.7 | 310 676 | 33.1 | 47.9 | 19.0 | 20.4 | 103 063 | 141.9 | 29 562 |
| District 11 | 4.6 | 2.8 | 2.4 | 394 181 | 35 368 | 9.0 | 358 813 | 51.2 | 36.9 | 11.9 | 9.0 | 132 655 | 183.0 | 6 667 |
| District 12 | 9.1 | 6.8 | 5.8 | 393 819 | 41 404 | 10.5 | 352 415 | 44.5 | 39.5 | 16.0 | 14.5 | 121 360 | 165.8 | 13 450 |
| NEW MEXICO | 21.5 | 16.6 | 15.4 | 979 399 | 109 626 | 11.2 | 869 773 | 35.5 | 43.8 | 20.7 | 22.7 | 382 366 | 183.6 | 63 381 |
| District 1 | 20.7 | 16.0 | 15.1 | 349 733 | 37 857 | 10.8 | 311 876 | 40.6 | 44.3 | 15.1 | 20.2 | 121 427 | 173.9 | 18 227 |
| District 2 | 23.2 | 17.8 | 17.5 | 308 595 | 35 536 | 11.5 | 273 059 | 29.6 | 43.3 | 27.1 | 23.1 | 134 866 | 191.9 | 23 812 |
| District 3 | 20.7 | 15.9 | 13.4 | 321 071 | 36 233 | 11.3 | 284 838 | 35.7 | 43.9 | 20.4 | 24.9 | 126 073 | 185.2 | 21 342 |
| NEW YORK | 16.0 | 12.3 | 15.2 | 9 907 450 | 948 435 | 9.6 | 8 959 015 | 38.1 | 45.0 | 16.9 | 13.0 | 3 394 309 | 174.4 | 696 894 |
| District 1 | 7.0 | 4.6 | 5.2 | 367 546 | 24 216 | 6.6 | 343 330 | 38.2 | 43.6 | 18.2 | 10.6 | 142 894 | 198.4 | 11 066 |
| District 2 | 5.4 | 3.7 | 7.0 | 389 549 | 31 794 | 8.2 | 357 755 | 33.3 | 45.3 | 21.4 | 12.0 | 128 836 | 177.9 | 11 276 |
| District 3 | 4.8 | 3.1 | 3.8 | 363 323 | 26 592 | 7.3 | 336 731 | 49.9 | 39.6 | 10.5 | 7.7 | 143 747 | 198.5 | 8 628 |
| District 4 | 9.0 | 6.5 | 6.4 | 371 039 | 28 554 | 7.7 | 342 485 | 41.0 | 43.9 | 15.1 | 11.5 | 131 448 | 183.6 | 11 103 |
| District 5 | 14.5 | 12.2 | 18.6 | 381 202 | 44 976 | 11.8 | 336 226 | 26.8 | 54.3 | 18.9 | 17.5 | 98 666 | 133.3 | 28 615 |
| District 6 | 13.3 | 11.4 | 10.1 | 358 324 | 31 289 | 8.7 | 327 035 | 38.5 | 46.1 | 15.4 | 18.7 | 108 989 | 154.0 | 24 302 |
| District 7 | 28.5 | 25.5 | 27.7 | 359 043 | 36 805 | 10.3 | 322 238 | 32.3 | 49.7 | 18.1 | 20.0 | 82 106 | 113.3 | 42 487 |
| District 8 | 25.7 | 22.3 | 26.3 | 345 371 | 52 666 | 15.2 | 292 705 | 34.2 | 50.5 | 15.2 | 14.4 | 103 026 | 143.9 | 52 005 |
| District 9 | 20.6 | 17.7 | 22.5 | 372 184 | 47 294 | 12.7 | 324 890 | 37.4 | 48.6 | 14.0 | 13.6 | 91 187 | 123.3 | 36 528 |
| District 10 | 16.6 | 13.0 | 11.1 | 389 347 | 29 092 | 7.5 | 360 255 | 56.8 | 34.5 | 8.6 | 10.8 | 100 545 | 140.4 | 27 045 |
| District 11 | 13.2 | 10.0 | 13.5 | 347 999 | 30 455 | 8.8 | 317 544 | 36.8 | 46.2 | 17.0 | 10.1 | 121 081 | 167.1 | 27 654 |
| District 12 | 12.9 | 8.5 | 7.4 | 451 172 | 32 356 | 7.2 | 418 816 | 63.3 | 31.5 | 5.2 | 11.6 | 102 617 | 144.9 | 17 202 |
| District 13 | 28.4 | 25.9 | 32.2 | 372 837 | 55 656 | 14.9 | 317 181 | 30.5 | 54.1 | 15.5 | 20.3 | 99 938 | 135.2 | 61 869 |
| District 14 | 19.2 | 16.6 | 17.2 | 376 158 | 34 403 | 9.1 | 341 755 | 25.4 | 53.4 | 21.2 | 25.2 | 90 796 | 127.5 | 25 837 |

1. Percent of civilian labor force.   2. Persons 16 years old and over.   3. Per 1,000 resident population estimated in the 2011 American Community Survey.

| STATE District | Representative, 113th Congress | Land area,[1] 2010 (sq km) | Total persons | Per square kilometer | White | Black | American Indian, Alaska Native | Asian and Pacific Islander | Some other race | Two or more races | Hispanic or Latino[2] | Non-Hispanic White alone | Percent female | Percent foreign born | Percent born in state of residence |
|---|---|---|---|---|---|---|---|---|---|---|---|---|---|---|---|
| | | 1 | 2 | 3 | 4 | 5 | 6 | 7 | 8 | 9 | 10 | 11 | 12 | 13 | 14 |
| **NEW YORK—Cont'd** | | | | | | | | | | | | | | | |
| District 15 | José E. Serrano (D) | 38 | 731 101 | 19 417.7 | 16.9 | 34.3 | 0.7 | 1.5 | 43.1 | 3.4 | 66.1 | 2.3 | 53.4 | 34.6 | 51.0 |
| District 16 | Eliot L. Engel (D) | 203 | 721 008 | 3 552.0 | 48.3 | 32.4 | 0.2 | 4.7 | 11.0 | 3.4 | 23.4 | 39.2 | 53.2 | 28.5 | 58.1 |
| District 17 | Nita M. Lowey (D) | 991 | 724 191 | 730.8 | 70.3 | 10.8 | 0.2 | 6.1 | 10.0 | 2.7 | 20.7 | 61.9 | 51.0 | 23.3 | 61.3 |
| District 18 | Sean Patrick Maloney (D) | 3 505 | 726 712 | 207.3 | 77.2 | 9.0 | 0.3 | 3.2 | 7.1 | 3.3 | 15.2 | 70.6 | 50.4 | 12.8 | 70.5 |
| District 19 | Christopher P. Gibson (R) | 20 557 | 710 597 | 34.6 | 89.7 | 4.2 | 0.2 | 1.5 | 2.1 | 2.3 | 6.7 | 85.8 | 49.7 | 6.5 | 74.4 |
| District 20 | Paul Tonko (D) | 3 189 | 720 133 | 225.8 | 82.3 | 9.0 | 0.2 | 3.6 | 1.5 | 3.4 | 5.5 | 79.3 | 51.4 | 7.1 | 78.1 |
| District 21 | William L. Owens (D) | 39 147 | 717 663 | 18.3 | 92.6 | 3.0 | 0.8 | 0.9 | 1.0 | 1.8 | 3.1 | 91.0 | 48.8 | 3.7 | 77.1 |
| District 22 | Richard L. Hanna (R) | 13 151 | 720 201 | 54.8 | 90.9 | 3.4 | 0.5 | 2.3 | 0.7 | 2.2 | 3.2 | 89.0 | 50.5 | 4.8 | 80.3 |
| District 23 | Tom Reed (R) | 19 092 | 717 909 | 37.6 | 91.6 | 2.9 | 0.7 | 2.2 | 0.9 | 1.7 | 3.3 | 89.4 | 50.2 | 3.9 | 75.3 |
| District 24 | Daniel B. Maffei (D) | 6 186 | 713 010 | 115.3 | 85.7 | 8.2 | 0.5 | 2.2 | 0.8 | 2.5 | 3.9 | 83.2 | 51.0 | 5.9 | 79.1 |
| District 25 | Louise McIntosh Slaughter (D) | 1 321 | 717 475 | 543.0 | 75.4 | 15.7 | 0.2 | 3.4 | 2.5 | 2.8 | 7.7 | 71.5 | 51.8 | 8.1 | 74.4 |
| District 26 | Brian Higgins (D) | 568 | 719 909 | 1 268.4 | 74.0 | 17.6 | 0.4 | 3.1 | 2.1 | 2.9 | 5.3 | 71.5 | 52.2 | 7.2 | 79.6 |
| District 27 | Chris Collins(R) | 10 290 | 713 175 | 69.3 | 93.5 | 2.4 | 0.7 | 1.2 | 0.7 | 1.5 | 2.6 | 92.1 | 50.1 | 3.5 | 84.9 |
| **NORTH CAROLINA** | | 125 920 | 9 656 401 | 76.7 | 70.1 | 21.7 | 1.2 | 2.2 | 2.7 | 2.1 | 8.6 | 64.9 | 51.5 | 7.3 | 58.0 |
| District 1 | G. K. Butterfield (D) | 14 230 | 739 665 | 52.0 | 40.3 | 52.1 | 0.7 | 1.3 | 3.6 | 2.0 | 8.4 | 35.7 | 52.8 | 6.2 | 69.9 |
| District 2 | Renee Ellmers (R) | 8 409 | 744 671 | 88.6 | 74.0 | 16.0 | 0.9 | 3.6 | 2.9 | 2.6 | 10.7 | 66.8 | 50.4 | 9.0 | 52.7 |
| District 3 | Walter B. Jones (R) | 20 228 | 749 823 | 37.1 | 74.0 | 20.6 | 0.7 | 1.3 | 1.5 | 2.0 | 5.8 | 70.5 | 49.9 | 3.9 | 53.4 |
| District 4 | David E. Price (D) | 2 707 | 758 619 | 280.2 | 54.8 | 33.1 | 0.5 | 5.4 | 3.7 | 2.5 | 11.9 | 47.4 | 52.4 | 13.2 | 45.9 |
| District 5 | Virginia Foxx (R) | 9 251 | 726 638 | 78.5 | 81.1 | 12.6 | 0.3 | 1.4 | 2.7 | 1.9 | 9.1 | 75.3 | 51.9 | 7.2 | 63.1 |
| District 6 | Howard Coble (R) | 9 517 | 749 909 | 78.8 | 77.1 | 15.9 | 0.3 | 1.7 | 2.8 | 2.1 | 5.9 | 74.3 | 51.6 | 5.2 | 64.3 |
| District 7 | Mike McIntyre (D) | 15 959 | 745 559 | 46.7 | 74.6 | 17.8 | 1.7 | 0.3 | 3.7 | 1.8 | 9.7 | 69.2 | 51.4 | 5.6 | 62.3 |
| District 8 | Richard Hudson (R) | 11 688 | 750 059 | 64.2 | 68.1 | 18.8 | 7.1 | 0.8 | 3.0 | 2.2 | 8.7 | 63.0 | 51.2 | 5.7 | 69.4 |
| District 9 | Robert Pittenger (R) | 2 219 | 750 582 | 338.2 | 78.8 | 13.7 | 0.3 | 4.1 | 0.9 | 2.1 | 6.8 | 73.8 | 51.3 | 9.5 | 40.1 |
| District 10 | Patrick T. McHenry (R) | 6 670 | 740 773 | 111.1 | 82.4 | 11.8 | 0.4 | 1.6 | 1.9 | 1.9 | 5.5 | 79.2 | 52.0 | 4.8 | 64.4 |
| District 11 | Mark Meadows (D) | 17 711 | 730 469 | 41.2 | 91.2 | 3.0 | 1.4 | 1.1 | 1.3 | 2.0 | 5.8 | 87.5 | 51.2 | 4.3 | 60.4 |
| District 12 | Melvin L. Watt (D) | 1 424 | 737 200 | 517.8 | 39.6 | 49.0 | 0.4 | 4.5 | 4.4 | 2.2 | 15.2 | 29.9 | 51.4 | 13.7 | 54.1 |
| District 13 | George Holding (R) | 5 907 | 732 434 | 124.0 | 75.7 | 16.7 | 0.2 | 1.9 | 3.3 | 2.2 | 8.0 | 71.6 | 51.5 | 7.0 | 54.1 |
| **NORTH DAKOTA** | | 178 711 | 683 932 | 3.8 | 89.8 | 1.0 | 5.6 | 1.1 | 0.6 | 1.9 | 2.2 | 88.5 | 49.7 | 2.4 | 67.7 |
| At Large | Kevin Cramer (R) | 178 711 | 683 932 | 3.8 | 89.8 | 1.0 | 5.6 | 1.1 | 0.6 | 1.9 | 2.2 | 88.5 | 49.7 | 2.4 | 67.7 |
| **OHIO** | | 105 829 | 11 544 951 | 109.1 | 82.9 | 12.1 | 0.2 | 1.7 | 0.9 | 2.3 | 3.2 | 80.9 | 51.1 | 4.0 | 75.1 |
| District 1 | Steve Chabot (R) | 1 779 | 729 005 | 409.7 | 72.9 | 22.0 | 0.1 | 2.4 | 0.4 | 2.1 | 2.9 | 70.7 | 51.2 | 5.2 | 73.1 |
| District 2 | Brad R. Wenstrup (R) | 8 344 | 716 833 | 85.9 | 87.8 | 8.2 | 0.0 | 1.3 | 0.5 | 2.2 | 1.5 | 86.8 | 51.1 | 2.7 | 74.5 |
| District 3 | Joyce Beatty (D) | 591 | 732 258 | 1 240.0 | 58.8 | 32.1 | 0.2 | 2.7 | 2.5 | 3.8 | 6.1 | 55.4 | 51.5 | 9.9 | 66.3 |
| District 4 | Jim Jordan (R) | 12 082 | 721 717 | 59.7 | 90.4 | 5.6 | 0.2 | 0.7 | 0.6 | 2.4 | 3.3 | 88.3 | 49.9 | 1.7 | 81.6 |
| District 5 | Robert E. Latta (R) | 14 572 | 714 435 | 49.0 | 92.6 | 2.8 | 0.2 | 1.0 | 1.4 | 2.1 | 4.3 | 90.4 | 51.7 | 2.4 | 79.2 |
| District 6 | Bill Johnson (R) | 18 687 | 717 143 | 38.4 | 95.3 | 2.4 | 0.1 | 0.3 | 0.3 | 1.5 | 0.8 | 94.9 | 50.6 | 0.8 | 70.4 |
| District 7 | Bob Gibbs (R) | 10 010 | 726 076 | 72.5 | 93.2 | 3.6 | 0.1 | 0.6 | 0.5 | 2.1 | 1.7 | 92.1 | 51.2 | 1.9 | 83.0 |
| District 8 | John A. Boehner (R) | 6 347 | 726 266 | 114.4 | 89.5 | 5.9 | 0.2 | 1.7 | 0.9 | 1.8 | 3.1 | 87.4 | 50.9 | 3.1 | 74.8 |
| District 9 | Marcy Kaptur (D) | 1 203 | 718 027 | 596.6 | 76.4 | 15.3 | 0.3 | 1.5 | 2.5 | 4.1 | 9.8 | 70.5 | 50.7 | 4.7 | 75.7 |
| District 10 | Michael R. Turner (R) | 2 926 | 725 479 | 247.9 | 77.3 | 17.1 | 0.2 | 2.2 | 0.8 | 2.5 | 2.3 | 76.0 | 51.8 | 4.0 | 67.6 |
| District 11 | Marcia L. Fudge (D) | 633 | 705 659 | 1 114.5 | 40.1 | 54.2 | 0.3 | 2.3 | 0.9 | 2.2 | 3.6 | 37.9 | 53.5 | 5.5 | 72.8 |
| District 12 | Patrick J. Tiberi (R) | 5 884 | 727 728 | 123.7 | 89.2 | 4.6 | 0.2 | 3.0 | 0.6 | 2.4 | 2.0 | 87.8 | 50.7 | 4.5 | 73.0 |
| District 13 | Tim Ryan (D) | 2 316 | 723 713 | 312.5 | 83.7 | 11.8 | 0.2 | 1.3 | 0.6 | 2.4 | 2.7 | 82.0 | 51.4 | 3.0 | 78.5 |
| District 14 | David P. Joyce (R) | 5 059 | 716 967 | 141.7 | 92.7 | 3.7 | 0.1 | 1.7 | 0.3 | 1.5 | 2.5 | 90.8 | 51.0 | 5.3 | 75.6 |
| District 15 | Steve Stivers (R) | 12 274 | 719 537 | 58.6 | 91.4 | 3.1 | 0.2 | 2.5 | 0.8 | 2.1 | 1.8 | 90.4 | 49.7 | 3.4 | 77.0 |
| District 16 | James B. Renacci (R) | 3 122 | 724 108 | 232.0 | 94.3 | 1.6 | 0.1 | 2.0 | 0.3 | 1.7 | 2.0 | 92.7 | 51.3 | 5.3 | 78.2 |
| **OKLAHOMA** | | 177 660 | 3 791 508 | 21.3 | 73.6 | 7.3 | 6.9 | 1.8 | 2.4 | 8.0 | 9.2 | 68.2 | 50.5 | 5.5 | 61.1 |
| District 1 | Jim Bridenstine (R) | 4 226 | 764 815 | 181.0 | 73.2 | 9.1 | 5.9 | 2.3 | 2.7 | 6.9 | 10.1 | 66.7 | 51.3 | 6.9 | 58.0 |
| District 2 | Markwayne Mullin (R) | 54 378 | 753 014 | 13.8 | 67.7 | 3.4 | 13.2 | 0.5 | 1.5 | 13.6 | 4.6 | 65.8 | 50.3 | 1.7 | 61.9 |
| District 3 | Frank D. Lucas (R) | 88 362 | 745 941 | 8.4 | 80.4 | 3.8 | 5.3 | 1.6 | 2.8 | 6.1 | 8.4 | 76.0 | 49.7 | 4.3 | 64.7 |
| District 4 | Tom Cole (R) | 25 323 | 765 183 | 30.2 | 77.6 | 6.3 | 5.3 | 2.2 | 1.6 | 7.0 | 7.8 | 72.9 | 50.1 | 4.5 | 60.8 |
| District 5 | James Lankford (R) | 5 371 | 762 555 | 142.0 | 69.3 | 13.7 | 4.7 | 2.8 | 3.3 | 6.2 | 14.9 | 59.6 | 51.0 | 10.1 | 60.1 |
| **OREGON** | | 248 608 | 3 871 859 | 15.6 | 84.7 | 1.8 | 1.3 | 4.3 | 4.3 | 3.5 | 12.0 | 77.9 | 50.6 | 9.8 | 46.2 |
| District 1 | Suzanne Bonamici (D) | 7 788 | 775 806 | 99.6 | 79.4 | 1.6 | 1.2 | 7.4 | 7.1 | 3.2 | 14.0 | 73.6 | 50.6 | 13.8 | 44.1 |
| District 2 | Greg Walden (R) | 179 856 | 770 403 | 4.3 | 90.4 | 0.6 | 1.9 | 1.5 | 2.3 | 3.2 | 12.8 | 81.2 | 50.4 | 5.9 | 44.5 |
| District 3 | Earl Blumenauer (D) | 2 783 | 782 486 | 281.2 | 79.4 | 5.3 | 0.9 | 7.1 | 3.8 | 3.4 | 10.9 | 73.0 | 50.5 | 14.3 | 45.2 |
| District 4 | Peter A. DeFazio (D) | 44 740 | 770 184 | 17.2 | 90.1 | 0.6 | 1.7 | 2.4 | 1.6 | 3.6 | 6.8 | 85.5 | 50.6 | 5.3 | 46.4 |
| District 5 | Kurt Schrader (D) | 13 441 | 772 980 | 57.5 | 84.3 | 0.8 | 1.0 | 3.2 | 6.8 | 3.9 | 15.6 | 76.3 | 50.8 | 9.3 | 51.0 |
| **PENNSYLVANIA** | | 115 883 | 12 742 886 | 110.0 | 82.3 | 10.8 | 0.1 | 2.8 | 2.0 | 1.9 | 5.9 | 79.1 | 51.2 | 5.9 | 74.0 |
| District 1 | Robert A. Brady (D) | 202 | 678 723 | 3 363.8 | 48.2 | 33.7 | 0.2 | 6.9 | 8.4 | 2.7 | 15.9 | 42.2 | 52.1 | 12.4 | 68.3 |
| District 2 | Chaka Fattah (D) | 192 | 726 364 | 3 782.9 | 31.7 | 58.6 | 0.2 | 4.6 | 3.0 | 1.9 | 5.5 | 29.4 | 54.3 | 8.8 | 67.2 |
| District 3 | Mike Kelly (R) | 9 974 | 705 049 | 70.7 | 92.4 | 4.6 | 0.1 | 0.8 | 0.5 | 1.6 | 2.1 | 91.2 | 51.0 | 2.2 | 82.2 |

1. Dry land or land partially or temporarily covered by water.　　2. May be of any race.

# Table E. Congressional Districts 113th Congress — Age and Education

| STATE District | Population and population characteristics, 2011 (cont.) — Age (percent) | | | | | | | | | | Education, 2011 | Attainment[2] (percent) | |
|---|---|---|---|---|---|---|---|---|---|---|---|---|---|
| | Under 5 years | 5 to 17 years | 18 to 24 years | 25 to 34 years | 35 to 44 years | 45 to 54 years | 55 to 64 years | 65 to 74 years | 75 years and over | Median age | Total Enrollment[1] | High school graduate or more | Bachelor's degree or more |
| | 15 | 16 | 17 | 18 | 19 | 20 | 21 | 22 | 23 | 24 | 25 | 26 | 27 |
| NEW YORK—Cont'd | | | | | | | | | | | | | |
| District 15 | 8.5 | 20.9 | 12.7 | 14.8 | 12.7 | 12.7 | 9.0 | 5.0 | 3.5 | 29.9 | 224 050 | 60.4 | 10.5 |
| District 16 | 6.4 | 16.8 | 8.9 | 12.8 | 13.4 | 14.9 | 12.1 | 7.4 | 7.1 | 38.7 | 191 482 | 85.3 | 37.4 |
| District 17 | 6.5 | 18.4 | 8.7 | 11.2 | 13.3 | 15.2 | 12.3 | 7.3 | 7.1 | 39.6 | 201 096 | 87.1 | 44.0 |
| District 18 | 5.8 | 19.5 | 9.9 | 10.1 | 13.7 | 16.4 | 12.1 | 6.8 | 5.8 | 39.2 | 210 690 | 88.6 | 33.7 |
| District 19 | 4.7 | 15.2 | 10.3 | 9.9 | 11.8 | 16.8 | 15.3 | 8.8 | 7.1 | 43.5 | 168 343 | 87.8 | 25.5 |
| District 20 | 5.2 | 15.7 | 11.9 | 12.9 | 12.4 | 14.6 | 13.0 | 6.9 | 7.5 | 39.1 | 196 374 | 91.9 | 35.7 |
| District 21 | 5.7 | 15.8 | 10.6 | 12.0 | 12.6 | 15.6 | 13.1 | 8.0 | 6.6 | 40.1 | 169 075 | 88.1 | 21.7 |
| District 22 | 5.3 | 15.9 | 11.3 | 11.4 | 11.6 | 15.4 | 13.2 | 8.2 | 7.7 | 40.6 | 188 208 | 88.2 | 23.8 |
| District 23 | 5.2 | 15.5 | 12.7 | 11.5 | 11.3 | 15.0 | 13.5 | 8.0 | 7.3 | 40.0 | 188 426 | 88.5 | 23.3 |
| District 24 | 5.8 | 16.5 | 10.9 | 11.7 | 12.0 | 15.5 | 13.2 | 7.2 | 7.1 | 40.2 | 190 671 | 87.9 | 28.4 |
| District 25 | 5.7 | 16.3 | 11.5 | 12.7 | 12.1 | 14.7 | 12.7 | 7.2 | 7.0 | 38.1 | 196 716 | 88.9 | 35.4 |
| District 26 | 5.4 | 14.9 | 11.7 | 13.7 | 11.2 | 14.6 | 13.2 | 7.3 | 8.2 | 38.9 | 187 101 | 87.4 | 28.8 |
| District 27 | 5.3 | 17.0 | 8.4 | 9.8 | 13.0 | 16.5 | 14.1 | 8.4 | 7.4 | 42.6 | 174 518 | 91.5 | 26.9 |
| NORTH CAROLINA | 6.5 | 17.3 | 10.0 | 12.9 | 13.7 | 14.2 | 12.3 | 7.6 | 5.6 | 37.3 | 2 557 304 | 84.7 | 26.9 |
| District 1 | 6.9 | 16.5 | 11.3 | 12.7 | 11.8 | 14.3 | 12.7 | 7.4 | 6.5 | 37.5 | 195 938 | 78.1 | 18.3 |
| District 2 | 7.3 | 19.2 | 9.1 | 13.2 | 14.3 | 13.5 | 10.9 | 7.1 | 5.5 | 36.0 | 206 980 | 87.2 | 27.0 |
| District 3 | 6.7 | 15.4 | 15.2 | 13.3 | 11.5 | 12.4 | 12.2 | 7.8 | 5.5 | 34.5 | 204 238 | 87.1 | 22.2 |
| District 4 | 7.0 | 16.0 | 13.9 | 17.7 | 13.9 | 12.2 | 10.0 | 5.3 | 4.0 | 31.9 | 238 975 | 87.2 | 38.7 |
| District 5 | 5.5 | 16.5 | 10.1 | 11.6 | 13.5 | 14.2 | 13.2 | 8.6 | 6.8 | 39.6 | 185 746 | 83.9 | 25.1 |
| District 6 | 5.3 | 17.2 | 8.9 | 10.8 | 13.2 | 15.7 | 13.9 | 8.2 | 6.8 | 41.2 | 193 728 | 85.1 | 28.5 |
| District 7 | 6.2 | 17.0 | 8.7 | 11.9 | 13.6 | 14.2 | 13.6 | 8.9 | 5.8 | 40.0 | 186 118 | 83.2 | 21.9 |
| District 8 | 6.6 | 18.8 | 9.2 | 12.4 | 13.3 | 15.0 | 12.5 | 7.0 | 5.1 | 37.5 | 197 786 | 79.9 | 16.2 |
| District 9 | 6.8 | 19.4 | 6.8 | 13.4 | 16.2 | 15.5 | 11.2 | 6.3 | 4.4 | 37.6 | 206 181 | 93.2 | 47.5 |
| District 10 | 6.1 | 16.3 | 8.4 | 11.6 | 14.0 | 14.7 | 13.8 | 8.5 | 6.5 | 40.4 | 173 494 | 84.1 | 23.4 |
| District 11 | 5.1 | 15.2 | 8.5 | 10.4 | 12.4 | 14.4 | 14.5 | 10.9 | 8.6 | 43.7 | 164 969 | 82.9 | 21.4 |
| District 12 | 8.1 | 17.3 | 12.7 | 16.6 | 14.5 | 12.4 | 9.5 | 4.9 | 3.9 | 31.9 | 204 269 | 79.6 | 22.0 |
| District 13 | 6.8 | 19.0 | 7.3 | 12.1 | 15.3 | 15.9 | 12.0 | 7.0 | 4.6 | 38.4 | 198 882 | 89.9 | 37.5 |
| NORTH DAKOTA | 6.8 | 15.4 | 12.4 | 13.7 | 11.0 | 13.8 | 12.6 | 7.0 | 7.4 | 36.6 | 172 936 | 90.7 | 26.3 |
| At Large | 6.8 | 15.4 | 12.4 | 13.7 | 11.0 | 13.8 | 12.6 | 7.0 | 7.4 | 36.6 | 172 936 | 90.7 | 26.3 |
| OHIO | 6.1 | 15.4 | 9.6 | 12.3 | 12.6 | 14.8 | 13.1 | 7.5 | 6.7 | 38.9 | 3 077 214 | 88.3 | 24.7 |
| District 1 | 6.8 | 17.9 | 10.0 | 13.2 | 12.9 | 15.0 | 12.2 | 6.4 | 5.5 | 36.5 | 210 422 | 88.2 | 30.0 |
| District 2 | 6.3 | 17.6 | 8.0 | 12.7 | 12.7 | 15.3 | 13.2 | 7.4 | 6.9 | 39.7 | 183 735 | 86.9 | 29.1 |
| District 3 | 7.9 | 17.0 | 13.2 | 17.0 | 13.2 | 13.2 | 9.9 | 4.7 | 4.0 | 31.7 | 214 198 | 85.2 | 25.0 |
| District 4 | 5.9 | 17.8 | 9.3 | 11.8 | 12.5 | 14.9 | 13.2 | 7.8 | 6.7 | 39.3 | 188 353 | 88.8 | 15.8 |
| District 5 | 6.0 | 17.2 | 9.9 | 11.4 | 12.0 | 14.7 | 13.8 | 7.7 | 7.4 | 39.7 | 192 073 | 91.0 | 22.9 |
| District 6 | 5.3 | 16.3 | 8.4 | 11.1 | 12.2 | 15.2 | 14.7 | 9.1 | 7.7 | 42.3 | 164 479 | 86.0 | 14.5 |
| District 7 | 6.4 | 18.4 | 8.3 | 11.2 | 12.2 | 14.8 | 13.4 | 8.1 | 7.2 | 40.2 | 183 803 | 86.9 | 18.4 |
| District 8 | 6.5 | 18.1 | 9.8 | 11.7 | 12.7 | 14.7 | 12.9 | 7.4 | 6.2 | 38.3 | 194 156 | 88.3 | 21.0 |
| District 9 | 6.4 | 16.5 | 10.0 | 13.2 | 12.8 | 14.8 | 12.6 | 6.9 | 6.7 | 38.2 | 190 109 | 85.5 | 20.2 |
| District 10 | 6.1 | 16.4 | 10.7 | 12.5 | 11.8 | 14.2 | 13.1 | 8.0 | 7.4 | 39.1 | 207 971 | 88.1 | 26.2 |
| District 11 | 6.1 | 16.7 | 10.3 | 12.8 | 11.5 | 14.3 | 13.5 | 7.3 | 7.5 | 38.9 | 194 614 | 83.8 | 25.0 |
| District 12 | 6.2 | 18.1 | 8.6 | 12.3 | 14.1 | 15.1 | 13.1 | 7.0 | 5.6 | 38.6 | 203 977 | 92.4 | 37.0 |
| District 13 | 5.7 | 15.4 | 10.7 | 11.8 | 11.7 | 14.7 | 14.1 | 7.8 | 8.0 | 40.7 | 186 592 | 88.3 | 19.8 |
| District 14 | 5.4 | 17.4 | 7.6 | 10.4 | 12.7 | 16.3 | 14.0 | 8.4 | 7.8 | 42.4 | 180 443 | 91.2 | 31.2 |
| District 15 | 5.9 | 16.7 | 10.2 | 13.8 | 13.4 | 14.7 | 12.3 | 7.5 | 5.5 | 37.7 | 196 505 | 89.3 | 27.9 |
| District 16 | 5.2 | 17.4 | 7.9 | 10.1 | 12.7 | 15.6 | 14.3 | 9.0 | 7.7 | 42.6 | 185 784 | 92.4 | 30.5 |
| OKLAHOMA | 7.0 | 17.7 | 10.2 | 13.6 | 12.3 | 13.6 | 12.1 | 7.6 | 6.0 | 36.3 | 994 523 | 86.3 | 23.8 |
| District 1 | 7.2 | 18.3 | 9.4 | 13.8 | 13.1 | 13.7 | 11.9 | 6.8 | 5.8 | 36.1 | 202 394 | 89.1 | 29.4 |
| District 2 | 6.6 | 17.8 | 9.4 | 11.5 | 11.7 | 13.8 | 13.0 | 9.5 | 6.8 | 39.3 | 184 261 | 83.2 | 16.2 |
| District 3 | 6.7 | 17.4 | 10.7 | 13.0 | 11.7 | 14.0 | 12.4 | 7.8 | 6.4 | 37.0 | 194 302 | 85.2 | 20.4 |
| District 4 | 6.6 | 17.4 | 11.4 | 14.2 | 12.9 | 13.3 | 11.4 | 7.2 | 5.5 | 35.2 | 210 225 | 88.7 | 24.1 |
| District 5 | 7.7 | 17.7 | 10.2 | 15.0 | 12.1 | 13.2 | 11.7 | 6.8 | 5.6 | 34.4 | 203 341 | 85.3 | 29.0 |
| OREGON | 6.2 | 16.1 | 9.4 | 13.7 | 13.0 | 13.7 | 13.6 | 7.9 | 6.3 | 38.7 | 973 213 | 89.4 | 29.3 |
| District 1 | 6.6 | 17.5 | 8.2 | 14.8 | 14.9 | 14.1 | 12.2 | 6.6 | 5.1 | 37.1 | 201 375 | 90.8 | 37.0 |
| District 2 | 6.2 | 16.3 | 8.2 | 12.1 | 11.5 | 13.6 | 14.6 | 9.6 | 7.7 | 40.9 | 181 137 | 88.3 | 23.1 |
| District 3 | 6.5 | 14.7 | 9.4 | 17.6 | 14.8 | 13.5 | 12.6 | 5.8 | 5.0 | 35.9 | 193 591 | 88.6 | 34.8 |
| District 4 | 5.2 | 14.5 | 12.4 | 11.7 | 10.8 | 13.2 | 15.1 | 9.4 | 7.6 | 40.9 | 202 846 | 90.7 | 24.1 |
| District 5 | 6.3 | 17.4 | 9.0 | 12.3 | 12.6 | 14.0 | 13.8 | 8.1 | 6.5 | 39.3 | 194 264 | 88.4 | 27.6 |
| PENNSYLVANIA | 5.7 | 16.0 | 9.9 | 12.1 | 12.4 | 15.1 | 13.3 | 7.8 | 7.7 | 40.3 | 3 177 813 | 88.6 | 27.0 |
| District 1 | 7.1 | 15.9 | 11.7 | 16.1 | 13.3 | 13.3 | 11.4 | 6.0 | 5.2 | 34.4 | 178 701 | 78.4 | 22.3 |
| District 2 | 6.3 | 14.8 | 15.5 | 16.3 | 10.9 | 12.3 | 11.0 | 6.7 | 6.2 | 32.7 | 217 326 | 84.7 | 31.5 |
| District 3 | 5.5 | 16.1 | 9.8 | 10.9 | 12.2 | 15.2 | 13.9 | 8.3 | 8.1 | 41.5 | 168 453 | 89.4 | 22.9 |

1. All persons 3 years old and over enrolled in nursery school through college and graduate or professional school.  2. Persons 25 years old and over.

# Table E. Congressional Districts 113th Congress — Households and Group Quarters

| STATE District | Households, 2011 | | | | | | Group quarters, 2010 | | | | | |
| --- | --- | --- | --- | --- | --- | --- | --- | --- | --- | --- | --- | --- |
| | Number | Persons per household | Family households (percent) | Married-couple family (percent) | Female family householder[1] | One person households (percent) | Total in group quarters | Percent 65 years and over | Persons in correctional institutions | Persons in nursing homes | Persons in college dormitories | Persons in military quarters |
| | 28 | 29 | 30 | 31 | 32 | 33 | 34 | 35 | 36 | 37 | 38 | 39 |
| **NEW YORK—Cont'd** | | | | | | | | | | | | |
| District 15 | 233 954 | 3.05 | 69.0 | 22.4 | 38.3 | 26.8 | 18 002 | 8.9 | 981 | 2 145 | 2 352 | 0 |
| District 16 | 266 067 | 2.65 | 65.6 | 41.7 | 18.9 | 30.8 | 16 738 | 41.8 | 0 | 7 221 | 5 113 | 0 |
| District 17 | 240 270 | 2.91 | 74.1 | 58.7 | 11.1 | 22.4 | 24 814 | 23.3 | 3 245 | 4 756 | 8 571 | 0 |
| District 18 | 249 532 | 2.80 | 70.5 | 54.8 | 11.9 | 24.5 | 28 817 | 14.3 | 8 143 | 3 627 | 7 046 | 4 409 |
| District 19 | 271 176 | 2.47 | 64.8 | 49.6 | 10.3 | 28.4 | 39 083 | 13.1 | 9 986 | 4 771 | 12 644 | 3 |
| District 20 | 286 788 | 2.40 | 59.1 | 43.1 | 12.5 | 32.8 | 30 326 | 16.3 | 1 298 | 4 651 | 18 920 | 0 |
| District 21 | 281 184 | 2.40 | 66.0 | 50.1 | 11.4 | 27.3 | 40 088 | 10.4 | 18 001 | 3 692 | 11 032 | 3 614 |
| District 22 | 279 381 | 2.45 | 62.0 | 45.8 | 12.1 | 32.2 | 34 547 | 18.0 | 6 104 | 6 243 | 17 830 | 0 |
| District 23 | 289 041 | 2.33 | 63.4 | 47.7 | 11.4 | 28.8 | 41 101 | 13.9 | 6 988 | 5 257 | 23 896 | 0 |
| District 24 | 276 202 | 2.47 | 63.4 | 45.7 | 13.1 | 29.5 | 27 512 | 17.7 | 4 484 | 4 882 | 14 806 | 0 |
| District 25 | 285 715 | 2.42 | 61.0 | 42.7 | 14.3 | 31.6 | 26 098 | 20.7 | 1 499 | 4 931 | 14 361 | 0 |
| District 26 | 306 493 | 2.28 | 57.5 | 36.9 | 16.0 | 35.8 | 20 695 | 20.0 | 926 | 3 778 | 11 661 | 0 |
| District 27 | 278 497 | 2.46 | 68.0 | 52.8 | 10.7 | 26.9 | 27 105 | 20.3 | 13 255 | 5 336 | 5 224 | 0 |
| **NORTH CAROLINA** | 3 683 364 | 2.55 | 66.7 | 48.5 | 13.9 | 28.0 | 257 246 | 16.6 | 61 680 | 46 638 | 89 795 | 26 326 |
| District 1 | 286 379 | 2.48 | 61.8 | 34.7 | 22.6 | 33.3 | 35 516 | 15.6 | 13 922 | 6 285 | 10 496 | 594 |
| District 2 | 270 656 | 2.70 | 70.2 | 53.5 | 12.9 | 25.8 | 13 273 | 21.8 | 1 132 | 3 214 | 1 773 | 5 949 |
| District 3 | 273 459 | 2.60 | 66.6 | 50.1 | 12.3 | 26.6 | 39 450 | 6.2 | 6 616 | 2 817 | 8 725 | 19 749 |
| District 4 | 290 467 | 2.49 | 60.5 | 40.4 | 16.3 | 31.9 | 34 239 | 7.0 | 5 518 | 2 406 | 22 784 | 0 |
| District 5 | 286 880 | 2.47 | 66.6 | 50.6 | 12.0 | 27.8 | 18 132 | 18.3 | 2 268 | 3 598 | 10 492 | 0 |
| District 6 | 297 765 | 2.45 | 68.3 | 51.4 | 12.3 | 26.9 | 14 844 | 23.6 | 2 493 | 3 811 | 6 738 | 0 |
| District 7 | 288 086 | 2.55 | 68.9 | 51.6 | 12.4 | 26.1 | 10 808 | 29.2 | 5 511 | 3 495 | 9 | 33 |
| District 8 | 269 642 | 2.72 | 70.5 | 50.8 | 15.1 | 24.9 | 17 025 | 17.1 | 8 325 | 3 469 | 3 449 | 0 |
| District 9 | 282 694 | 2.63 | 69.7 | 56.0 | 10.3 | 25.5 | 5 898 | 45.8 | 50 | 2 736 | 2 155 | 1 |
| District 10 | 285 613 | 2.54 | 67.3 | 50.4 | 12.6 | 27.9 | 15 408 | 30.8 | 2 503 | 4 741 | 4 033 | 0 |
| District 11 | 294 789 | 2.41 | 66.2 | 52.2 | 10.1 | 29.3 | 19 106 | 23.1 | 5 915 | 4 622 | 4 965 | 0 |
| District 12 | 280 942 | 2.54 | 60.2 | 33.5 | 21.0 | 32.3 | 26 561 | 10.1 | 4 648 | 3 049 | 13 560 | 0 |
| District 13 | 275 992 | 2.62 | 70.4 | 56.3 | 10.9 | 25.3 | 6 986 | 28.6 | 2 779 | 2 395 | 616 | 0 |
| **NORTH DAKOTA** | 283 440 | 2.32 | 61.8 | 50.2 | 7.9 | 31.1 | 25 056 | 25.3 | 2 489 | 6 433 | 10 570 | 1 380 |
| At Large | 283 440 | 2.32 | 61.8 | 50.2 | 7.9 | 31.1 | 25 056 | 25.3 | 2 489 | 6 433 | 10 570 | 1 380 |
| **OHIO** | 283 440 | 2.48 | 64.2 | 47.1 | 12.9 | 30.1 | 306 266 | 25.3 | 76 590 | 83 019 | 106 042 | 571 |
| District 1 | 275 055 | 2.58 | 64.8 | 46.4 | 15.0 | 29.5 | 22 047 | 17.7 | 6 431 | 4 486 | 7 060 | 0 |
| District 2 | 281 655 | 2.51 | 65.1 | 48.8 | 11.6 | 30.0 | 9 458 | 55.0 | 880 | 5 887 | 712 | 0 |
| District 3 | 281 759 | 2.53 | 55.3 | 32.1 | 18.8 | 36.3 | 20 391 | 10.7 | 2 353 | 2 793 | 11 851 | 0 |
| District 4 | 274 605 | 2.52 | 68.6 | 51.2 | 11.8 | 25.7 | 28 804 | 17.6 | 15 892 | 5 563 | 5 261 | 0 |
| District 5 | 282 475 | 2.47 | 65.9 | 51.2 | 10.4 | 28.4 | 16 472 | 31.9 | 971 | 6 014 | 8 367 | 0 |
| District 6 | 279 899 | 2.48 | 67.4 | 52.3 | 10.7 | 27.5 | 21 997 | 30.8 | 9 881 | 6 354 | 3 595 | 0 |
| District 7 | 276 717 | 2.57 | 69.8 | 53.9 | 11.4 | 25.8 | 15 183 | 35.8 | 795 | 6 223 | 5 129 | 0 |
| District 8 | 274 420 | 2.59 | 68.4 | 51.5 | 12.6 | 25.8 | 15 976 | 24.8 | 1 369 | 4 682 | 8 537 | 0 |
| District 9 | 296 092 | 2.38 | 59.3 | 37.4 | 16.6 | 34.3 | 15 306 | 26.5 | 1 894 | 4 930 | 5 512 | 0 |
| District 10 | 297 096 | 2.34 | 62.2 | 44.6 | 13.7 | 32.2 | 23 489 | 21.5 | 1 997 | 5 845 | 12 267 | 547 |
| District 11 | 299 974 | 2.27 | 53.4 | 28.7 | 20.8 | 41.0 | 24 734 | 21.5 | 3 906 | 6 243 | 7 446 | 0 |
| District 12 | 282 312 | 2.51 | 67.6 | 54.7 | 9.3 | 26.6 | 17 410 | 19.4 | 6 071 | 3 929 | 6 352 | 0 |
| District 13 | 296 606 | 2.37 | 60.8 | 40.5 | 16.0 | 33.6 | 22 930 | 20.6 | 5 134 | 5 394 | 10 204 | 0 |
| District 14 | 279 176 | 2.53 | 67.6 | 54.8 | 9.4 | 27.9 | 10 784 | 40.5 | 2 076 | 5 260 | 1 338 | 24 |
| District 15 | 276 995 | 2.49 | 65.1 | 52.2 | 9.0 | 27.9 | 31 105 | 11.1 | 16 670 | 3 476 | 9 591 | 0 |
| District 16 | 283 719 | 2.51 | 68.2 | 56.0 | 8.7 | 27.1 | 10 180 | 51.7 | 270 | 5 940 | 2 820 | 0 |
| **OKLAHOMA** | 1 442 731 | 2.55 | 66.4 | 49.6 | 12.2 | 28.3 | 112 017 | 24.0 | 40 562 | 21 678 | 30 148 | 7 203 |
| District 1 | 298 000 | 2.53 | 66.2 | 48.7 | 13.3 | 28.3 | 11 017 | 28.8 | 2 371 | 3 656 | 2 981 | 0 |
| District 2 | 283 184 | 2.58 | 69.2 | 51.9 | 12.9 | 26.9 | 22 805 | 19.9 | 9 915 | 5 506 | 4 623 | 0 |
| District 3 | 284 298 | 2.51 | 66.9 | 51.9 | 10.2 | 27.9 | 33 193 | 13.8 | 15 091 | 4 818 | 10 089 | 463 |
| District 4 | 284 443 | 2.59 | 67.7 | 51.4 | 11.6 | 26.9 | 27 619 | 12.1 | 7 991 | 3 797 | 7 490 | 6 740 |
| District 5 | 292 806 | 2.55 | 62.1 | 44.2 | 12.7 | 31.6 | 17 383 | 18.8 | 5 194 | 3 901 | 4 965 | 0 |
| **OREGON** | 1 516 979 | 2.50 | 63.1 | 48.4 | 10.0 | 28.4 | 86 642 | 18.0 | 22 203 | 11 491 | 23 704 | 178 |
| District 1 | 293 270 | 2.60 | 66.4 | 52.6 | 9.5 | 26.3 | 14 357 | 20.7 | 4 641 | 1 964 | 3 338 | 127 |
| District 2 | 308 490 | 2.43 | 65.5 | 50.5 | 9.7 | 28.1 | 18 743 | 19.0 | 8 762 | 2 660 | 1 775 | 13 |
| District 3 | 311 169 | 2.46 | 55.7 | 40.9 | 10.7 | 32.0 | 19 005 | 15.5 | 2 065 | 2 399 | 6 604 | 0 |
| District 4 | 312 356 | 2.41 | 61.4 | 47.5 | 9.3 | 28.7 | 18 307 | 16.5 | 1 354 | 2 067 | 8 825 | 21 |
| District 5 | 291 694 | 2.59 | 66.9 | 50.9 | 10.8 | 26.8 | 16 230 | 19.1 | 5 381 | 2 401 | 3 162 | 17 |
| **PENNSYLVANIA** | 4 937 333 | 2.49 | 64.7 | 48.1 | 12.1 | 29.7 | 426 113 | 21.0 | 97 820 | 87 775 | 177 332 | 259 |
| District 1 | 257 386 | 2.56 | 54.1 | 28.1 | 19.8 | 39.0 | 25 825 | 9.2 | 10 896 | 2 024 | 7 108 | 14 |
| District 2 | 277 515 | 2.48 | 50.7 | 24.3 | 21.8 | 41.3 | 36 155 | 13.8 | 680 | 4 909 | 23 446 | 0 |
| District 3 | 280 169 | 2.42 | 65.5 | 50.0 | 11.5 | 29.4 | 26 866 | 19.5 | 6 328 | 5 188 | 11 315 | 11 |

1. No spouse present.

# Table E. Congressional Districts 113th Congress — Housing and Money Income

| STATE District | Housing units, 2011 | | | | | | Money income, 2011 | | |
| | Total | Occupied units | | | | | Households | | |
| | | | Owner-occupied | | | Renter-occupied | | | |
| | | Percent Occupied | Percent | Median value[1] (dollars) | Percent valued at $500,000 or more | Median rent[2] | Per capita income (dollars) | Median income (dollars) | Percent with income of $100,000 or more |
| | 40 | 41 | 42 | 43 | 44 | 45 | 46 | 47 | 48 |
| **NEW YORK—Cont'd** | | | | | | | | | |
| District 15 | 255 487 | 91.6 | 8.8 | 369 900 | 19.5 | 919 | 12 274 | 23 894.0 | 5.3 |
| District 16 | 291 276 | 91.3 | 48.5 | 447 600 | 42.9 | 1 174 | 36 632 | 59 849.0 | 29.8 |
| District 17 | 255 921 | 93.9 | 68.0 | 460 800 | 42.1 | 1 351 | 40 896 | 84 664.0 | 43.0 |
| District 18 | 272 181 | 91.7 | 70.2 | 302 500 | 16.6 | 1 132 | 33 600 | 71 399.0 | 35.7 |
| District 19 | 361 436 | 75.0 | 72.1 | 204 800 | 7.3 | 862 | 27 460 | 53 769.0 | 20.8 |
| District 20 | 324 676 | 88.3 | 61.7 | 198 400 | 3.5 | 855 | 29 764 | 56 811.0 | 23.6 |
| District 21 | 367 986 | 76.4 | 70.8 | 130 700 | 3.8 | 772 | 23 990 | 48 759.0 | 14.5 |
| District 22 | 323 834 | 86.3 | 68.9 | 107 500 | 1.6 | 662 | 23 568 | 45 578.0 | 15.7 |
| District 23 | 340 908 | 84.8 | 67.6 | 94 600 | 2.3 | 667 | 23 145 | 44 518.0 | 14.3 |
| District 24 | 310 789 | 88.9 | 68.6 | 122 600 | 2.1 | 729 | 26 112 | 51 724.0 | 19.2 |
| District 25 | 310 211 | 92.1 | 63.7 | 134 200 | 1.9 | 778 | 26 715 | 49 343.0 | 18.8 |
| District 26 | 345 145 | 88.8 | 59.0 | 106 500 | 1.3 | 682 | 24 236 | 41 018.0 | 14.7 |
| District 27 | 302 989 | 91.9 | 77.2 | 134 700 | 2.4 | 688 | 28 349 | 55 340.0 | 20.7 |
| **NORTH CAROLINA** | 4 362 956 | 84.4 | 66.5 | 153 700 | 5.3 | 745 | 24 107 | 43 916 | 16.2 |
| District 1 | 341 401 | 83.9 | 54.6 | 107 900 | 2.1 | 678 | 17 999 | 32 009 | 7.9 |
| District 2 | 306 828 | 88.2 | 68.9 | 156 600 | 5.1 | 772 | 24 339 | 48 077 | 19.2 |
| District 3 | 364 377 | 75 | 64.9 | 161 400 | 5.4 | 799 | 22 499 | 44 871 | 13.1 |
| District 4 | 326 027 | 89.1 | 53.3 | 176 700 | 7.9 | 827 | 26 359 | 47 242 | 19.2 |
| District 5 | 347 574 | 82.5 | 69.7 | 149 600 | 4.3 | 667 | 23 565 | 41 781 | 14.2 |
| District 6 | 332 936 | 89.4 | 73.9 | 151 600 | 3.5 | 691 | 25 473 | 46 927 | 17.4 |
| District 7 | 364 910 | 78.9 | 69.7 | 147 700 | 5.2 | 733 | 23 559 | 41 935 | 14.9 |
| District 8 | 315 111 | 85.6 | 70.1 | 121 000 | 2.5 | 660 | 18 603 | 38 549 | 10.1 |
| District 9 | 304 839 | 92.7 | 73.6 | 225 000 | 12.7 | 909 | 37 073 | 65 681 | 32.9 |
| District 10 | 334 158 | 85.5 | 68.7 | 140 900 | 5.1 | 691 | 23 031 | 41 582 | 14.2 |
| District 11 | 396 799 | 74.3 | 72.7 | 149 900 | 5.0 | 636 | 21 688 | 39 322 | 11.1 |
| District 12 | 323 291 | 86.9 | 48.4 | 116 000 | 1.9 | 742 | 18 770 | 33 891 | 9.1 |
| District 13 | 304 705 | 90.6 | 76.1 | 197 400 | 6.9 | 827 | 30 278 | 61 234 | 27.1 |
| **NORTH DAKOTA** | 320 888 | 88.3 | 65.7 | 128 600 | 1.9 | 626 | 28 055 | 51 704 | 18.6 |
| At Large | 320 888 | 88.3 | 65.7 | 128 600 | 1.9 | 626 | 28 055 | 51 704 | 18.6 |
| **OHIO** | 5 133 528 | 88.4 | 67.0 | 129 600 | 2.4 | 692 | 24 750 | 45 749 | 16.3 |
| District 1 | 319 920 | 86.0 | 63.2 | 150 600 | 4.1 | 677 | 25 961 | 49 645 | 20.3 |
| District 2 | 323 565 | 87.0 | 69.4 | 137 900 | 3.8 | 697 | 27 128 | 48 066 | 19.3 |
| District 3 | 332 485 | 84.7 | 45.9 | 116 100 | 2.1 | 740 | 21 012 | 37 667 | 11.8 |
| District 4 | 306 454 | 89.6 | 70.6 | 115 400 | 1.8 | 641 | 22 338 | 45 326 | 13.6 |
| District 5 | 309 205 | 91.4 | 72.9 | 123 600 | 1.7 | 659 | 24 377 | 48 211 | 15.5 |
| District 6 | 323 607 | 86.5 | 75.5 | 99 600 | 2.0 | 552 | 21 404 | 41 355 | 11.0 |
| District 7 | 305 090 | 90.7 | 73.3 | 128 600 | 1.3 | 644 | 23 004 | 45 910 | 13.7 |
| District 8 | 301 974 | 90.9 | 71.3 | 137 900 | 1.3 | 716 | 23 608 | 48 452 | 17.3 |
| District 9 | 349 502 | 84.7 | 59.5 | 101 000 | 1.5 | 656 | 21 128 | 37 749 | 10.5 |
| District 10 | 334 034 | 88.9 | 62.5 | 122 800 | 1.6 | 714 | 24 859 | 42 813 | 15.4 |
| District 11 | 374 474 | 80.1 | 51.3 | 97 300 | 3.4 | 673 | 22 250 | 32 014 | 11.3 |
| District 12 | 304 191 | 92.8 | 72.1 | 173 000 | 3.7 | 763 | 31 809 | 61 304 | 26.6 |
| District 13 | 337 273 | 87.9 | 65.0 | 96 500 | 0.6 | 628 | 21 261 | 38 697 | 10.3 |
| District 14 | 303 752 | 91.9 | 76.5 | 168 700 | 4.3 | 767 | 30 555 | 56 506 | 23.6 |
| District 15 | 303 659 | 91.2 | 68.7 | 153 500 | 2.9 | 777 | 26 676 | 53 239 | 20.1 |
| District 16 | 304 343 | 93.2 | 76.0 | 157 600 | 2.1 | 754 | 28 589 | 56 251 | 21.5 |
| **OKLAHOMA** | 1 674 724 | 86.1 | 67.0 | 112 600 | 2.4 | 675 | 23 016 | 43 225 | 14.5 |
| District 1 | 334 676 | 89.0 | 65.3 | 133 200 | 3.0 | 717 | 26 303 | 47 211 | 18.4 |
| District 2 | 349 310 | 81.1 | 71.9 | 87 500 | 2.2 | 576 | 18 865 | 37 364 | 9.4 |
| District 3 | 331 450 | 85.8 | 69.5 | 100 300 | 1.8 | 618 | 21 721 | 42 953 | 13.4 |
| District 4 | 326 710 | 87.1 | 68.7 | 121 000 | 1.4 | 716 | 23 653 | 47 170 | 15.5 |
| District 5 | 332 578 | 88.0 | 60.0 | 123 500 | 3.8 | 721 | 24 445 | 42 029 | 15.7 |
| **OREGON** | 1 684 244 | 90.1 | 60.8 | 232 900 | 9.7 | 840 | 25 228 | 46 816 | 16.5 |
| District 1 | 320 623 | 91.5 | 63.2 | 269 100 | 12.1 | 915 | 30 009 | 60 868 | 24.1 |
| District 2 | 357 079 | 86.4 | 62.6 | 185 000 | 9.0 | 778 | 22 267 | 40 670 | 12.1 |
| District 3 | 331 516 | 93.9 | 54.9 | 255 700 | 10.6 | 878 | 26 601 | 47 378 | 17.8 |
| District 4 | 344 026 | 90.8 | 60.8 | 203 600 | 6.9 | 773 | 21 359 | 40 197 | 11.1 |
| District 5 | 331 000 | 88.1 | 62.7 | 237 900 | 10.5 | 832 | 25 843 | 49 677 | 17.7 |
| **PENNSYLVANIA** | 5 579 394 | 88.5 | 69.5 | 164 800 | 5.1 | 786 | 26 933 | 50 228 | 19.4 |
| District 1 | 299 393 | 86.0 | 56.2 | 133 900 | 4.5 | 871 | 21 236 | 35 702 | 12.5 |
| District 2 | 329 936 | 84.1 | 51.2 | 143 300 | 10.5 | 843 | 24 085 | 33 543 | 14.2 |
| District 3 | 316 284 | 88.6 | 72.6 | 115 800 | 2.1 | 612 | 24 222 | 44 092 | 14.4 |

1. Specified owner-occupied units.　　2. Specified renter-occupied units.

| STATE District | Poverty, 2011 (percent) | | | Civilian labor force, 2011 | | | Civilian employment,[2] 2011 | | | | | Social Security beneficiaries, December 2012 | | |
|---|---|---|---|---|---|---|---|---|---|---|---|---|---|---|
| | | | | | Unemployment | | | Percent | | | | | | |
| | Persons below poverty level | Families below poverty level | Households receiving food stamps in past 12 months | Total | Total | Rate[1] | Total | Management, professional, and related occupations | Service, sales, and office | Construction and production | Persons under age 65 with no health insurance, 2010 (percent) | Number | Rate[3] | Supplemental Security Income recipients, December 2012 |
| | 49 | 50 | 51 | 52 | 53 | 54 | 55 | 56 | 57 | 58 | 59 | 60 | 61 | 62 |
| NEW YORK—Cont'd | | | | | | | | | | | | | | |
| District 15 | 39.4 | 37.2 | 51.5 | 313 508 | 57 647 | 18.4 | 255 861 | 15.8 | 64.6 | 19.6 | 18.7 | 84 344 | 115.4 | 70 602 |
| District 16 | 13.3 | 11.0 | 15.1 | 363 568 | 39 970 | 11.0 | 323 598 | 39.1 | 46.2 | 14.7 | 12.3 | 122 600 | 170.0 | 23 313 |
| District 17 | 10.4 | 7.1 | 7.0 | 372 675 | 31 248 | 8.4 | 341 427 | 44.4 | 42.0 | 13.6 | 13.1 | 123 510 | 170.5 | 11 535 |
| District 18 | 11.6 | 7.7 | 9.1 | 366 448 | 34 342 | 9.4 | 332 106 | 40.0 | 42.3 | 17.7 | 11.5 | 124 440 | 171.2 | 12 487 |
| District 19 | 12.4 | 7.7 | 11.0 | 365 247 | 37 988 | 10.4 | 327 259 | 35.8 | 42.0 | 22.1 | 11.3 | 157 055 | 221.0 | 17 556 |
| District 20 | 13.3 | 9.5 | 11.0 | 388 264 | 30 690 | 7.9 | 357 574 | 41.3 | 44.4 | 14.4 | 8.0 | 144 507 | 200.7 | 19 659 |
| District 21 | 15.5 | 11.1 | 14.5 | 341 338 | 32 132 | 9.4 | 309 206 | 32.9 | 43.3 | 23.8 | 10.6 | 158 521 | 220.9 | 21 410 |
| District 22 | 16.2 | 10.9 | 14.9 | 349 719 | 29 516 | 8.4 | 320 203 | 35.1 | 43.4 | 21.5 | 10.5 | 162 607 | 225.8 | 23 181 |
| District 23 | 17.7 | 12.4 | 14.6 | 351 867 | 27 305 | 7.8 | 324 562 | 34.6 | 40.5 | 24.9 | 11.0 | 159 350 | 222.0 | 22 035 |
| District 24 | 16.1 | 10.8 | 13.6 | 354 718 | 27 464 | 7.7 | 327 254 | 38.0 | 41.3 | 20.7 | 10.5 | 148 355 | 208.1 | 21 703 |
| District 25 | 17.2 | 12.2 | 14.9 | 365 329 | 29 883 | 8.2 | 335 446 | 41.3 | 43.8 | 14.9 | 9.1 | 146 342 | 204.0 | 26 162 |
| District 26 | 18.7 | 15.2 | 19.4 | 365 948 | 38 211 | 10.4 | 327 737 | 35.5 | 47.9 | 16.6 | 10.1 | 157 562 | 218.9 | 30 250 |
| District 27 | 9.2 | 6.5 | 9.4 | 363 727 | 25 891 | 7.1 | 337 836 | 34.8 | 41.4 | 23.7 | 7.9 | 159 240 | 223.3 | 11 384 |
| NORTH CAROLINA | 17.9 | 13.2 | 14.7 | 4 751 695 | 555 887 | 11.7 | 4 195 808 | 35.6 | 41.2 | 23.1 | 18.7 | 1 859 520 | 192.6 | 230 691 |
| District 1 | 27.8 | 21.8 | 27.0 | 345 471 | 53 631 | 15.5 | 291 840 | 30.4 | 42.8 | 26.9 | 21.8 | 155 356 | 210.0 | 36 485 |
| District 2 | 14.9 | 11.8 | 11.2 | 341 575 | 37 775 | 11.1 | 303 800 | 36.9 | 40.1 | 23.0 | 17.3 | 132 811 | 178.3 | 14 815 |
| District 3 | 18.0 | 12.6 | 14.3 | 344 481 | 38 921 | 11.3 | 305 560 | 32.4 | 44.4 | 23.2 | 16.6 | 139 840 | 186.5 | 16 564 |
| District 4 | 18.2 | 13.6 | 12.6 | 394 534 | 43 656 | 11.1 | 350 878 | 45.7 | 39.1 | 15.2 | 18.9 | 102 625 | 135.3 | 16 060 |
| District 5 | 18.7 | 12.7 | 11.6 | 364 010 | 39 523 | 10.9 | 324 487 | 33.1 | 41.1 | 25.8 | 18.7 | 159 468 | 219.5 | 14 177 |
| District 6 | 15.0 | 10.3 | 11.3 | 377 952 | 36 143 | 9.6 | 341 809 | 37.3 | 40.4 | 22.3 | 15.9 | 160 191 | 213.6 | 13 491 |
| District 7 | 17.9 | 12.9 | 16.1 | 361 979 | 46 586 | 12.9 | 315 393 | 31.7 | 42.0 | 26.3 | 19.8 | 163 263 | 219.0 | 20 314 |
| District 8 | 20.7 | 15.9 | 19.3 | 349 671 | 48 014 | 13.7 | 301 657 | 27.7 | 40.4 | 31.9 | 22.5 | 150 178 | 200.2 | 21 302 |
| District 9 | 8.2 | 5.5 | 7.1 | 409 938 | 38 571 | 9.4 | 371 367 | 47.7 | 38.4 | 13.9 | 12.3 | 106 468 | 141.8 | 6 639 |
| District 10 | 16.6 | 12.5 | 15.7 | 370 378 | 46 408 | 12.5 | 323 970 | 31.7 | 41.6 | 26.6 | 19.4 | 166 112 | 224.2 | 17 794 |
| District 11 | 18.2 | 13.0 | 13.3 | 332 172 | 36 823 | 11.1 | 295 349 | 29.5 | 44.6 | 25.9 | 21.7 | 195 980 | 268.3 | 17 500 |
| District 12 | 27.2 | 22.6 | 23.7 | 377 531 | 57 750 | 15.3 | 319 781 | 28.7 | 46.4 | 25.0 | 24.8 | 106 778 | 144.8 | 24 536 |
| District 13 | 11.6 | 9.1 | 8.5 | 382 003 | 32 086 | 8.4 | 349 917 | 44.9 | 37.1 | 18.0 | 13.8 | 120 450 | 164.5 | 11 014 |
| NORTH DAKOTA | 12.2 | 7.9 | 8.8 | 382 841 | 12 011 | 3.1 | 370 830 | 34.6 | 40.4 | 25.0 | 11.3 | 122 084 | 178.5 | 8 481 |
| At Large | 12.2 | 7.9 | 8.8 | 382 841 | 12 011 | 3.1 | 370 830 | 34.6 | 40.4 | 25.0 | 11.3 | 122 084 | 178.5 | 8 481 |
| OHIO | 16.4 | 12.0 | 15.2 | 5 820 387 | 606 934 | 10.4 | 5 213 453 | 34.2 | 42.4 | 23.4 | 13.8 | 2 204 269 | 190.9 | 304 064 |
| District 1 | 17.6 | 13.3 | 15.6 | 377 072 | 44 805 | 11.9 | 332 267 | 37.0 | 45.1 | 17.9 | 13.3 | 121 026 | 166.0 | 19 941 |
| District 2 | 14.9 | 11.8 | 13.9 | 361 841 | 38 219 | 10.6 | 323 622 | 38.1 | 41.0 | 20.9 | 14.3 | 139 738 | 194.9 | 20 629.0 |
| District 3 | 25.6 | 20.7 | 21.5 | 378 722 | 45 733 | 12.1 | 332 989 | 32.9 | 47.9 | 19.2 | 18.8 | 99 847 | 136.4 | 27 597.0 |
| District 4 | 15.7 | 11.3 | 15.0 | 355 044 | 37 153 | 10.5 | 317 891 | 28.5 | 40.1 | 31.3 | 12.7 | 145 771 | 202.0 | 14 973 |
| District 5 | 12.9 | 8.7 | 11.0 | 371 060 | 36 876 | 9.9 | 334 184 | 33.0 | 38.5 | 28.4 | 11.1 | 141 529 | 198.1 | 10 343 |
| District 6 | 16.4 | 11.7 | 16.6 | 325 606 | 33 352 | 10.2 | 292 254 | 27.9 | 41.4 | 30.7 | 15.0 | 166 698 | 232.4 | 25 759 |
| District 7 | 14.7 | 10.9 | 13.2 | 363 176 | 36 363 | 10.0 | 326 813 | 28.9 | 40.1 | 31.0 | 16.8 | 149 382 | 205.7 | 14 424 |
| District 8 | 14.8 | 10.8 | 13.5 | 366 087 | 37 270 | 10.2 | 328 817 | 31.3 | 41.9 | 26.8 | 12.3 | 137 134 | 188.8 | 14 040 |
| District 9 | 22.6 | 17.8 | 22.1 | 361 191 | 46 168 | 12.8 | 315 023 | 28.6 | 46.6 | 24.8 | 16.7 | 136 895 | 190.7 | 30 310 |
| District 10 | 18.4 | 13.5 | 15.4 | 350 241 | 37 407 | 10.7 | 312 834 | 36.9 | 43.9 | 19.2 | 13.2 | 139 697 | 192.6 | 18 757 |
| District 11 | 27.4 | 21.7 | 25.5 | 334 327 | 59 160 | 17.7 | 275 167 | 35.6 | 45.8 | 18.6 | 16.6 | 137 153 | 194.4 | 42 481 |
| District 12 | 10.5 | 7.3 | 11.2 | 384 557 | 25 029 | 6.5 | 359 528 | 42.1 | 40.1 | 17.8 | 10.0 | 120 917 | 166.2 | 11 587 |
| District 13 | 19.8 | 14.8 | 17.6 | 360 267 | 39 887 | 11.1 | 320 380 | 28.3 | 45.5 | 26.2 | 15.7 | 154 983 | 214.1 | 22 036 |
| District 14 | 9.7 | 6.7 | 8.5 | 378 889 | 29 147 | 7.7 | 349 742 | 38.2 | 39.6 | 22.2 | 11.3 | 145 581 | 203.1 | 9 204 |
| District 15 | 13.6 | 9.0 | 13.3 | 366 686 | 30 338 | 8.3 | 336 348 | 38.0 | 41.6 | 20.4 | 10.7 | 123 893 | 172.2 | 14 607 |
| District 16 | 8.4 | 5.8 | 7.4 | 385 621 | 30 027 | 7.8 | 355 594 | 39.3 | 40.3 | 20.4 | 11.3 | 144 025 | 198.9 | 7 376 |
| OKLAHOMA | 17.2 | 12.8 | 14.3 | 1 818 689 | 136 930 | 7.5 | 1 681 759 | 32.9 | 42.1 | 25.0 | 21.5 | 730 022 | 192.5 | 97 169 |
| District 1 | 15.0 | 11.1 | 12.4 | 388 253 | 26 405 | 6.8 | 361 848 | 36.0 | 42.4 | 21.6 | 20.1 | 134 673 | 176.1 | 16 426 |
| District 2 | 20.7 | 15.8 | 18.5 | 324 223 | 33 887 | 10.5 | 290 336 | 28.8 | 41.3 | 30.0 | 26.4 | 179 038 | 237.8 | 27 804 |
| District 3 | 16.0 | 11.5 | 12.5 | 357 311 | 27 404 | 7.7 | 329 907 | 30.7 | 40.2 | 29.1 | 19.8 | 147 107 | 197.2 | 15 473 |
| District 4 | 14.4 | 10.3 | 11.9 | 371 813 | 20 929 | 5.6 | 350 884 | 32.5 | 42.8 | 24.6 | 17.6 | 138 352 | 180.8 | 15 991 |
| District 5 | 20.0 | 15.2 | 16.1 | 377 089 | 28 305 | 7.5 | 348 784 | 35.5 | 43.5 | 21.0 | 23.7 | 130 852 | 171.6 | 21 475 |
| OREGON | 17.5 | 11.9 | 18.9 | 1 942 971 | 232 635 | 12.0 | 1 710 336 | 36.0 | 42.6 | 21.4 | 18.2 | 757 029 | 195.5 | 81 019 |
| District 1 | 13.4 | 9.9 | 13.8 | 416 967 | 39 737 | 9.5 | 377 230 | 40.1 | 39.8 | 20.1 | 15.8 | 120 499 | 155.3 | 10 722 |
| District 2 | 17.7 | 12.4 | 20.9 | 367 326 | 53 130 | 14.5 | 314 196 | 33.0 | 43.2 | 23.8 | 21.4 | 181 827 | 236.0 | 16 538 |
| District 3 | 19.4 | 13.9 | 20.3 | 429 690 | 46 411 | 10.8 | 383 279 | 38.0 | 42.8 | 19.2 | 18.2 | 118 931 | 152.0 | 19 946 |
| District 4 | 21.4 | 12.5 | 21.3 | 355 856 | 46 884 | 13.2 | 308 972 | 32.5 | 44.0 | 23.5 | 18.7 | 182 886 | 237.5 | 19 185 |
| District 5 | 15.5 | 11.2 | 17.9 | 373 132 | 46 473 | 12.5 | 326 659 | 35.1 | 43.7 | 21.2 | 17.3 | 152 886 | 197.8 | 14 628 |
| PENNSYLVANIA | 13.8 | 9.6 | 12.7 | 6 458 914 | 605 594 | 9.4 | 5 853 320 | 35.7 | 42.2 | 22.1 | 11.8 | 2 660 338 | 208.8 | 376 894 |
| District 1 | 27.2 | 22.4 | 24.2 | 323 767 | 50 502 | 15.6 | 273 265 | 34.2 | 48.6 | 17.1 | 16.9 | 112 256 | 165.4 | 50 303 |
| District 2 | 30.7 | 22.2 | 25.2 | 325 238 | 52 099 | 16.0 | 273 139 | 43.2 | 45.9 | 10.9 | 14.0 | 122 678 | 168.9 | 49 843 |
| District 3 | 14.2 | 10.7 | 16.2 | 347 634 | 29 949 | 8.6 | 317 685 | 30.7 | 43.8 | 25.5 | 12.2 | 165 093 | 234.2 | 25 129 |

1. Percent of civilian labor force.  2. Persons 16 years old and over.  3. Per 1,000 resident population estimated in the 2011 American Community Survey.

| STATE District | Representative, 113th Congress | Land area,[1] 2010 (sq km) | Total persons | Per square kilometer | White | Black | American Indian, Alaska Native | Asian and Pacific Islander | Some other race | Two or more races | Hispanic or Latino[2] | Non-Hispanic White alone | Percent female | Percent foreign born | Percent born in state of residence |
|---|---|---|---|---|---|---|---|---|---|---|---|---|---|---|---|
| | | 1 | 2 | 3 | 4 | 5 | 6 | 7 | 8 | 9 | 10 | 11 | 12 | 13 | 14 |
| PENNSYLVANIA—Cont'd | | | | | | | | | | | | | | | |
| District 4 | Scott Perry (R) | 3 931 | 710 196 | 180.7 | 84.9 | 8.0 | 0.1 | 1.9 | 2.6 | 2.4 | 6.1 | 82.5 | 50.6 | 4.5 | 65.9 |
| District 5 | Glenn Thompson (R) | 27 742 | 706 147 | 25.5 | 94.2 | 2.3 | 0.3 | 1.7 | 0.3 | 1.2 | 1.7 | 93.1 | 49.2 | 3.1 | 79.8 |
| District 6 | Jim Gerlach (R) | 2 229 | 727 295 | 326.3 | 88.2 | 4.3 | 0.1 | 4.2 | 1.3 | 2.0 | 4.7 | 85.2 | 51.2 | 6.4 | 72.6 |
| District 7 | Patrick Meehan (R) | 2 234 | 692 866 | 310.1 | 88.4 | 5.6 | 0.1 | 4.0 | 0.5 | 1.5 | 3.2 | 85.9 | 50.8 | 6.7 | 74.5 |
| District 8 | Michael G. Fitzpatrick (R) | 1 831 | 704 485 | 384.8 | 89.6 | 3.7 | 0.1 | 4.0 | 1.1 | 1.5 | 4.3 | 86.7 | 51.0 | 8.0 | 69.2 |
| District 9 | Bill Shuster (R) | 14 841 | 707 435 | 47.7 | 94.5 | 3.1 | 0.2 | 0.6 | 0.4 | 1.3 | 1.8 | 93.3 | 51.0 | 1.8 | 80.9 |
| District 10 | Tom Marino (R) | 21 699 | 712 217 | 32.8 | 93.8 | 3.2 | 0.1 | 0.7 | 0.6 | 1.6 | 3.6 | 91.1 | 50.1 | 3.2 | 69.9 |
| District 11 | Lou Barletta (R) | 8 693 | 705 197 | 81.1 | 89.9 | 4.9 | 0.1 | 1.4 | 1.7 | 2.0 | 4.7 | 87.2 | 51.0 | 4.0 | 78.7 |
| District 12 | Keith J. Rothfus (R) | 5 602 | 703 764 | 125.6 | 93.7 | 3.1 | 0.1 | 1.3 | 0.4 | 1.4 | 1.0 | 93.1 | 51.0 | 2.4 | 84.0 |
| District 13 | Allyson Y. Schwartz (D) | 402 | 728 897 | 1 813.6 | 66.9 | 18.0 | 0.2 | 8.3 | 4.1 | 2.5 | 10.7 | 61.3 | 51.7 | 15.7 | 70.1 |
| District 14 | Michael F. Doyle (D) | 542 | 703 257 | 1 297.4 | 71.8 | 21.8 | 0.2 | 2.9 | 0.6 | 2.7 | 2.1 | 70.7 | 52.3 | 5.0 | 79.2 |
| District 15 | Charles W. Dent (R) | 3 328 | 723 086 | 217.3 | 87.0 | 4.1 | 0.1 | 2.4 | 3.7 | 2.9 | 13.2 | 79.1 | 50.9 | 7.2 | 68.3 |
| District 16 | Joseph R. Pitts (R) | 2 584 | 702 245 | 271.8 | 83.5 | 6.2 | 0.2 | 1.6 | 5.7 | 2.7 | 16.8 | 74.3 | 51.4 | 6.7 | 70.8 |
| District 17 | Matt Cartwright (D) | 4 489 | 694 123 | 154.6 | 88.7 | 5.9 | 0.1 | 1.7 | 1.8 | 1.8 | 7.6 | 83.8 | 50.8 | 5.8 | 68.8 |
| District 18 | Tim Murphy(R) | 5 368 | 711 540 | 132.5 | 94.3 | 2.4 | 0.2 | 1.7 | 0.2 | 1.4 | 1.4 | 93.3 | 51.3 | 2.8 | 81.5 |
| RHODE ISLAND | | 2 678 | 1 051 302 | 392.6 | 81.7 | 6.0 | 0.4 | 3.2 | 5.9 | 2.7 | 12.8 | 75.8 | 51.6 | 13.5 | 58.5 |
| District 1 | David Cicilline (D) | 695 | 524 097 | 753.7 | 79.3 | 7.8 | 0.2 | 3.7 | 5.9 | 3.1 | 14.7 | 71.7 | 52.0 | 16.3 | 53.3 |
| District 2 | James R. Langevin (D) | 1 982 | 527 205 | 266.0 | 84.1 | 4.3 | 0.6 | 2.6 | 6.0 | 2.3 | 11.0 | 80.0 | 51.3 | 10.7 | 63.7 |
| SOUTH CAROLINA | | 77 857 | 4 679 230 | 60.1 | 67.0 | 27.9 | 0.3 | 1.4 | 1.6 | 1.8 | 5.3 | 63.9 | 51.4 | 4.7 | 59.4 |
| District 1 | Mark Sanford (R) | 4 009 | 667 388 | 166.5 | 75.2 | 18.6 | 0.3 | 2.0 | 1.9 | 2.1 | 6.9 | 70.5 | 52.0 | 7.1 | 42.3 |
| District 2 | Joe Wilson (R) | 7 827 | 676 492 | 86.4 | 69.8 | 24.9 | 0.2 | 1.8 | 1.7 | 1.6 | 5.0 | 67.0 | 51.1 | 4.4 | 55.1 |
| District 3 | Jeff Duncan (R) | 13 645 | 666 024 | 48.8 | 77.8 | 17.7 | 0.2 | 0.8 | 1.0 | 2.5 | 4.0 | 75.1 | 50.6 | 3.1 | 69.2 |
| District 4 | Trey Gowdy (R) | 3 365 | 671 222 | 199.5 | 74.8 | 19.7 | 0.3 | 2.2 | 1.1 | 1.9 | 7.4 | 69.4 | 51.7 | 7.2 | 57.7 |
| District 5 | Mick Mulvaney (R) | 14 259 | 662 829 | 46.5 | 67.6 | 27.9 | 0.4 | 1.1 | 1.9 | 1.2 | 4.1 | 65.6 | 51.4 | 3.9 | 60.0 |
| District 6 | James E. Clyburn (D) | 20 883 | 667 523 | 32.0 | 38.4 | 56.9 | 0.3 | 0.9 | 2.0 | 1.5 | 4.7 | 36.4 | 51.0 | 3.8 | 71.1 |
| District 7 | Tom Rice (R) | 13 868 | 667 752 | 48.1 | 65.4 | 29.6 | 0.4 | 1.0 | 1.9 | 1.8 | 3.9 | 63.4 | 52.0 | 3.8 | 60.7 |
| SOUTH DAKOTA | | 196 350 | 824 082 | 4.2 | 85.9 | 1.2 | 8.7 | 1.0 | 0.9 | 2.4 | 2.8 | 84.6 | 50.2 | 2.7 | 64.7 |
| At Large | Kristi Noem (R) | 196 350 | 824 082 | 4.2 | 85.9 | 1.2 | 8.7 | 1.0 | 0.9 | 2.4 | 2.8 | 84.6 | 50.2 | 2.7 | 64.7 |
| TENNESSEE | | 106 798 | 6 403 353 | 60.0 | 77.9 | 16.7 | 0.3 | 1.4 | 1.7 | 1.9 | 4.7 | 75.3 | 51.3 | 4.8 | 61.4 |
| District 1 | David P. Roe (R) | 10 728 | 707 424 | 65.9 | 94.4 | 2.3 | 0.3 | 0.6 | 0.8 | 1.7 | 3.2 | 92.1 | 51.3 | 3.1 | 63.2 |
| District 2 | John J. Duncan Jr. (R) | 6 011 | 712 089 | 118.5 | 89.0 | 6.9 | 0.2 | 1.7 | 0.7 | 1.5 | 3.0 | 86.8 | 51.4 | 4.0 | 60.6 |
| District 3 | Chuck Fleischmann (R) | 11 837 | 715 757 | 60.5 | 85.3 | 10.9 | 0.3 | 1.1 | 0.8 | 1.5 | 3.4 | 83.1 | 51.2 | 3.6 | 65.1 |
| District 4 | Scott DesJarlais (R) | 15 501 | 708 356 | 45.7 | 86.3 | 8.3 | 0.4 | 1.4 | 1.0 | 2.7 | 5.4 | 82.5 | 50.3 | 4.9 | 62.0 |
| District 5 | Jim Cooper (D) | 3 234 | 713 990 | 220.8 | 64.8 | 24.8 | 0.3 | 2.6 | 5.0 | 2.4 | 9.1 | 61.0 | 51.5 | 10.7 | 53.4 |
| District 6 | Diane Black (R) | 16 768 | 713 928 | 42.6 | 91.9 | 4.4 | 0.5 | 0.8 | 1.2 | 1.3 | 3.7 | 89.8 | 51.3 | 3.2 | 62.9 |
| District 7 | Marsha Blackburn (R) | 23 725 | 714 187 | 30.1 | 85.0 | 9.8 | 0.5 | 1.4 | 0.8 | 2.5 | 4.3 | 82.0 | 50.5 | 4.1 | 54.3 |
| District 8 | Stephen Lee Fincher (R) | 17 743 | 706 748 | 39.8 | 76.4 | 19.5 | 0.1 | 1.8 | 0.6 | 1.6 | 2.6 | 74.7 | 51.4 | 3.4 | 67.0 |
| District 9 | Steve Cohen (D) | 1 252 | 710 874 | 567.8 | 28.2 | 63.8 | 0.2 | 1.9 | 4.0 | 1.9 | 7.0 | 25.9 | 52.6 | 6.1 | 64.1 |
| TEXAS | | 676 587 | 25 674 681 | 37.9 | 74.6 | 11.7 | 0.5 | 4.0 | 6.9 | 2.3 | 38.1 | 44.7 | 50.4 | 16.4 | 60.6 |
| District 1 | Louie Gohmert (R) | 20 354 | 703 177 | 34.5 | 77.1 | 18.4 | 0.3 | 1.1 | 2.0 | 1.1 | 16.4 | 63.4 | 51.2 | 8.3 | 69.8 |
| District 2 | Ted Poe (R) | 800 | 721 185 | 901.9 | 70.1 | 12.6 | 0.5 | 6.5 | 8.0 | 2.3 | 29.6 | 49.5 | 49.7 | 18.8 | 51.3 |
| District 3 | Sam Johnson (R) | 1 245 | 728 269 | 584.7 | 73.3 | 8.2 | 0.5 | 12.7 | 2.4 | 3.0 | 14.6 | 61.7 | 50.6 | 18.0 | 45.6 |
| District 4 | Ralph M. Hall (R) | 26 218 | 704 984 | 26.9 | 87.0 | 11.5 | 0.8 | 1.1 | 3.4 | 2.2 | 12.6 | 72.6 | 51.0 | 6.3 | 67.8 |
| District 5 | Jeb Hensarling (R) | 13 064 | 719 368 | 55.1 | 75.8 | 13.8 | 0.4 | 1.9 | 5.7 | 2.4 | 26.4 | 56.3 | 50.4 | 13.8 | 66.3 |
| District 6 | Joe Barton (R) | 5 564 | 722 452 | 129.8 | 69.0 | 19.3 | 0.7 | 5.3 | 3.4 | 2.2 | 22.7 | 51.3 | 50.5 | 14.4 | 60.1 |
| District 7 | John Abney Culberson (R) | 419 | 726 696 | 1 732.6 | 65.2 | 12.5 | 0.2 | 9.9 | 9.4 | 2.8 | 31.5 | 44.6 | 49.7 | 27.5 | 47.3 |
| District 8 | Kevin Brady (R) | 15 679 | 720 727 | 46.0 | 84.3 | 8.0 | 0.5 | 2.0 | 2.7 | 2.5 | 20.2 | 68.0 | 49.1 | 10.8 | 60.6 |
| District 9 | Al Green (D) | 429 | 691 497 | 1 611.8 | 39.4 | 38.6 | 0.2 | 9.4 | 10.4 | 2.1 | 37.2 | 13.6 | 52.0 | 31.5 | 51.8 |
| District 10 | Michael T. McCaul (R) | 13 134 | 709 456 | 54.0 | 75.2 | 9.7 | 0.4 | 5.0 | 7.2 | 2.4 | 25.9 | 57.9 | 49.9 | 15.1 | 58.5 |
| District 11 | K. Michael Conaway (R) | 72 085 | 700 744 | 9.7 | 88.5 | 4.0 | 0.5 | 0.7 | 4.4 | 1.9 | 34.0 | 60.1 | 50.4 | 8.1 | 70.3 |
| District 12 | Kay Granger (R) | 3 733 | 710 406 | 190.3 | 83.1 | 7.8 | 1.2 | 2.8 | 2.3 | 2.8 | 20.9 | 66.2 | 51.6 | 9.5 | 61.1 |
| District 13 | Mac Thornberry (R) | 99 324 | 698 612 | 7.0 | 86.2 | 5.5 | 0.8 | 1.8 | 2.7 | 3.1 | 25.4 | 65.4 | 49.3 | 8.0 | 68.1 |
| District 14 | Randy K. Weber, Sr. (R) | 6 323 | 708 198 | 112.0 | 71.7 | 20.6 | 0.3 | 2.7 | 3.3 | 1.4 | 23.3 | 52.3 | 49.3 | 9.7 | 66.6 |
| District 15 | Rubén Hinojosa (D) | 20 212 | 722 529 | 35.7 | 90.2 | 1.7 | 0.2 | 1.3 | 5.3 | 1.2 | 80.2 | 16.4 | 50.4 | 24.7 | 62.8 |
| District 16 | Beto O'Rourke (D) | 1 840 | 707 375 | 384.5 | 80.9 | 3.8 | 0.3 | 1.4 | 11.1 | 2.4 | 79.3 | 15.3 | 51.3 | 25.2 | 53.9 |
| District 17 | Bill Flores (R) | 19 816 | 710 793 | 35.9 | 76.0 | 13.4 | 0.4 | 4.1 | 4.1 | 2.1 | 22.9 | 58.0 | 50.7 | 11.4 | 68.2 |
| District 18 | Sheila Jackson-Lee (D) | 609 | 707 139 | 1 160.8 | 47.0 | 38.6 | 0.4 | 3.9 | 8.2 | 1.8 | 41.0 | 15.9 | 51.0 | 21.4 | 60.4 |
| District 19 | Randy Neugebauer (R) | 66 914 | 708 642 | 10.6 | 83.0 | 6.1 | 0.6 | 1.5 | 5.8 | 3.1 | 34.7 | 56.2 | 49.4 | 8.4 | 72.3 |
| District 20 | Joaquin Castro (D) | 517 | 716 759 | 1 386.0 | 78.7 | 4.7 | 0.8 | 2.6 | 9.7 | 3.6 | 66.3 | 24.7 | 50.6 | 14.7 | 64.3 |
| District 21 | Lamar Smith (R) | 15 335 | 723 750 | 47.2 | 85.3 | 3.4 | 0.5 | 2.8 | 5.2 | 2.8 | 27.7 | 64.1 | 50.7 | 9.6 | 58.0 |
| District 22 | Pete Olson (R) | 2 675 | 720 879 | 269.5 | 64.4 | 12.0 | 0.3 | 17.1 | 3.7 | 2.5 | 25.2 | 44.4 | 50.3 | 23.8 | 53.6 |
| District 23 | Pete P. Gallego (D) | 150 373 | 725 874 | 4.8 | 84.2 | 2.4 | 0.8 | 1.2 | 9.6 | 1.7 | 70.8 | 24.8 | 50.4 | 17.3 | 64.3 |
| District 24 | Kenny Marchant (R) | 681 | 719 185 | 1 056.8 | 68.7 | 10.9 | 0.3 | 10.5 | 6.9 | 2.7 | 24.4 | 52.3 | 50.6 | 21.1 | 46.1 |

1. Dry land or land partially or temporarily covered by water.    2. May be of any race.

# Table E. Congressional Districts 113th Congress — **Age and Education**

| STATE District | Population and population characteristics, 2011 (cont.) | | | | | | | | | | | Education, 2011 | | |
| | Age (percent) | | | | | | | | | | | Attainment[2] (percent) | | |
| | Under 5 years | 5 to 17 years | 18 to 24 years | 25 to 34 years | 35 to 44 years | 45 to 54 years | 55 to 64 years | 65 to 74 years | 75 years and over | Median age | Total Enrollment[1] | High school graduate or more | Bachelor's degree or more |
| | 15 | 16 | 17 | 18 | 19 | 20 | 21 | 22 | 23 | 24 | 25 | 26 | 27 |
|---|---|---|---|---|---|---|---|---|---|---|---|---|---|
| **PENNSYLVANIA—Cont'd** | | | | | | | | | | | | | |
| District 4 | 5.9 | 16.7 | 9.1 | 11.7 | 13.4 | 15.2 | 13.3 | 7.6 | 7.1 | 40.3 | 172 769 | 89.1 | 24.5 |
| District 5 | 4.9 | 14.4 | 14.1 | 10.9 | 11.6 | 14.5 | 13.4 | 8.3 | 7.8 | 40.4 | 186 927 | 90.0 | 21.3 |
| District 6 | 5.6 | 18.2 | 8.8 | 10.7 | 13.8 | 16.5 | 12.6 | 7.4 | 6.4 | 40.3 | 198 157 | 92.0 | 40.5 |
| District 7 | 6.0 | 17.1 | 8.8 | 11.0 | 12.0 | 16.1 | 13.4 | 7.3 | 8.4 | 41.2 | 179 996 | 92.2 | 38.9 |
| District 8 | 5.2 | 17.2 | 7.6 | 10.5 | 13.1 | 17.3 | 14.1 | 7.8 | 7.2 | 42.4 | 177 706 | 93.1 | 34.6 |
| District 9 | 5.4 | 15.4 | 9.8 | 10.9 | 12.3 | 14.6 | 14.0 | 9.0 | 8.5 | 41.9 | 158 912 | 87.0 | 16.5 |
| District 10 | 5.2 | 16.0 | 9.1 | 10.3 | 12.2 | 15.9 | 14.0 | 9.3 | 7.8 | 42.9 | 165 846 | 87.0 | 19.9 |
| District 11 | 5.4 | 15.7 | 9.9 | 11.4 | 12.5 | 14.8 | 13.9 | 8.5 | 7.8 | 41.2 | 167 307 | 88.5 | 21.4 |
| District 12 | 4.8 | 15.4 | 7.7 | 10.6 | 11.7 | 16.5 | 14.9 | 8.8 | 9.6 | 44.8 | 154 683 | 91.5 | 29.2 |
| District 13 | 6.3 | 17.1 | 8.5 | 14.9 | 12.8 | 14.2 | 12.1 | 6.5 | 7.7 | 37.4 | 188 910 | 88.3 | 32.4 |
| District 14 | 5.6 | 13.1 | 11.8 | 15.1 | 11.1 | 13.4 | 13.8 | 7.7 | 8.5 | 39.0 | 173 455 | 90.6 | 27.4 |
| District 15 | 5.7 | 16.2 | 9.9 | 11.8 | 12.5 | 15.4 | 13.5 | 7.7 | 7.4 | 40.3 | 180 476 | 87.1 | 26.6 |
| District 16 | 7.2 | 17.8 | 9.7 | 12.2 | 12.3 | 14.1 | 12.1 | 7.2 | 7.4 | 37.6 | 177 220 | 83.2 | 22.1 |
| District 17 | 4.9 | 15.6 | 9.6 | 10.8 | 13.0 | 15.7 | 13.3 | 8.4 | 8.7 | 41.9 | 166 875 | 88.0 | 19.6 |
| District 18 | 4.8 | 15.3 | 7.9 | 10.7 | 12.7 | 16.2 | 14.7 | 8.6 | 9.0 | 44.0 | 164 094 | 93.5 | 33.0 |
| **RHODE ISLAND** | 5.3 | 15.5 | 11.4 | 12.3 | 12.7 | 15.2 | 12.9 | 7.2 | 7.4 | 39.5 | 277 923 | 84.8 | 31.1 |
| District 1 | 5.5 | 15.4 | 11.2 | 12.9 | 12.8 | 14.6 | 12.5 | 7.4 | 7.8 | 39.2 | 134 406 | 82.7 | 31.6 |
| District 2 | 5.1 | 15.7 | 11.6 | 11.7 | 12.7 | 15.7 | 13.4 | 7.0 | 7.1 | 39.9 | 143 517 | 86.8 | 30.7 |
| **SOUTH CAROLINA** | 6.5 | 16.6 | 10.4 | 12.7 | 12.9 | 13.9 | 13.0 | 8.2 | 5.8 | 38.0 | 1 199 462 | 84.2 | 24.1 |
| District 1 | 6.5 | 16.3 | 9.5 | 14.4 | 13.2 | 13.3 | 12.7 | 8.5 | 5.7 | 36.8 | 165 679 | 90.9 | 34.9 |
| District 2 | 6.0 | 18.0 | 9.6 | 13.0 | 13.6 | 14.4 | 12.8 | 7.4 | 5.2 | 37.3 | 183 195 | 88.6 | 29.2 |
| District 3 | 6.3 | 16.1 | 10.8 | 11.6 | 12.3 | 14.0 | 13.6 | 8.7 | 6.6 | 39.8 | 167 257 | 80.9 | 19.0 |
| District 4 | 7.0 | 17.3 | 9.9 | 12.5 | 13.5 | 14.5 | 12.1 | 7.6 | 5.6 | 37.6 | 178 731 | 85.1 | 27.5 |
| District 5 | 6.5 | 17.6 | 9.1 | 11.9 | 13.8 | 14.2 | 13.0 | 8.1 | 5.8 | 38.8 | 170 561 | 82.1 | 21.2 |
| District 6 | 6.9 | 15.2 | 14.5 | 13.7 | 11.2 | 13.5 | 12.3 | 7.4 | 5.3 | 34.8 | 183 818 | 77.8 | 16.4 |
| District 7 | 6.1 | 16.1 | 9.5 | 11.2 | 13.0 | 13.5 | 14.4 | 9.9 | 6.2 | 40.9 | 150 221 | 83.2 | 19.8 |
| **SOUTH DAKOTA** | 7.1 | 17.4 | 10.3 | 12.7 | 11.7 | 14.0 | 12.3 | 7.3 | 7.3 | 37.1 | 219 022 | 90.6 | 26.3 |
| At Large | 7.1 | 17.4 | 10.3 | 12.7 | 11.7 | 14.0 | 12.3 | 7.3 | 7.3 | 37.1 | 219 022 | 90.6 | 26.3 |
| **TENNESSEE** | 6.2 | 17.0 | 9.7 | 13.0 | 13.1 | 14.4 | 12.7 | 7.8 | 5.9 | 38.3 | 1 594 654 | 84.2 | 23.6 |
| District 1 | 5.3 | 15.8 | 8.4 | 11.4 | 13.1 | 14.8 | 14.1 | 9.9 | 7.2 | 41.9 | 154 383 | 81.4 | 17.9 |
| District 2 | 5.6 | 16.0 | 10.6 | 12.5 | 12.8 | 14.5 | 13.1 | 8.6 | 6.5 | 39.5 | 170 125 | 87.2 | 27.7 |
| District 3 | 5.9 | 15.6 | 9.0 | 11.8 | 12.9 | 14.7 | 14.0 | 9.1 | 7.1 | 41.2 | 164 942 | 82.6 | 19.9 |
| District 4 | 6.4 | 17.5 | 10.4 | 13.2 | 13.4 | 14.1 | 12.3 | 7.5 | 5.3 | 37.0 | 181 065 | 83.1 | 20.7 |
| District 5 | 6.9 | 15.0 | 10.8 | 17.6 | 13.5 | 13.7 | 11.5 | 5.9 | 4.9 | 34.7 | 176 888 | 85.8 | 32.5 |
| District 6 | 6.0 | 17.5 | 8.5 | 11.4 | 13.4 | 14.8 | 13.2 | 8.9 | 6.2 | 40.1 | 171 678 | 83.4 | 18.9 |
| District 7 | 6.4 | 19.2 | 8.6 | 12.9 | 13.2 | 14.9 | 12.1 | 7.4 | 5.4 | 37.4 | 186 331 | 84.5 | 24.4 |
| District 8 | 6.1 | 18.7 | 8.8 | 10.7 | 12.9 | 14.9 | 13.5 | 8.3 | 6.0 | 39.9 | 189 072 | 86.6 | 28.0 |
| District 9 | 7.7 | 17.9 | 11.7 | 15.5 | 13.1 | 13.4 | 11.1 | 5.1 | 4.5 | 32.9 | 200 170 | 83.8 | 22.8 |
| **TEXAS** | 7.6 | 19.5 | 10.3 | 14.3 | 13.7 | 13.4 | 10.6 | 6.0 | 4.6 | 33.7 | 7 320 055 | 81.1 | 26.4 |
| District 1 | 7.1 | 18.2 | 11.1 | 12.4 | 11.7 | 13.1 | 12.0 | 7.8 | 6.7 | 36.1 | 190 531 | 82.8 | 19.7 |
| District 2 | 7.5 | 18.4 | 9.2 | 16.2 | 15.4 | 12.9 | 11.8 | 5.5 | 3.3 | 34.4 | 199 555 | 87.8 | 38.4 |
| District 3 | 7.4 | 20.5 | 7.5 | 14.1 | 16.6 | 15.4 | 10.0 | 5.3 | 2.9 | 35.3 | 212 719 | 92.9 | 51.4 |
| District 4 | 6.3 | 18.8 | 8.7 | 11.6 | 12.7 | 14.6 | 12.5 | 8.6 | 6.2 | 38.6 | 180 072 | 84.3 | 19.8 |
| District 5 | 7.8 | 19.5 | 8.9 | 13.5 | 13.4 | 13.8 | 11.2 | 7.0 | 5.0 | 35.2 | 187 378 | 77.8 | 18.1 |
| District 6 | 7.6 | 20.2 | 9.8 | 14.4 | 14.4 | 13.7 | 10.8 | 5.5 | 3.6 | 33.6 | 217 437 | 87.3 | 27.0 |
| District 7 | 7.5 | 18.4 | 8.6 | 17.0 | 15.3 | 13.7 | 10.5 | 5.2 | 3.8 | 33.9 | 201 227 | 88.0 | 45.7 |
| District 8 | 7.0 | 18.8 | 9.4 | 12.4 | 13.9 | 15.1 | 11.8 | 6.9 | 4.7 | 36.7 | 196 026 | 85.5 | 26.2 |
| District 9 | 7.9 | 19.2 | 11.1 | 16.0 | 14.2 | 13.4 | 10.3 | 4.5 | 3.4 | 32.3 | 204 944 | 75.4 | 22.5 |
| District 10 | 7.4 | 18.9 | 8.7 | 14.3 | 14.8 | 13.8 | 11.4 | 6.1 | 4.5 | 35.5 | 196 988 | 87.4 | 35.3 |
| District 11 | 7.0 | 18.2 | 10.0 | 12.7 | 11.4 | 13.4 | 12.3 | 8.2 | 6.8 | 36.7 | 173 708 | 79.6 | 18.9 |
| District 12 | 7.1 | 18.8 | 9.2 | 14.5 | 14.5 | 14.0 | 11.4 | 5.7 | 4.8 | 35.4 | 191 919 | 88.0 | 28.0 |
| District 13 | 7.2 | 18.4 | 10.3 | 13.0 | 12.0 | 13.8 | 11.8 | 7.2 | 6.4 | 35.8 | 179 051 | 82.8 | 19.6 |
| District 14 | 7.3 | 17.7 | 9.4 | 13.9 | 12.9 | 15.1 | 12.0 | 6.5 | 5.2 | 36.3 | 184 227 | 84.6 | 22.4 |
| District 15 | 9.0 | 23.1 | 11.0 | 14.1 | 13.0 | 11.4 | 8.5 | 5.5 | 4.4 | 30.0 | 227 970 | 67.4 | 19.0 |
| District 16 | 7.7 | 20.8 | 11.4 | 13.9 | 12.9 | 12.8 | 9.6 | 5.8 | 5.1 | 32.0 | 227 404 | 76.4 | 22.6 |
| District 17 | 6.3 | 16.8 | 17.9 | 14.5 | 11.8 | 12.3 | 9.6 | 5.9 | 4.8 | 30.7 | 238 486 | 85.7 | 26.9 |
| District 18 | 9.1 | 18.4 | 11.3 | 17.4 | 13.2 | 12.5 | 9.9 | 4.7 | 3.4 | 30.8 | 194 435 | 72.6 | 19.3 |
| District 19 | 7.2 | 17.6 | 14.0 | 13.6 | 11.8 | 12.6 | 10.7 | 6.7 | 6.0 | 33.0 | 210 919 | 79.5 | 20.9 |
| District 20 | 7.3 | 19.5 | 12.1 | 15.7 | 13.4 | 12.8 | 9.6 | 5.2 | 4.5 | 31.6 | 219 494 | 79.8 | 23.2 |
| District 21 | 5.9 | 15.1 | 11.2 | 15.5 | 12.5 | 13.9 | 12.5 | 7.3 | 6.1 | 36.8 | 194 177 | 91.7 | 43.6 |
| District 22 | 7.3 | 21.3 | 7.9 | 13.5 | 16.2 | 14.8 | 10.5 | 5.2 | 3.3 | 35.0 | 216 997 | 89.3 | 39.3 |
| District 23 | 8.2 | 21.5 | 10.4 | 13.0 | 13.5 | 12.2 | 10.4 | 6.6 | 4.2 | 32.6 | 215 974 | 73.0 | 20.7 |
| District 24 | 6.3 | 17.8 | 7.6 | 17.9 | 14.7 | 15.4 | 10.8 | 5.5 | 4.0 | 35.3 | 192 874 | 88.9 | 42.7 |

1.  All persons 3 years old and over enrolled in nursery school through college and graduate or professional school.    2.  Persons 25 years old and over.

# Table E. Congressional Districts 113th Congress — Households and Group Quarters

| STATE District | Households, 2011 | | | | | | Group quarters, 2010 | | | | | |
|---|---|---|---|---|---|---|---|---|---|---|---|---|
| | Number | Persons per household | Family households (percent) | Married-couple family (percent) | Female family householder[1] | One person households (percent) | Total in group quarters | Percent 65 years and over | Persons in correctional institutions | Persons in nursing homes | Persons in college dormitories | Persons in military quarters |
| | 28 | 29 | 30 | 31 | 32 | 33 | 34 | 35 | 36 | 37 | 38 | 39 |
| PENNSYLVANIA—Cont'd | | | | | | | | | | | | |
| District 4 | 277 249 | 2.48 | 67.7 | 50.9 | 11.9 | 27.5 | 20 161 | 20.4 | 6 485 | 3 922 | 7 205 | 37 |
| District 5 | 276 529 | 2.39 | 63.3 | 51.0 | 8.1 | 29.9 | 45 259 | 11.4 | 14 533 | 5 088 | 23 276 | 0 |
| District 6 | 274 433 | 2.57 | 68.3 | 56.6 | 8.2 | 25.8 | 18 822 | 24.0 | 3 336 | 4 461 | 7 424 | 0 |
| District 7 | 252 682 | 2.65 | 69.7 | 57.8 | 8.3 | 26.0 | 24 838 | 21.2 | 5 890 | 5 118 | 10 160 | 0 |
| District 8 | 261 924 | 2.65 | 71.0 | 57.1 | 9.6 | 24.6 | 8 976 | 46.3 | 1 039 | 4 098 | 1 569 | 0 |
| District 9 | 277 720 | 2.46 | 67.1 | 51.2 | 11.0 | 28.1 | 23 946 | 23.8 | 6 117 | 5 134 | 8 771 | 0 |
| District 10 | 271 289 | 2.51 | 68.1 | 54.3 | 9.3 | 26.5 | 29 624 | 15.5 | 11 878 | 4 486 | 10 876 | 0 |
| District 11 | 276 383 | 2.45 | 67.3 | 50.0 | 12.2 | 27.3 | 26 184 | 22.1 | 7 333 | 6 231 | 9 991 | 6 |
| District 12 | 283 966 | 2.43 | 67.1 | 52.9 | 10.2 | 28.9 | 15 433 | 32.7 | 4 480 | 4 694 | 3 073 | 6 |
| District 13 | 268 007 | 2.68 | 64.6 | 45.0 | 14.3 | 29.3 | 11 132 | 57.8 | 2 | 6 384 | 1 329 | 121 |
| District 14 | 309 362 | 2.18 | 52.1 | 32.3 | 15.4 | 40.5 | 28 190 | 15.0 | 4 663 | 4 194 | 15 905 | 0 |
| District 15 | 273 070 | 2.55 | 68.6 | 52.8 | 11.5 | 25.4 | 24 819 | 21.1 | 1 424 | 5 210 | 13 039 | 63 |
| District 16 | 260 773 | 2.61 | 67.5 | 51.1 | 12.1 | 27.1 | 18 879 | 27.5 | 1 132 | 5 327 | 9 156 | 0 |
| District 17 | 269 777 | 2.48 | 66.7 | 49.6 | 11.8 | 27.9 | 23 878 | 25.7 | 7 876 | 6 346 | 7 783 | 1 |
| District 18 | 289 099 | 2.39 | 66.7 | 52.8 | 10.6 | 29.0 | 17 126 | 30.3 | 3 728 | 4 961 | 5 906 | 0 |
| RHODE ISLAND | 412 259 | 2.45 | 62.1 | 44.0 | 13.4 | 30.6 | 42 663 | 18.5 | 3 783 | 8 420 | 24 687 | 1 385 |
| District 1 | 208 330 | 2.41 | 61.1 | 41.8 | 14.6 | 31.6 | 21 863 | 21.3 | 350 | 4 996 | 13 035 | 1 385 |
| District 2 | 203 929 | 2.48 | 63.2 | 46.3 | 12.2 | 29.6 | 20 800 | 15.5 | 3 433 | 3 424 | 11 652 | 0 |
| SOUTH CAROLINA | 1 768 834 | 2.57 | 67.9 | 48.3 | 15.1 | 27.3 | 139 154 | 13.0 | 41 649 | 19 020 | 46 463 | 19 413 |
| District 1 | 259 618 | 2.53 | 66.5 | 50.4 | 11.3 | 27.3 | 9 798 | 15.4 | 531 | 1 662 | 2 560 | 4 436 |
| District 2 | 260 798 | 2.52 | 69.0 | 50.2 | 15.1 | 26.3 | 17 312 | 12.8 | 1 458 | 2 391 | 823 | 11 567 |
| District 3 | 247 569 | 2.60 | 69.6 | 51.8 | 13.1 | 26.6 | 22 329 | 14.3 | 7 044 | 3 116 | 9 817 | 0 |
| District 4 | 254 465 | 2.57 | 69.4 | 51.2 | 15.3 | 26.4 | 18 665 | 14.5 | 3 776 | 2 832 | 9 668 | 0 |
| District 5 | 253 743 | 2.56 | 71.4 | 51.3 | 15.2 | 25.1 | 13 372 | 20 | 5 318 | 2 792 | 3 289 | 611 |
| District 6 | 237 806 | 2.62 | 62.6 | 36.6 | 20.8 | 31.6 | 44 801 | 6.5 | 18 400 | 3 087 | 17 383 | 2 799 |
| District 7 | 254 835 | 2.58 | 66.9 | 46.2 | 15.2 | 28.4 | 12 877 | 22.4 | 5 122 | 3 140 | 2 923 | 0 |
| SOUTH DAKOTA | 323 215 | 2.44 | 65.2 | 50.5 | 9.7 | 28.8 | 34 050 | 21.1 | 6 327 | 7 005 | 10 248 | 597 |
| At Large | 323 215 | 2.44 | 65.2 | 50.5 | 9.7 | 28.8 | 34 050 | 21.1 | 6 327 | 7 005 | 10 248 | 597 |
| TENNESSEE | 2 467 428 | 2.53 | 65.9 | 48.2 | 13.3 | 29.0 | 153 472 | 19.8 | 46 957 | 33 041 | 53 136 | 1 544 |
| District 1 | 290 801 | 2.38 | 68.6 | 53.3 | 11.0 | 26.6 | 15 573 | 26.7 | 4 577 | 4 466 | 4 176 | 0 |
| District 2 | 289 152 | 2.40 | 63.7 | 49.2 | 10.2 | 31.1 | 17 930 | 19.1 | 1 901 | 3 686 | 10 443 | 0 |
| District 3 | 281 450 | 2.48 | 66.6 | 49.9 | 12.4 | 28.9 | 16 674 | 23.8 | 4 913 | 4 071 | 4 884 | 3 |
| District 4 | 264 202 | 2.62 | 68.6 | 51.7 | 12.6 | 25.3 | 14 848 | 21.1 | 3 301 | 3 584 | 6 619 | 0 |
| District 5 | 283 405 | 2.43 | 56.3 | 38.5 | 14.2 | 35.8 | 26 770 | 9.0 | 6 769 | 2 588 | 13 660 | 0 |
| District 6 | 275 551 | 2.55 | 70.5 | 54.4 | 11.4 | 25.1 | 9 262 | 36.4 | 2 385 | 3 730 | 2 283 | 0 |
| District 7 | 262 427 | 2.66 | 71.9 | 57.1 | 11.1 | 24.6 | 17 000 | 21.2 | 8 311 | 3 918 | 2 350 | 1 250 |
| District 8 | 257 572 | 2.67 | 68.7 | 51.9 | 12.9 | 27.4 | 18 318 | 21.3 | 7 494 | 4 158 | 4 748 | 10 |
| District 9 | 262 868 | 2.64 | 58.4 | 27.7 | 24.7 | 35.9 | 17 097 | 14.0 | 7 306 | 2 840 | 3 973 | 281 |
| TEXAS | 8 850 370 | 2.84 | 69.7 | 50.1 | 14.5 | 25.0 | 581 139 | 14.9 | 267 405 | 94 278 | 119 834 | 35 260 |
| District 1 | 256 961 | 2.64 | 67.8 | 49.2 | 13.9 | 27.9 | 24 869 | 17.3 | 8 132 | 5 093 | 9 123 | 0 |
| District 2 | 254 606 | 2.80 | 68.5 | 51.7 | 11.5 | 24.2 | 8 443 | 18.4 | 2 441 | 1 873 | 2 921 | 0 |
| District 3 | 263 517 | 2.75 | 74.8 | 58.2 | 11.6 | 20.4 | 3 651 | 31.9 | 1 061 | 1 326 | 387 | 0 |
| District 4 | 254 156 | 2.70 | 72.3 | 54.2 | 13.5 | 24.4 | 17 048 | 25.8 | 8 850 | 5 078 | 2 237 | 0 |
| District 5 | 245 401 | 2.84 | 72.2 | 51.8 | 15.2 | 23.9 | 24 325 | 14.9 | 17 768 | 3 964 | 938 | 0 |
| District 6 | 249 163 | 2.87 | 73.1 | 52.5 | 15.3 | 21.8 | 6 320 | 32.8 | 689 | 2 419 | 2 137 | 0 |
| District 7 | 275 793 | 2.63 | 63.4 | 47.7 | 10.8 | 30.7 | 1 277 | 58.1 | 3 | 774 | 5 | 0 |
| District 8 | 245 032 | 2.81 | 73.2 | 55.1 | 12.5 | 22.6 | 28 693 | 8.5 | 23 107 | 2 021 | 2 615 | 0 |
| District 9 | 235 688 | 2.92 | 67.7 | 40.6 | 20.3 | 27.3 | 4 346 | 32.7 | 154 | 1 629 | 1 520 | 0 |
| District 10 | 255 466 | 2.73 | 69.6 | 55.1 | 9.9 | 24.7 | 11 828 | 25.7 | 2 453 | 3 156 | 4 344 | 0 |
| District 11 | 261 228 | 2.60 | 68.8 | 51.5 | 12.9 | 27.2 | 20 885 | 18.3 | 9 050 | 3 721 | 3 615 | 1 924 |
| District 12 | 262 217 | 2.65 | 67.7 | 49.9 | 13.3 | 27.5 | 14 385 | 20.3 | 5 807 | 3 540 | 3 405 | 202 |
| District 13 | 252 387 | 2.64 | 69.5 | 52.8 | 12.1 | 27.0 | 31 928 | 11.8 | 17 511 | 4 208 | 2 479 | 5 487 |
| District 14 | 254 973 | 2.66 | 68.4 | 48.3 | 15.0 | 26.7 | 30 381 | 9.5 | 22 748 | 2 861 | 2 869 | 40 |
| District 15 | 210 578 | 3.37 | 79.2 | 56.8 | 17.3 | 17.7 | 13 142 | 14.6 | 8 632 | 2 035 | 1 514 | 0 |
| District 16 | 230 560 | 3.01 | 72.5 | 47.1 | 19.3 | 23.1 | 15 283 | 9.8 | 6 076 | 1 482 | 491 | 5 683 |
| District 17 | 254 723 | 2.68 | 61.0 | 44.3 | 12.9 | 29.1 | 28 879 | 11.1 | 8 355 | 3 792 | 14 831 | 0 |
| District 18 | 240 434 | 2.85 | 63.7 | 34.6 | 22.2 | 30.5 | 25 069 | 3.8 | 12 624 | 783 | 5 661 | 0 |
| District 19 | 250 420 | 2.65 | 65.0 | 47.5 | 13.2 | 27.7 | 38 471 | 10.0 | 19 845 | 4 073 | 10 748 | 621 |
| District 20 | 242 711 | 2.89 | 66.9 | 43.3 | 18.8 | 26.7 | 17 573 | 11.9 | 4 | 2 081 | 4 846 | 9 322 |
| District 21 | 292 488 | 2.42 | 59.8 | 46.8 | 9.4 | 32.1 | 19 486 | 19.9 | 600 | 4 024 | 7 505 | 3 793 |
| District 22 | 236 224 | 3.03 | 80.7 | 63.9 | 12.2 | 16.4 | 6 573 | 21.6 | 4 494 | 1 409 | 4 | 0 |
| District 23 | 220 360 | 3.20 | 77.7 | 56.4 | 16.2 | 18.6 | 20 419 | 7.6 | 16 613 | 1 566 | 193 | 877 |
| District 24 | 287 155 | 2.49 | 62.3 | 45.9 | 11.7 | 31.9 | 2 583 | 65.8 | 53 | 1 913 | 480 | 0 |

1. No spouse present.

| STATE District | Housing units, 2011 | | | | | | Money income, 2011 | | |
|---|---|---|---|---|---|---|---|---|---|
| | | | Occupied units | | | | | Households | |
| | | | Owner-occupied | | | Renter-occupied | | | |
| | Total | Percent Occupied | Percent | Median value[1] (dollars) | Percent valued at $500,000 or more | Median rent[2] | Per capita income (dollars) | Median income (dollars) | Percent with income of $100,000 or more |
| | 40 | 41 | 42 | 43 | 44 | 45 | 46 | 47 | 48 |
| PENNSYLVANIA—Cont'd | | | | | | | | | |
| District 4 | 299 620 | 92.5 | 71.0 | 175 000 | 2.9 | 803 | 27 082 | 54 291 | 19.5 |
| District 5 | 340 907 | 81.1 | 71.4 | 109 800 | 2.0 | 649 | 22 747 | 43 583 | 12.8 |
| District 6 | 288 325 | 95.2 | 75.3 | 249 700 | 11.3 | 1 020 | 35 089 | 69 570 | 32.7 |
| District 7 | 266 970 | 94.6 | 77.7 | 280 100 | 14.5 | 1 030 | 37 154 | 73 638 | 36.2 |
| District 8 | 278 291 | 94.1 | 76.1 | 305 000 | 13.9 | 1 112 | 34 920 | 71 404 | 33.6 |
| District 9 | 319 156 | 87.0 | 73.6 | 113 100 | 1.9 | 629 | 21 440 | 42 277 | 11.3 |
| District 10 | 346 263 | 78.3 | 75.5 | 153 900 | 3.2 | 677 | 23 199 | 46 590 | 14.4 |
| District 11 | 319 643 | 86.5 | 70.8 | 150 300 | 2.2 | 726 | 25 146 | 49 085 | 16.5 |
| District 12 | 315 597 | 90.0 | 76.8 | 135 900 | 2.9 | 648 | 29 777 | 53 080 | 21.8 |
| District 13 | 290 032 | 92.4 | 65.2 | 223 200 | 5.4 | 954 | 28 788 | 56 222 | 23.8 |
| District 14 | 365 586 | 84.6 | 55.2 | 89 000 | 1.6 | 682 | 24 206 | 37 307 | 12.2 |
| District 15 | 293 984 | 92.9 | 71.2 | 193 200 | 3.7 | 866 | 27 723 | 54 470 | 20.8 |
| District 16 | 278 490 | 93.6 | 66.1 | 179 200 | 3.9 | 824 | 23 785 | 49 910 | 17.2 |
| District 17 | 316 930 | 85.1 | 70.9 | 140 200 | 2.3 | 698 | 23 777 | 46 722 | 15.3 |
| District 18 | 313 987 | 92.1 | 75.3 | 152 800 | 3.4 | 722 | 30 111 | 55 553 | 23.5 |
| RHODE ISLAND | 464 741 | 88.7 | 60.6 | 245 500 | 10.1 | 875 | 29 277 | 53 636 | 23.5 |
| District 1 | 233 552 | 89.2 | 55.6 | 248 500 | 11.9 | 844 | 28 205 | 50 672 | 21.6 |
| District 2 | 231 189 | 88.2 | 65.6 | 243 200 | 8.5 | 926 | 30 343 | 57 448 | 25.5 |
| SOUTH CAROLINA | 2 157 063 | 82.0 | 69.2 | 136 000 | 5.6 | 741 | 22 598 | 42 367 | 14.8 |
| District 1 | 323 191 | 80.3 | 69.1 | 212 800 | 15.3 | 977 | 28 435 | 56 079 | 21.6 |
| District 2 | 292 306 | 89.2 | 72.7 | 140 100 | 4.5 | 799 | 26 254 | 50 575 | 19.5 |
| District 3 | 301 899 | 82.0 | 72.2 | 118 100 | 3.7 | 655 | 20 220 | 39 922 | 11.8 |
| District 4 | 288 120 | 88.3 | 67.2 | 142 100 | 5.1 | 705 | 24 266 | 45 108 | 17.2 |
| District 5 | 287 323 | 88.3 | 71.6 | 120 600 | 3.4 | 689 | 22 088 | 41 942 | 13.6 |
| District 6 | 295 878 | 80.4 | 60.7 | 94 900 | 2.5 | 718 | 16 810 | 31 313 | 8.0 |
| District 7 | 368 346 | 69.2 | 70.1 | 124 200 | 4.3 | 713 | 20 051 | 36 940 | 11.3 |
| SOUTH DAKOTA | 366 521 | 88.2 | 68.5 | 131 400 | 2.5 | 612 | 24 701 | 48 321 | 15.0 |
| At Large | 366 521 | 88.2 | 68.5 | 131 400 | 2.5 | 612 | 24 701 | 48 321 | 15.0 |
| TENNESSEE | 2 829 125 | 87.2 | 67.3 | 138 300 | 4.1 | 715 | 23 320 | 41 693 | 14.4 |
| District 1 | 346 870 | 83.8 | 70.4 | 123 600 | 2.5 | 614 | 20 981 | 37 197 | 10.8 |
| District 2 | 320 846 | 90.1 | 68.4 | 151 900 | 4.9 | 727 | 25 174 | 43 576 | 15.8 |
| District 3 | 321 675 | 87.5 | 70.3 | 132 200 | 3.2 | 672 | 22 179 | 38 020 | 13.0 |
| District 4 | 298 838 | 88.4 | 70.3 | 136 300 | 2.7 | 666 | 21 601 | 42 506 | 13.2 |
| District 5 | 317 988 | 89.1 | 56.1 | 161 100 | 7.2 | 796 | 26 799 | 43 623 | 15.8 |
| District 6 | 311 743 | 88.4 | 73.3 | 147 100 | 3.1 | 662 | 22 638 | 41 842 | 12.7 |
| District 7 | 304 149 | 86.3 | 72.9 | 144 500 | 7.3 | 732 | 24 447 | 46 442 | 17.9 |
| District 8 | 293 320 | 87.8 | 73.7 | 146 000 | 4.4 | 658 | 26 836 | 48 792 | 20.3 |
| District 9 | 313 696 | 83.8 | 50.1 | 97 400 | 1.3 | 796 | 19 215 | 36 142 | 10.1 |
| TEXAS | 10 099 242 | 87.6 | 62.9 | 127 700 | 3.9 | 813 | 24 682 | 49 392 | 20.4 |
| District 1 | 299 778 | 85.7 | 68.0 | 106 400 | 2.1 | 728 | 21 969 | 41 834 | 13.9 |
| District 2 | 280 098 | 90.9 | 62.1 | 157 700 | 5.2 | 962 | 34 601 | 69 181 | 31.3 |
| District 3 | 278 049 | 94.8 | 65.9 | 212 900 | 7.2 | 1 003 | 37 245 | 83 724 | 41.7 |
| District 4 | 299 490 | 84.9 | 72.2 | 104 200 | 3.2 | 722 | 22 683 | 46 846 | 17.1 |
| District 5 | 285 542 | 85.9 | 64.3 | 110 100 | 2.8 | 785 | 21 047 | 42 887 | 15.0 |
| District 6 | 274 203 | 90.9 | 66.9 | 133 600 | 2.0 | 868 | 25 451 | 55 788 | 23.2 |
| District 7 | 304 675 | 90.5 | 51.9 | 186 600 | 17.7 | 953 | 40 847 | 63 282 | 32.7 |
| District 8 | 284 077 | 86.3 | 71.1 | 148 400 | 6.2 | 878 | 27 406 | 56 919 | 25.8 |
| District 9 | 277 357 | 85.0 | 52.1 | 105 600 | 0.9 | 775 | 19 549 | 41 354 | 13.0 |
| District 10 | 289 414 | 88.3 | 66.2 | 165 200 | 5.8 | 885 | 29 272 | 58 080 | 26.2 |
| District 11 | 321 356 | 81.3 | 69.4 | 98 000 | 3.1 | 715 | 24 055 | 44 607 | 16.0 |
| District 12 | 296 698 | 88.4 | 64.2 | 133 400 | 3.6 | 834 | 28 137 | 56 155 | 23.6 |
| District 13 | 299 861 | 84.2 | 69.9 | 94 100 | 1.8 | 685 | 22 349 | 45 739 | 15.7 |
| District 14 | 299 013 | 85.3 | 67.1 | 121 300 | 1.9 | 773 | 25 523 | 50 178 | 21.5 |
| District 15 | 238 622 | 88.2 | 69.4 | 91 100 | 1.2 | 619 | 16 008 | 37 000 | 13.7 |
| District 16 | 245 507 | 93.9 | 59.3 | 121 100 | 1.5 | 710 | 19 507 | 41 434 | 14.4 |
| District 17 | 301 159 | 84.6 | 55.5 | 128 900 | 2.4 | 816 | 21 957 | 41 989 | 15.3 |
| District 18 | 285 716 | 84.2 | 49.4 | 98 200 | 1.6 | 746 | 20 153 | 37 079 | 12.7 |
| District 19 | 290 254 | 86.3 | 63.7 | 87 000 | 1.2 | 689 | 20 745 | 41 186 | 13.6 |
| District 20 | 266 842 | 91.0 | 56.6 | 112 000 | 0.7 | 790 | 19 800 | 42 934 | 13.5 |
| District 21 | 329 027 | 88.9 | 57.3 | 205 400 | 8.9 | 901 | 33 229 | 57 219 | 25.9 |
| District 22 | 255 766 | 92.4 | 74.9 | 188 700 | 3.8 | 970 | 33 165 | 81 392 | 39.0 |
| District 23 | 257 245 | 85.7 | 73.8 | 97 100 | 3.9 | 722 | 21 314 | 46 232 | 19.0 |
| District 24 | 310 625 | 92.4 | 50.6 | 185 300 | 7.5 | 883 | 34 925 | 59 229 | 27.6 |

1. Specified owner-occupied units.    2. Specified renter-occupied units.

# Table E. Congressional Districts 113th Congress — Poverty, Labor Force, Employment, and Social Security

| STATE District | Poverty, 2011 (percent) | | | Civilian labor force, 2011 | | | Civilian employment,[2] 2011 | | | | | Social Security beneficiaries, December 2012 | | |
|---|---|---|---|---|---|---|---|---|---|---|---|---|---|---|
| | | | | | Unemployment | | | Percent | | | | | | |
| | Persons below poverty level | Families below poverty level | Households receiving food stamps in past 12 months | Total | Total | Rate[1] | Total | Management, professional, and related occupations | Service, sales, and office | Construction and production | Persons under age 65 with no health insurance, 2010 (percent) | Number | Rate[3] | Supplemental Security Income recipients, December 2012 |
| | 49 | 50 | 51 | 52 | 53 | 54 | 55 | 56 | 57 | 58 | 59 | 60 | 61 | 62 |
| PENNSYLVANIA—Cont'd | | | | | | | | | | | | | | |
| District 4 | 11.2 | 7.8 | 10.2 | 378 200 | 35 309 | 9.3 | 342 891 | 34.2 | 40.1 | 25.6 | 11.8 | 142 266 | 200.3 | 14 144 |
| District 5 | 15.1 | 8.6 | 12.4 | 344 880 | 28 063 | 8.1 | 316 817 | 32.0 | 40.9 | 27.1 | 11.1 | 157 742 | 223.4 | 17 993 |
| District 6 | 6.7 | 3.9 | 5.4 | 389 921 | 27 629 | 7.1 | 362 292 | 42.8 | 39.8 | 17.4 | 8.0 | 130 029 | 178.8 | 7 011 |
| District 7 | 5.2 | 3.7 | 4.6 | 366 039 | 26 301 | 7.2 | 339 738 | 44.3 | 38.0 | 17.7 | 9.0 | 136 916 | 197.6 | 6 705 |
| District 8 | 6.2 | 4.7 | 5.1 | 387 625 | 29 873 | 7.7 | 357 752 | 41.0 | 40.3 | 18.7 | 7.9 | 137 098 | 194.6 | 7 666 |
| District 9 | 15.1 | 10.2 | 14.6 | 334 965 | 30 139 | 9.0 | 304 826 | 28.0 | 42.7 | 29.3 | 14.1 | 170 910 | 241.6 | 26 170 |
| District 10 | 13.2 | 9.1 | 10.9 | 343 064 | 30 579 | 8.9 | 312 485 | 30.7 | 40.1 | 29.2 | 14.5 | 163 059 | 228.9 | 15 740 |
| District 11 | 12.4 | 9.2 | 11.3 | 357 804 | 28 486 | 8.0 | 329 318 | 30.6 | 43.7 | 25.7 | 10.9 | 162 795 | 230.9 | 16 758 |
| District 12 | 9.7 | 7.0 | 10.7 | 354 713 | 22 854 | 6.4 | 331 859 | 38.6 | 40.6 | 20.8 | 8.7 | 172 657 | 245.3 | 15 931 |
| District 13 | 13.0 | 10.5 | 12.2 | 386 187 | 47 164 | 12.2 | 339 023 | 38.7 | 43.4 | 17.9 | 13.7 | 121 764 | 167.1 | 24 066 |
| District 14 | 19.8 | 14.9 | 18.3 | 361 929 | 38 723 | 10.7 | 323 206 | 37.3 | 46.0 | 16.7 | 12.1 | 151 990 | 216.1 | 32 380 |
| District 15 | 12.3 | 8.5 | 10.1 | 379 429 | 35 681 | 9.4 | 343 748 | 32.9 | 42.4 | 24.7 | 11.8 | 148 554 | 205.4 | 16 024 |
| District 16 | 15.1 | 11.4 | 13.7 | 360 783 | 33 065 | 9.2 | 327 718 | 30.4 | 41.9 | 27.7 | 14.2 | 136 722 | 194.7 | 19 047 |
| District 17 | 13.1 | 9.4 | 14.1 | 346 820 | 34 240 | 9.9 | 312 580 | 30.8 | 43.4 | 25.8 | 12.4 | 163 775 | 235.9 | 19 181 |
| District 18 | 8.2 | 5.6 | 8.5 | 369 916 | 24 938 | 6.7 | 344 978 | 39.4 | 40.6 | 20.0 | 8.5 | 164 034 | 230.5 | 12 803 |
| RHODE ISLAND | 14.7 | 10.6 | 14.6 | 569 816 | 58 581 | 10.3 | 511 235 | 37.2 | 45.6 | 17.3 | 12.5 | 210 949 | 200.7 | 32 737 |
| District 1 | 15.9 | 12.0 | 16.7 | 279 249 | 28 351 | 10.2 | 250 898 | 36.5 | 46.3 | 17.2 | 13.6 | 105 320 | 201.0 | 18 988 |
| District 2 | 13.6 | 9.1 | 12.5 | 290 567 | 30 230 | 10.4 | 260 337 | 37.8 | 44.9 | 17.3 | 11.5 | 105 629 | 200.4 | 13 749 |
| SOUTH CAROLINA | 18.9 | 14.3 | 15.4 | 2 235 219 | 266 294 | 11.9 | 1 968 925 | 31.6 | 43.8 | 24.6 | 19.4 | 986 256 | 210.8 | 117 115 |
| District 1 | 13.1 | 10.2 | 9.3 | 333 872 | 34 066 | 10.2 | 299 806 | 35.5 | 44.1 | 20.4 | 17.9 | 133 073 | 199.4 | 9 389 |
| District 2 | 15.3 | 12.1 | 12.7 | 334 050 | 28 414 | 8.5 | 305 636 | 37.4 | 41.3 | 21.3 | 15.0 | 123 914 | 183.2 | 12 678 |
| District 3 | 18.8 | 13.4 | 15.2 | 301 732 | 37 281 | 12.4 | 264 451 | 28.8 | 40.8 | 30.3 | 18.4 | 158 208 | 237.5 | 15 521 |
| District 4 | 17.2 | 13.2 | 13.0 | 335 996 | 35 038 | 10.4 | 300 958 | 34.8 | 43.0 | 22.2 | 18.0 | 135 404 | 201.7 | 14 547 |
| District 5 | 18.9 | 14.3 | 17.0 | 316 633 | 41 454 | 13.1 | 275 179 | 30.0 | 42.3 | 27.7 | 17.4 | 143 633 | 216.7 | 16 574 |
| District 6 | 26.5 | 20.4 | 24.3 | 303 313 | 49 777 | 16.4 | 253 536 | 25.5 | 47.7 | 26.8 | 23.7 | 130 341 | 195.3 | 27 489 |
| District 7 | 22.8 | 17.4 | 17.4 | 309 623 | 40 264 | 13.0 | 269 359 | 27.4 | 47.6 | 24.9 | 25.5 | 161 683 | 242.1 | 20 917 |
| SOUTH DAKOTA | 13.9 | 9.6 | 10.6 | 439 730 | 24 107 | 5.5 | 415 623 | 34.8 | 42.3 | 22.9 | 13.8 | 159 439 | 193.5 | 14 682 |
| At Large | 13.9 | 9.6 | 10.6 | 439 730 | 24 107 | 5.5 | 415 623 | 34.8 | 42.3 | 22.9 | 13.8 | 159 439 | 193.5 | 14 682 |
| TENNESSEE | 18.3 | 13.7 | 17.6 | 3 113 007 | 328 545 | 10.6 | 2 784 462 | 33.1 | 42.3 | 24.5 | 16.9 | 1 321 955 | 206.4 | 182 957 |
| District 1 | 19.3 | 14.5 | 19.1 | 329 603 | 31 958 | 9.7 | 297 645 | 28.9 | 42.7 | 28.5 | 17.7 | 189 914 | 268.5 | 23 541 |
| District 2 | 15.5 | 11.4 | 14.1 | 356 865 | 29 715 | 8.3 | 327 150 | 36.3 | 42.2 | 21.6 | 14.6 | 152 725 | 214.5 | 18 091 |
| District 3 | 19.9 | 14.9 | 18.4 | 334 461 | 37 492 | 11.2 | 296 969 | 32.4 | 41.8 | 25.8 | 16.5 | 168 226 | 235.0 | 23 392 |
| District 4 | 16.4 | 11.4 | 16.1 | 350 439 | 35 905 | 10.2 | 314 534 | 29.2 | 42.9 | 27.9 | 16.8 | 143 645 | 202.8 | 17 304 |
| District 5 | 19.0 | 14.2 | 16.0 | 389 169 | 35 792 | 9.2 | 353 377 | 38.0 | 44.3 | 17.7 | 18.5 | 110 859 | 155.3 | 16 945 |
| District 6 | 17.2 | 12.9 | 16.9 | 336 732 | 32 234 | 9.6 | 304 498 | 32.1 | 41.6 | 26.4 | 16.7 | 163 268 | 228.7 | 17 607 |
| District 7 | 16.4 | 12.8 | 16.8 | 324 904 | 39 068 | 12.0 | 285 836 | 35.7 | 39.5 | 24.7 | 15.0 | 139 374 | 195.2 | 16 286 |
| District 8 | 14.6 | 11.0 | 15.6 | 332 923 | 33 723 | 10.1 | 299 200 | 36.5 | 38.8 | 24.7 | 12.9 | 145 985 | 206.6 | 18 011 |
| District 9 | 26.4 | 21.8 | 25.9 | 357 911 | 52 658 | 14.7 | 305 253 | 28.3 | 46.9 | 24.7 | 22.5 | 107 959 | 151.9 | 31 780 |
| TEXAS | 18.5 | 14.4 | 13.6 | 12 520 343 | 1 065 274 | 8.5 | 11 455 069 | 34.7 | 42.5 | 22.7 | 25.4 | 3 657 877 | 142.5 | 657 026 |
| District 1 | 18.2 | 13.2 | 12.8 | 323 885 | 26 196 | 8.1 | 297 689 | 30.8 | 42.7 | 27.0 | 23.7 | 140 204 | 199.4 | 21 472 |
| District 2 | 12.7 | 10.0 | 7.4 | 390 400 | 25 834 | 6.6 | 364 566 | 43.2 | 42.2 | 20.1 | 19.8 | 81 513 | 113.0 | 9 634 |
| District 3 | 9.1 | 7.1 | 4.2 | 395 365 | 24 170 | 6.1 | 371 195 | 53.4 | 41.8 | 10.4 | 15.3 | 75 367 | 103.5 | 6 574 |
| District 4 | 15.7 | 11.7 | 13.9 | 327 727 | 28 466 | 8.7 | 299 261 | 32.0 | 42.9 | 26.8 | 23.6 | 144 867 | 205.5 | 20 135 |
| District 5 | 19.4 | 15.3 | 13.5 | 328 483 | 27 729 | 8.4 | 300 754 | 28.0 | 44.3 | 28.3 | 31.1 | 119 854 | 166.6 | 18 148 |
| District 6 | 15.6 | 12.8 | 10.7 | 383 572 | 34 769 | 9.1 | 348 803 | 36.2 | 41.6 | 21.7 | 21.6 | 96 097 | 133.0 | 13 170 |
| District 7 | 16.1 | 12.8 | 6.6 | 405 713 | 29 437 | 7.3 | 376 276 | 47.6 | 39.5 | 15.5 | 23.9 | 76 694 | 105.5 | 9 587 |
| District 8 | 15.5 | 12.5 | 10.4 | 338 868 | 29 633 | 8.7 | 309 235 | 34.9 | 38.8 | 22.7 | 23.2 | 118 253 | 164.1 | 13 129 |
| District 9 | 21.6 | 18.9 | 17.3 | 365 481 | 39 052 | 10.7 | 326 429 | 28.2 | 46.9 | 22.2 | 34.3 | 74 540 | 107.8 | 26 929 |
| District 10 | 12.3 | 8.7 | 8.7 | 369 221 | 26 610 | 7.2 | 342 611 | 41.2 | 42.7 | 18.9 | 20.3 | 96 414 | 135.9 | 11 480 |
| District 11 | 15.5 | 11.6 | 11.7 | 327 320 | 18 497 | 5.7 | 308 823 | 30.3 | 42.2 | 27.3 | 27.2 | 134 273 | 191.6 | 16 959 |
| District 12 | 13.9 | 10.5 | 9.4 | 367 176 | 29 694 | 8.1 | 337 482 | 37.5 | 41.8 | 21.9 | 20.8 | 105 048 | 147.9 | 11 678 |
| District 13 | 15.1 | 11.3 | 11.7 | 329 906 | 20 933 | 6.3 | 308 973 | 30.2 | 42.9 | 28.1 | 23.2 | 123 596 | 176.9 | 14 314 |
| District 14 | 16.4 | 13.6 | 14.5 | 336 240 | 32 950 | 9.8 | 303 290 | 33.2 | 44.3 | 26.4 | 22.9 | 117 614 | 166.1 | 18 806 |
| District 15 | 32.5 | 27.4 | 28.7 | 312 038 | 31 185 | 10.0 | 280 853 | 27.6 | 41.6 | 22.5 | 36.9 | 93 504 | 129.4 | 32 977 |
| District 16 | 22.4 | 19.5 | 21.5 | 304 601 | 23 318 | 7.7 | 281 283 | 33.3 | 39.5 | 20.1 | 28.8 | 102 590 | 145.0 | 25 394 |
| District 17 | 22.9 | 14.5 | 12.3 | 359 052 | 29 743 | 8.3 | 329 309 | 36.5 | 38.8 | 20.7 | 21.4 | 101 650 | 143.0 | 16 672 |
| District 18 | 27.6 | 24.4 | 19.7 | 346 522 | 40 158 | 11.6 | 306 364 | 27.6 | 46.9 | 29.1 | 29.8 | 85 988 | 121.6 | 29 605 |
| District 19 | 19.6 | 13.9 | 13.6 | 335 274 | 24 539 | 7.3 | 310 735 | 29.7 | 42.7 | 24.4 | 23.7 | 117 738 | 166.1 | 17 678 |
| District 20 | 19.7 | 15.5 | 15.9 | 341 610 | 30 205 | 8.8 | 311 405 | 32.5 | 42.2 | 19.9 | 25.0 | 102 645 | 143.2 | 23 779 |
| District 21 | 12.7 | 7.7 | 7.3 | 385 478 | 24 293 | 6.3 | 361 185 | 46.9 | 41.8 | 13.0 | 19.9 | 122 545 | 169.3 | 9 042 |
| District 22 | 8.6 | 6.6 | 7.4 | 369 873 | 17 335 | 4.7 | 352 538 | 47.6 | 42.9 | 15.0 | 19.2 | 74 619 | 103.5 | 9 841 |
| District 23 | 20.3 | 16.4 | 18.4 | 317 742 | 28 003 | 8.8 | 289 739 | 30.2 | 44.3 | 26.4 | 25.8 | 111 553 | 153.7 | 26 347 |
| District 24 | 10.0 | 7.4 | 5.9 | 413 490 | 24 869 | 6.0 | 388 621 | 42.3 | 41.6 | 15.6 | 21.8 | 78 361 | 109.0 | 7 189 |

1. Percent of civilian labor force.   2. Persons 16 years old and over.   3. Per 1,000 resident population estimated in the 2011 American Community Survey.

# Table E. Congressional Districts 113th Congress — **Land Area and Population Characteristics**

| STATE District | Representative, 113th Congress | Land area,[1] 2010 (sq km) | Total persons | Per square kilometer | White | Black | American Indian, Alaska Native | Asian and Pacific Islander | Some other race | Two or more races | Hispanic or Latino[2] | Non-Hispanic White alone | Percent female | Percent foreign born | Percent born in state of residence |
|---|---|---|---|---|---|---|---|---|---|---|---|---|---|---|---|
| | | 1 | 2 | 3 | 4 | 5 | 6 | 7 | 8 | 9 | 10 | 11 | 12 | 13 | 14 |
| **TEXAS—Cont'd** | | | | | | | | | | | | | | | |
| District 25 | Roger Williams (R) | 19 738 | 714 682 | 36.2 | 84.4 | 7.5 | 0.7 | 2.8 | 2.5 | 2.1 | 16.9 | 70.7 | 50.2 | 7.8 | 58.8 |
| District 26 | Michael C. Burgess (R) | 2 350 | 722 749 | 307.6 | 82.2 | 6.6 | 0.7 | 5.1 | 2.1 | 3.2 | 16.1 | 69.6 | 50.8 | 11.3 | 54.4 |
| District 27 | Blake Farenthold (R) | 23 642 | 701 765 | 29.7 | 85.7 | 5.1 | 0.5 | 1.5 | 4.2 | 3.0 | 50.8 | 41.4 | 50.5 | 8.3 | 75.7 |
| District 28 | Henry Cuellar (D) | 24 290 | 710 260 | 29.2 | 87.2 | 4.2 | 0.5 | 0.9 | 5.3 | 2.0 | 78.4 | 15.9 | 50.8 | 22.4 | 63.7 |
| District 29 | Gene Green (D) | 485 | 718 379 | 1 482.7 | 68.2 | 9.8 | 0.6 | 1.7 | 18.7 | 1.0 | 76.4 | 12.1 | 49.6 | 32.1 | 57.4 |
| District 30 | Eddie Bernice Johnson (D) | 923 | 694 383 | 752.5 | 41.0 | 44.6 | 0.4 | 1.9 | 10.8 | 1.4 | 35.7 | 16.9 | 50.8 | 17.2 | 64.0 |
| District 31 | John R. Carter (R) | 5 580 | 721 698 | 129.3 | 77.0 | 11.2 | 0.5 | 4.6 | 3.0 | 3.8 | 23.1 | 58.8 | 50.9 | 10.0 | 51.9 |
| District 32 | Pete Sessions (R) | 481 | 711 796 | 1 480.2 | 62.6 | 10.9 | 0.2 | 7.2 | 14.8 | 4.2 | 28.3 | 50.7 | 50.6 | 20.3 | 51.9 |
| District 33 | Marc A. Veasey (D) | 549 | 710 945 | 1 295.2 | 64.8 | 15.6 | 0.5 | 2.6 | 14.9 | 1.7 | 65.0 | 16.0 | 48.7 | 32.8 | 55.2 |
| District 34 | Filemon Vela (D) | 21 213 | 702 624 | 33.1 | 89.6 | 1.5 | 0.2 | 0.6 | 6.9 | 1.2 | 82.6 | 15.2 | 51.2 | 20.3 | 68.9 |
| District 35 | Lloyd Doggett (D) | 1 538 | 724 271 | 471.0 | 64.0 | 9.6 | 0.6 | 1.7 | 21.7 | 2.4 | 64.0 | 23.8 | 49.6 | 17.8 | 64.8 |
| District 36 | Steve Stockman (R) | 18 456 | 712 433 | 38.6 | 78.7 | 10.1 | 0.7 | 2.4 | 6.4 | 1.6 | 22.9 | 62.9 | 49.9 | 11.1 | 67.6 |
| **UTAH** | | 212 818 | 2 817 222 | 13.2 | 88.3 | 1.2 | 1.1 | 3.0 | 4.0 | 2.5 | 13.2 | 79.9 | 49.7 | 8.4 | 61.7 |
| District 1 | Rob Bishop (R) | 50 662 | 699 943 | 13.8 | 88.5 | 1.2 | 0.9 | 1.5 | 5.3 | 2.6 | 11.5 | 83.2 | 49.5 | 5.8 | 65.7 |
| District 2 | Chris Stewart (R) | 103 568 | 705 688 | 6.8 | 87.0 | 1.4 | 1.3 | 3.7 | 4.2 | 2.4 | 14.5 | 77.5 | 49.5 | 9.5 | 59.1 |
| District 3 | Jason Chaffetz (R) | 51 982 | 708 809 | 13.6 | 90.7 | 0.7 | 1.6 | 2.4 | 2.2 | 2.3 | 10.6 | 82.7 | 50.1 | 7.9 | 59.1 |
| District 4 | Jim Matheson (D) | 6 605 | 702 782 | 106.4 | 86.8 | 1.4 | 0.7 | 4.3 | 4.4 | 2.5 | 16.3 | 76.1 | 49.7 | 10.5 | 62.8 |
| **VERMONT** | | 23 871 | 626 431 | 26.2 | 95.2 | 0.8 | 0.3 | 1.3 | 0.2 | 2.2 | 1.5 | 94.0 | 50.8 | 3.9 | 50.7 |
| At Large | Peter Welch (D) | 23 871 | 626 431 | 26.2 | 95.2 | 0.8 | 0.3 | 1.3 | 0.2 | 2.2 | 1.5 | 94.0 | 50.8 | 3.9 | 50.7 |
| **VIRGINIA** | | 102 279 | 8 096 604 | 79.2 | 69.4 | 19.5 | 0.3 | 5.7 | 2.1 | 3.0 | 8.2 | 64.3 | 50.9 | 11.1 | 50.3 |
| District 1 | Robert J. Wittman (R) | 9 542 | 743 824 | 77.9 | 73.0 | 17.5 | 0.4 | 3.5 | 3.0 | 2.6 | 9.5 | 67.1 | 50.7 | 8.5 | 44.5 |
| District 2 | Scott Rigell (R) | 2 568 | 710 769 | 276.7 | 67.9 | 21.9 | 0.4 | 5.1 | 1.3 | 3.5 | 7.3 | 63.2 | 50.7 | 8.0 | 43.6 |
| District 3 | Robert C. "Bobby" Scott (D) | 2 453 | 744 369 | 303.5 | 35.8 | 57.2 | 0.3 | 2.2 | 1.3 | 3.3 | 5.2 | 33.1 | 51.6 | 4.9 | 61.1 |
| District 4 | J. Randy Forbes (R) | 11 164 | 736 977 | 66.0 | 62.3 | 31.4 | 0.3 | 2.2 | 1.1 | 2.7 | 4.7 | 59.2 | 50.0 | 4.7 | 61.1 |
| District 5 | Robert Hurt (R) | 25 977 | 726 376 | 28.0 | 75.0 | 21.0 | 0.2 | 1.4 | 0.7 | 1.6 | 2.9 | 72.9 | 51.6 | 3.7 | 67.0 |
| District 6 | Bob Goodlatte (R) | 15 359 | 734 204 | 47.8 | 83.7 | 11.5 | 0.1 | 1.7 | 0.8 | 2.2 | 3.9 | 81.1 | 51.6 | 4.7 | 66.2 |
| District 7 | Eric Cantor (R) | 7 191 | 733 911 | 102.1 | 77.2 | 14.5 | 0.3 | 4.1 | 1.5 | 2.3 | 5.0 | 74.2 | 51.7 | 8.6 | 55.0 |
| District 8 | James P. Moran (D) | 387 | 742 531 | 1 921.0 | 63.6 | 14.3 | 0.3 | 11.1 | 6.6 | 4.1 | 18.0 | 53.9 | 50.8 | 28.3 | 25.0 |
| District 9 | Morgan Griffith (R) | 23 605 | 725 764 | 30.7 | 91.4 | 5.9 | 0.2 | 1.2 | 0.4 | 1.0 | 1.7 | 90.0 | 50.3 | 2.8 | 66.6 |
| District 10 | Frank R. Wolf (R) | 3 554 | 750 886 | 211.3 | 73.6 | 7.5 | 0.2 | 11.8 | 2.9 | 3.9 | 12.2 | 65.1 | 49.9 | 19.4 | 35.0 |
| District 11 | Gerald E. Connolly (D) | 479 | 746 993 | 1 558.2 | 60.3 | 12.3 | 0.4 | 17.7 | 3.9 | 5.4 | 17.3 | 49.1 | 50.5 | 27.9 | 28.7 |
| **WASHINGTON** | | 172 119 | 6 830 038 | 39.7 | 78.4 | 3.5 | 1.3 | 7.9 | 4.1 | 4.7 | 11.6 | 71.9 | 50.1 | 13.3 | 47.3 |
| District 1 | Suzan K. DelBene (D) | 16 023 | 686 848 | 42.9 | 82.6 | 1.1 | 1.0 | 9.1 | 2.0 | 4.1 | 8.1 | 77.0 | 49.8 | 14.9 | 49.3 |
| District 2 | Rick Larsen (D) | 2 629 | 678 014 | 257.9 | 81.0 | 2.2 | 1.4 | 8.3 | 2.7 | 4.4 | 10.3 | 74.2 | 50.3 | 13.6 | 48.8 |
| District 3 | Jaime Herrera Beutler (R) | 23 605 | 680 915 | 28.8 | 87.8 | 1.4 | 1.0 | 3.4 | 2.2 | 4.3 | 8.0 | 82.7 | 50.6 | 7.6 | 40.4 |
| District 4 | Doc Hastings (R) | 49 858 | 690 421 | 13.8 | 72.4 | 1.0 | 2.1 | 2.1 | 19.2 | 3.3 | 36.8 | 56.3 | 49.6 | 16.9 | 53.6 |
| District 5 | Cathy McMorris Rodgers (R) | 40 075 | 676 030 | 16.9 | 88.9 | 1.8 | 1.8 | 2.5 | 1.2 | 3.8 | 5.8 | 85.2 | 50.3 | 6.4 | 52.8 |
| District 6 | Derek Kilmer (D) | 17 878 | 674 679 | 37.7 | 81.3 | 3.7 | 2.3 | 4.9 | 1.9 | 5.9 | 6.7 | 77.6 | 49.8 | 7.7 | 47.4 |
| District 7 | Jim McDermott (D) | 373 | 683 158 | 1 830.0 | 76.0 | 5.3 | 0.9 | 11.0 | 2.1 | 4.8 | 7.3 | 71.6 | 50.0 | 15.9 | 42.0 |
| District 8 | David G. Reichert (R) | 19 062 | 681 117 | 35.7 | 82.2 | 2.4 | 0.9 | 7.3 | 2.8 | 4.4 | 9.2 | 76.4 | 50.5 | 11.4 | 52.2 |
| District 9 | Adam Smith (D) | 475 | 693 596 | 1 460.0 | 56.9 | 10.8 | 0.8 | 22.4 | 3.8 | 5.4 | 12.4 | 49.4 | 49.7 | 28.6 | 38.3 |
| District 10 | Denny Heck (D) | 2 141 | 685 260 | 320.1 | 75.9 | 5.4 | 1.3 | 8.1 | 2.7 | 6.7 | 10.5 | 69.8 | 50.5 | 9.8 | 48.0 |
| **WEST VIRGINIA** | | 62 259 | 1 855 364 | 29.8 | 93.9 | 3.0 | 0.2 | 0.6 | 0.2 | 2.1 | 1.3 | 93.1 | 50.7 | | 71.0 |
| District 1 | David McKinley (R) | 16 254 | 614 309 | 37.8 | 95.1 | 2.3 | 0.1 | 0.8 | 0.1 | 1.5 | 1.0 | 94.3 | 50.3 | 1.1 | 69.4 |
| District 2 | Shelley Moore Capito (R) | 20 765 | 626 469 | 30.2 | 92.3 | 3.2 | 0.2 | 0.6 | 0.4 | 3.2 | 1.7 | 91.2 | 50.7 | 1.7 | 65.4 |
| District 3 | Nick J. Rahall II (D) | 25 240 | 614 586 | 24.3 | 94.2 | 3.5 | 0.1 | 0.4 | 0.2 | 1.5 | 0.7 | 93.8 | 51.1 | 1.1 | 78.1 |
| **WISCONSIN** | | 140 268 | 5 711 767 | 40.7 | 87.2 | 6.2 | 0.8 | 2.3 | 1.4 | 2.0 | 6.1 | 83.0 | 50.4 | 4.7 | 71.8 |
| District 1 | Paul Ryan (R) | 4 475 | 710 310 | 158.7 | 88.8 | 5.6 | 0.3 | 1.9 | 1.7 | 1.7 | 9.0 | 81.7 | 50.1 | 5.2 | 67.7 |
| District 2 | Mark Pocan (D) | 11 750 | 720 334 | 61.3 | 88.1 | 4.4 | 0.3 | 3.6 | 1.3 | 2.5 | 5.9 | 83.9 | 50.5 | 6.5 | 66.3 |
| District 3 | Ron Kind (D) | 28 779 | 710 796 | 24.7 | 94.2 | 0.9 | 0.6 | 2.1 | 0.6 | 1.6 | 2.0 | 92.9 | 49.6 | 2.5 | 71.8 |
| District 4 | Gwen Moore (D) | 332 | 715 895 | 2 153.6 | 54.0 | 33.7 | 0.6 | 3.2 | 4.7 | 3.8 | 16.3 | 43.9 | 51.8 | 9.9 | 64.8 |
| District 5 | F. James Sensenbrenner Jr. (R) | 4 897 | 713 261 | 145.7 | 93.5 | 1.8 | 0.2 | 2.2 | 0.8 | 1.6 | 4.8 | 89.8 | 51.3 | 4.3 | 77.4 |
| District 6 | Thomas E. Petri (R) | 12 739 | 709 417 | 55.7 | 93.6 | 1.6 | 0.4 | 2.1 | 0.9 | 1.5 | 4.0 | 91.0 | 49.8 | 3.5 | 79.4 |
| District 7 | Sean P. Duffy (R) | 59 666 | 713 509 | 12.0 | 93.9 | 0.5 | 2.1 | 1.4 | 0.3 | 1.8 | 1.8 | 92.6 | 49.6 | 2.1 | 68.1 |
| District 8 | Reid J. Ribble (R) | 17 629 | 718 245 | 40.7 | 91.6 | 1.3 | 2.2 | 2.2 | 0.7 | 2.0 | 4.4 | 88.5 | 50.2 | 3.7 | 78.6 |
| **WYOMING** | | 251 470 | 568 158 | 2.3 | 90.7 | 0.9 | 2.2 | 0.9 | 2.6 | 2.8 | 9.1 | 85.6 | 49.1 | 3.2 | 40.7 |
| At Large | Cynthia M. Lummis (R) | 251 470 | 568 158 | 2.3 | 90.7 | 0.9 | 2.2 | 0.9 | 2.6 | 2.8 | 9.1 | 85.6 | 49.1 | 3.2 | 40.7 |

1. Dry land or land partially or temporarily covered by water.    2. May be of any race.

Items 1—14

# Table E. Congressional Districts 113th Congress — **Age and Education**

| STATE District | Population and population characteristics, 2011 (cont.) — Age (percent) | | | | | | | | | | Education, 2011 | Attainment[2] (percent) | |
| --- | --- | --- | --- | --- | --- | --- | --- | --- | --- | --- | --- | --- | --- |
| | Under 5 years | 5 to 17 years | 18 to 24 years | 25 to 34 years | 35 to 44 years | 45 to 54 years | 55 to 64 years | 65 to 74 years | 75 years and over | Median age | Total Enrollment[1] | High school graduate or more | Bachelor's degree or more |
| | 15 | 16 | 17 | 18 | 19 | 20 | 21 | 22 | 23 | 24 | 25 | 26 | 27 |
| TEXAS—Cont'd | | | | | | | | | | | | | |
| District 25 | 7.0 | 18.4 | 10.9 | 12.8 | 13.7 | 13.5 | 11.9 | 7.0 | 4.8 | 35.6 | 201 438 | 89.1 | 35.9 |
| District 26 | 8.1 | 21.0 | 9.8 | 13.9 | 15.8 | 14.6 | 9.3 | 5.0 | 2.5 | 33.0 | 235 238 | 93.3 | 40.6 |
| District 27 | 7.0 | 19.0 | 9.5 | 12.3 | 12.0 | 14.1 | 12.5 | 7.5 | 6.2 | 37.1 | 183 504 | 79.9 | 19.1 |
| District 28 | 9.2 | 23.7 | 9.9 | 12.2 | 14.1 | 11.5 | 9.2 | 5.7 | 4.5 | 30.6 | 228 092 | 68.8 | 15.5 |
| District 29 | 9.4 | 22.2 | 11.9 | 15.2 | 13.0 | 12.7 | 8.1 | 4.6 | 2.8 | 29.3 | 208 247 | 58.5 | 9.1 |
| District 30 | 7.9 | 19.8 | 11.1 | 14.1 | 14.2 | 13.5 | 10.1 | 5.5 | 3.8 | 32.9 | 190 382 | 75.0 | 19.7 |
| District 31 | 7.9 | 20.0 | 9.3 | 15.2 | 15.3 | 13.1 | 9.8 | 5.5 | 3.9 | 33.3 | 209 947 | 90.6 | 32.5 |
| District 32 | 7.1 | 19.1 | 9.7 | 15.2 | 14.9 | 13.8 | 10.4 | 5.0 | 4.7 | 34.1 | 200 372 | 85.0 | 39.9 |
| District 33 | 10.1 | 21.4 | 10.9 | 16.2 | 13.8 | 12.0 | 8.3 | 4.3 | 3.1 | 29.6 | 195 765 | 57.4 | 8.4 |
| District 34 | 8.5 | 22.5 | 9.8 | 13.0 | 12.5 | 11.6 | 10.1 | 6.7 | 5.4 | 31.6 | 213 682 | 64.6 | 13.4 |
| District 35 | 8.2 | 19.1 | 13.1 | 16.0 | 13.4 | 12.4 | 9.5 | 4.6 | 3.7 | 30.7 | 208 052 | 72.3 | 15.0 |
| District 36 | 6.9 | 19.6 | 8.2 | 13.3 | 13.1 | 14.4 | 12.5 | 6.7 | 5.2 | 36.6 | 190 824 | 82.5 | 17.7 |
| UTAH | 9.3 | 22.0 | 11.6 | 15.7 | 12.3 | 10.8 | 9.1 | 5.1 | 4.1 | 29.6 | 926 365 | 90.3 | 29.7 |
| District 1 | 9.6 | 22.5 | 10.9 | 15.4 | 12.3 | 11.3 | 9.5 | 4.7 | 3.8 | 29.8 | 224 550 | 90.5 | 28.0 |
| District 2 | 8.5 | 21.2 | 10.8 | 15.6 | 12.4 | 11.1 | 9.3 | 6.0 | 5.1 | 30.8 | 223 262 | 88.8 | 29.3 |
| District 3 | 9.3 | 22.4 | 14.9 | 14.3 | 11.5 | 10.2 | 8.6 | 5.2 | 3.7 | 27.3 | 259 743 | 93.0 | 35.2 |
| District 4 | 9.8 | 21.8 | 9.9 | 17.6 | 13.2 | 10.7 | 9.1 | 4.3 | 3.7 | 29.9 | 218 810 | 89.3 | 27.0 |
| VERMONT | 4.9 | 15.2 | 10.5 | 11.2 | 12.4 | 15.9 | 14.9 | 8.3 | 6.7 | 42.0 | 155 911 | 91.8 | 35.4 |
| At Large | 4.9 | 15.2 | 10.5 | 11.2 | 12.4 | 15.9 | 14.9 | 8.3 | 6.7 | 42.0 | 155 911 | 91.8 | 35.4 |
| VIRGINIA | 6.3 | 16.6 | 10.2 | 13.6 | 13.7 | 14.9 | 12.3 | 7.1 | 5.4 | 37.6 | 2 156 250 | 87.8 | 35.1 |
| District 1 | 6.5 | 18.4 | 9.0 | 12.7 | 13.5 | 15.4 | 11.8 | 7.4 | 5.2 | 37.9 | 200 891 | 90.4 | 34.0 |
| District 2 | 6.4 | 16.4 | 11.8 | 15.3 | 12.4 | 14.2 | 11.6 | 6.6 | 5.4 | 35.1 | 195 090 | 92.0 | 31.2 |
| District 3 | 6.9 | 15.3 | 14.8 | 15.7 | 11.5 | 13.4 | 11.3 | 5.9 | 5.1 | 32.7 | 203 189 | 82.4 | 21.4 |
| District 4 | 5.9 | 18.4 | 9.3 | 12.2 | 14.1 | 15.9 | 12.3 | 7.0 | 4.9 | 38.2 | 200 112 | 85.8 | 24.2 |
| District 5 | 5.4 | 15.1 | 10.9 | 10.7 | 12.1 | 14.5 | 14.6 | 9.3 | 7.4 | 41.6 | 184 047 | 83.4 | 25.8 |
| District 6 | 5.5 | 15.3 | 12.5 | 11.6 | 12.4 | 14.1 | 13.0 | 8.5 | 7.2 | 39.6 | 195 559 | 84.3 | 24.2 |
| District 7 | 6.1 | 17.8 | 8.2 | 12.1 | 13.6 | 16.5 | 12.7 | 7.2 | 5.8 | 39.9 | 187 911 | 90.9 | 39.2 |
| District 8 | 7.1 | 14.0 | 7.7 | 20.8 | 16.8 | 13.5 | 10.6 | 5.3 | 4.2 | 35.2 | 178 550 | 90.8 | 59.8 |
| District 9 | 5.1 | 13.9 | 12.0 | 10.8 | 12.6 | 14.6 | 14.2 | 9.5 | 7.4 | 41.6 | 181 444 | 80.9 | 18.5 |
| District 10 | 7.2 | 21.0 | 7.3 | 11.3 | 16.5 | 16.5 | 11.6 | 5.2 | 3.5 | 37.1 | 223 070 | 92.5 | 51.7 |
| District 11 | 6.9 | 16.9 | 8.6 | 16.6 | 14.9 | 14.8 | 11.7 | 6.0 | 3.7 | 35.7 | 206 387 | 92.6 | 53.7 |
| WASHINGTON | 6.4 | 16.7 | 9.8 | 14.0 | 13.4 | 14.3 | 12.8 | 7.1 | 5.5 | 37.3 | 1 710 462 | 90.1 | 31.9 |
| District 1 | 6.0 | 18.1 | 7.7 | 13.2 | 15.1 | 15.8 | 12.8 | 7.0 | 4.5 | 38.7 | 177 256 | 92.6 | 38.8 |
| District 2 | 6.0 | 15.3 | 11.1 | 14.5 | 12.7 | 14.4 | 13.2 | 6.8 | 5.9 | 37.4 | 162 092 | 91.5 | 28.5 |
| District 3 | 6.3 | 18.3 | 8.2 | 11.8 | 13.3 | 14.2 | 13.9 | 8.2 | 5.7 | 39.1 | 169 667 | 89.5 | 23.1 |
| District 4 | 8.6 | 20.9 | 9.6 | 13.5 | 12.4 | 12.4 | 11.0 | 6.7 | 5.1 | 33.3 | 182 381 | 78.0 | 20.8 |
| District 5 | 6.0 | 16.3 | 12.7 | 12.7 | 11.4 | 13.8 | 13.1 | 7.6 | 6.5 | 37.2 | 181 963 | 92.3 | 28.3 |
| District 6 | 5.3 | 14.9 | 9.8 | 12.5 | 11.5 | 14.6 | 15.4 | 9.2 | 6.9 | 41.8 | 152 074 | 92.0 | 27.2 |
| District 7 | 5.6 | 10.8 | 11.1 | 19.4 | 15.1 | 13.1 | 12.5 | 6.9 | 5.4 | 36.8 | 161 924 | 93.8 | 54.8 |
| District 8 | 6.4 | 19.2 | 8.6 | 11.7 | 14.7 | 16.0 | 13.0 | 6.0 | 4.6 | 38.0 | 184 687 | 91.6 | 30.4 |
| District 9 | 6.8 | 15.9 | 8.6 | 16.3 | 14.4 | 15.1 | 11.4 | 5.9 | 5.5 | 36.6 | 165 036 | 87.6 | 37.1 |
| District 10 | 7.3 | 17.3 | 10.3 | 14.8 | 13.1 | 13.3 | 11.9 | 6.7 | 5.3 | 35.3 | 173 382 | 91.5 | 26.4 |
| WEST VIRGINIA | 5.6 | 15.2 | 9.4 | 11.8 | 12.6 | 14.5 | 14.7 | 9.0 | 7.3 | 41.4 | 420 204 | 84.2 | 18.5 |
| District 1 | 5.2 | 14.7 | 11.4 | 11.9 | 12.0 | 14.1 | 14.4 | 8.8 | 7.5 | 41.0 | 148 265 | 87.8 | 20.3 |
| District 2 | 5.9 | 16.0 | 8.0 | 11.6 | 13.1 | 15.1 | 14.5 | 9.0 | 6.7 | 41.6 | 137 837 | 85.5 | 20.1 |
| District 3 | 5.8 | 15.0 | 8.8 | 11.7 | 12.6 | 14.2 | 15.2 | 9.2 | 7.6 | 41.7 | 134 102 | 79.4 | 15.0 |
| WISCONSIN | 6.1 | 17.0 | 9.7 | 12.8 | 12.5 | 15.1 | 12.9 | 7.2 | 6.7 | 38.7 | 1 506 580 | 90.4 | 26.5 |
| District 1 | 6.0 | 18.3 | 8.5 | 12.2 | 12.8 | 16.1 | 13.1 | 7.1 | 5.9 | 39.2 | 184 008 | 90.5 | 25.5 |
| District 2 | 6.2 | 16.1 | 11.9 | 14.6 | 13.1 | 14.2 | 12.4 | 6.2 | 5.5 | 35.9 | 205 682 | 93.0 | 37.6 |
| District 3 | 5.6 | 15.8 | 13.1 | 11.7 | 11.4 | 14.4 | 13.0 | 7.6 | 7.2 | 38.3 | 196 383 | 90.6 | 22.5 |
| District 4 | 7.8 | 18.1 | 12.4 | 15.8 | 12.5 | 12.4 | 10.4 | 5.2 | 5.3 | 32.0 | 215 002 | 83.1 | 25.9 |
| District 5 | 5.8 | 17.2 | 7.7 | 12.5 | 12.7 | 16.1 | 13.3 | 7.1 | 7.6 | 40.5 | 183 948 | 93.3 | 33.3 |
| District 6 | 5.5 | 16.8 | 8.8 | 11.7 | 12.5 | 15.8 | 13.5 | 7.9 | 7.6 | 41.1 | 175 041 | 90.6 | 23.8 |
| District 7 | 5.9 | 16.8 | 7.1 | 11.3 | 11.9 | 15.9 | 14.4 | 9.0 | 7.7 | 42.8 | 164 202 | 90.2 | 20.1 |
| District 8 | 6.1 | 17.5 | 8.3 | 12.6 | 12.5 | 16.0 | 12.8 | 7.4 | 6.7 | 39.7 | 182 314 | 90.9 | 23.2 |
| WYOMING | 6.9 | 16.9 | 10.1 | 14.0 | 11.7 | 14.2 | 13.6 | 7.2 | 5.4 | 36.8 | 145 877 | 92.0 | 24.7 |
| At Large | 6.9 | 16.9 | 10.1 | 14.0 | 11.7 | 14.2 | 13.6 | 7.2 | 5.4 | 36.8 | 145 877 | 92.0 | 24.7 |

1. All persons 3 years old and over enrolled in nursery school through college and graduate or professional school.    2. Persons 25 years old and over.

| STATE District | Households, 2011 | | | | | | Group quarters, 2010 | | | | | |
|---|---|---|---|---|---|---|---|---|---|---|---|---|
| | Number | Persons per household | Family households (percent) | Married-couple family (percent) | Female family householder[1] | One person households (percent) | Total in group quarters | Percent 65 years and over | Persons in correctional institutions | Persons in nursing homes | Persons in college dormitories | Persons in military quarters |
| | 28 | 29 | 30 | 31 | 32 | 33 | 34 | 35 | 36 | 37 | 38 | 39 |
| TEXAS—Cont'd | | | | | | | | | | | | |
| District 25 | 251 218 | 2.72 | 70.8 | 55.6 | 10.9 | 22.3 | 30 683 | 9.6 | 11 967 | 3 274 | 10 926 | 2 822 |
| District 26 | 245 244 | 2.90 | 73.1 | 59.0 | 9.0 | 20.3 | 10 539 | 14.1 | 1 179 | 1 636 | 6 475 | 0 |
| District 27 | 248 760 | 2.77 | 69.4 | 48.2 | 16.4 | 25.2 | 11 886 | 31.7 | 3 832 | 4 197 | 1 365 | 103 |
| District 28 | 203 814 | 3.45 | 81.0 | 57.9 | 18.7 | 16.2 | 8 208 | 32.3 | 3 252 | 2 888 | 740 | 146 |
| District 29 | 205 836 | 3.48 | 75.6 | 49.2 | 17.9 | 19.3 | 2 449 | 36.1 | 31 | 1 008 | 0 | 0 |
| District 30 | 238 809 | 2.84 | 64.9 | 37.6 | 21.3 | 29.8 | 19 335 | 9.2 | 11 108 | 2 286 | 2 507 | 0 |
| District 31 | 248 288 | 2.86 | 72.8 | 56.3 | 12.1 | 22.8 | 13 176 | 16.1 | 3 442 | 2 183 | 2 041 | 4 084 |
| District 32 | 264 009 | 2.68 | 64.1 | 47.9 | 11.8 | 29.0 | 4 965 | 38.4 | 22 | 2 226 | 2 437 | 0 |
| District 33 | 213 357 | 3.31 | 71.0 | 42.7 | 20.2 | 23.2 | 5 683 | 19.3 | 2 147 | 1 389 | 534 | 0 |
| District 34 | 205 591 | 3.32 | 78.9 | 54.5 | 19.2 | 18.2 | 19 738 | 13.7 | 13 244 | 2 881 | 2 180 | 41 |
| District 35 | 241 934 | 2.91 | 62.8 | 36.8 | 18.9 | 29.1 | 22 186 | 9.9 | 7 971 | 2 563 | 5 761 | 115 |
| District 36 | 251 269 | 2.77 | 71.5 | 53.3 | 12.6 | 24.5 | 16 434 | 16.7 | 12 140 | 2 926 | 0 | 0 |
| UTAH | 884 253 | 3.13 | 74.9 | 60.4 | 10.2 | 19.8 | 46 152 | 10.4 | 12 666 | 5 854 | 15 666 | 523 |
| District 1 | 224 758 | 3.07 | 76.9 | 62.8 | 10.1 | 18.1 | 9 250 | 10.6 | 1 892 | 1 190 | 3 227 | 488 |
| District 2 | 232 252 | 2.98 | 70.4 | 55.5 | 10.6 | 23.6 | 12 157 | 12.1 | 3 459 | 1 763 | 3 443 | 35 |
| District 3 | 208 072 | 3.34 | 78.4 | 65.1 | 9.4 | 16.3 | 14 790 | 7.5 | 441 | 1 279 | 8 960 | 0 |
| District 4 | 219 171 | 3.16 | 74.3 | 58.6 | 10.7 | 21.0 | 9 955 | 12.4 | 6 874 | 1 622 | 36 | 0 |
| VERMONT | 257 358 | 2.34 | 62.8 | 49.8 | 8.6 | 27.6 | 25 329 | 15.0 | 1 592 | 3 588 | 16 895 | 5 |
| At Large | 257 358 | 2.34 | 62.8 | 49.8 | 8.6 | 27.6 | 25 329 | 15.0 | 1 592 | 3 588 | 16 895 | 5 |
| VIRGINIA | 2 990 650 | 2.63 | 62.8 | 50.8 | 12.2 | 26.3 | 239 834 | 12.0 | 1 592 | 30 324 | 84 048 | 37 568 |
| District 1 | 262 627 | 2.76 | 75.7 | 58.9 | 12.3 | 19.7 | 17 625 | 13.8 | 4 215 | 2 568 | 6 380 | 3 351 |
| District 2 | 266 532 | 2.58 | 66.0 | 48.9 | 13.2 | 26.2 | 19 908 | 11.2 | 1 685 | 2 534 | 7 086 | 7 370 |
| District 3 | 277 518 | 2.55 | 58.5 | 31.4 | 21.5 | 32.7 | 49 326 | 5.4 | 6 045 | 3 045 | 11 014 | 24 287 |
| District 4 | 253 470 | 2.79 | 72.3 | 52.3 | 14.8 | 23.5 | 27 389 | 10.2 | 19 352 | 2 662 | 2 942 | 316 |
| District 5 | 278 750 | 2.49 | 66.5 | 51.1 | 11.9 | 27.7 | 29 183 | 13.8 | 10 972 | 4 052 | 12 206 | 0 |
| District 6 | 282 703 | 2.47 | 65.5 | 49.4 | 11.8 | 27.8 | 33 024 | 12.6 | 4 623 | 4 349 | 19 615 | 1 398 |
| District 7 | 274 284 | 2.63 | 68.5 | 55.2 | 10.5 | 25.6 | 12 723 | 19.8 | 4 500 | 2 649 | 3 721 | 0 |
| District 8 | 295 156 | 2.49 | 56.2 | 44.1 | 8.2 | 35.2 | 6 486 | 28.6 | 944 | 2 026 | 1 084 | 846 |
| District 9 | 288 861 | 2.41 | 64.7 | 48.7 | 11.1 | 29.6 | 31 178 | 13.1 | 10 091 | 4 288 | 14 085 | 0 |
| District 10 | 248 377 | 3.00 | 76.7 | 65.5 | 8.5 | 18.1 | 4 693 | 18.7 | 1 606 | 907 | 1 068 | 0 |
| District 11 | 262 372 | 2.82 | 72.0 | 56.1 | 10.8 | 21.0 | 8 299 | 13.6 | 1 207 | 1 244 | 4 847 | 0 |
| WASHINGTON | 2 632 621 | 2.54 | 64.6 | 49.5 | 10.6 | 27.5 | 139 375 | 18.6 | 31 960 | 22 156 | 35 534 | 12 385 |
| District 1 | 256 919 | 2.64 | 70.8 | 58.8 | 7.8 | 22.6 | 6 885 | 23.7 | 2 676 | 1 313 | 620 | 0 |
| District 2 | 268 752 | 2.47 | 62.8 | 47.3 | 11.7 | 27.8 | 13 727 | 20.5 | 1 754 | 2 323 | 3 862 | 2 504 |
| District 3 | 259 922 | 2.59 | 68.1 | 51.4 | 12.0 | 24.9 | 6 124 | 35.8 | 1 539 | 1 617 | 0 | 14 |
| District 4 | 231 583 | 2.94 | 71.7 | 54.1 | 11.6 | 23.2 | 8 872 | 25.7 | 4 028 | 2 246 | 382 | 4 |
| District 5 | 266 752 | 2.43 | 63.5 | 48.6 | 10.3 | 28.1 | 26 124 | 11.8 | 5 656 | 2 927 | 13 048 | 513 |
| District 6 | 270 310 | 2.41 | 63.1 | 48.7 | 9.9 | 29.4 | 21 965 | 16 | 8 063 | 3 211 | 1 022 | 5 694 |
| District 7 | 309 843 | 2.13 | 48.5 | 37.8 | 7.6 | 40.0 | 23 413 | 13.6 | 1 851 | 2 700 | 10 456 | 362 |
| District 8 | 249 759 | 2.70 | 71.6 | 57.5 | 10.1 | 21.9 | 6 454 | 24.8 | 839 | 1 305 | 2 155 | 0 |
| District 9 | 261 618 | 2.61 | 62.5 | 44.9 | 13.0 | 27.9 | 11 714 | 26.9 | 3 031 | 2 422 | 1 348 | 0 |
| District 10 | 257 163 | 2.61 | 67.4 | 49.2 | 13.0 | 26.0 | 14 097 | 17.9 | 2 523 | 2 092 | 2 641 | 3 294 |
| WEST VIRGINIA | 735 408 | 2.46 | 65.0 | 48.5 | 11.7 | 30.1 | 49 382 | 18.9 | 16 591 | 9 748 | 17 113 | 79 |
| District 1 | 241 111 | 2.46 | 62.9 | 48.3 | 9.9 | 32.0 | 22 849 | 15.8 | 6 965 | 3 632 | 10 300 | 0 |
| District 2 | 248 976 | 2.47 | 66.1 | 48.2 | 12.9 | 29.4 | 11 019 | 23.6 | 2 583 | 2 791 | 3 447 | 79 |
| District 3 | 245 321 | 2.44 | 65.9 | 49.0 | 12.2 | 29.0 | 15 514 | 20.1 | 7 043 | 3 325 | 3 366 | 0 |
| WISCONSIN | 2 275 352 | 2.44 | 64.3 | 49.8 | 10.1 | 28.8 | 150 214 | 23.1 | 38 102 | 33 808 | 56 773 | 132 |
| District 1 | 270 678 | 2.57 | 68.3 | 53.4 | 10.4 | 25.3 | 14 266 | 21.6 | 6 723 | 3 632 | 2 368 | 0 |
| District 2 | 295 563 | 2.38 | 61.4 | 47.6 | 9.2 | 29.3 | 16 252 | 19.7 | 2 269 | 2 791 | 8 805 | 0 |
| District 3 | 281 542 | 2.41 | 63.0 | 50.6 | 8.2 | 28.5 | 32 501 | 15.5 | 6 311 | 3 325 | 18 297 | 122 |
| District 4 | 277 680 | 2.51 | 56.0 | 30.7 | 19.4 | 35.8 | 19 762 | 17.5 | 2 539 | 3 173 | 9 814 | 0 |
| District 5 | 286 664 | 2.44 | 66.0 | 53.6 | 8.7 | 28.5 | 15 298 | 33.1 | 1 490 | 4 832 | 5 703 | 0 |
| District 6 | 283 306 | 2.42 | 65.6 | 53.1 | 8.4 | 28.4 | 26 096 | 20.2 | 12 174 | 5 078 | 6 097 | 0 |
| District 7 | 294 430 | 2.38 | 66.8 | 54.8 | 8.2 | 27.5 | 11 805 | 42.6 | 3 541 | 5 073 | 1 198 | 0 |
| District 8 | 285 489 | 2.46 | 67.1 | 54.7 | 8.3 | 27.4 | 14 234 | 31.5 | 3 055 | 4 742 | 4 491 | 10 |
| WYOMING | 222 539 | 2.49 | 64.1 | 51.4 | 8.7 | 27.0 | 13 712 | 18.4 | 3 576 | 2 450 | 4 443 | 503 |
| At Large | 222 539 | 2.49 | 64.1 | 51.4 | 8.7 | 27.0 | 13 712 | 18.4 | 3 576 | 2 450 | 4 443 | 503 |

1. No spouse present.

# Table E. Congressional Districts 113th Congress — Housing and Money Income

| STATE District | Housing units, 2011 | | | | | | Money income, 2011 | | |
|---|---|---|---|---|---|---|---|---|---|
| | | Occupied units | | | | | | Households | |
| | | | Owner-occupied | | | Renter-occupied | | | |
| | Total | Percent Occupied | Percent | Median value¹ (dollars) | Percent valued at $500,000 or more | Median rent² | Per capita income (dollars) | Median income (dollars) | Percent with income of $100,000 or more |
| | 40 | 41 | 42 | 43 | 44 | 45 | 46 | 47 | 48 |
| TEXAS—Cont'd | | | | | | | | | |
| District 25 | 289 282 | 86.8 | 68.0 | 173 300 | 11.2 | 892 | 30 347 | 57 538 | 25.7 |
| District 26 | 265 308 | 92.4 | 71.5 | 177 600 | 4.1 | 957 | 31 891 | 75 069 | 35.9 |
| District 27 | 303 599 | 81.9 | 64.6 | 105 900 | 2.8 | 784 | 22 579 | 45 011 | 16.3 |
| District 28 | 235 109 | 86.7 | 69.4 | 101 400 | 2.5 | 745 | 15 602 | 39 603 | 12.0 |
| District 29 | 235 595 | 87.4 | 54.1 | 90 000 | 0.4 | 714 | 14 552 | 36 490 | 9.0 |
| District 30 | 269 469 | 88.6 | 55.2 | 98 900 | 1.0 | 821 | 19 040 | 40 107 | 12.1 |
| District 31 | 285 200 | 87.1 | 62.5 | 164 200 | 1.9 | 911 | 26 956 | 58 960 | 24.8 |
| District 32 | 292 556 | 90.2 | 57.8 | 170 700 | 12.7 | 931 | 35 362 | 61 356 | 28.6 |
| District 33 | 239 749 | 89.0 | 50.1 | 81 700 | 0.5 | 717 | 13 355 | 32 316 | 5.7 |
| District 34 | 251 253 | 81.8 | 67.9 | 74 700 | 1.5 | 642 | 14 814 | 32 333 | 10.2 |
| District 35 | 271 147 | 89.2 | 51.6 | 102 000 | 0.7 | 787 | 17 245 | 36 792 | 9.8 |
| District 36 | 290 601 | 86.5 | 73.6 | 111 300 | 2.2 | 784 | 24 415 | 50 790 | 20.0 |
| UTAH | 993 125 | 89.0 | 69.4 | 207 500 | 6.2 | 822 | 22 497 | 55 869 | 19.7 |
| District 1 | 261 782 | 85.9 | 74.2 | 188 200 | 5.9 | 751 | 23 381 | 56 973 | 20.8 |
| District 2 | 268 815 | 86.4 | 65.5 | 194 500 | 6.1 | 777 | 22 382 | 49 178 | 16.8 |
| District 3 | 229 145 | 90.8 | 68.2 | 237 300 | 9.3 | 837 | 22 563 | 59 687 | 22.8 |
| District 4 | 233 383 | 93.9 | 69.7 | 213 600 | 3.7 | 885 | 21 665 | 57 124 | 18.8 |
| VERMONT | 324 385 | 79.3 | 71.3 | 213 700 | 6.9 | 849 | 28 089 | 52 776 | 18.8 |
| At Large | 324 385 | 79.3 | 71.3 | 213 700 | 6.9 | 849 | 28 089 | 52 776 | 18.8 |
| VIRGINIA | 3 387 801 | 88.3 | 67.3 | 243 100 | 15.3 | 1 062 | 32 123 | 61 882 | 28.5 |
| District 1 | 298 096 | 88.1 | 72.9 | 277 200 | 11.5 | 1 201 | 33 247 | 74 283 | 34.6 |
| District 2 | 302 721 | 88.0 | 63.6 | 244 300 | 9.4 | 1 107 | 29 328 | 60 101 | 23.9 |
| District 3 | 322 329 | 86.1 | 51.2 | 172 600 | 3.2 | 866 | 21 219 | 40 304 | 11.1 |
| District 4 | 286 551 | 88.5 | 72.1 | 220 600 | 4.1 | 1 010 | 26 012 | 59 061 | 24.1 |
| District 5 | 343 029 | 81.3 | 72.8 | 176 200 | 9.0 | 780 | 25 153 | 48 187 | 17.8 |
| District 6 | 325 944 | 86.7 | 68.9 | 178 900 | 4.9 | 716 | 23 931 | 46 350 | 14.5 |
| District 7 | 300 417 | 91.3 | 73.7 | 244 900 | 8.9 | 1 034 | 33 029 | 68 596 | 30.0 |
| District 8 | 326 545 | 90.4 | 52.4 | 471 100 | 45.9 | 1 516 | 49 671 | 91 027 | 45.5 |
| District 9 | 343 867 | 84.0 | 70.6 | 114 600 | 3.2 | 610 | 21 055 | 36 634 | 9.9 |
| District 10 | 262 768 | 94.5 | 79.0 | 419 500 | 39.1 | 1 384 | 46 752 | 109 505 | 55.6 |
| District 11 | 275 534 | 95.2 | 66.1 | 409 600 | 33.4 | 1 571 | 43 102 | 100 146 | 50.1 |
| WASHINGTON | 2 907 605 | 90.5 | 62.8 | 256 300 | 13.3 | 930 | 29 278 | 56 835 | 23.3 |
| District 1 | 283 754 | 90.5 | 72.7 | 338 900 | 20.3 | 1 171 | 37 164 | 77 382 | 35.7 |
| District 2 | 299 879 | 89.6 | 59.6 | 268 200 | 11.6 | 995 | 27 961 | 54 964 | 20.7 |
| District 3 | 286 394 | 90.8 | 66.8 | 210 500 | 5.1 | 847 | 25 378 | 51 366 | 18.4 |
| District 4 | 256 063 | 90.4 | 64.1 | 166 600 | 3.2 | 723 | 20 979 | 47 594 | 16.3 |
| District 5 | 296 219 | 90.1 | 64.6 | 183 900 | 4.8 | 707 | 23 523 | 45 714 | 14.5 |
| District 6 | 313 562 | 86.2 | 65.8 | 240 200 | 12.3 | 894 | 28 454 | 51 982 | 19.6 |
| District 7 | 335 347 | 92.4 | 49.5 | 397 700 | 33.4 | 1 030 | 40 149 | 61 747 | 30.0 |
| District 8 | 277 489 | 90.0 | 73.6 | 281 300 | 14.9 | 992 | 31 228 | 67 046 | 30.6 |
| District 9 | 279 482 | 93.6 | 54.5 | 322 800 | 22.4 | 1 029 | 32 246 | 62 381 | 27.4 |
| District 10 | 279 416 | 92.0 | 60.2 | 232 200 | 5.3 | 942 | 25 621 | 54 917 | 19.0 |
| WEST VIRGINIA | 881 821 | 83.4 | 72.3 | 99 300 | 1.9 | 599 | 22 060 | 38 482 | 12.4 |
| District 1 | 288 326 | 83.6 | 72.1 | 99 000 | 2.0 | 584 | 21 888 | 39 170 | 13.2 |
| District 2 | 294 139 | 84.6 | 71.2 | 122 700 | 2.3 | 662 | 24 153 | 41 260 | 14.2 |
| District 3 | 299 356 | 81.9 | 73.4 | 83 000 | 1.4 | 554 | 20 099 | 34 826 | 9.8 |
| WISCONSIN | 2 634 806 | 86.4 | 67.9 | 166 700 | 3.6 | 739 | 26 212 | 50 395 | 17.3 |
| District 1 | 302 631 | 89.4 | 70.8 | 190 500 | 3.5 | 809 | 27 521 | 56 022 | 22.4 |
| District 2 | 317 169 | 93.2 | 63.0 | 199 300 | 5.3 | 843 | 29 715 | 56 089 | 21.4 |
| District 3 | 318 540 | 88.4 | 69.2 | 141 600 | 2.6 | 678 | 23 385 | 46 448 | 13.4 |
| District 4 | 314 001 | 88.4 | 46.2 | 144 500 | 2.1 | 741 | 20 339 | 35 729 | 11.4 |
| District 5 | 306 464 | 93.5 | 70.3 | 213 600 | 5.8 | 843 | 31 576 | 61 272 | 23.9 |
| District 6 | 320 548 | 88.4 | 72.4 | 156 500 | 3.9 | 646 | 27 586 | 51 995 | 16.9 |
| District 7 | 414 749 | 71.0 | 76.7 | 144 500 | 2.8 | 634 | 23 994 | 45 868 | 12.7 |
| District 8 | 340 704 | 83.8 | 73.8 | 152 100 | 2.6 | 651 | 25 580 | 51 914 | 15.8 |
| WYOMING | 265 554 | 83.8 | 70.6 | 179 900 | 4.8 | 759 | 27 973 | 56 322 | 20.7 |
| At Large | 265 554 | 83.8 | 70.6 | 179 900 | 4.8 | 759 | 27 973 | 56 322 | 20.7 |

1. Specified owner-occupied units.    2. Specified renter-occupied units.

| STATE District | Poverty, 2011 (percent) | | | Civilian labor force, 2011 | | | Civilian employment,[2] 2011 | | | | Persons under age 65 with no health insurance, 2010 (percent) | Social Security beneficiaries, December 2012 | | Supplemental Security Income recipients, December 2012 |
|---|---|---|---|---|---|---|---|---|---|---|---|---|---|---|
| | | | | | Unemployment | | | Percent | | | | | | |
| | Persons below poverty level | Families below poverty level | Households receiving food stamps in past 12 months | Total | Total | Rate[1] | Total | Management, professional, and related occupations | Service, sales, and office | Construction and production | | Number | Rate[3] | |
| | 49 | 50 | 51 | 52 | 53 | 54 | 55 | 56 | 57 | 58 | 59 | 60 | 61 | 62 |
| TEXAS—Cont'd | | | | | | | | | | | | | | |
| District 25 | 13.9 | 9.7 | 10.9 | 330 791 | 28 594 | 8.6 | 302 197 | 42.2 | 39.5 | 18.2 | 17.7 | 109 906 | 153.8 | 11 322 |
| District 26 | 9.1 | 5.3 | 5.1 | 398 006 | 29 742 | 7.5 | 368 264 | 43.8 | 38.8 | 15.2 | 13.3 | 75 768 | 104.8 | 5 762 |
| District 27 | 19.2 | 15.0 | 17.3 | 334 227 | 28 674 | 8.6 | 305 553 | 28.6 | 46.9 | 26.1 | 25.1 | 130 245 | 185.6 | 23 471 |
| District 28 | 29.8 | 25.2 | 28.1 | 288 837 | 22 501 | 7.8 | 266 336 | 26.0 | 42.7 | 25.4 | 34.0 | 100 707 | 141.8 | 31 187 |
| District 29 | 27.1 | 23.5 | 20.5 | 328 335 | 35 478 | 10.8 | 292 857 | 15.8 | 42.2 | 41.1 | 38.7 | 70 446 | 98.1 | 20 300 |
| District 30 | 23.4 | 19.8 | 18.0 | 331 168 | 38 838 | 11.7 | 292 330 | 29.5 | 41.8 | 27.5 | 32.5 | 94 449 | 136.0 | 29 367 |
| District 31 | 10.3 | 7.6 | 8.3 | 356 478 | 33 480 | 9.4 | 322 998 | 40.7 | 42.9 | 18.0 | 17.6 | 96 346 | 133.5 | 10 585 |
| District 32 | 14.9 | 11.2 | 8.4 | 394 375 | 33 458 | 8.5 | 360 917 | 41.4 | 44.3 | 16.7 | 23.5 | 88 614 | 124.5 | 11 219 |
| District 33 | 30.7 | 27.5 | 23.6 | 327 481 | 43 613 | 13.3 | 283 868 | 14.3 | 41.6 | 41.2 | 41.1 | 74 218 | 104.4 | 22 503 |
| District 34 | 33.0 | 27.8 | 27.6 | 271 325 | 29 129 | 10.7 | 242 196 | 26.8 | 39.5 | 25.3 | 35.4 | 107 541 | 153.1 | 37 934 |
| District 35 | 25.1 | 20.6 | 22.4 | 356 365 | 38 118 | 10.7 | 318 247 | 24.6 | 38.8 | 25.4 | 28.5 | 92 653 | 127.9 | 26 050 |
| District 36 | 15.5 | 11.8 | 13.0 | 327 918 | 36 031 | 11.0 | 291 887 | 30.9 | 46.9 | 30.0 | 25.3 | 121 457 | 170.5 | 16 787 |
| UTAH | 13.5 | 10.4 | 9.9 | 1 370 085 | 109 279 | 8.0 | 1 260 806 | 36.0 | 42.5 | 21.5 | 16.7 | 346 962 | 123.2 | 30 747 |
| District 1 | 11.0 | 8.1 | 10.0 | 336 978 | 24 558 | 7.3 | 312 420 | 34.6 | 41.3 | 24.1 | 14.3 | 83 247 | 118.9 | 7 325 |
| District 2 | 17.3 | 12.5 | 11.4 | 338 816 | 33 106 | 9.8 | 305 710 | 35.5 | 42.6 | 21.9 | 20.0 | 102 733 | 145.6 | 9 120 |
| District 3 | 13.3 | 10.6 | 8.6 | 336 800 | 25 610 | 7.6 | 311 190 | 39.8 | 42.7 | 17.5 | 15.2 | 82 507 | 116.4 | 6 666 |
| District 4 | 12.5 | 10.6 | 9.4 | 357 491 | 26 005 | 7.3 | 331 486 | 34.2 | 43.1 | 22.7 | 17.5 | 78 475 | 111.7 | 7 636 |
| VERMONT | 11.5 | 6.9 | 13.7 | 349 718 | 22 416 | 6.4 | 327 302 | 40.5 | 38.5 | 21.0 | 7.7 | 135 597 | 216.5 | 15 889 |
| At Large | 11.5 | 6.9 | 13.7 | 349 718 | 22 416 | 6.4 | 327 302 | 40.5 | 38.5 | 21.0 | 7.7 | 135 597 | 216.5 | 15 889 |
| VIRGINIA | 11.5 | 8.2 | 9.6 | 4 175 698 | 315 567 | 7.6 | 3 860 131 | 42.3 | 39.8 | 17.9 | 14.1 | 1 353 676 | 167.2 | 153 267 |
| District 1 | 7.8 | 5.8 | 6.6 | 377 673 | 25 259 | 6.7 | 352 414 | 41.1 | 41.4 | 17.5 | 11.2 | 117 179 | 157.5 | 8 053 |
| District 2 | 10.2 | 7.4 | 7.6 | 366 101 | 26 325 | 7.2 | 339 776 | 39.0 | 42.8 | 18.2 | 14.1 | 107 950 | 151.9 | 10 339 |
| District 3 | 22.0 | 18.0 | 18.9 | 368 418 | 48 308 | 13.1 | 320 110 | 29.1 | 48.1 | 22.8 | 18.7 | 128 049 | 172.0 | 29 848 |
| District 4 | 10.2 | 8.0 | 11.9 | 361 726 | 33 855 | 9.4 | 327 871 | 35.0 | 42.1 | 22.9 | 13.3 | 127 089 | 172.4 | 14 934 |
| District 5 | 15.7 | 10.6 | 12.9 | 346 171 | 30 071 | 8.7 | 316 100 | 35.6 | 40.2 | 24.2 | 15.3 | 169 570 | 233.4 | 19 040 |
| District 6 | 14.3 | 9.8 | 11.4 | 366 459 | 26 610 | 7.3 | 339 849 | 32.9 | 44.5 | 22.6 | 15.4 | 157 986 | 215.2 | 15 895 |
| District 7 | 7.7 | 5.1 | 6.1 | 389 827 | 25 227 | 6.5 | 364 600 | 45.4 | 39.5 | 15.2 | 11.6 | 126 603 | 172.5 | 7 983 |
| District 8 | 7.9 | 5.4 | 4.2 | 446 093 | 22 416 | 5.0 | 423 677 | 58.9 | 31.5 | 9.6 | 15.5 | 70 711 | 95.2 | 7 702 |
| District 9 | 19.1 | 12.4 | 16.3 | 328 615 | 30 188 | 9.2 | 298 427 | 31.5 | 41.6 | 26.9 | 15.7 | 194 369 | 267.8 | 25 958 |
| District 10 | 5.8 | 3.9 | 3.9 | 398 557 | 22 125 | 5.6 | 376 432 | 54.5 | 33.6 | 11.9 | 10.7 | 82 613 | 110.0 | 5 733 |
| District 11 | 7.1 | 5.1 | 5.1 | 426 058 | 25 183 | 5.9 | 400 875 | 51.9 | 37.3 | 10.8 | 14.1 | 71 557 | 95.8 | 7 782 |
| WASHINGTON | 13.9 | 9.4 | 14.5 | 3 477 743 | 359 745 | 10.3 | 3 117 998 | 38.5 | 41.1 | 20.5 | 16.1 | 1 164 420 | 170.5 | 147 491 |
| District 1 | 8.1 | 5.5 | 8.7 | 364 877 | 32 566 | 8.9 | 332 311 | 44.8 | 37.7 | 17.5 | 11.8 | 102 238 | 148.9 | 8 460.0 |
| District 2 | 14.2 | 9.4 | 14.6 | 358 128 | 39 276 | 11.0 | 318 852 | 34.0 | 45.1 | 20.9 | 17.2 | 118 321 | 174.5 | 13 302.0 |
| District 3 | 14.7 | 11.3 | 19.0 | 324 471 | 39 926 | 12.3 | 284 545 | 33.1 | 41.4 | 25.5 | 16.3 | 139 231 | 204.5 | 16 491.0 |
| District 4 | 20.1 | 14.9 | 19.7 | 315 383 | 30 880 | 9.8 | 284 503 | 29.9 | 36.9 | 33.2 | 23.5 | 113 142 | 163.9 | 17 043.0 |
| District 5 | 17.0 | 10.9 | 17.6 | 327 044 | 35 505 | 10.9 | 291 539 | 37.5 | 44.0 | 18.5 | 15.6 | 134 173 | 198.5 | 18 460.0 |
| District 6 | 12.7 | 8.1 | 14.2 | 316 199 | 40 666 | 12.9 | 275 533 | 35.1 | 44.1 | 20.8 | 16.7 | 148 027 | 219.4 | 18 163.0 |
| District 7 | 13.0 | 6.5 | 9.9 | 408 824 | 28 800 | 7.0 | 380 024 | 53.0 | 36.4 | 10.6 | 12.9 | 99 987 | 146.4 | 12 811.0 |
| District 8 | 10.9 | 6.6 | 10.5 | 350 406 | 32 409 | 9.2 | 317 997 | 38.3 | 39.2 | 22.5 | 13.2 | 97 901 | 143.7 | 8 675.0 |
| District 9 | 14.7 | 10.9 | 16.2 | 381 417 | 39 982 | 10.5 | 341 435 | 39.7 | 42.9 | 17.5 | 18.4 | 95 787 | 138.1 | 18 661.0 |
| District 10 | 13.6 | 10.6 | 15.9 | 330 994 | 39 735 | 12.0 | 291 259 | 33.7 | 44.9 | 21.5 | 15.5 | 115 613 | 168.7 | 15 425.0 |
| WEST VIRGINIA | 18.6 | 13.7 | 16.0 | 821 367 | 72 809 | 8.9 | 748 558 | 32.0 | 42.6 | 25.3 | 17.7 | 455 810 | 245.7 | 80 089 |
| District 1 | 17.6 | 12.1 | 13.6 | 282 334 | 23 653 | 8.4 | 258 681 | 32.2 | 42.3 | 25.5 | 16.6 | 143 169 | 233.1 | 21 179 |
| District 2 | 17.6 | 12.8 | 13.9 | 295 760 | 28 892 | 9.8 | 266 868 | 32.7 | 44.1 | 23.3 | 18.6 | 146 747 | 234.2 | 22 033 |
| District 3 | 20.5 | 16.0 | 20.6 | 243 273 | 20 264 | 8.3 | 223 009 | 31.1 | 41.3 | 27.6 | 17.9 | 165 894 | 269.9 | 36 877 |
| WISCONSIN | 13.1 | 8.8 | 12.7 | 3 070 131 | 250 654 | 8.2 | 2 819 477 | 33.5 | 40.8 | 25.8 | 10.3 | 1 110 161 | 194.4 | 114 135 |
| District 1 | 10.9 | 7.8 | 13.0 | 379 201 | 36 722 | 9.7 | 342 479 | 34.0 | 40.5 | 25.6 | 9.8 | 135 745 | 191.1 | 12 713 |
| District 2 | 13.2 | 8.6 | 10.9 | 417 362 | 27 346 | 6.6 | 390 016 | 41.7 | 39.8 | 18.5 | 8.2 | 118 837 | 165.0 | 11 237 |
| District 3 | 14.6 | 8.4 | 12.0 | 380 003 | 26 463 | 7.0 | 353 540 | 30.4 | 41.3 | 28.3 | 11.1 | 147 217 | 207.1 | 12 597 |
| District 4 | 26.2 | 21.9 | 26.3 | 359 881 | 51 898 | 14.4 | 307 983 | 32.8 | 45.6 | 21.5 | 15.9 | 112 982 | 157.8 | 38 476 |
| District 5 | 7.8 | 4.9 | 8.3 | 396 233 | 25 595 | 6.5 | 370 638 | 37.1 | 40.6 | 22.3 | 6.6 | 137 750 | 193.1 | 6 812 |
| District 6 | 9.6 | 6.1 | 10.5 | 380 215 | 26 621 | 7.0 | 353 594 | 30.3 | 39.5 | 30.2 | 9.1 | 148 010 | 208.6 | 9 409 |
| District 7 | 12.4 | 8.5 | 11.8 | 367 847 | 29 465 | 8.0 | 338 382 | 30.3 | 38.9 | 30.8 | 12.0 | 167 765 | 235.1 | 12 190 |
| District 8 | 9.8 | 6.8 | 9.7 | 389 389 | 26 544 | 6.8 | 362 845 | 30.3 | 40.3 | 29.4 | 9.7 | 141 855 | 197.5 | 10 701.0 |
| WYOMING | 11.3 | 7.9 | 5.9 | 305 529 | 15 553 | 5.1 | 289 976 | 31.3 | 39.7 | 29.0 | 17.5 | 96 294 | 169.5 | 6 708.0 |
| At Large | 11.3 | 7.9 | 5.9 | 305 529 | 15 553 | 5.1 | 289 976 | 31.3 | 39.7 | 29.0 | 17.5 | 96 294 | 169.5 | 6 708.0 |

1. Percent of civilian labor force.    2. Persons 16 years old and over.    3. Per 1,000 resident population estimated in the 2011 American Community Survey.

# APPENDIX A
# GEOGRAPHIC CONCEPTS AND CODES

## GEOGRAPHIC AREAS COVERED

*County and City Extra* presents data for states (Table A), states and counties (Table B), metropolitan areas (Table C), cities with populations of 25,000 or more in 2010 (Table D), and congressional districts (Table E).

## STATES AND COUNTIES

Data are presented for each of the 50 states, the District of Columbia, and the United States as a whole. The states are arranged alphabetically and counties in Table B are arranged alphabetically within each state. Data are presented for 3,143 counties and county equivalents.

## County equivalents

In Louisiana, the primary divisions of the state are known as parishes rather than counties. In Alaska, the county equivalents are the organized boroughs, together with the census areas that were developed for general statistical purposes by the state of Alaska and the U.S. Census Bureau. Four states—Maryland, Missouri, Nevada, and Virginia—have one or more incorporated places that are legally independent of any county and thus constitute primary divisions of their states. Within each state, independent cities are listed alphabetically following the list of counties. The District of Columbia is not divided into counties or county equivalents—data for the entire district are presented as a county equivalent. New York City contains five counties: Bronx, Kings, New York, Queens, and Richmond.

## County changes since the 2000 census

- Broomfield County, CO, was created from parts of Adams, Boulder, Jefferson, and Weld Counties, effective November 15, 2001. The boundaries of Broomfield County reflect the boundaries of Broomfield city legally in effect on that date.
- Clifton Forge city, VA, formerly an independent city, became a town within Alleghany County, effective July 1, 2001.
- Effective June 20, 2007, the Skagway-Hoonah-Angoon Census Area in Alaska was divided into the Skagway Municipality and the Hoonah-Angoon Census Area.
- In May and June, 2008, the Wrangell-Petersburg and Prince of Wales-Outer Ketchikan Census Areas were dissolved and replaced by Wrangell City and Borough, Petersburg Census Area, and Prince of Wales Census Area. Some territory from the Prince of Wales Outer Ketchikan Census Area became part of the existing Ketchikan Gateway Borough.

## METROPOLITAN AREAS

Table C presents data for 366 metropolitan statistical areas and 29 metropolitan divisions, which are located within the 11 largest metropolitan statistical areas. The metropolitan statistical areas are listed alphabetically, and the metropolitan divisions are listed alphabetically under the metropolitan statistical area of which they are components.

The U.S. Office of Management and Budget (OMB) defines metropolitan and micropolitan statistical areas according to published standards. The major purpose of defining these areas is to enable all U.S. government agencies to use the same geographic definitions in tabulating and publishing data. The general concept of a metropolitan or micropolitan statistical area is that of a core area containing a substantial population nucleus, together with adjacent communities that have a high degree of economic and social integration with the core. Currently defined metropolitan and micropolitan statistical areas are based on application of the new 2000 standards to 2000 decennial census data. Current metropolitan and micropolitan statistical area definitions were announced by OMB effective December 1, 2009.

New delineations based on the 2010 census were released in February 2013. In the next few years, federal agencies will begin to use these new definitions of metropolitan and micropolitan areas, but Table C in this book continues to use the 2009 definitions. Appendix C, however, lists the new metropolitan and micropolitan areas, together with their 2010 census populations and their 2012 estimated populations.

Standard definitions of metropolitan areas were first issued in 1949 by the Bureau of the Budget (the predecessor of OMB), under the designation "standard metropolitan area" (SMA). The term was changed to "standard metropolitan statistical area" (SMSA) in 1959, and to "metropolitan statistical area" (MSA) in 1983. The term "metropolitan area" (MA) was adopted in 1990 and referred collectively to metropolitan statistical areas (MSAs), consolidated metropolitan statistical areas (CMSAs), and primary metropolitan statistical areas (PMSAs). The term "core based statistical area" (CBSA) became effective in 2000 and refers collectively to metropolitan and micropolitan statistical areas.

The 2000 standards provide that each CBSA must contain at least one urban area of 10,000 or more population. Each metropolitan statistical area must have at least one urbanized area of 50,000 or more inhabitants. Each micropolitan statistical area must have at least one urban cluster of at least 10,000 but less than 50,000 people.

Under the standards, the county (or counties) in which at least 50 percent of the population resides within urban areas of 10,000 or more population, or that contain at least 5,000 people residing within a single urban area of 10,000 or more population, is identified as a "central county" (counties). Additional "outlying counties" are included in the CBSA if they meet specified requirements of commuting to or from the central counties. Counties or equivalent entities form the geographic "building blocks" for metropolitan and micropolitan statistical areas throughout the United States.

If specified criteria are met, a metropolitan statistical area containing a single core with a population of 2.5 million or more may be subdivided to form smaller groupings of counties referred to as "metropolitan divisions."

As of December 1, 2009, there were 366 metropolitan statistical areas and 576 micropolitan statistical areas in the United States. Table C includes the 366 metropolitan statistical areas and the 29 metropolitan divisions. The metropolitan areas and metropolitan divisions (as of December 2009) are listed in Appendix B with their 2010 census population counts. Under the new 2013 delineations, there are 381 metropolitan statistical areas, 31 metropolitan divisions, and 536 micropolitan areas. These are listed in Appendix C with their 2010 census populations and their 2012 estimated popualations.

The largest city in each metropolitan or micropolitan statistical area is designated a "principal city." Additional cities qualify if specified requirements are met concerning population size and employment. The title of each metropolitan or micropolitan statistical area consists of the names of up to three of its principal cities and the name of each state into which the metropolitan or micropolitan statistical area extends. Titles of metropolitan divisions also typically are based on principal city names, but in certain cases consist of county names. The principal city need not be an incorporated place if it meets the requirements of population size and employment. Usually such a principal city is a census designated place in decennial census data, but it is not included in most other data sources and is not in Table D (cities) in this volume.

In view of the importance of cities and towns in New England, the 2000 and 2010 standards also provide for a set of geographic areas that are defined using cities and towns in the six New England states. These New England city and town areas (NECTAs) are not included in this volume.

Appendix B lists the 366 metropolitan statistical areas, together with their component metropolitan divisions, where appropriate, the component counties of each area, and their 2010 census populations Appendix C provides the same information for the 381 newly delineated 2013 metropolitan areas and it also includes the 536 new micropolitan statistical areas. Maps showing the metropolitan and micropolitan areas within each state can be found in Appendix D.

## CITIES

Table D presents data for 1,436 cities with 2010 census populations of 25,000 or more. Corresponding data for states are also provided. The states are arranged alphabetically and the cities are ordered alphabetically within each state.

As used in this volume, the term *city* refers to places that have been incorporated as cities, boroughs, towns, or villages under the laws of their respective states. Towns in the New England states and New York are treated as minor civil divisions (MCDs) and are not included in the cities database. For Hawaii, data for the census designated places (CDPs) are included in the cities table, since the Census Bureau does not recognize any incorporated places in Hawaii. CDPs are delineated by the Census Bureau, in cooperation with states and localities, as statistical counterparts of incorporated places for purposes of the decennial census. CDPs comprise densely settled concentrations of population that are identifiable by name but are not legally incorporated as places.

Appendix E lists the 1,436 cities followed by the county where each city is located. If a city includes portions of more than one county, the population in each part is specified.

A consolidated city is an incorporated place that has combined its government functions with a county or subcounty entity but contains one or more other semi-independent incorporated places that continue to function as local governments within the consolidated government. Each consolidated city contains a core city, the area of a consolidated city not included in another separately incorporated place. The census geographic term for this core is the "balance" of the consolidated city. Thus the "balance" is essentially the core city of the consolidated government. This volume includes the consolidated city data where possible, but some data sources include numbers only for the "balance" and others do not specify which entity is represented.

Consolidated cities included in this volume are Milford, CT; Athens-Clarke County, GA; Augusta-Richmond County, GA; Indianapolis, IN; Louisville-Jefferson County, KY; Butte-Silver Bow, MT; and Nashville-Davidson, TN.

Appendix E lists these seven consolidated cities, followed by the component places and their 2010 census populations.

## CONGRESSIONAL DISTRICTS

The congressional districts shown in this volume are the districts used for the election of the 113th Congress, which convened in January 2013. These are the districts that were established following the 2010 Census and are based on population data from that census. Data are shown for the 435 regular districts plus the District of Columbia, which has a non-voting delegate, but no representative. Corresponding data for each state also are included. States are listed alphabetically and districts numerically within each state. A map showing congressional districts for the 113th Congress is included in Appendix D.

## GEOGRAPHIC CODES

Tables A, B, C, and D provide, in one or more columns at the beginning of the table, a geographic code or codes for each area.

In Table B (states and counties), a five-digit state and county code is given for each state and county. The first two digits indicate the state; the remaining three represent the county. Within each state, the counties are listed in order, beginning with 001, with even numbers usually omitted. Independent cities follow the counties and begin with the number 510. In the second column of Table B, a five-digit core based statistical area (CBSA) code is given for those counties that are within metropolitan and micropolitan areas. In Table A, a two-digit state code is provided. The state code is a sequential numbering, with some gaps, of the states and the District of Columbia in alphabetical order from Alabama (01) to Wyoming (56).

These codes have been established by the U.S. government as Federal Information Processing Standards and are often referred to as *FIPS codes*. They are used by U.S. government agencies and many other organizations for data presentation. The codes are provided in this volume for use in matching the data given here with other data sources in which counties are identified by FIPS code. The metro area codes will also enable the user to identify the metro area of which a county is a component. Table C (metropolitan areas) provides the same metro area codes for each metropolitan area, as well as metropolitan division codes where appropriate.

Table D (cities) provides, in the first column, a seven-digit state and place code. The first two digits identify the state and are the same as the FIPS codes described above. The remaining five digits are the place FIPS codes established by the U.S. government.

## INDEPENDENT CITIES

The following independent cities are not included in any county; their data are presented separately in this volume.

### MARYLAND
Baltimore (separate from Baltimore County)

### MISSOURI
St. Louis (separate from St. Louis County)

### NEVADA
Carson City

### VIRGINIA

| | |
|---|---|
| Alexandria | Manassas |
| Bedford | Manassas Park |
| Bristol | Martinsville |
| Buena Vista | Newport News |
| Charlottesville | Norfolk |
| Chesapeake | Norton |
| Colonial Heights | Petersburg |
| Covington | Poquoson |
| Danville | Portsmouth |
| Emporia | Radford |
| Fairfax | Richmond |
| Falls Church | Roanoke |
| Franklin | Salem |
| Fredericksburg | Staunton |
| Galax | Suffolk |
| Hampton | Virginia Beach |
| Harrisonburg | Waynesboro |
| Hopewell | Williamsburg |
| Lexington | Winchester |
| Lynchburg | |

## COUNTY TYPE

Table B (states and counties) provides, in the third column, a *county type* code that identifies each county by its metropolitan/nonmetropolitan status and its size. These are the "rural-urban continuum codes" developed by the Economic Research Service of the U.S. Department of Agriculture.

The 2003 rural-urban continuum codes form a classification scheme that distinguishes metropolitan counties by size and non-metropolitan counties by degree of urbanization and proximity to metro areas. The standard OMB metro and nonmetro categories have been subdivided into three metro and six nonmetro categories, resulting in a nine-part county codification. This scheme was originally developed in 1974. The codes were updated in 1983 and 1993, and slightly revised in 1988. The 1988 revision was first published in 1990. This scheme allows researchers to break county data into finer residential groups, beyond metro and nonmetro, particularly for the analysis of trends in nonmetro areas that are related to population density and metro influence. The 2003 rural-urban continuum codes are not directly comparable with the codes from previous years because of the new methodology used in developing the 2003 metropolitan areas.

### Metropolitan counties
1. Counties in metro areas of 1 million population or more.
2. Counties in metro areas of 250,000 to 1 million population.
3. Counties in metro areas of fewer than 250,000 population.

### Nonmetropolitan counties
4. Urban population of 20,000 or more, adjacent to a metro area.
5. Urban population of 20,000 or more, not adjacent to a metro area.
6. Urban population of 2,500 to 19,999, adjacent to a metro area.
7. Urban population of 2,500 to 19,999, not adjacent to a metro area.
8. Completely rural or less than 2,500 urban population, adjacent to a metro area.
9. Completely rural or less than 2,500 urban population, not adjacent to a metro area.

# APPENDIX B
# METROPOLITAN STATISTICAL AREAS, METROPOLITAN DIVISIONS, AND COMPONENTS
## (as defined December 2009)

| Core based statistical area | State/ County FIPS code | Title and Geographic Components | 2010 Census Population | Core based statistical area | State/ County FIPS code | Title and Geographic Components | 2010 Census Population |
|---|---|---|---|---|---|---|---|
| 10180 | | Abilene, TX Metro SA ............................ | 165 252 | 11500 | | Anniston-Oxford, AL Metro SA...................... | 118 572 |
| | 48 059 | Callahan County, TX.......................... | 13 544 | | 01 015 | Calhoun County, AL .................................... | 118 572 |
| | 48 253 | Jones County, TX............................... | 20 202 | | | | |
| | 48 441 | Taylor County, TX.............................. | 131 506 | 11540 | | Appleton, WI Metro SA ............................ | 225 666 |
| | | | | | 55 015 | Calumet County, WI........................... | 48 971 |
| 10420 | | Akron, OH Metro SA ............................ | 703 200 | | 55 087 | Outagamie County, WI........................ | 176 695 |
| | 39 133 | Portage County, OH........................... | 161 419 | | | | |
| | 39 153 | Summit County, OH............................ | 541 781 | 11700 | | Asheville, NC Metro SA ......................... | 424 858 |
| | | | | | 37 021 | Buncombe County, NC ........................ | 238 318 |
| 10500 | | Albany, GA Metro SA ............................ | 157 308 | | 37 087 | Haywood County, NC........................... | 59 036 |
| | 13 007 | Baker County, GA.............................. | 3 451 | | 37 089 | Henderson County, NC ....................... | 106 740 |
| | 13 095 | Dougherty County, GA ........................ | 94 565 | | 37 115 | Madison County, NC ........................... | 20 764 |
| | 13 177 | Lee County, GA................................. | 28 298 | | | | |
| | 13 273 | Terrell County, GA............................. | 9 315 | 12020 | | Athens-Clarke County, GA Metro SA ............. | 192 541 |
| | 13 321 | Worth County, GA.............................. | 21 679 | | 13 059 | Clarke County, GA............................. | 116 714 |
| | | | | | 13 195 | Madison County, GA .......................... | 28 120 |
| 10580 | | Albany-Schenectady-Troy, NY Metro SA......... | 870 716 | | 13 219 | Oconee County, GA ........................... | 32 808 |
| | 36 001 | Albany County, NY ............................ | 304 204 | | 13 221 | Oglethorpe County, GA ...................... | 14 899 |
| | 36 083 | Rensselaer County, NY ...................... | 159 429 | | | | |
| | 36 091 | Saratoga County, NY ......................... | 219 607 | 12060 | | Atlanta-Sandy Springs-Marietta, GA Metro SA | 5 268 860 |
| | 36 093 | Schenectady County, NY ..................... | 154 727 | | 13 013 | Barrow County, GA............................. | 69 367 |
| | 36 095 | Schoharie County, NY ........................ | 32 749 | | 13 015 | Bartow County, GA............................. | 100 157 |
| | | | | | 13 035 | Butts County, GA............................... | 23 655 |
| 10740 | | Albuquerque, NM Metro SA ...................... | 887 077 | | 13 045 | Carroll County, GA ............................ | 110 527 |
| | 35 001 | Bernalillo County, NM......................... | 662 564 | | 13 057 | Cherokee County, GA ......................... | 214 346 |
| | 35 043 | Sandoval County, NM.......................... | 131 561 | | 13 063 | Clayton County, GA ........................... | 259 424 |
| | 35 057 | Torrance County, NM.......................... | 16 383 | | 13 067 | Cobb County, GA............................... | 688 078 |
| | 35 061 | Valencia County, NM........................... | 76 569 | | 13 077 | Coweta County, GA............................ | 127 317 |
| | | | | | 13 085 | Dawson County, GA ........................... | 22 330 |
| 10780 | | Alexandria, LA Metro SA ......................... | 153 922 | | 13 089 | DeKalb County, GA ............................ | 691 893 |
| | 22 043 | Grant Parish, LA............................... | 22 309 | | 13 097 | Douglas County, GA ........................... | 132 403 |
| | 22 079 | Rapides Parish, LA............................ | 131 613 | | 13 113 | Fayette County, GA ........................... | 106 567 |
| | | | | | 13 117 | Forsyth County, GA ........................... | 175 511 |
| 10900 | | Allentown-Bethlehem-Easton, PA-NJ Metro SA .... | 821 173 | | 13 121 | Fulton County, GA............................. | 920 581 |
| | 34 041 | Warren County, NJ............................. | 108 692 | | 13 135 | Gwinnett County, GA .......................... | 805 321 |
| | 42 025 | Carbon County, PA............................. | 65 249 | | 13 143 | Haralson County, GA .......................... | 28 780 |
| | 42 077 | Lehigh County, PA............................. | 349 497 | | 13 149 | Heard County, GA ............................. | 11 834 |
| | 42 095 | Northampton County, PA...................... | 297 735 | | 13 151 | Henry County, GA ............................. | 203 922 |
| | | | | | 13 159 | Jasper County, GA ............................ | 13 900 |
| 11020 | | Altoona, PA Metro SA ............................ | 127 089 | | 13 171 | Lamar County, GA ............................ | 18 317 |
| | 42 013 | Blair County, PA ............................... | 127 089 | | 13 199 | Meriwether County, GA ....................... | 21 992 |
| | | | | | 13 217 | Newton County, GA ........................... | 99 958 |
| 11100 | | Amarillo, TX Metro SA ........................... | 249 881 | | 13 223 | Paulding County, GA .......................... | 142 324 |
| | 48 011 | Armstrong County, TX......................... | 1 901 | | 13 227 | Pickens County, GA ........................... | 29 431 |
| | 48 065 | Carson County, TX............................. | 6 182 | | 13 231 | Pike County, GA ............................... | 17 869 |
| | 48 375 | Potter County, TX.............................. | 121 073 | | 13 247 | Rockdale County, GA .......................... | 85 215 |
| | 48 381 | Randall County, TX............................ | 120 725 | | 13 255 | Spalding County, GA .......................... | 64 073 |
| | | | | | 13 297 | Walton County, GA ............................ | 83 768 |
| 11180 | | Ames, IA Metro SA ............................... | 89 542 | 12100 | | Atlantic City-Hammonton, NJ Metro SA........... | 274 549 |
| | 19 169 | Story County, IA ............................... | 89 542 | | 34 001 | Atlantic County, NJ............................ | 274 549 |
| | | | | | | | |
| 11260 | | Anchorage, AK Metro SA......................... | 380 821 | 12220 | | Auburn-Opelika, AL Metro SA...................... | 140 247 |
| | 02 020 | Anchorage Municipality, AK................... | 291 826 | | 01 081 | Lee County, AL................................. | 140 247 |
| | 02 170 | Matanuska-Susitna Borough, AK .............. | 88 995 | | | | |
| | | | | 12260 | | Augusta-Richmond County, GA-SC Metro SA | 556 877 |
| 11300 | | Anderson, IN Metro SA .......................... | 131 636 | | 13 033 | Burke County, GA.............................. | 23 316 |
| | 18 095 | Madison County, IN ........................... | 131 636 | | 13 073 | Columbia County, GA ......................... | 124 053 |
| | | | | | 13 189 | McDuffie County, GA .......................... | 21 875 |
| 11340 | | Anderson, SC Metro SA.......................... | 187 126 | | 13 245 | Richmond County, GA ......................... | 200 549 |
| | 45 007 | Anderson County, SC.......................... | 187 126 | | 45 003 | Aiken County, SC .............................. | 160 099 |
| | | | | | 45 037 | Edgefield County, SC ......................... | 26 985 |
| 11460 | | Ann Arbor, MI Metro SA.......................... | 344 791 | | | | |
| | 26 161 | Washtenaw County, MI ........................ | 344 791 | | | | |

# Metropolitan Statistical Areas, Metropolitan Divisions, and Components (as defined December 2009)–*Continued*

| Core based statistical area | State/County FIPS code | Title and Geographic Components | 2010 Census Population |
|---|---|---|---|
| 12420 | | Austin-Round Rock-San Marcos, TX Metro SA... | 1716 289 |
| | 48 021 | Bastrop County, TX | 74 171 |
| | 48 055 | Caldwell County, TX | 38 066 |
| | 48 209 | Hays County, TX | 157 107 |
| | 48 453 | Travis County, TX | 1024 266 |
| | 48 491 | Williamson County, TX | 422 679 |
| 12540 | | Bakersfield-Delano, CA Metro SA | 839 631 |
| | 06 029 | Kern County, CA | 839 631 |
| 12580 | | Baltimore-Towson, MD Metro SA | 2710 489 |
| | 24 003 | Anne Arundel County, MD | 537 656 |
| | 24 005 | Baltimore County, MD | 805 029 |
| | 24 013 | Carroll County, MD | 167 134 |
| | 24 025 | Harford County, MD | 244 826 |
| | 24 027 | Howard County, MD | 287 085 |
| | 24 035 | Queen Anne's County, MD | 47 798 |
| | 24 510 | Baltimore city, MD | 620 961 |
| 12620 | | Bangor, ME Metro SA | 153 923 |
| | 23 019 | Penobscot County, ME | 153 923 |
| 12700 | | Barnstable Town, MA Metro SA | 215 888 |
| | 25 001 | Barnstable County, MA | 215 888 |
| 12940 | | Baton Rouge, LA Metro SA | 802 484 |
| | 22 005 | Ascension Parish, LA | 107 215 |
| | 22 033 | East Baton Rouge Parish, LA | 440 171 |
| | 22 037 | East Feliciana Parish, LA | 20 267 |
| | 22 047 | Iberville Parish, LA | 33 387 |
| | 22 063 | Livingston Parish, LA | 128 026 |
| | 22 077 | Pointe Coupee Parish, LA | 22 802 |
| | 22 091 | St. Helena Parish, LA | 11 203 |
| | 22 121 | West Baton Rouge Parish, LA | 23 788 |
| | 22 125 | West Feliciana Parish, LA | 15 625 |
| 12980 | | Battle Creek, MI Metro SA | 136 146 |
| | 26 025 | Calhoun County, MI | 136 146 |
| 13020 | | Bay City, MI Metro SA | 107 771 |
| | 26 017 | Bay County, MI | 107 771 |
| 13140 | | Beaumont-Port Arthur, TX Metro SA | 388 745 |
| | 48 199 | Hardin County, TX | 54 635 |
| | 48 245 | Jefferson County, TX | 252 273 |
| | 48 361 | Orange County, TX | 81 837 |
| 13380 | | Bellingham, WA Metro SA | 201 140 |
| | 53 073 | Whatcom County, WA | 201 140 |
| 13460 | | Bend, OR Metro SA | 157 733 |
| | 41 017 | Deschutes County, OR | 157 733 |
| 13740 | | Billings, MT Metro SA | 158 050 |
| | 30 009 | Carbon County, MT | 10 078 |
| | 30 111 | Yellowstone County, MT | 147 972 |
| 13780 | | Binghamton, NY Metro SA | 251 725 |
| | 36 007 | Broome County, NY | 200 600 |
| | 36 107 | Tioga County, NY | 51 125 |
| 13820 | | Birmingham-Hoover, AL Metro SA | 1128 047 |
| | 01 007 | Bibb County, AL | 22 915 |
| | 01 009 | Blount County, AL | 57 322 |
| | 01 021 | Chilton County, AL | 43 643 |
| | 01 073 | Jefferson County, AL | 658 466 |
| | 01 115 | St. Clair County, AL | 83 593 |
| | 01 117 | Shelby County, AL | 195 085 |
| | 01 127 | Walker County, AL | 67 023 |
| 13900 | | Bismarck, ND Metro SA | 108 779 |
| | 38 015 | Burleigh County, ND | 81 308 |
| | 38 059 | Morton County, ND | 27 471 |
| 13980 | | Blacksburg-Christiansburg-Radford, VA Metro SA | 162 958 |
| | 51 071 | Giles County, VA | 17 286 |
| | 51 121 | Montgomery County, VA | 94 392 |
| | 51 155 | Pulaski County, VA | 34 872 |
| | 51 750 | Radford city, VA | 16 408 |
| 14020 | | Bloomington, IN Metro SA | 192 714 |
| | 18 055 | Greene County, IN | 33 165 |
| | 18 105 | Monroe County, IN | 137 974 |
| | 18 119 | Owen County, IN | 21 575 |
| 14060 | | Bloomington-Normal, IL Metro SA | 169 572 |
| | 17 113 | McLean County, IL | 169 572 |
| 14260 | | Boise City-Nampa, ID Metro SA | 616 561 |
| | 16 001 | Ada County, ID | 392 365 |
| | 16 015 | Boise County, ID | 7 028 |
| | 16 027 | Canyon County, ID | 188 923 |
| | 16 045 | Gem County, ID | 16 719 |
| | 16 073 | Owyhee County, ID | 11 526 |
| 14460 | | Boston-Cambridge-Quincy, MA-NH Metro SA. | 4552 402 |
| | | Boston-Quincy, MA Metro Div 14484 | 1887 792 |
| | 25 021 | Norfolk County, MA | 670 850 |
| | 25 023 | Plymouth County, MA | 494 919 |
| | 25 025 | Suffolk County, MA | 722 023 |
| | | Cambridge-Newton-Framingham, MA Metro Div 15764 | 1503 085 |
| | 25 017 | Middlesex County, MA | 1503 085 |
| | | Peabody, MA Metro Div 37764 | 743 159 |
| | 25 009 | Essex County, MA | 743 159 |
| | | Rockingham County-Strafford County, NH Metro Div 40484 | 418 366 |
| | 33 015 | Rockingham County, NH | 295 223 |
| | 33 017 | Strafford County, NH | 123 143 |
| 14500 | | Boulder, CO Metro SA | 294 567 |
| | 08 013 | Boulder County, CO | 294 567 |
| 14540 | | Bowling Green, KY Metro SA | 125 953 |
| | 21 061 | Edmonson County, KY | 12 161 |
| | 21 227 | Warren County, KY | 113 792 |
| 14740 | | Bremerton-Silverdale, WA Metro SA | 251 133 |
| | 53 035 | Kitsap County, WA | 251 133 |
| 14860 | | Bridgeport-Stamford-Norwalk, CT Metro SA.... | 916 829 |
| | 09 001 | Fairfield County, CT | 916 829 |

| Core based statistical area | State/ County FIPS code | Title and Geographic Components | 2010 Census Population | Core based statistical area | State/ County FIPS code | Title and Geographic Components | 2010 Census Population |
|---|---|---|---|---|---|---|---|
| 15180 | | Brownsville-Harlingen, TX Metro SA............... | 406 220 | 16740 | | Charlotte-Gastonia-Rock Hill, NC-SC Metro SA............ | 1758 038 |
| | 48 061 | Cameron County, TX.................................... | 406 220 | | 37 007 | Anson County, NC.................................... | 26 948 |
| 15260 | | Brunswick, GA Metro SA ............................. | 112 370 | | 37 025 | Cabarrus County, NC .............................. | 178 011 |
| | 13 025 | Brantley County, GA................................... | 18 411 | | 37 071 | Gaston County, NC .................................. | 206 086 |
| | 13 127 | Glynn County, GA....................................... | 79 626 | | 37 119 | Mecklenburg County, NC .......................... | 919 628 |
| | 13 191 | McIntosh County, GA ................................. | 14 333 | | 37 179 | Union County, NC..................................... | 201 292 |
| 15380 | | Buffalo-Niagara Falls, NY Metro SA ............... | 1135 509 | | 45 091 | York County, SC ..................................... | 226 073 |
| | 36 029 | Erie County, NY......................................... | 919 040 | 16820 | | Charlottesville, VA Metro SA....................... | 201 559 |
| | 36 063 | Niagara County, NY.................................... | 216 469 | | 51 003 | Albemarle County, VA .............................. | 98 970 |
| 15500 | | Burlington, NC Metro SA .............................. | 151 131 | | 51 065 | Fluvanna County, VA ................................ | 25 691 |
| | 37 001 | Alamance County, NC ................................. | 151 131 | | 51 079 | Greene County, VA .................................. | 18 403 |
| 15540 | | Burlington-South Burlington, VT Metro SA ...... | 211 261 | | 51 125 | Nelson County, VA ................................... | 15 020 |
| | 50 007 | Chittenden County, VT ............................... | 156 545 | | 51 540 | Charlottesville city, VA............................... | 43 475 |
| | 50 011 | Franklin County, VT ................................... | 47 746 | 16860 | | Chattanooga, TN-GA Metro SA .................... | 528 143 |
| | 50 013 | Grand Isle County, VT................................ | 6 970 | | 13 047 | Catoosa County, GA ................................. | 63 942 |
| 15940 | | Canton-Massillon, OH Metro SA .................... | 404 422 | | 13 083 | Dade County, GA ..................................... | 16 633 |
| | 39 019 | Carroll County, OH .................................... | 28 836 | | 13 295 | Walker County, GA.................................... | 68 756 |
| | 39 151 | Stark County, OH ...................................... | 375 586 | | 47 065 | Hamilton County, TN ................................. | 336 463 |
| 15980 | | Cape Coral-Fort Myers, FL Metro SA............. | 618 754 | | 47 115 | Marion County, TN ................................... | 28 237 |
| | 12 071 | Lee County, FL ......................................... | 618 754 | | 47 153 | Sequatchie County, TN ............................. | 14 112 |
| 16020 | | Cape Girardeau-Jackson, MO-IL Metro SA..... | 96 275 | 16940 | | Cheyenne, WY Metro SA............................ | 91 738 |
| | 17 003 | Alexander County, IL.................................. | 8 238 | | 56 021 | Laramie County, WY ................................. | 91 738 |
| | 29 017 | Bollinger County, MO ................................. | 12 363 | 16980 | | Chicago-Joliet-Naperville, IL-IN-WI Metro SA.. | 9461 105 |
| | 29 031 | Cape Girardeau County, MO....................... | 75 674 | | | Chicago-Joliet-Naperville, IL Metro Div 16974 | 7883 147 |
| 16180 | | Carson City, NV Metro SA ........................... | 55 274 | | 17 031 | Cook County, IL ....................................... | 5194 675 |
| | 32 510 | Carson City, NV ........................................ | 55 274 | | 17 037 | DeKalb County, IL .................................... | 105 160 |
| 16220 | | Casper, WY Metro SA.................................. | 75 450 | | 17 043 | DuPage County, IL .................................... | 916 924 |
| | 56 025 | Natrona County, WY................................... | 75 450 | | 17 063 | Grundy County, IL .................................... | 50 063 |
| 16300 | | Cedar Rapids, IA Metro SA ......................... | 257 940 | | 17 089 | Kane County, IL ....................................... | 515 269 |
| | 19 011 | Benton County, IA ..................................... | 26 076 | | 17 093 | Kendall County, IL .................................... | 114 736 |
| | 19 105 | Jones County, IA ...................................... | 20 638 | | 17 111 | McHenry County, IL .................................. | 308 760 |
| | 19 113 | Linn County, IA ........................................ | 211 226 | | 17 197 | Will County, IL ........................................ | 677 560 |
| 16580 | | Champaign-Urbana, IL Metro SA.................... | 231 891 | | | Gary, IN Metro Div 23844 .......................... | 708 070 |
| | 17 019 | Champaign County, IL................................. | 201 081 | | 18 073 | Jasper County, IN..................................... | 33 478 |
| | 17 053 | Ford County, IL ......................................... | 14 081 | | 18 089 | Lake County, IN ....................................... | 496 005 |
| | 17 147 | Piatt County, IL ........................................ | 16 729 | | 18 111 | Newton County, IN .................................... | 14 244 |
| 16620 | | Charleston, WV Metro SA............................. | 304 284 | | 18 127 | Porter County, IN ..................................... | 164 343 |
| | 54 005 | Boone County, WV .................................... | 24 629 | | | Lake County-Kenosha County, IL-WI Metro Div 29404................................................ | 869 888 |
| | 54 015 | Clay County, WV ...................................... | 9 386 | | 17 097 | Lake County, IL ....................................... | 703 462 |
| | 54 039 | Kanawha County, WV ................................ | 193 063 | | 55 059 | Kenosha County, WI.................................. | 166 426 |
| | 54 043 | Lincoln County, WV ................................... | 21 720 | 17020 | | Chico, CA Metro SA................................... | 220 000 |
| | 54 079 | Putnam County, WV ................................... | 55 486 | | 06 007 | Butte County, CA ..................................... | 220 000 |
| 16700 | | Charleston-North Charleston-Summerville, SC Metro SA ........................................... | 664 607 | | | | |
| | 45 015 | Berkeley County, SC ................................. | 177 843 | | | | |
| | 45 019 | Charleston County, SC............................... | 350 209 | | | | |
| | 45 035 | Dorchester County, SC............................... | 136 555 | | | | |

# Metropolitan Statistical Areas, Metropolitan Divisions, and Components (as defined December 2009)–*Continued*

| Core based statistical area | State/ County FIPS code | Title and Geographic Components | 2010 Census Population | Core based statistical area | State/ County FIPS code | Title and Geographic Components | 2010 Census Population |
|---|---|---|---|---|---|---|---|
| 17140 | | Cincinnati-Middletown, OH-KY-IN Metro SA.... | 2130 151 | 18020 | | Columbus, IN Metro SA ................................ | 76 794 |
| | 18 029 | Dearborn County, IN.................................. | 50 047 | | 18 005 | Bartholomew County, IN............................. | 76 794 |
| | 18 047 | Franklin County, IN.................................... | 23 087 | | | | |
| | 18 115 | Ohio County, IN........................................ | 6 128 | 18140 | | Columbus, OH Metro SA ............................ | 1836 536 |
| | 21 015 | Boone County, KY...................................... | 118 811 | | 39 041 | Delaware County, OH................................ | 174 214 |
| | 21 023 | Bracken County, KY................................... | 8 488 | | 39 045 | Fairfield County, OH................................. | 146 156 |
| | 21 037 | Campbell County, KY................................. | 90 336 | | 39 049 | Franklin County, OH................................. | 1163 414 |
| | 21 077 | Gallatin County, KY................................... | 8 589 | | 39 089 | Licking County, OH................................... | 166 492 |
| | 21 081 | Grant County, KY...................................... | 24 662 | | 39 097 | Madison County, OH................................. | 43 435 |
| | 21 117 | Kenton County, KY.................................... | 159 720 | | 39 117 | Morrow County, OH.................................. | 34 827 |
| | 21 191 | Pendleton County, KY............................... | 14 877 | | 39 129 | Pickaway County, OH............................... | 55 698 |
| | 39 015 | Brown County, OH.................................... | 44 846 | | 39 159 | Union County, OH.................................... | 52 300 |
| | 39 017 | Butler County, OH.................................... | 368 130 | | | | |
| | 39 025 | Clermont County, OH............................... | 197 363 | 18580 | | Corpus Christi, TX Metro SA ...................... | 428 185 |
| | 39 061 | Hamilton County, OH............................... | 802 374 | | 48 007 | Aransas County, TX.................................. | 23 158 |
| | 39 165 | Warren County, OH.................................. | 212 693 | | 48 355 | Nueces County, TX................................... | 340 223 |
| | | | | | 48 409 | San Patricio County, TX............................ | 64 804 |
| 17300 | | Clarksville, TN-KY Metro SA ....................... | 273 949 | | | | |
| | 21 047 | Christian County, KY................................ | 73 955 | 18700 | | Corvallis, OR Metro SA .............................. | 85 579 |
| | 21 221 | Trigg County, KY...................................... | 14 339 | | 41 003 | Benton County, OR .................................. | 85 579 |
| | 47 125 | Montgomery County, TN............................ | 172 331 | | | | |
| | 47 161 | Stewart County, TN................................... | 13 324 | 18880 | | Crestview-Fort Walton Beach-Destin, FL Metro SA .............................................. | 180 822 |
| 17420 | | Cleveland, TN Metro SA ............................. | 115 788 | | 12 091 | Okaloosa County, FL.................................. | 180 822 |
| | 47 011 | Bradley County, TN................................... | 98 963 | | | | |
| | 47 139 | Polk County, TN....................................... | 16 825 | 19060 | | Cumberland, MD-WV Metro SA....................... | 103 299 |
| | | | | | 24 001 | Allegany County, MD................................. | 75 087 |
| 17460 | | Cleveland-Elyria-Mentor, OH Metro SA.......... | 2077 240 | | 54 057 | Mineral County, WV.................................. | 28 212 |
| | 39 035 | Cuyahoga County, OH ............................... | 1280 122 | | | | |
| | 39 055 | Geauga County, OH .................................. | 93 389 | 19100 | | Dallas-Fort Worth-Arlington, TX Metro SA...... | 6371 773 |
| | 39 085 | Lake County, OH...................................... | 230 041 | | | Dallas-Plano-Irving, TX Metro Div 19124..... | 4235 751 |
| | 39 093 | Lorain County, OH.................................... | 301 356 | | 48 085 | Collin County, TX..................................... | 782 341 |
| | 39 103 | Medina County, OH.................................. | 172 332 | | 48 113 | Dallas County, TX.................................... | 2368 139 |
| | | | | | 48 119 | Delta County, TX..................................... | 5 231 |
| 17660 | | Coeur d'Alene, ID Metro SA ........................ | 138 494 | | 48 121 | Denton County, TX................................... | 662 614 |
| | 16 055 | Kootenai County, ID.................................. | 138 494 | | 48 139 | Ellis County, TX....................................... | 149 610 |
| | | | | | 48 231 | Hunt County, TX...................................... | 86 129 |
| 17780 | | College Station-Bryan, TX Metro SA .............. | 228 660 | | 48 257 | Kaufman County, TX................................. | 103 350 |
| | 48 041 | Brazos County, TX.................................... | 194 851 | | 48 397 | Rockwall County, TX................................. | 78 337 |
| | 48 051 | Burleson County, TX................................. | 17 187 | | | Fort Worth-Arlington, TX Metro Div 23104... | 2136 022 |
| | 48 395 | Robertson County, TX................................ | 16 622 | | 48 251 | Johnson County, TX.................................. | 150 934 |
| | | | | | 48 367 | Parker County, TX.................................... | 116 927 |
| 17820 | | Colorado Springs, CO Metro SA..................... | 645 613 | | 48 439 | Tarrant County, TX................................... | 1809 034 |
| | 08 041 | El Paso County, CO .................................. | 622 263 | | 48 497 | Wise County, TX...................................... | 59 127 |
| | 08 119 | Teller County, CO..................................... | 23 350 | | | | |
| | | | | 19140 | | Dalton, GA Metro SA ................................ | 142 227 |
| 17860 | | Columbia, MO Metro SA.............................. | 172 786 | | 13 213 | Murray County, GA.................................... | 39 628 |
| | 29 019 | Boone County, MO.................................... | 162 642 | | 13 313 | Whitfield County, GA................................. | 102 599 |
| | 29 089 | Howard County, MO.................................. | 10 144 | | | | |
| | | | | 19180 | | Danville, IL Metro SA ................................ | 81 625 |
| 17900 | | Columbia, SC Metro SA............................... | 767 598 | | 17 183 | Vermilion County, IL.................................. | 81 625 |
| | 45 017 | Calhoun County, SC.................................. | 15 175 | | | | |
| | 45 039 | Fairfield County, SC.................................. | 23 956 | 19260 | | Danville, VA Metro SA ............................... | 106 561 |
| | 45 055 | Kershaw County, SC.................................. | 61 697 | | 51 143 | Pittsylvania County, VA.............................. | 63 506 |
| | 45 063 | Lexington County, SC................................ | 262 391 | | 51 590 | Danville city, VA...................................... | 43 055 |
| | 45 079 | Richland County, SC................................. | 384 504 | | | | |
| | 45 081 | Saluda County, SC.................................... | 19 875 | 19340 | | Davenport-Moline-Rock Island, IA-IL Metro SA........................................................ | 379 690 |
| 17980 | | Columbus, GA-AL Metro SA ........................ | 294 865 | | 17 073 | Henry County, IL...................................... | 50 486 |
| | 01 113 | Russell County, AL.................................... | 52 947 | | 17 131 | Mercer County, IL.................................... | 16 434 |
| | 13 053 | Chattahoochee County, GA......................... | 11 267 | | 17 161 | Rock Island County, IL .............................. | 147 546 |
| | 13 145 | Harris County, GA..................................... | 32 024 | | 19 163 | Scott County, IA...................................... | 165 224 |
| | 13 197 | Marion County, GA.................................... | 8 742 | | | | |
| | 13 215 | Muscogee County, GA................................ | 189 885 | | | | |

| Core based statistical area | State/ County FIPS code | Title and Geographic Components | 2010 Census Population | Core based statistical area | State/ County FIPS code | Title and Geographic Components | 2010 Census Population |
|---|---|---|---|---|---|---|---|
| 19380 | | Dayton, OH Metro SA .................................. | 841 502 | 20500 | | Durham-Chaspel Hill, NC Metro SA ............... | 504 357 |
| | 39 057 | Greene County, OH............................... | 161 573 | | 37 037 | Chatham County, NC .................................. | 63 505 |
| | 39 109 | Miami County, OH ................................. | 102 506 | | 37 063 | Durham County, NC................................... | 267 587 |
| | 39 113 | Montgomery County, OH.......................... | 535 153 | | 37 135 | Orange County, NC.................................... | 133 801 |
| | 39 135 | Preble County, OH ................................ | 42 270 | | 37 145 | Person County, NC.................................... | 39 464 |
| 19460 | | Decatur, AL Metro SA.................................. | 153 829 | 20740 | | Eau Claire, WI Metro SA.............................. | 161 151 |
| | 01 079 | Lawrence County, AL .............................. | 34 339 | | 55 017 | Chippewa County, WI ................................ | 62 415 |
| | 01 103 | Morgan County, AL ................................ | 119 490 | | 55 035 | Eau Claire County, WI................................ | 98 736 |
| 19500 | | Decatur, IL Metro SA .................................. | 110 768 | 20940 | | El Centro, CA Metro SA............................... | 174 528 |
| | 17 115 | Macon County, IL ................................... | 110 768 | | 06 025 | Imperial County, CA .................................. | 174 528 |
| 19660 | | Deltona-Daytona Beach-Ormond Beach, FL Metro SA ................................................. | 494 593 | 21060 | | Elizabethtown, KY Metro SA.......................... | 119 736 |
| | | | | | 21 093 | Hardin County, KY .................................... | 105 543 |
| | 12 127 | Volusia County, FL ................................. | 494 593 | | 21 123 | Larue County, KY ..................................... | 14 193 |
| 19740 | | Denver-Aurora-Broomfield, CO Metro SA....... | 2543 482 | 21140 | | Elkhart-Goshen, IN Metro SA ........................ | 197 559 |
| | 08 001 | Adams County, CO ................................. | 441 603 | | 18 039 | Elkhart County, IN .................................... | 197 559 |
| | 08 005 | Arapahoe County, CO .............................. | 572 003 | | | | |
| | 08 014 | Broomfield County, CO............................. | 55 889 | 21300 | | Elmira, NY Metro SA.................................. | 88 830 |
| | 08 019 | Clear Creek County, CO ........................... | 9 088 | | 36 015 | Chemung County, NY................................. | 88 830 |
| | 08 031 | Denver County, CO ................................. | 600 158 | | | | |
| | 08 035 | Douglas County, CO................................ | 285 465 | 21340 | | El Paso, TX Metro SA................................. | 800 647 |
| | 08 039 | Elbert County, CO .................................. | 23 086 | | 48 141 | El Paso County, TX ................................... | 800 647 |
| | 08 047 | Gilpin County, CO................................... | 5 441 | | | | |
| | 08 059 | Jefferson County, CO............................... | 534 543 | 21500 | | Erie, PA Metro SA...................................... | 280 566 |
| | 08 093 | Park County, CO .................................... | 16 206 | | 42 049 | Erie County, PA ....................................... | 280 566 |
| 19780 | | Des Moines-West Des Moines, IA Metro SA... | 569 633 | 21660 | | Eugene-Springfield, OR Metro SA................... | 351 715 |
| | 19 049 | Dallas County, IA .................................. | 66 135 | | 41 039 | Lane County, OR...................................... | 351 715 |
| | 19 077 | Guthrie County, IA ................................. | 10 954 | | | | |
| | 19 121 | Madison County, IA ................................ | 15 679 | 21780 | | Evansville, IN-KY Metro SA ........................... | 358 676 |
| | 19 153 | Polk County, IA ..................................... | 430 640 | | 18 051 | Gibson County, IN .................................... | 33 503 |
| | 19 181 | Warren County, IA .................................. | 46 225 | | 18 129 | Posey County, IN ..................................... | 25 910 |
| | | | | | 18 163 | Vanderburgh County, IN.............................. | 179 703 |
| 19820 | | Detroit-Warren-Livonia, MI Metro SA.............. | 4296 250 | | 18 173 | Warrick County, IN ................................... | 59 689 |
| | | Detroit-Livonia-Dearborn, MI Metro Div 19804............................................... | 1820 584 | | 21 101 | Henderson County, KY................................ | 46 250 |
| | 26 163 | Wayne County, MI ................................. | 1820 584 | | 21 233 | Webster County, KY .................................. | 13 621 |
| | | Warren-Troy-Farmington Hills, MI Metro Div 47644........................................... | 2475 666 | 21820 | | Fairbanks, AK Metro SA ............................... | 97 581 |
| | 26 087 | Lapeer County, MI .................................. | 88 319 | | 02 090 | Fairbanks North Star Borough, AK............... | 97 581 |
| | 26 093 | Livingston County, MI .............................. | 180 967 | 22020 | | Fargo, ND-MN Metro SA .............................. | 208 777 |
| | 26 099 | Macomb County, MI ................................ | 840 978 | | 27 027 | Clay County, MN ...................................... | 58 999 |
| | 26 125 | Oakland County, MI ................................ | 1202 362 | | 38 017 | Cass County, ND...................................... | 149 778 |
| | 26 147 | St. Clair County, MI ................................ | 163 040 | | | | |
| | | | | 22140 | | Farmington, NM Metro SA ............................ | 130 044 |
| 20020 | | Dothan, AL Metro SA.................................. | 145 639 | | 35 045 | San Juan County, NM ................................ | 130 044 |
| | 01 061 | Geneva County, AL ................................. | 26 790 | | | | |
| | 01 067 | Henry County, AL ................................... | 17 302 | 22180 | | Fayetteville, NC Metro SA.............................. | 366 383 |
| | 01 069 | Houston County, AL ................................ | 101 547 | | 37 051 | Cumberland County, NC ............................. | 319 431 |
| | | | | | 37 093 | Hoke County, NC...................................... | 46 952 |
| 20100 | | Dover, DE Metro SA .................................. | 162 310 | | | | |
| | 10 001 | Kent County, DE...................................... | 162 310 | 22220 | | Fayetteville-Springdale-Rogers, AR-MO Metro SA.......................................................... | 463 204 |
| 20220 | | Dubuque, IA Metro SA ............................... | 93 653 | | 05 007 | Benton County, AR.................................... | 221 339 |
| | 19 061 | Dubuque County, IA ................................ | 93 653 | | 05 087 | Madison County, AR .................................. | 15 717 |
| | | | | | 05 143 | Washington County, AR .............................. | 203 065 |
| 20260 | | Duluth, MN-WI Metro SA ............................. | 279 771 | | 29 119 | McDonald County, MO ............................... | 23 083 |
| | 27 017 | Carlton County, MN ................................. | 35 386 | | | | |
| | 27 137 | St. Louis County, MN ............................... | 200 226 | 22380 | | Flagstaff, AZ Metro SA................................. | 134 421 |
| | 55 031 | Douglas County, WI................................. | 44 159 | | 04 005 | Coconino County, AZ ................................. | 134 421 |

| Core based statistical area | State/ County FIPS code | Title and Geographic Components | 2010 Census Population | Core based statistical area | State/ County FIPS code | Title and Geographic Components | 2010 Census Population |
|---|---|---|---|---|---|---|---|
| 22420 | | Flint, MI Metro SA .......................... | 425 790 | 24540 | | Greeley, CO Metro SA ...................................... | 252 825 |
| | 26 049 | Genesee County, MI.................................... | 425 790 | | 08 123 | Weld County, CO..................................... | 252 825 |
| 22500 | | Florence, SC Metro SA .......................... | 205 566 | 24580 | | Green Bay, WI Metro SA ............................... | 306 241 |
| | 45 031 | Darlington County, SC............................ | 68 681 | | 55 009 | Brown County, WI................................... | 248 007 |
| | 45 041 | Florence County, SC ............................. | 136 885 | | 55 061 | Kewaunee County, WI............................... | 20 574 |
| | | | | | 55 083 | Oconto County, WI.................................... | 37 660 |
| 22520 | | Florence-Muscle Shoals, AL Metro SA............ | 147 137 | | | | |
| | 01 033 | Colbert County, AL................................ | 54 428 | 24660 | | Greensboro-High Point, NC Metro SA.......... | 723 801 |
| | 01 077 | Lauderdale County, AL............................ | 92 709 | | 37 081 | Guilford County, NC ............................... | 488 406 |
| | | | | | 37 151 | Randolph County, NC.............................. | 141 752 |
| 22540 | | Fond du Lac, WI Metro SA ............................ | 101 633 | | 37 157 | Rockingham County, NC........................... | 93 643 |
| | 55 039 | Fond du Lac County, WI ............................ | 101 633 | | | | |
| | | | | 24780 | | Greenville-Mauldin-Easley, NC Metro SA....... | 189 510 |
| 22660 | | Fort Collins-Loveland, CO Metro SA .............. | 299 630 | | 37 079 | Greene County, NC................................... | 21 362 |
| | 08 069 | Larimer County, CO............................... | 299 630 | | 37 147 | Pitt County, NC...................................... | 168 148 |
| 22900 | | Fort Smith, AR-OK Metro SA......................... | 298 592 | 24860 | | Greenville, SC Metro SA............................. | 636 986 |
| | 05 033 | Crawford County, AR............................... | 61 948 | | 45 045 | Greenville County, SC.............................. | 451 225 |
| | 05 047 | Franklin County, AR ............................... | 18 125 | | 45 059 | Laurens County, SC................................ | 66 537 |
| | 05 131 | Sebastian County, AR............................. | 125 744 | | 45 077 | Pickens County, SC................................ | 119 224 |
| | 40 079 | Le Flore County, OK............................... | 50 384 | | | | |
| | 40 135 | Sequoyah County, OK............................. | 42 391 | 25060 | | Gulfport-Biloxi, MS Metro SA....................... | 248 820 |
| | | | | | 28 045 | Hancock County, MS............................... | 43 929 |
| 23060 | | Fort Wayne, IN Metro SA............................ | 416 257 | | 28 047 | Harrison County, MS............................... | 187 105 |
| | 18 003 | Allen County, IN.................................... | 355 329 | | 28 131 | Stone County, MS ................................ | 17 786 |
| | 18 179 | Wells County, IN................................... | 27 636 | | | | |
| | 18 183 | Whitley County, IN................................. | 33 292 | 25180 | | Hagerstown-Martinsburg, MD-WV Metro SA... | 269 140 |
| | | | | | 24 043 | Washington County, MD............................ | 147 430 |
| 23420 | | Fresno, CA Metro SA............................... | 930 450 | | 54 003 | Berkeley County, WV .............................. | 104 169 |
| | 06 019 | Fresno County, CA ............................... | 930 450 | | 54 065 | Morgan County, WV................................ | 17 541 |
| 23460 | | Gadsden, AL Metro SA............................. | 104 430 | 25260 | | Hanford-Corcoran, CA Metro SA .................. | 152 982 |
| | 01 055 | Etowah County, AL................................ | 104 430 | | 06 031 | Kings County, CA................................... | 152 982 |
| 23540 | | Gainesville, FL Metro SA............................ | 264 275 | 25420 | | Harrisburg-Carlisle, PA Metro SA .................. | 549 475 |
| | 12 001 | Alachua County, FL................................ | 247 336 | | 42 041 | Cumberland County, PA............................ | 235 406 |
| | 12 041 | Gilchrist County, FL................................ | 16 939 | | 42 043 | Dauphin County, PA................................ | 268 100 |
| | | | | | 42 099 | Perry County, PA.................................... | 45 969 |
| 23580 | | Gainesville, GA Metro SA............................ | 179 684 | | | | |
| | 13 139 | Hall County, GA.................................... | 179 684 | 25500 | | Harrisonburg, VA Metro SA ........................ | 125 228 |
| | | | | | 51 165 | Rockingham County, VA ........................... | 76 314 |
| 24020 | | Glens Falls, NY Metro SA.......................... | 128 923 | | 51 660 | Harrisonburg city, VA.............................. | 48 914 |
| | 36 113 | Warren County, NY................................. | 65 707 | | | | |
| | 36 115 | Washington County, NY........................... | 63 216 | 25540 | | Hartford-West Hartford-East Hartford, CT Metro SA ................................ | 1212 381 |
| 24140 | | Goldsboro, NC Metro SA........................... | 122 623 | | 09 003 | Hartford County, CT ................................ | 894 014 |
| | 37 191 | Wayne County, NC................................. | 122 623 | | 09 007 | Middlesex County, CT.............................. | 165 676 |
| | | | | | 09 013 | Tolland County, CT................................. | 152 691 |
| 24220 | | Grand Forks, ND-MN Metro SA.................... | 98 461 | | | | |
| | 27 119 | Polk County, MN................................... | 31 600 | 25620 | | Hattiesburg, MS Metro SA......................... | 142 842 |
| | 38 035 | Grand Forks County, ND........................... | 66 861 | | 28 035 | Forrest County, MS................................ | 74 934 |
| | | | | | 28 073 | Lamar County, MS.................................. | 55 658 |
| 24300 | | Grand Junction, CO Metro SA..................... | 146 723 | | 28 111 | Perry County, MS................................... | 12 250 |
| | 08 077 | Mesa County, CO.................................. | 146 723 | | | | |
| | | | | 25860 | | Hickory-Lenoir-Morganton, NC Metro SA....... | 365 497 |
| 24340 | | Grand Rapids-Wyoming, MI Metro SA ........... | 774 160 | | 37 003 | Alexander County, NC.............................. | 37 198 |
| | 26 015 | Barry County, MI................................... | 59 173 | | 37 023 | Burke County, NC.................................. | 90 912 |
| | 26 067 | Ionia County, MI................................... | 63 905 | | 37 027 | Caldwell County, NC............................... | 83 029 |
| | 26 081 | Kent County, MI.................................... | 602 622 | | 37 035 | Catawba County, NC............................... | 154 358 |
| | 26 123 | Newaygo County, MI ............................... | 48 460 | | | | |
| | | | | 25980 | | Hinesville-Fort Stewart, GA Metro SA ............ | 77 917 |
| 24500 | | Great Falls, MT Metro SA.......................... | 81 327 | | 13 179 | Liberty County, GA................................. | 63 453 |
| | 30 013 | Cascade County, MT............................... | 81 327 | | 13 183 | Long County, GA................................... | 14 464 |

# Metropolitan Statistical Areas, Metropolitan Divisions, and Components (as defined December 2009)–*Continued*

| Core based statistical area | State/ County FIPS code | Title and Geographic Components | 2010 Census Population | Core based statistical area | State/ County FIPS code | Title and Geographic Components | 2010 Census Population |
|---|---|---|---|---|---|---|---|
| 26100 | | Holland-Grand Haven, MI Metro SA | 263 801 | 27140 | | Jackson, MS Metro SA | 539 057 |
| | 26 139 | Ottawa County, MI | 263 801 | | 28 029 | Copiah County, MS | 29 449 |
| 26180 | | Honolulu, HI Metro SA | 953 207 | | 28 049 | Hinds County, MS | 245 285 |
| | 15 003 | Honolulu County, HI | 953 207 | | 28 089 | Madison County, MS | 95 203 |
| 26300 | | Hot Springs, AR Metro SA | 96 024 | | 28 121 | Rankin County, MS | 141 617 |
| | 05 051 | Garland County, AR | 96 024 | | 28 127 | Simpson County, MS | 27 503 |
| 26380 | | Houma-Bayou Cane-Thibodaux, LA Metro SA | 208 178 | 27180 | | Jackson, TN Metro SA | 115 425 |
| | 22 057 | Lafourche Parish, LA | 96 318 | | 47 023 | Chester County, TN | 17 131 |
| | 22 109 | Terrebonne Parish, LA | 111 860 | | 47 113 | Madison County, TN | 98 294 |
| 26420 | | Houston-Sugar Land-Baytown, TX Metro SA | 5 946 800 | 27260 | | Jacksonville, FL Metro SA | 1 345 596 |
| | 48 015 | Austin County, TX | 28 417 | | 12 003 | Baker County, FL | 27 115 |
| | 48 039 | Brazoria County, TX | 313 166 | | 12 019 | Clay County, FL | 190 865 |
| | 48 071 | Chambers County, TX | 35 096 | | 12 031 | Duval County, FL | 864 263 |
| | 48 157 | Fort Bend County, TX | 585 375 | | 12 089 | Nassau County, FL | 73 314 |
| | 48 167 | Galveston County, TX | 291 309 | | 12 109 | St. Johns County, FL | 190 039 |
| | 48 201 | Harris County, TX | 4 092 459 | | | | |
| | 48 291 | Liberty County, TX | 75 643 | 27340 | | Jacksonville, NC Metro SA | 177 772 |
| | 48 339 | Montgomery County, TX | 455 746 | | 37 133 | Onslow County, NC | 177 772 |
| | 48 407 | San Jacinto County, TX | 26 384 | 27500 | | Janesville, WI Metro SA | 160 331 |
| | 48 473 | Waller County, TX | 43 205 | | 55 105 | Rock County, WI | 160 331 |
| 26580 | | Huntington-Ashland, WV-KY-OH Metro SA | 287 702 | 27620 | | Jefferson City, MO Metro SA | 149 807 |
| | 21 019 | Boyd County, KY | 49 542 | | 29 027 | Callaway County, MO | 44 332 |
| | 21 089 | Greenup County, KY | 36 910 | | 29 051 | Cole County, MO | 75 990 |
| | 39 087 | Lawrence County, OH | 62 450 | | 29 135 | Moniteau County, MO | 15 607 |
| | 54 011 | Cabell County, WV | 96 319 | | 29 151 | Osage County, MO | 13 878 |
| | 54 099 | Wayne County, WV | 42 481 | 27740 | | Johnson City, TN Metro SA | 198 716 |
| | | | | | 47 019 | Carter County, TN | 57 424 |
| 26620 | | Huntsville, AL Metro SA | 417 593 | | 47 171 | Unicoi County, TN | 18 313 |
| | 01 083 | Limestone County, AL | 82 782 | | 47 179 | Washington County, TN | 122 979 |
| | 01 089 | Madison County, AL | 334 811 | 27780 | | Johnstown, PA Metro SA | 143 679 |
| 26820 | | Idaho Falls, ID Metro SA | 130 374 | | 42 021 | Cambria County, PA | 143 679 |
| | 16 019 | Bonneville County, ID | 104 234 | 27860 | | Jonesboro, AR Metro SA | 121 026 |
| | 16 051 | Jefferson County, ID | 26 140 | | 05 031 | Craighead County, AR | 96 443 |
| 26900 | | Indianapolis-Carmel, IN Metro SA | 1 756 241 | | 05 111 | Poinsett County, AR | 24 583 |
| | 18 011 | Boone County, IN | 56 640 | | | | |
| | 18 013 | Brown County, IN | 15 242 | 27900 | | Joplin, MO Metro SA | 175 518 |
| | 18 057 | Hamilton County, IN | 274 569 | | 29 097 | Jasper County, MO | 117 404 |
| | 18 059 | Hancock County, IN | 70 002 | | 29 145 | Newton County, MO | 58 114 |
| | 18 063 | Hendricks County, IN | 145 448 | | | | |
| | 18 081 | Johnson County, IN | 139 654 | 28020 | | Kalamazoo-Portage, MI Metro SA | 326 589 |
| | 18 097 | Marion County, IN | 903 393 | | 26 077 | Kalamazoo County, MI | 250 331 |
| | 18 109 | Morgan County, IN | 68 894 | | 26 159 | Van Buren County, MI | 76 258 |
| | 18 133 | Putnam County, IN | 37 963 | | | | |
| | 18 145 | Shelby County, IN | 44 436 | 28100 | | Kankakee-Bradley, IL Metro SA | 113 449 |
| 26980 | | Iowa City, IA Metro SA | 152 586 | | 17 091 | Kankakee County, IL | 113 449 |
| | 19 103 | Johnson County, IA | 130 882 | | | | |
| | 19 183 | Washington County, IA | 21 704 | | | | |
| 27060 | | Ithaca, NY Metro SA | 101 564 | | | | |
| | 36 109 | Tompkins County, NY | 101 564 | | | | |
| 27100 | | Jackson, MI Metro SA | 160 248 | | | | |
| | 26 075 | Jackson County, MI | 160 248 | | | | |

# Metropolitan Statistical Areas,
# Metropolitan Divisions,
# and Components
# (as defined December 2009)–*Continued*

| Core based statistical area | State/ County FIPS code | Title and Geographic Components | 2010 Census Population | Core based statistical area | State/ County FIPS code | Title and Geographic Components | 2010 Census Population |
|---|---|---|---|---|---|---|---|
| 28140 | | Kansas City, MO-KS Metro SA | 2035 334 | 29420 | | Lake Havasu City-Kingman, AZ Metro SA | 200 186 |
| | 20 059 | Franklin County, KS | 25 992 | | 04 015 | Mohave County, AZ | 200 186 |
| | 20 091 | Johnson County, KS | 544 179 | | | | |
| | 20 103 | Leavenworth County, KS | 76 227 | 29460 | | Lakeland-Winter Haven, FL Metro SA | 602 095 |
| | 20 107 | Linn County, KS | 9 656 | | 12 105 | Polk County, FL | 602 095 |
| | 20 121 | Miami County, KS | 32 787 | | | | |
| | 20 209 | Wyandotte County, KS | 157 505 | 29540 | | Lancaster, PA Metro SA | 519 445 |
| | 29 013 | Bates County, MO | 17 049 | | 42 071 | Lancaster County, PA | 519 445 |
| | 29 025 | Caldwell County, MO | 9 424 | | | | |
| | 29 037 | Cass County, MO | 99 478 | 29620 | | Lansing-East Lansing, MI Metro SA | 464 036 |
| | 29 047 | Clay County, MO | 221 939 | | 26 037 | Clinton County, MI | 75 382 |
| | 29 049 | Clinton County, MO | 20 743 | | 26 045 | Eaton County, MI | 107 759 |
| | 29 095 | Jackson County, MO | 674 158 | | 26 065 | Ingham County, MI | 280 895 |
| | 29 107 | Lafayette County, MO | 33 381 | | | | |
| | 29 165 | Platte County, MO | 89 322 | 29700 | | Laredo, TX Metro SA | 250 304 |
| | 29 177 | Ray County, MO | 23 494 | | 48 479 | Webb County, TX | 250 304 |
| | | | | | | | |
| 28420 | | Kennewick-Pasco-Richland, WA Metro SA | 253 340 | 29740 | | Las Cruces, NM Metro SA | 209 233 |
| | 53 005 | Benton County, WA | 175 177 | | 35 013 | Dona Ana County, NM | 209 233 |
| | 53 021 | Franklin County, WA | 78 163 | | | | |
| | | | | 29820 | | Las Vegas-Paradise, NV Metro SA | 1951 269 |
| 28660 | | Killeen-Temple-Fort Hood, TX Metro SA | 405 300 | | 32 003 | Clark County, NV | 1951 269 |
| | 48 027 | Bell County, TX | 310 235 | | | | |
| | 48 099 | Coryell County, TX | 75 388 | 29940 | | Lawrence, KS Metro SA | 110 826 |
| | 48 281 | Lampasas County, TX | 19 677 | | 20 045 | Douglas County, KS | 110 826 |
| | | | | | | | |
| 28700 | | Kingsport-Bristol-Bristol, TN-VA Metro SA | 309 544 | 30020 | | Lawton, OK Metro SA | 124 098 |
| | 47 073 | Hawkins County, TN | 56 833 | | 40 031 | Comanche County, OK | 124 098 |
| | 47 163 | Sullivan County, TN | 156 823 | | | | |
| | 51 169 | Scott County, VA | 23 177 | 30140 | | Lebanon, PA Metro SA | 133 568 |
| | 51 191 | Washington County, VA | 54 876 | | 42 075 | Lebanon County, PA | 133 568 |
| | 51 520 | Bristol city, VA | 17 835 | | | | |
| | | | | 30300 | | Lewiston, ID-WA Metro SA | 60 888 |
| 28740 | | Kingston, NY Metro SA | 182 493 | | 16 069 | Nez Perce County, ID | 39 265 |
| | 36 111 | Ulster County, NY | 182 493 | | 53 003 | Asotin County, WA | 21 623 |
| | | | | | | | |
| 28940 | | Knoxville, TN Metro SA | 698 030 | 30340 | | Lewiston-Auburn, ME Metro SA | 107 702 |
| | 47 001 | Anderson County, TN | 75 129 | | 23 001 | Androscoggin County, ME | 107 702 |
| | 47 009 | Blount County, TN | 123 010 | | | | |
| | 47 093 | Knox County, TN | 432 226 | 30460 | | Lexington-Fayette, KY Metro SA | 472 099 |
| | 47 105 | Loudon County, TN | 48 556 | | 21 017 | Bourbon County, KY | 19 985 |
| | 47 173 | Union County, TN | 19 109 | | 21 049 | Clark County, KY | 35 613 |
| | | | | | 21 067 | Fayette County, KY | 295 803 |
| 29020 | | Kokomo, IN Metro SA | 98 688 | | 21 113 | Jessamine County, KY | 48 586 |
| | 18 067 | Howard County, IN | 82 752 | | 21 209 | Scott County, KY | 47 173 |
| | 18 159 | Tipton County, IN | 15 936 | | 21 239 | Woodford County, KY | 24 939 |
| | | | | | | | |
| 29100 | | La Crosse, WI-MN Metro SA | 133 665 | 30620 | | Lima, OH Metro SA | 106 331 |
| | 27 055 | Houston County, MN | 19 027 | | 39 003 | Allen County, OH | 106 331 |
| | 55 063 | La Crosse County, WI | 114 638 | | | | |
| | | | | 30700 | | Lincoln, NE Metro SA | 302 157 |
| 29140 | | Lafayette, IN Metro SA | 201 789 | | 31 109 | Lancaster County, NE | 285 407 |
| | 18 007 | Benton County, IN | 8 854 | | 31 159 | Seward County, NE | 16 750 |
| | 18 015 | Carroll County, IN | 20 155 | | | | |
| | 18 157 | Tippecanoe County, IN | 172 780 | 30780 | | Little Rock-North Little Rock-Conway, AR Metro SA | 699 757 |
| | | | | | 05 045 | Faulkner County, AR | 113 237 |
| 29180 | | Lafayette, LA Metro SA | 273 738 | | 05 053 | Grant County, AR | 17 853 |
| | 22 055 | Lafayette Parish, LA | 221 578 | | 05 085 | Lonoke County, AR | 68 356 |
| | 22 099 | St. Martin Parish, LA | 52 160 | | 05 105 | Perry County, AR | 10 445 |
| | | | | | 05 119 | Pulaski County, AR | 382 748 |
| 29340 | | Lake Charles, LA Metro SA | 199 607 | | 05 125 | Saline County, AR | 107 118 |
| | 22 019 | Calcasieu Parish, LA | 192 768 | | | | |
| | 22 023 | Cameron Parish, LA | 6 839 | | | | |

# Metropolitan Statistical Areas, Metropolitan Divisions, and Components (as defined December 2009)–*Continued*

| Core based statistical area | State/County FIPS code | Title and Geographic Components | 2010 Census Population | Core based statistical area | State/County FIPS code | Title and Geographic Components | 2010 Census Population |
|---|---|---|---|---|---|---|---|
| 30860 | | Logan, UT-ID Metro SA | 125 442 | 31700 | | Manchester-Nashua, NH Metro SA | 400 721 |
| | 16 041 | Franklin County, ID | 12 786 | | 33 011 | Hillsborough County, NH | 400 721 |
| | 49 005 | Cache County, UT | 112 656 | | | | |
| | | | | 31740 | | Manhattan, KS Metro SA | 127 081 |
| 30980 | | Longview, TX Metro SA | 214 369 | | 20 061 | Geary County, KS | 34 362 |
| | 48 183 | Gregg County, TX | 121 730 | | 20 149 | Pottawatomie County, KS | 21 604 |
| | 48 401 | Rusk County, TX | 53 330 | | 20 161 | Riley County, KS | 71 115 |
| | 48 459 | Upshur County, TX | 39 309 | | | | |
| | | | | 31860 | | Mankato-North Mankato, MN Metro SA | 96 740 |
| 31020 | | Longview, WA Metro SA | 102 410 | | 27 013 | Blue Earth County, MN | 64 013 |
| | 53 015 | Cowlitz County, WA | 102 410 | | 27 103 | Nicollet County, MN | 32 727 |
| 31100 | | Los Angeles-Long Beach-Santa Ana, CA Metro SA | 12828 837 | 31900 | | Mansfield, OH Metro SA | 124 475 |
| | | Los Angeles-Long Beach-Glendale, CA Metro Div 31084 | 9818 605 | | 39 139 | Richland County, OH | 124 475 |
| | 06 037 | Los Angeles County, CA | 9818 605 | 32580 | | McAllen-Edinburg-Mission, TX Metro SA | 774 769 |
| | | Santa Ana-Anaheim-Irvine, CA Metro Div 42044 | 3010 232 | | 48 215 | Hidalgo County, TX | 774 769 |
| | 06 059 | Orange County, CA | 3010 232 | 32780 | | Medford, OR Metro SA | 203 206 |
| | | | | | 41 029 | Jackson County, OR | 203 206 |
| 31140 | | Louisville-Jefferson County, KY-IN Metro SA | 1283 566 | 32820 | | Memphis, TN-MS-AR Metro SA | 1316 100 |
| | 18 019 | Clark County, IN | 110 232 | | 05 035 | Crittenden County, AR | 50 902 |
| | 18 043 | Floyd County, IN | 74 578 | | 28 033 | DeSoto County, MS | 161 252 |
| | 18 061 | Harrison County, IN | 39 364 | | 28 093 | Marshall County, MS | 37 144 |
| | 18 175 | Washington County, IN | 28 262 | | 28 137 | Tate County, MS | 28 886 |
| | 21 029 | Bullitt County, KY | 74 319 | | 28 143 | Tunica County, MS | 10 778 |
| | 21 103 | Henry County, KY | 15 416 | | 47 047 | Fayette County, TN | 38 413 |
| | 21 111 | Jefferson County, KY | 741 096 | | 47 157 | Shelby County, TN | 927 644 |
| | 21 163 | Meade County, KY | 28 602 | | 47 167 | Tipton County, TN | 61 081 |
| | 21 179 | Nelson County, KY | 43 437 | | | | |
| | 21 185 | Oldham County, KY | 60 316 | 32900 | | Merced, CA Metro SA | 255 793 |
| | 21 211 | Shelby County, KY | 42 074 | | 06 047 | Merced County, CA | 255 793 |
| | 21 215 | Spencer County, KY | 17 061 | 33100 | | Miami-Fort Lauderdale-Pompano Beach, FL Metro SA | 5564 635 |
| | 21 223 | Trimble County, KY | 8 809 | | | Fort Lauderdale-Pompano Beach-Deerfield Beach, FL Metro Div 22744 | 1748 066 |
| 31180 | | Lubbock, TX Metro SA | 284 890 | | 12 011 | Broward County, FL | 1748 066 |
| | 48 107 | Crosby County, TX | 6 059 | | | Miami-Miami Beach-Kendall, FL Metro Div 33124 | 2496 435 |
| | 48 303 | Lubbock County, TX | 278 831 | | 12 086 | Miami-Dade County, FL | 2496 435 |
| 31340 | | Lynchburg, VA Metro SA | 252 634 | | | West Palm Beach-Boca Raton-Boynton Beach, FL Metro Div 48424 | 1320 134 |
| | 51 009 | Amherst County, VA | 32 353 | | 12 099 | Palm Beach County, FL | 1320 134 |
| | 51 011 | Appomattox County, VA | 14 973 | | | | |
| | 51 019 | Bedford County, VA | 68 676 | 33140 | | Michigan City-La Porte, IN Metro SA | 111 467 |
| | 51 031 | Campbell County, VA | 54 842 | | 18 091 | LaPorte County, IN | 111 467 |
| | 51 515 | Bedford city, VA | 6 222 | | | | |
| | 51 680 | Lynchburg city, VA | 75 568 | 33260 | | Midland, TX Metro SA | 136 872 |
| 31420 | | Macon, GA Metro SA | 232 293 | | 48 329 | Midland County, TX | 136 872 |
| | 13 021 | Bibb County, GA | 155 547 | | | | |
| | 13 079 | Crawford County, GA | 12 630 | 33340 | | Milwaukee-Waukesha-West Allis, WI Metro SA | 1555 908 |
| | 13 169 | Jones County, GA | 28 669 | | 55 079 | Milwaukee County, WI | 947 735 |
| | 13 207 | Monroe County, GA | 26 424 | | 55 089 | Ozaukee County, WI | 86 395 |
| | 13 289 | Twiggs County, GA | 9 023 | | 55 131 | Washington County, WI | 131 887 |
| 31460 | | Madera-Chowchilla, CA Metro SA | 150 865 | | 55 133 | Waukesha County, WI | 389 891 |
| | 06 039 | Madera County, CA | 150 865 | | | | |
| 31540 | | Madison, WI Metro SA | 568 593 | | | | |
| | 55 021 | Columbia County, WI | 56 833 | | | | |
| | 55 025 | Dane County, WI | 488 073 | | | | |
| | 55 049 | Iowa County, WI | 23 687 | | | | |

# Metropolitan Statistical Areas, Metropolitan Divisions, and Components (as defined December 2009)–*Continued*

| Core based statistical area | State/ County FIPS code | Title and Geographic Components | 2010 Census Population | Core based statistical area | State/ County FIPS code | Title and Geographic Components | 2010 Census Population |
|---|---|---|---|---|---|---|---|
| 33460 | | Minneapolis-St. Paul-Bloomington, MN-WI Metro SA | 3279 833 | 34940 | | Naples-Marco Island, FL Metro SA | 321 520 |
| | 27 003 | Anoka County, MN | 330 844 | | 12 021 | Collier County, FL | 321 520 |
| | 27 019 | Carver County, MN | 91 042 | | | | |
| | 27 025 | Chisago County, MN | 53 887 | 34980 | | Nashville-Davidson—Murfreesboro—Franklin, TN Metro SA | 1589 934 |
| | 27 037 | Dakota County, MN | 398 552 | | 47 015 | Cannon County, TN | 13 801 |
| | 27 053 | Hennepin County, MN | 1152 425 | | 47 021 | Cheatham County, TN | 39 105 |
| | 27 059 | Isanti County, MN | 37 816 | | 47 037 | Davidson County, TN | 626 681 |
| | 27 123 | Ramsey County, MN | 508 640 | | 47 043 | Dickson County, TN | 49 666 |
| | 27 139 | Scott County, MN | 129 928 | | 47 081 | Hickman County, TN | 24 690 |
| | 27 141 | Sherburne County, MN | 88 499 | | 47 111 | Macon County, TN | 22 248 |
| | 27 163 | Washington County, MN | 238 136 | | 47 147 | Robertson County, TN | 66 283 |
| | 27 171 | Wright County, MN | 124 700 | | 47 149 | Rutherford County, TN | 262 604 |
| | 55 093 | Pierce County, WI | 41 019 | | 47 159 | Smith County, TN | 19 166 |
| | 55 109 | St. Croix County, WI | 84 345 | | 47 165 | Sumner County, TN | 160 645 |
| 33540 | | Missoula, MT Metro SA | 109 299 | | 47 169 | Trousdale County, TN | 7 870 |
| | 30 063 | Missoula County, MT | 109 299 | | 47 187 | Williamson County, TN | 183 182 |
| | | | | | 47 189 | Wilson County, TN | 113 993 |
| 33660 | | Mobile, AL Metro SA | 412 992 | 35300 | | New Haven-Milford, CT Metro SA | 862 477 |
| | 01 097 | Mobile County, AL | 412 992 | | 09 009 | New Haven County, CT | 862 477 |
| 33700 | | Modesto, CA Metro SA | 514 453 | 35380 | | New Orleans-Metairie-Kenner, LA Metro SA | 1167 764 |
| | 06 099 | Stanislaus County, CA | 514 453 | | 22 051 | Jefferson Parish, LA | 432 552 |
| | | | | | 22 071 | Orleans Parish, LA | 343 829 |
| 33740 | | Monroe, LA Metro SA | 176 441 | | 22 075 | Plaquemines Parish, LA | 23 042 |
| | 22 073 | Ouachita Parish, LA | 153 720 | | 22 087 | St. Bernard Parish, LA | 35 897 |
| | 22 111 | Union Parish, LA | 22 721 | | 22 089 | St. Charles Parish, LA | 52 780 |
| | | | | | 22 095 | St. John the Baptist Parish, LA | 45 924 |
| 33780 | | Monroe, MI Metro SA | 152 021 | | 22 103 | St. Tammany Parish, LA | 233 740 |
| | 26 115 | Monroe County, MI | 152 021 | 35620 | | New York-Northern NJ-Long Island, NY-NJ-PA Metro SA | 18897 109 |
| 33860 | | Montgomery, AL Metro SA | 374 536 | | | | |
| | 01 001 | Autauga County, AL | 54 571 | | | Edison-New Brunswick, NJ Metro Div 20764 | 2340 249 |
| | 01 051 | Elmore County, AL | 79 303 | | 34 023 | Middlesex County, NJ | 809 858 |
| | 01 085 | Lowndes County, AL | 11 299 | | 34 025 | Monmouth County, NJ | 630 380 |
| | 01 101 | Montgomery County, AL | 229 363 | | 34 029 | Ocean County, NJ | 576 567 |
| 34060 | | Morgantown, WV Metro SA | 129 709 | | 34 035 | Somerset County, NJ | 323 444 |
| | 54 061 | Monongalia County, WV | 96 189 | | | Nassau-Suffolk, NY Metro Div 35004 | 2832 882 |
| | 54 077 | Preston County, WV | 33 520 | | 36 059 | Nassau County, NY | 1339 532 |
| | | | | | 36 103 | Suffolk County, NY | 1493 350 |
| 34100 | | Morristown, TN Metro SA | 136 608 | | | Newark-Union, NJ-PA Metro Div 35084 | 2147 727 |
| | 47 057 | Grainger County, TN | 22 657 | | 34 013 | Essex County, NJ | 783 969 |
| | 47 063 | Hamblen County, TN | 62 544 | | 34 019 | Hunterdon County, NJ | 128 349 |
| | 47 089 | Jefferson County, TN | 51 407 | | 34 027 | Morris County, NJ | 492 276 |
| | | | | | 34 037 | Sussex County, NJ | 149 265 |
| 34580 | | Mount Vernon-Anacortes, WA Metro SA | 116 901 | | 34 039 | Union County, NJ | 536 499 |
| | 53 057 | Skagit County, WA | 116 901 | | 42 103 | Pike County, PA | 57 369 |
| 34620 | | Muncie, IN Metro SA | 117 671 | | | New York-White Plains-Wayne, NY-NJ Metro Div 35644 | 11576 251 |
| | 18 035 | Delaware County, IN | 117 671 | | 34 003 | Bergen County, NJ | 905 116 |
| | | | | | 34 017 | Hudson County, NJ | 634 266 |
| 34740 | | Muskegon-Norton Shores, MI Metro SA | 172 188 | | 34 031 | Passaic County, NJ | 501 226 |
| | 26 121 | Muskegon County, MI | 172 188 | | 36 005 | Bronx County, NY | 1385 108 |
| | | | | | 36 047 | Kings County, NY | 2504 700 |
| 34820 | | Myrtle Beach-North Myrtle Beach-Conway, SC Metro SA | 269 291 | | 36 061 | New York County, NY | 1585 873 |
| | 45 051 | Horry County, SC | 269 291 | | 36 079 | Putnam County, NY | 99 710 |
| | | | | | 36 081 | Queens County, NY | 2230 722 |
| 34900 | | Napa, CA Metro SA | 136 484 | | 36 085 | Richmond County, NY | 468 730 |
| | 06 055 | Napa County, CA | 136 484 | | 36 087 | Rockland County, NY | 311 687 |
| | | | | | 36 119 | Westchester County, NY | 949 113 |

| Core based statistical area | State/ County FIPS code | Title and Geographic Components | 2010 Census Population | Core based statistical area | State/ County FIPS code | Title and Geographic Components | 2010 Census Population |
|---|---|---|---|---|---|---|---|
| 35660 | | Niles-Benton Harbor, MI Metro SA ................. | 156 813 | 37340 | | Palm Bay-Melbourne-Titusville, FL Metro SA.. | 543 376 |
| | 26 021 | Berrien County, MI........................................ | 156 813 | | 12 009 | Brevard County, FL ..................................... | 543 376 |
| 35840 | | North Port-Bradenton-Sarasota, FL Metro SA. | 702 281 | 37380 | | Palm Coast, FL Metro SA............................... | 95 696 |
| | 12 081 | Manatee County, FL..................................... | 322 833 | | 12 035 | Flagler County, FL ....................................... | 95 696 |
| | 12 115 | Sarasota County, FL.................................... | 379 448 | 37460 | | Panama City-Lynn Haven-Panama City | |
| 35980 | | Norwich-New London, CT Metro SA............... | 274 055 | | | Beach, FL Metro SA...................................... | 168 852 |
| | 09 011 | New London County, CT ............................... | 274 055 | | 12 005 | Bay County, FL ............................................ | 168 852 |
| 36100 | | Ocala, FL Metro SA ....................................... | 331 298 | 37620 | | Parkersburg-Marietta-Vienna, WV-OH Metro | |
| | 12 083 | Marion County, FL........................................ | 331 298 | | | SA................................................................. | 162 056 |
| 36140 | | Ocean City, NJ Metro SA............................... | 97 265 | | 39 167 | Washington County, OH................................ | 61 778 |
| | 34 009 | Cape May County, NJ .................................. | 97 265 | | 54 073 | Pleasants County, WV.................................. | 7 605 |
| 36220 | | Odessa, TX Metro SA .................................... | 137 130 | | 54 105 | Wirt County, WV........................................... | 5 717 |
| | 48 135 | Ector County, TX ......................................... | 137 130 | | 54 107 | Wood County, WV......................................... | 86 956 |
| 36260 | | Ogden-Clearfield, UT Metro SA ...................... | 547 184 | 37700 | | Pascagoula, MS Metro SA ............................. | 162 246 |
| | 49 011 | Davis County, UT ......................................... | 306 479 | | 28 039 | George County, MS...................................... | 22 578 |
| | 49 029 | Morgan County, UT ...................................... | 9 469 | | 28 059 | Jackson County, MS..................................... | 139 668 |
| | 49 057 | Weber County, UT........................................ | 231 236 | 37860 | | Pensacola-Ferry Pass-Brent, FL Metro SA ..... | 448 991 |
| 36420 | | Oklahoma City, OK Metro SA ......................... | 1252 987 | | 12 033 | Escambia County, FL.................................... | 297 619 |
| | 40 017 | Canadian County, OK.................................... | 115 541 | | 12 113 | Santa Rosa County, FL................................. | 151 372 |
| | 40 027 | Cleveland County, OK................................... | 255 755 | 37900 | | Peoria, IL Metro SA........................................ | 379 186 |
| | 40 051 | Grady County, OK......................................... | 52 431 | | 17 123 | Marshall County, IL....................................... | 12 640 |
| | 40 081 | Lincoln County, OK....................................... | 34 273 | | 17 143 | Peoria County, IL.......................................... | 186 494 |
| | 40 083 | Logan County, OK......................................... | 41 848 | | 17 175 | Stark County, IL............................................ | 5 994 |
| | 40 087 | McClain County, OK...................................... | 34 506 | | 17 179 | Tazewell County, IL....................................... | 135 394 |
| | 40 109 | Oklahoma County, OK................................... | 718 633 | | 17 203 | Woodford County, IL...................................... | 38 664 |
| 36500 | | Olympia, WA Metro SA ................................... | 252 264 | 37980 | | Philadelphia-Camden-Wilmington, PA-NJ-DE- | |
| | 53 067 | Thurston County, WA.................................... | 252 264 | | | MD Metro SA.................................................. | 5965 343 |
| 36540 | | Omaha-Council Bluffs, NE-IA Metro SA .......... | 865 350 | | | Camden, NJ Metro Div 15804 ....................... | 1250 679 |
| | 19 085 | Harrison County, IA ...................................... | 14 928 | | 34 005 | Burlington County, NJ................................... | 448 734 |
| | 19 129 | Mills County, IA............................................ | 15 059 | | 34 007 | Camden County, NJ...................................... | 513 657 |
| | 19 155 | Pottawattamie County, IA ............................. | 93 158 | | 34 015 | Gloucester County, NJ ................................. | 288 288 |
| | 31 025 | Cass County, NE.......................................... | 25 241 | | | Philadelphia, PA Metro Div 37964 ............... | 4008 994 |
| | 31 055 | Douglas County, NE...................................... | 517 110 | | 42 017 | Bucks County, PA......................................... | 625 249 |
| | 31 153 | Sarpy County, NE......................................... | 158 840 | | 42 029 | Chester County, PA...................................... | 498 886 |
| | 31 155 | Saunders County, NE ................................... | 20 780 | | 42 045 | Delaware County, PA .................................... | 558 979 |
| | 31 177 | Washington County, NE ................................ | 20 234 | | 42 091 | Montgomery County, PA ............................... | 799 874 |
| 36740 | | Orlando-Kissimmee-Sanford, FL Metro SA ..... | 2134 411 | | 42 101 | Philadelphia County, PA................................ | 1526 006 |
| | 12 069 | Lake County, FL........................................... | 297 052 | | | Wilmington, DE-MD-NJ Metro Div 48864..... | 705 670 |
| | 12 095 | Orange County, FL........................................ | 1145 956 | | 10 003 | New Castle County, DE.................................. | 538 479 |
| | 12 097 | Osceola County, FL...................................... | 268 685 | | 24 015 | Cecil County, MD.......................................... | 101 108 |
| | 12 117 | Seminole County, FL..................................... | 422 718 | | 34 033 | Salem County, NJ......................................... | 66 083 |
| 36780 | | Oshkosh-Neenah, WI Metro SA....................... | 166 994 | 38060 | | Phoenix-Mesa-Glendale, AZ Metro SA............ | 4192 887 |
| | 55 139 | Winnebago County, WI.................................. | 166 994 | | 04 013 | Maricopa County, AZ..................................... | 3817 117 |
| 36980 | | Owensboro, KY Metro SA............................... | 114 752 | | 04 021 | Pinal County, AZ........................................... | 375 770 |
| | 21 059 | Daviess County, KY...................................... | 96 656 | 38220 | | Pine Bluff, AR Metro SA ................................ | 100 258 |
| | 21 091 | Hancock County, KY ..................................... | 8 565 | | 05 025 | Cleveland County, AR................................... | 8 689 |
| | 21 149 | McLean County, KY....................................... | 9 531 | | 05 069 | Jefferson County, AR .................................... | 77 435 |
| 37100 | | Oxnard-Thousand Oaks-Ventura, CA Metro | | | 05 079 | Lincoln County, AR........................................ | 14 134 |
| | | SA.................................................................. | 823 318 | | | | |
| | 06 111 | Ventura County, CA...................................... | 823 318 | | | | |

# Metropolitan Statistical Areas, Metropolitan Divisions, and Components (as defined December 2009)–*Continued*

| Core based statistical area | State/ County FIPS code | Title and Geographic Components | 2010 Census Population | Core based statistical area | State/ County FIPS code | Title and Geographic Components | 2010 Census Population |
|---|---|---|---|---|---|---|---|
| 38300 | | Pittsburgh, PA Metro SA | 2356 285 | 39540 | | Racine, WI Metro SA | 195 408 |
| | 42 003 | Allegheny County, PA | 1223 348 | | 55 101 | Racine County, WI | 195 408 |
| | 42 005 | Armstrong County, PA | 68 941 | | | | |
| | 42 007 | Beaver County, PA | 170 539 | 39580 | | Raleigh-Cary, NC Metro SA | 1130 490 |
| | 42 019 | Butler County, PA | 183 862 | | 37 069 | Franklin County, NC | 60 619 |
| | 42 051 | Fayette County, PA | 136 606 | | 37 101 | Johnston County, NC | 168 878 |
| | 42 125 | Washington County, PA | 207 820 | | 37 183 | Wake County, NC | 900 993 |
| | 42 129 | Westmoreland County, PA | 365 169 | | | | |
| | | | | 39660 | | Rapid City, SD Metro SA | 126 382 |
| 38340 | | Pittsfield, MA Metro SA | 131 219 | | 46 093 | Meade County, SD | 25 434 |
| | 25 003 | Berkshire County, MA | 131 219 | | 46 103 | Pennington County, SD | 100 948 |
| | | | | | | | |
| 38540 | | Pocatello, ID Metro SA | 90 656 | 39740 | | Reading, PA Metro SA | 411 442 |
| | 16 005 | Bannock County, ID | 82 839 | | 42 011 | Berks County, PA | 411 442 |
| | 16 077 | Power County, ID | 7 817 | | | | |
| | | | | 39820 | | Redding, CA Metro SA | 177 223 |
| 38860 | | Portland-South Portland-Biddeford, ME Metro SA | 514 098 | | 06 089 | Shasta County, CA | 177 223 |
| | 23 005 | Cumberland County, ME | 281 674 | 39900 | | Reno-Sparks, NV Metro SA | 425 417 |
| | 23 023 | Sagadahoc County, ME | 35 293 | | 32 029 | Storey County, NV | 4 010 |
| | 23 031 | York County, ME | 197 131 | | 32 031 | Washoe County, NV | 421 407 |
| | | | | | | | |
| 38900 | | Portland-Vancouver-Hillsboro, OR-WA Metro SA | 2226 009 | 40060 | | Richmond, VA Metro SA | 1258 251 |
| | 41 005 | Clackamas County, OR | 375 992 | | 51 007 | Amelia County, VA | 12 690 |
| | 41 009 | Columbia County, OR | 49 351 | | 51 033 | Caroline County, VA | 28 545 |
| | 41 051 | Multnomah County, OR | 735 334 | | 51 036 | Charles City County, VA | 7 256 |
| | 41 067 | Washington County, OR | 529 710 | | 51 041 | Chesterfield County, VA | 316 236 |
| | 41 071 | Yamhill County, OR | 99 193 | | 51 049 | Cumberland County, VA | 10 052 |
| | 53 011 | Clark County, WA | 425 363 | | 51 053 | Dinwiddie County, VA | 28 001 |
| | 53 059 | Skamania County, WA | 11 066 | | 51 075 | Goochland County, VA | 21 717 |
| | | | | | 51 085 | Hanover County, VA | 99 863 |
| 38940 | | Port St. Lucie, FL Metro SA | 424 107 | | 51 087 | Henrico County, VA | 306 935 |
| | 12 085 | Martin County, FL | 146 318 | | 51 097 | King and Queen County, VA | 6 945 |
| | 12 111 | St. Lucie County, FL | 277 789 | | 51 101 | King William County, VA | 15 935 |
| | | | | | 51 109 | Louisa County, VA | 33 153 |
| 39100 | | Poughkeepsie-Newburgh-Middletown, NY Metro SA | 670 301 | | 51 127 | New Kent County, VA | 18 429 |
| | 36 027 | Dutchess County, NY | 297 488 | | 51 145 | Powhatan County, VA | 28 046 |
| | 36 071 | Orange County, NY | 372 813 | | 51 149 | Prince George County, VA | 35 725 |
| | | | | | 51 183 | Sussex County, VA | 12 087 |
| 39140 | | Prescott, AZ Metro SA | 211 033 | | 51 570 | Colonial Heights city, VA | 17 411 |
| | 04 025 | Yavapai County, AZ | 211 033 | | 51 670 | Hopewell city, VA | 22 591 |
| | | | | | 51 730 | Petersburg city, VA | 32 420 |
| 39300 | | Providence-New Bedford-Fall River, RI-MA Metro SA | 1600 852 | | 51 760 | Richmond city, VA | 204 214 |
| | 25 005 | Bristol County, MA | 548 285 | 40140 | | Riverside-San Bernardino-Ontario, CA Metro SA | 4224 851 |
| | 44 001 | Bristol County, RI | 49 875 | | 06 065 | Riverside County, CA | 2189 641 |
| | 44 003 | Kent County, RI | 166 158 | | 06 071 | San Bernardino County, CA | 2035 210 |
| | 44 005 | Newport County, RI | 82 888 | 40220 | | Roanoke, VA Metro SA | 308 707 |
| | 44 007 | Providence County, RI | 626 667 | | 51 023 | Botetourt County, VA | 33 148 |
| | 44 009 | Washington County, RI | 126 979 | | 51 045 | Craig County, VA | 5 190 |
| | | | | | 51 067 | Franklin County, VA | 56 159 |
| 39340 | | Provo-Orem, UT Metro SA | 526 810 | | 51 161 | Roanoke County, VA | 92 376 |
| | 49 023 | Juab County, UT | 10 246 | | 51 770 | Roanoke city, VA | 97 032 |
| | 49 049 | Utah County, UT | 516 564 | | 51 775 | Salem city, VA | 24 802 |
| | | | | | | | |
| 39380 | | Pueblo, CO Metro SA | 159 063 | 40340 | | Rochester, MN Metro SA | 186 011 |
| | 08 101 | Pueblo County, CO | 159 063 | | 27 039 | Dodge County, MN | 20 087 |
| | | | | | 27 109 | Olmsted County, MN | 144 248 |
| 39460 | | Punta Gorda, FL Metro SA | 159 978 | | 27 157 | Wabasha County, MN | 21 676 |
| | 12 015 | Charlotte County, FL | 159 978 | | | | |

# Metropolitan Statistical Areas, Metropolitan Divisions, and Components (as defined December 2009)–*Continued*

| Core based statistical area | State/ County FIPS code | Title and Geographic Components | 2010 Census Population | Core based statistical area | State/ County FIPS code | Title and Geographic Components | 2010 Census Population |
|---|---|---|---|---|---|---|---|
| 40380 | | Rochester, NY Metro SA | 1054 323 | 41500 | | Salinas, CA Metro SA | 415 057 |
| | 36 051 | Livingston County, NY | 65 393 | | 06 053 | Monterey County, CA | 415 057 |
| | 36 055 | Monroe County, NY | 744 344 | | | | |
| | 36 069 | Ontario County, NY | 107 931 | 41540 | | Salisbury, MD Metro SA | 125 203 |
| | 36 073 | Orleans County, NY | 42 883 | | 24 039 | Somerset County, MD | 26 470 |
| | 36 117 | Wayne County, NY | 93 772 | | 24 045 | Wicomico County, MD | 98 733 |
| 40420 | | Rockford, IL Metro SA | 349 431 | 41620 | | Salt Lake City, UT Metro SA | 1124 197 |
| | 17 007 | Boone County, IL | 54 165 | | 49 035 | Salt Lake County, UT | 1029 655 |
| | 17 201 | Winnebago County, IL | 295 266 | | 49 043 | Summit County, UT | 36 324 |
| | | | | | 49 045 | Tooele County, UT | 58 218 |
| 40580 | | Rocky Mount, NC Metro SA | 152 392 | | | | |
| | 37 065 | Edgecombe County, NC | 56 552 | 41660 | | San Angelo, TX Metro SA | 111 823 |
| | 37 127 | Nash County, NC | 95 840 | | 48 235 | Irion County, TX | 1 599 |
| | | | | | 48 451 | Tom Green County, TX | 110 224 |
| 40660 | | Rome, GA Metro SA | 96 317 | | | | |
| | 13 115 | Floyd County, GA | 96 317 | 41700 | | San Antonio-New Braunfels, TX Metro SA | 2142 508 |
| 40900 | | Sacramento—Arden-Arcade—Roseville, CA Metro SA | 2149 127 | | 48 013 | Atascosa County, TX | 44 911 |
| | | | | | 48 019 | Bandera County, TX | 20 485 |
| | | | | | 48 029 | Bexar County, TX | 1714 773 |
| | 06 017 | El Dorado County, CA | 181 058 | | 48 091 | Comal County, TX | 108 472 |
| | 06 061 | Placer County, CA | 348 432 | | 48 187 | Guadalupe County, TX | 131 533 |
| | 06 067 | Sacramento County, CA | 1418 788 | | 48 259 | Kendall County, TX | 33 410 |
| | 06 113 | Yolo County, CA | 200 849 | | 48 325 | Medina County, TX | 46 006 |
| | | | | | 48 493 | Wilson County, TX | 42 918 |
| 40980 | | Saginaw-Saginaw Township North, MI Metro SA | 200 169 | 41740 | | San Diego-Carlsbad-San Marcos, CA Metro SA | 3095 313 |
| | 26 145 | Saginaw County, MI | 200 169 | | 06 073 | San Diego County, CA | 3095 313 |
| 41060 | | St. Cloud, MN Metro SA | 189 093 | | | | |
| | 27 009 | Benton County, MN | 38 451 | 41780 | | Sandusky, OH Metro SA | 77 079 |
| | 27 145 | Stearns County, MN | 150 642 | | 39 043 | Erie County, OH | 77 079 |
| 41100 | | St. George, UT Metro SA | 138 115 | 41860 | | San Francisco-Oakland-Fremont, CA Metro SA | 4335 391 |
| | 49 053 | Washington County, UT | 138 115 | | | Oakland-Fremont-Hayward, CA Metro Div 36084 | 2559 296 |
| 41140 | | St. Joseph, MO-KS Metro SA | 127 329 | | 06 001 | Alameda County, CA | 1510 271 |
| | 20 043 | Doniphan County, KS | 7 945 | | 06 013 | Contra Costa County, CA | 1049 025 |
| | 29 003 | Andrew County, MO | 17 291 | | | San Francisco-San Mateo-Redwood City, CA Metro Div 41884 | 1776 095 |
| | 29 021 | Buchanan County, MO | 89 201 | | 06 041 | Marin County, CA | 252 409 |
| | 29 063 | DeKalb County, MO | 12 892 | | 06 075 | San Francisco County, CA | 805 235 |
| 41180 | | St. Louis, MO-IL Metro SA | 2812 896 | | 06 081 | San Mateo County, CA | 718 451 |
| | 17 005 | Bond County, IL | 17 768 | | | | |
| | 17 013 | Calhoun County, IL | 5 089 | 41940 | | San Jose-Sunnyvale-Santa Clara, CA Metro SA | 1836 911 |
| | 17 027 | Clinton County, IL | 37 762 | | 06 069 | San Benito County, CA | 55 269 |
| | 17 083 | Jersey County, IL | 22 985 | | 06 085 | Santa Clara County, CA | 1781 642 |
| | 17 117 | Macoupin County, IL | 47 765 | | | | |
| | 17 119 | Madison County, IL | 269 282 | 42020 | | San Luis Obispo-Paso Robles, CA Metro SA | 269 637 |
| | 17 133 | Monroe County, IL | 32 957 | | 06 079 | San Luis Obispo County, CA | 269 637 |
| | 17 163 | St. Clair County, IL | 270 056 | | | | |
| | 29 071 | Franklin County, MO | 101 492 | 42060 | | Santa Barbara-Santa Maria-Goleta, CA Metro SA | 423 895 |
| | 29 099 | Jefferson County, MO | 218 733 | | 06 083 | Santa Barbara County, CA | 423 895 |
| | 29 113 | Lincoln County, MO | 52 566 | | | | |
| | 29 183 | St. Charles County, MO | 360 485 | | | | |
| | 29 189 | St. Louis County, MO | 998 954 | 42100 | | Santa Cruz-Watsonville, CA Metro SA | 262 382 |
| | 29 219 | Warren County, MO | 32 513 | | 06 087 | Santa Cruz County, CA | 262 382 |
| | 29 221 | Washington County, MO | 25 195 | | | | |
| | 29 510 | St. Louis city, MO | 319 294 | | | | |
| 41420 | | Salem, OR Metro SA | 390 738 | 42140 | | Santa Fe, NM Metro SA | 144 170 |
| | 41 047 | Marion County, OR | 315 335 | | 35 049 | Santa Fe County, NM | 144 170 |
| | 41 053 | Polk County, OR | 75 403 | | | | |

# Metropolitan Statistical Areas, Metropolitan Divisions, and Components (as defined December 2009)–*Continued*

| Core based statistical area | State/ County FIPS code | Title and Geographic Components | 2010 Census Population | Core based statistical area | State/ County FIPS code | Title and Geographic Components | 2010 Census Population |
|---|---|---|---|---|---|---|---|
| 42220 | | Santa Rosa-Petaluma, CA Metro SA............... | 483 878 | 44140 | | Springfield, MA Metro SA................................ | 692 942 |
| | 06 097 | Sonoma County, CA......................................... | 483 878 | | 25 011 | Franklin County, MA...................................... | 71 372 |
| 42340 | | Savannah, GA Metro SA.................................. | 347 611 | | 25 013 | Hampden County, MA..................................... | 463 490 |
| | 13 029 | Bryan County, GA........................................... | 30 233 | | 25 015 | Hampshire County, MA .................................. | 158 080 |
| | 13 051 | Chatham County, GA....................................... | 265 128 | 44180 | | Springfield, MO Metro SA ............................... | 436 712 |
| | 13 103 | Effingham County, GA..................................... | 52 250 | | 29 043 | Christian County, MO..................................... | 77 422 |
| 42540 | | Scranton—Wilkes-Barre, PA Metro SA .......... | 563 631 | | 29 059 | Dallas County, MO ........................................ | 16 777 |
| | 42 069 | Lackawanna County, PA ................................. | 214 437 | | 29 077 | Greene County, MO ....................................... | 275 174 |
| | 42 079 | Luzerne County, PA ....................................... | 320 918 | | 29 167 | Polk County, MO ........................................... | 31 137 |
| | 42 131 | Wyoming County, PA ...................................... | 28 276 | | 29 225 | Webster County, MO ..................................... | 36 202 |
| 42660 | | Seattle-Tacoma-Bellevue, WA Metro SA........ | 3 439 809 | 44220 | | Springfield, OH Metro SA............................... | 138 333 |
| | | Seattle-Bellevue-Everett, WA Metro Div 42644 ............................................................ | 2 644 584 | | 39 023 | Clark County, OH .......................................... | 138 333 |
| | 53 033 | King County, WA ............................................ | 1 931 249 | 44300 | | State College, PA Metro SA .......................... | 153 990 |
| | 53 061 | Snohomish County, WA .................................. | 713 335 | | 42 027 | Centre County, PA......................................... | 153 990 |
| | | Tacoma, WA Metro Div 45104 ...................... | 795 225 | 44600 | | Steubenville-Weirton, OH-WV Metro SA ........ | 124 454 |
| | 53 053 | Pierce County, WA ........................................ | 795 225 | | 39 081 | Jefferson County, OH..................................... | 69 709 |
| 42680 | | Sebastian-Vero Beach, FL Metro SA.............. | 138 028 | | 54 009 | Brooke County, WV ....................................... | 24 069 |
| | 12 061 | Indian River County, FL.................................. | 138 028 | | 54 029 | Hancock County, WV ..................................... | 30 676 |
| 43100 | | Sheboygan, WI Metro SA ............................... | 115 507 | 44700 | | Stockton, CA Metro SA.................................. | 685 306 |
| | 55 117 | Sheboygan County, WI.................................... | 115 507 | | 06 077 | San Joaquin County, CA................................ | 685 306 |
| 43300 | | Sherman-Denison, TX Metro SA .................... | 120 877 | 44940 | | Sumter, SC Metro SA .................................... | 107 456 |
| | 48 181 | Grayson County, TX........................................ | 120 877 | | 45 085 | Sumter County, SC........................................ | 107 456 |
| 43340 | | Shreveport-Bossier City, LA Metro SA ........... | 398 604 | 45060 | | Syracuse, NY Metro SA.................................. | 662 577 |
| | 22 015 | Bossier Parish, LA ......................................... | 116 979 | | 36 053 | Madison County, NY....................................... | 73 442 |
| | 22 017 | Caddo Parish, LA .......................................... | 254 969 | | 36 067 | Onondaga County, NY .................................... | 467 026 |
| | 22 031 | De Soto Parish, LA......................................... | 26 656 | | 36 075 | Oswego County, NY....................................... | 122 109 |
| 43580 | | Sioux City, IA-NE-SD Metro SA...................... | 143 577 | 45220 | | Tallahassee, FL Metro SA ............................. | 367 413 |
| | 19 193 | Woodbury County, IA...................................... | 102 172 | | 12 039 | Gadsden County, FL ...................................... | 46 389 |
| | 31 043 | Dakota County, NE......................................... | 21 006 | | 12 065 | Jefferson County, FL...................................... | 14 761 |
| | 31 051 | Dixon County, NE........................................... | 6 000 | | 12 073 | Leon County, FL............................................ | 275 487 |
| | 46 127 | Union County, SD........................................... | 14 399 | | 12 129 | Wakulla County, FL........................................ | 30 776 |
| 43620 | | Sioux Falls, SD Metro SA .............................. | 228 261 | 45300 | | Tampa-St. Petersburg-Clearwater, FL Metro SA........................................................ | 2 783 243 |
| | 46 083 | Lincoln County, SD......................................... | 44 828 | | 12 053 | Hernando County, FL..................................... | 172 778 |
| | 46 087 | McCook County, SD........................................ | 5 618 | | 12 057 | Hillsborough County, FL................................. | 1 229 226 |
| | 46 099 | Minnehaha County, SD ................................... | 169 468 | | 12 101 | Pasco County, FL .......................................... | 464 697 |
| | 46 125 | Turner County, SD.......................................... | 8 347 | | 12 103 | Pinellas County, FL........................................ | 916 542 |
| 43780 | | South Bend-Mishawaka, IN-MI Metro SA........ | 319 224 | 45460 | | Terre Haute, IN Metro SA.............................. | 172 425 |
| | 18 141 | St. Joseph County, IN .................................... | 266 931 | | 18 021 | Clay County, IN ............................................. | 26 890 |
| | 26 027 | Cass County, MI............................................. | 52 293 | | 18 153 | Sullivan County, IN........................................ | 21 475 |
| 43900 | | Spartanburg, SC Metro SA ............................ | 284 307 | | 18 165 | Vermillion County, IN...................................... | 16 212 |
| | 45 083 | Spartanburg County, SC................................. | 284 307 | | 18 167 | Vigo County, IN ............................................. | 107 848 |
| 44060 | | Spokane, WA Metro SA .................................. | 471 221 | 45500 | | Texarkana, TX-Texarkana, AR Metro SA........ | 136 027 |
| | 53 063 | Spokane County, WA...................................... | 471 221 | | 05 091 | Miller County, AR........................................... | 43 462 |
| 44100 | | Springfield, IL Metro SA................................. | 210 170 | | 48 037 | Bowie County, TX........................................... | 92 565 |
| | 17 129 | Menard County, IL.......................................... | 12 705 | 45780 | | Toledo, OH Metro SA..................................... | 651 429 |
| | 17 167 | Sangamon County, IL...................................... | 197 465 | | 39 051 | Fulton County, OH ......................................... | 42 698 |
| | | | | | 39 095 | Lucas County, OH ......................................... | 441 815 |
| | | | | | 39 123 | Ottawa County, OH ........................................ | 41 428 |
| | | | | | 39 173 | Wood County, OH .......................................... | 125 488 |

# Metropolitan Statistical Areas, Metropolitan Divisions, and Components (as defined December 2009)–*Continued*

| Core based statistical area | State/ County FIPS code | Title and Geographic Components | 2010 Census Population | Core based statistical area | State/ County FIPS code | Title and Geographic Components | 2010 Census Population |
|---|---|---|---|---|---|---|---|
| 45820 | | Topeka, KS Metro SA | 233 870 | 47260 | | Virginia Beach-Norfolk-Newport News, VA-NC Metro SA | 1671 683 |
| | 20 085 | Jackson County, KS | 13 462 | | 37 053 | Currituck County, NC | 23 547 |
| | 20 087 | Jefferson County, KS | 19 126 | | 51 073 | Gloucester County, VA | 36 858 |
| | 20 139 | Osage County, KS | 16 295 | | 51 093 | Isle of Wight County, VA | 35 270 |
| | 20 177 | Shawnee County, KS | 177 934 | | 51 095 | James City County, VA | 67 009 |
| | 20 197 | Wabaunsee County, KS | 7 053 | | 51 115 | Mathews County, VA | 8 978 |
| 45940 | | Trenton-Ewing, NJ Metro SA | 366 513 | | 51 181 | Surry County, VA | 7 058 |
| | 34 021 | Mercer County, NJ | 366 513 | | 51 199 | York County, VA | 65 464 |
| | | | | | 51 550 | Chesapeake city, VA | 222 209 |
| 46060 | | Tucson, AZ Metro SA | 980 263 | | 51 650 | Hampton city, VA | 137 436 |
| | 04 019 | Pima County, AZ | 980 263 | | 51 700 | Newport News city, VA | 180 719 |
| 46140 | | Tulsa, OK Metro SA | 937 478 | | 51 710 | Norfolk city, VA | 242 803 |
| | 40 037 | Creek County, OK | 69 967 | | 51 735 | Poquoson city , VA | 12 150 |
| | 40 111 | Okmulgee County, OK | 40 069 | | 51 740 | Portsmouth city, VA | 95 535 |
| | 40 113 | Osage County, OK | 47 472 | | 51 800 | Suffolk city, VA | 84 585 |
| | 40 117 | Pawnee County, OK | 16 577 | | 51 810 | Virginia Beach city, VA | 437 994 |
| | 40 131 | Rogers County, OK | 86 905 | | 51 830 | Williamsburg city, VA | 14 068 |
| | 40 143 | Tulsa County, OK | 603 403 | 47300 | | Visalia-Porterville, CA Metro SA | 442 179 |
| | 40 145 | Wagoner County, OK | 73 085 | | 06 107 | Tulare County, CA | 442 179 |
| 46220 | | Tuscaloosa, AL Metro SA | 219 461 | 47380 | | Waco, TX Metro SA | 234 906 |
| | 01 063 | Greene County, AL | 9 045 | | 48 309 | McLennan County, TX | 234 906 |
| | 01 065 | Hale County, AL | 15 760 | | | | |
| | 01 125 | Tuscaloosa County, AL | 194 656 | 47580 | | Warner Robins, GA Metro SA | 139 900 |
| 46340 | | Tyler, TX Metro SA | 209 714 | | 13 153 | Houston County, GA | 139 900 |
| | 48 423 | Smith County, TX | 209 714 | 47900 | | Washington-Arlington-Alexandria, DC-VA-MD-WV Metro SA | 5582 170 |
| 46540 | | Utica-Rome, NY Metro SA | 299 397 | | | Bethesda-Rockville-Frederick, MD Metro Div 13644 | 1205 162 |
| | 36 043 | Herkimer County, NY | 64 519 | | 24 021 | Frederick County, MD | 233 385 |
| | 36 065 | Oneida County, NY | 234 878 | | 24 031 | Montgomery County, MD | 971 777 |
| 46660 | | Valdosta, GA Metro SA | 139 588 | | | Washington-Arlington-Alexandria, DC-VA-MD-WV Metro Div 47894 | 4377 008 |
| | 13 027 | Brooks County, GA | 16 243 | | 11 001 | District of Columbia, DC | 601 723 |
| | 13 101 | Echols County, GA | 4 034 | | 24 009 | Calvert County, MD | 88 737 |
| | 13 173 | Lanier County, GA | 10 078 | | 24 017 | Charles County, MD | 146 551 |
| | 13 185 | Lowndes County, GA | 109 233 | | 24 033 | Prince George's County, MD | 863 420 |
| 46700 | | Vallejo-Fairfield, CA Metro SA | 413 344 | | 51 013 | Arlington County, VA | 207 627 |
| | 06 095 | Solano County, CA | 413 344 | | 51 043 | Clarke County, VA | 14 034 |
| | | | | | 51 059 | Fairfax County, VA | 1081 726 |
| 47020 | | Victoria, TX Metro SA | 115 384 | | 51 061 | Fauquier County, VA | 65 203 |
| | 48 057 | Calhoun County, TX | 21 381 | | 51 107 | Loudoun County, VA | 312 311 |
| | 48 175 | Goliad County, TX | 7 210 | | 51 153 | Prince William County, VA | 402 002 |
| | 48 469 | Victoria County, TX | 86 793 | | 51 177 | Spotsylvania County, VA | 122 397 |
| 47220 | | Vineland-Millville-Bridgeton, NJ Metro SA | 156 898 | | 51 179 | Stafford County, VA | 128 961 |
| | 34 011 | Cumberland County, NJ | 156 898 | | 51 187 | Warren County, VA | 37 575 |
| | | | | | 51 510 | Alexandria city, VA | 139 966 |
| | | | | | 51 600 | Fairfax city, VA | 22 565 |
| | | | | | 51 610 | Falls Church city, VA | 12 332 |
| | | | | | 51 630 | Fredericksburg city, VA | 24 286 |
| | | | | | 51 683 | Manassas city, VA | 37 821 |
| | | | | | 51 685 | Manassas Park city, VA | 14 273 |
| | | | | | 54 037 | Jefferson County, WV | 53 498 |
| | | | | 47940 | | Waterloo-Cedar Falls, IA Metro SA | 167 819 |
| | | | | | 19 013 | Black Hawk County, IA | 131 090 |
| | | | | | 19 017 | Bremer County, IA | 24 276 |
| | | | | | 19 075 | Grundy County, IA | 12 453 |
| | | | | 48140 | | Wausau, WI Metro SA | 134 063 |
| | | | | | 55 073 | Marathon County, WI | 134 063 |

# Metropolitan Statistical Areas,
# Metropolitan Divisions,
# and Components
# (as defined December 2009)–*Continued*

| Core based statistical area | State/ County FIPS code | Title and Geographic Components | 2010 Census Population | Core based statistical area | State/ County FIPS code | Title and Geographic Components | 2010 Census Population |
|---|---|---|---|---|---|---|---|
| 48300 | | Wenatchee-East Wenatchee, WA Metro SA ... | 110 884 | 49020 | | Winchester, VA-WVMetro SA ......................... | 128 472 |
| | 53 007 | Chelan County, WA .................................... | 72 453 | | 51 069 | Frederick County, VA ................................ | 78 305 |
| | 53 017 | Douglas County, WA ................................. | 38 431 | | 51 840 | Winchester city , VA ................................. | 26 203 |
| | | | | | 54 027 | Hampshire County, WV ............................. | 23 964 |
| 48540 | | Wheeling, WV-OH Metro SA........................ | 147 950 | | | | |
| | 39 013 | Belmont County, OH................................. | 70 400 | 49180 | | Winston-Salem, NC Metro SA ...................... | 477 717 |
| | 54 051 | Marshall County, WV ................................ | 33 107 | | 37 059 | Davie County, NC.................................... | 41 240 |
| | 54 069 | Ohio County, WV ..................................... | 44 443 | | 37 067 | Forsyth County, NC ................................. | 350 670 |
| 48620 | | Wichita, KS Metro SA................................ | 623 061 | | 37 169 | Stokes County, NC .................................. | 47 401 |
| | 20 015 | Butler County, KS .................................... | 65 880 | | 37 197 | Yadkin County, NC .................................. | 38 406 |
| | 20 079 | Harvey County, KS ................................... | 34 684 | 49340 | | Worcester, MA Metro SA ............................ | 798 552 |
| | 20 173 | Sedgwick County, KS ............................... | 498 365 | | 25 027 | Worcester County, MA .............................. | 798 552 |
| | 20 191 | Sumner County, KS .................................. | 24 132 | | | | |
| | | | | 49420 | | Yakima, WA Metro SA ................................ | 243 231 |
| 48660 | | Wichita Falls, TX Metro SA........................ | 151 306 | | 53 077 | Yakima County, WA ................................. | 243 231 |
| | 48 009 | Archer County, TX ................................... | 9 054 | | | | |
| | 48 077 | Clay County, TX ...................................... | 10 752 | 49620 | | York-Hanover, PA Metro SA........................ | 434 972 |
| | 48 485 | Wichita County, TX .................................. | 131 500 | | 42 133 | York County, PA ..................................... | 434 972 |
| 48700 | | Williamsport, PA Metro SA......................... | 116 111 | 49660 | | Youngstown-Warren-Boardman, OH-PA Metro SA ............................................. | 565 773 |
| | 42 081 | Lycoming County, PA ................................ | 116 111 | | 39 099 | Mahoning County, OH .............................. | 238 823 |
| 48900 | | Wilmington, NC Metro SA ........................... | 362 315 | | 39 155 | Trumbull County, OH................................ | 210 312 |
| | 37 019 | Brunswick County, NC............................... | 107 431 | | 42 085 | Mercer County, PA .................................. | 116 638 |
| | 37 129 | New Hanover County, NC ........................... | 202 667 | | | Yuba City, CA Metro SA ............................. | 166 892 |
| | 37 141 | Pender County, NC ................................... | 52 217 | 49700 | 06 101 | Sutter County, CA.................................... | 94 737 |
| | | | | | 06 115 | Yuba County, CA..................................... | 72 155 |
| | | | | 49740 | | Yuma, AZ Metro SA ................................... | 195 751 |
| | | | | | 04 027 | Yuma County, AZ ................................... | 195 751 |

# APPENDIX C
# CORE BASED STATISTICAL AREAS
## (Metropolitan and Micropolitan),
## METROPOLITAN DIVISIONS, AND COMPONENTS
## (as defined February 2013)

| Core Based Statistical Area | State/County FIPS Code | Title and Geographic Components | 2010 Census Population | 2012 Estimated Population | Core Based Statistical Area | State/County FIPS Code | Title and Geographic Components | 2010 Census Population | 2012 Estimated Population |
|---|---|---|---|---|---|---|---|---|---|
| 10100 | | Aberdeen, SD Micro area................ | 40 602 | 41 357 | 10820 | | Alexandria, MN Micro area.............. | 36 009 | 36 415 |
| | 46 013 | Brown County, SD.................... | 36 531 | 37 331 | | 27 041 | Douglas County, MN.................... | 36 009 | 36 415 |
| | 46 045 | Edmunds County, SD................ | 4 071 | 4 026 | 10860 | | Alice, TX Micro area...................... | 40 838 | 41 754 |
| 10140 | | Aberdeen, WA Micro area............... | 72 797 | 71 692 | | 48 249 | Jim Wells County, TX.................. | 40 838 | 41 754 |
| | 53 027 | Grays Harbor County, WA........... | 72 797 | 71 692 | 10900 | | Allentown-Bethlehem-Easton, PA-NJ Metro area...................... | 821 173 | 827 171 |
| 10180 | | Abilene, TX Metro area.................... | 165 252 | 166 963 | | 34 041 | Warren County, NJ.................... | 108 692 | 107 653 |
| | 48 059 | Callahan County, TX.................. | 13 544 | 13 517 | | 42 025 | Carbon County, PA..................... | 65 249 | 65 006 |
| | 48 253 | Jones County, TX..................... | 20 202 | 19 973 | | 42 077 | Lehigh County, PA..................... | 349 497 | 355 245 |
| | 48 441 | Taylor County, TX ..................... | 131 506 | 133 473 | | 42 095 | Northampton County, PA............. | 297 735 | 299 267 |
| 10220 | | Ada, OK Micro area....................... | 37 492 | 37 958 | 10940 | | Alma, MI Micro area...................... | 42 476 | 42 063 |
| | 40 123 | Pontotoc County, OK ................. | 37 492 | 37 958 | | 26 057 | Gratiot County, MI...................... | 42 476 | 42 063 |
| 10300 | | Adrian, MI Micro area..................... | 99 892 | 98 987 | 10980 | | Alpena, MI Micro area.................... | 29 598 | 29 234 |
| | 26 091 | Lenawee County, MI.................. | 99 892 | 98 987 | | 26 007 | Alpena County, MI..................... | 29 598 | 29 234 |
| 10420 | | Akron, OH Metro area .................... | 703 200 | 702 262 | 11020 | | Altoona, PA Metro area................... | 127 089 | 127 121 |
| | 39 133 | Portage County, OH................... | 161 419 | 161 451 | | 42 013 | Blair County, PA....................... | 127 089 | 127 121 |
| | 39 153 | Summit County, OH................... | 541 781 | 540 811 | 11060 | | Altus, OK Micro area ..................... | 26 446 | 26 237 |
| 10460 | | Alamogordo, NM Micro area............ | 63 797 | 66 041 | | 40 065 | Jackson County, OK .................. | 26 446 | 26 237 |
| | 35 035 | Otero County, NM ...................... | 63 797 | 66 041 | 11100 | | Amarillo, TX Metro area.................. | 251 933 | 257 578 |
| 10500 | | Albany, GA Metro area................... | 157 308 | 157 399 | | 48 011 | Armstrong County, TX................ | 1 901 | 1 944 |
| | 13 007 | Baker County, GA ..................... | 3 451 | 3 366 | | 48 065 | Carson County, TX.................... | 6 182 | 6 157 |
| | 13 095 | Dougherty County, GA................ | 94 565 | 94 501 | | 48 359 | Oldham County, TX................... | 2 052 | 2 060 |
| | 13 177 | Lee County, GA........................ | 28 298 | 28 746 | | 48 375 | Potter County, TX..................... | 121 073 | 122 335 |
| | 13 273 | Terrell County, GA..................... | 9 315 | 9 045 | | 48 381 | Randall County, TX................... | 120 725 | 125 082 |
| | 13 321 | Worth County, GA...................... | 21 679 | 21 741 | 11140 | | Americus, GA Micro area .............. | 37 829 | 36 544 |
| 10540 | | Albany, OR Metro area................... | 116 672 | 118 360 | | 13 249 | Schley County, GA.................... | 5 010 | 4 990 |
| | 41 043 | Linn County, OR........................ | 116 672 | 118 360 | | 13 261 | Sumter County, GA.................... | 32 819 | 31 554 |
| 10580 | | Albany-Schenectady-Troy, NY Metro area.......................... | 870 716 | 874 646 | 11180 | | Ames, IA Metro area...................... | 89 542 | 91 140 |
| | 36 001 | Albany County, NY..................... | 304 204 | 305 455 | | 19 169 | Story County, IA....................... | 89 542 | 91 140 |
| | 36 083 | Rensselaer County, NY............... | 159 429 | 159 835 | 11220 | | Amsterdam, NY Micro area............ | 50 219 | 49 941 |
| | 36 091 | Saratoga County, NY ................. | 219 607 | 222 133 | | 36 057 | Montgomery County, NY.............. | 50 219 | 49 941 |
| | 36 093 | Schenectady County, NY............. | 154 727 | 155 124 | 11260 | | Anchorage, AK Metro area............. | 380 821 | 392 535 |
| | 36 095 | Schoharie County, NY................ | 32 749 | 32 099 | | 02 020 | Anchorage Municipality, AK......... | 291 826 | 298 610 |
| 10620 | | Albemarle, NC Micro area.............. | 60 585 | 60 576 | | 02 170 | Matanuska-Susitna Borough, AK.. | 88 995 | 93 925 |
| | 37 167 | Stanly County, NC..................... | 60 585 | 60 576 | 11380 | | Andrews, TX Micro area................. | 14 786 | 16 117 |
| 10660 | | Albert Lea, MN Micro area............. | 31 255 | 31 054 | | 48 003 | Andrews County, TX.................. | 14 786 | 16 117 |
| | 27 047 | Freeborn County, MN................. | 31 255 | 31 054 | 11420 | | Angola, IN Micro area.................... | 34 185 | 34 124 |
| 10700 | | Albertville, AL Micro area................ | 93 019 | 94 776 | | 18 151 | Steuben County, IN................... | 34 185 | 34 124 |
| | 01 095 | Marshall County, AL................... | 93 019 | 94 776 | 11460 | | Ann Arbor, MI Metro area............... | 344 791 | 350 946 |
| 10740 | | Albuquerque, NM Metro area........... | 887 077 | 901 700 | | 26 161 | Washtenaw County, MI............... | 344 791 | 350 946 |
| | 35 001 | Bernalillo County, NM ................ | 662 564 | 673 460 | 11500 | | Anniston-Oxford-Jacksonville, AL Metro area............................. | 118 572 | 117 296 |
| | 35 043 | Sandoval County, NM................. | 131 561 | 135 588 | | 01 015 | Calhoun County, AL................... | 118 572 | 117 296 |
| | 35 057 | Torrance County, NM................. | 16 383 | 16 021 | 11540 | | Appleton, WI Metro area................. | 225 666 | 228 450 |
| | 35 061 | Valencia County, NM ................. | 76 569 | 76 631 | | 55 015 | Calumet County, WI................... | 48 971 | 49 634 |
| 10780 | | Alexandria, LA Metro area.............. | 153 922 | 154 441 | | 55 087 | Outagamie County, WI................ | 176 695 | 178 816 |
| | 22 043 | Grant Parish, LA....................... | 22 309 | 22 068 | | | | | |
| | 22 079 | Rapides Parish, LA ................... | 131 613 | 132 373 | | | | | |

| Core Based Statistical Area | State/County FIPS Code | Title and Geographic Components | 2010 Census Population | 2012 Estimated Population | Core Based Statistical Area | State/County FIPS Code | Title and Geographic Components | 2010 Census Population | 2012 Estimated Population |
|---|---|---|---|---|---|---|---|---|---|
| 11580 | | Arcadia, FL Micro area | 34 862 | 34 712 | | 13 211 | Morgan County, GA | 17 868 | 17 881 |
| | 12 027 | DeSoto County, FL | 34 862 | 34 712 | | 13 217 | Newton County, GA | 99 958 | 101 505 |
| 11620 | | Ardmore, OK Micro area | 47 557 | 48 085 | | 13 223 | Paulding County, GA | 142 324 | 144 800 |
| | 40 019 | Carter County, OK | 47 557 | 48 085 | | 13 227 | Pickens County, GA | 29 431 | 29 268 |
| 11660 | | Arkadelphia, AR Micro area | 22 995 | 22 936 | | 13 231 | Pike County, GA | 17 869 | 17 810 |
| | 05 019 | Clark County, AR | 22 995 | 22 936 | | 13 247 | Rockdale County, GA | 85 215 | 85 820 |
| 11680 | | Arkansas City-Winfield, KS Micro area | 36 311 | 36 288 | | 13 255 | Spalding County, GA | 64 073 | 63 865 |
| | 20 035 | Cowley County, KS | 36 311 | 36 288 | | 13 297 | Walton County, GA | 83 768 | 84 575 |
| 11700 | | Asheville, NC Metro area | 424 858 | 432 406 | 12100 | | Atlantic City-Hammonton, NJ Metro area | 274 549 | 275 422 |
| | 37 021 | Buncombe County, NC | 238 318 | 244 490 | | 34 001 | Atlantic County, NJ | 274 549 | 275 422 |
| | 37 087 | Haywood County, NC | 59 036 | 58 908 | 12140 | | Auburn, IN Micro area | 42 223 | 42 321 |
| | 37 089 | Henderson County, NC | 106 740 | 108 266 | | 18 033 | DeKalb County, IN | 42 223 | 42 321 |
| | 37 115 | Madison County, NC | 20 764 | 20 742 | 12180 | | Auburn, NY Micro area | 80 026 | 79 552 |
| 11740 | | Ashland, OH Micro area | 53 139 | 52 962 | | 36 011 | Cayuga County, NY | 80 026 | 79 552 |
| | 39 005 | Ashland County, OH | 53 139 | 52 962 | 12220 | | Auburn-Opelika, AL Metro area | 140 247 | 147 257 |
| 11780 | | Ashtabula, OH Micro area | 101 497 | 100 389 | | 01 081 | Lee County, AL | 140 247 | 147 257 |
| | 39 007 | Ashtabula County, OH | 101 497 | 100 389 | 12260 | | Augusta-Richmond County, GA-SC Metro area | 564 873 | 575 898 |
| 11820 | | Astoria, OR Micro area | 37 039 | 37 301 | | 13 033 | Burke County, GA | 23 316 | 23 125 |
| | 41 007 | Clatsop County, OR | 37 039 | 37 301 | | 13 073 | Columbia County, GA | 124 053 | 131 627 |
| 11860 | | Atchison, KS Micro area | 16 924 | 16 813 | | 13 181 | Lincoln County, GA | 7 996 | 7 737 |
| | 20 005 | Atchison County, KS | 16 924 | 16 813 | | 13 189 | McDuffie County, GA | 21 875 | 21 663 |
| 11900 | | Athens, OH Micro area | 64 757 | 64 304 | | 13 245 | Richmond County, GA | 200 549 | 202 587 |
| | 39 009 | Athens County, OH | 64 757 | 64 304 | | 45 003 | Aiken County, SC | 160 099 | 162 812 |
| 11940 | | Athens, TN Micro area | 52 266 | 52 416 | | 45 037 | Edgefield County, SC | 26 985 | 26 347 |
| | 47 107 | McMinn County, TN | 52 266 | 52 416 | 12300 | | Augusta-Waterville, ME Micro area | 122 151 | 121 853 |
| 11980 | | Athens, TX Micro area | 78 532 | 79 094 | | 23 011 | Kennebec County, ME | 122 151 | 121 853 |
| | 48 213 | Henderson County, TX | 78 532 | 79 094 | 12380 | | Austin, MN Micro area | 39 163 | 39 372 |
| 12020 | | Athens-Clarke County, GA Metro area | 192 541 | 196 425 | | 27 099 | Mower County, MN | 39 163 | 39 372 |
| | 13 059 | Clarke County, GA | 116 714 | 120 266 | 12420 | | Austin-Round Rock, TX Metro area | 1 716 289 | 1 834 303 |
| | 13 195 | Madison County, GA | 28 120 | 27 922 | | 48 021 | Bastrop County, TX | 74 171 | 74 763 |
| | 13 219 | Oconee County, GA | 32 808 | 33 619 | | 48 055 | Caldwell County, TX | 38 066 | 38 734 |
| | 13 221 | Oglethorpe County, GA | 14 899 | 14 618 | | 48 209 | Hays County, TX | 157 107 | 168 990 |
| 12060 | | Atlanta-Sandy Springs-Roswell, GA Metro area | 5 286 728 | 5 457 831 | | 48 453 | Travis County, TX | 1 024 266 | 1 095 584 |
| | 13 013 | Barrow County, GA | 69 367 | 70 169 | | 48 491 | Williamson County, TX | 422 679 | 456 232 |
| | 13 015 | Bartow County, GA | 100 157 | 100 661 | 12460 | | Bainbridge, GA Micro area | 27 842 | 27 509 |
| | 13 035 | Butts County, GA | 23 655 | 23 524 | | 13 087 | Decatur County, GA | 27 842 | 27 509 |
| | 13 045 | Carroll County, GA | 110 527 | 111 580 | 12540 | | Bakersfield, CA Metro area | 839 631 | 856 158 |
| | 13 057 | Cherokee County, GA | 214 346 | 221 315 | | 06 029 | Kern County, CA | 839 631 | 856 158 |
| | 13 063 | Clayton County, GA | 259 424 | 265 888 | 12580 | | Baltimore-Columbia-Towson, MD Metro area | 2 710 489 | 2 753 149 |
| | 13 067 | Cobb County, GA | 688 078 | 707 442 | | 24 003 | Anne Arundel County, MD | 537 656 | 550 488 |
| | 13 077 | Coweta County, GA | 127 317 | 130 929 | | 24 005 | Baltimore County, MD | 805 029 | 817 455 |
| | 13 085 | Dawson County, GA | 22 330 | 22 422 | | 24 013 | Carroll County, MD | 167 134 | 167 217 |
| | 13 089 | DeKalb County, GA | 691 893 | 707 089 | | 24 025 | Harford County, MD | 244 826 | 248 622 |
| | 13 097 | Douglas County, GA | 132 403 | 133 971 | | 24 027 | Howard County, MD | 287 085 | 299 430 |
| | 13 113 | Fayette County, GA | 106 567 | 107 524 | | 24 035 | Queen Anne's County, MD | 47 798 | 48 595 |
| | 13 117 | Forsyth County, GA | 175 511 | 187 928 | | 24 510 | Baltimore city, MD | 620 961 | 621 342 |
| | 13 121 | Fulton County, GA | 920 581 | 977 773 | 12620 | | Bangor, ME Metro area | 153 923 | 153 746 |
| | 13 135 | Gwinnett County, GA | 805 321 | 842 046 | | 23 019 | Penobscot County, ME | 153 923 | 153 746 |
| | 13 143 | Haralson County, GA | 28 780 | 28 400 | 12660 | | Baraboo, WI Micro area | 61 976 | 62 597 |
| | 13 149 | Heard County, GA | 11 834 | 11 633 | | 55 111 | Sauk County, WI Micro area | 61 976 | 62 597 |
| | 13 151 | Henry County, GA | 203 922 | 209 053 | 12680 | | Bardstown, KY Micro area | 43 437 | 44 319 |
| | 13 159 | Jasper County, GA | 13 900 | 13 630 | | 21 179 | Nelson County, KY | 43 437 | 44 319 |
| | 13 171 | Lamar County, GA | 18 317 | 18 057 | | | | | |
| | 13 199 | Meriwether County, GA | 21 992 | 21 273 | | | | | |

# Core Based Statistical Areas (Metropolitan and Micropolitan), Metropolitan Divisions, and Components (as defined February 2013)–*Continued*

| Core Based Statistical Area | State/ County FIPS Code | Title and Geographic Components | 2010 Census Population | 2012 Estimated Population | Core Based Statistical Area | State/ County FIPS Code | Title and Geographic Components | 2010 Census Population | 2012 Estimated Population |
|---|---|---|---|---|---|---|---|---|---|
| 12700 | | Barnstable Town, MA Metro area..... | 215 888 | 215 423 | 13460 | | Bend-Redmond, OR Metro area....... | 157 733 | 162 277 |
| | 25 001 | Barnstable County, MA ................ | 215 888 | 215 423 | | 41 017 | Deschutes County, OR ................ | 157 733 | 162 277 |
| 12740 | | Barre, VT Micro area ..................... | 59 534 | 59 465 | 13500 | | Bennettsville, SC Micro area ........... | 28 933 | 28 145 |
| | 50 023 | Washington County, VT ................ | 59 534 | 59 465 | | 45 069 | Marlboro County, SC.................... | 28 933 | 28 145 |
| 12780 | | Bartlesville, OK Micro area .............. | 50 976 | 51 633 | 13540 | | Bennington, VT Micro area............... | 37 125 | 36 697 |
| | 40 147 | Washington County, OK............... | 50 976 | 51 633 | | 50 003 | Bennington County, VT ............... | 37 125 | 36 697 |
| 12820 | | Bastrop, LA Micro area................... | 27 979 | 27 559 | 13620 | | Berlin, NH-VT Micro area................ | 39 361 | 38 322 |
| | 22 067 | Morehouse Parish, LA.................. | 27 979 | 27 559 | | 33 007 | Coos County, NH .................... | 33 055 | 32 096 |
| 12860 | | Batavia, NY Micro area.................. | 60 079 | 59 977 | | 50 009 | Essex County, VT ...................... | 6 306 | 6 226 |
| | 36 037 | Genesee County, NY ................. | 60 079 | 59 977 | 13660 | | Big Rapids, MI Micro area ............... | 42 798 | 43 318 |
| 12900 | | Batesville, AR Micro area .............. | 36 647 | 37 025 | | 26 107 | Mecosta County, MI ..................... | 42 798 | 43 318 |
| | 05 063 | Independence County, AR ........... | 36 647 | 37 025 | 13700 | | Big Spring, TX Micro area .............. | 36 238 | 36 667 |
| 12940 | | Baton Rouge, LA Metro area........... | 802 484 | 815 298 | | 48 173 | Glasscock County, TX................ | 1 226 | 1 259 |
| | 22 005 | Ascension Parish, LA.................. | 107 215 | 112 286 | | 48 227 | Howard County, TX.................... | 35 012 | 35 408 |
| | 22 033 | East Baton Rouge Parish, LA....... | 440 171 | 444 526 | 13720 | | Big Stone Gap, VA Micro area ........ | 61 313 | 60 676 |
| | 22 037 | East Feliciana Parish, LA............. | 20 267 | 20 008 | | 51 051 | Dickenson County, VA ............... | 15 903 | 15 690 |
| | 22 047 | Iberville Parish, LA.................... | 33 387 | 33 228 | | 51 195 | Wise County, VA...................... | 41 452 | 40 918 |
| | 22 063 | Livingston Parish, LA.................. | 128 026 | 131 942 | | 51 720 | Norton city, VA........................ | 3 958 | 4 068 |
| | 22 077 | Pointe Coupee Parish, LA............ | 22 802 | 22 726 | 13740 | | Billings, MT Metro area.................. | 158 934 | 162 848 |
| | 22 091 | St. Helena Parish, LA.................. | 11 203 | 11 071 | | 30 009 | Carbon County, MT ................... | 10 078 | 10 127 |
| | 22 121 | West Baton Rouge Parish, LA...... | 23 788 | 24 106 | | 30 037 | Golden Valley County, MT ........... | 884 | 839 |
| | 22 125 | West Feliciana Parish, LA............ | 15 625 | 15 405 | | 30 111 | Yellowstone County, MT .............. | 147 972 | 151 882 |
| 12980 | | Battle Creek, MI Metro area ............ | 136 146 | 135 099 | 13780 | | Binghamton, NY Metro area............. | 251 725 | 248 538 |
| | 26 025 | Calhoun County, MI ..................... | 136 146 | 135 099 | | 36 007 | Broome County, NY ................... | 200 600 | 198 060 |
| 13020 | | Bay City, MI Metro area............... | 107 771 | 106 935 | | 36 107 | Tioga County, NY....................... | 51 125 | 50 478 |
| | 26 017 | Bay County, MI........................ | 107 771 | 106 935 | 13820 | | Birmingham-Hoover, AL Metro area. | 1 128 047 | 1 136 650 |
| 13060 | | Bay City, TX Micro area ................ | 36 702 | 36 547 | | 01 007 | Bibb County, AL ...................... | 22 915 | 22 597 |
| | 48 321 | Matagorda County, TX.................. | 36 702 | 36 547 | | 01 009 | Blount County, AL ..................... | 57 322 | 57 826 |
| 13100 | | Beatrice, NE Micro area .................. | 22 311 | 21 806 | | 01 021 | Chilton County, AL ..................... | 43 643 | 43 819 |
| | 31 067 | Gage County, NE Micro area....... | 22 311 | 21 806 | | 01 073 | Jefferson County, AL................... | 658 466 | 660 009 |
| 13140 | | Beaumont-Port Arthur, TX Metro | | | | 01 115 | St. Clair County, AL ................... | 83 593 | 85 237 |
| | | area...................................... | 403 190 | 404 180 | | 01 117 | Shelby County, AL ..................... | 195 085 | 200 941 |
| | 48 199 | Hardin County, TX...................... | 54 635 | 55 190 | | 01 127 | Walker County, AL ..................... | 67 023 | 66 221 |
| | 48 245 | Jefferson County, TX ................... | 252 273 | 251 813 | 13900 | | Bismarck, ND Metro area ................ | 114 778 | 120 060 |
| | 48 351 | Newton County, TX..................... | 14 445 | 14 200 | | 38 015 | Burleigh County, ND ................... | 81 308 | 85 774 |
| | 48 361 | Orange County, TX ..................... | 81 837 | 82 977 | | 38 059 | Morton County, ND .................... | 27 471 | 28 101 |
| 13180 | | Beaver Dam, WI Micro area ............ | 88 759 | 88 415 | | 38 065 | Oliver County, ND ...................... | 1 846 | 1 838 |
| | 55 027 | Dodge County, WI........................ | 88 759 | 88 415 | | 38 085 | Sioux County, ND....................... | 4 153 | 4 347 |
| 13220 | | Beckley, WV Metro area................. | 124 898 | 124 890 | 13940 | | Blackfoot, ID Micro area ................. | 45 607 | 45 474 |
| | 54 019 | Fayette County, WV .................... | 46 039 | 45 869 | | 16 011 | Bingham County, ID.................... | 45 607 | 45 474 |
| | 54 081 | Raleigh County, WV ..................... | 78 859 | 79 021 | 13980 | | Blacksburg-Christiansburg-Radford, | | |
| 13260 | | Bedford, IN Micro area .................. | 46 134 | 46 078 | | | VA Metro area............................ | 178 237 | 178 933 |
| | 18 093 | Lawrence County, IN.................... | 46 134 | 46 078 | | 51 063 | Floyd County, VA ...................... | 15 279 | 15 390 |
| 13300 | | Beeville, TX Micro area ................. | 31 861 | 32 527 | | 51 071 | Giles County, VA ....................... | 17 286 | 16 928 |
| | 48 025 | Bee County, TX........................ | 31 861 | 32 527 | | 51 121 | Montgomery County, VA.............. | 94 392 | 95 194 |
| 13340 | | Bellefontaine, OH Micro area ........... | 45 858 | 45 474 | | 51 155 | Pulaski County, VA .................... | 34 872 | 34 736 |
| | 39 091 | Logan County, OH ...................... | 45 858 | 45 474 | | 51 750 | Radford city, VA ....................... | 16 408 | 16 685 |
| 13380 | | Bellingham, WA Metro area............. | 201 140 | 205 262 | 14010 | | Bloomington, IL Metro area ............. | 186 133 | 188 715 |
| | 53 073 | Whatcom County, WA.................... | 201 140 | 205 262 | | 17 039 | De Witt County, IL...................... | 16 561 | 16 434 |
| 13420 | | Bemidji, MN Micro area ................. | 44 442 | 45 375 | | 17 113 | McLean County, IL...................... | 169 572 | 172 281 |
| | 27 007 | Beltrami County, MN................... | 44 442 | 45 375 | 14020 | | Bloomington, IN Metro area............. | 159 549 | 162 399 |
| | | | | | | 18 105 | Monroe County, IN ..................... | 137 974 | 141 019 |
| | | | | | | 18 119 | Owen County, IN........................ | 21 575 | 21 380 |

# Core Based Statistical Areas (Metropolitan and Micropolitan), Metropolitan Divisions, and Components (as defined February 2013)–Continued

| Core Based Statistical Area | State/County FIPS Code | Title and Geographic Components | 2010 Census Population | 2012 Estimated Population |
|---|---|---|---|---|
| 14100 | | Bloomsburg-Berwick, PA Metro area | 85 562 | 85 243 |
| | 42 037 | Columbia County, PA | 67 295 | 66 887 |
| | 42 093 | Montour County, PA | 18 267 | 18 356 |
| 14140 | | Bluefield, WV-VA Micro area | 107 342 | 106 791 |
| | 51 185 | Tazewell County, VA | 45 078 | 44 268 |
| | 54 055 | Mercer County, WV | 62 264 | 62 523 |
| 14180 | | Blytheville, AR Micro area | 46 480 | 45 562 |
| | 05 093 | Mississippi County, AR | 46 480 | 45 562 |
| 14220 | | Bogalusa, LA Micro area | 47 168 | 46 670 |
| | 22 117 | Washington Parish, LA | 47 168 | 46 670 |
| 14260 | | Boise City, ID Metro area | 616 561 | 637 896 |
| | 16 001 | Ada County, ID | 392 365 | 409 061 |
| | 16 015 | Boise County, ID | 7 028 | 6 835 |
| | 16 027 | Canyon County, ID | 188 923 | 193 888 |
| | 16 045 | Gem County, ID | 16 719 | 16 673 |
| | 16 073 | Owyhee County, ID | 11 526 | 11 439 |
| 14340 | | Boone, IA Micro area | 26 306 | 26 195 |
| | 19 015 | Boone County, IA | 26 306 | 26 195 |
| 14380 | | Boone, NC Micro area | 51 079 | 51 871 |
| | 37 189 | Watauga County, NC | 51 079 | 51 871 |
| 14420 | | Borger, TX Micro area | 22 150 | 21 922 |
| | 48 233 | Hutchinson County, TX | 22 150 | 21 922 |
| 14460 | | Boston-Cambridge Newton, MA-NH Metro area | 4 552 402 | 4 640 802 |
| 14460 | | Boston, MA Metro Div 14454 | 1 887 792 | 1 926 030 |
| | 25 021 | Norfolk County, MA | 670 850 | 681 845 |
| | 25 023 | Plymouth County, MA | 494 919 | 499 759 |
| | 25 025 | Suffolk County, MA | 722 023 | 744 426 |
| 14460 | | Cambridge-Newton-Framingham, MA Metro Div 15764 | 2 246 244 | 2 292 833 |
| | 25 009 | Essex County, MA | 743 159 | 755 618 |
| | 25 017 | Middlesex County, MA | 1 503 085 | 1 537 215 |
| 14460 | | Rockingham County-Strafford County-NH Metro Div 40484 | 418 366 | 421 939 |
| | 33 015 | Rockingham County, NH | 295 223 | 297 820 |
| | 33 017 | Strafford County, NH | 123 143 | 124 119 |
| 14500 | | Boulder, CO Metro area | 294 567 | 305 318 |
| | 08 013 | Boulder County, CO | 294 567 | 305 318 |
| 14540 | | Bowling Green, KY Metro area | 158 599 | 162 231 |
| | 21 003 | Allen County, KY | 19 956 | 20 210 |
| | 21 031 | Butler County, KY | 12 690 | 12 840 |
| | 21 061 | Edmonson County, KY | 12 161 | 12 071 |
| | 21 227 | Warren County, KY | 113 792 | 117 110 |
| 14580 | | Bozeman, MT Micro area | 89 513 | 92 614 |
| | 30 031 | Gallatin County, MT | 89 513 | 92 614 |
| 14620 | | Bradford, PA Micro area | 43 450 | 43 127 |
| | 42 083 | McKean County, PA | 43 450 | 43 127 |
| 14660 | | Brainerd, MN Micro area | 91 067 | 91 239 |
| | 27 021 | Cass County, MN | 28 567 | 28 357 |
| | 27 035 | Crow Wing County, MN | 62 500 | 62 882 |
| 14700 | | Branson, MO Micro area | 83 877 | 84 524 |
| | 29 209 | Stone County, MO Micro area | 32 202 | 31 568 |
| | 29 213 | Taney County, MO Micro area | 51 675 | 52 956 |
| 14720 | | Breckenridge, CO Micro area | 27 994 | 28 044 |
| | 08 117 | Summit County, CO | 27 994 | 28 044 |
| 14740 | | Bremerton-Silverdale, WA Metro area | 251 133 | 254 991 |
| | 53 035 | Kitsap County, WA | 251 133 | 254 991 |
| 14780 | | Brenham, TX Micro area | 33 718 | 34 093 |
| | 48 477 | Washington County, TX | 33 718 | 34 093 |
| 14820 | | Brevard, NC Micro area | 33 090 | 32 849 |
| | 37 175 | Transylvania County, NC | 33 090 | 32 849 |
| 14860 | | Bridgeport-Stamford-Norwalk, CT Metro area | 916 829 | 933 835 |
| | 09 001 | Fairfield County, CT | 916 829 | 933 835 |
| 15020 | | Brookhaven, MS Micro area | 34 869 | 34 900 |
| | 28 085 | Lincoln County, MS | 34 869 | 34 900 |
| 15060 | | Brookings, OR Micro area | 22 364 | 22 248 |
| | 41 015 | Curry County, OR | 22 364 | 22 248 |
| 15100 | | Brookings, SD Micro area | 31 965 | 32 629 |
| | 46 011 | Brookings County, SD | 31 965 | 32 629 |
| 15180 | | Brownsville-Harlingen, TX Metro area | 406 220 | 415 557 |
| | 48 061 | Cameron County, TX | 406 220 | 415 557 |
| 15220 | | Brownwood, TX Micro area | 38 106 | 37 825 |
| | 48 049 | Brown County, TX | 38 106 | 37 825 |
| 15260 | | Brunswick, GA Metro area | 112 370 | 113 448 |
| | 13 025 | Brantley County, GA | 18 411 | 18 587 |
| | 13 127 | Glynn County, GA | 79 626 | 81 022 |
| | 13 191 | McIntosh County, GA | 14 333 | 13 839 |
| 15340 | | Bucyrus, OH Micro area | 43 784 | 42 849 |
| | 39 033 | Crawford County, OH | 43 784 | 42 849 |
| 15380 | | Buffalo-Cheektowaga-Niagara Falls, NY Metro area | 1 135 509 | 1 134 210 |
| | 36 029 | Erie County, NY | 919 040 | 919 086 |
| | 36 063 | Niagara County, NY | 216 469 | 215 124 |
| 15420 | | Burley, ID Micro area | 43 021 | 43 286 |
| | 16 031 | Cassia County, ID | 22 952 | 23 249 |
| | 16 067 | Minidoka County, ID | 20 069 | 20 037 |
| 15460 | | Burlington, IA-IL Micro area | 47 656 | 47 383 |
| | 17 071 | Henderson County, IL | 7 331 | 7 043 |
| | 19 057 | Des Moines County, IA | 40 325 | 40 340 |
| 15500 | | Burlington, NC Metro area | 151 131 | 153 920 |
| | 37 001 | Alamance County, NC | 151 131 | 153 920 |
| 15540 | | Burlington-South Burlington, VT Metro area | 211 261 | 213 701 |
| | 50 007 | Chittenden County, VT | 156 545 | 158 504 |
| | 50 011 | Franklin County, VT | 47 746 | 48 214 |
| | 50 013 | Grand Isle County, VT | 6 970 | 6 983 |
| 15580 | | Butte-Silver Bow, MT Micro area | 34 200 | 34 403 |
| | 30 093 | Silver Bow County, MT | 34 200 | 34 403 |

# Core Based Statistical Areas (Metropolitan and Micropolitan), Metropolitan Divisions, and Components (as defined February 2013)–*Continued*

| Core Based Statistical Area | State/County FIPS Code | Title and Geographic Components | 2010 Census Population | 2012 Estimated Population | Core Based Statistical Area | State/County FIPS Code | Title and Geographic Components | 2010 Census Population | 2012 Estimated Population |
|---|---|---|---|---|---|---|---|---|---|
| 15620 | | Cadillac, MI Micro area.................... | 47 584 | 47 639 | 16460 | | Centralia, IL Micro area ................... | 39 437 | 38 894 |
| | 26 113 | Missaukee County, MI................ | 14 849 | 15 031 | | 17 121 | Marion County, IL....................... | 39 437 | 38 894 |
| | 26 165 | Wexford County, MI .................... | 32 735 | 32 608 | 16500 | | Centralia, WA Micro area ............... | 75 455 | 75 621 |
| 15660 | | Calhoun, GA Micro area................. | 55 186 | 55 766 | | 53 041 | Lewis County, WA...................... | 75 455 | 75 621 |
| | 13 129 | Gordon County, GA..................... | 55 186 | 55 766 | 16540 | | Chambersburg-Waynesboro, PA Metro area................ | 149 618 | 151 275 |
| 15680 | | California-Lexington Park, MD Metro area................ | 105 151 | 108 987 | | 42 055 | Franklin County, PA .................... | 149 618 | 151 275 |
| | 24 037 | St. Mary's County, MD................. | 105 151 | 108 987 | 16580 | | Champaign-Urbana, IL Metro area... | 231 891 | 233 788 |
| 15700 | | Cambridge, MD Micro area ............. | 32 618 | 32 551 | | 17 019 | Champaign County, IL................. | 201 081 | 203 276 |
| | 24 019 | Dorchester County, MD............... | 32 618 | 32 551 | | 17 053 | Ford County, IL ......................... | 14 081 | 14 008 |
| 15740 | | Cambridge, OH Micro area.............. | 40 087 | 39 817 | | 17 147 | Piatt County, IL......................... | 16 729 | 16 504 |
| | 39 059 | Guernsey County, OH................. | 40 087 | 39 817 | 16620 | | Charleston, WV Metro area............ | 227 078 | 225 954 |
| 15780 | | Camden, AR Micro area................. | 31 488 | 30 703 | | 54 005 | Boone County, WV...................... | 24 629 | 24 478 |
| | 05 013 | Calhoun County, AR.................... | 5 368 | 5 307 | | 54 015 | Clay County, WV....................... | 9 386 | 9 297 |
| | 05 103 | Ouachita County, AR................... | 26 120 | 25 396 | | 54 039 | Kanawha County, WV ................. | 193 063 | 192 179 |
| 15820 | | Campbellsville, KY Micro area.......... | 24 512 | 24 691 | 16660 | | Charleston-Mattoon, IL Micro area... | 64 921 | 64 623 |
| | 21 217 | Taylor County, KY ...................... | 24 512 | 24 691 | | 17 029 | Coles County, IL........................ | 53 873 | 53 655 |
| 15860 | | Cañon City, CO Micro area ............. | 46 824 | 46 788 | | 17 035 | Cumberland County, IL ................ | 11 048 | 10 968 |
| | 08 043 | Fremont County, CO.................... | 46 824 | 46 788 | 16700 | | Charleston-North Charleston, SC Metro area................ | 664 607 | 697 439 |
| 15900 | | Canton, IL Micro area................... | 37 069 | 36 651 | | 45 015 | Berkeley County, SC.................... | 177 843 | 189 781 |
| | 17 057 | Fulton County, IL........................ | 37 069 | 36 651 | | 45 019 | Charleston County, SC ................ | 350 209 | 365 162 |
| 15940 | | Canton-Massillon, OH Metro area.... | 404 422 | 403 455 | | 45 035 | Dorchester County, SC ................ | 136 555 | 142 496 |
| | 39 019 | Carroll County, OH...................... | 28 836 | 28 587 | 16740 | | Charlotte-Concord-Gastonia, NC-SC Metro area................ | 2 217 012 | 2 296 569 |
| | 39 151 | Stark County, OH ...................... | 375 586 | 374 868 | | 37 025 | Cabarrus County, NC.................. | 178 011 | 184 498 |
| 15980 | | Cape Coral-Fort Myers, FL Metro area................ | 618 754 | 645 293 | | 37 071 | Gaston County, NC..................... | 206 086 | 208 049 |
| | 12 071 | Lee County, FL........................... | 618 754 | 645 293 | | 37 097 | Iredell County, NC...................... | 159 437 | 162 708 |
| 16020 | | Cape Girardeau, MO-IL Metro area . | 96 275 | 97 080 | | 37 109 | Lincoln County, NC..................... | 78 265 | 79 313 |
| | 17 003 | Alexander County, IL................... | 8 238 | 7 748 | | 37 119 | Mecklenburg County, NC.............. | 919 628 | 969 031 |
| | 29 017 | Bollinger County, MO.................. | 12 363 | 12 382 | | 37 159 | Rowan County, NC..................... | 138 428 | 138 180 |
| | 29 031 | Cape Girardeau County, MO ....... | 75 674 | 76 950 | | 37 179 | Union County, NC ...................... | 201 292 | 208 520 |
| 16060 | | Carbondale-Marion, IL Metro area ... | 126 575 | 126 745 | | 45 023 | Chester County, SC.................... | 33 140 | 32 546 |
| | 17 077 | Jackson County, IL...................... | 60 218 | 60 071 | | 45 057 | Lancaster County, SC ................. | 76 652 | 79 089 |
| | 17 199 | Williamson County, IL .................. | 66 357 | 66 674 | | 45 091 | York County, SC ....................... | 226 073 | 234 635 |
| 16100 | | Carlsbad-Artesia, NM Micro area ..... | 53 829 | 54 419 | 16820 | | Charlottesville, VA Metro area.......... | 218 705 | 222 860 |
| | 35 015 | Eddy County, NM........................ | 53 829 | 54 419 | | 51 003 | Albemarle County, VA................. | 98 970 | 102 251 |
| 16180 | | Carson City, NV Metro area ............ | 55 274 | 54 838 | | 51 029 | Buckingham County, VA .............. | 17 146 | 17 088 |
| | 32 510 | Carson City, NV Metro area......... | 55 274 | 54 838 | | 51 065 | Fluvanna County, VA.................. | 25 691 | 25 967 |
| 16220 | | Casper, WY Metro area................. | 75 450 | 78 621 | | 51 079 | Greene County, VA..................... | 18 403 | 18 771 |
| | 56 025 | Natrona County, WY ................... | 75 450 | 78 621 | | 51 125 | Nelson County, VA ..................... | 15 020 | 14 827 |
| 16260 | | Cedar City, UT Micro area................ | 46 163 | 46 750 | | 51 540 | Charlottesville city, VA ................ | 43 475 | 43 956 |
| | 49 021 | Iron County, UT......................... | 46 163 | 46 750 | 16860 | | Chattanooga, TN-GA Metro area ..... | 528 143 | 537 889 |
| 16300 | | Cedar Rapids, IA Metro area............ | 257 940 | 261 761 | | 13 047 | Catoosa County, GA ................... | 63 942 | 65 046 |
| | 19 011 | Benton County, IA...................... | 26 076 | 25 827 | | 13 083 | Dade County, GA....................... | 16 633 | 16 490 |
| | 19 105 | Jones County, IA........................ | 20 638 | 20 639 | | 13 295 | Walker County, GA .................... | 68 756 | 68 094 |
| | 19 113 | Linn County, IA.......................... | 211 226 | 215 295 | | 47 065 | Hamilton County, TN................... | 336 463 | 345 545 |
| 16340 | | Cedartown, GA Micro area ............. | 41 475 | 41 188 | | 47 115 | Marion County, TN..................... | 28 237 | 28 291 |
| | 13 233 | Polk County, GA......................... | 41 475 | 41 188 | | 47 153 | Sequatchie County, TN................ | 14 112 | 14 423 |
| 16380 | | Celina, OH Micro area................... | 40 814 | 40 875 | 16940 | | Cheyenne, WY Metro area ............. | 91 738 | 94 483 |
| | 39 107 | Mercer County, OH ..................... | 40 814 | 40 875 | | 56 021 | Laramie County, WY ................... | 91 738 | 94 483 |
| | | | | | 16980 | | Chicago-Naperville-Elgin, IL-IN-WI Metro area................ | 9 461 105 | 9 522 434 |

# Core Based Statistical Areas (Metropolitan and Micropolitan), Metropolitan Divisions, and Components (as defined February 2013)–*Continued*

| Core Based Statistical Area | State/County FIPS Code | Title and Geographic Components | 2010 Census Population | 2012 Estimated Population | Core Based Statistical Area | State/County FIPS Code | Title and Geographic Components | 2010 Census Population | 2012 Estimated Population |
|---|---|---|---|---|---|---|---|---|---|
| 16980 | | Chicago-Naperville-Arlington Heights, IL Metro Div 16974............ | 7 262 718 | 7 318 387 | 17380 | | Cleveland, MS Micro area ................ | 34 145 | 33 904 |
| | 17 031 | Cook County, IL.......................... | 5 194 675 | 5 231 351 | | 28 011 | Bolivar County, MS ...................... | 34 145 | 33 904 |
| | 17 043 | DuPage County, IL...................... | 916 924 | 927 987 | 17420 | | Cleveland, TN Metro area ............... | 115 788 | 117 820 |
| | 17 063 | Grundy County, IL....................... | 50 063 | 50 281 | | 47 011 | Bradley County, TN..................... | 98 963 | 101 134 |
| | 17 093 | Kendall County, IL...................... | 114 736 | 118 105 | | 47 139 | Polk County, TN ......................... | 16 825 | 16 686 |
| | 17 111 | McHenry County, IL..................... | 308 760 | 308 145 | 17460 | | Cleveland-Elyria, OH Metro area...... | 2 077 240 | 2 063 535 |
| | 17 197 | Will County, IL ........................... | 677 560 | 682 518 | | 39 035 | Cuyahoga County, OH.................. | 1 280 122 | 1 265 111 |
| | | | | | | 39 055 | Geauga County, OH..................... | 93 389 | 93 680 |
| 16980 | | Elgin, IL Metro Div 20994 ................ | 620 429 | 627 191 | | 39 085 | Lake County, OH........................ | 230 041 | 229 582 |
| | 17 037 | DeKalb County, IL....................... | 105 160 | 104 704 | | 39 093 | Lorain County, OH ...................... | 301 356 | 301 478 |
| | 17 089 | Kane County, IL ......................... | 515 269 | 522 487 | | 39 103 | Medina County, OH..................... | 172 332 | 173 684 |
| 16980 | | Gary, IN Metro Div 23844................ | 708 070 | 706 800 | 17500 | | Clewiston, FL Micro area ................ | 39 140 | 37 447 |
| | 18 073 | Jasper County, IN ...................... | 33 478 | 33 456 | | 12 051 | Hendry County, FL....................... | 39 140 | 37 447 |
| | 18 089 | Lake County, IN ......................... | 496 005 | 493 618 | 17540 | | Clinton, IA Micro area.................... | 49 116 | 48 717 |
| | 18 111 | Newton County, IN ..................... | 14 244 | 14 044 | | 19 045 | Clinton County, IA ...................... | 49 116 | 48 717 |
| | 18 127 | Porter County, IN ....................... | 164 343 | 165 682 | 17580 | | Clovis, NM Micro area ................... | 48 376 | 49 938 |
| 16980 | | Lake County-Kenosha County, IL-WI Metro Div 29404 | 869 888 | 870 056 | | 35 009 | Curry County, NM ...................... | 48 376 | 49 938 |
| | 17 097 | Lake County, IL.......................... | 703 462 | 702 120 | 17660 | | Coeur d'Alene, ID Metro area........... | 138 494 | 142 357 |
| | 55 059 | Kenosha County, WI.................... | 166 426 | 167 936 | | 16 055 | Kootenai County, ID..................... | 138 494 | 142 357 |
| 17020 | | Chico, CA Metro area ..................... | 220 000 | 221 539 | 17700 | | Coffeyville, KS Micro area ............... | 35 471 | 34 459 |
| | 06 007 | Butte County, CA........................ | 220 000 | 221 539 | | 20 125 | Montgomery County, KS ............... | 35 471 | 34 459 |
| 17060 | | Chillicothe, OH Micro area............... | 78 064 | 77 429 | 17740 | | Coldwater, MI Micro area ................ | 45 248 | 43 868 |
| | 39 141 | Ross County, OH........................ | 78 064 | 77 429 | | 26 023 | Branch County, MI ...................... | 45 248 | 43 868 |
| 17140 | | Cincinnati, OH-KY-IN Metro area ..... | 2 114 580 | 2 128 603 | 17780 | | College Station-Bryan, TX Metro area | 228 660 | 234 501 |
| | 18 029 | Dearborn County, IN ................... | 50 047 | 49 831 | | 48 041 | Brazos County, TX...................... | 194 851 | 200 665 |
| | 18 115 | Ohio County, IN.......................... | 6 128 | 6 079 | | 48 051 | Burleson County, TX.................... | 17 187 | 17 291 |
| | 18 161 | Union County, IN ........................ | 7 516 | 7 362 | | 48 395 | Robertson County, TX.................. | 16 622 | 16 545 |
| | 21 015 | Boone County, KY....................... | 118 811 | 123 316 | 17820 | | Colorado Springs, CO Metro area.... | 645 613 | 668 353 |
| | 21 023 | Bracken County, KY..................... | 8 488 | 8 494 | | 08 041 | El Paso County, CO..................... | 622 263 | 644 964 |
| | 21 037 | Campbell County, KY.................... | 90 336 | 90 908 | | 08 119 | Teller County, CO ....................... | 23 350 | 23 389 |
| | 21 077 | Gallatin County, KY..................... | 8 589 | 8 479 | 17860 | | Columbia, MO Metro area ............... | 162 642 | 168 535 |
| | 21 081 | Grant County, KY........................ | 24 662 | 24 485 | | 29 019 | Boone County, MO...................... | 162 642 | 168 535 |
| | 21 117 | Kenton County, KY...................... | 159 720 | 161 711 | 17900 | | Columbia, SC Metro area ............... | 767 598 | 784 745 |
| | 21 191 | Pendleton County, KY.................. | 14 877 | 14 604 | | 45 017 | Calhoun County, SC .................... | 15 175 | 14 910 |
| | 39 015 | Brown County, OH ...................... | 44 846 | 44 381 | | 45 039 | Fairfield County, SC..................... | 23 956 | 23 363 |
| | 39 017 | Butler County, OH....................... | 368 130 | 370 589 | | 45 055 | Kershaw County, SC.................... | 61 697 | 62 343 |
| | 39 025 | Clermont County, OH................... | 197 363 | 199 085 | | 45 063 | Lexington County, SC................... | 262 391 | 270 406 |
| | 39 061 | Hamilton County, OH................... | 802 374 | 802 038 | | 45 079 | Richland County, SC.................... | 384 504 | 393 830 |
| | 39 165 | Warren County, OH..................... | 212 693 | 217 241 | | 45 081 | Saluda County, SC...................... | 19 875 | 19 893 |
| 17200 | | Claremont-Lebanon, NH-VT Micro area | 218 466 | 217 390 | 17980 | | Columbus, GA-AL Metro area ......... | 294 865 | 310 531 |
| | 33 009 | Grafton County, NH..................... | 89 118 | 89 181 | | 01 113 | Russell County, AL...................... | 52 947 | 57 820 |
| | 33 019 | Sullivan County, NH.................... | 43 742 | 43 074 | | 13 053 | Chattahoochee County, GA .......... | 11 267 | 13 037 |
| | 50 017 | Orange County, VT...................... | 28 936 | 28 924 | | 13 145 | Harris County, GA....................... | 32 024 | 32 550 |
| | 50 027 | Windsor County, VT..................... | 56 670 | 56 211 | | 13 197 | Marion County, GA...................... | 8 742 | 8 711 |
| 17220 | | Clarksburg, WV Micro area ............. | 94 196 | 94 310 | | 13 215 | Muscogee County, GA.................. | 189 885 | 198 413 |
| | 54 017 | Doddridge County, WV ................ | 8 202 | 8 178 | 18020 | | Columbus, IN Metro area ............... | 76 794 | 79 129 |
| | 54 033 | Harrison County, WV ................... | 69 099 | 69 141 | | 18 005 | Bartholomew County, IN ............... | 76 794 | 79 129 |
| | 54 091 | Taylor County, WV ...................... | 16 895 | 16 991 | 18060 | | Columbus, MS Micro area................ | 59 779 | 59 670 |
| 17260 | | Clarksdale, MS Micro area ............. | 26 151 | 25 709 | | 28 087 | Lowndes County, MS ................... | 59 779 | 59 670 |
| | 28 027 | Coahoma County, MS .................. | 26 151 | 25 709 | 18100 | | Columbus, NE Micro area ............... | 32 237 | 32 681 |
| 17300 | | Clarksville, TN-KY Metro area.......... | 260 625 | 274 342 | | 31 141 | Platte County, NE........................ | 32 237 | 32 681 |
| | 21 047 | Christian County, KY..................... | 73 955 | 75 427 | | | | | |
| | 21 221 | Trigg County, KY......................... | 14 339 | 14 447 | | | | | |
| | 47 125 | Montgomery County, TN............... | 172 331 | 184 468 | | | | | |
| 17340 | | Clearlake, CA Micro area ................ | 64 665 | 63 983 | | | | | |
| | 06 033 | Lake County, CA......................... | 64 665 | 63 983 | | | | | |

# Core Based Statistical Areas (Metropolitan and Micropolitan), Metropolitan Divisions, and Components (as defined February 2013)–*Continued*

| Core Based Statistical Area | State/County FIPS Code | Title and Geographic Components | 2010 Census Population | 2012 Estimated Population | Core Based Statistical Area | State/County FIPS Code | Title and Geographic Components | 2010 Census Population | 2012 Estimated Population |
|---|---|---|---|---|---|---|---|---|---|
| 18140 | | Columbus, OH Metro area................ | 1 901 974 | 1 944 002 | 18900 | | Crossville, TN Micro area................ | 56 053 | 57 029 |
| | 39 041 | Delaware County, OH.................... | 174 214 | 181 061 | | 47 035 | Cumberland County, TN ............. | 56 053 | 57 029 |
| | 39 045 | Fairfield County, OH..................... | 146 156 | 147 474 | | | | | |
| | 39 049 | Franklin County, OH..................... | 1 163 414 | 1 195 537 | 18980 | | Cullman, AL Micro area................. | 80 406 | 80 440 |
| | 39 073 | Hocking County, OH..................... | 29 380 | 29 273 | | 01 043 | Cullman County, AL .................... | 80 406 | 80 440 |
| | 39 089 | Licking County, OH...................... | 166 492 | 167 537 | | | | | |
| | 39 097 | Madison County, OH..................... | 43 435 | 43 053 | 19000 | | Cullowhee, NC Micro area............... | 40 271 | 40 448 |
| | 39 117 | Morrow County, OH...................... | 34 827 | 34 938 | | 37 099 | Jackson County, NC .................... | 40 271 | 40 448 |
| | 39 127 | Perry County, OH......................... | 36 058 | 36 015 | | | | | |
| | 39 129 | Pickaway County, OH.................... | 55 698 | 56 399 | 19060 | | Cumberland, MD-WV Metro area..... | 103 299 | 101 968 |
| | 39 159 | Union County, OH......................... | 52 300 | 52 715 | | 24 001 | Allegany County, MD ................... | 75 087 | 74 012 |
| 18180 | | Concord, NH Micro area................ | 146 445 | 146 761 | | 54 057 | Mineral County, WV .................... | 28 212 | 27 956 |
| | 33 013 | Merrimack County, NH................... | 146 445 | 146 761 | 19100 | | Dallas-Fort Worth-Arlington, TX Metro area................................ | 6 426 214 | 6 700 991 |
| 18220 | | Connersville, IN Micro area ............ | 24 277 | 24 029 | | | | | |
| | 18 041 | Fayette County, IN ....................... | 24 277 | 24 029 | 19100 | | Dallas-Plano-Irving, TX Metro Div 19124 ..................................... | 4 230 520 | 4 426 611 |
| 18260 | | Cookeville, TN Micro area............... | 106 042 | 106 860 | | 48 085 | Collin County, TX ....................... | 782 341 | 834 642 |
| | 47 087 | Jackson County, TN ..................... | 11 638 | 11 441 | | 48 113 | Dallas County, TX ...................... | 2 368 139 | 2 453 843 |
| | 47 133 | Overton County, TN ..................... | 22 083 | 22 190 | | 48 121 | Denton County, TX ...................... | 662 614 | 707 304 |
| | 47 141 | Putnam County, TN...................... | 72 321 | 73 229 | | 48 139 | Ellis County, TX......................... | 149 610 | 153 969 |
| 18300 | | Coos Bay, OR Micro area............... | 63 043 | 62 534 | | 48 231 | Hunt County, TX......................... | 86 129 | 87 079 |
| | 41 011 | Coos County, OR......................... | 63 043 | 62 534 | | 48 257 | Kaufman County, TX.................... | 103 350 | 106 753 |
| | | | | | | 48 397 | Rockwall County, TX.................... | 78 337 | 83 021 |
| 18380 | | Cordele, GA Micro area................ | 23 439 | 23 606 | 19100 | | Fort Worth-Arlington, TX Metro Div 23104 ..................................... | 2 195 694 | 2 274 380 |
| | 13 081 | Crisp County, GA ........................ | 23 439 | 23 606 | | 48 221 | Hood County, TX......................... | 51 182 | 52 044 |
| 18420 | | Corinth, MS Micro area.................. | 37 057 | 37 164 | | 48 251 | Johnson County, TX..................... | 150 934 | 153 441 |
| | 28 003 | Alcorn County, MS ...................... | 37 057 | 37 164 | | 48 367 | Parker County, TX....................... | 116 927 | 119 712 |
| | | | | | | 48 425 | Somervell County, TX ................. | 8 490 | 8 598 |
| 18460 | | Cornelia, GA Micro area................ | 43 041 | 43 520 | | 48 439 | Tarrant County, TX...................... | 1 809 034 | 1 880 153 |
| | 13 137 | Habersham County, GA................ | 43 041 | 43 520 | | 48 497 | Wise County, TX......................... | 59 127 | 60 432 |
| 18500 | | Corning, NY Micro area.................. | 98 990 | 99 063 | 19140 | | Dalton, GA Metro area.................... | 142 227 | 142 751 |
| | 36 101 | Steuben County, NY ..................... | 98 990 | 99 063 | | 13 213 | Murray County, GA ..................... | 39 628 | 39 392 |
| | | | | | | 13 313 | Whitfield County, GA.................... | 102 599 | 103 359 |
| 18580 | | Corpus Christi, TX Metro area.......... | 428 185 | 437 109 | | | | | |
| | 48 007 | Aransas County, TX ..................... | 23 158 | 23 818 | 19180 | | Danville, IL Metro area .................. | 81 625 | 80 727 |
| | 48 355 | Nueces County, TX...................... | 340 223 | 347 691 | | 17 183 | Vermilion County, IL..................... | 81 625 | 80 727 |
| | 48 409 | San Patricio County, TX................ | 64 804 | 65 600 | | | | | |
| | | | | | 19220 | | Danville, KY Micro area.................. | 53 174 | 53 119 |
| 18620 | | Corsicana, TX Micro area................ | 47 735 | 47 979 | | 21 021 | Boyle County, KY ........................ | 28 432 | 28 658 |
| | 48 349 | Navarro County, TX ..................... | 47 735 | 47 979 | | 21 137 | Lincoln County, KY....................... | 24 742 | 24 461 |
| 18660 | | Cortland, NY Micro area ................ | 49 336 | 49 474 | 19260 | | Danville, VA Micro area.................. | 106 561 | 105 803 |
| | 36 023 | Cortland County, NY .................... | 49 336 | 49 474 | | 51 143 | Pittsylvania County, VA................ | 63 506 | 62 807 |
| | | | | | | 51 590 | Danville city, VA ......................... | 43 055 | 42 996 |
| 18700 | | Corvallis, OR Metro area................ | 85 579 | 86 430 | | | | | |
| | 41 003 | Benton County, OR....................... | 85 579 | 86 430 | 19300 | | Daphne-Fairhope-Foley, AL Metro area........................................ | 182 265 | 190 790 |
| 18740 | | Coshocton, OH Micro area.............. | 36 901 | 36 779 | | 01 003 | Baldwin County, AL...................... | 182 265 | 190 790 |
| | 39 031 | Coshocton County, OH ................ | 36 901 | 36 779 | | | | | |
| 18780 | | Craig, CO Micro area.................... | 13 795 | 13 200 | 19340 | | Davenport-Moline-Rock Island, IA-IL Metro area................................ | 379 690 | 382 630 |
| | 08 081 | Moffat County, CO ...................... | 13 795 | 13 200 | | 17 073 | Henry County, IL ......................... | 50 486 | 50 155 |
| | | | | | | 17 131 | Mercer County, IL........................ | 16 434 | 16 219 |
| 18820 | | Crawfordsville, IN Micro area ........... | 38 124 | 38 254 | | 17 161 | Rock Island County, IL................. | 147 546 | 147 457 |
| | 18 107 | Montgomery County, IN .............. | 38 124 | 38 254 | | 19 163 | Scott County, IA ......................... | 165 224 | 168 799 |
| 18860 | | Crescent City, CA Micro area........... | 28 610 | 28 290 | 19380 | | Dayton, OH Metro area .................. | 799 232 | 800 972 |
| | 06 015 | Del Norte County, CA ................... | 28 610 | 28 290 | | 39 057 | Greene County, OH ..................... | 161 573 | 163 587 |
| | | | | | | 39 109 | Miami County, OH ....................... | 102 506 | 103 060 |
| 18880 | | Crestview-Fort Walton Beach-Destin, FL Metro area.................... | 235 865 | 247 665 | | 39 113 | Montgomery County, OH ............. | 535 153 | 534 325 |
| | 12 091 | Okaloosa County, FL .................... | 180 822 | 190 083 | 19420 | | Dayton, TN Micro area................... | 31 809 | 32 247 |
| | 12 131 | Walton County, FL ....................... | 55 043 | 57 582 | | 47 143 | Rhea County, TN ........................ | 31 809 | 32 247 |

# Core Based Statistical Areas (Metropolitan and Micropolitan), Metropolitan Divisions, and Components (as defined February 2013)–*Continued*

| Core Based Statistical Area | State/ County FIPS Code | Title and Geographic Components | 2010 Census Population | 2012 Estimated Population | Core Based Statistical Area | State/ County FIPS Code | Title and Geographic Components | 2010 Census Population | 2012 Estimated Population |
|---|---|---|---|---|---|---|---|---|---|
| 19460 | | Decatur, AL Metro area | 153 829 | 154 233 | 19980 | | Dodge City, KS Micro area | 33 848 | 34 752 |
| | 01 079 | Lawrence County, AL | 34 339 | 33 838 | | 20 057 | Ford County, KS | 33 848 | 34 752 |
| | 01 103 | Morgan County, AL | 119 490 | 120 395 | 20020 | | Dothan, AL Metro area | 145 639 | 147 620 |
| 19500 | | Decatur, IL Metro area | 110 768 | 110 122 | | 01 061 | Geneva County, AL | 26 790 | 26 931 |
| | 17 115 | Macon County, IL | 110 768 | 110 122 | | 01 067 | Henry County, AL | 17 302 | 17 287 |
| | | | | | | 01 069 | Houston County, AL | 101 547 | 103 402 |
| 19540 | | Decatur, IN Micro area | 34 387 | 34 365 | | | | | |
| | 18 001 | Adams County, IN | 34 387 | 34 365 | 20060 | | Douglas, GA Micro area | 42 356 | 43 170 |
| | | | | | | 13 069 | Coffee County, GA | 42 356 | 43 170 |
| 19580 | | Defiance, OH Micro area | 39 037 | 38 677 | | | | | |
| | 39 039 | Defiance County, OH | 39 037 | 38 677 | 20100 | | Dover, DE Metro area | 162 310 | 167 626 |
| | | | | | | 10 001 | Kent County, Delaware | 162 310 | 167 626 |
| 19620 | | Del Rio, TX Micro area | 48 879 | 48 705 | | | | | |
| | 48 465 | Val Verde County, TX | 48 879 | 48 705 | 20140 | | Dublin, GA Micro area | 58 414 | 57 938 |
| | | | | | | 13 167 | Johnson County, GA | 9 980 | 9 897 |
| 19660 | | Deltona-Daytona Beach-Ormond Beach, FL Metro area | 590 289 | 595 309 | | 13 175 | Laurens County, GA | 48 434 | 48 041 |
| | 12 035 | Flagler County, FL | 95 696 | 98 359 | 20180 | | DuBois, PA Micro area | 81 642 | 81 184 |
| | 12 127 | Volusia County, FL | 494 593 | 496 950 | | 42 033 | Clearfield County, PA | 81 642 | 81 184 |
| 19700 | | Deming, NM Micro area | 25 095 | 25 041 | 20220 | | Dubuque, IA Metro area | 93 653 | 95 097 |
| | 35 029 | Luna County, NM | 25 095 | 25 041 | | 19 061 | Dubuque County, IA | 93 653 | 95 097 |
| 19740 | | Denver-Aurora-Lakewood, CO Metro area | 2 543 482 | 2 645 209 | 20260 | | Duluth, MN-WI Metro area | 279 771 | 279 452 |
| | 08 001 | Adams County, CO | 441 603 | 459 598 | | 27 017 | Carlton County, MN | 35 386 | 35 348 |
| | 08 005 | Arapahoe County, CO | 572 003 | 595 546 | | 27 137 | St. Louis County, MN | 200 226 | 200 319 |
| | 08 014 | Broomfield County, CO | 55 889 | 58 298 | | 55 031 | Douglas County, WI | 44 159 | 43 785 |
| | 08 019 | Clear Creek County, CO | 9 088 | 9 026 | 20300 | | Dumas, TX Micro area | 21 904 | 22 313 |
| | 08 031 | Denver County, CO | 600 158 | 634 265 | | 48 341 | Moore County, TX | 21 904 | 22 313 |
| | 08 035 | Douglas County, CO | 285 465 | 298 215 | | | | | |
| | 08 039 | Elbert County, CO | 23 086 | 23 383 | 20340 | | Duncan, OK Micro area | 45 048 | 44 779 |
| | 08 047 | Gilpin County, CO | 5 441 | 5 491 | | 40 137 | Stephens County, OK | 45 048 | 44 779 |
| | 08 059 | Jefferson County, CO | 534 543 | 545 358 | | | | | |
| | 08 093 | Park County, CO | 16 206 | 16 029 | 20380 | | Dunn, NC Micro area | 114 678 | 122 135 |
| | | | | | | 37 085 | Harnett County, NC | 114 678 | 122 135 |
| 19760 | | DeRidder, LA Micro area | 35 654 | 36 281 | | | | | |
| | 22 011 | Beauregard Parish, LA | 35 654 | 36 281 | 20420 | | Durango, CO Micro area | 51 334 | 52 401 |
| | | | | | | 08 067 | La Plata County, CO | 51 334 | 52 401 |
| 19780 | | Des Moines-West Des Moines, IA Metro area | 569 633 | 588 999 | 20460 | | Durant, OK Micro area | 42 416 | 43 399 |
| | 19 049 | Dallas County, IA | 66 135 | 71 967 | | 40 013 | Bryan County, OK | 42 416 | 43 399 |
| | 19 077 | Guthrie County, IA | 10 954 | 10 777 | | | | | |
| | 19 121 | Madison County, IA | 15 679 | 15 654 | 20500 | | Durham-Chapel Hill, NC Metro area | 504 357 | 522 826 |
| | 19 153 | Polk County, IA | 430 640 | 443 710 | | 37 037 | Chatham County, NC | 63 505 | 65 976 |
| | 19 181 | Warren County, IA | 46 225 | 46 891 | | 37 063 | Durham County, NC | 267 587 | 279 641 |
| | | | | | | 37 135 | Orange County, NC | 133 801 | 137 941 |
| 19820 | | Detroit-Warren-Dearborn, MI Metro area | 4 296 250 | 4 292 060 | | 37 145 | Person County, NC | 39 464 | 39 268 |
| 19820 | | Detroit-Dearborn-Livonia, MI Metro Div 19804 | 1 820 584 | 1 792 365 | 20540 | | Dyersburg, TN Micro area | 38 335 | 38 255 |
| | 26 163 | Wayne County, MI | 1 820 584 | 1 792 365 | | 47 045 | Dyer County, TN | 38 335 | 38 255 |
| 19820 | | Warren-Troy-Farmington Hills, MI Metro Div 47664 | 2 475 666 | 2 499 695 | 20580 | | Eagle Pass, TX Micro area | 54 258 | 55 365 |
| | 26 087 | Lapeer County, MI | 88 319 | 88 173 | | 48 323 | Maverick County, TX | 54 258 | 55 365 |
| | 26 093 | Livingston County, MI | 180 967 | 182 838 | 20660 | | Easton, MD Micro area | 37 782 | 38 098 |
| | 26 099 | Macomb County, MI | 840 978 | 847 383 | | 24 041 | Talbot County, MD | 37 782 | 38 098 |
| | 26 125 | Oakland County, MI | 1 202 362 | 1 220 657 | | | | | |
| | 26 147 | St. Clair County, MI | 163 040 | 160 644 | 20700 | | East Stroudsburg, PA Metro area | 169 842 | 168 798 |
| | | | | | | 42 089 | Monroe County, PA | 169 842 | 168 798 |
| 19860 | | Dickinson, ND Micro area | 24 199 | 26 771 | 20740 | | Eau Claire, WI Metro area | 161 151 | 163 599 |
| | 38 089 | Stark County, ND | 24 199 | 26 771 | | 55 017 | Chippewa County, WI | 62 415 | 62 922 |
| | | | | | | 55 035 | Eau Claire County, WI | 98 736 | 100 677 |
| 19940 | | Dixon, IL Micro area | 36 031 | 35 037 | 20780 | | Edwards, CO Micro area | 52 197 | 51 874 |
| | 17 103 | Lee County, IL | 36 031 | 35 037 | | 08 037 | Eagle County, CO | 52 197 | 51 874 |

# Core Based Statistical Areas (Metropolitan and Micropolitan), Metropolitan Divisions, and Components (as defined February 2013)–*Continued*

| Core Based Statistical Area | State/County FIPS Code | Title and Geographic Components | 2010 Census Population | 2012 Estimated Population | Core Based Statistical Area | State/County FIPS Code | Title and Geographic Components | 2010 Census Population | 2012 Estimated Population |
|---|---|---|---|---|---|---|---|---|---|
| 20820 | | Effingham, IL Micro area | 34 242 | 34 353 | 21700 | | Eureka-Arcata-Fortuna, CA Micro area | 134 623 | 134 827 |
| | 17 049 | Effingham County, IL | 34 242 | 34 353 | | 06 023 | Humboldt County, CA | 134 623 | 134 827 |
| 20900 | | El Campo, TX Micro area | 41 280 | 41 285 | 21740 | | Evanston, WY Micro area | 21 118 | 21 025 |
| | 48 481 | Wharton County, TX | 41 280 | 41 285 | | 56 041 | Uinta County, WY | 21 118 | 21 025 |
| 20940 | | El Centro, CA Metro area | 174 528 | 176 948 | 21780 | | Evansville, IN-KY Metro area | 311 552 | 313 433 |
| | 06 025 | Imperial County, CA | 174 528 | 176 948 | | 18 129 | Posey County, IN | 25 910 | 25 599 |
| 20980 | | El Dorado, AR Micro area | 41 639 | 40 867 | | 18 163 | Vanderburgh County, IN | 179 703 | 180 858 |
| | 05 139 | Union County, AR | 41 639 | 40 867 | | 18 173 | Warrick County, IN | 59 689 | 60 463 |
| 21020 | | Elizabeth City, NC Micro area | 64 094 | 64 244 | | 21 101 | Henderson County, KY | 46 250 | 46 513 |
| | 37 029 | Camden County, NC | 9 980 | 10 090 | 21820 | | Fairbanks, AK Metro area | 97 581 | 100 272 |
| | 37 139 | Pasquotank County, NC | 40 661 | 40 591 | | 02 090 | Fairbanks North Star Borough, AK | 97 581 | 100 272 |
| | 37 143 | Perquimans County, NC | 13 453 | 13 563 | | | | | |
| 21060 | | Elizabethtown-Fort Knox, KY Metro area | 148 338 | 150 413 | 21840 | | Fairfield, IA Micro area | 16 843 | 16 867 |
| | 21 093 | Hardin County, KY | 105 543 | 107 025 | | 19 101 | Jefferson County, IA | 16 843 | 16 867 |
| | 21 123 | Larue County, KY | 14 193 | 14 151 | 21900 | | Fairmont, WV Micro area | 56 418 | 56 678 |
| | 21 163 | Meade County, KY | 28 602 | 29 237 | | 54 049 | Marion County, WV | 56 418 | 56 678 |
| 21120 | | Elk City, OK Micro area | 22 119 | 23 081 | 21980 | | Fallon, NV Micro area | 24 877 | 24 375 |
| | 40 009 | Beckham County, OK | 22 119 | 23 081 | | 32 001 | Churchill County, NV | 24 877 | 24 375 |
| 21140 | | Elkhart-Goshen, IN Metro area | 197 559 | 199 619 | 22020 | | Fargo, ND-MN Metro area | 208 777 | 216 312 |
| | 18 039 | Elkhart County, IN | 197 559 | 199 619 | | 27 027 | Clay County, MN | 58 999 | 60 155 |
| 21180 | | Elkins, WV Micro area | 29 405 | 29 384 | | 38 017 | Cass County, ND | 149 778 | 156 157 |
| | 54 083 | Randolph County, WV | 29 405 | 29 384 | 22060 | | Faribault-Northfield, MN Micro area | 64 142 | 64 854 |
| 21220 | | Elko, NV Micro area | 50 805 | 53 217 | | 27 131 | Rice County, MN | 64 142 | 64 854 |
| | 32 007 | Elko County, NV | 48 818 | 51 216 | 22100 | | Farmington, MO Micro area | 65 359 | 65 917 |
| | 32 011 | Eureka County, NV | 1 987 | 2 001 | | 29 187 | St. Francois County, MO | 65 359 | 65 917 |
| 21260 | | Ellensburg, WA Micro area | 40 915 | 41 672 | 22140 | | Farmington, NM Metro area | 130 044 | 128 529 |
| | 53 037 | Kittitas County, WA | 40 915 | 41 672 | | 35 045 | San Juan County, NM | 130 044 | 128 529 |
| 21300 | | Elmira, NY Metro area | 88 830 | 88 911 | 22180 | | Fayetteville, NC Metro area | 366 383 | 374 585 |
| | 36 015 | Chemung County, NY | 88 830 | 88 911 | | 37 051 | Cumberland County, NC | 319 431 | 324 049 |
| 21340 | | El Paso, TX Metro area | 804 123 | 830 735 | | 37 093 | Hoke County, NC | 46 952 | 50 536 |
| | 48 141 | El Paso County, TX | 800 647 | 827 398 | 22220 | | Fayetteville-Springdale-Rogers, AR-MO Metro area | 463 204 | 482 200 |
| | 48 229 | Hudspeth County, TX | 3 476 | 3 337 | | 05 007 | Benton County, AR | 221 339 | 232 268 |
| 21380 | | Emporia, KS Micro area | 33 690 | 33 748 | | 05 087 | Madison County, AR | 15 717 | 15 645 |
| | 20 111 | Lyon County, KS | 33 690 | 33 748 | | 05 143 | Washington County, AR | 203 065 | 211 411 |
| 21420 | | Enid, OK Micro area | 60 580 | 61 189 | | 29 119 | McDonald County, MO | 23 083 | 22 876 |
| | 40 047 | Garfield County, OK | 60 580 | 61 189 | 22260 | | Fergus Falls, MN Micro area | 57 303 | 57 288 |
| 21460 | | Enterprise, AL Micro area | 49 948 | 51 252 | | 27 111 | Otter Tail County, MN | 57 303 | 57 288 |
| | 01 031 | Coffee County, AL | 49 948 | 51 252 | 22280 | | Fernley, NV Micro area | 51 980 | 51 327 |
| 21500 | | Erie, PA Metro area | 280 566 | 280 646 | | 32 019 | Lyon County, NV | 51 980 | 51 327 |
| | 42 049 | Erie County, PA | 280 566 | 280 646 | 22300 | | Findlay, OH Micro area | 74 782 | 75 671 |
| 21540 | | Escanaba, MI Micro area | 37 069 | 36 884 | | 39 063 | Hancock County, OH | 74 782 | 75 671 |
| | 26 041 | Delta County, MI | 37 069 | 36 884 | 22340 | | Fitzgerald, GA Micro area | 17 634 | 17 538 |
| 21580 | | Española, NM Micro area | 40 246 | 40 318 | | 13 017 | Ben Hill County, GA | 17 634 | 17 538 |
| | 35 039 | Rio Arriba County, NM | 40 246 | 40 318 | 22380 | | Flagstaff, AZ Metro area | 134 421 | 136 011 |
| 21660 | | Eugene, OR Metro area | 351 715 | 354 542 | | 04 005 | Coconino County, AZ | 134 421 | 136 011 |
| | 41 039 | Lane County, OR | 351 715 | 354 542 | 22420 | | Flint, MI Metro area | 425 790 | 418 408 |
| | | | | | | 26 049 | Genesee County, MI | 425 790 | 418 408 |

# Core Based Statistical Areas (Metropolitan and Micropolitan), Metropolitan Divisions, and Components (as defined February 2013)–*Continued*

| Core Based Statistical Area | State/County FIPS Code | Title and Geographic Components | 2010 Census Population | 2012 Estimated Population | Core Based Statistical Area | State/County FIPS Code | Title and Geographic Components | 2010 Census Population | 2012 Estimated Population |
|---|---|---|---|---|---|---|---|---|---|
| 22500 | | Florence, SC Metro area .................. | 205 566 | 206 087 | 23420 | | Fresno, CA Metro area .................... | 930 450 | 947 895 |
| | 45 031 | Darlington County, SC ................. | 68 681 | 68 139 | | 06 019 | Fresno County, CA..................... | 930 450 | 947 895 |
| | 45 041 | Florence County, SC..................... | 136 885 | 137 948 | 23460 | | Gadsden, AL Metro area ................. | 104 430 | 104 392 |
| 22520 | | Florence-Muscle Shoals, AL Metro area .. | 147 137 | 146 988 | | 01 055 | Etowah County, AL ...................... | 104 430 | 104 392 |
| | 01 033 | Colbert County, AL .................... | 54 428 | 54 446 | 23500 | | Gaffney, SC Micro area ................. | 55 342 | 55 662 |
| | 01 077 | Lauderdale County, AL ............... | 92 709 | 92 542 | | 45 021 | Cherokee County, SC ................ | 55 342 | 55 662 |
| 22540 | | Fond du Lac, WI Metro area ............ | 101 633 | 101 843 | 23540 | | Gainesville, FL Metro area ............ | 264 275 | 268 232 |
| | 55 039 | Fond du Lac County, WI................ | 101 633 | 101 843 | | 12 001 | Alachua County, FL................ | 247 336 | 251 417 |
| 22580 | | Forest City, NC Micro area............. | 67 810 | 67 323 | | 12 041 | Gilchrist County, FL................ | 16 939 | 16 815 |
| | 37 161 | Rutherford County, NC................. | 67 810 | 67 323 | 23580 | | Gainesville, GA Metro area ............ | 179 684 | 185 416 |
| 22620 | | Forrest City, AR Micro area ........... | 28 258 | 27 858 | | 13 139 | Hall County, GA ....................... | 179 684 | 185 416 |
| | 05 123 | St. Francis County, AR ................ | 28 258 | 27 858 | 23620 | | Gainesville, TX Micro area ............ | 38 437 | 38 688 |
| 22660 | | Fort Collins, CO Metro area ............ | 299 630 | 310 487 | | 48 097 | Cooke County, TX...................... | 38 437 | 38 688 |
| | 08 069 | Larimer County, CO ................... | 299 630 | 310 487 | 23660 | | Galesburg, IL Micro area............... | 52 919 | 52 247 |
| 22700 | | Fort Dodge, IA Micro area.............. | 38 013 | 37 273 | | 17 095 | Knox County, IL....................... | 52 919 | 52 247 |
| | 19 187 | Webster County, IA..................... | 38 013 | 37 273 | 23700 | | Gallup, NM Micro area.................. | 71 492 | 73 016 |
| 22780 | | Fort Leonard Wood, MO Micro area | 52 274 | 53 259 | | 35 031 | McKinley County, NM................... | 71 492 | 73 016 |
| | 29 169 | Pulaski County, MO .................... | 52 274 | 53 259 | 23780 | | Garden City, KS Micro area ............ | 40 753 | 41 168 |
| 22800 | | Fort Madison-Keokuk, IA-IL-MO Micro area .. | 62 105 | 61 477 | | 20 055 | Finney County, KS ..................... | 36 776 | 37 200 |
| | 17 067 | Hancock County, IL..................... | 19 104 | 18 891 | | 20 093 | Kearny County, KS..................... | 3 977 | 3 968 |
| | 19 111 | Lee County, IA ......................... | 35 862 | 35 617 | 23820 | | Gardnerville Ranchos, NV Micro area .. | 46 997 | 46 996 |
| | 29 045 | Clark County, MO...................... | 7 139 | 6 969 | | 32 005 | Douglas County, NV................... | 46 997 | 46 996 |
| 22820 | | Fort Morgan, CO Micro area ........... | 28 159 | 28 472 | 23860 | | Georgetown, SC Micro area ............ | 60 158 | 60 189 |
| | 08 087 | Morgan County, CO ................... | 28 159 | 28 472 | | 45 043 | Georgetown County, SC .............. | 60 158 | 60 189 |
| 22860 | | Fort Polk South, LA Micro area........ | 52 334 | 53 869 | 23900 | | Gettysburg, PA Metro area............. | 101 407 | 101 482 |
| | 22 115 | Vernon Parish, LA ..................... | 52 334 | 53 869 | | 42 001 | Adams County, PA...................... | 101 407 | 101 482 |
| 22900 | | Fort Smith, AR-OK Metro area........ | 280 467 | 280 521 | 23940 | | Gillette, WY Micro area................. | 46 133 | 47 874 |
| | 05 033 | Crawford County, AR .................. | 61 948 | 61 946 | | 56 005 | Campbell County, WY.................. | 46 133 | 47 874 |
| | 05 131 | Sebastian County, AR .................. | 125 744 | 127 304 | 23980 | | Glasgow, KY Micro area................ | 52 272 | 52 600 |
| | 40 079 | Le Flore County, OK ................... | 50 384 | 49 873 | | 21 009 | Barren County, KY ..................... | 42 173 | 42 631 |
| | 40 135 | Sequoyah County, OK ................. | 42 391 | 41 398 | | 21 169 | Metcalfe County, KY ................... | 10 099 | 9 969 |
| 23060 | | Fort Wayne, IN Metro area.............. | 416 257 | 421 406 | 24020 | | Glens Falls, NY Metro area.............. | 128 923 | 128 472 |
| | 18 003 | Allen County, IN ....................... | 355 329 | 360 412 | | 36 113 | Warren County, NY .................... | 65 707 | 65 538 |
| | 18 179 | Wells County, IN ...................... | 27 636 | 27 652 | | 36 115 | Washington County, NY.............. | 63 216 | 62 934 |
| | 18 183 | Whitley County, IN .................... | 33 292 | 33 342 | 24060 | | Glenwood Springs, CO Micro area... | 73 537 | 74 216 |
| 23140 | | Frankfort, IN Micro area................ | 33 224 | 33 022 | | 08 045 | Garfield County, CO................... | 56 389 | 56 953 |
| | 18 023 | Clinton County, IN ..................... | 33 224 | 33 022 | | 08 097 | Pitkin County, CO...................... | 17 148 | 17 263 |
| 23180 | | Frankfort, KY Micro area ................ | 70 706 | 71 532 | 24100 | | Gloversville, NY Micro area ............ | 55 531 | 54 925 |
| | 21 005 | Anderson County, KY.................. | 21 421 | 21 728 | | 36 035 | Fulton County, NY..................... | 55 531 | 54 925 |
| | 21 073 | Franklin County, KY .................... | 49 285 | 49 804 | 24140 | | Goldsboro, NC Metro area ............ | 122 623 | 124 246 |
| 23240 | | Fredericksburg, TX Micro area........ | 24 837 | 25 153 | | 37 191 | Wayne County, NC .................... | 122 623 | 124 246 |
| | 48 171 | Gillespie County, TX ................... | 24 837 | 25 153 | 24220 | | Grand Forks, ND-MN Metro area..... | 98 461 | 98 888 |
| 23300 | | Freeport, IL Micro area................. | 47 711 | 46 959 | | 27 119 | Polk County, MN ...................... | 31 600 | 31 416 |
| | 17 177 | Stephenson County, IL................. | 47 711 | 46 959 | | 38 035 | Grand Forks County, ND ............. | 66 861 | 67 472 |
| 23340 | | Fremont, NE Micro area ................. | 36 691 | 36 427 | 24260 | | Grand Island, NE Metro area .......... | 81 850 | 83 472 |
| | 31 053 | Dodge County, NE .................... | 36 691 | 36 427 | | 31 079 | Hall County, NE........................ | 58 607 | 60 345 |
| 23380 | | Fremont, OH Micro area................. | 60 944 | 60 510 | | 31 081 | Hamilton County, NE.................. | 9 124 | 9 011 |
| | 39 143 | Sandusky County, OH.................. | 60 944 | 60 510 | | 31 093 | Howard County, NE ................... | 6 274 | 6 336 |
| | | | | | | 31 121 | Merrick County, NE.................... | 7 845 | 7 780 |

| Core Based Statistical Area | State/County FIPS Code | Title and Geographic Components | 2010 Census Population | 2012 Estimated Population | Core Based Statistical Area | State/County FIPS Code | Title and Geographic Components | 2010 Census Population | 2012 Estimated Population |
|---|---|---|---|---|---|---|---|---|---|
| 24300 | | Grand Junction, CO Metro area ....... | 146 723 | 147 848 | 24980 | | Grenada, MS Micro area ................ | 21 906 | 21 682 |
| | 08 077 | Mesa County, CO......................... | 146 723 | 147 848 | | 28 043 | Grenada County, MS .................. | 21 906 | 21 682 |
| 24340 | | Grand Rapids-Wyoming, MI Metro area.................................. | 988 938 | 1 005 648 | 25060 | | Gulfport-Biloxi-Pascagoula, MS Metro area.............................. | 370 702 | 379 582 |
| | 26 015 | Barry County, MI ....................... | 59 173 | 58 990 | | 28 045 | Hancock County, MS ................. | 43 929 | 45 255 |
| | 26 081 | Kent County, MI ........................ | 602 622 | 614 462 | | 28 047 | Harrison County, MS ................. | 187 105 | 194 029 |
| | 26 117 | Montcalm County, MI.................. | 63 342 | 63 097 | | 28 059 | Jackson County, MS ................. | 139 668 | 140 298 |
| | 26 139 | Ottawa County, MI ..................... | 263 801 | 269 099 | 25100 | | Guymon, OK Micro area................ | 20 640 | 21 498 |
| 24380 | | Grants, NM Micro area ................ | 27 213 | 27 334 | | 40 139 | Texas County, OK ..................... | 20 640 | 21 498 |
| | 35 006 | Cibola County, NM..................... | 27 213 | 27 334 | 25180 | | Hagerstown-Martinsburg, MD-WV Metro area.............................. | 251 599 | 256 278 |
| 24420 | | Grants Pass, OR Metro area........... | 82 713 | 82 930 | | 24 043 | Washington County, MD ............. | 147 430 | 149 180 |
| | 41 033 | Josephine County, OR................. | 82 713 | 82 930 | | 54 003 | Berkeley County, WV ................. | 104 169 | 107 098 |
| 24460 | | Great Bend, KS Micro area ............ | 27 674 | 27 557 | 25200 | | Hailey, ID Micro area.................. | 27 701 | 27 500 |
| | 20 009 | Barton County, KS ..................... | 27 674 | 27 557 | | 16 013 | Blaine County, ID ..................... | 21 376 | 21 146 |
| 24500 | | Great Falls, MT Metro area ............ | 81 327 | 81 723 | | 16 025 | Camas County, ID ..................... | 1 117 | 1 077 |
| | 30 013 | Cascade County, MT ................... | 81 327 | 81 723 | | 16 063 | Lincoln County, ID..................... | 5 208 | 5 277 |
| 24540 | | Greeley, CO Metro area ................ | 252 825 | 263 691 | 25220 | | Hammond, LA Metro area .............. | 121 097 | 123 441 |
| | 08 123 | Weld County, CO ...................... | 252 825 | 263 691 | | 22 105 | Tangipahoa Parish, LA................ | 121 097 | 123 441 |
| 24580 | | Green Bay, WI Metro area .............. | 306 241 | 311 098 | 25260 | | Hanford-Corcoran, CA Metro area ... | 152 982 | 151 364 |
| | 55 009 | Brown County, WI ...................... | 248 007 | 253 032 | | 06 031 | Kings County, CA....................... | 152 982 | 151 364 |
| | 55 061 | Kewaunee County, WI ................. | 20 574 | 20 624 | 25300 | | Hannibal, MO Micro area .............. | 38 948 | 39 022 |
| | 55 083 | Oconto County, WI ..................... | 37 660 | 37 442 | | 29 127 | Marion County, MO .................... | 28 781 | 28 745 |
| 24620 | | Greeneville, TN Micro area............. | 68 831 | 68 819 | | 29 173 | Ralls County, MO ...................... | 10 167 | 10 277 |
| | 47 059 | Greene County, TN ..................... | 68 831 | 68 819 | 25420 | | Harrisburg-Carlisle, PA Metro area .. | 549 475 | 553 980 |
| 24640 | | Greenfield Town, MA Micro area...... | 71 372 | 71 540 | | 42 041 | Cumberland County, PA .............. | 235 406 | 238 614 |
| | 25 011 | Franklin County, MA.................... | 71 372 | 71 540 | | 42 043 | Dauphin County, PA ................... | 268 100 | 269 665 |
| 24660 | | Greensboro-High Point, NC Metro area.................................. | 723 801 | 736 065 | | 42 099 | Perry County, PA ...................... | 45 969 | 45 701 |
| | 37 081 | Guilford County, NC.................... | 488 406 | 500 879 | 25460 | | Harrison, AR Micro area ............... | 45 233 | 45 413 |
| | 37 151 | Randolph County, NC ................. | 141 752 | 142 466 | | 05 009 | Boone County, AR ..................... | 36 903 | 37 327 |
| | 37 157 | Rockingham County, NC.............. | 93 643 | 92 720 | | 05 101 | Newton County, AR..................... | 8 330 | 8 086 |
| 24700 | | Greensburg, IN Micro area ............ | 25 740 | 26 042 | 25500 | | Harrisonburg, VA Metro area........... | 125 228 | 128 372 |
| | 18 031 | Decatur County, IN...................... | 25 740 | 26 042 | | 51 165 | Rockingham County, VA.............. | 76 314 | 77 391 |
| 24740 | | Greenville, MS Micro area ............. | 51 137 | 49 750 | | 51 660 | Harrisonburg city, VA ................. | 48 914 | 50 981 |
| | 28 151 | Washington County, MS ............. | 51 137 | 49 750 | 25540 | | Hartford-West Hartford-East Hartford, CT Metro area .............. | 1 212 381 | 1 214 400 |
| 24780 | | Greenville, NC Metro area.............. | 168 148 | 172 554 | | 09 003 | Hartford County, CT.................... | 894 014 | 897 259 |
| | 37 147 | Pitt County, NC ......................... | 168 148 | 172 554 | | 09 007 | Middlesex County, CT................. | 165 676 | 165 602 |
| 24820 | | Greenville, OH Micro area ............. | 52 959 | 52 507 | | 09 013 | Tolland County, CT .................... | 152 691 | 151 539 |
| | 39 037 | Darke County, OH...................... | 52 959 | 52 507 | 25580 | | Hastings, NE Micro area............... | 31 364 | 31 459 |
| 24860 | | Greenville-Anderson-Mauldin, SC Metro area.............................. | 824 112 | 842 853 | | 31 001 | Adams County, NE...................... | 31 364 | 31 459 |
| | 45 007 | Anderson County, SC ................. | 187 126 | 189 355 | 25620 | | Hattiesburg, MS Metro area ........... | 142 842 | 146 766 |
| | 45 045 | Greenville County, SC................. | 451 225 | 467 605 | | 28 035 | Forrest County, MS ................... | 74 934 | 76 894 |
| | 45 059 | Laurens County, SC.................... | 66 537 | 66 223 | | 28 073 | Lamar County, MS .................... | 55 658 | 57 786 |
| | 45 077 | Pickens County, SC.................... | 119 224 | 119 670 | | 28 111 | Perry County, MS...................... | 12 250 | 12 086 |
| 24900 | | Greenwood, MS Micro area............ | 42 914 | 41 371 | 25700 | | Hays, KS Micro area.................... | 28 452 | 29 053 |
| | 28 015 | Carroll County, MS..................... | 10 597 | 10 423 | | 20 051 | Ellis County, KS ....................... | 28 452 | 29 053 |
| | 28 083 | Leflore County, MS .................... | 32 317 | 30 948 | 25720 | | Heber, UT Micro area .................. | 23 530 | 25 273 |
| 24940 | | Greenwood, SC Micro area............ | 95 078 | 94 857 | | 49 051 | Wasatch County, UT .................. | 23 530 | 25 273 |
| | 45 001 | Abbeville County, SC ................. | 25 417 | 25 101 | 25740 | | Helena, MT Micro area ................. | 74 801 | 76 277 |
| | 45 047 | Greenwood County, SC............... | 69 661 | 69 756 | | 30 043 | Jefferson County, MT.................. | 11 406 | 11 401 |
| | | | | | | 30 049 | Lewis and Clark County, MT........ | 63 395 | 64 876 |

# Core Based Statistical Areas (Metropolitan and Micropolitan), Metropolitan Divisions, and Components (as defined February 2013)–*Continued*

| Core Based Statistical Area | State/County FIPS Code | Title and Geographic Components | 2010 Census Population | 2012 Estimated Population |
|---|---|---|---|---|
| 25760 | | Helena-West Helena, AR Micro area | 21 757 | 20 784 |
| | 05 107 | Phillips County, AR | 21 757 | 20 784 |
| 25780 | | Henderson, NC Micro area | 45 422 | 45 132 |
| | 37 181 | Vance County, NC | 45 422 | 45 132 |
| 25820 | | Hereford, TX Micro area | 19 372 | 19 360 |
| | 48 117 | Deaf Smith County, TX | 19 372 | 19 360 |
| 25840 | | Hermiston-Pendleton, OR Micro area | 87 062 | 88 064 |
| | 41 049 | Morrow County, OR | 11 173 | 11 244 |
| | 41 059 | Umatilla County, OR | 75 889 | 76 820 |
| 25860 | | Hickory-Lenoir-Morganton, NC Metro area | 365 497 | 363 627 |
| | 37 003 | Alexander County, NC | 37 198 | 36 853 |
| | 37 023 | Burke County, NC | 90 912 | 90 505 |
| | 37 027 | Caldwell County, NC | 83 029 | 81 930 |
| | 37 035 | Catawba County, NC | 154 358 | 154 339 |
| 25880 | | Hillsdale, MI Micro area | 46 688 | 46 229 |
| | 26 059 | Hillsdale County, MI | 46 688 | 46 229 |
| 25900 | | Hilo, HI Micro area | 185 079 | 189 191 |
| | 15 001 | Hawaii County, HI | 185 079 | 189 191 |
| 25940 | | Hilton Head Island-Bluffton-Beaufort, SC Metro area | 187 010 | 193 882 |
| | 45 013 | Beaufort County, SC | 162 233 | 168 049 |
| | 45 053 | Jasper County, SC | 24 777 | 25 833 |
| 25980 | | Hinesville, GA Metro area | 77 917 | 81 519 |
| | 13 179 | Liberty County, GA | 63 453 | 65 471 |
| | 13 183 | Long County, GA | 14 464 | 16 048 |
| 26020 | | Hobbs, NM Micro area | 64 727 | 66 338 |
| | 35 025 | Lea County, NM | 64 727 | 66 338 |
| 26090 | | Holland, MI Micro area | 111 408 | 112 039 |
| | 26 005 | Allegan County, MI | 111 408 | 112 039 |
| 26140 | | Homosassa Springs, FL Metro area | 141 236 | 139 360 |
| | 12 017 | Citrus County, FL | 141 236 | 139 360 |
| 26220 | | Hood River, OR Micro area | 22 346 | 22 584 |
| | 41 027 | Hood River County, OR | 22 346 | 22 584 |
| 26300 | | Hot Springs, AR Metro area | 96 024 | 96 903 |
| | 05 051 | Garland County, AR | 96 024 | 96 903 |
| 26340 | | Houghton, MI Micro area | 38 784 | 38 735 |
| | 26 061 | Houghton County, MI | 36 628 | 36 520 |
| | 26 083 | Keweenaw County, MI | 2 156 | 2 215 |
| 26380 | | Houma-Thibodaux, LA Metro area | 208 178 | 208 922 |
| | 22 057 | Lafourche Parish, LA | 96 318 | 97 029 |
| | 22 109 | Terrebonne Parish, LA | 111 860 | 111 893 |
| 26420 | | Houston-The Woodlands-Sugar Land, TX Metro area | 5 920 416 | 6 177 035 |
| | 48 015 | Austin County, TX | 28 417 | 28 618 |
| | 48 039 | Brazoria County, TX | 313 166 | 324 769 |
| | 48 071 | Chambers County, TX | 35 096 | 36 196 |
| | 48 157 | Fort Bend County, TX | 585 375 | 627 293 |
| | 48 167 | Galveston County, TX | 291 309 | 300 484 |
| | 48 201 | Harris County, TX | 4 092 459 | 4 253 700 |
| | 48 291 | Liberty County, TX | 75 643 | 76 571 |
| | 48 339 | Montgomery County, TX | 455 746 | 485 047 |
| | 48 473 | Waller County, TX | 43 205 | 44 357 |

| Core Based Statistical Area | State/County FIPS Code | Title and Geographic Components | 2010 Census Population | 2012 Estimated Population |
|---|---|---|---|---|
| 26460 | | Hudson, NY Micro area | 63 096 | 62 499 |
| | 36 021 | Columbia County, NY | 63 096 | 62 499 |
| 26500 | | Huntingdon, PA Micro area | 45 913 | 45 943 |
| | 42 061 | Huntingdon County, PA | 45 913 | 45 943 |
| 26540 | | Huntington, IN Micro area | 37 124 | 36 987 |
| | 18 069 | Huntington County, IN | 37 124 | 36 987 |
| 26580 | | Huntington-Ashland, WV-KY-OH Metro area | 364 908 | 364 665 |
| | 21 019 | Boyd County, KY | 49 542 | 49 164 |
| | 21 089 | Greenup County, KY | 36 910 | 36 707 |
| | 39 087 | Lawrence County, OH | 62 450 | 62 109 |
| | 54 011 | Cabell County, WV | 96 319 | 96 974 |
| | 54 043 | Lincoln County, WV | 21 720 | 21 627 |
| | 54 079 | Putnam County, WV | 55 486 | 56 435 |
| | 54 099 | Wayne County, WV | 42 481 | 41 649 |
| 26620 | | Huntsville, AL Metro area | 417 593 | 430 734 |
| | 01 083 | Limestone County, AL | 82 782 | 87 654 |
| | 01 089 | Madison County, AL | 334 811 | 343 080 |
| 26660 | | Huntsville, TX Micro area | 82 446 | 82 717 |
| | 48 455 | Trinity County, TX | 14 585 | 14 309 |
| | 48 471 | Walker County, TX | 67 861 | 68 408 |
| 26700 | | Huron, SD Micro area | 17 398 | 17 753 |
| | 46 005 | Beadle County, SD | 17 398 | 17 753 |
| 26740 | | Hutchinson, KS Micro area | 64 511 | 64 438 |
| | 20 155 | Reno County, KS | 64 511 | 64 438 |
| 26780 | | Hutchinson, MN Micro area | 36 651 | 36 053 |
| | 27 085 | McLeod County, MN | 36 651 | 36 053 |
| 26820 | | Idaho Falls, ID Metro area | 133 265 | 136 108 |
| | 16 019 | Bonneville County, ID | 104 234 | 106 684 |
| | 16 023 | Butte County, ID | 2 891 | 2 740 |
| | 16 051 | Jefferson County, ID | 26 140 | 26 684 |
| 26860 | | Indiana, PA Micro area | 88 880 | 88 218 |
| | 42 063 | Indiana County, PA | 88 880 | 88 218 |
| 26900 | | Indianapolis-Carmel-Anderson, IN Metro area | 1 887 877 | 1 928 982 |
| | 18 011 | Boone County, IN | 56 640 | 58 944 |
| | 18 013 | Brown County, IN | 15 242 | 15 083 |
| | 18 057 | Hamilton County, IN | 274 569 | 289 495 |
| | 18 059 | Hancock County, IN | 70 002 | 70 933 |
| | 18 063 | Hendricks County, IN | 145 448 | 150 434 |
| | 18 081 | Johnson County, IN | 139 654 | 143 191 |
| | 18 095 | Madison County, IN | 131 636 | 130 348 |
| | 18 097 | Marion County, IN | 903 393 | 918 977 |
| | 18 109 | Morgan County, IN | 68 894 | 69 356 |
| | 18 133 | Putnam County, IN | 37 963 | 37 750 |
| | 18 145 | Shelby County, IN | 44 436 | 44 471 |
| 26940 | | Indianola, MS Micro area | 29 450 | 28 431 |
| | 28 133 | Sunflower County, MS | 29 450 | 28 431 |
| 26960 | | Ionia, MI Micro area | 63 905 | 63 941 |
| | 26 067 | Ionia County, MI | 63 905 | 63 941 |
| 26980 | | Iowa City, IA Metro area | 152 586 | 158 231 |
| | 19 103 | Johnson County, IA | 130 882 | 136 317 |
| | 19 183 | Washington County, IA | 21 704 | 21 914 |

# Core Based Statistical Areas (Metropolitan and Micropolitan), Metropolitan Divisions, and Components (as defined February 2013)–*Continued*

| Core Based Statistical Area | State/County FIPS Code | Title and Geographic Components | 2010 Census Population | 2012 Estimated Population | Core Based Statistical Area | State/County FIPS Code | Title and Geographic Components | 2010 Census Population | 2012 Estimated Population |
|---|---|---|---|---|---|---|---|---|---|
| 27020 | | Iron Mountain, MI-WI Micro area...... | 30 591 | 30 702 | 27700 | | Jesup, GA Micro area..................... | 30 099 | 30 305 |
| | 26 043 | Dickinson County, MI................ | 26 168 | 26 220 | | 13 305 | Wayne County, GA ...................... | 30 099 | 30 305 |
| | 55 037 | Florence County, WI .................. | 4 423 | 4 482 | 27740 | | Johnson City, TN Metro area .......... | 198 716 | 200 684 |
| 27060 | | Ithaca, NY Metro area .................... | 101 564 | 102 554 | | 47 019 | Carter County, TN....................... | 57 424 | 57 355 |
| | 36 109 | Tompkins County, NY .................. | 101 564 | 102 554 | | 47 171 | Unicoi County, TN....................... | 18 313 | 18 235 |
| 27100 | | Jackson, MI Metro area.................. | 160 248 | 160 309 | | 47 179 | Washington County, TN................ | 122 979 | 125 094 |
| | 26 075 | Jackson County, MI..................... | 160 248 | 160 309 | 27780 | | Johnstown, PA Metro area .............. | 143 679 | 141 584 |
| 27140 | | Jackson, MS Metro area.................. | 567 122 | 576 800 | | 42 021 | Cambria County, PA ...................... | 143 679 | 141 584 |
| | 28 029 | Copiah County, MS..................... | 29 449 | 28 955 | 27860 | | Jonesboro, AR Metro area.............. | 121 026 | 124 042 |
| | 28 049 | Hinds County, MS....................... | 245 285 | 248 643 | | 05 031 | Craighead County, AR ................. | 96 443 | 99 735 |
| | 28 089 | Madison County, MS.................... | 95 203 | 98 468 | | 05 111 | Poinsett County, AR..................... | 24 583 | 24 307 |
| | 28 121 | Rankin County, MS...................... | 141 617 | 145 165 | 27900 | | Joplin, MO Metro area.................. | 175 518 | 174 327 |
| | 28 127 | Simpson County, MS.................... | 27 503 | 27 374 | | 29 097 | Jasper County, MO....................... | 117 404 | 115 258 |
| | 28 163 | Yazoo County, MS ...................... | 28 065 | 28 195 | | 29 145 | Newton County, MO..................... | 58 114 | 59 069 |
| 27160 | | Jackson, OH Micro area.................. | 33 225 | 32 954 | 27920 | | Junction City, KS Micro area........... | 34 362 | 38 013 |
| | 39 079 | Jackson County, OH .................... | 33 225 | 32 954 | | 20 061 | Geary County, KS ....................... | 34 362 | 38 013 |
| 27180 | | Jackson, TN Metro area .................. | 130 011 | 130 450 | 27940 | | Juneau, AK Micro area.................... | 31 275 | 32 556 |
| | 47 023 | Chester County, TN..................... | 17 131 | 17 171 | | 02 110 | Juneau City and Borough, AK ...... | 31 275 | 32 556 |
| | 47 033 | Crockett County, TN.................... | 14 586 | 14 623 | 27980 | | Kahului-Wailuku-Lahaina, HI Metro area........................................ | 154 924 | 158 316 |
| | 47 113 | Madison County, TN.................... | 98 294 | 98 656 | | 15 005 | Kalawao County, HI...................... | 90 | 90 |
| 27220 | | Jackson, WY-ID Micro area.............. | 31 464 | 31 727 | | 15 009 | Maui County, HI........................... | 154 834 | 158 226 |
| | 16 081 | Teton County, ID ........................ | 10 170 | 10 052 | 28020 | | Kalamazoo-Portage, MI Metro area . | 326 589 | 330 034 |
| | 56 039 | Teton County, WY ....................... | 21 294 | 21 675 | | 26 077 | Kalamazoo County, MI................. | 250 331 | 254 580 |
| 27260 | | Jacksonville, FL Metro area.............. | 1 345 596 | 1 377 850 | | 26 159 | Van Buren County, MI.................. | 76 258 | 75 454 |
| | 12 003 | Baker County, FL ....................... | 27 115 | 27 086 | 28060 | | Kalispell, MT Micro area.................. | 90 928 | 91 633 |
| | 12 019 | Clay County, FL ......................... | 190 865 | 194 345 | | 30 029 | Flathead County, MT.................... | 90 928 | 91 633 |
| | 12 031 | Duval County, FL ....................... | 864 263 | 879 602 | 28100 | | Kankakee, IL Metro area................. | 113 449 | 113 040 |
| | 12 089 | Nassau County, FL ..................... | 73 314 | 74 629 | | 17 091 | Kankakee County, IL.................... | 113 449 | 113 040 |
| | 12 109 | St. Johns County, FL .................. | 190 039 | 202 188 | 28140 | | Kansas City, MO-KS Metro area...... | 2 009 342 | 2 038 724 |
| 27300 | | Jacksonville, IL Micro area .............. | 40 902 | 40 562 | | 20 091 | Johnson County, KS .................... | 544 179 | 559 913 |
| | 17 137 | Morgan County, IL...................... | 35 547 | 35 272 | | 20 103 | Leavenworth County, KS .............. | 76 227 | 77 739 |
| | 17 171 | Scott County, IL.......................... | 5 355 | 5 290 | | 20 107 | Linn County, KS ......................... | 9 656 | 9 441 |
| 27340 | | Jacksonville, NC Metro area.............. | 177 772 | 183 263 | | 20 121 | Miami County, KS ....................... | 32 787 | 32 612 |
| | 37 133 | Onslow County, NC ..................... | 177 772 | 183 263 | | 20 209 | Wyandotte County, KS................. | 157 505 | 159 129 |
| 27380 | | Jacksonville, TX Micro area.............. | 50 845 | 51 206 | | 29 013 | Bates County, MO....................... | 17 049 | 16 709 |
| | 48 073 | Cherokee County, TX................... | 50 845 | 51 206 | | 29 025 | Caldwell County, MO................... | 9 424 | 9 145 |
| 27420 | | Jamestown, ND Micro area ............. | 21 100 | 20 934 | | 29 037 | Cass County, MO........................ | 99 478 | 100 376 |
| | 38 093 | Stutsman County, ND .................. | 21 100 | 20 934 | | 29 047 | Clay County, MO......................... | 221 939 | 227 577 |
| 27460 | | Jamestown-Dunkirk-Fredonia, NY Micro area...................................... | 134 905 | 133 539 | | 29 049 | Clinton County, MO..................... | 20 743 | 20 508 |
| | 36 013 | Chautauqua County, NY .............. | 134 905 | 133 539 | | 29 095 | Jackson County, MO.................... | 674 158 | 677 377 |
| 27500 | | Janesville-Beloit, WI Metro area....... | 160 331 | 160 418 | | 29 107 | Lafayette County, MO.................. | 33 381 | 33 080 |
| | 55 105 | Rock County, WI ........................ | 160 331 | 160 418 | | 29 165 | Platte County, MO....................... | 89 322 | 92 054 |
| 27540 | | Jasper, IN Micro area ..................... | 54 734 | 54 837 | | 29 177 | Ray County, MO.......................... | 23 494 | 23 064 |
| | 18 037 | Dubois County, IN ...................... | 41 889 | 42 071 | 28180 | | Kapaa, HI Micro area...................... | 67 091 | 68 434 |
| | 18 125 | Pike County, IN ......................... | 12 845 | 12 766 | | 15 007 | Kauai County, HI......................... | 67 091 | 68 434 |
| 27600 | | Jefferson, GA Micro area................. | 60 485 | 60 571 | 28260 | | Kearney, NE Micro area ................. | 52 591 | 53 948 |
| | 13 157 | Jackson County, GA ................... | 60 485 | 60 571 | | 31 019 | Buffalo County, NE...................... | 46 102 | 47 463 |
| 27620 | | Jefferson City, MO Metro area ........ | 149 807 | 150 151 | | 31 099 | Kearney County, NE.................... | 6 489 | 6 485 |
| | 29 027 | Callaway County, MO................... | 44 332 | 44 305 | 28300 | | Keene, NH Micro area................... | 77 117 | 76 851 |
| | 29 051 | Cole County, MO......................... | 75 990 | 76 363 | | 33 005 | Cheshire County, NH ................... | 77 117 | 76 851 |
| | 29 135 | Moniteau County, MO.................. | 15 607 | 15 625 | 28340 | | Kendallville, IN Micro area.............. | 47 536 | 47 582 |
| | 29 151 | Osage County, MO...................... | 13 878 | 13 858 | | 18 113 | Noble County, IN......................... | 47 536 | 47 582 |

# Core Based Statistical Areas (Metropolitan and Micropolitan), Metropolitan Divisions, and Components (as defined February 2013)–*Continued*

| Core Based Statistical Area | State/County FIPS Code | Title and Geographic Components | 2010 Census Population | 2012 Estimated Population | Core Based Statistical Area | State/County FIPS Code | Title and Geographic Components | 2010 Census Population | 2012 Estimated Population |
|---|---|---|---|---|---|---|---|---|---|
| 28380 | | Kennett, MO Micro area .................. | 31 953 | 31 826 | 29100 | | La Crosse-Onalaska, WI-MN Metro area.............................................. | 133 665 | 135 298 |
| | 29 069 | Dunklin County, MO...................... | 31 953 | 31 826 | | 27 055 | Houston County, MN.................... | 19 027 | 18 837 |
| 28420 | | Kennewick-Richland, WA Metro area.............................................. | 253 340 | 268 243 | | 55 063 | La Crosse County, WI.................. | 114 638 | 116 461 |
| | 53 005 | Benton County, WA...................... | 175 177 | 182 398 | 29180 | | Lafayette, LA Metro area.................. | 466 750 | 474 415 |
| | 53 021 | Franklin County, WA..................... | 78 163 | 85 845 | | 22 001 | Acadia Parish, LA........................ | 61 773 | 61 912 |
| 28500 | | Kerrville, TX Micro area.................. | 49 625 | 49 786 | | 22 045 | Iberia Parish, LA......................... | 73 240 | 73 999 |
| | 48 265 | Kerr County, TX ........................... | 49 625 | 49 786 | | 22 055 | Lafayette Parish, LA.................... | 221 578 | 227 055 |
| 28540 | | Ketchikan, AK Micro area............... | 13 477 | 13 779 | | 22 099 | St. Martin Parish, LA................... | 52 160 | 52 726 |
| | 02 130 | Ketchikan Gateway Borough, AK.. | 13 477 | 13 779 | | 22 113 | Vermilion Parish, LA.................... | 57 999 | 58 723 |
| 28580 | | Key West, FL Micro area................. | 73 090 | 74 809 | 29200 | | Lafayette-West Lafayette, IN Metro area.............................................. | 201 789 | 206 412 |
| | 12 087 | Monroe County, FL....................... | 73 090 | 74 809 | | 18 007 | Benton County, IN....................... | 8 854 | 8 804 |
| 28620 | | Kill Devil Hills, NC Micro area ......... | 38 327 | 38 911 | | 18 015 | Carroll County, IN....................... | 20 155 | 20 095 |
| | 37 055 | Dare County, NC.......................... | 33 920 | 34 573 | | 18 157 | Tippecanoe County, IN ............... | 172 780 | 177 513 |
| | 37 177 | Tyrrell County, NC....................... | 4 407 | 4 338 | 29260 | | La Grande, OR Micro area.............. | 25 748 | 25 759 |
| 28660 | | Killeen-Temple, TX Metro area........ | 405 300 | 420 375 | | 41 061 | Union County, OR........................ | 25 748 | 25 759 |
| | 48 027 | Bell County, TX ........................... | 310 235 | 323 037 | 29300 | | LaGrange, GA Micro area .............. | 67 044 | 68 468 |
| | 48 099 | Coryell County, TX...................... | 75 388 | 77 231 | | 13 285 | Troup County, GA........................ | 67 044 | 68 468 |
| | 48 281 | Lampasas County, TX.................. | 19 677 | 20 107 | 29340 | | Lake Charles, LA Metro area .......... | 199 607 | 201 195 |
| 28700 | | Kingsport-Bristol-Bristol, TN-VA Metro area........................... | 309 544 | 309 006 | | 22 019 | Calcasieu Parish, LA................... | 192 768 | 194 493 |
| | 47 073 | Hawkins County, TN..................... | 56 833 | 56 587 | | 22 023 | Cameron Parish, LA.................... | 6 839 | 6 702 |
| | 47 163 | Sullivan County, TN..................... | 156 823 | 156 786 | 29380 | | Lake City, FL Micro area................. | 67 531 | 67 966 |
| | 51 169 | Scott County, VA.......................... | 23 177 | 22 781 | | 12 023 | Columbia County, FL ................... | 67 531 | 67 966 |
| | 51 191 | Washington County, VA............... | 54 876 | 55 190 | 29420 | | Lake Havasu City-Kingman, AZ Metro area.............................................. | 200 186 | 203 334 |
| | 51 520 | Bristol city, VA............................ | 17 835 | 17 662 | | 04 015 | Mohave County, AZ ..................... | 200 186 | 203 334 |
| 28740 | | Kingston, NY Metro area ................. | 182 493 | 181 791 | 29460 | | Lakeland-Winter Haven, FL Metro area.............................................. | 602 095 | 616 158 |
| | 36 111 | Ulster County, NY ....................... | 182 493 | 181 791 | | 12 105 | Polk County, FL.......................... | 602 095 | 616 158 |
| 28780 | | Kingsville, TX Micro area............... | 32 477 | 32 456 | 29500 | | Lamesa, TX Micro area .................. | 13 833 | 13 640 |
| | 48 261 | Kenedy County, TX...................... | 416 | 431 | | 48 115 | Dawson County, TX..................... | 13 833 | 13 640 |
| | 48 273 | Kleberg County, TX...................... | 32 061 | 32 025 | 29540 | | Lancaster, PA Metro area............... | 519 445 | 526 823 |
| 28820 | | Kinston, NC Micro area.................. | 59 495 | 59 227 | | 42 071 | Lancaster County, PA .................. | 519 445 | 526 823 |
| | 37 107 | Lenoir County, NC....................... | 59 495 | 59 227 | 29620 | | Lansing-East Lansing, MI Metro area | 464 036 | 465 732 |
| 28860 | | Kirksville, MO Micro area................ | 30 038 | 29 951 | | 26 037 | Clinton County, MI...................... | 75 382 | 76 001 |
| | 29 001 | Adair County, MO........................ | 25 607 | 25 581 | | 26 045 | Eaton County, MI ........................ | 107 759 | 108 008 |
| | 29 197 | Schuyler County, MO................... | 4 431 | 4 370 | | 26 065 | Ingham County, MI...................... | 280 895 | 281 723 |
| 28900 | | Klamath Falls, OR Micro area ......... | 66 380 | 65 912 | 29660 | | Laramie, WY Micro area ................. | 36 299 | 37 276 |
| | 41 035 | Klamath County, OR .................... | 66 380 | 65 912 | | 56 001 | Albany County, WY...................... | 36 299 | 37 276 |
| 28940 | | Knoxville, TN Metro area ................. | 837 571 | 848 350 | 29700 | | Laredo, TX Metro area ................... | 250 304 | 259 172 |
| | 47 001 | Anderson County, TN................... | 75 129 | 75 416 | | 48 479 | Webb County, TX......................... | 250 304 | 259 172 |
| | 47 009 | Blount County, TN....................... | 123 010 | 124 177 | 29740 | | Las Cruces, NM Metro area ........... | 209 233 | 214 445 |
| | 47 013 | Campbell County, TN................... | 40 716 | 40 420 | | 35 013 | Doña Ana County, NM.................. | 209 233 | 214 445 |
| | 47 057 | Grainger County, TN.................... | 22 657 | 22 706 | 29780 | | Las Vegas, NM Micro area.............. | 29 393 | 28 891 |
| | 47 093 | Knox County, TN.......................... | 432 226 | 441 311 | | 35 047 | San Miguel County, NM................ | 29 393 | 28 891 |
| | 47 105 | Loudon County, TN...................... | 48 556 | 49 793 | 29820 | | Las Vegas-Henderson-Paradise, NV Metro area......................................... | 1 951 269 | 2 000 759 |
| | 47 129 | Morgan County, TN..................... | 21 987 | 21 931 | | 32 003 | Clark County, NV ........................ | 1 951 269 | 2 000 759 |
| | 47 145 | Roane County, TN....................... | 54 181 | 53 469 | | | | | |
| | 47 173 | Union County, TN........................ | 19 109 | 19 127 | | | | | |
| 29020 | | Kokomo, IN Metro area ................... | 82 752 | 82 849 | 29860 | | Laurel, MS Micro area .................... | 84 823 | 85 164 |
| | 18 067 | Howard County, IN....................... | 82 752 | 82 849 | | 28 061 | Jasper County, MS....................... | 17 062 | 16 523 |
| 29060 | | Laconia, NH Micro area.................. | 60 088 | 60 327 | | 28 067 | Jones County, MS........................ | 67 761 | 68 641 |
| | 33 001 | Belknap County, NH...................... | 60 088 | 60 327 | | | | | |

# Core Based Statistical Areas (Metropolitan and Micropolitan), Metropolitan Divisions, and Components (as defined February 2013)–*Continued*

| Core Based Statistical Area | State/County FIPS Code | Title and Geographic Components | 2010 Census Population | 2012 Estimated Population | Core Based Statistical Area | State/County FIPS Code | Title and Geographic Components | 2010 Census Population | 2012 Estimated Population |
|---|---|---|---|---|---|---|---|---|---|
| 29900 | | Laurinburg, NC Micro area .............. | 36 157 | 36 094 | 30780 | | Little Rock-North Little Rock- | | |
| | 37 165 | Scotland County, NC.................. | 36 157 | 36 094 | | | Conway, AR Metro area .................. | 699 757 | 717 666 |
| 29940 | | Lawrence, KS Metro area................ | 110 826 | 112 864 | | 05 045 | Faulkner County, AR.................... | 113 237 | 118 704 |
| | 20 045 | Douglas County, KS.................... | 110 826 | 112 864 | | 05 053 | Grant County, AR........................ | 17 853 | 17 986 |
| 29980 | | Lawrenceburg, TN Micro area ......... | 41 869 | 42 086 | | 05 085 | Lonoke County, AR.................... | 68 356 | 69 839 |
| | 47 099 | Lawrence County, TN ................. | 41 869 | 42 086 | | 05 105 | Perry County, AR...................... | 10 445 | 10 339 |
| 30020 | | Lawton, OK Metro area .................. | 130 291 | 132 545 | | 05 119 | Pulaski County, AR.................... | 382 748 | 388 953 |
| | 40 031 | Comanche County, OK................ | 124 098 | 126 390 | | 05 125 | Saline County, AR...................... | 107 118 | 111 845 |
| | 40 033 | Cotton County, OK...................... | 6 193 | 6 155 | 30820 | | Lock Haven, PA Micro area.............. | 39 238 | 39 517 |
| 30060 | | Lebanon, MO Micro area ............... | 35 571 | 35 417 | | 42 035 | Clinton County, PA...................... | 39 238 | 39 517 |
| | 29 105 | Laclede County, MO................... | 35 571 | 35 417 | 30860 | | Logan, UT-ID Metro area................ | 125 442 | 128 306 |
| 30140 | | Lebanon, PA Metro area ................ | 133 568 | 135 251 | | 16 041 | Franklin County, ID ................... | 12 786 | 12 786 |
| | 42 075 | Lebanon County, PA................... | 133 568 | 135 251 | | 49 005 | Cache County, UT...................... | 112 656 | 115 520 |
| 30220 | | Levelland, TX Micro area............... | 22 935 | 23 072 | 30880 | | Logan, WV Micro area.................. | 36 743 | 36 168 |
| | 48 219 | Hockley County, TX .................... | 22 935 | 23 072 | | 54 045 | Logan County, WV..................... | 36 743 | 36 168 |
| 30260 | | Lewisburg, PA Micro area ............. | 44 947 | 44 952 | 30900 | | Logansport, IN Micro area .............. | 38 966 | 38 581 |
| | 42 119 | Union County, PA........................ | 44 947 | 44 952 | | 18 017 | Cass County, IN........................ | 38 966 | 38 581 |
| 30280 | | Lewisburg, TN Micro area ............. | 30 617 | 30 883 | 30940 | | London, KY Micro area.................. | 126 369 | 126 696 |
| | 47 117 | Marshall County, TN .................. | 30 617 | 30 883 | | 21 121 | Knox County, KY....................... | 31 883 | 31 735 |
| 30300 | | Lewiston, ID-WA Metro area ........... | 60 888 | 61 419 | | 21 125 | Laurel County, KY..................... | 58 849 | 59 462 |
| | 16 069 | Nez Perce County, ID ................. | 39 265 | 39 531 | | 21 235 | Whitley County, KY ................... | 35 637 | 35 499 |
| | 53 003 | Asotin County, WA..................... | 21 623 | 21 888 | 30980 | | Longview, TX Metro area ............... | 214 369 | 216 679 |
| 30340 | | Lewiston-Auburn, ME Metro area..... | 107 702 | 107 609 | | 48 183 | Gregg County, TX...................... | 121 730 | 122 658 |
| | 23 001 | Androscoggin County, ME ........... | 107 702 | 107 609 | | 48 401 | Rusk County, TX....................... | 53 330 | 54 026 |
| 30380 | | Lewistown, PA Micro area.............. | 46 682 | 46 773 | | 48 459 | Upshur County, TX.................... | 39 309 | 39 995 |
| | 42 087 | Mifflin County, PA...................... | 46 682 | 46 773 | 31020 | | Longview, WA Metro area............... | 102 410 | 101 996 |
| 30420 | | Lexington, NE Micro area............... | 26 370 | 26 249 | | 53 015 | Cowlitz County, WA ................... | 102 410 | 101 996 |
| | 31 047 | Dawson County, NE.................... | 24 326 | 24 220 | 31060 | | Los Alamos, NM Micro area............ | 17 950 | 18 159 |
| | 31 073 | Gosper County, NE.................... | 2 044 | 2 029 | | 35 028 | Los Alamos County, NM .............. | 17 950 | 18 159 |
| 30460 | | Lexington-Fayette, KY Metro area.... | 472 099 | 485 023 | 31080 | | Los Angeles-Long Beach-Anaheim, CA Metro area ................................ | 12 828 837 | 13 052 921 |
| | 21 017 | Bourbon County, KY ................... | 19 985 | 19 978 | 31080 | | Anaheim-Santa Ana-Irvine, CA Metro Div 11244 ............................ | 3 010 232 | 3 090 132 |
| | 21 049 | Clark County, KY....................... | 35 613 | 35 787 | | 06 059 | Orange County, CA.................... | 3 010 232 | 3 090 132 |
| | 21 067 | Fayette County, KY.................... | 295 803 | 305 489 | 31080 | | Los Angeles-Long Beach-Glendale, CA Metro Div 31084 ...................... | 9 818 605 | 9 962 789 |
| | 21 113 | Jessamine County, KY ............... | 48 586 | 49 635 | | 06 037 | Los Angeles County, CA.............. | 9 818 605 | 9 962 789 |
| | 21 209 | Scott County, KY....................... | 47 173 | 49 057 | 31140 | | Louisville/Jefferson County, KY-IN Metro area................................ | 1 235 708 | 1 251 351 |
| | 21 239 | Woodford County, KY................. | 24 939 | 25 077 | | 18 019 | Clark County, IN........................ | 110 232 | 111 951 |
| 30580 | | Liberal, KS Micro area.................. | 22 952 | 23 547 | | 18 043 | Floyd County, IN ....................... | 74 578 | 75 283 |
| | 20 175 | Seward County, KS.................... | 22 952 | 23 547 | | 18 061 | Harrison County, IN................... | 39 364 | 39 134 |
| 30620 | | Lima, OH Metro area .................... | 106 331 | 105 141 | | 18 143 | Scott County, IN ....................... | 24 181 | 23 791 |
| | 39 003 | Allen County, OH ...................... | 106 331 | 105 141 | | 18 175 | Washington County, IN............... | 28 262 | 27 921 |
| 30660 | | Lincoln, IL Micro area ................... | 30 305 | 30 013 | | 21 029 | Bullitt County, KY ..................... | 74 319 | 75 896 |
| | 17 107 | Logan County, IL........................ | 30 305 | 30 013 | | 21 103 | Henry County, KY ..................... | 15 416 | 15 318 |
| 30700 | | Lincoln, NE Metro area.................. | 302 157 | 310 342 | | 21 111 | Jefferson County, KY................. | 741 096 | 750 828 |
| | 31 109 | Lancaster County, NE................. | 285 407 | 293 407 | | 21 185 | Oldham County, KY ................... | 60 316 | 61 412 |
| | 31 159 | Seward County, NE.................... | 16 750 | 16 935 | | 21 211 | Shelby County, KY .................... | 42 074 | 43 614 |
| | | | | | | 21 215 | Spencer County, KY................... | 17 061 | 17 416 |
| | | | | | | 21 223 | Trimble County, KY ................... | 8 809 | 8 787 |
| | | | | | 31180 | | Lubbock, TX Metro area.................. | 290 805 | 297 669 |
| | | | | | | 48 107 | Crosby County, TX.................... | 6 059 | 6 126 |
| | | | | | | 48 303 | Lubbock County, TX.................... | 278 831 | 285 760 |
| | | | | | | 48 305 | Lynn County, TX ....................... | 5 915 | 5 783 |

| Core Based Statistical Area | State/ County FIPS Code | Title and Geographic Components | 2010 Census Population | 2012 Estimated Population | Core Based Statistical Area | State/ County FIPS Code | Title and Geographic Components | 2010 Census Population | 2012 Estimated Population |
|---|---|---|---|---|---|---|---|---|---|
| 31220 | | Ludington, MI Micro area.................. | 28 705 | 28 680 | 31930 | | Marietta, OH Micro area ................... | 61 778 | 61 475 |
| | 26 105 | Mason County, MI..................... | 28 705 | 28 680 | | 39 167 | Washington County, OH ............... | 61 778 | 61 475 |
| 31260 | | Lufkin, TX Micro area ...................... | 86 771 | 87 597 | 31940 | | Marinette, WI-MI Micro area............ | 65 778 | 65 378 |
| | 48 005 | Angelina County, TX ..................... | 86 771 | 87 597 | | 26 109 | Menominee County, MI................ | 24 029 | 23 815 |
| 31300 | | Lumberton, NC Micro area .............. | 134 168 | 135 496 | | 55 075 | Marinette County, WI................ | 41 749 | 41 563 |
| | 37 155 | Robeson County, NC..................... | 134 168 | 135 496 | 31980 | | Marion, IN Micro area ...................... | 70 061 | 69 330 |
| 31340 | | Lynchburg, VA Metro area................ | 252 634 | 255 342 | | 18 053 | Grant County, IN ......................... | 70 061 | 69 330 |
| | 51 009 | Amherst County, VA..................... | 32 353 | 32 384 | 32000 | | Marion, NC Micro area .................... | 44 996 | 44 998 |
| | 51 011 | Appomattox County, VA.............. | 14 973 | 15 128 | | 37 111 | McDowell County, NC.................. | 44 996 | 44 998 |
| | 51 019 | Bedford County, VA ..................... | 68 676 | 69 590 | | | | | |
| | 51 031 | Campbell County, VA................... | 54 842 | 55 163 | 32020 | | Marion, OH Micro area ................... | 66 501 | 66 238 |
| | 51 515 | Bedford city, VA ........................... | 6 222 | 5 964 | | 39 101 | Marion County, OH ..................... | 66 501 | 66 238 |
| | 51 680 | Lynchburg city, VA ...................... | 75 568 | 77 113 | 32100 | | Marquette, MI Micro area ............... | 67 077 | 67 906 |
| 31380 | | Macomb, IL Micro area.................... | 32 612 | 32 537 | | 26 103 | Marquette County, MI.................. | 67 077 | 67 906 |
| | 17 109 | McDonough County, IL ............... | 32 612 | 32 537 | | | | | |
| 31420 | | Macon, GA Metro area ..................... | 232 293 | 232 723 | 32140 | | Marshall, MN Micro area ................ | 25 857 | 25 543 |
| | 13 021 | Bibb County, GA ......................... | 155 547 | 156 462 | | 27 083 | Lyon County, MN ........................ | 25 857 | 25 543 |
| | 13 079 | Crawford County, GA .................. | 12 630 | 12 600 | 32180 | | Marshall, MO Micro area ............... | 23 370 | 23 339 |
| | 13 169 | Jones County, GA ....................... | 28 669 | 28 577 | | 29 195 | Saline County, MO...................... | 23 370 | 23 339 |
| | 13 207 | Monroe County, GA ..................... | 26 424 | 26 637 | | | | | |
| | 13 289 | Twiggs County, GA ...................... | 9 023 | 8 447 | 32220 | | Marshall, TX Micro area ................. | 65 631 | 67 450 |
| 31460 | | Madera, CA Metro area.................... | 150 865 | 152 218 | | 48 203 | Harrison County, TX..................... | 65 631 | 67 450 |
| | 06 039 | Madera County, CA...................... | 150 865 | 152 218 | 32260 | | Marshalltown, IA Micro area............ | 40 648 | 40 857 |
| 31500 | | Madison, IN Micro area ................... | 32 428 | 32 554 | | 19 127 | Marshall County, IA..................... | 40 648 | 40 857 |
| | 18 077 | Jefferson County, IN ................... | 32 428 | 32 554 | 32280 | | Martin, TN Micro area ................... | 35 021 | 34 793 |
| 31540 | | Madison, WI Metro area................... | 605 435 | 620 778 | | 47 183 | Weakley County, TN ................... | 35 021 | 34 793 |
| | 55 021 | Columbia County, WI................... | 56 833 | 56 539 | 32300 | | Martinsville, VA Micro area............. | 67 972 | 66 702 |
| | 55 025 | Dane County, WI.......................... | 488 073 | 503 523 | | 51 089 | Henry County, VA ....................... | 54 151 | 52 969 |
| | 55 045 | Green County, WI........................ | 36 842 | 36 909 | | 51 690 | Martinsville city, VA ................... | 13 821 | 13 733 |
| | 55 049 | Iowa County, WI.......................... | 23 687 | 23 807 | 32340 | | Maryville, MO Micro area................. | 23 370 | 23 419 |
| 31580 | | Madisonville, KY Micro area............. | 46 920 | 46 718 | | 29 147 | Nodaway County, MO................... | 23 370 | 23 419 |
| | 21 107 | Hopkins County, KY ..................... | 46 920 | 46 718 | 32380 | | Mason City, IA Micro area............... | 51 749 | 51 307 |
| 31620 | | Magnolia, AR Micro area................. | 24 552 | 24 473 | | 19 033 | Cerro Gordo County, IA ............... | 44 151 | 43 788 |
| | 05 027 | Columbia County, AR.................... | 24 552 | 24 473 | | 19 195 | Worth County, IA......................... | 7 598 | 7 519 |
| 31660 | | Malone, NY Micro area.................... | 51 599 | 51 795 | 32460 | | Mayfield, KY Micro area .................. | 37 121 | 37 544 |
| | 36 033 | Franklin County, NY ..................... | 51 599 | 51 795 | | 21 083 | Graves County, KY...................... | 37 121 | 37 544 |
| 31680 | | Malvern, AR Micro area.................... | 32 923 | 33 394 | 32500 | | Maysville, KY Micro area ................. | 17 490 | 17 512 |
| | 05 059 | Hot Spring County, AR.................. | 32 923 | 33 394 | | 21 161 | Mason County, KY ...................... | 17 490 | 17 512 |
| 31700 | | Manchester-Nashua, NH Metro area | 400 721 | 402 922 | 32540 | | McAlester, OK Micro area ............... | 45 837 | 45 048 |
| | 33 011 | Hillsborough County, NH............... | 400 721 | 402 922 | | 40 121 | Pittsburg County, OK ................... | 45 837 | 45 048 |
| 31740 | | Manhattan, KS Metro area .............. | 92 719 | 97 810 | 32580 | | McAllen-Edinburg-Mission, TX Metro area.................................... | 774 769 | 806 552 |
| | 20 149 | Pottawatomie County, KS............. | 21 604 | 22 302 | | 48 215 | Hidalgo County, TX...................... | 774 769 | 806 552 |
| | 20 161 | Riley County, KS........................ | 71 115 | 75 508 | 32620 | | McComb, MS Micro area.................. | 53 535 | 53 057 |
| 31820 | | Manitowoc, WI Micro area............... | 81 442 | 80 671 | | 28 005 | Amite County, MS ....................... | 13 131 | 12 957 |
| | 55 071 | Manitowoc County, WI................. | 81 442 | 80 671 | | 28 113 | Pike County, MS ........................ | 40 404 | 40 100 |
| 31860 | | Mankato-North Mankato, MN Metro area........................................ | 96 740 | 98 020 | 32660 | | McMinnville, TN Micro area............. | 39 839 | 39 839 |
| | 27 013 | Blue Earth County, MN ................ | 64 013 | 65 091 | | 47 177 | Warren County, TN ..................... | 39 839 | 39 839 |
| | 27 103 | Nicollet County, MN .................... | 32 727 | 32 929 | 32700 | | McPherson, KS Micro area............. | 29 180 | 29 356 |
| 31900 | | Mansfield, OH Metro area ............... | 124 475 | 122 673 | | 20 113 | McPherson County, KS................. | 29 180 | 29 356 |
| | 39 139 | Richland County, OH .................... | 124 475 | 122 673 | | | | | |

# Core Based Statistical Areas (Metropolitan and Micropolitan), Metropolitan Divisions, and Components (as defined February 2013)–*Continued*

| Core Based Statistical Area | State/ County FIPS Code | Title and Geographic Components | 2010 Census Population | 2012 Estimated Population | Core Based Statistical Area | State/ County FIPS Code | Title and Geographic Components | 2010 Census Population | 2012 Estimated Population |
|---|---|---|---|---|---|---|---|---|---|
| 32740 | | Meadville, PA Micro area.................. | 88 765 | 87 598 | 33340 | | Milwaukee-Waukesha-West Allis, WI Metro area............................. | 1 555 908 | 1 566 981 |
| | 42 039 | Crawford County, PA .................... | 88 765 | 87 598 | | 55 079 | Milwaukee County, WI ................. | 947 735 | 955 205 |
| 32780 | | Medford, OR Metro area.................. | 203 206 | 206 412 | | 55 089 | Ozaukee County, WI .................... | 86 395 | 86 823 |
| | 41 029 | Jackson County, OR ...................... | 203 206 | 206 412 | | 55 131 | Washington County, WI ............... | 131 887 | 132 661 |
| 32820 | | Memphis, TN-MS-AR Metro area..... | 1 324 829 | 1 341 690 | | 55 133 | Waukesha County, WI .................. | 389 891 | 392 292 |
| | 05 035 | Crittenden County, AR ................. | 50 902 | 50 021 | 33420 | | Mineral Wells, TX Micro area .......... | 28 111 | 27 856 |
| | 28 009 | Benton County, MS...................... | 8 729 | 8 730 | | 48 363 | Palo Pinto County, TX................. | 28 111 | 27 856 |
| | 28 033 | DeSoto County, MS ...................... | 161 252 | 166 234 | 33460 | | Minneapolis-St. Paul-Bloomington, MN Metro area........................... | 3 348 859 | 3 422 264 |
| | 28 093 | Marshall County, MS .................... | 37 144 | 36 612 | | 27 003 | Anoka County, MN ....................... | 330 844 | 336 414 |
| | 28 137 | Tate County, MS ......................... | 28 886 | 28 490 | | 27 019 | Carver County, MN ...................... | 91 042 | 93 707 |
| | 28 143 | Tunica County, MS....................... | 10 778 | 10 475 | | 27 025 | Chisago County, MN .................... | 53 887 | 53 452 |
| | 47 047 | Fayette County, TN ...................... | 38 413 | 38 659 | | 27 037 | Dakota County, MN...................... | 398 552 | 405 088 |
| | 47 157 | Shelby County, TN ....................... | 927 644 | 940 764 | | 27 053 | Hennepin County, MN .................. | 1 152 425 | 1 184 576 |
| | 47 167 | Tipton County, TN ........................ | 61 081 | 61 705 | | 27 059 | Isanti County, MN........................ | 37 816 | 38 248 |
| 32860 | | Menomonie, WI Micro area ............. | 43 857 | 44 072 | | 27 079 | Le Sueur County, MN .................. | 27 703 | 27 677 |
| | 55 033 | Dunn County, WI.......................... | 43 857 | 44 072 | | 27 095 | Mille Lacs County, MN................. | 26 097 | 25 740 |
| 32900 | | Merced, CA Metro area ................... | 255 793 | 262 305 | | 27 123 | Ramsey County, MN .................... | 508 640 | 520 152 |
| | 06 047 | Merced County, CA...................... | 255 793 | 262 305 | | 27 139 | Scott County, MN ........................ | 129 928 | 135 152 |
| 32940 | | Meridian, MS Micro area ................. | 107 449 | 107 111 | | 27 141 | Sherburne County, MN ................ | 88 499 | 89 455 |
| | 28 023 | Clarke County, MS ...................... | 16 732 | 16 556 | | 27 143 | Sibley County, MN ...................... | 15 226 | 15 123 |
| | 28 069 | Kemper County, MS...................... | 10 456 | 10 335 | | 27 163 | Washington County, MN .............. | 238 136 | 244 088 |
| | 28 075 | Lauderdale County, MS ............... | 80 261 | 80 220 | | 27 171 | Wright County, MN ...................... | 124 700 | 127 336 |
| 32980 | | Merrill, WI Micro area ..................... | 28 743 | 28 392 | | 55 093 | Pierce County, WI ....................... | 41 019 | 40 814 |
| | 55 069 | Lincoln County, WI....................... | 28 743 | 28 392 | | 55 109 | St. Croix County, WI ................... | 84 345 | 85 242 |
| 33020 | | Mexico, MO Micro area ................... | 25 529 | 25 621 | 33500 | | Minot, ND Micro area..................... | 69 540 | 73 146 |
| | 29 007 | Audrain County, MO..................... | 25 529 | 25 621 | | 38 049 | McHenry County, ND.................... | 5 395 | 5 789 |
| 33060 | | Miami, OK Micro area..................... | 31 848 | 32 236 | | 38 075 | Renville County, ND..................... | 2 470 | 2 559 |
| | 40 115 | Ottawa County, OK ...................... | 31 848 | 32 236 | | 38 101 | Ward County, ND......................... | 61 675 | 64 798 |
| 33100 | | Miami-Fort Lauderdale-West Palm Beach, FL Metro area...................... | 5 564 635 | 5 762 717 | 33540 | | Missoula, MT Metro area................. | 109 299 | 110 977 |
| | | | | | | 30 063 | Missoula County, MT ................... | 109 299 | 110 977 |
| 33100 | | Fort Lauderdale-Pompano Beach-Deerfield Beach, FL Metro Div 22744 ............................................... | 1 748 066 | 1 815 137 | 33580 | | Mitchell, SD Micro area ................. | 22 835 | 23 146 |
| | 12 011 | Broward County, FL ..................... | 1 748 066 | 1 815 137 | | 46 035 | Davison County, SD..................... | 19 504 | 19 769 |
| | | | | | | 46 061 | Hanson County, SD ..................... | 3 331 | 3 377 |
| 33100 | | Miami-Miami Beach-Kendall, FL Metro Div 33124 ............................ | 2 496 435 | 2 591 035 | 33620 | | Moberly, MO Micro area .................. | 25 414 | 25 330 |
| | 12 086 | Miami-Dade County, FL ............... | 2 496 435 | 2 591 035 | | 29 175 | Randolph County, MO................... | 25 414 | 25 330 |
| | | | | | 33660 | | Mobile, AL Metro area .................... | 412 992 | 413 936 |
| 33100 | | West Palm Beach-Boca Raton-Delray Beach, FL Metro Div 48424 .. | 1 320 134 | 1 356 545 | | 01 097 | Mobile County, AL ....................... | 412 992 | 413 936 |
| | 12 099 | Palm Beach County, FL................ | 1 320 134 | 1 356 545 | 33700 | | Modesto, CA Metro area ................. | 514 453 | 521 726 |
| | | | | | | 06 099 | Stanislaus County, CA ................. | 514 453 | 521 726 |
| 33140 | | Michigan City-La Porte, IN Metro area | 111 467 | 111 246 | 33740 | | Monroe, LA Metro area.................... | 176 441 | 177 782 |
| | 18 091 | LaPorte County, IN....................... | 111 467 | 111 246 | | 22 073 | Ouachita Parish, LA .................... | 153 720 | 155 363 |
| 33180 | | Middlesborough, KY Micro area ....... | 28 691 | 28 183 | | 22 111 | Union Parish, LA ......................... | 22 721 | 22 419 |
| | 21 013 | Bell County, KY ........................... | 28 691 | 28 183 | 33780 | | Monroe, MI Metro area.................... | 152 021 | 151 048 |
| 33220 | | Midland, MI Metro area ................... | 83 629 | 83 822 | | 26 115 | Monroe County, MI....................... | 152 021 | 151 048 |
| | 26 111 | Midland County, MI ...................... | 83 629 | 83 822 | 33860 | | Montgomery, AL Metro area............ | 374 536 | 377 149 |
| 33260 | | Midland, TX Metro area ................... | 141 671 | 151 662 | | 01 001 | Autauga County, AL...................... | 54 571 | 55 514 |
| | 48 317 | Martin County, TX ........................ | 4 799 | 5 017 | | 01 051 | Elmore County, AL ...................... | 79 303 | 80 629 |
| | 48 329 | Midland County, TX....................... | 136 872 | 146 645 | | 01 085 | Lowndes County, AL .................... | 11 299 | 10 857 |
| 33300 | | Milledgeville, GA Micro area............ | 55 149 | 55 363 | | 01 101 | Montgomery County, AL ............... | 229 363 | 230 149 |
| | 13 009 | Baldwin County, GA..................... | 45 720 | 46 367 | 33940 | | Montrose, CO Micro area ................ | 41 276 | 40 725 |
| | 13 141 | Hancock County, GA.................... | 9 429 | 8 996 | | 08 085 | Montrose County, CO .................. | 41 276 | 40 725 |
| | | | | | 33980 | | Morehead City, NC Micro area........ | 66 469 | 67 632 |
| | | | | | | 37 031 | Carteret County, NC..................... | 66 469 | 67 632 |

| Core Based Statistical Area | State/ County FIPS Code | Title and Geographic Components | 2010 Census Population | 2012 Estimated Population | Core Based Statistical Area | State/ County FIPS Code | Title and Geographic Components | 2010 Census Population | 2012 Estimated Population |
|---|---|---|---|---|---|---|---|---|---|
| 34020 | | Morgan City, LA Micro area............ | 54 650 | 53 697 | 34860 | | Nacogdoches, TX Micro area.......... | 64 524 | 66 034 |
| | 22 101 | St. Mary Parish, LA..................... | 54 650 | 53 697 | | 48 347 | Nacogdoches County, TX............ | 64 524 | 66 034 |
| 34060 | | Morgantown, WV Metro area........... | 129 709 | 134 164 | 34900 | | Napa, CA Metro area..................... | 136 484 | 139 045 |
| | 54 061 | Monongalia County, WV .............. | 96 189 | 100 332 | | 06 055 | Napa County, CA ...................... | 136 484 | 139 045 |
| | 54 077 | Preston County, WV................... | 33 520 | 33 832 | 34940 | | Naples-Immokalee-Marco Island, FL Metro area................................ | 321 520 | 332 427 |
| 34100 | | Morristown, TN Metro area............. | 113 951 | 114 937 | | 12 021 | Collier County, FL ...................... | 321 520 | 332 427 |
| | 47 063 | Hamblen County, TN................... | 62 544 | 62 746 | 34980 | | Nashville-Davidson-Murfreesboro-Franklin, TN Metro area............... | 1 670 890 | 1 726 693 |
| | 47 089 | Jefferson County, TN................... | 51 407 | 52 191 | | 47 015 | Cannon County, TN .................... | 13 801 | 13 811 |
| 34140 | | Moscow, ID Micro area................. | 37 244 | 38 184 | | 47 021 | Cheatham County, TN ................. | 39 105 | 39 271 |
| | 16 057 | Latah County, ID ...................... | 37 244 | 38 184 | | 47 037 | Davidson County, TN.................. | 626 681 | 648 295 |
| 34180 | | Moses Lake, WA Micro area........... | 89 120 | 91 723 | | 47 043 | Dickson County, TN ................... | 49 666 | 50 381 |
| | 53 025 | Grant County, WA...................... | 89 120 | 91 723 | | 47 081 | Hickman County, TN .................. | 24 690 | 24 170 |
| 34220 | | Moultrie, GA Micro area................ | 45 498 | 46 137 | | 47 111 | Macon County, TN ..................... | 22 248 | 22 498 |
| | 13 071 | Colquitt County, GA ................... | 45 498 | 46 137 | | 47 119 | Maury County, TN ..................... | 80 956 | 81 990 |
| 34260 | | Mountain Home, AR Micro area....... | 41 513 | 41 048 | | 47 147 | Robertson County, TN ................. | 66 283 | 66 931 |
| | 05 005 | Baxter County, AR ..................... | 41 513 | 41 048 | | 47 149 | Rutherford County, TN................. | 262 604 | 274 454 |
| 34300 | | Mountain Home, ID Micro area ........ | 27 038 | 26 223 | | 47 159 | Smith County, TN ...................... | 19 166 | 19 102 |
| | 16 039 | Elmore County, ID...................... | 27 038 | 26 223 | | 47 165 | Sumner County, TN ................... | 160 645 | 166 123 |
| 34340 | | Mount Airy, NC Micro area............. | 73 673 | 73 561 | | 47 169 | Trousdale County, TN ................. | 7 870 | 7 795 |
| | 37 171 | Surry County, NC ...................... | 73 673 | 73 561 | | 47 187 | Williamson County, TN................. | 183 182 | 192 911 |
| 34380 | | Mount Pleasant, MI Micro area ........ | 70 311 | 70 617 | | 47 189 | Wilson County, TN...................... | 113 993 | 118 961 |
| | 26 073 | Isabella County, MI ................... | 70 311 | 70 617 | 35020 | | Natchez, MS-LA Micro area ............ | 53 119 | 52 487 |
| 34420 | | Mount Pleasant, TX Micro area........ | 32 334 | 32 663 | | 22 029 | Concordia Parish, LA .................. | 20 822 | 20 365 |
| | 48 449 | Titus County, TX ....................... | 32 334 | 32 663 | | 28 001 | Adams County, MS ..................... | 32 297 | 32 122 |
| 34460 | | Mount Sterling, KY Micro area ........ | 44 396 | 44 924 | 35060 | | Natchitoches, LA Micro area ........... | 39 566 | 39 436 |
| | 21 011 | Bath County, KY....................... | 11 591 | 11 802 | | 22 069 | Natchitoches Parish, LA............... | 39 566 | 39 436 |
| | 21 165 | Menifee County, KY ................... | 6 306 | 6 220 | 35100 | | New Bern, NC Metro area.............. | 126 802 | 128 119 |
| | 21 173 | Montgomery County, KY .............. | 26 499 | 26 902 | | 37 049 | Craven County, NC ..................... | 103 505 | 104 770 |
| 34500 | | Mount Vernon, IL Micro area........... | 38 827 | 38 720 | | 37 103 | Jones County, NC ...................... | 10 153 | 10 275 |
| | 17 081 | Jefferson County, IL.................... | 38 827 | 38 720 | | 37 137 | Pamlico County, NC.................... | 13 144 | 13 074 |
| 34540 | | Mount Vernon, OH Micro area......... | 60 921 | 60 705 | 35140 | | Newberry, SC Micro area ............... | 37 508 | 37 576 |
| | 39 083 | Knox County, OH ...................... | 60 921 | 60 705 | | 45 071 | Newberry County, SC ................. | 37 508 | 37 576 |
| 34580 | | Mount Vernon-Anacortes, WA Metro area....................................... | 116 901 | 118 222 | 35220 | | New Castle, IN Micro area ............. | 49 462 | 49 345 |
| | 53 057 | Skagit County, WA..................... | 116 901 | 118 222 | | 18 065 | Henry County, IN........................ | 49 462 | 49 345 |
| 34620 | | Muncie, IN Metro area.................. | 117 671 | 117 364 | 35260 | | New Castle, PA Micro area ............ | 91 108 | 89 871 |
| | 18 035 | Delaware County, IN................... | 117 671 | 117 364 | | 42 073 | Lawrence County, PA .................. | 91 108 | 89 871 |
| 34660 | | Murray, KY Micro area.................. | 37 191 | 37 655 | 35300 | | New Haven-Milford, CT Metro area.. | 862 477 | 862 813 |
| | 21 035 | Calloway County, KY .................. | 37 191 | 37 655 | | 09 009 | New Haven County, CT .............. | 862 477 | 862 813 |
| 34700 | | Muscatine, IA Micro area............... | 42 745 | 42 879 | 35380 | | New Orleans-Metairie, LA Metro area....................................... | 1 189 866 | 1 227 096 |
| | 19 139 | Muscatine County, IA.................. | 42 745 | 42 879 | | 22 051 | Jefferson Parish, LA.................... | 432 552 | 433 676 |
| 34740 | | Muskegon, MI Metro area.............. | 172 188 | 170 182 | | 22 071 | Orleans Parish, LA ..................... | 343 829 | 369 250 |
| | 26 121 | Muskegon County, MI.................. | 172 188 | 170 182 | | 22 075 | Plaquemines Parish, LA............... | 23 042 | 23 921 |
| 34780 | | Muskogee, OK Micro area.............. | 70 990 | 70 596 | | 22 087 | St. Bernard Parish, LA................. | 35 897 | 41 635 |
| | 40 101 | Muskogee County, OK................. | 70 990 | 70 596 | | 22 089 | St. Charles Parish, LA................. | 52 780 | 52 681 |
| 34820 | | Myrtle Beach-Conway-North Myrtle Beach, NC-SC Metro area............ | 376 722 | 394 542 | | 22 093 | St. James Parish, LA .................. | 22 102 | 21 722 |
| | 37 019 | Brunswick County, NC ................. | 107 431 | 112 257 | | 22 095 | St. John the Baptist Parish, LA..... | 45 924 | 44 758 |
| | 45 051 | Horry County, SC ...................... | 269 291 | 282 285 | | 22 103 | St. Tammany Parish, LA.............. | 233 740 | 239 453 |
| | | | | | 35420 | | New Philadelphia-Dover, OH Micro area....................................... | 92 582 | 92 392 |
| | | | | | | 39 157 | Tuscarawas County, OH.............. | 92 582 | 92 392 |
| | | | | | 35440 | | Newport, OR Micro area............... | 46 034 | 46 151 |
| | | | | | | 41 041 | Lincoln County, OR .................... | 46 034 | 46 151 |

| Core Based Statistical Area | State/County FIPS Code | Title and Geographic Components | 2010 Census Population | 2012 Estimated Population | Core Based Statistical Area | State/County FIPS Code | Title and Geographic Components | 2010 Census Population | 2012 Estimated Population |
|---|---|---|---|---|---|---|---|---|---|
| 35460 | | Newport, TN Micro area ................. | 35 662 | 35 571 | 35860 | | North Vernon, IN Micro area ........... | 28 525 | 28 161 |
| | 47 029 | Cocke County, TN...................... | 35 662 | 35 571 | | 18 079 | Jennings County, IN..................... | 28 525 | 28 161 |
| 35500 | | Newton, IA Micro area..................... | 36 842 | 36 602 | 35900 | | North Wilkesboro, NC Micro area..... | 69 340 | 69 306 |
| | 19 099 | Jasper County, IA...................... | 36 842 | 36 602 | | 37 193 | Wilkes County, NC ....................... | 69 340 | 69 306 |
| 35580 | | New Ulm, MN Micro area ............... | 25 893 | 25 425 | 35940 | | Norwalk, OH Micro area................. | 59 626 | 59 280 |
| | 27 015 | Brown County, MN....................... | 25 893 | 25 425 | | 39 077 | Huron County, OH....................... | 59 626 | 59 280 |
| 35620 | | New York-Newark-Jersey City, NY-NJ-PA Metro area ...................... | 19 567 410 | 19 831 858 | 35980 | | Norwich-New London, CT Metro area................................ | 274 055 | 274 170 |
| 35620 | | Dutchess County-Putnam County, NY Metro Div 20524 | 397 198 | 396 929 | | 09 011 | New London County, CT.............. | 274 055 | 274 170 |
| | 36 027 | Dutchess County, NY................. | 297 488 | 297 322 | 36020 | | Oak Harbor, WA Micro area........... | 78 506 | 79 177 |
| | 36 079 | Putnam County, NY .................... | 99 710 | 99 607 | | 53 029 | Island County, WA ..................... | 78 506 | 79 177 |
| 35620 | | Nassau County-Suffolk County, NY Metro Div 35004 | 2 832 882 | 2 848 506 | 36100 | 12 083 | Ocala, FL Metro area...................... Marion County, FL....................... | 331 298 331 298 | 335 125 335 125 |
| | 36 059 | Nassau County, NY..................... | 1 339 532 | 1 349 233 | | | | | |
| | 36 103 | Suffolk County, NY...................... | 1 493 350 | 1 499 273 | 36140 | | Ocean City, NJ Metro area.............. | 97 265 | 96 304 |
| 35620 | | Newark, NJ-PA Metro Div 35084 ..... | 2 471 171 | 2 488 817 | | 34 009 | Cape May County, NJ.................. | 97 265 | 96 304 |
| | 34 013 | Essex County, NJ....................... | 783 969 | 787 744 | 36220 | | Odessa, TX Metro area ................... | 137 130 | 144 325 |
| | 34 019 | Hunterdon County, NJ................. | 128 349 | 127 050 | | 48 135 | Ector County, TX........................ | 137 130 | 144 325 |
| | 34 027 | Morris County, NJ ...................... | 492 276 | 497 999 | 36260 | | Ogden-Clearfield, UT Metro area ..... | 597 159 | 612 441 |
| | 34 035 | Somerset County, NJ.................. | 323 444 | 327 707 | | 49 003 | Box Elder County, UT ................. | 49 975 | 50 171 |
| | 34 037 | Sussex County, NJ..................... | 149 265 | 147 442 | | 49 011 | Davis County, UT ....................... | 306 479 | 315 809 |
| | 34 039 | Union County, NJ ....................... | 536 499 | 543 976 | | 49 029 | Morgan County, UT..................... | 9 469 | 9 821 |
| | 42 103 | Pike County, PA.......................... | 57 369 | 56 899 | | 49 057 | Weber County, UT ...................... | 231 236 | 236 640 |
| 35620 | | New York-Jersey City-White Plains, NY-NJ Metro Div 35614................... | 13 866 159 | 14 097 606 | 36300 | | Ogdensburg-Massena, NY Micro area................................ | 111 944 | 112 232 |
| | 34 003 | Bergen County, NJ..................... | 905 116 | 918 888 | | 36 089 | St. Lawrence County, NY............. | 111 944 | 112 232 |
| | 34 017 | Hudson County, NJ..................... | 634 266 | 652 302 | | | | | |
| | 34 023 | Middlesex County, NJ................. | 809 858 | 823 041 | 36340 | | Oil City, PA Micro area................... | 54 984 | 54 272 |
| | 34 025 | Monmouth County, NJ ................. | 630 380 | 629 384 | | 42 121 | Venango County, PA................... | 54 984 | 54 272 |
| | 34 029 | Ocean County, NJ....................... | 576 567 | 580 470 | 36380 | | Okeechobee, FL Micro area............ | 39 996 | 39 467 |
| | 34 031 | Passaic County, NJ..................... | 501 226 | 502 885 | | 12 093 | Okeechobee County, FL .............. | 39 996 | 39 467 |
| | 36 005 | Bronx County, NY....................... | 1 385 108 | 1 408 473 | 36420 | | Oklahoma City, OK Metro area........ | 1 252 987 | 1 296 565 |
| | 36 047 | Kings County, NY........................ | 2 504 700 | 2 565 635 | | 40 017 | Canadian County, OK ................. | 115 541 | 122 560 |
| | 36 061 | New York County, NY.................. | 1 585 873 | 1 619 090 | | 40 027 | Cleveland County, OK................. | 255 755 | 265 638 |
| | 36 071 | Orange County, NY..................... | 372 813 | 374 512 | | 40 051 | Grady County, OK...................... | 52 431 | 53 118 |
| | 36 081 | Queens County, NY .................... | 2 230 722 | 2 272 771 | | 40 081 | Lincoln County, OK..................... | 34 273 | 34 189 |
| | 36 085 | Richmond County, NY.................. | 468 730 | 470 728 | | 40 083 | Logan County, OK...................... | 41 848 | 43 666 |
| | 36 087 | Rockland County, NY.................. | 311 687 | 317 757 | | 40 087 | McClain County, OK.................... | 34 506 | 35 613 |
| | 36 119 | Westchester County, NY.............. | 949 113 | 961 670 | | 40 109 | Oklahoma County, OK ................. | 718 633 | 741 781 |
| 35660 | 26 021 | Niles-Benton Harbor, MI Metro area Berrien County, MI ...................... | 156 813 156 813 | 156 067 156 067 | 36460 | 36 009 | Olean, NY Micro area..................... Cattaraugus County, NY ............. | 80 317 80 317 | 79 458 79 458 |
| 35700 | | Nogales, AZ Micro area.................. | 47 420 | 47 303 | | | | | |
| | 04 023 | Santa Cruz County, AZ................ | 47 420 | 47 303 | 36500 | 53 067 | Olympia-Tumwater, WA Metro area. Thurston County, WA.................. | 252 264 252 264 | 258 332 258 332 |
| 35740 | | Norfolk, NE Micro area.................... | 48 271 | 48 286 | | | | | |
| | 31 119 | Madison County, NE................... | 34 876 | 35 031 | 36540 | | Omaha-Council Bluffs, NE-IA Metro area................................ | 865 350 | 885 624 |
| | 31 139 | Pierce County, NE....................... | 7 266 | 7 166 | | 19 085 | Harrison County, IA .................... | 14 928 | 14 548 |
| | 31 167 | Stanton County, NE .................... | 6 129 | 6 089 | | 19 129 | Mills County, IA.......................... | 15 059 | 14 837 |
| 35820 | | North Platte, NE Micro area ............ | 37 590 | 37 373 | | 19 155 | Pottawattamie County, IA............. | 93 158 | 92 913 |
| | 31 111 | Lincoln County, NE..................... | 36 288 | 36 099 | | 31 025 | Cass County, NE........................ | 25 241 | 25 133 |
| | 31 113 | Logan County, NE....................... | 763 | 765 | | 31 055 | Douglas County, NE.................... | 517 110 | 531 265 |
| | 31 117 | McPherson County, NE................ | 539 | 509 | | 31 153 | Sarpy County, NE....................... | 158 840 | 165 853 |
| 35840 | | North Port-Sarasota-Bradenton, FL Metro area................................ | 702 281 | 720 042 | | 31 155 | Saunders County, NE.................. | 20 780 | 20 823 |
| | 12 081 | Manatee County, FL.................... | 322 833 | 333 895 | | 31 177 | Washington County, NE............... | 20 234 | 20 252 |
| | 12 115 | Sarasota County, FL ................... | 379 448 | 386 147 | 36580 | 36 077 | Oneonta, NY Micro area.................. Otsego County, NY...................... | 62 259 62 259 | 61 709 61 709 |

# Core Based Statistical Areas (Metropolitan and Micropolitan), Metropolitan Divisions, and Components (as defined February 2013)–*Continued*

| Core Based Statistical Area | State/County FIPS Code | Title and Geographic Components | 2010 Census Population | 2012 Estimated Population | Core Based Statistical Area | State/County FIPS Code | Title and Geographic Components | 2010 Census Population | 2012 Estimated Population |
|---|---|---|---|---|---|---|---|---|---|
| 36620 | | Ontario, OR-ID Micro area............... | 53 936 | 53 269 | 37220 | | Pahrump, NV Micro area................. | 43 946 | 42 963 |
| | 16 075 | Payette County, ID..................... | 22 623 | 22 639 | | 32 023 | Nye County, NV ............................ | 43 946 | 42 963 |
| | 41 045 | Malheur County, OR .................... | 31 313 | 30 630 | 37260 | | Palatka, FL Micro area ................... | 74 364 | 73 263 |
| 36660 | | Opelousas, LA Micro area............... | 83 384 | 83 662 | | 12 107 | Putnam County, FL...................... | 74 364 | 73 263 |
| | 22 097 | St. Landry Parish, LA.................... | 83 384 | 83 662 | 37300 | | Palestine, TX Micro area................. | 58 458 | 58 190 |
| 36700 | | Orangeburg, SC Micro area ........... | 92 501 | 91 476 | | 48 001 | Anderson County, TX.................. | 58 458 | 58 190 |
| | 45 075 | Orangeburg County, SC.............. | 92 501 | 91 476 | 37340 | | Palm Bay-Melbourne-Titusville, FL Metro area............... | 543 376 | 547 307 |
| 36740 | | Orlando-Kissimmee-Sanford, FL Metro....... | 2 134 411 | 2 223 674 | | 12 009 | Brevard County, FL....................... | 543 376 | 547 307 |
| | 12 069 | Lake County, FL...................... | 297 052 | 303 186 | 37420 | | Pampa, TX Micro area.................... | 22 535 | 22 978 |
| | 12 095 | Orange County, FL...................... | 1 145 956 | 1 202 234 | | 48 179 | Gray County, TX ........................ | 22 535 | 22 978 |
| | 12 097 | Osceola County, FL...................... | 268 685 | 287 416 | 37460 | | Panama City, FL Metro area ........... | 184 715 | 187 621 |
| | 12 117 | Seminole County, FL.................... | 422 718 | 430 838 | | 12 005 | Bay County, FL........................... | 168 852 | 171 903 |
| 36780 | | Oshkosh-Neenah, WI Metro area..... | 166 994 | 168 794 | | 12 045 | Gulf County, FL........................... | 15 863 | 15 718 |
| | 55 139 | Winnebago County, WI ................ | 166 994 | 168 794 | 37500 | | Paragould, AR Micro area ............. | 42 090 | 43 163 |
| 36820 | | Oskaloosa, IA Micro area ............... | 22 381 | 22 443 | | 05 055 | Greene County, AR...................... | 42 090 | 43 163 |
| | 19 123 | Mahaska County, IA..................... | 22 381 | 22 443 | 37540 | | Paris, TN Micro area ...................... | 32 330 | 32 341 |
| 36830 | | Othello, WA Micro area ................ | 18 728 | 19 005 | | 47 079 | Henry County, TN........................ | 32 330 | 32 341 |
| | 53 001 | Adams County, WA.................... | 18 728 | 19 005 | 37580 | | Paris, TX Micro area ...................... | 49 793 | 49 811 |
| 36840 | | Ottawa, KS Micro area .................. | 25 992 | 25 906 | | 48 277 | Lamar County, TX........................ | 49 793 | 49 811 |
| | 20 059 | Franklin County, KS .................... | 25 992 | 25 906 | 37620 | | Parkersburg-Vienna, WV Metro area....... | 92 673 | 92 548 |
| 36860 | | Ottawa-Peru, IL Micro area ............. | 154 908 | 153 182 | | 54 105 | Wirt County, WV.......................... | 5 717 | 5 847 |
| | 17 011 | Bureau County, IL...................... | 34 978 | 34 323 | | 54 107 | Wood County, WV........................ | 86 956 | 86 701 |
| | 17 099 | LaSalle County, IL...................... | 113 924 | 112 973 | 37660 | | Parsons, KS Micro area.................. | 21 607 | 21 284 |
| | 17 155 | Putnam County, IL...................... | 6 006 | 5 886 | | 20 099 | Labette County, KS...................... | 21 607 | 21 284 |
| 36900 | | Ottumwa, IA Micro area................. | 44 378 | 44 055 | 37740 | | Payson, AZ Micro area .................... | 53 597 | 53 144 |
| | 19 051 | Davis County, IA ........................ | 8 753 | 8 689 | | 04 007 | Gila County, AZ.......................... | 53 597 | 53 144 |
| | 19 179 | Wapello County, IA .................... | 35 625 | 35 366 | 37780 | | Pecos, TX Micro area ..................... | 13 783 | 13 798 |
| 36940 | | Owatonna, MN Micro area............. | 36 576 | 36 322 | | 48 389 | Reeves County, TX....................... | 13 783 | 13 798 |
| | 27 147 | Steele County, MN...................... | 36 576 | 36 322 | 37860 | | Pensacola-Ferry Pass-Brent, FL Metro area............... | 448 991 | 461 227 |
| 36980 | | Owensboro, KY Metro area............. | 114 752 | 116 030 | | 12 033 | Escambia County, FL................... | 297 619 | 302 715 |
| | 21 059 | Daviess County, KY..................... | 96 656 | 97 847 | | 12 113 | Santa Rosa County, FL............... | 151 372 | 158 512 |
| | 21 091 | Hancock County, KY .................... | 8 565 | 8 677 | 37900 | | Peoria, IL Metro area...................... | 379 186 | 380 447 |
| | 21 149 | McLean County, KY ..................... | 9 531 | 9 506 | | 17 123 | Marshall County, IL ..................... | 12 640 | 12 327 |
| 37020 | | Owosso, MI Micro area.................. | 70 648 | 69 232 | | 17 143 | Peoria County, IL ........................ | 186 494 | 187 254 |
| | 26 155 | Shiawassee County, MI ............... | 70 648 | 69 232 | | 17 175 | Stark County, IL.......................... | 5 994 | 5 946 |
| 37060 | | Oxford, MS Micro area .................. | 47 351 | 49 495 | | 17 179 | Tazewell County, IL...................... | 135 394 | 135 949 |
| | 28 071 | Lafayette County, MS................... | 47 351 | 49 495 | | 17 203 | Woodford County, IL.................... | 38 664 | 38 971 |
| 37080 | | Oxford, NC Micro area................... | 59 916 | 60 436 | 37940 | | Peru, IN Micro area ....................... | 36 903 | 36 486 |
| | 37 077 | Granville County, NC .................. | 59 916 | 60 436 | | 18 103 | Miami County, IN........................ | 36 903 | 36 486 |
| 37100 | | Oxnard-Thousand Oaks-Ventura, CA Metro area............... | 823 318 | 835 981 | 37980 | | Philadelphia-Camden-Wilmington, PA-NJ-DE-MD Metro area............... | 5 965 343 | 6 018 800 |
| | 06 111 | Ventura County, CA ..................... | 823 318 | 835 981 | 37980 | | Camden, NJ Metro Div 15804......... | 1 250 679 | 1 254 461 |
| 37120 | | Ozark, AL Micro area.................... | 50 251 | 50 444 | | 34 005 | Burlington County, NJ .................. | 448 734 | 451 336 |
| | 01 045 | Dale County, AL......................... | 50 251 | 50 444 | | 34 007 | Camden County, NJ..................... | 513 657 | 513 539 |
| 37140 | | Paducah, KY-IL Micro area ............. | 98 762 | 98 539 | | 34 015 | Gloucester County, NJ................. | 288 288 | 289 586 |
| | 17 127 | Massac County, IL ...................... | 15 429 | 15 234 | | | | | |
| | 21 007 | Ballard County, KY ...................... | 8 249 | 8 333 | | | | | |
| | 21 139 | Livingston County, KY ................. | 9 519 | 9 423 | | | | | |
| | 21 145 | McCracken County, KY................. | 65 565 | 65 549 | | | | | |

| Core Based Statistical Area | State/ County FIPS Code | Title and Geographic Components | 2010 Census Population | 2012 Estimated Population | Core Based Statistical Area | State/ County FIPS Code | Title and Geographic Components | 2010 Census Population | 2012 Estimated Population |
|---|---|---|---|---|---|---|---|---|---|
| 37980 | | Montgomery County-Bucks County-Chester County, PA Metro Div 33874 ................ | 1 924 009 | 1 942 088 | 38580 | | Point Pleasant, WV-OH Micro area .. | 58 258 | 57 887 |
| | 42 017 | Bucks County, PA ................ | 625 249 | 627 053 | | 39 053 | Gallia County, OH ................ | 30 934 | 30 708 |
| | 42 029 | Chester County, PA ................ | 498 886 | 506 575 | | 54 053 | Mason County, WV ................ | 27 324 | 27 179 |
| | 42 091 | Montgomery County, PA ............ | 799 874 | 808 460 | 38620 | | Ponca City, OK Micro area .............. | 46 562 | 45 831 |
| 37980 | | Philadelphia, PA Metro Div 37964.... | 2 084 985 | 2 108 705 | | 40 071 | Kay County, OK ................ | 46 562 | 45 831 |
| | 42 045 | Delaware County, PA ................ | 558 979 | 561 098 | 38700 | | Pontiac, IL Micro area.................... | 38 950 | 38 647 |
| | 42 101 | Philadelphia County, PA .............. | 1 526 006 | 1 547 607 | | 17 105 | Livingston County, IL.............. | 38 950 | 38 647 |
| 37980 | | Wilmington, DE-MD-NJ Metro Div 48864 ................ | 705 670 | 713 546 | 38740 | 29 023 | Poplar Bluff, MO Micro area ............ | 42 794 | 43 053 |
| | | | | | | | Butler County, MO.............. | 42 794 | 43 053 |
| | 10 003 | New Castle County, Delaware...... | 538 479 | 546 076 | 38780 | | Portales, NM Micro area................ | 19 846 | 20 419 |
| | 24 015 | Cecil County, MD ................ | 101 108 | 101 696 | | 35 041 | Roosevelt County, NM ................ | 19 846 | 20 419 |
| | 34 033 | Salem County, NJ ................ | 66 083 | 65 774 | 38820 | | Port Angeles, WA Micro area.......... | 71 404 | 71 863 |
| 38060 | | Phoenix-Mesa-Scottsdale, AZ Metro area ................ | 4 192 887 | 4 329 534 | | 53 009 | Clallam County, WA .................... | 71 404 | 71 863 |
| | 04 013 | Maricopa County, AZ ................ | 3 817 117 | 3 942 169 | 38840 | | Port Clinton, OH Micro area ............ | 41 428 | 41 339 |
| | 04 021 | Pinal County, AZ ................ | 375 770 | 387 365 | | 39 123 | Ottawa County, OH ................ | 41 428 | 41 339 |
| 38100 | | Picayune, MS Micro area ................ | 55 834 | 55 295 | 38860 | | Portland-South Portland, ME Metro area ................ | 514 098 | 518 117 |
| | 28 109 | Pearl River County, MS ................ | 55 834 | 55 295 | | 23 005 | Cumberland County, ME............ | 281 674 | 283 921 |
| 38180 | | Pierre, SD Micro area.................... | 21 361 | 21 846 | | 23 023 | Sagadahoc County, ME .............. | 35 293 | 35 191 |
| | 46 065 | Hughes County, SD ................ | 17 022 | 17 450 | | 23 031 | York County, ME ................ | 197 131 | 199 005 |
| | 46 117 | Stanley County, SD ................ | 2 966 | 2 969 | 38900 | | Portland-Vancouver-Hillsboro, OR-WA Metro area................ | 2 226 009 | 2 289 800 |
| | 46 119 | Sully County, SD................ | 1 373 | 1 427 | | 41 005 | Clackamas County, OR.............. | 375 992 | 383 857 |
| 38220 | | Pine Bluff, AR Metro area.............. | 100 258 | 97 451 | | 41 009 | Columbia County, OR ................ | 49 351 | 49 286 |
| | 05 025 | Cleveland County, AR ................ | 8 689 | 8 627 | | 41 051 | Multnomah County, OR.............. | 735 334 | 759 256 |
| | 05 069 | Jefferson County, AR ................ | 77 435 | 74 723 | | 41 067 | Washington County, OR ............ | 529 710 | 547 672 |
| | 05 079 | Lincoln County, AR ................ | 14 134 | 14 101 | | 41 071 | Yamhill County, OR.................... | 99 193 | 100 255 |
| 38240 | | Pinehurst-Southern Pines, NC Micro area ................ | 88 247 | 90 302 | | 53 011 | Clark County, WA.................... | 425 363 | 438 287 |
| | 37 125 | Moore County, NC ................ | 88 247 | 90 302 | | 53 059 | Skamania County, WA ................ | 11 066 | 11 187 |
| 38260 | | Pittsburg, KS Micro area.............. | 39 134 | 39 361 | 38920 | | Port Lavaca, TX Micro area............ | 21 381 | 21 609 |
| | 20 037 | Crawford County, KS ................ | 39 134 | 39 361 | | 48 057 | Calhoun County, TX................ | 21 381 | 21 609 |
| 38300 | | Pittsburgh, PA Metro area .............. | 2 356 285 | 2 360 733 | 38940 | | Port St. Lucie, FL Metro area .......... | 424 107 | 432 683 |
| | 42 003 | Allegheny County, PA ................ | 1 223 348 | 1 229 338 | | 12 085 | Martin County, FL.................... | 146 318 | 148 817 |
| | 42 005 | Armstrong County, PA ................ | 68 941 | 68 409 | | 12 111 | St. Lucie County, FL .................... | 277 789 | 283 866 |
| | 42 007 | Beaver County, PA................ | 170 539 | 170 245 | 39020 | | Portsmouth, OH Micro area............ | 79 499 | 78 477 |
| | 42 019 | Butler County, PA.................... | 183 862 | 184 970 | | 39 145 | Scioto County, OH ................ | 79 499 | 78 477 |
| | 42 051 | Fayette County, PA ................ | 136 606 | 135 660 | 39060 | | Pottsville, PA Micro area ................ | 148 289 | 147 063 |
| | 42 125 | Washington County, PA ................ | 207 820 | 208 716 | | 42 107 | Schuylkill County, PA ................ | 148 289 | 147 063 |
| | 42 129 | Westmoreland County, PA............ | 365 169 | 363 395 | 39140 | | Prescott, AZ Metro area ................ | 211 033 | 212 637 |
| 38340 | | Pittsfield, MA Metro area ................ | 131 219 | 130 016 | | 04 025 | Yavapai County, AZ ................ | 211 033 | 212 637 |
| | 25 003 | Berkshire County, MA ................ | 131 219 | 130 016 | 39220 | | Price, UT Micro area................ | 21 403 | 21 246 |
| 38380 | | Plainview, TX Micro area.................... | 36 273 | 36 385 | | 49 007 | Carbon County, UT ................ | 21 403 | 21 246 |
| | 48 189 | Hale County, TX.................... | 36 273 | 36 385 | 39260 | | Prineville, OR Micro area................ | 20 978 | 20 729 |
| 38420 | | Platteville, WI Micro area................ | 51 208 | 51 087 | | 41 013 | Crook County, OR.................... | 20 978 | 20 729 |
| | 55 043 | Grant County, WI ................ | 51 208 | 51 087 | 39300 | | Providence-Warwick, RI-MA Metro area ................ | 1 600 852 | 1 601 374 |
| 38460 | | Plattsburgh, NY Micro area .............. | 82 128 | 81 654 | | 25 005 | Bristol County, MA ................ | 548 285 | 551 082 |
| | 36 019 | Clinton County, NY ................ | 82 128 | 81 654 | | 44 001 | Bristol County, RI ................ | 49 875 | 49 144 |
| 38500 | | Plymouth, IN Micro area................ | 47 051 | 47 024 | | 44 003 | Kent County, RI ................ | 166 158 | 164 843 |
| | 18 099 | Marshall County, IN.................... | 47 051 | 47 024 | | 44 005 | Newport County, RI.................... | 82 888 | 82 036 |
| 38540 | | Pocatello, ID Metro area.................... | 82 839 | 83 800 | | 44 007 | Providence County, RI ................ | 626 667 | 628 323 |
| | 16 005 | Bannock County, ID ................ | 82 839 | 83 800 | | 44 009 | Washington County, RI ................ | 126 979 | 125 946 |

# Core Based Statistical Areas (Metropolitan and Micropolitan), Metropolitan Divisions, and Components (as defined February 2013)–*Continued*

| Core Based Statistical Area | State/County FIPS Code | Title and Geographic Components | 2010 Census Population | 2012 Estimated Population | Core Based Statistical Area | State/County FIPS Code | Title and Geographic Components | 2010 Census Population | 2012 Estimated Population |
|---|---|---|---|---|---|---|---|---|---|
| 39340 | | Provo-Orem, UT Metro area............ | 526 810 | 550 845 | 40060 | | Richmond, VA Metro area................ | 1 208 101 | 1 231 980 |
| | 49 023 | Juab County, UT........................ | 10 246 | 10 341 | | 51 007 | Amelia County, VA........................ | 12 690 | 12 759 |
| | 49 049 | Utah County, UT........................ | 516 564 | 540 504 | | 51 033 | Caroline County, VA..................... | 28 545 | 28 972 |
| | | | | | | 51 036 | Charles City County, VA .............. | 7 256 | 7 157 |
| 39380 | | Pueblo, CO Metro area................... | 159 063 | 160 852 | | 51 041 | Chesterfield County, VA................ | 316 236 | 323 856 |
| | 08 101 | Pueblo County, CO..................... | 159 063 | 160 852 | | 51 053 | Dinwiddie County, VA.................. | 28 001 | 27 994 |
| | | | | | | 51 075 | Goochland County, VA................. | 21 717 | 21 347 |
| 39420 | | Pullman, WA Micro area.................. | 44 776 | 46 606 | | 51 085 | Hanover County, VA .................... | 99 863 | 100 668 |
| | 53 075 | Whitman County, WA................... | 44 776 | 46 606 | | 51 087 | Henrico County, VA...................... | 306 935 | 314 932 |
| | | | | | | 51 101 | King William County, VA.............. | 15 935 | 15 981 |
| 39460 | | Punta Gorda, FL Metro area ........... | 159 978 | 162 449 | | 51 127 | New Kent County, VA................... | 18 429 | 19 169 |
| | 12 015 | Charlotte County, FL................... | 159 978 | 162 449 | | 51 145 | Powhatan County, VA................... | 28 046 | 28 123 |
| | | | | | | 51 149 | Prince George County, VA........... | 35 725 | 36 941 |
| 39500 | | Quincy, IL-MO Micro area ............. | 77 314 | 77 371 | | 51 183 | Sussex County, VA....................... | 12 087 | 11 972 |
| | 17 001 | Adams County, IL...................... | 67 103 | 67 197 | | 51 570 | Colonial Heights city, VA............ | 17 411 | 17 479 |
| | 29 111 | Lewis County, MO...................... | 10 211 | 10 174 | | 51 670 | Hopewell city, VA....................... | 22 591 | 22 348 |
| | | | | | | 51 730 | Petersburg city, VA ..................... | 32 420 | 31 973 |
| 39540 | | Racine, WI Metro area.................... | 195 408 | 194 797 | | 51 760 | Richmond city, VA....................... | 204 214 | 210 309 |
| | 55 101 | Racine County, WI...................... | 195 408 | 194 797 | 40080 | | Richmond-Berea, KY Micro area...... | 99 972 | 101 792 |
| 39580 | | Raleigh, NC Metro area................... | 1 130 490 | 1 188 564 | | 21 151 | Madison County, KY ................... | 82 916 | 84 786 |
| | 37 069 | Franklin County, NC................... | 60 619 | 61 475 | | 21 203 | Rockcastle County, KY ............... | 17 056 | 17 006 |
| | 37 101 | Johnston County, NC................... | 168 878 | 174 938 | 40100 | | Rio Grande City, TX Micro area....... | 60 968 | 61 615 |
| | 37 183 | Wake County, NC ....................... | 900 993 | 952 151 | | 48 427 | Starr County, TX........................ | 60 968 | 61 615 |
| 39660 | | Rapid City, SD Metro area .............. | 134 598 | 138 738 | 40140 | | Riverside-San Bernardino-Ontario, CA ...................................... | 4 224 851 | 4 350 096 |
| | 46 033 | Custer County, SD ...................... | 8 216 | 8 339 | | 06 065 | Riverside County, CA.................. | 2 189 641 | 2 268 783 |
| | 46 093 | Meade County, SD ...................... | 25 434 | 26 052 | | 06 071 | San Bernardino County, CA.......... | 2 035 210 | 2 081 313 |
| | 46 103 | Pennington County, SD................ | 100 948 | 104 347 | 40180 | | Riverton, WY Micro area ................ | 40 123 | 41 110 |
| 39700 | | Raymondville, TX Micro area .......... | 22 134 | 22 058 | | 56 013 | Fremont County, WY.................... | 40 123 | 41 110 |
| | 48 489 | Willacy County, TX...................... | 22 134 | 22 058 | 40220 | | Roanoke, VA Metro area................ | 308 707 | 310 118 |
| 39740 | | Reading, PA Metro area................... | 411 442 | 413 491 | | 51 023 | Botetourt County, VA .................. | 33 148 | 33 154 |
| | 42 011 | Berks County, PA....................... | 411 442 | 413 491 | | 51 045 | Craig County, VA........................ | 5 190 | 5 213 |
| 39780 | | Red Bluff, CA Micro area................ | 63 463 | 63 406 | | 51 067 | Franklin County, VA.................... | 56 159 | 56 411 |
| | 06 103 | Tehama County, CA..................... | 63 463 | 63 406 | | 51 161 | Roanoke County, VA................... | 92 376 | 92 901 |
| 39820 | | Redding, CA Metro area.................. | 177 223 | 178 586 | | 51 770 | Roanoke city, VA........................ | 97 032 | 97 469 |
| | 06 089 | Shasta County, CA..................... | 177 223 | 178 586 | | 51 775 | Salem city, VA........................... | 24 802 | 24 970 |
| 39860 | | Red Wing, MN Micro area.............. | 46 183 | 46 336 | 40260 | | Roanoke Rapids, NC Micro area...... | 76 790 | 75 434 |
| | 27 049 | Goodhue County, MN .................. | 46 183 | 46 336 | | 37 083 | Halifax County, NC...................... | 54 691 | 54 006 |
| 39900 | | Reno, NV Metro area...................... | 425 417 | 433 843 | | 37 131 | Northampton County, NC............. | 22 099 | 21 428 |
| | 32 029 | Storey County, NV...................... | 4 010 | 3 935 | 40300 | | Rochelle, IL Micro area.................. | 53 497 | 52 848 |
| | 32 031 | Washoe County, NV.................... | 421 407 | 429 908 | | 17 141 | Ogle County, IL ......................... | 53 497 | 52 848 |
| 39940 | | Rexburg, ID Micro area .................. | 50 778 | 50 413 | 40340 | | Rochester, MN Metro area .............. | 206 877 | 209 607 |
| | 16 043 | Fremont County, ID..................... | 13 242 | 12 957 | | 27 039 | Dodge County, MN...................... | 20 087 | 20 231 |
| | 16 065 | Madison County, ID..................... | 37 536 | 37 456 | | 27 045 | Fillmore County, MN ................... | 20 866 | 20 834 |
| 39980 | | Richmond, IN Micro area................ | 68 917 | 68 346 | | 27 109 | Olmsted County, MN................... | 144 248 | 147 066 |
| | 18 177 | Wayne County, IN....................... | 68 917 | 68 346 | | 27 157 | Wabasha County, MN.................. | 21 676 | 21 476 |
| | | | | | 40380 | | Rochester, NY Metro area.............. | 1 079 671 | 1 082 284 |
| | | | | | | 36 051 | Livingston County, NY................. | 65 393 | 64 810 |
| | | | | | | 36 055 | Monroe County, NY..................... | 744 344 | 747 813 |
| | | | | | | 36 069 | Ontario County, NY.................... | 107 931 | 108 519 |
| | | | | | | 36 073 | Orleans County, NY.................... | 42 883 | 42 836 |
| | | | | | | 36 117 | Wayne County, NY...................... | 93 772 | 92 962 |
| | | | | | | 36 123 | Yates County, NY....................... | 25 348 | 25 344 |
| | | | | | 40420 | | Rockford, IL Metro area................... | 349 431 | 346 009 |
| | | | | | | 17 007 | Boone County, IL ....................... | 54 165 | 53 940 |
| | | | | | | 17 201 | Winnebago County, IL................. | 295 266 | 292 069 |
| | | | | | 40460 | | Rockingham, NC Micro area ........... | 46 639 | 46 627 |
| | | | | | | 37 153 | Richmond County, NC.................. | 46 639 | 46 627 |

# Core Based Statistical Areas (Metropolitan and Micropolitan), Metropolitan Divisions, and Components (as defined February 2013)–*Continued*

| Core Based Statistical Area | State/ County FIPS Code | Title and Geographic Components | 2010 Census Population | 2012 Estimated Population | Core Based Statistical Area | State/ County FIPS Code | Title and Geographic Components | 2010 Census Population | 2012 Estimated Population |
|---|---|---|---|---|---|---|---|---|---|
| 40540 | | Rock Springs, WY Micro area .......... | 43 806 | 45 267 | 41180 | | St. Louis, MO-IL Metro area ............ | 2 787 701 | 2 795 794 |
| | 56 037 | Sweetwater County, WY ............... | 43 806 | 45 267 | | 17 005 | Bond County, IL ............... | 17 768 | 17 644 |
| 40580 | | Rocky Mount, NC Metro area.......... | 152 392 | 151 662 | | 17 013 | Calhoun County, IL.............. | 5 089 | 5 014 |
| | 37 065 | Edgecombe County, NC .............. | 56 552 | 55 954 | | 17 027 | Clinton County, IL.............. | 37 762 | 38 061 |
| | 37 127 | Nash County, NC ..................... | 95 840 | 95 708 | | 17 083 | Jersey County, IL ............... | 22 985 | 22 742 |
| 40620 | | Rolla, MO Micro area................. | 45 156 | 44 987 | | 17 117 | Macoupin County, IL .......... | 47 765 | 47 231 |
| | 29 161 | Phelps County, MO ................. | 45 156 | 44 987 | | 17 119 | Madison County, IL ............ | 269 282 | 267 883 |
| 40660 | | Rome, GA Metro area ..................... | 96 317 | 96 177 | | 17 133 | Monroe County, IL ............. | 32 957 | 33 357 |
| | 13 115 | Floyd County, GA..................... | 96 317 | 96 177 | | 17 163 | St. Clair County, IL............. | 270 056 | 268 858 |
| 40700 | | Roseburg, OR Micro area................ | 107 667 | 107 164 | | 29 071 | Franklin County, MO ........... | 101 492 | 101 412 |
| | 41 019 | Douglas County, OR .................. | 107 667 | 107 164 | | 29 099 | Jefferson County, MO ......... | 218 733 | 220 209 |
| 40740 | | Roswell, NM Micro area................ | 65 645 | 65 784 | | 29 113 | Lincoln County, MO ........... | 52 566 | 53 354 |
| | 35 005 | Chaves County, NM.................. | 65 645 | 65 784 | | 29 183 | St. Charles County, MO ............... | 360 485 | 368 666 |
| 40780 | | Russellville, AR Micro area.............. | 83 939 | 84 697 | | 29 189 | St. Louis County, MO........... | 998 954 | 1 000 438 |
| | 05 115 | Pope County, AR ...................... | 61 754 | 62 765 | | 29 219 | Warren County, MO ............ | 32 513 | 32 753 |
| | 05 149 | Yell County, AR ....................... | 22 185 | 21 932 | | 29 510 | St. Louis city, MO............... | 319 294 | 318 172 |
| 40820 | | Ruston, LA Micro area..................... | 46 735 | 46 953 | 41220 | | St. Marys, GA Micro area............... | 50 513 | 51 402 |
| | 22 061 | Lincoln Parish, LA ................... | 46 735 | 46 953 | | 13 039 | Camden County, GA................... | 50 513 | 51 402 |
| 40860 | | Rutland, VT Micro area................... | 61 642 | 60 869 | 41400 | | Salem, OH Micro area................. | 107 841 | 106 507 |
| | 50 021 | Rutland County, VT................... | 61 642 | 60 869 | | 39 029 | Columbiana County, OH .............. | 107 841 | 106 507 |
| 40900 | | Sacramento-Roseville-Arden-Arcade, CA Metro area.......... | 2 149 127 | 2 196 482 | 41420 | | Salem, OR Metro area................. | 390 738 | 396 338 |
| | 06 017 | El Dorado County, CA.................. | 181 058 | 180 561 | | 41 047 | Marion County, OR ................... | 315 335 | 319 985 |
| | 06 061 | Placer County, CA..................... | 348 432 | 361 682 | | 41 053 | Polk County, OR ..................... | 75 403 | 76 353 |
| | 06 067 | Sacramento County, CA .............. | 1 418 788 | 1 450 121 | 41460 | | Salina, KS Micro area................... | 61 697 | 62 060 |
| | 06 113 | Yolo County, CA......................... | 200 849 | 204 118 | | 20 143 | Ottawa County, KS................... | 6 091 | 6 072 |
| 40940 | | Safford, AZ Micro area ................... | 37 220 | 37 416 | | 20 169 | Saline County, KS ................... | 55 606 | 55 988 |
| | 04 009 | Graham County, AZ ................... | 37 220 | 37 416 | 41500 | | Salinas, CA Metro area ................ | 415 057 | 426 762 |
| 40980 | | Saginaw, MI Metro area ................. | 200 169 | 198 353 | | 06 053 | Monterey County, CA.................. | 415 057 | 426 762 |
| | 26 145 | Saginaw County, MI................... | 200 169 | 198 353 | 41540 | | Salisbury, MD-DE Metro area.......... | 373 802 | 381 868 |
| 41060 | | St. Cloud, MN Metro area.............. | 189 093 | 190 471 | | 10 005 | Sussex County, DE................... | 197 145 | 203 390 |
| | 27 009 | Benton County, MN................... | 38 451 | 38 865 | | 24 039 | Somerset County, MD.............. | 26 470 | 26 253 |
| | 27 145 | Stearns County, MN................. | 150 642 | 151 606 | | 24 045 | Wicomico County, MD.............. | 98 733 | 100 647 |
| 41100 | | St. George, UT Metro area.............. | 138 115 | 144 809 | | 24 047 | Worcester County, MD............. | 51 454 | 51 578 |
| | 49 053 | Washington County, UT.............. | 138 115 | 144 809 | 41620 | | Salt Lake City, UT Metro area.......... | 1 087 873 | 1 123 712 |
| 41140 | | St. Joseph, MO-KS Metro area........ | 127 329 | 127 927 | | 49 035 | Salt Lake County, UT.................. | 1 029 655 | 1 063 842 |
| | 20 043 | Doniphan County, KS................... | 7 945 | 7 864 | | 49 045 | Tooele County, UT..................... | 58 218 | 59 870 |
| | 29 003 | Andrew County, MO.................... | 17 291 | 17 417 | 41660 | | San Angelo, TX Metro area.......... | 111 823 | 114 854 |
| | 29 021 | Buchanan County, MO.................. | 89 201 | 89 706 | | 48 235 | Irion County, TX ................... | 1 599 | 1 573 |
| | 29 063 | DeKalb County, MO.................. | 12 892 | 12 940 | | 48 451 | Tom Green County, TX............... | 110 224 | 113 281 |
| | | | | | 41700 | | San Antonio-New Braunfels, TX Metro........ | 2 142 508 | 2 234 003 |
| | | | | | | 48 013 | Atascosa County, TX ................... | 44 911 | 46 446 |
| | | | | | | 48 019 | Bandera County, TX.................... | 20 485 | 20 537 |
| | | | | | | 48 029 | Bexar County, TX..................... | 1 714 773 | 1 785 704 |
| | | | | | | 48 091 | Comal County, TX..................... | 108 472 | 114 384 |
| | | | | | | 48 187 | Guadalupe County, TX................... | 131 533 | 139 841 |
| | | | | | | 48 259 | Kendall County, TX................... | 33 410 | 35 956 |
| | | | | | | 48 325 | Medina County, TX................... | 46 006 | 46 765 |
| | | | | | | 48 493 | Wilson County, TX................... | 42 918 | 44 370 |
| | | | | | 41740 | | San Diego-Carlsbad, CA Metro area | 3 095 313 | 3 177 063 |
| | | | | | | 06 073 | San Diego County, CA.................. | 3 095 313 | 3 177 063 |
| | | | | | 41760 | | Sandpoint, ID Micro area............... | 40 877 | 40 476 |
| | | | | | | 16 017 | Bonner County, ID...................... | 40 877 | 40 476 |
| | | | | | 41780 | | Sandusky, OH Micro area .............. | 77 079 | 76 398 |
| | | | | | | 39 043 | Erie County, OH.......................... | 77 079 | 76 398 |

# Core Based Statistical Areas (Metropolitan and Micropolitan), Metropolitan Divisions, and Components (as defined February 2013)–*Continued*

| Core Based Statistical Area | State/County FIPS Code | Title and Geographic Components | 2010 Census Population | 2012 Estimated Population | Core Based Statistical Area | State/County FIPS Code | Title and Geographic Components | 2010 Census Population | 2012 Estimated Population |
|---|---|---|---|---|---|---|---|---|---|
| 41820 | | Sanford, NC Micro area | 57 866 | 59 715 | 42620 | | Searcy, AR Micro area | 77 076 | 78 493 |
| | 37 105 | Lee County, NC | 57 866 | 59 715 | | 05 145 | White County, AR | 77 076 | 78 493 |
| 41860 | | San Francisco-Oakland-Hayward, CA Metro area | 4 335 391 | 4 455 560 | 42660 | | Seattle-Tacoma-Bellevue, WA Metro area | 3 439 809 | 3 552 157 |
| 41860 | | Oakland-Hayward-Berkeley, CA Metro Div 36084 | 2 559 296 | 2 634 317 | 42660 | | Seattle-Bellevue-Everett, WA Metro Div 42644 | 2 644 584 | 2 740 476 |
| | 06 001 | Alameda County, CA | 1 510 271 | 1 554 720 | | 53 033 | King County, WA | 1 931 249 | 2 007 440 |
| | 06 013 | Contra Costa County, CA | 1 049 025 | 1 079 597 | | 53 061 | Snohomish County, WA | 713 335 | 733 036 |
| 41860 | | San Francisco-Redwood City-South San Francisco, CA Metro Div 41884 | 1 523 686 | 1 565 174 | 42660 | | Tacoma-Lakewood, WA Metro Div 45104 | 795 225 | 811 681 |
| | 06 075 | San Francisco County, CA | 805 235 | 825 863 | | 53 053 | Pierce County, WA | 795 225 | 811 681 |
| | 06 081 | San Mateo County, CA | 718 451 | 739 311 | 42680 | | Sebastian-Vero Beach, FL Metro area | 138 028 | 140 567 |
| 41860 | | San Rafael, CA Metropolitan Div 42034 | 252 409 | 256 069 | | 12 061 | Indian River County, FL | 138 028 | 140 567 |
| | 06 041 | Marin County, CA | 252 409 | 256 069 | 42700 | | Sebring, FL Metro area | 98 786 | 98 128 |
| 41940 | | San Jose-Sunnyvale-Santa Clara, CA Metro area | 1 836 911 | 1 894 388 | | 12 055 | Highlands County, FL | 98 786 | 98 128 |
| | 06 069 | San Benito County, CA | 55 269 | 56 884 | 42740 | | Sedalia, MO Micro area | 42 201 | 42 319 |
| | 06 085 | Santa Clara County, CA | 1 781 642 | 1 837 504 | | 29 159 | Pettis County, MO | 42 201 | 42 319 |
| 42020 | | San Luis Obispo-Paso Robles-Arroyo Grande, CA Metro area | 269 637 | 274 804 | 42780 | | Selinsgrove, PA Micro area | 39 702 | 39 672 |
| | 06 079 | San Luis Obispo County, CA | 269 637 | 274 804 | | 42 109 | Snyder County, PA | 39 702 | 39 672 |
| 42100 | | Santa Cruz-Watsonville, CA Metro area | 262 382 | 266 776 | 42820 | | Selma, AL Micro area | 43 820 | 42 864 |
| | 06 087 | Santa Cruz County, CA | 262 382 | 266 776 | | 01 047 | Dallas County, AL | 43 820 | 42 864 |
| 42140 | | Santa Fe, NM Metro area | 144 170 | 146 375 | 42860 | | Seneca, SC Micro area | 74 273 | 74 627 |
| | 35 049 | Santa Fe County, NM | 144 170 | 146 375 | | 45 073 | Oconee County, SC | 74 273 | 74 627 |
| 42200 | | Santa Maria-Santa Barbara, CA Metro | 423 895 | 431 249 | 42900 | | Seneca Falls, NY Micro area | 35 251 | 35 305 |
| | 06 083 | Santa Barbara County, CA | 423 895 | 431 249 | | 36 099 | Seneca County, NY | 35 251 | 35 305 |
| 42220 | | Santa Rosa, CA Metro area | 483 878 | 491 829 | 42940 | | Sevierville, TN Micro area | 89 889 | 92 512 |
| | 06 097 | Sonoma County, CA | 483 878 | 491 829 | | 47 155 | Sevier County, TN | 89 889 | 92 512 |
| 42300 | | Sault Ste. Marie, MI Micro area | 38 520 | 38 917 | 42980 | | Seymour, IN Micro area | 42 376 | 43 083 |
| | 26 033 | Chippewa County, MI | 38 520 | 38 917 | | 18 071 | Jackson County, IN | 42 376 | 43 083 |
| 42340 | | Savannah, GA Metro area | 347 611 | 361 941 | 43020 | | Shawano, WI Micro area | 46 181 | 45 947 |
| | 13 029 | Bryan County, GA | 30 233 | 32 214 | | 55 078 | Menominee County, WI | 4 232 | 4 340 |
| | 13 051 | Chatham County, GA | 265 128 | 276 434 | | 55 115 | Shawano County, WI | 41 949 | 41 607 |
| | 13 103 | Effingham County, GA | 52 250 | 53 293 | 43060 | | Shawnee, OK Micro area | 69 442 | 70 760 |
| 42380 | | Sayre, PA Micro area | 62 622 | 62 792 | | 40 125 | Pottawatomie County, OK | 69 442 | 70 760 |
| | 42 015 | Bradford County, PA | 62 622 | 62 792 | 43100 | | Sheboygan, WI Metro area | 115 507 | 115 009 |
| 42420 | | Scottsbluff, NE Micro area | 38 971 | 39 039 | | 55 117 | Sheboygan County, WI | 115 507 | 115 009 |
| | 31 007 | Banner County, NE | 690 | 760 | 43140 | | Shelby, NC Micro area | 98 078 | 97 474 |
| | 31 157 | Scotts Bluff County, NE | 36 970 | 36 964 | | 37 045 | Cleveland County, NC | 98 078 | 97 474 |
| | 31 165 | Sioux County, NE | 1 311 | 1 315 | 43180 | | Shelbyville, TN Micro area | 45 058 | 45 573 |
| 42460 | | Scottsboro, AL Micro area | 53 227 | 53 019 | | 47 003 | Bedford County, TN | 45 058 | 45 573 |
| | 01 071 | Jackson County, AL | 53 227 | 53 019 | 43220 | | Shelton, WA Micro area | 60 699 | 60 832 |
| 42540 | | Scranton-Wilkes-Barre-Hazleton, PA Metro area | 563 631 | 563 629 | | 53 045 | Mason County, WA | 60 699 | 60 832 |
| | 42 069 | Lackawanna County, PA | 214 437 | 214 477 | 43260 | | Sheridan, WY Micro area | 29 116 | 29 596 |
| | 42 079 | Luzerne County, PA | 320 918 | 321 027 | | 56 033 | Sheridan County, WY | 29 116 | 29 596 |
| | 42 131 | Wyoming County, PA | 28 276 | 28 125 | 43300 | | Sherman-Denison, TX Metro area | 120 877 | 121 935 |
| | | | | | | 48 181 | Grayson County, TX | 120 877 | 121 935 |
| | | | | | 43320 | | Show Low, AZ Micro area | 107 449 | 107 094 |
| | | | | | | 04 017 | Navajo County, AZ | 107 449 | 107 094 |

| Core Based Statistical Area | State/County FIPS Code | Title and Geographic Components | 2010 Census Population | 2012 Estimated Population | Core Based Statistical Area | State/County FIPS Code | Title and Geographic Components | 2010 Census Population | 2012 Estimated Population |
|---|---|---|---|---|---|---|---|---|---|
| 43340 | | Shreveport-Bossier City, LA Metro area | 439 811 | 447 193 | 44100 | | Springfield, IL Metro area | 210 170 | 211 993 |
| | 22 015 | Bossier Parish, LA | 116 979 | 122 197 | | 17 129 | Menard County, IL | 12 705 | 12 722 |
| | 22 017 | Caddo Parish, LA | 254 969 | 257 093 | | 17 167 | Sangamon County, IL | 197 465 | 199 271 |
| | 22 031 | De Soto Parish, LA | 26 656 | 26 963 | 44140 | | Springfield, MA Metro area | 621 570 | 625 718 |
| | 22 119 | Webster Parish, LA | 41 207 | 40 940 | | 25 013 | Hampden County, MA | 463 490 | 465 923 |
| | | | | | | 25 015 | Hampshire County, MA | 158 080 | 159 795 |
| 43380 | | Sidney, OH Micro area | 49 423 | 49 167 | | | | | |
| | 39 149 | Shelby County, OH | 49 423 | 49 167 | 44180 | | Springfield, MO Metro area | 436 712 | 444 617 |
| | | | | | | 29 043 | Christian County, MO | 77 422 | 79 824 |
| 43420 | | Sierra Vista-Douglas, AZ Metro area | 131 346 | 132 088 | | 29 059 | Dallas County, MO | 16 777 | 16 799 |
| | 04 003 | Cochise County, AZ | 131 346 | 132 088 | | 29 077 | Greene County, MO | 275 174 | 280 626 |
| | | | | | | 29 167 | Polk County, MO | 31 137 | 31 017 |
| 43460 | | Sikeston, MO Micro area | 39 191 | 39 139 | | 29 225 | Webster County, MO | 36 202 | 36 351 |
| | 29 201 | Scott County, MO | 39 191 | 39 139 | 44220 | | Springfield, OH Metro area | 138 333 | 137 206 |
| 43500 | | Silver City, NM Micro area | 29 514 | 29 388 | | 39 023 | Clark County, OH | 138 333 | 137 206 |
| | 35 017 | Grant County, NM | 29 514 | 29 388 | 44260 | | Starkville, MS Micro area | 47 671 | 48 192 |
| 43580 | | Sioux City, IA-NE-SD Metro area | 168 563 | 168 921 | | 28 105 | Oktibbeha County, MS | 47 671 | 48 192 |
| | 19 149 | Plymouth County, IA | 24 986 | 24 907 | 44300 | | State College, PA Metro area | 153 990 | 155 171 |
| | 19 193 | Woodbury County, IA | 102 172 | 102 323 | | 42 027 | Centre County, PA | 153 990 | 155 171 |
| | 31 043 | Dakota County, NE | 21 006 | 20 918 | 44340 | | Statesboro, GA Micro area | 70 217 | 72 694 |
| | 31 051 | Dixon County, NE | 6 000 | 5 918 | | 13 031 | Bulloch County, GA | 70 217 | 72 694 |
| | 46 127 | Union County, SD | 14 399 | 14 855 | 44420 | | Staunton-Waynesboro, VA Metro area | 118 502 | 118 686 |
| 43620 | | Sioux Falls, SD Metro area | 228 261 | 237 251 | | 51 015 | Augusta County, VA | 73 750 | 73 658 |
| | 46 083 | Lincoln County, SD | 44 828 | 48 296 | | 51 790 | Staunton city, VA | 23 746 | 23 921 |
| | 46 087 | McCook County, SD | 5 618 | 5 610 | | 51 820 | Waynesboro city, VA | 21 006 | 21 107 |
| | 46 099 | Minnehaha County, SD | 169 468 | 175 037 | | | | | |
| | 46 125 | Turner County, SD | 8 347 | 8 308 | 44460 | | Steamboat Springs, CO Micro area | 23 509 | 23 334 |
| | | | | | | 08 107 | Routt County, CO | 23 509 | 23 334 |
| 43660 | | Snyder, TX Micro area | 16 921 | 17 126 | 44500 | | Stephenville, TX Micro area | 37 890 | 39 321 |
| | 48 415 | Scurry County, TX | 16 921 | 17 126 | | 48 143 | Erath County, TX | 37 890 | 39 321 |
| 43700 | | Somerset, KY Micro area | 63 063 | 63 593 | 44540 | | Sterling, CO Micro area | 22 709 | 22 631 |
| | 21 199 | Pulaski County, KY | 63 063 | 63 593 | | 08 075 | Logan County, CO | 22 709 | 22 631 |
| 43740 | | Somerset, PA Micro area | 77 742 | 76 957 | 44580 | | Sterling, IL Micro area | 58 498 | 57 846 |
| | 42 111 | Somerset County, PA | 77 742 | 76 957 | | 17 195 | Whiteside County, IL | 58 498 | 57 846 |
| 43760 | | Sonora, CA Micro area | 55 365 | 54 008 | 44620 | | Stevens Point, WI Micro area | 70 019 | 70 433 |
| | 06 109 | Tuolumne County, CA | 55 365 | 54 008 | | 55 097 | Portage County, WI | 70 019 | 70 433 |
| 43780 | | South Bend-Mishawaka, IN-MI Metro area | 319 224 | 318 586 | 44660 | | Stillwater, OK Micro area | 77 350 | 78 399 |
| | 18 141 | St. Joseph County, IN | 266 931 | 266 344 | | 40 119 | Payne County, OK | 77 350 | 78 399 |
| | 26 027 | Cass County, MI | 52 293 | 52 242 | 44700 | | Stockton-Lodi, CA Metro area | 685 306 | 702 612 |
| 43900 | | Spartanburg, SC Metro area | 313 268 | 316 997 | | 06 077 | San Joaquin County, CA | 685 306 | 702 612 |
| | 45 083 | Spartanburg County, SC | 284 307 | 288 745 | 44740 | | Storm Lake, IA Micro area | 20 260 | 20 592 |
| | 45 087 | Union County, SC | 28 961 | 28 252 | | 19 021 | Buena Vista County, IA | 20 260 | 20 592 |
| 43940 | | Spearfish, SD Micro area | 24 097 | 24 397 | 44780 | | Sturgis, MI Micro area | 61 295 | 60 796 |
| | 46 081 | Lawrence County, SD | 24 097 | 24 397 | | 26 149 | St. Joseph County, MI | 61 295 | 60 796 |
| 43980 | | Spencer, IA Micro area | 16 667 | 16 599 | 44860 | | Sulphur Springs, TX Micro area | 35 161 | 35 469 |
| | 19 041 | Clay County, IA | 16 667 | 16 599 | | 48 223 | Hopkins County, TX | 35 161 | 35 469 |
| 44020 | | Spirit Lake, IA Micro area | 16 667 | 16 972 | 44900 | | Summerville, GA Micro area | 26 015 | 25 725 |
| | 19 059 | Dickinson County, IA | 16 667 | 16 972 | | 13 055 | Chattooga County, GA | 26 015 | 25 725 |
| 44060 | | Spokane-Spokane Valley, WA Metro area | 527 753 | 532 253 | 44920 | | Summit Park, UT Micro area | 36 324 | 38 003 |
| | 53 051 | Pend Oreille County, WA | 13 001 | 12 980 | | 49 043 | Summit County, UT | 36 324 | 38 003 |
| | 53 063 | Spokane County, WA | 471 221 | 475 735 | | | | | |
| | 53 065 | Stevens County, WA | 43 531 | 43 538 | | | | | |

# Core Based Statistical Areas (Metropolitan and Micropolitan), Metropolitan Divisions, and Components (as defined February 2013)–*Continued*

| Core Based Statistical Area | State/County FIPS Code | Title and Geographic Components | 2010 Census Population | 2012 Estimated Population | Core Based Statistical Area | State/County FIPS Code | Title and Geographic Components | 2010 Census Population | 2012 Estimated Population |
|---|---|---|---|---|---|---|---|---|---|
| 44940 | | Sumter, SC Metro area..................... | 107 456 | 108 052 | 45700 | | Tifton, GA Micro area ...................... | 40 118 | 41 064 |
| | 45 085 | Sumter County, SC ...................... | 107 456 | 108 052 | | 13 277 | Tift County, GA.............................. | 40 118 | 41 064 |
| 44980 | | Sunbury, PA Micro area ................. | 94 528 | 94 428 | 45740 | | Toccoa, GA Micro area................... | 26 175 | 25 891 |
| | 42 097 | Northumberland County, PA ........ | 94 528 | 94 428 | | 13 257 | Stephens County, GA ................. | 26 175 | 25 891 |
| 45000 | | Susanville, CA Micro area .............. | 34 895 | 33 658 | 45780 | | Toledo, OH Metro area.................... | 610 001 | 608 711 |
| | 06 035 | Lassen County, CA ...................... | 34 895 | 33 658 | | 39 051 | Fulton County, OH ...................... | 42 698 | 42 513 |
| 45020 | | Sweetwater, TX Micro area ............. | 15 216 | 14 924 | | 39 095 | Lucas County, OH ....................... | 441 815 | 437 998 |
| | 48 353 | Nolan County, TX.......................... | 15 216 | 14 924 | | 39 173 | Wood County, OH ....................... | 125 488 | 128 200 |
| 45060 | | Syracuse, NY Metro area ................ | 662 577 | 660 934 | 45820 | | Topeka, KS Metro area ................... | 233 870 | 234 566 |
| | 36 053 | Madison County, NY ..................... | 73 442 | 72 382 | | 20 085 | Jackson County, KS..................... | 13 462 | 13 449 |
| | 36 067 | Onondaga County, NY.................. | 467 026 | 466 852 | | 20 087 | Jefferson County, KS .................. | 19 126 | 18 945 |
| | 36 075 | Oswego County, NY..................... | 122 109 | 121 700 | | 20 139 | Osage County, KS ...................... | 16 295 | 16 142 |
| 45140 | | Tahlequah, OK Micro area .............. | 46 987 | 48 150 | | 20 177 | Shawnee County, KS................... | 177 934 | 178 991 |
| | 40 021 | Cherokee County, OK.................. | 46 987 | 48 150 | | 20 197 | Wabaunsee County, KS............... | 7 053 | 7 039 |
| 45180 | | Talladega-Sylacauga, AL Micro area | 93 830 | 92 728 | 45860 | | Torrington, CT Micro area .............. | 189 927 | 187 530 |
| | 01 037 | Coosa County, AL ....................... | 11 539 | 10 966 | | 09 005 | Litchfield County, CT.................... | 189 927 | 187 530 |
| | 01 121 | Talladega County, AL................... | 82 291 | 81 762 | 45900 | | Traverse City, MI Micro area........... | 143 372 | 145 283 |
| 45220 | | Tallahassee, FL Metro area............. | 367 413 | 375 371 | | 26 019 | Benzie County, MI........................ | 17 525 | 17 465 |
| | 12 039 | Gadsden County, FL.................... | 46 389 | 46 528 | | 26 055 | Grand Traverse County, MI ......... | 86 986 | 89 112 |
| | 12 065 | Jefferson County, FL.................... | 14 761 | 14 256 | | 26 079 | Kalkaska County, MI.................... | 17 153 | 17 099 |
| | 12 073 | Leon County, FL.......................... | 275 487 | 283 769 | | 26 089 | Leelanau County, MI.................... | 21 708 | 21 607 |
| | 12 129 | Wakulla County, FL...................... | 30 776 | 30 818 | 45940 | | Trenton, NJ Metro area .................. | 366 513 | 368 303 |
| 45300 | | Tampa-St. Petersburg-Clearwater, FL Metro area | 2 783 243 | 2 842 878 | | 34 021 | Mercer County, NJ ...................... | 366 513 | 368 303 |
| | 12 053 | Hernando County, FL................... | 172 778 | 173 422 | 45980 | | Troy, AL Micro area ....................... | 32 899 | 33 182 |
| | 12 057 | Hillsborough County, FL............... | 1 229 226 | 1 277 746 | | 01 109 | Pike County, AL .......................... | 32 899 | 33 182 |
| | 12 101 | Pasco County, FL........................ | 464 697 | 470 391 | 46020 | | Truckee-Grass Valley, CA Micro area | 98 764 | 98 292 |
| | 12 103 | Pinellas County, FL...................... | 916 542 | 921 319 | | 06 057 | Nevada County, CA ..................... | 98 764 | 98 292 |
| 45340 | | Taos, NM Micro area ...................... | 32 937 | 32 779 | 46060 | | Tucson, AZ Metro area.................... | 980 263 | 992 394 |
| | 35 055 | Taos County, NM ......................... | 32 937 | 32 779 | | 04 019 | Pima County, AZ......................... | 980 263 | 992 394 |
| 45380 | | Taylorville, IL Micro area ................ | 34 800 | 34 638 | 46100 | | Tullahoma-Manchester, TN Micro area | 100 210 | 100 333 |
| | 17 021 | Christian County, IL...................... | 34 800 | 34 638 | | 47 031 | Coffee County, TN ...................... | 52 796 | 53 222 |
| 45460 | | Terre Haute, IN Metro area ............. | 172 425 | 172 493 | | 47 051 | Franklin County, TN..................... | 41 052 | 40 772 |
| | 18 021 | Clay County, IN............................ | 26 890 | 26 837 | | 47 127 | Moore County, TN....................... | 6 362 | 6 339 |
| | 18 153 | Sullivan County, IN...................... | 21 475 | 21 188 | 46140 | | Tulsa, OK Metro area...................... | 937 478 | 951 880 |
| | 18 165 | Vermillion County, IN................... | 16 212 | 16 040 | | 40 037 | Creek County, OK........................ | 69 967 | 70 651 |
| | 18 167 | Vigo County, IN........................... | 107 848 | 108 428 | | 40 111 | Okmulgee County, OK ................. | 40 069 | 39 625 |
| 45500 | | Texarkana, TX-AR Metro area ......... | 149 198 | 149 701 | | 40 113 | Osage County, OK ...................... | 47 472 | 47 917 |
| | 05 081 | Little River County, AR................. | 13 171 | 12 919 | | 40 117 | Pawnee County, OK..................... | 16 577 | 16 474 |
| | 05 091 | Miller County, AR........................ | 43 462 | 43 634 | | 40 131 | Rogers County, OK...................... | 86 905 | 88 367 |
| | 48 037 | Bowie County, TX ....................... | 92 565 | 93 148 | | 40 143 | Tulsa County, OK ........................ | 603 403 | 613 816 |
| 45520 | | The Dalles, OR Micro area............... | 25 213 | 25 487 | | 40 145 | Wagoner County, OK................... | 73 085 | 75 030 |
| | 41 065 | Wasco County, OR ...................... | 25 213 | 25 487 | 46180 | | Tupelo, MS Micro area ................... | 136 268 | 138 976 |
| 45540 | | The Villages, FL Metro area............. | 93 420 | 101 620 | | 28 057 | Itawamba County, MS................... | 23 401 | 23 340 |
| | 12 119 | Sumter County, FL....................... | 93 420 | 101 620 | | 28 081 | Lee County, MS .......................... | 82 910 | 85 042 |
| 45580 | | Thomaston, GA Micro area ............. | 27 153 | 26 630 | | 28 115 | Pontotoc County, MS................... | 29 957 | 30 594 |
| | 13 293 | Upson County, GA ...................... | 27 153 | 26 630 | 46220 | | Tuscaloosa, AL Metro area ............. | 230 162 | 233 389 |
| 45620 | | Thomasville, GA Micro area ............ | 44 720 | 44 724 | | 01 065 | Hale County, AL .......................... | 15 760 | 15 388 |
| | 13 275 | Thomas County, GA ..................... | 44 720 | 44 724 | | 01 107 | Pickens County, AL...................... | 19 746 | 19 405 |
| 45660 | | Tiffin, OH Micro area ...................... | 56 745 | 56 018 | | 01 125 | Tuscaloosa County, AL................. | 194 656 | 198 596 |
| | 39 147 | Seneca County, OH ..................... | 56 745 | 56 018 | 46300 | | Twin Falls, ID Micro area................. | 99 604 | 101 094 |
| | | | | | | 16 053 | Jerome County, ID ...................... | 22 374 | 22 499 |
| | | | | | | 16 083 | Twin Falls County, ID ................... | 77 230 | 78 595 |

# Core Based Statistical Areas (Metropolitan and Micropolitan), Metropolitan Divisions, and Components (as defined February 2013)–*Continued*

| Core Based Statistical Area | State/ County FIPS Code | Title and Geographic Components | 2010 Census Population | 2012 Estimated Population | Core Based Statistical Area | State/ County FIPS Code | Title and Geographic Components | 2010 Census Population | 2012 Estimated Population |
|---|---|---|---|---|---|---|---|---|---|
| 46340 | | Tyler, TX Metro area......................... | 209 714 | 214 821 | 47260 | | Virginia Beach-Norfolk-Newport News, VA-NC Metro area................ | 1 676 822 | 1 699 925 |
| | 48 423 | Smith County, TX........................... | 209 714 | 214 821 | | 37 053 | Currituck County, NC................... | 23 547 | 24 077 |
| 46380 | | Ukiah, CA Micro area ...................... | 87 841 | 87 428 | | 37 073 | Gates County, NC...................... | 12 197 | 11 869 |
| | 06 045 | Mendocino County, CA ................ | 87 841 | 87 428 | | 51 073 | Gloucester County, VA................ | 36 858 | 36 886 |
| 46460 | | Union City, TN-KY Micro area.......... | 38 620 | 37 865 | | 51 093 | Isle of Wight County, VA............. | 35 270 | 35 399 |
| | 21 075 | Fulton County, KY........................ | 6 813 | 6 525 | | 51 095 | James City County, VA............... | 67 009 | 68 967 |
| | 47 131 | Obion County, TN........................ | 31 807 | 31 340 | | 51 115 | Mathews County, VA................... | 8 978 | 8 884 |
| 46500 | | Urbana, OH Micro area .................. | 40 097 | 39 565 | | 51 199 | York County, VA......................... | 65 464 | 66 146 |
| | 39 021 | Champaign County, OH............... | 40 097 | 39 565 | | 51 550 | Chesapeake city, VA.................. | 222 209 | 228 417 |
| 46520 | | Urban Honolulu, HI Metro area ....... | 953 207 | 976 372 | | 51 650 | Hampton city, VA........................ | 137 436 | 136 836 |
| | 15 003 | Honolulu County, HI.................... | 953 207 | 976 372 | | 51 700 | Newport News city, VA ............... | 180 719 | 180 726 |
| 46540 | | Utica-Rome, NY Metro area ............ | 299 397 | 298 064 | | 51 710 | Norfolk city, VA.......................... | 242 803 | 245 782 |
| | 36 043 | Herkimer County, NY .................. | 64 519 | 64 508 | | 51 735 | Poquoson city, VA...................... | 12 150 | 12 097 |
| | 36 065 | Oneida County, NY...................... | 234 878 | 233 556 | | 51 740 | Portsmouth city, VA.................... | 95 535 | 96 470 |
| 46620 | | Uvalde, TX Micro area..................... | 26 405 | 26 752 | | 51 800 | Suffolk city, VA........................... | 84 585 | 85 181 |
| | 48 463 | Uvalde County, TX ...................... | 26 405 | 26 752 | | 51 810 | Virginia Beach city, VA............... | 437 994 | 447 021 |
| 46660 | | Valdosta, GA Metro area................ | 139 588 | 144 343 | | 51 830 | Williamsburg city, VA ................. | 14 068 | 15 167 |
| | 13 027 | Brooks County, GA ..................... | 16 243 | 15 403 | 47300 | | Visalia-Porterville, CA Metro area .... | 442 179 | 451 977 |
| | 13 101 | Echols County, GA...................... | 4 034 | 3 988 | | 06 107 | Tulare County, CA...................... | 442 179 | 451 977 |
| | 13 173 | Lanier County, GA....................... | 10 078 | 10 400 | 47340 | | Wabash, IN Micro area.................... | 32 888 | 32 361 |
| | 13 185 | Lowndes County, GA................... | 109 233 | 114 552 | | 18 169 | Wabash County, IN..................... | 32 888 | 32 361 |
| 46700 | | Vallejo-Fairfield, CA Metro area ...... | 413 344 | 420 757 | 47380 | | Waco, TX Metro area ..................... | 252 772 | 256 317 |
| | 06 095 | Solano County, CA...................... | 413 344 | 420 757 | | 48 145 | Falls County, TX......................... | 17 866 | 17 610 |
| 46740 | | Valley, AL Micro area ..................... | 34 215 | 34 064 | | 48 309 | McLennan County, TX ................ | 234 906 | 238 707 |
| | 01 017 | Chambers County, AL.................. | 34 215 | 34 064 | 47420 | | Wahpeton, ND-MN Micro area ........ | 22 897 | 22 802 |
| 46780 | | Van Wert, OH Micro area ............... | 28 744 | 28 744 | | 27 167 | Wilkin County, MN...................... | 6 576 | 6 585 |
| | 39 161 | Van Wert County, OH .................. | 28 744 | 28 744 | | 38 077 | Richland County, ND................... | 16 321 | 16 217 |
| 46820 | | Vermillion, SD Micro area............... | 13 864 | 14 131 | 47460 | | Walla Walla, WA Metro area ........... | 62 859 | 63 399 |
| | 46 027 | Clay County, SD......................... | 13 864 | 14 131 | | 53 013 | Columbia County, WA................. | 4 078 | 3 995 |
| 46860 | | Vernal, UT Micro area .................... | 32 588 | 34 524 | | 53 071 | Walla Walla County, WA............. | 58 781 | 59 404 |
| | 49 047 | Uintah County, UT....................... | 32 588 | 34 524 | 47540 | | Wapakoneta, OH Micro area........... | 45 949 | 45 831 |
| 46900 | | Vernon, TX Micro area.................... | 13 535 | 13 258 | | 39 011 | Auglaize County, OH.................. | 45 949 | 45 831 |
| | 48 487 | Wilbarger County, TX.................. | 13 535 | 13 258 | 47580 | | Warner Robins, GA Metro area....... | 179 605 | 185 478 |
| 46980 | | Vicksburg, MS Micro area .............. | 58 377 | 57 433 | | 13 153 | Houston County, GA................... | 139 900 | 146 136 |
| | 28 021 | Claiborne County, MS.................. | 9 604 | 9 349 | | 13 225 | Peach County, GA ..................... | 27 695 | 27 622 |
| | 28 149 | Warren County, MS...................... | 48 773 | 48 084 | | 13 235 | Pulaski County, GA .................... | 12 010 | 11 720 |
| 47020 | | Victoria, TX Metro area................... | 94 003 | 96 620 | 47620 | | Warren, PA Micro area.................... | 41 815 | 41 146 |
| | 48 175 | Goliad County, TX....................... | 7 210 | 7 351 | | 42 123 | Warren County, PA ..................... | 41 815 | 41 146 |
| | 48 469 | Victoria County, TX..................... | 86 793 | 89 269 | 47660 | | Warrensburg, MO Micro area.......... | 52 595 | 54 397 |
| 47080 | | Vidalia, GA Micro area.................... | 36 346 | 36 228 | | 29 101 | Johnson County, MO .................. | 52 595 | 54 397 |
| | 13 209 | Montgomery County, GA.............. | 9 123 | 8 913 | 47700 | | Warsaw, IN Micro area................... | 77 358 | 77 609 |
| | 13 279 | Toombs County, GA.................... | 27 223 | 27 315 | | 18 085 | Kosciusko County, IN.................. | 77 358 | 77 609 |
| 47180 | | Vincennes, IN Micro area ............... | 38 440 | 38 122 | 47780 | | Washington, IN Micro area.............. | 31 648 | 32 064 |
| | 18 083 | Knox County, IN........................... | 38 440 | 38 122 | | 18 027 | Daviess County, IN ..................... | 31 648 | 32 064 |
| 47220 | | Vineland-Bridgeton, NJ Metro area .. | 156 898 | 157 785 | 47820 | | Washington, NC Micro area ............ | 47 759 | 47 507 |
| | 34 011 | Cumberland County, NJ.............. | 156 898 | 157 785 | | 37 013 | Beaufort County, NC................... | 47 759 | 47 507 |
| 47240 | | Vineyard Haven, MA Micro area ...... | 16 535 | 17 041 | 47900 | | Washington-Arlington-Alexandria, DC-VA-MD-WV Metro area ............. | 5 636 232 | 5 860 342 |
| | 25 007 | Dukes County, MA ...................... | 16 535 | 17 041 | 47900 | | Silver Spring-Frederick-Rockville, MD Metro Div 43524...................... | 1 205 162 | 1 244 291 |
| | | | | | | 24 021 | Frederick County, MD ................ | 233 385 | 239 582 |
| | | | | | | 24 031 | Montgomery County, MD ............. | 971 777 | 1 004 709 |

# Core Based Statistical Areas (Metropolitan and Micropolitan), Metropolitan Divisions, and Components (as defined February 2013)–*Continued*

| Core Based Statistical Area | State/County FIPS Code | Title and Geographic Components | 2010 Census Population | 2012 Estimated Population | Core Based Statistical Area | State/County FIPS Code | Title and Geographic Components | 2010 Census Population | 2012 Estimated Population |
|---|---|---|---|---|---|---|---|---|---|
| 47900 | | Washington-Arlington-Alexandria, DC-VA-MD-WV Metro Div 47894 ..... | 4 431 070 | 4 616 051 | 48460 | | West Plains, MO Micro area............ | 40 400 | 40 629 |
| | 11 001 | District of Columbia, DC............... | 601 723 | 632 323 | | 29 091 | Howell County, MO ...................... | 40 400 | 40 629 |
| | 24 009 | Calvert County, MD...................... | 88 737 | 89 628 | 48540 | | Wheeling, WV-OH Metro area......... | 147 950 | 146 420 |
| | 24 017 | Charles County, MD...................... | 146 551 | 150 592 | | 39 013 | Belmont County, OH ................... | 70 400 | 69 671 |
| | 24 033 | Prince George's County, MD ........ | 863 420 | 881 138 | | 54 051 | Marshall County, WV .................. | 33 107 | 32 674 |
| | 51 013 | Arlington County, VA..................... | 207 627 | 221 045 | | 54 069 | Ohio County, WV ....................... | 44 443 | 44 075 |
| | 51 043 | Clarke County, VA........................ | 14 034 | 14 323 | | | | | |
| | 51 047 | Culpeper County, VA .................... | 46 689 | 47 911 | 48580 | | Whitewater-Elkhorn, WI Micro area.. | 102 228 | 102 851 |
| | 51 059 | Fairfax County, VA........................ | 1 081 726 | 1 118 602 | | 55 127 | Walworth County, WI .................. | 102 228 | 102 851 |
| | 51 061 | Fauquier County, VA..................... | 65 203 | 66 542 | | | | | |
| | 51 107 | Loudoun County, VA..................... | 312 311 | 336 898 | 48620 | | Wichita, KS Metro area................ | 630 919 | 636 105 |
| | 51 153 | Prince William County, VA............ | 402 002 | 430 289 | | 20 015 | Butler County, KS....................... | 65 880 | 65 827 |
| | 51 157 | Rappahannock County, VA............ | 7 373 | 7 456 | | 20 079 | Harvey County, KS...................... | 34 684 | 34 852 |
| | 51 177 | Spotsylvania County, VA............... | 122 397 | 125 684 | | 20 095 | Kingman County, KS................... | 7 858 | 7 863 |
| | 51 179 | Stafford County, VA...................... | 128 961 | 134 352 | | 20 173 | Sedgwick County, KS.................. | 498 365 | 503 889 |
| | 51 187 | Warren County, VA....................... | 37 575 | 38 070 | | 20 191 | Sumner County, KS ..................... | 24 132 | 23 674 |
| | 51 510 | Alexandria city, VA....................... | 139 966 | 146 294 | | | | | |
| | 51 600 | Fairfax city, VA............................ | 22 565 | 23 461 | 48660 | | Wichita Falls, TX Metro area.......... | 151 306 | 150 829 |
| | 51 610 | Falls Church city, VA.................... | 12 332 | 13 229 | | 48 009 | Archer County, TX ..................... | 9 054 | 8 735 |
| | 51 630 | Fredericksburg city, VA................. | 24 286 | 27 307 | | 48 077 | Clay County, TX ........................ | 10 752 | 10 535 |
| | 51 683 | Manassas city, VA........................ | 37 821 | 40 605 | | 48 485 | Wichita County, TX ..................... | 131 500 | 131 559 |
| | 51 685 | Manassas Park city, VA................. | 14 273 | 15 798 | 48700 | | Williamsport, PA Metro area.......... | 116 111 | 117 168 |
| | 54 037 | Jefferson County, WV................... | 53 498 | 54 504 | | 42 081 | Lycoming County, PA................... | 116 111 | 117 168 |
| 47920 | | Washington Court House, OH Micro area....................................... | 29 030 | 28 880 | 48780 | | Williston, ND Micro area............... | 22 398 | 26 697 |
| | 39 047 | Fayette County, OH ..................... | 29 030 | 28 880 | | 38 105 | Williams County, ND.................... | 22 398 | 26 697 |
| 47940 | | Waterloo-Cedar Falls, IA Metro area | 167 819 | 168 747 | 48820 | | Willmar, MN Micro area................ | 42 239 | 42 379 |
| | 19 013 | Black Hawk County, IA ................ | 131 090 | 131 820 | | 27 067 | Kandiyohi County, MN................. | 42 239 | 42 379 |
| | 19 017 | Bremer County, IA........................ | 24 276 | 24 479 | | | | | |
| | 19 075 | Grundy County, IA........................ | 12 453 | 12 448 | 48900 | | Wilmington, NC Metro area............ | 254 884 | 263 429 |
| | | | | | | 37 129 | New Hanover County, NC............ | 202 667 | 209 234 |
| 47980 | | Watertown, SD Micro area ............. | 27 227 | 27 606 | | 37 141 | Pender County, NC ..................... | 52 217 | 54 195 |
| | 46 029 | Codington County, SD ................. | 27 227 | 27 606 | | | | | |
| | | | | | 48940 | | Wilmington, OH Micro area............ | 42 040 | 41 886 |
| 48020 | | Watertown-Fort Atkinson, WI Micro area....................................... | 83 686 | 84 498 | | 39 027 | Clinton County, OH .................... | 42 040 | 41 886 |
| | 55 055 | Jefferson County, WI.................... | 83 686 | 84 498 | 48980 | | Wilson, NC Micro area.................. | 81 234 | 81 867 |
| | | | | | | 37 195 | Wilson County, NC...................... | 81 234 | 81 867 |
| 48060 | | Watertown-Fort Drum, NY Metro area....................................... | 116 229 | 120 262 | 49020 | | Winchester, VA-WV Metro area ....... | 128 472 | 130 907 |
| | 36 045 | Jefferson County, NY................... | 116 229 | 120 262 | | 51 069 | Frederick County, VA.................. | 78 305 | 80 317 |
| | | | | | | 51 840 | Winchester city, VA.................... | 26 203 | 26 881 |
| 48100 | | Wauchula, FL Micro area ................ | 27 731 | 27 514 | | 54 027 | Hampshire County, WV............... | 23 964 | 23 709 |
| | 12 049 | Hardee County, FL....................... | 27 731 | 27 514 | 49080 | | Winnemucca, NV Micro area........... | 16 528 | 17 048 |
| | | | | | | 32 013 | Humboldt County, NV ................. | 16 528 | 17 048 |
| 48140 | | Wausau, WI Metro area.................. | 134 063 | 134 735 | 49100 | | Winona, MN Micro area................ | 51 461 | 51 629 |
| | 55 073 | Marathon County, WI................... | 134 063 | 134 735 | | 27 169 | Winona County, MN..................... | 51 461 | 51 629 |
| 48180 | | Waycross, GA Micro area............... | 55 070 | 54 665 | 49180 | | Winston-Salem, NC Metro area....... | 640 595 | 647 697 |
| | 13 229 | Pierce County, GA ...................... | 18 758 | 18 844 | | 37 057 | Davidson County, NC.................. | 162 878 | 163 260 |
| | 13 299 | Ware County, GA ........................ | 36 312 | 35 821 | | 37 059 | Davie County, NC ...................... | 41 240 | 41 433 |
| 48220 | | Weatherford, OK Micro area............ | 27 469 | 28 536 | | 37 067 | Forsyth County, NC.................... | 350 670 | 358 137 |
| | 40 039 | Custer County, OK....................... | 27 469 | 28 536 | | 37 169 | Stokes County, NC..................... | 47 401 | 46 783 |
| 48260 | | Weirton-Steubenville, WV-OH Metro area....................................... | 124 454 | 122 547 | | 37 197 | Yadkin County, NC...................... | 38 406 | 38 084 |
| | 39 081 | Jefferson County, OH.................. | 69 709 | 68 389 | 49220 | | Wisconsin Rapids-Marshfield, WI Micro area................................ | 74 749 | 74 424 |
| | 54 009 | Brooke County, WV..................... | 24 069 | 23 853 | | 55 141 | Wood County, WI ....................... | 74 749 | 74 424 |
| | 54 029 | Hancock County, WV................... | 30 676 | 30 305 | | | | | |
| 48300 | | Wenatchee, WA Metro area............. | 110 884 | 113 037 | 49260 | | Woodward, OK Micro area ............ | 20 081 | 20 548 |
| | 53 007 | Chelan County, WA...................... | 72 453 | 73 687 | | 40 153 | Woodward County, OK ............... | 20 081 | 20 548 |
| | 53 017 | Douglas County, WA.................... | 38 431 | 39 350 | | | | | |

# Core Based Statistical Areas (Metropolitan and Micropolitan), Metropolitan Divisions, and Components (as defined February 2013)–*Continued*

| Core Based Statistical Area | State/ County FIPS Code | Title and Geographic Components | 2010 Census Population | 2012 Estimated Population |
|---|---|---|---|---|
| 49300 | | Wooster, OH Micro area................. | 114 520 | 114 848 |
| | 39 169 | Wayne County, OH ...................... | 114 520 | 114 848 |
| 49340 | | Worcester, MA-CT Metro area ........ | 916 980 | 923 762 |
| | 09 015 | Windham County, CT.................. | 118 428 | 117 599 |
| | 25 027 | Worcester County, MA ................ | 798 552 | 806 163 |
| 49380 | | Worthington, MN Micro area............ | 21 378 | 21 487 |
| | 27 105 | Nobles County, MN ...................... | 21 378 | 21 487 |
| 49420 | | Yakima, WA Metro area ................. | 243 231 | 246 977 |
| | 53 077 | Yakima County, WA..................... | 243 231 | 246 977 |
| 49460 | | Yankton, SD Micro area ................. | 22 438 | 22 603 |
| | 46 135 | Yankton County, SD..................... | 22 438 | 22 603 |
| 49620 | | York-Hanover, PA Metro area .......... | 434 972 | 437 846 |
| | 42 133 | York County, PA........................... | 434 972 | 437 846 |
| 49660 | | Youngstown-Warren-Boardman, OH-PA Metro area........................... | 565 773 | 558 206 |
| | 39 099 | Mahoning County, OH.................. | 238 823 | 235 145 |
| | 39 155 | Trumbull County, OH ................... | 210 312 | 207 406 |
| | 42 085 | Mercer County, PA....................... | 116 638 | 115 655 |
| 49700 | | Yuba City, CA Metro area ............... | 166 892 | 167 948 |
| | 06 101 | Sutter County, CA ....................... | 94 737 | 95 022 |
| | 06 115 | Yuba County, CA ........................ | 72 155 | 72 926 |
| 49740 | | Yuma, AZ Metro area ..................... | 195 751 | 200 022 |
| | 04 027 | Yuma County, AZ......................... | 195 751 | 200 022 |
| 49780 | | Zanesville, OH Micro area............... | 86 074 | 85 950 |
| | 39 119 | Muskingum County, OH............... | 86 074 | 85 950 |
| 49820 | | Zapata, TX Micro area..................... | 14 018 | 14 290 |
| | 48 505 | Zapata County, TX........................ | 14 018 | 14 290 |

# APPENDIX D
# MAPS OF CONGRESSIONAL DISTRICTS AND STATES

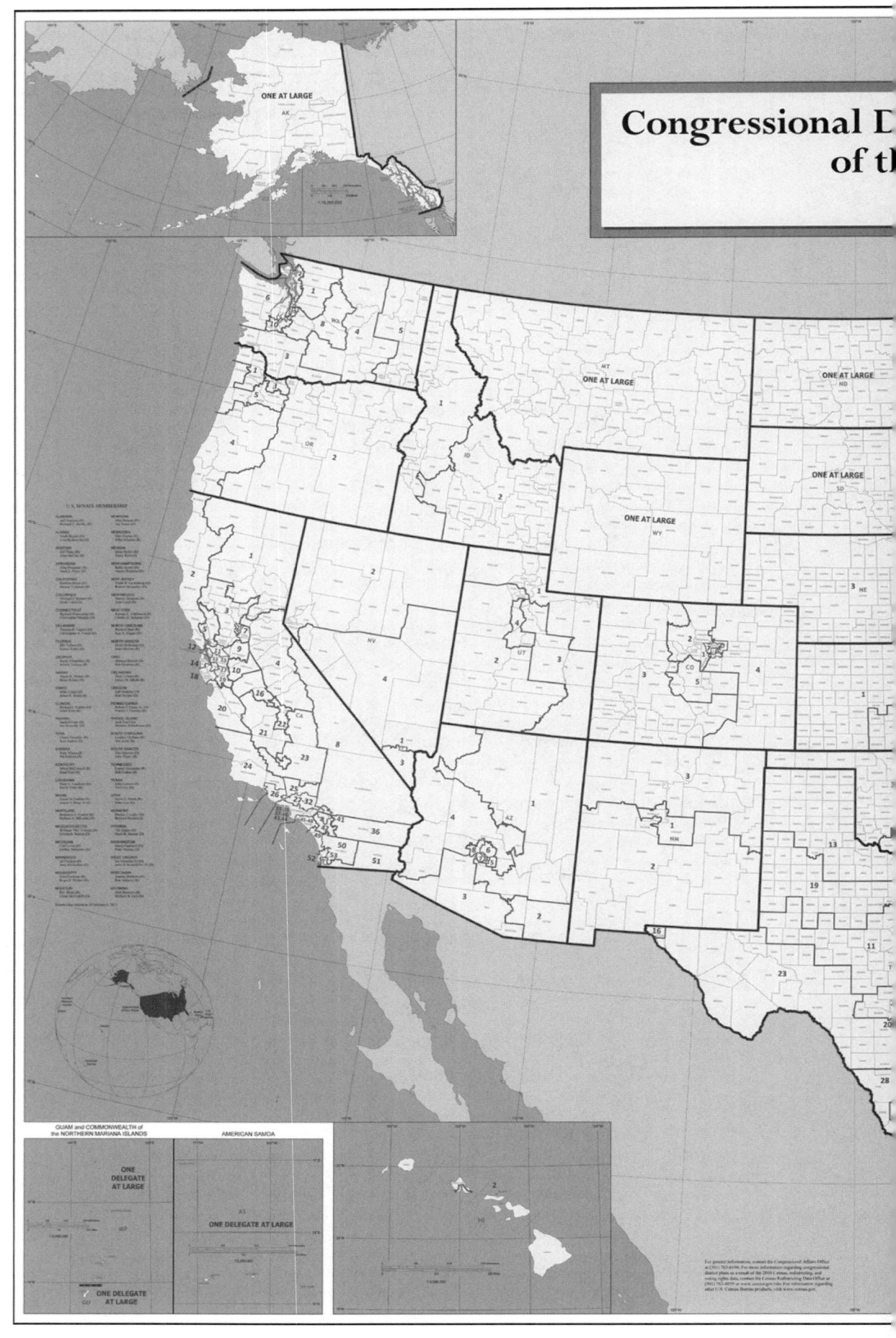

**Congressional D**
**of t**

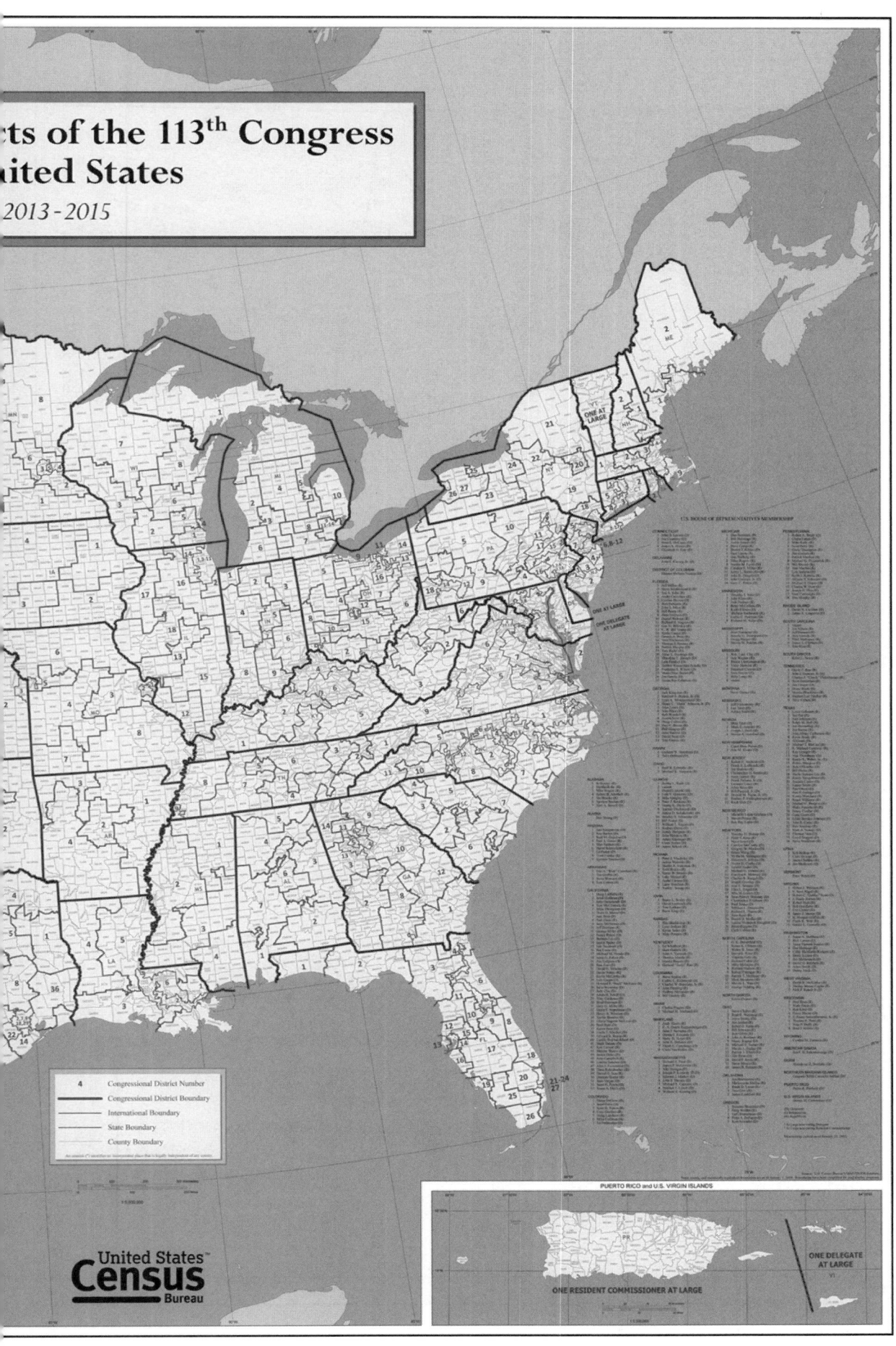

Districts of the 113th Congress
United States
2013-2015

United States Census Bureau

# ALABAMA - Core Based Statistical Areas and Counties

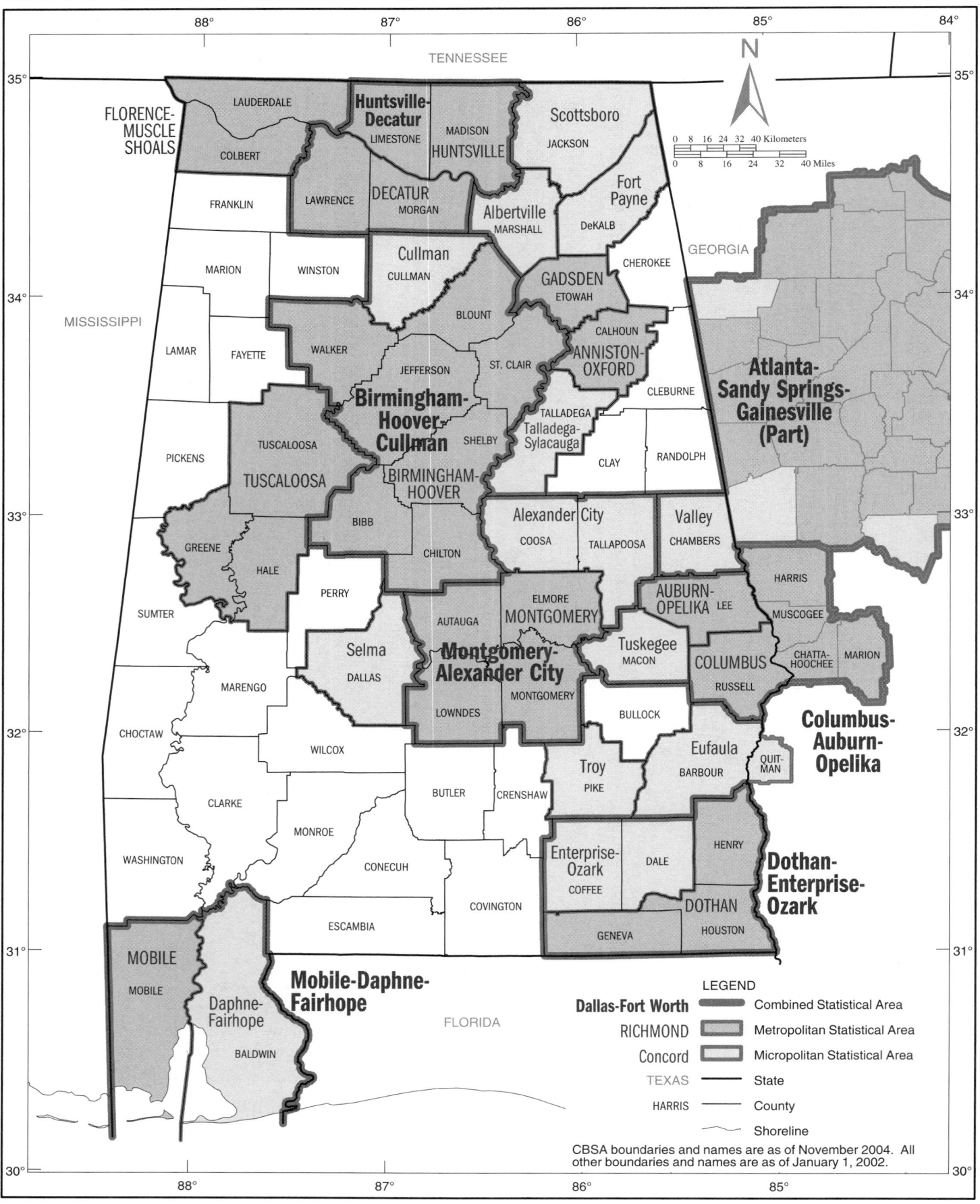

# ALASKA - Core Based Statistical Areas, Boroughs, and Census Areas

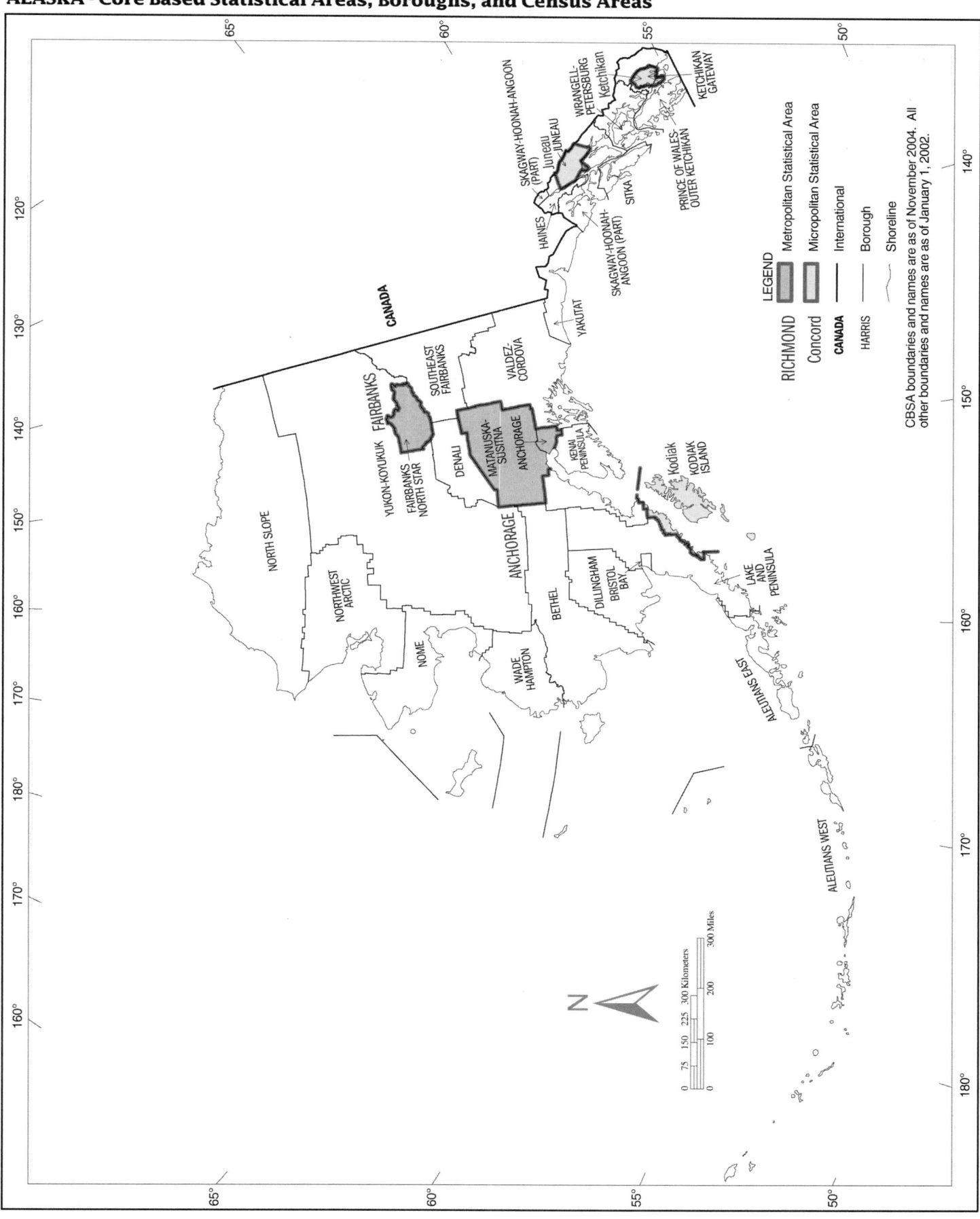

# ARIZONA - Core Based Statistical Areas and Counties

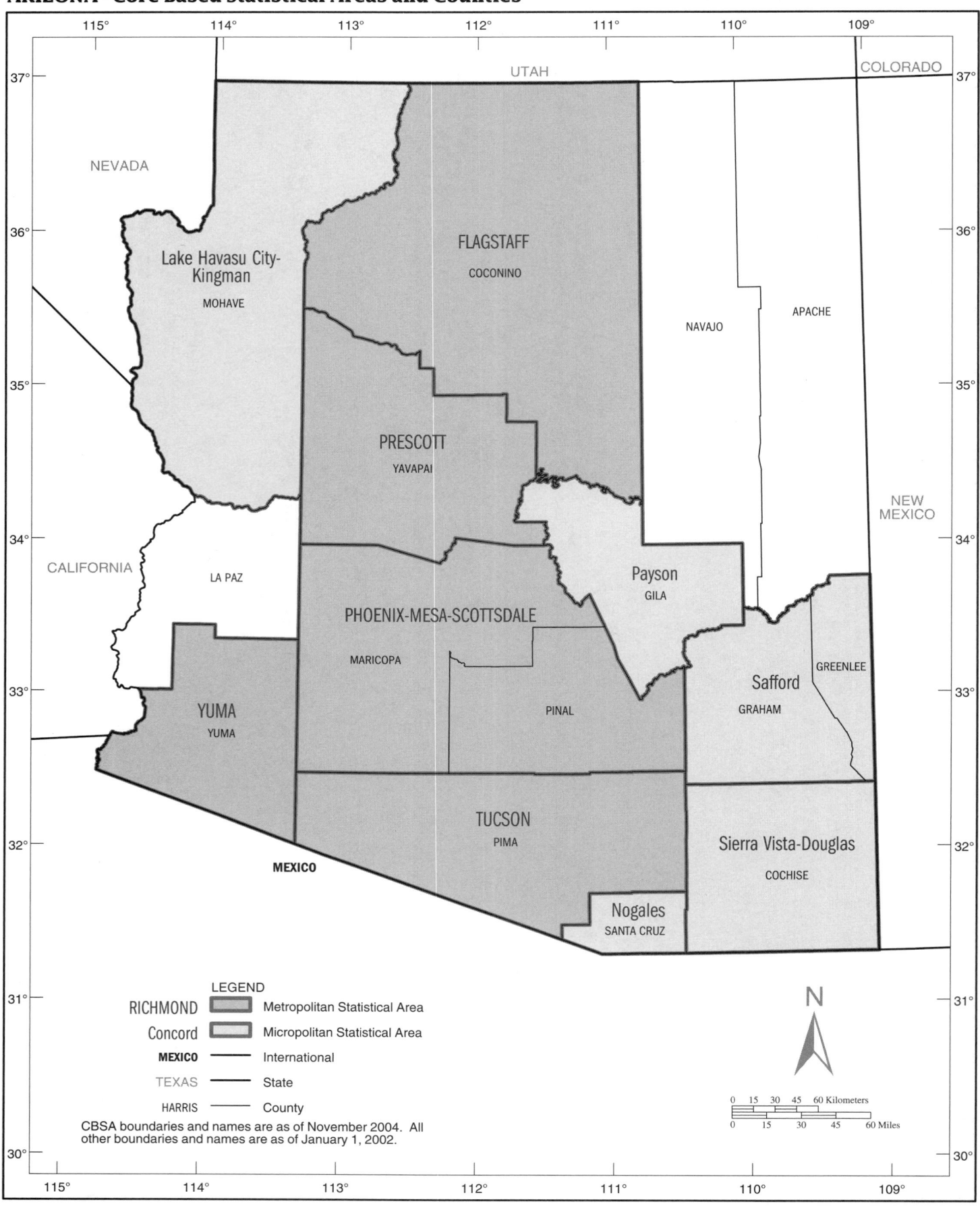

LEGEND

RICHMOND — Metropolitan Statistical Area

Concord — Micropolitan Statistical Area

**MEXICO** — International

TEXAS — State

HARRIS — County

CBSA boundaries and names are as of November 2004. All other boundaries and names are as of January 1, 2002.

U.S. DEPARTMENT OF COMMERCE Economics and Statistics Administration U.S. Census Bureau

# ARKANSAS - Core Based Statistical Areas and Counties

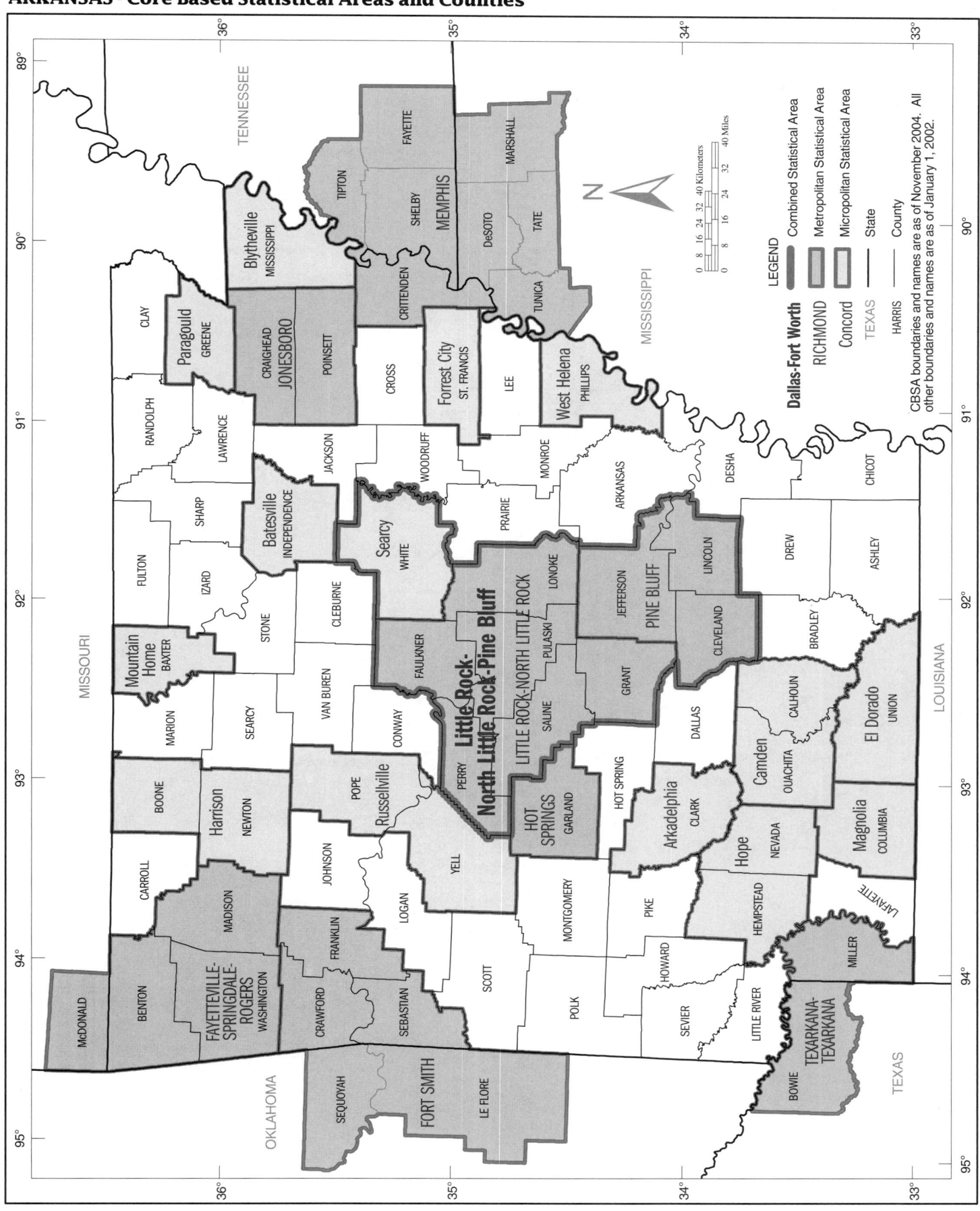

LEGEND

- Combined Statistical Area
- Metropolitan Statistical Area
- Micropolitan Statistical Area
- State
- County

**Dallas-Fort Worth**
RICHMOND
Concord
TEXAS
HARRIS

CBSA boundaries and names are as of November 2004. All other boundaries and names are as of January 1, 2002.

U.S. DEPARTMENT OF COMMERCE Economics and Statistics Administration U.S. Census Bureau

# CALIFORNIA - Core Based Statistical Areas and Counties

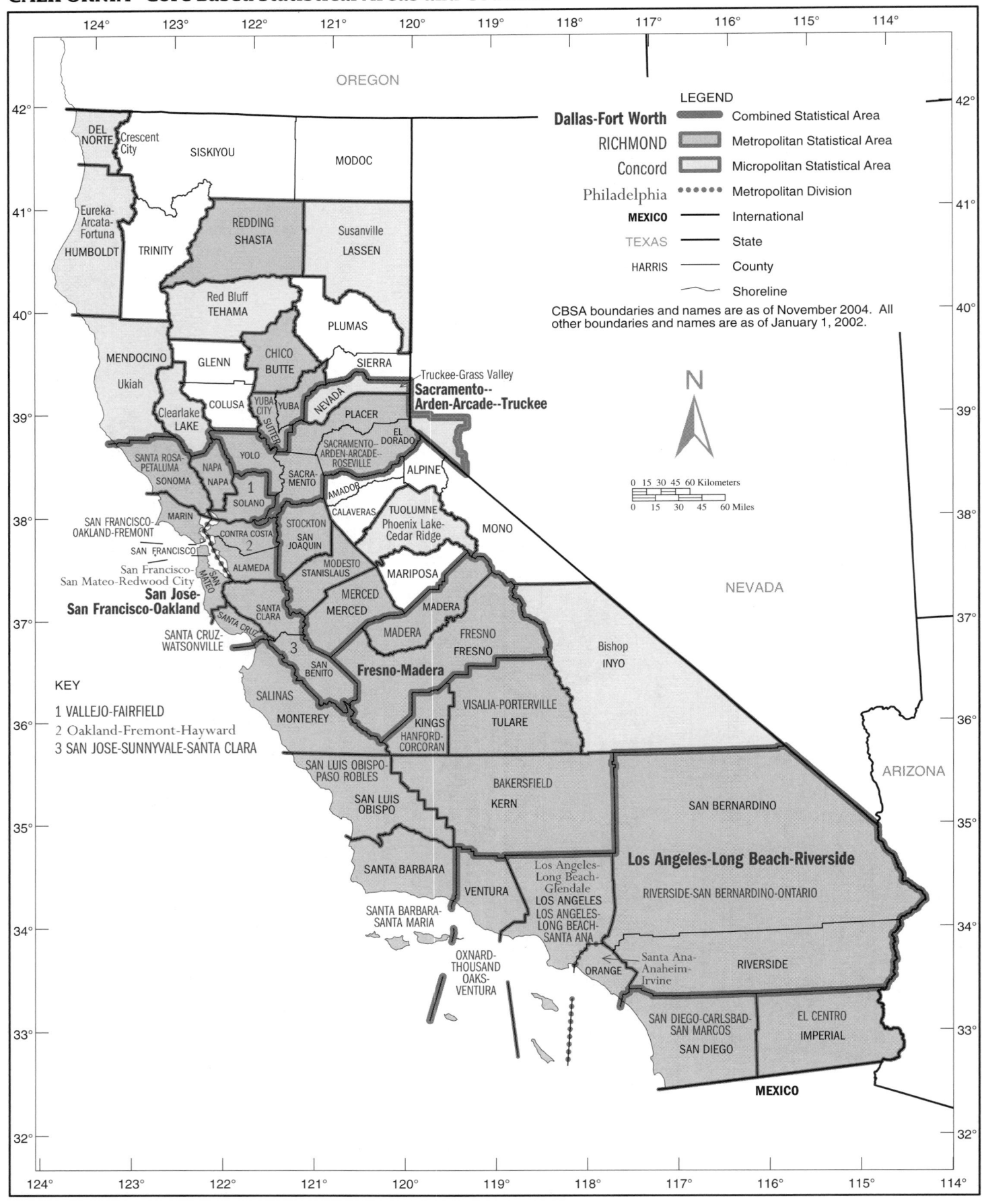

LEGEND

| | |
|---|---|
| **Dallas-Fort Worth** | Combined Statistical Area |
| RICHMOND | Metropolitan Statistical Area |
| Concord | Micropolitan Statistical Area |
| Philadelphia | ·····  Metropolitan Division |
| **MEXICO** | International |
| TEXAS | State |
| HARRIS | County |
| | Shoreline |

CBSA boundaries and names are as of November 2004. All other boundaries and names are as of January 1, 2002.

0  15  30  45  60 Kilometers
0  15  30  45  60 Miles

KEY

1 VALLEJO-FAIRFIELD
2 Oakland-Fremont-Hayward
3 SAN JOSE-SUNNYVALE-SANTA CLARA

# COLORADO - Core Based Statistical Areas and Counties

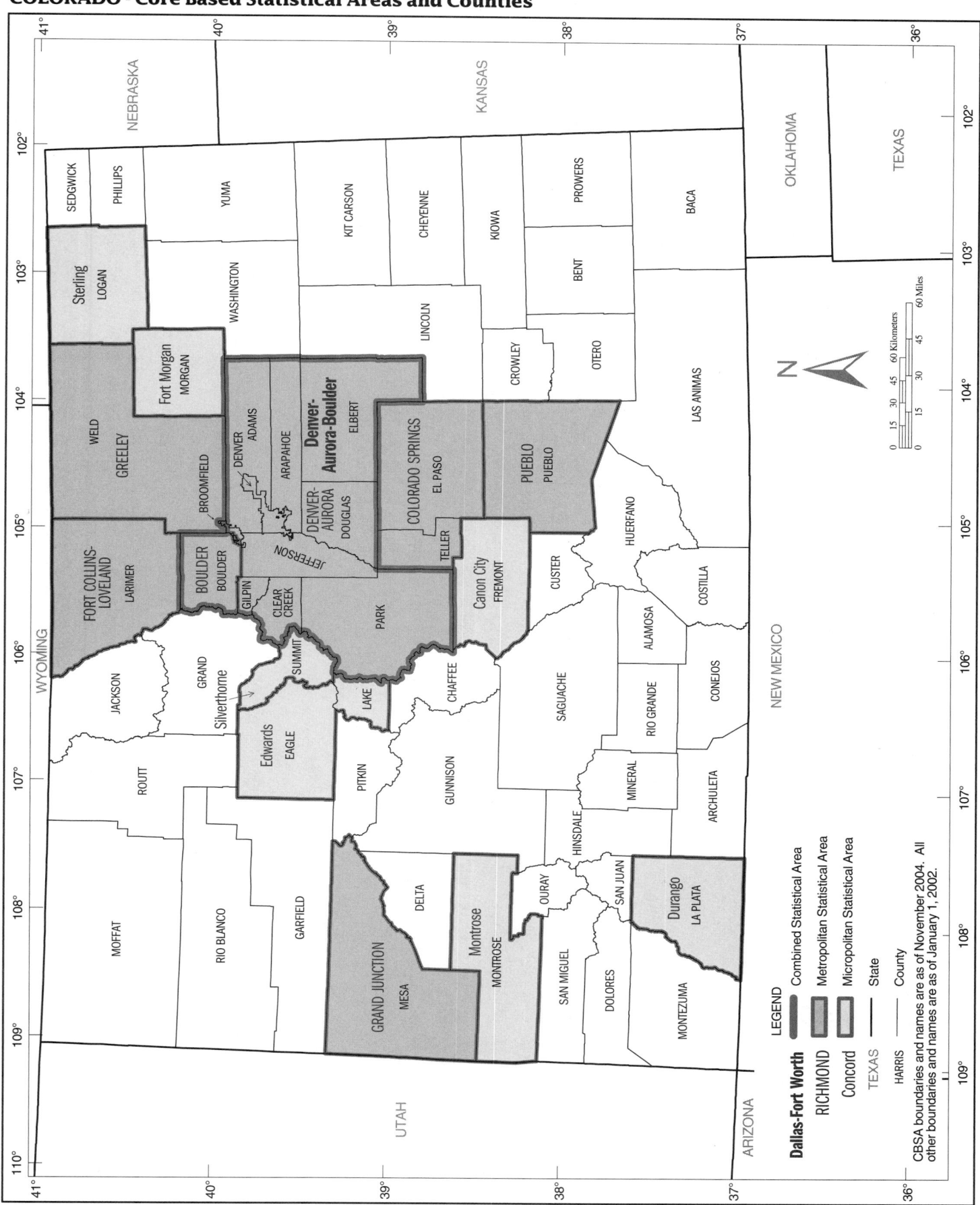

U.S. DEPARTMENT OF COMMERCE Economics and Statistics Administration  U.S. Census Bureau

Appendix D

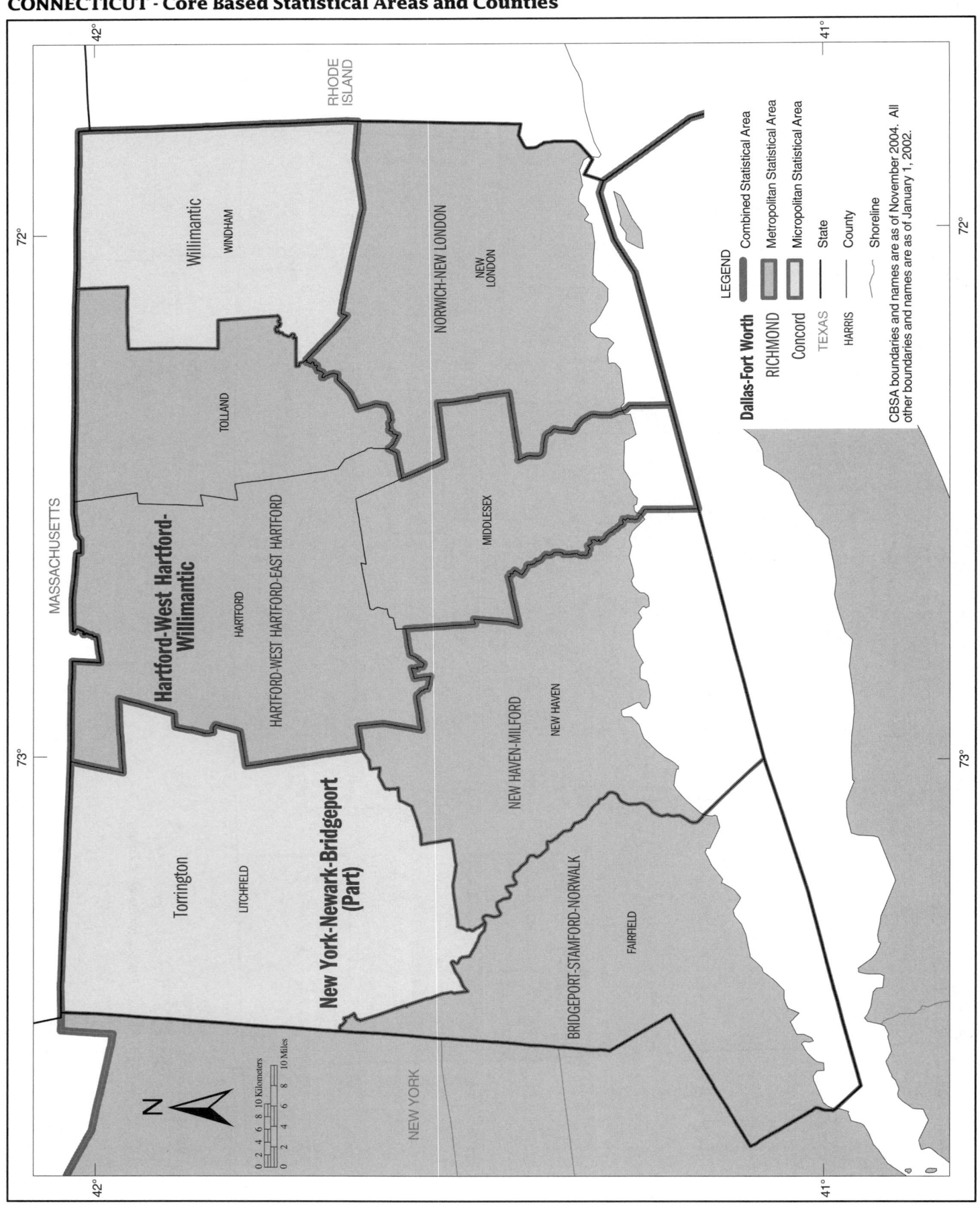

# DELAWARE - Core Based Statistical Areas and Counties

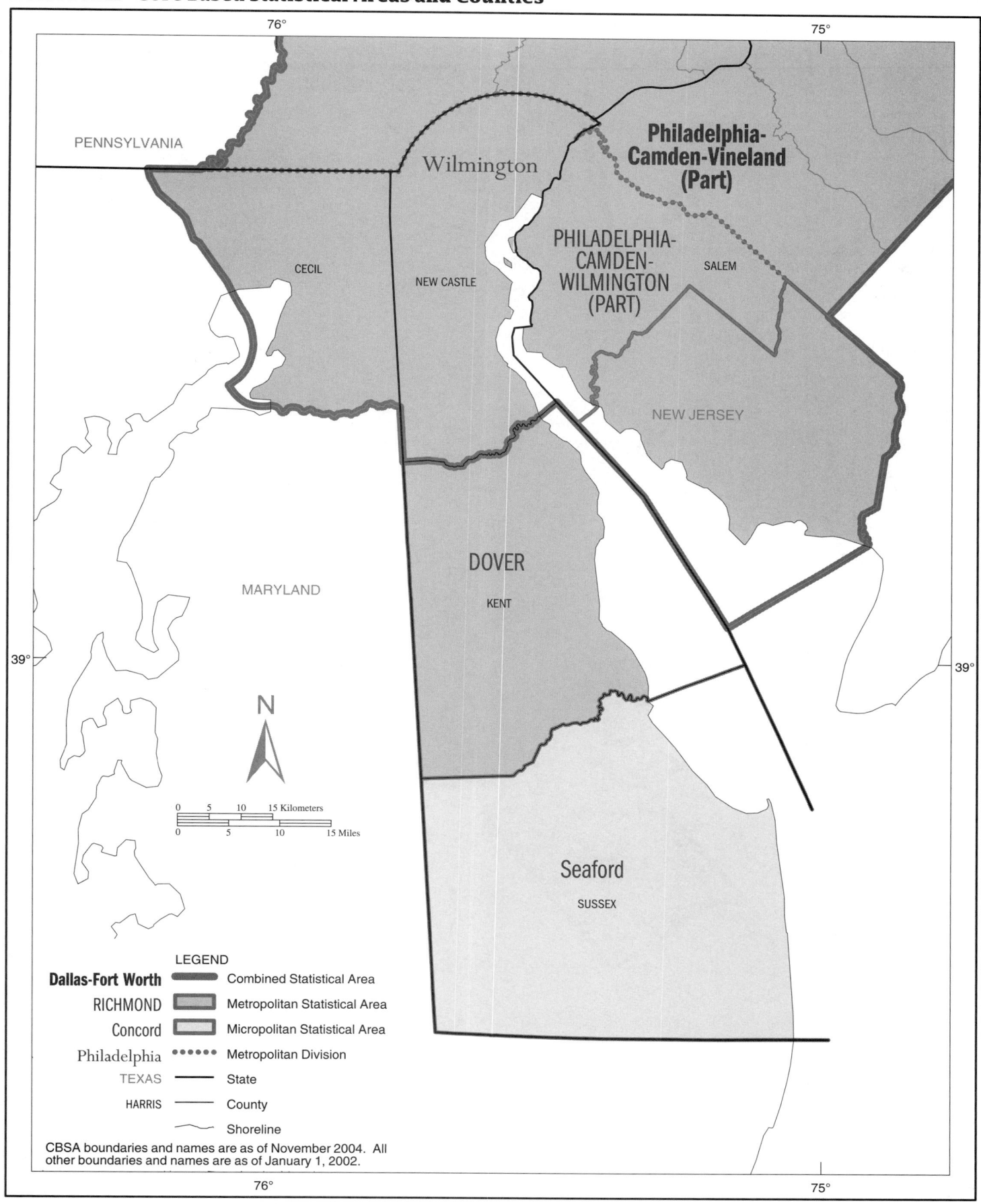

**Philadelphia-Camden-Vineland (Part)**

Wilmington

PENNSYLVANIA

CECIL

NEW CASTLE

PHILADELPHIA-CAMDEN-WILMINGTON (PART)

SALEM

NEW JERSEY

MARYLAND

DOVER

KENT

N

0  5  10  15 Kilometers
0  5  10  15 Miles

Seaford

SUSSEX

39°

39°

76°

75°

LEGEND

| | |
|---|---|
| **Dallas-Fort Worth** | Combined Statistical Area |
| RICHMOND | Metropolitan Statistical Area |
| Concord | Micropolitan Statistical Area |
| Philadelphia | •••••• Metropolitan Division |
| TEXAS | State |
| HARRIS | County |
| | Shoreline |

CBSA boundaries and names are as of November 2004. All other boundaries and names are as of January 1, 2002.

76°                                          75°

# DISTRICT OF COLUMBIA - Core Based Statistical Areas, Counties, and Independent Cities

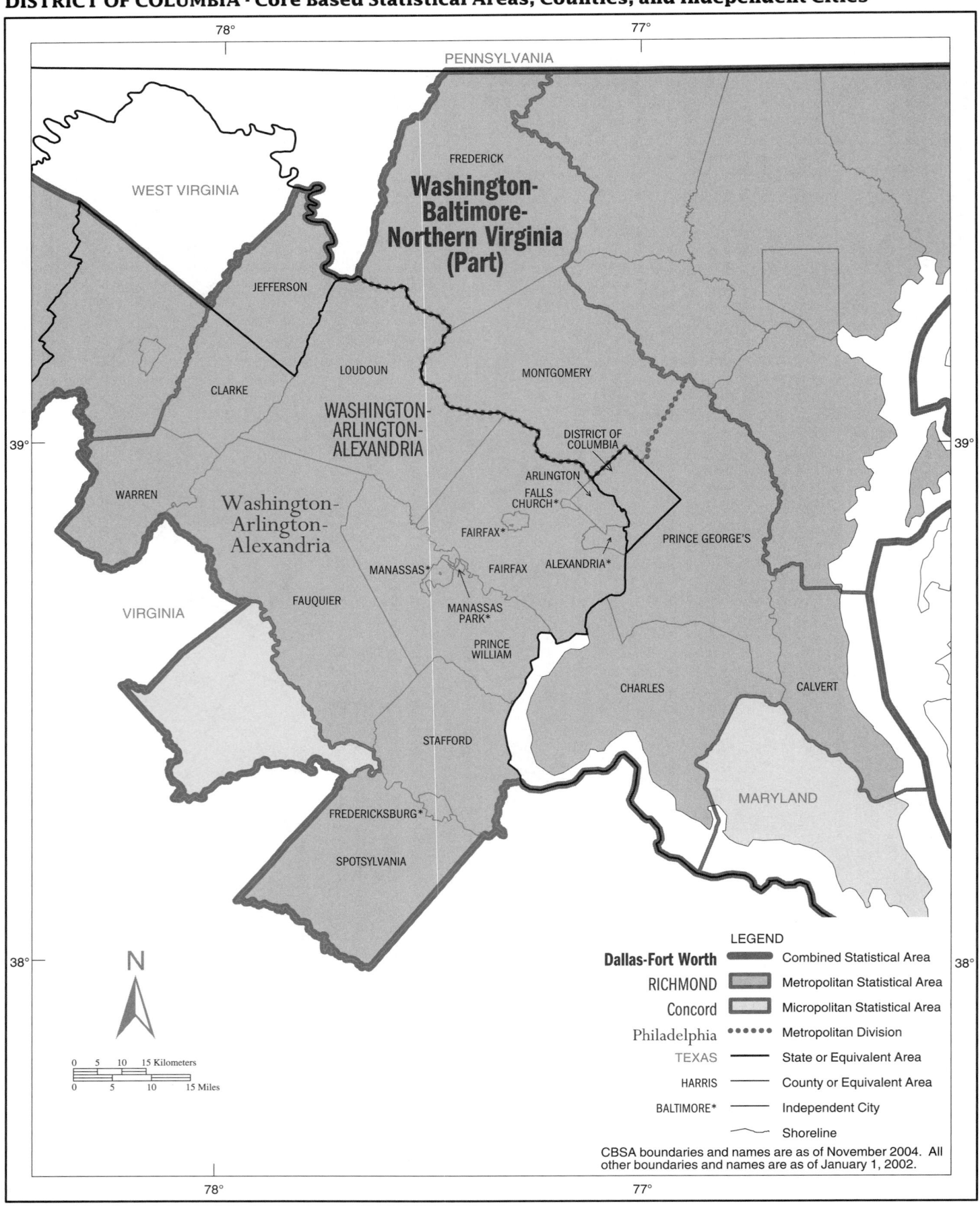

# FLORIDA - Core Based Statistical Areas and Counties

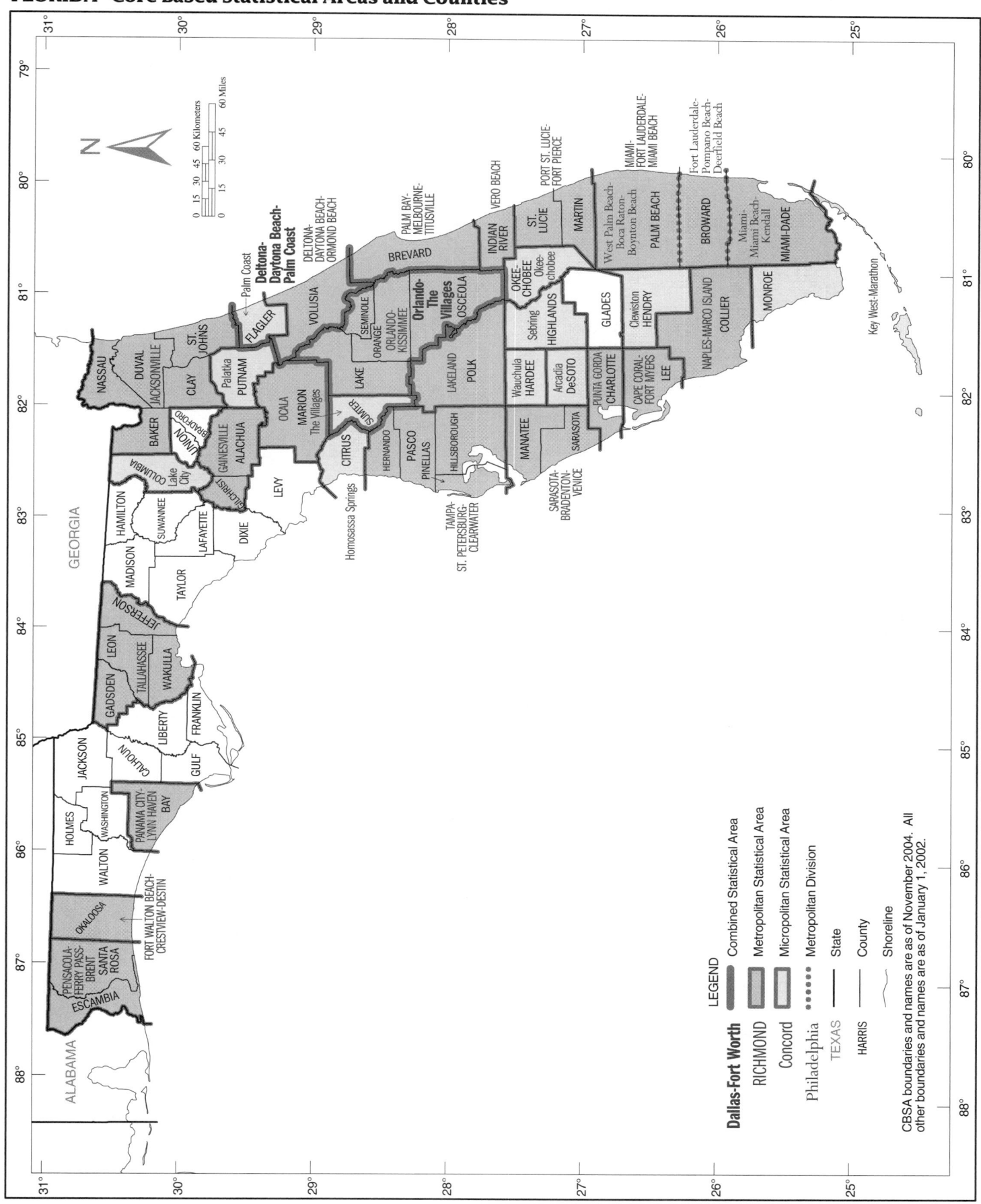

LEGEND

**Dallas-Fort Worth** Combined Statistical Area
RICHMOND Metropolitan Statistical Area
Concord Micropolitan Statistical Area
•••••• Metropolitan Division
Philadelphia State
TEXAS County
HARRIS Shoreline

CBSA boundaries and names are as of November 2004. All other boundaries and names are as of January 1, 2002.

# GEORGIA - Core Based Statistical Areas and Counties

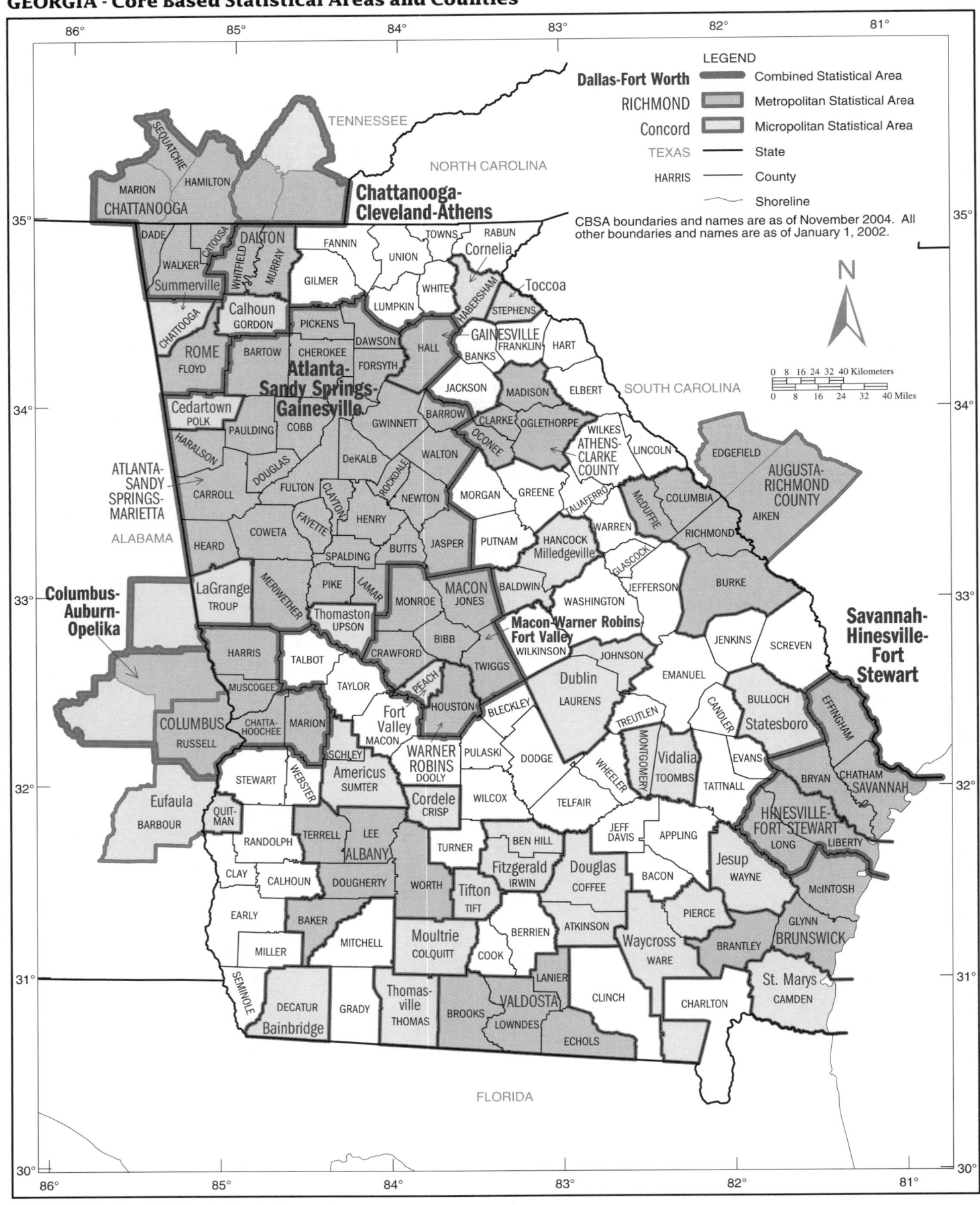

# HAWAII - Core Based Statistical Areas and Counties

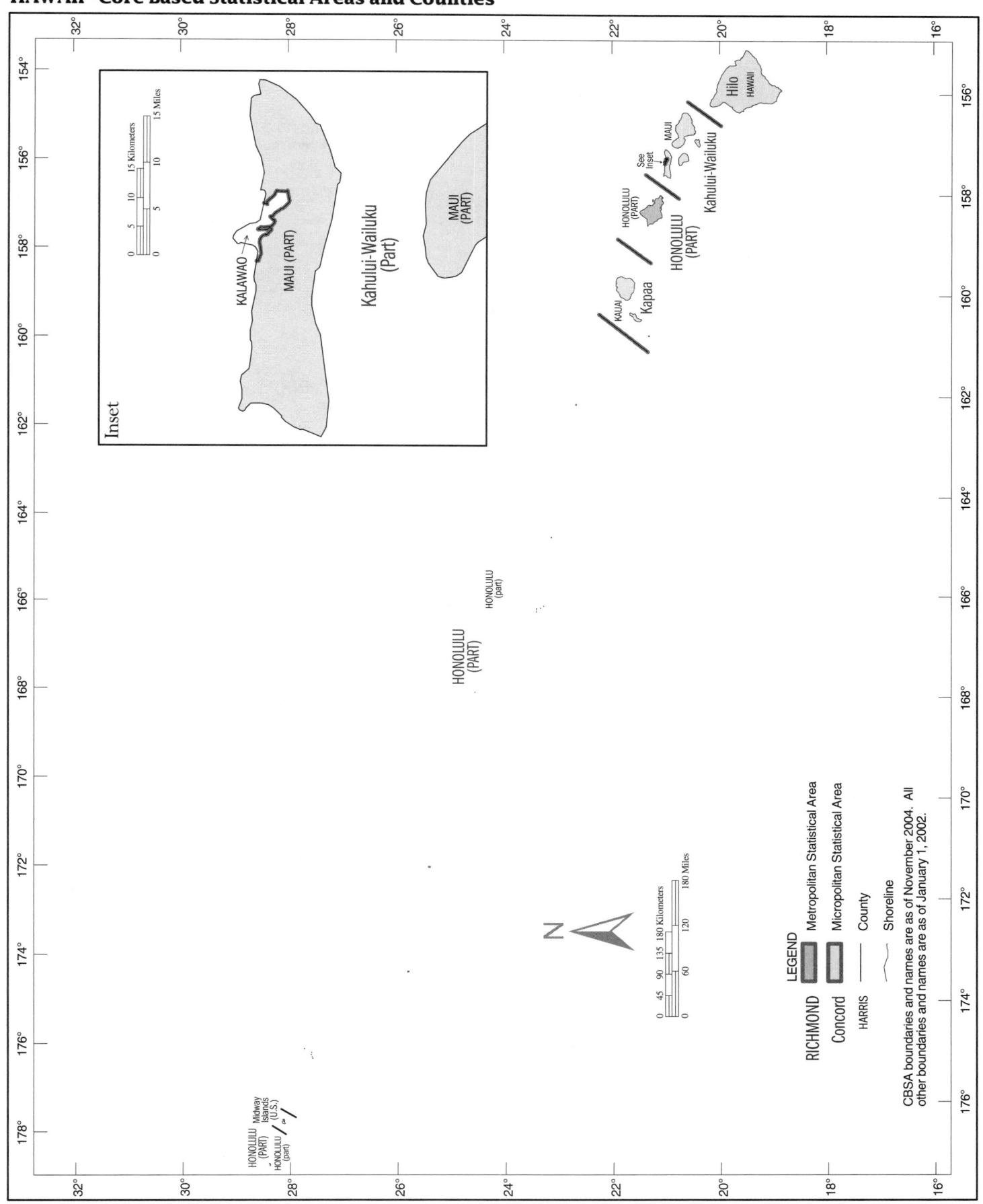

# IDAHO - Core Based Statistical Areas and Counties

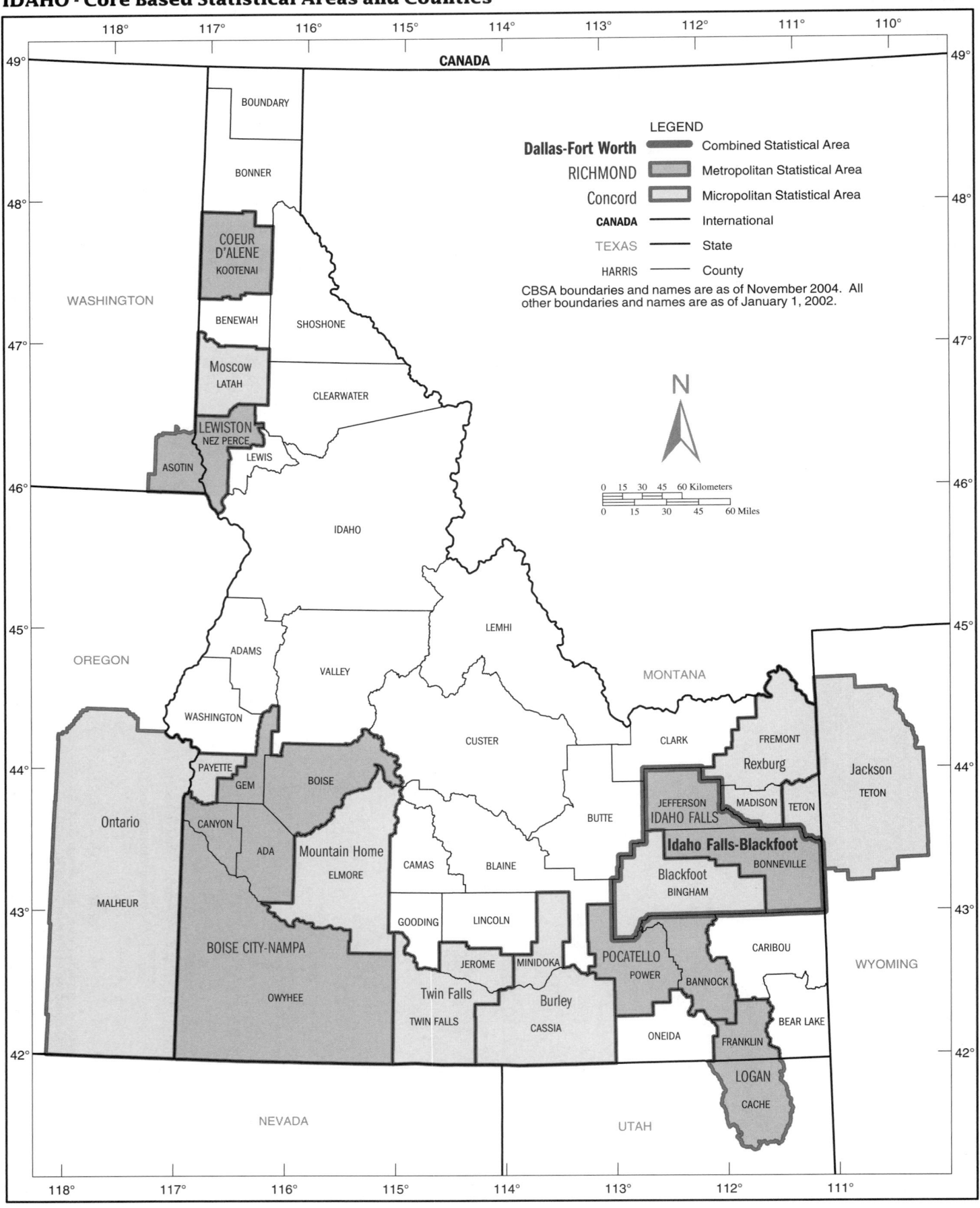

U.S. DEPARTMENT OF COMMERCE Economics and Statistics Administration  U.S. Census Bureau

# ILLINOIS - Core Based Statistical Areas, Counties, and Independent City

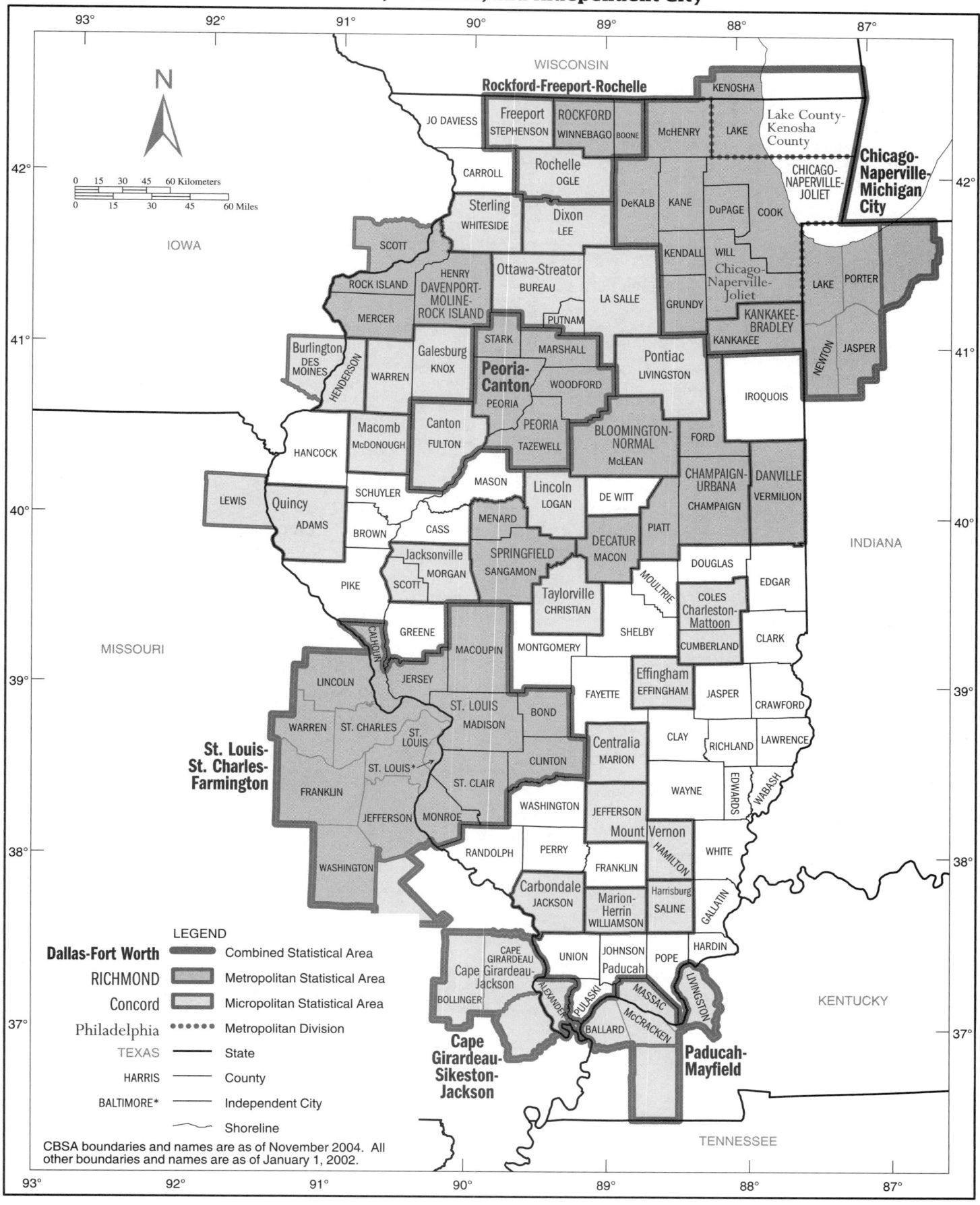

LEGEND

**Dallas-Fort Worth** — Combined Statistical Area
RICHMOND — Metropolitan Statistical Area
Concord — Micropolitan Statistical Area
Philadelphia ••••• Metropolitan Division
TEXAS —— State
HARRIS —— County
BALTIMORE* —— Independent City
—— Shoreline

CBSA boundaries and names are as of November 2004. All other boundaries and names are as of January 1, 2002.

# INDIANA - Core Based Statistical Areas and Counties

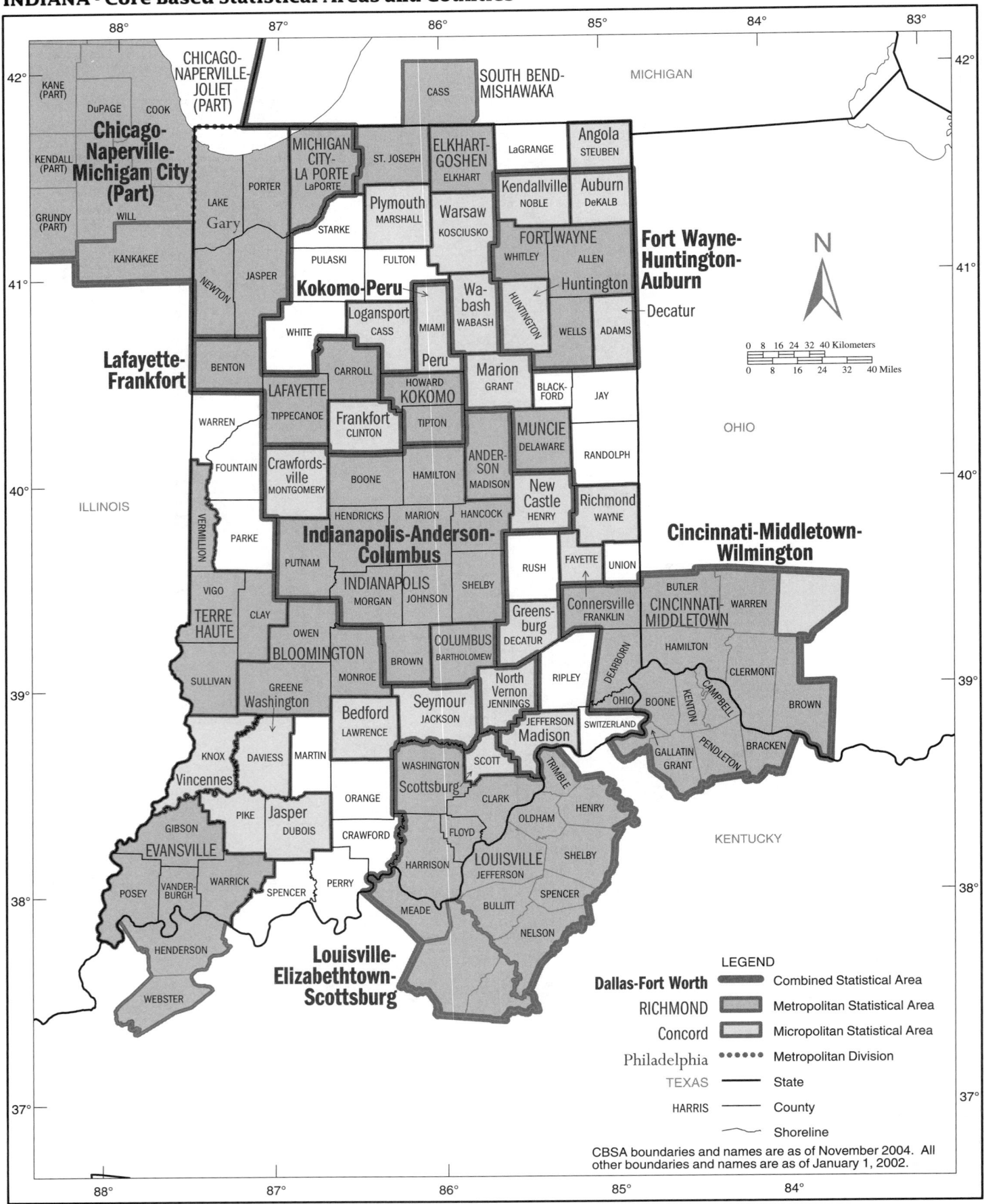

## LEGEND

| | |
|---|---|
| **Dallas-Fort Worth** | Combined Statistical Area |
| RICHMOND | Metropolitan Statistical Area |
| Concord | Micropolitan Statistical Area |
| Philadelphia | •••••• Metropolitan Division |
| TEXAS | ——— State |
| HARRIS | ——— County |
| | ～～ Shoreline |

CBSA boundaries and names are as of November 2004. All other boundaries and names are as of January 1, 2002.

# IOWA - Core Based Statistical Areas and Counties

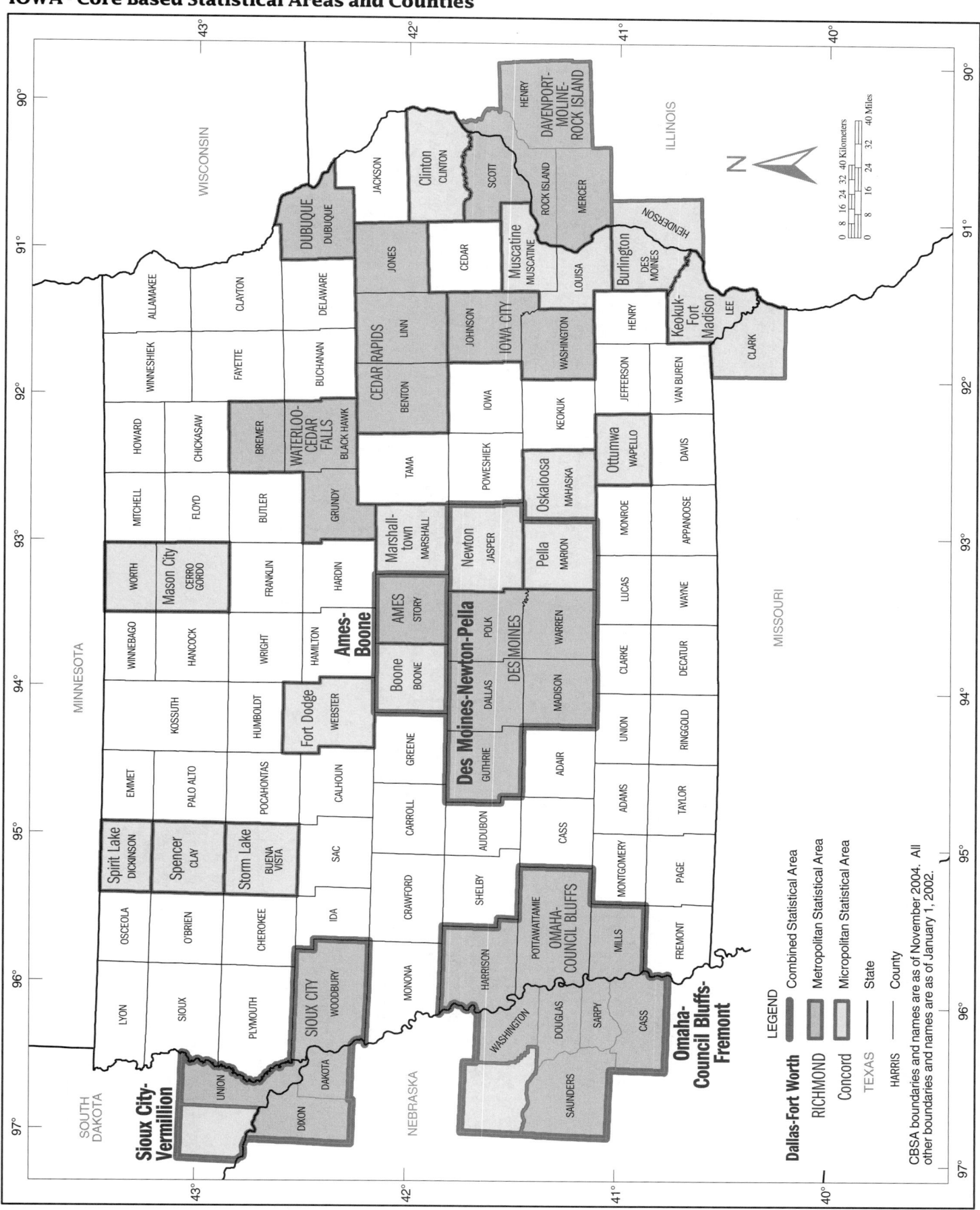

U.S. DEPARTMENT OF COMMERCE Economics and Statistics Administration  U.S. Census Bureau

Appendix D

**D-19**

# KANSAS - Core Based Statistical Areas and Counties

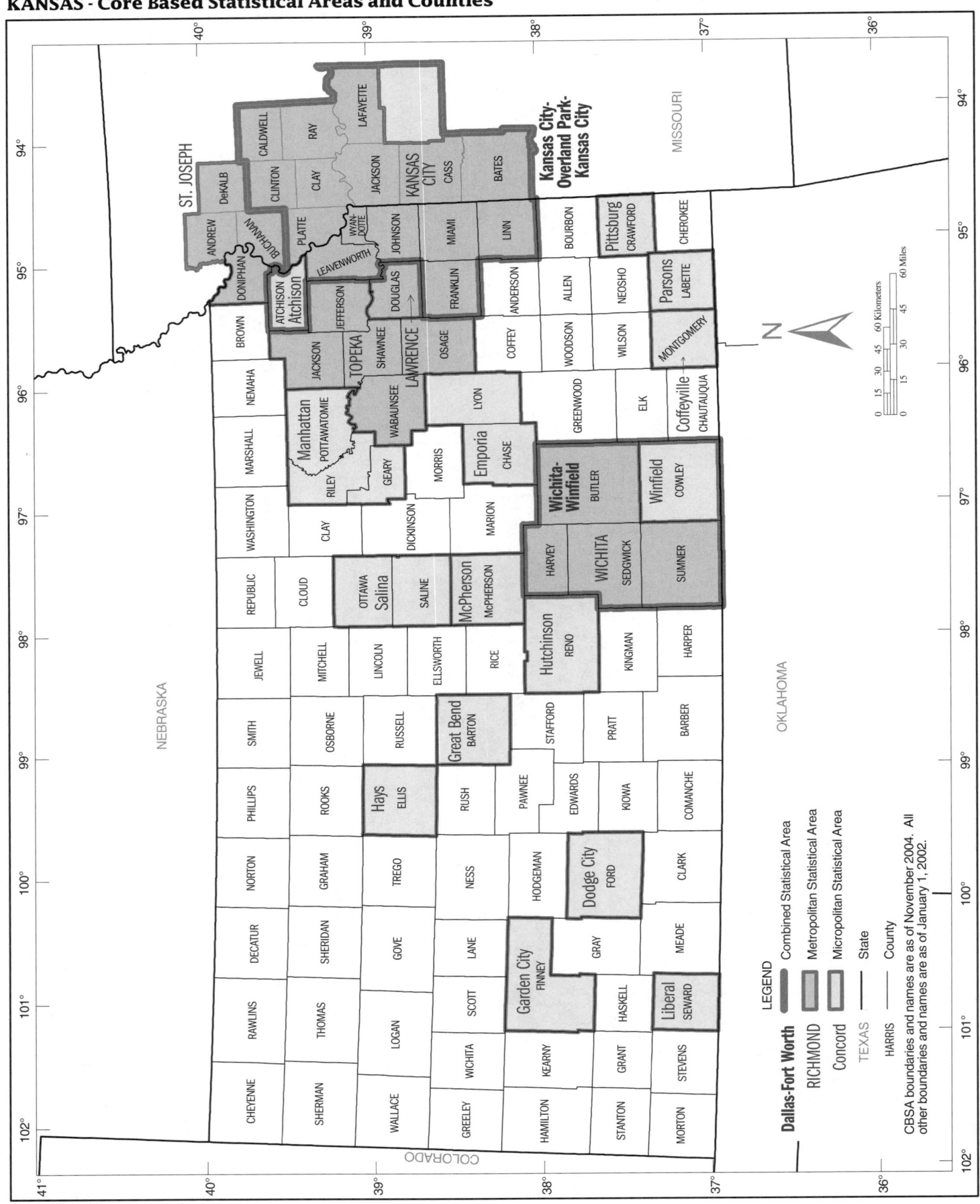

# KENTUCKY - Core Based Statistical Areas and Counties

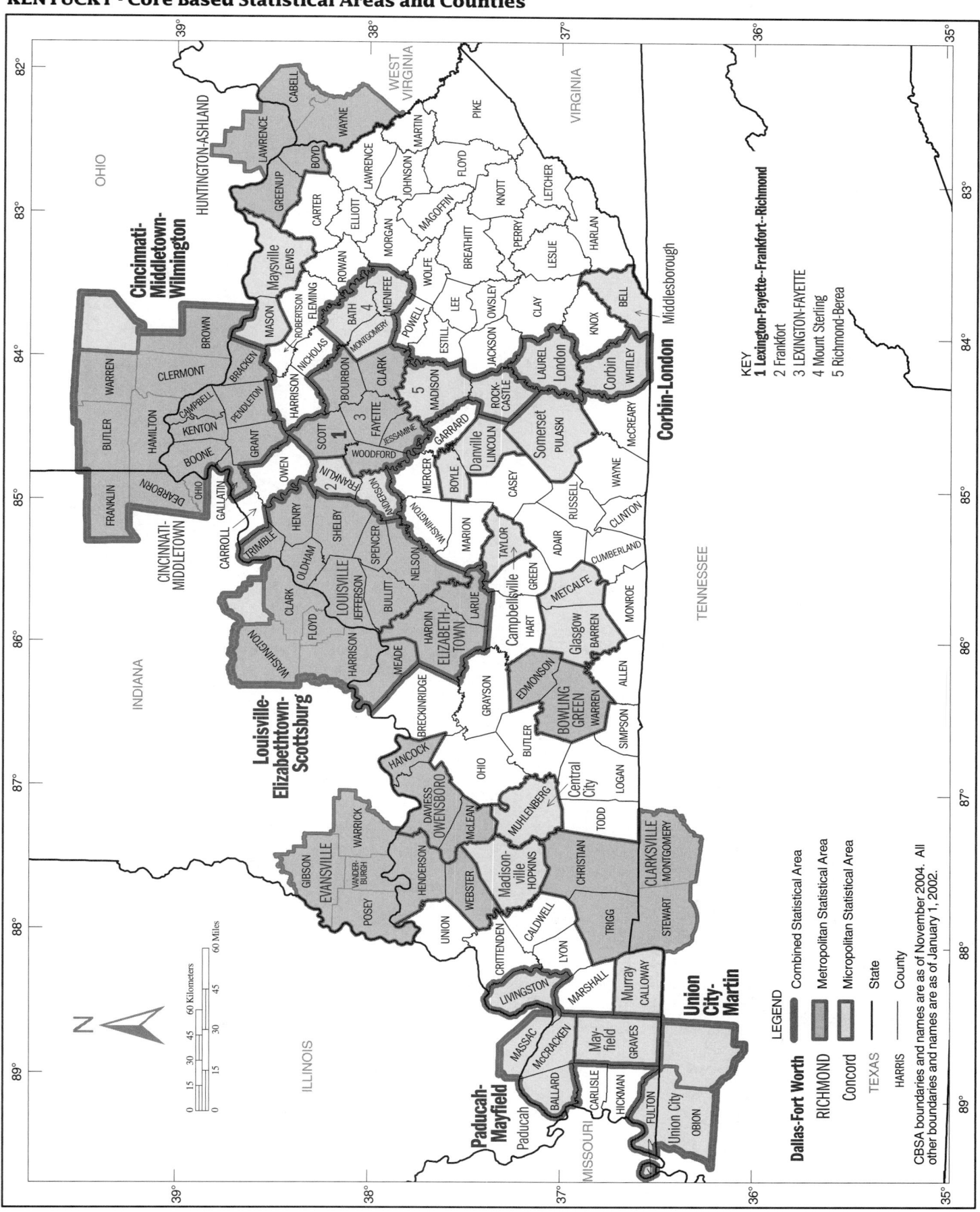

KEY
**1 Lexington-Fayette-Frankfort--Richmond**
2 Frankfort
3 LEXINGTON-FAYETTE
4 Mount Sterling
5 Richmond-Berea

LEGEND

**Dallas-Fort Worth** — Combined Statistical Area
**RICHMOND** — Metropolitan Statistical Area
Concord — Micropolitan Statistical Area
TEXAS — State
HARRIS — County

CBSA boundaries and names are as of November 2004. All
other boundaries and names are as of January 1, 2002.

# LOUISIANA - Core Based Statistical Areas and Parishes

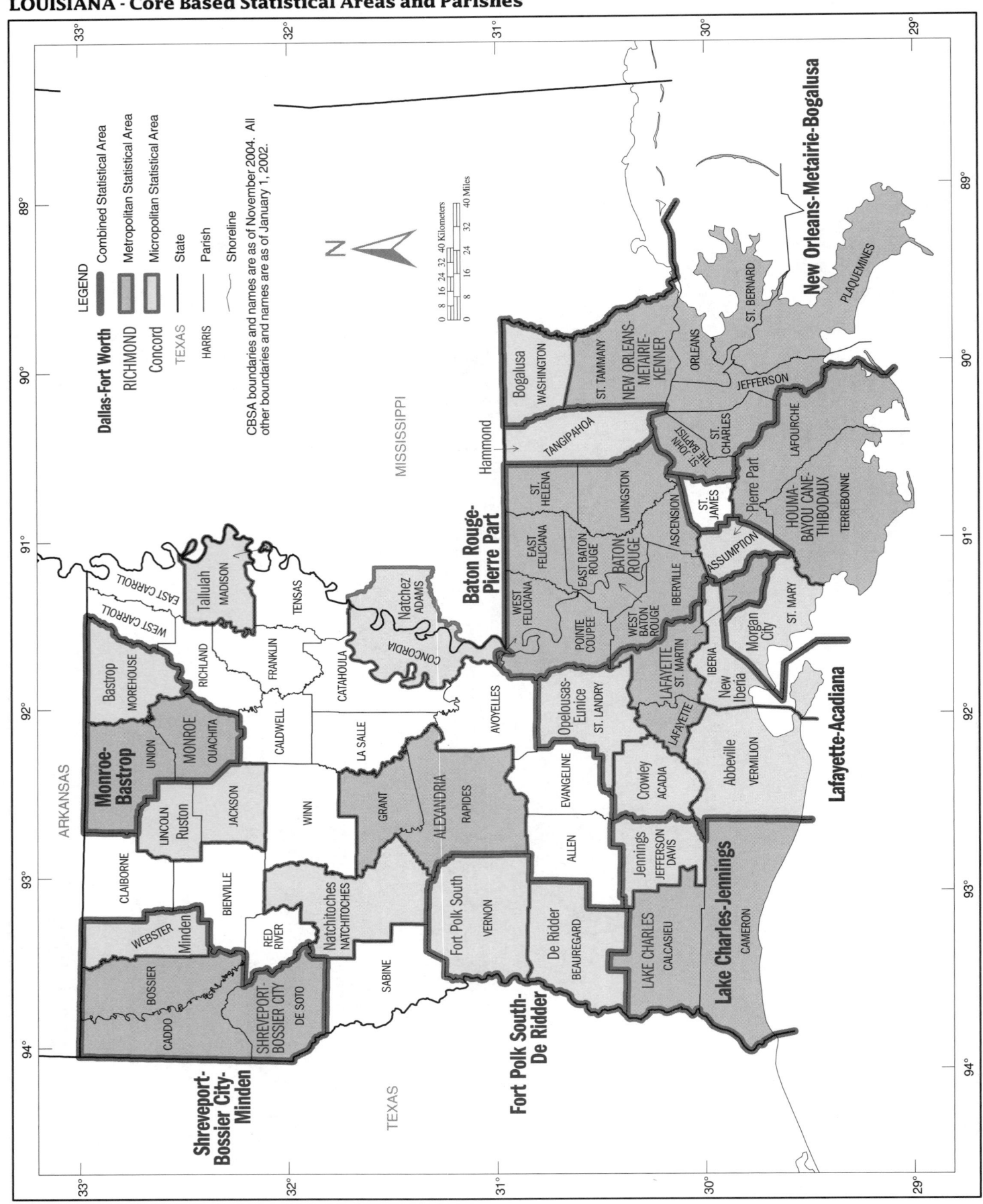

# MAINE - Core Based Statistical Areas and Counties

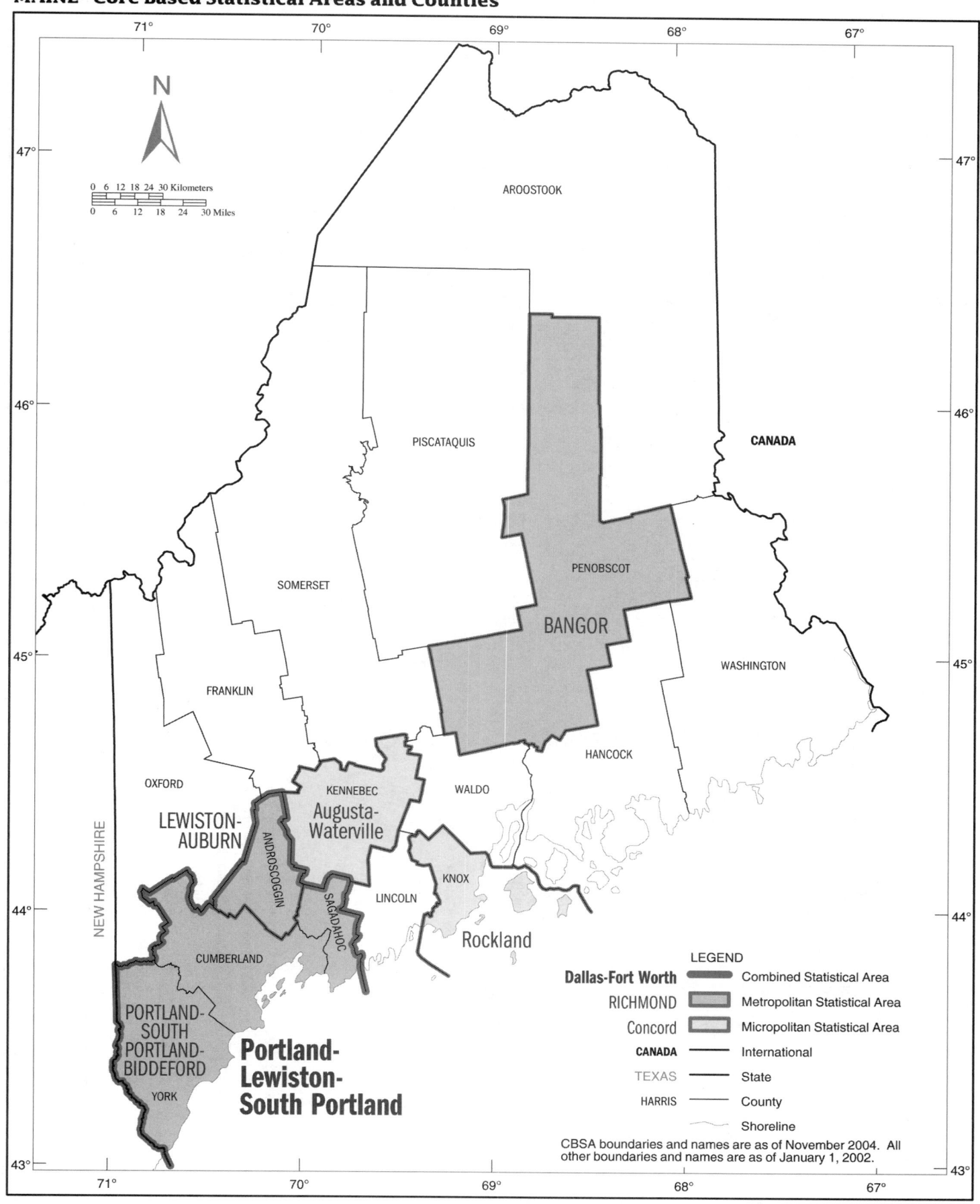

LEGEND

**Dallas-Fort Worth** — Combined Statistical Area

RICHMOND — Metropolitan Statistical Area

Concord — Micropolitan Statistical Area

**CANADA** — International

TEXAS — State

HARRIS — County

— Shoreline

CBSA boundaries and names are as of November 2004. All other boundaries and names are as of January 1, 2002.

U.S. DEPARTMENT OF COMMERCE Economics and Statistics Administration  U.S. Census Bureau

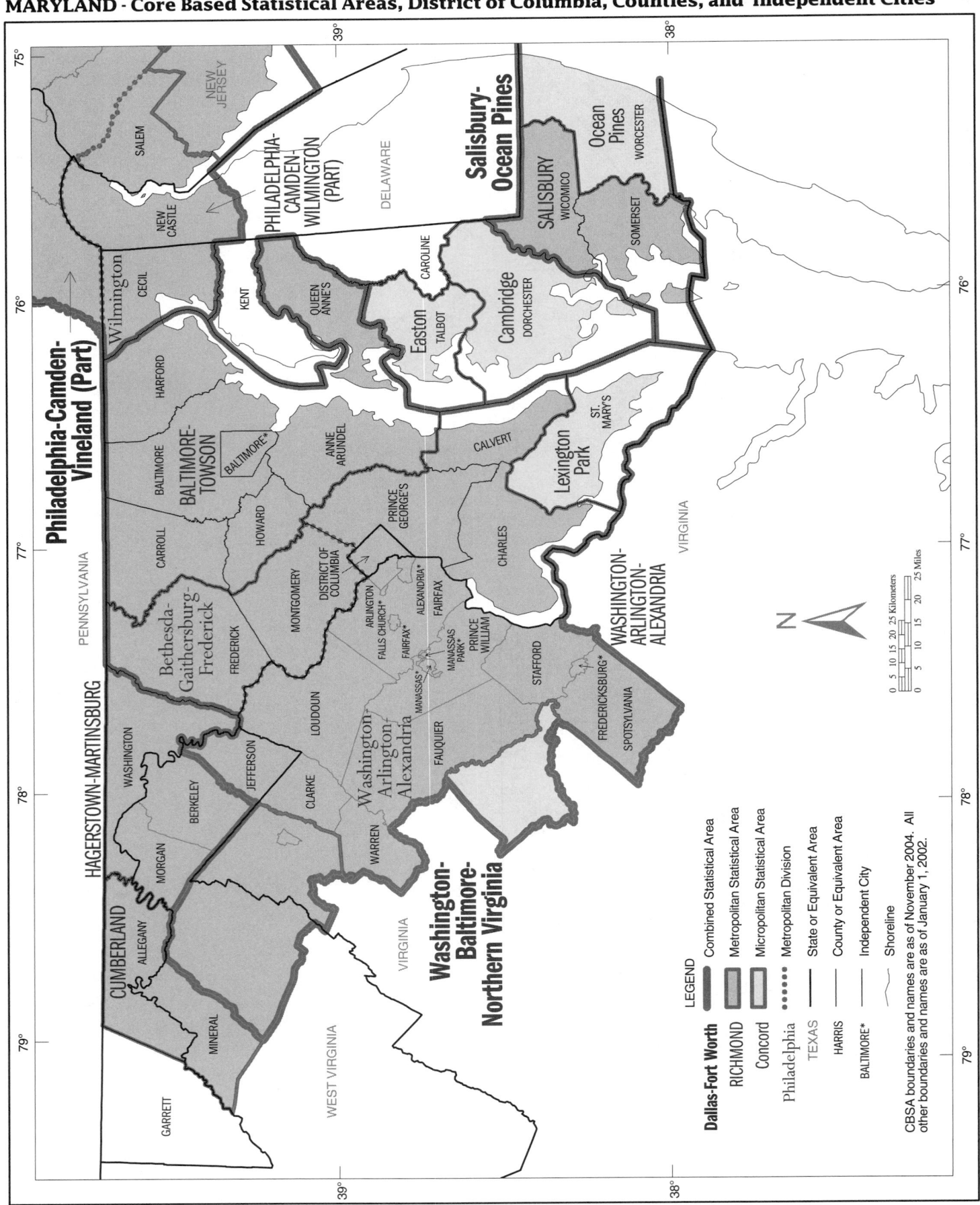

# MASSACHUSETTS - Core Based Statistical Areas and Counties

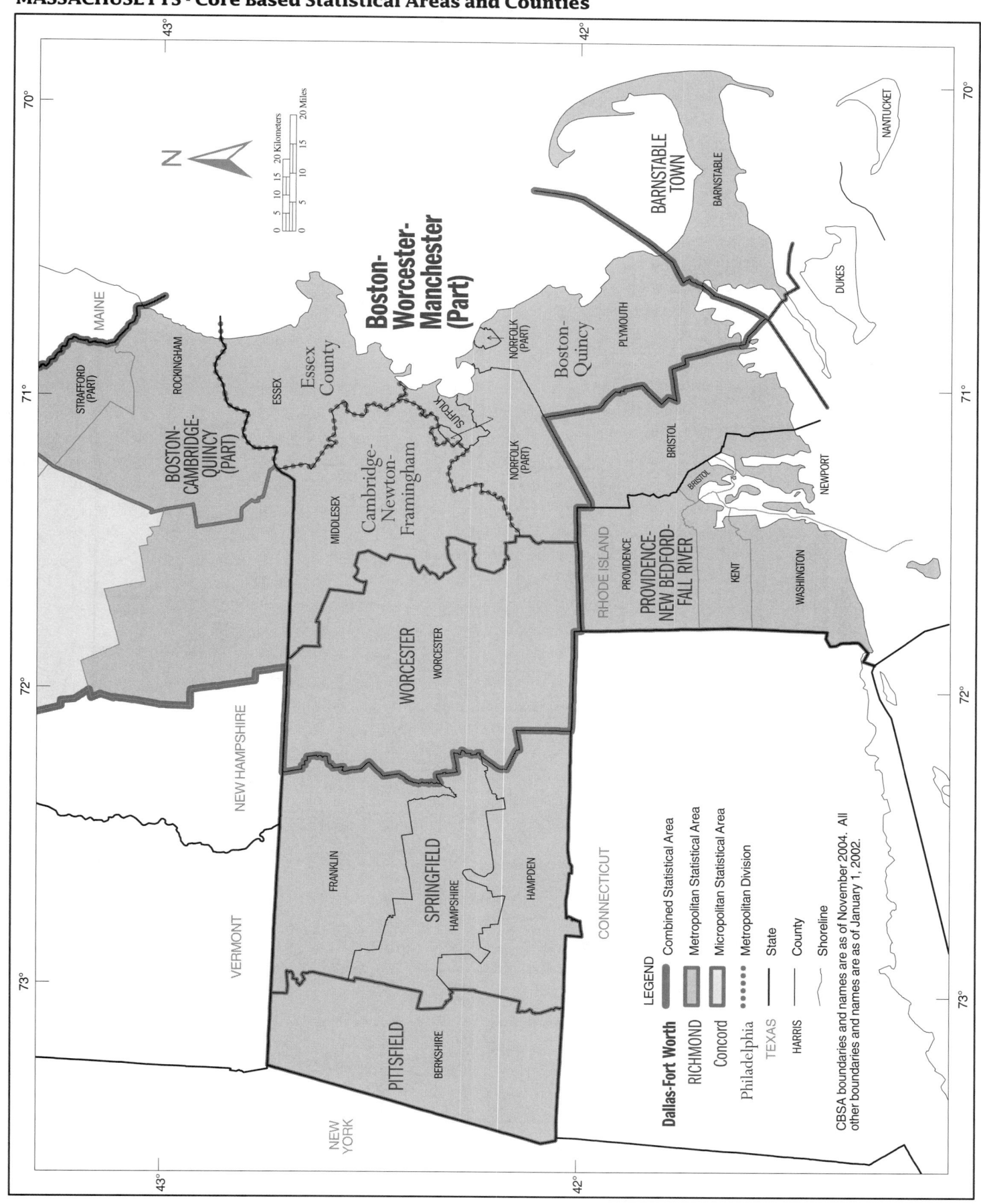

# MICHIGAN - Core Based Statistical Areas and Counties

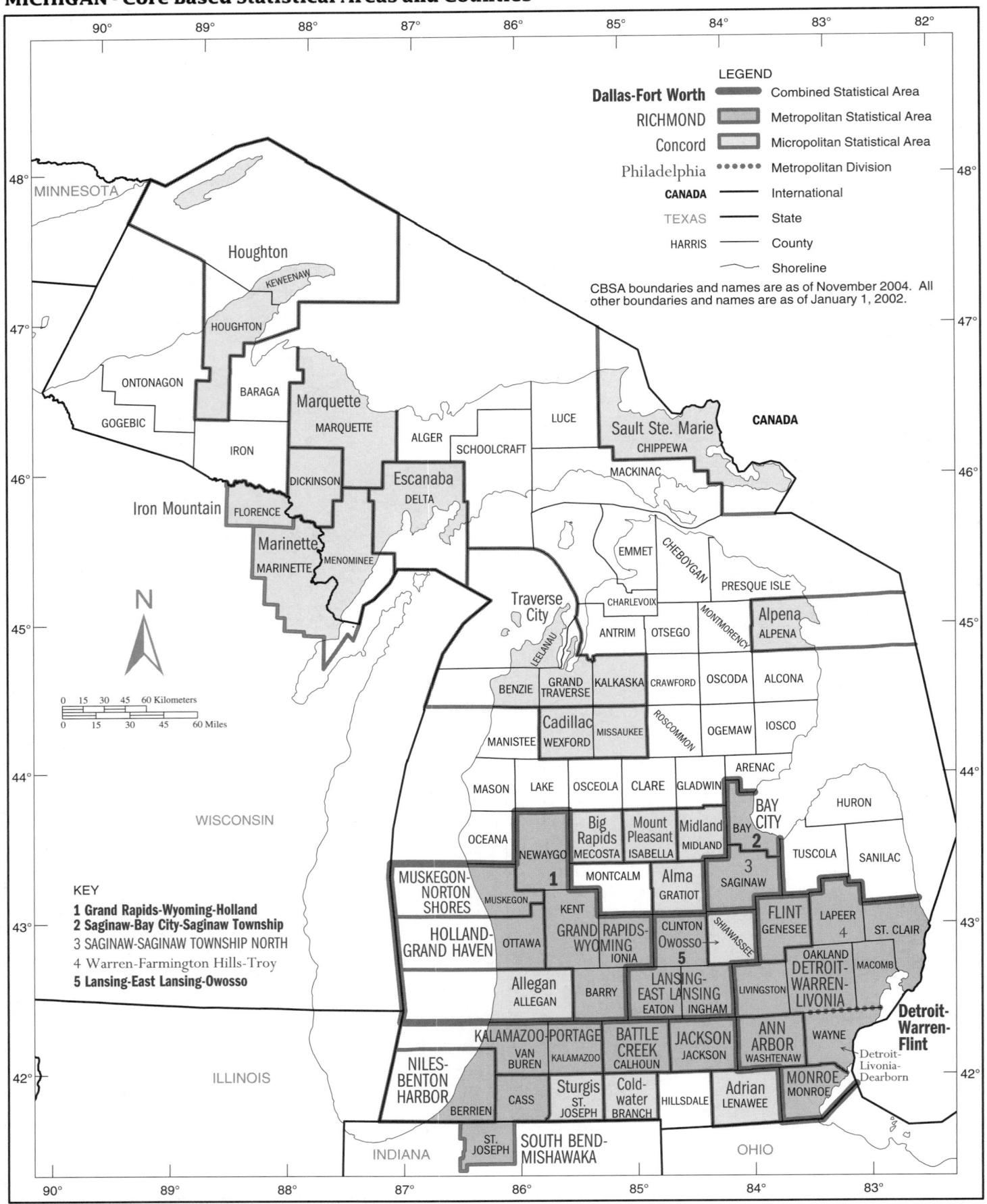

LEGEND

**Dallas-Fort Worth** — Combined Statistical Area
RICHMOND — Metropolitan Statistical Area
Concord — Micropolitan Statistical Area
Philadelphia ••••• Metropolitan Division
**CANADA** — International
TEXAS — State
HARRIS — County
— Shoreline

CBSA boundaries and names are as of November 2004. All other boundaries and names are as of January 1, 2002.

KEY

**1 Grand Rapids-Wyoming-Holland**
**2 Saginaw-Bay City-Saginaw Township**
3 SAGINAW-SAGINAW TOWNSHIP NORTH
4 Warren-Farmington Hills-Troy
**5 Lansing-East Lansing-Owosso**

# MINNESOTA - Core Based Statistical Areas and Counties

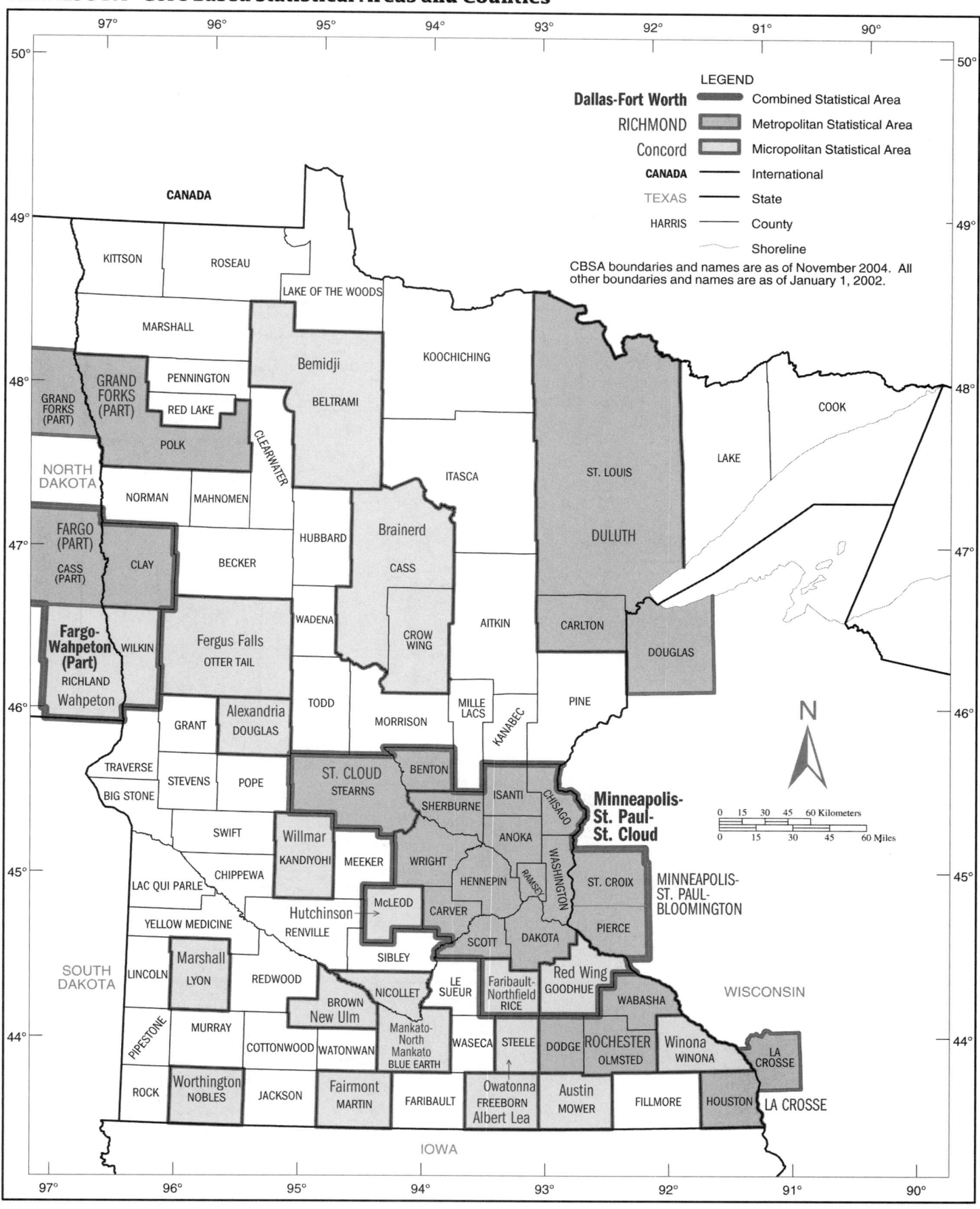

**LEGEND**

| Dallas-Fort Worth | Combined Statistical Area |
| RICHMOND | Metropolitan Statistical Area |
| Concord | Micropolitan Statistical Area |
| **CANADA** | International |
| TEXAS | State |
| HARRIS | County |
| | Shoreline |

CBSA boundaries and names are as of November 2004. All other boundaries and names are as of January 1, 2002.

# MISSISSIPPI - Core Based Statistical Areas and Counties

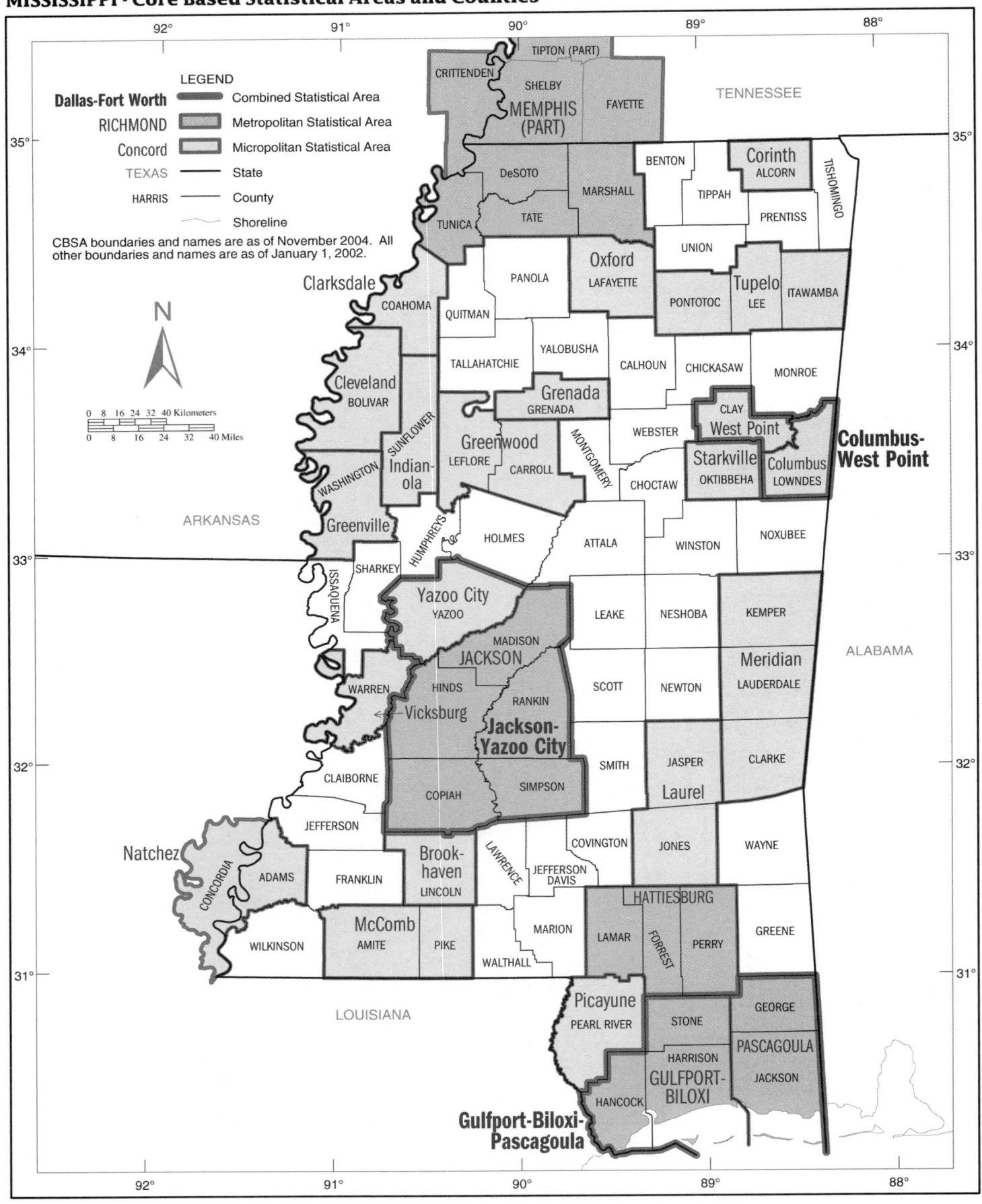

U.S. DEPARTMENT OF COMMERCE Economics and Statistics Administration  U.S. Census Bureau

# MISSOURI - Core Based Statistical Areas, Counties, and Independent City

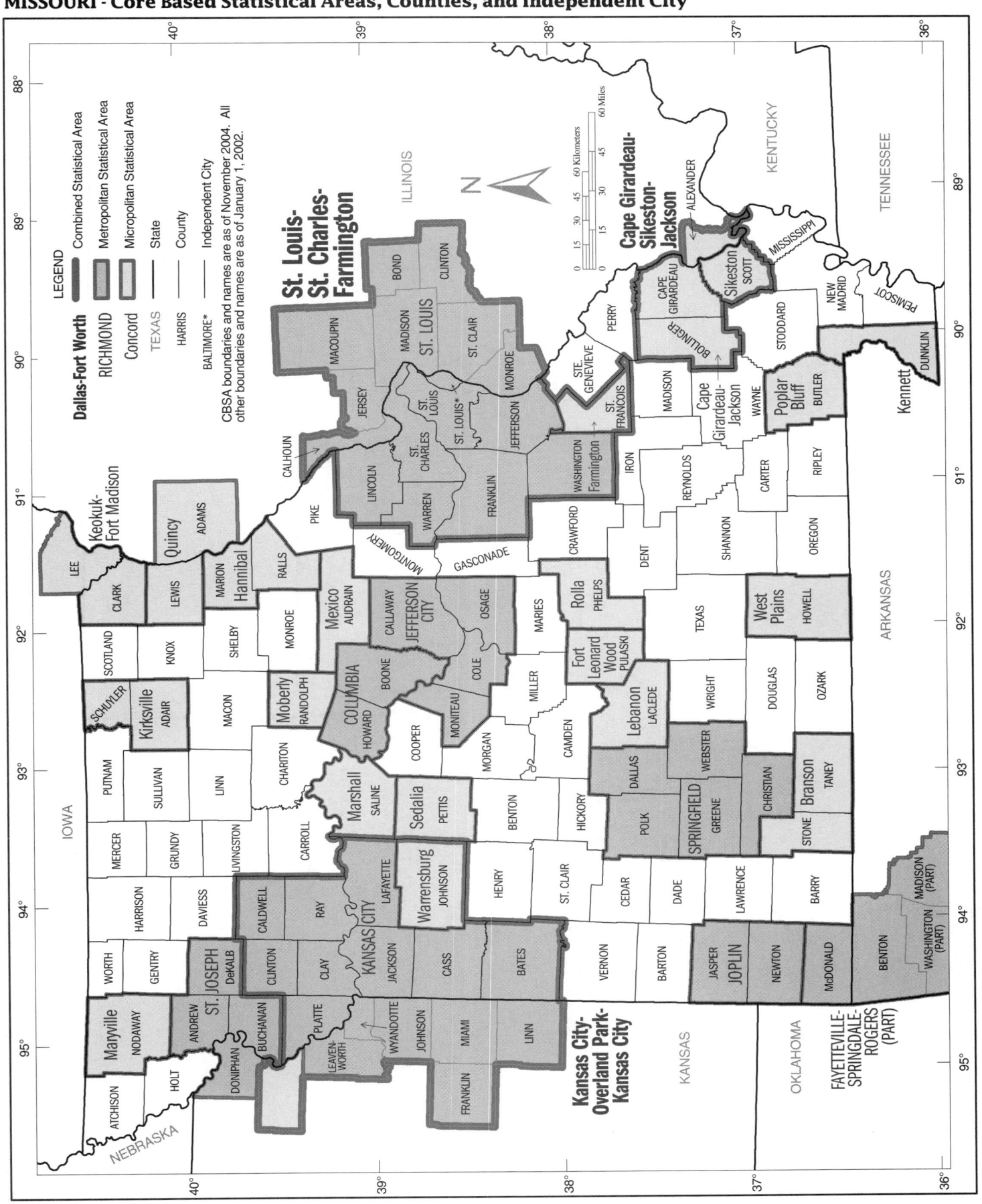

# MONTANA - Core Based Statistical Areas and Counties

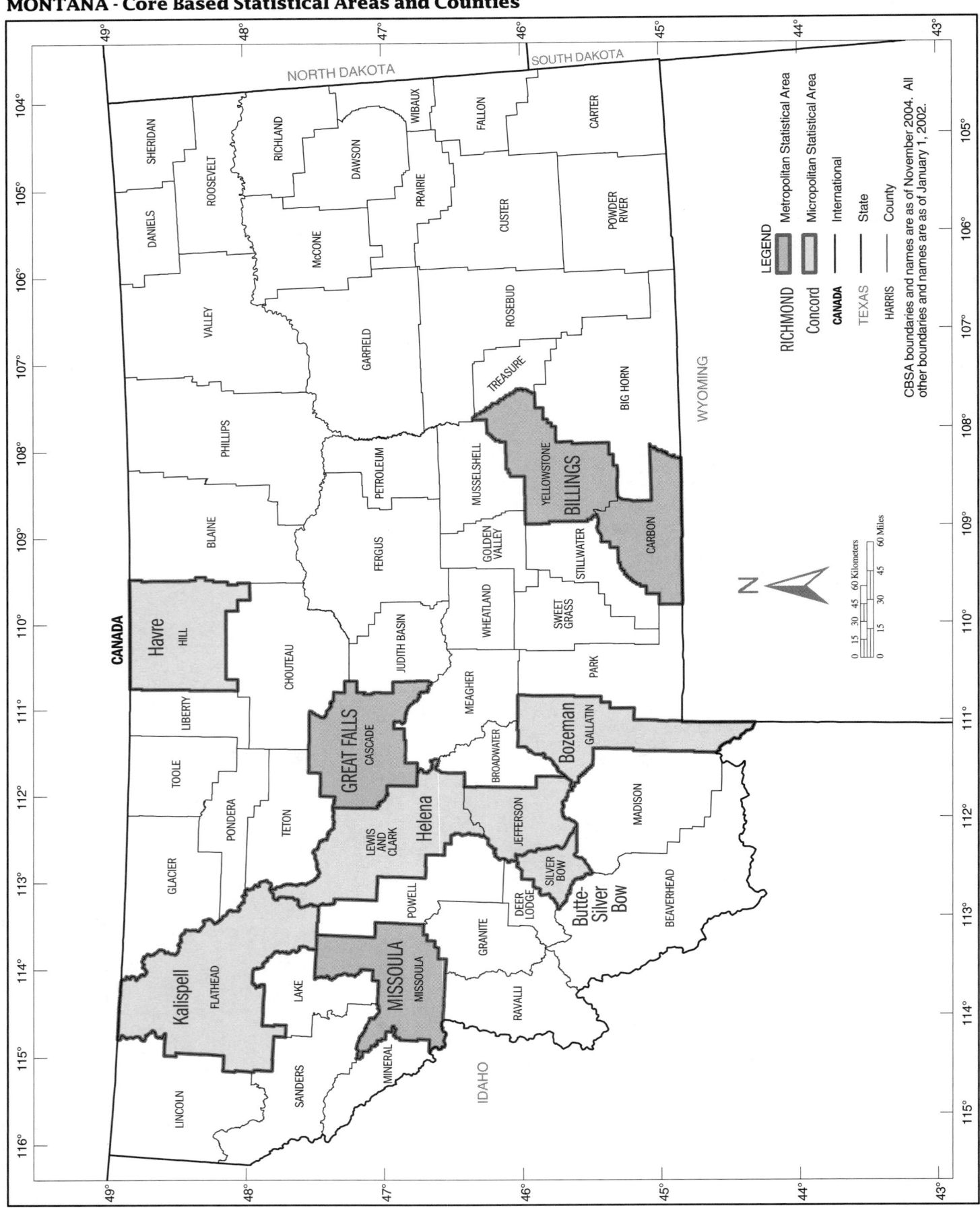

# NEBRASKA - Core Based Statistical Areas and Counties

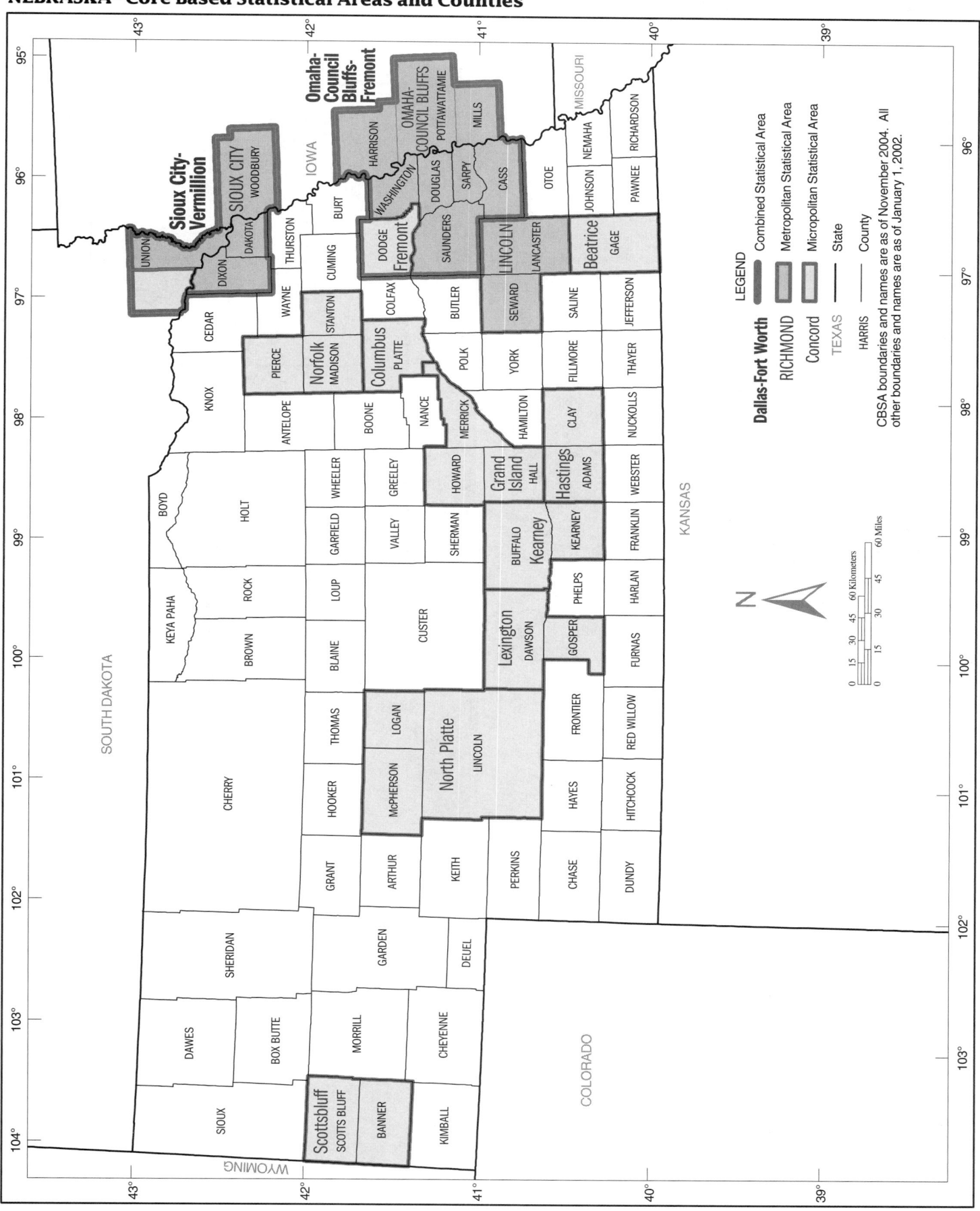

# NEVADA - Core Based Statistical Areas, Counties, and Independent City

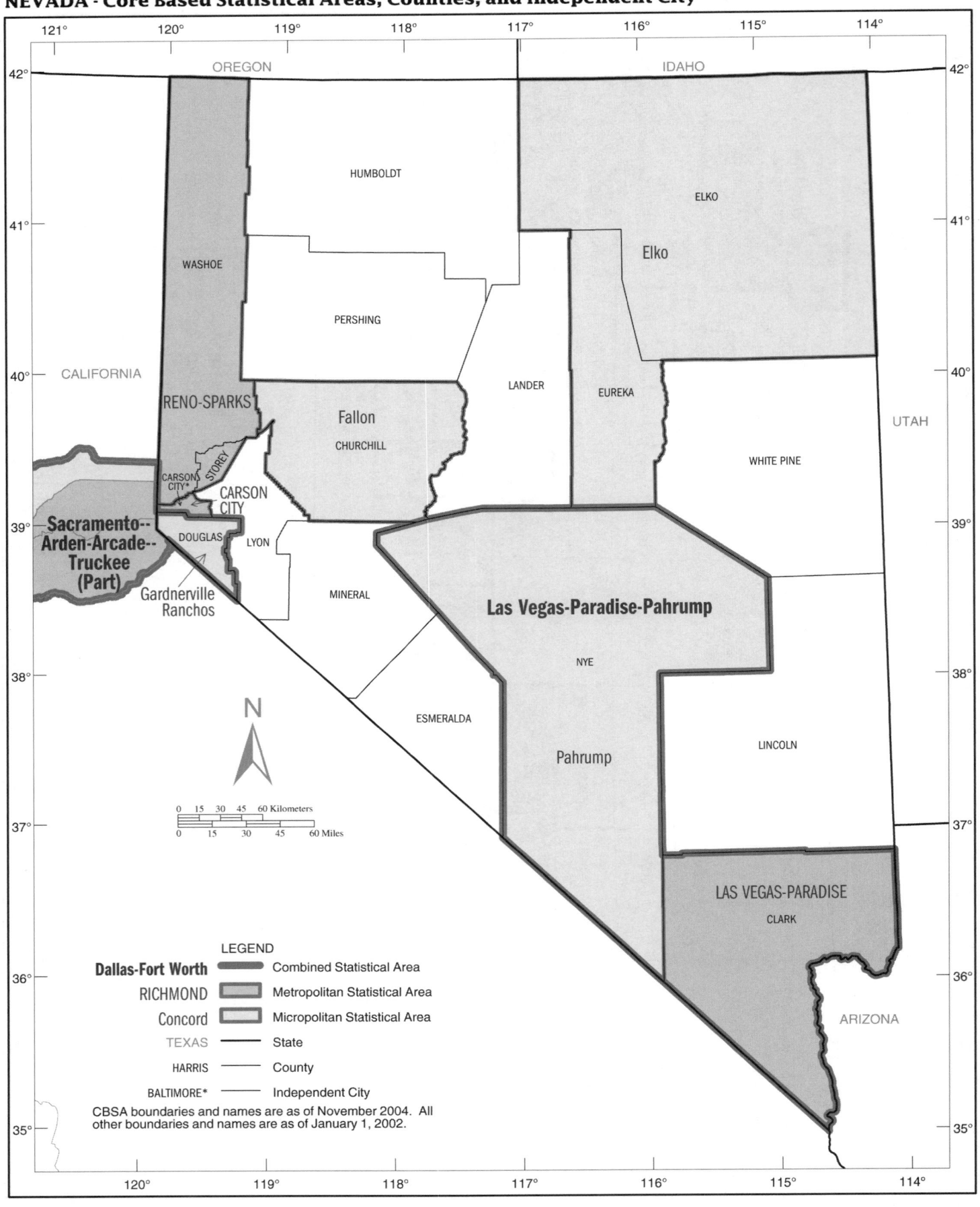

LEGEND

**Dallas-Fort Worth** ▬ Combined Statistical Area

RICHMOND ▬ Metropolitan Statistical Area

Concord ▯ Micropolitan Statistical Area

TEXAS ── State

HARRIS ── County

BALTIMORE* ── Independent City

CBSA boundaries and names are as of November 2004. All other boundaries and names are as of January 1, 2002.

# NEW HAMPSHIRE - Core Based Statistical Areas and Counties

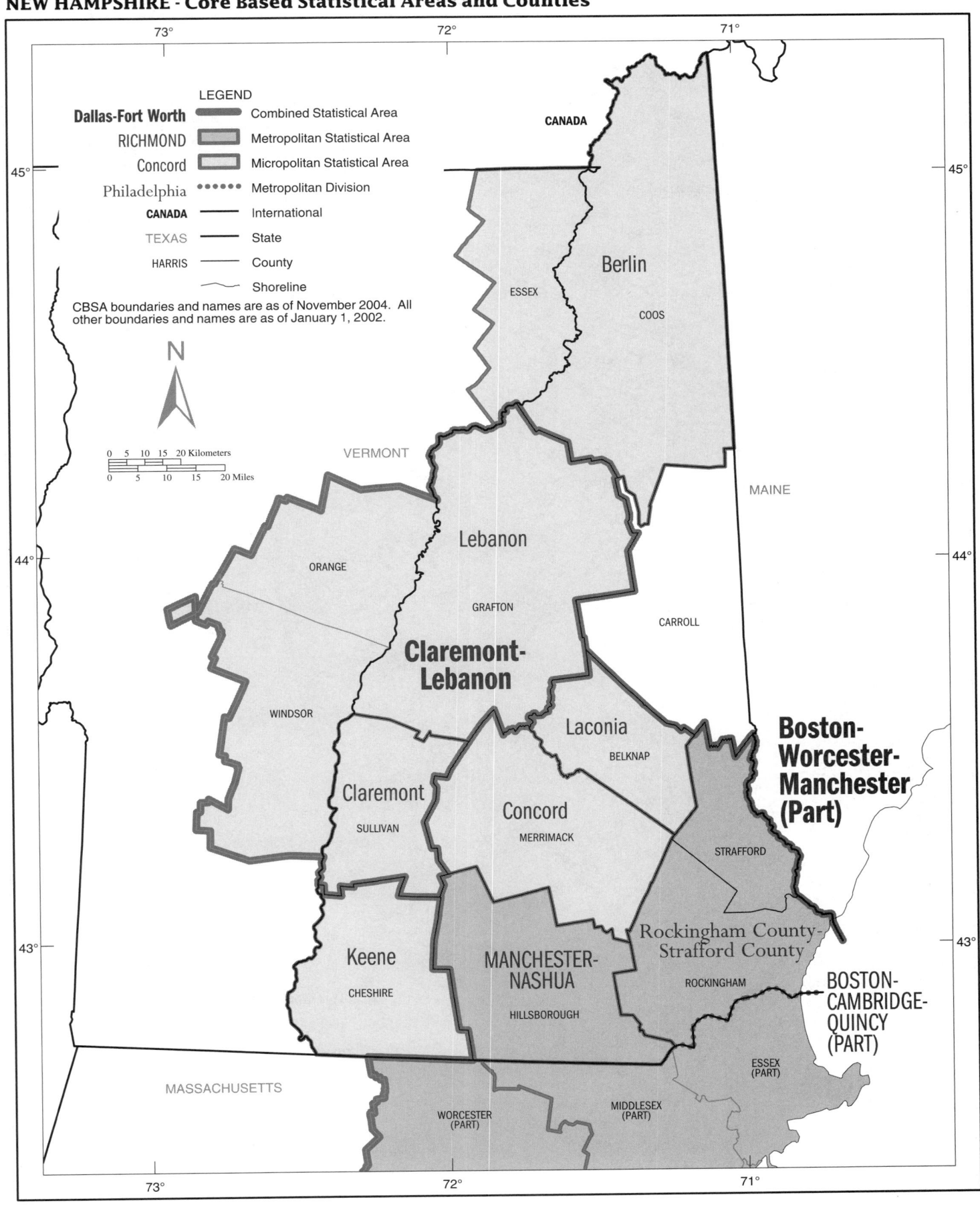

LEGEND

**Dallas-Fort Worth** — Combined Statistical Area
RICHMOND — Metropolitan Statistical Area
Concord — Micropolitan Statistical Area
Philadelphia ••••• Metropolitan Division
**CANADA** — International
TEXAS — State
HARRIS — County
— Shoreline

CBSA boundaries and names are as of November 2004. All other boundaries and names are as of January 1, 2002.

N

0  5  10  15  20 Kilometers
0  5  10  15  20 Miles

CANADA

VERMONT

MAINE

MASSACHUSETTS

**Berlin**
ESSEX
COOS

**Lebanon**
ORANGE
GRAFTON

CARROLL

**Claremont-Lebanon**

WINDSOR

**Laconia**
BELKNAP

**Boston-Worcester-Manchester (Part)**

**Claremont**
SULLIVAN

**Concord**
MERRIMACK

STRAFFORD

*Rockingham County-Strafford County*

**Keene**
CHESHIRE

**MANCHESTER-NASHUA**
HILLSBOROUGH

ROCKINGHAM

BOSTON-CAMBRIDGE-QUINCY (PART)

ESSEX (PART)

WORCESTER (PART)

MIDDLESEX (PART)

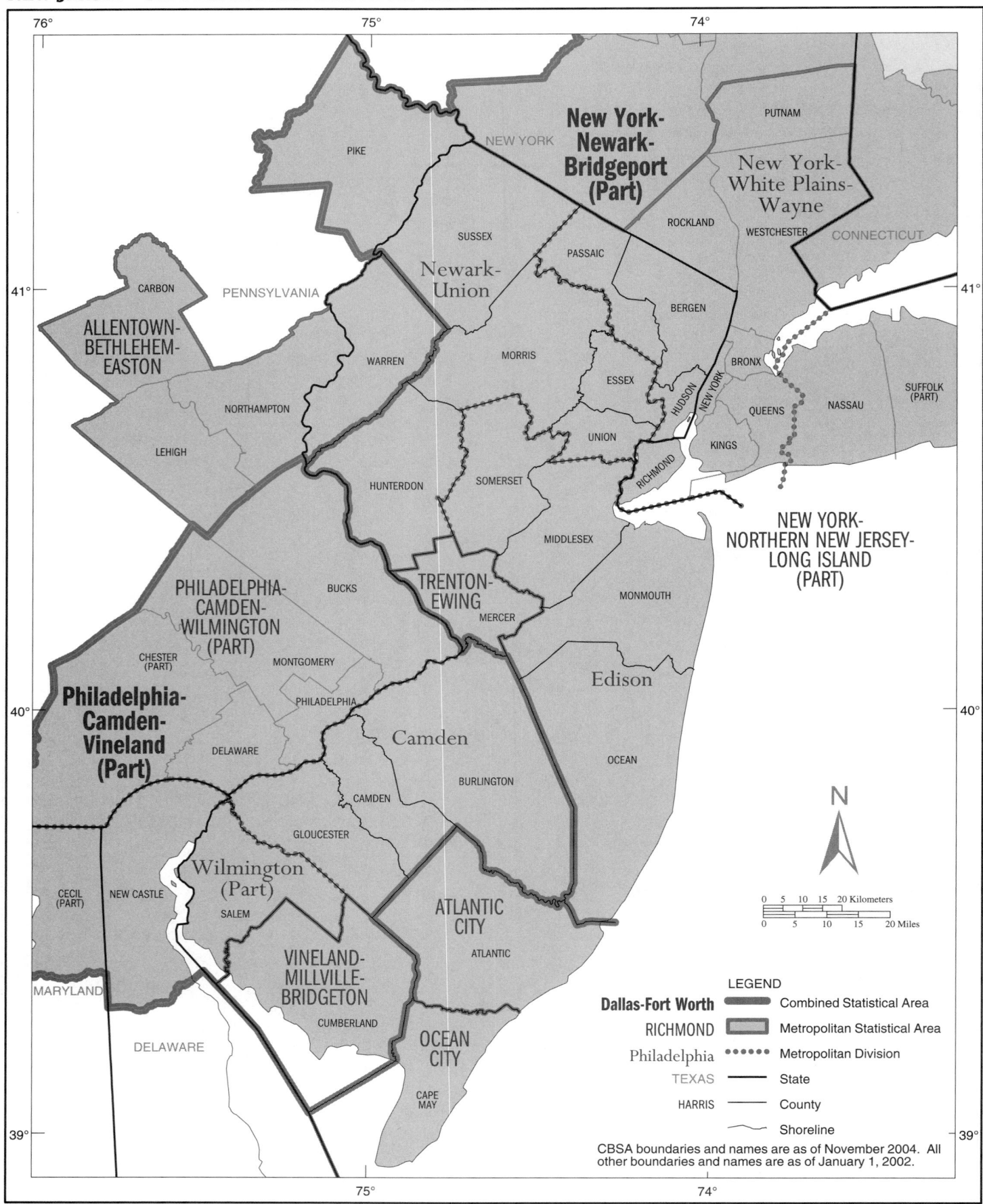

# NEW MEXICO - Core Based Statistical Areas and Counties

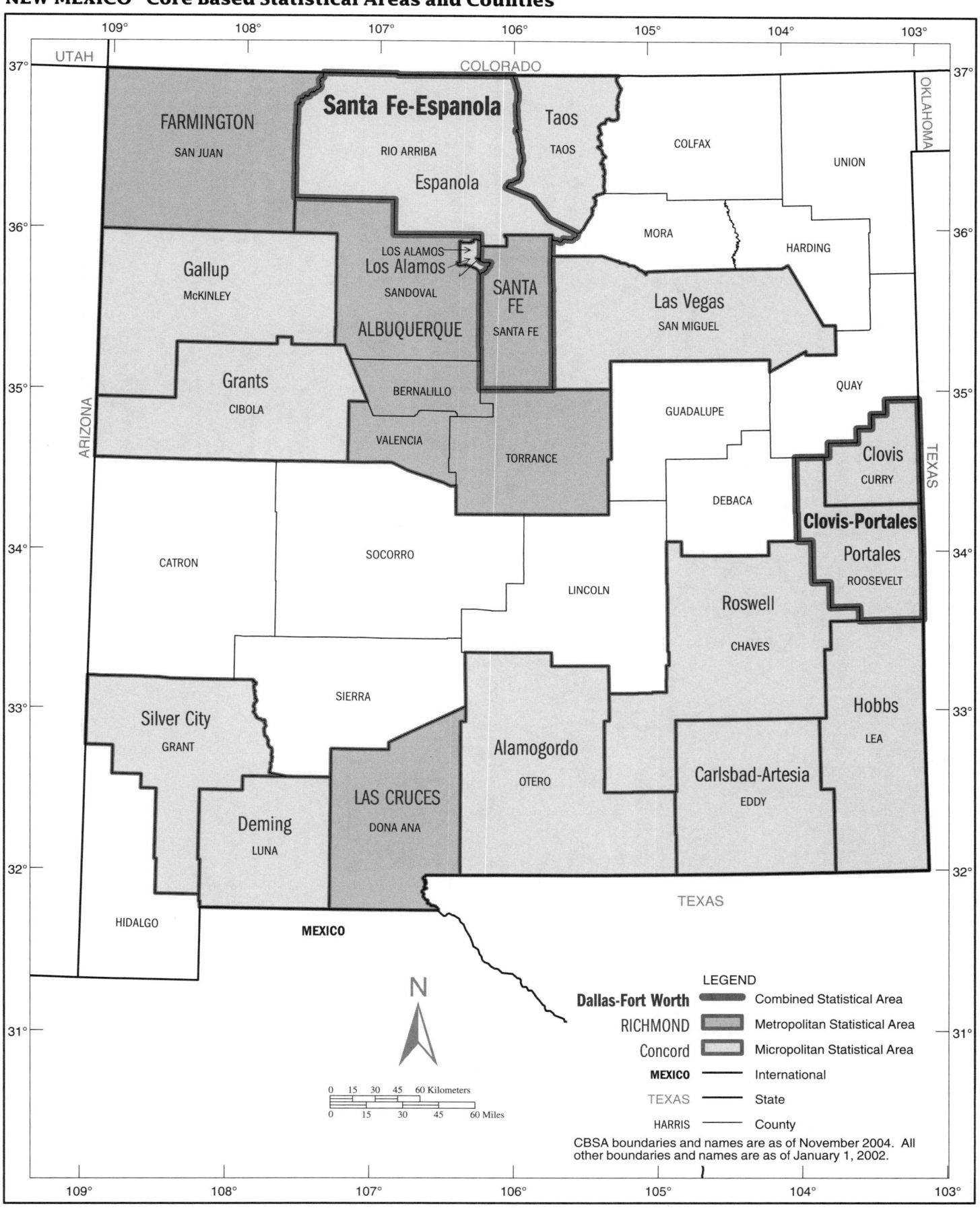

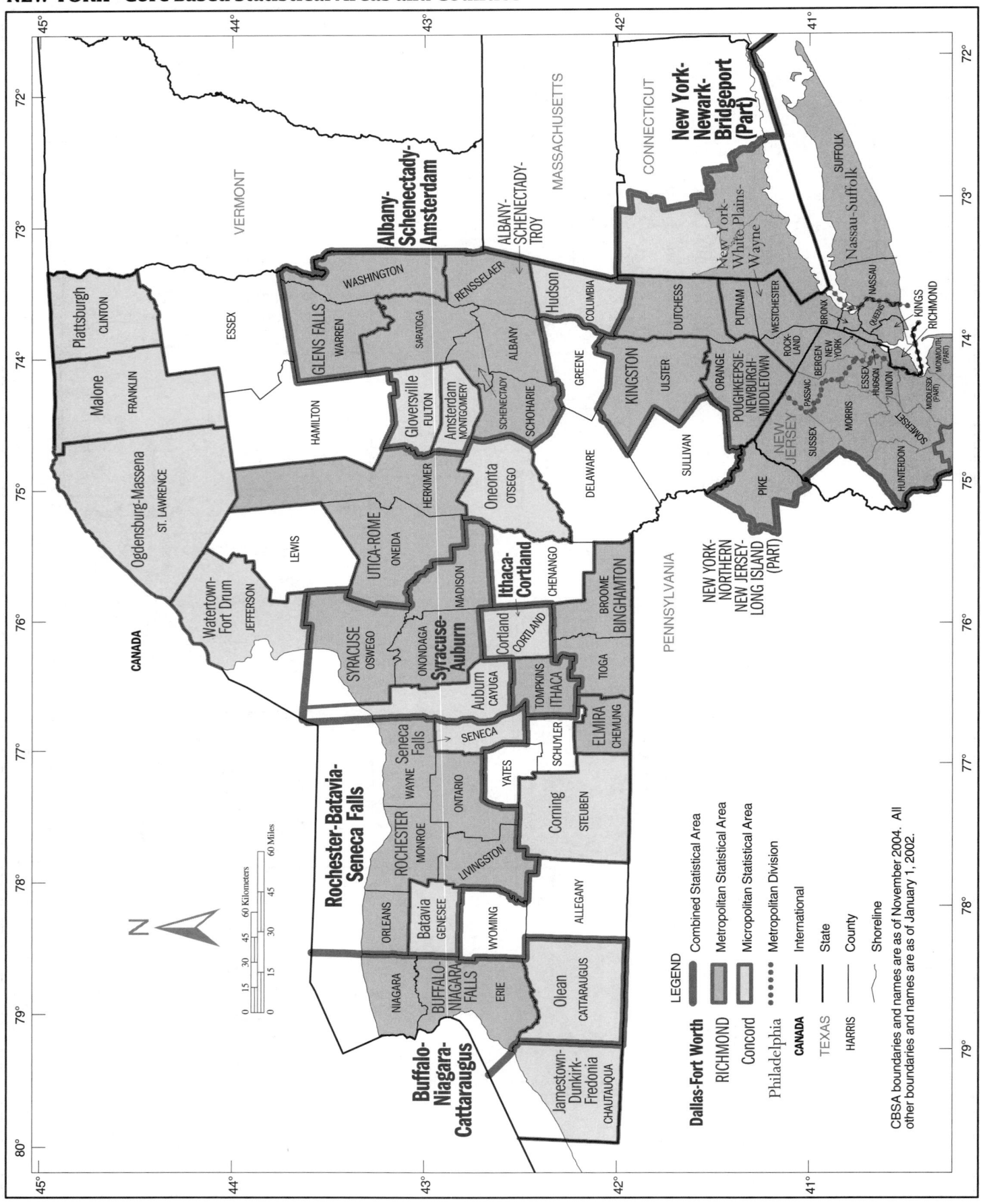

# NORTH CAROLINA - Core Based Statistical Areas, Counties, and Independent Cities

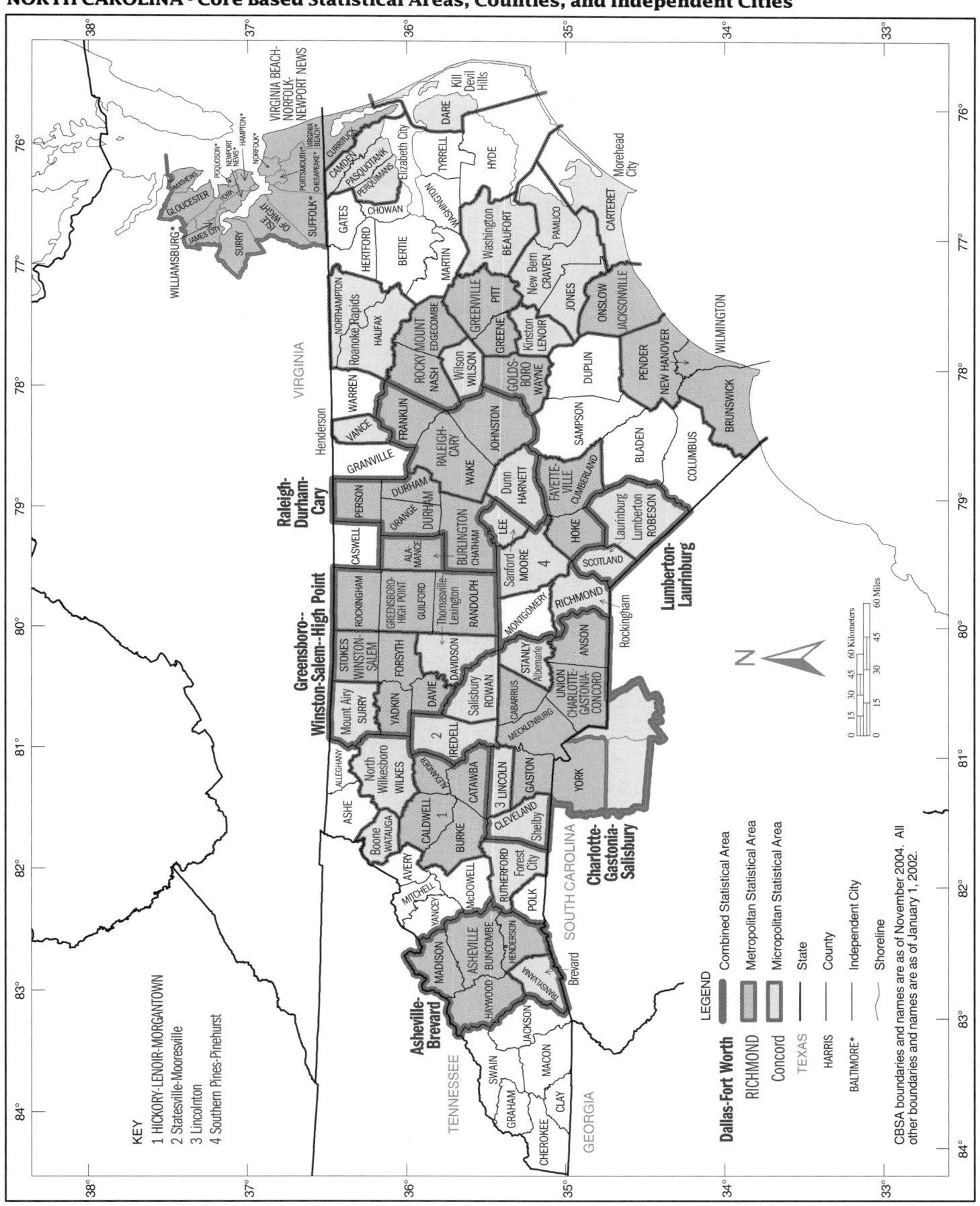

KEY
1 HICKORY-LENOIR-MORGANTOWN
2 Statesville-Mooresville
3 Lincolnton
4 Southern Pines-Pinehurst

LEGEND

**Dallas-Fort Worth** Combined Statistical Area
RICHMOND Metropolitan Statistical Area
Concord Micropolitan Statistical Area
State
County
HARRIS Independent City
BALTIMORE* Shoreline

CBSA boundaries and names are as of November 2004. All other boundaries and names are as of January 1, 2002.

# NORTH DAKOTA - Core Based Statistical Areas and Counties

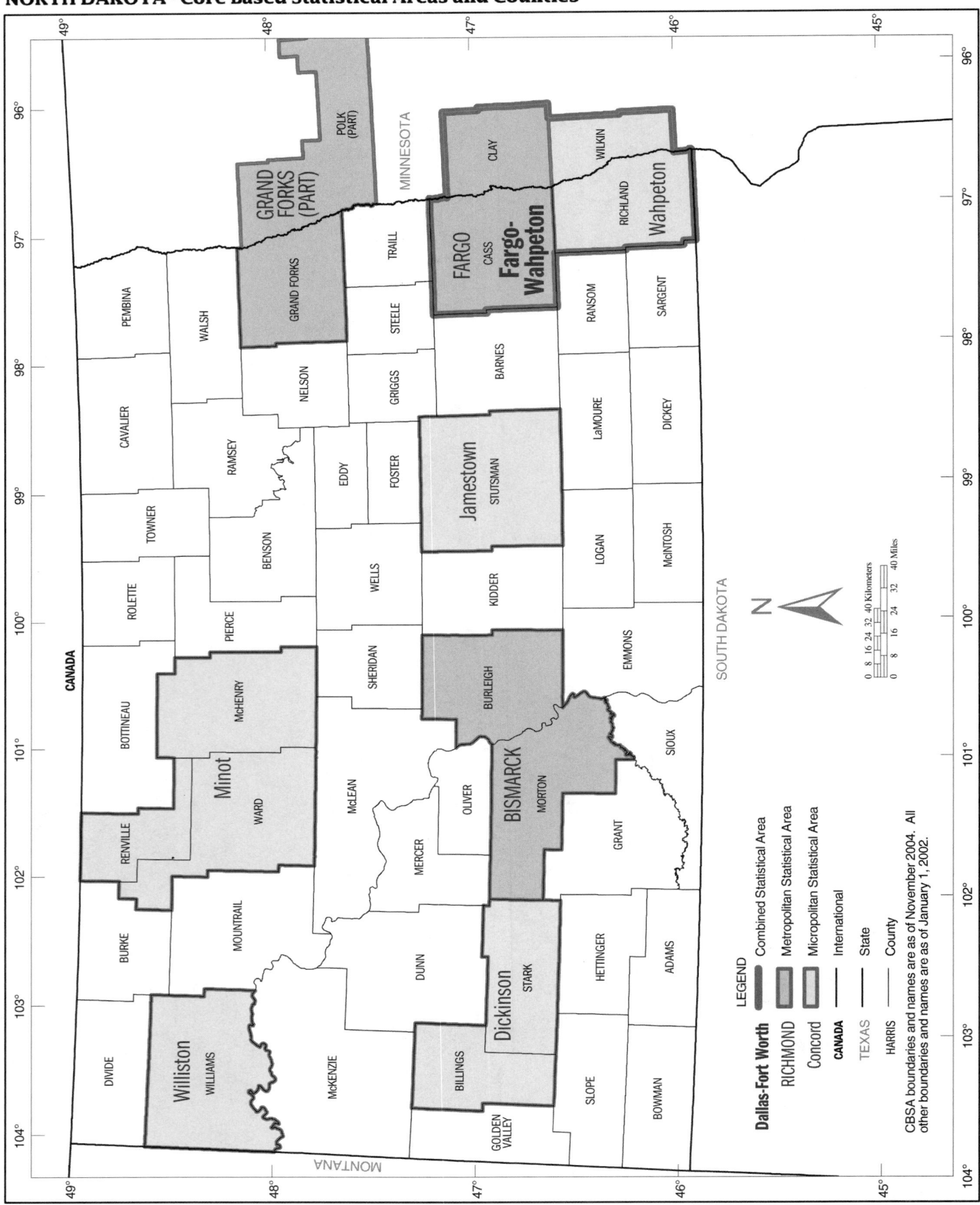

# OHIO - Core Based Statistical Areas and Counties

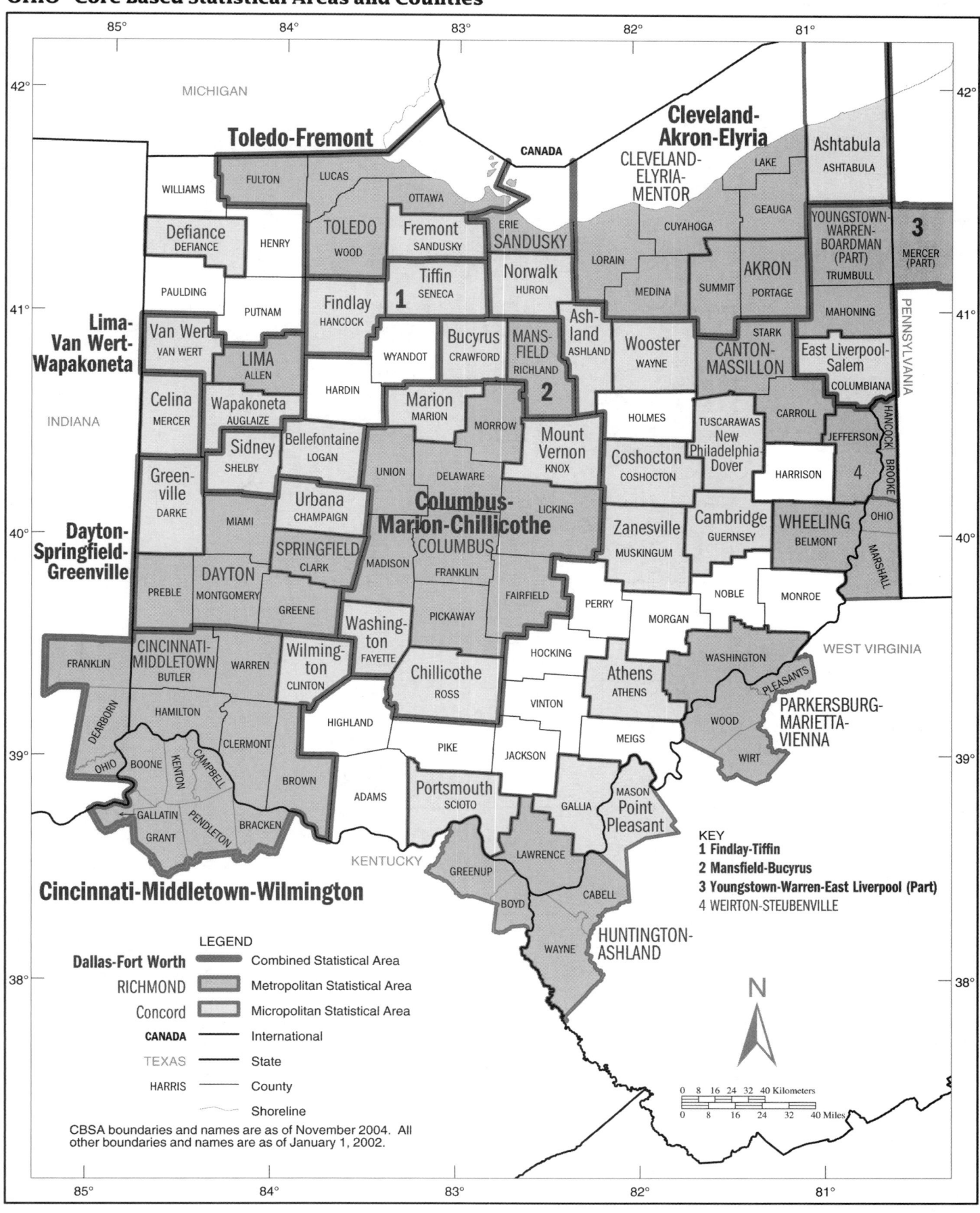

**Toledo-Fremont**

**Cleveland-Akron-Elyria**

CLEVELAND-ELYRIA-MENTOR

Ashtabula

ASHTABULA

MICHIGAN

CANADA

WILLIAMS
FULTON
LUCAS
OTTAWA
TOLEDO
WOOD
Fremont
SANDUSKY
ERIE
SANDUSKY
Norwalk
HURON
LORAIN
CUYAHOGA
LAKE
GEAUGA

Defiance
DEFIANCE
HENRY

**Lima-Van Wert-Wapakoneta**

PAULDING
PUTNAM

Tiffin
SENECA

Findlay
HANCOCK

**1**

MEDINA
SUMMIT
Akron
PORTAGE

YOUNGSTOWN-WARREN-BOARDMAN (PART)
TRUMBULL

**3**
MERCER (PART)

PENNSYLVANIA

Van Wert
VAN WERT

LIMA
ALLEN

WYANDOT

Bucyrus
CRAWFORD

MANS-FIELD
RICHLAND

Ash-land
ASHLAND

Wooster
WAYNE

MAHONING

STARK

CANTON-MASSILLON

East Liverpool-Salem
COLUMBIANA

INDIANA

HARDIN

**2**

Celina
MERCER

Wapakoneta
AUGLAIZE

Marion
MARION

MORROW

Mount Vernon
KNOX

HOLMES

Coshocton
COSHOCTON

New Philadelphia-Dover
TUSCARAWAS

CARROLL

HARRISON

JEFFERSON

**4**

HANCOCK
BROOKE

Sidney
SHELBY

Bellefontaine
LOGAN

UNION

DELAWARE

Greenville
DARKE

MIAMI

Urbana
CHAMPAIGN

**Columbus-Marion-Chillicothe**

COLUMBUS

LICKING

Zanesville
MUSKINGUM

Cambridge
GUERNSEY

**WHEELING**
BELMONT

OHIO

**Dayton-Springfield-Greenville**

PREBLE

SPRINGFIELD
CLARK

DAYTON
MONTGOMERY

GREENE

MADISON

Franklin
FRANKLIN

FAIRFIELD

PERRY

MORGAN

NOBLE

MONROE

MARSHALL

WEST VIRGINIA

FRANKLIN

CINCINNATI-MIDDLETOWN
BUTLER

WARREN

Wilmington
CLINTON

Washington
FAYETTE

PICKAWAY

HOCKING

Athens
ATHENS

Washington
WOOD

PLEASANTS

**PARKERSBURG-MARIETTA-VIENNA**

HAMILTON

CLERMONT

HIGHLAND

Chillicothe
ROSS

VINTON

MEIGS

WIRT

DEARBORN

OHIO
BOONE
KENTON
CAMPBELL

PIKE

JACKSON

PARKERSBURG-MARIETTA-VIENNA

PELLASANTS

GALLATIN
GRANT
PENDLETON
BRACKEN

BROWN

ADAMS

Portsmouth
SCIOTO

GALLIA

MASON

Point Pleasant

**KEY**
1 Findlay-Tiffin
2 Mansfield-Bucyrus
3 Youngstown-Warren-East Liverpool (Part)
4 WEIRTON-STEUBENVILLE

**Cincinnati-Middletown-Wilmington**

KENTUCKY

GREENUP

LAWRENCE

CABELL

BOYD

WAYNE

**HUNTINGTON-ASHLAND**

N

## LEGEND

| | |
|---|---|
| **Dallas-Fort Worth** | Combined Statistical Area |
| RICHMOND | Metropolitan Statistical Area |
| Concord | Micropolitan Statistical Area |
| **CANADA** | International |
| TEXAS | State |
| HARRIS | County |
| | Shoreline |

CBSA boundaries and names are as of November 2004. All other boundaries and names are as of January 1, 2002.

0  8  16  24  32  40 Kilometers
0  8  16  24  32  40 Miles

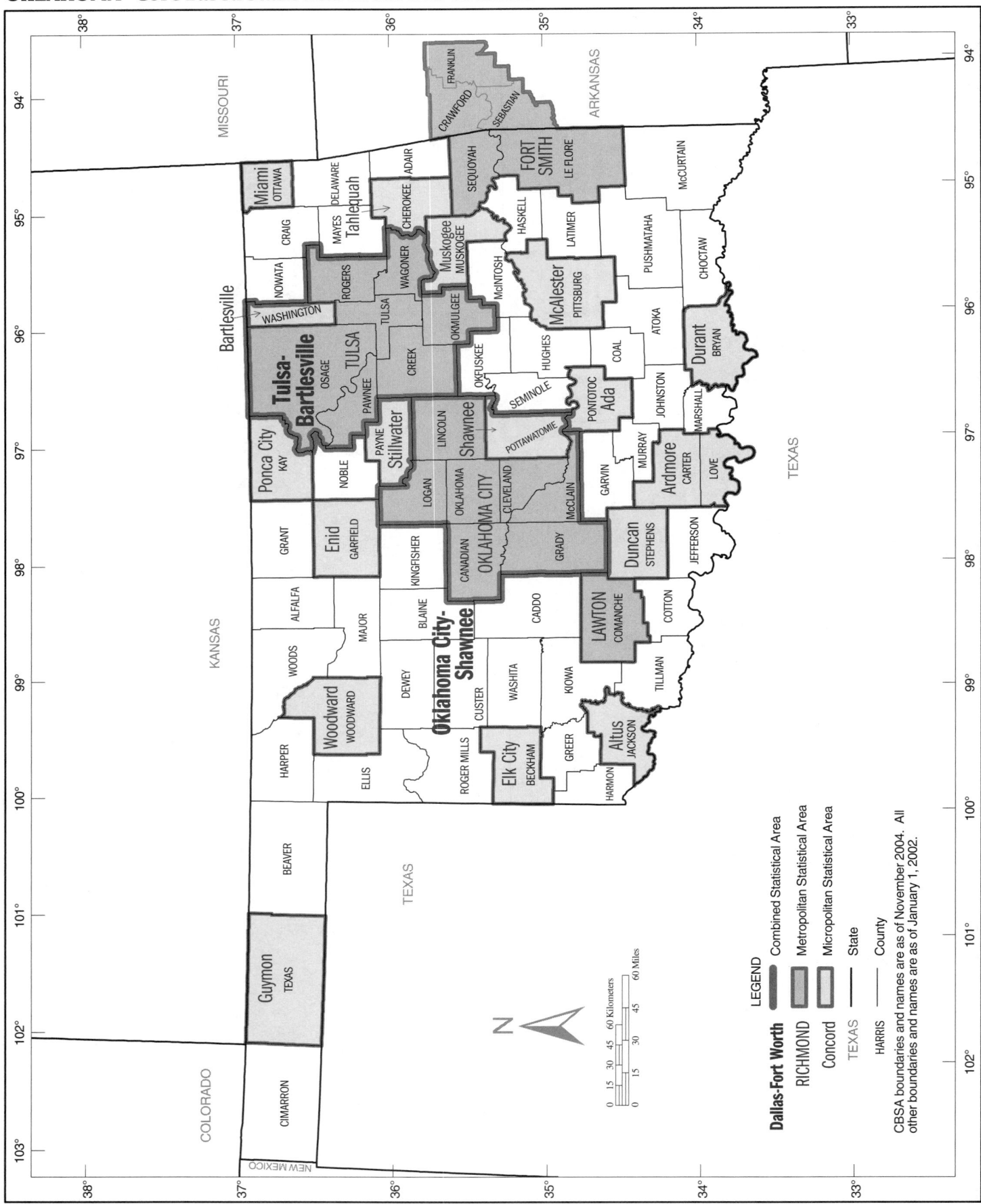

# OREGON - Core Based Statistical Areas and Counties

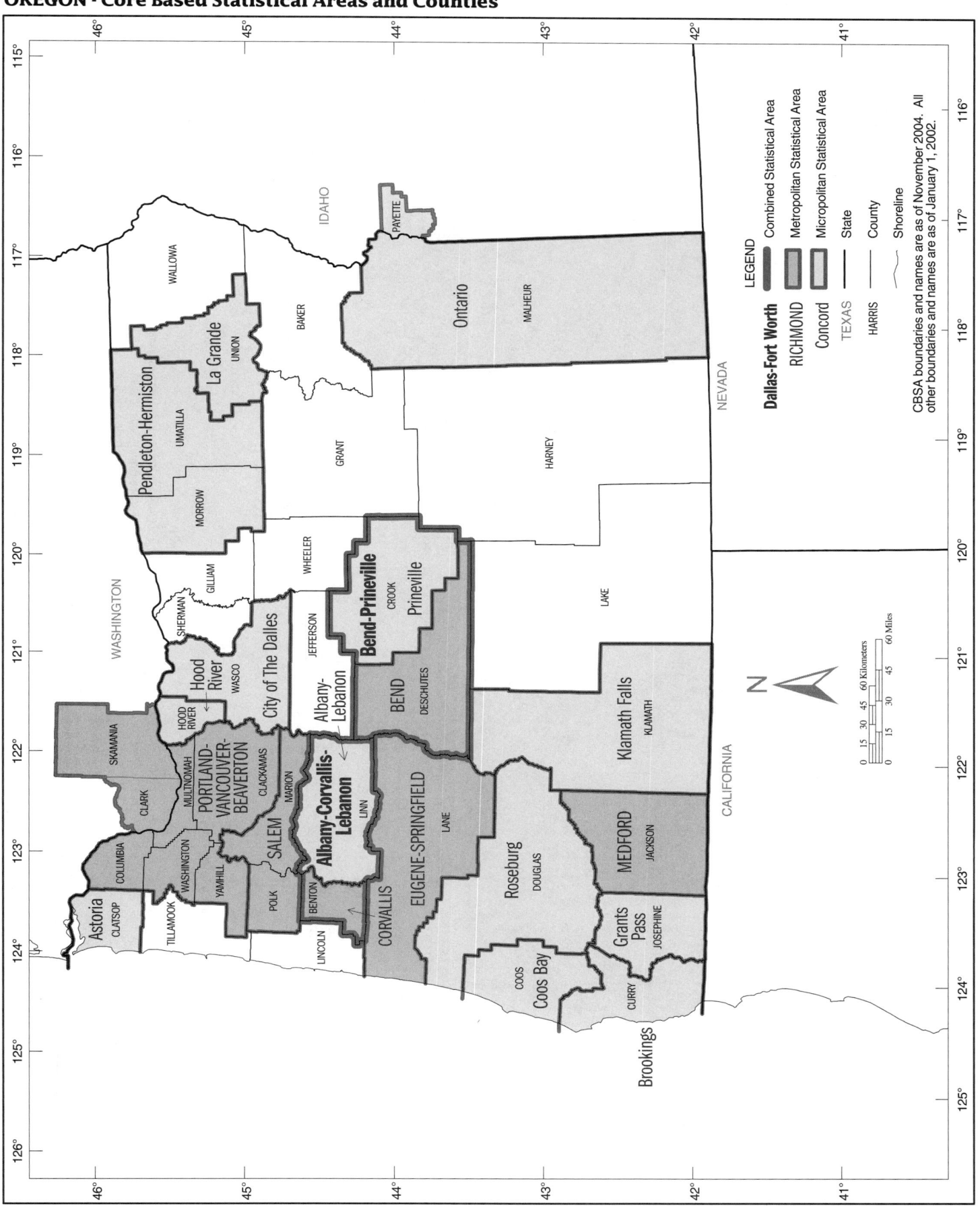

# PENNSYLVANIA - Core Based Statistical Areas and Counties

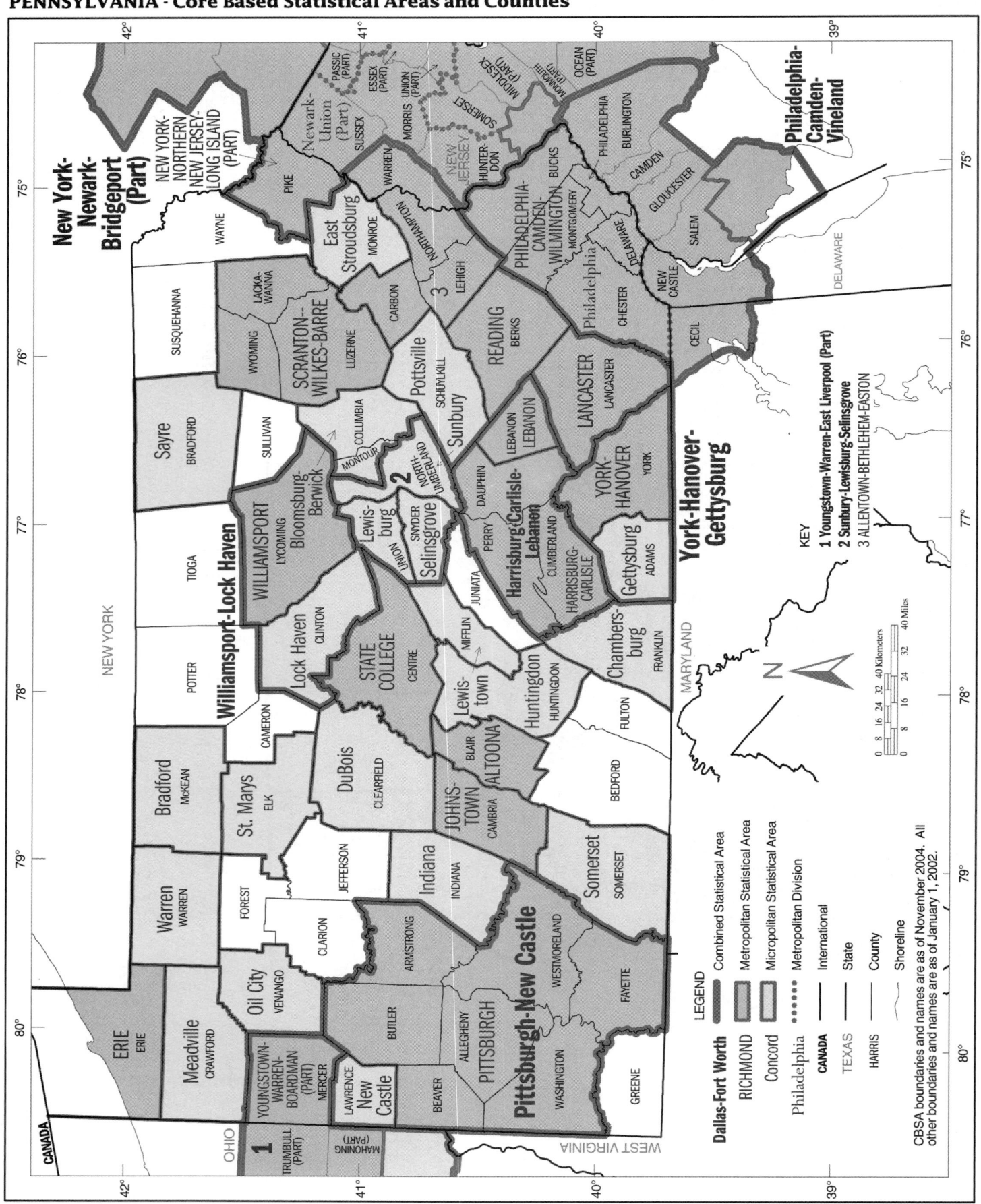

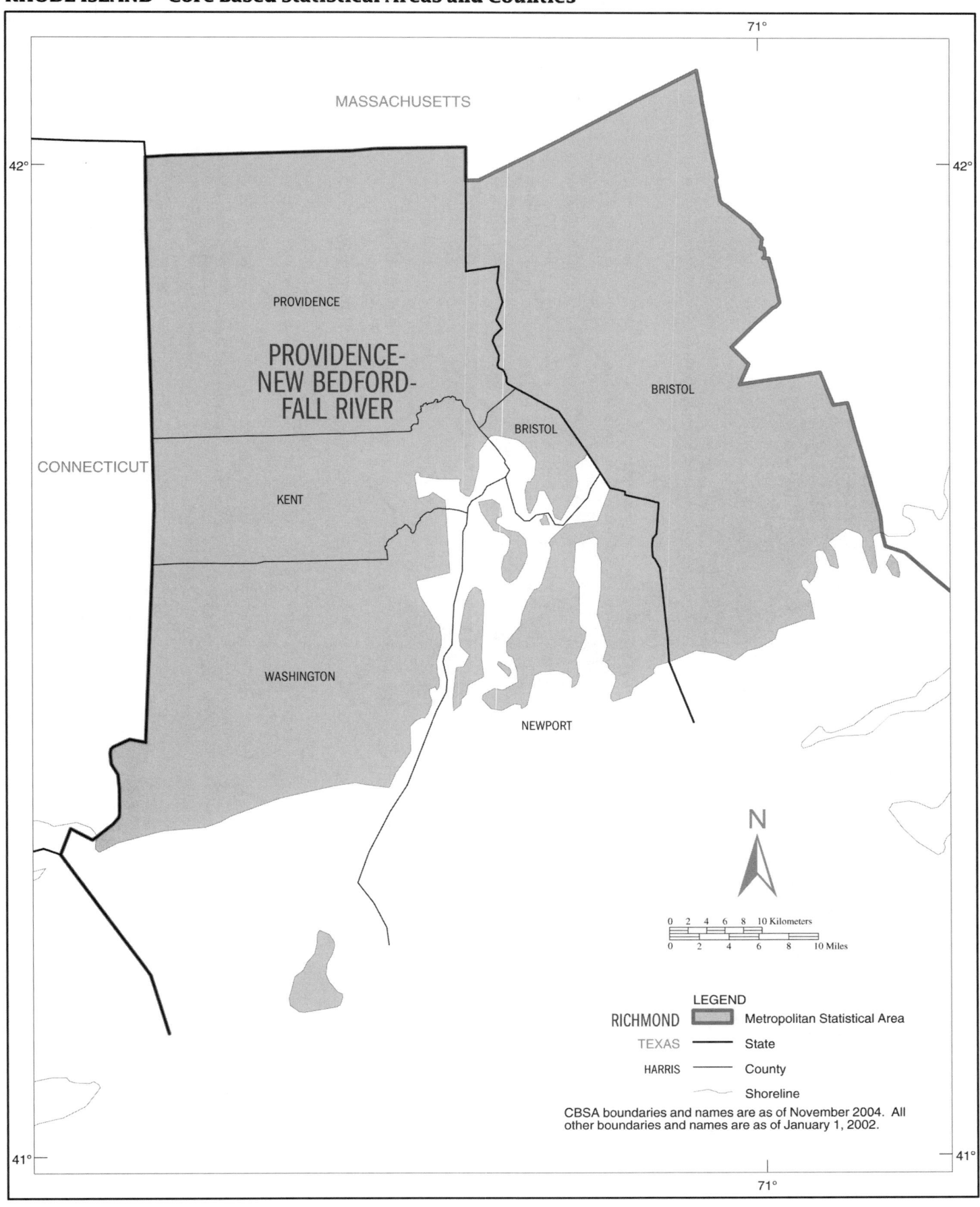

MASSACHUSETTS

PROVIDENCE

**PROVIDENCE-
NEW BEDFORD-
FALL RIVER**

BRISTOL

BRISTOL

CONNECTICUT

KENT

WASHINGTON

NEWPORT

N

| 0 | 2 | 4 | 6 | 8 | 10 Kilometers |
| 0 | 2 | 4 | 6 | 8 | 10 Miles |

LEGEND

RICHMOND — Metropolitan Statistical Area

TEXAS — State

HARRIS — County

Shoreline

CBSA boundaries and names are as of November 2004. All other boundaries and names are as of January 1, 2002.

# SOUTH CAROLINA - Core Based Statistical Areas and Counties

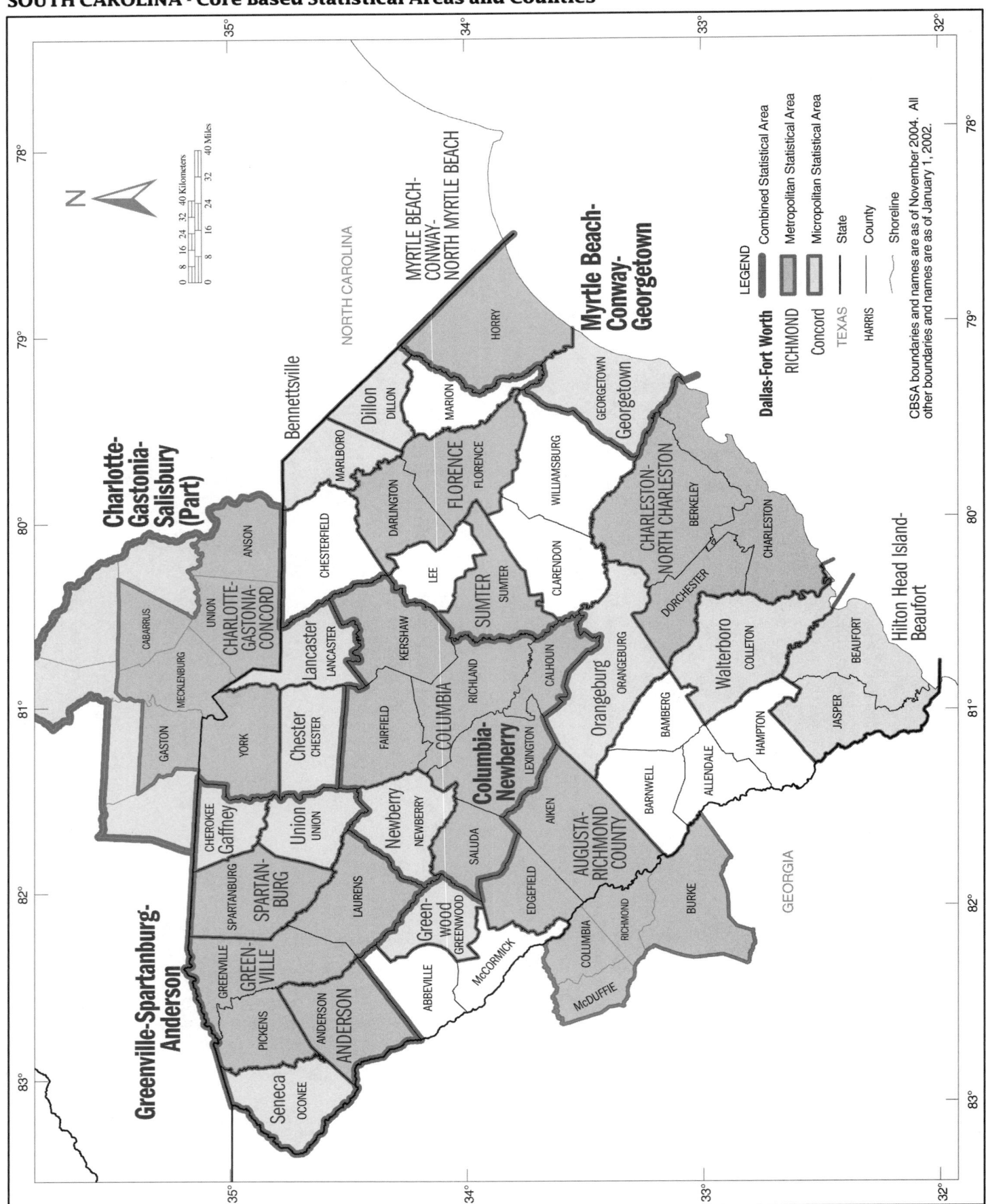

Charlotte-Gastonia-Salisbury (Part)

Greenville-Spartanburg-Anderson

Myrtle Beach-Conway-North Myrtle Beach

Myrtle Beach-Conway-Georgetown

Columbia-Newberry

Hilton Head Island-Beaufort

NORTH CAROLINA

GEORGIA

### LEGEND

**Dallas-Fort Worth** Combined Statistical Area
**RICHMOND** Metropolitan Statistical Area
Concord Micropolitan Statistical Area
State
County
Shoreline

TEXAS State
HARRIS County

CBSA boundaries and names are as of November 2004. All other boundaries and names are as of January 1, 2002.

# SOUTH DAKOTA - Core Based Statistical Areas and Counties

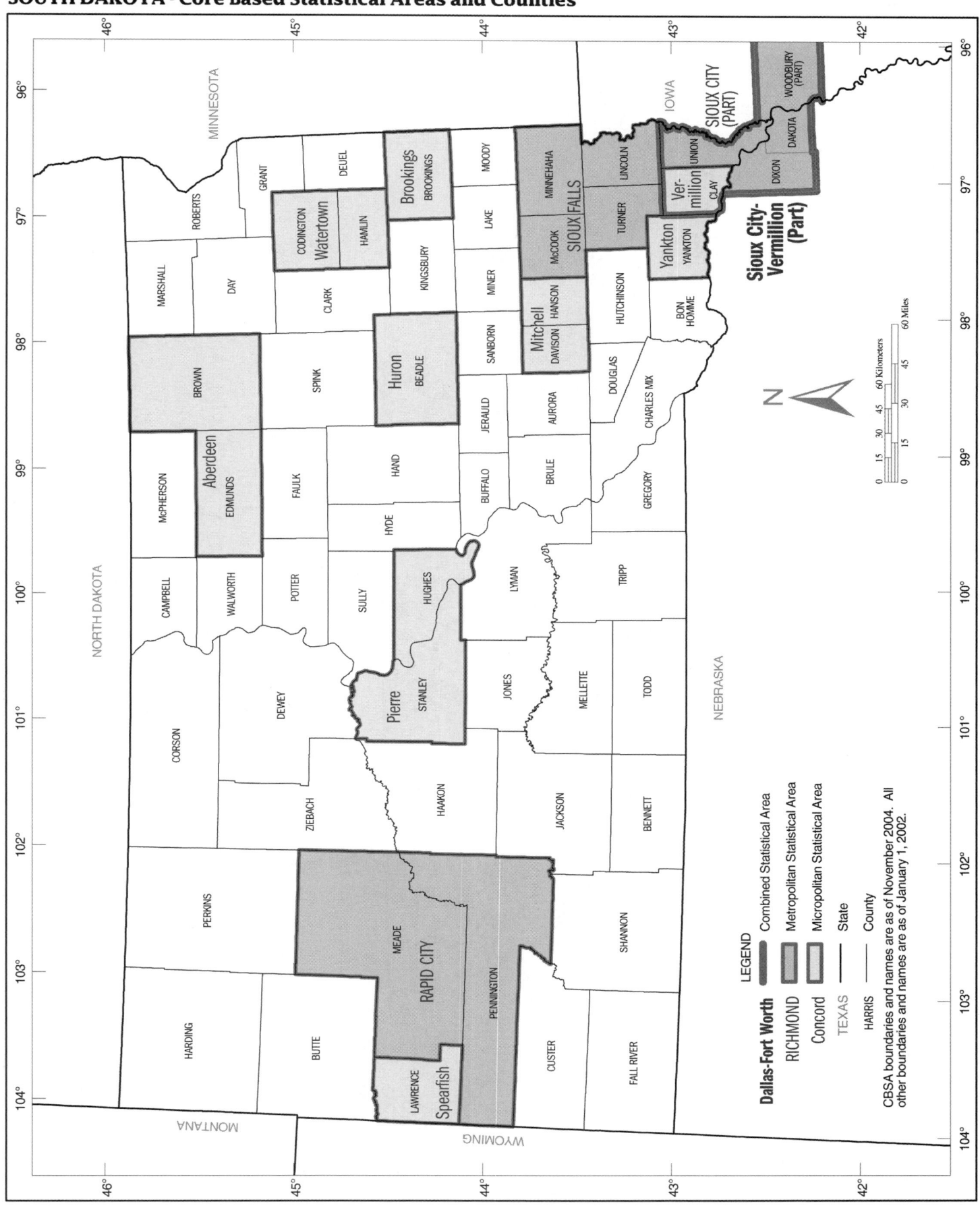

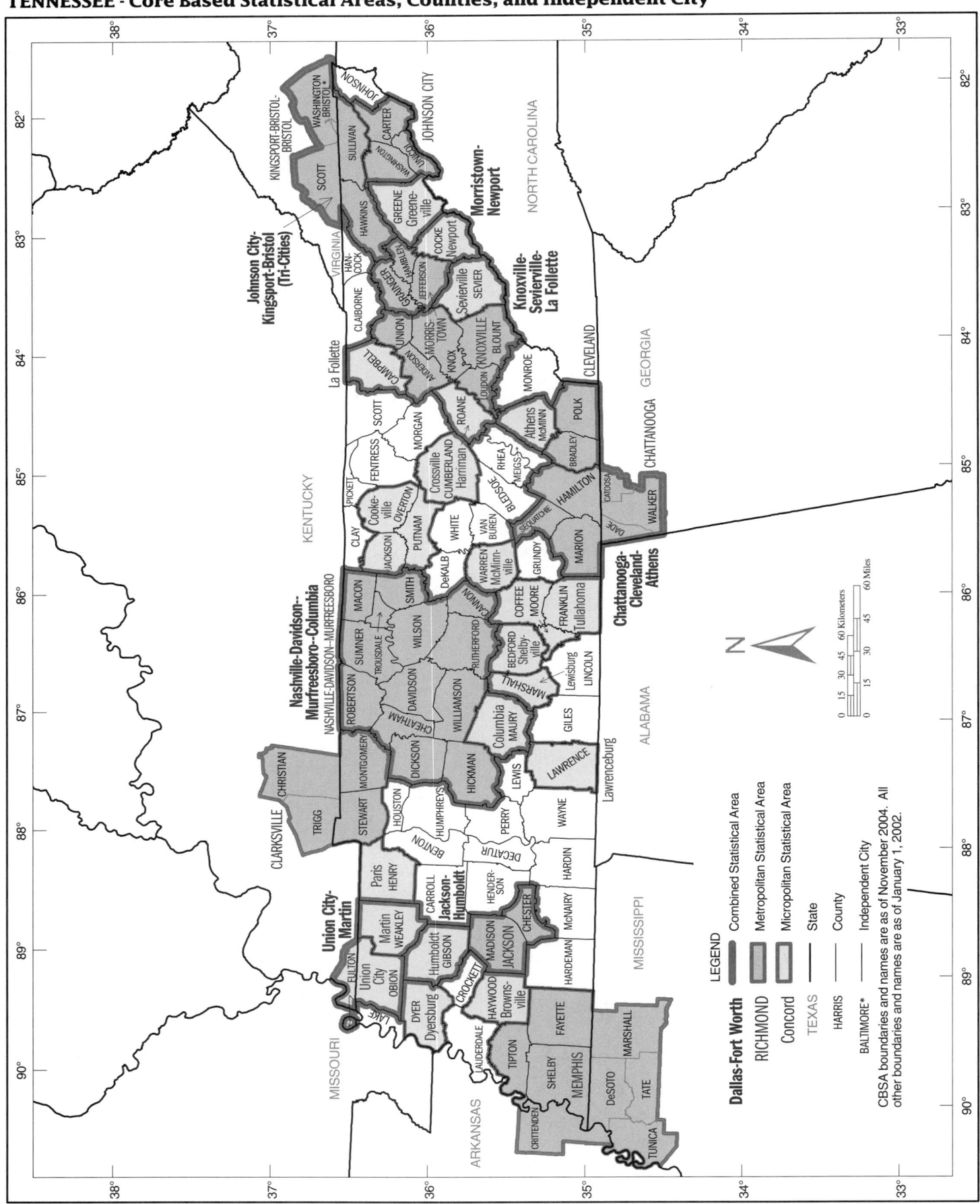

# TEXAS - Core Based Statistical Areas and Counties

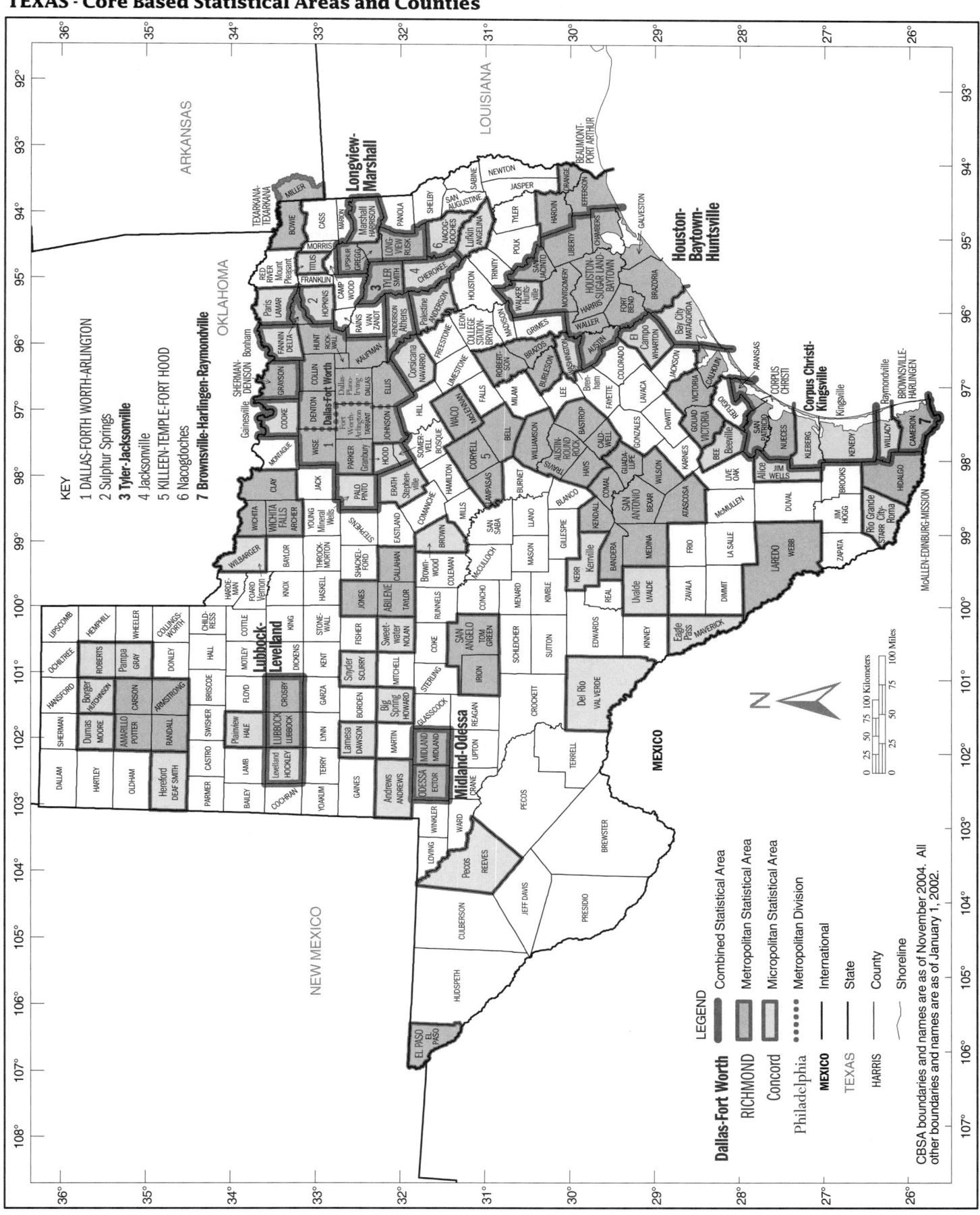

# UTAH - Core Based Statistical Areas and Counties

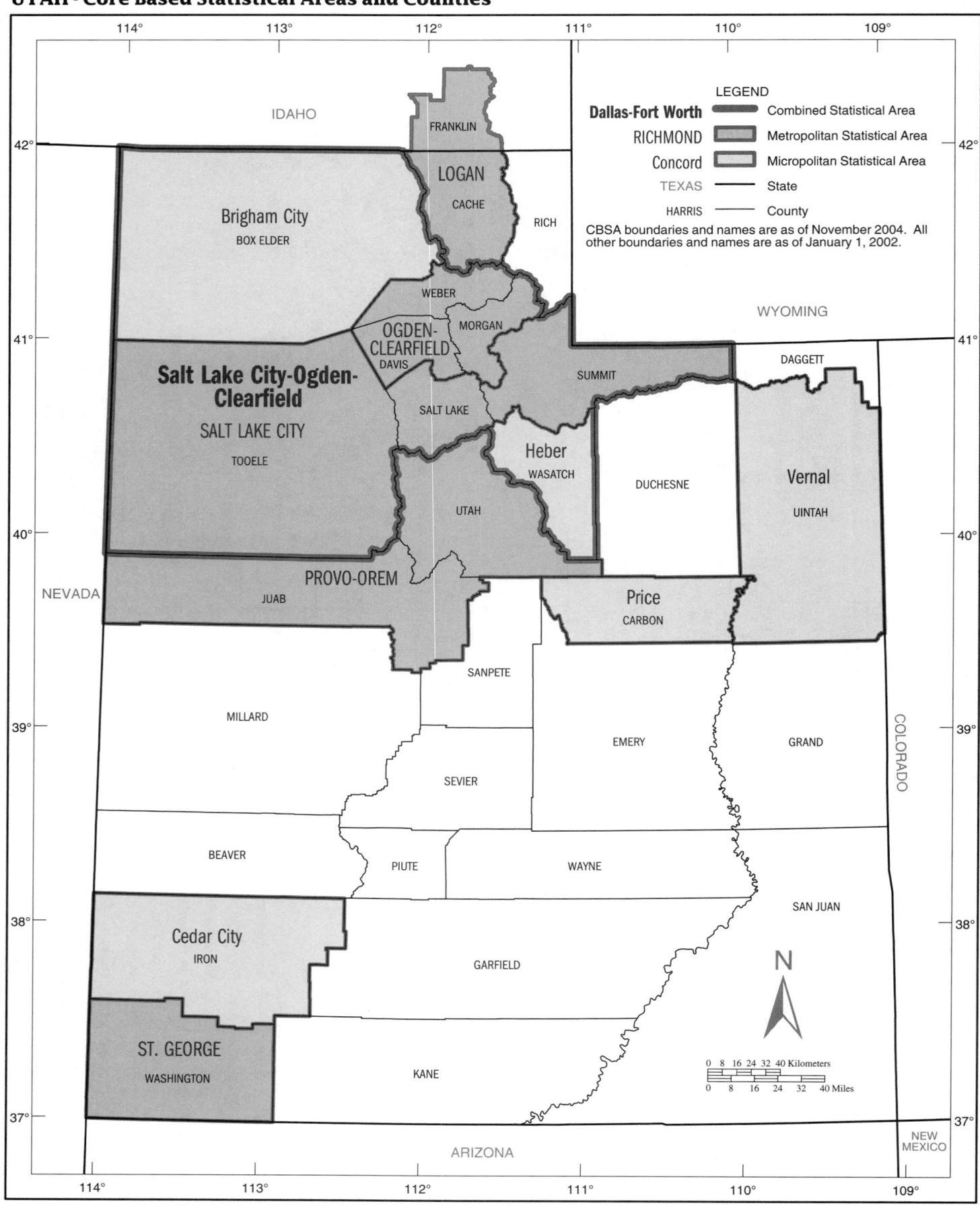

# VERMONT - Core Based Statistical Areas and Counties

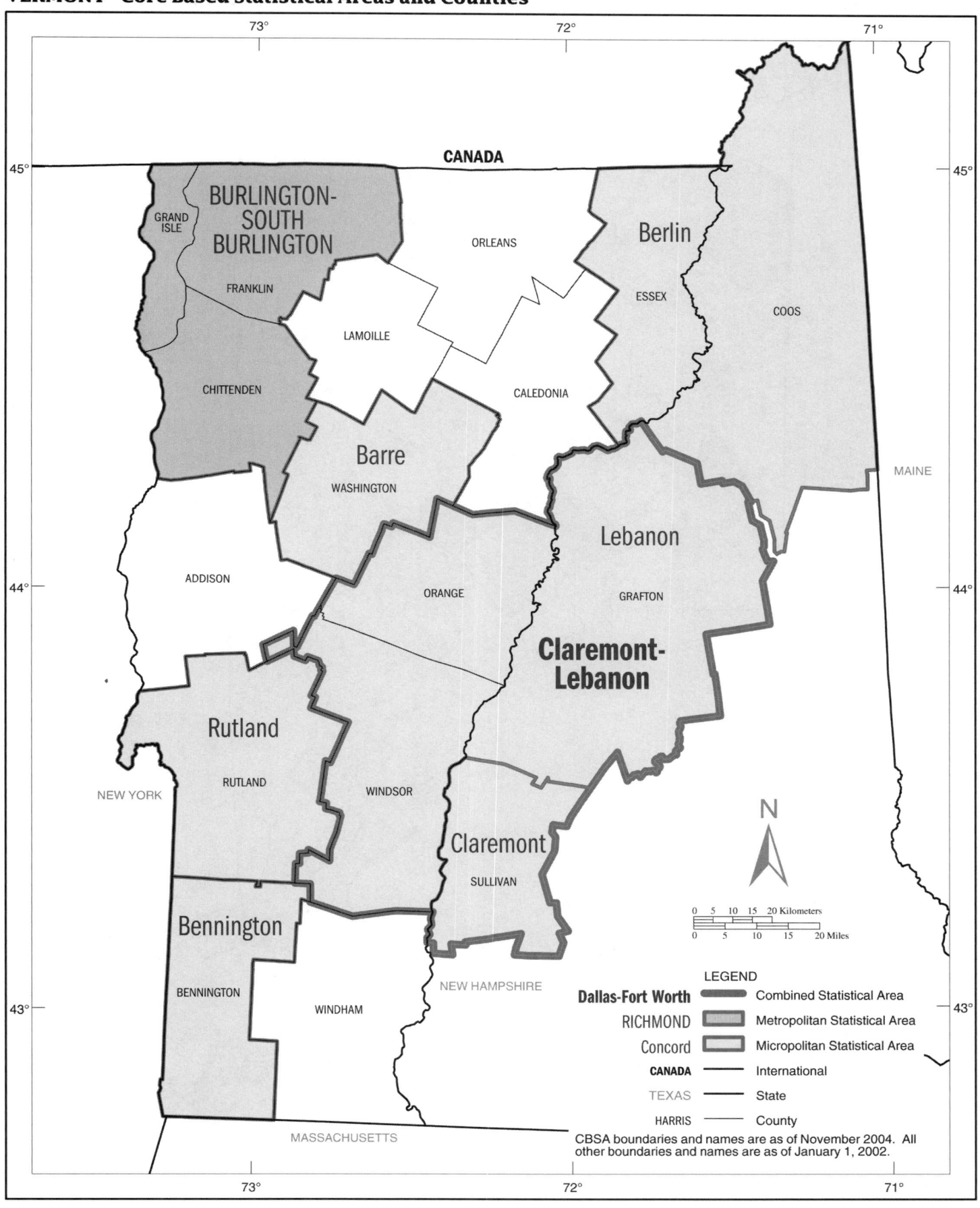

CANADA

BURLINGTON-SOUTH BURLINGTON

GRAND ISLE

ORLEANS

Berlin

FRANKLIN

ESSEX

COOS

LAMOILLE

MAINE

CHITTENDEN

CALEDONIA

Barre

WASHINGTON

Lebanon

ADDISON

GRAFTON

ORANGE

Claremont-Lebanon

Rutland

NEW YORK

RUTLAND

WINDSOR

Claremont

SULLIVAN

Bennington

NEW HAMPSHIRE

BENNINGTON

WINDHAM

MASSACHUSETTS

N

0  5  10  15  20 Kilometers
0  5  10  15  20 Miles

## LEGEND

**Dallas-Fort Worth** ━━ Combined Statistical Area

RICHMOND ▢ Metropolitan Statistical Area

Concord ▢ Micropolitan Statistical Area

**CANADA** ── International

TEXAS ── State

HARRIS ── County

CBSA boundaries and names are as of November 2004. All other boundaries and names are as of January 1, 2002.

U.S. DEPARTMENT OF COMMERCE Economics and Statistics Administration U.S. Census Bureau

# VIRGINIA - Core Based Statistical Areas, District of Columbia, Counties, and Independent Cities

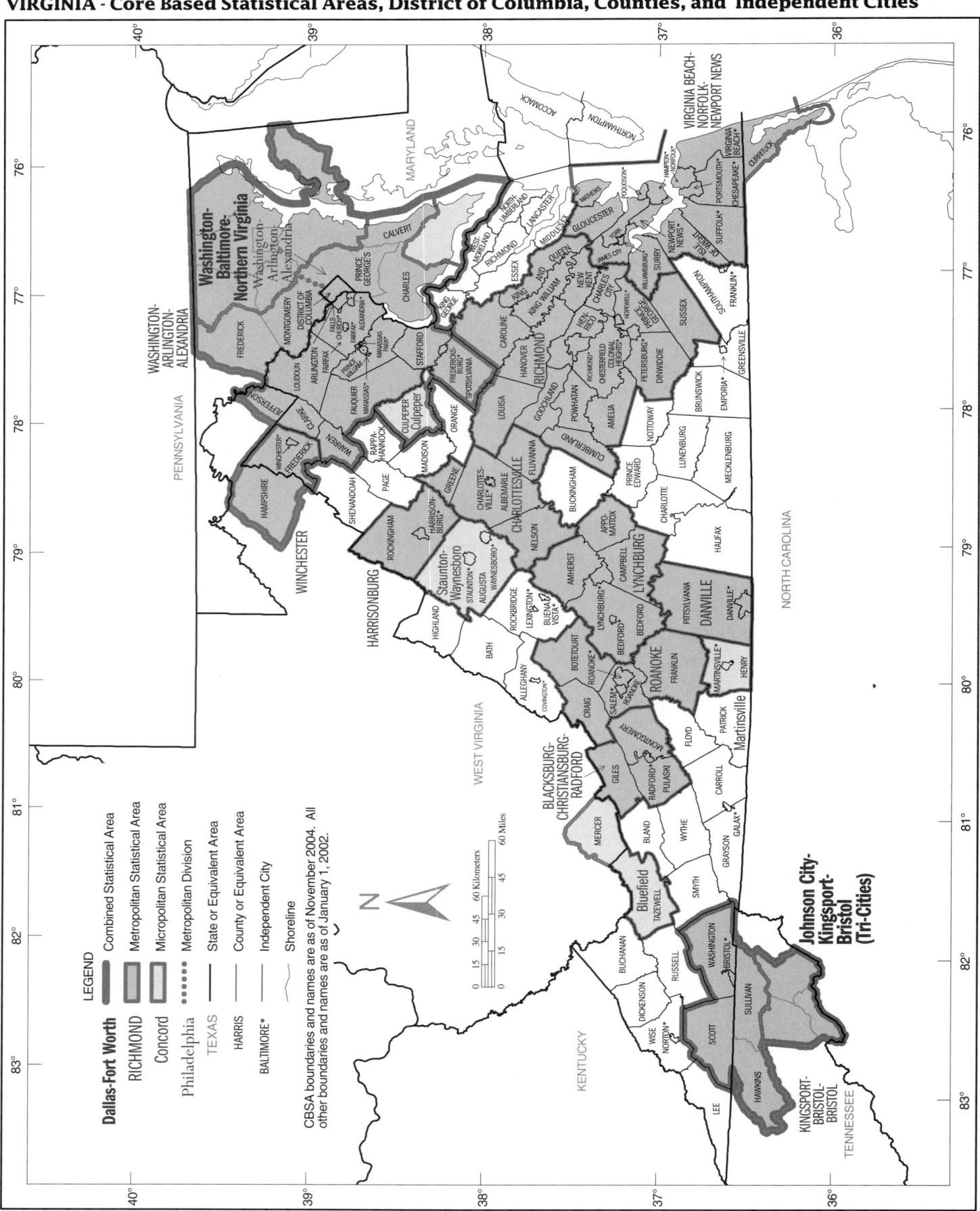

# WASHINGTON - Core Based Statistical Areas and Counties

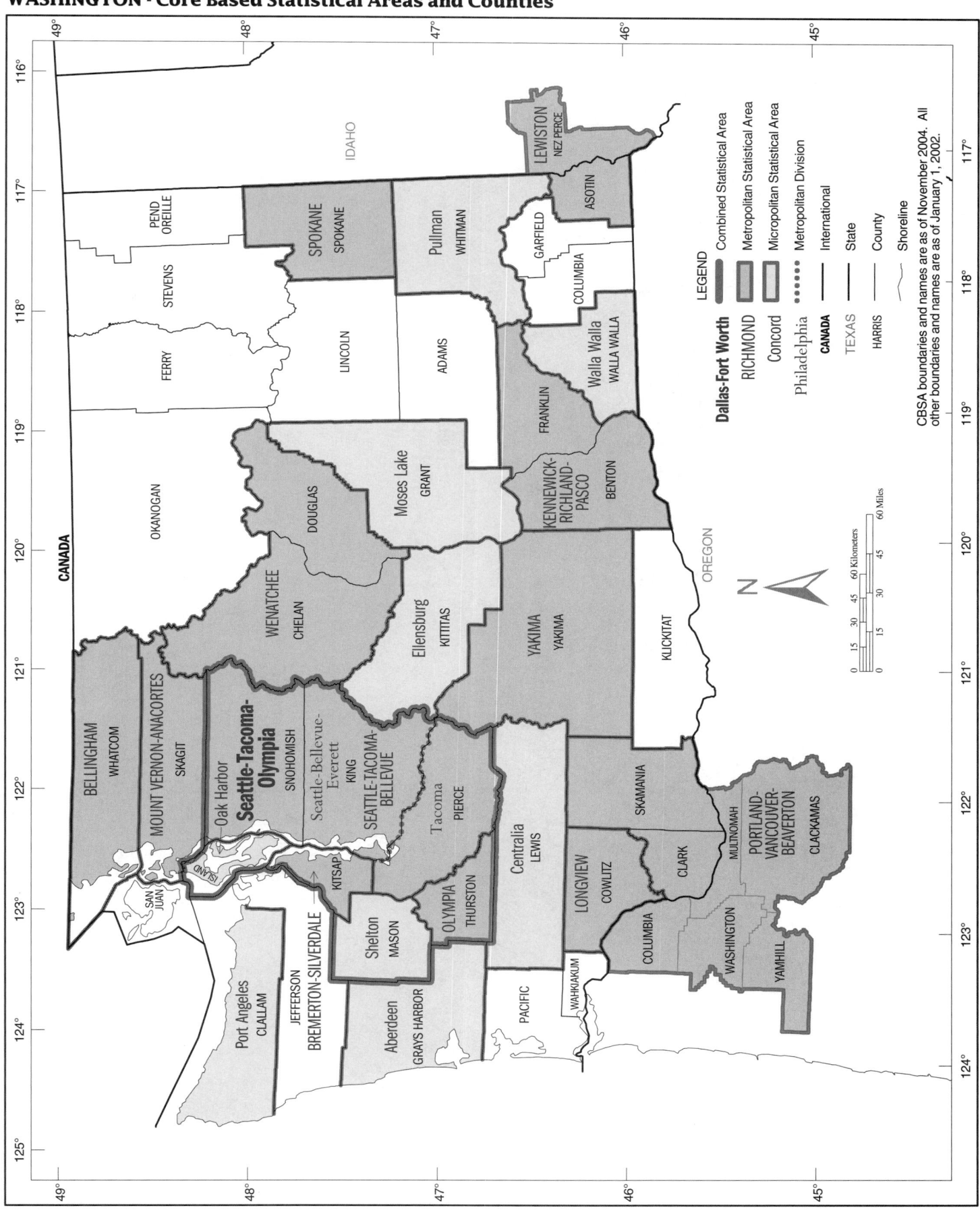

LEGEND

Combined Statistical Area
Metropolitan Statistical Area
Micropolitan Statistical Area
Metropolitan Division

**Dallas-Fort Worth** Combined Statistical Area
RICHMOND Metropolitan Statistical Area
Concord Micropolitan Statistical Area
Philadelphia Metropolitan Division

CANADA International
TEXAS State
HARRIS County
Shoreline

CBSA boundaries and names are as of November 2004. All other boundaries and names are as of January 1, 2002.

# WEST VIRGINIA - Core Based Statistical Areas, District of Columbia, Counties, and Independent Cities

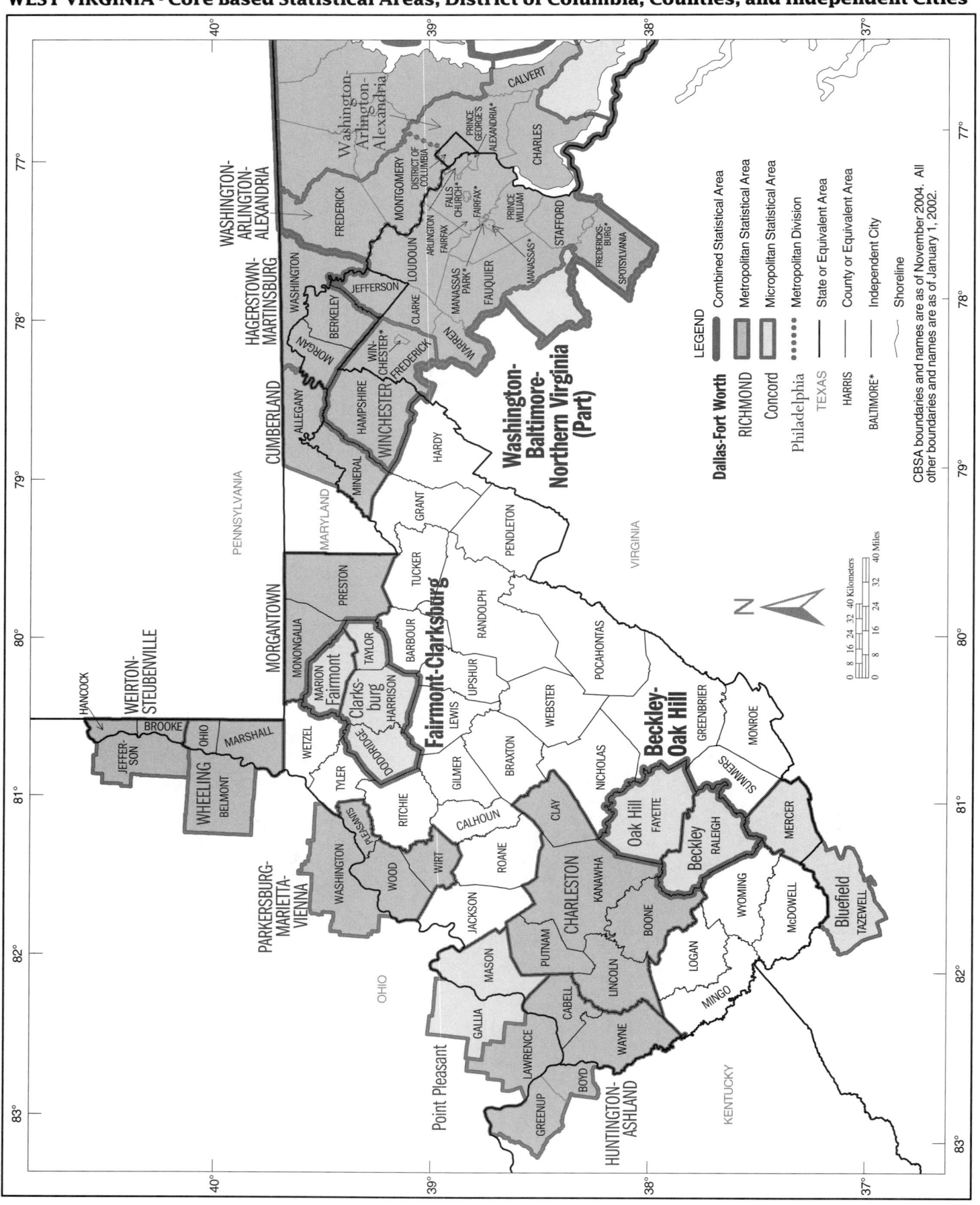

# WISCONSIN - Core Based Statistical Areas and Counties

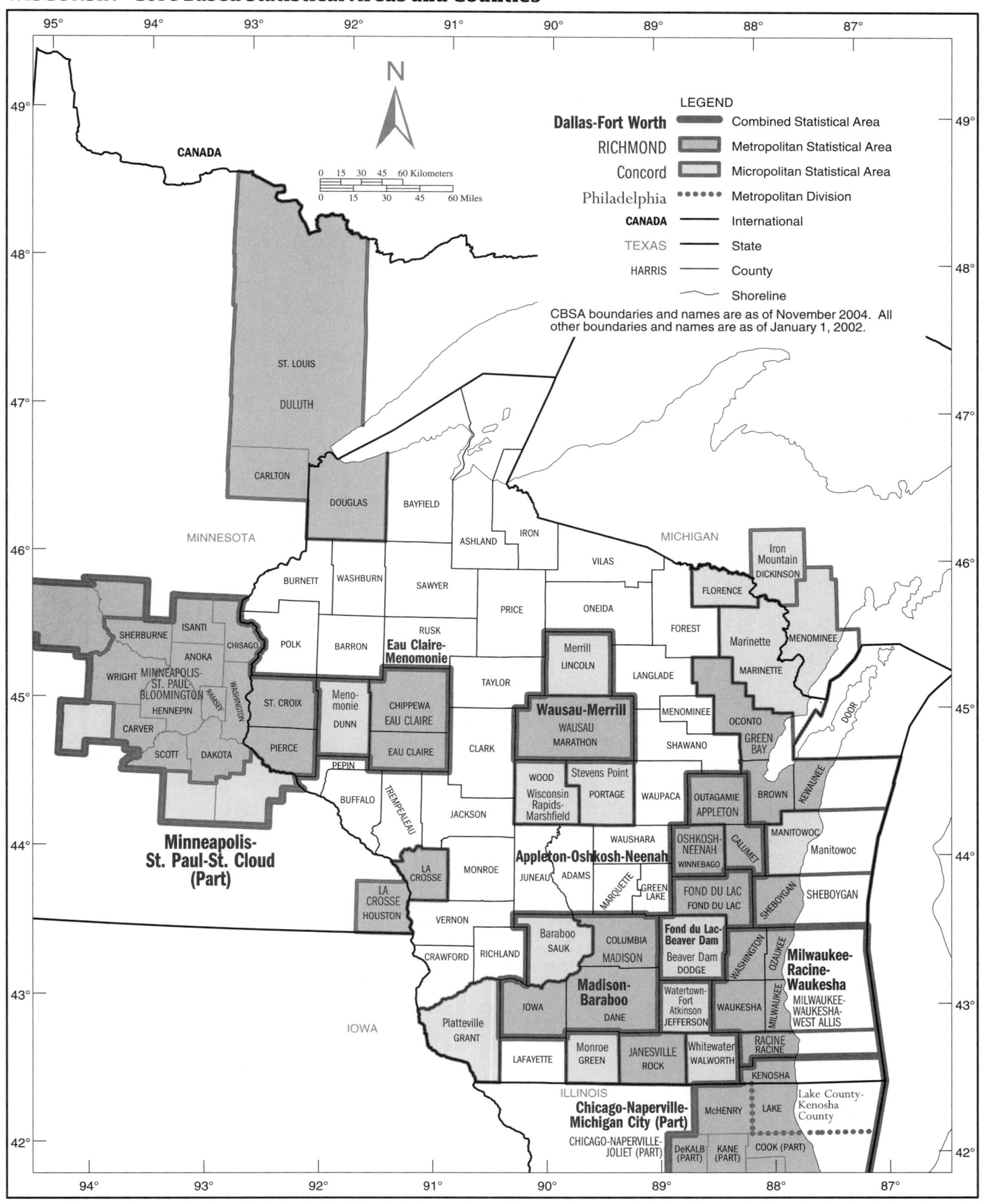

# WYOMING - Core Based Statistical Areas and Counties

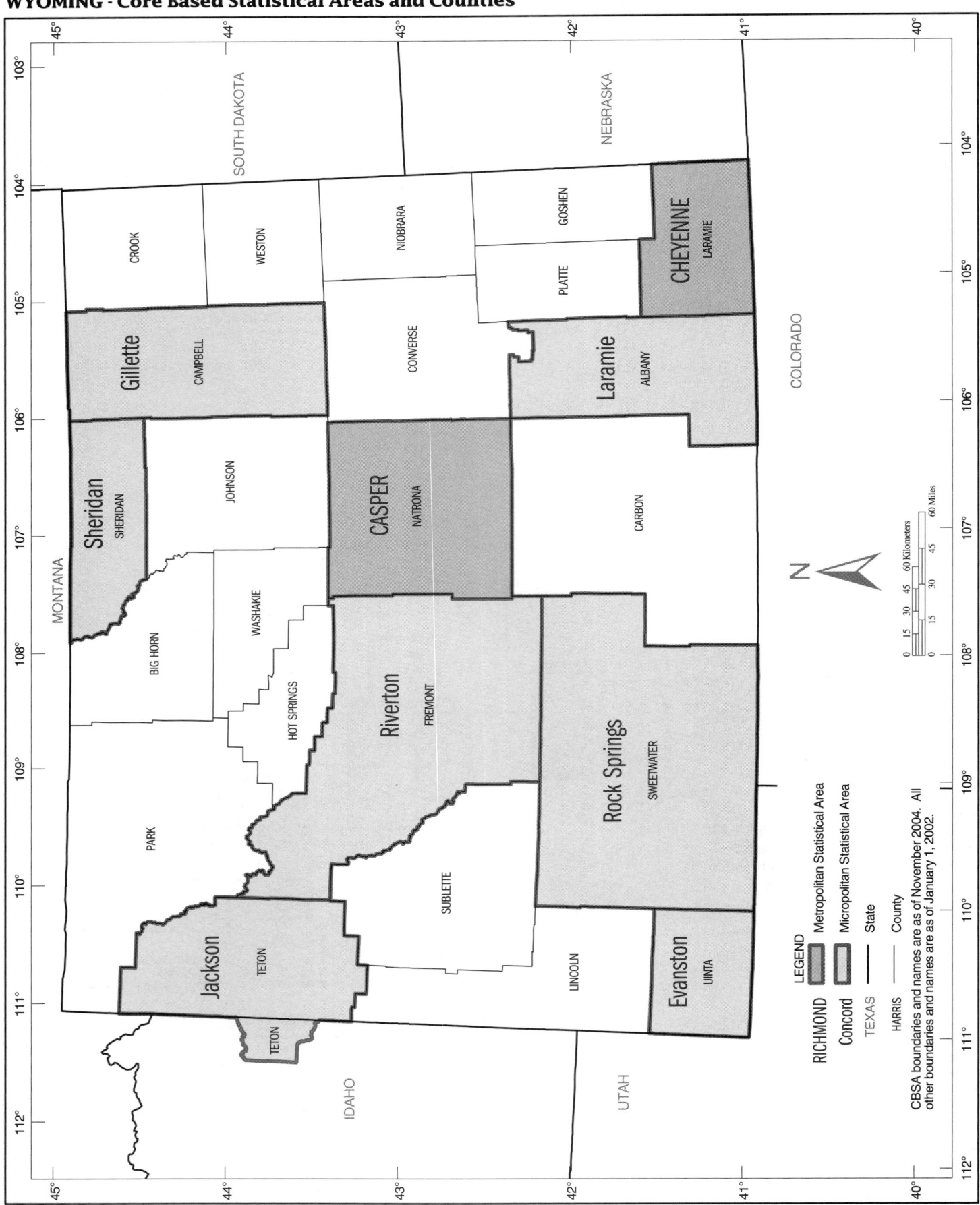

# APPENDIX E
# CITIES BY COUNTY

The following table is arranged alphabetically by state. Under each state heading are listed all cities with a 2010 census population over 25,000 along with their component counties and the population in each component.

| State Code | Place Code | County Code | Geographic Area Name | 2010 Census Population | State Code | Place Code | County Code | Geographic Area Name | 2010 Census Population |
|---|---|---|---|---|---|---|---|---|---|
| 01 | | | **ALABAMA** | 4 779 736 | 01 | 78552 | | Vestavia Hills city | 34 033 |
| 01 | 00820 | | Alabaster city | 30 352 | 01 | 78552 | 073 | Jefferson County | 34 019 |
| 01 | 00820 | 117 | Shelby County | 30 352 | 01 | 78552 | 117 | Shelby County | 14 |
| 01 | 03076 | | Auburn city | 53 380 | 02 | | | **ALASKA** | 710 231 |
| 01 | 03076 | 081 | Lee County | 53 380 | 02 | 03000 | | Anchorage municipality | 291 826 |
| 01 | 05980 | | Bessemer city | 27 456 | 02 | 03000 | 020 | Anchorage Municipality | 291 826 |
| 01 | 05980 | 073 | Jefferson County | 27 456 | 02 | 24230 | | Fairbanks city | 31 535 |
| 01 | 07000 | | Birmingham city | 212 237 | 02 | 24230 | 090 | Fairbanks North Star Borough | 31 535 |
| 01 | 07000 | 073 | Jefferson County | 210 609 | | | | | |
| 01 | 07000 | 117 | Shelby County | 1 628 | 02 | 36400 | | Juneau city and borough | 31 275 |
| | | | | | 02 | 36400 | 110 | Juneau City and Borough | 31 275 |
| 01 | 20104 | | Decatur city | 55 683 | 04 | | | **ARIZONA** | 6 392 017 |
| 01 | 20104 | 083 | Limestone County | 84 | 04 | 02830 | | Apache Junction city | 35 840 |
| 01 | 20104 | 103 | Morgan County | 55 599 | 04 | 02830 | 013 | Maricopa County | 294 |
| | | | | | 04 | 02830 | 021 | Pinal County | 35 546 |
| 01 | 21184 | | Dothan city | 65 496 | | | | | |
| 01 | 21184 | 045 | Dale County | 887 | 04 | 04720 | | Avondale city | 76 238 |
| 01 | 21184 | 067 | Henry County | 5 | 04 | 04720 | 013 | Maricopa County | 76 238 |
| 01 | 21184 | 069 | Houston County | 64 604 | 04 | 07940 | | Buckeye town | 50 876 |
| 01 | 24184 | | Enterprise city | 26 562 | 04 | 07940 | 013 | Maricopa County | 50 876 |
| 01 | 24184 | 031 | Coffee County | 26 139 | | | | | |
| 01 | 24184 | 045 | Dale County | 423 | 04 | 08220 | | Bullhead City city | 39 540 |
| | | | | | 04 | 08220 | 015 | Mohave County | 39 540 |
| 01 | 26896 | | Florence city | 39 319 | | | | | |
| 01 | 26896 | 077 | Lauderdale County | 39 319 | 04 | 10530 | | Casa Grande city | 48 571 |
| | | | | | 04 | 10530 | 021 | Pinal County | 48 571 |
| 01 | 28696 | | Gadsden city | 36 856 | | | | | |
| 01 | 28696 | 055 | Etowah County | 36 856 | 04 | 12000 | | Chandler city | 236 123 |
| | | | | | 04 | 12000 | 013 | Maricopa County | 236 123 |
| 01 | 35800 | | Homewood city | 25 167 | | | | | |
| 01 | 35800 | 073 | Jefferson County | 25 167 | 04 | 22220 | | El Mirage city | 31 797 |
| | | | | | 04 | 22220 | 013 | Maricopa County | 31 797 |
| 01 | 35896 | | Hoover city | 81 619 | | | | | |
| 01 | 35896 | 073 | Jefferson County | 58 582 | 04 | 23620 | | Flagstaff city | 65 870 |
| 01 | 35896 | 117 | Shelby County | 23 037 | 04 | 23620 | 005 | Coconino County | 65 870 |
| 01 | 37000 | | Huntsville city | 180 105 | 04 | 23760 | | Florence town | 25 536 |
| 01 | 37000 | 083 | Limestone County | 1 521 | 04 | 23760 | 021 | Pinal County | 25 536 |
| 01 | 37000 | 089 | Madison County | 178 584 | | | | | |
| | | | | | 04 | 27400 | | Gilbert town | 208 453 |
| 01 | 45784 | | Madison city | 42 938 | 04 | 27400 | 013 | Maricopa County | 208 453 |
| 01 | 45784 | 083 | Limestone County | 3 453 | | | | | |
| 01 | 45784 | 089 | Madison County | 39 485 | 04 | 27820 | | Glendale city | 226 721 |
| | | | | | 04 | 27820 | 013 | Maricopa County | 226 721 |
| 01 | 50000 | | Mobile city | 195 111 | | | | | |
| 01 | 50000 | 097 | Mobile County | 195 111 | 04 | 28380 | | Goodyear city | 65 275 |
| | | | | | 04 | 28380 | 013 | Maricopa County | 65 275 |
| 01 | 51000 | | Montgomery city | 205 764 | | | | | |
| 01 | 51000 | 101 | Montgomery County | 205 764 | 04 | 37620 | | Kingman city | 28 068 |
| | | | | | 04 | 37620 | 015 | Mohave County | 28 068 |
| 01 | 57048 | | Opelika city | 26 477 | | | | | |
| 01 | 57048 | 081 | Lee County | 26 477 | 04 | 39370 | | Lake Havasu City city | 52 527 |
| | | | | | 04 | 39370 | 015 | Mohave County | 52 527 |
| 01 | 59472 | | Phenix City city | 32 822 | | | | | |
| 01 | 59472 | 081 | Lee County | 4 153 | 04 | 44270 | | Marana town | 34 961 |
| 01 | 59472 | 113 | Russell County | 28 669 | 04 | 44270 | 019 | Pima County | 34 961 |
| | | | | | 04 | 44270 | 021 | Pinal County | 0 |
| 01 | 62328 | | Prattville city | 33 960 | | | | | |
| 01 | 62328 | 001 | Autauga County | 32 168 | 04 | 44410 | | Maricopa city | 43 482 |
| 01 | 62328 | 051 | Elmore County | 1 792 | 04 | 44410 | 021 | Pinal County | 43 482 |
| 01 | 77256 | | Tuscaloosa city | 90 468 | 04 | 46000 | | Mesa city | 439 041 |
| 01 | 77256 | 125 | Tuscaloosa County | 90 468 | 04 | 46000 | 013 | Maricopa County | 439 041 |

| State Code | Place Code | County Code | Geographic Area Name | 2010 Census Population | State Code | Place Code | County Code | Geographic Area Name | 2010 Census Population |
|---|---|---|---|---|---|---|---|---|---|
| 04 | 51600 | | Oro Valley town | 41 011 | 05 | 41000 | | Little Rock city | 193 524 |
| 04 | 51600 | 019 | Pima County | 41 011 | 05 | 41000 | 119 | Pulaski County | 193 524 |
| | | | | | | | | | |
| 04 | 54050 | | Peoria city | 154 065 | 05 | 50450 | | North Little Rock city | 62 304 |
| 04 | 54050 | 013 | Maricopa County | 154 058 | 05 | 50450 | 119 | Pulaski County | 62 304 |
| 04 | 54050 | 025 | Yavapai County | 7 | | | | | |
| | | | | | 05 | 53390 | | Paragould city | 26 113 |
| 04 | 55000 | | Phoenix city | 1 445 632 | 05 | 53390 | 055 | Greene County | 26 113 |
| 04 | 55000 | 013 | Maricopa County | 1 445 632 | | | | | |
| | | | | | 05 | 55310 | | Pine Bluff city | 49 083 |
| 04 | 57380 | | Prescott city | 39 843 | 05 | 55310 | 069 | Jefferson County | 49 083 |
| 04 | 57380 | 025 | Yavapai County | 39 843 | | | | | |
| | | | | | 05 | 60410 | | Rogers city | 55 964 |
| 04 | 57450 | | Prescott Valley town | 38 822 | 05 | 60410 | 007 | Benton County | 55 964 |
| 04 | 57450 | 025 | Yavapai County | 38 822 | | | | | |
| | | | | | 05 | 61670 | | Russellville city | 27 920 |
| 04 | 58150 | | Queen Creek town | 26 361 | 05 | 61670 | 115 | Pope County | 27 920 |
| 04 | 58150 | 013 | Maricopa County | 25 912 | | | | | |
| 04 | 58150 | 021 | Pinal County | 449 | 05 | 63800 | | Sherwood city | 29 523 |
| | | | | | 05 | 63800 | 119 | Pulaski County | 29 523 |
| 04 | 62140 | | Sahuarita town | 25 259 | | | | | |
| 04 | 62140 | 019 | Pima County | 25 259 | 05 | 66080 | | Springdale city | 69 797 |
| | | | | | 05 | 66080 | 007 | Benton County | 6 054 |
| 04 | 63470 | | San Luis city | 25 505 | 05 | 66080 | 143 | Washington County | 63 743 |
| 04 | 63470 | 027 | Yuma County | 25 505 | | | | | |
| | | | | | 05 | 68810 | | Texarkana city | 29 919 |
| 04 | 65000 | | Scottsdale city | 217 385 | 05 | 68810 | 091 | Miller County | 29 919 |
| 04 | 65000 | 013 | Maricopa County | 217 385 | | | | | |
| | | | | | 05 | 74540 | | West Memphis city | 26 245 |
| 04 | 66820 | | Sierra Vista city | 43 888 | 05 | 74540 | 035 | Crittenden County | 26 245 |
| 04 | 66820 | 003 | Cochise County | 43 888 | | | | | |
| | | | | | 06 | | | **CALIFORNIA** | 37 253 956 |
| 04 | 71510 | | Surprise city | 117 517 | 06 | 00296 | | Adelanto city | 31 765 |
| 04 | 71510 | 013 | Maricopa County | 117 517 | 06 | 00296 | 071 | San Bernardino County | 31 765 |
| | | | | | | | | | |
| 04 | 73000 | | Tempe city | 161 719 | 06 | 00562 | | Alameda city | 73 812 |
| 04 | 73000 | 013 | Maricopa County | 161 719 | 06 | 00562 | 001 | Alameda County | 73 812 |
| | | | | | | | | | |
| 04 | 77000 | | Tucson city | 520 116 | 06 | 00884 | | Alhambra city | 83 089 |
| 04 | 77000 | 019 | Pima County | 520 116 | 06 | 00884 | 037 | Los Angeles County | 83 089 |
| | | | | | | | | | |
| 04 | 85540 | | Yuma city | 93 064 | 06 | 00947 | | Aliso Viejo city | 47 823 |
| 04 | 85540 | 027 | Yuma County | 93 064 | 06 | 00947 | 059 | Orange County | 47 823 |
| | | | | | | | | | |
| 05 | | | **ARKANSAS** | 2 915 918 | 06 | 02000 | | Anaheim city | 336 265 |
| 05 | 04840 | | Bella Vista town | 26 461 | 06 | 02000 | 059 | Orange County | 336 265 |
| 05 | 04840 | 007 | Benton County | 26 461 | | | | | |
| | | | | | 06 | 02252 | | Antioch city | 102 372 |
| 05 | 05290 | | Benton city | 30 681 | 06 | 02252 | 013 | Contra Costa County | 102 372 |
| 05 | 05290 | 125 | Saline County | 30 681 | | | | | |
| | | | | | 06 | 02364 | | Apple Valley town | 69 135 |
| 05 | 05320 | | Bentonville city | 35 301 | 06 | 02364 | 071 | San Bernardino County | 69 135 |
| 05 | 05320 | 007 | Benton County | 35 301 | | | | | |
| | | | | | 06 | 02462 | | Arcadia city | 56 364 |
| 05 | 15190 | | Conway city | 58 908 | 06 | 02462 | 037 | Los Angeles County | 56 364 |
| 05 | 15190 | 045 | Faulkner County | 58 908 | | | | | |
| | | | | | 06 | 03064 | | Atascadero city | 28 310 |
| 05 | 23290 | | Fayetteville city | 73 580 | 06 | 03064 | 079 | San Luis Obispo County | 28 310 |
| 05 | 23290 | 143 | Washington County | 73 580 | | | | | |
| | | | | | 06 | 03162 | | Atwater city | 28 168 |
| 05 | 24550 | | Fort Smith city | 86 209 | 06 | 03162 | 047 | Merced County | 28 168 |
| 05 | 24550 | 131 | Sebastian County | 86 209 | | | | | |
| | | | | | 06 | 03386 | | Azusa city | 46 361 |
| 05 | 33400 | | Hot Springs city | 35 193 | 06 | 03386 | 037 | Los Angeles County | 46 361 |
| 05 | 33400 | 051 | Garland County | 35 193 | | | | | |
| | | | | | 06 | 03526 | | Bakersfield city | 347 483 |
| 05 | 34750 | | Jacksonville city | 28 364 | 06 | 03526 | 029 | Kern County | 347 483 |
| 05 | 34750 | 119 | Pulaski County | 28 364 | | | | | |
| | | | | | 06 | 03666 | | Baldwin Park city | 75 390 |
| 05 | 35710 | | Jonesboro city | 67 263 | 06 | 03666 | 037 | Los Angeles County | 75 390 |
| 05 | 35710 | 031 | Craighead County | 67 263 | | | | | |

| State Code | Place Code | County Code | Geographic Area Name | 2010 Census Population | State Code | Place Code | County Code | Geographic Area Name | 2010 Census Population |
|---|---|---|---|---|---|---|---|---|---|
| 06 | 03820 | | Banning city | 29 603 | 06 | 13214 | | Chino Hills city | 74 799 |
| 06 | 03820 | 065 | Riverside County | 29 603 | 06 | 13214 | 071 | San Bernardino County | 74 799 |
| 06 | 04758 | | Beaumont city | 36 877 | 06 | 13392 | | Chula Vista city | 243 916 |
| 06 | 04758 | 065 | Riverside County | 36 877 | 06 | 13392 | 073 | San Diego County | 243 916 |
| 06 | 04870 | | Bell city | 35 477 | 06 | 13588 | | Citrus Heights city | 83 301 |
| 06 | 04870 | 037 | Los Angeles County | 35 477 | 06 | 13588 | 067 | Sacramento County | 83 301 |
| 06 | 04982 | | Bellflower city | 76 616 | 06 | 13756 | | Claremont city | 34 926 |
| 06 | 04982 | 037 | Los Angeles County | 76 616 | 06 | 13756 | 037 | Los Angeles County | 34 926 |
| 06 | 04996 | | Bell Gardens city | 42 072 | 06 | 14218 | | Clovis city | 95 631 |
| 06 | 04996 | 037 | Los Angeles County | 42 072 | 06 | 14218 | 019 | Fresno County | 95 631 |
| 06 | 05108 | | Belmont city | 25 835 | 06 | 14260 | | Coachella city | 40 704 |
| 06 | 05108 | 081 | San Mateo County | 25 835 | 06 | 14260 | 065 | Riverside County | 40 704 |
| 06 | 05290 | | Benicia city | 26 997 | 06 | 14890 | | Colton city | 52 154 |
| 06 | 05290 | 095 | Solano County | 26 997 | 06 | 14890 | 071 | San Bernardino County | 52 154 |
| 06 | 06000 | | Berkeley city | 112 580 | 06 | 15044 | | Compton city | 96 455 |
| 06 | 06000 | 001 | Alameda County | 112 580 | 06 | 15044 | 037 | Los Angeles County | 96 455 |
| 06 | 06308 | | Beverly Hills city | 34 109 | 06 | 16000 | | Concord city | 122 067 |
| 06 | 06308 | 037 | Los Angeles County | 34 109 | 06 | 16000 | 013 | Contra Costa County | 122 067 |
| 06 | 08100 | | Brea city | 39 282 | 06 | 16350 | | Corona city | 152 374 |
| 06 | 08100 | 059 | Orange County | 39 282 | 06 | 16350 | 065 | Riverside County | 152 374 |
| 06 | 08142 | | Brentwood city | 51 481 | 06 | 16532 | | Costa Mesa city | 109 960 |
| 06 | 08142 | 013 | Contra Costa County | 51 481 | 06 | 16532 | 059 | Orange County | 109 960 |
| 06 | 08786 | | Buena Park city | 80 530 | 06 | 16742 | | Covina city | 47 796 |
| 06 | 08786 | 059 | Orange County | 80 530 | 06 | 16742 | 037 | Los Angeles County | 47 796 |
| 06 | 08954 | | Burbank city | 103 340 | 06 | 17568 | | Culver City city | 38 883 |
| 06 | 08954 | 037 | Los Angeles County | 103 340 | 06 | 17568 | 037 | Los Angeles County | 38 883 |
| 06 | 09066 | | Burlingame city | 28 806 | 06 | 17610 | | Cupertino city | 58 302 |
| 06 | 09066 | 081 | San Mateo County | 28 806 | 06 | 17610 | 085 | Santa Clara County | 58 302 |
| 06 | 09710 | | Calexico city | 38 572 | 06 | 17750 | | Cypress city | 47 802 |
| 06 | 09710 | 025 | Imperial County | 38 572 | 06 | 17750 | 059 | Orange County | 47 802 |
| 06 | 10046 | | Camarillo city | 65 201 | 06 | 17918 | | Daly City city | 101 123 |
| 06 | 10046 | 111 | Ventura County | 65 201 | 06 | 17918 | 081 | San Mateo County | 101 123 |
| 06 | 10345 | | Campbell city | 39 349 | 06 | 17946 | | Dana Point city | 33 351 |
| 06 | 10345 | 085 | Santa Clara County | 39 349 | 06 | 17946 | 059 | Orange County | 33 351 |
| 06 | 11194 | | Carlsbad city | 105 328 | 06 | 17988 | | Danville town | 42 039 |
| 06 | 11194 | 073 | San Diego County | 105 328 | 06 | 17988 | 013 | Contra Costa County | 42 039 |
| 06 | 11530 | | Carson city | 91 714 | 06 | 18100 | | Davis city | 65 622 |
| 06 | 11530 | 037 | Los Angeles County | 91 714 | 06 | 18100 | 113 | Yolo County | 65 622 |
| 06 | 12048 | | Cathedral City city | 51 200 | 06 | 18394 | | Delano city | 53 041 |
| 06 | 12048 | 065 | Riverside County | 51 200 | 06 | 18394 | 029 | Kern County | 53 041 |
| 06 | 12524 | | Ceres city | 45 417 | 06 | 18996 | | Desert Hot Springs city | 25 938 |
| 06 | 12524 | 099 | Stanislaus County | 45 417 | 06 | 18996 | 065 | Riverside County | 25 938 |
| 06 | 12552 | | Cerritos city | 49 041 | 06 | 19192 | | Diamond Bar city | 55 544 |
| 06 | 12552 | 037 | Los Angeles County | 49 041 | 06 | 19192 | 037 | Los Angeles County | 55 544 |
| 06 | 13014 | | Chico city | 86 187 | 06 | 19766 | | Downey city | 111 772 |
| 06 | 13014 | 007 | Butte County | 86 187 | 06 | 19766 | 037 | Los Angeles County | 111 772 |
| 06 | 13210 | | Chino city | 77 983 | 06 | 20018 | | Dublin city | 46 036 |
| 06 | 13210 | 071 | San Bernardino County | 77 983 | 06 | 20018 | 001 | Alameda County | 46 036 |

| State Code | Place Code | County Code | Geographic Area Name | 2010 Census Population | State Code | Place Code | County Code | Geographic Area Name | 2010 Census Population |
|---|---|---|---|---|---|---|---|---|---|
| 06 | 20956 | | East Palo Alto city | 28 155 | 06 | 32548 | | Hawthorne city | 84 293 |
| 06 | 20956 | 081 | San Mateo County | 28 155 | 06 | 32548 | 037 | Los Angeles County | 84 293 |
| 06 | 21712 | | El Cajon city | 99 478 | 06 | 33000 | | Hayward city | 144 186 |
| 06 | 21712 | 073 | San Diego County | 99 478 | 06 | 33000 | 001 | Alameda County | 144 186 |
| 06 | 21782 | | El Centro city | 42 598 | 06 | 33182 | | Hemet city | 78 657 |
| 06 | 21782 | 025 | Imperial County | 42 598 | 06 | 33182 | 065 | Riverside County | 78 657 |
| 06 | 22020 | | Elk Grove city | 153 015 | 06 | 33434 | | Hesperia city | 90 173 |
| 06 | 22020 | 067 | Sacramento County | 153 015 | 06 | 33434 | 071 | San Bernardino County | 90 173 |
| 06 | 22230 | | El Monte city | 113 475 | 06 | 33588 | | Highland city | 53 104 |
| 06 | 22230 | 037 | Los Angeles County | 113 475 | 06 | 33588 | 071 | San Bernardino County | 53 104 |
| 06 | 22300 | | El Paso de Robles (Paso Robles) | 29 793 | 06 | 34120 | | Hollister city | 34 928 |
| 06 | 22300 | 079 | San Luis Obispo County | 29 793 | 06 | 34120 | 069 | San Benito County | 34 928 |
| 06 | 22678 | | Encinitas city | 59 518 | 06 | 36000 | | Huntington Beach city | 189 992 |
| 06 | 22678 | 073 | San Diego County | 59 518 | 06 | 36000 | 059 | Orange County | 189 992 |
| 06 | 22804 | | Escondido city | 143 911 | 06 | 36056 | | Huntington Park city | 58 114 |
| 06 | 22804 | 073 | San Diego County | 143 911 | 06 | 36056 | 037 | Los Angeles County | 58 114 |
| 06 | 23042 | | Eureka city | 27 191 | 06 | 36294 | | Imperial Beach city | 26 324 |
| 06 | 23042 | 023 | Humboldt County | 27 191 | 06 | 36294 | 073 | San Diego County | 26 324 |
| 06 | 23182 | | Fairfield city | 105 321 | 06 | 36448 | | Indio city | 76 036 |
| 06 | 23182 | 095 | Solano County | 105 321 | 06 | 36448 | 065 | Riverside County | 76 036 |
| 06 | 24638 | | Folsom city | 72 203 | 06 | 36546 | | Inglewood city | 109 673 |
| 06 | 24638 | 067 | Sacramento County | 72 203 | 06 | 36546 | 037 | Los Angeles County | 109 673 |
| 06 | 24680 | | Fontana city | 196 069 | 06 | 36770 | | Irvine city | 212 375 |
| 06 | 24680 | 071 | San Bernardino County | 196 069 | 06 | 36770 | 059 | Orange County | 212 375 |
| 06 | 25338 | | Foster City city | 30 567 | 06 | 39220 | | Laguna Hills city | 30 344 |
| 06 | 25338 | 081 | San Mateo County | 30 567 | 06 | 39220 | 059 | Orange County | 30 344 |
| 06 | 25380 | | Fountain Valley city | 55 313 | 06 | 39248 | | Laguna Niguel city | 62 979 |
| 06 | 25380 | 059 | Orange County | 55 313 | 06 | 39248 | 059 | Orange County | 62 979 |
| 06 | 26000 | | Fremont city | 214 089 | 06 | 39290 | | La Habra city | 60 239 |
| 06 | 26000 | 001 | Alameda County | 214 089 | 06 | 39290 | 059 | Orange County | 60 239 |
| 06 | 27000 | | Fresno city | 494 665 | 06 | 39486 | | Lake Elsinore city | 51 821 |
| 06 | 27000 | 019 | Fresno County | 494 665 | 06 | 39486 | 065 | Riverside County | 51 821 |
| 06 | 28000 | | Fullerton city | 135 161 | 06 | 39496 | | Lake Forest city | 77 264 |
| 06 | 28000 | 059 | Orange County | 135 161 | 06 | 39496 | 059 | Orange County | 77 264 |
| 06 | 28168 | | Gardena city | 58 829 | 06 | 39892 | | Lakewood city | 80 048 |
| 06 | 28168 | 037 | Los Angeles County | 58 829 | 06 | 39892 | 037 | Los Angeles County | 80 048 |
| 06 | 29000 | | Garden Grove city | 170 883 | 06 | 40004 | | La Mesa city | 57 065 |
| 06 | 29000 | 059 | Orange County | 170 883 | 06 | 40004 | 073 | San Diego County | 57 065 |
| 06 | 29504 | | Gilroy city | 48 821 | 06 | 40032 | | La Mirada city | 48 527 |
| 06 | 29504 | 085 | Santa Clara County | 48 821 | 06 | 40032 | 037 | Los Angeles County | 48 527 |
| 06 | 30000 | | Glendale city | 191 719 | 06 | 40130 | | Lancaster city | 156 633 |
| 06 | 30000 | 037 | Los Angeles County | 191 719 | 06 | 40130 | 037 | Los Angeles County | 156 633 |
| 06 | 30014 | | Glendora city | 50 073 | 06 | 40340 | | La Puente city | 39 816 |
| 06 | 30014 | 037 | Los Angeles County | 50 073 | 06 | 40340 | 037 | Los Angeles County | 39 816 |
| 06 | 30378 | | Goleta city | 29 888 | 06 | 40354 | | La Quinta city | 37 467 |
| 06 | 30378 | 083 | Santa Barbara County | 29 888 | 06 | 40354 | 065 | Riverside County | 37 467 |
| 06 | 31960 | | Hanford city | 53 967 | 06 | 40830 | | La Verne city | 31 063 |
| 06 | 31960 | 031 | Kings County | 53 967 | 06 | 40830 | 037 | Los Angeles County | 31 063 |

| State Code | Place Code | County Code | Geographic Area Name | 2010 Census Population | State Code | Place Code | County Code | Geographic Area Name | 2010 Census Population |
|---|---|---|---|---|---|---|---|---|---|
| 06 | 40886 | | Lawndale city | 32 769 | 06 | 48788 | | Montclair city | 36 664 |
| 06 | 40886 | 037 | Los Angeles County | 32 769 | 06 | 48788 | 071 | San Bernardino County | 36 664 |
| 06 | 41124 | | Lemon Grove city | 25 320 | 06 | 48816 | | Montebello city | 62 500 |
| 06 | 41124 | 073 | San Diego County | 25 320 | 06 | 48816 | 037 | Los Angeles County | 62 500 |
| 06 | 41474 | | Lincoln city | 42 819 | 06 | 48872 | | Monterey city | 27 810 |
| 06 | 41474 | 061 | Placer County | 42 819 | 06 | 48872 | 053 | Monterey County | 27 810 |
| 06 | 41992 | | Livermore city | 80 968 | 06 | 48914 | | Monterey Park city | 60 269 |
| 06 | 41992 | 001 | Alameda County | 80 968 | 06 | 48914 | 037 | Los Angeles County | 60 269 |
| 06 | 42202 | | Lodi city | 62 134 | 06 | 49138 | | Moorpark city | 34 421 |
| 06 | 42202 | 077 | San Joaquin County | 62 134 | 06 | 49138 | 111 | Ventura County | 34 421 |
| 06 | 42524 | | Lompoc city | 42 434 | 06 | 49270 | | Moreno Valley city | 193 365 |
| 06 | 42524 | 083 | Santa Barbara County | 42 434 | 06 | 49270 | 065 | Riverside County | 193 365 |
| 06 | 43000 | | Long Beach city | 462 257 | 06 | 49278 | | Morgan Hill city | 37 882 |
| 06 | 43000 | 037 | Los Angeles County | 462 257 | 06 | 49278 | 085 | Santa Clara County | 37 882 |
| 06 | 43280 | | Los Altos city | 28 976 | 06 | 49670 | | Mountain View city | 74 066 |
| 06 | 43280 | 085 | Santa Clara County | 28 976 | 06 | 49670 | 085 | Santa Clara County | 74 066 |
| 06 | 44000 | | Los Angeles city | 3 792 621 | 06 | 50076 | | Murrieta city | 103 466 |
| 06 | 44000 | 037 | Los Angeles County | 3 792 621 | 06 | 50076 | 065 | Riverside County | 103 466 |
| 06 | 44028 | | Los Banos city | 35 972 | 06 | 50258 | | Napa city | 76 915 |
| 06 | 44028 | 047 | Merced County | 35 972 | 06 | 50258 | 055 | Napa County | 76 915 |
| 06 | 44112 | | Los Gatos town | 29 413 | 06 | 50398 | | National City city | 58 582 |
| 06 | 44112 | 085 | Santa Clara County | 29 413 | 06 | 50398 | 073 | San Diego County | 58 582 |
| 06 | 44574 | | Lynwood city | 69 772 | 06 | 50916 | | Newark city | 42 573 |
| 06 | 44574 | 037 | Los Angeles County | 69 772 | 06 | 50916 | 001 | Alameda County | 42 573 |
| 06 | 45022 | | Madera city | 61 416 | 06 | 51182 | | Newport Beach city | 85 186 |
| 06 | 45022 | 039 | Madera County | 61 416 | 06 | 51182 | 059 | Orange County | 85 186 |
| 06 | 45400 | | Manhattan Beach city | 35 135 | 06 | 51560 | | Norco city | 27 063 |
| 06 | 45400 | 037 | Los Angeles County | 35 135 | 06 | 51560 | 065 | Riverside County | 27 063 |
| 06 | 45484 | | Manteca city | 67 096 | 06 | 52526 | | Norwalk city | 105 549 |
| 06 | 45484 | 077 | San Joaquin County | 67 096 | 06 | 52526 | 037 | Los Angeles County | 105 549 |
| 06 | 46114 | | Martinez city | 35 824 | 06 | 52582 | | Novato city | 51 904 |
| 06 | 46114 | 013 | Contra Costa County | 35 824 | 06 | 52582 | 041 | Marin County | 51 904 |
| 06 | 46492 | | Maywood city | 27 395 | 06 | 53000 | | Oakland city | 390 724 |
| 06 | 46492 | 037 | Los Angeles County | 27 395 | 06 | 53000 | 001 | Alameda County | 390 724 |
| 06 | 46842 | | Menifee city | 77 519 | 06 | 53070 | | Oakley city | 35 432 |
| 06 | 46842 | 065 | Riverside County | 77 519 | 06 | 53070 | 013 | Contra Costa County | 35 432 |
| 06 | 46870 | | Menlo Park city | 32 026 | 06 | 53322 | | Oceanside city | 167 086 |
| 06 | 46870 | 081 | San Mateo County | 32 026 | 06 | 53322 | 073 | San Diego County | 167 086 |
| 06 | 46898 | | Merced city | 78 958 | 06 | 53896 | | Ontario city | 163 924 |
| 06 | 46898 | 047 | Merced County | 78 958 | 06 | 53896 | 071 | San Bernardino County | 163 924 |
| 06 | 47766 | | Milpitas city | 66 790 | 06 | 53980 | | Orange city | 136 416 |
| 06 | 47766 | 085 | Santa Clara County | 66 790 | 06 | 53980 | 059 | Orange County | 136 416 |
| 06 | 48256 | | Mission Viejo city | 93 305 | 06 | 54652 | | Oxnard city | 197 899 |
| 06 | 48256 | 059 | Orange County | 93 305 | 06 | 54652 | 111 | Ventura County | 197 899 |
| 06 | 48354 | | Modesto city | 201 165 | 06 | 54806 | | Pacifica city | 37 234 |
| 06 | 48354 | 099 | Stanislaus County | 201 165 | 06 | 54806 | 081 | San Mateo County | 37 234 |
| 06 | 48648 | | Monrovia city | 36 590 | 06 | 55156 | | Palmdale city | 152 750 |
| 06 | 48648 | 037 | Los Angeles County | 36 590 | 06 | 55156 | 037 | Los Angeles County | 152 750 |

| State Code | Place Code | County Code | Geographic Area Name | 2010 Census Population | State Code | Place Code | County Code | Geographic Area Name | 2010 Census Population |
|---|---|---|---|---|---|---|---|---|---|
| 06 | 55184 | | Palm Desert city | 48 445 | 06 | 60466 | | Rialto city | 99 171 |
| 06 | 55184 | 065 | Riverside County | 48 445 | 06 | 60466 | 071 | San Bernardino County | 99 171 |
| 06 | 55254 | | Palm Springs city | 44 552 | 06 | 60620 | | Richmond city | 103 701 |
| 06 | 55254 | 065 | Riverside County | 44 552 | 06 | 60620 | 013 | Contra Costa County | 103 701 |
| 06 | 55282 | | Palo Alto city | 64 403 | 06 | 60704 | | Ridgecrest city | 27 616 |
| 06 | 55282 | 085 | Santa Clara County | 64 403 | 06 | 60704 | 029 | Kern County | 27 616 |
| 06 | 55520 | | Paradise town | 26 218 | 06 | 62000 | | Riverside city | 303 871 |
| 06 | 55520 | 007 | Butte County | 26 218 | 06 | 62000 | 065 | Riverside County | 303 871 |
| 06 | 55618 | | Paramount city | 54 098 | 06 | 62364 | | Rocklin city | 56 974 |
| 06 | 55618 | 037 | Los Angeles County | 54 098 | 06 | 62364 | 061 | Placer County | 56 974 |
| 06 | 56000 | | Pasadena city | 137 122 | 06 | 62546 | | Rohnert Park city | 40 971 |
| 06 | 56000 | 037 | Los Angeles County | 137 122 | 06 | 62546 | 097 | Sonoma County | 40 971 |
| 06 | 56700 | | Perris city | 68 386 | 06 | 62896 | | Rosemead city | 53 764 |
| 06 | 56700 | 065 | Riverside County | 68 386 | 06 | 62896 | 037 | Los Angeles County | 53 764 |
| 06 | 56784 | | Petaluma city | 57 941 | 06 | 62938 | | Roseville city | 118 788 |
| 06 | 56784 | 097 | Sonoma County | 57 941 | 06 | 62938 | 061 | Placer County | 118 788 |
| 06 | 56924 | | Pico Rivera city | 62 942 | 06 | 64000 | | Sacramento city | 466 488 |
| 06 | 56924 | 037 | Los Angeles County | 62 942 | 06 | 64000 | 067 | Sacramento County | 466 488 |
| 06 | 57456 | | Pittsburg city | 63 264 | 06 | 64224 | | Salinas city | 150 441 |
| 06 | 57456 | 013 | Contra Costa County | 63 264 | 06 | 64224 | 053 | Monterey County | 150 441 |
| 06 | 57526 | | Placentia city | 50 533 | 06 | 65000 | | San Bernardino city | 209 924 |
| 06 | 57526 | 059 | Orange County | 50 533 | 06 | 65000 | 071 | San Bernardino County | 209 924 |
| 06 | 57764 | | Pleasant Hill city | 33 152 | 06 | 65028 | | San Bruno city | 41 114 |
| 06 | 57764 | 013 | Contra Costa County | 33 152 | 06 | 65028 | 081 | San Mateo County | 41 114 |
| 06 | 57792 | | Pleasanton city | 70 285 | 06 | 65042 | | San Buenaventura (Ventura) | 106 433 |
| 06 | 57792 | 001 | Alameda County | 70 285 | 06 | 65042 | 111 | Ventura County | 106 433 |
| 06 | 58072 | | Pomona city | 149 058 | 06 | 65070 | | San Carlos city | 28 406 |
| 06 | 58072 | 037 | Los Angeles County | 149 058 | 06 | 65070 | 081 | San Mateo County | 28 406 |
| 06 | 58240 | | Porterville city | 54 165 | 06 | 65084 | | San Clemente city | 63 522 |
| 06 | 58240 | 107 | Tulare County | 54 165 | 06 | 65084 | 059 | Orange County | 63 522 |
| 06 | 58520 | | Poway city | 47 811 | 06 | 66000 | | San Diego city | 1 307 402 |
| 06 | 58520 | 073 | San Diego County | 47 811 | 06 | 66000 | 073 | San Diego County | 1 307 402 |
| 06 | 59444 | | Rancho Cordova city | 64 776 | 06 | 66070 | | San Dimas city | 33 371 |
| 06 | 59444 | 067 | Sacramento County | 64 776 | 06 | 66070 | 037 | Los Angeles County | 33 371 |
| 06 | 59451 | | Rancho Cucamonga city | 165 269 | 06 | 67000 | | San Francisco city | 805 235 |
| 06 | 59451 | 071 | San Bernardino County | 165 269 | 06 | 67000 | 075 | San Francisco County | 805 235 |
| 06 | 59514 | | Rancho Palos Verdes city | 41 643 | 06 | 67042 | | San Gabriel city | 39 718 |
| 06 | 59514 | 037 | Los Angeles County | 41 643 | 06 | 67042 | 037 | Los Angeles County | 39 718 |
| 06 | 59587 | | Rancho Santa Margarita city | 47 853 | 06 | 67112 | | San Jacinto city | 44 199 |
| 06 | 59587 | 059 | Orange County | 47 853 | 06 | 67112 | 065 | Riverside County | 44 199 |
| 06 | 59920 | | Redding city | 89 861 | 06 | 68000 | | San Jose city | 945 942 |
| 06 | 59920 | 089 | Shasta County | 89 861 | 06 | 68000 | 085 | Santa Clara County | 945 942 |
| 06 | 59962 | | Redlands city | 68 747 | 06 | 68028 | | San Juan Capistrano city | 34 593 |
| 06 | 59962 | 071 | San Bernardino County | 68 747 | 06 | 68028 | 059 | Orange County | 34 593 |
| 06 | 60018 | | Redondo Beach city | 66 748 | 06 | 68084 | | San Leandro city | 84 950 |
| 06 | 60018 | 037 | Los Angeles County | 66 748 | 06 | 68084 | 001 | Alameda County | 84 950 |
| 06 | 60102 | | Redwood City city | 76 815 | 06 | 68154 | | San Luis Obispo city | 45 119 |
| 06 | 60102 | 081 | San Mateo County | 76 815 | 06 | 68154 | 079 | San Luis Obispo County | 45 119 |

# Cities by County–*Continued*

| State Code | Place Code | County Code | Geographic Area Name | 2010 Census Population | State Code | Place Code | County Code | Geographic Area Name | 2010 Census Population |
|---|---|---|---|---|---|---|---|---|---|
| 06 | 68196 | | San Marcos city | 83 781 | 06 | 75630 | | Suisun City city | 28 111 |
| 06 | 68196 | 073 | San Diego County | 83 781 | 06 | 75630 | 095 | Solano County | 28 111 |
| 06 | 68252 | | San Mateo city | 97 207 | 06 | 77000 | | Sunnyvale city | 140 081 |
| 06 | 68252 | 081 | San Mateo County | 97 207 | 06 | 77000 | 085 | Santa Clara County | 140 081 |
| 06 | 68294 | | San Pablo city | 29 139 | 06 | 78120 | | Temecula city | 100 097 |
| 06 | 68294 | 013 | Contra Costa County | 29 139 | 06 | 78120 | 065 | Riverside County | 100 097 |
| 06 | 68364 | | San Rafael city | 57 713 | 06 | 78148 | | Temple City city | 35 558 |
| 06 | 68364 | 041 | Marin County | 57 713 | 06 | 78148 | 037 | Los Angeles County | 35 558 |
| 06 | 68378 | | San Ramon city | 72 148 | 06 | 78582 | | Thousand Oaks city | 126 683 |
| 06 | 68378 | 013 | Contra Costa County | 72 148 | 06 | 78582 | 111 | Ventura County | 126 683 |
| 06 | 69000 | | Santa Ana city | 324 528 | 06 | 80000 | | Torrance city | 145 438 |
| 06 | 69000 | 059 | Orange County | 324 528 | 06 | 80000 | 037 | Los Angeles County | 145 438 |
| 06 | 69070 | | Santa Barbara city | 88 410 | 06 | 80238 | | Tracy city | 82 922 |
| 06 | 69070 | 083 | Santa Barbara County | 88 410 | 06 | 80238 | 077 | San Joaquin County | 82 922 |
| 06 | 69084 | | Santa Clara city | 116 468 | 06 | 80644 | | Tulare city | 59 278 |
| 06 | 69084 | 085 | Santa Clara County | 116 468 | 06 | 80644 | 107 | Tulare County | 59 278 |
| 06 | 69088 | | Santa Clarita city | 176 320 | 06 | 80812 | | Turlock city | 68 549 |
| 06 | 69088 | 037 | Los Angeles County | 176 320 | 06 | 80812 | 099 | Stanislaus County | 68 549 |
| 06 | 69112 | | Santa Cruz city | 59 946 | 06 | 80854 | | Tustin city | 75 540 |
| 06 | 69112 | 087 | Santa Cruz County | 59 946 | 06 | 80854 | 059 | Orange County | 75 540 |
| 06 | 69196 | | Santa Maria city | 99 553 | 06 | 80994 | | Twentynine Palms city | 25 048 |
| 06 | 69196 | 083 | Santa Barbara County | 99 553 | 06 | 80994 | 071 | San Bernardino County | 25 048 |
| 06 | 70000 | | Santa Monica city | 89 736 | 06 | 81204 | | Union City city | 69 516 |
| 06 | 70000 | 037 | Los Angeles County | 89 736 | 06 | 81204 | 001 | Alameda County | 69 516 |
| 06 | 70042 | | Santa Paula city | 29 321 | 06 | 81344 | | Upland city | 73 732 |
| 06 | 70042 | 111 | Ventura County | 29 321 | 06 | 81344 | 071 | San Bernardino County | 73 732 |
| 06 | 70098 | | Santa Rosa city | 167 815 | 06 | 81554 | | Vacaville city | 92 428 |
| 06 | 70098 | 097 | Sonoma County | 167 815 | 06 | 81554 | 095 | Solano County | 92 428 |
| 06 | 70224 | | Santee city | 53 413 | 06 | 81666 | | Vallejo city | 115 942 |
| 06 | 70224 | 073 | San Diego County | 53 413 | 06 | 81666 | 095 | Solano County | 115 942 |
| 06 | 70280 | | Saratoga city | 29 926 | 06 | 82590 | | Victorville city | 115 903 |
| 06 | 70280 | 085 | Santa Clara County | 29 926 | 06 | 82590 | 071 | San Bernardino County | 115 903 |
| 06 | 70742 | | Seaside city | 33 025 | 06 | 82954 | | Visalia city | 124 442 |
| 06 | 70742 | 053 | Monterey County | 33 025 | 06 | 82954 | 107 | Tulare County | 124 442 |
| 06 | 72016 | | Simi Valley city | 124 237 | 06 | 82996 | | Vista city | 93 834 |
| 06 | 72016 | 111 | Ventura County | 124 237 | 06 | 82996 | 073 | San Diego County | 93 834 |
| 06 | 72520 | | Soledad city | 25 738 | 06 | 83332 | | Walnut city | 29 172 |
| 06 | 72520 | 053 | Monterey County | 25 738 | 06 | 83332 | 037 | Los Angeles County | 29 172 |
| 06 | 73080 | | South Gate city | 94 396 | 06 | 83346 | | Walnut Creek city | 64 173 |
| 06 | 73080 | 037 | Los Angeles County | 94 396 | 06 | 83346 | 013 | Contra Costa County | 64 173 |
| 06 | 73220 | | South Pasadena city | 25 619 | 06 | 83542 | | Wasco city | 25 545 |
| 06 | 73220 | 037 | Los Angeles County | 25 619 | 06 | 83542 | 029 | Kern County | 25 545 |
| 06 | 73262 | | South San Francisco city | 63 632 | 06 | 83668 | | Watsonville city | 51 199 |
| 06 | 73262 | 081 | San Mateo County | 63 632 | 06 | 83668 | 087 | Santa Cruz County | 51 199 |
| 06 | 73962 | | Stanton city | 38 186 | 06 | 84200 | | West Covina city | 106 098 |
| 06 | 73962 | 059 | Orange County | 38 186 | 06 | 84200 | 037 | Los Angeles County | 106 098 |
| 06 | 75000 | | Stockton city | 291 707 | 06 | 84410 | | West Hollywood city | 34 399 |
| 06 | 75000 | 077 | San Joaquin County | 291 707 | 06 | 84410 | 037 | Los Angeles County | 34 399 |

| State Code | Place Code | County Code | Geographic Area Name | 2010 Census Population | State Code | Place Code | County Code | Geographic Area Name | 2010 Census Population |
|---|---|---|---|---|---|---|---|---|---|
| 06 | 84550 | | Westminster city | 89 701 | 08 | 31660 | | Grand Junction city | 58 566 |
| 06 | 84550 | 059 | Orange County | 89 701 | 08 | 31660 | 077 | Mesa County | 58 566 |
| | | | | | | | | | |
| 06 | 84816 | | West Sacramento city | 48 744 | 08 | 32155 | | Greeley city | 92 889 |
| 06 | 84816 | 113 | Yolo County | 48 744 | 08 | 32155 | 123 | Weld County | 92 889 |
| | | | | | | | | | |
| 06 | 85292 | | Whittier city | 85 331 | 08 | 43000 | | Lakewood city | 142 980 |
| 06 | 85292 | 037 | Los Angeles County | 85 331 | 08 | 43000 | 059 | Jefferson County | 142 980 |
| | | | | | | | | | |
| 06 | 85446 | | Wildomar city | 32 176 | 08 | 45255 | | Littleton city | 41 737 |
| 06 | 85446 | 065 | Riverside County | 32 176 | 08 | 45255 | 005 | Arapahoe County | 39 328 |
| | | | | | 08 | 45255 | 035 | Douglas County | 28 |
| 06 | 85922 | | Windsor town | 26 801 | 08 | 45255 | 059 | Jefferson County | 2 381 |
| 06 | 85922 | 097 | Sonoma County | 26 801 | | | | | |
| | | | | | 08 | 45970 | | Longmont city | 86 270 |
| 06 | 86328 | | Woodland city | 55 468 | 08 | 45970 | 013 | Boulder County | 86 240 |
| 06 | 86328 | 113 | Yolo County | 55 468 | 08 | 45970 | 123 | Weld County | 30 |
| | | | | | | | | | |
| 06 | 86832 | | Yorba Linda city | 64 234 | 08 | 46465 | | Loveland city | 66 859 |
| 06 | 86832 | 059 | Orange County | 64 234 | 08 | 46465 | 069 | Larimer County | 66 859 |
| | | | | | | | | | |
| 06 | 86972 | | Yuba City city | 64 925 | 08 | 54330 | | Northglenn city | 35 789 |
| 06 | 86972 | 101 | Sutter County | 64 925 | 08 | 54330 | 001 | Adams County | 35 777 |
| | | | | | 08 | 54330 | 123 | Weld County | 12 |
| 06 | 87042 | | Yucaipa city | 51 367 | | | | | |
| 06 | 87042 | 071 | San Bernardino County | 51 367 | 08 | 57630 | | Parker town | 45 297 |
| | | | | | 08 | 57630 | 035 | Douglas County | 45 297 |
| 08 | | | **COLORADO** | 5 029 196 | | | | | |
| 08 | 03455 | | Arvada city | 106 433 | 08 | 62000 | | Pueblo city | 106 595 |
| 08 | 03455 | 001 | Adams County | 2 849 | 08 | 62000 | 101 | Pueblo County | 106 595 |
| 08 | 03455 | 059 | Jefferson County | 103 584 | | | | | |
| | | | | | 08 | 77290 | | Thornton city | 118 772 |
| 08 | 04000 | | Aurora city | 325 078 | 08 | 77290 | 001 | Adams County | 118 772 |
| 08 | 04000 | 001 | Adams County | 39 871 | 08 | 77290 | 123 | Weld County | 0 |
| 08 | 04000 | 005 | Arapahoe County | 285 090 | | | | | |
| 08 | 04000 | 035 | Douglas County | 117 | 08 | 83835 | | Westminster city | 106 114 |
| | | | | | 08 | 83835 | 001 | Adams County | 63 696 |
| 08 | 07850 | | Boulder city | 97 385 | 08 | 83835 | 059 | Jefferson County | 42 418 |
| 08 | 07850 | 013 | Boulder County | 97 385 | | | | | |
| | | | | | 08 | 84440 | | Wheat Ridge city | 30 166 |
| 08 | 08675 | | Brighton city | 33 352 | 08 | 84440 | 059 | Jefferson County | 30 166 |
| 08 | 08675 | 001 | Adams County | 33 009 | | | | | |
| 08 | 08675 | 123 | Weld County | 343 | 09 | | | **CONNECTICUT** | 3 574 097 |
| | | | | | 09 | 08000 | | Bridgeport city | 144 229 |
| 08 | 09280 | | Broomfield city | 55 889 | 09 | 08000 | 001 | Fairfield County | 144 229 |
| 08 | 09280 | 014 | Broomfield County | 55 889 | | | | | |
| | | | | | 09 | 08420 | | Bristol city | 60 477 |
| 08 | 12415 | | Castle Rock town | 48 231 | 09 | 08420 | 003 | Hartford County | 60 477 |
| 08 | 12415 | 035 | Douglas County | 48 231 | | | | | |
| | | | | | 09 | 18430 | | Danbury city | 80 893 |
| 08 | 12815 | | Centennial city | 100 377 | 09 | 18430 | 001 | Fairfield County | 80 893 |
| 08 | 12815 | 005 | Arapahoe County | 100 377 | | | | | |
| | | | | | 09 | 37000 | | Hartford city | 124 775 |
| 08 | 16000 | | Colorado Springs city | 416 427 | 09 | 37000 | 003 | Hartford County | 124 775 |
| 08 | 16000 | 041 | El Paso County | 416 427 | | | | | |
| | | | | | 09 | 46450 | | Meriden city | 60 868 |
| 08 | 16495 | | Commerce City city | 45 913 | 09 | 46450 | 009 | New Haven County | 60 868 |
| 08 | 16495 | 001 | Adams County | 45 913 | | | | | |
| | | | | | 09 | 47290 | | Middletown city | 47 648 |
| 08 | 20000 | | Denver city | 600 158 | 09 | 47290 | 007 | Middlesex County | 47 648 |
| 08 | 20000 | 031 | Denver County | 600 158 | | | | | |
| | | | | | 09 | 49880 | | Naugatuck borough | 31 862 |
| 08 | 24785 | | Englewood city | 30 255 | 09 | 49880 | 009 | New Haven County | 31 862 |
| 08 | 24785 | 005 | Arapahoe County | 30 255 | | | | | |
| | | | | | 09 | 50370 | | New Britain city | 73 206 |
| 08 | 27425 | | Fort Collins city | 143 986 | 09 | 50370 | 003 | Hartford County | 73 206 |
| 08 | 27425 | 069 | Larimer County | 143 986 | | | | | |
| | | | | | 09 | 52000 | | New Haven city | 129 779 |
| 08 | 27865 | | Fountain city | 25 846 | 09 | 52000 | 009 | New Haven County | 129 779 |
| 08 | 27865 | 041 | El Paso County | 25 846 | | | | | |
| | | | | | 09 | 52280 | | New London city | 27 620 |
| | | | | | 09 | 52280 | 011 | New London County | 27 620 |

| State Code | Place Code | County Code | Geographic Area Name | 2010 Census Population | State Code | Place Code | County Code | Geographic Area Name | 2010 Census Population |
|---|---|---|---|---|---|---|---|---|---|
| 09 | 55990 | | Norwalk city | 85 603 | 12 | 14125 | | Cooper City city | 28 547 |
| 09 | 55990 | 001 | Fairfield County | 85 603 | 12 | 14125 | 011 | Broward County | 28 547 |
| 09 | 56200 | | Norwich city | 40 493 | 12 | 14250 | | Coral Gables city | 46 780 |
| 09 | 56200 | 011 | New London County | 40 493 | 12 | 14250 | 086 | Miami-Dade County | 46 780 |
| 09 | 68100 | | Shelton city | 39 559 | 12 | 14400 | | Coral Springs city | 121 096 |
| 09 | 68100 | 001 | Fairfield County | 39 559 | 12 | 14400 | 011 | Broward County | 121 096 |
| 09 | 73000 | | Stamford city | 122 643 | 12 | 15968 | | Cutler Bay town | 40 286 |
| 09 | 73000 | 001 | Fairfield County | 122 643 | 12 | 15968 | 086 | Miami-Dade County | 40 286 |
| 09 | 76500 | | Torrington city | 36 383 | 12 | 16335 | | Dania Beach city | 29 639 |
| 09 | 76500 | 005 | Litchfield County | 36 383 | 12 | 16335 | 011 | Broward County | 29 639 |
| 09 | 80000 | | Waterbury city | 110 366 | 12 | 16475 | | Davie town | 91 992 |
| 09 | 80000 | 009 | New Haven County | 110 366 | 12 | 16475 | 011 | Broward County | 91 992 |
| 09 | 82800 | | West Haven city | 55 564 | 12 | 16525 | | Daytona Beach city | 61 005 |
| 09 | 82800 | 009 | New Haven County | 55 564 | 12 | 16525 | 127 | Volusia County | 61 005 |
| 10 | | | **DELAWARE** | 897 934 | 12 | 16725 | | Deerfield Beach city | 75 018 |
| 10 | 21200 | | Dover city | 36 047 | 12 | 16725 | 011 | Broward County | 75 018 |
| 10 | 21200 | 001 | Kent County | 36 047 | | | | | |
| | | | | | 12 | 16875 | | DeLand city | 27 031 |
| 10 | 50670 | | Newark city | 31 454 | 12 | 16875 | 127 | Volusia County | 27 031 |
| 10 | 50670 | 003 | New Castle County | 31 454 | | | | | |
| | | | | | 12 | 17100 | | Delray Beach city | 60 522 |
| 10 | 77580 | | Wilmington city | 70 851 | 12 | 17100 | 099 | Palm Beach County | 60 522 |
| 10 | 77580 | 003 | New Castle County | 70 851 | | | | | |
| | | | | | 12 | 17200 | | Deltona city | 85 182 |
| 11 | | | **DISTRICT OF COLUMBIA** | 601 723 | 12 | 17200 | 127 | Volusia County | 85 182 |
| 11 | 50000 | | Washington city | 601 723 | | | | | |
| 11 | 50000 | 001 | District of Columbia | 601 723 | 12 | 17935 | | Doral city | 45 704 |
| | | | | | 12 | 17935 | 086 | Miami-Dade County | 45 704 |
| 12 | | | **FLORIDA** | 18 801 310 | | | | | |
| 12 | 00950 | | Altamonte Springs city | 41 496 | 12 | 18575 | | Dunedin city | 35 321 |
| 12 | 00950 | 117 | Seminole County | 41 496 | 12 | 18575 | 103 | Pinellas County | 35 321 |
| 12 | 01700 | | Apopka city | 41 542 | 12 | 24000 | | Fort Lauderdale city | 165 521 |
| 12 | 01700 | 095 | Orange County | 41 542 | 12 | 24000 | 011 | Broward County | 165 521 |
| 12 | 02681 | | Aventura city | 35 762 | 12 | 24125 | | Fort Myers city | 62 298 |
| 12 | 02681 | 086 | Miami-Dade County | 35 762 | 12 | 24125 | 071 | Lee County | 62 298 |
| 12 | 07300 | | Boca Raton city | 84 392 | 12 | 24300 | | Fort Pierce city | 41 590 |
| 12 | 07300 | 099 | Palm Beach County | 84 392 | 12 | 24300 | 111 | St. Lucie County | 41 590 |
| 12 | 07525 | | Bonita Springs city | 43 914 | 12 | 25175 | | Gainesville city | 124 354 |
| 12 | 07525 | 071 | Lee County | 43 914 | 12 | 25175 | 001 | Alachua County | 124 354 |
| 12 | 07875 | | Boynton Beach city | 68 217 | 12 | 27322 | | Greenacres city | 37 573 |
| 12 | 07875 | 099 | Palm Beach County | 68 217 | 12 | 27322 | 099 | Palm Beach County | 37 573 |
| 12 | 07950 | | Bradenton city | 49 546 | 12 | 28452 | | Hallandale Beach city | 37 113 |
| 12 | 07950 | 081 | Manatee County | 49 546 | 12 | 28452 | 011 | Broward County | 37 113 |
| 12 | 10275 | | Cape Coral city | 154 305 | 12 | 30000 | | Hialeah city | 224 669 |
| 12 | 10275 | 071 | Lee County | 154 305 | 12 | 30000 | 086 | Miami-Dade County | 224 669 |
| 12 | 11050 | | Casselberry city | 26 241 | 12 | 32000 | | Hollywood city | 140 768 |
| 12 | 11050 | 117 | Seminole County | 26 241 | 12 | 32000 | 011 | Broward County | 140 768 |
| 12 | 12875 | | Clearwater city | 107 685 | 12 | 32275 | | Homestead city | 60 512 |
| 12 | 12875 | 103 | Pinellas County | 107 685 | 12 | 32275 | 086 | Miami-Dade County | 60 512 |
| 12 | 12925 | | Clermont city | 28 742 | 12 | 35000 | | Jacksonville city | 821 784 |
| 12 | 12925 | 069 | Lake County | 28 742 | 12 | 35000 | 031 | Duval County | 821 784 |
| 12 | 13275 | | Coconut Creek city | 52 909 | 12 | 35875 | | Jupiter town | 55 156 |
| 12 | 13275 | 011 | Broward County | 52 909 | 12 | 35875 | 099 | Palm Beach County | 55 156 |

| State Code | Place Code | County Code | Geographic Area Name | 2010 Census Population | State Code | Place Code | County Code | Geographic Area Name | 2010 Census Population |
|---|---|---|---|---|---|---|---|---|---|
| 12 | 36950 | | Kissimmee city | 59 682 | 12 | 54075 | | Palm Beach Gardens city | 48 452 |
| 12 | 36950 | 097 | Osceola County | 59 682 | 12 | 54075 | 099 | Palm Beach County | 48 452 |
| 12 | 38250 | | Lakeland city | 97 422 | 12 | 54200 | | Palm Coast city | 75 180 |
| 12 | 38250 | 105 | Polk County | 97 422 | 12 | 54200 | 035 | Flagler County | 75 180 |
| 12 | 39075 | | Lake Worth city | 34 910 | 12 | 54700 | | Panama City city | 36 484 |
| 12 | 39075 | 099 | Palm Beach County | 34 910 | 12 | 54700 | 005 | Bay County | 36 484 |
| 12 | 39425 | | Largo city | 77 648 | 12 | 55775 | | Pembroke Pines city | 154 750 |
| 12 | 39425 | 103 | Pinellas County | 77 648 | 12 | 55775 | 011 | Broward County | 154 750 |
| 12 | 39525 | | Lauderdale Lakes city | 32 593 | 12 | 55925 | | Pensacola city | 51 923 |
| 12 | 39525 | 011 | Broward County | 32 593 | 12 | 55925 | 033 | Escambia County | 51 923 |
| 12 | 39550 | | Lauderhill city | 66 887 | 12 | 56975 | | Pinellas Park city | 49 079 |
| 12 | 39550 | 011 | Broward County | 66 887 | 12 | 56975 | 103 | Pinellas County | 49 079 |
| 12 | 43125 | | Margate city | 53 284 | 12 | 57425 | | Plantation city | 84 955 |
| 12 | 43125 | 011 | Broward County | 53 284 | 12 | 57425 | 011 | Broward County | 84 955 |
| 12 | 43975 | | Melbourne city | 76 068 | 12 | 57550 | | Plant City city | 34 721 |
| 12 | 43975 | 009 | Brevard County | 76 068 | 12 | 57550 | 057 | Hillsborough County | 34 721 |
| 12 | 45000 | | Miami city | 399 457 | 12 | 58050 | | Pompano Beach city | 99 845 |
| 12 | 45000 | 086 | Miami-Dade County | 399 457 | 12 | 58050 | 011 | Broward County | 99 845 |
| 12 | 45025 | | Miami Beach city | 87 779 | 12 | 58575 | | Port Orange city | 56 048 |
| 12 | 45025 | 086 | Miami-Dade County | 87 779 | 12 | 58575 | 127 | Volusia County | 56 048 |
| 12 | 45060 | | Miami Gardens city | 107 167 | 12 | 58715 | | Port St. Lucie city | 164 603 |
| 12 | 45060 | 086 | Miami-Dade County | 107 167 | 12 | 58715 | 111 | St. Lucie County | 164 603 |
| 12 | 45100 | | Miami Lakes town | 29 361 | 12 | 60975 | | Riviera Beach city | 32 488 |
| 12 | 45100 | 086 | Miami-Dade County | 29 361 | 12 | 60975 | 099 | Palm Beach County | 32 488 |
| 12 | 45975 | | Miramar city | 122 041 | 12 | 62100 | | Royal Palm Beach village | 34 140 |
| 12 | 45975 | 011 | Broward County | 122 041 | 12 | 62100 | 099 | Palm Beach County | 34 140 |
| 12 | 49425 | | North Lauderdale city | 41 023 | 12 | 62625 | | St. Cloud city | 35 183 |
| 12 | 49425 | 011 | Broward County | 41 023 | 12 | 62625 | 097 | Osceola County | 35 183 |
| 12 | 49450 | | North Miami city | 58 786 | 12 | 63000 | | St. Petersburg city | 244 769 |
| 12 | 49450 | 086 | Miami-Dade County | 58 786 | 12 | 63000 | 103 | Pinellas County | 244 769 |
| 12 | 49475 | | North Miami Beach city | 41 523 | 12 | 63650 | | Sanford city | 53 570 |
| 12 | 49475 | 086 | Miami-Dade County | 41 523 | 12 | 63650 | 117 | Seminole County | 53 570 |
| 12 | 49675 | | North Port city | 57 357 | 12 | 64175 | | Sarasota city | 51 917 |
| 12 | 49675 | 115 | Sarasota County | 57 357 | 12 | 64175 | 115 | Sarasota County | 51 917 |
| 12 | 50575 | | Oakland Park city | 41 363 | 12 | 69700 | | Sunrise city | 84 439 |
| 12 | 50575 | 011 | Broward County | 41 363 | 12 | 69700 | 011 | Broward County | 84 439 |
| 12 | 50750 | | Ocala city | 56 315 | 12 | 70600 | | Tallahassee city | 181 376 |
| 12 | 50750 | 083 | Marion County | 56 315 | 12 | 70600 | 073 | Leon County | 181 376 |
| 12 | 51075 | | Ocoee city | 35 579 | 12 | 70675 | | Tamarac city | 60 427 |
| 12 | 51075 | 095 | Orange County | 35 579 | 12 | 70675 | 011 | Broward County | 60 427 |
| 12 | 53000 | | Orlando city | 238 300 | 12 | 71000 | | Tampa city | 335 709 |
| 12 | 53000 | 095 | Orange County | 238 300 | 12 | 71000 | 057 | Hillsborough County | 335 709 |
| 12 | 53150 | | Ormond Beach city | 38 137 | 12 | 71900 | | Titusville city | 43 761 |
| 12 | 53150 | 127 | Volusia County | 38 137 | 12 | 71900 | 009 | Brevard County | 43 761 |
| 12 | 53575 | | Oviedo city | 33 342 | 12 | 75812 | | Wellington village | 56 508 |
| 12 | 53575 | 117 | Seminole County | 33 342 | 12 | 75812 | 099 | Palm Beach County | 56 508 |
| 12 | 54000 | | Palm Bay city | 103 190 | 12 | 76582 | | Weston city | 65 333 |
| 12 | 54000 | 009 | Brevard County | 103 190 | 12 | 76582 | 011 | Broward County | 65 333 |

# Cities by County–*Continued*

| State Code | Place Code | County Code | Geographic Area Name | 2010 Census Population | State Code | Place Code | County Code | Geographic Area Name | 2010 Census Population |
|---|---|---|---|---|---|---|---|---|---|
| 12 | 76600 | | West Palm Beach city | 99 919 | 13 | 55020 | | Newnan city | 33 039 |
| 12 | 76600 | 099 | Palm Beach County | 99 919 | 13 | 55020 | 077 | Coweta County | 33 039 |
| 12 | 78250 | | Winter Garden city | 34 568 | 13 | 59724 | | Peachtree City city | 34 364 |
| 12 | 78250 | 095 | Orange County | 34 568 | 13 | 59724 | 113 | Fayette County | 34 364 |
| 12 | 78275 | | Winter Haven city | 33 874 | 13 | 66668 | | Rome city | 36 303 |
| 12 | 78275 | 105 | Polk County | 33 874 | 13 | 66668 | 115 | Floyd County | 36 303 |
| 12 | 78300 | | Winter Park city | 27 852 | 13 | 67284 | | Roswell city | 88 346 |
| 12 | 78300 | 095 | Orange County | 27 852 | 13 | 67284 | 121 | Fulton County | 88 346 |
| 12 | 78325 | | Winter Springs city | 33 282 | 13 | 68516 | | Sandy Springs city | 93 853 |
| 12 | 78325 | 117 | Seminole County | 33 282 | 13 | 68516 | 121 | Fulton County | 93 853 |
| 13 | | | **GEORGIA** | 9 687 653 | 13 | 69000 | | Savannah city | 136 286 |
| 13 | 01052 | | Albany city | 77 434 | 13 | 69000 | 051 | Chatham County | 136 286 |
| 13 | 01052 | 095 | Dougherty County | 77 434 | 13 | 71492 | | Smyrna city | 51 271 |
| 13 | 01696 | | Alpharetta city | 57 551 | 13 | 71492 | 067 | Cobb County | 51 271 |
| 13 | 01696 | 121 | Fulton County | 57 551 | 13 | 73256 | | Statesboro city | 28 422 |
| 13 | 04000 | | Atlanta city | 420 003 | 13 | 73256 | 031 | Bulloch County | 28 422 |
| 13 | 04000 | 089 | DeKalb County | 28 292 | 13 | 73704 | | Stockbridge city | 25 636 |
| 13 | 04000 | 121 | Fulton County | 391 711 | 13 | 73704 | 151 | Henry County | 25 636 |
| 13 | 19000 | | Columbus city | 189 885 | 13 | 78800 | | Valdosta city | 54 518 |
| 13 | 19000 | 215 | Muscogee County | 189 885 | 13 | 78800 | 185 | Lowndes County | 54 518 |
| 13 | 21380 | | Dalton city | 33 128 | 13 | 80508 | | Warner Robins city | 66 588 |
| 13 | 21380 | 313 | Whitfield County | 33 128 | 13 | 80508 | 153 | Houston County | 66 224 |
| 13 | 23900 | | Douglasville city | 30 961 | 13 | 80508 | 225 | Peach County | 364 |
| 13 | 23900 | 097 | Douglas County | 30 961 | 15 | | | **HAWAII** | 1 360 301 |
| 13 | 24600 | | Duluth city | 26 600 | 15 | 06290 | | East Honolulu CDP | 49 914 |
| 13 | 24600 | 135 | Gwinnett County | 26 600 | 15 | 06290 | 003 | Honolulu County | 49 914 |
| 13 | 24768 | | Dunwoody city | 46 267 | 15 | 14650 | | Hilo CDP | 43 263 |
| 13 | 24768 | 089 | DeKalb County | 46 267 | 15 | 14650 | 001 | Hawaii County | 43 263 |
| 13 | 25720 | | East Point city | 33 712 | 15 | 22700 | | Kahului CDP | 26 337 |
| 13 | 25720 | 121 | Fulton County | 33 712 | 15 | 22700 | 009 | Maui County | 26 337 |
| 13 | 31908 | | Gainesville city | 33 804 | 15 | 23150 | | Kailua CDP | 38 635 |
| 13 | 31908 | 139 | Hall County | 33 804 | 15 | 23150 | 003 | Honolulu County | 38 635 |
| 13 | 38964 | | Hinesville city | 33 437 | 15 | 28250 | | Kaneohe CDP | 34 597 |
| 13 | 38964 | 179 | Liberty County | 33 437 | 15 | 28250 | 003 | Honolulu County | 34 597 |
| 13 | 42425 | | Johns Creek city | 76 728 | 15 | 51050 | | Mililani Town CDP | 27 629 |
| 13 | 42425 | 121 | Fulton County | 76 728 | 15 | 51050 | 003 | Honolulu County | 27 629 |
| 13 | 43192 | | Kennesaw city | 29 783 | 15 | 62600 | | Pearl City CDP | 47 698 |
| 13 | 43192 | 067 | Cobb County | 29 783 | 15 | 62600 | 003 | Honolulu County | 47 698 |
| 13 | 44340 | | LaGrange city | 29 588 | 15 | 71550 | | Urban Honolulu CDP | 337 256 |
| 13 | 44340 | 285 | Troup County | 29 588 | 15 | 71550 | 003 | Honolulu County | 337 256 |
| 13 | 45488 | | Lawrenceville city | 28 546 | 15 | 79700 | | Waipahu CDP | 38 216 |
| 13 | 45488 | 135 | Gwinnett County | 28 546 | 15 | 79700 | 003 | Honolulu County | 38 216 |
| 13 | 49000 | | Macon city | 91 351 | 16 | | | **IDAHO** | 1 567 582 |
| 13 | 49000 | 021 | Bibb County | 90 885 | 16 | 08830 | | Boise City city | 205 671 |
| 13 | 49000 | 169 | Jones County | 466 | 16 | 08830 | 001 | Ada County | 205 671 |
| 13 | 49756 | | Marietta city | 56 579 | 16 | 12250 | | Caldwell city | 46 237 |
| 13 | 49756 | 067 | Cobb County | 56 579 | 16 | 12250 | 027 | Canyon County | 46 237 |
| 13 | 51670 | | Milton city | 32 661 | 16 | 16750 | | Coeur d'Alene city | 44 137 |
| 13 | 51670 | 121 | Fulton County | 32 661 | 16 | 16750 | 055 | Kootenai County | 44 137 |

# Cities by County–*Continued*

| State Code | Place Code | County Code | Geographic Area Name | 2010 Census Population | State Code | Place Code | County Code | Geographic Area Name | 2010 Census Population |
|---|---|---|---|---|---|---|---|---|---|
| 16 | 39700 | | Idaho Falls city | 56 813 | 17 | 09447 | | Buffalo Grove village | 41 496 |
| 16 | 39700 | 019 | Bonneville County | 56 813 | 17 | 09447 | 031 | Cook County | 13 644 |
| | | | | | 17 | 09447 | 097 | Lake County | 27 852 |
| 16 | 46540 | | Lewiston city | 31 894 | | | | | |
| 16 | 46540 | 069 | Nez Perce County | 31 894 | 17 | 09642 | | Burbank city | 28 925 |
| | | | | | 17 | 09642 | 031 | Cook County | 28 925 |
| 16 | 52120 | | Meridian city | 75 092 | | | | | |
| 16 | 52120 | 001 | Ada County | 75 092 | 17 | 10487 | | Calumet City city | 37 042 |
| | | | | | 17 | 10487 | 031 | Cook County | 37 042 |
| 16 | 56260 | | Nampa city | 81 557 | | | | | |
| 16 | 56260 | 027 | Canyon County | 81 557 | 17 | 11163 | | Carbondale city | 25 902 |
| | | | | | 17 | 11163 | 077 | Jackson County | 25 902 |
| 16 | 64090 | | Pocatello city | 54 255 | 17 | 11163 | 199 | Williamson County | 0 |
| 16 | 64090 | 005 | Bannock County | 54 239 | | | | | |
| 16 | 64090 | 077 | Power County | 16 | 17 | 11332 | | Carol Stream village | 39 711 |
| | | | | | 17 | 11332 | 043 | DuPage County | 39 711 |
| 16 | 64810 | | Post Falls city | 27 574 | | | | | |
| 16 | 64810 | 055 | Kootenai County | 27 574 | 17 | 11358 | | Carpentersville village | 37 691 |
| | | | | | 17 | 11358 | 089 | Kane County | 37 691 |
| 16 | 67420 | | Rexburg city | 25 484 | | | | | |
| 16 | 67420 | 065 | Madison County | 25 484 | 17 | 12385 | | Champaign city | 81 055 |
| | | | | | 17 | 12385 | 019 | Champaign County | 81 055 |
| 16 | 82810 | | Twin Falls city | 44 125 | | | | | |
| 16 | 82810 | 083 | Twin Falls County | 44 125 | 17 | 14000 | | Chicago city | 2 695 598 |
| | | | | | 17 | 14000 | 031 | Cook County | 2 695 598 |
| 17 | | | **ILLINOIS** | 12 830 632 | 17 | 14000 | 043 | DuPage County | 0 |
| 17 | 00243 | | Addison village | 36 942 | | | | | |
| 17 | 00243 | 043 | DuPage County | 36 942 | 17 | 14026 | | Chicago Heights city | 30 276 |
| | | | | | 17 | 14026 | 031 | Cook County | 30 276 |
| 17 | 00685 | | Algonquin village | 30 046 | | | | | |
| 17 | 00685 | 089 | Kane County | 8 433 | 17 | 14351 | | Cicero town | 83 891 |
| 17 | 00685 | 111 | McHenry County | 21 613 | 17 | 14351 | 031 | Cook County | 83 891 |
| | | | | | | | | | |
| 17 | 01114 | | Alton city | 27 865 | 17 | 15599 | | Collinsville city | 25 579 |
| 17 | 01114 | 119 | Madison County | 27 865 | 17 | 15599 | 119 | Madison County | 22 573 |
| | | | | | 17 | 15599 | 163 | St. Clair County | 3 006 |
| 17 | 02154 | | Arlington Heights village | 75 101 | | | | | |
| 17 | 02154 | 031 | Cook County | 75 101 | 17 | 17887 | | Crystal Lake city | 40 743 |
| 17 | 02154 | 097 | Lake County | 0 | 17 | 17887 | 111 | McHenry County | 40 743 |
| | | | | | | | | | |
| 17 | 03012 | | Aurora city | 197 899 | 17 | 18563 | | Danville city | 33 027 |
| 17 | 03012 | 043 | DuPage County | 49 433 | 17 | 18563 | 183 | Vermilion County | 33 027 |
| 17 | 03012 | 089 | Kane County | 130 976 | | | | | |
| 17 | 03012 | 093 | Kendall County | 6 019 | 17 | 18823 | | Decatur city | 76 122 |
| 17 | 03012 | 197 | Will County | 11 471 | 17 | 18823 | 115 | Macon County | 76 122 |
| | | | | | | | | | |
| 17 | 04013 | | Bartlett village | 41 208 | 17 | 19161 | | DeKalb city | 43 862 |
| 17 | 04013 | 031 | Cook County | 16 797 | 17 | 19161 | 037 | DeKalb County | 43 862 |
| 17 | 04013 | 043 | DuPage County | 24 411 | | | | | |
| 17 | 04013 | 089 | Kane County | 0 | 17 | 19642 | | Des Plaines city | 58 364 |
| | | | | | 17 | 19642 | 031 | Cook County | 58 364 |
| 17 | 04078 | | Batavia city | 26 045 | | | | | |
| 17 | 04078 | 043 | DuPage County | 0 | 17 | 20591 | | Downers Grove village | 47 833 |
| 17 | 04078 | 089 | Kane County | 26 045 | 17 | 20591 | 043 | DuPage County | 47 833 |
| | | | | | | | | | |
| 17 | 04845 | | Belleville city | 44 478 | 17 | 22255 | | East St. Louis city | 27 006 |
| 17 | 04845 | 163 | St. Clair County | 44 478 | 17 | 22255 | 163 | St. Clair County | 27 006 |
| | | | | | | | | | |
| 17 | 05092 | | Belvidere city | 25 585 | 17 | 23074 | | Elgin city | 108 188 |
| 17 | 05092 | 007 | Boone County | 25 585 | 17 | 23074 | 031 | Cook County | 24 032 |
| | | | | | 17 | 23074 | 089 | Kane County | 84 156 |
| 17 | 05573 | | Berwyn city | 56 657 | | | | | |
| 17 | 05573 | 031 | Cook County | 56 657 | 17 | 23256 | | Elk Grove Village village | 33 127 |
| | | | | | 17 | 23256 | 031 | Cook County | 33 127 |
| 17 | 06613 | | Bloomington city | 76 610 | 17 | 23256 | 043 | DuPage County | 0 |
| 17 | 06613 | 113 | McLean County | 76 610 | | | | | |
| | | | | | 17 | 23620 | | Elmhurst city | 44 121 |
| 17 | 07133 | | Bolingbrook village | 73 366 | 17 | 23620 | 031 | Cook County | 0 |
| 17 | 07133 | 043 | DuPage County | 1 571 | 17 | 23620 | 043 | DuPage County | 44 121 |
| 17 | 07133 | 197 | Will County | 71 795 | | | | | |
| | | | | | 17 | 24582 | | Evanston city | 74 486 |
| | | | | | 17 | 24582 | 031 | Cook County | 74 486 |

| State Code | Place Code | County Code | Geographic Area Name | 2010 Census Population | State Code | Place Code | County Code | Geographic Area Name | 2010 Census Population |
|---|---|---|---|---|---|---|---|---|---|
| 17 | 27884 | | Freeport city | 25 638 | 17 | 53234 | | Normal town | 52 497 |
| 17 | 27884 | 177 | Stephenson County | 25 638 | 17 | 53234 | 113 | McLean County | 52 497 |
| 17 | 28326 | | Galesburg city | 32 195 | 17 | 53481 | | Northbrook village | 33 170 |
| 17 | 28326 | 095 | Knox County | 32 195 | 17 | 53481 | 031 | Cook County | 33 170 |
| 17 | 29730 | | Glendale Heights village | 34 208 | 17 | 53559 | | North Chicago city | 32 574 |
| 17 | 29730 | 043 | DuPage County | 34 208 | 17 | 53559 | 097 | Lake County | 32 574 |
| 17 | 29756 | | Glen Ellyn village | 27 450 | 17 | 54638 | | Oak Forest city | 27 962 |
| 17 | 29756 | 043 | DuPage County | 27 450 | 17 | 54638 | 031 | Cook County | 27 962 |
| 17 | 29938 | | Glenview village | 44 692 | 17 | 54820 | | Oak Lawn village | 56 690 |
| 17 | 29938 | 031 | Cook County | 44 692 | 17 | 54820 | 031 | Cook County | 56 690 |
| 17 | 30926 | | Granite City city | 29 849 | 17 | 54885 | | Oak Park village | 51 878 |
| 17 | 30926 | 119 | Madison County | 29 849 | 17 | 54885 | 031 | Cook County | 51 878 |
| 17 | 32018 | | Gurnee village | 31 295 | 17 | 55249 | | O'Fallon city | 28 281 |
| 17 | 32018 | 097 | Lake County | 31 295 | 17 | 55249 | 163 | St. Clair County | 28 281 |
| 17 | 32746 | | Hanover Park village | 37 973 | 17 | 56640 | | Orland Park village | 56 767 |
| 17 | 32746 | 031 | Cook County | 20 636 | 17 | 56640 | 031 | Cook County | 56 583 |
| 17 | 32746 | 043 | DuPage County | 17 337 | 17 | 56640 | 197 | Will County | 184 |
| 17 | 33383 | | Harvey city | 25 282 | 17 | 56887 | | Oswego village | 30 355 |
| 17 | 33383 | 031 | Cook County | 25 282 | 17 | 56887 | 093 | Kendall County | 30 355 |
| 17 | 34722 | | Highland Park city | 29 763 | 17 | 57225 | | Palatine village | 68 557 |
| 17 | 34722 | 097 | Lake County | 29 763 | 17 | 57225 | 031 | Cook County | 68 557 |
| | | | | | 17 | 57225 | 097 | Lake County | 0 |
| 17 | 35411 | | Hoffman Estates village | 51 895 | | | | | |
| 17 | 35411 | 031 | Cook County | 51 895 | 17 | 57875 | | Park Ridge city | 37 480 |
| 17 | 35411 | 089 | Kane County | 0 | 17 | 57875 | 031 | Cook County | 37 480 |
| 17 | 38570 | | Joliet city | 147 433 | 17 | 58447 | | Pekin city | 34 094 |
| 17 | 38570 | 093 | Kendall County | 9 749 | 17 | 58447 | 143 | Peoria County | 0 |
| 17 | 38570 | 197 | Will County | 137 684 | 17 | 58447 | 179 | Tazewell County | 34 094 |
| 17 | 38934 | | Kankakee city | 27 537 | 17 | 59000 | | Peoria city | 115 007 |
| 17 | 38934 | 091 | Kankakee County | 27 537 | 17 | 59000 | 143 | Peoria County | 115 007 |
| 17 | 41183 | | Lake in the Hills village | 28 965 | 17 | 60287 | | Plainfield village | 39 581 |
| 17 | 41183 | 111 | McHenry County | 28 965 | 17 | 60287 | 093 | Kendall County | 2 079 |
| | | | | | 17 | 60287 | 197 | Will County | 37 502 |
| 17 | 42028 | | Lansing village | 28 331 | | | | | |
| 17 | 42028 | 031 | Cook County | 28 331 | 17 | 62367 | | Quincy city | 40 633 |
| | | | | | 17 | 62367 | 001 | Adams County | 40 633 |
| 17 | 44407 | | Lombard village | 43 165 | | | | | |
| 17 | 44407 | 043 | DuPage County | 43 165 | 17 | 65000 | | Rockford city | 152 871 |
| | | | | | 17 | 65000 | 201 | Winnebago County | 152 871 |
| 17 | 45694 | | McHenry city | 26 992 | | | | | |
| 17 | 45694 | 111 | McHenry County | 26 992 | 17 | 65078 | | Rock Island city | 39 018 |
| | | | | | 17 | 65078 | 161 | Rock Island County | 39 018 |
| 17 | 48242 | | Melrose Park village | 25 411 | | | | | |
| 17 | 48242 | 031 | Cook County | 25 411 | 17 | 65442 | | Romeoville village | 39 680 |
| | | | | | 17 | 65442 | 197 | Will County | 39 680 |
| 17 | 49867 | | Moline city | 43 483 | | | | | |
| 17 | 49867 | 161 | Rock Island County | 43 483 | 17 | 66040 | | Round Lake Beach village | 28 175 |
| | | | | | 17 | 66040 | 097 | Lake County | 28 175 |
| 17 | 51089 | | Mount Prospect village | 54 167 | | | | | |
| 17 | 51089 | 031 | Cook County | 54 167 | 17 | 66703 | | St. Charles city | 32 974 |
| | | | | | 17 | 66703 | 043 | DuPage County | 543 |
| 17 | 51349 | | Mundelein village | 31 064 | 17 | 66703 | 089 | Kane County | 32 431 |
| 17 | 51349 | 097 | Lake County | 31 064 | | | | | |
| | | | | | 17 | 68003 | | Schaumburg village | 74 227 |
| 17 | 51622 | | Naperville city | 141 853 | 17 | 68003 | 031 | Cook County | 74 227 |
| 17 | 51622 | 043 | DuPage County | 94 533 | 17 | 68003 | 043 | DuPage County | 0 |
| 17 | 51622 | 197 | Will County | 47 320 | | | | | |
| | | | | | 17 | 70122 | | Skokie village | 64 784 |
| 17 | 53000 | | Niles village | 29 803 | 17 | 70122 | 031 | Cook County | 64 784 |
| 17 | 53000 | 031 | Cook County | 29 803 | | | | | |

| State Code | Place Code | County Code | Geographic Area Name | 2010 Census Population | State Code | Place Code | County Code | Geographic Area Name | 2010 Census Population |
|---|---|---|---|---|---|---|---|---|---|
| 17 | 72000 | | Springfield city | 116 250 | 18 | 28386 | | Goshen city | 31 719 |
| 17 | 72000 | 167 | Sangamon County | 116 250 | 18 | 28386 | 039 | Elkhart County | 31 719 |
| 17 | 73157 | | Streamwood village | 39 858 | 18 | 29898 | | Greenwood city | 49 791 |
| 17 | 73157 | 031 | Cook County | 39 858 | 18 | 29898 | 081 | Johnson County | 49 791 |
| 17 | 75484 | | Tinley Park village | 56 703 | 18 | 31000 | | Hammond city | 80 830 |
| 17 | 75484 | 031 | Cook County | 49 236 | 18 | 31000 | 089 | Lake County | 80 830 |
| 17 | 75484 | 197 | Will County | 7 467 | 18 | 34114 | | Hobart city | 29 059 |
| 17 | 77005 | | Urbana city | 41 250 | 18 | 34114 | 089 | Lake County | 29 059 |
| 17 | 77005 | 019 | Champaign County | 41 250 | 18 | 38358 | | Jeffersonville city | 44 953 |
| 17 | 77694 | | Vernon Hills village | 25 113 | 18 | 38358 | 019 | Clark County | 44 953 |
| 17 | 77694 | 097 | Lake County | 25 113 | 18 | 40392 | | Kokomo city | 45 468 |
| 17 | 79293 | | Waukegan city | 89 078 | 18 | 40392 | 067 | Howard County | 45 468 |
| 17 | 79293 | 097 | Lake County | 89 078 | 18 | 40788 | | Lafayette city | 67 140 |
| 17 | 80060 | | West Chicago city | 27 086 | 18 | 40788 | 157 | Tippecanoe County | 67 140 |
| 17 | 80060 | 043 | DuPage County | 27 086 | 18 | 42426 | | Lawrence city | 46 001 |
| 17 | 81048 | | Wheaton city | 52 894 | 18 | 42426 | 097 | Marion County | 46 001 |
| 17 | 81048 | 043 | DuPage County | 52 894 | 18 | 46908 | | Marion city | 29 948 |
| 17 | 81087 | | Wheeling village | 37 648 | 18 | 46908 | 053 | Grant County | 29 948 |
| 17 | 81087 | 031 | Cook County | 37 642 | 18 | 48528 | | Merrillville town | 35 246 |
| 17 | 81087 | 097 | Lake County | 6 | 18 | 48528 | 089 | Lake County | 35 246 |
| 17 | 82075 | | Wilmette village | 27 087 | 18 | 48798 | | Michigan City city | 31 479 |
| 17 | 82075 | 031 | Cook County | 27 087 | 18 | 48798 | 091 | LaPorte County | 31 479 |
| 17 | 83245 | | Woodridge village | 32 971 | 18 | 49932 | | Mishawaka city | 48 252 |
| 17 | 83245 | 031 | Cook County | 0 | 18 | 49932 | 141 | St. Joseph County | 48 252 |
| 17 | 83245 | 043 | DuPage County | 32 949 | 18 | 51876 | | Muncie city | 70 085 |
| 17 | 83245 | 197 | Will County | 22 | 18 | 51876 | 035 | Delaware County | 70 085 |
| 18 | | | **INDIANA** | 6 483 802 | 18 | 52326 | | New Albany city | 36 372 |
| 18 | 01468 | | Anderson city | 56 129 | 18 | 52326 | 043 | Floyd County | 36 372 |
| 18 | 01468 | 095 | Madison County | 56 129 | 18 | 54180 | | Noblesville city | 51 969 |
| 18 | 05860 | | Bloomington city | 80 405 | 18 | 54180 | 057 | Hamilton County | 51 969 |
| 18 | 05860 | 105 | Monroe County | 80 405 | 18 | 60246 | | Plainfield town | 27 631 |
| 18 | 10342 | | Carmel city | 79 191 | 18 | 60246 | 063 | Hendricks County | 27 631 |
| 18 | 10342 | 057 | Hamilton County | 79 191 | 18 | 61092 | | Portage city | 36 828 |
| 18 | 14734 | | Columbus city | 44 061 | 18 | 61092 | 127 | Porter County | 36 828 |
| 18 | 14734 | 005 | Bartholomew County | 44 061 | 18 | 64260 | | Richmond city | 36 812 |
| 18 | 16138 | | Crown Point city | 27 317 | 18 | 64260 | 177 | Wayne County | 36 812 |
| 18 | 16138 | 089 | Lake County | 27 317 | 18 | 68220 | | Schererville town | 29 243 |
| 18 | 19486 | | East Chicago city | 29 698 | 18 | 68220 | 089 | Lake County | 29 243 |
| 18 | 19486 | 089 | Lake County | 29 698 | 18 | 71000 | | South Bend city | 101 168 |
| 18 | 20728 | | Elkhart city | 50 949 | 18 | 71000 | 141 | St. Joseph County | 101 168 |
| 18 | 20728 | 039 | Elkhart County | 50 949 | 18 | 75428 | | Terre Haute city | 60 785 |
| 18 | 22000 | | Evansville city | 117 429 | 18 | 75428 | 167 | Vigo County | 60 785 |
| 18 | 22000 | 163 | Vanderburgh County | 117 429 | 18 | 78326 | | Valparaiso city | 31 730 |
| 18 | 23278 | | Fishers town | 76 794 | 18 | 78326 | 127 | Porter County | 31 730 |
| 18 | 23278 | 057 | Hamilton County | 76 794 | 18 | 82700 | | Westfield town | 30 068 |
| 18 | 25000 | | Fort Wayne city | 253 691 | 18 | 82700 | 057 | Hamilton County | 30 068 |
| 18 | 25000 | 003 | Allen County | 253 691 | 18 | 82862 | | West Lafayette city | 29 596 |
| 18 | 27000 | | Gary city | 80 294 | 18 | 82862 | 157 | Tippecanoe County | 29 596 |
| 18 | 27000 | 089 | Lake County | 80 294 | | | | | |

# Cities by County–*Continued*

| State Code | Place Code | County Code | Geographic Area Name | 2010 Census Population | State Code | Place Code | County Code | Geographic Area Name | 2010 Census Population |
|---|---|---|---|---|---|---|---|---|---|
| 19 | | | **IOWA** | 3 046 355 | 20 | 25325 | | Garden City city | 26 658 |
| 19 | 01855 | | Ames city | 58 965 | 20 | 25325 | 055 | Finney County | 26 658 |
| 19 | 01855 | 169 | Story County | 58 965 | | | | | |
| | | | | | 20 | 33625 | | Hutchinson city | 42 080 |
| 19 | 02305 | | Ankeny city | 45 582 | 20 | 33625 | 155 | Reno County | 42 080 |
| 19 | 02305 | 153 | Polk County | 45 582 | | | | | |
| | | | | | 20 | 36000 | | Kansas City city | 145 786 |
| 19 | 06355 | | Bettendorf city | 33 217 | 20 | 36000 | 209 | Wyandotte County | 145 786 |
| 19 | 06355 | 163 | Scott County | 33 217 | | | | | |
| | | | | | 20 | 38900 | | Lawrence city | 87 643 |
| 19 | 09550 | | Burlington city | 25 663 | 20 | 38900 | 045 | Douglas County | 87 643 |
| 19 | 09550 | 057 | Des Moines County | 25 663 | | | | | |
| | | | | | 20 | 39000 | | Leavenworth city | 35 251 |
| 19 | 11755 | | Cedar Falls city | 39 260 | 20 | 39000 | 103 | Leavenworth County | 35 251 |
| 19 | 11755 | 013 | Black Hawk County | 39 260 | | | | | |
| | | | | | 20 | 39075 | | Leawood city | 31 867 |
| 19 | 12000 | | Cedar Rapids city | 126 326 | 20 | 39075 | 091 | Johnson County | 31 867 |
| 19 | 12000 | 113 | Linn County | 126 326 | | | | | |
| | | | | | 20 | 39350 | | Lenexa city | 48 190 |
| 19 | 14430 | | Clinton city | 26 885 | 20 | 39350 | 091 | Johnson County | 48 190 |
| 19 | 14430 | 045 | Clinton County | 26 885 | | | | | |
| | | | | | 20 | 44250 | | Manhattan city | 52 281 |
| 19 | 16860 | | Council Bluffs city | 62 230 | 20 | 44250 | 149 | Pottawatomie County | 146 |
| 19 | 16860 | 155 | Pottawattamie County | 62 230 | 20 | 44250 | 161 | Riley County | 52 135 |
| | | | | | 20 | 52575 | | Olathe city | 125 872 |
| 19 | 19000 | | Davenport city | 99 685 | 20 | 52575 | 091 | Johnson County | 125 872 |
| 19 | 19000 | 163 | Scott County | 99 685 | | | | | |
| | | | | | 20 | 53775 | | Overland Park city | 173 372 |
| 19 | 21000 | | Des Moines city | 203 433 | 20 | 53775 | 091 | Johnson County | 173 372 |
| 19 | 21000 | 153 | Polk County | 203 419 | | | | | |
| 19 | 21000 | 181 | Warren County | 14 | 20 | 62700 | | Salina city | 47 707 |
| | | | | | 20 | 62700 | 169 | Saline County | 47 707 |
| 19 | 22395 | | Dubuque city | 57 637 | | | | | |
| 19 | 22395 | 061 | Dubuque County | 57 637 | 20 | 64500 | | Shawnee city | 62 209 |
| | | | | | 20 | 64500 | 091 | Johnson County | 62 209 |
| 19 | 28515 | | Fort Dodge city | 25 206 | | | | | |
| 19 | 28515 | 187 | Webster County | 25 206 | 20 | 71000 | | Topeka city | 127 473 |
| | | | | | 20 | 71000 | 177 | Shawnee County | 127 473 |
| 19 | 38595 | | Iowa City city | 67 862 | | | | | |
| 19 | 38595 | 103 | Johnson County | 67 862 | 20 | 79000 | | Wichita city | 382 368 |
| | | | | | 20 | 79000 | 173 | Sedgwick County | 382 368 |
| 19 | 49485 | | Marion city | 34 768 | 21 | | | **KENTUCKY** | 4 339 367 |
| 19 | 49485 | 113 | Linn County | 34 768 | 21 | 08902 | | Bowling Green city | 58 067 |
| | | | | | 21 | 08902 | 227 | Warren County | 58 067 |
| 19 | 49755 | | Marshalltown city | 27 552 | | | | | |
| 19 | 49755 | 127 | Marshall County | 27 552 | 21 | 17848 | | Covington city | 40 640 |
| | | | | | 21 | 17848 | 117 | Kenton County | 40 640 |
| 19 | 50160 | | Mason City city | 28 079 | | | | | |
| 19 | 50160 | 033 | Cerro Gordo County | 28 079 | 21 | 24274 | | Elizabethtown city | 28 531 |
| | | | | | 21 | 24274 | 093 | Hardin County | 28 531 |
| 19 | 60465 | | Ottumwa city | 25 023 | | | | | |
| 19 | 60465 | 179 | Wapello County | 25 023 | 21 | 27982 | | Florence city | 29 951 |
| | | | | | 21 | 27982 | 015 | Boone County | 29 951 |
| 19 | 73335 | | Sioux City city | 82 684 | | | | | |
| 19 | 73335 | 149 | Plymouth County | 6 | 21 | 28900 | | Frankfort city | 25 527 |
| 19 | 73335 | 193 | Woodbury County | 82 678 | 21 | 28900 | 073 | Franklin County | 25 527 |
| 19 | 79950 | | Urbandale city | 39 463 | 21 | 30700 | | Georgetown city | 29 098 |
| 19 | 79950 | 049 | Dallas County | 6 337 | 21 | 30700 | 209 | Scott County | 29 098 |
| 19 | 79950 | 153 | Polk County | 33 126 | | | | | |
| 19 | 82425 | | Waterloo city | 68 406 | 21 | 35866 | | Henderson city | 28 757 |
| 19 | 82425 | 013 | Black Hawk County | 68 406 | 21 | 35866 | 101 | Henderson County | 28 757 |
| | | | | | 21 | 37918 | | Hopkinsville city | 31 577 |
| 19 | 83910 | | West Des Moines city | 56 609 | 21 | 37918 | 047 | Christian County | 31 577 |
| 19 | 83910 | 049 | Dallas County | 11 569 | | | | | |
| 19 | 83910 | 153 | Polk County | 44 999 | 21 | 40222 | | Jeffersontown city | 26 595 |
| 19 | 83910 | 181 | Warren County | 41 | 21 | 40222 | 111 | Jefferson County | 26 595 |
| 20 | | | **KANSAS** | 2 853 118 | | | | | |
| 20 | 18250 | | Dodge City city | 27 340 | | | | | |
| 20 | 18250 | 057 | Ford County | 27 340 | | | | | |

| State Code | Place Code | County Code | Geographic Area Name | 2010 Census Population | State Code | Place Code | County Code | Geographic Area Name | 2010 Census Population |
|---|---|---|---|---|---|---|---|---|---|
| 21 | 46027 | | Lexington-Fayette urban county | 295 803 | 24 | 04000 | | Baltimore city | 620 961 |
| 21 | 46027 | 067 | Fayette County | 295 803 | 24 | 04000 | 510 | Baltimore city | 620 961 |
| 21 | 56136 | | Nicholasville city | 28 015 | 24 | 08775 | | Bowie city | 54 727 |
| 21 | 56136 | 113 | Jessamine County | 28 015 | 24 | 08775 | 033 | Prince George's County | 54 727 |
| 21 | 58620 | | Owensboro city | 57 265 | 24 | 18750 | | College Park city | 30 413 |
| 21 | 58620 | 059 | Daviess County | 57 265 | 24 | 18750 | 033 | Prince George's County | 30 413 |
| 21 | 58836 | | Paducah city | 25 024 | 24 | 30325 | | Frederick city | 65 239 |
| 21 | 58836 | 145 | McCracken County | 25 024 | 24 | 30325 | 021 | Frederick County | 65 239 |
| 21 | 65226 | | Richmond city | 31 364 | 24 | 31175 | | Gaithersburg city | 59 933 |
| 21 | 65226 | 151 | Madison County | 31 364 | 24 | 31175 | 031 | Montgomery County | 59 933 |
| 22 | | | **LOUISIANA** | 4 533 372 | 24 | 36075 | | Hagerstown city | 39 662 |
| 22 | 00975 | | Alexandria city | 47 723 | 24 | 36075 | 043 | Washington County | 39 662 |
| 22 | 00975 | 079 | Rapides Parish | 47 723 | 24 | 45900 | | Laurel city | 25 115 |
| 22 | 05000 | | Baton Rouge city | 229 493 | 24 | 45900 | 033 | Prince George's County | 25 115 |
| 22 | 05000 | 033 | East Baton Rouge Parish | 229 493 | 24 | 67675 | | Rockville city | 61 209 |
| 22 | 08920 | | Bossier City city | 61 315 | 24 | 67675 | 031 | Montgomery County | 61 209 |
| 22 | 08920 | 015 | Bossier Parish | 61 315 | 24 | 69925 | | Salisbury city | 30 343 |
| 22 | 13960 | | Central city | 26 864 | 24 | 69925 | 045 | Wicomico County | 30 343 |
| 22 | 13960 | 033 | East Baton Rouge Parish | 26 864 | 25 | | | **MASSACHUSETTS** | 6 547 629 |
| 22 | 36255 | | Houma city | 33 727 | 25 | 00840 | | Agawam Town city | 28 438 |
| 22 | 36255 | 109 | Terrebonne Parish | 33 727 | 25 | 00840 | 013 | Hampden County | 28 438 |
| 22 | 39475 | | Kenner city | 66 702 | 25 | 02690 | | Attleboro city | 43 593 |
| 22 | 39475 | 051 | Jefferson Parish | 66 702 | 25 | 02690 | 005 | Bristol County | 43 593 |
| 22 | 40735 | | Lafayette city | 120 623 | 25 | 03690 | | Barnstable Town city | 45 193 |
| 22 | 40735 | 055 | Lafayette Parish | 120 623 | 25 | 03690 | 001 | Barnstable County | 45 193 |
| 22 | 41155 | | Lake Charles city | 71 993 | 25 | 05595 | | Beverly city | 39 502 |
| 22 | 41155 | 019 | Calcasieu Parish | 71 993 | 25 | 05595 | 009 | Essex County | 39 502 |
| 22 | 51410 | | Monroe city | 48 815 | 25 | 07000 | | Boston city | 617 594 |
| 22 | 51410 | 073 | Ouachita Parish | 48 815 | 25 | 07000 | 025 | Suffolk County | 617 594 |
| 22 | 54035 | | New Iberia city | 30 617 | 25 | 07740 | | Braintree Town city | 35 744 |
| 22 | 54035 | 045 | Iberia Parish | 30 617 | 25 | 07740 | 021 | Norfolk County | 35 744 |
| 22 | 55000 | | New Orleans city | 343 829 | 25 | 09000 | | Brockton city | 93 810 |
| 22 | 55000 | 071 | Orleans Parish | 343 829 | 25 | 09000 | 023 | Plymouth County | 93 810 |
| 22 | 70000 | | Shreveport city | 199 311 | 25 | 11000 | | Cambridge city | 105 162 |
| 22 | 70000 | 015 | Bossier Parish | 2 702 | 25 | 11000 | 017 | Middlesex County | 105 162 |
| 22 | 70000 | 017 | Caddo Parish | 196 609 | 25 | 13205 | | Chelsea city | 35 177 |
| 22 | 70805 | | Slidell city | 27 068 | 25 | 13205 | 025 | Suffolk County | 35 177 |
| 22 | 70805 | 103 | St. Tammany Parish | 27 068 | 25 | 13660 | | Chicopee city | 55 298 |
| 23 | | | **MAINE** | 1 328 361 | 25 | 13660 | 013 | Hampden County | 55 298 |
| 23 | 02795 | | Bangor city | 33 039 | 25 | 21990 | | Everett city | 41 667 |
| 23 | 02795 | 019 | Penobscot County | 33 039 | 25 | 21990 | 017 | Middlesex County | 41 667 |
| 23 | 38740 | | Lewiston city | 36 592 | 25 | 23000 | | Fall River city | 88 857 |
| 23 | 38740 | 001 | Androscoggin County | 36 592 | 25 | 23000 | 005 | Bristol County | 88 857 |
| 23 | 60545 | | Portland city | 66 194 | 25 | 23875 | | Fitchburg city | 40 318 |
| 23 | 60545 | 005 | Cumberland County | 66 194 | 25 | 23875 | 027 | Worcester County | 40 318 |
| 23 | 71990 | | South Portland city | 25 002 | 25 | 25172 | | Franklin Town city | 31 635 |
| 23 | 71990 | 005 | Cumberland County | 25 002 | 25 | 25172 | 021 | Norfolk County | 31 635 |
| 24 | | | **MARYLAND** | 5 773 552 | 25 | 26150 | | Gloucester city | 28 789 |
| 24 | 01600 | | Annapolis city | 38 394 | 25 | 26150 | 009 | Essex County | 28 789 |
| 24 | 01600 | 003 | Anne Arundel County | 38 394 | | | | | |

| State Code | Place Code | County Code | Geographic Area Name | 2010 Census Population | State Code | Place Code | County Code | Geographic Area Name | 2010 Census Population |
|---|---|---|---|---|---|---|---|---|---|
| 25 | 29405 | | Haverhill city | 60 879 | 25 | 76030 | | Westfield city | 41 094 |
| 25 | 29405 | 009 | Essex County | 60 879 | 25 | 76030 | 013 | Hampden County | 41 094 |
| 25 | 30840 | | Holyoke city | 39 880 | 25 | 77890 | | West Springfield Town city | 28 391 |
| 25 | 30840 | 013 | Hampden County | 39 880 | 25 | 77890 | 013 | Hampden County | 28 391 |
| 25 | 34550 | | Lawrence city | 76 377 | 25 | 78972 | | Weymouth Town city | 53 743 |
| 25 | 34550 | 009 | Essex County | 76 377 | 25 | 78972 | 021 | Norfolk County | 53 743 |
| 25 | 35075 | | Leominster city | 40 759 | 25 | 81035 | | Woburn city | 38 120 |
| 25 | 35075 | 027 | Worcester County | 40 759 | 25 | 81035 | 017 | Middlesex County | 38 120 |
| 25 | 37000 | | Lowell city | 106 519 | 25 | 82000 | | Worcester city | 181 045 |
| 25 | 37000 | 017 | Middlesex County | 106 519 | 25 | 82000 | 027 | Worcester County | 181 045 |
| 25 | 37490 | | Lynn city | 90 329 | 26 | | | **MICHIGAN** | 9 883 640 |
| 25 | 37490 | 009 | Essex County | 90 329 | 26 | 01380 | | Allen Park city | 28 210 |
| | | | | | 26 | 01380 | 163 | Wayne County | 28 210 |
| 25 | 37875 | | Malden city | 59 450 | | | | | |
| 25 | 37875 | 017 | Middlesex County | 59 450 | 26 | 03000 | | Ann Arbor city | 113 934 |
| | | | | | 26 | 03000 | 161 | Washtenaw County | 113 934 |
| 25 | 38715 | | Marlborough city | 38 499 | | | | | |
| 25 | 38715 | 017 | Middlesex County | 38 499 | 26 | 05920 | | Battle Creek city | 52 347 |
| | | | | | 26 | 05920 | 025 | Calhoun County | 52 347 |
| 25 | 39835 | | Medford city | 56 173 | | | | | |
| 25 | 39835 | 017 | Middlesex County | 56 173 | 26 | 06020 | | Bay City city | 34 932 |
| | | | | | 26 | 06020 | 017 | Bay County | 34 932 |
| 25 | 40115 | | Melrose city | 26 983 | | | | | |
| 25 | 40115 | 017 | Middlesex County | 26 983 | 26 | 12060 | | Burton city | 29 999 |
| | | | | | 26 | 12060 | 049 | Genesee County | 29 999 |
| 25 | 40710 | | Methuen Town city | 47 255 | | | | | |
| 25 | 40710 | 009 | Essex County | 47 255 | 26 | 21000 | | Dearborn city | 98 153 |
| | | | | | 26 | 21000 | 163 | Wayne County | 98 153 |
| 25 | 45000 | | New Bedford city | 95 072 | | | | | |
| 25 | 45000 | 005 | Bristol County | 95 072 | 26 | 21020 | | Dearborn Heights city | 57 774 |
| | | | | | 26 | 21020 | 163 | Wayne County | 57 774 |
| 25 | 45560 | | Newton city | 85 146 | | | | | |
| 25 | 45560 | 017 | Middlesex County | 85 146 | 26 | 22000 | | Detroit city | 713 777 |
| | | | | | 26 | 22000 | 163 | Wayne County | 713 777 |
| 25 | 46330 | | Northampton city | 28 549 | | | | | |
| 25 | 46330 | 015 | Hampshire County | 28 549 | 26 | 24120 | | East Lansing city | 48 579 |
| | | | | | 26 | 24120 | 037 | Clinton County | 1 969 |
| 25 | 52490 | | Peabody city | 51 251 | 26 | 24120 | 065 | Ingham County | 46 610 |
| 25 | 52490 | 009 | Essex County | 51 251 | | | | | |
| | | | | | 26 | 24290 | | Eastpointe city | 32 442 |
| 25 | 53960 | | Pittsfield city | 44 737 | 26 | 24290 | 099 | Macomb County | 32 442 |
| 25 | 53960 | 003 | Berkshire County | 44 737 | | | | | |
| | | | | | 26 | 27440 | | Farmington Hills city | 79 740 |
| 25 | 55745 | | Quincy city | 92 271 | 26 | 27440 | 125 | Oakland County | 79 740 |
| 25 | 55745 | 021 | Norfolk County | 92 271 | | | | | |
| | | | | | 26 | 29000 | | Flint city | 102 434 |
| 25 | 56585 | | Revere city | 51 755 | 26 | 29000 | 049 | Genesee County | 102 434 |
| 25 | 56585 | 025 | Suffolk County | 51 755 | | | | | |
| | | | | | 26 | 31420 | | Garden City city | 27 692 |
| 25 | 59105 | | Salem city | 41 340 | 26 | 31420 | 163 | Wayne County | 27 692 |
| 25 | 59105 | 009 | Essex County | 41 340 | | | | | |
| | | | | | 26 | 34000 | | Grand Rapids city | 188 040 |
| 25 | 62535 | | Somerville city | 75 754 | 26 | 34000 | 081 | Kent County | 188 040 |
| 25 | 62535 | 017 | Middlesex County | 75 754 | | | | | |
| | | | | | 26 | 38640 | | Holland city | 33 051 |
| 25 | 67000 | | Springfield city | 153 060 | 26 | 38640 | 005 | Allegan County | 7 016 |
| 25 | 67000 | 013 | Hampden County | 153 060 | 26 | 38640 | 139 | Ottawa County | 26 035 |
| | | | | | | | | | |
| 25 | 69170 | | Taunton city | 55 874 | 26 | 40680 | | Inkster city | 25 369 |
| 25 | 69170 | 005 | Bristol County | 55 874 | 26 | 40680 | 163 | Wayne County | 25 369 |
| | | | | | | | | | |
| 25 | 72600 | | Waltham city | 60 632 | 26 | 41420 | | Jackson city | 33 534 |
| 25 | 72600 | 017 | Middlesex County | 60 632 | 26 | 41420 | 075 | Jackson County | 33 534 |
| | | | | | | | | | |
| 25 | 73440 | | Watertown Town city | 31 915 | 26 | 42160 | | Kalamazoo city | 74 262 |
| 25 | 73440 | 017 | Middlesex County | 31 915 | 26 | 42160 | 077 | Kalamazoo County | 74 262 |

| State Code | Place Code | County Code | Geographic Area Name | 2010 Census Population | State Code | Place Code | County Code | Geographic Area Name | 2010 Census Population |
|---|---|---|---|---|---|---|---|---|---|
| 26 | 42820 | | Kentwood city | 48 707 | 26 | 84000 | | Warren city | 134 056 |
| 26 | 42820 | 081 | Kent County | 48 707 | 26 | 84000 | 099 | Macomb County | 134 056 |
| | | | | | | | | | |
| 26 | 46000 | | Lansing city | 114 297 | 26 | 86000 | | Westland city | 84 094 |
| 26 | 46000 | 045 | Eaton County | 4 734 | 26 | 86000 | 163 | Wayne County | 84 094 |
| 26 | 46000 | 065 | Ingham County | 109 563 | | | | | |
| | | | | | 26 | 88900 | | Wyandotte city | 25 883 |
| 26 | 47800 | | Lincoln Park city | 38 144 | 26 | 88900 | 163 | Wayne County | 25 883 |
| 26 | 47800 | 163 | Wayne County | 38 144 | | | | | |
| | | | | | 26 | 88940 | | Wyoming city | 72 125 |
| 26 | 49000 | | Livonia city | 96 942 | 26 | 88940 | 081 | Kent County | 72 125 |
| 26 | 49000 | 163 | Wayne County | 96 942 | 27 | | | **MINNESOTA** | 5 303 925 |
| 26 | 50560 | | Madison Heights city | 29 694 | 27 | 01486 | | Andover city | 30 598 |
| 26 | 50560 | 125 | Oakland County | 29 694 | 27 | 01486 | 003 | Anoka County | 30 598 |
| | | | | | | | | | |
| 26 | 53780 | | Midland city | 41 863 | 27 | 01900 | | Apple Valley city | 49 084 |
| 26 | 53780 | 017 | Bay County | 157 | 27 | 01900 | 037 | Dakota County | 49 084 |
| 26 | 53780 | 111 | Midland County | 41 706 | | | | | |
| | | | | | 27 | 06382 | | Blaine city | 57 186 |
| 26 | 56020 | | Mount Pleasant city | 26 016 | 27 | 06382 | 003 | Anoka County | 57 186 |
| 26 | 56020 | 073 | Isabella County | 26 016 | 27 | 06382 | 123 | Ramsey County | 0 |
| | | | | | | | | | |
| 26 | 56320 | | Muskegon city | 38 401 | 27 | 06616 | | Bloomington city | 82 893 |
| 26 | 56320 | 121 | Muskegon County | 38 401 | 27 | 06616 | 053 | Hennepin County | 82 893 |
| | | | | | | | | | |
| 26 | 59440 | | Novi city | 55 224 | 27 | 07948 | | Brooklyn Center city | 30 104 |
| 26 | 59440 | 125 | Oakland County | 55 224 | 27 | 07948 | 053 | Hennepin County | 30 104 |
| | | | | | | | | | |
| 26 | 59920 | | Oak Park city | 29 319 | 27 | 07966 | | Brooklyn Park city | 75 781 |
| 26 | 59920 | 125 | Oakland County | 29 319 | 27 | 07966 | 053 | Hennepin County | 75 781 |
| | | | | | | | | | |
| 26 | 65440 | | Pontiac city | 59 515 | 27 | 08794 | | Burnsville city | 60 306 |
| 26 | 65440 | 125 | Oakland County | 59 515 | 27 | 08794 | 037 | Dakota County | 60 306 |
| | | | | | | | | | |
| 26 | 65560 | | Portage city | 46 292 | 27 | 13114 | | Coon Rapids city | 61 476 |
| 26 | 65560 | 077 | Kalamazoo County | 46 292 | 27 | 13114 | 003 | Anoka County | 61 476 |
| | | | | | | | | | |
| 26 | 65820 | | Port Huron city | 30 184 | 27 | 13456 | | Cottage Grove city | 34 589 |
| 26 | 65820 | 147 | St. Clair County | 30 184 | 27 | 13456 | 163 | Washington County | 34 589 |
| | | | | | | | | | |
| 26 | 69035 | | Rochester Hills city | 70 995 | 27 | 17000 | | Duluth city | 86 265 |
| 26 | 69035 | 125 | Oakland County | 70 995 | 27 | 17000 | 137 | St. Louis County | 86 265 |
| | | | | | | | | | |
| 26 | 69800 | | Roseville city | 47 299 | 27 | 17288 | | Eagan city | 64 206 |
| 26 | 69800 | 099 | Macomb County | 47 299 | 27 | 17288 | 037 | Dakota County | 64 206 |
| | | | | | | | | | |
| 26 | 70040 | | Royal Oak city | 57 236 | 27 | 18116 | | Eden Prairie city | 60 797 |
| 26 | 70040 | 125 | Oakland County | 57 236 | 27 | 18116 | 053 | Hennepin County | 60 797 |
| | | | | | | | | | |
| 26 | 70520 | | Saginaw city | 51 508 | 27 | 18188 | | Edina city | 47 941 |
| 26 | 70520 | 145 | Saginaw County | 51 508 | 27 | 18188 | 053 | Hennepin County | 47 941 |
| | | | | | | | | | |
| 26 | 70760 | | St. Clair Shores city | 59 715 | 27 | 22814 | | Fridley city | 27 208 |
| 26 | 70760 | 099 | Macomb County | 59 715 | 27 | 22814 | 003 | Anoka County | 27 208 |
| | | | | | | | | | |
| 26 | 74900 | | Southfield city | 71 739 | 27 | 31076 | | Inver Grove Heights city | 33 880 |
| 26 | 74900 | 125 | Oakland County | 71 739 | 27 | 31076 | 037 | Dakota County | 33 880 |
| | | | | | | | | | |
| 26 | 74960 | | Southgate city | 30 047 | 27 | 35180 | | Lakeville city | 55 954 |
| 26 | 74960 | 163 | Wayne County | 30 047 | 27 | 35180 | 037 | Dakota County | 55 954 |
| | | | | | | | | | |
| 26 | 76460 | | Sterling Heights city | 129 699 | 27 | 39878 | | Mankato city | 39 309 |
| 26 | 76460 | 099 | Macomb County | 129 699 | 27 | 39878 | 013 | Blue Earth County | 39 305 |
| | | | | | 27 | 39878 | 079 | Le Sueur County | 4 |
| 26 | 79000 | | Taylor city | 63 131 | 27 | 39878 | 103 | Nicollet County | 0 |
| 26 | 79000 | 163 | Wayne County | 63 131 | | | | | |
| | | | | | 27 | 40166 | | Maple Grove city | 61 567 |
| 26 | 80700 | | Troy city | 80 980 | 27 | 40166 | 053 | Hennepin County | 61 567 |
| 26 | 80700 | 125 | Oakland County | 80 980 | | | | | |
| | | | | | 27 | 40382 | | Maplewood city | 38 018 |
| | | | | | 27 | 40382 | 123 | Ramsey County | 38 018 |

| State Code | Place Code | County Code | Geographic Area Name | 2010 Census Population | State Code | Place Code | County Code | Geographic Area Name | 2010 Census Population |
|---|---|---|---|---|---|---|---|---|---|
| 27 | 43000 | | Minneapolis city | 382 578 | 28 | 36000 | | Jackson city | 173 514 |
| 27 | 43000 | 053 | Hennepin County | 382 578 | 28 | 36000 | 049 | Hinds County | 172 891 |
| | | | | | 28 | 36000 | 089 | Madison County | 622 |
| 27 | 43252 | | Minnetonka city | 49 734 | 28 | 36000 | 121 | Rankin County | 1 |
| 27 | 43252 | 053 | Hennepin County | 49 734 | | | | | |
| | | | | | 28 | 46640 | | Meridian city | 41 148 |
| 27 | 43864 | | Moorhead city | 38 065 | 28 | 46640 | 075 | Lauderdale County | 41 148 |
| 27 | 43864 | 027 | Clay County | 38 065 | | | | | |
| | | | | | 28 | 54040 | | Olive Branch city | 33 484 |
| 27 | 47680 | | Oakdale city | 27 378 | 28 | 54040 | 033 | DeSoto County | 33 484 |
| 27 | 47680 | 163 | Washington County | 27 378 | | | | | |
| | | | | | 28 | 55760 | | Pearl city | 25 092 |
| 27 | 49300 | | Owatonna city | 25 599 | 28 | 55760 | 121 | Rankin County | 25 092 |
| 27 | 49300 | 147 | Steele County | 25 599 | | | | | |
| | | | | | 28 | 69280 | | Southaven city | 48 982 |
| 27 | 51730 | | Plymouth city | 70 576 | 28 | 69280 | 033 | DeSoto County | 48 982 |
| 27 | 51730 | 053 | Hennepin County | 70 576 | | | | | |
| | | | | | 28 | 74840 | | Tupelo city | 34 546 |
| 27 | 54214 | | Richfield city | 35 228 | 28 | 74840 | 081 | Lee County | 34 546 |
| 27 | 54214 | 053 | Hennepin County | 35 228 | | | | | |
| | | | | | 29 | | | **MISSOURI** | 5 988 927 |
| 27 | 54880 | | Rochester city | 106 769 | 29 | 03160 | | Ballwin city | 30 404 |
| 27 | 54880 | 109 | Olmsted County | 106 769 | 29 | 03160 | 189 | St. Louis County | 30 404 |
| 27 | 55852 | | Roseville city | 33 660 | 29 | 06652 | | Blue Springs city | 52 575 |
| 27 | 55852 | 123 | Ramsey County | 33 660 | 29 | 06652 | 095 | Jackson County | 52 575 |
| 27 | 56896 | | St. Cloud city | 65 842 | 29 | 11242 | | Cape Girardeau city | 37 941 |
| 27 | 56896 | 009 | Benton County | 6 396 | 29 | 11242 | 031 | Cape Girardeau County | 37 941 |
| 27 | 56896 | 141 | Sherburne County | 6 785 | 29 | 11242 | 201 | Scott County | 0 |
| 27 | 56896 | 145 | Stearns County | 52 661 | | | | | |
| | | | | | 29 | 13600 | | Chesterfield city | 47 484 |
| 27 | 57220 | | St. Louis Park city | 45 250 | 29 | 13600 | 189 | St. Louis County | 47 484 |
| 27 | 57220 | 053 | Hennepin County | 45 250 | | | | | |
| | | | | | 29 | 15670 | | Columbia city | 108 500 |
| 27 | 58000 | | St. Paul city | 285 068 | 29 | 15670 | 019 | Boone County | 108 500 |
| 27 | 58000 | 123 | Ramsey County | 285 068 | | | | | |
| | | | | | 29 | 24778 | | Florissant city | 52 158 |
| 27 | 58738 | | Savage city | 26 911 | 29 | 24778 | 189 | St. Louis County | 52 158 |
| 27 | 58738 | 139 | Scott County | 26 911 | | | | | |
| | | | | | 29 | 27190 | | Gladstone city | 25 410 |
| 27 | 59350 | | Shakopee city | 37 076 | 29 | 27190 | 047 | Clay County | 25 410 |
| 27 | 59350 | 139 | Scott County | 37 076 | | | | | |
| | | | | | 29 | 31276 | | Hazelwood city | 25 703 |
| 27 | 59998 | | Shoreview city | 25 043 | 29 | 31276 | 189 | St. Louis County | 25 703 |
| 27 | 59998 | 123 | Ramsey County | 25 043 | | | | | |
| | | | | | 29 | 35000 | | Independence city | 116 830 |
| 27 | 71032 | | Winona city | 27 592 | 29 | 35000 | 047 | Clay County | 0 |
| 27 | 71032 | 169 | Winona County | 27 592 | 29 | 35000 | 095 | Jackson County | 116 830 |
| 27 | 71428 | | Woodbury city | 61 961 | 29 | 37000 | | Jefferson City city | 43 079 |
| 27 | 71428 | 163 | Washington County | 61 961 | 29 | 37000 | 027 | Callaway County | 22 |
| 28 | | | **MISSISSIPPI** | 2 967 297 | 29 | 37000 | 051 | Cole County | 43 057 |
| 28 | 06220 | | Biloxi city | 44 054 | | | | | |
| 28 | 06220 | 047 | Harrison County | 44 054 | 29 | 37592 | | Joplin city | 50 150 |
| | | | | | 29 | 37592 | 097 | Jasper County | 43 955 |
| 28 | 14420 | | Clinton city | 25 216 | 29 | 37592 | 145 | Newton County | 6 195 |
| 28 | 14420 | 049 | Hinds County | 25 216 | | | | | |
| | | | | | 29 | 38000 | | Kansas City city | 459 787 |
| 28 | 29180 | | Greenville city | 34 400 | 29 | 38000 | 037 | Cass County | 197 |
| 28 | 29180 | 151 | Washington County | 34 400 | 29 | 38000 | 047 | Clay County | 113 415 |
| | | | | | 29 | 38000 | 095 | Jackson County | 302 499 |
| 28 | 29700 | | Gulfport city | 67 793 | 29 | 38000 | 165 | Platte County | 43 676 |
| 28 | 29700 | 047 | Harrison County | 67 793 | | | | | |
| | | | | | 29 | 39044 | | Kirkwood city | 27 540 |
| 28 | 31020 | | Hattiesburg city | 45 989 | 29 | 39044 | 189 | St. Louis County | 27 540 |
| 28 | 31020 | 035 | Forrest County | 41 000 | | | | | |
| 28 | 31020 | 073 | Lamar County | 4 989 | 29 | 41348 | | Lee's Summit city | 91 364 |
| | | | | | 29 | 41348 | 037 | Cass County | 1 917 |
| 28 | 33700 | | Horn Lake city | 26 066 | 29 | 41348 | 095 | Jackson County | 89 447 |
| 28 | 33700 | 033 | DeSoto County | 26 066 | | | | | |

# Cities by County–*Continued*

| State Code | Place Code | County Code | Geographic Area Name | 2010 Census Population | State Code | Place Code | County Code | Geographic Area Name | 2010 Census Population |
|---|---|---|---|---|---|---|---|---|---|
| 29 | 42032 | | Liberty city | 29 149 | 32 | | | **NEVADA** | 2 700 551 |
| 29 | 42032 | 047 | Clay County | 29 149 | 32 | 09700 | | Carson City | 55 274 |
| | | | | | 32 | 09700 | 510 | Carson City | 55 274 |
| 29 | 46586 | | Maryland Heights city | 27 472 | | | | | |
| 29 | 46586 | 189 | St. Louis County | 27 472 | 32 | 31900 | | Henderson city | 257 729 |
| | | | | | 32 | 31900 | 003 | Clark County | 257 729 |
| 29 | 54074 | | O'Fallon city | 79 329 | | | | | |
| 29 | 54074 | 183 | St. Charles County | 79 329 | 32 | 40000 | | Las Vegas city | 583 756 |
| | | | | | 32 | 40000 | 003 | Clark County | 583 756 |
| 29 | 60788 | | Raytown city | 29 526 | | | | | |
| 29 | 60788 | 095 | Jackson County | 29 526 | 32 | 51800 | | North Las Vegas city | 216 961 |
| | | | | | 32 | 51800 | 003 | Clark County | 216 961 |
| 29 | 64082 | | St. Charles city | 65 794 | | | | | |
| 29 | 64082 | 183 | St. Charles County | 65 794 | 32 | 60600 | | Reno city | 225 221 |
| | | | | | 32 | 60600 | 031 | Washoe County | 225 221 |
| 29 | 64550 | | St. Joseph city | 76 780 | | | | | |
| 29 | 64550 | 021 | Buchanan County | 76 780 | 32 | 68400 | | Sparks city | 90 264 |
| | | | | | 32 | 68400 | 031 | Washoe County | 90 264 |
| 29 | 65000 | | St. Louis city | 319 294 | | | | | |
| 29 | 65000 | 510 | St. Louis city | 319 294 | 33 | | | **NEW HAMPSHIRE** | 1 316 470 |
| | | | | | 33 | 14200 | | Concord city | 42 695 |
| 29 | 65126 | | St. Peters city | 52 575 | 33 | 14200 | 013 | Merrimack County | 42 695 |
| 29 | 65126 | 183 | St. Charles County | 52 575 | | | | | |
| | | | | | 33 | 18820 | | Dover city | 29 987 |
| 29 | 70000 | | Springfield city | 159 498 | 33 | 18820 | 017 | Strafford County | 29 987 |
| 29 | 70000 | 043 | Christian County | 2 | | | | | |
| 29 | 70000 | 077 | Greene County | 159 496 | 33 | 45140 | | Manchester city | 109 565 |
| | | | | | 33 | 45140 | 011 | Hillsborough County | 109 565 |
| 29 | 75220 | | University City city | 35 371 | | | | | |
| 29 | 75220 | 189 | St. Louis County | 35 371 | 33 | 50260 | | Nashua city | 86 494 |
| | | | | | 33 | 50260 | 011 | Hillsborough County | 86 494 |
| 29 | 78442 | | Wentzville city | 29 070 | | | | | |
| 29 | 78442 | 183 | St. Charles County | 29 070 | 33 | 65140 | | Rochester city | 29 752 |
| | | | | | 33 | 65140 | 017 | Strafford County | 29 752 |
| 29 | 79820 | | Wildwood city | 35 517 | | | | | |
| 29 | 79820 | 189 | St. Louis County | 35 517 | 34 | | | **NEW JERSEY** | 8 791 894 |
| | | | | | 34 | 02080 | | Atlantic City city | 39 558 |
| 30 | | | **MONTANA** | 989 415 | 34 | 02080 | 001 | Atlantic County | 39 558 |
| 30 | 06550 | | Billings city | 104 170 | | | | | |
| 30 | 06550 | 111 | Yellowstone County | 104 170 | 34 | 03580 | | Bayonne city | 63 024 |
| | | | | | 34 | 03580 | 017 | Hudson County | 63 024 |
| 30 | 08950 | | Bozeman city | 37 280 | | | | | |
| 30 | 08950 | 031 | Gallatin County | 37 280 | 34 | 05170 | | Bergenfield borough | 26 764 |
| | | | | | 34 | 05170 | 003 | Bergen County | 26 764 |
| 30 | 32800 | | Great Falls city | 58 505 | | | | | |
| 30 | 32800 | 013 | Cascade County | 58 505 | 34 | 07600 | | Bridgeton city | 25 349 |
| | | | | | 34 | 07600 | 011 | Cumberland County | 25 349 |
| 30 | 35600 | | Helena city | 28 190 | | | | | |
| 30 | 35600 | 049 | Lewis and Clark County | 28 190 | 34 | 10000 | | Camden city | 77 344 |
| | | | | | 34 | 10000 | 007 | Camden County | 77 344 |
| 30 | 50200 | | Missoula city | 66 788 | | | | | |
| 30 | 50200 | 063 | Missoula County | 66 788 | 34 | 13690 | | Clifton city | 84 136 |
| | | | | | 34 | 13690 | 031 | Passaic County | 84 136 |
| 31 | | | **NEBRASKA** | 1 826 341 | | | | | |
| 31 | 03950 | | Bellevue city | 50 137 | 34 | 19390 | | East Orange city | 64 270 |
| 31 | 03950 | 153 | Sarpy County | 50 137 | 34 | 19390 | 013 | Essex County | 64 270 |
| | | | | | | | | | |
| 31 | 17670 | | Fremont city | 26 397 | 34 | 21000 | | Elizabeth city | 124 969 |
| 31 | 17670 | 053 | Dodge County | 26 397 | 34 | 21000 | 039 | Union County | 124 969 |
| | | | | | | | | | |
| 31 | 19595 | | Grand Island city | 48 520 | 34 | 21480 | | Englewood city | 27 147 |
| 31 | 19595 | 079 | Hall County | 48 520 | 34 | 21480 | 003 | Bergen County | 27 147 |
| | | | | | | | | | |
| 31 | 25055 | | Kearney city | 30 787 | 34 | 22470 | | Fair Lawn borough | 32 457 |
| 31 | 25055 | 019 | Buffalo County | 30 787 | 34 | 22470 | 003 | Bergen County | 32 457 |
| | | | | | | | | | |
| 31 | 28000 | | Lincoln city | 258 379 | 34 | 24420 | | Fort Lee borough | 35 345 |
| 31 | 28000 | 109 | Lancaster County | 258 379 | 34 | 24420 | 003 | Bergen County | 35 345 |
| | | | | | | | | | |
| 31 | 37000 | | Omaha city | 408 958 | 34 | 25770 | | Garfield city | 30 487 |
| 31 | 37000 | 055 | Douglas County | 408 958 | 34 | 25770 | 003 | Bergen County | 30 487 |

# Cities by County–*Continued*

| State Code | Place Code | County Code | Geographic Area Name | 2010 Census Population | State Code | Place Code | County Code | Geographic Area Name | 2010 Census Population |
|---|---|---|---|---|---|---|---|---|---|
| 34 | 28680 | | Hackensack city | 43 010 | 35 | 16420 | | Clovis city | 37 775 |
| 34 | 28680 | 003 | Bergen County | 43 010 | 35 | 16420 | 009 | Curry County | 37 775 |
| 34 | 32250 | | Hoboken city | 50 005 | 35 | 25800 | | Farmington city | 45 877 |
| 34 | 32250 | 017 | Hudson County | 50 005 | 35 | 25800 | 045 | San Juan County | 45 877 |
| 34 | 36000 | | Jersey City city | 247 597 | 35 | 32520 | | Hobbs city | 34 122 |
| 34 | 36000 | 017 | Hudson County | 247 597 | 35 | 32520 | 025 | Lea County | 34 122 |
| 34 | 36510 | | Kearny town | 40 684 | 35 | 39380 | | Las Cruces city | 97 618 |
| 34 | 36510 | 017 | Hudson County | 40 684 | 35 | 39380 | 013 | Doña Ana County | 97 618 |
| 34 | 40350 | | Linden city | 40 499 | 35 | 63460 | | Rio Rancho city | 87 521 |
| 34 | 40350 | 039 | Union County | 40 499 | 35 | 63460 | 001 | Bernalillo County | 130 |
| 34 | 41310 | | Long Branch city | 30 719 | 35 | 63460 | 043 | Sandoval County | 87 391 |
| 34 | 41310 | 025 | Monmouth County | 30 719 | 35 | 64930 | | Roswell city | 48 366 |
| 34 | 46680 | | Millville city | 28 400 | 35 | 64930 | 005 | Chaves County | 48 366 |
| 34 | 46680 | 011 | Cumberland County | 28 400 | 35 | 70500 | | Santa Fe city | 67 947 |
| 34 | 51000 | | Newark city | 277 140 | 35 | 70500 | 049 | Santa Fe County | 67 947 |
| 34 | 51000 | 013 | Essex County | 277 140 | 36 | | | **NEW YORK** | 19 378 102 |
| 34 | 51210 | | New Brunswick city | 55 181 | 36 | 01000 | | Albany city | 97 856 |
| 34 | 51210 | 023 | Middlesex County | 55 181 | 36 | 01000 | 001 | Albany County | 97 856 |
| 34 | 55950 | | Paramus borough | 26 342 | 36 | 03078 | | Auburn city | 27 687 |
| 34 | 55950 | 003 | Bergen County | 26 342 | 36 | 03078 | 011 | Cayuga County | 27 687 |
| 34 | 56550 | | Passaic city | 69 781 | 36 | 06607 | | Binghamton city | 47 376 |
| 34 | 56550 | 031 | Passaic County | 69 781 | 36 | 06607 | 007 | Broome County | 47 376 |
| 34 | 57000 | | Paterson city | 146 199 | 36 | 11000 | | Buffalo city | 261 310 |
| 34 | 57000 | 031 | Passaic County | 146 199 | 36 | 11000 | 029 | Erie County | 261 310 |
| 34 | 58200 | | Perth Amboy city | 50 814 | 36 | 24229 | | Elmira city | 29 200 |
| 34 | 58200 | 023 | Middlesex County | 50 814 | 36 | 24229 | 015 | Chemung County | 29 200 |
| 34 | 59190 | | Plainfield city | 49 808 | 36 | 27485 | | Freeport village | 42 860 |
| 34 | 59190 | 039 | Union County | 49 808 | 36 | 27485 | 059 | Nassau County | 42 860 |
| 34 | 61530 | | Rahway city | 27 346 | 36 | 29113 | | Glen Cove city | 26 964 |
| 34 | 61530 | 039 | Union County | 27 346 | 36 | 29113 | 059 | Nassau County | 26 964 |
| 34 | 65790 | | Sayreville borough | 42 704 | 36 | 32402 | | Harrison village | 27 472 |
| 34 | 65790 | 023 | Middlesex County | 42 704 | 36 | 32402 | 119 | Westchester County | 27 472 |
| 34 | 74000 | | Trenton city | 84 913 | 36 | 33139 | | Hempstead village | 53 891 |
| 34 | 74000 | 021 | Mercer County | 84 913 | 36 | 33139 | 059 | Nassau County | 53 891 |
| 34 | 74630 | | Union City city | 66 455 | 36 | 38077 | | Ithaca city | 30 014 |
| 34 | 74630 | 017 | Hudson County | 66 455 | 36 | 38077 | 109 | Tompkins County | 30 014 |
| 34 | 76070 | | Vineland city | 60 724 | 36 | 38264 | | Jamestown city | 31 146 |
| 34 | 76070 | 011 | Cumberland County | 60 724 | 36 | 38264 | 013 | Chautauqua County | 31 146 |
| 34 | 79040 | | Westfield town | 30 316 | 36 | 42554 | | Lindenhurst village | 27 253 |
| 34 | 79040 | 039 | Union County | 30 316 | 36 | 42554 | 103 | Suffolk County | 27 253 |
| 34 | 79610 | | West New York town | 49 708 | 36 | 43335 | | Long Beach city | 33 275 |
| 34 | 79610 | 017 | Hudson County | 49 708 | 36 | 43335 | 059 | Nassau County | 33 275 |
| 35 | | | **NEW MEXICO** | 2 059 179 | 36 | 47042 | | Middletown city | 28 086 |
| 35 | 01780 | | Alamogordo city | 30 403 | 36 | 47042 | 071 | Orange County | 28 086 |
| 35 | 01780 | 035 | Otero County | 30 403 | 36 | 49121 | | Mount Vernon city | 67 292 |
| 35 | 02000 | | Albuquerque city | 545 852 | 36 | 49121 | 119 | Westchester County | 67 292 |
| 35 | 02000 | 001 | Bernalillo County | 545 852 | 36 | 50034 | | Newburgh city | 28 866 |
| 35 | 12150 | | Carlsbad city | 26 138 | 36 | 50034 | 071 | Orange County | 28 866 |
| 35 | 12150 | 015 | Eddy County | 26 138 | | | | | |

# Cities by County–*Continued*

| State Code | Place Code | County Code | Geographic Area Name | 2010 Census Population | State Code | Place Code | County Code | Geographic Area Name | 2010 Census Population |
|---|---|---|---|---|---|---|---|---|---|
| 36 | 50617 | | New Rochelle city | 77 062 | 37 | 10740 | | Cary town | 135 234 |
| 36 | 50617 | 119 | Westchester County | 77 062 | 37 | 10740 | 037 | Chatham County | 1 422 |
| | | | | | 37 | 10740 | 183 | Wake County | 133 812 |
| 36 | 51000 | | New York city | 8 175 133 | | | | | |
| 36 | 51000 | 005 | Bronx County | 1 385 108 | 37 | 11800 | | Chapel Hill town | 57 233 |
| 36 | 51000 | 047 | Kings County | 2 504 700 | 37 | 11800 | 063 | Durham County | 2 836 |
| 36 | 51000 | 061 | New York County | 1 585 873 | 37 | 11800 | 135 | Orange County | 54 397 |
| 36 | 51000 | 081 | Queens County | 2 230 722 | | | | | |
| 36 | 51000 | 085 | Richmond County | 468 730 | 37 | 12000 | | Charlotte city | 731 424 |
| | | | | | 37 | 12000 | 119 | Mecklenburg County | 731 424 |
| 36 | 51055 | | Niagara Falls city | 50 193 | | | | | |
| 36 | 51055 | 063 | Niagara County | 50 193 | 37 | 14100 | | Concord city | 79 066 |
| | | | | | 37 | 14100 | 025 | Cabarrus County | 79 066 |
| 36 | 53682 | | North Tonawanda city | 31 568 | | | | | |
| 36 | 53682 | 063 | Niagara County | 31 568 | 37 | 19000 | | Durham city | 228 330 |
| | | | | | 37 | 19000 | 063 | Durham County | 228 300 |
| 36 | 55530 | | Ossining village | 25 060 | 37 | 19000 | 135 | Orange County | 30 |
| 36 | 55530 | 119 | Westchester County | 25 060 | 37 | 19000 | 183 | Wake County | 0 |
| 36 | 59223 | | Port Chester village | 28 967 | 37 | 22920 | | Fayetteville city | 200 564 |
| 36 | 59223 | 119 | Westchester County | 28 967 | 37 | 22920 | 051 | Cumberland County | 200 564 |
| 36 | 59641 | | Poughkeepsie city | 32 736 | 37 | 25480 | | Garner town | 25 745 |
| 36 | 59641 | 027 | Dutchess County | 32 736 | 37 | 25480 | 183 | Wake County | 25 745 |
| 36 | 63000 | | Rochester city | 210 565 | 37 | 25580 | | Gastonia city | 71 741 |
| 36 | 63000 | 055 | Monroe County | 210 565 | 37 | 25580 | 071 | Gaston County | 71 741 |
| 36 | 63418 | | Rome city | 33 725 | 37 | 26880 | | Goldsboro city | 36 437 |
| 36 | 63418 | 065 | Oneida County | 33 725 | 37 | 26880 | 191 | Wayne County | 36 437 |
| 36 | 65255 | | Saratoga Springs city | 26 586 | 37 | 28000 | | Greensboro city | 269 666 |
| 36 | 65255 | 091 | Saratoga County | 26 586 | 37 | 28000 | 081 | Guilford County | 269 666 |
| 36 | 65508 | | Schenectady city | 66 135 | 37 | 28080 | | Greenville city | 84 554 |
| 36 | 65508 | 093 | Schenectady County | 66 135 | 37 | 28080 | 147 | Pitt County | 84 554 |
| 36 | 70420 | | Spring Valley village | 31 347 | 37 | 31060 | | Hickory city | 40 010 |
| 36 | 70420 | 087 | Rockland County | 31 347 | 37 | 31060 | 023 | Burke County | 66 |
| | | | | | 37 | 31060 | 027 | Caldwell County | 18 |
| 36 | 73000 | | Syracuse city | 145 170 | 37 | 31060 | 035 | Catawba County | 39 926 |
| 36 | 73000 | 067 | Onondaga County | 145 170 | | | | | |
| | | | | | 37 | 31400 | | High Point city | 104 371 |
| 36 | 75484 | | Troy city | 50 129 | 37 | 31400 | 057 | Davidson County | 5 310 |
| 36 | 75484 | 083 | Rensselaer County | 50 129 | 37 | 31400 | 067 | Forsyth County | 8 |
| | | | | | 37 | 31400 | 081 | Guilford County | 99 042 |
| 36 | 76540 | | Utica city | 62 235 | 37 | 31400 | 151 | Randolph County | 11 |
| 36 | 76540 | 065 | Oneida County | 62 235 | | | | | |
| | | | | | 37 | 33120 | | Huntersville town | 46 773 |
| 36 | 76705 | | Valley Stream village | 37 511 | 37 | 33120 | 119 | Mecklenburg County | 46 773 |
| 36 | 76705 | 059 | Nassau County | 37 511 | | | | | |
| | | | | | 37 | 33560 | | Indian Trail town | 33 518 |
| 36 | 78608 | | Watertown city | 27 023 | 37 | 33560 | 179 | Union County | 33 518 |
| 36 | 78608 | 045 | Jefferson County | 27 023 | | | | | |
| | | | | | 37 | 34200 | | Jacksonville city | 70 145 |
| 36 | 81677 | | White Plains city | 56 853 | 37 | 34200 | 133 | Onslow County | 70 145 |
| 36 | 81677 | 119 | Westchester County | 56 853 | | | | | |
| | | | | | 37 | 35200 | | Kannapolis city | 42 625 |
| 37 | | | **NORTH CAROLINA** | 9 535 483 | 37 | 35200 | 025 | Cabarrus County | 33 194 |
| 37 | 01520 | | Apex town | 37 476 | 37 | 35200 | 159 | Rowan County | 9 431 |
| 37 | 01520 | 183 | Wake County | 37 476 | | | | | |
| | | | | | 37 | 41960 | | Matthews town | 27 198 |
| 37 | 02080 | | Asheboro city | 25 012 | 37 | 41960 | 119 | Mecklenburg County | 27 198 |
| 37 | 02080 | 151 | Randolph County | 25 012 | | | | | |
| | | | | | 37 | 43920 | | Monroe city | 32 797 |
| 37 | 02140 | | Asheville city | 83 393 | 37 | 43920 | 179 | Union County | 32 797 |
| 37 | 02140 | 021 | Buncombe County | 83 393 | | | | | |
| | | | | | 37 | 44220 | | Mooresville town | 32 711 |
| 37 | 09060 | | Burlington city | 49 963 | 37 | 44220 | 097 | Iredell County | 32 711 |
| 37 | 09060 | 001 | Alamance County | 49 308 | | | | | |
| 37 | 09060 | 081 | Guilford County | 655 | 37 | 46340 | | New Bern city | 29 524 |
| | | | | | 37 | 46340 | 049 | Craven County | 29 524 |

| State Code | Place Code | County Code | Geographic Area Name | 2010 Census Population | State Code | Place Code | County Code | Geographic Area Name | 2010 Census Population |
|---|---|---|---|---|---|---|---|---|---|
| 37 | 55000 | | Raleigh city | 403 892 | 39 | 16014 | | Cleveland Heights city | 46 121 |
| 37 | 55000 | 063 | Durham County | 1 067 | 39 | 16014 | 035 | Cuyahoga County | 46 121 |
| 37 | 55000 | 183 | Wake County | 402 825 | | | | | |
| | | | | | 39 | 18000 | | Columbus city | 787 033 |
| 37 | 57500 | | Rocky Mount city | 57 477 | 39 | 18000 | 041 | Delaware County | 7 245 |
| 37 | 57500 | 065 | Edgecombe County | 17 524 | 39 | 18000 | 045 | Fairfield County | 9 666 |
| 37 | 57500 | 127 | Nash County | 39 953 | 39 | 18000 | 049 | Franklin County | 770 122 |
| 37 | 58860 | | Salisbury city | 33 662 | 39 | 19778 | | Cuyahoga Falls city | 49 652 |
| 37 | 58860 | 159 | Rowan County | 33 662 | 39 | 19778 | 153 | Summit County | 49 652 |
| 37 | 59280 | | Sanford city | 28 094 | 39 | 21000 | | Dayton city | 141 527 |
| 37 | 59280 | 105 | Lee County | 28 094 | 39 | 21000 | 113 | Montgomery County | 141 527 |
| 37 | 67420 | | Thomasville city | 26 757 | 39 | 21434 | | Delaware city | 34 753 |
| 37 | 67420 | 057 | Davidson County | 26 493 | 39 | 21434 | 041 | Delaware County | 34 753 |
| 37 | 67420 | 151 | Randolph County | 264 | | | | | |
| | | | | | 39 | 22694 | | Dublin city | 41 751 |
| 37 | 70540 | | Wake Forest town | 30 117 | 39 | 22694 | 041 | Delaware County | 4 018 |
| 37 | 70540 | 069 | Franklin County | 899 | 39 | 22694 | 049 | Franklin County | 35 367 |
| 37 | 70540 | 183 | Wake County | 29 218 | 39 | 22694 | 159 | Union County | 2 366 |
| 37 | 74440 | | Wilmington city | 106 476 | 39 | 25256 | | Elyria city | 54 533 |
| 37 | 74440 | 129 | New Hanover County | 106 476 | 39 | 25256 | 093 | Lorain County | 54 533 |
| 37 | 74540 | | Wilson city | 49 167 | 39 | 25704 | | Euclid city | 48 920 |
| 37 | 74540 | 195 | Wilson County | 49 167 | 39 | 25704 | 035 | Cuyahoga County | 48 920 |
| 37 | 75000 | | Winston-Salem city | 229 617 | 39 | 25914 | | Fairborn city | 32 352 |
| 37 | 75000 | 067 | Forsyth County | 229 617 | 39 | 25914 | 057 | Greene County | 32 352 |
| 38 | | | **NORTH DAKOTA** | 672 591 | 39 | 25970 | | Fairfield city | 42 510 |
| 38 | 07200 | | Bismarck city | 61 272 | 39 | 25970 | 017 | Butler County | 42 510 |
| 38 | 07200 | 015 | Burleigh County | 61 272 | 39 | 25970 | 061 | Hamilton County | 0 |
| 38 | 25700 | | Fargo city | 105 549 | 39 | 27048 | | Findlay city | 41 202 |
| 38 | 25700 | 017 | Cass County | 105 549 | 39 | 27048 | 063 | Hancock County | 41 202 |
| 38 | 32060 | | Grand Forks city | 52 838 | 39 | 29106 | | Gahanna city | 33 248 |
| 38 | 32060 | 035 | Grand Forks County | 52 838 | 39 | 29106 | 049 | Franklin County | 33 248 |
| 38 | 53380 | | Minot city | 40 888 | 39 | 29428 | | Garfield Heights city | 28 849 |
| 38 | 53380 | 101 | Ward County | 40 888 | 39 | 29428 | 035 | Cuyahoga County | 28 849 |
| 38 | 84780 | | West Fargo city | 25 830 | 39 | 31860 | | Green city | 25 699 |
| 38 | 84780 | 017 | Cass County | 25 830 | 39 | 31860 | 153 | Summit County | 25 699 |
| 39 | | | **OHIO** | 11 536 504 | 39 | 32592 | | Grove City city | 35 575 |
| 39 | 01000 | | Akron city | 199 110 | 39 | 32592 | 049 | Franklin County | 35 575 |
| 39 | 01000 | 153 | Summit County | 199 110 | | | | | |
| | | | | | 39 | 33012 | | Hamilton city | 62 477 |
| 39 | 03828 | | Barberton city | 26 550 | 39 | 33012 | 017 | Butler County | 62 477 |
| 39 | 03828 | 153 | Summit County | 26 550 | | | | | |
| | | | | | 39 | 35476 | | Hilliard city | 28 435 |
| 39 | 04720 | | Beavercreek city | 45 193 | 39 | 35476 | 049 | Franklin County | 28 435 |
| 39 | 04720 | 057 | Greene County | 45 193 | | | | | |
| | | | | | 39 | 36610 | | Huber Heights city | 38 101 |
| 39 | 07972 | | Bowling Green city | 30 028 | 39 | 36610 | 057 | Greene County | 0 |
| 39 | 07972 | 173 | Wood County | 30 028 | 39 | 36610 | 109 | Miami County | 959 |
| | | | | | 39 | 36610 | 113 | Montgomery County | 37 142 |
| 39 | 09680 | | Brunswick city | 34 255 | | | | | |
| 39 | 09680 | 103 | Medina County | 34 255 | 39 | 39872 | | Kent city | 28 904 |
| | | | | | 39 | 39872 | 133 | Portage County | 28 904 |
| 39 | 12000 | | Canton city | 73 007 | | | | | |
| 39 | 12000 | 151 | Stark County | 73 007 | 39 | 40040 | | Kettering city | 56 163 |
| | | | | | 39 | 40040 | 057 | Greene County | 467 |
| 39 | 15000 | | Cincinnati city | 296 943 | 39 | 40040 | 113 | Montgomery County | 55 696 |
| 39 | 15000 | 061 | Hamilton County | 296 943 | | | | | |
| | | | | | 39 | 41664 | | Lakewood city | 52 131 |
| 39 | 16000 | | Cleveland city | 396 815 | 39 | 41664 | 035 | Cuyahoga County | 52 131 |
| 39 | 16000 | 035 | Cuyahoga County | 396 815 | | | | | |

| State Code | Place Code | County Code | Geographic Area Name | 2010 Census Population |
|---|---|---|---|---|
| 39 | 41720 | | Lancaster city | 38 780 |
| 39 | 41720 | 045 | Fairfield County | 38 780 |
| 39 | 43554 | | Lima city | 38 771 |
| 39 | 43554 | 003 | Allen County | 38 771 |
| 39 | 44856 | | Lorain city | 64 097 |
| 39 | 44856 | 093 | Lorain County | 64 097 |
| 39 | 47138 | | Mansfield city | 47 821 |
| 39 | 47138 | 139 | Richland County | 47 821 |
| 39 | 47754 | | Marion city | 36 837 |
| 39 | 47754 | 101 | Marion County | 36 837 |
| 39 | 48188 | | Mason city | 30 712 |
| 39 | 48188 | 165 | Warren County | 30 712 |
| 39 | 48244 | | Massillon city | 32 149 |
| 39 | 48244 | 151 | Stark County | 32 149 |
| 39 | 48790 | | Medina city | 26 678 |
| 39 | 48790 | 103 | Medina County | 26 678 |
| 39 | 49056 | | Mentor city | 47 159 |
| 39 | 49056 | 085 | Lake County | 47 159 |
| 39 | 49840 | | Middletown city | 48 694 |
| 39 | 49840 | 017 | Butler County | 45 994 |
| 39 | 49840 | 165 | Warren County | 2 700 |
| 39 | 54040 | | Newark city | 47 573 |
| 39 | 54040 | 089 | Licking County | 47 573 |
| 39 | 56882 | | North Olmsted city | 32 718 |
| 39 | 56882 | 035 | Cuyahoga County | 32 718 |
| 39 | 56966 | | North Ridgeville city | 29 465 |
| 39 | 56966 | 093 | Lorain County | 29 465 |
| 39 | 57008 | | North Royalton city | 30 444 |
| 39 | 57008 | 035 | Cuyahoga County | 30 444 |
| 39 | 61000 | | Parma city | 81 601 |
| 39 | 61000 | 035 | Cuyahoga County | 81 601 |
| 39 | 66390 | | Reynoldsburg city | 35 893 |
| 39 | 66390 | 045 | Fairfield County | 910 |
| 39 | 66390 | 049 | Franklin County | 26 157 |
| 39 | 66390 | 089 | Licking County | 8 826 |
| 39 | 67468 | | Riverside city | 25 201 |
| 39 | 67468 | 113 | Montgomery County | 25 201 |
| 39 | 70380 | | Sandusky city | 25 793 |
| 39 | 70380 | 043 | Erie County | 25 793 |
| 39 | 71682 | | Shaker Heights city | 28 448 |
| 39 | 71682 | 035 | Cuyahoga County | 28 448 |
| 39 | 74118 | | Springfield city | 60 608 |
| 39 | 74118 | 023 | Clark County | 60 608 |
| 39 | 74944 | | Stow city | 34 837 |
| 39 | 74944 | 153 | Summit County | 34 837 |
| 39 | 75098 | | Strongsville city | 44 750 |
| 39 | 75098 | 035 | Cuyahoga County | 44 750 |
| 39 | 77000 | | Toledo city | 287 208 |
| 39 | 77000 | 095 | Lucas County | 287 208 |
| 39 | 77588 | | Troy city | 25 058 |
| 39 | 77588 | 109 | Miami County | 25 058 |
| 39 | 79002 | | Upper Arlington city | 33 771 |
| 39 | 79002 | 049 | Franklin County | 33 771 |
| 39 | 80892 | | Warren city | 41 557 |
| 39 | 80892 | 155 | Trumbull County | 41 557 |
| 39 | 83342 | | Westerville city | 36 120 |
| 39 | 83342 | 041 | Delaware County | 7 792 |
| 39 | 83342 | 049 | Franklin County | 28 328 |
| 39 | 83622 | | Westlake city | 32 729 |
| 39 | 83622 | 035 | Cuyahoga County | 32 729 |
| 39 | 86548 | | Wooster city | 26 119 |
| 39 | 86548 | 169 | Wayne County | 26 119 |
| 39 | 86772 | | Xenia city | 25 719 |
| 39 | 86772 | 057 | Greene County | 25 719 |
| 39 | 88000 | | Youngstown city | 66 982 |
| 39 | 88000 | 099 | Mahoning County | 66 971 |
| 39 | 88000 | 155 | Trumbull County | 11 |
| 39 | 88084 | | Zanesville city | 25 487 |
| 39 | 88084 | 119 | Muskingum County | 25 487 |
| 40 | | | **OKLAHOMA** | 3 751 351 |
| 40 | 04450 | | Bartlesville city | 35 750 |
| 40 | 04450 | 113 | Osage County | 3 |
| 40 | 04450 | 147 | Washington County | 35 747 |
| 40 | 09050 | | Broken Arrow city | 98 850 |
| 40 | 09050 | 143 | Tulsa County | 80 634 |
| 40 | 09050 | 145 | Wagoner County | 18 216 |
| 40 | 23200 | | Edmond city | 81 405 |
| 40 | 23200 | 109 | Oklahoma County | 81 405 |
| 40 | 23950 | | Enid city | 49 379 |
| 40 | 23950 | 047 | Garfield County | 49 379 |
| 40 | 41850 | | Lawton city | 96 867 |
| 40 | 41850 | 031 | Comanche County | 96 867 |
| 40 | 48350 | | Midwest City city | 54 371 |
| 40 | 48350 | 109 | Oklahoma County | 54 371 |
| 40 | 49200 | | Moore city | 55 081 |
| 40 | 49200 | 027 | Cleveland County | 55 081 |
| 40 | 50050 | | Muskogee city | 39 223 |
| 40 | 50050 | 101 | Muskogee County | 39 223 |
| 40 | 52500 | | Norman city | 110 925 |
| 40 | 52500 | 027 | Cleveland County | 110 925 |
| 40 | 55000 | | Oklahoma City city | 579 999 |
| 40 | 55000 | 017 | Canadian County | 44 541 |
| 40 | 55000 | 027 | Cleveland County | 63 723 |
| 40 | 55000 | 109 | Oklahoma County | 471 671 |
| 40 | 55000 | 125 | Pottawatomie County | 64 |
| 40 | 56650 | | Owasso city | 28 915 |
| 40 | 56650 | 131 | Rogers County | 2 614 |
| 40 | 56650 | 143 | Tulsa County | 26 301 |
| 40 | 59850 | | Ponca City city | 25 387 |
| 40 | 59850 | 071 | Kay County | 25 387 |

| State Code | Place Code | County Code | Geographic Area Name | 2010 Census Population | State Code | Place Code | County Code | Geographic Area Name | 2010 Census Population |
|---|---|---|---|---|---|---|---|---|---|
| 40 | 66800 | | Shawnee city | 29 857 | 41 | 74950 | | Tualatin city | 26 054 |
| 40 | 66800 | 125 | Pottawatomie County | 29 857 | 41 | 74950 | 005 | Clackamas County | 2 862 |
| | | | | | 41 | 74950 | 067 | Washington County | 23 192 |
| 40 | 70300 | | Stillwater city | 45 688 | | | | | |
| 40 | 70300 | 119 | Payne County | 45 688 | 41 | 80150 | | West Linn city | 25 109 |
| | | | | | 41 | 80150 | 005 | Clackamas County | 25 109 |
| 40 | 75000 | | Tulsa city | 391 906 | | | | | |
| 40 | 75000 | 113 | Osage County | 6 136 | 42 | | | **PENNSYLVANIA** | 12 702 379 |
| 40 | 75000 | 131 | Rogers County | 0 | 42 | 02000 | | Allentown city | 118 032 |
| 40 | 75000 | 143 | Tulsa County | 385 613 | 42 | 02000 | 077 | Lehigh County | 118 032 |
| 40 | 75000 | 145 | Wagoner County | 157 | | | | | |
| | | | | | 42 | 02184 | | Altoona city | 46 320 |
| 41 | | | **OREGON** | 3 831 074 | 42 | 02184 | 013 | Blair County | 46 320 |
| 41 | 01000 | | Albany city | 50 158 | | | | | |
| 41 | 01000 | 003 | Benton County | 6 463 | 42 | 06064 | | Bethel Park municipality | 32 313 |
| 41 | 01000 | 043 | Linn County | 43 695 | 42 | 06064 | 003 | Allegheny County | 32 313 |
| | | | | | | | | | |
| 41 | 05350 | | Beaverton city | 89 803 | 42 | 06088 | | Bethlehem city | 74 982 |
| 41 | 05350 | 067 | Washington County | 89 803 | 42 | 06088 | 077 | Lehigh County | 19 343 |
| | | | | | 42 | 06088 | 095 | Northampton County | 55 639 |
| 41 | 05800 | | Bend city | 76 639 | | | | | |
| 41 | 05800 | 017 | Deschutes County | 76 639 | 42 | 13208 | | Chester city | 33 972 |
| | | | | | 42 | 13208 | 045 | Delaware County | 33 972 |
| 41 | 15800 | | Corvallis city | 54 462 | | | | | |
| 41 | 15800 | 003 | Benton County | 54 462 | 42 | 21648 | | Easton city | 26 800 |
| | | | | | 42 | 21648 | 095 | Northampton County | 26 800 |
| 41 | 23850 | | Eugene city | 156 185 | | | | | |
| 41 | 23850 | 039 | Lane County | 156 185 | 42 | 24000 | | Erie city | 101 786 |
| | | | | | 42 | 24000 | 049 | Erie County | 101 786 |
| 41 | 30550 | | Grants Pass city | 34 533 | | | | | |
| 41 | 30550 | 033 | Josephine County | 34 533 | 42 | 32800 | | Harrisburg city | 49 528 |
| | | | | | 42 | 32800 | 043 | Dauphin County | 49 528 |
| 41 | 31250 | | Gresham city | 105 594 | | | | | |
| 41 | 31250 | 051 | Multnomah County | 105 594 | 42 | 33408 | | Hazleton city | 25 340 |
| | | | | | 42 | 33408 | 079 | Luzerne County | 25 340 |
| 41 | 34100 | | Hillsboro city | 91 611 | | | | | |
| 41 | 34100 | 067 | Washington County | 91 611 | 42 | 41216 | | Lancaster city | 59 322 |
| | | | | | 42 | 41216 | 071 | Lancaster County | 59 322 |
| 41 | 38500 | | Keizer city | 36 478 | | | | | |
| 41 | 38500 | 047 | Marion County | 36 478 | 42 | 42168 | | Lebanon city | 25 477 |
| | | | | | 42 | 42168 | 075 | Lebanon County | 25 477 |
| 41 | 40550 | | Lake Oswego city | 36 619 | | | | | |
| 41 | 40550 | 005 | Clackamas County | 34 066 | 42 | 50528 | | Monroeville municipality | 28 386 |
| 41 | 40550 | 051 | Multnomah County | 2 544 | 42 | 50528 | 003 | Allegheny County | 28 386 |
| 41 | 40550 | 067 | Washington County | 9 | | | | | |
| | | | | | 42 | 54656 | | Norristown borough | 34 324 |
| 41 | 45000 | | McMinnville city | 32 187 | 42 | 54656 | 091 | Montgomery County | 34 324 |
| 41 | 45000 | 071 | Yamhill County | 32 187 | | | | | |
| | | | | | 42 | 60000 | | Philadelphia city | 1 526 006 |
| 41 | 47000 | | Medford city | 74 907 | 42 | 60000 | 101 | Philadelphia County | 1 526 006 |
| 41 | 47000 | 029 | Jackson County | 74 907 | | | | | |
| | | | | | 42 | 61000 | | Pittsburgh city | 305 704 |
| 41 | 55200 | | Oregon City city | 31 859 | 42 | 61000 | 003 | Allegheny County | 305 704 |
| 41 | 55200 | 005 | Clackamas County | 31 859 | | | | | |
| | | | | | 42 | 61536 | | Plum borough | 27 126 |
| 41 | 59000 | | Portland city | 583 776 | 42 | 61536 | 003 | Allegheny County | 27 126 |
| 41 | 59000 | 005 | Clackamas County | 744 | | | | | |
| 41 | 59000 | 051 | Multnomah County | 581 485 | 42 | 63624 | | Reading city | 88 082 |
| 41 | 59000 | 067 | Washington County | 1 547 | 42 | 63624 | 011 | Berks County | 88 082 |
| | | | | | | | | | |
| 41 | 61200 | | Redmond city | 26 215 | 42 | 69000 | | Scranton city | 76 089 |
| 41 | 61200 | 017 | Deschutes County | 26 215 | 42 | 69000 | 069 | Lackawanna County | 76 089 |
| | | | | | | | | | |
| 41 | 64900 | | Salem city | 154 637 | 42 | 73808 | | State College borough | 42 034 |
| 41 | 64900 | 047 | Marion County | 130 398 | 42 | 73808 | 027 | Centre County | 42 034 |
| 41 | 64900 | 053 | Polk County | 24 239 | | | | | |
| | | | | | 42 | 85152 | | Wilkes-Barre city | 41 498 |
| 41 | 69600 | | Springfield city | 59 403 | 42 | 85152 | 079 | Luzerne County | 41 498 |
| 41 | 69600 | 039 | Lane County | 59 403 | | | | | |
| | | | | | 42 | 85312 | | Williamsport city | 29 381 |
| 41 | 73650 | | Tigard city | 48 035 | 42 | 85312 | 081 | Lycoming County | 29 381 |
| 41 | 73650 | 067 | Washington County | 48 035 | | | | | |

| State Code | Place Code | County Code | Geographic Area Name | 2010 Census Population | State Code | Place Code | County Code | Geographic Area Name | 2010 Census Population |
|---|---|---|---|---|---|---|---|---|---|
| 42 | 87048 | | York city | 43 718 | 45 | 70270 | | Summerville town | 43 392 |
| 42 | 87048 | 133 | York County | 43 718 | 45 | 70270 | 015 | Berkeley County | 3 643 |
| | | | | | 45 | 70270 | 019 | Charleston County | 1 010 |
| 44 | | | **RHODE ISLAND** | 1 052 567 | 45 | 70270 | 035 | Dorchester County | 38 739 |
| 44 | 19180 | | Cranston city | 80 387 | | | | | |
| 44 | 19180 | 007 | Providence County | 80 387 | 45 | 70405 | | Sumter city | 40 524 |
| | | | | | 45 | 70405 | 085 | Sumter County | 40 524 |
| 44 | 22960 | | East Providence city | 47 037 | | | | | |
| 44 | 22960 | 007 | Providence County | 47 037 | 46 | | | **SOUTH DAKOTA** | 814 180 |
| | | | | | 46 | 00100 | | Aberdeen city | 26 091 |
| 44 | 54640 | | Pawtucket city | 71 148 | 46 | 00100 | 013 | Brown County | 26 091 |
| 44 | 54640 | 007 | Providence County | 71 148 | | | | | |
| | | | | | 46 | 52980 | | Rapid City city | 67 956 |
| 44 | 59000 | | Providence city | 178 042 | 46 | 52980 | 103 | Pennington County | 67 956 |
| 44 | 59000 | 007 | Providence County | 178 042 | | | | | |
| | | | | | 46 | 59020 | | Sioux Falls city | 153 888 |
| 44 | 74300 | | Warwick city | 82 672 | 46 | 59020 | 083 | Lincoln County | 21 095 |
| 44 | 74300 | 003 | Kent County | 82 672 | 46 | 59020 | 099 | Minnehaha County | 132 793 |
| | | | | | | | | | |
| 44 | 80780 | | Woonsocket city | 41 186 | 47 | | | **TENNESSEE** | 6 346 105 |
| 44 | 80780 | 007 | Providence County | 41 186 | 47 | 03440 | | Bartlett city | 54 613 |
| | | | | | 47 | 03440 | 157 | Shelby County | 54 613 |
| 45 | | | **SOUTH CAROLINA** | 4 625 364 | | | | | |
| 45 | 00550 | | Aiken city | 29 524 | 47 | 08280 | | Brentwood city | 37 060 |
| 45 | 00550 | 003 | Aiken County | 29 524 | 47 | 08280 | 187 | Williamson County | 37 060 |
| | | | | | | | | | |
| 45 | 01360 | | Anderson city | 26 686 | 47 | 08540 | | Bristol city | 26 702 |
| 45 | 01360 | 007 | Anderson County | 26 686 | 47 | 08540 | 163 | Sullivan County | 26 702 |
| | | | | | | | | | |
| 45 | 13330 | | Charleston city | 120 083 | 47 | 14000 | | Chattanooga city | 167 674 |
| 45 | 13330 | 015 | Berkeley County | 8 095 | 47 | 14000 | 065 | Hamilton County | 167 674 |
| 45 | 13330 | 019 | Charleston County | 111 988 | | | | | |
| | | | | | 47 | 15160 | | Clarksville city | 132 929 |
| 45 | 16000 | | Columbia city | 129 272 | 47 | 15160 | 125 | Montgomery County | 132 929 |
| 45 | 16000 | 063 | Lexington County | 559 | | | | | |
| 45 | 16000 | 079 | Richland County | 128 713 | 47 | 15400 | | Cleveland city | 41 285 |
| | | | | | 47 | 15400 | 011 | Bradley County | 41 285 |
| 45 | 25810 | | Florence city | 37 056 | | | | | |
| 45 | 25810 | 041 | Florence County | 37 056 | 47 | 16420 | | Collierville town | 43 965 |
| | | | | | 47 | 16420 | 047 | Fayette County | 0 |
| 45 | 29815 | | Goose Creek city | 35 938 | 47 | 16420 | 157 | Shelby County | 43 965 |
| 45 | 29815 | 015 | Berkeley County | 35 933 | | | | | |
| 45 | 29815 | 019 | Charleston County | 5 | 47 | 16540 | | Columbia city | 34 681 |
| | | | | | 47 | 16540 | 119 | Maury County | 34 681 |
| 45 | 30850 | | Greenville city | 58 409 | | | | | |
| 45 | 30850 | 045 | Greenville County | 58 409 | 47 | 16920 | | Cookeville city | 30 435 |
| | | | | | 47 | 16920 | 141 | Putnam County | 30 435 |
| 45 | 30985 | | Greer city | 25 515 | | | | | |
| 45 | 30985 | 045 | Greenville County | 18 635 | 47 | 27740 | | Franklin city | 62 487 |
| 45 | 30985 | 083 | Spartanburg County | 6 880 | 47 | 27740 | 187 | Williamson County | 62 487 |
| | | | | | | | | | |
| 45 | 34045 | | Hilton Head Island town | 37 099 | 47 | 28540 | | Gallatin city | 30 278 |
| 45 | 34045 | 013 | Beaufort County | 37 099 | 47 | 28540 | 165 | Sumner County | 30 278 |
| | | | | | | | | | |
| 45 | 48535 | | Mount Pleasant town | 67 843 | 47 | 28960 | | Germantown city | 38 844 |
| 45 | 48535 | 019 | Charleston County | 67 843 | 47 | 28960 | 157 | Shelby County | 38 844 |
| | | | | | | | | | |
| 45 | 49075 | | Myrtle Beach city | 27 109 | 47 | 33280 | | Hendersonville city | 51 372 |
| 45 | 49075 | 051 | Horry County | 27 109 | 47 | 33280 | 165 | Sumner County | 51 372 |
| | | | | | | | | | |
| 45 | 50875 | | North Charleston city | 97 471 | 47 | 37640 | | Jackson city | 65 211 |
| 45 | 50875 | 015 | Berkeley County | 0 | 47 | 37640 | 113 | Madison County | 65 211 |
| 45 | 50875 | 019 | Charleston County | 78 393 | | | | | |
| 45 | 50875 | 035 | Dorchester County | 19 078 | 47 | 38320 | | Johnson City city | 63 152 |
| | | | | | 47 | 38320 | 019 | Carter County | 1 252 |
| 45 | 61405 | | Rock Hill city | 66 154 | 47 | 38320 | 163 | Sullivan County | 367 |
| 45 | 61405 | 091 | York County | 66 154 | 47 | 38320 | 179 | Washington County | 61 533 |
| | | | | | | | | | |
| 45 | 68290 | | Spartanburg city | 37 013 | 47 | 39560 | | Kingsport city | 48 205 |
| 45 | 68290 | 083 | Spartanburg County | 37 013 | 47 | 39560 | 073 | Hawkins County | 2 854 |
| | | | | | 47 | 39560 | 163 | Sullivan County | 45 351 |

| State Code | Place Code | County Code | Geographic Area Name | 2010 Census Population | State Code | Place Code | County Code | Geographic Area Name | 2010 Census Population |
|---|---|---|---|---|---|---|---|---|---|
| 47 | 40000 | | Knoxville city | 178 874 | 48 | 11428 | | Burleson city | 36 690 |
| 47 | 40000 | 093 | Knox County | 178 874 | 48 | 11428 | 251 | Johnson County | 29 111 |
| | | | | | 48 | 11428 | 439 | Tarrant County | 7 579 |
| 47 | 41200 | | La Vergne city | 32 588 | | | | | |
| 47 | 41200 | 149 | Rutherford County | 32 588 | 48 | 13024 | | Carrollton city | 119 097 |
| | | | | | 48 | 13024 | 085 | Collin County | 2 |
| 47 | 41520 | | Lebanon city | 26 190 | 48 | 13024 | 113 | Dallas County | 49 352 |
| 47 | 41520 | 189 | Wilson County | 26 190 | 48 | 13024 | 121 | Denton County | 69 743 |
| 47 | 46380 | | Maryville city | 27 465 | 48 | 13492 | | Cedar Hill city | 45 028 |
| 47 | 46380 | 009 | Blount County | 27 465 | 48 | 13492 | 113 | Dallas County | 44 477 |
| | | | | | 48 | 13492 | 139 | Ellis County | 551 |
| 47 | 48000 | | Memphis city | 646 889 | | | | | |
| 47 | 48000 | 157 | Shelby County | 646 889 | 48 | 13552 | | Cedar Park city | 48 937 |
| | | | | | 48 | 13552 | 453 | Travis County | 489 |
| 47 | 50280 | | Morristown city | 29 137 | 48 | 13552 | 491 | Williamson County | 48 448 |
| 47 | 50280 | 063 | Hamblen County | 29 131 | | | | | |
| 47 | 50280 | 089 | Jefferson County | 6 | 48 | 15364 | | Cleburne city | 29 337 |
| | | | | | 48 | 15364 | 251 | Johnson County | 29 337 |
| 47 | 51560 | | Murfreesboro city | 108 755 | | | | | |
| 47 | 51560 | 149 | Rutherford County | 108 755 | 48 | 15976 | | College Station city | 93 857 |
| | | | | | 48 | 15976 | 041 | Brazos County | 93 857 |
| 47 | 55120 | | Oak Ridge city | 29 330 | | | | | |
| 47 | 55120 | 001 | Anderson County | 26 271 | 48 | 16432 | | Conroe city | 56 207 |
| 47 | 55120 | 145 | Roane County | 3 059 | 48 | 16432 | 339 | Montgomery County | 56 207 |
| 47 | 69420 | | Smyrna town | 39 974 | 48 | 16612 | | Coppell city | 38 659 |
| 47 | 69420 | 149 | Rutherford County | 39 974 | 48 | 16612 | 113 | Dallas County | 37 905 |
| | | | | | 48 | 16612 | 121 | Denton County | 754 |
| 47 | 70580 | | Spring Hill city | 29 036 | | | | | |
| 47 | 70580 | 119 | Maury County | 7 023 | 48 | 16624 | | Copperas Cove city | 32 032 |
| 47 | 70580 | 187 | Williamson County | 22 013 | 48 | 16624 | 027 | Bell County | 0 |
| | | | | | 48 | 16624 | 099 | Coryell County | 31 457 |
| 48 | | | **TEXAS** | 25 145 561 | 48 | 16624 | 281 | Lampasas County | 575 |
| 48 | 01000 | | Abilene city | 117 063 | | | | | |
| 48 | 01000 | 253 | Jones County | 5 145 | 48 | 17000 | | Corpus Christi city | 305 215 |
| 48 | 01000 | 441 | Taylor County | 111 918 | 48 | 17000 | 007 | Aransas County | 0 |
| | | | | | 48 | 17000 | 273 | Kleberg County | 0 |
| 48 | 01924 | | Allen city | 84 246 | 48 | 17000 | 355 | Nueces County | 305 215 |
| 48 | 01924 | 085 | Collin County | 84 246 | 48 | 17000 | 409 | San Patricio County | 0 |
| 48 | 03000 | | Amarillo city | 190 695 | 48 | 19000 | | Dallas city | 1 197 816 |
| 48 | 03000 | 375 | Potter County | 105 486 | 48 | 19000 | 085 | Collin County | 46 885 |
| 48 | 03000 | 381 | Randall County | 85 209 | 48 | 19000 | 113 | Dallas County | 1 124 296 |
| | | | | | 48 | 19000 | 121 | Denton County | 26 579 |
| 48 | 04000 | | Arlington city | 365 438 | 48 | 19000 | 257 | Kaufman County | 0 |
| 48 | 04000 | 439 | Tarrant County | 365 438 | 48 | 19000 | 397 | Rockwall County | 56 |
| 48 | 05000 | | Austin city | 790 390 | 48 | 19624 | | Deer Park city | 32 010 |
| 48 | 05000 | 209 | Hays County | 2 | 48 | 19624 | 201 | Harris County | 32 010 |
| 48 | 05000 | 453 | Travis County | 754 691 | | | | | |
| 48 | 05000 | 491 | Williamson County | 35 697 | 48 | 19792 | | Del Rio city | 35 591 |
| | | | | | 48 | 19792 | 465 | Val Verde County | 35 591 |
| 48 | 06128 | | Baytown city | 71 802 | | | | | |
| 48 | 06128 | 071 | Chambers County | 4 116 | 48 | 19972 | | Denton city | 113 383 |
| 48 | 06128 | 201 | Harris County | 67 686 | 48 | 19972 | 121 | Denton County | 113 383 |
| 48 | 07000 | | Beaumont city | 118 296 | 48 | 20092 | | DeSoto city | 49 047 |
| 48 | 07000 | 245 | Jefferson County | 118 296 | 48 | 20092 | 113 | Dallas County | 49 047 |
| 48 | 07132 | | Bedford city | 46 979 | 48 | 21628 | | Duncanville city | 38 524 |
| 48 | 07132 | 439 | Tarrant County | 46 979 | 48 | 21628 | 113 | Dallas County | 38 524 |
| 48 | 08236 | | Big Spring city | 27 282 | 48 | 21892 | | Eagle Pass city | 26 248 |
| 48 | 08236 | 227 | Howard County | 27 282 | 48 | 21892 | 323 | Maverick County | 26 248 |
| 48 | 10768 | | Brownsville city | 175 023 | 48 | 22660 | | Edinburg city | 77 100 |
| 48 | 10768 | 061 | Cameron County | 175 023 | 48 | 22660 | 215 | Hidalgo County | 77 100 |
| 48 | 10912 | | Bryan city | 76 201 | 48 | 24000 | | El Paso city | 649 121 |
| 48 | 10912 | 041 | Brazos County | 76 201 | 48 | 24000 | 141 | El Paso County | 649 121 |

# Cities by County–*Continued*

| State Code | Place Code | County Code | Geographic Area Name | 2010 Census Population | State Code | Place Code | County Code | Geographic Area Name | 2010 Census Population |
|---|---|---|---|---|---|---|---|---|---|
| 48 | 24768 | | Euless city | 51 277 | 48 | 38632 | | Keller city | 39 627 |
| 48 | 24768 | 439 | Tarrant County | 51 277 | 48 | 38632 | 439 | Tarrant County | 39 627 |
| 48 | 25452 | | Farmers Branch city | 28 616 | 48 | 39148 | | Killeen city | 127 921 |
| 48 | 25452 | 113 | Dallas County | 28 616 | 48 | 39148 | 027 | Bell County | 127 921 |
| 48 | 26232 | | Flower Mound town | 64 669 | 48 | 39352 | | Kingsville city | 26 213 |
| 48 | 26232 | 121 | Denton County | 64 457 | 48 | 39352 | 273 | Kleberg County | 26 213 |
| 48 | 26232 | 439 | Tarrant County | 212 | | | | | |
| | | | | | 48 | 39952 | | Kyle city | 28 016 |
| 48 | 27000 | | Fort Worth city | 741 206 | 48 | 39952 | 209 | Hays County | 28 016 |
| 48 | 27000 | 121 | Denton County | 7 813 | | | | | |
| 48 | 27000 | 367 | Parker County | 7 | 48 | 40588 | | Lake Jackson city | 26 849 |
| 48 | 27000 | 439 | Tarrant County | 733 386 | 48 | 40588 | 039 | Brazoria County | 26 849 |
| 48 | 27000 | 497 | Wise County | 0 | | | | | |
| | | | | | 48 | 41212 | | Lancaster city | 36 361 |
| 48 | 27648 | | Friendswood city | 35 805 | 48 | 41212 | 113 | Dallas County | 36 361 |
| 48 | 27648 | 167 | Galveston County | 25 510 | | | | | |
| 48 | 27648 | 201 | Harris County | 10 295 | 48 | 41440 | | La Porte city | 33 800 |
| | | | | | 48 | 41440 | 201 | Harris County | 33 800 |
| 48 | 27684 | | Frisco city | 116 989 | | | | | |
| 48 | 27684 | 085 | Collin County | 72 489 | 48 | 41464 | | Laredo city | 236 091 |
| 48 | 27684 | 121 | Denton County | 44 500 | 48 | 41464 | 479 | Webb County | 236 091 |
| 48 | 28068 | | Galveston city | 47 743 | 48 | 41980 | | League City city | 83 560 |
| 48 | 28068 | 167 | Galveston County | 47 743 | 48 | 41980 | 167 | Galveston County | 81 998 |
| | | | | | 48 | 41980 | 201 | Harris County | 1 562 |
| 48 | 29000 | | Garland city | 226 876 | | | | | |
| 48 | 29000 | 085 | Collin County | 266 | 48 | 42016 | | Leander city | 26 521 |
| 48 | 29000 | 113 | Dallas County | 226 608 | 48 | 42016 | 453 | Travis County | 1 077 |
| 48 | 29000 | 397 | Rockwall County | 2 | 48 | 42016 | 491 | Williamson County | 25 444 |
| 48 | 29336 | | Georgetown city | 47 400 | 48 | 42508 | | Lewisville city | 95 290 |
| 48 | 29336 | 491 | Williamson County | 47 400 | 48 | 42508 | 113 | Dallas County | 841 |
| | | | | | 48 | 42508 | 121 | Denton County | 94 449 |
| 48 | 30464 | | Grand Prairie city | 175 396 | | | | | |
| 48 | 30464 | 113 | Dallas County | 123 487 | 48 | 43012 | | Little Elm city | 25 898 |
| 48 | 30464 | 139 | Ellis County | 45 | 48 | 43012 | 121 | Denton County | 25 898 |
| 48 | 30464 | 439 | Tarrant County | 51 864 | | | | | |
| | | | | | 48 | 43888 | | Longview city | 80 455 |
| 48 | 30644 | | Grapevine city | 46 334 | 48 | 43888 | 183 | Gregg County | 78 585 |
| 48 | 30644 | 113 | Dallas County | 0 | 48 | 43888 | 203 | Harrison County | 1 870 |
| 48 | 30644 | 121 | Denton County | 0 | | | | | |
| 48 | 30644 | 439 | Tarrant County | 46 334 | 48 | 45000 | | Lubbock city | 229 573 |
| | | | | | 48 | 45000 | 303 | Lubbock County | 229 573 |
| 48 | 30920 | | Greenville city | 25 557 | | | | | |
| 48 | 30920 | 231 | Hunt County | 25 557 | 48 | 45072 | | Lufkin city | 35 067 |
| | | | | | 48 | 45072 | 005 | Angelina County | 35 067 |
| 48 | 31928 | | Haltom City city | 42 409 | | | | | |
| 48 | 31928 | 439 | Tarrant County | 42 409 | 48 | 45384 | | McAllen city | 129 877 |
| | | | | | 48 | 45384 | 215 | Hidalgo County | 129 877 |
| 48 | 32312 | | Harker Heights city | 26 700 | | | | | |
| 48 | 32312 | 027 | Bell County | 26 700 | 48 | 45744 | | McKinney city | 131 117 |
| | | | | | 48 | 45744 | 085 | Collin County | 131 117 |
| 48 | 32372 | | Harlingen city | 64 849 | | | | | |
| 48 | 32372 | 061 | Cameron County | 64 849 | 48 | 46452 | | Mansfield city | 56 368 |
| | | | | | 48 | 46452 | 139 | Ellis County | 95 |
| 48 | 35000 | | Houston city | 2 099 451 | 48 | 46452 | 251 | Johnson County | 1 652 |
| 48 | 35000 | 157 | Fort Bend County | 38 124 | 48 | 46452 | 439 | Tarrant County | 54 621 |
| 48 | 35000 | 201 | Harris County | 2 057 280 | | | | | |
| 48 | 35000 | 339 | Montgomery County | 4 047 | 48 | 47892 | | Mesquite city | 139 824 |
| | | | | | 48 | 47892 | 113 | Dallas County | 139 731 |
| 48 | 35528 | | Huntsville city | 38 548 | 48 | 47892 | 257 | Kaufman County | 93 |
| 48 | 35528 | 471 | Walker County | 38 548 | | | | | |
| | | | | | 48 | 48072 | | Midland city | 111 147 |
| 48 | 35576 | | Hurst city | 37 337 | 48 | 48072 | 317 | Martin County | 0 |
| 48 | 35576 | 439 | Tarrant County | 37 337 | 48 | 48072 | 329 | Midland County | 111 147 |
| 48 | 37000 | | Irving city | 216 290 | 48 | 48768 | | Mission city | 77 058 |
| 48 | 37000 | 113 | Dallas County | 216 290 | 48 | 48768 | 215 | Hidalgo County | 77 058 |

| State Code | Place Code | County Code | Geographic Area Name | 2010 Census Population | State Code | Place Code | County Code | Geographic Area Name | 2010 Census Population |
|---|---|---|---|---|---|---|---|---|---|
| 48 | 48804 | | Missouri City city | 67 358 | 48 | 65600 | | San Marcos city | 44 894 |
| 48 | 48804 | 157 | Fort Bend County | 61 755 | 48 | 65600 | 055 | Caldwell County | 3 |
| 48 | 48804 | 201 | Harris County | 5 603 | 48 | 65600 | 187 | Guadalupe County | 0 |
| | | | | | 48 | 65600 | 209 | Hays County | 44 891 |
| 48 | 50256 | | Nacogdoches city | 32 996 | | | | | |
| 48 | 50256 | 347 | Nacogdoches County | 32 996 | 48 | 66128 | | Schertz city | 31 465 |
| | | | | | 48 | 66128 | 029 | Bexar County | 1 157 |
| 48 | 50820 | | New Braunfels city | 57 740 | 48 | 66128 | 091 | Comal County | 845 |
| 48 | 50820 | 091 | Comal County | 47 586 | 48 | 66128 | 187 | Guadalupe County | 29 463 |
| 48 | 50820 | 187 | Guadalupe County | 10 154 | | | | | |
| | | | | | 48 | 66644 | | Seguin city | 25 175 |
| 48 | 52356 | | North Richland Hills city | 63 343 | 48 | 66644 | 187 | Guadalupe County | 25 175 |
| 48 | 52356 | 439 | Tarrant County | 63 343 | | | | | |
| | | | | | 48 | 67496 | | Sherman city | 38 521 |
| 48 | 53388 | | Odessa city | 99 940 | 48 | 67496 | 181 | Grayson County | 38 521 |
| 48 | 53388 | 135 | Ector County | 98 270 | | | | | |
| 48 | 53388 | 329 | Midland County | 1 670 | 48 | 68636 | | Socorro city | 32 013 |
| | | | | | 48 | 68636 | 141 | El Paso County | 32 013 |
| 48 | 55080 | | Paris city | 25 171 | | | | | |
| 48 | 55080 | 277 | Lamar County | 25 171 | 48 | 69032 | | Southlake city | 26 575 |
| | | | | | 48 | 69032 | 121 | Denton County | 773 |
| 48 | 56000 | | Pasadena city | 149 043 | 48 | 69032 | 439 | Tarrant County | 25 802 |
| 48 | 56000 | 201 | Harris County | 149 043 | | | | | |
| | | | | | 48 | 70808 | | Sugar Land city | 78 817 |
| 48 | 56348 | | Pearland city | 91 252 | 48 | 70808 | 157 | Fort Bend County | 78 817 |
| 48 | 56348 | 039 | Brazoria County | 86 706 | | | | | |
| 48 | 56348 | 157 | Fort Bend County | 721 | 48 | 72176 | | Temple city | 66 102 |
| 48 | 56348 | 201 | Harris County | 3 825 | 48 | 72176 | 027 | Bell County | 66 102 |
| | | | | | | | | | |
| 48 | 57176 | | Pflugerville city | 46 936 | 48 | 72368 | | Texarkana city | 36 411 |
| 48 | 57176 | 453 | Travis County | 46 636 | 48 | 72368 | 037 | Bowie County | 36 411 |
| 48 | 57176 | 491 | Williamson County | 300 | | | | | |
| | | | | | 48 | 72392 | | Texas City city | 45 099 |
| 48 | 57200 | | Pharr city | 70 400 | 48 | 72392 | 071 | Chambers County | 0 |
| 48 | 57200 | 215 | Hidalgo County | 70 400 | 48 | 72392 | 167 | Galveston County | 45 099 |
| | | | | | | | | | |
| 48 | 58016 | | Plano city | 259 841 | 48 | 72530 | | The Colony city | 36 328 |
| 48 | 58016 | 085 | Collin County | 254 525 | 48 | 72530 | 121 | Denton County | 36 328 |
| 48 | 58016 | 121 | Denton County | 5 316 | | | | | |
| | | | | | 48 | 74144 | | Tyler city | 96 900 |
| 48 | 58820 | | Port Arthur city | 53 818 | 48 | 74144 | 423 | Smith County | 96 900 |
| 48 | 58820 | 245 | Jefferson County | 53 814 | | | | | |
| 48 | 58820 | 361 | Orange County | 4 | 48 | 75428 | | Victoria city | 62 592 |
| | | | | | 48 | 75428 | 469 | Victoria County | 62 592 |
| 48 | 61796 | | Richardson city | 99 223 | | | | | |
| 48 | 61796 | 085 | Collin County | 28 569 | 48 | 76000 | | Waco city | 124 805 |
| 48 | 61796 | 113 | Dallas County | 70 654 | 48 | 76000 | 309 | McLennan County | 124 805 |
| | | | | | | | | | |
| 48 | 62828 | | Rockwall city | 37 490 | 48 | 76816 | | Waxahachie city | 29 621 |
| 48 | 62828 | 397 | Rockwall County | 37 490 | 48 | 76816 | 139 | Ellis County | 29 621 |
| | | | | | | | | | |
| 48 | 63284 | | Rosenberg city | 30 618 | 48 | 76864 | | Weatherford city | 25 250 |
| 48 | 63284 | 157 | Fort Bend County | 30 618 | 48 | 76864 | 367 | Parker County | 25 250 |
| | | | | | | | | | |
| 48 | 63500 | | Round Rock city | 99 887 | 48 | 77272 | | Weslaco city | 35 670 |
| 48 | 63500 | 453 | Travis County | 1 362 | 48 | 77272 | 215 | Hidalgo County | 35 670 |
| 48 | 63500 | 491 | Williamson County | 98 525 | | | | | |
| | | | | | 48 | 79000 | | Wichita Falls city | 104 553 |
| 48 | 63572 | | Rowlett city | 56 199 | 48 | 79000 | 485 | Wichita County | 104 553 |
| 48 | 63572 | 113 | Dallas County | 49 188 | | | | | |
| 48 | 63572 | 397 | Rockwall County | 7 011 | 48 | 80356 | | Wylie city | 41 427 |
| | | | | | 48 | 80356 | 085 | Collin County | 39 957 |
| 48 | 64472 | | San Angelo city | 93 200 | 48 | 80356 | 113 | Dallas County | 415 |
| 48 | 64472 | 451 | Tom Green County | 93 200 | 48 | 80356 | 397 | Rockwall County | 1 055 |
| | | | | | | | | | |
| 48 | 65000 | | San Antonio city | 1 327 407 | 49 | | | **UTAH** | 2 763 885 |
| 48 | 65000 | 029 | Bexar County | 1 327 381 | 49 | 01310 | | American Fork city | 26 263 |
| 48 | 65000 | 091 | Comal County | 0 | 49 | 01310 | 049 | Utah County | 26 263 |
| 48 | 65000 | 325 | Medina County | 26 | | | | | |
| | | | | | 49 | 07690 | | Bountiful city | 42 552 |
| 48 | 65516 | | San Juan city | 33 856 | 49 | 07690 | 011 | Davis County | 42 552 |
| 48 | 65516 | 215 | Hidalgo County | 33 856 | | | | | |

| State Code | Place Code | County Code | Geographic Area Name | 2010 Census Population | State Code | Place Code | County Code | Geographic Area Name | 2010 Census Population |
|---|---|---|---|---|---|---|---|---|---|
| 49 | 11320 | | Cedar City city | 28 857 | 49 | 76680 | | Tooele city | 31 605 |
| 49 | 11320 | 021 | Iron County | 28 857 | 49 | 76680 | 045 | Tooele County | 31 605 |
| | | | | | | | | | |
| 49 | 13850 | | Clearfield city | 30 112 | 49 | 82950 | | West Jordan city | 103 712 |
| 49 | 13850 | 011 | Davis County | 30 112 | 49 | 82950 | 035 | Salt Lake County | 103 712 |
| | | | | | | | | | |
| 49 | 16270 | | Cottonwood Heights city | 33 433 | 49 | 83470 | | West Valley City city | 129 480 |
| 49 | 16270 | 035 | Salt Lake County | 33 433 | 49 | 83470 | 035 | Salt Lake County | 129 480 |
| | | | | | | | | | |
| 49 | 20120 | | Draper city | 42 274 | 50 | | | **VERMONT** | 625 741 |
| 49 | 20120 | 035 | Salt Lake County | 40 532 | 50 | 10675 | | Burlington city | 42 417 |
| 49 | 20120 | 049 | Utah County | 1 742 | 50 | 10675 | 007 | Chittenden County | 42 417 |
| | | | | | | | | | |
| 49 | 36070 | | Holladay city | 26 472 | 51 | | | **VIRGINIA** | 8 001 024 |
| 49 | 36070 | 035 | Salt Lake County | 26 472 | 51 | 01000 | | Alexandria city | 139 966 |
| | | | | | 51 | 01000 | 510 | Alexandria city | 139 966 |
| 49 | 40360 | | Kaysville city | 27 300 | | | | | |
| 49 | 40360 | 011 | Davis County | 27 300 | 51 | 07784 | | Blacksburg town | 42 620 |
| | | | | | 51 | 07784 | 121 | Montgomery County | 42 620 |
| 49 | 43660 | | Layton city | 67 311 | | | | | |
| 49 | 43660 | 011 | Davis County | 67 311 | 51 | 14968 | | Charlottesville city | 43 475 |
| | | | | | 51 | 14968 | 540 | Charlottesville city | 43 475 |
| 49 | 44320 | | Lehi city | 47 407 | | | | | |
| 49 | 44320 | 049 | Utah County | 47 407 | 51 | 16000 | | Chesapeake city | 222 209 |
| | | | | | 51 | 16000 | 550 | Chesapeake city | 222 209 |
| 49 | 45860 | | Logan city | 48 174 | | | | | |
| 49 | 45860 | 005 | Cache County | 48 174 | 51 | 21344 | | Danville city | 43 055 |
| | | | | | 51 | 21344 | 590 | Danville city | 43 055 |
| 49 | 49710 | | Midvale city | 27 964 | | | | | |
| 49 | 49710 | 035 | Salt Lake County | 27 964 | 51 | 35000 | | Hampton city | 137 436 |
| | | | | | 51 | 35000 | 650 | Hampton city | 137 436 |
| 49 | 53230 | | Murray city | 46 746 | | | | | |
| 49 | 53230 | 035 | Salt Lake County | 46 746 | 51 | 35624 | | Harrisonburg city | 48 914 |
| | | | | | 51 | 35624 | 660 | Harrisonburg city | 48 914 |
| 49 | 55980 | | Ogden city | 82 825 | | | | | |
| 49 | 55980 | 057 | Weber County | 82 825 | 51 | 44984 | | Leesburg town | 42 616 |
| | | | | | 51 | 44984 | 107 | Loudoun County | 42 616 |
| 49 | 57300 | | Orem city | 88 328 | | | | | |
| 49 | 57300 | 049 | Utah County | 88 328 | 51 | 47672 | | Lynchburg city | 75 568 |
| | | | | | 51 | 47672 | 680 | Lynchburg city | 75 568 |
| 49 | 60930 | | Pleasant Grove city | 33 509 | | | | | |
| 49 | 60930 | 049 | Utah County | 33 509 | 51 | 48952 | | Manassas city | 37 821 |
| | | | | | 51 | 48952 | 683 | Manassas city | 37 821 |
| 49 | 62470 | | Provo city | 112 488 | | | | | |
| 49 | 62470 | 049 | Utah County | 112 488 | 51 | 56000 | | Newport News city | 180 719 |
| | | | | | 51 | 56000 | 700 | Newport News city | 180 719 |
| 49 | 64340 | | Riverton city | 38 753 | | | | | |
| 49 | 64340 | 035 | Salt Lake County | 38 753 | 51 | 57000 | | Norfolk city | 242 803 |
| | | | | | 51 | 57000 | 710 | Norfolk city | 242 803 |
| 49 | 65110 | | Roy city | 36 884 | | | | | |
| 49 | 65110 | 057 | Weber County | 36 884 | 51 | 61832 | | Petersburg city | 32 420 |
| | | | | | 51 | 61832 | 730 | Petersburg city | 32 420 |
| 49 | 65330 | | St. George city | 72 897 | | | | | |
| 49 | 65330 | 053 | Washington County | 72 897 | 51 | 64000 | | Portsmouth city | 95 535 |
| | | | | | 51 | 64000 | 740 | Portsmouth city | 95 535 |
| 49 | 67000 | | Salt Lake City city | 186 440 | | | | | |
| 49 | 67000 | 035 | Salt Lake County | 186 440 | 51 | 67000 | | Richmond city | 204 214 |
| | | | | | 51 | 67000 | 760 | Richmond city | 204 214 |
| 49 | 67440 | | Sandy city | 87 461 | | | | | |
| 49 | 67440 | 035 | Salt Lake County | 87 461 | 51 | 68000 | | Roanoke city | 97 032 |
| | | | | | 51 | 68000 | 770 | Roanoke city | 97 032 |
| 49 | 70850 | | South Jordan city | 50 418 | | | | | |
| 49 | 70850 | 035 | Salt Lake County | 50 418 | 51 | 76432 | | Suffolk city | 84 585 |
| | | | | | 51 | 76432 | 800 | Suffolk city | 84 585 |
| 49 | 71290 | | Spanish Fork city | 34 691 | | | | | |
| 49 | 71290 | 049 | Utah County | 34 691 | 51 | 82000 | | Virginia Beach city | 437 994 |
| | | | | | 51 | 82000 | 810 | Virginia Beach city | 437 994 |
| 49 | 72280 | | Springville city | 29 466 | | | | | |
| 49 | 72280 | 049 | Utah County | 29 466 | 51 | 86720 | | Winchester city | 26 203 |
| | | | | | 51 | 86720 | 840 | Winchester city | 26 203 |
| 49 | 75360 | | Taylorsville city | 58 652 | | | | | |
| 49 | 75360 | 035 | Salt Lake County | 58 652 | | | | | |

# Cities by County–*Continued*

| State Code | Place Code | County Code | Geographic Area Name | 2010 Census Population | State Code | Place Code | County Code | Geographic Area Name | 2010 Census Population |
|---|---|---|---|---|---|---|---|---|---|
| 53 | | | **WASHINGTON** | 6 724 540 | 53 | 56625 | | Pullman city | 29 799 |
| 53 | 03180 | | Auburn city | 70 180 | 53 | 56625 | 075 | Whitman County | 29 799 |
| 53 | 03180 | 033 | King County | 62 761 | | | | | |
| 53 | 03180 | 053 | Pierce County | 7 419 | 53 | 56695 | | Puyallup city | 37 022 |
| | | | | | 53 | 56695 | 053 | Pierce County | 37 022 |
| 53 | 05210 | | Bellevue city | 122 363 | | | | | |
| 53 | 05210 | 033 | King County | 122 363 | 53 | 57535 | | Redmond city | 54 144 |
| | | | | | 53 | 57535 | 033 | King County | 54 144 |
| 53 | 05280 | | Bellingham city | 80 885 | | | | | |
| 53 | 05280 | 073 | Whatcom County | 80 885 | 53 | 57745 | | Renton city | 90 927 |
| | | | | | 53 | 57745 | 033 | King County | 90 927 |
| 53 | 07380 | | Bothell city | 33 505 | | | | | |
| 53 | 07380 | 033 | King County | 17 090 | 53 | 58235 | | Richland city | 48 058 |
| 53 | 07380 | 061 | Snohomish County | 16 415 | 53 | 58235 | 005 | Benton County | 48 058 |
| | | | | | | | | | |
| 53 | 07695 | | Bremerton city | 37 729 | 53 | 61115 | | Sammamish city | 45 780 |
| 53 | 07695 | 035 | Kitsap County | 37 729 | 53 | 61115 | 033 | King County | 45 780 |
| | | | | | | | | | |
| 53 | 08850 | | Burien city | 33 313 | 53 | 62288 | | SeaTac city | 26 909 |
| 53 | 08850 | 033 | King County | 33 313 | 53 | 62288 | 033 | King County | 26 909 |
| | | | | | | | | | |
| 53 | 17635 | | Des Moines city | 29 673 | 53 | 63000 | | Seattle city | 608 660 |
| 53 | 17635 | 033 | King County | 29 673 | 53 | 63000 | 033 | King County | 608 660 |
| | | | | | | | | | |
| 53 | 20750 | | Edmonds city | 39 709 | 53 | 63960 | | Shoreline city | 53 007 |
| 53 | 20750 | 061 | Snohomish County | 39 709 | 53 | 63960 | 033 | King County | 53 007 |
| | | | | | | | | | |
| 53 | 22640 | | Everett city | 103 019 | 53 | 67000 | | Spokane city | 208 916 |
| 53 | 22640 | 061 | Snohomish County | 103 019 | 53 | 67000 | 063 | Spokane County | 208 916 |
| | | | | | | | | | |
| 53 | 23515 | | Federal Way city | 89 306 | 53 | 67167 | | Spokane Valley city | 89 755 |
| 53 | 23515 | 033 | King County | 89 306 | 53 | 67167 | 063 | Spokane County | 89 755 |
| | | | | | | | | | |
| 53 | 33805 | | Issaquah city | 30 434 | 53 | 70000 | | Tacoma city | 198 397 |
| 53 | 33805 | 033 | King County | 30 434 | 53 | 70000 | 053 | Pierce County | 198 397 |
| | | | | | | | | | |
| 53 | 35275 | | Kennewick city | 73 917 | 53 | 73465 | | University Place city | 31 144 |
| 53 | 35275 | 005 | Benton County | 73 917 | 53 | 73465 | 053 | Pierce County | 31 144 |
| | | | | | | | | | |
| 53 | 35415 | | Kent city | 92 411 | 53 | 74060 | | Vancouver city | 161 791 |
| 53 | 35415 | 033 | King County | 92 411 | 53 | 74060 | 011 | Clark County | 161 791 |
| | | | | | | | | | |
| 53 | 35940 | | Kirkland city | 48 787 | 53 | 75775 | | Walla Walla city | 31 731 |
| 53 | 35940 | 033 | King County | 48 787 | 53 | 75775 | 071 | Walla Walla County | 31 731 |
| | | | | | | | | | |
| 53 | 36745 | | Lacey city | 42 393 | 53 | 77105 | | Wenatchee city | 31 925 |
| 53 | 36745 | 067 | Thurston County | 42 393 | 53 | 77105 | 007 | Chelan County | 31 925 |
| | | | | | | | | | |
| 53 | 37900 | | Lake Stevens city | 28 069 | 53 | 80010 | | Yakima city | 91 067 |
| 53 | 37900 | 061 | Snohomish County | 28 069 | 53 | 80010 | 077 | Yakima County | 91 067 |
| | | | | | | | | | |
| 53 | 38038 | | Lakewood city | 58 163 | 54 | | | **WEST VIRGINIA** | 1 852 994 |
| 53 | 38038 | 053 | Pierce County | 58 163 | 54 | 14600 | | Charleston city | 51 400 |
| | | | | | 54 | 14600 | 039 | Kanawha County | 51 400 |
| 53 | 40245 | | Longview city | 36 648 | | | | | |
| 53 | 40245 | 015 | Cowlitz County | 36 648 | 54 | 39460 | | Huntington city | 49 138 |
| | | | | | 54 | 39460 | 011 | Cabell County | 45 214 |
| 53 | 40840 | | Lynnwood city | 35 836 | 54 | 39460 | 099 | Wayne County | 3 924 |
| 53 | 40840 | 061 | Snohomish County | 35 836 | | | | | |
| | | | | | 54 | 55756 | | Morgantown city | 29 660 |
| 53 | 43955 | | Marysville city | 60 020 | 54 | 55756 | 061 | Monongalia County | 29 660 |
| 53 | 43955 | 061 | Snohomish County | 60 020 | | | | | |
| | | | | | 54 | 62140 | | Parkersburg city | 31 492 |
| 53 | 47560 | | Mount Vernon city | 31 743 | 54 | 62140 | 107 | Wood County | 31 492 |
| 53 | 47560 | 057 | Skagit County | 31 743 | | | | | |
| | | | | | 54 | 86452 | | Wheeling city | 28 486 |
| 53 | 51300 | | Olympia city | 46 478 | 54 | 86452 | 051 | Marshall County | 276 |
| 53 | 51300 | 067 | Thurston County | 46 478 | 54 | 86452 | 069 | Ohio County | 28 210 |
| | | | | | | | | | |
| 53 | 53545 | | Pasco city | 59 781 | | | | | |
| 53 | 53545 | 021 | Franklin County | 59 781 | | | | | |

# Cities by County–*Continued*

| State Code | Place Code | County Code | Geographic Area Name | 2010 Census Population | State Code | Place Code | County Code | Geographic Area Name | 2010 Census Population |
|---|---|---|---|---|---|---|---|---|---|
| 55 | | | **WISCONSIN** | 5 686 986 | 55 | 72975 | | Sheboygan city | 49 288 |
| 55 | 02375 | | Appleton city | 72 623 | 55 | 72975 | 117 | Sheboygan County | 49 288 |
| 55 | 02375 | 015 | Calumet County | 11 088 | | | | | |
| 55 | 02375 | 087 | Outagamie County | 60 045 | 55 | 77200 | | Stevens Point city | 26 717 |
| 55 | 02375 | 139 | Winnebago County | 1 490 | 55 | 77200 | 097 | Portage County | 26 717 |
| 55 | 06500 | | Beloit city | 36 966 | 55 | 78600 | | Sun Prairie city | 29 364 |
| 55 | 06500 | 105 | Rock County | 36 966 | 55 | 78600 | 025 | Dane County | 29 364 |
| 55 | 10025 | | Brookfield city | 37 920 | 55 | 78650 | | Superior city | 27 244 |
| 55 | 10025 | 133 | Waukesha County | 37 920 | 55 | 78650 | 031 | Douglas County | 27 244 |
| 55 | 22300 | | Eau Claire city | 65 883 | 55 | 84250 | | Waukesha city | 70 718 |
| 55 | 22300 | 017 | Chippewa County | 1 981 | 55 | 84250 | 133 | Waukesha County | 70 718 |
| 55 | 22300 | 035 | Eau Claire County | 63 902 | 55 | 84475 | | Wausau city | 39 106 |
| 55 | 25950 | | Fitchburg city | 25 260 | 55 | 84475 | 073 | Marathon County | 39 106 |
| 55 | 25950 | 025 | Dane County | 25 260 | 55 | 84675 | | Wauwatosa city | 46 396 |
| 55 | 26275 | | Fond du Lac city | 43 021 | 55 | 84675 | 079 | Milwaukee County | 46 396 |
| 55 | 26275 | 039 | Fond du Lac County | 43 021 | 55 | 85300 | | West Allis city | 60 411 |
| 55 | 27300 | | Franklin city | 35 451 | 55 | 85300 | 079 | Milwaukee County | 60 411 |
| 55 | 27300 | 079 | Milwaukee County | 35 451 | 55 | 85350 | | West Bend city | 31 078 |
| 55 | 31000 | | Green Bay city | 104 057 | 55 | 85350 | 131 | Washington County | 31 078 |
| 55 | 31000 | 009 | Brown County | 104 057 | 56 | | | **WYOMING** | 563 626 |
| 55 | 31175 | | Greenfield city | 36 720 | 56 | 13150 | | Casper city | 55 316 |
| 55 | 31175 | 079 | Milwaukee County | 36 720 | 56 | 13150 | 025 | Natrona County | 55 316 |
| 55 | 37825 | | Janesville city | 63 575 | 56 | 13900 | | Cheyenne city | 59 466 |
| 55 | 37825 | 105 | Rock County | 63 575 | 56 | 13900 | 021 | Laramie County | 59 466 |
| 55 | 39225 | | Kenosha city | 99 218 | 56 | 31855 | | Gillette city | 29 087 |
| 55 | 39225 | 059 | Kenosha County | 99 218 | 56 | 31855 | 005 | Campbell County | 29 087 |
| 55 | 40775 | | La Crosse city | 51 320 | 56 | 45050 | | Laramie city | 30 816 |
| 55 | 40775 | 063 | La Crosse County | 51 320 | 56 | 45050 | 001 | Albany County | 30 816 |
| 55 | 48000 | | Madison city | 233 209 | | | | | |
| 55 | 48000 | 025 | Dane County | 233 209 | | | | | |
| 55 | 48500 | | Manitowoc city | 33 736 | | | | | |
| 55 | 48500 | 071 | Manitowoc County | 33 736 | | | | | |
| 55 | 51000 | | Menomonee Falls village | 35 626 | | | | | |
| 55 | 51000 | 133 | Waukesha County | 35 626 | | | | | |
| 55 | 53000 | | Milwaukee city | 594 833 | | | | | |
| 55 | 53000 | 079 | Milwaukee County | 594 833 | | | | | |
| 55 | 53000 | 131 | Washington County | 0 | | | | | |
| 55 | 53000 | 133 | Waukesha County | 0 | | | | | |
| 55 | 54875 | | Mount Pleasant village | 26 197 | | | | | |
| 55 | 54875 | 101 | Racine County | 26 197 | | | | | |
| 55 | 55750 | | Neenah city | 25 501 | | | | | |
| 55 | 55750 | 139 | Winnebago County | 25 501 | | | | | |
| 55 | 56375 | | New Berlin city | 39 584 | | | | | |
| 55 | 56375 | 133 | Waukesha County | 39 584 | | | | | |
| 55 | 58800 | | Oak Creek city | 34 451 | | | | | |
| 55 | 58800 | 079 | Milwaukee County | 34 451 | | | | | |
| 55 | 60500 | | Oshkosh city | 66 083 | | | | | |
| 55 | 60500 | 139 | Winnebago County | 66 083 | | | | | |
| 55 | 66000 | | Racine city | 78 860 | | | | | |
| 55 | 66000 | 101 | Racine County | 78 860 | | | | | |

# Cities by County–*Continued*

The following consolidated cities are included in Table D. They are listed here with their 2010 census populations followed by the separate entities that make up the consolidated city. Data from the American Community Survey include only the "balance," the major city of each consolidated city.

| State Code | Place Code | County Code | Geographic Area Name | 2010 Census Population | State Code | Place Code | County Code | Geographic Area Name | 2010 Census Population |
|---|---|---|---|---|---|---|---|---|---|
| 09 | | | **CONNECTICUT** | 3 574 097 | 21 | 38818 | | Hurstbourne Acres city | 1 811 |
| 09 | 47500 | | Milford city | 52 759 | 21 | 39304 | | Indian Hills city | 2 868 |
| | | | Milford city (balance) | 51 271 | 21 | 40222 | | Jeffersontown city | 26 595 |
| | 88050 | | Woodmont borough | 1 488 | 21 | 42598 | | Kingsley city | 381 |
| | | | | | 21 | 43900 | | Langdon Place city | 936 |
| 13 | | | **GEORGIA** | 9 687 653 | 21 | 46540 | | Lincolnshire city | 148 |
| 13 | 03436 | | Athens-Clark county | 116 714 | 21 | 48006 | | Louisville/Jefferson County (balance) | 597 337 |
| 13 | 03440 | | Athens-Clark county (balance) | 115 452 | | | | | |
| 13 | 09068 | | Bogart town | 140 | 21 | 48558 | | Lyndon city | 11 002 |
| 13 | 83728 | | Winterville city | 1 122 | 21 | 48648 | | Lynnview city | 914 |
| | | | | | 21 | 49800 | | Manor Creek city | 140 |
| 13 | 04200 | | Augusta-Richmond county | 200 549 | 21 | 50412 | | Maryhill Estates city | 179 |
| 13 | 04204 | | Augusta-Richmond county (balance) | 195 844 | 21 | 51193 | | Meadowbrook Farm city | 136 |
| 13 | 09040 | | Blythe city | 694 | 21 | 51258 | | Meadow Vale city | 736 |
| 13 | 38040 | | Hephzibah city | 4 011 | 21 | 51294 | | Meadowview Estates city | 363 |
| | | | | | 21 | 51978 | | Middletown city | 7 218 |
| 18 | | | **INDIANA** | 6 483 802 | 21 | 52842 | | Mockingbird Valley city | 167 |
| 18 | 36000 | | Indianapolis city | 829 718 | 21 | 53328 | | Moorland city | 431 |
| 18 | 04204 | | Beech Grove city | 0 | 21 | 54660 | | Murray Hill city | 582 |
| 18 | 13492 | | Clermont town | 1 356 | 21 | 56550 | | Norbourne Estates city | 441 |
| 18 | 16156 | | Crows Nest town | 73 | 21 | 56730 | | Northfield city | 1 020 |
| 18 | 16336 | | Cumberland town | 2 597 | 21 | 56928 | | Norwood city | 370 |
| 18 | 34420 | | Homecroft town | 722 | 21 | 57658 | | Old Brownsboro Place city | 353 |
| 18 | 36003 | | Indianapolis city (balance) | 820 445 | 21 | 59322 | | Parkway Village city | 650 |
| 18 | 42426 | | Lawrence city | 42 | 21 | 61554 | | Plantation city | 832 |
| 18 | 48456 | | Meridian Hills town | 1 616 | 21 | 62370 | | Poplar Hills city | 362 |
| 18 | 54612 | | North Crows Nest town | 45 | 21 | 63264 | | Prospect city | 4 636 |
| 18 | 65556 | | Rocky Ripple town | 606 | 21 | 65208 | | Richlawn city | 405 |
| 18 | 72232 | | Spring Hill town | 98 | 21 | 65766 | | Riverwood city | 446 |
| 18 | 80234 | | Warren Park town | 1 480 | 21 | 66486 | | Rolling Fields city | 646 |
| 18 | 84374 | | Williams Creek town | 407 | 21 | 66504 | | Rolling Hills city | 959 |
| 18 | 85742 | | Wynnedale town | 231 | 21 | 67944 | | St. Matthews city | 17 472 |
| | | | | | 21 | 67998 | | St. Regis Park city | 1 454 |
| 21 | | | **KENTUCKY** | 4 339 367 | 21 | 69384 | | Seneca Gardens city | 696 |
| 21 | 46003 | | Louisville/Jefferson County | 741 096 | 21 | 70284 | | Shively city | 15 264 |
| 21 | 01504 | | Anchorage city | 2 348 | 21 | 72138 | | South Park View city | 7 |
| 21 | 02656 | | Audubon Park city | 1 473 | 21 | 72770 | | Spring Mill city | 287 |
| 21 | 03376 | | Bancroft city | 494 | 21 | 72790 | | Spring Valley city | 654 |
| 21 | 03556 | | Barbourmeade city | 1 218 | 21 | 74064 | | Strathmoor Manor city | 337 |
| 21 | 05068 | | Beechwood Village city | 1 324 | 21 | 74082 | | Strathmoor Village city | 648 |
| 21 | 05392 | | Bellemeade city | 865 | 21 | 75190 | | Sycamore city | 160 |
| 21 | 05464 | | Bellewood city | 321 | 21 | 75963 | | Ten Broeck city | 103 |
| 21 | 07858 | | Blue Ridge Manor city | 767 | 21 | 76380 | | Thornhill city | 178 |
| 21 | 09532 | | Briarwood city | 435 | 21 | 80913 | | Watterson Park city | 976 |
| 21 | 09847 | | Broeck Pointe city | 272 | 21 | 81372 | | Wellington city | 565 |
| 21 | 10162 | | Brownsboro Farm city | 648 | 21 | 81624 | | West Buechel city | 1 230 |
| 21 | 10198 | | Brownsboro Village city | 319 | 21 | 82164 | | Westwood city | 634 |
| 21 | 12066 | | Cambridge city | 175 | 21 | 83208 | | Wildwood city | 261 |
| 21 | 16395 | | Coldstream city | 1 100 | 21 | 83784 | | Windy Hills city | 2 385 |
| 21 | 18270 | | Creekside city | 305 | 21 | 84486 | | Woodland Hills city | 696 |
| 21 | 18766 | | Crossgate city | 225 | 21 | 84576 | | Woodlawn Park city | 942 |
| 21 | 22204 | | Douglass Hills city | 5 484 | 21 | 84891 | | Worthington Hills city | 1 446 |
| 21 | 22474 | | Druid Hills city | 308 | | | | | |
| 21 | 27262 | | Fincastle city | 817 | 30 | | | **MONTANA** | 989 415 |
| 21 | 28342 | | Forest Hills city | 444 | 30 | 11390 | | Butte-Silver Bow | 34 200 |
| 21 | 31348 | | Glenview city | 531 | 30 | 11397 | | Butte-Silver Bow (balance) | 33 525 |
| 21 | 31402 | | Glenview Hills city | 319 | 30 | 77650 | | Walkerville town | 675 |
| 21 | 31420 | | Glenview Manor city | 191 | | | | | |
| 21 | 31870 | | Goose Creek city | 294 | 47 | | | **TENNESSEE** | 6 346 105 |
| 21 | 32523 | | Graymoor-Devondale city | 2 870 | 47 | 52004 | | Nashville-Davidson | 626 681 |
| 21 | 32986 | | Green Spring city | 715 | 47 | 04620 | | Belle Meade city | 2 912 |
| 21 | 36102 | | Heritage Creek city | 1 076 | 47 | 05140 | | Berry Hill city | 537 |
| 21 | 36374 | | Hickory Hill city | 114 | 47 | 27020 | | Forest Hills city | 4 812 |
| 21 | 36865 | | Hills and Dales city | 142 | 47 | 29920 | | Goodlettsville city | 10 319 |
| 21 | 37576 | | Hollow Creek city | 783 | 47 | 40720 | | Lakewood city | 2 302 |
| 21 | 37630 | | Hollyvilla city | 537 | 47 | 52006 | | Nashville-Davidson (balance) | 601 222 |
| 21 | 38170 | | Houston Acres city | 507 | 47 | 54780 | | Oak Hill city | 4 529 |
| 21 | 38814 | | Hurstbourne city | 4 216 | 47 | 63140 | | Ridgetop city | 48 |

# APPENDIX F
# SOURCE NOTES AND EXPLANATIONS

The following documentation is provided in the order in which items appear in the tables. Internet addresses are provided for the sources of the data. Some of the links refer to the specific data tables. Others provide information about the general data source.

## TABLE A—STATES

Table A presents 355 items for the United States as a whole, for each individual state, and for the District of Columbia. The states are presented in alphabetical order.

## LAND AREA, Items 1 and 4
**Source: U.S. Census Bureau—Decennial Censuses and Population Estimates**
**http://www.census.gov/geo/www/2010census/statearea_intpt.html**

Land area measurements are shown to the nearest square kilometer. Land area includes dry land and land temporarily or partially covered by water, such as marshlands, swamps, and river floodplains.

## POPULATION AND COMPONENTS OF CHANGE, Items 2–4, 31–41
**Source: U.S. Census Bureau—Decennial Censuses and Population Estimates**
**http://www.census.gov/popest/estimates.html**
**http://2010.census.gov/2010census/data/**

The population data for 2012 are Census Bureau estimates of the resident population as of July 1, 2012.

The population data for 1990, 2000, and 2010 are from the decennial censuses and represent the resident population as of April 1 of those years.

The change in population between 2010 and 2012 is made up of (a) natural increase—births minus deaths, and (b) net migration—the difference between the number of persons moving into a particular state and the number of persons moving out of the state. Net migration is composed of internal and international migration.

## POPULATION PROJECTIONS, Items 42–44
**Source: U.S. Census Bureau—Population Projections Branch**
**http://www.census.gov/population/www/projections/index.html**

Projections are estimates of the population for future dates. They illustrate plausible courses of future population change based on assumptions about future births, deaths, international migration, and domestic migration. Projected numbers are based on an estimated population consistent with the most recent decennial census as enumerated. The Census Bureau does not have a current set of state population projections and currently has no plans to produce them. This volume includes projections released in 2005, based on the 2000 census. The Census Bureau notes that these projections should be used with caution because population trends may have changed substantially since their release.

## POPULATION AND POPULATION CHARACTERISTICS, Items 5–23 and 45–63
**Source: U.S. Census Bureau—Decennial Censuses and Population Estimates**
**http://www.census.gov/popest/estimates.html**
**http://2010.census.gov/2010census/data/**
**2011 American Community Survey**
**http://www.census.gov/acs/www/**

Data on age, sex, race, and Hispanic origin are from the 2011 estimates of the residential population as of July 1 and from the 2010 Census. Data on place of birth are from the 2011 American Community Survey, a nationwide continuous survey designed to replace the long form questionnaire used in previous censuses.

Data on race were derived from answers to the question on race that was asked of all persons. The concept of race, as used by the Census Bureau, reflects self-identification by respondents according to the race or races with which they most closely identify. These categories are sociopolitical constructs and should not be interpreted as being scientific or anthropological in nature. Furthermore, the race categories include both racial and national origin groups.

The **White** population is defined as persons who indicated their race as White, as well as persons who did not classify themselves in one of the specific race categories listed on the questionnaire but entered a nationality such as Irish, German, Italian, Lebanese, Near Easterner, Arab, or Polish.

The **Black** population includes persons who indicated their race as ''Black, African Am., or Negro,'' as well as persons who did not classify themselves in one of the specific race categories but reported entries such as African American, Afro American, Kenyan, Nigerian, or Haitian.

The **American Indian or Alaska Native** population includes persons who indicated their race as American Indian or Alaska Native, as well as persons who did not classify themselves in one of the specific race categories but reported entries such as Canadian Indian, French-American Indian, Spanish-American Indian, Eskimo, Aleut, Alaska Indian, or any of the American Indian or Alaska Native tribes.

The **Asian and Pacific Islander** population combines two census groupings: **Asian** and **Native Hawaiian or Other Pacific Islander**. The **Asian** population includes persons who indicated their race as Asian Indian, Chinese, Filipino, Japanese, Korean, Vietnamese, or ''Other Asian,'' as well as persons who provided write-in entries of such groups as Cambodian, Laotian, Hmong, Pakistani, or Taiwanese. The **Native Hawaiian or Other Pacific Islander** population includes persons who indicated their race as

"Native Hawaiian," "Guamanian or Chamorro," "Samoan," or "Other Pacific Islander," as well as persons who reported entries such as Part Hawaiian, American Samoan, Fijian, Melanesian, or Tahitian.

The Hispanic population is based on a question that asked respondents "Is this person Spanish/Hispanic/Latino?" Persons marking any one of the four Hispanic categories (i.e., Mexican, Puerto Rican, Cuban, or other Spanish) are collectively referred to as Hispanic.

Age is defined as age at last birthday (number of completed years since birth), as of April 1 of the census year.

The median age is the age that divides the population into two equal-size groups. Half of the population is older than the median age and half is younger. Median age is based on a standard distribution of the population by single years of age and is shown to the nearest tenth of a year.

The female population is shown as a percentage of total population.

The foreign-born population includes all persons who were not U.S. citizens at birth. Foreign-born persons are those who indicated they were either a U.S. citizen by naturalization or were not a citizen of the United States. Neither the census nor the American Community Survey asked about immigration status. The population surveyed included all persons who indicated that the United States was their usual place of residence. The foreign-born population consists of immigrants (legal permanent residents), temporary migrants (students), humanitarian migrants (refugees), and unauthorized migrants (persons illegally residing in the United States).

Percent born in state of residence is shown as a percentage of total population.

## IMMIGRANTS, Item 24
### Source: Department of Homeland Security, U.S. Citizenship and Immigration Services
http://www.dhs.gov/yearbook-immigration-statistics-2011–1

The number of immigrants by state of intended residence is summarized from the administrative records of the Citizenship and Immigration Services. This information is compiled from immigrant visas and forms granting legal permanent resident status.

An immigrant is an alien admitted to the United States as a lawful permanent resident. Immigrants are those persons lawfully accorded the privilege of residing permanently in the United States. They may be newly arrived individuals who were issued immigrant visas by the Department of State overseas, or they may be U.S. residents who were admitted to permanent resident status in 2011 by the U.S. Citizenship and Immigration Services.

## HOUSEHOLDS, Items 25–30 and 64–68
### Source: U.S. Census Bureau—2011 American Community Survey and 2010 Census
http://www.census.gov/acs/www/
http://2010.census.gov/2010census/data/

A household includes all of the persons who occupy a housing unit. Persons not living in households are classified as living in group quarters. A housing unit is a house, an apartment, a mobile home, a group of rooms, or a single room occupied (or, if vacant, intended for occupancy) as separate living quarters. Separate living quarters are those in which the occupants live separately from any other persons in the building and have direct access from the outside of the building or through a common hall. The occupants may be a single family, one person living alone, two or more families living together, or any other group of related or unrelated persons who share living quarters. The number of households is the same as the number of year-round occupied housing units.

The measure of persons per household is obtained by dividing the number of persons in households by the number of households or householders. One person in each household is designated as the householder. In most cases, this is the person, (or one of the persons) in whose name the house is owned, being bought, or rented. If there is no such person in the household, any adult household member 15 years old and over can be designated as the householder.

A family includes a householder and one or more other persons living in the same household who are related to the householder by birth, marriage, or adoption. All persons in a household who are related to the householder are regarded as members of his or her family. A family household may contain persons not related to the householder; thus, family households may include more members than families do. A household can contain only one family for the purposes of census tabulations. Not all households contain families, as a household may comprise a group of unrelated persons or one person living alone. Families are classified by type as either a "husband-wife family" or "other family" according to the presence of a spouse.

The category female family householder includes only female-headed family households with no spouse present.

## HOUSING, Items 69–92
### Source: U.S. Census Bureau—2010 and 2011 American Community Survey
http://www.census.gov/acs/www/

Housing data for 2010 and 2011 are from the American Community Survey, a nationwide continuous survey designed to replace the long form questionnaire used in previous censuses. A sample of households is surveyed to provide estimates.

A housing unit is a house, apartment, mobile home or trailer, group of rooms, or single room occupied or, if vacant, intended for occupancy as separate living quarters. Separate living quarters are those in which the occupants do not live and eat with any other person in the structure and which have direct access from the outside of the building or through a common hall. For vacant units, the criteria of separateness and direct access are applied to the intended occupants whenever possible. If that information cannot be obtained, the criteria are applied to the previous occupants.

The occupants of a housing unit may be a single family, one person living alone, two or more families living together, or any other group of related or unrelated persons who share living arrangements. Both occupied and vacant housing units are included in the housing inventory, although recreational vehicles, tents, caves, boats, railroad cars, and the like are included only if they are occupied as a person's usual place of residence.

A housing unit is classified as **occupied** if it is the usual place of residence of the person or group of persons living in it at the time of enumeration, or if the occupants are only temporarily absent (away on vacation). A household consists of all persons who occupy a housing unit as their usual place of residence.

**Housing cost**, as a percentage of income, is shown separately for owners with mortgages, owners without mortgages, and renters. Also shown is the percentage of mortgaged owners and renters who pay 30 percent or more of household income on selected monthly costs. Rent as a percent of income is a computed ratio of gross rent and monthly household income (total household income divided by 12). Selected owner costs include utilities and fuels, mortgage payments, insurance, taxes, etc. In each case, the ratio of housing cost to income is computed separately for each housing unit. The housing cost ratios for half of all units are above the median shown in this book, and half are below the median. Median monthly housing costs divides the monthly housing costs distribution into two equal parts, one-half of the cases falling below the median monthly housing costs and one-half above the median.

**Median value** is the dollar amount that divides the distribution of specified owner-occupied housing units into two equal parts, with half of all units below the median value and half above the median value. Value is defined as the respondent's estimate of what the house would sell for if it were for sale. Data are presented for single-family units on fewer than 10 acres of land that have no business or medical office on the property.

**Median rent** divides the distribution of renter-occupied housing units into two equal parts. The rent concept used in this volume is gross rent, which includes the amount of cash rent a renter pays (contract rent) plus the estimated average cost of utilities and fuels, if these are paid by the renter. The rent is the amount of rent only for living quarters and excludes any business or other space occupied. Single-family houses on lots of 10 or more acres of land are excluded.

**Substandard units** are occupied units that are overcrowded or lack complete plumbing facilities. For the purposes of this item, "overcrowded" is defined as having 1.01 persons or more per room. Complete plumbing facilities include hot and cold piped water, a flush toilet, and a bathtub or shower. These facilities must be located inside the housing unit, but do not have to be in the same room.

**Different house** includes all people 1 year old and over who, a year earlier, lived in a different house or apartment from the one they occupied at the time of interview.

## BUILDING PERMITS, Items 93–95
### Source: U.S. Census Bureau—Building Permits Survey
http://www.census.gov/construction/bps/

These figures represent private residential construction authorized by building permits in approximately 20,000 places in the United States. Valuation represents the expected cost of construction as recorded on the building permit. This figure usually excludes the cost of on-site and off-site development and improvements, as well as the cost of heating, plumbing, electrical, and elevator installations.

National, state, and county totals were obtained by adding the data for permit-issuing places within each jurisdiction. These totals thus are limited to permits issued in the 20,000 place universe covered by the Census Bureau and may not include all permits issued within a state. Current surveys indicate that construction is undertaken for all but a very small percentage of housing units authorized by building permits.

Residential building permits include buildings with any number of housing units. Housing units exclude group quarters (such as dormitories and rooming houses), transient accommodations (such as transient hotels, motels, and tourist courts), "HUD-code" manufactured (mobile) homes, moved or relocated units, and housing units created in an existing residential or nonresidential structure.

## MANUFACTURED HOUSING UNITS, Item 96
### Source: U.S. Census Bureau—Manufactured Housing Survey
http://www.census.gov/construction/mhs/placbystate.html

The Manufactured Housing Survey involves a monthly sample of new mobile homes shipped by manufacturers. The dealer to whom the sampled unit was shipped is contacted by telephone and asked about the status of the unit. This is done each month until that unit is reported as placed.

A mobile home, often referred to as a manufactured housing unit, is defined as a movable dwelling, 8 feet or more wide and 40 feet or more long, that is designed to be towed on its own chassis (with transportation gear integral to the unit when it leaves the factory) and without need of a permanent foundation. These mobile homes include multiwides, which are counted as single units, and expandable mobile homes. Excluded are travel trailers, motor homes, and modular housing.

There was not an increase in placements due to Hurricane Katrina, as federally owned FEMA units are not included in the private placement data collected by the Manufactured Housing Survey.

## BIRTHS AND DEATHS, Items 97–103
### Source: U.S. Centers for Disease Control and Prevention, National Center for Health Statistics
http://www.cdc.gov/nchs/data/nvsr/nvsr60/nvsr6001.pdf
http://www.cdc.gov/nchs/data/nvsr/nvsr59/nvsr5910.pdf

The registration of births, deaths, and other vital events in the United States is primarily a state and local function. The civil laws of every state provide for continuous and permanent birth and death registration systems. Through the National Vital Statistics System, the National Center for Health Statistics (NCHS) obtains data on births and deaths from the registration offices of each state, New York City, and the District of Columbia.

Birth and death statistics are limited to events occurring during the year. The data are by place of residence and exclude events for nonresidents of the United States. Births or deaths occurring outside the United States are excluded.

Birth and death rates represent the number of births and deaths per 1,000 resident population enumerated as of April 1 for decennial census years and estimated as of July 1 for other years.

Figures for infant deaths include deaths of children under 1 year of age but exclude fetal deaths. The infant death rate is per 1,000 live births.

The rates of almost all causes of disease, injury, and death vary by age. Age adjustment is a technique for "removing" the effects of age from crude rates, in order to allow meaningful comparisons across populations with different underlying age structures. For example, comparing the crude death rate in Florida to that of California is misleading, since the relatively older population in Florida will lead to a higher crude death rate. For such a comparison, age-adjusted death rates are preferable.

The population estimates were developed by the Census Bureau's Population Division using a traditional cohort component method. Starting with a basic population from the 2000 census, each component of population change—births, deaths, domestic migration, and international migration—is estimated separately for each birth cohort by sex, race, and Hispanic or Latino origin.

Age-adjusted rates are calculated by applying the age-specific rates of various populations to a single standard population. In this volume, the standard population is 2000. The Centers for Disease Control and Prevention recently switched to the year 2000, after many years of using the year 1940 as the standard population for age-adjusted death rates. For this reason, the 2009 age-adjusted rates are close to the actual death rates.

## PERSONS LACKING HEALTH INSURANCE, Items 104–105
**Source: U.S. Census Bureau—Current Population Survey**
http://www.census.gov/hhes/www/cpstables/032011/health/toc.htm

The data on which these estimates are based were gathered in March 2011 from a national sample of about 60,000 households Data are available for states but not for counties or cities.

Those lacking coverage are the percentage of the population of each state who were not covered by private health plans purchased directly or provided by an employer, Medicaid, Medicare, or military health care.

## MEDICARE ENROLLEES, Item 106
**Source: U.S. Department of Health and Human Services, Centers for Medicare and Medicaid Services**
http://www.cms.hhs.gov/DataCompendium/

The Centers for Medicare and Medicaid Services (CMS) administers Medicare, which provides health insurance to persons 65 years old and over, persons with permanent kidney failure, and certain persons with disabilities. Medicare has two parts: Hospital Insurance and Supplemental Medical Insurance. The numbers in this volume include persons enrolled in either or both parts of the program as of July 1 of the year shown, by their state of residence.

## CRIME, Items 107–110
**Source: U.S. Federal Bureau of Investigation—Uniform Crime Reports**
http://www.fbi.gov/ucr/ucr.htm

Crime data are as reported to the Federal Bureau of Investigation (FBI) by law enforcement agencies and have not been adjusted for underreporting. This may affect comparability between geographic areas or over time.

Through the voluntary contribution of crime statistics by law enforcement agencies across the United States, the Uniform Crime Reporting (UCR) Program provides periodic assessments of crime in the nation as measured by offenses that have come to the attention of the law enforcement community. The Committee on Uniform Crime Records of the International Association of Chiefs of Police initiated this voluntary national data-collection effort in 1930. The UCR Program contributors compile and submit their crime data either directly to the FBI or through state-level UCR Programs.

Seven offenses, because of their severity, frequency of occurrence, and likelihood of being reported to police, were initially selected to serve as an index for evaluating fluctuations in the volume of crime. These serious crimes were murder and nonnegligent manslaughter, forcible rape, robbery, aggravated assault, burglary, larceny-theft, and motor vehicle theft. By congressional mandate, arson was added as the eighth index offense in 1979. The totals shown in this volume do not include arson.

In 2004, the FBI discontinued the use of the Crime Index in the UCR Program and its publications, stating that the Crime Index was driven upward by the offense with the highest number of cases (in this case, larceny-theft) creating a bias against jurisdictions with a high number of larceny-thefts but a low number of other serious crimes, such as murder and forcible rape. The FBI is currently publishing a violent crime total and a property crime total until a more viable index is developed.

**Violent crimes** include four categories of offenses: (1) Murder and nonnegligent manslaughter, as defined in the UCR Program, is the willful (nonnegligent) killing of one human being by another. This offense excludes deaths caused by negligence, suicide, or accident; justifiable homicides; and attempts to murder or assaults to murder. (2) Forcible rape is the carnal knowledge of a female forcibly and against her will. Assaults or attempts to commit rape by force or threat of force are also included; however, statutory rape (without force) and other sex offenses are excluded. (3) Robbery is the taking or attempting to take anything of value from the care, custody, or control of a person or persons by force or threat of force or violence and/or by putting the victim in fear. (4) Aggravated assault is an unlawful attack by one person upon another for the purpose of inflicting severe or aggravated bodily injury. This type of assault is usually accompanied by the use of a weapon or by other means likely to produce death or great bodily harm. Attempts are included, since injury does not necessarily have to result when a gun, knife, or other weapon is used, as these incidents could and probably would result in a serious personal injury if the crime were successfully completed.

**Property crimes** include three categories: (1) Burglary, or breaking and entering, is the unlawful entry of a structure to commit a felony or theft, even though no force was used to gain entrance. (2) Larceny-theft is the unauthorized taking of the personal property of another, without the use of force. (3) Motor vehicle theft is the unauthorized taking of any motor vehicle.

Rates are based on population estimates provided by the FBI. For some states, reporting is not sufficiently complete to be representative of the state as a whole. The FBI has estimated state totals for those states.

## ELEMENTARY AND SECONDARY SCHOOL ENROLLMENT, Items 111 and 112
**Source: U.S. Department of Education, National Center for Education Statistics—Common Core of Data**
http://www.nces.ed.gov/ccd/

Data on public school enrollment is from the Common Core of Data 2010–2011 survey. Public school enrollment includes pre-kindergarten through grade 12 and ungraded students. The student/teacher ratio is calculated by dividing the number of students in all schools by the number of full-time equivalent teachers employed by all schools and agencies.

## EDUCATIONAL ATTAINMENT, Items 113–116
**Source: U.S. Census Bureau—2010 and 2011 American Community Survey**
http://www.census.gov/acs/www/

Data on **educational attainment** are tabulated for the population 25 years old and over. The data were derived from a question that asked respondents for the highest level of school completed or the highest degree received. Persons who had passed a high school equivalency examination were considered high school graduates. Schooling received in foreign schools was to be reported as the equivalent grade or years in the regular American school system. Vocational and technical training, such as barber school training; business, trade, technical, and vocational schools; or other training for a specific trade are specifically excluded.

**High school graduate or more.** This category includes persons whose highest degree was a high school diploma or its equivalent, and those who reported any level higher than a high school diploma.

**Bachelor's degree or more.** This category includes persons who have received bachelor's degrees, master's degrees, professional school degrees (such as law school or medical school degrees), and doctoral degrees.

## LOCAL GOVERNMENT EDUCATION EXPENDITURES, Items 117 and 118
**Source: U.S. Department of Education, National Center for Education Statistics—Common Core of Data**
http://www.nces.ed.gov/ccd/bat/

Total expenditure for education includes provision or support of schools and facilities for elementary and secondary education. It encompasses instructional, support, and auxiliary services (school lunch, student activities, and community service) offered by public school systems. Retirement benefits paid to former education employees and interest payments are not included. Current expenditure includes all components of total expenditure except capital outlay. Expenditure data are obtained by the Census Bureau through its annual survey of government finances and are supplied to the National Center for Education Statistics (NCES). Current expenditure per student is current expenditure divided by the number of students enrolled. The number of students enrolled is based on an annual "membership" count of students on or about October 1.

NCES uses the Common Core of Data (CCD) Survey system to acquire and maintain statistical data from each of the 50 states, the District of Columbia, and the outlying areas. State education agencies compile and submit data for approximately 94,000 schools and 17,000 local school districts. Typically, this results in varying interpretation of NCES definitions and different record keeping systems, leading to large amounts of missing data for several states; this absence is reflected in the data in this publication. The numbers in Table A reflect imputations and adjustments as published in *Revenues and Expenditures for Public Elementary and Secondary Education: School Year 2009–10 (Fiscal Year 2010)*.

## EXPORTS, Items 119–121
**Source: U.S. Department of Commerce, International Trade Administration**
http://www.census.gov/foreign-trade/statistics/state/origin-movement/index.html

The data on exports of goods by state of origin are based on the location of the exporter (the principal party responsible for exportation from the United States). Exporters are often intermediaries, so the data do not necessarily represent the states in which the goods were actually produced. The total includes re-exports of foreign goods.

## INCOME AND POVERTY, Items 122–133
**Source: U.S. Census Bureau—2011 American Community Survey**
http://www.census.gov/acs/www/

The data on income were derived from answers to questions which were asked of the population 15 years old and over. **Total income** is the sum of the amounts reported separately for wage or salary income; net self-employment income; interest, dividends, or net rental or royalty income or income from estates and trusts; Social Security or railroad retirement income; Supplemental Security Income (SSI); public assistance or welfare payments; retirement, survivor, or disability pensions; and all other income. Receipts from the following sources are not included as income: capital gains; money received from the sale of property (unless the recipient was engaged in the business of selling such property); the value of income "in kind" from food stamps, public housing subsidies, medical care, employer contributions for individuals, etc.; withdrawal of bank deposits; money borrowed; tax refunds; exchange of money between relatives living in the same household; and gifts and lump-sum inheritances, insurance payments, and other types of lump-sum receipts.

**Per capita income** is the mean income computed for every man, woman, and child in a particular group. It is derived by dividing the aggregate income of a particular group by the total population in that group. Per capita income is rounded to the nearest whole dollar.

**Household income** includes the income of the householder and all other individuals 15 years old and over in the household, whether or not they are related to the householder. Since many households consist of only one person, average household income is usually less than average family income. Although the household income statistics cover the past 12 months, the characteristics of individuals and the composition of households refer to the time of enumeration. Thus, the income of the household does not include amounts received by individuals who were members of the household during all or part of the past 12 months if these individuals no longer resided in the household at the time of interview. Similarly, income amounts reported by individuals who did not reside in the household during the past 12 months but who were members of the household at the time of interview are included. However, the composition of most households was the same during the past 12 months as at the time of interview.

**Median income** divides the income distribution into two equal parts, with half of all cases below the median income level and half of all cases above the median income level. For households and families, the median income is based on the distribution of the total number of households and families, including those with no income. Median income for households is computed on the basis of a standard distribution with a minimum value of less than $2,500 and a maximum value of $200,000 or more and is rounded to the nearest whole dollar.

For **family income**, the incomes of all household members 15 years old and over related to the householder are summed and treated as a single amount. Although the family income statistics cover the past 12 months, the characteristics of individuals and the composition of families refer to the time of interview. Thus, the income of the family does not include amounts received by individuals who were members of the family during all of part of the past 12 months if these individuals no longer resided with the family at the time of interview. Similarly, income amounts reported by individuals who did not reside with the family during the past 12 months but who were members of the family at the time of interview are included. However, the composition of most families was the same during the past 12 months as at the time of interview.

The **poverty status** data were derived from data collected on the number of persons in the household, each person's relationship to the householder, and the income data. The Social Security Administration (SSA) developed the original poverty definition in 1964, which federal interagency committees subsequently revised in 1969 and 1980. The Office of Management and Budget's (OMB) *Directive 14* prescribes the SSA's definition as the official poverty measure for federal agencies to use in their statistical work. Poverty statistics presented in American Community Survey products adhere to the standards defined by OMB in *Directive 14*.

The poverty thresholds vary depending on three criteria: size of family, number of children, and, for one- and two-person families, age of householder. In determining the poverty status of families and unrelated individuals, the Census Bureau uses thresholds (income cutoffs) arranged in a two-dimensional matrix. The matrix consists of family size (from one person to nine or more persons), cross-classified by presence and number of family members under 18 years old (from no children present to eight or more children present). Unrelated individuals and two-person families are further differentiated by age of reference person (under 65 years old and 65 years old and over). To determine a person's poverty status, the person's total family income in the last 12 months is compared to the poverty threshold appropriate for that person's family size and composition. If the total income of that person's family is less than the threshold appropriate for that family, then the person is considered poor or "below the poverty level," together with every member of his or her family. If a person is not living with anyone related by birth, marriage, or adoption, then the person's own income is compared with his or her poverty threshold. The total number of persons below the poverty level is the sum of persons in families and the number of unrelated individuals with incomes below the poverty level in the last 12 months. The average poverty threshold for a four-person family was $23,021 in 2011.

The data on **poverty status of households** were derived from answers to the income questions. Since poverty is defined at the family level and not the household level, the poverty status of the household is determined by the poverty status of the householder. Households are classified as poor when the total income of the householder's family in the previous 12 months is below the appropriate poverty threshold. (For nonfamily householders, the person's income is compared with the appropriate threshold.) The income of persons living in the household who are unrelated to the householder is not considered when determining the poverty status of a household, nor does their presence affect the family size in determining the appropriate threshold. The poverty thresholds vary depending upon three criteria: size of family, number of children, and, for one- and two-person families, age of the householder.

Poverty status of children by **family type** is the percentage of children living in that particular type of family that has a family income below the poverty threshold based on family size and composition.

## PERSONAL INCOME AND EARNINGS, Items 134–158

**Source: U.S. Bureau of Economic Analysis, Regional Economic Accounts**
**http://www.bea.gov/regional/index.htm#state**

**Total personal income** is the current income received by residents of an area from all sources. It is measured before deductions of income and other personal taxes but after deductions of personal contributions for Social Security, government retirement, and other social insurance programs. It consists of **wage and salary disbursements** (covering all employee earnings, including executive salaries, bonuses, commissions, payments-in-kind, incentive payments, and tips); various types of supplementary earnings, such as employers' contributions to pension funds (termed "other labor income" or "supplements to wages and salaries"); proprietors' income; rental income of persons; dividends; personal interest income; and government and business transfer payments.

**Proprietors' income** is the monetary income and income-in-kind of proprietorships and partnerships (including the independent professions), and the income of tax-exempt cooperatives. **Dividends** are cash payments by corporations to stockholders who are U.S. residents. **Interest** is the monetary and imputed interest income of persons from all sources. **Rent** is the monetary income of persons from the rental of real property, except the income of persons primarily engaged in the real estate business; the imputed net rental income of owner-occupants of nonfarm dwellings; and the royalties received by persons.

**Transfer payments** are income for which services are not currently rendered. They consist of both government and business transfer payments. Government transfer payments include payments under the following programs: Federal Old-Age, Survivors, and Disability Insurance ("Social Security"); Medicare and medical vendor payments; unemployment insurance; railroad and government retirement; federal- and state-government-insured workers' compensation; veterans' benefits, including veterans' life insurance; food stamps; black lung payments; Supplemental Security Income; and Temporary Assistance for Needy Families. Government payments to nonprofit institutions, other than for work under research and development contracts, are also included. Business transfer payments consist primarily of liability payments for personal injury and of corporate gifts to nonprofit institutions.

**Per capita personal income** is based on resident population estimated as of July 1 of the year shown.

**Personal tax payments** include taxes paid by individuals to federal, state, and local governments. Personal taxes include individual income taxes, estate and gift taxes, motor vehicle license taxes, and personal property taxes. Personal contributions to social insurance ("Social Security taxes") are not included, nor are sales taxes.

**Disposable personal income** equals personal income less personal tax payments. It is a measure of the income available to persons for spending or saving.

**Earnings** cover wage and salary disbursements, other labor income, and proprietors' income.

The data for earnings obtained from the Bureau of Economic Analysis (BEA) are based on place of work. In computing personal income, BEA makes an "adjustment for residence" to earnings based on commuting patterns; thus, personal income is presented on a place-of-residence basis.

**Farm earnings** include the income of farm workers (wages and salaries and other labor income) and farm proprietors. Farm proprietors' income includes only the income of sole proprietorships and partnerships.

Farm earnings estimates are benchmarked to data collected in the Census of Agriculture and the revised Department of Agriculture state totals of income and expense items.

**Goods-related** industries include mining, construction, and manufacturing. **Service-related** and other industries includes private-sector earnings in forestry, related activities, and other; utilities; transportation and warehousing; information; wholesale trade; retail trade; finance and insurance; real estate and rental and leasing; and services, which includes professional, scientific, and technical services; management of companies and enterprises; administrative and waste services; educational services; health care and social assistance; arts, entertainment, and recreation; accommodation and food services; and other services, except

public administration. Government earnings include all levels of government. Industries are categorized under the North American Industry Classification System (NAICS), and are not directly comparable to years prior to 2002.

## GROSS STATE PRODUCT, Item 159
**Source: U.S. Bureau of Economic Analysis, Regional Economic Accounts**
http://www.bea.gov/regional/index.htm#state

Gross state product (GSP) for a state is derived as the sum of gross state product originating in all industries in the state. In concept, an industry's GSP, referred to as its "value added," is equivalent to its gross output (sales or receipts and other operating income, commodity taxes, and inventory changes) minus its intermediate inputs (consumption of goods and services purchased from other industries or imported from other countries). As such, it is often referred to as the state counterpart to the nation's gross domestic product (GDP). In practice, GSP estimates are measured as the sum of distributions by industry of the components of gross domestic income—that is, the sum of the costs incurred (such as compensation of employees, net interest, and indirect business taxes) and the profits earned in production.

## SOCIAL SECURITY AND SUPPLEMENTAL SECURITY INCOME, Items 160–162
**Source: U.S. Social Security Administration**
http://www.ssa.gov/policy/docs/statcomps/oasdisc/
http://www.ssa.gov/policy/docs/statcomps/ssisc/

**Social Security beneficiaries** are persons receiving benefits under the Old-Age, Survivors, and Disability Insurance Program. These include retired or disabled workers covered by the program, their spouses and dependent children, and the surviving spouses and dependent children of deceased workers.

**Supplemental Security Income (SSI) recipients** are persons receiving SSI payments. The SSI program is a cash assistance program that provides monthly benefits to low-income aged, blind, or disabled persons.

Data are as of December of the year shown.

## CIVILIAN EMPLOYMENT, Items 163–166
**Source: U.S. Census Bureau—2011 American Community Survey**
http://www.census.gov/acs/www/

The data on occupation were derived from answers to questions that were asked of all persons 15 years old and over who had worked in the past 5 years. **Occupation** describes the kind of work the person does on the job. For employed persons, the data refer to the person's job during the previous week. For those who worked two or more jobs, the data refer to the job at which the person worked the greatest number of hours. For unemployed persons, the data refer to their last job. The American Community Survey uses the occupational classification system that was developed for the 2000 census and modified in 2002 and again in 2010. This system consists of 539 specific occupational categories for employed persons arranged into 23 major occupational groups.

This classification was developed based on the *Standard Occupational Classification (SOC) Manual: 2010*, published by the Executive Office of the President, Office of Management and Budget.

## CIVILIAN LABOR FORCE AND UNEMPLOYMENT, Items 167–171
### Source: U.S. Bureau of Labor Statistics—Local Areas Unemployment Statistics
http://www.bls.gov/lau/#tables

Data for the civilian labor force are the product of a federal-state cooperative program in which state employment security agencies prepare labor force and unemployment estimates under concepts, definitions, and technical procedures established by the Bureau of Labor Statistics (BLS). The **civilian labor force** consists of all civilians 16 years old and over who are either employed or unemployed.

**Unemployment** includes all persons who did not work during the survey week, made specific efforts to find a job during the prior four weeks, and were available for work during the survey week (except for temporary illness). Persons waiting to be called back to a job from which they had been laid off and those waiting to report to a new job within the next 30 days are included in unemployment figures.

## PRIVATE NONFARM EMPLOYMENT AND EARNINGS, Items 172–183
### Source: U.S. Bureau of Labor Statistics—Current Employment Survey
http://www.bls.gov/ces/#tables

Data for private nonfarm employment and earnings are compiled from payroll information reported monthly on a voluntary basis to the BLS and its cooperating state agencies. More than 350,000 establishments represent all industries except agriculture.

**Employment** is the annual average of monthly totals of persons who received pay for any part of the pay period including the 12th day of the month. Included are all full-time and part-time workers in nonfarm establishments. Not covered are government employees, proprietors, the self-employed, unpaid volunteers or family workers, farm workers, and domestic workers in households. The data by industry conform to the definitions established in the North American Industry Classification System (NAICS).

**Earnings** of **production workers** in **manufacturing** industries are derived from reports of gross payrolls and corresponding paid hours. Payroll is reported before deductions of any kinds. Total hours during the pay period include all hours worked (including overtime hours) and hours paid for holidays, vacations, and sick leave.

## AGRICULTURE, ITEMS 184–202
### Source: U.S. Department of Agriculture, National Agricultural Statistics Service—2007 Census of Agriculture
http://www.agcensus.usda.gov/Publications/2007/index.asp

The Census Bureau took a census of agriculture every 10 years from 1840 to 1920; since 1925, this census has been taken roughly once every 5 years. The 1997 Census of Agriculture was the first one conducted by the National Agricultural Statistics Service of the U.S. Department of Agriculture. Over time, the definition of a farm has varied. For recent censuses (including the 2007 census), a farm has been defined as any place from which $1,000 or more of agricultural products were produced and sold or normally would have been sold during the census year. Dollar figures are expressed in current dollars and have not been adjusted for inflation or deflation.

The term **operator** refers to a person who operates a farm by either doing the work or making day-to-day decisions about such activities as planting, harvesting, feeding, marketing, etc. The operator may be the owner, a member of the owner's household, a salaried manager, a tenant, a renter, or a sharecropper. If a person rents land to others or has land worked on shares by others, he/she is considered the operator only of the land that is retained for his/her own operation. The census collected information on the total number of operators, the total number of women operators, and demographic information for up to three operators per farm.

**Government payments** consists of direct payments as defined by the 2002 Farm Bill; payments from Conservation Reserve Program (CRP), Wetlands reserve Program (WRP), Farmable Wetlands Program (FWP), and Conservation Reserve Enhancement Program (CREP); loan deficiency payments; disaster payments; other conservation programs; and all other federal farm programs under which payments were made directly to farm operators. Commodity Credit Corporation (CCC) proceeds, amount from state and local federal crop insurance payments were not included in this category.

The acreage designated as **land in farms** consists primarily of agricultural land used for crops, pasture, or grazing. It also includes woodland and wasteland not actually under cultivation or used for pasture or grazing, provided that this land was part of the farm operator's total operation.

Land in farms is an operating-unit concept and includes all land owned and operated, as well as all land rented from others. Land used rent-free is classified as land rented from others. All land in Indian reservations used for growing crops or grazing livestock is classified as land in farms.

**Irrigated land** includes all land watered by any artificial or controlled means, such as sprinklers, flooding, furrows or ditches, sub-irrigation, and spreader dikes. Included are supplemental, partial, and preplant irrigation. Each acre was counted only once regardless of the number of times it was irrigated or harvested. Livestock lagoon waste water distributed by sprinkler or flood systems was also included.

**Total cropland** includes cropland harvested, cropland used only for pasture or grazing, cropland on which all crops failed or were abandoned, cropland in cultivated summer fallow, and cropland idle or used for cover crops or soil improvement but not harvested and not pastured or grazed.

Respondents were asked to report their estimate of the current market **value of land and buildings** owned, rented, or leased from others and rented and leased to others. Market value refers to the respondent's estimate of what the land and buildings would sell for under current market conditions.

The **value of machinery and equipment** was estimated by the respondent as the current market value of all cars, trucks, tractors, combines, balers, irrigation equipment, etc., used on the farm. This value is an estimate of what the machinery and equipment would sell for in its present condition and not the replacement of depreciated value. Share interests are reported at full value at the farm where the equipment and machinery are usually kept. Only equipment that was actually used in 2006 and 2007, or newly purchased but not yet used and physically located at the farm on December 31, 2007, is included.

Market **value of agricultural products sold** by farms represents the gross market value before taxes and the production expenses of all agricultural products sold or removed from the place in 2007, regardless of who received the payment. It is equivalent to total sales and it includes sales by the operator as well as the value of any share received by partners, landlords, contractors, and others associated with the operation. It includes value of direct sales and the value of commodities placed in the Commodity Credit Corporation (CCC) loan program. Market value of agricultural products sold does not include payments received for participation in other federal farm programs. Also, it does not include income from farm-related sources such as customwork and other agricultural services, or income from non-farm sources.

## LAND USE, ITEMS 203 to 205
**Source**: U.S. Department of Agriculture, Natural Resources Conservation Service—2007 National Resources Inventory
http://www.nrcs.usda.gov/technical/NRI/

The National Resources Inventory (NRI) has been conducted every five years since 1982. The 2007 NRI is based on a sample of about 800,000 locations throughout the United States (excluding Alaska and the District of Columbia). Acreages for federal land and total surface area are established through geospatial processes and administrative records. Total surface area of the contiguous United States is 1,937.7 million acres.

**Cropland** includes cultivated and non-cultivated cropland. **Federally-owned lands** include military bases, national forests, wildlife refuges, parks, grassland game preserves, scenic waterways, wilderness areas, monuments, lakeshore, parkways, battlefields, Bureau of Land Management lands, and other federal lands. **Developed land** includes any built-up area greater than one fourth of an acre. Built-up areas include residential, industrial, commercial, and institutional land; construction sites; public administrative sites; railroad yards; cemeteries; airports; golf courses; sanitary landfills; sewage treatment plants; water control structures and spillways; other land used for such purpose; small parks (fewer than 10 acres of land) within urban and built-up areas; and highways, railroads, and other transportation facilities that are surrounded by urban areas. Also included are tracts of fewer

than 10 acres that do not meet the above definition but are completely surrounded by urban and built-up land, as well as all highways, roads, railroads, and associated rights-of-way outside of urban and built-up areas (including private roads to farmsteads or ranch headquarters, logging roads, and other private roads).

## WATER CONSUMPTION, Item 206
**Source: U.S. Geological Survey, National Water Use Information Program—2005 Water Use Data**
http://pubs.usgs.gov/circ/1344/

Every five years, the U.S. Geological Survey compiles national water-use estimates. This volume includes the total fresh and saline water withdrawals expressed as million gallons per day. Estimate of withdrawals of ground and surface water are given for the following categories of use: public water supplies, domestic, commercial, irrigation, livestock, industrial, mining, and thermo-electric power.

## MANUFACTURES, Items 207–216
**Source: U.S. Census Bureau—2011 Annual Survey of Manufactures**
http://www.census.gov/manufacturing/asm/

The Annual Survey of Manufactures (ASM) has been conducted annually every year since 1949, except for years ending in ''2'' and ''7,'' at which time ASM data are included in the manufacturing sector of the Economic Census. The ASM provides statistics on employment, payroll, worker hours, payroll supplements, cost of materials, value added by manufacturing, capital expenditures, inventories, and energy consumption. It also provides estimates of value of shipments for over 1,400 classes of manufactured products. The Annual Survey of Manufactures includes approximately 50,000 establishments selected from the census universe of 350,000 manufacturing establishments.

The **all employees** number is the average number of production workers for the payroll periods including the 12th of March, May, August, and November plus the number of other employees in mid-March. Included are all persons on paid sick leave, paid holidays, and paid vacations during the pay period. Officers of corporations are included as employees, while proprietors and partners of unincorporated firms are excluded.

**Payroll** figures include the gross annual earnings of all employees on the payroll of operating manufacturing establishments. The definition, which is the same as the one used for calculating the federal withholding tax, includes all forms of compensation, such as salaries, wages, commissions, dismissal pay, bonuses, vacation and sick leave pay, and compensation-in-kind, prior to such deductions as employees' Social Security contributions, withholding taxes, group insurance, union dues, and savings bonds. The total includes salaries of officers of corporations; it excludes payments to proprietors or partners of unincorporated concerns. Also excluded are payments to members of armed forces and to pensioners carried on the active payrolls of manufacturing establishments.

**Production workers** include workers (up through the line-supervisor level) engaged in fabricating, processing, assembling, inspecting, receiving, storing, handling, packing, warehousing, shipping (but not delivering), maintenance, repair, janitorial and guard services, product development, auxiliary production for the plant's own use (for example, power plant), record keeping, and other services closely associated with these production operations at the establishment covered by the report. Employees above the working-supervisor level are excluded.

The number of production workers is the average for the payroll periods including the 12th of March, May, August, and November. Not included in this classification are all other employees, defined as non-production employees, including those engaged in factory supervision above the line-supervisor level.

Production worker hours cover hours worked or paid for at the manufacturing plant, including actual overtime hours (not straight-time equivalent hours). The data exclude hours paid for vacations, holidays, or sick leave when the employee is not at the establishment. Production wages represent all compensation paid to production workers.

**Value added** by manufacture is derived by subtracting the cost of materials, supplies, containers, fuel, purchased electricity, and contract work from the value of shipments (products manufactured plus receipts for services rendered). The result of this calculation is adjusted by the addition of value added by merchandising operations (the difference between the sales value and the cost of merchandise sold without further manufacture, processing, or assembly) plus the net change in finished goods and work-in-process between the beginning- and end-of-year inventories.

**Value of shipments** covers the received or receivable net selling values; free on board plant (excluding of freight and taxes), of all products shipped, both primary and secondary; and all miscellaneous receipts, such as receipts for contract work performed for others, installation and repair, sales of scrap, and sales of products bought and sold without further processing. Included are all items made by or for the establishments from material owned by it, whether sold, transferred to other plants of the same company, or shipped on consignment. The net selling value of products made in one plant on a contract basis from materials owned by another was reported by the plant providing the materials.

In the case of multi-unit companies, the manufacturer was asked to report the value of products transferred to other establishments of the same company at full economic or commercial value, including both the direct cost of production and a reasonable proportion of "all other costs" (including company overhead) and profit (interplant transfers).

The aggregate of the value of shipments figure for industry groups and for all manufacturing industries includes large amounts of duplications, as the products of some industries are used as materials by others. Estimates as to the overall extent of this duplication indicate that the value of manufactured products exclusive of such duplication (the value of finished manufactures) tends to approximate two-thirds of the total value of products reported in the census of manufactures.

**Total capital expenditures (new and used)** represents the total new and used capital expenditures reported by establishments in operation and any known plants under construction. These data include expenditures for (1) permanent additions and major alterations to manufacturing and mining establishments and (2) new and used machinery and equipment used for replacement and additions to plant capacity, if they are of the type for which depreciation, depletion accounts were ordinarily maintained.

Totals for expenditures include the costs of assets leased from nonmanufacturing concerns through capital leases. New facilities owned by the federal government but operated under contract by private companies and plant and equipment furnished to the manufacturer by communities and nonprofit organizations are excluded. These data exclude expenditures for land and mineral rights and cost of maintenance and repairs charged as current operating expenses.

For any equipment or structure transferred for the use for the reporting establishment by the parent company or one of its subsidiaries, the value at which it was transferred to the establishment was to be reported.

If an establishment changed ownership during the year, the cost of fixed assets (building and equipment) was to be reported.

## 2007 ECONOMIC CENSUS: OVERVIEW, Items 217–308
### Source: U.S. Census Bureau
### http://www.census.gov/econ/census07/

The Economic Census provides a detailed portrait of the nation's economy, from the national to the local level, once every five years. The 2007 Economic Census covers nearly all of the U.S. economy in its basic collection of establishment statistics. The 1997 Economic Census was the first major data source to use the new North American Industry Classification System (NAICS); therefore, data are not comparable to economic data from prior years, which were based on the Standard Industrial Classification (SIC) system.

NAICS, developed in cooperation with Canada and Mexico, classifies North America's economic activities at two-, three-, four-, and five-digit levels of detail; the U.S. version of NAICS further defines industries to a sixth digit. The Economic Census takes advantage of this hierarchy to publish data at these successive levels of detail: sector (two-digit); subsector (three-digit); industry group (four-digit); industry (five-digit); and U.S. industry (six-digit). Information in Table A is at the two-digit level, with a few three- and four-digit items.

Several key statistics are tabulated for all industries included in this volume: number of establishments (or companies); number of employees; payroll; and a measure of output (sales, receipts, revenue, value of shipments, or value of construction work done).

**Number of establishments.** An establishment is a single physical location at which business is conducted. It is not necessarily identical with a company or enterprise, which may consist of one establishment or more. Economic Census figures represent a summary of reports for individual establishments rather than companies. For cases in which a census report was received, separate information was obtained for each location where business was conducted. When administrative records of other federal agencies were used instead of a census report, no information was available on the number of locations operated. Each Economic Census establishment was tabulated according to the physical location at which the business was conducted. The count of establishments represents those in business at any time during 2007.

When two activities or more were carried on at a single location under a single ownership, all activities were generally grouped together as a single establishment. The entire establishment was classified on the basis of its major activity and all of its data were included in that classification. However, when distinct and separate economic activities (for which different industry classification codes were appropriate) were conducted at a single location under a single ownership, separate establishment reports for each of the different activities were obtained in the census.

**Number of employees.** Paid employees consist of the full-time and part-time employees, including salaried officers and executives of corporations. Included are employees on paid sick leave, paid holidays, and paid vacations; not included are proprietors and partners of unincorporated businesses. The definition of paid employees is the same as that used by the Internal Revenue Service (IRS) on form 941.

For some industries, the Economic Census gives codes representing the number of employees as a range of numbers (for example, ''100 to 249 employees'' or ''1,000 to 2,499'' employees). In this volume, those codes have been replaced by the standard suppression code ''D''.

**Payroll.** Payroll includes all forms of compensation, such as salaries, wages, commissions, dismissal pay, bonuses, vacation allowances, sick-leave pay, and employee contributions to qualified pension plans paid during the year to all employees. For corporations, payroll includes amounts paid to officers and executives; for unincorporated businesses, it does not include profit or other compensation of proprietors or partners. Payroll is reported before deductions for Social Security, income tax, insurance, union dues, etc. This definition of payroll is the same as that used on IRS form 941.

**Sales, shipments, receipts, revenue, or business done.** This measure includes the total sales, shipments, receipts, revenue, or business done by establishments within the scope of the Economic Census. The definition of each of these items is specific to the economic sector measured.

## CONSTRUCTION, Items 217–221
### Source: U.S. Census Bureau—2007 Economic Census (See Overview of 2007 Economic Census prior to Item 217)

The Construction sector (sector 23) comprises establishments primarily engaged in the construction of buildings and other structures, heavy construction (except buildings), additions, alterations, reconstruction, installation, and maintenance and repairs. Establishments engaged in the demolition or wrecking of buildings and other structures, the clearing of building sites, and the sale of materials from demolished structures are also included. This sector also contains those establishments engaged in blasting, test drilling, landfill, leveling, earthmoving, excavating, land drainage, and other land preparation. The industries within this sector have been defined on the basis of their unique production processes. As with all industries, the production processes are distinguished by their use of specialized human resources and specialized physical capital. Construction activities are generally administered or managed at a relatively fixed place of business, but the actual construction work can be performed at one or more different project sites. This sector is divided into three subsectors of construction activities: (1) building construction and land sub-division and land development; (2) heavy construction (except

buildings), such as highways, power plants, and pipelines; and (3) construction activity by special trade contractors.

## WHOLESALE TRADE, Items 222–226
### Source: U.S. Census Bureau—2007 Economic Census (See Overview of 2007 Economic Census prior to Item 217)

The Wholesale Trade sector (sector 42) comprises establishments engaged in wholesaling merchandise, generally without transformation, and rendering services incidental to the sale of merchandise. The wholesaling process is an intermediate step in the distribution of merchandise. Wholesalers are organized to sell or arrange the purchase or sale of (1) goods for resale (i.e., goods sold to other wholesalers or retailers), (2) capital or durable nonconsumer goods, and (3) raw and intermediate materials and supplies used in production.

Wholesalers sell merchandise to other businesses and normally operate from a warehouse or office. These warehouses and offices are characterized by having little or no display of merchandise. In addition, neither the design nor the location of the premises is intended to solicit walk-in traffic. Wholesalers do not normally use advertising directed to the general public. Customers are generally first reached via telephone, in-person marketing, or by specialized advertising that may include internet and other electronic means. Follow-up orders are either vendor-initiated or client-initiated, are usually based on previous sales, and typically exhibit strong ties between sellers and buyers. In fact, transactions are often conducted between wholesalers and clients that have long-standing business relationships.

This sector is made up of two main types of wholesalers: those that sell goods on their own account and those that arrange sales and purchases for others for a commission or fee.

(1) Establishments that sell goods on their own account are known as wholesale merchants, distributors, jobbers, drop shippers, import/export merchants, and sales branches. These establishments typically maintain their own warehouse, where they receive and handle goods for their customers. Goods are generally sold without transformation, but may include integral functions, such as sorting, packaging, labeling, and other marketing services.

(2) Establishments arranging for the purchase or sale of goods owned by others or purchasing goods on a commission basis are known as agents and brokers, commission merchants, import/export agents and brokers, auction companies, and manufacturers' representatives. These establishments operate from offices and generally do not own or handle the goods they sell.

Some wholesale establishments may be connected with a single manufacturer and/or promote and sell that particular manufacturer's products to a wide range of other wholesalers or retailers. Other wholesalers may be connected to a retail chain or a limited number of retail chains and only provide a variety of products needed by that particular retail operation(s). These wholesalers may obtain the products from a wide range of manufacturers. Still other wholesalers may not take title to the goods but act as agents and brokers for a commission.

Although, in general, wholesaling normally denotes sales in large volumes, durable nonconsumer goods may be sold in single units. Sales of capital or durable nonconsumer goods used in the production of goods and services, such as farm machinery, medium- and heavy-duty trucks, and industrial machinery, are always included in Wholesale Trade.

## RETAIL TRADE, Items 227–235
### Source: U.S. Census Bureau—2007 Economic Census (See Overview of 2007 Economic Census prior to Item 217)

The Retail Trade sector (44–45) is made up of establishments engaged in retailing merchandise, generally without transformation, and rendering services incidental to the sale of merchandise.

The retailing process is the final step in the distribution of merchandise; retailers are, therefore, organized to sell merchandise in small quantities to the general public. This sector comprises two main types of retailers: store and nonstore retailers.

Store retailers operate fixed point-of-sale locations, located and designed to attract a high volume of walk-in customers. In general, retail stores have extensive displays of merchandise and use mass-media advertising to attract customers. They typically sell merchandise to the general public for personal or household consumption; some also serve business and institutional clients. These include establishments, such as office supply stores, computer and software stores, building materials dealers, plumbing supply stores, and electrical supply stores. Catalog showrooms, gasoline service stations, automotive dealers, and mobile home dealers are treated as store retailers.

In addition to retailing merchandise, some types of store retailers are also engaged in the provision of after-sales services, such as repair and installation. For example, new automobile dealers, electronic and appliance stores, and musical instrument and supply stores often provide repair services. As a general rule, establishments engaged in retailing merchandise and providing after-sales services are classified in this sector.

Nonstore retailers, like store retailers, are organized to serve the general public, although their retailing methods differ. The establishments of this subsector reach customers and market merchandise with methods, such as the broadcasting of "infomercials," the broadcasting and publishing of direct-response advertising, the publishing of paper and electronic catalogs, door-to-door solicitation, in-home demonstration, selling from portable stalls (street vendors, except food), and distribution through vending machines. Establishments engaged in the direct sale (nonstore) of products, such as home heating oil dealers and home-delivery newspaper routes are included in this sector.

The buying of goods for resale is a characteristic of retail trade establishments that distinguishes them from establishments in the Agriculture, Manufacturing, and Construction sectors. For example, farms that sell their products at or from the point of production are classified in Agriculture instead of in Retail Trade. Similarly, establishments that both manufacture and sell their products to the general public are classified in Manufacturing instead of Retail Trade. However, establishments that engage in processing activities incidental to retailing are classified in retail.

Industries in the **Motor Vehicle and Parts Dealers** subsector (441) retail motor vehicle and parts merchandise from fixed point-of-sale locations. Establishments in this subsector typically operate from a showroom and/or an open lot where the vehicles are on display. The display of vehicles and the related parts require little by way of display equipment. Personnel generally include both sales and sales support staff familiar with the requirements for registering and financing a vehicle as well as a staff of parts experts and mechanics trained to provide vehicle repair and maintenance services. Specific industries have been included in this subsector to identify the type of vehicle being retailed. Sales of capital or durable nonconsumer goods, such as medium and heavy-duty trucks, are always included in the Wholesale Trade sector. These goods are virtually never sold through retail methods.

Industries in the **Food and Beverage Stores** subsector (445) usually retail food and beverage merchandise from fixed point-of-sale locations. Establishments in this subsector have special equipment (e.g., freezers, refrigerated display cases, and refrigerators) for displaying food and beverage goods. They have staff trained in the processing of food products to guarantee the proper storage and sanitary conditions, as mandated by regulatory authority.

Industries in the **Clothing and Clothing Accessories Stores** subsector (448) retail new clothing and clothing accessories merchandise from fixed point-of-sale locations. Establishments in this subsector have similar types of display equipment, as well as employees who are knowledgeable regarding fashion trends and who can match styles, colors, and combinations of clothing and accessories to the characteristics and tastes of the customer.

Industries in the **General Merchandise Stores** subsector (452) retail new general merchandise from fixed point-of-sale locations. Establishments in this subsector are unique in that they have the equipment and staff capable of retailing a large variety of goods from a single location. This includes a variety of display equipment and staff trained to provide information on many lines of products.

## INFORMATION, Items 236–246
### Source: U.S. Census Bureau—2007 Economic Census (See Overview of 2007 Economic Census prior to Item 217)

The Information sector (51) comprises establishments engaged in the following processes: (1) producing and distributing information and cultural products, (2) providing the means to transmit or distribute these products as well as data or communications, and (3) processing data.

The main components of this sector are the publishing industries, including software publishing; the motion picture and sound recording industries; the broadcasting and telecommunications industries; and the information services and data processing industries.

For the purpose of NAICS, the transformation of information into a commodity that is produced and distributed by a number of growing industries is at issue. The Information sector groups three types of establishments: (1) those engaged in producing and distributing information and cultural products; (2) those that provide the means to transmit or distribute these products as well as data or communications; and (3) those that process data. Cultural products are those that directly express attitudes, opinions, ideas, values, and artistic creativity; provide entertainment; or offer information and analysis concerning the past and present. Included in this definition are popular, mass-produced products, as well as cultural products that normally have a more limited audience, such as poetry books, literary magazines, or classical records. These activities were formerly classified throughout the existing national classifications. Traditional publishing was in manufacturing; broadcasting in communications; software production in business services; film production in amusement services; and so forth.

Industries in the **Publishing Industries, Except Internet** subsector (511) include establishments engaged in the publishing of newspapers, magazines, other periodicals, and books, as well as database and software publishing. In general, these establishments, which are known as publishers, issue copies of works for which they usually possess copyright. Works may be in one or more formats, including traditional print format, CD-ROM format, or online format. Publishers may publish works originally created by others for which they have obtained the rights and/or works that they have created in-house. Software publishing is included here because the activity (creation of a copyrighted product and bringing it to market) is equivalent to the creation process for other types of intellectual products.

In NAICS, publishing—the reporting, writing, editing, and other processes that are required to create an edition of a book or a newspaper—is treated as a major economic activity in its own right, rather than as a subsidiary activity to printing, which is a manufacturing activity. Thus, publishing is classified in the Information sector, while printing remains in the NAICS Manufacturing sector. In part, the NAICS classification reflects the fact that publishing increasingly takes place in establishments that are physically separate from the associated printing establishments. More crucially, the NAICS classification of book and newspaper publishing is intended to portray their roles in a modern economy—roles that do not resemble manufacturing activities.

Music publishers are not included in the Publishing Industries subsector, but can be found in the Motion Picture and Sound Recording Industries subsector. Reproduction of prepackaged software is treated in NAICS as a manufacturing activity; online distribution of software products is in the Information sector, and custom design of software to client specifications is included in the Professional, Scientific, and Technical Services sector. These distinctions arise because of the different ways that software is created, reproduced, and distributed.

The Information sector does not include products, such as manifold business forms. Information is not the essential component of these items. Establishments producing these items are included in subsector 323, Printing and Related Support Activities.

Industries in the **Motion Picture and Sound Recording Industries** subsector (512) group establishments involved in the production and distribution of motion pictures and sound recordings. While producers and distributors of motion pictures and sound recordings issue works for sale as traditional publishers do, the processes are different enough to warrant placing the establishments engaged in these activities in separate subsectors. Production is typically a complex process that involves several distinct types of establishments engaged in activities, such as contracting with performers, creating the film or sound content, and providing technical postproduction services. Film distribution is often to exhibitors, such as theaters and broadcasters, rather than to a wholesale or retail distribution chain. When the product

is in a mass-produced form, NAICS treats production and distribution as the major economic activity, rather than as a subsidiary activity to the manufacture of such products.

This subsector does not include establishments primarily engaged in the wholesale distribution of video cassettes and sound recordings, such as compact discs and audio tapes; these establishments are included in the Wholesale Trade sector. Reproduction of video cassettes and sound recordings that is carried out separately from establishments engaged in production and distribution is treated in NAICS as a manufacturing activity.

Industries in the **Broadcasting, except Internet** subsector (515) include establishments that create content or acquire the right to distribute and subsequently broadcast content. The industry groups (Radio and Television Broadcasting and Cable and Other Subscription Programming) are based on differences in the methods of communication and the nature of services provided. The Radio and Television Broadcasting industry group includes establishments that operate broadcasting studios and facilities for over-the-air or satellite delivery of radio and television programs, including entertainment, news, and talk programs. These establishments are often engaged in production and purchase of programs and generating revenues from the sale of air time to advertisers, as well as from donations, subsidies, and/or the sale of programs. The Cable and Other Subscription Programming industry group includes establishments that operate studios and facilities for the broadcasting of limited-format programs (such as news, sports, educational, and youth-oriented programs) that are typically narrowly-focused in nature; these programs are usually available on a subscription or fee basis. The distribution of cable and other subscription programming is included in subsector 517, Telecommunications.

Industries in the **Internet Publishing and Broadcasting and Web search portals** subsector (51913) consist of establishments that publish and/or broadcast content exclusively for the Internet. The unique combination of text, audio, video, and interactive features present in informational and/or cultural products on the internet justifies the separation of internet publishers and broadcasters from the more traditional publishers included in subsector 511, Publishing Industries, Except Internet, and subsector 515, Broadcasting, Except Internet.

Industries in the **Telecommunications** subsector (517) include establishments that provide telecommunications and services related to that activity. The Telecommunications subsector is primarily engaged in operating, maintaining, and/or providing access to facilities for the transmission of voice, data, text, sound, and video. A transmission facility may be based on a single technology or a combination of technologies. Establishments primarily engaged as independent contractors in the maintenance and installation of broadcasting and telecommunications systems are classified in sector 23, Construction.

Industries in the **Internet Service Providers, Web Search Portals, and Data Processing Services** subsector (518) group establishments that provide: (1) access to the Internet; (2) search facilities for the Internet; and (3) data processing, hosting, and related services. The industry groups (Internet Service Providers and Web Search Portals, Data Processing Hosting, and Related Services) are based on differences in the processes used to access information and process information. The Internet Service Providers and Web Search Portals industry group includes establishments that provide access to the internet or assist users in their navigations on the Web. The Data Processing, Hosting, and Related Services industry group includes establishments that process data. These establishments can transform data, prepare data for dissemination, or place data or content on the Internet for others. In addition, the shared use of computer resources is included in the Data Processing, Hosting, and Related Services industry group.

Establishments that are publishing exclusively on the internet are included in subsector 516, Internet Publishing and Broadcasting; establishments that sell goods over the internet are included in sector 44–45, Retail Trade.

## UTILITIES, Items 247–252
### Source: U.S. Census Bureau—2007 Economic Census (See Overview of 2007 Economic Census prior to Item 217)

The Utilities sector (22) comprises establishments engaged in the provision of the following utility services: electric power, natural gas, steam supply, water supply, and sewage removal. Within this sector, the specific activities associated with the utility services provided vary by utility: electric power includes generation, transmission, and distribution; natural gas includes distribution; steam supply includes provision and/or distribution; water supply includes treatment and distribution; and sewage removal includes collection, treatment, and disposal of waste through sewer systems and sewage treatment facilities.

Excluded from this sector are establishments primarily engaged in waste management. These services are classified in subsector 562, Waste Management and Remediation Services, which also collect, treat, and dispose of waste materials; however, establishments in this subsector do not use sewer systems or sewage treatment facilities.

## TRANSPORTATION AND WAREHOUSING, Items 252–256
### Source: U.S. Census Bureau—2007 Economic Census (See Overview of 2007 Economic Census prior to Item 217)

The Transportation and Warehousing sector (48–49) includes industries that provide transportation of passengers and cargo, warehousing and storage for goods, scenic and sightseeing transportation, and support activities related to modes of transportation. Establishments in these industries use transportation equipment or transportation related facilities as a productive asset. The type of equipment depends on the mode of transportation, which includes air, rail, water, road, and pipeline.

The transportation and warehousing sector distinguishes three basic types of activities: subsectors for each mode of transportation, a subsector for warehousing and storage, and a subsector for establishments providing support activities for transportation. In addition, there are subsectors for establishments that provide passenger transportation for scenic and sightseeing purposes, postal services, and courier services.

## FINANCE AND INSURANCE, Items 257–261
### Source: U.S. Census Bureau—2007 Economic Census (See Overview of 2007 Economic Census prior to Item 217)

The Finance and Insurance sector (52) comprises establishments primarily engaged in financial transactions (transactions involving the creation, liquidation, or change in ownership of financial assets) and/or in facilitating financial transactions. Three principal types of activities are identified:

(1) Raising funds by taking deposits and/or issuing securities and, in the process, incurring liabilities. Establishments engaged in this activity use raised funds to acquire financial assets by making loans and/or purchasing securities. Putting themselves at risk, they channel funds from lenders to borrowers and transform or repackage the funds with respect to maturity, scale and risk. This activity is known as financial intermediation.

(2) Pooling of risk by underwriting insurance and annuities. Establishments engaged in this activity collect fees, insurance premiums, or annuity considerations; build up reserves; invest those reserves; and make contractual payments. Fees are based on the expected incidence of the insured risk and the expected return on investment.

(3) Providing specialized services facilitating or supporting financial intermediation, insurance, and employee benefit programs.

In addition, monetary authorities charged with monetary control are included in this sector.

## REAL ESTATE AND RENTAL AND LEASING, Items 262–266
### Source: U.S. Census Bureau—2007 Economic Census (See Overview of 2007 Economic Census prior to Item 217)

The Real Estate and Rental and Leasing sector (53) comprises establishments primarily engaged in renting, leasing, or otherwise allowing the use of tangible or intangible assets, and establishments providing related services. The major portion of this sector comprises establishments that rent, lease, or otherwise allow the use of their own assets by others. The assets may be tangible, such as real estate and equipment, or intangible, such as patents and trademarks.

This sector also includes establishments primarily engaged in managing real estate for others, selling, renting, and/or buying real estate for others, and appraising real estate. These activities are closely related to this sector's main activity. In addition, a substantial proportion of property management is self-performed by lessors.

The main components of this sector are the real estate lessors industries; equipment lessors industries (including motor vehicles, computers, and consumer goods); and lessors of nonfinancial intangible assets (except copyrighted works).

## PROFESSIONAL, SCIENTIFIC, AND TECHNICAL SERVICES, Items 267–275

**Source: U.S. Census Bureau—2007 Economic Census (See Overview of 2007 Economic Census prior to Item 217)**

The Professional, Scientific, and Technical Services sector (54) is made up of establishments that specialize in performing professional, scientific, and technical activities for others. These activities require a high degree of expertise and training. The establishments in this sector specialize according to expertise and provide services to clients in a variety of industries (and, in some cases, to households). Activities performed include legal advice and representation; accounting, bookkeeping, and payroll services; architectural, engineering, and specialized design services; computer services; consulting services; research services; advertising services; photographic services; translation and interpretation services; veterinary services; and other professional, scientific, and technical services.

This sector excludes establishments primarily engaged in providing a range of day-to-day office administrative services, such as financial planning, billing and record keeping, personnel services, and physical distribution and logistics services. These establishments are classified in sector 56, Administrative and Support and Waste Management and Remediation Services.

**Legal Services** is a NAICS industry group (5411) that includes establishments classified in the following NAICS industries: 54111, Offices of Lawyers, and 54119, Other Legal Services.

**Accounting, Tax Preparation, Bookkeeping, and Payroll Services** is a NAICS industry group (5412) that comprises establishments primarily engaged in providing services such as auditing of accounting records, designing accounting systems, preparing financial statements, developing budgets, preparing tax returns, processing payrolls, bookkeeping, and billing.

**Architectural, Engineering, and Related Services** is a NAICS industry group (5413) that includes establishments classified in the following NAICS industries: 54131, Architectural Services; 54133, Engineering Services; 54134, Drafting Services; 54135, Building Inspection Services; 54136, Geophysical Surveying and Mapping Services; 54137, Surveying and Mapping (Except Geophysical) Services; and 54138, Testing Laboratories.

**Computer Systems Design and Related Services** is a NAICS industry group (5415) that consists of establishments primarily engaged in providing expertise in the field of information technologies through one or more of the following activities: (1) writing, modifying, testing, and supporting software to meet the needs of a particular customer; (2) planning and designing computer systems that integrate computer hardware, software, and communication technologies; (3) on-site management and operation of clients' computer systems and/or data processing facilities; and (4) other professional and technical computer-related advice and services.

## HEALTH CARE AND SOCIAL ASSISTANCE, Items 276–289

**Source: U.S. Census Bureau—2007 Economic Census (See Overview of 2007 Economic Census prior to Item 217)**

The Health Care and Social Assistance sector (62) consists of establishments that provide health care and social assistance services to individuals. The sector includes both health care and social assistance, because it is sometimes difficult to distinguish between the boundaries of these two activities. The industries in this sector are arranged on a continuum starting with those that provide medical care exclusively, continuing with those that provide health care and social assistance, and finishing with those that provide only social assistance. The services provided by establishments in this sector are delivered by trained professionals. All industries in the sector share this commonality of process—namely, labor inputs of health practitioners or social workers with the requisite expertise. Many of the industries in the sector are defined based on the educational degree held by the practitioners included in the industry.

In this volume, taxable and tax-exempt establishments are presented separately.

Excluded from this sector are aerobic classes, which can be found in subsector 713, Amusement, Gambling and Recreation Industries; and nonmedical diet and weight-reducing centers, which can be found in subsector 812, Personal and Laundry Services. Although these can be viewed as health services, they are not typically delivered by health practitioners.

Industries in the **Ambulatory Health Care Services** subsector (621) provide health care services directly or indirectly to ambulatory patients and do not typically provide inpatient services. Health practitioners in this subsector provide outpatient services, and facilities and equipment do not usually play the most significant part in this sector's production process.

Industries in the **Hospitals** subsector (622) provide medical, diagnostic, and treatment services, including physician, nursing, specialized accommodation, and other health services, to inpatients. Hospitals may provide outpatient services as a secondary activity. Many of the services provided by establishments in the Hospitals subsector require the use of specialized facilities and equipment, both of which form a significant and integral part of the production process.

## ARTS, ENTERTAINMENT, AND RECREATION, Items 290–294

**Source: U.S. Census Bureau—2007 Economic Census (See Overview of 2007 Economic Census prior to Item 217)**

The Arts, Entertainment, and Recreation sector (71) includes a wide range of establishments that operate facilities or provide services that meet the diverse cultural, entertainment, and recreational interests of their patrons. This sector is made up of: (1) establishments that are involved in producing, promoting, or participating in live performances, events, or exhibits intended for public viewing; (2) establishments that preserve and exhibit objects and sites of historical, cultural, or educational interest; and (3) establishments that operate facilities or provide services that enable patrons to participate in recreational activities or pursue amusement, hobby, and leisure time interests.

Some establishments that provide cultural, entertainment, or recreational facilities and services are classified in other sectors. Excluded from this sector are: (1) establishments that provide both accommodations and recreational facilities—such as hunting and fishing camps and resort and casino hotels—are classified in subsector 721, Accommodation; (2) restaurants and night clubs that provide live entertainment in addition to the sale of food and beverages are classified in subsector 722, Food Services and Drinking Places; (3) motion picture theaters, libraries and archives, and publishers of newspapers, magazines, books, periodicals, and computer software are classified in sector 51, Information; and (4) establishments that use transportation equipment to provide recreational and entertainment services, such as those operating sightseeing buses, dinner cruises, or helicopter rides, are classified in subsector 487, Scenic and Sightseeing Transportation.

## ACCOMMODATION AND FOOD SERVICES, Items 295–300

**Source: U.S. Census Bureau—2007 Economic Census (See Overview of 2007 Economic Census prior to Item 217)**

The Accommodation and Food Services sector (72) consists of establishments that provide customers with lodging and/or meals, snacks, and beverages for immediate consumption. The sector includes both accommodation and food services establishments because the two activities are often combined at the same establishment. Excluded from this sector are civic and social organizations, amusement and recreation parks, theaters, and other recreation or entertainment facilities providing food and beverage services.

Industries in the **Food Services and Drinking Places** subsector (722) prepare meals, snacks, and beverages to customer order for immediate on-premises and off-premises consumption. There is a wide range of establishments in these industries. Some provide food and drink only; while others provide various combinations of seating space, waiter/waitress services and incidental amenities, such as limited entertainment. The industries in the subsector are grouped based on the type and level of services provided. The industry groups are full-service restaurants; limited-service eating places; special food services, such as food service contractors, caterers, and mobile food services, and drinking places. Food services and drink activities at hotels and motels; amusement parks, theaters, casinos, country clubs, and similar recreational facilities; and civic and social organizations are included in this subsector only if these services are provided by a separate establishment primarily engaged in providing food and beverage services. Excluded from this subsector are establishments operating dinner cruises. These establishments are classified in subsector 487, Scenic and Sightseeing Transportation, because they utilize transportation equipment to provide scenic recreational entertainment.

## OTHER SERVICES, EXCEPT PUBLIC ADMINISTRATION Items 301–308

**Source: U.S. Census Bureau—2007 Economic Census (See Overview of 2007 Economic Census prior to Item 217)**

The Other Services, Except Public Administration sector (81) comprises establishments engaged in providing services not specifically categorized elsewhere in the classification system. Establishments in this sector are primarily engaged in activities such as equipment and machinery repairing, promoting or administering religious activities, grant making, and advocacy; this sector also includes establishments that provide dry-cleaning and laundry services, personal care services, death care services, pet care services, photofinishing services, temporary parking services, and dating services.

Private households that employ workers on or about the premises in activities primarily concerned with the operation of the household are included in this sector.

Excluded from this sector are establishments primarily engaged in retailing new equipment and performing repairs and general maintenance on equipment. These establishments are classified in sector 44–45, Retail Trade.

Industries in the **Repair and Maintenance** subsector (811) restore machinery, equipment, and other products to working order. These establishments also typically provide general or routine maintenance (i.e., servicing) on such products to ensure they work efficiently; this maintenance also helps prevent breakdowns and make certain repairs unnecessary.

The NAICS structure for this subsector brings together most types of repair and maintenance establishments and categorizes them based on production processes (i.e., on the type of repair and maintenance activity performed, and the necessary skills, expertise, and processes required for different repair and maintenance establishments). This NAICS classification does not delineate between repair services provided to businesses versus those provided to households. Although some industries primarily serve either businesses or households, separation by class of customer is limited by the fact that many establishments serve both types. Establishments that repair computers and consumer electronics products are examples of such overlap.

The Repair and Maintenance subsector does not include all establishments engaged in repair and maintenance. For example, a substantial amount of repair is done by establishments that also manufacture machinery, equipment, and other goods. These establishments are included in the Manufacturing sector in NAICS. In addition, the repairing of transportation equipment is often provided by or based at transportation facilities, such as airports and seaports; these activities are included in the Transportation and Warehousing sector.

A particularly unique situation exists with repair of buildings. Plumbing, electrical installation and repair, painting and decorating, and other construction-related establishments are often involved in performing installation or other work on new construction, while also providing repair services on existing structures. Although some establishments do specialize in repair, it is difficult to distinguish between these two types. Thus, all such establishments are included in the Construction sector.

Excluded from this subsector are establishments primarily engaged in rebuilding or remanufacturing machinery and equipment. These are classified in sector 31–33, Manufacturing. Also excluded are retail establishments that provide after-sale services and repair. These are classified in sector 44–45, Retail Trade.

Industries in the **Personal and Laundry Services** subsector (812) include establishments that provide personal and laundry services to individuals, households, and businesses. Services performed include personal care services, death care services, laundry and dry-cleaning services, and a wide range of other personal services, such as pet care (except veterinary) services, photofinishing services, temporary parking services, and dating services.

The Personal and Laundry Services subsector is by no means all-inclusive of the activities that could be termed personal services (i.e., those provided to individuals rather than businesses). There are many other sectors and subsectors that provide services to persons. Establishments providing legal, accounting, tax preparation, architectural, portrait photography, and similar professional services are classified in sector 54, Professional, Scientific, and Technical Services; those providing job placement, travel arrangement, home security, interior and exterior house cleaning, exterminating, lawn and garden care, and similar support services are classified in sector 56, Administrative and Support and Waste Management and Remediation Services; those providing health and social services are classified in sector 62, Health Care and Social Assistance; those providing amusement and recreation services are classified in sector 71, Arts, Entertainment and Recreation; those providing educational instruction are classified in sector 61, Educational Services; those providing repair services are classified in subsector 811, Repair and Maintenance; and those providing spiritual, civic, and advocacy services are classified in subsector 813, Religious, Grantmaking, Civic, Professional, and Similar Organizations.

Industries in the **Religious, Grantmaking, Civic, Professional, and Similar Organizations** subsector (813) include establishments that organize and promote religious activities, support various causes through grant making, advocate various social and political causes, and promote and defend the interests of their members. This category includes only tax-exempt establishments.

The industry groups within the subsector are defined in terms of their activities, separately grouping establishments that provide funding for specific causes or for a variety of charitable causes, establishments that advocate and actively promote causes and beliefs for the public good, and establishments that have an active membership structure to promote causes and represent the interests of their members. Establishments in this subsector may publish newsletters, books, and periodicals for distribution to their membership.

# GOVERNMENT EMPLOYMENT, Items 309–311
## Source: U.S. Bureau of Economic Analysis—Regional Economic Accounts
http://www.bea.gov/regional/index.htm#state

Employment is measured as the average annual sum of full-time and part-time jobs. The estimates are on a place-of-work basis. Data for federal civilian employment include civilian employees of the Department of Defense. Military employment includes all persons on active duty status.

# FEDERAL FUNDS, Items 312–330
## Source: U.S. Census Bureau—Consolidated Federal Funds Report
http://www.census.gov/govs/cffr/

Data on federal expenditure and obligations are obtained from a report prepared by the Census Bureau in accordance with the Consolidated Federal Funds Report (CFFR) Act of 1982 (P.L. 97-326). The data are for federal fiscal years beginning October 1 and ending the following September 30.

**Salaries and wages** represent actual federal expenditures during the fiscal year; the geographic distribution of these amounts by state and county was estimated based upon place of employment.

**Procurement contract awards** cover awards given by the United States Postal Service (USPS), as well as those given by all other federal agencies. Amounts provided by the USPS represent actual outlays for contractual commitments, while amounts for other agencies represent the value of obligations for contract actions and do not reflect actual federal government expenditures. In general, only current-year contract actions are included; however, multiple-year obligations may be reported for contract actions of less than 3 years' duration.

**Direct payments** for individuals include Social Security benefits, federal government retirement, Medicare, Supplemental Security Income, unemployment compensation, food stamps, agricultural and housing assistance, and other categories not shown separately. All data represent actual expenditures during the fiscal year.

Direct housing assistance primarily includes the Low Income Housing Assistance Program.

**Grants** data represent the federal obligations incurred at the time the grant is awarded. The amounts reported do not represent actual expenditures, since obligations in one time period may not result in outlays during the same period. Moreover, initial amounts obligated may be adjusted at a later date, through either enhancements or de-obligations.

Medicaid and other health-related grants include a variety of grants from the Department of Health and Human Services for health services and research.

Nutrition and family welfare grants include a variety of grants from the Department of Health and Human Services for child welfare, special programs for the aging, and related areas. The school lunch program and other nutritional assistance programs administered by the Department of Agriculture are also included in this category.

Disasters and emergency preparedness grants include assistance to fire-fighting and rescue organizations; community assistance for earthquakes, floods, hurricanes and other disasters; domestic preparedness programs; and similar activities.

Housing and community development grants include Community Development Block Grants, housing demonstration programs, rental housing rehabilitation, and other housing programs.

Employment and training grants include various job training programs, welfare-to-work grants, occupational safety and health grants, and similar employment related funds.

Energy and environment grants include grants from the Department of Energy for energy development, energy conservation, and nuclear waste disposal, as well as grants from the Environmental Protection Agency for a variety of pollution control and waste management activities.

## STATE GOVERNMENT FINANCES, Items 331–350
### Source: U.S. Census Bureau—State Government Finances
http://www.census.gov/govs/state/

Data are from an annual survey conducted by the Census Bureau and pertain to state government fiscal years ending on June 30, except for four states with other ending dates: Alabama and Michigan (September 30), New York (March 31), and Texas (August 31).

The state government finance data presented in this publication may differ from data published by state governments because the Census Bureau may be using a different definition of which organizations are covered under the term, "state government."

For the purpose of Census Bureau statistics, the term "state government" refers not only to the executive, legislative, and judicial branches of a given state, but it also includes agencies, institutions, commissions, and public authorities that operate separately or somewhat autonomously from the central state government but where the state government maintains administrative or fiscal control over their activities as defined by the Census Bureau.

Total **general revenue** includes all revenue except utility, liquor stores, and insurance trust revenue. All tax revenue and intergovernmental revenue, even if designated for employee-retirement or local utility purpose, are classified as general revenue.

**Intergovernmental revenue** covers amounts received from the federal government as fiscal aid, reimbursements for performance of general government functions and specific services for the paying government, or in lieu of taxes. It excludes any amounts received from other governments from the sale of property, commodities, and utility services.

**Taxes** consist of compulsory contributions exacted by governments for public purposes. However, this category excludes employer and employee payments for retirement and social insurance purposes, which are classified as insurance trust revenue; it also excludes special assessments, which are classified as non-tax general revenue. Sales and gross receipts taxes do not include dealer discounts, or "commissions" allowed to merchants for collection of taxes from consumers. General sales taxes and selected taxes on sales of motor fuels, tobacco products, and other particular commodities and services are included.

**General government expenditure** includes capital outlay, a major portion of which is commonly financed by borrowing. Government revenue does not include receipts from borrowing. Among other things, this distorts the relationship between totals of revenue and expenditure figures that are presented and renders it useless as a direct measure of the degree of budgetary "balance" (as that term is generally applied).

**Direct general expenditure** comprises all expenditures of the state governments, excluding utility, liquor stores, insurance trust expenditures, and any intergovernmental payments.

State government expenditure for **education** is mainly for the provision and general support of schools and other educational facilities and services, including those for educational institutions beyond high school. They cover such related services as student transportation; school lunch and other cafeteria operations; school health, recreation, and library services; and dormitories, dining halls, and bookstores operated by public institutions of higher education.

**Health and hospitals expenditure** includes health research; clinics; nursing; immunization; other categorical, environmental, and general health services provided by health agencies; establishment and operation of hospital facilities; provision of hospital care; and support of other public and private hospitals.

**Highways expenditure** is for the provision and maintenance of highway facilities, including toll turnpikes, bridges, tunnels, and ferries, as well as regular roads, highways, and streets. Also included are expenditures for street lighting and for snow and ice removal. Not included are highway policing and traffic control, which are considered part of police protection

**Public safety expenditure** includes police and correctional institution expenditures.

**Public welfare expenditure** covers support of and assistance to needy persons; this aid is contingent upon the person's needs. Included are cash assistance paid directly to needy persons under categorical (Old Age Assistance, Temporary Assistance for Needy Families, Aid to the Blind, and Aid to the Disabled) and other welfare programs; vendor payments made directly to private purveyors for medical care, burials, and other commodities and services provided under welfare programs; welfare institutions; and any intergovernmental or other direct expenditure for welfare purposes. Pensions to former employees and other benefits not contingent on need are excluded.

**Natural resources, parks, and recreation** includes expenditures for conservation, promotion, and development of natural resources (soil, water, energy, minerals, etc.) and the regulation of industries which develop, utilize, or affect natural resources. It also includes the provision and support of recreational and cultural-scientific facilities, such as golf courses, playgrounds, tennis courts, public beaches, swimming pools, play fields, parks, camping areas, recreational piers and marinas, galleries, museums, zoos, botanical gardens, auditoriums, stadiums, recreational centers, convention centers, exhibition halls, community music, drama, and celebrations.

**Debt outstanding** includes all long-term debt obligations of the government and its agencies (exclusive of utility debt) and all interest-bearing, short-term (repayable within one year) debt obligations remaining unpaid at the close of the fiscal year. It includes judgments, mortgages, and revenue bonds, as well as general obligation bonds, notes, and interest-bearing warrants. This category consists of non-interest-bearing, short-term obligations; inter-fund obligations; amounts owed in a trust or agency capacity; advances and contingent loans from other governments; and rights of individuals to benefit from government-administered employee-retirement funds.

## VOTING AND REGISTRATION, Items 351 and 352

**Source: U.S. Census Bureau—Current Population Survey**
**http://www.census.gov/hhes/www/socdemo/voting/index.html**

These estimates are based on the November 2012 Voting and Registration Supplement to the Current Population Survey (CPS).

Voting rates are calculated using the voting-age population, which includes both citizens and noncitizens. Statistics from surveys are subject to sampling and nonsampling error. The CPS estimate of overall turnout differs from the ''official'' turnout reported by the Clerk of the House of Representatives.

## ELECTION STATISTICS, Items 353–355

**Source: Election Data Services, Inc. Washington, DC (copyright)**
**http://www.electiondataservices.com/**

© 2013 Election Data Services, Inc. All rights reserved. This material is proprietary and the subject of copyright protection and other intellectual property rights owned by or licensed to Election Data Services, Inc. The use of this material is subject to the terms of a License Agreement. You will be held liable for any unauthorized copying or disclosure of this material.

Election results show the percentage of the total vote cast for the Democratic and Republican candidates, as well as the combined percentage for all other candidates in the 2012 presidential election.

# TABLE B—STATES AND COUNTIES

Table B presents 199 items for the United States as a whole, each individual state, and the District of Columbia; and every county, county equivalent, and independent city. The counties are presented in alphabetical order within each state, and the states are also presented in alphabetical order. Independent cities, which are found in Maryland, Missouri, Nevada, and Virginia, are placed in alphabetical order at the end of the list of counties for those states. The District of Columbia is included in Table B as both a county and a state. It is also included as a city in Table D.

## LAND AREA, Items 1 and 4
**Source: U.S. Census Bureau—2010 Census of Population and Housing**
**http://2010.census.gov/2010census/data/**

Land area measurements are shown to the nearest square kilometer. Land area includes dry land and land temporarily or partially covered by water, such as marshlands, swamps, and river floodplains.

## POPULATION, Items 2–4
**Source: U.S. Census Bureau—Population Estimates**
**http://www. census.gov.popest/estimates.html**

The population data are Census Bureau estimates of the resident population as of July 1 of the year shown. The ranks are shown for counties (including independent cities and the District of Columbia).

## POPULATION AND POPULATION CHARACTERISTICS, Items 5–19
**Source: U.S. Census Bureau—Population Estimates**
**http://www.census.gov/popest/estimates.html**

The concept of race, as used by the Census Bureau, reflects self-identification by persons according to the race or races with which they most closely identify. These categories are sociopolitical constructs and should not be interpreted as being scientific or anthropological in nature. Furthermore, race categories include both racial and national origin groups.

Beginning with the 2000 census, respondents were offered the option of selecting one or more races. This option was not available in prior censuses; thus, comparisons between censuses should be made with caution. In Table B, Columns 5 through 8 refer to individuals who identified with each racial category, either alone or in combination with other races. The estimates exclude persons of Hispanic or Latino origin from all race groups. Because respondents could include as many categories as they wished, and because the columns refer to the percentage of the population, the total will often exceed 100 percent.

The **White** population is defined as persons who indicated their race as White, as well as persons who did not classify themselves in one of the specific race categories listed on the questionnaire but entered a nationality such as Irish, German, Italian, Lebanese, Near Easterner, Arab, or Polish.

The **Black** population includes persons who indicated their race as ''Black, African Am., or Negro,'' as well as persons who did not classify themselves in one of the specific race categories but reported entries such as African American, Afro American, Kenyan, Nigerian, or Haitian.

The **American Indian or Alaska Native** population includes persons who indicated their race as American Indian or Alaska Native, as well as persons who did not classify themselves in one of the specific race categories but reported entries such as Canadian Indian, French-American Indian, Spanish-American Indian, Eskimo, Aleut, Alaska Indian, or any of the American Indian or Alaska Native tribes.

The **Asian and Pacific Islander** population combines two census groupings: **Asian** and **Native Hawaiian or Other Pacific Islander**. The **Asian** population includes persons who indicated their race as Asian Indian, Chinese, Filipino, Japanese, Korean, Vietnamese, or ''Other Asian,'' as well as persons who provided write-in entries of such groups as Cambodian, Laotian, Hmong, Pakistani, or Taiwanese. The **Native Hawaiian or Other Pacific Islander** population includes persons who indicated their race as ''Native Hawaiian,'' ''Guamanian or Chamorro,'' ''Samoan,'' or ''Other Pacific Islander,'' as well as persons who reported entries such as Part Hawaiian, American Samoan, Fijian, Melanesian, or Tahitian. Because this is a combined group, it sometimes double-counts persons who are both Asian and Native Hawaiian or Other Pacific Islander.

The **Hispanic population** is based on a question that asked respondents ''Is this person Spanish/Hispanic/Latino?'' Persons marking any one of the four Hispanic categories (i.e., Mexican, Puerto Rican, Cuban, or other Spanish) are collectively referred to as Hispanic.

In the census, the Hispanic origin question was placed before the race question and specific instructions indicated that both questions should be answered. These changes were designed to improve accuracy and may affect comparability with data prior to the 2000 census.

**Age** is defined as age at last birthday (number of completed years since birth), as of April 1 of the census year. The census also asked for the specific date of birth of the respondent, and census procedures used the birth date for deriving age data. For this reason, it is likely that the data have fewer problems than data from censuses prior to 2000, such as the tendency of respondents to round ages or to report their ages on the date the questionnaire was filled out rather than on April 1.

The **female** population is shown as a percentage of total population.

## POPULATION AND COMPONENTS OF CHANGE, Items 20–26
**Source: U.S. Census Bureau—Decennial Censuses and Population Estimates**
**http://www.census.gov/main/www/cen2000.html**
**http://www.census.gov/popest/estimates.html**
**http://2010.census.gov/2010census/data/**

The population data for 1990, 2000, and 2010 are from the decennial censuses and represent the resident population as of April 1 of those years. The components of change are based on Census Bureau estimates of the resident population as of July 1,

2012. The change in population between 2010 and 2012 is made up of (a) natural increase—births minus deaths, and (b) net migration—the difference between the number of persons moving into a particular area and the number of persons moving out of the area. Net migration is composed of internal and international migration.

Because the 2012 population estimates are based on a model that begins with a national population estimate, the county components of change do not always exactly add up to the difference between the 2010 census population and the 2012 estimates.

## HOUSEHOLDS, Items 27–31
### Source: U.S. Census Bureau—2010 Census of Population and Housing
### http://2010.census.gov/2010census/data/

A **household** includes all of the persons who occupy a housing unit. (Persons not living in households are classified as living in group quarters.) A housing unit is a house, an apartment, a mobile home, a group of rooms, or a single room occupied (or, if vacant, intended for occupancy) as separate living quarters. Separate living quarters are those in which the occupants live separately from any other persons in the building and have direct access from the outside of the building or through a common hall. The occupants may be a single family, one person living alone, two or more families living together, or any other group of related or unrelated persons who share living quarters. The number of households is the same as the number of year-round occupied housing units.

A **family** includes a householder and one or more other persons living in the same household who are related to the householder by birth, marriage, or adoption. All persons in a household who are related to the householder are regarded as members of his or her family. A **family household** may contain persons not related to the householder; thus, family households may include more members than families do. A household can contain only one family for the purposes of census tabulations. Not all households contain families, as a household may comprise a group of unrelated persons or of one person living alone. Families are classified by type as either a ''husband-wife family'' or ''other family,'' according to the presence or absence of a spouse.

The measure of **persons per household** is obtained by dividing the number of persons in households by the number of households or householders. One person in each household is designated as the householder. In most cases, this is the person (or one of the persons) in whose name the house is owned, being bought, or rented. If there is no such person in the household, any adult household member 15 years old and over can be designated as the householder.

The category **female family householder** includes only female-headed family households with no spouse present.

## GROUP QUARTERS, Item 32
### Source: U.S. Census Bureau—2010 Census of Population and Housing
### http://2010.census.gov/2010census/data/

The Census Bureau classifies all persons not living in households as living in group quarters; this category includes both the institutional and noninstitutional populations. The institutionalized population includes persons under formally authorized, supervised care or custody in institutions, such as correctional institutions, nursing homes, mental (psychiatric) hospitals, and juvenile institutions. The noninstitutionalized population includes persons who live in group quarters other than institutions, such as college dormitories, military quarters, and group homes. This volume includes the total number of persons in group quarters.

## DAYTIME POPULATION, Items 33 and 34
### Source: U.S. Census Bureau—American Community Survey, 2007–2011
### http://www.census.gov/acs/www/

Daytime population refers to the number of persons who are present in an area or place during normal business hours, including workers. This can be contrasted with the ''resident'' population, which is present during the evening and nighttime hours. The daytime population estimate is calculated by adding the total resident population and the total workers working in the area/place, and then subtracting the total workers living in the area/place from that result. Information on the expansion or contraction experienced by different communities between their nighttime and daytime populations is important for many planning purposes, especially those concerning transportation, disaster, and relief operations.

The employment/residence ratio is a measure of the total number of workers working in an area or place, relative to the total number of workers living in the area or place. It is often used as a rough indication of the jobs-workers balance in an area/place, although it does not take into account whether the resident workers possess the skills needed for the jobs available in their particular area/place. The employment/residence ratio is calculated by dividing the number of total workers working in an area/place by the number of total workers residing in the area/place.

## BIRTHS AND DEATHS, Items 35–38
### Source: U.S. Census Bureau—Population Estimates
### http://www.census.gov/popest/estimates.html

The numbers of births and deaths are from the Census Bureau's Population Estimates Program. They represent the total number of live births and deaths occurring to residents of an area as estimated using reports from the National Center for Health Statistics (NCHS) and the Federal-State Cooperative for Population Estimates (FSCPE). The rates measure births and deaths during the specified time period as a proportion of an area's population. Rates are expressed per 1,000 population estimated as of July 1. These numbers and rates do not represent the calendar year, but rather the year-long period ending on July 1.

## PERSONS UNDER 65 WITH NO HEALTH INSURANCE, Items 39 and 40
### Source: U.S. Census Bureau—Small Area Health Insurance Estimates
### http://www.census.gov/did/www/sahie/index.html

The Small Area Health Insurance Estimates (SAHIE) program develops model-based estimates of health insurance coverage for counties and states. This developmental program builds on the work of the Small Area Income and Poverty Estimates (SAIPE) program. The SAHIE program models health insurance coverage by combining survey data with population estimates and administrative records. The estimates are based on data from The Annual Social and Economic Supplement (ASEC) of the Current Population Survey (CPS); Demographic population estimates; Aggregated federal tax returns; Participation records for the Supplemental Nutrition Assistance Program (SNAP), formerly known as the Food Stamp program; County Business Patterns; Medicaid and Children's Health Insurance Program (CHIP) participation records; and Census 2000.

## MEDICARE ENROLLMENT, Items 41–43

**Source: U.S. Department of Health and Human Services, Centers for Medicare and Medicaid Services**
http://www.cms.hhs.gov/MCRAdvPartDEnrolData/
http://www.cms.hhs.gov/DataCompendium/

The Centers for Medicare and Medicaid Services (CMS) administers Medicare, which provides health insurance to persons 65 years old and over, persons with permanent kidney failure, and certain persons with disabilities. Original Medicare has two parts: Hospital Insurance and Supplemental Medical Insurance. In recent years, Medicare has been expanded to include two new programs: Medicare Advantage plans and prescription drug coverage. Medicare Advantage Plans are health plan options that are approved by Medicare but run by private companies. Medicare prescription drug plans can be part of Medicare Advantage plans or stand-alone drug plans.

Persons who are **eligible** for Medicare can enroll in Part A (Hospital Insurance) at no charge, and can choose to pay a monthly premium to enroll in Part B. Most eligible persons are enrolled in Part A, and more than 90 percent of enrollees in Part A are also enrolled in Part B (Supplemental Medical Insurance.) This table includes persons who were eligible as of December 2010.

**Medicare Advantage** enrollees were enrolled in a Medicare Advantage plan of some type at the end of 2010. These include Private Fee for Service plans, Preferred Provider Organizations, Health Maintenance Organizations, Medical Savings Account Plans, Demonstration plans, and Programs for All-Inclusive Care for the Elderly.

Persons enrolled in a **Medicare Prescription drug plan** were enrolled in stand-alone plans for prescription drug benefits. This number does not include Medicare enrollees who had prescription drug coverage through private or federal retiree health plans, through Medicare Advantage plans, or through Medicaid.

## CRIME, Items 44–47

**Source: U.S. Federal Bureau of Investigation—Uniform Crime Reports**
http://www.fbi.gov/ucr/ucr.htm

Crime data are as reported to the Federal Bureau of Investigation (FBI) by law enforcement agencies and have not been adjusted for underreporting. This may affect comparability between geographic areas or over time.

Through the voluntary contribution of crime statistics by law enforcement agencies across the United States, the Uniform Crime Reporting (UCR) Program provides periodic assessments of crime in the nation as measured by offenses that have come to the attention of the law enforcement community. The Committee on Uniform Crime Records of the International Association of Chiefs of Police initiated this voluntary national data collection effort in 1930. The UCR Program contributors compile and submit their crime data either directly to the FBI or through state-level UCR Programs.

Seven offenses, because of their severity, frequency of occurrence, and likelihood of being reported to police, were initially selected to serve as an index for evaluating fluctuations in the volume of crime. These serious crimes were murder and nonnegligent manslaughter, forcible rape, robbery, aggravated assault, burglary, larceny-theft, and motor vehicle theft. By congressional mandate, arson was added as the eighth index offense in 1979. The totals shown in this volume do not include arson.

In 2004, the FBI discontinued the use of the Crime Index in the UCR Program and its publications, stating that the Crime Index was driven upward by the offense with the highest number of cases (in this case, larceny-theft), creating a bias against jurisdictions with a high number of larceny-thefts but a low number of other serious crimes, such as murder and forcible rape. The FBI is currently publishing a violent crime total and property crime total until a more viable index is developed. This book includes the crime total, as well as violent crime and property crime rates.

**Violent crimes** include four categories of offenses: (1) Murder and nonnegligent manslaughter, as defined in the UCR Program, is the willful (nonnegligent) killing of one human being by another. This offense excludes deaths caused by negligence, suicide, or accident; justifiable homicides; and attempts to murder or assaults to murder. (2) Forcible rape is the carnal knowledge of a female forcibly and against her will. Assaults or attempts to commit rape by force or threat of force are also included; however, statutory rape (without force) and other sex offenses are excluded. (3) Robbery is the taking or attempting to take anything of value from the care, custody, or control of a person or persons by force or threat of force or violence and/or by putting the victim in fear. (4) Aggravated assault is an unlawful attack by one person upon another for the purpose of inflicting severe or aggravated bodily injury. This type of assault is usually accompanied by the use of a weapon or by other means likely to produce death or great bodily harm. Attempts are included, since injury does not necessarily have to result when a gun, knife, or other weapon is used, as these incidents could and probably would result in a serious personal injury if the crime were successfully completed.

**Property crimes** include three categories: (1) Burglary, or breaking and entering, is the unlawful entry of a structure to commit a felony or theft, even though no force was used to gain entrance. (2) Larceny-theft is the unauthorized taking of the personal property of another, without the use of force. (3) Motor vehicle theft is the unauthorized taking of any motor vehicle.

Rates are based on population estimates provided by the FBI. The county totals published in this volume were obtained by aggregating individual reporting units within each county and MSA. If the population total for the units aggregated was less than 75 percent of the county's population (as estimated by the Census Bureau), the total was not considered representative of the county as a whole and was not published. State and U.S. totals include FBI estimates for those areas. State and U.S. totals in this table are the adjusted totals as published in the FBI's *Crime in the United States*.

## EDUCATION—SCHOOL ENROLLMENT AND EDUCATIONAL ATTAINMENT, Items 48–51
**Source: U.S. Census Bureau—American Community Survey, 2007–2011**
**http://www.census.gov/acs/www/**

Persons were classified as enrolled in school if they reported attending a "regular" public or private school (or college) during the three months preceding the interview. The instructions were to include only nursery school, kindergarten, elementary school, and schooling which would lead to a high school diploma or a college degree as regular school. The Census Bureau defines a public school as "any school or college controlled and supported by a local, county, state, or federal government." Schools primarily supported and controlled by religious organizations or other private groups are defined as private schools.

Data on **educational attainment** are tabulated for the population 25 years old and over. The data were derived from a question that asked respondents for the highest level of school completed or the highest degree received. Persons who had passed a high school equivalency examination were considered high school graduates. Schooling received in foreign schools was to be reported as the equivalent grade or years in the regular American school system.

Vocational and technical training, such as barber school training; business, trade, technical, and vocational schools; or other training for a specific trade are specifically excluded.

**High school graduate or less**. This category includes persons whose highest degree was a high school diploma or its equivalent, and those who reported any level lower than a high school diploma.

**Bachelor's degree or more.** This category includes persons who have received bachelor's degrees, master's degrees, professional school degrees (such as law school or medical school degrees), and doctoral degrees.

## LOCAL GOVERNMENT EDUCATION EXPENDITURES, Items 52 and 53
**Source: U.S. Department of Education, National Center for Education Statistics—Common Core of Data**
**http://nces.ed.gov/ccd/f33agency.asp**

Total expenditure for education includes provision or support of schools and facilities for elementary and secondary education. It encompasses instructional, support, and auxiliary services (school lunch, student activities, and community service) offered by public school systems. Retirement benefits paid to former education employees and interest payments are not included. Current expenditure includes all components of total expenditure except capital outlay. Expenditure data are obtained by the Census Bureau through its annual survey of government finances and are supplied to the National Center for Education Statistics (NCES). Current expenditure per student is current expenditure divided by the number of students enrolled. The number of students

enrolled is based on an annual "membership" count of students on or about October 1.

NCES uses the Common Core of Data (CCD) Survey system to acquire and maintain statistical data from each of the 50 states, the District of Columbia, and the outlying areas. State education agencies compile and submit data for approximately 85,000 schools and 15,000 local school districts. Typically, this results in varying interpretation of NCES definitions and different record keeping systems, leading to large amounts of missing data for several states; this absence is reflected in the data in this publication. Schools and school districts are included in the county in which the school district offices (the local education agency) are located.

The state totals in this table are aggregated from the agencies in this file, sometimes resulting in different numbers from the state data in Table A.

## MONEY INCOME, Items 54–57
**Source: U.S. Census Bureau—American Community Survey, 2007–2011**
**http://www.census.gov/acs/www/**

**Total money income** is the sum of the amounts reported separately for wage or salary income; net self-employment income; interest, dividends, or net rental or royalty income or income from estates and trusts; Social Security or railroad retirement income; Supplemental Security Income (SSI); public assistance or welfare payments; retirement, survivor, or disability pensions; and all other income. Receipts from the following sources are not included as income: capital gains; money received from the sale of property (unless the recipient was engaged in the business of selling such property); the value of income "in kind" from food stamps, public housing subsidies, medical care, employer contributions for individuals, etc.; withdrawal of bank deposits; money borrowed; tax refunds; exchange of money between relatives living in the same household; and gifts, lump-sum inheritances, insurance payments, and other types of lump-sum receipts.

Money income differs in definition from personal income (item 62). For example, money income does not include the pension rights, employer provided health insurance, food stamps, or Medicare payments that are included in personal income.

**Per capita income** is the mean income computed for every man, woman, and child in a particular group. It is derived by dividing the aggregate income of a particular group by the resident population in that group as estimated in the American Community Survey. Per capita income is rounded to the nearest whole dollar.

**Household income** includes the income of the householder and all other individuals 15 years old and over in the household, whether or not they are related to the householder. Since many households consist of only one person, median household income is usually less than median family income. Although the household income statistics cover the 12 months preceding the interview, the characteristics of individuals and the composition of households refer to the date of interview. Thus, the income of the household does not include amounts received by individuals who were no longer residing in the household at the time of interview. Similarly, income amounts reported by individuals who did not reside in the household during all of the past 12 months but who were members of the household at the time of interview are included. However, the composition of most households was the same during those 12 months as it was at the time of interview.

**Median income** divides the income distribution into two equal parts, with half of all cases below the median income level and half of all cases above the median income level. For households, the median income is based on the distribution of the total number of households, including those with no income. Median income for households is computed on the basis of a standard distribution with a minimum value of less than $2,500 and a maximum value of $200,000 or more and is rounded to the nearest whole dollar. Median income figures are calculated using linear interpolation if the width of the interval containing the estimate is $2,500 or less. If the width of the interval containing the estimate is greater than $2,500, Pareto interpolation is used.

Income amounts have been adjusted for inflation to represent the final year of multi-year estimates, in this case 2007–2011 estimates. The constant-dollar figures are based on an annual average Consumer Price Index from the Bureau of Labor Statistics. Constant-dollar figures are estimates representing an effort to remove the effects of price changes from statistical series reported in dollar terms. However, the estimates do not reflect the price and cost-of-living differences that may exist between areas.

## INCOME AND POVERTY, Items 58–61

**Source: U.S. Census Bureau—Small Area Income and Poverty Estimates Program**
http://www.census.gov/did/www/saipe/index.html

The 2011 income and poverty estimates by county are constructed from statistical models that relate income and poverty to indicators based on summary data from federal income tax returns, data about participation in the Food Stamp program, and the previous census. A regression model predicts the number of people in poverty using county-level observations from the current year's American Community Survey (ACS) and administrative records and census data as the predictors. The 2005 estimates were the first to use the ACS. Prior year models were based on the Annual Social and Economic Supplement (ASEC) of the Current Population Survey (CPS). The ACS is a much larger survey than the ASEC, permitting income and poverty estimates based on a single year for many counties, Because of the differences between the two surveys, caution should be used when comparing these estimates with those from earlier years.

The **poverty status** data were derived from data collected on the number of persons in a household, each person's relationship to the householder, and income data. The Social Security Administration (SSA) developed the original poverty definition in 1964, which federal interagency committees subsequently revised in 1969 and 1980. The Office of Management and Budget's (OMB) *Directive 14* prescribes the SSA's definition as the official poverty measure for federal agencies to use in their statistical work. Poverty statistics presented in American Community Survey products adhere to the standards defined by OMB in *Directive 14*.

Poverty thresholds vary depending on three criteria: size of family, number of children, and, for one- and two-person families, age of householder. In determining the poverty status of families and unrelated individuals, the Census Bureau uses thresholds (income cutoffs) arranged in a two-dimensional matrix. The matrix consists of family size (from one person to nine or more persons), cross-classified by presence and number of family members under 18 years old (from no children present to eight or more children present). Unrelated individuals and two-person families are further differentiated by age of reference person (under 65 years old and 65 years old and over). To determine a person's poverty status, the person's total family income over the previous 12 months is compared with the poverty threshold appropriate for that person's family size and composition. If the total income of that person's family is less than the threshold appropriate for that family, then the person is considered poor or "below the poverty level," together with every member of his or her family. If a person is not living with anyone related by birth, marriage, or adoption, then the person's own income is compared with his or her poverty threshold. The total number of persons below the poverty level is the sum of persons in families and the number of unrelated individuals with incomes below the poverty level over the previous 12 months.

**Poverty Thresholds for 2011 by Size of Family and Number of Related Children Under 18 Years**

| Size of family unit | Weighted average thresholds |
|---|---|
| One person (unrelated individual) | 11,484 |
|     Under 65 years | 11,702 |
|     65 years and over | 10,788 |
| Two people | 14,657 |
|     Householder under 65 years | 15,139 |
|     Householder 65 years and over | 13,609 |
| Three people | 17,916 |
| Four people | 23,021 |
| Five people | 27,251 |
| Six people | 30,847 |
| Seven people | 35,085 |
| Eight people | 39,064 |
| Nine people or more | 46,572 |

**Source: U.S. Census Bureau.**

## PERSONAL INCOME AND EARNINGS, Items 62–83

**Source: U.S. Bureau of Economic Analysis, Regional Economic Accounts**
http://www.bea.gov/regional/index.htm#state

**Total personal income** is the current income received by residents of an area from all sources. It is measured before deductions of income and other personal taxes, but after deductions of personal contributions for Social Security, government retirement, and other social insurance programs. It consists of **wage and salary disbursements** (covering all employee earnings, including executive salaries, bonuses, commissions, payments-in-kind, incentive payments, and tips); various types of supplementary earnings, such as employers' contributions to pension funds (termed "other labor income" or "supplements to wages and salaries"); proprietors' income; rental income of persons; dividends; personal interest income; and government and business transfer payments.

**Per capita personal income** is based on the resident population estimated as of July 1 of the year shown.

**Proprietors' income** is the monetary income and income-in-kind of proprietorships and partnerships (including the independent professions) and the income of tax-exempt cooperatives. **Dividends** are cash payments by corporations to stockholders who are U.S. residents. **Interest** is the monetary and imputed interest income of persons from all sources. **Rent** is the monetary income of persons from the rental of real property, except the income of persons primarily engaged in the real estate business; the imputed net rental income of owner-occupants of nonfarm dwellings; and the royalties received by persons.

**Transfer payments** are income for which services are not currently rendered. They consist of both government and business transfer payments. Government transfer payments include payments under the following programs: Federal Old-Age, Survivors, and Disability Insurance (''Social Security''); Medicare and medical vendor payments; unemployment insurance; railroad and government retirement; federal- and state-government-insured workers' compensation; veterans' benefits, including veterans' life insurance; food stamps; black lung payments; Supplemental Security Income; and Temporary Assistance for Needy Families. Government payments to nonprofit institutions, other than for work under research and development contracts, are also included. Business transfer payments consist primarily of liability payments for personal injury and of corporate gifts to nonprofit institutions.

Personal income differs in definition from money income (items 54–57). For example, personal income includes pension rights, employer-provided health insurance, food stamps, and Medicare. These are not included in the definition of money income.

**Earnings** cover wage and salary disbursements, other labor income, and proprietors' income.

The data for earnings obtained from the Bureau of Economic Analysis (BEA) are based on place of work. In computing personal income, BEA makes an ''adjustment for residence'' to earnings, based on commuting patterns; personal income is thus presented on a place-of-residence basis.

**Farm** earnings include the income of farm workers (wages and salaries and other labor income) and farm proprietors. Farm proprietors' income includes only the income of sole proprietorships and partnerships. Farm earnings estimates are benchmarked to data collected in the Census of Agriculture and the revised Department of Agriculture statistical totals of income and expense items.

**Goods-related** industries include mining, construction, and manufacturing. **Service-related** and other industries include private-sector earnings in agricultural services, forestry, and fisheries; transportation and public utilities; wholesale trade; retail trade; finance, insurance, and real estate; and services. Government earnings include all levels of government. Industries are categorized under the North American Industry Classification System (NAICS), and are not comparable to years prior to 2002.

## SOCIAL SECURITY AND SUPPLEMENTAL SECURITY INCOME, Items 84–86

**Source: U.S. Social Security Administration**
http://www.ssa.gov/policy/docs/statcomps/oasdisc/
http://www.ssa.gov/policy/docs/statcomps/ssisc/

Social Security beneficiaries are persons receiving benefits under the Old-Age, Survivors, and Disability Insurance Program. These include retired or disabled workers covered by the program, their spouses and dependent children, and the surviving spouses and dependent children of deceased workers.

Supplemental Security Income (SSI) recipients are persons receiving SSI payments. The SSI program is a cash assistance program that provides monthly benefits to low-income aged, blind, or disabled persons.

Data are as of December of the year shown.

## HOUSING, Items 87–96

**Source: U.S. Census Bureau—2010 Census of Population and Housing**
http://2010.census.gov/2010census/data/
**Source: U.S. Census Bureau—American Community Survey, 2007–2011**
http://www.census.gov/acs/www/

Housing data for 2010 are from the 2010 census. Housing unit characteristics for 2007–2011 are from the American Community Survey.

A **housing unit** is a house, apartment, mobile home or trailer, group of rooms, or single room occupied or, if vacant, intended for occupancy as separate living quarters. Separate living quarters are those in which the occupants do not live and eat with any other person in the structure and which have direct access from the outside of the building or through a common hall.

The occupants of a housing unit may be a single family, one person living alone, two or more families living together, or any other group of related or unrelated persons who share living quarters. Both occupied and vacant housing units are included in the housing inventory, although recreational vehicles, tents, caves, boats, railroad cars, and the like are included only if they are occupied as a person's usual place of residence.

A housing unit is classified as occupied if it is the usual place of residence of the person or group of persons living in it at the time of enumeration, or if the occupants are only temporarily absent (away on vacation). A household consists of all persons who occupy a housing unit as their usual place of residence. Vacant units for sale or rent include units rented or sold but not occupied and any other units held off the market.

**Median value** is the dollar amount that divides the distribution of specified owner-occupied housing units into two equal parts, with half of all units below the median value and half of all units above the median value. Value is defined as the respondent's estimate of what the house would sell for if it were for sale. Data are presented for single-family units on fewer than 10 acres of land that have no business or medical offices on the property.

**Median rent** divides the distribution of renter-occupied housing units into two equal parts. The rent concept used in this volume is gross rent, which includes the amount of cash rent a renter pays (contract rent) plus the estimated average cost of utilities and fuels, if these are paid by the renter. The rent is the amount of rent only for living quarters and excludes amounts paid for any business or other space occupied. Single-family houses on lots of 10 or more acres of land are also excluded.

**Housing cost** as a percentage of income is shown separately for owners with mortgages, owners without mortgages, and renters. Rent as a percentage of income is a computed ratio of gross rent and monthly household income (total household income in 1999 divided by 12). Selected owner costs include utilities and fuels, mortgage payments, insurance, taxes, etc. In each case, the ratio of housing cost to income is computed separately for each housing unit. The housing cost ratios for half of all units are above the median shown in this book, and half are below the median shown in the book.

**Substandard units** are occupied units that are overcrowded or lack complete plumbing facilities. For the purposes of this item, ''overcrowded'' is defined as having 1.01 persons or more per room. Complete plumbing facilities include hot and cold piped water, a flush toilet, and a bathtub or shower. These facilities must be located inside the housing unit, but do not have to be in the same room.

## CIVILIAN LABOR FORCE AND UNEMPLOYMENT, Items 97–100
### Source: U.S. Bureau of Labor Statistics—Local Area Unemployment Statistics
http://www.bls.gov/lau/#tables

Data for the civilian labor force are the product of a federal-state cooperative program in which state employment security agencies prepare labor force and unemployment estimates under concepts, definitions, and technical procedures established by the Bureau of Labor Statistics (BLS). The civilian labor force consists of all civilians 16 years old and over who are either employed or unemployed.

Unemployment includes all persons who did not work during the survey week, made specific efforts to find a job during the previous four weeks, and were available for work during the survey week (except for temporary illness). Persons waiting to be called back to a job from which they had been laid off and those waiting to report to a new job within the next 30 days are included in unemployment figures.

Table B includes annual average data for the year shown. The Local Area Unemployment Statistics data are periodically updated to reflect revised inputs, reestimation, and controlling to new statewide totals.

## CIVILIAN EMPLOYMENT, Items 101–103
### Source: U.S. Census Bureau—American Community Survey, 2007–2011
http://www.census.gov/acs/www/

**Total employment** includes all civilians 16 years old and over who were either (1) ''at work''—those who did any work at all during the reference week as paid employees, worked in either their own business or profession, worked on their own farm, or worked 15 hours or more as unpaid workers in a family farm or business; or were (2) ''with a job, but not at work'' —those who

had a job but were not at work that week due to illness, weather, industrial dispute, vacation, or other personal reasons.

The **occupational categories** are based on the occupational classification system that was developed for the 2000 census and revised in 2002 and 2010. This system consists of 539 specific occupational categories for employed persons arranged into 23 major occupational groups. This classification was developed based on the *Standard Occupational Classification (SOC) Manual: 2000*, published by the Executive Office of the President, Office of Management and Budget.

## PRIVATE NONFARM EMPLOYMENT AND EARNINGS, Items 104–112
### Source: U.S. Bureau of Labor Statistics—County Business Patterns
http://www.census.gov/econ/cbp/index.html

Data for private nonfarm employment and earnings are compiled from the payroll information reported monthly in the Census Bureau publication *County Business Patterns*. The estimates are based on surveys conducted by the Census Bureau and administrative records from the Internal Revenue Service (IRS).

The following types of employment are excluded from the tables: government employment, self-employed persons, farm workers, and domestic service workers. Railroad employment jointly covered by Social Security and railroad retirement programs, employment on oceanborne vessels, and employment in foreign countries are also excluded.

Annual payroll is the combined amount of wages paid, tips reported, and other compensation (including salaries, vacation allowances, bonuses, commissions, sick-leave pay, and the value of payments-in-kind such as free meals and lodging) paid to employees before deductions for Social Security, income tax, insurance, union dues, etc. All forms of compensation are included, regardless of whether they are subject to income tax or the Federal Insurance Contributions Act tax, with the exception of annuities, third-party sick pay, and supplemental unemployment compensation benefits (even if income tax was withheld). For corporations, total annual payroll includes compensation paid to officers and executives; for unincorporated businesses, it excludes profit or other compensation of proprietors or partners.

## AGRICULTURE, ITEMS 113–132
### Source: U.S. Department of Agriculture, National Agricultural Statistics Service—2007 Census of Agriculture
http://www.agcensus.usda.gov/Publications/2007/index.asp

Data for the 2007 Census of Agriculture were collected in 2008, but pertain to the year 2007.

The Census Bureau took a census of agriculture every 10 years from 1840 to 1920; since 1925, this census has been taken roughly once every 5 years. The 1997 Census of Agriculture was the first one conducted by the National Agricultural Statistics Service of the U.S. Department of Agriculture. Over time, the definition of a farm has varied. For recent censuses (including the 2007 census), a farm has been defined as any place from which $1,000 or more of agricultural products were produced and sold or normally would have been sold during the census year. Dollar figures are expressed in current dollars and have not been adjusted for inflation or deflation.

The term **operator** refers to a person who operates a farm by either doing the work or making day-to-day decisions about such activities as planting, harvesting, feeding, marketing, etc. The operator may be the owner, a member of the owner's household, a salaried manager, a tenant, a renter, or a sharecropper. If a person rents land to others or has land worked on shares by others, he/she is considered the operator only of the land that is retained for his/her own operation. The census collected information on the total number of operators, the total number of women operators, and demographic information for up to three operators per farm.

The acreage designated as **land in farms** consists primarily of agricultural land used for crops, pasture, or grazing. It also includes woodland and wasteland not actually under cultivation or used for pasture or grazing, provided that this land was part of the farm operator's total operation. Land in farms is an operating-unit concept and includes all land owned and operated, as well as all land rented from others. Land used rent-free is classified as land rented from others. All land in Indian reservations used for growing crops or grazing livestock is classified as land in farms.

**Irrigated land** includes all land watered by any artificial or controlled means, such as sprinklers, flooding, furrows or ditches, sub-irrigation, and spreader dikes. Included are supplemental, partial, and preplant irrigation. Each acre was counted only once regardless of the number of times it was irrigated or harvested. Livestock lagoon waste water distributed by sprinkler or flood systems was also included.

**Total cropland** includes cropland harvested, cropland used only for pasture or grazing, cropland on which all crops failed or were abandoned, cropland in cultivated summer fallow, and cropland idle or used for cover crops or soil improvement but not harvested and not pastured or grazed.

Respondents were asked to report their estimate of the current market **value of land and buildings** owned, rented, or leased from others, and rented and leased to others. Market value refers to the respondent's estimate of what the land and buildings would sell for under current market conditions. If the value of land and buildings was not reported, it was estimated during processing by using the average value of land and buildings from similar farms in the same geographic area.

The **value of machinery and equipment** was estimated by the respondent as the current market value of all cars, trucks, tractors, combines, balers, irrigation equipment, etc., used on the farm. This value is an estimate of what the machinery and equipment would sell for in its present condition and not the replacement or depreciated value. Share interests are reported at full value at the farm where the equipment and machinery are usually kept. Only equipment that was actually used in 2006 and 2007, or newly purchased but not yet used and physically located at the farm on December 31, 2007, is included.

**Market value of agricultural products sold** by farms represents the gross market value before taxes and the production expenses of all agricultural products sold or removed from the place in 2007, regardless of who received the payment. It is equivalent to total sales and it includes sales by the operator as well as the value of any share received by partners, landlords, contractors, and others associated with the operation. It includes value of direct sales and the value of commodities placed in the Commodity Credit Corporation (CCC) loan program. Market value of agricultural products sold does not include payments received for participation in other federal farm programs. Also, it does not include income from farm-related sources such as customwork and other agricultural services, or income from non-farm sources.

**Government payments** consist of direct payments as defined by the 2002 Farm Bill; payments from Conservation Reserve Program (CRP), Wetlands Reserve Program (WRP), Farmable Wetlands Program (FWP), and Conservation Reserve Enhancement Program (CREP); loan deficiency payments; disaster payments; other conservation programs; and all other federal farm programs under which payments were made directly to farm operators. Commodity Credit Corporation (CCC) proceeds, amount from State and local federal crop insurance payments were not included in this category.

## WATER CONSUMPTION, Items 133–134
**Source: U.S. Geological Survey, National Water Information System—2005 Water Use Data**
**http://water.usgs.gov/watuse/data/2005/index.html**

Every ten years, the U.S. Geological Survey compiles county-level water-use estimates. This volume includes the total fresh and saline withdrawals expressed as million gallons per day. Estimate of withdrawals of ground and surface water are given for the following categories of use: public water supplies, domestic, commercial, irrigation, livestock, industrial, mining, and thermo-electric power. The number of gallons withdrawn per person is based on the county population but the water is not necessarily used locally, providing an indicator of counties that serve as major water sources.

## 2007 ECONOMIC CENSUS: OVERVIEW, Items 135–166
**Source: U.S. Census Bureau**
**http://www.census.gov/econ/census07/**

The Economic Census provides a detailed portrait of the nation's economy, from the national to the local level, once every five years. The 2007 Economic Census covers nearly all of the U.S. economy in its basic collection of establishment statistics. The 1997 Economic Census was the first major data source to use the new North American Industry Classification System (NAICS); therefore, data from this census are not comparable to economic data from prior years, which were based on the Standard Industrial Classification (SIC) system.

NAICS, developed in cooperation with Canada and Mexico, classifies North America's economic activities at two-, three-, four-, and five-digit levels of detail; the U.S. version of NAICS further defines industries to a sixth digit. The Economic Census takes advantage of this hierarchy to publish data at these successive levels of detail: sector (two-digit), subsector (three-digit), industry group (four-digit), industry (five-digit), and U.S. industry (six-digit). Information in Table A is at the two-digit level, with a few three- and four-digit items. The data in Table B are at the two-digit level.

Several key statistics are tabulated for all industries in this volume, including number of establishments (or companies), number of employees, payroll, and certain measures of output (sales, receipts, revenue, value of shipments, or value of construction work done).

**Number of establishments.** An establishment is a single physical location at which business is conducted. It is not necessarily identical with a company or enterprise, which may consist of one establishment or more. Economic Census figures represent a summary of reports for individual establishments rather than companies. For cases in which a census report was received, separate information was obtained for each location where business was conducted. When administrative records of other federal agencies were used instead of a census report, no information was available on the number of locations operated. Each Economic Census establishment was tabulated according to the physical location at which the business was conducted. The count of establishments represents those in business at any time during 2007.

When two activities or more were carried on at a single location under a single ownership, all activities were generally grouped together as a single establishment. The entire establishment was classified on the basis of its major activity and all of its data were included in that classification. However, when distinct and separate economic activities (for which different industry classification codes were appropriate) were conducted at a single location under a single ownership, separate establishment reports for each of the different activities were obtained in the census.

**Number of employees.** Paid employees consist of the full-time and part-time employees, including salaried officers and executives of corporations. Included are employees on paid sick leave, paid holidays, and paid vacations; not included are proprietors and partners of unincorporated businesses. The definition of paid employees is the same as that used by the Internal Revenue Service (IRS) on form 941.

For some industries, the Economic Census gives codes representing the number of employees as a range of numbers (for example, "100 to 249 employees" or "1,000 to 2,499" employees). In this volume, those codes have been replaced by the standard suppression code "D".

**Payroll.** Payroll includes all forms of compensation, such as salaries, wages, commissions, dismissal pay, bonuses, vacation allowances, sick-leave pay, and employee contributions to qualified pension plans paid during the year to all employees. For corporations, payroll includes amounts paid to officers and executives; for unincorporated businesses, it does not include profit or other compensation of proprietors or partners. Payroll is reported before deductions for Social Security, income tax, insurance, union dues, etc. This definition of payroll is the same as that used by on IRS form 941.

**Sales, shipments, receipts, revenue, or business done.** This measure includes the total sales, shipments, receipts, revenue, or business done by establishments within the scope of the Economic Census. The definition of each of these items is specific to the economic sector measured.

# WHOLESALE TRADE, Items 135–138
## Source: U.S. Census Bureau—2007 Economic Census (See Overview of 2007 Economic Census prior to Item 135)

The Wholesale Trade sector (sector 42) comprises establishments engaged in wholesaling merchandise, generally without transformation, and rendering services incidental to the sale of merchandise. The wholesaling process is an intermediate step in the distribution of merchandise.

Wholesalers are organized to sell or arrange the purchase or sale of (1) goods for resale (i.e., goods sold to other wholesalers or retailers), (2) capital or durable nonconsumer goods, and (3) raw and intermediate materials and supplies used in production.

Wholesalers sell merchandise to other businesses and normally operate from a warehouse or office. These warehouses and offices are characterized by having little or no display of merchandise. In addition, neither the design nor the location of the premises is intended to solicit walk-in traffic. Wholesalers do not normally use advertising directed to the general public. In general, customers are initially reached via telephone, in-person marketing, or specialized advertising, which may include the internet and other electronic means. Follow-up orders are either vendor-initiated or client-initiated, are usually based on previous sales, and typically exhibit strong ties between sellers and buyers. In fact, transactions are often conducted between wholesalers and clients that have long-standing business relationships.

This sector is made up of two main types of wholesalers: those that sell goods on their own account and those that arrange sales and purchases for others for a commission or fee.

(1) Establishments that sell goods on their own account are known as wholesale merchants, distributors, jobbers, drop shippers, import/export merchants, and sales branches. These establishments typically maintain their own warehouse, where they receive and handle goods for their customers. Goods are generally sold without transformation, but may include integral functions, such as sorting, packaging, labeling, and other marketing services.

(2) Establishments arranging for the purchase or sale of goods owned by others or purchasing goods on a commission basis are known as agents and brokers, commission merchants, import/export agents and brokers, auction companies, and manufacturers' representatives. These establishments operate from offices and generally do not own or handle the goods they sell.

Some wholesale establishments may be connected with a single manufacturer and promote and sell that particular manufacturer's products to a wide range of other wholesalers or retailers. Other wholesalers may be connected to a retail chain or a limited number of retail chains and only provide the products needed by the particular retail operation(s). These wholesalers may obtain the products from a wide range of manufacturers. Still other wholesalers may not take title to the goods, but act instead as agents and brokers for a commission.

Although wholesaling normally denotes sales in large volumes, durable nonconsumer goods may be sold in single units. Sales of capital or durable nonconsumer goods used in the production of goods and services, such as farm machinery, medium- and heavy-duty trucks, and industrial machinery, are always included in Wholesale Trade.

The county table includes only **Merchant wholesalers, except manufacturers' sales branches and offices,** establishments primarily engaged in buying and selling merchandise on their own account. Included here are such types of establishments as wholesale distributors and jobbers, importers, exporters, own-brand importers/marketers, terminal and country grain elevators, and farm products assemblers.

## RETAIL TRADE, Items 139–142
### Source: U.S. Census Bureau—2007 Economic Census (See Overview of 2007 Economic Census prior to Item 135)

The Retail Trade sector (44–45) is made up of establishments engaged in retailing merchandise, generally without transformation, and rendering services incidental to the sale of merchandise.

The retailing process is the final step in the distribution of merchandise; retailers are therefore organized to sell merchandise in small quantities to the general public. This sector comprises two main types of retailers: store and nonstore retailers.

Store retailers operate fixed point-of-sale locations, located and designed to attract a high volume of walk-in customers. In general, retail stores have extensive displays of merchandise and use mass-media advertising to attract customers. They typically sell merchandise to the general public for personal or household consumption; some also serve business and institutional clients. These include establishments such as office supply stores, computer and software stores, building materials dealers, plumbing supply stores, and electrical supply stores. Catalog showrooms, gasoline service stations, automotive dealers, and mobile home dealers are treated as store retailers.

In addition to retailing merchandise, some types of store retailers are also engaged in the provision of after-sales services, such as repair and installation. For example, new automobile dealers, electronic and appliance stores, and musical instrument and supply stores often provide repair services. As a general rule, establishments engaged in retailing merchandise and providing after-sales services are classified in this sector.

Nonstore retailers, like store retailers, are organized to serve the general public, although their retailing methods differ. The establishments of this subsector reach customers and market merchandise with methods including the broadcasting of "infomercials," the broadcasting and publishing of direct-response advertising, the publishing of paper and electronic catalogs, door-to-door solicitation, in-home demonstration, selling from portable stalls (street vendors, except food), and distribution through vending machines. Establishments engaged in the direct sale (nonstore) of products, such as home heating oil dealers and home-delivery newspaper routes are included in this sector.

The buying of goods for resale is a characteristic of retail trade establishments that distinguishes them from establishments in the Agriculture, Manufacturing, and Construction sectors. For example, farms that sell their products at or from the point of production are classified in Agriculture instead of in Retail Trade. Similarly, establishments that both manufacture and sell their products to the general public are classified in Manufacturing instead of Retail Trade. However, establishments that engage in processing activities incidental to retailing are classified in Retail Trade.

## REAL ESTATE AND RENTAL AND LEASING, Items 143–146
### Source: U.S. Census Bureau—2007 Economic Census (See Overview of 2007 Economic Census prior to Item 135)

The Real Estate and Rental and Leasing sector (53) comprises establishments primarily engaged in renting, leasing, or otherwise allowing the use of tangible or intangible assets, and establishments providing related services. The major portion of this sector is made up of establishments that rent, lease, or otherwise allow the use of their own assets by others. The assets may be tangible, such as real estate and equipment, or intangible, such as patents and trademarks.

This sector also includes establishments primarily engaged in managing real estate for others, selling, renting, and/or buying real estate for others, and appraising real estate. These activities are closely related to this sector's main activity. In addition, a substantial proportion of property management is self-performed by lessors.

The main components of this sector are the real estate lessors industries; equipment lessors industries (including motor vehicles, computers, and consumer goods); and lessors of nonfinancial intangible assets (except copyrighted works).

## PROFESSIONAL, SCIENTIFIC, AND TECHNICAL SERVICES, Items 147–150
### Source: U.S. Census Bureau—2007 Economic Census (See Overview of 2007 Economic Census prior to Item 135)

The Professional, Scientific, and Technical Services sector (54) is made up of establishments that specialize in performing professional, scientific, and technical activities for others. These activities require a high degree of expertise and training. The establishments in this sector specialize in one or more areas and provide services to clients in a variety of industries (and, in some cases, to households). Activities performed include legal advice and representation; accounting, bookkeeping, and payroll services; architectural, engineering, and specialized design services; computer services; consulting services; research services; advertising services; photographic services; translation and interpretation services; veterinary services; and other professional, scientific, and technical services.

Table B includes only those establishments subject to federal income tax.

This sector excludes establishments primarily engaged in providing a range of day-to-day office administrative services, such as financial planning, billing and record keeping, personnel services, and physical distribution and logistics services. These establishments are classified in sector 56, Administrative and Support and Waste Management and Remediation Services.

## MANUFACTURING, Items 151–154

**Source: U.S. Census Bureau—2007 Economic Census (See Overview of 2007 Economic Census prior to Item 135)**

The Manufacturing sector (31–33) is made up of establishments engaged in the mechanical, physical, or chemical transformation of materials, substances, or components into new products. The assembling of component parts of manufactured products is considered manufacturing, except in cases in which the activity is appropriately classified in the Construction sector. Establishments in the Manufacturing sector are often described as plants, factories, or mills, and characteristically use power-driven machines and materials-handling equipment. However, establishments that transform materials or substances into new products by hand or in the worker's home, and establishments engaged in selling to the general public products made on the same premises from which they are sold (such as bakeries, candy stores, and custom tailors) may also be included in this sector. Manufacturing establishments may process materials or contract with other establishments to process their materials for them. Both types of establishments are included in the Manufacturing sector.

The materials, substances, or components transformed by manufacturing establishments are raw materials that are products of agriculture, forestry, fishing, mining, or quarrying, or are products of other manufacturing establishments. The materials used may be purchased directly from producers, obtained through customary trade channels, or secured without recourse to the market by transferring the product from one establishment to another, under the same ownership. The new product of a manufacturing establishment may be finished (in the sense that it is ready for utilization or consumption), or it may be semifinished to become an input for an establishment engaged in further manufacturing. For example, the product of the alumina refinery is the input used in the primary production of aluminum; primary aluminum is the input used in an aluminum wire drawing plant; and aluminum wire is the input used in a fabricated wire product manufacturing establishment.

Data are included for counties with 500 or more employees in the Manufacturing sector.

## ACCOMMODATION AND FOOD SERVICES, Items 155–158

**Source: U.S. Census Bureau—2007 Economic Census (See Overview of 2007 Economic Census prior to Item 135)**

The Accommodation and Food Services sector (72) consists of establishments that provide customers with lodging and/or meals, snacks, and beverages for immediate consumption. This sector includes both accommodation and food services establishments because the two activities are often combined at the same establishment.

Excluded from this sector are civic and social organizations, amusement and recreation parks, theaters, and other recreation or entertainment facilities providing food and beverage services.

## HEALTH CARE AND SOCIAL ASSISTANCE, Items 159–162

**Source: U.S. Census Bureau—2007 Economic Census (See Overview of 2007 Economic Census prior to Item 135)**

The Health Care and Social Assistance sector (62) consists of establishments that provide health care and social assistance services to individuals. The sector includes both health care and social assistance because it is sometimes difficult to distinguish between the boundaries of these two activities. The industries in this sector are arranged on a continuum, starting with establishments that provide medical care exclusively, continuing with those that provide health care and social assistance, and finishing with those that provide only social assistance. The services provided by establishments in this sector are delivered by trained professionals. All industries in the sector share this commonality of process—namely, labor inputs of health practitioners or social workers with the requisite expertise. Many of the industries in the sector are defined based on the educational degree held by the practitioners included in the industry.

Excluded from this sector are aerobic classes, which can be found in subsector 713, Amusement, Gambling, and Recreation Industries; and nonmedical diet and weight-reducing centers, which can be found in subsector 812, Personal and Laundry Services. Although these can be viewed as health services, they are not typically delivered by health practitioners.

## OTHER SERVICES, EXCEPT PUBLIC ADMINISTRATION Items 163–166

**Source: U.S. Census Bureau—2007 Economic Census (See Overview of 2007 Economic Census prior to Item 135)**

The Other Services, Except Public Administration sector (81) comprises establishments engaged in providing services not specifically categorized elsewhere in the classification system. Establishments in this sector are primarily engaged in activities such as equipment and machinery repairing, promoting or administering religious activities, grant making, and advocacy; this sector also includes establishments that provide dry-cleaning and laundry services, personal care services, death care services, pet care services, photofinishing services, temporary parking services, and dating services.

Private households that employ workers on or about the premises in activities primarily concerned with the operation of the household are included in this sector.

Excluded from this sector are establishments primarily engaged in retailing new equipment and performing repairs and general maintenance on equipment. These establishments are classified in sector 44–45, Retail Trade.

## FEDERAL FUNDS, Items 167–177
### Source: U.S. Census Bureau—Consolidated Federal Funds Report
### http://www.census.gov/govs/cffr/

Data on federal expenditure and obligations are obtained from a report prepared by the Census Bureau in accordance with the Consolidated Federal Funds Report (CFFR) Act of 1982 (P.L. 97–326). The data are for federal fiscal years beginning October 1 and ending the following September 30. Dollar amounts reported can reflect expenditures or obligations. In some cases, dollar amounts are negative, representing de-obligations of financial assistance that had previously been awarded. Such amounts generally appear in the grant categories.

**Direct payments** for individuals include Social Security benefits, federal government retirement, Medicare, Supplemental Security Income, food stamps, educational and housing assistance, and other categories not shown separately. All data represent actual expenditures during the fiscal year.

**Salaries and wages** represent actual federal expenditures during the fiscal year; the geographic distribution of these amounts by state and county was estimated based upon place of employment.

**Procurement contract awards** cover awards given by the United States Postal Service (USPS), as well as those given by all other federal agencies. Amounts provided by the USPS represent actual outlays for contractual commitments, while amounts for other agencies represent the value of obligations for contract actions and do not reflect actual federal government expenditures. In general, only current-year contract actions are included; however, multiple-year obligations may be reported for contract actions of less than three years' duration.

**Grants** data represent the federal obligations incurred at the time the grant is awarded. The amounts reported do not represent actual expenditures, since obligations in one time period may not result in outlays during the same period. Moreover, initial amounts obligated may be adjusted at a later date, through either enhancements or de-obligations. For many grants, this recipient is the state government even though grants monies are subsequently distributed to county, municipal, or township governments.

**Medicaid and other health-related** grants include a variety of grants from the Department of Health and Human Services for health services and research.

**Nutrition and family welfare** grants include a variety of grants from the Department of Health and Human Services for child welfare, special programs for the aging, and related areas. The school lunch program and other nutritional assistance programs administered by the Department of Agriculture are also included in this category.

**Education** grants include a variety of grant programs relating to elementary, secondary, and postsecondary education; adult education; vocational education; faculty training; and related areas.

## BUILDING PERMITS, Items 178 and 179
### Source: U.S. Census Bureau—Building Permits Survey
### http://www.census.gov/const/www/permitsindex.html

These figures represent private residential construction authorized by building permits in approximately 20,000 places in the United States. Valuation represents the expected cost of construction as recorded on the building permit. This figure usually excludes the cost of on-site and off-site development and improvements, as well as the cost of heating, plumbing, electrical, and elevator installations.

National, state, and county totals were obtained by adding the data for permit-issuing places within each jurisdiction. Not all areas of the country require a building or zoning permit. The statistics only represent those areas that do require a permit. These totals thus are limited to permits issued in the 20,000 place universe covered by the Census Bureau and may not include all permits issued within a state. Current surveys indicate that construction is undertaken for all but a very small percentage of housing units authorized by building permits.

Residential building permits include buildings with any number of housing units. Housing units exclude group quarters (such as dormitories and rooming houses), transient accommodations (such as transient hotels, motels, and tourist courts), "HUD-code" manufactured (mobile) homes, moved or relocated units, and housing units created in an existing residential or nonresidential structure.

## LOCAL GOVERNMENT FINANCES, Items 180–193
### Source: U.S. Census Bureau—2007 Census of Governments
### http://www.census.gov/govs/cog/

Data on local government finances are based on result of the 2007 Census of Governments. For each county area, the financial data comprise amounts for all local governments—not only the county government, but also any municipalities, townships, school districts, and special districts within the county. Statistics from governmental units located in two or more county areas are assigned to the county area containing the administrative office.

Revenue and expenditure items include all amounts of money received and paid out, respectively, by a government and its agencies (net of correcting transactions such as recoveries of refunds), with the exception of amounts for debt issuance and retirement and for loan and investment, agency, and private transactions.

Payments among the various funds and agencies of a particular government are excluded from revenue and expenditure items as representing internal transfers. Therefore, a government's contribution to a retirement fund that it administers is not counted as expenditure, nor is the receipt of this contribution by the retirement fund counted as revenue.

Total **general revenue** includes all revenue except utility, liquor stores, and insurance trust revenue. All tax revenue and intergovernmental revenue, even if designated for employee-retirement or local utility purpose, are classified as general revenue.

**Intergovernmental revenue** covers amounts received from the federal government as fiscal aid, reimbursements for performance of general government functions and specific services for the paying government, or in lieu of taxes. It excludes any amounts received from other governments from the sale of property, commodities, and utility services.

**Taxes** consist of compulsory contributions exacted by governments for public purposes. However, this category excludes employer and employee payments for retirement and social insurance purposes, which are classified as insurance trust revenue; it also excludes special assessments, which are classified as non-tax general revenue. Property taxes are taxes conditioned on ownership of property and assessed by its value. Sales and gross receipts taxes do not include dealer discounts, or ''commissions'' allowed to merchants for collection of taxes from consumers. General sales taxes and selected taxes on sales of motor fuels, tobacco products, and other particular commodities and services are included.

**General government expenditure** includes capital outlay, a major portion of which is commonly financed by borrowing. Government revenue does not include receipts from borrowing. Among other things, this distorts the relationship between totals of revenue and expenditure figures that are presented and renders it useless as a direct measure of the degree of budgetary ''balance'' (as that term is generally applied).

**Direct general expenditure** comprises all expenditures of the local governments, excluding utility, liquor stores, insurance trust expenditures, and any intergovernmental payments.

Local government expenditure for **education** is mainly for the provision and general support of schools and other educational facilities and services, including those for educational institutions beyond high school. They cover such related services as student transportation; school lunch and other cafeteria operations; school health, recreation, and library services; and dormitories, dining halls, and bookstores operated by public institutions of higher education.

**Health and hospital expenditure** includes health research; clinics; nursing; immunization; other categorical, environmental, and general health services provided by health agencies; establishment and operation of hospital facilities; provision of hospital care; and support of other public and private hospitals.

**Police protection expenditure** includes police activities such as patrols, communications, custody of persons awaiting trial, and vehicular inspection.

**Public welfare expenditure** covers support of and assistance to needy persons; this aid is contingent upon the person's needs. Included are cash assistance paid directly to needy persons under categorical (Old Age Assistance, Temporary Assistance for Needy Families, Aid to the Blind, and Aid to the Disabled) and other welfare programs; vendor payments made directly to private purveyors for medical care, burials, and other commodities and services provided under welfare programs; welfare institutions; and any intergovernmental or other direct expenditure for welfare purposes. Pensions to former employees and other benefits not contingent on need are excluded.

**Highway expenditure** is for the provision and maintenance of highway facilities, including toll turnpikes, bridges, tunnels, and ferries, as well as regular roads, highways, and streets. Also included are expenditures for street lighting and for snow and ice removal. Not included are highway policing and traffic control, which are considered part of police protection

**Debt outstanding** includes all long-term debt obligations of the government and its agencies (exclusive of utility debt) and all interest-bearing, short-term (repayable within one year) debt obligations remaining unpaid at the close of the fiscal year. It includes judgments, mortgages, and revenue bonds, as well as general obligation bonds, notes, and interest-bearing warrants. This category consists of non-interest-bearing, short-term obligations; inter-fund obligations; amounts owed in a trust or agency capacity; advances and contingent loans from other governments; and rights of individuals to benefit from government-administered employee-retirement funds.

## GOVERNMENT EMPLOYMENT, Items 194–196
**Source: U.S. Bureau of Economic Analysis—Regional Economic Accounts**
**http://www.bea.gov/regional/index.htm#state**

Employment is measured as the average annual sum of full-time and part-time jobs. The estimates are on a place-of-work basis. State and local government employment includes person employed in all state and local government agencies and enterprises. Data for federal civilian employment include civilian employees of the federal government, including civilian employees of the Department of Defense. Military employment includes all persons on active duty status.

## ELECTION STATISTICS, Items 197–199
**Source: Election Data Services, Inc. Washington, DC (copyright)**
**http://www.electiondataservices.com/index.php?con tent = elecdata**

© 2013 Election Data Services, Inc. All rights reserved. This material is proprietary and the subject of copyright protection and other intellectual property rights owned by or licensed to Election Data Services, Inc. The use of this material is subject to the terms of a License Agreement. You will be held liable for any unauthorized copying or disclosure of this material.

Election results show the percentage of the total vote cast for the Democratic and Republican candidates, as well as the combined percentage for all other candidates in the 2012 presidential election.

# TABLE C—METROPOLITAN AREAS

Table C presents 199 items for the 366 metropolitan statistical areas (MSAs) and 29 metropolitan divisions in the United States. The metropolitan areas are presented in alphabetical order, and the metropolitan divisions are presented in alphabetical order within the appropriate metropolitan area. For many data items, the metropolitan area data have been aggregated from county data sources.

## LAND AREA, Items 1 and 4
**Source: U.S. Census Bureau—2010 Census of Population and Housing**
http://2010.census.gov/2010census/data/

Land area measurements are shown to the nearest square kilometer. Land area includes dry land and land temporarily or partially covered by water, such as marshlands, swamps, and river floodplains.

## POPULATION, Items 2–4
**Source: U.S. Census Bureau—Population Estimates**
http://www.census.gov/popest/estimates.html

The population data are Census Bureau estimates of the resident population as of July 1 of the year shown. The ranks are shown for metropolitan statistical areas, but exclude metropolitan divisions.

## POPULATION AND POPULATION CHARACTERISTICS, Items 5–19
**Source: U.S. Census Bureau—Population Estimates**
http://www.census.gov/popest/estimates.html

The concept of race, as used by the Census Bureau, reflects self-identification by persons according to the race or races with which they most closely identify. These categories are sociopolitical constructs and should not be interpreted as being scientific or anthropological in nature. Furthermore, race categories include both racial and national origin groups.

Beginning with the 2000 census, respondents were offered the option of selecting one or more races. This option was not available in prior censuses; thus, comparisons between censuses should be made with caution. In Table C, Columns 5 through 8 refer to individuals who identified with each racial category, either alone or in combination with other races. The estimates exclude persons of Hispanic or Latino origin from all race groups. Because respondents could include as many categories as they wished, and because the columns refer to the percentage of the population, the total will often exceed 100 percent.

The **White** population is defined as persons who indicated their race as White, as well as persons who did not classify themselves in one of the specific race categories listed on the questionnaire but entered a nationality such as Irish, German, Italian, Lebanese, Near Easterner, Arab, or Polish.

The **Black** population includes persons who indicated their race as "Black, African Am., or Negro," as well as persons who did not classify themselves in one of the specific race categories but reported entries such as African American, Afro American, Kenyan, Nigerian, or Haitian.

The **American Indian or Alaska Native** population includes persons who indicated their race as American Indian or Alaska Native, as well as persons who did not classify themselves in one of the specific race categories but reported entries such as Canadian Indian, French-American Indian, Spanish-American Indian, Eskimo, Aleut, Alaska Indian, or any of the American Indian or Alaska Native tribes.

The **Asian and Pacific Islander** population combines two census groupings: **Asian** and **Native Hawaiian or Other Pacific Islander**. The **Asian** population includes persons who indicated their race as Asian Indian, Chinese, Filipino, Japanese, Korean, Vietnamese, or "Other Asian," as well as persons who provided write-in entries of such groups as Cambodian, Laotian, Hmong, Pakistani, or Taiwanese. The **Native Hawaiian or Other Pacific Islander** population includes persons who indicated their race as "Native Hawaiian," "Guamanian or Chamorro," "Samoan," or "Other Pacific Islander," as well as persons who reported entries such as Part Hawaiian, American Samoan, Fijian, Melanesian, or Tahitian.

The **Hispanic population** is based on a complete-count question that asked respondents "Is this person Spanish/Hispanic/Latino?" Persons marking any one of the four Hispanic categories (i.e., Mexican, Puerto Rican, Cuban, or other Spanish) are collectively referred to as Hispanic.

In the 2000 census, the Hispanic origin question was placed before the race question and specific instructions indicated that both questions should be answered. These changes were designed to improve accuracy and may affect comparability with 1990 data.

**Age** is defined as age at last birthday (number of completed years since birth), as of April 1 of the census year. The 2000 census also asked for the specific date of birth of the respondent, and 2000 census procedures used the birth date for deriving age data. For this reason, it is likely that the 2000 data have fewer problems than data from prior censuses, such as the tendency of respondents to round ages or to report their ages on the date the questionnaire was filled out rather than on April 1.

The **female** population is shown as a percentage of total population.

## POPULATION AND COMPONENTS OF CHANGE, Items 20–26
**Source: U.S. Census Bureau—Decennial Censuses and Population Estimates**
http://www.census.gov/main/www/cen2000.html
http://www.census.gov/popest/estimates.html
http://2010.census.gov/2010census/data/

The population data for 2000 and 2010 are from the decennial censuses and represent the resident population as of April 1 of those years. The components of change are based on Census Bureau estimates of the resident population as of July 1 of 2012. The change in population between 2010 and 2012 is made up of (a) natural increase—births minus deaths, and (b) net migration—the difference between the number of persons moving into a particular area and the number of persons moving out of the area. Net migration is composed of internal and international migration.

Because the 2012 population estimates are based on a model that begins with a national population estimate, the county and msa components of change do not always exactly add up to the difference between the 2010 census population and the 2012 estimates.

## HOUSEHOLDS, Items 27–31
**Source: U.S. Census Bureau—2010 Census of Population and Housing http://2010.census.gov/2010census/data/**

A **household** includes all of the persons who occupy a housing unit. (Persons not living in households are classified as living in group quarters.) A housing unit is a house, an apartment, a mobile home, a group of rooms, or a single room occupied (or, if vacant, intended for occupancy) as separate living quarters. Separate living quarters are those in which the occupants live separately from any other persons in the building and have direct access from the outside of the building or through a common hall. The occupants may be a single family, one person living alone, two or more families living together, or any other group of related or unrelated persons who share living quarters. The number of households is the same as the number of year-round occupied housing units.

A **family** includes a householder and one or more other persons living in the same household who are related to the householder by birth, marriage, or adoption. All persons in a household who are related to the householder are regarded as members of his or her family. A **family household** may contain persons not related to the householder; thus, family households may include more members than families do. A household can contain only one family for the purposes of census tabulations. Not all households contain families, as a household may comprise a group of unrelated persons or of one person living alone. Families are classified by type as either a ''husband-wife family'' or ''other family,'' according to the presence or absence of a spouse.

The measure of **persons per household** is obtained by dividing the number of persons in households by the number of households or householders. One person in each household is designated as the householder. In most cases, this is the person (or one of the persons) in whose name the house is owned, being bought, or rented. If there is no such person in the household, any adult household member 15 years old and over can be designated as the householder.

The category **female family householder** includes only female-headed family households with no spouse present.

## GROUP QUARTERS, Item 32
**Source: U.S. Census Bureau—2010 Census of Population and Housing http://2010.census.gov/2010census/data/**

The Census Bureau classifies all persons not living in households as living in group quarters; this category includes both the institutional and noninstitutional populations. The institutionalized population includes persons under formally authorized, supervised care or custody in institutions, such as correctional institutions, nursing homes, mental (psychiatric) hospitals, and juvenile institutions. The noninstitutionalized population includes persons who live in group quarters other than institutions, such

as college dormitories, military quarters, and group homes. This volume includes the total number of persons in group quarters.

## DAYTIME POPULATION, Items 33 and 34
**Source: U.S. Census Bureau—American Community Survey, 2007–2011
http://www.census.gov/acs/www/**

Daytime population refers to the number of persons who are present in an area or place during normal business hours, including workers. This can be contrasted with the ''resident'' population, which is present during the evening and nighttime hours. The daytime population estimate is calculated by adding the total resident population and the total workers working in the area/place, and then subtracting the total workers living in the area/place from that result. Information on the expansion or contraction experienced by different communities between their nighttime and daytime populations is important for many planning purposes, especially those concerning transportation, disaster, and relief operations.

The employment/residence ratio is a measure of the total number of workers working in an area or place, relative to the total number of workers living in the area or place. It is often used as a rough indication of the jobs-workers balance in an area/place, although it does not take into account whether the resident workers possess the skills needed for the jobs available in their particular area/place. The employment/residence ratio is calculated by dividing the number of total workers working in an area/place by the number of total workers residing in the area/place.

## BIRTHS AND DEATHS, Items 35–38
**Source: U.S. Census Bureau—Population Estimates
http://www.census.gov/popest/estimates.html**

The numbers of births and deaths are from the Census Bureau's Population Estimates Program. They represent the total number of live births and deaths occurring to residents of an area as estimated using reports from the National Center for Health Statistics (NCHS) and the Federal-State Cooperative for Population Estimates (FSCPE). The rates measure births and deaths during the specified time period as a proportion of an area's population. Rates are expressed per 1,000 population estimated as of July 1. These numbers and rates do not represent the calendar year, but rather the year-long period ending on July 1.

## PERSONS UNDER 65 WITH NO HEALTH INSURANCE, Items 39 and 40
**Source: U.S. Census Bureau—Small Area Health Insurance Estimates
http://www.census.gov/did/www/sahie/index.html**

The Small Area Health Insurance Estimates (SAHIE) program develops model-based estimates of health insurance coverage for counties and states. This developmental program builds on the work of the Small Area Income and Poverty Estimates (SAIPE) program. The SAHIE program models health insurance coverage by combining survey data with population estimates and administrative records. The estimates are based on data from The Annual

Social and Economic Supplement (ASEC) of the Current Population Survey (CPS); Demographic population estimates; Aggregated federal tax returns; Participation records for the Supplemental Nutrition Assistance Program (SNAP), formerly known as the Food Stamp program; County Business Patterns; Medicaid and Children's Health Insurance Program (CHIP) participation records; and Census 2000.

## MEDICARE ENROLLMENT, Items 41–43
### Source: U.S. Department of Health and Human Services, Centers for Medicare and Medicaid Services
http://www.cms.hhs.gov/MCRAdvPartDEnrolData/
http://www.cms.hhs.gov/DataCompendium/

The Centers for Medicare and Medicaid Services (CMS) administers Medicare, which provides health insurance to persons 65 years old and over, persons with permanent kidney failure, and certain persons with disabilities. Original Medicare has two parts: Hospital Insurance and Supplemental Medical Insurance. In recent years, Medicare has been expanded to include two new programs: Medicare Advantage plans and prescription drug coverage. Medicare Advantage Plans are health plan options that are approved by Medicare but run by private companies. Medicare prescription drug plans can be part of Medicare Advantage plans or stand-alone drug plans.

Persons who are eligible for Medicare can enroll in Part A (Hospital Insurance) at no charge, and can choose to pay a monthly premium to enroll in Part B. Most eligible persons are enrolled in Part A, and more than 90 percent of enrollees in Part A are also enrolled in Part B (Supplemental Medical Insurance.) This table includes persons who were eligible as of December 2010.

Medicare Advantage enrollees were enrolled in a Medicare Advantage plan of some type at the end of 2010. These include Private Fee For Service plans, Preferred Provider Organizations, Health Maintenance Organizations, Medical Savings Account Plans, Demonstration plans, and Programs for All-Inclusive Care for the Elderly.

Persons enrolled in a Medicare Prescription drug plan were enrolled in stand-alone plans for prescription drug benefits. This number does not include Medicare enrollees who had prescription drug coverage through private or federal retiree health plans, through Medicare Advantage plans, or through Medicaid.

## CRIME, Items 44–47
### Source: U.S. Federal Bureau of Investigation—
Uniform Crime Reports http://www.fbi.gov/ucr/ucr.htm

Crime data are as reported to the Federal Bureau of Investigation (FBI) by law enforcement agencies and have not been adjusted for underreporting. This may affect comparability between geographic areas or over time.

Through the voluntary contribution of crime statistics by law enforcement agencies across the United States, the Uniform Crime Reporting (UCR) Program provides periodic assessments of crime in the nation as measured by offenses that have come to the attention of the law enforcement community. The Committee on Uniform Crime Records of the International Association of Chiefs of Police initiated this voluntary national data collection effort in 1930. The UCR Program contributors compile and submit their crime data either directly to the FBI or through state-level UCR Programs.

Seven offenses, because of their severity, frequency of occurrence, and likelihood of being reported to police, were initially selected to serve as an index for evaluating fluctuations in the volume of crime. These serious crimes were murder and nonnegligent manslaughter, forcible rape, robbery, aggravated assault, burglary, larceny-theft, and motor vehicle theft. By congressional mandate, arson was added as the eighth index offense in 1979. The totals shown in this volume do not include arson.

In 2004, the FBI discontinued the use of the Crime Index in the UCR Program and its publications, stating that the Crime Index was driven upward by the offense with the highest number of cases (in this case, larceny-theft), creating a bias against jurisdictions with a high number of larceny-thefts but a low number of other serious crimes, such as murder and forcible rape. The FBI is currently publishing a violent crime total and property crime total until a more viable index is developed. This book includes the crime total, as well as violent crime and property crime rates.

**Violent crimes** include four categories of offenses: (1) Murder and nonnegligent manslaughter, as defined in the UCR Program, is the willful (nonnegligent) killing of one human being by another. This offense excludes deaths caused by negligence, suicide, or accident; justifiable homicides; and attempts to murder or assaults to murder. (2) Forcible rape is the carnal knowledge of a female forcibly and against her will. Assaults or attempts to commit rape by force or threat of force are also included; however, statutory rape (without force) and other sex offenses are excluded. (3) Robbery is the taking or attempting to take anything of value from the care, custody, or control of a person or persons by force or threat of force or violence and/or by putting the victim in fear. (4) Aggravated assault is an unlawful attack by one person upon another for the purpose of inflicting severe or aggravated bodily injury. This type of assault is usually accompanied by the use of a weapon or by other means likely to produce death or great bodily harm. Attempts are included, since injury does not necessarily have to result when a gun, knife, or other weapon is used, as these incidents could and probably would result in a serious personal injury if the crime were successfully completed.

**Property crimes** include three categories: (1) Burglary, or breaking and entering, is the unlawful entry of a structure to commit a felony or theft, even though no force was used to gain entrance. (2) Larceny-theft is the unauthorized taking of the personal property of another, without the use of force. (3) Motor vehicle theft is the unauthorized taking of any motor vehicle.

Rates are based on population estimates provided by the FBI. The county and metropolitan area totals published in this volume were obtained by aggregating individual reporting units within each county and metropolitan area. If the population total for the units aggregated was less than 75 percent of the county's population (as estimated by the Census Bureau), the total was not considered representative of the county or metropolitan area as a whole and was not published.

## EDUCATION—SCHOOL ENROLLMENT AND EDUCATIONAL ATTAINMENT, Items 48–51

**Source: U.S. Census Bureau—American Community Survey, 2007–2011**
http://www.census.gov/acs/www/

Data on school enrollment and educational attainment were derived from a sample of the population. Persons were classified as enrolled in school if they reported attending a "regular" public or private school (or college) during the three months prior to the survey. The instructions were to "include only nursery school, kindergarten, elementary school, and schooling which would lead to a high school diploma or a college degree" as regular school. The Census Bureau defines a public school as "any school or college controlled and supported by a local, county, state, or federal government." Schools primarily supported and controlled by religious organizations or other private groups are defined as private schools.

Data on **educational attainment** are tabulated for the population 25 years old and over. The data were derived from a question that asked respondents for the highest level of school completed or the highest degree received. Persons who had passed a high school equivalency examination were considered high school graduates. Schooling received in foreign schools was to be reported as the equivalent grade or years in the regular American school system.

Vocational and technical training, such as barber school training; business, trade, technical, and vocational schools; or other training for a specific trade are specifically excluded.

**High school graduate or less.** This category includes persons whose highest degree was a high school diploma or its equivalent, and those who reported any level lower than a high school diploma.

**Bachelor's degree or more.** This category includes persons who have received bachelor's degrees, master's degrees, professional school degrees (such as law school or medical school degrees), and doctoral degrees.

## LOCAL GOVERNMENT EDUCATION EXPENDITURES, Items 52 and 53

**Source: U.S. Department of Education, National Center for Education Statistics—Common Core of Data**
http://nces.ed.gov/ccd/f33agency.asp

Total expenditure for education includes provision or support of schools and facilities for elementary and secondary education. It encompasses instructional, support, and auxiliary services (school lunch, student activities, and community service) offered by public school systems. Retirement benefits paid to former education employees and interest payments are not included. Current expenditure includes all components of total expenditure except capital outlay. Expenditure data are obtained by the Census Bureau through its annual survey of government finances and are supplied to the National Center for Education Statistics (NCES). Current expenditure per student is current expenditure divided by the number of students enrolled. The number of students enrolled is based on an annual "membership" count of students on or about October 1.

NCES uses the Common Core of Data (CCD) Survey system to acquire and maintain statistical data from each of the 50 states, the District of Columbia, and the outlying areas. State education agencies compile and submit data for approximately 85,000 schools and 15,000 local school districts. Typically, this results in varying interpretation of NCES definitions and different record keeping systems, leading to large amounts of missing data for several states; this absence is reflected in the data in this publication. Schools and school districts are included in the county in which the school district offices (the local education agency) are located.

## INCOME AND POVERTY Items 54–61

**Source: U.S. Census Bureau—American Community Survey, 2007–2011**
http://www.census.gov/acs/www/

The data on income were derived from responses of a sample of persons 15 years old and over. **Total money income** is the sum of the amounts reported separately for wage or salary income; net self-employment income; interest, dividends, or net rental or royalty income or income from estates and trusts; Social Security or railroad retirement income; Supplemental Security Income (SSI); public assistance or welfare payments; retirement, survivor, or disability pensions; and all other income. Receipts from the following sources are not included as income: capital gains; money received from the sale of property (unless the recipient was engaged in the business of selling such property); the value of income "in kind" from food stamps, public housing subsidies, medical care, employer contributions for individuals, etc.; withdrawal of bank deposits; money borrowed; tax refunds; exchange of money between relatives living in the same household; and gifts, lump-sum inheritances, insurance payments, and other types of lump-sum receipts.

Money income differs in definition from personal income (item 62). For example, money income does not include the pension rights, employer provided health insurance, food stamps, or Medicare payments that are included in personal income.

**Per capita income** is the mean income computed for every man, woman, and child in a particular group. It is derived by dividing the aggregate income of a particular group by the resident population in that group in the survey year. Per capita income is rounded to the nearest whole dollar.

**Household income** includes the income of the householder and all other individuals 15 years old and over in the household, whether or not they are related to the householder. Since many households consist of only one person, median household income is usually less than median family income. Although the household income statistics cover the year preceding the survey, the characteristics of individuals and the composition of households refer to the date of the survey. Thus, the income of the household does not include amounts received by individuals who were members of the household during the year if these individuals were no longer residing in the household at the time of the survey. Similarly, income amounts reported by individuals who did not reside in the household during the year but who were members of the household at the time of the survey are included. However, the composition of most households was the same during the year as it was at the time of the survey.

**Median income** divides the income distribution into two equal parts, with half of all cases below the median income level and half of all cases above the median income level. For households, the median income is based on the distribution of the total number of households, including those with no income. Median income for households is computed on the basis of a standard distribution with a minimum value of less than $2,500 and a maximum value of $200,000 or more and is rounded to the nearest whole dollar. Median income figures are calculated using linear interpolation if the width of the interval containing the estimate is $2,500 or less. If the width of the interval containing the estimate is greater than $2,500, Pareto interpolation is used.

Income components were reported for the 12 months preceding the interview month. Monthly Consumer Price Indices (CPI) factors were used to inflation-adjust these components to a reference calendar year (January through December). For example, a household interviewed in March 2008 reports their income for March 2007 through February 2008. Their income is adjusted to the 2008 reference calendar year by multiplying their reported income by 2008 average annual CPI (January–December 2008) and then dividing by the average CPI for March 2007–February 2008. However, the estimates do not reflect the price and cost-of-living differences that may exist between areas.

The **poverty status** data were derived from data collected on the number of persons in a household, each person's relationship to the householder, and income data. The Social Security Administration (SSA) developed the original poverty definition in 1964, which federal interagency committees subsequently revised in 1969 and 1980. The Office of Management and Budget's (OMB) *Directive 14* prescribes the SSA's definition as the official poverty measure for federal agencies to use in their statistical work. Poverty statistics presented in American Community Survey products adhere to the standards defined by OMB in *Directive 14*.

Poverty thresholds vary depending on three criteria: size of family, number of children, and, for one- and two-person families, age of householder. In determining the poverty status of families and unrelated individuals, the Census Bureau uses thresholds (income cutoffs) arranged in a two-dimensional matrix. The matrix consists of family size (from one person to nine or more persons), cross-classified by presence and number of family members under 18 years old (from no children present to eight or more children present). Unrelated individuals and two-person families are further differentiated by age of reference person (under 65 years old and 65 years old and over). To determine a person's poverty status, the person's total family income over the previous 12 months is compared with the poverty threshold appropriate for that person's family size and composition. If the total income of that person's family is less than the threshold appropriate for that family, then the person is considered poor or "below the poverty level," together with every member of his or her family. If a person is not living with anyone related by birth, marriage, or adoption, then the person's own income is compared with his or her poverty threshold. The total number of persons below the poverty level is the sum of persons in families and the number of unrelated individuals with incomes below the poverty level over the previous 12 months.

**Poverty Thresholds for 2011 by Size of Family and Number of Related Children Under 18 Years**

| Size of family unit | Weighted average thresholds |
|---|---|
| One person (unrelated individual) | 11,484 |
| Under 65 years | 11,702 |
| 65 years and over | 10,788 |
| | |
| Two people | 14,657 |
| Householder under 65 years | 15,139 |
| Householder 65 years and over | 13,609 |
| | |
| Three people | 17,916 |
| Four people | 23,021 |
| Five people | 27,251 |
| Six people | 30,847 |
| Seven people | 35,085 |
| Eight people | 39,064 |
| Nine people or more | 46,572 |

**Source: U.S. Census Bureau.**

## PERSONAL INCOME AND EARNINGS, Items 62–83

**Source: U.S. Bureau of Economic Analysis, Regional Economic Accounts**
**http://www.bea.gov/regional/index.htm#state**

**Total personal income** is the current income received by residents of an area from all sources. It is measured before deductions of income and other personal taxes, but after deductions of personal contributions for Social Security, government retirement, and other social insurance programs. It consists of **wage and salary disbursements** (covering all employee earnings, including executive salaries, bonuses, commissions, payments-in-kind, incentive payments, and tips); various types of supplementary earnings, such as employers' contributions to pension funds (termed "other labor income" or "supplements to wages and salaries"); proprietors' income; rental income of persons; dividends; personal interest income; and government and business transfer payments.

**Per capita personal income** is based on the resident population estimated as of July 1 of the year shown.

**Proprietors' income** is the monetary income and income-in-kind of proprietorships and partnerships (including the independent professions) and the income of tax-exempt cooperatives. **Dividends** are cash payments by corporations to stockholders who are U.S. residents. **Interest** is the monetary and imputed interest income of persons from all sources. **Rent** is the monetary income of persons from the rental of real property, except the income of persons primarily engaged in the real estate business; the imputed net rental income of owner-occupants of nonfarm dwellings; and the royalties received by persons.

**Transfer payments** are income for which services are not currently rendered. They consist of both government and business transfer payments. Government transfer payments include payments under the following programs: Federal Old-Age, Survivors, and Disability Insurance ("Social Security"); Medicare and medical vendor payments; unemployment insurance; railroad and government retirement; federal- and state-government-insured workers' compensation; veterans' benefits, including veterans' life insurance; food stamps; black lung payments; Supplemental Security Income; and Temporary Assistance for Needy Families. Government payments to nonprofit institutions, other than for work under research and development contracts, are also included. Business transfer payments consist primarily of liability payments for personal injury and of corporate gifts to nonprofit institutions.

Personal income differs in definition from money income (items 54–57). For example, personal income includes pension rights, employer-provided health insurance, food stamps, and Medicare. These are not included in the definition of money income.

**Earnings** cover wage and salary disbursements, other labor income, and proprietors' income.

The data for earnings obtained from the Bureau of Economic Analysis (BEA) are based on place of work. In computing personal income, BEA makes an "adjustment for residence" to earnings, based on commuting patterns; personal income is thus presented on a place-of-residence basis.

**Farm** earnings include the income of farm workers (wages and salaries and other labor income) and farm proprietors. Farm proprietors' income includes only the income of sole proprietorships and partnerships.

Farm earnings estimates are benchmarked to data collected in the Census of Agriculture and the revised Department of Agriculture statistical totals of income and expense items.

**Goods-related** industries include mining, construction, and manufacturing. In many metropolitan areas, small amounts for mining are suppressed for confidentiality reasons. **Service-related** and other industries include private-sector earnings in agricultural services, forestry, and fisheries; transportation and public utilities; wholesale trade; retail trade; finance, insurance, and real estate; and services. Government earnings include all levels of government. Industries are categorized under the North American Industry Classification System (NAICS), and are not comparable to years prior to 2002.

## SOCIAL SECURITY AND SUPPLEMENTAL SECURITY INCOME, Items 84–86
**Source: U.S. Social Security Administration**
http://www.ssa.gov/policy/docs/statcomps/oasdisc/
http://www.ssa.gov/policy/docs/statcomps/ssisc/

Social Security beneficiaries are persons receiving benefits under the Old-Age, Survivors, and Disability Insurance Program. These include retired or disabled workers covered by the program, their spouses and dependent children, and the surviving spouses and dependent children of deceased workers.

Supplemental Security Income (SSI) recipients are persons receiving SSI payments. The SSI program is a cash assistance program that provides monthly benefits to low-income aged, blind, or disabled persons.

Data are as of December of the year shown.

## HOUSING, Items 87–96
**Source: U.S. Census Bureau—2010 Census of Population and Housing**
**U.S. Census Bureau—American Community Survey, 2007–2011**
http://2010.census.gov/2010census/data/
http://www.census.gov/acs/www/

The housing unit counts in columns 87 and 88 are from the 2010 census. The characteristics of occupied housing units in 2007–2011 are from the American Community Survey.

A **housing unit** is a house, apartment, mobile home or trailer, group of rooms, or single room occupied or, if vacant, intended for occupancy as separate living quarters. Separate living quarters are those in which the occupants do not live and eat with any other person in the structure and which have direct access from the outside of the building through a common hall.

The occupants of a housing unit may be a single family, one person living alone, two or more families living together, or any other group of related or unrelated persons who share living quarters. Both occupied and vacant housing units are included in the housing inventory, although recreational vehicles, tents, caves, boats, railroad cars, and the like are included only if they are occupied as a person's usual place of residence.

A housing unit is classified as occupied if it is the usual place of residence of the person or group of persons living in it at the time of enumeration, or if the occupants are only temporarily absent (away on vacation). A household consists of all persons who occupy a housing unit as their usual place of residence. Vacant units for sale or rent include units rented or sold but not occupied and any other units held off the market.

**Median value** is the dollar amount that divides the distribution of specified owner-occupied housing units into two equal parts, with half of all units below the median value and half of all units above the median value. Value is defined as the respondent's estimate of what the house would sell for if it were for sale. Data are presented for single-family units on fewer than 10 acres of land that have no business or medical offices on the property.

**Median rent** divides the distribution of renter-occupied housing units into two equal parts. The rent concept used in this volume is gross rent, which includes the amount of cash rent a renter pays (contract rent) plus the estimated average cost of utilities and fuels, if these are paid by the renter. The rent is the amount of rent only for living quarters and excludes amounts paid for any business or other space occupied. Single-family houses on lots of 10 or more acres of land are also excluded.

**Housing cost** as a percentage of income is shown separately for owners with mortgages, owners without mortgages, and renters. Rent as a percentage of income is a computed ratio of gross rent and monthly household income (total household income in the past 12 months divided by 12). Selected owner costs include utilities and fuels, mortgage payments, insurance, taxes, etc. In each case, the ratio of housing cost to income is computed separately for each housing unit. The housing cost ratios for half of all units are above the median shown in this book, and half are below the median shown in the book.

**Substandard units** are occupied units that are overcrowded or lack complete plumbing facilities. For the purposes of this item, "overcrowded" is defined as having 1.01 persons or more per room. Complete plumbing facilities include hot and cold piped water, a flush toilet, and a bathtub or shower. These facilities must be located inside the housing unit, but do not have to be in the same room.

## CIVILIAN LABOR FORCE AND UNEMPLOYMENT, Items 97–100
### Source: U.S. Bureau of Labor Statistics—Local Area Unemployment Statistics
### http://www.bls.gov/lau/#tables

Data for the civilian labor force are the product of a federal-state cooperative program in which state employment security agencies prepare labor force and unemployment estimates under concepts, definitions, and technical procedures established by the Bureau of Labor Statistics (BLS). The civilian labor force consists of all civilians 16 years old and over who are either employed or unemployed.

Unemployment includes all persons who did not work during the survey week, made specific efforts to find a job during the previous four weeks, and were available for work during the survey week (except for temporary illness). Persons waiting to be called back to a job from which they had been laid off and those waiting to report to a new job within the next 30 days are included in unemployment figures.

Table C includes annual average data for the year shown. The Local Area Unemployment Statistics data are periodically updated to reflect revised inputs, reestimation, and controlling to new statewide totals.

## CIVILIAN EMPLOYMENT, Items 101–103
### Source: U.S. Census Bureau—American Community Survey, 2010
### http://www.census.gov/acs/www/

**Total employment** includes all civilians 16 years old and over who were either (1) "at work"—those who did any work at all during the reference week as paid employees, worked in either their own business or profession, worked on their own farm, or worked 15 hours or more as unpaid workers in a family farm or business; or were (2) "with a job, but not at work" —those who had a job but were not at work that week due to illness, weather, industrial dispute, vacation, or other personal reasons.

The **occupational categories** are based on the occupational classification system that was developed for the 2000 census. This system consists of 509 specific occupational categories for employed persons arranged into 23 major occupational groups. This classification was developed based on the *Standard Occupational Classification (SOC) Manual: 2000*, published by the Executive Office of the President, Office of Management and Budget.

## PRIVATE NONFARM EMPLOYMENT AND EARNINGS, Items 104–112
### Source: U.S. Bureau of Labor Statistics—County Business Patterns
### http://www.census.gov/econ/cbp/index.html

Data for private nonfarm employment and earnings are compiled from the payroll information reported monthly in the Census Bureau publication *County Business Patterns*. The estimates are based on surveys conducted by the Census Bureau and administrative records from the Internal Revenue Service (IRS).

The following types of employment are excluded from the tables: government employment, self-employed persons, farm workers, and domestic service workers. Railroad employment jointly covered by Social Security and railroad retirement programs, employment on oceanborne vessels, and employment in foreign countries are also excluded.

Annual payroll is the combined amount of wages paid, tips reported, and other compensation (including salaries, vacation allowances, bonuses, commissions, sick-leave pay, and the value of payments-in-kind such as free meals and lodging) paid to employees before deductions for Social Security, income tax, insurance, union dues, etc. All forms of compensation are included, regardless of whether they are subject to income tax or the Federal Insurance Contributions Act tax, with the exception of annuities, third-party sick pay, and supplemental unemployment compensation benefits (even if income tax was withheld). For corporations, total annual payroll includes compensation paid to officers and executives; for unincorporated businesses, it excludes profit or other compensation of proprietors or partners.

## AGRICULTURE, ITEMS 113–132
### Source: U.S. Department of Agriculture, National Agricultural Statistics Service—2007 Census of Agriculture
### http://www.agcensus.usda.gov/Publications/2007/index.asp

Data for the 2007 Census of Agriculture were collected in 2008, but pertain to the year 2007.

The Census Bureau took a census of agriculture every 10 years from 1840 to 1920; since 1925, this census has been taken roughly once every 5 years. The 1997 Census of Agriculture was the first one conducted by the National Agricultural Statistics Service of the U.S. Department of Agriculture. Over time, the definition of a farm has varied. For recent censuses (including the 2007 census), a farm has been defined as any place from which $1,000 or more of agricultural products were produced and sold or normally would have been sold during the census year. Dollar figures are expressed in current dollars and have not been adjusted for inflation or deflation.

The term **operator** refers to a person who operates a farm by either doing the work or making day-to-day decisions about such activities as planting, harvesting, feeding, marketing, etc. The operator may be the owner, a member of the owner's household, a salaried manager, a tenant, a renter, or a sharecropper. If a person rents land to others or has land worked on shares by others, he/she is considered the operator only of the land that is retained for his/her own operation. The census collected information on the total number of operators, the total number of women operators, and demographic information for up to three operators per farm.

The acreage designated as **land in farms** consists primarily of agricultural land used for crops, pasture, or grazing. It also includes woodland and wasteland not actually under cultivation or used for pasture or grazing, provided that this land was part of the farm operator's total operation. Land in farms is an operating-unit concept and includes all land owned and operated, as well as all land rented from others. Land used rent-free is classified as land rented from others. All land in Indian reservations used for growing crops or grazing livestock is classified as land in farms.

**Irrigated land** includes all land watered by any artificial or controlled means, such as sprinklers, flooding, furrows or ditches, sub-irrigation, and spreader dikes. Included are supplemental, partial, and preplant irrigation. Each acre was counted only once regardless of the number of times it was irrigated or harvested. Livestock lagoon waste water distributed by sprinkler or flood systems was also included.

**Total cropland** includes cropland harvested, cropland used only for pasture or grazing, cropland on which all crops failed or were abandoned, cropland in cultivated summer fallow, and cropland idle or used for cover crops or soil improvement but not harvested and not pastured or grazed.

Respondents were asked to report their estimate of the current market **value of land and buildings** owned, rented, or leased from others, and rented and leased to others. Market value refers to the respondent's estimate of what the land and buildings would sell for under current market conditions. If the value of land and buildings was not reported, it was estimated during processing by using the average value of land and buildings from similar farms in the same geographic area.

The **value of machinery and equipment** was estimated by the respondent as the current market value of all cars, trucks, tractors, combines, balers, irrigation equipment, etc., used on the farm. This value is an estimate of what the machinery and equipment would sell for in its present condition and not the replacement or depreciated value. Share interests are reported at full value at the farm where the equipment and machinery are usually kept. Only equipment that was actually used in 2006 and 2007, or newly purchased but not yet used and physically located at the farm on December 31, 2007, is included.

**Market value of agricultural products sold** by farms represents the gross market value before taxes and the production expenses of all agricultural products sold or removed from the place in 2007, regardless of who received the payment. It is equivalent to total sales and it includes sales by the operator as well as the value of any share received by partners, landlords, contractors, and others associated with the operation. It includes value of direct sales and the value of commodities placed in the Commodity Credit Corporation (CCC) loan program. Market value of agricultural products sold does not include payments received for participation in other federal farm programs. Also, it does not include income from farm-related sources such as customwork and other agricultural services, or income from non-farm sources.

**Government payments** consists of direct payments as defined by the 2002 Farm Bill; payments from Conservation Reserve Program (CRP), Wetlands Reserve Program (WRP), Farmable

Wetlands Program (FWP), and Conservation Reserve Enhancement Program (CREP); loan deficiency payments; disaster payments; other conservation programs; and all other federal farm programs under which payments were made directly to farm operators. Commodity Credit Corporation (CCC) proceeds, amount from State and local federal crop insurance payments were not included in this category.

## WATER CONSUMPTION, Items 133–134
**Source: U.S. Geological Survey, National Water Information System—2005 Water Use Data**
**http://water.usgs.gov/watuse/data/2005/index.html**

Every ten years, the U.S. Geological Survey compiles county-level water-use estimates. This volume includes the total fresh and saline withdrawals expressed as million gallons per day. Estimate of withdrawals of ground and surface water are given for the following categories of use: public water supplies, domestic, commercial, irrigation, livestock, industrial, mining, and thermo-electric power. The number of gallons withdrawn per person is based on the metropolitan area population but the water is not necessarily used locally, providing an indicator of metropolitan areas that serve as major water sources.

## 2007 Economic CENSUS: OVERVIEW, Items 135–166
**Source: U.S. Census Bureau**
**http://www.census.gov/econ/census07/**

The Economic Census provides a detailed portrait of the nation's economy, from the national to the local level, once every five years. The 2007 Economic Census covers nearly all of the U.S. economy in its basic collection of establishment statistics. The 1997 Economic Census was the first major data source to use the new North American Industry Classification System (NAICS); therefore, data from this census are not comparable to economic data from prior years, which were based on the Standard Industrial Classification (SIC) system.

NAICS, developed in cooperation with Canada and Mexico, classifies North America's economic activities at two-, three-, four-, and five-digit levels of detail; the U.S. version of NAICS further defines industries to a sixth digit. The Economic Census takes advantage of this hierarchy to publish data at these successive levels of detail: sector (two-digit), subsector (three-digit), industry group (four-digit), industry (five-digit), and U.S. industry (six-digit). Information in Table A is at the two-digit level, with a few three- and four-digit items. The data in Tables B and C are at the two-digit level.

Several key statistics are tabulated for all industries in this volume, including number of establishments (or companies), number of employees, payroll, and certain measures of output (sales, receipts, revenue, value of shipments, or value of construction work done).

**Number of establishments.** An establishment is a single physical location at which business is conducted. It is not necessarily identical with a company or enterprise, which may consist of one establishment or more. Economic Census figures represent a summary of reports for individual establishments rather than companies. For cases in which a census report was received, separate information was obtained for each location where business was conducted. When administrative records of other federal agencies were used instead of a census report, no information was available on the number of locations operated. Each Economic Census establishment was tabulated according to the physical location at which the business was conducted. The count of establishments represents those in business at any time during 2002.

When two activities or more were carried on at a single location under a single ownership, all activities were generally grouped together as a single establishment. The entire establishment was classified on the basis of its major activity and all of its data were included in that classification. However, when distinct and separate economic activities (for which different industry classification codes were appropriate) were conducted at a single location under a single ownership, separate establishment reports for each of the different activities were obtained in the census.

**Number of employees.** Paid employees consist of the full-time and part-time employees, including salaried officers and executives of corporations. Included are employees on paid sick leave, paid holidays, and paid vacations; not included are proprietors and partners of unincorporated businesses. The definition of paid employees is the same as that used by the Internal Revenue Service (IRS) on form 941.

For some industries, the Economic Census gives codes representing the number of employees as a range of numbers (for example, ''100 to 249 employees'' or ''1,000 to 2,499'' employees). In this volume, those codes have been replaced by the standard suppression code ''D''.

**Payroll.** Payroll includes all forms of compensation, such as salaries, wages, commissions, dismissal pay, bonuses, vacation allowances, sick-leave pay, and employee contributions to qualified pension plans paid during the year to all employees. For corporations, payroll includes amounts paid to officers and executives; for unincorporated businesses, it does not include profit or other compensation of proprietors or partners. Payroll is reported before deductions for Social Security, income tax, insurance, union dues, etc. This definition of payroll is the same as that used by on IRS form 941.

**Sales, shipments, receipts, revenue, or business done.** This measure includes the total sales, shipments, receipts, revenue, or business done by establishments within the scope of the Economic Census. The definition of each of these items is specific to the economic sector measured.

# WHOLESALE TRADE, Items 135–138
## Source: U.S. Census Bureau—2007 Economic Census (See Overview of 2007 Economic Census prior to Item 135)

The Wholesale Trade sector (sector 42) comprises establishments engaged in wholesaling merchandise, generally without transformation, and rendering services incidental to the sale of merchandise. The wholesaling process is an intermediate step in the distribution of merchandise.

Wholesalers are organized to sell or arrange the purchase or sale of (1) goods for resale (i.e., goods sold to other wholesalers or retailers), (2) capital or durable nonconsumer goods, and (3) raw and intermediate materials and supplies used in production.

Wholesalers sell merchandise to other businesses and normally operate from a warehouse or office. These warehouses and offices are characterized by having little or no display of merchandise. In addition, neither the design nor the location of the premises is intended to solicit walk-in traffic. Wholesalers do not normally use advertising directed to the general public. In general, customers are initially reached via telephone, in-person marketing, or specialized advertising, which may include the internet and other electronic means. Follow-up orders are either vendor-initiated or client-initiated, are usually based on previous sales, and typically exhibit strong ties between sellers and buyers. In fact, transactions are often conducted between wholesalers and clients that have long-standing business relationships.

This sector is made up of two main types of wholesalers: those that sell goods on their own account and those that arrange sales and purchases for others for a commission or fee.

(1) Establishments that sell goods on their own account are known as wholesale merchants, distributors, jobbers, drop shippers, import/export merchants, and sales branches. These establishments typically maintain their own warehouse, where they receive and handle goods for their customers. Goods are generally sold without transformation, but may include integral functions, such as sorting, packaging, labeling, and other marketing services.

(2) Establishments arranging for the purchase or sale of goods owned by others or purchasing goods on a commission basis are known as agents and brokers, commission merchants, import/export agents and brokers, auction companies, and manufacturers' representatives. These establishments operate from offices and generally do not own or handle the goods they sell.

Some wholesale establishments may be connected with a single manufacturer and promote and sell that particular manufacturer's products to a wide range of other wholesalers or retailers. Other wholesalers may be connected to a retail chain or a limited number of retail chains and only provide the products needed by the particular retail operation(s). These wholesalers may obtain the products from a wide range of manufacturers. Still other wholesalers may not take title to the goods, but act instead as agents and brokers for a commission.

Although wholesaling normally denotes sales in large volumes, durable nonconsumer goods may be sold in single units. Sales of capital or durable nonconsumer goods used in the production of goods and services, such as farm machinery, medium- and heavy-duty trucks, and industrial machinery, are always included in Wholesale Trade.

The metropolitan area table includes only **Merchant wholesalers, except manufacturers' sales branches and offices,** establishments primarily engaged in buying and selling merchandise on their own account. Included here are such types of establishments as wholesale distributors and jobbers, importers, exporters, own-brand importers/marketers, terminal and country grain elevators, and farm products assemblers.

## RETAIL TRADE, Items 139–142

Source: U.S. Census Bureau—2007 Economic Census
(See Overview of 2007 Economic Census prior to Item 135)

The Retail Trade sector (44–45) is made up of establishments engaged in retailing merchandise, generally without transformation, and rendering services incidental to the sale of merchandise.

The retailing process is the final step in the distribution of merchandise; retailers are therefore organized to sell merchandise in small quantities to the general public. This sector comprises two main types of retailers: store and nonstore retailers.

Store retailers operate fixed point-of-sale locations, located and designed to attract a high volume of walk-in customers. In general, retail stores have extensive displays of merchandise and use mass-media advertising to attract customers. They typically sell merchandise to the general public for personal or household consumption; some also serve business and institutional clients. These include establishments such as office supply stores, computer and software stores, building materials dealers, plumbing supply stores, and electrical supply stores. Catalog showrooms, gasoline service stations, automotive dealers, and mobile home dealers are treated as store retailers.

In addition to retailing merchandise, some types of store retailers are also engaged in the provision of after-sales services, such as repair and installation. For example, new automobile dealers, electronic and appliance stores, and musical instrument and supply stores often provide repair services. As a general rule, establishments engaged in retailing merchandise and providing after-sales services are classified in this sector.

Nonstore retailers, like store retailers, are organized to serve the general public, although their retailing methods differ. The establishments of this subsector reach customers and market merchandise with methods including the broadcasting of "infomercials," the broadcasting and publishing of direct-response advertising, the publishing of paper and electronic catalogs, door-to-door solicitation, in-home demonstration, selling from portable stalls (street vendors, except food), and distribution through vending machines. Establishments engaged in the direct sale (nonstore) of products, such as home heating oil dealers and home-delivery newspaper routes are included in this sector.

The buying of goods for resale is a characteristic of retail trade establishments that distinguishes them from establishments in the Agriculture, Manufacturing, and Construction sectors. For example, farms that sell their products at or from the point of production are classified in Agriculture instead of in Retail Trade. Similarly, establishments that both manufacture and sell their products to the general public are classified in Manufacturing instead of Retail Trade. However, establishments that engage in processing activities incidental to retailing are classified in Retail Trade.

## REAL ESTATE AND RENTAL AND LEASING, Items 143–146

Source: U.S. Census Bureau—2007 Economic Census
(See Overview of 2007 Economic Census prior to Item 135)

The Real Estate and Rental and Leasing sector (53) comprises establishments primarily engaged in renting, leasing, or otherwise allowing the use of tangible or intangible assets, and establishments providing related services. The major portion of this sector is made up of establishments that rent, lease, or otherwise allow the use of their own assets by others. The assets may be tangible, such as real estate and equipment, or intangible, such as patents and trademarks.

This sector also includes establishments primarily engaged in managing real estate for others, selling, renting, and/or buying real estate for others, and appraising real estate. These activities are closely related to this sector's main activity. In addition, a substantial proportion of property management is self-performed by lessors.

The main components of this sector are the real estate lessors industries; equipment lessors industries (including motor vehicles, computers, and consumer goods); and lessors of nonfinancial intangible assets (except copyrighted works).

## PROFESSIONAL, SCIENTIFIC, AND TECHNICAL SERVICES, Items 147–150

Source: U.S. Census Bureau—2007 Economic Census
(See Overview of 2007 Economic Census prior to Item 135)

The Professional, Scientific, and Technical Services sector (54) is made up of establishments that specialize in performing professional, scientific, and technical activities for others. These activities require a high degree of expertise and training. The establishments in this sector specialize in one or more areas and provide services to clients in a variety of industries (and, in some cases, to households). Activities performed include legal advice and representation; accounting, bookkeeping, and payroll services; architectural, engineering, and specialized design services; computer services; consulting services; research services; advertising services; photographic services; translation and interpretation services; veterinary services; and other professional, scientific, and technical services.

Table C includes only those establishments subject to federal income tax.

This sector excludes establishments primarily engaged in providing a range of day-to-day office administrative services, such as financial planning, billing and record keeping, personnel services, and physical distribution and logistics services. These establishments are classified in sector 56, Administrative and Support and Waste Management and Remediation Services.

## MANUFACTURING, Items 151–154
Source: U.S. Census Bureau—2007 Economic Census
(See Overview of 2007 Economic Census prior to Item 135)

The Manufacturing sector (31–33) is made up of establishments engaged in the mechanical, physical, or chemical transformation of materials, substances, or components into new products. The assembling of component parts of manufactured products is considered manufacturing, except in cases in which the activity is appropriately classified in the Construction sector. Establishments in the Manufacturing sector are often described as plants, factories, or mills, and characteristically use power-driven machines and materials-handling equipment. However, establishments that transform materials or substances into new products by hand or in the worker's home, and establishments engaged in selling to the general public products made on the same premises from which they are sold (such as bakeries, candy stores, and custom tailors) may also be included in this sector. Manufacturing establishments may process materials or contract with other establishments to process their materials for them. Both types of establishments are included in the Manufacturing sector.

The materials, substances, or components transformed by manufacturing establishments are raw materials that are products of agriculture, forestry, fishing, mining, or quarrying, or are products of other manufacturing establishments. The materials used may be purchased directly from producers, obtained through customary trade channels, or secured without recourse to the market by transferring the product from one establishment to another, under the same ownership. The new product of a manufacturing establishment may be finished (in the sense that it is ready for utilization or consumption), or it may be semifinished to become an input for an establishment engaged in further manufacturing. For example, the product of the alumina refinery is the input used in the primary production of aluminum; primary aluminum is the input used in an aluminum wire drawing plant; and aluminum wire is the input used in a fabricated wire product manufacturing establishment.

Data are included for counties with 500 or more employees in the Manufacturing sector.

## ACCOMMODATION AND FOOD SERVICES, Items 155–158
Source: U.S. Census Bureau—2007 Economic Census
(See Overview of 2007 Economic Census prior to Item 135)

The Accommodation and Food Services sector (72) consists of establishments that provide customers with lodging and/or meals, snacks, and beverages for immediate consumption. This sector includes both accommodation and food services establishments because the two activities are often combined at the same establishment.

Excluded from this sector are civic and social organizations, amusement and recreation parks, theaters, and other recreation or entertainment facilities providing food and beverage services.

## HEALTH CARE AND SOCIAL ASSISTANCE, Items 159–162
Source: U.S. Census Bureau—2007 Economic Census
(See Overview of 2007 Economic Census prior to Item 135)

The Health Care and Social Assistance sector (62) consists of establishments that provide health care and social assistance services to individuals. The sector includes both health care and social assistance because it is sometimes difficult to distinguish between the boundaries of these two activities. The industries in this sector are arranged on a continuum, starting with establishments that provide medical care exclusively, continuing with those that provide health care and social assistance, and finishing with those that provide only social assistance. The services provided by establishments in this sector are delivered by trained professionals. All industries in the sector share this commonality of process—namely, labor inputs of health practitioners or social workers with the requisite expertise. Many of the industries in the sector are defined based on the educational degree held by the practitioners included in the industry.

Excluded from this sector are aerobic classes, which can be found in subsector 713, Amusement, Gambling, and Recreation Industries; and nonmedical diet and weight-reducing centers, which can be found in subsector 812, Personal and Laundry Services. Although these can be viewed as health services, they are not typically delivered by health practitioners.

## OTHER SERVICES, EXCEPT PUBLIC ADMINISTRATION Items 163–166
Source: U.S. Census Bureau—2007 Economic Census
(See Overview of 2007 Economic Census prior to Item 135)

The Other Services, Except Public Administration sector (81) comprises establishments engaged in providing services not specifically categorized elsewhere in the classification system. Establishments in this sector are primarily engaged in activities such as equipment and machinery repairing, promoting or administering religious activities, grant making, and advocacy; this sector also includes establishments that provide dry-cleaning and laundry services, personal care services, death care services, pet care services, photofinishing services, temporary parking services, and dating services.

Private households that employ workers on or about the premises in activities primarily concerned with the operation of the household are included in this sector.

Excluded from this sector are establishments primarily engaged in retailing new equipment and performing repairs and general maintenance on equipment. These establishments are classified in sector 44–45, Retail Trade.

## FEDERAL FUNDS, Items 167–177

**Source: U.S. Census Bureau—Consolidated Federal Funds Report**
http://www.census.gov/govs/cffr/

Data on federal expenditure and obligations are obtained from a report prepared by the Census Bureau in accordance with the Consolidated Federal Funds Report (CFFR) Act of 1982 (P.L. 97–326). The data are for federal fiscal years beginning October 1 and ending the following September 30. Dollar amounts reported can reflect expenditures or obligations. In some cases, dollar amounts are negative, representing de-obligations of financial assistance that had previously been awarded. Such amounts generally appear in the grant categories.

**Direct payments** for individuals include Social Security benefits, federal government retirement, Medicare, Supplemental Security Income, food stamps, educational and housing assistance, and other categories not shown separately. All data represent actual expenditures during the fiscal year.

**Salaries and wages** represent actual federal expenditures during the fiscal year; the geographic distribution of these amounts by state and county was estimated based upon place of employment.

**Procurement contract awards** cover awards given by the United States Postal Service (USPS), as well as those given by all other federal agencies. Amounts provided by the USPS represent actual outlays for contractual commitments, while amounts for other agencies represent the value of obligations for contract actions and do not reflect actual federal government expenditures. In general, only current-year contract actions are included; however, multiple-year obligations may be reported for contract actions of less than three years' duration.

**Grants** data represent the federal obligations incurred at the time the grant is awarded. The amounts reported do not represent actual expenditures, since obligations in one time period may not result in outlays during the same period. Moreover, initial amounts obligated may be adjusted at a later date, through either enhancements or de-obligations. For many grants, this recipient is the state government even though grants monies are subsequently distributed to county, municipal, or township governments.

**Medicaid and other health-related** grants include a variety of grants from the Department of Health and Human Services for health services and research.

**Nutrition and family welfare** grants include a variety of grants from the Department of Health and Human Services for child welfare, special programs for the aging, and related areas. The school lunch program and other nutritional assistance programs administered by the Department of Agriculture are also included in this category.

**Education** grants include a variety of grant programs relating to elementary, secondary, and postsecondary education; adult education; vocational education; faculty training; and related areas.

## BUILDING PERMITS, Items 178 and 179

**Source: U.S. Census Bureau—Building Permits Survey**
http://www.census.gov/const/www/permitsindex.html

These figures represent private residential construction authorized by building permits in approximately 20,000 places in the United States. Valuation represents the expected cost of construction as recorded on the building permit. This figure usually excludes the cost of on-site and off-site development and improvements, as well as the cost of heating, plumbing, electrical, and elevator installations.

National, state, and county totals were obtained by adding the data for permit-issuing places within each jurisdiction. Not all areas of the country require a building or zoning permit. The statistics only represent those areas that do require a permit. These totals thus are limited to permits issued in the 20,000 place universe covered by the Census Bureau and may not include all permits issued within a state. Current surveys indicate that construction is undertaken for all but a very small percentage of housing units authorized by building permits.

Residential building permits include buildings with any number of housing units. Housing units exclude group quarters (such as dormitories and rooming houses), transient accommodations (such as transient hotels, motels, and tourist courts), "HUD-code" manufactured (mobile) homes, moved or relocated units, and housing units created in an existing residential or nonresidential structure.

## LOCAL GOVERNMENT FINANCES, Items 180–193

**Source: U.S. Census Bureau—2007 Census of Governments**
http://www.census.gov/govs/cog/

Data on local government finances are based on result of the 2002 Census of Governments. For each county area, the financial data comprise amounts for all local governments—not only the county government, but also any municipalities, townships, school districts, and special districts within the county. Statistics from governmental units located in two or more county areas are assigned to the county area containing the administrative office.

Revenue and expenditure items include all amounts of money received and paid out, respectively, by a government and its agencies (net of correcting transactions such as recoveries of refunds), with the exception of amounts for debt issuance and retirement and for loan and investment, agency, and private transactions.

Payments among the various funds and agencies of a particular government are excluded from revenue and expenditure items as representing internal transfers. Therefore, a government's contribution to a retirement fund that it administers is not counted as expenditure, nor is the receipt of this contribution by the retirement fund counted as revenue.

Total **general revenue** includes all revenue except utility, liquor stores, and insurance trust revenue. All tax revenue and intergovernmental revenue, even if designated for employee-retirement or local utility purpose, are classified as general revenue.

**Intergovernmental revenue** covers amounts received from the federal government as fiscal aid, reimbursements for performance of general government functions and specific services for the paying government, or in lieu of taxes. It excludes any amounts received from other governments from the sale of property, commodities, and utility services.

**Taxes** consist of compulsory contributions exacted by governments for public purposes. However, this category excludes employer and employee payments for retirement and social insurance purposes, which are classified as insurance trust revenue; it also excludes special assessments, which are classified as non-tax general revenue. Property taxes are taxes conditioned on ownership of property and assessed by its value. Sales and gross receipts taxes do not include dealer discounts, or ''commissions'' allowed to merchants for collection of taxes from consumers. General sales taxes and selected taxes on sales of motor fuels, tobacco products, and other particular commodities and services are included.

**General government expenditure** includes capital outlay, a major portion of which is commonly financed by borrowing. Government revenue does not include receipts from borrowing. Among other things, this distorts the relationship between totals of revenue and expenditure figures that are presented and renders it useless as a direct measure of the degree of budgetary ''balance'' (as that term is generally applied).

**Direct general expenditure** comprises all expenditures of the local governments, excluding utility, liquor stores, insurance trust expenditures, and any intergovernmental payments.

Local government expenditure for **education** is mainly for the provision and general support of schools and other educational facilities and services, including those for educational institutions beyond high school. They cover such related services as student transportation; school lunch and other cafeteria operations; school health, recreation, and library services; and dormitories, dining halls, and bookstores operated by public institutions of higher education.

**Health and hospital expenditure** includes health research; clinics; nursing; immunization; other categorical, environmental, and general health services provided by health agencies; establishment and operation of hospital facilities; provision of hospital care; and support of other public and private hospitals.

**Police protection expenditure** includes police activities such as patrols, communications, custody of persons awaiting trial, and vehicular inspection.

**Public welfare expenditure** covers support of and assistance to needy persons; this aid is contingent upon the person's needs. Included are cash assistance paid directly to needy persons under categorical (Old Age Assistance, Temporary Assistance for Needy Families, Aid to the Blind, and Aid to the Disabled) and other welfare programs; vendor payments made directly to private purveyors for medical care, burials, and other commodities and services provided under welfare programs; welfare institutions; and any intergovernmental or other direct expenditure for welfare purposes. Pensions to former employees and other benefits not contingent on need are excluded.

**Highway expenditure** is for the provision and maintenance of highway facilities, including toll turnpikes, bridges, tunnels, and ferries, as well as regular roads, highways, and streets. Also included are expenditures for street lighting and for snow and ice removal. Not included are highway policing and traffic control, which are considered part of police protection

**Debt outstanding** includes all long-term debt obligations of the government and its agencies (exclusive of utility debt) and all interest-bearing, short-term (repayable within one year) debt obligations remaining unpaid at the close of the fiscal year. It includes judgments, mortgages, and revenue bonds, as well as general obligation bonds, notes, and interest-bearing warrants. This category consists of non-interest-bearing, short-term obligations; inter-fund obligations; amounts owed in a trust or agency capacity; advances and contingent loans from other governments; and rights of individuals to benefit from government-administered employee-retirement funds.

## GOVERNMENT EMPLOYMENT, Items 194–196
**Source: U.S. Bureau of Economic Analysis—Regional Economic Accounts**
**http://www.bea.gov/regional/index.htm#state**

Employment is measured as the average annual sum of full-time and part-time jobs. The estimates are on a place-of-work basis. The estimates are on a place-of-work basis. State and local government employment includes person employed in all state and local government agencies and enterprises. Data for federal civilian employment include civilian employees of the federal government, including civilian employees of the Department of Defense. Military employment includes all persons on active duty status.

## ELECTION STATISTICS, Items 197–199
**Source: Election Data Services, Inc. Washington, DC (copyright)**
**http://www.electiondataservices.com/ index.php?content=elecdata**

© 2013 Election Data Services, Inc. All rights reserved. This material is proprietary and the subject of copyright protection and other intellectual property rights owned by or licensed to Election Data Services, Inc. The use of this material is subject to the terms of a License Agreement. You will be held liable for any unauthorized copying or disclosure of this material.

Election results show the percentage of the total vote cast for the Democratic and Republican candidates, as well as the combined percentage for all other candidates in the 2012 presidential election.

# TABLE D—CITIES

Table D present 147 items of data for cities with populations of 25,000 or more at the time of the 2010 census.

## LAND AREA, Items 1 and 4
### Source: U.S. Census Bureau—2010 Census of Population and Housing
http://2010.census.gov/2010census/data/

Land area measurements are shown to the nearest square kilometer. Land area includes dry land and land temporarily or partially covered by water, such as marshlands, swamps, and river floodplains.

## POPULATION, Items 2–4
### Source: U.S. Census Bureau—Population Estimates
http://www.census.gov/popest/estimates.html

The population data are Census Bureau estimates of the resident population as of July 1 of the year shown.

## POPULATION AND POPULATION CHARACTERISTICS, Items 5–22
### Source: U.S. Census Bureau—2010 Census of Population and Housing
http://2010.census.gov/2010census/data/
### 2007–2011 American Community Survey
http://www.census.gov/acs/www/

Data on age, sex, race, and Hispanic origin are from the 2010 Census. Data on place of birth are from the 2007–2011 American Community Survey, a nationwide continuous survey designed to replace the long form questionnaire used in previous censuses.

Data on race were derived from answers to the question on race that was asked of all persons. The concept of race, as used by the Census Bureau, reflects self-identification by respondents according to the race or races with which they most closely identify. These categories are sociopolitical constructs and should not be interpreted as being scientific or anthropological in nature. Furthermore, the race categories include both racial and national origin groups.

On the American Community Survey, respondents were offered the option of selecting one or more races. This option was not available prior to the 2000 census; thus, comparisons between censuses should be made with caution. In this table, Columns 5 through 9 refer to individuals who identified with each racial category, either alone or in combination with other races. Because respondents could include as many categories as they wished, and because the columns refer to the percentage of the population, the total will often exceed 100 percent.

The **White** population is defined as persons who indicated their race as White, as well as persons who did not classify themselves in one of the specific race categories listed on the questionnaire but entered a nationality such as Irish, German, Italian, Lebanese, Near Easterner, Arab, or Polish.

The **Black** population includes persons who indicated their race as "Black, African Am., or Negro," as well as persons who did not classify themselves in one of the specific race categories but reported entries such as African American, Afro American, Kenyan, Nigerian, or Haitian.

The **American Indian or Alaska Native** population includes persons who indicated their race as American Indian or Alaska Native, as well as persons who did not classify themselves in one of the specific race categories but reported entries such as Canadian Indian, French-American Indian, Spanish-American Indian, Eskimo, Aleut, Alaska Indian, or any of the American Indian or Alaska Native tribes.

The **Asian and Pacific Islander** population combines two census groupings: **Asian** and **Native Hawaiian or Other Pacific Islander**. Because two separate groups are combined, this category occasionally represents more than 100 percent of a city's population. The **Asian** population includes persons who indicated their race as Asian Indian, Chinese, Filipino, Japanese, Korean, Vietnamese, or "Other Asian," as well as persons who provided write-in entries of such groups as Cambodian, Laotian, Hmong, Pakistani, or Taiwanese. The **Native Hawaiian or Other Pacific Islander** population includes persons who indicated their race as "Native Hawaiian," "Guamanian or Chamorro," "Samoan," or "Other Pacific Islander," as well as persons who reported entries such as Part Hawaiian, American Samoan, Fijian, Melanesian, or Tahitian.

The **Some other race** category includes all persons who indicated "Some other race," as well as persons who wrote in a category not included in race categories describe above, including entries such as multiracial, mixed, interracial, or a Hispanic/Latino group such as Mexican, Puerto Rican, or Cuban in the "Some other race" write-in space.

The **Hispanic population** is based on a separate question that asked respondents "Is this person Spanish/Hispanic/Latino?" Persons marking any one of the four Hispanic categories (i.e., Mexican, Puerto Rican, Cuban, or other Spanish) are collectively referred to as Hispanic.

The Hispanic origin question was placed before the race question and specific instructions indicated that both questions should be answered.

The **foreign-born** population includes all persons who were not U.S. citizens at birth. Foreign-born persons are those who indicated they were either a U.S. citizen by naturalization or were not a citizen of the United States. The foreign-born population consists of immigrants (legal permanent residents), temporary migrants (students), humanitarian migrants (refugees), and unauthorized migrants (persons illegally residing in the United States).

**Age** is defined as age at last birthday (number of completed years since birth), at the time of the interview. The American Community Survey also asked for the specific date of birth of the respondent. Both age and date of birth are used in combination to calculate the most accurate age at the time of the interview.

The **female** population is shown as a percentage of total population.

## POPULATION CHANGE, Items 23–26

Source: U.S. Census Bureau—Decennial Censuses
U.S. Census Bureau—Population Estimateshttp://
www.census.gov/main/www/cen2000.html
http://2010.census.gov/2010census/data/
http://www.census.gov/popest/estimates.html

The population data for 2000 and 2010 are from the decennial censuses and represent the resident population as of April 1 of those years. The data for 2012 are from the Census Bureau's Population Estimates Program and represent the estimated resident population as of July 1.

The change in population from 2000 to 2010 is calculated from census data based on city boundaries as they existed in 2000 and 2010, respectively. No attempt was made to adjust the data to reflect boundary changes.

## HOUSEHOLDS, Items 27–30

Source: U.S. Census Bureau—2010 Census of
Population and Housing
http://2010.census.gov/2010census/data/

A **household** includes all of the persons who occupy a housing unit. (Persons not living in households are classified as living in group quarters.) A housing unit is a house, an apartment, a mobile home, a group of rooms, or a single room occupied (or, if vacant, intended for occupancy) as separate living quarters. Separate living quarters are those in which the occupants live separately from any other persons in the building and have direct access from the outside of the building or through a common hall. The occupants may be a single family, one person living alone, two or more families living together, or any other group of related or unrelated persons who share living quarters. The number of households is the same as the number of year-round occupied housing units.

A **family** includes a householder and one or more other persons living in the same household who are related to the householder by birth, marriage, or adoption. All persons in a household who are related to the householder are regarded as members of his or her family. A **family household** may contain persons not related to the householder; thus, family households may include more members than families do. A household can contain only one family for the purposes of census tabulations. Not all households contain families, as a household may comprise a group of unrelated persons or of one person living alone. Families are classified by type as either a ''husband-wife family'' or ''other family,'' according to the presence or absence of a spouse.

The measure of **persons per household** is obtained by dividing the number of persons in households by the number of households or householders. One person in each household is designated as the householder. In most cases, this is the person (or one of the persons) in whose name the house is owned, being bought, or rented. If there is no such person in the household, any adult household member 15 years old and over can be designated as the householder.

The category **female family householder** includes only female-headed family households with no spouse present.

## GROUP QUARTERS, Item 31–34

Source: U.S. Census Bureau—2010 Census of
Population and Housing
http://2010.census.gov/2010census/data/

The Census Bureau classifies all persons not living in households as living in group quarters; this category includes both the institutional and noninstitutional populations. This volume includes the total number of persons in group quarters and in selected types of group quarters.

The **institutionalized population** includes persons who are primarily ineligible, unable, or unlikely to participate in the labor force while residents, including those in correctional institutions, skilled-nursing facilities, mental (psychiatric) hospitals, and juvenile institutions.

**Nursing facilities** include facilities licensed to provide medical care with 7-day, 24-hour coverage for people requiring long-term non-acute care. People in these facilities require nursing care, regardless of age.. Included in this category are skilled-nursing facilities, intermediate-care facilities, long-term care rooms in wards or buildings on the grounds of hospitals, or long-term care rooms/nursing wings in congregate housing facilities. Also included are nursing, convalescent, and rest homes, such as soldiers', veterans', and fraternal or religious homes for the aged, with or without nursing care.

The **noninstitutionalized population** includes persons who live in group quarters other than institutions, such as college dormitories, military quarters, and group homes.

## CRIME, Items 35–38

Source: U.S. Federal Bureau of Investigation—
Uniform Crime Reports
http://www.fbi.gov/ucr/ucr.htm

Crime data are as reported to the Federal Bureau of Investigation (FBI) by law enforcement agencies and have not been adjusted for underreporting. This may affect comparability between geographic areas or over time.

Through the voluntary contribution of crime statistics by law enforcement agencies across the United States, the Uniform Crime Reporting (UCR) Program provides periodic assessments of crime in the nation as measured by offenses that have come to the attention of the law enforcement community. The Committee on Uniform Crime Records of the International Association of Chiefs of Police initiated this voluntary national data collection effort in 1930. The UCR Program contributors compile and submit their crime data either directly to the FBI or through state-level UCR Programs.

Seven offenses, because of their severity, frequency of occurrence, and likelihood of being reported to police, were initially selected to serve as an index for evaluating fluctuations in the volume of crime. These serious crimes were murder and nonnegligent manslaughter, forcible rape, robbery, aggravated assault, burglary, larceny-theft, and motor vehicle theft. By congressional mandate, arson was added as the eighth index offense in 1979. The totals shown in this volume do not include arson.

In 2004, the FBI discontinued the use of the Crime Index in the UCR Program and its publications, stating that the Crime Index was driven upward by the offense with the highest number of cases (in this case, larceny-theft), creating a bias against jurisdictions with a high number of larceny-thefts but a low number of other serious crimes, such as murder and forcible rape. The FBI is currently publishing a violent crime total and property crime total until a more viable index is developed. This book includes the total Crime Index, as well as violent crime and property crime rates.

**Violent crimes** include four categories of offenses: (1) Murder and nonnegligent manslaughter, as defined in the UCR Program, is the willful (nonnegligent) killing of one human being by another. This offense excludes deaths caused by negligence, suicide, or accident; justifiable homicides; and attempts to murder or assaults to murder. (2) Forcible rape is the carnal knowledge of a female forcibly and against her will. Assaults or attempts to commit rape by force or threat of force are also included; however, statutory rape (without force) and other sex offenses are excluded. (3) Robbery is the taking or attempting to take anything of value from the care, custody, or control of a person or persons by force or threat of force or violence and/or by putting the victim in fear. (4) Aggravated assault is an unlawful attack by one person upon another for the purpose of inflicting severe or aggravated bodily injury. This type of assault is usually accompanied by the use of a weapon or by other means likely to produce death or great bodily harm. Attempts are included, since injury does not necessarily have to result when a gun, knife, or other weapon is used, as these incidents could and probably would result in a serious personal injury if the crime were successfully completed.

**Property crimes** include three categories: (1) Burglary, or breaking and entering, is the unlawful entry of a structure to commit a felony or theft, even though no force was used to gain entrance. (2) Larceny-theft is the unauthorized taking of the personal property of another, without the use of force. (3) Motor vehicle theft is the unauthorized taking of any motor vehicle.

Rates are based on population estimates provided by the FBI. If a city is not in the UCR database, or if the population total for the units aggregated was less than 75 percent of the city's population (as estimated by the Census Bureau), the total was not considered representative of the city as a whole and was not published. State and U.S. totals include FBI estimates for those areas.

## EDUCATIONAL ATTAINMENT, Items 39–41
**Source: U.S. Census Bureau—American Community Survey, 2007–2011**
**http://www.census.gov/acs/www/**

Data on **educational attainment** are tabulated for the population 25 years old and over. The data were derived from a question that asked respondents for the highest level of school completed or the highest degree received. Persons who had passed a high school equivalency examination were considered high school graduates. Schooling received in foreign schools was to be reported as the equivalent grade or years in the regular American school system.

Vocational and technical training, such as barber school training; business, trade, technical, and vocational schools; or other training for a specific trade are specifically excluded.

**High school graduate or less.** This category includes persons whose highest degree was a high school diploma or its equivalent, and those who reported any level lower than a high school diploma.

**Bachelor's degree or more.** This category includes persons who have received bachelor's degrees, master's degrees, professional school degrees (such as law school or medical school degrees), and doctoral degrees.

## INCOME AND POVERTY, Items 42–46
**Source: U.S. Census Bureau—American Community Survey, 2007–2011**
**http://www.census.gov/acs/www/**

**Total money income** is the sum of the amounts reported separately for wage or salary income; net self-employment income; interest, dividends, or net rental or royalty income or income from estates and trusts; Social Security or railroad retirement income; Supplemental Security Income (SSI); public assistance or welfare payments; retirement, survivor, or disability pensions; and all other income. Receipts from the following sources are not included as income: capital gains; money received from the sale of property (unless the recipient was engaged in the business of selling such property); the value of income "in kind" from food stamps, public housing subsidies, medical care, employer contributions for individuals, etc.; withdrawal of bank deposits; money borrowed; tax refunds; exchange of money between relatives living in the same household; and gifts, lump-sum inheritances, insurance payments, and other types of lump-sum receipts.

**Per capita income** is the mean income computed for every man, woman, and child in a particular group. It is derived by dividing the aggregate income of a particular group by the resident population in that group in the survey year. Per capita income is rounded to the nearest whole dollar.

**Household income** includes the income of the householder and all other individuals 15 years old and over in the household, whether or not they are related to the householder. Since many households consist of only one person, median household income is usually less than median family income. Although the household income statistics cover the twelve months prior to the survey, the characteristics of individuals and the composition of households refer to the date of the interview. Thus, the income of the household does not include amounts received by individuals who were members of the household during all or part of the year if these individuals were no longer residing in the household at the time of the interview. Similarly, income amounts reported by individuals who did not reside in the household during full year but who were members of the household at the time of the interview are included. However, the composition of most households was the same during the year as it was at the time of the interview.

**Median income** divides the income distribution into two equal parts, with half of all cases below the median income level and half of all cases above the median income level. For households, the median income is based on the distribution of the total number of households, including those with no income. Median income for households is computed on the basis of a standard distribution with a minimum value of less than $2,500 and a maximum value of $200,000 or more and is rounded to the nearest whole dollar. Median income figures are calculated using linear interpolation if the width of the interval containing the estimate is $2,500 or less. If the width of the interval containing the estimate is greater than $2,500, Pareto interpolation is used.

Income components were reported for the 12 months preceding the interview month. Monthly Consumer Price Index (CPI) factors were used to inflation-adjust these components to a reference calendar year (January through December). For example, a household interviewed in March 2007 reports their income for March 2006 through February 2007. Their income is adjusted to the 2007 reference calendar year by multiplying their reported income by 2007 average annual CPI (January–December 2007) and then dividing by the average CPI for March 2006–February 2007. In addition, the 3-year estimates are inflation-adjusted to the final year. However, the estimates do not reflect the price and cost-of-living differences that may exist between areas.

The **poverty status** data were derived from data collected on the number of persons in a household, each person's relationship to the householder, and each person's income during the past twelve months. The Social Security Administration (SSA) developed the original poverty definition in 1964, which federal inter-agency committees subsequently revised in 1969 and 1980. The Office of Management and Budget's (OMB) *Directive 14* prescribes the SSA's definition as the official poverty measure for federal agencies to use in their statistical work.

Poverty thresholds vary depending on three criteria: size of family, number of children, and, for one- and two-person families, age of householder. In determining the poverty status of families and unrelated individuals, the Census Bureau uses thresholds (income cutoffs) arranged in a two-dimensional matrix. The matrix consists of family size (from one person to nine or more persons), cross-classified by presence and number of family members under 18 years old (from no children present to eight or more children present). Unrelated individuals and two-person families are further differentiated by age of reference person (under 65 years old and 65 years old and over). To determine a person's poverty status, the person's total family income over the previous 12 months is compared with the poverty threshold appropriate for that person's family size and composition. If the total income of that person's family is less than the threshold appropriate for that family, then the person is considered poor or "below the poverty level," together with every member of his or her family. If a person is not living with anyone related by birth, marriage, or adoption, then the person's own income is compared with his or her poverty threshold. The total number of persons below the poverty level is the sum of persons in families and the number of unrelated individuals with incomes below the poverty level.

**Poverty Thresholds for 2011 by Size of Family and Number of Related Children Under 18 Years**

| Size of family unit | Weighted average thresholds |
|---|---|
| One person (unrelated individual) | 11,484 |
|     Under 65 years | 11,702 |
|     65 years and over | 10,788 |
| Two people | 14,657 |
|     Householder under 65 years | 15,139 |
|     Householder 65 years and over | 13,609 |
| Three people | 17,916 |
| Four people | 23,021 |
| Five people | 27,251 |
| Six people | 30,847 |
| Seven people | 35,085 |
| Eight people | 39,064 |
| Nine people or more | 46,572 |

Source: U.S. Census Bureau.

# HOUSING, Items 47–57
**Source: U.S. Census Bureau—2010 Census of Population and Housing**
http://2010.census.gov/2010census/data/Source:
**American Community Survey, 2007–2011**
http://www.census.gov/acs/www/

The housing unit counts in columns 47 through 49 are from the 2010 census. The characteristics of occupied housing units are from the 2007–2011 American Community Survey.

A **housing unit** is a house, apartment, mobile home or trailer, group of rooms, or single room occupied or, if vacant, intended for occupancy as separate living quarters. Separate living quarters are those in which the occupants do not live and eat with any other person in the structure and which have direct access from the outside of the building through a common hall. For vacant units, the criteria of separateness and direct access are applied to the intended occupants whenever possible. If that information cannot be obtained, the criteria are applied to the previous occupants.

The occupants of a housing unit may be a single family, one person living alone, two or more families living together, or any other group of related or unrelated persons who share living quarters. Both occupied and vacant housing units are included in the housing inventory, although recreational vehicles, tents, caves, boats, railroad cars, and the like are included only if they are occupied as a person's usual place of residence.

A housing unit is classified as occupied if it is the usual place of residence of the person or group of persons living in it at the time of enumeration, or if the occupants are only temporarily absent (away on vacation). A household consists of all persons who occupy a housing unit as their usual place of residence. Vacant units for sale or rent include units rented or sold but not occupied and any other units held off the market.

The percent change represents the difference in the number of total housing units in a specified area from 2000 to 2010.

A housing unit is **owner occupied** if the owner or co-owner lives in the unit, even if it is mortgaged or not fully paid for. The owner or co-owner must live in the unit and is usually the first person listed on the census or ACS questionnaire.

All occupied housing units that are not owner occupied, whether they are rented for cash rent or occupied without payment of cash rent, are classified as **renter occupied**.

**Median value** is the dollar amount that divides the distribution of specified owner-occupied housing units into two equal parts, with half of all units below the median value and half of all units above the median value. Value is defined as the respondent's estimate of what the house would sell for if it were for sale. Data are presented for single-family units on fewer than 10 acres of land that have no business or medical offices on the property.

**Median rent** divides the distribution of renter-occupied housing units into two equal parts. The rent concept used in this volume is gross rent, which includes the amount of cash rent a renter pays (contract rent) plus the estimated average cost of utilities and fuels, if these are paid by the renter. The rent is the amount of rent only for living quarters and excludes amounts paid for any business or other space occupied. Single-family houses on lots of 10 or more acres of land are also excluded.

**Housing cost** as a percentage of income is shown separately for owners with mortgages, owners without mortgages, and renters. Rent as a percentage of income is a computed ratio of gross rent and monthly household income (total household income during the year divided by 12). Selected owner costs include utilities and fuels, mortgage payments, insurance, taxes, etc. In each case, the ratio of housing cost to income is computed separately for each housing unit. The housing cost ratios for half of all units are above the median shown in this book, and half are below the median shown in the book.

**Substandard units** are occupied units that are overcrowded or lack complete plumbing facilities. For the purposes of this item, "overcrowded" is defined as having 1.01 persons or more per room. Complete plumbing facilities include hot and cold piped water, a flush toilet, and a bathtub or shower. These facilities must be located inside the housing unit, but do not have to be in the same room.

## PERCENT WITH NO VEHICLES AVAILABLE, Item 58
**Source: U.S. Census Bureau—American Community Survey, 2007–2011**
**http://www.census.gov/acs/www/**

The data on vehicles available show the number of passenger cars, vans, and pickup or panel trucks of one-ton capacity or less kept at home and available for the use of household members. Vehicles rented or leased for one month or more, company vehicles, and police and government vehicles are included if kept at home and used for non-business purposes. Dismantled or immobile vehicles are excluded. Vehicles kept at home but used only for business purposes also are excluded

## MIGRATION, Items 59 and 60
**Source: U.S. Census Bureau—American Community Survey, 2007–2011**
**http://www.census.gov/acs/www/**

**Residence one year ago** is used in conjunction with location of current residence to determine the extent of residential mobility of the population and the resulting redistribution of the population across the various states, metropolitan areas, and regions of the country. **Same house** includes all people 1 year old and over who, a year before the survey date, lived in the same house or apartment that they occupied at the time of interview.

The **percent who lived outside this city** includes all persons who did not live in the listed city 1 year before the interview, whether their previous residence was in the same state, a different state, Puerto Rico, or abroad.

## CIVILIAN LABOR FORCE AND UNEMPLOYMENT, Items 61–64
**Source: U.S. Bureau of Labor Statistics—Local Areas Unemployment Statistics**
**http://www.bls.gov/lau/#tables**

Data for the civilian labor force are the product of a federal-state cooperative program in which state employment security agencies prepare labor force and unemployment estimates under concepts, definitions, and technical procedures established by the Bureau of Labor Statistics (BLS). The civilian labor force consists of all civilians 16 years old and over who are either employed or unemployed.

Unemployment includes all persons who did not work during the survey week, made specific efforts to find a job during the previous four weeks, and were available for work during the survey week (except for temporary illness). Persons waiting to be called back to a job from which they had been laid off and those waiting to report to a new job within the next 30 days are included in unemployment figures.

Table D includes annual average data for the year shown. The Local Area Unemployment Statistics data are periodically updated to reflect revised inputs, reestimation, and controlling to new statewide totals.

## CIVILIAN EMPLOYMENT, Items 65–68
**Source: U.S. Census Bureau—American Community Survey, 2007–2011**
**http://www.census.gov/acs/www/**

The **labor force** includes all persons 16 years old and over who were either (1) "at work"—those who did any work at all during the reference week as paid employees, worked in either their own business or profession, worked on their own farm, or worked 15 hours or more as unpaid workers in a family farm or business; or were (2) "with a job, but not at work"—those who had a job but were not at work that week due to illness, weather, industrial dispute, vacation, or other personal reasons.

**Full-year, Full-Time Workers** includes all people 16 years old and over who usually worked 35 hours or more per week for 50 to 52 weeks in the past 12 months.

**Households with no workers** includes households where all members "Did not work in the past 12 months." Workers include all people 16 years old and over who, for one or more weeks, did any work for pay or profit (including paid vacation and paid sick leave) or worked without pay on a family farm or in a family business. Weeks of active service in the Armed Forces are also included.

## BUILDING PERMITS, Items 69–71
**Source: U.S. Census Bureau—Building Permits Survey**
**http://www.census.gov/const/www/permitsindex.html**

These figures represent private residential construction authorized by building permits in approximately 20,000 places in the United States. Valuation represents the expected cost of construction as recorded on the building permit. This figure usually excludes the cost of on-site and off-site development and improvements, as well as the cost of heating, plumbing, electrical, and elevator installations.

National, state, and county totals were obtained by adding the data for permit-issuing places within each jurisdiction. These totals thus are limited to permits issued in the 20,000 place universe covered by the Census Bureau and may not include all permits issued within a state. Current surveys indicate that construction is undertaken for all but a very small percentage of housing units authorized by building permits.

Residential building permits include buildings with any number of housing units. Housing units exclude group quarters (such as dormitories and rooming houses), transient accommodations (such as transient hotels, motels, and tourist courts), "HUD-code" manufactured (mobile) homes, moved or relocated units, and housing units created in an existing residential or nonresidential structure.

## 2007 Economic CENSUS: OVERVIEW, Items 72–107
**Source: U.S. Census Bureau**
**http://www.census.gov/econ/census07/**

The Economic Census provides a detailed portrait of the nation's economy, from the national to the local level, once every five years. The 2007 Economic Census covers nearly all of the U.S. economy in its basic collection of establishment statistics. The 1997 Economic Census was the first major data source to use the new North American Industry Classification System (NAICS); therefore, data from this census are not comparable to economic data from prior years, which were based on the Standard Industrial Classification (SIC) system.

NAICS, developed in cooperation with Canada and Mexico, classifies North America's economic activities at two-, three-, four-, and five-digit levels of detail; the U.S. version of NAICS further defines industries to a sixth digit. The Economic Census takes advantage of this hierarchy to publish data at these successive levels of detail: sector (two-digit), subsector (three-digit), industry group (four-digit), industry (five-digit), and U.S. industry (six-digit). Information in Table A is at the two-digit level, with

a few three- and four-digit items. The data in Table D are at the two-digit level.

Several key statistics are tabulated for all industries in this volume, including number of establishments (or companies), number of employees, payroll, and certain measures of output (sales, receipts, revenue, value of shipments, or value of construction work done).

**Number of establishments.** An establishment is a single physical location at which business is conducted. It is not necessarily identical with a company or enterprise, which may consist of one establishment or more. Economic Census figures represent a summary of reports for individual establishments rather than companies. For cases in which a census report was received, separate information was obtained for each location where business was conducted. When administrative records of other federal agencies were used instead of a census report, no information was available on the number of locations operated. Each Economic Census establishment was tabulated according to the physical location at which the business was conducted. The count of establishments represents those in business at any time during 2002.

When two activities or more were carried on at a single location under a single ownership, all activities were generally grouped together as a single establishment. The entire establishment was classified on the basis of its major activity and all of its data were included in that classification. However, when distinct and separate economic activities (for which different industry classification codes were appropriate) were conducted at a single location under a single ownership, separate establishment reports for each of the different activities were obtained in the census.

**Number of employees.** Paid employees consist of the full-time and part-time employees, including salaried officers and executives of corporations. Included are employees on paid sick leave, paid holidays, and paid vacations; not included are proprietors and partners of unincorporated businesses. The definition of paid employees is the same as that used by the Internal Revenue Service (IRS) on form 941. For some industries, the Economic Census gives codes representing the number of employees as a range of numbers (for example, "100 to 249 employees" or "1,000 to 2,499" employees). In this volume, those codes have been replaced by the standard suppression code "D".

**Payroll.** Payroll includes all forms of compensation, such as salaries, wages, commissions, dismissal pay, bonuses, vacation allowances, sick-leave pay, and employee contributions to qualified pension plans paid during the year to all employees. For corporations, payroll includes amounts paid to officers and executives; for unincorporated businesses, it does not include profit or other compensation of proprietors or partners. Payroll is reported before deductions for Social Security, income tax, insurance, union dues, etc. This definition of payroll is the same as that used by on IRS form 941.

**Sales, shipments, receipts, revenue, or business done.** This measure includes the total sales, shipments, receipts, revenue, or business done by establishments within the scope of the Economic Census. The definition of each of these items is specific to the economic sector measured.

## WHOLESALE TRADE, Items 72–75

Source: U.S. Census Bureau—2007 Economic Census (See Overview of 2007 Economic Census prior to Item 72)

The Wholesale Trade sector (sector 42) comprises establishments engaged in wholesaling merchandise, generally without transformation, and rendering services incidental to the sale of merchandise. The wholesaling process is an intermediate step in the distribution of merchandise.

Wholesalers are organized to sell or arrange the purchase or sale of (1) goods for resale (i.e., goods sold to other wholesalers or retailers), (2) capital or durable nonconsumer goods, and (3) raw and intermediate materials and supplies used in production.

Wholesalers sell merchandise to other businesses and normally operate from a warehouse or office. These warehouses and offices are characterized by having little or no display of merchandise. In addition, neither the design nor the location of the premises is intended to solicit walk-in traffic. Wholesalers do not normally use advertising directed to the general public. In general, customers are initially reached via telephone, in-person marketing, or specialized advertising, which may include the internet and other electronic means. Follow-up orders are either vendor-initiated or client-initiated, are usually based on previous sales, and typically exhibit strong ties between sellers and buyers. In fact, transactions are often conducted between wholesalers and clients that have long-standing business relationships.

This sector is made up of two main types of wholesalers: those that sell goods on their own account and those that arrange sales and purchases for others for a commission or fee.

(1) Establishments that sell goods on their own account are known as wholesale merchants, distributors, jobbers, drop shippers, import/export merchants, and sales branches. These establishments typically maintain their own warehouse, where they receive and handle goods for their customers. Goods are generally sold without transformation, but may include integral functions, such as sorting, packaging, labeling, and other marketing services.

(2) Establishments arranging for the purchase or sale of goods owned by others or purchasing goods on a commission basis are known as agents and brokers, commission merchants, import/export agents and brokers, auction companies, and manufacturers' representatives. These establishments operate from offices and generally do not own or handle the goods they sell.

Some wholesale establishments may be connected with a single manufacturer and promote and sell that particular manufacturer's products to a wide range of other wholesalers or retailers. Other wholesalers may be connected to a retail chain or a limited number of retail chains and only provide the products needed by the particular retail operation(s). These wholesalers may obtain the products from a wide range of manufacturers. Still other wholesalers may not take title to the goods, but act instead as agents and brokers for a commission.

Although wholesaling normally denotes sales in large volumes, durable nonconsumer goods may be sold in single units. Sales of capital or durable nonconsumer goods used in the production of goods and services, such as farm machinery, medium- and heavy-duty trucks, and industrial machinery, are always included in Wholesale Trade.

The city table includes only **Merchant wholesalers, except manufacturers' sales branches and offices,** establishments primarily engaged in buying and selling merchandise on their own account. Included here are such types of establishments as wholesale distributors and jobbers, importers, exporters, own-brand importers/marketers, terminal and country grain elevators, and farm products assemblers.

## RETAIL TRADE, Items 76–79

Source: U.S. Census Bureau—2007 Economic Census (See Overview of 2007 Economic Census prior to Item 72)

The Retail Trade sector (44–45) is made up of establishments engaged in retailing merchandise, generally without transformation, and rendering services incidental to the sale of merchandise.

The retailing process is the final step in the distribution of merchandise; retailers are therefore organized to sell merchandise in small quantities to the general public. This sector comprises two main types of retailers: store and nonstore retailers.

Store retailers operate fixed point-of-sale locations, located and designed to attract a high volume of walk-in customers. In general, retail stores have extensive displays of merchandise and use mass-media advertising to attract customers. They typically sell merchandise to the general public for personal or household consumption; some also serve business and institutional clients. These include establishments such as office supply stores, computer and software stores, building materials dealers, plumbing supply stores, and electrical supply stores. Catalog showrooms, gasoline service stations, automotive dealers, and mobile home dealers are treated as store retailers.

In addition to retailing merchandise, some types of store retailers are also engaged in the provision of after-sales services, such as repair and installation. For example, new automobile dealers, electronic and appliance stores, and musical instrument and supply stores often provide repair services. As a general rule, establishments engaged in retailing merchandise and providing after-sales services are classified in this sector.

Nonstore retailers, like store retailers, are organized to serve the general public, although their retailing methods differ. The establishments of this subsector reach customers and market merchandise with methods including the broadcasting of ''infomercials,'' the broadcasting and publishing of direct-response advertising, the publishing of paper and electronic catalogs, door-to-door solicitation, in-home demonstration, selling from portable stalls (street vendors, except food), and distribution through vending machines. Establishments engaged in the direct sale (nonstore) of products, such as home heating oil dealers and home-delivery newspaper routes are included in this sector.

The buying of goods for resale is a characteristic of retail trade establishments that distinguishes them from establishments in the Agriculture, Manufacturing, and Construction sectors. For example, farms that sell their products at or from the point of production are classified in Agriculture instead of in Retail Trade. Similarly, establishments that both manufacture and sell their products to the general public are classified in Manufacturing instead of Retail Trade. However, establishments that engage in processing activities incidental to retailing are classified in Retail Trade.

## REAL ESTATE AND RENTAL AND LEASING, Items 80–83

**Source: U.S. Census Bureau—2007 Economic Census (See Overview of 2007 Economic Census prior to Item 72)**

The Real Estate and Rental and Leasing sector (53) comprises establishments primarily engaged in renting, leasing, or otherwise allowing the use of tangible or intangible assets, and establishments providing related services. The major portion of this sector is made up of establishments that rent, lease, or otherwise allow the use of their own assets by others. The assets may be tangible, such as real estate and equipment, or intangible, such as patents and trademarks.

This sector also includes establishments primarily engaged in managing real estate for others, selling, renting, and/or buying real estate for others, and appraising real estate. These activities are closely related to this sector's main activity. In addition, a substantial proportion of property management is self-performed by lessors.

The main components of this sector are the real estate lessors industries; equipment lessors industries (including motor vehicles, computers, and consumer goods); and lessors of nonfinancial intangible assets (except copyrighted works).

## PROFESSIONAL, SCIENTIFIC, AND TECHNICAL SERVICES, Items 84–87

**Source: U.S. Census Bureau—2007 Economic Census (See Overview of 2007 Economic Census prior to Item 72)**

The Professional, Scientific, and Technical Services sector (54) is made up of establishments that specialize in performing professional, scientific, and technical activities for others. These activities require a high degree of expertise and training. The establishments in this sector specialize in one or more areas and provide services to clients in a variety of industries (and, in some cases, to households). Activities performed include legal advice and representation; accounting, bookkeeping, and payroll services; architectural, engineering, and specialized design services; computer services; consulting services; research services; advertising services; photographic services; translation and interpretation services; veterinary services; and other professional, scientific, and technical services.

Table D includes only those establishments subject to federal income tax.

This sector excludes establishments primarily engaged in providing a range of day-to-day office administrative services, such as financial planning, billing and record keeping, personnel services, and physical distribution and logistics services. These establishments are classified in sector 56, Administrative and Support and Waste Management and Remediation Services.

## MANUFACTURING, Items 88–91

**Source: U.S. Census Bureau—2007 Economic Census (See Overview of 2007 Economic Census prior to Item 72)**

The Manufacturing sector (31–33) is made up of establishments engaged in the mechanical, physical, or chemical transformation of materials, substances, or components into new products. The assembling of component parts of manufactured products is considered manufacturing, except in cases in which the activity is appropriately classified in the Construction sector. Establishments in the Manufacturing sector are often described as plants, factories, or mills, and characteristically use power-driven machines and materials-handling equipment. However, establishments that transform materials or substances into new products by hand or in the worker's home, and establishments engaged in selling to the general public products made on the same premises from which they are sold (such as bakeries, candy stores, and custom tailors) may also be included in this sector. Manufacturing establishments may process materials or contract with other establishments to process their materials for them. Both types of establishments are included in the Manufacturing sector.

The materials, substances, or components transformed by manufacturing establishments are raw materials that are products of agriculture, forestry, fishing, mining, or quarrying, or are products of other manufacturing establishments. The materials used may be purchased directly from producers, obtained through customary trade channels, or secured without recourse to the market by transferring the product from one establishment to another, under the same ownership. The new product of a manufacturing establishment may be finished (in the sense that it is ready for utilization or consumption), or it may be semifinished to become an input for an establishment engaged in further manufacturing. For example, the product of the alumina refinery is the input used in the primary production of aluminum; primary aluminum is the input used in an aluminum wire drawing plant; and aluminum wire is the input used in a fabricated wire product manufacturing establishment.

Data are included for cities with 500 or more employees in the Manufacturing sector.

## ACCOMMODATION AND FOOD SERVICES, Items 92–95

**Source: U.S. Census Bureau—2007 Economic Census (See Overview of 2007 Economic Census prior to Item 72)**

The Accommodation and Food Services sector (72) consists of establishments that provide customers with lodging and/or meals, snacks, and beverages for immediate consumption. This sector includes both accommodation and food services establishments because the two activities are often combined at the same establishment.

Excluded from this sector are civic and social organizations, amusement and recreation parks, theaters, and other recreation or entertainment facilities providing food and beverage services.

## ARTS, ENTERTAINMENT, AND RECREATION, Items 96–99

### Source: U.S. Census Bureau—2007 Economic Census (See Overview of 2007 Economic Census prior to Item 72)

The Arts, Entertainment, and Recreation sector (71) includes a wide range of establishments that operate facilities or provide services that meet the diverse cultural, entertainment, and recreational interests of their patrons. This sector is made up of: (1) establishments that are involved in producing, promoting, or participating in live performances, events, or exhibits intended for public viewing; (2) establishments that preserve and exhibit objects and sites of historical, cultural, or educational interest; and (3) establishments that operate facilities or provide services that enable patrons to participate in recreational activities or pursue amusement, hobby, and leisure time interests.

Some establishments that provide cultural, entertainment, or recreational facilities and services are classified in other sectors. Excluded from this sector are: (1) establishments that provide both accommodations and recreational facilities—such as hunting and fishing camps and resort and casino hotels—are classified in subsector 721, Accommodation; (2) restaurants and night clubs that provide live entertainment in addition to the sale of food and beverages are classified in subsector 722, Food Services and Drinking Places; (3) motion picture theaters, libraries and archives, and publishers of newspapers, magazines, books, periodicals, and computer software are classified in sector 51, Information; and (4) establishmentsthat use transportation equipment to provide recreational and entertainment services, such as those operating sightseeing buses, dinner cruises, or helicopter rides, are classified in subsector 487, Scenic and Sightseeing Transportation.

Table D includes only those establishments subject to federal tax.

## HEALTH CARE AND SOCIAL ASSISTANCE, Items 100–103

### Source: U.S. Census Bureau—2007 Economic Census (See Overview of 2007 Economic Census prior to Item 72)

The Health Care and Social Assistance sector (62) consists of establishments that provide health care and social assistance services to individuals. The sector includes both health care and social assistance because it is sometimes difficult to distinguish between the boundaries of these two activities. The industries in this sector are arranged on a continuum, starting with establishments that provide medical care exclusively, continuing with those that provide health care and social assistance, and finishing with those that provide only social assistance. The services provided by establishments in this sector are delivered by trained professionals. All industries in the sector share this commonality of process—namely, labor inputs of health practitioners or social workers with the requisite expertise. Many of the industries in the sector are defined based on the educational degree held by the practitioners included in the industry.

Excluded from this sector are aerobic classes, which can be found in subsector 713, Amusement, Gambling, and Recreation

Industries; and nonmedical diet and weight-reducing centers, which can be found in subsector 812, Personal and Laundry Services. Although these can be viewed as health services, they are not typically delivered by health practitioners.

Table D includes only those establishments subject to federal tax.

## OTHER SERVICES, EXCEPT PUBLIC ADMINISTRATION Items 104–107

### Source: U.S. Census Bureau—2007 Economic Census (See Overview of 2007 Economic Census prior to Item 72)

The Other Services, Except Public Administration sector (81) comprises establishments engaged in providing services not specifically categorized elsewhere in the classification system. Establishments in this sector are primarily engaged in activities such as equipment and machinery repairing, promoting or administering religious activities, grant making, and advocacy; this sector also includes establishments that provide dry-cleaning and laundry services, personal care services, death care services, pet care services, photofinishing services, temporary parking services, and dating services.

Private households that employ workers on or about the premises in activities primarily concerned with the operation of the household are included in this sector.

In Table D, only firms subject to federal tax are included.

Excluded from this sector are establishments primarily engaged in retailing new equipment and performing repairs and general maintenance on equipment. These establishments are classified in sector 44–45, Retail Trade.

## FEDERAL FUNDS, Items 108–116

### Source: U.S. Census Bureau—Consolidated Federal Funds Report
### http://www.census.gov/govs/cffr/

Data on federal expenditure and obligations are obtained from a report prepared by the Census Bureau in accordance with the Consolidated Federal Funds Report (CFFR) Act of 1982 (P.L. 97–326). The data are for federal fiscal years beginning October 1 and ending the following September 30.

Only selected categories of data from the CFFR are identified at the city level. The city items shown in this book are "selected" federal funds and do not represent all federal funds received by individuals and entities within the city.

Dollar amounts reported can reflect expenditures or obligations. In some cases, dollar amounts are negative, representing de-obligations of financial assistance that had previously been awarded. Such amounts generally appear in the grant categories. Many categories are assigned only to state and county levels and never assigned to cities.

**Procurement contract awards** cover awards given by the United States Postal Service (USPS), as well as those given by all other federal agencies. Amounts provided by the USPS represent actual outlays for contractual commitments, while amounts for other agencies represent the value of obligations for contract actions and do not reflect actual federal government expenditures.

In general, only current-year contract actions are included; however, multiple-year obligations may be reported for contract actions of less than three years' duration. The procurement contract data for cities are relatively complete.

**Grants** data represent the federal obligations incurred at the time the grant is awarded. The amounts reported do not represent actual expenditures, since obligations in one time period may not result in outlays during the same period. Moreover, initial amounts obligated may be adjusted at a later date, through either enhancements or de-obligations. All grant awards were reported by state, county, and city of the initial recipient. For many grants, this recipient is the state government even though grants monies are subsequently distributed to county, municipal, or township governments.

**Medicaid and other health-related** grants include a variety of grants from the Department of Health and Human Services for health services and research.

**Nutrition and family welfare** grants include a variety of grants from the Department of Health and Human Services for child welfare, special programs for the aging, and related areas. The school lunch program and other nutritional assistance programs administered by the Department of Agriculture are also included in this category.

**Energy and environment** grants include grants from the Department of Energy for energy development, energy conservation, and nuclear waste disposal, as well as grants from the Environmental Protection Agency for a variety of pollution control and waste management activities.

**Disaster and emergency** preparedness grants include assistance to fire-fighting and rescue organizations; community assistance for earthquakes, floods, hurricanes and other disasters; domestic preparedness programs; and similar activities.

**Housing and community development** grants include Community Development Block Grants, housing demonstration programs, rental housing rehabilitation, and other housing programs.

**Employment and** training grants include various job training programs, welfare-to-work grants, occupational safety and health grants, and similar employment related funds.

## CITY GOVERNMENT FINANCES, Items 117–139

### Source: U.S. Census Bureau—2007 Census of Governments
http://www.census.gov/govs/cog

Revenue and expenditure data are included in Table D for city governments only. The data do not include funds of any special district governments located in the city.

Total **general revenue** includes all revenue except utility, liquor stores, and insurance trust revenue. All tax revenue and intergovernmental revenue, even if designated for employee-retirement or local utility purpose, are classified as general revenue.

**Intergovernmental revenue** covers amounts received from other governments as fiscal aid in the form of shared revenues and grants-in-aid, as reimbursements for the performance of general government functions and specific services for the paying government (for example, care of prisoners or contractual research), or in lieu of taxes. It excludes any amounts received from other

governments from the sale of property, commodities, and utility services. All intergovernmental revenue is classified as general revenue. Intergovernmental revenue from the state governments includes amounts originally from the federal government but channeled through the state.

**Taxes** consist of compulsory contributions exacted by governments for public purposes. However, this category excludes employer and employee payments for retirement and social insurance purposes, which are classified as insurance trust revenue. All tax revenue is classified as general revenue and comprises amounts received (including interest and penalties, but excluding protested amounts and refunds) from all taxes imposed by a government. Note that local government tax revenue excludes any amounts from shares of state-imposed and collected taxes, which are classified as intergovernmental revenue.

**Property taxes** are based on ownership of property and measured by its value. They include general property taxes related to property as a whole—real and personal, tangible or intangible—whether taxed at a single rate or at classified rates. Also included are taxes on selected types of property, such as motor vehicles or certain or all intangibles.

**Sales and gross receipts taxes** include "licenses" at more than nominal rates, based on volume or value of transfers of goods or services; taxes upon gross receipts or upon gross income; and related taxes based upon the use, storage, production (other than the severance of natural resources), importation, or consumption of goods. Dealer discounts "commissions," which are allowed to merchants for the collection of taxes from consumers, are excluded.

Total **general expenditure** includes all city expenditure other than specifically enumerated kinds of expenditure, including utility, liquor store, and employee-retirement and other insurance trust expenditures.

**Capital outlays** are direct expenditures for contract of force account construction or buildings, roads, and other improvements, and for purchases of equipment, land, and existing structures. They include amounts for additions, replacements, and major alterations to fixed work and structures. Expenditures for repair to such works and structures, however, is classified as current operation expenditure.

A major portion of capital outlay is commonly financed by borrowing, while governmental revenue does not include receipts from borrowing. Among other things, this distorts the relationship between the totals presented for revenue and expenditure and renders this relationship useless as a direct measure of the degree of budgetary "balance" (as that term is generally applied).

**Public welfare expenditure** covers support of and assistance to needy persons; this aid is contingent upon the person's needs. Included are cash assistance paid directly to needy persons; vendor payments made directly to private purveyors for medical care, burials, and other commodities and services provided under welfare programs; welfare institutions; and any intergovernmental or other direct expenditure for welfare purposes. Pensions to former employees and other benefits not contingent on need are excluded.

**Highway expenditure** is for the provision and maintenance of highway facilities, including toll turnpikes, bridges, tunnels, and ferries, as well as regular roads, highways, and streets. Also included are expenditures for street lighting and for snow and ice removal. Not included are highway policing and traffic control, which are considered part of police protection

**Parking facilities** include the construction, purchase, maintenance, and operation of public-use parking lots, garages, parking meters, and other distinctive parking facilities on a commercial basis.

**Education** is mainly for the provision and general support of schools and other educational facilities and services, including those for educational institutions beyond high school. Elementary and secondary education includes the provision of public kindergarten through high school education by local governments. It encompasses instructional, support, and auxiliary services (school lunch, student activities, and community services) offered by public school systems. Higher education consists of all local institutions of higher education.

**Health expenditures** include outpatient health services other than hospital care, such as public health administration; research and education; categorical health programs; treatment and immunization clinics; nursing; environmental health activities, such as air and water pollution control; ambulance service if provided separately from fire protection services; and other general public health activities, such as mosquito abatement. School health services provided by health agencies (rather than school agencies) are included here. Not included are sewage treatment operations, which are classified as part of sewerage and sanitation. **Hospital expenditures** include financing, construction, acquisition, maintenance and operation of hospital facilities, provision of hospital care, and support of public or private hospitals.

**Police protection** encompasses expenditures for the preservation of law and order, as well as for traffic safety. It includes police patrols and communications, crime prevention activities, detention and custody of persons awaiting trial, traffic safety, and vehicular inspection.

**Sewerage and recreation** include sanitary and storm sewers, sewage disposal facilities and services, and other government activities for such purposes. Street cleaning and the collection and disposal of garbage and other waste are also included.

**Parks and recreation** includes cultural and scientific activities, such as museums and art galleries; organized recreation, including playgrounds and playing fields, swimming pools, and bathing beaches; and municipal parks and special recreation facilities, such as auditoriums, stadiums, auto camps, recreation piers, and boat harbors.

**Housing and community development** includes city housing and redevelopment projects and the regulation, promotion, and support of private housing and redevelopment activities. Data from Arizona, Kentucky, Michigan, New Mexico, New York, and Virginia generally include municipal housing authorities. Housing authorities for other cities are usually classified as independent governments, and data from them are not included.

**Interest** on debt is the amount paid for the use of borrowed money.

Total **debt outstanding** is the total of debt obligations remaining unpaid on the date specified. **Debt issued during the year** is the amount of the outstanding debt that was recently borrowed.

# CITY GOVERNMENT EMPLOYMENT, Item 140

**Source: U.S. Census Bureau—Survey of Governments, 2011: Employment Statistics**
**http://www.census.gov/govs/apes/**

The data are from an annual survey conducted by the Census Bureau and represent paid employment by city governments during March 2011. Full-time equivalent employment is a computed statistic representing the number of full-time employees that would have been employed if the hours worked by the part-time employees were converted to full-time equivalents.

# CLIMATE, Items 141–147

**Source: National Oceanic and Atmospheric Administration**
**http://cdo.ncdc.noaa.gov/cgi-bin/climatenormals/climatenormals.pl**

All climate data are average values for the 30-year period from 1971 to 2000.

Mean temperatures for January and July were determined by adding the average daily maximum temperatures and the average daily minimum temperatures and dividing by two.

Temperature limits represent average daily minimum for January and average daily maximum for July.

Annual precipitation values are the average annual water equivalent of all precipitation for the 30-year period.

Heating and cooling degree days are used as relative measures of the energy required for heating and cooling buildings. One heating degree day is accumulated for each whole degree that the mean daily temperature is below 65 degrees Fahrenheit (a mean daily temperature of 62 degrees Fahrenheit will produce three heating degree days). Cooling degree days are accumulated in similar fashion for deviations of the mean daily temperature above 65 degrees Fahrenheit.

# TABLE E—CONGRESSIONAL DISTRICTS OF THE 113TH CONGRESS

**Members of the House of Representatives** are for the 113th Congress.

## LAND AREA, Items 1 and 3
**Source: U.S. Census Bureau—2010 Census of Population and Housing**
**http://2010.census.gov/2010census/data/**

Land area measurements are shown to the nearest square kilometer. Land area includes dry land and land temporarily or partially covered by water, such as marshlands, swamps, and river floodplains.

## POPULATION AND POPULATION CHARACTERISTICS, Items 2–24
**Source: U.S. Census Bureau—American Community Survey, 2011**
**http://www.census.gov/acs/www/**

The population data and population characteristics are estimates from the 2011 American Community Survey.

Data on race were derived from answers to the question on race that was asked of all respondents. The concept of race, as used by the Census Bureau, reflects self-identification by people according to the race or races with which they most closely identify. These categories are sociopolitical constructs and should not be interpreted as being scientific or anthropological in nature. Furthermore, the race categories include both racial and national origin groups.

In Table E, Columns 4 through 8 refer to individuals who identified with each racial category alone, while column 9 includes persons who identified with two or more races.

The **White** population is defined as persons who indicated their race as White, as well as persons who did not classify themselves in one of the specific race categories listed on the questionnaire but entered a nationality such as Irish, German, Italian, Lebanese, Near Easterner, Arab, or Polish.

The **Black** population includes persons who indicated their race as "Black, African Am., or Negro," as well as persons who did not classify themselves in one of the specific race categories but reported entries such as African American, Afro American, Kenyan, Nigerian, or Haitian.

The **American Indian or Alaska Native** population includes persons who indicated their race as American Indian or Alaska Native, as well as persons who did not classify themselves in one of the specific race categories but reported entries such as Canadian Indian, French-American Indian, Spanish-American Indian, Eskimo, Aleut, Alaska Indian, or any of the American Indian or Alaska Native tribes.

The **Asian and Pacific Islander** population combines two census groupings: **Asian** and **Native Hawaiian or Other Pacific Islander**. The **Asian** population includes persons who indicated their race as Asian Indian, Chinese, Filipino, Japanese, Korean, Vietnamese, or "Other Asian," as well as persons who provided write-in entries of such groups as Cambodian, Laotian, Hmong, Pakistani, or Taiwanese. The **Native Hawaiian or Other Pacific Islander** population includes persons who indicated their race as "Native Hawaiian," "Guamanian or Chamorro," "Samoan," or "Other Pacific Islander," as well as persons who reported entries such as Part Hawaiian, American Samoan, Fijian, Melanesian, or Tahitian.

The **Hispanic population** is based on a question that asked respondents "Is this person Spanish/Hispanic/Latino?" Persons marking any one of the four Hispanic categories (i.e., Mexican, Puerto Rican, Cuban, or other Spanish) are collectively referred to as Hispanic.

The **Non-Hispanic White alone** number in Column 11 includes only those persons who were not Hispanic and whose race was "White only."

The **female** population is shown as a percentage of total population.

The **foreign-born** population includes all persons who were not U.S. citizens at birth. Foreign-born persons are those who indicated they were either a U.S. citizen by naturalization or were not a citizen of the United States. The foreign-born population consists of immigrants (legal permanent residents), temporary migrants (students), humanitarian migrants (refugees), and unauthorized migrants (persons illegally residing in the United States).

**Percent born in state of residence** is shown as a percentage of total population.

**Age** is defined as age at last birthday (number of completed years since birth).

## EDUCATION—SCHOOL ENROLLMENT AND EDUCATIONAL ATTAINMENT, Items 25–27
**Source: U.S. Census Bureau—American Community Survey, 2011**
**http://www.census.gov/acs/www/**

Data on school enrollment and educational attainment were derived from a sample of the population. Persons were classified as enrolled in school if they reported attending a "regular" public or private school (or college) during the year. The instructions were to "include only nursery school, kindergarten, elementary school, and schooling which would lead to a high school diploma or a college degree" as regular school. The Census Bureau defines a public school as "any school or college controlled and supported by a local, county, state, or federal government." Schools primarily supported and controlled by religious organizations or other private groups are defined as private schools.

Data on **educational attainment** are tabulated for the population 25 years old and over. The data were derived from a question that asked respondents for the highest level of school completed or the highest degree received. Persons who had passed a high school equivalency examination were considered high school graduates. Schooling received in foreign schools was to be reported as the equivalent grade or years in the regular American school system.

Vocational and technical training, such as barber school training; business, trade, technical, and vocational schools; or other training for a specific trade are specifically excluded.

**High school graduate or more.** This category includes persons who have received a high school diploma or its equivalent, and those who reported any level higher than a high school diploma.

**Bachelor's degree or more.** This category includes persons who have received bachelor's degrees, master's degrees, professional school degrees (such as law school or medical school degrees), and doctoral degrees.

## HOUSEHOLDS, Items 28–33
**Source: U.S. Census Bureau—American Community Survey, 2011**
**http://www.census.gov/acs/www/**

A **household** includes all persons who occupy a housing unit. (Persons not living in households are classified as living in group quarters.) A housing unit is a house, an apartment, a mobile home, a group of rooms, or a single room occupied (or, if vacant, intended for occupancy) as separate living quarters. Separate living quarters are those in which the occupants live separately from any other persons in the building and have direct access from the outside of the building or through a common hall. The occupants may be a single family, one person living alone, two or more families living together, or any other group of related or unrelated persons who share living quarters. The number of households is the same as the number of year-round occupied housing units.

A **family** includes a householder and one or more other persons living in the same household who are related to the householder by birth, marriage, or adoption. All persons in a household who are related to the householder are regarded as members of his or her family. A **family household** may contain persons not related to the householder; thus, family households may include more members than families do. A household can contain only one family for the purposes of census tabulations. Not all households contain families, as a household may comprise a group of unrelated persons or of one person living alone. Families are classified by type as either a ''husband-wife family'' or ''other family,'' according to the presence or absence of a spouse.

The measure of **persons per household** is obtained by dividing the number of persons in households by the number of households or householders. One person in each household is designated as the householder. In most cases, this is the person (or one of the persons) in whose name the house is owned, being bought, or rented. If there is no such person in the household, any adult household member 15 years old and over can be designated as the householder.

The category **female family householder** includes only female-headed family households with no spouse present.

## GROUP QUARTERS, Items 34–39
**Source: U.S. Census Bureau—2010 Census of Population and Housing**
**http://2010.census.gov/2010census/data/**

The Census Bureau classifies all people not living in households as living in **group quarters**. There are two types of group quarters: institutional, including correctional facilities, nursing homes, and mental hospitals; and non-institutional, including college dormitories, military quarters, group homes, missions, and shelters.

## HOUSING, Items 40–45
**Source: U.S. Census Bureau—American Community Survey, 2011**
**http://www.census.gov/acs/www/**

A **housing unit** is a house, apartment, mobile home or trailer, group of rooms, or single room occupied or, if vacant, intended for occupancy as separate living quarters. Separate living quarters are those in which the occupants do not live and eat with any other person in the structure and which have direct access from the outside of the building or through a common hall. For vacant units, the criteria of separateness and direct access are applied to the intended occupants whenever possible. If that information cannot be obtained, the criteria are applied to the previous occupants.

The occupants of a housing unit may be a single family, one person living alone, two or more families living together, or any other group of related or unrelated persons who share living quarters. Both occupied and vacant housing units are included in the housing inventory, although recreational vehicles, tents, caves, boats, railroad cars, and the like are included only if they are occupied as a person's usual place of residence.

A housing unit is classified as **occupied** if it is the usual place of residence of the person or group of persons living in it at the time of interview, or if the occupants are only temporarily absent (away on vacation). A household consists of all persons who occupy a housing unit as their usual place of residence. Vacant units for sale or rent include units rented or sold but not occupied and any other units held off the market.

A housing unit is **owner occupied** if the owner or co-owner lives in the unit, even if it is mortgaged or not fully paid for. The owner or co-owner must live in the unit and is usually the first person listed on the census questionnaire

All occupied housing units that are not owner occupied, whether they are rented for cash rent or occupied without payment of cash rent, are classified as **renter occupied**.

**Median value** is the dollar amount that divides the distribution of specified owner-occupied housing units into two equal parts, with half of all units below the median value and half of all units above the median value. Value is defined as the respondent's estimate of what the house would sell for if it was for sale. Data are presented for single-family units on fewer than 10 acres of land that have no business or medical offices on the property.

**Median rent** divides the distribution of renter-occupied housing units into two equal parts. The rent concept used in this volume is gross rent, which includes the amount of cash rent a renter pays (contract rent) plus the estimated average cost of utilities and fuels, if these are paid by the renter. The rent is the amount of rent only for living quarters and excludes amounts paid for any business or other space occupied. Single-family houses on lots of 10 or more acres of land are also excluded.

**Housing cost** as a percentage of income is shown separately for owners with mortgages, owners without mortgages, and renters. Rent as a percentage of income is a computed ratio of gross rent and monthly household income (total household income the past 12 months divided by 12). Selected owner costs include utilities and fuels, mortgage payments, insurance, taxes, etc. In each case, the ratio of housing cost to income is computed separately for each housing unit. The housing cost ratios for half of all units are above the median shown in this book, and half are below the median shown in the book.

**Substandard units** are occupied units that are overcrowded or lack complete plumbing facilities. For the purposes of this item, "overcrowded" is defined as having 1.01 persons or more per room. Complete plumbing facilities include hot and cold piped water, a flush toilet, and a bathtub or shower. These facilities must be located inside the housing unit, but do not have to be in the same room.

## INCOME AND POVERTY, Items 46–51
### Source: U.S. Census Bureau—American Community Survey, 2011
### http://www.census.gov/acs/www/

The data on income were derived from responses of a sample of persons 15 years old and over. **Total money income** is the sum of the amounts reported separately for wage or salary income; net self-employment income; interest, dividends, or net rental or royalty income or income from estates and trusts; Social Security or railroad retirement income; Supplemental Security Income (SSI); public assistance or welfare payments; retirement, survivor, or disability pensions; and all other income. Receipts from the following sources are not included as income: capital gains; money received from the sale of property (unless the recipient was engaged in the business of selling such property); the value of income "in kind" from food stamps, public housing subsidies, medical care, employer contributions for individuals, etc.; withdrawal of bank deposits; money borrowed; tax refunds; exchange of money between relatives living in the same household; and gifts, lump-sum inheritances, insurance payments, and other types of lump-sum receipts.

**Per capita income** is the mean income computed for every man, woman, and child in a particular group. It is derived by dividing the aggregate income of a particular group by the resident population in that group. Per capita income is rounded to the nearest whole dollar.

**Household income** includes the income of the householder and all other individuals 15 years old and over in the household, whether or not they are related to the householder. Since many households consist of only one person, median household income is usually less than median family income.

The **poverty status** data were derived from data collected on the number of persons in a household, from questionnaire item 3, which provided data on each person's relationship to the householder, and questionnaire items 41 and 42, which were also used to derive the income data. The Social Security Administration (SSA) developed the original poverty definition in 1964, which federal interagency committees subsequently revised in 1969 and 1980. The Office of Management and Budget's (OMB) *Directive 14* prescribes the SSA's definition as the official poverty measure for federal agencies to use in their statistical work. Poverty statistics presented in American Community Survey products adhere to the standards defined by OMB in *Directive 14*.

Poverty thresholds vary depending on three criteria: size of family, number of children, and, for one- and two-person families, age of householder. In determining the poverty status of families and unrelated individuals, the Census Bureau uses thresholds (income cutoffs) arranged in a two-dimensional matrix. The matrix consists of family size (from one person to nine or more persons), cross-classified by presence and number of family members under 18 years old (from no children present to eight or more children present). Unrelated individuals and two-person families are further differentiated by age of reference person (under 65 years old and 65 years old and over). To determine a person's poverty status, the person's total family income over the previous 12 months is compared with the poverty threshold appropriate for that person's family size and composition. If the total income of that person's family is less than the threshold appropriate for that family, then the person is considered poor or "below the poverty level," together with every member of his or her family. If a person is not living with anyone related by birth, marriage, or adoption, then the person's own income is compared with his or her poverty threshold. The total number of persons below the poverty level is the sum of persons in families and the number of unrelated individuals with incomes below the poverty level over the previous 12 months. The average poverty threshold for a four-person family was $23,021 in 2011.

The data on participation in the Food Stamp Program are designed to identify households in which one or more of the current members received food stamps during the past 12 months. Once a food stamp household was identified, a question was asked about the total value of all food stamps received by the household during that 12-month period. The Food Stamp Act of 1977 defines this federally funded program as one intended to "permit low-income households to obtain a more nutritious diet." (From title XIII of P.L. 95–113, The Food Stamp Act of 1977, declaration of policy.) Providing eligible households with coupons that can be used to purchase food increases food purchasing power. The Food and Nutrition Service (FNS) of the U.S. Department of Agriculture (USDA) administers the Food Stamp program through state and local welfare offices. The Food Stamp program is the major national income support program to which all low-income and low-resource households, regardless of household characteristics, are eligible.

## CIVILIAN LABOR FORCE, UNEMPLOYMENT, AND EMPLOYMENT, Items 52–58
### Source: U.S. Census Bureau—American Community Survey, 2011
### http://www.census.gov/acs/www/

The **civilian labor force** consists of all civilians 16 years old and over who are either employed or unemployed.

**Unemployment** includes all persons who did not work during the survey week, made specific efforts to find a job during the previous four weeks, and were available for work during the survey week (except for temporary illness). Persons waiting to be called back to a job from which they had been laid off and those waiting to report to a new job within the next 30 days are included in unemployment figures.

**Total employment** includes all civilians 16 years old and over who were either (1) "at work"—those who did any work at all during the reference week as paid employees, worked in either their own business or profession, worked on their own farm, or worked 15 hours or more as unpaid workers in a family farm or business; or were (2) "with a job, but not at work"—those who had a job but were not at work that week due to illness, weather, industrial dispute, vacation, or other personal reasons.

The **occupational categories** are based on the occupational classification system that was developed for the 2000 census. This system consists of 539 specific occupational categories for employed persons arranged into 23 major occupational groups. This classification was developed based on the *Standard Occupational Classification (SOC) Manual: 2010*, published by the Executive Office of the President, Office of Management and Budget.

## PERSONS WITH NO HEALTH INSURANCE, Item 59
**Source: U.S. Census Bureau—American Community Survey, 2011**
**http://www.census.gov/acs/www/**

The percentage of persons under age 65 with no **health insurance** shows the percentage of the population of each congressional district who were not covered by private health plans purchased directly or provided by an employer, Medicaid, Medicare, or military health care.

## SOCIAL SECURITY AND SUPPLEMENTAL SECURITY INCOME, Items 60–62
**Source: U.S. Social Security Administration**
**Source: U.S. Social Security Administration**
**http://www.ssa.gov/policy/docs/factsheets/cong/stats/**

**Social Security beneficiaries** are persons receiving benefits under the Old-Age, Survivors, and Disability Insurance Program. These include retired or disabled workers covered by the program, their spouses and dependent children, and the surviving spouses and dependent children of deceased workers.

**Supplemental Security Income (SSI) recipients** are persons receiving SSI payments. The SSI program is a cash assistance program that provides monthly benefits to low-income aged, blind, or disabled persons.

Data are as of December of the year shown.